THE AUTHORITY SINCE 1868

THE WORLD ALMANAC®

AND BOOK OF FACTS

2003

WORLD ALMANAC BOOKS

THE WORLD ALMANAC®
AND BOOK OF FACTS
2003

Editorial Director: William A. McGeveran Jr.
Managing Editor: Lori P. Wiesenfeld
Desktop Production Manager: Elizabeth J. Lazzara
Senior Editor: Kevin Seabrooke
Associate Editors: Mette A. Bahde, Christopher Larson, Olivia Jane Smith
Desktop Publishing Associate: Lloyd Sabin
Contributing Editors: Elizabeth Barden, Peter S. Falcier, Jacqueline Laks Gorman, Richard Hantula, Kate Hill, Jane Hogan, Geoffrey M. Horn, Andrea J. Pitluk, Jane Reynolds, Mark J. Schepp, Dr. Lee T. Shapiro, Donald Young
Research: Sean J. Alfano, Cassandra L. Capo, Rachael Mason, Catherine McHugh
Cover: Jay Jaffe/Bill SMITH STUDIO

WORLD ALMANAC EDUCATION GROUP
Chief Executive Officer, WRC Media Inc.: Martin E. Kenney Jr.
President: Robert Jackson
Publisher: Ken Park
Director–Purchasing and Production: Edward A. Thomas
Associate Editor: Ileana Parvulescu; **Desktop Publishing Assistant:** Erik C. Gopel
Director of Indexing Services: Marjorie B. Bank; **Index Editor:** Walter Kronenberg
Facts On File World News Digest: Marion Farrier, Editor in Chief; Jonathan Taylor, Managing Editor
World Almanac Reference Database@*FACTS.com*: Louise Bloomfield, Dennis La Beau

WORLD ALMANAC BOOKS
Vice President–Sales and Marketing: James R. Keenley
Marketing Coordinator: Sarah De Vos

We acknowledge with thanks the many helpful letters and e-mails from readers of THE WORLD ALMANAC. Because of the volume of mail, it is not possible to reply to each one. However, every communication is read by the editors, and all suggestions receive careful attention. THE WORLD ALMANAC's e-mail address is Walmanac@waegroup.com.

The first edition of THE WORLD ALMANAC, a 120-page volume with 12 pages of advertising, was published by the New York World in 1868. Annual publication was suspended in 1876. Joseph Pulitzer, publisher of the *New York World*, revived THE WORLD ALMANAC in 1886 with the goal of making it a "compendium of universal knowledge." It has been published annually since then. THE WORLD ALMANAC does not decide wagers.

COVER PHOTOS: Front cover: Soccer players, Brian Bahr/Getty Images; Wright Brothers' plane, Library of Congress, Prints & Photographs Division [reproduction number LC-DIG-ppprs-00626]; Wall St. tickers, AP/Wide World Photos; Sarah Hughes, Jamie Squire/Getty Images; Towers of Light, © Photo by Edward A. Thomas. Back cover: Colin Powell, U.S. Dept. of State.

THE WORLD ALMANAC and BOOK OF FACTS 2003

Library of Congress Catalog Card Number 4-3781
International Standard Serial Number (ISSN) 0084-1382
ISBN (softcover) 0-88687-882-9
ISBN (hardcover) 0-88687-883-7
Printed in the United States of America
The softcover and hardcover editions are distributed to the book trade by St. Martin's Press.

WORLD ALMANAC BOOKS
A Division of World Almanac Education Group, Inc.
A WRC Media Company
512 Seventh Avenue
New York, NY 10018

CONTENTS

The World Almanac
and Book of Facts
2003

THE TOP TEN NEWS STORIES OF 2002

1. The U.S. and its allies continued their **war on terrorism** seeking to rout out members of the **al-Qaeda** terror network, held responsible for the Sept. 11, 2001, attacks in which some 3,000 people were killed, and their Afghan **Taliban supporters**. Despite some success, the whereabouts and fate of al-Qaeda leader Osama bin Laden and of Taliban leader Mullah Mohammed Omar remained unknown as of mid-Oct., and there were renewed terrorist attacks, including an Oct. 12 bombing in a tourist district of Bali, Indonesia, that killed more than 180 people. Some al-Qaeda were taken into custody by the U.S. and detained at its naval base in Guantanamo Bay, Cuba. Suspected terrorists were arrested in many countries, including Pakistan, Germany, Italy, Singapore, Sudan, Spain, and the U.S. The stability of **Afghanistan's new government** remained at risk, underlined by a Sept. 5 assassination attempt on Pres. Hamid Karzai. **At home,** U.S. leaders sought policies to better protect against attacks. The federal government Feb. 17 took control of security at commercial airports; Pres. George W. Bush June 6 proposed a cabinet-level Dept. of Homeland Security to coordinate domestic antiterrorism efforts; and U.S. lawmakers investigated evidence of pre-Sept. 11 intelligence lapses. Amid concerns about civil liberties, federal courts made conflicting rulings over whether to release names of hundreds detained in the antiterrorism drive.

2. Congress passed a resolution Oct. 10-11 giving Pres. Bush a broad mandate to use **military force** against "the continuing threat" posed by the regime of Saddam Hussein in **Iraq**; the vote was 77-23 in the Senate and 296-133 in the House. As of mid-Oct., the UN Security Council was still trying to reach agreements to return international inspectors to Iraq, in an attempt to verify whether Iraq had weapons of mass destruction and perhaps avoid war.

3. **Violence between Israelis and Palestinians** continued, with little progress toward a peace settlement. A 2-year cycle of Palestinian attacks (frequently suicide bombings) and Israeli military incursions and targeted attacks on militant leaders had left about 600 Israelis and 1,600 Palestinians dead by Oct. 2002.

4. The U.S. corporate community was battered by **accounting scandals and bankruptcies** that led to congressional hearings and arrests, and further undermined a weakening **stock market**—which hit 5-year lows in early Oct. Telecommunications giant **WorldCom Inc.**, July 21, filed the U.S.'s largest-ever bankruptcy; it eventually disclosed more than $7 billion in accounting irregularities. A probe into the Dec. 2001 bankruptcy of energy trader **Enron Corp.** led to congressional hearings, the June 15 conviction of its outside auditor, **Arthur Andersen LLP,** on federal obstruction of justice charges, and the Oct. 2 arrest of its former CFO on fraud and other charges. Congress passed and Pres. Bush on July 30 signed a measure aimed at overhauling the federal accounting, securities fraud, and corporate governance laws.

5. The U.S. Roman Catholic Church was engulfed in a scandal over its handling of **sexual abuse of minors** by priests. Following up on a meeting in April between Pope John Paul II and U.S. cardinals in Rome, the U.S. Conference of Catholic Bishops, in Dallas, TX, June 13-15, agreed to stringent steps, including removing from ministry any priest credibly accused of sexually abusing a minor; however, the Vatican Oct. 18 called for revision of these policies. In Sept. the Boston archdiocese agreed to pay $10 million to settle a suit by 86 plaintiffs against defrocked priest John Geoghan.

6. Control of the U.S. Congress was at stake in **midterm elections** set for Nov. 5. There were 34 races for seats in the Senate, currently split 50-49 in favor of the Democrats. Also at stake were all 435 House seats, and 36 governorships. *For election results*, visit www.worldalmanac.com/2002elections.

7. The **Washington, DC, suburbs** were terrorized by a series of **sniper shootings,** beginning Oct. 2. The attacker or attackers, firing single shots with a high-powered rifle, usually from far away, killed 9 people and injured 2 through Oct. 14; as of that date police had not made an arrest in the case.

8. Rising tensions in May between **India and Pakistan** aroused fears that their longstanding dispute over the Kashmir region would erupt into a full-fledged war between the 2 nuclear-armed nations, but steps taken in June reduced this threat.

9. Pres. Bush Mar. 26 signed a **campaign-finance reform bill,** capping a 7-year effort by sponsors Sen. John McCain (R, AZ) and Russell Feingold (D, WI) to impose a ban on unregulated "soft money" contributions to political parties and restrict so-called issue ads by interest groups. It was the most comprehensive campaign-finance overhaul since 1974, when Pres. Gerald Ford signed landmark post-Watergate reforms.

10. The **North Korean government** of Kim Jong Il admitted it has been pursuing a **clandestine nuclear weapons program,** U.S. officials disclosed Oct.16. Officials said the U.S. would withdraw from a 1994 pact under which the West provided aid to North Korea in exchange for a freeze in nuclear arms development.

The Ongoing War Against Terrorism

By Geoffrey M. Horn

Geoffrey M. Horn, a freelance writer and editor, writes about U.S. politics and current affairs.

More than a year after the attacks of Sept. 11, 2001, the war against terrorism continued to dominate the American agenda. Even as the U.S. turned its attention toward another Near East nemesis—Iraqi leader Saddam Hussein—a spate of deadly attacks in October from Kuwait to Bali and the Philippines gave evidence that the al-Qaeda terrorist network, though weakened by its defeat by Alliance forces in Afghanistan, was beginning to regroup.

Al-Qaeda's October resurgence came despite damage to its highest echelon. Training director Mohammed Atef of Egypt was believed to have been killed Nov. 13, 2001, in a U.S. bombing raid near Kabul, and the man believed to be Atef's successor, Abu Zubaydah, a Palestinian born in Saudi Arabia, had been captured Mar. 28, 2002, in Pakistan and detained for questioning by the U.S. There was no hard evidence that al-Qaeda leader Osama bin Laden remained alive (though the failure to capture either Bin Laden or Taliban leader Mullah Mohammed Omar meant that they might still be active).

International Battlefront

One top aide to Bin Laden who survived the U.S. onslaught was Ayman al-Zawahiri, an Egyptian surgeon and the founder of Egyptian Islamic Jihad, who called the Sept. 11 attacks "a great victory" in a videotape broadcast Apr. 15, 2002. Release of the video followed by 4 days a truck bombing at a synagogue on the Tunisian island of Djerba in which at least 17 people were killed, many of them German tourists. "We've sent a message to Germany," Zawahiri said in an audiotape aired Oct. 8.

That message (together with communications purporting to come from Bin Laden) coincided with the wave of terrorist operations in which many analysts saw the hand of al-Qaeda and its allies. On the S Philippine island of Mindanao—where U.S. forces and Filipino government troops were fighting Abu Sayyaf, an Islamic guerrilla group linked with al-Qaeda—a nail bomb mounted on a motorcycle exploded Oct. 2, killing an American Green Beret and 3 other people. An explosion and fire Oct. 6 damaged a French oil tanker, killed one crew member, and spilled 90,000 barrels of oil into the Gulf of Aden, off Yemen. An attack Oct. 8 by Kuwaiti gunmen killed one U.S. marine and wounded another. A huge blast and fire Oct. 12 claimed the lives of at least 180 people, many of them young Australian tourists, in the Kuta beach district of Bali, Indonesia. The Bali explosion was attributed to al-Qaeda "with the cooperation of local terrorists" by Indonesian Defense Minister Matori Abdul Jalil.

Repair, Rebuild, Remember

The war on terrorism in Afghanistan resulted in the overthrow of oppressive Taliban rule and the installation of a functioning government, with a mission to rebuild the country. Meanwhile, at home, Americans sought to honor the heroes and victims of the 2001 attacks, repair and rebuild the sites struck by the hijackers, revive the damaged U.S. economy, and determine why U.S. intelligence and law enforcement agencies had been unable to prevent the terrorist acts that had killed more than 3,000 people.

At Wedge 1 of the Pentagon, where 125 workers died, the Phoenix Project construction team completed repairs June 11 to the limestone facade through which American Airlines Flight 77 had crashed. Thirteen thousand people gathered for a special ceremony in front of the rebuilt section on Sept. 11, 2002—one of many hundreds of commemorations held in churches, town squares, and other places throughout the U.S. on that day.

At the site where World Trade Center had stood, the task of removing 1.62 million tons of rubble while searching for human remains officially ended July 15, 2002. New York City's official list of the dead and missing had been pared to 2,801 by Sept. 11, 2002, when all the names were read at a ceremony held at the site. Discussions of how to redevelop the area revealed divisions between those who wanted to replace the lost office space (and the economic benefit it represented) and those (including many of the victims' families) who regarded the site as holy ground fit only for a permanent memorial.

A report released Sept. 4 by the New York City comptroller, *One Year Later: The Fiscal Impact of 9/11 on New York City*, estimated that the overall cost to the city of the terrorist attacks could reach as high as $95 billion. Other financial statistics were equally sobering. The sluggish economy, declining tax revenues, plunging stock prices (exacerbated by an epidemic of corporate scandals), and increased spending on national defense and homeland security combined to transform a federal budget surplus of $127 billion for the 2001 fiscal year to a deficit of $157 billion in fiscal 2002. Revenues had suffered their largest percentage drop in 50 years and spending had shown its most rapid increase in two decades. Forty-six state governments had to address budget shortfalls totalling $37.2 billion for the fiscal year ended June 30, according to the National Conference of State Legislatures.

What Went Wrong?

A crucial question confronting Congress was whether government intelligence and law enforcement could have anticipated and prevented the Sept. 2001 attacks. Beginning Sept. 18, 2002, a series of joint hearings by the House and Senate Intelligence Committees presented a portrait of an overworked and stressed-out intelligence community that had overlooked some clues, undervalued others, and failed to share information effectively. The initial report noted that although Director of Central Intelligence George Tenet had declared "war" against al-Qaeda as early as Dec. 1998, neither the Central Intelligence Agency nor the Federal Bureau of Investigation had reallocated its resources accordingly. Former FBI Director Louis J. Freeh responded that Congress had not appropriated the funds that he had sought to fight terrorism.

A 2nd report, released 2 days later, argued that by Jan. 2000, the CIA had good reason to be suspicious of Khalid al-Mihdhar and Nawaf al-Hazmi, 2 Saudi citizens who were among the 5 hijackers who crashed Flight 77 into the Pentagon. However, the CIA did not circulate an alarm until Aug. 23, 2001, by which time the 2 men were already in the U.S.

The joint committee also focused on the failure of FBI higher-ups to heed an urgent warning from an agent in Phoenix, AZ, who contended in an electronic memo on July 10, 2001, that Bin Laden had launched a coordinated effort to send students to the U.S. for civil aviation training. Also unheeded was a high-priority request from an FBI supervisor in Minneapolis, MN, for a warrant to search the laptop computer of Zacarias Moussaoui, who was detained Aug. 16 after arousing suspicions at a local flight school.

Facts Related to the War Against Terrorism

(All figures latest as of Oct. 2002, unless otherwise indicated.)

- **Victims of the Sept. 11 attacks:** 3,021. Official count for the World Trade Center disaster was 2,797 (4 fewer than the number of names read at Ground Zero ceremonies on Sept. 11, 2002). Including the 147 on board the 2 aircraft that crashed into the Twin Towers.
  - The New York City listing included 1,411 victims who had been identified. Other victims: 184 at the Pentagon (of whom 59 were on board American Flight 77) and 40 on board United Flight 93, which crashed near Shanksville, PA.
  - Victim figures do not include the 19 hijackers, all presumed to have died that day.
- **Average initial Victim's Compensation Fund payment:** $1.56 million. 749 claims; 67 award letters issued, of which 41 were accepted as of mid-Oct.
- **Projected increase in annual U.S. defense spending:** 43.4% between the 2001 and 2007 fiscal years. Defense expenditures were forecast to rise from $309 billion in fiscal 2001 to $379 billion by fiscal 2003 and $442.5 billion by fiscal 2007.
- **Persons with terrorist connections:** more than 70,000 on the U.S. State Dept. "watch list."
- **Suspected terrorists arrested worldwide:** more than 2,400 in 90 countries since Sept. 2001.
- **Prisoners held at Guantánamo Bay Naval Base, Cuba:** about 550. These al-Qaeda and Taliban fighters captured in Afghanistan are classified as "enemy combatants" by the U.S. government.
- **Items seized at U.S. commercial airports:** more than 3 million items, such as guns, knives, box cutters, scissors, razors, and other prohibited objects, with 720 people held for weapons violations, from Feb. 17, 2002, when the federal government took over security, to Sept. 30, 2002.
- **U.S. troops deployed to combat terrorism:** more than 60,000, including those assigned to Afghanistan, the Philippines, Georgia, and Yemen.
- **U.S. military casualties, worldwide in terror war:** 52 deaths, more than 200 injured, as of Sept. 2002.
- **Afghan casualties:** Unknown; estimates of civilian dead range from below 1,000 to over 3,000.
- **Bombs dropped in Afghanistan by the U.S. and its allies:** 24,000 as of Sept. 2002; of these, 13,000 were precision guided.
- **Refugees returned to Afghanistan:** about 2 million. In addition, 630,000 internally displaced persons had returned to their homes. A year earlier, at the start of U.S. bombing, more than 3.5 million Afghans were living in refugee camps in neighboring countries, and over 1.3 million were internally displaced.
- **Food delivered to Afghanistan:** more than 575,000 metric tons since Oct. 2001.
- **International aid pledges to Afghanistan for 2002:** $2 billion, of which about $1.3 billion had been used or was expected to become available before the end of 2002. Afghanistan's national budget for 2002 was $460 million, for a national population of about 28 million.

Search for Security

Both at home and overseas, the Bush administration and Congress moved to bolster American security. Legislation signed by Pres. Bush on Nov. 19, 2001, authorized a federal force to screen passengers and baggage at major airports, increased the number of sky marshals, and provided for the strengthening of cockpit doors to ward off intruders. On Mar. 12, 2002, Homeland Security Director Tom Ridge unveiled a five-step, color-coded alert system ranging from green (low risk of attack) up to red (severe risk); the level remained at yellow (elevated risk) throughout the spring and summer but was raised to orange (high risk) for a 2-week period while the U.S. marked the 1st anniversary of the Sept. 11 attacks.

Pres. Bush June 6 proposed the creation of a new cabinet-level Department of Homeland Security, comprising some 22 separate agencies with about 170,000 employees. Included in the new department would be the INS, the Coast Guard, the Secret Service, the Customs Service, and the Federal Emergency Management Agency, along with the Transportation Security Administration, which had been established the previous November. The proposal—the most ambitious executive branch reorganization since the creation of the Department of Defense in the late 1940s—passed the House of Representatives 7 weeks later, by a vote of 295-132, but stalled in the Senate because of a wrangle over the employees' civil service and collective bargaining rights.

By autumn, new Coast Guard maritime safety and security teams were patrolling the harbors of Seattle, Los Angeles, Houston/Galveston, and Chesapeake, VA. The computer network of the Centers for Disease Control and Prevention was linked with those of some 2,000 local health agencies, while programs to combat bioterrorism received a fourfold increase in the budget for the 2003 fiscal year.

Another approach to securing the homeland was cutting the flow of funds to terrorists. According to the U.S. State Dept., more than 160 countries have frozen the financial assets of suspected terrorists. A UN report leaked to the *Washington Post* in Aug. 2002 suggested that about $100 million in assets had been blocked from Sept. through Dec. 2001, but only about $10 million since that time. By Jan. 2002 more than 50 countries, not including the U.S., had detained at least 800 terrorist suspects. Documents released 8 months later, however, indicated that the State Department's "watch list" of persons with terrorist connectons exceeded 70,000 and was expanding at a rate of about 2,000 a month.

To tighten enforcement of immigration laws, the names of over 300,000 foreigners living in the U.S. who had ignored deportation orders were entered into a national FBI crime database; the INS acknowledged, however, that it would not be able to meet a congressionally mandated deadline for tracking the more than 500,000 foreign nationals who hold student visas. On Oct. 1, 2002, immigration authorities began implementing a controversial policy of routinely registering, fingerprinting, and photographing men entering the U.S. from certain Middle Eastern and North African countries.

Some government actions raised concerns among civil liberties advocates. About 1,200 people—nearly all men of Middle Eastern or South Asian origin—were secretly arrested and held in the immediate aftermath of the Sept. 11 attacks. Civil and human rights groups filed suit calling on the Justice Dept. to release the names of the detainees, and in August a district court judge ordered the names released (the order was stayed pending appeal); by that time fewer than 100 reportedly remained in custody, with most having been deported. Concerns were also raised about the indefinite detention of Taliban and al-Qaeda prisoners at a prison camp at Guantánamo Bay, Cuba.

In pursuing the war on terrorism abroad, the U.S. to some extent downplayed human rights considerations. Pakistan's military ruler Pervez Musharraf emerged as an invaluable ally, and the U.S. also tightened defense ties with some Central Asian regimes with poor human rights records, such as Uzbekistan and Tajikistan. Concerns about continued American vulnerability to terrorist attacks in part prompted a shift in global defense strategy, as outlined in the administration's *National Security Strategy,* released in Sept. 2002. This document argued that the policy of deterrence, pursued effectively against the Soviet Union during the cold war, was no longer viable. Mindful of Sept. 11, the Bush administration placed new emphasis on possible preemptive action against terrorist groups and rogue states. The policy was controversial, but Congress appeared to endorse it when, on Oct. 10-11, the House and Senate approved a resolution authorizing Pres. Bush to use military force against Iraq "as he determines to be necessary and appropriate" to defend national security and enforce UN resolutions.

Legal Cases Related to the War Against Terrorism

The following are some of the major cases, with their status as of mid-Oct. 2002.

- **Enaam Arnaout**, U.S. citizen born 1962 in Syria, executive director of Benevolence International Foundation (BIF), an Illinois-based Islamic charity. Indicted Oct. 9 on racketeering and fraud charges for allegedly funneling charitable donations to al-Qaeda.
- **Ramzi bin al-Shibh**, born 1972 in Yemen. Alleged al-Qaeda leader and key planner of Sept. 11 attacks. Roommate of hijacker Mohamed Atta in Hamburg, Germany, 1998-99. Fled Germany Sept. 5, 2001. Indicted in Germany in absentia for the murder of over 3,000 on Sept. 11. Captured in Karachi, Pakistan, Sept. 11, 2002. Transferred Sept. 16 to U.S. custody.
- **Yaser Esam Hamdi**, born 1980 to Saudi parents in East Baton Rouge, LA. Taken into custody in Afghanistan and detained at U.S. naval base, Guantánamo Bay, Cuba. Transferred as an enemy combatant Apr. 5, 2002, to Navy brig at Norfolk (VA), after claiming U.S. citizenship.
- **John Walker Lindh**, the "American Taliban"; born 1981 in Washington, DC. Fought in 2001 with Taliban against Northern Alliance in Afghanistan. Indicted Jan. 15, 2002, in U.S. federal court; pleaded guilty July 15 to serving as a soldier for the Taliban. Sentenced to 20 years in prison.
- **Zacarias Moussaoui**, sometimes called the "20th hijacker"; French citizen of Moroccan descent; born 1968. Detained on immigration charges Aug. 16, 2001, after a Minneapolis, MN, flight school suspected his motives in seeking to fly a commercial jetliner. Indicted Dec. 12 for conspiracy to carry out Sept. 11 attacks. Trial postponed to June 30, 2003.
- **José Padilla**, also known as Abdullah Al Muhajir; born 1970 in Brooklyn, NY. Arrested May 8, 2002, in Chicago in connection with a plot to detonate a "dirty bomb" containing radioactive materials. Classified as an enemy combatant June 9, and held in a Navy brig in Charleston, SC.
- **Richard Reid**, known as the "shoe bomber"; British citizen born 1973 in suburban London. Subdued Dec. 22, 2001, by flight attendants and passengers on an American Airlines flight from Paris, France, to Miami, FL, as he tried to ignite plastic explosives hidden in the soles of his shoes. Indicted Jan. 16 on multiple charges, including attempted murder. Pleaded guilty Oct. 4, declaring that he was a member of al-Qaeda, a follower of Bin Laden, and an enemy of the U.S.
- **Earnest James Ujaama**, born 1965 in Denver, CO, as James Earnest Thompson; known in Seattle, WA, as entrepreneur and community leader. Detained July 22, 2002, in Alexandria, VA, as material witness in federal terror investigation. Indicted Aug. 28 in Seattle for conspiring to set up a terrorist training camp in Bly, OR.
- **Suspected U.S. Terrorist Cells:** Five **Detroit** area residents (Karim Koubriti, Ahmed Hannan, Youssef Hmimssa, Ahmed Hannan, Farouk Ali-Haimoud, and a man known only as Abdella) were indicted Aug. 28 and accused of being part of a "sleeper operational combat cell." The first 4 were in federal custody; Abdella, the alleged ringleader, was still at large at that time. Five U.S. citizens of Yemeni ancestry (Yahya Goba, Sahim Alwan, Shafal Mosed, Yasein Taher, and Faysal Galab), all living in Lackawanna, N.Y., a suburb of **Buffalo**, were arrested Sept. 13-14 and charged with receiving terrorist training at an al-Qaeda camp near Kandahar, Afghanistan. A 6th suspect in the case, Mukhtar al-Bakri, was arrested Sept. 15 in Bahrain. Six residents of **Portland, OR** (Jeffrey Leon Battle, October Martinique Lewis, Patrice Lumumba Ford, Muhammad Ibrahim Bilal, Ahmed Ibrahim Bilal, and Habis Abdulla al Saoub) were indicted Oct. 3 on charges of conspiring to assist al-Qaeda. The first 4 were arrested Oct. 4; the other 2 were at large and believed to be overseas.

Nuclear Terrorism: Assessing the Risk

By Richard Hantula

Richard Hantula is a freelance editor and writer who frequently covers scientific and technical topics.

The nuclear bomb was used as a weapon for the first and, to date, last time in the bombing of Japan that ended World War II. The bombs dropped on Hiroshima and Nagasaki in Aug. 1945, each the equivalent of some 20,000 tons (20 kilotons) of TNT, destroyed a large part of both cities and killed more than 100,000 people within days. After that, the balance of power in the world and fears of massive retaliation deterred the small body of nuclear nations from using this weapon again.

But the suicide attacks that killed 3,000 people in the U.S. on Sept. 11, 2001, focused attention on a new threat: an apparently well-financed worldwide network of fanatical Islamic terrorists who might not shrink from using radiation as a weapon, perhaps even exploding a nuclear device if they could. Without a definable homeland, such terrorists would not be deterred by fear of massive retaliation—and they probably would not fear the serious health risks from handling nuclear materials.

The Availability of Weapons

Nuclear weapons rank among the most fearsome options potentially available to terrorists. The more powerful devices among today's fission and fusion weapons are many times more destructive than the bombs that hit Japan. Besides their direct damage, they release radiation—which if it does not kill quickly may cause disease and a slow and painful death. However, such weapons are generally kept under tight control. Terrorists would find it difficult to acquire one— though not necessarily impossible; they might steal one, or buy it from corrupt officials, or get it from a nation willing to use terrorism to advance its foreign policy objectives.

According to the Center for Defense Information (CDI), a nonpartisan research group based in Washington, DC, as of early 2002 the number of nuclear warheads in world stockpiles, including smaller tactical weapons as well as powerful strategic devices, exceeded 20,000. It was believed that Russia and the U.S. each had more than 10,000, China about 400, France 350, Britain 200, Israel perhaps 100-200, India 60 or more, and Pakistan at least 2 dozen. North Korea in Oct. 2002 admitted it had been pursuing a clandestine nuclear arms program.

Concerns over the security of these nuclear devices have been voiced particularly about Pakistan, where Muslim extremists enjoy significant popular support, and Russia, which inherited the bulk of the formidable Soviet arsenal after the Soviet Union's 1991 disintegration but found it difficult to finance strict security procedures. The late Gen. Aleksandr Lebed, who once served as secretary of Russia's Security Council, claimed in 1997 that 84 "suitcase" nuclear devices were found to be missing in the 1990s, though some senior Russian officials have denied this. These small, portable bombs could produce an explosion equivalent to perhaps 1,000 tons of TNT, with a blast radius of 1,600 ft. The al-Qaeda terrorist network has reportedly spent heavily on efforts to acquire portable nuclear devices from the former Soviet Union.

Besides North Korea, Iran and Iraq are suspected of having secret nuclear weapons programs, and may have the necessary materials for making them. If terrorists purchased or stole these ingredients, they might be able to do the same. According to the CDI, some 90 lbs. of enriched uranium and plutonium suitable for weapons have been stolen from nuclear facilities in the former Soviet Union since its 1991 collapse; most of the material was recovered, but not all.

Alternatively, terrorists might opt to build a small, primitive weapon from lower-grade ingredients. According to a 2002 report issued by the Oxford Research Group, a British think tank, terrorists could "relatively easily" make a modest nuclear explosive by obtaining reactor-grade plutonium from MOX, a mixture of plutonium oxide and uranium oxide used for reactor fuel in some countries. According to the report's author, the chemistry involved in separating out the plutonium "is less sophisticated than that required for the illicit preparation of designer drugs." Such a device would be far weaker than the bombs dropped on Japan. But the blast, heat, and radiation even from a bomb equivalent to 100 tons of TNT could wreak havoc, especially in urban areas. The spread of radioactive particles would depend on meteorological conditions and on the height at which the explosion occurred, but the report's author estimated the lethal area for radiation emitted in the first minute after the blast at about ½ mile.

> **Radiation's Havoc in One City**
>
> A 1987 incident in Goiânia, Brazil, a city of close to 1 million people at the time, gives an idea of how even unintentional exposure to medical-grade radioactive material can wreak havoc. An abandoned radiation therapy machine containing powdered radioactive cesium-137 was found by scavengers looking for scrap metal. The cesium capsule was cut open, and the "pretty" powder ended up being distributed about the city. Some 250 people experienced significant contamination, over 2 dozen had radiation burns, and 4 eventually died. Over 100,000 were subjected to monitoring. The cleanup operation produced 125,000 drums and 1,470 boxes of contaminated clothing, furniture, dirt, and other materials; about 85 houses were destroyed.

Radiation Terrorism

An easier alternative to obtaining or building a nuclear bomb of some kind is so-called radiation terrorism. In the eyes of many experts this is a more likely path for terrorists. It covers a range of options that fall short of bringing about "mass destruction" but can release enough radiation to induce panic. A piece of highly radioactive material can be transformed into a weapon of terror by merely leaving it in a public place. Terrorists could generate mass fear by hijacking a truck full of radioactive waste and using it to, say, contaminate a public water supply. Or they could seek to release significant amounts of radiation by sabotaging a nuclear power plant or by exploding a so-called radiological, or radiation, dispersal device, or "dirty bomb." This is an ordinary explosive device to which radioactive material (e.g., nuclear reactor wastes or radioactive substances from industrial or medical equipment) has been added. The blast spreads the radioactive particles, which may then be inhaled or ingested, and can remain a lingering source of contamination. While a dirty bomb's toll in death and destruction would probably be small (compared to a true nuclear device), it could create a powerful psychological shock and bring long-term economic and social disruption—the affected area would likely need to be evacuated and decontaminated even if the immediate health risks were judged to be only moderate. Material suitable for radiation terrorism is relatively common. Radioactive waste from nuclear reactors, for example, could be used; it is found around the world and tends to be less well guarded than nuclear weapons. Another potential source is industrial and medical equipment using certain radioactive substances.

The first known instance of radiation terrorism occurred in 1995, when rebels from the separatist Russian region of Chechnya buried a dirty bomb in Izmailovo Park in downtown Moscow. The device, reportedly consisting of dynamite plus cesium-137, was not detonated, and was removed by Russian authorities after the Chechens announced its presence. The cesium was believed to have been stolen from an industrial facility in the Urals.

Al-Qaeda has reportedly worked on development of a dirty bomb. Abu Zubaydah, who was al-Qaeda's operations chief until captured in Pakistan in Mar. 2002, reportedly told U.S. investigators that the organization had the ability to make a dirty bomb and also get it into the U.S. Officials were skeptical, however.

Radiation and Its Effects

There are various kinds of radiation, harmful or not, whether in the form of electromagnetic waves, like X rays or gamma rays, or in the form of particles, such as in cosmic rays. Light, for example, is a form of electromagnetic radiation that does not, so far as is known, harm living tissue, except in very high doses. A nuclear bomb blast generates a super-sized dose of light, but it also produces ionizing radiation, which can damage living tissue even at lower doses. Such radiation has sufficiently high energy to affect atoms that it hits, causing neutral atoms to gain or lose electrons and thereby become "ions." Ionizing radiation is also produced by the radioactive materials used in terrorism.

What to Do in a Radiation Emergency

In the event of a radiation emergency, the U.S. Centers for Disease Control and Prevention (CDC) recommends that you find shelter in a stable building and check your radio or TV for emergency-alert information. If you live near a nuclear power plant, you should have a copy of its emergency plan, avaliable from the plant. Every household should also have its own emergency plan.

Officials may advise you to "shelter in place," in which case you should avoid opening doors and windows, close fireplace dampers, and turn off fans, air conditioners, and heating units that draw in outside air; it's generally safer in an inner room or basement. If possible, change your clothes, sealing the potentially contaminated clothes in a plastic bag. Showering or washing yourself will reduce any radioactive particles on the skin. It's a good idea to always keep an emergency kit on hand, with items such as flashlight, portable radio, extra batteries, bottled water, canned and packaged food, hand-operated can opener, first-aid kit, and needed prescription drugs and personal items. If told to evacuate to another location, it is useful to bring such items, plus cash and credit cards. You may have to leave pets behind, since they are often not allowed in emergency shelters.

Some common forms of ionizing radiation—including alpha particles and, to a lesser extent, beta particles—can generally be readily blocked. Alpha particles are relatively large particles, the nuclei of helium atoms, and travel short distances; they can be stopped by a piece of paper. They ordinarily present a danger only if their source is within the body, as a result, say, of inhalation or ingestion. The much smaller and lighter beta particles, which are electrons, usually won't penetrate more than a few inches into the body and can be blocked by thin layers of metal or plastic. They can cause a type of skin injury that doctors sometimes call a "beta burn," and present a danger inside the body. Other kinds of ionizing radiation—such as high-energy neutrons and gamma rays—have much greater penetrating power.

Highly penetrating neutrons and gamma rays typically make up the radiation released immediately by a nuclear explosion; the relatively large neutrons account for the bulk of the tissue damage wrought. Also associated with a nuclear blast, however, is residual radiation released by the radioactive decay of atoms in the fallout. This longer-term radiation threat is also found in the weapons used in radiation terrorism. Generally speaking, it includes alpha and beta particles, along with, to some degree, neutrons and gamma rays. The precise nature of the radiation emitted, and the length of time the hazard lingers, depends on the radioactive substances involved. Some have a half-life (that is, time needed for half of a given amount of the substance to spontaneously decay) measured in seconds or minutes. Others pose a longer-term danger. The half-life of iodine-131, for example, is 8 days, that of cesium-137 about 30 years.

The damage to cells varies greatly, depending on such factors as the kind of radiation, the dose, and the rate at which the dose is delivered, as well as the cells' sensitivity to the radiation and their ability to recover from radiation-caused injury. The average person experiences in daily life a small amount of "background" ionizing radiation, and many experts believe that exposure to up to 20 times the annual background dose is usually harmless. But exposure to up to 1,000 times the background amount can lead to nausea, vomiting, hair loss, immune system impairment, and blood disease. Generally, if the whole body experiences a rapid, heavy radiation dose, death may follow in hours or days. Less extreme exposure may lead to impairment of organs or body functions, gangrene, birth defects, or cancer.

Countermeasures

Experts point to several ways of reducing the risk of nuclear terrorism. One, of course, is to upgrade the intelligence collected on terrorist groups. Also important is spotting terrorist nuclear devices or materials that are in transit. In the wake of Sept. 11, U.S. authorities began building a network of detectors at key transportation locations, among them airports, seaports, and border crossings. The federal government also stepped up research to improve devices and procedures for detecting nuclear materials, including those whose radiation may be masked by shielding. Sept. 11 also prompted some countries, including U.S. and U.K., to expand their stocks of the drug potassium iodide, which can help prevent thyroid cancer if taken immediately prior to, or right after, exposure.

Also helpful are tighter controls on nuclear weapon, nuclear materials used for other purposes, and nuclear waste. The U.S. government after Sept. 11 pushed for tightened security at private nuclear power plants. However, a Sept. 2002 report by the Project on Government Oversight (POGO), a Washington, DC-based watchdog group, found that security forces at many nuclear power plants were inadequately equipped and trained, and suffered from low morale and overwork. A proposed bipartisan Nuclear Security Act would mandate measures to upgrade power plant security such as introducing new hiring and training standards for security staff, assigning a federal security coordinator to each plant, and authorizing plant security officers to use deadly force.

At the G8 summit of major powers in June 2002, Western leaders agreed to contribute $20 billion over the next decade, including $10 billion from the U.S., to projects aimed at countering "the spread of weapons and materials of mass destruction." Nuclear weapons and materials in Russia were a major focus of this initiative, which included "dismantlement of decommissioned nuclear submarines, the disposition of fissile materials, and the employment of former weapons scientists"—this last point reflected concern that highly skilled but now jobless engineers and scientists might accept work from terrorists. Outside Russia, highly enriched uranium can be found at well over 300 research reactors in nearly 60 countries, in some cases under very lax security.

Further Information

For more information on radiation and its effects, visit the Univ. of Michigan's Radiation and Health Physics Page, www.umich.edu/~radinfo, as well as websites of the Health Physics Society, www.hps.org/publicinformation/ate; National Center for Environmental Health at the CDC, www.cdc.gov/nceh/radiation; National Council on Radiation Protection and Measurements, www.ncrp.com; and the U.S. Environmental Protection Agency, www.epa.gov/radiation/understand

In Aug. 2002 hundreds of Yugoslav scientists, technicians, and officials, with the aid of U.S., Russian, and International Atomic Energy Agency (IAEA) specialists and under the watchful protection of Yugoslav Army helicopters and troops, removed nearly 100 lb of weapons-grade uranium—enough for 2 or 3 bombs—from a decrepit research institute in Belgrade. This was the first of what many hoped would be a series of multinational operations to secure such materials.

A June 2002 report by the IAEA noted that security problems extend far beyond the relatively few facilities with plutonium or enriched uranium. Many governmental, educational, and industrial facilities around the world have other radioactive materials that could be used in a dirty bomb. According to the report, over 100 countries lack adequate controls to prevent, or detect the theft of, these materials. Since 1996, U.S. companies have lost track of some 1,500 radioactive sources, according to the U.S. Nuclear Regulatory Commission. Contentious talks under UN auspices have been under way since the late 1990s on an international Draft Convention on Nuclear Terrorism. Such a pact, if agreed upon, could help standardize and streamline procedures for suppressing nuclear terrorism.

The Threat from Biological and Chemical Weapons

By Richard Hantula

Richard Hantula is a freelance editor and writer who frequently covers scientific and technical topics.

The terrorist attacks of Sept. 11, 2001, and the subsequent discovery of letters laced with anthrax, heightened concerns about the possibility of terrorist or state-sponsored attacks using biological or chemical agents.

A variety of microorganisms and chemicals, many of them extremely difficult to detect, could be employed for that purpose. Some, such as the virus that causes the highly contagious disease smallpox, could be considered weapons of mass destruction because of their power to kill thousands, even millions. Experts estimate that if terrorists could infect 100,000 individuals with highly contagious smallpox, as many as 30 million deaths could ensue within 4 months.

Most harmful biological and chemical agents don't match smallpox in their capacity to cause widespread illness and death, but many may still suit the needs of terrorists who aim to weaken their enemy by generating panic among its population or sabotaging its economy. Not long after the Sept. 11 attacks, a few individuals in the media, Congress, and elsewhere received envelopes containing spores of the bacterium that causes anthrax, sent by an unknown person or group. Fewer than 2 dozen confirmed or suspected cases resulted, and 5 people died. Nonetheless, the anthrax cases precipitated widespread social disruption. Public health agencies were inundated with samples of spore-like powder and with worried people describing suspicious symptoms. Buildings were closed for decontamination, and the U.S. Postal Service irradiated mail sent to some government offices. Stores saw a run on gas masks, and the demand for antibiotics used in treating anthrax threatened to exhaust the supply in some areas. People were afraid.

Historical Perspective

Rudimentary biological and chemical weapons were used in antiquity. In the 5th century B.C., the Scythians dipped the heads of their arrows with blood from decaying corpses, and toxic fumes were put to military use in Greece's Peloponnesian War. In the mid-14th century A.D., besieging Mongols tossed plague-ridden corpses over the walls of the Crimean city of Kaffa. During the French and Indian Wars of the 18th century, the British may have given hostile Indians blankets in which smallpox victims had been wrapped. But not until the 20th century did large-scale research into and production of biological and chemical weapons get under way. Poison gases such as tear gas, chlorine, the lung irritant phosgene, and the blistering agent known as mustard gas were first used in World War I. Also during that war, Germany used anthrax and the horse disease glanders to infect sheep, horses, and mules intended for use by the Allies. The 1930s saw the use of biological weapons by Japan in China and the development of the nerve gases tabun and sarin by Germany. Several other countries mounted substantial biological and chemical weapon programs beginning in World War II, among them Britain, the Soviet Union, and the U.S.

An international convention banning biological weapons came into force in the mid-1970s, followed some 2 decades later by a pact banning chemical weapons. The chemical weapons treaty included a mechanism for verifying compliance. The biological pact, however, did not, and the Soviet Union (and perhaps some other signatories) continued secret production of bioweapons, manufacturing, for instance, enormous quantities of weaponized anthrax and smallpox.

Potential Biological Weapons

- **Anthrax.** The bacterium *Bacillus anthracis* causes anthrax, which normally afflicts grazing animals, such as sheep or cows. It enters the body through skin wounds or abrasions, or by inhalation or ingestion. Natural human cases occur relatively rarely. After an incubation period of several days or longer, the **inhalational** form of the disease attacks quickly, typically leading to overwhelming infection and often respiratory failure, if antibiotic treatment is not provided in time. So-called **cutaneous anthrax** is less likely to be fatal if untreated.

  For maximum casualties, the most effective way to distribute anthrax spores in a biological attack would probably be as an aerosol spray. The spores, which are extremely durable and can survive harsh conditions, could cover a great distance. A 1993 estimate by the U.S. Congress's Office of Technology Assessment put the number of potential deaths resulting from the release of 100 kg (220 lb) of spores at 130,000 to 3 million. After the accidental release of aerosolized anthrax spores in 1979 at a military biology facility in Sverdlovsk (now Yekaterinburg), Russia, as many as 250 cases may have occurred, of which some 100 were fatal.

  As of late 2002, anthrax vaccine existed only in limited quantities in the U.S. and was not available to the public. In Oct., the U.S. Dept. of Health and Human Services said it had contracted with 2 companies to produce 25 million doses of an improved vaccine.
- **Botulism.** Botulism is a rare but serious paralytic illness resulting from a toxin produced by the bacterium *Clostridium botulinum.* Classic symptoms include double or blurred vision, drooping eyelids, slurred speech, difficulty swallowing, dry mouth, and muscle weakness. If untreated, the illness may progress to paralysis of the arms, legs, trunk, and respiratory muscles. In severe cases a person may need to be kept on a breathing machine (ventilator) for weeks. With botulism spread via an aerosol, symptoms would typically appear 12 to 72 hours after exposure. If diagnosed early, botulism can be treated with an antitoxin.
- **Plague.** The Black Death, which killed about 25 million people in Europe in the mid-14th century, was a form of plague. It comes from the bacterium *Yersinia pestis,* usually transmitted by fleas that fed on bacteria-infected rodents. Symptoms, generally appearing in 2 to 10 days, include high fever, malaise, headaches, and extremely tender, swollen lymph nodes. Treatment with antibiotics should begin within 24 hours of the first symptoms. Otherwise, respiratory failure, shock, and death may follow.
- **Smallpox.** Smallpox, caused by the virus variola, gets its name from the characteristic blisters it causes. It can spread through the air. The incubation period is about 12 days. Within 2 weeks of developing the first symptom, a red rash, about 30% of victims die. Although there are no known treatments, a prototype for an effective vaccine was developed in 1798. Vaccination programs from 1967 to 1980 eradicated the disease worldwide, leading to the dismantling of production facilities for vaccines. Virus samples were to be kept in 2 laboratories, one in the U.S. and one in Russia. Some nations or groups, however, may have preserved secret supplies, perhaps in weaponized form. If an outbreak occurred, it would be hard to contain.

  Few Americans born after 1973 have been vaccinated, and since experts are unsure how long smallpox inoculation remains effective, people vaccinated years ago may be vulnerable again. The U.S. has or will soon have enough vaccine to vaccinate every American. As of Oct. 2002 the White House was considering offering the vaccine to the public; however, mass vaccinations would entail some risk: research from the 1960s suggested that a proportion of those vaccinated, 1 out of every 150,000, would develop serious complications, and 1 or 2 in a million would die.
- **Tularemia.** The bacterium *Francisella tularensis,* which causes tularemia, is one of the most infectious known. In nature, tularemia affects primarily animals, and human-to-human transmission has not been documented. Aerosol dissemination in a populated area would be expected to result in many cases of acute, nonspecific feverish illness in a few days (normal incubation range, 1-14 days), with inflammation of the lung sacs often developing. Without antibiotic treatment, the disease could progress to respiratory failure, shock, and, or in 30% or more of inhalational cases, death.
- **Viral hemorrhagic fever (VHF).** This is actually a group of illnesses, some of them life threatening, caused by several distinct families of viruses. Some, such as Ebola and Marburg, can spread from one person to another. Initial symptoms often include marked fever, fatigue, dizziness, muscle aches, loss of strength, and exhaustion. Severe cases commonly show signs of bleeding under the skin, in internal organs, or from body orifices. There is no cure. Vaccines exist only for yellow fever and Argentine hemorrhagic fever. Depending on the strain of virus, up to 90% of Ebola cases lead to death within a week.

According to the Center for Nonproliferation Studies at the Monterey (CA) Institute of International Studies, by the end of the century up to 20 countries were developing a chemical weapons capability, and more than a dozen were conducting bioweapon programs. Countries currently belonging to neither weapons pact include Egypt, Israel, and Syria.

Iraq acceded to the biological convention after its 1991 defeat in the Persian Gulf War but did not agree to a chemical weapons pact. In the mid-1980s Iraq reportedly did use chemical weapons—mustard and nerve agents—to suppress its Kurdish population and also in war against Iran. Following the Gulf War, UN arms inspectors worked in Iraq until 1998, by which time it had been established that among the weapons in Iraq's arsenal were a number of bioweapons, including anthrax, botulinum toxin, ricin, aflatoxin, wheat cover smut, and the potent nerve agent VX. Some experts suspect Iraq may currently have a stockpile of smallpox, perhaps developed from a natural outbreak there in 1971-72.

Military and Terrorist Use

By and large biological and chemical weapons were used only sporadically in the 20th century. A 1925 League of Nations curb may have helped limit their use, as well as a fear of enemy retaliation in kind, and practical problems, such as the unpredictability of winds, which makes weapons disseminated in the form of an aerosol, or tiny airborne particles, difficult to control. Bioweapons also do not usually produce instant results. An incubation period must pass before an infected person begins to show symptoms.

While such disadvantages constitute an obstacle for the military, they may not bother terrorists. A group with access to the necessary skills and/or money may undertake to construct biological or chemical weapons on its own. That's what the cult Aum Shinrikyo did near the end of the 20th century in Japan. More recently, documents found in Afghanistan indicated that the al-Qaeda terrorist network has carried on research toward developing biological and chemical weapons. It takes considerable expertise, however, to produce some of the more devastating weapons (as well as to store and distribute them effectively). Terrorists may be able to obtain efficient biological or chemical weapons in simpler ways—by theft, purchase, or gift, from the arsenals of rogue states such as Iraq or from inadequately guarded stocks remaining after the 1991 dissolution of the Soviet Union.

Biological Agents

Many infectious organisms could be made into bioweapons, but certain agents are of particular concern because they are especially deadly, can be distributed or transmitted relatively easily, and could create severe social disruption. The U.S. Centers for Disease Control and Prevention (CDC) classifies several as such "Category A" threats (*see box*, page 9).

Chemical Agents

Certain deadly industrial chemicals are amenable to widespread dissemination through the air. In 1984 the accidental release of methyl isocyanate gas from a Union Carbide pesticide plant in Bhopal, India, resulted in some 14,000 deaths. According to a 2001 study by the U.S. Army surgeon general, a terrorist attack on a chemical plant that unleashed deadly gas over a heavily populated urban area could cause up to 2.4 million deaths and injuries. A less devastating but perhaps easier option for terrorists is to employ common poisonous substances, like pesticides or mercury, as weapons. More sophisticated agents that can be used include those shown in the *box* below.

Defensive Measures

Preventive vaccines exist for some diseases that can be used as bioweapons. But the only defense against most chemical weapons is protective clothing and masks that can prevent exposure. Experts do not recommend, however, that most individuals buy a simple gas mask to keep on hand as a precaution. A gas mask has to be airtight, and so should fit its wearer precisely. Special training is needed in order to use it properly. Furthermore, there is almost no way of knowing in advance when you might be exposed.

Detection of a bioattack in time to avert casualties is a major concern. If authorities have to wait until an unusual wave of symptoms appears, and until they analyze the cases correctly, it may be too late to take effective countermeasures.

Among measures recently taken to upgrade U.S. capability to discover the existence of an attack, the CDC has set up a Rapid Response and Advanced Technology Laboratory for quick identification of naturally occurring biological agents (such as anthrax) ordinarily seldom seen in the U.S. In Oct. 2002 the CDC announced the funding of a pilot early-warning system to continually scan existing managed-care networks for suspicious disease clusters. Researchers are exploring expanded use of environmental monitors, such as the electronic noses used to detect chemicals like explosives. Creating a sensing system that can distinguish between ordinary dust and smoke, harmless microorganisms, and dangerous pathogens is, however, an extremely tough job, and the difficulty is compounded if the sensor has to work quickly.

For further information, visit the website for U.S. Centers for Disease Control, www.bt.cdc.gov; the Center for Nonproliferation Studies at the Monterey Institute of International Studies, cns.miis.edu/research/cbw; Henry L. Stimson Center, www.stimson.org/cbw; and MEDLINEplus at the U.S. National Library of Medicine, www.nlm.nih.gov/medlineplus/biologicalandchemicalweapons.html

Chemical Agents

- **Blood Agents.** These interfere with the absorption of oxygen into the bloodstream. The chemicals, which include hydrogen cyanide and cyanogen chloride, can be stored as a liquid in shells, converting to a thick gas upon detonation. In high concentrations, cyanide inhalation kills quickly, within minutes after exposure. Antidotes, which must be intravenously administered immediately after exposure, are highly effective. Because the chemicals used in blood agents are highly volatile and are lethal only in large doses, their military usefulness is considered limited.
- **Nerve Agents.** Sarin, tabun, soman, GF, VX and related nerve agents are among the most toxic of all known chemicals. When they touch the skin or are inhaled, nerve agents can cause death within minutes. The chemicals disable enzymes needed for the transmission of nerve impulses. Initial symptoms may include runny nose, watery eyes, drooling, excessive sweating, tightness of the chest, and difficulty in breathing. Strong doses may lead to the loss of consciousness, convulsions, and death within 10 minutes.

  Although antidotes exist, the extremely rapid action of nerve agents often demands immediate treatment. As a result, most U.S. soldiers facing possible chemical attack carry the necessary drugs with them. Aum Shinrikyo used sarin in a 1994 terrorist attack in Matsumoto that killed 7 people and a 1995 attack on the Tokyo subway system that left 12 dead and thousands injured. The low casualty figures were presumably due to the fact that the group lacked expertise.
- **Pulmonary (Choking) Agents.** Choking agents, such as phosgene and chlorine, are dispersed when a liquid-filled shell explodes, creating a cloud of gas. When the gas is inhaled, the lungs become filled with liquid, making breathing increasingly difficult. Victims often choke to death or die from a respiratory infection.

  Depending on which chemical agent is used, lethal effects can be felt anywhere from 10 minutes to 24 hours after exposure. There are no treatments or cures for choking agents.
- **Vesicant (Blister) Agents.** Mustard, the best-known vesicant weapon, has been considered a major military threat since its widespread use in gas form during World War I. It is easily deliverable by rockets, bombs, and artillery shells, and makes the affected territory temporarily unusable by the enemy.

  In both liquid and gas forms, mustard causes burning blisters on the skin, eyes, and lungs within 2 to 24 hours after exposure. Respiratory failure, pneumonia, and immune system failure may result from high doses. Mustard is less deadly than nerve agents but can cause permanent injury and may lead to cancer and birth defects.

  Other vesicants, such as lewisite, have similar effects and act more rapidly. Although no specific antidote for vesicants exists, the effects of the attack can often be lessened through the application of ointments and antibiotics on the blisters, or by rinsing exposed flesh with water.

SPECIAL SECTION: FOCUS ON THE ELDERLY

Older Americans: Living Longer, Living Better

By Donna E. Shalala

Dr. Donna E. Shalala is president of the University of Miami. As secretary of Health and Human Services for a record-setting eight years, she oversaw programs including Medicare, Social Security, Medicaid and the National Institutes of Health.

We have transformed what it means to grow old in America. My own mother, a 91-year-old lawyer, vividly illustrates this transformation. She has an active law practice. She played on the senior amateur tennis circuit until just a few years ago. She participates in classes and trips sponsored by the Institute for Retired Professionals.

In the past, aging was often feared as a steep descent into a nightmare of disability, depression, and isolation. Today—though seniors still face challenges—we know that this nightmare is far from reality. The fact is: older Americans are now living not only longer but also *better*.

"Active Aging"

The lives of the elderly have changed partly because more people are adopting the idea of "active aging."Active aging means encouraging—and supporting—seniors to remain involved and engaged. Now the seniors of my mother's generation, and the legions to come as the baby boomers age, will continue to make major contributions to our society:

They will work full time in every field.

They will start businesses and second careers.

They will raise children and grandchildren.

They will volunteer in our communities.

In short, they will enrich the lives of all Americans.

Active aging means preserving curiosity and contributing even more to the world. It is a time to celebrate the wisdom and the peace of a life well lived—and a life worth living.

Just ask the seniors' grandchildren, and their great-grandchildren. When I was secretary of Health and Human Services, I received a collection of essays written by second-graders at Meadow Lane Elementary School outside Kansas City, explaining what it means to grow old:

"When people get old they get wrinkles on their face … but their brain gets smarter," wrote Justin Pannullo.

"Older people like to fish and they go to church," wrote Matt Sherman.

Tyler Willis said, "My grandma runs a lot and has a man."

And Cole Julo summed it up: "Growing old means you don't have to brush your teeth anymore. You just take them out at night."

Government's Role

By the middle of this century, the United Nations estimates, 1 in 5 people in the world will be 60 or older, and more than 2 million people will be 100 or older. The world's fastest-growing age group, by percent, is 80 and older.

With the transformation of what it means to be elderly in the U.S. has come an evolving role for government. Medicare, which provides health insurance to virtually all older Americans, and Social Security are pillars of the American dream. These landmark initiatives say to all Americans: Work hard and play by the rules, and this country will provide you with security when you retire.

Like Social Security, Medicare is a "social insurance" program: it offers health care protection to all eligible elderly and disabled people no matter what their income or medical history. People contribute to Medicare while working so they will have health insurance when they retire.

In providing security for older Americans, Medicare and Social Security also benefit their children. Without this help from the government, middle-class Americans might exhaust their savings—and dreams—paying for the medical care of older family members. They might not be able to send their children to college or buy their own homes.

Max Frankel, a reporter for the *New York Times* who later became the newspaper's executive editor, was present in Independence, MO, when Pres. Lyndon Johnson signed the Medicare legislation in 1965. Johnson went to Independence so he could hand Harry Truman, who had long fought for national health insurance for the elderly, and his wife, Bess, the first two Medicare cards. As the ceremony ended, Frankel said to the president, "My mother thanks you."

"No," Johnson replied, "it is *you* who should be thanking me."

Indeed, Medicare has emancipated children as it cares for their parents. But Johnson meant more. He saw that Medicare is a living program, one whose promise will be just as important for each succeeding generation of Americans.

Needs to be Met

More must be done. Essentially, we must create a seamless system of supports for America's aging population. These supports must reach across retirement systems to health care systems to care-giving systems to our national infrastructures—from our highways to our sidewalks—to help seniors live longer and live better. These supports must include technological advances that promote greater independence and provide greater dignity for older Americans.

The enormous increases in the elderly population mean all our programs, including Medicare, must continue to be reinvented. The 1 in 10 Medicare beneficiaries over age 85 belong to a group with high levels of chronic illnesses and conditions requiring medical care. Dr. Carl Eisdorfer, chairman of Psychiatry at the University of Miami and an internationally known expert on aging, has come up with a formula he calls Eisdorfer's Rule: For every five years of life after 65, we see a doubling of medical morbidity. A 10-year increase in life expectation means a four-fold increase in medical problems. So it is of no small significance that the number of Medicare beneficiaries 85 and older is predicted to more than double by the year 2030.

While we have made huge gains in providing security for older Americans, it is a national tragedy that significant numbers of them still do not get enough to eat. Elderly women on their own are particularly vulnerable to poverty. We need a national strategy for long-term care that guarantees a safe, dignified quality of life for our oldest citizens.

Depression is a widespread, and widely undiagnosed, problem in the elderly. The symptoms—isolation, loneliness, pain—are too often thought to be an unavoidable part of growing old. This failure to diagnose and treat depression has formidable consequences: People 65 and older have the highest suicide rates of any age group. Those over 85 have a rate nearly double the overall national rate. We must raise the index of suspicion that part of an elderly patient's problem may be mental health, and follow up with appropriate treatment.

The elderly themselves are not the only ones affected by the physical and emotional ravages of aging. Their caregivers, most often untrained family members, face overwhelming psychological and physical challenges. Dr. Eisdorfer found in research on caregivers of Alzheimer's patients, for example, that clinical depression affects about 60% of all wives and daughters, 33% of husbands, and 28% of sons.

In the face of this suffering, there is ample reason for hope. We are on the verge of discovering the causes and cures of many of the most intractable diseases. Biomedical research is bringing us ever closer to figuring out how to protect against neurodegeneration, how to predict disease risk, how to repair and replace human tissue.

Government programs must keep pace with the promise of medicine, with ever-accelerating technological and scientific breakthroughs, so that all Americans have access to the most sophisticated care.

A Moral Test

As Vice Pres. Hubert H. Humphrey said at the 1977 dedication of the Health and Human Services headquarters building that bears his name: "The moral test of a government is how that government treats those who are in the dawn of life—the children; the twilight of life—the elderly; and the shadows of life—the sick, the needy, and the handicapped."

Through Medicare and Social Security, this nation continues to pass Humphrey's moral test. Our enduring commitment to that challenge means the seniors of today—and for generations to come—will continue to chart new territories and explore for all of us how to live a long and fulfilled life.

The Wonderful World of Longevity

By Robert N. Butler, M.D.

Dr. Robert N. Butler, 75, a noted gerontologist, is the president and CEO of the International Longevity Center and was director of the National Institute on Aging at the U.S. National Institutes of Health (NIH) from 1976 to 1982. He received a Pulitzer Prize in 1976 for his book Why Survive? Being Old in America.

The world has experienced three waves of increasing longevity, and in the 21st century we are likely to experience a fourth. The first occurred between 2.5 million and 100,000 years ago, when evidence suggests a doubling of the length of life as hominids evolved to *Homo sapiens*.

The second wave happened 12,000 years ago, during the Neolithic period, when animal husbandry and agriculture became established. Humankind no longer had to survive as hunter-gatherers. But greater density of settlements brought closer contact with animals and insects, and therefore with diseases; life expectancy may have been about 20 years.

Beginning in the 18th century, the Industrial Revolution resulted in major increases in longevity. For example, in 1776 in the U.S., average life expectancy was 35. In 1900, it was 47. Today it is 77. So, in the U.S., we have gained 40 years of life expectancy since the American Revolution and 30 years since the beginning of the 20th century. The last increase exceeds what had been attained during the whole preceding 5,000 years of human history! This revolution in longevity is occurring throughout the world.

In the 21st century, following effective biomedical research, we're likely to experience a fourth wave of longevity gains. There are new possibilities for retarding the process of aging. Finding biological methods to commit embryonic stem cells to specific tissue and organ destinations will give birth to regenerative medicine. Less likely—but possible, and even more exciting—would be the discovery and usability of genes that determine the length of life of our species.

We're living better as well as longer. Deaths from cardiovascular disease and stroke dropped 60% between 1950 and 2000 in the U.S., and disability rates have also declined significantly

We need to prepare individuals and society for population aging and longevity and to do so in *positive and productive ways*. Three big tasks lie ahead: to improve and maintain the expectation of a continuing healthy life into great old age, to extend the productive work life, and, of course, to contribute to the adaptation of the changing family. We may soon have large numbers of four- to five-generation families.

At the same time as we address the issues of public pension and health care costs, we must also look to the worlds of work and health. We must look more broadly at the implications of the great social upheaval likely to parallel and follow the revolution of longevity. It is instructive to think back to 1900 when the normal workweek was 60 hours and the average life expectancy was 47. Now we have a 40-hour workweek, or less, and average life expectancy is 77. We must conclude that individuals and society are not fully prepared for this longevity.

For one thing, we haven't yet successfully facilitated new careers for older workers. And we have yet to establish affordable, community-based long-term care, at least in the United States. (The Netherlands, Germany, and Japan are making rapid advances in this area.)

The United States and other countries lack geriatric specialization. Only 4 of the over 100 American medical schools have departments of geriatrics. We have a long way to go, too, in developing "magic bullets" that cure specific diseases without untoward side effects.

Who Is Responsible?

Who is responsible for old age? The family, government, civil society, and business all have a role. For example, the National Institute on Aging has helped us confront Alzheimer's disease, as well as other debilitating conditions. National and international associations concerned with Alzheimer's disease have grown, and pharmaceutical company laboratories are focusing on this devastating disease.

But finally, it is the individual who must prepare. People need to plan for aging in a variety of ways. They need financial planning, intellectual stimulation, and a sense of purpose. Meaningful social interactions are especially important. One reason women live longer than men—by about 5 years in the U.S.—is that women tend to have more intimate social support systems than men. Social interaction also contributes to our maintaining intellectual function.

Happily the prescription for longevity also encompasses robust exercise for the brain: brain jogging. People need to remain intellectually active. This includes anything from enrollment in adult education classes and Elderhostel trips to crossword puzzles and bridge and book clubs, to the development of new interests and the acquisition of new skills.

Productive Aging

In some ways retirement has been a 20th century aberration. It was required when the majority of workers labored in mines, factories, and farms, and it continues to be humane and necessary for individuals who have reasons to stop working after a lifetime of drudgery. But for many of us, retirement must be marked by a new kind of *responsible aging*. It is unimaginable that public benefits can be maintained if people are in retirement for 2 to 3 decades. Through paid and unpaid work, people must continue to contribute to society. Since older workers are more expensive, employers need to be offered financial incentives.

The Dependency Ratio

Frequent references are made to the "dependency ratio"—that is, the rising numbers of older persons compared to people employed in the traditional workforce. It is suggested that the aging of the population forces the workforce to shoulder an unfair burden in paying for their care. However, the *total dependency ratio*, which counts in everyone under 18 as well as those over 65, offers more insight to the situation. And when we look at this ratio, the striking decline in birth rates in most developed nations comes into play.

In the U.S., for example, we end up with the same total dependency ratio for 2050 as existed in 1900. Moreover, while in the U.S. very few children under 18 are significant wage earners, a considerable number of people over 65 are economically able to take care of themselves. And the cost of raising a child to age 18 can be conservatively put at at least $200,000 (or, with college, at least $300,000), while the average cost of a nursing home is about $60,000 a year (with an average stay of 2-3 years).

Most important, dependency ratios matter less than *productivity per capita* in evaluating the economic health of the population. One example: at the turn of the century, 37% of the population worked in agriculture in the U.S. Today, that number is 2%, but we enjoy a more plentiful food supply.

The longevity in the 20th century has been extraordinary, accompanied by improved quality of life. In fact, economists David E. Bloom and David Canning contend (*Science*, February 2000) that *longevity has brought greater wealth to our world*. This runs counter to the worry that population aging will lead to economic stagnation. Improving health and longevity are associated with growing national wealth.

Conclusion

What will 2100 bring? Conceivably people will live for 120 years. (Most gerontologists believe the maximum life span is genetically determined to be 110-120 years.) Perhaps people will work a 30-hour workweek until they are 90, with many choosing to work at home. Perhaps a National Youth Community Service will delay entry into the workforce. Maybe many people will go on sabbaticals, as is already true in Australia and Norway.

This is the first time in human history that the prospect of living a long, healthy, and productive life has become reality for the majority of people in most parts of the world. What was once the special advantage of the few has become the destiny of many. And it is likely that this increase in longevity will continue. As important as is liberation by health, as powerful as is liberation by law, older people must be liberated, too, from stereotypes that limit their horizons. We are in the midst of the wonderful new world of longevity. It is in our power to make it a celebration.

THE ELDERLY: A STATISTICAL PORTRAIT

World Population

The number of people in the world aged 65 and over (65 +) is growing by 800,000 a month. As people around the world live longer and fertility rates decline in the developed nations and flatten in the developing world, the average age of the population is advancing. By 2050, the number of people aged 60 and over worldwide is expected to exceed the number under 15 for the first time in the history of the human race. The aging of the population is and will be especially pronounced in developed nations, especially in Western Europe.

Population 65 and Older: Selected Regions and Countries, 2002, 2030

Source: U.S. Bureau of the Census, International Data Base

	2002 Total pop. 65 +	2002 % 65+	2030 Total pop. 65 +	2030 % 65+
WORLD	440,616,212	7.1	967,425,774	11.9
Less dev. countries	264,772,222	5.3	686,169,082	9.9
More dev. countries	175,843,990	14.8	281,256,692	22.7
Continent or region				
Africa	26,766,824	3.2	61,549,369	4.5
Sub-Saharan Africa	20,398,304	2.9	43,212,702	3.7
Northern Africa	6,368,520	4.3	18,336,667	8.7
Near East	8,159,756	4.6	23,621,157	7.8
Asia (whole continent)	230,331,429	6.1	576,345,892	11.7
North America	48,407,730	9.8	104,111,706	16.4
Latin America and Caribbean	30,262,410	5.7	80,426,075	11.6
South America only	21,268,240	6.0	55,634,713	12.4
Europe	110,623,341	15.2	163,087,155	23.1
Western Europe	65,327,890	16.6	98,917,401	25.2
Eastern Europe	16,210,191	13.4	24,598,744	21.4
Baltics	1,080,216	14.6	1,413,781	20.9
Commonwealth of Independent States	32,810,336	11.6	47,662,371	16.2
Oceania	3,218,648	10.2	6,696,939	16.3
Most populous countries				
China	93,217,096	7.3	237,021,465	16.0
India	49,240,979	4.7	128,836,480	9.0
United States	35,302,936	12.6	70,319,071	20.0
Indonesia	11,118,407	4.8	34,136,543	10.9
Brazil	9,855,251	5.6	26,799,815	13.2
Russia	19,070,586	13.2	27,191,862	20.5
Pakistan	6,113,790	4.1	14,689,556	6.5
Bangladesh	4,514,130	3.4	13,207,711	7.2
Japan	22,896,026	18.0	33,049,579	28.3
Nigeria	3,676,803	2.8	8,138,686	3.7

Countries with Highest Proportion of People 65+, 2002

Source: U.S. Bureau of the Census, International Data Base

	Country	% 65+
1.	Monaco	22.4
2.	Italy	18.6
3.	Japan	18.0
4.	Greece	18.0
5.	Spain	17.4
6.	Sweden	17.3
7.	Belgium	17.1
8.	Germany	17.0
9.	Bulgaria	16.9
10.	France	16.2

Note: In the U.S., 12.6% of the population was 65 or older.

Countries with Biggest Projected Increase in Elderly, 2000-2030

Source: Bureau of the Census, U.S. Dept. of Commerce

	Country	% 65+
1.	Singapore	372
2.	Malaysia	277
3.	Colombia	250
4.	Costa Rica	240
5.	Philippines	240
6.	Indonesia	227
7.	Mexico	216
8.	South Korea	210
9.	Egypt	207
10.	Bangladesh	206
11.	Peru	197
12.	Thailand	196
13.	Guatemala	193
14.	Morocco	193
15.	Brazil	192
16.	Chile	183
17.	Sri Lanka	178
18.	Turkey	177
19.	India	174
20.	Tunisia	171

Note: The projected increase was 102% for the U.S. and Israel, which put them in 28th place.

U.S. Population

In the U.S., there were 35 million people 65 or older, as of the 2000 census. This was a 12% increase over 1990. It is estimated that by 2040, the proportion of elderly will peak at 20.7% of the total U.S. population. Those age 85 and over are expected to make up 4.8% of the population by then.

While 14.1% of whites are 65 years or over, only 7.9% of African Americans fall into that group. The median age of whites (37.3) is significantly higher than that for blacks (29.5) or Hispanics (25.8).

In 2000, there were approximately 20.6 million women 65 or older, compared with 14.4 million men, or 70 men per 100 women. That ratio keeps dropping at higher-aged groups among the elderly.

Breakdown of Population 65+ by Age, 1990, 2000

Source: Bureau of the Census, U.S. Dept. of Commerce

	1990		2000		% of U.S. total		% change,
Age	Number	Percent	Number	Percent	1990	2000	1990 to 2000
65 years and over	**31,241,831**	**100.0**	**34,991,753**	**100.0**	**12.6**	**12.4**	**12.0**
65-74 years	18,106,558	58.0	18,390,986	52.6	7.3	6.5	1.6
65-69 years	10,111,735	32.4	9,533,545	27.2	4.1	3.4	–5.7
70-74 years	7,994,823	25.6	8,857,441	25.3	3.2	3.1	10.8
75-84 years	10,055,108	32.2	12,361,180	35.3	4.0	4.4	22.9
75-79 years	6,121,369	19.6	7,415,813	21.2	2.5	2.6	21.1
80-94 years	3,933,739	12.6	4,945,367	14.1	1.6	1.8	25.7
85-95 years	2,829,728	9.1	3,902,349	11.2	1.1	1.4	37.9
85 to 89 years	2,060,247	6.6	2,789,818	8.0	0.8	1.0	35.4
90-94 years	769,481	2.5	1,112,531	3.2	0.3	0.4	44.6
95 years and over	250,437	0.8	337,238	1.0	0.1	0.1	34.7

Number of Males per 100 Females, by Age, 2000

Source: Bureau of the Census, U.S. Dept. of Commerce

Age	Ratio
All Ages	96.3
Under 5	104.8
Under 18	105.2
18-64	98.9
65+	70.0
65-74	82.3
75-84	65.2
85+	40.7

States with the Highest Proportion of Elderly[1]

Source: Administration on Aging, U.S. Dept. of Health and Human Services; Bureau of the Census, U.S. Dept. of Commerce

	Total pop. 65+	% 65+		Total pop. 65+	% 65+		Total pop. 65+	% 65+
Florida	2,848,438	17.4	North Dakota	93,756	14.8	South Dakota	107,805	14.2
Pennsylvania	1,908,159	15.5	Maine	184,857	14.4	Arkansas	374,035	13.9
West Virginia	275,556	15.3	Rhode Island	152,289	14.4	Connecticut	470,472	13.7
Iowa	432,944	14.8						

(1) As of July 2001 (estimated).

U.S. Elderly Population by Age, 2000-2040

Source: Administration on Aging, U.S. Dept. of Health and Human Services; Bureau of the Census, U.S. Dept. of Commerce

Census year	65-74 years Number in thousands	65-74 years % of total pop.	75-84 years Number in thousands	75-84 years %	85+ years Number in thousands	85+ years %	65 and over Number in thousands	65 and over %	Total, all ages
2000	18,391	6.5	12,361	4.4	4,240	1.5	34,992	12.4	281,422
2020	30,910	9.5	15,480	4.7	6,959	2.1	53,348	16.4	325,942
2040	33,968	9.1	29,206	7.9	13,840	3.7	77,014	20.7	371,505

Note: Data are July 1 projections and are Middle Series (middle fertility, mortality, and immigration assumptions).

Social Security Contributors vs. Beneficiaries, 1950-2030

Source: Social Security Administration.

The ratio of covered workers to those drawing Social Security benefits has decreased sharply since 1950, and is projected to decrease further in the 21st century. By 2030 there will only be 2 workers for every beneficiary. (Asterisks indicate projected values.)

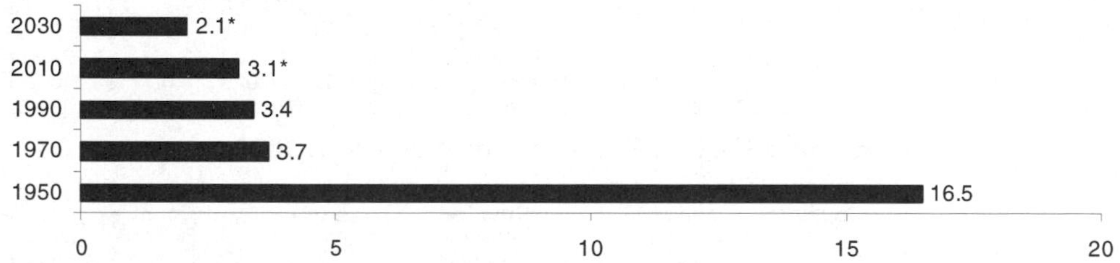

U.S. Vital Statistics

The 65-year-old woman in the U.S., as of 2000, could expect to live another 19.2 years; a man the same age, 16.3 years. (For life expectancy at various ages, see Vital Statistics chapter.)

In 2000, there were 3.9 million multigenerational families in the U.S., defined as families where grandparents lived with 2 or more generations of descendants. However, many older Americans live alone. As of 2000, 39.6% of U.S. women 65 or older, but only 17.0% of men those ages, lived alone. For those 75 or older, the figure was 40.4% for women, 21.4% for men. As of 1999, 18.3% of Americans 85 or older lived in a nursing home. (The figure was 11.7% for men and 21.1% for women.)

Marital Status, U.S. Population 60+, 2000

Source: Bureau of the Census, U.S. Dept. of Commerce

(in thousands)

Marital status and sex	Total 60-85+ years NUMBER	Total 60-85+ years %	60-64 years NUMBER	60-64 years %	65-74 years NUMBER	65-74 years %	75-84 years NUMBER	75-84 years %	85+ years NUMBER	85+ years %
BOTH SEXES										
Married, spouse present	25,202	58.4	7,375	70.1	11,327	63.6	5,699	48.8	801	25.5
Married, spouse absent[1]	630	1.5	146	1.4	248	1.4	169	1.4	67	2.1
Widowed	11,518	26.7	1,034	9.8	3,722	20.9	4,704	40.3	2,058	65.5
Divorced	3,481	8.0	1,287	12.2	1,530	8.6	571	4.9	93	2.9
Separated	544	1.3	183	1.7	257	1.4	91	0.8	13	0.4
Never married	1,764	4.1	494	4.7	711	4.0	451	3.9	108	3.4
Male totals	18,918	100.0	5,032	100.0	8,049	100.0	4,796	100.0	1,041	100.0
Married, spouse present	13,980	73.9	3,896	77.4	6,170	76.7	3,367	70.2	547	52.6
Married, spouse absent[1]	269	1.4	73	1.4	100	1.2	71	1.5	25	2.4
Widowed	2,165	11.4	171	3.4	667	8.3	936	19.5	391	37.5
Divorced	1,398	7.4	549	10.9	624	7.8	195	4.1	30	2.8
Separated	249	1.3	78	1.6	139	1.7	25	0.5	7	0.7
Never married	855	4.5	265	5.3	348	4.3	201	4.2	41	3.9
Female totals	24,222	100.0	5,487	100.0	9,747	100.0	6,889	100.0	2,099	100.0
Married, spouse present	11,221	46.3	3,479	63.4	5,156	52.9	2,332	33.9	254	12.1
Married, spouse absent[1]	362	1.5	74	1.3	148	1.5	98	1.4	42	2.0
Widowed	9,353	38.6	863	15.7	3,055	31.3	3,768	54.7	1,667	79.4
Divorced	2,082	8.6	738	13.5	906	9.3	375	5.4	63	3.0
Separated	295	1.2	105	1.9	119	1.2	66	1.0	5	0.3
Never married	909	3.8	229	4.2	363	3.7	250	3.6	67	3.2

(1) Excludes separated.

Education

Nearly 36% of all people in the U.S. age 65 and over graduated from high school and did not pursue further education, compared with 33% of all those 25 and over. Another 18% of the elderly had attended some college or received an associate degree (compared with 25% of all those age 25 and over), 10% received a bachelor's degree (compared with 17% of all those age 25 and over), and 6% received an advanced degree (compared with 9% of all those age 25 and over); about 31% did not graduate from high school.

Some elderly people in the U.S. are continuing their education, with about 80,000 Americans age 60 and over taking courses of some kind, according to Census Bureau figures from 2000.

Labor Force

Despite being of what many consider "retirement age," 13.1% of people in the U.S. age 65 and over are in the work force and 12.7% are employed. Older men (17.2%) are more likely to be employed than older women (9.4%).

Employment Status of U.S. Civilians by Age and Sex, 2001

Source: Bureau of Labor Statistics, U.S. Dept. of Labor; average for the year; remainder of population not in work force.

Age	% Working	% Unemployed
TOTAL		
16+	63.8	4.8
55-59	67.0	3.0
60-64	47.5	3.1
65+	12.7	3.0
65-69	24.0	3.2
70-74	13.7	2.8
75+	5.2	2.8

Age	% Working	% Unemployed
Men		
16+	70.8	4.8
55-59	74.8	3.2
60-64	54.5	3.6
65+	17.2	3.0
65-69	29.3	3.3
70-74	17.6	2.8
75+	8.2	2.7

Age	% Working	% Unemployed
Women		
16+	57.3	4.7
55-59	59.9	2.8
60-64	41.3	2.5
65+	9.4	2.9
65-69	19.4	3.0
70-74	10.5	2.8
75+	3.3	2.8

Income

The 2000 U.S. median household income for those 65 and over was $23,048. This contrasts with the overall U.S. median household income of $42,148, and of $44,992 for those age 55-64. For people 65 and over reporting income in 2000, about 34% received $9,999 or less, 42% received $10,000 to $24,999, and 16% received $25,000 to $49,999; another 8% received more than that. The major sources of income were Social Security (reported by 90%) and assets (reported by 59%).

Percent of Elderly with Income from Various Sources, 2000

Source: Social Security Administration

Source of Income	55-61 years	62-64 years	65 years and over: TOTAL	65-69	70-74	75-79	80-84	85+
Earnings	80%	64%	22%	44%	26%	14%	7%	4%
Wages and salaries	76	59	19	39	22	12	6	3
Self-employment	13	10	5	9	6	3	2	1
Retirement benefits	26	62	93	89	93	94	96	95
Social Security[1]	13	53	90	86	91	91	94	93
Other public pensions	7	12	15	15	15	14	15	13
Private pensions or annuities	10	20	29	28	31	31	28	22
Income from assets	61	60	59	60	59	60	62	55
Interest	57	57	57	57	57	57	59	52
Dividends	33	31	24	27	26	22	22	17
Rent or royalties	11	10	9	11	9	8	8	7
Veterans' benefits	2	2	4	4	4	6	6	3
Unemployment compensation	4	3	1	2	1	0	0	0
Workers' compensation	2	2	1	1	1	0	0	0
Public assistance	5	6	5	5	5	4	3	6
Supplemental Security Income	5	5	5	5	5	4	3	6
TOTAL POPULATION (in thousands)	**12,430**	**4,049**	**25,230**	**6,508**	**6,154**	**5,689**	**3,841**	**3,038**

(1) Social security includes retired-worker benefits, dependents' or survivors' benefits, disabiltiy benefits, and special age-72 benefits.

Poverty

In 2000, the poverty rate among those 65 and over was 10.1%, compared with 11.7% for all people in the U.S. The poverty rate was higher (11.2%), for those 75 and over. The rate was higher still for selected groups, including women 65 and over (12.4%), blacks 65 and over (21.9%), black men 65 and over (15.6%), and black women 65 and over (26.1%).

Health

While elderly Americans are healthier and living longer than in the past, they are still more likely than younger people to suffer from chronic conditions and from disabilities. Almost all older Americans have health insurance coverage of some type; a sizeable portion, however, are protected only by Medicare, which does not cover all costs and as of Oct. 2002 excluded the cost of prescription drugs. 36% of the elderly did not have private health insurance as of 1999.

Selected Chronic Conditions, per 1,000 Americans, by Sex and Age, 1995

Source: National Center for Health Statistics, U.S. Dept. of Health and Human Services

	MALE					FEMALE				
			65 years +					65 years +		
Type of chronic condition	Under 45 years	45–64 years	Total	65-74 years	75 years and over	Under 45 years	45–64 years	Total	65-74 years	75 years and over
Arthritis	22.4	176.7	404.7	385.5	437.0	36.0	285.4	550.2	498.2	616.1
Cataracts	1.8	16.8	125.1	72.1	214.0	1.1	21.6	182.8	132.1	247.0
Hearing impairment	41.4	203.6	366.8	332.8	423.5	26.3	89.7	224.5	159.0	307.3
Deformity or orthopedic impairment	90.0	186.6	165.9	167.1	163.9	101.3	165.2	186.8	168.0	210.5
Back problems	42.4	110.3	77.8	69.9	91.0	68.8	102.6	109.1	96.9	124.5
Ulcer	10.4	29.9	19.2	19.9	17.9	12.0	27.7	30.3	38.7	19.6
Diabetes	6.2	62.1	123.6	131.4	110.6	9.7	65.4	128.4	134.3	121.1
Anemia	3.7	5.1	15.5	15.2	16.1	25.0	31.6	23.9	9.9	41.8
Prostate disease	1.9	34.9	118.0	125.0	106.1	—	—	—	—	—
Disease of female genital organs	—	—	—	—	—	39.7	54.5	19.9	25.9	12.1
Heart disease	24.0	143.1	362.4	316.3	439.4	34.0	100.0	268.5	229.3	318.0
High blood pressure	34.0	233.2	349.3	352.0	344.5	30.3	212.9	442.1	423.8	465.3
Hardening of the arteries	0.5	12.8	44.7	31.5	67.0	.3	6.1	38.6	26.6	53.7
Varicose veins (lower extremities)	4.1	17.1	44.7	46.9	41.1	23.3	73.4	107.5	101.6	115.0

— = not applicable

Percent of Persons Age 65 and Over with Disabilities

Source: Administration on Aging, U.S. Dept. of Health and Human Services; as of 1997

Age	With any disability	With severe disability	Need assistance
65-69 years	44.9	30.7	8.1
70-74 years	46.6	28.3	10.5
75-79 years	57.7	38.0	16.9
80+ years	73.6	57.6	34.9

Deaths and Death Rates for Leading Causes, for Americans 65+, 2000[1]

Source: National Center for Health Statistics, U.S. Dept. of Health and Human Services

Cause of death	Number	Rate
ALL CAUSES	**1,805,187**	**5,190.8**
Heart disease	595,440	1,712.2
Cancer	392,082	1,127.4
Cerebrovascular disease	146,725	421.9
Chronic lower respiratory diseases	107,888	310.2
Influenza and pneumonia	60,261	173.3
Diabetes	52,102	149.8
Alzheimer's disease	48,492	139.4
Kidney disease	31,588	90.8
Accidents	31,332	90.1
Motor vehicle accidents	7,165	20.6
All other accidents	24,167	69.5
Blood poisoning	25,143	72.3

(1) Preliminary data; rates are per 100,000 people 65 and older.

Leisure Activities

According to a survey by the American Association of Retired Persons, 3 out of 4 people in the U.S. age 50-79 consider themselves to be in good health and 6 out of 10 say they are physically active on a regular basis, with walking the most popular form of exercise. Four out of 5 report that they frequently spend time with family, while 3 out of 10 report that they make love frequently. According to Census Bureau surveys, exercise programs and home improvement are among the most common leisure activities for all ages.

Participation in Various Leisure Activities, by Sex and Age, 1997

Source: Bureau of the Census, U.S. Dept. of Commerce
(in percent, except where indicated)

	ATTENDANCE AT...			PARTICIPATION IN...					ACTIVITIES								
	Movies	Sports events	Amusement park	Exercise program	Playing sports	Charity work	Home improvement /repair	Computer hobbies	Playing classical music	Modern dancing[1]	Drawing	Pottery Work[2]	Weaving	Photography[3]	Creative writing	Buying art work	Singing in groups
ALL AGES	66%	41%	57%	76%	45%	43%	66%	40%	1%	13%	16%	15%	28%	17%	12%	35%	10%
Sex																	
Male	66	49	58	75	56	40	71	44	9	13	15	16	5	16	10	36	9
Female	65	34	57	77	35	46	61	37	13	12	17	14	49	18	14	34	12
Age																	
45-54	65	42	53	77	40	46	75	40	15	11	13	18	29	18	10	37	13
55-64	46	33	40	69	19	44	71	23	9	8	9	10	29	10	5	31	11
65-74	38	21	29	65	23	40	55	11	6	14	7	10	32	10	5	23	10
75+	28	16	18	56	13	40	44	7	6	9	4	3	28	5	6	8	7

(1) Dancing other than ballet (e.g. folk and tap). (2) Includes ceramics, jewelry, leatherwork, and metalwork. (3) Includes making movies or videos as an artistic activity.

Health-Related Activities Reported in Past 12 Months by Persons 50-79, 2002[1]

Source: American Association of Retired Persons

Activity	% TOTAL	GENDER % Men	GENDER % Women	AGE % 50-59	AGE % 60-69	AGE % 70-79
Had blood pressure checked	93	92	94	91	96	94
Discussed health issues with a doctor	82	80	84	77	86	86
Tried to control their weight	78	75	80	79	79	74
Had cholesterol checked	76	74	78	70	82	81
Tried to manage stress	73	65	79	77	71	66
Read books or articles on health	68	59	75	64	73	67
Ate more healthy foods than last year	62	52	70	66	60	56
Took a specifc action to prevent disease	59	55	63	56	64	60
Learned how to avoid accidents while driving	57	57	56	53	63	57
Had prostate or skin cancer screening	53	52	55	49	59	55
Changed what they ate to prevent disease	51	45	56	55	49	44
Started an exercise program	43	44	41	44	44	37
Made changes in their home to prevent falls and accidents	33	28	38	31	32	39
Used Internet for health information	29	28	29	41	24	11

(1) Percentages based on survey with 1,000 respondents—375 men, 625 women; 379 aged 50-59, 339 aged 60-69, 282 aged 70-79.

WORLD ALMANAC QUICK QUIZ

A 65-year-old American woman in 2000 has a life expectancy of what age?

(a) 72 (b) 77 (c) 84 (d) 89

For the answer look in this chapter, or see page 1008.

YEAR IN REVIEW

This section on events and highlights of the year contains the following features:

CHRONOLOGY OF EVENTS

Reported Month by Month, Oct. 11, 2001 to Oct. 15, 2002

OCTOBER 11-31, 2001

National

Three More Die of Anthrax, As Concern Over Terrorism Continues—On **Oct. 15** a letter from Trenton, NJ, opened at the U.S. Capitol by aides of Sen. Tom Daschle (D, SD), the Senate majority leader, was found to be contaminated with anthrax. Preliminary test results 2 days later showed that over 30 people who worked on Capitol Hill had been exposed to anthrax spores. All 6 Senate and House office buildings were closed for screening. A number of Washington, DC, postal workers also fell ill from anthrax, and on **Oct. 22**, 2 of them died.

These deaths followed by about 2 weeks the nation's first known anthrax death, in Boca Raton, FL, on **Oct. 5**. Robert Stevens, a photo editor for American Media Inc., publisher of *The National Enquirer* and other tabloids, had fallen ill after opening an anthrax-contaminated letter sent to his office. Federal officials acknowledged **Oct. 24** that they had underestimated the threat to postal workers just from proximity to unopened mail at processing centers. On **Oct. 26** anthrax spores were also found in the Washington, DC, area in mail centers serving the CIA, Supreme Court, and Walter Reed Medical Center. Officials theorized that the Daschle letter alone was probably not responsible for all cases in the capital.

On **Oct. 31**, a New York City hospital worker died of anthrax; hers was the 4th anthrax death, all from pulmonary, or inhalation, anthrax, the more severe form, obtained by inhaling anthrax spores. By the end of the month, 5 others had been diagnosed with inhalation anthrax. Apparent sources included offices of ABC and CBS News and the *New York Post*.

New Anti-Terrorism Law Is Enacted—The U.S. House **Oct. 24** (356–66) and Senate **Oct. 25** (98–1) passed a federal antiterrorism bill designed to make authorizing of wiretaps easier and allow detention, without charges, of immigrations suspected of involvement in or knowledge of terrorist activities; it also contained provisions aimed at curbing money laundering in financing of terrorist operations. The final bill, signed by Pres. George W. Bush on **Oct. 26**, did not, however contain all the provisions sought by the administration; notably, it did not allow for unlimited detention of persons not charged with specific crimes

On **Oct. 29** Atty. Gen. John Ashcroft warned that new terrorist attacks against the U.S. or U.S. interests abroad were being planned and could take place within a week; he said the administration viewed this information as credible, and was sending a "terrorist threat advisory" to 18,000 state and local law enforcement agencies, but did not know anything about the nature or specific targets of the attacks. A similar warning had been issued **Oct. 11**; no attack followed after either announcement.

Largest Military Contract Ever Goes to Lockheed Martin—On **Oct. 26**, the Pentagon declared Lockheed Martin the winner of a contract purportedly worth over $200 billion to build a new generation of supersonic jet fighters—more than 3,000 in all—for the U.S. military over 20 years. The decision was a major blow to Boeing, already facing 30,000 layoffs in its commercial aircraft division.

International

UN and Sec. Gen. Annan Win Peace Prize—On **Oct. 12** it was announced that the United Nations and its secretary general, Kofi Annan, would receive the Nobel Peace Prize. In its citation, the Norwegian Nobel Committee said Annan, who had been unanimously reelected in June, "has been preeminent in bringing new life to the organization."

U.S. Responds to Terrorist Attacks—Sec. of State Colin Powell and Pres. Pervez Musharraf, in Pakistan, **Oct. 16**, pledged to seek a coalition government in Afghanistan that might include moderate Taliban leaders. The Afghan conflict entered a new phase **Oct. 19**, when U.S. commandos participated in an assault at Kandahar, site of a Taliban base. Their targets included an airfield and a headquarters compound of Mullah Muhammed Omar, the Taliban leader. Two U.S. soldiers were killed that day in Pakistan, when a helicopter involved in that mission crashed.

U.S. planes attacked front-line Taliban troops north of Kabul **Oct. 21**. Sec. of Defense Donald Rumsfeld said **Oct. 22** that air attacks on Taliban positions were in support of the anti-Taliban forces; these attacks continued, amid reports that coordination between U.S. forces and Northern Alliance fighters was intensifying. In some cases, however, bombs missed their apparent targets or were targeted incorrectly, as on **Oct. 26**, when U.S. planes bombed a Red Cross warehouse facility in Kabul.

On **Oct. 26**, Taliban officials announced they had captured and summarily executed Abdul Haq and 2 associates; the former guerrilla commander, a foe of the Taliban, had been a key figure in inducing defections from Taliban ranks. The same day, a Czech government official said Mohammed Atta, a ringleader in the Sept. 11 attacks, had met in Prague with an Iraqi intelligence official 5 months beforehand.

Israeli-Palestinian Strife Continues—On **Oct. 17**, a gunman shot to death the Israeli tourism minister, Rehavam Zeevi, in a Jerusalem hotel. Zeevi had announced his resignation, effective that day, having charged that Prime Min. Ariel Sharon's stand against Palestinian violence was weakening. The Palestinian National Authority, **Oct. 18**, rejected Israeli demands to hand over those involved in the killing. Also on **Oct. 18**, a Palestinian militia leader and 2 others were killed by a car bomb; Israel did not directly claim responsibility, but alleged he had been responsible for 5 Israeli deaths. On **Oct. 19-20** Israeli tanks and troops invaded Palestinian-controlled territory in the West Bank and occupied Bethlehem and several other urban areas, in the largest military offensive since 1994; at least 35 Palestinians were killed over the next few days. Pres. Bush demanded that Israel withdraw immediately; Israel refused, saying Palestinians had not cracked down on militants.

Israeli troops **Oct. 24** attacked the Palestinian town of Beit Rima, killing at least 5 people and arresting at least 11, including 2 who Israelis said had helped kill Zeevi. On **Oct. 28**, Palestinians sprayed gunfire on a busy street in the Israeli city of Hadera, killing 4 women. That night, Israel, acceding to pressures from the U.S., withdrew its forces from Bethlehem and Beit Jala, but intensified its military presence in other West Bank towns. On **Oct. 31**, Israeli strikes in the West Bank killed 6 Palestinian militants.

4 Get Life in Prison in 1998 Embassy Bombings—Four men convicted in connection with the bombing of U.S. embassies in Kenya and Tanzania in 1998 were sentenced **Oct. 18** in Manhattan to life in prison without parole. The 4 had been convicted in May of conspiring with al-Qaeda leader Osama bin Laden to bomb the embassies, in which 224 people were killed and thousands injured.

Bush Meets World Leaders in Shanghai—Pres. Bush met with Pres. Jiang Zemin of China in Shanghai, **Oct. 19**. In their public statements they appeared to steer clear of potential matters of discord, including Taiwan and Bush's plan for an antimissile shield. Bush met with leaders of 21 nations at the Asia-Pacific Economic Cooperation forum in

Shanghai **Oct. 20**. He met with Russian Pres. Vladimir Putin in Shanghai **Oct. 21**.

Violence Erupts in Nigeria as Army Shoots Hundreds—In some of the worst violence since the end of military government in 1999, the Nigerian army attacked villages throughout the eastern state of Benue on **Oct. 22**. Many viewed the attacks as retaliation for the killings of 19 soldiers in the area earlier in the month. The state governor said a "conservative estimate" of the dead was around 500; officials in the capital claimed the soldiers had acted in self-defense.

IRA Says It Is Disarming—The Irish Republican Army said **Oct. 23** that, in order to prevent the collapse of the peace agreement in Northern Ireland, it would begin to give up its weapons. Sinn Fein, the political wing of the IRA, had urged **Oct. 22** that the weapons be surrendered. David Trimble, the Ulster Unionist leader, said **Oct. 23** that he believed his Protestant allies could now rejoin the home-rule government they had left days earlier. Britain **Oct. 24** began to reduce its military presence in Northern Ireland.

Terrorists Attack Christian Worshippers in Pakistan—On **Oct. 28**, in Bahawalpur, Pakistan, gunmen opened fire at a Sunday morning service by Protestants in a Catholic Church; 16 worshippers were killed.

General

Alpine Tunnel Blaze Kills 11—The St. Gotthard Tunnel, a key link between Italy and Northern Europe, was shut down **Oct. 24** when 2 trucks collided head-on deep inside the tunnel. Fire and smoke trapped motorists in 23 vehicles; 11 people were confirmed dead.

Diamondbacks and Yankees Advance—On **Oct. 21**, the Arizona Diamondbacks beat the Atlanta Braves, 3-2, to win the National League Championship Series, 4 games to 1, and advance to the World Series. Arizona outfielder Craig Counsell was named MVP. The New York Yankees advanced to the Series by winning the American League Championship Series, 4 games to 1, clinching the title with a 12-3 win over the Cleveland Indians **Oct. 22**. The ALCS MVP was New York pitcher Andy Pettitte.

San Jose Takes Soccer Crown; Tiznow Repeats as Breeders' Champ—The San Jose Earthquakes defeated the L.A. Galaxy in overtime, 2-1, to take the 2001 Major League Soccer Cup at Columbus (OH) Crew Stadium on **Oct. 21**.

At the World Thoroughbred Championships **Oct. 27** at Belmont Park, Tiznow became the first horse ever to repeat as champion of the Breeders' Cup Classic. Tiznow, the 2000 Horse of the Year, held off runner-up Sakhee by a nose.

NOVEMBER 2001

National

Microsoft, U.S. Reach Tentative Agreement—The Microsoft Corp. and the U.S. Justice Dept. worked out a tentative settlement **Nov. 2** of their antitrust controversy. In the latest phase of a fight that had raged in the courts for years, Microsoft agreed not to restrict makers of personal computers from installing software it did not make. The company also agreed to share technical information with rivals seeking to create products that would function with Microsoft's Windows program. Under the agreement, Microsoft could not retaliate against manufacturers who created competing software. On **Nov. 6**, 9 states and the District of Columbia said they would continue their antitrust suit against the company. Nine other states went along with the new agreement, which required court approval.

Unemployment at 5-Year High; Recession Declared—On **Nov. 2**, the Labor Dept. reported that unemployment in October had jumped to 5.4%, the highest in 5 years. The department also said that 415,000 nonfarm jobs had been lost in October, the highest for any month since 1980. On **Nov. 26** the National Bureau of Economic Research declared that the country had officially been in recession since March.

U.S. Seeks to Disrupt Financing of Terrorists—The Bush administration said **Nov. 2** that the assets of 22 groups on its list of terrorist organizations would be subject to seizure. Under an executive order, foreign banks that did not cooperate in the effort could face sanctions. The list of groups included names familiar from the Mideast struggle—Hezbollah, Hamas, Islamic Jihad, and the Popular Front for the Liberation of Palestine.

Addressing the UN General Assembly **Nov. 10** in New York City, Pres. George W. Bush said that every member country was a potential target of terrorists and that all had an obligation to cut off any financing of terrorism and share intelligence information. Bush said **Nov. 10** that a $1 billion U.S. aid package would go to Pakistan for its support in the current conflict. Bush, **Nov. 13,** signed an order that would allow special, closed-door military tribunals to try persons accused of engaging in terrorism.

In Spain **Nov. 18,** 8 men were charged with engaging in terrorism-related crimes. The U.S. sought the extradition of the men but ran into resistance from the Spanish government, which opposed the death penalty or the use of military tribunals to try suspected terrorists.

Democrats Pick up 2 Governorships; New York Elects GOP Mayor—Scattered elections on **Nov. 6** provided some gains for the Democrats, who took away 2 governorships from the Republicans. In New Jersey, Woodbridge Mayor James McGreevey (D) defeated former Jersey City Mayor Bret Schundler (R), 56% to 42%. In Virginia, Mark Warner, a venture capitalist, defeated his GOP opponent, former state Atty. Gen. Mark Earley.

Running as a Republican, billionaire businessman Michael Bloomberg won the mayoralty in heavily Democratic New York, to succeed another Republican, Rudolph Giuliani. Giuliani, whose popularity skyrocketed after the Sept. 11 terrorist attack, ultimately endorsed Bloomberg, who spent an estimated $40 million or more of his own money on the campaign.

Elsewhere, Democrats did well in mayoral races. Democrats reelected included Thomas Menino (Boston), Charles Luken (Cincinnati), and Tom Murphy (Pittsburgh). Newly elected Democrats included Shirley Clarke Franklin (Atlanta), Jane Campbell (Cleveland), and Kwame Kilpatrick (Detroit). In a runoff in Miami **Nov. 13,** Manny Diaz, a Cuban-American lawyer, defeated former Mayor Maurice Ferre, an independent. Diaz had represented Miami relatives of Elián González. On **Dec. 1**, Mayor Lee Brown (D) of Houston won a 52%–48% runoff battle against Orlando Sanchez (R).

Airliner Crashes in New York City, Killing 265—An American Airlines plane crashed in the New York City borough of Queens **Nov. 12,** just minutes after taking off from John F. Kennedy International Airport. All 260 aboard Flight 587, bound for Santo Domingo, in the Dominican Republic, were killed. The Airbus A-300 plunged into the neighborhood of Belle Harbor on the Rockaway Peninsula. About a dozen homes were destroyed, and 5 people were killed on the ground. No evidence pointed to foul play.

Congress Toughens Security Measures at Airports—On **Nov. 19,** Pres. Bush signed a bill that would change the way baggage was inspected at airports. The House **Nov. 1** had voted, 286–139, for a Democrat-sponsored bill that would increase federal oversight over security measures taken at airports; it differed from a version approved unanimously by the Senate on **Oct. 11**, which required in addition that the inspectors be federal employees. Under current law the airlines contracted the screening of luggage to private companies. Although Republican leaders, including Bush, opposed the creation of a federal security force, a Senate–House conference committee, **Nov. 15,** agreed, as part of the new changes, to federalizing workers to screen baggage, for at least 3 years.

Anthrax Mystery Deepens as 5th Victim Dies—The mystery of who was mailing lethal anthrax spores through the U.S. mail remained unsolved as a 5th fatality occurred on **Nov. 21** under seemingly inexplicable circumstances. The 5th person to die was Ottilie Lundgren, a 94-year-old widow who lived quietly in Oxford, CT, population 9,800, and seldom went far from home. Investigators found no trace of anthrax at her home or in 2 nearby postal facilities.

By **Nov. 1,** 4 of 10 suffering from pulmonary anthrax had died, and 6 nonfatal cases of cutaneous anthrax had been reported. In all, as of **Nov. 1,** 19 sites in the Washington, DC, area had tested positive for the anthrax bacteria. The Centers for Disease Control and Prevention said **Nov. 1** that 2 anthrax letters had been mailed about **Sept. 18** and one about **Oct. 9**. The first letters, according to the CDC, contained a brown granular substance, while the Oct. 9 letter contained a white powder that could more easily float through a person's nostrils into the lungs. James Caruso of the FBI told a Senate subcommittee **Nov. 6** that little headway had been made in solving the anthrax mystery. FBI scientists confirmed **Nov. 19** that a letter sent to Sen. Patrick Leahy (D, VT) contained anthrax. It was discovered on **Nov. 16** in a batch of unopened mail sent to the Capitol. It appeared to bear the same handwriting found on an anthrax-laced letter postmarked the same day (**Oct. 9**) to Sen. Tom Daschle (D, SD).

Persons Held After Terrorist Attacks Top 1,200—As of late November, more than 1,200 individuals had been detained in the U.S. following the September terrorist attacks, and about 650 were still in custody. Atty. Gen. John Ashcroft announced **Nov. 27** that those still held were primarily of Middle Eastern descent and in most cases were being detained on immigration violations, including overstaying their visas. Ashcroft, under pressure from civil libertarians, released the identities of 93 of the 104 persons charged with federal crimes. He also released nationalities and charges against 548 others, but not the names. Ashcroft claimed that divulging a complete list of names would aid al-Qaeda's "effort to kill Americans." Senior Justice Dept. officials conceded on **Nov. 29** that only a handful of those detained were suspected of links to al-Qaeda.

International

Off Center Stage, Israeli–Palestinian Fight Goes On—With international attention focused elsewhere, Israeli-Palestinian violence added to the death toll on both sides. Prime Min. Tony Blair met separately **Nov. 1** with Prime Min. Ariel Sharon of Israel and Palestinian leader Yasir Arafat, urging Sharon to withdraw troops from Palestinian cities. The Israelis pulled out of 2 Palestinian cities **Nov. 5** and **7**. Sharon said **Nov. 5** that the Israelis had killed 79 Palestinians and arrested 85 during their occupation. Firing missiles at a van from the air, the Israelis, **Nov. 23,** killed Mahmoud Abu Hanoud, a top leader of Hamas whom the Israelis said had planned 1997 suicide bombings that had killed 21.

U.S. Planes, Rebel Fighters Gain in Afghanistan—The Islamic fundamentalist Taliban regime in Afghanistan, which had sheltered terrorist mastermind Osama bin Laden and his al-Qaeda organization, collapsed under the pressure of U.S. bombs and attacks by the rebel army of the Northern Alliance. Bin Laden's whereabouts remained unknown. From a tape given to it, the Qatar-based al-Jazeera television network played a message from Bin Laden **Nov. 3** in which he called the U.S.-led attack a war against Islam.

After nearly a month of aerial pounding, U.S. planes **Nov. 4** began dropping so-called Daisy Cutter bombs on Taliban positions; the fuel-air explosion bombs could kill everything within hundreds of yards. The Pentagon **Nov. 5** reported a step-up in the bombing of caves and tunnels used by the Taliban and al-Qaeda. Defense Sec. Donald Rumsfeld said **Nov. 6** that 31 U.S. commandos had been injured in an **Oct. 19** raid in southern Afghanistan. Via satellite, **Nov. 6,** Pres. George W. Bush spoke to a 17-nation antiterrorist summit in Warsaw, Poland; for the first time he said bin Laden was trying to get chemical, biological, and nuclear weapons. At the White House, Bush met with Pres. Jacques Chirac of France (**Nov. 6**) and Prime Min. Tony Blair of Britain (**Nov. 7**). Since the terrorist attacks in September, Blair had met with 54 world leaders in his effort to rally the international coalition.

The Northern Alliance, which had previously held less than 10% of Afghanistan, reported **Nov. 6** and **7** capturing several districts on the road to Mazar-e Sharif, a key crossroads. That city fell to the rebels **Nov. 9.** Many Taliban soldiers joined the rebels. The Alliance reported the capture of other northern cities **Nov. 10** and **11**. On **Nov. 11**, Taliban leader Mullah Muhammad Omar reportedly ordered his forces to pull out of the capital, Kabul, and move south toward the Taliban heartland. The withdrawal was underway **Nov. 12**. Northern Alliance forces rolled into Kabul **Nov. 13**, to be greeted enthusiastically by the population, which had been subjected to severe restrictions under Taliban rule.

Eight foreign aid workers, including 2 American women, were rescued from southern Afghanistan by U.S. military helicopters **Nov. 14**, 3 months after the Taliban regime had charged them with preaching Christianity. Negotiations with the Taliban reportedly played a role in their release.

American officials said **Nov. 15** that U.S. commandos were on the ground in southern Afghanistan, carrying out covert operations behind Taliban lines and searching for al Qaeda leaders. By **Nov. 15** it appeared that 80% of Afghanistan was in control of the Alliance and other anti-Taliban forces. On **Nov. 15**, more than 150 American and British special-force troops landed north of Kabul.

U.S. officials said **Nov. 16** that a bomb had killed Muhammad Atef, one of bin Laden's oldest and closest strategists, who was thought to have helped plan the September terrorist attacks. Under direct U.S. pressure, Alliance leaders agreed **Nov. 19** to support establishment of a broad-based government in the capital. Four journalists were seized and shot to death **Nov. 19** by armed gunmen as they traveled between Kabul and Jalalabad.

Although the Taliban trapped in Kunduz agreed to surrender the city, fierce fighting broke out **Nov. 22** between them and Alliance troops. Within the city the defenders were feuding among themselves, amid reports that foreign supporters of the Taliban were killing Afghan Taliban seeking to surrender or change sides. On **Nov. 24**, the surrender of the Taliban was well underway at Kunduz; 300 Afghans were greeted as friends as they gave up, but 400 foreigners were detained in a fort. Alliance commanders said **Nov. 25** that they had captured the northern city of Kunduz and that some Taliban fighters had escaped and fled west. At a prison outside Mazar-e Sharif, hundreds of Taliban captives revolted **Nov. 25**, overpowered their guards, and put up a fierce fight. U.S. planes bombed the prison. The Pentagon said **Nov. 26** that 5 Americans had been injured near the prison when a bomb exploded close to them; one CIA operative, Johnny Michael ("Mike") Spann, was killed. Alliance soldiers claimed **Nov. 27** that the revolt had been crushed, with most of the 400 prisoners killed.

Hundreds of U.S. Marines **Nov. 25** landed near Kandahar, the Taliban political base, and secured an airfield. A large Taliban military force occupied the city. The Marines directed air attacks on an armored column. U.S. planes **Nov. 27** bombed a Taliban compound southeast of Kandahar that Sec. of Defense Rumsfeld said was "clearly a leadership area."

In Bonn, Germany, **Nov. 27**, representatives of 4 Afghan factions began talks on establishing an interim government.

Nicaraguan Leftist Fails in Comeback Bid—Former Pres. Daniel Ortega of Nicaragua failed in his bid **Nov. 5** to reclaim the presidency. He lost, 54% to 45%, to Enrique Bolanos, a wealthy businessman once jailed by Ortega's Sandinista government who had served as vice president from 1997 to 2000. Ortega had run a Marxist-oriented government from 1979 to 1990.

Australian Prime Minister Wins Another Term—The ruling Liberal Party of Australian Prime Min. John Howard retained power in parliamentary elections **Nov. 10**. The Liberals (a conservative party) and their junior partner, the National Party, prevailed over the Labor Party led by Kim Beazley. In his bid for a 3rd term, Howard had supported the U.S. fight against terrorism and strongly opposed illegal immigration.

Bush, Putin Agree to Reduce Nuclear Stockpiles—Pres. Bush and Pres. Vladimir Putin of Russia, meeting in Washington, DC, **Nov. 13**, both promised to reduce their stockpiles of nuclear warheads by about two-thirds. Putin said he favored putting this agreement in a treaty; Bush preferred an informal approach. Putin declined to agree to changes in the 1972 Antiballistic Missile Treaty that would allow the U.S. to proceed with a missile defense system. On **Nov. 14-15**, Putin visited the Bushes in Texas.

General

Arizona Defeats Yankees in 7-Game World Series—The Arizona Diamondbacks, in only their 4th season as a National League expansion team, prevailed over the New

York Yankees in a thrilling 7-game world series. Arizona won 3 games easily (9–1, 4–0, and 15-2) and the Yankees squeezed out 3 wins (2–1, 4–3, 3–2). Because of regular-season games postponed after the terrorist attacks, the series ran later than usual. The final game was in Phoenix **Nov. 4**. Arizona came to bat in the last of the 9th, down 2-1. Yankee ace reliever Mariano Rivera was on the mound. Mark Grace singled to center. On a bunt, Rivera attempted to get out the lead runner but threw the ball away. On another bunt, the lead runner was thrown out at 3rd. Tony Womack doubled to score Midre Cummings, a pinch runner. Rivera hit the next batter, loading the bases. Luis Gonzalez hit a bloop single to win the game. Diamondback starting pitchers Randy Johnson and Curt Schilling were named co-MVPs.

Harry Potter Hits Theaters—The much-anticipated movie version of *Harry Potter and the Sorcerer's Stone*, the first book in J.K. Rowling's series, opened **Nov. 16** on one quarter of North American movie screens. It grossed $90.3 mil. in its first 3 days, breaking the record set by *The Lost World: Jurassic Park* in 1997, and soon toppled records for 5-day grosses, the shortest trip to $150 mil. and the most lucrative week ever at the box office.

Company Says It Created Human Embryo—A Massachusetts biotechnology company announced **Nov. 25** that it had created the first-ever human embryos by cloning. Its objective was to produce stem cells that could serve as replacement tissue to combat disease. Scientists at Advanced Cell Technology in Worcester said that the embryos had died quickly. Pres. Bush **Nov. 26** said he considered the work on human cloning to be immoral.

DECEMBER 2001

National

Enron Largest Firm Ever to File for Bankruptcy—Houston-based Enron, the 7th-largest U.S. corporation, filed for bankruptcy **Dec. 2.** The energy-trading company, whose stock, now nearly worthless, once traded for $90 a share, specialized in the buying and selling of natural gas and electricity. With assets of $50 billion, it was the largest company ever to seek bankruptcy protection. Dynegy, another Houston company, had agreed to buy Enron, then backed out. Enron sued Dynegy, saying that changing its mind damaged Enron. Enron also sought a court order preventing Dynegy from taking possession of a natural gas pipeline that Dynegy claimed it owned in return for a $1.5 billion investment in Enron. Dynegy said it pulled out of the buyout because of Enron's abrupt decline and its misrepresentations.

Nearly a Million Jobs Lost in 3 Months—The Labor Dept. reported **Dec. 7** that 300,000 jobs had been lost in November, bringing the 3-month total to nearly 1 million. The unemployment rate in November rose to 5.7% from 5.4% in October. In 13 months, the rate had climbed from 3.9%, a 30-year low, to its highest in 6 years.

U.S. Charges French Citizen in Sept. 11 Plot—The U.S. government **Dec. 11** filed its first charges in connection with the **Sept. 11** terrorist attacks. In an indictment, the government asserted that Zacarias Moussaoui, a French citizen of Moroccan descent, had conspired with others to carry out the assault. Moussaoui had been arrested in Minnesota in August on immigration charges after raising suspicion while training at a flying school. Alleged terrorist mastermind Osama bin Laden, the 19 hijackers killed **Sept. 11**, and 3 others were named unindicted co-conspirators.

Officials believed he had been intended to be the 5th hijacker on the plane that crashed **Sept. 11** near Pittsburgh with 4 terrorists aboard.

House Majority Leader Announces Retirement—Rep. Dick Armey (R, TX), the majority leader of the U.S. House, announced **Dec. 12** that he would not seek reelection in 2002.

U.S. Pulls Out of Antiballistic Missile Treaty—Pres. Bush announced **Dec. 13** that the U.S. was withdrawing from the 1972 Antiballistic Missile Treaty which he called a Cold War relic. The withdrawal opened the way for the Defense Dept. to test and deploy a missile-defense system without restraints. Pres. Vladimir Putin, who had objected to the planned U.S. withdrawal but conferred extensively with Bush prior to the final decision, issued a mild statement **Dec. 13**, calling the U.S. decision "erroneous."

Airline Passengers Prevent Shoe Bomb Attempt—A man aboard an American Airlines jetliner bound for Miami, FL, from Paris, tried to light a match and detonate powerful explosives contained in his sneakers, **Dec. 22**. Flight attendants and passengers overpowered the man, later identified as Richard Reid, a 28-year-old unemployed British citizen. It was confirmed **Dec. 26** that Reid had attended the same London mosque as Zacarias Moussaoui, a defendant charged with conspiracy in the Sept. 11 terrorist attacks.

Bush Grants Trade Status to China—Pres. Bush, **Dec. 28**, formally granted permanent normal trade status to China, as of Jan. 1, 2002, changing a 20-year policy of using access to U.S. markets as an annual enticement to China to expand freedoms. Congress had previously approved such a move, over objections from many human rights activists; China in return had pledged to open up markets more fully to U.S. goods.

U.S. Economy at a Glance: Calendar Year 2001	
Unemployment rate	4.8%
Consumer prices (change over 2000)	+1.6%
Producer prices (change over 2000)	−1.8%
Trade deficit	$346.3 bil.
Dow Jones high (May 21)	11,337.92
Dow Jones low (Sept. 21)	8,235.81
GDP (change over 2000)	+1.2%

International

Search for Bin Laden Continues—As the U.S. and its allies continued to crush the remnants of the Taliban regime in Afghanistan, the whereabouts of alleged terrorist mastermind Osama bin Laden remained a mystery. One of the Taliban's last stands was in Kandahar, their religious capital, which US B-52s pounded **Dec. 1–2** in some of the heaviest attacks of the war. U.S. Marines, joined by forces from Britain and Australia, began to move toward Kandahar **Dec. 4**.

Three American soldiers were killed north of Kandahar **Dec. 5** when an errant bomb from a B-52 struck their position. Five Afghan soldiers were killed, and 20 Americans and 18 Afghans were injured. The Americans were advising troops led by Hamid Karzai, newly chosen head of the interim Afghan government, who was slightly injured.

Taliban leader Mullah Muhammad Omar **Dec. 6** yielded power in Kandahar to a local tribal chief. Fighting continued in the mountainous eastern region of Tora Bora, where bin Laden was thought to be holed up in a cave. Anti-Taliban fighters occupied Kandahar **Dec. 7**, but Omar was not found. Some Taliban fighters continued to resist for awhile, and 2 occupying Pashtun factions fought between themselves.

On **Dec. 13**, the U.S. government released a tape of bin Laden and others believed to have been made **Nov. 9** in Kandahar. On the hour-long tape, bin Laden expressed surprise and pleasure at the number of "enemy" killed in the Sept. 11 attack. He said of the terrorists, "We asked each of them to go to America," but added that they did not have details of the attack until they arrived at the airports. The administration **Dec. 14** began wide international distribution of the tape, offering it as proof of bin Laden's complicity in the terrorist attack and disregard for human life. Many Muslims abroad claimed the tape was a fabrication.

By **Dec. 15**, U.S. and British commandos and local Afghan fighters believed they had the last remnants of bin Laden's al-Qaeda force trapped in mountains near the Pakistan border, with Pakistani patrols blocking attempts to flee across the border. Sec. of State Colin Powell said **Dec. 16**, "We've destroyed al-Qaeda in Afghanistan." However, by **Dec. 17**, it appeared that hundreds of bin Laden's men were escaping through the mountains into Pakistan. U.S. officials said they had lost track of bin Laden. Meanwhile, the U.S. Embassy building reopened in Kabul, the Afghan capital, **Dec. 17** for the first time since 1989.

On **Dec. 20**, an advance contingent of 53 British Royal Marines landed near Kabul. The same day, the UN Security Council approved placing a British-led multinational security force in Afghanistan. The Arab TV network al-Jazeera played a tape of bin Laden **Dec. 27** thought to have been made around **Dec. 1**; bin Laden appeared gaunt and never moved his left hand, though he is left-handed. He said he wanted to destroy the U.S. economy.

Arafat Pressured to Crack Down on Terrorists— Prime Min. Ariel Sharon of Israel and Pres. George W. Bush were among those demanding that Palestinian leader Yasir Arafat do more to stop Palestinians from committing terrorist acts. On **Dec. 1**, 2 suicide bombers killed themselves and 10 other people in Jerusalem. Another bomber in Haifa **Dec. 2** killed himself and 15 others in an explosion on a bus. Arafat's lieutenants said the same day that they would move against Hamas and Islamic Jihad, 2 militant organizations, and began arresting suspects. The Palestinian Authority declared a state of emergency in the West Bank and Gaza and suspended due process.

Israel retaliated **Dec. 3**, striking into the West Bank with planes, helicopter gunships, tanks, and bulldozers. In the Gaza Strip, Arafat's helicopters were destroyed. In Ramallah, **Dec. 4,** Israeli soldiers moved to within 200 yards of Arafat's headquarters, into which helicopters fired 3 missiles. Sheik Ahmad Yassin, founder and spiritual leader of Hamas, which had claimed responsibility for the latest Palestinian attacks, was put under house arrest by the Palestinian authority, **Dec. 5**. Killings continued almost daily. The Israelis, **Dec. 10**, killed 2 boys, 13 and 2, during an attempt in Hebron to kill a leader of Islamic Jihad. On **Dec. 12**, members of Hamas bombed a bus in the West Bank and shot at survivors who sought to flee; 10 were killed. On **Dec. 13** the Israeli government decided to sever all communications with Arafat; the same day the Palestinian Authority suspended its crackdown on terrorists, saying the pounding by the Israeli military made police pursuit of the extremists impossible. On Palestinian TV **Dec. 16**, Arafat appealed for an end to all armed attacks on Israelis, while also charging that Sharon was waging a "brutal war" against the people in Gaza and the West Bank.

American Fighting for Taliban Is Captured—John Walker Lindh, 20, a U.S. citizen who had converted to a radical brand of Islam and was fighting with the Taliban, was captured by U.S. forces in Afghanistan, it was reported **Dec. 2**. He was among those who survived a prison revolt in Mazar-e Sharif. Lindh, from San Anselmo, CA, had studied at an Islamic school in Yemen, then traveled to Pakistan before joining the Taliban and receiving military training.

Afghan Factions Agree on Interim Government—After 9 days of intense negotiations in Bonn, Germany, representatives of 4 Afghan factions agreed **Dec. 5** on the makeup of an interim government, with most posts going to the Northern Alliance. Hamid Karzai, wounded by a stray B-52 bomb on the day he was chosen, was a Pashtun tribal leader and relative of Zahir Shah, Afghanistan's exiled king. The government was installed **Dec. 22.**

14 Killed as Gunmen Attack Indian Parliament—A wild gunfight and flurry of explosions ended with 14 dead **Dec. 13** outside the Parliament building in New Delhi, capital of India. Five men had driven onto the grounds and opened fire with rifles, plastic explosives, and grenades; police and security forces fired back, shooting 4 attackers dead. The 5th, who had explosives on his body, was blown up. No group claimed responsibility for the attack. Indian police said **Dec. 16** that they had arrested 4 suspects, who named Pakistan-based terrorist groups as responsible. On **Dec. 20**, Pres. Bush moved to freeze the assets of one of these groups, Lashkar-e-Taiba, which has been linked to al-Qaeda. As tensions between India and Pakistan grew, both began mobilizing troops along their border. The 2 sides exchanged artillery fire **Dec. 25**. India moved short-range ballistic missiles to the border, defense officials said **Dec. 27**.

Argentine President Resigns Amid Chaos—Confronted with mass protest demonstrations, Pres. Fernando de la Rua of Argentina resigned **Dec. 20**, but the chaos gripping the country did not relax, with unemployment at 18% and a default on foreign debt a possibility. De la Rua, **Dec. 1**, had limited cash withdrawals from banks to $250 a week. After the International Monetary Fund **Dec. 5** froze payment of a $1.3 billion loan installment, the government next day had seized $3.2 billion in private pension funds to pay expenses. On **Dec. 17** the government had announced budget cuts to reassure the IMF, which was demanding austerity. Ramon Puerta, head of the senate, automatically became acting president on **Dec. 20.** Adolfo Rodriguez Saa was chosen interim president Dec. 23; he declared default on the $132 billion foreign debt, then resigned **Dec. 30**, saying he was unable to govern. Puerta, again president, resigned the next day, leaving the presidency to the head of the lower house of Congress, Eduardo Camano. By then some 30 people had been killed during rioting in Buenos Aires and other cities

JANUARY 2002

National

Student Pilot, 15, Flies Plane into Tampa Building—A 15-year-old student pilot, flying alone, crashed a single-engine Cessna into the 28th floor of the Bank of America building in Tampa, FL, **Jan. 5**. The pilot, Charles Bishop, got into the plane at St. Petersburg–Clearwater International Airport without his instructor and took off. He was killed in the crash, but no one else was hurt.

Bush Signs Education Bill—Pres. George W. Bush **Jan. 8** signed into law a major education bill, fulfilling goals that he made central in his presidential campaign. The measure, signed at Hamilton High School, Hamilton, OH, mandated annual testing of students in grades 3 to 8, provided for tutors in poor schools, and emphasized early development of reading skills. In its final form the bill had received bipartisan support, but it did not include a voucher program for private schools, as Bush had wanted.

Ford to Cut 35,000 Employees, Car Models—The Ford Motor Co. announced **Jan. 11** that it was planning to lay off 35,000 employees, close 4 plants, and drop 4 models. The closing of 5 of 44 North American plants would occur within the next several years.

Enemy Fighters Flown to U.S. Base in Cuba—Taliban and al-Qaeda fighters captured in Afghanistan were flown to the U.S. Naval Base at Guantanamo Bay in Cuba, with the first 20 arriving **Jan. 11**. Defense Sec. Donald Rumsfeld called them "unlawful combatants" rather than prisoners of war. The captives, regarded as dangerous and fanatical, received food and medical attention but were closely guarded and kept in individual 8x8-foot chain link cages. International human rights organizations raised questions about their treatment and about the initial U.S. conclusion that the captives were not subject to the Geneva Convention and not POWs. Representatives of the International Committee of the Red Cross arrived **Jan. 17** to see the prisoners; the Red Cross subsequently said the U.S. might have violated the Geneva Convention by releasing photos showing prisoners kneeling and shackled.

The Pentagon **Jan. 23** suspended any further transfers from Afghanistan, as prisoner interrogations began. A U.S. congressional delegation, after visiting the prison **Jan. 25**, said treatment of detainees appeared humane. The Bush administration said **Feb. 7** that Geneva Convention rules would be applied to the Taliban captives but not to the al-Qaeda prisoners. None, however, would be classified as POWs.

American Accused of Conspiring with Terrorists— John Walker Lindh, the 20-year-old American seized with the Taliban near Mazar-e Sharif, Afghanistan, in December 2001, was charged **Jan. 15** with conspiring to kill U.S. citizens and abetting terrorist groups. Lindh was flown back to the U.S. **Jan. 23** and taken to a detention center in Alexandria, VA. He appeared in court **Jan. 24** to hear the charges against him, and saw his parents for the first time in 2 years. On Feb. 5 he was indicted by a federal grand jury; he later pleaded not guilty.

U.S. Seeks 5 Linked to a New Terrorist Plot—The U.S. Justice Dept. **Jan. 17** began an international manhunt for 5 suspected al-Qaeda members believed to be plotting a new suicide attack. Videotapes in which the men discussed their plans were found in the rubble of a compound in Afghanistan that had been occupied by an aide to Osama bin Laden. Their photographs were distributed throughout the world.

Airlines Begin to Inspect Checked Luggage—As mandated by Congress, U.S. airlines **Jan. 18** began to inspect every piece of luggage checked by passengers. The carriers would determine that the owner of a bag did in fact board the plane, but would not verify whether the owner boarded successive connecting flights. Use of sniffing dogs and expensive explosive-detection machines was being planned.

Kmart Files for Bankruptcy—Kmart, the nation's 3rd-largest discount retailer, filed for bankruptcy **Jan. 22**. The company had been in a cash squeeze and had disappointing holiday sales. Since August 2000, Kmart stock had declined in value from $13.16 to about 70 cents.

Congress Opens Enron Probe—Committees in both houses of Congress **Jan. 24** began public hearings into the bankruptcy of the Enron Corp. Savings of many employees who had bought company stock were wiped out when the stock plummeted from a high of $90 to less than $1 a share. It was reported that top Enron executives had sold more than $1 billion in stock near its peak.

Enron had contributed large sums to candidates in both parties, but mostly to Republicans, including Pres. Bush. The White House said **Jan. 10** that Enron CEO Kenneth Lay phoned 2 cabinet secretaries as the company plunged toward bankruptcy, but it was not clear whether he had sought help. In subsequent days other reports emerged of contacts between Enron and government officials. Arthur Andersen & Co., Enron's accounting firm, admitted **Jan. 10** that it had shredded Enron documents in September after the Securities and Exchange Commission announced an investigation into Enron. Andersen **Jan. 15** fired David Duncan, its partner in charge of the Enron account.

A House committee **Jan. 14** released portions of an August 2001 letter from Sherron Watkins, an Enron employee, to Lay warning him that because of improper accounting practices the company could "implode" in scandal. A former Enron executive, Maureen Castaneda, said **Jan. 21** that Enron employees were shredding documents as recently as the previous week. Pres. Bush said **Jan. 22** that his mother-in-law had lost 99% of an $8,000 investment in Enron. Lay resigned as Enron's CEO **Jan. 23**.

On **Jan. 24**, appearing before a House subcommittee, Duncan declined, on the ground of possible self-incrimination, to answer questions about shredding of documents. J. Clifford Baxter, a former Enron vice chairman who left the company in 2001 after warning about its questionable financial practices, was found shot to death in his automobile near Houston **Jan. 25**; police ruled his death a suicide.

Bush Focuses on Terrorism in State of the Union Address—Receiving a warm welcome for his first State of the Union address, delivered to Congress **Jan. 29**, Pres. Bush stressed that the U.S. "war against terror" was still only beginning, with tens of thousands of al-Qaeda-trained potential terrorists "spread throughout the world like ticking time bombs." He issued new warnings to Iran, Iraq, and North Korea, calling states that shield terrorists an "axis of evil." Taking a cautious outlook toward the economy, he said he would use the national unity forged by the Sept. 11 assault to focus on creating jobs for victims of recession and promoting national service.

International

12 European Countries Get a New Currency—The biggest currency change in world history got underway **Jan. 1** in 12 European countries. The 12, all members of the European Union, began to surrender their own currencies in favor of a common one, the euro. The changeover had been put in motion by the Maastricht (Netherlands) Treaty in 1991. The objective was to facilitate commerce, tourism, and financial dealings within the EU. Participating countries were Austria, Belgium, Finland, France, Germany, Greece, Ireland, Italy, Luxembourg, the Netherlands, Portugal, and Spain. Historically important currencies such as the franc, mark, drachma, and lira were now a part of history themselves. Three EU members—Great Britain, Denmark, and Sweden—declined to participate.

Argentina Gets 5th President in 2 Weeks—Congress **Jan. 1** picked Eduardo Duhalde, an influential senator in the Peronist Party, to become Argentina's 5th president in 2 weeks. He faced the same headache as his predecessors: the nation's worst-ever economic crisis, including a $132 billion public debt and a recession. Duhalde **Jan. 4** asked Congress for sweeping power to deal with the crisis. He proposed devaluing the peso, now fixed at 1 U.S. dollar. Congress approved the devaluation **Jan. 6**. On **Jan. 11**, after a bank holiday, the value of the peso fell sharply against the dollar.

Major Taliban Resistance Put Down in Afghanistan—In the largest U.S. ground operation in the war up to then, some 200 marines **Jan. 1-2** made a sweep of a deserted terrorist training camp in southern Afghanistan. They found a few weapons and documents but no trace of top terrorist leaders. In Kabul, the capital, Afghanistan and Britain **Jan. 4** formally signed an agreement to bring in 4,500 peacekeeping troops. The 17 nations that would contribute troops had already approved it.

On **Jan. 4**, Sgt. 1st Class Nathan Chapman of San Antonio became the first U.S. soldier to die from enemy fire in Afghanistan. He was shot by unidentified assailants near the towns of Khost and Gardez, while seeking information about terrorist leaders. A CIA officer was wounded in the same attack. Ten other Americans had thus far been killed in or near Afghanistan.

Afghan officials said **Jan. 5** that the surrender of Taliban fighters in a mountainous region in southern Afghanistan—in what was then said to be their last redoubt—had been completed. However, Mullah Muhammad Omar had escaped. A U.S. military transport plane crashed in Pakistan **Jan. 9**, killing all 7 marines aboard. Two marines were killed and 5 wounded **Jan. 20** when their helicopter crashed in northern Afghanistan.

On **Jan. 28**, Afghan troops stormed a hospital in Kandahar where 6 pro-Taliban Arab fighters had been holding out for 7 weeks. All the Arabs were killed. U.S. Special Operations forces directed the attack.

Zambia Inaugurates President Amid Protests—Amid protests, Zambia, **Jan. 2**, got its 3rd president since independence in 1964. Levy Mwanawasa, the choice of outgoing Pres. Frederick Chiluba, had been declared winner of the Dec. 27 election, with 29% of the vote, as against 27% for the closest of 11 opposition candidates. On **Jan. 2** more than 1,000 persons, claiming the election was rigged, stormed the Supreme Court building, site of the inauguration; their bricks were met with tear gas. A judge **Jan. 3** declined to delay the inauguration for an investigation.

Militant's Death Revives Mideast Violence—On **Jan. 14**, Raed-al-Karmi, leader of a Palestinian militia, was killed by a bomb near his home in Tulkarm in the West Bank. His followers blamed Israel and, hours later, killed an Israeli soldier. Palestinian militants **Jan. 15** killed 2 Israeli civilians, the first in a month. A gunman opened fire in a crowded reception hall in Hadera, **Jan. 17**, killing 6 Israelis and wounding 25; he was killed. On **Jan. 21**, the Israeli army seized control of the entire city of Tulkarm, and in a raid in Nablus killed 4 men at what was said to be a bomb-making factory. A Palestinian shot and wounded 22 in a Jerusalem shopping district **Jan. 22**. A Hamas leader and 5 other Palestinians were killed in separate incidents **Jan. 24**.

Australian Fires Extinguished—The last of hundreds of fires that had burned forests and farmlands surrounding Sydney, Australia, since **Dec. 24** were extinguished by rains **Jan. 16**. No lives were lost, but an estimated 1.6 million acres were burned and 170 homes destroyed by the fires, many of which were believed set by vandals.

Volcano Devastates Town in Congo—Mount Nyiragongo, a volcano near the town of Goma in the eastern part of the Democratic Republic of Congo, erupted **Jan. 17**, leaving an estimated 55,000 people homeless and causing at least 45 deaths. Lava from the volcano covered nearly one-half of the town. On **Jan. 21**, at least 50 were killed when hot lava caused an explosion at a gas station where local residents were looting fuel.

Hundreds Die in Nigeria After Explosions at Depot—A fire at an army weapons depot in a crowded residential area of Lagos, Nigeria, **Jan. 27**, spawned huge explosions and a mass evacuation, with many fleeing across two nearby canals. The death toll was put at more than 1,000.

General

New Clonings Point Toward Organ Transplants—Successful pig clonings, announced **Jan. 2-3,** moved science closer to the day when animal organs could be successfully transplanted into humans. The new cloned pigs lacked 1 or 2 copies of a gene whose presence would cause the human body to reject a transplanted organ. Pigs are candidates for transplanting because they are easily bred, but the presence of the gene had posed a major obstacle. The announcements were made by Scotland's PPL Therapeutics and the University of Missouri in collaboration with Immerge BioTherapeutics, Charlestown, MA.

Miami Hurricanes Win NCAA Football Title—The University of Miami Hurricanes defeated the Nebraska Cornhuskers, 37–14, **Jan. 3**, in the Rose Bowl in Pasadena, CA, and claimed the Division 1 NCAA football championship. The two teams had been matched based on polls and computer calculations made at the end of the regular season. Miami was led by quarterback Ken Dorsey, who completed 22 of 35 passes for 362 yards and 3 touchdowns. The Canes' back Clinton Portis ran for 104 yards and a TD. In polls after the game, the Oregon Ducks, who finished with an 11–1 record, were ranked 2nd in the nation.

Father Convicted in Beating Death at Hockey Rink—A father who killed another father in a fight, after a hockey practice in which their sons participated, was convicted of involuntary manslaughter **Jan. 11**. Thomas Junta was sentenced to 6 to 10 years in prison **Jan. 25**. He had killed Michael Costin at a Reading, MA, hockey rink, in July 2000.

FEBRUARY 2002

National

Enron Executives Criticized in Report and Called Before Congressional Committees—A report requested by the board of directors of the Enron Corp., released **Feb. 2**, blamed top executives for the company's bankruptcy. William Powers, dean of the University of Texas Law School, led the investigation. The report asserted that executives had inflated profits by almost $1 billion, enriched themselves at the expense of stockholders, and disregarded federal securities laws. It cited partnerships controlled by then-Chief Financial Officer Andrew Fastow that had no purpose other than to misrepresent profits. Other failures of responsibility were attributed to Kenneth Lay, former chairman and chief executive officer, and Jeffrey Skilling, who was CEO before resigning in August 2001. The report also criticized Enron lawyers and Arthur Andersen, Enron's accounting firm, for going along with improper procedures.

Andersen, **Feb. 3,** announced that Paul Volcker, former chairman of the Federal Reserve Board, would head an independent oversight panel that would review the firm's policies.

The same day, Lay's lawyer announced that he would not be appearing before congressional committees as promised, and on **Feb. 4,** Lay ended his connection with Enron by resigning from its board. On **Feb. 7,** Skilling testified before a House subcommittee, declaring he had been unaware of dubious financial practices. Fastow and other executives appeared but declined to testify, citing 5th Amendment rights. On **Feb. 12,** responding to a subpoena, Lay did appear before the Senate Commerce Committee, but like others declined to testify on 5th Amendment grounds. Sherron Watkins, an Enron executive who had warned of an accounting scandal in August 2001, testified **Feb. 14** that she had tried to inform Lay of improprieties but that he did not seem to appreciate their seriousness. She put blame mainly on Skilling and Fastow.

Bush Budget Boosts Military Spending, Cuts Taxes—On **Feb. 4,** Pres. George W. Bush submitted to Congress a $2.13 trillion budget for the 2003 fiscal year. He proposed a 14% increase ($48 billion) in defense spending, and more than doubled spending on homeland security overall. The latter would entail preparedness for bioterrorism and an increase in border security ($38 billion overall). Bush also called for more tax cuts, including a permanent extension of the $1.35 trillion, 10-year tax cut that he got from Congress in 2001. Democrats said they would seek more funding for health, education, and environmental programs. They also objected to the plan to dip into the Social Security surplus.

Campaign-Finance Reform Bill Advances in Congress—Campaign finance reform edged closer to approval **Feb. 14** when the House endorsed the Shays-Meehan bill, 240-189. The GOP leadership was unable to prevent 41 Republicans from supporting the bill; only 12 Democrats opposed it. The bill would bar national political parties from accepting so-called soft money, the large unregulated contributions that are not supposed to be used for particular candidates but in effect often are. The bill would increase from $1,000 to $2,000 the amount an individual could give to an individual candidate. Unions, corporations, and not-for-profit organizations would be barred from paying for broadcast ads in the last 60 days of a general-election campaign.

In April 2001, the Senate had passed a similar, but not identical, bill; further Senate action was pending.

More Than 300 Bodies Found Near Crematory—Investigators found hundreds of bodies in a wooded area near a crematory in northwest Georgia. A woman walking a dog **Feb. 15** reported seeing a human skull, and as of **Mar. 11** authorities had found remains of some 340 bodies piled in sheds and in the woods. Funeral homes in the area had given these remains to the Tri-State Crematory in Noble, near the borders with Tennessee and Alabama, and relatives had received urns that were supposed to have contained ashes. Police **Feb. 16** charged Ray Brent Marsh, manager of the crematory, with multiple counts of theft by deception.

General Accounting Office Sues Vice President—The General Accounting Office, the investigative arm of Congress, sued Vice Pres. Dick Cheney **Feb. 22**. The suit, filed in Federal District Court in Washington, DC, sought information from Cheney on who had met with him and other members of his task force as they developed a proposed national energy policy. Cheney contended that the names and views of such advisers should be kept secret so as to allow them to offer candid advice.

International

Milosevic War Crimes Trial Begins—The war crimes trial of Slobodan Milosevic, former president of Yugoslavia, began **Feb. 12** at The Hague, the Netherlands. An appeals panel of the international UN tribunal ruled **Feb. 1** that he would face a single trial on charges related to the wars in Kosovo, Bosnia, and Croatia. The chief prosecutor, Carla del Ponte, addressing the tribunal **Feb. 12,** attributed to Milosevic "a calculated cruelty that went beyond the bounds of legitimate warfare" and said Milosevic was motivated by a lust for power. The prosecution **Feb. 13** continued to outline a long account of ethnic cleansing, executions, deportations, and other alleged human-rights abuses. Milosevic, who was acting as his own counsel, responded that the prosecution and the media were engaged in "a parallel lynch process." He spoke for several hours on **Feb. 14-15,** charging the Clinton administration with genocide against Serbia and vowing to call world leaders, including ex-Pres. Bill Clinton, to the stand.

***Wall Street Journal* Reporter Murdered by Captors in Pakistan**—A videotape delivered to Pakistani officials **Feb. 20** reportedly provided graphic evidence that Daniel Pearl, a *Wall Street Journal* reporter abducted by terrorists in Pakistan on **Jan. 23,** had been murdered sometime thereafter. Pearl had been the subject of an intense search. A telephoned demand for a $2 million ransom was made **Feb. 1.** An e-mail sent to news organizations that day claimed Pearl had been killed, but amid conflicting indications the FBI and Pakistani officials continued to search for him. Pakistani police said **Feb. 13** that the chief suspect, Ahmed Omar Sheikh, who had been arrested, had provided no solid information on Pearl's fate.

Near-War Between Israel, Palestinians Continues—Exchanges that approached outright warfare continued between Israelis and Palestinians. In retaliation for an attack on a Jewish settlement and a military outpost, Israel, **Feb. 2,** shelled a naval base in the Gaza Strip. Israel **Feb. 4** denied responsibility for an explosion that killed 5 Palestinians riding in a car in the Gaza Strip. A mother and child were among 3 Israelis killed in a **Feb. 6** attack by militants on a remote settlement. Israeli planes then bombed a compound of the Palestinian Authority.

After meeting with Pres. George W. Bush in the White House, **Feb. 7,** Prime Min. Ariel Sharon said he expected that a Palestinian state would emerge from the current conflict. Hamas militants launched 2 rockets at towns in southern Israel, **Feb. 10,** and Israeli planes then attacked a Palestinian security compound in the Gaza Strip. Israelis in armored vehicles and tanks raided 3 towns in Gaza, **Feb. 13,** killing 5 Palestinians. Three Israeli soldiers were killed **Feb. 14** when a bomb exploded under their tank at Karni Crossing. Two Israeli teenagers died in a suicide bombing at a Jewish settlement in the West Bank **Feb. 16.** Israeli police averted a suicide bombing **Feb. 17,** killing one occupant of a stolen car; the other occupant died when it exploded. A suicide bomber shot and killed an Israeli woman in Gaza **Feb. 18,** then blew himself up, killing 2 soldiers.

After a 24-hour period in which 16 were killed on both sides, Palestinian gunmen **Feb. 19** killed 6 Israeli soldiers at a West Bank outpost. On **Feb. 20,** Israelis attacked the official compound of Palestinian leader Yasir Arafat in Gaza City, killing 4 guards. Arafat was in Ramallah, where his movements were restricted by Israeli tanks.

Venezuelan Currency Plunges in Value—The bolivar, the currency of Venezuela, skidded in value after Pres. Hugo Chávez **Feb. 12** abandoned a controlled devaluation plan and allowed the currency to float against other currencies. To attack an $8 billion budget deficit, he announced a 7% cut in government spending. By **Feb. 13** the bolivar had fallen 19% from its level the previous Friday.

Afghan Minister Killed—The violent death **Feb. 14** of Afghanistan's minister of air transport and tourism underscored sharp divisions within the country's post-Taliban leadership. Abdul Rahman had reportedly been killed after being pulled from a plane by pilgrims angered by a delay in their departure for the holy city of Mecca, Saudi Arabia. On **Feb. 15,** Hamid Karzai, chairman of the interim government, claimed that senior government officials pursuing a vendetta had been responsible. At least 4 officials allegedly involved were arrested in Kabul **Feb. 16,** and 3 others, who had fled to Saudi Arabia, were arrested there.

On **Feb. 17,** the U.S. Central Command in Afghanistan said that U.S. planes **Feb. 16-17** had bombed "enemy troops" who were attacking forces loyal to the Afghan interim government. For the first time, the targets of U.S. bombings were not al-Qaeda or Taliban but rather militias opposed to the Karzai government.

Communist Rebel Action Flares in Nepal—Maoists made a series of attacks in Nepal **Feb. 17** that killed at least 137 people. The rebellion had claimed 2,400 lives since 1996. Prime Min. Sher Bahadur Deuba had imposed a state of emergency in November 2001. In their latest attack, the rebels killed soldiers, police officers, and civilians at a district headquarters and airport in northwestern Nepal. On **Feb. 19,** the government deployed the army against the rebels, and a major operation **Feb. 20** reportedly resulted in 48 rebel deaths. Officials reported **Feb. 22** that rebels had killed 32 policemen at a remote post.

Bush Visits Japan, South Korea, and China—Pres. Bush, on the first stop of an Asian trip **Feb. 18** in Japan, met with Prime Min. Junichiro Koizumi. In private, the leaders discussed Japan's economic problems. At a joint press conference, Koizumi was more conciliatory than Bush toward North Korea, which Bush had described as part of an "axis of evil." Addressing the Japanese parliament **Feb. 19,** Bush predicted that the next 100 years would be the "Pacific century" and that the U.S. would, if necessary, come to the defense of South Korea, the Philippines, and Taiwan.

In Seoul, South Korea, **Feb. 20,** Bush said that the U.S. had no intention of attacking North Korea and that he supported reunification efforts by both Koreas. Bush and Pres. Jiang Zemin of China met **Feb. 21** and agreed to work together to unify Korea. In a **Feb. 22** speech at Beijing's Tsinghua University, broadcast across China, Bush said religious freedom should be welcomed, not feared.

Angolan Rebel Leader Jonas Savimbi Is Killed—Jonas Savimbi, who had fought for decades to free Angola from Portuguese rule and then to overthrow its black governments, was killed in an ambush in Moxico province, according to a report **Feb. 22** by local government officials. Savimbi had led the rebel group known as UNITA (Union for the Total Independence of Angola).

General

Patriots' Field Goal as Time Expires Wins Super Bowl—The underdog New England Patriots won arguably the most exciting Super Bowl game ever, **Feb. 3**, when Adam Vinatieri kicked a 48-yard field goal as time ran out. They defeated the St. Louis Rams, champions just 2 years earlier, 20-17. St. Louis had trailed 17-3 with 10 minutes to play, but scored 2 touchdowns, the second with 1 minute and 30 seconds left, to tie the score. New England then moved the ball from their own 17-yard line to the St. Louis 30, and Vinatieri kicked the decisive 3-pointer. New England quarterback Tom Brady, who completed 16 of 27 passes, was named most valuable player. Security at the game in the New Orleans Superdome was tight.

2002 Winter Olympics

The Olympic Winter Games were declared open by Pres. George W. Bush on **Feb. 8** in Salt Lake City, UT, before a crowd of 50,000 people at Rice-Eccles Stadium. A tattered American flag recovered from the World Trade Center after the September 11 attack was borne into the stadium at the beginning of the ceremonies. Athletes from 77 nations marched in. The Olympic cauldron was lit by members of the 1980 U.S. men's hockey team that had upset the Soviet Union and won a gold medal. Among the highlights:

- In snowboarding, in the women's halfpipe, Kelly Clark prevailed **Feb. 10** with a score of 47.9 and the first U.S. gold medal. American Ross Powers matched her gold with his own in the men's halfpipe, **Feb. 11,** scoring 46.1. Danny Kass and Jarret Thomas won the silver and bronze, respectively, in the halfpipe, accomplishing the first U.S. medals sweep of a Winter Olympics event since men's figure skating in 1956.
- On **Feb. 11,** the judging of the figure skating pairs created an international uproar (see story).
- The American Casey FitzRandolph prevailed by 0.03 of a second to win the gold in the men's 500-meter speedskating, **Feb. 12.**
- Aleksei Yagudin, a Russian, won the men's figure-skating competition on **Feb. 14.**
- Derek Parra (U.S.) won the men's 1,500-meter speedskating title, **Feb. 19.**
- In the first Olympics to include the event, Americans Jill Bakken (pilot) and Vonetta Flowers (brakewoman) won the 2-woman bobsled gold medal **Feb. 19.** Flowers was the first black athlete ever to win gold in a winter Olympics.
- American Jack Shea Jr., a 3rd-generation winter Olympian, reintroduced Skeleton, and won a gold medal in the event **Feb. 20.**
- In a stunning upset, American Sarah Hughes, 16, won the women's figure skating gold **Feb. 21.**
- Canada won the women's hockey gold **Feb. 21,** defeating the U.S. in the final, 3-2.
- On **Feb. 22,** Janica Kostelic of Croatia became the first alpine skier to win 4 medals in a single Olympic games after capturing the gold in the women's giant slalom.
- Canada took the men's hockey title, **Feb. 24,** defeating the U.S., 5-2.

In the end Germany won 35 medals; the U.S. was close behind, with 34, and Norway came in 3rd, with 24. The gold-medal count was even closer: Germany 12, Norway 11, and the U.S. 10.

Russia, Canada Share Figure-Skating Gold After Furor—On **Feb. 11,** 5 of 9 judges named Russians Yelena Berezhnaya and Anton Sikharulidze as winners in Olympic figure skating, leaving the silver medal to Canadians Jamie Salé and David Pelletier, the overwhelming crowd favorites. The crowd booed the decision. On Feb. 13, Didier Gailhaguet, head of the French Olympic Committee, said that the French judge, Marie Reine Le Gougne, had been pressured to "act in a certain way." The International Skating Union voted Feb. 14 to award duplicate gold medals to the 2 Canadian skaters.

Ex-Priest Sentenced; Child Abuse Scandal Spreads—A former Roman Catholic priest was sentenced to prison **Feb. 21** for child molestation, as a widening scandal involving alleged sexual abuse of children by priests brought anguish to the Church in the U.S. and elsewhere. John Geoghan was convicted **Jan. 18** by a jury in Cambridge, MA, of having molested a 10-year-old boy at a swimming pool in 1991. Cardinal Bernard Law of Boston had moved Geoghan from parish to parish after learning of complaints against him; Geoghan was defrocked in 1998. The Boston archdiocese and others were under fire for alleged insufficient action in response to such charges and faced heavy financial costs as a result of civil suits.

MARCH 2002

National

Congressman Linked to Missing Intern Defeated—Rep. Gary Condit (D, CA), who had admitted having had a "very close" relationship with Chandra Levy, a missing government intern, lost his bid for renomination in his redrawn district, **Mar. 5**. The winner in the Democratic primary was Dennis Cardoza, 55% to 37%. Statewide, in the Republican gubernatorial primary, businessman Bill Simon Jr. upset former Los Angeles Mayor Richard Riordan, whom many GOP voters apparently viewed as too moderate. Simon spent $5.5 million of his own money and benefited from a $10 million advertising blitz aimed at Riordan by Gov. Gray Davis, a Democrat, who preferred to face a more conservative candidate in the general election.

Pres. Bush Imposes Tariffs on Steel Imports—Pres. George W. Bush **Mar. 5** imposed tariffs of up to 30% on steel imported from Europe, Asia, and South America. The tariffs, which took effect **Mar. 20** and were set to last three years, are among the U.S. government's most sweeping anti-import measures in two decades. Countries most affected are Brazil, China, Germany, Japan, South Korea, and Taiwan; Mexico, Canada, and developing countries are exempt. The tariffs aim to bolster the beleaguered U.S. steel industry while it restructures itself in an attempt to cope with the economic downturn and soaring costs of retiree benefits. U.S. consumer groups and manufacturers that depend on steel for their products opposed the tariffs, which will raise the cost of U.S. steel 10%. The European Union denounced the measure and filed a complaint with the World Trade Organization (WTO) **Mar. 7**, and China followed suit **Mar. 15**.

2 Reports End Investigations of Clinton—Two reports issued by the office of Robert Ray, who succeeded Kenneth Starr as independent counsel investigating former Pres. Bill Clinton, appeared to conclude Clinton's legal troubles. In a report released **Mar. 6**, Ray said there was enough evidence to convict the former president of perjury and obstruction of justice for his actions in connection with his involvement with Monica Lewinsky, a former White House intern. However, Clinton had agreed on Jan. 19, 2001, to admit he had given false testimony under oath, and with that avoided prosecution.

In another report **Mar. 20**, Ray's office said there was not enough evidence that either the former president or his wife, Hillary Rodham Clinton, had committed any crimes in connection with the failed Whitewater real-estate venture in Arkansas. The investigation had sought to determine whether the Clintons knew of, or had been involved with, crimes committed by one of their business partners in the development, James McDougal.

Enron's Accountant Indicted for Obstruction of Justice—The Justice Dept. announced **Mar. 14** that the accounting firm Arthur Andersen had been indicted for destroying thousands of documents related to the investigation into the collapse of a client, Enron, the energy-trading company. The indictment alleged there had been a concerted effort in 4 cities to shred documents on a wide scale. Andersen denied any wrongdoing. Paul Volker, a former Federal Reserve chairman who was heading an oversight committee seeking to reform Andersen, proposed a management shakeup **Mar. 22**. On **Mar. 26**, Andersen CEO Joseph Berardino announced that he would resign in order to help restore confidence in the firm.

5 Killed in Separate Army and Navy Training Exercises—Five U.S. military personnel were killed and five others injured in two separate training accidents in March. The first occurred about 1 P.M. on **Mar. 21**, when a Navy HH-1 Huey helicopter crashed into a crevice near the peak of Split Mountain, in the Sequoia National Forest, killing two crew members and injuring four. Three soldiers were killed **Mar. 22** when a 120-millimeter mortar round exploded while being fired from an armored vehicle in a nighttime exercise at the Army National Training Center at Fort Irwin, in the Mohave Desert east of Los Angeles.

Energy Dept. Policy Records Released—The Energy Dept. **Mar. 25** released thousands of records documenting the development of Pres. Bush's energy policy. The move was in response to a court-order resulting from lawsuits insisting the records be made public under the Freedom of Information Act (FOIA). Although many records were still withheld, the documents made available supported critics' accusations that the policy was developed with significant input from corporations that donated money to the Republican party, and little from environmental groups.

Campaign-Finance Reform Bill Signed by Bush—Pres. Bush **Mar. 27** signed into law the campaign-finance reform bill approved by the House in February and the Senate **Mar. 20**. To avoid having to send the bill to conference committee, Senate supporters brought the House-passed bill to a vote, and prevailed by a 60-40 margin. Prior to the final vote, the Senate had voted, 68-32, to end a filibuster against the bill. Senate sponsors John McCain (R, AZ) and Russell Feingold (D, WI) had first introduced a bill in 1995, but the issue did not seem to catch on until McCain made reform the centerpiece of his spirited, if unsuccessful, run for the 2000 GOP presidential nomination. The collapse of the Enron Corp., which had made huge political donations, gave further impetus to the bill. Opponents of the bill said they would challenge its constitutionality in court.

U.S. Continues War on Terrorism—The Justice Dept. announced **Mar. 28** that it would seek the death penalty for Zacarias Moussaoui, the only person yet charged as a co-conspirator in the Sept. 11 terrorist attacks. A French citizen of Moroccan descent, Moussaoui allegedly had received training aimed at allowing him to participate in the attacks, but was being held on immigration charges at the time. Also on **Mar. 28**, a team of American agents stormed several houses in Pakistan, and captured 5 Taliban fighters and 25 Arabs suspected of having links to al-Qaeda.

U.S. Economy at a Glance: March 2002	
Unemployment rate	5.7%
Consumer prices (12 mo. change)	1.5%
Producer prices (12 mo. change)	–4.5%
Trade deficit (12 mos. through Mar.)	$356.6 bil.
Dow Jones high (1st quarter: Mar. 19)	10,635.25
Dow Jones low (1st quarter: Jan. 29)	9,618.24
1st-quarter GDP (annual rate)	+5.0%

International

Mideast Violence Escalates—Violence continued at a quickening pace in the Middle East. Over three days ending **Mar. 2**, Israeli ground forces raided Palestinian refugee camps, killing 30 people at 2 locations, while losing 2 soldiers. A suicide bomber killed himself and 9 others in Jerusalem **Mar. 2**; a sniper killed 7 Israeli soldiers and 3 civilians at a West Bank checkpoint **Mar. 3**; and a gunman was shot dead at a Tel Aviv nightclub **Mar. 4** after killing 3 and wounding 30. In retaliatory raids by Israel, the wife and 3 children of a spokesman for Hamas, the militant Palestinian group, were killed **Mar. 4**. Israeli Prime Min. Ariel Sharon said the same day that he aimed to kill as many Palestinians as possible in order to force them to negotiate. U.S. Sec. of State Colin Powell said **Mar. 6** that this approach was not likely to lead anywhere, and the Bush administration backed off from unqualified support of Sharon's policy. Scattered incidents claimed 24 lives on both sides on **Mar. 5-6**. After 5 Israeli teenagers were killed **Mar. 8**, Israeli retaliation claimed 40 lives. Two terror attacks in Jerusalem and Netanya, **Mar. 9**, took the lives of 14 Israelis. Palestinians reported that 17 died during a **Mar. 12** Israeli incursion into the Jabaliya refugee camp.

On **Mar. 12,** as Israeli attacks killed 31 Palestinians, UN Sec. Gen. Kofi Annan declared that Israel must end its "illegal occupation" of Palestinian land. That night, the UN Security Council, 14-0, passed a resolution demanding an immediate cease-fire. Pres. George W. Bush the next day called the Israeli assaults "not helpful." On **Mar. 14**, after a demand from Powell that the Israelis pull out of the Palestinian territories, Sharon announced that the army would leave Ramallah. By the next day the Israelis had left all West Bank towns except Bethlehem. Gen. Anthony Zinni, the U.S. mediator, met separately with Israeli and Palestinian leaders **Mar. 15**. U.S. Vice Pres. Dick Cheney met with Sharon in Israel **Mar. 18**. The Israeli army pulled out of Bethlehem **Mar. 19**. A suicide bomber killed 7 Israelis on a bus **Mar. 20**, and another killed 3 in Jerusalem **Mar. 21**.

Arafat said **Mar. 26** that he would not attend an Arab summit in Beirut, Lebanon, because Sharon had threatened to prevent him from returning to the West Bank. The summit was deliberating a proposal by Crown Prince Abdullah of Saudi Arabia for Arab nations to accept "normal relations" with Israel in return for Israeli withdrawal from the occupied territories. Abdullah, **Mar. 27**, detailed his proposal in Beirut. It also called for creation of a Palestinian state and the return of Palestinian refugees. Arafat, speaking by satellite, endorsed it. That night, in Netanya, a suicide bomber killed himself and 19 Israelis attending a Passover meal at a hotel; more than 100 were wounded. In response, Israeli ground troops stormed Yasir Arafat's compound in the West Bank city of Ramallah **Mar. 29**, smashing through walls and battling from room to room, as Arafat holed up with aides in an office on the 2nd floor. A Tel Aviv cafe was the scene of another suicide bombing **Mar. 30**, leaving dozens injured. In back-to-back suicide bombings, 15 Israelis were killed on **Mar. 31**, leading Prime Min. Ariel Sharon to denounce Yasir Arafat as "the enemy of the entire free world."

8 U.S. Troops Killed During Fight in Afghanistan— Eight U.S. troops were killed during an assault by Americans and their Afghan allies against Taliban and al-Qaeda forces in the Shah-i-Kot Valley and surrounding mountains in eastern Afghanistan. Seeking to clear the region of their foes, hundreds of U.S. and Afghan troops entered the area at night, **Mar. 2**, and were attacked by enemy fighters armed with mortars, machine guns, and artillery. One American was killed in the initial action. On **Mar. 4**, a rocket-propelled grenade hit a U.S. helicopter, knocking a member of the Navy Seals out of the craft. A second copter brought U.S. soldiers in to rescue him. They were attacked on the ground; 6 were killed and 11 wounded. Other rescuers retrieved the bodies, including that of the American who fell from the helicopter. By **Mar. 6**, 1,200 U.S. troops were involved in the mission, Operation Anaconda. In subsequent days the enemy forces were subjected to heavy aerial pounding, and U.S. and Afghan ground forces entering the defended area **Mar. 12** declared victory. It was unclear how many enemy had been killed and how many may have fled.

Hundreds Die in Hindu–Muslim Violence in India— More than 600 people were reported dead by **Mar. 7,** after several days of Hindu-Muslim violence in the state of Gujarat, India. Hindu rioters had rampaged across the state, after Muslims attacked and burned a train carrying Hindu activists in the city of Godhra **Feb. 27.**

Mugabe Reelected in Zimbabwe Amid Turmoil—Pres. Robert Mugabe was reelected president of Zimbabwe, **Mar. 9-11**. The reported returns showed him well ahead of his challenger, Morgan Tsvangirai. Although highly esteemed when he first came to power 22 years earlier, Mugabe had been widely criticized in recent years for allegedly condoning political violence and suppressing opposition. Police reportedly intimidated voters in the 2002 election, and a judge extended the voting to a 3rd day to allow more to participate. Mugabe's supporters declared victory, **Mar. 13**, but Tsvangirai denounced the election as a fraud. Pres. Bush said the U.S. would not recognize the validity of Mugabe's election. Canada, **Mar. 14**, and Germany, **Mar. 15**, cut off aid to Zimbabwe. The Commonwealth—a 54-nation body consisting mostly of former British colonies—**Mar. 19** suspended Zimbabwe from membership for a year.

Cheney on Trip Seeks Support Against Iraq—Vice Pres. Dick Cheney traveled abroad in an effort to build international support for possible U.S. action against the Iraqi regime of Saddam Hussein. In London **Mar. 11**, Prime Min. Tony Blair of Great Britain agreed that Saddam's efforts to gain weapons of mass destruction might require military action by the West, but international support for action against Iraq appeared weak. In Amman, Jordan, **Mar. 12**, King Abdullah II warned Cheney that a U.S. attack on Iraq could destabilize the region, and he urged the U.S. to seek a peaceful settlement. At a meeting with Cheney **Mar. 13**, Pres. Hosni Mubarak of Egypt said he would seek to defuse the Iraqi crisis by urging Iraq to readmit UN weapons inspectors. In Yemen **Mar. 14**, Pres. Ali Abdullah Saleh told Cheney he opposed any U.S. attack on Iraq. Crown Prince Abdullah, the de facto leader of Saudi Arabia, said **Mar. 16** upon Cheney's arrival that it was not in the best interests of the U.S. or the region for the U.S. to attack Iraq.

2 Americans Among 5 Killed in Church in Pakistan— Two men threw grenades inside a church in Islamabad, Pakistan, **Mar. 17**, during Sunday services, killing 5 people and wounding at least 40. The attack in the nondenominational Protestant International Church occurred near the U.S. Embassy. The dead included 2 Americans, an Embassy employee and her daughter.

Bombing at Embassy Precedes Bush's Peru Visit—A visit by Pres. Bush to Peru was preceded, **Mar. 20**, by a car bomb explosion outside the U.S. Embassy in Lima that killed 9 and injured 30. Bush had begun his Latin trip in Monterrey, Mexico, at a conference on aid to developing nations attended by 50 world leaders. He and Mexico's Pres. Vicente Fox announced plans, **Mar. 21**, to improve security measures along their 2,000-mile common border. In a speech **Mar. 22**, Bush said rich nations should aid only poor nations that undertake a wide range of reforms.

In Lima **Mar. 23**, Bush told Pres. Alejandro Toledo he would help Peru fight Marxist guerrillas and end drug trafficking in the Andes region. Bush, the 1st U.S. president to visit Peru while in office, restated his commitment to an Andean trade accord awaiting the U.S. Senate approval.

General

More Catholic Clergy Linked to Abuse of Children— Revelations of sexual abuse of children by Roman Catholic clergy continued to emerge. Since the current flurry of accusations, which began in January, dozens of priests across the U.S. had resigned or been suspended. Many dioceses began turning over to prosecutors reports of complaints about abuse. On **Mar. 8**, the bishop of Palm Beach, FL, Anthony O'Connell, resigned after admitting he had abused a teenage seminary student in the 1970s. His predecessor had resigned in 1999 after admitting that he had molested 5 boys. In 1996, O'Connell's victim had won a $125,000 settlement that was not made public at the time.

The Boston archdiocese said **Mar. 12** that its insurance would not cover the estimated $100 million in settlements of lawsuits against priests resulting from instances of sexual abuse. The archdiocese said it would sell Church property, take out loans, and seek donations from wealthy supporters.

In a letter released **Mar. 21**, Pope John Paul II, referring briefly to the scandal, wrote that "a dark shadow of suspicion" had fallen over all priests because of the behavior of those who had succumbed to "the most grievous forms . . . of the mystery of evil." He said priests must "commit ourselves more fully to the search for holiness." On **Mar. 28** the pope accepted the resignation of the archbishop of Poznan,

Poland, Juliusz Paetz, who had been accused of molesting teen-age seminarians, a charge Paetz denied.

Mother Who Drowned 5 Children Gets Life in Prison—Andrea Pia Yates, who confessed to drowning her 5 children, was found guilty of capital murder **Mar. 12**. Tried in Houston, TX, for 3 of the deaths, she had pleaded not guilty by reason of insanity. The jury **Mar. 15** recommended that she be sentenced to life in prison.

U.S. Report Blames Egyptian Copilot in Crash—The U.S. National Transportation Safety Board issued a report **Mar. 21** concluding that the copilot of an EgyptAir plane was responsible for the Oct. 31, 1999, crash that killed all 217 aboard. The Boeing 767 had taken off from Kennedy Airport in New York City for Cairo. The report found that "manipulation of the controls by the copilot, Gamil al-Batouti," had brought the plane down. A recording of cockpit conversation indicated he had played a role in the disaster. The report did not suggest a motive; however, there were indications al-Batouti had learned shortly beforehand that he would be taken off the route because of accusations of sexual misconduct.

History Made at 73rd Academy Awards—Halle Berry made history on **Mar. 24** when she became the first African-American woman to win the Academy Award for Best Actress, for her role in *Monster's Ball*. Berry was the 3rd black actress ever to receive an Oscar. The others won in the Best Supporting Actress category: Hattie McDaniel for *Gone With the Wind* (1939) and Whoopi Goldberg for *Ghost* (1990). Denzel Washington became the 2nd African-American actor to win Best Actor, for his role in *Training Day*. Veteran actor Sidney Poitier, who was presented with an Honorary Award at the 2002 ceremonies, was the first African-American man ever to take the top acting award; he won for *Lilies of the Field* (1963). Washington had earned a Best Supporting Actor Oscar in 1989 for *Glory*.

A Beautiful Mind, the story of mathematical genius John Nash, who struggles through life with schizophrenia but nonetheless wins a Nobel Prize, was a big Oscar winner in 2002. It took 4 awards: Best Picture, Best Director (Ron Howard), Best Supporting Actress (Jennifer Connelly), and Best Adapted Screenplay (Akiva Goldsman). Jim Broadbent was named Best Supporting Actor for *Iris*. In the Foreign Language Film category, Bosnia and Herzegovina had its first win ever, with *No Man's Land*. *Shrek* won for Animated Feature Film, and Randy Newman won for Best Original Song, for "If I Didn't Have You." It was Newman's first Oscar, after 15 nominations.

Earthquake Devastates Rural Area of Afghanistan—A 6.1-magnitude earthquake centered in northern Afghanistan's mountainous Burka region **Mar. 25** left at least 600 confirmed dead, perhaps more than 1,200 dead in all, with tens of thousands homeless or cut off from food supplies. Some 80 villages were decimated, including Nahrin, 100 mi. north of Kabul, an early focus of relief efforts.

APRIL 2002

National

First Guilty Plea Entered in Enron Investigation—David Duncan, a former partner with Arthur Andersen, accounting firm for the Enron Corp., pleaded guilty **Apr. 9** to obstruction of justice. As investigations of Enron and Andersen moved forward, Duncan, who admitted to having orchestrated an effort to destroy Enron files at Andersen, became the first person to enter a guilty plea in the case. He acknowledged before Judge Melinda Harmon in U.S. District Court in Houston, TX, that he had sought to thwart an investigation by the Securities and Exchange Commission.

Ohio U.S. Representative Convicted of Racketeering—Rep. James Traficant (D, OH) was convicted **Apr. 11** by a jury in Cleveland of racketeering and corruption. Though not a lawyer, the Youngstown congressman chose to act as his own attorney, and was convicted on all 10 counts. One ex-staff member testified that Traficant had demanded a $2,500-a-month kickback for hiring him.

Senate Rejects Oil Drilling in Arctic Refuge—The U.S. Senate **Apr. 18** defeated a component of Pres. George W. Bush's energy program. On a procedural motion, the Senate voted 54-46 not to end debate on the issue, effectively killing the proposal to open the Arctic National Wildlife Refuge to oil drilling. Eight Republicans and an independent joined 45 Democrats in the majority. Environmentalists had made the issue a top priority.

International

Terrorist Leader Captured in Pakistan—U.S. and Pakistani officials announced **Apr. 1** that a top al-Qaeda leader had been seized **Mar. 28**. Raids by FBI agents and Pakistani police in Lahore and Faisalabad had rounded up about 20 suspected al-Qaeda figures and 40 Pakistanis. The al-Qaeda leader, Abu Zubaydah, was thought to have succeeded Muhammed Atef as head of operations for the organization, after the latter was killed by U.S. bombing in November. U.S. officials said **Apr. 19** that Zubaydah claimed terrorists planned to attack U.S. financial institutions.

Bush Steps Up Efforts to Stop Mideast Bloodshed—Pres. George W. Bush became more involved in seeking to stop the Israeli-Palestinian conflict. In early April, as more suicide bombings occurred, Israeli forces, seeking to root out terrorists, expanded their incursion into Palestinian territory, raiding or occupying Bethlehem, Nablus, Jenin, and other West Bank cities. On **Apr. 2**, as Israel lifted a curfew in Ramallah, where Palestinian leader Yasir Arafat and 200 staffers and supporters were surrounded, Prime Min. Ariel Sharon of Israel suggested that Arafat use a "one-way ticket" into exile. Israeli troops **Apr. 2** surrounded the Church of the Nativity, at the reputed site of Christ's birth, now occupied by some 250 Palestinian fighters.

The Hezbollah **Apr. 2** fired mortars and missiles from Lebanon into Israel. In retaliation, Israeli planes **Apr. 2** attacked Lebanese villages. As thousands in Cairo and elsewhere in the Arab world demonstrated for the Palestinians, Egypt **Apr. 3** suspended ties with Israel.

On **Apr. 4**, as Israel invaded Hebron, Bush demanded that Israel end its attacks and pull back, and also end construction of settlements in Palestinian territory. He asked Arafat, for his part, to denounce terrorism. The International Committee of the Red Cross, **Apr. 5**, called Israel's attacks on its vehicles and facilities "totally unacceptable," and the Red Cross and other agencies said a humanitarian crisis was occurring in the occupied cities. On **Apr. 7**, Israel said it had detained 2,000 Palestinians. In Jenin, where Palestinian casualties were large, 13 Israeli soldiers were killed in an ambush **Apr. 9**. Heavy fighting occurred in Nablus and at the refugee camp in Jenin, where Palestinians claimed Israeli troops were massacring civilians.

In Rabat, Morocco, on **Apr. 7**, the eve of the first stop on a peace mission by U.S. Sec. of State Colin Powell, over 500,000 people demonstrated for the Palestinians. Powell met there **Apr. 8** with King Mohammed VI and Saudi Crown Prince Abdullah bin Abdul Aziz al-Saud. In Bethlehem, the 2 sides exchanged fire at the Church of the Nativity **Apr. 8**. Sharon said the same day that he would not withdraw from the Palestinian areas, although a pullout from 2 towns did occur the day after. On **Apr. 10** a bomber killed himself and 8 Israelis near Haifa.

Powell met **Apr. 10** in Madrid with European foreign ministers, who demanded an immediate Israeli pullback. After a stop in Jordan **Apr. 11**, Powell met in Jerusalem **Apr. 12** with Sharon, but they failed to agree on a timetable for Israeli withdrawal from the West Bank. After a Palestinian woman blew herself up and killed 6 people in Jerusalem the same day, Powell postponed a meeting with Arafat. The meeting did take place **Apr. 14**, at Arafat's battered office in Ramallah, with Israeli soldiers close at hand. Arafat told Powell that no cease-fire was possible until Israel ended its military operation and pulled back.

In Ramallah **Apr. 15**, Israel arrested Marwan Barghouti, a top Arafat aide, and charged him with planning terrorist attacks. Powell met with Arafat again **Apr. 17**, afterward stating that no cease-fire was possible until Israel withdrew from Palestinian cities. In Cairo, **Apr. 17**, Pres. Hosni Mubarak of Egypt declined to meet with Powell. When Israelis **Apr. 17** allowed Palestinians to return to their refugee camp in Jenin, the residents dug through the rubble in search of possible survivors of the army's attack.

The Israeli government said **Apr. 23** that it would delay the arrival in Jenin of UN fact finders until Israel had approved the members of the delegation. Three Palestinian boys were shot dead by Israeli soldiers **Apr. 23** as they prepared to attack an Israeli settlement near Gaza City. On **Apr. 25**, Bush met with Crown Prince Abdullah in Crawford, TX. Abdullah reportedly told Bush the U.S. had to do more to stop Israeli incursions in Palestinian territory or lose credibility in the Middle East. He presented a peace proposal to Bush; it called for U.S. help in reconstructing the Palestinian territories, a renunciation of violence by both sides, and an end to new Israeli settlements on Palestinian land. On **Apr. 27**, three gunmen fled—one was later killed—after killing 4 people, including a girl, 5, at the settlement of Adora.

On **Apr. 28**, Israel and the Palestinians agreed to a Bush administration compromise in which 6 Palestinians wanted by Israel would be taken from Arafat's compound and confined under the observation of U.S. and British wardens. Israel wanted 5 of the 6 in connection with the 2001 assassination of the Israeli minister of tourism. Under the agreement, Arafat would be free to travel again. At the same time, on **Apr. 29** Israel killed at least 8 in an assault on Hebron, the largest West Bank city, in retaliation for the Palestinian attack on the nearby Adora settlement. On **Apr. 30** the Israeli cabinet refused to let a UN fact-finding mission probe alleged Israeli atrocities at the Jenin refugee camp unless a series of stringent conditions could be met.

Angolan Government Signs Cease-fire With Rebels—The end of a 27-year civil war in Angola appeared at hand **Apr. 4** when the government and the rebel leadership of the National Union for the Total Independence of Angola (UNITA) signed a cease-fire. The death in battle in February of Jonas Savimbi, UNITA's leader, had opened the door to negotiations. Under the agreement, signed in Luanda, the capital, the government recognized UNITA as a legitimate political movement whose leaders could serve in the government. UNITA agreed to demobilize its 50,000 fighters.

Attack on Minister Linked to Plot to Topple Afghan Regime—Afghanistan's defense minister, Muhammad Qassim Fahim, escaped an assassination attempt **Apr. 8**, days after the government had sought to break up an alleged plot against it. On **Apr. 3**, officials said they had arrested hundreds for attempting to subvert the government; the next day they said they had released 140 of a total of 300 people arrested. The government **Apr. 4** also announced an initiative, quite unpopular in some quarters, to eradicate cultivation of opium poppies. In Jalalabad **Apr. 8**, a bomb exploded on the route of Fahim's motorcade, killing 5 people but leaving the minister unscathed.

Four American soldiers were killed **Apr. 15** in the desert near Kandahar when a rocket exploded while they were in the process of destroying it and other captured weapons. Four Canadian soldiers were killed before dawn **Apr. 18** when a laser-guided bomb from a U.S. plane was dropped on them unintentionally.

Exiled Afghan King Mohammad Zahir Shah returned to Afghanistan **Apr. 18** amid tight security. He had been living in Italy since his ouster in 1973.

The U.S. announced **Apr. 30** a new deployment of 1,000 troops in eastern Afghanistan, along the Pakistan border, in an effort to prevent Taliban and al-Qaeda forces from regrouping.

IRA Decommissions More Weapons—The peace process in Northern Ireland moved forward **Apr. 8** when it was announced that the Provisional Irish Republican Army had decommissioned a 2nd set of weapons. The decommissioning, a requirement of the peace settlement, had gotten underway in October 2001. The announcement by the Independent International Commission on Decommissioning said that the IRA had "put a varied and substantial quantity of ammunition, arms, and explosive material beyond use."

Iraq Halts Oil Exports to Hurt U.S. Economy—Pres. Saddam Hussein of Iraq halted his country's oil exports **Apr. 8** as a means, he said, of damaging the U.S. economy. The move, announced as temporary, was a protest against U.S. support for Israel in the Middle East crisis. Hussein called on other Middle East oil producers to follow his lead, but none did. After Iraq's move, oil prices rose. Exports were resumed in early May. On **Apr. 27**, Iraq celebrated Hussein's 65th birthday.

Venezuela President Ousted and Then Restored—Pres. Hugo Chavez of Venezuela was overthrown in a military coup **Apr. 12** but regained power **Apr. 14**, riding a wave of popular sentiment. His feud with the national oil company, Petroleos de Venezuela SA (PDVSA), heretofore largely autonomous, had angered many business, labor, and military leaders. Viewing PDVSA as a "state within a state" whose profits went disproportionately to the rich, Chavez in February had replaced its president and named 5 board members sympathetic to him. Groups opposed to Chavez initiated a nationwide strike **Apr. 9** that turned into a push for his resignation. Brig. Gen. Nestor Gonzalez said Chavez was politicizing the armed forces and supporting leftists in Colombia.

On **Apr. 11**, hundreds of thousands of protestors marched on the presidential palace. Shots fired at the crowd killed at least 14 and wounded more than 100. Some top generals called for Chavez's resignation. Early on **Apr. 12**, Chavez stepped down at a meeting with military officers and was arrested and placed in their custody. Later that day, a businessman, Pedro Carmona, was sworn in as interim president. But an outpouring of protests from the poorer masses forced the military to back down. Chavez returned to his palace in triumph, resuming his duties **Apr. 14**. Bush administration officials conceded **Apr. 15** that they had met in recent months with opponents of Chavez and agreed that he should be removed from office. On **Apr. 15**, Mayor Alfredo Pena said that at least 40 people in all had been killed in the uprising. As part of his reorganization of the armed forces, Chavez, **Apr. 17**, named Gen. Luis Acevedo commander of the air force. However, on **Apr. 19**, Acevedo and 3 other generals were killed when their helicopter crashed.

Dutch Government Resigns After Report on Massacre—Premier Wim Kok of the Netherlands and all the members of his governing 3-party coalition resigned **Apr. 16** after a report faulted the government—as well as the United Nations—for a massacre of 7,500 Muslim men and boys in Srebrenica, Bosnia and Herzegovina, in 1995. The army commander, Lt. Gen. Ad van Baal, resigned **Apr. 17.** The Dutch government had sent 200 troops to protect Muslims in Srebrenica, a UN-designated "safe area." The town was overrun by Serbian forces, who assembled Muslim civilians and killed them. Drastically outnumbered, the Dutch offered little resistance to the atrocity. A newly issued report by the Netherlands Institute for War Documentation found that the Dutch peacekeeping mission had been "ill-conceived" and that the troops were poorly armed and unprepared. It said the failure of the Dutch troops was "tantamount to collaborating with ethnic cleansing."

Right-Winger in Runoff for President of France—National Front candidate Jean-Marie Le Pen, a longtime crusader for far right-wing causes, scored a major upset **Apr. 21** when he qualified for the runoff to choose the next president of France. He was slated to oppose the incumbent president, Jacques Chirac, of the Rally for the Republic Party (RPR). LePen, a foe of immigration who has also decried the alleged adverse economic impact of France's affiliation with the European Union, saw himself as a spokesman for "you little people." In the large field of candidates, Chirac received 20%, LePen 17%, and the Socialist candidate Prime Min. Lionel Jospin, who had been expected to easily make the runoff, 16%.

General

Maryland Wins NCAA Men's Basketball Title—The University of Maryland Terrapins won their first national men's basketball championship in Atlanta **Apr. 1** with a 64-52 victory over the Indiana University Hoosiers. Maryland, capping a 32-4 season, was led by Juan Dixon, who was named the most outstanding player of the Final Four. The Hoosiers, winners of 5 previous titles, had lost 11 games during the regular season before upsetting Duke and Oklahoma in the tournament.

The University of Connecticut woman's team completed a 39-0 season **Mar. 31** by defeating Oklahoma 82-70 in San Antonio, TX. Claiming their 3rd national title, the Connecticut women were led by Sue Bird, who had been voted national player of the year.

Kenyans Dominate Boston Marathon—In the 106th Boston Marathon, **Apr. 15**, Rodgers Rop of Kenya won in 2:09:02. Kenyans took the top 4 places and 6 out of the top 10. In the women's race, Kenya's Margaret Okayo set a course record of 2:20:43.

Pope, U.S. Cardinals Discuss Abuses by Priests—In extraordinary meetings at the Vatican **Apr. 23-24**, Pope John Paul II and U.S. cardinals discussed an unfolding scandal caused by widespread reports of abuses of children and young people by Roman Catholic priests, and alleged inaction and cover-ups by some U.S. church leaders.

The Archdiocese of New York, under attack for failure to do so, announced **Apr. 3** that it had given the U.S. district attorney's office a list of priests accused over a 40-year period of sexually abusing minors. Documents released **Apr. 8** revealed that high Church officials in Boston, including Cardinal Bernard Law, had known for many years that a priest, Paul Shanley, was abusing boys, but allowed him to continue to have contacts with children. By **Apr. 9**, calls were being heard for Law's resignation from some priests, political leaders, and lay Catholics; Law indicated **Apr. 12** that he would not resign.

Vatican officials announced **Apr. 15** that Pope John Paul had summoned U.S. cardinals to Rome to discuss the sex abuse scandal. On **Apr. 20**, the pope said bishops must "diligently investigate accusations" against priests who had broken their vows of celibacy. At his first meeting with the cardinals, **Apr. 23**, the pope expressed an apology to victims of abuse, saying that what had happened to them was a crime and "an appalling sin in the eyes of God." After meeting with the pope again on **Apr. 24**, the U.S. cardinals issued proposals for dealing with the removal of priests who abused minors. They appeared to distinguish between priests "guilty of the serial, predatory sexual abuse of minors"—and hence subject to zero tolerance—and those whose cases "might be less clear-cut." The Associated Press reported **Apr. 28** that at least 177 U.S. priests had either resigned or been removed from their duties since the sexual abuse scandal gained wide attention in January.

Tiger Woods Takes 3rd Masters—Tiger Woods won his 2nd straight Masters tournament, and his 3rd Masters overall, at Augusta, GA, **Apr. 14**, with a 12-under-par score of 276. He finished 3 strokes ahead of Retief Goosen. This was Woods's 7th major professional title; no other golfer had reached that total at Woods's age, 26.

Plane Crashes Into Milan Skyscraper—A small plane crashed into the tallest building in Milan, Italy, **Apr. 18**, killing 3 people and injuring about 60. The pilot, who was the only person in the plane, was among the dead. He had taken off for Milan from Locarno, Switzerland, in a Rockwell Commander 112, and had reported having trouble lowering his wheels. The plane struck the 25th and 26th floors of the 30-floor Pirelli Tower. Almost everyone evacuated the building, some with the help of firefighters. The government said the crash appeared to be an accident.

Actor Arrested in Wife's Murder—Police in Los Angeles **Apr. 18** arrested actor Robert Blake in connection with the murder of his wife, Bonny Lee Bakley, in May 2001. Blake's former bodyguard and chauffeur, Earle Caldwell, was also arrested. The actor claimed that after dining with his wife in a restaurant he had walked her to their car, then returned to the restaurant to retrieve a pistol he carried to protect her. According to Blake, when he returned to the car he found her shot. On **Apr. 22,** Blake was formally charged with shooting his wife, and he and Caldwell were charged with conspiracy. Both pleaded not guilty.

17 Die in German School Shooting—A German youth who had been expelled from the Gutenberg school in Erfurt, Germany, returned to the school **Apr. 26** and shot 16 people to death. The gunman, Robert Steinhaeuser, 19, who used a rifle and a handgun in his rampage, also shot himself to death. A policeman who had rushed to the scene was among the victims. Most of the others who died were teachers.

MAY 2002

National

Unemployment Hits 8-Year High—Despite some signs of a gradual economic recovery, it was reported **May 3** that the national unemployment rate, often regarded as a lagging economic indicator, had hit 6.0% in April, the highest rate since summer 1994.

Clues to Attacks Were Available Before Sept. 11—Revelations in May suggested that the Sept. 11 terrorist attacks might have been anticipated and possibly averted if officials had collated and analyzed reports on suspicious activity. Robert S. Mueller III, who became FBI director a few days before the terrorists struck, told a Senate committee **May 8** that the FBI had paid insufficient heed to a July 2001 memo from an FBI agent in Phoenix. The agent, Kenneth Williams, warned that Arab men with possible terrorist ties were taking flight lessons, and called for a nationwide review. Mueller testified that he did not believe agents investigating Zacarias Moussaoui, the so-called 20th hijacker, arrested in August 2001, had been told of Williams's report.

The White House said **May 15** that Pres. George W. Bush had received a CIA briefing in August 2001 warning that Osama bin Laden was planning to hijack planes, but that the warning did not predict the planes would be crashed into buildings. Condoleezza Rice, Bush's national security adviser, said **May 16** that the government had received many threats during the summer of 2001, but that the information was nonspecific. House Minority Leader Dick Gephardt (D, MO) and other Democrats called for an investigation, while maintaining that their aim was to better guard against future attacks, rather than to cast blame on Bush and others.

Mueller warned **May 20** that suicide-bomber attacks similar to those in Israel were "inevitable" in the U.S. On **May 23** he ordered an internal inquiry into charges by Coleen Rowley, a Minneapolis FBI agent, that the Sept. 11 terror attacks could have been thwarted. It was reported **May 25** that, according to Rowley's letter, a request from the FBI in Minneapolis for a warrant to search Moussaoui's computer had been watered down by an unidentified Washington FBI agent, resulting in a denial of the search. Mueller acknowledged **May 29** that the attacks might have been prevented if the FBI had acted on the available information. He announced a new primary mission for the agency—preventing terrorist attacks—and said more than 400 analysts would be added to "a redesigned and refocused FBI."

Atty. Gen. John Ashcroft announced **May 30** that the FBI would have expanded powers to monitor religious, political, and other organizations, as well as internet and other media, to gain knowledge about possible terrorist threats. Unless engaged in an explicit criminal investigation, agents had been barred from such monitoring, under guidelines adopted to prevent infringements of civil liberties such as had occurred under former FBI chief J. Edgar Hoover. Ashcroft said the old guidelines hampered agents "from taking the initiative to detect and prevent future terrorist attacks." Some civil rights advocates voiced concern about the new changes.

Ex-FBI Agent Gets Life in Prison for Spying—Robert Hanssen, the FBI agent who had spied for the Soviet Union and Russia, off and on, for more than 20 years before his arrest in 2001, was sentenced on **May 10** to life in prison without possibility of parole. The sentence, imposed by Chief Judge Claude Hilton in U.S. District Court in Alexandria, VA, resulted from a plea bargain with the government in which Hanssen, in order to escape the death penalty, had agreed to cooperate in telling the story of his espionage.

Bush Signs Farm Subsidy Bill—Pres. Bush **May 13** signed a bill that would increase federal payments to farmers by at least $83 billion over 10 years. Congressional critics called it a budget-buster. Bush argued that the bill, backed by farm-state politicians alarmed at falling prices, would provide a safety net without encouraging overproduction.

Last Suspect in 1963 Killing of 4 Black Girls Convicted—An Alabama jury closed the book on a 39-year-old murder case, **May 22,** convicting a former member of the Ku Klux Klan in a 1963 bombing at a Birmingham, AL, Baptist church that killed 4 young black girls. The defendant, Bobby Frank Cherry, 71, was found guilty of 4 counts of murder and would remain in prison for the rest of his life. Two other defendants were convicted in 1977 and 2001; a 4th suspect died without being tried. Cherry's conviction, by a Jefferson County jury of 9 whites and 3 blacks, was subject to an automatic appeal.

Remains of Missing Intern Found in DC Park—A year-long mystery took a dramatic turn **May 22** with the discovery of the remains of Chandra Levy, a 24-year-old government intern last seen Apr. 30, 2001. A man walking his dog and looking for turtles saw a skull in an unfrequented spot in Rock Creek Park, in Washington, DC. Police found scattered bones and pieces of a woman's clothing; dental records confirmed the identification. During the past year, police had questioned Rep. Gary Condit (D, CA) several times; he acknowledged having had a close relationship with Levy. He was defeated for renomination to the U.S. House in a March 2002 primary. On **May 28**, the District's chief medical examiner, Dr. Jonathan Arden, ruled Levy's death a homicide, but could not say how she had been killed.

International

Israel Frees Arafat; Bombings Continue—Israeli forces pulled out of the West Bank city of Ramallah on **May 2,** allowing Palestinian leader Yasir Arafat to leave his compound.

Meanwhile, fire broke out briefly **May 1** in the compound of the Church of the Nativity, in Bethlehem, after Palestinians inside exchanged shots with Israelis. The same day, UN Sec. Gen. Kofi Annan said he would disband an investigation into the conduct of Israeli forces at the Jenin refugee camp. Israel had challenged the makeup of the proposed mission and had demanded immunity from prosecution for Israeli soldiers and officials. On **May 2** the U.S. Senate, 94–2, and House, 352–21, supported resolutions backing Israel's recent military operations.

A meeting in Washington, DC, **May 7** between Israeli Prime Min. Ariel Sharon and Pres. George W. Bush was jarringly interrupted by news of a suicide bombing in Rishon le Zion, Israel. The explosion, at a gambling and billiards club, killed 15 and injured 58; Sharon quickly returned home. Arafat **May 8** ordered his forces to "confront and prevent all terrorist attacks against Israeli civilians." On **May 9,** Palestinian forces arrested 16 members of Hamas, thought to be responsible for the bombing. Israeli tanks moved toward the Gaza Strip, where Hamas was based.

Most Palestinians left the Church of the Nativity **May 9** after an agreement with Israel that 26 would be sent to the Gaza Strip; 13 Israeli-described "senior terrorists" also eventually left, to be dispersed throughout Europe. On **May 10,** Israeli forces ended a 39-day siege and left Bethlehem.

On **May 12,** the Likud Party, the main component of Israel's ruling coalition government, approved a resolution never to allow creation of a Palestinian state. In Netanya **May 19,** a bomber disguised as an Israeli soldier killed himself and 3 others and wounded more than 50 in a crowded market. In the following days, more bombings and attempted bombings occurred. Israeli forces went back into Bethlehem **May 27.**

French President Reelected, Routing Right-Winger—Pres. Jacques Chirac of France was reelected **May 5** with 82% of the vote. He defeated Jean-Marie Le Pen, a right-wing extremist who had qualified for the runoff in an upset. Chirac drew broad support, even from the political left, which had been left with no viable alternative.

Foe of Myanmar Regime Released from House Arrest—A longtime advocate of democracy in Myanmar was freed from house arrest, the government said **May 6.** Aung San Suu Kyi, who won the 1991 Nobel Peace Prize, had been barred from organizing a political opposition to the authoritarian regime. In 1990, her party had won a landslide victory in parliamentary elections, which the military government had rejected. Many of her political allies had been arrested. The government drew international condemnation and received economic sanctions as a result.

Dutch Candidate for Prime Minister Assassinated—Pim Fortuyn, a candidate for prime minister in the Netherlands, was shot dead **May 6** after giving an interview in Hilversum. Fortuyn had labeled Islam a "backward culture" and opposed immigration by Muslims; he had also criticized environmentalists. Generally seen as a populist, he was openly gay and had hoped to become the country's first gay prime minister. Police **May 6** arrested Volkert van der Graaf, an animal rights advocate, for the shooting. In parliamentary elections held **May 15,** Fortuyn's party ran a surprisingly strong 2nd, behind the conservative Christian Democrats.

Tensions Heighten Between India and Pakistan—In India's Gujarat state, 16 were killed and nearly 50 wounded **May 7-8** in Hindu-Muslim violence. On **May 14,** in Jammu, capital of the disputed state of Kashmir, 3 gunmen killed 34 and wounded almost 50. Indian officials blamed a Pakistan-based militant group. Militants killed 3 soldiers and a policeman, as soldiers from both countries exchanged fire in the mountains of Kashmir. By **May 20,** as reports came of combat deaths and killings from several sectors, thousands of villagers in Kashmir fled, seeking safety. On **May 21,** a moderate Kashmiri leader, Abdul Goni Lone, was assassinated, with India and Pakistan blaming each other for the killing. Prime Min. Atal Behari Vajpayee of India told his army **May 22** to prepare for a "decisive battle" against terrorism. On **May 23,** Pakistan said it would shift troops from the search for al-Qaeda and Taliban fighters to the Kashmir front. Pakistan **May 25** began a series of missile tests.

In St. Petersburg, Russia, **May 25,** Pres. Bush urged Musharraf to "stop the incursions" by militants into Kashmir, while Russian Pres. Vladimir Putin criticized Pakistan's missile tests. There were widespread concerns that war could break out between India and Pakistan, 2 bitter adversaries with nuclear capability. A million soldiers from both sides were already facing each other along an 1,800-mile border.

On **May 1,** Pakistani Pres. Pervez Musharraf had claimed victory in an Apr. 30 referendum that extended his term for 5 years. Opponents disputed the government's assertion that 71% of the people had voted, 98% for Musharraf.

Terrorist Bombers Strike in Pakistan and Russia—A bomber stopped his car next to a bus and set off an explosion in Karachi, Pakistan, **May 8,** killing 14 and injuring more than 20. Most of the victims were French civilians working on a submarine project.

A bomb exploded next to a military marching band in Kaspiisk, in the Russian republic of Dagestan **May 9,** killing 42, at least 17 of whom were children, and injuring more than 100. Dagestan borders the breakaway province of Chechnya.

Carter Visits Cuba—Former Pres. Jimmy Carter arrived in Cuba **May 12,** becoming the first U.S. president in or out of office to visit the island since the Communists seized power there in 1959. On **May 13** he visited a biological research center, where he said that his briefings by the Bush administration had not touched upon any allegations that Cuba was developing biological weapons—despite public U.S. State Dept. charges that such weapons were being developed. The same day Carter also met with Cuban dissidents. Allowed by Cuban Pres. Fidel Castro to speak live and uncensored on television **May 14,** Carter, in Spanish, criticized Castro's one-party rule and urged the regime to allow opposition movements and other basic freedoms. He called on the U.S. to end its trade embargo and ease travel restrictions. In Miami on **May 20,** on the 100th anniversary of Cuban independence, Pres. Bush declared he would not lift the embargo until Cuba made progress toward democracy.

U.S., Russia Agree to Cut Nuclear Warheads—Pres. Bush announced **May 13** that he and Pres. Putin of Russia would sign a treaty committing the two nations to reduce their nuclear arsenals by two-thirds. The reductions, over 10 years, would leave each with 1,700 to 2,200 strategic warheads. Decommissioned warheads would not be destroyed, but placed in storage. Bush and Putin signed a formal treaty in the Kremlin **May 24;** Bush said the event marked the end of "a long chapter of confrontation."

On **May 28,** in Rome, NATO leaders signed an agreement to admit Russia as a sort of junior partner. Russia did not formally join the recently expanded 19-member organization, and was not bound by its collective defense agreement, but would have a seat at the table to join NATO members in dealing with terrorism and other common issues.

Ireland Returns Prime Minister to Power—Prime Min. Bertie Ahern of Ireland was assured of retaining office after his Fianna Fail party ran far ahead of Fine Gael in general elections **May 17**. Sinn Fein, the political arm of the Irish Republican Army, won 5 seats. Ahern had played a principal role in advancing the peace process in Northern Ireland.

East Timor Joins Roster of Nations—East Timor, a small and poor Pacific Ocean nation, became independent **May 20**. Portugal had pulled out in 1975, and neighboring Indonesia had then annexed the area, allegedly practicing widespread repression and fueling civil unrest that led to massive numbers of deaths in the largely Roman Catholic population. In a 1999 UN-organized referendum, 78% of the voters had supported independence. Pres. Megawati Sukarnoputri of Indonesia and former U.S. Pres. Bill Clinton were among those at the independence ceremony.

Bush, in Europe, Defends Anti-Terror Strategy—Pres. Bush arrived in Berlin **May 22,** beginning a European trip in which he defended his handling of the war on terrorism. Addressing the German parliament in the historic Reichstag building **May 23,** he likened contemporary terrorist groups to those who had killed in the past in the name of racial purity—an apparent reference to Nazis. He said Europe, Russia, and the U.S. must defeat rogue nations that would give weapons of mass destruction to terrorists. In Paris, **May 26,** Bush downplayed differences with Europe on the environment, relations with Iraq, and other issues. On **May 27,** Memorial Day in the U.S., he visited the Normandy battlefield. On **May 28,** he met in the Vatican with Pope John Paul II.

Colombians Elect Hard-Line Foe of Rebels—Alvaro Uribe, a former mayor of Medellin who had promised to step up efforts to defeat leftist rebels, was elected president of Colombia **May 26**. He won a majority in the first round of voting, finishing more than 20 percentage points ahead of Horacio Serpa of the Liberal Party, his nearest challenger.

General

Boston Archdiocese Renounces Abuse Settlement; More Catholic Clerics Implicated—On **May 3,** the finance council of the Roman Catholic archdiocese of Boston withdrew from an agreement to settle claims by 86 sexual abuse victims against a former priest, John Geoghan. The council said the archdiocese, led by Cardinal Bernard Law, could not afford the agreement, which would cost up to $30 million, while at the same time facing large numbers of additional claims from alleged victims.

The Rev. Paul Shanley, a former priest arrested in April, pleaded not guilty in Cambridge, MA, **May 7** to 3 counts of raping a boy. The next day, in Malden, MA, another retired priest, Ronald Pacquin, pleaded not guilty to a similar charge. Cardinal Law, responding in a court-ordered deposition **May 8** in Boston, said he had known in 1984 of accusations against Geoghan but had turned the inquiry over to aides and never followed up. He said he took the advice of a deputy and doctors when he assigned Geoghan to a new parish 2 months after having removed him from another parish following complaints.

On **May 13,** Rev. Maurice Blackwell was wounded by 3 shots outside his home in Baltimore; Dontee Stokes, arrested by police, said the priest had abused him when he was 17. A Connecticut priest, Rev. Alfred Bietighofer, hanged himself **May 16** at the St. Luke Institute in Silver Spring, MD, a treatment center for priests accused of molestation.

On **May 23,** Archbishop Rembert Weakland of Milwaukee acknowledged having paid $450,000 in church funds in response to a claim that he had sexually assaulted a graduate student, then 33; the acknowledgement came hours after the secret 1998 settlement was reported on television. Though he denied any sexual misconduct, Weakland, 75, asked the Vatican to grant him immediate retirement, which was approved **May 24**.

Student Arrested for Planting Pipe Bombs—Luke John Helder, 21, a student at the University of Wisconsin at Menomonie, was arrested **May 7** near Reno, NV, for planting pipe bombs in or near rural mailboxes. Eight bombs had been found in Illinois and Iowa **May 3**. Six had detonated, injuring 4 mail carriers and 2 residents. An anti-government message left with the bombs had promised more "attention-getters." Seven bombs were found in Nebraska **May 4** and **5,** and one each in Nebraska, Colorado, and Texas **May 6.**

Ceremony Marks End of WTC Clean-Up—A ceremonial last girder was removed **May 30** from the site in lower Manhattan where the World Trade Center towers had stood before the Sept. 11 terrorist attack, signaling the end of a massive clean-up and recovery operation. The solemn event began at 10:29 A.M., the time the second tower had collapsed. There were no speeches. As public officials and thousands of others looked on in silence, workers filed out and an empty stretcher was carried out of the pit, followed by a truck hauling the flag-draped 58-ton steel column. The clean-up had involved the removal—and sifting for human remains—of some 1.8 million tons of debris.

War Emblem Wins Two out of Three—War Emblem led from the gate to the finish line to win the 128th Kentucky Derby in Louisville **May 4.** Prevailing by 4 lengths in 2:01.13, the horse, ridden by Victor Espinoza, trained by Bob Baffert, and owned by Saudi Prince Ahmed bin Salman of Saudi Arabia, won an $875,000 prize. War Emblem's bid for the Triple Crown reached the two-thirds mark **May 18** when the colt won the Preakness Stakes in Baltimore by three-quarters of a length in 1:56.36. However, on **June 8,** in the Belmont Stakes in New York, War Emblem stumbled out of the starting gate to finish 8th. The winner, in 2:29.71, was Sarava, a 70-1 long shot.

2 Smash Science Fiction Movies Pack In the Fans—*Spider-Man,* a sci-fi adventure based on the comic-strip character, broke box office records **May 3-5,** raking in $114.8 million on its opening 3-day weekend. The previous high, $90.3 million, was set in 2001 by *Harry Potter and the Sorcerer's Stone.* Released by Columbia Pictures, *Spider-Man* starred Tobey Maguire as the adolescent superhero.

Star Wars: Episode 2—Attack of the Clones, which opened on Thursday, **May 16,** tallied $116.3 million in ticket sales over its first 4 days. *Spider-Man* had gotten good reviews, but *Star Wars*—the 5th in the sequence despite its subtitle—was panned by many critics.

Castroneves Wins Indy 500 Race Again—Helio Castroneves won the Indianapolis 500 Mile Race for the 2nd year in a row, **May 26,** in a car owned by Roger Penske.

JUNE 2002

National

Bush Proposes Cabinet-level Security Department—On **June 6,** in a televised address, Pres. George W. Bush proposed creation of a cabinet-level Dept. of Homeland Security combining 22 existing federal agencies and charged with responsibility for preventing terrorist attacks. Agencies transferred to the new department would include the Coast Guard, Secret Service, Immigration and Naturalization Service, and Customs Service. The Federal Bureau of Investigation and the Central Intelligence Agency would remain outside, but the new department would review their intelligence. Bush's proposal required approval by Congress.

On **June 6,** Coleen Rowley, the lawyer in the Minneapolis FBI office who had written a letter in May protesting actions by FBI higher-ups in Washington, DC, testified before the Senate Intelligence Committee. She said reports from FBI field offices often got swallowed up by a many-tiered hierarchy in Washington. She also testified that Washington agents had prevented efforts by Minneapolis agents to obtain a warrant to search the computer of Zacarias Moussaoui, an alleged conspirator arrested in August 2001. She said his computer contained the phone number of one of the principal Sept. 11 hijackers and data on the configuration of airplane cockpits.

The Justice Dept. said **June 10** that it had thwarted a plot to explode a "dirty bomb"—a conventional bomb with radioactive material added in that would be spread in an explosion—within the U.S. Attorney Gen. John Ashcroft, in

Moscow, announced that on **May 8,** at O'Hare International Airport in Chicago, authorities had arrested a U.S. citizen arriving from Pakistan who was connected to the plot: Jose Padilla, who now called himself Abdullah al-Muhajir. The arrest was said to be based on leads from the interrogation of a captured al-Qaeda leader, Abu Zubaydah. The plot was said to be in its early stages, with no evidence indicating Padilla or his confederates had obtained radioactive material.

Accounting Firm Guilty of Obstructing Justice—Arthur Andersen, heretofore one of the nation's "Big 5" accounting firms, was convicted of obstruction of justice by a federal jury, **June 15,** after 10 days of deliberation. Andersen, once the accounting firm for the now-bankrupt Enron Corp., had been charged with hindering a Securities and Exchange Commission investigation into Enron, in part by destroying thousands of records related to its Enron audit.

On **June 13,** in a controversial ruling, U.S. Federal District Judge Melinda Harmon had told jurors they could convict the firm even if they could not agree on which individual Andersen employee(s) acted with corrupt intent. While the destruction of documents assumed a central role in the prosecution case, several jurors later said they had reached their verdict because of finding that an Andersen partner and lawyer, Nancy Temple, prescribed crucial deletions from a memo by David Duncan, Andersen's chief auditor for Enron. Duncan had pleaded guilty in April to obstructing justice.

After the Enron scandal broke, many of Andersen's clients had deserted it, and Andersen's U.S. payroll had shrunk from 27,000 to 10,000. After the verdict, which Andersen said it would appeal, the company voluntarily agreed to relinquish auditing public companies in the U.S., effectively ending its 89 years in business.

Ventura Won't Seek Reelection—Jesse Ventura, elected governor of Minnesota in 1998 on the Refom Party ticket, announced **June 18** that he would not seek a 2nd term. The outspoken former wrestler, who rode a wave of discontent to win the governorship, became frustrated by a hostile legislature and a $2 billion budget deficit, as well as by what he considered media intrusions into his family's privacy.

WorldCom Admits $3.8 Billion Cash-Flow Error—WorldCom, the nation's 2nd-largest long-distance communications carrier, announced **June 25** that it had overstated its cash flow by $3.8 billion during the past 15 months. WorldCom operated a network for Internet, data, and telephone services in 65 countries; its MCI unit, acquired in 1998, had 20 million U.S. long-distance customers. Its auditor was Arthur Andersen. Chief Executive Bernard Ebbers, who owed the company more than $400 million for loans and loan guarantees, had resigned in April. In May, as WorldCom struggled to refinance $30 billion in debt, its bonds were reduced to junk status. Since the beginning of the year its stock had lost more than 90% of its value. On **June 25** WorldCom announced it had dismissed its CFO, Scott Sullivan, and would lay off 17,000 of its 85,000 employees. The Securities and Exchange Commission, **June 26,** filed fraud charges against the company; Pres. Bush called WorldCom's overstatement of earnings "outrageous" and said responsible people would be held accountable.

Appeals Court Calls Pledge of Allegiance Unconstitutional—A 3-judge panel of the U.S Court of Appeals for the Ninth Circuit ruled 2–1, **June 26,** in San Francisco that recitation in schools of the Pledge of Allegiance was unconstitutional because the phrase "under God," added by Congress in 1954, violated the First Amendment prohibition against "laws respecting establishment of religion." Under the ruling, which was stayed pending appeal, schools in the 9 Western states covered by the circuit would be barred from reciting the pledge. The lawsuit was brought by Michael Newdow, an atheist whose daughter attended a California public school. An appeal of the ruling seemed certain.

Supreme Court OK's Vouchers—In a major decision on **June 27,** the U.S. Supreme Court, ruling 5-4, upheld a 6-year-old program in Cleveland, OH, providing for public money to help parents pay tuition in nonpublic schools. According to 1999-2000 statistics, some 3,700 of the district's 75,000 children were using vouchers of up to $2,250 each to attend nonpublic schools, 96% of which were religious. The Cleveland program also provided for magnet public schools that parents could choose. A federal appeals court in December 2000 had stricken down the program, concluding it had the "impermissible effect of promoting sectarian schools." The Supreme Court's majority opinion, written by Chief Justice William Rehnquist, contended that the Ohio program was "entirely neutral with respect to religion" in that it allowed "genuine choice among options public and private, secular and religious."

The ruling appeared to move the focus of the school choice controversy back toward the states, where more voucher plans might be considered in legislatures and referenda, leaving state courts to decide whether they were permissible under the state constitution.

U.S. Economy at a Glance: June 2002	
Unemployment rate	5.9%
Consumer prices (12 mo. change)	1.1%
Producer prices (12 mo. change)	–3.2%
Trade deficit (12 mos. through June)	$373.7 bil.
Dow Jones high (2nd quarter: Apr. 10)	10,381.73
Dow Jones low (2nd quarter: June 26)	9,120.11
2nd-quarter GDP (annual rate)	+1.3%

International

As Terrorism Against Israel Continues, U.S. Repudiates Arafat—Israeli forces, sweeping through Nablus, in the West Bank, claimed **June 2** that they had found a large explosives factory in a refugee camp. They raided other cities in the following days. Palestinian Authority chairman Yasir Arafat met **June 4** with CIA Director George Tenet in Ramallah and presented a plan to reform the Palestinian security forces. Meanwhile, on **June 5** a Palestinian militant stopped his car next to a bus in northern Israel and detonated explosives that killed himself and 17 Israelis, including 13 soldiers. Israel responded the next day by surrounding Arafat's compound in Ramallah and pounding it in a new assault that left 2 people dead.

Pres. George W. Bush met with Prime Min. Ariel Sharon of Israel at the White House, **June 10,** and told reporters, "Israel has a right to defend herself." On **June 18,** a suicide bomber detonated an explosion on a bus in Jerusalem, killing himself and 19 others; in a 2nd bombing in Jerusalem, **June 19,** a bomber killed himself and 6 Israelis at a bus stop. Palestinian gunmen, **June 20,** killed 5 Israelis in a raid on the settlement of Itamar. The next day, Israeli forces began occupying portions of the West Bank, under a policy of seizing and holding territory until bombings stopped.

In a major speech **June 24,** Bush declared for the first time that the U.S. would not support creation of an independent Palestine until Arafat departed as the Palestinian leader. Bush also called for reforms by Palestinians, including free elections and an end to terrorism and corruption. The next day, Arafat, while endorsing these calls, brushed aside the repudiation of his leadership, stating that the Palestinian people would decide who their leaders would be. On **June 26,** the Palestinian Authority announced it would hold elections for president and legislative positions in January 2003.

In a raid **June 30** on a house in Nablus, Israeli special forces killed Mohaned Tahir, described by Israeli officials as a top Hamas bomb-maker, responsible for the deaths of more than 100 Israelis in suicide attacks. The same day Israeli Defense Min. Benyamin Ben-Eliezer said Israel had begun construction of an electronic fence designed to block off 3 sides of Jerusalem from the West Bank. The fence around Jerusalem was similar to a barrier begun earlier in the month farther to the northwest, separating part of Israel from the West Bank. Israeli plans, opposed by many Palestinians and by some Israelis (especially settlers in the West Bank), called for eventually building barriers that would separate all of Israel from the West Bank.

Britain Celebrates Queen's Jubilee—Britain in early June celebrated the Golden Jubilee of Queen Elizabeth II, who had succeeded to the throne on the death of her father, George VI, in 1952. On **June 2,** festivities at Buckingham Palace were disrupted when a fire forced the evacuation of hundreds of people. A **June 3** concert featured performances by Sir Paul McCartney, Eric Clapton, and others. The final day of celebrations, **June 4,** included marching bands, a carnival at the palace, and a wave by the queen from the balcony to 1.2 million cheering admirers.

Tensions Between India and Pakistan Ease—After appearing to be near the brink of nuclear war in May, India and Pakistan took some steps toward easing their confrontation over Kashmir. In speeches on **June 4** at a regional conference in Kazakhstan, Pres. Pervez Musharraf of Pakistan and Prime Min. Atal Bihari Vajpayee of India blamed each other for the crisis. Russian Pres. Vladimir Putin met with both and sought without success to find some common ground. On **June 8,** however, the Indian government applauded a promise by Musharraf to end infiltration by Muslim militants across the Line of Control into the Indian province of Jammu and Kashmir. And on **June 10,** India lifted a ban on Pakistani commercial aircraft flying over India and withdrew naval vessels from Pakistan's coast.

American Hostage Killed in Philippines—Martin Burnham, a U.S. missionary captured in the Philippines by the Abu Sayyaf Muslim group in May 2001, was fatally shot **June 7** during a rescue attempt by Filipino soldiers on Mindanao. The victim's wife, Gracia Burnham, was wounded but rescued; a Filipino nurse also being held hostage was killed. As part of the worldwide struggle against terrorism, the Bush administration had sent weapons to the Filipino army, and on Jan. 31 U.S. troops had begun arriving in the islands to provide anti-terror training.

Grand Council OKs Plan for Afghan Government—Delegates to a *loya jirga,* or grand council, assembled in the Afghan capital of Kabul **June 10** to establish a constitutional framework for a permanent government. The 86-year-old former king, Mohammad Zahir Shah, and former Pres. Burhanuddin Rabbani threw their support for president behind Hamid Karzai, the interim leader, and on **June 13,** Karzai was elected with 1,295 of 1,575 ballots. On **June 24,** a new cabinet, put together with difficulty among the various factions, was sworn in.

Terrorists Strike Again in Pakistan—A car bombing in front of the U.S. consulate in Karachi, Pakistan, **June 14** claimed at least 12 lives.

General

Kennedy Kin Convicted of 1975 Murder—After 4 days of deliberation, a Norwalk, CT, jury **June 7** convicted Michael Skakel, 41, nephew of the late Sen. Robert Kennedy, in the 1975 murder of Martha Moxley, his 15-year-old neighbor. Moxley had been bludgeoned to death on her family's Greenwich, CT, estate with a golf club owned by the Skakel family, but investigators failed in initial efforts to construct a solid case against any suspect. When, 25 years later, Skakel was first charged, he was indicted as a juvenile, but a juvenile court in 2001 ordered that he be charged as an adult.

Wildfires Ravage Western U.S.—Wildfires in June consumed large acreages in Colorado, Arizona, California, and other western states. A welding accident in northern Los Angeles County on **June 6** started one fire, which destroyed 7 homes and forced 1,100 people to flee their homes. On **June 8,** 4,000 were evacuated from Glenwood Springs, in western Colorado, as a fire threatened. As winds rose to 40 mph and with temperatures in the 90s, fires spread throughout Colorado **June 9.** On **June 10,** the largest of 8 fires, which had burned 75,000 acres, came within 50 miles of Denver; clouds of smoke rose 20,000 feet and covered the city. As of **June 10,** 22 major fires in 7 states had burned 780 square miles.

On **June 15,** an 18-year veteran of the Forest Service, Terry Lynn Barton, said she had accidentally started the biggest Colorado fire—which had now consumed 100,000 acres—when she burned a letter from her estranged husband. She had reported the fire herself, claiming at first to have discovered it at a campsite. On **June 16,** several charges were filed against her. Gradually, the fire near Denver was contained.

A major fire in Arizona began when a lost hiker started a small fire as a signal. A nearby fire began **June 18** and by **June 21** had consumed 120,000 acres and driven 8,000 from their homes. The fires merged **June 23**. By **June 24,** this fire, having consumed 330,000 acres, was moving close to Show Low, pop. 8,000, now evacuated. Pres. Bush toured the fire area **June 25** and met with evacuees at Eagar, AZ.

On **June 30,** Leonard Gregg, 29, a part-time firefighter, was charged with deliberately setting the **June 18** fire near his home, reportedly in order to earn money fighting it.

Catholic Bishops Debate Sex-Abuse Scandal—Roman Catholic cardinals and bishops from across the U.S. met in Dallas, TX, in June to discuss what to do about the scandal in the church relating to sexual abuse of minors by priests.

On **June 12,** more than a dozen victims of abuse met with Church leaders, described their experiences, and demanded that the bishops support a zero-tolerance policy for abusers. Three men and a woman spoke to the bishops **June 13,** describing how their lives had been devastated by the abuse and by subsequent ill treatment by the Church. Bishop Wilton Gregory of Belleville, IL, president of the conference, said the bishops were responsible for the tragedy, for allowing guilty priests to remain in the ministry and reassigning them. The bishops **June 14** approved a new set of policies for all dioceses, which called for removing from active duties any priest found to have abused a minor and reporting all accusations of abuse to civil authorities. An outside review board headed by Gov. Frank Keating of Oklahoma would monitor compliance. The new policies, in order to become official church law, require approval by the Vatican.

On **June 21,** a Catholic priest was arrested in Texas on charges that 2 years earlier, in Brooklyn, NY, he had raped a woman who was seeking his advice. The priest, Cyriacus Udegbulem, was dismissed in Brooklyn but later found work in a church and hospital in Laredo, TX.

Lakers Win 3rd Straight NBA Title—The Los Angeles Lakers, led again by Shaquille O'Neal, won the National Basketball Assn. championship for the 3rd straight year, **June 12.** Their victims, the New Jersey Nets, fell in 4 straight games, including the final one, in East Rutherford, NJ, 113-107. The Nets had never before reached the title series. O'Neal, named the series' MVP for the 3rd time, scored 34 points in the final; Kobe Bryant added 25. Phil Jackson was the championship coach for the 9th time—he had won 6 times with the Chicago Bulls—tying him with former Boston Celtics coach Red Auerbach for most titles.

Tiger Woods Wins His 2nd U.S. Open Title—Tiger Woods captured the U.S. Open Golf title for the 2nd time, **June 16,** shooting a 3-under-par 277 in Farmingdale, NY.

Brazil Takes World Cup—Brazil defeated Germany, 2-0, in the finals of the World Cup soccer tournament, **June 30** in Yokohama, Japan, to win its 5th global soccer title. Earlier, the U.S. made an unusually strong showing, qualifying for the 16-team single-elimination rounds and advancing to the quarter-finals, **June 17,** by defeating Mexico, 2-0; Germany then defeated the U.S., 1-0, on **June 21**.

JULY 2002

National

Watts Not Running—On **July 1,** Rep. J. C. Watts (R, OK), chairman of the House Republican Conference, and the only black Republican in the House, announced he would not seek reelection in Nov. 2002.

Gunman Kills 2 at L.A. Airport—On **July 4**, with the nation on alert for possible terrorist attacks on the holiday, a gunman shot 2 people to death at the international airport in Los Angeles, near the ticket counter for El Al, the Israeli airline. He was shot dead by an El Al guard. Israel called the incident a terrorist act, but the FBI found no immediate evidence for that. Authorities **July 5** identified the gunman as Hesham Mohamed Hadayet, the Egyptian-born owner of a limousine service.

Stocks Plummet Amid Demands for Reform—On **July 9** amid corporate accounting scandals and a continued drop in U.S. stock market averages, Pres. George W. Bush spoke at a hotel near the New York Stock Exchange. Denouncing a climate of greed among some top business executives, he asked Congress to grant the Securities and Exchange Commission $100 million in additional funds to enforce securities laws. Bush also called for a corporate fraud task force to prosecute criminal acts, longer prison sentences for fraud by corporate officers and directors, and shareholder approval of stock-option plans, and asked corporate boards to forbid loans to executives. Even as Bush spoke, the Dow Jones industrial average was tumbling; it ended **July 9** at 9096.09, down 178.81.

On **July 10** the Dow declined 282.59 points to 8813.50, and the Standard & Poor's 500-stock index and the Nasdaq index fell to their lowest levels since 1997. The Nasdaq, in which technology companies are heavily represented, had lost almost 75% of its value since 2000. By week's end, **July 12,** the Dow had declined to 8684.53. The market's fall impacted the federal government's bottom line. Although the government recorded a $127 billion surplus in the fiscal year ending Sept. 30, 2001, the Bush administration said **July 13** that fiscal year 2002 would see a deficit of $165 billion. On **July 15**, for the first time in 2 years, the euro came out ahead of the slumping U.S. dollar, reaching $1.0055.

Testifying before the Senate Banking Committee **July 16**, Federal Reserve Chairman Alan Greenspan blamed the decline in investor confidence on "an infectious greed" that "seemed to grip much of our business community." During the week of **July 15-19**, the market slump accelerated, with the Dow closing Friday at 8019.26. The slide continued through **July 23,** when it closed at 7702.34. Then, on **July 24,** it jumped 488.95, its 2nd-highest one-day point increase. After another surge of 447.49 points, **July 29,** the Dow stood at 8711.88. The Commerce Dept. **July 31** released a report estimating economic growth in the 2nd quarter at a meager 1.1%. The report also gave revised figures showing that the recession of 2001 had been worse than originally estimated.

AOL Time Warner announced **July 31** that the Justice Dept. had launched an investigation of accounting practices at the media giant's AOL division. That probe came just a week after the start of an inquiry by the SEC. The company said its outside auditors, Ernst & Young, had approved its accounting repeatedly. In a separate development, General Electric said **July 31** that it would abandon a common but frequently criticized accounting practice, and begin to count stock options for executives as an expense.

Bush **July 30** signed a bill reforming corporate fraud, accounting and security laws. The legislation set new rules for prosecuting corporate misdeeds and provided lengthy jail terms for executives who deliberately mislead investors. Bush said the law represented the most important reform of U.S. business practices since the time of Franklin D. Roosevelt. Bush had opposed some of the provisions a few weeks earlier, but mushrooming corporate scandals had altered the political landscape. Both the House and the Senate had overwhelmingly approved the legislation, based on a bill proposed by Sen. Paul Sarbanes (D, MD).

Earlier, on **July 21**, WorldCom displaced the Enron Corp. as the largest U.S. company to declare bankruptcy. WorldCom had disclosed **July 1** that its profits might have been overstated as far back as 1999, 2 years earlier than acknowledged in June. In its **July 21** filing, WorldCom listed $107 billion in assets and $41 billion in debt. The bankruptcy was not expected to have any immediate impact on the 20 million people who used its MCI long-distance service, but WorldCom stock, worth $60 a share in 1999, was now essentially worthless.

On **July 24**, John Rigas, 78, who had built Adelphia, the nation's 6th largest cable company, from scratch, was arrested in New York City, 4 weeks after the firm declared bankruptcy. Rigas's sons, Michael and Timothy, and 2 others were also arrested. The Rigases were charged with fraud; prosecutors said they had used the company for their "personal piggy bank," taking away more than $1 billion.

American Who Fought With Taliban Admits Guilt—John Walker Lindh, an American captured by the U.S. military in Afghanistan in late 2001 while with Taliban forces, admitted **July 15** that he had fought as a soldier with them. The plea bargain ended his trial in Alexandria, VA. Lindh, now 21, had gone to the Middle East to study Islam and had joined the Taliban, the radical Muslim group that previously controlled most of Afghanistan. He was originally indicted for conspiring to kill Americans and engaging in terrorism, among other crimes. Lindh said he had carried a rifle and 2 grenades while doing so, a circumstance for which he had not been charged. All other charges were dropped, including those linking him with the death of CIA agent Johnny Michael Spann, killed in a prison uprising shortly after he interviewed Lindh. Lindh, who agreed to cooperate with the U.S. investigation into the terrorist network, was sentenced **Oct. 4** to 20 years in prison.

Judge Rejects Guilty Plea by 9/11 Defendant—Zacarias Moussaoui, the only person charged in connection with the Sept. 11 attack on the U.S., told U.S. District Judge Leonie Brinkema **July 18** that he wanted to plead guilty. The government indictment had described him as the 20th hijacker, who missed a date with destiny because he had been arrested and imprisoned in August 2001. Moussaoui, who was representing himself, told the court he was a member of al-Qaeda and a loyal supporter of Osama bin Laden. He also said he had knowledge of the attacks—information he would provide to a grand jury. The judge declined to accept the plea and told him to think about it for a week. On **July 25**, Moussaoui withdrew his guilty plea after the judge told him he would be required to admit detailed involvement in the Sept. 11 plot.

19 Million Pounds of Ground Beef Recalled—The U.S. Agriculture Dept. **July 19** announced a recall of 19 million pounds of ground beef that was potentially contaminated with the *E. coli* bacterium. Nineteen people from 6 states had become ill—several were hospitalized—after consuming the hamburger, which was traced to a ConAgra Beef Co. plant in Greeley, CO. Ann Veneman, the secretary of agriculture, stressed **July 19** the need to cook ground beef thoroughly at 160 degrees in order to kill pathogens.

U.S. House Expels a Member—The U.S. House **July 24** expelled James Traficant (D, OH), by a vote of 420-1. (The one "nay" vote was cast by Gary Condit, D, CA.) In April he had been convicted of bribery, racketeering, and corruption. Traficant, who had represented the Youngstown area for 9 terms, was the 5th member of the House, and only the 2nd since the Civil War, to be expelled. On **July 30** he was sentenced to 8 years in prison.

New Jersey Senator Admonished—Sen. Robert Torricelli (D, NJ) was "severely admonished" **July 30** in a letter from the Senate Ethics Committee, for accepting expensive gifts from a businessman, David Chang, while taking "official actions of benefit" to him. Torricelli, in a tight reelection campaign, apologized the same day, in a speech to colleagues and constituents.

International

U.S. Fire Kills Many Civilians in Afghanistan—Bombs and/or cannon fire from a U.S. Air Force AC-130 struck a town in southern Afghanistan **July 1**, killing around 50 to 80 people. Many victims were members of a wedding party. Pres. Hamid Karzai, who had not previously protested publicly against the accidental killings of Afghans by the U.S. military, called for an explanation of the tragedy. U.S. officials in Afghanistan said the plane had reported being fired upon, but this was in dispute. Some reports suggested the Americans had misinterpreted the celebratory gunshots that traditionally accompany Afghan weddings.

In a blow to the Afghan government, gunmen **July 6** shot dead a vice president, Haji Abdul Qadir, in Kabul.

Former Chilean Dictator Won't Face Trial—Gen. Augusto Pinochet, 86, who had been linked to human rights violations when he was president of Chile, was spared any further legal action **July 1**. The Supreme Court ruled, 4-1, that he was mentally incompetent and unable to defend himself. He had been accused of approving and then covering up the torture and killing of large numbers of leftists.

4 Convicted in Pakistan in Death of U.S. Reporter—A judge in Pakistan **July 15** found 4 men guilty in the kidnapping and murder of Daniel Pearl, a reporter for the *Wall Street Journal.* One defendant, Ahmed Omar Sheikh, was sentenced to death; 3 others received prison sentences.

Mideast Violence Resumes—In the first attack on Israeli civilians in almost a month, Palestinians **July 16** set off a bomb near a bus near a Jewish settlement in the West Bank, killing 9 and wounding 16. Two suicide bombers killed themselves and 3 others **July 17** when they ignited explosives near a bus station in Tel Aviv. On **July 23**, a laser-guided bomb fired from an Israeli warplane hit the home in Gaza City of Sheik Salah Shehada, a founder of the military wing of Hamas, killing him. The strike, in a densely populated area, killed 14 others, including 9 children, and wounded more than 140. It prompted international criticism, including an unusual display of displeasure from the Bush administration, which termed it "heavy handed." Four Jewish settlers in the West Bank were shot to death in an ambush **July 26**. After a funeral for one of the victims of the shooting, Jewish settlers rampaged in a Palestinian neighborhood **July 28** and killed a 14-year-old Palestinian girl.

Seven people, including 5 Americans, died **July 31** when a bomb hidden in a bag exploded in a crowded cafeteria in Hebrew University in Jerusalem. More than 70 were injured. A Hamas spokesman termed it reprisal for the Israeli air strike in Gaza City on **July 23**. On **July 30**, Palestinian gunmen had killed 2 Israeli brothers in Jamain on the West Bank. The al-Aqsa Martyrs Brigades reportedly claimed responsibility. The same day a 17-year-old Palestinian blew himself up in a suicide bombing in Jerusalem; 5 Israelis were wounded.

In Beirut, Lebanon, 8 people died **July 31** when a disgruntled employeed shot at an Education Ministry building.

Congo, Rwanda Sign Peace Pact—The presidents of Rwanda and the Democratic Republic of Congo **July 30** signed a peace agreement intended to end the hostilities between the 2 countries after Rwandan Hutu rebels fled to the Congo (then called Zaire). The Hutus had been involved in extensive massacres of their ethnic rivals, the Tutsis, in Rwanda. War between Rwanda and the Congo had gone on for 4 years, reportedly costing the lives of 2 million people. The peace accord, signed in Pretoria, South Africa, provided for the Congo to disarm and arrest the Hutu rebels, while Rwanda promised to remove soldiers from the eastern regions of the Congo. Observers noted, however, that Congolese forces would not have an easy time disarming the Hutu militias, and in fact an organization representing Rwandan Hutu rebels rejected the agreement.

General

71 Die as Planes Collide Over Germany—In a rare high-altitude accident, a passenger airliner and a cargo plane collided over Germany, **July 1**, killing all 71 persons. Wreckage fell over 20 square miles near Lake Constance at the Swiss border. The crash involved a Russian Tupolev operated by Bashkirian Airlines, with a crew of 12 and 57 passengers, and a Boeing 757 operated by the DHL Worldwide courier network, with 2 pilots. Fifty-two of the dead on the Russian plane were children from the city of Ufa on their way to a vacation in Spain. Skyguide, the Swiss company running the country's air-traffic control system, acknowledged **July 3** that one of 2 controllers responsible for the planes had taken a break, and that controllers had disabled an alarm system to perform maintenance. Information from plane flight recorders, released **July 8**, showed that the Russian pilot followed an order from a Swiss air traffic controller to descend, although the plane's collision-avoidance system was urging the pilot to climb.

First Solo Global Balloon Flight Completed—After 5 previous unsuccessful attempts, Steve Fossett of the U.S. completed a round-the-world balloon flight **July 2** reaching Queensland in the Australian outback. Strong winds delayed his landing until **July 4**. He had lifted off from Northam, east of Perth, in Western Australia **June 19** and traveled 19,428 miles.

Baseball's Season of Discontent—On **July 5**, baseball great Ted Williams, the last player to hit .400 for a season (.406 in 1941), died at 83. Mixed with the sadness over Williams's passing was a note of the bizarre; reports surfaced by **July 8** that his son, John Henry Williams, had sent the body from a funeral home in Florida to a cryonics facility, the Alcor Life Extension Foundation, in Scottsdale, AZ. John's half sister, Barbara Williams, charged that he hoped to freeze the body and sell DNA from it to prospective parents who wanted a Ted Williams of their own.

The All-Star Game, on **July 9** in Milwaukee, featured outstanding plays and an exciting contest, but ended on a sour note when Baseball Commissioner Bud Selig halted play after 11 innings, with the score tied at 7, saying the teams had run out of pitchers. Fans howled in protest.

Also casting a pall over the season were the threat of a players' strike and rumors of alleged widespread use by players of steroids and other performance-enhancing drugs. The players' union executive board declined **July 8** to set a date for a strike. Besides salary issues, players objected to a plan by owners to test them for steroid use 3 times a year. They also opposed a plan by owners to unilaterally eliminate 2 major league teams for economic reasons.

Williams Sisters Rule Wimbledon—Serena Williams and her older sister, Venus, continued to dominate women's tennis at the annual All-England tournament in Wimbledon. Venus had won the last 2 women's titles there, but on **July 6** she lost the final to Serena, 7-6 (4), 6-3. For Serena, winner of the French Open in June, it was her 2nd grand slam tournament victory in 2 months. On **July 7,** the Williams sisters won the women's doubles, defeating Virginia Ruano Pascual of Spain and Paola Suarez of Argentina, 6-2, 7-5. In a contest of youth, Lleyton Hewitt, 21, of Australia, defeated David Nalbandian, 20, of Argentina, 6-1, 6-3, 6-2, to win the men's title **July 7.** Hewitt was the world's top-ranked player; Nalbandian was competing at Wimbledon for the first time.

Russian "Crime Boss" Nabbed in Olympics Scheme—U.S. federal prosecutors said **July 31** that Alimzan Tokhtakhounov, a Russian who was a reputed organized crime leader, had been arrested at his resort in northern Italy for allegedly attempting to fix the outcome of 2 ice skating events at the Olympics in Salt Lake City, UT. Tokhtakhounov allegedly sought to influence the judging to secure gold medals for the Russian competitors in the pairs event and the French team in the ice dancing competition. The judging in the pairs events had indeed been at the center of a scandal, with a French judge admitting she had given in to pressure; as a consequence, 2 teams had received gold medals.

Kidnappings Draw National Publicity—Several kidnappings of young girls around the U.S. in the summer generated heavy press coverage and fed people's anxieties.

On **July 19**, authorities announced they had arrested a suspect in the kidnapping and murder of 5-year-old Samantha Runnion. She had been seized **July 15** in the courtyard at an apartment complex in Stanton, CA, where she lived. The body of the victim, who had been sexually assaulted, was found **July 16** near the town of Lake Elsinore, which was also the home of the suspect, Alejandro Avila. On **July 22**, charges were filed against Avila.

Another child, Erica Pratt, escaped from her captors **July 23**. She was seized outside her Philadelphia home **July 22** and taken to an abandoned house 12 miles away. The kidnappers demanded a $150,000 ransom. Erica chewed through duct tape, broke through a wooden panel on a basement door, broke a window, and cried for help. Two boys led police officers to her. Two men were arrested in the kidnapping **July 25**.

On **July 26**, 6-year-old Cassandra Williamson was kidnapped in Valley Park, a St. Louis, MO, suburb. Her body was found several hours later. Johnny Johnson, who had stayed with the family overnight, was charged.

A kidnapping on **June 5** continued to baffle police in Salt Lake City. Elizabeth Smart, 14, was taken from her bedroom during the night. Her sister, 9, the sole witness, gave conflicting accounts of the incident. Hundreds of volunteers joined the search for Elizabeth, but she was not found, and, although a suspect was investigated, no charges were filed.

Doctor Found to Have Murdered 215 Patients—An English judge announced **July 19**, after conducting an investigation, that a family doctor had killed 215 patients over a period of 23 years. The doctor, Harold Shipman, practiced in a suburb of Manchester named Hyde (evoking a "Dr. Jekyll and Mr. Hyde" concept). Typically, his victims were elderly women to whom he gave lethal injections of diamorphine, a painkiller. Previously convicted of killing 15 people, he had already been sentenced to life in prison in 2000.

Els Wins British Open—Ernie Els, a native of South Africa, tied with 3 other golfers for first place in the British Open, **July 18-21**, then won the title in a playoff. The Open, in Gullane, Scotland, ended a Grand Slam bid by Tiger Woods, who had won the 2 previous Grand Slam events.

Ailing Pope Attends World Youth Day—Pope John Paul II, though weakened by Parkinson's disease, arrived in Toronto, Canada, **July 23** to begin an 11-day trip. Toronto was host to World Youth Day, a weeklong Roman Catholic festival. Speaking to hundreds of thousands of young people **July 25**, he urged them to turn to Christ, "the path of forgiveness and reconciliation in a world often laid waste by violence and terror." In a homily at an outdoor mass **July 28**, the pope said that the crimes and misbehaviors of some priests were a source of shame.

Visiting Guatemala City, Guatemala, **July 30**, the pope presided at a ceremony canonizing Pedro de San Jose Betancur, Central America's first saint. In Mexico City **July 31**, an exhausted-appearing pope officiated at a ceremony canonizing Juan Diego. The new saint—whose existence was questioned by some scholars—was according to the Church a 16th-century peasant whose visions of the Madonna played a role in the conversion of Mexico's Indian population; he was the first Native American to be declared a saint.

Woman Arrested in Fire Near Giant Trees—A woman was arrested **July 24** in connection with a fire burning near 2 groves of giant sequoia trees in central California. The woman, Peri Van Brunt, reportedly had stated in a convenience store that she had started a fire after having a quarrel with her boyfriend. The fire, within view of Johnsondale, covered 85 square miles.

9 Men Trapped in Coal Mine Are Rescued—A dramatic rescue operation saved the lives of 9 coal miners after several days trapped 240 feet underground in southwest Pennsylvania. The miners were inundated by water from an abandoned mine **July 25** when a wall collapsed. They survived with their heads in an air pocket. A bit on the high-powered drill used in the rescue effort broke off **July 26** and had to be replaced. The drill reached the miners **July 27**, and by early the next day all had been brought to the surface. All were thought to be in good condition.

Crash at Air Show Kills 83—In one of the worst-ever air show tragedies, 83 people were killed near Lviv, Ukraine, **July 27**, when a Ukrainian jet fighter crashed to the ground amid spectators. The 2 crew members ejected safely, but were injured. The state prosecutor, **July 29**, blamed the accident on criminal negligence. Four military officials were being detained.

Lance Armstrong Wins Tour de France 4th Time—Lance Armstrong of the U.S. won the 2,036-mile Tour de France **July 28** for the 4th straight year. His time was 82 hours, 5 minutes, and 12 seconds.

AUGUST 2002

National

Bush Gains Fast-Track Trade Power—Pres. George W. Bush **Aug. 6** signed a fast-track trade bill that strengthened his hand in negotiating trade pacts with other countries. The measure, approved by the House, **July 27**, 215-212, and the Senate, **Aug. 1**, 64-34, limited Congress to up or down votes on trade agreements negotiated by the executive branch, with no modifications allowed. This system had also been in effect from 1975 to 1994. The new bill also provided $12 billion to help U.S. workers who lose jobs because of foreign competition related to a trade agreement.

U.S. House Members Face Tough Primaries—A number of U.S. House incumbents were challenged in primaries, especially in districts merged or redrawn following results of the 2000 census. Among them, John Dingell (D, MI), a U.S. representative for longer than any other current member, faced strong opposition from fellow incumbent Lynn Rivers, but defeated her in the **Aug. 6** Democratic primary. On **Aug. 20**, Rep. Bob Barr, matched in the same district with Rep. John Linder, lost to Linder; Barr is a conservative known as a vehement critic of Pres. Bill Clinton. In another high-profile Georgia race, Rep. Cynthia McKinney, known for strong pro-Palestinian views, lost the Democratic primary to Denise Majette, a former state judge regarded as a moderate; both candidates are African-Americans.

Corporate Executives Face Trouble—The founder and former CEO of ImClone, a biotechnology company, was indicted **Aug. 7** on charges of insider trading. Prosecutors alleged that the executive, Samuel Waksal, had told relatives to sell their ImClone shares just before it became publicly known that the Food and Drug Administration was not considering ImClone's application for a new cancer drug. TV personality-entrepreneur Martha Stewart, head of Martha Stewart Living Omnimedia Inc., also came under congressional investigation for insider trading in connection with the sale of ImClone shares on **Dec. 27, 2001**, a day before the FDA decision became public.

A former Enron Corp. executive pleaded guilty in Houston **Aug. 21** to conspiracy to commit wire fraud and money laundering. Michael Kopper was the 1st employee of the bankrupt energy giant to plead guilty or be convicted in the case. In his plea bargain, Kopper agreed to cooperate with the investigation and pay the government $12 million obtained through criminal activity. He admitted having paid kickbacks to Andrew Fastow, then Enron's CFO, from money he got for managing a partnership created to conceal company debt and inflate profits.

On **Aug. 28**, 2 men were indicted in connection with an investigation into WorldCom. Scott Sullivan, its former CFO, and Buford Yates Jr., the former director of general accounting, were charged with conspiring to hide billions of dollars of losses at the company.

US Airways Files for Bankruptcy—US Airways, the nation's 6th largest airline, filed for bankruptcy protection **Aug. 11**. Like other airlines, US Airways had been hard-hit by the terrorist attack of Sept. 11; the company lost $2 billion in 2001. The airline expected to continue flying, but with altered schedules.

Bush Convenes Economic Summit—At an economic forum he convened in Waco, TX, **Aug. 13**, Pres. Bush said he was concerned but optimistic about the future of the U.S. economy; most of the 240 invited guests echoed his views. Democratic critics said the forum fell short of being a serious reexamination of economic policy.

U.S. Indicts 5 on Terrorist-Related Charges—Four Arab men were indicted in federal court in Detroit, **Aug. 28**, on charges that they were part of a terrorist unit operating in the area; 3 of them worked at Detroit Metropolitan Airport. In Seattle, **Aug. 28**, the government indicted a Muslim man, alleging he had tried to set up a terrorist training camp in Oregon. The same day, German authorities charged a Moroccan man with supporting a cell of terrorists in Hamburg thought to have had a role in planning the Sept. 11 attacks.

International

Mideast Death Toll Continues to Climb—Retaliating for a bombing at Hebrew University in Jerusalem, the Israeli army swept through Nablus, in the West Bank, **Aug. 2**, killing 3 Palestinians and arresting 50. The army, **Aug. 4**, blew up the homes of 9 suicide bombers. A bomb destroyed a bus near Safed, Israel, **Aug. 4**, killing the bomber and 9 others, and injuring more than 40. Violent incidents continued throughout the month. On **Aug. 29**, shells from an Israeli tank struck a house in Gaza, killing a woman, her 2 sons, and a cousin. Israeli helicopter gunships ambushed a car in the West Bank on **Aug. 31**, killing 3 Palestinian militants and 2 children On **Aug. 1**, the UN reported it had not found evidence that the Israeli army massacred Palestinian refugees in Jenin in April, as was charged by Palestinians.

Shells in Colombia Kill 19 at Inauguration—Alvaro Uribe Vélez was sworn in **Aug. 7** as president of Colombia, but the occasion in the capital, Bogotá, was marred by mortar shells that landed nearby. Nineteen people were killed and more than 60 wounded. Authorities believed the attack came from the nation's largest rebel group, the Revolutionary Armed Forces of Colombia. Uribe campaigned on a promise to defeat the rebels, who had been fighting the government for 38 years.

Terrorist Leader Dies of Gunshot Wounds—Abu Nidal, once one of the most feared of Palestinian terrorists, died of gunshot wounds in Baghdad, Iraq, a Palestinian newspaper reported **Aug. 19**. Long at odds with Palestinian leader Yasir Arafat, he led an extremist organization, Fatah Revolutionary Council, which reportedly received backing from Iraq. Acts attributed to Nidal included the bombing of a TWA airliner over the Aegean Sea (1974; 88 killed), the hijacking of an Egyptian airliner (1985; 66 killed), and shootings at airline ticket desks in Rome and Vienna (1985; 18 killed). Iraqi Deputy Prime Min. Tariq Aziz said **Aug. 20** that Nidal had committed suicide. The French newswire service Agence France-Presse reported that he had shot himself after officials came to arrest him on charges of trying to overthrow the Iraqi government.

Russian Copter Crash in Chechnya Kills 117—A Russian military helicopter crash-landed in a minefield near the main Russian military base in rebellious Chechnya, **Aug. 19**. The pilot of the Mi-26 transport had reported an engine fire moments before. In all, 117 of the 147 aboard were killed in the crash or by mine explosions as they sought to flee. Pres. Vladimir Putin blamed the military, **Aug. 22**, for the disaster, noting that the Ministry of Defense had banned use of the Mi-26 for transporting troops; on **Sept. 7** it was announced that 1 general had been dismissed and 4 others reprimanded.

Iraqi Opposition Group Takes Hostages in Berlin—Iraqis who opposed the regime of Saddam Hussein briefly seized control of the Iraqi embassy in Berlin **Aug. 20**. They held members of the staff hostage for 5 hours before German police broke into the compound, arrested 5 men, and freed their captives.

Bush Administration Supports "Regime Change" in Iraq—Pres. George W. Bush reiterated statements that the U.S. was considering an attack on Iraq but indicated that no final decision had been made. On **Aug. 21,** he said he was weighing all options on Iraq, while adding, "Regime change is in the interest of the world."

Sanctions imposed on Iraq after its defeat in the Gulf War in 1991 required Iraq to destroy any nuclear, biological, and chemical weapons and allow arms inspection; U.S. administration officials have maintained that Iraq had failed to cooperate with UN arms inspection teams and continued to develop weapons of mass destruction.

Foreign support for a military campaign appeared scant, while domestic opinion was divided on whether a case had yet been made. Some leading Republicans opposed intervention or urged caution, among them Rep. Dick Armey (TX), the House majority leader; Brent Scowcroft, national security adviser under Bush's father; former Sec. of State Lawrence Eagleburger; and Sen. Chuck Hagel (NE). Vice Pres. Dick Cheney, in an **Aug. 26** speech favoring U.S. military action, argued that the risks of inaction "are far greater than the risk of action." He said Iraq would have nuclear weapons "fairly soon."

Prime Minister of Canada to Retire—Prime Min. Jean Chrétien of Canada announced **Aug. 21** that he would not seek a 4th term and would step down in February 2004. Leader of the country for 9 years, he had recently been embroiled in infighting within the ruling Liberal Party. The economy had done well, but scandals involving favors from corporations to cabinet ministers had surfaced, and polls indicated his popularity was declining.

General

Heads of Siamese Twins Separated Surgically—Two one-year-old twin girls from Guatemala, who had been joined at their heads at birth, survived a 22-hour operation, **Aug. 5-6**, with apparently favorable results. A team of 13 doctors performed the procedure at Mattel Children's Hospital at the University of California at Los Angeles. Few who underwent similar procedures in the past had survived without serious brain damage.

Floods Slash Through Central Europe and Asia—More than a week of nearly constant rain sent floodwaters tearing through central Europe and southwestern Russia. By **Aug. 12** the death toll in Russia was 58. The Vlitava River inundated parts of central Prague, in the Czech Republic, forcing the evacuation of 50,000 and menacing the historic area. The autobahn between Munich, Germany, and Salzburg, Austria, was under up to 5 feet of water. By **Aug. 14**, 200,000 Czechs had fled their homes. In Dresden, Germany, the Elbe River jeopardized paintings in the famed Zwinger Palace (they were carried to the upper floors). In Austria, the Danube River overflowed in several places.

Meanwhile, in Asia, monsoon rains and resultant landslides took many lives. The death toll in China was put at 800 **Aug. 14**, and in Southeast Asia—Bangladesh, India, and Nepal—about 880 lives had been lost by that time.

West Nile Virus Spreads in U.S.—The U.S. Centers for Disease Control confirmed, **Aug. 15,** that the U.S. was experiencing its worst outbreak of the mosquito-borne West Nile virus since the virus 1st appeared in the nation (in New York City) in 1999. Most of those infected have only mild flu-like symptoms, but some suffer serious, even life-threatening complications. From June through early October, 2,946 cases were reported, with 160 deaths. Illinois had the most cases (661) and deaths (41), followed by Michigan (409, 28).

Baseball Strike Averted—Major League Baseball owners and players agreed to a new contract, **Aug. 30**, averting what would have been the sport's 9th work stoppage since 1972. It was the 1st time the 2 sides had settled their differences without a strike or a lockout. The deal, which runs through the 2006 season, stipulated that no teams would be eliminated.

SEPTEMBER 2002

National

Primaries Are Held; Florida Experiences Another Voting Snafu—Major primary elections were held in Florida, New York, and New Hampshire **Sept. 10**. In Florida, one important contest ran afoul of voting problems similar to those that snarled the 2000 presidential election. Voting machine malfunctions were reported in 14 counties, and some poll workers were unable to operate new touch-screen machines. The tight contest for the Democratic gubernatorial nomination remained in doubt for days; finally, on **Sept. 17**, former U.S. Atty. Gen. Janet Reno, who was behind by 4,800 votes, conceded to Bill McBride, a lawyer, who was slated to challenge Gov. Jeb Bush's reelection bid in November.

In New York, state Comptroller H. Carl McCall easily won the Democratic primary for governor after his opponent, Andrew Cuomo, son of the former governor and himself a former secretary of Housing and Urban Development, on **Sept. 3**, withdrew his name from consideration. (McCall was to face Gov. George Pataki (R) in November.

In New Hampshire, Sen. Bob Smith (R, NH) was defeated for renomination by Rep. John Sununu. Smith, a maverick, had briefly left the GOP in 1999, complaining that it was not conservative enough. In Washington, DC, Mayor Anthony Williams won the Democratic primary with write-in votes, after his nominating papers were found to have forged signatures and his name was removed from the ballot.

U.S. Observes Sept. 11 Anniversary—The 1st anniversary of the **Sept. 11, 2001**, terrorist attacks on the U.S., in which more than 3,000 people died, was observed with somber ceremonies. Pres. George W. Bush attended memorials at the 3 places where hijacked airplanes had crashed—the Pentagon; a field near Shanksville, PA; and the site of the World Trade Center in Manhattan. In London, a service remembered 67 Britons killed in the attacks. Earlier, on **Sept. 6**, Congress held a one-day joint session at Federal Hall, a few blocks from the New York attack site, to honor victims. Congress had not met in New York since 1790, when the capital was moved from New York to Philadelphia. Just before the anniversary, on **Sept. 10**, Atty. Gen. John Ashcroft announced an orange alert, up from yellow, meaning that the country faced an elevated risk of attack. Threats against U.S. embassies abroad were cited. Vice Pres. Dick Cheney went to a secure, undisclosed location.

3 Former Execs at Tyco Are Indicted—Charges were filed **Sept. 12** in state court in New York City against 3 former leaders of Tyco International Ltd. The 3 were former CEO L. Dennis Kozlowski, former CFO Mark Swarts, and Mark Belnik, who was general counsel. They were charged with having defrauded Tyco of millions of dollars. Tyco **Sept. 12** filed a civil suit against Kozlowski.

Dow Falls to 4-Year Low—After bouncing up from a low in late July, stock averages slid again in September. On **Sept. 24**, the Dow Jones industrial average fell 189.02 points and closed at 7,683.13, its lowest standing since October 1998.

U.S. Economy at a Glance: September 2002	
Unemployment rate	5.6%
Consumer prices (12 mo. change)	1.3%
Producer prices (12 mo. change)	–1.0%
Trade deficit (12 mo. through July)	$374.4 bil.
Dow Jones high (3rd quarter: July 5)	9,739.50
Dow Jones low (3rd quarter: Sept. 30)	7,591.93

International

Environmental Summit Held in South Africa—More than 100 heads of state met in Johannesburg, South Africa, **Aug. 25-Sept. 4** at a UN World Summit on Sustainable Development, which drew 40,000, including over 100 heads of state. The meeting was a follow-up on the Earth Summit in Brazil in 1992. The Bush administration was widely criticized for its environmental policies, and Sec. of State Colin Powell, who represented the U.S. at the conference, was heckled by activists during his speech **Sept. 4.** A document adopted **Sept. 4** made pledges to halve the number of people in the world lacking safe drinking water and adequate sanitation, increase use of renewable energy sources, minimize adverse effects of chemicals, replenish global fish stocks, and protect endangered species.

Bush Rounds Up Support for Action Against Iraq—Pres. Bush said **Sept. 4** that he would seek congressional approval for any military move against Iraq. He also promised to consult U.S. allies, many of whom opposed his plan to seek "regime change" in Iraq, where Pres. Saddam Hussein remained in power. German Chancellor Gerhard Schröder, in the midst of a reelection campaign, said **Sept. 4** that Germany would not support an attack on Iraq even if it had UN authorization.

Addressing the UN General Assembly **Sept. 12**, Bush said he would work with the UN Security Council to meet the challenge from Iraq, but added that the world must move decisively to deal with the threat posed by Iraq's weapons of mass destruction. Iraq **Sept. 16** asserted that it would allow weapons inspectors back into the country "without conditions," but U.S. and other authorities were skeptical. Hans Blix, head of the UN inspection commission, met with Iraqi officials **Sept. 17**. Defense Sec. Donald Rumsfeld said **Sept. 19** that a number of countries had pledged military support for offensive action against Iraq; the same day, Bush asked Congress to give him authority to use force against Iraq. Israeli Prime Min. Ariel Sharon was reported, **Sept. 21**, to have informed the Bush administration that Israel would strike back if attacked by Iraq, a move which many feared could inflame the Arab world; Israel had not responded to Iraqi Scud missile attacks during the Persian Gulf war.

Rumsfeld said **Sept. 27** that the U.S. had solid evidence of links between al-Qaeda and the Iraqi government. On **Sept. 28**, Iraq rejected a draft proposal from the U.S. and Britain to the Security Council for a resolution calling on Iraq to make full disclosure of weapons of mass destruction within 30 days; Iraq said it would refuse to accept any new conditions outlined by others.

Afghan Leader Escapes Assassination—An attempt to assassinate Pres. Hamid Karzai failed **Sept. 5** in Kandahar. A gunman opened fire on a car in which he was traveling, missing Karzai but slightly wounding a passenger. U.S. Special Forces troops, firing back, killed the gunman as well as 2 others. Also on **Sept. 5**, a car bomb in Kabul, the capital, killed 30 people.

UN Admits Switzerland and East Timor—Switzerland **Sept. 10** became the 190th member of the United Nations. Switzerland had not applied for UN membership in the past, as part of an effort to maintain neutrality in international affairs. But a number of UN and other international entities were based in Switzerland, and Swiss voters in a March referendum had supported joining the UN. East Timor, newly independent, also joined, becoming the 191st member **Sept. 27**.

Arrests Made on Terrorism Charges—Ramzi bin al-Shibh, who had already been indicted in Germany on 3,000 counts of murder after the Sept. 11, 2001, attacks, was arrested in Pakistan on **Sept. 10-11**, along with others with alleged ties to al-Qaeda. The U.S. took custody of al-Shibh, who was a Yemeni, and flew him to an unnamed military base **Sept. 16**. On **Sept. 13-14** the FBI arrested 5 U.S. citizens of Yemeni descent in Lackawanna, NY; they were charged in federal court in Buffalo, NY, **Sept. 14** with providing "material support" to terrorists. A 6th man was arrested in Bahrain **Sept. 15** and extradited to Buffalo. A 7th, described as the ringleader of the group, was believed to be living in Yemen.

2 U.S. Pilots Charged in Deaths of Canadians—Two U.S. F-16 fighter pilots whose bombs had killed 4 Canadian soldiers in Afghanistan in April were charged **Sept. 13** with involuntary manslaughter and assault. The pilots reportedly had thought they were under fire from the ground; the Canadians were conducting a training exercise. A U.S.-Canadian investigation found that Majors Harry Schmidt and William Umbach had acted with "reckless disregard."

Japanese Premier Makes Historic Visit to North Korea—Two countries lacking diplomatic relations since 1948 took a step toward reconciliation **Sept. 17**. Japanese Prime Min. Junichiro Koizumi met with North Korean leader Kim Jong Il in the latter's capital, Pyongyang, where they agreed to open talks on normalizing relations. In a **Sept. 17** agreement, Japan apologized for abuses during its colonial rule, 1910-45, and pledged to provide compensation, perhaps as much as $10 billion. North Korea, for its part, admitted that it had kidnapped 12 Japanese citizens in the 1970s and 1980s; Kim said that 4 of these, known to be alive in North Korea, would be returned to Japan.

North Korea agreed to extend indefinitely its moratorium on ballistic missile tests, and Koizumi said North Korea would adhere to a 1994 agreement to allow international inspection to determine if it was producing weapons of mass destruction.

Israelis Demolish Arafat's Compound—Israeli forces **Sept. 20** demolished all but one building in the office compound of Palestinian leader Yasir Arafat. Israel's renewed attack followed a suicide bombing on a bus in Tel Aviv, **Sept. 19**, in which the bomber killed himself and 6 others and injured scores. Israel demanded that 50 or so Palestinians (among 200 inside the compound) that Israel had linked to terrorist acts be handed over. On **Sept. 29**, under U.S. pressure, Israel pulled its forces back despite the demand; Arafat, claiming victory, left the building. Nine more Palestinians, including 6 civilians, were killed by Israeli forces in Gaza **Sept. 24**.

Earlier, on **Sept. 1**, Israel said it would investigate 3 incidents on **Aug. 29-Sept. 1** in which Israeli forces killed a total of 12 Palestinian civilians. On **Sept. 11**, Arafat's cabinet resigned as it faced a vote of no-confidence by the Palestinian Legislative Council.

German Chancellor Retains Power in Close Vote—Chancellor Gerhard Schröder clung to power after a close parliamentary election, **Sept. 22**. His party, the Social Democrats, and the conservative coalition (Christian Democratic Union and Christian Social Union), whose candidate was Edmund Stoiber, each won 38.5% of the popular vote. However, another party allied with Schröder, the Greens, won 8.6% (their best showing ever), while the Free Democrats, who supported Stoiber, managed only 7.4%. That difference would produce an edge in Parliament of about 10 seats for the winning coalition. Schröder had strongly opposed any U.S. military action in Iraq, leaving a strained state of relations between the 2 countries. Contrary to the usual custom, Bush declined to make a congratulatory phone call to Schröder after his victory.

Assailants Kill 29 in Hindu Temple in India—Assailants armed with automatic weapons attacked a Hindu temple in Gandhinagar, India, **Sept. 24**, killing 29 and wounding 74. Infantry commandos killed 2 attackers.

General

Sampras, Serena Williams Win U.S. Open Titles—Serena Williams defeated her sister Venus, **Sept. 7**, 6-4, 6-3, to win the women's U.S. Open tennis title in New York. The victory was the 3rd straight for Serena Williams in a grand slam event, and in all 3 she had defeated her sister in the final. On **Sept. 8**, Pete Sampras won his 5th men's U.S. open title, defeating Andre Agassi, 6-3, 6-4, 5-7, 6-4.

OCTOBER 1-15, 2002

National

Lautenberg Replaces Torricelli on Jersey Ballot—On **Oct. 1**, just 5 weeks before elections, former Sen. Frank Lautenberg, a senator for 18 years prior to his retirement in 2001, agreed to appeals by New Jersey Democrats to allow his name to be placed on the state ballot as the party's candidate for Senate. He replaced incumbent Democratic Sen. Robert Torricelli; Torricelli had bowed out of the race **Sept. 30,** as his prospects continued to dim in the wake of allegations he had accepted improper gifts from a contributor. Republicans had challenged the substitution so late in the campaign as a violation of state election law, but the state Supreme Court ruled against them, 7–0, **Oct. 2,** and on **Oct. 7**, the U.S. Supreme Court declined to hear the case.

Former Enron Executive Charged With Fraud—The former CFO of Enron, the bankrupt energy-trading company, was charged **Oct. 2** with fraud, conspiracy, and money laundering. The government's complaint, in Houston, alleged that Andrew Fastow had made use of off-the-books partnerships to hide Enron's falling financial situation and obtain millions of dollars of the company's cash himself. Meanwhile, on **Oct. 7,** Buford Yates became the 2nd (after David Myers) former official of WorldCom, another megabankruptcy, to plead guilty to securities fraud.

"Shoe Bomber" Pleads Guilty—Richard Reid, a British national nicknamed the "Shoe Bomber," pleaded guilty **Oct. 4,** in federal district court in Boston, to all charges against him relating to an incident aboard a Paris-to-Miami flight in Dec. 2001. Prosecutors said he had attempted to ignite explosives concealed in his sneakers, before being subdued by flight attendants and passengers.

Citizens Arrested in Al-Qaeda Plot—Four U.S. citizens living in Portland, OR, were arrested **Oct. 4** and charged with plotting to join al-Qaeda and Taliban forces against the U.S. The FBI began a search for 2 others thought to be linked with the Portland cell. One of the 2 was arrested in Malaysia **Oct. 8.** On **Oct. 9,** the head of the Benevolence International Foundation, Enaam Arnaout, was indicted for conspiracy and racketeering; the indictment charged that he had funneled donations to al-Qaeda contributed by unwitting benefactors.

Bush Acts to Reopen West Coast Docks—Pres. George W. Bush **Oct. 8** invoked the Taft–Hartley Act to get West Coast longshoremen back to work. The employers had shut down the docks 11 days earlier, after negotiations over a new contract seemed to be going nowhere. The cost of the shutdown was put as high as $10 billion.

Stocks Bounce Back After Another Plunge—Stock market prices continued to fluctuate widely. On **Oct. 9**, the Dow Jones industrial average closed at 7286.27, a 5-year low. Just 4 trading days later, on **Oct. 15,** the Dow had rebounded to 8255.68.

ImClone Founder Admits Fraud, Other Crimes—Samuel Waksal, founder of ImClone Systems, pleaded guilty **Oct. 15**, to federal charges of securities fraud, perjury, obstruction of justice, conspiracy, and bank fraud. Most charges filed against him related to the sale of ImClone stock prior to the public announcement of news adverse to the company.

International

U.S., Iraq Continue Sparring Over Inspections—The U.S. continued to pressure Iraq to agree to allow UN weapons inspectors unfettered access to all sites that might contain weapons of mass destruction. Iraq, in agreeing **Oct. 1** that inspectors could return in 2 weeks, declined to agree to allow access to some areas, including numerous presidential palace complexes. On **Oct. 4,** Hans Blix, the chief UN weapons inspector, backed a U.S. demand that Iraq disclose all of its weapons programs before the inspectors returned.

In a speech in Cincinnati, **Oct. 7,** Pres. Bush said that only Saddam Hussein's removal from office would end the confrontation with Iraq. He set out a detailed case for resorting to military action if other efforts failed. He said that the Iraqi regime had ties to al-Qaeda terrorists and that Iraq could attack the U.S. at any time with chemical or biological weapons.

The House, 296-133, on **Oct. 10,** and the Senate, 77-23, on **Oct. 11,** passed a measure giving Bush its backing for using military force against Iraq. All but 6 Republicans in the House backed the measure, while Democrats were split, with 81 supporting it and 126 against. In the Senate, 29 Democrats and all but 1 (Lincoln Chafee, RI) of the 49 Republicans voted in favor; 21 Democrats and 1 independent voted against it.

Ex-President of Bosnian Serbs Pleads Guilty—A former president of the Bosnian Serbs pleaded guilty **Oct. 2** to crimes against humanity. As part of her agreement with the international tribunal at The Hague, other charges against the former official, Biljana Plavsic, including genocide, were to be dropped. During the 1992–95 war in Bosnia, thousands of people were killed, imprisoned, or forced from their homes. The only woman accused of war crimes by the tribunal, Plavsic had been vice president during the war, and president later; she expressed remorse for what she had done.

Strikes Launched in Philippines and Kuwait—An American soldier and a Filipino were killed **Oct. 2** in Zamboanga City, in southern Philippines, when a bomb exploded in front of a karaoke bar. A U.S. Marine was killed and a second was wounded **Oct. 8,** in an attack by 2 gunmen on a Kuwaiti island. The 2 assailants were shot dead; 1 left behind a videotape indicating he was an al-Qaeda member.

Explosion Sets Oil Tanker Afire—A French oil tanker exploded off the coast of Yemen **Oct. 6**. French sources speculated that a terrorist attack was responsible. All but one of the ship's 25 crew members were rescued; thousands of barrels of oil spilled into the sea.

13 Palestinians Killed in Israeli Raid—Israeli tanks and helicopters struck Khan Yunis, in the Gaza Strip, **Oct. 7;** 13 Palestinians were killed and more than 100 wounded. The town is a stronghold of the militant group Hamas.

Bomb Blamed on Terrorists Kills Hundreds in Bali—A bomb exploded near 2 crowded discothèques on the island of Bali, in Indonesia, **Oct. 12.** More than 180 people were believed killed. The Islamic militant group Jemaah Islamiah, was believed responsible for the attack, which occurred in a resort area popular with foreign tourists; many Australians and Europeans were among the victims. A link to al-Qaeda was suspected.

General

Sniper Terrorizes Washington Suburbs—A skilled shooter, firing from a distance, struck terror into residents of the Washington, DC, suburbs. Between **Oct. 2** and **Oct. 14,** 9 people were killed and 2, including a 13-year-old boy shot at the entrance to his school, were wounded. No pattern was discernible among the victims, who were struck down while going about routine activities such as cutting grass, pumping gas, or shopping at a mall, mostly at long range, by a single shot from a high powered rifle. Hundreds of police were involved in the hunt for the killer; as of mid-Oct., few clues had surfaced, and there was no evidence of a linkage to a terrorist group.

Jimmy Carter Wins Nobel Peace Prize—Former Pres. Jimmy Carter was named as winner of the 2002 Nobel Peace Prize on **Oct. 10**. The Nobel committee cited his efforts as president to bring peace to the Middle East and his post-presidential commitment to human rights and the promotion of democratic values around the world. Gunnar Berge, chairman of the Nobel committee, generated controversy by saying that the award should be interpreted as an implied criticism of the position taken by the Bush administration toward military action in Iraq.

Notable Supreme Court Decisions, 2001-2002

During the Supreme Court's 2001-2002 term, which ended June 27, 79 decisions were announced, of which 21 (a large proportion, as has been typical in recent years) were decided by 5-4 votes. Chief Justice William H. Rehnquist and Justices Antonin Scalia and Clarence Thomas tended to vote as a conservative bloc, often finding themselves at odds with the court's more liberal wing—Justices Ruth Bader Ginsburg, Stephen G. Breyer, John Paul Stevens, and David H. Souter. Justices Sandra Day O'Connor and Anthony M. Kennedy were considered swing votes, although they both sided with the conservatives in most of the close cases. Following are some of the major rulings of the term.

Criminal Law: The justices June 20 ruled, 6–3, that the execution of mentally retarded felons violated the Eighth Amendment ban on cruel and unusual punishment *[Atkins v. Virginia]*.

The court June 24 ruled, 7–2, that only a jury, not a judge, could determine whether to impose the death penalty *[Ring v. Arizona]*.

The court June 10 held, 5–4, that prison rehabilitation programs for sex offenders could penalize participants who refused to admit guilt and confess to any undisclosed crimes, even though those admissions would expose them to possible further prosecution *[McKune v. Lile]*.

The court, in an expansion of the right to counsel May 20 ruled, 5–4, that a state could not impose even a suspended sentence on a defendant who had not had a lawyer at trial *[Alabama v. Shelton]*.

Education: The court June 27 held, 5–4, that the separation of church and state was not violated by publicly funded tuition vouchers that could be used at religious schools *[Zelman v. Simmons-Harris]*.

Speech and Press: The justices Apr. 16 voided portions of the 1996 Child Pornography Prevention Act that banned "virtual" child pornography. The vote was 7–2 against the ban on using young-looking adults to depict minors engaged in sexual activity, and 6–3 against the ban on computer-generated images *[Ashcroft v. Free Speech Coalition]*.

The court, in an 8–1 ruling May 13, partially upheld the 1998 Child Online Protection Act, in allowing commercial World Wide Web sites on the Internet to be banned from displaying sexually explicit images that would be "harmful to minors." *[Ashcroft v. American Civil Liberties Union]*.

The court, in a 5–4 decision, June 27 ruled that Minnesota could not bar candidates in judicial elections from announcing their views on "disputed legal or political issues" *[Republican Party of Minnesota v. White]*.

Search and Seizure: The court, in a 5–4 decision, June 27 held that public schools could require students to submit to random drug tests as a condition of participating in extracurricular activities *[Board of Education of Independent School District No. 92 of Pottawatomie County v. Earls]*.

The court June 17 ruled, 6–3, that police officers could conduct random searches of bus passengers for contraband without having to tell the passengers that they could refuse to cooperate *[U.S. v. Drayton]*.

Disabilities: The justices, in a 5–4 decision Apr. 29, ruled that the federal Americans With Disabilities Act (ADA) did not require an employer to override a workplace seniority system in order to accommodate a disabled employee's need to transfer to a different position *[U.S. Airways v. Barnett]*.

The court June 10 unanimously ruled that under the ADA an employer could refuse to hire a disabled applicant if the job would exacerbate the person's disability or otherwise pose a special health risk to him or her *[Chevron USA Inc. v. Echazabal]*.

The court Jan. 8 unanimously ruled that an impairment was not entitled to workplace accommodation under the ADA unless it substantially affected the performance of basic everyday activities, rather than merely hindering the plaintiff's ability to do a particular job *[Toyota Motor Manufacturing v. Williams]*.

Labor Issues: The court Mar. 27 ruled, 5-4, that the National Labor Relations Board could not force an employer to give back pay to illegal immigrants unlawfully fired for trying to unionize. *[Hoffman Plastic Compounds Inc. v. NLRB]*.

Property Rights: The court Mar. 26 ruled, 8–0, that public housing authorities could evict a tenant for drug use by any family member or guest, whether or not the illegal activity was within the tenant's knowledge or control *[Department of Housing and Urban Development v. Rucker]*.

Federalism: The court May 28 held, 5–4, that the 11th Amendment gave states immunity from private lawsuits adjudicated by federal administrative agencies *[Federal Maritime Commission v. South Carolina State Ports Authority]*.

The court May 20 ruled, 8–0, that telecommunications companies could sue states in federal court to challenge how state regulators were implementing the 1996 Telecommunications Act, a federal law designed to promote competition in the local telephone service market *[Verizon Maryland v. Public Service Commission of Maryland]*.

The 2002 Nobel Prizes

The 2002 Nobel Prize winners were announced Oct. 7-11. Each prize consisted of a large solid gold medal and a cash award of 10 million Swedish kronor (about $1 million).

Chemistry: John B. Fenn of the U.S. and Koichi Tanaka of Japan shared one-half of the award for adapting the techniques of mass spectrometry to identify and analyze the large protein molecules found in all living organisms. Kurt Wüthrich of Switzerland received the other half for using nuclear magnetic resonance to map the structure of proteins.

Economics: Vernon L. Smith of the U.S. and Daniel Kahneman of the U.S. and Israel shared the Bank of Sweden Prize in Economic Sciences in Memory of Alfred Nobel, for applying the tools of laboratory experimentation and psychological research to studies of economic decision making.

Literature: Imre Kertész, a Hungarian novelist and Holocaust survivor, received the award for the novel *Fateless* and other works that uphold "the fragile experience of the individual against the barbaric arbitrariness of history."

Peace: Former U.S. Pres. Jimmy Carter was honored for "his decades of untiring effort to find peaceful solutions to international conflicts, to advance democracy and human rights, and to promote economic and social development."

Physics: Raymond Davis Jr., of the U.S. and Masatoshi Koshiba of Japan shared one-half of the prize for detecting cosmic neutrinos, which are formed in the thermonuclear fusion process that powers the sun and other stars. Riccardo Giacconi of the U.S. received the other half for developing X-ray astronomy and making the first X-ray telescopes.

Physiology or Medicine: H. Robert Horvitz of the U.S. and Sydney Brenner and John E. Sulston of the United Kingdom were honored for studying the genes that regulate organ development and the natural process of "programmed cell death," shedding light on the development of many illnesses.

WORLD ALMANAC QUICK QUIZ

Which of the following never won a Nobel Peace Prize?

(a) Albert Schweitzer (b) Woodrow Wilson (c) Rev. Martin Luther King Jr. (d) Mahatma Gandhi

For the answer look in the Awards chapter, page 288, or see page 1008.

Major Actions of the 107th Congress

The 107th Congress convened Jan. 3, 2001, with the 2 chambers more evenly divided that at any time since the 1950s. In the House of Representatives, Republicans held 221 seats and Democrats 211, with 2 independents and 1 vacancy. The speaker of the House was J. Dennis Hastert (R, IL). Other high-ranking House members included Majority Leader Dick Armey (R, TX) and Minority Leader Richard A. (Dick) Gephardt (D, MO).

Senate Switch. In the Senate, Republicans and Democrats each held 50 seats. For the first 17 days of the session, while Vice Pres. Al Gore, a Democrat, remained in office and was capable of breaking a Senate tie, the chamber was under Democratic control. With the inauguration of Vice Pres. Dick Cheney, a Republican, on Jan. 20, 2001, the Senate passed into Republican hands, with Trent Lott (R, MS) as majority leader and Tom Daschle (D, SD) as minority leader. The ceremonial role of president pro tempore was filled by Strom Thurmond (R, SC); first elected to the Senate in 1954, Thurmond (born Dec. 5, 1902) was the longest-serving senator in history and the oldest person ever to serve in Congress.

On May 24, 2001, James M. (Jim) Jeffords (VT) announced that he planned to leave the Republican Party and become an independent, voting with the Democrats on organizational matters. When the Jeffords switch became official June 5, the balance of the Senate shifted in favor of the Democrats, and Daschle became majority leader and Lott minority leader. The president pro tempore was Robert C. Byrd (D, WV), who was first elected to the Senate in 1958.

Impact of Terrorism. The Capitol was evacuated and senior congressional leaders transported to a secure location shortly after 2 hijacked aircraft crashed into the World Trade Center and one slammed into the Pentagon Sept. 11, 2001. After a letter sent to Daschle containing highly refined anthrax spores was discovered Oct. 15, he and other senators and staff members were treated for anthrax exposure. The following month, the U.S. Postal Service began irradiating mail addressed to Congress. The Hart Senate Office Building, where Daschle's office was located, remained closed until Jan. 22, 2002, and the majority leader's office did not reopen until Apr. 3. To mark the anniversary of the attack on the World Trade Center, Congress met Sept. 6, 2002, in New York City for the first time in 212 years.

Ethics. On July 24, 2002, by a vote of 420-1 (with Rep. Gary Condit [D, CA] dissenting), the House expelled James Traficant (D, OH), who had been convicted Apr. 11 on federal charges of fraud, bribery, and racketeering. The occasion marked the 5th time in its history—and only the 2nd time since the Civil War—that the House had voted to expel a member. The Senate Ethics Committee July 30 "severely admonished" Robert Torricelli (D, NJ) for improperly accepting gifts from and doing favors for a campaign contributor, David Chang. Torricelli announced Sept. 30 that he was abandoning his bid for a 2nd term.

Unfinsished Business. Although the 2003 fiscal year began Oct. 1, 2002, none of the 13 major appropriations bills for fiscal 2003 had been enacted by that date. Instead, Congress passed, and Pres. George W. Bush signed, a series of stopgap measures to continue funding government operations. As of mid-October, Congress had also failed to pass the centerpiece of the Bush administration's legislative program for 2002: a major executive branch reorganization that included creation of a cabinet-level Department of Homeland Security. After recessing in mid-October, Congress was expected to return after the Nov. elections.

For Further Information. Following is a summary of major legislation passed by the 107th Congress through Oct. 20, 2002. Measures that have become law are identified by their Public Law (PL) number. Detailed legislative information may be accessed via the Internet at thomas.loc.gov

2001

Tax Cut. Reduces federal tax revenues by an estimated $1.35 trillion over a 10-year period. Passed by the House May 26, 240-154; passed by the Senate May 26, 58-33; signed by Pres. Bush June 7 (PL 107-16).

War Against Terrorism. Authorizes the president to use force against those who perpetrated or assisted in the Sept. 11 attacks against the U.S. Passed without objection by the House Sept. 14; passed by the Senate Sept. 14, 98-0; signed by Pres. Bush Sept. 18 (PL 107-40).

Airline Bailout. Provides $5 billion in aid and $10 billion in loan guarantees to ease the impact of the Sept. 11 attacks on airlines. Sets up compensation fund for victims of the attacks who elect not to sue. Passed by the House Sept. 21, 356-54; passed 96-1 by the Senate, Sept. 21; signed by Pres. Bush Sept. 22 (PL 107-42).

USA Patriot Act. Strengthens powers of police to wiretap telephones, monitor Internet and e-mail use, and search the homes of suspected terrorists. Without the filing of any charges, allows the detention for up to 7 days of any foreigner suspected of terrorism. Passed by the House Oct. 24, 357-66; passed by the Senate Oct. 25, 98-1; signed by Pres. Bush Oct. 26 (PL 107-56).

Aviation Security. Establishes Transportation Security Administration within the Dept. of Transportation. Creates a federal force to screen passengers and baggage at major airports, replacing private screeners. Imposes fee on air travelers to pay for security measures. Passed by the House Nov. 16, 410-9; passed by the Senate Nov. 16 by voice vote; signed by Pres. Bush Nov. 19 (PL 107-71).

Education Reform. Requires annual standardized tests in reading and mathematics in grades 3-8 by 2005-06, and makes federal education aid to schools contingent on students' scores. Authorizes $26.5 billion in federal spending on education programs in fiscal 2002, up $8 billion from 2001. Passed by the House Dec. 13, 381-41; passed by the Senate Dec. 18, 87-10; signed by Pres. Bush Jan. 8, 2002 (PL 107-110).

2002

Campaign Finance Reform. Bars donations of unregulated "soft money" to political parties. Restricts campaign "issue ads" paid for by special interest groups. Raises limits on direct contributions to candidates. Passed by the House Feb. 14, 240-189; passed by the Senate Mar. 20, 60-40; signed by Pres. Bush Mar. 27 (PL 107-155).

Farm Bill. Provides $248.6 billion in aid to agriculture over a 6-year period, including increased subsidies for grain, cotton, peanuts, and other commodities. Passed by the House May 2, 280-141; passed by the Senate May 8, 64-35; signed by Pres. Bush May 13 (PL 107-171).

National Debt. Increases public debt limit from $5.95 trillion to $6.4 trillion. Passed by the House June 27, 215-214 (1 present); passed by the Senate June 11, 68-29; signed by Pres. Bush June 28 (PL 107-199).

Corporate Accountability. Strengthens regulation of accounting and securities industries and toughens laws against corporate fraud. Passed by the House July 25, 423-3; passed by the Senate July 25, 99-0; signed by Pres. Bush July 30 (PL 107-204).

Trade Authority. Restores "fast track" presidential authority to negotiate international trade agreements that Congress may approve or reject but not amend. Passed by the House July 27, 215-212; passed by the Senate Aug. 1, 64-34; signed by Pres. Bush Aug. 6 (PL 107-210).

Military Action Against Iraq. Authorizes the president to use force against Iraq to protect U.S. security and enforce UN Security Council resolutions. Passed by the House Oct. 10, 296-133; passed by the Senate Oct. 11, 77-23; signed by Pres. Bush Oct. 16 (PL 107-243).

Election Reform. Authorizes nearly $4 billion to upgrade voting machines, educate voters, and train poll workers. Requires states to create computerized voter registration systems, improve voting access for the disabled, and protect against vote fraud. Passed by the House Oct. 10, 357-48; passed by the Senate Oct. 16, 92-2.

Notable Quotes in 2002

September 11 Remembered

"In the ruins of two towers, under a flag unfurled at the Pentagon, at the funerals of the lost, we have made a sacred promise to ourselves and to the world: We will not relent until justice is done, and our nation is secure. What our enemies have begun, we will finish."

Pres. George W. Bush at Ellis Island, Sept. 11, 2002.

"Gordon M. Aamoth Jr."

Former New York City Mayor *Giuliani*, reading the first name on the list of 2,801 World Trade Center victims read in a ceremony at Ground Zero on Sept. 11, 2002.

"I'll be sprinkling my husband's ashes that day."

Marian Fontana, widow of New York City firefighter David Fontana, on Sept. 11, the day both of David's death and their wedding anniversary.

"Our work is done here."

Ronald Werner, New York City Fire Department battalion chief, as the World Trade Center recovery effort ended.

"Every time I've seen videotapes, listened to audio recordings, or read the accounts of firefighters and their actions on Sept. 11, I've felt the same thing: an extraordinary sense of awe at their incredible professionalism and bravery."

New York City Fire Commissioner *Nicholas Scoppetta,* commenting in Aug. 2002 on an audiotape of firefighters inside the twin towers Sept. 11, 2001.

"It was an excruciating and incomparable experience."

Alice Hoglan, in April, after hearing audiotape of United Flight 93, on which her son Mark Bingham was a passenger when it crashed in Pennsylvania.

The War on Terror

"States like those [Iraq, Iran and North Korea] and their terrorist allies, constitute an axis of evil, aiming to threaten the peace of the world."

Pres. George W. Bush in his 2002 State of the Union address, Jan. 29, 2002.

"They were either asleep, or inept, or both."

Sen. Richard Shelby (R, AL) commenting on the FBI's failure to follow up on warnings that possible terrorists had enrolled in flight schools.

"He was the most treasured thing I could give my country."

Ricky Crosse, on his son, Sgt. Bradley Crosse, who was killed in March 2002, during antiterrorism operations in Afghanistan.

"The threat environment we find ourselves in today is as bad as it was last summer, the summer before Sept. 11."

CIA Director *George Tenet* testifying before Congress, Oct. 17.

"Al-Qaeda maintains a hidden but active presence in the United States, waiting to strike again."

Attorney General *John Ashcroft,* testifying July 11, at a congressional hearing on homeland security.

"Al-Qaeda has many tentacles, but one of them has just been cut off."

White House spokesman *Ari Fleischer,* Apr. 2, on the arrest of top al-Qaeda operative Abu Zubaydah.

"I miss my sons, but there was nothing to eat."

Akhtar Muhammad, Afghan father who sold two of his sons for bags of wheat.

"I pray. . . to Allah for the destruction of the United States."

Zacarias Moussaoui, the so-called 20th hijacker, at a federal court hearing, Apr. 22.

"So long as people remain on this planet, I think this will remain."

Exiled Tibetan spiritual leader *Dalai Lama,* in May, on the possibility of completely eliminating terrorism.

Iraq

"When states decide to use force to deal with broader threats to international peace and security, there is no substitute for the unique legitimacy provided by the United Nations."

Kofi Annan, UN secretary-general, Sept. 2, introducing Pres. Bush to the General Assembly.

"Will the United Nations serve the purpose of its founding, or will it be irrelevant?"

Pres. George W. Bush, in his speech Sept. 12 before the UN General Assembly on the need for action against Iraq.

"If Allah Almighty, in his great wisdom and for reasons beyond our comprehension, decides to put you again to the test of fighting on a large scale, the Almighty, the nation, and history will expect you to deliver an effective stand."

Iraqi *Pres. Saddam Hussein,* Oct. 17, speaking before the Iraqi National Parliament.

"It is less important to have unanimity than it is to be making the right decisions and doing the right thing."

Sec. of Defense *Donald Rumsfeld,* in August, on seeking international support for U.S. military action against Iraq.

"This is the guy that tried to kill my dad."

Pres. Bush, in Sept., on Saddam Hussein.

"There is no country in the world that supports it. There is no international sanction for it. There is no coalition for it."

Adel Jubeir, adviser to Saudi Arabia's Crown Prince Abdullah, in August, on the possible U.S. military action in Iraq.

"The United Nations has done nothing for four years . . . It has been this president, President George Bush, that has taken the initiative to go not only to the American people but to the whole world and very carefully and methodically told the world we should be on alert. We cannot do nothing."

Sen. John Warner (R, VA), Oct. 4, in the Senate debate on backing possible military action against Iraq.

"I have searched for that single piece of evidence that would convince me that the president must have in his hands, before the month is out, open-ended congressional authorization to deliver an unprovoked attack on Iraq. I remain unconvinced."

Sen. Robert Byrd (D, WV) in an op-ed piece for the *New York Times*, Oct. 10.

Palestinian-Israeli Conflict

"I look at the sky. I look at the people."

20-year-old Palestinian student *Arien Ahmed,* in June, on her decision not to set off a bomb she was carrying in a backpack to a mall in the Israeli city Rishon le Zion.

"If you declare war against the Palestinians thinking that you can solve the problem by seeing how many Palestinians can be killed, I don't know that that leads us anywhere."

Sec. of State *Colin Powell,* in March, responding to Israeli Prime Min. Ariel Sharon's expressed desire to "increase the number of losses on the other side."

"As long as there is occupation, there will be resistance."

Hamas spokesman *Abdel Aziz Rantisi,* in March, expressing his group's opposition to the existence of the state of Israel.

"We all strive to end the terrible, bloody conflict with the Palestinians. We can—we can—achieve peace. But will the present Palestinian leadership want to abandon their scheme to eliminate Israel, and instead, choose to live with us in peace?"

Israeli Prime Min. *Ariel Sharon,* at the opening of the Knesset winter session, Oct. 14.

Economy and Business

"I am concerned about the economy. I was the first one laid off."

Former Vice Pres. *Al Gore,* July 24.

"You are perhaps the most accomplished confidence man since Charles Ponzi. I'd say you were a carnival barker, but that wouldn't be fair to carnival barkers."

Sen. Peter Fitzgerald (R, IL), to former Enron CEO Ken Lay, at Senate hearings, Feb. 12.

"Enron robbed the bank, Arthur Andersen provided the getaway car, and they say you were at the wheel."

Rep. Jim Greenwood (R, PA), speaking to fired Andersen auditor David Duncan, who had pleaded the Fifth Amendment at hearings on Enron, Jan. 24.

"Such a piece of crap."

A Merrill Lynch analyst's comment in a private e-mail June 3, about the stock of Excite@home, which Merrill Lynch had publicly given a "buy" rating.

"I have been the subject of very favorable reporting and very unfavorable reporting throughout the years. This is not new to me. And I choose to go ahead with my work. . . . And we will continue to do that, and I want focus on my salad."

Martha Stewart, in an interview with CBS *Early Show* anchor Jane Clayson, June 25.

Other News

"My concept of human rights has grown to include not only the right to live in peace, but also to adequate health care, shelter, food, and to economic opportunity. I hope this award reflects a universal acceptance and even embrace of this broad-based concept of human rights."

Former Pres. Jimmy Carter, in a statement posted on the Carter Center website after he was named as the recipient of 2002 Nobel Peace Prize.

"We've been waiting for you."

Unidentified miner, one of 9 trapped for 3 days in a flooded mineshaft in Somerset, PA, when rescuers first made contact. All 9 were safely rescued July 28.

"God is in control. I believe he will vindicate me."

Amina Lawal Kurami, the northern Nigeria woman sentenced by an Islamic court to die by stoning for giving birth out of wedlock.

"He never promised me a Rose Garden."

Sen. John McCain (R, AZ), on the lack of fanfare surrounding Pres. Bush's Mar. 27 signing of the campaign finance reform bill, which McCain had nurtured and championed.

"This is Martha's day."

Dorthy Moxley, after a jury June 7 found Kennedy relative Michael Skakel guilty of murdering her daughter in 1975.

"The priesthood lost me but kept the perpetrator."

Michael Blend, psychologist and former priest, in June, about the aftermath of his abuse by a priest as a teenager.

"I'm 71 years old and I have never had sexual relations with anybody—man, woman or child. And that can go on the record."

Cardinal Theodore McCarrick, archbishop of Washington, DC.

"There is no strike."

Atlanta Braves pitcher *Tom Glavine,* the National League player representative, after an all-night session led to a settlement averting a Major League baseball strike.

"The kids who are fat are getting really fatter."

Dr. Nazrat Mirza of Children's National Medical Center, Washington, DC, on the rising rate of child obesity.

"We sell seats, and if you consume more than one seat, you have to buy more than one seat."

Beth Harbin, a Southwest Airlines spokeswoman, defending a policy of charging large passengers for two seats.

"I am glad I stayed in my seat on a Montgomery, Alabama, bus, Dec. 1, 1955. . . . I would also like you to keep your seat."

Rosa Parks, in a note July 1 to Rep. J.C. Watts (R, OK), urging him to run for reelection as the GOP's only African-American congressman. Watts chose not to seek reelection.

"A rodent could do a lot worse than live out its life span in research facilities."

Sen. Jesse Helms (R, NC), in February, on federal protections for rats, mice, and birds used in lab experiments.

Arts/Personalities

"A cigarette in the hands of a Hollywood star on-screen is a gun aimed at a 12- or 14-year-old."

Joe Eszterhas, screenwriter, now suffering from throat cancer, apologizing for putting so much smoking in movies like *Basic Instinct.*

"Being Irish, if you get eight nominations and got no awards they wouldn't let you back in the country, so this is a public-safety issue."

U2 lead singer *Bono,* joking about his winning a 2002 Grammy award on Feb. 27.

"I feel like 45. I don't look too bad for someone my age, with my history of illnesses and operations and all those anesthetics. When they knock you out, it gives you time to catch up on your beauty sleep."

Actress *Elizabeth Taylor,* on turning 70 Feb. 27.

"Wop bop a loo bop—that's rock and roll. You don't have to regurgitate on anybody."

Old-time rock singer *Little Richard,* on shock rock.

"I'm 30 years old now. Three kids. A wife. A mom. Brothers. Artists . . . They all need me. They all depend on me."

Rapper *Snoop Dogg, High Times* 2002 Stoner of the Year, Sept. 3, on his decision to keep away from drugs and alcohol.

"It's a paltry honor. He's joining the brown-noses. I said, 'Hold out for the lordship, mate.'"

Rolling Stone *Keith Richards,* on bandmate Mick Jagger's being knighted by the queen.

On the Lighter Side

"You will be glad to know the President is practicing safe snacks."

First Lady Laura Bush, Feb. 27, after a pretzel caused Pres. Bush to faint.

"I do hope we get the bronze, too, so we can get the entire collection."

Canadian skater *David Pelletier,* who with Jamie Salé, was given first silver and then a duplicate gold medal at the Salt Lake City Olympics for pairs skating because of a judging scandal.

"I didn't think I had a chance, so I just skated for myself."

Sixteen-year-old figure skater *Sarah Hughes,* Feb. 21, after a surprise victory in the Olympic figure skating competition.

"We weren't alerted by her."

Detroit Public Schools CFO *Ken Forrest,* on a city teacher who was erroneously given $4,015,624.80, after taxes, for 18 minutes of work.

Miscellaneous Facts

He's Still the King! Twenty-five years after his death, Elvis was on top of the charts again with the release of *Elvis: 30 #1 Hits*. It was the first time an Elvis album had debuted at the top spot in the U.S., as sales hit over 500,000 units.

Yodel, Hey, He . . . How Many? For a full minute they held the melody; when they were done, 937 German and Swiss yodelers, at a mass concert in southern Germany in Oct. 2002, had set a new world record for the "largest simultaneous yodel." The old record of 807 was set in Dublin earlier in the year.

An Eponymous Nut by Any Other Name . . . Since 1999, Bolivia, not Brazil, has been the world's top producer of Brazil nuts. Unique to the Amazonian rain forest, the shelled nuts add about $44 million annually to the South American economy. In 2000, the U.S. imported $21.1 milllion worth of the shelled nuts. The U.K. followed with $12.1 million, and Germany was 3rd, with $5.4 million.

The Last Camaro—Introduced in 1966, the muscle car that fueled a million high school dreams is no more. The last 2 of over 4 million rolled off the line in August. The penultimate car, a red Z-28 with a T-top, was auctioned off for charity, fetching $71,500. Chevrolet put the last one in its museum.

Who Knew They Still Made Them? Nearly 20 years after the home VCR wars of the mid-1980s left VHS as the dominant format, Sony Corp. announced Aug. 27, that it would stop making Betamax VCRs by the end of 2002. Sales of Betamax VCRs had peaked at 2.3 million units in fiscal 1984, and had dwindled to 2,800 units by 2001.

When They Do Come Marching In, It Might Take a While. Through Oct. 2002, when Mother Teresa was officially canonized, Pope John Paul II had recognized a record 464 saints in 24 years—more than all of the popes of the past 4 centuries combined. The current total of Roman Catholic saints stands at nearly 10,000.

Offbeat News Stories, 2002

Calling All Dunlops. In the so-called Dunlop "Tired of Your Name Challenge," Dunlop Tires of Canada put up $25,000 (Canadian) to be split among all Canadian adults named Dunlop who agreed to legally change their name from plain Dunlop to the moniker Dunlop Tires. There are at least 1,000 adults in Canada with the surname Dunlop. More than 100 contacted the company, and in the end 4 Dunlops provided proof that they had extended their names as required. They each took home Can$6,250, plus reimbursement for legal costs, and a brand new name.

Tricentennial, Plus or Minus One. As part of the events around Pennsylvania in 2002 marking the 225th anniversary of Revolutionary War battles in the region, the town of Downingtown, PA, known as Milltown in Revolutionary times, decided to stage a re-enactment Aug. 17 of a 1777 skirmish with British troops. One catch: the battle never took place. As it happened, the people of Downingtown were also celebrating the 300th anniversary of the town's 1701 founding. Another catch: since it was 2002, the town was actually 301 years old. Glenn Usher, chairman of the Downingtown Historical and Parks commission, cleared the matter up for reporters: "To tell you the truth, the 300th anniversary was last year, but we forgot about it."

Marriage of Convenience, Thank Heaven. Randy Kimball, a former 7-Eleven manager, married his former employee, Sharon Stehli, at the Fort Myers, FL, 7-Eleven store where they met in the summer of 2000. They were wed at 7:11 A.M. on July 11. An assistant manager of another 7-Eleven, who's also a notary, presided over the brief ceremony. The post-nuptial beverage: coffee in a 7-Eleven foam cup. "I figured if I got married at 7:11 on 7/11 in 7-Eleven, it'd be hard to forget my anniversary," said Kimball.

Bone Chips for Sale. Seattle Mariners relief pitcher Jeff Nelson put a little piece of himself on the line for charity. Literally. Nelson offered bone chips, removed from his elbow during surgery, for sale on eBay. The bidding reached $23,600 before eBay employees removed the offer; Kevin Pursglove, senior director of communications for eBay, said the bone chips violated a company policy prohibiting the sale of body parts.

That's Using Your Head, Sort Of. Professional bowler Kim Adler did a little better on eBay, when she had a brainstorm of sorts. She gets to the televised finals of most of the tournaments she enters, so why not try for some ad revenue? So she auctioned off an 8" x 8" space on the back of her skirt on eBay, and Pacific Pools, an indoor swimming pool manufacturer, put in a winning bid of $14,389!

Tennis players, golfers, skiers, and race-car drivers wear commercial logos on their clothes and uniforms, and boxers Bernard Hopkins and Eric "Butterbean" Esch have been paid to have ads for a gambling Website inked onto their backs. But an eBay spokesman said Adler may have been the first athlete to use a Website to auction off ad space on clothes. She planned to model the ad for one year, starting with a Sept. 15 tournament in Pittsburgh.

Using Your Head, Part 2. Jesper Parnevik, the son of Sweden's most famous comedian, is a professional golfer, with a twist. Part of his "trademark" look is that he wears a hat with the brim turned up. At a tournament in Las Vegas in Oct., he was promoting the new film *Analzye That* on the upturned brim. On other days it was Nexium, a heartburn medication.

In a Class by Herself. David Letterman, host of *The Late Show* on CBS, invited anyone graduating in 2002 from Harrold High School in Harrold, SD, to appear on his late night TV show May 22. Luckily for Dave, that narrowed it down to one student, April Kleinschmidt. The lone graduate was thrilled about her TV appearance, and unfazed by the notion that Dave would poke fun at her home state and town (population 209). Kleinschmidt was already well on her way to validating her "Most Likely to Succeed" award; she planned to attend Black Hills State, on a 4-year scholarship.

Richard M. Nixon, the Ultimate Comeback? Richard M. Nixon recently applied to run as a Republican candidate for agriculture commissioner in the state of Alabama. That is, Richard Milton Nixon, who is well known in Pell City, AL. Nixon runs a restaurant, and used to be a golf pro. When his name was first presented to state Republican leaders, they suspected a prank. But Nixon's identity was verified. He was added to the ballot but lost against J. Lee Alley, a veterinarian, in the June 4 party primary.

Frozen Dead Guy Weekend. You may have heard of quirky local celebrations such as strawberry days, beer or asparagus festivals. . .there's even a Cow Appreciation Day in Vermont. But only one town observes "Frozen Dead Guy" weekend, which fell on Mar. 9-10 in 2002. Residents of Nederland, CO, got this cool idea after the body of Bredo Morstoel, a Norwegian who died in 1989, was brought to Nederland by his grandson, Trygve Bauge, to be preserved frozen in a shed serving as a makeshift cryogenics facility. Bauge eventually had to return to Norway, but his grandfather's body is still preserved, at –109 °F, using dry ice in the backyard shed. The festival features tours of the shed, a coffin race, and a "grandpa look-alike" contest. A portion of the festival proceeds go toward keeping the body frozen.

A Typo Can Make a Difference. You don't need to tell that to officials in Kansas's Riley County, where a house in the town of Manhattan, KS, valued at $59,000, was accidentally entered into the county database as being worth $200,059,000. That's a difference of $200 million! The error, discovered by the county appraiser in Aug. 2002, caused the town's overall property value to be overestimated by 6.5%. Riley County officials had based their budget on the tax revenue generated from those inflated figures; now they have a shortfall to make up.

World's Funniest Joke. The British Association for the Advancement of Science did an Internet survey that received more than 40,000 entries from 70 countries. The survey found that people from Ireland, UK, and New Zealand liked jokes involving word play, the Scots liked jokes about death, and Americans and Canadians liked jokes that make people look stupid, as well as marriage-mocking jokes.

Designated the top joke among Americans was the following:

> *A man and a friend are playing golf one day. One of the guys is about to chip onto the green when he sees a long funeral procession on the road next to the course.*
>
> *He stops in in mid-swing, takes off his golf cap, closes his eyes, and bows down in prayer. His friend says: "Wow, that is the most thoughtful and touching thing I have ever seen. You are truly a kind man."*
>
> *The man then replies: "Yeah, well, we were married 35 years."*

After sifting through lots of laughs, the following joke was proclaimed the overall winner:

> *Two hunters are out in the woods when one of them collapses. He doesn't seem to be breathing and his eyes are glazed.*
>
> *The other man pulls out his phone and calls emergency services. He gasps to the operator: "My friend is dead! What can I do?"*
>
> *The operator in a calm, soothing voice replies: "Take it easy. I can help. First, let's make sure he's dead."*
>
> *There is a silence, then a shot is heard. Back on the phone, the hunter says, "OK, now what?"*

Historical Anniversaries

1903 — 100 Years Ago

Pres. Theodore Roosevelt creates the 9th U.S cabinet office, the Dept. of Commerce and Labor, on **Feb. 14**.

On **Feb. 23**, in *Champion v. Ames,* the U.S. Supreme Court, in an important assertion of federal power, upholds a federal law barring states from sending lottery tickets interstate through the mail.

Dissident Serbian army officers assassinate the king of Serbia, Alexander I Obrenovich, and his wife, Draga, on **June 10** at the royal palace in Belgrade.

Henry Ford founds the Ford Motor Company on **June 16,** and becomes its 1st president.

On **July 4**, Pres. Roosevelt sends the 1st official message over the new cable across the Pacific Ocean, from San Francisco to Manila. He receives a reply 12 minutes later.

Pope Leo XIII dies on **July 20**. Pius X is elected to replace him, **Aug. 4**.

Vladimir Ilyich Lenin is elected leader of the Russian Bolshevik party during a Socialist Congress held in London **July 30-Aug. 23**. The Bolsheviks call for a revolution in their homeland with rule by the proleteriat.

In races **Aug. 22–Sept. 2**, the American yacht *Reliance* successfully defends the America's Cup from the British craft *Shamrock*, defeating it in three straight races.

The first-ever World Series game is played on **Oct. 1.** The series featured the American League's Boston Red Stockings and the National League's Pittsburgh Pirates. The Red Stockings win the best-of-9 series, 5-3.

With U.S. support, Panama declares its independence from Colombia on **Nov. 3**. The Hay-Bunau Varilla Treaty, signed **Nov. 18**, gives the U.S. full control of a 10-mile zone around the Panama Canal for a down payment of $10 million and an annual fee of $250,000.

Orville Wright makes the 1st sustained flight in a heavier than-air machine at the beach in Kitty Hawk, NC, on **Dec. 17**. The flight, which lasted 12 seconds, covered 120 feet. His brother, Wilbur, flew 852 feet later that day.

Some 600 people die in a fire in Chicago's Iroquois Theatre during a performance of *Mr. Bluebeard* on **Dec. 30**. Many exit doors were locked, and others became jammed as patrons tried to flee.

Art. Picasso's *The Old Guitarist*; Rousseau's *Child With Puppet.*

Literature. Samuel Butler's *The Way of All Flesh*; Henry James's *The Ambassadors*; Jack London's *The Call of the Wild*; Frank Norris's *The Pit.*

Movies. *The Great Train Robbery*, the 1st motion picture with a plot, makes its debut.

Music. Bruckner's *Symphony No. 9* (posthumous); Eugene D'Albert's opera *Tiefland*; Frederick Delius's *Sea Drift*; Leoncavallo's *Pagliacci* becomes the 1st complete opera recorded for phonographs.

Nonfiction. W. E. B. DuBois's *The Souls of Black Folk*; Helen Keller's *The Story of My Life*; G. E. Moore's *Principia Ethica.*

Popular Songs. "Sweet Adeline" by Henry Armstrong; "Ida, Sweet as Apple Cider" by Eddie Leonard; "Dear Old Girl" by Theodore F. More; "Bedelia" by Jean Schwartz.

Science and Technology. The electrocardiograph (EKG), a machine used to monitor the heart's activity, is invented by Dutch physiologist Willhelm Einthoven; Valdemar Poulsen, a Danish electrical engineer, invents a device able to generate continuous radio waves, which is crucial for radio communication.

Sports. Frenchman M. Garin of France wins the first-ever Tour de France bicycle race; Willie Anderson wins the U.S. Open Golf Tournament; Britain defeats the United States four matches to one in the Davis Cup international tennis challenge.

Theatre. *Babes in Toyland* by Victor Herbert; George Bernard Shaw's *Man and Superman.*

Miscellaneous. King C. Gillette begins production on safety razors with disposable blades in Boston. British activist Emmeline Pankhurst founds the Women's Social and Political Union to advance women's rights.

1953 — 50 Years Ago

Dwight D Eisenhower is inaugurated 34th president of the U.S. on **Jan. 20.**

A federal jury in New York convicts 13 Communist leaders on **Jan. 21** for conspiring to advocate the overthrow of the U.S. government.

Soviet Prem. Joseph R. Stalin dies **Mar. 5**. He is succeeded the next day by Georgi Malenkov.

The U.S. Communist Party, **Apr. 20**, is ordered to register with the Justice Dept. as an organization controlled by a foreign power.

An earthquake registering 7.2 on the Richter scale hits northeast Turkey on **Mar. 18**, leaving some 1,200 people dead and 50,000 homeless.

On **May 29**, Edmund Hillary (NZ) and his Sherpa guide, Tenzing Norgay, become the first humans to reach the top of Mt. Everest, the highest spot on Earth.

Queen Elizabeth II is crowned at Westminster Abbey on **June 2**.

The worst air accident to date occurs on **June 18** near Tokyo, Japan, when a U.S. Air Force C-124 plane crashes, killing 129.

Julius and Ethel Rosenberg are executed on **June 19**. They were convicted of espionage after allegedly passing nuclear secrets to the USSR. They become the only civilians ever executed in the U.S. for espionage.

The Korean Armistice is signed on **July 27** at Panmunjom by UN, North Korean, and Chinese delegates.

The USSR explodes its 1st thermonuclear (hydrogen or "H") bomb, in Kazakhstan, **Aug. 29**.

Playwright Eugene O'Neill dies **Nov. 27** at age 65.

General Electric announces **Dec. 9** that all Communist employees will be discharged.

Chuck Yeager sets the new airborne speed record on **Dec. 16**, when he flies a Bell X-1A rocket-fueled jet over 1,600 miles per hour.

Art. Francis Bacon's *Papal Portraits of 1953*; Henry Moore's *King and Queen*; Jackson Pollock's *Blue Poles.*

Literature. James Baldwin's *Go Tell It on the Mountain*; Saul Bellow's *The Adventures of Augie March*; James Michener's *The Bridges at Toko-Ri;* Leon Uris's *Battle Cry*; Ernest Hemingway wins the Pulitzer Prize for *The Old Man and the Sea.*

Movies. *From Here to Eternity* starring Burt Lancaster and Deborah Kerr; *Roman Holiday* starring Audrey Hepburn.

Music. Britten's *Gloriana*; Shostakovich's *10th Symphony*; Stravinsky's *Canticum Sacrum*; Vaughan Williams's *7th Symphony.*

Nonfiction. Margaret Mead's *Cultural Patterns and Technical Change*; B.F. Skinner's *Science and Human Behavior.*

Popular Songs. "Rags to Riches" by Richard Adler; "That Doggie in the Window" by Bob Merrill; "I'm Walking Behind You" by Billy Reid; "That's Amore" by Henry Warren.

Science and Technology. Francis Crick (Brit.) and James Watson (U.S.) construct a model of the DNA molecule; Jonas Salk reports success in clinical trials of a polio vaccine.

Sports. Minneapolis Lakers beat the New York Knicks in the NBA championship, 4 games to 1. The Boston Braves baseball franchise moves to Milwaukee, and the St. Louis Browns move to Baltimore (and become the Orioles) before the start of the 1954 season; the New York Yankees beat the Brooklyn Dodgers 4 games to 2 in the World Series. Indiana defeats Kansas in the NCAA basketball finals, 69-68. The Detroit Lions defeat the Cleveland Browns 17-16 to win the NFL championship.

Theatre. Robert Anderson's *Tea and Sympathy*; William Inge's *Picnic*; Arthur Miller's *The Crucible*; Dylan Thomas's made-for-radio play *Under Milk Wood*; Samuel Beckett's *Waiting for Godot* is performed for the 1st time, in Paris **Jan. 5**; *Wonderful Town* opens on Broadway with Rosalind Russell.

Miscellaneous. Libya signs a 20-year treaty with Great Britain, allowing military bases in return for an annual subsidy. Gale winds devastate coastal areas in the Netherlands, Belgium, and Britain, killing approximately 2,000 people.

OBITUARIES

Deaths, Nov. 1, 2001–Oct. 15, 2002

A

Abbott, Jack Henry, 58, prison memoirist (*In the Belly of the Beast*, 1981) who, after being paroled in 1981, committed murder and was re-incarcerated; Alden, NY, Feb. 10, 2002.

Abu Nidal, 65, nom de guerre of radical Palestinian leader Sabri al-Banna, linked to terrorist attacks in the 1970s and 1980s; Baghdad, Iraq, Aug. 16, 2002.

Ambrose, Stephen, 66, prolific biographer and historian whose books on World War II were best-sellers; accused early in 2002 of occasional plagiarism; Bay St. Louis, MS, Oct. 13, 2002.

Annenberg, Walter, 96, publishing magnate whose holdings included *TV Guide* and the *Philadelphia Inquirer;* well-known as a philanthropist, art collector, and Nixon friend; Wynnewood, PA, Oct. 1, 2002.

Ash, Mary Kay, 83, creator, in 1963, of Mary Kay cosmetics; Dallas, TX, Nov. 22, 2001.

B

Balaguer, Joaquin, 95, longtime president of the Dominican Republic; Santo Domingo, Dom. Republic, July 14, 2002.

Banzer Suarez, Hugo, 75, Bolivia's military dictator (1971-78); later (1997-2001) served as elected president; Santa Cruz, Bolivia, May 5, 2002.

Belaunde Terry, Fernando, 89, architect turned politician who was president of Peru, 1963-68 and 1980-85; Lima, Peru, June 4, 2002.

Berle, Milton, 93, comedian nicknamed "Mr. Television"; star of one of TV's earliest weekly shows, in the late 1940s and 1950s; his 88-year career also included stints in vaudeville, nightclubs, radio, and movies; Los Angeles, CA, Mar. 27, 2002.

Blass, Bill, 79, fashion designer whose elegant yet understated clothes were known for their distinctly American look; Preston, CT, June 12, 2002.

Boland, Edward P., 90, U.S. representative (D, MA, 1953-89); his 1980s amendment sought to curtail funding to overthrow Nicaragua's Sandinistas; Springfield, MA, Nov. 4, 2001.

Bonanno, Joseph, 97, founder of the New York City-based Bonanno crime family and its leader for 3 decades; Tucson, AZ, May 11, 2002.

Boreman, Linda, 53, who, as Linda Lovelace, starred in the 1972 pornographic film *Deep Throat*; later became an antiporn crusader; Denver, CO, Apr. 22, 2002.

Bosch, Juan, 92, Dominican writer, academic, opposition leader; served briefly as president; Santo Domingo, Dominican Republic, Nov. 1, 2001.

Brown, Claude, 64, author of the landmark work *Manchild in the Promised Land* (1965), on growing up in Harlem; New York, NY, Feb. 2, 2002.

Brown, Norman O., popular Freudian-oriented philosopher who wrote *Life Against Death* (1959); Santa Cruz, CA, Oct. 2, 2002.

Brown, Ray, 75, jazz bassist known for his swinging style; accompanied such singers as Frank Sinatra and Ella Fitzgerald, to whom he was once married; Indianapolis, IN, July 2, 2002.

Buck, Jack, 77, sportscaster; longtime voice of the St. Louis Cardinals baseball team; St. Louis, MO, June 18, 2002.

Buono Jr., Angelo, 67, the "Hillside Strangler"; convicted in 1983 of murdering 9 young Los Angeles-area women; Calipatria, CA, Sept. 21, 2002.

C

Cannon, Howard, 90, 4-term Democratic U.S. senator from Nevada (1959-83); Las Vegas, NV, Mar. 6, 2002.

Cela, Camilo José, 85, Spanish author whose realistic fiction won him the 1989 Nobel Prize for literature; Madrid, Spain, Jan. 17, 2002.

Clooney, Rosemary, 74, popular 1950s pop singer and actress who had a distinguished career later as a jazz stylist; Beverly Hills, CA, June 29, 2002.

Conniff, Ray, 85, longtime big band leader whose best-selling albums included "We Wish You a Merry Christmas" (1962); Escondido, CA, Oct. 12, 2002.

D

Dale, Alan, 73, crooner; his hits included "Cherry Pink (and Apple Blossom White)" (1955) and "Heart of My Heart" (1956); New York, NY, Apr. 20, 2002.

Davenport, Willie, 59, won the 110m high hurdles at the 1968 Olympics and competed in bobsled in the 1980 Winter Games; Chicago, IL, June 17, 2002.

Davis Jr., Benjamin O., 89, leader of the black World War II combat pilots known as the Tuskegee Airmen; later the U.S. Air Force's first black general; Washington, DC, July 4, 2002.

Dillard, William T., 87, founder of Dillard's department store chain; Little Rock, AR, Feb. 8, 2002.

E

Elizabeth, the Queen Mother, 101, who became Britain's queen consort in 1936, and won the hearts of the British by staying in London during World War II; Windsor, England, Mar. 27, 2002.

Entwistle, John, 57, bass player for the British rock group The Who; Las Vegas, NV, June 27, 2002.

F

Farrell, Eileen, 82, dramatic soprano who excelled in everything from opera to jazz to show tunes; Park Ridge, NJ, Mar. 23, 2002.

Felix, Maria, 87, glamorous Mexican and international actress; Mexico City, Mexico, Apr. 8, 2002.

Frankenheimer, John, 72, director of such films as *Birdman of Alcatraz* (1962) and *The Manchurian Candidate* (1964); also did award-winning work in TV; Los Angeles, CA, July 6, 2002.

G

Gardner, John W., 89, founder of the citizens' lobby Common Cause; Palo Alto, CA, Feb. 16, 2002.

Ginzburg, Alexander I., 65, journalist and human rights campaigner who spent 9 years in Soviet prisons and labor camps before being expelled in 1979; Paris, France, July 19, 2002.

Gotti, John, 61, New York City mobster known as the "Dapper Don" and, until convicted of murder and racketeering in 1992, as the "Teflon Don"; Springfield, MO, June 10, 2002.

Gould, Stephen Jay, 60, Harvard Univ. evolutionary biologist who also wrote widely for the general public; New York, NY, May 20, 2002.

Gray, Dolores, 78, actress of 1950s musical theater and film; New York, NY, June 26, 2002.

H

Hampton, Lionel, 94, jazz icon who played the vibraphone in groundbreaking recordings with Benny Goodman and others; New York, NY, Aug. 31, 2002.

Handler, Ruth, 85, cofounded Mattel toy company; created the Barbie doll (1959); Los Angeles, CA, Apr. 27, 2002.

Harrison, George, 58, guitarist and songwriter; the "quiet" Beatle; wrote "While My Guitar Gently Weeps," "Here Comes the Sun," and "Something"; Los Angeles, CA, Nov. 29, 2001.

Hawthorne, Sir Nigel, 72, British actor; played a conniving civil servant in the 1980s TV series *Yes, Minister*; Hertfordshire, England, Dec. 26, 2001.

Hayes, Bob, 59, champion sprinter; became a star wide receiver for the Dallas Cowboys; only Olympic gold medalist to earn a Super Bowl ring; Jacksonville, FL, Sept. 18, 2002.

Hearn, Chick, 85, long-time broadcaster for the L.A. Lakers basketball team, credited with coining "slam dunk" and "air ball"; Northridge, CA, Aug 5, 2002.

Heckart, Eileen, 82, gravelly-voiced Tony- and Emmy-award-winning actress, won an Oscar for *Butterflies Are Free* (1972); Norwalk, CT, Dec. 31, 2001.

Heineken, Alfred Henry, 78, Dutch industrialist who headed one of the world's biggest breweries; Amsterdam, the Netherlands, Jan. 3, 2002.

Heyerdahl, Thor, 87, Norwegian explorer; his chronicle of a 1947 trans-Pacific journey aboard a raft, the *Kon-Tiki*, was an international best-seller; near Colla Michari, Italy, Apr. 18, 2002.

Howard, Edward Lee, 50, onetime CIA agent; defected to the USSR in the mid-1980s after eluding arrest on spy charges; Moscow, Russia, July 12, 2002.

Hunter, Kim, 79 actress who in 1947 originated the role of Stella in a *Streetcar Named Desire*; won an Oscar for reprising the role in the 1951 film version; New York, NY, Sept. 11, 2002.

J

Jennings, Waylon, 64, leader of country music's 1970s "outlaw" movement; Chandler, AZ, Feb. 14, 2002.

Jones, Chuck, 89, animator who helped create Bugs Bunny and Daffy Duck and invented Road Runner and Wile E. Coyote; Corona del Mar, Calif., Feb. 22, 2002.

Jovanovich, William, 81, publisher who transformed a small literary press into giant Harcourt Brace Jovanovich; San Diego, CA, Dec. 4, 2001.

Jurado, Katy, 78, Mexican actress who was an Oscar nominee for the western *Broken Lance* (1954); Cuernavaca, Mexico, July 5, 2002.

K

Kesey, Ken, 66, author whose first and best-known novel was *One Flew Over the Cuckoo's Nest* (1962); Eugene, OR, Nov. 10, 2001.

Kile, Darryl, 33, ace pitcher for the St. Louis Cardinals baseball team; Chicago, IL, June 22, 2002.

Knef, Hildegard, 76, German actress who, as Hildegarde Neff, made her mark in Hollywood and on Broadway in the 1950s; Berlin, Germany, Feb. 1, 2002.

Koch, Kenneth, 77, witty, erudite poet of the 1950s New York School; New York, NY, July 6, 2002.

L

Landers, Ann, 83, pen name of Eppie Lederer; her advice column appeared in more than 1,200 newspapers worldwide; Chicago, IL, June 22, 2002.

Lebed, Aleksandr, 52, ex-Russian general who helped foil a 1991 coup and in 1996 negotiated an end to Russia's first war against Chechen separatists; near Abakan, Russia, Apr. 28, 2002.

Lee, Peggy, 81, U.S. pop vocalist hailed for decades for her understated style and her ability to sound sultry and cool at the same time; Los Angeles, CA, Jan. 21, 2002.

Leone, Giovanni, 93, Italian president, 1971-78; lost office because of a bribery scandal involving Lockheed Aircraft Corp.; near Rome, Italy, Nov. 9, 2001.

LeNoire, Rosetta, 90, black actress and theater producer who starred in the TV show *Family Matters*; Teaneck, NJ, Mar. 17, 2002.

Lindgren, Astrid, 94, Swedish author who created the character of Pippi Longstocking in children's literature; Stockholm, Sweden, Jan. 28, 2002.

Littlewood, Joan, 87, British theater producer of *Oh What a Lovely War* (1963), London, England, Sept. 20, 2002.

Lomax, Allen, 87, musicologist who played a major role in preserving and disseminating folk and roots music; Safety Harbor, FL, July 19, 2002.

Lopes, Lisa, 30, rapper and songwriter who was the "L" in TLC, the rhythm-and-blues trio that was the best-selling female group (in albums) ever; Roma, Honduras, Apr. 25, 2002.

Lord, Walter, 84, popular historian whose *A Night to Remember* (1955) dealt with the 1912 sinking of the *Titanic*; New York, NY, May 19, 2002.

M

Marcus, Stanley, 96, department-store heir who oversaw creation of the Neiman-Marcus retailing empire; Dallas, TX, Jan. 22, 2002.

Margaret, Princess, 71, Queen Elizabeth's younger sister; made headlines when she gave up on marrying divorced Group Capt. Peter Townsend in 1955; London, England, Feb. 9, 2002.

McIntire, Carl, 95, fiery conservative radio evangelist once listened to by millions; forced off the air by the FCC in 1973; Voorhees, NJ, Mar. 19, 2002.

McKay, Gardner, 69, star of TV's *Adventures in Paradise* series (1959-62); Honolulu, HI, Nov. 21, 2001.

McKern, Leo, 82, actor who played curmudgeonly barrister Horace Rumpole in the TV series *Rumpole of the Bailey;* Bath, England, July 23, 2002.

Milligan, Spike, 83, star and main author of the *Goon Show*, an absurdist 1950s BBC radio series; near Rye, England, Feb. 27, 2002.

Milstein, Cesar, 74, Cambridge Univ. chemist; shared a 1984 Nobel for his contribution to immunology; Cambridge, England, Mar. 24, 2002.

Mink, Patsy Takemoto, 74, liberal Democratic U.S. representative from Hawaii; Honolulu, HI, Sept. 28, 2002.

Moore, Dudley, 66, diminutive British-born actor and comedian who gained fame in the satirical revue *Beyond the Fringe*, and starred in such movies as *10* and *Arthur;* Plainfield, NJ, Mar. 27, 2002.

N

Nozick, Robert, 63, Harvard political philosopher whose *Anarchy, State, and Utopia* (1974) became a classic; Cambridge, MA, Jan. 23, 2002.

P

Perutz, Max F., 87, Cambridge Univ.-based biochemist who in 1962 won a Nobel Prize for elucidating the molecular structure of hemoglobin; Cambridge, England, Feb. 6, 2002.

Phillips, Julia, 57, onetime film producer who skewered Hollywood figures in her memoir *You'll Never Eat Lunch in This Town Again* (1991); West Hollywood, CA, Jan. 1, 2002

Posner, Victor, 83, U.S. corporate raider who amassed a fortune but was eventually barred from involvement with public companies; Miami Beach, FL, Feb. 11, 2002.

Potok, Chaim, 73, rabbi turned author best-selling novels about religious Jews battling temptations of secularism; Merion, PA, July 23, 2002.

Pusey, Nathan M., 94, Harvard Univ. president from the 1950s (when he opposed McCarthyism) through the turbulent unrest of the 60s; New York, NY, Nov. 14, 2001.

R

Ramone, Dee Dee, 49, bassist and songwriter; a founding member of the punk rock group the Ramones; Los Angeles, CA, June 5, 2002.

Riesman, David, 92, Harvard sociologist whose book *The Lonely Crowd* (1950) portrayed modern Americans as "other-directed" conformists; Binghamton, NY, May 10, 2002.

Riopelle, Jean-Paul, 78, Canada's best-known 20th-century painter; Ile-aux-Grues, Quebec, Mar. 12, 2002.

Rivers, Larry, 78, painter and sculptor whose work helped usher in Pop Art; also a jazz saxophonist; Southhampton, NY, Aug. 14, 2002.

Rosenberg, William, 86, food franchising pioneer who founded Dunkin' Donuts chain; Mashpee, MA, Sept. 20, 2002.

Russell, Harold, 88, disabled World War II vet who won 2 Oscars (best supporting actor and a special Oscar) for his role in *The Best Years of Our Lives* (1946); Needham, MA, Jan. 29, 2002.

S

Savimbi, Jonas, 67, longtime leader of the Angolan rebel group UNITA ; killed in battle with government troops, Moxico province, Angola, Feb. 22, 2002.

Schaap, Dick, 67, sports journalist, radio and TV broadcaster, and author; New York, NY, Dec. 21, 2001.

Senghor, Léopold, 95, first president of post-colonial Senegal; a noted poet; helped found the *négritude* movement; Normandy, France, Dec. 20, 2001.

Shuster, Frank, 85, half of the Wayne and Shuster comedy duo, known as the "kings of Canadian Comedy"; Toronto, Canada, Jan. 13, 2002.

Sidney, George, 85, leading director of Hollywood musicals during the golden age of the genre at MGM studios; Las Vegas, NV, May 5, 2002.

Slaughter, Enos, 86, baseball Hall of Famer; his dash from 1st to home scored the winning run for the St. Louis Cardinals in the 1946 World Series; Durham, NC, Aug. 12, 2002.

Smith, Howard K., 87, broadcast journalist who in 1960 moderated the first televised presidential debate; Bethesda, MD, Feb. 15, 2002.

Snead, Sam, 89, star golfer who won a record 82 PGA Tour events and shot a 66 at age 67; Hot Springs, VA, May 23, 2002.

Steiger, Rod, 77, actor known for such films as *On the Waterfront* (1954) and *In the Heat of the Night* (1967), for which he won an Oscar; Los Angeles, CA, July 9, 2002.

Stone, W. Clement, 100, Illinois insurance executive and philanthropist; single largest contributor to Richard Nixon's campaigns in 1968 and 1972; Evanston, IL, Sept. 3, 2002.

T

Talmadge, Herman, 88, Georgia governor (1948-55) and U.S. senator (1957-81); once a staunch segregationist, he gradually moved closer to the political center; Hampton, GA, Mar. 21, 2002.

Thaw, John, 60, British actor who played the title character in the "Inspector Morse" TV detective series; London, England, Feb. 21, 2002.

Thomas, Dave, 69, founder and pitchman of the Wendy's International chain of fast-food restaurants; Fort Lauderdale, FL, Jan. 8, 2002.

Tobin, James, 84, Nobel Prize-winning U.S. economist; a leading advocate of the theories of John Maynard Keynes; New Haven, CT, Mar. 11, 2002.

Trigère, Pauline, 93, French-born U.S. fashion designer prominent from the 1940s into the 1990s; New York, NY, Feb. 13, 2002.

U

Unitas, Johnny, 69, NFL Hall of Fame quarterback; played with the Baltimore Colts for 17 seasons; widely regarded as the top quarterback in NFL history; Towson, MD, Sept. 11, 2002.

Urich, Robert, 55, star of the TV detective series *Vega$* (1978-81) and *Spencer: For Hire* (1985-88); Thousand Oaks, CA, Apr. 16, 2002.

V

Vance, Cyrus R., 84, U.S. secretary of state under Pres. Jimmy Carter, 1977-1980; New York, NY, Jan. 12, 2002.

Von Amsberg, Claus, 76, husband of Queen Beatrix of the Netherlands; Amsterdam, Oct. 6, 2002.

W

Walters, Vernon A., 85, U.S. diplomat and military officer who served as CIA deputy director and U.S. ambassador to the UN; West Palm Beach, FL, Feb. 10, 2002.

Warfield, William, 82, bass-baritone who played Porgy in George Gershwin's *Porgy and Bess,* often opposite his then-wife, soprano Leontyne Price; Chicago, IL, Aug. 25, 2002.

Wasserman, Lew, 89, longtime Hollywood mogul who helped build MCA into a huge entertainment empire, Beverly Hills, CA, June 3, 2002.

Weaver, Sylvester (Pat), 93, pioneer NBC TV executive; created the *Today* and *Tonight* shows; Santa Barbara, CA, Mar. 15, 2002.

Webster, Mike, 50, Hall of Fame center for the Steelers in the 1970s; later diagnosed with brain damage from hits to the head; Pittsburgh, PA, Sept. 24, 2002.

Weinstock, Arnold (Baron Weinstock of Bowden), 77, British industrialist; longtime managing director of General Electric Co. (GEC); Wiltshire, England, July 23, 2002.

White, Byron, 84, onetime college and professional football star (known as "Whizzer" White) who became a U.S. Supreme Court justice in 1962 and served for 31 years; Denver, CO, Apr. 15, 2002.

Wilder, Billy, 95, writer and director who won 6 Oscars; his films ranged from *Double Indemnity* (1945) to *The Apartment* (1960); Beverly Hills, CA, Mar. 27, 2002.

Wilhelm, Hoyt, 80, knuckleball-throwing pitcher; first pitcher admitted to the Hall of Fame mainly for his work as a reliever; Sarasota, FL, Aug. 23, 2002.

Williams, Harrison A., Jr., 81, Democratic senator from New Jersey, 1959-82; convicted of bribery in the Abscam scandal (1981); Denville, NJ, Nov. 17, 2001.

Williams, Ted, 83, arguably the greatest pure hitter of Major League Baseball and the sport's last .400-plus hitter, with a .406 batting average in 1941; Inverness, FL, July 5, 2002.

Worth, Irene, 85 (?), U.S.-born actress, best known for theater; she rose to fame in London, thereafter had a splendid transatlantic career; New York, NY, Mar. 10, 2002.

UNITED STATES GOVERNMENT

EXECUTIVE BRANCH	LEGISLATIVE BRANCH	JUDICIAL BRANCH
PRESIDENT **Vice President** **Executive Office of the President** White House Office Office of the Vice President Council of Economic Advisers Council on Environmental Quality National Security Council Office of Administration Office of Management and Budget Office of National Drug Control Policy Office of Policy Development Office of Science and Technology Policy Office of the U.S. Trade Representative	**CONGRESS** **Senate House** Architect of the Capitol U.S. Botanic Garden General Accounting Office Government Printing Office Library of Congress Congressional Budget Office	**Supreme Court of the United States** Courts of Appeals District Courts Territorial Courts Court of International Trade Court of Federal Claims Tax Court Court of Appeals for Veterans Claims Administrative Office of the Courts Federal Judicial Center Sentencing Commission

The Bush Administration

As of Oct. 2002; mailing addresses are for Washington, DC.

Terms of office of the president and vice president: Jan. 20, 2001, to Jan. 20, 2005.

President — George W. Bush receives an annual salary of $400,000 (taxable), and an annual expense allowance of $50,000 (nontaxable) for costs resulting from official duties. In addition, up to $100,000 a year may be spent on travel expenses and $19,000 on official entertainment (both nontaxable), available for allocation within the Executive Office of the President.
Website: www.whitehouse.gov/president
E-mail: president@whitehouse.gov

Vice President — Dick Cheney receives an annual salary of $192,600 (taxable), plus $90,000 for official entertainment expenses (nontaxable).
Website: www.whitehouse.gov/vicepresident
E-mail: vice.president@whitehouse.gov

The Cabinet Department Heads

(Salary: $166,700 per year)

Secretary of State — Colin L. Powell
Secretary of the Treasury — Paul H. O'Neill
Secretary of Defense — Donald H. Rumsfeld
Attorney General — John Ashcroft
Secretary of the Interior — Gale Norton
Secretary of Agriculture — Ann M. Veneman
Secretary of Commerce — Donald L. Evans
Secretary of Labor — Elaine L. Chao
Secretary of Health and Human Services — Tommy Thompson
Secretary of Housing and Urban Development — Mel Martinez
Secretary of Transportation — Norman Y. Mineta
Secretary of Energy — Spencer Abraham
Secretary of Education — Roderick R. Paige
Secretary of Veterans Affairs — Anthony Principi

The White House Staff

1600 Pennsylvania Ave. NW 20500
Website: www.whitehouse.gov

Chief of Staff to the President — Andrew H. Card Jr.
Asst. to the President & Deputy Chief of Staff for Operations — Joseph W. Hagin II
Asst. to the President & Deputy Chief of Staff for Policy — Joshua Bolten
Office of Homeland Security — Tom Ridge, dir.
Assistants to the President:
Counsel to the President — Alberto R. Gonzalez
Deputy Counsel to the President — Timothy Flanigan
Domestic Policy Council — Margaret LaMontagne
Presidential Personnel — Clay S. Johnson
Press Secretary — L. Ari Fleischer
Legislative Affairs — Nicholas Calio
Communications — Dan Bartlett, dir.
Counselor to the President — Karen Hughes
National Economic Council — Lawrence Lindsay, dir.
Intergovernmental Affairs — Ruben S. Barrales
National Security — Condoleezza Rice
Staff Secretary — Harriet Miers
Political Affairs — Kenneth B. Mehlman
Public Liaison — Barbara Chaffee
Management & Administration — Hector F. Irastorza Jr.
Cabinet Secretary — Albert Hawkins
Director of Presidential Scheduling — Bradley Blakeman
Director of Speechwriting — Michael Gerson
Chief of Staff to the First Lady — Andi Ball
E-mail: first.lady@whitehouse.gov
Senior Advisor to the President — Karl Rove
Director of Advance — Brian D. Montgomery
Oval Office Operations — Linda Gambatesa
Faith-Based and Community Initiatives — Jim Towey
Office of National AIDS Policy — Scott Evertz

Executive Agencies

Council of Economic Advisers — Glenn Hubbard, chair
Website: www.whitehouse.gov/cea/index.html
Office of Administration — Philip Larsen, dir.
Website: www.whitehouse.gov/oa/index.html
Office of Science & Technology Policy — John H. Marburger III, Ph.D.
Website: www.ostp.gov
Office of Natl. Drug Control Policy — John P. Walters, dir.
Website: www.whitehousedrugpolicy.gov
Office of Management and Budget — Mitchell E. Daniels Jr., dir.
Website: www.whitehouse.gov/omb/index.html
U.S. Trade Representative — Robert B. Zoellick
Website: www.ustr.gov
Council on Environ. Quality — James L. Connaughton, chair
Website: www.whitehouse.gov/ceq/index.html

Department of State

2201 C St. NW 20520
Website: www.state.gov

Secretary of State — Colin L. Powell
Deputy Secretary — Richard L. Armitage
Chief of Staff — Bill Smullen
U.S. Ambassador to the United Nations — John D. Negroponte
Under Sec. for Political Affairs — Marc Grossman
Under Sec. for Management — Grant S. Green
Under Sec. for Global Affairs — Paula J. Dobriansky
Under Sec. for Economic, Business, & Agricultural Affairs — Alan P. Larson
Under Sec. for Arms Control & International Security Affairs — John R. Bolton
Policy Planning Director — Richard N. Haass
Chief of Protocol — Donald B. Ensenat
Inspector General — Clark Kent Ervin
Legal Adviser — William H. Taft IV
Director General of the Foreign Service & Director of Personnel — Ruth Davis
Assistant Secretaries for:
Administration — Willliam A. Eaton
African Affairs — Walter H. Kansteiner
Consular Affairs — Mary A. Ryan
Democracy, Human Rights, & Labor — Lorne W. Craner
Diplomatic Security — David Carpenter
East Asian & Pacific Affairs — James A. Kelly

Economic & Business Affairs — Earl Anthony Wayne
European & Canadian Affairs — A. Elizabeth Jones
Intelligence & Research — Carl W. Ford Jr.
International Narcotics & Law — Rand Beers
International Organization Affairs — David Welch
Legislative Affairs — Paul V. Kelly
Near Eastern Affairs — William Joseph Burns
Oceans, International Environmental, & Scientific Affairs — John F. Turner
Political-Military Affairs — Lincoln P. Bloomfield
Population, Refugees, & Migration — Arthur E. Dewey
Public Affairs — Richard A. Boucher
South Asian Affairs — Christina B. Rocca
Afghan Coordinator — David T. Johnson

Department of the Treasury

1500 Pennsylvania Ave. NW 20220
Website: www.ustreas.gov

Secretary of the Treasury — Paul H. O'Neill
Deputy Sec. of the Treasury — Kenneth Dam
Under Sec. for Domestic Finance — Peter R. Fisher
Under Sec. for International Affairs — John Taylor
Under Sec. for Enforcement — Jimmy Gurule
General Counsel — David Aufhauser
Inspector General — Jeffrey Rush Jr.
Inspector General for Tax Administration — David Williams
Assistant Secretaries for:
Economic Policy — Richard H. Clarida
Enforcement — Kenneth E. Lawson
Financial Institutions — J. Patrick Cave, act.
Fiscal Affairs — Donald Hammond
International Affairs — Randy K. Quarles
Legislative Affairs — John Duncan
Management — Edward R. Kingman Jr.
Public Affairs — Michele Davis
Tax Policy — Pamela F. Olson, act.
Treasurer of the U.S. — Rosario Marin
Bureaus:
Alcohol, Tobacco, & Firearms — Bradley A. Buckles, dir.
Comptroller of the Currency — John Hawke Jr., comm.
Customs — Robert Bonner
Engraving & Printing — Tom Ferguson, dir.
Federal Law Enforcement Training Center — John C. Dooher, act.
Financial Management Service — Richard Gregg, comm.
Internal Revenue Service — Charles Rossotti, comm.
Mint — Henrietta Fore
Office of Thrift Supervision — James Gilleron
Public Debt — Van Zeck, comm.
U.S. Secret Service — Brian L. Stafford, dir.

Department of Defense

The Pentagon 20301
Website: www.defenselink.mil

Secretary of Defense — Donald H. Rumsfeld
Deputy Secretary — Paul D. Wolfowitz
Under Sec. for Acquis. and Technol. — E. C. "Pete" Aldridge
Under Sec. for Personnel & Readiness — David S. C. Chu
Under Sec. for Policy — Douglas J. Feith
Assistant Secretaries for:
Command, Control, Communications, & Intelligence — John P. Stenbit
Force Management — Charles S. Abell
Health Affairs — William Winkenwerder Jr., MD
International Security Affairs — Peter W. Rodman
International Security Policy — Dr. J. D. Crouch II
Legislative Affairs — Powell A. Moore
Public Affairs — Victoria Clarke
Reserve Affairs — Craig W. Duehring, act.
Special Operations & Low-Intensity Conflict — vacant
Program Analysis & Evaluation — Stephen A. Cambone
Inspector General — Joseph E. Schmitz
Comptroller — Dov S. Zakheim
General Counsel — William J. Haynes II
Intelligence Oversight — George B. Lotz II
Operational Test & Evaluation — Thomas P. Christie, dir.
Chairman, Joint Chiefs of Staff — Gen. Richard B. Myers
Secretary of the Army — Thomas E. White
Secretary of the Navy — Gordon R. England
Commandant of the Marine Corps — James Jones
Secretary of the Air Force — James G. Roche

Department of Justice

Constitution Ave. & 10th St. NW 20530
Website: www.usdoj.gov

Attorney General — John Ashcroft
Deputy Attorney General — Larry Thompson
Associate Attorney General — Jay Stephens
Office of Dispute Resolution — Jeffrey M. Senger
Solicitor General — Theodore B. Olson
Office of Inspector General — Glenn Fine
Assistants:
Administration — Janis Sposato
Antitrust Division — Charles James
Civil Division — Robert McCallum Jr.
Civil Rights Division — Ralph Boyd Jr.
Criminal Division — Michael Chertoff
Environ. & Nat. Resources Division — Thomas Sansonetti
Justice Programs — Deborah Daniels
Legal Counsel — William Haynes
Legislative Affairs — Daniel J. Bryant
Legal Policy — Viet Dinh
Tax Division — Eileen O'Connor
Executive Secretariat — Kathie Harting
Office of Public Affairs — Barbara Comstock
Office of Information & Privacy — Richard L. Huff/Daniel J. Metcalfe
Community Oriented Policing Services — Carl R. Peed
Federal Bureau of Investigation — Robert S. Mueller III
Exec. Off. for Immigration Review — Kevin D. Rooney, dir.
Bureau of Prisons — Kathleen Hawk Sawyer, dir.
Community Relations Service — Sharee M. Freeman, dir.
Drug Enforcement Admin. — Asa Hutchinson
Office of Intelligence Policy & Review — James Baker
Office of Professional Responsibility — H. Marshall Jarrett, counsel
Exec. Off. for U.S. Trustees — Lawrence Friedman, dir.
Foreign Claims Settlement Comm. — Mauricio J. Tamargo
Exec. Office for U.S. Attorneys — Guy A. Lewis, dir.
Immigration & Naturalization Service — James W. Ziglar
Pardon Attorney — Roger C. Adams
U.S. Parole Commission — Edward F. Reilly Jr.
U.S. Marshals Service — Benigno G. Regna
U.S. Natl. Cen. Bureau of INTERPOL — Edgar A. Adamson
Office of Intergovernmental and Public Liaison — Lori Sharpe Day
Office of Tribal Justice — Todd Araujo
Violence Against Women Office — Catherine Pierce
National Drug Intelligence Center — Michael T. Horn, dir.

Department of the Interior

1849 C St. NW 20240
Website: www.doi.gov

Secretary of the Interior — Gale Norton
Deputy Secretary — J. Steven Griles
Assistant Secretaries for:
Fish, Wildlife, & Parks — Craig Manson
Indian Affairs — Neal A. McCaleb
Land & Minerals — Rebecca W. Watson
Policy, Management, & Budget — P. Lynn Scarlett
Water & Science — Bennett Raley
Bureau of Land Management — Kathleen Clarke
Bureau of Reclamation — John W. Keys III
Fish & Wildlife Service — Steven A. Williams
Geological Survey — Charles Groat
Minerals Management Service — R.M. "Johnnie" Burton
National Park Service — Fran P. Mainella, dir.
Surf. Mining Reclam. & Enforcement — Jeffrey Jarrett
Communications — Eric Ruff, dir.
Congressional & Legislative Affairs — David L. Bernhardt
Solicitor — William G. Myers
External Affairs — Kit Kimball
Exec. Secretariat & Regulatory Affairs — Fay Iudicello

Department of Agriculture

1400 Independence Ave. SW 20250
Website: www.usda.gov

Secretary of Agriculture — Ann M. Veneman
Deputy Secretary — James R. "Jim" Moseley
Under Secretaries for:
Farm & Foreign Agric. Services — J. B. Penn
Food, Nutrition, & Consumer Services — Eric M. Bost
Food Safety — Elsa A. Murano
Marketing & Regulatory Programs — William T. "Bill" Hawk
Natural Resources & Environment — Mark E. Rey
Research, Education, & Economics — Joseph Jen
Rural Development — Tom Dorr
Assistant Secretaries for:
Administration — Lou Gallegos
Congressional Relations — Mary Waters
General Counsel — Nancy S. Bryson
Inspector General — Joyce N. Fleischman, act.
Chief Financial Officer — Edward R. McPherson
Chief Information Officer — Scott Charbo
Chief Economist — Keith Collins
Communications — Kevin Herglotz
Press Secretary — Alisa Harrison

Department of Commerce

14th St. between Constitution & Pennsylvania Ave. NW 20230
Website: www.doc.gov

Secretary of Commerce — Donald L. Evans
Deputy Secretary — Samuel Bodman
Chief of Staff — Phil Bond
General Counsel — Ted Kassinger
Assistant Secretaries:
Chief Financial Officer & Asst. Secretary for Admin. — Otto Wolff
Economic Development Admin. — David Sampson
Export Admin. — Jim Jochun
Export Enforcement — Michael Garcia
Import Administration — Faryar Shirzad
Legislative Affairs — Brenda Becker
Market Access & Compliance — William Lash
National Telecomm. Information Administration — Nancy Victory
Oceans & Atmosphere — James Mahoney
Patent & Trademark Office — James Rogan
Trade Development — Linda Conlin
U.S. & Foreign Commercial Service — Maria Cino
Bureau of the Census — Charles Louis Kincannon
Under Sec. for Oceans & Atmosphere — Vice Admiral Conrad Lautenbacher
Under Sec. for Industry & Security — Kenneth Juster
Under Sec. for International Trade — Grant Aldonas
Under Sec. for Econ. Affairs — Kathleen Cooper
Under Sec. for Technology — Phil Bond
Natl. Institute of Standards & Tech. — Arden Bement
Minority Business Dev. Agency — Ronald Langston
Public Affairs — Mary Crawford

Department of Labor

200 Constitution Ave. NW 20210
Website: www.dol.gov

Secretary of Labor — Elaine L. Chao
Deputy Secretary — D. Cameron Findlay
Chief of Staff — Steven J. Law
Assistant Secretaries for:
Admin. & Management — Patrick Pizzella
Congressional & Intergov. Affairs — Kristine Iverson
Employment & Training — Emily Stover DeRocco
Employment Standards — Victoria Lipnic
Occupational Safety & Health — John Henshaw
Mine Safety & Health — David Lauriski
Pension & Welfare Benefits — Ann Combs
Policy — Christopher Spear
Public Affairs — Kathleen Harrington
Veterans Employment & Training — Frederico Juarbe Jr.
Solicitor of Labor — Eugene Scalia
Bureau of International Affairs — Thomas B. Moorhead
Women's Bureau — Shinae Chun
Inspector General — Gordon S. Heddell
Bureau of Labor Statistics — Kathleen P. Utgoff

Department of Health and Human Services

200 Independence Ave. SW 20201
Website: www.os.dhhs.gov

Secretary of Health & Human Services — Tommy Thompson
Deputy Secretary — Claude A. Allen
Chief of Staff — Robert Wood
Assistant Secretaries for:
Aging — Josefina Carbonell
Children & Families — vacant
Health — Carolyn M. Clancy, act.
Legislation — Scott Whitaker
Administration & Management — Ed Sontag
Planning & Evaluation — Bobby Piyush Jindal
Public Affairs — Kevin Keane
General Counsel — Alex Azar
Inspector General — Janet Rehnquist
Office for Civil Rights — Robinsue Frohboese, act. dir.
Surgeon General — Richard Carmona
Centers for Medicare and Medicaid Services — Tom Scully

Department of Housing and Urban Development

451 7th St. SW 20410
Website: www.hud.gov

Secretary of Housing & Urban Development — Mel Martinez
Deputy Secretary — Alphonso R. Jackson
Chief of Staff — Frank R. Jimenez
Assistant Secretaries for:
Community Planning & Development — Roy A. Bernardi
Congressional & Intergov. Relations — vacant
Fair Housing & Equal Opportunity — vacant
Housing & Federal Housing Comm. — John C. Weicher
Policy Development & Research — vacant
Public & Indian Housing — Michael Liu
General Counsel — Richard A. Hauser
Chief Information Officer — Gloria R. Parker
Inspector General — Kevin M. Donohue
Chief Financial Officer — Angela Antonelli
Government National Mortgage Assn. — Ronald Rosenfeld
Off. of Federal Housing Enterprise Oversight — Armando Falcon Jr.

Department of Transportation

400 7th St. SW 20590
Website: www.dot.gov

Secretary of Transportation — Norman Y. Mineta
Deputy Secretary — Michael P. Jackson
Assistant Secretaries for:
Administration — Melissa Allen
Aviation & International Affairs — Read Van de Water
Budget & Programs — Donna McLean
Governmental Affairs — Sean B. O'Hollaren
Public Affairs — Chet Lunner
Transportation Policy — Emil H. Frankel
U.S. Coast Guard Commandant — Adm. Thomas H. Collins
Federal Aviation Admin. — Marion C. Blakey
Federal Highway Admin. — Mary Peters
Federal Railroad Admin. — Allan Rutter
Maritime Admin. — Capt. William Schubert
Natl. Highway Traffic Safety Admin. — Dr. Jeffrey W. Runge
Federal Transit Admin. — Jennifer L. Dorn
Research & Special Programs Admin. — Ellen G. Engleman
St. Lawrence Seaway Devel. Corp. — Albert Jacquez

Department of Energy

1000 Independence Ave. SW 20585
Website: www.energy.gov

Secretary of Energy — Spencer Abraham
Deputy Secretary — Frank Blake
Under Secretary — Robert Card
Chief of Staff — Kyle McSlarrow
General Counsel — Lee Otis
Inspector General — Gregory Friedman

Assistant Secretaries for:
Administration & Human Resource Management — Richard Farrell
Congressional & Intergov. Affairs — Dan Brouillette
Defense Programs — Linton Brooks, act.
Energy Efficiency & Renewable Energy — David Garman
Environment, Safety, & Health — Beverly Cook
Environmental Management — Jessie Roberson
Fossil Energy — Carl Michael Smith
International Affairs — Vicky A. Bailey
Oversight & Performance Assurance — Glenn Podonsky
Nuclear Energy — Bill Magwood
Energy Information Admin. — Mary Hutzler, act.
Economic Impact & Diversity — Theresa Speake
Hearings & Appeals — George Breznay, dir.
Science & Technology — Walter L. Warnick, dir.
Civilian Radioactive Waste Management — Lake H. Barrett, act. dir.
Nonproliferation & National Security — Joseph P. Indusi
Chief Financial Officer — Bruce Carnes
Energy Advisory Board — M. Peter McPherson
Office of Public Affairs — Jeanne Lopatto

Department of Education

400 Maryland Ave., SW 20202
Website: www.ed.gov

Secretary of Education — Roderick R. Paige
Deputy Secretary — William D. Hansen
Chief of Staff — John M. Danielson
Inspector General — John P. Higgins Jr.
General Counsel — Brian W. Jones
Assistant Secretaries for:
Adult & Vocational Education — Carol D'Amico
Civil Rights — Gerald Reynolds
Educational Research & Improvement — Grover J. "Russ" Whitehurst
Elementary & Secondary Educ. — Susan B. Neuman
Intergov. & Interagency Affairs — Laurie M. Rich
Legislative & Congressional Affairs — Clayton Boothby, act.
Postsecondary Education — Sally L. Stroup
Special Educ. & Rehab. Services — Robert H. Pasternack
Bilingual Education & Minority Language Affairs — Arthur Love
Rehab. Services Admin. — Joanne M. Wilson, comm.
Education Statistics — Dr. Gary Phillips, act. comm.

Department of Veterans Affairs

810 Vermont Ave. NW 20420
Website: www.va.gov

Secretary of Veterans Affairs — Anthony Principi
Deputy Secretary — Leo Mackay Jr.
Assistant Secretaries for:
Congressional Affairs — Gordon Mansfield
Management — vacant
Human Resources & Admin. — Jacob Lozada, PhD.
Policy & Planning — Claude Kicklighter
Public & Intergovernmental Affairs — Maureen Cragin
Inspector General — Richard J. Griffin
Under Sec. for Benefits — Daniel L. Cooper
Under Sec. for Health — Robert H. Roswell, M.D.
Under Sec. for Memorial Affairs — Robin Higgins
General Counsel — Tim McClain
Board of Veterans Appeals — Eligah Dane Clark, chair
Board of Contract Appeals — Guy H. McMichael III, chairman
Small & Disadvantaged Business Utilization — Scott S. Denniston, dir.
Veterans Service Organization Liaison — Allen F. Kent

Notable U.S. Government Agencies

Source: *The U.S. Government Manual*; National Archives and Records Administration; World Almanac research

All addresses are Washington, DC, unless otherwise noted; as of Oct. 2002
* = independent agency

Bureau of Alcohol, Tobacco, and Firearms — Bradley A. Buckles, dir. (Dept. of Treas., 650 Mass. Ave NW, 20226).
Website: www.atf.treas.gov

Bureau of the Census — Charles Louis Kincannon, dir. (Dept. of Commerce, 4700 Silver Hill Rd., Suitland, MD 20746).
Website: www.census.gov

Bureau of Economic Analysis — J. Steven Landefeld, dir. (Dept. of Commerce, 1441 L St. NW, 20230).
Website: www.bea.gov

Bureau of Indian Affairs — Neal A. McCaleb, asst. sec. (Dept. of the Interior, 1849 C St. NW, 20240).
Website: www.doi.gov/bureau-indian-affairs.html

Bureau of Prisons — Kathleen Hawk Sawyer, dir. (Dept. of Justice, 320 First St. NW, 20534).
Website: www.bop.gov

Centers for Disease Control & Prevention — Dr. Julie Louise Gerberding, dir. (Dept. of HHS, 1600 Clifton Rd. NE, Atlanta, GA 30333).
Website: www.cdc.gov

*__Central Intelligence Agency__ — George J. Tenet, dir. (Wash., DC 20505).
Website: www.cia.gov

*__Commission on Civil Rights__ — Mary Frances Berry, chair (624 9th St. NW, 20425).
Website: www.usccr.gov

*__Commodity Futures Trading Commission__ — James E. Newsome, chair (3 Lafayette Centre, 1155 21st St. NW, 20581).
Website: www.cftc.gov

*__Consumer Product Safety Commission__ — Hal Stratton, chair (East-West Towers, 4330 East West Hwy., Bethesda, MD 20814).
Website: www.cpsc.gov

*__Environmental Protection Agency__ — Christine Todd Whitman, adm. (Ariel Rios Bldg., 1200 Pennsylvania Ave. NW, 20460).
Website: www.epa.gov

*__Equal Employment Opportunity Commission__ — Cari M. Dominguez, chair (1801 L St. NW, 20507).
Website: www.eeoc.gov

*__Export-Import Bank of the United States__ — vacant (811 Vermont Avenue NW, 20571).
Website: www.exim.gov

*__Farm Credit Administration__ — Michael M. Reyna, chair, Farm Credit Administration Board (1501 Farm Credit Drive, McLean, VA 22102).
Website: www.fca.gov

Federal Aviation Administration — Marion C. Blakey, adm. (Dept. of Trans., 800 Independence Ave. SW, 20591).
Website: www.faa.gov

Federal Bureau of Investigation — Robert S. Mueller III, dir. (Dept. of Justice, 935 Pennsylvania Ave. NW, 20535).
Website: www.fbi.gov

*__Federal Communications Commission__ — Michael K. Powell, chair (445 12th St. SW, 20554).
Website: www.fcc.gov

*__Federal Deposit Insurance Corporation__ — Donald E. Powell, chair (550 17th St. NW, 20429).
Website: www.fdic.gov

*__Federal Election Commission__ — David M. Mason, chair (999 E St. NW, 20463).
Website: www.fec.gov

*__Federal Emergency Management Agency__ — Joe M. Allbaugh, dir. (500 C St. SW, 20472).
Website: www.fema.gov

*__Federal Energy Regulatory Commission__ — Pat Wood III, chair (888 1st St. NE, 20426).
Website: www.ferc.fed.us

Federal Highway Administration — Mary E. Peters, adm. (Dept. of Trans., 400 7th St. SW, 20590).
Website: www.fhwa.dot.gov

*__Federal Maritime Commission__ — Steven R. Blust, chair (800 N. Capitol St. NW, 20573).
Website: www.fmc.gov

*__Federal Mine Safety & Health Review Commission__ — Robert H. Beatty Jr., comm. (1730 K St. NW, 20006).
Website: www.fmshrc.gov

*__Federal Reserve System__ — Alan Greenspan, chair, Board of Governors (20th St. & Constitution Ave. NW, 20551).
Website: www.federalreserve.gov

*__Federal Trade Commission__ — Timothy J. Muris, chair (600 Pennsylvania Ave. NW, 20580).
Website: www.ftc.gov

Fish & Wildlife Service — Steven A. Williams, dir. (Dept. of the Interior, 1849 C St. NW, 20240).
Website: www.fws.gov

Food and Drug Administration — Lester M. Crawford Jr., dep. comm. (5600 Fishers Lane, Rockville, MD 20857).
Website: www.fda.gov

Forest Service — Dale N. Bosworth, chief (Dept. of Agriculture, 201 14th St. SW, 20250).
Website: www.fs.fed.us

General Accounting Office — (cong. agency) David Michael Walker, comptroller gen. (441 G St. NW, 20548).
Website: www.gao.gov

*__General Services Administration__ — Stephen A. Perry, adm. (1941 Jefferson Davis Hwy., Arlington, VA 22202).
Website: www.gsa.gov

Government Printing Office — (cong. agency) Michael F. DiMario, public printer (732 N. Capitol St. NW, 20401).
Website: www.gpo.gov

Immigration & Naturalization Service — James W. Ziglar, comm. (Dept. of Justice, 425 I St. NW, 20536).
Website: www.ins.usdoj.gov

*__Inter-American Foundation__ — Frank Yturria, chair (901 N Stuart St., 10th floor, Arlington, VA 22203).
Website: www.iaf.gov

Internal Revenue Service — Charles O. Rossotti, comm. (Dept. of Treas., 1111 Constitution Ave. NW, 20224).
Website: www.irs.gov

Library of Congress — (cong. agency) Dr. James H. Billington, Librarian of Congress (101 Indep. Ave. SE, 20540).
Website: www.loc.gov

*__National Aeronautics and Space Administration__ — Sean O'Keefe, adm. (300 E St. SW, 20546).
Website: www.nasa.gov

*__National Archives & Records Administration__ — John W. Carlin, archivist (700 Pennsylvania Ave. NW, 20408).
Website: www.nara.gov

*__National Endowment for the Arts__ — vacant (1100 Pennsylvania Ave. NW, 20506).
Website: www.arts.gov

*__National Endowment for the Humanities__ — Bruce Cole, chair (1100 Pennsylvania Ave. NW, 20506).
Website: www.neh.fed.us

National Institutes of Health — Dr. Elias Zerhouni, dir. (9000 Rockville Pike, Bethesda, MD 20892).
Website: www.nih.gov

*__National Labor Relations Board__ — vacant (1099 14th St. NW, 20570).
Website: www.nlrb.gov

National Oceanic and Atmospheric Administration — Vice Adm. Conrad C. Lautenbacher Jr., adm. (Dept. of Commerce, 14th & Constitution Ave. NW, 20230).
Website: www.noaa.gov

National Park Service — Fran B. Mainella, dir. (Dept. of the Interior, 1849 C St. NW, 20240).
Website: www.nps.gov

*__National Railroad Passenger Corp. (Amtrak)__ — David Gunn, pres. (60 Mass. Ave. NE, 20002).
Website: www.amtrak.com

*__National Science Foundation__ — Dr. Rita Colwell, dir., National Science Foundation; Dr. Warren M. Washington, chair, National Science Board (4201 Wilson Blvd., Arlington, VA 22230).
Website: www.nsf.gov

*__National Transportation Safety Board__ — Carol J. Carmody, act. chair (490 L'Enfant Plaza SW, 20594).
Website: www.ntsb.gov

*__Nuclear Regulatory Commission__ — Richard A. Meserve, chair (11555 Rockville Pike, Rockville, MD 20852).
Website: www.nrc.gov

Occupational Safety & Health Administration — John L. Henshaw, asst. sec. (Dept. of Labor, 200 Constitution Ave. NW, 20210).
Website: www.osha.gov

*__Occupational Safety & Health Review Commission__ — W. Scott Railton, chair (1120 20th St. NW, 9th Floor, 20036).
Website: www.oshrc.gov

*__Office of Government Ethics__ — Amy L. Comstock, dir. (1201 New York Ave. NW, Suite 500, 20005).
Website: www.usoge.gov

*__Office of Personnel Management__ — Kay Coles James, dir. (1900 E St. NW, 20415-0001).
Website: www.opm.gov

*__Office of Special Counsel__ — Elaine D. Kaplan, special counsel (1730 M St. NW, Suite 300, 20036).
Website: www.osc.gov

*__Peace Corps__ — Gaddi H. Vasquez, dir. (1111 20th St., NW, 20526).
Website: www.peacecorps.gov

*__Postal Rate Commission__ — George A. Omas, chair (1333 H St. NW, Suite 300, 20268).
Website: www.prc.gov

*__Securities and Exchange Commission__ — Harvey L. Pitt, chair (450 5th St. NW, 20549).
Website: www.sec.gov

*__Selective Service System__ — Alfredo V. Rascon, dir. (National Headquarters, 1515 Wilson Blvd., Arlington, VA 22209-2425).
Website: www.sss.gov

*__Small Business Administration__ — Hector V. Barreto, adm. (409 Third St. SW, 20416).
Website: www.sba.gov

Smithsonian Institution — (quasi-official agency) Lawrence M. Small, sec. (1000 Jefferson Dr. SW, Rm. 354, 20560-0033).
Website: www.si.edu

*__Social Security Administration__ — Jo Anne B. Barnhart, comm. (6401 Security Blvd., Baltimore, MD 21235).
Website: www.ssa.gov

Surgeon General — Dr. Richard Carmona (Dept. of HHS, 5600 Fishers Ln., Rm. 18-66, Rockville, MD 20857).
Website: www.surgeongeneral.gov

*__Tennessee Valley Authority__ — Glenn L. McCollough Jr., chair, Board of Directors (400 W. Summit Hill Dr., Knoxville, TN 37902, and One Mass. Ave. NW, Suite 300, 20444).
Website: www.tva.gov

*__Trade and Development Agency__ — Thelma J. Askey, dir. (1621 N. Kent St., Suite 200, Arlington, VA 22209).
Website: www.tda.gov

United States Coast Guard — Adm. Thomas H. Collins, commandant (Dept. of Trans., 2100 2nd St. SW, 20593).
Website: www.uscg.mil

United States Customs Service — Robert C. Bonner, comm. (1300 Pennsylvania Ave. NW, 20229).
Website: www.customs.gov

United States Geological Survey — Charles G. Groat, dir. (Dept. of the Interior, 12201 Sunrise Valley Dr., Reston, VA 20192).
Website: www.usgs.gov

United States International Trade Commission — Deanna Tanner Okun, chair (500 E St. SW, 20436).
Website: www.usitc.gov

United States Mint — Henrietta Holsman Fore, dir. (U.S. Mint Headquarters, 801 9th St., NW, 20002).
Website: www.usmint.gov

*__United States Postal Service__ — John E. Potter, Postmaster General (475 L'Enfant Plaza SW, 20260).
Website: www.usps.com

United States Secret Service — Brian L. Stafford, dir. (Dept. of Treas., 950 H St. NW, Ste. 8000, 20001).
Website: www.ustreas.gov/usss

CABINETS OF THE U.S.

The U.S. Cabinet and Its Role

The heads of major executive departments of government constitute the Cabinet. This institution, not provided for in the U.S. Constitution, developed as an advisory body out of the desire of presidents to consult on policy matters. Aside from its advisory role, the Cabinet as a body has no function and wields no executive authority. Individual members exercise authority as heads of their departments, reporting to the president.

In addition to the heads of federal departments as listed below, the Cabinet commonly includes other officials designated by the president as of Cabinet rank.

The officials so designated by Pres. George W. Bush include: Vice Pres. Dick Cheney, Chief of Staff to the President Andrew H. Card Jr., Environmental Protection Agency Administrator Christine Todd Whitman, Office of Management and Budget Director Mitchell E. Daniels Jr., Office of National Drug Control Policy Director John Walters, United States Trade Representative Robert B. Zoellick, and Office of Homeland Security Director Tom Ridge.

The Cabinet meets at times set by the president. Members of Pres. Bush's Cabinet listed in this chapter are as of Oct. 15, 2002.

Secretaries of State

The Department of Foreign Affairs was created by act of Congress on July 27, 1789, and the name changed to Department of State on Sept. 15, 1789.

President	Secretary	Home	Apptd.
Washington	Thomas Jefferson	VA	1789
	Edmund Randolph	VA	1794
	Timothy Pickering	PA	1795
Adams, J.	Timothy Pickering	PA	1797
	John Marshall	VA	1800
Jefferson	James Madison	VA	1801
Madison	Robert Smith	MD	1809
	James Monroe	VA	1811
Monroe	John Quincy Adams	MA	1817
Adams, J.Q.	Henry Clay	KY	1825
Jackson	Martin Van Buren	NY	1829
	Edward Livingston	LA	1831
	Louis McLane	DE	1833
	John Forsyth	GA	1834
Van Buren	John Forsyth	GA	1837
Harrison, W.H.	Daniel Webster	MA	1841
Tyler	Daniel Webster	MA	1841
	Abel P. Upshur	VA	1843
	John C. Calhoun	SC	1844
Polk	John C. Calhoun	SC	1845
	James Buchanan	PA	1845
Taylor	James Buchanan	PA	1849
	John M. Clayton	DE	1849
Fillmoe	John M. Clayton	DE	1850
	Daniel Webster	MA	1850
	Edward Everett	MA	1852
Pierce	William L. Marcy	NY	1853
Buchanan	William L. Marcy	NY	1857
	Lewis Cass	MI	1857
	Jeremiah S. Black	PA	1860
Lincoln	Jeremiah S. Black	PA	1861
	William H. Seward	NY	1861
Johnson, A.	William H. Seward	NY	1865
Grant	Elihu B. Washburne	IL	1869
	Hamilton Fish	NY	1869
Hayes	Hamilton Fish	NY	1877
	William M. Evarts	NY	1877
Garfield	William M. Evarts	NY	1881
	James G. Blaine	ME	1881
Arthur	James G. Blaine	ME	1881
	F.T. Frelinghuysen	NJ	1881
Cleveland	F.T. Frelinghuysen	NJ	1885
	Thomas F. Bayard	DE	1885
Harrison, B.	Thomas F. Bayard	DE	1889
Harrison, B.	James G. Blaine	ME	1889
	John W. Foster	IN	1892
Cleveland	Walter Q. Gresham	IN	1893
	Richard Olney	MA	1895
McKinley	Richard Olney	MA	1897
	John Sherman	OH	1897
	William R. Day	OH	1898
	John Hay	DC	1898
Roosevelt, T.	John Hay	DC	1901
	Elihu Root	NY	1905
	Robert Bacon	NY	1909
Taft	Robert Bacon	NY	1909
	Philander C. Knox	PA	1909
Wilson	Philander C. Knox	PA	1913
	William J. Bryan	NE	1913
	Robert Lansing	NY	1915
	Bainbridge Colby	NY	1920
Harding	Charles E. Hughes	NY	1921
Coolidge	Charles E. Hughes	NY	1923
	Frank B. Kellogg	MN	1925
Hoover	Frank B. Kellogg	MN	1929
	Henry L. Stimson	NY	1929
Roosevelt, F.D.	Cordell Hull	TN	1933
	E.R. Stettinius Jr.	VA	1944
Truman	E.R. Stettinius Jr.	VA	1945
	James F. Byrnes	SC	1945
	George C. Marshall	PA	1947
	Dean G. Acheson	CT	1949
Eisenhower	John Foster Dulles	NY	1953
	Christian A. Herter	MA	1959
Kennedy	Dean Rusk	NY	1961
Johnson, L.B.	Dean Rusk	NY	1963
Nixon	William P. Rogers	NY	1969
	Henry A. Kissinger	DC	1973
Ford	Henry A. Kissinger	DC	1974
Carter	Cyrus R. Vance	NY	1977
	Edmund S. Muskie	ME	1980
Reagan	Alexander M. Haig Jr.	CT	1981
	George P. Shultz	CA	1982
Bush, G.H.W.	James A. Baker 3rd	TX	1989
	Lawrence S. Eagleburger	MI	1992
Clinton	Warren M. Christopher	CA	1993
	Madeleine K. Albright	DC	1997
Bush, G.W.	Colin L. Powell	NY	2001

Secretaries of the Treasury

The Treasury Department was organized by act of Congress on Sept. 2, 1789.

President	Secretary	Home	Apptd.
Washington	Alexander Hamilton	NY	1789
	Oliver Wolcott	CT	1795
Adams, J.	Oliver Wolcott	CT	1797
	Samuel Dexter	MA	1801
Jefferson	Samuel Dexter	MA	1801
	Albert Gallatin	PA	1801
Madison	Albert Gallatin	PA	1809
	George W. Campbell	TN	1814
	Alexander J. Dallas	PA	1814
	William H. Crawford	GA	1816
Monroe	William H. Crawford	GA	1817
Adams, J.Q.	Richard Rush	PA	1825
Jackson	Samuel D. Ingham	PA	1829
	Louis McLane	DE	1831
	William J. Duane	PA	1833
	Roger B. Taney	MD	1833
	Levi Woodbury	NH	1834
Van Buren	Levi Woodbury	NH	1837
Harrison, W.H.	Thomas Ewing	OH	1841
Tyler	Thomas Ewing	OH	1841
	Walter Forward	PA	1841
	John C. Spencer	NY	1843
	George M. Bibb	KY	1844
Polk	Robert J. Walker	MS	1845
Taylor	William M. Meredith	PA	1849
Fillmore	Thomas Corwin	OH	1850
Pierce	James Guthrie	KY	1853
Buchanan	Howell Cobb	GA	1857
	Phillip F. Thomas	MD	1860
	John A. Dix	NY	1861
Lincoln	Salmon P. Chase	OH	1861
	William P. Fessenden	ME	1864
	Hugh McCulloch	IN	1865
Johnson, A.	Hugh McCulloch	IN	1865

President	Secretary	Home	Apptd.
Grant	George S. Boutwell	MA	1869
	William A. Richardson	MA	1873
	Benjamin H. Bristow	KY	1874
	Lot M. Morrill	ME	1876
Hayes	John Sherman	OH	1877
Garfield	William Windom	MN	1881
Arthur	Charles J. Folger	NY	1881
	Walter Q. Gresham	IN	1884
	Hugh McCulloch	IN	1884
Cleveland	Daniel Manning	NY	1885
	Charles S. Fairchild	NY	1887
Harrison, B.	William Windom	MN	1889
	Charles Foster	OH	1891
Cleveland	John G. Carlisle	KY	1893
McKinley	Lyman J. Gage	IL	1897
Roosevelt, T.	Lyman J. Gage	IL	1901
	Leslie M. Shaw	IA	1902
	George B. Cortelyou	NY	1907
Taft	Franklin MacVeagh	IL	1909
Wilson	William G. McAdoo	NY	1913
	Carter Glass	VA	1918
	David F. Houston	MO	1920
Harding	Andrew W. Mellon	PA	1921
Coolidge	Andrew W. Mellon	PA	1923
Hoover	Andrew W. Mellon	PA	1929
	Ogden L. Mills	NY	1932
Roosevelt, F.D.	William H. Woodin	NY	1933
	Henry Morgenthau, Jr.	NY	1934
Truman	Fred M. Vinson	KY	1945
	John W. Snyder	MO	1946
Eisenhower	George M. Humphrey	OH	1953
	Robert B. Anderson	CT	1957
Kennedy	C. Douglas Dillon	NJ	1961
Johnson, L.B.	C. Douglas Dillon	NJ	1963
	Henry H. Fowler	VA	1965
	Joseph W. Barr	IN	1968
Nixon	David M. Kennedy	IL	1969
	John B. Connally	TX	1971
	George P. Shultz	IL	1972
	William E. Simon	NJ	1974
Ford	William E. Simon	NJ	1974
Carter	W. Michael Blumenthal	MI	1977
	G. William Miller	RI	1979
Reagan	Donald T. Regan	NY	1981
	James A. Baker 3rd	TX	1985
	Nicholas F. Brady	NJ	1988
Bush, G.H.W.	Nicholas F. Brady	NJ	1989
Clinton	Lloyd Bentsen	TX	1993
	Robert E. Rubin	NY	1995
	Lawrence H. Summers	CT	1999
Bush, G.W.	Paul H. O'Neill	PA	2001

Secretaries of Defense

The Department of Defense, originally designated the National Military Establishment, was created on Sept. 18, 1947. It is headed by the secretary of defense, who is a member of the president's Cabinet. The departments of the army, of the navy, and of the air force function within the Defense Department, and since 1947 the secretaries of these departments have not been members of the president's Cabinet.

President	Secretary	Home	Apptd.
Truman	James V. Forrestal	NY	1947
	Louis A. Johnson	WV	1949
	George C. Marshall	PA	1950
	Robert A. Lovett	NY	1951
Eisenhower	Charles E. Wilson	MI	1953
	Neil H. McElroy	OH	1957
	Thomas S. Gates Jr.	PA	1959
Kennedy	Robert S. McNamara	MI	1961
Johnson, L.B.	Robert S. McNamara	MI	1963
	Clark M. Clifford	MD	1968
Nixon	Melvin R. Laird	WI	1969
	Elliot L. Richardson	MA	1973
	James R. Schlesinger	VA	1973
Ford	James R. Schlesinger	VA	1974
	Donald H. Rumsfeld	IL	1975
Carter	Harold Brown	CA	1977
Reagan	Caspar W. Weinberger	CA	1981
	Frank C. Carlucci	PA	1987
Bush, G.H.W.	Richard B. Cheney	WY	1989
Clinton	Les Aspin	WI	1993
	William J. Perry	CA	1994
	William S. Cohen	ME	1997
Bush, G.W.	Donald H. Rumsfeld	IL	2001

Secretaries of War

The War Department (which included jurisdiction over the navy until 1798) was created by act of Congress on Aug. 7, 1789, and Gen. Henry Knox was commissioned secretary of war under that act on Sept. 12, 1789.

President	Secretary	Home	Apptd.
Washington	Henry Knox	MA	1789
	Timothy Pickering	PA	1795
	James McHenry	MD	1796
Adams, J.	James McHenry	MD	1797
	Samuel Dexter	MA	1800
Jefferson	Henry Dearborn	MA	1801
Madison	William Eustis	MA	1809
	John Armstrong	NY	1813
	James Monroe	VA	1814
	William H. Crawford	GA	1815
Monroe	John C. Calhoun	SC	1817
Adams, J.Q.	James Barbour	VA	1825
	Peter B. Porter	NY	1828
Jackson	John H. Eaton	TN	1829
	Lewis Cass	MI	1831
	Benjamin F. Butler	NY	1837
Van Buren	Joel R. Poinsett	SC	1837
Harrison, W.H.	John Bell	TN	1841
Tyler	John Bell	TN	1841
	John C. Spencer	NY	1841
	James M. Porter	PA	1843
	William Wilkins	PA	1844
Polk	William L. Marcy	NY	1845
Taylor	George W. Crawford	GA	1849
Fillmore	Charles M. Conrad	LA	1850
Pierce	Jefferson Davis	MS	1853
Buchanan	John B. Floyd	VA	1857
	Joseph Holt	KY	1861
Lincoln	Simon Cameron	PA	1861
	Edwin M. Stanton	PA	1862
Johnson, A.	Edwin M. Stanton	PA	1865
	John M. Schofield	IL	1868
Grant	John A. Rawlins	IL	1869
	William T. Sherman	OH	1869
	William W. Belknap	IA	1869
	Alphonso Taft	OH	1876
	James D. Cameron	PA	1876
Hayes	George W. McCrary	IA	1877
	Alexander Ramsey	MN	1879
Garfield	Robert T. Lincoln	IL	1881
Arthur	Robert T. Lincoln	IL	1881
Cleveland	William C. Endicott	MA	1885
Harrison, B.	Redfield Proctor	VT	1889
	Stephen B. Elkins	WV	1891
Cleveland	Daniel S. Lamont	NY	1893
McKinley	Russel A. Alger	MI	1897
	Elihu Root	NY	1899
Roosevelt, T.	Elihu Root	NY	1901
	William H. Taft	OH	1904
	Luke E. Wright	TN	1908
Taft	Jacob M. Dickinson	TN	1909
	Henry L. Stimson	NY	1911
Wilson	Lindley M. Garrison	NJ	1913
	Newton D. Baker	OH	1916
Harding	John W. Weeks	MA	1921
Coolidge	John W. Weeks	MA	1923
	Dwight F. Davis	MO	1925
Hoover	James W. Good	IL	1929
	Patrick J. Hurley	OK	1929
Roosevelt, F.D.	George H. Dern	UT	1933
	Harry H. Woodring	KS	1937
	Henry L. Stimson	NY	1940
Truman	Robert P. Patterson	NY	1945
	Kenneth C. Royall[1]	NC	1947

(1) Last member of the Cabinet with this title. The War Department became the Department of the Army and became a branch of the Department of Defense in 1947.

Secretaries of the Navy

The Navy Department was created by act of Congress on Apr. 30, 1798.

President	Secretary	Home	Apptd.
Adams, J.	Benjamin Stoddert	MD	1798
Jefferson	Benjamin Stoddert	MD	1801
	Robert Smith	MD	1801
Madison	Paul Hamilton	SC	1809
	William Jones	PA	1813
	Benjamin W. Crowninshield	MA	1814
Monroe	Benjamin W. Crowninshield	MA	1817
	Smith Thompson	NY	1818
	Samuel L. Southard	NJ	1823
Adams, J.Q.	Samuel L. Southard	NJ	1825
Jackson	John Branch	NC	1829
	Levi Woodbury	NH	1831
	Mahlon Dickerson	NJ	1834
Van Buren	Mahlon Dickerson	NJ	1837
	James K. Paulding	NY	1838
Harrison, W.H.	George E. Badger	NC	1841
Tyler	George E. Badger	NC	1841
	Abel P. Upshur	VA	1841
	David Henshaw	MA	1843
	Thomas W. Gilmer	VA	1844
	John Y. Mason	VA	1844
Polk	George Bancroft	MA	1845
	John Y. Mason	VA	1846
Taylor	William B. Preston	VA	1849
Fillmore	William A. Graham	NC	1850
	John P. Kennedy	MD	1852
Pierce	James C. Dobbin	NC	1853
Buchanan	Isaac Toucey	CT	1857
Lincoln	Gideon Welles	CT	1861
Johnson, A.	Gideon Welles	CT	1865
Grant	Adolph E. Borie	PA	1869
	George M. Robeson	NJ	1869
Hayes	Richard W. Thompson	IN	1877
	Nathan Goff Jr.	WV	1881
Garfield	William H. Hunt	LA	1881
Arthur	William E. Chandler	NH	1882
Cleveland	William C. Whitney	NY	1885
Harrison, B.	Benjamin F. Tracy	NY	1889
Cleveland	Hilary A. Herbert	AL	1893
McKinley	John D. Long	MA	1897
Roosevelt, T.	John D. Long	MA	1901
	William H. Moody	MA	1902
	Paul Morton	IL	1904
	Charles J. Bonaparte	MD	1905
	Victor H. Metcalf	CA	1906
	Truman H. Newberry	MI	1908
Taft	George von L. Meyer	MA	1909
Wilson	Josephus Daniels	NC	1913
Harding	Edwin Denby	MI	1921
Coolidge	Edwin Denby	MI	1923
	Curtis D. Wilbur	CA	1924
Hoover	Charles Francis Adams	MA	1929
Roosevelt, F.D.	Claude A. Swanson	VA	1933
	Charles Edison	NJ	1940
	Frank Knox	IL	1940
	James V. Forrestal	NY	1944
Truman	James V. Forrestal[1]	NY	1945

(1) Last member of Cabinet with this title. The Navy Department became a branch of the Department of Defense when the latter was created on Sept. 18, 1947.

Attorneys General

The Office of Attorney General was established by act of Congress on Sept. 24, 1789. It officially reached Cabinet rank in Mar. 1792, when the first attorney general, Edmund Randolph, attended his initial Cabinet meeting. The Department of Justice, headed by the attorney general, was created June 22, 1870.

President	Attorney General	Home	Apptd.
Washington	Edmund Randolph	VA	1789
	William Bradford	PA	1794
	Charles Lee	VA	1795
Adams, J.	Charles Lee	VA	1797
Jefferson	Levi Lincoln	MA	1801
	John Breckenridge	KY	1805
	Caesar A. Rodney	DE	1807
Madison	Caesar A. Rodney	DE	1807
	William Pinkney	MD	1811
	Richard Rush	PA	1814
Monroe	Richard Rush	PA	1817
	William Wirt	VA	1817
Adams, J.Q.	William Wirt	VA	1825
Jackson	John M. Berrien	GA	1829
	Roger B. Taney	MD	1831
	Benjamin F. Butler	NY	1833
Van Buren	Benjamin F. Butler	NY	1837
	Felix Grundy	TN	1838
	Henry D. Gilpin	PA	1840
Harrison, W.H.	John J. Crittenden	KY	1841
Tyler	John J. Crittenden	KY	1841
	Hugh S. Legare	SC	1841
	John Nelson	MD	1843
Polk	John Y. Mason	VA	1845
	Nathan Clifford	ME	1846
	Isaac Toucey	CT	1848
Taylor	Reverdy Johnson	MD	1849
Fillmore	John J. Crittenden	KY	1850
Pierce	Caleb Cushing	MA	1853
Buchanan	Jeremiah S. Black	PA	1857
	Edwin M. Stanton	PA	1860
Lincoln	Edward Bates	MO	1861
	James Speed	KY	1864
Johnson, A.	James Speed	KY	1865
	Henry Stanbery	OH	1866
	William M. Evarts	NY	1868
Grant	Ebenezer R. Hoar	MA	1869
	Amos T. Akerman	GA	1870
	George H. Williams	OR	1871
	Edwards Pierrepont	NY	1875
	Alphonso Taft	OH	1876
Hayes	Charles Devens	MA	1877
Garfield	Wayne MacVeagh	PA	1881
Arthur	Benjamin H. Brewster	PA	1882
Cleveland	Augustus Garland	AR	1885
Harrison, B.	William H. H. Miller	IN	1889
Cleveland	Richard Olney	MA	1893
	Judson Harmon	OH	1895
McKinley	Joseph McKenna	CA	1897
	John W. Griggs	NJ	1898
	Philander C. Knox	PA	1901
Roosevelt, T.	Philander C. Knox	PA	1901
	William H. Moody	MA	1904
	Charles J. Bonaparte	MD	1906
Taft	George W. Wickersham	NY	1909
Wilson	J.C. McReynolds	TN	1913
	Thomas W. Gregory	TX	1914
	A. Mitchell Palmer	PA	1919
Harding	Harry M. Daugherty	OH	1921
Coolidge	Harry M. Daugherty	OH	1923
	Harlan F. Stone	NY	1924
	John G. Sargent	VT	1925
Hoover	William D. Mitchell	MN	1929
Roosevelt, F.D.	Homer S. Cummings	CT	1933
	Frank Murphy	MI	1939
	Robert H. Jackson	NY	1940
	Francis Biddle	PA	1941
Truman	Thomas C. Clark	TX	1945
	J. Howard McGrath	RI	1949
	J.P. McGranery	PA	1952
Eisenhower	Herbert Brownell Jr.	NY	1953
	William P. Rogers	MD	1957
Kennedy	Robert F. Kennedy	MA	1961
Johnson, L.B.	Robert F. Kennedy	MA	1963
	N. de B. Katzenbach	IL	1964
	Ramsey Clark	TX	1967
Nixon	John N. Mitchell	NY	1969
	Richard G. Kleindienst	AZ	1972
	Elliot L. Richardson	MA	1973
	William B. Saxbe	OH	1974
Ford	William B. Saxbe	OH	1974
	Edward H. Levi	IL	1975
Carter	Griffin B. Bell	GA	1977
	Benjamin R. Civiletti	MD	1979
Reagan	William French Smith	CA	1981
	Edwin Meese 3rd	CA	1985
	Richard Thornburgh	PA	1988
Bush, G.H.W.	Richard Thornburgh	PA	1989
	William P. Barr	NY	1991
Clinton	Janet Reno	FL	1993
Bush, G.W.	John Ashcroft	MO	2001

Secretaries of the Interior

The Department of the Interior was created by act of Congress on Mar. 3, 1849.

President	Secretary	Home	Apptd.
Taylor	Thomas Ewing	OH	1849
Fillmore	Thomas M. T. McKennan	PA	1850
	Alex H. H. Stuart	VA	1850
Pierce	Robert McClelland	MI	1853
Buchanan	Jacob Thompson	MS	1857
Lincoln	Caleb B. Smith	IN	1861
	John P. Usher	IN	1863
Johnson, A.	John P. Usher	IN	1865
	James Harlan	IA	1865
	Orville H. Browning	IL	1866
Grant	Jacob D. Cox	OH	1869
	Columbus Delano	OH	1870
	Zachariah Chandler	MI	1875
Hayes	Carl Schurz	MO	1877
Garfield	Samuel J. Kirkwood	IA	1881
Arthur	Henry M. Teller	CO	1882
Cleveland	Lucius Q.C. Lamar	MS	1885
	William F. Vilas	WI	1888
Harrison, B.	John W. Noble	MO	1889
Cleveland	Hoke Smith	GA	1893
	David R. Francis	MO	1896
McKinley	Cornelius N. Bliss	NY	1897
	Ethan A. Hitchcock	MO	1898
Roosevelt, T.	Ethan A. Hitchcock	MO	1901
	James R. Garfield	OH	1907
Taft	Richard A. Ballinger	WA	1909
	Walter L. Fisher	IL	1911
Wilson	Franklin K. Lane	CA	1913
	John B. Payne	IL	1920
Harding	Albert B. Fall	NM	1921
	Hubert Work	CO	1923
Coolidge	Hubert Work	CO	1923
	Roy O. West	IL	1929
Hoover	Ray Lyman Wilbur	CA	1929
Roosevelt, F.D.	Harold L. Ickes	IL	1933
Truman	Harold L. Ickes	IL	1945
	Julius A. Krug	WI	1946
	Oscar L. Chapman	CO	1949
Eisenhower	Douglas McKay	OR	1953
	Fred A. Seaton	NE	1956
Kennedy	Stewart L. Udall	AZ	1961
Johnson, L.B.	Stewart L. Udall	AZ	1963
Nixon	Walter J. Hickel	AK	1969
	Rogers C.B. Morton	MD	1971
Ford	Rogers C.B. Morton	MD	1971
	Stanley K. Hathaway	WY	1975
	Thomas S. Kleppe	ND	1975
Carter	Cecil D. Andrus	ID	1977
Reagan	James G. Watt	CO	1981
	William P. Clark	CA	1983
	Donald P. Hodel	OR	1985
Bush, G.H.W.	Manuel Lujan	NM	1989
Clinton	Bruce Babbitt	AZ	1993
Bush, G.W.	Gale Norton	CO	2001

Secretaries of Agriculture

The Department of Agriculture was created by act of Congress on May 15, 1862. On Feb. 8, 1889, its commissioner was renamed secretary of agriculture and became a member of the Cabinet.

President	Secretary	Home	Apptd.
Cleveland	Norman J. Colman	MO	1889
Harrison, B.	Jeremiah M. Rusk	WI	1889
Cleveland	J. Sterling Morton	NE	1893
McKinley	James Wilson	IA	1897
Roosevelt, T.	James Wilson	IA	1901
Taft	James Wilson	IA	1909
Wilson	David F. Houston	MO	1913
	Edwin T. Meredith	IA	1920
Harding	Henry C. Wallace	IA	1921
Coolidge	Henry C. Wallace	IA	1923
	Howard M. Gore	WV	1924
	William M. Jardine	KS	1925
Hoover	Arthur M. Hyde	MO	1929
Roosevelt, F.D.	Henry A. Wallace	IA	1933
	Claude R. Wickard	IN	1940
Truman	Clinton P. Anderson	NM	1945
Truman	Charles F. Brannan	CO	1948
Eisenhower	Ezra Taft Benson	UT	1953
Kennedy	Orville L. Freeman	MN	1961
Johnson, L.B.	Orville L. Freeman	MN	1963
Nixon	Clifford M. Hardin	IN	1969
	Earl L. Butz	IN	1971
Ford	Earl L. Butz	IN	1974
	John A. Knebel	VA	1976
Carter	Bob Bergland	MN	1977
Reagan	John R. Block	IL	1981
	Richard E. Lyng	CA	1986
Bush, G.H.W.	Clayton K. Yeutter	NE	1989
	Edward Madigan	IL	1991
Clinton	Mike Espy	MS	1993
	Dan Glickman	KS	1995
Bush, G.W.	Ann M. Veneman	CA	2001

Secretaries of Commerce and Labor

The Department of Commerce and Labor, created by Congress on Feb. 14, 1903, was divided by Congress Mar. 4, 1913, into separate departments of Commerce and Labor. The secretary of each was made a Cabinet member.

Secretaries of Commerce and Labor

President	Secretary	Home	Apptd.
Roosevelt, T.	George B. Cortelyou	NY	1903
	Victor H. Metcalf	CA	1904
	Oscar S. Straus	NY	1906
Taft	Charles Nagel	MO	1909

Secretaries of Labor

President	Secretary	Home	Apptd.
Wilson	William B. Wilson	PA	1913
Harding	James J. Davis	PA	1921
Coolidge	James J. Davis	PA	1923
Hoover	James J. Davis	PA	1929
	William N. Doak	VA	1930
Roosevelt, F.D.	Frances Perkins	NY	1933
Truman	L.B. Schwellenbach	WA	1945
	Maurice J. Tobin	MA	1949
Eisenhower	Martin P. Durkin	IL	1953
	James P. Mitchell	NJ	1953
Kennedy	Arthur J. Goldberg	IL	1961
	W. Willard Wirtz	IL	1962
Johnson, L.B.	W. Willard Wirtz	IL	1963
Nixon	George P. Shultz	IL	1969
	James D. Hodgson	CA	1970
	Peter J. Brennan	NY	1973
Ford	Peter J. Brennan	NY	1974
	John T. Dunlop	CA	1975
	W.J. Usery Jr.	GA	1976
Carter	F. Ray Marshall	TX	1977
Reagan	Raymond J. Donovan	NJ	1981
	William E. Brock	TN	1985
	Ann D. McLaughlin	DC	1987
Bush, G.H.W.	Elizabeth Hanford Dole	NC	1989
	Lynn Martin	IL	1991
Clinton	Robert B. Reich	MA	1993
	Alexis M. Herman	AL	1997
Bush, G.W.	Elaine L. Chao	KY	2001

Secretaries of Commerce

President	Secretary	Home	Apptd.
Wilson	William C. Redfield	NY	1913
	Joshua W. Alexander	MO	1919
Harding	Herbert C. Hoover	CA	1921
Coolidge	Herbert C. Hoover	CA	1923
	William F. Whiting	MA	1928
Hoover	Robert P. Lamont	IL	1929
	Roy D. Chapin	MI	1932
Roosevelt, F.D.	Daniel C. Roper	SC	1933
	Harry L. Hopkins	NY	1939
	Jesse Jones	TX	1940
	Henry A. Wallace	IA	1945
Truman	Henry A. Wallace	IA	1945
	W. Averell Harriman	NY	1947
	Charles Sawyer	OH	1948
Eisenhower	Sinclair Weeks	MA	1953
	Lewis L. Strauss	NY	1958
	Frederick H. Mueller	MI	1959

President	Secretary	Home	Apptd.
Kennedy	Luther H. Hodges	NC	1961
Johnson, L.B.	Luther H. Hodges	NC	1963
	John T. Connor	NJ	1965
	Alex B. Trowbridge	NJ	1967
	Cyrus R. Smith	NY	1968
Nixon	Maurice H. Stans	MN	1969
	Peter G. Peterson	IL	1972
	Frederick B. Dent	SC	1973
Ford	Frederick B. Dent	SC	1974
	Rogers C.B. Morton	MD	1975
	Elliot L. Richardson	MA	1975
Carter	Juanita M. Kreps	NC	1977
	Philip M. Klutznick	IL	1979
Reagan	Malcolm Baldrige	CT	1981
	C. William Verity Jr.	OH	1987
Bush, G.H.W.	Robert A. Mosbacher	TX	1989
	Barbara H. Franklin	PA	1992
Clinton	Ronald H. Brown	DC	1993
	Mickey Kantor	CA	1996
	William M. Daley	IL	1997
	Norman Y. Mineta	CA	2000
Bush, G.W.	Donald L. Evans	TX	2001

Secretaries of Housing and Urban Development

The Department of Housing and Urban Development was created by act of Congress on Sept. 9, 1965.

President	Secretary	Home	Apptd.
Johnson, L.B.	Robert C. Weaver	WA	1966
	Robert C. Wood	MA	1969
Nixon	George W. Romney	MI	1969
	James T. Lynn	OH	1973
Ford	James T. Lynn	OH	1974
	Carla Anderson Hills	CA	1975
Carter	Patricia Roberts Harris	DC	1977
	Moon Landrieu	LA	1979
Reagan	Samuel R. Pierce Jr.	NY	1981
Bush, G.H.W.	Jack F. Kemp	NY	1989
Clinton	Henry G. Cisneros	TX	1993
	Andrew M. Cuomo	NY	1997
Bush, G.W.	Mel Martinez	FL	2001

Secretaries of Transportation

The Department of Transportation was created by act of Congress on Oct. 15, 1966.

President	Secretary	Home	Apptd.
Johnson, L.B.	Alan S. Boyd	FL	1966
Nixon	John A. Volpe	MA	1969
	Claude S. Brinegar	CA	1973
Ford	Claude S. Brinegar	CA	1974
	William T. Coleman Jr.	PA	1975
Carter	Brock Adams	WA	1977
	Neil E. Goldschmidt	OR	1979
Reagan	Andrew L. Lewis Jr.	PA	1981
	Elizabeth Hanford Dole	NC	1983
	James H. Burnley	NC	1987
Bush, G.H.W.	Samuel K. Skinner	IL	1989
	Andrew H. Card Jr.	MA	1992
Clinton	Federico F. Peña	CO	1993
	Rodney E. Slater	AR	1997
Bush, G.W.	Norman Y. Mineta	CA	2001

Secretaries of Energy

The Department of Energy was created by federal law on Aug. 4, 1977.

President	Secretary	Home	Apptd.
Carter	James R. Schlesinger	VA	1977
	Charles Duncan Jr.	WY	1979
Reagan	James B. Edwards	SC	1981
	Donald P. Hodel	OR	1982
	John S. Herrington	CA	1985
Bush, G.H.W.	James D. Watkins	CA	1989
Clinton	Hazel R. O'Leary	MN	1993
	Federico F. Peña	CO	1997
	Bill Richardson	NM	1998
Bush, G.W.	Spencer Abraham	MI	2001

Secretaries of Health, Education, and Welfare

The Department of Health, Education, and Welfare was created by Congress on Apr. 11, 1953. On Sept. 27, 1979, it was divided by Congress into the departments of Education and of Health and Human Services, with the secretary of each being a Cabinet member.

President	Secretary	Home	Apptd.
Eisenhower	Oveta Culp Hobby	TX	1953
	Marion B. Folsom	NY	1955
	Arthur S. Flemming	OH	1958
Kennedy	Abraham A. Ribicoff	CT	1961
	Anthony J. Celebrezze	OH	1962
Johnson, L.B.	Anthony J. Celebrezze	OH	1963
	John W. Gardner	NY	1965
	Wilbur J. Cohen	MI	1968
Nixon	Robert H. Finch	CA	1969
	Elliot L. Richardson	MA	1970
	Caspar W. Weinberger	CA	1973
Ford	Caspar W. Weinberger	CA	1974
	Forrest D. Mathews	AL	1975
Carter	Joseph A. Califano Jr.	DC	1977
	Patricia Roberts Harris	DC	1979

Secretaries of Health and Human Services

President	Secretary	Home	Apptd.
Carter	Patricia Roberts Harris	DC	1979
Reagan	Richard S. Schweiker	PA	1981
	Margaret M. Heckler	MA	1983
Reagan	Otis R. Bowen	IN	1985
Bush, G.H.W.	Louis W. Sullivan	GA	1989
Clinton	Donna E. Shalala	WI	1993
Bush, G.W.	Tommy Thompson	WI	2001

Secretaries of Education

President	Secretary	Home	Apptd.
Carter	Shirley Hufstedler	CA	1979
Reagan	Terrel Bell	UT	1981
	William J. Bennett	NY	1985
	Lauro F. Cavazos	TX	1988
Bush, G.H.W.	Lauro F. Cavazos	TX	1989
	Lamar Alexander	TN	1991
Clinton	Richard W. Riley	SC	1993
Bush, G.W.	Roderick R. Paige	TX	2001

Secretaries of Veterans Affairs

The Department of Veterans Affairs was created on Oct. 25, 1988, when Pres. Ronald Reagan signed a bill that made the Veterans Administration into a Cabinet department, effective Mar. 15, 1989.

President	Secretary	Home	Apptd.
Bush, G.H.W.	Edward J. Derwinski	IL	1989
Clinton	Jesse Brown	IL	1993
Clinton	Togo D. West Jr.	NC	1998
	Hershel W. Gober (acting)	AR	2000
Bush, G.W.	Anthony Principi	CA	2001

CONGRESS

The One Hundred and Seventh Congress

The 107th Congress convened on Jan. 3, 2001, and was to be succeeded by the 108th Congress in Jan. 2003.

The Senate, as of Oct. 2002

Dem., 50; Rep., 49; Ind., 1; Total, 100.

Terms are for 6 years and end Jan. 3 of the year preceding the senator's name in the following table. Among those senators with terms ending in 2003, those with an asterisk (*) were running for reelection in Nov. 2002; for election results see www.worldalmanac.com/2002elections. Annual salary, $150,000; President Pro Tempore, Majority Leader, and Minority Leader, $166,700. To be eligible for the Senate, one must be at least 30 years old, a U.S. citizen for at least 9 years, and a resident of the state from which chosen. Congress must meet annually on Jan. 3, unless it has, by law, appointed a different day.

The ZIP code of the Senate is 20510; the telephone number is 202-224-3121; the website is www.senate.gov

Senate officials in 2002 were: President Pro Tempore, Robert C. Byrd (WV); Majority Leader, Tom Daschle (SD); Majority Whip, Harry Reid (NV); Minority Leader, Trent Lott (MS); Minority Whip, Don Nickles (OK).

D-Democrat; R-Republican; I-Independent

Term ends	Senator (Party); Service from[1]
	Alabama
2003	Jeff Sessions* (R); 1/7/97
2005	Richard Shelby (R); 1/6/87
	Alaska
2003	Ted Stevens* (R); 12/24/68
2005	Frank H. Murkowski (R); 1981
	Arizona
2005	John McCain (R); 1/6/87
2007	Jon Kyl(R); 1/4/95
	Arkansas
2003	Tim Hutchinson* (R); 1/7/97
2005	Blanche Lambert Lincoln (D);1/6/99
	California
2005	Barbara Boxer (D); 1993
2007	Dianne Feinstein (D); 11/10/92
	Colorado
2003	Wayne Allard* (R); 1/7/97
2005	Ben Nighthorse Campbell (R);1993
	Connecticut
2005	Christopher J. Dodd (D); 1981
2007	Joe Lieberman (D); 1989
	Delaware
2003	Joseph R. Biden, Jr.* (D); 1973
2007	Thomas R. Carper (D); 2001
	Florida
2005	Bob Graham (D); 1/6/87
2007	Bill Nelson (D); 2001
	Georgia
2003	Max Cleland* (D); 1/7/97
2005	Zell Miller (D); 7/24/00
	Hawaii
2005	Daniel K. Inouye (D); 1963
2007	Daniel K. Akaka (D); 4/28/90
	Idaho
2003	Larry E. Craig* (R); 1991
2005	Mike Crapo (R); 1/6/99
	Illinois
2003	Richard J. Durbin* (D); 1/7/97
2005	Peter G. Fitzgerald (R); 1/6/99
	Indiana
2005	Evan Bayh (D); 1/6/99
2007	Richard G. Lugar (R); 1977
	Iowa
2003	Tom Harkin* (D); 1985
2005	Chuck Grassley (R); 1981
	Kansas
2003	Pat Roberts* (R); 1/7/97
2005	Sam Brownback (R); 1/7/97
	Kentucky
2003	Mitch McConnell* (R); 1985
2005	Jim Bunning (R); 1/6/99
	Louisiana
2003	Mary L. Landrieu* (D); 1/7/97
2005	John B. Breaux (D); 1/6/87
	Maine
2003	Susan M. Collins* (R); 1/7/97
2007	Olympia J. Snowe (R); 1/4/95
	Maryland
2005	Barbara Ann Mikulski (D); 1/6/87
2007	Paul S. Sarbanes (D); 1977
	Massachusetts
2003	John F. Kerry* (D); 1/2/85
2007	Edward M. Kennedy (D); 11/7/62
	Michigan
2003	Carl Levin* (D); 1979
2007	Debbie Stabenow (D); 2001
	Minnesota
2003	Paul David Wellstone* (D); 1991
2007	Mark Dayton (D); 2001
	Mississippi
2003	Thad Cochran* (R); 12/27/78
2007	Trent Lott (R); 1989
	Missouri
2005	Christopher (Kit) Bond (R); 1/6/87
2003	Jean Carnahan* (D); 2001
	Montana
2003	Max Baucus* (D); 12/15/78
2007	Conrad Burns (R); 1989
	Nebraska
2003	Chuck Hagel* (R); 1/7/97
2007	Ben Nelson (D); 2001
	Nevada
2005	Harry Reid (D); 1/6/87
2007	John Ensign (R); 2001
	New Hampshire
2003	Robert Smith (R); 12/7/90
2005	Judd Gregg (R); 1993
	New Jersey
2003	Robert G. Torricelli (D); 1/7/97
2007	Jon S. Corzine (D); 2001
	New Mexico
2003	Pete V. Domenici* (R); 1973
2007	Jeff Bingaman (D); 1983
	New York
2005	Charles E. Schumer (D); 1/6/99
2007	Hillary Rodham Clinton (D) 2001
	North Carolina
2003	Jesse Helms (R); 1973
2005	John Edwards (D); 1/6/99
	North Dakota
2005	Byron L. Dorgan (D); 12/14/92
2007	Kent Conrad (D); 1/6/87
	Ohio
2005	George V. Voinovich (R); 1/6/99
2007	Mike DeWine (R); 1/4/95
	Oklahoma
2003	James M. Inhofe* (R); 11/21/94
2005	Don Nickles (R); 1981
	Oregon
2003	Gordon Smith* (R); 1/7/97
2005	Ron Wyden (D); 2/6/96
	Pennsylvania
2005	Arlen Specter (R); 1981
2007	Rick Santorum (R); 1/4/95
	Rhode Island
2003	John F. Reed* (D); 1/7/97
2007	Lincoln D. Chafee (R); 11/2/99
	South Carolina
2003	Strom Thurmond (R); 11/7/56
2005	Ernest Hollings (D); 11/9/66
	South Dakota
2003	Tim Johnson* (D); 1/7/97
2005	Tom Daschle (D); 1/6/87
	Tennessee
2003	Fred Thompson (R); 12/9/94
2007	Bill Frist (R); 1/4/95
	Texas
2003	Phil Gramm (R); 1985
2007	Kay Bailey Hutchison (R); 6/5/93
	Utah
2005	Robert F. Bennett (R); 1993
2007	Orrin G. Hatch (R); 1977
	Vermont
2005	Patrick Leahy (D); 1975
2007	James M. Jeffords (I); 1989
	Virginia
2003	John W. Warner* (R); 1/2/79
2007	George F. Allen (R); 2001
	Washington
2005	Patty Murray (D); 1993
2007	Maria Cantwell (D); 2001
	West Virginia
2003	John D. Rockefeller IV* (D);1/15/85
2007	Robert C. Byrd (D); 1959
	Wisconsin
2005	Russ Feingold (D); 1993
2007	Herbert H. Kohl (D); 1989
	Wyoming
2003	Michael B. Enzi* (R); 1/7/97
2007	Craig Thomas (R); 1/4/95

(1) Jan. 3, unless otherwise noted.

The House of Representatives, as of Oct. 2002

Rep., 223; Dem., 208; Ind., 1; Vacant, 3; Total, 435.

All terms are for 2 years ending Jan. 3, 2003. **Asterisk (*) denotes members running for reelection in Nov. 2002.** In some cases, because of redistricting, they were running in new districts. For election results, see www.worldalmanac.com/2002elections. Annual salary for regular members, $150,000; Speaker of the House, $192,600; Majority Leader and Minority Leader, $166,700. To be eligible to run for membership, a person must be at least 25 years of age, a U.S. citizen for at least 7 years, and a resident of the state from which he or she is chosen.

The ZIP code of the House is 20515; the telephone number is 202-225-3121. The website is www.house.gov

House officials in 2002 were: Speaker, J. Dennis Hastert (IL); Majority Leader, Dick Armey (TX); Majority Whip, Tom DeLay (TX); Minority Leader, Richard A. Gephardt (MO); Minority Whip, Nancy Pelosi (CA).

D-Democrat; R-Republican; I-Independent

Dist.	Representative (Party)
Alabama	
1.	H. L. "Sonny" Callahan (R)
2.	Terry Everett* (R)
3.	Bob Riley (R)
4.	Robert Aderholt* (R)
5.	Bud Cramer* (D)
6.	Spencer Bachus* (R)
7.	Earl F. Hilliard (D)
Alaska	
	Don E. Young* (R)
Arizona	
1.	Jeff Flake* (R)
2.	Ed Pastor* (D)
3.	Bob Stump (R)
4.	John Shadegg* (R)
5.	Jim Kolbe* (R)
6.	J.D. Hayworth* (R)
Arkansas	
1.	Marion Berry* (D)
2.	Vic Snyder* (D)
3.	John Boozman* (R)[1]
4.	Mike Ross* (D)
California	
1.	Mike Thompson* (D)
2.	Wally Herger* (R)
3.	Doug Ose* (R)
4.	John T. Doolittle* (R)
5.	Robert T. Matsui* (D)
6.	Lynn Woolsey* (D)
7.	George Miller* (D)
8.	Nancy Pelosi* (D)
9.	Barbara Lee* (D)
10.	Ellen O. Tauscher* (D)
11.	Richard W. Pombo* (R)
12.	Tom Lantos* (D)
13.	Fortney Pete Stark* (D)
14.	Anna G. Eshoo* (D)
15.	Mike Honda* (D)
16.	Zoe Lofgren* (D)
17.	Sam Farr* (D)
18.	Gary A. Condit (D)
19.	George Randanovich* (R)
20.	Cal Dooley* (D)
21.	Bill Thomas* (R)
22.	Lois Capps* (D)
23.	Elton W. Gallegly* (R)
24.	Brad Sherman* (D)
25.	Howard P. "Buck" McKeon* (R)
26.	Howard L. Berman* (D)
27.	Adam Schiff* (D)
28.	David Dreier* (R)
29.	Henry A. Waxman* (D)
30.	Xavier Becerra* (D)
31.	Hilda L. Solis* (D)
32.	Diane E. Watson* (D)
33.	Lucille Roybal-Allard* (D)
34.	Grace Flores Napolitano* (D)
35.	Maxine Waters* (D)
36.	Jane Harman* (D)
37.	Juanita Millender-McDonald* (D)
38.	Steve Horn (R)
39.	Ed Royce* (R)
40.	Jerry Lewis* (R)
41.	Gary G. Miller* (R)
42.	Joe Baca* (D)
43.	Ken Calvert* (R)
44.	Mary Bono* (R)
45.	Dana Rohrabacher* (R)
46.	Loretta Sanchez* (D)
47.	Christopher Cox* (R)
48.	Darrell Issa* (R)
49.	Susan A. Davis* (D)
50.	Bob Filner* (D)
51.	Randy "Duke" Cunningham* (R)
52.	Duncan Hunter* (R)
Colorado	
1.	Diana DeGette* (D)
2.	Mark Udall* (D)
3.	Scott McInnis* (R)
4.	Bob Schaffer (R)
5.	Joel Hefley* (R)
6.	Tom Tancredo* (R)
Connecticut	
1.	John B. Larson* (D)
2.	Rob Simmons* (R)
3.	Rosa L. DeLauro* (D)
4.	Christopher Shays* (R)
5.	Jim Maloney* (D)
6.	Nancy L. Johnson* (R)
Delaware	
	Michael N. Castle* (R)
Florida	
1.	Jeff Miller* (R)[2]
2.	Allen Boyd* (D)
3.	Corrine Brown* (D)
4.	Ander Crenshaw* (R)
5.	Karen L. Thurman* (D)
6.	Clifford (Cliff) B. Stearns* (R)
7.	John L. Mica* (R)
8.	Ric Keller* (R)
9.	Michael Bilirakis* (R)
10.	C. W. Bill Young* (R)
11.	Jim Davis* (D)
12.	Adam H. Putnam* (R)
13.	Dan Miller (R)
14.	Porter Goss* (R)
15.	Dave Weldon* (R)
16.	Mark Foley* (R)
17.	Carrie P. Meek (D)
18.	Ileana Ros-Lehtinen* (R)
19.	Robert Wexler* (D)
20.	Peter Deutsch* (D)
21.	Lincoln Diaz-Balart* (R)
22.	Clay Shaw* (R)
23.	Alcee L. Hastings* (D)
Georgia	
1.	Jack Kingston* (R)
2.	Sanford Dixon Bishop, Jr.* (D)
3.	Michael A. (Mac) Collins* (R)
4.	Cynthia McKinney (D)
5.	John Lewis* (D)
6.	Johnny Isakson* (R)
7.	Bob Barr (R)
8.	Saxby Chambliss (R)
9.	Nathan Deal* (R)
10.	Charlie Norwood* (R)
11.	John Linder* (R)
Hawaii	
1.	Neil Abercrombie* (D)
2.	Vacant[3]
Idaho	
1.	C. L. "Butch" Otter* (R)
2.	Michael Simpson* (R)
Illinois	
1.	Bobby L. Rush* (D)
2.	Jesse L. Jackson, Jr.* (D)
3.	William O. Lipinski* (D)
4.	Luis V. Gutierrez* (D)
5.	Rod R. Blagojevich (D)
6.	Henry J. Hyde* (R)
7.	Danny K. Davis* (D)
8.	Philip M. Crane* (R)
9.	Jan Schakowsky* (D)
10.	Mark Steven Kirk* (R)
11.	Gerald C. "Jerry" Weller* (R)
12.	Jerry F. Costello* (D)
13.	Judy Biggert* (R)
14.	J. Dennis Hastert* (R)
15.	Tim Johnson* (R)
16.	Donald A. Manzullo* (R)
17.	Lane A. Evans* (D)
18.	Ray LaHood* (R)
19.	Dave Phelps* (D)
20.	John M. Shimkus* (R)

Dist.	Representative (Party)
Indiana	
1.	Peter J. Visclosky* (D)
2.	Mike Pence* (R)
3.	Tim Roemer (D)
4.	Mark E. Souder* (R)
5.	Steve Buyer* (R)
6.	Dan Burton* (R)
7.	Brian D. Kerns (R)
8.	John N. Hostettler* (R)
9.	Baron Hill* (D)
10.	Julia M. Carson* (D)
Iowa	
1.	Jim Leach* (R)
2.	Jim Nussle* (R)
3.	Leonard L. Boswell* (D)
4.	Greg Ganske (R)
5.	Tom Latham* (R)
Kansas	
1.	Jerry Moran* (R)
2.	Jim Ryun* (R)
3.	Dennis Moore* (D)
4.	Todd Tiahrt* (R)
Kentucky	
1.	Edward Whitfield* (R)
2.	Ron Lewis* (R)
3.	Anne Meagher Northup* (R)
4.	Ken Lucas* (D)
5.	Harold “Hal” Rogers* (R)
6.	Ernest Fletcher* (R)
Louisiana	
1.	David Vitter* (R)
2.	William J. Jefferson* (D)
3.	W.J. “Billy” Tauzin* (R)
4.	“Jim” McCrery* (R)
5.	John C. Cooksey (R)
6.	Richard H. Baker* (R)
7.	Chris John* (D)
Maine	
1.	Thomas H. Allen* (D)
2.	John E. Baldacci (D)
Maryland	
1.	Wayne T. Gilchrest* (R)
2.	Robert L. Ehrlich Jr. (R)
3.	Benjamin L. Cardin* (D)
4.	Albert R. Wynn* (D)
5.	Steny H. Hoyer* (D)
6.	Roscoe G. Bartlett* (R)
7.	Elijah E. Cummings* (D)
8.	Constance A. Morella* (R)
Massachusetts	
1.	John W. Olver* (D)
2.	Richard E. Neal* (D)
3.	James P. McGovern* (D)
4.	Barney Frank* (D)
5.	Martin T. Meehan* (D)
6.	John F. Tierney* (D)
7.	Edward J. Markey* (D)
8.	Michael E. Capuano* (D)
9.	Stephen F. Lynch* (D)[4]
10.	William D. Delahunt* (D)

Dist.	Representative (Party)
Michigan	
1.	Bart Stupak* (D)
2.	Peter Hoekstra* (R)
3.	Vernon Ehlers* (R)
4.	Dave Camp* (R)
5.	James A. Barcia* (D)
6.	Fred Upton* (R)
7.	Nick Smith* (R)
8.	Mike Rogers* (R)
9.	Dale E. Kildee* (D)
10.	David E. Bonior (D)
11.	Joe Knollenberg* (R)
12.	Sander Levin* (D)
13.	Lynn Nancy Rivers (D)
14.	John Conyers, Jr.* (D)
15.	Carolyn Cheeks Kilpatrick* (D)
16.	John D. Dingell* (D)
Minnesota	
1.	Gil Gutknecht* (R)
2.	Mark Kennedy* (R)
3.	Jim Ramstad* (R)
4.	Betty McCollum* (D)
5.	Martin Olav Sabo* (D)
6.	Bill Luther* (D)
7.	Collin C. Peterson* (D)
8.	James L. Oberstar* (D)
Mississippi	
1.	Roger F. Wicker* (R)
2.	Bennie G. Thompson* (D)
3.	Charles W. “Chip” Pickering, Jr.* (R)
4.	Ronnie Shows* (D)
5.	Gene Taylor* (D)
Missouri	
1.	William Lacy Clay, Jr.* (D)
2.	Todd Akin* (R)
3.	Richard A. Gephardt* (D)
4.	Ike Skelton* (D)
5.	Karen McCarthy* (D)
6.	Samuel B. (Sam) Graves, Jr.* (R)
7.	Roy Blunt* (R)
8.	Jo Ann Emerson* (R)
9.	Kenny Hulshof* (R)
Montana	
	Dennis Rehberg* (R)
Nebraska	
1.	Doug Bereuter* (R)
2.	Lee Terry* (R)
3.	Tom Osborne* (R)
Nevada	
1.	Shelley Berkley* (D)
2.	Jim Gibbons* (R)
New Hampshire	
1.	John E. Sununu (R)
2.	Charles Bass* (R)
New Jersey	
1.	Robert E. Andrews* (D)
2.	Frank A. LoBiondo* (R)
3.	Jim Saxton* (R)
4.	Christopher H. Smith* (R)

Dist.	Representative (Party)
5.	Marge Roukema (R)
6.	Frank Pallone, Jr.* (D)
7.	Mike Ferguson* (R)
8.	Bill J. Pascrell, Jr.* (D)
9.	Steven R. Rothman* (D)
10.	Donald M. Payne* (D)
11.	Rodney P. Frelinghuysen* (R)
12.	Rush Holt* (D)
13.	Robert Menendez* (D)
New Mexico	
1.	Heather A. Wilson* (R)
2.	Joe R. Skeen (R)
3.	Tom Udall* (D)
New York	
1.	Felix J. Grucci, Jr.* (R)
2.	Steve J. Israel* (D)
3.	Peter T. King* (R)
4.	Carolyn McCarthy* (D)
5.	Gary L. Ackerman* (D)
6.	Gregory W. Meeks* (D)
7.	Joseph Crowley* (D)
8.	Jerrold L. Nadler* (D)
9.	Anthony D. Weiner* (D)
10.	Edolphus Towns* (D)
11.	Major R. Owens* (D)
12.	Nydia M. Velazquez* (D)
13.	Vito J. Fossella* (R)
14.	Carolyn B. Maloney* (D)
15.	Charles B. Rangel* (D)
16.	Jose E. Serrano* (D)
17.	Eliot L. Engel* (D)
18.	Nita M. Lowey* (D)
19.	Sue W. Kelly* (R)
20.	Benjamin A. Gilman (R)
21.	Michael R. McNulty* (D)
22.	John E. Sweeney* (R)
23.	Sherwood L. Boehlert* (R)
24.	John M. McHugh* (R)
25.	James T. Walsh* (R)
26.	Maurice D. Hinchey* (D)
27.	Thomas M. Reynolds* (R)
28.	Louise M. Slaughter* (D)
29.	John J. La Falce (D)
30.	Jack Quinn* (R)
31.	Amo Houghton* (R)
North Carolina	
1.	Eva M. Clayton (D)
2.	Bob Etheridge* (D)
3.	Walter B. Jones* (R)
4.	David Price* (D)
5.	Richard M. Burr* (R)
6.	Howard Coble* (R)
7.	Mike McIntyre* (D)
8.	Robert C. (Robin) Hayes* (R)
9.	Sue Myrick* (R)
10.	T. Cass Ballenger* (R)
11.	Charles H. Taylor* (R)
12.	Mel Watt* (D)
North Dakota	
	Earl Pomeroy* (D)

Dist.	Representative (Party)

Ohio

1. Steve Chabot* (R)
2. Rob Portman* (R)
3. Vacant[5]
4. Michael G. Oxley* (R)
5. Paul E. Gillmor* (R)
6. Ted Strickland* (D)
7. Dave Hobson* (R)
8. John A. Boehner* (R)
9. Marcy Kaptur* (D)
10. Dennis J. Kucinich* (D)
11. Stephanie Tubbs-Jones* (D)
12. Pat Tiberi (R)
13. Sherrod Brown* (D)
14. Thomas C. Sawyer (D)
15. Deborah Pryce* (R)
16. Ralph Regula* (R)
17. Vacant[6]
18. Bob Ney* (R)
19. Steven C. LaTourette* (R)

Oklahoma

1. John Sullivan* (R)[7]
2. Brad Carson* (D)
3. Wes Watkins (R)
4. J.C. Watts, Jr. (R)
5. Ernest Istook* (R)
6. Frank D. Lucas* (R)

Oregon

1. David Wu* (D)
2. Greg Walden* (R)
3. Earl Blumenauer* (D)
4. Peter A. DeFazio* (D)
5. Darlene Hooley* (D)

Pennsylvania

1. Robert A. Brady* (D)
2. Chaka Fattah* (D)
3. Robert A. Borski (D)
4. Melissa Hart* (R)
5. John E. Peterson* (R)
6. Tim Holden* (D)
7. Curt Weldon* (R)
8. Jim Greenwood* (R)
9. Bill Shuster* (R)
10. Don Sherwood* (R)
11. Paul E. Kanjorski* (D)
12. John P. Murtha* (D)
13. Joseph M. Hoeffel* (D)
14. William J. Coyne (D)
15. Pat Toomey* (R)
16. Joseph R. Pitts* (R)
17. George W. Gekas* (R)
18. Mike Doyle* (D)
19. Todd Platts* (R)
20. Frank Mascara (D)
21. Phil English* (R)

Rhode Island

1. Patrick J. Kennedy* (D)
2. James R. Langevin (D)

South Carolina

1. Henry Brown* (R)
2. Joe Wilson* (R)[8]
3. Lindsey Graham (R)
4. Jim DeMint* (R)
5. John Spratt* (D)
6. James E. "Jim" Clyburn* (D)

South Dakota

John R. Thune (R)

Tennessee

1. William L. "Bill" Jenkins* (R)
2. John J. Duncan, Jr.* (R)
3. Zach Wamp* (R)
4. Van Hilleary (R)
5. Bob Clement (D)
6. Bart Gordon* (D)
7. Ed Bryant (R)
8. John S. Tanner* (D)
9. Harold E. Ford, Jr.* (D)

Texas

1. Max Sandlin* (D)
2. Jim Turner* (D)
3. Sam Johnson* (R)
4. Ralph M. Hall* (D)
5. Pete Sessions* (R)
6. Joe Barton* (R)
7. John Culberson (R)
8. Kevin Brady* (R)
9. Nick Lampson* (D)
10. Lloyd Doggett* (D)
11. Chet Edwards* (D)
12. Kay Granger* (R)
13. William "Mac" Thornberry* (R)
14. Ron Paul* (R)
15. Ruben Hinojosa* (D)
16. Silvestre Reyes* (D)
17. Charles Stenholm* (D)
18. Sheila Jackson Lee* (D)
19. Larry Combest* (R)
20. Charles A. Gonzalez* (D)
21. Lamar Smith* (R)
22. Tom DeLay* (R)
23. Henry Bonilla* (R)
24. Martin Frost* (D)
25. Ken Bentsen (D)
26. Dick Armey (R)
27. Solomon P. Ortiz* (D)
28. Ciro D. Rodriguez* (D)
29. Gene Green* (D)
30. Eddie Bernice Johnson* (D)

Utah

1. James V. Hansen (R)
2. Jim Matheson* (D)
3. Chris Cannon* (R)

Vermont

Bernard Sanders* (I)

Virginia

1. Jo Ann S. Davis* (R)
2. Edward L. "Ed" Schrock (R)
3. Robert C. "Bobby" Scott* (D)
4. J. Randy Forbes* (R)
5. Virgil H. Goode, Jr.* (R)[9]
6. Robert W. "Bob" Goodlatte* (R)
7. Eric I. Cantor* (R)
8. James P. Moran, Jr.* (D)
9. Frederick C. "Rick" Boucher* (D)
10. Frank R. Wolf* (R)
11. Thomas M. Davis, III* (R)

Washington

1. Jay Inslee* (D)
2. Rick Larsen* (D)
3. Brian Baird* (D)
4. Doc Hastings* (R)
5. George R. Nethercutt, Jr.* (R)
6. Norm Dicks* (D)
7. Jim McDermott* (D)
8. Jennifer Dunn* (R)
9. Adam Smith* (D)

West Virginia

1. Alan B. Mollohan* (D)
2. Shelley Moore Capito (R)
3. Nick Joe Rahall, II* (D)

Wisconsin

1. Paul D. Ryan* (R)
2. Tammy Baldwin* (D)
3. Ron Kind* (D)
4. Jerry Kleczka* (D)
5. Tom Barrett (D)
6. Tom Petri* (R)
7. David R. Obey* (D)
8. Mark Green* (R)
9. F. James Sensenbrenner, Jr.* (R)

Wyoming

Barbara Cubin* (R)

The following members of Congress are nonvoting: Aníbal Acevedo-Vilá (Popular Democratic Party), resident commissioner, Puerto Rico; Eleanor Holmes Norton (D), District of Columbia; Robert A. Underwood (D), Guam; Eni F. H. Faleomavaega (D), American Samoa; Donna M. Christian-Christensen (D), Virgin Islands.

(1) John Boozman won a special election Nov. 20, 2001, to fill seat left vacant by the resignation of Asa Hutchinson on Aug. 6, 2001. (2) Jeff Miller won a special election Oct. 16, 2001, to fill seat left vacant by the resignation of Joe Scarborough on Sept. 5, 2001. (3) Seat fell vacant after the death of Patsy Takemoto Mink on Sept. 28, 2002. The Hawaii Supreme Court ruled that her name would remain on the ballot for the Nov. 5, 2002, election, and that a special election was to be held Jan. 4, 2003, if she won. A special election was also to be held Nov. 30, 2002, to fill the seat for the remainder of her term. (4) Stephen F. Lynch won a special election Oct. 16, 2001, to fill seat left vacant after the death of John Joseph Moakley on May 28, 2001. (5) Seat fell vacant after Tony P. Hall resigned on Sept. 9, 2002, to become U.S. ambassador to the UN Food and Agriculture Organization. The seat was to be filled on Election Day, Nov. 5, 2002. (6) Seat fell vacant after the expulsion of James A. Traficant, Jr., on July 25, 2002. The seat was to be filled on Election Day, Nov. 5, 2002. (7) John Sullivan won a special election Jan. 8, 2002, to fill seat left vacant by the resignation of Steve Largent effective Feb. 15, 2002. (8) Joe Wilson won a special election Dec. 18, 2001, to fill seat left vacant after the death of Floyd Spence on Aug. 16, 2001. (9) Virgil H. Goode, Jr. changed his party designation to Republican on Aug. 1, 2002.

WORLD ALMANAC QUICK QUIZ

What U.S. president vetoed the most pieces of legislation during his time in the White House?

(a) Ronald Reagan (b) Harry Truman (c) Franklin D. Roosevelt (d) Andrew Johnson

For the answer look in this chapter, or see page 1008.

Political Divisions of the U.S. Senate and House of Representatives, 1901-2002

Source: *Congressional Directory*; Senate Library

(all figures reflect immediate post-election party breakdown; **boldface** denotes party in majority immediately after the election.)

		SENATE					HOUSE OF REPRESENTATIVES				
Congress	Years	Total Sens.	Demo-crats	Repub-licans	Other parties	Vacant	Total Members	Demo-crats	Repub-licans	Other parties	Vacant
57th	1901-03	90	29	*56	3	2	357	153	*198	5	1
58th	1903-05	90	32	**58**			386	178	**207**		1
59th	1905-07	90	32	**58**			386	136	**250**		
60th	1907-09	92	29	**61**		2	386	164	**222**		
61st	1909-11	92	32	**59**		1	391	172	**219**		
62nd	1911-13	92	42	**49**		1	391	**228**	162	1	
63rd	1913-15	96	**51**	44	1		435	**290**	127	18	
64th	1915-17	96	**56**	39	1		435	**231**	193	8	3
65th	1917-19	96	**53**	42	1		435	210[1]	**216**	9	
66th	1919-21	96	47	**48**	1		435	191	**237**	7	
67th	1921-23	96	37	**59**			435	132	**300**	1	2
68th	1923-25	96	43	**51**	2		435	207	**225**	3	
69th	1925-27	96	40	**54**	1	1	435	183	**247**	5	
70th	1927-29	96	47	**48**	1		435	195	**237**	3	
71st	1929-31	96	39	**56**	1		435	163	**267**	1	4
72nd	1931-33	96	47	**48**	1		435	216[2]	**218**	1	
73rd	1933-35	96	**59**	36	1		435	**313**	117	5	
74th	1935-37	96	**69**	25	2		435	**322**	103	10	
75th	1937-39	96	**75**	17	4		435	**333**	89	13	
76th	1939-41	96	**69**	23	4		435	**262**	169	4	
77th	1941-43	96	**66**	28	2		435	**267**	162	6	
78th	1943-45	96	**57**	38	1		435	**222**	209	4	
79th	1945-47	96	**57**	38	1		435	**243**	190	2	
80th	1947-49	96	45	**51**			435	188	**246**	1	
81st	1949-51	96	**54**	42			435	**263**	171	1	
82nd	1951-53	96	**48**	47	1		435	**234**	199	2	
83rd	1953-55	96	46	**48**	2		435	213	**221**	1	
84th	1955-57	96	**48**	47	1		435	**232**	203		
85th	1957-59	96	**49**	47			435	**234**	201		
86th	1959-61	98	**64**	34			436[3]	**283**	153		
87th	1961-63	100	**64**	36			437[4]	**262**	175		
88th	1963-65	100	**67**	33			435	**258**	176		1
89th	1965-67	100	**68**	32			435	**295**	140		
90th	1967-69	100	**64**	36			435	**248**	187		
91st	1969-71	100	**58**	42			435	**243**	192		
92nd	1971-73	100	**54**	44	2		435	**255**	180		
93rd	1973-75	100	**56**	42	2		435	**242**	192	1	
94th	1975-77	100	**60**	37	2		435	**291**	144	1	
95th	1977-79	100	**61**	38	1		435	**292**	143		
96th	1979-81	100	**58**	41	1		435	**277**	158		
97th	1981-83	100	46	**53**	1		435	**242**	192	1	
98th	1983-85	100	46	**54**			435	**269**	166		
99th	1985-87	100	47	**53**			435	**253**	182		
100th	1987-89	100	**55**	45			435	**258**	177		
101st	1989-91	100	**55**	45			435	**260**	175		
102nd	1991-93	100	**56**	44			435	**267**	167	1	
103rd	1993-95	100	**57**	43			435	**258**	176	1	
104th	1995-97	100	48	**52**			435	204	**230**	1	
105th	1997-99	100	45	**55**			435	207	**227**	1	
106th	1999-2001	100	45	**55**			435	211	**223**	1	
107th	2001-03	100	50	**50**[5]			435	212	**221**	2	

(1) Democrats organized the House with help of other parties. (2) Democrats organized House because of Republican deaths. (3) Proclamation declaring Alaska a state issued Jan. 3, 1959. (4) Proclamation declaring Hawaii a state issued Aug. 21, 1959. (5) Republican Sen. James M. Jeffords (VT) changed his party designation to Independent on June 5, 2001, switching control of the Senate to Democrats from Republicans.

Floor Leaders in the U.S. Senate Since the 1920s

Majority Leaders

Name	Party	State	Tenure
Charles Curtis[1]	R	KS	1925-1929
James E. Watson	R	IN	1929-1933
Joseph T. Robinson	D	AR	1933-1937
Alben W. Barkley	D	KY	1937-1947
Wallace H. White	R	ME	1947-1949
Scott W. Lucas	D	IL	1949-1951
Ernest W. McFarland	D	AZ	1951-1953
Robert A. Taft	R	OH	1953
William F. Knowland	R	CA	1953-1955
Lyndon B. Johnson	D	TX	1955-1961
Mike Mansfield	D	MT	1961-1977
Robert C. Byrd	D	WV	1977-1981
Howard H. Baker Jr.	R	TN	1981-1985
Robert J. Dole	R	KS	1985-1987
Robert C. Byrd	D	WV	1987-1989
George J. Mitchell	D	ME	1989-1995
Robert J. Dole	R	KS	1995-1996
Trent Lott	R	MS	1996-2001
Thomas A. Daschle	D	SD	2001-

Minority Leaders

Name	Party	State	Tenure
Oscar W. Underwood[2]	D	AL	1920-1923
Joseph T. Robinson	D	AR	1923-1933
Charles L. McNary	R	OR	1933-1944
Wallace H. White	R	ME	1944-1947
Alben W. Barkley	D	KY	1947-1949
Kenneth S. Wherry	R	NE	1949-1951
Henry Styles Bridges	R	NH	1951-1953
Lyndon B. Johnson	D	TX	1953-1955
William F. Knowland	R	CA	1955-1959
Everett M. Dirksen	R	IL	1959-1969
Hugh D. Scott	R	PA	1969-1977
Howard H. Baker Jr.	R	TN	1977-1981
Robert C. Byrd	D	WV	1981-1987
Robert J. Dole	R	KS	1987-1995
Thomas A. Daschle	D	SD	1995-2001
Trent Lott	R	MS	2001-

Note: The offices of party (majority and minority) leaders in the Senate did not evolve until the early 20th century. (1) First Republican to be designated floor leader. (2) First Democrat to be designated floor leader.

Speakers of the House of Representatives

(through Oct. 2002)

Party designations: A, American; D, Democratic; DR, Democratic-Republican; F, Federalist; R, Republican; W, Whig

Name	Party	State	Tenure
Frederick Muhlenberg	F	PA	1789-1791
Jonathan Trumbull	F	CT	1791-1793
Frederick Muhlenberg	F	PA	1793-1795
Jonathan Dayton	F	NJ	1795-1799
Theodore Sedgwick	F	MA	1799-1801
Nathaniel Macon	DR	NC	1801-1807
Joseph B. Varnum	DR	MA	1807-1811
Henry Clay	DR	KY	1811-1814
Langdon Cheves	DR	SC	1814-1815
Henry Clay	DR	KY	1815-1820
John W. Taylor	DR	NY	1820-1821
Philip P. Barbour	DR	VA	1821-1823
Henry Clay	DR	KY	1823-1825
John W. Taylor	D	NY	1825-1827
Andrew Stevenson	D	VA	1827-1834
John Bell	D	TN	1834-1835
James K. Polk	D	TN	1835-1839
Robert M. T. Hunter	D	VA	1839-1841
John White	W	KY	1841-1843
John W. Jones	D	VA	1843-1845
John W. Davis	D	IN	1845-1847
Robert C. Winthrop	W	MA	1847-1849
Howell Cobb	D	GA	1849-1851
Linn Boyd	D	KY	1851-1855
Nathaniel P. Banks	A	MA	1856-1857
James L. Orr	D	SC	1857-1859
William Pennington	R	NJ	1860-1861
Galusha A. Grow	R	PA	1861-1863
Schuyler Colfax	R	IN	1863-1869
Theodore M. Pomeroy	R	NY	1869
James G. Blaine	R	ME	1869-1875
Michael C. Kerr	D	IN	1875-1876
Samuel J. Randall	D	PA	1876-1881
Joseph W. Keifer	R	OH	1881-1883
John G. Carlisle	D	KY	1883-1889
Thomas B. Reed	R	ME	1889-1891
Charles F. Crisp	D	GA	1891-1895
Thomas B. Reed	R	ME	1895-1899
David B. Henderson	R	IA	1899-1903
Joseph G. Cannon	R	IL	1903-1911
Champ Clark	D	MO	1911-1919
Frederick H. Gillett	R	MA	1919-1925
Nicholas Longworth	R	OH	1925-1931
John N. Garner	D	TX	1931-1933
Henry T. Rainey	D	IL	1933-1935
Joseph W. Byrns	D	TN	1935-1936
William B. Bankhead	D	AL	1936-1940
Sam Rayburn	D	TX	1940-1947
Joseph W. Martin Jr.	R	MA	1947-1949
Sam Rayburn	D	TX	1949-1953
Joseph W. Martin Jr.	R	MA	1953-1955
Sam Rayburn	D	TX	1955-1961
John W. McCormack	D	MA	1962-1971
Carl Albert	D	OK	1971-1977
Thomas P. O'Neill Jr.	D	MA	1977-1987
James Wright	D	TX	1987-1989
Thomas S. Foley	D	WA	1989-1995
Newt Gingrich	R	GA	1995-1999
J. Dennis Hastert	R	IL	1999-

Congressional Bills Vetoed, 1789-2002

Source: Senate Library

President	Regular vetoes	Pocket vetoes	Total vetoes	Vetoes overridden
Washington	2	—	2	—
John Adams	—	—	—	—
Jefferson	—	—	—	—
Madison	5	2	7	—
Monroe	1	—	1	—
John Q. Adams	—	—	—	—
Jackson	5	7	12	—
Van Buren	—	1	1	—
William Harrison	—	—	—	—
Tyler	6	4	10	1
Polk	2	1	3	—
Taylor	—	—	—	—
Fillmore	—	—	—	—
Pierce	9	—	9	5
Buchanan	4	3	7	—
Lincoln	2	4	6	—
Andrew Johnson	21	8	29	15
Grant	45	48	93	4
Hayes	12	1	13	1
Garfield	—	—	—	—
Arthur	4	8	12	1
Cleveland[1]	304	110	414	2
Benjamin Harrison	19	25	44	1
Cleveland[2]	42	128	170	5
McKinley	6	36	42	—
Theodore Roosevelt	42	40	82	1
Taft	30	9	39	1
Wilson	33	11	44	6
Harding	5	1	6	—
Coolidge	20	30	50	4
Hoover	21	16	37	3
Franklin Roosevelt	372	263	635	9
Truman	180	70	250	12
Eisenhower	73	108	181	2
Kennedy	12	9	21	—
Lyndon Johnson	16	14	30	—
Nixon	26	17	43	7
Ford	48	18	66	12
Carter	13	18	31	2
Reagan	39	39	78	9
George H. W. Bush[3]	29	15	44	1
Clinton[4]	36	1	37	2
George W. Bush[5]	—	—	—	—
Total[3,4]	**1,484**	**1,065**	**2,549**	**106**

— = 0. (1) First term only. (2) Second term only. (3) Excluded from the figures are 2 additional bills, which Pres. George H. W. Bush claimed to be vetoed but Congress considered enacted into law because the president failed to return them to Congress during a recess period. (4) Does not include line-item veto, which was ruled unconstitutional by the Supreme Court on June 25, 1998. (5) As of Oct. 1, 2002.

Librarians of Congress

Librarian	Served	Appointed by President
John J. Beckley	1802-1807	Jefferson
Patrick Magruder	1807-1815	Jefferson
George Watterston	1815-1829	Madison
John Silva Meehan	1829-1861	Jackson
John G. Stephenson	1861-1864	Lincoln
Ainsworth Rand Spofford	1864-1897	Lincoln
John Russell Young	1897-1899	McKinley
Herbert Putnam	1899-1939	McKinley
Archibald MacLeish	1939-1944	F. D. Roosevelt
Luther H. Evans	1945-1953	Truman
L. Quincy Mumford	1954-1974	Eisenhower
Daniel J. Boorstin	1975-1987	Ford
James H. Billington	1987-	Reagan

IT'S A FACT: The Library of Congress, founded in 1800, is the oldest federal cultural institution in the U.S. and the biggest library in the world. It houses more than 120 million items, including about 18 million books, covering 532 miles of bookshelves. The library, on Capitol Hill in Washington, DC, is open to all members of the public above high school age and has about 1 million visitors a year. For further information, visitors can also go to www.loc.gov

U.S. JUDICIARY

(data as of Sept. 2002)

Justices of the U.S. Supreme Court

The Supreme Court comprises the chief justice of the U.S. and 8 associate justices, all appointed for life by the president with advice and consent of the Senate. Names of chief justices are in **boldface.** Salaries: chief justice, $192,600; associate justice, $184,400. The U.S. Supreme Court Bldg. is at 1 First St. NE, Washington, DC 20543. The Court website is www.supremecourtus.gov

Members at start of 2002-2003 term (Oct. 7, 2002): Chief justice: William H. Rehnquist; assoc. justices: Stephen G. Breyer, Ruth Bader Ginsburg, Anthony M. Kennedy, Sandra Day O'Connor, Antonin Scalia, David H. Souter, John Paul Stevens, Clarence Thomas.

	Service			
Name, apptd. from	Term	Yrs	Born	Died
John Jay, NY	1789-1795	5	1745	1829
John Rutledge, SC[1]	1789-1791	1	1739	1800
William Cushing, MA	1789-1810	20	1732	1810
James Wilson, PA	1789-1798	8	1742	1798
John Blair, VA	1789-1796	6	1732	1800
James Iredell, NC	1790-1799	9	1751	1799
Thomas Johnson, MD	1791-1793	1	1732	1819
William Paterson, NJ	1793-1806	13	1745	1806
John Rutledge, SC[2,3]	1795	—	1739	1800
Samuel Chase, MD	1796-1811	15	1741	1811
Oliver Ellsworth, CT	1796-1800	4	1745	1807
Bushrod Washington, VA	1798-1829	31	1762	1829
Alfred Moore, NC	1799-1804	4	1755	1810
John Marshall, VA	1801-1835	34	1755	1835
William Johnson, SC	1804-1834	30	1771	1834
Henry B. Livingston, NY	1806-1823	16	1757	1823
Thomas Todd, KY	1807-1826	18	1765	1826
Joseph Story, MA	1811-1845	33	1779	1845
Gabriel Duval, MD	1811-1835	22	1752	1844
Smith Thompson, NY	1823-1843	20	1768	1843
Robert Trimble, KY	1826-1828	2	1777	1828
John McLean, OH	1829-1861	32	1785	1861
Henry Baldwin, PA	1830-1844	14	1780	1844
James M. Wayne, GA	1835-1867	32	1790	1867
Roger B. Taney, MD	1836-1864	28	1777	1864
Philip P. Barbour, VA	1836-1841	4	1783	1841
John Catron, TN	1837-1865	28	1786	1865
John McKinley, AL	1837-1852	15	1780	1852
Peter V. Daniel, VA	1841-1860	19	1784	1860
Samuel Nelson, NY	1845-1872	27	1792	1873
Levi Woodbury, NH	1845-1851	5	1789	1851
Robert C. Grier, PA	1846-1870	23	1794	1870
Benjamin R. Curtis, MA	1851-1857	6	1809	1874
John A. Campbell, AL	1853-1861	8	1811	1889
Nathan Clifford, ME	1858-1881	23	1803	1881
Noah H. Swayne, OH	1862-1881	18	1804	1884
Samuel F. Miller, IA	1862-1890	28	1816	1890
David Davis, IL	1862-1877	14	1815	1886
Stephen J. Field, CA	1863-1897	34	1816	1899
Salmon P. Chase, OH	1864-1873	8	1808	1873
William Strong, PA	1870-1880	10	1808	1895
Joseph P. Bradley, NJ	1870-1892	21	1813	1892
Ward Hunt, NY	1872-1882	9	1810	1886
Morrison R. Waite, OH	1874-1888	14	1816	1888
John M. Harlan, KY	1877-1911	34	1833	1911
William B. Woods, GA	1880-1887	6	1824	1887
Stanley Matthews, OH	1881-1889	7	1824	1889
Horace Gray, MA	1881-1902	20	1828	1902
Samuel Blatchford, NY	1882-1893	11	1820	1893
Lucius Q.C. Lamar, MS	1888-1893	5	1825	1893
Melville W. Fuller, IL	1888-1910	21	1833	1910
David J. Brewer, KS	1889-1910	20	1837	1910
Henry B. Brown, MI	1890-1906	15	1836	1913
George Shiras Jr., PA	1892-1903	10	1832	1924
Howell E. Jackson, TN	1893-1895	2	1832	1895
Edward D. White, LA[1]	1894-1910	16	1845	1921
Rufus W. Peckham, NY	1895-1909	13	1838	1909
Joseph McKenna, CA	1898-1925	26	1843	1926
Oliver W. Holmes, MA	1902-1932	29	1841	1935
William R. Day, OH	1903-1922	19	1849	1923
William H. Moody, MA	1906-1910	3	1853	1917
Horace H. Lurton, TN	1909-1914	4	1844	1914
Charles E. Hughes, NY[1]	1910-1916	5	1862	1948
Willis Van Devanter, WY	1910-1937	26	1859	1941
Joseph R. Lamar, GA	1910-1916	5	1857	1916
Edward D. White, LA[2]	1910-1921	10	1845	1921
Mahlon Pitney, NJ	1912-1922	10	1858	1924
James C. McReynolds, TN	1914-1941	26	1862	1946
Louis D. Brandeis, MA	1916-1939	22	1856	1941
John H. Clarke, OH	1916-1922	5	1857	1945
William H. Taft, CT	1921-1930	8	1857	1930
George Sutherland, UT	1922-1938	15	1862	1942
Pierce Butler, MN	1922-1939	16	1866	1939
Edward T. Sanford, TN	1923-1930	7	1865	1930
Harlan F. Stone, NY[1]	1925-1941	16	1872	1946
Charles E. Hughes, NY[2]	1930-1941	11	1862	1948
Owen J. Roberts, PA	1930-1945	15	1875	1955
Benjamin N. Cardozo, NY	1932-1938	6	1870	1938
Hugo L. Black, AL	1937-1971	34	1886	1971
Stanley F. Reed, KY	1938-1957	19	1884	1980
Felix Frankfurter, MA	1939-1962	23	1882	1965
William O. Douglas, CT	1939-1975	36[4]	1898	1980
Frank Murphy, MI	1940-1949	9	1890	1949
Harlan F. Stone, NY[2]	1941-1946	5	1872	1946
James F. Byrnes, SC	1941-1942	1	1879	1972
Robert H. Jackson, NY	1941-1954	12	1892	1954
Wiley B. Rutledge, IA	1943-1949	6	1894	1949
Harold H. Burton, OH	1945-1958	13	1888	1964
Fred M. Vinson, KY	1946-1953	7	1890	1953
Tom C. Clark, TX	1949-1967	18	1899	1977
Sherman Minton, IN	1949-1956	7	1890	1965
Earl Warren, CA	1953-1969	16	1891	1974
John Marshall Harlan, NY	1955-1971	16	1899	1971
William J. Brennan Jr., NJ	1956-1990	33	1906	1997
Charles E. Whittaker, MO	1957-1962	5	1901	1973
Potter Stewart, OH	1958-1981	23	1915	1985
Byron R. White, CO	1962-1993	31	1917	2002
Arthur J. Goldberg, IL	1962-1965	3	1908	1990
Abe Fortas, TN	1965-1969	4	1910	1982
Thurgood Marshall, NY	1967-1991	24	1908	1993
Warren E. Burger, VA	1969-1986	17	1907	1995
Harry A. Blackmun, MN	1970-1994	24	1908	1999
Lewis F. Powell Jr., VA	1971-1987	16	1907	1998
William H. Rehnquist, AZ[1]	1971-1986	15	1924	
John Paul Stevens, IL	1975-		1920	
Sandra Day O'Connor, AZ	1981-		1930	
William H. Rehnquist, AZ[2]	1986-		1924	
Antonin Scalia, VA	1986-		1936	
Anthony M. Kennedy, CA	1988-		1936	
David H. Souter, NH	1990-		1939	
Clarence Thomas, VA	1991-		1948	
Ruth Bader Ginsburg, DC	1993-		1933	
Stephen G. Breyer, MA	1994-		1938	

(1) Later, chief justice, as listed. (2) Formerly assoc. justice. (3) Named as acting chief justice; confirmation rejected by the Senate. (4) Longest term of service.

IT'S A FACT: Byron R. "Whizzer" White, who retired from the Supreme Court in 1993 and died in April 2002, was an All-American athlete in college, where he was a running back for the Univ. of Colorado Buffaloes (and later played pro football). Off the field he was a Phi Beta Kappa and Rhodes Scholar who went on to win 2 Bronze Stars during World War II; he became one of the youngest justices ever, at 44, when he was named to the Court by Pres. John F. Kennedy in 1962.

U.S. Courts of Appeals

(Salaries, $159,100, as of Jan. 2002. CJ means Chief Judge)

Federal Circuit — Haldane Robert Mayer, CJ; Pauline Newman, Paul R. Michel, Alan D. Lourie, Raymond C. Clevenger III, Randall R. Rader, Alvin A. Schall, William C. Bryson, Richard Linn, Timothy B. Dyk, Sharon Prost, Arthur J. Gajarsa; Clerk's Office, Washington, DC 20439.

District of Columbia Circuit — Douglas Ginsburg, CJ; Harry T. Edwards, David B. Sentelle, Karen LeCraft Henderson, A. Raymond Randolph, Judith W. Rogers, David S. Tatel, Merrick B. Garland; Clerk's Office, Washington, DC 20001.

First Circuit (ME, MA, NH, RI, Puerto Rico) — Juan R. Torrvella, CJ; Bruce M. Selya, Michael Boudin, Norman H. Stahl, Sandra Lynch, Kermit Lipez, Bailey Aldrich; Clerk's Office, Boston, MA 02210.

Second Circuit (CT, NY, VT) — John M. Walker, CJ; Dennis Jacobs, Guido Calabresi, José A. Cabranes, Fred I. Parker, Chester J. Straub, Rosemary S. Pooler, Robert D. Sack, Sonia Sotomayor, Robert A. Katzmann, Barrington Daniels Parker Jr.; Clerk's Office, New York, NY 10007.

Third Circuit (DE, NJ, PA, Virgin Islands) — Edward R. Becker, CJ; Dolores K. Sloviter, Anthony J. Scirica, Richard L. Nygaard, Samuel A. Alito Jr., Jane R. Roth, Theodore A. McKee, Marjorie O. Rendell, Thomas L. Ambro, Maryanne Trump Barry, Julio M. Fuentes; Clerk's Office, Philadelphia, PA 19106.

Fourth Circuit (MD, NC, SC, VA, WV) — J. Harvie Wilkinson III, CJ; H. Emory Widener Jr., William W. Wilkins Jr., Paul V. Niemeyer, J. Michael Luttig, Karen J. Williams, M. Blane Michael, Diana Gribbon Motz, William B. Traxler Jr., Robert B. King, Roger L. Gregory; Clerk's Office, Richmond, VA 23219.

Fifth Circuit (LA, MS, TX) — Carolyn Dineen King, CJ; E. Grady Jolly, Patrick E. Higginbotham, W. Eugene Davis, Edith H. Jones, Jerry E. Smith, Jacques L. Wiener Jr., Rhesa H. Barksdale, Emilio M. Garza, Harold R. DeMoss Jr., Fortunato P. Benavides, Carl E. Stewart, Robert M. Parker, James L. Dennis, Edith Brown Clement; Clerk's Office, New Orleans, LA 70130.

Sixth Circuit (KY, MI, OH, TN) — Boyce F. Martin Jr., CJ; Danny J. Boggs, Alice M. Batchelder, Martha Craig Daughtrey, Karen Nelson Moore, R. Guy Cole Jr., Eric L. Clay, Ronald Lee Gilman, Julia Smith Gibbons; Clerk's Office, Cincinnati, OH 45202.

Seventh Circuit (IL, IN, WI) — Joel M. Flaum, CJ; Richard A. Posner, John L. Coffey, Frank H. Easterbrook, Kenneth F. Ripple, Daniel A. Manion, Michael S. Kanne, Ilana D. Rovner, Diane P. Wood, Terence T. Evans, Ann Claire Williams; Clerk's Office, Chicago, IL 60604.

Eighth Circuit (AR, IA, MN, MO, NE, ND, SD) — David R. Hansen, CJ; Pasco M. Bowman, Roger L. Wollman, Theodore McMillian, James B. Loken, Morris S. Arnold, Diana E. Murphy, Kermit Edward Bye, William J. Riley, Michael Joseph Melloy, Lavenski R. Smith; Clerk's Office, St. Louis, MO 63101.

Ninth Circuit (AK, AZ, CA, HI, ID, MT, NV, OR, WA, Guam, N. Mariana Islands) — Mary M. Schroeder, CJ; William A. Fletcher, Susan P. Graber, Michael Daly Hawkins, Andrew J. Kleinfeld, Alex Kozinski, M. Margaret McKeown, Thomas G. Nelson, Diarmuid F. O'Scannlain, Harry Pregerson, Stephen Reinhardt, Pamela Ann Rymer, Barry G. Silverman, A. Wallace Tashima, Sidney R. Thomas, Stephen S. Trott, Kim M. Wardlaw, Richard A. Paez, Raymond C. Fisher, Ronald Murray Gould, Marsha L. Berzon, Richard C. Tallman, Johnnie B. Rawlinson, Richard R. Clifton; Clerk's Office, San Francisco, CA 94119.

Tenth Circuit (CO, KS, NM, OK, UT, WY) — Deanell R. Tacha, CJ; Stephanie K. Seymour, David M. Ebel, Paul J. Kelly, Robert H. Henry, Mary Beck Briscoe, Carlos Lucero, Michael R. Murphy, Harris L. Hartz, Terence L. O'Brien, Clerk's Office, Denver, CO 80257.

Eleventh Circuit (AL, FL, GA) — J. L. Edmondson, CJ; R. Lanier Anderson III, Gerald B. Tjoflat, Stanley F. Birch Jr., Joel F. Dubina, Susan H. Black, Ed Carnes, Rosemary Barkett, Frank M. Hull, Stanley Marcus, Charles R. Wilson; Clerk's Office, Atlanta GA 30303.

U.S. District Courts

(Salaries, $150,000, as of Jan. 2002. CJ means Chief Judge)

Alabama — Northern: U. W. Clemon, CJ; Edwin Nelson, Inge Johnson, Sharon L. Blackburn, C. Lynwood Smith Jr., Karon O. Bowdre; Clerk's Office, Birmingham 35203. **Middle:** W. Harold Albritton, CJ; Myron H. Thompson; Clerk's Office, Montgomery 36101. **Southern:** Charles R. Butler Jr., CJ; Callie V. Granade; Clerk's Office, Mobile 36602.

Alaska — James K. Singleton, CJ; H. Russel Holland, John W. Sedwick; Clerk's Office, Anchorage 99513.

Arizona — Stephen M. McNamee, CJ; Paul G. Rosenblatt, Roslyn Silver, Mary Murguia, Susan Bolton, Frederick J. Martone; Clerk's Office, Phoenix 85025.

Arkansas — Eastern: Susan Webber Wright, CJ; Stephen M. Reasoner; George Howard Jr., William R. Wilson Jr., James M. Moody, G. Thomas Eisele; Clerk's Office, Little Rock 72201-3325. **Western:** Jimm Larry Hendren, CJ; Robert T. Dawson, Harry F. Barnes; Clerk's Office, Fort Smith 72902-1547.

California — Northern: Marilyn H. Patel, CJ; Vaughn R. Walker, James Ware, Saundra Brown Armstrong, Ronald M. Whyte, Claudia Wilken, Maxine M. Chesney, Susan Illston, Charles R. Breyer, Jeremy Fogel, William Alsup, Phyllis J. Hamilton; Clerk's Office, San Francisco 94102. **Eastern:** William B. Shubb, CJ; David F. Levi, Garland E. Burrell, Frank C. Damrell Jr., Morrison C. England Jr.; Clerk's Office, Sacramento 95814. **Central:** Consuelo B. Marshall, CJ; Alicemarie H. Stotler, Stephen V. Wilson, Dickran Tevrizian, Terry J. Hatter Jr., Ronald S. W. Lew, Gary L. Taylor, Lourdes G. Baird, Audrey B. Collins, Robert J. Timlin, George H. King, Dean D. Pregerson, Christina A. Snyder, Margaret M. Morrow, A. Howard Matz, David O. Carter, Nora M. Manella, Gary A. Feess, Manuel L. Real, Florence-Marie Cooper, Virginia A. Philips, Percy Anderson, John F. Walter; Clerk's Office, Los Angeles 90012. **Southern:** Marilyn L. Huff, CJ; Judith N. Keep, Irma E. Gonzalez, Napoleon A. Jones Jr., Barry T. Moskowitz, Jeffrey T. Miller, Thomas J. Whelan, Howard B. Turrentine, William B. Enright, John S. Rhoades, Rudi M. Brewster, M. James Lorenz; Gordon Thompson Jr., Clerk's Office, San Diego 92101-8900.

Colorado — Lewis T. Babcock, CJ; Richard P. Matsch, Edward W. Nottingham, Daniel B. Sparr, Wiley Y. Daniel, Walker D. Miller, Marcia S. Krieger, Robert E. Blackburn; Clerk's Office, Denver 80294.

Connecticut — Alfred V. Covello, CJ; Robert N. Chatigny, Dominic J. Squatrito, Alvin W. Thompson, Janet Bond Arterton, Janet C. Hall, Christopher F. Droney, Stefan Underhill; Clerk's Offices, Bridgeport 06604, Hartford 06103, New Haven 06510.

Delaware — Sue L. Robinson, CJ; Joseph J. Farnan Jr., Gregory M. Sleet; Clerk's Office, Wilmington 19801.

District of Columbia — Thomas F. Hogan, CJ, Royce C. Lamberth, Gladys Kessler, Paul L. Friedman, Ricardo M. Urbina, Emmet G. Sullivan, James Robertson, Colleen Kollar-Kotelly, Henry H. Kennedy Jr., Richard W. Roberts, Ellen S. Huvelle, Reggie B. Walton, John D. Bates, Richard J. Leon; Clerk's Office, Washington DC 20001.

Florida — Northern: C. Roger Vinson, CJ; Lacey A. Collier, Robert L. Hinkle, Stephan Mickle; Clerk's Office, Tallahassee 32301. **Middle:** Elizabeth A. Kovachevich, CJ; Patricia C. Fawsett, Harvey E. Schlesinger, Ralph W. Nimmons Jr., Anne C. Conway, Steven D. Merryday, Susan C. Bucklew, Henry Lee Adams Jr., Richard A. Lazzara, James D. Whittemore, John Antoon II, John E. Steele, James S. Moody Jr., Gregory A. Presnell; Clerk's Office, Tampa 33602. **Southern:** William J. Zloch, CJ; Federico A. Moreno, Shelby Highsmith, Donald L. Graham, K. Michael Moore, Ursula Ungaro-Benages, Wilkie D. Ferguson Jr., Daniel T. K. Hurley, Joan A. Lenard, Donald M. Middlebrooks, Alan S. Gold, William P. Dimitrouleas, Patricia A. Seitz, Adalberto J. Jordan, Paul C. Huck; Clerk's Office, Miami 33128.

Georgia — Northern: Orinda D. Evans, CJ; Harold L. Murphy, J. Owen Forrester, Jack T. Camp, Julie E. Carnes, Clarence Cooper, Willis B. Hunt Jr., Thomas W. Thrash Jr., Richard W. Story, Charles A. Pannell Jr., Beverly B. Martin; Clerk's Office, Atlanta 30303. **Middle:** W. Louis Sands, CJ; Hugh Lawson, Clay D. Land, C. Ashley Royal; Clerk's Office, Macon 31202. **Southern:** Dudley H. Bowen Jr., CJ; B. Avant Edenfield, William T. Moore Jr.; Clerk's Office, Savannah 31412.

Hawaii — David Alan Ezra, CJ; Helen Gillmor, Susan Oki Mollway; Clerk's Office, Honolulu 96850.

Idaho — B. Lynn Winmill, CJ; Edward J. Lodge; Clerk's Office, Boise 83724.

Illinois — Northern: Charles P. Kocoras, CJ; Charles R. Norgle Sr, James F. Holderman, James B. Zagel, Suzanne B. Conlon, Wayne R. Andersen, Philip G. Reinhard, Ruben Castillo, Blanche M. Manning, David H. Coar, Robert W. Gettleman, Elaine E. Bucklo, Joan B. Gottschall, Rebecca R. Pallmeyer, William J. Hibbler, Matthew F. Kennelly, Ronald A. Guzman, Joan H. Lefkow, John W. Darrah, Amy J. St. Eve; Clerk's Office, Chicago 60604. **Central:** Joe Billy McDade, CJ; Michael M. Mihm, Michael P. McCuskey, Jeanne E. Scott, Richard H. Mills, Harold A . Baker; Clerk's Office, Springfield 62701. **Southern:** G. Patrick Murphy, CJ; J. Phil Gilbert, David R. Herndon, James L. Foreman, William D. Stiehl, Michael J. Reagan; Clerk's Office, East St. Louis 62202.

Indiana — Northern: William C. Lee, CJ; Allen Sharp, James T. Moody, Robert L. Miller Jr., Rudy Lozano; Clerk's Office, South Bend 46601. **Southern:** Larry J. McKinney, CJ; S. Hugh Dillin, Sarah E. Barker, John Daniel Tinder, David F. Hamilton, Richard L. Young; Clerk's Office, Indianapolis 46204.

Iowa — Northern: Mark W. Bennett, CJ; Michael J. Melloy; Clerk's Office, Cedar Rapids 52401. **Southern:** Ronald E. Longstaff, CJ; Charles R. Wolle, Robert W. Pratt; Clerk's Office, Des Moines 50306-9344.

Kansas — John W. Lungstrum, CJ; Monti L. Belot, G. Thomas Van Bebber, Kathryn H. Vratil, J. Thomas Marten, Carlos Murguia, Julie A. Robinson; Clerk's Office, Kansas City 66101.

Kentucky — Eastern: Karl S. Forester, CJ; Joseph M. Hood, Jennifer B. Coffman, Karen K. Caldwell, Danny C. Reeves, David L. Bunning; Clerk's Office, Lexington 40588-3074. **Western:** Charles R. Simpson III, CJ; John G. Heyburn II, Jennifer B. Coffman, Thomas B. Russell, Joseph H. McKinley Jr.; Clerk's Office, Louisville 40202.

Louisiana — Eastern: Helen Ginger Berrigan, CJ; Martin L. C. Feldman, Stanwood R. Duval, Eldon E. Fallon, Sarah S. Vance, Mary Ann Vial Lemmon, G. Thomas Porteous Jr., Ivan L. R. Lemelle, Carl J. Barbier, Kurt D. Engelhardt, Jay C. Zainey, Lance M. Africk; Clerk's Office, New Orleans 70130. **Middle:** Frank J. Polozola, CJ; Ralph E. Tyson, James J. Brady; Clerk's Office, Baton Rouge 70801. **Western:** Richard T. Haik, CJ; F. A. Little Jr., Rebecca F. Doherty, James T. Trimble Jr., Donald E. Walter, Tucker L. Melançon, Robert G. James; Clerk's Office, Shreveport 71101.

Maine — D. Brock Hornby, CJ; Gene Carter, George Z. Singal; Clerk's Office, Portland 04101.

Maryland — Frederic N. Smalkin, CJ; J. Frederick Motz, William M. Nickerson, Marvin J. Garbis, Benson Everett Legg, Catherine C. Blake, Andre M. Davis, Deborah K. Chasanow, Peter J. Messitte, Alexander Williams Jr., Edward S. Northrop, Alexander Harvey II, Joseph H. Young, Walter E. Black Jr.; Herbert N. Maletz; Clerk's Office, Baltimore 21201.

Massachusetts — William G. Young, CJ; Joseph L. Tauro, Robert E. Keeton, Mark L. Wolf, Douglas P. Woodlock, Nathaniel M. Gorton, Richard G. Stearns, Reginald C. Lindsay, Patti B. Saris, Nancy Gertner, George A. O'Toole, Rya W. Zobel, Michael A. Ponsor; Clerk's Office, Boston 02210.

Michigan — Eastern: Lawrence P. Zatkoff, CJ; Avern Cohn, Patrick J. Duggan, Bernard A. Friedman, Paul V. Gadola, Gerald E. Rosen, Robert H. Cleland, Nancy G. Edmunds, Denise Page Hood, Paul D. Borman, John Corbett O'Meara, Arthur J. Tarnow, Victoria A. Roberts, George C. Steeh, Julian A. Cook Jr., Stewart A. Newblatt, Anna Johnston Diggs Taylor, George E. Woods, Marianne O. Battani, David M. Lawson; Clerk's Office, Detroit 48226. **Western:** Robert H. Bell, CJ; Richard A. Enslen, David W. McKeague, Gordon J. Quist; Clerk's Office, Grand Rapids 49503.

Minnesota — James M. Rosenbaum, CJ; Richard H. Kyle, Donovan W. Frank, Michael J. Davis, John R. Tunheim, Ann D. Montgomery, Joan E. Lancaster; Clerk's Offices, Minneapolis 55415, St. Paul 55101.

Mississippi — Northern: Glen H. Davidson, CJ; W. Allen Pepper Jr., Michael P. Mills; Clerk's Office, Oxford 38655. **Southern:** Tom S. Lee, CJ; William H. Barbour Jr., Henry T. Wingate, Walter J. Gex III, Charles W. Pickering Sr., David Bramlette; Clerk's Office, Jackson 39201.

Missouri — Eastern: Carol E. Jackson, CJ; Donald J. Stohr, Charles A. Shaw, Catherine D. Perry, E. Richard Webber, Rodney W. Sippel, Jean C. Hamilton; Clerk's Office, St. Louis 63101. **Western:** Dean Whipple, CJ; Fernando J. Gaitan Jr., Ortrie D. Smith, Gary A. Fenner, Nanette Laughrey, Richard E. Dorr; Clerk's Office, Kansas City 64106.

Montana — Donald W. Molloy, CJ; Richard F. Cebull, Sam E. Haddon; Clerk's Office, Billings 59101.

Nebraska — Richard G. Kopf, CJ; Thomas M. Shanahan, Joseph F. Batallion; Clerk's Office, Omaha 68101.

Nevada — Howard D. McKibben, CJ; Philip M. Pro, David W. Hagen, Roger L. Hunt, Kent J. Dawson, Larry R. Hicks, James C. Mahan; Clerk's Office, Las Vegas 89101, Reno 89501.

New Hampshire — Paul J. Barbadoro, CJ; Joseph A. DiClerico, Steven J. McAuliffe; Clerk's Office, Concord 03301.

New Jersey — John W. Bissell, CJ; Anne E. Thompson, Garrett E. Brown Jr., Alfred M. Wolin, John C. Lifland, William G. Bassler, Mary L. Cooper, Joseph E. Irenas, Jerome B. Simandle, William H. Walls, Stephen M. Orlofsky, Joseph A. Greenaway Jr., Katharine S. Hayden, Faith S. Hochberg, Joel A. Pisano, Dennis M. Cavanaugh; Clerk's Office, Newark 07101.

New Mexico — James A. Parker, CJ; C. Leroy Hansen, Martha Vázquez, Bruce D. Black, M. Christina Armijo, William P. Johnson, E.L. Mechem; Clerk's Office, Albuquerque 87102.

New York — Northern: Frederick J. Scullin Jr., CJ; Lawrence E. Kahn, David N. Hurd, Neal P. McCurn, Thomas J. McAvoy; Clerk's Office, Syracuse 13261-7367. **Eastern:** Edward R. Korman, CJ; Raymond J. Dearie, Reena Raggi, Arthur D. Spatt, Carol Bagley Amon, Sterling Johnson Jr., Denis R. Hurley, David G. Trager, Joanna Seybert, Allyne R. Ross, John Gleeson, Nina Gershon, Fredric Block, Nicholas Garaufis; Clerk's Office, Brooklyn 11201. **Southern:** Michael B. Mukasey, CJ; Thomas P. Griesa, Charles L. Brieant, John E. Sprizzo, Lewis A. Kaplan, Kimba Wood, Robert P. Patterson Jr., Lawrence McKenna, John S. Martin Jr., Loretta A. Preska, Harold Baer Jr., Deborah A. Batts, Denny Chin, Denise L. Cote, John Koeltl, Allen G. Schwartz, Shira A. Scheindlin, Sidney H. Stein, Jed S. Rakoff, Barbara S. Jones, Richard C. Casey, Constance B. Motley, Milton Pollack, Whitman Knapp, Robert L. Carter, Kevin T. Duffy, Robert J. Ward, William C. Conner, Richard Owen, Charles S. Haight Jr., Robert W. Sweet, Leonard B. Sand, Shirley Wohl Kram, John F. Keenan, Peter K. Leisure, Louis L. Stanton, Miriam G. Cedarbaum, Richard M. Berman, Alvin K. Hellerstein, Colleen McMahon, William H. Pauley III, Naomi R. Buchwald, Victor Marrero, George B. Daniels, Gerard E. Lynch, Laura Taylor Swain; Clerk's Office New York City 10007. **Western:** David G. Larimer, CJ; Richard J. Arcara, William M. Skretny, Charles J. Siragusa; Clerk's Office, Buffalo 14202, Rochester 14614.

North Carolina — Eastern: Terrence W. Boyle, CJ; Malcolm J. Howard; Clerk's Office, Raleigh 27611. **Middle:** N. Carlton Tilley Jr., CJ; Frank W. Bullock, William L. Osteen Sr, James A. Beaty Jr.; Clerk's Office, Greensboro 27402. **Western:** Graham C. Mullen, CJ; Richard L.

Voorhees, Lacy H. Thornburg; Clerk's Office, Asheville 28801, Charlotte 28202, Statesville 28687.

North Dakota — Rodney S. Webb, CJ; Patrick A. Conmy; Clerk's Office, Bismarck 58502.

Ohio — Northern: Paul R. Matia, CJ; Lesley Brooks Wells, James G. Carr, Solomon Oliver Jr., David A. Katz, Kathleen McDonald O'Malley, Peter C. Economus, Donald C. Nugent, Patricia A. Gaughan, James S. Gwin, Dan Aaron Polster; Clerk's Office, Cleveland 44114. **Southern:** Walter Herbert Rice, CJ; James L. Graham, Sandra S. Beckwith, Edmund A. Sargus Jr., Susan J. Dlott, Algenon L. Marbley, Thomas M. Rose; Clerk's Office, Columbus 43215.

Oklahoma — Northern: Terry C. Kern, CJ; Sven Erik Holmes, Claire Eagan, James H. Payne; Clerk's Office, Tulsa 74103. **Eastern:** Frank H. Seay, CJ; James H. Payne; Clerk's Office, Muskogee 74402. **Western:** Robin J. Cauthron, CJ; David L. Russell, Timothy Leonard, Vicki Miles-LaGrange, Stephen P. Friot, Joe Heaton; Clerk's Office, Oklahoma City 73102.

Oregon — Ancer L. Haggerty, CJ; Garr M. King, Ann L. Aiken, Michael R. Hogan, Anna J. Brown; Clerk's Office, Portland 97204.

Pennsylvania — Eastern: James T. Giles, CJ; Franklin S. Van Antwerpen, Herbert J. Hutton, Jay C. Waldman, Ronald L. Buckwalter, William H. Yohn Jr., Harvey Bartle III, Stewart Dalzell, John R. Padova, J. Curtis Joyner, Eduardo C. Robreno, Anita B. Brody, Bruce W. Kauffman, Emanuel M. Troutman, John B. Hannum, John W. Ditter Jr., Mary A. McLaughlin, Petrese B. Tucker, Berle M. Schiller, R. Barclay Surrick, Legrome D. Davis, Cynthia M. Rufe, Michael M. Baylson, Timothy J. Savage; Clerk's Office, Philadelphia 19106-1797. **Middle:** Thomas I. Vanaskie, CJ; A. Richard Caputo, James M. Munley, Yvette Kane, Christopher C. Conner, John E. Jones III; Clerk's Office, Scranton 18501. **Western:** Donetta W. Ambrose, CJ; Gary L. Lancaster, Robert J. Cindrich, Sean J. McLaughlin, Joy Flowers Conti, David Stewart Cercone; Clerk's Office, Pittsburgh 15230.

Rhode Island — Ernest C. Torres, CJ; Mary M. Lisi; Clerk's Office, Providence 02903.

South Carolina — Joseph F. Anderson Jr., CJ; G. Ross Anderson Jr., C. Weston Houck, David C. Norton, Dennis W. Shedd, Henry M. Herlong Jr., Cameron McGowan Currie, Patrick Michael Duffy, Margaret B. Seymour, Terry L. Wooten; Clerk's Office, Columbia 29201.

South Dakota — Lawrence L. Piersol, CJ; Charles B. Kornmann, Karen E. Schreier, Richard H. Battey; Clerk's Office, Rapid City 57701.

Tennessee — Eastern: R. Allan Edgar, CJ; James H. Jarvis, Thomas G. Hull, R. Leon Jordan, Curtis L. Collier; Clerk's Office, Knoxville 37902. **Middle:** Robert L. Echols, CJ; Todd J. Campbell, Aleta A. Trauger, William J. Haynes Jr.; Clerk's Office, Nashville 37203. **Western:** James D. Todd, CJ; Julia S. Gibbons, Bernice B. Donald, Robert H. Cleland, Samuel H. Mays Jr.; Clerk's Office, Memphis 38103.

Texas — Northern: A. Joe Fish, CJ; Mary Lou Robinson, Jerry Buchmeyer, Sidney A. Fitzwater, Samuel R. Cummings, John H. McBryde, Jorge A. Solis, Terry Means, Sam A. Lindsay, David C. Godbey, Barbara M. Lynn; Clerk's Office, Dallas 75242. **Southern:** George P. Kazen, CJ; Hayden W. Head Jr., Ricardo H. Hinojosa, Lynn N. Hughes, David Hittner, Kenneth M. Hoyt, Simeon T. Lake, Melinda Harmon, John D. Rainey, Samuel B. Kent, Ewing Werlein Jr., Lee H. Rosenthal, Janis Graham Jack, Vanessa D. Gilmore, Nancy F. Atlas, Hilda G. Tagle, Keith P. Ellison; Clerk's Office, Houston 77002. **Eastern:** John Hannah Jr., CJ; Richard A. Schell, David Folsom, Thad Heartfield, T. John Ward, Leonard E. Davis; Clerk's Office, Tyler 75702. **Western:** James R. Nowlin, CJ; David Briones, Edward C. Prado, Fred Biery, Orlando L. Garcia, Sam Sparks, Walter S. Smith Jr., W. Royal Furgeson Jr., Philip R. Martinez; Clerk's Office, San Antonio 78206.

Utah — Dee Benson, CJ; Tena Campbell, Dale A. Kimball, Brian Theodore "Ted" Stewart, Paul G. Cassell; Clerk's Office, Salt Lake City 84101.

Vermont — William K. Sessions III, CJ; J. Garran Murtha; Clerk's Office, Burlington 05402.

Virginia — Eastern: Claude M. Hilton, CJ; James R. Spencer, Thomas S. Ellis III, Rebecca Beach Smith, Henry Coke Morgan Jr., Robert E. Payne, Raymond A. Jackson, Leonie M. Brinkema, Jerome B. Friedman, Gerald Bruce Lee; Clerk's Office, Alexandria 22314. **Western:** Samuel G. Wilson, CJ; James C. Turk, James P. Jones, Norman K. Moon; Clerk's Office, Roanoke 24006.

Washington — Eastern: Fred Van Sickle, CJ; Wm. Fremming Nielsen; Robert H. Whaley, Edward F. Shea; Clerk's Office, Spokane 99210. **Western:** John C. Coughenour, CJ; Barbara Jacobs Rothstein, Thomas S. Zilly, Franklin D. Burgess, Robert S. Lasnik, Marsha J. Pechman; Clerk's Office, Seattle 98104, Tacoma 98402.

West Virginia — Northern: Irene M. Keeley, CJ; Frederick P. Stamp Jr., W. Craig Broadwater; Clerk's Office, Wheeling 26003. **Southern:** Charles H. Haden II, CJ; John T. Copenhaver Jr., David A. Faber, Joseph R. Goodwin, Robert C. Chambers; Clerk's Office, Charleston 25329.

Wisconsin — Eastern: J. P. Stadtmueller, CJ; Rudolph T. Randa, , Charles N. Clevert Jr., Lynn S. Adelman, William C. Griesbach; Clerk's Office, Milwaukee 53202. **Western:** Barbara B. Crabb; CJ; John C. Shabaz; Clerk's Office, Madison 53701.

Wyoming — William F. Downes, CJ; Alan B. Johnson, Clarence A. Brimmer; Clerk's Office, Cheyenne 82001.

U.S. Territorial District Courts

Guam — John S. Unpingco, CJ; Clerk's Office, Hagatña 96910.

Northern Mariana Islands — Alex R. Munson, CJ; Clerk's Office, Saipan MP 96950.

Puerto Rico — Hector M. Laffitte, CJ; Juan M. Perez-Gimenez, Jose Antonio Fuste, Salvador E. Casellas, Daniel R. Dominguez, Carmen C. Cerezo, Jay A. Garcia-Gregory; Clerk's Office, Hato Rey 00918.

Virgin Islands — Raymond L. Finch, CJ; Thomas K. Moore; Clerk's Office, St. Croix 00820.

U.S. Court of International Trade

New York, NY 10278-0001
(Salaries, $150,000, as of Jan. 2002)

Chief Judge — Gregory W. Carman

Judges — Jane A. Restani, Thomas J. Aquilino Jr., Donald C. Pogue, Evan J. Wallach, Judith M. Barzilay, Delissa A. Ridgway, Richard K. Eaton.

U.S. Court of Federal Claims

Washington, DC 20005 (Salaries, $150,000, as of Jan. 2002)

Chief Judge — Edward J. Damich

Judges — Christine Odell Cook Miller, Bohdan A. Futey, James T. Turner, Robert H. Hodges, Diane Gilbert Sypolt, Lawrence M. Baskir, Francis M. Allegra, Lynn J. Bush, Nancy B. Firestone, Emily C. Hewitt, Sarah L. Wilson.

U.S. Tax Court

Washington, DC 20217 (Salaries, $150,000 as of Jan. 2002)

Chief Judge — Mary Ann Cohen

Judges — Renato Beghe, Herbert L. Chabot, John O. Colvin, Joel Gerber, Julian I. Jacobs, Carolyn Miller Parr, Robert P. Ruwe, James S. Halpern, Carolyn P. Chiechi, David Laro, Stephen J. Swift, Thomas B. Wells, Laurence J. Whalen, Maurice B. Foley, Juan F. Vasquez, Joseph H. Gale, L. Paige Marvel, Michael B. Thornton.

U.S. Court of Appeals for Veterans Claims

Washington, DC 20004 (Salaries, $150,000 as of Jan. 2002)

Chief Judge — Frank Q. Nebeker

Judges — Kenneth B. Kramer, John J. Farley 3d, Ronald M. Holdaway, Donald L. Ivers, Jonathan R. Steinberg, William P. Greene Jr.

STATE GOVERNMENT

Governors of States and Puerto Rico

As of Oct. 2002. For Nov. 2002 election results, see www.worldalmanac.com/2002elections

State	Capital, ZIP Code	Governor	Party	Term years	Term expires	Annual salary[1]
Alabama	Montgomery 36130	Don Siegelman*	Dem.	4	Jan. 2003	$94,655
Alaska**	Juneau 99811	Tony Knowles	Dem.	4	Dec. 2002	85,776
Arizona**	Phoenix 85007	Jane Dee Hull	Rep.	4	Jan. 2003	95,000
Arkansas	Little Rock 72201	Mike Huckabee*	Rep.	4	Jan. 2003	71,738
California	Sacramento 95814	Gray Davis*	Dem.	4	Jan. 2003	175,000
Colorado	Denver 80203	Bill Owens*	Rep.	4	Jan. 2003	90,000
Connecticut	Hartford 06106	John G. Rowland*	Rep.	4	Jan. 2003	78,000
Delaware	Dover 19901	Ruth Ann Minner	Dem.	4	Jan. 2005	114,000
Florida	Tallahassee 32399	Jeb Bush*	Rep.	4	Jan. 2003	123,175
Georgia	Atlanta 30334	Roy E. Barnes*	Dem.	4	Jan. 2003	127,303
Hawaii**	Honolulu 96813	Ben Cayetano	Dem.	4	Dec. 2002	94,780
Idaho	Boise 83720	Dirk Kempthorne*	Rep.	4	Jan. 2003	101,500
Illinois**	Springfield 62706	George H. Ryan	Rep.	4	Jan. 2003	150,691
Indiana	Indianapolis 46204	Frank O'Bannon	Dem.	4	Jan. 2005	95,000
Iowa	Des Moines 50319	Tom Vilsack*	Dem.	4	Jan. 2003	104,352
Kansas**	Topeka 66612	Bill Graves	Rep.	4	Jan. 2003	96,877
Kentucky**	Frankfort 40601	Paul Patton	Dem.	4	Dec. 2003	104,619
Louisiana	Baton Rouge 70804	M. J. "Mike" Foster Jr.	Rep.	4	Jan. 2004	95,000
Maine**	Augusta 04333	Angus S. King Jr.	Ind.	4	Jan. 2003	70,000
Maryland**	Annapolis 21401	Parris N. Glendening	Dem.	4	Jan. 2003	120,000
Massachusetts**	Boston 02133	Jane Swift	Rep.	4	Jan. 2003	135,000
Michigan**	Lansing 48909	John Engler	Rep.	4	Jan. 2003	177,000
Minnesota**	St. Paul 55155	Jesse Ventura	IPM[2]	4	Jan. 2003	120,303
Mississippi	Jackson 39205	Ronnie Musgrove	Dem.	4	Jan. 2004	101,800
Missouri	Jefferson City 65102	Bob Holden	Dem.	4	Jan. 2005	120,087
Montana	Helena 59620	Judy Martz	Rep.	4	Jan. 2005	88,190
Nebraska	Lincoln 68509	Mike Johanns*	Rep.	4	Jan. 2003	85,000
Nevada	Carson City 89710	Kenny C. Guinn*	Rep.	4	Jan. 2003	117,000
New Hampshire**	Concord 03301	Jeanne Shaheen	Dem.	2	Jan. 2003	100,690
New Jersey	Trenton 08625	James E. McGreevey	Dem.	4	Jan. 2006	83,333
New Mexico**	Santa Fe 87503	Gary E. Johnson	Rep.	4	Jan. 2003	150,000
New York	Albany 12224	George E. Pataki*	Rep.	4	Jan. 2003	179,000
North Carolina	Raleigh 27603	Mike Easley	Dem.	4	Jan. 2005	118,430
North Dakota	Bismarck 58505	John Hoeven	Rep.	4	Jan. 2005	85,506
Ohio	Columbus 43266	Bob Taft*	Rep.	4	Jan. 2003	122,800
Oklahoma**	Oklahoma City 73105	Frank Keating	Rep.	4	Jan. 2003	110,299
Oregon**	Salem 97310	John Kitzhaber	Dem.	4	Jan. 2003	93,600
Pennsylvania**	Harrisburg 17120	Mark Schweiker	Rep.	4	Jan. 2003	142,142
Rhode Island**	Providence 02903	Lincoln C. Almond	Rep.	4	Jan. 2003	95,000
South Carolina	Columbia 29211	Jim Hodges*	Dem.	4	Jan. 2003	106,078
South Dakota**	Pierre 57501	William J. Janklow	Rep.	4	Jan. 2003	98,250
Tennessee**	Nashville 37243	Don Sundquist	Rep.	4	Jan. 2003	85,000
Texas	Austin 78711	Rick Perry*	Rep.	4	Jan. 2003	115,345
Utah	Salt Lake City 84114	Michael O. Leavitt	Rep.	4	Jan. 2005	100,600
Vermont**	Montpelier 05609	Howard Dean	Dem.	2	Jan. 2003	125,572
Virginia	Richmond 23219	Mark R. Warner	Dem.	4	Jan. 2006	124,855
Washington	Olympia 98504	Gary Locke	Dem.	4	Jan. 2005	142,286
West Virginia	Charleston 25305	Bob Wise	Dem.	4	Jan. 2005	90,000
Wisconsin	Madison 53707	Scott McCallum*	Rep.	4	Jan. 2003	122,406
Wyoming**	Cheyenne 82002	Jim Geringer	Rep.	4	Jan. 2003	95,000
Puerto Rico	San Juan 00936	Sila Calderón	PDP[3]	4	Jan. 2005	70,000

*Running for reelection, Nov. 2002. **Election in Nov. 2002; incumbent not running. (1) Salary in effect in 2002. (2) Independence Party of Minnesota. (3) Popular Democratic Party.

State Officials, Salaries, Party Membership

As of Oct. 2002; I=independent

Alabama

Governor — Don Siegelman, D, $94,655
Lt. Gov. — Steve Windom, R, $12 per day, plus $50 per day expenses, plus $3,780 per mo expenses
Sec. of State — Jim Bennett, R, $66,722
Atty. Gen. — William Pryor, R, $124,951
Treasurer — Lucy Baxley, D, $66,722
Legislature: meets annually at Montgomery the 1st Tues. in Mar., 1st year of term of office; 1st Tues. in Feb., 2nd and 3rd yr; 2nd Tues. in Jan., 4th yr. Members receive $10 per day salary, plus $50 per day expenses, plus $2,280 per mo expenses.
Senate — Dem., 24; Rep., 11. Total, 35
House — Dem., 67; Rep., 38. Total, 105

Alaska

Governor — Tony Knowles, D, $85,776
Lt. Gov — Fran Ulmer, D, $80,040
Atty. General — Bruce Botelho, D, $91,200
Legislature: meets annually in Jan. at Juneau for 120 days with a 10-day extension possible upon 2/3 vote. First session in odd years. Members receive $24,012 annually, plus $202 per diem.
Senate — Dem., 6; Rep., 14. Total, 20
House — Dem., 10; Rep., 30. Total, 40

Arizona

Governor — Jane Dee Hull, R, $95,000
Sec. of State — Betsey Bayless, R, $70,000
Atty. Gen. — Janet Napolitano, D, $90,000
Treasurer — Carol Springer, R, $70,000
Legislature: meets annually in Jan. at Phoenix. Each member receives an annual salary of $24,000.
Senate — Dem., 15; Rep., 15. Total, 30
House — Dem., 24; Rep., 36. Total, 60

Arkansas

Governor — Mike Huckabee, R, $71,738
Lt. Gov. — Winthrop P. Rockefeller, R, $34,673
Sec. of State — Sharon Priest, D, $44,836
Atty. Gen. — Mark Pryor, D, $59,781
Treasurer — Jimmie Lou Fisher, D, $44,836
Auditor — Gus Wingfield, D, $44,836
General Assembly: meets odd years in Jan. at Little Rock. Members receive $13,442 annually.
Senate — Dem., 28; Rep., 7. Total, 35
House — Dem., 70; Rep., 30. Total, 100

California

Governor — Gray Davis, D, $175,000
Lt. Gov. — Cruz Bustamante, D, $131,250
Sec. of State — Bill Jones, R, $131,250
Controller — Kathleen Connell, D, $140,000
Treasurer — Phil Angelides, D, $140,000
Atty. Gen. — Bill Lockyer, D, $148,750
Legislature: meets at Sacramento on the 1st Mon. in Dec. of even-numbered years; each session lasts 2 years. Members receive $99,000 annually, plus $121 per diem.
Senate — Dem., 26; Rep., 14. Total, 40
Assembly — Dem., 50; Rep., 30. Total, 80

Colorado
Governor — Bill Owens, R, $90,000
Lt. Gov. — Joe Rogers, R, $68,500
Sec. of State — Donetta Davidson, R, $68,500
Atty. Gen. — Ken Salazar, D, $80,000
Treasurer — Mike Coffman, R, $68,500
General Assembly: meets annually in Jan. at Denver. Members receive $30,000 annually plus $99 per diem for attendance at interim committee meetings.
Senate — Dem., 18; Rep., 17. Total, 35
House — Dem., 30; Rep., 35. Total, 65

Connecticut
Governor — John G. Rowland, R, $78,000
Lt. Gov. — M. Jodi Rell, R, $71,500
Sec. of State — Susan Bysiewicz, D, $65,000
Treasurer — Denise Nappier, D, $70,000
Comptroller — Nancy S. Wyman, D, $65,000
Atty. Gen. — Richard Blumenthal, D, $75,000
General Assembly: meets annually odd years in Jan. and even years in Feb., at Hartford. Members receive $28,000 annually, plus $5,500 (senator), $4,500 (representative) per year for expenses.
Senate — Dem., 21; Rep., 15. Total, 36
House — Dem., 100; Rep., 51. Total, 151

Delaware
Governor — Ruth Ann Minner, D, $114,000
Lt. Gov. — John C. Carney Jr., D, $62,400
Sec. of State — Harriet Smith Windsor, D, $106,000
Atty. Gen. — M. Jane Brady, R, $116,700
Treasurer — Jack A. Markell, D, $94,000
General Assembly: meets annually the 2nd Tues. in Jan. and continues each Tues., Wed., and Thurs. until June 30, at Dover. Members receive $34,800 annually.
Senate — Dem., 13; Rep., 8. Total, 21
House — Dem., 15; Rep., 26. Total, 41

Florida
Governor — Jeb Bush, R, $123,175
Lt. Gov. — Frank T. Brogan, R, $117,990
Sec. of State* — Jim Smith, R, $121,931
Comptroller — Robert F. Milligan, R, $121,931
Atty. Gen. — Robert Butterworth, D, $121,931
Treasurer — Tom Gallagher, R, $121,931
Legislature: meets annually at Tallahassee. Members receive $27,900 annually, plus expense allowance.
Senate — Dem., 15; Rep., 25. Total, 40
House — Dem., 43; Rep., 77. Total, 120
*Dept. was to become an agency under the Gov.'s office in Jan. 2003.

Georgia
Governor — Roy E. Barnes, D, $127,303
Lt. Gov. — Mark Taylor, D, $83,148
Sec. of State — Cathy Cox, D, $112,776
Atty. Gen. — Thurbert Baker, D, $125,871
General Assembly: meets annually at Atlanta on 2nd Mon. in Jan. Members receive $16,200 annually ($128 per diem and $7,000 annual expense reimbursement).
Senate — Dem., 32; Rep., 22. Total, 54
House — Dem., 105; Rep., 73; 1 ind. Total, 179

Hawaii
Governor — Ben Cayetano, D, $94,780
Lt. Gov. — Mazie K. Hirono, D, $90,041
Atty. Gen. — Earl I. Anzai, $85,302
Comptroller — Mary Alice Evans, $85,302
Dir. of Budget & Finance — Stanley T. Shiraki, $85,302
Legislature: meets annually on 3rd Wed. in Jan. at Honolulu. Members receive $32,000 annually; presiding officers receive $37,000.
Senate — Dem., 22; Rep., 3. Total, 25
House — Dem., 32; Rep., 19. Total, 51

Idaho
Governor — Dirk Kempthorne, R, $101,500
Lt. Gov. — Jack Riggs, R, $26,750
Sec. of State — Pete T. Cenarrusa, R, $82,500
Treasurer — Ron Crane, R, $82,500
Atty. Gen. — Alan Lance, R, $91,500
Legislature: meets annually the Mon. on or nearest Jan. 9 at Boise. Members receive $15,646 annually, plus $99 per day during session if required to maintain a 2nd residence, $38 if no 2nd residence; plus $50 per day when engaged in legislative business when legislature is not in session.
Senate — Dem., 3, Rep., 32. Total, 35
House — Dem., 9; Rep., 61. Total, 70

Illinois
Governor — George H. Ryan, R, $150,691
Lt. Gov. — Corinne Wood, R, $115,235
Sec. of State — Jesse White, D, $132,963
Comptroller — Daniel Hynes, D, $115,235
Atty. Gen. — James Ryan, R, $132,963
Treasurer — Judy Baar Topinka, R, $115,235
General Assembly: meets annually in Nov. and Jan. at Springfield. Members receive $57,619 annually.
Senate — Dem., 27; Rep., 32. Total, 59
House — Dem., 62; Rep., 56. Total, 118

Indiana
Governor — Frank O'Bannon, D, $95,000
Lt. Gov. — Joseph E. Kernan, D, $76,000
Sec. of State — Sue Anne Gilroy, R, $66,000
Atty. Gen. — Steve Carter, R, $79,400
Treasurer — Tim Berry, R, $66,000
Auditor — Connie Kay Nass, R, $66,000
General Assembly: meets annually on the Tues. after the 2nd Mon. in Jan. at Indianapolis. Members receive $11,600 annually, plus $112 per day while in session, $25 per day while not in session.
Senate — Dem., 18; Rep., 32. Total, 50
House — Dem., 53; Rep., 47. Total, 100

Iowa
Governor — Tom Vilsack, D, $104,352
Lt. Gov. — Sally Pederson, D, $73,046
Sec. of State — Chester J. Culver D, $83,590
Atty. Gen. — Tom Miller, D, $102,740
Treasurer — Michael L. Fitzgerald, D, $85,429
Auditor — Richard D. Johnson, R, $85,429
Sec. of Agriculture — Patty Judge, D, $85,429
General Assembly: meets annually in Jan. at Des Moines. Members receive $21,381 annually, plus expense allowance.
Senate — Dem., 21; Rep., 29. Total, 50
House — Dem., 44; Rep., 56 Total, 100

Kansas
Governor — Bill Graves, R, $96,877
Lt. Gov. — Gary Sherrer, R, $109,870
Sec. of State — Ron Thornburgh, R, $75,259
Atty. Gen. — Carla Stovall, R, $86,546
Treasurer — Tim Shallenburger, R, $75,259
Insurance Commissioner — Kathleen Sebelius, D, $75,259
Legislature: meets annually on the 2nd Mon. of Jan. at Topeka. Members receive $78.75 per day salary, plus $85 per day expenses while in session, $5,400 total allowance while not in session.
Senate — Dem., 10; Rep., 30. Total, 40
House — Dem., 40, Rep., 79. Total, 125

Kentucky
Governor — Paul Patton, D, $104,619
Lt. Gov. — Steve Henry, D, $88,941
Sec. of State — John Y. Brown III, D, $88,941
Atty. Gen. — A. B. Chandler III, D, $88,941
Treasurer — Jonathan Miller, D, $88,941
Auditor — Ed Hatchett, D, $88,941
Sec. of Economic Dev. — Gene Strong, $162,750
General Assembly: meets annually on the 1st Tues. after the 1st Mon. in Jan. at Frankfort. Members receive $164 per day, plus $94 per day expenses during session and $1,554 per month for expenses for interim.
Senate — Dem., 18; Rep., 20. Total, 38
House — Dem., 66; Rep., 34. Total, 100

Louisiana
Governor — M. J. "Mike" Foster Jr., R, $95,000
Lt. Gov. — Kathleen Babineaux Blanco, D, $85,000
Sec. of State — W. Fox McKeithen, R, $85,000
Atty. Gen. — Richard Ieyoub, D, $85,000
Treasurer — John Kennedy, D, $85,000
Legislature: meets in odd-numbered years at Baton Rouge starting last Mon. in Mar., for 60 legislative days of 85 calendar days; meets in even-numbered years on last Mon. in Apr. for 30 days of 45 calendar days. Members receive $16,800 annually, plus $97 per day expenses while in session and $500 per month as an unvouchered expense allowance.
Senate — Dem., 27; Rep., 12. Total, 39
House — Dem., 75; Rep., 30. Total, 105

Maine
Governor — Angus S. King Jr., I, $70,000
Sec. of State — Dan A. Gwadosky, D, $79,768
Atty. Gen. — G. Steven Rowe, D, $87,755
Treasurer — Dale McCormick, D, $79,768
State Auditor — Gail M. Chase, D, $86,798
Legislature: meets in odd-numbered years at Augusta on first Wed. in Dec.; meets in even-numbered years on Wed. after first Tues. in Jan. Members receive $10,815 for first regular session, $7,725 for 2nd, plus a daily expense allowance.
Senate — Dem., 19; Rep., 15; 1 ind. Total, 35
House — Dem., 89; Rep., 61; 1 ind. Total, 151

Maryland
Governor — Parris N. Glendening, D, $120,000
Lt. Gov. — Kathleen Kennedy Townsend, D, $100,000
Comptroller — William Donald Schaefer, D, $100,000
Atty. Gen. — J. Joseph Curran Jr., D, $100,000
Sec. of State — John Willis, D, $70,000
Treasurer — Nancy Kopp, D, $100,000

General Assembly: meets 90 consecutive days annually beginning on 2nd Wed. in Jan. at Annapolis. Members receive $31,509 annually, plus expenses.
Senate — Dem., 33; Rep., 14. Total, 47
House — Dem., 106; Rep., 35. Total, 141

Massachusetts

Governor — Jane Swift, R, $135,000
Lt. Gov. — vacant
Sec. of the Commonwealth — William F. Galvin, D, $120,000
Atty. Gen. — Thomas F. Reilly, D, $122,500
Treasurer and Receiver General — Shannon P. O'Brien, D, $120,000
State Auditor — A. Joseph DeNucci, D, $120,000
General Court (legislature): meets Jan. annually in Boston. Members receive $49,710 annually.
Senate — Dem., 34; Rep., 6. Total, 40
House — Dem., 134; Rep., 22; 4 vacancies. Total, 160

Michigan

Governor — John Engler, R, $177,000
Lt. Gov. — Dick Posthumus, R, $123,900
Sec. of State — Candice S. Miller, R, $124,900
Atty. Gen. — Jennifer M. Granholm, D, $124,900
Treasurer — Doug Roberts (appointed), $153,000
Legislature: meets annually in Jan. at Lansing. Members receive $79,650 annually.
Senate — Dem., 15; Rep., 23. Total, 38
House — Dem., 52; Rep., 58. Total, 110

Minnesota

(IPM=Independence Party of Minnesota; DFL=Democratic-Farmer-Labor Party)

Governor — Jesse Ventura, IPM, $120,303
Lt. Gov. — Mae Schunk, IPM, $66,168
Sec. of State — Mary Kiffmeyer, R, $66,168
Atty. Gen. — Michael Hatch, DFL, $93,983
Treasurer — Carol C. Johnson, DFL, $66,168
Auditor — Judith H. Dutcher, DFL, $72,187
Legislature: meets for a total of 120 days within every 2 years, at St. Paul. Members receive $31,140 annually, plus expense allowance during session.
Senate — DFL, 39; R, 27; 1 ind. Total, 67
House — DFL, 65; R, 69. Total, 134

Mississippi

Governor — Ronnie Musgrove, D, $101,800
Lt. Gov. — Amy Tuck, D, $60,000
Sec. of State — Eric Clark, D, $75,000
Atty. Gen. — Mike Moore, D, $90,800
Treasurer — Marshall Bennett, D, $75,000
Auditor — Phil Bryant, R, $75,000
Legislature: meets annually in Jan. at Jackson. Members receive $10,000 per regular session, plus travel allowance, and $1,500 per month when not in session.
Senate — Dem., 32; Rep., 19; 1 vacancy. Total, 52
House — Dem., 86; Rep., 33; 3 ind. Total, 122

Missouri

Governor — Bob Holden, D, $120,087
Lt. Gov. — Joe Maxwell, D, $77,184
Sec. of State — Matt Blunt, R, $96,455
Atty. Gen. — Jeremiah W. Nixon, D, $104,332
Treasurer — Nancy Farmer, D, $96,455
State Auditor — Claire McCaskill, D, $96,455
General Assembly: meets annually at Jefferson City beginning 1st Wed. after 1st Mon. in Jan. Members receive $31,351 annually.
Senate — Dem., 18; Rep., 15; 1 vacancy. Total, 34
House — Dem., 85; Rep., 75; 3 vacancies. Total, 163

Montana

Governor — Judy Martz, R, $88,190
Lt. Gov. — Karl Ohs, R, $62,471
Sec. of State — Bob Brown, R, $67,485
Atty. Gen. — Mike McGrath, D, $75,550
Legislative Assembly: meets odd years in Jan. at Helena. Members receive $71.83 per legislative day, plus $87.25 per day for expenses while in session.
Senate — Dem., 19; Rep., 31. Total, 50
House — Dem., 42; Rep., 58. Total, 100

Nebraska

Governor — Mike Johanns, R, $85,000
Lt. Gov. — David Heineman, R, $60,000
Sec. of State — John A. Gale, R, $65,000
Atty. Gen. — Don Stenberg, R, $75,000
Treasurer — Lorelee Byrd, R, $60,000
State Auditor — Kate Witek, R, $60,000
Legislature: Unicameral body composed of 49 members who are elected on a nonpartisan ballot and are called senators; meets annually in Jan. at Lincoln. Members receive $12,000 annually, plus expenses.

Nevada

Governor — Kenny C. Guinn, R, $117,000
Lt. Gov. — Lorraine Hunt, R, $50,000
Sec. of State — Dean Heller, R, $80,000
Controller — Kathy Augustine, R, $80,000
Atty. Gen. — Frankie Sue Del Papa, D, $110,000
Treasurer — Brian Krolicki, R, $80,000
Legislature: meets at Carson City odd years starting on 1st Mon. in Feb. for 120 days. Members receive $130 per day salary, plus $80 per day expenses, while in session.
Senate — Dem., 9; Rep., 12. Total, 21
Assembly — Dem., 27; Rep., 15. Total, 42

New Hampshire

Governor — Jeanne Shaheen, D, $100,690
Sec. of State — William M. Gardner, D, $87,380
Atty. Gen. — Philip T. McLaughlin, D, $97,370
Treasurer — Michael A. Ablowich, R, $78,640
General Court (Legislature): meets every year in Jan. at Concord. Members receive $200, presiding officers $250, biannually.
Senate — Dem., 11; Rep., 13. Total, 24
House — Rep., 249; Dem., 140; 1 ind.; 10 vacancies. Total, 400

New Jersey

Governor — James E. McGreevey, D, $83,333
Sec. of State — Regena L. Thomas, D, $133,000
Atty. Gen. — David Samson, D, $133,000
Treasurer — John E. McCormac, $133,000
Legislature: meets throughout the year at Trenton. Members receive $35,000 annually, except president of Senate and speaker of Assembly, who receive 1/3 more.
Senate — Dem., 20; Rep., 20. Total, 40
Assembly — Dem., 44; Rep., 35; 1 vacancy. Total, 80

New Mexico

Governor — Gary E. Johnson, R, $150,000
Lt. Gov. — Walter Bradley, R, $90,000
Sec. of State — Rebecca Vigil-Giron, D, $90,000
Atty. Gen. — Patricia Madrid, D, $100,000
Treasurer — Michael A. Montoya, D, $90,000
Legislature: meets starting on the 3rd Tues. in Jan. at Santa Fe; odd years for 60 days, even years for 30 days. Members receive $145 per day while in session.
Senate — Dem., 24; Rep., 18. Total, 42
House — Dem., 42; Rep., 28. Total, 70

New York

Governor — George E. Pataki, R, $179,000
Lt. Gov. — Mary O. Donohue, R, $151,500
Sec. of State — Randy A. Daniels, D, $120,800
Comptroller — H. Carl McCall, D, $151,500
Atty. Gen. — Eliot Spitzer, D, $151,500
Legislature: meets annually on the 1st Wed. after the 1st Mon. in Jan. at Albany. Members receive $79,500 annually, plus $138 per day expenses.
Senate — Dem., 25; Rep., 36. Total, 61
Assembly — Dem., 99; Rep., 51. Total, 150

North Carolina

Governor — Mike Easley, D, $118,430
Lt. Gov. — Beverly Perdue, D, $104,523
Sec. of State — Elaine F. Marshall, D, $104,523
Atty. Gen. — Roy Cooper, D, $104,523
Treasurer — Richard H. Moore, D, $104,523
General Assembly: meets odd years starting on the 3rd Wed. following the 2nd Mon. in Jan. at Raleigh. Members receive $13,951 annually and an expense allowance of $559 per month, plus subsistence and travel allowance while in session. Also meets in even years for a short session (about 6-8 weeks), usually in May.
Senate — Dem., 35; Rep., 15. Total, 50
House — Dem., 62; Rep., 58. Total, 120

North Dakota

Governor — John Hoeven, R, $85,506
Lt. Gov. — John S. Dalrymple III, R, $66,380
Sec. of State — Alvin A. Jaeger, R, $68,018
Atty. Gen. — Wayne Stenehjem, R, $74,668
Treasurer — Kathi Gilmore, D, $64,235
Legislative Assembly: meets odd years in Jan. at Bismarck. Members receive $250 per month salary, plus $125 per calendar day salary during session and $45 per day expenses plus any additional state or local taxes on lodging, with a limit of $650 per month.
Senate — Dem., 17; Rep., 32. Total, 49
House — Dem., 29; Rep., 69. Total, 98

Ohio

Governor — Bob Taft, R, $122,800
Lt. Gov. — Maureen O'Connor, R, $64,375
Sec. of State — J. Kenneth Blackwell, R, $90,725
Atty. Gen. — Betty D. Montgomery, R, $90,725
Treasurer — Joseph T. Deters, R, $90,725
Auditor — Jim Petro, R, $90,725
General Assembly: begins odd years at Columbus starting on 1st Mon. in Jan. Members receive $51,674 annually.
Senate — Dem., 12; Rep., 21. Total, 33
House — Dem., 40; Rep., 59. Total, 99

Oklahoma

Governor — Frank Keating, R, $110,299
Lt. Gov. — Mary Fallin, R, $85,500
Sec. of State — Mike Hunter, R, $65,000
Atty. Gen. — Drew Edmondson, D, $103,109
Treasurer — Robert Butkin, D, $87,875
Auditor — Clifton Scott, D, $87,875
Legislature: meets annually at noon the first Mon. in Feb. at Oklahoma City. In odd-numbered years, the session includes one day (1st Tuesday after 1st Monday) in Jan. Members receive $38,400 annually.
Senate — Dem., 30; Rep., 18. Total, 48
House — Dem., 52; Rep., 49. Total, 101

Oregon

Governor — John Kitzhaber, D, $93,600
Sec. of State — Bill Bradbury, D, $72,000
Atty. Gen. — Hardy Myers, D, $77,200
Treasurer — Randall Edwards, D, $72,000
Legislative Assembly: meets odd years in Jan. at Salem. Members receive $1,283 monthly, $85 expenses per day during session and when attending meetings during the interim, plus between $450 and $550 expense account during interim.
Senate — Dem., 14; Rep., 16. Total, 30
House — Dem., 28; Rep., 32. Total, 60

Pennsylvania

Governor — Mark Schweiker, R, $142,142
Lt. Gov. — Robert C. Jubelirer, R, $119,399
Sec. of the Commonwealth — C. Michael Weaver, R, $102,343
Atty. Gen. — Mike Fisher, R, $118,262
Treasurer — Barbara Hafer, R, $118,262
General Assembly: convenes annually on the 1st Tues. in Jan. at Harrisburg. Members receive $63,629 annually, plus expenses.
Senate — Dem., 21; Rep., 28; 1 vacancy. Total, 50
House — Dem., 98; Rep., 105. Total, 203

Rhode Island

Governor — Lincoln C. Almond, R, $95,000
Lt. Gov. — Charles J. Fogarty, D, $80,000
Sec. of State — Edward S. Inman III, D, $80,000
Atty. Gen. — Sheldon Whitehouse, D, $85,000
Treasurer — Paul J. Tavares, D, $80,000
General Assembly: meets annually in Jan. at Providence. Members receive $10,000 annually.
Senate — Dem., 44; Rep., 6. Total, 50
House — Dem., 85; Rep., 15. Total, 100

South Carolina

Governor — Jim Hodges, D, $106,078
Lt. Gov. — Robert L. Peeler, R, $46,545
Sec. of State — Jim Miles, R, $92,007
Comptroller Gen. — James A. Lander, D, $92,007
Atty. Gen. — Charles M. Condon, R, $92,007
Treasurer — Grady L. Patterson Jr., $92,007
General Assembly: meets annually on the 2nd Tues. in Jan. at Columbia. Members receive $10,400 annually, plus $130 per day for expenses.
Senate — Dem., 21; Rep., 24; 1 vacancy. Total, 46
House — Dem., 54; Rep., 70. Total, 124

South Dakota

Governor — William J. Janklow, R, $98,250
Lt. Gov. — Carole Hillard, R, $71,321
Sec. of State — Joyce Hazeltine, R, $66,757
Treasurer — Dick Butler, D, $66,757
Atty. Gen. — Mark Barnett, R, $83,425
Auditor — Vernon Larson, R, $66,757
Comm. of School & Public Lands — Curt Johnson, D, $66,757
Legislature: meets annually beginning the 2nd Tues. in Jan. at Pierre, for 40-day session in odd-numbered years, and 35-day session in even-numbered years. Members receive $12,000 per 2-year term plus $110 per legislative day or $110 for a statute committee.
Senate — Dem., 11; Rep., 24. Total, 35
House — Dem., 20; Rep., 50. Total, 70

Tennessee

Governor — Don Sundquist, R, $85,000
Lt. Gov. — John S. Wilder, D, $49,500
Sec. of State — Riley C. Darnell, D, $124,200
Comptroller — John Morgan, D, $124,200
Atty. Gen. — Paul Summers, D, $114,528
General Assembly: meets annually on the 2nd Tues. in Jan. at Nashville. Members receive $16,500 annual salary, plus $114 per day expenses while in session.
Senate — Dem., 18; Rep., 15. Total, 33
House — Dem., 57; Rep., 42. Total, 99

Texas

Governor — Rick Perry, R, $115,345
Lt. Gov. — Bill Ratliff, R, $7,200
Sec. of State — Gwyn Shea, R, $117,516
Comptroller — Carole Keeton Rylander, R, $92,217
Atty. Gen. — John Cornyn, R, $92,217
Railroad Commissioners — Michael L. Williams, R, Chair; Tony Garza, R; Charles R. Matthews, R; $92,217
Legislature: meets odd years in Jan. at Austin. Members receive $7,200 annually, plus $95 per day expenses while in session.
Senate — Dem., 15; Rep., 16. Total, 31
House — Dem., 78; Rep., 72. Total, 150

Utah

Governor — Michael O. Leavitt, R, $100,600
Lt. Gov. — Olene S. Walker, R, $78,200
Atty. Gen. — Mark Shurtleff, R, $84,600
Auditor — Auston G. Johnson, R, $80,700
Treasurer — Edward T. Alter, R, $78,200
Legislature: convenes for 45 days on 3rd Mon. in Jan. each year at Salt Lake City. Members receive $120 per day, plus $38 a day expenses.
Senate — Dem., 9; Rep., 20. Total, 29
House — Dem., 24; Rep., 51. Total, 75

Vermont

Governor — Howard Dean, D, $125,572
Lt. Gov. — Douglas A. Racine, D, $53,303
Sec. of State — Deborah L. Markowitz, D, $79,624
Atty. Gen. — William H. Sorrell, D, $95,322
Treasurer — James H. Douglas, R, $79,624
Auditor — Elizabeth M. Ready, D, $79,624
General Assembly: meets in Jan. at Montpelier (annual and biennial session). Members receive $536 per week while in session plus $105 per day for special session, plus expenses.
Senate — Dem., 16; Rep., 14. Total, 30
House — Dem., 63; Rep., 82; Prog. Coalition, 4; 1 ind. Total, 150

Virginia

Governor — Mark R. Warner, D, $124,855
Lt. Gov. — Timothy M. Kaine, D, $36,321
Atty. Gen. — Jerry W. Kilgore, R, $110,667
Sec. of the Commonwealth — Anita A. Rimler, D, $124,435
Treasurer — Jody M. Wagner, D, $112,653
General Assembly: meets annually in Jan. at Richmond. Members receive $18,000 (senate), $17,640 (assembly) annually, plus expense and mileage allowances.
Senate — Dem., 17; Rep., 22, 1 vacancy. Total, 40
House — Dem., 34; Rep., 63; 2 ind.; 1 vacancy. Total, 100

Washington

Governor — Gary Locke, D, $142,286
Lt. Gov. — Brad Owen, D, $74,377
Sec. of State — Sam Reed, R, $91,048
Atty. Gen. — Christine Gregoire, D, $129,351
Treasurer — Mike Murphy, D, $99,708
Legislature: meets annually in Jan. at Olympia. Members receive $33,556 annually, plus $82 per diem while in session, and $82 per diem for attending meetings during interim.
Senate — Dem., 25; Rep., 24. Total, 49
House — Dem., 50; Rep., 48. Total, 98

West Virginia

Governor — Bob Wise, D, $90,000
Sec. of State — Joe Manchin III, D, $65,000
Atty. Gen. — Darrell McGraw, D, $75,000
Treasurer — John D. Perdue, D, $70,000
Comm. of Agric. — Gus Douglass, D, $70,000
Auditor — Glen B. Gainer III, D, $75,000
Legislature: meets annually in Jan. at Charleston, except after gubernatorial elections, when the legislature meets in Feb. Members receive $15,000 annually.
Senate — Dem., 28; Rep., 6. Total, 34
House — Dem., 75; Rep., 25. Total, 100

Wisconsin

Governor — Scott McCallum, R, $122,406
Lt. Gov. — Margaret A. Farrow, R, $60,183
Sec. of State — Douglas La Follette, D, $54,610
Treasurer — Jack Voight, R, $54,610
Atty. Gen. — James E. Doyle, D, $112,274
Legislature: meets in Jan. at Madison. Members receive $44,233 annually, plus $88 per day expenses.
Senate — Dem., 18; Rep., 15. Total, 33
Assembly — Dem., 44; Rep., 53; 2 vacancies. Total, 99

Wyoming

Governor — Jim Geringer, R, $95,000
Sec. of State — Joseph B. Meyer, R, $77,500
Atty. Gen. — Horace MacMillan, R, $95,000
Treasurer — Cynthia Lummis, R, $77,500
State Auditor — Max Maxfield, R, $77,500
Legislature: meets odd years in Jan., even years in Feb., at Cheyenne. Members receive $125 per day while in session, plus $80 per day for expenses.
Senate — Dem., 10; Rep., 20. Total, 30
House — Dem., 14; Rep., 46. Total, 60

VITAL STATISTICS

Recent Trends in Vital Statistics

Source: National Center for Health Statistics, U.S. Dept. of Health and Human Services; latest years available

Highlights

Provisional data for 2001 reported by the National Center for Health Statistics show that the teen birth rate continued to decline for the 10th straight year (45.9 births per 1,000 women aged 15-19 years in 2001, compared with 62.1 in 1991). Marriage rates have declined slightly, as have divorce rates, according to provisional 2001 data. Life expectancy for all Americans at birth rose to 76.9 in 2000, up from the previous all-time high of 76.7 years reached in 1998 and again in 1999.

Births

An estimated 4,028,000 babies were born in the U.S. in 2001, a drop from 4,058,814 births in 2000. The birth rate declined to 14.5 per 1,000 population in 2001, compared to 14.7 in 2000. The fertility rate (number of live births per 1,000 women aged 15-44 years) for 2001 was estimated at 67.0, down from the 2000 rate of 67.5.

Deaths

The number of deaths during 2001 was estimated at 2,419,000, slightly higher than during the previous year (2,403,351). Provisional data for 2001 showed a death rate of 8.7 per 1,000 population, unchanged from the previous year. The provisional infant mortality rate of 6.9 infant deaths per 1,000 live births in 2001 was the same as the revised number for 2000.

Natural Increase

As a result of natural increase (the excess of births over deaths) by itself, an estimated 1,609,000 persons were added to the population in 2001. The rate of increase (5.8 per 1,000 population) was down slightly from 2000 (6.0). The drop reflected a falling off in the fertility rate and the birth rate, according to provisional 2001 data.

Marriages

An estimated 2,327,000 marriages were performed in 2001, a minute drop (less than 1/10 of a percent) from the 2,329,000 performed in 2000. The marriage rate for 2001 (8.4 per 1,000 population) was down from the 2000 rate of 8.5 (since the population was larger in 2001, essentially the same number of marriages was led to a slightly lower rate).

Divorces

Provisional 2001 data give a divorce rate of 4.0 per 1,000 population, down from the 4.1 of 2000, and a low-water mark for the last quarter century. The NCHS no longer publishes U.S. totals. California, Colorado, Indiana and Louisiana are not included in calculations of the divorce rate.

Births and Deaths in the U.S.

Source: National Center for Health Statistics, U.S. Dept. of Health and Human Services

BIRTHS

Year	Total number	Rate
1960	4,257,850	23.7
1970	3,731,386	18.4
1980	3,612,258	15.9
1990	4,158,212	16.7
1991	4,110,907	16.3
1992	4,065,014	15.9
1993	4,000,240	15.5
1994	3,952,767	15.2
1995	3,899,589	14.8
1996	3,891,494	14.7
1997	3,880,894	14.5
1998	3,941,553	14.6
1999	3,959,417	14.5
2000	4,058,814	14.7
2001 (P)	4,028,000	14.5

DEATHS

Year	Total number	Rate
1960	1,711,982	9.5
1970	1,921,031	9.5
1980	1,989,841	8.7
1990	2,148,463	8.6
1991	2,169,518	8.6
1992	2,175,613	8.5
1993	2,268,000	8.8
1994	2,278,994	8.8
1995	2,312,132	8.8
1996	2,314,690	8.7
1997	2,314,245	8.6
1998	2,337,258	8.7
1999	2,391,399	8.8
2000	2,403,351	8.7
2001 (P)	2,419,000	8.7

(P) = provisional data. **NOTE:** Statistics cover only events occurring within the U.S. and exclude fetal deaths. Rates per 1,000 population; enumerated as of Apr. 1 for 1960 and 1970; estimated as of July 1 for all other years. Beginning 1970 statistics exclude births and deaths occurring to nonresidents of the U.S. Data include revisions.

Marriage and Divorce Rates, 1921-2001

Source: National Center for Health Statistics, U.S. Dept. of Health and Human Services

The U.S. marriage rate dipped during the Depression and peaked sharply just after World War II; the trend after that has been more gradual. The divorce rate has generally risen since the 1920s; it peaked at 5.3 per 1,000 in 1981, before declining somewhat. The graph below shows marriage and divorce rates per 1,000 population since 1921. Some data provisional.

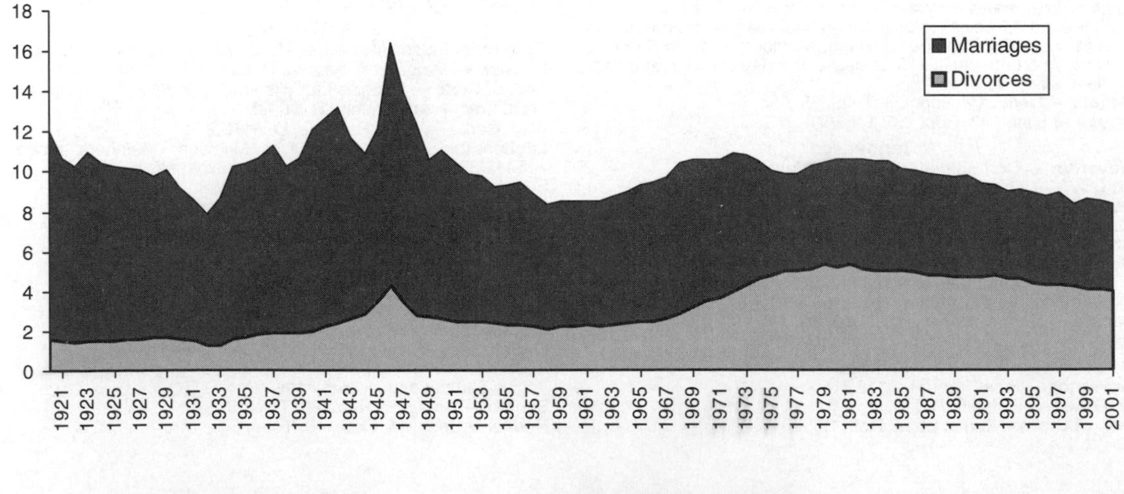

Births and Deaths, by States, 1999-2000

Source: National Center for Health Statistics, U.S. Dept. of Health and Human Services

	LIVE BIRTHS				DEATHS			
	2000		1999		2000		1999	
	Number	Rate	Number	Rate	Number	Rate	Number	Rate
Alabama	63,299	14.4	62,122	14.2	45,062	1,027.0	44,806	1,025.3
Alaska	9,974	16.0	9,950	16.1	2,914	468.4	2,708	437.1
Arizona	85,273	17.5	81,145	17.0	40,500	829.5	40,050	838.2
Arkansas	37,783	14.7	36,729	14.4	28,217	1,095.2	27,925	1,094.5
California	531,959	15.8	518,508	15.6	229,551	682.5	229,380	692.0
Colorado	65,438	15.8	62,167	15.3	27,288	659.7	27,114	668.5
Connecticut	43,026	13.0	43,310	13.2	30,129	913.8	29,446	897.2
Delaware	11,051	14.5	10,676	14.2	6,875	902.0	6,666	884.6
District of Columbia	7,666	14.8	7,522	14.5	6,001	1,157.7	6,076	1,170.7
Florida	204,125	13.3	197,023	13.0	164,395	1,072.2	163,224	1,080.1
Georgia	132,644	16.7	126,717	16.3	63,870	804.1	62,028	796.4
Hawaii	17,551	14.9	17,038	14.4	8,290	703.0	8,270	697.6
Idaho	20,366	16.0	19,872	15.9	9,563	751.1	9,579	765.3
Illinois	185,036	15.2	182,068	15.0	106,634	875.1	108,436	894.1
Indiana	87,699	14.7	86,031	14.5	55,469	928.1	55,303	930.6
Iowa	38,266	13.3	37,558	13.1	28,060	975.2	28,411	990.1
Kansas	39,666	14.9	38,782	14.6	24,717	927.2	24,472	922.1
Kentucky	56,029	14.1	54,403	13.7	39,504	991.2	39,321	992.7
Louisiana	67,898	15.5	67,136	15.4	41,138	040.0	41,238	043.2
Maine	13,603	10.8	13,616	10.9	12,354	981.6	12,261	978.5
Maryland	74,316	14.2	71,967	13.9	43,753	838.4	43,089	833.2
Massachusetts	81,614	13.2	80,939	13.1	56,681	913.6	55,840	904.3
Michigan	136,171	13.7	133,607	13.5	86,953	876.7	87,232	884.4
Minnesota	67,604	14.0	65,990	13.8	37,690	780.7	38,537	807.0
Mississippi	44,075	15.8	42,684	15.4	28,654	1,028.1	28,185	1,018.0
Missouri	76,463	13.9	75,432	13.8	54,865	997.1	55,931	1,022.8
Montana	10,957	12.3	10,785	12.2	8,096	911.8	8,128	920.7
Nebraska	24,646	14.8	23,907	14.3	14,992	897.5	15,579	935.1
Nevada	30,829	16.4	29,362	16.2	15,261	811.6	15,082	833.6
New Hampshire	14,609	12.0	14,041	11.7	9,697	797.5	9,537	794.0
New Jersey	115,632	14.1	114,105	14.0	74,800	911.7	73,981	908.5
New Mexico	27,223	15.6	27,191	15.6	13,425	768.1	13,676	786.0
New York	258,737	14.2	255,612	14.0	158,203	865.5	159,927	878.9
North Carolina	120,311	15.5	113,795	14.9	71,905	928.5	69,600	909.7
North Dakota	7,676	12.2	7,639	12.1	5,856	930.6	6,103	963.1
Ohio	155,472	13.8	152,584	13.6	108,125	959.4	108,517	964.0
Oklahoma	49,782	14.7	49,010	14.6	35,079	1,037.8	34,700	1,033.3
Oregon	45,804	13.7	45,204	13.6	29,552	884.5	29,422	887.2
Pennsylvania	146,281	12.2	145,347	12.1	130,813	1,091.5	130,283	1,086.2
Rhode Island	12,505	12.6	12,366	12.5	10,027	1,006.6	9,708	979.8
South Carolina	56,114	14.3	54,948	14.1	36,948	941.5	36,053	927.8
South Dakota	10,345	14.0	10,524	14.4	7,021	952.3	6,953	948.4
Tennessee	79,611	14.4	77,803	14.2	55,246	998.4	53,765	980.5
Texas	363,414	17.8	349,245	17.4	149,939	735.4	146,858	732.7
Utah	47,353	21.9	46,290	21.7	12,364	571.2	12,058	566.1
Vermont	6,500	10.9	6,567	11.1	5,127	857.6	4,993	840.9
Virginia	98,938	14.2	95,469	13.9	56,282	807.4	55,320	804.9
Washington	81,036	13.9	79,586	13.8	43,941	756.2	43,865	762.0
West Virginia	20,865	11.6	20,728	11.5	21,114	1,171.5	21,049	1,164.9
Wisconsin	69,326	13.1	68,208	13.0	46,461	877.4	46,672	888.9
Wyoming	6,253	13.0	6,129	12.8	3,920	815.1	4,042	842.8
United States	**4,058,814**	**14.7**	**3,959,417**	**14.5**	**2,403,351**	**873.1**	**2,391,399**	**877.0**

Note: Births are per 1,000 population. Death rates are per 100,000 population.

Birth Rates; Fertility Rates by Age of Mother, 1950-2000

Source: National Center for Health Statistics, U.S. Dept. of Health and Human Services

			AGE OF MOTHER									
			10-14 years	15-19 years			20-24 years	25-29 years	30-34 years	35-39 years	40-44 years	45-49 years
	Birth rate[1]	Fertility rate[2]		Total	15-17	18-19						
			Live births per 1,000 women by age group									
1950	24.1	106.2	1.0	81.6	40.7	132.7	196.6	166.1	103.7	52.9	15.1	1.2
1960	23.7	118.0	0.8	89.1	43.9	166.7	258.1	197.4	112.7	56.2	15.5	0.9
1970	18.4	87.9	1.2	68.3	38.8	114.7	167.8	145.1	73.3	31.7	8.1	0.5
1980	15.9	68.4	1.1	53.0	32.5	82.1	115.1	112.9	61.9	19.8	3.9	0.2
1990	16.7	70.9	1.4	59.9	37.5	88.6	116.5	120.2	80.8	31.7	5.5	0.2
1991	16.3	69.6	1.4	62.1	38.7	94.4	115.7	118.2	79.5	32.0	5.5	0.2
1992	15.9	68.9	1.4	60.7	37.8	94.5	114.6	117.4	80.2	32.5	5.9	0.3
1993	15.5	67.6	1.4	59.6	37.8	92.1	112.6	115.5	80.8	32.9	6.1	0.3
1994	15.2	66.7	1.4	58.9	37.6	91.5	111.1	113.9	81.5	33.7	6.4	0.3
1995	14.8	65.6	1.3	56.8	36.0	89.1	109.8	112.2	82.5	34.3	6.6	0.3
1996	14.7	65.3	1.2	54.4	33.8	86.0	110.4	113.1	83.9	35.3	6.8	0.3
1997	14.5	65.0	1.1	52.3	32.1	83.6	110.4	113.8	85.3	36.1	7.1	0.4
1998	14.6	65.6	1.0	51.1	30.4	82.0	111.2	115.9	87.4	37.4	7.3	0.4
1999	14.5	65.9	0.9	49.6	28.7	80.3	111.0	117.8	89.6	38.3	7.4	0.4
2000	14.7	67.5	0.9	48.5	27.4	79.2	112.3	121.4	94.1	40.4	7.9	0.5

(1) Live births per 1,000 population. (2) Live births per 1,000 women 15-44 years of age.

Nonmarital Childbearing in the U.S., 1970-2000

Source: National Center for Health Statistics, U.S. Dept. of Health and Human Services

Race of Mother	1970	1975	1980	1985	1990	1993	1994	1995	1996	1997	1998	1999	2000
	Percent of live births to unmarried mothers												
All races	10.7	14.3	18.4	22.0	28.0	31.0	32.6	32.2	32.4	32.4	32.8	33.0	33.2
White	5.5	7.1	11.2	14.7	20.4	23.6	25.4	25.3	25.7	25.8	26.3	26.8	27.1
Black	37.5	49.5	56.1	61.2	66.5	68.7	70.4	69.9	69.8	69.2	69.1	68.9	68.5
American Indian or Alaska Native	22.4	32.7	39.2	46.8	53.6	55.8	57.0	57.2	58.0	58.7	59.3	58.9	58.4
Asian or Pacific Islander	—	—	7.3	9.5	13.2	15.7	16.2	16.3	16.7	15.6	15.6	15.4	14.8
Hispanic origin (selected states)[1,2]	—	—	23.6	29.5	36.7	40.0	43.1	40.8	40.7	40.9	41.6	42.2	42.7
White, non-Hispanic (selected states)[1]	—	—	9.6	12.4	16.9	19.5	20.8	21.2	21.5	21.5	21.9	22.1	22.1
Black, non-Hispanic (selected states)[1]	—	—	57.3	62.1	66.7	68.9	70.7	70.0	70.0	69.4	69.3	69.1	68.7
Live births to unmarried mothers (in thousands)	399	448	666	828	1,165	1,240	1,290	1,254	1,260	1,257	1,294	1,309	1,347
Maternal age	**Percent distribution of live births to unmarried mothers**												
Under 20 years	50.1	52.1	40.8	33.8	30.9	29.7	30.5	30.9	30.4	30.7	30.1	29.3	28.0
20–24 years	31.8	29.9	35.6	36.3	34.7	35.4	34.8	34.5	34.2	34.9	35.6	36.4	37.4
25 years and over	18.1	18.0	23.5	29.9	34.4	34.9	34.6	34.7	35.3	34.4	34.3	34.3	34.6
	Live births per 1,000 unmarried women 15–44 years of age[3]												
All races and origins	26.4	24.5	29.4	32.8	43.8	45.3	46.9	45.1	44.8	44.0	44.3	44.4	45.2
White[4]	13.9	12.4	18.1	22.5	32.9	35.9	38.3	37.5	37.6	37.0	37.5	38.1	38.9
Black[4]	95.5	84.2	81.1	77.0	90.5	84.0	82.1	75.9	74.4	73.4	73.3	71.5	72.5
Hispanic origin (selected states)[1,2]	—	—	—	—	89.6	95.2	101.2	95.0	93.2	91.4	90.1	93.4	97.3
White, non-Hispanic	—	—	—	—	—	—	28.5	28.2	28.3	27.0	27.4	27.9	27.9

— Data not available. (1) Data for Hispanics and non-Hispanics are affected by expansion of the reporting area for an Hispanic-origin item on the birth certificate and by immigration. These 2 factors affect numbers of events, composition of the Hispanic population, and maternal and infant health characteristics. The states in the reporting area increased from 22 in 1980, to 23 and the District of Columbia in 1983, 48 and DC by 1990, and 50 and DC by 1993. (2) Includes mothers of all races. (3) Rates computed by relating births to unmarried mothers, regardless of mother's age, to unmarried women 15–44 years of age. (4) For 1970 and 1975, birth rates are by race of child.

Top 20 Countries for U.S. Foreign Adoptions, 1991-2001

Source: Holt International Children's Service

Country	2001	2000	1999	1998	1997	1996	1995	1994	1993	1992	1991
China	4,681	5,053	4,101	4,206	3,597	3,333	2,130	787	330	206	61
Russia	4,279	4,269	4,348	4,491	3,816	2,454	1,896	1,530	746	324	0
South Korea	1,770	1,794	2,008	1,829	1,654	1,516	1,666	1,795	1,775	1,840	1,818
Guatemala	1,609	1,518	1,002	911	788	427	449	436	512	418	329
Ukraine	1,246	659	321	180	NA	1	4	164	273	55	0
Romania	782	1,122	895	406	621	555	275	199	97	121	2,594
Vietnam	737	724	709	603	425	354	318	220	110	22	37
Kazakhstan	672	399	113	NA	NA	0	0	0	0	0	0
India	543	503	499	478	349	380	371	412	331	352	445
Cambodia	407	402	249	249	66	32	10	3	1	15	60
Bulgaria	297	214	221	151	148	163	110	97	133	91	9
Colombia	266	246	231	351	233	255	350	351	426	404	521
Philippines	219	173	195	200	163	229	298	314	360	357	393
Haiti	192	131	96	121	144	68	49	61	51	16	49
Ethiopia	158	95	103	96	82	44	63	54	30	37	15
Poland	86	83	97	77	78	62	30	94	70	109	92
Thailand	74	88	77	84	NA	55	53	47	69	86	131
Mexico	73	106	137	168	152	76	83	85	91	91	97
Jamaica	51	NA	NA	NA	NA	NA	NA	NA	NA	NA	NA
Liberia	51	NA	NA	NA	NA	NA	NA	NA	NA	NA	NA

NA = Not available.

Numbers of Multiple Births in the U.S., 1990-2000

Source: National Center for Health Statistics, U.S. Dept. of Health and Human Services

The general upward trend in multiple births reflects greater numbers of births to older women and increased use of fertility drugs.

Year	Twins	Triplets	Quadruplets	Quintuplets and higher
1990	93,865	2,830	185	13
1992	95,372	3,547	310	26
1993	96,445	3,834	277	57
1994	97,064	4,233	315	46
1995	96,736	4,551	365	57
1996	100,750	5,298	560	81
1997	104,137	6,148	510	79
1998	110,670	6,919	627	79
1999	114,307	6,742	512	67
2000	118,916	6,742	506	77

10 Leading Causes of Infant Death in the U.S., 2000

Source: National Center for Health Statistics, U.S. Dept. of Health and Human Services

Cause	Number	Rate[1]	% change 1999-2000[2]
Congenital malformations, deformations, and chromosomal abnormalities	5,743	141.5	2.4
Disorders relating to short gestation and low birthweight, not elsewhere classified	4,397	108.3	–2.3
Sudden infant death syndrome	2,523	62.2	–7.0
Newborn affected by maternal complications of pregnancy	1,404	34.6	–2.0
Newborn affected by complications of placenta, cord, and membranes	1,062	26.2	–12.1
Respiratory distress of newborn	999	24.6	1.2
Accidents (unintentional injuries)	881	21.7	1.9
Bacterial sepsis[3] of newborn	768	18.9	8.0
Diseases of the circulatory system	663	16.3	–3.0
Intrauterine hypoxia and birth asphyxia	630	15.5	—
All other causes	8,965	220.9	NA
All causes	**28,035**	**690.7**	**–2.1**

NA = Not applicable. — = no change. (1) Infant deaths per 100,000 live births. (2) Refers to change in mortality rates from 1999 to 2000. (3) Toxic condition resulting from the spread of bacteria.

U.S. Infant Mortality Rates, by Race and Sex, 1960-2000

Source: National Center for Health Statistics, U.S. Dept. of Health and Human Services

Year	ALL RACES Total	ALL RACES Male	ALL RACES Female	WHITE Total	WHITE Male	WHITE Female	BLACK Total	BLACK Male	BLACK Female
1960	26.0	29.3	22.6	22.9	26.0	19.6	44.3	49.1	39.4
1970	20.0	22.4	17.5	17.8	20.0	15.4	32.6	36.2	29.0
1980	12.6	13.9	11.2	11.0	12.3	9.6	21.4	23.3	19.4
1985	10.6	11.9	9.3	9.3	10.6	8.0	18.2	19.9	16.5
1986	10.4	11.5	9.1	8.9	10.0	7.8	18.0	20.0	16.0
1987	10.1	11.2	8.9	8.6	9.6	7.6	17.9	19.6	16.0
1988	10.0	11.0	8.9	8.5	9.5	7.4	17.6	19.0	16.1
1989	9.8	10.8	8.8	8.1	9.0	7.1	18.6	20.0	17.2
1990	9.2	10.3	8.1	7.6	8.5	6.6	18.0	19.6	16.2
1991	8.9	10.0	7.8	7.3	8.3	6.3	17.6	19.4	15.7
1992	8.5	9.4	7.6	6.9	7.7	6.1	16.8	18.4	15.3
1993	8.4	9.3	7.4	6.8	7.6	6.0	16.5	18.3	14.7
1994	8.0	8.8	7.2	6.6	7.2	5.9	15.8	17.5	14.1
1995	7.6	8.3	6.8	6.3	7.0	5.6	15.1	16.3	13.9
1996	7.3	8.0	6.6	6.1	6.7	5.4	14.7	16.0	13.3
1997	7.2	8.0	6.5	6.0	6.7	5.4	14.2	15.5	12.8
1998	7.2	7.8	6.5	6.0	6.5	5.4	14.3	15.7	12.8
1999	7.1	7.7	6.4	5.8	6.4	5.2	14.6	15.9	13.2
2000	6.9	7.6	6.2	5.7	6.2	5.1	14.1	15.5	12.6

Note: Rates per 1,000 live births.

Years of Life Expected at Birth in U.S., 1900-2000

Source: National Center for Health Statistics, U.S. Dept. of Health and Human Services

Year[1]	ALL RACES Total	ALL RACES Male	ALL RACES Female	WHITE Total	WHITE Male	WHITE Female	BLACK Total	BLACK Male	BLACK Female
1900	47.3	46.3	48.3	47.6	46.6	48.7	NA	NA	NA
1910	50.0	48.4	51.8	50.3	48.6	52.0	NA	NA	NA
1920	54.1	53.6	54.6	54.9	54.4	55.6	NA	NA	NA
1930	59.7	58.1	61.6	61.4	59.7	63.5	NA	NA	NA
1940	62.9	60.8	65.2	64.2	62.1	66.6	NA	NA	NA
1950	68.2	65.6	71.1	69.1	66.5	72.2	NA	NA	NA
1960	69.7	66.6	73.1	70.6	67.4	74.1	NA	NA	NA
1970	70.8	67.1	74.7	71.7	68.0	75.6	64.1	60.0	68.3
1975	72.6	68.8	76.6	73.4	69.5	77.3	68.8	62.4	71.3
1980	73.7	70.0	77.5	74.4	70.7	78.1	68.1	63.8	72.5
1981	74.2	70.4	77.8	74.8	71.1	78.4	68.9	64.5	73.2
1982	74.5	70.9	78.1	75.1	71.5	78.7	69.4	65.1	73.6
1983	74.6	71.0	78.1	75.2	71.7	78.7	69.4	65.2	73.5
1984	74.7	71.2	78.2	75.3	71.8	78.7	69.5	65.3	73.6
1985	74.7	71.2	78.2	75.3	71.9	78.7	69.3	65.0	73.4
1986	74.8	71.3	78.3	75.4	72.0	78.8	69.1	64.8	73.4
1987	75.0	71.5	78.4	75.6	72.2	78.9	69.1	64.7	73.4
1988	74.9	71.5	78.3	75.6	72.3	78.9	68.9	64.4	73.2
1989	75.1	71.7	78.5	75.9	72.5	79.2	68.8	64.3	73.3
1990	75.4	71.8	78.8	76.1	72.9	79.4	69.1	64.5	73.6
1991	75.5	72.0	78.9	76.3	72.9	79.2	69.3	64.6	73.8
1992	75.5	72.1	78.9	76.4	73.0	79.5	69.6	65.0	73.9
1993	75.5	72.1	78.9	76.3	73.0	79.5	69.2	64.6	73.7
1994	75.7	72.4	79.0	76.5	73.3	79.6	69.5	64.9	73.9
1995	75.8	72.5	78.9	76.5	73.4	79.6	69.6	65.2	73.9
1996	76.1	73.1	79.1	76.8	73.9	79.7	70.2	66.1	74.2
1997	76.5	73.6	79.4	77.1	74.3	79.9	71.1	67.2	74.7
1998	76.7	73.8	79.5	77.3	74.5	80.0	71.3	67.6	74.8
1999	76.7	73.9	79.4	77.3	74.6	79.9	71.4	67.8	74.7
2000	76.9	74.1	79.5	77.4	74.8	80.0	71.7	68.2	74.9

NA = Not available. (1) Data prior to 1940 for death-registration states only.

U.S. Life Expectancy at Selected Ages, 2000

Source: National Center for Health Statistics, U.S. Dept. of Health and Human Services

Exact age in years	ALL RACES[1] Both sexes	ALL RACES[1] Male	ALL RACES[1] Female	WHITE Both sexes	WHITE Male	WHITE Female	BLACK Both sexes	BLACK Male	BLACK Female
0	76.9	74.1	79.5	77.4	74.8	80.0	71.7	68.2	74.9
1	76.4	73.7	79.0	76.9	74.3	79.4	71.7	68.3	74.9
5	72.5	69.8	75.1	73.0	70.3	75.5	67.9	64.4	71.0
10	67.6	64.9	70.1	68.0	65.4	70.5	63.0	59.5	66.1
15	62.6	59.9	65.2	63.1	60.5	65.6	58.1	54.6	61.2
20	57.8	55.2	60.3	58.3	55.7	60.7	53.3	49.9	56.3
25	53.1	50.6	55.4	53.5	51.1	55.8	48.7	45.5	51.5
30	48.3	45.9	50.6	48.7	46.4	50.9	44.1	41.1	46.8
35	43.6	41.3	45.8	44.0	41.7	46.1	39.6	36.6	42.1
40	38.9	36.7	41.0	39.3	37.1	41.3	35.1	32.3	37.5
45	34.4	32.2	36.3	34.7	32.6	36.6	30.8	28.1	33.1
50	30.0	27.9	31.8	30.2	28.2	32.0	26.8	24.2	28.9
55	25.7	23.8	27.4	25.9	24.0	27.5	23.0	20.7	24.9
60	21.6	19.9	23.1	21.8	20.0	23.2	19.4	17.5	21.0
65	17.9	16.3	19.2	17.9	16.3	19.2	16.2	14.5	17.4
70	14.4	13.0	15.5	14.4	13.0	15.5	13.1	11.7	14.1
75	11.3	10.1	12.1	11.3	10.1	12.1	10.5	9.4	11.2
80	8.6	7.6	9.1	8.5	7.6	9.1	8.2	7.3	8.6
85	6.3	5.6	6.7	6.2	5.5	6.6	6.3	5.7	6.5
90	4.7	4.1	4.8	4.5	4.0	4.7	4.8	4.5	4.8
95	3.5	3.1	3.5	3.3	2.9	3.3	3.7	3.6	3.6
100	2.6	2.4	2.7	2.4	2.2	2.4	2.8	2.9	2.7

(1) Includes races other than white and black.

The 10 Leading Causes of Death, 2000

Source: National Center for Health Statistics, U.S. Dept. of Health and Human Services

	Number	Death rate[1]	Percentage of total deaths
ALL CAUSES	**2,403,351**	**873.1**	**100.0**
1. Heart disease	710,760	258.2	29.6
2. Cancer	553,091	200.9	23.0
3. Stroke	167,661	60.9	7.0
4. Chronic lower respiratory diseases	122,009	44.3	5.1
5. Accidents (unintentional injuries)	97,900	35.6	4.1
6. Diabetes mellitus	69,301	25.2	2.9
7. Influenza and pneumonia	65,313	23.7	2.7
8. Alzheimer's disease	49,558	18.0	2.1
9. Kidney disease	37,251	13.5	1.5
10. Blood poisoning	31,224	11.3	1.3

(1) Per 100,000 population.

U.S. Abortions, by State, 1992-96

Source: Alan Guttmacher Institute, New York, NY; latest year reported

	Number of reported abortions[1]			Rate per 1,000 women[2]			% change
	1992	1995	1996	1992	1995	1996	1992-96
TOTAL U.S.	**1,528,930**	**1,363,690**	**1,365,730**	**25.9**	**22.9**	**22.9**	**–12**
Alabama	17,450	14,580	15,150	18.2	15.0	15.6	–15
Alaska	2,370	1,990	2,040	16.5	14.2	14.6	–11
Arizona	20,600	18,120	19,310	24.1	19.1	19.8	–18
Arkansas	7,130	6,010	6,200	13.5	11.1	11.4	–15
California	304,230	240,240	237,830	42.1	33.4	33.0	–22
Colorado	19,880	15,690	18,310	23.6	18.0	20.9	–12
Connecticut	19,720	16,680	16,230	26.2	23.0	22.5	–14
Delaware	5,730	5,790	4,090	35.2	34.4	24.1	–32
District of Columbia	21,320	21,090	20,790	138.4	151.7	154.5	12
Florida	84,680	87,500	94,050	30.0	30.0	32.0	7
Georgia	39,680	36,940	37,320	24.0	21.2	21.1	–12
Hawaii	12,190	7,510	6,930	46.0	29.3	27.3	–41
Idaho	1,710	1,500	1,600	7.2	5.8	6.1	–15
Illinois	68,420	68,160	69,390	25.4	25.6	26.1	3
Indiana	15,840	14,030	14,850	12.0	10.6	11.2	–7
Iowa	6,970	6,040	5,780	11.4	9.8	9.4	–17
Kansas	12,570	10,310	10,630	22.4	18.3	18.9	–16
Kentucky	10,000	7,770	8,470	11.4	8.8	9.6	–16
Louisiana	13,600	14,820	14,740	13.4	14.7	14.7	10
Maine	4,200	2,690	2,700	14.7	9.6	9.7	–34
Maryland	31,260	30,520	31,310	26.4	25.6	26.3	0
Massachusetts	40,660	41,190	41,160	28.4	29.2	29.3	3
Michigan	55,580	49,370	48,780	25.2	22.6	22.3	–11
Minnesota	16,180	14,910	14,660	15.6	14.2	13.9	–11
Mississippi	7,550	3,420	4,490	12.4	5.5	7.2	–42
Missouri	13,510	10,540	10,810	11.6	8.9	9.1	–21
Montana	3,300	3,010	2,900	18.2	16.2	15.6	–14
Nebraska	5,580	4,360	4,460	15.7	12.1	12.3	–22
Nevada	13,300	15,600	15,450	44.2	46.7	44.6	1
New Hampshire	3,890	3,240	3,470	14.6	12.0	12.7	–13
New Jersey	55,320	61,130	63,100	31.0	34.5	35.8	16
New Mexico	6,410	5,450	5,470	17.7	14.4	14.4	–19
New York	195,390	176,420	167,600	46.2	42.8	41.1	–11
North Carolina	36,180	34,600	33,550	22.4	21.0	20.2	–10
North Dakota	1,490	1,330	1,290	10.7	9.6	9.4	–13
Ohio	49,520	40,940	42,870	19.5	16.2	17.0	–13
Oklahoma	8,940	9,130	8,400	12.5	12.9	11.8	–5
Oregon	16,060	15,590	15,050	23.9	22.6	21.6	–10
Pennsylvania	49,740	40,760	39,520	18.6	15.5	15.2	–18
Rhode Island	6,990	5,720	5,420	30.0	25.5	24.4	–19
South Carolina	12,190	11,020	9,940	14.2	12.9	11.6	–19
South Dakota	1,040	1,040	1,030	6.8	6.6	6.5	–4
Tennessee	19,060	18,240	17,990	16.2	15.2	14.8	–8
Texas	97,400	89,240	91,270	23.1	20.5	20.7	–10
Utah	3,940	3,740	3,700	9.3	8.1	7.8	–16
Vermont	2,900	2,420	2,300	21.2	17.9	17.1	–19
Virginia	35,020	31,480	29,940	22.7	20.0	18.9	–16
Washington	33,190	25,190	26,340	27.7	20.2	20.9	–24
West Virginia	3,140	3,050	2,610	7.7	7.6	6.6	–14
Wisconsin	15,450	13,300	14,160	13.6	11.6	12.3	–9
Wyoming	460	280	280	4.3	2.7	2.7	–37

(1) Rounded to the nearest 10. (2) Only for women aged 15-44 years old.

Contraceptive Use in the U.S

Source: National Center for Health Statistics, U.S. Dept. of Health and Human Services; as of 1995

Age	15-44	15-19	20-24	25-29	30-34	35-39	40-44
	Percent of women in each age group						
Using contraception (any method)	64.2	29.8	63.4	69.3	72.7	72.9	71.5
Female sterilization	17.8	0.1	2.5	11.8	21.4	29.8	35.6
Male sterilization	7.0	—	0.7	3.1	7.6	13.6	14.5
Pill	17.3	13.0	33.1	27.0	20.7	8.1	4.2
Implant	0.9	0.8	2.4	1.4	0.5	0.2	0.1
Injectable	1.9	2.9	3.9	2.9	1.3	0.8	0.2
Intrauterine device (IUD)	0.5	—	0.2	0.5	0.6	0.7	0.9
Diaphragm	1.2	0.0	0.4	0.6	1.7	2.2	1.9

Age	15-44	15-19	20-24	25-29	30-34	35-39	40-44
Condom	13.1	10.9	16.7	16.8	13.4	12.3	8.8
Female condom	0.0	—	0.1	—	—	—	—
Periodic abstinence	1.5	0.4	0.6	1.2	2.3	2.1	1.8
Natural family planning	0.2	—	0.1	0.2	0.3	0.4	0.2
Withdrawal	2.0	1.2	2.1	2.6	2.1	2.3	1.4
Other methods[1]	1.0	0.3	0.9	1.2	1.3	0.9	1.8

(1) Includes morning-after pill, foam, cervical cap, Today sponge, suppository, jelly or cream (without diaphragm), and other methods not shown separately.

U.S. Median Age at First Marriage, 1890-2000

Source: Bureau of the Census, U.S. Dept. of Commerce

Year[1]	Men	Women	Year[1]	Men	Women	Year[1]	Men	Women	Year[1]	Men	Women	Year[1]	Men	Women
2000	26.8	25.1	1995	26.9	24.5	1990	26.1	23.9	1965	22.8	20.6	1920	24.6	21.2
1999	26.8	25.1	1994	26.7	24.5	1985	25.5	23.3	1960	22.8	20.3	1910	25.1	21.6
1998	26.7	25.0	1993	26.5	24.5	1980	24.7	22.0	1950	22.8	20.3	1900	25.9	21.9
1997	26.8	25.0	1992	26.5	24.4	1975	23.5	21.1	1940	24.3	21.5	1890	26.1	22.0
1996	27.1	24.8	1991	26.3	24.1	1970	23.2	20.8	1930	24.3	21.3			

(1) Figures after 1940 based on Current Population Survey data; figures for 1900-40 based on decennial censuses.

Cigarette Use in the U.S., 1985-2001

Source: Substance Abuse and Mental Health Services Administration (SAMHSA), U.S. Dept. of Health and Human Services

(percentage reporting use in the month prior to the survey; figures exclude persons under age 12)

	1985	1999	2000	2001
TOTAL	**38.7**	**25.8**	**24.9**	**24.9**
Sex				
Male	43.4	28.3	26.9	27.1
Female	34.5	23.4	23.1	23.0
Age group				
12-17	29.4	14.9	13.4	13.0
18-25	47.4	39.7	38.3	39.1
26-34	45.7	24.9[1]	24.2[1]	24.2[1]
35 and older	35.5	NA	NA	NA

	1985	1999	2000	2001
Race/Ethnicity				
White	38.9	27.0	25.9	26.1
Black	38.0	22.5	23.3	23.9
Hispanic	40.0	22.6	20.7	20.9
Education[2]				
Non-high school graduate	37.3	39.9	32.4	33.8
High school graduate	37.0	36.4	31.1	32.1
Some college	32.6	32.5	27.7	26.7
College graduate	23.0	18.2	13.9	13.8

NA = Not available. (1) Figures are for all persons aged 26 and older. (2) Estimates for Education are for persons aged 18 and older.

Drug Use in the General U.S. Population, 2001

Source: Substance Abuse and Mental Health Services Administration (SAMHSA), U.S. Dept. of Health and Human Services

According to the Substance Abuse and Mental Health Services Administration's 2001 National Household Survey on Drug Abuse, an estimated 94 million Americans 12 years of age and older (41.7%) had used an illicit drug at least once during their lifetimes, 12.6% had used one during the previous year, and 7.1% had used one in the month before the survey was conducted.

The rate of current illicit drug use for men was 8.7% in 2001 (up from 7.7% the year before), while for women the rate of current illicit drug use was 5.5% (up from 5.0% in 2000). An estimated 25.6% of Americans 12 or older (57.8 million) had at least once in their life used an illicit drug other than marijuana.

The Substance Abuse and Mental Health Services Administration's Drug Abuse Warning Network (DAWN) reported 638,484 drug-related episodes in hospital emergency departments in the coterminous U.S in 2001, a 6% increase from 2000. Cocaine was a factor in 30% of the emergency department episodes, and alcohol in combination with illegal or nonmedical use of legal drugs was a factor in 34% in 2001.

Drug Use: America's Middle and High School Students, 2001

Use of illicit drugs by American young people held fairly steady in 2001, according to the University of Michigan's 27th annual survey of high school seniors and 11th annual survey of 8th and 10th graders.

While drug use was lower than the recent peaks in 1996 and 1997, there was no significant decline from 2000. The percentage of 10th and 12th graders who had used any illicit drug in the 30 days before the survey rose slightly in 2001 (from 22.5% in 2000 to 22.7% for 10th graders and from 24.9% in 2000 to 25.7% for 12th graders). The rate dropped modestly for 8th graders (from 11.9% in 2000 to 11.7% in 2001). The percent of 8th graders who had used an illicit drug in the past 30 days was about double what it had been in 1991, when it stood at 5.7%. The percentages of 10th and 12th graders using an illicit drug in the past 30 days were also markedly higher in 1991, when for 10th graders the percent was 11.6% and for 12th graders it was 16.4%.

Percentages of students who had used an illicit drug at some time in the past year were also considerably higher than a decade ago; in 2001, these percentages were 41.4% for 12th graders (compared with 29.4% in 1991), 37.2% for 10th graders (21.4% in 1991), and 19.5% for 8th graders (11.3% in 1991)

Marijuana remained the most commonly used illegal drug for all 3 grade levels. In 2001, the proportion of students that reported using marijuana the past year changed little from the previous survey: it was 15.4% for 8th graders (down 0.1 percentage points from 2000), 32.7% for 10th graders (up 0.5 percentage points), and 37.0% of 12th graders (up 0.5 percentage points). Use of marijuana on a daily basis went up for 10th graders—to 4.5% (1 in 22) in 2001 from 3.8% (1 in 26) in 2000. About 1.3% of 8th graders (1 in 77) were daily users (no change from the year before), while 5.8% (1 in 17) of high school seniors (a drop of 0.2 percentage points) used marijuana daily.

The percentage of seniors who had used LSD in the last 30 days rose to 2.3% in 2001 from 1.6% in 2000; for other grades and for use in the past year, percentages held steady or declined very slightly. Use of hallucinogens other than LSD essentially held steady or dropped slightly, except for ecstasy, where all three grade levels showed increased use on an annual basis. Inhalant use dropped slightly for all grades, while use of stimulants in general increased modestly. Heroin use remained fairly low, declining for all grades (when asked about use in the past year). Both 8th and 10th graders showed small declines in use of alcohol, while for 12th graders alcohol use held about steady.

Cigarette smoking declined for all three grades. 5.5% of 8th graders, 12.2% of 10th graders and 19.0% of seniors said they smoked daily in the past month; these numbers were between 1.5 and 2 percentage points lower than figures for 2000.

In 2001 about 16,800 8th graders, 14,300 10th graders, and 13,300 seniors from 424 schools took part in the survey. It should be noted that the surveys missed the 3-6% of a class group that drops out of school early, and about 9-17% who were absentees. These populations tend to have higher rates of drug use overall.

Drug Use: America's High School Seniors, 1975-2001

Source: *Monitoring the Future,* Univ. of Michigan Inst. for Social Research and National Inst. on Drug Abuse

	PERCENTAGE EVER USED										
	Class of 1975	Class of 1980	Class of 1985	Class of 1990	Class of 1995	Class of 1997	Class of 1998	Class of 1999	Class of 2000	Class of 2001	'00-'01 change
Marijuana/hashish	47.3	60.3	54.2	40.7	41.7	49.6	49.1	49.7	48.8	49.0	+0.2
Inhalants[1]	NA	17.3	18.1	18.5	17.8	16.9	16.5	16.0	14.2	13.0	–1.2
Amyl & butyl nitrites	NA	11.1	7.9	2.1	1.5	2.0	2.7	1.7	0.8	1.9	+1.1
Hallucinogens[2]	NA	15.6	12.1	9.7	12.7	15.1	14.1	13.7	13.0	12.8	–0.2
LSD	11.3	9.3	7.5	8.7	11.7	13.6	12.6	12.2	11.1	10.9	–0.2
PCP	NA	9.6	4.9	2.8	2.7	3.9	3.9	3.4	3.4	3.5	+0.2
Ecstasy	NA	NA	NA	NA	NA	6.9	5.8	8.0	11.0	11.7	+0.7
Cocaine	9.0	15.7	17.3	9.4	6.0	8.7	9.3	9.8	8.6	8.2	–0.4
Crack	NA	NA	NA	3.5	3.0	3.9	4.4	4.6	3.9	3.7	–0.2
Heroin[3]	2.2	1.1	1.2	1.3	1.6	2.1	2.0	2.0	2.4	1.8	–0.6
Other opiates[4]	9.0	9.8	10.2	8.3	7.2	9.7	9.8	10.2	10.6	9.9	–0.8
Stimulants[4,5]	22.3	26.4	26.2	17.5	15.3	16.5	16.4	16.3	15.6	16.2	+0.6
Sedatives[4]	18.2	14.9	11.8	7.5	7.6	8.7	9.2	9.5	NA	NA	NA
Barbiturates[4]	16.9	11.0	9.2	6.8	7.4	8.1	8.7	8.9	9.2	8.7	–0.5
Methaqualone[4]	8.1	9.5	6.7	2.3	1.2	1.7	1.6	1.8	NA	NA	NA
Tranquilizers[4]	17.0	15.2	11.9	7.2	7.1	7.8	8.5	9.3	8.9	9.2	+0.4
Alcohol[6]	90.4	93.2	92.2	89.5	80.7	81.7	81.4	80.0	80.3	79.7	–0.6
Cigarettes	73.6	71.0	68.8	64.4	64.2	65.4	65.3	64.6	62.5	61.0	–1.5
Steroids	NA	NA	NA	2.9	2.3	2.4	2.7	2.9	2.5	3.7	+1.2

NA = Not available. (1) Adjusted for underreporting of amyl and butyl nitrites. (2) Adjusted for underreporting of PCP. (3) Reflects use with or without injection. (4) Includes only drug use that was not under a doctor's orders. (5) Data for 1990-2001 are not directly comparable to prior years. (6) Data for 1994-2001 are not directly comparable to prior years.

Alcohol Use by 8th and 12th Graders, 1980-2001

Source: *Monitoring the Future,* Univ. of Michigan Inst. for Social Research and National Inst. on Drug Abuse

	1980	1990	1991	1992	1993	1994	1995	1996	1997	1998	1999	2000	2001
ALCOHOL[1]	Percent using alcohol in the month before the survey												
All 12th graders	72.0	57.1	54.0	51.3	51.0	50.1	51.3	50.8	52.7	52.0	51.0	50.0	49.8
Male	77.4	61.3	58.4	55.8	54.9	55.5	55.7	54.8	56.2	57.3	55.3	54.0	54.7
Female	66.8	52.3	49.0	46.8	46.7	45.2	47.0	46.9	48.9	46.9	46.8	46.1	45.1
White	75.4	63.8	60.0	56.8	55.6	54.0	54.5	54.8	56.4	57.7	56.3	55.1	55.3
Black	47.6	35.8	33.7	31.7	32.4	33.8	35.2	36.5	34.3	33.3	32.2	30.0	29.4
All 8th graders	—	—	25.1	26.1	26.2	25.5	24.6	26.2	24.5	23.0	24.0	22.4	21.5
Male	—	—	26.3	26.3	26.7	26.5	25.0	26.6	25.2	24.0	24.8	22.5	22.3
Female	—	—	23.8	25.9	26.1	24.7	24.0	25.8	23.9	21.9	23.3	22.0	20.6
White	—	—	—	26.6	27.1	25.3	25.4	26.6	26.7	24.8	24.7	24.7	23.2
Black	—	—	—	18.6	19.7	19.4	18.7	18.1	17.9	16.1	16.0	16.0	15.0
HEAVY ALCOHOL[2]	Percent heavily using the 2 weeks before the survey												
All 12th graders	41.2	32.2	29.8	27.9	27.5	28.2	29.8	30.2	31.3	31.5	30.8	30.0	29.7
Male	52.1	39.1	37.8	35.6	34.6	37.0	36.9	37.0	37.9	39.2	38.1	36.7	36.0
Female	30.5	24.4	21.2	20.3	20.7	20.2	23.0	23.5	24.4	24.0	23.6	23.5	23.7
White	44.3	36.6	34.6	32.1	31.3	31.5	32.3	33.4	35.1	36.4	35.7	34.6	34.5
Black	17.7	14.4	11.7	11.3	12.6	14.4	14.9	15.3	13.4	12.3	12.3	11.5	11.8
All 8th graders	—	—	12.9	13.4	13.5	14.5	14.5	15.6	14.5	13.7	15.2	14.1	13.2
Male	—	—	14.3	13.9	14.8	16.0	15.1	16.5	15.3	14.4	16.4	14.4	13.7
Female	—	—	11.4	12.8	12.3	13.0	13.9	14.5	13.5	12.7	13.9	13.6	12.4
White	—	—	—	12.7	12.6	12.9	13.9	15.1	15.1	14.1	14.3	14.9	13.8
Black	—	—	—	9.6	10.7	11.8	10.8	10.4	9.8	9.0	9.9	10.0	9.0

— Data not available. **Note**: *Monitoring the Future* study excludes high school dropouts (about 3-6% of the class group, according to a 1996 report) and absentees (about 16-17% of 12th graders and about 9-10% of 8th graders). High school dropouts and absentees have higher alcohol usage than those included in the survey. (1) In 1993 the alcohol question was changed to indicate that a "drink" meant "more than a few sips." (2) Five or more drinks in a row at least once in the prior 2-week period.

Principal Types of Accidental Deaths in the U.S., 1970-2001

Source: National Safety Council

Year	Motor vehicle	Falls	Poisoning	Drowning	Fires, flames, smoke	Ingestion of food, object	Firearms	Mechanical Suffocation
1970	54,633	16,926	5,299	7,860	6,718	2,753	2,406	NA
1980	53,172	13,294	4,331	7,257	5,822	3,249	1,955	NA
1985	45,901	12,001	5,170	5,316	4,938	3,551	1,649	NA
1990	46,814	12,313	5,803	4,685	4,175	3,303	1,416	NA
1991	43,536	12,662	6,434	4,818	4,120	3,240	1,441	NA
1992	40,982	12,646	7,082	3,542	3,958	3,182	1,409	NA
1993	41,893	13,141	8,537	3,807	3,900	3,160	1,521	NA
1994	42,524	13,450	8,994	3,942	3,986	3,065	1,356	NA
1995	43,363	13,986	9,072	4,350	3,761	3,185	1,225	NA
1996	43,649	14,986	9,510	3,959	3,741	3,206	1,134	NA
1997	43,458	15,447	10,163	4,051	3,490	3,275	981	NA
1998	43,501	16,274	10,801	4,406	3,255	3,515	866	NA
1999[1]	42,401	13,162[3]	12,186[3]	3,529[3]	3,348	3,885	824	1,618[3]
2000[1]	42,500	12,900	12,700	3,300	3,900	4,300	800	1,500
2001[2]	42,900	14,200	14,500	3,300	3,900	4,200	800	1,300
	Death rates per 100,000 population							
1970	26.8	8.3	2.6	3.9	3.3	1.4	1.2	NA
1980	23.4	5.9	1.9	3.2	2.6	1.4	0.9	NA
1985	19.3	5.0	2.2	2.2	2.1	1.5	0.7	NA
1990	18.8	4.9	2.3	1.9	1.7	1.3	0.6	NA
1991	17.3	5.0	2.6	1.8	1.6	1.3	0.6	NA
1992	16.1	5.0	2.7	1.4	1.6	1.2	0.6	NA

Year	Motor vehicle	Falls	Poisoning	Drowning	Fires, flames, smoke	Ingestion of food, object	Firearms	Mechanical Suffocation
1993	16.3	5.1	3.4	1.5	1.5	1.2	0.6	NA
1994	16.3	5.2	3.5	1.5	1.5	1.2	0.5	NA
1995	16.5	5.3	3.4	1.7	1.4	1.2	0.5	NA
1996	16.5	5.6	3.5	1.5	1.4	1.2	0.4	NA
1997	16.2	5.8	3.8	1.5	1.3	1.2	0.4	NA
1998	16.1	6.0	4.0	1.6	1.2	1.3	0.3	NA
1999[1]	15.5	4.8[3]	4.5[3]	1.3[3]	1.2	1.4	0.3	0.6[3]
2000[1]	15.4	4.7	4.6	1.2	1.4	1.6	0.3	0.5
2001[2]	15.4	5.1	5.2	1.2	1.4	1.5	0.3	0.5

NA = Not available. **Note:** There were 12,900 other accidental deaths in 2001; the most frequently occurring types involved struck by or against an object, machinery, electric current, and air, rail and water transport. (1) Revised figures. (2) Preliminary figures. (3) Data for this year and later not comparable with earlier data because of classification changes.

U.S. Motor Vehicle Accidents

Source: National Safety Council

Motor vehicle deaths in the U.S. rose 1% from 2000 to 2001 (after holding essentially steady from 1999 to 2000). Among the 193,300,000 licensed drivers in 2001, there were slightly more male drivers than female (97,100,000 male vs 96,200,000 female), but males accounted for an estimated 62% of all miles driven. About 12,700,000 male drivers and 8,600,000 female drivers were involved in some type of accident in 2001.

Male drivers were involved in more fatal accidents than female drivers. About 40,800 men and 14,900 women drivers were involved in fatal accidents. The rate of involvement in fatal accidents was also higher for men (24 per billion miles driven) than for women (14).

However, women had higher total accident involvement rates. These rates were 74 per 10 million miles driven for men and 82 per 10 million miles driven for women.

In 2000, about 40% of all traffic fatalities involved an intoxicated or alcohol-impaired driver or nonoccupant. (For comparison, in 1987 alcohol-related fatalities accounted for 51% of all traffic deaths.) Of the 16,653 alcohol-related traffic fatalities (a 4% increase from 1999, but a 25% drop from 1990), an estimated 12,892 occurred in accidents where a driver or pedestrian was intoxicated; the remainder involved a driver or pedestrian who had been drinking but was not legally intoxicated. Alcohol was a factor in about 8% of all traffic accidents.

	Death total 2001	Percentage change from 2000	Death rate 2001[1]
All motor vehicle accidents	42,900	+1	15.4
Collision between motor vehicles	18,400	–4	6.6
Collision with fixed object	12,300	+4	4.4
Pedestrian accidents	5,800	+4	2.1

	Death total 2001	Percentage change from 2000	Death rate 2001[1]
Noncollision accidents	5,100	+9	1.8
Collision with pedalcycle	800	0	0.3
Collision with railroad train	400	0	0.1
Other collision (animal, animal-drawn vehicles)	100	0	(2)

(1) Deaths per 100,000 population. (2) Death rate was less than 0.05.

Improper Driving Reported in Accidents, 1999-2001

Source: National Safety Council

Type	Percentage of fatal accidents			Percentage of injury accidents			Percentage of all accidents		
	2001	2000	1999	2001	2000	1999	2001	2000	1999
Improper driving	**59.5**	**61.6**	**72.6**	**57.1**	**60.3**	**67.2**	**54.1**	**57.8**	**62.2**
Speed too fast or unsafe	23.0	18.6	23.0	14.6	16.3	13.0	11.7	13.6	10.6
Right of way	17.9	10.1	20.1	18.5	19.9	25.8	18.3	20.1	22.9
Failed to yield	9.4	4.6	10.8	13.8	15.0	19.2	11.7	12.7	13.8
Disregarded signal	4.9	8.2	4.7	3.4	1.3	4.9	4.7	2.2	5.9
Passed stop sign	3.6	3.8	4.6	1.3	3.6	1.7	1.9	5.3	3.2
Drove left of center	6.3	0.7	9.6	0.9	1.1	1.7	0.9	1.0	1.3
Improper overtaking	0.9	0.9	1.1	0.6	2.0	0.9	0.8	2.4	1.2
Made improper turn	0.8	0.7	1.2	1.8	0.6	2.4	2.3	0.9	3.0
Followed too closely	0.4	0.9	0.5	4.2	4.3	3.4	5.4	5.7	6.3
Other improper driving	10.2	9.0	17.1	16.5	16.1	20.3	14.7	14.1	16.9
No improper driving stated	**40.5**	**38.4**	**27.4**	**42.9**	**39.7**	**32.8**	**45.9**	**42.2**	**37.8**

Note: Based on reports from 9 state traffic authorities. When a driver was under the influence of alcohol or drugs, the accident was considered a result of the driver's physical condition—not a driving error. For this reason, accidents in which the driver was reported to be under the influence are included under "no improper driving stated."

Risk Behaviors in High School Students, 2001

Source: CDC, *Youth Risk Behavior Surveillance—United States, 2001*

	Percent rarely or never wear seatbelts[1]			Percent rarely or never wear bicycle helmets[2]			Percent who rode with a driver who had been drinking alcohol[3]		
	Female	Male	Total	Female	Male	Total	Female	Male	Total
Race									
Non-Hispanic White	9.7	17.7	13.6	81.1	85.5	83.6	29.4	31.2	30.3
Non-Hispanic Black	12.2	20.3	16.1	90.4	90.9	90.7	24.2	31.2	27.6
Hispanic	11.3	17.7	14.5	86.9	90.6	88.9	39.3	37.1	38.3
Grade									
9	10.8	19.4	14.9	80.4	86.0	83.3	31.3	29.2	30.4
10	10.3	16.6	13.3	81.5	85.0	83.5	29.9	31.5	30.6
11	9.7	17.5	13.6	86.2	87.7	87.1	25.4	32.8	29.1
12	9.4	18.6	13.9	85.1	87.1	86.3	31.3	34.5	32.8
Total	10.2	18.1	14.1	82.6	86.3	84.7	29.6	31.8	30.7

(1) When riding in a car or truck driven by someone else. (2) Among the 65.1% of students who rode bicycles during the 12 months preceding the survey. (3) One or more times during the 30 days preceding the survey.

Sexual Activity of High School Students, 2001

Source: CDC, *Youth Risk Behavior Surveillance—United States, 2001*

	Ever had sexual intercourse			First sexual intercourse before age 13			Currently sexually active[1]			Responsible sexual behavior[2]		
	Female	Male	Total	Female	Male	Total	Female	Male	Total	Female	Male	Total
Race/Ethnicity												
White[3]	41.3	45.1	43.2	3.3	6.2	4.7	32.3	30.0	31.3	84.2	89.3	86.6
Black[3]	53.4	68.8	60.8	7.6	25.7	16.3	39.5	52.3	45.6	84.8	85.9	85.2
Hispanic	44.0	53.0	48.4	4.1	11.4	7.6	34.5	37.3	35.9	82.1	85.2	83.6
Grade												
9	29.1	40.5	34.4	5.4	13.7	9.2	19.9	25.9	22.7	93.5	92.2	92.8
10	39.3	42.2	40.8	4.7	10.6	7.5	30.7	28.6	29.7	85.4	91.4	88.3
11	49.7	54.0	51.9	2.9	6.4	4.6	38.1	37.8	38.1	82.1	87.0	84.5
12	60.1	61.0	60.5	2.2	5.0	3.6	51.0	44.6	47.9	70.1	81.9	75.8
Total	**42.9**	**48.5**	**45.6**	**4.0**	**9.3**	**6.6**	**33.4**	**33.4**	**33.4**	**83.9**	**88.5**	**86.1**

(1) Sexual intercourse during the 3 months preceding the survey. (2) This includes students who had never had sexual intercourse, had had sexual intercourse but not during the 3 months preceeding the survey, or had used a condom the last time they had sexual intercourse during the 3 months preceding the survey. (3) Non-Hispanic.

Deaths in the U.S. Involving Firearms, by Age, 1999

Source: National Safety Council

	All ages	Under 5	5-14	15-19	20-24	25-44	45-64	65-74	75 & over
Total firearms deaths[1]	**28,874**	**73**	**416**	**2,896**	**3,899**	**11,209**	**6,028**	**2,034**	**2,319**
Male	24,700	41	308	2,560	3,496	9,385	5,008	1,786	2,116
Female	4,174	32	108	336	403	1,824	1,020	248	203
Unintentional	824	12	76	126	125	279	140	33	33
Male	707	7	60	115	114	234	119	31	27
Female	117	5	16	11	11	45	21	2	6
Suicides	16,599	0	103	975	1,340	5,718	4,537	1,791	2,135
Male	14,479	0	80	867	1,216	4,856	3,845	1,615	2,000
Female	2120	0	23	108	124	862	692	176	135
Homicides	10,828	58	224	1,708	2,330	4,916	1,266	193	133
Male	8,944	31	155	1,498	2,071	4,023	970	124	72
Female	1,884	27	69	210	259	893	296	69	61
Undetermined[2]	324	3	12	68	59	108	42	15	17
Male	277	3	12	61	50	89	32	14	16
Female	47	0	0	7	9	19	10	1	1

(1) Figures exclude firearms deaths by legal intervention. These deaths totaled 299 in 1999. (2) "Undetermined" means that the intention involved (whether accident, suicide, or homicide) could not be determined.

Home Accident Deaths in the U.S., 1950-2001

Source: National Safety Council

Year	Total	Falls	Poisoning	Fires, burns[1]	Suffoc.: ingesting object	Suffoc.: mechanical	Firearms	Drowning	Natural heat/cold	All other
1950	29,000	14,800	2,550	5,000	(2)	1,600	950	(2)	(2)	4,100
1960	28,000	12,300	2,450	6,350	1,850	1,500	1,200	(2)	(2)	2,550
1970	27,000	9,700	4,100	5,600	1,800[3]	1,100[3]	1,400[3]	(2)	(2)	3,300[3]
1980	22,800	7,100	3,200	4,800	2,000	500	1,100	(2)	(2)	4,100[4]
1990	21,500	6,700	4,500	3,400	2,300	600	800	(2)	(2)	3,200
1991	22,100	6,900	5,000	3,400	2,200	700	800	(2)	(2)	3,100
1992	24,000	7,700	5,200	3,700	1,500	700	1,000	900	(2)	3,300
1993	26,100	7,900	6,500	3,700	1,700	700	1,100	900	(2)	3,600
1994	26,300	8,100	6,800	3,700	1,600	800	900	900	(2)	3,500
1995	27,200	8,400	7,000	3,500	1,500	800	900	900	(2)	4,200
1996	27,500	9,000	7,300	3,500	1,500	800	800	900	(2)	3,700
1997	27,700	9,100	7,800	3,200	1,500	800	700	900	(2)	3,500
1998	29,000	9,500	8,400	2,900	1,800	800	600	1,000	(2)	4,000
1999[3,5]	30,500	7,600	9,300	3,000	1,900	1,100	600	900	700	5,400
2000[5]	30,900	8,000	9,900	3,500	2,200	1,100	500	1,000	500	4,200
2001[6]	33,200	9,000	11,500	3,500	2,200	1,000	600	900	600	3,900

(1) Includes deaths resulting from conflagration, regardless of nature of injury. (2) Included under "All other" category. (3) Data for this year and later not comparable with earlier data because of classification changes. (4) Includes about 1,000 deaths attributed to summer heat wave. (5) Revised figures. (6) Data for 2001 are preliminary.

Worldwide Airline Fatalities, 1986-2001[1]

Source: National Safety Council.

Year	Aircraft accidents[2]	Passenger deaths	Death rate[3]
1986	24	641	0.04
1987	25	900	0.06
1988	29	742	0.04
1989	29	879	0.05
1990	27	544	0.03
1991	29	638	0.03
1992	28	1,070	0.06
1993	33	864	0.04
1994	27	1,170	0.05
1995	25	711	0.03
1996	24	1,146	0.05
1997	25	921	0.04
1998	20	904	0.03
1999	21	499	0.02
2000	18	757	0.03
2001[4]	13	577	0.02

(1) Some figures have been revised from previous figures. (2) Involving 1 or more fatalities only. (3) Passenger deaths per 100 mil passenger mi. (4) Preliminary; excluding accidents caused by terrorism or sabotage.

WORLD ALMANAC QUICK QUIZ

What was the life expectancy at birth of a baby born in the U.S. in 1900?

(a) 38 (b) 47 (c) 52 (d) 58

For the answer look in this chapter, or see page 1008.

U.S. Fires, 2001

Source: National Fire Protection Assn.

Fires

- Public fire departments responded to 1,734,500 fires in 2001, an increase of 1.6% from 2000.
- There were 521,500 structure fires in 2001, an increase of 3.2% from the 2000 figure.
- 76% of all structure fires, or 396,500 fires, occurred in residential properties.
- There were 351,500 vehicle fires in 2001, a modest increase of 0.8% from the previous year.
- There were 861,500 fires in outside properties, a slight increase of 0.9% from 2000.

Civilian deaths

- There were 6,196 civilian fire deaths in 2001. 2,451 of the deaths occurred because of the 9/11 terrorist attack; the other 3,745 civilian deaths were not related to 9/11. In the previous year there were 4,045 civilian fire deaths.
- The number of deaths from fire in the home dropped by 9.1%, to 3,110. Of civilian fire deaths not related to 9/11, about 83% occurred in the home.
- Nationwide, someone died in a home fire every 170 minutes.

Civilian injuries

- There were an estimated 21,100 civilian fire injuries in 2001, of which 800 occurred because of 9/11. In 2000 there were an estimated 22,350 civilian fire injuries. These estimate are traditionally low because of underreporting of civilian fire injuries to the fire service.
- Residential properties were the site of 15,575 civilian fire injuries, or 76.7% of all injuries not related to 9/11; there were 1,650 injuries (apart from the 800 related to 9/11) in nonresidential structure fires.
- Nationwide, a civilian was injured in a fire in the home every 34 minutes.

Property damage

- Property damage resulting from fires amounted to an estimated $44,023,000,000. About 3/4 of this number—$33,440,000,000—relates to the events of 9/11. Non-9/11 property damage totalled an estimated $10,583,000,000.
- Excluding the events of 9/11, structure fires accounted for $8,874,000,000 of property damage, or approximately 84%.
- Property loss in residential properties came to $5,643,000,000 for 2001.

Intentionally set fires

- There were an estimated 45,500 intentionally set structure fires in 2001. This number was comparable to the number of fires termed "incendiary" in 2000. The NFPA survey no longer tracked "suspicious" fires; in 2000, suspicious and incendiary fires together had amounted to 75,000.
- Intentionally set structure fires resulted in 2,781 civilian deaths; of this number, 2,451 were due to 9/11 and 330 occurred in other set structure fires. Property damage from intentionally set structure fires totalled $34,453,000,000. The lion's share of this—$33,440,000,000—was due to the events of 9/11, while $1,013,000,000 related to other set structure fires.
- The number of intentionally set vehicle fires in 2001 was 39,500, a drop of 15.1% from the number of incendiary vehicle fires in 2000. The intentionally set vehicle fires caused an estimated $219 million in property damage, an increase of 17.7% from 2000.

Physicians by Age, Sex, and Specialty, 2000

Source: American Medical Assn., as of Dec. 31, 2000

	Total Physicians[1]		Under 35 yrs		35-44 yrs		45-54 yrs		55-64 yrs	
	Male	Female	Male	Female	Male	Female	Male	Female	Male	Female
All Specialties	**618,233**	**195,537**	**81,473**	**55,231**	**145,043**	**66,830**	**156,782**	**44,864**	**102,522**	**16,086**
Aerospace Medicine	442	31	8	4	78	8	144	13	101	5
Allergy & Immunology	3,115	883	111	106	689	328	981	283	733	107
Anaesthesiology	28,364	7,335	2,908	1,076	10,555	2,881	8,192	2,013	4,093	982
Cardiovascular Disease	19,402	1,623	1,612	286	5,748	688	6,475	472	3,514	124
Child Psychiatry	3,654	2,504	229	244	834	924	1,142	788	785	344
Colon/Rectal Surgery	1,036	91	60	24	302	49	342	16	198	2
Dermatology	6,486	3,189	636	820	1,343	1,262	1,927	800	1,609	230
Diagnostic Radiology	16,975	4,129	2,849	983	4,826	1,607	5,191	1,201	3,157	278
Emergency Medicine	18,713	4,351	3,786	1,427	5,222	1,499	6,617	1,094	2,181	261
Family Practice	51,234	20,401	7,959	7,076	14,070	7,521	17,064	4,494	6,095	934
Forensic Pathology	409	168	27	10	88	61	119	57	92	25
Gastroenterology	9,700	927	810	167	3,111	452	3,364	251	1,744	53
General Practice	12,875	2,338	54	23	660	305	2,138	730	2,993	679
General Preventive Med.	1,132	586	95	98	345	244	315	176	183	42
General Surgery	32,633	4,017	6,496	1,862	6,906	1,249	7,421	719	6,261	128
Internal Medicine	97,466	37,073	18,548	12,260	25,955	13,405	28,624	8,512	13,964	2,108
Medical Genetics	199	162	23	22	54	58	64	53	37	23
Neurological Surgery	4,764	233	718	79	1,120	87	1,152	55	1,043	9
Neurology	9,724	2,609	920	518	2,568	994	3,358	804	1,879	208
Nuclear Medicine	1,200	248	75	23	221	67	370	89	312	51
Obstetrics/Gynecology	26,117	14,124	2,159	4,646	5,342	5,013	7,789	3,118	6,095	997
Occupational Medicine	2,500	490	6	5	356	162	795	205	481	71
Ophthalmology	15,498	2,628	1,430	607	3,754	1,062	4,284	695	3,702	195
Orthopedic Surgery	21,513	774	3,273	270	5,344	279	5,774	178	4,579	31
Otolaryngology	8,579	838	1,225	277	2,118	330	2,112	191	1,995	24
Pathology-Anat./Clin.	12,812	5,408	973	787	2,804	1,856	3,566	1,583	2,863	819
Pediatric Cardiology	1,146	390	123	76	383	179	307	73	201	36
Pediatrics	32,063	30,322	5,810	9,930	7,897	10,083	8,899	6,770	5,479	2,574
Physical Med./Rehab.	4,366	2,142	699	408	1,640	857	1,082	506	525	250
Plastic Surgery	5,590	610	400	114	1,538	234	1,694	198	1,342	47
Psychiatry	27,809	11,648	1,838	1,673	5,066	3,491	7,380	3,568	6,601	1,720
Public Health	1,134	516	4	5	114	88	360	165	311	110
Pulmonary Diseases	7,609	1,097	791	243	2,315	522	2,821	231	1,207	63
Radiation Oncology	3,047	857	337	131	979	336	829	253	594	103
Radiology	7,525	1,136	485	92	1,476	370	1,300	347	2,303	225
Thoracic Surgery	4,821	132	178	10	1,235	60	1,387	55	1,161	7
Transplantation Surgery	59	7	1	0	32	6	20	1	4	0
Urological Surgery	9,968	334	1,151	132	2,221	126	2,564	65	2,582	6
Other	4,896	898	57	16	505	187	1,198	286	1,204	186
Not Classified	29,515	15,621	9,175	6,478	12,520	6,256	3,808	1,768	2,252	808
Unspecified	5,390	2,937	3,077	1,970	1,094	593	676	242	250	79

(1) Includes physicians 65 and older, "Inactive," "Address Unknown," and certain specialties with very few practitioners

U.S. Health Expenditures, 1960-2000

Source: *Health, United States, 2002,* National Center for Health Statistics, U.S. Dept. of Health and Human Services

	1960	1965	1970	1975	1980	1985	1990	1995	1998	1999	2000
						Amount in billions					
National health expenditures	**$26.7**	**$41.0**	**$73.1**	**$129.8**	**$245.8**	**$426.5**	**$696.0**	**$990.3**	**$1,149.8**	**$1,215.6**	**$1,299.5**
						Percent distribution					
Health services and supplies	**93.6**	**91.1**	**92.2**	**93.2**	**95.0**	**95.8**	**96.2**	**96.7**	**96.7**	**96.7**	**96.6**
Personal health care	87.6	84.7	86.5	87.0	87.3	87.3	87.6	87.4	87.8	87.4	87.0
Hospital care	34.4	33.7	37.8	40.0	41.3	39.1	36.5	34.7	33.0	32.3	31.7
Professional services	31.3	30.3	28.3	27.8	27.4	29.4	31.2	32.0	32.7	32.7	32.5
Physician and clinical services	20.1	20.3	19.1	19.1	19.2	21.1	22.6	22.3	22.3	22.2	22.0
Other professional services	1.5	1.3	1.0	1.1	1.5	2.0	2.6	2.9	3.1	3.0	3.0
Dental services	7.4	6.8	6.4	6.1	5.4	5.1	4.5	4.5	4.6	4.6	4.6
Other personal health care	2.4	1.9	1.7	1.5	1.3	1.2	1.4	2.3	2.6	2.8	2.8
Home health care	0.2	0.2	0.3	0.5	1.0	1.3	1.8	3.1	2.9	2.7	2.5
Nursing home care	3.2	3.6	5.8	6.7	7.2	7.2	7.6	7.5	7.7	7.3	7.1
Retail outlet sales of medical products	18.6	16.9	14.3	12.0	10.5	10.4	10.5	10.2	11.5	12.5	13.2
Government administration and net cost of private health insurance	4.5	4.9	3.8	3.9	4.9	5.8	5.7	6.1	5.5	5.9	6.2
Government public health activities[1]	1.5	1.5	1.9	2.3	2.7	2.7	2.9	3.2	3.3	3.4	3.4
Investment	6.4	8.9	7.8	6.8	5.0	4.2	3.8	3.3	3.3	3.3	3.4
Research	2.6	3.7	2.7	2.6	2.2	1.9	1.8	1.7	1.8	1.9	2.0
Construction	3.8	5.2	5.2	4.3	2.8	2.2	2.0	1.6	1.5	1.4	1.4
						Average annual percent change from previous year shown					
National health expenditures	**NA**	**9.0**	**12.2**	**12.2**	**13.6**	**11.7**	**11.0**	**7.3**	**5.4**	**5.7**	**6.9**
Health services and supplies	**NA**	**8.4**	**12.5**	**12.4**	**14.1**	**11.9**	**11.1**	**7.4**	**5.5**	**5.7**	**6.9**
Personal health care	NA	8.2	12.7	12.3	13.7	11.7	11.0	7.3	5.3	5.2	6.4
Hospital care	NA	8.5	14.9	13.4	14.4	10.4	9.6	6.2	3.2	3.4	5.1
Physician and clinical services	NA	9.2	10.9	12.2	13.7	13.8	12.8	7.0	6.6	5.2	6.0
Other professional services	NA	6.3	6.9	13.2	21.1	18.6	17.5	9.5	6.4	3.3	6.3
Dental services	NA	7.3	10.8	11.2	10.9	10.2	9.0	7.1	6.0	6.1	6.3
Other personal health care	NA	4.2	10.2	9.4	10.5	10.0	11.4	18.9	8.8	11.7	8.9
Home health care	NA	9.6	19.7	23.2	30.7	18.9	18.1	19.4	–2.8	–3.7	0.3
Nursing home care	NA	11.6	23.4	15.5	15.3	11.7	11.5	7.2	4.7	0.2	3.3
Retail outlet sales of medical products	NA	7.0	8.6	8.3	10.5	11.4	11.1	6.5	10.4	14.8	13.0
Government administration and net cost of private health insurance	NA	10.6	6.7	12.8	19.2	15.4	12.7	8.6	7.5	12.3	13.1
Government public health activities[1]	NA	9.6	16.9	16.7	18.1	11.4	11.6	9.2	6.8	7.8	8.3
Investment	NA	16.5	9.5	9.1	6.7	7.6	8.0	4.3	2.9	5.8	8.4
Research	NA	17.1	5.1	11.2	10.4	8.7	8.8	6.2	10.1	11.9	10.0
Construction	NA	16.1	12.2	8.0	4.2	6.7	7.3	2.4	–4.4	–1.3	6.4

Note: NA = Not applicable. Numbers may not add to totals because of rounding. (1) Includes personal care services delivered by government public health agencies.

IT'S A FACT: In 1960 there were about 51,000 married U.S. couples in which one spouse was white and one black, or 1 out of about 800 married couples. In 2000, there were some 363,000 black-white couples, or 1 in 160.

Ownership of Life Insurance in the U.S. and Assets of U.S. Life Insurance Companies, 1940-2001

Source: American Council of Life Insurance

(amounts in millions)

	PURCHASES OF LIFE INSURANCE				INSURANCE IN FORCE					
Year	**Ordinary**	**Group**	**Industrial**	**Total**	**Ordinary**	**Group**	**Industrial**	**Credit**	**Total**	**Assets**
1940	$6,689	$691	$3,350	$10,730	$79,346	$14,938	$20,866	$380	$115,530	$30,802
1950	17,326	6,068	5,402	28,796	149,116	47,793	33,415	3,844	234,168	64,020
1960	52,883	14,645	6,880	74,408	341,881	175,903	39,563	29,101	586,448	119,576
1970	122,820	63,690[1]	6,612	193,122[1]	734,730	551,357	38,644	77,392	1,402,123	207,254
1975	188,003	95,190[1]	6,729	289,922[1]	1,083,421	904,695	39,423	112,032	2,139,571	289,304
1980	385,575	183,418	3,609	572,602	1,760,474	1,579,355	35,994	165,215	3,541,038	479,210
1985	910,944	319,503[2]	722	1,231,169[2]	3,247,289	2,561,595	28,250	215,973	6,053,107	825,901
1990	1,069,660	459,271	220	1,529,151	5,366,982	3,753,506	24,071	248,038	9,392,597	1,408,208
1991	1,041,508	573,953[1]	198	1,615,659[1]	5,677,777	4,057,606	22,475	228,478	9,986,336	1,551,201
1992	1,048,135	440,143	222	1,488,500	5,941,810	4,240,919	20,973	202,090	10,405,792	1,664,531
1993	1,101,327	576,823	149	1,678,299	6,428,434	4,456,338	20,451	199,518	11,104,741	1,839,127
1994	1,056,976	560,232	257	1,617,465	6,429,811	4,443,179	18,947	189,398	11,081,335	1,942,273
1995	1,039,102	537,828	156	1,577,086	6,872,252	4,604,856	18,134	201,083	11,696,325	2,143,544
1996	1,089,137	614,565	130	1,703,832	7,407,682	5,067,804	18,064	210,746	12,704,296	2,327,924
1997	1,203,552	688,589	128	1,892,269	7,854,570	5,279,042	17,991	212,255	13,363,858	2,579,078
1998	1,324,565	739,508	106	2,064,179	8,505,894	5,735,273	17,365	212,917	14,471,449	2,826,522
1999[3]	1,399,848	966,858	—	2,508,019	9,172,397	6,110,218	—	213,453	15,496,069	3,070,653
2000[3]	1,593,907	921,001	—	2,681,234	9,376,370	6,376,127	—	200,770	15,953,267	3,181,736
2001[3]	1,600,471	1,172,080	—	2,938,702	9,345,723	6,765,074	—	178,851	16,289,648	3,269,019

Note: — = Data not available. Ordinary purchases, ordinary in force, and group in force numbers were revised for 1994-97. (1) Includes Servicemen's Group Life Insurance, which amounted to $17.1 billion in 1970, $1.7 billion in 1975, and $166.7 billion in 1991. (2) Includes Federal Employees' Group Life Insurance of $10.8 billion. (3) For 1999 and later, category of "ordinary" is combined with data for "industrials." Also, totals for purchases from 1999 on include the category "Credit," not listed here.

IT'S A FACT: According to a federal government study, the average hospital charge for treating a heart attack victim rose by about a third from 1993 to 2000—from $20,578 to $28,663—while the average hospital stay for a heart attack dropped from 7.4 days to 5.5 days. New technologies and higher medication costs were major reasons for the cost hike.

Health Insurance Coverage,[1] by State, 1990, 2000-2001

Source: Bureau of the Census, U.S. Dept. of Commerce

	2001		2000		1990			2001		2000		1990	
	Not covered[2]	% not covered	Not covered[2]	% not covered	Not covered[2]	% not covered		Not covered[2]	% not covered	Not covered[2]	% not covered	Not covered[2]	% not covered
AL	573	13.1	582	13.3	710	17.4	MT	121	13.6	150	16.8	115	14.0
AK	100	15.7	117	18.7	77	15.4	NE	160	9.5	154	9.1	138	8.5
AZ	950	17.9	869	16.7	547	15.5	NV	344	16.1	344	16.8	201	16.5
AR	428	16.1	379	14.3	421	17.4	NH	119	9.4	103	8.4	107	9.9
CA	6,718	19.5	6,299	18.5	5,683	19.1	NJ	1,109	13.1	1,021	12.2	773	10.0
CO	687	15.6	620	14.3	495	14.7	NM	373	20.7	435	24.2	339	22.2
CT	346	10.2	330	9.8	226	6.9	NY	2,916	15.5	3,056	16.3	2,176	12.1
DE	73	9.2	72	9.3	96	13.9	NC	1,167	14.4	1,084	13.6	883	13.8
DC	70	12.7	78	14.0	109	19.2	ND	60	9.6	71	11.3	40	6.3
FL	2,856	17.5	2,829	17.7	2,376	18.0	OH	1,248	11.2	1,248	11.2	1,123	10.3
GA	1,376	16.6	1,166	14.3	971	15.3	OK	620	18.3	641	18.9	574	18.6
HI	117	9.6	113	9.4	81	7.3	OR	443	12.8	433	12.7	360	12.4
ID	210	16.0	199	15.4	159	15.2	PA	1,119	9.2	1,047	8.7	1,218	10.1
IL	1,676	13.6	1,704	13.9	1,272	10.9	RI	80	7.7	77	7.4	105	11.1
IN	714	11.8	674	11.2	587	10.7	SC	493	12.3	480	12.1	550	16.2
IA	216	7.5	253	8.8	225	8.1	SD	69	9.3	81	11.0	81	11.6
KS	301	11.4	289	10.9	272	10.8	TN	640	11.3	615	10.9	673	13.7
KY	492	12.3	545	13.6	480	13.2	TX	4,960	23.5	4,748	22.9	3,569	21.1
LA	845	19.3	789	18.1	797	19.7	UT	335	14.8	281	12.5	156	9.0
ME	132	10.3	138	10.9	139	11.2	VT	58	9.6	52	8.6	54	9.5
MD	653	12.3	547	10.4	601	12.7	VA	771	10.9	814	11.6	990	15.7
MA	520	8.2	540	8.7	530	9.1	WA	780	13.1	792	13.5	557	11.4
MI	1,028	10.4	901	9.2	865	9.4	WV	234	13.2	250	14.1	249	13.8
MN	392	8.0	399	8.1	389	8.9	WI	409	7.7	406	7.6	321	6.7
MS	459	16.4	380	13.6	531	19.9	WY	78	15.9	76	15.7	58	12.5
MO	565	10.2	524	9.5	665	12.7	**U.S.**	**41,207**	**14.6**	**39,804**	**14.2**	**34,719**	**13.9**

(1) For population, all ages, including those 65 or over, an age group largely covered by Medicare. (2) In thousands.

Persons Not Covered by Health Insurance, by Selected Characteristics, 2001

Source: Bureau of the Census, U.S. Dept. of Commerce

	Number[1]	%
Total	**41,207**	**14.6**
Sex		
Male	21,722	15.8
Female	19,485	13.5
Race and Ethnicity		
White	31,193	13.6
Non-Hispanic	19,409	10.0
Black	6,833	19.0
Asian and Pacific Islander	2,278	18.2
Hispanic[2]	12,417	33.2
Age		
Under 18 years	8,509	11.7
18 to 24 years	7,673	28.1
25 to 34 years	9,051	23.4
35 to 44 years	7,131	16.1
45 to 64 years	8,571	13.1
65 years and over	272	0.8
Nativity		
Native	30,364	12.2
Foreign born	10,843	33.4
Naturalized citizen	2,060	17.2
Not a citizen	8,782	42.9
Region		
Northeast	6,399	12.0
Midwest	6,840	10.7
South	16,712	16.6
West	11,257	17.5
Household Income		
Less than $25,000	14,474	23.3
$25,000 to $49,999	13,516	17.7
$50,000 to $74,999	6,595	11.3
$75,000 or more	6,623	7.7
Education (18 years and older)		
Total	32,698	15.6
No high school diploma	9,776	27.6
High school graduate only	11,618	17.4
Some college, no degree	5,815	14.4
Associate degree	1,754	10.8
Bachelor's degree or higher	3,734	7.3

(1) In thousands. (2) Persons of Hispanic origin may be of any race.

Health Coverage for Persons Under 65, by Characteristics, 1984, 1998-2000

Source: *Health, United States, 2002,* National Center for Health Statistics, U.S. Dept. of Health and Human Services

	PRIVATE INSURANCE				MEDICAID[1]				NOT COVERED[2]			
	1984	1998[3]	1999	2000	1984	1998[3]	1999	2000	1984	1998[3]	1999	2000
	Percent of each population group											
Age												
Under 18 years	72.6	68.4	68.8	67.0	11.9	17.1	18.1	19.4	13.9	12.7	11.9	12.4
18-44 years	76.5	71.1	72.0	70.9	5.1	5.8	5.7	5.6	17.1	21.4	21.0	22.0
45-64 years	83.3	79.0	79.3	78.7	3.4	4.5	4.4	4.5	9.6	12.2	12.2	12.7
Race and Hispanic origin[4,5]												
White, non-Hispanic	80.1	75.9	76.8	75.8	4.6	6.7	6.9	7.2	13.4	15.2	14.6	15.2
Black, non-Hispanic	59.2	55.9	58.1	56.9	18.9	19.6	18.7	19.4	20.0	20.7	19.5	20.0
All Hispanic	57.1	49.9	50.3	49.0	12.2	14.1	14.1	14.2	29.1	34.0	33.9	35.4
Percent of poverty level[4]												
Below 100%	33.0	24.1	26.1	25.8	30.5	37.9	36.8	37.2	34.7	34.6	34.4	34.2
100-149%	61.8	43.3	40.1	39.5	7.5	16.0	18.6	20.3	27.0	36.5	35.8	36.5
150-199%	77.2	61.4	59.4	58.4	3.1	7.2	9.8	10.8	17.4	26.7	27.7	27.3
200% or more	91.6	88.3	88.7	87.2	0.6	1.8	2.0	2.3	5.8	8.0	7.7	8.7
Geographic region[4]												
Northeast	80.7	76.4	77.1	76.5	8.5	9.8	10.1	10.5	10.1	12.3	12.2	12.1
Midwest	80.9	79.1	80.2	78.9	7.2	7.5	7.3	7.9	11.1	11.9	11.5	12.3
South	74.5	67.8	68.0	67.0	5.0	8.6	8.9	9.4	17.4	20.0	19.8	20.4
West	72.3	67.8	68.9	67.1	6.9	9.7	10.3	10.2	17.8	19.9	18.6	20.2

Note: Data based on household interviews of a sample of the civilian noninstitutionalized population. Percents do not add to 100 because other types of health insurance (e.g., Medicare, military) are not shown and persons with both private insurance and Medicaid appear in both columns. (1) Includes Medicaid or other public assistance. In 2000, the age-adjusted percent of the population under 65 covered by Medicaid was 8.1%; 0.7% were covered by state-sponsored health plans and 0.6% were covered by Child Health Insurance Program (CHIP). (2) Includes persons not covered by private insurance, Medicaid or other public assistance, Medicare, or military plans. (3) In 1997 the questionnaire changed compared with previous years. (4) Age adjusted. (5) Changed reporting methods make percentages for race before 1999 not strictly comparable with those from 1999 on.

Enrollment in Health Maintenance Organizations (HMOs), 1976-2001

Source: *Health, United States, 2002,* National Center for Health Statistics, U.S. Dept. of Health and Human Services

	1976	1980	1990	1993	1994	1995	1996	1997	1998	1999	2000	2001
	Number of enrolled in millions											
TOTAL	**6.0**	**9.1**	**33.0**	**38.4**	**45.1**	**50.9**	**59.1**	**66.8**	**76.6**	**81.3**	**80.9**	**79.5**
Model type[1]												
Individual practice assoc.[2]	0.4	1.7	13.7	15.3	17.8	20.1	26.0	26.7	32.6	32.8	33.4	33.1
Group[3]	5.6	7.4	19.3	15.4	13.9	13.3	14.1	11.0	13.8	15.9	15.2	15.6
Mixed	—	—	—	7.7	13.4	17.6	19.0	29.0	30.1	32.6	32.3	30.9
Federal program[4]												
Medicaid[5]	—	0.3	1.2	1.7	2.6	3.5	4.7	5.6	7.8	10.4	10.8	11.4
Medicare	—	0.4	1.8	2.2	2.5	2.9	3.7	4.8	5.7	6.5	6.6	6.1
	Percent of population enrolled in HMOs											
TOTAL	**2.8**	**4.0**	**13.4**	**15.1**	**17.3**	**19.4**	**22.3**	**25.2**	**28.6**	**30.1**	**30.0**	**28.3**
Geographic region												
Northeast	2.0	3.1	14.6	18.0	20.8	24.4	25.9	32.4	37.8	36.7	36.5	35.1
Midwest	1.5	2.8	12.6	13.2	15.2	16.4	18.8	19.5	22.7	23.3	23.2	21.7
South	0.4	0.8	7.1	8.4	10.2	12.4	15.2	17.9	21.0	23.9	22.6	21.0
West	9.7	12.2	23.2	25.1	27.4	28.6	33.2	36.4	39.1	41.4	41.7	40.7

— = Not available. **Note:** Data as of June 30 in 1976-80, Jan. 1 from 1990 onwards. HMOs in Guam included starting in 1994; Puerto Rico, 1998; Guam HMO enrollment was 97,000 in 2001 and Puerto Rico enrollment was 1,265,000 in 2001. Open-ended enrollment in HMO plans, amounting to 9 million on Jan. 1, 2001, included from 1994 onwards. (1) Enrollment may not equal total because some plans did not report these characteristics. (2) This type of HMO contracts with an association of physicians from various settings (a mixture of solo and group practices) to provide health services. (3) Group includes staff, group, and network model types. (4) Enrollment by Medicaid or Medicare beneficiaries, where the Medicaid or Medicare program contracts directly with the HMO to pay the premium. (5) Data for 1990 and later include enrollment in managed-care health insuring organizations.

Health Care Visits, by Selected Characteristics, 1999, 2000

Source: Centers for Disease Control and Prevention, National Center for Health Statistics. National Health Interview Survey, family core and sample adult questionnaires.

	No visits		1-3 visits		4-9 visits		10 or more visits	
	1999	2000	1999	2000	1999	2000	1999	2000
	Percent distribution							
All persons	**17.5**	**16.6**	**45.8**	**45.4**	**23.3**	**24.7**	**13.4**	**13.3**
Age								
Under 6 years	5.9	6.3	45.9	44.3	36.8	38.3	11.3	11.2
6–17 years	15.5	15.1	58.5	58.2	19.4	20.7	6.7	6.0
18–24 years	24.8	24.3	46.1	45.6	17.8	18.8	11.4	11.2
25–44 years	24.0	22.9	45.7	45.2	17.8	19.3	12.6	12.6
45–54 years	18.4	16.4	43.2	45.3	22.8	23.7	15.7	14.6
55–64 years	14.7	12.8	41.1	40.6	28.4	28.8	15.8	17.8
65–74 years	8.6	9.0	36.9	34.5	33.2	34.4	21.3	22.1
75 years and over	7.2	5.8	31.1	29.3	35.1	39.3	26.6	25.6
Sex								
Male	23.1	21.5	45.5	46.0	20.6	22.4	10.8	10.1
Female	12.0	11.9	46.1	44.8	25.9	27.0	15.9	16.4
Race and Hispanic origin								
White, non-Hispanic	15.5	14.5	46.0	45.4	24.5	26.0	14.1	14.1
Black, non-Hispanic	18.4	17.2	46.2	46.9	21.9	23.4	13.5	12.6
Hispanic[1]	26.2	26.5	44.3	41.8	19.2	20.0	10.3	11.7
Geographic region								
Northeast	12.8	12.4	46.4	46.2	25.6	27.3	15.2	14.0
Midwest	16.2	14.4	46.7	46.2	23.8	25.6	13.3	13.9
South	18.9	18.4	45.5	44.7	22.5	24.1	13.2	12.9
West	20.9	20.0	44.8	44.9	21.9	22.2	12.4	12.8

(1) Persons of Hispanic origin may be of any race.

Major Reasons Given by Patients for Emergency Room Visits, 2000

Source: National Center for Health Statistics, U.S. Dept. of Health and Human Services

Principal reason for visit	Number of visits (in thousands)	Percent distribution
All visits	**108,017**	**100.0**
Stomach and abdominal pain, cramps, and spasms	6,759	6.3
Chest pain and related symptoms	5,798	5.4
Fever	4,383	4.1
Headache, pain in head	2,962	2.7
Shortness of breath	2,701	2.5
Back symptoms	2,595	2.4
Cough	2,592	2.4
Pain, site not referable to a specific body system	2,335	2.2
Laceration and cuts—upper extremity	2,322	2.1
Symptoms referable to throat	2,043	2.1
Vomiting	2,001	1.9
Accident, not otherwise specified	1,869	1.7
Labored or difficult breathing (dyspnea)	1,813	1.7
Earache or ear infection	1,798	1.7
Skin rash	1,638	1.5
Motor vehicle accident, type of injury unspecified	1,575	1.5
Low back symptoms	1,564	1.4
Injury, other and unspecified type—head, neck, and face	1,523	1.4
Laceration and cuts—facial area	1,439	1.3
Neck symptoms	1,436	1.3
ALL OTHER REASONS	**56,871**	**52.6**

Top 20 Reasons Given by Patients for Physicians' Office Visits, 2000

Source: National Center for Health Statistics, U.S. Dept. of Health and Human Services

	Number of visits (1,000)	PERCENT DISTRIBUTION Total	Female	Male
ALL VISITS	**823,542**	**100.0**	**100.0**	**100.0**
1. General medical examination	63,952	7.8	7.5	8.1
2. Progress visit, not otherwise specified	32,776	4.0	3.8	4.2
3. Cough	22,360	2.7	2.5	3.1
4. Routine prenatal examination	22,085	2.7	4.5	—
5. Postoperative visit	21,178	2.6	2.7	2.4
6. Symptoms referable to throat	17,519	2.1	2.2	2.0
7. Skin rash	13,365	1.6	1.4	1.9
8. Vision dysfunctions	12,965	1.6	1.7	1.5
9. Knee symptoms	12,533	1.5	1.4	1.7
10. Back symptoms	12,464	1.5	1.5	1.6
11. Well-baby examination	12,457	1.5	1.3	1.9
12. Stomach pain, cramps, and spasms	12,275	1.5	1.6	1.4
13. Medication, other and unspecified kinds	11,424	1.4	1.3	1.6
14. Earache or ear infection	11,288	1.4	1.2	1.6
15. Hypertension	10,398	1.3	1.1	1.4
16. Depression	10,043	1.2	1.3	1.1
17. Headache, pain in head	9,320	1.1	1.4	0.8
18. Nasal congestion	8,857	1.1	0.9	1.3
19. Chest pain and related symptoms	8,833	1.1	1.0	1.2
20. Fever	8,801	1.1	0.9	1.3
ALL OTHER REASONS	**400,650**	**59.3**	**58.0**	**60.2**

Drugs Most Frequently Prescribed in Physicians' Offices, 2000

Source: National Center for Health Statistics, U.S. Dept. of Health and Human Services; *Physicians' Desk Reference*; in thousands

Rank	Name of drug (prinicipal generic substance)[1]	Times prescribed	Therapeutic use
1.	Claritin (loratadine)	17,145	Antihistamine
2.	Lipitor (atorvastatin calcium)	16,267	Lowers cholesterol
3.	Synthroid (levothyroxine)	15,999	Thyroid hormone therapy
4.	Premarin (estrogens)	14,775	Estrogen replacement therapy
5.	Amoxicillin	13,068	Antibiotic
6.	Tylenol (acetaminophen)	12,789	Analgesic (for pain relief)
7.	Lasix (furosemide)	12,577	Diuretic, antihypertensive
8.	Celebrex (celecoxib)	12,161	Anti-inflammatory agent
9.	Glucophage (metformin)	11,468	Blood glucose regulator
10.	Albuterol sulfate	10,862	Antiasthmatic/bronchodilator
11.	Vioxx (rofecoxib)	10,801	Anti-inflammatory agent
12.	Prilosec (omeprazole)	10,751	For duodenal or gastric ulcer
13.	Norvasc (amlodipine besylate)	10,635	For high blood pressure
14.	Atenolol	10,372	For high blood pressure
15.	Influenza virus vaccine	10,197	Vaccine
16.	Prednisone	10,049	Steroid replacement therapy, anti-inflammatory agent
17.	Amoxil (amoxicillin)	9,719	Antibiotic
18.	Prevacid (lansoprazole)	9,268	For duodenal or gastric ulcer
19.	Zocor (simvastatin)	9,202	Lowers cholesterol
20.	Zoloft (sertraline hydrochloride)	9,183	Antidepressant
	ALL OTHER	**1,026,216**	

(1) The trade or generic name used by the physician on the prescription or other medical records. The use of trade names is for identification only and does not imply endorsement by the Public Health Service or the U.S. Dept. of Health and Human Services.

Hospitals and Nursing Homes in the U.S., 2000

Source: *Hospital Statistics™ 2002* edition, Health Forum, LLC, An American Hospital Association Company, copyright 2002; *Health, United States, 2002*

For information on choosing a nursing home, go to the website www.medicare.gov/nursing/overview.asp

STATE	Hospitals[1]	% of beds occupied[1]	Nursing homes	% of beds occupied	STATE	Hospitals[1]	% of beds occupied[1]	Nursing homes	% of beds occupied
AL	108	60.0	225	91.4	MT	52	67.3	104	77.9
AK	18	56.8	15	72.5	NE	85	59.1	236	83.8
AZ	61	63.1	150	75.9	NV	22	70.8	51	65.9
AR	83	58.6	255	75.1	NH	28	58.5	83	91.3
CA	389	65.9	1,369	80.8	NJ	80	68.6	361	87.8
CO	69	58.0	225	84.2	NM	35	57.6	80	89.2
CT	35	75.0	259	91.4	NY	215	78.7	665	93.7
DE	5	75.3	43	79.5	NC	113	69.5	410	88.6
DC	11	73.9	20	92.9	ND	42	59.6	88	91.2
FL	202	60.7	732	82.8	OH	163	61.2	1,009	78.0
GA	151	75.9	363	91.8	OK	108	56.2	392	70.3
HI	21	62.9	84	88.8	OR	59	59.3	150	74.0
ID	42	52.6	45	75.1	PA	207	68.4	770	88.2
IL	196	60.1	869	75.5	RI	11	71.5	99	88.0
IN	109	56.4	564	74.6	SC	63	69.4	178	86.9
IA	115	57.8	467	78.9	SD	48	65.4	114	90.0
KS	129	52.7	392	82.1	TN	121	56.3	349	89.9
KY	105	61.6	307	89.7	TX	403	59.4	1,215	68.2
LA	123	55.7	337	77.9	UT	42	56.1	93	74.5
ME	37	64.2	126	88.5	VT	14	66.8	44	89.5
MD	49	73.3	255	81.4	VA	88	67.6	278	88.5
MA	80	70.9	526	88.9	WA	84	59.8	277	81.7
MI	146	64.9	439	84.1	WV	57	61.0	139	90.5
MN	135	67.1	433	92.1	WI	118	59.5	420	83.9
MS	95	59.0	190	92.7	WY	24	56.1	40	83.5
MO	119	58.1	551	70.4	**U.S.**	**4,915**	**64.0**	**16,886**	**82.4**

(1) Community hospitals (excludes federal hospitals, hospital units of institutions, facilities for the mentally retarded, and alcoholism and chemical dependency hospitals).

Expected New Cancer Cases and Deaths, by Sex, for Leading Sites, 2002

Source: American Cancer Society

The estimates of expected new cases are offered as a rough guide only. They exclude basal and squamous cell skin cancers and in situ carcinomas, except urinary bladder. Carcinoma in situ of the breast accounts for about 54,300 new cases annually, melanoma carcinoma in situ for about 34,300. More than 1 million cases of basal cell and squamous cell cancer, which are highly curable forms of skin cancer, occur annually. About 2,200 nonmelanoma skin cancer deaths are included among deaths expected in all sites.

EXPECTED NEW CASES

Both sexes		Women		Men	
Breast	205,000	Breast	203,500	Prostate	189,000
Prostate	189,000	Lung	79,200	Lung	90,200
Lung	169,400	Colorectal	75,700	Colorectal	72,600
Colorectal	148,300	Endometrium (uterus)	39,300	Urinary bladder	41,500
Urinary bladder	56,500	Non-Hodgkin's lymphoma	25,700	Melanoma-skin	30,100
ALL SITES	**1,284,900**	**ALL SITES**	**647,400**	**ALL SITES**	**637,500**

EXPECTED DEATHS

Both sexes		Women		Men	
Lung	154,900	Lung	65,700	Lung	89,200
Colorectal	56,600	Breast	39,600	Prostate	30,200
Breast	40,000	Colorectal	28,800	Colorectal	27,800
Prostate	30,200	Pancreas	15,200	Pancreas	14,500
Pancreas	29,700	Ovary	13,900	Non-Hodgkin's lymphoma	12,700
ALL SITES	**555,500**	**ALL SITES**	**267,300**	**ALL SITES**	**288,200**

U.S. Cancer Incidence for Top 15 Sites, 1992-99

Source: Surveillance, Epidemiology, and End Results (SEER) Program, National Cancer Institute

	Rate[1]	Average yearly % change		Rate[1]	Average yearly % change		Rate[1]	Average yearly % change
ALL SITES	**475.8**	**–0.9**	Non-Hodgkin's lymphoma	19.0	+0.1	Oral cavity and pharynx	11.4	–2.1
Prostate	178.9	–4.2	Ovary	17.1	–0.9	Pancreas	11.0	–0.6
Breast (female)	132.1	+1.1	Melanoma of the skin	15.5	+2.8	Kidney and renal pelvis	10.7	+0.9
Lung	63.9	–1.3	Leukemia	12.2	–1.6	Stomach	9.3	–1.3
Colon and rectum	54.3	–0.6				Thyroid	6.3	+3.2
Uterus	24.5	+0.3						
Urinary bladder	20.2	–0.4						

(1) Per 100,000 population; rates for prostate, breast, and ovary are sex-specific; rates age-adjusted to the 2000 population, and so not comparable with previously published rates; annual average for 8-year period.

U.S. Cancer Mortality for Top 15 Sites, 1992-99

Source: Surveillance, Epidemiology, and End Results (SEER) Program, National Cancer Institute

	Rate[1]	Average yearly % change[2]		Rate[1]	Average yearly % change[2]		Rate[1]	Average yearly % change[2]
ALL SITES	**208.7**	**–0.9**	Ovary	9.1	–0.9	Liver and intraheptic bile duct	4.4	+2.4
Lung	58.2	–0.7	Non-Hodgkin's lymphoma	8.6	+0.6	Urinary bladder	4.4	–0.3
Prostate	35.7	–3.5	Leukemia	7.9	–0.5	Esophagus	4.3	+0.7
Breast (female)	29.7	–2.4	Stomach	5.2	–2.8	Kidney and renal pelvis	4.3	–0.2
Colon and rectum	22.3	–1.7	Brain and other nervous system	4.8	–0.5	Myeloma (bone marrow)	3.9	–0.1
Pancreas	10.6	–0.1						

(1) Per 100,000 population; rates age-adjusted to the 2000 population, and so not comparable with previously published rates; annual average for 8-year period. (2) For 1992-99.

Cardiovascular Diseases Statistical Summary, 2000

Source: American Heart Association

Prevalence — An estimated 61,800,000 Americans had one or more forms of heart and blood vessel disease in 2000.
- hypertension (high blood pressure) — 50,000,000
- coronary heart disease — 12,900,000
- stroke — 4,700,000
- congestive heart failure — 4,900,000

Mortality — 945,836 in 2000 (39.4% of all deaths).
- Someone died from cardiovascular disease every 33 seconds in the U.S. in 2000.

Congenital or inborn heart defects —
- Mortality from such heart defects was 4,310 in 2000.

Coronary heart disease (heart attack and angina pectoris) — caused 515,204 deaths in 2000.
- 12,700,000 Americans had a history of heart attack and/or angina pectoris.
- As many as 1,100,000 Americans had coronary attacks in 2000.

Congestive heart failure — killed 51,546 in 2000.
Stroke — killed 167,661 Americans in 2000.
Rheumatic heart disease — killed 3,582 in 2000.

Transplant Waiting List, Oct. 2002*

Source: United Network for Organ Sharing

Type of transplant	Patients waiting
Kidney	53,145
Liver	17,295
Pancreas	1,322
Pancreas islet cell	320
Kidney-pancreas	2,493
Intestine	193
Heart	3,966
Heart-lung	203
Lung	3,832
Total[1]	**80,319**

* As of Oct. 4, 2002. (1) Some patients are waiting for more than one organ; therefore total number of patients waiting is less than the sum of patients waiting for each organ.

Transplants Performed, 2001

Source: United Network for Organ Sharing

Type of transplant	Number
Kidney	14,184
Liver	5,181
Pancreas	466
Kidney-pancreas	886
Intestine	111
Heart	2,202
Heart-lung	27
Lung	1,053
Total	**24,110**

AIDS Deaths and New AIDS Cases in the U.S., 1985-2001

Source: *Health, United States, 2002; HIV/AIDS Surveillance Report,* Vol. 13, No. 2, covering through 2001; National Center for Health Statistics, U.S. Dept. of Health and Human Services

	Percent Distribution	All Years[2]	1985	1990	1995	1998	1999	2000	1st ½ 2001	2001 rate[3]
TOTAL DEATHS[1]	**—**	**467,910**	**6,996**	**31,836**	**51,414**	**18,148**	**16,762**	**14,499**	**NA**	**NA**
						NEW AIDS CASES				
All races	—	767,023	8,159	41,465	70,519	45,881	44,700	40,421	19,094	14.3
MALE										
All males, 13 years and over	100.0	629,429	7,504	36,193	56,776	35,104	34,094	30,251	14,304	27.2
Race										
White, non-Hispanic	48.7	306,373	4,749	20,835	26,065	13,827	12,721	11,370	5,293	13.8
Black, non-Hispanic	34.7	218,150	1,709	10,237	20,858	14,602	14,849	13,115	6,354	106.7
Hispanic[4]	15.5	97,337	989	4,748	9,130	6,176	6,069	5,300	2,412	42.8
American Indian or Alaska Native[5]	0.3	1,955	8	81	198	119	135	135	71	18.3
Asian or Pacific Islander[5]	0.8	5,088	49	263	490	322	298	290	155	7.4
Age										
13-19 years	0.4	2,338	27	107	222	141	131	146	88	1.3
20-29 years	15.7	99,050	1,501	6,923	8,396	4,248	3,960	3,332	1,551	17.9
30-39 years	45.2	284,310	3,588	16,673	25,719	15,168	14,444	12,554	5,739	57.7
40-49 years	27.4	172,420	1,632	8,833	16,181	10,859	10,884	9,724	4,719	45.8
50-59 years	8.4	52,881	597	2,647	4,702	3,494	3,491	3,403	1,633	22.7
60 years and over	2.9	18,430	159	1,010	1,556	1,194	1,184	1,092	574	5.6
FEMALE										
All females, 13 years and over	100.0	129,005	524	4,547	12,998	10,410	10,352	9,979	4,698	8.4
White, non-Hispanic	22.5	29,002	143	1,227	3,043	2,003	1,901	1,872	875	2.2
Black, non-Hispanic	60.5	78,064	280	2,559	7,605	6,700	6,740	6,493	3,151	46.1
Hispanic[4]	16.0	20,675	98	728	2,235	1,604	1,602	1,464	614	11.2
American Indian or Alaska Native[5]	0.3	447	2	9	38	32	41	70	19	6.1
Asian or Pacific Islander[5]	0.6	732	1	20	73	56	62	75	32	1.5
Age										
13-19 years	1.3	1,694	5	66	155	142	167	171	74	1.2
20-29 years	21.1	27,236	178	1,119	2,672	1,919	1,892	1,734	785	9.2
30-39 years	44.4	57,321	232	2,088	5,948	4,426	4,255	4,002	1,822	18.3
40-49 years	23.3	30,086	45	781	3,070	2,850	2,795	2,856	1,405	13.1
50-59 years	6.6	8,550	26	274	818	788	922	873	438	5.6
60 years and over	3.2	4,118	38	219	335	285	321	343	174	1.4
CHILDREN										
All children, under 13 years	100.0	8,589	131	725	745	367	254	191	92	0.4
Race										
White, non-Hispanic	18.2	1,564	26	157	117	59	31	30	16	0.1
Black, non-Hispanic	61.4	5,273	87	390	483	234	170	125	57	1.7
Hispanic[4]	19.3	1,656	18	169	135	71	48	31	18	0.4
American Indian or Alaska Native[5]	0.4	31	0	5	2	0	2	1	0	0.0
Asian or Pacific Islander[5]	0.6	52	0	4	5	2	2	3	1	0.1
Age										
Under 1 year	39.0	3,352	63	318	268	96	89	66	24	1.5
1-12 years	61.0	5,237	68	407	477	271	165	125	68	0.3

NA = Not available. **Note:** The definition of AIDS cases for reporting purposes was expanded in 1985, 1987, and 1993, as more was learned about the spectrum of human immunodeficiency virus-associated diseases. Data exclude residents of U.S. territories. Figures were updated June 30, 2001 to include temporarily delayed case reports and may differ from previous reports of *Health, United States.* (1) Based on preliminary figures and subject to revision. (2) Revised figures; includes cases and deaths prior to 1985 and for years not shown. Through Dec. 2001. (3) Rate is per 100,000 pop. (4) Persons of Hispanic origin may be of any race. (5) Excludes persons of Hispanic origin.

New AIDS Cases in the U.S., 1985-2001, by Transmission Category

Source: *Health, United States, 2002,* CDC, National Center for HIV, STD, and TB Prevention, Div. of HIV/AIDS Prevention

TRANSMISSION CATEGORY	Percent distribution	All years[1]	1985	1990	1995	1998	1999	2000	1st ½ 2001
All males 13 years and older	**100.0**	**629,429**	**7,504**	**36,193**	**56,776**	**35,104**	**34,094**	**30,251**	**14,304**
Men who have sex with men	56.8	357,583	5,348	23,658	30,944	16,878	15,632	13,648	6,241
Injecting drug use	21.0	132,238	1,103	6,923	13,376	7,440	6,893	5,554	2,215
Men who have sex with men and injecting drug use	7.6	48,132	661	2,943	4,185	2,224	1,929	1,587	657
Hemophilia/coagulation disorder	0.8	4,893	68	332	438	153	143	93	45
Heterosexual contact[2]	4.5	28,430	32	715	2,924	2,723	2,947	2,537	1,077
Sex with injecting drug user	1.4	8,931	25	454	871	645	634	514	228
Transfusion[3]	0.8	4,944	102	440	319	151	137	146	54
Undetermined[4]	8.5	53,209	190	1,182	4,590	5,535	6,413	6,686	4,015
All females 13 years and older	**100.0**	**129,005**	**524**	**4,547**	**12,998**	**10,410**	**10,352**	**9,979**	**4,698**
Injecting drug use	40.3	52,009	287	2,347	5,426	3,251	2,985	2,545	954
Hemophilia/coagulation disorder	0.2	278	3	15	29	24	13	5	3
Heterosexual contact[2]	39.8	51,339	119	1,538	5,555	4,401	4,397	4,025	1,680
Sex with injecting drug user	15.1	19,437	82	1,030	1,923	1,249	1,135	976	383
Transfusion[3]	2.9	3,754	63	330	253	126	131	151	42
Undetermined[4]	16.8	21,625	52	317	1,735	2,608	2,826	3,253	2,019

Note: The definition of AIDS cases for reporting purposes was expanded in 1985, 1987, and 1993, as more was learned about the spectrum of human immunodeficiency virus-associated diseases. Data exclude residents of U.S. territories. Figures were updated June 30, 2001 to include temporarily delayed case reports and may differ from previous reports of Health, United States. (1) Includes cases prior to 1985 and for years not shown. (2) Includes persons who have had heterosexual contact with a person with human immunodeficiency virus (HIV) infection or at risk of HIV infection. (3) Receipt of blood transfusion, blood components, or tissue. (4) Includes persons for whom risk information is incomplete, persons still under investigation, men reported only to have had heterosexual contact with prostitutes, and interviewed persons for whom no specific risk is identified.

HEALTH

Basic First Aid

Source: American Red Cross

NOTE: This information is not intended to be a substitute for formal training. It is recommended that you contact your local American Red Cross chapter to sign-up for a First Aid/CPR/AED course.

Knowing what to do for an injured victim until a doctor or other trained person gets to the accident scene can save a life, especially in cases of severe bleeding, stoppage of breathing, poisoning, and shock. It is important to get medical assistance as soon as possible.

People with special medical problems, such as diabetes, cardiovascular disease, epilepsy, or allergy, are urged to wear some sort of emblem identifying the problem, as a safeguard against receiving medication that might be harmful or even fatal. Emblems may be obtained from Medic Alert Foundation, 2323 Colorado Ave., Turlock, CA 95382; 800-344-3226.

Animal bite — Wash wound with soap under running water and apply antibiotic ointment and dressing. When possible, the animal should be caught alive for rabies testing.

Asphyxiation — Call 9-1-1, or the local emergency number, then start rescue breathing.

Bleeding — Elevate the wound above the heart if possible. Apply direct pressure to the wound with sterile compress until bleeding stops. Call 9-1-1, or the local emergency number if bleeding is severe.

Burn — If mild, with skin unbroken and no blisters, flush with cool water until pain subsides. Apply a loose sterile dry dressing if necessary. If severe, call 9-1-1 or the local emergency number. Apply sterile compresses and keep patient comfortably warm until advanced medical assistance arrives. Do not try to clean burn or break blisters.

Chemical in eye — Call or have someone call 9-1-1 or the local emergency number. With the victim's head turned to the side, continuously flush the injured eye with water, letting the water run away from the other eye.

Choking — See **Abdominal Thrust**.

Convulsions — Place person on back on bed or rug. Loosen clothing. Turn head to side. Do not place a blunt object between the patient's teeth. If convulsions do not stop, get medical attention immediately.

Cut (minor) — Apply mild antiseptic and sterile compress after washing with soap under warm running water.

Fainting — If victim feels faint, lower him or her to the ground. Lay the victim down on his or her back. If there are no signs of a spinal injury or nausea, elevate the victim's legs approximately 12 inches. Loosen any restrictive clothing and check for any other signs of injury. Call 9-1-1 or the local emergency number if the victim remains unconscious for more than a few minutes.

Foreign body in eye — Try to remove the object by having the victim blink several times. If the object doesn't come out, try gently flushing the eye with water. Do not rub the eye. If the object still doesn't come out, the victim should receive professional medical attention.

Frostbite — Handle frostbitten area gently. Do not rub. Soak affected area in warm water (100–105° F). Do not allow frostbitten area to touch the container. Soak until frostbitten part looks red and feels warm. Loosely bandage with dry, sterile dressings. If fingers or toes are frostbitten, put sterile gauze between them.

Heat Stroke and Heat Exhaustion — Remove the victim from the heat. Loosen any tight clothing and apply cool, wet cloths to the skin. If the victim is conscious give him or her cool water, to drink slowly. Call 9-1-1 or the local emergency number if the victim becomes unconscious.

Hypothermia — Call 9-1-1 or the local emergency number. Move victim to a warm place. Remove wet clothing and dry victim, if necessary. Warm victim gradually by wrapping the person in warm blankets or clothing. Apply heat pads or other heat sources if available, but not directly to the body. Give the victim warm, non-alcoholic and decaffeinated liquids to drink.

Loss of Limb — If a limb is severed, it is important to properly protect the limb so that it can possibly be reattached. After the victim is cared for, the limb should be wrapped in a sterile gauze or clean material and placed in a clean plastic bag, garbage can or other suitable container. Pack ice around the limb on the OUTSIDE of the bag to keep the limb cold. Call ahead to the hospital to alert staff there of the situation.

Poisoning — Call 9-1-1 or the local emergency number and Poison Control Center (800-222-1222) and follow their directions. Do not give the victim any food or drink or induce vomiting, unless specified by the Poison Control Center.

Shock (injury-related) — Monitor breathing and consciousness. Help the victim rest as comfortably as possible. If uncertain as to his or her injuries, keep the victim flat on the back. Otherwise elevate feet and legs 12 inches. Maintain normal body temperature; if the weather is cold or damp, place blankets or extra clothing over and under the victim; if weather is hot, provide shade.

Snakebite — Call 9-1-1 or the local emergency number. Wash the injury. Keep the area still and at a lower level than the heart. Keep the victim quiet. If the victim cannot get professional medical help within 30 minute, consider using a snakebite kit if available.

Sprains and fractures — Apply ice to reduce swelling and pain. Do not try to straighten or move broken limbs. Apply a splint to immobilize the injured area if the victim must be transported. If you suspect a serious injury, call 9-1-1 or the local emergency number.

Sting from insect — If possible, remove stinger by scraping it away or using tweezers. Wash the area with soap and water; cover it to keep it clean. Apply a cold pack to reduce pain and swelling. Call 9-1-1 or the local emergency number immediately if body swells, patient collapses, or you know that the victim is allergic to the sting.

Unconsciousness — Call 9-1-1 or the local emergency number immediately. If the person has signs of circulation, place him or her in the recovery position (i.e., lying on his or her side, with head supported, so that the airway is open —but do not move if a spinal injury is suspected).

Abdominal Thrust (Heimlich Maneuver)

The recommended first aid for conscious choking victims is the abdominal thrust, also known as the Heimlich maneuver, after its creator, Dr. Henry Heimlich.

- Get behind the victim and wrap your arms around him or her about 1-2 inches above the navel.
- Make a fist with one hand and place it, with the thumb knuckle pressing inward at the abdomen.
- Grasp the fist with the other hand and give upward thrusts until object is removed or help arrives.

Rescue Breathing

- Determine consciousness by tapping the victim on the shoulder and asking loudly, "Are you okay?"
- Tilt the victim's head back so that the chin is pointing upward. Do not press on the soft tissue under the chin, as this might obstruct the airway. If you suspect that an accident victim might have neck or back injuries, open the airway by placing the tips of your index and middle fingers on the corners of the person's jaw, and your thumbs on the victim's cheekbones, to lift the jaw forward without tilting the head.
- Place your cheek and ear close to the victim's mouth and nose. Look at the chest to see if it rises and falls. Listen and feel for air to be exhaled for about 5 seconds.
- If there is no breathing, pinch the victim's nostrils shut with the thumb and index finger of your hand that is pressing on the victim's forehead. Another way to prevent leakage of air when the lungs are inflated is to press your cheek against the victim's nose.
- Blow air into the mouth by taking a deep breath and then sealing your mouth tightly around the victim's mouth. Initially, give 2 rescue (approx. 2 seconds each) breaths.
- Watch for the victim's chest to see if it rises.
- Stop when the chest is expanded. Raise your mouth; turn your head to the side and listen for exhalation.
- Watch the chest to see if it falls. Check for signs of circulation, including movement or coughing in response to the rescue breaths. If there are signs of circulation, but no breathing, continue rescue breathing. If there are no signs of circulation, begin CPR.
- Repeat giving 1 breath every 5 seconds until the victim starts breathing or advanced medical help arrives and takes over. Recheck for breathing and movement about every minute

Note: Infants (up to 1 year) and children (1 to 8 years) should be treated as described above, except for the following:

- Do not tilt the head as far back as an adult's head.
- Both the mouth and nose of an infant should be sealed by the mouth.
- Blow into the infant's mouth and nose once every 3 seconds with less pressure and volume than for a child.

Heart and Blood Vessel Disease

Source: American Heart Association, 7272 Greenville Ave., Dallas, TX 75231-4596; phone: (800) 242-8721

Warning Signs

Of Heart Attack

- Uncomfortable pressure, fullness, squeezing, or pain in the center of the chest lasting 2 minutes or longer
- Pain may radiate to the shoulder, arm, neck, or jaw
- Sweating may accompany pain or discomfort
- Nausea and vomiting also may occur
- Shortness of breath, dizziness, or fainting may accompany other signs

The American Heart Association advises immediate action at the onset of these symptoms. The association points out that more than half of heart attack victims die within 1 hour of the onset of symptoms and before they have reached the hospital.

Of Stroke

- Sudden numbness or weakness of face, arm or leg, especially on one side of the body
- Sudden confusion, trouble speaking or understanding
- Sudden trouble seeing in one or both eyes
- Sudden trouble walking, dizziness, loss of balance or coordination
- Sudden severe headache with no known cause

Some Major Risk Factors

Blood pressure—High blood pressure increases the risk of stroke, heart attack, kidney failure, and congestive heart failure.

Cholesterol—A blood cholesterol level over 240 mg/dl (milligrams of cholesterol per deciliter of blood) approximately doubles the risk of coronary heart disease; over 40 mil have a cholesterol level above 240 mg/dl. Levels between 200 and 240 mg/dl are in a zone of moderate and increasing risk.

Diabetes—¾ of people with diabetes mellitus die of some form of heart or blood vessel disease.

Smoking—Cigarette smokers have more than twice the risk of heart attack and 2-4 times the risk of sudden cardiac death as nonsmokers. Young smokers have a higher risk for early death from stroke.

Obesity—Using a body mass index (BMI) of 25 and higher for overweight and 30 and higher for obesity, 111.8 mil Americans age 20 and over are overweight and 45.6 mil are obese.

Understanding Blood Pressure

High blood pressure, or hypertension, affects people of all races, sexes, ethnic origins, and ages. Various causes can trigger this often symptomless disease. Since hypertension can increase one's risk for stroke, heart attack, kidney failure, and congestive heart failure, it is recommended that individuals have a blood pressure reading at least once every 2 years (more often if advised by a physician).

A blood pressure reading is really two measurements in one, with one written over the other, such as 122/78. The **upper number (systolic pressure)** represents the amount of pressure in the blood vessels when the heart contracts (beats) and pushes blood through the circulatory system. The **lower number (diastolic pressure)** represents the pressure in the blood vessels between beats, when the heart is resting. According to National Institutes of Health guidelines, normal blood pressure is below 130/85 and "high normal" is between 130/85 and 139/89.

High blood pressure is divided into 3 stages, based upon severity:

- **Stage 1** is from 140/90 through 159/99
- **Stage 2** is from 160/100 through 179/109
- **Stage 3** is 180/110 or greater

The diagnosis of hypertension can be based on either the systolic or the diastolic reading.

High blood pressure usually cannot be cured, but it can be controlled in a variety of ways, including lifestyle modifications and medication. Treatment always should be at the direction and under the supervision of a physician.

Examples of Moderate[1] Amounts of Exercise

Source: *Physical Activity and Health: A Report of the Surgeon General*, U.S. Dept. of Health and Human Services, 1996

ACTIVITY	DURATION[2] (min)
Washing and waxing a car	45-60
Washing windows or floors	45-60
Playing touch football	30-45
Wheeling self in wheelchair	30-40
Walking 1 ¾ mi (20 min/mi)	35
Basketball (shooting baskets)	30
Bicycling 5 mi	30
Dancing fast (social)	30
Raking leaves	30
Walking 2 mi (15 min/mi)	30
Swimming laps	20
Basketball (playing a game)	15-20
Bicycling 4 mi	15
Jumping rope	15
Running 1 ½ mi (10 min/mi)	15
Shoveling snow	15

Note: The activities are arranged from less vigorous, and using more time, to more vigorous, and using less time. (1) A "moderate" amount of physical activity uses about 150 calories (kcal), or 1,000 if done daily for a week. (2) Activities can be performed at various intensities; the suggested durations are based on the expected intensity of effort.

Finding Your Target Heart Rate

Source: Carole Casten, EdD, *Aerobics Today;* Peg Jordan, RN, Aerobics and Fitness Assoc. of America

The target heart rate is the heartbeat rate a person should have during aerobic exercise (such as running, fast walking, cycling, or cross-country skiing) to get the full benefit of the exercise for cardiovascular conditioning.

First, determine the intensity level at which one would like to exercise. A sedentary person may want to begin an exercise regimen at the 60% level and work up gradually to the 70% level. Athletes and highly fit individuals must work at the 85-95% level to receive benefits.

Second, calculate the target heart rate. One common way of doing this is by using the American College of Sports Medicine Method.

To obtain cardiovascular fitness benefits from aerobic exercise, it is recommended that an individual participate in an aerobic activity at least 3-5 times a week for 20-30 minutes per session, although cardiac patients and very sedentary individuals can obtain benefits with shorter periods (15-20 minutes). Generally, training changes occur in 4-6 weeks, but they can occur in as little as 2 weeks.

The American College of Sports Medicine Method

Using the American College of Sports Medicine Method to calculate one's target heart rate, an individual should subtract his or her age from 220, then multiply by the desired intensity level of the workout. Then divide the answer by 6 for a 10-second pulse count. (The 10-second pulse count is useful for checking whether the target heart rate is being achieved during the workout. One can easily check one's pulse—at the wrist or side of the neck—counting the number of beats in 10 seconds.)

For example, a 20-year-old wishing to exercise at 70% intensity would employ the following steps:

Maximum Heart Rate	220 – 20 = 200
Target Heart Rate	200 × .70 = 140
10-second Pulse Count	140 6 = 23

To work at the desired level of intensity, this 20 year-old would strive for a target heart rate of 140 beats per minute, or a 10-second pulse count of 23.

Cancer Prevention

Source: American Cancer Society, 1599 Clifton Road NE, Atlanta, GA 30329-4251; phone: (800) 227-2345

PRIMARY PREVENTION: Modifiable determinants of cancer risk.

Smoking	Lung cancer mortality rates are about 22 times higher for current male smokers, and 12 times higher for current female smokers, than for those who have never smoked. Smoking accounts for about 30% of all cancer deaths in the U.S. Tobacco use is responsible for nearly 1 in 5 deaths in the U.S. Smoking is associated with cancer of the lung, mouth, pharynx, larynx, esophagus, pancreas, uterine cervix, kidney, and bladder.
Nutrition and Diet	Risk for colon, rectum, breast (among postmenopausal women), kidney, prostate, and endometrial cancers increases in obese people. While a diet high in fat may be a factor in the development of certain cancers, particularly cancer of the colon and rectum, prostate, and endometrium, the link between obesity and cancer is more the result of an imbalance between caloric intake and energy expenditure than fat per se. Eating 5 or more servings of fruits and vegetables each day, and eating other foods from plant sources (especially grains and beans), may reduce risk for many cancers. Physical activity can help protect against some cancers, and help to maintain a healthy weight.
Sunlight	Many of the one million skin cancers that are expected to be diagnosed in 2001 could have been prevented by protection from the sun's rays. Epidemiological evidence shows that sun exposure is a major factor in the development of melanoma and that the incidence rates are increasing around the world.
Alcohol	Heavy drinking, especially when accompanied by cigarette smoking or smokeless tobacco use, increases risk of cancers of the mouth, larynx, pharynx, esophagus, and liver. Studies have also noted an association between regular alcohol consumption and an increased risk of breast cancer.
Smokeless Tobacco	Use of chewing tobacco or snuff increases risk of cancers of the mouth and pharynx. The excess risk of cancer of the cheek and gum may reach nearly 50-fold among long-term snuff users.
Estrogen	Estrogen replacement therapy (ERT) to control menopausal symptoms can increase the risk of endometrial cancer. However, adding progesterone to estrogen (hormone replacement therapy, or HRT) helps to minimize this risk. Most studies suggest that long-term use (5 years or more) of HRT after menopause increases the risk of breast cancer, and recent studies suggest that risks from taking HRT exceed benefits. The benefits and risks of the use of HRT or ERT by menopausal women should be discussed carefully by the woman and her doctor. Research in this area continues.
Radiation	Excessive exposure to ionizing radiation can increase cancer risk. Medical and dental X rays are adjusted to deliver the lowest dose possible without sacrificing image quality. Excessive radon exposure in the home may increase lung cancer risk, especially in cigarette smokers. If levels are found to be too high, remedial actions should be taken.
Environmental Hazards	Exposure to various chemicals (including benzene, asbestos, vinyl chloride, arsenic, and aflatoxin) increases risk of various cancers. Risk of lung cancer from asbestos is greatly increased when combined with smoking. Pesticides, low-frequency radiation, toxic wastes, and proximity to nuclear power plants have not been proven to cause cancer.

Cancer-Detection Guidelines

Source: American Cancer Society, 1599 Clifton Road NE, Atlanta, GA 30329-4251; phone: (800) 227-2345

SECONDARY PREVENTION: Steps to diagnose a cancer or precursor as early as possible after it has developed.

A cancer-related checkup is recommended every 3 years for people aged 20-40 and every year for people 40 years of age and older. This exam should include health counseling and, depending on a person's age, might include examinations for cancers of the thyroid, oral cavity, skin, lymph nodes, testes, and ovaries, as well as for some nonmalignant diseases. Special tests for certain cancer sites for individuals at average risk are recommended as outlined below:

Breast Cancer	Breast self-exam monthly, beginning at age 20. Breast clinical physical examination for women aged 20-39, every 3 years; 40 and over, every year. Mammography for women aged 40 and over, every year.
Cervical Cancer	Annual Pap test and pelvic exam for women who are or have been sexually active or have reached age 18. After 3 or more consecutive satisfactory normal annual exams, the Pap test may be performed less frequently at the discretion of the physician.
Colorectal Cancer	Beginning at age 50, both men and women should follow one of these testing schedules: Yearly fecal occult blood test, or Flexible sigmoidoscopy every five years, or Yearly fecal occult blood test, plus flexible sigmoidoscopy every 5 years, or Colonoscopy every 10 years, or Double-contrast barium enema every 5-10 years.
Endometrial Cancer	For women with or at high risk of hereditary nonpolyposis colon cancer (HNPCC), annual screening including endometrial biopsy should be obtained beginning at age 35.
Prostate Cancer	Both Prostate-Specific Antigen (PSA) and Digital Rectal Examination (DRE) should be offered annually, beginning at age 50, to men who have at least a 10-year life expectancy. Men at high risk, such as African-Americans and men who have a first-degree relative (father, brother, or son) diagnosed with prostate cancer at an early age, should begin testing at age 45. Health care professionals should give men the opportunity to openly discuss the benefits and risks of testing at annual checkups. Men should actively participate in the decision by learning about prostate cancer and the pros and cons of early detection and treatment of prostate cancer, so that they can make an informed decision about testing.
Skin Cancer	Adults should practice skin self-exam regularly. Suspicious lesions should be evaluated promptly by a physician.

IT'S A FACT: Chefs and cooks should keep their fingernails short, researchers from the University of Georgia said at the 2002 annual conference of the International Association for Food Protection. Even thorough hand washing often failed to remove bacteria that breed under the nails, the scientists said.

Breast Cancer

Source: American Cancer Society, Inc., 1599 Clifton Road NE, Atlanta, GA 30329-4251; phone: (800) 227-2345

It is estimated that, in 2002, about 203,500 women and 1,500 men in the United States will be diagnosed with breast cancer, and about 39,600 women and 400 men will die from it. Breast cancer is the second largest cause of cancer death for women in the U.S. (lung cancer ranks first), but mortality rates have been declining, especially among younger women, probably because of earlier detection and improved treatment.

The risk for breast cancer increases as a woman ages. The risk is also higher for women with a personal or family history; a long menstrual history (menstrual periods that started early and ended late in life); recent use of oral contraceptives (birth control pills) long-term use of postmenopausal hormone replacement therapy; and no children or no live birth until age 30 or older. Other risk factors for the disease include alcohol consumption and obesity. Inherited mutations such as in the BRCA1 and BRCA2 genes greatly increase a woman's risk for breast cancer, but these mutations probably account for less than 10% of all breast cancers. By far, the majority of women who develop breast cancer have no family history.

Breast cancer is often manifested first as an abnormality that appears on a mammogram, which is a special type of x-ray. Physical signs and symptoms that show up later, which may be detectable by a woman or her doctor, include a breast lump and, less commonly, breast thickening, swelling, distortion, or tenderness; skin irritation or dimpling; or pain, scaliness, or retraction of the nipple. Breast pain is more commonly associated with benign (noncancerous) conditions.

Studies show that **early detection** increases survival and treatment options. The American Cancer Society (ACS) recommends that women 40 and older should have an annual mammogram, have an annual clinical breast exam by a health care professional, and perform monthly breast self-examinations. The ACS recommends that women ages 20-39 should have a clinical breast exam every 3 years and should also perform monthly breast self-examinations. Although most breast lumps that are detected are noncancerous, any suspicious lump needs to be biopsied.

Treatment for breast cancer may involve lumpectomy (local removal of a tumor), mastectomy (surgical removal of the breast), radiation therapy, chemotherapy, hormone therapy, immunotherapy, or some combination of these. For early-stage breast cancer, long-term survival rates following lumpectomy plus radiation therapy are similar to survival rates after modified radical mastectomy.

Numerous **drugs** that may **prevent** breast cancer or improve its treatment are being studied. One is **tamoxifen**, a synthetic hormone that blocks the action of estrogen in the breast. Already used for treating breast cancer, it has been shown to reduce the likelihood of developing the disease in women considered at higher than average risk, including women age 60 and older. Unfortunately, tamoxifen also has dangerous side effects, such as increased risk of uterine cancer and blood clots in the lungs. Research is also being done on another drug, **Raloxifene**, which is approved for preventing osteoporosis in postmenopausal women. It is now being directly compared to tamoxifen in a large clinical study to evaluate its effect on breast cancer risk.

Trends in Daily Use of Cigarettes, for U.S. 8th, 10th, and 12th Graders

Source: *Monitoring the Future*, Univ. of Michigan Inst. for Social Research and National Inst. on Drug Abuse

(percent who smoked daily in last 30 days; change 2000-2001 in percentage points)

	8th grade						10th grade						12th grade					
	1997	1998	1999	2000	2001	'00-'01 change	1997	1998	1999	2000	2001	'00-'01 change	1997	1998	1999	2000	2001	'00-'01 change
TOTAL	9.0	8.8	8.1	7.4	5.5	–1.9	18.0	15.8	15.9	14.0	12.2	–1.8	24.6	22.4	23.1	20.6	19.0	–1.6
Sex																		
Male	9.0	8.1	7.4	7.0	5.9	–1.1	17.2	14.7	15.6	13.7	12.4	–1.3	24.8	22.7	23.6	20.9	18.4	–2.5
Female	8.7	9.0	8.4	7.5	4.9	–2.5	18.5	16.8	15.9	14.1	11.9	–2.2	23.6	21.5	22.2	19.7	18.9	–0.8
College plans																		
None or under 4 yrs.	25.4	25.2	25.2	21.7	17.7	–4.0	35.4	31.7	32.1	28.8	27.3	–1.5	35.6	34.6	34.2	31.7	30.1	–1.6
Complete 4 yrs.	6.9	6.6	5.9	5.6	3.9	–1.6	15.0	12.9	13.2	11.6	9.6	–2.0	20.6	18.4	19.5	16.6	15.5	–1.1
Region																		
Northeast	8.8	6.1	7.2	6.9	6.1	–0.8	18.0	18.7	17.7	14.1	11.0	–3.2	29.4	23.4	23.2	22.8	21.9	–0.9
North central	10.3	11.2	11.5	9.0	6.4	–2.6	19.5	17.3	19.6	16.3	13.2	–3.1	28.0	27.8	25.9	23.6	25.2	1.6
South	9.5	10.2	8.5	7.8	6.1	–1.6	20.5	17.1	16.3	15.7	14.3	–1.3	22.6	21.8	24.2	19.4	15.5	–3.9
West	6.8	5.8	3.8	4.9	2.6	–2.3	11.1	8.8	9.1	7.8	7.0	–0.7	17.5	15.5	17.3	16.9	13.4	–3.6
Race/Ethnicity[1]																		
White	11.4	10.4	9.7	9.0	7.5	–1.5	21.4	20.3	19.1	17.7	15.5	–2.2	27.8	28.3	26.9	25.7	23.8	–2.0
Black	3.7	3.8	3.8	3.2	2.8	–0.4	5.6	5.8	5.3	5.2	5.2	0.0	7.2	7.4	7.7	8.0	7.5	–0.5
Hispanic	8.1	8.4	8.5	7.1	5.0	–2.1	10.8	9.4	9.1	8.8	7.4	–1.4	14.0	13.6	14.0	15.7	12.0	–3.7

(1) For each of these groups, data for the specified year and previous year have been combined to increase sample size and thus provide a more reliable estimate.

Some Benefits of Quitting Smoking

Source: American Cancer Society, Inc., 1599 Clifton Road NE, Atlanta, GA 30329-4251; phone: (800) 227-2345

Within 20 Minutes
- Blood pressure drops to a level close to that before the last cigarette
- Temperature of hands and feet increases to normal

Within 8 Hours
- Carbon monoxide level in the blood drops to normal

Within 24 Hours
- Chance of heart attack decreases

Within 2 Weeks to 3 Months
- Circulation improves
- Lung function increases up to 30%

Within 1 to 9 Months
- Coughing, sinus congestion, fatigue, and shortness of breath decrease
- Cilia regain normal function in the lungs, increasing the ability to handle mucus, clean the lungs, reduce infection

Within 1 Year
- Excess risk of coronary heart disease is half that of a smoker's

Within 5 Years
- Stroke risk is reduced to that of a nonsmoker 5-15 years after quitting

Within 10 Years
- Lung cancer death rate about half that of a continuing smoker's
- Risk of cancer of the mouth, throat, esophagus, bladder, kidney, and pancreas decreases

Within 15 Years
- Risk of coronary heart disease is that of a nonsmoker's

Diabetes

Source: American Diabetes Association, 1701 N Beauregard St., Alexandria, VA 22311; phone: (800) 342-2382

Diabetes is a chronic disease in which the body does not produce or properly use **insulin**, a hormone needed to convert sugar, starches, and other foods into energy necessary for daily life. Both genetics and environment appear to play roles in the onset of diabetes. This disease, which has no cure, is the 5th-leading cause of death by disease in the U.S. According to death certificate data, diabetes contributed to 210,000 deaths in 1999. It is estimated that there are 17 million Americans with diabetes, 5.9 million of whom are undiagnosed.

In 1997, the American Diabetes Association issued **new guidelines for diagnosing diabetes**. The recommendations include: lowering the acceptable level of blood sugar in a fasting glucose test from 140 mg of glucose/deciliter of blood to 126 mg/deciliter; testing all adults 45 years and older, and then every 3 years if normal; and testing at a younger age, or more frequently, in high-risk individuals. The American Diabetes Association supports studies that have proven that detection at an earlier stage and modest lifestyle changes will help prevent or delay complications of diabetes.

There are 2 major types of diabetes:

Type 1 (formerly known as insulin dependent, or juvenile diabetes). The body produces very little or no insulin; disease most often begins in childhood or early adulthood. People with type 1 diabetes must take daily insulin injections to stay alive.

Type 2 (formerly known as non-insulin dependent, or adult-onset diabetes). The body does not produce enough or cannot properly use insulin. It is the most common form of the disease (90-95% of cases in people over age 20) and often begins later in life.

Warning Signs of Diabetes

Type 1 Diabetes (usually occurs suddenly):

frequent urination	unusual weight loss
unusual thirst	extreme fatigue
extreme hunger	irritability

Type 2 Diabetes (occurs less suddenly):

any type 1 symptoms	cuts/bruises slow to heal
frequent infections	tingling/numbness in hands or feet
blurred vision	recurring skin, gum, or bladder infections

Pre-Diabetes

Among U.S. adults 40-74 years of age, at least 16.0 million (15.6% of the population) have **pre-diabetes**, the state that occurs when a person's blood glucose levels are higher than normal but not high enough for a diagnosis of diabetes.

In a recent study, about 11% of people with pre-diabetes developed type 2 diabetes during each year of the study. Other studies show that most people with pre-diabetes develop type 2 diabetes in 10 years.

Complications of Diabetes

People often have diabetes many years before it is diagnosed. During that time, serious complications have a chance to develop. Potential complications include:

Blindness. Diabetes is the leading cause of blindness in people ages 20-74. Each year, from 12,000 to 24,000 people lose their sight because of diabetes.

Kidney disease. 10% to 21% of all people with diabetes develop kidney disease. In 1999, more than 38,160 people initiated treatment for end-stage renal disease (kidney failure) because of diabetes.

Amputations. Diabetes is the most frequent cause of non-traumatic lower limb amputations. The risk of a leg amputation is 15 to 40 times greater for a person with diabetes than for the average American. Each year, an estimated 80,000 people lose a foot or leg as a result of complications brought on by diabetes.

Heart disease and stroke. People with diabetes are 2 to 4 times more likely to have heart disease (more than 77,000 deaths due to heart disease annually). And they are 2 to 4 times more likely to suffer a stroke.

Health-care and related costs for the treatment of the disease, added to the cost of lost productivity, total nearly $100 billion annually in the U.S.

Alzheimer's Disease

Source: Alzheimer's Association, 919 N Michigan Ave., Suite 1100, Chicago, IL 60611-1676; phone: (800) 272-3900

Alzheimer's disease, the most common form of dementia, is a progressive, degenerative disease of the brain in which nerve cells deteriorate and die for unknown reasons. Its first symptoms usually involve impaired memory and confusion about recent events. As the disease advances, it results in greater impairment of memory, thinking, behavior, and physical health.

The **rate of progression** of Alzheimer's varies, ranging from 3 to 20 years; the average length of time from onset of symptoms until death is 8 years. Eventually, affected individuals lose their ability to care for themselves and become susceptible to infections of the lungs, urinary tract, or other organs as they grow progressively more debilitated.

Alzheimer's disease affects an estimated 4 million Americans, striking men and women of all ethnic groups. Although most people diagnosed with Alzheimer's are older than age 60, some cases occur in people in their 40s and 50s. By age 65, an estimated 10 percent of the population has Alzheimer's, and the disease affects almost half of those over 85. In the United States, annual costs of diagnosis, treatment, and long-term care are estimated at $100 billion.

Diagnosis involves a comprehensive evaluation that may include a complete health history, a physical examination, neurological and mental status assessments, and other testing as needed. Skilled health care professionals can generally diagnose Alzheimer's with about 90 percent accuracy. Other conditions that can cause similar symptoms include depression, drug interactions, nutritional imbalances, infections such as AIDS, meningitis, and syphilis, and other forms of dementia, such as those associated with stroke, Huntington's disease, Parkinson's disease, frontotemporal dementia, and vascular disease. Absolute confirmation of diagnosis requires a brain biopsy or autopsy.

Treatments for cognitive and behavioral symptoms are available, but no intervention has yet been developed that prevents Alzheimer's or reverses its course. Providing care for people with Alzheimer's is physically and psychologically demanding. Nearly 70 percent of affected individuals live at home, where family or friends care for them. In advanced stages of the disease, many individuals require care in a nursing home. Nearly half of all nursing home residents in the United States have Alzheimer's.

People with Alzheimer's need a safe, stable environment and a regular daily schedule offering appropriate stimulation. Physical exercise and social interaction are important, as is proper nutrition. Security is also a consideration, because many people with Alzheimer's tend to wander. An identification bracelet listing the person's name, address, and condition may help ensure the safe return of an individual who wanders.

Warning Signs of Alzheimer's Disease

- Recent memory loss that affects job performance
- Inability to learn new information
- Difficulty with everyday tasks such as cooking or dressing oneself
- Inability to remember simple words
- Use of inappropriate words when communicating
- Disorientation of time and place
- Poor or decreased judgment
- Problems with abstract thinking
- Putting objects in inappropriate places
- Rapid changes in mood or behavior
- Increased irritability, anxiety, depression, confusion, and restlessness
- Prolonged loss of initiative

Acquired Immune Deficiency Syndrome

Source: Centers for Disease Control and Prevention

AIDS (Acquired Immune Deficiency Syndrome) is caused by the human immunodeficiency virus (**HIV**). HIV kills or disables crucial cells of the immune system, progressively destroying the body's ability to fight disease.

HIV is commonly spread through unprotected sexual contact with an infected partner. HIV is also spread through contact with infected blood. Where modern screening techniques are used it is rare to contract HIV from transfusion, but it can be contracted when intravenous drug users share syringes. Though HIV can be spread through semen, vaginal fluids, and breast milk, there is no evidence it can be spread through saliva. About one-quarter of untreated HIV-positive pregnant women transmit HIV to their fetuses, but with drug treatment that risk can be reduced to about 1%. Studies have indicated no evidence of HIV transmission through casual contact such as the sharing of food utensils, towels and bedding, telephones, or toilet seats.

Some people experience flu-like symptoms a short time after infection with HIV, and scientists estimate that about half of those infected by HIV develop more serious, often chronic symptoms within ten years. Even when symptoms are not present, HIV is active in the body, multiplying, infecting, and killing CD4+ T cells, or "T-helper cells," the crucial immune cells that signal other cells in the immune system to perform their functions.

The term **AIDS** applies to the most advanced stages of HIV infection. According to the official definition set by the Centers for Disease Control and Prevention (CDC), an HIV–infected person with fewer than 200 CD4+ T cells can be said to have AIDS. (Healthy adults usually have 1,000 or more). An HIV-infected person, regardless of T cell count, is diagnosed with AIDS if he or she develops one of 26 conditions that typically affect people with advanced HIV. Most of these conditions are "opportunistic infections" that occur when the immune system is so ravaged by HIV that the body cannot fight off certain bacteria, viruses and microbes.

Months or years prior to the onset of AIDS, many people experience such symptoms as swollen glands, lack of energy, fevers and sweats, and skin rashes. People with full-blown AIDS may develop infections of the intestinal tract, lungs, brain, eyes, and other organs, with a variety of symptoms, and may become severely debilitated. They also are prone to developing certain cancers, especially those caused by viruses, such as Kaposi's sarcoma, cervical cancer, and lymphoma. Children with AIDS may have delayed development or failure to thrive.

HIV is primarily **detected** by testing a person's blood for the presence of antibodies (disease-fighting proteins) to HIV. In about 5% of infected individuals, HIV antibodies take as long as six months after exposure to reach detectable levels, but in most cases the antibodies are detectable in about six weeks. HIV testing may also be performed on oral fluid and urine samples.

The **U.S. Food and Drug Administration** has approved a number of **drugs** that may slow down the growth of HIV in the body and treat the infections and cancers associated with AIDS. The first group of drugs used to treat HIV, called nucleoside analog reverse transcriptase inhibitors (NRTIs), include the drug zidovudine (commonly known as AZT). Non-nucleoside reverse transcriptase inhibitors (NNRTIs) have also been approved to treat HIV. A third class of drugs, called protease inhibitors, are approved as well for the treatment of HIV. Patients are typically given a combination of different drugs, because HIV can much more easily become resistant to a single drug. While these drugs extend the period between HIV infection and serious illness, they do not prevent the spread of the disease to others, and can have severe side effects.

Since there is no vaccine or cure for AIDS, the only protection is to avoid activities that carry a risk. When it cannot be known with certainty whether a sexual partner has HIV, the virus that causes AIDS, the CDC recommends abstinence (the only certain protection), mutual monogamy with an uninfected partner, or correct and consistent use of male latex condoms.

Allergies and Asthma

Source: Asthma and Allergy Foundation of America, 1233 20th St., NW, Suite 402, Washington, DC 20036; phone: (800) 7-ASTHMA

One out of five Americans suffers from **allergies**. People with allergies have extra-sensitive immune systems that react to normally harmless substances. Allergens that may produce this reaction include plant pollens, dust mites, or animal dander; plants such as poison ivy; certain drugs, such as penicillin; and certain foods such as eggs, milk, nuts, or seafood.

The tendency to develop allergies is usually inherited, and allergies usually begin to appear in childhood, but they can show up at any age. Common allergies for infants include food allergies and eczema (patches of dry skin). Older children and adults may often develop allergic rhinitis (hay fever), a reaction to an inhaled allergen; common symptoms include nasal congestion, runny nose, and sneezing.

It is best to avoid contact with the allergen, if feasible. In some cases, medications such as antihistamines are used to decrease the reaction, and there are treatments aimed at gradually desensitizing the patient to the allergen. Other effective allergy treatments include decongestants, eye drops, and ointments.

Some people with allergies also have **asthma**, and allergens are a common asthma trigger. Asthma is a disease of chronic inflammation, affecting the passages that carry air into and out of the lungs. It is most often seen in children but can develop at any age.

People with asthma have inflamed, supersensitive airways that tighten and become filled with mucus during an asthma episode. Wheezing, difficulty in breathing, tightening of the chest, and coughing are common symptoms. Asthma can progress through stages to become life-threatening if not controlled. Emergency symptoms of asthma include a bluish cast to the face and lips, severe anxiety, increased pulse rate, and sweating.

Besides common allergens, tobacco smoke, cold air, and pollution can trigger an asthma attack, as can viral infections or physical exercise that taxes the breathing. Of course, an accurate diagnosis by a physician is important. Although there is no cure for asthma or allergies, they can be controlled with medications and lifestyle changes. Allergy vaccines are available which can be effective in many patients.

IT'S A FACT: The Great Influenza Pandemic of 1918-19 killed between 20 and 50 million people, far more than died in World War I. The death toll probably exceeded the 25 million thought to have been killed by the plague in Europe in the 14th century.

Arthritis

Source: Arthritis Foundation, 1330 West Peachtree Street, Atlanta, GA 30309; phone: (800) 283-7800

The term "arthritis" refers to more than 100 different diseases that cause pain, stiffness, swelling, and restricted movement in joints. The condition is usually chronic. Nearly 43 million people in the U.S. have some form of arthritis—about 23 million are women and almost 300,000 are children. The cause for most types of arthritis is unknown; scientists are studying the roles played by genetics, lifestyle, and the environment.

Symptoms of arthritis may develop either slowly or suddenly. A visit to the doctor is indicated when pain, stiffness, or swelling in a joint or difficulty in moving a joint persists for more than two weeks. To make a diagnosis of arthritis, the doctor records the patient's symptoms and examines joints, looking for any swelling or limited movement. In addition, the doctor checks for other signs often seen with arthritis, such as rashes, mouth sores, or eye involvement. Finally, the doctor may test the blood, urine, or joint fluid, or take X rays of the joints.

Medications to treat arthritis include drugs that relieve pain and swelling, such as analgesics, anti-inflammatory drugs, biologic response modifiers, glucocorticoids, or disease-modifying antirheumatic drugs, which tend to slow the disease process. Most treatment programs call for exercise; use of heat or cold; and joint-protection techniques (such as avoiding excess stress on joints, using assistive devices, and controlling weight). In some cases, surgery can help when other treatments fail.

Of the three most prevalent forms of arthritis, **osteoarthritis** is the most common, affecting more than 20 million Americans; it usually occurs after age 45. In this type, which is also called degenerative arthritis, the protective cartilage of joints is lost and changes occur in the bone, leading to pain and stiffness. It usually occurs in the fingers, knees, feet, hips, and back.

Fibromyalgia, another common arthritis condition, affects more than 2 million Americans and affects more women than men. In this form, widespread pain and tenderness occur in muscles and their attachments to the bone. Common symptoms include fatigue, disturbed sleep, stiffness, and psychological distress.

Rheumatoid arthritis, which also affects more than 2 million people in the U.S., is one of the most serious and disabling forms of the disease. In this type, which is also more common in women, inflammation of the joints leads to damage of the cartilage and bone. The areas of the body that can be affected are the hands, wrists, feet, knees, ankles, shoulders, neck, jaw, and elbows.

Other forms of arthritis and related conditions include lupus, gout, ankylosing spondylitis, and scleroderma; also related are bursitis and tendinitis, which may result from injuring or overusing a joint.

Depression

Source: National Institute of Mental Health

Depression is a serious illness that affects thoughts, feelings, and the ability to function in everyday life. It strikes across all age groups, and often goes unrecognized. Studies sponsored by the National Institute of Mental Health estimate that 6% of 9- to 17-year-olds in the U.S. and almost 10% of American adults, or about 19 million people age 18 and older, experience some form of depression every year.

Women are more vulnerable than men. Nearly twice as many women as men suffer from a depressive illness in a given year, and at some point in their lives, as many as 20% have at least one episode of depression that should be treated. Although conventional wisdom holds that depression is most closely associated with menopause, in fact, the childbearing years are marked by the highest rates of depression, followed by the years prior to menopause. The influence of hormones on depression in women has been an active area of NIMH research.

In a given year, 1-2% of people over age 65 living in the community (outside of institutions) suffer from major depression. Depression frequently occurs with other physical illnesses, including heart disease, stroke, cancer, and diabetes. It is not a normal part of aging.

In more than 4 out of 5 cases of depression, the treatments that are available will alleviate symptoms, but less than half of all people with depression seek the help they need. Often these people—and those around them—fail to realize that they have an illness or that they could benefit from medical help.

Symptoms and Types of Depression

Symptoms of depression include the following:

- persistent sad mood;
- loss of interest or pleasure in activities once enjoyed;
- significant change in appetite or body weight;
- difficulty sleeping or oversleeping;
- physical slowing or agitation;
- loss of energy;
- feelings of worthlessness or inappropriate guilt;
- difficulty thinking or concentrating;
- recurrent thoughts of death or suicide.

A diagnosis of *major depressive disorder* (or *unipolar major depression*) is made if an individual has 5 or more of these symptoms during the same two-week period. Unipolar major depression typically comes to the fore in episodes that recur during a person's lifetime.

Bipolar disorder (or *manic-depressive illness*) is characterized by episodes of major depression as well as episodes of mania—abnormally and persistently elevated mood or irritability, accompanied by such symptoms as inflated self-esteem, less need for sleep, increased talkativeness, racing thoughts, distractibility, physical agitation, and excessive involvement in pleasurable activities that have a high potential for painful consequences. While sharing some of the features of major depression, bipolar disorder is a distinct illness.

Dysthymic disorder (or *dysthymia*), a less severe yet typically more chronic form of depression, is diagnosed when a depressed mood persists for at least two years in adults (one year in children or adolescents) and is accompanied by at least 2 other depressive symptoms. Many people with dysthymic disorder also experience major depressive episodes.

In contrast to the normal experiences of sadness, loss, or passing moods, depression is extreme and persistent and can interfere significantly with an individual's ability to function. A recent study sponsored by the World Health Organization and the World Bank found unipolar major depression to be the leading cause of disability in the U.S. and worldwide.

Treatments for Depression

A variety of **drugs** are used to treat depression. These drugs influence the functioning of certain neurotransmitters in the brain, primarily serotonin and norepinephrine, known as monoamines. Older drugs—so-called tricyclic antidepressants (TCAs) and monoamine oxidase inhibitors (MAOIs)—affect the functioning of both of these neurotransmitters. But they can have strong side effects or, in the case of MAOIs, require dietary restrictions. Newer medications, such as the selective serotonin reuptake inhibitors (SSRIs), have fewer side effects. All of these medications can be effective, but some people respond to one type and not another.

NIMH research has shown that certain types of **psychotherapy**, particularly cognitive-behavioral therapy (CBT) and interpersonal therapy (IPT), can help relieve depression. CBT helps patients change the negative styles of thinking and behaving often associated with depression. IPT focuses on working through disturbed personal relationships that may contribute to depression. Both kinds of psychotherapy work by changing the way the brain functions. Studies of adults have shown that while psychotherapy alone is rarely sufficient to treat moderate to severe depression, it may provide relief in combination with antidepressant drugs.

Electroconvulsive therapy (ECT) has been found effective in treating 80-90% of cases of severe depression. ECT involves producing a seizure in the brain of a patient under general anesthesia by applying electrical stimulation to the brain through electrodes placed on the scalp. Memory loss and other cognitive problems are common, but typically short-lived, side effects.

For more information, start with the website www.nimh.nih.gov/publicat/depressionmenu.cfm

Complementary and Alternative Medicine

Source: National Center for Complementary and Alternative Medicine, National Institutes of Health (NIH)

Complementary and alternative medicine (CAM) comprises a wide variety of healing philosophies, approaches, and therapies. It includes treatments and health care practices not widely taught in medical schools, not generally used in hospitals, and not usually reimbursed by health insurance companies. While some scientific evidence exists regarding some therapies, for most there are key questions that are yet to be answered through well-designed scientific studies--questions such as whether they are safe and whether they work for the diseases or medical conditions for which they are used. The National Institutes of Health cautions people not to seek alternative therapies without the consultation of a licensed health care provider.

The National Center for Complementary and Alternative Medicine (NCCAM), a part of the National Institutes of Health, distinguishes between **complementary medicine**, used together with conventional medicine (as, for instance, the use of aromatherapy to lessen discomfort after surgery) and **alternative medicine**, used in place of conventional medicine (as, for instance, adopting a special diet to treat cancer instead of using the conventional approaches of chemotherapy, radiation, or surgery). The list of what is considered to be CAM changes continually, as therapies proven to be safe and effective become adopted into conventional health care and as new approaches to health care emerge. Worldwide, only about 10-30% of health care is provided by conventional practitioners; the remaining 70-90% involves alternative practices. An estimated 1 in 3 Americans uses some form of alternative medicine.

The NCCAM classifies CAM in 5 categories:

Alternative medical systems are built upon complete systems of theory and practice. Often, these systems have evolved apart from and earlier than the conventional medical approach used in the U.S. Examples of alternative medical systems that have developed in Western cultures include homeopathic medicine and naturopathic medicine. Systems that have developed in non-Western cultures include traditional Chinese medicine and Ayurveda.

Mind-body medicine uses a variety of techniques designed to enhance the mind's capacity to affect bodily function and symptoms. Some techniques that were considered CAM in the past have become mainstream (for example, patient support groups and cognitive-behavioral therapy). Other mind-body techniques are still considered CAM, including meditation, prayer, mental healing, and therapies that use creative outlets such as art, music, or dance.

Biologically based therapies in CAM use substances found in nature, such as herbs, foods, and vitamins. Some examples include dietary supplements, herbal products, and other so-called "natural" but as yet scientifically unproven therapies (for example, using shark cartilage to treat cancer).

Manipulative and body-based methods in CAM are based on manipulation and/or movement of one or more parts of the body. Some examples include chiropractic or osteopathic manipulation and massage.

Energy therapies involve the use of energy fields. They are of two types:

—*Biofield therapies* are intended to affect energy fields that purportedly surround and penetrate the human body. The existence of such fields has not yet been proven. Some forms of energy therapy manipulate biofields by applying pressure and/or manipulating the body by placing the hands in, or through, these fields. Examples include qi gong, Reiki, and Therapeutic Touch.

—*Bioelectromagnetic-based therapies* involve the unconventional use of electromagnetic fields, such as pulsed fields, magnetic fields, or alternating current or direct current fields.

Alternative Health Services in the U.S., 2001

Source: *Nutrition Business Journal*

HEALTH CARE PRACTICE	Licensed practitioners	Lay or other practitioners	Total revenues[1]
Acupuncture	15,800	5,000	$ 2,050
Chiropractic	65,100	3,500	14,430
Homeopathy	1,000	5,400	470
Massage therapy	70,000	190,000	8,250
Naturopathy	2,400	3,000	$ 630
Traditional Oriental medicine	13,000	15,000	3,450
TOTAL	**167,300**	**221,900**	**$29,280**

(1) In millions of dollars.

Top-Selling Medicinal Herbs in the U.S., 1997–2001

Source: *Nutrition Business Journal*; dollars in millions

HERB	Sales in 1997	Sales in 1998	Sales in 1999	Sales in 2000	Sales in 2001
Echinacea	$201	$214	$213	$196	$189
Ginkgo Biloba[1]	223	307	296	234	181
Garlic[1]	213	203	175	163	153
Ginseng	224	222	191	162	130
Saw palmetto	85	107	116	122	123
Noni/Morinda	15	22	33	87	121
St. John's wort	98	315	232	158	105
Soy	$18	$ 25	$ 36	$ 60	$ 76
Mahuang	19	25	29	38	58
Milk Thistle	21	35	42	45	53
other singles	747	781	984	910	939
total single herbs	1,865	2,255	2,348	2,176	2,127
combination herbs	1,659	1,705	1,722	1,943	2,049
TOTAL	**$ 3,524**	**$3,960**	**$4,070**	**$4,119**	**$4,176**

(1) Does not include nonmedicinal use.

Performance of Global Health Systems

Source: *The World Health Report 2000,* World Health Organization

Health Expenditure Per Capita

Rank	Top 25	Rank	Top 25	Rank	Bottom 25	Rank	Bottom 25
1	United States	14	Iceland	191	Somalia	178	Central African Rep.
2	Switzerland	15	Belgium	190	Madagascar	177	Rwanda
3	Germany	16	Norway	189	Ethiopia	176	Nigeria
4	France	17	Australia	188	Dem. Rep. of the Congo	175	Chad
5	Luxembourg	18	Finland	187	Eritrea	174	Tanzania
6	Austria	19	Israel	186	Burundi	173	Burkina Faso
7	Sweden	20	New Zealand	185	Niger	172	Dem. People's Rep. of Korea
8	Denmark	21	San Marino	184	Afghanistan	171	Benin
9	Netherlands	22	Bahamas	183	Sierra Leone	170	Nepal
10	Canada	23	Andorra	182	Yemen	169	Sudan
11	Italy	24	Spain	181	Liberia	168	Uganda
12	Monaco	25	Ireland	180	Togo	167	São Tomé and Príncipe
13	Japan			179	Mali		

Overall Goal Attainment[1]

Rank	Top 25	Rank	Top 25	Rank	Bottom 25	Rank	Bottom 25
1	Japan	14	Germany	191	Sierra Leone	179	Dem. Rep. of the Congo
2	Switzerland	15	United States	190	Central African Republic	178	Mali
3	Norway	16	Iceland	189	Somalia	177	Chad
4	Sweden	17	Andorra	188	Niger	176	Eritrea
5	Luxembourg	18	Monaco	187	Liberia	175	Myanmar (Burma)
6	France	19	Spain	186	Ethiopia	174	Zambia
7	Canada	20	Denmark	185	Mozambique	173	Lesotho
8	Netherlands	21	San Marino	184	Nigeria	172	Guinea
9	United Kingdom	22	Finland	183	Afghanistan	171	Rwanda
10	Austria	23	Greece	182	Malawi	170	Djibouti
11	Italy	24	Israel	181	Angola	169	Mauritania
12	Australia	25	Ireland	180	Guinea-Bissau	168	Botswana
13	Belgium					167	Madagascar

(1) A composite measure that factors in level of health, distribution of health based on the equality of child survival, responsiveness to the needs of disadvantaged groups, and financial fairness, based on in-depth surveys of health care practitioners.

WORLD ALMANAC QUICK QUIZ

Three of these food choices have about 350 calories. Which has only about 160?

(a) A chocolate milkshake (10 oz.)
(b) Lemon meringue pie ($^1/_6$ of a pie)
(c) A bagel with 1 $^1/_2$ oz cream cheese
(d) Mashed potatoes (1 cup)

For the answer look in this chapter, or see page 1008.

Food Guide Pyramid

The Food Guide Pyramid was developed by the U.S. Dept. of Agriculture and was revised for the year 2000. The Pyramid is an outline of what to eat each day. It is not meant as a rigid prescription, but as a general guide to help in choosing a healthful diet. It calls for eating a variety of foods to get needed nutrients and at the same time the right amount of calories to maintain or improve your weight. The Pyramid focuses heavily on fat because most Americans' diets are too high in fat, especially saturated fat.

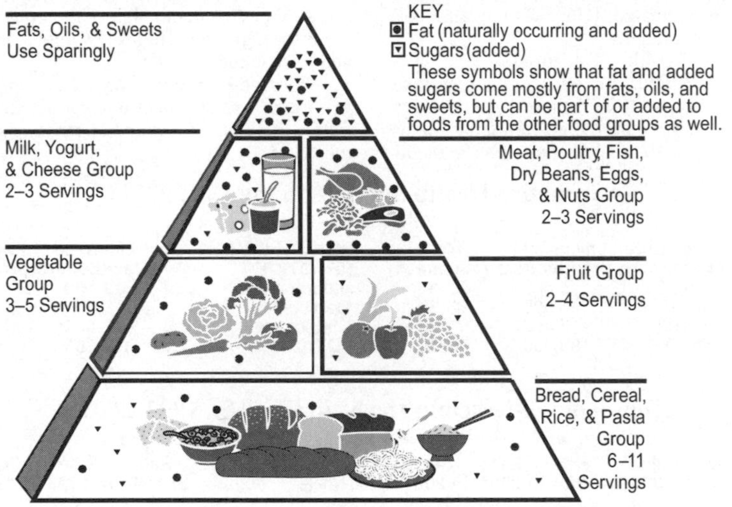

What Counts as a Serving?

Bread, Cereal, Rice, and Pasta
- 1 slice of bread
- 1 ounce of ready to-eat cereal
- ½ cup of cooked cereal, rice, or pasta

Vegetable
- 1 cup of raw leafy vegetables
- ½ cup of other vegetables, cooked or chopped raw
- ¾ cup of vegetable juice

Fruit
- 1 medium apple, banana, orange
- ½ cup of chopped, cooked, or canned fruit
- ¾ cup of fruit juice

Milk, Yogurt, and Cheese
- 1 cup of milk or yogurt
- 1-1/2 ounces of natural cheese
- 2 ounces of process cheese

Meat, Poultry, Fish, Dry Beans, Eggs, and Nuts
- 2-3 ounces of cooked lean meat, poultry, or fish
- ½ cup of cooked dry beans or 1 egg counts as 1 ounce of lean meat.
- 2 tablespoons of peanut butter or $^1/_3$ cup of nuts count as 1 ounce of meat.

Food and Nutrition

In a report issued in Sept. 2002, the Food and Nutrition Board of the National Academy of Sciences' Institute of Medicine recommended increased levels of physical activity and more flexible guidelines for eating. Adults and children should engage in moderately intense physical activity for an hour a day, the study said, a level twice the minimum goal set by the 1996 Surgeon General's report. Caloric intake should be geared to activity level, offering recommended calorie totals for individuals according to a scheme that takes into account height, weight, sex ,and four different exertion levels (for example, a daily average of 1,800-2,000 calories was recommended for a 30-year-old woman weighing 111-150 pounds and 5 feet 5 inches tall with a sedentary lifestyle, while a very active woman, with other characteristics the same, might consume 2,500-2,800 calories a day).

The study said carbohydrates should make up 45-65% of an adult's calories, with fat providing 20-35% and protein 10-35%. The ranges were intended to allow people to accommodate their preferences while making healthy and realistic choices. Guidelines for children were similar, although the range for fat was slightly higher: it was recommended that 25-40% of a child's calories come from fat. Adults and children, it said, should have at least 130 grams of carbohydrates a day to provide necessary glucose for brain functions; most people, however, consume much more. The study contained the Food and Nutrition Board's first specific recommendations for daily intake of fiber [see below] and reaffirmed earlier recommended levels for protein, 0.8 grams per kilogram of body weight for adults. The report noted that mono- and polyunsaturated fats can play a positive role in the diet, while cautioning against saturated fats and excessive intake of added sugar.

The study was called *Dietary Reference Intakes for Energy, Carbohydrates, Fiber, Fat, Protein and Amino Acids (Macronutrients)*. Earlier Food and Nutrition Board reports had set Dietary Reference Intakes (DRIs) for vitamins and minerals. The DRIs, based on extensive scientific research, were intended to promote health at all stages of life, and not just guard against nutritional deficiencies.

PROTEIN

Proteins, composed of amino acids, are essential to good nutrition. They build, maintain, and repair the body. Best sources: eggs, milk, fish, meat, poultry, soybeans, nuts. High-quality proteins such as eggs, meat, or fish supply all 8 amino acids needed in the diet. Plant foods can be combined to meet protein needs as well: whole grain breads and cereals, rice, oats, soybeans, other beans, split peas, and nuts.

FATS

Fats provide energy by furnishing calories to the body, and they also carry vitamins A, D, E, and K. They are the most concentrated source of energy in the diet. Best sources of polyunsaturated and monounsaturated fats: margarine, vegetable/plant oils, nuts. Meats, cheeses, butter, cream, egg yolks, lard are concentrated sources of saturated fats.

CARBOHYDRATES

Carbohydrates provide energy for body function and activity by supplying immediate calories. The carbohydrate group includes sugars, starches, fiber, and starchy vegetables. Best sources: grains, legumes, potatoes, vegetables, fruits.

FIBER

The portion of plant foods that our bodies cannot digest is known as fiber. There are 2 basic types: *insoluble* ("roughage") and *soluble*. Insoluble fibers help move food materials through the digestive tract, soluble fibers tend to slow them down. Both types absorb water, thus prevent and treat constipation by softening and increasing the bulk of the undigested food components passing through the digestive tract. Soluble fibers have also been reported to be helpful in reducing blood cholesterol levels. Best sources: beans, bran, fruits, whole grains, vegetables. New recommendations from the Food and Nutrition Board call for men 50 and younger to have 38 grams of fiber a day and women to have 25 grams; 30 and 21 grams a day are proposed, respectively, for older men and women (because of reduced food intake). Fiber is also recommended for children and teenagers.

WATER

Water dissolves and transports other nutrients throughout the body, aiding the processes of digestion, absorption, circulation, and excretion. It helps regulate body temperature.

VITAMINS

Vitamin A—promotes good eyesight and helps keep the skin and mucous membranes resistant to infection. Best sources: liver, sweet potatoes, carrots, kale, cantaloupe, turnip greens, collard greens, broccoli, fortified milk.

Vitamin B_1 (thiamine)—prevents beriberi. Essential to carbohydrate metabolism and health of nervous system. Best sources: pork, enriched cereals, grains, soybeans, nuts.

Vitamin B_2 (riboflavin)—protects the skin, mouth, eyes, eyelids, and mucous membranes. Essential to protein and energy metabolism. Best sources: milk, meat, poultry, cheese, broccoli, spinach.

Vitamin B_6 (pyridoxine)—important in the regulation of the central nervous system and in protein metabolism. Best sources: whole grains, meats, fish, poultry, nuts, brewers' yeast.

Vitamin B_{12} (cobalamin)—needed to form red blood cells. Best sources: meat, fish, poultry, eggs, dairy products.

Niacin—maintains health of skin, tongue, digestive system. Best sources: poultry, peanuts, fish, enriched flour and bread.

Folic acid (folacin)—required for normal blood cell formation, growth, and reproduction and for important chemical reactions in body cells. Best sources: yeast, orange juice, green leafy vegetables, wheat germ, asparagus, broccoli, nuts.

Other B vitamins—biotin, pantothenic acid.

Vitamin C (ascorbic acid)—maintains collagen, a protein necessary for the formation of skin, ligaments, and bones. It helps heal wounds and mend fractures and aids in resisting some types of viral and bacterial infections. Best sources: citrus fruits and juices, cantaloupe, broccoli, brussels sprouts, potatoes and sweet potatoes, tomatoes, cabbage.

Vitamin D—important for bone development. Best sources: sunlight, fortified milk and milk products, fish-liver oils, egg yolks.

Vitamin E (tocopherol)—helps protect red blood cells. Best sources: vegetable oils, wheat germ, whole grains, eggs, peanuts, margarine, green leafy vegetables.

Vitamin K—necessary for formation of prothrombin, which helps blood to clot. Also made by intestinal bacteria. Best dietary sources: green leafy vegetables, tomatoes.

MINERALS

Calcium—works with phosphorus in building and maintaining bones and teeth. Best sources: milk and milk products, cheese, blackstrap molasses, some types of tofu.

Phosphorus—performs more functions than any other mineral, and plays a part in nearly every chemical reaction in the body. Best sources: cheese, milk, meats, poultry, fish, tofu.

Iron—Necessary for the formation of myoglobin, which is a reservoir of oxygen for muscle tissue, and hemoglobin, which transports oxygen in the blood. Best sources: lean meats, beans, green leafy vegetables, shellfish, enriched breads and cereals, whole grains.

Other minerals—chromium, cobalt, copper, fluorine, iodine, magnesium, manganese, molybdenum, potassium, selenium, sodium, sulfur, and zinc.

Understanding Food Label Claims

Source: Food Labeling Education Information Center, Beltville, MD

The federal Nutrition Labeling and Education Act of 1990 provides that manufacturers can make certain claims on processed food labels only if they meet the definitions specified here:

SUGAR

Sugar free: less than 0.5 g per serving

No added sugar; Without added sugar; No sugar added:

- No sugars added during processing or packing, including ingredients that contain sugars (for example, fruit juices, applesauce, or dried fruit).
- Processing does not increase sugar content above the amount naturally in the ingredients. (A functionally insignificant increase in sugars is acceptable from processes used for purposes other than increasing sugar content.)
- The food for which it substitutes normally contains added sugars.

Reduced sugar: at least 25% less sugar than reference food

CALORIES

Low calorie: 40 calories or less per serving; if the serving is 30 g or less or 2 tablespoons or less, 40 calories or less per 50 g of food

Calorie free: under 5 calories per serving

Reduced or Fewer calories: at least 25% fewer calories than reference food

FAT

Fat free: less than 0.5 g of fat per serving

Saturated fat free: less than 0.5 g of saturated fat per serving, and the level of trans fatty acids does not exceed 1% of total fat

Low fat: 3 g or less per serving and, if the serving is 30 g or less or 2 tbs or less, per 50 g of the food

Low saturated fat: 1 g or less per serving and not more than 15% of calories from saturated fatty acids

Reduced or Less fat: at least 25% less per serving than reference food

CHOLESTEROL

Cholesterol free: less than 2 mg of cholesterol and 2 g or less of saturated fat per serving

Low cholesterol: 20 mg or less and 2 g or less of saturated fat per serving and, if the serving is 30 g or less or 2 tbs or less, per 50 g of the food

Reduced or Less cholesterol: at least 25% less than reference food

SODIUM

Sodium free: less than 5 mg per serving

Low sodium: 140 mg or less per serving and, if the serving is 30 g or less or 2 tbs or less, per 50 g of the food

Very low sodium: 35 mg or less per serving and, if the serving is 30 g or less or 2 tbs or less, per 50 g of the food

Reduced or Less sodium: at least 25% less per serving than reference food

FIBER

High fiber: 5 g or more per serving. (Also, must meet low-fat definition, or must state level of total fat.)

Good source of fiber: 2.5 g to 4.9 g per serving

More or Added fiber: at least 2.5 g more per serving than reference food

Nutritive Value of Food (Calories, Proteins, etc.)

Source: *Home and Garden Bulletin No. 72;* U.S. Dept. of Agriculture

FOOD	Measure	Grams	Food Energy (calories)	Protein (grams)	Fat (grams)	Saturated fats (grams)	Carbohydrate (grams)	Calcium (milligrams)	Iron (milligrams)	Sodium (milligrams)	Vitamin A (I.U.)	Ascorbic Acid (milligrams)
DAIRY PRODUCTS												
Cheese, cheddar, cut pieces	1 oz.	28	115	7	9	6.0	T	204	0.2	176	300	0
Cheese, cottage, small curd	1 cup	210	215	26	9	6.0	6	126	0.3	850	340	T
Cheese, cream	1 oz.	28	100	2	10	6.2	1	23	0.3	84	400	0
Cheese, Swiss	1 oz.	28	95	7	7	4.5	1	219	0.2	388	230	0
Half-and-half	1 tbsp.	15	20	T	2	1.1	1	16	T	6	70	T
Cream, sour	1 tbsp.	12	25	T	3	1.6	1	14	T	6	90	T
Milk, whole	1 cup	244	150	8	8	5.1	11	291	0.1	120	310	2
Milk, nonfat (skim)	1 cup	245	85	8	T	0.3	12	302	0.1	126	500	2
Milkshake, chocolate	10 oz.	283	355	9	8	4.8	60	374	0.9	314	240	0
Ice cream, hardened	1 cup	133	270	5	14	8.9	32	176	0.1	116	540	1
Sherbet	1 cup	193	270	2	4	2.4	59	103	0.3	88	190	4
Yogurt, fruit-flavored	8 oz.	227	230	10	2	1.6	43	345	0.2	133	100	1
EGGS												
Fried in margarine	1	46	90	6	7	1.9	1	25	0.7	162	390	0
Hard-cooked	1	50	75	6	5	1.6	1	25	0.6	62	280	0
Scrambled (milk added) in margarine	1	61	100	7	7	2.2	1	44	0.7	171	420	T
FATS & OILS												
Butter, salted	1 tbsp.	14	100	T	11	7.1	T	3	T	116	430	0
Margarine, salted	1 tbsp.	14	100	T	11	2.2	T	4	T	132	460	T
Olive oil	1 tbsp.	14	125	0	14	1.9	0	0	0	0	0	0
Salad dressing, blue cheese	1 tbsp.	15	75	1	8	1.5	1	12	T	164	30	T
Salad dressing, French, regular	1 tbsp.	16	85	T	9	1.4	1	2	T	188	T	T
Salad dressing, French, low calorie	1 tbsp.	16	25	T	2	0.2	2	6	T	306	T	T
Salad dressing, Italian	1 tbsp.	15	80	T	9	1.3	1	1	T	162	30	T
Mayonnaise	1 tbsp.	14	100	T	11	1.7	T	3	0.1	80	40	0
FISH, MEAT, POULTRY												
Clams, raw, meat only	3 oz.	85	65	11	1	0.3	2	59	2.6	102	90	9
Crabmeat, canned	1 cup	135	135	23	3	0.5	1	61	1.1	1,350	50	0
Fish sticks, frozen, reheated	1 fish stick	28	70	6	3	0.8	4	11	0.3	53	20	0
Salmon canned (pink), solids and liquid	3 oz.	85	120	17	5	0.9	0	167	0.7	443	60	0
Sardines, Atlantic, canned in oil, drained solids	3 oz.	85	175	20	9	2.1	0	371	2.6	425	190	0
Shrimp, French fried	3 oz.	85	200	16	10	2.5	11	61	2.0	384	90	0
Trout, broiled, with butter and lemon juice	3 oz.	85	175	21	9	4.1	T	26	1.0	122	230	1
Tuna, canned in oil	3 oz.	85	165	24	7	1.4	0	7	1.6	303	70	0
Bacon, broiled or fried crisp	3 slices	19	110	6	9	3.3	T	2	0.3	303	0	6
Ground beef, broiled, regular	3 oz.	85	245	20	18	6.9	0	9	2.1	70	T	0
Roast beef, relatively lean (lean only)	2.6 oz.	75	135	22	5	1.9	0	3	1.5	46	T	0
Beef steak, lean and fat	3 oz.	85	240	23	15	6.4	0	9	2.6	53	T	0
Beef & vegetable stew	1 cup	245	220	16	11	4.4	15	29	2.9	292	5,690	17
Lamb, chop, broiled loin, lean and fat	2.8 oz.	80	235	22	16	7.3	0	16	1.4	62	T	0
Liver, beef, fried	3 oz.	85	185	23	7	2.5	7	9	5.3	90	30,690	23
Ham, light cure, roasted, lean and fat	3 oz.	85	205	18	14	5.1	0	6	0.7	1,009	0	0
Pork, chop, broiled, lean and fat	3.1 oz.	87	275	24	19	7.0	0	3	0.7	61	10	T
Bologna	2 slices	57	180	7	16	6.1	2	7	0.9	581	0	12
Frankfurter, pork, cooked	1	45	145	5	13	4.8	1	5	0.5	504	0	12
Sausage, pork link, cooked	1 link	13	50	3	4	1.4	T	4	0.2	168	0	T
Veal, cutlet, braised or broiled	3 oz.	85	185	23	9	4.1	0	9	0.8	56	T	0
Chicken, drumstick, fried, bones removed	2.5 oz.	72	195	16	11	3.0	6	12	1.0	194	60	0
Chicken, roasted, half breast, without skin	3 oz.	86	140	27	3	0.9	0	13	0.9	64	20	0
Turkey, roasted, chopped light and dark meat	1 cup	140	240	41	7	2.3	0	35	2.5	98	0	0
Frankfurter, chicken, cooked	1	45	115	6	9	2.5	3	43	0.9	616	60	0
FRUITS & FRUIT PRODUCTS												
Apple, raw, 2-3/4 in. diam.	1	138	80	T	T	0.1	21	10	0.2	T	70	8
Apple juice	1 cup	248	115	T	T	T	29	17	0.9	7	T	2
Apricots, raw	3	106	50	1	T	T	12	15	0.6	1	2,770	11
Banana, raw	1	114	105	1	1	0.2	27	7	0.4	1	90	10
Cherries, sweet, raw	10	68	50	1	1	0.1	11	10	0.3	T	150	5
Cranberry juice cocktail, sweetened	1 cup	253	145	T	T	T	38	8	0.4	10	10	108
Fruit cocktail, canned, in heavy syrup	1 cup	255	185	1	T	T	48	15	0.7	15	520	5
Grapefruit, raw, medium, white	1/2	120	40	1	T	T	10	14	0.1	T	10	41
Grapes, Thompson seedless	10	50	35	T	T	0.1	9	6	0.1	1	40	5
Lemonade, frozen, unsweetened	6 oz.	244	55	1	1	0.1	16	20	0.3	2	30	77
Cantaloupe, 5-in. diam.	1/2	267	95	2	1	0.1	22	29	0.6	24	8,610	113
Orange, 2-5/8 in. diam.	1	131	60	1	T	T	15	52	0.1	T	270	70
Orange juice, frozen, diluted	1 cup	249	110	2	T	T	27	22	0.2	2	190	97
Peach, raw, 2-1/2 in. diam.	1	87	35	1	T	T	10	4	0.1	T	470	6
Raisins, seedless	1 cup	145	435	5	1	0.2	115	71	3.0	17	10	5
Strawberries, whole	1 cup	149	45	1	1	T	10	21	0.6	1	40	84
Tomatoes, raw	1	123	25	1	T	T	5	9	0.6	10	1,390	22
Watermelon, 4 by 8 in. wedge	1 piece	482	155	3	2	0.3	35	39	0.8	10	1,760	46
GRAIN PRODUCTS												
Bagel, plain	1	68	200	7	2	0.3	38	29	1.8	245	0	0
Biscuit, 2 in. diam., from home recipe	1	28	100	2	5	1.2	13	47	0.7	195	10	T
Bread, pita, enriched, white, 6-1/2 in. diam	1 pita	60	165	6	1	0.1	12	15	0.7	124	0	0
Bread, white, enriched	1 slice	25	65	2	1	0.3	12	32	0.7	129	T	T
Bread, whole-wheat	1 slice	28	70	3	1	0.4	13	20	1.0	180	T	T
Oatmeal or rolled oats, without added salt	1 cup	234	145	6	2	0.4	25	19	1.6	2	40	0
Bran flakes (40% bran), added sugar, salt, iron, vitamins	1 oz.	28	90	4	1	0.1	22	14	8.1	264	1,250	0
Corn flakes, added sugar, salt, iron, vitamins	1 oz.	28	110	2	T	T	24	1	1.8	351	1,250	15
Rice, puffed, added iron, thiamine, niacin	1 oz.	28	110	2	T	T	25	4	1.8	340	1,250	15
Wheat, shredded, plain, 1 biscuit or 2/3 cup	1 oz.	28	100	3	1	0.1	23	11	1.2	3	0	0
Bulgur, uncooked	1 cup	170	600	19	3	1.2	129	49	9.5	7	0	0
Cake, angel food, 1/12 of cake	1	53	125	3	T	T	29	44	0.2	269	0	0
Cupcake, 2-1/2 in. diam., with chocolate icing	1	35	120	2	4	1.8	20	21	0.7	92	50	T

FOOD	Measure	Grams	Food Energy (calories)	Protein (grams)	Fat (grams)	Saturated fats (grams)	Carbohydrate (grams)	Calcium (milligrams)	Iron (milligrams)	Sodium (milligrams)	Vitamin A (I.U.)	Ascorbic Acid (milligrams)
Plain sheet cake with white, uncooked frosting, 1/9 of cake	1	121	445	4	14	4.6	77	61	1.2	275	240	T
Fruitcake, dark, 1/32 of loaf	1	43	165	2	7	1.5	25	41	1.2	67	50	16
Cake, pound, 1/17 of loaf	1	29	110	2	5	3.0	15	8	0.5	108	160	0
Cheesecake, 1/12 of 9-in. diam. cake	1	92	280	5	18	9.9	26	52	0.4	204	230	5
Brownies, with nuts, from commercial recipe	1	25	100	1	4	1.6	16	13	0.6	59	70	T
Cookies, chocolate chip, from home recipe	4	40	185	2	11	3.9	26	13	1.0	82	20	0
Crackers, graham, 2-1/2 in. squares	2	14	60	1	1	0.4	11	6	0.4	86	0	0
Crackers, saltines	4	12	50	1	1	0.5	9	3	0.5	165	0	0
Danish pastry, round piece	1	57	220	4	12	3.6	26	60	1.1	218	60	T
Doughnut, cake type	1	50	210	3	12	2.8	24	22	1.0	192	20	T
Macaroni, firm stage (hot)	1 cup	130	190	7	1	0.1	39	14	2.1	1	0	0
Muffin, bran, commercial mix	1	45	140	3	4	1.3	24	27	1.7	385	100	0
Muffin, corn, from home recipe	1	45	145	3	5	1.5	21	66	0.9	169	80	T
Noodles, enriched, cooked	1 cup	160	200	7	2	0.5	37	16	2.6	3	110	0
Pie, apple, 1/6 of pie	1	158	405	3	18	4.6	60	13	1.6	476	50	2
Pie, cherry, 1/6 of pie	1	158	410	4	18	4.7	61	22	1.6	480	700	0
Pie, lemon meringue, 1/6 of pie	1	140	355	5	14	4.3	53	20	1.4	395	240	4
Pie, pecan, 1/6 of pie	1	138	575	7	32	4.7	71	65	4.6	305	220	0
Popcorn, air-popped, plain	1 cup	8	30	1	T	T	6	1	0.2	T	10	0
Pretzels, stick	10	3	10	T	T	T	2	1	0.1	48	0	0
Rolls, enriched, brown & serve	1	28	85	2	2	0.5	14	33	0.8	155	T	T
Rolls, frankfurter & hamburger	1	40	115	3	2	0.5	20	54	1.2	241	T	T
Tortillas, corn	1	30	65	2	1	0.1	13	42	0.6	1	80	0
LEGUMES, NUTS, SEEDS												
Beans, Black	1 cup	171	225	15	1	0.1	41	47	2.9	1	T	0
Beans, Great Northern, cooked	1 cup	180	210	14	1	0.1	38	90	4.9	13	0	0
Peanuts, roasted in oil, salted	1 cup	145	840	39	71	9.9	27	125	2.8	626	0	0
Peanut butter	1 tbsp.	16	95	5	8	1.4	3	5	0.3	75	0	0
Refried beans, canned	1 cup	290	295	18	3	0.4	51	141	5.1	1,228	0	17
Tofu	1 piece	120	85	9	5	0.7	3	108	2.3	8	0	0
Sunflower seeds, hulled	1 oz.	28	160	6	14	1.5	5	33	1.9	1	10	T
MIXED FOODS												
Chop suey with beef and pork, home recipe	1 cup	250	300	26	17	4.3	13	60	4.8	1,053	600	33
Enchilada	1	230	235	20	16	7.7	24	97	3.3	1,332	2,720	T
Pizza, cheese, 1/8 of 15 in.-diam. pie	1	120	290	15	9	4.1	39	220	1.6	699	750	2
Spaghetti with meatballs & tomato sauce	1 cup	248	330	19	12	3.9	39	124	3.7	1,009	1,590	22
SUGARS & SWEETS												
Candy, caramels	1 oz.	28	115	1	3	2.2	22	42	0.4	64	T	T
Candy, milk chocolate	1 oz.	28	145	2	9	5.4	16	50	0.4	23	30	T
Fudge, chocolate	1 oz.	28	115	1	3	2.1	21	22	0.3	54	T	T
Gelatin dessert, from prepared powder	1/2 cup	120	70	2	0	0.0	17	2	T	55	0	0
Candy, hard	1 oz.	28	110	0	0	0.0	28	T	0.1	7	0	0
Honey	1 tbsp.	21	65	T	0	0.0	17	1	0.1	1	0	T
Jams & preserves	1 tbsp.	20	55	T	T	0.0	14	4	0.2	2	T	T
Popsicle, 3 fl. oz.	1	95	70	0	0	0.0	18	0	T	11	0	0
Sugar, white, granulated	1 tbsp.	12	45	0	0	0.0	12	T	T	T	0	0
VEGETABLES												
Asparagus, spears, cooked from raw	4 spears	60	15	2	T	T	3	14	0.4	2	500	16
Beans, green, from frozen, cuts	1 cup	135	35	2	T	T	8	61	1.1	18	710	11
Broccoli, cooked from raw	1 spear	180	50	5	1	0.1	10	82	2.1	20	2,540	113
Cabbage, raw, coarsely shredded or sliced	1 cup	70	15	1	T	T	4	33	0.4	13	90	33
Carrots, raw, 7-1/2 by 1-1/8 in.	1	72	30	1	T	T	7	19	0.4	25	20,250	7
Cauliflower, cooked, drained, from raw	1 cup	125	30	2	T	T	6	34	0.5	8	20	69
Celery, raw	1 stalk	40	5	T	T	T	1	14	0.2	35	50	3
Collards, cooked from raw	1 cup	190	25	2	T	0.1	5	148	0.8	36	4,220	19
Corn, sweet, yellow, cooked from raw	1 ear	77	85	3	1	0.2	19	2	0.5	13	170	5
Eggplant, cooked, steamed	1 cup	96	25	1	T	T	6	6	0.3	3	60	1
Lettuce, iceberg, chopped	1 cup	55	5	1	T	T	1	10	0.3	5	180	2
Lettuce, looseleaf (such as romaine)	1 cup	56	10	1	T	T	2	38	0.8	5	1,060	10
Mushrooms, raw	1 cup	70	20	1	T	T	3	4	0.9	3	0	2
Onions, raw, chopped	1 cup	160	55	2	T	0.1	12	40	0.6	3	0	13
Peas, green, frozen, cooked	1 cup	160	125	8	T	0.1	23	38	2.5	139	1,070	16
Potatoes, baked, peeled	1	156	145	3	T	T	34	8	0.5	8	0	20
Potatoes, frozen, French fried (oven-heated)	10	50	110	2	4	2.1	17	5	0.7	16	0	5
Potatoes, mashed, milk added	1 cup	210	160	4	1	0.7	37	55	0.6	636	40	14
Potato chips	10	20	105	1	7	1.8	10	5	0.2	94	0	8
Potato salad	1 cup	250	360	7	21	3.6	28	48	1.6	1,323	520	25
Spinach, drained, cooked from raw	1 cup	180	40	5	T	0.1	7	245	6.4	126	14,740	18
Sweet potatoes, baked in skin, peeled	1	114	115	2	T	T	28	32	0.5	11	24,880	28
Vegetable juice cocktail, canned	1 cup	242	45	2	T	T	11	27	1.0	883	2,830	67
MISCELLANEOUS												
Beer, regular	12 fl. oz.	360	150	1	0	0.0	13	14	0.1	18	0	0
Gin, rum, vodka, whisky, 86 proof	1½ fl. oz.	42	105	0	0	0.0	T	T	T	T	0	0
Wine, table, white	3½ fl. oz.	102	80	T	0	0.0	3	9	0.3	5	(1)	0
Cola-type beverage	12 fl. oz.	369	160	0	0	0.0	41	11	0.2	18	0	0
Ginger ale	12 fl. oz	366	125	0	0	0.0	32	11	0.1	29	0	0
Coffee, brewed	6 fl. oz.	180	T	T	T	T	T	4	T	2	0	0
Tea, brewed	8 fl. oz.	240	T	T	T	T	T	0	T	1	0	0
Catsup	1 tbsp.	15	15	T	T	T	4	3	0.1	156	210	2
Mustard, prepared, yellow	1 tsp.	5	5	T	T	T	T	4	0.1	63	0	T
Olives, canned, green	4 medium	13	15	T	2	0.2	T	8	0.2	312	40	0
Pickles, dill, whole	1	65	5	T	T	T	1	17	0.7	928	70	4
Relish, finely chopped, sweet	1 tbsp.	15	20	T	T	T	5	3	0.1	107	20	1
Soup, tomato, prepared with milk	1 cup	248	160	6	6	2.9	22	159	1.8	932	850	68
Soup, chicken noodle, prepared with water	1 cup	241	75	4	2	0.7	9	17	0.8	1,106	710	T
Soup, green pea, prepared with water	1 cup	250	165	9	3	1.4	27	28	2.0	988	200	2
Soup, vegetarian, prepared with water	1 cup	241	70	2	2	0.3	12	22	1.1	822	3,010	1

T — Indicates trace. (1) — Value not determined. **NOTE:** Values shown here for these foods may be from several different manufacturers and, therefore, may differ somewhat from the values provided by one source.

U.S. Per Capita Consumption of Selected Foods, 1909-99

Source: Economic Research Service, U.S. Dept. of Agriculture

	Whole milk[1]	Low-fat & skim milk[1]	Butter[2]	Margarine[2]	Red meat[2]	Poultry[2]	Fish & shellfish[2]
1909	26.85	7.30	17.9	1.2	101.7	11.2	11.0
1939	29.24	4.79	17.4	2.3	86.9	11.9	10.8
1969	26.60	5.46	5.6	10.7	129.5	32.9	11.2
1999	8.0	13.90	4.8	8.1	117.2	68.3	15.2

(1) Gallons. (2) Pounds.

Dietary Requirements

The Food and Nutrition Board of the National Academy of Sciences' Institute of Medicine, in a series of reports published from 1997 to 2001, set **Dietary Reference Intakes (DRIs)** for vitamins and elements (often called minerals). The DRIs, based on recent scientific research, establish daily consumption values that aim to optimize health at all stages of life, not just to guard against, nutritional deficiencies.

The DRIs include 4 categories of values. The **Recommended Dietary Allowance (RDA)** gives an intake that meets the nutrient requirements of almost all (97-98%) healthy individuals in a specified group. The **Estimated Average Requirement (EAR)** is the intake that meets the estimated nutrient need of half the individuals in a specified group, while the **Adequate Intake (AI)** is the value given when adequate scientific evidence is not available to calculate an EAR. For healthy breastfed infants, the AI is the mean intake; for other life stage groups the AI is thought to cover the needs of all individuals in the group, but lack of data or uncertainty in the data prevents the percentage of individuals covered from being specified with confidence. The **Tolerable Upper Intake Level (UL)** designates the maximum intake that is unlikely to pose risks of adverse health effects in almost all healthy individuals in a specified group; taking the nutrient above that level could be bad for one's health. RDAs and AIs may both be used as goals for individual intake.

The following two tables give the RDA or, where not available, the AI, followed by an asterisk(*).

Recommended Levels for Vitamins

Source: Food and Nutrition Board, National Academy of Sciences—Institute of Medicine, 2001

in milligrams per day (mg/d) or in micrograms per day (µg/d)

	Vitamin A (µg/d)[1]	Vitamin C (mg/d)	Vitamin D (µg/d)[2]	Vitamin E (mg/d)	Vitamin K (µg/d)	Thiamin (mg/d)	Riboflavin (mg/d)	Niacin (mg/d)[3]	Vitamin B_6 (mg/d)	Folate (µg/d)[4]	Vitamin B_{12} (µg/d)	Pantothenic Acid (mg/d)	Biotin (µg/d)	Choline (mg/d)[5]
Infants														
0-6 mos	400*	40*	5*	4*	2.0*	0.2*	0.3*	2*	0.1*	65*	0.4*	1.7*	5*	125*
7-12 mos	500*	50*	5*	5*	2.5*	0.3*	0.4*	4*	0.3*	80*	0.5*	1.8*	6*	150*
Children														
1-3 yrs	300	15	5*	6	30*	0.5	0.5	6	0.5	150	0.9	2*	8*	200*
4-8 yrs	400	25	5*	7	55*	0.6	0.6	8	0.6	200	1.2	3*	12*	250*
Males														
9-13 yrs	600	45	5*	11	60*	0.9	0.9	12	1.0	300	1.8	4*	20*	375*
14-18 yrs	900	75	5*	15	75*	1.2	1.3	16	1.3	400	2.4	5*	25*	550*
19-30 yrs	900	90	5*	15	120*	1.2	1.3	16	1.3	400	2.4	5*	30*	550*
31-50 yrs	900	90	5*	15	120*	1.2	1.3	16	1.3	400	2.4	5*	30*	550*
51-70 yrs	900	90	10*	15	120*	1.2	1.3	16	1.7	400	2.4[6]	5*	30*	550*
over 70 yrs	900	90	15*	15	120*	1.2	1.3	16	1.7	400	2.4[6]	5*	30*	550*
Females														
9-13 yrs	600	45	5*	11	60*	0.9	0.9	12	1.0	300	1.8	4*	20*	375*
14-18 yrs	700	65	5*	15	75*	1.0	1.0	14	1.2	400[7]	2.4	5*	25*	400*
19-30 yrs	700	75	5*	15	90*	1.1	1.1	14	1.3	400[7]	2.4	5*	30*	425*
31-50 yrs	700	75	5*	15	90*	1.1	1.1	14	1.3	400[7]	2.4	5*	30*	425*
51-70 yrs	700	75	10*	15	90*	1.1	1.1	14	1.5	400	2.4[6]	5*	30*	425*
over 70 yrs	700	75	15*	15	90*	1.1	1.1	14	1.5	400	2.4[6]	5*	30*	425*
Pregnancy														
18 yrs. or less	750	80	5*	15	75*	1.4	1.4	18	1.9	600[8]	2.6	6*	30*	450*
19-30 yrs.	770	85	5*	15	90*	1.4	1.4	18	1.9	600[8]	2.6	6*	30*	450*
31-50 yrs.	770	85	5*	15	90*	1.4	1.4	18	1.9	600[8]	2.6	6*	30*	450*
Lactation														
18 yrs. or less	1,200	115	5*	19	75*	1.4	1.6	17	2.0	500	2.8	7*	35*	550*
19-30 yrs.	1,300	120	5*	19	90*	1.4	1.6	17	2.0	500	2.8	7*	35*	550*
31-50 yrs.	1,300	120	5*	19	90*	1.4	1.6	17	2.0	500	2.8	7*	35*	550*

NOTE: For healthy breastfed infants, the AI is the mean intake. The AI for other life stage and gender groups is believed to cover needs of all individuals in the group, but lack of data or uncertainty in the data prevent being able to specify with confidence the percentage of individuals covered by this intake. (1) As retinol activity equivalents. (2) In the absence of adequate exposure to sunlight. (3) As niacin equivalents (NE). 1 mg of niacin = 60 mg of tryptophan; 0-6 months = preformed niacin (not NE). (4) As dietary folate equivalents (DFE). 1 DFE = 1 µg food folate = 0.6 µg of folic acid from fortified food or as a supplement consumed with food = 0.5 µg of a supplement taken on an empty stomach. (5) Although AIs have been set for choline, there are few data to assess whether a dietary supply of choline is needed at all stages of the life cycle, and it may be that the choline requirement can be met by endogenous synthesis at some of these stages. (6) Because 10-30% of older people may malabsorb food-bound B_{12}, it is advisble for those older than 50 years to meet their RDA mainly by consuming foods fortified with B_{12} or a supplement containing B_{12}. (7) In view of evidence linking folate intake with neural tube defects in the fetus, it is recommended that all women capable of becoming pregnant consume 400 µg from supplements or fortified foods in addition to intake of food folate from a varied diet. (8) It is assumed that women will continue consuming 400 µg from supplements or fortified food until their pregnancy is confirmed and they enter prenatal care, which ordinarily occurs after the end of the periconceptional period—the critical time for formation of the neural tube.

Recommended Levels for Elements (Minerals)

Source: Food and Nutrition Board, National Academy of Sciences—Institute of Medicine, 2001
in milligrams per day (mg/d) or in micrograms per day (μg/d)

	Calcium (mg/d)	Chromium (μg/d)	Copper (μg/d)	Fluoride (mg/d)	Iodine (μg/d)	Iron (mg/d)	Magnesium (mg/d)	Manganese (mg/d)	Molybdenum (μg/d)	Phosphorus (mg/d)	Selenium (μg/d)	Zinc (mg/d)
Infants												
0-6 mos	210*	0.2*	200*	0.01*	110*	0.27*	30*	0.003*	2*	100*	15*	2*
7-12 mos	270*	5.5*	220*	0.5*	130*	11	75*	0.6*	3*	275*	20*	3
Children												
1-3 yrs	500*	11*	340	0.7*	90	7	80	1.2*	17	460	20	3
4-8 yrs	800*	15*	440	1*	90	10	130	1.5*	22	500	30	5
Males												
9-13 yrs	1,300*	25*	700	2*	120	8	240	1.9*	34	1,250	40	8
14-18 yrs	1,300*	35*	890	3*	150	11	410	2.2*	43	1,250	55	11
19-30 yrs	1,000*	35*	900	4*	150	8	400	2.3*	45	700	55	11
31-50 yrs	1,000*	35*	900	4*	150	8	420	2.3*	45	700	55	11
51-70 yrs	1,200*	30*	900	4*	150	8	420	2.3*	45	700	55	11
over 70 yrs	1,200*	30*	900	4*	150	8	420	2.3*	45	700	55	11
Females												
9-13 yrs	1,300*	21*	700	2*	120	8	240	1.6*	34	1,250	40	8
14-18 yrs	1,300*	24*	890	3*	150	15	360	1.6*	43	1,250	55	9
19-30 yrs	1,000*	25*	900	3*	150	18	310	1.8*	45	700	55	8
31-50 yrs	1,000*	25*	900	3*	150	18	320	1.8*	45	700	55	8
51-70 yrs	1,200*	20*	900	3*	150	8	320	1.8*	45	700	55	8
over 70 yrs	1,200*	20*	900	3*	150	8	320	1.8*	45	700	55	8
Pregnancy												
18 yrs or less	1,300*	29*	1,000	3*	220	27	400	2.0*	50	1,250	60	12
19-30 yrs	1,000*	30*	1,000	3*	220	27	350	2.0*	50	700	60	11
31-50 yrs	1,000*	30*	1,000	3*	220	27	360	2.0*	50	700	60	11
Lactation												
18 yrs or less	1,300*	44*	1,300	3*	290	10	360	2.6*	50	1,250	70	13
19-30 yrs	1,000*	45*	1,300	3*	290	9	310	2.6*	50	700	70	12
31-50 yrs	1,000*	45*	1,300	3*	290	9	320	2.6*	50	700	70	12

Weight Guidelines for Adults

Source: *Clinical Guidelines on the Identification, Evaluation, and Treatment of Overweight and Obesity in Adults,* National Heart, Lung, and Blood Institute, National Institutes of Health, 1998

Guidelines on identification, evaluation, and treatment of overweight and obesity in adults were released in June 1998 by the National Heart, Lung, and Blood Institute (NHLBI), in cooperation with the National Institute of Diabetes and Digestive and Kidney Diseases. The guidelines, based on research into risk factors in heart disease, stroke, and other conditions, define degrees of overweight and obesity in terms of **body mass index (BMI)**, which is based on weight and height and is strongly correlated with total body fat content. A BMI of 25-29 is said to indicate **overweight**; a BMI of 30 or above is said to indicate **obesity**. Weight reduction is advised for persons with a BMI of 25 or higher. (Previous guidelines have been less stringent.) Factors such as large waist circumference, high blood pressure or cholesterol, and a family history of obesity-related disease may increase risk.

Despite the perceived need by Americans to control their weight, an increasing percentage of adults are overweight or obese, according to a 1999-2000 National Health and Nutrition Examination Survey published in Oct. 2002. Nearly two-thirds—64.5%—of adults (120 million people) are overweight or obese; of these, 59 million, or 31% of all adults, are obese. 5% of adults qualified as extremely obese (having a BMI of 40 or higher). A companion study also found that weight was increasingly a problem for children, with 15% (9 million) of children aged 6 to 19 found to be overweight. These numbers were increases across-the-board from previous years, and were seen as portending serious health problems for the country.

The table given here shows the BMI for certain heights and weights. For weight reduction tips, write to the NHLBI Information Center, PO Box 30105, Bethesda, MD 20824-0105. See also the NHLBI website: www.nhlbi.nih.gov/index.htm

Weight (lbs)

Height	HEALTHY						OVERWEIGHT					OBESE								
4'10"	91	96	100	105	110	115	119	124	129	134	138	143	148	153	158	162	167	172	177	181
4'11"	94	99	104	109	114	119	124	128	133	138	143	148	153	158	163	168	173	178	183	188
5'0"	97	102	107	112	118	123	128	133	138	143	148	153	158	163	168	174	179	184	189	194
5'1"	100	106	111	116	122	127	132	137	143	148	153	158	164	169	174	180	185	190	195	201
5'2"	104	109	115	120	126	131	136	142	147	153	158	164	169	175	180	186	191	196	202	207
5'3"	107	113	118	124	130	135	141	146	152	158	163	169	175	180	186	191	197	203	208	214
5'4"	110	116	122	128	134	140	145	151	157	163	169	174	180	186	192	197	204	209	215	221
5'5"	114	120	126	132	138	144	150	156	162	168	174	180	186	192	198	204	210	216	222	228
5'6"	118	124	130	136	142	148	155	161	167	173	179	186	192	198	204	210	216	223	229	235
5'7"	121	127	134	140	146	153	159	166	172	178	185	191	198	204	211	217	223	230	236	242
5'8"	125	131	138	144	151	158	164	171	177	184	190	197	203	210	216	223	230	236	243	249
5'9"	128	135	142	149	155	162	169	176	182	189	195	203	209	216	223	230	236	243	250	257
5'10"	132	139	146	153	160	167	174	181	188	195	202	209	216	222	229	236	243	250	257	264
5'11"	136	143	150	157	165	172	179	186	193	200	208	215	222	229	236	243	250	257	265	272
6'0"	140	147	154	162	169	177	184	191	199	206	213	221	228	235	242	250	258	265	272	279
6'1"	144	151	159	166	174	182	189	197	204	212	219	227	235	242	250	257	265	272	280	288
6'2"	148	155	163	171	179	186	194	202	210	218	225	233	241	249	256	264	272	280	287	295
6'3"	152	160	168	176	184	192	200	208	216	224	232	240	248	256	264	272	279	287	295	303
6'4"	156	164	172	180	189	197	205	213	221	230	238	246	254	263	271	279	287	295	304	312
BMI[1]	**19**	**20**	**21**	**22**	**23**	**24**	**25**	**26**	**27**	**28**	**29**	**30**	**31**	**32**	**33**	**34**	**35**	**36**	**37**	**38**

(1) The BMI numbers apply to both men and women. Some very muscular people may have a high BMI without health risks.

Where to Get Help

Source: Based on Health & Medical Year Book. © by Collier Newfield, Inc.; additional data, World Almanac research

Listed here are some of the major U.S. and Canadian organizations providing information about good health practices generally, or about specific conditions and how to deal with them. (Canadian sources are identified as such.) Where a toll-free number is not available, an address is given when possible.

Some entries conclude with an e-mail address for the organization and/or an address for its Internet site, where you can also obtain useful information. In addition to these selected sites, there is a vast array of medical information on the Internet; however, it is very important to be certain that the source of information is reliable and accurate. Always check with a physician before embarking on any new health-related undertaking.

General Sources

Centers for Disease Control and Prevention Voice Information System
800-311-3435
Recorded information about public health topics, such as AIDS and Lyme disease. Also, you can request to talk with a CDC expert or have information faxed to you.
Website: www.cdc.gov

National Health Information Center
800-336-4797; in Maryland, 301-565-4167
Phone numbers for more than 1,000 health-related organizations in the United States. Printed materials offered.
E-mail: nhicinfo@health.org

National Institutes of Health
301-496-4000
Free information, including the latest research findings, on many diseases.
E-mail: NIHinfo@O.D.NIH.GOV
Website: www.nih.gov

Tel-Med
Check the phone book for local listings or call Tel-Med at 909-478-0330.
Recorded information on over 600 health topics. Sponsored by local medical societies, health organizations, or hospitals.
E-mail: telmed@ix.netcom.com
Website: www.tel-med.com

Aging

National Association of Area Agencies on Aging's Eldercare Locator Line
800-677-1116
Information and assistance on a wide range of services and programs including adult day-care and respite services, consumer fraud, hospital and nursing home information, legal services, elder abuse/protective services, Medicaid/Medigap information, tax assistance, and transportation.
Hours 9 AM-8 PM EST M-F.
Website: www.eldercare.gov

National Institute on Aging
800-222-2225
Information and publications about disabling conditions, support groups, and community resources.
E-mail: KARPF@nia.nih.gov
Website: www.nia.nih.gov

AIDS

AIDS Clinical Trials Information Service
800-874-2572
Information on federally and privately sponsored clinical trials for patients with AIDS or HIV.
E-mail: actis@actis.org
Website: www.actis.org

Canadian AIDS Society
613-230-3580
Written materials and referrals.
Website: www.cdnaids.ca
E-mail: CASinfo@cdnaids.ca

Centers for Disease Control and Prevention National AIDS/HIV Hotline
800-342-AIDS 24 hours; in Spanish, 800-344-SIDA, everyday, 8 AM-2 AM; for the hearing impaired, 800-AIDS-TTY, M-F, 10 AM-10 PM
Information on the prevention and spread of AIDS, along with referrals.
E-mail: hivmail@cdc.gov
Website: www.cdc.gov/hiv/hivinfo/nah.htm

HIV-AIDS Treatment Information Service
800-HIV-0440
Treatment information to people with AIDS, their families, and health care providers.
E-mail: atis@hivatis.org
Website: www.hivatis.org

Alcoholism and Drug Abuse

Wellplace
800-821-4357, 24 hours
Referrals to local facilities
Website: www.wellplace.com

Alcoholics Anonymous
212-870-3400
Worldwide support groups for alcoholics. Check phone book for local chapters.
Websites: www.alcoholics-anonymous.org or www.AA.org

American Council on Alcoholism
800-527-5344
Treatment referrals and counseling for recovering alcoholics.
E-mail: aca2@earthlink.net
Website: www.aca-usa.org

National Clearinghouse for Alcohol and Drug Information
800-729-6686
Provides written materials on alcohol and drug-related subjects.
E-mail: info@health.org
Website: www.health.org

National Council on Alcoholism and Drug Dependence Hopeline
800-622-2255
An answering machine for callers to request information.
Website: www.resourcedirectory.com
E-mail: griddick@resourcedirectory.com

DrugHelp
800-DRUGHELP
Answers questions on substance abuse and provides referrals to treatment centers. Operates 24 hours.
Website: www.drughelp.org

Alzheimer's Disease

Alzheimer's Association
800-272-3900
Gives referrals to local chapters and support groups; offers information on publications available from the association.
E-mail: info@alz.org
Website: www.alz.org

Alzheimer's Society of Canada
416-488-8772
Gives phone numbers for local support chapters. Publishes support materials.
E-mail: info@alzheimer.ca
Website: www.alzheimer.ca

Amyotrophic Lateral Sclerosis

ALS Association
800-782-4747; in the San Fernando Valley, 818-880-9007
Information about ALS (Lou Gehrig's Disease) and referrals to ALS specialists, local chapters and support groups.
Website: www.alsa.org

Arthritis

Arthritis Foundation
800-283-7800
Information, publications, and referrals to local groups.
Website: www.arthritis.org

Arthritis Society (Canada)
393 University Ave., Suite 1700
Toronto, ON M5G 1E6
416-979-7228; in Ontario only, 800-321-1433
Phone numbers for local chapters.
E-mail: info@arthritis.ca
Website: www.arthritis.ca

National Arthritis and Musculoskeletal and Skin Diseases Information Clearinghouse
877-226-4267
Subject searches and resource referrals.
E-mail: niamsinfo@mail.nih.gov
Website: www.niams.nih.gov

Asthma and Allergies

See also *Lung Diseases*

Asthma and Allergy Foundation of America
800-7-ASTHMA
Written information.
E-mail: info@aafa.org
Website: www.aafa.org

American Academy of Allergy, Asthma, and Immunology Referral Line
800-822-ASMA, 24 hours
Written materials on asthma and allergies.
E-mail: info@aaaai.org
Website: www.aaaai.org

Blindness and Eye Care

Canadian National Institute for the Blind
416-486-2500 or contact your local chapter.
National office offers training and library with braille books and audiotapes. Local chapters provide core services: orientation in mobility, sight enhancement, counseling, referrals, career aid, technology services.
Website: www.cnib.ca

Foundation Fighting Blindness
888-394-3937; for the hearing impaired, 800-683-5551
Answers questions about retinal degenerative diseases; has written materials.
Website: www.blindness.org

Library of Congress National Library Service for the Blind and Physically Handicapped
800-424-9100; in Spanish, 800-345-8901; in Washington, DC, 202-707-5100; for the hearing impaired, 202-707-0744
Information on libraries that offer talking books and books in braille.
E-mail: nls@loc.gov
Website: lcweb.loc.gov

National Association for Parents of the Visually Impaired
800-562-6265
Support and information for parents of individuals who are visually impaired.
Website: www.napvi.org

Blood Disorders

Cooley's Anemia Foundation
800-522-7222
Information on patient care and support groups; makes referrals to local chapters.
E-mail: info@cooleysanemia.org
Website: www.thalassemia.org

Sickle Cell Disease Association of America
800-421-8453; in California, 310-216-6363
Genetic counseling and information packet.
E-mail: scdaa@sicklecelldisease.org
Website: www.sicklecelldisease.org

Burns

Phoenix Society
800-888-2876
Counseling for burn survivors and information on self-help services for burn survivors and their families.
E-mail: info@phoenix-society.org
Website: www.phoenix-society.org

Cancer

American Cancer Society
800-ACS-2345
Publications and information about cancer and coping with cancer; makes referrals to local chapters for support services.
E-mail: ACS@aol.com
Website: www.cancer.org

Canadian Cancer Information Service
888-939-3333, in Canada only, 9 AM-6PM, Mon.-Fri.
Information on prevention, treatment, drugs, clinical trails, local services.

National Cancer Institute's Cancer Information Service
800-4-CANCER
Information about clinical trials, treatments, symptoms, prevention, referrals to support groups, and screening.
Website: cis.nci.nih.gov

Y-Me Breast Cancer Support Program
800-221-2141, 24 hours
Information and literature on breast cancer, counseling, and referrals.
E-mail: help@y-me.org
Website: www.y-me.org

Cerebral Palsy

Ontario Federation for Cerebral Palsy
877-244-9686; 416-244-9686
Canada does not have a national cerebral palsy organization, but the provincial organizations offer information on housing, services, and coping with life, and each one will provide contact numbers for the others.
E-mail: info@ofcp.on.ca
Website: www.ofcp.on.ca

United Cerebral Palsy Associations
877-835-7335; in Washington, DC, 202-776-0406
Written materials.
Website: www.ucpa.org

Child Abuse

See *Domestic Violence*

Children

American Academy of Pediatrics
847-228-5005
Child-care publications and materials; referrals to pediatricians.
E-mail: kidsdocs@aap.org
Website: www.aap.org

Childhelp's USA National Child Abuse Hotline
800-4-A-CHILD
Crisis intervention, professional counseling, referrals to local groups and shelters for runaways, and literature. Operates 24 hours.
Website: www.childhe/pusa.org

National Center for Missing and Exploited Children
800-843-5678; for the hearing impaired, 800-826-7653
Hotline for reporting missing children and sightings of missing children.
Website: www.missingkids.org

Chronic Fatigue Syndrome

CFIDS Association of America
800-442-3437
Literature and a list of support groups.
E-mail: info@cfids.org
Website: www.cfids.org

Crisis

National Runaway Switchboard
800-621-4000
Crisis intervention and referrals for runaways. Runaways can leave messages for parents, and vice versa. Operates 24 hours.
E-mail: info@nrscrisisline.org
Website: nrscrisisline.org

Cystic Fibrosis

Canadian Cystic Fibrosis Foundation
416-485-9149; in Canada only, 800-378-2233
Information and brochures; makes referrals to local chapters.
E-mail: info@cysticfibrosis.ca
Website: www.cysticfibrosis.ca

Cystic Fibrosis Foundation
800-FIGHT-CF
Answers questions and offers literature and referrals to local clinics.
E-mail: info@cff.org
Website: www.cff.org

Diabetes

American Diabetes Association
800-342-2383; in Virginia and Washington, DC, 703-549-1500
Information about diabetes, nutrition, exercise, and treatment; offers referrals.
Website: www.diabetes.org

Canadian Diabetes Association
416-363-3373; 800-226-8464
E-mail: info@diabetes.ca
Website: www.diabetes.ca

Juvenile Diabetes Foundation Hotline
800-533-2873; in NY: 212-785-9500
Answers questions, provides literature (some in Spanish). Offers referrals to local chapters, physicians, and clinics.
E-mail: info@jdf.org
Website: www.jdf.org

Digestive Diseases

Crohn's and Colitis Foundation of America
800-932-2423; in New York, 212-685-3440
Educational materials; offers referrals to local chapters, which can provide referrals to support groups and physicians.
E-mail: info@ccfa.org
Website: www.ccfa.org

Crohn's and Colitis Foundation of Canada
60 St. Clair Avenue East, Suite 600, Toronto, ON M4T 1L9
416-920-5035; in Canada only, 800-387-1479
Will send out educational materials upon request.
Website: www.ccfc.ca

Domestic Violence

National Council on Child Abuse and Family Violence
in Washington, DC, 202-429-6695
A recording provides toll-free numbers to call for information or referrals.
E-mail: info@NCCAFV.org
Website: www.nccafv.org

Down Syndrome

National Down Syndrome Congress
800-232-6372; in Georgia, 770-604-9500
Answers questions on all aspects of Down syndrome. Provides referrals.
E-mail: info@ndsccenter.com
Website: www.ndsCcenter.org

National Association for Down Syndrome
630-325-9112 (Chicago area only)
Counseling and support; advocacy, referral, and information services.
Website: www.nads.org

Drug Abuse

See *Alcoholism and Drug Abuse*

Dyslexia

International Dyslexia Association
800-ABCD-123; in Maryland, 410-296-0232
Information on testing, tutoring, and computers used to aid people with dyslexia and related disorders.
E-mail: info@interdys.org
Website: www.interdys.org

Eating Disorders

National Association of Anorexia Nervosa and Associated Disorders
847-831-3438
Written materials, referrals to health professionals treating eating disorders, telephone counseling, offers 3 self-help groups and information on how to set up a self-help group.
E-mail: anad20@aol.com
Website: www.anad.org

Endometriosis

Endometriosis Association
800-992-ENDO; in Canada, 800-426-2END
An answering machine for callers to request information.
E-mail: endo@endometriosisassn.org
Website: www.endometriosisassn.org

Epilepsy

Epilepsy and Seizure Disorder Service at the Epilepsy Foundation of America
800-332-1000, Mon. through Thurs., 9 am to 5 pm (EST), Fri., 9 am to 3 pm.
Information and referrals to local chapters.
Website: www.efa.org

Food Safety and Nutrition

Meat and Poultry Hotline of the U.S. Department of Agriculture's Food, Safety, and Inspection Service
800-535-4555
Information on prevention of food-borne illness and the proper handling, preparation, storage, labeling, and cooking of meat, poultry, and eggs.
E-mail: MPHotline.fsis@usda.gov
Website: www.fsis.usda.gov

FDA Center for Food Safety and Applied Nutrition Outreach & Information Center
800-SAFE-FOOD
Information on how to buy and use food products and on their proper handling and storage, women's health, and cosmetics & colors. Callers may speak to food specialists, Mon. through Fri., 10 am to 4 PM (EST).
Website: www.cfsan.fda.gov

Headaches

National Headache Foundation
888-NHF-5552
Literature on headaches and treatment.
E-mail: info@headaches.org
Website: www.headaches.org

Heart Disease and Stroke

American Heart Association
800-242-8721
Information, publications, and referrals to organizations.
Website: www.americanheart.org

National Institute of Neurological Disorders and Stroke
800-352-9424
Literature and information.
Website: www.ninds.nih.gov

National Stroke Association
800-787-6537
Information on support networks for stroke victims and their families; referrals to local support groups.
Website: www.stroke.org

Hospices

Children's Hospice International
800-242-4453; in Virginia, 703-684-0330
Information, referrals to children's hospices.
E-mail: chiorg@aol.com
Website: www.chionline.org

Hospice Education Institute Hospicelink
800-331-1620; in Maine, 207-255-8800
Information, referrals to local programs.
E-mail: hospiceall@aol.com
Website: www.hospiceworld.org

Huntington's Disease

Huntington's Disease Society of America
800-345-4372; in New York, 212-242-1968
Information and referrals to physicians and support groups.
E-mail: hdsainfo@hdsa.org
Website: www.hdsa.org

Huntington Society of Canada
519-749-7063, in Canada only, 800-998-7398
Information, including telephone numbers of local services; publications and referrals.
E-mail: info@hsc-ca.org
Website: www.hsc-ca.org

Impotence

Impotence Information Center
800-843-4315
Information on treatment of impotence, incontinence, and prostate problems.

Impotence World Association
800-669-1603
Written materials, physician referrals, and telephone numbers of local Impotents Anonymous chapters.
Website: www.impotenceworld.org

Kidney Diseases

Kidney Foundation of Canada
514-369-4806; In Canada only, 800-361-7494
Educational materials and general information.
Website: www.kidney.ca

National Kidney and Urologic Diseases Information Clearinghouse
301-654-4415
Information, referrals to organizations.
Website: www.niddk.nih.gov

National Kidney Foundation
800-622-9010
Information and referrals.
E-mail: info@kidney.org
Website: www.kidney.org

Lead Exposure

National Lead Information Center
800-424-LEAD
Recommendations (in English and Spanish) for reducing a child's exposure to lead. Referrals to state and local agencies.
E-mail: info@kidney.org
Website: www.epa.gov/lead

Liver Diseases

American Liver Foundation
800-465-7837; in NJ, 973-256-2550
Information on hepatitis, liver disease, and gallbladder disease.
E-mail: info@liverfoundation.org
Website: www.liverfoundation.org

Lung Diseases

See also *Asthma and Allergies*

American Lung Association
Check the phone book for local listings or call the national office at 800-LUNG-USA for automatic connection to the office nearest you. Answers questions about asthma and lung diseases; publications and referrals.
E-mail: info@lungusa.org
Website: www.lungusa.org

Lung Line Information Service at the National Jewish Medical and Research Center
800-222-LUNG; outside the U.S.: 303-388-4461
Answers questions on asthma, emphysema, allergies, smoking, and other respiratory and immune system disorders.
E-mail: lungline@njc.org
Website: www.njc.org

Lupus

Lupus Foundation of America
800-558-0121; in Colorado, 301-670-9292
Sends information to those who leave name and address on answering machine.
E-mail: info@lupus.org
Website: www.lupus.org

Lyme Disease

Lyme Disease Foundation
800-886-LYME, 24 hours
Written information; doctor referrals.
E-mail: lymefind@aol.com
Website: www.lyme.org

Mental Health

National Depressive and Manic Depressive Association
800-826-3632
Support for patients and families, provides publications, and makes referrals to affiliated organizations.
E-mail: questions@ndmda.org
Website: www.ndmda.org

National Foundation for Depressive Illness
800-239-1265, 24 hours
Recorded message describing the symptoms of depression and offering an address for more information and physician referral.
Website: www.depression.org

National Institute of Mental Health
301-443-4513
Information on a range of topics, from children's mental disorders to schizophrenia, depression, eating disorders, and others.
E-mail: nimhinfo@nih.gov
Website: www.nimh.nih.gov

National Mental Health Association
800-969-6642
Referrals to mental health groups.
E-mail: infoctr@nmha.org
Website: www.nmha.org

Multiple Sclerosis

Multiple Sclerosis Society of Canada
416-922-6065
Counseling, literature, and referrals to local chapters.
E-mail: info@mssociety.ca
Website: www.mssociety.ca

National Multiple Sclerosis Society
800-344-4867
Information about local chapters.
Website: www.nmss.org

Muscular Dystrophy

Muscular Dystrophy Association
800-572-1717
Written materials on 40 neuromuscular diseases, including muscular dystrophy. Will give information over the phone about such matters as MDA clinics, support groups, summer camps, and wheelchair purchase assistance.
E-mail: mda@mdausa.org
Website: www.mdausa.org

Nutrition

See *Food Safety and Nutrition*

Organ Donation

Living Bank
800-528-2971, 24 hours
A registry and referral service for people wanting to commit organs to transplantation or research.
E-mail: info@livingbank.org
Website: www.livingbank.org

Osteoporosis

National Osteoporosis Foundation
800-223-9994, in Washington, DC, 202-223-2226
Information packet available on request.
Website: www.nof.org

Pain

National Chronic Pain Outreach Association
540-862-9437
Information packet available on request.

Parkinson's Disease

National Parkinson Foundation
800-327-4545; in Florida, 800-433-7022; in Miami, 305-547-6666
Answers questions, makes physician referrals, and provides written information in English and Spanish.
E-mail: mailbox@parkinson.org
Website: www.parkinson.org

Parkinson Society Canada
800-565-3000, Canada only
Information; referrals to support groups.
E-mail: General.info@parkinso.ca
Website: www.parkinson.ca

Plastic Surgery

Plastic Surgery Information Service
888-475-2784
Referrals to board-certified plastic surgeons in the U.S. and Canada; general information.
Website: www.plasticsurgery.org

Polio

International Polio Network
4207 Lindell Blvd., #110
St. Louis, MO 63108-2915
314-534-0475
Information on coping with the late effects of polio; referrals to other organizations.
E-mail: gini_intl@msn.com
Website: www.post-polio.org

Prostate Problems

American Foundation for Urologic Disease
800-242-2383
Information and publications.
E-mail: admin@afud.org
Website: www.afud.org

Rare Disorders

National Organization for Rare Disorders
800-999-6673
Information on diseases and networking programs; referrals to organizations for specific disorders.
E-mail: orphan@rarediseases.org
Website: www.rarediseases.org

Rehabilitation

National Rehabilitation Information Center
800-34-NARIC; in Maryland, 301-459-5900
Research referrals and information on rehabilitation issues.
E-mail: naricinfo@heitechservices.com
Website: www.naric.com

Scleroderma

United Scleroderma Foundation
800-722-4673
Referrals to local support groups and treatment centers, as well as information on scleroderma and related skin disorders.
E-mail: sfinfo@scleroderma.org
Website: www.scleroderma.org

Sexually Transmitted Diseases

See also *AIDS*

National STD Hotline
800-227-8922
Information; confidential referrals.
E-mail: std-hivnet@ashastd.org
Website: www.ashastd.org

Sjogren's Syndrome

Sjogren's Syndrome Foundation
800-475-6473; in New York, 516-933-6365
Provides an answering machine for callers to request treatment literature.
Website: www.sjogrens.org

Skin Problems

National Psoriasis Foundation
800-723-9166
Information and referrals.
E-mail: getinfo@npfusa.org
Website: www.psoriasis.org

Speech and Hearing

American Speech-Language-Hearing Association Action Center
800-638-8255 (also TTY)
Materials on speech and language disorders and hearing impairment; referrals.
E-mail: actioncenter@asha.org
Website: www.asha.org

Canadian Hard of Hearing Association
800-263-8068, Canada only; TTY 613-526-2692
Publications; answers general questions.
E-mail: chhanational@chha.ca
Website: www.chha.ca

Dial a Hearing Screening Test
800-222-EARS
Answers questions on hearing problems. Makes referrals to local telephone numbers for a two-minute hearing test. Also to ear, nose, and throat specialists and to organizations that can provide specialized ear and hearing aid information. 9 AM-5 PM EST
E-mail: dahst@aol.com
Website: dialatest.com

Hearing Aid Helpline
800-521-5247, ext. 333
Information and distributes a directory of hearing aid specialists certified by the International Hearing Society.
Website: www.hearingihs.org

National Center for Stuttering
800-221-2483; in New York, 212-532-1460
Information on stuttering in all age groups.
Website: www.stuttering.com

Stuttering Foundation of America
800-992-9392
Referrals to speech pathologists; resource lists, publications.
E-mail: stutter@vantek.net
Website: www.stutteringhelp.org

Spinal Injuries

National Spinal Cord Injury Association
800-962-9629; in Maryland, 301-588-6959
Peer counseling; referrals to local chapters and other organizations.
E-mail: nscia@aol.com
Website: www.spinalcord.org

Stroke

See *Heart Disease and Stroke*

Sudden Infant Death Syndrome

American Sudden Infant Death Syndrome Institute
800-232-SIDS
Answers questions; literature; referrals to other organizations.
E-mail: prevent@sids.org
Website: www.sids.org

National SIDS Foundation
800-221-SIDS; in Maryland, 410-653-8226
Literature on medical information, referrals, and support groups.
E-mail: info@sidsalliance.org
Website: www.sidsalliance.org

Tourette Syndrome

Tourette Syndrome Association
718-224-2999
Printed information.
E-mail: ts@tsa-usa.org
Website: tsa-usa.org

Urinary Incontinence

National Association for Continence
800-BLADDER
Information on bladder control, services available for incontinence, and assistive devices.
E-mail: memberservices@nafc.org
Website: www.nafc.org

Simon Foundation for Continence
800-23-SIMON
Support and literature on incontinence.
E-mail: Simoninfo@simonfoundations.org
Website: www.simonfoundation.org

Women's Health

National Women's Health Network
202-347-1140; 202-628-7814 (clearinghouse)
Information and referrals on more than 70 women's health concerns.
Website: www.womenshealthnetwork.org

National Women's Health Resource Center
877-986-9472
A national clearinghouse for women's health information.
E-mail: info@healthywomen.org
Website: www.healthywomen.org

ECONOMICS

Consumer Price Index

The Consumer Price Index (CPI) is a measure of the average change in prices over time of one or more kinds of basic consumer goods and services.

From Jan. 1978, the Bureau of Labor Statistics began publishing CPIs for 2 population groups: (1) a CPI for all urban consumers (CPI-U), which covers about 87% of the total population; and (2) a CPI for urban wage earners and clerical workers (CPI-W), which covers about 32% of the total population. The CPI-U includes, in addition to wage earners and clerical workers, groups such as professional, managerial, and technical workers, the self-employed, short-term workers, the unemployed, retirees, and others not in the labor force.

The CPI is based on prices of food, clothing, shelter, and fuels; transportation fares; charges for doctors' and dentists' services; drug prices; and prices of other goods and services bought for day-to-day living. The index currently measures price changes from a designated reference period, 1982-84, which equals 100.0. Use of this reference period began in Jan. 1988.

U.S. Consumer Price Indexes, 2001-2002

Source: Bureau of Labor Statistics, U.S. Dept. of Labor

(Data are semiannual averages of monthly figures. For all urban consumers; 1982-84 = 100.)

	1st half 2001	% change 2nd half 2000 to 1st half 2001	2nd half 2001	% change 1st half 2001 to 2nd half 2001	1st half 2002	% change 2nd half 2001 to 1st half 2002
ALL ITEMS	**176.6**	**1.7**	**177.5**	**0.5**	**178.9**	**0.8**
Food, beverages	172.4	1.7	174.8	1.4	170.5	1.0
Housing	175.5	2.4	177.3	1.0	179.2	1.1
Apparel	129.0	0.2	125.5	–2.7	125.1	–0.3
Transportation	156.1	1.0	152.4	–2.4	151.4	–0.7
Medical care	270.1	2.6	275.4	2.0	282.4	2.5
Recreation	104.6	0.8	105.2	0.6	106.1	0.9
Other goods, services	278.9	1.9	286.4	2.7	290.8	1.5
Services	201.9	2.3	205.0	1.5	208.1	1.5
SPECIAL INDEXES						
All items less food	177.5	1.8	178.1	0.3	179.4	0.7
Commodities less food	140.5	0.6	137.2	–2.3	135.7	–1.1
Nondurables	161.3	1.3	159.8	–0.9	160.2	0.3
Energy	134.6	4.5	124.0	–7.9	118.1	–4.8
All items less energy	182.4	1.5	184.7	1.3	186.9	1.2

U.S. Consumer Price Indexes (CPI-U),[1] Annual Percent Change, 1990-2001

Source: Bureau of Labor Statistics, U.S. Dept. of Labor

	1990	1991	1992	1993	1994	1995	1996	1997	1998	1999	2000	2001
ALL ITEMS	**5.4**	**4.2**	**3.0**	**3.0**	**2.6**	**2.8**	**3.0**	**2.3**	**1.6**	**2.2**	**3.4**	**2.8**
Food	5.8	2.9	1.2	2.2	2.4	2.8	3.3	2.6	2.2	2.1	2.3	3.2
Shelter	5.4	4.5	3.3	3.0	3.1	3.2	3.2	3.1	3.3	2.9	3.3	3.7
Rent, residential	5.6	6.1	2.5	2.3	2.5	2.5	2.7	2.9	3.2	3.1	3.6	4.5
Fuel and other utilities	3.5	3.3	2.2	3.0	1.0	0.7	3.1	2.6	–1.8	0.2	7.1	8.9
Apparel and upkeep	4.6	3.7	2.5	1.4	–0.2	–1.0	–0.2	0.9	0.1	–1.3	–1.3	–1.8
Private transportation	5.2	2.6	2.2	2.3	3.1	3.7	2.7	0.7	–2.2	1.9	6.1	0.6
New cars	1.8	3.8	2.5	2.4	3.4	2.2	1.7	0.2	–0.6	–0.3	–0.1	–0.5
Gasoline	14.1	–1.8	–0.2	–1.3	0.5	1.6	6.1	–0.1	–13.4	9.3	28.5	–3.6
Public transportation	10.1	4.4	1.7	10.3	3.0	2.3	3.4	2.6	1.9	3.9	6.0	0.5
Medical care	9.0	8.7	7.4	5.9	4.8	4.5	3.5	2.8	3.2	3.5	4.1	4.6
Entertainment	4.7	4.5	2.8	2.5	2.9	2.5	3.4	2.1	1.5	0.9	1.3	1.5
Commodities	5.2	4.2	2.0	1.9	1.7	1.9	2.6	1.4	0.1	1.8	3.3	1.0

(1) The Consumer Price Index CPI-U measures the average change in prices of goods and services purchased by all urban consumers.

Consumer Price Index, 1915-2002

Source: Bureau of Labor Statistics, U.S. Dept. of Labor

(1967 = 100. Annual averages of monthly figures, specified for all urban consumers.)

Prices as measured by the U.S. Consumer Price Index have risen steadily since World War II. What cost $1.00 in 1967 (the reference year) cost about 30 cents in 1915, 54 cents in 1945, and $5.36 by 2002.

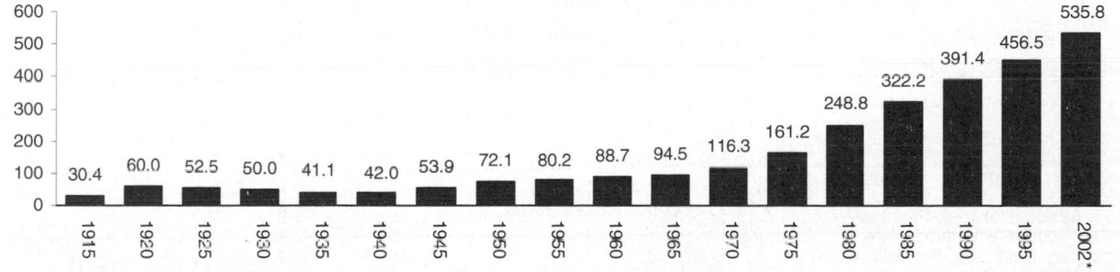

*Average for 1st half 2002.

U.S. Consumer Price Indexes for Selected Items and Groups, 1970-2001

Source: Bureau of Labor Statistics, U.S. Dept. of Labor

(1982-84 = 100, unless otherwise noted. Annual averages of monthly figures. For all urban consumers.)

	1970	1975	1980	1985	1990	1995	1998	1999	2000	2001
ALL ITEMS	**38.8**	**53.8**	**82.4**	**107.6**	**130.7**	**152.4**	**163.0**	**166.6**	**172.2**	**177.1**
Food and beverages	**40.1**	**60.2**	**86.7**	**105.6**	**132.1**	**148.9**	**161.1**	**164.6**	**168.4**	**173.6**
Food	39.2	59.8	86.8	105.6	132.4	148.4	160.7	164.1	167.8	173.1
Food at home	39.9	61.8	88.4	104.3	132.3	148.8	161.1	164.2	167.9	173.4
Cereals and bakery products	37.1	62.9	83.9	107.9	140.0	167.5	181.1	185.0	188.3	193.8
Meats, poultry, fish, and eggs	44.6	67.0	92.0	100.1	130.0	138.8	147.3	147.9	154.5	161.3
Dairy products	44.7	62.6	90.9	103.2	126.5	132.8	150.8	159.6	160.7	167.1
Fruits and vegetables	37.8	56.9	82.1	106.4	149.0	177.7	198.2	203.1	204.6	212.2
Sugar and sweets	30.5	65.3	90.5	105.8	124.7	137.5	150.2	152.3	154.0	155.7
Fats and oils	39.2	73.5	89.3	106.9	126.3	137.3	146.9	148.3	147.4	155.7
Nonalcoholic beverages	27.1	41.3	91.4	104.3	113.5	131.7	133.0	134.3	137.8	139.2
Other foods	39.6	58.9	83.6	106.4	131.2	151.1	165.5	168.9	172.2	176.0
Food away from home	37.5	54.5	83.4	108.3	133.4	149.0	161.1	165.1	169.0	173.9
Alcoholic beverages	52.1	65.9	86.4	106.4	129.3	153.9	165.7	169.7	174.7	179.3
Housing	**36.4**	**50.7**	**81.1**	**107.7**	**128.5**	**148.5**	**160.4**	**163.9**	**169.6**	**176.4**
Shelter	35.5	48.8	81.0	109.8	140.0	165.7	182.1	187.3	193.4	200.6
Rent of primary residence[1]	46.5	58.0	80.9	111.8	138.4	157.8	172.1	177.5	183.9	192.1
Fuel and other utilities[1]	29.1	45.4	75.4	106.5	111.6	123.7	128.5	128.8	137.9	150.2
Gas (piped) and electricity	25.4	40.1	71.4	107.1	109.3	119.2	121.2	120.9	128.0	142.4
Household furnishings and operations	46.8	63.4	86.3	103.8	113.3	123.0	126.6	126.7	128.2	129.1
Apparel	**59.2**	**72.5**	**90.9**	**105.0**	**124.1**	**132.0**	**133.0**	**131.3**	**129.6**	**127.3**
Men's and boys'	62.2	75.5	89.4	105.0	120.4	126.2	131.8	131.1	129.7	125.7
Women's and girls'	71.8	85.5	96.0	104.9	122.6	126.9	126.0	123.3	121.5	119.3
Footwear	56.8	69.6	91.8	102.3	117.4	125.4	128.0	125.7	123.8	123.0
Transportation	**37.5**	**50.1**	**83.1**	**106.4**	**120.5**	**139.1**	**141.6**	**144.4**	**153.3**	**154.3**
Private	37.5	50.6	84.2	106.2	118.8	136.3	137.9	140.5	149.1	150.0
New vehicles	53.0	62.9	88.4	106.1	121.4	139.0	143.4	142.9	142.8	142.1
Used cars and trucks	31.2	43.8	62.3	113.7	117.6	156.5	150.6	152.0	155.8	158.7
Gasoline	27.9	45.1	97.5	98.6	101.0	99.8	91.6	100.1	128.6	124.0
Public	35.2	43.5	69.0	110.5	142.6	175.9	190.3	197.7	209.6	210.6
Medical care	**34.0**	**47.5**	**74.9**	**113.5**	**162.8**	**220.5**	**242.1**	**250.6**	**260.8**	**272.8**
Entertainment	**47.5**	**62.0**	**83.6**	**107.9**	**132.4**	**153.9**	— [2]	— [2]	— [2]	— [2]
Other goods and services	**40.9**	**53.9**	**75.2**	**114.5**	**159.0**	**206.9**	**237.7**	**258.3**	**271.1**	**282.6**
Tobacco products	43.1	54.7	72.0	116.7	181.5	225.7	274.8	355.8	394.9	425.2
Personal care	43.5	57.9	81.9	106.3	130.4	147.1	156.7	161.1	165.6	170.5
Personal care products	42.7	58.0	79.6	107.6	128.2	143.1	148.3	151.8	153.7	155.1
Personal care services	44.2	57.7	83.7	108.9	132.8	151.5	166.0	171.4	178.1	184.3

(1) Dec. 1982 = 100. (2) The BLS stopped tracking this category after 1997, and began tracking a category classified as Recreation. The Recreation index for 1998 is 99.6, for 1999 is 102.0, for 2000 is 103.3, for 2001 is 104.9.

Consumer Price Indexes by Region and Selected Cities, 2000-2002[1]

Source: Bureau of Labor Statistics, U.S. Dept. of Labor

(1982-84 = 100, unless otherwise noted)

	Semiannual averages				Percent change from preceding semiannual average			
	2nd half 2000	1st half 2001	2nd half 2001	1st half 2002	2nd half 2000	1st half 2001	2nd half 2001	1st half 2002
U.S. CITY AVERAGE	**173.6**	**176.6**	**177.5**	**178.9**	**1.6**	**1.7**	**0.5**	**0.8**
Northeast urban	**180.7**	**183.8**	**184.9**	**186.9**	**1.5**	**1.7**	**0.6**	**1.1**
Size A—More than 1,500,000	181.6	184.7	186.2	188.4	1.6	1.7	0.8	1.2
Size B/C—50,000 to 1,500,000[2]	108.5	110.4	110.6	111.3	1.3	1.8	0.2	0.6
Midwest urban	**169.6**	**172.8**	**172.9**	**173.8**	**1.6**	**1.9**	**0.1**	**0.5**
Size A—More than 1,500,000	171.1	174.3	174.6	176.2	1.5	1.9	0.2	0.9
Size B/C—50,000 to 1,500,000[2]	108.3	110.4	110.3	110.3	1.4	1.9	–0.1	0
Size D—Nonmetro. (less than 50,000)	164.2	166.9	166.7	167.5	1.9	1.6	–0.1	0.5
South urban	**168.3**	**170.9**	**171.4**	**172.3**	**1.3**	**1.5**	**0.3**	**0.5**
Size A—More than 1,500,000	168.3	171.1	172.5	173.5	1.7	1.7	0.8	0.6
Size B/C—50,000 to 1,500,000[2]	108.0	109.6	109.6	110.2	1.2	1.5	0	0.5
Size D—Nonmetro. (less than 50,000)	167.6	170.0	169.4	170.0	0.8	1.4	–0.4	0.4
West urban	**176.5**	**180.2**	**182.1**	**184.0**	**2.0**	**2.1**	**1.1**	**1.0**
Size A—More than 1,500,000	178.3	182.3	184.2	186.3	2.2	2.2	1.0	1.1
Size B/C—50,000 to 1,500,000[2]	108.7	110.6	111.7	112.6	1.7	1.7	1.0	0.8
SELECTED AREAS								
Atlanta, GA	171.9	176.1	176.4	177.6	1.6	2.4	0.2	0.7
Boston–Brockton–Nashua, MA–NH–ME–CT	185.4	190.5	192.6	194.4	2.0	2.8	1.1	0.9
Chicago–Gary–Kenosha, IL–IN–WI	175.1	178.5	178.2	180.1	1.4	1.9	–0.2	1.1
Cleveland–Akron, OH	169.6	172.6	173.3	172.9	2.0	1.8	0.4	–0.2
Dallas–Fort Worth, TX	166.7	168.9	171.8	172.1	2.5	1.3	1.7	0.2
Detroit–Ann Arbor–Flint, MI	171.2	174.1	174.6	177.6	1.7	1.7	0.3	1.7
Houston–Galveston–Brazoria, TX	155.7	158.9	158.6	157.8	2.0	2.1	–0.2	–0.5
L.A.–Riverside–Orange County, CA	173.0	176.5	178.2	181.1	1.7	2.0	1.0	1.6
Miami–Fort Lauderdale, FL	169.0	172.4	173.6	174.7	1.4	2.0	0.7	0.6
New York, NY–Northern NJ–Long Island, NY–NJ–CT–PA	184.0	186.5	187.8	190.7	1.7	1.4	0.7	1.5
Philadelphia–Wilmington–Atlantic City, PA–DE–NJ–MD	177.6	180.5	182.1	183.3	1.3	1.6	0.9	0.7
San Francisco–Oakland–San Jose, CA	182.6	188.7	191.1	192.3	2.8	3.3	1.3	0.6
Seattle–Tacoma–Bremerton, WA	181.1	184.4	186.9	188.3	2.1	1.8	1.4	0.7
Washington–Baltimore, DC–MD–VA–WV[3]	108.6	109.7	111.1	112.1	1.9	1.0	1.3	0.9

(1) For all urban consumers. (2) Dec. 1996 = 100. (3) Nov. 1996 = 100.

Percentage Change in Consumer Prices in Selected Countries

Source: International Monetary Fund

(annual averages)

COUNTRY	1975-1980	1980-1985	1992-1993	1993-1994	1994-1995	1995-1996	1996-1997	1997-1998	1998-1999	1999-2000[R]	2000-2001
Canada	8.7	7.4	1.8	0.2	2.2	1.6	1.6	1.0	1.7	2.7	2.6
France	10.5	9.6	2.1	1.7	1.8	2.0	1.2	0.7	0.5	1.7	1.7
Germany	4.1	3.9	4.1	3.0	1.8	1.5	1.8	1.0	0.6	1.9	2.5
Italy	16.3	13.7	4.5	4.0	5.2	4.0	2.0	2.0	1.7	2.5	2.7
Japan	6.5	2.7	1.3	0.7	–0.1	0.1	1.7	0.6	–0.3	–0.7	–0.7
Spain	18.6	12.2	4.6	4.7	4.7	3.6	2.0	1.8	2.3	3.4	NA
Sweden	10.5	9.0	4.6	2.2	2.5	0.5	0.5	–0.1	0.5	0.9	2.4
Switzerland	2.3	4.3	3.3	0.8	1.8	0.8	0.5	0.1	0.7	1.5	1.0
United Kingdom	14.4	7.2	1.6	2.5	3.4	2.4	3.1	3.4	1.6	3.0	1.8
United States	8.9	5.5	3.0	2.6	2.8	3.0	2.3	1.6	2.2	3.4	2.8

R = Revised. NA = Not available.

Index of Leading Economic Indicators

Source: The Conference Board

The index of leading economic indicators is used to project the U.S. economy's performance. The index is made up of 10 measurements of economic activity that tend to change direction in advance of the overall economy. The index has predicted economic downturns from 8 to 20 months in advance and recoveries from 1 to 10 months in advance; however, it can be inconsistent, and has occasionally shown "false signals" of recessions.

Components

- Average weekly hours of production workers in manufacturing
- Average weekly initial claims for unemployment insurance, state programs
- Manufacturers' new orders for consumer goods and materials, adjusted for inflation
- Vendor performance (slower deliveries diffusion index)
- Manufacturers' new orders, nondefense capital goods industries, adjusted for inflation
- New private housing units authorized by local building permits
- Stock prices, 500 common stocks
- Money supply: M-2, adjusted for inflation
- Interest rate spread, 10-yr Treasury bonds less federal funds
- Consumer expectations (researched by Univ. of Michigan)

U.S. Gross Domestic Product, Gross National Product, Net National Product, National Income, and Personal Income

Source: Bureau of Economic Analysis, U.S. Dept. of Commerce

(billions of current dollars)

	1960	1970	1980	1990	2000[R]	2001
GROSS DOMESTIC PRODUCT	—	—	—	$5,546.1	$9,824.6	$10,082.2
GROSS NATIONAL PRODUCT	$515.3	$1,015.5	$2,732.0	5,567.8	9,848.0	10,104.1
Less: Consumption of fixed capital	46.4	88.8	303.8	602.7	1,228.9	1,329.3
Equals: Net national product	468.9	926.6	2,428.1	4,965.1	8,619.1	8,774.8
Less: Indirect business tax and nontax liability	45.3	94.0	213.3	444.0	753.6	774.8
Business transfer payments	2.0	4.1	12.1	26.8	43.7	42.5
Statistical discrepancy	–2.8	–1.1	4.9	7.8	–128.5	–117.3
Plus: Subsidies less current surplus of government enterprises	0.4	2.9	5.7	4.5	34.1	47.3
Equals: National income	424.9	832.6	2,203.5	4,491.0	7,984.4	8,122.0
Less: Corporate profits with inventory valuation and capital consumption adjustments	49.5	74.7	177.2	380.6	788.1	731.6
Net interest	11.3	41.2	200.9	463.7	611.5	649.8
Contributions for social insurance	21.9	62.2	216.5	503.1	701.3	726.1
Wage accruals less disbursements	0.0	0.0	0.0	0.1	0.0	0.0
Plus: Personal interest income	27.5	81.8	312.6	666.3	1,077.0	1,091.3
Personal dividend income	24.9	69.3	271.9	698.2	375.7	409.2
Government transfer payments to persons	12.9	22.2	52.9	144.4	1,037.3	1,137.0
Business transfer payments to persons	2.0	4.1	12.1	21.3	33.0	33.4
Equals: PERSONAL INCOME	409.4	831.8	2,258.5	4,673.8	8,406.6	8,685.3

Note: R = Revised.

U.S. Gross Domestic Product

Source: Bureau of Economic Analysis, U.S. Dept. of Commerce

(billions of current dollars)

	1991	2001	2nd Quarter 2002[1]
Gross domestic product	5,986.2	10,082.2	10,376.9
Personal consumption expenditures	3,971.2	6,987.0	7,254.7
Durable goods	443.0	835.9	856.9
Nondurable goods	1,278.8	2,041.3	2,108.2
Services	2,249.4	4,109.9	4,289.5
Gross private domestic investment	800.2	1,586.0	1,588.0
Fixed investment	800.4	1,646.3	1,584.6
Nonresidential	608.9	1,201.6	1,115.8
Structures	183.4	324.5	275.2
Equipment and software	425.4	877.1	840.7
Residential	191.5	444.8	468.7
Change in private inventories	–0.2	–60.3	3.4

	1991	2001	2nd Quarter 2002[1]
Net exports of goods and services	–20.7	–348.9	–425.6
Exports	601.6	1,034.1	1,018.1
Goods	426.4	733.5	709.4
Services	175.2	300.6	308.8
Imports	622.3	1,383.0	1,443.7
Goods	500.7	1,167.2	1,202.9
Services	121.6	215.8	240.8
Government consumption expenditures and gross investment	1,235.5	1,858.0	1,959.8
Federal	527.4	628.1	688.2
National defense	384.5	399.9	442.1
Nondefense	142.9	228.2	246.1
State and local	708.1	1,229.9	1,271.6

(1) Seasonally adjusted at annual rates.

Countries With Highest Gross Domestic Product and Per Capita GDP[1]

Source: Central Intelligence Agency, *The World Factbook 2002*

Gross Domestic Product

(billions of dollars; 2001 estimates)

Rank	Country	GDP	Rank	Country	GDP
1.	U.S.	$10,082.0	21.	South Africa	$412.0
2.	China[2]	5,560.0	22.	Thailand	410.0
3.	Japan	3,450.0	23.	Taiwan	386.0
4.	India	2,500.0	24.	Poland	339.6
5.	Germany	2,174.0	25.	Philippines	335.0
6.	France	1,510.0	26.	Pakistan	299.0
7.	U.K.	1,470.0	27.	Belgium	267.7
8.	Italy	1,402.0	28.	Egypt	258.0
9.	Brazil	1,340.0	29.	Colombia	255.0
10.	Russia	1,200.0	30.	Saudi Arabia	241.0
11.	Mexico	920.0	31.	Bangladesh	230.0
12.	Canada	875.0	32.	Switzerland	226.0
13.	South Korea	865.0	33.	Austria	220.0
14.	Spain	757.0	34.	Sweden	219.0
15.	Indonesia	687.0	35.	Ukraine	205.0
16.	Australia	465.9	36.	Malaysia	200.0
17.	Argentina	453.0	37.	Greece	189.7
18.	Turkey	443.0	38.	Algeria	177.0
19.	Iran	426.0	39.	Portugal	174.1
20.	Netherlands	413.0	40.	Vietnam	168.1

Per Capita Gross Domestic Product[3]

(dollars; 2001 estimates unless otherwise noted)

Rank	Country	Per capita GDP	Rank	Country	Per capita GDP
1.	Luxembourg	$43,400	21.	Italy	$24,300
2.	U.S.	36,300	22.	Australia	24,000
3.	San Marino	34,600	23.	Liechtenstein	23,000[4]
4.	Switzerland	31,100	24.	Qatar	21,200
5.	Norway	30,800	25.	U.A.E.	21,100
6.	Denmark	28,000	26.	Israel	20,000
7.	Canada	27,700	27.	New Zealand	19,500
8.	Ireland	27,300	28.	Andorra	19,000[5]
9.	Japan	27,200	29.	Spain	18,900
10.	Austria	27,000	30.	Brunei	18,000
	Monaco	27,000[4]		South Korea	18,000
12.	Germany	26,200	32.	Greece	17,900
13.	Belgium	26,100	33.	Portugal	17,300
14.	Finland	25,800	34.	Taiwan	17,200[5]
	Netherlands	25,800	35.	The Bahamas	16,800
16.	France	25,400	36.	Slovenia	16,000
17.	Iceland	24,800[5]	37.	Kuwait	15,100
18.	Singapore	24,700	38.	Malta	15,000
	Sweden	24,700	39.	Barbados	14,500
	U.K.	24,700	40.	Czech Republic	14,440

(1) U.S. data from *The World Factbook* may differ from data from the U.S. Bureau of Economic Analysis. International GDP estimates derive from purchasing power parity calculations, which involve the use of intl. dollar price weights applied to quantities of goods and services produced in a given economy. (2) Chinese government figures may substantially overstate the GDP. Hong Kong, a special administrative region of China since July 1, 1997, had a GDP of $180.0 billion and a per capita GDP of $25,000 in 2001. (3) These territories or former territories had large per capita GDPs: Bermuda (UK, 2001) $34,800, Cayman Islands (UK, 1999) $30,000, Aruba (Neth., 2000) $28,000, Guam (U.S., 2000) $21,000, Greenland (Den., 2001) $20,000, Faroe Islands (Den., 2000) $20,000, Macao (Port., 2001) $17,600, Gibraltar (UK, 1997) $17,500. (4) 1998 est. (5) 2000 est.

U.S. National Income by Industry[1]

Source: Bureau of Economic Analysis, U.S. Dept. of Commerce

(billions of current dollars)

	1960	1970	1980	1990	1995	1998	1999	2000R	2001
National income without capital consumption adjustment	**$428.6**	**$835.1**	**$2,263.9**	**$4,640.5**	**$5,884.4**	**$7,013.2**	**$7,424.5**	**$7,958.7**	**$8,053.5**
Domestic industries	**425.1**	**827.8**	**2,216.3**	**4,611.6**	**5,864.0**	**7,016.6**	**7,401.8**	**7,935.3**	**8,031.5**
Private industries	**371.6**	**695.4**	**1,894.5**	**3,929.0**	**5,039.9**	**6,101.6**	**6,448.5**	**6,928.0**	**6,969.4**
Agriculture, forestry, fisheries	17.8	25.9	61.4	89.0	86.9	102.4	111.3	109.7	111.1
Mining	5.6	8.4	43.8	40.8	45.7	54.2	48.6	62.9	69.5
Construction	22.5	47.4	126.6	230.5	266.7	349.6	389.4	422.9	438.9
Manufacturing	125.3	215.6	532.1	879.0	1,058.5	1,145.4	1,180.5	1,250.7	1,132.2
Durable goods	73.4	127.7	313.7	498.1	606.8	671.0	688.0	729.2	640.5
Nondurable goods	52.0	87.9	218.4	380.9	451.6	474.4	492.6	521.4	491.8
Transportation, public utilities	35.8	64.4	177.3	330.5	440.7	495.9	511.4	530.5	529.9
Transportation	18.5	31.5	85.8	138.7	183.9	224.6	234.0	243.7	236.6
Communications	8.2	17.6	48.1	94.2	129.4	142.8	144.1	149.4	148.4
Electric, gas, sanitary services	9.1	86.8	43.4	97.6	127.3	128.5	133.2	137.4	144.9
Wholesale trade	25.0	47.5	143.3	266.0	328.2	420.5	444.4	481.1	458.4
Retail trade	41.3	79.9	189.4	385.3	481.8	585.6	619.3	659.1	686.1
Finance, insurance, real estate	51.3	96.4	279.5	738.5	1,013.5	1,309.5	1,379.3	1,521.5	1,571.1
Services	46.9	109.8	341.0	969.5	1,318.1	1,638.6	1,764.2	1,889.8	1,972.0
Government	**53.5**	**132.4**	**321.8**	**682.6**	**824.2**	**915.1**	**953.3**	**1,007.3**	**1,062.1**

NOTE: R = revised. (1) Figures may not add because of rounding. Total national income also includes income from outside the U.S.

U.S. National Income by Type of Income[1]

Source: Bureau of Economic Analysis, U.S. Dept. of Commerce

(billions of current dollars)

	1960	1970	1980	1990	1995	1998	1999	2000R	2001
NATIONAL INCOME[2]	**427.5**	**837.5**	**2,243.0**	**4,642.1**	**5,876.7**	**7,041.4**	**7,468.7**	**7,984.4**	**8,122.0**
Compensation of employees	**296.4**	**617.2**	**1,651.7**	**3,351.0**	**4,202.5**	**4,989.6**	**5,308.8**	**5,723.4**	**5,874.9**
Wage and salary accruals	272.8	551.5	1,377.4	2,754.6	3,441.1	4,192.1	4,475.6	4,836.3	4,950.6
Government	49.2	117.1	261.2	516.8	622.7	692.7	724.2	768.9	810.8
Other	223.7	434.3	1,116.2	2,237.9	2,818.4	3,499.4	3,751.4	4,067.4	4,139.8
Supplements to wages and salaries	23.6	65.7	274.3	596.4	761.4	797.5	833.2	887.1	924.3
Employer contributions for social insurance	9.3	23.8	88.9	206.5	264.5	306.9	323.0	342.9	353.9
Other labor income	14.4	41.9	185.4	390.0	497.0	490.6	510.2	544.2	570.4
Proprietors' income with inventory valuation and capital consumption adjustments	**51.9**	**79.8**	**177.6**	**381.0**	**497.7**	**623.8**	**678.4**	**714.8**	**727.9**
Farm	11.4	14.3	13.1	31.1	22.2	25.6	27.7	22.6	19.0
Nonfarm	40.4	65.5	164.5	349.9	475.5	598.2	650.7	692.2	708.8
Rental income of persons with capital consumption adjustment	16.2	20.3	31.3	49.1	117.9	138.6	149.1	146.6	137.9
Corporate profits with inventory valuation and capital consumption adjustments	**52.3**	**81.6**	**198.5**	**408.6**	**668.8**	**777.4**	**805.8**	**788.1**	**731.6**
Corporate profits with inventory valuation adjustment	51.4	74.0	209.3	388.6	650.2	739.4	757.9	767.3	675.1
Profits before tax	51.5	80.6	251.4	401.5	668.5	721.1	762.1	782.3	670.2
Profits tax liability	22.7	34.4	84.8	140.6	211.0	238.8	247.8	259.4	199.3
Profits after tax	28.8	46.2	166.6	260.9	457.5	482.3	514.3	522.9	470.9
Dividends	13.4	24.3	64.1	165.6	254.2	348.7	328.4	376.1	409.6
Undistributed profits	15.5	21.9	102.6	95.3	203.3	133.6	185.9	146.8	61.2
Inventory valuation adjustment	–0.2	–6.6	–42.1	–12.9	–18.3	18.3	–4.2	–15.0	5.0
Net interest	**10.7**	**38.4**	**183.9**	**452.4**	**389.8**	**511.9**	**526.6**	**611.5**	**649.8**

NOTE: R = revised. (1) Figures do not add, because of rounding and incomplete enumeration. (2) National income is the aggregate of labor and property earnings that arises in the production of goods and services. It is the sum of employee compensation, proprietors' income, rental income, adjusted corporate profits, and net interest. It measures the total factor costs of goods and services produced by the economy. Income is measured before deduction of taxes. Total national income figures include adjustments not itemized.

Selected Personal Consumption Expenditures in the U.S., 1994-2001[1]

Source: Bureau of Economic Analysis, U.S. Dept. of Commerce

(billions of dollars)

	1994	1995	1996	1997	1998	1999	2000	2001
Personal consumption expenditures	**$4,716.4**	**$4,969.0**	**$5,237.5**	**$5,529.3**	**$5,856.0**	**$6,246.5**	**$6,683.7**	**$6,987.0**
Food and tobacco	**773.6**	**802.5**	**834.1**	**862.0**	**906.9**	**964.7**	**1,027.2**	**1,068.7**
Food purchased for off-premise consumption	445.5	459.8	476.7	486.5	507.9	537.7	568.6	589.0
Purchased meals and beverages	274.5	287.5	300.5	316.6	335.4	351.5	376.5	393.2
Food furnished to employees (incl. milit.) and produced/consumed on farms	8.1	8.5	8.7	9.0	9.3	9.6	9.9	10.2
Tobacco products	45.4	46.7	48.2	49.8	54.4	65.9	72.2	76.3
Clothing, accessories, and jewelry	**307.2**	**317.3**	**333.3**	**348.0**	**367.2**	**391.2**	**409.8**	**412.6**
Shoes	35.8	37.1	38.8	40.1	42.4	44.7	46.3	47.0
Clothing and accessories except shoes	204.6	210.4	219.5	231.3	242.0	256.1	267.1	267.9
Women's and children's	132.3	135.5	140.8	148.0	154.6	164.1	171.9	172.6
Men's and boys'	72.3	74.9	78.6	83.3	87.4	92.0	95.2	95.3
Jewelry and watches	36.2	38.1	40.3	41.2	44.3	48.5	51.1	51.0
Other	30.5	31.7	34.7	35.5	38.5	41.9	45.3	46.7
Personal care (toilet articles, barbershops, health clubs)	**63.3**	**67.4**	**71.6**	**76.1**	**79.9**	**84.0**	**87.8**	**89.1**
Housing	**704.7**	**740.8**	**772.5**	**810.5**	**859.7**	**912.6**	**960.0**	**1,014.5**
Owner-occupied nonfarm dwellings–space rent	502.6	529.3	555.4	585.5	625.0	666.4	704.9	751.0
Tenant-occupied nonfarm dwellings–rent	169.3	177.0	180.6	186.1	194.0	202.8	207.8	217.1
Rental value of farm dwellings	5.9	6.0	6.2	6.4	6.7	7.2	7.6	8.0
Other	27.0	28.5	30.2	32.5	34.0	36.1	39.6	38.5
Household operation	**528.2**	**555.0**	**589.2**	**617.8**	**642.9**	**677.7**	**723.9**	**747.3**
Furniture, including mattresses and bedsprings	45.1	47.5	50.9	53.8	56.7	60.3	64.4	64.0
Kitchen and other household appliances	27.5	29.1	30.0	30.8	32.1	34.1	35.7	36.1
China, glassware, tableware, and utensils	22.5	23.8	25.4	27.2	29.1	31.4	33.3	34.1
Other durable house furnishings	45.1	47.7	50.5	53.5	57.1	61.6	65.1	66.4
Semidurable house furnishings	28.5	29.7	31.0	33.1	34.5	36.8	38.3	38.7
Cleaning and polishing preparations, and miscellaneous household supplies and paper products	45.4	47.3	49.8	51.4	53.5	56.9	59.3	61.7
Stationery and writing supplies	16.7	17.7	18.8	20.0	21.3	22.6	23.4	23.5
Household utilities (oil, gas, electricity, water, sanitary)	169.5	175.0	185.0	188.1	186.2	190.1	209.2	221.7
Telephone and telegraph	82.7	87.8	97.1	105.0	112.9	122.3	130.6	136.5
Other	45.3	49.4	50.7	55.1	59.7	61.5	64.5	64.6
Medical care	**838.1**	**888.6**	**932.3**	**984.4**	**1,041.7**	**1,097.9**	**1,171.1**	**1,270.2**
Drug preparations and sundries	85.8	92.1	100.3	110.6	122.1	139.2	156.3	176.4
Ophthalmic products and orthopedic appliances	15.0	15.8	17.6	19.1	20.6	21.6	22.9	21.6
Physicians	181.0	192.4	199.1	208.8	220.5	230.3	244.3	266.7
Dentists	42.9	46.5	48.4	51.9	55.1	58.3	62.7	67.5
Other professional services	103.6	112.9	119.7	125.9	132.1	137.0	142.8	153.5
Hospitals and nursing homes	353.9	370.9	390.8	408.9	427.8	445.8	471.5	509.6
Health insurance	55.8	58.0	56.6	59.3	63.6	65.7	70.6	75.0
Personal business	**381.6**	**406.8**	**435.1**	**489.0**	**529.8**	**575.2**	**632.5**	**634.3**
Transportation	**532.1**	**560.3**	**594.6**	**626.7**	**649.9**	**707.8**	**768.9**	**794.8**
User-operated transportation	492.3	517.8	550.2	578.9	599.2	654.7	711.9	742.0
New autos	86.5	82.2	81.9	82.5	87.9	98.4	105.5	105.9
Net purchases of used autos	43.0	50.0	51.4	53.1	54.9	57.7	59.4	60.6
Other motor vehicles	77.7	80.2	84.3	89.0	104.5	118.7	125.9	149.0
Tires, tubes, accessories, and other parts	35.2	36.9	38.7	39.6	41.5	44.4	45.9	45.8
Repair, greasing, washing, parking, storage, rental, and leasing	110.0	122.2	134.2	146.3	153.6	165.1	175.5	181.6
Gasoline and oil	109.0	113.3	124.2	128.1	114.8	129.3	164.4	162.1
Bridge, tunnel, ferry, and road tolls	3.3	3.4	3.7	4.0	4.0	4.4	4.6	4.9
Insurance	27.8	29.7	31.8	36.3	38.0	36.8	30.7	32.1
Purchased local transportation	10.0	10.4	11.2	11.6	12.3	12.4	12.7	13.2
Mass transit systems	7.1	7.1	7.7	7.8	8.3	8.6	9.1	9.5
Taxicab	3.0	3.2	3.5	3.7	4.1	3.8	3.6	3.7
Purchased intercity transportation	29.8	32.1	33.3	36.2	38.4	40.7	44.3	39.7
Railway	0.6	0.6	0.6	0.7	0.7	0.7	0.8	0.9
Bus	1.5	1.6	1.8	1.8	1.9	2.0	1.5	1.5
Airline	23.7	25.5	26.2	29.0	30.8	32.7	36.7	32.4
Other	4.0	4.3	4.7	4.7	4.9	5.3	5.2	4.8
Recreation	**368.7**	**401.6**	**429.6**	**456.6**	**489.1**	**526.5**	**564.7**	**593.9**
Books, maps, magazines, sheet music	45.7	49.3	52.5	55.4	59.2	63.3	67.4	70.3
Wheel goods, toys, sports and photographic equipment and supplies, boats, and pleasure aircraft	78.6	85.7	91.1	96.0	102.7	110.8	118.0	127.5
Video and audio goods, including musical instruments, and computer goods	71.0	77.0	80.0	83.7	90.3	98.1	106.3	105.6
Other (plants and seeds, clubs, spectator admissions, etc.)	173.2	189.8	205.9	221.5	236.9	254.3	272.9	290.4
Education and research	**107.2**	**114.5**	**122.3**	**130.5**	**140.2**	**152.1**	**164.0**	**174.9**
Religious and welfare activities	**127.9**	**134.9**	**146.8**	**149.5**	**163.9**	**172.9**	**190.1**	**199.6**
Foreign travel and other, net	**-16.2**	**-20.7**	**-24.1**	**-21.8**	**-15.1**	**-16.0**	**-16.1**	**-12.9**
Foreign travel by U.S. residents	53.0	54.1	57.6	63.6	68.8	72.3	80.9	76.3
Expenditures abroad by U.S. residents	2.4	2.3	2.2	2.9	3.1	3.2	3.3	3.6
Less: Expenditures in the United States by nonresidents	69.9	75.4	82.4	86.7	85.4	89.6	98.3	90.6
Less: Personal remittances in kind to nonresidents	1.6	1.6	1.5	1.6	1.6	1.9	2.0	2.2

(1) Subtotals may not add to total, due to rounding.

Distribution of U.S. Total Personal Income[1]

Source: Bureau of Economic Analysis, U.S. Dept. of Commerce
(billions of current dollars)

Year	Personal income	Personal taxes and nontax payments	Disposable personal income	Personal outlays	Personal Savings: Amount	Personal Savings: As pct. of disposable income
1960	$411.7	$48.7	$362.9	$339.6	$23.3	6.4%
1965	555.8	61.9	493.9	456.2	37.8	7.6
1970	836.1	109.0	727.1	666.1	61.0	8.4
1975	1,315.6	156.4	1,159.2	1,054.8	104.4	9.0
1980	2,285.7	312.4	1,973.3	1,811.5	161.8	8.2
1985	3,439.6	437.7	3,002.0	2,795.8	206.2	6.9
1990	4,791.6	624.8	4,166.8	3,958.1	208.7	5.0
1991	4,968.5	624.8	4,343.7	4,097.4	246.4	5.7
1992	5,264.2	650.5	4,613.7	4,341.0	272.6	5.9
1995	6,072.1	795.0	5,277.0	5,097.2	179.8	3.4
1996	6,425.2	890.5	5,534.7	5,376.2	158.5	2.9
1997	6,784.0	989.0	5,795.1	5,674.1	121.0	2.1
1998	7,391.0	1,070.9	6,320.0	6,054.7	265.4	4.2
1999	7,777.3	1,159.2	6,618.0	6,457.2	160.9	2.4
2000R	8,406.6	1,286.4	7,120.2	6,918.6	201.5	2.8
2001	8,685.3	1,292.1	7,393.2	7,223.5	169.7	2.3

R = revised. (1) Personal income minus taxes/nontax payments=disposable income; disposable income minus outlays=savings. Figures may not add because of rounding.

Banks in the U.S.—Number, Deposits

Source: Federal Deposit Insurance Corp. (as of Dec. 2000)
Comprises all FDIC-insured commercial and savings banks, including savings and loan institutions (S&Ls).

	TOTAL NUMBER OF BANKS					TOTAL DEPOSITS (millions of dollars)				
		Commercial banks[1]					Commercial banks[1]			
Year	ALL BANKS	Natl.	State	Non-members	All savings	ALL DEPOSITS	Natl.	State	Non-members	All savings
1935	**15,295**	5,386	1,001	7,735	1,173	**$45,102**[2]	$24,802	$13,653	$5,669	$978[2]
1940	**15,772**	5,144	1,342	6,956	2,330	**67,494**	35,787	20,642	7,040	4,025
1945	**15,969**	5,017	1,864	6,421	2,667	**151,524**	77,778	41,865	16,307	15,574
1950	**16,500**	4,958	1,912	6,576	3,054	**171,963**	84,941	41,602	19,726	25,694
1955	**17,001**	4,692	1,847	6,698	3,764	**235,211**	102,796	55,739	26,198	50,478
1960	**17,549**	4,530	1,641	6,955	4,423	**310,262**	120,242	65,487	34,369	90,164
1965	**18,384**	4,815	1,405	7,327	4,837	**467,633**	185,334	78,327	51,982	151,990
1970	**18,205**	4,621	1,147	7,743	4,694	**686,901**	285,436	101,512	95,566	204,367
1975	**18,792**	4,744	1,046	8,595	4,407	**1,157,648**	450,308	143,409	187,031	376,900
1980	**18,763**	4,425	997	9,013	4,328	**1,832,716**	656,752	191,183	344,311	640,470
1985	**18,033**	4,959	1,070	8,378	3,626	**3,140,827**	1,241,875	354,585	521,628	1,022,739
1990	**15,158**	3,979	1,009	7,355	2,815	**3,637,292**	1,558,915	397,797	693,438	987,142
1995	**11,970**	2,858	1,042	6,040	2,030	**3,769,477**	1,695,817	614,924	716,829	741,907
1996	**11,670**	2,763	1,024	5,902	1,981	**3,788,905**	1,795,110	567,809	698,497	727,489
1997	**10,922**	2,597	992	5,554	1,779	**4,125,811**	2,004,855	729,009	687,832	704,115
1998	**10,463**	2,456	994	5,324	1,689	**4,386,298**	2,137,946	810,471	733,027	704,855
1999	**10,221**	2,363	1,010	5,207	1,641	**4,538,036**	2,154,259	899,252	777,264	707,261
2000	**9,905**	2,230	991	5,094	1,590	**4,914,808**	2,250,464	1,032,110	894,000	738,234
2001	**9,631**	2,137	972	4,971	1,533	**5,189,444**	2,384,462	1,079,388	927,772	797,822

(1) "Nonmembers" are banks that are not members of the Federal Reserve System; "National" and "State" institutions are members.
(2) Figures for 1935 do not include data for S&Ls (not available).

50 Largest U.S. Bank Holding Companies

Source: *American Banker* (as of Dec. 31, 2001)

Company Name	Total Assets ($ in thousands)
Citigroup Inc., New York, NY	$1,051,450,000
J.P. Morgan Chase & Co., New York, NY	693,575,000
Bank of America Corp., Charlotte, NC	621,764,000
Wachovia Corp., Charlotte, NC	330,452,000
Wells Fargo & Co., San Francisco, CA	307,569,000
Bank One Corp., Chicago, IL	268,954,000
MetLife Inc., New York, NY	256,897,467
Taunus Corp., New York, NY	227,229,000
Washington Mutual Inc., Seattle, WA	207,659,811
FleetBoston Financial Corp., Boston, MA	203,638,000
U.S. Bancorp, Minneapolis, MN	171,390,000
National City Corp., Cleveland, OH	106,894,340
SunTrust Banks Inc., Atlanta, GA	104,740,644
Bank of New York Co. Inc., New York, NY	81,025,323
KeyCorp, Cleveland, OH	80,399,503
Fifth Third Bancorp, Cincinnati, OH	71,026,340
Bank and Trust Corp., Winston-Salem, NC	70,869,945
State Street Corp., Boston, MA	69,895,857
PNC Financial Services Group, Pittsburgh, PA	69,570,206
Golden West Financial Corp., Oakland, CA	58,443,622
Golden State Bancorp Inc., Glendale, CA	56,555,539
Comerica Inc., Detroit, MI	50,949,608
SouthTrust Corp., Birmingham, AL	48,754,548
Regions Financial Corp., Birmingham, AL	45,545,287
MBNA Corp., Wilmington, DE	45,450,837
Charles Schwab Corp., San Francisco, CA	40,463,921
Northern Trust Corp., Chicago, IL	$39,664,457
AmSouth Bancorp, Birmingham, AL	38,622,252
Charter One Financial Inc., Cleveland, OH	38,221,017
Countrywide Credit Industries, Calabasas, CA	37,216,805
Mellon Financial Corp., Pittsburgh, PA	35,771,807
Sovereign Bancorp Inc., Wyomissing, PA	35,631,606
Union Planters Corp., Memphis, TN	33,197,604
M&T Bank Corp., Buffalo, NY	31,450,196
Popular Inc., San Juan, PR	30,731,000
Huntington Bancshares Inc., Columbus, OH	28,496,659
Dime Bancorp Inc., New York, NY	27,971,169
Marshall & Ilsley Corp., Milwaukee, WI	27,272,753
Zions Bancorp, Salt Lake City, UT	24,304,164
Compass Bancshares, Birmingham, AL	23,078,952
Astoria Financial Corp., Lake Success, NY	22,463,688
BancWest Corp., Honolulu, HI	21,646,514
Banknorth Group Inc., Portland, ME	21,095,424
First Tennessee National Corp., Memphis, TN	20,618,320
Greenpoint Financial Corp., New York, NY	20,186,070
National Commerce Financial Corp., Memphis, TN	19,278,386
North Fork Bancorp, Melville, NY	17,232,103
Synovus Financial Corp., Columbus, GA	16,657,947
Hibernia Corp., New Orleans, LA	16,618,176
Provident Financial Group, Cincinnati, OH	15,793,507

U.S. Bank Failures

Source: Federal Deposit Insurance Corp.

Comprises all FDIC-insured commercial and savings banks, including savings and loan institutions (S&Ls) 1980 and after.

Year	Closed or assisted	Year	Closed or assisted	Year	Closed or assisted	Year	Closed or assisted	Year	Closed or assisted	Year	Closed or assisted
1934	9	1955	5	1967	4	1978	7	1986	204	1994	15
1935	26	1959	3	1969	9	1979	10	1987	262	1995	8
1936	69	1960	1	1970	7	1980	22	1988	465	1996	6
1937	77	1961	5	1971	7	1981	40	1989	534	1997	1
1938	74	1963	2	1972	2	1982	119	1990	382	1998	3
1939	60	1964	7	1973	6	1983	99	1991	271	1999	8
1940	43	1965	5	1975	13	1984	106	1992	181	2000	7
		1966	7	1976	17	1985	180	1993	50	2001	4

World's 50 Largest Banking Companies[1]

Source: *American Banker* (as of Dec. 31, 2001)

	Assets[2] (millions)
Mizuho Holdings, Japan	$1,281,389
Citigroup Inc., U.S.	1,051,450
Sumitomo Mitsui Banking Corp., Japan	924,146
Mitsubishi Tokyo Financial Group, Japan	854,749
Deutsche Bank, Germany	815,126
Allianz AG, Germany	805,433
UBS AG, Switzerland	753,833
BNP Paribas, France	734,833
HSBC Holdings PLC, United Kingdom	694,590
J.P. Morgan Chase & Co., U.S.	693,575
Bayerische Hypo-und Vereinsbanken AG, Germany	638,544
ING Group NV, Netherlands	628,590
Bank of America Corp. U.S.	621,764
Credit Suisse Group, Switzerland	608,781
UFJ Holdings, Japan	601,000
Royal Bank of Scotland Group PLC, United Kingdom	536,799
ABN Amro Holding NV, Netherlands	531,695
Barclays PLC, United Kingdom	519,130
Norinchukin Bank, Japan	476,538
Societe Generale, France	456,899
HBOS PLC, United Kingdom	454,540
Commerzbank, Germany	444,454
Credit Agricole SA, France	441,124
Axa, France	432,481
Fortis, Netherlands	428,471
Westdeutsche Landesbank Girozentrale, Germany	372,200
Lloyds TSB Group PLC, United Kingdom	$344,273
Wachovia, U.S.	330,452
Rabobank Group, Netherlands	324,154
Dexia, Belgium	313,144
Abbey National PLC, United Kingdom	312,759
Santander Central Hispano, Spain	312,119
Wells Fargo & Co., U.S.	307,569
Bayerische Landesbank Girozentrale, Germany	287,385
BBV Argenteria, Spain	271,813
Bank One Corp., U.S.	268,954
Washington Mutual, U.S.	242,506
Almanij NV, Belgium	231,171
Royal Bank of Canada, Canada	225,403
Nordea Bank AB, Sweden	215,285
Intesa, Italy	211,471
FleetBoston Financial Corp., U.S.	203,638
KBC Bank and Insurance Holding Co. NV, Belgium	203,333
UniCredito Italiano SpA, Italy	194,269
National Australia Bank Ltd., Australia	183,501
Toronto-Dominion Bank, Canada	181,145
Canadian Imperial Bank of Commerce, Canada	180,550
Credit Lyonnais SA, France	180,411
Bank of Nova Scotia, Canada	178,479
Norddeutsche Landesbank Girozentrale, Germany	177,072

(1) Includes bank holding companies and commercial and savings banks. (2) Exchange rates at end of fiscal year used in currency conversions. **NOTE:** Data for U.S. companies listed include assets not included in "50 Largest U.S. Bank Holding Companies" table.

Federal Deposit Insurance Corporation (FDIC)

The Federal Deposit Insurance Corporation (FDIC) is the independent deposit insurance agency created by Congress to maintain stability and public confidence in the nation's banking system. In its unique role as deposit insurer of banks and savings associations, and in cooperation with other federal and state regulatory agencies, the FDIC seeks to promote the safety and soundness of insured depository institutions in the U.S. financial system by identifying, monitoring, and addressing risks to the deposit insurance funds. The FDIC aims at promoting public understanding and sound public policies by providing financial and economic information and analyses. It seeks to minimize disruptive effects from the failure of banks and savings associations. It seeks to ensure fairness in the sale of financial products and the provision of financial services.

The FDIC's income comes from assessments on insured banks and income from investments. The Corporation may borrow from the U.S. Treasury, not to exceed $30 billion outstanding, but the agency has made no such borrowings since it was organized in 1933. The FDIC's Bank Insurance Fund was $31.2 billion (unaudited) and the Savings Association Insurance Fund stood at $11.3 billion (unaudited), as of June 30, 2002.

Federal Reserve Board Discount Rate

The discount rate is the rate of interest set by the Federal Reserve that member banks are charged when borrowing money through the Federal Reserve System. Includes any changes through Oct. 20, 2002.

Effective date	Rate
1980:	
Feb. 15	13
May 30	12
June 13	11
July 28	10
Sept. 26	11
Nov. 17	12
Dec. 5	13
1981:	
May 5	14
Nov. 2	13
Dec. 4	12
1982:	
July 20	11½
Aug. 2	11
Aug. 16	10
Aug. 27	10
Oct. 12	9½
Nov. 22	9
Dec. 15	8½
1984:	
April 9	9
Nov. 21	8½
Dec. 24	8
1985:	
May 20	7½
1986:	
March 7	7
April 21	6½
July 11	6
Aug. 21	5½
1987:	
Sept. 4	6
1988:	
Aug. 9	6½
1989:	
Feb. 24	7
1990:	
Dec. 18	6½
1991:	
Apr. 30	5½
Sept. 13	5
Nov. 6	4½
Dec. 20	3½
1992:	
July 2	3
1994:	
May 17	3½
Aug. 16	4
Nov. 15	4¾
1995:	
Feb. 1	5¼
1996:	
Jan. 31	5
1998:	
Oct. 15	4¾
Nov. 17	4½
1999:	
Aug. 24	4¾
Nov. 16	5
2000:	
Feb. 2	5¼
Mar. 21	5½
May 16	6
2001:	
Jan. 3	5¾
Jan. 31	5
Mar. 20	4½
Apr. 18	4
May 15	3½
June 27	3¼
Aug. 21	3
Sept. 17	2½
Oct. 2	2
Nov. 6	1½
Dec. 11	1¼

Federal Reserve System

The Federal Reserve System is the central bank for the U.S. The system was established on Dec. 23, 1913, originally to give the country an elastic currency, to provide facilities for discounting commercial paper, and to improve the supervision of banking. Since then, the system's responsibilities have been broadened. Over the years, stability and growth of the economy, a high level of employment, stability in the purchasing power of the dollar, and reasonable balance in transactions with other countries have come to be recognized as primary objectives of governmental economic policy.

The Federal Reserve System consists of the Board of Governors, the 12 District Reserve Banks and their branch offices, and the Federal Open Market Committee. Several advisory councils help the board meet its varied responsibilities.

The hub of the system is the 7-member Board of Governors in Washington. The members of the board are appointed by the president and confirmed by the Senate, to serve 14-year terms. The president also appoints the chairman and vice chairman of the board from among the board members for 4-year terms that may be renewed. As of June 2001 the board members were: Alan Greenspan, Chair; Roger W. Ferguson Jr., Vice Chair; Edward W. Kelley Jr.; Laurence H. Meyer; and Edward M. Gramlich; there were two vacancies.

The board is the policy-making body. In addition to those responsibilities, it supervises the budget and operations of the Reserve Banks, approves the appointments of their presidents, and appoints 3 of each District Bank's directors, including the chairman and vice chairman of each Reserve Bank's board.

The 12 Reserve Banks and their branch offices serve as the decentralized portion of the system, carrying out day-to-day operations such as circulating currency and coin and providing fiscal agency functions and payments mechanism services. The District Banks are in Boston, New York, Philadelphia, Cleveland, Richmond, Atlanta, Chicago, St. Louis, Minneapolis, Kansas City, Dallas, and San Francisco.

The system's principal function is monetary policy, which it controls using 3 tools: reserve requirements, the discount rate, and open market operations. Uniform reserve requirements, set by the board, are applied to the transaction accounts and nonpersonal time deposits of all depository institutions.

Responsibility for setting the discount rate (the interest rate at which depository institutions can borrow money from the Reserve Banks) is shared by the Board of Governors and the Reserve Banks. Changes in the discount rate are recommended by the individual boards of directors of the Reserve Banks and are subject to approval by the Board of Governors.

The most important tool of monetary policy is open market operations (the purchase and sale of government securities). Responsibility for influencing the cost and availability of money and credit through the purchase and sale of government securities lies with the Federal Open Market Committee (FOMC), which is composed of the 7 members of the Board of Governors, the president of the Federal Reserve Bank of New York, and 4 other Federal Reserve Bank presidents, who each serve one-year terms on a rotating basis. The committee bases its decisions on economic and financial developments and outlook, setting yearly growth objectives for key measures of money supply and credit. The decisions of the committee are carried out by the Domestic Trading Desk of the Federal Reserve Bank of New York.

The Federal Reserve Act prescribes a Federal Advisory Council, consisting of 1 member from each Federal Reserve District, who is elected annually by the Board of Directors of each of the 12 Federal Reserve Banks. The council meets with the Federal Reserve Board 4 times a year to discuss business and financial conditions, as well as to make advisory recommendations.

The Consumer Advisory Council is a statutory body, including both consumer and creditor representatives, which advises the Board of Governors on its implementation of consumer regulations and other consumer-related matters.

Following the congressional passage of the Monetary Control Act of 1980, the Federal Reserve System's Board of Governors established the Thrift Institutions Advisory Council to provide information and perspectives on the special needs and problems of thrift institutions. This group is composed of representatives of mutual savings banks, savings and loan associations, and credit unions.

United States Mint

Source: United States Mint, U.S. Dept. of the Treasury

The United States Mint was created on Apr. 2, 1792, by an act of Congress, which established the U.S. national coinage system. Supervision of the mint was a function of the secretary of state, but in 1799 the mint became an independent agency reporting directly to the president. The mint was made a statutory bureau of the Treasury Department in 1873, with a director appointed by the president to oversee its operations.

The mint manufactures and ships all U.S. coins for circulation to Federal Reserve banks and branches, which in turn issue coins to the public and business community through depository institutions. The mint also safeguards the Treasury Department's stored gold and silver, as well as other monetary assets.

The composition of dimes, quarters, and half dollars, traditionally produced from silver, was changed by the Coinage Act of 1965, which mandated that these coins from here on in be minted from a cupronickel-clad alloy and reduced the silver content of the half dollar to 40%. In 1970, legislative action mandated that the half dollar and a dollar coin be minted from the same alloy.

The Eisenhower dollar was minted from 1971 through 1978, when legislation called for the minting of the smaller Susan B. Anthony dollar coin. The Anthony dollar, which was minted from 1979 through 1981, marked the first time that a woman, other than a mythical figure, appeared on a U.S. coin produced for general circulation. Authorized by the U.S. Dollar Coin Act of 1997 to replace the Susan B. Anthony dollar in 2000, is the Golden Dollar Coin. Golden in color, with a smooth edge and wide border, the obverse side depicts Sacagawea (a Shoshone woman who helped guide Lewis and Clark) and her infant son. The reverse shows an American eagle and 17 stars, one for each of the states at the time of the Lewis and Clark expedition.

Mint headquarters are in Washington, DC. Mint production facilities are in Philadelphia, Denver, San Francisco, and West Point, NY. In addition, the mint is responsible for the U.S. Bullion Depository at Fort Knox, KY.

Proof coin sets, silver proof coin sets, and uncirculated coin sets are available from the mint. The mint also produces ongoing series of national and historic medals in honor of significant persons, events, and sites.

Since 1982, the mint has produced the following congressionally authorized commemorative coins: 1982 George Washington half dollar; 1984 U.S. Olympic coins; 1986 U.S. Statue of Liberty coins; 1987 Bicentennial of the U.S. Constitution coins; 1989 U.S. Congressional coins; 1990 Eisenhower Centennial coin; 1991 United Services Organization 59th Anniversary coin; 1991 Korean War Memorial coin; 1991 Mount Rushmore Anniversary coins; 1992 U.S. Olympic coins; 1992 White House 200th Anniversary coin; 1992 Christopher Columbus Quincentenary coins; 1993 Bill of Rights coins; 1993 World War II 50th Anniversary coins; 1994 World Cup USA coins; Thomas Jefferson 250th Anniversary coin; U.S. Veterans coins (featuring the Prisoner of War coin, Vietnam Veterans Memorial coin, and Women in Military Service for America coin); Bicentennial of the U.S. Capitol Commemorative Silver Dollar; 1995 Civil War Battlefield coins; 1995/1996 U.S. Olympic Games of the Atlanta Centennial Games; 1997 U.S. Botanic Garden Silver

Dollar; 1997 Franklin Delano Roosevelt Gold coin; 1997 Gold and Silver Jackie Robinson Commemorative coins; 1997 National Law Enforcement Memorial Silver Dollar; Black Revolutionary War Patriots Silver Dollar; Robert F. Kennedy Silver Dollar; National Law Enforcement Officers Memorial Silver Dollar; 1999 Yellowstone National Park Silver Dollar; 1999 George Washington five-dollar gold coin; the Dolley Madison Silver Dollar; 2000 U.S. Leif Ericson Proof Silver Dollar; 2000 Icelandic Leif Ericson Proof Silver Krønur; the 2000 Library of Congress Commemorative Coin Program featuring the Proof Silver Dollar and the Proof Bi-metallic Gold and Platinum $10 coin; the 2001 American Buffalo Proof Siver Dollar; the 2001 U.S. Capitol Visitor Center Commemorative Coin Program, featuring the Half Dollar Clad Proof coin, the Proof Silver Dollar, and the Proof Gold $5 coin; the 2002 Olympic Winter Games Silver Dollar and Gold $5 coins; and the 2002 West Point Bicentennial Commemorative Silver Dollar.

The congressionally authorized American Eagle gold, platinum, and silver bullion coins are available through dealers worldwide. The gold and platinum eagles are sold in one-ounce, half-ounce, quarter-ounce, and one-tenth-ounce sizes. The American eagle silver bullion coin contains one troy ounce of .999 fine silver and is priced according to the daily market value of silver. These coins also are available directly from the mint in proof condition, separately priced.

The mint offers free public tours and operates sales centers at the U.S. mints in Denver and Philadelphia; it also operates a sales center at Union Station, in Washington, DC.

Further information is available from the U.S. Mint, Customer Care Center, 801 9th St., NW, Washington, DC 20220.

Telephone number: (800) USA-MINT.

Website: www. usmint.gov

Denominations of U.S. Currency

Since 1969 the largest denomination of U.S. currency that has been issued is the $100 bill. As larger-denomination bills reach the Federal Reserve Bank, they are removed from circulation. Because some discontinued currency is expected to be in the hands of holders for many years, the description of the various denominations below is continued.

Amt.	Portait	Embellishment on Back	Amt.	Portait	Embellishment on Back
$1	Washington	Great Seal of U.S.	$100	B. Franklin	Independence Hall
2	Jefferson	Signers of Declaration	500	McKinley	Ornate denominational marking
5	Lincoln	Lincoln Memorial	1,000	Cleveland	Ornate denominational marking
10	Hamilton	U.S. Treasury	5,000	Madison	Ornate denominational marking
20	Jackson	White House	10,000	Salmon Chase	Ornate denominational marking
50	Grant	U.S. Capitol	100,000*	Wilson	Ornate denominational marking

*For use only in transactions between Federal Reserve System and Treasury Department.

New Commemorative State Quarters, 1999-2008

Source: United States Mint, U.S. Dept. of the Treasury

Beginning in Jan. 1999, a series of five quarter dollars with new reverses are being issued each year through 2008, celebrating each of the 50 states. To make room on the reverse of the commemorative quarters for each state's design, certain design elements have been moved, thereby creating a new obverse design as well. The coins are being issued in the sequence the states became part of the Union (date each state entered the union is shown below).

1999	2000	2001	2002	2003
Delaware Dec. 7, 1787	Massachusetts Feb. 6, 1788	New York July 26, 1788	Tennessee June 1, 1796	Illinois Dec. 3, 1818
Pennsylvania Dec. 12, 1787	Maryland Apr. 28, 1788	North Carolina Nov. 21, 1789	Ohio Mar. 1, 1803	Alabama Dec. 14, 1819
New Jersey Dec. 18, 1787	South Carolina May 23, 1788	Rhode Island May 29, 1790	Louisiana Apr. 30, 1812	Maine Mar. 15, 1820
Georgia Jan. 2, 1788	New Hampshire June 21, 1788	Vermont Mar. 4, 1791	Indiana Dec. 11, 1816	Missouri Aug. 10, 1821
Connecticut Jan. 9, 1788	Virginia June 25, 1788	Kentucky June 1, 1792	Mississippi Dec. 10, 1817	Arkansas June 15, 1836
2004	**2005**	**2006**	**2007**	**2008**
Michigan Jan. 26, 1837	California Sept. 9, 1850	Nevada Oct. 31, 1864	Montana Nov. 8, 1889	Oklahoma Nov. 16, 1907
Florida Mar. 3, 1845	Minnesota May 11, 1858	Nebraska Mar. 1, 1867	Washington Nov. 11, 1889	New Mexico Jan. 6, 1912
Texas Dec. 29, 1845	Oregon Feb. 14, 1859	Colorado Aug. 1, 1876	Idaho July 3, 1890	Arizona Feb. 14, 1912
Iowa Dec. 28, 1846	Kansas Jan. 29, 1861	North Dakota Nov. 2, 1889	Wyoming July 10, 1890	Alaska Jan. 3, 1959
Wisconsin May 29, 1848	West Virginia June 20, 1863	South Dakota Nov. 2, 1889	Utah Jan. 4, 1896	Hawaii Aug. 21, 1959

Portraits on U.S. Treasury Bills, Bonds, Notes, and Savings Bonds

Denomination	Savings bonds	Treasury bills*	Treasury bonds*	Treasury notes*
$50	Washington		Jefferson	
75	Adams			
100	Jefferson		Jackson	
200	Madison			
500	Hamilton		Washington	
1,000	B. Franklin	H. McCulloch	Lincoln	Lincoln
5,000	P. Revere	J. G. Carlisle	Monroe	Monroe
10,000	J. Wilson	J. Sherman	Cleveland	Cleveland
50,000	C. Glass			
100,000		A. Gallatin	Grant	Grant
1,000,000		O. Wolcott	T. Roosevelt	T. Roosevelt
100,000,000				Madison
500,000,000				McKinley

*The U.S. Treasury discontinued issuing treasury bill, bond, and note certificates in 1986. Since then, all issues of marketable treasury securities have been available only in book-entry form, although some certificates remain in circulation.

U.S. Currency and Coin

Source: Financial Management Service, U.S. Dept. of the Treasury (June 30, 2002)

Amounts Outstanding and in Circulation

Currency	Total currency and coin	Total currency	Federal Reserve notes[1]	U.S. notes	Currency no longer issued
Amounts outstanding	$786,132,402,212	$752,652,072,504	$752,137,355,941	$262,775,016	$251,941,547
Less amounts held by:					
Treasury	371,120,625	19,845,625	19,635,669	20,739	189,217
Federal Reserve banks	127,837,579,484	126,889,832,454	126,889,830,643	—	1,811
Amounts in circulation	$657,923,702,103	$625,742,394,425	$625,227,889,629	$262,754,277	$251,750,519

Coins[2]	Total	Dollars[3]	Fractional coins
Amounts outstanding	$33,480,329,708	$3,492,929,008	$29,987,400,700
Less amounts held by:			
Treasury	351,275,000	300,825,000	50,450,000
Federal Reserve banks	947,747,030	196,462,163	751,284,867
Amounts in circulation	$32,181,307,678	$2,995,641,845	$29,185,665,833

(1) Issued on or after July 1, 1929. (2) Excludes coins sold to collectors at premium prices. (3) Includes $481,781,898 in standard silver dollars.

Currency in Circulation by Denominations

(June 30, 2002)

Denomination	Total currency in circulation	Federal Reserve notes[1]	U.S. notes	Currency no longer issued
$1	$7,607,195,706	$7,461,125,222	$143,481	$145,927,003
$2	1,280,733,254	1,148,369,985	132,351,066	12,576
$5	8,846,548,605	8,707,036,985	109,707,610	29,804,010
$10	13,990,099,800	13,968,224,200	5,950	21,869,650
$20	96,856,498,360	96,836,393,160	3,380	20,101,820
$50	56,272,791,100	56,261,297,950	—	11,493,150
$100	440,574,178,500	440,531,643,000	20,542,700	21,992,800
$500	142,932,500	142,744,500	—	188,000
$1,000	166,221,000	166,015,000	—	206,000
$5,000	1,755,000	1,700,000	—	55,000
$10,000	3,440,000	3,340,000	—	100,000
Fractional parts	485	—	—	485
Partial notes[2]	115	—	90	25
TOTAL CURRENCY	**$625,742,394,425**	**$625,227,889,629**	**$262,754,277**	**$251,750,519**

(1) Issued on or after July 1, 1929. (2) Represents the value of certain partial denominations not presented for redemption.

Comparative Totals of Money in Circulation — Selected Dates

Date	Dollars (in millions)	Per capita[1]	Date	Dollars (in millions)	Per capita[1]
Mar. 31, 2002	$641,909.0	$2,238.45	June 30, 1965	$39,719.8	$204.14
Mar. 30, 2001	585,916.0	2,121.82	June 30, 1960	32,064.6	177.47
Mar. 31, 2000	562,949.0	2,050.00	June 30, 1955	30,229.3	182.90
Mar. 31, 1999	517,829.0	1,902.21	June 30, 1950	27,156.3	179.03
Mar. 31, 1998	474,979.0	1,762.42	June 30, 1945	26,746.4	191.14
Mar. 31, 1997	444,534.0	1,664.58	June 30, 1940	7,847.5	59.40
Mar. 31, 1996	416,280.0	1,573.15	June 30, 1935	5,567.1	43.75
Mar. 31, 1995	401,610.0	1,531.39	June 30, 1930	4,522.0	36.74
Mar. 31, 1990	257,664.4	1,028.71	June 30, 1925	4,815.2	41.56
June 30, 1985	185,890.7	778.58	June 30, 1920	5,467.6	51.36
June 30, 1980	127,097.2	558.28	June 30, 1915	3,319.6	33.01
June 30, 1975	81,196.4	380.08	June 30, 1910	3,148.7	34.07
June 30, 1970	54,351.0	265.39			

(1) Based on Bureau of the Census estimates of population. The requirement for a gold reserve against U.S. notes was repealed by Public Law 90-269, approved Mar. 18, 1968. Silver certificates issued on and after July 1, 1929, became redeemable from the general fund on June 24, 1968. The amount of security after those dates has been reduced accordingly.

IT'S A FACT: The original U.S. Mint building was the first building to be erected by the federal government under the Constitution. In 1793 it made its first delivery of coins—11,178 copper cents, amounting to $111.78.

New U.S. Currency Designs

On Mar. 25, 1996, the U.S. Treasury issued a redesigned $100 note incorporating many new and modified anticounterfeiting features. It was the first of the U.S. currency series to be redesigned. A new $50 note was issued Oct. 27, 1997, a new $20 bill was released into circulation Sept. 24, 1998, and new $10 and $5 notes were issued May 24, 2000; a new $1 note with a more modest redesign was to come next. Old notes are being removed from circulation as they are returned to the Federal Reserve.

The new $100 bill has a larger portrait, moved off-center; a watermark (seen only when held up to the light) to the right of the portrait, depicting the same person (Benjamin Franklin); a security thread that glows red when exposed to ultraviolet light in a dark environment; color-shifting ink that changes from green to black when viewed at different angles, to appear in the numeral on the lower, front right-hand corner of the bill; microprinting in the numeral in the note's lower, front left-hand corner and on the portrait; and other features for security, machine authentication, and processing of the currency. The redesigned $5, $10, $20, and $50 bills incorporate the same features as the $100 bill, with the notable addition of a low-vision feature, a large (14-mm high, as compared to 7.8-mm on the old design), dark numeral on a light background on the back of the note. (The security thread glows yellow in the $50, green in the $20, orange in the $10, and blue in the $5. There is no color-shifting ink on the $5 note.) More new currency information is available on the U.S. Treasury's website: www.ustreas.gov

Summary of Receipts, Outlays, and Surpluses or Deficits, 1936-2002

Source: Financial Management Service, U.S. Dept. of the Treasury

(millions of current dollars)

Fiscal Year[1]	Receipts	Outlays	Surplus or Deficit (–)[2]	Fiscal Year[1]	Receipts	Outlays	Surplus or Deficit (–)[2]
1936	$3,923	$8,228	$–4,304	1970	$192,807	$195,649	$–2,842
1937	5,387	7,580	–2,193	1971	187,139	210,172	–23,033
1938	6,751	6,840	–89	1972	207,309	230,681	–23,373
1939	6,295	9,141	–2,846	1973	230,799	245,707	–14,908
1940	6,548	9,468	–2,920	1974	263,224	269,359	–6,135
1941	8,712	13,653	–4,941	1975	279,090	332,332	–53,242
1942	14,634	35,137	–20,503	1976	298,060	371,779	–73,719
1943	24,001	78,555	–54,554	Transition quarter[3]	81,232	95,973	–14,741
1944	43,747	91,304	–47,557	1977	355,559	409,203	–53,644
1945	45,159	92,712	–47,553	1978	399,561	458,729	–59,168
1946	39,296	55,232	–15,936	1979	463,302	503,464	–40,162
1947	38,514	34,496	4,018	1980	517,112	590,920	–73,808
1948	41,560	29,764	11,796	1981	599,272	678,209	–78,936
1949	39,415	38,835	580	1982	617,766	745,706	–127,940
1950	39,443	42,562	–3,119	1983	600,562	808,327	–207,764
1951	51,616	45,514	6,102	1984	666,457	851,781	–185,324
1952	66,167	67,686	–1,519	1985	734,057	946,316	–212,260
1953	69,608	76,101	–6,493	1986	769,091	990,231	–221,140
1954	69,701	70,855	–1,154	1987	854,143	1,003,804	–149,661
1955	65,451	68,444	–2,993	1988	908,166	1,063,318	–155,151
1956	74,587	70,640	3,947	1989	990,701	1,144,020	–153,319
1957	79,990	76,578	3,412	1990	1,031,308	1,251,776	–220,469
1958	79,636	82,405	–2,769	1991	1,054,265	1,323,757	–269,492
1959	79,249	92,098	–12,849	1992	1,090,453	1,380,794	–290,340
1960	92,492	92,191	301	1993	1,153,226	1,408,532	–255,306
1961	94,388	97,723	–3,335	1994	1,257,451	1,460,553	–203,102
1962	99,676	106,821	–7,146	1995	1,351,495	1,515,412	–163,917
1963	106,560	111,316	–4,756	1996	1,452,763	1,560,094	–107,331
1964	112,613	118,528	–5,915	1997	1,578,955	1,600,911	–21,957
1965	116,817	118,228	–1,411	1998	1,721,421	1,652,224	+70,039
1966	130,835	134,532	–3,698	1999	1,827,302	1,704,942	+124,360
1967	148,822	157,464	–8,643	2000	2,025,060	1,788,143	+236,917
1968	152,973	178,134	–25,161	2001R	1,990,930	1,863,909	+127,021
1969	186,882	183,640	3,242	2002E	1,946,136	2,052,320	–106,184

R = Revised. E = Estimated. (1) Fiscal years 1936 to 1976 end June 30; after 1976, fiscal years end Sept. 30. (2) May not equal difference between figures shown, because of rounding. (3) Transition quarter covers July 1, 1976-Sept. 30, 1976.

Budget Receipts and Outlays, 1789-1935

Source: U.S. Dept. of the Treasury; annual statements for years ending June 30 unless otherwise noted

(thousands of dollars)

Yearly Average	Receipts	Outlays	Yearly Average	Receipts	Outlays	Yearly Average	Receipts	Outlays
1789-1800[1]	$5,717	$5,776	1866-1870	$447,301	$377,642	1901-1905	$559,481	$535,559
1801-1810[2]	13,056	9,086	1871-1875	336,830	287,460	1906-1910	628,507	639,178
1811-1820[2]	21,032	23,943	1876-1880	288,124	255,598	1911-1915	710,227	720,252
1821-1830[2]	21,928	16,162	1881-1885	366,961	257,691	1916-1920	3,483,652	8,065,333
1831-1840[2]	30,461	24,495	1886-1890	375,448	279,134	1921-1925	4,306,673	3,578,989
1841-1850[2]	28,545	34,097	1891-1895	352,891	363,599	1926-1930	4,069,138	3,182,807
1851-1860	60,237	60,163	1896-1900	434,877	457,451	1931-1935	2,770,973	5,214,874
1861-1865	160,907	683,785						

(1) Average for period March 4, 1789, to Dec. 31, 1800. (2) Years from 1801 to 1842 end Dec. 31; average for 1841-1850 is for the period Jan. 1, 1841, to June 30, 1850.

Public Debt of the U.S.

Source: Bureau of Public Debt, U.S. Dept. of the Treasury; World Almanac research

Fiscal year	Debt (billions)	Debt per cap. (dollars)	Interest paid (billions)	% of federal outlays	Fiscal year	Debt (billions)	Debt per cap. (dollars)	Interest paid (billions)	% of federal outlays
1870	$2.4	$61.06	—	—	1983	$1,377.2	$5,870	$128.8	15.9
1880	2.0	41.60	—	—	1984	1,572.3	6,640	153.8	18.1
1890	1.1	17.80	—	—	1985	1,823.1	7,598	178.9	18.9
1900	1.2	16.60	—	—	1986	2,125.3	8,774	190.2	19.2
1910	1.1	12.41	—	—	1987	2,350.3	9,615	195.4	19.5
1920	24.2	228	—	—	1988	2,602.3	10,534	214.1	20.1
1930	16.1	131	—	—	1989	2,857.4	11,545	240.9	21.0
1940	43.0	325	$1.0	10.5	1990	3,233.3	13,000	264.8	21.1
1950	256.1	1,688	5.7	13.4	1991	3,665.3	14,436	285.5	21.6
1955	272.8	1,651	6.4	9.4	1992	4,064.6	15,846	292.3	21.2
1960	284.1	1,572	9.2	10.0	1993	4,411.5	17,105	292.5	20.8
1965	313.8	1,613	11.3	9.6	1994	4,692.8	18,025	296.3	20.3
1970	370.1	1,814	19.3	9.9	1995	4,974.0	18,930	332.4	22.0
1975	533.2	2,475	32.7	9.8	1996	5,224.8	19,805	344.0	22.0
1976	620.4	2,852	37.1	10.0	1997	5,413.1	20,026	355.8	22.2
1977	698.8	3,170	41.9	10.2	1998	5,526.2	20,443	363.8	22.0
1978	771.5	3,463	48.7	10.6	1999	5,656.3	20,746	353.5	20.7
1979	826.5	3,669	59.8	11.9	2000	5,674.2	20,591	362.0	20.3
1980	907.7	3,985	74.9	12.7	2001	5,807.5	20,353	359.5	19.3
1981	997.9	4,338	95.6	14.1	2002[1]	6,228.2	21,603	332.5	16.4
1982	1,142.0	4,913	117.4	15.7					

Note: As of end of fiscal year. Through 1976 the fiscal year ended June 30. From 1977 on, the fiscal year ends Sept. 30. (1) Estimated.

U.S. Budget Receipts and Outlays, 1997-2002

Source: Financial Management Service, U.S. Dept. of the Treasury

As of Sept. 2002, the estimate from the Congressional Budget Office of the total U.S. budget deficit for the fiscal year 2002 was $106 billion, or 1% of GDP. This was to be the first budget deficit since FY 1997, when the deficit was $21,957 billion.

(in millions of current dollars; many figures do not add to totals because of independent rounding or omitted subcategories, including some subcategories with negative values.)

	Fiscal 1997[1]	Fiscal 1998[1]	Fiscal 1999[1]	Fiscal 2000[1]	Fiscal 2001[1,2]	Fiscal 2002[1,2]
NET RECEIPTS						
Individual income taxes	$737,466	$828,597	$879,480	$1,004,461	$994,339	$949,239
Corporation income taxes	182,294	188,677	184,680	207,288	151,075	201,445
Social insurance taxes and contributions:						
Federal old-age and survivors insurance	336,728	358,784	383,559	411,676	434,057	—
Federal disability insurance	55,261	57,016	60,910	68,907	73,463	—
Federal hospital insurance	110,710	119,863	132,268	135,528	149,650	—
Railroad retirement fund	4,051	4,353	4,143	4,336	4,272	4,260
Total employment taxes and contributions	506,750	540,015	580,880	620,447	661,442	—
Other insurance and retirement:						
Unemployment	28,202	27,484	26,480	27,641	27,812	30,288
Federal employees retirement	4,344	4,261	4,399	4,693	4,647	4,550
Non-federal employees	74	74	73	70	66	62
Total social insurance taxes and contributions	**539,371**	**571,835**	**611,832**	**652,851**	**693,967**	**708,035**
Excise taxes	56,926	57,669	70,412	68,866	66,232	66,871
Estate and gift taxes	19,845	24,076	27,782	29,010	28,400	27,490
Customs duties	17,927	18,297	18,336	19,913	19,616	18,666
Deposits of earnings by Federal Reserve Banks	19,636	24,540	25,917	32,293	26,124	25,596
All other miscellaneous receipts	5,491	5,027	5,112	5,807	11,426	10,794
Net Budget Receipts	**1,578,955**	**1,721,421**	**1,827,302**	**2,025,038**	**1,990,930**	**1,946,136**
NET OUTLAYS						
Legislative Branch	2,362	2,600	2,612	2,913	3,029	3,625
The Judiciary	3,259	3,463	3,793	4,087	4,409	4,977
Executive Office of the President:						
The White House Office	39	46	51	53	52	—
Office of Management and Budget	56	56	59	64	64	—
Total Executive Office	**219**	**236**	**416**	**284**	**280**	**464**
International Assistance Program:						
International security assistance	4,403	4,950	5,405	6,534	6,783	—
Multilateral assistance	2,141	1,850	1,857	1,759	2,166	—
Agency for International Development	2,814	2,435	2,337	2,622	2,764	—
International Development Assistance	2,902	2,494	2,410	2,953	2,895	—
Total International Assistance Program	**10,128**	**8,980**	**10,061**	**12,083**	**11,767**	**13,287**
Agriculture Department:						
Food stamp program	22,857	20,141	19,005	18,295	19,097	—
Farm Service Agency	7,417	10,421	19,508	33,353	22,974	—
Forest Service	3,209	3,399	3,423	3,978	4,225	—
Total Agriculture Department	**52,549**	**53,950**	**62,839**	**75,728**	**68,156**	**76,565**
Commerce Department:						
Bureau of the Census	282	542	1,131	4,214	1,025	—
Total Commerce Department	**3,780**	**4,047**	**5,036**	**7,931**	**5,017**	**5,495**
Defense Department—Military:						
Military personnel	69,722	68,976	69,503	75,950	73,977	—
Operation and maintenance	92,465	93,473	96,420	105,871	112,019	—
Procurement	47,691	48,207	48,824	51,616	54,991	—
Research, development, test, evaluation	37,026	37,421	37,362	37,608	40,462	—
Military construction	6,188	6,046	5,519	5,111	4,978	—
Total Defense Department—Military	**258,330**	**256,124**	**261,379**	**281,233**	**290,980**	**330,553**
Defense Department—Civil	30,282	31,216	32,008	32,019	34,161	35,537
Education Department	30,014	31,498	32,435	33,308	35,959	47,587
Energy Department	14,470	14,444	16,054	15,010	16,420	19,093
Health and Human Services Department:						
Public Health Service	21,755	23,680	25,554	28,281	32,667	—
Health Care Financing Adm.	369,714	379,950	390,181	413,124	450,751	—
Food and Drug Administration	873	838	951	1,023	1,075	—
National Institutes of Health	11,199	12,501	13,815	15,415	17,254	—
Total Health and Human Services Dept.	**339,541**	**350,571**	**359,700**	**382,627**	**426,444**	**459,366**
Housing and Urban Development Department	27,525	30,224	32,736	30,830	33,937	30,948
Interior Department	6,722	7,232	7,814	8,036	8,024	10,290
Justice Department:						
Federal Bureau of Investigation	2,700	2,949	3,040	3,088	20,810	—
Drug Enforcement Administration	969	1,099	1,203	1,339	3,208	—
Immigration and Naturalization Service	2,770	3,593	3,775	4,163	4,558	—
Federal Prison System	2,939	2,682	3,204	3,708	4,205	—
Total Justice Department	**14,315**	**16,169**	**18,318**	**19,561**	**20,810**	—
Labor Department:						
Unemployment Trust Fund	24,299	23,408	24,870	24,149	31,530	—
Total Labor Department	**30,461**	**30,002**	**32,459**	**31,354**	**39,280**	**58,579**
State Department	5,245	5,373	6,463	6,849	7,446	11,132
Transportation Department:						
Federal Aviation Administration	8,815	9,242	9,507	9,561	10,731	—
Total Transportation Department	**39,835**	**39,467**	**41,836**	**46,030**	**54,075**	**60,788**
Treasury Department:						
Internal Revenue Service	31,386	33,153	37,087	37,986	38,695	—
Interest on the public debt	355,796	363,824	353,511	362,118	359,508	338,833
Total Treasury Department	**379,345**	**390,094**	**386,703**	**390,813**	**389,944**	**382,616**
Veterans Affairs Department	39,277	41,776	43,169	47,087	45,043	51,451
Environmental Protection Agency	6,167	6,288	6,752	7,236	7,390	7,790

	Fiscal 1997[1]	Fiscal 1998[1]	Fiscal 1999[1]	Fiscal 2000[1]	Fiscal 2001[1,2]	Fiscal 2002[1,2]
General Services Administration	$1,083	$1,095	$–46	$25	$–8	$586
National Aeronautics and Space Administration	14,358	14,206	13,665	13,442	14,094	14,484
Office of Personnel Management	45,404	46,307	47,515	48,660	50,915	54,277
Small Business Administration	334	–78	58	–422	-569	1,073
Social Security Administration	393,309	408,202	419,790	441,810	461,748	492,671
Other independent agencies:						
Corporation for Natl. and Community Service	564	591	609	604	757	—
Corporation for Public Broadcasting	260	250	281	316	360	—
District of Columbia	717	818	–2,910	312	539	—
Equal Employment Opportunity Commission	231	244	255	290	289	—
Export-Import Bank of the U.S.	–114	–208	–159	–743	–1,749	—
Federal Communications Commission	1,001	1,769	3,293	4,073	4,011	—
Federal Deposit Insurance Corporation	–14,181	–4,122	–5,025	–2,837	–1,220	—
Legal Services Corporation	282	285	298	301	320	—
National Archives & Records Adm.	198	210	225	201	217	—
National Foundation on the Arts and Humanities	230	207	217	218	223	—
National Labor Relations Board	175	177	182	198	220	—
National Science Foundation	3,131	3,188	3,285	3,487	3,691	4,564
Nuclear Regulatory Commission	51	38	37	33	31	—
Railroad Retirement Board	4,870	4,837	4,830	4,992	5,541	—
Securities and Exchange Commission	–20	–231	–255	–506	–330	—
Smithsonian Institution	491	488	486	517	561	—
Tennessee Valley Authority	–337	–784	2	–307	–662	—
Total other independent agencies	–2,489	10,653	6,943	10,526	12,581	—
Undistributed offsetting receipts	–154,970	–161,036	–159,080	–172,844	–190,946	—
NET BUDGET OUTLAYS	**$1,000,911**	**$1,652,224**	**$1,704,942**	**$1,788,045**	**$1,863,909**	**$2,052,320**
Less net receipts	1,578,955	1,721,421	1,827,302	2,025,038	1,990,930	1,946,136
DEFICIT (-) OR SURPLUS (+)	**$–21,957**	**$+70,039**	**$+124,360**	**$+236,993**	**$+127,021**	**$–106,184**

— = Not available. (1) Fiscal year ends Sept. 30. (2) Figures for some agencies are preliminary.

State Finances: Revenue, Expenditures, Debt, and Taxes

Source: Census Bureau, U.S. Dept. of Commerce

(fiscal year 2000)

STATE	Revenue (millions)	Expenditures (millions)	Debt (millions)	Per capita debt	Per capita taxes	Per capita expenditures
Alabama	$16,857	$15,873	$5,292	$1,190	$1,448	$3,569
Alaska	8,584	6,611	4,150	6,620	2,270	10,544
Arizona	16,781	16,574	3,101	604	1,579	3,230
Arkansas	10,789	9,589	2,746	1,027	1,822	3,587
California	172,481	149,772	57,170	1,688	2,474	4,422
Colorado	17,060	13,930	4,431	1,030	1,645	3,239
Connecticut	18,007	16,723	18,456	5,419	2,986	4,910
Delaware	5,162	4,211	3,261	4,159	2,720	5,371
Florida	51,621	45,208	18,181	1,138	1,553	2,829
Georgia	29,630	24,813	7,086	866	1,651	3,031
Hawaii	6,941	6,605	5,592	4,614	2,751	5,449
Idaho	5,576	4,493	2,279	1,761	1,837	3,472
Illinois	48,524	41,183	28,828	2,321	1,835	3,316
Indiana	20,456	20,289	7,894	1,298	1,662	3,337
Iowa	11,340	11,453	2,362	807	1,772	3,914
Kansas	10,394	9,124	1,912	711	1,804	3,394
Kentucky	19,451	15,682	7,753	1,918	1,904	3,880
Louisiana	18,788	16,554	7,770	1,739	1,457	3,704
Maine	6,294	5,448	4,060	3,185	2,087	4,273
Maryland	21,366	19,370	11,365	2,146	1,955	3,657
Massachusetts	32,011	29,478	38,961	6,137	2,544	4,643
Michigan	49,512	42,749	19,445	1,957	2,290	4,302
Minnesota	26,889	23,326	5,602	1,139	2,712	4,742
Mississippi	12,181	10,972	3,222	1,133	1,656	3,857
Missouri	20,309	17,293	9,820	1,755	1,532	3,091
Montana	4,204	3,718	2,557	2,835	1,564	4,122
Nebraska	6,185	5,772	1,680	982	1,742	3,374
Nevada	7,285	6,047	2,990	1,497	1,860	3,027
New Hampshire	4,993	4,366	5,499	4,449	1,372	3,532
New Jersey	42,341	34,783	28,938	3,439	2,157	4,134
New Mexico	10,570	8,701	3,625	1,993	2,058	4,783
New York	111,397	96,925	78,616	4,143	2,199	5,108
North Carolina	34,361	29,615	9,336	1,160	1,903	3,679
North Dakota	3,295	2,856	1,520	2,367	1,826	4,448
Ohio	55,274	44,631	18,087	1,593	1,733	3,931
Oklahoma	13,116	10,630	5,663	1,641	1,692	3,080
Oregon	21,321	15,776	6,235	1,823	1,738	4,612
Pennsylvania	54,517	47,682	18,595	1,514	1,829	3,883
Rhode Island	5,589	4,648	5,681	5,421	1,942	4,435
South Carolina	15,966	16,237	7,057	1,759	1,591	4,047
South Dakota	2,901	2,403	2,305	3,053	1,228	3,183
Tennessee	18,970	16,853	3,292	579	1,360	2,962
Texas	72,323	60,425	19,228	922	1,315	2,898
Utah	10,227	8,592	3,885	1,740	1,782	3,848
Vermont	3,292	3,219	2,165	3,555	2,435	5,286
Virginia	29,409	24,314	12,011	1,697	1,787	3,435
Washington	30,616	25,902	11,734	1,991	2,132	4,395
West Virginia	8,591	7,552	3,730	2,063	1,849	4,177
Wisconsin	32,119	23,027	11,454	2,135	2,344	4,293
Wyoming	5,740	2,553	1,250	2,529	1,951	5,167
ALL STATES[1]	**$1,261,607**	**$1,084,548**	**$547,876**	**$1,951**	**$1,922**	**$3,862**

(1) Totals may not add because of rounding.

State and Local Government Receipts and Current Expenditures

Source: Bureau of Economic Analysis, U.S. Dept. of Commerce

(billions of current dollars)

	1999R	2000R	2001
RECEIPTS	**$1,144.1**	**$1,214.2**	**$1,261.3**
Personal tax and nontax receipts	255.8	2,77.5	281.2
Income taxes	199.7	2,18.1	218.7
Nontaxes	36.1	39.0	41.9
Other	20.0	20.4	20.6
Corporate profits tax accruals	34.8	35.6	29.1
Indirect business tax and nontax accruals	612.7	644.5	664.4
Sales taxes	300.6	314.3	321.2
Property taxes	239.2	248.1	257.4
Other	72.9	82.1	85.8
Contributions for social insurance	9.7	9.2	9.2
Federal grants–in–aid	231.0	247.5	277.4
CURRENT EXPENDITURES	**1,105.8**	**1,196.2**	**1,292.6**
Consumption expenditures	864.7	937.9	993.7
Transfer payments to persons	$ 252.7	$271.3	$ 304.4

	1999R	2000R	2001
Net interest paid	–0.7	–2.8	–2.1
Interest paid	78.7	81.4	83.3
Less: Interest received by government	79.4	84.2	85.4
Less: Dividends received by government	0.4	0.4	0.4
Subsidies less current surplus of government enterprises	–10.5	–9.7	–3.1
Subsidies	0.4	0.4	7.8
Less: Current surplus of government enterprises	10.9	10.2	10.9
Less: Wage accruals less disbursements	0.0	0.0	0.0
CURRENT SURPLUS or DEFICIT (–)	**38.3**	**18.0**	**–31.3**

(R) Revised figures.

State and Local Government Current Expenditures and Gross Investment, by Function

Source: Bureau of Economic Analysis, U.S. Dept. of Commerce

(millions of dollars)

	1997			1998		
	Total[1]	Current Expends	Gross Investment[2]	Total[1]	Current Expends.	Gross Investment[2]
TOTAL	**$1,135,758**	**$960,147**	**$175,611**	**$1,028,681**	**$1,212,200**	**$183,519**
Central executive, legislative, and judicial activities	**71,725**	**68,150**	**3,575**	**71,502**	**76,521**	**5,019**
Administrative, legislative, and judicial activities	38,921	36,593	2,328	40,258	43,286	3,028
Tax collection and financial management	32,804	31,557	1,247	31,244	33,235	1,991
Civilian safety	**118,689**	**110,537**	**8,152**	**119,773**	**128,429**	**8,656**
Police	53,218	50,390	2,828	55,977	59,129	3,152
Fire	20,297	18,613	1,684	20,145	21,682	1,537
Correction	45,174	41,534	3,640	43,651	47,618	3,967
Education	**407,721**	**367,955**	**39,766**	**396,141**	**442,174**	**46,033**
Elementary and secondary	312,962	284,993	27,969	306,202	338,991	32,789
Higher	70,195	59,693	10,502	64,606	76,530	11,924
Libraries	5,747	5,104	643	5,906	6,704	798
Other	18,817	18,165	652	19,427	19,949	522
Health and hospitals	**27,450**	**21,827**	**5,623**	**23,936**	**32,575**	**8,639**
Health	26,408	24,406	2,002	25,578	27,990	2,412
Hospitals	1,042	–2,579	3,621	–1,642	4,585	6,227
Income support, social security, and welfare	**255,974**	**255,216**	**758**	**267,027**	**268,290**	**1,263**
Govt. employees retirement and disability	1,768	1,768	—	—	—	—
Workers' compensation and temporary disability insurance	10,021	10,021	—	13,138	13,138	0
Medical care	169,123	169,123	—	173,951	173,951	0
Welfare and social services	75,062	74,304	758	79,938	81,201	1,263
Veterans' benefits and services	**277**	**260**	**17**	**309**	**356**	**47**
Housing and community services	**30,877**	**5,525**	**25,352**	**6,588**	**30,451**	**23,863**
Housing, comm. dev., urban renewal	6,852	2,899	3,953	5,978	9,800	3,822
Water	6,308	–3,428	9,736	–4,445	4,758	9,203
Sewerage	10,612	597	10,015	–1,332	7,776	9,108
Sanitation	7,105	5,457	1,648	6,387	8,117	1,730
Recreational and cultural activities	**17,142**	**12,388**	**4,754**	**14,163**	**19,539**	**5,376**
Energy	**–3,250**	**–7,688**	**4,438**	**–7,658**	**–4,336**	**3,322**
Gas utilities	–1,139	–1,404	265	–679	–262	417
Electric utilities	–2,111	–6,284	4,173	–6,979	–4,074	2,905
Agriculture	**4,643**	**4,379**	**264**	**4,857**	**5,218**	**361**
Natural resources	**11,897**	**9,331**	**2,566**	**9,005**	**11,552**	**2,547**
Transportation	**134,408**	**67,866**	**66,542**	**76,950**	**139,958**	**63,008**
Highways	106,923	54,610	52,313	64,149	113,466	49,317
Water	1,705	71	1,634	–256	868	1,124
Air	2,741	–1,268	4,009	–2,062	2,073	4,135
Transit and railroad	23,039	14,453	8,586	15,119	23,551	8,432
Economic development, regulation, and services	**8,488**	**8,103**	**385**	**7,443**	**7,952**	**509**
Labor training and services	**5,474**	**5,345**	**129**	**5,744**	**5,990**	**246**
Commercial activities	**–13,919**	**–14,224**	**305**	**–14,641**	**–14,290**	**351**
Publicly owned liquor store systems	–648	–658	10	–726	–712	14
Govt.-administered lotteries, parimutuels	–13,527	–13,527	—	–13,744	–13,744	—
Other	256	-39	295	171	166	337
Net interest paid[2]	**–6,452**	**–6,452**	—	**–2,345**	**–2,345**	—
Other and unallocable	**64,614**	**51,629**	**12,985**	**49,887**	**64,166**	**14,279**

(1) Sum of current expenditures and gross investment. (2) Excludes interest received by social insurance funds, which is netted against expenditures for the appropriate functions.

Top U.S. Charities by Donations, 2001

Source: The Chronicle of Philanthropy

(in millions of dollars)

Rank	Organization	Private Support[1]	Total Income
1	Salvation Army (Alexandria, VA)	$1,440.4	$2,792.8
2	Fidelity Investments Charitable Gift Fund (Boston, MA)	1,087.7	1,260.5
3	YMCA of the USA (Chicago, IL)	812.1	3,987.5
4	American Cancer Society (Atlanta, GA)	746.4	812.3
5	Lutheran Services in America (St. Paul, MN)	710.3	6,909.1
6	American Red Cross (Washington, DC)	637.7	2,492.4
7	Gifts in Kind International (Alexandria, VA)	601.9	605.1
8	Stanford University (Palo Alto, CA)	580.5	3,781.1
9	Harvard University (Cambridge, MA)	485.2	5,967.2
10	Nature Conservancy (Arlington, VA)	445.3	784.3
11	Boys & Girls Clubs of America (Atlanta, GA)	425.1	894.9
12	America's Second Harvest (Chicago, IL)	421.7	424.2
13	Catholic Charities USA (Alexandria, VA)	414.4	2,342.2
14	Duke University (Durham, NC)	$408.0	$2,742.5
15	American Heart Association (Dallas, TX)	396.4	471.6
16	Feed the Children (Oklahoma City, OK)	395.6	398.5
17	World Vision (Federal Way, WA)	372.0	468.0
18	Habitat for Humanity International (Americus, GA)	371.1	548.9
19	Yale University (New Haven, CT)	358.1	3,081.9
20	AmeriCares Foundation (New Canaan, CT)	326.4	328.1
21	Campus Crusade for Christ Intl. (Orlando, FL)	325.8	374.0
22	Cornell University (Ithaca, NY)	308.7	2,148.2
23	Johns Hopkins University (Baltimore, MD)	304.0	2,065.6
24	Columbia University (New York, NY)	292.3	2,366.4
25	University of Pennsylvania (Philadelphia, PA)	288.2	2,380.7

(1) Private support consists of donations from individuals, foundations, and corporations. Total income also includes government funding and fees charged.

IT'S A FACT: According to *The Chronicle of Philanthropy,* America's most generous donors in 2001 were Gordon and Betty Moore, who gave or pledged a total of $6.1 billion to higher education, scientific research, and the environment. (Gordon Moore was a co-founder of the Intel Corp.) In the number 2 spot were Bill and Melinda Gates, who donated or pledged $2.0 billion in 2001.

Consumer Credit Outstanding, 1999-2001

Source: Federal Reserve System

(billions of dollars)

Estimated amounts of credit outstanding as of end of year. Not seasonally adjusted.

	1999	2000	2001
TOTAL	**$1,446.1**	**$1,593.1**	**$1,701.9**
Major Holders			
Commercial banks	499.8	541.5	558.4
Finance companies	201.5	219.8	236.6
Credit unions	184.4	184.4	189.6
Savings institutions	61.6	64.6	69.1
Nonfinancial business	82.7	82.7	68.0
Pools of securitized assets[1]	500.1	500.1	580.3
Major Types of Credit[2]			
Revolving	693.0	693.0	727.3
Commercial banks	189.4	218.1	224.9
Finance companies	32.5	37.6	31.5
Credit unions	20.6	22.2	22.3
Savings institutions	15.8	16.6	17.8
Nonfinancial business	42.8	42.4	29.8
Pools of securitized assets[1]	356.1	356.1	401.1
Nonrevolving	824.2	900.1	974.6
Commercial banks	323.4	323.4	333.5
Finance companies	182.2	182.2	205.0
Credit unions	162.2	162.2	167.3
Savings institutions	48.0	48.0	51.3
Nonfinancial business	40.2	40.2	38.2
Pools of securitized assets[1]	144.0	144.0	179.2

(1) Outstanding balances of pools upon which securities have been issued; these balances are no longer carried on the balance sheets of the loan originators. (2) Includes estimates for holders that do not separately report consumer credit holding by type.

Leading U.S. Businesses in 2001

Source: Data from FORTUNE Magazine

(millions of dollars in revenues)

Advertising, Marketing	
Omnicom Group	$6,889
Interpublic Group	6,727
Aerospace	
Boeing	$58,198
United Technologies	27,897
Lockheed Martin	24,793
Honeywell Intl.	23,652
Raytheon	16,867
Northrop Grumman	13,558
Textron	12,321
General Dynamics	12,163
Airlines	
AMR	$18,963
UAL	16,138
Delta Air Lines	13,879
NWA	9,905
Continental Airlines	8,969
US Airways Group	8,288
Southwest Airlines	5,555
Alaska Air Group	2,141
America West Holdings	2,066
Apparel	
Nike	$9,489
VF	5,519
Levi Strauss	4,259
Jones Apparel Group	4,073
Liz Claiborne	3,449
Reebok International	2,993
Kellwood	2,282
Polo Ralph Lauren	2,226
Phillips-Van Heusen	1,432
Timberland	1,184
Automotive Retailing, Services	
AutoNation	$19,989
Beverages	
PepsiCo	$26,935
Coca-Cola	20,092
Coca-Cola Enterprises	15,700
Anheuser-Busch	12,912
The Pepsi Bottling Group	8,443
Pepsi Americas	3,171
Adolph Coors	2,430
Building Materials, Glass	
Owens-Corning	$4,762
USG	3,296
Armstrong Holdings	3,135
Vulcan Materials	3,019
Texas Industries	1,252
Chemicals	
Dow Chemical	$27,805
E. I. du Pont de Nemours	25,370
Ashland	8,547
PPG Industries	8,169
Rohm & Haas	5,896
Air Products & Chem.	5,723
Commercial Banks	
Bank of America Corp.	$52,641
J.P. MorganChase	50,429
Wells Fargo	26,891
Bank One Corp.	24,527
Wachovia Corp.	22,396
Fleet Boston	19,190
U.S. Bancorp	16,443
Computer and Data Services	
Electronic Data Systems	$21,543
Computer Sciences	10,524
Automatic Data Proc.	7,018
First Data	6,451
Science Applications Intl.	6,163
Unisys	6,018
Computer Peripherals	
EMC	$7,091
Quantum	4,452
Lexmark International	4,143
Maxtor	3,797
Computers, Office Equipment	
IBM	$85,866
Hewlett-Packard	45,226
Compaq Computer	33,554
Dell Computer	31,168
Sun Microsystems	18,250
Xerox	16,502
Gateway	6,080
NCR	5,917
Computer Software	
Microsoft	$25,296
Oracle	10,860
Computer Assoc. Intl.	4,198

Diversified Financials

General Electric	$125,913
Citigroup	112,022
Fannie Mae	50,803
Freddie Mac	35,523
American Express	22,582

Electronics, Electrical Equip.

Emerson Electric	$15,480
Whirlpool	10,343
Eaton	7,299
Maytag	4,564

Energy

Enron	$138,718
American Electric Power	61,257
Duke Energy	59,503
El Paso	57,475
Reliant Energy	46,226
Aquila	40,377

Engineering, Construction

Fluor	$8,972
Jacobs Engineering Grp.	3,957

Entertainment

AOL Time Warner	$38,234
Walt Disney	25,269
Viacom	23,223

Food

ConAgra	$27,194
Sara Lee	17,747
H. J. Heinz	9,430
Kellogg	8,853
General Mills	7,078
Campbell Soup	6,664
Smithfield Foods	5,900
Dole Food	4,688

Food and Drug Stores

Kroger	$50,098
Albertson's	37,931
Safeway	34,301
Walgreen	24,623
CVS	22,241
Rite Aid	15,297
Publix Super Markets	15,284
Winn-Dixie Stores	12,903

Food Production

Archer Daniels Midland	20,051
Farmland Industries	11,763
Tyson Foods	10,751

Food Services

McDonald's	$14,870
Tricon Global Restaurants	6,953
Darden Restaurants	4,021
Starbucks	2,649

Forest and Paper Products

International Paper	$26,363
Georgia-Pacific	25,309
Weyerhaeuser	14,545
Boise Cascade	7,422
Williamette Industries	4,454
MeadWestvaco	3,984

Furniture

Leggett & Platt	$4,114
Steelcase	3,886
La-Z-Boy	2,256
Herman Miller	2,236

General Merchandisers

Wal-Mart Stores	$219,812
Sears Roebuck	41,078
Target	39,888
Kmart	36,910
J. C. Penney	32,004
Federated Dept. Stores	16,895
May Dept. Stores	14,175

Health Care

Aetna	$25,191
UnitedHealth Group	23,454
Cigna	19,115
HCA	17,953

Home Equipment, Furnishings

Masco	$8,358
Newell Rubbermaid	6,909
Fortune Brands	5,318
U.S. Industries	2,453

Hotels, Casinos, Resorts

Marriott International	$10,152
Park Place Entertainment	4,631
MGM Mirage	4,010
Starwood Hotels & Resorts	3,967

Household and Personal Products

Procter & Gamble	$39,244
Kimberly-Clark	14,524
Colgate-Palmolive	9,428
Gillette	8,084
Avon Products	5,995
Estee Lauder	4,608
Clorox	3,903

Industrial and Farm Equip.

Caterpillar	$20,450
Deere	13,293
Illinois Tool Works	9,698
American Standard	7,465
Parker Hannifin	5,980

Insurance (Life and Health)

MetLife[1]	$31,928
Prudential Financial[1]	27,177
New York Life (Mutual)	25,678
TIAA-CREF (Mut.)[2]	24,231
Mass. Mutual Life Ins.	19,340
Northwestern Mutual	16,212
AFLAC	9,598

Insurance (Property and Casualty)

American International Group	$62,402
State Farm (Mutual)	46,705
Berkshire Hathaway	37,668
Allstate	28,865
Loews	18,799
Hartford Financial Services	15,147
Nationwide	15,118
Liberty Mutual Group	14,256

Mail, Pkg., Freight Delivery

United Parcel Service	$30,646
FedEx	19,629

Metals

Alcoa	$22,859
Nucor	4,139
Phelps Dodge	4,002
AK Steel Holding	3,994
LTV	3,956

Mining, Crude-Oil Production

Occidental Petroleum	$14,126
Andarko	8,369

Motor Vehicles and Parts

General Motors	$177,260
Ford Motor	162,412
Delphi	26,088
Johnson Controls	18,427
Visteon	17,843

Network and Other Communications

Motorola	$30,004
Lucent Technologies	25,132
Cisco Systems	22,293

Petroleum Refining

Exxon Mobil	$191,581
ChevronTexaco	99,699
Marathon Oil	35,041
Conoco	32,795
Phillips Petroleum	24,189

Pharmaceuticals

Merck	$47,716
Johnson & Johnson	33,004
Pfizer	32,259
Bristol-Myers Squibb	21,717
Pharmacia	19,299
Abbott Laboratories	16,285
Wyeth	14,129
Eli Lilly	11,543
Schering-Plough	9,802

Pipelines

Dynegy	$42,242
Williams	11,055
Plains All Amer. Pipeline	6,868

Publishing & Printing

Gannett	$6,344
R.R. Donnelley & Sons	5,298
Tribune	5,253
McGraw-Hill	4,646
New York Times	3,043
Knight-Ridder	2,900

Railroads

Union Pacific	$11,973
Burlington Northern Santa Fe	9,208
CSX	8,110
Norfolk Southern	6,170

Scientific, Photo., and Control Equip.

Eastman Kodak	$13,234
Agilent Technologies	9,161
Danaher	3,782

Securities

Morgan Stanley/Dean Witter	$43,727
Merrill Lynch	38,793
Goldman Sachs Group	31,138
Lehman Bros. Holdings	22,392

Semiconductors and Other Electron.

Intel	$26,539
Solectron	18,692
SCI Systems	8,714

Specialty Retailers

Home Depot	$53,553
Costco Wholesale	34,797
Lowe's	22,111
Best Buy	15,327
Gap	13,848
Circuit City Stores	12,959
Office Depot	11,154
Toys "R" Us	11,019
Staples	10,744
TJX	10,709

Telecommunications

Verizon	$67,190
AT&T	59,142
SBC Communications	45,908
WorldCom	35,179
Sprint	26,071
BellSouth	24,130
Qwest Communications	19,743

Temporary Help

Manpower	$10,484
Kelly Services	4,257
Spherion	2,713

Textiles

Mohawk Industries	$3,446
WestPoint Stevens	1,765
Burlington Industries	1,404

Tobacco

Philip Morris	$72,944
R.J. Reynolds Tobacco	8,585
Universal	3,018

Toys, Sporting Goods

Mattel	$4,804
Hasbro	2,856

Transportation Equipment

Brunswick	$3,684
Harley-Davidson	3,363
Trinity Industries	1,904

Utilities: Gas and Electric

TXU	$27,927
PG&E Corp.	22,959
Excelon	15,140
Xcel Energy	15,028
Edison International	12,184
Dominion Resources	10,558

Waste Management

Waste Management	$11,322
Allied Waste Industries	5,565
Republic Services	2,258

Wholesalers

Genuine Parts	$8,221
W. W. Grainger	4,754
Wesco International	3,658
Core-Mark International	3,425
Hughes Supply	3,038
TruServ	2,909

(1) Not a stock company, but reported financial data according to Generally Accepted Accounting Principle. (2) Not a mutual company, but reported financial data based on statutory accounting.

25 U.S. Corporations With Largest Revenues in 2001

Source: FORTUNE Magazine
(millions of dollars)

Company, headquarters	Revenues
Wal-Mart Stores, Bentonville, AR	$219,812
ExxonMobil, Irving, TX	191,581
General Motors, Detroit, MI	177,260
Ford Motor, Dearborn, MI	162,412
Enron, Houston, TX	138,718
General Electric, Fairfield, CT	125,913
Citigroup, New York, NY	112,022
ChevronTexaco, San Francisco, CA	99,699
IBM, Armonk, NY	85,866
Philip Morris, New York, NY	72,944
Verizion Communications, New York, NY	67,190
American International Group, New York, NY	62,402
American Electric Power, Columbus, OH	61,257
Duke Energy, Charlotte, NC	$59,503
AT&T, New York, NY	59,142
Boeing, Seattle, WA	58,198
El Paso, Houston, TX	57,475
Home Depot, Atlanta, GA	53,553
Bank of America Corp., Charlotte, NC	52,641
Fannie Mae, Washington, DC	50,803
J.P. Morgan Chase, New York, NY	50,429
Kroger, Cincinnati, OH	50,098
Cardinal Health, Dublin, OH	47,948
Merck, Whitehouse Station, NJ	47,716
State Farm Insurance, Bloomington, IL	46,705

Fastest-Growing U.S. Franchises in 2001[1]

Source: *Entrepreneur* Magazine

Company	Business	Minimum start-up cost[2]
Kumon Math & Reading Centers	Supplemental education	$5,900
7-Eleven Inc.	Convenience stores	varies
Curves for Women	Women's fitness and weight loss centers	25,600
Coverall Cleaning Concepts	Commercial cleaning	6,300
Subway	Submarine sandwiches and salads	63,400
Jani-King	Commercial cleaning	8,200
Jackson Hewitt Tax Service	Computerized tax preparation/electronic filing services	47,400
KFC Corp.	Chicken	1.1 mil
McDonald's	Hamburgers, chicken, salads	489,000
Budget Rent A Car Corp.	Auto & truck rentals	166,700
RE/MAX Int'l. Inc.	Real estate	20,000
CleanNet USA Inc.	Commercial office cleaning	3,900
The Quizno's Franchise Co.	Submarine sandwiches, soups, salads	170,000
Management Recruiters/ Sales Consult./MRI Worldwide	Personnel placement/ search & recruiting services	114,000
am/pm Convenience Stores	Convenience food stores	$1 mil
Yogen Fruz Worldwide	Frozen yogurt & ice cream	25,000
Holiday Inn Worldwide	Hotels	varies
Baskin-Robbins USA Co.	Ice cream & yogurt	132,800
WSI Internet	Internet Services	40,000
Mail Boxes Etc.	Postal/business/communications services	140,990
Jazzercise Inc.	Dance/exercise classes	1,800
Results Travel	Travel services	10,700
Denny's Inc.	Full-service family restaurant	901,000
Great Clips Inc.	Family hair salons	88,600
Popeye's Chicken & Biscuits	Cajun-style fried chicken and biscuits	700,000
Choice Hotels Int'l	Hotels, inns, suites, & resorts	4 mil
Snap on Tools	Professional tools & equipment	17,800
Party Land Inc.	Party supplies & balloons	234,000
Merry Maids	Residential cleaning	32,500
Century 21 Real Estate Corp.	Real estate	10,100

(1) Ranked by number of new franchise units added. (2) Not including franchise fee, which varies.

Largest Corporate Mergers or Acquisitions in U.S.

Source: Securities Data Co.
(as of Oct. 2002; * denotes an announced merger or acquisition not yet complete; year = year effective or announced)

Company	Acquirer	Dollars (in billions)	Year
Time Warner	America Online, Inc.	$181.6	2001
Warner-Lambert	Pfizer Inc.	88.8	2000
Mobil Corp.	Exxon Corp.	86.4	1999
Citicorp	Travelers Group Inc.	72.6	1998
Ameritech Corp	SBC Communications Inc.	72.4	1999
AT&T Broadband & Internet Services	Comcast Corp.*	72.0	2001
GTE Corp.	Bell Atlantic Corp.	71.3	2000
Tele Communications	AT&T	69.9	1999
AirTouch Communications	Vodafone Group PLC	65.8	1999
BankAmerica Corp.	NationsBank Corp.	61.6	1998
Pharmacia Corp.	Pfizer, Inc.*	61.3	2001
US West	Qwest Communication	56.3	2000
Amoco Corp.	British Petroleum Co. PLC	55.0	1998
MediaOne Group	AT&T	51.9	2000
Liberty Media Group (AT&T)	shareholders	46.0	2001
Texaco	Chevron	43.3	2001
MCI Communications	WorldCom Inc.	41.4	1998
SDL Inc.	JDS Uniphase Corp.	41.0	2001
CBS Corp.	Viacom	40.9	2000
Chrysler Corp	Daimler-Benz AG.	40.5	1998
Wells Fargo & Co.	Norwest Corp.	34.4	1998
VoiceStream Wireless Corp.	Deutsche Telekom AG	34.1	2001
ARCO	BP Amoco PLC	33.7	2000
J.P. Morgan & Co.	Chase Manhattan	33.6	2000
US West Media Group	shareholders	31.7	1998
Agilent Technologies	shareholders	$31.2	2000
Associates First Capital	Citigroup	31.0	2000
NYNEX	Bell Atlantic	30.8	1997
Electronic Data Syst.	shareholders	29.7	1996
First Chicago NBD	BANC ONE Corp.	29.6	1998
RJR Nabisco	Kohlberg Kravis Roberts	29.4	1989
Pharmacia & Upjohn	Monsanto Co.	26.9	2000
Hughes Electronics Corp	EchoStar Communications Corp.*	26.6	2001
Associates First Capital	shareholders	26.6	1998
Conoco	Phillips Petroleum	24.8	2002
Lucent Technologies (AT&T)	shareholders	24.1	1996
Bestfoods	Unilever PLC	23.7	2000
Compaq Computer	Hewlett-Packard	23.5	2002
Amer. General Corp.	American Int'l. Group	23.4	2001
AMFM, Inc.	Clear Channel Communications	22.7	2000
Pacific Telesis Group	SBC Communications	22.4	1997
General Re Corp.	Berkshire Hathaway Inc.	22.3	1998
US Bancorp, MN	Firstar Corp.	21.1	2001
Ascend Communications	Lucent Technologies	21.1	1999
Network Solutions, Inc.	VeriSign, Inc.	20.8	2000
Waste Management	USA Waste Services	20.0	1998
Nabisco Holdings	Philip Morris	19.4	2000
AT&T Wireless Serv.	shareholders	18.8	2001
Capital Cities/ABC Inc.	Walt Disney	18.3	1996
SunAmerica Inc.	American Int'l. Group	18.1	1999

2002 Federal Corporate Tax Rates

Taxable Income Amount	Tax Rate	Taxable Income Amount	Tax Rate	Taxable Income Amount	Tax Rate
Not more than $50,000 . . .	15%	$100,001 to $335,000	39%	$15,000,001 to $18,333,333	38%
$50,001 to $75,000	25%	$335,001 to $10,000,000. .	34%	More than $18,333,333. . . .	35%
$75,001 to $100,000	34%	$10,000,001 to $15,000,000	35%		

Personal service corporations (used by incorporated professionals such as attorneys and doctors) pay a flat rate of 35%.

U.S. Capital Gains Tax, 1960-2002

Source: George W. Smith IV, CPA, Partner, George W. Smith & Company. P.C.

The following shows how the maximum tax rate on net long-term capital gains for individuals has changed since 1960.

Year	Max %	Year	Max %	Year	Max %	Year	Max %	Year	Max %	Year	Max %
1960 . . .	25.0	1972 . . .	35.0[1]	1981 . . .	20.0	1988 . . .	33.0[2]	1997 . . .	20.0[4]	2001 . . .	20/18[6]
1970 . . .	29.5	1978 . . .	28.0	1987 . . .	28.0	1990 . . .	28.0[3]	1999 . . .	20.0[5]		
1971 . . .	32.5										

(1) From 1972 to 1976, the interplay of minimum tax and maximum tax resulted in a marginal rate of 49.125%. (2) Statutory maximum of 28%, but "phase-out" notch increased marginal rate to 33%; interplay of all "phase-outs" could have increased the effective marginal rate to 49.5%. (3) The Budget Act of 1990 increased the statutory rate to 31% and capped the marginal rate at 28%; however, some taxpayers faced effective marginal rates of more than 34% because of the phase-out of personal exemptions and itemized deductions. (4) New rate is for those who, after July 28, 1997, sell capital assets held for more than 18 mos (12 mos for sales after Dec. 31, 1997). A 10% capital gains rate applies to individuals in the 15% income tax bracket. (Those who, after July 28, 1997, but before Jan. 1, 1998, sell capital assets held between 12 and 18 mos will be taxed at the old top rate of 28%. Those who sold capital assets after May 6, 1997, but before July 29, 1997, will be taxed at the 20% rate, so long as such assets were held for at least a year.) (5) The IRS Restructuring and Reform Act of 1998 repealed the more-than-18-month holding period for sales after Dec. 31, 1997. Beginning Jan. 1, 1998, capital assets need only be held 12 months to have the 20%/10% capital gains rates apply. (6) For capital assets bought after Dec. 31, 2000, and held for more than 5 years, the 20% minimum capital gains rate will be lowered to 18%. The 10% rate will be lowered to 8%, regardless of when the assets were bought. The capital gains rate for the sale of collectibles such as antiques remains 28%. Capital gains on the sale of certain depreciable real estate will be taxed at 25%.

Global Stock Markets

Source: The Conference Board; not seasonally adjusted

Stock price indexes (1990=100):	June 1, 1960	June 1, 1970	June 1, 1980	June 1, 1990	2001		2002	
					Jan. 1	June 1	Jan. 1	June 1
United States	17.1	21.9	34.3	107.6	410.6	368.0	339.7	297.5
Japan	4.4	7.3	23.8	110.8	48.0	45.0	34.7	36.8
Germany	36.1	27.5	30.5	111.1	401.8	358.2	302.0	259.1
France	16.3	15.6	23.8	112.0	330.0	287.5	245.5	214.5
United Kingdom	8.2	11.6	24.9	108.2	279.9	252.0	230.6	209.1
Italy.	28.9	20.6	15.9	117.3	303.3	254.1	223.6	196.7
Canada.	14.8	25.0	60.3	103.6	272.5	226.1	223.6	208.9

U.S. Holdings of Foreign Stocks[1]

Source: Bureau of Economic Analysis, U.S. Dept. of Commerce

(billions of dollars)

	1999	2000	2001
Western Europe	**$1,167.8**	**$1,119.7**	**$932.7**
Of which: United Kingdom.	374.8	365.7	335.0
Finland.	58.4	51.4	39.4
France	183.2	183.3	140.4
Germany	117.6	94.7	91.0
Ireland	18.2	16.8	14.4
Italy	53.5	50.1	38.2
Netherlands	141.9	137.8	103.8
Spain	35.7	30.7	24.8
Sweden	74.8	65.9	53.0
Switzerland	64.3	75.5	57.2
Canada	100.7	123.3	99.6
Japan.	273.7	182.2	143.5

	1999	2000	2001
Latin America.	$89.1	$73.7	$60.2
Of which: Argentina	11.3	9.7	8.1
Brazil.	28.9	27.7	23.1
Mexico	30.2	25.1	20.0
Other W. Hemisphere	129.0	144.2	141.7
Of which: Bermuda.	45.9	36.3	34.8
Netherlands Antilles . .	26.7	34.4	28.3
Other countries and territories	266.3	189.3	187.0
Of which: Australia	39.2	35.1	37.9
Hong Kong	38.7	34.3	32.2
Singapore	16.3	8.6	4.0
TOTAL HOLDINGS	**$2,026.6**	**$1,832.4**	**$1,564.7**

(1) As of year end.

Gold Reserves of Central Banks and Governments

Source: International Financial Statistics, IMF; million fine troy ounces

Year end	All countries[1]	United States	Belgium	Canada	France	Germany[2]	Italy	Japan	Nether-lands	Switzer-land	United Kingdom
1975. .	1,018.71	274.71	42.17	21.95	100.93	117.61	82.48	21.11	54.33	83.20	21.03
1980. .	952.99	264.32	34.18	20.98	81.85	95.18	66.67	24.23	43.94	83.28	18.84
1985. .	949.39	262.65	34.18	20.11	81.85	95.18	66.67	24.33	43.94	83.28	19.03
1990. .	939.01	261.91	30.23	14.76	81.85	95.18	66.67	24.23	43.94	83.28	18.94
1995. .	908.79	261.70	20.54	3.41	81.85	95.18	66.67	24.23	34.77	83.28	18.43
1996. .	906.10	261.66	15.32	3.09	81.85	95.18	66.67	24.23	34.77	83.28	18.43
1997. .	890.57	261.64	15.32	3.09	81.89	95.18	66.67	24.23	27.07	83.28	18.42
1998. .	966.15	261.61	9.52	2.49	102.37	118.98	83.36	24.23	33.83	83.28	23.00
1999. .	940.51	261.67	8.30	1.81	97.24	111.52	78.83	24.23	31.57	83.28	20.55
2000. .	950.63	261.61	8.30	1.18	97.25	111.52	78.83	24.55	29.32	77.79	15.67
2001. .	941.43	262.00	8.30	1.05	97.25	111.13	78.83	24.60	28.44	70.68	11.42

(1) Covers IMF members with reported gold holdings. For countries not listed above, see International Monetary Fund's *International Financial Statistics Report.* (2) West Germany prior to 1991.

Record One-Day Gains and Losses on the Dow Jones Industrial Average

Source: Dow Jones & Co., Inc.; as of Sept. 30, 2002

GREATEST POINT GAINS

Rank	Date	Close	Net Chg	% Chg
1.	3/16/2000	10630.60	499.19	4.93
2.	7/24/2002	8191.29	488.95	6.35
3.	7/29/2002	8711.88	447.49	5.41
4.	4/5/2001	9918.05	402.63	4.23
5.	4/18/2001	10615.83	399.10	3.91
6.	9/8/1998	8020.78	380.53	4.98
7.	9/24/2001	8603.86	368.05	4.47
8.	10/1/2002	7938.79	346.86	4.57
9.	5/16/2001	11215.92	342.95	3.15
10.	12/5/2000	10898.72	338.62	3.21

GREATEST POINT LOSSES

Rank	Date	Close	Net Chg	% Chg
1.	9/17/2001	8920.70	–684.81	–7.13
2.	4/14/2000	10305.77	–617.78	–5.66
3.	10/27/1997	7161.15	–554.26	–7.19
4.	8/31/1998	7539.07	512.61	–6.37
5.	10/19/1987	1738.74	–508.00	–22.61
6.	3/13/2001	10208.25	–436.37	–4.1
7.	7/19/2002	8019.26	–390.23	–4.63
8.	9/20/2001	8376.21	–382.92	–4.37
9.	10/12/2000	10034.58	–379.21	–3.64
10.	3/7/2000	9796.03	–374.47	–3.68

GREATEST % GAINS

Rank	Date	Close	Net Chg	% Chg
1.	10/6/1931	99.34	12.86	14.87
2.	10/30/1929	258.47	28.40	12.34
3.	9/21/1932	75.16	7.67	11.36
4.	10/21/1987	2,027.85	186.84	10.15
5.	8/3/1932	58.22	5.06	9.52
6.	2/11/3192	78.60	6.80	9.47
7.	11/14/1929	217.28	18.59	9.36
8.	12/18/1931	80.69	6.90	9.35
9.	2/13/1932	85.82	7.22	9.19
10.	5/6/1932	59.01	4.91	9.08

GREATEST % LOSSES

Rank	Date	Close	Net Chg	% Chg
1.	10/19/1987	1,738.74	–508.00	–22.61
2.	10/28/1929	260.54	–38.33	–12.82
3.	10/29/1929	230.07	–30.57	–11.73
4.	11/6/1929	232.13	–25.55	–9.92
5.	12/18/1899	58.27	–5.57	–8.72
6.	8/12/1932	63.11	–5.79	–8.40
7.	3/14/1907	76.23	–6.89	–8.29
8.	10/25/1987	1,793.93	–156.83	–8.04
9.	7/21/1933	88.71	–7.55	–7.84
10.	10/18/1937	125.73	–10.57	–7.75

Dow Jones Industrial Average Since 1963

High		YEAR	Low	
Dec. 18	767.21	**1963**	Jan. 2	646.79
Nov. 18	891.71	**1964**	Jan. 2	766.08
Dec. 31	969.26	**1965**	June 28	840.59
Feb. 9	995.15	**1966**	Oct. 7	744.32
Sept. 25	943.08	**1967**	Jan. 3	786.41
Dec. 3	985.21	**1968**	Mar. 21	825.13
May 14	968.85	**1969**	Dec. 17	769.93
Dec. 29	842.00	**1970**	May 6	631.16
Apr. 28	950.82	**1971**	Nov. 23	797.97
Dec. 11	1036.27	**1972**	Jan. 26	889.15
Jan. 11	1051.70	**1973**	Dec. 5	788.31
Mar. 13	891.66	**1974**	Dec. 6	577.60
July 15	881.81	**1975**	Jan. 2	632.04
Sept. 21	1014.79	**1976**	Jan. 2	858.71
Jan. 3	999.75	**1977**	Nov. 2	800.85
Sept. 8	907.74	**1978**	Feb. 28	742.12
Oct. 5	897.61	**1979**	Nov. 7	796.67
Nov. 20	1000.17	**1980**	Apr. 21	759.13
Apr. 27	1024.05	**1981**	Sept. 25	824.01
Dec. 27	1070.55	**1982**	Aug. 12	776.92
Nov. 29	1287.20	**1983**	Jan. 3	1027.04
Jan. 6	1286.64	**1984**	July 24	1086.57
Dec. 16	1553.10	**1985**	Jan. 4	1184.96
Dec. 2	1955.57	**1986**	Jan. 22	1502.29
Aug. 25	2722.42	**1987**	Oct. 19	1738.74
Oct. 21	2183.50	**1988**	Jan. 20	1879.14
Oct. 9	2791.41	**1989**	Jan. 3	2144.64
July 16	2999.75	**1990**	Oct. 11	2365.10
Dec. 31	3168.83	**1991**	Jan. 9	2470.30
June 1	3413.21	**1992**	Oct. 9	3136.58
Dec. 29	3701.33	**1993**	Jan. 20	3241.95
Jan. 31	3978.36	**1994**	Apr. 4	3593.35
Dec. 13	5216.47	**1995**	Jan. 30	3832.08
Dec. 27	6560.91	**1996**	Jan. 10	5032.94
Aug. 6	8259.31	**1997**	Apr. 11	6391.69
Nov. 23	9374.27	**1998**	Aug. 31	7539.07
Dec. 31	11497.12	**1999**	Jan. 22	9120.67
Jan. 14	11722.98	**2000**	Mar. 7	9796.03
May 21	11337.92	**2001**	Sept. 21	8235.84

Milestones of the Dow Jones Industrial Average

(as of Sept. 30, 2002)

First close over...	
100	Jan. 12, 1906
500	Mar. 12, 1956
1000	Nov. 14, 1972
1500	Dec. 11, 1985
2000	Jan. 8, 1987
2500	July 17, 1987
3000	April 17, 1991
3500	May 19, 1993
4000	Feb. 23, 1995
4500	June 16, 1995
5000	Nov. 21, 1995
5500	Feb. 8, 1996
6000	Oct. 14, 1996
6500	Nov. 25, 1996
7000	Feb. 13, 1997
7500	June 10, 1997
8000	July 16, 1997
8100	July 24, 1997
8200	July 30, 1997
8100	July 24, 1997
8200	July 30, 1997
8300	Feb. 12, 1998
8400	Feb. 18, 1998
8300	Feb. 12, 1998
8400	Feb. 18, 1998
8500	Feb. 27, 1998
8600	Mar. 10, 1998
8700	Mar. 16, 1998
8800	Mar. 19, 1998
8900	Mar. 20, 1998
9000	Apr. 6, 1998
9100	Apr. 14, 1998
9200	May 13, 1998
9300	July 16, 1998
9500	Jan. 6, 1999*
9600	Jan. 8, 1999
9700	Mar. 5, 1999
9800	Mar. 11, 1999
9900	Mar. 15, 1999
10000	Mar. 29, 1999
10100	Apr. 8, 1999
10300	Apr. 12, 1999*
10400	Apr. 14, 1999
10500	Apr. 21, 1999
10700	Apr. 22, 1999*
10800	Apr. 27, 1999
11000	May 3, 1999*
11100	May 13, 1999
11200	July 12, 1999
11300	Aug. 25, 1999
11400	Dec. 23, 1999
11500	Jan. 7, 2000
11700	Jan. 14, 2000*

*9400, 10200, 10600, 10900, and 11600 are not listed because the Dow had risen another 100 points or more by the time the market closed for the day.

Components of the Dow Jones Averages

(as of Sept. 30, 2002)

Dow Jones Industrial Average

Aluminum Co. of America (Alcoa)
American Express
AT&T
Boeing
Caterpillar
Citigroup
Coca-Cola
DuPont
Eastman Kodak
Exxon Mobil
General Electric
General Motors
Hewlett-Packard
Home Depot
Honeywell International
IBM
Intel*
International Paper
J.P. Morgan
Johnson & Johnson
McDonald's
Merck
Microsoft*
Philip Morris
Procter & Gamble
SBC Communications
3M
United Technologies
Wal-Mart
Walt Disney

*The inclusion in 1999 of Intel and Microsoft, both traded on the Nasdaq stock market, marked the first time a DJIA component has not been listed on the NYSE since the Dow's inception in 1896.

Dow Jones Utility Average

AES Corp.
American Electric Power
CenterPoint Energy
Consolidated Edison
Dominion Resources
Duke Energy
Edison International
Exelon
FirstEnergy Corp.
NiSource
PG&E
Public Service Enterprise Group
Southern Co.
TXU
Williams Cos.

Dow Jones Transportation Average

Airborne
Alexander & Baldwin
AMR (American Airlines)
Burlington Northern Santa Fe
CNF Transportation
Continental Airlines
CSX
Delta Air Lines
FedEx
GATX
J.B. Hunt Transportation
Norfolk Southern
Northwest Airlines
Roadway Corp.
Ryder System
Southwest Airlines
UAL (United Air Lines)
Union Pacific
USFreightways
Yellow Corp.

Record One-Day Gains and Losses on the Nasdaq Stock Market

Source: Nasdaq Stock Market; as of Sept. 30, 2002

GREATEST POINT GAINS

Rank	Date	Point Change
1.	1/3/01	324.83
2.	12/5/00	274.05
3.	4/18/00	254.41
4.	5/30/00	254.37
5.	10/19/00	247.04
6.	10/13/00	242.09
7.	6/2/00	230.88
8.	4/25/00	228.75
9.	4/17/00	217.87
10.	6/1/00	181.59

GREATEST % GAINS

Rank	Date	% Change
1.	1/3/01	12.41%
2.	12/5/00	9.48%
3.	4/5/01	8.19%
4.	4/18/01	7.51%
5.	5/30/00	7.35%
6.	10/21/87	7.34%
7.	10/13/00	7.30%
8.	10/19/00	7.23%
9.	5/8/02	7.22%
10.	12/22/00	7.03%

GREATEST POINT LOSSES

Rank	Date	Point Change
1.	4/14/00	–355.49
2.	4/3/00	–349.15
3.	4/12/00	–28.27
4.	4/10/00	–258.25
5.	1/4/00	–229.46
6.	3/14/00	–200.61
7.	5/10/00	–200.28
8.	5/23/00	–199.66
9.	10/25/00	–190.22
10.	3/29/00	–189.22

GREATEST % LOSSES

Rank	Date	% Change
1.	10/19/87	–11.35%
2.	4/14/00	–10.70%
3.	8/31/98	–9.37%
4.	10/20/87	–9.00%
5.	10/26/87	–9.00%
6.	4/3/00	–8.27%
7.	1/2/01	–7.80%
8.	12/20/00	–7.67%
9.	4/12/00	–7.59%
10.	10/27/97	–7.55%

Nasdaq Stock Market Since 1971

High	YEAR	Low	High	YEAR	Low	High	YEAR	Low	High	YEAR	Low
114.12	**1971**	99.68	152.29	**1979**	117.84	456.27	**1987**	288.49	1072.82	**1995**	740.53
135.15	**1972**	113.65	208.29	**1980**	124.09	397.54	**1988**	329.00	1328.45	**1996**	978.17
136.84	**1973**	88.67	223.96	**1981**	170.80	487.60	**1989**	376.87	1748.62	**1997**	1194.39
96.53	**1974**	54.87	241.63	**1982**	158.92	470.30	**1990**	322.93	2200.63	**1998**	1357.09
88.00	**1975**	60.70	329.11	**1983**	229.88	586.35	**1991**	352.85	4090.61	**1999**	2193.13
97.88	**1976**	78.06	288.41	**1984**	223.91	676.95	**1992**	545.85	5048.62	**2000**	2332.78
105.05	**1977**	93.66	325.53	**1985**	245.82	790.56	**1993**	645.02	2892.36	**2001**	1387.06
139.25	**1978**	99.09	411.21	**1986**	322.14	803.93	**1994**	691.23			

Milestones of the Nasdaq Stock Market

Source: Nasdaq Stock Market; as of Oct. 15, 2002

First close over...

100 . . . . Feb. 8, 1971
200 . . . . Nov. 13, 1980
300 . . . . May 6, 1986
400 . . . . May 30, 1986
500 . . . . Apr. 12, 1991

First close over...

1,000 . . . . July 17, 1995
1,500 . . . . July 11, 1997
2,000 . . . . July 16, 1998
2,500 . . . . Jan. 29, 1999
3,000 . . . . Nov. 3, 1999

First close over...

3,500 . . . . Dec. 3, 1999
4,000 . . . . Dec. 29, 1999
4,500 . . . . Feb. 17, 2000
5,000 . . . . Mar. 9, 2000

Standard & Poor's 500 Index, 1991-2002

Source: *Facts On File World News Digest;* monthly closing levels

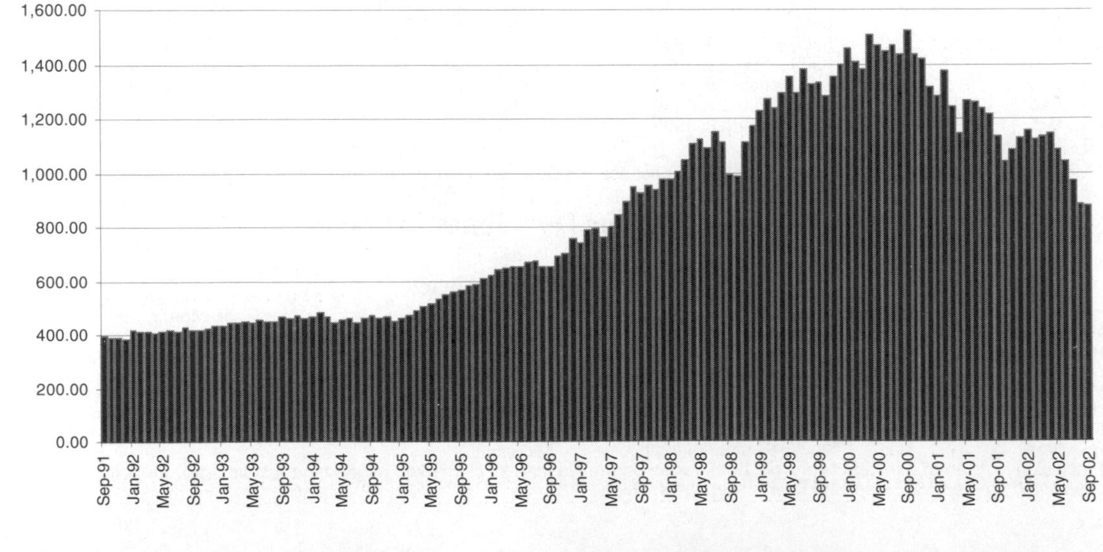

Most Active Common Stocks in 2001

New York Exchange Volume (millions of shares)	
General Electric	4,363.4
Lucent Technologies	4,264.1
EMC Corp.	3,864.1
Nortel Networks	3,541.8
AOL Time Warner	3,444.8
Nokia Corp.	2,950.8
Citigroup Inc.	2,836.6
Pfizer Inc.	2,759.3
Compaq Computer	2,743.6
AT&T Corp.	2,649.4

American Exchange Volume (millions of shares)	
Nabors Industries	570.9
IVAX Corp.	363.6
Devon Energy Corp.	302.2
Grey Wolf, Inc.	270.1
E-MedSoft.com	200.4
Kinross Gold Corp.	104.9
Bema Gold Corp.	82.4
Titan Pharmaceuticals	79.1
Xcelera, Inc.	76.7
Ultra Petroleum Corp.	64.6

NASDAQ Volume (millions of shares)	
Cisco Systems, Inc.	21,295.7
Intel Corp.	13,427.9
Sun Microsystems, Inc.	12,831.9
Oracle Corp.	11,870.8
Microsoft Corp.	9,607.4
JDS Uniphase Corp.	8,977.8
Dell Computer Corp.	7,890.8
WorldCom, Inc.	7,628.9
Juniper Networks, Inc.	5,744.5
CIENA Corp.	5,469.9

Average Yields of Long-Term Treasury, Corporate, and Municipal Bonds

Source: Office of Market Finance, U.S. Dept. of the Treasury

Period	Treasury 30-year bonds(1)	New Aa corporate bonds(2)	New Aa municipal bonds(3)
1986			
June	7.57	9.39	7.75
Dec.	7.37	8.87	6.70
1987			
June	8.57	9.64	7.69
Dec.	9.12	10.22	7.83
1988			
June	9.00	10.08	7.67
Dec.	9.01	10.05	7.40
1989			
June	8.27	9.24	6.94
Dec.	7.90	9.23	6.76
1990			
June	8.46	9.69	6.98
Dec.	8.24	9.55	6.85
1991			
June	8.47	9.37	6.90
Dec.	7.70	8.55	6.43

Period	Treasury 30-year bonds(1)	New Aa corporate bonds(2)	New Aa municipal bonds(3)
1992			
June	7.84	8.45	6.32
Dec.	7.44	8.12	6.02
1993			
June	6.81	7.48	5.54
Dec.	6.25	7.22	5.27
1994			
June	7.40	8.16	5.96
Dec.	7.87	8.66	6.63
1995			
June	6.57	7.42	5.61
Dec.	6.06	7.02	5.46
1996			
June	7.06	8.00	5.82
Dec.	6.55	7.45	5.47
1997			
June	6.77	7.71	5.39
Dec.	5.99	6.68	5.07

Period	Treasury 30-year bonds(1)	New Aa corporate bonds(2)	New Aa municipal bonds(3)
1998			
Jun	5.70	6.43	5.01
Dec	5.06	6.13	4.90
1999			
Jun.	6.04	7.21	5.31
Dec.	6.35	7.55	5.91
2000			
June	5.93	7.75	5.74
Dec.	5.49	7.21	5.23
2001			
June	5.67	7.11	5.18
Dec.	5.48	6.80	5.22
2002			
Jan.	5.45	6.75	5.09
March	5.93	6.79	5.07
June	5.65	6.57	5.02

(1) Treasury bond rate is for a 30-year maturity prior to Feb. 2002 and for a 20-year maturity thereafter. (2) Treasury series based on 3-week moving average of reoffering yields of new corporate bonds rated Aa by Moody's Investors Service with an original maturity of at least 20 years. (3) Index of new reoffering yields on 20-year general obligations rated Aa by Moody's Investors Service.

Performance of Mutual Funds by Type, 2002

Source: Thomson Financial, Rockville, MD, 800-232-2285
(data for period ending Sept. 30, 2002)

Fund Type/Fund Objective	AVERAGE RETURN 1–year	3–year	5–year
Diversified Stock			
Aggressive Growth	–21.08%	–15.35%	–6.78%
Equity Income	–15.84	–7.73	–2.3
Growth–Domestic	–19.39	–12.19	–3.46
Growth & Income	–17.39	–8.62	–1.9
Mid Cap	–12.94	–5.79	–0.4
S&P 500 Index	–18.61	–12.71	–1.89
Small Cap	–10.48	–2.64	–1.65
Specialty Stock			
Sector–Energy/Natural Res	2.13	1.24	–3.09
Sector–Financial Services	–10.72	2.01	2.53
Sector–Precious Metals	47.12	8.38	–1.63
Sector–Health/Biotechnology	–24.25	4.14	3.95
Sector–Other	–12.91	–8.24	–2.6
Sector–Real Estate	7.7	12.18	2.91
Sector–Tech/Communications	–33.76	–31.02	–10.03
Sector–Utilities	–30.22	–14.02	–3.18
World Stock			
Emerging Market Equity	6.99	–8.06	–10.15
Global Equity	–16.74	–12.36	–4.89
Non–US Equity	–11.46	–12.35	–6.52
Emerging Market Income	5.72	9.08	1.01
Hybrid			
Asset Allocation–Domestic	–10.08	–4.71	0.09
Asset Allocation–Global	–11.4%	–6.36%	–2.59%
Balanced–Domestic	–9.53	–3.77	0.47
Balanced–Global	–12.56	–8.21	–2.6
Bond			
Corporate–High Yield	–2.66	–4.75	–2.51
Corporate–Investment Grade	5.8	7.05	5.79
Convertible	–6.67	–2.64	0.21
General Bd–Investment Grade	5.37	7.06	5.8
General Bd–Long	6.37	7.71	5.98
General Bd–Short & Interm	4.7	6.61	5.8
General Mortgage	6.22	7.55	6.26
Global Income	6.1	3.78	2.85
Loan Participation	–0.07	2.15	3.89
Multi–Sector Bond	5.13	4.53	3.56
US Government/Agency	7.26	8.09	6.43
US Government–Long	9.12	9.4	7.33
US Government–Short & Interm	6.37	7.53	6.2
US Treasury	9.39	9.46	7.6
Municipal Bond			
Municipal–High Yield	5.94	4.55	3.95
Municipal–Insured	8.42	7.78	5.63
Municipal–National	7.03	6.78	5.11
Municipal–Single State	7.48	7.08	5.23

The Richest 400

The Sept. 30, 2002, issue of *Forbes* contained the magazine's latest annual roster of the 400 wealthiest Americans. Here are the top ten (with *Forbes*'s estimate of their net worth):

1 Microsoft chief Bill Gates, $43 bil.
2 Berkshire Hathaway magnate Warren Buffett $36 bil.
3 Microsoft co-founder Paul Allen, $21 bil.
4-8 Heirs of Wal-Mart founder Sam Walton—Alice L. Walton, Helen R. Walton, Jim C. Walton, John T. Walton, S. Robson Walton, each $18.8 bil.
9 Oracle chief Larry Ellison, $15.2 bil.
10 Microsoft exec. Steve Ballmer, $11.9 bil.

The total estimated net worth of all 400 on the list came to $872 bil, down from $946 bil in 2001 and $1.2 tril in 2000.

Chicago Board of Trade, Contracts Traded 1992, 2001

Source: Chicago Board of Trade

	1992	2001	% change 1992-2001
FUTURES GROUP			
Agricultural	31,783,316	49,021,270	54.2
Financial	89,121,811	156,024,293	75.1
Stock index	360,879	4,926,973	1365.3
Metals	63,548	15,466	–75.7
Total futures	**121,329,766**	**209,988,002**	**73.1**
OPTIONS GROUP			
Agricultural	5,145,395	11,779,493	128.9
Financial	23,533,861	38,277,207	62.6
Stock index	2,215	288,364	12918.7
Metals	20,105	4	–100.0
PCS insurance	50	—	–100.0
Total options	**28,701,626**	**50,345,068**	**75.4**
COMBINED FUTURES AND OPTIONS			
Agricultural	36,928,711	60,800,763	64.6
Financial	112,655,672	194,301,500	72.5
Stock index	363,094	5,215,337	1336.4
Metals	83,653	15,470	–81.5
PCS insurance	262	—	–100.0
GRAND TOTAL	**150,031,392**	**260,333,070**	**73.5**

U.S. Mutual Fund Shareholders[1]

Source: The Investment Company Institute

Shareholder Characteristics, 2001	
Median age[2]	46
Median annual household Income	$62,100
Median household financial assets	$100,000
Median number of funds owned	4
Median year of first fund purchase	1990
Employed[2]	78%
Married or living with a partner	67%
Spouse or partner employed	77%
Four-year college degree or more[2]	52%
Owning:	
Equity funds	88%
Bond funds	37%
Hybrid funds	34%
Money market funds	48%

Year	**Households owning mutual funds (in millions)[3]**
1980	4.6
1984	10.2
1988	22.2
1992	25.8
1994	30.2
1996	36.8
1998	44.4
1999	48.4
2000	50.6
2001	54.2

(1) Data include households owning mutual funds inside and outside employer-sponsored retirement plans. (2) Refers to the household's responding financial decision maker for mutual fund investments. (3) Data from 1980-1988 exclude households owning mutual funds solely through employer-sponsored retirement plans.

Distribution of Financial Assets of U.S. Families[1]

Source: Federal Reserve System (by type of asset, in percent)

	1989	1992	1995	1998
TOTAL	100	100	100	100
Certificates of deposit	10.2	8.1	5.7	4.3
U.S. savings bonds	1.5	1.1	1.3	0.7
Bonds	10.2	8.4	6.3	4.3
Stocks	15.0	16.5	15.7	22.7
Mutual funds (excl. money market)	5.3	7.7	12.7	12.5
Retirement accounts	21.5	25.5	27.9	27.5
Cash value of life insurance	6.0	6.0	7.2	6.4
Other managed assets	6.6	5.4	5.9	8.6
Other financial	4.8	3.8	3.4	1.7
Financial assets as a percentage of total assets	30.4	31.5	36.6	40.6

(1) Data is from the triennial *Survey of Consumer Finances*; 2001 survey to be released in Feb. 2003.

Stock Ownership of U.S. Families, by Income and Age, 1989, 1992, 1995, and 1998[1]

Source: Federal Reserve System

(in percent, except as noted)

		Families having direct or indirect stock holdings[2]				Median value of portfolios for families with stock holdings (thousands of 1998 dollars)				Stock holdings as share of financial assets[3]			
		1989	1992	1995	1998	1989	1992	1995	1998	1989	1992	1995	1998
All families		**31.6%**	**36.7%**	**40.4%**	**48.8%**	**$10.8**	**$12.0**	**$15.4**	**$25.0**	**27.8%**	**33.7%**	**40.0%**	**53.9%**
Annual Income (in thousands of dollars):	Under $10	*	6.8	5.4	7.7	*	6.2	3.2	4.0	*	15.9	12.9	24.8
	$10-25	12.7	17.8	22.2	24.7	6.4	4.6	6.4	9.0	11.7	15.3	26.7	27.5
	$25-50	31.5	40.2	45.4	52.7	6.0	7.2	8.5	11.5	16.9	23.7	30.3	39.1
	$50-100	51.5	62.5	65.4	74.3	10.2	15.4	23.6	35.7	23.2	33.5	39.9	48.8
	Over $100	81.8	78.3	81.6	91.0	53.5	71.9	85.5	150.0	35.3	40.2	46.4	63.0
By age of family head (years):	Under 35	22.4	28.3	36.6	40.7	3.8	4.0	5.4	7.0	20.2	24.8	27.2	44.8
	35-44	38.9	42.4	46.4	56.5	6.6	8.6	10.6	20.0	29.2	31.0	39.5	54.7
	45-54	41.8	46.4	48.9	58.6	16.7	17.1	27.6	38.0	33.5	40.6	42.9	55.7
	55-64	36.2	45.3	40.0	55.9	23.4	28.5	32.9	47.0	27.6	37.3	44.4	58.3
	65-74	26.7	30.2	34.4	42.6	25.8	18.3	36.1	56.0	26.0	31.6	35.8	51.3
	75 +	25.9	25.7	27.9	29.4	31.8	28.5	21.2	60.0	25.0	25.4	39.8	48.7

*Denotes insufficient data. (1) Data is from the triennial *Survey of Consumer Finances*; 2001 survey to be released in Feb. 2003. (2) Indirect holdings are those in mutual funds, retirement accounts, and other managed assets. (3) Among stock holding families.

Minerals

Source: U.S. Geological Survey, U.S. Dept. of the Interior; as of mid-2002; minerals.usgs.gov/minerals

Aluminum: the 2nd-most-abundant metallic element in the earth's crust. Bauxite is the main source of aluminum. Guinea, Brazil, and Australia have 60% of the world's reserves. Main uses in the U.S. are transportation (35%), packaging (25%), and construction (15%).

Chromium: most of the world's production of chromium ore is in India, Kazakhstan, and South Africa. The chemical and metallurgical industries use about 90% of the chromite consumed in the world.

Cobalt: used in superalloys for jet engines, chemicals, permanent magnets, tool steels, and cemented carbides for cutting tools. Congo (Kinshasa), Zambia, Australia, Canada, and Russia account for most of the world cobalt production.

Construction Aggregates: construction sand and gravel and crushed stone are 2 of the most accessible natural resources in the world. Construction sand and gravel is produced in every U.S. state, and crushed stone is mined in every state except Delaware. They are used in construction, agriculture, chemicals, and metallurgy and are produced worldwide.

Copper: main uses of copper in the U.S. are in building construction (42%), electrical and electronic products (26%), transportation (11%), industrial machinery and equipment (11%), and consumer and general products (10%). The leading mine producers are Chile, the U.S. (in Arizona, Utah, and New Mexico), Indonesia, Australia, Peru, Canada, and China.

Gold: used in the U.S. in jewelry and the arts (85%), dentistry (11%), electrical applications and electronics, and other industries (4%). South Africa has about half of the world's resources; significant quantities are also present in the U.S. (mined in most western states and Alaska), Australia, Russia, Uzbekistan, Canada, and Brazil.

Gypsum: used in wallboard and plaster products, cement production, and agriculture. Leading producers are the U.S., Iran, Canada, Mexico, and Spain.

Iron ore: the source of primary iron for the world's iron and steel industries. Major iron ore producers include Brazil, Australia, China, India, Russia, Ukraine, and the U.S.

Lead: Australia, China, the U.S., and Peru are the world's largest producers of lead. Major end uses in the U.S. are transportation (with 75% used in batteries, bearings, casting metals, and solders), other batteries, construction sheeting, sporting ammunition, and power cable coverings. The U.S. produces and consumes about 22% and 25%, respectively, of the world's lead metal (primary and recycled).

Manganese: essential to iron and steel production. South Africa and the former Soviet Union have over 80% of the world's identified resources.

Nickel: vital to the stainless steel industry; and used to make superalloys. Leading producers are Russia, Australia, Canada, New Caledonia, and Indonesia.

Platinum-Group Metals: this group consists of 6 metals: platinum, palladium, rhodium, ruthenium, iridium, and osmium. They commonly occur together in nature and are among the scarcest of the metallic elements. In the U.S., the automotive and chemical industries use PGMs mainly as catalysts. They also are consumed in electrical and electronic, dental, and medical industries. Russia and South Africa have most of the world's reserves.

Phosphate Rock: used in fertilizers, animal feed supplements, chemicals, and food. Phosphorus is an essential element for plant and animal nutrition. The U.S., Morocco, China, Russia, and Tunisia are the world's leading producers.

Salt: used in chemicals, highway de-icing, industry, agriculture, food, and water treatment. Leading producers are the U.S., China, Germany, India, and Canada.

Silver: used in photography, electrical and electronic products, sterlingware, electroplated ware, and jewelry in the U.S. Silver is mined in more than 60 countries. Nevada produces more than 40% of U.S. silver, and Idaho 16%.

Soda Ash: a raw material for glass, chemicals, and detergents, it can be mined or produced synthetically. The U.S. is, by far, the world's leading producer of natural soda ash.

Sulfur: used in agricultural chemicals production, oil refining, metal mining, and many other industries. It is produced as a byproduct of oil refining, natural gas processing, and nonferrous metal smelting. Leading producers are Canada, the U.S., Russia, China, and Japan.

Titanium: ilmenite and rutile are the major mineral sources of titanium. About 95% of titanium minerals is used to produce TiO_2 pigments. The remainder is mainly used to produce metals, chemicals, and ceramics. Major mining operations are in Australia, Canada, Norway, and South Africa. U.S. mine production is in Florida and Virginia.

Zinc: used as a protective coating on steel, as diecastings, as an alloying metal with copper to make brass, and as a component of chemical compounds in rubber and paints. Leading producers are China, Australia, Peru, Canada, the U.S. (in Alaska, Tennessee, and Missouri), and Mexico.

World Mineral Reserve Base, 2001

Source: U.S. Geological Survey, U.S. Dept. of the Interior; as of year-end 2001

Mineral	Reserve Base[1]
Aluminum	34,000 mil metric tons[2]
Chromium	7,600 mil metric tons[3]
Cobalt	10 mil metric tons
Copper	650 mil metric tons
Gold	78,000 metric tons[4]
Iron Ore	310,000 mil metric tons
Lead	130 mil metric tons
Manganese	5,000 mil metric tons
Nickel	160 mil metric tons
Phosphate Rock	47,000 mil metric tons
Platinum-Group Metals	73,000 metric tons
Silver	430,000 metric tons
Soda Ash (Natural)	40,000 mil metric tons
Titanium (ilmenite/rutile)	540 mil metric tons[5]
Zinc	440 mil metric tons

(1) Includes demonstrated reserves that are currently economic or marginally economic, plus some that are currently subeconomic. (2) Bauxite. (3) Chromite ore. (4) Excludes China and some other countries for which reliable data were not available. (5) Titanium dioxide (TiO_2) content of ilmenite and rutile.

U.S. Nonfuel Mineral Production—10 Leading States in 2001

Source: U.S. Geological Survey, U.S. Dept. of the Interior

Rank	State	Value (in mil $)	Percent of U.S. total	Principal minerals, in order of value
1.	California	3,250	8.35	Sand & gravel (construction), cement, boron minerals, stone (crushed), gold
2.	Nevada	2,930	7.53	Gold, sand & gravel (construction), silver, lime, cement
3.	Texas	2,210	5.68	Cement, stone (crushed), sand & gravel (construction), salt, lime
4.	Arizona	2,110	5.43	Copper, sand & gravel (construction), cement, stone (crushed), lime
5.	Florida	1,750	4.50	Phosphate rock, stone (crushed), cement, sand & gravel (construction)
6.	Michigan	1,620	4.17	Cement, iron ore, sand & gravel (construction), stone (crushed), magnesium compounds
7.	Georgia	1,610	4.13	Clays, stone (crushed), cement, sand & gravel (construction)
8.	Minnesota	1,440	3.70	Iron ore, sand & gravel (construction), stone (crushed & dimension), sand & gravel (industrial)
9.	Missouri	1,340	3.45	Stone (crushed), cement, lead, lime, zinc
10.	Utah	1,310	3.36	Copper, gold, cement, sand & gravel (construction), salt

U.S. Nonfuel Minerals Production

Source: U.S. Geological Survey, U.S. Dept. of the Interior

Production as measured by mine shipments, sales, or marketable production (including consumption by producers).

		1996	1997	1998	1999	2000	2001
Beryllium (metal equivalent)	metric tons	211	231	243	200	180	100
Copper (recoverable content of ores, etc.)	thousand metric tons	1,920	1,940	1,860	1,600	1,440	1,340
Gold (recoverable content of ores, etc.)	metric tons	326.0	362.0	366.0	341.0	353.0	335
Iron ore, usable (includes byproduct material)	million metric tons	62.1	63.0	62.9	57.7	63.1	46.2
Lead (in concentrate)	thousand metric tons	426	448	481	503	457	454
Magnesium metal (primary)	thousand metric tons	133	125	106	W	W	W
Molybdenum (content of ore and concentrate)	metric tons	56,000	58,900	53,300	43,000	41,000	37,600
Nickel (content of ore and concentrate)	metric tons	1,333	—	—	—	—	—
Silver (recoverable content of ores, etc.)	metric tons	1,570	2,180	2,060	1,950	1,860	1,740
Zinc (recoverable content of ores, etc.)	thousand metric tons	586	592	709	808	786	799
Asbestos	thousand metric tons	10	7	6	7	5	5
Barite	thousand metric tons	662	692	476	434	392	400
Boron minerals	thousand metric tons	581	604	587	618	564	536
Bromine	million kilograms	227	247	230	239	228	212
Cement (portland, masonry, etc.)	thousand metric tons	79,266	82,582	83,931	86,600[E]	87,846	88,861
Clays	thousand metric tons	43,100	41,800	41,900	42,200	40,800	40,600
Diatomite	thousand metric tons	729	773	725	747	677	644
Feldspar	thousand metric tons	890	900[E]	820[E]	875[E]	790[E]	800[E]
Fluorspar	thousand metric tons	8	—	—	—	—	NA
Garnet (industrial)	metric tons	60,900	64,900	74,000	60,700	60,200	52,700
Gemstones	million dollars	43.6	25.0	14.3	16.1	17.2	15.1
Gypsum	thousand metric tons	17,500	18,600	19,000	22,400	19,500	16,300
Helium (extracted from natural gas)	million cubic meters	103	116	112.0	118[E]	117[E]	100[E]
Helium (Grade A sold)	million cubic meters	95	107	112.0	108[E]	125[E]	137[E]
Iodine	thousand kilograms	1,270	1,320	1,490	1,620	1,470	1,290
Lime	thousand metric tons	19,225	19,678	20,132	19,565	19,555	18,941
Mica (scrap & flake)	thousand metric tons	97	114	87	104	101	97
Peat	thousand metric tons	549	661	685	731	755	870
Perlite (sold and used by producers)	thousand metric tons	684	706	685	711	672	588
Phosphate rock (marketable product)	thousand metric tons	45,400	45,900	44,200	40,600	38,600	31,900
Potash (K2O equivalent)	thousand metric tons	1,390	1,400	1,300	1,200	1,300	1,200
Pumice and pumicite	thousand metric tons	612	577	583	643	697	618
Salt	thousand metric tons	42,900	40,600	40,800	41,000	43,300	42,200
Sand and gravel (construction)	thousand metric tons	914,000	961,000	1,080,000	1,080,000[E]	1,120	1,120
Sand and gravel (industrial)	thousand metric tons	27,800	28,500	28,200	28,900	28,400	27,900
Soda ash (sodium carbonate)	thousand metric tons	10,200	10,700	10,100	10,200	10,200	10,300
Sodium sulfate (natural)	thousand metric tons	306	318	290	NA	NA	NA
Stone (crushed)	million metric tons	1,330	1,410	1,510	1,560[E]	1,560	1,600
Stone (dimension)	thousand metric tons	1,150	1,180	1,140	1,250[E]	1,254	1,280
Sulfur (in all forms)	thousand metric tons	12,000	12,000	11,600[E]	11,300	10,300	9,250
Talc	thousand metric tons	994	1,050	971	925	851	853

(W) Withheld to avoid disclosing company proprietary data. (—) No production. (E) Estimated. (NA) Not available.

U.S. Reliance on Foreign Supplies of Minerals

Source: U.S. Geological Survey, U.S. Dept. of the Interior

Mineral	% Imported in 2001	Major sources (1997-2000)	Major Uses
Arsenic (trioxide)	100%	China, Chile, Mexico	Wood preservatives, nonferrous alloys
Asbestos	100	Canada	Roofing products, gaskets, friction products
Bauxite & alumina	100	Australia, Guinea, Jamaica, Brazil	Aluminum production, refractories, abrasives, chemicals
Columbium (niobium)	100	Brazil, Canada, Germany, Russia	Steelmaking, superalloys
Fluorspar	100	China, S. Africa, Mexico	Hydrofluoric acid, aluminum fluoride, steelmaking
Graphite (natural)	100	China, Mexico, Canada, Brazil	Refractories, brake linings, pencils
Manganese	100	S. Africa, Gabon, Australia, Mexico	Steelmaking, batteries, agricultural chemicals
Mica, sheet (natural)	100	India, Belgium, Germany, China	Electronic & electrical equipment
Quartz crystal	100	Brazil, Germany, Madagascar	Electronics, optical applications
Strontium	100	Mexico, Germany	Television picture tubes, ferrite magnets, pyrotechnics
Thallium	100	Belgium, Canada, Germany, UK, France	Electronics, alloys, glass
Thorium	100	France, Canada, Japan, Singapore	Ceramics, catalysts, welding electrodes
Vanadium	100	Canada, S. Africa, China, Austria	Steelmaking, catalysts
Yttrium	100	China, Japan, UK, Germany	Television phosphors, fluorescent lights, oxygen sensors
Gemstones	99	Israel, India, Belgium	Jewelry, carvings, gem & mineral collections
Bismuth	95	Belgium, Mexico, UK, China	Pharmaceuticals, chemicals, alloys, metallurgical additives
Indium	95	Canada, China, Russia, France	Coatings, solders, alloys, electrical components
Tin	88	China, Peru, Indonesia, Brazil, Bolivia	Solder, tinplate, chemicals, alloys
Barite	87	China, India, Canada, Mexico	Oil & gas well drilling fluids, chemicals
Palladium	87	Russia, S. Africa, Belgium, UK	Catalysts, dental, electronics, electrical
Antimony	86	China, Mexico, S. Africa, Belgium, Bolivia	Flame retardants, batteries, chemicals, ceramics & glass
Diamond (natural)	83	UK, Switzerland, Ireland, Belgium	Abrasives
Potash	80	Canada, Russia, Belarus	Fertilizers, chemicals
Stone (dimension)	80	Italy, Brazil, Canada, India	Construction, monuments
Tantalum	80	Australia, China, Thailand, Japan	Capacitors, superalloys, cemented carbide tools
Chromium	78	S. Africa, Kazakhstan, Russia, Turkey, Zimbabwe	Steel, chemicals, refractories
Cobalt	78	Finland, Norway, Canada, Russia	Superalloys, cemented carbides, magnetic alloys, chemicals
Iodine	72	Chile, Japan,Russia	Sanitation, pharmaceuticals, heat stabilizers, catalysts
Titanium concent.	72	S. Africa, Australia, Canada, Ukraine	Pigment, welding rod coatings, metal, carbides, chemicals
Rhenium	71	Chile, Kazakhstan, Germany, Russia	Superalloys, petroleum-reforming catalysts
Rare earths	68	China, France, Japan, UK	Catalysts, glass polishing, ceramics, magnets, metallurgy
Platinum	66	S. Africa, UK, Germany, Russia	Catalysts, jewelry, dental & medical alloys
Zinc	60	Canada, Mexico, Peru	Galvanizing, zinc-base alloys, brass & bronze
Tungsten	59	China, Russia, Germany, Portugal	Cemented carbides, electrical & electronic components
Titanium (sponge)	58	Russia, Japan, Kazakhstan	Aerospace, armor, chemical processing, power generation
Nickel	56	Canada, Norway, Russia, Australia	Stainless and alloy steel, nonferrous and super alloys
Peat	50	Canada	Horticulture, agriculture

U.S. Copper, Lead, and Zinc Production, 1950-2001

Source: U.S. Geological Survey, U.S. Dept. of the Interior

Year	Copper Quantity (metric tons) (1,000)	Copper Value ($1,000)	Lead Quantity (metric tons)	Lead Value ($1,000)	Zinc Quantity (metric tons)	Zinc Value ($1,000)	Year	Copper Quantity (metric tons) (1,000)	Copper Value ($1,000)	Lead Quantity (metric tons)	Lead Value ($1,000)	Zinc Quantity (metric tons)	Zinc Value ($1,000)
1950	827	379,122	390,839	113,078	565,516	167,000	1993	1,800	3,635,000	355,185	248,540	488,283	490,795
1960	1,037	733,706	223,774	57,722	395,013	112,365	1994	1,850	4,430,000	363,000	298,000	570,000	619,000
1970	1,560	1,984,484	518,698	178,609	484,560	163,650	1995	1,850	5,640,000	386,000	359,000	603,000	756,000
1975	1,282	1,814,763	563,783	267,230	425,792	366,097	1996	1,920	4,610,000	426,000	459,000	586,000	660,000
1980	1,181	2,666,931	550,366	515,189	317,103	261,671	1997	1,940	4,570,000	448,000	460,000	605,000	860,000
1985	1,105	1,631,000	413,955	174,008	226,545	201,607	1998	1,860	3,235,000	481,000	480,000	722,000	819,000
1990	1,586	431,000	483,704	490,750	515,355	847,485	1999	1,600	2,680,000	503,000	485,000	808,000	953,000
1991	1,630	3,931,000	465,931	343,907	517,804	602,426	2000	1,440	2,800,000	449,000	430,000	805,000	987,000
1992	1,760	4,179,000	397,076	307,337	523,430	673,800	2001	1,340	2,270,000	454,000	440,000	799,000	774,000

U.S. Pig Iron and Raw Steel Output, 1940-2000

Source: American Iron and Steel Institute
(net tons)

Year	Total pig iron	Raw steel[1]	Year	Total pig iron	Raw steel[1]	Year	Total pig iron	Raw steel[1]
1940	46,071,666	66,982,686	1975	79,923,000	116,642,000	1994	54,426,000	100,579,000
1945	53,223,169	79,701,648	1980	68,721,000	111,835,000	1995	56,097,000	104,930,000
1950	64,586,907	96,836,075	1985	50,446,000	88,259,000	1996	54,485,000	105,309,478
1955	76,857,417	117,036,085	1990	54,750,000	98,906,000	1997	54,079,000	108,561,182
1960	66,480,648	99,281,601	1991	48,637,000	87,896,000	1998	53,164,000	108,752,334
1965	88,184,901	131,461,601	1992	52,224,000	92,949,000	1999	51,002,000	107,395,010
1970	91,435,000	131,514,000	1993	53,082,000	97,877,000	2000	52,787,000	112,242,000

(1) Steel figures include only that portion of the capacity and production of steel for castings used by foundries operated by companies producing steel ingots.

World Gold Production, 1975-2001[1]

Source: U.S. Geological Survey, U.S. Dept. of the Interior
(thousands of troy ounces)

		Africa			North and South America				Other			
Year	World prod.	South Africa	Ghana	Congo Dem. Rep.	United States	Canada	Mexico	Colombia	Australia	China	Philip-pines	USSR/ Russia[2]
1975	38,476	22,938	524	116	1,052	1,654	145	309	527	NA	503	NA
1980	39,197	21,669	353	96	970	1,627	106	510	548	NA	753	8,425
1985	49,284	21,565	299	257	2,427	2,815	266	1,142	1,881	1,950	1,063	8,700
1990	70,207	19,454	541	299	9,458	5,447	311	944	7,849	3,215	791	9,710
1991	70,423	19,326	846	283	9,454	5,676	326	1,120	7,530	3,858	833	8,359
1992	73,530	19,743	998	225	10,617	5,189	318	1,033	7,825	4,501	730	8,232
1993	73,300	19,908	1,250	280	10,642	4,917	357	883	7,948	5,144	509	8,228
1994	72,500	16,650	1,400	357	10,500	4,710	447	668	8,237	4,240	870	8,173
1995	71,800	16,800	1,710	322	10,200	4,890	652	680	8,150	4,500	873	4,250
1996	73,600	16,000	1,580	264	10,500	5,350	787	710	9,310	4,660	970	3,960
1997	78,900	15,800	1,760	13	11,600	5,510	836	605	10,100	5,630	1,050	3,990
1998	80,400	14,900	2,330	5	11,800	5,320	817	605	10,000	5,720	1,090	3,690
1999	82,300	14,500	2,570	7	11,000	5,070	764	1,410	9,680	5,560	1,000	4,050
2000	82,900	13,800	2,320	2	11,300	5,020	848	1,190	9,530	5,790	965	4,600
2001	82,600	12,900	2,210	2	10,800	5,130	846	701	9,160	5,950	965	4,890

(1) Figures are rounded. (2) Figures for 1975-94 are for USSR as constituted prior to Dec. 1991; after 1994, Russia only. NA = Not available.

U.S. and World Silver Production, 1930-2001

Source: U.S. Geological Survey, U.S. Dept. of the Interior
(metric tons)

Year[1]	United States	World	Year[1]	United States	World	Year[1]	United States	World	Year[1]	United States	World
1930	1,578	7,736	1960	1,120	7,505	1990	2,120	16,600	1996	1,570	15,100
1935	1,428	6,865	1965	1,238	8,007	1991	1,860	15,600	1997	2,180	16,500
1940	2,164	8,565	1970	1,400	9,670	1992	1,800	14,600	1998	2,060	16,200
1945	904	5,039	1975	1,087	9,428	1993	1,640	14,300	1999	1,950	16,600
1950	1,347	6,323	1980	1,006	10,556	1994	1,490	14,000	2000	1,860	18,300
1955	1,134	9,967	1985	1,227	13,051	1995	1,560	15,100	2001	1,740	18,400

(1) Largest production of silver in the United States was in 1915—2,332 metric tons.

Aluminum Summary, 1980-2001

Source: U.S. Geological Survey, U.S. Dept. of the Interior

Item	Unit	1980	1985	1990	1995	1996[4]	1997[4]	1998[4]	1999[4]	2000[4]	2001[4]
U.S. production	1,000 metric tons	6,231	5,262	6,441	6,563	6,860	7,150	7,150	7,530	7,120	5,620
Primary aluminum	1,000 metric tons	4,654	3,500	4,048	3,375	3,577	3,603	3,713	3,779	3,668	2,637
Secondary aluminum[1]	1,000 metric tons	1,577	1,762	2,393	3,188	3,310	3,550	3,440	3,750	3,450	2,980
Primary aluminum value	Billion dollars	7.8	3.8	6.6	6.4	5.6	6.1	5.4	5.5	6.0	4.0
Price (Primary aluminum)[2]	Cents/pound	76.1	48.8	74.0	85.9	71.3	77.1	65.5	65.7	74.6	68.8
Imports for consumption[3]	1,000 metric tons	647	1,420	1,514	2,975	2,810	3,080	3,550	4,000	3,910	3,740
Exports[3]	1,000 metric tons	1,346	908	1,659	1,610	1,500	1,570	1,590	1,650	1,760	1,590
World production	1,000 metric tons	15,383	15,398	19,299	19,700	20,700	21,600	22,500	23,100	24,000	24,400

(1) Recoverable metal content from purchased scrap, old and new. (2) Average prices for primary aluminum, quoted by *Metals Week*. (3) Crude and semicrude (incl. metal and alloys, plates, bars, etc., and scrap). (4) All tonnage data, except primary production, have been rounded to 3 significant figures.

Economic and Financial Glossary

Source: Reviewed by William M. Gentry, Graduate School of Business, Columbia University

Annuity contract: An investment vehicle sold by insurance companies. Annuity buyers can elect to receive periodic payments for the rest of their lives. Annuities provide insurance against outliving one's wealth.

Arbitrage: A form of hedged investment meant to capture slight differences in the prices of 2 related securities—for example, buying gold in London and selling it at a higher price in New York.

Balanced budget: A budget is balanced when receipts equal expenditures. When receipts exceed expenditures, there is a **surplus;** when they fall short of expenditures, there is a **deficit.**

Balance of payments: The difference between all payments, for some categories of transactions, made to and from foreign countries over a set period of time. A *favorable* balance of payments exists when more payments are coming in than going out; an *unfavorable* balance of payments obtains when the reverse is true. Payments may include gold, the cost of merchandise and services, interest and dividend payments, money spent by travelers, and repayment of principal on loans.

Balance of trade (trade gap): The difference between exports and imports, in both actual funds and credit. A nation's balance of trade is *favorable* when exports exceed imports and *unfavorable* when the reverse is true.

Bear market: A market in which prices are falling.

Bearer bond: A bond issued in bearer form rather than being registered in a specific owner's name. Ownership is determined by possession.

Bond: A written promise, or IOU, by the issuer to repay a fixed amount of borrowed money on a specified date and generally to pay interest at regular intervals in the interim.

Bull market: A market in which prices are on the rise.

Capital gain (loss): An increase (decrease) in the market value of an asset over some period of time. For tax purposes, capital gains are typically calculated from when an asset is bought to when it is sold.

Commercial paper: An extremely short-term corporate IOU, generally due in 270 days or less.

Convertible bond: A corporate bond (see below) that may be converted into a stated number of shares of common stock. Its price tends to fluctuate along with fluctuations in the price of the stock and with changes in interest rates.

Consumer price index (CPI): A statistical measure of the change in the price of consumer goods.

Corporate bond: A bond issued by a corporation. The bond normally has a stated life and pays a fixed rate of interest. Considered safer than the common or preferred stock of the same company.

Cost of living: The cost of maintaining a standard of living measured in terms of purchased goods and services. Inflation typically measures changes in the cost of living.

Cost-of-living adjustments: Changes in promised payments, such as retirement benefits, to account for changes in the cost of living.

Credit crunch (liquidity crisis): A situation in which cash for lending is in short supply.

Debenture: An unsecured bond backed only by the general credit of the issuing corporation.

Deficit spending: Government spending in excess of revenues, generally financed with the sale of bonds. A deficit increases the government debt.

Deflation: A decrease in the level of prices.

Depression: A long period of economic decline when prices are low, unemployment is high, and there are many business failures.

Derivatives: Financial contracts, such as options, whose values are based on, or *derived* from, the price of an underlying financial asset or indicator such as a stock or an interest rate.

Devaluation: The official lowering of a nation's currency, decreasing its value in relation to foreign currencies.

Discount rate: The rate of interest set by the Federal Reserve that member banks are charged when borrowing money through the Federal Reserve System.

Disposable income: Income after taxes that is available to persons for spending and saving.

Diversification: Investing in more than one asset in order to reduce the riskiness of the overall asset portfolio. By holding more than one asset, losses on some assets may be offset by gains realized on other assets.

Dividend: Discretionary payment by a corporation to its shareholders, usually in the form of cash or stock shares.

Dow Jones Industrial Average: An index of stock market prices, based on the prices of 30 companies, 28 of which are on the New York Stock Exchange.

Econometrics: The use of statistical methods to study economic and financial data.

Federal Deposit Insurance Corporation (FDIC): A U.S. government-sponsored corporation that insures accounts in national banks and other qualified institutions against bank failures.

Federal Reserve System: The entire banking system of the U.S., incorporating 12 Federal Reserve banks (one in each of 12 Federal Reserve districts), 25 Federal Reserve branch banks, all national banks, and state-chartered commercial banks and trust companies that have been admitted to its membership. The governors of the system greatly influence the nation's monetary and credit policies.

Full employment: The economy is said to be at full employment when everyone who wishes to work at the going wage-rate for his or her type of labor is employed, save only for the small amount of unemployment due to the time it takes to switch from one job to another.

Futures: A futures contract is an agreement to buy or sell a specific amount of a commodity or financial instrument at a particular price at a set date in the future. For example, futures based on a stock index (such as the Dow Jones Industrial Average) are bets on the future price of that group of stocks.

Golden parachute: Provisions in contracts of some high-level executives guaranteeing substantial severance benefits if they lose their position in a corporate takeover.

Government bond: A bond issued by the U.S. Treasury, considered a safe investment. Government bonds are divided into 2 categories—those that are not marketable and those that are. *Savings bonds* cannot be bought and sold once the original purchase is made. Marketable bonds fall into several categories. *Treasury bills* are short-term U.S. obligations, maturing in 3, 6, or 12 months. *Treasury notes* mature in up to 10 years. *Treasury bonds* mature in 10 to 30 years. *Indexed bonds* are adjusted for inflation.

Greenmail: A company buying back its own shares for more than the going market price to avoid a threatened hostile takeover.

Gross domestic product (GDP): The market value of all goods and services that have been bought for final use during a period of time. It became the official measure of the size of the U.S. economy in 1991, replacing *gross national product (GNP),* in use since 1941. GDP covers workers and capital employed within the nation's borders. GNP covers production by U.S. residents regardless of where it takes place. The switch aligned U.S. terminology with that of most other industrialized countries.

Hedge fund: A flexible investment fund for a limited number of large investors (the minimum investment is typically $1 million). Hedge funds use a variety of investment techniques, including those forbidden to mutual funds, such as short-selling and heavy leveraging.

Hedging: Taking 2 positions whose gains and losses will offset each other if prices change, in order to limit risk.

Individual retirement account (IRA): A self-funded tax-advantaged retirement plan that allows employed individuals to contribute up to a maximum yearly sum. With a *traditional* IRA, individuals contribute pre-tax earnings and defer income taxes until retirement. With a *Roth* IRA, individuals contribute after-tax earnings but do not pay taxes on future withdrawals (the interest is never taxed). *401(k) plans* are employer-sponsored plans similar to traditional IRAs, but having higher contribution limits.

Inflation: An increase in the level of prices.

Insider information: Important facts about the condition or plans of a corporation that have not been released to the general public.

Interest: The cost of borrowing money.

Investment bank: A financial institution that arranges the initial issuance of stocks and bonds and offers companies advice about acquisitions and divestitures.

Junk bonds: Bonds issued by companies with low credit ratings. They typically pay relatively high interest rates because of the fear of default.

Leading indicators: A series of 11 indicators from different segments of the economy used by the U.S. Commerce Department to predict when changes in the level of economic activity will occur.

Leverage: The extent to which a purchase was paid for with borrowed money. Amplifies the potential gain or loss for the purchaser.

Leveraged buyout (LBO): An acquisition of a company in which much of the purchase price is borrowed, with the debt to be repaid from future profits or by subsequently selling off company assets. A leveraged buyout is typically carried out by a small group of investors, often including incumbent management.

Liquid assets: Assets consisting of cash and/or items that are easily converted into cash.

Margin account: A brokerage account that allows a person to trade securities on credit. A **margin call** is a demand for more collateral on the account.

Money supply: The currency held by the public, plus checking accounts in commercial banks and savings institutions.

Mortgage-backed securities: Created when a bank, builder, or government agency gathers together a group of mortgages and then sells bonds to other institutions and the public. The investors receive their proportionate share of the interest payments on the loans as well as the principal payments. Usually, the mortgages in question are guaranteed by the government.

Municipal bond: Issued by governmental units such as states, cities, local taxing authorities, and other agencies. Interest is exempt from U.S.—and sometimes state and local—income tax. *Municipal bond unit investment trusts* offer a portfolio of many different municipal bonds chosen by professionals. The income is exempt from federal income taxes.

Mutual fund: A portfolio of professionally bought and managed financial assets in which you pool your money along with that of many other people. A share price is based on net asset value, or the value of all the investments owned by the funds, less any debt, and divided by the total number of shares. The major advantage, relative to investing individually in only a small number of stocks, is less risk—the holdings are spread out over many assets and if one or two do badly the remainder may shield you from the losses. *Bond funds* are mutual funds that deal in the bond market exclusively. *Money market mutual funds* buy in the so-called money market—institutions that need to borrow large sums of money for short terms. These funds often offer special checking account advantages.

National debt: The debt of the national government, as distinguished from the debts of political subdivisions of the nation and of private business and individuals.

National debt ceiling: Total borrowing limit set by Congress beyond which the U.S. national debt cannot rise. This limit is periodically raised by congressional vote.

Option: A type of contractual agreement between a buyer and a seller to buy or sell shares of a security. A **call** option contract gives the right to purchase shares of a specific stock at a stated price within a given period of time. A **put** option contract gives the buyer the right to sell shares of a specific stock at a stated price within a given period of time.

Per capita income: The total income of a group divided by the number of people in the group.

Prime interest rate: The rate charged by banks on short-term loans to large commercial customers with the highest credit rating.

Producer price index: A statistical measure of the change in the price of wholesale goods. It is reported for 3 different stages of the production chain: crude, intermediate, and finished goods.

Program trading: Trading techniques involving large numbers and large blocks of stocks, usually used in conjunction with computer programs. Techniques include *index arbitrage,* in which traders profit from price differences between stocks and futures contracts on stock indexes, and *portfolio insurance,* which is the use of stock-index futures to protect stock investors from potentially large losses when the market drops.

Public debt: The total of a nation's debts owed by state, local, and national government. Increases in this sum, reflected in public-sector deficits, indicate how much of the nation's spending is being financed by borrowing rather than by taxation.

Recession: A mild decrease in economic activity marked by a decline in real (inflation-adjusted) GDP, employment, and trade, usually lasting from 6 months to a year, and marked by widespread decline in many sectors of the economy.

Savings Association Insurance Fund (SAIF): Created in 1989 to insure accounts in savings and loan associations up to $100,000.

Seasonal adjustment: Statistical changes made to compensate for regular fluctuations in data that are so great they tend to distort the statistics and make comparisons meaningless. For instance, seasonal adjustments are made for a slowdown in housing construction in midwinter and for the rise in farm income in the fall after summer crops are harvested.

Short-selling: Borrowing shares of stock from a brokerage firm and selling them, hoping to buy the shares back at a lower price, return them, and realize a profit from the decline in prices.

Stagnation: Economic slowdown in which there is little growth in the GDP, capital investment, and real income.

Stock: *Common stocks* are shares of ownership in a corporation. For publicly held firms, the stock typically trades on an exchange, such as the New York Stock Exchange; for closely held firms, the founders and managers own most of the stock. There can be wide swings in the prices of this kind of stock. *Preferred stock* is a type of stock on which a fixed dividend must be paid before holders of common stock are issued their share of the issuing corporation's earnings. Preferred stock is less risky than common stock. *Convertible preferred stock* can be converted into the common stock of the company that issued the preferred. *Over-the-counter stock* is not traded on the major or regional exchanges, but rather through dealers from whom you buy directly. *Blue chip* stocks are so called because they have been leading stocks for a long time. *Growth* stocks are from companies that reinvest their earnings, rather than pay dividends, with the expectation of future stock price appreciation.

Supply-side economics: A school of thinking about economic policy holding that lowering income tax rates will inevitably lead to enhanced economic growth and general revitalization of the economy.

Takeover: Acquisition of one company by another company or group by sale or merger. A *friendly takeover* occurs when the acquired company's management is agreeable to the merger; when management is opposed to the merger, it is a *hostile* takeover.

Tender offer: A public offer to buy a company's stock; usually priced at a premium above the market.

Zero coupon bond: A corporate or government bond that is issued at a deep discount from the maturity value and pays no interest during the life of the bond. It is redeemable at face value.

AGRICULTURE

U.S. Farms—Number and Acreage by State, 1995, 2000, 2001

Source: National Agricultural Statistics Service, U.S. Dept. of Agriculture

STATE	No. of farms (1,000) 2001	2000	Acreage in farms (mil.) 2001	2000	Acreage per farm 2001	2000
AL	47	47	8.9	9	189.4	191.5
AK	0.58	0.58	0.92	0.92	1,586.2	1,586.2
AZ	7.3	7.5	26.6	26.7	3,643.8	3,560
AR	48	48	14.6	14.6	304.2	304,2
CA	88	87.5	27.7	27.8	314.8	317.7
CO	30	29.5	31.3	31.6	1,043.3	1,071.2
CT	3.9	3.9	0.36	0.36	92.3	92.3
DE	2.5	2.6	0.57	0.58	228	223.1
FL	44	44	10.2	10.3	231.8	234.1
GA	50	50	11	11.1	220	222
HI	5.3	5.5	1.44	1.44	271.7	261.8
ID	24	24.5	11.9	11.9	495.8	485.7
IL	76	78	27.7	27.7	364.5	355.1
IN	63	64	15.4	15.5	244.4	242.2
IA	93.5	95	32.7	32.8	349.7	345.3
KS	63	64	47.4	47.5	752.4	742.2
KY	88	90	13.6	13.6	154.5	151.1
LA	29	29.5	8.05	8.1	277.6	274.6
ME	6.7	6.8	1.26	1.27	188.1	186.8
MD	12.4	12.4	2.1	2.1	169.4	169.4
MA	6	6.1	0.56	0.57	93.3	93.4
MI	52	52	10.4	10.4	200	200
MN	79	79	28.5	28.6	360.8	362
MS	42	43	11	11.1	261.9	258.1
MO	108	109	29.9	30	276.9	275.2
MT	26.6	27.6	56.5	56.7	2,124.1	2,054.3
NE	53	54	46.4	46.4	875.5	859.3
NV	3	3	6.8	6.8	2,266.7	2,266.7
NH	3.1	3.1	0.42	0.42	135.5	135.5
NJ	9.6	9.6	0.83	0.83	86.5	86.5
NM	15	15.2	44	44	2,933.3	2,894.7
NY	37.5	38	7.6	7.7	202.7	202.6
NC	56	57	9.1	9.2	162.5	161.4
ND	30.3	30.3	39.4	39.4	1,300.3	1,300.3
OH	78	80	14.8	14.9	189.7	186.3
OK	86	85	34	34	395.3	400
OR	40	40	17.2	17.2	430	430
PA	59	59	7.7	7.7	130.5	130.5
RI	0.7	0.7	0.06	0.06	85.7	85.7
SC	24	24	4.8	4.8	200	200
SD	32.5	32.5	44	44	1,353.8	1,353.8
TN	91	90	11.8	11.7	129.7	130
TX	227	226	130	130	572.7	575.2
UT	15	15.5	11.6	11.6	773.3	748.4
VT	6.6	6.7	1.34	1.34	203	200
VA	49	49	8.7	8.7	177.6	177.6
WA	39	40	15.7	15.7	402.6	392.5
WV	20.5	20.5	3.6	3.6	175.6	175.6
WI	77	77	16.2	16.2	210.4	210.4
WY	9.2	9.2	34.6	34.6	3,760.9	3,760.9
U.S.	**2,158**	**2,172**	**941.2**	**943.1**	**436.2**	**434.1**

U.S. Farms, 18940-2001

Source: National Agricultural Statistics Service, U.S. Dept. of Agriculture

The number of farms declined in 2001 (by about 1%), while the size of the average farm increased very slightly (by about 0.5%). These changes continued a decades-long trend toward fewer, but larger farming operations.

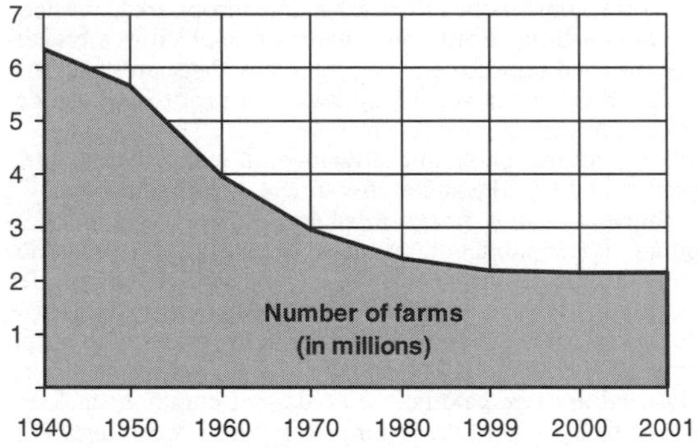

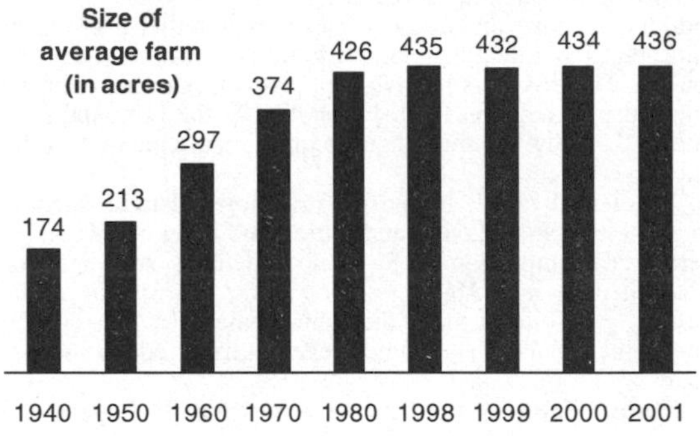

Decline in U.S. Farm Workers, 1820-1994*

Source: U.S. Dept. of Agriculture, Economic Research Service

Of the approximately 2.9 mil workers in the U.S. in 1820, 71.8%, or about 2.1 mil, were employed in farm occupations. The percentage of U.S. workers in farm occupations had declined drastically by the turn of the century, and by 1994 only 2.5% of all U.S. workers were employed in farm occupations.

(percent of total U.S. workers in farm occupations)

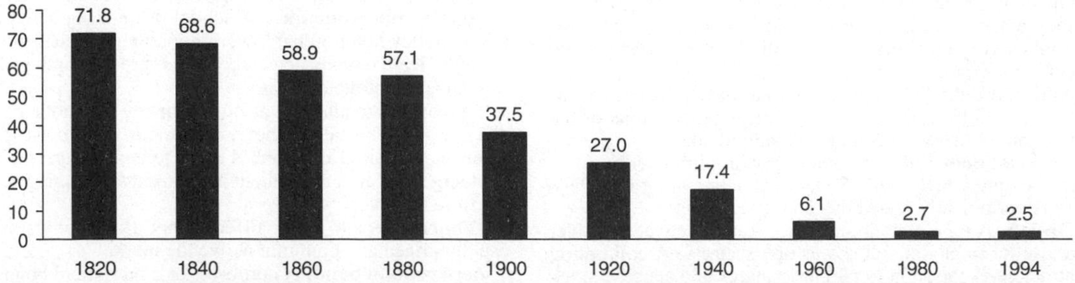

* Figures not compiled for years after 1994. Total workers for 1994 are employed workers age 15 and older; total workers for 1980 are members of the experienced civilian labor force ages 16 and older; total workers for 1900 to 1960 are members of the experienced civilian labor force 14 and older; total workers for 1820 to 1880 are gainfully employed workers 10 and older.

Eggs: U.S. Production, Price, and Value, 2000-2001[1]

Source: National Agricultural Statistics Service, U.S. Dept. of Agriculture

STATE	Eggs produced 2000 (mil)	Eggs produced 2001 (mil)	Price per dozen[2] 2000 (dollars)	Price per dozen[2] 2001 (dollars)	Value of Production 2000 (1,000 dollars)	Value of Production 2001 (1,000 dollars)	STATE	Eggs produced 2000 (mil)	Eggs produced 2001 (mil)	Price per dozen[2] 2000 (dollars)	Price per dozen[2] 2001 (dollars)	Value of Production 2000 (1,000 dollars)	Value of Production 2001 (1,000 dollars)
AL	2,371	2,359	1.310	1.350	258,834	265,388	MT	84	95	.460	.410	3,220	3,246
AR	3,559	3,427	1.060	1.060	314,378	302,718	NC	2,501	2,535	1.070	1.100	223,006	232,375
CA	6,293	5,996	.453	.472	237,561	235,843	NE	2,999	3,001	.375	.382	93,719	95,532
CO	988	946	.697	.612	57,386	48,246	NH	39	42	.859	.861	2,792	3,014
CT	863	883	.555	.568	39,914	41,795	NJ	574	556	.527	.531	25,208	24,603
DE	386	369	.670	.676	21,552	20,787	NY	1,113	1,143	.564	.567	52,311	54,007
FL	2,716	2,737	.478	.536	108,187	122,253	OH	8,163	7,900	.503	.491	342,166	323,242
GA	5,114	5,086	.868	.868	369,913	367,887	OK	931	926	.838	.843	65,015	65,052
HI	143	129	.890	.894	10,598	9,640	OR	805	818	.482	.600	32,334	40,900
IA	7,554	8,676	.383	.390	241,099	281,970	PA	6,309	6,662	.545	.547	286,534	303,676
ID	249	251	.611	.586	12,678	12,257	SC	1,245	1,416	.642	.674	66,608	79,532
IL	944	888	.472	.486	37,131	35,964	SD	580	575	.354	.350	17,110	16,771
IN	6,098	6,025	.516	.515	262,214	258,573	TN	278	294	1.240	1.300	28,727	31,850
KS	416	434	.390	.376	13,520	13,599	TX	4,423	4,734	.697	.677	256,903	267,077
KY	940	933	.904	.935	70,813	72,696	UT	712	853	.434	.440	25,751	31,277
LA	493	480	.810	.793	33,278	31,720	VA	824	766	.963	.961	66,126	61,344
MA	93	80	.627	.657	4,859	4,380	VT	68	62	.598	.626	3,389	3,234
MD	845	870	.598	.607	42,109	44,008	WA	1,306	1,337	.549	.560	59,750	62,393
ME	1,135	1,100	.596	.618	56,372	56,650	WI	1,225	1,235	.479	.500	48,898	51,458
MI	1,617	1,677	.419	.437	56,460	61,071	WV	217	205	1.400	1.410	30,052	27,613
MN	3,271	3,112	.428	.435	116,666	112,810	WY	3.6	3.6	.550	.560	165	168
MO	1,614	1,789	.520	.507	69,940	75,585	Other[3]	668	719	.441	.465	24,549	27,861
MS	1,581	1,550	1.180	1.260	155,465	162,750	**U.S.[4]**	**84,386**	**85,702**	**.618**	**.622**	**4,345,879**	**4,442,220**

(1) Estimates cover the 12-month period from Dec. 1 of the previous year through Nov. 30. (2) Average of all eggs sold by producers, including hatching eggs. (3) AK, AZ, NM, NV, ND, and RI combined to avoid disclosure of individual operations; totals listed under "other." (4) Total states may not equal U.S. total because of rounding.

Livestock on Farms in the U.S., 1900-2002

Source: National Agricultural Statistics Service, U.S. Dept. of Agriculture

(in thousands)

Year (On Jan. 1)	All cattle[1]	Milk cows	Sheep and lambs	Hogs and pigs[2]	Year (On Jan. 1)	All cattle[1]	Milk cows	Sheep and lambs	Hogs and pigs[2]
1900	59,739	16,544	48,105	51,055	1990	95,816	10,015	11,358	53,700
1910	50,993	19,450	50,239	48,072	1991	96,393	9,966	11,174	54,416
1920	70,400	21,455	40,743	60,159	1992	97,556	9,688	10,797	57,649
1930	61,003	23,032	51,565	55,705	1993	99,176	9,581	10,906	58,795
1940	68,309	24,940	52,107	61,165	1994	100,974	9,494	9,836	60,847
1950	77,963	23,853	29,826	58,937	1995	102,755	9,487	8,886	57,150
1955	96,592	23,462	31,582	50,474	1996	103,487	9,416	8,461	56,124
1960	96,236	19,527	33,170	59,026	1997	101,656	9,318	8,024	57,366
1965	109,000	16,981	25,127	56,106	1998	99,744	9,199	7,825	62,213
1970	112,369	12,091	20,423	57,046	1999	99,115	9,133	7,215	60,896
1975	132,028	11,220	14,515	54,693	2000	98,198	9,190	7,032	59,117
1980	111,242	10,758	12,699	67,318	2001	97,227	9,183	6,965	58,603
1985	109,582	10,777	10,716	54,073	2002	96,704	9,110	6,685	60,188

(1) From 1970, includes milk cows and heifers that have calved. (2) 1900-95, as of Dec. 1 of preceding year; 1996-2002 as of June 1 of same year.

U.S. Meat Production and Consumption, 1940-2001

Source: Economic Research Service, U.S. Dept. of Agriculture

(in millions of pounds)

	Beef		Veal		Lamb and mutton		Pork		All red meats[1]		All Poultry	
Year	Production	Consumption[2]	Production	Consumption[2]	Production	Consumption[2]	Production	Consumption[2]	Production	Consumption[2]	Production	Consumption[2]
1940	7,175	7,257	981	981	876	873	10,044	9,701	19,076	18,812	NA	NA
1950	9,534	9,529	1,230	1,206	597	596	10,714	10,390	22,075	21,721	3,174	3,097
1960	14,728	15,465	1,109	1,118	769	857	13,905	14,057	30,511	31,497	6,310	6,168
1970	21,684	23,451	588	613	551	669	14,699	14,957	37,522	39,689	10,193	9,981
1980	21,643	23,560	400	420	318	351	16,617	16,838	38,978	41,170	14,173	13,525
1990	22,743	24,030	327	325	363	397	15,354	16,025	38,787	40,778	23,468	22,152
1991	22,917	24,115	306	305	363	397	15,999	16,392	39,585	41,209	24,701	23,272
1992	23,086	24,262	310	311	348	388	17,233	17,462	40,977	42,423	26,201	24,394
1993	23,049	24,006	285	286	337	381	17,088	17,408	40,759	42,081	27,328	25,097
1994	24,386	25,128	293	291	308	346	17,696	17,812	42,683	43,577	29,113	25,754
1995	25,222	25,534	319	319	285	346	17,849	17,768	43,675	43,967	30,393	25,944
1996	25,525	25,861	378	378	268	333	17,117	16,797	43,288	43,369	32,015	26,760
1997	25,490	25,611	334	333	260	332	17,274	16,823	43,358	43,099	32,964	27,261
1998	25,760	26,305	262	265	251	360	19,010	18,308	45,283	45,237	33,352	27,821
1999	26,493	26,937	235	235	248	358	19,308	18,946	46,284	46,476	35,252	29,584
2000	26,888	27,377	225	225	234	354	18,952	18,643	46,299	46,559	36,087	30,031
2001	26,107	27,022	205	204	227	368	19,160	18,499	45,804	46,802	38,839	30,087

(1) Meats may not add to total because of rounding. (2) Consumption (also called total disappearance) is estimated as: production plus beginning stocks, plus imports, minus exports, minus ending stocks. NA = Not available.

Total U.S. Government Agricultural Payments, by State, 1990-2001

Source: Economic Research Service, U.S. Dept. of Agriculture

(in thousands of dollars)

STATE	1990	1995	1997	1999	2000	2001
Alabama	$82,226	$54,140	$65,784	$179,505	$170,852	$230,734
Alaska	1,117	1,735	1,490	1,766	1,672	2,173
Arizona	43,349	9,456	46,575	107,899	107,066	99,254
Arkansas	312,696	383,783	274,938	815,267	900,648	832,545
California	252,333	239,809	220,475	668,501	667,466	586,761
Colorado	236,723	167,661	175,637	374,202	351,116	319,599
Connecticut	2,123	2,382	1,383	8,708	18,143	7,540
Delaware	3,213	3,150	5,725	19,850	25,028	25,004
Florida	37,155	55,778	19,044	76,859	56,741	108,011
Georgia	130,593	67,332	109,156	361,827	380,057	427,261
Hawaii	519	947	554	820	11,927	3,860
Idaho	133,431	89,482	110,401	210,657	261,297	207,664
Illinois	506,603	543,753	552,452	1,798,822	1,943,916	1,849,769
Indiana	244,170	246,026	265,132	852,051	938,464	925,278
Iowa	753,733	786,652	712,839	2,061,881	2,302,094	1,971,677
Kansas	834,746	422,226	529,786	1,401,286	1,231,923	1,068,706
Kentucky	81,610	67,382	83,056	232,109	448,473	293,379
Louisiana	154,631	164,251	157,343	420,630	451,831	434,612
Maine	6,982	14,114	4,191	11,650	13,851	7,819
Maryland	17,386	15,241	19,489	68,265	88,470	86,626
Massachusetts	3,023	2,490	1,196	10,186	10,973	10,138
Michigan	168,831	151,055	121,289	401,436	381,056	352,766
Minnesota	511,759	467,807	417,041	1,409,859	1,502,230	1,242,141
Mississippi	185,969	133,544	169,868	440,837	463,901	517,007
Missouri	299,065	256,629	278,025	717,096	869,390	817,044
Montana	299,599	189,809	230,857	492,057	490,002	476,158
Nebraska	624,646	507,302	454,549	1,411,884	1,406,971	1,297,623
Nevada	5,347	4,264	2,133	2,676	3,918	5,864
New Hampshire	1,856	1,216	890	3,944	4,768	2,815
New Jersey	15,744	5,491	3,629	10,258	22,481	16,403
New Mexico	63,840	55,134	38,995	92,378	79,495	93,729
New York	59,304	43,563	39,623	120,397	159,876	114,039
North Carolina	73,255	41,476	87,743	290,453	447,096	330,730
North Dakota	545,378	296,215	361,478	975,583	1,170,234	944,591
Ohio	197,006	167,351	186,431	650,237	678,104	681,651
Oklahoma	319,040	164,662	205,603	532,263	439,851	392,822
Oregon	89,137	52,145	63,461	105,641	137,401	104,946
Pennsylvania	41,414	41,096	35,470	95,717	147,848	103,462
Rhode Island	191	317	122	877	1,218	292
South Carolina	62,637	34,586	43,050	127,788	144,499	130,287
South Dakota	332,851	245,016	268,087	791,124	789,895	715,264
Tennessee	91,029	47,405	76,201	227,205	298,873	247,485
Texas	974,702	643,119	648,444	1,961,835	1,647,066	1,703,168
Utah	34,897	25,045	20,094	30,521	36,181	39,754
Vermont	5,793	4,334	3,093	12,221	26,093	7,877
Virginia	32,378	25,967	30,589	100,980	152,452	117,158
Washington	205,425	116,062	147,263	270,594	352,503	298,784
West Virginia	6,049	5,268	5,675	11,269	23,509	9,842
Wisconsin	181,243	184,350	176,552	503,046	603,213	415,110
Wyoming	31,283	31,432	22,390	40,203	34,302	50,272
UNITED STATES	**$9,298,030**	**$7,279,451**	**$7,495,294**	**$21,513,119**	**$22,896,433**	**$20,727,496**

U.S. Federal Food Assistance Programs, 1990-2001[1]

Source: Food and Nutrition Service, U.S. Dept. of Agriculture

(in millions of dollars)

	1990	1995	1996	1997	1998	1999	2000	2001
Food stamps[2]	$15,491	$24,620	$24,327	$21,487	$18,893	$17,698	$17,058	$17,797
Puerto Rico nutrition asst.[3]	937	1,131	1,143	1,174	1,204	1,236	1,268	1,296
Natl. school lunch[4]	3,834	5,160	5,355	5,554	5,830	6,019	6,149	6,475
School breakfast[5]	596	1,048	1,119	1,214	1,272	1,345	1,393	1,450
WIC[6]	2,122	3,440	3,695	3,844	3,890	3,940	3,981	4,150
Summer food service[7]	164	237	250	244	263	268	267	272
Child/adult care[7]	813	1,464	1,534	1,572	1,553	1,621	1,684	1,739
Special milk	19	17	17	17	17	16	15	16
Nutrition for the elderly[4]	142	148	145	145	141	140	137	152
Food distrib. to Indian reserv.[7]	66	65	70	71	72	76	72	68
Commodity supp. food prog.[7]	85	99	100	99	94	98	95	103
Food dist.—charitable inst.[8]	104	64	11	6	9	3	2	7
Emergency food assistance[9]	334	135	44	192	234	270	225	377
TOTAL[10]	**$24,707**	**$37,628**	**$37,810**	**$35,619**	**$33,472**	**$32,730**	**$32,346**	**$33,902**

(1) All data are for fiscal (not calendar) years. (2) Includes federal share of state administrative expenses and other federal costs. (3) Puerto Rico participated in the Food Stamp Program from FY 1975 until July 1982, when it initiated a separate grant program. (4) Includes cash payments and commodity costs (entitlement, bonus, and cash in lieu). (5) Excludes startup costs. (6) Includes the WIC Farmers Market Nutrition Program, program studies and special grants. (7) Includes commodity costs and administrative expenditures. (8) Includes summer camps. (9) Includes the Emergency Food Assistance Program (TEFAP) for all years, and the Soup Kitchens/Food Banks Program (1989-96). (10) Excludes Food Program Administration (federal) costs. Totals may not add because of rounding.

U.S. Farm Marketings by State, 2000-2001

Source: Economic Research Service, U.S. Dept. of Agriculture

(in thousands of dollars)

STATE	RANK, 2001	2001 FARM MARKETINGS Total	2001 Crops	2001 Livestock and products	2000 FARM MARKETINGS Total	2000 Crops	2000 Livestock and products
Alabama	(23)	$3,519,731	$705,210	$2,814,515	$3,205,251	$559,622	$2,645,629
Alaska	(49)	51,865	23,853	28,012	51,885	20,327	31,558
Arizona	(29)	2,574,698	1,409,090	1,165,608	2,287,294	1,216,878	1,070,416
Arkansas	(13)	5,131,964	1,624,569	3,507,395	4,737,768	1,482,678	3,255,090
California	(1)	25,892,319	18,545,880	7,346,439	25,683,196	19,431,128	6,252,068
Colorado	(16)	4,728,954	1,354,465	3,374,489	4,611,563	1,281,138	3,330,425
Connecticut	(44)	476,150	298,829	177,321	495,632	327,518	168,114
Delaware	(39)	847,718	185,719	661,999	736,360	178,753	557,607
Florida	(9)	6,415,882	4,957,896	1,457,986	6,777,113	5,401,907	1,375,206
Georgia	(11)	5,514,952	1,975,220	3,539,732	5,098,526	1,991,455	3,107,071
Hawaii	(42)	510,507	419,298	91,209	521,771	429,517	92,254
Idaho	(21)	3,847,926	1,787,513	2,060,413	3,371,855	1,743,566	1,628,289
Illinois	(8)	7,547,087	5,704,242	1,842,845	7,126,795	5,416,123	1,710,672
Indiana	(14)	5,105,437	3,235,048	1,870,389	4,584,456	2,882,969	1,701,487
Iowa	(3)	11,550,109	5,614,520	5,935,589	10,803,640	5,047,008	5,756,632
Kansas	(5)	8,121,044	2,585,380	5,535,664	8,018,974	2,519,386	5,499,588
Kentucky	(22)	3,548,328	1,280,795	2,267,533	3,649,098	1,276,927	2,372,171
Louisiana	(33)	1,817,088	1,115,957	701,131	1,787,089	1,134,649	652,440
Maine	(43)	485,064	210,774	274,290	501,573	241,662	259,911
Maryland	(36)	1,596,085	646,712	949,373	1,450,729	614,909	835,820
Massachusetts	(47)	366,611	272,925	93,686	388,008	294,779	93,229
Michigan	(24)	3,469,122	1,979,799	1,489,323	3,321,666	1,987,798	1,333,868
Minnesota	(6)	8,101,875	3,813,440	4,288,435	7,463,087	3,579,972	3,883,115
Mississippi	(26)	3,146,582	871,056	2,275,526	2,727,435	690,989	2,036,446
Missouri	(15)	4,824,141	2,144,809	2,679,332	4,613,903	1,933,479	2,680,424
Montana	(34)	1,785,002	657,248	1,127,754	1,843,581	737,098	1,106,483
Nebraska	(4)	9,488,580	3,402,349	6,086,231	8,992,509	3,075,546	5,916,963
Nevada	(45)	424,596	153,300	271,296	387,286	150,075	237,211
New Hampshire	(48)	155,478	89,644	65,834	150,986	90,871	60,115
New Jersey	(40)	821,070	617,316	203,754	826,042	634,530	191,512
New Mexico	(31)	2,215,122	545,019	1,670,103	2,113,502	500,395	1,613,107
New York	(25)	3,419,790	1,199,163	2,220,627	3,121,511	1,190,784	1,930,727
North Carolina	(7)	7,730,633	3,086,554	4,644,079	7,340,127	3,040,248	4,299,879
North Dakota	(28)	2,978,548	2,258,615	719,933	2,706,065	2,076,681	629,384
Ohio	(17)	4,682,011	2,818,473	1,863,538	4,369,995	2,615,784	1,754,211
Oklahoma	(20)	4,026,680	873,802	3,152,878	4,293,314	852,649	3,440,665
Oregon	(27)	3,122,641	2,297,688	824,953	3,093,158	2,263,794	829,364
Pennsylvania	(18)	4,454,979	1,308,750	3,146,229	4,062,998	1,297,151	2,765,847
Rhode Island	(50)	47,438	39,735	7,703	46,039	38,418	7,621
South Carolina	(35)	1,646,020	763,677	882,343	1,520,669	727,767	792,902
South Dakota	(19)	4,107,879	1,852,454	2,255,425	3,805,544	1,768,888	2,036,656
Tennessee	(32)	2,160,707	1,033,948	1,126,759	1,996,706	1,006,907	989,799
Texas	(2)	13,795,618	4,456,153	9,339,465	13,370,108	4,210,776	9,159,332
Utah	(37)	1,116,343	263,082	853,261	1,019,621	247,586	772,035
Vermont	(41)	556,779	66,719	490,060	500,459	68,924	431,535
Virginia	(30)	2,443,987	770,785	1,673,202	2,284,562	735,482	1,549,080
Washington	(12)	5,191,920	3,464,259	1,727,661	5,117,215	3,407,899	1,709,316
West Virginia	(46)	407,570	59,315	348,255	396,990	57,505	339,485
Wisconsin	(10)	5,896,293	1,432,106	4,464,187	5,364,473	1,498,143	3,866,330
Wyoming	(38)	982,545	145,086	837,459	957,169	156,811	800,358
UNITED STATES		**$202,849,408**	**$96,418,236**	**$106,431,172**	**$193,695,232**	**$94,135,840**	**$99,559,392**

Value of U.S. Agricultural Exports and Imports, 1977-2001

Source: Economic Research Service, U.S. Dept. of Agriculture

(in billions of dollars, except percent)

Year[1]	Trade surplus	Agric. exports	% of all exports	Agric. imports	% of all imports
1977	10.6	24.0	20	13.4	9
1978	13.4	27.3	21	13.9	8
1979	15.8	32.0	19	16.2	8
1980	23.2	40.5	19	17.3	7
1981	26.4	43.8	19	17.3	7
1982	23.6	39.1	18	15.5	6
1983	18.5	34.8	18	16.3	7
1984	19.1	38.0	18	18.9	6
1985	11.5	31.2	15	19.7	6
1986	5.4	26.3	13	20.9	6
1987	7.2	27.9	12	20.7	5
1988	14.3	35.3	12	21.0	5
1989	18.1	39.7	12	21.6	5
1990	17.7	40.4	11	22.7	5
1991	15.1	37.8	10	22.7	5
1992	18.2	42.6	10	24.5	5
1993	18.3	42.9	10	24.6	4
1994	17.4	44.0	9	26.6	4
1995	24.9	54.7	10	29.9	4
1996	27.3	59.9	10	32.6	4
1997	21.6	57.4	9	35.8	4
1998	16.6	53.6	8	37.0	4
1999	11.8	49.1	8	37.2	4
2000[2]	11.9	50.9	7	38.9	3
2001[3]	13.9	52.9	7	39.0	3

(1) Fiscal year (Oct.-Sept.). (2) Revised. (3) Preliminary.

Farm Business Real Estate Debt Outstanding, by Lender Groups,[1] 1960-2001

Source: Economic Research Service, U.S. Dept. of Agriculture
(in millions of dollars)

		AMOUNTS HELD BY PRINCIPAL LENDER GROUPS				
Dec. 31	Total farm real estate debt[2]	Farm Credit System[2]	Farm Services Agency[3]	Life insurance companies[4]	All operating banks	Other[5]
1960	$11,310	$2,222	$624	$2,652	$1,356	$4,456
1970	27,506	6,420	2,180	5,123	3,329	10,455
1980	89,692	33,225	7,435	11,998	7,765	27,813
1985	100,076	42,169	9,821	11,273	10,732	25,775
1990	74,732	25,924	7,639	9,704	16,288	15,169
1991	74,944	25,305	7,041	9,546	17,417	15,632
1992	75,421	25,408	6,394	8,765	18.757	16,095
1993	76,036	24,900	5,837	8,985	19,595	16,719
1994	77,680	24,597	5,465	9,025	21,079	17,514
1995	79,287	24,851	5,055	9,092	22,277	18,012
1996	81,657	25,730	4,702	9,468	23,276	18,481
1997	85,359	27,098	4,373	9,699	25,240	18,950
1998	89,615	28,888	4,073	10,723	27,168	18,763
1999	94,226	30,302	3,872	11,490	29,799	18,763
2000	97,474	31,766	3,657	11,826	31,836	18,389
2001[6]	103,052	35,507	3,557	12,001	33,225	18,763

(1) Exclude operator households. (2) Includes data for joint stock land banks and real estate loans by Agricultural Credit Assn. (3) Includes loans made directly by Farm Services Agency for farm ownership, soil and water loans to individuals, Native American tribe land acquisition, grazing associations, and half of economic emergency loans. Also includes loans for rural housing on farm tracts and labor housing. (4) American Council of Life Insurance members. (5) Estimated by ERS, USDA. Includes Commodity Credit Corporation storage and drying facility loans. (6) Preliminary

Grain, Hay, Potato, Cotton, Soybean, Tobacco Production, by State, 2001

Source: National Agricultural Statistics Service, U.S. Dept. of Agriculture

STATE	Barley (1,000 bu)	Corn, grain (1,000 bu)	Cotton (Upland) (1,000 b)	All hay (1,000 t)	Oats (1,000 bu)	Potatoes (1,000 cwt)	Soybeans (1,000 bu)	Tobacco (1,000 lb)	All wheat (1,000 bu)
Alabama	—	16,050	890	2,392	NE	624	4,725	—	3,360
Alaska	—	—	—	—	—	—	—	—	—
Arizona	4,400	5,824	690.0	1,862	—	2,214	—	—	8,517
Arkansas	—	26,825	1,825	2,792	NE	—	91,200	—	50,440
California	5,830	27,200	1,800	8,915	900	12,788	—	—	35,105
Colorado	8,560	149,800	—	4,780	1,920	23,274	—	—	69,168
Connecticut	—	NE	—	117	—	—	—	3,908	—
Delaware	2,002	23,652	—	49	—	1,161	7,839	—	3,477
Florida	—	2,262	169	756	—	9,295	261	11,700	369
Georgia	—	29,480	2,200	1,950	2,275	—	4,185	64,395	10,600
Hawaii	—	—	—	—	—	—	—	—	—
Idaho	50,250	6,750	—	4,938	1,360	127,980	—	—	85,150
Illinois	—	1,649,200	—	2,670	3,200	1,855	477,900	—	43,920
Indiana	—	884,520	—	2,048	1,280	928	273,910	9,450	25,080
Iowa	—	1,664,400	—	5,565	9,100	NE	480,480	—	972
Kansas	400	387,350	23.0	7,980	2,120	720	87,360	—	328,00
Kentucky	680	156,200	—	5,545	—	—	48,800	262,335	23,760
Louisiana	—	45,436	1,030	1,260	—	—	20,130	—	8,000
Maine	1,820	NE	—	202	2,325	16,120	—	—	—
Maryland	3,825	55,760	—	522	NE	1,175	20,085	2,755	11,025
Massachusetts	—	NA	—	185	—	742	—	1,986	—
Michigan	1,008	199,500	—	3,790	3,520	14,030	63,900	—	35,840
Minnesota	7,975	806,000	—	6,195	12,600	18,425	266,400	—	79,655
Mississippi	—	50,050	2,360	1,950	—	—	36,960	—	11,700
Missouri	—	345,800	720	7,853	1,000	1,904	186,200	3,304	41,040
Montana	29,520	1,924	—	4,445	2,400	3,040	—	—	96,570
Nebraska	180	1,139,250	—	7,578	3,660	8,512	222,950	—	59,200
Nevada	90	NE	—	1,584	—	2,340	—	—	NE
New Hampshire	—	NE	—	99	—	—	—	—	270
New Jersey	216	7,392	—	255	—	638	3,131	—	1,215
New Mexico	—	8,280	120	1,592	—	2,198	—	—	8,160
New York	612	56,700	—	3,548	5,520	5,942	5,214	—	6,360
North Carolina	1,206	78,125	1620	1,578	1,680	3,515	43,200	388,780	18,330
North Dakota	79,750	81,075	—	5,065	14,880	26,400	71,740	—	292,400
Ohio	380	437,460	—	4,275	6,205	984	187,780	11,956	60,300
Oklahoma	NE	26,250	210	3,964	380	—	5,035	—	122,100
Oregon	4,500	2,520	—	3,052	1,925	20,730	—	—	33,250
Pennsylvania	4,200	97,020	—	3,439	7,475	3,173	14,175	6,166	8,320
Rhode Island	—	NE	—	14	—	135	—	—	—
South Carolina	NE	25,290	425	640	1,425	—	9,460	78,400	9,030
South Dakota	4,056	370,600	—	9,150	7,800	648	138,570	—	76,766
Tennessee	—	81,840	975	4,757	7,200	—	35,700	84,465	18,360
Texas	NE	167,560	4,150	10,837	390	5,190	5,670	—	108,800
Utah	4,420	2,130	—	2,536	—	345	—	—	6,034
Vermont	—	NE	—	400	—	—	—	—	—
Virginia	3,750	40,590	199	2,741	—	1,386	17,280	66,015	10,200
Washington	21,000	10,450	—	3,088	660	94,400	—	—	132,580
West Virginia	—	3,120	—	1,079	NE	—	672	1,885	464
Wisconsin	1,820	330,200	—	4,790	12,480	31,955	59,660	3,436	10,708
Wyoming	7,140	6,375	—	1,881	1,176	NE	—	—	3,048
UNITED STATES	**249,590**	**9,506,840**	**19,406**	**156,703**	**116,856**	**444,766**	**2,890,572**	**1,000,936**	**1,957,643**

NE = Not estimated, bu = bushels, b = bales (480-lbs), t = tons, cwt = hundredweight.

Production of Principal U.S. Crops, 1989-2001

Source: National Agricultural Statistics Service, U.S. Dept. of Agriculture

Year	Corn for grain (1,000 bu)	Oats (1,000 bu)	Barley (1,000 bu)	Sorghum for grain (1,000 bu)	All wheat (1,000 bu)	Rye (1,000 bu)	Flaxseed (1,000 bu)	Upland Cotton (1,000 b)	Cottonseed (1,000 t)
1989	7,531,953	373,587	404,203	615,420	2,036,618	13,647	1,215	12,196.6	4,677.4
1990	7,934,028	357,654	422,196	573,303	2,729,778	10,176	3,812	15,505.4	5,968.5
1991	7,474,765	243,851	464,326	584,860	1,980,139	9,734	6,200	17,614.3	6,925.5
1992	9,476,698	294,229	455,090	875,022	2,466,798	11,440	3,288	16,219.5	6,230.1
1993	6,336,470	206,770	398,041	534,172	2,396,440	10,340	3,480	16,134.6	6,343.2
1994	10,102,735	229,008	374,862	649,206	2,320,981	11,341	2,922	19,662.0	7,603.9
1995	7,373,876	162,027	359,562	460,373	2,182,591	10,064	2,211	17,532.2	6,848.7
1996	9,293,435	155,273	395,751	802,974	2,285,133	9,016	1,602	18,413.5	7,143.5
1997	9,206,832	167,246	359,878	633,545	2,481,466	8,132	2,420	18,245.0	6,934.6
1998	9,758,685	165,981	352,125	519,933	2,547,321	12,161	6,708	13,475.9	5,365.4
1999	9,430,612	146,193	280,292	595,166	2,299,010	11,038	7,864	16,293.7	6,354.0
2000[1]	9,915,051	149,545	318,728	470,526	2,232,460	8,386	10,730	16,799.2	6,435.6
2001	9,506,840	116,856	249,590	514,524	1,957,643	6,971	11,455	19,406.0	7,533.0

Year	Tobacco (1,000 lb)	All hay (1,000 t)	Beans, dry edible (1,000 cwt)	Peas, dry edible (1,000 cwt)	Peanuts[2] (1,000 lb)	Soybeans[3] (1,000 bu)	Potatoes (1,000 cwt)	Sweet potatoes (1,000 cwt)
1989	1,367,188	144,706	23,729	3,883	3,989,995	1,923,666	370,444	11,358
1990	1,626,380	146,212	32,379	2,372	3,602,770	1,925,947	402,110	12,594
1991	1,664,372	152,073	33,765	3,715	4,926,570	1,986,539	417,622	11,203
1992	1,721,671	146,903	22,615	2,535	4,284,416	2,190,354	425,367	12,005
1993	1,613,319	146,700	21,913	3,292	3,392,415	1,870,958	428,693	11,053
1994	1,582,896	150,060	29,028	2,255	4,247,455	2,516,694	467,054	13,395
1995	1,268,538	154,166	30,812	4,765	4,247,455	2,176,814	443,606	12,906
1996	1,517,334	149,457	27,960	2,671	3,661,205	2,382,364	498,633	13,456
1997	1,787,399	152,536	29,370	5,752	3,539,380	2,688,750	467,091	13,327
1998	1,479,867	151,780	30,418	5,934	3,963,440	2,741,014	475,771	12,382
1999	1,292,692	159,707	33,085	4,773	3,829,490	2,653,758	478,216	12,234
2000[1]	1,052,998	151,921	26,409	3,499	3,265,505	2,757,810	513,621	13,794
2001	1,000,936	156,703	19,541	3,779	4,239,450	2,890,572	444,766	14,355

Year	Rice (1,000 cwt)	Sugarcane (1,000 t)	Sugar beets (1,000 t)	Pecans[4] (1,000 lb)	Apples (1,000 t)	Grapes (1,000 t)	Peaches (1,000 t)	Oranges[5] (1,000 bx)	Grapefruit[5] (1,000 bx)
1989	154,487	29,426	25,131	250,500	4,958.4	5,930.9	1,181.5	209,050	69,500
1990	156,088	28,136	27,513	205,000	4,828.4	5,659.9	1,121.1	184,415	49,300
1991	159,367	30,252	28,203	299,000	4,853.4	5,555.9	1,347.8	178,950	55,500
1992	179,658	30,363	29,143	166,000	5,284.3	6,052.1	1,336.0	209,010	55,265
1993	156,110	31,101	26,249	365,000	5,342.4	6,023.2	1,330.1	255,760	68,375
1994	197,779	30,929	31,853	199,000	5,667.8	5,870.6	1,253.3	240,450	65,100
1995	173,871	30,944	27,954	268,000	5,292.5	5,922.3	1,150.8	263,605	71,050
1996	171,321	29,462	26,680	221,500	5,196.0	5,554.3	1,058.2	263,890	66,200
1997	182,992	31,709	29,886	335,000	5,161.9	7,290.9	1,312.3	292,620	70,200
1998	184,443	32,743	32,499	73,200	5,381.3	5,816.4	1,162.8	315,525	63,150
1999	206,027	35,299	33,420	203,100	5,223.3	6,234.8	1,216.7	224,580	61,200
2000[1]	190,872	36,114	32,541	209,850	5,324.4	7,658.0	1,299.9	299,760	66,980
2001	213,045	34,801	25,754	318,300	4,780.2	6,471.9	1,268.7	285,435	59,950

(1) Revised. (2) Harvested for nuts. (3) Harvested for beans. (4) Utilized production only. (5) Crop year ending in year cited.

Principal U.S. Crops: Area Planted and Harvested, 1995, 2000, 2001

Source: National Agricultural Statistics Service, U.S. Dept. of Agriculture

(in thousand acres)

STATE	Area Planted[1] 1995	Area Planted[1] 2000	Area Planted[1] 2001	Area Harvested[1] 1995	Area Harvested[1] 2000	Area Harvested[1] 2001
AL	2,204	2,075	2,236	2,093	1,885	2,116
AK	30	27	34	29	22	30
AZ	795	745	772	787	738	763
AR	8,435	8,490	8,396	8,198	8,184	8,188
CA	5,220	4,794	4,582	4,660	4,395	4,115
CO	6,104	6,454	6,362	5,748	5,996	5,800
CT	112	103	97	107	100	95
DE	507	500	487	499	493	476
FL	1,070	1,101	1,074	1,027	1,047	1,054
GA	4,237	3,860	3,872	3,864	3,273	3,409
HI	53	32	23	53	32	23
ID	4,483	4,502	4,348	4,306	4,324	4,099
IL	23,221	23,671	23,396	22,526	23,533	23,228
IN	11,942	12,547	12,442	11,785	12,452	12,383
IA	23,502	24,990	24,615	22,872	24,828	24,348
KS	22,428	22,929	23,904	21,363	21,657	21,849
KY	5,709	5,783	5,476	5,454	5,506	5,259
LA	3,857	3,775	3,723	3,786	3,653	3,641
ME	364	282	280	358	276	274
MD	1,548	1,531	1,496	1,463	1,495	1,467
MA	134	124	124	131	119	121
MI	6,790	6,718	6,604	6,647	6,593	6,435
MN	19,578	20,398	19,359	18,976	19,895	18,937
MS	4,850	4,750	4,555	4,739	4,587	4,464
MO	12,056	13,678	13,494	11,689	13,368	13,237
MT	9,697	8,883	9,211	9,245	8,079	7,596
NE	18,280	19,196	19,263	17,769	18,636	18,750
NV	516	523	524	512	518	509
NH	85	73	72	83	72	71
NJ	452	368	342	413	359	334
NM	1,282	1,279	1,303	869	880	1,014
NY	3,045	2,924	3,132	2,981	2,888	3,101
NC	4,639	4,909	4,847	4,351	4,645	4,557
ND	20,707	21,712	20,477	20,120	20,266	19,557
OH	10,025	10,657	10,587	9,883	10,546	10,441
OK	10,621	10,417	9,960	8,635	7,859	7,511
OR	2,389	2,355	2,233	2,260	2,291	2,134
PA	4,146	4,227	3,978	4,050	4,169	3,896
RI	11	12	11	11	12	11
SC	1,976	1,674	1,651	1,871	1,598	1,587
SD	14,334	17,264	17,671	13,947	16,824	16,302
TN	4,892	5,056	5,085	4,530	4,845	4,884
TX	22,600	23,311	23,776	17,870	16,150	17,945
UT	1,099	1,089	1,082	1,042	1,019	988
VT	387	320	330	379	315	325
VA	2,910	2,831	2,773	2,748	2,757	2,697
WA	4,130	4,180	4,056	3,997	4,094	3,918
WV	650	685	660	642	679	654
WI	8,194	7,859	7,617	7,792	7,637	7,438
WY	1,883	1,698	1,636	1,820	1,618	1,520
U.S.[2]	**323,964**	**328,325**	**324,928**	**308,135**	**307,519**	**303,818**

(1) Crops included in area planted are corn, sorghum, oats, barley, winter wheat, rye, durum wheat, other spring wheat, rice, soybeans, peanuts, sunflower, cotton, dry edible beans, potatoes, canola, millet, and sugarbeets. Harvested acreage is used for all hay, tobacco, and sugarcane in computing total area planted. Includes double-cropped acres and unharvested small grains planted as cover crops. (2) State figures do not add to U.S. totals because of sunflower and canola unallocated acreage.

Average Prices Received by U.S. Farmers, 1940-2001

Source: National Agricultural Statistics Service, U.S. Dept. of Agriculture

Figures below represent dollars per 100 lb for hogs, beef cattle, veal calves, sheep, lamb, and milk (wholesale); dollars per head for milk cows; cents per lb for chickens, broilers, turkeys, and wool; cents per dozen for eggs; weighted calendar year prices for livestock and livestock products other than wool. For 1943-63, wool prices are weighted on marketing year basis. The marketing year was changed in 1964 from a calendar year to a Dec.-Nov. basis for hogs, chickens, broilers, and eggs.

Year	Hogs	Cattle (beef)	Calves (veal)	Sheep	Lambs	Milk cows	Milk	Chickens (excl. broilers)	Broilers	Turkeys	Eggs	Wool
1940...	5.39	7.56	8.83	3.95	8.10	61	1.82	13.0	17.3	15.2	18.0	28.4
1950...	18.00	23.30	26.30	11.60	25.10	198	3.89	22.2	27.4	32.8	36.3	62.1
1960...	15.30	20.40	22.90	5.61	17.90	223	4.21	12.2	16.9	25.4	36.1	42.0
1970...	22.70	27.10	34.50	7.51	26.40	332	5.71	9.1	13.6	22.6	39.1	35.4
1975...	46.10	32.20	27.20	11.30	42.10	412	8.75	9.9	26.3	34.8	54.5	44.8
1980...	38.00	62.40	76.80	21.30	63.60	1,190	13.05	11.0	27.7	41.3	56.3	88.1
1985...	44.00	53.70	62.10	23.90	67.70	860	12.76	14.8	30.1	49.1	57.1	63.3
1986...	49.30	52.60	61.10	25.60	69.00	820	12.51	12.5	34.5	47.1	61.6	66.8
1987...	51.20	61.10	78.50	29.50	77.60	920	12.54	11.0	28.7	34.8	54.9	91.7
1988...	42.30	66.60	89.20	25.60	69.10	990	12.26	9.2	33.1	38.6	52.8	138.0
1989...	42.50	69.50	90.80	24.40	66.10	1,030	13.56	14.9	36.6	40.9	68.9	124.0
1990...	53.70	74.60	95.60	23.20	55.50	1,160	13.74	9.3	32.6	39.4	70.9	80.0
1991...	49.10	72.70	98.00	19.70	52.20	1,100	12.27	7.1	30.8	38.4	67.8	55.0
1992...	41.60	71.30	89.00	25.80	59.50	1,130	13.15	8.6	31.8	37.7	57.6	74.0
1993...	45.20	72.60	91.20	28.60	64.40	1,160	12.84	10.0	34.0	39.0	63.4	51.0
1994...	39.90	66.70	87.20	30.90	65.60	1,170	13.01	7.6	35.0	40.4	61.4	78.0
1995...	40.50	61.80	73.10	28.00	78.20	1,130	12.78	6.5	34.4	41.6	62.4	104.0
1996...	51.90	58.70	58.40	29.90	82.20	1,090	14.75	6.6	38.1	43.3	74.9	70.0
1997...	52.90	63.10	78.90	37.90	90.30	1,100	13.36	7.7	37.7	39.9	70.3	84.0
1998...	34.40	59.60	78.80	30.60	72.30	1,120	15.41	8.0	39.3	38.0	65.5	60.0
1999...	30.30	63.40	87.70	31.10	74.50	1,280	14.38	7.1	37.1	40.8	62.2	38.0
2000[1]..	42.30	68.60	104.0	34.30	79.80	1,340	12.40	5.7	33.6	40.7	61.8	33.0
2001...	44.30	71.30	106.0	34.6	66.9	1,500	15.05	4.5	39.3	39.0	62.2	36.0

Figures below represent cents per lb for cotton, apples, and peanuts; dollars per bushel for oats, wheat, corn, barley, and soybeans; dollars per 100 lb for rice, sorghum, and potatoes; dollars per ton for cottonseed and baled hay; weighted crop year prices. The marketing year is described as follows: apples, June-May; wheat, oats, barley, hay, and potatoes, July-June; cotton, rice, peanuts, and cottonseed, Aug.-July; soybeans, Sept.-Aug.; and corn and sorghum grain, Oct.-Sept.

Year	Corn	Wheat	Upland cotton*	Oats	Barley	Rice	Soy-beans	Sor-ghum	Peanuts	Cotton-seed	Hay	Pota-toes	Apples
1940...	0.62	0.67	9.8	0.30	0.39	1.80	0.89	0.87	3.7	21.70	9.78	0.85	NA
1950...	1.52	2.00	39.9	0.79	1.19	5.09	2.47	1.88	10.9	86.60	21.10	1.50	NA
1960...	1.00	1.74	30.1	0.60	0.84	4.55	2.13	1.49	10.0	42.50	21.70	2.00	2.7
1970...	1.33	1.33	21.9	0.62	0.97	5.17	2.85	2.04	12.8	56.40	26.10	2.21	6.5
1975...	2.54	3.55	51.1	1.45	2.42	8.35	4.92	4.21	19.0	97.00	52.10	4.48	8.8
1980...	3.11	3.91	74.4	1.79	2.86	12.80	7.57	5.25	25.1	129.00	71.00	6.55	12.1
1985...	2.23	3.08	56.8	1.23	1.98	6.53	5.05	3.45	24.4	66.00	67.60	3.92	17.3
1986...	1.50	2.42	51.5	1.21	1.61	3.75	4.78	2.45	29.2	80.00	59.70	5.03	19.1
1987...	1.94	2.57	63.7	1.56	1.81	7.27	5.88	3.04	28.0	82.50	65.00	4.38	12.7
1988...	2.54	3.72	55.6	2.61	2.80	6.83	7.42	4.05	28.0	118.00	85.20	6.02	17.4
1989...	2.36	3.72	63.6	1.49	2.42	7.35	5.69	3.75	28.0	105.00	85.40	7.36	13.9
1990...	2.28	2.61	67.1	1.14	2.14	6.68	5.74	3.79	34.7	121.00	80.60	6.08	20.9
1991...	2.37	3.00	56.8	1.21	2.10	7.58	5.58	4.01	28.3	71.00	71.20	4.96	25.1
1992...	2.07	3.24	53.7	1.32	2.04	5.89	5.56	3.38	30.0	97.50	74.30	5.52	19.5
1993...	2.50	3.26	58.1	1.36	1.99	7.98	6.40	4.13	30.4	113.00	84.70	6.18	18.4
1994...	2.26	3.45	72.0	1.22	2.03	6.78	5.48	3.80	28.9	101.00	86.70	5.58	18.6
1995...	3.24	4.55	75.4	1.67	2.89	9.15	6.72	5.69	29.3	106.00	82.20	6.77	24.0
1996...	2.71	4.30	69.3	1.96	2.74	9.96	7.35	4.17	28.1	126.00	95.80	4.93	20.8
1997...	2.43	3.38	65.2	1.60	2.38	9.70	6.47	3.95	28.3	121.00	100.00	5.62	22.1
1998...	1.90	2.65	64.2	1.10	1.98	8.50	5.35	3.10	25.7	129.00	84.60	5.24	17.1
1999...	1.82	2.48	45.0	1.12	2.13	5.93	4.63	2.80	25.4	89.00	76.90	5.77	21.3
2000[1]..	1.85	2.62	49.8	1.10	2.11	5.61	4.54	3.37	27.4	105.00	85.00	5.08	17.8
2001...	2.00	2.80	32.4	1.50	2.25	4.25	4.30	3.50	23.4	89.50	97.30	6.60	22.9

*Beginning in 1964, 480-lb net weight bales. NA = Not available. (1) Revised.

Off-Farm Grain Storage Facilities, by State[1]

Source: National Agricultural Statistics Service, U.S. Dept. of Agriculture

State	No. of facilities	Total capacity (1,000 bu)	State	No. of facilities	Total capacity (1,000 bu)	State	No. of facilities	Total capacity (1,000 bu)	State	No. of facilities	Total capacity (1,000 bu)
AL.....	89	26,617	IA......	490	1,040,000	New Eng.	26	7,945	SD.....	268	145,000
AZ.....	25	18,300	KS.....	803	890,000	NJ.....	17	2,880	TN.....	207	56,084
AR....	185	230,300	KY.....	191	58,650	NM.....	27	15,460	TX.....	530	630,000
CA....	170	121,980	LA.....	41	97,400	NY.....	59	38,890	UT.....	38	19,000
CO....	126	120,950	MD.....	60	45,600	NC.....	204	66,000	VA.....	90	31,301
DE....	19	22,400	MI......	245	146,000	ND.....	385	240,130	WA....	272	213,390
FL.....	26	7,131	MN.....	623	506,500	OH.....	467	353,030	WI.....	385	214,812
GA....	188	46,350	MS.....	85	53,500	OK.....	260	235,600	WY....	18	9,100
ID.....	150	112,400	MO.....	420	224,860	OR.....	98	62,580	Unalloc.[2]	10	923
IL.....	995	1,127,400	MT.....	171	66,740	PA.....	201	30,280			
IN.....	425	370,080	NE.....	519	690,156	SC.....	87	24,161	**TOTAL..**	**9,695**	**8,419,880**

(1) Data as of Dec. 1, 2001; excludes AK and HI. Off-farm capacity includes all elevators, warehouse terminals, merchant mills, other storage, and oilseed crushers which store grains, soybeans, sunflowers, or flaxseed. (2) Unallocated includes NV and WV.

World Wheat, Rice, and Corn Production, 2001

Source: UN Food and Agriculture Organization; in thousands of metric tons

COUNTRY	Wheat	Rice[1]	Corn
Algeria	1,980	<1	2
Argentina	17,723	855	15,350
Australia	23,760	1,239	420
Austria	1,508	—	420
Bangladesh	2,000	39,112	2
Belgium-Lux.	1,442	—	439
Bosnia and Herz.	640	—	269
Brazil	3,203	10,207	41,411
Bulgaria	3,800	7	520
Cambodia	—	4,099	174
Canada	21,282	—	8,171
Chile	1,780	143	778
China	93,500	181,515	115,805
Colombia	43	2,107	1,351
Croatia	800	—	2,008
Cuba	—	350	205
Czech Rep.	4,546	—	350
Denmark	4,500	—	—
Ecuador	20	1,377	642
Egypt	6,255	5,700	6,450
Ethiopia	1,600	—	2,500
Finland	489	—	—
France	31,695	110	16,472
Germany	22,009	—	3,618
Greece	1,764	160	1,658
Hungary	5,176	—	7,686
India	68,478	131,900	11,836
Indonesia	—	50,096	9,090
Iran	7,500	2,200	800
Iraq	550	130	60
Ireland	760	—	—
Italy	6,503	1,222	10,588
Japan	700	11,320	<1
Kazakhstan	12,910	300	346
Kenya	180	55	2,700
Korea, North	117	2,060	1,482
Korea, South	3	7,316	80
Laos	—	2,202	117
Madagascar	9	2,300	150
Malaysia	—	2,215	67
Mexico	3,278	259	18,616
Moldova	980	—	—
Morocco	3,316	40	54
Myanmar	103	20,600	350
Nepal	1,158	4,216	1,484
Netherlands	1,090	—	150
New Zealand	364	—	177
Nigeria	103	3,298	5,598
Pakistan	18,955	6,750	1,600
Peru	190	2,019	1,418
Philippines	—	12,955	4,525
Poland	9,393	—	1,375
Portugal	123	151	975
Romania	7,000	7	7,500
Russian Federation	46,871	497	831
Slovakia	1,894	—	721
South Africa	2,132	3	71,00
Spain	5,019	888	5,108
Sri Lanka	—	2,868	31
Sweden	2,362	—	—
Switzerland	520	—	222
Syria	4,745	—	216
Thailand	1	25,200	4,673
Turkey	16,000	354	2,100
Turkmenistan	1,200	34	20
Ukraine	21,333	100	3,300
United Kingdom	11,570	—	—
United States	53,278	9,664	241,485
Uruguay	324	—	263
Uzbekistan	3,127	—	118
Venezuela	1	690	1,200
Vietnam	—	31,925	2,118
Zimbabwe	250	—	1,622
WORLD, TOTAL	**582,692**	**592,831**	**609,182**

— production is small or nonexistent. Because not all countries are reported on this table, country totals do not add to world totals.
(1) Rice paddy

Wheat, Rice, and Corn—Exports/Imports of 10 Leading Countries, 2000, 1995

Source: UN Food and Agriculture Organization

(export and import figures in thousands of metric tons; by marketing years)

Wheat

TOP EXPORTERS 2000		TOP EXPORTERS 1995		TOP IMPORTERS 2000		TOP IMPORTERS 1995	
U.S.	27,830,150	U.S.	32,420,000	Brazil	7,523,008	China	12,601,814
Canada	18,771,740	Canada	16,960,000	Italy	6,860,443	Brazil	6,135,235
France	18,034,060	France	16,310,000	Iran	6,577,877	Japan	5,965,296
Australia	17,724,360	Australia	7,818,000	Japan	5,853	Italy	5,078,844
Argentina	11,019,021	Argentina	6,913,286	Algeria	5,367,044	Egypt	4,054,203
Kazakhstan	4,989,634	Germany	3,681,597	Egypt	4,956,958	Indonesia	4,054,203
Germany	4,569,373	Hungary	2,764,541	Indonesia	3,588,729	Algeria	3,504,679
U.K.	3,526,823	U.K.	2,669,090	Belgium	3,581,041	Iran	3,100,000
Turkey	1,782,048	Kazakhstan	2,485,588	Morocco	3,441,163	Spain	2,757,498
Belgium	1,093,209	Denmark	1,540,179	South Korea	3,329,318	Belgium-Lux.	2,719,024

Rice

TOP EXPORTERS 2000		TOP EXPORTERS 1995		TOP IMPORTERS 2000		TOP IMPORTERS 1995	
Thailand	6,140,314	Thailand	6,197,990	Indonesia	1,355,038	Indonesia	3,157,700
Vietnam	3,477,000	India	4,913,156	Iraq	1,200,000	China	1,645,837
China	3,070,644	U.S.	3,083,609	Iran	1,129,000	Iran	1,633,000
U.S.	2,736,462	Vietnam	1,988,000	Saudi Arabia	936,603	Bangladesh	995,946
Pakistan	2,016,273	Pakistan	1,852,267	Nigeria	785,745	Brazil	870,506
India	1,532,598	Australia	541,848	Brazil	659,508	South Korea	587,000
Uruguay	741,369	Italy	523,898	Japan	655,760	U. Arab Em.	540,888
Italy	666,336	Uruguay	462,471	Philippines	642,273	Saudi Arabia	522,942
Australia	621,666	Argentina	390,091	Senegal	536,871	Côte d'Ivoire	483,688
Argentina	466,960	Myanmar	353,800	South Africa	523,356	South Africa	466,154

Corn

TOP EXPORTERS 2000		TOP EXPORTERS 1995		TOP IMPORTERS 2000		TOP IMPORTERS 1995	
U.S.	47,970,790	U.S.	60,240,000	Japan	16,111,190	Japan	16,580,000
Argentina	10,846,503	France	6,474,138	Korea (South)	8,714,506	China	11,702,350
China	10,465,990	Argentina	6,000,873	Mexico	5,347,618	South Korea	9,035,169
France	7,947,828	South Africa	1,508,450	Egypt	5,161,556	Spain	2,912,371
Hungary	1,007,202	Hungary	600,950	China	4,944,841	Mexico	2,686,921
South Africa	616,848	Canada	443,612	Spain	3,483,609	Egypt	2,425,162
Germany	553,373	Belgium-Lux.	442,645	Malaysia	2,310,900	Malaysia	2,383,267
Canada	273,850	Zimbabwe	287,818	Brazil	1,771,194	Belg.-Lux.	1,815,945
Paraguay	214,905	Germany	244,000	Canada	1,530,339	Netherlands	1,589,800
Italy	187,133	Paraguay	203,430	Algeria	1,481,981	U.K.	1,501,563

IT'S A FACT: The U.S. leads the world in cranberry production, growing about 85% of the annual crop. The biggest cranberry state is Wisconsin, which produced 284 million lbs, or about 45% of the world total (633 mil lbs), in 2001; Massachusetts came in 2nd, with 142 mil lbs.

World Commercial Catch of Fish, Crustaceans, and Mollusks, by Major Fishing Areas, 1995-2000

Source: Food and Agriculture Organization of the United Nations (FAO); in metric tons

(in thousands of metric tons; live weight)

AREA	1995	1996	1997	1998	1999	2000
Marine						
Pacific Ocean	62,022	63,671	62,894	57,428	63,862	65,734
Atlantic Ocean	24,944	24,937	26,092	25,276	25,172	25,427
Indian Ocean	8,218	8,269	8,542	8,579	8,952	9,032
TOTAL						
Inland Waters						
N. America	539	564	600	597	627	618
S. America	445	447	462	475	522	541
Europe	836	830	815	847	892	882
Former USSR	419	412	388	430	493	488
Asia	17,340	19,508	21,095	22,429	24,357	25,647
Africa	2,047	1,950	2,018	2,132	2,243	2,527
Oceania	23	22	24	25	26	26
TOTAL	**21,228**	**23,322**	**25,014**	**26,507**	**28,666**	**30,241**
GRAND TOTAL	**116,412**	**120,199**	**122,542**	**117,790**	**126,652**	**130,434**

Note: Data for marine mammals and aquatic plants are excluded. Totals include areas or territories not shown. Details may not equal totals due to rounding.

Commercial Catch of Fish, Crustaceans, and Mollusks, for 20 Leading Countries, 1995-2000[1]

Source: U.S. Dept. of Commerce, Natl. Oceanic and Atmospheric Admin., Natl. Marine Fisheries Service

(in thousands of metric tons; live weight; ranked for 1999)

COUNTRY	2000	1999	1998	1997	1996	1995	COUNTRY	2000	1999	1998	1997	1996	1995
China	41,568	40,030	39,545	36,529	33,320	29,912	Korean Rep.	2,146	2,423	2,354	2,596	2,772	2,688
Peru	10,665	8,437	4,346	7,877	9,522	8,943	Philippines	2,281	2,201	2,146	2,136	2,133	2,222
Japan	5,752	5,961	6,030	6,733	6,763	6,787	Vietnam	1,952	1,854	1,653	1,573	1,461	1,452
India	5,689	5,592	5,245	5,379	5,258	4,906	Iceland	1,986	1,740	1,686	2,210	2,064	1,616
Chile	4,692	5,325	3,558	6,083	6,909	7,591	Bangladesh	1,661	1,579	1,354	1,262	1,194	1,109
U.S.[2]	5,174	5,228	5,154	5,422	5,395	5,638	Spain	1,289	1,511	1,529	1,389	1,363	1.372
Indonesia	4,929	4,736	4,595	4,453	4,291	4,145	Denmark	1,578	1,448	1,560	1,867	1,723	2,044
Russian Fed.	4,048	4,210	4,518	4,715	4,730	4,374	Malaysia	1,441	1,407	1,287	1,281	1,239	1,245
Thailand	3,631	3,621	3,508	3,417	3,561	3,573	Mexico	1,368	1,251	1,216	1,529	1,495	1,355
Norway	3,191	3,096	3,259	3,224	2,970	2,802	Taiwan	1,338	1,347	1,105	1,052	976	914

(1) Includes aquaculture. (2) Includes weight of clam, oyster, scallop, and other mollusk shells. This weight is not included in U.S. landings statistics shown elsewhere.

U.S. Commercial Landings of Fish and Shellfish, 1986-2001[1]

Source: U.S. Dept. of Commerce, Natl. Oceanic and Atmospheric Admin., Natl. Marine Fisheries Service

	Landings for human food		Landings for industrial purposes[2]		TOTAL	
YEAR	mil lb	mil dollars	mil lb	mil dollars	mil lb	mil dollars
1986	3,393	$2,641	2,638	$122	6,031	$2,763
1987	3,946	2,979	2,950	136	6,896	3,115
1988	4,588	3,362	2,604	158	7,192	3,520
1989	6,204	3,111	2,259	127	8,463	3,238
1990	7,041	3,366	2,363	156	9,404	3,522
1991	7,031	3,169	2,453	139	9,484	3,308
1992	7,618	3,531	2,019	147	9,637	3,678
1993	8,214	3,317	2,253	154	10,467	3,471
1994	7,936	3,751	2,525	95	10,461	3,846
1995	7,667	3,625	2,121	145	9,788	3,770
1996	7,474	3,355	2,091	132	9,565	3,487
1997	7,244	3,285	2,598	163	9,842	3,448
1998	7,173	3,009	2,021	119	9,194	3,128
1999	6,832	3,265	2,507	202	9,339	3,467
2000	6,912	3,398	2,157	152	9,069	3,550
2001	7,314	3,074	2,178	154	9,492	3,228

Note: Data does not include products of aquaculture, except oysters and clams. (1) Statistics on landings are shown in round weight for all items except univalve and bivalve mollusks such as clams, oysters, and scallops, which are shown in weight of meats (excluding the shell). All data are preliminary. (2) Processed into meal, oil, solubles, and shell products or used as bait or animal food.

U.S. Domestic Landings, by Regions, 2000-2001[1]

Source: U.S. Dept. of Commerce, Natl. Oceanic and Atmospheric Admin., Natl. Marine Fisheries Service

	2000		2001	
REGION	1,000 lb	1,000 dollars	1,000 lb	1,000 dollars
New England	576,600	$688,703	632,437	$634,946
Middle Atlantic	220,674	174,268	218,089	172,676
Chesapeake	492,111	172,211	617,244	174,968
South Atlantic	220,961	217,200	193,197	161,256
Gulf	1,793,477	994,241	1,608,502	803,765
Pacific Coast and Alaska	5,810,665	1,398,607	6,199,874	1.247.920
Great Lakes	22,176	18,404	18,722	17,687
Hawaii	32,531	68,477	23,870	54,561
TOTAL	**9,136,664**	**$3,663,433**	**9,488,065**	**$3,213,218**

(1) Landings reported in round (live) weight items except for univalve and bivalve mollusks (e.g., clams, oysters, scallops), which are reported in weight of meats (excluding shell). Landings for Mississippi River Drainage Area states not included (not available).

EMPLOYMENT

Employment and Unemployment in the U.S., 1900-2001

Source: Bureau of Labor Statistics, U.S. Dept. of Labor

(civilian labor force, persons 16 years of age and older; annual averages; in thousands)

Year[1]	Employed	Unemployed	Unemployment rate	Year[1]	Employed	Unemployed	Unemployment rate
1900[2]	26,956	1,420	5.0%	1988	114,968	6,701	5.5%
1910[2]	34,599	2,150	5.9	1989	117,342	6,528	5.3
1920[2]	39,208	2,132	5.2	1990[3]	118,793	7,047	5.6
1930[2]	44,183	4,340	8.9	1991	117,718	8,628	6.8
1940[2]	47,520	8,120	14.6	1992	118,492	9,613	7.5
1950	58,918	3,288	5.0	1993	120,259	8,940	6.9
1955	62,170	2,852	4.4	1994[4]	123,060	7,996	6.1
1960	65,778	3,852	5.5	1995	124,900	7,404	5.6
1965	71,088	3,366	4.5	1996	126,708	7,236	5.4
1970	78,678	4,093	4.9	1997[5]	129,558	6,739	4.9
1975	85,846	7,929	8.5	1998[5]	131,463	6,210	4.5
1980	99,303	7,637	7.1	1999[6]	133,488	5,880	4.2
1985	107,150	8,312	7.2	2000[7]	135,208	5,655	4.0
1986	109,597	8,237	7.0	2001[7]	135,073	6,742	4.8
1987	112,440	7,425	6.2				

(1) **Other early unemployment rates:** 1905, 4.3; 1915, 8.5; 1925, 3.2; 1935, 20.3; 1936, 16.9; 1937, 14.3; 1938, 19.0; 1939, 17.2. 1945, 1.9; all for 14 years of age and older. (2) Persons 14 years of age and older. (3) Beginning in 1990, data incorporate 1990 census-based population controls, adjusted for estimated undercount. (4) Beginning in 1994, not strictly comparable with prior years, because of major redesign of the survey used. (5) Not strictly comparable with 1994-96 because of revisions in population controls used in household survey. (6) Data not strictly comparable with 1998 and earlier years because of further revisions in population controls used in household survey. (7) Beginning in Jan. 2000, not strictly comparable with earlier years because of revisions to the controls used in the survey.

Unemployment Insurance Data, by State, 2001

Source: Employment and Training Admin., U.S. Dept. of Labor; state programs only

STATE	Monetarily eligible claimants	First payments	Final payments	Initial claims	Benefits paid	Average weekly benefit	Employers subject to state law
AL	188,887	164,210	37,120	377,039	275,825,917	164.17	86,494
AK	47,342	44,017	17,256	88,384	102,863,761	193.01	16,336
AZ	148,019	113,334	29,660	233,399	265,180,546	172.74	105,436
AR	147,343	115,116	31,496	275,086	266,383,968	220.10	59,590
CA	1,696,334	1,289,136	427,497	2,781,983	3,217,030,870	172.01	955,173
CO	139,231	94,146	31,127	163,489	319,931,240	291.47	136,547
CT	168,228	147,056	30,575	257,643	489,600,210	277.09	96,852
DE	27,236	29,531	6,050	61,399	90,282,171	220.71	25,220
DC	22,646	22,703	8,436	21,106	89,442,213	261.56	26,478
FL	427,748	336,088	112,932	517,261	924,469,607	223.24	389,375
GA	367,033	269,538	72,221	649,033	592,872,210	228.42	191,549
HI	52,485	40,245	7,478	108,637	134,794,876	296.97	28,436
ID	69,677	57,109	14,541	127,733	140,699,578	223.46	40,149
IL	511,644	446,294	129,770	825,811	1,841,964,192	268.68	279,323
IN	261,746	206,761	61,037	413,781	495,278,397	243.98	125,123
IA	134,677	113,983	21,356	211,769	306,267,520	249.57	68,778
KS	92,631	69,886	18,629	154,408	215,264,220	260.89	67,559
KY	164,121	145,026	26,814	343,376	403,449,496	234.32	89,410
LA	113,393	87,044	26,755	186,880	220,452,041	193.94	95,803
ME	56,357	34,545	8,747	79,569	96,829,556	215.83	38,875
MD	164,893	124,289	31,446	247,708	373,225,891	235.27	131,814
MA	321,031	271,897	69,684	481,022	1,319,389,712	334.72	169,276
MI	614,116	525,766	120,730	1,102,604	1,594,985,782	260.73	213,399
MN	208,220	164,690	40,674	311,938	633,839,220	306.73	129,709
MS	108,557	82,333	23,372	206,657	177,062,864	162.99	53,557
MO	246,637	174,147	49,515	405,578	470,749,117	200.49	128,948
MT	34,621	26,187	8,175	55,651	67,435,554	194.19	33,022
NE	54,807	38,498	11,320	76,601	89,993,212	204.80	44,906
NV	103,344	93,051	26,595	185,350	287,524,794	228.46	45,831
NH	42,133	26,728	1,922	61,622	64,964,969	240.59	39,538
NJ	382,401	312,865	133,631	555,548	1,478,196,792	308.91	275,799
NM	42,568	34,903	9,878	64,912	91,777,184	193.23	41,711
NY	753,233	624,207	245,313	1,161,678	2,576,227,027	268.99	471,015
NC	486,590	382,640	74,072	1,169,536	918,969,154	248.00	173,868
ND	21,011	13,383	4,336	32,613	42,519,369	218.17	18,641
OH	453,244	364,626	80,264	806,512	1,213,018,150	247.65	232,070
OK	84,975	61,786	17,935	144,766	171,108,613	227.88	74,868
OR	235,593	203,344	51,655	483,454	649,716,287	255.97	99,872
PA	640,962	545,596	128,679	1,256,629	2,045,299,465	281.52	263,172
PR	128,694	131,291	61,052	234,679	258,117,986	93.62	50,936
RI	53,330	44,154	13,579	96,419	173,382,967	289.12	33,020
SC	216,273	161,564	38,957	481,863	374,324,077	205.88	89,034
SD	14,343	10,945	1,001	22,419	22,767,059	189.91	22,679
TN	238,869	247,085	70,324	516,035	565,964,950	197.81	109,958
TX	808,477	484,532	210,515	957,475	1,492,925,293	241.35	389,889
UT	80,373	60,270	16,545	98,889	172,702,043	252.84	53,522
VT	29,508	25,236	2,965	44,635	60,735,900	232.93	21,140
VI	2,431	2,277	556	3,162	5,758,341	225.74	3,110
VA	219,934	150,664	30,116	388,488	383,617,021	234.63	162,648
WA	373,874	272,761	70,512	636,119	1,198,882,513	311.27	194,407
WV	59,969	51,251	9,790	81,356	126,886,321	202.14	38,085
WI	374,514	327,155	55,913	743,570	788,155,515	241.71	121,997
WY	24,439	11,559	2,571	18,899	25,455,845	215.31	19,021
U.S.	**12,460,742**	**9,877,448**	**2,833,089**	**21,012,173**	**30,404,561,577**	**238.07**	**6,872,962**

Unemployment Rates, by Selected Country, 1970-2002

Source: Bureau of Labor Statistics, U.S. Dept. of Labor; civilian labor force, seasonally adjusted; May 2002

Time period	U.S.	Australia	Canada	France	Germany[1]	Italy[2]	Japan	Sweden	UK
1970	4.9	1.6	5.7	2.5	0.5	3.2	1.2	1.5	3.1
1975	8.5	4.9	6.9	4.2	3.4	3.4	1.9	1.6	4.6
1980	7.1	6.1	7.5	6.5	2.8	4.4	2.0	2.0	7.0
1981	7.6	5.8	7.6	7.6	4.0	4.9	2.2	2.5	10.5
1982	9.7	7.2	11.0	8.3	5.6	5.4	2.4	3.1	11.3
1983	9.6	10.0	11.9	8.6	6.9[3]	5.9	2.7	3.5	11.8
1984	7.5	9.0	11.3	10.0	7.1	5.9	2.8	3.1	11.7
1985	7.2	8.3	10.7	10.5	7.2	6.0	2.6	2.8	11.2
1986	7.0	8.1	9.6	10.6	6.6	7.5[3]	2.8	2.6	11.2
1987	6.2	8.1	8.8	10.8	6.3	7.9	2.9	2.2[3]	10.3
1988	5.5	7.2	7.8	10.3	6.3	7.9	2.5	1.9	8.6
1989	5.3	6.2	7.5	9.6	5.7	7.8	2.3	1.6	7.2
1990	5.6[3]	6.9	8.1	9.1	5.0	7.0	2.1	1.8	6.9
1991	6.8	9.6	10.3	9.6	5.6	6.9[3]	2.1	3.1	8.8
1992	7.5	10.8	11.2	9.9[3]	6.7	7.3	2.2	5.6	10.1
1993	6.9	10.9	11.4	11.3	7.9	10.2[3]	2.5	9.3	10.5
1994	6.1[3]	9.7	10.4	11.8	8.5	11.2	2.9	9.6	9.7
1995	5.6	8.5	9.4	11.3	8.2	11.8	3.2	9.1	8.7
1996	5.4	8.6	9.6	11.9	8.9	11.7	3.4	9.9	8.2
1997	4.9	8.6	9.1	11.8	9.9	11.9	3.4	10.1	7.0
1998	4.5	8.0	8.3	11.3	9.4	12.0	4.1	8.4	6.3
1999	4.2	7.2	6.8	10.6	8.7	11.5	4.7	7.1	6.0
2000	4.0	6.3	6.1	9.1	8.1	10.7	4.8	5.8	5.5
2001	4.8	6.7	6.4	8.5	8.0	9.6	5.1	5.0	5.1
2002 1st quarter	5.6	6.6	7.1	8.6	8.2	9.2	5.3	5.0	5.1
2002 2nd quarter	5.9	6.3	7.0	8.7	8.4	9.2	5.4	4.9	5.2

NA = Not available. **NOTE:** Some data for 2001-2002 are preliminary. For the sake of comparisons, U.S. unemployment rate concepts were applied to unemployment data for other countries. Quarterly and monthly figures for France and Germany were calculated by applying annual adjustment factors to current published data and are less precise indicators of unemployment under U.S. concepts than the annual figures. (1) For former West Germany only, through 1994; from 1995 on figures are for unified Germany and not adjusted by BLS. (2) Quarterly rates are for first month of quarter. (3) As a result of revisions in survey methodology, there are breaks in the data series for the U.S. (1994, 1997-2000), France (1992), Germany (1983, 1991), Italy (1986, 1991, 1993), and Sweden (1987); data prior to a survey change are not fully comparable to data after a survey change.

Employed Persons in the U.S., by Occupation and Sex, 1996, 2001

Source: Bureau of Labor Statistics, U.S. Dept. of Labor

(in thousands)

	Total 16 years and older		Men 16 years and older		Women 16 years and older	
	1996	2001	1996	2001	1996	2001
TOTAL	**126,708**	**135,073**	**68,207**	**72,080**	**58,501**	**62,992**
Managerial and professional specialty	36,497	41,894	18,744	20,966	17,754	20,928
Executive, administrative, and managerial	17,746	20,338	9,979	10,990	7,767	9,348
Officials and administrators, public administration	716	830	384	427	332	403
Other executive, administrative, and managerial	12,656	14,369	7,703	8,437	4,953	5,932
Management-related occupations	4,374	5,139	1,892	2,125	2,481	3,014
Professional specialty	18,752	21,556	8,764	9,976	9,987	11,580
Engineers	1,960	2,122	1,793	1,902	167	221
Mathematical and computer scientists	1,345	2,103	933	1,470	412	633
Natural scientists	536	582	379	382	157	200
Health diagnosing occupations	960	1,090	715	778	245	312
Health assessment and treating occupations	2,812	3,052	403	423	2,409	2,629
Teachers, college and university	889	1,003	502	568	387	435
Teachers, except college and university	4,724	5,473	1,207	1,375	3,517	4,098
Lawyers and judges	911	966	647	682	264	283
Other professional specialty occupations	4,616	5,164	2,186	2,396	2,430	2,769
Technical, sales, and administrative support	37,683	39,044	13,489	14,167	24,194	24,877
Technicians and related support	3,926	4,497	1,865	2,097	2,061	2,400
Sales occupations	15,404	16,044	7,782	8,120	7,622	7,924
Administrative support, including clerical	18,353	18,503	3,842	3,950	14,511	14,553
Service occupations	17,177	18,359	6,967	7,263	10,210	11,096
Precision production, craft, and repair	13,587	14,833	12,368	13,545	1,219	1,287
Mechanics and repairers	4,521	4,807	4,335	4,571	185	237
Construction trades	5,108	6,253	4,981	6,099	127	153
Other precision production, craft, and repair	3,959	3,772	3,052	2,875	906	897
Operators, fabricators, and laborers	18,197	17,698	13,750	13,569	4,447	4,129
Machine operators, assemblers, and inspectors	7,874	6,734	4,902	4,286	2,972	2,448
Transportation and material moving occupations	5,302	5,638	4,799	5,049	504	589
Motor vehicle operators	4,025	4,356	3,575	3,827	450	529
Other transportation and material moving occupations	1,277	1,282	1,223	1,222	54	60
Handlers, equipment cleaners, helpers, and laborers	5,021	5,326	4,049	4,234	971	1,092
Construction laborers	809	1,024	778	988	31	36
Other handlers, equipment cleaners, etc.	4,212	4,302	3,272	3,246	940	1,055
Farming, forestry, and fishing	3,566	3,245	2,889	2,570	677	675
Farm operators and managers	NA	1,108	NA	828	NA	281
Other farming, forestry, and fishing occupations	NA	2,136	NA	1,742	NA	394

NA = Not available. **NOTE:** Beginning in Jan. 2000, data reflect revised population controls used in the household survey. Totals may not add because of independent rounding.

Elderly in the Labor Force, 1890-2000

Source: Bureau of the Census, U.S. Dept. of Commerce

The percentage of men 65 years of age and older in the labor force steadily declined between 1890 and 1990 dropping 74% in 100 years, but then increased slightly by 2000. The percentage of women 65 or older in the work force has barely changed at all.

(labor force participation rate; figs. for 1910 not available)

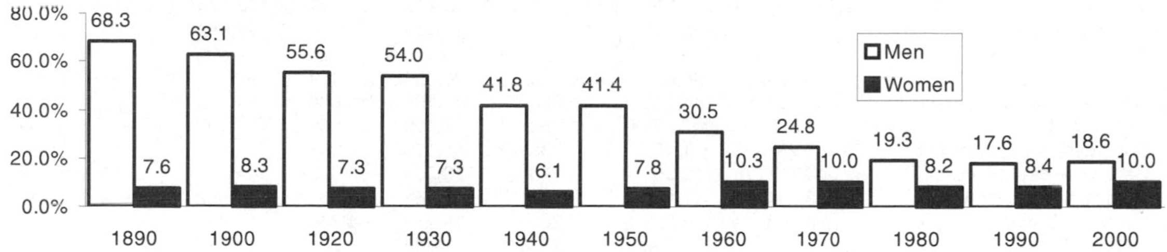

Unemployment Insurance

Source: Unemployment Insurance Service, U.S. Dept. of Labor

Unlike old-age and survivors insurance, which is entirely a federal program, unemployment insurance in the U.S. is a federal-state system that provides insured wage earners partial replacement for lost wages during a period of involuntary unemployment. The program protects most wage and salary workers. During fiscal year 2000, 127 million workers in commerce, industry, agriculture, and government were covered under the federal-state system.

Each state, as well as the District of Columbia, Puerto Rico, and the Virgin Islands, has its own law and operates its own program. The amount and duration of the weekly benefits are determined by state laws and are based on prior wages and length of employment. States are required to extend the duration of benefits when unemployment in the state rises to and remains above specified levels; costs of extended benefits are shared by the state and federal governments.

Under the Federal Unemployment Tax Act, the federal tax rate is 6.2% on the first $7,000 paid to each employee of employers with one or more employees in 20 weeks of the year or with a quarterly payroll of $1,500 or more. A credit of up to 5.4% is allowed for taxes paid under state unemployment insurance laws that meet certain criteria, for a net federal rate of 0.8%; subject employers also pay a state unemployment tax. Governmental agencies and certain nonprofit organizations are not subject to the federal tax; these employers reimburse states for benefits paid to former employees.

The secretary of labor certifies states for administrative grants to operate the program (under the Social Security Act) and for employer tax credit (under the Federal Unemployment Tax Act).

Benefits are financed solely by employer contributions, except in Alaska, New Jersey, and Pennsylvania, where employees also contribute. Benefits are paid through the states' public employment offices, at which unemployed workers must register for work and to which they must report regularly for referral to a possible job during the time when they are drawing weekly benefit payments.

During fiscal year 2000, $20.9 billion in benefits were paid under all unemployment insurance programs to 6.9 million beneficiaries. They received an average payment of $212 weekly for total unemployment, which lasted an average of 14.2 weeks.

U.S. Unemployment Rates by Selected Characteristics, 1960-2002

Source: Bureau of Labor Statistics, U.S. Dept. of Labor; seasonally adjusted, quarterly averages

	1960	1970	1980	1990	2000	2001				2002	
						I	II	III	IV	I	II
TOTAL (all civilian workers)	**5.5**	**4.9**	**7.1**	**5.6**	**4.0**	**4.2**	**4.5**	**4.8**	**5.6**	**5.6**	**5.9**
Men, 20 years and older	4.7	3.5	5.9	5.0	3.3	3.6	4.0	4.3	5.0	5.1	5.3
Women, 20 years and older	5.1	4.8	6.4	4.9	3.6	3.6	3.8	4.2	5.0	4.9	5.2
Both sexes, 16 to 19 years	14.7	15.3	17.8	15.5	13.1	13.6	14.1	15.2	15.8	16.0	17.1
White	5.0	4.5	6.3	4.8	3.5	3.7	3.9	4.2	4.9	5.0	5.2
Black	NA	NA	14.3	11.4	6.7	8.0	8.2	8.7	9.9	10.1	10.7
Black and other	10.2	8.2	13.1	10.1	7.7	7.0	7.2	7.8	8.8	9.0	9.5
Hispanic origin	NA	NA	10.1	8.2	5.7	6.1	6.4	6.4	7.5	7.5	7.4
Married men, spouse present	3.7	2.6	4.2	3.4	2.0	2.3	2.5	2.7	3.3	3.4	3.9
Married women, spouse present	5.2	4.9	5.8	3.8	2.7	2.6	2.9	3.1	3.6	3.6	3.9
Women who maintain families	NA	5.4	9.2	8.3	5.9	6.2	6.3	6.7	7.6	7.7	8.3
OCCUPATION											
Managerial and professional specialty	NA	NA	NA	2.1	1.7	1.8	2.1	2.4	2.8	3.0	3.2
Technical, sales, and administrative support	NA	NA	NA	4.3	3.6	3.6	3.9	4.3	5.0	5.1	5.3
Precision production, craft, and repair	NA	NA	NA	5.9	3.6	3.7	4.4	4.7	5.7	5.9	6.1
Operators, fabricators, and laborers	NA	NA	NA	8.7	6.3	7.1	7.4	7.6	8.9	9.0	9.2
Farming, forestry, and fishing	NA	NA	NA	6.4	6.0	7.5	6.9	7.7	6.8	8.0	6.2
INDUSTRY											
Nonagricultural private wage and salary workers	6.2	5.2	7.4	5.8	4.1	4.4	4.6	5.1	6.0	6.0	6.4
Goods-producing industries	7.5	6.1	9.4	7.0	4.4	5.1	5.4	6.1	7.1	7.3	7.6
Mining	9.7	3.1	6.4	4.8	4.0	3.6	5.2	4.5	5.7	5.6	6.1
Construction	13.5	9.7	14.1	11.1	6.4	6.6	6.9	7.5	8.7	8.7	9.1
Manufacturing	6.2	5.6	8.5	5.8	3.5	4.5	4.8	5.5	6.4	6.8	6.9
Durable goods	6.4	5.7	8.9	5.8	3.4	4.3	4.7	5.5	6.9	7.3	7.0
Nondurable goods	6.1	5.4	7.9	5.8	4.0	4.7	4.9	5.4	5.6	5.9	6.7
Service-producing industries	5.1	4.5	6.1	5.2	4.0	4.1	4.4	4.7	5.6	5.5	6.0
Transportation and public utilities	4.6	3.2	4.9	3.9	3.1	3.0	3.9	3.7	6.1	5.8	5.9
Wholesale and retail trade	5.9	5.3	7.4	6.4	5.0	5.1	5.3	5.6	6.5	6.4	6.9
Finance, insurance, and real estate	2.4	2.8	3.4	3.0	2.3	2.4	2.5	2.9	3.1	2.7	3.8
Services	5.1	4.7	5.9	5.0	3.8	4.0	4.2	4.7	5.4	5.4	5.7
Government workers	NA	NA	4.1	2.7	2.1	2.0	2.1	2.1	2.4	2.6	2.5
Agricultural wage/salary workers	8.3	7.5	11.0	9.8	7.6	9.8	9.1	9.4	9.3	10.7	8.8

NA = Not available.

Civilian Employment of the Federal Government, May 2001

Source: Statistical Analysis and Services Division, U.S. Office of Personnel Management

(payroll in thousands of dollars)

	ALL AREAS		UNITED STATES		WASH., D.C., MSA[2]		OVERSEAS	
	Employ-ment	Payroll	Employ-ment	Payroll	Employ-ment	Payroll	Employ-ment	Payroll
TOTAL, all agencies[1]	**2,704,015***	**$10,529,616***	**2,614,584***	**$10,216,145***	**322,633***	**$1,592,373***	**89,431***	**$313,471***
Legislative Branch	**30,199***	**133,544***	**30,191***	**133,481***	**29,104***	**127,682***	**8***	**63***
Congress	17,124	70,975	17,124	70,975	17,124	70,975	—	—
U.S. Senate	6,464	26,823	6,464	26,823	6,464	26,823	—	—
House of Representatives	10,660	44,152	10,660	44,152	10,660	44,152	—	—
Architect of the Capitol	1,950	7,199	1,950	7,199	1,950	7,199	—	—
Congressional Budget Ofc	232	1,458	232	1,458	232	1,458	—	—
General Accounting Ofc	3,117	19,562	3,116	19,556	2,338	14,818	1	6
Government Printing Ofc	3,044	12,461	3,044	12,461	2,766	11,502	—	—
Library of Congress	4,268	19,530	4,261	19,473	4,240	19,395	7	57
U.S. Tax Court	241	1,438	241	1,438	241	1,438	—	—
Judicial Branch	**32,957**	**150,648**	**32,548**	**148,985**	**1,904**	**10,308**	**409**	**1,663**
Supreme Court	418	1,415	418	1,415	418	1,415	—	—
U.S. Courts	32,539	149,233	32,130	147,570	1,486	8,893	409	1,663
Executive Branch	**2,640,859***	**10,245,424***	**2,551,845***	**9,933,679***	**291,625***	**1,454,383***	**89,014***	**311,745***
Exec Ofc of the President	1,566	10,570	1,557	10,507	1,557	10,507	9	63
White House Office	369	2,061	369	2,061	369	2,061	—	—
Ofc of Vice President	15	116	15	116	15	116	—	—
Ofc of Mgmt & Budget	490	3,883	490	3,883	490	3,883	—	—
Ofc of Administration	182	1,100	182	1,100	182	1,100	—	—
Council Economic Advisors	30	170	30	170	30	170	—	—
Ofc of Policy Development	31	145	31	145	31	145	—	—
National Security Council	47	301	47	301	47	301	—	—
Ofc of Natl Drug Control	109	795	109	795	109	795	—	—
Ofc of U.S. Trade Rep	173	1,262	164	1,199	164	1,199	9	63
Executive Departments	1,593,855	6,527,928	1,512,051	6,244,115	218,226	1,082,600	81,804	283,813
State	28,054	147,512	10,586	55,906	9,295	47,026	17,468	91,606
Treasury	159,274	639,368	157,898	632,876	22,538	123,053	1,376	6,492
Defense, Total	670,568	2,390,373	616,772	2,242,590	63,119	233,318	53,796	147,783
Defense, Mil Function	645,849	2,323,444	592,127	2,175,761	62,398	231,479	53,722	147,683
Defense, Civ Function	24,719	66,929	24,645	66,829	721	1,839	74	100
Dept of the Army	227,870	629,053	205,062	563,591	19,003	40,749	22,808	65,462
Army, Mil Function	203,152	562,125	180,418	496,763	18,282	38,910	22,734	65,362
Army, Civil Function	24,718	66,928	24,644	66,828	721	1,839	74	100
Corps of Engineers	24,699	66,880	24,625	66,780	702	1,791	74	100
Dept of the Navy	182,557	739,163	174,527	706,456	24,660	99,855	8,030	32,707
Dept of the Air Force	154,438	624,766	147,651	597,306	5,123	20,737	6,787	27,460
Defense Logist. Agency	23,680	89,067	22,942	85,749	2,007	8,921	738	3,318
Other Defense Activities	82,023	308,324	66,590	289,488	12,326	63,056	15,433	18,836
Justice	126,711	613,108	124,162	600,322	21,831	132,058	2,549	12,786
Interior	72,982	271,041	72,601	269,722	7,936	37,267	381	1,319
Agriculture	100,084	369,032	98,797	365,085	11,213	55,138	1,287	3,947
Commerce	39,151	171,637	38,381	168,339	20,074	103,643	770	3,298
Labor	16,016	74,725	15,973	74,554	5,364	27,622	43	171
Health & Human Services	63,323	309,912	63,064	308,371	28,227	151,882	259	1,541
Housing & Urban Dev	10,154	55,056	10,067	54,627	3,059	18,159	87	429
Transportation	64,131	431,276	63,629	428,252	10,487	67,425	502	3,024
Energy	15,689	92,019	15,681	91,959	5,230	33,547	8	60
Education	4,581	24,268	4,576	24,247	3,195	17,579	5	21
Veterans Affairs	223,137	938,601	219,864	927,265	6,658	34,883	3,273	11,336
Independent Agencies	1,045,438*	3,706,926*	1,038,237*	3,679,057*	71,842*	361,276*	7,201*	27,869*
Bd of Gov, Fed Rsrv Sys	1,650	9,814	1,650	9,814	1,650	9,814	—	—
Environmtl Protect Agcy	17,968	98,190	17,919	97,933	6,019	35,576	49	257
Equal Employ Opp Comm	2,746	12,828	2,746	12,828	655	3,510	—	—
Federal Communic Comm	1,946	11,425	1,944	11,411	1,620	9,764	2	14
Federal Deposit Ins Corp	6,532	40,743	6,524	40,692	2,442	16,608	8	51
Fed. Emerg. Mgmt Agency	4,826	20,294	4,763	19,941	2,150	9,247	63	353
General Svcs Admin	13,921	65,322	13,836	64,971	4,734	25,266	85	351
Natl Aero & Space Admin	18,850	110,569	18,829	110,428	3,984	24,123	21	141
Natl Fnd Arts & Humanities	363	1,908	363	1,908	363	1,908	—	—
Peace Corps	1,004	3,889	584	2,511	472	2,134	420	1,378
Securities & Exch. Comm	2,946	17,558	2,946	17,558	1,806	10,754	—	—
Small Business Adm.	3,968	18,688	3,876	18,386	823	4,666	92	302
Smithsonian Inst.	5,082*	19,825*	5,054*	19,649*	4,636*	17,879*	28*	176*
Social Security Admin	63,997	262,696	63,491	260,730	1,743	7,568	506	1,966
U.S. Postal Service	856,550	2,779,914	852,520	2,764,579	21,065	78,582	4,030	15,335

NOTE: * denotes figures that are preliminary or are based in whole or part on figures for the previous month. (1) Totals include agencies not listed. (2) Metropolitan Statistical Area.

U.S. Occupational Illnesses, by Industry and Type of Illness, 2000

Source: Bureau of Labor Statistics, U.S. Dept. of Labor

(percent distribution)

		GOODS PRODUCING				SERVICE PRODUCING				
	All private sector[1]	Agri-culture[2]	Mining[3]	Con-struc-tion	Manu-facturing	Trans. and pub. utilities	Whole-sale	Retail	Finance[4]	Service
Total [1,664,018 cases]	**100.0**	**100.0**	**100.0**	**100.0**	**100.0**	**100.0**	**100.0**	**100.0**	**100.0**	**100.0**
Nature of injury or illness:										
Sprains, strains	43.8	33.7	39.4	38.4	38.5	50.6	45.2	41.5	39.4	50.6
Bruises, contusions	9.1	9.1	11.3	7.9	8.6	10.4	9.6	10.4	6.8	8.6
Cuts, lacerations	7.3	9.0	6.9	9.0	8.7	4.1	7.0	10.9	4.5	4.4
Fractures	7.0	10.0	12.8	11.1	6.9	5.6	8.0	6.8	8.1	5.0
Heat burns	1.5	1.1	1.3	1.4	1.6	.4	.7	3.1	.8	1.1
Carpal tunnel syndrome	1.7	.6	.5	.5	2.9	1.0	1.2	1.3	6.7	1.4
Tendonitis	.9	.3	.1	.5	1.5	.5	.6	.7	1.4	.9
Chemical burns	.6	.3	.4	.5	.7	.4	.4	.7	.5	.5
Amputations	.6	1.9	.9	.6	1.2	.2	.8	.4	.3	.1
Multiple traumatic injuries	3.6	3.7	6.1	4.2	3.1	3.3	3.5	3.8	3.6	3.5
Part of body affected by the injury or illness:										
Head	6.6	8.6	8.3	7.8	7.5	6.0	6.2	6.3	6.0	5.7
Neck	1.7	1.2	1.8	1.2	1.5	2.7	1.6	1.4	1.8	2.0
Trunk	37.2	29.3	39.2	34.5	34.8	39.7	40.3	34.4	31.7	41.6
Upper extremities	23.0	27.6	21.3	22.9	30.7	16.0	21.6	25.5	24.2	17.4
Lower extremities	20.9	23.6	21.6	23.8	17.6	24.0	21.1	21.7	20.6	20.2
Body systems	1.3	1.3	.5	.7	1.2	1.3	1.0	.9	4.1	1.7
Multiple parts	8.7	7.8	7.1	8.1	6.3	9.6	7.8	9.4	10.9	10.7
Source of injury or illness:										
Chemicals and chemical products	1.5	1.3	5.7	1.0	2.1	1.0	1.3	1.3	1.4	1.6
Containers	14.4	7.8	6.2	5.3	13.6	22.0	24.5	21.2	12.1	8.8
Furniture and fixtures	3.4	.6	.9	1.6	2.6	2.1	2.6	5.4	5.0	4.7
Machinery	6.7	9.2	10.6	6.1	11.9	2.5	7.5	6.5	5.9	3.8
Parts and materials	11.0	8.6	23.6	23.2	18.0	8.6	10.4	6.6	3.3	3.3
Worker motion or position	15.5	15.4	4.7	14.2	18.7	14.3	13.7	13.5	22.9	15.5
Floors, walkways, ground surfaces	16.7	16.5	15.4	19.3	10.8	16.4	14.1	20.2	24.3	19.1
Tools, instruments, and equipment	6.2	6.6	10. 7	10.8	6.4	4.0	4.3	6.9	3.9	5.2
Vehicles	8.3	8.0	5.5	5.9	5.3	18.1	12.4	6.8	5.7	7.5
Health care patient	4.5	—	—	—	(5)	.7	—	.2	1.3	18.6
Event or exposure leading to injury or illness:										
Contact with objects and equipment	26.7	31.2	40.1	32.3	34.1	22.3	28.6	28.5	16.9	17.0
Struck by object	13.5	15.6	22.9	17.7	14.4	12.0	15.2	15.7	8.3	9.3
Struck against object	6.5	6.8	7.3	6.9	7.5	5.6	6.3	8.0	5.3	4.7
Caught in equipment or object	4.5	6.4	7.7	3.8	9.1	2.9	5.2	3.2	1.5	2.0
Fall to lower level	5.7	7.8	7.9	12.5	3.4	6.6	5.9	4.6	7.1	4.5
Fall on same level	12.0	9.8	7.2	7.5	8.3	10.0	9.7	16.9	18.0	15.7
Slip, trip, loss of balance—without fall	3.2	3.6	1.9	2.9	2.7	3.7	2.8	3.4	4.4	3.4
Overexertion	27.3	16.2	31.3	22.1	25.9	30.1	29.8	25.2	21.1	32.2
Overexertion in lifting	15.4	9.4	13.6	12.1	13.6	17.0	18.2	17.2	11.7	16.8
Repetitive motion	4.1	1.4	.9	1.4	8.1	2.2	3.1	3.1	11.5	3.2
Exposure to harmful substances	4.2	4.8	3.5	3.3	4.9	3.2	2.7	4.8	4.5	4.3
Transportation accidents	4.4	5.6	1.6	4.1	2.0	9.0	6.4	2.8	4.4	4.9
Fires and explosions	.2	.5	.5	.5	.2	.1	.2	.3	.2	.1
Assaults and violent acts by person	1.1	—	—	.2	.1	.4	.2	1.2	.9	3.3

NOTE: Dashes (—) indicate data are not available or do not meet publication guidelines. Because of rounding and classifications not shown, percentages may not add to 100. All injuries and illnesses reported involved days away from work. (1) Private sector includes all industries except government, but excludes farms with fewer than 11 employees. (2) Agriculture includes forestry and fishing, but excludes farms with fewer than 11 employees. (3) Data conforming to OSHA definition for mining operators in coal, metal, and nonmetal mining and for employers in railroad transportation are provided by the Mine Safety and Health Administration, U.S. Dept. of Labor, and by the Federal Railroad Administration, U.S. Dept. of Transportation. Independent mining contractors are excluded from the coal, metal, and nonmetal industries. (4) Finance includes insurance and real estate. (5) Less than 0.1%.

Fatal Occupational Injuries, 2001

Source: Bureau of Labor Statistics, U.S. Dept. of Labor

	FATALITIES Number	FATALITIES Percent
TRANSPORTATION INCIDENTS	**2,517**	**43**
Highway	1,404	24
Collision between vehicles, mobile equipment	723	12
Noncollision	339	6
Nonhighway (farm, industrial premises)	324	5
Aircraft	247	4
Worker struck by a vehicle	383	6
Water vehicle	90	2
Rail vehicle	62	1
ASSAULTS AND VIOLENT ACTS	**902**	**15**
Homicides	639	11
Shooting	505	9
Stabbing	58	1
Self-inflicted injuries	228	4
CONTACT WITH OBJECTS AND EQUIPMENT	**962**	**16**
Struck by object	553	9
Struck by falling object	343	6
Struck by flying object	60	1
Caught in or compressed by equipment or objects	266	5
Caught in running equipment or machinery	144	2
Caught in or crushed in collapsing materials	122	2
Falls	**808**	14
EXPOSURE TO HARMFUL SUBSTANCE OR ENVIRONMENTS	**499**	**8**
Contact with electric current	285	5
Contact with overhead power lines	124	2
Contact with temperature extremes	35	1
Exposure to caustic, noxious, or allergenic substances	96	2
Oxygen deficiency	83	1
FIRES AND EXPLOSIONS	**188**	**3**
OTHER EVENTS OR EXPOSURES	**24**	—
TOTAL	**5,900**	**100**
TOTAL, with fatalities from Sept. 11	**8,786**	—

NOTE: Totals for categories may include subcategories not shown separately. Percentages based on incidence rate per total fatalities. Dashes (—) indicate less than 0.5% or unavailable data.

U.S. Wage and Salary Workers Paid Hourly Rates, Second Quarter 2002

Source: Bureau of Labor Statistics, U.S. Dept. of Labor; unpublished tabulations from Current Population Survey; pay rates per hour

(in thousands)

SEX AND AGE	Total hourly workers	$5.15[1] or less	% of workers earning $5.15[1] or less	Less than $10.00	% of workers earning less than $10.00	$10.00 or more	% of workers earning $10.00 or more
Total, 16 years and older	**71,482**	**2,221**	**3.1**	**30,114**	**42.1**	**41,448**	**58.0**
16 to 24 years	16,274	1,226	7.5	12,083	74.2	4,190	25.7
20 to 24 years	10,332	617	6.0	6,732	65.2	3,600	34.8
25 years and older	55,208	995	1.8	17,929	32.5	37,256	67.5
25 to 54 years	46,669	774	1.7	14,615	31.3	32,054	68.7
25 to 34 years	15,761	379	2.4	5,751	36.5	10,011	63.5
35 to 44 years	17,172	247	1.4	4,985	29.0	12,186	71.0
45 to 54 years	13,735	148	1.1	3,878	28.2	9,857	71.8
55 years and older	8,540	221	2.6	3,337	39.1	5,204	60.9
55 to 64 years	6,627	112	1.7	2,301	34.7	4,324	65.2
65 years and older	1,913	109	5.7	1,034	54.1	879	45.9
Men, 16 years and older	35,407	856	2.4	12,287	34.7	23,119	65.3
16 to 24 years	8,185	476	5.8	5,614	68.6	2,571	31.4
20 to 24 years	5,279	267	5.1	2,903	55.0	2,175	41.2
25 years and older	27,222	381	1.4	6,674	24.5	20,548	75.5
Women, 16 years and older	36,075	1,365	3.8	17,766	49.2	18,329	50.8
16 to 24 years	8,089	750	9.3	6,469	80.0	1,619	20.0
20 to 24 years	5,053	350	6.9	3,607	71.4	1,425	28.2
25 years and older	27,986	615	2.2	12,276	43.9	18,710	66.9
RACE AND HISPANIC ORIGIN							
White							
Total, 16 years and older	58,247	1,804	3.1	24,070	41.3	34,178	58.7
Men	29,125	654	2.2	9,812	33.7	19,314	66.3
Women	29,122	1,151	4.0	14,218	48.8	14,864	51.0
Black							
Total, 16 years and older	9,776	322	3.3	4,307	44.1	5,266	53.9
Men	4,595	156	3.4	1,857	40.4	2,737	59.6
Women	5,181	167	3.2	2,673	51.6	2,528	48.8
Hispanic origin							
Total, 16 years and older	10,079	304	3.0	5,453	54.1	4,627	45.9
Men	5,779	128	2.2	2,666	46.1	3,113	53.9
Women	4,300	176	4.1	2,787	64.8	1,514	35.2
FULL- AND PART-TIME STATUS							
Full-time workers							
Total, 16 years and older	53,986	891	1.7	18,127	33.6	35,860	66.4
Men	29,698	407	1.4	8,045	27.1	21,654	72.9
Women	24,288	483	2.0	10,083	41.5	14,206	58.5
Part-time workers							
Total, 16 years and older	17,389	1,317	7.6	11,835	68.1	5,554	31.9
Men	5,657	445	7.9	4,216	74.5	1,441	25.5
Women	11,732	873	7.4	7,619	64.9	4,113	35.1

NOTE: Data refer to the sole or principal job, exclude the self-employed, and are not seasonally adjusted. Totals may not add because of independent rounding or because all subcategories are not listed. Full- or part-time status on the principal job is not identifiable for some multiple jobholders. Data for other races are not presented, and Hispanics are included in both white and black population groups. The data are from unpublished work tables and should not be considered part of an official BLS news release. (1) $5.15 = minimum hourly wage starting Sept. 1, 1997.

Federal Minimum Hourly Wage Rates Since 1950

Source: Bureau of Labor Statistics, U.S. Dept. of Labor

The Fair Labor Standards Act of 1938 and subsequent amendments provide for minimum wage-coverage applicable to nonprofessional workers in specified nonsupervisory employment categories.

EFFECTIVE DATE	NONFARM WORKERS: Under laws prior to 1966[1]	Percent of avg. earnings[2]	Under 1966 and later provis.[3]	FARM WORKERS[4]
Jan. 25, 1950	$0.75	54	NA	NA
Mar. 1, 1956	1.00	52	NA	NA
Sept. 3, 1961	1.15	50	NA	NA
Sept. 3, 1963	1.25	51	NA	NA
Feb. 1, 1967	1.40	50	$1.00	$1.00
Feb. 1, 1968	1.60	54	1.15	1.15
Feb. 1, 1969	(5)	(5)	1.30	1.30
Feb. 1, 1970	(5)	(5)	1.45	(5)
Feb. 1, 1971	(5)	(5)	1.60	(5)
May 1, 1974	2.00	46	1.90	1.60
Jan. 1, 1975	2.10	45	2.00	1.80
Jan. 1, 1976	$2.30	46	$2.20	$2.00
Jan. 1, 1977	(5)	(5)	2.30	2.20
Jan. 1, 1978	2.65	44	2.65	2.65
Jan. 1, 1979	2.90	45	2.90	2.90
Jan. 1, 1980	3.10	43	3.10	3.10
Jan. 1, 1981	3.35	42	3.35	3.35
Apr. 1, 1990	3.80[6]	35	3.80	3.80[6]
Apr. 1, 1991	4.25[6]	38	4.25	4.25[6]
Oct. 1, 1996	4.75[7]	37	4.75	4.75[7]
Sept. 1, 1997	5.15[7]	39	5.15	5.15[7]

NA = not applicable. (1) Applies to workers covered prior to 1961 Amendments and, after Sept. 1965, to workers covered by 1961 Amendments. Rates set by 1961 Amendments were: Sept. 1961, $1.00; Sept. 1964, $1.15; and Sept. 1965, $1.25. (2) Percent of gross average hourly earnings of production workers in manufacturing. (3) Applies to workers newly covered by Amendments of 1966, 1974, and 1977, and Title IX of Education Amendments of 1972. (4) Included in coverage as of 1966, 1974, and 1977 Amendments. (5) No change in rate. (6) Training wage for workers age 16-19 in first 6 months of first job: Apr. 1, 1990, $3.35; Apr. 1, 1991, $3.62. The training wage expired Mar. 31, 1993. (7) Under 1996 legislation, a subminimum training wage of $4.25 an hour was established for employees under 20 years of age during their first 90 consecutive calendar days of employment with an employer. For workers receiving gratuities, the minimum wage remained $2.13 per hour.

Hourly Compensation Costs[1], by Selected Country, 1975-2001

Source: Bureau of Labor Statistics, U.S. Dept. of Labor

(in U.S. dollars, compensation for production workers in manufacturing)

Country/Territory	1975	1985	1990	2001
Australia	$5.62	$8.21	$13.24	$13.15
Austria	4.51	7.58	17.75	19.40
Belgium	6.41	8.97	19.17	21.04
Canada	5.96	10.95	15.95	15.64
Denmark	6.28	8.13	18.04	21.98
Finland	4.66	8.25	21.25	19.94
France	4.52	7.52	15.49	15.88
Germany[2]	6.29	9.50	21.81	22.86
Greece	1.69	3.66	6.76	—
Hong Kong[3]	0.76	1.73	3.23	5.96
Ireland	3.03	5.99	11.81	13.28
Israel	2.25	4.06	8.55	13.53
Italy	4.67	7.63	17.45	13.76
Japan	3.00	6.34	12.80	19.59
Korea, South	0.32	1.23	3.71	8.09
Luxembourg	$6.26	$7.49	$16.04	$17.37
Mexico	1.47	1.59	1.58	2.34
Netherlands	6.58	8.75	18.06	19.29
New Zealand	3.15	4.38	8.17	7.74
Norway	6.77	10.37	21.47	23.13
Portugal	1.58	1.53	3.77	—
Singapore	0.84	2.47	3.78	7.77
Spain	2.53	4.66	11.38	10.88
Sri Lanka	0.28	0.28	0.35	—
Sweden	7.18	9.66	20.93	18.35
Switzerland	6.09	9.66	20.86	21.84
Taiwan	0.38	1.49	3.90	5.70
United Kingdom	3.37	6.27	12.70	16.14
United States	6.36	13.01	14.91	20.32

— Data not available. (1) Compensation includes all direct pay (including bonuses, etc.), paid benefits, and for some countries, labor taxes. (2) 1975, 1985, and 1990 data are for area covered by the former West Germany. 2001 is for unified Germany. (3) Now part of China.

Top 15 U.S. Metropolitan Areas, by Average Annual Salary, 2000

Source: Bureau of Labor Statistics, U.S. Dept. of Labor

Rank	Metropolitan area	Average annual salary[1]
1.	San Jose, CA	$76,076
2.	San Francisco, CA	59,314
3.	New York, NY	56,377
4.	New Haven–Bridgeport–Stamford–Danbury–Waterbury, CT	50,585
5.	Middlesex-Somerset-Hunterdon, NJ	48,977
6.	Newark, NJ	48,733
7.	Jersey City, NJ	47,514
8.	Boulder-Longmont, CO	45,565
9.	Washington, DC–MD–VA–WV	$45,333
10.	Boston-Worcester–Lawrence–Lowell-Brockton, MA–NH	45,191
11.	Seattle–Bellevue–Everett, WA	45,171
12.	Trenton, NJ	44,576
13.	Oakland, CA	44,170
14.	Bergen–Passaic, NJ	43,789
15.	Hartford, CT	42,349

NOTE: Jacksonville, NC, recorded the **lowest average annual pay** among U.S. metropolitan areas in 2000—$21,057—followed by Yuma, AZ ($21,487), Brownsville–Harlingen–San Benito, TX ($21,561), McAllen–Edinburg–Mission, TX ($21,695), and Myrtle Beach, SC ($22,881). The nationwide metropolitan average was $36,986. (1) Data are preliminary and include workers covered by Unemployment Insurance and Unemployment Compensation for Federal Employees programs.

Average Hours and Earnings of U.S. Production Workers, 1969-2001[1]

Source: Bureau of Labor Statistics, U.S. Dept. of Labor

(annual averages)

Year	Weekly hours	Hourly earnings	Weekly earnings
1969	37.7	$3.04	$114.61
1970	37.1	3.23	119.83
1971	36.9	3.45	127.31
1972	37.0	3.70	136.90
1973	36.9	3.94	145.39
1974	36.5	4.24	154.76
1975	36.1	4.53	163.53
1976	36.1	4.86	175.45
1977	36.0	5.25	189.00
1978	35.8	5.69	203.70
1979	35.7	6.16	219.91
1980	35.3	6.66	235.10
1981	35.2	7.25	255.20
1982	34.8	7.68	267.26
1983	35.0	8.02	280.70
1984	35.2	8.32	292.86
1985	34.9	8.57	299.09
1986	34.8	$8.76	$304.85
1987	34.8	8.98	312.50
1988	34.7	9.28	322.02
1989	34.6	9.66	334.24
1990	34.5	10.01	345.35
1991	34.3	10.32	353.98
1992	34.4	10.57	363.61
1993	34.5	10.83	373.64
1994	34.7	11.12	385.86
1995	34.5	11.43	394.34
1996	34.4	11.82	406.61
1997	34.6	12.28	424.89
1998	34.6	12.78	442.19
1999	34.5	13.24	456.78
2000	34.5	13.76	474.72
2001	34.2	14.32	489.74

(1) Private-industry production workers in mining and manufacturing; construction workers; nonsupervisory workers in services, transportation, and public utilities; wholesale or retail trade; finance, insurance, or real estate. Figures may be revised.

Median Income, by Sex, Race, Age, and Education, 2000, 2001

Source: Bureau of the Census, U.S. Dept. of Commerce

	2000	2001
MALE	**$28,318**	**$29,101**
Race		
White	29,797	30,240
Black	21,343	21,466
Hispanic origin[1]	19,498	20,189
Age		
Under 65 years	30,612	30,951
65 and over	19,411	19,688
Educational attainment		
Less than 9th grade	14,131	14,594
9th-12th grade (no diploma)	18,915	19,434
High school graduate	27,480	28,343
Some college, no degree	33,039	33,777
Associate degree	38,026	38,870
Bachelor's degree or more	53,488	54,069
FEMALE	**$16,063**	**$16,614**
Race		
White	16,079	16,652
Black	15,881	16,282
Hispanic origin[1]	12,248	12,583
Age		
Under 65 years	18,295	18,976
65 and over	11,023	11,313
Educational attainment		
Less than 9th grade	8,546	8,846
9th-12th grade (no diploma)	10,063	10,330
High school graduate	15,153	15,665
Some college, no degree	20,166	20,101
Associate degree	23,124	22,638
Bachelor's degree or more	33,148	33,842

NOTE: Includes both full-time and part-time year-round workers, 15 years old and over as of Mar. of the following year. (1) May be of any race.

Median Weekly Earnings of Wage and Salary Workers in the U.S. by Age, Sex, and Union Affiliation, 1996, 2001

Source: Bureau of Labor Statistics, U.S. Dept. of Labor

	1996				2001			
SEX AND AGE	TOTAL	Members of unions[1]	Represented by unions[2]	Non-union	TOTAL	Members of unions[1]	Represented by unions[2]	Non-union
Total, 16 years and older	$490	$615	$610	$462	$597	$718	$712	$575
16 to 24 years	298	371	362	294	376	473	475	370
25 years and older	520	625	621	498	632	733	728	612
25 to 34 years	463	554	548	447	579	654	646	563
35 to 44 years	559	636	632	530	658	743	738	637
45 to 54 years	594	687	686	552	693	776	774	663
55 to 64 years	535	620	616	505	640	744	744	613
65 years and older	384	510	510	367	472	607	605	440
Men, 16 years and older	557	653	651	520	672	765	761	647
16 to 24 years	307	375	369	303	392	482	488	387
25 years and older	599	669	668	580	722	781	779	705
25 to 34 years	499	591	587	485	621	699	691	610
35 to 44 years	632	683	683	617	755	799	794	744
45 to 54 years	698	718	721	682	799	814	813	790
55 to 64 years	643	667	664	633	766	801	807	748
65 years and older	477	589	593	424	548	686	705	520
Women, 16 years and older	418	549	543	398	511	643	639	494
16 to 24 years	284	358	339	280	354	458	456	348
25 years and older	444	560	555	420	542	656	652	519
25 to 34 years	415	497	495	405	514	600	597	503
35 to 44 years	463	561	556	439	545	643	641	523
45 to 54 years	481	620	616	445	588	721	715	554
55 to 64 years	420	524	523	395	539	656	659	512
65 years and older	334	417	413	321	372	497	487	358

Note: Data refer to the sole or principal job of full-time workers. Excluded are self-employed workers regardless of whether or not their businesses are incorporated. (1) Including members of an employee association similar to a union. (2) Including members of a labor union or employee association similar to a union, and others whose jobs are covered by a union or an employee-association contract.

Work Stoppages (Strikes and Lockouts) in the U.S., 1960-2001

Source: Bureau of Labor Statistics, U.S. Dept. of Labor; involving 1,000 workers or more

Year	Number of stoppages[1]	Workers involved[1] (thousands)	Work days idle[1] (thousands)	Year	Number of stoppages[1]	Workers involved[1] (thousands)	Work days idle[1] (thousands)
1960	222	896	13,260	1985	54	324	7,079
1965	268	999	15,140	1986	69	533	11,861
1970	381	2,468	52,761	1987	46	174	4,481
1971	298	2,516	35,538	1988	40	118	4,381
1972	250	975	16,764	1989	51	452	16,996
1973	317	1,400	16,260	1990	44	185	5,926
1974	424	1,796	31,809	1991	40	392	4,584
1975	235	965	17,563	1992	35	364	3,989
1976	231	1,519	23,962	1993	35	182	3,981
1977	298	1,212	21,258	1994	45	322	5,020
1978	219	1,006	23,774	1995	31	192	5,771
1979	235	1,021	20,409	1996	37	273	4,889
1980	187	795	20,844	1997	29	339	4,497
1981	145	729	16,908	1998	34	387	5,116
1982	96	656	9,061	1999	17	73	1,996
1983	81	909	17,461	2000	39	394	20,419
1984	62	376	8,499	2001	29	99	1,151

(1) Numbers cover stoppages that began in the year indicated. Days of idleness include all stoppages in effect. Workers are counted more than once if they are involved in more than 1 stoppage during the year.

Work Stoppages Involving 5,000 Workers or More Beginning in 2001

Source: Bureau of Labor Statistics, U.S. Dept. of Labor

EMPLOYER; LOCATION; UNION	Began	Ended	Workers involved[1]	Estimated days idle in 2001[1]
Department of Education; Hawaii; National Education Association	4/5	4/23	12,400	161,200
Seattle Public Schools; Seattle, WA; National Education Association	5/1	5/1	6,900	6,900
State of Minnesota; Minnesota; American Federation of State, County, and Municipal Employees and Minnesota Association of Professional Employees	10/1	10/14	24,900	242,500
Pratt and Whitney, United Technologies Corporation; Connecticut; Machinists	12/3	12/13	5,000	45,000

(1) Workers and days idle are rounded to the nearest 100.

Labor Union Directory

Source: Bureau of Labor Statistics, U.S. Dept. of Labor; AFL-CIO; World Almanac research.

(*) Independent union; all others affiliated with AFL-CIO.

Actors and Artistes of America, Associated (AAAA), 165 W 46th St., Suite 500, New York, NY 10036; founded 1919; Theodore Bikel, Pres.; no individual members, 7 National Performing Arts Unions are affiliates; approx. 100,000 combined membership.

Actors' Equity Association, 165 W 46th St., New York, NY 10036; founded 1913; Patrick Quinn, Pres. (since 2000); 40,000 active members.

Air Line Pilots Association, 535 Herndon Pkwy., Herndon, VA 20170; founded 1931; Capt. Duane Woerth, Pres. (since 1999); 66,000+ members, 43 airlines.

American Federation of Labor & Congress of Industrial Organizations (AFL-CIO), 815 16th St. NW, Washington, DC 20006; founded 1955; John J. Sweeney, Pres. (since 1995); 13 mil. members.

Automobile, Aerospace & Agricultural Implement Workers of America, International Union, United (UAW), 8000 E Jefferson Ave., Detroit, MI 48214; founded 1935; Ron Gettelfinger, Pres. (since 2002); 710,000 active (500,000 ret.) members, 950+ locals.

Bakery, Confectionery, Tobacco Workers and Grain Millers International Union (BCTGM), 10401 Connecticut Ave., Kensington, MD 20895; founded 1886; Frank Hurt, Pres. (since 1992); 125,000 members.

Boilermakers, Iron Ship Builders, Blacksmiths, Forgers and Helpers, International Brotherhood of (IBBISB/BF&H), 753 State Ave., Suite 565, Kansas City, KS 66101; founded 1880; Charles W. Jones, Int'l Pres. (since 1983); 100,000+ members, 420 locals.

Bricklayers and Allied Craftworkers, International Union of, 1776 Eye St. NW, Washington, DC 20006; founded 1865; John J. Flynn, Pres. (since 1999); 100,000 members, 200 locals.

Carpenters and Joiners of America, United Brotherhood of, 101 Constitution Ave., NW, Washington, DC 20001; founded 1881; Douglas J. McCarron, Gen. Pres. (since 1995); 525,000 members, 1,000 locals.

Communications Workers of America (IUE-CWA), 501 3rd St. NW, Washington, DC 20001; founded 1938; Morton Bahr, Pres. (since 1985); 740,000 members, 1,200 locals. (Merged with the Intl. Union of Electronic, Electrical, Salaried, Machine, and Furniture Workers 10/1/00.)

***Education Association, National,** 1201 16th St. NW, Washington, DC 20036; founded 1857; Reg Weaver, Pres. (since 2002); 2.7 mil. members, 14,000+ affiliates.

Electrical Workers, International Brotherhood of (IBEW), 1125 15th St. NW, Washington, DC 20005; founded 1891; Edwin D. Hill, Pres. (since 2001); 727,836 members, 1,019 locals.

Engineers, International Union of Operating (IUOE), 1125 17th St. NW, Washington, DC 20036; founded 1896; Frank Hanley, Pres.; 400,000 members, 170 locals.

Farm Workers of America, United (UFW), 29700 Woodford-Tehachapi Rd., PO Box 62, Keene, CA 93531; founded 1962; Arturo S. Rodríguez, Pres. (since 1993); 50,000 members.

***Federal Employees, Federal District 1, National Federation of (NFFE FD1, IAMAW, AFL-CIO),** 1016 16th St. NW, Suite 300, Washington, DC 20036; founded 1917; Richard N. Brown, Pres. (1998); 120,000 members, 290 locals.

Fire Fighters, International Association of, 1750 New York Ave. NW, Washington, DC 20006; founded 1918; Harold Schaitberger, Pres. (since 2000); 250,000 members, 2,700 locals.

Firemen and Oilers, National Conference of, 1023 15th St. NW, 10th Floor, Washington, DC 20035; founded 1898; George J. Francisco, Jr., Pres.; 26,000 members, 133 locals.

Flight Attendants, Association of, 1275 K St. NW, Washington, DC 20005; founded 1945; Patricia A. Friend, Int'l Pres.; 50,000 members, 26 carriers.

Food and Commercial Workers International Union, United (UFCW), 1775 K St. NW, Washington, DC 20006-1598; founded 1979 following merger; Douglas H. Dority, Intl. Pres. (since 1994); 1.4 mil. members, 997 locals.

Glass, Molders, Pottery, Plastics & Allied Workers Intl. Union (GMP), 608 E Baltimore Pike, PO Box 607, Media, PA 19063; founded 1842; James H. Rankin, Pres. (since 1997); 51,000 members, 370 locals.

Government Employees, American Federation of (AFGE), 80 F St. NW, Washington, DC 20001; founded 1932; Bobby L. Harnage Sr., Pres. (since 1997); 600,000 members, 1,100 locals.

Graphic Communications International Union (GCIU), 1900 L St. NW, Washington, DC 20036; founded 1983; James J. George Tedeschi, Pres. (since 2000); 150,000 members, 321 locals.

Hotel Employees and Restaurant Employees International Union, 1219 28th St. NW, Washington, DC 20007; John W. Wilhelm, Gen. Pres. (since 1998); 265,000 members, 11 locals.

Iron Workers, International Association of Bridge, Structural, Ornamental and Reinforcing, 1750 New York Ave. NW, Suite 400, Washington, DC 20006; founded 1896; Joseph Hunt, Gen. Pres. (since 2001); 120,000 members, 242 locals.

Laborers' International Union of North America (LIUNA), 905 16th St. NW, Washington, DC 20006-1765; founded 1903; Terence M. O'Sullivan, Pres. (since 2000); 800,000 members.

Leather Goods, Plastics Novelty, and Service Workers' Union, International, 265 W 14th St., Suite 711, New York, NY 10011; 5,500 members, 80 locals.

Letter Carriers, National Association of (NALC), 100 Indiana Ave. NW, Washington, DC 20001-2144; founded 1889; Vincent R. Sombrotto, Pres. (since 1978); 312,500 members, 2,723 locals.

Locomotive Engineers, Brotherhood of (BLE), The Standard Bldg. Mezzanine, 1370 Ontario St., Cleveland, OH 44113-1702; founded 1863; Don M. Hahs, Pres. (since 2001); 58,000 members, 600+ divisions.

Longshore & Warehouse Union, International (ILWU), 1188 Franklin St., San Francisco, CA 94109-6800; founded 1937; James Spinosa, Pres. (since 2000); 60,000 members, 60 locals, 16 units of locals.

Longshoremen's Association, International (ILA), 17 Battery Pl., Suite 1530, New York, NY 10004; John M. Bowers, Pres. (since 1987); 65,000 members.

Machinists and Aerospace Workers, International Association of (IAMAW), 9000 Machinists Pl., Upper Marlboro, MD 20772-2687; founded 1888; R. Thomas Buffenbarger, Pres. (since 1997); 780,000 members, 1,194 locals.

Maintenance of Way Employes, Brotherhood of (BMWE), 26555 Evergreen Rd., Suite 200, Southfield, MI 48076; founded 1887; M. A. "Mac" Fleming, Pres. (since 1990); 55,000 members, 790 locals.

Marine Engineers' Beneficial Assn. (MEBA), 444 N Capitol St. NW, Suite 800, Washington, DC 20001; founded 1875; Ron Daris, Pres. (since 2002).

Mine Workers of America, United (UMWA), 8315 Lee Highway, Fairfax, VA 22031; founded 1890; Cecil E. Roberts, Pres. (since 1995); 130,000 members, 600 locals.

Musicians of the United States and Canada, American Federation of (AFM), 1501 Broadway, Suite 600, New York, NY 10036; founded 1896; Thomas F. Lee, Pres. (since 2001); 125,000 members, 250+ locals.

Needletrades, Industrial, and Textile Employees, Union of (UNITE), 1710 Broadway, New York, NY 10019; founded 1995; Bruce S. Raynor, Pres. (since 2001); 250,000 members, 900 locals.

Newspaper Guild-Communications Workers of America (CWA), The, 501 3d St. NW, Suite 250, Washington, DC 20001-2797; founded 1933; Linda K. Foley, Pres. (since 1995); 35,000 members, 90 locals.

WORLD ALMANAC QUICK QUIZ

What percentage of the labor force today are members of labor unions?

(a)13.5% (b) 23.5
(c) 29.5% (d) 33.5%

For the answer look in this chapter, or see page 1008.

***Nurses Association, American (ANA),** 600 Maryland Ave. SW, Suite 100-W, Washington, DC 20024-2571; founded 1897; Mary E. Foley, Pres.; 177,000 members, 53 constituent state & territorial assns.

Office and Professional Employees International Union (OPEIU), 265 W 14th St., Suite 610, New York, NY 10011; founded 1945 (AFL Charter); Michael Goodwin, Pres. (since 1994); 130,000 members, 200 locals.

PACE International Union, AFL-CIO, CLC (PACE), 3340 Perimeter Hill Dr., PO Box 1475, Nashville, TN 37202; founded 1884; Boyd D. Young, Pres. (since 1999); 320,000 members, 1,600 locals.

Painters and Allied Trades, International Union of (IUPAT), 1750 New York Ave. NW, Washington, DC 20006; founded 1887; Michael E. Monroe, Gen. Pres.; 130,000 members, 425 locals.

Plasterers' and Cement Masons' International Association of the United States and Canada, Operative, 14405 Laurel Pl., Suite 300, Laurel, MD 20707; founded 1864; John J. Dougherty, Pres.; 40,000 members, 100 locals.

Plumbing and Pipe Fitting Industry of the United States and Canada, United Association of Journeymen and Apprentices of the, 901 Massachusetts Ave. NW, PO Box 37800, Washington, DC 20013; founded 1889; Martin J. Maddaloni, Gen. Pres. (since 1997); 307,000 members, 333 locals.

***Police, National Fraternal Order of,** 1410 Donelson Pike, A-17, Nashville, TN 37217; Steve Young, Natl. Pres. (since 2001); 290,000 members, 2,000+ affiliates.

Police Associations, International Union of, 1421 Prince St., Suite 400, Alexandria, VA 22314; Samuel Cabral, Pres. (since 1995); 80,000 members, 500 locals.

***Postal Supervisors, National Association of,** 1727 King St., Suite 400, Alexandria, VA 22314-2753; Vincent Palladino, Pres. (since 1992); 36,000 members, 400 locals.

Postal Workers Union, American (APWU), 1300 L St. NW, Washington, DC 20005; founded 1971; WIlliam Burrus, Pres. (since 2001); 350,000 members, 1,600+ locals.

Roofers, Waterproofers & Allied Workers, United Union of, 1660 L St. NW, Suite 800, Washington, DC 20036; founded 1906; Earl J. Kruse, Pres. (since 1985); 25,000 members, 86 locals.

***Rural Letter Carriers' Association, National,** 1630 Duke St., 4th Fl., Alexandria, VA 22314; founded 1903; Gus Baffa, Pres. (since 2001); 100,000 members; 50 state org.

Seafarers International Union of North America (SIU), 5201 Auth Way and Britannia Way, Camp Springs, MD 20746; founded 1938; Michael Sacco, Pres. (since 1988); 85,000 members, 18 affiliates.

***Security, Police, and Fire Professionals of America (SPFPA),** 25510 Kelly Rd., Roseville, MI 48066; founded 1948; David L. Hickey, Pres. (since 2000); 12,000 members, 160 locals.

Service Employees International Union (SEIU), 1313 L St. NW, Washington, DC 20005; founded 1921; Andrew L. Stern, Pres. (since 1996); 1.4 million members, 350 locals.

Sheet Metal Workers' International Association (SMWIA), 1750 New York Ave. NW, Washington, DC 20006; founded 1888; Michael J. Sullivan, Pres. (since 1999); 150,000 members, 194 locals.

State, County, and Municipal Employees, American Federation of (AFSCME), 1625 L St. NW, Washington, DC 20036; Gerald W. McEntee, Pres. (since 1981); 1.3 mil. members, 3,617 locals.

Steelworkers of America, United (USWA), 5 Gateway Center, Pittsburgh, PA 15222; founded 1936; Leo W. Gerard, Pres. (since 2001); 700,000+ members, 2,000 locals.

Teachers, American Federation of (AFT), 555 New Jersey Ave. NW, Washington, DC 20001; founded 1916; Sandra Feldman, Pres. (since 1997); 1 mil.+ members, 3,000 locals.

Teamsters, International Brotherhood of (IBT), 25 Louisiana Ave. NW, Washington, DC 20001; founded 1903; James P. Hoffa, Gen. Pres. (since 1999); 1.5 mil. members, 569 locals.

Television and Radio Artists, American Federation of, (AFTRA) 260 Madison Ave., 7th fl., New York, NY 10016; founded 1937; John Connolly, Natl. Pres. (since 2001); 75,000 members, 35 locals.

Theatrical Stage Employees, Moving Picture Technicians, Artists and Allied Crafts of the United States, Its Territories, and Canada, International Alliance of (IATSE), 1430 Broadway, 20th floor, New York, NY 10018; founded 1893; Thomas C. Short, Pres. (since 1994); 95,000 members, 555+ locals.

Transit Union, Amalgamated (ATU), 5025 Wisconsin Ave. NW, 3rd Fl., Washington, DC 20016; founded 1892; James La Sala, Pres. (since 1986); 165,000 members, 285 locals.

Transportation-Communications International Union (TCU), 3 Research Place, Rockville, MD 20850; founded 1899; Robert A. Scardelletti, Pres. (since 1991); 100,000 members.

Transportation Union, United (UTU), 14600 Detroit Ave., Cleveland, OH 44107; founded 1969; Byron A. Boyd Jr., Pres. (since 2001); 135,000 members, 680 locals.

Transport Workers Union of America, 80 West End Ave., 5th Fl., New York, NY 10023; founded 1934; Sonny Hall, Int'l. Pres. (since 1993); 125,000+ members, 92 locals.

***Treasury Employees Union, National (NTEU),** 901 E St. NW, Suite 600, Washington, DC 20004; founded 1938; Colleen M. Kelley, Natl. Pres. (since 1999); 155,000 represented, 270+ chapters.

***University Professors, American Association of (AAUP),** 1012 14th St. NW, Suite 500, Washington, DC 20005; founded 1915; Jane Buck, Pres.; 44,000 members, 600 chapters.

Utility Workers Union of America (UWUA), 815 16th St. NW, Washington, DC 20006; founded 1945; Donald Wightman, Pres. (since 1996); 43,000 members, 250 locals.

U.S. Union Membership, 1930-2001

Source: Bureau of Labor Statistics, U.S. Dept. of Labor

Year	Labor force[1] (thousands)	Union members[2] (thousands)	Percentage of labor force	Year	Labor force[1] (thousands)	Union members[2] (thousands)	Percentage of labor force
1930	29,424	3,401	11.6	1988	101,407	17,002	16.8
1935	27,053	3,584	13.2	1989	103,480	16,960	16.4
1940	32,376	8,717	26.9	1990	103,905	16,740	16.1
1945	40,394	14,322	35.5	1991	102,786	16,568	16.1
1950	45,222	14,267	31.5	1992	103,688	16,390	15.8
1955	50,675	16,802	33.2	1993	105,067	16,598	15.8
1960	54,234	17,049	31.4	1994	107,989	16,748	15.5
1965	60,815	17,299	28.4	1995	110,038	16,360	14.9
1970	70,920	19,381	27.3	1996	111,960	16,269	14.5
1975	76,945	19,611	25.5	1997	114,533	16,110	14.1
1980	90,564	19,843	21.9	1998	116,730	16,211	13.9
1985	94,521	16,996	18.0	1999	118,963	16,477	13.9
1986	96,903	16,975	17.5	2000	120,786	16,258	13.5
1987	99,303	16,913	17.0	2001	120,760	16,275	13.5

(1) Does not include agricultural employment; from 1985, does not include self employed or unemployed persons. (2) From 1930 to 1980, includes dues-paying members of traditional trade unions, regardless of employment status; after that includes employed only. From 1985, includes members of employee associations that engage in collective bargaining with employers.

TAXES

Federal Income Tax

Source: George W. Smith III, CPA, Nationally Syndicated Tax Author and Columnist

In June 2001, Pres. Geroge W. Bush signed into law the largest federal income tax cut in more than 2 decades. In March 2002, a smaller package of cuts, primarily for businesses, became law.

The Job Creation and Worker Assistance Act of 2002

This measure became law on Mar. 9, 2002, and contains over $38 billion in tax cuts spread over 10 years. Through 2004, the new law provides taxpayers over $120 billion in tax breaks and incentives. After that date some of the provisions reverse themselves and become revenue raisers.

Classroom Materials. Elementary and secondary school teachers, principals, and counselors who purchase school books or other teaching materials and supplies with their own money can deduct up to $250 of these expenses. This is a page-one deduction that begins in 2002 and expires after 2003. Taxpayers do not have to itemize to take advantage of this deduction.

Depreciation. Businesses that purchase new qualifying property after Sept. 10, 2001, and before Sept. 10, 2004, can take an additional first-year depreciation deduction equal to 30% of the property's basis. This deduction is in addition to any amount expensed under Section 179.

Business vehicles are limited to inflation-adjusted dollar caps for their depreciation deduction. Previously, the maximum on first-year depreciation was $3,060. The new law increases this amount to $7,660 for new vehicles placed in service after Sept. 10, 2001, and before Sept. 10, 2004.

Operating Loss. Businesses and individuals with an operating loss in taxable years ending in 2001 and 2002 may carry the loss back 5 years, instead of 2 under prior legislation.

Reconstruction. The new law gives New York City businesses and individuals in the "Liberty Zone" (southern Manhattan) temporary tax breaks including a depreciation bonus of 30%, special rebuilding bonds, and certain involuntary conversion expense. It also increases the small business Section 179 expensing election up to $35,000.

Other Measures. The new law clarifies when a taxpayer can qualify as head of household or surviving spouse if a child is kidnapped or missing. The definition of qualified foster care payments excludable from income has been expanded. Payors may send Miscellaneous Income Form 1099 to recipients electronically.

The Economic Growth and Tax Relief Reconciliation Act of 2001 (Tax Relief Act)

On May 26, 2001, Congress passed the massive $1.35 trillion, 10-year Tax Relief Act. President Bush signed this tax package into law on June 7, 2001. This legislation added 440 changes to the Internal Revenue Tax Code.

Individual Tax Rates. Again in 2002 the Tax Relief Act reduces tax rates for individuals. The former 39.1% tax rate in 2001 is reduced to 38.6%, 35.5% drops to 35.0%, 30.5% lowers to 30.0%, and the 27.5% rate falls to 27.0%. The top tax rate eventually decreases to 35%, in 2006, but the bottom rate, 15%, remains the same. However, there is a new, lower 10% rate beginning Jan. 1, 2002. This rate covers the first $6,000 of taxable income for those filing as single, $10,000 for heads of households, and $12,000 for married persons filing jointly.

Child Credits. This credit increased from $500 to $600 beginning in 2001 and remains the same through 2004 for each qualifying child. The credit increases to $700 in 2005, $800 for 2009, and finally $1,000 in 2010. A credit reduces a taxpayer's income tax liability. Generally, any unused credit is not refundable. One exception: for lower-income taxpayers the Act makes the child tax credit partially refundable even if no income tax was paid.

Starting in 2003, the maximum expense eligible for the dependent care tax credit increases from $2,400 to $3,000 for one qualifying child or other dependent incapable of self-care, and from $4,800 to $6,000 for 2 or more. Special income phase-out limitations also increase.

Adoption Credit. Beginning in 2002 both the maximum dollar limitation for the adoption credit and the exclusion from income of employer-provided adoption assistance increases to $10,000 per eligible child. The income phase-out limitations also increase. For the following year, 2003, a credit can be claimed for a special needs adoption whether or not the taxpayer has qualified adoption expenses.

Education IRA. The maximum annual contribution increased in 2002 from $500 to $2,000. Funds may be used for elementary and secondary education expenses, whether for a public, private, or religious school. Qualifying distributions are not taxable to the recipient. The phase-out maximum for joint filers increases to twice that of single filers. Contributions are not tax deductible.

Student Loans. Starting in 2002, the Tax Relief Act increases the income phase-out range for the interest deduction on student loans to $50,000-$65,000 for single taxpayers and $100,000-$130,000 for married taxpayers. Beginning in 2003, these ranges will be adjusted annually for inflation. The provision also repeals the 60-month time limitation for the number of months during which interest paid is deductible.

College Education. For the years 2002 and 2003, a $3,000 deduction for qualified tuition and related expenses is available to individual taxpayers even if the taxpayer does not itemize. The amount increases to $4,000 for 2004 and 2005. Generally, any accredited public, nonprofit, or proprietary post-secondary institution is considered an eligible education institution. These dollar amounts are phased-out for higher-income taxpayers. The Tax Relief Act terminates this deduction after 2005.

Joint Filers' Standard Deductions. The standard deduction available to married taxpayers filing a joint return will gradually increase over a 5-year period starting in 2005, until 2009, when the amount reaches 200% of that allowed for single taxpayers. The upper limit of the 15% bracket for married taxpayers filing a joint return also will increase beginning in 2005.

Higher Income. Levels for phasing out personal exemptions and Schedule A itemized deductions for higher income taxpayers will fall by 1/3 in 2006 and 2007, and by 2/3 in 2008 and 2009. They will be eliminated in 2010.

Estate Exclusion. The estate tax exclusion increased from $675,000 to $1 million in 2002 and 2003. The exclusion increases in 2004 and 2005 to $1.5 million, then to $2 million in 2006 through 2008, and $3.5 millon in 2009. The Tax Relief Act repeals all estate taxes for the year 2010.

Note: Unless Congress passes new legislation, most of the above changes enacted in the Economic Growth and Tax Relief Reconciliation Act of 2001 will go out of existence at the end of 2010, when the measure expires.

New Legislation, IRS Rulings, and Other Tax Matters

Weight Loss. The Internal Revenue Service (IRS) decided to allow medical deductions for costs of certain weight-loss programs. Participation must be for treatment of a physician-diagnosed disease (including obesity). No deduction is allowed for purely cosmetic reasons or special diet foods.

Eye Surgery. The IRS now allows the cost of certain kinds of eye surgery (radial keratomy, lasik, etc.) to improve vision as a medical deduction since the treatment is considered corrective, not cosmetic.

Smoking. The IRS will now allow taxpayers to deduct two types of treatments for quitting cigarette smoking as a medical expense: (1) participation in a smoking-cessation program, and (2) prescription drugs to alleviate the effects of nicotine withdrawal. However, over-the-counter products such as nicotine patches and chewing gum remain nondeductible.

Medical Conference. An IRS ruling allowed a taxpayer with a chronically ill dependent to take a medical deduction for expenses paid to attend a medical conference recommended by the dependent's physician.

Funeral Expenses. Funeral expenses are not deductible on an individual's income tax return. However, they are deductible on the federal estate tax return (Form 706) of the deceased.

IT'S A FACT: The IRS is testing a new internet-based service that will allow taxpayers to check the status of their refunds at anytime from anywhere. The web application is expected to be fully operational for the 2003 filing season. The main IRS website is www.irs.gov

Frequent Flyers. IRS Announcement 2002-18 says, "The IRS will not assert that any taxpayer has understated his federal tax liability by reason of the receipt or personal use of frequent flyer miles or other in-kind promotional benefits attributable to the taxpayer's business or official travel."

Garage Sale. Revenues received from a garage sale usually do not result in taxable income. In most cases, the item that was sold cost more than the revenue received for it. By the same token, the losses do not result from a trade or business and, therefore, are considered personal and not deductible.

Day Camp. If both spouses work, the cost of summer day camp may qualify for the child care credit.

Gambling. Lottery and other gambling winnings are reported on page l, Form 1040. Gambling expenses are reported on Schedule A. The expenses are deductible to the extent of the winnings reported on page 1. No winnings, no deduction.

Divorce. Legal fees paid to collect taxable alimony or to seek tax advice during a divorce are deductible.

Rent Free. Rental income is not taxable if the taxpayers home is rented for fewer than 15 days during the year. Expenses attributed to the rental are not deductible.

Fines. Penalties and fines paid to a governmental agency or department are not deductible. This includes parking and speeding tickets. This also is true for penalties resulting for late filing of an individual's tax return.

Profit Motive. A recent U.S. Tax Court decision ruled that married taxpayers who organized a deep-sea fishing tournament could not deduct losses in excess of income generated by the activity because it was not for profit. Since they had no income, no expense was allowed as a deduction.

Being Frivolous. An IRS news release dated Apr. 3, 2002, states, "Taxpayers who file frivolous income tax returns face a $500 penalty and may be subject to civil penalties of 20-75% of the underpaid tax. Those who pursue frivolous tax cases in the courts may face a penalty of up to $25,000, in addition to the taxes, interest, and civil penalties that they may owe."

Tax Highlights

Medical Insurance. The page 1, Form 1040 deduction for medical insurance premiums paid in 2002 for self-employed individuals, spouses, and dependents rises to 70%, and becomes a 100% page-one deduction for 2003. The remaining portion of the premium not used is deductible as a medical expense on Schedule A subject to the 7.5% limitation rule. For more information call the IRS at 1-800-829-3676 and ask for Publication 535, Business Expense. It's free.

Death Benefits. Qualified accelerated death benefits paid under a life insurance contract to terminally ill persons (certified as expected to die within 24 months) are excludable from gross income. A similar exclusion applies to the sale or assignment of insurance death benefits to another person. Starting in 2002 accelerated death benefits paid to a chronically ill person under a long-term care rider are tax-free up to $210 per day and will continue to be indexed annually for inflation.

Sale of Residence. Married couples who lived in their principal residence for at least 2 years during a 5-year period ending on the date of sale and file a joint income tax return may exclude up to $500,000 in gain from the sale of their residence. This deduction is reusable every 2 years. Single taxpayers may exclude a gain up to $250,000. Married couples who do not share a principal residence but continue to file a joint return also may claim up to the $250,000 exclusion for a qualifying sale or exchange of each spouse's principal residence.

Homeowners who have lived in their home fewer than 2 years and must sell because of a change in place of work may prorate the exclusion based on amount of time lived there.

House Closing Points. The IRS has ruled that taxpayers need not deduct points in the year of purchase of a home. They may amortize the points over the life of the loan. This ruling could help first-time home buyers who may not have sufficient deductions to itemize.

Home Office. A deduction is allowed for taxpayers who set up an office at home to take care of the administrative or management side of their business. The home is considered a principal place of business in such cases. Follow the instructions on Form 8829, Expenses for Business Use of Your Home.

Domestic Workers. The annual threshold dollar amount in 2002 for reporting and paying Social Security and federal unemployment taxes on domestic employees, including nannies and housekeepers, is $1,300. Household workers under 18 are exempt unless household work is their principal occupation. Household employers must apply for an employer federal ID number and issue W-2 wage statements.

Mileage. The mileage allowance deduction for driving to obtain medical treatment or for automobile costs incurred in a job-related move increased to 13 cents per mile for 2002, up from 12 cents in 2001. For individuals using their automobile in volunteer work for qualified charities the deduction remains at 14 cents per mile. The standard mileage rate for business use of an automobile including leased cars increased from 34.5 cents in 2001 to 36.5 cents for 2002.

Investment Expenses. Investors can take a miscellaneous deduction on Schedule A for investment and custodial fees, trust administration fees, investment advice, financial newspapers and reports and other expenses paid for managing their investment portfolio that produces taxable income (or loss). However, they cannot deduct expenses for attending a convention, seminar, or similar meeting for investment purposes.

Innocent Spouse Relief. The IRS Reform Act of 1998 provides a separate liability section for taxpayers who are divorced, legally separated, or living apart for at least 12 months. In effect, this legislation prevents a spouse from being held liable for the other spouse's tax liability.

Children's Income. Parents may elect to include on their income tax return the dividends and interest income of a dependent child under age 14 whose unearned income is more than $750 and whose gross income is less than $7,500. Form 8814, Parent's Election to Report Child's Interest and Dividends, must be attached to the parents' tax return. The election is not available if estimated tax payments were made or investments were sold in the child's name during the year.

If a dependent child with taxable income cannot file an income tax return, the parent, guardian, or other legally responsible person must file a return for the child.

An individual may not claim a dependency exemption in the year 2002 for a child who qualifies as a full-time student and is over age 23 at the end of the year, unless the child's gross income is less than $3,000.

Capital Gains. The long-term capital gains tax rate for individual taxpayers is 20% for qualified investments held more than 12 months. For taxpayers in the 10% or 15% tax bracket, the maximum long-term capital gains rate is 10%.

For investments purchased after Dec. 31, 2000, and held more than 5 years, Congress lowered the capital gains rate to 18%; if the taxpayer is in the 10% or 15% tax bracket the rate is 8% for investments held more than 5 years.

Hobbies. Qualifying long-term gains for collectibles such as art, antiques, jewelry, stamps, and coins are taxed at a maximum 28%.

Filing and Payment Dates

Filing Dates. The due date for filing a timely 2002 U.S. individual income tax return is Tue., Apr. 15, 2003.

Estimated Taxes. Due dates for individual quarterly federal estimated tax payments for 2003 are: 1st quarter, Tue., Apr. 15, 2003; 2nd quarter, Mon., June 16; 3rd quarter, Mon., Sept. 15; 4th quarter, Thur., Jan. 15, 2004. Different filing dates may apply for state and local quarterly estimated tax payments.

Refunds. Individuals can call the IRS toll-free at 1-800-829-4477 for a recorded message to check on the status of their expected refund. Taxpayers may have refunds deposited directly into their bank account.

Need More Time? Individuals who cannot file their 2002 tax return by the Apr 15, 2003 due date, may apply for a 4-month extension of time. Although the extension is automatic, they must file Form 4868 no later than midnight Apr. 15, 2003, to qualify. Some 8 million individuals filed for an extension in 2002.

Payments. Taxpayers may use their VISA, MasterCard, Discover, or American Express credit cards for tax payments. To pay by credit card, call 1-888-2-PAY-TAX. There is a "convenience fee" charged by the credit card company based on the size of the payment. Estimated tax payments can be made this way instead of filing Form 1040-ES payment vouchers. Federal income taxes now may be paid via the Internet.

Depending on the tax owed, taxpayers may apply for monthly installment payments by attaching Form 9465 to their tax return. There is a nominal filing fee if the request is approved.

Timely Postmark. When a tax return postmarked on time, the IRS must accept the postmark as the filing date even if IRS receives it weeks later. The postmark of qualified couriers such as UPS and FedEx also is proof of timely mailing. *Caution:* When the return is mailed after the filing due date of Apr. 15, 2003, or after the extended due date, the IRS considers a return as filed on the date it is received by the IRS, not the date of postmark.

Statute of Limitations. Taxpayers have until Apr. 15, 2003, to file their 1999 federal tax return to claim a refund. After that date any tax or withholding refund for 1999 including the refundable earned income tax credit they may have coming will be lost . . . forever.

Filing Penalties. The IRS can levy 2 potential penalties when a tax return is filed after the due date with a balance owing. One penalty is for failing to file a timely tax return. The second is for failure to pay the tax when due. Interest will be charged on any unpaid tax balance.

Taxpayer Privacy. To protect the taxpayer's privacy, Social Security numbers no longer appear on mailing labels.

Free IRS Services. Federal tax forms, tax legislation, relevant court decisions, and other information and resources are available from the IRS via the following:

Internet website: www.irs.gov
Telnet: iris.irs.gov
File Transfer Protocol: ftp.irs.gov
Fax: 1-703-368-9694
Forms/Publications: 1-800-829-3676

English/Spanish. The IRS provides videotaped instructions both in English and Spanish at participating libraries. Many IRS publications and tax forms including instructions also are printed in Spanish. For more information, call 1-800-TAX-FORM and ask for the free IRS Publication 1SP, Derechos del Contribuyente.

Hearing Impaired. The IRS telephone service for hearing impaired persons is available for taxpayers with access to TDD equipment. The toll-free telephone number is 1-800-829-4059.

Who Must File a Tax Return

Most U.S. citizens and resident aliens will have to file a 2002 income tax return if their gross income for the year is at least as much as the amount shown in the following table:

Filing Status	2002 Gross Income
Single	
Under 65	$7,700
65 or older	8,850
Married filing jointly	
Both spouses under 65	13,850
One spouse 65 or older	14,750
Both spouses 65 or older	15,650
Married filing separately	3,000
Head of household	
Under 65	9,900
65 or older	11,050
Qualifying widow(er)	
Under 65	10,850
65 or older	11,750

Regardless of the above amounts, a tax return must also be filed if:

- Taxpayer had net earnings of $400 or more from self-employment for the year.
- Taxpayer received advance earned income credit payments during the year from an employer or is entitled to receive a refundable earned income credit.
- Taxpayer paid estimated income tax payments during the year 2002 or expects an income tax refund.
- Taxpayer has losses to be carried back or forward.

Additional taxes are owed for:
— Social Security tax on unreported tips.
— Alternative minimum tax.
— Recapture of investment credit.
— Excise tax attributable to qualified retirement distributions including IRAs, annuities, and modified endowment contracts.

Which Tax Return Form to File

Most U.S. citizens can use one of the following income tax forms: Form 1040, 1040A, or 1040EZ. Forms 1040A and 1040EZ are shorter and simpler to use than Form 1040.

You may be able to use the shortest tax return, Form 1040EZ, if:

- You are single or married filing jointly and do not claim any dependents.
- You are not 65 or older or blind.
- Your only income is from wages, salaries, tips, taxable scholarships or fellowships, unemployment compensation or Alaska Permanent Fund dividends.
- Your taxable income is less than $50,000 and you do not have over $400 of taxable interest income.
- You do not claim a student loan interest deduction or an education credit.
- You do not itemize deductions, claim any adjustments to income or have tax credits other than the earned income credit.
- You received no advance earned income credit payments.
- You did not make any estimated tax payments.

Form 1040A may be used if:

- You have income only from wages, salaries, tips, taxable scholarships or fellowships, interest and dividends, IRA distributions, pensions, annuities, unemployment compensation and/or taxable Social Security or railroad retirement benefits.
- Your taxable income is less than $50,000.
- You do not itemize deductions.
- You claim a deduction for qualified IRA contributions.
- You claim a credit for child and dependent care expenses, credit for the elderly or the disabled, the earned income credit, the adoption credit, child tax credit or education credits.
- You report employment taxes on wages paid to household employees on Schedule H.
- You take the education exclusion for interest income earned from Series EE U.S. Savings Bonds.
- You received advance earned income credit payments.
- You owe alternative minimum tax.
- You have made estimated tax payments.

You must file Form 1040 if any of these apply:

- Your taxable income is $50,000 or more. (However, you also may use Form 1040 for lower income amounts.)
- You plan to itemize deductions.
- You received any nontaxable dividends or capital gain distributions.
- You have foreign bank accounts and/or foreign trusts.
- You have taxable refunds from state or local income taxes.
- You have business, farm, or rental income or losses.
- You sold or exchanged capital assets or business property.
- You have miscellaneous income such as alimony that is reportable on Form 1040A or 1040EZ.
- You have additional adjustments to income such as payments for alimony or moving expenses.
- You are allowed a foreign tax credit or certain other credits.
- You have other taxes to pay, such as self-employment tax or Social Security tax on tips.
- You have losses that are to be carried back or forward.
- You are required to file additional forms such as Form 2106, Employee Business Expenses; Form 2555, Foreign Earned Income; Form 3903, Moving Expenses; Form 4972, Tax on Lump-Sum Distributions.

Filing separately vs. jointly

Married taxpayers can file separate income tax returns. If they later change their minds, they may amend their tax returns and file jointly. However, once a joint return is filed, they cannot later file separate returns.

Individual Income Tax Rates for Year 2002

Single

Tax Rate	Taxable Income
10%	$1 to $6,000
15%	$6,001 to 27,950
27%	$27,951 to $67,700
30%	$67,701 to $141,250
35%	$141,251 to $307,050
38.6%	More than $307,050

Married Filing Jointly or Qualifying Widow(er)

Tax Rate	Taxable Income
10%	$1 to $12,000
15%	$12,001 to $46,700
27%	$46,701 to $112,850
30%	$112,851 to $171,950
35%	$171,951 to $307,050
38.6%	More than $307,050

Married Filing Separately

Tax Rate	Taxable Income
10%	$1 to $6,000
15%	$6,001 to $23,350
27%	$23,351 to $56,425
30%	$56,426 to $85,975
35%	$85,976 to $153,525
38.6%	More than $153,525

Head of Household

Tax Rate	Taxable Income
10%	$1 to $10,000
15%	$10,001 to $37,450
27%	$37,451 to $96,700
30%	$96,701 to $156,600
35%	$156,601 to $307,050
38.6%	More than $307,050

Estates and Trusts

Tax Rate	Taxable Income
15%	$0 to $1,850
27%	$1,851 to $4,400
30%	$4,401 to $6,750
35%	$6,751 to $9,200
38.6%	More than $9,200

"Kiddie Tax." If a child under age 14 has net investment income exceeding $1,500 for 2002, the excess is taxed at the parents' top marginal tax rate.

Exemptions

Dollar Amounts. The personal exemption amount for each taxpayer, spouse and dependent for 2002 is $3,000, up from $2,900 for 2001. These exemptions amounts are adjusted each year for any cost of living increase.

Phaseout. The exemption deduction for higher income taxpayers begins to be phased out when their income exceeds certain threshold dollar amounts. These threshold amounts are adjusted for a cost of living increase. Each exemption is reduced by 2% for each $2,500 ($1,250 for married persons filing separately) or fraction thereof by which adjusted gross income for year 2002 exceeds the following:

Married filing jointly	$206,000
Qualifying widow(er)	$206,000
Head of household	$171,650
Single	$137,300
Married filing separately	$103,000

Exemptions for the year 2002 are fully phased out when adjusted gross income is more than $122,500 ($61,250 for married filing separately) over the above threshold amount.

Standard Deduction

The standard deduction is a flat dollar amount that is subtracted from the adjusted gross income (AGI) of taxpayers who do not itemize deductions. The amount allowed depends on filing status and is adjusted annually for inflation.

2002 Standard Deduction Amount

Single	$4,700
Married filing jointly or qualifying widow(er)	$7,850
Married filing separately	$3,925
Head of household	$6,900

These figures are not applicable if an individual can be claimed as a dependent on another person's tax return.

Standard Deduction for Dependents. An individual reported as a dependent on another person's 2002 income tax return generally may claim on his or her own tax return only the greater of $750 or the sum of $250 plus earned income not to exceed $4,700. A blind dependent may add $1,150 to this amount. Earned income includes wages, salaries, commissions and tips. Earned income also includes net profit from self-employment and any part of a scholarship or fellowship grant that must be included in gross income.

Taxpayers who are 65 or older and/or blind may claim an additional standard deduction:

2002 Additional Standard Deduction Amount

Single or head of household, 65 or older OR blind	$1,150
Single or head of household, 65 or older AND blind	$2,300
Married filing jointly or qualifying widow(er), 65 or older OR blind (per person)	$900
Married filing jointly or qualifying widow(er), 65 or older AND blind (per person)	$1,800
Married filing separately, 65 or older OR blind	$900
Married filing separately, 65 or older AND blind	$1,800

Adjustments to Income

IRA Deduction. The maximum tax-deferred Individual Retirement Arrangement (IRA) contribution for a married couple filing jointly increased in 2002 to $6,000, but not to exceed total earned income if less than $6,000. Each spouse can contribute up to $3,000 annually even if one spouse had little or no income. Individuals age 50 or older can fund an additional "catch-up" amount of $500, starting in 2002. However, there are income limitations.

IRA Withdrawals. There is a 10% early withdrawal penalty for IRA distributions before age 59½ unless it qualifies for one of the following exceptions:

- Distributions paid to the beneficiary after the death of the owner.
- Payments paid due to the disability of the owner.
- Part of a series of substantially equal periodic payments.
- Payments made to an employee following separation from employment after age 55. This exception does not apply if a qualified distribution from a pension plan is rolled into an IRA.
- Used to pay certain unreimbursed medical expenses.
- Used to pay certain qualifying higher education expenses.
- Used to pay certain qualified first time home buyer acquisition costs (up to $10,000).

The Roth IRA. Although contributions paid into a Roth IRA are not deductible, distributions of funds including investment earnings held in the account for 5 years or longer and distributed after age 59½ are free both of income tax and the 10% early withdrawal penalty at the time of distribution.

Any funds paid from the Roth IRA after the 5-year exclusion period to an estate or decedent's beneficiary on or after an individual's death, including funds paid to an individual who is disabled, are tax and penalty free regardless of age. This includes withdrawals of up to $10,000 for a first-time home purchase.

Withdrawals from a Roth IRA held less than 5 years are subject both to income tax and the 10% withdrawal penalty regardless of age. However, earnings withdrawn for "qualified higher education expenses" of the taxpayer, spouse, or any child or grandchild of the taxpayer or spouse are taxable but not subject to the early withdrawal penalty.

For more information on IRAs call the IRS at 1-800-829-3676 for a free copy of Publication 590, Individual Retirement Arrangements (IRA).

Moving Expenses. Taxpayers who change jobs or are transferred usually can deduct part of their moving expenses including travel and the cost of moving of household goods, but not meals. For 2002, the mileage rate for automobiles used in the move increased to 13 cents per mile plus parking and tolls.

To take a deduction, the new job must be at least 50 miles farther from the former home than the old job. Employees must work full-time for at least 39 weeks during the first 12 months after they arrive in the general area of their new job.

IT'S A FACT: After an earlier version was declared unconstitutional, an income tax was authorized in the U.S. by the 16th Amendment, ratified in 1913. The basic rate of the first tax was 1% of income over $3,000 for singles and over $4,000 for married couples.

Itemized Deductions

If the total amount of itemized deductions is more than the standard deduction, taxpayers generally should itemize their deductions on Schedule A, Form 1040. *Only the total amount of medical expenses that exceeds 7.5% of the taxpayer's adjusted gross income is deductible.* The following examples are just a few of the deductions that may be itemized; some of these deductions are subject to income limitations:

- Medicines, birth control pills, and insulin are deductible if prescribed by a doctor.
- Long-term care insurance premiums are deductible up to certain annual limits based on age.The maximum premium allowed in 2002 as a medical expense deduction is: $240 if age 40 or less; $450 from 41 to 50; $900, 51 to 60; $2,390, 61 to 70, and $2,990 if over age 70. Any long-term benefits received under a qualifying policy are tax-free subject to per diem restrictions.
- Cosmetic surgery for congenital abnormality, personal injury resulting from an accident or trauma, or a disfiguring disease is allowed as a medical deduction.
- Most mortgage interest paid on a primary residence or a second home is fully deductible. However, there are limitations on mortgages in excess of $1,000,000.
- Interest paid on home equity loans is deductible but only on the first $100,000 of equity debt.
- Borrowers generally can deduct points paid on their principal home mortgage loan on Schedule A.
- Investment interest expense is deductible only to the extent of net investment income. Any investment interest expense not currently deducted is carried over to future years.
- State and local income taxes, real estate taxes, and personal property taxes are fully deductible. *Sales taxes are not deductible.*
- Casualty and theft losses are deductible subject to the $100 and 10% limitation rule for each occurrence.
- Taxpayers deducting individual charitable contributions of $250 or more must obtain written substantiation from the charity. If the amount is $75 or more, the charity must include a breakdown of the payment indicating how much was a (deductible) contribution and what (if any) was the (nondeductible) value of goods, meals or services received.
- Miscellaneous expenses including union and professional dues, tax preparation fees, safe-deposit box rental fees, and employee business expenses are deductible insofar as they exceed 2% of adjusted gross income.
- Unreimbursed employee business expenses including travel, automobile, telephone, and gifts are deductible on Schedule A as miscellaneous itemized deductions. Only 50% of the cost of customer meals and entertainment is deductible and it is further subject to the 2% rule.
- Employment fees paid to agencies, resume costs, postage, travel, and other expenses to look for a new job in your present occupation are deductible even if you do not get a new job. *Credit card interest is considered personal and not deductible.*

Threshold Reduction. Many itemized deductions otherwise allowed are further reduced by the smaller of these two figures: 3% of a taxpayer's 2002 adjusted gross income in excess of the threshold amount of $137,300 ($68,650 for married taxpayers filing separately) OR 80% of the amount of these itemized deductions otherwise allowable for the year. This provision does not apply to medical expenses, investment interest expense, casualty losses, or gambling expenses. The dollar amount was adjusted for the cost-of-living increase in 2002. The threshold reduction amount is phased out over a five year period by the Tax Relief Act, starting in 2006.

Business Expenses

Business Equipment. The election to expense currently the cost of certain business machinery and other assets instead of depreciating them over a period of years is called a "Section 179 Expense Election." The maximum amount deductible for 2002 is $24,000. The expensing limit is scheduled to increase in 2003 to $25,000. Higher amounts apply to businesses in the reconstruction "Liberty Zone" of New York City.

Business Trips Within the U.S. If the primary purpose of a trip is to transact business, taxpayers may deduct all of the costs of transportation to and from the area, lodging, and 50% of meal expenses, even if some time is spent vacationing. If the employer extends the individual's business trip over a weekend to take advantage of discount airfares that require a Saturday night stayover, taxpayers may deduct the additional cost of meals, lodging and other incidental expenses.

Dues. Dues paid to business, social, athletic, luncheon, sporting, and country clubs, including airport and hotel clubs, are no longer deductible. However, dues paid to the Chamber of Commerce, business economic clubs, and trade associations remain deductible.

Tax Credits

A tax deduction such as for a charitable contribution results in a reduction in one's taxable income. Whereas, tax credits are reductions in the amount of taxed owed.

Adoption Credit. Beginning in 2002 the Tax Relief Act increases the adoption credit from $5,000 to $10,000 of qualified expenses and the phase-out starting point at $150,000 of adjusted gross income. Starting in 2003 the phase-out amount will be adjusted for inflation. The credit limit is per person, not per year.

Earned Income Credit. The Tax Relief Act of 2001 increases the phaseout range of the earned income credit for joint filers by an additional $1,000 starting in 2002 up to a maximum increase of $3,000 in 2008. After 2008 the credit will be adjusted for the cost of living.

Lower income workers who maintain a household may be eligible for a refundable earned income credit. The credit is based on total earned income such as wages, commissions, and tips.

Congress further simplified the rules by redefining earned income, extending the definition of qualifying children to include descendents of stepchildren and eliminating the one-year residency requirement for foster children. Unless Congress decides otherwise, all these changes will be repealed after Dec. 31, 2010.

Individuals may qualify for the credit even if they are not required to file a return. However, a tax return must be filed to receive the earned income credit refund. The IRS will assist individuals filing for the credit if they would like help.

Education Credits. The Hope Scholarship Credit applies to qualified tuition and expenses for the first 2 years of postsecondary education in a degree or certificate program at an eligible educational institution. However, it does not apply to room and board or cost of books. The credit can be as high as $1,500 per student.

The Lifetime Learning Credit is available for taxpayers whose postsecondary education expenses are not eligible for the Hope credit. The credit is 20% of tuition and other qualifying expenses paid for by the taxpayer, spouse or dependents. Taxpayers can deduct up to $1,000 ($5,000 of expenses x 20%) for all entitled students who are enrolled in an eligible educational institution. After 2003, this credit increases to $2,000 ($10,000 x 20%).

The Lifetime Learning Credit is allowed only for years in which the Hope credit is not used. Neither credit may be taken in any year in which funds are withdrawn from a Coverdell education savings account (formerly known as an Educational IRA) for the same expenses. The credit begins to phase out when modified AGI exceeds $41,000 for singles and $82,000 on a joint return, with full phaseout at $51,000 for singles and $102,000 on joint returns.

These credits are deducted from the individual's federal income tax and reported on Form 8863, Education Credits (Hope and Lifetime Learning Credits). Any excess credit not used is nonrefundable.

Taxable Social Security Benefits

Earnings Limitations. Age 62 to 65: Starting in 2002 individuals in this age group lose $1 of their Social Security benefits for every $2 of earned income over $11,280.

Age 65 or Over: As a result of The Senior Citizen's Freedom to Work Act, individuals 65 or over receiving Social Security benefits no longer are subject to an earnings limitation.

Taxable Benefits. Up to 50% of Social Security benefits may be taxable income if the person's total income is: over $25,000 but less than $34,000 for a single individual, head of household, qualifying widow(er), or a married person who is filing separately if spouses lived apart all year; or over $32,000 but less than $44,000 for married individuals filing jointly.

For incomes exceeding these maximums, 85% of Social Security benefits may become taxable. If a taxpayer is married and filing separately and lived with a spouse at any time during the year, the percentage amounts are reduced to zero.

Most Social Security benefits will not be taxable if they are the only income received during the year 2002.

Retirement Planning

The SIMPLE Plan. A very popular retirement plan is called the Savings Incentive Match Plan for Employees (SIMPLE). This plan is available for businesses with 100 or fewer employees including self-employed individuals, and generally is easier to implement and more cost-effective to administrate than a traditional 401(k) plan.

Beginning in 2002, employees can defer up to $7,000 in compensation, an increase of $500 from 2001 and $1,000 over 2000. The Tax Relief Act increases the amount annually thereafter by $1,000 until $10,000 is reached in 2005. A SIMPLE retirement plan can operate either as an IRA or as a 401(k). The tax liability on these amounts is deferred until a future date.

Profit-Sharing Plans. This plan limits the total employer and employee contributions to the lesser of 25% of compensation or $40,000 for 2002, $35,000 for last year.

Age 70½ Plus. The owner of a traditional IRA must begin receiving distributions from the IRA by Apr. 1 of the calendar year following the year in which he or she reaches age 70½, even if the individual is not retired. However, any employee who works beyond age 70½ and is not a 5% or more owner of the business can continue to defer his or her profit sharing and pension retirement plan distributions to a later date.

Retired and Moved. States may not impose an income tax on retirement income if the person is no longer a resident of that state.

IRS Tax Audit

The IRS projects that well over 230 million individual income tax returns will be filed in 2003. Only about 1 out of every 100 will be selected for audit. That is good news...unless that one return happens to be yours!

Needless to say, the agency is very good at selecting returns that will yield additional taxes. If the IRS concludes that you owe more and you disagree with the findings, you can meet with a supervisor. If you still do not agree, you can appeal to a separate Appeals Office or to the U.S. Tax Court.

More than 20% of recent IRS tax audits resulted in no change for the taxpayer. "Too high," says the IRS. As a consequence the IRS has proposed a "National Research Program." This includes about 50,000 special audits designed to catch abusive filing and improve its audit-selection process.

For more information about income tax audits, call the IRS at 1-800-829-3676 for its free Publication 556, Examination of Returns, Appeal Rights, and Claims for Refund. Or, visit www.irs.gov

Your Rights as a Taxpayer

Several years ago Congress enacted the Taxpayer Bill of Rights 1. It required the IRS to explain in easy-to-understand language any actions it proposes taking against a taxpayer, as well as to modify some audit and collection procedures. Congress later passed the Taxpayer Bill of Rights 2, creating an Office of the Taxpayer Advocate within the IRS, with authority to order IRS personnel to issue refund checks and meet deadlines for resolving disputes. Taxpayers Advocates can be contacted by calling 1-877-777-4778 (1-800-829-4059 for TTY/TDD). The IRS also must pay legal fees if the taxpayer wins the case and the IRS cannot show it was "substantially justified" in pursuing the matter.

More recently, Congress created a 9-member oversight board to watch over the IRS management. The legislation shifts the burden of proof to the IRS under certain circumstances in disputes dealing with income, estate, and gift taxes. Further, it establishes procedures designed to ensure due process when the IRS seeks to collect taxes by levy.

Individuals who want to confidentially report misconduct, waste, fraud, or abuse by an IRS employee, can call 1-800-366-4484. All discussions can remain anonymous.

For more information ask for IRS Publication 1, Your Rights as a Taxpayer, by calling 1-800-TAX-FORM for a free copy.

Federal Outlays to States Per Dollar of Tax Revenue Received

Source: The Tax Foundation

(figures for fiscal year 2001; ranked highest to lowest)

State	Outlay	State	Outlay	State	Outlay	State	Outlay
District of Columbia	$5.73	Louisiana	$1.42	Vermont	$1.12	Delaware	$0.86
New Mexico	2.08	Kentucky	1.38	Rhode Island	1.11	Washington	0.84
North Dakota	1.95	Maine	1.31	Utah	1.11	Massachusetts	0.84
Mississippi	1.78	South Carolina	1.30	Pennsylvania	1.07	New York	0.83
West Virginia	1.73	Missouri	1.29	North Carolina	1.06	Colorado	0.82
Montana	1.67	Maryland	1.26	Florida	1.05	California	0.82
Alaska	1.63	Idaho	1.24	Ohio	1.01	Minnesota	0.81
Hawaii	1.54	Tennessee	1.20	Georgia	1.01	Illinois	0.78
Alabama	1.53	Iowa	1.17	Oregon	1.00	Nevada	0.76
South Dakota	1.50	Nebraska	1.17	Indiana	0.99	New Hampshire	0.71
Oklahoma	1.48	Wyoming	1.14	Texas	0.92	Connecticut	0.67
Arkansas	1.45	Kansas	1.14	Wisconsin	0.89	New Jersey	0.67
Virginia	1.45	Arizona	1.12	Michigan	0.86		

Tax Burden in Selected Countries[1]

Source: Organization for Economic Cooperation and Development, 2000

Country	Income tax (%)	Social Security (%)	Total payment[2] (%)	Country	Income tax (%)	Social Security (%)	Total payment[2] (%)
Denmark	32	12	44	**United States**	**18**	**8**	**26**
Germany	21	21	42	United Kingdom	16	8	24
Belgium	28	14	42	Czech Republic	11	13	23
Netherlands	8	29	36	Australia	23	0	23
Finland	27	7	34	Iceland	21	0	21
Sweden	26	7	33	Switzerland	10	12	21
Hungary	20	13	32	Ireland	15	5	20
Poland	7	25	31	Slovak Republic	7	13	20
Norway	21	8	29	New Zealand	19	0	19
Turkey	15	14	29	Spain	12	6	18
Italy	19	9	29	Greece	2	16	18
Austria	10	18	28	Portugal	7	11	18
France	13	13	27	Japan	6	10	16
Canada	21	6	27	Korea	2	7	9
Luxembourg	13	14	27	Mexico	1	2	3

(1) Does not include taxes not listed, such as sales tax or VAT. Rates shown apply to a single person with average earnings. (2) Totals may not add due to rounding.

State Government Personal Income Tax Rates, 2002

Source: Reproduced with permission from *CCH State Tax Guide*, published and copyrighted by CCH Inc., 2700 Lake Cook Road, Riverwoods, IL 60015

Below are basic state tax rates on taxable income, for 2002 unless otherwise indicated. Alaska, Florida, Nevada, South Dakota, Texas, Washington, and Wyoming did not have state income taxes and are thus not listed. For further details, see notes which follow.

Alabama

Single, Head of household, & Married filing separately
- $0 to $500 .... 2%
- $500 to $3,000 .... 4%
- $3,000 and over 5%

Married filing jointly
- $0 to $1,000 .... 2%
- $1,000 to $6,000 .... 4%
- $6,000 and over 5%

Arizona[1]

Single & Married filing separately
- $0 to $10,000 .... 2.87%
- $10,000 to $25,000 .... 3.2%
- $25,000 to $50,000 ... 3.74%
- $50,000 to $150,000 .. 4.72%
- $150,000 and over ... 5.04%

Married filing jointly and Head of household
- $0 to $20,000 .... 2.87%
- $20,000 to $50,000 .... 3.2%
- $50,000 to $100,000 .. 3.74%
- $100,000 to $300,000 . 4.72%
- $300,000 and over ... 5.04%

Arkansas[2]

Single, Head of household, Married filing jointly, & Married filing separately
- $0 to $3,199 .... 1%
- $3,199 to $6,399 ...... 2.5%
- $6,399 to $9,599 ...... 3.5%
- $9,599 to $15,999 ..... 4.5%
- $15,999 to $26,699 ..... 6%
- $26,699 and over 7%

California[1,2,3]

Single or Married filing separately
- $0 to $5,748 .... 1%
- $5,748 to $13,625 ...... 2%
- $13,625 to $21,503 ..... 4%
- $21,503 to $29,850 ..... 6%
- $29,850 to $37,725 ..... 8%
- $37,725 and over 9.3%

Head of household
- $0 to $11,500 .... 1%
- $11,500 to $27,250 ..... 2%
- $27,250 to $35,126 ..... 4%
- $35,126 to $43,473 ..... 6%
- $43,473 to $51,350 ..... 8%
- $51,350 and over 9.3%

Married filing jointly
- $0 to $11,496 .... 1%
- $11,496 to $27,250 ..... 2%
- $27,250 to $43,006 ..... 4%
- $43,006 to $59,700 ..... 6%
- $59,700 to $75,450 ..... 8%
- $75,450 and over 9.3%

Colorado

4.63% of federal taxable income.

Connecticut

Single & Married filing separately
- $0 to $10,000 .... 3%
- $10,000 and over 4.5%

Head of household
- $0 to $16,000 .... 3%
- $16,000 and over 4.5%

Married filing jointly
- $0 to $20,000 .... 3%
- $20,000 and over 4.5%

Delaware

Single, Head of household, Married filing jointly, & Married filing separately
- $2,000 to $5,000 ...... 2.2%
- $5,000 to $10,000 ..... 3.9%
- $10,000 to $20,000 .... 4.8%
- $20,000 to $25,000 .... 5.2%
- $25,000 to $60,000 ... 5.55%
- $60,000 and over 5.95%

District Of Columbia

Single, Head of household, Married filing jointly, & Married filing separately
- $0 to $10,000 .... 5%
- $10,000 to $30,000 ..... 7%
- $30,000 and over 9%

Georgia

Single
- $0 to $750 .... 1%
- $750 to $2,250 .... 2%
- $2,250 to $3,750 .... 3%
- $3,750 to $5,250 .... 4%
- $5,250 to $7,000 .... 5%
- $7,000 and over 6%

Head of household & Married filing jointly
- $0 to $1,000 .... 1%
- $1,000 to $3,000 .... 2%
- $3,000 to $5,000 .... 3%
- $5,000 to $7,000 .... 4%
- $7,000 to $10,000 ...... 5%
- $10,000 and over 6%

Married filing separately
- $0 to $500 .... 1%
- $500 to $1,500 .... 2%
- $1,500 to $2,500 .... 3%
- $2,500 to $3,500 .... 4%
- $3,500 to $5,000 .... 5%
- $5,000 and over 6%

Hawaii

Single & Married filing separately
- $0 to $2,000 ....1.4%
- $2,000 to $4,000 ......3.2%
- $4,000 to $8,000 ......5.5%
- $8,000 to $12,000 .....6.4%
- $12,000 to $16,000 ....6.8%
- $16,000 to $20,000 ....7.2%
- $20,000 to $30,000 ....7.6%
- $30,000 to $40,000 ....7.9%
- $40,000 and over 8.25%

Head of household
- $0 to $3,000 ....1.4%
- $3,000 to $6,000 ......3.2%
- $6,000 to $12,000 .....5.5%
- $12,000 to $18,000 ....6.4%
- $18,000 to $24,000 ....6.8%
- $24,000 to $30,000 ....7.2%
- $30,000 to $45,000 ....7.6%
- $45,000 to $60,000 ....7.9%
- $60,000 and over 8.25%

Married filing jointly
- $0 to $4,000 ....1.4%
- $4,000 to $8,000 ......3.2%
- $8,000 to $16,000 .....5.5%
- $16,000 to $24,000 ....6.4%
- $24,000 to $32,000 ....6.8%
- $32,000 to $40,000 ....7.2%
- $40,000 to $60,000 ....7.6%
- $60,000 to $80,000 ....7.9%
- $80,000 and over 8.25%

Idaho[1,2]

Single & Married filing separately
- $0 to $1,087 ....1.6%
- $1,087 to $2,173 ......3.6%
- $2,173 to $3,260 ......4.1%
- $3,260 to $4,346 ......5.1%
- $4,346 to $5,433 ......6.1%
- $5,433 to $8,149 ......7.1%
- $8,149 to $21,730 .....7.4%
- $21,730 and over 7.8%

Head of household & Married filing jointly
- $0 to $2,173 ....1.6%
- $2,173 to $4,346 ......3.6%
- $4,346 to $6,519 ......4.1%
- $6,519 to $8,692 ......5.1%
- $8,692 to $10,865 .....6.1%
- $10,865 to $16,298 ....7.1%
- $16,298 to $43,460 ....7.4%
- $43,460 and over 7.8%

Illinois

3% of taxable net income

Indiana

3.4% of adjusted gross income

Iowa[2]

Single, Head of household, Married filing jointly, & Married filing separately
- $0 to $1,211 ....0.36%
- $1,211 to $2,422 ....0.72%
- $2,422 to $4,844 ....2.43%
- $4,844 to $10,899 .....4.5%
- $10,899 to $18,165 ..6.12%
- $18,165 to $24,200... 6.48%
- $24,200 to $36,330.... 6.8%
- $36,330 to $54,495 .. 7.92%
- $54,495 and over 8.98%

Kansas

Single, Head of household, & Married filing separately
- $0 to $15,000 .... 3.5%
- $15,000 to $30,000... 6.25%
- $30,000 and over 6.45%

Married filing jointly
- $0 to $30,000 .... 3.5%
- $30,000 to $60,000... 6.25%
- $60,000 and over 6.45%

Kentucky

Single, Head of household, Married filing jointly, & Married filing separately
- $0 to $3,000 ....2%
- $3,000 to $4,000........3%
- $4,000 to $5,000........4%
- $5,000 to $8,000........5%
- $8,000 and over 6%

Louisiana[1]

Single, Head of household, Married filing jointly, & Married filing separately
- $0 to $10,000 ....2%
- $10,000 to $50,000......4%
- $50,000 and over 6%

Maine[2]

Single & Married filing separately
- $0 to $4,200 ....2%
- $4,200 to $8,350...... 4.5%
- $8,350 to $16,700.......7%
- $16,700 and over 8.5%

Head of household
- $0 to $6,300 ....2%
- $6,300 to $12,500..... 4.5%
- $12,500 to $25,050......7%
- $25,050 and over 8.5%

Married filing jointly
- $0 to $8,400 ....2%
- $8,400 to $16,700..... 4.5%
- $16,700 to $33,400......7%
- $33,400 and over 8.5%

Maryland

Single, Head of household, Married filing jointly, & Married filing separately
- $0 to $1,000 ....2%
- $1,000 to $2,000........3%
- $2,000 to $3,000........4%
- $3,000 and over 4.75%

Massachusetts

- Short-term capital gains... 12%
- 6 Classes of capital gain income ...... 0% to 5%
- All other income......... 5.3%

Michigan

4.1% of taxable income

Minnesota[2]

Single
- $0 to $18,710 .... 5.35%
- $18,710 to $61,460... 7.05%
- $61,460 and over 7.85%

Head of household
- $0 to $23,040 .... 5.35%
- $23,040 to $92,560... 7.05%
- $92,560 and over 7.85%

Married filing jointly
- $0 to $27,350 .... 5.35%
- $27,350 to $108,660.. 7.05%
- $108,660 and over ... 7.85%

Married filing separately
- $0 to $13,680 .... 5.35%
- $13,680 to $54,330... 7.05%
- $54,330 and over 7.85%

Mississippi

Single, Head of household, Married filing jointly, & Married filing separately
- $0 to $5,000 ....3%
- $5,000 to $10,000.......4%
- $10,000 and over 5%

Missouri[2]

Single, Head of household, Married filing jointly, & Married filing separately
- $0 to $1,000 .... 1.5%
- $1,000 to $2,000........2%
- $2,000 to $3,000...... 2.5%
- $3,000 to $4,000........3%
- $4,000 to $5,000...... 3.5%
- $5,000 to $6,000........4%
- $6,000 to $7,000...... 4.5%
- $7,000 to $8,000........5%
- $8,000 to $9,000...... 5.5%
- $9,000 and over 6%

Montana[2,3]

Single, Head of household, Married filing jointly, & Married filing separately
- $0 to $2,200 ....2%
- $2,200 to $4,300........3%
- $4,300 to $8,600........4%
- $8,600 to $12,900.......5%
- $12,900 to $17,200......6%
- $17,200 to $21,500......7%
- $21,500 to $30,200......8%
- $30,200 to $43,100......9%
- $43,100 to $75,400.....10%
- $75,400 and over 11%

Nebraska

Single
- $0 to $2,400 .... 2.51%
- $2,400 to $17,000.... 3.49%
- $17,000 to $26,500... 5.01%
- $26,500 and over 6.68%

Head of household
- $0 to $3,800 .... 2.51%
- $3,800 to $24,000.... 3.49%
- $24,000 to $35,000... 5.01%
- $35,000 and over 6.68%

Married filing jointly
- $0 to $4,000 .... 2.51%
- $4,000 to $30,000.... 3.49%
- $30,000 to $46,750... 5.01%
- $46,750 and over 6.68%

Married filing separately
- $0 to $2,000 .... 2.51%
- $2,000 to $15,000.... 3.49%
- $15,000 to $23,375... 5.01%
- $23,375 and over 6.68%

New Hampshire

5% on interest and dividends only

New Jersey

Single & Married filing separately
- $0 to $20,000 .... 1.4%
- $20,000 to $35,000... 1.75%
- $35,000 to $40,000.... 3.5%
- $40,000 to $75,000.. 5.525%
- $75,000 and over 6.37%

Head of household & Married filing jointly
- $0 to $20,000 .... 1.4%
- $20,000 to $50,000... 1.75%
- $50,000 to $70,000... 2.45%
- $70,000 to $80,000.... 3.5%
- $80,000 to $150,000. 5.525%
- $150,000 and over ... 6.37%

New Mexico[1]

Single
- $0 to $5,500 .... 1.7%
- $5,500 to $11,000..... 3.2%
- $11,000 to $16,000.... 4.7%
- $16,000 to $26,000......6%
- $26,000 to $42,000.... 7.1%
- $42,000 to $65,000.... 7.9%
- $65,000 and over 8.2%

Head of household
- $0 to $7,000 .... 1.7%
- $7,000 to $14,000..... 3.2%
- $14,000 to $20,000.... 4.7%
- $20,000 to $33,000......6%
- $33,000 to $53,000.... 7.1%
- $53,000 to $83,000.... 7.9%
- $83,000 and over 8.2%

Married filing jointly
- $0 to $8,000 .... 1.7%
- $8,000 to $16,000 .... 3.2%
- $16,000 to $24,000 .... 4.7%
- $24,000 to $40,000 ..... 6%
- $40,000 to $64,000 .... 7.1%
- $64,000 to $100,000 ... 7.9%
- $100,000 and over 8.2%

Married filing separately
- $0 to $4,000 .... 1.7%
- $4,000 to $8,000 ...... 3.2%
- $8,000 to $12,000 ..... 4.7%
- $12,000 to $20,000 ..... 6%
- $20,000 to $32,000 .... 7.1%
- $32,000 to $50,000 .... 7.9%
- $50,000 and over 8.2%

New York

Single & Married filing separately
- $0 to $8,000 .... 4%
- $8,000 to $11,000 ..... 4.5%
- $11,000 to $13,000 ... 5.25%
- $13,000 to $20,000 .... 5.9%
- $20,000 and over 6.85%

Head of household
- $0 to $11,000 .... 4%
- $11,000 to $15,000 .... 4.5%
- $15,000 to $17,000 ... 5.25%
- $17,000 to $30,000 .... 5.9%
- $30,000 and over 6.85%

Married filing jointly
- $0 to $16,000 .... 4%
- $16,000 to $22,000 .... 4.5%
- $22,000 to $26,000 ... 5.25%
- $26,000 to $40,000 .... 5.9%
- $40,000 and over 6.85%

North Carolina

Single
- $0 to $12,750 .... 6%
- $12,750 to $60,000 ..... 7%
- $60,000 to $120,000 .. 7.75%
- $120,000 and over ... 8.25%

Head of household
- $0 to $17,000 .... 6%
- $17,000 to $80,000 ..... 7%
- $80,000 to $160,000 .. 7.75%
- $160,000 and over ... 8.25%

Married filing jointly
- $0 to $21,250 .... 6%
- $21,250 to $100,000 .... 7%
- $100,000 to $200,000 . 7.75%
- $200,000 and over ... 8.25%

Married filing separately
- $0 to $10,625 .... 6%
- $10,625 to $50,000 ..... 7%
- $50,000 to $100,000 .. 7.75%
- $100,000 and over .. 8.25%

North Dakota[2,3]

Single
- $0 to $27,050 .... 2.1%
- $27,050 to $65,550 ... 3.92%
- $65,550 to $136,750 .. 4.34%
- $136,750 to $297,350 . 5.04%
- $297,350 and over 5.54%

Head of Household
- $0 to $36,250 .... 2.1%
- $36,250 to $93,650 ... 3.92%
- $93,650 to $151,650 .. 4.34%
- $151,650 to $297,350 . 5.04%
- $297,350 and over 5.54%

Married filing jointly
- $0 to $45,200 .... 2.1%
- $45,200 to $109,250 .. 3.92%
- $109,250 to $166,500 . 4.34%
- $166,500 to $297,350 . 5.04%
- $297,350 and over 5.54%

Married filing separately
- $0 to $22,600 .... 2.1%
- $22,600 to $54,625 ... 3.92%
- $54,625 to $83,250 ... 4.34%
- $83,250 to $148,675 .. 5.04%
- $148,675 and over 5.54%

Ohio

Single, Head of household, Married filing jointly, & Married filing separately
- $0 to $5,000 .... 0.743%
- $5,000 to $10,000 ... 1.486%
- $10,000 to $15,000 .. 2.972%
- $15,000 to $20,000 .. 3.715%
- $20,000 to $40,000 .. 4.457%
- $40,000 to $80,000 .. 5.201%
- $80,000 to $100,000 . 5.943%
- $100,000 to $200,000 .. 6.9%
- $200,000 and over 7.5%

Oklahoma

Single & Married filing separately
- $0 to $1,000 .... 0.5%
- $1,000 to $2,500 .... 1%
- $2,500 to $3,750 .... 2%
- $3,750 to $4,900 .... 3%
- $4,900 to $6,200 .... 4%
- $6,200 to $7,700 .... 5%
- $7,700 to $10,000 ...... 6%
- $10,000 and over 7%

Head of household & Married filing jointly
- $0 to $2,000 .... 0.5%
- $2,000 to $5,000 .... 1%
- $5,000 to $7,500 .... 2%
- $7,500 to $9,800 .... 3%
- $9,800 to $12,200 .... 4%
- $12,200 to $15,000 ...... 5%
- $15,000 to $21,000 ...... 6%
- $21,000 and over 7%

Oregon[2]

Single & Married filing separately
- $0 to $2,500 .... 5%
- $2,500 to $6,250 .... 7%
- $6,250 and over 9%

Married filing jointly and Head of household
- $0 to $5,000 .... 5%
- $5,000 to $12,500 ..... 7%
- $12,500 and over 9%

Pennsylvania

2.8% of taxable compensation, net profits, net gains from the sale of property, rent, royalties, dividends, interest, etc.

Rhode Island

Generally, 25% of the federal income tax liability

South Carolina[2]

Single, Head of household, Married filing jointly, & Married filing separately
- $0 to $2,400 .... 2.5%
- $2,400 to $4,800 ...... 3%
- $4,800 to $7,200 ...... 4%
- $7,200 to $9,600 ...... 5%
- $9,600 to $12,000 ..... 6%
- $12,000 and over 7%

Tennessee

6% of interest and dividends

Utah

Single & Married filing separately
- $0 to $750 .... 2.3%
- $750 to $1,500 .... 3.3%
- $1,500 to $2,250 ..... 4.2%
- $2,25 0 to $3,000 ..... 5.2%
- $3,000 to $3,750 ...... 6%
- $3,750 and over 7%

Head of household & Married filing jointly
- $0 to $1,500 .... 2.3%
- $1,500 to $3,000 ...... 3.3%
- $3,000 to $4,500 ...... 4.2%
- $4,500 to $6,000 ...... 5.2%
- $6,000 to $7,500 .... 6%
- $7,500 and over 7%

Vermont

24% of federal income tax liability

Virginia

Single, Head of household, Married filing jointly, & Married filing separately
- $0 to $3,000 .... 2%
- $3,000 to $5,000 .... 3%
- $5,000 to $17,000 .... 5%
- $17,000 and over 5.75%

West Virginia

Single, Head of household, & Married filing jointly
- $0 to $10,000 .... 3%
- $10,000 to $25,000 ...... 4%
- $25,000 to $40,000 .... 4.5%
- $40,000 to $60,000 ...... 6%
- $60,000 and over 6.5%

Married filing separately
- $0 to $5,000 .... 3%
- $to 5,000 to $12,500 ..... 4%
- $12,500 to $20,000 .... 4.5%
- $20,000 to $30,000 ...... 6%
- $30,000 and over 6.5%

Wisconsin[1,2]

Single and Head of household
- $0 to $8,280 .... 4.6%
- $8,280 to $16,560 .... 6.15%
- $16,560 to $124,200 ... 6.5%
- $124,000 and over ... 6.75%

Married filing jointly
- $0 to $11,040 .... 4.6%
- $11,040 to $22,080 ... 6.15%
- $22,080 to $165,600 ... 6.5%
- $165,600 and over ... 6.75%

Married filing separately
- $0 to $5,520 .... 4.6%
- $5,520 to $11,040 .... 6.15%
- $11,040 to $82,800 .... 6.5%
- $82,800 and over 6.75%

(1) Arizona, Idaho, Louisiana, New Mexico, Wisconsin: Community property states in which one-half of the community income is usually taxable to each spouse. (2) Brackets indexed for inflation annually. (3) 2002 adjusted brackets not currently available. Bracketed rates listed are for 2001.

Colorado: Alternative minimum tax imposed. Qualified taxpayers may pay alternative tax of 0.5% of gross receipts from sales.

Connecticut: Resident estates and trusts are subject to the 4.5% income tax rate on all of their income. Additional state minimum tax imposed on resident individuals, trusts, and estates is equal to the amount by which the minimum tax exceeds the basic income tax (the lesser of (a) 19% of adjusted federal tentative minimum tax, or (b) 5% of adjusted federal alternative minimum taxable income). Separate provisions apply for non- and part-year resident individuals, trusts and estates.

District of Columbia: The tax on unincorporated business is 9.3%. Minimum tax is $100.

Idaho: Each person (joint returns deemed one person) filing a return pays additional $10.

Illinois: Additional personal property replacement tax of 1.5% of net income is imposed on partnerships, trusts, and S corporations.

Indiana: Counties may impose an adjusted gross income tax on residents at .5%, .75% or 1% and at .25% on nonresidents or a county option income tax at rates ranging between .2% and 1%, with the rate on nonresidents equal to one-fourth of the rate on residents.

Iowa: An alternative minimum tax is imposed to equal 75% of the maximum state individual income tax rate for the tax year of the state alternative minimum taxable income.

Louisiana: The amount of tax due is determined from tax tables. These amounts are doubled (rates remain the same) for taxpayers filing joint returns.

Maine: Additional state minimum tax is imposed equal to the amount by which the state minimumtax (27% of adjusted federal tentative minimum tax) exceeds Maine income tax liability, other than withholding tax liability.

Massachusetts: For tax years after 2001, rate on all other income is reduced to 5.3%; for tax years beginning after 2002, to 5%.

Michigan: Persons with business activity allocated or apportioned to Michigan are also subject to a single business tax on an adjusted tax base.

Minnesota: A 6.4% alternative minimum tax is imposed.

Montana: Minimum tax, $1.

Nebraska: The tax rates in the schedules are determined by multiplying the primary rate set by the legislature by the following factors for the brackets, from lowest to highest bracket. For tax years beginning on January 1, 2003, and before January 1, 2004, the respective factors are: 0.6932, 0.9646, 1.3846, and 1.848. For tax years beginning before January 1, 2003, and for tax years beginning on or after January 1, 2004, the respective factors are: 0.6784, 0.9432, 1.3541, and 1.8054. The figure obtained for each bracket is rounded to the nearest tenth of 1%. One rate schedule is to be established for each federal filing status (Sec. 77-2715.02).

New Mexico: Qualified taxpayers may pay alternative tax of 0.75% of gross receipts for New Mexico sales.

New York: A tax table benefit recapture supplemental tax is imposed equal to a taxpayer's tax table benefit multiplied by a fraction, the numerator of which is the lesser of $50,000 or the excess of the taxpayer's New York adjusted gross income for the tax year over $100,000 and the denominator of which is $50,000.

Wisconsin: A temporary recycling surcharge is imposed on individuals, estates, partnerships, trusts, and exempt trusts, except those entities engaged only in farming, at the rate of the greater of $25 or .2173% of net business income. The maximum surcharge is $9,800. An individual, estate, trust, exempt trut, or partnership engaged in farming is subject to a surcharge of $25.

ENERGY

U.S. Energy Overview, 1960-2001

Source: Energy Information Administration, U.S. Dept. of Energy, Internationl Energy Database, Sept. 2002; in quadrillion Btu

	1960	1965	1970	1975	1980	1985	1990[1]	1995	2000	2001[P]
Production	**42.80**	**50.68**	**63.50**	**61.36**	**67.24**	**67.72**	**70.84**	**71.30**	**71.60**	**72.48**
Fossil fuels	39.87	47.23	59.19	54.73	59.01	57.54	58.56	57.46	57.05	58.38
Coal	10.82	13.06	14.61	14.99	18.60	19.33	22.46	22.03	22.62	23.63
Natural gas (dry)	12.66	15.78	21.67	19.64	19.91	16.98	18.36	19.10	19.46	19.92
Crude oil[2]	14.93	16.52	20.40	17.73	18.25	18.99	15.57	13.89	12.36	12.28
Natural gas plant liquids (NGPL)	1.46	1.88	2.51	2.37	2.25	2.24	2.17	2.44	2.61	2.55
Nuclear electric power	0.01	0.04	0.24	1.90	2.74	4.15	6.16	7.18	8.01	8.17
Hydroelectric pumped storage[3]	(4)	(4)	(4)	(4)	(4)	(4)	–0.04	–0.03	–0.06	–0.09
Renewable energy	2.93	3.40	4.08	4.72	5.49	6.03	6.15	6.69	6.60	6.03
Conventional hydroelectric power[5]	1.61	2.06	2.63	3.15	2.90	2.97	3.05	3.21	2.88	2.24
Geothermal energy	0.001	0.004	0.01	0.07	0.11	0.20	0.34	0.31	0.32	0.31
Wood, waste, alcohol[6]	1.32	1.34	1.43	1.50	2.49	2.86	2.66	3.07	3.28	3.34
Solar	NA	NA	NA	NA	NA	(*)	0.06	0.07	0.07	0.07
Wind	NA	NA	NA	NA	NA	(*)	0.03	0.03	0.05	0.06
Imports	**4.23**	**5.92**	**8.39**	**14.11**	**15.97**	**12.10**	**18.95**	**22.57**	**29.31**	**30.45**
Coal	0.01	(*)	(*)	0.02	0.03	0.05	0.07	0.24	0.31	0.49
Natural gas	0.16	0.47	0.85	0.98	1.01	0.95	1.55	2.90	3.87	4.10
All crude oil and petroleum prods.[7]	4.00	5.40	7.47	12.95	14.66	10.61	17.12	18.88	24.53	25.40
Other[8]	0.06	0.04	0.07	0.16	0.28	0.49	0.22	0.55	0.60	0.46
Exports	**1.48**	**1.85**	**2.66**	**2.36**	**3.72**	**4.23**	**4.87**	**4.54**	**4.11**	**3.89**
Coal	1.02	1.38	1.94	1.76	2.42	2.44	2.77	2.32	1.53	1.27
Natural gas	0.01	0.03	0.07	0.07	0.05	0.06	0.09	0.16	0.25	0.37
All crude oil and petroleum prods.[7]	0.43	0.39	0.55	0.44	1.16	1.66	1.82	1.99	2.15	2.04
Other[8]	0.02	0.06	0.11	0.08	0.09	0.08	0.18	0.07	0.18	0.21
Consumption[9]	**45.12**	**54.02**	**67.86**	**72.04**	**78.43**	**76.78**	**84.34**	**90.94**	**98.77**	**96.34**
Fossil fuels	42.14	50.58	63.52	65.35	69.98	66.22	72.03	76.92	84.09	82.22
Coal	9.84	11.58	12.26	12.66	15.42	17.48	19.25	20.03	22.36	21.77
Coal coke net imports	–0.01	–0.02	–0.06	0.01	–0.04	–0.01	(*)	0.06	0.07	0.03
Natural gas[10]	12.39	15.77	21.79	19.95	20.39	17.83	19.30	22.16	23.11	22.00
Petroleum[11]	19.92	23.25	29.52	32.73	34.20	30.92	33.55	34.55	38.40	38.33
Nuclear electric power	0.01	0.04	0.24	1.90	2.74	4.15	6.16	7.18	8.01	8.17
Hydroelectric pumped storage[3]	(4)	(4)	(4)	(4)	(4)	(4)	–0.04	–0.03	–0.06	–0.09
Renewable energy	2.98	3.40	4.10	4.79	5.71	6.46	6.25	6.99	6.87	6.19
Conventional hydroelectric power[5,12]	1.66	2.06	2.65	3.22	3.12	3.40	3.15	3.48	3.15	2.40
Geothermal energy[13]	0.001	0.004	0.01	0.07	0.11	0.20	0.36	0.33	0.32	0.31
Wood, waste, alcohol[6]	1.32	1.34	1.43	1.50	2.49	2.86	2.66	3.07	3.28	3.34
Solar energy	NA	NA	NA	NA	NA	(*)	0.06	0.07	0.07	0.07
Wind energy	NA	NA	NA	NA	NA	(*)	0.03	0.03	0.05	0.06

(1) Starting in 1990, expanded coverage of nonelectric utility use of renewable energy resulted in an increase in total production and consumption figures. (2) Incl. lease condensate. (3) Total pumped storage facility production minus energy used for pumping. (4) Included in conventional hydroelectric power. (5) Starting in 1990, pumped storage is removed and expanded coverage of industrial use of hydroelectric power is included. (6) Substituted in 2000 for former "Biofuels" category; figures for 1960-99 were recalculated. Alcohol is ethanol blended into motor gasoline. (7) Incl. imports of crude oil for the Strategic Petroleum Reserve, which began in 1977. (8) Coal coke and small amts. of electricity transmitted across borders with Canada and Mexico. (9) Starting in 1990, "Consumption" includes net imports of electricity from nonrenewable energy sources. (10) Incl. supplemental gaseous fuels. (11) Petroleum products supplied, incl. natural gas plant liquids and crude oil burned as fuel. (12) Starting in 1990, includes only the part of net imports of electricity derived from hydroelectric power. (13) Incl. electricity imports from Mexico derived from geothermal energy. NA = Not available. P = preliminary. (*) = Less than 0.005 quadrillion Btu. Some figures here have been revised.

U.S. Energy Flow, 2001

Source: Energy Information Administration, U.S. Dept. of Energy, *Monthly Energy Review, August 2002*; in quadrillion Btu

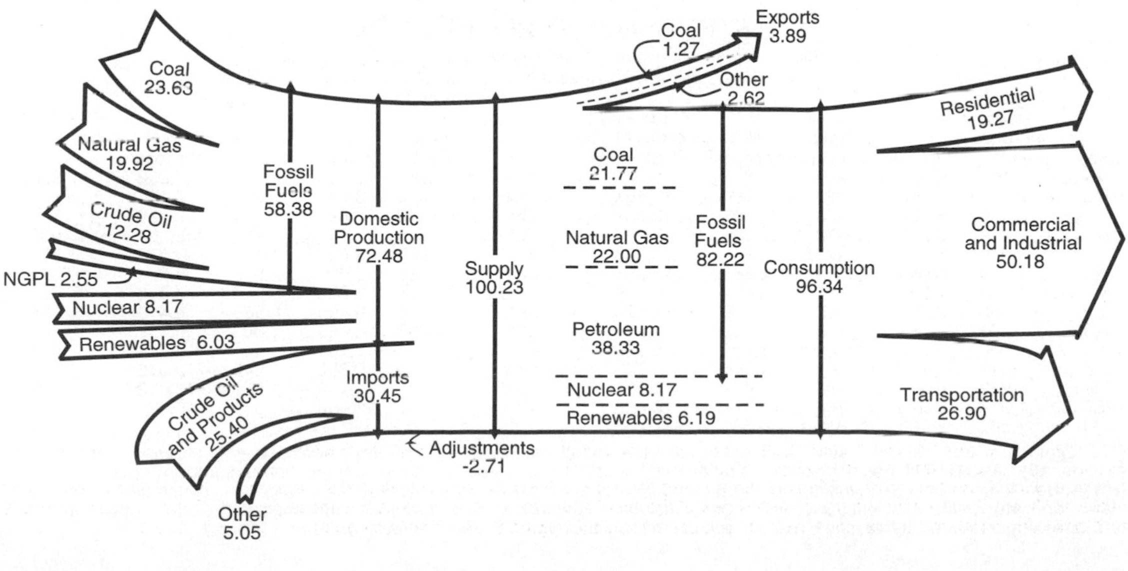

World Energy Consumption and Production Trends, 2000

Source: Energy Information Administration, U.S. Dept. of Energy, International Energy Database, Sept. 2002

The world's **consumption** of primary energy—petroleum, natural gas, coal, net hydroelectric, nuclear, geothermal, solar, wind, and wood and waste electric power, and other wood and waste—increased from 390 quadrillion Btu in 1999 to 397 quadrillion Btu in 2000.

The 30 countries of the Organization for Economic Cooperation and Development (OECD), which includes most of the world's most developed economies (the United States, Japan, and Germany), continued to dominate global energy use. OECD nations accounted for 58% of the world's primary energy consumption in 2000, unchanged from 1999.

World **production** of primary energy increased from 388 quadrillion Btu in 1999 to 397 quadrillion Btu in 2000. World production of petroleum in 2000 was over 74 million barrels per day, or 155 quadrillion Btu, up almost 4%; petroleum remained the most heavily used source of energy.

In 2000, 3 countries—the United States, Russia, and China—were the world's leading producers (38%) and consumers (41%) of energy. Russia and the United States alone supplied 29% of the world total. The United States alone accounted for 25% of the world's energy consumption. The United States consumed 38% more energy than it produced—an imbalance of 27 quadrillion Btu.

World's Major Consumers of Primary Energy, 2000

Source: Energy Information Administration, International Energy Database; quadrillion Btu

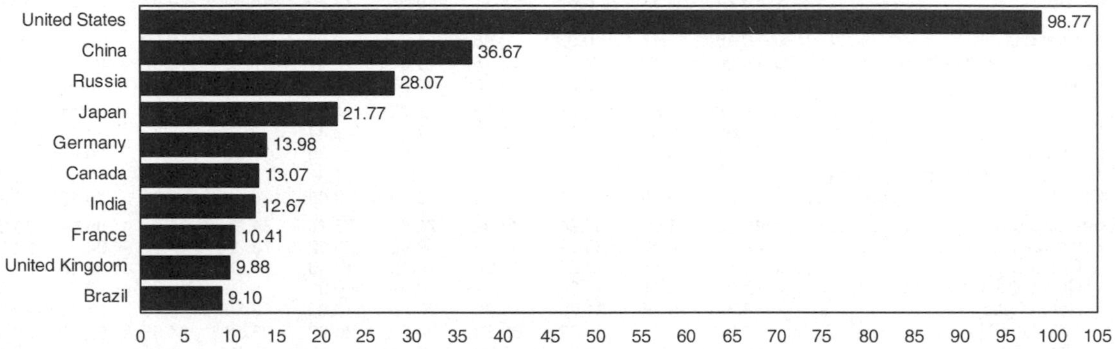

World's Major Producers of Primary Energy, 2000

Source: Energy Information Administration, International Energy Database; quadrillion Btu

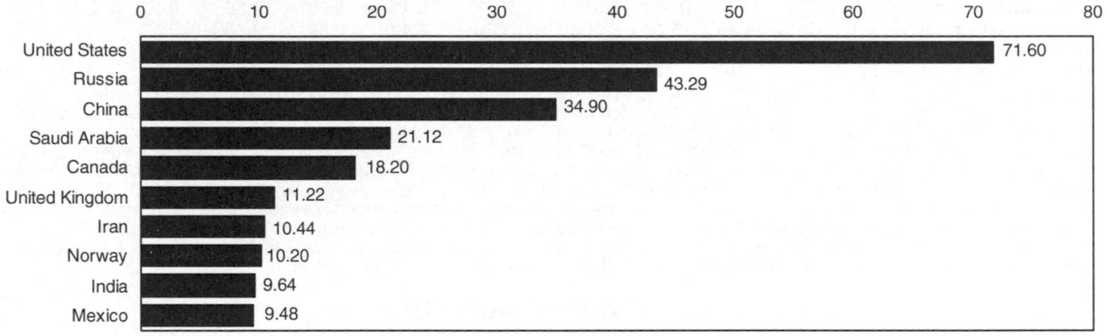

U.S. Petroleum Trade, 1975-2001

Source: Energy Information Administration, U.S. Dept. of Energy, *Monthly Energy Review,* Aug. 2002

(in thousands of barrels per day; average for the year)

Year	Imports from Persian Gulf[1]	Total imports	Total exports	Net imports[2]	Petroleum products supplied[3]
1975	1,165	6,056	209	5,846	16,322
1976	1,840	7,313	223	7,090	17,461
1977	2,448	8,807	243	8,565	18,431
1978	2,219	8,363	362	8,002	18,847
1979	2,069	8,456	471	7,985	18,513
1980	1,519	6,909	544	6,365	17,056
1981	1,219	5,996	595	5,401	16,058
1982	696	5,113	815	4,298	15,296
1983	442	5,051	739	4,312	15,231
1984	506	5,437	722	4,715	15,726
1985	311	5,067	781	4,286	15,726
1986	912	6,224	785	5,439	16,281
1987	1,077	6,678	764	5,914	16,665
1988	1,541	7,402	815	6,587	17,283
1989	1,861	8,061	859	7,202	17,325
1990	1,966	8,018	857	7,161	16,988
1991	1,845	7,627	1,001	6,626	16,714
1992	1,778	7,888	950	6,938	17,033
1993	1,782	8,620	1,003	7,618	17,237
1994	1,728	8,996	942	8,054	17,718
1995	1,573	8,835	949	7,886	17,725
1996	1,604	9,399	981	8,419	18,234
1997	1,755	10,162	1,003	9,158	18,620
1998	2,136	10,708	945	9,764	18,917
1999	2,464	10,852	940	9,912	19,519
2000	2,488	11,459	1,040	10,419	19,701
2001	2,761	11,459	971	10,900	19,649

(1) Bahrain, Iran, Iraq, Kuwait, Qatar, Saudi Arabia, and the United Arab Emirates. (2) Net imports are total imports minus total exports. (3) Basically includes domestic production and imports minus change in stocks, refinery imports, and exports.

Notes: Beginning in Oct. 1977, imports for the Strategic Petroleum Reserves are included. U.S. geographic coverage includes the 50 states and the District of Columbia. U.S. exports include shipments to U.S. territories, and imports include receipts from U.S. territories. Figures in this table may not add, because of rounding. Some figures are revised.

Energy Consumption, Total and Per Capita, by State, 1999

Source: Energy Information Administration, U.S. Dept. of Energy, State Energy Data Report 1999

TOTAL CONSUMPTION

Rank/State	Trillion Btu	Rank/State	Trillion Btu
1. Texas	11,501.0	28. Arkansas	1,203.7
2. California	8,375.4	29. Colorado	1,155.5
3. Ohio	4,323.4	30. Iowa	1,121.7
4. New York	4,283.0	31. Oregon	1,109.2
5. Illinois	3,882.6	32. Kansas	1,050.0
6. Florida	3,852.9	33. Connecticut	839.3
7. Pennsylvania	3,715.5	34. West Virginia	735.4
8. Louisiana	3,615.4	35. Alaska	694.7
9. Michigan	3,239.6	36. Utah	693.9
10. Georgia	2,798.1	37. New Mexico	635.0
11. Indiana	2,735.8	38. Nevada	615.3
12. New Jersey	2,588.7	39. Nebraska	602.0
13. North Carolina	2,446.9	40. Maine	528.6
14. Washington	2,240.8	41. Idaho	518.3
15. Virginia	2,227.3	42. Wyoming	421.8
16. Tennessee	2,070.5	43. Montana	412.4
17. Alabama	2,004.8	44. North Dakota	365.7
18. Kentucky	1,830.2	45. New Hampshire	335.4
19. Wisconsin	1,810.5	46. Delaware	278.8
20. Missouri	1,768.0	47. Rhode Island	261.1
21. Minnesota	1,675.3	48. Hawaii	241.4
22. Massachusetts	1,569.1	49. South Dakota	239.0
23. South Carolina	1,493.0	50. District of Columbia	169.8
24. Maryland	1,378.2	51. Vermont	165.0
25. Oklahoma	1,377.5	**TOTAL U.S.**	**95,682.4**
26. Arizona	1,219.8		
27. Mississippi	1,208.5		

CONSUMPTION PER CAPITA

Rank/State	Million Btu	Rank/State	Million Btu
1. Alaska	1,121.5	28. Nevada	340.1
2. Wyoming	879.4	29. Oregon	334.5
3. Louisiana	826.9	30. Michigan	328.4
4. North Dakota	577.1	31. District of Columbia	327.1
5. Texas	573.8	32. South Dakota	326.0
6. Arkansas	471.8	33. Utah	325.8
7. Montana	467.1	34. Virginia	324.1
8. Kentucky	462.1	35. Missouri	323.3
9. Indiana	460.3	36. Illinois	320.1
10. Alabama	458.8	37. North Carolina	319.8
11. Mississippi	436.5	38. New Jersey	317.9
12. Maine	421.9	39. Pennsylvania	309.8
13. Idaho	414.1	40. Colorado	284.9
14. Oklahoma	410.2	41. New Hampshire	279.2
15. West Virginia	407.0	42. Vermont	277.9
16. Kansas	395.6	43. Maryland	266.5
17. Iowa	390.9	44. Rhode Island	263.5
18. Washington	389.3	45. Connecticut	255.7
19. South Carolina	384.2	46. Arizona	255.3
20. Ohio	384.1	47. Florida	255.0
21. Tennessee	377.6	48. Massachusetts	254.1
22. Delaware	370.0	49. California	252.7
23. New Mexico	365.0	50. New York	235.4
24. Nebraska	361.3	51. Hawaii	203.7
25. Georgia	359.3	**TOTAL U.S.**	**350.9**
26. Minnesota	350.8		
27. Wisconsin	344.8		

Gasoline Retail Prices, U.S. City Average, 1974-2002

Source: Energy Information Administration, U.S. Dept. of Energy, *Monthly Energy Review,* Aug. 2002

(cents per gallon, including taxes)

AVERAGE	Leaded regular	Unleaded regular	Unleaded premium	All types[1]	AVERAGE	Leaded regular	Unleaded regular	Unleaded premium	All types[1]
1974	53.2	NA	NA	NA	1989	99.8	102.1	119.7	106.0
1975	56.7	NA	NA	NA	1990	114.9	116.4	134.9	121.7
1976	59.0	61.4	NA	NA	1991	NA	114.0	132.1	119.6
1977	62.2	65.6	NA	NA	1992	NA	112.7	131.6	119.0
1978	62.6	67.0	NA	65.2	1993	NA	110.8	130.2	117.3
1979	85.7	90.3	NA	88.2	1994	NA	111.2	130.5	117.4
1980	119.1	124.5	NA	122.1	1995	NA	114.7	133.6	120.5
1981[2]	131.1	137.8	147.03[3]	135.3	1996	NA	123.1	141.3	128.8
1982	122.2	129.6	141.5	128.1	1997	NA	123.4	141.6	129.1
1983	115.7	124.1	138.3	122.5	1998	NA	105.9	125.0	111.5
1984	112.9	121.2	136.6	119.8	1999	NA	116.5	135.7	122.1
1985	111.5	120.2	134.0	119.6	2000	NA	151.0	169.3	156.3
1986	85.7	92.7	108.5	93.1	2001	NA	146.1	165.7	153.1
1987	89.7	94.8	109.3	95.7	2002 (Jan.-June)	NA	129.0	149.3	137.2
1988	89.9	94.6	110.7	96.3					

Until unleaded gas became available in 1976, leaded was the only type used in automobiles. Average retail prices (in cents per gallon) for selected years preceding those in the table above were as follows: 1950: .27; 1955: .29; 1960: .31; 1965: .31; 1970: .36. (1) Also includes types of motor gasoline not shown separately. (2) In Sept. 1981, the Bureau of Labor Statistics changed the weights in the calculation of average motor gasoline prices. Starting in Sept. 1981, gasohol is included in average for all types, and unleaded premium is weighted more heavily. (3) Based on Sept. through Dec. data only. **NOTE:** Geographic coverage for 1974-77 is 56 urban areas; for 1978 and later, 85 urban areas. NA = Not applicable.

Gasoline Retail Prices in Selected Countries, 1990-2001

Source: Energy Information Administration, U.S. Dept. of Energy

(average price of unleaded regular gas; dollars per gallon, including taxes)

Year	Australia	Brazil	Canada	China	Germany	Japan	Mexico	Taiwan	U.S.
1990	NA	$3.82	$1.87	NA	$2.65	$3.17	$1.00	$2.49	$1.16
1991	$1.96	2.91	1.92	NA	2.90	3.46	1.29	2.39	1.14
1992	1.89	2.92	1.73	NA	3.27	3.59	1.50	2.42	1.13
1993	1.73	2.40	1.57	NA	3.07	4.02	1.56	2.27	1.11
1994	1.84	2.80	1.45	$0.96	3.52	4.39	1.48	2.14	1.11
1995	1.95	2.16	1.53	1.03	3.96	4.43	1.12	2.23	1.15
1996	2.12	2.31	1.61	1.03	3.94	3.65	1.26	2.15	1.23
1997	2.05	2.61	1.62	1.07	3.54	3.27	1.47	2.23	1.23
1998	1.63	2.80	1.38	1.08	3.34	2.82	1.50	1.86	1.06
1999	1.72	NA	1.51	NA	3.42	3.27	1.80	1.86	1.17
2000	1.94	NA	1.86	NA	3.45	3.74	2.02	NA	1.51
2001	1.71	NA	1.72	NA	3.40	3.35	2.21	NA	1.46

NA = Not available.

Major U.S. Coal Producers, 2000

Source: Energy Information Administration

Rank	Company Name	Production (thousand short tons)	Percent of total production
1.	Peabody Coal Sales Co.	140,552	13.1
2.	Arch Coal, Inc.	108,749	10.1
3.	Kennecott Energy & Coal Co.	106,690	9.9
4.	Consol Energy Inc.	73,718	6.9
5.	RAG American Coal Holding, Inc.	62,809	5.9
6.	AEI Resources Inc	51,642	4.8
7.	A.T. Massey Coal Co., Inc	40,286	3.8
8.	Vulcan Partners, L.P.	33,040	3.1
9.	North American Coal Corp.	27,208	2.5
10.	TXU Corporation	25,927	2.4
11.	Westmoreland Coal Sales Co.	18,791	1.8
12.	Robert Murray	16,049	1.5
13.	Black Beauty Coal Co.	16,021	1.5
14.	Pacificorp	15,568	1.5
15.	BHP Minerals Group	14,711	1.4
16.	Alliance Coal Co.	13,928	1.3
17.	James River Coal Co	11,922	1.1
18.	Peter Kiewit/Kennecott	9,932	.9
19.	Quaker Coal Co.	9,130	.9
20.	Pittston Co.	8,404	.8
21.	Lodestar Energy Inc.	7,526	.7
22.	Coastal Coal Co., L.L.C.	7,362	.7
23.	Walter Industries, Inc.	6,787	.6
24.	ALCOA Inc	6,624	.6
25.	Chevron Corp	6,546	.6
26.	Pittsburg & Midway Coal Mining Co	6,330	.6
27.	Andalex Resources, Inc.	5,980	.6
	All other coal producers	**221,380**	**20.6**
	U.S. Total	**1,073,612**	**100.0**

Note: The company is the firm controlling the coal, particularly the sale of the coal. Usually it is also the owner of the mine.

Major U.S. Coal Mines, 2000

Source: Energy Information Administration

Rank	Mine Name/Company	Mine Type	State	Production (short tons)
1.	Rochelle Mine Complex/Powder River Coal	Surface	Wyoming	70,769,071
2.	Black Thunder/Thunder Basin Coal	Surface	Wyoming	60,102,031
3.	Cordero/Cordero Mining	Surface	Wyoming	38,698,196
4.	Jacobs Ranch/Jacobs Ranch Coal	Surface	Wyoming	28,307,022
5.	Caballo/Caballo Coal	Surface	Wyoming	25,595,660
6.	Antelope/Antelope Coal	Surface	Wyoming	22,971,230
7.	Eagle Butte/RAG Coal West	Surface	Wyoming	18,622,992
8.	North Rochelle/Triton Coal Co.	Surface	Wyoming	17,206,504
9.	Freedom Mine/Coteau Properties	Surface	North Dakota	16,125,847
10.	Buckskin/Triton Coal	Surface	Wyoming	15,833,179
11.	Belle Ayr/RAG Coal West	Surface	Wyoming	15,015,064
12.	Spring Creek/Spring Creek Coal Co	Surface	Montana	11,302,150
13.	Rosebud No 6/Western Energy Co.	Surface	Montana	10,430,858
14.	Decker/Decker Coal	Surface	Montana	9,932,166
15.	Bailey No 1/Consol PA Coal Co.	Underground	Pennsylvania	9,863,772
16.	Enlow Fork/Consol PA Coal Co.	Underground	Pennsylvania	9,521,262
17.	Navajo/BHP Minerals	Surface	New Mexico	8,489,100
18.	Keyenta/Peabody Western Coal	Surface	Arizona	8,485,952
19.	Jewett/Northwestern Resources	Surface	Texas	7,987,833
20.	Falkirik/Falkirk Mining	Surface	North Dakota	7,633,171
21.	Galatia/American Coal Company	Underground	Illinois	7,348,369
22.	Foidel Creek/Twenty Mile Coal	Underground	Colorado	7,221,704
23.	Oak Hill/Texas Utilities Mining	Surface	Texas	6,885,681
24.	McElroy/McElroy Coal Co.	Underground	West Virginia	6,763,483
25.	Sandow-Rockdale/ALCOA	Surface	Texas	6,624,060
	All Other Mines			**625,875,204**
	U.S. Total			**1,073,611,561**

Note: The company is the firm operating the mine.

Ten Largest Oil Fields in the United States

Source: Energy Information Administration, *Petroleum: An Energy Profile, 1999*
(as of Jan. 1, 1999, by size of total recoverable resources)

Oil Field	Location	Year Discovered	Cumulative Production	Remaining Reserves	Recoverable Resources
				(billion barrels)	
Prudhoe Bay	Alaska	1968	9.7	3.3	13
East Texas	Texas	1930	5.3	(s)	5.4
Wilmington	California	1932	2.5	0.3	2.8
Midway-Sunset	California	1894	2.4	0.3	2.7
Kuparuk River	Alaska	1969	1.6	1	2.6
Wasson	Texas	1936	2.0	0.1	2.1
Kern River	California	1899	1.7	0.4	2.1
Yates	Texas	1926	1.4	0.6	2
Panhandle	Texas	1921	1.5	(s)	1.5
Elk Hills	California	1911	1.1	0.3	1.4

(s) = less than 100 million barrels

Production of Crude Oil, by Major States, 2001

Source: Energy Information Administration, *Petroleum Supply Annual 2001*
(thousand barrels)

Rank	State	Total
1.	Texas	424,295
2.	Alaska	351,412
3.	California	260,665
4.	Louisiana	104,608
5.	Oklahoma	68,531
6.	New Mexico	68,001
7.	Wyoming	57,432
8.	Kansas	33,942
9.	North Dakota	31,691
10.	Mississippi	19,530
11.	Colorado	16,518
12.	Montana	15,919
13.	Utah	15,251
14.	Illinois	10,092
15.	Alabama	9,333
16.	Arkansas	7,591
17.	Michigan	7,374
18.	Ohio	6,050
19.	Florida	4,426
20.	Kentucky	2,970
21.	Nebraska	2,922
22.	Indiana	2,022
23.	Pennsylvania	1,620
24.	South Dakota	1,255
25.	West Virginia	1,225
26.	Nevada	571
27.	Tennessee	349
28.	New York	166
29.	Missouri	90
30.	Arizona	60
31.	Virginia	12
	U.S. TOTAL	**2,117,511**

World Crude Oil and Natural Gas Reserves, Jan. 1, 2001

Sources: Energy Information Administration, U.S. Dept. of Energy, *U.S. Crude Oil and Natural Gas Liquids Reserves, Dec. 2001; Oil and Gas Journal (OGJ),* Dec. 2000; *World Oil (WO),* Aug. 2001

	Crude oil (billion barrels)		Natural gas (trillion cubic feet)	
	OGJ	*WO*	*OGJ*	*WO*
North America	**55.0**	**54.6**	**268.8**	**281.0**
Canada	4.7	5.6	61.0	62.2
Mexico	28.3	26.9	30.4	41.4
United States	22.0	22.0	177.4	177.4
Central and South America	**94.5**	**67.5**	**244.6**	**234.4**
Argentina	3.1	3.0	26.4	27.4
Bolivia	0.4	0.2	18.3	6.6
Brazil	8.1	8.5	8.2	7.8
Colombia	2.0	2.6	6.9	6.9
Ecuador	2.1	3.1	3.7	4.2
Peru	0.3	0.9	8.7	8.7
Trinidad and Tobago	0.7	0.7	21.4	23.5
Venezuela	76.9	47.6	146.8	147.6
Other	1.0	1.0	4.2	1.8
Western Europe	**17.4**	**17.6**	**161.8**	**150.0**
Denmark	1.1	1.1	3.4	2.6
Germany	0.4	0.3	11.5	9.3
Italy	0.6	0.6	8.1	7.0
Netherlands	0.1	0.1	62.5	58.4
Norway	9.4	10.1	44.0	41.8
United Kingdom	5.0	4.7	26.8	26.0
Other	0.7	0.7	5.4	4.9
Eastern Europe and Former USSR	**58.9**	**66.1**	**1,999.2**	**1,944.0**
Hungary	0.1	0.1	2.9	1.1
Kazakhstan	5.4	NA	65.0	NA
Romania	1.4	1.2	13.2	4.9
Russia	48.6	54.3	1,700.0	1,695.0
Other[1]	3.3	10.6	218.1	243.0
Middle East	**683.5**	**654.6**	**1,854.8**	**1,985.3**
Bahrain	0.1	NA	3.9	NA
Iran	89.7	96.4	812.3	929.1
Iraq	112.5	115.0	109.8	112.6
Kuwait	96.5	98.8	52.7	56.6
Oman	5.5	5.8	29.3	30.3
Qatar	13.2	5.6	393.8	400.0
Saudi Arabia	261.7	265.3	213.8	214.0
Syria	2.5	2.2	8.5	8.4
United Arab Emirates	97.8	62.8	212.1	204.1
Yemen	4.0	2.1	16.9	17.0
Other	(2)	0.5	1.7	13.2
Africa	**74.9**	**86.4**	**394.2**	**413.7**
Algeria	9.2	12.7	159.7	155.6
Angola	5.4	9.0	1.6	4.0
Cameroon	0.4	NA	3.9	NA
Congo Republic	1.5	1.7	3.2	4.2
Egypt	2.9	3.6	35.2	50.6
Libya	29.5	30.0	46.4	46.4
Nigeria	22.5	24.1	124.0	125.0
Tunisia	0.3	0.3	2.8	2.8
Other	3.1	5.1	17.4	25.2
Asia and Oceania	**44.0**	**57.2**	**365.1**	**441.8**
Australia	2.0	2.8	44.6	44.0
Brunei	1.4	1.2	13.8	8.8
China	24.0	30.6	48.3	42.0
India	4.7	3.3	22.8	15.9
Indonesia	5.0	9.7	72.3	146.9
Malaysia	3.9	5.1	81.7	81.7
New Zealand	0.1	0.2	2.5	3.0
Pakistan	0.2	0.3	21.6	25.1
Papua New Guinea	0.4	0.6	7.9	16.9
Thailand	0.4	0.6	11.8	12.7
Other	1.1	2.9	37.9	44.8
WORLD	**1,028.1**	**1,004.1**	**5,288.5**	**5,450.2**

NA = Not available. (1) Albania, Azerbaijan, Belarus, Bulgaria, Czech Republic, Georgia, Kyrgyzstan, Lithuania, Poland, Slovakia, Tajikistan, Turkmenistan, Ukraine, Uzbekistan. (2) Less than 50 million barrels. **NOTE:** Data for Kuwait and Saudi Arabia include one-half of the reserves in the Neutral Zone between Kuwait and Saudi Arabia. All reserve figures except those for the former USSR and natural gas reserves in Canada are *proved reserves* recoverable with present technology and prices at the time of estimation. Former USSR and Canadian natural gas figures include *proved* and some *probable reserves*. Totals may not equal sum of components as a result of independent rounding.

Nuclear Electricity Generation by Selected Country, 2001

Source: Energy Information Administration, U.S. Dept. of Energy, *Monthly Energy Review*, Aug. 2002

(Generation for 2001, in billion kilowatt-hours; E = estimate)

Country	Generation
Argentina	7.0E
Armenia	2.0E
Belgium	45.8
Brazil	17.8E
Bulgaria	19.6
Canada	64.1E
China	13.7E
Czech Republic	14.8E
Finland	22.8
France	421.1
Germany	171.3
Hungary	14.2E
India	19.2E
Japan	324.9E
Korea, South	113.3E
Lithuania	10.2E
Mexico	8.7
Netherlands	4.0
Pakistan	2.2
Romania	5.4E
Russia	134.4
Slovakia	17.5E
Slovenia	5.3
South Africa	11.3
Spain	63.7
Sweden	72.8E
Switzerland	26.7
Taiwan	35.5
Ukraine	74.6E
United Kingdom	90.3E
United States	800.6E

Nations Most Reliant on Nuclear Energy, 2001

Source: International Atomic Energy Agency, Oct. 2002

(Nuclear electricity generation as % of total electricity generated)

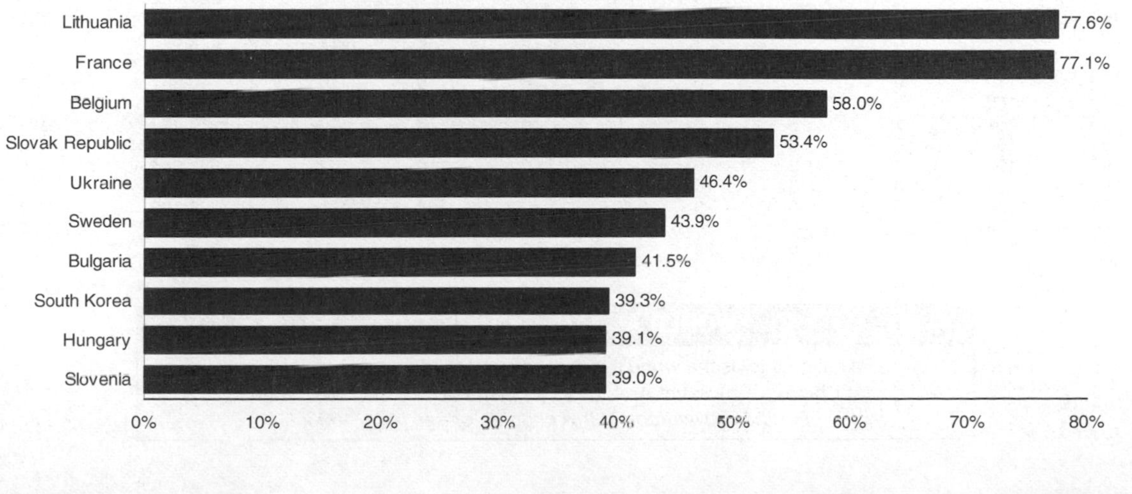

World Nuclear Power Summary, 2002

Source: International Atomic Energy Agency, Power Reactor Information System, Jan. 2002

Country	Reactors in operation: No. of units	Reactors in operation: Total MW(e)	Reactors under construction: No. of units	Reactors under construction: Total MW(e)	Nuclear electricity supplied in 2001: TW(e).h[1]	Nuclear electricity supplied in 2001: % of nation's total	Total operating experience[2]: Years	Total operating experience[2]: Months
Argentina	2	935	1	692	6.54	8.19	46	7
Armenia	1	376	—	—	1.99	34.82	34	3
Belgium	7	5,712	—	—	44.10	58.03	177	7
Brazil	2	1,901	—	—	14.35	4.34	21	3
Bulgaria	6	3,538	—	—	18.24	41.55	119	2
Canada	14	10,018	—	—	72.35	12.85	447	2
China	3	2,167	8	6,426	16.68	1.14	26	5
Czech Republic	5	2,560	1	912	14.75	19.76	63	9
Finland	4	2,656	—	—	21.88	30.54	91	4
France	59	63,073	—	—	401.30	77.07	1,228	2
Germany	19	21,283	—	—	162.30	30.52	610	1
Hungary	4	1,755	—	—	14.13	39.09	66	2
India	14	2,503	2	980	17.32	3.72	195	5
Iran	—	—	2	2,111	—	—	—	—
Japan	54	44,289	3	3,696	321.94	34.26	1,016	4
Korea, South	16	12,990	4	3,820	112.13	39.32	185	2
Lithuania	2	2,370	—	—	11.36	77.58	32	6
Mexico	2	1,360	—	—	8.11	3.66	19	11
Netherlands	1	450	—	—	3.75	4.16	57	0
Pakistan	2	425	—	—	1.98	2.86	31	10
Romania	1	655	1	650	5.05	10.46	5	6
Russia	30	20,793	2	1,875	125.36	15.40	701	4
Slovakia	6	2,408	2	776	17.10	53.44	91	0
Slovenia	1	676	—	—	5.03	38.98	20	3
South Africa	2	1,800	—	—	13.34	6.65	34	3
Spain	9	7,524	—	—	61.07	26.88	201	2
Sweden	11	9,432	—	—	69.20	43.85	289	1
Switzerland	5	3,200	—	—	25.29	35.96	133	10
Taiwan	6	4,884	2	2,700	34.09	21.57	122	1
Ukraine	13	11,207	4	3,800	71.67	46.36	253	10
United Kingdom	33	12,498	—	—	82.34	22.44	1,270	2
United States	104	97,860	—	—	768.83	20.35	2,663	8
TOTAL	**438**	**353,298**	**32**	**28,438**	**2,543.57**	—	**10,256**	**3**

(1) 1 terawatt-hour [TW(e).h] = 10^6 megawatt-hour [MW(e).h]. For an average power plant, 1 TW(e).h = 0.39 megatons of coal equivalent (input) and 0.23 megatons of oil equivalent (input). (2) Through Dec. 31, 2001.

U.S. Nuclear Reactor Units and Power Plant Operations, 1978-2001

Source: Energy Information Administration, U.S. Dept. of Energy, Aug. 2002

Year	Number of reactor units: Licensed for operation: Operable	Licensed for operation: In startup	Construction permits: Granted	Construction permits: Pending	On order	Announced	Total	Total design capacity (million KWs)	Nuclear-based electricity generation (million net KW-hrs)	Nuclear portion of domestic electricity generation (percent)
1978	70	0	88	32	5	0	195	191	276,403	12.5
1979	69	0	90	24	3	0	185	180	255,155	11.4
1980	71	1	82	12	3	0	168	162	251,116	11.0
1981	75	0	76	11	2	0	163	157	272,674	11.9
1982	78	2	60	3	2	0	144	134	282,773	12.6
1983	81	3	53	0	2	0	138	129	293,677	12.7
1984	87	6	38	0	2	0	132	123	327,634	13.6
1985	96	3	30	0	2	0	130	121	383,691	15.5
1986	101	7	19	0	2	0	128	119	414,038	16.6
1987	107	4	14	0	2	0	127	119	455,270	17.7
1988	109	3	12	0	0	0	123	115	526,973	19.5
1989	111	1	10	0	0	0	121	113	529,402	17.8
1990	112	0	8	0	0	0	119	111	576,974	19.1
1991	111	0	8	0	0	0	119	111	612,642	19.9
1992	109	0	8	0	0	0	117	111	618,841	20.1
1993	110	0	7	0	0	0	116	110	610,367	19.1
1994	109	0	7	0	0	0	116	110	640,492	19.7
1995	109	1	6	0	0	0	116	110	673,402	20.1
1996	109	0	6	0	0	0	116	110	674,729	19.6
1997	107	0	3	0	0	0	110	102	628,644	18.0
1998	104	0	3	0	0	0	107	99	673,702	18.6
1999	104	0	0	0	0	0	104	NA	728,198	19.8
2000	104	0	0	0	0	0	104	NA	753,893	19.8
2001	104	0	0	0	0	0	104	NA	768,826	20.5

NA = Not available.

WORLD ALMANAC QUICK QUIZ

What country is the world's biggest producer of energy?

(a) China (b) Saudi Arabia (c) Canada (d) United States

For the answer look in this chapter, or see page 1008.

ENVIRONMENT

Greenhouse Effect and Global Warming

Source: U.S. Environmental Protection Agency

The Earth naturally absorbs incoming solar radiation and emits thermal radiation back into space. Some of the thermal radiation is trapped by so-called greenhouse gases in the atmosphere, which increases warming of the Earth's surface and atmosphere. In recent years, carbon dioxide (CO_2), a naturally occurring greenhouse gas, has been building up as a result of activities such as the burning of fossil fuels (coal, oil, natural gas) and deforestation. Water vapor, methane (CH_4), nitrous oxide (N_2O), and ozone (O_3) are also naturally occurring greenhouse gases. Greenhouse gases that are mostly human-made include chlorofluorocarbons (CFCs), hydrochlorofluorocarbons (HCFCs), hydrofluorocarbons (HFCs), perfluorocarbons (PFCs), and sulfur hexafluoride (SF_6). Several nongreenhouse gases (carbon monoxide [CO], oxides of nitrogen [NOx], and nonmethane volatile organic compounds [NMVOCs]) contribute indirectly to the greenhouse effect by producing greenhouse gases during chemical transformations or by influencing the atmospheric lifetimes of greenhouse gases.

Since the start of the industrial revolution, atmospheric concentrations of CO_2, CH_4, and N_2O have increased by 30%, 145%, and 15%, respectively. This buildup is believed by many scientists to be the major cause of higher than normal average global temperatures in the 1990s and into the 21st century; 2001 was the 2nd-warmest year on record. The hottest was 1998, the 3rd-hottest was 1997, and 9 of the 10 hottest on record have occurred since 1990. Over the 20th century, Earth's average temperature has risen by about 1°F, and some scientists believe that it could rise by 2° to 6°F over the 21st century. This global warming could speed the melting of polar ice caps, inundate coastal lowlands, and cause major changes in crop production and in natural habitat. The U.S. is the world's leading producer of CO_2, followed by China, Russia, Japan, India, and Germany.

In Dec. 1997, at a UN summit on global warming in Kyoto, Japan, delegates from over 150 nations adopted a treaty to limit emissions of CO_2, CH_4, N_2O, HFCs, PFCs, and SF_6. The so-called Kyoto Protocol called for cutting emissions 5.2% below 1990 levels by 2012 for all 38 industrialized countries that signed the accord. Developing nations were not bound. The 15 EU nations agreed to binding reductions of 8%, the U.S. to 7%, and Japan to 6%.

The U.S. signed the treaty on Nov. 12, 1998, but Pres. Bill Clinton did not send it to the Senate for ratification because of dim prospects for approval. The current administration opposes the treaty, calling it unfair to developed countries and anti-growth. A report submitted to the UN by the Bush administration in May 2002 acknowledged a link between human activity and global warming, forecasting a 43% increase in U.S. greenhouse gas emissions from 2000 to 2002. However, the administration favored a voluntary approach, including tax incentives, rather than mandatory controls. At a meeting in Bonn, Germany in July 2001 delegates agreed, despite U.S. opposition, on binding guidelines and timetables for achieving the Kyoto-mandated reductions. Under the agreement, high-emissions nations could meet their targets by purchasing pollution credits from nations that exceed targets, and gain credits for "sinks," such as forests and croplands, that absorb CO_2 from the atmosphere. At the World Summit on Sustainable Development, in Johannesburg, South Africa, in Aug.-Sept. 2002, Russia indicated it would soon ratify the Kyoto Protocol; the treaty could then take effect, having received approval from enough major greenhouse gas producers.

U.S. Greenhouse Gas Emissions From Human Activities, 1990-2000

Source: U.S. Environmental Protection Agency

GAS AND SOURCE	1990	1995	1996	1997	1998	1999	2000
Carbon dioxide (CO_2)	**4,998.5**	**5,305.9**	**5,483.7**	**5,568.0**	**5,575.1**	**5,665.5**	**5,840.0**
Fossil fuel combustion	4,779.8	5,085.0	5,266.6	5,339.6	5,356.2	5,448.6	5,623.3
Methane (CH_4)	**651.3**	**657.6**	**643.7**	**633.3**	**627.1**	**620.5**	**614.5**
Coal mining	87.1	73.5	68.4	68.1	67.9	63.7	61.0
Landfills	213.4	216.6	211.5	206.4	201.0	203.1	203.5
Natural gas systems	121.2	125.7	126.6	122.7	122.2	118.6	116.4
Enteric fermentation[1]	127.9	133.2	129.6	126.8	124.9	124.5	123.9
Nitrous oxide (N_2O)	**387.3**	**419.8**	**430.5**	**429.8**	**426.3**	**423.5**	**425.3**
Agricultural soil management	267.1	283.4	292.6	297.5	298.4	296.3	297.6
Hydrofluorocarbons (HFCs), perfluorocarbons (PFCs), and sulfur hexafluoride (SF_6)[2]	**93.6**	**98.5**	**111.9**	**116.9**	**127.7**	**120.0**	**121.3**
TOTAL U.S. EMISSIONS	**6,130.7**	**6,481.8**	**6,669.8**	**6,748.1**	**6,756.2**	**6,829.5**	**7,001.2**
NET U.S. EMISSIONS[3]	**5,033.0**	**5,371.8**	**5,561.7**	**5,860.5**	**5,870.3**	**5,933.1**	**6,098.7**

Note: Emissions given in terms of equivalent emissions of carbon dioxide (CO_2), using units of teragrams of carbon dioxide equivalents (Tg CO_2 Eq.). Before 1999, emissions were given in units of million metric tons of carbon equivalents (MMTCE). (1) Digestive process of ruminent animals, such as cattle and sheep, producing methane as a by-product. (2) These gases have extremely high global warming potential, and PFCs and SF_6 have long atmospheric lifetimes. (3) Total emissions minus carbon dioxide absorbed by forests or other means.

U.S. Greenhouse Gas Emissions, 2000

Source: U.S. Environmental Protection Agency

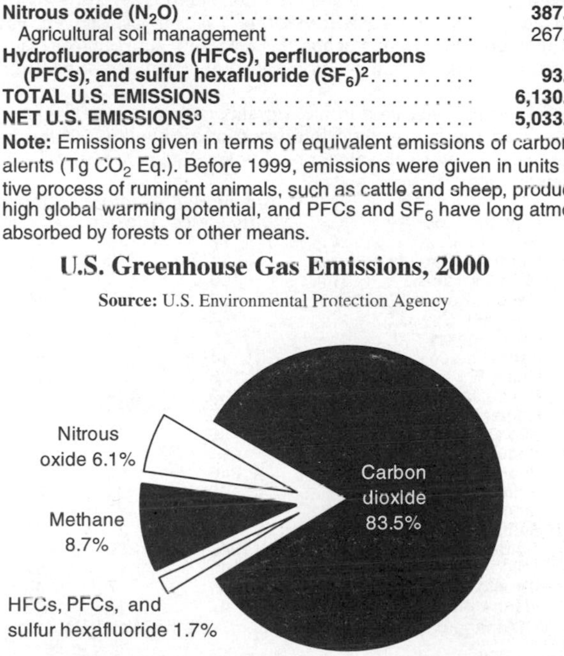

World Carbon Dioxide Emissions From the Use of Fossil Fuels, 2000

Source: Energy Information Administration

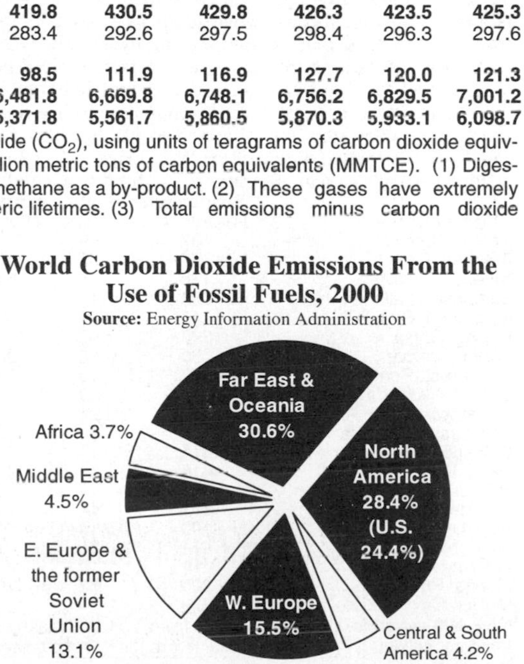

Average Global Temperatures, 1900-2000

Source: National Oceanic and Atmospheric Administration; in degrees Fahrenheit

1900-09 .. 56.52	1920-29 .. 56.74	1940-49 .. 57.13	1960-69 .. 57.05	1980-89 ... 57.36	2000 ..... 57.60
1910-19 .. 56.57	1930-39 .. 57.00	1950-59 .. 57.06	1970-79 .. 57.04	1990-99 ... 57.64	

Toxics Release Inventory, U.S., 1999-2000

Source: U.S. Environmental Protection Agency

Releases of toxic chemicals into the environment by major manufacturing facilities and by what the EPA classifies as "new" industries (chiefly, mining facilities and power plants), for which monitoring began in 1998. In the "old" industries for which data are available for a longer period, there has been a 48% drop in toxic releases since 1988. Totals below may not add because of rounding.

	1999 mil lb	2000 mil lb
Pollutant releases		
Air releases	2,029	1,904
Surface water releases	259	261
Underground injection	258	279
On-site land releases	4,747	4,131
Off-site releases	479	525
TOTAL on- and off-site releases	**7,772**	**7,101**
Pollutant transfers		
To recycling	2,112	2,095
To energy recovery	778	800
To treatment	293	282
To publicly owned treatment works	324	341
Other transfers	0	11
Off-site to disposal	594	611
TOTAL	**4,101**	**4,140**

	1999	2000
Top industries, total releases		
Metal mining	51.2%	47.3%
Manufacturing industries	29.9	32.2
Electric utilities	15.0	16.2
Hazardous waste/solvent recovery	3.7	4.0
Coal mining	0.2	0.2
Other[1]	0.13	0.12
Top carcinogens, air/water/land releases	**mil lb**	**mil lb**
Styrene	61	60
Dichloromethane	37	32
Formaldehyde	24	25
Acetaldehyde	13	14
Trichloroethylene	11	10
Ethylbenzene	10	9

(1) Includes petroleum terminals and bulk storage and chemical wholesale distributors.

Top 10 States, Total Toxics Releases, 1998-2000

Source: U.S. Environmental Protection Agency

State	2000 mil lb	1999 mil lb	1998 mil lb
Nevada	1,008	1,168	1,272
Utah	956	1,162	574
Arizona	745	963	1,069
Alaska	535	433	307
Texas	302	314	312
Ohio	283	303	336
Pennsylvania	226	253	216
Indiana	204	199	189
Tennessee	163	144	139
North Carolina	157	158	133
Total, all states*	**7,101**	**7,772**	**7,307**

* Total includes District of Columbia, Puerto Rico, American Samoa, Guam, Northern Marianas, and the Virgin Islands.

Air Pollution

Source: World Bank, *World Development Indicators 2001*

Air pollution is a major threat to health and the environment. **Winter smog**—made up of soot, dust, and sulfur dioxide—has long been associated with temporary increases in deaths. Prolonged exposure to **particulate pollution** can lead to chronic respiratory illnesses and exacerbates heart disease and other conditions. Particulate pollution causes an estimated 500,000 premature deaths in the world each year.

Emissions of sulfur dioxide and nitrogen oxides lead to **acid rain,** which spreads over long distances, upsetting the chemical balance of soils, trees, and plants. Direct exposure to high levels of sulfur dioxide or acid deposition causes **defoliation.**

Where **coal** is a primary fuel, high levels of urban air pollution may result. If the coal has a high sulfur content, widespread acid deposition may result. Combustion of **petroleum** products is another important cause of air pollution.

Air Pollution in 40 Selected World Cities[1]

In the table below, **suspended particulates** refers to smoke, soot, dust, and liquid droplets from combustion that are in the air. The level of particulates indicates the quality of the air and the level of technology and pollution controls. **Sulfur dioxide** is an air pollutant formed when fossil fuels containing sulfur are burned. **Nitrogen dioxide** is a poisonous, pungent gas formed when nitric oxide combines with hydrocarbons and sunlight, producing a photochemical reaction. Nitrogen oxides are emitted by bacteria, nitrogenous fertilizers, aerobic decomposition of organic matter, biomass combustion and, especially, burning fuel for motor vehicles and industrial activities.

Data are based on reports from urban monitoring sites. Annual means (measured in micrograms per cubic meter, mpcm) are average concentrations observed at various sites; resulting figures give a general indication of air quality, but results should be interpreted with caution.World Health Organization standards for acceptable air quality are 90 mpcm for total suspended particulates and 50 mpcm for sulfur dioxide and nitrogen dioxide.

City and Country	Suspended Particulates	Sulfur Dioxide	Nitrogen Dioxide
Accra, Ghana	137	NA	NA
Ankara, Turkey	57	55	46
Athens, Greece	178	34	64
Bangkok, Thailand	223	11	23
Barcelona, Spain	117	11	43
Beijing, China	377	90	122
Berlin, Germany	50	18	26
Bucharest, Romania	82	10	71
Calcutta (Kolkata), India	375	49	34
Capetown, South Africa	NA	21	72
Caracas, Venezuela	53	33	57
Chicago, U.S.	NA	14	57
Delhi, India	415	24	41
Frankfurt, Germany	36	11	45
Jakarta, Indonesia	271	NA	NA
Kiev, Ukraine	100	14	51
London, UK	NA	25	77
Los Angeles, U.S.	NA	9	74
Manila, Philippines	200	33	NA
Mexico City, Mexico	279	74	130
Milan, Italy	77	31	248
Montreal, Canada	34	10	42
Moscow, Russia	100	109	NA
Nairobi, Kenya	69	NA	NA
New York City, U.S.	NA	26	79
Oslo, Norway	15	8	43
Paris, France	14	14	57
Quito, Ecuador	175	22	NA
Rio de Janeiro, Brazil	139	129	NA
Rome, Italy	73	NA	NA
São Paulo, Brazil	86	43	83
Seoul, South Korea	84	44	60
Shanghai, China	246	53	73
Sofia, Bulgaria	195	39	122
Stockholm, Sweden	9	3	20
Sydney, Australia	54	28	81
Tehran, Iran	248	209	NA
Tokyo, Japan	49	18	68
Toronto, Canada	36	17	43
Vienna, Austria	47	14	42

NA = Not available. (1) Data derived from WHO's Healthy Cities Air Management Information System and the World Resources Institute, collected in 1998 or, if earlier, are the latest available.

Emissions of Principal Air Pollutants in the U.S., 1970-2000

Source: U.S. Environmental Protection Agency, Office of Air Quality Planning and Standards; in thousand short tons; estimated

Source	1970	1975	1980	1985	1990	1995	1997	1998	1999	2000
Carbon monoxide	129,444	116,757	117,434	117,013	99,119	94,058	105,466	101,246	102,356	109,300
Lead	220,869	159,659	74,153	22,890	4,975	3,929	4,137	4,057	4,199	4,228
Nitrogen oxides[1]	20,928	22,632	24,384	23,198	24,170	25,051	25,910	25,572	24,970	24,442
Volatile organic compounds[1]	30,982	26,079	26,336	24,428	21,053	20,918	20,305	19,258	19,421	20,366
Particulate matter[2]	12,325	7,108	6,258	3,662	3,340	3,165	2,963	2877	2,889	2,937
Sulfur dioxide	31,161	28,011	25,905	23,658	23,679	19,188	19,925	20,045	19,335	18,187
TOTAL[3]	**445,709**	**360,156**	**274,470**	**214,849**	**176,335**	**166,309**	**178,706**	**173,055**	**173,170**	**179,460**

(1) Ozone, a major air pollutant and the primary constituent of smog, is not emitted directly to the air but is formed by sunlight acting on emissions of nitrogen oxides and volatile organic compounds. (2) Does not include natural sources. (3) Totals are rounded, as are components of totals.

Carbon Monoxide Emission Estimates, 1970-2000

Source: U.S. Environmental Protection Agency, Office of Air Quality Planning and Standards; in thousand short tons

Source	1970	1975	1980	1985	1990	1995	1997	1998	1999	2000
Fuel combustion[1]	4,632	4,480	7,302	8,485	5,510	5,934	4,336	4,337	4,348	4,590
Industrial processes	16,899	10,770	9,250	7,215	5,852	5,790	7,348	7,362	7,343	7,521
Transportation	100,004	96,243	92,538	93,386	76,635	75,035	81,308	80,244	77,779	76,383
Miscellaneous	7,909	5,263	8,344	7,927	11,122	7,298	12,474	9,303	12,886	20,806
TOTAL[2]	**129,444**	**116,757**	**117,434**	**117,013**	**99,119**	**94,058**	**105,466**	**101,246**	**102,356**	**109,300**

(1) Does not include Transportation or Industrial processes. (2) Totals may not add because of rounding.

Lead Emission Estimates, 1970-2000

Source: U.S. Environmental Protection Agency, Office of Air Quality Planning and Standards; in short tons

Source	1970	1975	1980	1985	1990	1995	1997	1998	1999	2000
Fuel combustion[1]	10,616	10,347	4,299	515	500	490	493	494	501	501
Industrial processes	28,554	12,976	5,148	3,402	3,278	2,875	3,121	3,045	3,162	3,162
Transportation	181,698	136,336	64,706	18,973	1,197	564	523	518	536	565
TOTAL[2]	**220,869**	**159,659**	**74,153**	**22,890**	**4,975**	**3,929**	**4,137**	**4,057**	**4,199**	**4,228**

(1) Does not include Transportation or Industrial processes. (2) Totals may not add because of rounding.

Nitrogen Oxides Emission Estimates, 1970-2000

Source: U.S. Environmental Protection Agency, Office of Air Quality Planning and Standards; in thousand short tons

Source	1970	1975	1980	1985	1990	1995	1997	1998	1999	2000
Fuel combustion[1]	10,061	10,486	11,320	10,048	10,895	10,827	10,563	10,389	9,964	9,649
Industrial processes	1,215	697	666	891	892	873	923	933	933	967
Transportation	9,322	11,284	12,150	11,948	12,014	13,085	14,023	13,932	13,731	13,251
Miscellaneous	330	165	248	310	369	267	401	318	343	576
TOTAL[2]	**20,928**	**22,632**	**24,384**	**23,198**	**24,170**	**25,051**	**25,910**	**25,572**	**24,970**	**24,442**

(1) Does not include Transportation or Industrial processes. (2) Totals may not add because of rounding.

Air Quality of Selected U.S. Metropolitan Areas, 1990-2000

Source: U.S. Environmental Protection Agency, Office of Air Quality Planning and Standards

Data indicate the number of days metropolitan statistical areas failed to meet acceptable air-quality standards. All figures were revised based on new standards set in 1998.

Metropolitan statistical area	1990	1991	1992	1993	1994	1995	1996	1997	1998	1999	2000
Atlanta, GA	42	23	20	36	15	35	25	31	50	61	26
Bakersfield, CA	99	113	100	97	98	105	109	55	76	89	82
Baltimore, MD	29	50	23	48	41	36	28	30	51	40	16
Boston, MA–NH	7	13	9	5	9	11	4	8	8	7	1
Chicago, IL	4	25	6	3	8	23	7	9	10	14	0
Dallas, TX	24	2	12	14	27	36	12	20	28	23	20
Denver, CO	9	6	11	6	2	3	0	0	7	3	2
Detroit, MI	11	27	7	5	11	14	13	11	17	15	3
El Paso, TX	19	7	10	7	11	8	7	4	6	6	3
Fresno, CA	62	83	69	59	55	61	70	75	67	81	78
Hartford, CT	13	23	15	14	18	14	5	10	10	18	7
Houston, TX	51	36	32	27	38	65	26	47	38	50	42
Las Vegas, NV–AZ	4	0	3	3	3	0	4	0	3	0	0
Los Angeles–Long Beach, CA	173	168	175	134	139	113	94	60	56	27	48
Miami, FL	1	1	3	6	1	2	1	3	8	5	0
Minneapolis–St. Paul, MN–WI	4	2	1	0	2	5	0	0	1	0	0
New Haven–Meriden, CT	17	29	10	17	14	14	8	19	10	16	6
New York, NY	36	49	10	19	21	19	15	23	17	24	12
Orange County, CA	45	35	35	25	15	9	9	3	6	1	4
Philadelphia, PA–NJ	39	49	27	62	37	38	38	38	37	32	18
Phoenix–Mesa, AZ	12	11	11	15	10	22	15	12	14	10	10
Pittsburgh, PA	19	21	9	13	19	25	11	21	39	23	4
Riverside–San Bernardino, CA	159	154	174	168	149	124	119	105	95	93	98
Sacramento, CA	61	44	51	20	37	41	44	17	29	39	29
St. Louis, MO–IL	23	24	14	9	32	36	20	15	23	29	14
Salt Lake City–Ogden, UT	5	20	9	5	12	4	8	1	12	2	6
San Diego, CA	96	67	66	59	46	48	31	14	33	16	14
San Francisco, CA	0	0	0	0	0	2	0	0	0	0	0
Seattle–Bellevue–Everett, WA	9	4	3	0	3	0	6	1	3	1	1
Ventura, CA	70	87	54	43	63	66	62	45	29	22	27
Washington, DC–MD–VA–WV	25	48	14	52	22	32	18	30	47	39	11

Hazardous Waste Sites in the U.S., 2002

Source: U.S. Environmental Protection Agency, *National Priorities List*, Sept. 2002

State/Territory	Total proposed Gen	Total proposed Fed	Total final Gen	Total final Fed	Total
Alabama	2	0	10	3	15
Alaska	0	0	1	6	7
Arizona	0	0	7	2	9
Arkansas	0	0	12	0	12
California	2	0	73	24	99
Colorado	2	0	12	3	17
Connecticut	1	0	14	1	16
Delaware	0	0	15	1	16
District of Columbia	0	0	0	1	1
Florida	2	0	45	6	53
Georgia	1	0	12	2	15
Hawaii	0	0	1	2	3
Idaho	4	0	4	2	10
Illinois	5	1	35	4	45
Indiana	1	0	28	0	29
Iowa	1	0	12	1	14
Kansas	1	1	9	1	12
Kentucky	0	0	13	1	14
Louisiana	2	0	12	1	15
Maine	0	0	10	3	13
Maryland	1	0	9	9	19
Massachusetts	1	0	24	7	32
Michigan	1	1	67	0	69
Minnesota	0	0	22	2	24
Mississippi	2	0	2	0	4
Missouri	0	0	20	3	23
Montana	2	0	13	0	15
Nebraska	1	0	9	1	11
Nevada	0	0	1	0	1
New Hampshire	1	0	17	1	19
New Jersey	2	0	105	8	115
New Mexico	1	0	11	1	13
New York	1	0	86	4	91
North Carolina	1	0	25	2	28
North Dakota	0	0	0	0	0
Ohio	3	2	26	3	34
Oklahoma	1	0	9	1	11
Oregon	2	0	9	2	13
Pennsylvania	2	0	88	6	96
Rhode Island	0	0	10	2	12
South Carolina	0	0	23	2	25
South Dakota	0	0	1	1	2
Tennessee	0	1	9	3	13
Texas	3	0	36	4	43
Utah	5	0	12	4	21
Vermont	0	0	9	0	9
Virginia	0	0	19	11	30
Washington	0	0	34	14	48
West Virginia	0	0	7	2	9
Wisconsin	1	0	39	0	40
Wyoming	0	0	1	1	2
American Samoa	0	0	0	0	0
Commonwealth of Marianas	0	0	0	0	0
Guam	0	0	1	1	2
Puerto Rico	1	0	8	0	9
Trust Territories	0	0	0	0	0
Virgin Islands	0	0	2	0	2
Total	**56**	**6**	**1,079**	**159**	**1,300**

Note: Gen = general superfund sites; Fed = federal facility sites.

Watersheds in the U.S.

Source: U.S. Environmental Protection Agency

A **watershed** is a water drainage area, or land areas bounded by ridges that catch rain and snow and drain to rivers, lakes, and groundwater within the drainage area. In a comprehensive assessment of watersheds in the continental U.S. released in Sept. 1999, the Environmental Protection Agency (EPA) concluded that 15% of the 2,262 watersheds had good water quality, 36% had moderate water quality, and 23% had less acceptable water quality. There was insufficient information to characterize the remaining 26%. The data indicate that polluted runoff from urban and rural areas is a major contributor to water quality problems, threatening water quality even in currently healthy watersheds.

The EPA categorized the watersheds by combining nationally available data from 15 databases, from both public and private sources, into a single Index of Watershed Indicators. The indicators include 7 to assess watershed quality and 8 to assess vulnerability to degradation from pollution. You can find information about your own watershed by going to the following website: www.epa.gov/surf3/index.html

Renewable Water Resources

Source: World Resources Institute

Globally, water supplies are abundant, but they are unevenly distributed among and within countries. In some areas, water withdrawals are so high, relative to supply, that surface water supplies are shrinking and groundwater reserves are being depleted faster than they can be replenished by precipitation. The U.S. has a total of 2,460.0 cubic kilometers of internal renewable water resources, or 8,838 cubic meters per capita. Totals for the world are 42,655.0 cubic kilometers, or 7,045 cubic meters per capita.

Countries With Most Resources

(ranked by per capita resources)

Country	Total cubic km	Cubic meters per capita
Iceland	170.0	605,049
Suriname	200.0	479,467
Guyana	241.0	279,799
Papua New Guinea	801.0	166,644
Gabon	164.0	133,754
Canada	2,740.0	87,971
Norway	382.0	85,560
New Zealand	327.0	84,673
Congo	221.9	75,387
Peru	1,746.0	68,039
Belize	16.0	66,470
Equatorial Guinea	30.0	66,275
Liberia	200.0	63,412
Chile	928.0	61,007
Panama	147.4	51,616
Colombia	2,133.0	50,400
Bhutan	95.0	44,728
Central African Rep.	141.0	39,001
Bolivia	316.0	37,941
Nicaragua	190.2	37,484

Countries With Least Resources*

(ranked by per capita resources)

Country	Total cubic km	Cubic meters per capita
Egypt	1.8	26
United Arab Emirates	0.2	61
Jordan	0.7	102
Saudi Arabia	2.4	111
Libya	0.8	143
Mauritania	0.4	150
Yemen	4.1	226
Moldova	1.0	228
Turkmenistan	1.4	305
Israel	1.9	312
Niger	3.5	326
Tunisia	3.5	367
Oman	1.0	388
Syria	7.0	434
Algeria	13.9	442
Burundi	3.6	538
Pakistan	84.7	541
Somalia	6.0	594
Hungary	6.0	598
Uzbekistan	16.3	672
Kenya	20.2	672

* Data not available from all nations.

Frontier Forests

Only 1/5 of the Earth's forest cover from 8,000 years ago survives unfragmented, in large unspoiled tracts called **frontier forests**. These forests are big enough to provide stable habitats for a rich diversity of plant and animal species. Most are in the far north or the tropics (2/3 of their acreage is in Russia, Canada, or Brazil); most are also under threat from development or other causes.

Percentage of Frontier Forest Under Moderate or High Threat of Destruction

Source: World Resources Institute

Europe	100	Africa	77	Asia	60	North America	26
Central America	87	Oceania	76	South America	54	World	39

U.S. List of Endangered and Threatened Species

Source: Fish and Wildlife Service, U.S. Dept. of Interior; as of Aug. 2002

Group	Endangered U.S.	Endangered Foreign	Threatened U.S.	Threatened Foreign	Total species	Total species with recovery plans
Mammals	65	251	9	17	342	53
Birds	78	175	14	6	273	75
Reptiles	14	64	22	15	115	32
Amphibians	12	8	9	1	30	13
Fishes	71	11	44	0	126	95
Clams	62	2	8	0	72	56
Snails	21	1	11	0	33	21
Insects	35	4	9	0	48	29
Arachnids	12	0	0	0	12	5
Crustaceans	18	0	3	0	21	12
Animal subtotal	**388**	**516**	**129**	**39**	**1,072**	**391**
Flowering plants	568	1	144	0	713	555
Conifers and cycads	2	0	1	2	5	2
Ferns and allies	24	0	2	0	26	26
Lichens	2	0	0	0	2	2
Plant subtotal	**596**	**1**	**147**	**2**	**746**	**585**
GRAND TOTAL	**984**	**517**	**276**	**41**	**1,818***	**976**

(1) Some species are classified as both endangered and threatened. The table tallies these "dual status" species only once, as endangered, except for the olive ridley sea turtle, which is dual status but tallied as a U.S. threatened species. The other dual status species, all tallied as endangered, are: (U.S.) chinook salmon, gray wolf, green sea turtle, piping plover, roseate tern, sockeye salmon, steelhead, Steller sea-lion; (non-U.S.) argali, chimpanzee, leopard, saltwater crocodile.

Some Endangered Animal Species

Source: Fish and Wildlife Service, U.S. Dept. of the Interior

Common name	Scientific name	Range
Armadillo, giant	Pridontes maximus	Venezuela, Guyana to Argentina
Babirusa	Babyrousa babyrussa	Indonesia
Bandicoot, desert	Perameles eremiana	Australia
Bat, gray	Myotis grisescens	Central, southeastern U.S.
Bear, brown (grizzly)	Ursus arctos arctos	Palearctic
Bison, wood	Bison bison athabascae	Canada, northwestern U.S.
Bobcat, Mexican	Felis rufus escuinapae	Central Mexico
Camel, Bactrian	Camelus bactrianus	Mongolia, China
Caribou, woodland	Rangifer tarandus caribou	U.S., Canada
Cheetah	Acinonyx jubatus	Africa to India
Chimpanzee, pygmy	Pan paniscus	Congo (formerly Zaire)
Condor, California	Gymnogyps californianus	U.S. (AZ, CA, OR), Mexico (Baja California)
Crane, whooping	Grus americana	Canada, Mexico, U.S. (Rocky Mts. to Carolinas)
Crocodile, American	Crocodylus acutus	U.S. (FL), Mexico, Caribbean Sea, Central and S America
Deer, Columbian white-tailed	Odocoileus virginianus leucurus	U.S. (OR, WA)
Dolphin, Chinese river	Lipotes vexillifer	China
Dugong	Dugong dugon	East Africa to southern Japan
Elephant, Asian	Elephas maximus	S central and southeastern Asia
Fox, northern swift	Vulpes velox hebes	U.S., Canada
Gorilla	Gorilla gorilla	Central and W Africa
Hawk, Hawaiian	Buteo solitarius	U.S. (HI)
Hyena, brown	Hyaena brunnea	Southern Africa
Kangaroo, Tasmanian forester	Macropus giganteus tasmaniensis	Australia (Tasmania)
Leopard	Panthera pardus	Africa and Asia
Lion, Asiatic	Panthera leo persica	Turkey to India
Manatee, West Indian	Trichechus manatus	Southeastern U.S., Caribbean Sea, S America
Monkey, spider	Ateles geoffroyi frontatus	Costa Rica, Nicaragua
Ocelot	Felis pardalis	U.S. (AZ, TX) to Central and S America
Orangutan	Pongo pygmaeus	Borneo, Sumatra
Ostrich, West African	Struthio camelus spatzi	W Sahara
Otter, marine	Lutra felina	Peru south to Straits of Magellan
Panda, giant	Ailuropoda melanoleuca	China
Panther, Florida	Felis concolor coryi	U.S. (LA, AR east to SC, FL)
Parakeet, golden	Aratinga guarouba	Brazil
Parrot, imperial	Amazona imperialis	West Indies (Dominica)
Penguin, Galapagos	Spheniscus mendiculus	Ecuador (Galapagos Islands)
Puma, eastern	Puma concolor couguar	Eastern N America
Python, Indian	Python molurus molurus	Sri Lanka, India
Rhinoceros, black	Diceros bicornis	Sub-Saharan Africa
Rhinoceros, northern white	Ceratotherium simum cottoni	Congo (formerly Zaire), Sudan, Uganda, Central African Republic
Salamander, Chinese giant	Andrias davidianus davidianus	Western China
Squirrel, Carolina northern flying	Glaucomys sabrinus coloratus	U.S. (NC, TN)
Stork, oriental white	Ciconia ciconia boyciana	China, Japan, Korea, Russia

IT'S A FACT: Scientists have found that predator animals and their prey are governed by one ratio that holds for many different species: for every 90 kilograms of predator (whether it's wolves or weasels), there have to be 10,000 kilograms of prey. This doesn't mean the predators must eat that much, but they need that much prey in the field to survive.

Common name	Scientific name	Range
Tiger	Panthera tigris	Asia
Tortoise, Galapagos	Geochelone elephantopus	Ecuador (Galapagos Islands)
Turtle, Plymouth red-bellied	Pseudemys rubriventris bangsi	U.S. (MA)
Whale, gray	Eschrichtius robustus	N Pacific Ocean
Whale, humpback	Megaptera novaeangliae	Oceania
Wolf, red	Canis rufus	Southeastern U.S. to central TX
Woodpecker, ivory-billed	Campephilus principalis	S central and southeastern U.S., Cuba
Yak, wild	Bos grunniens mutus	China (Tibet), India
Zebra, mountain	Equus zebra zebra	South Africa

Classification

Source: *Funk & Wagnalls New Encyclopedia*

In biology, classification is the identification, naming, and grouping of organisms into a formal system. The 2 fields that are most directly concerned with classification are taxonomy and systematics. Although the 2 disciplines overlap considerably, taxonomy is more concerned with nomenclature (naming) and with constructing hierarchical systems, and systematics with uncovering evolutionary relationships. Two kingdoms of living forms, Plantae and Animalia, have been recognized since Aristotle established the first taxonomy in the 4th century BC. In addition, there are the following 3 kingdoms: Protista (one-celled organisms), Monera (bacteria and blue-green algae; also known as the kingdom Procaryotae), and Fungi. The 7 basic categories of classification (from most general to most specific) are: kingdom, phylum (or division), class, order, family, genus, and species. Below are 2 examples:

ZOOLOGICAL HIERARCHY

Kingdom	Phylum	Class	Order	Family	Genus	Species name	Common name
Animalia	Chordata	Mammalia	Primates	Hominidae	Homo	Homo sapiens	Human

BOTANICAL HIERARCHY

Kingdom	Division*	Class	Order	Family	Genus	Species name	Common name
Plantae	Magnoliophyta	Magnoliopsida	Magnoliales	Magnoliaceae	Magnolia	M. virginiana	Sweet Bay

* In botany, the division is generally used in place of the phylum.

Gestation, Longevity, and Incubation of Animals

Information reviewed and updated by Ronald M. Nowak, author *Walker's Mammals of the World* (6th ed., Johns Hopkins University Press, 1999). Average longevity figures supplied by Ronald T. Reuther. These apply to animals in captivity; the potential life span of animals is rarely attained in nature. Figures on gestation and incubation are averages based on estimates.

ANIMAL	Gestation (days)	Average longevity (years)	Maximum longevity (yr-mo)
Ass	365	12	47
Baboon	187	20	45
Bear: Black	219	18	36-10
Grizzly	225	25	50
Polar	240	20	45
Beaver	105	5	50
Bison	285	15	40
Camel	406	12	50
Cat (domestic)	63	12	28
Chimpanzee	230	20	60
Chipmunk	31	6	10
Cow	284	15	30
Deer (white-tailed)	201	8	20
Dog (domestic)	61	12	20
Elephant (African)	660	35	70
Elephant (Asian)	645	40	77
Elk	250	15	26-8
Fox (red)	52	7	14
Giraffe	457	10	36-2
Goat (domestic)	151	8	18
Gorilla	258	20	54
Guinea pig	68	4	8
Hippopotamus	238	41	61
Horse	330	20	50
Kangaroo (gray)	36	7	24
Leopard	98	12	23
Lion	100	15	30
Monkey (rhesus)	166	15	37
Moose	240	12	27
Mouse (meadow)	21	3	4
Mouse (dom. white)	19	3	6
Opossum (American)	13	1	5
Pig (domestic)	112	10	27
Puma	90	12	20
Rabbit (domestic)	31	5	13
Rhinoceros (black)	450	15	45-10
Rhinoceros (white)	480	20	50
Sea lion (California)	350	12	34
Sheep (domestic)	154	12	20
Squirrel (gray)	44	10	23-6
Tiger	105	16	26-3
Wolf (maned)	63	5	15-8
Zebra (Grant's)	365	15	50

Incubation time (days)

Chicken	21
Duck	30
Goose	30
Pigeon	18
Turkey	26

Speeds of Animals

Source: *Natural History* magazine. © The American Museum of Natural History

ANIMAL	mph
Cheetah	70
Pronghorn antelope	61
Wildebeest	50
Lion	50
Thomson's gazelle	50
Quarterhorse	47.5
Elk	45
Cape hunting dog	45
Coyote	43
Gray fox	42
Hyena	40
Zebra	40
Mongolian wild ass	40
Greyhound	39.35
Whippet	35.50
Rabbit (domestic)	35
Mule deer	35
Jackal	35
Reindeer	32
Giraffe	32
White-tailed deer	30
Wart hog	30
Grizzly bear	30
Cat (domestic)	30
Human	27.89
Elephant	25
Black mamba snake	20
Six-lined race runner (lizard)	18
Wild turkey	15
Squirrel	12
Pig (domestic)	11
Chicken	9
Spider (Tegenaria atrica)	1.17
Giant tortoise	0.17
Three-toed sloth	0.15
Garden snail	0.03

Most of these measurements are for maximum speeds over approximate quarter-mile distances. Exceptions are the lion and elephant, whose speeds were clocked in the act of charging; the whippet, which was timed over a 200-yd course; the cheetah, timed over a 100-yd distance; and the black mamba, six-lined race runner, spider, giant tortoise, three-toed sloth, and garden snail, which were measured over various small distances.

Major Venomous Animals

Snakes

Asian pit viper — from 2 ft to 5 ft long; throughout Asia; reactions and mortality vary, but most bites cause tissue damage, and mortality is generally low.

Australian brown snake — 4 ft to 7 ft long; very slow onset of cardiac or respiratory distress; moderate mortality, but because death can be sudden and unexpected, it is the most dangerous of the Australian snakes; antivenom.

Barba Amarilla or fer-de-lance — up to 7 ft long; from tropical Mexico to Brazil; severe tissue damage common; moderate mortality; antivenom.

Black mamba — up to 14 ft long, fast-moving; S and C Africa; rapid onset of dizziness, difficulty breathing, erratic heartbeat; mortality high, nears 100% without antivenom.

Boomslang — less than 6 ft long; in African savannahs; rapid onset of nausea and dizziness, often followed by slight recovery and then sudden death from internal hemorrhaging; bites rare, mortality high; antivenom.

Bushmaster — up to 12 ft long; wet tropical forests of C and S America; few bites occur, but mortality rate is high.

Common or Asian cobra — 4 ft to 8 ft long; throughout southern Asia; considerable tissue damage, sometimes paralysis; mortality probably not more than 10%; antivenom.

Copperhead — less than 4 ft long; from New England to Texas; pain and swelling; very seldom fatal; antivenom seldom needed.

Coral snake — 2 ft to 5 ft long; in Americas south of Canada; bite may be painless; slow onset of paralysis, impaired breathing; mortalities rare, but high without antivenom and mechanical respiration.

Cottonmouth water moccasin — up to 5 ft long; wetlands of southern U.S. from Virginia to Texas. Rapid onset of severe pain, swelling; mortality low, but tissue destruction can be extensive; antivenom.

Death adder — less than 3 ft long; Australia; rapid onset of faintness, cardiac and respiratory distress; at least 50% mortality without antivenom.

Desert horned viper — in dry areas of Africa and western Asia; swelling and tissue damage; low mortality; antivenom.

European viper — 1 ft to 3 ft long; bleeding and tissue damage; mortality low; antivenom.

Gaboon viper — more than 6 ft long; fat; 2-in. fangs; south of the Sahara; massive tissue damage, internal bleeding; few recorded bites.

King cobra — up to 16 ft long; throughout southern Asia; rapid swelling, dizziness, loss of consciousness, difficulty breathing, erratic heartbeat; mortality varies sharply with amount of venom involved, but most bites involve nonfatal amounts; antivenom.

Krait — up to 5 ft long; in SE Asia; rapid onset of sleepiness; numbness; as much as 50% mortality even with use of antivenom.

Puff adder — up to 5 ft long; fat; south of the Sahara and throughout the Middle East; rapid large swelling, great pain, dizziness; moderate mortality, often from internal bleeding; antivenom.

Rattlesnake — 2 ft to 6 ft long; throughout W Hemisphere; rapid onset of severe pain, swelling; mortality low, but amputation of affected digits is sometimes necessary; antivenom. Mojave rattler may produce temporary paralysis.

Ringhals, or spitting, cobra — 5 ft to 7 ft long; southern Africa; squirts venom through holes in front of fangs as a defense; venom is severely irritating, can cause blindness.

Russell's viper or tic-polonga — more than 5 ft long; throughout Asia; internal bleeding; bite reports common; moderate mortality rate; antivenom.

Saw-scaled or carpet viper — as much as 2 ft long; in dry areas from India to Africa; severe bleeding, fever; high mortality, causes more human fatalities than any other snake; antivenom.

Sea snakes — throughout Pacific, Indian oceans except NE Pacific; almost painless bite, variety of muscle pain, paralysis; mortality rate low, many bites not envenomed; some antivenoms.

Sharp-nosed pit viper or one hundred pace snake — up to 5 ft long; in S Vietnam, Taiwan, and China; the most toxic of Asian pit vipers; very rapid onset of swelling and tissue damage, internal bleeding; moderate mortality; antivenom.

Taipan — up to 11 ft long; in Australia and New Guinea; rapid paralysis with severe breathing difficulty; mortality nears 100% without antivenom.

Tiger snake — 2 ft to 6 ft long; S Australia; pain, numbness, mental disturbances with rapid onset of paralysis; may be the deadliest of all land snakes, although antivenom is quite effective.

Yellow or Cape cobra — 7 ft long; in S Africa; most toxic venom of any cobra; rapid onset of swelling, breathing and cardiac difficulties; mortality is high without treatment; antivenom.

Note: Not all bites by venomous snakes are actually envenomed. Any animal bite, however, carries the danger of tetanus, and anyone suffering a venomous snake bite should seek medical attention. Antivenoms do not cure; they are only an aid in the treatment of bites. Mortality rates above are for envenomed bites; low mortality, c. 2% or less; moderate, 2%-5%; high, 5%-15%.

Lizards

Gila monster — as much as 24 in. long, with heavy body and tail; in high desert in SW U.S. and N Mexico; immediate severe pain and transient low blood pressure; no recent mortality.

Mexican beaded lizard — similar to Gila monster, Mexican west coast; reaction and mortality rate similar to Gila monster.

Insects

Ants, bees, wasps, hornets, etc. Global distribution. Usual reaction is piercing pain in area of sting. Not directly fatal, except in cases of massive multiple stings. However, many people suffer allergic reactions — swelling and rashes — and a few may die within minutes from severe sensitivity to the venom (anaphylactic shock).

Spiders, Scorpions

Atrax spider — also known as funnel web spider; several varieties, often large; in Australia; slow onset of breathing, circulation difficulties; low mortality; antivenom.

Black widow — small, round-bodied with red hourglass marking; the widow and its relatives are found in tropical and temperate zones; severe musculoskeletal pain, weakness, breathing difficulty, convulsions; may be more serious in small children; low mortality; antivenom. The **redback** spider of Australia has the hourglass marking on its back, rather than on its front, but is otherwise identical to the black widow.

Brown recluse, or fiddleback, spider — small, oblong body; throughout U.S.; pain with later ulceration at place of bite; in severe cases fever, nausea, and stomach cramps; ulceration may last months; very low mortality.

Scorpion — crablike body with stinger in tail, various sizes, many varieties throughout tropical and subtropical areas; various symptoms may include severe pain spreading from the wound, numbness, severe agitation, cramps; severe reaction may include respiratory failure; low mortality, usually in children; antivenoms.

Tarantula — large, hairy spider found around the world; the American tarantula, and probably all other tarantulas, are harmless to humans, though their bite may cause some pain and swelling.

Sea Life

Cone-shell — mollusk in small, beautiful shell; in the S Pacific and Indian oceans; shoots barbs into victims; paralysis; low mortality.

Octopus — global distribution, usually in warm waters; all varieties produce venom, but only a few can cause death; rapid onset of paralysis with breathing difficulty.

Portuguese man-of-war — jellyfishlike, with tentacles up to 70 ft long; in most warm water areas; immediate severe pain; not directly fatal, though shock may cause death in rare cases.

Sea wasp — jellyfish, with tentacles up to 30 ft long, in the S Pacific; very rapid onset of circulatory problems; high mortality because of speed of toxic reaction; antivenom.

Stingray — several varieties of differing sizes; found in tropical and temperate seas and some fresh water; severe pain, rapid onset of nausea, vomiting, breathing difficulties; wound area may ulcerate, gangrene may appear; seldom fatal.

Stonefish — brownish fish that lies motionless as a rock on bottom in shallow water; throughout S Pacific and Indian oceans; extraordinary pain, rapid paralysis; low mortality; antivenom available, amount determined by number of puncture wounds; warm water relieves pain.

Major U.S. Public Zoological Parks

Source: *World Almanac* questionnaire, 2002; budget and attendance in millions

Zoo	Budget	Attendance	Acres	Species	Some major attractions/information
Arizona-Sonora Desert Museum (Tucson, AZ)	$6.0	0.5	100	300+	Desert Loop Trail, Hummingbird Aviary, Pollination Gardens *(520) 883-2702; www.desertmuseum.org*
Audubon Zoo (New Orleans)	NA	0.9	58	350+	Jaguar Jungle, Monkey Treehouse, white tigers *(866) ITS-AZOO; www.auduboznoo.org*
Baltimore Zoo	NA	0.6	161	305	Children's zoo, African Watering Hole, Keeper Encounters *(410) 396-7102; www.baltimorezoo.org*
Bronx Zoo/Wildlife Conservation Park (N.Y.C.)	38.0	2.2	265	500+	Congo Gorilla Forest, African Plains, Jungle World *(718) 367-1010; www.wcs.org/home/zoos/bronxzoo*
Brookfield Zoo (Chicago area)	48.0	2.0	216	479	Family Play Zoo, Living Coast, Habitat Africa, Tropic World *(708) 485-0263; www.brookfieldzoo.org*
Buffalo (NY) Zoological Gardens	4.8	0.4	24	200	Indian Rhino Pavilion, Gorilla Rainforest, Vanishing Animals *(716) 837-3900; www.buffalozoo.org*
Cincinnati Zoo and Botanical Garden	18.8	1.3	96	633	Wings of Wonder, Jungle Trails, Manatee Springs *(800) 94-HIPPO; www.cincinnatizoo.org*
Cleveland Metroparks Zoo	12.1	1.3	168	625	Rainforest, Wolf Wilderness, Australian Adventure *(216) 661-6500; www.clemetzoo.com*
Columbus Zoo and Aquarium (Powell, OH)	20.0	1.3	580	700	Manatee Coast, Discovery Reef, African Forest *(800) MONKEYS; www.colszoo.org*
Dallas Zoo	13.0	0.6	95	400	Endangered Tiger Habitat, Wilds of Africa, Children's Zoo *(214) 670-5656; www.dallaszoo.org*
Denver Zoo	15.3	1.7	80	715	Komodo Dragon habitat, okapi, black rhino, primates *(303) 376-4800; www.denverzoo.org*
Detroit Zoological Park (Royal Oak, MI)	12.8	1.3	125	581	Arctic Ring of Life, Wild Adventure, Natl. Amphibian Center *(248) 398-0900; www.detroitzoo.org*
The Houston Zoo	NA	1.5	55	700+	Indochinese Tigers, primates, Reptile House, sun bears *(713) 533-6500; www.houstonzoo.org*
Lincoln Park Zoological Gardens (Chicago)	17.0	3.0	35	208	Farm-in-the-Zoo, Kovler Lion House, Primate House *(312) 742-2000; www.lpzoo.org*
Los Angeles Zoo and Botanical Gardens	16.0	1.5	80	370	Dragons of Komodo, Chimpanzees of Mahale Mountains *(323) 644-6400; www.lazoo.org*
Louisville (KY) Zoo	10.3	0.8	135	134	African Petting Zoo, Islands Exhibit, Gorilla Forest *(502) 459-2181; www.louisvillezoo.org*
Memphis (TN) Zoo	8.0	0.7	70+	500+	China Exhibit, Cat Country, Primate Canyon *(901) 276-WILD; www.memphiszoo.org*
Miami Metrozoo	8.4	0.4	300	303	Komodo dragons, meerkats, Dr. Wilde's Rainforest Museum *(305) 251-0400; www.zsf.org*
Milwaukee County Zoo	16.0	1.3	200	350	Apes of Africa, Aquatic and Reptile Center, Siberian Tigers *(414) 256-5412; www.milwaukeezoo.org*
Minnesota Zoo (Apple Valley)	17.8	1.0	500	400	Coral Reef, Dolphin shows, Tiger Lair, Family Farm *(800) 366-7811; www.mnzoo.org*
The National Zoo (Washington, DC)[1]	28.6	3.0	163	475	Giant pandas, Sumatran tigers, Great Cats Exchange *(202) 673-4800; www.fonz.org*
Oklahoma City Zoological Park & Botanical Garden	10.5	0.7	110	600	Aquaticus, Cat Forest, Lion Overlook, Great EscApe *(405) 424-3344; www.okczoo.com*
Omaha's Henry Doorly Zoo	16.0	1.2	130	857	Desert Dome, Cat Complex, indoor rain forest, aquarium *(402) 733-8401; www.omahazoo.org*
Oregon Zoo (Portland)	28.6	1.3	64	200	Penguinarium, Africa Rainforest, Steller Cove, Alaska Tundra *(503) 226-1561; www.oregonzoo.org*
Philadelphia Zoo	19.1	1.2	42	330	PECO Primate Reserve, Reptile and Amphibian House *(215) 243-1100; www.phillyzoo.org*
Phoenix (AZ) Zoo	15.0	1.2	125	250	Arizona Trail, Discovery Trail, Africa Trail, Tropics Trail *(602) 273-1341; www.phoenixzoo.org*
Point Defiance Zoo & Aquarium (Tacoma, WA)	6.4	0.4	27	300	Polar bears, sharks, elephants, leopards, petting farm *(253) 591-5337; www.pdza.org*
Rio Grande Zoo (Albuquerque, NM)	9.0	1.0	64	200	Animals of Africa, Australia, and the Americas, waterfalls *(505) 764-6200; www.cabq.gov/biopark*
Riverbanks Zoo & Garden (Columbia, SC)	6.2	0.9	170	350	Ndoki Forest, Koala Knockabout, African Plains, Birdhouse *(803) 779-8717; www.riverbanks.org*
St. Louis Zoo	33.9	2.7	90	767	Big Cat Country, Jungle of the Apes, Monsanto Insectarium *(314) 781-0900; www.stlzoo.org*
San Diego Wild Animal Park	NA	1.5	1,800	400	Condor Ridge, Heart of Africa, Wgasa Bush Line Railway *(619) 234-6541; www.sandiegozoo.org/wap*
San Diego Zoo	NA	3.5	100	800	Panda research station, Polar Bear Plunge, Gorilla Tropics *(619) 231-1515; www.sandiegozoo.org*
San Francisco Zoo	16.0	0.9	100	225	Gorilla World, Koala Crossing, Penguin Island, Lemur Forest *(415) 753-7080; www.sfzoo.org*
Toledo (OH) Zoo	15.0	1.0	62	700	Hippoquarium, Frogtown, Arctic Encounter, Africa! *(419) 385-5721; www.toledozoo.org*
Tulsa (OK) Zoo and Living Museum	NA	0.6	82	500	North American Rain Forest, Elephant Encounter, North American Living Museum *(918) 669-6600; www.tulsazoo.org*
Woodland Park Zoo (Seattle)	21.0	1.0	9	290	Baby Asian elephant, Tropical Rain Forest, Northern Trail *(206) 684-4800; www.zoo.org*
Zoo Atlanta	15.8	0.7	39	221	Gorillas of the Ford African Rain Forest, Orkin Children's Zoo *(404) 624-5600; www.zooatlanta.org*

Note: NA = Not available. (1) 2001 data.

Major Canadian Public Zoological Parks

Source: *World Almanac* questionnaire, 2002; budget in millions of dollars (Canadian), attendance in millions

Zoo	Budget	Attendance	Acres	Species	Some major attractions/information
Assiniboine Park Zoo (Winnipeg)	$3.0	0.4	95	333	Snow leopards, polar and grizzly bears, Tropical House *(204) 986-2327; www.zoosociety.com*
Calgary Zoo	NA	0.9	136	254	Botanical Garden, Prehistoric Park, Canadian Wilds *(403) 232-9300; www.calgaryzoo.ab.ca*
Granby Zoo (Quebec)	11.7	0.5	100	225	Exotic Animal collection, AMAZOO water park *(877) GRANBYZOO; www.zoogranby.ca*
Toronto Zoo	31.0	1.2	710	500	Gorilla Rainforest, African Savanna, polar bears *(416) 392-5900; www.torontozoo.com*

Top 50 American Kennel Club Registrations

Source: American Kennel Club, New York, NY; covers (new) dogs registered during calendar year shown

Breed	2001 Rank	2001 Number registered	2000 Rank	2000 Number registered
Labrador Retriever	1	165,970	1	172,841
Golden Retriever	2	62,497	2	66,300
German Shepherd Dog	3	51,625	3	57,660
Dachshund	4	50,478	4	54,773
Beagle	5	50,419	5	52,026
Yorkshire Terrier	6	42,025	7	43,574
Poodle	7	40,550	6	45,868
Boxer	8	37,035	9	38,803
Chihuahua	9	36,627	8	43,096
Shih Tzu	10	33,240	10	37,599
Rottweiler	11	29,269	11	37,355
Pomeranian	12	28,495	12	33,568
Miniature Schnauzer	13	27,587	13	30,472
Cocker Spaniel	14	25,445	14	29,393
Pug	15	23,769	15	24,373
Shetland Sheepdog	16	20,899	16	23,866
Miniature Pinscher	17	19,072	17	22,020
Boston Terrier	18	18,100	18	19,922
Bulldog	19	15,501	21	15,215
Maltese	20	15,214	20	17,446
Siberian Husky	21	14,015	19	17,551
German Shorthaired Pointer	22	12,884	24	13,224
Basset Hound	23	12,850	22	14,427
Doberman Pinscher	24	12,570	23	13,874
Bichons Frise	25	10,969	25	11,750
Pembroke Welsh Corgi	26	10,344	27	10,301
English Springer Spaniel	27	10,180	26	10,918
Great Dane	28	9,629	28	10,210
Weimaraner	29	8,964	32	9,126
West Highland White Terrier	30	8,716	30	9,364
Brittany	31	8,405	31	9,230
Pekingese	32	7,798	29	9,749
Collie	33	7,340	34	8,042
Lhasa Apso	34	6,584	33	8,122
Australian Shepherd	35	6,158	35	6,905
Saint Bernard	36	5,722	36	6,561
Mastiff	37	5,434	39	5,576
Chinese Shar-Pei	38	5,416	37	6,299
Akita	39	4,904	38	5,927
Papillon	40	4,438	43	4,128
Chesapeake Bay Retriever	41	4,400	41	4,665
Cairn Terrier	42	4,333	40	4,887
Scottish Terrier	43	3,958	42	4,396
Cavalier King Charles Spaniel	44	3,612	54	2,719
Vizsla	45	3,235	47	3,224
Airedale Terrier	46	3,055	46	3,431
Great Pyrenees	47	3,033	45	3,569
Bloodhound	48	3,010	50	3,056
Bullmastiff	49	2,987	52	2,954
Newfoundland	50	2,911	53	2,900

Cat Breeds, 2002

Source: The Cat Fanciers' Association, Manasquan, NJ

Only a small percentage of house cats in the U.S. are pedigreed or registered with one of the official registering bodies. The largest is the Cat Fanciers' Assn., Inc., with 655 member clubs. The Cat Fanciers' Association recognized 40 breeds as of Oct. 1, 2002 (in order of registration totals): Persian, Maine Coon, Exotic, Siamese, Abyssinian, Oriental, American Shorthair, Burmese, Birman, Tonkinese, Cornish Rex, Scottish Fold, Devon Rex, Ocicat, Russian Blue, Ragdoll, Norwegian Forest Cat, British Shorthair, Colorpoint Shorthair, Somali, Egyptian Mau, Manx, Chartreux, Japanese Bobtail, Turkish Angora, Selkirk Rex, American Curl, American Bobtail, Singapura, Turkish Van, Sphynx, Bombay, Balinese, Korat, European Burmese, Siberian, Havana Brown, Javanese, American Wirehair, and La Perm.

Trees of the U.S.

Source: American Forests, Washington, DC

Approximately 826 native and naturalized species of trees are grown in the U.S. The oldest living tree is believed to be a bristlecone pine tree in California named Methuselah, estimated to be 4,700 years old. The world's largest known living tree, the General Sherman giant sequoia in California, weighs more than 6,167 tons—as much as 41 blue whales or 740 elephants.

American Forests recognizes and lists the "National Champion" (largest known) of each U.S. tree species. Anyone can nominate candidates for the 2003-2004 *National Register of Big Trees*; for information, write to American Forests, PO Box 2000, Washington, DC 20013, or check their website: www.americanforests.org

Listed here are 10 largest National Champion trees selected by American Forests.

10 Largest National Champion Trees

Tree Type	Girth at 4.5 ft. (in.)	Height (ft.)	Crown Spread (ft.)	Total Points	Location
Giant sequoia (Gen. Sherman tree)	1,024	261	108	1,312	Sequoia National Park, CA
Coast redwood	950	321	80	1,291	Jedidiah Smith State Park, CA
Western redcedar	761	159	45	931	Olympic National Park, WA
Sitka spruce	707	191	96	922	Olympic National Park, WA
Coast Douglas-fir	505	281	71	804	Olympic National Forest, WA
Bluegum eucalyptus	586	141	126	759	Petrolia, CA
Common baldcypress	644	83	85	748	Cat Island, LA
California-laurel	546	108	118	684	Grass Valley, CA
Sugar pine	442	232	29	681	Dorrington, CA
Port-Orford-cedar	451	219	39	680	Siskiyou National Forest, OR

METEOROLOGY

National Weather Service Watches and Warnings

Source: National Weather Service, NOAA, U.S. Dept. of Commerce; *Glossary of Meteorology,* American Meteorological Society

National Weather Service forecasters issue a *Severe Thunderstorm* or *Tornado Watch* for a specific area when a severe convective storm that usually covers a relatively small geographic area or moves in a narrow path is sufficiently intense to threaten life and/or property. Examples include thunderstorms with large hail, damaging winds, and/or tornadoes. Excessive localized convective rains are not classified as severe storms but are often the product of severe local storms. Such rainfall may result in phenomena that threaten life and property, such as flash floods. Although cloud-to-ground lightning is not a criterion for severe local storms, it is acknowledged to be a leading cause of storm deaths and injuries.

A *Watch* alerts people that threatening weather is likely. Under a Watch, they should remain alert for approaching storms, activate a plan for action, and monitor ongoing events closely. A *Warning* means that severe weather is occurring or has been indicated by radar; immediate action should be taken by people in the storm's path.

Severe Thunderstorm—a thunderstorm that produces a tornado, winds of at least 50 knots (58 mph), and/or hail at least 3/4 inch in diameter. A thunderstorm with winds of at least 35 knots (40 mph) and/or hail at least ½ inch in diameter is defined as approaching severe. A *Severe Thunderstorm Watch* is issued for a specific area where such storms are most likely to develop. A *Severe Thunderstorm Warning* indicates that a severe thunderstorm has been sighted or indicated by radar.

Tornado—a violent rotating column of air (winds over 200 mph), usually pendant to a cumulonimbus cloud, with circulation reaching the ground. A tornado nearly always starts as a funnel cloud and may be accompanied by a loud roaring noise. On a local scale, it is the most destructive of all atmospheric phenomena. Tornado paths have varied in length from a few feet to more than 100 miles (avg. 5 mi); in diameter from a few feet to more than a mile (avg. 220 yd); average forward speed, 30 mph.

Cyclone—an atmospheric circulation of winds rotating counterclockwise in the northern hemisphere and clockwise in the southern hemisphere. Tornadoes, hurricanes, and the lows shown on weather maps are all examples of cyclones of various size and intensity. Cyclones are usually accompanied by precipitation or stormy weather.

Subtropical Storm—an atmospheric circulation of one-minute sustained surface winds, 34 knots (39 mph) or more. Depending on its characteristics and intensity, it can develop into a tropical storm or a hurricane.

Tropical Storm—an atmospheric circulation of one-minute sustained surface winds within a range of 34 to 63 knots (39 to 73 mph). A *Tropical Storm Watch* is an announcement that a tropical storm or tropical storm conditions may pose a threat to coastal areas generally within 36 hours. A *Tropical Storm Warning* is an announcement that tropical storm conditions pose a threat along a specified segment of coastline within 24 hours.

Hurricane—a severe cyclone originating over tropical ocean waters and having one-minute sustained surface winds 64 knots (73 mph) or higher. (West of the international date line, in the western Pacific, such storms are known as *typhoons.*) The area of hurricane-force winds forms a circle or an oval, sometimes as wide as 300 mi in diameter. In the lower latitudes, hurricanes usually move west or northwest at 10 to 15 mph. When the center approaches 25° to 30° North Latitude, the direction of motion often changes to northeast, with increased forward speed.

Blizzard—a severe weather condition characterized by strong winds bearing a great amount of snow. The National Weather Service specifies winds of 35 mph or higher and sufficient falling and/or blowing snow to frequently reduce visibility to less than ¼ mi. for at least 3 hours.

Flood—Flooding takes many forms. *River Flooding:* This natural process occurs when rains, sometimes coupled with melting snow, fill river basins with too much water too quickly; torrential rains from decaying hurricanes or tropical systems can also be a major cause of river flooding. *Coastal Flooding:* Winds from tropical storms and hurricanes or intense offshore low pressure systems can drive ocean water inland and cause significant flooding. Coastal floods can also be produced by sea waves called *tsunamis,* sometimes referred to as tidal waves; these waves are produced by earthquakes or volcanic activity. *Flash Flooding:* Usually due to copious amounts of rain falling in a short time, flash flooding typically occurs within 6 hours of the rain event. Flash floods account for the majority of flood deaths in the U.S. *Urban Flooding:* Urbanization significantly increases runoff over what would occur on natural terrain, making flash flooding in these areas extremely dangerous. Streets can become swift-moving rivers, and basements can become death traps as they fill with water. *Ice Jam Flooding:* Ice can accumulate at natural or artificial obstructions and stop the flow of water. As the water flow is stopped, water builds up and flooding can occur upstream. If the jam suddenly gives way, the gush of ice and water can cause serious downstream flash flooding.

Flash Flood or Flood Watch: Flash flooding or flooding is possible within a designated area.

Flash Flood or Flood Warning: Flash flooding or flooding has been reported or is imminent; all necessary precautions should be taken immediately.

Urban and Small Stream Advisory: Small streams, streets, and low-lying areas such as railroad underpasses and urban storm drains are flooding.

National Weather Service Marine Warnings and Advisories

Small Craft Advisory alerts mariners to sustained (exceeding 2 hours) weather and/or sea conditions, either present or forecast, potentially hazardous to small boats. Although "small craft" is not defined, hazardous conditions generally include winds of 18 to 33 knots and/or dangerous wave conditions. It is the responsibility of the mariner, based on experience and on the location and size or type of boat, to determine whether conditions are hazardous to the boat. Upon receiving word of a Small Craft Advisory, the mariner should immediately obtain the latest marine forecast to determine the reason for the advisory.

Gale Warning indicates that winds within the range 34 to 47 knots, not directly associated with a tropical storm, are forecast for the area.

Tropical Storm Warning indicates that winds within the range of 34 to 63 knots are forecast in a specified coastal area to occur within 24 hours or less. Issued only for winds of tropical weather systems.

Storm Warning indicates that winds 48 knots or above, not directly associated with a tropical storm, are forecast for the area.

Hurricane Warning indicates that winds 64 knots or greater are forecast for the area within 24 hours. Issued only for winds produced by tropical weather systems.

Special Marine Warning indicates potentially hazardous weather conditions, usually of short duration (2 hours or less) and producing wind speeds of 34 knots or more, not adequately covered by existing marine warnings.

Primary sources of dissemination are commercial radio, TV, U.S. Coast Guard radio stations, and NOAA VHF-FM broadcasts. These NOAA broadcasts on 162.40 to 162.55 MHz can usually be received 20-40 mi from the transmitting antenna site, depending on terrain and quality of the receiver used. Where transmitting antennas are on high ground, the range may be somewhat greater, reaching 60 mi or more.

IT'S A FACT: The U.S. record for the greatest burst of rain in a short time was set in Uniondale, NJ, on July 4, 1956, when 1.23 inches of rain fell in 1 minute.

Monthly Normal Temperatures, Precipitation

Source: National Climatic Data Center, NESDIS, NOAA, U.S. Dept. of Commerce

The temperatures given here are based on records for the 30-year period 1971-2000. For stations that did not have continuous records from the same site for the entire 30 years, the means have been adjusted to the record at the present site.

Figures are for airport stations unless otherwise indicated. * = city station. T = temp. in Fahrenheit; P = precipitation in inches.

	Jan.		Feb.		Mar.		Apr.		May		June		July		Aug.		Sept.		Oct.		Nov.		Dec.	
Station	T	P	T	P	T	P	T	P	T	P	T	P	T	P	T	P	T	P	T	P	T	P	T	P
Albany, NY	22	2.7	25	2.3	35	3.2	47	3.3	58	3.7	66	3.7	71	3.5	69	3.7	61	3.3	49	3.2	39	3.3	28	2.8
Albuquerque, NM	36	0.5	41	0.4	48	0.6	56	0.5	65	0.6	75	0.7	79	1.3	76	1.7	69	1.1	57	1.0	44	0.6	36	0.5
Anchorage, AK	16	0.7	19	0.7	26	0.7	36	0.5	47	0.7	55	1.1	58	1.7	56	2.9	48	2.9	34	2.1	22	1.1	18	1.1
Asheville, NC	36	3.1	39	3.2	46	3.9	54	3.2	62	3.5	69	3.2	73	3.0	72	3.3	66	3.0	55	2.4	46	2.9	39	2.6
Atlanta, GA	43	5.0	47	4.7	54	5.4	62	3.6	70	4.0	77	3.6	80	5.1	79	3.7	73	4.1	63	3.1	53	4.1	45	3.8
Atlantic City, NJ	32	3.6	34	2.9	42	4.1	51	3.5	61	3.4	70	2.7	75	3.9	74	4.3	66	3.1	55	2.9	46	3.3	37	3.2
Baltimore, MD	32	3.5	36	3.0	44	3.9	53	3.0	63	3.9	72	3.4	77	3.9	75	3.7	67	4.0	55	3.2	46	3.1	37	3.4
Barrow, AK	–14	0.1	–16	0.1	–14	0.1	–1	0.1	20	0.1	35	0.3	40	0.9	39	1.0	31	0.7	15	0.4	–1	0.2	–11	0.1
Birmingham, AL	43	5.5	47	4.2	55	6.1	61	4.7	69	4.8	76	3.8	80	5.1	80	3.5	74	4.1	63	3.2	53	4.6	46	4.5
Bismarck, ND	10	0.5	18	0.5	30	0.9	43	1.5	56	2.2	65	2.6	70	2.6	69	2.2	58	1.6	45	1.3	28	0.7	15	0.4
Boise, ID	30	1.4	37	1.1	44	1.4	51	1.3	59	1.3	67	0.7	75	0.4	74	0.3	64	0.8	53	0.8	40	1.4	31	1.4
Boston, MA	29	3.9	32	3.3	39	3.9	48	3.6	59	3.2	68	3.2	74	3.1	72	3.4	65	3.5	54	3.8	45	4.0	35	3.7
Buffalo, NY	25	3.2	26	2.4	34	3.0	45	3.0	57	3.4	66	3.8	71	3.1	69	3.9	62	3.8	51	3.2	40	3.9	30	3.8
Burlington, VT	18	2.2	20	1.7	31	2.3	44	2.9	57	3.3	66	3.4	71	4.0	68	4.0	59	3.8	48	3.1	37	3.1	25	2.2
Caribou, ME	10	3.0	13	2.1	25	2.6	38	2.6	52	3.3	61	3.3	66	3.9	63	4.2	54	3.3	43	3.0	31	3.1	16	3.2
Charleston, SC	48	4.1	51	3.1	58	4.0	64	2.8	72	3.7	78	5.9	82	6.1	81	6.9	76	6.0	66	3.1	58	2.7	51	3.2
Charleston, WV	33	3.3	37	3.2	45	3.9	54	3.3	62	4.3	70	4.1	74	4.9	73	4.1	66	3.5	55	2.7	46	3.7	38	3.3
Chicago, IL	22	1.8	27	1.6	37	2.7	48	3.7	59	3.4	68	3.6	73	3.5	72	4.6	64	3.3	52	2.7	39	3.0	27	2.4
Cleveland, OH	26	2.5	28	2.3	38	2.9	48	3.4	59	3.5	68	3.9	72	3.5	70	3.7	63	3.8	52	2.7	42	3.4	31	3.1
Columbus, OH	28	2.5	32	2.2	42	2.9	52	3.3	63	3.9	71	4.1	75	4.6	74	3.7	67	2.9	55	2.3	44	3.2	34	2.9
Dallas–Ft. Worth, TX	44	1.9	49	2.4	57	3.1	65	3.2	73	5.2	81	3.2	85	2.1	84	2.0	78	2.4	67	4.1	55	2.6	47	2.6
Denver, CO	29	0.5	33	0.5	40	1.3	48	1.9	57	2.3	68	1.6	73	2.2	72	1.8	62	1.1	51	1.0	38	1.0	30	0.6
Des Moines, IA	20	1.0	27	1.2	38	2.2	51	3.6	62	4.3	71	4.6	76	4.2	74	4.5	65	3.2	53	2.6	38	2.1	25	1.3
Detroit, MI	25	1.9	27	1.9	37	2.5	48	3.1	60	3.1	69	3.6	74	3.2	72	3.1	64	3.3	52	2.2	41	2.7	30	2.5
Dodge City, KS	30	0.6	36	0.7	44	1.8	54	2.3	64	3.0	74	3.2	80	3.2	78	2.7	69	1.7	57	1.5	42	1.0	33	0.8
Duluth, MN	8	1.1	15	0.8	25	1.7	39	2.1	52	3.0	60	4.3	66	4.2	64	4.2	55	4.1	44	2.5	28	2.1	14	0.9
Fairbanks, AK	–10	0.6	–4	0.4	11	0.3	32	0.2	49	0.6	60	1.4	62	1.7	56	1.7	45	1.1	24	1.0	2	0.7	–6	0.7
Fresno, CA	46	2.2	51	2.1	56	2.2	61	0.8	69	0.4	76	0.2	81	0.0	80	0.0	75	0.3	65	0.7	53	1.1	45	1.3
Galveston, TX*	56	4.1	58	2.6	64	2.8	70	2.6	77	3.7	82	4.0	84	3.5	84	4.2	81	5.8	74	3.5	65	3.6	58	3.5
Grand Rapids, MI	22	2.0	25	1.5	35	2.6	46	3.5	58	3.4	67	3.7	71	3.6	69	3.8	61	4.3	50	2.8	38	3.4	28	2.7
Hartford, CT	26	3.8	29	3.0	38	3.9	49	3.9	60	4.4	69	3.9	74	3.7	72	4.0	63	4.1	52	3.9	42	4.1	31	3.6
Helena, MT	20	0.5	26	0.4	35	0.6	44	0.9	53	1.8	61	1.8	68	1.3	67	1.3	56	1.1	45	0.7	31	0.5	21	0.5
Honolulu, HI	73	2.7	73	2.4	74	1.9	76	1.1	77	0.8	80	0.4	81	0.5	82	0.5	82	0.7	80	2.2	78	2.3	75	2.9
Houston, TX	52	3.7	55	3.0	62	3.4	69	3.6	76	5.2	81	5.4	84	3.2	83	3.8	79	4.3	70	4.5	61	4.2	54	3.7
Huron, SD	14	0.5	21	0.6	33	1.7	46	2.3	58	3.0	68	3.3	73	2.9	72	2.1	61	1.8	48	1.6	31	0.9	19	0.4
Indianapolis, IN	27	2.5	31	2.4	42	3.4	52	3.6	63	4.4	72	4.1	75	4.4	74	3.8	66	2.9	55	2.8	43	3.6	32	3.0
Jackson, MS	45	5.7	49	4.5	57	5.7	63	5.0	72	4.9	79	3.8	81	4.7	81	3.7	76	3.2	64	3.4	55	5.0	48	5.3
Jacksonville, FL	53	3.7	56	3.2	62	3.9	67	3.1	73	3.5	79	5.4	82	6.0	81	6.9	78	7.9	69	3.9	62	2.3	55	2.6
Juneau, AK	26	4.8	29	4.0	34	3.5	41	3.0	48	3.5	54	3.4	57	4.1	56	5.4	50	7.6	42	8.3	33	5.4	29	5.4
Kansas City, MO	27	1.2	33	1.3	44	2.4	54	3.4	64	5.4	74	4.4	79	4.4	77	3.5	68	4.6	57	3.3	43	2.3	31	1.6
Knoxville, TN	38	4.6	42	4.0	50	5.2	58	4.0	66	4.7	74	4.0	78	4.7	77	2.9	71	3.0	59	2.7	49	4.0	41	4.5
Lander, WY	20	0.5	26	0.5	36	1.2	44	2.1	53	2.4	64	1.2	71	0.8	69	0.6	59	1.1	46	1.4	30	1.0	21	0.6
Lexington, KY	32	3.3	36	3.3	46	4.4	55	3.7	64	4.8	72	4.6	76	4.8	75	3.8	68	3.1	57	2.7	46	3.4	36	4.0
Little Rock, AR	40	3.6	45	3.3	53	4.9	61	5.5	70	5.1	78	4.0	82	3.3	81	2.9	74	3.7	63	4.3	52	5.7	43	4.7
Los Angeles, CA*	57	3.0	58	3.1	58	2.4	61	0.6	63	0.2	66	0.1	69	0.0	71	0.1	70	0.3	67	0.4	62	1.1	58	1.8
Louisville, KY	33	3.3	38	3.3	47	4.4	56	3.9	66	4.9	74	3.8	78	4.3	77	3.4	70	3.1	59	2.8	48	3.8	38	3.7
Marquette, MI*	12	2.6	15	1.9	24	3.1	36	2.8	50	3.1	59	3.2	64	3.0	62	3.6	54	3.7	43	3.7	29	3.3	17	2.4
Memphis, TN	40	4.2	45	4.3	54	5.6	62	5.8	71	5.2	79	4.3	83	4.2	81	3.0	75	3.3	64	3.3	52	5.8	43	5.7
Miami, FL	68	1.9	69	2.1	72	2.6	76	3.4	80	5.5	82	8.5	84	5.8	84	8.6	82	8.4	79	6.2	74	3.4	70	2.2
Milwaukee, WI	21	1.9	25	1.7	35	2.6	45	3.8	56	3.1	66	3.6	72	3.6	71	4.0	63	3.3	51	2.5	38	2.7	26	2.2
Minneapolis, MN	13	1.0	20	0.8	32	1.9	47	2.3	59	3.2	68	4.3	73	4.0	71	4.1	61	2.7	49	2.1	33	1.9	19	1.0
Mobile, AL	61	5.8	65	5.1	71	7.2	77	5.1	84	6.1	89	5.0	91	6.5	91	6.2	87	6.0	79	3.3	70	5.4	63	4.7
Moline, IL	21	1.6	27	1.5	39	2.9	51	3.8	62	4.3	71	4.6	75	4.0	73	4.4	65	3.2	53	2.8	39	2.7	26	2.2
Nashua, NH	23	3.9	26	3.1	35	4.1	46	3.9	57	3.7	66	3.9	71	3.7	69	3.8	61	3.6	49	3.9	39	4.2	28	3.7
Nashville, TN	37	4.0	41	3.7	50	4.9	59	3.9	67	5.1	75	4.1	79	3.8	78	3.3	71	3.6	60	2.9	49	4.5	41	4.5
Newark, NJ	31	4.0	34	3.0	42	4.2	52	3.9	63	4.5	72	3.4	77	4.7	76	4.0	68	4.0	56	3.2	46	3.9	36	3.6
New Orleans, LA	53	5.9	56	5.5	62	5.2	68	5.0	76	4.6	81	6.8	83	6.2	83	6.2	79	5.6	70	3.1	61	5.1	55	5.1
New York, NY*	33	3.6	35	2.8	42	3.9	52	3.7	62	4.2	72	3.6	77	4.4	76	4.1	69	3.8	58	3.3	48	3.7	38	3.5
Norfolk, VA	40	3.9	42	3.3	49	4.1	57	3.4	66	3.7	75	3.8	79	5.2	77	4.8	72	4.1	61	3.5	52	3.0	44	3.0
Oklahoma City, OK	37	1.3	42	1.6	51	2.9	60	3.0	68	5.4	77	4.6	82	2.9	81	2.5	73	4.0	62	3.6	49	2.1	40	1.9
Omaha, NE	22	0.8	28	0.8	39	2.1	51	2.9	62	4.4	72	4.0	77	3.9	75	3.2	65	3.2	53	2.2	38	1.8	26	0.9
Philadelphia, PA	32	3.5	35	2.7	43	3.8	53	3.5	64	3.9	72	3.3	78	4.4	76	3.8	69	3.9	57	2.8	47	3.2	37	3.3
Phoenix, AZ	54	0.8	58	0.8	63	1.1	70	0.3	79	0.2	89	0.1	93	1.0	91	0.9	86	0.8	75	0.8	62	0.7	54	0.9
Pittsburgh, PA	28	2.7	31	2.4	40	3.2	50	3.0	60	3.8	68	4.1	73	4.0	71	3.4	64	3.2	53	2.3	42	3.0	33	2.9
Portland, ME	22	4.1	25	3.1	34	4.1	44	4.3	54	3.8	63	3.3	69	3.3	67	3.1	59	3.4	48	4.4	38	4.7	28	4.2
Portland, OR	40	5.1	43	4.2	47	3.7	51	2.6	57	2.4	63	1.6	68	0.7	69	0.9	64	1.7	54	2.9	46	5.6	40	5.7
Providence, RI	29	4.4	31	3.5	39	4.4	49	4.2	59	3.7	68	3.4	73	3.2	72	3.9	64	3.7	53	3.7	44	4.4	34	4.1
Raleigh, NC	40	4.0	43	3.5	51	4.0	59	2.8	67	3.8	75	3.4	79	4.3	77	3.8	71	4.3	60	3.2	51	3.0	43	3.0
Rapid City, SD	22	0.4	27	0.5	35	1.0	45	1.9	55	3.0	65	2.8	72	2.0	71	1.6	61	1.1	48	1.4	33	0.6	25	0.4
Reno, NV	34	1.1	39	1.1	43	0.9	49	0.4	56	0.6	65	0.5	71	0.2	70	0.3	62	0.5	52	0.4	41	0.8	34	0.9
Richmond, VA	36	3.6	40	3.0	48	4.1	57	3.2	65	4.0	74	3.5	78	4.7	76	4.2	70	4.0	58	3.6	49	3.1	40	3.1
St. Louis, MO	30	2.1	35	2.3	46	3.6	57	3.7	67	4.1	77	3.8	80	3.9	78	3.0	70	3.0	58	2.8	45	3.7	34	2.9
Salt Lake City, UT	29	1.4	35	1.3	43	1.9	50	2.0	59	2.1	69	0.8	77	0.7	76	0.8	65	1.3	53	1.6	40	1.4	30	1.2
San Antonio, TX	51	1.7	55	1.8	63	1.9	69	2.6	76	4.7	81	4.3	84	2.0	84	2.6	79	3.0	71	3.9	60	2.6	53	2.0
San Diego, CA	58	2.3	59	2.0	60	2.3	63	0.8	65	0.2	67	0.1	71	0.0	73	0.1	72	0.2	68	0.4	62	1.1	58	1.3
San Francisco, CA	49	4.5	52	4.0	54	3.3	56	1.2	59	0.4	61	0.1	63	0.0	64	0.1	64	0.2	61	1.0	55	2.5	50	2.9
San Juan, PR	77	3.0	77	2.3	78	2.1	79	3.7	81	5.3	82	3.5	82	4.2	82	5.2	82	5.6	82	5.1	80	6.2	78	4.6
Santa Fe, NM	29	0.6	35	0.5	41	0.8	48	0.7	57	1.3	66	1.2	70	2.3	68	2.1	62	1.7	51	1.3	38	1.1	30	0.7
Savannah, GA	49	4.0	53	2.9	59	3.6	65	3.3	73	3.6	79	5.5	82	6.0	81	7.2	77	5.1	67	3.1	59	2.4	51	2.8
Seattle, WA	41	5.1	43	4.2	46	3.8	50	2.6	56	1.8	61	1.5	65	0.8	66	1.0	61	1.6	53	3.2	45	5.9	41	5.6
Spokane, WA	27	1.8	33	1.5	40	1.5	47	1.3	54	1.6	62	1.2	69	0.8	69	0.7	59	0.8	47	1.1	35	2.2	27	2.3
Springfield, MO	32	2.1	37	2.3	46	3.8	56	4.3	65	4.6	73	5.0	79	3.6	78	3.4	69	4.8	58	3.5	46	4.5	36	3.2
Syracuse, NY	23	2.6	25	2.1	34	3.0	45	3.3	57	3.4	66	3.7	71	4.0	69	3.6	61	4.1	50	3.2	40	3.8	29	3.1
Tampa, FL	61	2.3	63	2.7	67	2.9	72	1.8	78	2.9	82	5.5	83	6.5	83	7.6	82	6.5	76	2.3	69	1.6	63	2.3
Washington, DC	34	3.6	36	2.8	44	3.9	54	3.3	64	4.3	73	3.6	78	4.2	76	3.9	69	4.1	57	3.4	47	3.3	38	3.2
Wilmington, DE	32	3.4	34	2.8	43	4.0	52	3.4	63	4.1	72	4.0	77	4.3	75	3.5	68	4.0	56	3.0	46	3.2	36	3.4

Normal High and Low Temperatures, Precipitation

Source: National Climatic Data Center, NESDIS, NOAA, U.S. Dept. of Commerce

The normal temperatures and precipitation given here are based on records for the 30-year period 1971-2000. The extreme temperatures (through 1990 only) are listed for the stations shown and may not agree with the state records shown on page 178.

Figures are for airport stations unless otherwise indicated. * = city station. Temperatures are Fahrenheit.

State	Station	NORMAL TEMPERATURE January Max.	January Min.	July Max.	July Min.	EXTREME TEMPERATURE Highest	Lowest	AVG. ANNUAL PRECIPITATION (inches)
Alabama	Mobile	61	40	91	72	104	3	66.29
Alaska	Anchorage	22	9	65	52	85	–34	16.08
Alaska	Barrow	–8	–20	47	34	79	–56	4.16
Alaska	Juneau	31	21	64	49	—	—	58.33
Arizona	Phoenix	65	43	104	81	122	17	8.29
Arkansas	Little Rock	50	31	93	72	112	–5	50.93
California	Los Angeles*	66	49	75	63	112	28	13.15
California	San Francisco	56	43	71	55	106	20	20.11
Colorado	Denver	43	15	88	59	104	–30	15.81
Connecticut	Hartford	34	17	85	62	102	–26	46.16
Delaware	Wilmington	39	24	86	67	102	–14	42.81
District of Columbia	Washington–National	43	24	89	67	104	–5	43.70
Florida	Jacksonville	64	42	91	72	105	7	52.34
Florida	Miami	77	60	91	77	98	30	58.53
Georgia	Atlanta	52	34	89	71	105	–8	50.20
Georgia	Savannah	60	38	92	72	105	3	49.58
Hawaii	Honolulu	80	66	88	74	94	53	18.29
Idaho	Boise	37	24	89	60	111	–25	12.19
Illinois	Chicago	30	14	84	63	104	–27	36.27
Indiana	Indianapolis	35	19	86	65	104	–23	40.95
Iowa	Des Moines	29	12	86	66	108	–24	34.72
Kansas	Dodge City	41	19	97	67	—	—	22.35
Kentucky	Lexington	40	24	86	66	103	–21	45.91
Kentucky	Louisville	41	25	87	70	105	–20	44.54
Louisiana	New Orleans	62	43	91	74	102	11	64.16
Maine	Caribou	19	0	76	55	96	–41	37.44
Maine	Portland	31	13	79	59	103	–39	45.83
Maryland	Baltimore	41	24	87	66	105	–7	41.94
Massachusetts	Boston	37	22	82	66	102	–12	42.53
Michigan	Detroit	31	18	83	64	104	–21	32.89
Michigan	Grand Rapids	29	16	82	61	—	—	37.13
Michigan	Sault Ste. Marie*	22	5	76	52	98	–36	34.67
Minnesota	Duluth	18	–1	76	55	97	–39	31.00
Minnesota	Minneapolis-St. Paul	22	4	83	63	105	–34	29.41
Mississippi	Jackson	55	35	91	71	106	2	55.95
Missouri	Kansas City	36	18	89	68	109	–23	37.98
Missouri	St. Louis	38	21	90	71	107	–18	38.75
Montana	Helena	31	10	83	52	105	–42	11.32
Nebraska	Omaha	32	12	87	66	114	–23	30.22
Nevada	Reno	46	22	91	51	105	–16	7.48
New Hampshire	Nashua	33	12	83	59	—	—	45.43
New Jersey	Atlantic City	41	23	85	65	106	–11	40.59
New Mexico	Albuquerque	48	24	92	65	105	–17	9.47
New Mexico	Santa Fe	43	16	86	54	—	—	14.22
New York	Albany	31	13	82	60	100	–28	38.60
New York	Buffalo	31	18	80	62	99	–20	40.54
New York	New York–La Guardia	39	27	85	70	107	–3	44.36
North Carolina	Raleigh	50	30	89	69	105	–9	43.05
North Dakota	Bismarck	21	–1	85	56	109	–44	16.84
Ohio	Cleveland	33	19	81	62	104	–19	38.71
Ohio	Columbus	36	20	85	65	102	–19	38.52
Oklahoma	Oklahoma City	47	26	93	71	—	—	35.85
Oregon	Portland	46	34	79	57	107	–3	37.07
Pennsylvania	Philadelphia	39	26	86	70	104	–7	42.05
Pennsylvania	Pittsburgh	35	20	83	62	103	–18	37.85
Puerto Rico	San Juan	82	71	87	77	—	—	50.76
Rhode Island	Providence	37	20	83	64	104	–13	46.45
South Carolina	Charleston	59	37	91	73	104	6	51.53
South Dakota	Huron	25	4	86	61	112	–39	20.90
South Dakota	Rapid City	34	11	86	58	110	–30	16.64
Tennessee	Memphis	49	31	92	73	108	–13	54.65
Tennessee	Nashville	46	28	89	70	107	–17	48.11
Texas	Galveston*	62	50	89	80	101	8	43.84
Texas	Houston	62	41	94	74	107	7	47.84
Utah	Salt Lake City	37	21	91	63	107	–30	16.50
Vermont	Burlington	27	9	81	60	101	–30	36.05
Virginia	Norfolk	48	32	87	71	104	–3	45.74
Virginia	Richmond	45	28	88	68	105	–12	43.91
Washington	Seattle-Tacoma	46	36	75	55	99	0	37.07
Washington	Spokane	33	22	83	55	108	–25	16.67
West Virginia	Charleston	43	24	85	63	—	—	44.05
Wisconsin	Milwaukee	28	13	81	63	103	–26	34.81
Wyoming	Lander	32	9	86	55	101	–37	13.42

Mean Annual Snowfall (inches) based on record through 1990: Boston, MA, 42; Sault Ste. Marie, MI, 113; Albany, NY, 65.2; Burlington, VT, 78.6; Lander, WY, 66; Juneau, AK, 105.8. **Wettest Spot:** Mount Waialeale, HI, on the island of Kauai, is the rainiest place in the world and in the U.S., according to the National Geographic Society; it has an average annual rainfall of 460 inches.
Temperature Extremes: A temperature of 136° F observed at El Azizia (Al Aziziyah), near Tripoli, Libya, on Sept. 13, 1922, is generally accepted as the world's highest temperature recorded under standard conditions. The record high in the U.S. was 134° F in Death Valley, CA, July 10, 1913. A record low of –129° F was recorded at the Soviet Antarctica station of Vostok on July 21, 1983.The record low in the United States was –80° F at Prospect Creek, AK, Jan. 23, 1971.

Annual Climatological Data, 2001

Source: National Climatic Data Center, NESDIS, NOAA, U.S. Dept. of Commerce

Station	Elev. (ft.)	Temperature °F				Precipitation[1]			Sleet or snow			Fastest[2] wind		No. of Days	
		Highest	Date	Lowest	Date	Total (in.)	Greatest in 24 hours	Date	Total (in.)	Greatest in 24 hours	Date	MPH	Date	Prec. .01 in. or more	Snow, sleet 1 in. or more
Albany, NY	278	96	8/09	1	1/02	28.59	1.30	3/05-06	62.0	12.5	3/05-3/06	40	2/17	121	20
Albuquerque, NM	5,305	98	7/01	17	1/18	6.50	.84	8/13-8/14	4.3	1.4	1/27	48	6/19	63	1
Anchorage, AK	130	75	6/28	–15	12/17+	12.52	2.37	7/04-7/05	89.1	7.3	10/17	33	4/03	114	24
Asheville, NC	2,171	89	8/09	10	1/03	34.49	1.5	3/20-3/21	7.4	6.1	3/20	47	3/06	117	1
Atlanta, GA	971	93	8/24	17	1/03	38.39	2.86	6/01	0.1	0.1	1/01	48	2/16	111	0
Atlantic City, NJ	114	103	8/09	8	1/04	27.21	2.47	6/17	9.6	8.0	2/22	38	2/17	105	2
Baltimore, MD	193	98	8/10+	14	1/03	34.57	3.23	8/30	7.4	3.7	2/22	40	2/10	114	3
Barrow, AK	35	68	7/16	–36	3/13	5.25	.62	1/08	47.5	7.3	1/08	53	1/08	75	9
Birmingham, AL	636	95	7/09	12	1/03	66.73	4.13	4/03	—	—	—	51	2/16	123	0
Bismarck, ND	1,651	103	9/05	–23	2/27	21.34	2.99	7/26-7/27	25.4	4.5	1/14	64	7/19	90	6
Boise, ID	2,858	106	7/03	7	1/30	8.54	.75	4/11-4/12	26.7	3.0	12/31	40	4/30	78	11
Boston, MA	19	97	8/09	10	2/12	30.72	2.85	3/21-3/22	46.4	6.4	1/21	45	3/30	108	15
Buffalo, NY	714	93	8/05	5	1/02	35.18	2.30	12/24-12/25	145.9	35.4	12/27-12/28	46	10/25	160	27
Burlington, VT	345	99	8/09	–7	1/21	23.27	2.20	9/31-10/01	93.6	14.8	3/05	37	2/10	127	26
Caribou, ME	627	91	8/06	–28	3/02	29.10	1.82	3/31	97.1	18.8	3/31	41	11/07	152	27
Charleston, SC	45	97	7/09	19	1/04	39.98	4.66	7/27-7/28	—	—	—	38	4/01	111	0
Chicago, IL	655	95	8/09+	–2	2/02	45.77	4.31	8/30	9.8	4.0	3/16	38	2/25	134	3
Cleveland, OH	802	94	8/08	7	1/09	31.38	1.90	5/21-5/22	40.4	7.7	3/25	44	2/09	150	16
Columbus, OH	846	93	8/09+	6	1/03+	36.85	2.39	7/24-7/25	13.3	2.1	1/26	47	12/14	130	4
Dallas-Ft. Worth, TX	559	102	8/05	19	1/20+	38.13	3.83	7/01	—	—	—	47	2/24	84	0
Denver, CO	5,379	101	7/01	–15	2/09	16.46	1.44	7/23	—	—	—	53	4/11	86	0
Des Moines, IA	968	99	7/22	–9	2/02	28.45	3.11	9/07-9/08	—	—	—	52	9/07	110	0
Detroit, MI	628	99	8/08	4	1/09	34.45	1.92	10/16	17.5	2.4	3/16	47	4/12	149	5
Duluth, MN	1,426	93	8/05	–19	2/21	30.22	2.60	4/22-4/23	83.3	11.7	2/24	46	8/08	136	23
Fairbanks, AK	461	82	7/19	–41	12/19	8.48	.51	7/28	49.3	6.1	5/04-/05	30	2/27	103	15
Fresno, CA	372	110	7/03	29	1/17	12.02	1.15	4/06-4/07	—	—	—	30	11/24	53	0
Grand Rapids, MI	785	94	8/08	–2	1/02	40.49	4.32	5/14-5/15	70.2	11.9	12/26	44	10/25	146	15
Hartford, CT	162	102	8/09	–3	1/03	33.03	2.14	6/17	—	—	—	38	2/17	117	0
Helena, MT	3,864	102	8/03	–9	1/29	10.31	1.26	9/05-9/06	—	—	—	47	7/13	81	0
Honolulu, HI	15	92	9/15	59	2/07	9.14	3.67	11/26-11/27	—	—	—	35	12/12	84	0
Houston, TX	118	101	8/05	26	1/20+	71.19	11.02	6/08-6/09	—	—	—	38	6/28	115	0
Huron, SD	1,281	100	9/04	–21	2/10+	26.78	3.87	6/12-6/13	69.8	19.5	1/29-1/30	48	6/09	85	14
Indianapolis, IN	794	92	8/22+	3	1/03	41.89	1.91	6/05-6/06	3.8	1.9	1/26	46	2/09	105	1
Jackson, MS	293	96	7/21	14	1/03	64.22	5.49	7/25-7/26	—	—	—	33	2/24	111	0
Jacksonville, FL	31	96	7/12	22	1/02+	49.14	7.02	9/12-9/13	—	—	—	38	6/16	118	0
Kansas City, MO	1,005	100	8/21	–6	1/02	53.50	4.54	9/16-9/17	11.0	4.8	2/27	48	4/11	104	2
Knoxville, TN	979	93	7/24	11	1/03	42.50	2.60	1/18-1/19	—	—	—	43	10/24	115	0
Lander, WY	5,557	100	8/06	–14	2/09	5.38	0.74	9/14	5.25	0.4	5/20	51	5/01	52	18
Lexington, KY	977	92	8/23	5	1/21+	38.97	2.18	7/25-7/26	—	—	—	39	12/14	131	0
Los Angeles, CA	323	84	2/04	41	2/15+	17.01	3.04	1/10-1/11	—	—	—	38	12/09	44	0
Louisville, KY	481	96	7/08	6	1/03	43.99	2.26	11/28-11/29	5.7	2.5	1/20	40	10/24	116	2
Marquette, MI	1,415	96	8/06	–18	2/22	34.24	2.46	11/26-11/27	218.8	24.4	11/26-11/27	—	—	169	54
Memphis, TN	283	96	8/22	11	1/03+	66.01	7.30	11/28-11/29	—	—	—	37	5/20	105	0
Miami, FL	26	94	8/26	39	1/05	72.03	5.23	9/28-9/29	—	—	—	35	9/27+	135	0
Milwaukee, WI	677	95	8/09+	1	2/02	36.73	1.92	2/08-2/09	9.4	1.5	2/14	47	6/11	124	1
Minn.-St. Paul, MN	871	99	8/06	–13	2/02	34.23	2.51	6/12-6/13	—	—	—	45	6/13	116	0
Mobile, AL	209	95	7/24+	21	1/04+	54.65	4.83	3/02-3/03	—	—	—	45	6/11	116	0
Moline, IL	604	96	7/31	–5	2/02	40.25	2.13	8/02	13.5	3.0	3/16	49	6/14	131	5
Nashville, TN	571	95	7/08	8	1/03	48.56	3.46	11/29	—	—	—	37	4/15	113	0
Newark, NJ	25	105	8/09	12	1/03	31.44	1.96	3/21-3/22	24.4	5.5	2/22	39	7/01	113	6
New Orleans, LA	4	94	7/24	25	1/03+	69.51	6.05	6/05-6/06	—	—	—	37	7/11	108	0
New York, NY	158	103	8/09	16	2/12	35.65	2.37	3/29-3/30	21.6	6.0	1/21	36	3/30+	107	6
Norfolk, VA	66	96	8/10+	19	1/05+	33.36	4.39	6/16	—	—	—	33	12/14	98	0
North Little Rock, AR	563	102	7/11	14	1/03+	50.26	3.80	12/16-12/17	—	—	—	—	—	98	0
Oklahoma City, OK	1,281	107	7/12	14	1/03+	29.10	3.19	5/29-5/30	8.1	3.4	1/16-1/17	47	5/27	76	4
Philadelphia, PA	59	101	8/09	15	1/03	31.01	3.34	6/16-6/17	15.6	7.0	2/22	39	1/30	101	4
Phoenix, AZ	1,103	116	7/2	36	12/14	6.72	.88	4/05-4/06	—	—	—	51	4/21	33	0
Pittsburgh, PA	1,172	92	8/07+	7	1/26	35.74	1.87	8/28	30.7	5.2	1/20	46	8/28	133	13
Portland, ME	69	95	8/09	–2	2/04	33.11	3.39	3/22-3/23	85.5	16.5	3/05-3/06	44	2/10	116	20
Portland, OR	220	98	8/09	26	2/10+	30.44	1.41	11/28	—	—	—	38	12/01	152	0
Providence, RI	50	100	8/09	10	2/12	40.19	2.92	9/21-9/22	32.3	5.6	1/21	39	3/06	11	11
Raleigh, NC	427	100	8/09	12	1/03	34.78	2.45	7/27	0.3	0.3	2/22	36	8/11	109	0
Rapid City, SD	3,150	104	8/07	–16	2/09	14.29	1.28	6/08-6/09	—	—	—	54	6/09	82	0
Reno, NV	4,404	102	7/02	14	2/08	4.35	1.19	12/02	—	—	—	46	12/01	50	0
Richmond, VA	164	98	8/10+	12	1/03	31.52	3.12	8/12	3.3	2.5	2/22	35	4/24+	97	0
St. Louis, MO	707	100	8/22	0	1/02	35.29	1.55	2/23-2/24	2.9	0.7	2/27+	43	10/24	107	0
Salt Lake City, UT	4,221	104	7/04	7	12/25+	15.04	1.53	11/22-/11/23	73.5	10.4	11/25	48	6/12	89	23
San Antonio, TX	818	102	8/06	26	1/20	36.72	3.50	8/29-8/30	—	—	—	37	6/14	89	0
San Diego, CA	78	85	9/25	41	1/17	8.47	1.13	1/10-1/11	—	—	—	33	2/13	39	0
San Francisco, CA	86	95	5/30	37	1/27+	26.14	2.89	12/01-12/02	—	—	—	46	11/24	77	0
San Juan, PR	7	94	9/30+	46	10/31	56.06	3.19	12/21-12/22	—	—	—	37	10/13	202	0
Sault Ste. Marie, MI	724	92	8/07	–8	1/08	38.46	2.11	9/09-9/10	—	—	—	39	2/25	162	0
Savannah, GA	48	96	8/17	17	1/04	31.64	2.16	9/30-10/01	—	—	—	43	3/29	105	0
Scottsbluff, NE	3,946	101	6/23	–9	2/09	13.02	1.78	4/02	29.9	6.0	4/22	43	7/04	70	11
Seattle, WA	447	88	8/10	26	2/07	37.56	3.40	11/13-11/14	—	—	—	33	12/01	155	0
Spokane, WA	2,381	99	8/12	7	2/07	13.71	0.76	11/16-11/17	57.7	5.3	11/28	40	12/01	110	20
Springfield, MO	1,277	97	7/23	–6	1/02	45.29	2.92	2/23-2/24	—	—	—	39	8/18	113	0
Syracuse, NY	414	100	8/09	4	3/04	34.30	3.07	9/24-9/25	109.4	12.5	3/04-3/05	49	2/10	158	29
Tampa, FL	8	95	6/15	32	1/01	39.75	6.77	9/14-9/15	—	—	—	39	9/14	96	0
Washington, DC	10	97	8/09+	20	1/03	29.95	1.77	6/15-6/16	5.4	2.8	2/22	37	4/09	107	3
Wilmington, DE	92	99	8/09	12	1/23	33.85	2.78	6/16-6/17	10.5	4.5	2/22	39	9/04	110	3

(T) Trace. (—) Data not available or incomplete. (1) Where one date is shown, it is the starting date of the storm. (2) Sustained for at least 2 minutes, not peak gust.

Record Temperatures by State

Source: National Climatic Data Center, NESDIS, NOAA, U.S. Dept. of Commerce, through Dec. 2000

State	Lowest °F	Highest °F	Latest date	Station	Approx. elevation in feet
Alabama	–27		Jan. 30, 1966	New Market	760
		112	*Sept. 5, 1925*	*Centerville*	*345*
Alaska	–80		Jan. 23, 1971	Prospect Creek	1,100
		100	*June 27, 1915*	*Fort Yukon*	*420*
Arizona	–40		Jan. 7, 1971	Hawley Lake	8,180
		128	*June 29, 1994*[1]	*Lake Havasu City*	*505*
Arkansas	–29		Feb. 13, 1905	Pond	1,250
		120	*Aug. 10, 1936*	*Ozark*	*396*
California	–45		Jan. 20, 1937	Boca	5,532
		134	*July 10, 1913*	*Greenland Ranch*	*–178*
Colorado	–61		Feb. 1, 1985	Maybell	5,920
		118	*July 11, 1888*	*Bennett*	*5,484*
Connecticut	–32		Feb. 16, 1943	Falls Village	585
		106	*July 15, 1995*	*Danbury*	*450*
Delaware	–17		Jan. 17, 1893	Millsboro	20
		110	*July 21, 1930*	*Millsboro*	*20*
Florida	–2		Feb. 13, 1899	Tallahassee	193
		109	*June 29, 1931*	*Monticello*	*207*
Georgia	–17		Jan. 27, 1940	CCC Camp F-16	1,000
		112	*July 24, 1952*	*Louisville*	*132*
Hawaii	12		May 17, 1979	Mauna Kea Obs. 111.2	13,770
		100	*Apr. 27, 1931*	*Pahala*	*850*
Idaho	–60		Jan. 18, 1943	Island Park Dam	6,285
		118	*July 28, 1934*	*Orofino*	*1,027*
Illinois	–36		Jan. 5, 1999	Congerville	635
		117	*July 14, 1954*	*East St. Louis*	*410*
Indiana	–36		Jan. 19, 1994	New Whiteland	785
		116	*July 14, 1936*	*Collegeville*	*672*
Iowa	–47		Feb. 3, 1996[1]	Elkader	770
		118	*July 20, 1934*	*Keokuk*	*614*
Kansas	–40		Feb. 13, 1905	Lebanon	1,812
		121	*July 24, 1936*[1]	*Alton (near)*	*1,651*
Kentucky	–37		Jan. 19, 1994	Shelbyville	730
		114	*July 28, 1930*	*Greensburg*	*581*
Louisiana	–16		Feb. 13, 1899	Minden	194
		114	*Aug. 10, 1936*	*Plain Dealing*	*268*
Maine	–48		Jan. 19, 1925	Van Buren	510
		105	*July 10, 1911*[1]	*North Bridgton*	*450*
Maryland	–40		Jan. 13, 1912	Oakland	2,461
		109	*July 10, 1936*[1]	*Cumberland; Frederick*	*623; 325*
Massachusetts	–35		Jan. 12, 1981	Chester	640
		107	*Aug. 2, 1975*	*Chester; New Bedford*	*640; 120*
Michigan	–51		Feb. 9, 1934	Vanderbilt	785
		112	*July 13, 1936*	*Mio*	*963*
Minnesota	–60		Feb. 2, 1996	Tower	1,430
		114	*July 6, 1936*[1]	*Moorhead*	*904*
Mississippi	–19		Jan. 30, 1966	Corinth	420
		115	*July 29, 1930*	*Holly Springs*	*600*
Missouri	–40		Feb. 13, 1905	Warsaw	700
		118	*July 14, 1954*[1]	*Warsaw; Union*	*700; 560*
Montana	–70		Jan. 20, 1954	Rogers Pass	5,470
		117	*July 5, 1937*	*Medicine Lake*	*1,950*
Nebraska	–47		Feb. 12, 1899	Camp Clarke	3,700
		118	*July 24, 1936*[1]	*Minden*	*2,169*
Nevada	–50		Jan. 8, 1937	San Jacinto	5,200
		125	*June 29, 1994*[1]	*Laughlin*	*605*
New Hampshire	–46		Jan. 28 1925	Pittsburg	1,575
		106	*July 4, 1911*	*Nashua*	*125*
New Jersey	–34		Jan. 5, 1904	River Vale	70
		110	*July 10, 1936*	*Runyon*	*18*
New Mexico	–50		Feb. 1, 1951	Gavilan	7,350
		122	*June 27, 1994*	*Waste Isolat. Pilot Plt.*	*3,418*
New York	–52		Feb. 18, 1979[1]	Old Forge	1,720
		108	*July 22, 1926*	*Troy*	*35*
North Carolina	–34		Jan. 21, 1985	Mt. Mitchell	6,525
		110	*Aug. 21, 1983*	*Fayetteville*	*213*
North Dakota	–60		Feb. 15, 1936	Parshall	1,929
		121	*July 6, 1936*	*Steele*	*1,857*
Ohio	–39		Feb. 10, 1899	Milligan	800
		113	*July 21, 1934*[1]	*Gallipolis (near)*	*673*
Oklahoma	–27		Jan. 18, 1930	Watts	958
		120	*June 27, 1994*[1]	*Tipton*	*1,350*
Oregon	–54		Feb. 10, 1933[1]	Seneca	4,700
		119	*Aug. 10, 1898*	*Pendleton*	*1,074*
Pennsylvania	–42		Jan. 5, 1904	Smethport	1,500
		111	*July 10, 1936*[1]	*Phoenixville*	*100*
Rhode Island	–25		Feb. 5, 1996	Greene	425
		104	*Aug. 2, 1975*	*Providence*	*51*
South Carolina	–19		Jan. 21, 1985	Caesars Head	3,115
		111	*June 28, 1954*[1]	*Camden*	*170*
South Dakota	–58		Feb. 17, 1936	McIntosh	2,277
		120	*July 5, 1936*	*Gannvalley*	*1,750*
Tennessee	–32		Dec. 30, 1917	Mountain City	2,471
		113	*Aug. 9, 1930*[1]	*Perryville*	*377*
Texas	–23		Feb. 8, 1933[1]	Seminole	3,275
		120	*Aug. 12, 1936*	*Seymour*	*1,291*

State	Lowest °F	Highest °F	Latest date	Station	Approx. elevation in feet
Utah	–69		Feb. 1, 1985	Peter's Sink	8,092
		117	*Jul. 5, 1985*	*Saint George*	*2,880*
Vermont	–50		Dec. 30, 1933	Bloomfield	915
		105	*July 4, 1911*	*Vernon*	*310*
Virginia	–30		Jan. 22, 1985	Mountain Lake Bio. Station	3,870
		110	*July 15, 1954*	*Balcony Falls*	*725*
Washington	–48		Dec. 30, 1968	Mazama; Winthrop	2,120; 1,755
		118	*Aug. 5, 1961[1]*	*Ice Harbor Dam*	*475*
West Virginia	–37		Dec. 30, 1917	Lewisburg	2,200
		112	*July 10, 1936[1]*	*Martinsburg*	*435*
Wisconsin	–54		Jan. 24, 1922	Danbury	908
		114	*July 13, 1936*	*Wisconsin Dells*	*900*
Wyoming	–66		Feb. 9, 1933	Riverside R.S.	6,650
		114	*July 12, 1900*	*Basin*	*3,5003*

(1) Also on earlier dates at the same or other places.

World Temperature and Precipitation

Source: World Meteorological Organization

Average daily maximum and minimum temperatures and annual precipitation are based on records for the 30-year period 1961-90. The length of record of extreme temperatures includes all available years of data for a given location and is usually for a longer period; record temperatures may have been measured at a different location within the city. Surface elevations are supplied by the WMO and may differ from city elevation figures in other sections of *The World Almanac*. NA = Not available.

		Temperature °F						
		AVERAGE DAILY				EXTREME		
	Surface elevation	January		July				Average annual precipitation
Station	(feet)	Max.	Min.	Max.	Min.	Max.	Min.	(inches)
Algiers, Algeria	82	61.7	42.6	87.1	65.3	NA	NA	27.0
Athens, Greece	49	56.1	44.6	88.9	73.0	NA	NA	14.6
Auckland, New Zealand	20	74.8	61.2	58.5	46.4	NA	NA	49.4
Bangkok, Thailand	66	89.6	69.8	90.9	77.0	104	51	59.0
Berlin, Germany	190	35.2	26.8	73.6	55.2	107	–4	23.3
Bogotá, Colombia	8,357	67.3	41.7	64.6	45.5	75	21	32.4
Bombay (Mumbai), India	36	85.3	66.7	86.2	77.5	110	46	85.4
Bucharest, Romania	298	34.7	22.1	83.8	60.1	105	–18	23.4
Budapest, Hungary	456	34.2	24.8	79.7	59.7	103	–10	20.3
Buenos Aires, Argentina	82	85.8	67.3	59.7	45.7	104	22	45.2
Cairo, Egypt	243	65.8	48.2	93.9	71.1	118	34	1.0
Cape Town, South Africa	138	79.0	60.3	63.3	44.6	105	28	20.5
Caracas, Venezuela	2,739	79.9	60.8	81.3	66.0	96	45	36.1
Casablanca, Morocco	203	62.8	47.1	77.7	66.7	NA	NA	16.8
Copenhagen, Denmark	16	35.6	28.4	68.9	55.0	NA	NA	NA
Damascus, Syria	2,004	54.3	32.9	97.2	61.9	NA	NA	5.6
Dublin, Ireland	279	45.7	36.5	66.0	52.5	86	8	28.8
Geneva, Switzerland	1,364	38.3	27.9	76.3	53.2	101	–3	35.6
Havana, Cuba	164	78.4	65.5	88.3	74.8	NA	NA	46.9
Hong Kong, China	203	65.5	56.5	88.7	79.9	97	32	87.2
Istanbul, Turkey	108	47.8	37.2	82.8	65.3	105	7	27.4
Jerusalem, Israel	2,483	53.4	39.4	83.8	63.0	107	26	23.2
Lagos, Nigeria	125	90.0	72.3	82.8	72.1	NA	NA	59.3
Lima, Peru	43	79.0	66.9	66.4	59.4	NA	NA	0.2
London, England	203	44.1	32.7	71.1	52.3	99	2	29.7
Manila, Philippines	79	85.8	74.8	89.1	76.8	NA	NA	49.6
Mexico City, Mexico	7,570	70.3	43.7	73.8	53.2	NA	NA	33.4
Montreal, Canada	118	21.6	5.2	79.2	59.7	100	–36	37.0
Nairobi, Kenya	5,897	77.9	50.9	71.6	48.6	NA	NA	41.9
Paris, France	213	42.8	33.6	75.2	55.2	105	–1	25.6
Prague, Czech Republic	1,197	32.7	22.5	73.9	53.2	98	–16	20.7
Reykjavik, Iceland	200	35.4	26.6	55.9	46.9	76	–3	31.5
Rome, Italy	79	53.8	35.4	88.2	62.1	NA	NA	33.0
San Salvador, El Salvador	2,037	86.5	61.3	86.2	66.4	105	45	68.3
São Paulo, Brazil	2,598	81.1	65.7	71.2	53.1	NA	NA	57.4
Shanghai, China	23	45.9	32.9	88.9	76.6	104	10	43.8
Singapore	52	85.8	73.6	87.4	75.6	NA	NA	84.6
Stockholm, Sweden	171	30.7	23.0	71.4	56.1	97	–26	21.2
Sydney, Australia	10	79.5	65.5	62.4	43.9	114	32	46.4
Tehran, Iran	3,906	45.0	30.0	98.2	75.2	109	–5	9.1
Tokyo, Japan	118	49.1	34.2	83.8	72.1	NA	NA	55.4
Toronto, Canada	567	27.5	12.0	80.2	57.6	105	–26	30.8

Hurricane and Tornado Classifications

Source: National Weather Service, NOAA, U.S. Dept. of Commerce

The Saffir-Simpson Hurricane Scale is a 1-5 rating based on a hurricane's intensity. The scale is used to give an estimate of the potential property damage and flooding expected along the coast from a hurricane landfall. Wind speed is the determining factor in the scale. The Fujita (or F) Scale, created by T. Theodore Fujita, is used to classify tornadoes. The F Scale uses rating numbers from 0 to 5, based on the amount and type of wind damage.

Saffir-Simpson Scale (Hurricanes)

Category	Wind Speed	Severity	Storm Surge[1]
1	74-95 MPH	Weak	4-5 feet
2	96-110 MPH	Moderate	6-8 feet
3	111-130 MPH	Strong	9-12 feet
4	131-155 MPH	Very Strong	13-18 feet
5	above 155 MPH	Devastating	above 18 feet

Fujita Scale (Tornadoes)

Rank	Wind Speed	Damage	Strength
F-0	40-72 MPH	Light	Weak
F-1	73-112 MPH	Moderate	Weak
F-2	113-157 MPH	Considerable	Strong
F-3	158-206 MPH	Severe	Strong
F-4	207-260 MPH	Devastating	Violent
F-5	above 261 MPH	Incredible	Violent

(1) Above normal tides.

Hurricane Names in 2003

Source: National Weather Service, NOAA, U.S. Dept. of Commerce

Atlantic hurricanes — Ana, Bill, Claudette, Danny, Erika, Fabian, Grace, Henri, Isabel, Juan, Kate, Larry, Mindy, Nicholas, Odette, Peter, Rose, Sam, Teresa, Victor, Wanda.

Eastern Pacific hurricanes — Andres, Blanca, Carlos, Dolores, Enrique, Felicia, Guillermo, Hilda, Ignacio, Jimena, Kevin, Linda, Marty, Nora, Olaf, Patricia, Rick, Sandra, Terry, Vivian, Waldo, Xina, York, Zelda.

Tides and Their Causes

Source: U.S. Dept. of Commerce, Natl. Oceanic & Atmospheric Admin. (NOAA), Natl. Ocean Service (NOS)

The tides are a natural phenomenon involving the alternating rise and fall in the large fluid bodies of the earth caused by the combined gravitational attraction of the sun and moon. The combination of these 2 variable influences produces the complex recurrent cycle of the tides. Tides may occur in both oceans and seas, to a limited extent in large lakes, in the atmosphere, and, to a very minute degree, in the earth itself. The length of time between succeeding tides varies as the result of many factors.

The tide-generating force represents the difference between (1) the centrifugal force produced by the revolution of the earth around the common center-of-gravity of the earth-moon system and (2) the gravitational attraction of the moon acting upon the earth's overlying waters. The moon is about 400 times closer than the sun; so despite its smaller mass, the moon's tide-raising force is 2.5 times greater.

The tide-generating forces of the moon and sun acting tangentially to the earth's surface tend to cause a maximum accumulation of waters at 2 diametrically opposite positions on the surface of the earth and to withdraw compensating amounts of water from all points 90° removed from these tidal bulges. As the earth rotates beneath the maxima and minima of these tide-generating forces, a sequence of 2 high tides, separated by 2 low tides, ideally is produced each day (semidiurnal tide).

Twice in each month, when the sun, moon, and earth are directly aligned, with the moon between the earth and sun (at new moon) or on the opposite side of the earth from the sun (at full moon), the sun and moon exert gravitational force in a mutual or additive fashion. The highest high tides and lowest low tides are produced at these times. These are called *spring* tides. At 2 positions 90° in between, the gravitational forces of the moon and sun—imposed at right angles—counteract each other to the greatest extent, and the range between high and low tides is reduced. These are called *neap* tides. This semi-monthly variation between spring and neap tides is called the *phase inequality*.

The inclination to the equator of the moon's monthly orbit and the inclination of the sun to the equator during the earth's yearly orbit produce a difference in the height of succeeding high tides and in the extent of depression of succeeding low tides that is known as the *diurnal inequality*. In most cases, this produces a so-called *mixed tide*. In extreme cases, these phenomena may result in only one high tide and one low tide each (*diurnal tide*). There are other monthly and yearly variations in the tide because of the elliptical shape of the orbits themselves.

U.S. convention distinguishes between Mean Higher High Water (MHHW), Mean High Water (MHW), Mean Tide Level (MTL), Mean Sea Level (MSL), Mean Low Water (MLW), and Mean Lower Low Water (MLLW). Diurnal range of tide is the difference in height between MHHW and MLLW. Mean range of tide is the difference between MHW and MLW.

The range of tide in the open ocean is less than in shoreline regions. However, as the ocean tide approaches shoal waters and its effects are augmented, the tidal range may be greatly increased. In Nova Scotia along the narrow channel of the Bay of Fundy, the range of tides, or difference between high and low waters, may reach 43½ feet or more (under spring tide conditions).

In every case, actual high or low tide can vary considerably from the average, as a result of weather conditions such as strong winds, abrupt barometric pressure changes, or prolonged periods of extreme high or low pressure.

Average Rise and Fall of Tides[1]

Places	Ft.	In.	Places	Ft.	In.	Places	Ft.	In.	Places	Ft.	In.
Baltimore, MD	1	8	Galveston, TX	1	5	Newport, RI	3	11	San Diego, CA	5	9
Boston, MA	10	4	Halifax, N.S.	4	5[2]	New York, NY	5	1	Sandy Hook, NJ	5	2
Charleston, SC	5	10	Hampton Roads, VA	2	10	Philadelphia, PA	6	9	San Francisco, CA	5	10
Cristobal, Panama	1	1	Key West, FL	1	10	Portland, ME	9	11	Seattle, WA	11	4
Eastport, ME	19	4	Mobile, AL	1	6	St. John's, Nfld.	2	7[2]	Vancouver, B.C.	10	6
Ft. Pulaski, GA	7	6	New London, CT	3	1	St. Petersburg, FL	2	3	Washington, DC	3	2

(1) Diurnal range. (2) Mean range.

Speed of Winds in the U.S.

Source: National Climatic Data Center, NESDIS, NOAA, U.S. Dept. of Commerce

In miles per hour; through 2000.

Station	Avg.	High	Station	Avg.	High	Station	Avg.	High
Albuquerque, NM	8.9	52	Honolulu, HI	11.3	46	Mt. Washington, NH	35.2	231
Anchorage, AK	7.1	75	Houston, TX	7.7	51	New Orleans, LA	8.2	69
Atlanta, GA	9.1	60	Indianapolis, IN	9.6	49	New York, NY(b)	9.3	40
Baltimore, MD	8.9	80	Jacksonville, FL	7.9	57	Omaha, NE	10.5	58
Bismarck, ND	10.2	55	Kansas City, MO	10.6	58	Philadelphia, PA	9.5	73
Boston, MA	12.4	54	Las Vegas, NV	9.3	56	Phoenix, AZ	6.2	43
Buffalo, NY	11.8	91	Lexington, KY	9.1	47	Pittsburgh, PA	9.0	58
Cape Hatteras, NC	10.9	60	Little Rock, AR	7.8	65	Portland, OR	7.9	88
Casper, WY	12.8	81	Los Angeles, CA	6.0	49	St. Louis, MO	9.7	52
Chicago, IL	10.4	58	Louisville, KY	8.3	56	Salt Lake City, UT	8.8	71
Denver, CO	8.6	46	Memphis, TN	8.8	51	San Diego, CA	7.0	56
Des Moines, IA	10.7	76	Miami, FL	9.2	86(a)	San Francisco, CA	8.7	47
Detroit, MI	10.3	53	Milwaukee, WI	11.5	54	Seattle, WA	8.9	66
Hartford, CT	8.4	46	Minn.-St. Paul, MN	10.5	51	Spokane, WA	8.9	59
Helena, MT	7.7	73	Mobile, AL	8.8	63	Washington, DC	9.4	49

(a) Highest velocity ever recorded in Miami area was 132 mph, at former station in Miami Beach in Sept. 1926. (b) Data for Central Park; Battery Place data through 1960, avg. 14.5, high 113.

El Niño

Source: National Weather Service, NOAA, U.S. Dept. of Commerce

El Niño is a climate phenomenon characterized by warmer-than-normal ocean temperatures in the equatorial E Pacific and along the tropical W coasts of Central and South America. The term *El Niño*, Spanish for "the Christ Child," was originally used by fishermen to refer to a warm ocean current appearing around Christmas and lasting several months. The term has come to be reserved for exceptionally strong, warm currents that bring heavy rains.

El Niño episodes generally occur every 2 to 6 years and last 12 to 18 months. The intensity of El Niño events varies; some are strong such as the 1982-83 and 1997-98 events; others are considerably weaker, based on intensity and area encompassed by the abnormally warm ocean temperatures. The eastward extent of warmer than normal water varies from episode to episode. Both global characteristics affect the patterns of temperature and precipitation.

El Niño influences weather around the globe, and its impacts are most clearly seen in the winter. During El Niño years, winter temperatures in the continental U.S. tend to be warmer than normal in the N and W coast states and cooler than normal in the SE. Conditions tend to be wetter than normal over central and southern California, the SW states and across much of the South, and drier than normal over the N portions of the Rocky Mountains and in the Ohio valley. Globally, El Niño brings wetter than normal conditions to Peru and Chile and dry conditions to Australia and Indonesia. It should be noted that El Niño is only one of a number of factors influencing seasonal variations of climate.

The opposite of El Niño is La Niña, with colder than normal sea surface temperatures in the tropical Pacific. La Niña typically brings wetter than normal conditions to the Pacific NW and warmer than normal temperatures to much of the southern U.S. during winter.

El Niño and La Niña episodes are monitored by observing systems, including satellites, moored buoys, and drifting buoys released by volunteer ships crossing the Pacific Ocean. Highly sophisticated numerical computer models of the global ocean and atmosphere use data from the observing systems to predict the onset and evolution of El Niño.

Lightning

Source: National Weather Service

There are an estimated 25 million cloud-to-ground lightning bolts in the U.S. each year, killing an annual average of 73 people. This is a small number compared to deaths from fire (about 4,000 a year) and motor vehicle accidents (about 40,000), but still significant. By way of comparison with other weather phenomena, tornadoes cause an average of 68 deaths a year, and hurricanes an average of 16. Documented injuries from lightning in the U.S. number about 300 a year.

Lightning is a result of ice in storm clouds. As ice particles rise and sink in the cloud, numerous collisions between them cause a separation of electrical charge. Positively charged crystals rise to the top, while negatively charged crystals drop to lower parts. As the storm travels, a pool of positive charges gathers in the ground below and follows along, traveling up objects like trees and telephone poles. In a common form of lightning, the negatively charged area in the storm sends charges downward; these are attracted to positively charged objects, and a channel develops, with an electrical transfer that you see as lightning. Lightning can travel miles away from the area of a storm.

The transfer of charges in lightning generates a huge amount of heat, sending the temperature in the channel to 30,000 degrees Fahrenheit and causing the air within it to expand rapidly; the sound of that expansion is thunder. Sound travels more slowly than light, so you usually see lightning before you hear thunder. A rule of thumb for gauging one's danger is the 30-30 rule. In good visibility, count the time between a lightning flash and the crack of thunder. If it's less than 30 seconds, it's time to seek shelter from the storm, which is within 6 miles. The threat of more lightning does not stop right away; you need to wait about 30 minutes after the last flash of the storm to be sure.

Most lightning deaths and injuries occur in the summer months when people are outdoors; when a storm threatens people need to move to a safe place promptly. Even indoors people are advised to stay away from windows and avoid contact with anything conducting electricity.

For more information about lightning, try the website www.lightningsafety.noaa.gov/overview.htm

Wind Chill Table

Source: National Weather Service, NOAA, U.S. Dept. of Commerce

Temperature and wind combine to cause heat loss from body surfaces. The following table shows that, for example, a temperature of 5° degrees Fahrenheit, plus a wind of 10 miles per hour, causes a body heat loss equal to that in minus 10 degrees temperature with no wind. In other words, a 10-mph wind makes 5° degrees feel like minus 10.

The National Weather Service issued new wind chill calculations in 2002. The top line of figures shows temperatures in degrees Fahrenheit. The column at far left shows wind speeds up to 45 mph. (Wind speeds greater than 45 mph have little additional chilling effect.) At wind chills in the shaded area, frostbite occurs in 15 minutes or less.

Calm	**40**	**35**	**30**	**25**	**20**	**15**	**10**	**5**	**0**	**–5**	**–10**	**–15**	**–20**	**–25**	**–30**	**–35**	**–40**	**–45**
5	36	31	25	19	13	7	1	–5	–11	–16	–22	–28	–34	–40	–46	–52	–57	–63
10	34	27	21	15	9	3	–4	–10	–16	–22	–28	–35	–41	–47	–53	–59	–66	–72
15	32	25	19	13	6	0	–7	–13	–19	–26	–32	–39	–45	–51	–58	–64	–71	–77
20	30	24	17	11	4	–2	–9	–15	–22	–29	–35	–42	–48	–55	–61	–68	–74	–81
25	29	23	16	9	3	–4	–11	–17	–24	–31	–37	–44	–51	–58	–64	–71	–78	–84
30	28	22	15	8	1	–5	–12	–19	–26	–33	–39	–46	–53	–60	–67	–73	–80	–87
35	28	21	14	7	0	–7	–14	–21	–27	–34	–41	–48	–55	–62	–69	–76	–82	–89
40	27	20	13	6	–1	–8	–15	–22	–29	–36	–43	–50	–57	–64	–71	–78	–84	–91

Heat Index

The heat index is a measure of the contribution high humidity makes, in combination with abnormally high temperatures, to reducing the body's ability to cool itself. For example, the index shows that an air temperature of 100° Fahrenheit with a relative humidity of 50% has the same effect on the human body as a temperature of 120° . Sunstroke and heat exhaustion are likely when the heat index reaches 105. This index is a measure of what hot weather "feels like" to the average person.

					Air Temperature*						
	70	**75**	**80**	**85**	**90**	**95**	**100**	**105**	**110**	**115**	**120**
Relative Humidity					**Apparent Temperature***						
0%	64	69	73	78	83	87	91	95	99	103	107
10%	65	70	75	80	85	90	95	100	105	111	116
20%	66	72	77	82	87	93	99	105	112	120	130
30%	67	73	78	84	90	96	104	113	123	135	148
40%	68	74	79	86	93	101	110	123	137	151	
50%	69	75	81	88	96	107	120	135	150		
60%	70	76	82	90	100	114	132	149			
70%	70	77	85	93	106	124	144				
80%	71	78	86	97	113	136					
90%	71	79	88	102	122						
100%	72	80	91	108							

*Degrees Fahrenheit

Ultraviolet (UV) Index Forecast

Source: National Weather Service, NOAA, U.S. Dept. of Commerce

The National Weather Service (NWS), Environmental Protection Agency (EPA), and Centers for Disease Control and Prevention (CDC) developed and began offering a UV index on June 28, 1994, in response to increasing incidence of skin cancer, cataracts, and other effects from exposure to the sun's harmful rays. The UV Index is now a regular element of NWS atmospheric forecasts.

UV Index number and forecast. The UV Index number, ranging from 0 to 10+, is an indication of the amount of UV radiation reaching the earth's surface over the one-hour period around noon. The lower the number, the less the radiation. The UV Index forecast is produced for 58 cities by the NWS Climate Prediction Center. The index number is based on several factors: latitude, day of year, time of day, total atmospheric ozone, elevation, and predicted cloud conditions. The index is valid for a radius of about 30 miles around a listed city; however, adjustments should be made for a number of factors.

Ozone. Ozone is measured by a NOAA polar orbiting satellite. The more ozone, the lower the UV radiation at the surface.

Cloudiness. Increased cloudiness lowers the Index number.

Reflectivity. Reflective surfaces intensify UV exposure. As an example, grass reflects 2.5% to 3% of UV radiation reaching the surface; sand, 20% to 30%; snow and ice, 80% to 90%; water, up to 100% (depending on reflection angle).

Elevation. At higher elevations, UV radiation travels a shorter distance to reach the surface so there is less atmosphere to absorb the rays. For every 4,000 ft. one travels above sea level, the UV Index increases by 1 unit. Snow and lack of pollutants intensify UV exposure at higher altitudes.

Latitude. The closer to the equator, the higher the UV radiation level.

Accuracy. After gathering data from 20 UV sensors (during June-Oct. 1994), the NWS determined that 32% of UV Index forecasts for that period were correct, 76% were within ±1 UV Index unit, and about 90% were within ±2 units. Unpredictable cloudiness, haze, and pollution contribute to forecast error.

SPF number. The UV Index is not linked in any way to the SPF number on suntan lotions and sunscreens. For an explanation of the SPF factor, contact the product's manufacturer or the Food and Drug Administration.

Further information. For precautions to take after learning the UV Index number, call the U.S. EPA hotline (800-296-1996) or your doctor. For questions on scientific aspects, call the NWS at 301-713-0622.

Global Measured Extremes of Temperature and Precipitation

Source: National Climatic Data Center

Highest Temperature Extremes

Continent	Highest Temp. (deg F)	Place	Elevation (Feet)	Date
Africa	136	El Azizia, Libya	367	Sept. 13, 1922
North America	134	Death Valley, CA (Greenland Ranch)	–178	July 10, 1913
Asia	129	Tirat Tsvi, Israel	–722	June 21, 1942
Australia	128	Cloncurry, Queensland	622	Jan. 16, 1889
Europe	122	Seville, Spain	26	Aug. 4, 1881
South America	120	Rivadavia, Argentina	676	Dec. 11, 1905
Oceania	108	Tuguegarao, Philippines	72	Apr. 29, 1912
Antarctica	59	Vanda Station, Scott Coast	49	Jan. 5, 1974

Lowest Temperature Extremes

Continent	Lowest Temp. (deg F)	Place	Elevation (Feet)	Date
Antarctica	–129.0	Vostok	11,220	July 21, 1983
Asia	–90.0	Oimekon, Russia	2,625	Feb. 6, 1933
Asia	–90.0	Verkhoyansk, Russia	350	Feb. 7, 1892
Greenland	–87.0	Northice	7,687	Jan. 9, 1954
North America	–81.4	Snag, Yukon, Canada	2,120	Feb. 3, 1947
Europe	–67.0	Ust'Shchugor, Russia	279	Jan.*
South America	–27.0	Sarmiento, Argentina	879	June 1, 1907
Africa	–11.0	Ifrane, Morocco	5,364	Feb. 11, 1935
Australia	–9.4	Charlotte Pass, NSW	5,758	June 29, 1994
Oceania	14.0	Haleakala Summit, Maui, HI	9,750	Jan. 2, 1961

* Exact day and year unknown.

Highest Average Annual Precipitation Extremes

Continent	Highest Avg. (Inches)	Place	Elevation (Feet)	Years of Data
South America	523.6[1,2]	Lloro, Colombia	520[3]	29
Asia	467.4[1]	Mawsynram, India	4,597	38
Oceania	460.0[1]	Mt. Waialeale, Kauai, HI	5,148	30
Africa	405.0	Debundscha, Cameroon	30	32
South America	354.0[2]	Quibdo, Colombia	120	16
Australia	340.0	Bellenden Ker, Queensland	5,102	9
North America	256.0	Henderson Lake, British Columbia	12	14
Europe	183.0	Crkvica, Bosnia-Herzegovina	3,337	22

(1) The value given is continent's highest and possibly the world's depending on measurement practices, procedures, and period of record variations. (2) The official greatest average annual precipitation for South America is 354 inches at Quibdo, Colombia. The 523.6 inches average at Lloro, Colombia (14 miles SE and at a higher elevation than Quibdo) is an estimated amount. (3) Approximate elevation.

Lowest Average Annual Precipitation Extremes

Continent	Lowest Avg. (Inches)	Place	Elevation (Feet)	Years of Data
South America	0.03	Arica, Chile	95	59
Africa	<0.1	Wadi Halfa, Sudan	410	39
Antarctica	0.8[1]	Amundsen-Scott South Pole Station	9,186	10
North America	1.2	Batagues, Mexico	16	14
Asia	1.8	Aden, Yemen	22	50
Australia	4.05	Mulka (Troudaninna), South Australia	160[2]	42
Europe	6.4	Astrakhan, Russia	45	25
Oceania	8.93	Puako, Hawaii	5	13

(1) The value given is the average amount of solid snow accumulating in one year as indicated by snow markers. The liquid content of the snow is undetermined. (2) Approximate elevation.

DISASTERS

As of Oct. 1, 2002. Listings in this chapter are selective and may not include acts of terrorism, war related disasters, or disasters with relatively low fatalities.

Some Notable Shipwrecks Since 1854

(Figures indicate estimated lives lost. Does not include most military disasters.)

1854, Mar.—City of Glasgow; Brit. steamer missing in N Atlantic; 480.
1854, Sept. 27—Arctic; U.S. (Collins Line) steamer sunk in collision with French steamer *Vesta* near Cape Race; 285-351.
1856, Jan. 23—Pacific; U.S. (Collins Line) steamer missing in N Atlantic; 186-286.
1858, Sept. 23—Austria; German steamer destroyed by fire in N Atlantic; 471.
1863, Apr. 27—Anglo-Saxon; Brit. steamer wrecked at Cape Race; 238.
1865, Apr. 27—Sultana; Mississippi River steamer blew up near Memphis, TN; 1,450.
1869, Oct. 27—Stonewall; steamer burned on Mississippi River below Cairo, IL; 200.
1870, Jan. 25—City of Boston; Brit. (Inman Line) steamer vanished between New York and Liverpool; 177.
1870, Oct. 19—Cambria; Brit. steamer wrecked off N Ireland; 196.
1872, Nov. 7—Mary Celeste; U.S. half-brig sailed from New York for Genoa; found abandoned; loss of life unknown.
1873, Jan. 22—Northfleet; Brit. steamer foundered off Dungeness, England; 300.
1873, Apr. 1—Atlantic; Brit. (White Star) steamer wrecked off Nova Scotia; 585.
1873, Nov. 23—Ville du Havre; French steamer sank after collision with Brit. sailing ship *Loch Earn*; 226.
1875, May 7—Schiller; German steamer wrecked off Scilly Isles; 312.
1875, Nov. 4—Pacific; U.S. steamer sank after collision off Cape Flattery; 236.
1878, Sept. 3—Princess Alice; Brit. steamer sank after collision in Thames River; 700.
1878, Dec. 18—Byzantin; French steamer sank after collision in Dardanelles; 210.
1881, May 24—Victoria; steamer capsized in Thames River, Canada; 200.
1883, Jan. 19—Cimbria; German steamer sank in collision with Brit. steamer *Sultan* in North Sea; 389.
1887, Nov. 15—Wah Yeung; Brit. steamer burned at sea; 400.
1890, Feb. 17—Duburg; Brit. steamer wrecked, China Sea; 400.
1890, Sept. 19—Ertogrul; Turkish frigate wrecked off Japan; 540.
1891, Mar. 17—Utopia; Brit. steamer sank in collision with Brit. ironclad *Anson* off Gibraltar; 562.
1895, Jan. 30—Elbe; German steamer sank in collision with Brit. steamer *Craithie* in North Sea; 332.
1895, Mar. 11—Reina Regenta; Spanish cruiser foundered near Gibraltar; 400.
1898, Feb. 15—Maine; U.S. battleship blown up in Havana Harbor; 260.
1898, July 4—La Bourgogne; French steamer sank in collision with Brit. sailing ship *Cromartyshire* off Nova Scotia; 549.
1898, Nov. 26—Portland; U.S. steamer wrecked off Cape Cod; 157.
1904, June 15—General Slocum; excursion steamer burned in East River, New York City; 1,030.
1904, June 28—Norge; Danish steamer wrecked on Rockall Island, Scotland; 620.
1906, Aug. 4—Sirio; Italian steamer wrecked off Cape Palos, Spain; 350.
1908, Mar. 23—Matsu Maru; Japanese steamer sank in collision near Hakodate, Japan; 300.
1909, Aug. 1—Waratah; Brit. steamer, Sydney to London, vanished; 300.
1910, Feb. 9—General Chanzy; French steamer wrecked off Minorca, Spain; 200.
1911, Sept. 25—Liberté; French battleship exploded at Toulon, 285.
1912, Mar. 5—Principe de Asturias; Spanish steamer wrecked off Spain; 500.
1912, Apr. 14-15—Titanic; Brit. (White Star) steamer hit iceberg in N Atlantic; 1,503.
1912, Sept. 28—Kichemaru; Japanese steamer sank off Japanese coast; 1,000.
1914, May 29—Empress of Ireland; Brit. (Canadian Pacific) steamer sunk in collision with Norwegian collier in St. Lawrence River; 1,014.
1915, May 7—Lusitania; Brit. (Cunard Line) steamer torpedoed and sunk by German submarine off Ireland; 1,198.
1915, July 24—Eastland; excursion steamer capsized in Chicago River; 812.
1916, Feb. 26—Provence; French cruiser sank in Mediterranean; 3,100.
1916, Mar. 3—Principe de Asturias; Spanish steamer wrecked near Santos, Brazil; 558.
1916, Aug. 29—Hsin Yu; Chinese steamer sank off Chinese coast; 1,000.
1917, Dec. 6—Mont Blanc, Imo; French ammunition ship and Belgian steamer collided in Halifax Harbor; 1,600.
1918, Apr. 25—Kiang-Kwan; Chinese steamer sank in collision off Hankow; 500.
1918, July 12—Kawachi; Japanese battleship blew up in Tokayama Bay; 500.
1918, Oct. 25—Princess Sophia; Canadian steamer sank off Alaskan coast; 398.
1919, Jan. 17—Chaonia; French steamer lost in Straits of Messina, Italy; 460.
1919, Sept. 9—Valbanera; Spanish steamer lost off Florida coast; 500.
1921, Mar. 18—Hong Kong; steamer wrecked in South China Sea; 1,000.
1922, Aug. 26—Niitaka; Japanese cruiser sank in storm off Kamchatka, USSR; 300.
1924, June 12—USS Mississippi; U.S. battleship; explosions in gun turret, off San Pedro, CA; 48.
1927, Oct. 25—Principessa Mafalda; Italian steamer blew up, sank off Porto Seguro, Brazil; 314.
1928, Nov. 12—Vestris; Brit. steamer sank off Virginia; 113.
1934, Sept. 8—Morro Castle; U.S. steamer, Havana to New York, burned off Asbury Park, NJ; 134.
1939, May 23—Squalus; U.S. submarine sank off Portsmouth, NH; 26.
1939, June 1—Thetis; submarine sank, Liverpool Bay; 99.
1942, Feb. 18—Truxtun and **Pollux;** U.S. destroyer and cargo ship ran aground, sank off Newfoundland; 204.
1942, Oct. 2—Curacao; Brit. cruiser sank after collision with liner *Queen Mary;* 338.
1944, Dec. 17-18—3 U.S. Third Fleet destroyers sank during typhoon in Philippine Sea; 790.
1947, Jan. 19—Himera; Greek steamer hit a mine off Athens; 392.
1947, Apr. 16—Grandcamp; French freighter exploded in Texas City, TX, harbor, starting fires; 510.
1948, Nov.—Chinese army evacuation ship exploded and sank off S Manchuria; 6,000.
1948, Dec. 3—Kiangya; Chinese refugee ship wrecked in explosion S of Shanghai; 1,100+.
1949, Sept. 17—Noronic; Canadian Great Lakes Cruiser burned at Toronto dock; 130.
1952, Apr. 26—Hobson and Wasp; U.S. destroyer and aircraft carrier collided in Atlantic; 176.
1954, May 26—Pennington; sank off Rhode Island; 103.
1954, Sept. 26—Toya Maru; Japanese ferry sank in Tsugaru Strait, Japan; 1,172.
1956, July 26—Andrea Doria and **Stockholm;** Italian liner and Swedish liner collided off Nantucket; 51.
1957, July 14—Eshghabad; Soviet ship ran aground in Caspian Sea; 270.
1960, Dec. 19—Constellation; U.S. aircraft carrier caught fire in Brooklyn Navy Yard, NY; 49.
1961, Apr. 8—Dara; British ocean liner exploded in Persian Gulf; 236.
1961, July 8—Save; Portuguese ship ran aground off Mozambique; 259.
1963, Apr. 10—Thresher; U.S. Navy atomic submarine sank in N Atlantic; 129.
1964, Feb. 10—Australian destroyer *Voyager* sank after collision with aircraft carrier *Melbourne* off New South Wales; 82.
1965, Nov. 13—Yarmouth Castle; Panamanian registered cruise ship burned and sank off Nassau; 89.
1967, July 29—Forrestal; U.S. aircraft carrier caught fire off N Vietnam; 134.
1968, Jan. 25—Dakar; Israeli submarine vanished in Mediterranean Sea; 69.
1968, late May—Scorpion; U.S. nuclear submarine sank in Atlantic near Azores; 99 (located Oct. 31).
1969, June 2—Evans; U.S. destroyer cut in half by Australian carrier *Melbourne*, S China Sea; 74.
1970, Mar. 4—Eurydice; French submarine sank in Mediterranean near Toulon; 57.
1970, Dec. 15—Namyong-Ho; South Korean ferry sank in Korea Strait; 308.
1974, May 1—Motor launch capsized off Bangladesh; 250.
1974, Sept. 26—Soviet destroyer sank in Black Sea; 200+.
1975, Nov. 10—Edmund Fitzgerald; U.S. cargo ship sank during storm on Lake Superior; 29.
1976, Oct. 20—George Prince and **Frosta;** ferryboat and Norwegian tanker collided on Mississippi R. at Luling, LA; 77.
1976, Dec. 25—Patria; Egyptian liner caught fire and sank in the Red Sea; 100.
1979, Aug. 14—23 yachts competing in Fastnet yacht race sank or abandoned during storm in S Irish Sea; 18.
1980, Sept. 9—Derbyshire; British bulk carrier sank in typhoon in Pacific Ocean near Okinawa, Japan; 44.
1981, Jan. 27—Tamponas II; Indonesian passenger ship caught fire and sank in Java Sea; 580.
1981, May 26—Nimitz; U.S. Marine combat jet crashed on deck of U.S. aircraft carrier; 14.
1983, Feb. 12—Marine Electric; coal freighter sank during storm off Chincoteague, VA; 33.
1983, May 25—10th of Ramadan; Nile steamer caught fire and sank in Lake Nasser; 357.

1986, Apr. 20—ferry sank near Barisal, Bangladesh; 262.
1986, Aug. 31—Soviet passenger ship *Admiral Nakhimov* and Soviet freighter *Pyotr Vasev* collided in Black Sea; 398.
1987, Mar. 6—British ferry capsized off Zeebrugge, Belgium; 189.
1987, Dec. 20—Philippine ferry *Dona Paz* and oil tanker *Victor* collided in Tablas Strait; 4,341.
1988, Aug. 6—Indian ferry capsized on Ganges R.; 400+.
1989, Apr. 19—USS Iowa; explosion in gun turret; 47.
1989, Aug. 20—Brit. barge *Bowbelle* struck Brit. pleasure cruiser *Marchioness* on Thames R. in central London; 56.
1989, Sept. 10—Romanian pleasure boat and Bulgarian barge collided on Danube R.; 161.
1991, Apr. 10—Auto ferry and oil tanker collided outside Livorno Harbor, Italy; 140.
1991, Dec. 14—Salem Express; ferry rammed coral reef near Safaga, Egypt; 462.
1993, Feb. 17—Neptune; ferry capsized off Port-au-Prince, Haiti; 500+.
1993, Oct. 10—West Sea Ferry; capsized in Yellow Sea near W South Korea during storm; 285.
1994, Sept. 28—Estonia; ferry sank in Baltic Sea; 1,049.
1996, May 21—Bukoba; ferry sank in Lake Victoria (Africa); 500.
1997, Feb. 20—Tamil refugee boat sank off Sri Lanka; 165.
1997, Mar. 28—Albanian refugee boat sank in Adriatic Sea after being rammed by Italian navy warship *Sibilla*; 83.
1997, Sept. 8—Pride of la Gonâve; Haitian ferry sank off Montrouis, Haiti; 200+.
1998, Apr. 4—passenger boat capsized off coast near Ibaka beach, Nigeria; 280.
1998, Sept. 2—2 passenger boats capsized on Lake Kivu, near Bukavu, Congo; 200+.
1998, Sept. 18—ferry sank S of Manila; 97.
1999, Feb. 6—Harta Rimba; cargo ship sank off Indonesia; 280+.
1999, Mar. 26—passenger boat overturned off coast, Sierra Leone; 150+.
1999, Apr. 2—passenger ferry sank off coast of Nigeria; 100+.
1999, May 1—amphibious excursion boat sank in Lake Hamilton, AR; 13.
1999, May 8—passenger ferry capsized off Bangladesh; 200+.
1999, Nov. 24—Dashun; passenger ferry capsized near Yantai, China; 280.
2000, May 3—2 ferries capsized in storm in Meghna R., Bangladesh; 72+.
2000, June 29—overloaded ferry capsized in storm off Sulawesi Island, Indonesia; 500+.
2000, Aug. 12—Kursk; Russian submarine sank in Barents Sea; 118.
2000, Sept. 26—Express Samina; Greek ferry sank off Paros, Greece; 81+.
2001, Feb. 9—Ehime Maru; Japanese trawler sunk by surfacing U.S. submarine *Greeneville*, near Hawaii; 9.
2001, Dec. 22—North Korean spy ship sank after exchanging fire with Japanese coast guard; 15.
2002, May 4—Bangladesh ferry sunk in storm on Meghna R.; 370+.
2002, May 26—barge struck Interstate highway bridge over Arkansas R. in Oklahoma; 13+.
2002, Sept. 26—overloaded Senegalese ferry capsized in ocean off The Gambia; 950+

Some Notable Aircraft Disasters Since 1937

Date	Aircraft	Site of accident	Deaths
1937, May 6	German zeppelin Hindenburg	Burned at mooring, Lakehurst, NJ	36*
1944, Aug. 23	U.S. Air Force B-24 Liberator bomber	Hit school, Freckleton, England	61*
1945, July 28	U.S. Army B-25	Hit Empire State Building, New York, NY	14*
1952, Dec. 20	U.S. Air Force C-124	Fell, burned, Moses Lake, WA	87
1953, Mar. 3	Canadian Pacific Comet Jet	Karachi, Pakistan	11[1]
1953, June 18	U.S. Air Force C-124	Crashed, burned near Tokyo	129
1955, Oct. 6	United Airlines DC-4	Crashed in Medicine Bow Peak, WY	66
1955, Nov. 1	United Airlines DC-6B	Exploded, crashed near Longmont, CO	44[2]
1956, June 20	Venezuelan Super-Constellation	Crashed in Atlantic off Asbury Park, NJ	74
1956, June 30	TWA Super-Const., United DC-7	Collided over Grand Canyon, AZ	128
1960, Dec. 16	United DC-8 jet, TWA Super-Const.	Collided over New York City	134[3]
1962, Mar. 16	Flying Tiger Super-Constellation	Vanished in W Pacific	107
1962, June 3	Air France Boeing 707 jet	Crashed on takeoff from Paris	130
1962, June 22	Air France Boeing 707 jet	Crashed in storm, Guadeloupe, W.I.	113
1963, June 3	Chartered Northwest Airlines DC-7	Crashed in Pacific off British Columbia	101
1963, Nov. 29	Trans-Canada Airlines DC-8F	Crashed after takeoff from Montreal	118
1965, May 20	Pakistani Boeing 720-B	Crashed at Cairo, Egypt, airport	121
1966, Jan. 24	Air India Boeing 707 jetliner	Crashed on Mont Blanc, France-Italy	117
1966, Feb. 4	All-Nippon Boeing 727	Plunged into Tokyo Bay	133
1966, Mar. 5	BOAC Boeing 707 jetliner	Crashed on Mount Fuji, Japan	124
1966, Dec. 24	U.S. military-chartered CL-44	Crashed into village in South Vietnam	129*
1967, Apr. 20	Swiss Britannia turboprop	Crashed at Nicosia, Cyprus	126
1967, July 19	Piedmont Boeing 727, Cessna 310	Collided in air, Hendersonville, NC	82
1968, Apr. 20	S. African Airways Boeing 707	Crashed on takeoff, Windhoek, South-West Africa	122
1968, May 3	Braniff International Electra	Crashed in storm near Dawson, TX	85
1969, Mar. 16	Venezuelan DC-9	Crashed after takeoff from Maracaibo, Venezuela	155[4]
1969, Dec. 8	Olympic Airways DC-6B	Crashed near Athens in storm	93
1970, Feb. 15	Dominican DC-9	Crashed into sea on takeoff from Santo Domingo	102
1970, July 3	British chartered jetliner	Crashed near Barcelona, Spain	112
1970, July 5	Air Canada DC-8	Crashed near Toronto International Airport	108
1970, Aug. 9	Peruvian turbojet	Crashed after takeoff from Cuzco, Peru	101*
1970, Nov. 14	Southern Airways DC-9	Crashed in mountains near Huntington, WV	75[5]
1971, July 30	All-Nippon Boeing 727 and Japanese Air Force F-86	Collided over Morioka, Japan	162[6]
1971, Sept. 4	Alaska Airlines Boeing 727	Crashed into mountain near Juneau, AK	111
1972, Aug. 14	East German Ilyushin-62	Crashed on takeoff, East Berlin	156
1972, Oct. 13	Aeroflot Ilyushin-62	Crashed near Moscow	176
1972, Dec. 3	Chartered Spanish airliner	Crashed on takeoff, Canary Islands	155
1972, Dec. 29	Eastern Airlines Lockheed Tristar	Crashed on approach to Miami Intl. Airport	101
1973, Jan. 22	Chartered Boeing 707	Burst into flames during landing, Kano Airport, Nigeria	176
1973, Feb. 21	Libyan jetliner	Shot down by Israeli fighter planes over Sinai	108
1973, Apr. 10	British Vanguard turboprop	Crashed during snowstorm at Basel, Switzerland	104
1973, June 3	Soviet Supersonic TU-144	Crashed near Goussainville, France	14[7]
1973, July 11	Brazilian Boeing 707	Crashed on approach to Orly Airport, Paris	122
1973, July 31	Delta Airlines jetliner	Crashed, landing in fog at Logan Airport, Boston	89
1973, Dec. 23	French Caravelle jet	Crashed in Morocco	106
1974, Mar. 3	Turkish DC-10 jet	Crashed at Ermenonville near Paris	346
1974, Apr. 23	Pan American 707 jet	Crashed in Bali, Indonesia	107
1974, Dec. 1	TWA-727	Crashed in storm, Upperville, VA	92
1974, Dec. 4	Dutch-chartered DC-8	Crashed in storm near Colombo, Sri Lanka	191
1975, Apr. 4	Air Force Galaxy C-5A	Crashed near Saigon, S Viet., after takeoff (carrying orphans)	172
1975, June 24	Eastern Airlines 727 jet	Crashed in storm, JFK Airport, NY	113
1975, Aug. 3	Chartered 707	Hit mountainside, Agadir, Morocco	188
1976, Sept. 10	British Airways Trident, Yugoslav DC-9	Collided near Zagreb, Yugoslavia	176
1976, Sept. 19	Turkish 727	Hit mountain, S Turkey	155
1976, Oct. 13	Bolivian 707 cargo jet	Crashed in Santa Cruz, Bolivia	100[8]
1977, Mar. 27	KLM 747, Pan American 747	Collided on runway, Tenerife, Canary Islands	582[9]
1977, Nov. 19	TAP Boeing 727	Crashed on Madeira	130

Date	Aircraft	Site of accident	Deaths
1977, Dec. 4	Malaysian Boeing 737	Hijacked, then exploded in mid-air over Straits of Johore	100
1977, Dec. 13	U.S. DC-3	Crashed after takeoff at Evansville, IN	29[10]
1978, Jan. 1	Air India 747	Exploded, crashed into sea off Bombay	213
1978, Sept. 25	Boeing 727, Cessna 172	Collided in air, San Diego, CA	150
1978, Nov. 15	Chartered DC-8	Crashed near Colombo, Sri Lanka	183
1979, May 25	American Airlines DC-10	Crashed after takeoff at O'Hare Intl. Airport, Chicago	275[11]
1979, Aug. 17	Two Soviet Aeroflot jetliners	Collided over Ukraine	173
1979, Nov. 26	Pakistani Boeing 707	Crashed near Jidda, Saudi Arabia	156
1979, Nov. 28	New Zealand DC-10	Crashed into mountain in Antarctica	257
1980, Mar. 14	Polish Ilyushin 62	Crashed making emergency landing, Warsaw	87[12]
1980, Aug. 19	Saudi Arabian Tristar	Burned after emergency landing, Riyadh	301
1981, Dec. 1	Yugoslavian DC-9	Crashed into mountain in Corsica	178
1982, Jan. 13	Air Florida Boeing 737	Crashed into Potomac R. after takeoff	78
1982, July 9	Pan Am Boeing 727	Crashed after takeoff in Kenner, LA	153[13]
1983, Sept. 1	S. Korean Boeing 747	Shot down after violating Soviet airspace	269
1983, Nov. 27	Colombian Boeing 747	Crashed near Barajas Airport, Madrid	183
1985, Feb. 19	Spanish Boeing 727	Crashed into Mt. Oiz, Spain	148
1985, June 23	Air-India Boeing 747	Crashed into Atlantic Ocean S of Ireland	329
1985, Aug. 2	Delta Air Lines L-1011	Crashed at Dallas-Ft. Worth Intl. Airport	137
1985, Aug. 12	Japan Air Lines Boeing 747	Crashed into Mt. Ogura, Japan	520[14]
1985, Dec. 12	Arrow Air DC-8	Crashed after takeoff in Gander, Newfoundland	256[15]
1986, Mar. 31	Mexican Boeing 727	Crashed NW of Mexico City	166
1986, Aug. 31	Aeromexico DC-9	Collided with Piper PA-28 over Cerritos, CA	82[16]
1987, May 9	Polish Ilyushin 62M	Crashed after takeoff in Warsaw, Poland	183
1987, Aug. 16	Northwest Airlines MD-82	Crashed after takeoff in Romulus, MI	156
1987, Nov. 28	S. African Boeing 747	Crashed into Indian Ocean near Mauritius	159
1987, Nov. 29	S. Korean Boeing 707	Exploded over Thai-Burmese border	155
1988, Mar. 17	Colombian Boeing 707	Crashed into mountainside near Venezuela border	137
1988, July 3	Iranian A300 Airbus	Shot down by U.S. Navy warship *Vincennes* over Persian Gulf	290
1988, Dec. 21	Pan Am Boeing 747	Exploded and crashed in Lockerbie, Scotland	270[17]
1989, Feb. 8	U.S. Boeing 707	Crashed into mountain in Azores Islands off Portugual	144
1989, June 7	Suriname DC-8	Crashed near Paramaribo Airport, Suriname	168
1989, July 19	United Airlines DC-10	Crashed while landing in Sioux City, IA	111
1989, Sept. 19	French DC-10	Exploded in air over Niger	171
1990, Oct. 2	Chinese airline Boeing 737	Hijacked; upon landing in Guangzhou, crashed on ground	132
1991, May 26	Lauda-Air Boeing 767-300	Exploded over rural Thailand	223
1991, July 11	Nigerian DC-8	Crashed while landing at Jidda, Saudi Arabia	261
1991, Oct. 5	Indonesian military transport	Crashed after takeoff from Jakarta	137*
1992, July 31	Thai Airbus A-300-310	Crashed into mountain S. of Kathmandu, Nepal	113
1992, Oct. 4	El Al Boeing 747-200F	Crashed into 2 apartment bldgs., Amsterdam, Netherlands	120*
1994, Jan. 3	Aeroflot TU-154	Crashed and exploded after takeoff in Irkhutsk, Russia	125[18]
1994, Apr. 26	China Airlines Airbus A-300-600R	Crashed at Japan's Nagoya Airport	264
1994, June 16	China Northwest Airlines TU-154	Crashed 10 min. after takeoff	160
1994, Sept. 8	USAir Boeing 737-300	Crashed in Aliquippa, PA, near Pittsburgh Intl. Airport	132
1994, Oct. 31	American Eagle ATR-72-210	Crashed in field near Roselawn, IN	68
1995, Aug. 11	Aviateca Boeing 737	Crashed into Chichontepec volcano, El Salvador	65
1995, Dec. 20	American Airlines Boeing 757	Crashed into mountain 50 mi N of Cali, Colombia	160
1996, Jan. 8	Antonova 32 cargo jet	Crashed into central market, Kinshasa, Zaire	350+*
1996, Feb. 6	Turkish Boeing 757	Crashed into Atlantic Ocean, off Dominican Republic	189
1996, Apr. 25	T-43, a military version of a Boeing 737	Crashed into mountain near Dubrovnik, Croatia	35[19]
1996, May 11	ValuJet DC-9	Crashed into the Florida Everglades after takeoff	110
1996, July 17	Trans World Airlines Boeing 747	Exploded and crashed in Atlantic Ocean, off Long Isl., NY	230
1996, Aug. 29	Vnukovo TU-154	Crashed into mountain on Arctic island of Spitsbergen	141
1996, Oct. 2	Aeroperu Boeing 757	Crashed in Pacific after takeoff from Lima, Peru	70
1996, Oct. 31	Brazilian TAM Fokker-100	Crashed into houses in São Paulo, Brazil	98[20]
1996, Nov. 7	Nigerian Boeing 727	Crashed into a lagoon 40 mi SE of Lagos, Nigeria	143
1996, Nov. 12	Saudi Arabian Boeing 747, Kazakh Ilyushin-76 cargo plane	Collided in midair near New Delhi, India	349[21]
1996, Nov. 23	Ethiopian Boeing 767	Hijacked, then crashed in Indian Ocean off the Comoros	127
1997, Jan. 9	Comair Embraer 120	Crashed on approach into Detroit Metro. Airport	29
1997, Feb. 4	2 Sikorsky CH-53 transport helicopters	Collided in midair over northern Galilee, Israel	73
1997, May 8	China Southern Airlines Boeing 737	Crashed on approach into Shenzhen's Huangtian Airport	35
1997, July 11	Cubana de Aviación Antonov-24	Crashed into the Caribbean off SE Cuba	44
1997, Aug. 6	Korean Air Boeing 747-300	Crashed into jungle on Guam on approach into airport	228
1997, Sept. 3	Vietnamese Airlines Tupolev TU-134	Crashed on approach into Phnom Penh airport	64
1997, Sept. 14	U.S. C-141 cargo plane, Ger. TU-154	Collided in midair off SW Africa	33
1997, Sept. 26	Indonesian Airbus A-300	Crashed near Medan, Indonesia, airport	234
1997, Oct. 10	Austral Airlines DC-9-32	Crashed and exploded near Neuvo Berlin, Uruguay	74
1997, Dec. 6	Russian AN-124 transport cargo plane	Crashed into apartment complex near Irkutsk, Siberia	67*
1997, Dec. 15	Chartered TU-154 from Tajikistan	Crashed in desert near Sharja, U.A.E., airport	85
1997, Dec. 17	Chartered Yakovlev-42 from Ukraine	Crashed in mountains near Katerini, Greece	70
1997, Dec. 19	SilkAir Boeing 737-300	Crashed in Musi River, Sumatra, Indonesia	104
1998, Jan. 14	Afghan cargo plane	Crashed into mountain, SW Pakistan	50+
1998, Feb. 2	Cebu Pacific Air DC-9-32	Crashed into mountain near Cagayan de Oro, Philippines	104
1998, Feb. 16	China Airlines Airbus 300-622R	Crashed on approach to airport, Taipei, Taiwan	203[22]
1998, Apr. 20	Air France Boeing 727-200	Crashed into mountain after takeoff from Bogotá, Colombia	53
1998, Sept. 2	Swissair MD-11	Crashed into Atlantic Ocean off Halifax, Nova Scotia	229
1998, Sept. 25	Pauknair BAE146	Crashed into hillside in Morocco	38
1998, Oct. 11	Congo Air Lines Boeing 727	Shot down by rebels in Kindu, Congo	40
1998, Dec. 11	Thai Airways Airbus A310-200	Crashed short of runway at Surat Thani airport, southern Thailand	101
1999, Feb. 24	China Southwest Airlines TU-154	Crashed on approach to Wenzhou airport, eastern China	61
1999, Sept. 1	LAPA Boeing 737-200	Crashed on takeoff from Jorge Newbery Airport, Buenos Aires	74[23]
1999, Oct. 31	EgyptAir Boeing 767-300	Crashed off Nantucket, MA	217
2000, Apr. 8	Marine Corps V-22 Osprey	Crashed landing at Marana, AZ	19
2000, Jan. 31	Alaska Airlines MD-83	Crashed into Pacific Ocean NW of Malibu, CA	88
2000, Apr. 19	Air Philippines Boeing 737-200	Crashed by Davao airport	131
2000, May 21	Chartered Jetstream 31	Crashed near Wilkes-Barre, PA	19
2000, July 25	Air France Concorde	Crashed into hotel after takeoff from Paris	113[25]
2000, Aug. 9	Piper Navajo and Piper Seminole	Collided over a housing development in Burlington, NJ	11
2000, Aug. 23	Gulf Air Airbus A320	Crashed into Persian Gulf near Manama, Bahrain	143

Date	Aircraft	Site of accident	Deaths
2000, Oct. 31	Singapore Airlines 747-400	Crashed immediately after takeoff, Taipei, Taiwan	81
2000, Oct. 31	Chartered Antonov 26	Exploded after takeoff in northern Angola	50
2000, Nov. 15	Chartered Antonov 24	Crashed after takeoff from Luanda, Angola	40+
2001, Jan. 27	Chartered Beechcraft King Air 200	Crashed after takeoff from Boulder, CO	10[26]
2001, Mar. 3	C23 Sherpa mil. transp.	Crashed in storm, central GA	21
2001, Mar. 29	Chartered Gulfstream III jet	Crashed into hillside on approach to Aspen, CO	18
2001, Apr. 7	M-17 helicopter	Crashed into mountain S. of Hanoi, Vietnam	16[27]
2001, July 3	Vladivostokavia Tu-154	Crashed on approach to landing at Irkutsk, Russia	145
2001, Sept. 11	2 Boeing 767s, 2 Boeing 757s	see below[28]	265[28]
2001, Oct. 4	Sibir Airlines Tupelov Tu-154	Crashed into Black Sea, struck by errant Ukrainian missile	78
2001, Oct. 8	Twin-engine Cessna, Scandinavian Airlines System (SAS) jetliner	Collided in heavy fog during takeoff from Milan, Italy	118*
2001, Nov. 12	American Airlines Airbus A-300	Crashed after takeoff from JFK Airport, New York, NY	265*
2002, Jan. 17	Petroproduccion Fairchild FH-227E	Crashed into mountain in S Colombia	26
2002, Jan. 28	Ecuadoran airline Boeing 727-100	Crashed in Andes mountains in southern Colombia	92
2002, Feb. 12	Iran Air Tours Tu-154	Crashed before landing in Khorramabad, Iran	119
2002, Apr. 15	Air China Boeing 767-200	Crashed into hillside amid rain and fog near Pusan, South Korea	122
2002, Apr. 18	4-seat Rockwell Commander	Crashed into Pirelli building, tallest skyscraper in Milan, Italy	3*
2002, May 4	EAS Airlines BAC 1-11-500	Crashed in suburb of Kano, Nigeria, shortly after takeoff	148+*
2002, May 7	China Northern MD-82	Plunged into Yellow Sea near Dalian, China, after fire in cabin	112
2002, May 25	China Airlines Boeing 747-200	Broke apart in mid-air and plunged into Taiwan Strait	225
2002, July 1	Bashkirian Airlines Tupolev Tu-154 and DHL (German cargo) Boeing 757	Collided over S Germany	71
2002, July 4	Prestige Airlines Cargo Boeing B-707	Crashed short of runway in Bangui, Central African Rep.	25
2002, July 27	Ukraine Air Force Sukhoi SU-27	Crashed into spectators at airshow in Lviv, Ukraine	85
2002, Aug. 19	Russian Mi-26 helicopter	Troop-carrier hit by Chechen missile near Grozny	118+

*Including those on ground and in buildings. (1) First fatal crash of commercial jet plane. (2) Caused by bomb planted by John G. Graham in insurance plot to kill his mother, a passenger. (3) Incl. all 128 aboard planes and 6 on ground. (4) Killed 84 on plane and 71 on ground. (5) Incl. 43 Marshall Univ. football players and coaches. (6) Airliner-fighter crash; pilot of fighter parachuted to safety, was arrested for negligence. (7) First supersonic plane crash; killed 6 crew and 8 on ground; there were no passengers. (8) Crew of 3 killed; 97, mostly children, killed on the ground. (9) World's worst airline disaster. (10) Incl. Univ. of Evansville basketball team. (11) Incl. 2 on ground. Highest death toll in U.S. aviation history. (12) Incl. 22 members of U.S. boxing team. (13) Incl. 8 on ground. (14) Worst single-plane disaster. (15) Incl. 248 members of U.S. 101st Airborne Division. (16) Incl. 15 on ground. (17) Incl. 11 on ground. (18) Incl. 1 on ground. (19) Incl. U.S. Sec. of Commerce Ron Brown. (20) Incl. 2 on ground. (21) World's worst midair collision. (22) Incl. 6 on ground. (23) Incl. 10 on ground. (24) Incl. 4 on ground. (25) World's first Concorde crash; deaths incl. 5 on ground. (26) Incl. 7 players and staff of Oklahoma State Univ. men's basketball team. (27) Carried U.S. mil. personnel, searching for MIAs from Vietnam War. (28) 4 planes were hijacked and crashed, with all on board (265, including 19 hijackers) killed: American Airlines Flight 11, a Boeing 767-200, with 81 passengers plus 11 crew, crashed into Tower 1 of the World Trade Center in NYC; United Airlines Flight 175, a Boeing 767-200, with 56 passengers plus 9 crew, crashed into Tower 2 of the World Trade Center; American Airlines Flight 77, a Boeing 757-200, with 58 passengers plus 6 crew, crashed into the Pentagon outside Washington, DC; United Air Lines Flight 93, a Boeing 757-200, with 37 passengers plus 7 crew, crashed near Shanksville, PA. In addition, according to Oct. 2002 estimates, about 2,600 people died on the ground in the 2 World Trade Center towers, and 125 in the Pentagon.

Some Notable Railroad Disasters

Date	Location	Deaths
1876, Dec. 29	Ashtabula, OH	92
1880, Aug. 11	Mays Landing, NJ	40
1887, Aug. 10	Chatsworth, IL	81
1888, Oct. 10	Mud Run, PA	55
1889, June 12	Amagh, Ireland	80
1891, June 14	Nr. Basel, Switzerland	100
1896, July 30	Atlantic City, NJ	60
1903, Dec. 23	Laurel Run, PA	53
1904, Aug. 7	Eden, CO	96
1904, Sept. 24	New Market, TN	56
1906, Mar. 16	Florence, CO	35
1906, Oct. 28	Atlantic City, NJ	40
1906, Dec. 30	Washington, DC	53
1907, Jan. 2	Volland, KS	33
1907, Jan. 19	Fowler, IN	29
1907, Feb. 16	New York, NY	22
1907, Feb. 23	Colton, CA	26
1907, May 11	Lompoc, CA	36
1907, July 20	Salem, MI	33
1908, Sept. 25	Young's Point, MT	21
1909, Jan. 15	Dotsero, CO	21
1910, Mar. 1	Wellington, WA	96
1910, Mar. 21	Green Mountain, IA	55
1911, Aug. 25	Manchester, NY	29
1912, July 4	East Corning, NY	39
1912, July 5	Ligonier, PA	23
1914, Aug. 5	Tipton Ford, MO	43
1914, Sept. 15	Lebanon, MO	28
1915, May 22	Nr. Gretna, Scotland	227
1916, Mar. 29	Amherst, OH	27
1917, Sept. 28	Kellyville, OK	23
1917, Dec. 12	Modane, France	543
1917, Dec. 20	Shepherdsville, KY	46
1918, June 22	Ivanhoe, IN	68
1918, July 9	Nashville, TN	101
1918, Nov. 1	Brooklyn, NY	97
1919, Jan. 12	South Byron, NY	22
1919, Dec. 20	Onawa, ME	23
1921, Feb. 27	Porter, IN	37
1921, Dec. 5	Woodmont, PA	27
1922, Aug. 5	Sulphur Spring, MO	34
1922, Dec. 13	Humble, TX	22
1923, Sept. 27	Lockett, WY	31
1925, June 16	Hackettstown, NJ	50
1925, Oct. 27	Victoria, MS	21
1926, Sept. 5	Waco, CO	30
1937, July 16	Nr. Patna, India	107
1938, June 19	Saugus, MT	47
1939, Aug. 12	Harney, NV	24
1939, Dec. 22	Near Magdeburg, Germany	132
1939, Dec. 22	Near Friedrichshafen, Germany	99
1940, Apr. 19	Little Falls, NY	31
1940, July 31	Cuyahoga Falls, OH	43
1943, Aug. 29	Wayland, NY	27
1943, Sept. 6	Frankford Junction, Philad. PA	79
1943, Dec. 16	Between Rennert and Buie, NC	72
1944, Jan. 16	Leon Prov., Spain	500
1944, Mar. 2	Salerno, Italy	521
1944, July 6	High Bluff, TN	35
1944, Aug. 4	Near Stockton, GA	47
1944, Sept. 14	Dewey, IN	29
1944, Dec. 31	Bagley, UT	50
1945, Aug. 9	Michigan, ND	34
1946, Mar. 20	Aracaju, Mexico	185
1946, Apr. 25	Naperville, IL	45
1947, Feb. 18	Gallitzin, PA	24
1949, Oct. 22	Nr. Dwor, Poland	200+
1950, Feb. 17	Rockville Centre, NY	31
1950, Sept. 11	Coshocton, OH	33
1950, Nov. 22	Richmond Hill, NY	79
1951, Feb. 6	Woodbridge, NJ	84
1952, Mar. 4	Nr. Rio de Janeiro, Brazil	119
1952, July 9	Rzepin, Poland	160
1952, Oct. 8	Harrow, England	112
1953, Mar. 27	Conneaut, OH	21
1955, Apr. 3	Guadalajara, Mexico	300
1956, Jan. 22	Los Angeles, CA	30
1957, Sept. 1	Kendal, Jamaica	178
1957, Sept. 29	Montgomery, W Pakistan	250
1957, Dec. 4	London, England	90
1958, May 8	Rio de Janeiro, Brazil	128
1958, Sept. 15	Elizabethport, NJ	48
1960, Nov. 14	Pardubice, Czech.	110
1962, Jan. 8	Woerden, Netherlands	91
1962, May 3	Tokyo, Japan	163
1964, July 26	Porto, Portugal	94
1970, Feb. 1	Buenos Aires, Argentina	236
1972, June 16	Vierzy, France	107
1972, July 21	Seville, Spain	76
1972, Oct. 6	Saltillo, Mexico	208

Date	Location	Deaths
1972, Oct. 30	Chicago, IL	45
1974, Aug. 30	Zagreb, Yugoslavia	153
1975, Feb. 28	London subway train	41
1977, Jan. 18	Granville, Australia	83
1981, June 6	Bihar, India	700+
1982, Jan. 27	El Asnam, Algeria	130
1982, July 11	Tepic, Mexico	120
1983, Feb. 19	Empalme, Mexico	100
1987, July 2	Kasumbalesha Shaba, Zaire	125
1988, Dec. 12	London, England	115
1989, Jan. 15	Maizdi Khan, Bangladesh	110+
1990, Jan. 4	Sindh Prov., Pakistan	210+
1991, May 14	Shigaraki, Japan	42
1993, Sept. 22	Big Bayou Conot, AL	47
1994, Mar. 8	Nr. Durban, South Africa	63
1994, Sept. 22	Tolunda, Angola	300
1995, Aug. 20	Firozabad, India	358
1997, Mar. 3	Punjab State, Pakistan	125
1997, Mar. 31	Huarte Arakil, Spain	21
1997, Apr. 29	Hunan, China	58
1997, May 4	Rwanda	100+
1997, Sept. 14	Central India	77
1998, June 3	Eschede, Germany	102
1998, Feb. 19	Yaounde, Cameroon	100+
1999, Mar. 15	Bourbonnais, IL	11
1999, Mar. 24	Nairobi, Kenya	32+
1999, Aug. 2	Gauhati, India	285+
1999, Oct. 5	London, England	31
2000, Jan. 4	Rena, Norway	35
2000, July 28	São Paulo, Brazil	12
2000, Nov. 11	Kaprun, Austria	155
2001, Feb. 28	Great Heck, England	13
2001, Mar. 18	Nr. Des Moines, IA	1
2002, Feb. 20	South of Cairo, Egypt	373
2002, Apr. 18	Seville, FL	4
2002, Apr. 23	Placentia, CA	2
2002, May 10	Potter's Bar, England	7
2002, May 25	Muamba, Mozambique	196+
2002, June 24	Igandu, Tanzania	281+

Principal U.S. Mine Disasters Since 1900

Source: Bureau of Mines, U.S. Dept. of the Interior; Mine Safety and Health Admin., U.S. Dept. of Labor

(All are bituminous-coal mines unless otherwise noted.)

Date	Location	Deaths
1900, May 1	Scofield, UT	200
1902, May 19	Coal Creek, TN	184
1902, July 10	Johnstown, PA	112
1903, June 30	Hanna, WY	169
1904, Jan. 25	Cheswick, PA	179
1905, Feb. 26	Virginia City, AL	112
1907, Jan. 29	Stuart, WV	84
1907, Dec. 6	Monongah, WV	361
1907, Dec. 19	Jacobs Creek, PA	239
1908, Nov. 28	Marianna, PA	154
1909, Nov. 13	Cherry, IL	259
1910, Jan. 31	Primero, CO	75
1910, May 5	Palos, AL	90
1910, Nov.8	Delagua, CO	79
1911, Apr. 8	Littleton, AL	128
1911, Dec. 9	Briceville, TN	84
1912, Mar. 26	Jed, WV	83
1913, Apr. 23	Finleyville, PA	96
1913, Oct. 22	Dawson, NM	263
1914, Apr. 28	Eccles, WV	181
1915, Mar. 2	Layland, WV	112
1917, Apr. 27	Hastings, CO	121
1917, June 8	Butte, MT[1]	163
1919, June 5	Wilkes-Barre, PA[2]	92
1922, Nov. 6	Spangler, PA	77
1922, Nov. 22	Dolomite, AL	90
1923, Feb. 8	Dawson, NM	120
1923, Aug. 14	Kemmerer, WY	99
1924, Mar. 8	Castle Gate, UT	171
1924, Apr. 28	Benwood, WV	119
1926, Jan. 13	Wilburton, OK	91
1927, Apr. 30	Everettville, WV	97
1928, May 19	Mather, PA	195
1930, Nov. 5	Millfield, OH	82
1940, Jan. 10	Bartley, WV	91
1947, Mar. 25	Centralia, IL	111
1951, Dec. 21	West Frankfort, IL	119
1959, Jan. 22	Port Griffith, PA	12
1968, Nov. 20	Farmington, WV	78
1970, Dec. 30	Hyden, KY	38
1972, May 2	Kellogg, ID[1]	91
1976, Mar. 9	Oven Fork, KY	15
1981, Apr. 15	Redstone, CO	15
1981, Dec. 8	Whitwell, TN	13
1984, Dec. 19	Huntington, UT	27
1989, Sept. 13	Sturgis, KY	10
2001, Sept. 23	Brookwood, AL	13

Note: World's worst mine disaster killed 1,549 workers in Manchuria, Apr. 25, 1942. (1) Metal mine. (2) Anthracite mine.

Some Notable U.S. Tornadoes Since 1925

Date	Location	Deaths
1925, Mar. 18	MO, IL, IN	689
1927, Apr. 12	Rock Springs, TX	74
1927, May 9	AR, Poplar Bluff, MO	92
1927, Sept. 29	St. Louis, MO	90
1930, May 6	Hill, Navarro, Ellis Co., TX	41
1932, Mar. 21	AL (series of tornadoes)	268
1936, Apr. 5	MS, GA	455
1936, Apr. 6	Gainesville, GA	203
1938, Sept. 29	Charleston, SC	32
1942, Mar. 16	Central to NE Mississippi	75
1942, Apr. 27	Rogers and Mayes Co., OK	52
1944, June 23	OH, PA, WV, MD	150
1945, Apr. 12	OK-AR	102
1947, Apr. 9	TX, OK, KS	169
1948, Mar. 19	Bunker Hill and Gillespie, IL	33
1949, Jan. 3	LA and AR	58
1952, Mar. 21	AR, MO, TN (series)	208
1953, May 11	Waco, TX	114
1953, June 8	MI, OH	142
1953, June 9	Worcester and vicinity, MA	90
1953, Dec. 5	Vicksburg, MS	38
1955, May 25	KS, MO, OK, TX	115
1957, May 20	KS, MO	48
1958, June 4	NW Wisconsin	30
1959, Feb. 10	St. Louis, MO	21
1960, May 5, 6	Southeastern OK, AR	30
1965, Apr. 11	IN, IL, OH, MI, WI	271
1966, Mar. 3	Jackson, MS	57
1966, Mar. 3	MS, AL	61
1967, Apr. 21	IL, MI	33
1968, May 15	Midwest	71
1969, Jan. 23	MS	32
1971, Feb. 21	Mississippi delta	110
1973, May 26-27	South, Midwest (series)	47
1974, Apr. 3-4	AL, GA, TN, KY, OH	315
1977, Apr. 4	AL, MS, GA	22
1979, Apr. 10	TX, OK	60
1984, Mar. 28	NC, SC	57
1985, May 31	NY, PA, OH, Ont. (series)	75
1987, May 22	Saragosa, TX	29
1989, Nov. 15	Huntsville, AL	18
1990, Aug. 28	Northern IL	25
1991, Apr. 26	KS, OK	23
1992, Nov. 21-23	South, Midwest	26
1994, Mar. 27-28	AL, TN, GA, NC, SC (series)	52
1995, May 6-7	Southern OK, northern TX	23
1997, Mar. 1	Central AR	26
1997, May 27	Jarrell, TX	27
1998, Feb. 22-23	Central FL	42
1998, Mar. 20	Northeast GA	12
1998, Mar. 24	Eastern India	145
1998, Apr. 8	AL, GA, MS	39
1998, Apr. 16	AK, KY, TN	10
1998, May 30	Spencer, SD	6
1999, Jan. 17	Western TN	8
1999, Jan. 21	AK, TN	8
1999, Apr. 3	Northwestern LA	6
1999, Apr. 9	OH, IL, IN, MO	6
1999, May 3-4	OK, KS	42
2000, Feb. 14	Southwest GA	22+
2000, Mar. 28	TX	5
2000, July 14	Alberta	11
2000, Dec. 16	AL	12
2001, Feb. 24	Pontotoc, MS	8
2001, Nov. 23-24	AL, AR, MS (series)	13
2002, Apr. 27-28	IL, KY, MD, MO	6

Some Notable Hurricanes, Typhoons, Blizzards, Other Storms

H.—hurricane; T.—typhoon

Date	Location	Deaths
1888, Mar. 11-14	Blizzard, eastern U.S.	400
1900, Sept. 8	H., Galveston, TX	6,000+
1906, Sept. 19-24	H., LA, MS	350
1906, Sept. 18	Typhoon, Hong Kong	10,000
1915, Sept. 29	H., LA	500
1926, Sept. 11-22	H., FL, AL	243
1926, Oct. 20	H., Cuba	600
1928, Sept. 6-20	H., southern FL	1,836
1930, Sept. 3	H., Dominican Republic	2,000
1935, Aug. 29-Sept. 10	H., Caribbean, southeastern U.S.	400+
1938, Sept. 21	H., Long Island, NY; New England	600
1940, Nov. 11-12	Blizzard, NE, Midwest U.S.	144
1942, Oct. 15-16	H., Bengal, India	40,000
1944, Sept. 9-16	H., NC to New England	46
1947, Dec. 26	Blizzard, NYC, N Atlantic states	55
1952, Oct. 22	Typhoon, Philippines	440
1954, Aug. 30	H. *Carol,* northeastern U.S.	68
1954, Oct. 5-18	H. *Hazel,* E Canada, U.S.; Haiti	347
1955, Aug. 12-13	H. *Connie,* NC, SC, VA, MD	43
1955, Aug. 7-21	H. *Diane,* eastern U.S.	400
1955, Sept. 19	H. *Hilda,* Mexico	200
1955, Sept. 22-28	H. *Janet,* Caribbean	500
1956, Feb. 1-29	Blizzard, W Europe	1,000
1957, June 25-30	H. *Audrey,* TX to AL	390
1958, Feb. 15-16	Blizzard, northeastern U.S.	171
1959, Sept. 17-19	T. *Sarah,* Japan, S. Korea	2,000
1959, Sept. 26-27	T. *Vera,* Honshu, Japan	4,466
1960, Sept. 4-12	H. *Donna,* Caribbean, E U.S.	148
1961, Sept. 11-14	H. *Carla,* TX	46
1961, Oct. 31	H. *Hattie,* Br. Honduras	400
1963, May 28-29	Windstorm, Bangladesh	22,000
1963, Oct. 4-8	H. *Flora,* Caribbean	6,000
1964, Oct. 4-7	H. *Hilda,* LA, MS, GA	38
1964, June 30	T. *Winnie,* N Philippines	107
1964, Sept. 5	T. *Ruby,* Hong Kong and China	735
1965, May 11-12	Windstorm, Bangladesh	17,000
1965, June 1-2	Windstorm, Bangladesh	30,000
1965, Sept. 7-12	H. *Betsy,* FL, MS, LA	74
1965, Dec. 15	Windstorm, Bangladesh	10,000
1966, June 4-10	H. *Alma,* Honduras, SE U.S.	51
1966, Sept. 24-30	H. *Inez,* Carib., FL, Mexico	293
1967, July 9	T. *Billie,* SW Japan	347
1967, Sept. 5-23	H. *Beulah,* Carib., Mex., TX	54
1967, Dec. 12-20	Blizzard, Southwest U.S.	51
1968, Nov. 18-28	T. *Nina,* Philippines	63
1969, Aug. 17-18	H. *Camille,* MS, LA	256
1970, Aug. 20-21	H. *Dorothy,* Martinique	42
1970, Sept. 15	T. *Georgia,* Philippines	300
1970, Oct. 14	T. *Sening,* Philippines	583
1970, Oct. 15	T. *Titang,* Philippines	526
1970, Nov. 13	Cyclone, Bangladesh	300,000
1971, Aug. 1	T. *Rose,* Hong Kong	130
1972, June 19-29	H. *Agnes,* FL to NY	118
1972, Dec. 3	T. *Theresa,* Philippines	169
1973, June-Aug.	Monsoon rains, India	1,217
1974, June 11	Storm Dinah, Luzon Isl., Phil.	71
1974, July 11	T. *Gilda,* Japan, S. Korea	108
1974, Sept. 19-20	H. *Fifi,* Honduras	2,000
1974, Dec. 25	Cyclone leveled Darwin, Austral.	50
1975, Sept. 13-27	H. *Eloise,* Caribbean, NE U.S.	71
1976, May 20	T. *Olga,* floods, Philippines	215
1978, Oct. 27	T. *Rita,* Philippines	c. 400
1979, Aug. 30 - Sept. 7	H. *David,* Caribbean, E U.S.	1,100
1980, Aug. 4-11	H. *Allen,* Caribbean, TX	272
1981, Nov. 25	T. *Irma,* Luzon Isl., Phil.	176
1983, June	Monsoon, India	900
1984, Sept. 2	T. *Ike,* S Philippines	1,363
1985, May 25	Cyclone, Bangladesh	10,000
1985, Oct. 26-Nov. 6	H. *Juan,* SE U.S.	97
1987, Nov. 25	T. *Nina,* Philippines	650
1988, Sept. 10-17	H. *Gilbert,* Caribbean, Gulf of Mexico	260
1989, Sept. 16-22	H. *Hugo,* Caribbean, SE U.S.	504
1990, May 6-11	Cyclones, SE India	450
1991, Apr. 30	Cyclone, Bangladesh	139,000
1991, Nov. 5	Tropical storm, Philippines	7,000+
1992, Aug. 24-26	H. *Andrew,* southern FL, LA	23
1993, Mar. 13-14	Blizzard, eastern U.S.	200
1993, June	Monsoon, Bangladesh	2,000
1994, Nov. 8-18	Storm Gordon, Caribbean, FL	830
1995, Oct. 2-4	H. *Opal,* S Mexico, FL, AL	59
1995, Nov. 2-3	T. *Angela,* Philippines	600+
1996, Jan. 7-8	Blizzard, northeastern U.S.	100
1996, July 8-13	H. *Bertha,* Carib., eastern U.S.	15
1996, Aug. 22	Blizzard, Himalayas, N India	239
1996, Aug. 29-Sept. 6	H. *Fran,* Carib., NC, VA, WV.	28
1996, Sept. 9-10	H. *Hortense,* Caribbean	24
1996, Sept. 9	T. *Sally,* S China	114
1996, Nov. 6	Cyclone, Andhra Pradesh, India	1,000+
1996, Nov. 24-25	Ice storms, TX to MO	26
1996, Dec. 25	Tropical storm, E Malaysia	100+
1997, May 19	Cyclone, Bangladesh	108
1997, July 2	Storms, southeastern MI	16
1997, Aug. 18	Typhoon, Taiwan	24
1997, Oct. 8-10	H. *Pauline,* SW Mexico	230
1998, Feb. 4-6	Blizzard, KY, WV	10+
1998, June 9	Cyclone, Gujarat, India	1,320
1998, Aug.	Monsoon, Bangladesh	326
1998, Sept. 21-23	H. *Georges,* Caribbean, FL Keys, U.S. Gulf Coast	600+
1998, Oct. 27-29	H. *Mitch,* Honduras, Nicaragua, Guatemala, El Salvador	10,866+
1999, Sept. 4-17	H. *Floyd,* Bahamas, eastern seaboard, U.S.	69+
1999, Oct. 29	Cyclone, Eastern India	9,392
1999, Dec. 26-29	Gales, France, Switzerland, Germany	120
2000, Dec. 27	TX, OK, AR	40+
2001, June 6-17	Tropical storm *Allison*, SE U.S.	47
2001, July 30	Typhoon, Taiwan	200
2001, Oct. 8-9	H. *Iris*, Belize	22
2001, Nov. 2-5	H. *Michelle*, Cuba, Jamaica	17
2001, Nov. 6-12	T. *Lingling*, S Philippines, central Vietnam	220+
2002, July 1-11	T. *Chata'an*, Micronesia, Philippines, Japan	70+
2002, Aug.-Sept.	T. *Rusa*, S. and N. Korea	115+

IT'S A FACT: Heat waves kill far more people in the U.S. than all other natural disasters. About 1,500 Americans—mostly poor or old—die each year from the heat, compared with an average annual toll of 200 for earthquakes, floods, and tornadoes combined.

Some Notable Floods, Tidal Waves

Date	Location	Deaths
1228	Holland	100,000
1642	China	300,000
1883, Aug. 27	Indonesia	36,000
1887	Huang He River, China	900,000
1889, May 31	Johnstown, PA	2,209
1903, June 15	Heppner, OR	325
1911	Chang Jiang River, China	100,000
1913, Mar. 25-27	OH, IN	732
1915, Aug. 17	Galveston, TX	275
1928, Mar. 13	Dam collapse, Saugus, CA	450
1928, Sept. 13	Lake Okeechobee, FL	2,000
1931, Aug.	Huang He River, China	3,700,000
1937, Jan. 22	OH, MS Valleys	250
1939	N China	200,000
1946, Apr. 1	HI, AK	159
1947, Sept. 20	Honshu Island, Japan	1,900
1951, Aug.	Manchuria	1,800
1953, Jan. 31	W Europe	2,000
1954, Aug. 17	Farahzad, Iran	2,000
1955, Oct. 7-12	India, Pakistan	1,700
1959, Nov. 1	W Mexico	2,000
1959, Dec. 2	Frejus, France	412
1960, Oct. 10	Bangladesh	6,000
1960, Oct. 31	Bangladesh	4,000
1962, Feb. 17	North Sea coast, Germany	343
1962, Sept. 27	Barcelona, Spain	445
1963, Oct. 9	Dam collapse, Vaiont, Italy	1,800
1966, Nov. 3-4	Florence, Venice, Italy	113
1967, Jan. 18-24	E Brazil	894
1967, Mar. 19	Rio de Janeiro, Brazil	436
1967, Nov. 26	Lisbon, Portugal	464
1968, Aug. 7-14	Gujarat State, India	1,000
1968, Oct. 7	NE India	780
1969, Jan. 18-26	Southern CA	100

Date	Location	Deaths
1969, Mar. 17	Mundau Valley, Alagoas, Brazil	218
1969, Aug. 20-22	Western VA	189
1969, Sept. 15	South Korea	250
1969, Oct. 1-8	Tunisia	500
1970, May 20	Central Romania	160
1970, July 22	Himalayas, India	500
1971, Feb. 26	Rio de Janeiro, Brazil	130
1972, Feb. 26	Buffalo Creek, WV	118
1972, June 9	Rapid City, SD	236
1972, Aug. 7	Luzon Isl., Philippines	454
1972, Aug. 19-31	Pakistan	1,500
1974, Mar. 29	Tubaro, Brazil	1,000
1974, Aug. 12	Monty-Long, Bangladesh	2,500
1976, June 5	Teton Dam collapse, ID	11
1976, July 31	Big Thompson Canyon, CO	139
1976, Nov. 17	East Java, Indonesia	136
1977, July 19-20	Johnstown, PA	68
1977, Nov. 6	Toccoa, GA	39
1978, June-Sept.	N India	1,200
1979, Jan.-Feb.	Brazil	204
1979, July 17	Lomblem Isl., Indonesia	539
1979, Aug. 11	Morvi, India	15,000
1980, Feb. 13-22	Southern CA, AZ	26
1981, Apr.	N China	550
1981, July	Sichuan, Hubei Prov., China	1,300
1982, Jan. 23	Nr. Lima, Peru	600
1982, May 12	Guangdong, China	430
1982, Sept. 17-21	El Salvador, Guatemala	1,300+
1984, Aug-Sept.	South Korea	200+
1985, July 19	Dam collapse, N Italy	361
1987, Aug.-Sept.	N Bangladesh	1,000+
1988, Sept.	N India	1,000+
1990, June 14	Shadyside, OH	23
1991, Dec. 18-26	TX	18
1993, July-Aug.	Midwest	48
1994, July	GA, AL	32
1995, Jan. 30-Feb. 9	NW Europe	40
1995, July	Hunan Province, China	1,200
1995, Aug. 19	SW Morocco	136
1995, Dec. 25	KwaZulu Natal, South Africa	166
1996, Jan.	Northeastern U.S.	15+
1996, Feb. 17	Biak Isl., Indonesia	105
1996, April	Afghanistan	100+
1996, June-July	S China	950+
1996, Aug. 7	Pyrenees Mts., Spain	71
1996, Dec.-1997, Jan.	Northwestern U.S.	29
1997, Mar.	Ohio R. Valley	35
1997, July	Poland, Czech Republic	98
1997, Nov.	Spanish-Portuguese border	31+
1997, Nov.	Bardera, Somalia	1,300+
1998, Jan.	Kenya	86
1998, Feb.	California to Tijuana, Mexico	30+
1998, Mar.	SW Pakistan	300+
1998, July-Aug.	China	4,150
1998, July-Sept.	Bangladesh	1,441
1998, July 17	Papua New Guinea	3,000
1998, Aug. 24	S Texas, Mexico	16
1999, Aug. 1-4	S. Korea, Philippines, Vietnam, Thailand	188+
1999, Sept.-Oct.	NE Mexico	350+
1999, Oct.-Dec.	Central Vietnam	700+
1999, Feb. 6-11	Botswana	70+
1999, Dec.	Venezuela	9,000+
2000, Feb.-Mar.	Madagascar	150+
2000, Feb.-Mar.	Mozambique	700
2000, May 17	Timor Island	50+
2000, May 31	Gansu, China	36
2000, June 7	Sichaun, China	38
2000, June 8-12	Uttar Pradesh, India	43+
2000, Aug. 2	Himachal Pradesh, India	120+
2000, Aug. 2	Bhutan	200+
2000, Sept. 19-30	India, Bangladesh	1,000+
2000, Oct. 12-17	France, Brit., Italy, Switz.	35
2001, Jan.-Feb.	Mozambique	84+
2001, Aug.-Nov.	S.Vietnam and Cambodia	360+
2001, Aug. 1-6	Taiwan	100+
2001, Aug. 10-12	Northeastern Iran	247
2001, Aug.	Northern Thailand	170
2001, Nov. 9-10	Northern Algeria	711+
2001, Dec. 23-31	Rio de Janeiro	66
2002, Jan. 30-Feb. 15	Java Isl., Indonesia	147
2002, Feb. 19	La Paz, Bolivia	65
2002, Apr.-May	East Africa	150+
2002, early May	MO, IL, IN	9
2002, early May	WV, VA KY	11
2002, Apr.-Aug.	China	000+
2002, July-Aug.	India, Nepal, Bangladesh	1,100+
2002, Aug.	Russia	110
2002, Aug.	Germany, Hungary, Austria, Czech Rep.	100+

Some Major Earthquakes

Source: Global Volcanism Network, Smithsonian Institution; U.S. Geological Survey, Dept. of the Interior; World Almanac research

Magnitude of earthquakes (Mag.) is measured on the Richter scale; each higher number represents a tenfold increase in energy. Adopted in 1935, the scale is applied to earthquakes as far back as reliable seismograms are available.

Date	Location	Deaths	Mag.
526, May 20	Antioch, Syria	250,000	NA
856	Corinth, Greece	45,000	"
1057	Chihli, China	25,000	"
1169, Feb. 11	Near Mt. Etna, Sicily	15,000[1]	"
1268	Cilicia, Asia Minor	60,000	"
1290, Sept. 27	Chihli, China	100,000	"
1293, May 20	Kamakura, Japan	30,000	"
1531, Jan. 26	Lisbon, Portugal	30,000	"
1556, Jan. 24	Shaanxi, China	830,000	"
1667, Nov.	Shemaka, Caucasia	80,000	"
1693, Jan. 11	Catania, Italy	60,000	"
1730, Dec. 30	Hokkaido, Japan	137,000	"
1737, Oct. 11	India, Calcutta	300,000	"
1755, June 7	N Persia	40,000	"
1755, Nov. 1	Lisbon, Portugal	60,000	8.75*
1783, Feb. 4	Calabria, Italy	30,000	NA
1797, Feb. 4	Quito, Ecuador	41,000	"
1811-12	New Madrid, MO (series)	NA	8.7*
1822, Sept. 5	Asia Minor, Aleppo	22,000	NA
1828, Dec. 28	Echigo, Japan	30,000	"
1868, Aug. 13-15	Peru, Ecuador	40,000	"
1875, May 16	Venezuela, Colombia	16,000	"
1886, Aug. 31	Charleston, SC	60	6.6
1896, June 15	Japan, sea wave	27,120	NA
1905, Apr. 4	Kangra, India	19,000	8.6
1906, Apr. 18-19	San Francisco, CA	503[2]	8.3
1906, Aug. 17	Valparaiso, Chile	20,000	8.6
1907, Oct. 21	Central Asia	12,000	8.1
1908, Dec. 28	Messina, Italy	83,000	7.5
1915, Jan. 13	Avezzano, Italy	29,980	7.5
1918, Oct. 11	Mona Passage, P.R.	116	7.5
1920, Dec. 16	Gansu, China	200,000	8.6
1923, Sept. 1	Yokohama, Japan	143,000	8.3
1925, Mar. 16	Yunnan, China	5,000	7.1
1927, May 22	Nan-Shan, China	200,000	8.3
1932, Dec. 25	Gansu, China	70,000	7.6
1933, Mar. 2	Japan	2,990	8.9
1933, Mar. 10	Long Beach, CA	115	6.2
1934, Jan. 15	India, Bihar-Nepal	10,700	8.4
1935, Apr. 21	Taiwan (Formosa)	3,276	7.4
1935, May 30	Quetta, India	50,000	7.5
1939, Jan. 25	Chillan, Chile	28,000	8.3
1939, Dec. 26	Erzincan, Turkey	30,000	8.0
1946, Dec. 20	Honshu, Japan	1,330	8.4
1948, June 28	Fukui, Japan	5,390	7.3
1949, Aug. 5	Pelileo, Ecuador	6,000	6.8
1950, Aug. 15	Assam, India	1,530	8.7
1953, Mar. 18	NW Turkey	1,200	7.2
1956, June 10-17	N Afghanistan	2,000	7.7
1957, July 2	N Iran	1,200	7.4
1957, Dec. 13	W Iran	1,130	7.3
1960, Feb. 29	Agadir, Morocco	12,000	5.9
1960, May 21-30	S Chile	5,000	9.5
1962, Sept. 1	NW Iran	12,230	7.3
1963, July 26	Skopje, Yugoslavia	1,100	6.0
1964, Mar. 27	Alaska	131	9.2
1966, Aug. 19	E Turkey	2,520	7.1
1968, Aug. 31	NE Iran	12,000	7.3
1970, Jan. 5	Yunnan Prov., China	15,621	7.7
1970, Mar. 28	W Turkey	1,100	7.3
1970, May 31	N Peru	66,000	7.8
1971, Feb. 9	San Fernando Val., CA	65	6.6
1972, Apr. 10	S Iran	5,054	7.1
1972, Dec. 23	Managua, Nicaragua	5,000	6.2
1974, Dec. 28	Pakistan (9 towns)	5,200	6.3
1975, Sept. 6	Turkey (Lice, etc.)	2,300	6.7
1976, Feb. 4	Guatemala	23,000	7.5
1976, May 6	NE Italy	1,000	6.5
1976, June 25	Irian Jaya, New Guinea	422	7.1
1976, July 27	Tangshan, China	255,000	8.0

Date	Location	Deaths	Mag.
1976, Aug. 16	Mindanao, Philippines	8,000	7.8
1976, Nov. 24	NW Iran-USSR border	5,000	7.3
1977, Mar. 4	Romania	1,500	7.2
1977, Aug. 19	Indonesia	200	8.0
1977, Nov. 23	NW Argentina	100	8.2
1978, Sept. 16	NE Iran	15,000	7.8
1979, Sept. 12	Indonesia	100	8.1
1979, Dec. 12	Colombia, Ecuador	800	7.9
1980, Oct. 10	NW Algeria	3,500	7.7
1980, Nov. 23	S Italy	3,000	7.2
1981, June 11	S Iran	3,000	6.9
1981, July 28	S Iran	1,500	7.3
1982, Dec. 13	W Arabian Peninsula	2,800	6.0
1983, May 26	N Honshu, Japan	81	7.7
1983, Oct. 30	E Turkey	1,342	6.9
1985, Mar. 3	Chile	146	7.8
1985, Sept. 19	Michoacan, Mexico	9,500	8.1
1986, Oct. 10	El Salvador	1,000+	5.5
1987, Mar. 6	Colombia-Ecuador	4,000+	7.0
1988, Aug. 20	India-Nepal border	1,450	6.6
1988, Nov. 6	China-Burma border	1,000	7.3
1988, Dec. 7	Soviet Armenia	55,000	7.0
1989, Oct. 17	San Francisco Bay area	62	7.1
1990, May 30	N Peru	115	6.3
1990, June 20	W Iran	40,000+	7.7
1990, July 16	Luzon, Philippines	1,621	7.8
1991, Feb. 1	Pakistan, Afgh. border	1,200	6.8
1991, Oct. 19	N India	2,000	7.0
1992, Mar. 13, 15	E Turkey	4,000	6.2/6.0
1992, June 28	S California	1	7.5/6.6
1992, Dec. 12	Flores Isl., Indonesia	2,500	7.5
1993, July 12	off Hokkaido, Japan	200+	7.7
1992, Sept. 1	SW Nicaragua	116	7.0
1992, Oct. 12	Cairo, Egypt	450	5.9
1993, Sept. 30	Maharashtra, S India	9,748(3)	6.3
1994, Jan. 17	Northridge, CA	61	6.8
1994, Feb. 15	S Sumatra, Indon.	215	7.0
1994, June 6	Cauca, SW Colombia	1,000	6.8

Date	Location	Deaths	Mag.
1994, Aug. 19	N Algeria	164	6.0
1995, Jan. 16	Kobe, Japan	5,502	6.9
1995, May 27	Sakhalin Isl., Russia	1,989	7.5
1995, Oct. 1	SW Turkey	73	6.0
1996, Feb. 3	SW China	200+	7.0
1996, Feb. 17	Irian Jaya, Indonesia	53	7.5
1997, Feb. 4	Turkmen.-Iran border	79	6.9
1997, Feb. 27	W Pakistan	100+	7.3
1997, Feb. 28	NW Iran	1,000+	6.1
1997, May 10	N Iran	1,560	7.5
1997, July 9	NE Venezuela	82	6.9
1997, Sept. 26	Central Italy	11	5.5/5.7
1998, Jan. 10	Zhangbei, China	50	6.2
1998, Feb. 4, 8	Takhar province, NE Afghanistan	2,323	6.1
1998, May 22	Central Bolivia	105	6.5
1998, May 30	NE Afghanistan	4,700+	6.9
1998, June 27	Adana, Turkey	144	6.3
1999, Jan. 25	Armenia, Colombia	1,185+	6.0
1999, Feb. 11	Central Afghanistan	60	6.0
1999, Mar. 28	Uttar Pradesh, India	87	6.8
1999, Aug. 17	Western Turkey	17,200+	7.4
1999, Sept. 7	Athens, Greece	143	5.9
1999, Sept. 21	Taichung, Taiwan	2,474	7.6
1999, Nov. 12	Duzce, Turkey	675+	7.2
2000, June 4	Sumatra, Indonesia	103	7.9
2001, Jan. 13	San Vicente, El Salvador	800+	7.6
2001, Jan. 26	Gujarat, India	20,000+	7.9
2001, Feb. 13	San Vicente, El Salvador	255	6.6
2001, Mar. 24	Hiroshima, Japan	2	6.4
2001, June 23	Arequipa, Peru	102	8.1
2002, Feb. 3	Central Turkey	44+	6.5
2002, Mar. 3	N Afghanistan	150+	7.4
2002, Mar. 25-26	Nahrin, N Afghanistan	1,000+	6.1
2002, Mar. 31	Hualien, Taiwan	5	7.1
2002, Apr. 1	E New Guinea	36	5.0
2002, Apr. 12	Hindu Kush, Afghanistan	50+	5.9
2002, June 22	W Iran	261+	6.5

(*) estimated from earthquake intensity. NA = Not available. (1) Once thought to have been a volcanic eruption; evidence indicates a destructive earthquake and tsunami occurred on this date. (2) With subsequent fires, death toll rose to 700; some estimates of the death toll are much higher. (3) Official death toll as released by Indian government. Other sources reported estimates of about 30,000 deaths.

Some Notable Fires Since 1835

(See also Some Notable Explosions Since 1910.)

Date	Location	Deaths
1835, Dec. 16	New York, NY, 500 bldgs. destroyed	—
1845, May	Canton, China, theater	1,670
1871, Oct. 8	Chicago, $196 million loss; 17,000 bldgs. destroyed	250
1871, Oct. 8	Peshtigo, WI, forest fire	1,182
1872, Nov. 9	Boston, 800 bldgs. destroyed	—
1876, Dec. 5	Brooklyn, NY, theater	295
1877, June 20	St. John, New Brunswick	100
1881, Dec. 8	Ring Theater, Vienna	850
1887, May 25	Opera Comique, Paris	200
1887, Sept. 4	Exeter, England, theater	200
1894, Sept. 1	MN, forest fire	413
1897, May 4	Paris, charity bazaar	150
1900, June 30	Hoboken, NJ, docks	326
1902, Sept. 20	Birmingham, AL, church	115
1903, Dec. 30	Iroquois Theater, Chicago	602
1908, Jan. 13	Rhoads Theater, Boyertown, PA	170
1908, Mar. 4	Collinwood, OH, school	176
1911, Mar. 25	Triangle Shirtwaist factory, NY, NY	146
1913, Oct. 14	Mid Glamorgan, Wales, colliery	439
1918, Apr. 13	Norman, OK, state hospital	38
1918, Oct. 12	Cloquet, MN, forest fire	400
1919, June 20	Mayagüez Theater, San Juan, P.R.	150
1923, May 17	Camden, SC, school	76
1924, Dec. 24	Babb's Switch, OK, school	35
1929, May 15	Cleveland, OH, clinic	125
1930, Apr. 21	Columbus, OH, penitentiary	320
1931, July 24	Pittsburgh, PA, home for aged	48
1934, Dec. 11	Hotel Kerns, Lansing, MI	34
1938, May 16	Atlanta, GA, Terminal Hotel	35
1940, Apr. 23	Natchez, MS, dance hall	198
1942, Nov. 28	Cocoanut Grove, Boston	491
1942, Dec. 12	St. John's, Nfld., hostel	100
1943, Sept. 7	Gulf Hotel, Houston, TX	55
1944, July 6	Ringling Circus, Hartford, CT	168
1946, June 5	LaSalle Hotel, Chicago	61
1946, Dec. 7	Winecoff Hotel, Atlanta	119
1946, Dec. 12	NY, NY, ice plant, tenement	37
1949, Apr. 5	Effingham, IL, hospital	77
1950, Jan. 7	Davenport, IA, Mercy Hospital	41
1953, Mar. 29	Largo, FL, nursing home	35
1953, Apr. 16	Chicago, metalworking plant	35
1957, Feb. 17	Warrenton, MO, home for aged	72

Date	Location	Deaths
1958, Mar. 19	New York, NY, loft building	24
1958, Dec. 1	Chicago, parochial school	95
1958, Dec. 16	Bogotá, Colombia, store	83
1959, June 23	Stalheim, Norway, resort hotel	34
1960, Mar. 12	Pusan, Korea, chemical plant	68
1960, July 14	Guatemala City, mental hospital	225
1960, Nov. 13	Amude, Syria, movie theater	152
1961, Jan. 6	Thomas Hotel, San Francisco	20
1961, Dec. 8	Hartford, CT, hospital	16
1961, Dec. 17	Niteroi, Brazil, circus	323
1963, May 4	Diourbel, Senegal, theater	64
1963, Nov. 18	Surfside Hotel, Atlantic City, NJ	25
1963, Nov. 23	Fitchville, OH, rest home	63
1963, Dec. 29	Roosevelt Hotel, Jacksonville, FL	22
1964, May 8	Manila, apartment bldg.	30
1964, Dec. 18	Fountaintown, IN, nursing home	20
1965, Mar. 1	LaSalle, Quebec, apartment	28
1965, Aug. 11-16	Watts riot fires, CA	30+
1966, Mar. 11	Numata, Japan, 2 ski resorts	31
1966, Aug. 13	Melbourne, Australia, hotel	29
1966, Oct. 17	New York, NY, bldg. (firefighters)	12
1966, Dec. 7	Erzurum, Turkey, barracks	68
1967, Feb. 7	Montgomery, AL, restaurant	25
1967, May 22	Brussels, Belgium, store	322
1967, July 16	Jay, FL, state prison	37
1968, May 11	Vijayawada, India, wedding hall	58
1969, Dec. 2	Notre Dame, Can., nursing home	54
1970, Jan. 9	Marietta, OH, nursing home	27
1970, Nov. 1	Grenoble, France, dance hall	145
1970, Dec. 20	Tucson, AZ, hotel	28
1971, Mar. 6	Burghoezli, Switzerland, psychiatric clinic	28
1971, Dec., 25	Seoul, South Korea, hotel	162
1972, May 13	Osaka, Japan, nightclub	116
1972, July 5	Sherborne, England, hospital	30
1973, June 24	New Orleans, LA, bar	32
1973, Aug. 3	Isle of Man, Eng., amusement park	51
1973, Sept. 1	Copenhagen, Denmark, hotel	35
1973, Nov. 6	Fukui, Japan, train	28
1973, Nov. 29	Kumamoto, Japan, dept. store	107
1973, Dec. 2	Seoul, South Korea, theater	50
1974, Feb. 1	São Paulo, Brazil, bank building	189
1974, June 30	Port Chester, NY, discotheque	24

Date	Location	Deaths
1974, Nov. 3	Seoul, S. Korea, hotel, disco	88
1975, Dec. 12	Mina, Saudi Arabia, tent city	138
1976, Oct. 24	Bronx, NY, social club	25
1977, Feb. 25	Moscow, Russia, Rossiya hotel	45
1977, May 28	Southgate, KY, nightclub	164
1977, June 9	Abidjan, Ivory Coast, nightclub	41
1977, June 26	Columbia, TN, jail	42
1977, Nov. 14	Manila, Philippines, hotel	47
1978, Jan. 28	Kansas City, Coates House Hotel	16
1978, Aug. 19	Abadan, Iran, movie theater	425+
1979, July 14	Saragossa, Spain, hotel	80
1979, Dec. 31	Chapais, Quebec, social club	42
1980, May 20	Kingston, Jamaica, nursing home	157
1980, Nov. 21	MGM Grand Hotel, Las Vegas	84
1980, Dec. 4	Stouffer Inn, Harrison, NY	26
1981, Jan. 9	Keansburg, NJ, boarding home	30
1981, Feb. 10	Las Vegas Hilton	8
1981, Feb. 14	Dublin, Ireland, discotheque	44
1982, Sept. 4	Los Angeles, apartment house	24
1982, Nov. 8	Biloxi, MS, county jail	29
1983, Feb. 13	Turin, Italy, movie theater	64
1983, Dec. 17	Madrid, Spain, discotheque	83
1984, May 11	Great Adventure Amusement Pk., NJ	8
1985, Apr. 21	Tabaco, Phil., movie theater	44
1985, Apr. 26	Buenos Aires, Argentina, hospital	79
1985, May 11	Bradford, England, soccer stadium	53
1986, Dec. 31	Puerto Rico, Dupont Plaza Hotel	96
1987, May 6-June 2	N China, forest fire	193
1987, Nov. 17	London, England, subway	30
1988, Mar. 20	Lashio, Burma, 2,000 buildings	134
1990, Mar. 25	Bronx, NY, social club	87
1991, Mar. 3	Addis Ababa, Ethiopia, munitions dump	260+
1991, Sept. 3	Hamlet, NC, processing plant	25
1991, Oct. 20-21	Oakland, Berkeley, CA, wildfire	24
1993, Apr. 19	Waco, TX, cult compound	72
1994, May 10	Bangkok, Thailand, toy factory	213
1994, July 4-10	Glenwood Springs, CO (firefighters)	14
1994, Dec. 10	Karamay, China, theater	300
1994, Nov. 2	Durunka, Egypt, burning fuel flood	500
1995, Oct. 28	Baku, Azerbaijan, subway train	300
1995, Dec. 23	Mandi Dabwali, India, school	500+
1996, Mar. 19	Quezon City, Philippines, nightclub	150+
1996, Mar. 28	Bogor, Indonesia, shopping mall	78
1996, Oct. 22	Caracas, Venezuela, jail	25
1996, Nov. 20	Hong Kong, building	39
1997, Feb. 23	Baripada, India, worship site	164
1997, Apr. 15	Mina, Saudi Arabia, encampment	343
1997, June 7	Thanjavur, India, temple	60+
1997, June 13	New Delhi, India, movie theater	60
1997, July 11	Pattaya, Thailand, hotel	90
1997, Sept. 29	Home for retarded children, near Colina, Chile	30
1998, Dec. 3	Manila, Philippines, orphanage	28
1999, Mar. 24	France and Italy, Mont Blanc tunnel	40
1999, Oct. 30	Inchon, S. Korea, karaoke salon	55+
2000, Mar. 17	Kanungu, Uganda, church	530
2000, Oct. 20	Mexico City, Mexico, nightclub	20
2000, Dec. 25	Luoyang, China, shopping center	309
2001, Jan. 1	Volendam, Netherlands, cafe	10
2001, Mar. 6	Central China, school	41
2001, Mar. 26	Machakos, Kenya, school	64
2001, Aug. 6	Madras, India, home for mentally ill	27
2001, Aug. 18	Quezon City, Philippines, hotel	73
2001, Sept. 1	Tokyo, Japan, nightclub	44
2001, Oct. 24	Swiss Alps, St. Gotthard Tunnel	11
2001, Dec. 29	Lima, Peru, fireworks accident	291
2002, Mar. 11	Mecca, Saudi Arabia, girls' school	15
2002, June 16	Beijing, China, internet cafe	24
2002, July 7	Donetsk region, Ukraine, coal mine	34+
2002, July 20	Lima, Peru, disco	25+
2002, July 31	Donetsk region, Ukraine, coal mine	20

Some Notable Explosions Since 1910

(See also Principal U.S. Mine Disasters Since 1900.) Many bombings related to the Arab-Israeli conflict not included here; see coverage in the Chronology chapter and Nations of the World: Israel.

Date	Location	Deaths
1910, Oct. 1	Los Angeles Times Bldg.	21
1913, Mar. 7	Dynamite, Baltimore harbor	55
1915, Sept. 27	Gasoline tank car, Ardmore, OK	47
1917, Apr. 10	Munitions plant, Eddystone, PA	133
1917, Dec. 6	Halifax Harbor, Canada	1,654
1918, May 18	Chemical plant, Oakdale, PA	193
1918, July 2	Explosives, Split Rock, NY	50
1918, Oct. 4	Shell plant, Morgan Station, NJ	64
1919, May 22	Food plant, Cedar Rapids, IA	44
1920, Sept. 16	Wall Street, NY, NY, bomb	30
1921, Sept. 21	Chem. storage facility, Oppau, Ger.	561
1924, Jan. 3	Food plant, Pekin, IL	42
1927, May 18	Bath school, Lansing, MI	38
1928, April 13	Dance hall, West Plains, MO	40
1937, Mar. 18	New London, TX, school	311
1940, Sept. 12	Hercules Powder, Kenvil, NJ	55
1942, June 5	Ordnance plant, Elwood, IL	49
1944, Apr. 14	Bombay, India, harbor	700
1944, July 17	Port Chicago, CA, pier	322
1944, Oct. 21	Liquid gas tank, Cleveland	135
1947, Apr. 16	Texas City, TX, pier	576
1948, July 28	Farben works, Ludwigshafen, Ger.	184
1950, May 19	Munitions barges, S. Amboy, NJ	30
1956, Aug. 7	Dynamite trucks, Cali, Colombia	1,100
1958, Apr. 18	Sunken munitions ship, Okinawa, Japan	40
1958, May 22	Nike missiles, Leonardo, NJ	10
1959, Apr. 10	World War II bomb, Philippines	38
1959, June 28	Rail tank cars, Meldrim, GA	25
1959, Aug. 7	Dynamite truck, Roseburg, OR	13
1959, Nov. 2	Jamuri Bazar, India, explosives	46
1959, Dec. 13	2 apt. bldgs., Dortmund, Ger.	26
1960, Mar. 4	Belgian munitions ship, Havana, Cuba	100
1960, Oct. 25	Gas, Windsor, Ont., store	11
1962, Jan. 16	Gas pipeline, Edson, Alberta	8
1962, Oct. 3	Telephone Co. office, NY, NY	23
1963, Jan. 2	Packing plant, Terre Haute, IN	16
1963, Mar. 9	Dynamite plant, S. Africa	45
1963, Aug. 13	Explosives dump, Gauhaiti, India	32
1963, Oct. 31	State Fair Coliseum, Indianapolis, IN	73
1964, July 23	Bone, Algeria, harbor munitions	100
1965, Mar. 4	Gas pipeline, Natchitoches, LA	17
1965, Aug. 9	Missile silo, Searcy, AR	53
1965, Oct. 21	Bridge, Tila Bund, Pakistan	80
1965, Oct. 30	Cartagena, Colombia	48
1965, Nov. 24	Armory, Keokuk, IA	20
1967, Dec. 25	Apartment bldg., Moscow, USSR	20
1968, Apr. 6	Sports store, Richmond, IN	43
1970, Apr. 8	Subway construction, Osaka, Japan	73
1971, June 24	Tunnel, Sylmar, CA	17
1973, Feb., 10	Liquid gas tank, Staten Island, NY	40
1975, Dec. 27	Coal mine, Chasnala, India	431
1976, Apr. 13	Lapua, Finland, munitions works	40
1977, Nov. 11	Freight train, Iri, South Korea	57
1977, Dec. 22	Grain elevator, Westwego, LA	35
1978, Feb. 24	Derailed tank car, Waverly, TN	12
1978, July 11	Propylene tank truck, Spanish coastal campsite	150
1980, Oct. 23	School, Ortuella, Spain	64
1982, Apr. 25	Antiques exhibition, Todi, Italy	33
1982, Nov. 2	Salang Tunnel, Afghanistan	1,000+
1984, Feb. 25	Oil pipeline, Cubatao, Brazil	508
1984, June 21	Naval supply depot, Severomorsk, USSR	200+
1984, Nov. 19	Gas storage area, NE Mexico City	334
1984, Dec. 3	Chemical plant, Bhopal, India	3,849
1984, Dec. 5	Coal mine, Taipei, Taiwan	94
1985, June 25	Fireworks factory, Hallett, OK	21
1988, Apr. 10	Pakistani army ammunitions dump near Rawalpindi and Islamabad	100
1988, July 6	Oil rig, North Sea	167
1989, June 3	Gas pipeline, between Ufa, Asha, USSR	650+
1992, Mar. 3	Coal mine, Kozlu, Turkey	270+
1992, Apr. 22	Sewer, Guadalajara, Mexico	190
1992, May 9	Coal mine, Plymouth, Nova Scotia	26
1993, Feb. 26	World Trade Center, NY, NY	6
1994, July 18	Jewish community center, Buenos Aires, Argentina	100
1995, Apr. 19	Fed'l. office building, Oklahoma City	168
1995, Apr. 29	Subway construction, South Korea	110
1995, Nov. 13	Military facility, Riyadh, Saudi Arabia	7
1996, Jan. 31	Bank, Colombo, Sri Lanka	53
1996, Feb. 25	Jerusalem and Ashkelon, Israel	27
1996, Mar. 3-4	Jerusalem and Tel Aviv, Israel	33
1996, June 25	U.S. military housing complex, near Dhahran, Saudi Arabia	19
1996, July 24	Train, Colombo, Sri Lanka	86
1996, Nov. 16	Russian military apartment, Dagestan region, Russia	68
1996, Nov. 21	Building, San Juan, Puerto Rico	29
1996, Nov. 27	Coal mine, Shanxi province, China	91+
1996, Dec. 30	Train, Assam, India	59+
1997, Jan. 18	Near courthouse, Lahore, Pakistan	25
1997, Mar. 19	Ammunition depot, Jalalabad, Afgh.	16
1997, July 8	Train, Punjab, India	36

Date	Location	Deaths
1997, Nov. 19	Car, Hyderabad, India	23
1997, Dec. 2	Coal mine, Novokuznetsk, Siberia	68
1997, Dec. 6	Trains, southern India	10+
1998, Jan. 17	Coal mine, Sokobanja, Serbia	29
1998, Feb. 14	Oil tankers (2), Yaounde, Cameroon	120
1998, Feb. 14	17 bombs, Coimbatore, India	50
1998, Mar. 5	Bus, Colombo, Sri Lanka	32
1998, Apr. 4	Coal mine, Donetsk, Ukraine	63
1998, Aug. 7	Bomb, U.S. Embassy, Nairobi, Kenya	213
	Bomb, U.S. Embassy, Dar-es-Salaam, Tanzania	11
1998, Aug. 15	Car bomb, Omagh, Ireland	29
1998, Sept. 8	Two buses, Sao Paulo, Brazil	59
1998, Oct. 17	Oil pipeline, Jesse, Nigeria	700+
1999, May 16	Fuel truck, Punjab province, Pakistan	75
1999, July 29	Gold mine, Carletonville, S. Africa	17
1999, Sept. 10	Apartment building, Moscow	94
1999, Sept. 13	Apartment building, Moscow	118
1999, Sept. 16	Apartment building, Moscow	18
1999, Sept. 26	Fireworks factory, Celaya, Mexico	56
2000, Feb. 25	Two buses with bombs, Ozamis, Philippines	41
2000, Mar. 11	Coal mine, Krasnodon, Ukraine	80
2000, Apr. 16	Airport hangar, Congo, Dem. Rep. of	100+
2000, July 16	Oil pipeline, Warri, Nigeria	30
2000, Aug. 19	Train derailed in Nairobi, Kenya	25
2000, Aug. 20	Natural gas pipeline, Carlsbad, NM	10
2000, Sept. 9	Truck explodes in Urumqi, China	60
2000, Sept. 13	Bomb, Jakarta, Indonesia	15
2000, Sept. 19	Bomb, Islamabad, Pakistan	16
2000, Oct. 12	U.S. destroyer, Yemen	17
2001, Mar. 6	School, Wanzai County China	41
2001, Apr. 21	Coal mine, Shaanxi, China	51
2001, June 1	Dance club, Tel Aviv, Israel	21
2001, July 17	Coal mine, Guanxi, China	76+
2001, Aug. 19	Coal mine, Donetsk region, Ukraine	52
2001, Sept. 21	Chem. plant, Toulouse, France	29
2002, Jan. 21	Volcanic lava causes gas station blast in Goma, Dem. Rep. of the Congo	50+
2002, Jan. 27	Munitions dump, Lagos, Nigeria	1,000+
2002, Mar. 17	Grenade at church near U.S. embassy, Islamabad, Pakistan	5
2002, Mar. 21	Car bomb near U.S. embassy, Lima, Peru	9
2002, Apr. 11	Truck outside Ghriba synagogue, Djerba, Tunisia	17
2002, Apr. 21	Bomb outside department store, Mindanao, Philippines	14
2002, Apr. 26	Bomb at mosque, central Pakistan	12
2002, May 8	Suicide bomber on bus outside hotel, Karachi, Pakistan	14
2002, May 9	Land mine during parade, Kaspiisk, Russia	34+
2002, June 14	Car bomb outside U.S. consulate, Karachi, Pakistan	12
2002, June 18	Bomb on bus, Jerusalem, Israel	20
2002, July 5	Bomb in market, Larba, Algeria	35+
2002, Aug. 9	Explosion at road construction company, Jalalabad, Afghanistan	25+
2002, Sept. 5	Car bomb, Kabul, Afghanistan	30

Notable Nuclear Accidents

Oct. 7, 1957 — A fire in the Windscale plutonium production reactor N of Liverpool, England, released radioactive material; later blamed for 39 cancer deaths.

Jan. 3, 1961 — A reactor at a federal installation near Idaho Falls, ID, killed 3 workers. Radiation contained.

Oct. 5, 1966 — A sodium cooling system malfunction caused a partial core meltdown at the Enrico Fermi demonstration breeder reactor, near Detroit, MI. Radiation contained.

Jan. 21, 1969 — A coolant malfunction from an experimental underground reactor at Lucens Vad, Switzerland, released a large amount of radiation into a cavern, which was then sealed.

Mar. 22, 1975 — Fire at the Brown's Ferry reactor in Decatur, AL, caused dangerous lowering of cooling water levels.

Mar. 28, 1979 — The worst commercial nuclear accident in the U.S. occurred as equipment failures and human mistakes led to a loss of coolant and a partial core meltdown at the Three Mile Island reactor in Middletown, PA.

Feb. 11, 1981 — Eight workers were contaminated when more than 100,000 gallons of radioactive coolant fluid leaked into the containment building of TVA's Sequoyah 1 plant in Tennessee.

Apr. 25, 1981 — Some 100 workers were exposed to radiation during repairs of a nuclear plant at Tsuruga, Japan.

Jan. 6, 1986 — A cylinder of nuclear material burst after being improperly heated at a Kerr-McGee plant at Gore, OK. One worker died; 100 were hospitalized.

Apr. 26, 1986 — In the worst accident in the history of nuclear power, fires and explosions resulting from an unauthorized experiment at the Chernobyl nuclear power plant near Kiev, USSR (now in Ukraine), left at least 31 dead in the immediate aftermath and spread radioactive material over much of Europe. An estimated 135,000 people were evacuated from areas around Chernobyl, some of which were uninhabitable for years. As a result of the radiation released, tens of thousands of excess cancer deaths (as well as increased birth defects) were expected.

Sept. 30, 1999 — Japan's worst nuclear accident ever occurred at a uranium-reprocessing facility in Tokaimura, NE of Tokyo, when workers accidentally overloaded a container with uranium, thereby exposing workers and area residents to extremely high radiation levels.

On Dec. 24, 1984, in the worst industrial accident in history, more than 3,000 people were killed within hours when toxic gas leaked from a storage tank in a Union Carbide insecticide factory in a heavily populated section of Bhopal, India. An estimated 14,000 or more people were eventually killed, and more than 100,000 suffered injuries, including severe damage to eyes, lungs, and kidneys.

Record Oil Spills

The number of tons can be multiplied by 7 to estimate roughly the number of barrels spilled; the exact number of barrels in a ton varies with the type of oil. Each barrel contains 42 gallons.

Name, place	Date	Cause	Tons
Ixtoc I oil well, S Gulf of Mexico	June 3, 1979	Blowout	600,000
Nowruz oil field, Persian Gulf	Feb. 1983	Blowout	600,000 (est.)
Atlantic Empress & *Aegean Captain*, off Trinidad and Tobago	July 19, 1979	Collision	300,000
Castillo de Bellver, off Cape Town, South Africa	Aug. 6, 1983	Fire	250,000
Amoco Cadiz, near Portsall, France	Mar. 16, 1978	Grounding	223,000
Torrey Canyon, off Land's End, England	Mar. 18, 1967	Grounding	119,000
Sea Star, Gulf of Oman	Dec. 19, 1972	Collision	115,000
Urquiola, La Coruna, Spain	May 12, 1976	Grounding	100,000
Hawaiian Patriot, N Pacific	Feb. 25, 1977	Fire	99,000
Othello, Tralhavet Bay, Sweden	Mar. 20, 1970	Collision	60,000-100,000

Other Notable Oil Spills

Name, place	Date	Cause	Gallons
Persian Gulf	began Jan. 23, 1991	Spillage by Iraq	130,000,000[1]
Braer, off Shetland Islands	Jan. 5, 1993	Grounding	26,000,000
Aegean Sea, off N Spain	Dec. 3, 1992	Unknown	21,500,000
Sea Empress, off SW Wales	Feb. 15, 1996	Grounding	18,000,000
World Glory, off South Africa	June 13, 1968	Hull failure	13,524,000
Exxon Valdez, Prince William Sound, AK	Mar. 24, 1989	Grounding	10,080,000
Keo, off MA	Nov. 5, 1969	Hull failure	8,820,000
Storage tank, Sewaren, NJ	Nov. 4, 1969	Tank rupture	8,400,000
Ekofisk oil field, North Sea	Apr. 22, 1977	Well blowout	8,200,000
Argo Merchant, Nantucket, MA	Dec. 15, 1976	Grounding	7,700,000
Pipeline, West Delta, LA	Oct. 15, 1967	Dragging anchor	6,720,000
Tanker off Japan	Nov. 30, 1971	Ship broke in half	6,258,000

(1) Est. by Saudi Arabia. Some estimates as low as 25 mil gal.

THE YEAR IN PICTURES

VINCENT LAFORET/THE NEW YORK TIMES

AP/WIDE WORLD PHOTOS

▲ SEPTEMBER 11, 2002

During a ceremony at the site where New York City's World Trade Center stood, the names of 2,801 people believed lost there were read out over 2½ hours. Mourners (right) left flowers. Commemorations were also held at the Pentagon, in Shanksville, PA, and around the nation and world for the 3,000 people killed in terrorist attacks one year earlier.

AP/WIDE WORLD PHOTOS

AP/WIDE WORLD PHOTOS

PROBING 9-11

FBI Agent Coleen Rowley (left) appears before a Senate committee June 6; she charged that Washington bureau heads hindered field agents investigating Zacarias Moussaoui in August 2001. Prosecutors later alleged that Moussaoui (right) had conspired with the 19 hijackers in the 9-11 attacks and might have participated had he not been in detention on immigration charges.

AP/WIDE WORLD PHOTOS

AP/WIDE WORLD PHOTOS

AP/WIDE WORLD PHOTOS

▲ HOMELAND SECURITY

In the wake of 9-11, the nation sought to tighten security procedures. Above left, passengers undergo screening at Denver International Airport. On Capitol Hill (above, from left), Attorney Gen. John Ashcroft, Defense Sec. Donald H. Rumsfeld, Treasury Sec. Paul O'Neill, and Sec. of State Colin Powell testify July 11 before a House committee about Pres. George W. Bush's plan to consolidate federal agencies involved in protecting against domestic terrorism.

▼ WAR ON TERRORISM

U.S. paratroopers arrive in July at Kandahar Airfield as part of Operation Enduring Freedom, aimed at uprooting al-Qaeda terrorists and their Taliban backers in Afghanistan. At left, Hamid Karzai, who became interim leader of Afghanistan in December 2001 once the Taliban were ousted from the capital city, arrives there for a *Loya Jirga*, or grand council meeting, June 14, after being voted in as head of a transitional government.

AP/WIDE WORLD PHOTOS

U.S. ARMY

AP/WIDE WORLD PHOTOS

AP/WIDE WORLD PHOTOS

▲ CORPORATE SCANDALS

Above, a worker leaves WorldCom offices outside Atlanta, June 28. The telecommunications giant announced 17,000 layoffs and later reported $7 billion in overstated earnings; its bankruptcy filing was the largest in U.S. history. Above right, former Enron CEO Jeffrey Skilling (right) and VP Sherron Watkins are sworn in Feb. 28 before a Senate committee probing accounting improprieties at the now-bankrupt energy-trading conglomerate.

AP/WIDE WORLD PHOTOS

WALL STREET WOES ►

A seemingly distraught trader at the New York Stock Exchange rests his order book on his forehead July 18. Major stock indexes fell to 4-year lows in mid-July.

AP/WIDE WORLD PHOTOS

◄ BUSH SEEKS ACTION ON IRAQ
Addressing the General Assembly Sept. 12, Pres. George W. Bush called on the UN to force Iraq to comply with UN resolutions, including eliminating weapons of mass destruction. The president said that if Iraq did not comply, "action will be unavoidable."

AP/WIDE WORLD PHOTOS

CAMPAIGN FINANCE REFORM ►
Sen. John McCain (right; R, AZ) and Sen. Russ Feingold (D, WI) enjoy a long-sought victory, Mar. 20, after a crucial Senate vote ensured passage of their Campaign Finance Reform Bill banning "soft money" contributions to political parties.

AP/WIDE WORLD PHOTOS

◄ SUMMIT ON ABUSE
Pope John Paul II reads his opening message Apr. 23, at a 2-day closed-door meeting with American cardinals at the Vatican. The meeting was called to address the growing scandal involving sexual abuse of minors by priests.

AP/WIDE WORLD PHOTOS

ALL NINE ALIVE! ►
The last of 9 miners trapped 240 feet underground for 3 days in the Quecreek Mine in southwestern Pennsylvania is brought safely to the surface in a special steel capsule early on July 28, to the cheers of relieved rescuers.

▼ WESTERN WILDFIRES
The Missionary Ridge fire burns in mid-June around the Vallecito Reservoir in southwestern Colorado. More than 6 million acres across the drought-stricken western U.S. were scorched during June, July, and August, with large fires sweeping through Oregon, Arizona, and Colorado. About half the country was affected by drought conditions over the summer, with western states experiencing their driest June-August on record, according to the National Climactic Data Center.

AP/WIDE WORLD PHOTOS

AFP

▲ DENZEL & HALLE
Halle Berry (left) and Denzel Washington won best actress and actor awards at Oscar ceremonies Mar. 24. She was the 1st African-American woman to win it; he was the 2nd African-American man.

AP/WIDE WORLD PHOTOS

▲ SPRINGSTEEN RISING
Rocker Bruce Springsteen (left) reunites with Steven Van Zandt and the E Street Band at a concert in Washington, DC, Aug. 10. His new album, *The Rising*, which focused on Sept. 11 and its aftermath, debuted at #1.

▼ SPIDER-MAN CLIMBS CHARTS
Tobey Maguire (left), as Spider-Man, drops in on Kirsten Dunst. The film, based on the Marvel comic, took in a record $114 million its opening weekend. By September it was the 5th-highest-grossing film ever, passing $400 million.

MICHAEL YARISH, COURTESY OF MTV

FATHER KNOWS BEST?! ►
Heavy metal rocker Ozzy Osbourne and family (clockwise from top: Sharon, Kelly, Jack, Ozzy) became the unlikely stars of a heavily censored (for language) hit MTV reality show, *The Osbournes*.

2003 FAREWELLS

MILTON BERLE ►
Milton Berle died Mar. 27 at 93. A former vaudeville and radio comic, he debuted on TV in 1948, becoming the medium's first superstar.

AP/WIDE WORLD PHOTOS

AP/WIDE WORLD PHOTOS

◄ STEPHEN JAY GOULD
Harvard paleontologist, evolutionary theorist, and popular writer Stephen Jay Gould died May 20 at 60.

AP/WIDE WORLD PHOTOS

▲ ANN LANDERS
Eppie Lederer, known to the world as Ann Landers, died June 22 at 83. Her advice column ran in some 1,200 newspapers.

▼ QUEEN MOTHER
Britain's queen mother Elizabeth, especially beloved for her morale-boosting efforts during World War II, died Mar. 30 at 101.

AP/WIDE WORLD PHOTOS

AP/WIDE WORLD PHOTOS

▲ SAM SNEAD
Three-time Masters champ Sam Snead, shown at the 2002 Masters, died May 23 at 89. He won a record 82 PGA tournaments.

AP/WIDE WORLD PHOTOS

◄ BILLY WILDER
Oscar-winning writer-director Billy Wilder died Mar. 27 at 95. His films include *Sunset Boulevard*, *Some Like It Hot*, and *The Apartment*.

TED WILLIAMS ►
Boston Red Sox star and Hall of Famer Ted Williams died July 5 at 83. He was the last Major League player to hit over .400 (.406 in 1941).

AP/WIDE WORLD PHOTOS

NATIONAL DEFENSE

Chief Commanding Officers of the U.S. Military

Chairman, Joint Chiefs of Staff
Gen. Richard B. Myers (USAF)
Vice Chairman
Gen. Peter Pace (USN)

The Joint Chiefs of Staff consists of the Chairman and Vice Chairman of the Joint Chiefs of Staff; the Chief of Staff, U.S. Army; the Chief of Naval Operations; the Chief of Staff, U.S. Air Force; and the Commandant of the Marine Corps.

Army

Chief of Staff	Date of Rank
Eric K. Shinseki	Aug. 5, 1997
Other Generals	
Abrams, John N.	Sept. 14, 1998
Coburn, John G.	May 14, 1999
Franks, Tommy R.	July 6, 2000
Hendrix, John W.	Nov. 23, 1999
Keane, John M.	Jan. 22, 1999
Kernan, William F.	July 2000
Meigs, Montgomery C.	Nov. 10, 1998
Schoomaker, Peter J.	Oct. 24, 1997
Schwartz, Thomas A.	Aug. 31, 1998
Shelton, Henry H.	Mar. 1, 1996

Air Force

Chief of Staff	Date of Rank
John P. Jumper	Nov. 17, 1997
Other Generals	
Cook, Donald G.	Dec, 17, 2001
Eberhart, Ralph E.	Aug. 1, 1997
Foglesong, Robert H.	Nov. 5, 2001
Handy, John W.	July 1, 2000
Holland, Charles R.	Dec. 1, 2000
Hornburg, Hal M.	Aug. 1, 2000
Jumper, John P.	Nov. 17, 1997
Lord, Lance W.	Apr. 19, 2002
Lyles, Lester L.	July 1, 1999
Martin, Gregory S.	June 1, 2000
Myers, Richard B.	Sept. 1, 1997
Ralston, Joseph W.	July 1, 1995

Navy

Chief of Naval Operations	Date of Rank
Clark, Vernon E. (surface warfare)	Nov. 1, 1999
Other Admirals	
Bowman, Frank L. (submariner)	Oct. 1, 1996
Doran, Walter F. (surface warfare)	May 4, 2002
Ellis, James O., Jr. (aviator)	Jan. 1, 1999
Fallon, William J. (aviator)	Nov. 1, 2000
Fargo, Thomas B. (submariner)	Dec. 1, 1999
Giambastiani, Edmund P., Jr. (submariner)	Oct. 2, 2002
Johnson, Gregory G. (aviator)	Feb. 1, 2002
Natter, Robert J. (surface warfare)	Sept. 1, 2000

Marine Corps

Commandant of the Marine Corps (CMC)	Date of Rank
Gen. James L. Jones	July 1, 1999
Other Generals	
Fulford Jr, Carlton W.	Oct. 1, 2000
Nyland, William L.	Sept. 4, 2002
Pace, Peter	Nov. 1, 2000
Williams, Michael J.	Nov. 1, 2000

Coast Guard

Commandant, with rank of Admiral	Date of Rank
Thomas H. Collins	May 30, 2002
Vice Commandant, with rank of Vice Admiral	
Thomas J. Barrett	NA

Unified Combatant Commands Commanders in Chief

U.S. European Command, Stuttgart-Vaihingen, Germany — Gen. Joseph W. Ralston (USAF) (concurrently NATO Supreme Allied Commander, Europe)
U.S. Pacific Command, Honolulu, HI — Adm. Thomas B. Fargo (USN)
U.S. Joint Forces Command, Norfolk, VA — Gen. William F. Kernan (U.S. Army) (concurrently NATO Supreme Allied Commander, Atlantic)
U.S. Special Operations Command, MacDill AFB, Florida — Gen. Charles R. Holland (USAF)
U.S. Transportation Command, Scott AFB, Illinois — Gen. John W. Handy (USAF)
U.S. Central Command, MacDill AFB, Florida — Gen. Tommy R. Franks (U.S. Army)
U.S. Southern Command, Miami, FL — Maj. Gen. Gary D. Speer (U.S. Army), *acting*
U.S. Northern Command, Peterson AFB, Colorado — Gen. Ralph E. Eberhart (USAF)
U.S. Strategic Command, Offutt AFB, Nebraska — Adm. James O. Ellis Jr. (USN)

North Atlantic Treaty Organization International Commands

NATO Headquarters:
Chairman, NATO Military Committee — Gen. Harald Kujat (Germany)

Strategic Command:
Allied Command Europe (ACE) — Gen. Joseph W. Ralston (USAF), Supreme Allied Commander, Europe

Subordinate Command:
Allied Forces South Europe (AFSOUTH) — Adm. James D. Ellis Jr. (USN), Commander-in-Chief, South
Allied Forces North Europe (AFNORTH) — Gen. Sir John Deverell KCB OBE (Royal Army, UK), Commander-in-Chief, North

Strategic Command:
Allied Command Atlantic (ACLANT) — Gen. William F. Kernan (U.S. Army), Supreme Allied Commandor, Atlantic

Subordinate Commands:
Western Atlantic (WESTLANT) — Adm. Robert J. Natter (USN), Commander-in-Chief, Western Atlantic
Southern Atlantic (SOUTHLANT) — Vice Adm. Americo da Silva Santos (Portuguese Navy), Commander-in-Chief, Southern Atlantic
Eastern Atlantic (EASTLANT) — Adm. Alan West KCB DSC, (Royal Navy, UK), Commander-in-Chief, Eastern Atlantic

Principal U.S. Military Training Centers

Army

Name, PO address	ZIP	Nearest city
Aberdeen Proving Ground, MD	21005	Aberdeen
Carlisle Barracks, PA	17013	Carlisle
Fort Benning, GA	31905	Columbus
Fort Bliss, TX	79916	El Paso
Fort Bragg, NC	28307	Fayetteville
Fort Gordon, GA	30905	Augusta
Fort Huachuca, AZ	85613	Sierra Vista
Fort Jackson, SC	29207	Columbia
Fort Knox, KY	40121	Radcliff
Fort Leavenworth, KS	66027	Leavenworth
Fort Lee, VA	23801	Petersburg
Fort McClellan, AL	36205	Anniston
Fort Rucker, AL	36362	Dothan
Fort Sill, OK	73503	Lawton
Fort Leonard Wood, MO	65473	St. Robert
Joint Readiness Training Center, Ft. Polk, LA	71459	Leesville
National Training Center, Ft. Irwin, CA	92311	Barstow, CA
The Judge Advocate General School, VA	22901	Charlottesville

Navy

Name, PO address	ZIP	Nearest city	Name, PO address	ZIP	Nearest city
Naval Education & Training Ctr.	32508	Pensacola, FL	Naval Post Graduate School	93943	Monterey, CA
Naval Air Training Center	78419	Corpus Christi,TX	Naval Submarine School	06349	Groton, CT
Training Command Fleet	23511	Norfolk, VA	Naval Training Ctr., Great Lakes	60088	N. Chicago, IL
Training Command Fleet	92113	San Diego, CA	Naval War College	02841	Newport, RI
Naval Aviation Schools Command	32508	Pensacola, FL	Naval Air Tech. Training Ctr.	32508	Pensacola, FL
Naval Education & Training Ctr.	02841	Newport, RI	Fleet Antisubmarine Warfare	92147	San Diego, CA

Marine Corps

Name, PO address	ZIP	Nearest city	Name, PO address	ZIP	Nearest city
MCB Camp Lejeune, NC	28542	Jacksonville	MCAS Cherry Point, NC	28533	Havelock
MCBCamp Pendleton, CA	92055	Oceanside	MCAS Miramar, CA	92145	San Diego
MCB Kaneohe Bay, HI	96863	Kailua	MCAS New River, NC	28545	Jacksonville
MCAGCCTwentynine Palms, CA	92278	Palm Springs	MCAS Beaufort, SC	29904	Beaufort
MCCDC Quantico, VA	22134	Quantico	MCAS Yuma, AZ	85369	Yuma
MCRD Parris Island, SC.	29905	Beaufort	MCMWTC Bridgeport, CA.	93517	Bridgeport
MCRD San Diego, CA	92140	San Diego			

MCB = Marine Corps Base. MCCDC = Marine Corps Combat Development Command. MCAS = Marine Corps Air Station. MCRD = Marine Corps Recruit Depot. MCAGCC = Marine Corps Air-Ground Combat Center. MCMWTC = Marine Corps Mountain Warfare Training Center.

Air Force

Name, PO address	ZIP	Nearest city	Name, PO address	ZIP	Nearest city
Goodfellow AFB, TX	76908	San Angelo	Maxwell AFB, AL	36112	Montgomery
Keesler AFB, MS	39534	Biloxi	Sheppard AFB, TX	76311	Wichita Falls
Lackland AFB, TX	78236	San Antonio			

All are Air Education and Training Command Bases.

Personal Salutes and Honors, U.S.

The U.S. national salute, 21 guns, is also the salute to a national flag. U.S. independence is commemorated by the salute to the Union—one gun for each state—fired at noon July 4, at all military posts provided with suitable artillery.

A 21-gun salute on arrival and departure, with 4 ruffles and flourishes, is rendered to the **president** of the United States, to an ex-president, and to a president-elect. The national anthem or "Hail to the Chief," as appropriate, is played for the president, and the national anthem for the others. A 21-gun salute on arrival and departure, with 4 ruffles and flourishes, also is rendered to the **sovereign or chief of state** of a foreign country or a member of a reigning royal family, and the national anthem of his or her country is played. The music is considered an inseparable part of the salute and immediately follows the ruffles and flourishes without pause. For the Honors March, generals receive the "General's March," admirals receive the "Admiral's March," and all others receive the 32-bar medley of "The Stars and Stripes Forever."

GRADE, TITLE, OR OFFICE	SALUTE (IN GUNS) Arriving	Leaving	Ruffles and flourishes	Music
Vice president of United States	19		4	Hail, Columbia
Speaker of the House	19		4	Honors March
U.S. or foreign ambassador	19		4	Nat. anthem of official
Premier or prime minister	19		4	Nat. anthem of official
Secretary of Defense, Army, Navy, or Air Force	19	19	4	Honors March
Other cabinet members, Senate president pro tempore, governor, or chief justice of U.S.	19		4	Honors March
Chairman, Joint Chiefs of Staff	19	19	4	
Army chief of staff, chief of naval operations, Air Force chief of staff, Marine commandant	19	19	4	Honors March
General of the Army, general of the Air Force, fleet admiral	19	19	4	
Generals, admirals	17	17	4	
Assistant secretaries of Defense, Army, Navy, or Air Force	17	17	4	Honors March
Chair of a committee of Congress	17		4	Honors March

OTHER SALUTES (on arrival only) include: 15 guns, with 3 ruffles and flourishes, for U.S. envoys or ministers and foreign envoys or ministers accredited to the U.S.; 15 guns, for a lieutenant general or vice admiral; 13 guns, with 2 ruffles and flourishes, for a major general or rear admiral (upper half) and for U.S. ministers resident and ministers resident accredited to the U.S.; 11 guns, with 1 ruffle and flourish, for a brigadier general or rear admiral (lower half) and for U.S. charges d'affaires and like officials accredited to the U.S.; 11 guns, no ruffles and flourishes, for consuls general accredited to the U.S.

Military Units, U.S. Army and Air Force

ARMY UNITS. Squad: In infantry usually 10 enlisted personnel under a staff sergeant. **Platoon:** In infantry 4 squads under a lieutenant. **Company:** Headquarters section and 3 platoons under a captain. (Company-size unit in the artillery is a battery; in the cavalry, a troop.) **Battalion:** Hdqts. and 4 or more companies under a lieutenant colonel. (Battalion-size unit in the cavalry is a squadron.) **Brigade:** Hdqts. and 3 or more battalions under a colonel. **Division:** Hdqts. and 3 brigades with artillery, combat support, and combat service support units under a major general. **Army Corps:** Two or more divisions with corps troops under a lieutenant general. **Field Army:** Hdqts. and 2 or more corps with field Army troops under a general.

AIR FORCE UNITS. Flight: Numerically designated flights are the lowest level unit in the Air Force. They are used primarily where there is a need for small mission elements to be incorporated into an organized unit. **Squadron:** A squadron is the basic unit in the Air Force. It is used to designate the mission units in operational commands. **Group:** The group is a flexible unit composed of 2 or more squadrons whose functions may be operational, support, or administrative in nature. **Wing:** An operational wing normally has 2 or more assigned mission squadrons in an area such as combat, flying training, or airlift. **Numbered Air Forces:** Normally an operationally oriented agency, the numbered air force is designed for the control of 2 or more wings with the same mission and/or geographical location. **Major Command:** A major subdivision of the Air Force that is assigned a major segment of the USAF mission.

The Federal Service Academies

U.S. Military Academy, West Point, NY. Founded 1802. Awards BS degree and Army commission for a 5-year service obligation. For admissions information, write Admissions Office, Bldg. 606, USMA, West Point, NY 10996.

U.S. Naval Academy, Annapolis, MD. Founded 1845. Awards BS degree and Navy or Marine Corps commission for a 5-year service obligation. For admissions information, write Candidate Guidence Office, Naval Academy, Annapolis, MD 21402-5018.

U.S. Air Force Academy, Colorado Springs, CO. Founded 1954. Awards BS degree and Air Force commission for a 6-year service obligation. For admissions information, write Registrar, U.S. Air Force Academy, CO 80840-5025.

U.S. Coast Guard Academy, New London, CT. Founded 1876. Awards BS degree and Coast Guard commission for a 5-year service obligation. For admissions information, write Director of Admissions, Coast Guard Academy, New London, CT 06320-8103.

U.S. Merchant Marine Academy, Kings Point, NY. Founded 1943. Awards BS degree, a license as a deck, engineer, or dual officer, and a U.S. Naval Reserve commission. Service obligations vary according to options taken by the graduate. For admissions information, write Admission Office, U.S. Merchant Marine Academy, Kings Point, NY 11024.

U.S. Army, Navy, Air Force, Marine Corps, and Coast Guard Insignia

Source: Dept. of the Army, Dept. of the Navy, Dept. of the Air Force, U.S. Dept. of Defense

Army

General of the Armies — Gen. John J. Pershing (1860-1948), the only person to have held this rank, in life, was authorized to prescribe his own insignia, but never wore in excess of four stars. The rank originally was established posthumously by Congress for George Washington in 1799, and he was promoted to the rank by joint resolution of Congress, approved by Pres. Gerald Ford, Oct. 19, 1976.

General of the Army — Five silver stars fastened together in a circle and the coat of arms of the United States in gold color metal with shield and crest enameled.

General	Four silver stars
Lieutenant General	Three silver stars
Major General	Two silver stars
Brigadier General	One silver star
Colonel	Silver eagle
Lieutenant Colonel	Silver maple leaf
Major	Gold maple leaf
Captain	Two silver bars
First Lieutenant	One silver bar
Second Lieutenant	One gold bar

Warrant Officers

Grade Five — Silver bar with 4 enamel silver squares
Grade Four — Silver bar with 4 enamel black squares
Grade Three — Silver bar with 3 enamel black squares
Grade Two — Silver bar with 2 enamel black squares
Grade One — Silver bar with 1 enamel black squares

Noncommissioned Officers

Sergeant Major of the Army (E-9) — Three chevrons above 3 arcs, with an American Eagle centered on the chevrons, flanked by 2 stars—one star on each side of the eagle. Also wears distinctive red and white shield collar insignia.

Command Sergeant Major (E-9) — Three chevrons above 3 arcs with a 5-pointed star with a wreath around the star between the chevrons and arcs.

Sergeant Major (E-9) — Three chevrons above 3 arcs with a 5-pointed star between the chevrons and arcs.

First Sergeant (E-8) — Three chevrons above 3 arcs with a lozenge between the chevrons and arcs.

Master Sergeant (E-8) — Three chevrons above 3 arcs.
Sergeant First Class (E-7) — Three chevrons above 2 arcs.
Staff Sergeant (E-6) — Three chevrons above 1 arc.
Sergeant (E-5) — Three chevrons.
Corporal (E-4) — Two chevrons.

Specialists

Specialist (E-4) — Eagle device only.

Other enlisted

Private First Class (E-3) — One chevron above one arc.
Private (E-2) — One chevron.
Private (E-1) — None.

Air Force

Insignia for Air Force officers are identical to those of the Army. Insignia for enlisted personnel are worn on both sleeves and consist of a star and an appropriate number of rockers. Chevrons appear above 5 rockers for the top 3 noncommissioned officer ranks, as follows (in ascending order): Master Sergeant, 1 chevron; Senior Master Sergeant, 2 chevrons; and Chief Master Sergeant, 3 chevrons. The insignia of the Chief Master Sergeant of the Air Force has 3 chevrons and a wreath around the star design.

Navy

The following stripes are worn on the lower sleeves of the Service Dress Blue uniform. They are of gold embroidery.

Rank	Insignia
Fleet Admiral*	1 two inch with 4 one-half inch
Admiral	1 two inch with 3 one-half inch
Vice Admiral	1 two inch with 2 one-half inch
Rear Admiral (upper half)	1 two inchwith 1 one-half inch
Rear Admiral (lower half)	1 two inch
Captain	4 one-half inch
Commander	3 one-half inch
Lieutenant Commander	2 one-half inch with 1 one-quarter inch between
Lieutenant	2 one-half inch
Lieutenant (j.g.)	1 one-half inch with one-quarter inch above
Ensign	1 one-half inch

Warrant Officer-W-4 — ½″ stripe with 1 break
Warrant Officer W-3 — ½″ stripe with 2 breaks, 2″ apart
Warrant Officer W-2 — ½″ stripe with 3 breaks, 2″ apart

Enlisted personnel (noncommissioned petty officers)—A rating badge worn on the upper left sleeve, consisting of a spread eagle, appropriate number of chevrons, and centered specialty mark.

*The rank of Fleet Admiral is reserved for wartime use only.

Marine Corps

Marine Corps' distinctive cap and collar ornament is the Marine Corps Emblem—a combination of the American eagle, a globe, and an anchor. Marine Corps and Army officer insignia are similar. Marine Corps enlisted insignia, although basically similar to the Army's, feature crossed rifles beneath the chevrons. Marine Corps enlisted rank insignia are as follows:

Sergeant Major of the Marine Corps (E-9) — Same as Sergeant Major (below) but with Marine Corps emblem in the center with a 5-pointed star on both sides of the emblem.

Sergeant Major (E-9) — Three chevrons above 4 rockers with a 5-pointed star in the center.

Master Gunnery Sergeant (E-9) — Three chevrons above 4 rockers with a bursting bomb insignia in the center.

First Sergeant (E-8) — Three chevrons above 3 rockers with a diamond in the middle.

Master Sergeant (E-8) — Three chevrons above 3 rockers with crossed rifles in the middle.

Gunnery Sergeant (E-7) — Three chevrons above 2 rockers with crossed rifles in the middle.

Staff Sergeant (E-6) — Three chevrons above 1 rocker with crossed rifles in the middle.

Sergeant (E-5) — Three chevrons above crossed rifles.
Corporal (E-4) — Two chevrons above crossed rifles.
Lance Corporal (E-3) — One chevron above crossed rifles.
Private First Class (E-2) — One chevron.
Private (E-1) — None.

Coast Guard

Coast Guard insignia follow Navy custom, with certain minor changes such as the officer cap insignia. The Coast Guard shield is worn on both sleeves of officers and on the right sleeve of all enlisted personnel.

U.S. Army Personnel on Active Duty[1]

Source: Dept. of the Army, U.S. Dept. of Defense

Date[2]	Total strength[3]	Commissioned officers: Total	Commissioned officers: Male	Commissioned officers: Female[4]	Warrant officers: Male[5]	Warrant officers: Female	Enlisted personnel: Total	Enlisted personnel: Male	Enlisted personnel: Female
1940	267,767	17,563	16,624	939	763	—	249,441	249,441	—
1942	3,074,184	203,137	190,662	12,475	3,285	—	2,867,762	2,867,762	—
1943	6,993,102	557,657	521,435	36,222	21,919	—	6,413,526	6,358,200	55,325
1944	7,992,868	740,077	692,351	47,726	36,893	10	7,215,888	7,144,601	71,287
1945	8,266,373	835,403	772,511	62,892	56,216	44	7,374,710	7,283,930	90,780
1946	1,889,690	257,300	240,643	16,657	9,826	18	1,622,546	1,605,847	16,699
1950	591,487	67,784	63,375	4,409	4,760	22	518,921	512,370	6,551
1955	1,107,606	111,347	106,173	5,174	10,552	48	985,659	977,943	7,716
1960	871,348	91,056	86,832	4,224	10,141	39	770,112	761,833	8,279
1965	967,049	101,812	98,029	3,783	10,285	23	854,929	846,409	8,520
1970	1,319,735	143,704	138,469	5,235	23,005	13	1,153,013	1,141,537	11,476
1975	781,316	89,756	85,184	4,572	13,214	22	678,324	640,621	37,703
1980 (Sept. 30)	772,661	85,339	77,843	7,496	13,265	113	673,944	612,593	61,351
1985 (Sept. 30)	776,244	94,103	83,563	10,540	15,296	288	666,557	598,639	67,918
1990 (Mar. 31)	746,220	91,330	79,520	11,810	15,177	470	639,713	567,015	72,698
1995	521,036	72,646	62,250	10,396	12,053	599	435,807	377,832	57,975
1996 (May 31)	493,330	68,850	58,875	9,975	11,456	660	408,511	351,669	56,842
1997 (May 31)	487,297	67,986	58,270	9,716	11,021	719	403,072	342,817	60,255
1998	491,707	67,048	56,650	10,398	10,989	661	402,000	345,149	56,851
1999	479,100	66,613	56,952	9,661	10,767	757	388,211	329,803	58,408
2000	471,633	66,344	56,391	9,953	10,608	781	393,900	333,947	59,953
2001	478,918	76,882[6]	NA	NA	NA	NA	398,983	NA	NA
2002	485,536	78,170[6]	NA	NA	NA	NA	404,363	NA	NA

NA = Not available. (1) Represents strength of the active Army, including Philippine Scouts, retired Regular Army personnel on extended active duty, and National Guard and Reserve personnel on extended active duty; excludes U.S. Military Academy cadets, contract surgeons, and National Guard and Reserve personnel not on extended active duty. (2) June 30, unless otherwise noted. (3) Data for 1940 to 1946 include personnel in the Army Air Forces and its predecessors (Air Service and Air Corps). (4) Includes women doctors, dentists, and Medical Service Corps officers for 1946 and subsequent years, women in the Army Nurse Corps for all years, and the Women's Army Corps and Women's Medical Specialists Corps (dietitians, physical therapists, and occupational specialists) for 1943 and subsequent years. (5) Act of Congress approved Apr. 27, 1926, directed the appointment as warrant officers of field clerks still in active service. Includes flight officers as follows: 1943, 5,700; 1944, 13,615; 1945, 31,117; 1946, 2,580. (6) Includes warrant officers.

U.S. Navy Personnel on Active Duty

Source: Dept. of the Navy, U.S. Dept. of Defense

(As of June 30, 2002)

Date	Officers	Nurses	Enlisted	Officer Candidates	Total
1940 (June)	13,162	442	144,824	2,569	160,997
1945 (June)	320,293	11,086	2,988,207	61,231	3,380,817
1950 (June)	42,687	1,964	331,860	5,037	381,538
1960 (June)	67,456	2,103	544,040	4,385	617,984
1970 (June)	78,488	2,273	605,899	6,000	692,660
1980 (June)[1]	63,100	—	464,100	—	527,200
1990 (Sept.)	74,429	—	530,133	—	604,562
1993 (Mar.)	66,787	—	445,409	—	512,196
1994 (Apr.)	64,430	—	418,378	—	482,808
1995 (May)	61,075	—	402,626	—	463,701
1996 (June)	60,013	—	376,595	—	436,608
1997 (June)	57,341	—	340,616	—	397,957
1998 (Sept.)	55,007	—	326,196	—	381,203
1999 (June)	55,726	—	322,372	—	378,098
2000 (Oct.)	53,698	—	320,212	—	373,910
2001 (Aug.)	54,177	—	317,100	—	375,618
2002 (June)	55,506	—	324,712	—	384,576

(1) Starting in 1980, "Nurses" are included with "Officers," and "Officer Candidates" are included with "Enlisted."

U.S. Marine Corps Personnel on Active Duty

Source: Dept. of the Marines, U.S. Dept. of Defense

(As of June 30, 2002)

Year	Officers	Enlisted	Total
1940	1,800	26,545	28,345
1945	37,067	437,613	474,680
1950	7,254	67,025	74,279
1960	16,203	154,418	170,621
1970	24,941	234,796	259,737
1980	18,198	170,271	188,469
1990	19,958	176,694	196,652
1991	19,753	174,287	194,040
1992	19,132	165,397	184,529
1993	18,878	161,205	180,083
1994	18,430	159,949	178,379
1995	18,017	153,929	171,946
1996	18,146	154,141	172,287
1997	18,089	154,240	172,329
1998	17,984	154,648	172,632
1999	17,892	155,250	173,142
2000	17,897	154,744	172,641
2001	18,072	152,559	170,631
2002	18,472	154,913	173,385

U.S. Air Force Personnel on Active Duty

Source: Air Force Dept., U.S. Dept. of Defense

(as of June 30, 2002)

Year[1]	Strength
1918	195,023
1920	9,050
1930	13,531
1940	51,165
1941	152,125
1942	764,415
1943	2,197,114
1944	2,372,292
1945	2,282,259
1950	411,277
1960	814,213
1970	791,078
1980	557,969
1986	608,200
1990	535,233
1991	510,432
1992	470,315
1993	444,351
1994	426,327
1995	400,051
1996	389,400
1997	378,681
1998	363,479
1999	357,929
2000	357,777
2001	351,935
2002	369,721

(1) Prior to 1947, data are for U.S. Army Air Corps and Air Service of the Signal Corps.

U.S. Coast Guard Personnel on Active Duty

Source: U.S. Coast Guard, U.S. Dept. of Defense

(midyear personnel figures)

Year	Total	Officers	Cadets	Enlisted
1970	37,689	5,512	653	31,524
1980	39,381	6,463	877	32,041
1985	38,595	6,775	733	31,087
1990	37,308	6,475	820	29,860
1992	39,185	7,348	919	30,918
1993	38,832	7,724	691	30,417
1994	37,284	7,401	881	29,002
1995	36,731	7,489	841	28,401
1996	35,229	7,270	830	27,129
1997	34,717	7,079	868	26,770
1998	34,890	7,140	805	26,945
1999	35,266	7,135	880	27,251
2000	35,712	7,154	863	27,695
2001	35,328	7,112	631	27,585
2002	37,166	7,267	694	29,205

Chairmen of the Joint Chiefs of Staff, 1949-2002

Gen. of the Army Omar N. Bradley, USA	8/16/49 –8/14/53
Adm. Arthur W. Radford, USN	8/15/53 – 8/14/57
Gen. Nathan F. Twining, USAF	8/15/57 – 9/30/60
Gen. Lyman L. Lemnitzer, USA	10/1/60 – 10/30/62
Gen. Maxwell D. Taylor, USA	10/1/62 – 7/3/64
Gen. Earle G. Wheeler, USA	7/3/64 – 7/2/70
Adm. Thomas H. Moorer, USN	7/3/70 – 6/30/74
Gen. George S. Brown, USAF	7/1/74 – 6/20/78
Gen. David C. Jones, USAF	6/21/78 – 6/18/82
Gen. John W. Vessey Jr., USA	6/18/82 – 9/30/85
Adm. William J. Crowe, Jr., USN	10/1/85 – 9/30/89
Gen. Colin L. Powell, USA	10/1/89 – 9/30/93
Gen. John M. Shalikashvili, USA	10/1/93 – 9/30/97
Gen. Henry H. Shelton, USA	10/1/97 – 9/30/01
Gen. Richard B. Myers	10/1/01 –

Women in the U.S. Armed Forces

Source: U.S. Dept. of Defense

Women in the Army, Navy, Air Force, Marines, and Coast Guard are fully integrated with male personnel. Expansion of military women's programs began in the Department of Defense in fiscal year 1973.

Admission of women to the service academies began in the fall of 1976.

Under rules instituted in 1993, women were allowed to fly combat aircraft and serve aboard warships. Women remained restricted from service in ground combat units.

Between Apr. 1993 and July 1994, almost 260,000 positions in the armed forces were opened to women. By the mid-1990s, 80% of all jobs and more than 90% of all career fields in the military had been opened to women. By mid-2000, women made up 14% of the armed forces.

Women Active Duty Troops in 2000

Service	% Women
Army	15.1
Navy	14.0
Marines	5.9
Air Force	19.0
Coast Guard	10.2

Women on Active Duty, All Services*: 1973-2000

Year	% Women
1973	2.5
1975	4.6
1981	8.9
1987	10.2
1993	11.6
2000	14.4

*Not including the Coast Guard, which is a part of the Dept. of Transportation.

For Further Information on the U.S. Armed Forces

Army — Office of the Chief of Public Affairs, Attention: Media Relations Division—MRD, Army 1500, Wash., DC 20310-1500. **Website:** www.army.mil

Navy — Chief of Information, 1200 Navy Pentagon, Wash., DC 20350-1200. **Website:** www.navy.mil

Air Force — Office of Public Affairs, 1690 Air Force, Pentagon, Wash., DC 20330-1690. **Website:** www.af.mil

Marine Corps — Commandant of the Marine Corps (Code PA), Headquarters, U.S. Marine Corps, Wash. DC 20380-1775. **Website:** www.usmc.mil

Coast Guard — Commandant (G-IPA), U.S. Coast Guard, 2100 Second St. SW, Wash., DC 20593-0001. **Website:** www.uscg.mil

Additional information on all the U.S. Armed Forces branches, as well as many other related organizations, can be accessed through DefenseLINK, the official Internet site of the Dept. of Defense: www.defenselink.mil

African American Service in U.S. Wars

American Revolution. About 5,000 African Americans served in the Continental Army, mostly in integrated units, some in all-black combat units.

Civil War. Some 200,000 African Americans served in the Union Army; 38,000 were killed, and 22 won the Medal of Honor (the nation's highest award).

World War I. About 367,000 African Americans served in the armed forces, 100,000 in France.

World War II. Over 1 mil African Americans served in the armed forces; all-black fighter and bomber AAF units and infantry divisions gave distinguished service. (By 1954, armed forces were completely desegregated.)

Korean War. Approximately 3,100 African Americans lost their lives in combat.

Vietnam War. 274,937 African Americans served in the armed forces (1965-74); 5,681 were killed in combat.

Persian Gulf War. About 104,000 African Americans served in the Kuwaiti theater—20% of all U.S. troops, compared with 8.7% of all troops for World War II and 9.8% for Vietnam.

Defense Contracts, 2000

Source: U.S. Dept. of Defense

(in thousands of dollars)

Listed are the 50 companies (including their subsidiaries) or organizations receiving the largest dollar volume of prime contract awards from the U.S. Department of Defense during fiscal year 2000.

Lockheed Martin	$15,125,846
Boeing	12,041,420
Raytheon	6,330,613
General Dynamics	4,195,923
Northrop Grumman	3,079,615
Litton Industries	2,737,284
United Technologies	2,071,536
TRW	2,004,857
General Electric	1,609,329
Science Applications Intl.	1,522,077
Carlyle Group	1,194,713
Computer Sciences	1,164,634
Textron	1,164,465
Marconi	997,339
Honeywell International	951,255
Newport News Shipbuilding	789,900
Dyncorp	771,235
Bechtel Group, Inc.	694,717
Government of Canada	$676,881
National Amusements	619,696
Morrison Knudsen	596,635
Halliburton	595,070
BP Amoco	591,953
Energy, U.S. Dept. of	590,631
ITT Industries	553,972
Health Net	550,580
IT Group	493,335
Rockwell International	473,668
Alliant Techsystems	470,397
Longbow Limited Liability	468,091
FED EX	452,385
Maersk	426,798
Stewart & Stevenson Services	424,051
Booz Allen & Hamilton	419,576
Mitre	409,217
Federal Republic of Germany	$408,004
Raytheon Lockheed Martin	401,584
Jacobs Engineering Group	387,343
Boeing Sikorsky Comanche Team	384,751
L-3 Communications Holding	377,662
Oshkosh Truck	372,526
AT&T	352,547
Johns Hopkins Univ.	351,776
Mass. Inst. of Technology	347,197
Triwest Healthcore Alliance	335,878
Philipp Holzmann Aktiengesells	334,703
Aerospace Corporation	334,194
Renco Group	330,064
Electronic Data Systems	329,554
Exxon Mobil	324,816

U.S. Veteran Population

Source: U.S. Dept. of Veterans Affairs; as of September 30, 2002

TOTAL VETERANS IN CIVILIAN LIFE[1]	**24,934,117**
Total wartime veterans[2]	**18,765,511**
Total Gulf War	3,231,627
Gulf War with service in Vietnam era	303,207
Gulf War with no prior wartime service	2,928,231
Total Vietnam era	8,381,801
Vietnam era with service in Korean conflict	265,868
Vietnam era with no prior wartime service	7,658,077
Total Korean conflict	3,727,550
Korean conflict with service in WWII	348,585
Korean conflict with no prior wartime service	2,958,449
World War II	4,651,144
World War I	347
Total peacetime veterans	**6,168,607**
Service between Vietnam era and Gulf War only	3,389,027
Service between Korean conflict and Vietnam era only	2,672,656
Other peacetime	106,923

NOTE: Details may not add to total shown because of rounding. (1) There are an indeterminate number of Mexican Border period veterans, 5 of whom were receiving benefits in August 2002. (2) The total for "wartime veterans" consists only of veterans from each listed war that had no prior wartime service. Figures are for U.S. veterans worldwide. Source: VetPop2001, VA Office of the Actuary

Veterans Compensation and Pension Case Payments

Source: 1900-1980: Dept. of Veterans Affairs; 1990-2001: Natl. Center for Veteran Analysis and Statistics

Fiscal year	Living veteran cases	Deceased veteran cases	Total cases	Total expenditures (dollars)
1900	752,510	241,019	993,529	$138,462,130
1910	602,622	318,461	921,083	159,974,056
1920	419,627	349,916	769,543	316,418,030
1930	542,610	298,223	840,833	418,432,809
1940	610,122	239,176	849,298	429,138,465
1950	2,368,238	658,123	3,026,361	2,009,462,298
1960	3,008,935	950,802	3,959,737	3,314,761,383
1970	3,127,338	1,487,176	4,614,514	5,253,839,611
1980	3,195,395	1,450,785	4,646,180	11,046,637,368
1990	2,746,329	837,596	3,583,925	$14,674,411,000
1995	2,668,576	661,679	3,330,255	17,765,045,000
1996	2,671,026	637,232	3,308,258	17,055,809,000
1997	2,666,785	613,976	3,280,761	19,284,287,000
1998	2,668,030	594,782	3,262,812	20,164,598,000
1999	2,673,167	578,508	3,251,675	21,023,864,000
2000	2,672,407	563,754	3,236,161	21,963,216,000
2001	2,669,156	548,589	3,217,745	23,198,139,000

Active Duty U.S. Military Personnel Strengths, Worldwide, 2001

Source: U.S. Dept. of Defense

(as of Dec. 31, 2001)

U.S. TERRITORIES & SPEC. LOCATIONS	
U.S., 48 contiguous states	947,955
Alaska	15,926
Hawaii	33,191
Guam	3,398
Puerto Rico	2,525
Transients	27,208
Afloat	99,485
Regional Total[1]	**1,129,747**
EUROPE	
Belgium	1,554
Bosnia and Herzegovina	3,1098
Germany	71,434
Greece	526
Greenland	153
Iceland	1,713
Italy	11,854
Macedonia, F.Y.R. of	346
Netherlands	696
Norway	187
Portugal	992
Serbia (incl. Kosovo)	5,200
Spain	1,778
Turkey	2,170
United Kingdom	11,361
Afloat	4,728
Regional Total[1]	**118,149**
EAST ASIA & PACIFIC	
Australia	188
Japan	39,691
Korea, South	37,972
Singapore	160
Thailand	114
Afloat	12,503
Regional Total[1]	**90,822**
SUB-SAHARAN AFRICA TOTAL[1]	**259**
FORMER SOVIET UNION TOTAL	**151**
NORTH AFRICA, NEAR EAST, & SOUTH ASIA*	
Bahrain	1,280
Diego Garcia	537
Egypt	665
Kuwait	4,300
Oman	560
Saudi Arabia	4,802
United Arab Emirates	207
Afloat	13,559
Regional Total[1]	**26,172**
OTHER WESTERN HEMISPHERE	
Canada	165
Cuba (Guantánamo)	461
Honduras	426
Afloat	12,013
Regional Total[1]	13,556
TOTAL WORLDWIDE[2]	**1,384,812**

*Special Forces personnel involved in Operation Enduring Freedom not reported by Dept. of Defense. (1) Countries and areas with fewer than 100 assigned U.S. military members not listed; regional totals include personnel stationed in those countries and areas not shown. (2) Total worldwide also includes undistributed personnel.

The Medal of Honor

The Medal of Honor is the highest military award for bravery that can be given to any individual in the United States. The first Army Medals were awarded on Mar. 25, 1863, and the first Navy Medals went to sailors and Marines on Apr. 3, 1863.

On Dec. 21, 1861, Pres. Abraham Lincoln signed into law a bill to create the Navy Medal of Honor. Lincoln later (July 14, 1862) approved a resolution providing for the presentation of Medals of Honor to enlisted men of the Army and Voluntary Forces, making it a law. The law was amended on March 3, 1863 to extend its provisions to include officers as well as enlisted men.

The Medal of Honor is awarded in the name of Congress to a person who, while a member of the armed forces, distinguishes himself or herself conspicuously by gallantry and intrepidity at the risk of life above and beyond the call of duty while engaged in an action against any enemy of the United States; while engaged in military operations involving conflict with an opposing foreign force; or while serving with friendly foreign forces engaged in an armed conflict against an opposing armed force in which the United States is not a belligerent party. The deed performed must have been one of personal bravery or self-sacrifice so conspicuous as to clearly distinguish the individual above his or her comrades and must have involved risk of life. Incontestable proof of the performance of service is required, and each recommendation for award of this decoration is considered on the standard of extraordinary merit.

Prior to World War I, the 2,625 Army Medal of Honor awards up to that time were reviewed to determine which past awards met new stringent criteria. The Army removed 911 names from the list, most of them former members of a volunteer infantry group during the Civil War who had been induced to extend their enlistments when they were promised the medal. However, in 1977 a medal was restored to Dr. Mary Walker, and in 1989 medals were restored to Buffalo Bill Cody and 7 other Indian scouts.

Since that review, Medals of Honor have been awarded in the following numbers:

World War I	125	Korean War	131
Peacetime (1920-40)	18	Vietnam War	241
World War II	441	Somalia	2

The figure for World War II includes 7 African-American soldiers who were awarded Medals of Honor (6 of them posthumously) in Jan. 1997. Previously, no black soldier had received the medal for World War II service; an Army inquiry begun in 1993 concluded that the prevailing political climate and Army practices of the time had prevented proper recognition of heroism on the part of black soldiers in that war.

On May 1, 2002, the medal was posthumously awarded to Captain Jon Swanson, a helicopter pilot who died in 1971 on active duty in Vietnam, and Captain Ben Salomon, who was killed in 1944 while serving as a surgeon in the Marianas Islands during World War II.

Nations With Largest Armed Forces, by Active-Duty Troop Strength[1]

Source: *The Military Balance*. 2001-2002 (International Institute for Strategic Studies, published by Oxford University Press, UK)

	Troop strength				Navy		Combat aircraft	
	Active troops (thousands)	Reserve troops (thousands)	Defense expend. ($ bil)	Tanks (MBT) (army only)	Cruisers/ Frigates/ Destroyers	Sub-marines	FGA (air force only)	Fighters (air force only)
1. CHINA	2,310.0	500–600	42	8,000	41F/21D	69	1,020	874
2. UNITED STATES	1,368.7	1,200.6	291.2	7,620	27C/35F/54D*	73	36 tactical fighter squadrons	
3. India	1,263.0	535	65.5	3,414	8F/11D*	16	21 sqn	19 sqn
4. N. Korea	1,082.0	4,700.0	2.1	3,500	3F	26	15 rgt FGA/FTR	
5. RUSSIA	977.1	20,000	60	21,820	7C/10F/17D*	56	586	952
6. S. Korea	683.0	4,500.0	12.0	1,000	9F/6D	19		7 tact ftr wgs
7. Turkey	515.1	378.7	10.8	4,205	22F	10	11 sqn	7 sqn
8. Iran	513.0	350.0	5.7	1,565	3F	6	9 sqn	7 sqn
9. Pakistan	620.0	513.0	3.5	2,300+	8F	7	6 sqn	12 sqn
10. Vietnam	484.0	3,000.0	.9	1,215	6F	2	2 rgt	6 rgt
11. Egypt	443.0	254.0	3.0	3,860	10F/1D	4	7 sqn	22 sqn
12. Iraq	424.0	650.0	1.4	2,200	—	—	130	180
13. Afghanistan	—	—	.25	1,000	—	0	20	—
14. Taiwan	370.0	1,657.5	15.0	926	21F/11D	4	20 sqn FGA/FTR	
15. Myanmar	440.0	—	2.0	100	—	—	2 sqn	3 sqn
16. Germany	308.4	363.5	31.1	2,521	12F/2D	14	5 wg	4 wg
17. Ethiopia	252.5	—	.4	300+	—	—	24	—
18. FRANCE	273.7	419.0	37.1	1,618	1C/30F/3D*	10	6 sqn	6 sqn
19. Syria	321.0	354.0	1.0	4,700	2F	—	9-10 sqn	17 sqn
20. Ukraine	303.8	1,000.0	1.4	3,937	1C/2F	1	2 rgt	8 rgt
21. Thailand	306.0	200.0	2.6	333	12F*	—	3 sqn	2 sqn
22. Indonesia	297.0	400.0	1.5	—	17F	2	5 sqn	1 sqn
23. Brazil	287.6	1,115.0	16.0	178	14F*	4	3 sqn	2 sqn
24. Italy	230.4	65.2	22.0	1,349	1C/16F/4D*	7	8 sqn	6 sqn
25. Japan	239.8	47.4	40.8	1,050	12F/42D	16	1 sqn	9 sqn
26. Poland	206.0	406.0	3.2	1,677	2F/1D	3	9 sqn	1 sqn
27. UNITED KINGDOM	211.4	247.1	36.4	636	20F/11D*	16	10 sqn	5 sqn
28. Romania	103.0	470.0	.6	1,373	6F/1D	1	4 rgt	1 rgt
29. Eritrea	171.9	120.0	.4	100	—	—	10 FGA/FTR	
30. Morocco	198.5	150.0	1.8	744	1F	—	43	15

Nations with known strategic nuclear capability are shown in all capital letters. India and Pakistan HAVE tested nuclear devices. MBT = main battle tank. FGA = fighter, ground attack; rgt = regiment; sqn = squadron (12-24 aircraft); wg = wing (72 fighter aircraft). *Denotes navies with aircraft carriers, as follows: United States 12, United Kingdom 3, France 1, India 1, Italy 1, Russian 1, Brazil 1, Spain 1, Thailand 1. (1) All figures are for 2000. — = not available.

Directors of the Central Intelligence Agency

In 1942, Pres. Franklin D. Roosevelt established the Office of Strategic Services (OSS); it was disbanded in 1945. In 1946, Pres. Harry Truman established the Central Intelligence Group (CIG) to operate under the National Intelligence Authority (NIA). A 1947 law replaced the NIA with the National Security Council and the CIG with the Central Intelligence Agency.

Director	Served	Appointed by President
Adm. Sidney W. Souers	1946	Truman
Gen. Hoyt S. Vandenberg	1946 -1947	Truman
Adm. Roscoe H. Hillenkoetter	1947-1950	Truman
Gen. Walter Bedell Smith	1950-1953	Truman
Allen W. Dulles	1953 -1961	Eisenhower
John A. McCone	1961-1965	Kennedy
Adm. William F. Raborn Jr.	1965-1966	Johnson
Richard Helms	1966 -1973	Johnson
James R. Schlesinger	1973	Nixon
William E. Colby	1973 -1976	Nixon
George Bush	1976 -1977	Ford
Adm. Stansfield Turner	1977-1981	Carter
William J. Casey	1981-1987	Reagan
William H. Webster	1987-1991	Reagan
Robert M. Gates	1991-1993	Bush
R. James Woolsey	1993 -1995	Clinton
John M. Deutch	1995 -1997	Clinton
George J. Tenet	1997-	Clinton

Nuclear Arms Treaties and Negotiations: A Historical Overview

Aug. 5, 1963—Limited Test Ban Treaty signed in Moscow by U.S., USSR, and Britain; prohibited testing of nuclear weapons in space, above ground, and under water.

Jan. 27, 1967—Outer Space Treaty banned the introduction of other weapons of mass destruction in space.

July 1, 1968—Nuclear Nonproliferation Treaty, with U.S., USSR, and Great Britain as major signers, limited spread of nuclear material for military purposes by agreement not to help nonnuclear nations get or make nuclear weapons.

May 26, 1972—Strategic Arms Limitation Treaty (SALT I) signed in Moscow by U.S. and USSR. This short-term agreement imposed a 5-year freeze on both testing and deployment of intercontinental ballistic missiles (ICBMs) as well as submarine-launched ballistic missiles (SLBMs). In the area of defensive nuclear weapons, the separate **ABM Treaty,** signed on the same occasion, limited antiballistic missiles to 2 sites of 100 antiballistic missile launchers in each country (amended in 1974 to 1 site in each country).

July 3, 1974—ABM Treaty Revision (protocol on antiballistic missile systems) and **Threshold Test Ban Treaty** on limiting underground testing of nuclear weapons to 150 kilotons were signed by U.S. and USSR in Moscow.

Sept. 1977—U.S. and USSR agreed to continue to abide by **SALT I**, despite its expiration date.

June 18, 1979—SALT II signed in Vienna by the U.S. and USSR, constrained offensive nuclear weapons, limiting each side to 2,400 missile launchers and heavy bombers; ceiling to apply until Jan. 1, 1985. Treaty also set a subceiling of 1,320 ICBMs and SLBMs with multiple warheads on each side. SALT II never reached the Senate floor for ratification because Pres. Jimmy Carter withdrew support following Dec. 1979 Soviet invasion of Afghanistan.

Dec. 8, 1987—Intermediate-Range Nuclear Forces (INF) Treaty signed in Washington, DC, by U.S. and USSR, eliminating all U.S. and Soviet intermediate- and shorter-range nuclear missiles from Europe and Asia. Ratified, with conditions, by U.S. Senate May 27, 1988; by USSR.June 1, 1988. Entered into force June 1, 1988.

July 31, 1991—Strategic Arms Reduction Treaty (START I) signed in Moscow by USSR and U.S. to reduce strategic offensive arms by about 30% in 3 phases over 7 years. START I was the first treaty to mandate reductions by the superpowers. Treaty was approved by U.S. Senate Oct. 1, 1992.

With the Soviet Union breakup in Dec. 1991, 4 former Soviet republics became independent nations with strategic nuclear weapons—Russia, Ukraine, Kazakhstan, and Belarus. The last 3 agreed in principle in 1992 to transfer their nuclear weapons to Russia and ratify START I. The Russian Supreme Soviet voted to ratify, Nov. 4, 1992, but Russia decided not to provide instruments of ratification until the other 3 republics ratified START I and acceded to the Nuclear Nonproliferation Treaty (NPT) as nonnuclear nations. By late 1994, all 3 nations had done so, and NPT entered into force on Dec. 5, 1994.

Jan. 3, 1993—START II signed in Moscow by U.S. and Russia, called for both sides to reduce their long-range nuclear arsenals to about one-third of their then-current levels within a decade and disable and dismantle launching systems. The U.S. ratified START II Jan. 26, 1996; Russia ratified it Apr. 13, 2000. On Sept. 26, 1997, the U.S. and Russia signed an agreement that would delay the dismantling of launching systems under START II to the end of 2007.

Sept. 24, 1996—Comprehensive Test Ban Treaty (CTBT) signed by U.S. and Russia. The CTBT banned all nuclear weapon tests and other nuclear explosions. It was intended to help prevent the nuclear powers from developing more advanced weapons, while limiting the ability of other states to acquire such devices. As of Oct. 2002, the CTBT had been signed by 166 nations, including China, Russia, the U.S., the U.K, and France. It had been ratified by 96, including France, Russia, and the U.K., but not the U.S. or China. The treaty will enter into force after 44 nuclear-capable states ratify it. As of Oct. 1, 2002, 31 of the 44 had done so.

Sept. 1997—ABM Treaty amended to allow greater flexibility in development of shorter-range nuclear weapons.

May 24, 2002—Nuclear Arms Reduction Pact (Treaty of Moscow) signed by U.S. and Russia in Moscow, committed both countries to cutting nuclear arsenals to 1,700 to 2,200 warheads each, down from about 6,000, by 2012. No intermediate timetable established, but joint committee set up for monitoring implementation; either side allowed to back out with 90 days notice.

June 2002—U.S. formally withdrew from the **ABM Treaty**, effective June 13, with the intent of developing a defensive missile system. Russia, June 14, announced its withdrawal from **START II**, stating that U.S. withdrawal from the ABM Treaty effectively invalidated START II.

Monthly Military Pay Scale[1]

Source: U.S. Dept. of Defense; effective Jan. 1, 2002

	Years of Service													
Grade	<2	2	4	6	8	10	12	14	16	18	20	22	24	26
Commissioned officers														
O-10.	NA	NA	NA	NA	NA	NA	NA	NA	NA	NA	$11,517	$11,517	$11,517	$11,517
O-9 .	NA	NA	NA	NA	NA	NA	NA	NA	NA	NA	10,148	10,294	10,505	10,874
O-8. .	$7,180	$7,415	$7,615	$7,809	$8,135	$8,211	$8,520	$8,609	$8,874	$9,260	9,615	9,852	9,852	9,852
O-7. .	5,966	6,372	6,418	6,658	6,840	7,051	7,262	7,473	8,135	8,695	8,695	8,695	8,695	8,739
O-6. .	4,422	4,858	5,177	5,197	5,419	5,449	5,449	5,629	6,306	6,627	6,948	7,131	7,316	7,675
O-5. .	3,537	4,153	4,494	4,673	4,673	4,814	5,073	5,414	5,756	5,919	6,080	6,263	6,263	6,263
O-4. .	3,024	3,682	3,983	4,211	4,396	4,696	4,930	5,093	5,256	5,311	5,311	5,311	5,311	5,311
O-3. .	2,797	3,170	3,699	3,876	4,070	4,232	4,441	4,550	4,550	4,550	4,550	4,550	4,550	4,550
O-2. .	2,416	2,752	3,276	3,344	3,344	3,344	3,344	3,344	3,344	3,344	3,344	3,344	3,344	3,344
O-1. .	2,098	2,183	2,639	2,639	2,639	2,639	2,639	2,639	2,639	2,639	2,639	2,639	2,639	2,639
Commissioned officers with over 4 years active duty service as enlisted member or warrant officer														
O-3E.	NA	NA	3,699	3,876	4,070	4,232	4,441	4,617	4,718	4,855	4,855	4,855	4,855	4,855
O-2E.	NA	NA	3,276	3,344	3,450	3,630	3,769	3,872	3,872	3,872	3,872	3,872	3,872	3,872
O-1E.	NA	NA	2,639	2,818	2,922	3,029	3,133	3,276	3,276	3,276	3,276	3,276	3,276	3,276
Warrant officers														
W-5. .	NA	NA	NA	NA	NA	NA	NA	NA	NA	NA	4,966	5,136	5,307	5,479
W-4. .	2,890	3,109	3,286	3,437	3,587	3,738	3,885	4,038	4,184	4,334	4,481	4,633	4,782	4,935
W-3. .	2,639	2,862	2,899	3,017	3,152	3,331	3,440	3,558	3,694	3,829	3,964	4,098	4,233	4,369
W-2. .	2,321	2,454	2,654	2,726	2,875	2,984	3,094	3,200	3,318	3,439	3,560	3,680	3,801	3,801
W-1. .	2,050	2,218	2,403	2,512	2,625	2,738	2,850	2,964	3,077	3,190	3,275	3,275	3,275	3,275
Enlisted members														
E-9 . .	NA	NA	NA	NA	NA	3,424	3,501	3,599	3,715	3,830	3,944	4,098	4,251	4,467
E-8 . .	NA	NA	NA	NA	2,858	2,941	3,018	3,110	3,210	3,315	3,420	3,573	3,725	3,938
E-7 . .	1,987	2,169	2,333	2,417	2,563	2,645	2,726	2,808	2,893	2,975	3,057	3,200	3,293	3,527
E-6 . .	1,701	1,871	2,034	2,117	2,255	2,337	2,417	2,499	2,558	2,603	2,603	2,603	2,603	2,603
E-5 . .	1,562	1,665	1,829	1,913	2,030	2,110	2,193	2,193	2,193	2,193	2,193	2,193	2,193	2,193
E-4 . .	1,444	1,518	1,680	1,752	1,752	1,752	1,752	1,752	1,752	1,752	1,752	1,752	1,752	1,752
E-3 . .	1,304	1,385	1,469	1,469	1,469	1,469	1,469	1,469	1,469	1,469	1,469	1,469	1,469	1,469
E-2 . .	1,239	1,239	1,239	1,239	1,239	1,239	1,239	1,239	1,239	1,239	1,239	1,239	1,239	1,239
E-1>4[2]	1,106	1,106	1,106	1,106	1,106	1,106	1,106	1,106	1,106	1,106	1,106	1,106	1,106	1,106
E-1<4[2]	1,023	NA	NA	NA	NA	NA	NA	NA	NA	NA	NA	NA	NA	NA

NA = Not applicable. (1) Basic pay is limited for O-7 to O-10 to $11,516.70 per month, and for O-6 and below to $10,133.40 per month. (2) E-1>4 = E-1 grade personnel with 4 or more months service. E-1<4 = E-1 grade personnel with less than 4 months service.

Casualties in Principal Wars of the U.S.

Source: U.S. Dept. of Defense, U.S. Coast Guard

Data prior to World War I are based on incomplete records in many cases. Casualty data are confined to dead and wounded personnel and, therefore, exclude personnel captured or missing in action who were subsequently returned to military control. Dash (—) indicates information is not available. off. = officers.

			CASUALTIES			
WAR	**Branch of service**	**Number serving**	**Battle deaths**	**Other deaths**	**Wounds not mortal[7]**	**Total[13]**
Revolutionary War	**Total**	—	**4,435**	—	**6,188**	**10,623**
1775-83	Army	184,000	4,044	—	6,004	10,048
	Navy	to	342	—	114	456
	Marines	250,000	49	—	70	119
War of 1812	**Total**	**286,730[8]**	**2,260**	—	**4,505**	**6,765**
1812-15	Army	—	1,950	—	4,000	5,950
	Navy	—	265	—	439	704
	Marines	—	45	—	66	111
Mexican War	**Total**	**78,789[8]**	**1,733**	**11,550**	**4,152**	**17,435**
1846-48	Army	—	1,721	11,550	4,102	17,373
	Navy	—	1	—	3	4
	Marines	—	11	—	47	58
	Coast Guard[12]	71 off.	—	—	—	—
Civil War						
Union forces	**Total**	**2,213,363[8]**	**140,415**	**224,097**	**281,881**	**646,392**
1861-65	Army	2,128,948	138,154	221,374	280,040	630,568
	Navy	—	2,112	2,411	1,710	6,233
	Marines	84,415	148	312	131	591
Confederate forces	**Total**	—	**74,524**	**59,297**	—	**133,821**
(estimate)[1]	Army	600,000	—	—	—	—
1863-66	Navy	to	—	—	—	—
	Marines	1,500,000	—	—	—	—
	Coast Guard[12]	219 off.	1	—	—	1
Spanish-American War	**Total**	**307,420**	**385**	**2,061**	**1,662**	**4,108**
1898	Army[3]	280,564	369	2,061	1,594	4,024
	Navy	22,875	10	0	47	57
	Marines	3,321	6	0	21	27
	Coast Guard[12]	660	0	—	—	—
World War I	**Total**	**4,743,826**	**53,513**	**63,195**	**204,002**	**320,710**
April 6, 1917 - Nov. 11, 1918	Army[4]	4,057,101	50,510	55,868	193,663	300,041
	Navy	599,051	431	6,856	819	8,106
	Marines	78,839	2,461	390	9,520	12,371
	Coast Guard	8,835	111	81		192
World War II	**Total**	**16,353,659**	**292,131**	**115,185**	**671,846**	**1,079,162**
Dec. 7, 1941 - Dec. 31, 1946[2]	Army[5]	11,260,000	234,874	83,400	565,861	884,135
	Navy[6]	4,183,466	36,950	25,664	37,778	100,392
	Marines	669,100	19,733	4,778	68,207	91,718
	Coast Guard	241,093	574	1,343	—	1,917
Korean War[9]	**Total**	**5,764,143**	**33,667**	**3,249**	**103,284**	**140,200**
June 25, 1950 - July 27, 1953	Army	2,834,000	27,709	2,452	77,596	107,757
	Navy	1,177,000	493	160	1,576	2,226
	Marines	424,000	4,267	339	23,744	28,353
	Air Force	1,285,000	1,198	298	368	1,864
	Coast Guard	44,143	—	—	—	—
Vietnam War[10]	**Total**	**8,752,000**	**47,393**	**10,800**	**153,363**	**211,556**
Aug. 4, 1964 - Jan. 27, 1973	Army	4,368,000	30,929	7,272	96,802	135,003
	Navy	1,842,000	1,631	931	4,178	6,740
	Marines	794,000	13,085	1,753	51,392	66,230
	Air Force	1,740,000	1,741	842	931	3,514
	Coast Guard	8,000	7	2	60	69
Persian Gulf War	**Total**	**467,939[11]**	**148**	**151**	**467**	**766**
1991	Army	246,682	98	105	—	203
	Navy	98,852	6	14	—	20
	Marines	71,254	24	26	—	50
	Air Force	50,751	20	6	—	26
	Coast Guard	400	—	—	—	—

(1) Authoritative statistics for the Confederate forces are not available. An estimated 26,000-31,000 Confederate personnel died in Union prisons. (2) Data are for Dec. 1, 1941, through Dec. 31, 1946, when hostilities were officially terminated by Presidential Proclamation; few battle deaths or wounds not mortal were incurred after Japanese acceptance of Allied peace terms on Aug. 14,1945. Numbers serving Dec. 1, 1941-Aug. 31, 1945, were: Total—14,903,213; Army—10,420,000; Navy—3,883,520; Marine Corps—599,693. (3) Number serving covers the period April 21-Aug. 13, 1898, while dead and wounded data are for the period May 1-Aug. 31, 1898. Active hostilities ceased on Aug. 13, 1898, but ratifications of the treaty of peace were not exchanged between the United States and Spain until April 11, 1899. (4) Includes Army Air Forces battle deaths and wounds not mortal, as well as casualties suffered by American forces in northern Russia to Aug. 25, 1919, and in Siberia to April 1, 1920. Other deaths covered the period April 1, 1917-Dec. 31, 1918. (5) Includes Army Air Forces. (6) Battle deaths and wounds not mortal include casualties incurred in Oct. 1941 due to hostile action. (7) Marine Corps data for World War II, the Spanish-American War, and prior wars represent the number of individuals wounded, whereas all other data in this column represent the total number (incidence) of wounds. (8) As was reported by the Commissioner of Pensions in his Annual Report for Fiscal Year 1903. (9) As a result of an ongoing Dept. of Defense review of available Korean War casualty record information, updates to previously reported figures for battle deaths and other deaths are reflected in this table. (10) Number serving covers the period Aug. 4, 1964-Jan. 27, 1973 (date of ceasefire). Includes casualties incurred in Mayaguez Incident. Wounds not mortal exclude 150,332 persons not requiring hospital care. (11) Estimated. (12) Actually the U.S. Revenue Cutter Services, predecessor to the U.S. Coast Guard. (13) Totals do not include categories for which no data are listed.

AEROSPACE

Memorable Moments in Human Spaceflight

Sources: National Aeronautics and Space Administration; Congressional Research Service; World Almanac research

Note: Listed are selected notable U.S. missions by the National Aeronautics and Space Administration (NASA), plus non-U.S. missions (shown with an asterisk), sponsored by the USSR or, later, the Commonwealth of Independent States. Dates are Eastern standard time. EVA = extravehicular activity. ASTP = Apollo-Soyuz Test Project. STS = Space Transportation System, NASA's name for the overall Shuttle program. Number of total flights by each crew member is given in parentheses when flight listed is not the first.

Launch Date	Mission[1]	Crew (no. of flights)	Duration (hr:min)	Remarks
4/12/61	*Vostok 1	Yuri A. Gagarin	1:48	**1st human orbital flight**
5/5/61	Mercury-Redstone 3	Alan B. Shepard Jr.	0:15	**1st American in space**
7/21/61	Mercury-Redstone 4	Virgil I. Grissom	0:15	Spacecraft sank, Grissom rescued
8/6/61	*Vostok 2	Gherman S. Titov	25:18	1st spaceflight of more than 24 hrs
2/20/62	Mercury-Atlas 6	John H. Glenn Jr.	4:55	**1st American in orbit**; 3 orbits
5/24/62	Mercury-Atlas 7	M. Scott Carpenter	4:56	Manual retrofire error caused 250-mi landing overshoot
8/11/62	*Vostok 3	Andrian G. Nikolayev	94:22	Vostok 3 and 4 made 1st group flight
8/12/62	*Vostok 4	Pavel R. Popovich	70:57	On 1st orbit, it came within 3 mi of Vostok 3
10/3/62	Mercury-Atlas 8	Walter M. Schirra Jr.	9:13	Landed 5 mi from target
5/15/63	Mercury-Atlas 9	L. Gordon Cooper	34:19	1st U.S. evaluation of effects of one day in space on a person; 22 orbits
6/14/63	*Vostok 5	Valery F. Bykovsky	119:06	Vostok 5 and 6 made 2nd group flight
6/16/63	*Vostok 6	Valentina V. Tereshkova	70:50	**1st woman in space**; passed within 3 mi of Vostok 5
10/12/64	*Voskhod 1	Vladimir M. Komarov, Konstantin P. Feoktistov, Boris B. Yegorov	24:17	1st 3-person orbital flight; 1st without space suits
3/18/65	*Voskhod 2	Pavel I. Belyayev, Aleksei A. Leonov	26:02	Leonov made **1st "space walk"** (10 min)
3/23/65	Gemini-Titan 3	Grissom (2), John W. Young	4:53	1st piloted spacecraft to change its orbital path
6/3/65	Gemini-Titan 4	James A. McDivitt, Edward H. White 2nd	97:56	White was 1st American to "walk in space" (36 min)
8/21/65	Gemini-Titan 5	Cooper (2), Charles Conrad Jr.	190:55	Longest-duration human flight to date
12/15/65	Gemini-Titan 6A	Schirra (2), Thomas P. Stafford	25:51	Completed 1st U.S. space rendezvous, with Gemini 7
12/4/65	Gemini-Titan 7	Frank Borman, James A. Lovell	330:35	Longest-duration Gemini flight
3/16/66	Gemini-Titan 8	Neil A. Armstrong, David R. Scott	10:41	1st docking of one space vehicle with another; mission aborted, control malfunction; 1st Pacific landing
6/3/66	Gemini-Titan 9A	Stafford (2), Eugene A. Cernan	72:21	Performed simulation of lunar module rendezvous
7/18/66	Gemini-Titan 10	Young (2), Michael Collins	70:47	1st use of Agena target vehicle's propulsion systems; 1st orbital docking
9/12/66	Gemini-Titan 11	Conrad (2), Richard F. Gordon Jr.	71:17	1st tethered flight; highest Earth-orbit altitude (850 mi)
11/11/66	Gemini-Titan 12	Lovell (2), Edwin E. "Buzz" Aldrin Jr.	94:34	Final Gemini mission; 5-hr EVA
4/23/67	*Soyuz 1	Komarov (2)	26:40	Crashed on reentry, killing Komarov
10/11/68	Apollo-Saturn 7	Schirra (3), Donn F. Eisele, R. Walter Cunningham	260:09	1st piloted flight of Apollo spacecraft command-service module only; live TV footage of crew
12/21/68	Apollo-Saturn 8	Borman (2), Lovell (3), William A. Anders	147:00	**1st lunar orbit** and piloted lunar return reentry (command-service module only); views of lunar surface televised to Earth
1/14/69	*Soyuz 4	Vladimir A. Shatalov	71:21	Docked with Soyuz 5
1/15/69	*Soyuz 5	Boris V. Volyanov, Aleksei S. Yeliseyev, Yevgeny V. Khrunov	72:54	Docked with 4; Yeliseyev and Khrunov transferred to Soyuz 4 via a spacewalk
3/3/69	Apollo-Saturn 9	McDivitt (2), D. Scott (2), Russell L. Schweickart	241:00	1st piloted flight of lunar module
5/18/69	Apollo-Saturn 10	Stafford (3), Young (3), Cernan (2)	192:03	1st lunar module orbit of Moon, 50,000 ft from Moon surface
7/16/69	Apollo-Saturn 11	Armstrong (2), Collins (2), Aldrin (2)	195:18	**1st lunar landing** made by Armstrong and Aldrin (7/20); collected 48.5 lb of soil, rock samples; lunar stay time 21:36:21
10/11/69	*Soyuz 6	Georgi S. Shonin, Valery N. Kubasov	118:43	1st welding of metals in space
10/12/69	*Soyuz 7	Anatoly V. Flipchenko, Vladislav N. Volkov, Viktor V. Gorbatko	118:40	Space lab construction test made; Soyuz 6, 7, and 8: 1st time 3 spacecraft, 7 crew members orbited the Earth at once
10/13/69[2]	*Soyuz 8	Shatalov (2), Yeliseyev (2)	118:51	Part of space lab construction team
11/14/69	Apollo-Saturn 12	Conrad (3), Richard F. Gordon Jr. (2), Alan L. Bean	244:36	Conrad and Bean made 2nd Moon landing (11/18); collected 74.7 lb of samples, lunar stay time 31:31
4/11/70	Apollo-Saturn 13	Lovell (4), Fred W. Haise Jr., John L. Swigert Jr.	142:54	Aborted after service module oxygen tank ruptured; crew returned in lunar module
6/1/70	*Soyuz 9	Nikolayev (2), Vitaliy I. Sevastyanov	424:59	Longest human spaceflight to date
1/31/71	Apollo-Saturn 14	A. Shepard (2), Stuart A. Roosa, Edgar D. Mitchell	216:01	Shepard and Mitchell made 3rd Moon landing (2/3); collected 96 lb of lunar samples; lunar stay 33:31
4/19/71[2]	*Salyut 1[3]	(Occupied by Soyuz 11 crew)		**1st space station**
4/22/71[2]	*Soyuz 10	Shatalov (3), Yeliseyev (3), Nikolay N. Rukavishnikov	47:46	1st successful docking with a space station; failed to enter space station

Launch Date	Mission[1]	Crew (no. of flights)	Duration (hr:min)	Remarks
6/6/71	*Soyuz 11	Georgi T. Dobrovolskiy, V. Volkov (2), Viktor I. Patsayev	570:22	Docked and entered Salyut 1 space station; crew died during reentry from loss of pressurization
7/26/71	Apollo-Saturn 15	D. Scott (3), James B. Irwin, Alfred M. Worden	295:12	Scott and Irwin made 4th Moon landing (7/30); 1st lunar rover use; 1st deep space walk; 170 lb of samples; 66:55 stay
4/16/72	Apollo-Saturn 16	Young (4), Charles M. Duke Jr., Thomas K. Mattingly 2nd	265:51	Young and Duke made 5th Moon landing (4/20); collected 213 lb of lunar samples; lunar stay 71:2
12/7/72	Apollo-Saturn 17	Cernan (3), Ronald E. Evans, Harrison H. Schmitt	301:51	Cernan and Schmitt made 6th and **last lunar landing** (12/11); collected 243 lb of samples; record lunar stay over 75 hrs
5/14/73[2]	Skylab 1[4]	(Occupied by Skylab 2, 3, and 4 crews)		**1st U.S. space station**
5/25/73	Skylab 2	Conrad (4), Joseph P. Kerwin, Paul J. Weitz	672:49	1st Amer. piloted orbiting space station; crew repaired damage caused in boost
7/28/73	Skylab 3	Bean (2), Owen K. Garriott, Jack R. Lousma	1,427:09	Crew systems and operational tests; exceeded pre-mission plans for scientific activities; 3 EVAs, 13:44
11/16/73	Skylab 4	Gerald P. Carr, Edward G. Gibson, William Pogue	2,017:15	Final Skylab mission
7/15/75	*Soyuz 19 (ASTP)	Leonov (2), Kubasov (2)	143:31	U.S.-USSR joint flight; crews linked up in space (7/17), conducted experiments, shared meals, held a joint news conf.
7/15/75	Apollo (ASTP)	Vance Brand, Stafford (4), Donald K. Slayton	217:28	Joint flight with Soyuz 19
12/10/77[2]	*Soyuz 26	Yuri V. Romanenko, Georgiy M. Grechko (2)	2,314:00	1st multiple docking to a space station (Soyuz 26 and 27 docked at Salyut 6)
1/10/78[2]	*Soyuz 27	Vladimir A. Dzhanibekov	142:59	*See Soyuz 26*
3/2/78[2]	*Soyuz 28	Aleksei A. Gubarev (2), Vladimir Remek	190:16	1st international crew launch; Remek was 1st Czech in space
4/12/81	Columbia (STS-1)	Young (5), Robert L. Crippen	54:21	**1st space shuttle** to fly into Earth's orbit
11/12/81	Columbia (STS-2)	Joe H. Engle, Richard H. Truly	54:13	1st scientific payload; 1st reuse of space shuttle
11/11/82	Columbia (STS-5)	Brand (2), Robert Overmyer, William Lenoir, Joseph Allen	122:14	1st 4-person crew
6/18/83	Challenger (STS-7)	Crippen (2), Frederick Hauck, Sally K. Ride, John M. Fabian, Norman Thagard	146:24	Ride was **1st U.S. woman in space**; 1st 5-person crew
6/27/83[2]	*Soyuz T-9	Vladimir A. Lyakhov (2), Aleksandr Pavlovich Aleksandrov	3,585:48	Docked at Salyut 7; 1st construction in space
8/30/83	Challenger (STS-8)	Truly (2), Daniel Brandenstein, William Thornton, Guion Bluford, Dale Gardner	145:09	Bluford was 1st African-American in space
11/28/83	Columbia (STS-9)	Young (6), Brewster Shaw Jr., Robert Parker, Garriott (2), Byron Lichtenberg, Ulf Merbold	247:47	1st 6-person crew; 1st Spacelab mission
2/3/84	Challenger (41-B)	Brand (3), Robert Gibson, Ronald McNair, Bruce McCandless, Robert Stewart	191:16	1st untethered EVA
2/8/84	*Soyuz T-10B	Leonid Kizim, Vladimir Solovyov, Oleg Atkov	1,510:43	Docked with Salyut 7; crew set space duration record of 237 days
4/3/84	*Soyuz T-11	Yury Malyshev (2), Gennady Strekalov (3), Rakesh Sharma	4,365:48	Docked with Salyut 7; Sharma 1st Indian in space
4/6/84	Challenger (41-C)	Crippen (3), Francis R. Scobee, George D. Nelson, Terry J. Hart, James D. van Hoften	167:40	1st in-orbit satellite repair
7/17/84[2]	*Soyuz T-12	Dzhanibekov (4), Svetlana Y. Savitskaya (2), Igor P. Volk	283:14	Docked at Salyut 7; Savitskaya was 1st woman to perform EVA
8/30/84	Discovery (41-D)	Henry W. Hartsfield (2), Michael L. Coats, Richard M. Mullane, Steven A. Hawley, Judith A. Resnik, Charles D. Walker	144:56	1st flight of U.S. nonastronaut (Walker)
10/5/84	Challenger (41-G)	Crippen (4), Jon A. McBride, Kathryn D. Sullivan, Ride (2), Marc Garneau, David C. Leestma, Paul D. Scully-Power	197:24	1st 7-person crew
11/8/84	Discovery (51-A)	Hauck (2); David M. Walker, Dr. Anna L. Fisher, J. Allen (2), D. Gardner (2)	191:45	1st satellite retrieval/repair
4/12/85	Discovery (51-D)	Karol J. Bobko, Donald E. Williams, Jake Garn, C. Walker (2), Jeffrey A. Hoffman, S. David Griggs, M. Rhea Seddon	167:55	Garn (R, UT) was 1st U.S. senator in space
6/17/85	Discovery (51-G)	Brandenstein (2), John O. Creighton, Shannon W. Lucid, Steven R. Nagel, Fabian (2), Prince Sultan Salman al-Saud, Patrick Baudry	169:39	Launched 3 satellites; Salman al-Saud was 1st Arab in space; Baudry was 1st French person on U.S. mission
10/3/85	Atlantis (51-J)	Bobko (3), Ronald J. Grabe, David C. Hilmers, Stewart (2), William A. Pailes	97:47	1st Atlantis flight
10/30/85	Challenger (61-A)	Hartsfield (3), Nagel (2), Buchli (2), Bluford (2), Bonnie J. Dunbar, Wubbo J. Ockels, Richard Furrer, Ernst Messerschmid	168:45	1st 8-person crew; 1st German Spacelab mission
1/12/86	Columbia (61-C)	R. Gibson (2), Charles F. Bolden Jr., Hawley (2), G. Nelson (2), Franklin R. Chang-Diaz, Robert J. Cenker, Bill Nelson	146:04	B. Nelson was 1st U.S. representative in space; material and astronomy experiments conducted
1/28/86	Challenger (51-L)	Scobee (2), Michael J. Smith, Resnik (2), Ellison S. Onizuka (2), Ronald E. McNair, Gregory B. Jarvis, Christa McAuliffe	—	**Exploded 73 sec after liftoff**; all were killed
2/20/86[2]	*Mir[3]	—	—	***Mir* space station** with 6 docking ports **launched**
3/13/86[2]	*Soyuz T-15	Kizim (3), Solovyov (2)	3,000:01	Ferry between stations; docked at *Mir*

Launch Date	Mission[1]	Crew (no. of flights)	Duration (hr:min)	Remarks
2/5/87	*Soyuz TM-2	Romanenko (3), Aleksandr I. Laveikin	7,835:38	Romanenko set endurance record, since broken
7/22/87	*Soyuz TM-3	Aleksandr Viktorenko, Aleksandr Pavlovich Aleksandrov (2), Mohammed Faris	3,847:16	Docked with *Mir*; Faris 1st Syrian in space
12/21/87	*Soyuz TM-4	V. Titov (2), Muso Manarov, Anatoly Levchenko	8,782:39	Docked with *Mir*
6/7/88	*Soyuz TM-5	Viktor Savinykh (3), Anatoly Solovyev, Aleksandr Panayotov Aleksandrov	236:13	Docked with *Mir*; Aleksandrov 1st Bulgarian in space
9/29/88	Discovery (STS-26)	Hauck (3), Richard O. Covey (2), Hilmers (2), G. Nelson (2), John M. Lounge (2)	97:00	1st shuttle flight since *Challenger* explosion 1/28/86
5/4/89	Atlantis (STS-30)	D. Walker (2), Grabe (2), Thagard (2), Mary L. Cleave (2), Mark C. Lee	96:56	Launched Venus orbiter *Magellan*
10/18/89	Atlantis (STS-34)	Donald E. Williams (2), Michael J. McCulley, Lucid (2), Chang-Diaz (2), Ellen S. Baker	119:39	Launched Jupiter probe and orbiter *Galileo*
4/24/90	Discovery (STS-31)	McCandless (2), Sullivan (2), Loren J. Shriver (2), Bolden (2), Hawley (3)	121:16	**Launched Hubble Space Telescope**
10/6/90	Discovery (STS-41)	Richard N. Richards (2), Robert D. Cabana, Bruce E. Melnick, William M. Shepherd (2), Thomas D. Akers	98:10	Launched *Ulysses* spacecraft to investigate interstellar space and the Sun
4/5/91	Atlantis (STS-37)	Nagel (3), Kenneth D. Cameron, Linda Godwin, Jerry L. Ross (3), Jay Apt	144:32	Launched Gamma Ray Observatory to measure celestial gamma rays
5/18/91	*Soyuz TM-12	Anatoly Artsebarskiy, Sergei Krikalev (2) (to *Mir*), Helen Sharman	3,471:22	Docked with *Mir;* Sharman 1st from United Kingdom in space
3/17/92	*Soyuz TM-14	Viktorenko (3) (to *Mir*), Alexandr Kaleri (to *Mir*), Klaus-Dietrich Flade, Aleksandr Volkov (3) (from *Mir*), Krikalev (2) (from *Mir*)	3,495:11	First human CIS space mission; docked with *Mir* 3/19; Viktorenko and Kaleri to *Mir*, Volkov and Krikalev from *Mir;* Krikalev was in space 313 days
5/7/92	Endeavour (STS-49)	Brandenstein (4), Kevin C. Chilton, Melnick (2), Pierre J. Thuot (2), Richard J. Hieb (2), Kathryn Thornton (2), Akers (2)	213:30	1st 3-person EVA; satellite recovery and redeployment
9/12/92	Endeavour (STS-47)	R. Gibson (4), Curtis L. Brown Jr., Lee (2), Apt (2), N. Jan Davis, Mae Carol Jemison, Mamoru Mohri	190:30	Jemison was 1st black woman in space; Lee and Davis were 1st married couple to travel together in space; 1st Japanese Spacelab
6/21/93	Endeavour (STS-57)	Grabe (4), Brian J. Duffy (2), G. David Low (3), Nancy J. Sherlock, Peter J. K. Wisoff, Janice E. Voss	239:46	Carried Spacelab commercial payload module
12/2/93	Endeavour (STS-61)	Covey (3), Kenneth D. Bowersox (2), Claude Nicollier (2), Story Musgrave (5), Akers (3), K. Thornton (3), Hoffman (4)	259:58	Hubble Space Telescope repaired; Akers set new U.S. EVA duration record (29 hr, 40 min)
2/3/94	Discovery (STS-60)	Bolden (3), Kenneth S. Reightier Jr. (2), Davis (2), Chang-Diaz (3), Ronald M. Sega, Krikalev (3)	199:10	Krikalev was 1st Russian on U.S. shuttle
4/9/94	Endeavour (STS-59)	Sidney M. Gutierrez (2), Chilton (2), Apt (3), Michael R. Clifford (2), Godwin (2), Thomas D. Jones	269:50	Gathered data about Earth and the effects humans have on its carbon, water, and energy cycles
7/1/94	*Soyuz TM-19	Yuri I. Malenchenko, Talgat A. Musabayev, Merbold (2) (from *Mir*)	3,022:53	Docked with *Mir;* Merbold from *Mir*
9/9/94	Discovery (STS-64)	Richards (4), L. Blaine Hammond Jr. (2), Jerry M. Linenger, Susan J. Helms (2), Carl J. Meade (3), Lee (3)	262:50	Performed atmospheric research; 1st untethered EVA in over 10 years
2/3/95	Discovery (STS-63)	James D. Wetherbee (3), Eileen M. Collins, Bernard A. Harris (2), C. Michael Foale (3), Janice E. Voss (2), V. Titov (4)	198:29	*Discovery* and Russian space station rendezvous
3/2/95	Endeavour (STS-67)	Stephen S. Oswald (3), William G. Gregory, Samuel T. Durrance (2), Ronald Parise (2), Wendy B. Lawrence, Tamara E. Jernigan (3), John M. Grunsfeld	399:09	Shuttle data made available on the Internet; astronomy research conducted
3/14/95	*Soyuz TM-21	Thagard (2), Vladimir Dezhurov, Strekalov (5)	2,688[5]	Docked with *Mir* 3/16/95; Thagard was 1st Amer. on the Russ. spacecraft; Valery Polyakov returned to Earth, 3/22/95, after record stay in space (439 days)
6/27/95	Atlantis (STS-71)	R. Gibson (5), Charles J. Precourt (2), E. Baker (3), Gregory J. Harbaugh (3), Dunbar (4), Solovyev (4) (to *Mir*), Nikolai M. Budarin (to *Mir*), Thagard (5) (from *Mir*), Strekalov (from *Mir*), Dezhurov (from *Mir*)	269:47	**1st shuttle-*Mir* docking**; exchanged crew members with *Mir;* Thagard, with his stay on *Mir,* had spent 115 days in space
11/8/95	Atlantis (STS-74)	Cameron (3), James D. Halsell Jr. (2), Chris Hadfield, Ross (5), William S. McArthur (2)	196:30	2nd shuttle-*Mir* docking (11/15-11/18); erected a 15-ft permanent docking tunnel to *Mir* for future use by U.S. orbiters
2/22/96	Columbia (STS-75)	Andrew M. Allen (3), Scott J. Horowitz, Chang-Diaz (5), Umberto Guidoni, Hoffman (5), Maurizio Cheli, Nicollier (3)	377:40	Lost an Italian satellite when its tether was severed; microgravity experiments performed; singe marks found on 2 O-rings
3/22/96	Atlantis (STS-76)	Chilton (3), Richard A. Searfoss (2), Sega (2), Clifford (3) Godwin (3), Lucid (5) (to *Mir*)	221:15	3rd shuttle-*Mir* docking (5 days); Lucid to *Mir*, 2-person EVA
9/16/96	Atlantis (STS-79)	Apt (4), Terry Wilcutt (2), William Readdy (3), Akers (4), Carl E. Walz (3), Lucid (5) (from *Mir*), John E. Blaha (5) (to *Mir*)	243:19	Docked with *Mir* 9/18/96; exchanged crew members, including Lucid, who set U.S. and women's individual duration in space record (188 days)
11/19/96	Columbia (STS-80)	Kenneth D. Cockrell (3), Kent V. Rominger (2), Jernigan (4), Jones (3), Musgrave (6)	423:53	Longest-duration shuttle flight; Musgrave was oldest person to fly in space; 2 science satellites deployed and retrieved

Launch Date	Mission[1]	Crew (no. of flights)	Duration (hr:min)	Remarks
1/12/97	Atlantis (STS-81)	Michael A. Baker (4), Brent W. Jett (2), Wisoff (3), Grunsfeld (2), Marsha Ivins (4), Linenger (2) (to *Mir*), Blaha (5) (from *Mir*)	243:30	Docked with *Mir* 1/14-1/19/97; Linenger to *Mir;* Blaha from *Mir,* spent 128 days in space
2/11/97	Discovery (STS-82)	Bowersox (4), Horowitz (2), Joe Tanner (2), Hawley (4), Harbaugh (4), Lee (4), Steve Smith (2)	238:47	Increased capabilities of Hubble Space Telescope; 5 EVAs used to service it
5/15/97	Atlantis (STS-84)	Precourt (3), E. Collins (2), Jean-François Clervoy (2), Carlos Noriega, Ed Lu, Elena Kondakova, Foale (4) (to *Mir*), Linenger (2) (from *Mir*)	221:20	Docked with *Mir* 5/16-5/21; Foale to *Mir;* Linenger from *Mir,* 132 days in space, 2nd-longest time for an American; stay on *Mir* marked by troubles incl. fire 2/23
8/5/97	*Soyuz TM-26	Solovyev (5), Pavel Vinogradov	4,743:35	Docked with *Mir* 8/7/97; repaired damaged space station
8/7/97	Discovery (STS-85)	Brown (4), Rominger (3), Davis (3), Robert L. Curbeam Jr., Stephen K. Robinson, Bjarni V. Tryggvason	284:27	Deployed and retrieved satellite designed to study Earth's middle atmosphere; demonstrated robotic arm
9/25/97	Atlantis (STS-86)	Wetherbee (4), Michael J. Bloomfield, V. Titov (4), Scott Parazynski (2), Jean-Loup Chrétien (3), Lawrence (2), David A. Wolf (2) (to *Mir*), Foale (4) (from *Mir*)	236:24	Docked with *Mir* 9/27-10/3/97; delivered new computer to *Mir;* Wolf to *Mir;* Foale from *Mir;* stay on *Mir* marked by major collision with cargo ship 6/25
1/22/98	Endeavour (STS-89)	Wilcutt (3), Joe F. Edwards Jr., Dunbar (5), Michael P. Anderson, James F. Reilly II, Salizhan Sharipov, Andrew Thomas (2) (to *Mir*), Wolf (2) (from *Mir*)	211:48	Docked with *Mir* 1/24-1/29/98; delivered water and cargo; Thomas to *Mir; W*olf from *Mir,* 128 days in space
1/29/98	*Soyuz TM-27	Musabayev (2), Budarin (2), Leopold Eyharts	4,923:36	Docked with *Mir* 1/31/98
4/17/98	Columbia (STS-90)	Searfoss (3), Scott D. Altman, Richard M. Linnehan (2), Dafydd Rhys Williams, Kathryn P. Hire, Jay C. Buckey, James A. Pawelczyk	381:50	Studied effects of microgravity on the nervous systems of the crew and over 2,000 live animals; 1st surgery in space on animals meant to survive
6/2/98	Discovery (STS-91)	Precourt (4), Dominic L. Gorie, Lawrence (3), Chang-Diaz (6), Janet L. Kavandi, Valery Ryumin (4), A. Thomas (2) (from *Mir*)	235:53	Final docking mission with *Mir;* Thomas from *Mir,* 141 days in space
10/29/98	Discovery (STS-95)	Brown (5), Steven W. Lindsey (2), Parazynski (3), Robinson (2), Pedro Duque, Chiaki Mukai (2), Glenn (2)	213:44	Sen. John Glenn (D, OH), 77, was **oldest person to fly in space**; Duque was 1st Spaniard in space; experiments to study aging performed on Glenn
12/4/98	Endeavour (STS-88)	Cabana (4), Frederick W. Sturckow, Nancy J. Currie (3), Ross (6), James H. Newman (3), Krivalev (4)	283:18	**1st assembly of International Space Station (ISS)**; attached U.S.-built *Unity* connecting module to Russian-built *Zarya* control module; 1st crew to enter ISS
7/23/99	Columbia (STS-93)	E. Collins (3), Jeffrey S. Ashby, Hawley (5), Catherine G. Coleman (2), Michel Tognini (2)	118:50	Collins was 1st woman to command a space shuttle; deployed Chandra X-ray Observatory telescope
12/19/99	Discovery (STS-103)	Brown (6), Scott Kelly, S. Smith (3), Foale (5), Grunsfeld (3), Nicollier (4), Clervoy (3)	191:10	Replaced equipment on and upgraded Hubble Space Telescope; 3 EVAs
2/11/00	Endeavour (STS-99)	Kevin Kregel (4), Gorie (2), Kavandi (2), Janice E. Voss (5), Mohri (2), Gerhard P.J. Thiele	269:38	Used radar to make most complete topographic map of Earth's surface ever produced
5/19/00	Atlantis (STS-101)	Halsell (5), Horowitz (3), Helms (4), Yury Usachev (3), James S. Voss (4), Mary Ellen Weber (2), Jeffrey N. Williams	236:09	Serviced and resupplied ISS; boosted orbit of ISS to an altitude of about 238 mi; 1 EVA
9/8/00	Atlantis (STS-106)	Wilcutt (4), Altman (2), Lu (2), Richard A. Mastracchio, Daniel C. Burbank, Malenchenko (2), Boris V. Morukov	283:10	Prepared ISS for 1st permanent crew; 1 EVA by all 7 crew members
10/11/00	Discovery (STS-92)	Duffy (4), Pamela A. Melroy, Koichi Wakata (2), Leroy Chiao (3), Wisoff (4), Michael Lopez-Alegria (2), McArthur (3)	309:43	Installed framework structure on ISS, setting the stage for future additions; 4 EVAs
10/31/00[2]	*Soyuz TM-204	Shepherd (4), Yuri Gidzenko (2), Krikalev (5)	—	Established **1st permanent manning of ISS** with 3-person crew for a 4-month stay
11/30/00	Endeavour (STS-97)	Jett (3), Bloomfield (2), Tanner (3), Marc Garneau (3), Noriega (2)	259:57	Delivered 17-ton solar arrays, batteries, and radiators to ISS; 3 EVAs
2/7/01	Atlantis (STS-98)	Cockrell (4), Ivins (5), Jones (4), Curbeam (2), Mark L. Polansky	309:20	Installed U.S. Destiny Laboratory Module on the ISS; 3 EVAs
3/8/01	Discovery (STS-102)	Wetherbee (5), James M. Kelly, Helms (4) (to ISS), James S. Voss (5) (to ISS), Paul Richards, Andrew S.W. Thomas (2), Usachev (4) (to ISS), Shepherd (4) (from ISS), Gidzenko (2) (from ISS), Krikalev (5) (from ISS)	307:49	Transported 2nd permanent crew (Voss, Helms, Usachev) to ISS and returned 1st crew to Earth; 2 EVAs
4/19/01	Endeavour (STS-100)	Rominger (5), John L. Phillips, Hadfield (2), Ashby (2), Parazynski (4), Guidoni (2), Yuri V. Lonchakov	285:30	Installed the Canadarm2, a robotic arm, and delivered supplies to ISS; 2 EVAs
7/12/01	Atlantis (STS-104)	Lindsey (3), Charles O. Hobaugh, Michael L. Gernhardt (4), Kavandi (3), Reilly (2)	259:58	Installed a Joint Airlock, with nitrogen and oxygen tanks to permit future spacewalks from the ISS; 3 EVAs
8/10/01	Discovery (STS-105)	Horowitz (4), Sturckow (2), Daniel Barry (3), Patrick G. Forrester, Culbertson (3) (to ISS), Dezhurov (2) (to ISS), Mikhail Tyurin (to ISS), Usachev, (4), Voss (5) (from ISS), Helms (5) (from ISS)	285:13	Transported Expedition Three crew to ISS (Culbertson, Tyurin, Dezhurov) and returned Expedition Two crew to Earth; 2 EVAs
12/5/01	Endeavour (STS-108)	Gorie (3), Mark Kelly, Godwin (4), Daniel Tani, Yury Onufrienko (2) (to ISS), Daniel Bursch (4) (to ISS), Walz (4) (to ISS), Culbertson (3) (from ISS), Dezhurov (2) (from ISS), Tyurin (from ISS)	283:36	Transported Expedition Four crew to ISS (Onufrienko, Bursch, Walz) and returned Expedition Three crew to Earth; deployed STARSHINE 2 satellite; 1 EVA
3/1/02	Columbia (STS-109)	Altman (3), Duane G. Carey, Grunsfeld (4), Currie (4), Linnehan (3), Newman (4), Michael J. Massimino	262:10	Installed powerful new camera and upgraded other equipment on Hubble Space Telescope; 5 EVAs

Launch Date	Mission[1]	Crew (no. of flights)	Duration (hr:min)	Remarks
4/8/02	Atlantis (STS-110)	Bloomfield (3), Stephen N. Frick, Rex J. Walheim, Ellen Ochoa (4), Lee M.E. Morin, Ross (7), S. Smith (4)	259:42	Installed S0 Truss, backbone for expansion of ISS; Ross set records with 7th spaceflight, 9th spacewalk; 4 EVAs
6/5/02	Endeavour (STS-111)	Cockrell (5), Paul Lockhart, Chang-Diaz (7), Philippe Perrin, Valery Korzun (2) (to ISS), Peggy Whitson (to ISS), Sergei Treschev (to ISS), Onufrienko (2) (from ISS), Bursch (4) (from ISS), Walz (4) (from ISS)	332:35	Transported Expedition Five crew to ISS (Korzun, Whitson, Treschev) and returned Expedition Four crew to Earth; brought platform for ISS robot arm; 3 EVAs

Note: As of Sept. 2002, there have been 110 space shuttle flights, 85 since the 1986 *Challenger* explosion. Active shuttles include the *Columbia* (27 flights), the *Discovery* (30), the *Atlantis* (25), and the *Endeavour* (18). (The *Challenger* completed 9 missions.) Four Soviets are known to have died in spaceflights: Komarov was killed on Soyuz 1 (1967) when the parachute lines tangled during descent; the 3-person Soyuz 11 crew (1971) was asphyxiated. Seven Americans died in the *Challenger* explosion, and 3 astronauts—Virgil I. Grissom, Edward H. White, and Roger B. Chaffee—died in the Jan. 27, 1967, Apollo 1 fire on the ground at Cape Kennedy, FL. (1) For space shuttle flights, the mission name is in parentheses following the name of the orbiter. (2) Launch date. (3) Space stations, such as the *Salyuts* and *Mir*, were used to house crews starting in 1971. (4) Skylab 1 deteriorated and fell from orbit without burning up upon entering the atmosphere. Pieces fell on Australia and into the Indian Ocean; no one was injured. (5) The approximate crew duration for Thagard's stay. Crew did not return together.

International Space Station

The International Space Station (ISS) is considered the largest cooperative scientific project in history.

16 cooperating nations: U.S., Russia, Canada, Belgium, Denmark, France, Germany, Italy, Netherlands, Norway, Spain, Sweden, Switzerland, United Kingdom, Japan, and Brazil

The station when completed:

- mass of 1,040,000 lb
- 356' x 290', with almost an acre of solar panels
- internal volume roughly equivalent to passenger cabin of a 747 jumbo jet
- 6 laboratories; living space for up to 7 people

Assembly:

- 11/20/98: U.S.-owned, Russian-built *Zarya* ("sunrise") control module launched by rocket from Kazakhstan—1st step in assembly of the station
- 12/4/98: U.S.-built *Unity* connecting module launched on space shuttle *Endeavour*; shuttle crew attached *Unity* and *Zarya*
- 5/27/99: space shuttle *Discovery* launched, bringing supplies; 1st docking with ISS
- 7/26/00: Russian-built *Zvezda* ("star") service module, the primary Russian contribution to the ISS, connected with the station
- 11/2/00: 1st permanent crew arrives for 4-month stay
- 2/9/00: U.S. Destiny Laboratory Module delivered
- 4/21/01: A robotic arm, Canadarm2, delivered
- 4/11/02: The S0 Truss, backbone of future expansion of the ISS, installed
- to be completed by 2005, after 44 total missions

Examples of research planned:

- growing living cells for research in an environment free of gravity
- studying the effects on humans of long-term exposure to reduced gravity
- studying large-scale long-term changes in Earth's environment by observing Earth from orbit

Summary of Worldwide Successful Launches, 1957-2001

Source: National Aeronautics and Space Administration

Year	Total[1]	Russia[2]	United States	Japan	European Space Agency	China	France	India	United Kingdom	Germany	Canada
1957-59 . . .	24	6	18	—	—	—	—	—	—	—	—
1960-69 . . .	1,035	399	614	—	2	—	4	—	1	—	—
1970-79 . . .	1,366	1,028	247	18	5	8	14	1	6	3	4
1980-89 . . .	1,431	1,132	191	26	14	16	5	9	4	7	5
1990-99 . . .	1,045	542	300	23	55	33	16	11	7	6	4
2000.	81	35	29	0	12	5	0	0	0	0	0
2001.	57	23	23	1	7	1	0	2	0	0	0
TOTAL	**5,039**	**3,165**	**1,422**	**68**	**95**	**63**	**39**	**23**	**18**	**16**	**13**

(1) Includes launches sponsored by countries not shown. (2) Figures covering 1957-96 apply to the the Soviet Union, or, after 1991, to the Commonwealth of Independent States.

Space Junk

Source: National Aeronautics and Space Administration; North American Aerospace Defense Command

Space junk, or space debris, consists of objects that have spun off from space missions since Sputnik-1 in 1957 and orbit the Earth at high speeds, posing an increasing risk to space missions and functioning space satellites.

- NORAD keeps track of about 8,300 orbiting artifacts, baseball-size (about 10 cm) and larger. Some 7% of these are functioning satellites, while the remainder (about 7,700 items) are rocket bodies or fragmentary objects. In all, there are at least 110,000 objects 1 cm or larger in size orbiting the Earth.
- Space junk includes derelict satellites, upper stages of rockets that carry payloads into orbit, specks and beads of slag from rocket exhaust, metal bolts, and garbage left by Earth-orbiting missions and space stations.
- 80% of space junk that could damage active satellites or space shuttles orbits the planet at an altitude of about 1,200 miles above Earth—what scientists call a near-Earth orbit.
- Even minuscule objects pose a threat to space missions, as they travel at speeds around 16,500 miles per hour—40 times faster than a bullet shot from a .38 caliber pistol.

Notable Proposed Space Missions

Source: National Aeronautics and Space Administration

Planned Launch date	Mission	Purpose
Jan. 2003	Space InfraRed Telescope Facility (SIRTF)	Make high-sensitivity observations of celestial sources
Jan. 2003	The International Rosetta Mission	Rendezvous with comet 46 P/Wirtanen in 2011 to study the object's nucleus and environment
Apr. 2003	Gravity Probe B (GP-B)	Attempt to prove Einstein's Theory of General Relativity by measuring minute "twisting" in space-time caused by the rotation of the Earth
May-July 2003	Mars Exploration Rovers	Land 2 robot "rovers" to explore the geology and study the history of water on the planet
2007	Planck-Herschel Satellite	Study the origins of the Universe and "dark matter"; collect data to study whether the Universe is finite or infinite

IT'S A FACT: During the Dec. 2001 mission of Space Shuttle *Endeavour*, NASA honored the victims of the Sept. 11 terrorist attacks by sending nearly 6,000 small U.S. flags into orbit on the shuttle, part of the "Flags for Heroes and Families" campaign; the flags were later given to 9-11 survivors and families of those killed.

Notable U.S. Planetary Science Missions

Source: National Aeronautics and Space Administration

Spacecraft	Launch date (Coordinated Universal Time)	Mission	Remarks
Mariner 2	Aug. 27, 1962	Venus	Passed within 22,000 mi of Venus 12/14/62; contact lost 1/3/63 at 54 million mi
Ranger 7	July 28, 1964	Moon	Yielded over 4,000 photos of lunar surface
Mariner 4	Nov. 28, 1964	Mars	Passed behind Mars 7/14/65; took 22 photos from 6,000 mi
Ranger 8	Feb. 17, 1965	Moon	Yielded over 7,000 photos of lunar surface
Surveyor 3	Apr. 17, 1967	Moon	Scooped and tested lunar soil
Mariner 5	June 14, 1967	Venus	In solar orbit; closest Venus flyby 10/19/67
Mariner 6	Feb. 24, 1969	Mars	Came within 2,000 mi of Mars 7/31/69; collected data, photos
Mariner 7	Mar. 27, 1969	Mars	Came within 2,000 mi of Mars 8/5/69
Mariner 9	May 30, 1971	Mars	First craft to orbit Mars 11/13/71; sent back over 7,000 photos
Pioneer 10	Mar. 2, 1972	Jupiter	Passed Jupiter 12/4/73; exited the planetary system 6/13/83; transmission ended 3/31/97 at 6.39 billion mi
Pioneer 11	Apr. 5, 1973	Jupiter, Saturn	Passed Jupiter 12/3/74; Saturn 9/1/79; discovered an additional ring and 2 moons around Saturn; operating in outer solar system; transmission ended 9/95
Mariner 10	Nov. 3, 1973	Venus, Mercury	Passed Venus 2/5/74; arrived Mercury 3/29/74. 1st time gravity of 1 planet (Venus) used to whip spacecraft toward another (Mercury)
Viking 1	Aug. 20, 1975	Mars	Landed on Mars 7/20/76; did scientific research, sent photos; functioned 6 years
Viking 2	Sept. 9, 1975	Mars	Landed on Mars 9/3/76; functioned 3 years
Voyager 1	Sept. 5, 1977	Jupiter, Saturn	Encountered Jupiter 3/5/79, provided evidence of Jupiter ring; passed near Saturn 11/12/80
Voyager 2	Aug. 20, 1977	Jupiter, Saturn, Uranus, Neptune	Encountered Jupiter 7/9/79; Saturn 8/25/81; Uranus 1/24/86; Neptune 8/25/89
Pioneer Venus 1	May 20, 1978	Venus	Entered Venus orbit 12/4/78; spent 14 years studying planet; ceased operating 10/19/92
Pioneer Venus 2	Aug. 8, 1978	Venus	Encountered Venus 12/9/78; probes impacted on surface
Magellan	May 4, 1989	Venus	Landed on Venus 8/10/90; orbited and mapped Venus; monitored geological activity on surface; ceased operating 10/11/94
Galileo	Oct. 18, 1989	Jupiter	Used Earth's gravity to propel it toward Jupiter; encountered Venus Feb. 1990; encountered Jupiter 12/7/95; released probe to Jovian surface; encountered moons Ganymede, Europa, Io, and Callisto
Mars Observer	Sept. 25, 1992	Mars	Communication was lost 8/21/93
Near Earth Asteroid Rendezvous (NEAR)	Feb. 17, 1996	Asteroid Eros	Rendezvoused with Eros 4/00; began orbiting and studying the asteroid; communication ceased 2/28/01
Mars Global Surveyor	Nov. 7, 1996	Mars	Began orbiting Mars 9/11/97; began 2-year mapping survey of entire Martian surface 3/9/99; discovered magnetism on planet; observed Martian moon Phobos; discovered evidence of liquid water in geologically recent past 6/22/00
Mars Pathfinder	Dec. 4, 1996	Mars	Landed on Mars 7/4/97; rover Sojourner made measurements of the Martian climate and soil composition, sending thousands of surface images; ceased operating 9/27/97
Cassini	Oct. 15, 1997	Saturn	Scheduled to reach Saturn in 2004; 4-year mission to study planet's atmosphere, rings, and moons; probe will land on moon Titan
Lunar Prospector	Jan. 6, 1998	Moon	Began orbiting Moon 1/11/98; mapped abundance of 11 elements on Moon's surface; discovered evidence of water-ice at both lunar poles; made 1st precise gravity map of entire lunar surface; crashed into crater near Moon's south pole 7/31/99 to end mission
Mars Climate Orbiter	Dec. 11, 1998	Mars	Communication was lost 9/23/99
Mars Polar Lander	Jan. 3, 1999	Mars	Communication was lost 12/3/99
Stardust	Feb. 7, 1999	Comet Wild-2	Scheduled to reach comet in 2004; to gather dust samples and return them to Earth in 2006
2001 Mars Odyssey	Apr. 7, 2001	Mars	Reached Mars 10/24/01; mission through 8/04 to study climate and geologic history.
Genesis	Aug. 8, 2001	Sun	Scheduled to travel to the Sun and collect particles from solar wind and return them to Earth in 2004.

Passenger Traffic at World Airports, 2001[1]

Source: Airports Council International-Geneva, Switzerland

AIRPORT LOCATION (NAME)[1]	Passenger Arrivals and Departures	AIRPORT LOCATION (NAME)[1]	Passenger Arrivals and Departures
London, UK (Heathrow)	60,743,154	Munich, Germany (Munich)	23,646,900
Tokyo/Haneda, Japan (Tokyo Intl.)	58,692,688	Paris, France (Orly)	23,028,736
Frankfurt, Germany (Rhein/Main)	48,559,980	Seoul, South Korea (Kimpo Intl.)	22,062,248
Paris, France (Charles De Gaulle)	47,996,223	Zurich, Switzerland (Zurich)	20,978,639
Amsterdam, Netherlands (Schiphol)	39,538,483	Barcelona, Spain (El Prat)	20,746,260
Madrid, Spain (Barajas)	33,984,413	Mexico City, Mexico (Mexico City)	20,599,064
Hong Kong, China (Hong Kong Intl.)	32,553,000	Brussels, Belgium (Brussels Intl.)	19,635,635
London, UK (Gatwick)	31,182,361	Manchester, UK (Manchester)	19,554,531
Bangkok, Thailand (Bangkok Intl.)	30,623,764	Osaka, Japan (Kansai Intl.)	19,341,525
Singapore (Changi)	28,093,759	Palma De Mallorca, Spain (Palma de Mallorca)	19,202,092
Toronto, Ontario (Lester B. Pearson Intl.)	28,042,692	Milan, Italy (Malpensa)	18,570,494
Rome, Italy (Fiumicino)	25,563,927	Taipei, Taiwan (Chiang Kai-Shek)	18,460,827
Tokyo, Japan (Narita)	25,379,370	Stockholm, Sweden (Arlanda)	18,284,340
Sydney, Australia (Kingsford Smith)	24,303,024	Copenhagen, Denmark (Copenhagen)	18,034,697
Beijing, China (Beijing Capital Intl.)	24,176,495	Melbourne, Australia (Melbourne)	17,019,571

(1) Excludes U.S. airports (see page 216). Includes only airports participating in the Airports Council Intl. Airport Traffic Statistics collection.

Passenger Traffic at U.S. Airports, 2001

Source: Airports Council International-North America

AIRPORT	Passenger Arrivals and Departures	AIRPORT	Passenger Arrivals and Departures
Hartsfield Atlanta (ATL)	75,858,500	Detroit (DTW)	32,294,121
Chicago O'Hare (ORD)	67,448,064	Miami (MIA)	31,668,450
Los Angeles (LAX)	61,606,204	Newark (EWR)	30,558,000
Dallas/Ft. Worth (DFW)	55,150,693	JFK-New York (JFK)	29,349,000
Denver (DEN)	36,092,806	Orlando (MCO)	28,253,248
Las Vegas (LAS	35,180,960	Seattle-Tacoma (SEA)	27,036,073
Houston (IAH)	34,803,580	St. Louis (STL)	26,695,019
San Francisco (SFO)	34,632,474	Boston Logan (BOS)	24,199,930
Phoenix Sky Harbor (PHX)	34,338,544	Philadelphia (PHL)	23,953,052
Minneapolis/St. Paul (MSP)	34,308,389	Charlotte (CLT)	23,177,555

U.S. Scheduled Airline Traffic, 1990-2001

Source: Courtesy of Air Transport Association of America, Inc. Reprinted with permission.

(in thousands, except where otherwise noted)

	1990	1995	2000	2001*
Revenue passengers enplaned	465,600	547,800	666,200	622,100
Revenue passenger miles	457,926,000	540,656,000	692,757,000	651,663,000
Available seat miles	733,375,000	807,078,000	956,950,000	930,486,000
% of seating utilized	62.4	67.0	72.4	70.0
Cargo traffic (ton miles)	12,549,000	16,921,000	23,888,000	21,997,000
Passenger revenue	$58,453,000	$69,594,000	$93,622,000	$80,936,000
Net profit	–$3,921,000	$2,314,000	$2,486,000	–$7,710,000
Employees	545,809	546,987	679,967	670,730

*Financial results include cash compensation from government after Sept. 2001 terrorist attacks.

Leading U.S. Passenger Airlines, 2001

Source: Courtesy of Air Transport Association of America, Inc. Reprinted with permission.

(in thousands)

Airline	Passengers	Airline	Passengers	Airline	Passengers	Airline	Passengers
American*	98,742	America West	19,578	American Trans Air	6,515	Air Wisconsin	4,101
Delta	94,045	Alaska	13,639	Mesaba	5,909	Spirit	3,187
United	75,138	American Eagle	11,984	Hawaiian	5,459	JetBlue	3,056
Southwest	73,629	Continental Express	8,305	Comair	4,753	Frontier	2,998
US Airways	56,105	AirTran	8,303	Horizon Air	4,668	Midway	2,392
Northwest	52,271	Atlantic Southeast	6,666	Aloha	4,598	National	2,350
Continental	42,357						

*Data include TWA.

U.S. Airline Safety, Scheduled Commercial Carriers, 1985-2001

Source: Courtesy of Air Transport Association of America, Inc. Reprinted with permission.

	Departures (millions)	Fatal accidents	Fatalities	Accident rate[2]
1985	5.8	4	197	0.069
1986[1]	6.4	2	5	0.016
1987[1]	6.6	4	231	0.046
1988[1]	6.7	3	285	0.030
1989	6.6	8	131	0.121
1990	6.9	6	39	0.087
1991	6.8	4	62	0.059
1992	7.1	4	33	0.057
1993	7.2	1	1	0.014
1994	7.5	4	239	0.053
1995	8.1	2	166	0.025
1996	8.2	3	342	0.036
1997	8.2	3	3	0.037
1998	8.3	1	1[3]	0.012
1999	8.6	2	12	0.023
2000	9.0	3	92	0.033
2001[1]	8.8	6	531	0.023

(1) Sabotage-caused accidents are included in the number of fatal accidents and fatalities, but not in the calculation of accident rates. (2) Fatal accidents per 100,000 departures. (3) On-ground employee fatality.

Aircraft Operating Statistics, 2001

Source: Courtesy of Air Transport Association of America, Inc. Reprinted with permission.
 Figures are averages for most commonly used models

	No. of seats	Speed airborne (mph)	Flight length (mi)	Fuel (gal per hr)	Operating cost per hr
B747-400	369	537	4,445	3,429	$8,158
B747-200/300	357	522	3,386	3,536	8,080
B747-F	0	506	2,519	3,518	6,700
L-1011	339	493	1,396	2,140	8,721
DC-10-10	309	513	2,476	2,491	5,000
DC-10-40	284	491	1,516	2,580	6,544
B-777	266	525	3,557	2,134	4,878
MD-11	270	525	3,648	2,181	7,474
DC-10-30	273	520	3,292	2,651	6,388
A300-600	228	479	1,513	1,743	5,145
B767-300ER	207	499	2,274	1,401	3,823
B767-200ER	176	487	2,083	1,459	4,406
MD-90	149	441	811	927	2,590
B727-200	147	439	756	1,278	3,435
B737-800	148	454	1,058	834	2,255
A320-100/200	146	454	1,090	822	2,492
B737-400	141	407	663	784	$2,948
MD-80	135	431	780	960	2,725
B737-300/700	131	408	580	785	2,417
DC-9-50	126	365	333	913	1,954
A319	122	445	933	758	1,987
B737-100/200	117	401	537	901	2,601
B717-200	106	374	331	629	2,212
DC-9-40	111	380	465	850	1,845
B737-500	109	410	600	704	2,397
DC-9-30	97	392	509	827	2,218
F-100	88	380	473	658	3,015
DC-9-10	69	389	477	748	2,227
CRJ 145	50	389	488	358	1,033
ERJ-145	50	362	382	357	1,151
ERJ-135	37	363	400	310	1,028

WORLD ALMANAC QUICK QUIZ

Who is the only astronaut to fly in all three of the nation's pioneering space programs: Mercury, Gemini, and Apollo?
(a) Neil Armstrong (b) John Glenn (c) Buzz Aldrin (d) Walter Schirra

For the answer look in this chapter, or see page 1008.

Some Notable Aviation Firsts[1]

1903 — On Dec. 17, near Kitty Hawk, NC, brothers Wilbur and Orville Wright made the 1st human-carrying, powered flight. Each made 2 flights; the longest, about 852 ft, lasted 59 sec.

1907 — U.S. airplane manufacturing company formed by Glenn H. Curtiss.

1908 — 1st airplane passenger, Lt. Frank P. Lahm, rode with Wilbur Wright in a brief (6 min, 24 sec) flight.

1911 — 1st transportation of mail by airplane officially approved by the U.S. Postal Service began on Sept. 23. It lasted one week. In 1918, limited scheduled air mail service began. By 1921, scheduled transcontinental airmail service began between New York City and San Francisco.

1914 — 1st scheduled passenger airline service began. It operated between St. Petersburg and Tampa, FL.

1919 — 1st airline food, a basket lunch, was served as part of a commercial airline service.

1930 — Ellen Church became 1st flight attendant.

(1) Excludes notable around-the-world and international trips.

1939 — On Aug. 27, the German Heinkel He 178 made the 1st successful flight powered by a jet engine.

1947 — Mach 1, the sound barrier, was broken by Amer. Charles E. ("Chuck") Yeager in a Bell X-1 rocket-powered aircraft.

1947 — Largest airplane ever flown, Howard Hughes's "Spruce Goose," flew 1 mi at an altitude of 80 ft.

1953 — Jacqueline Cochran became 1st woman to fly faster than sound.

1960 — Convair B-58, 1st supersonic bomber, was introduced.

1968 — The supersonic speed of Mach 2 was accomplished for 1st time, in a Tupolev Tu-144. The plane had an approximate maximum speed of 1,200 mph.

1970 — The Tupolev Tu-144, during commercial transport, exceeded Mach 2. It reached about 1,335 mph at 53,475 ft.

1976 — The Concorde began 1st scheduled supersonic commercial service.

Some Notable Around-the-World and Intercontinental Trips

Aviator or Craft	From/To	Miles	Time	Date
Nellie Bly	New York/New York		72d 06h 11m	1889
George Francis Train	New York/New York		67d 12h 03m	1890
Charles Fitzmorris	Chicago/Chicago		60d 13h 29m	1901
J. W. Willis Sayre	Seattle/Seattle		54d 09h 42m	1903
J. Alcock-A.W. Brown [1]	Newfoundland/Ireland	1,960	16h 12m	June 14-15, 1919
2 U.S. Army airplanes	Seattle/Seattle	26,103	35d 01h 11m	1924
Richard E. Byrd, Floyd Bennett [2]	Spitsbergen (Nor.)/N. Pole	1,545	15h 30m	May 9, 1926
Amundsen-Ellsworth-Nobile Polar Expedition (in a dirigible)	Spitsbergen (Nor.)/over N. Pole to Teller, Alaska		80h	May 11-14,1926
E.S. Evans and L. Wells (*New York World*)	New York/New York	18,410[3]	28d 14h 36m 05s	June 16-July 14, 1926
Charles Lindbergh[4]	New York/Paris	3,610	33h 29m 30s	May 20-21, 1927
Amelia Earhart, W. Stultz, L. Gordon	Newfoundland/Wales		20h 40m	June 17-18, 1928
Graf Zeppelin	Friedrichshafen, Ger./Lakehurst, NJ	6,630	4d 15h 46m	Oct. 11-15, 1928
Graf Zeppelin	Friedrichshafen, Ger./Lakehurst, NJ	21,700	20d 04h	Aug. 14-Sept. 4, 1929
Wiley Post and Harold Gatty (Monoplane Winnie Mae)	New York/New York	15,474	8d 15h 51m	July 1, 1931
C. Pangborn-H. Herndon Jr.[5]	Misawa, Japan/Wenatchee, Wash.	4,458	41h 34m	Oct. 3-5, 1931
Amelia Earhart [6]	Newfoundland/Ireland	2,026	14h 56m	May 20-21, 1932
Wiley Post (Monoplane Winnie Mae)[7]	New York/New York	15,596	115h 36m 30s	July 15-22, 1933
Hindenburg Zeppelin	Lakehurst, NJ/Frankfort, Ger.		42h 53m	Aug. 9-11, 1936
Howard Hughes and 4 assistants	New York/New York	14,824	3d 19h 08m 10s	July 10-13, 1938
America, Pan American 4-engine Lockheed Constellation[8]	New York/New York	22,219	101h 32m	June 17-30, 1947
Col. Edward Eagan	New York/New York	20,559	147h 15m	Dec. 13, 1948
USAF B-50 Lucky Lady II (Capt. James Gallagher) [9]	Ft. Worth, TX/Ft. Worth, TX	23,452	94h 01m	Mar. 2, 1949
Col. D. Schilling, USAF [10]	England/Limestone, ME	3,300	10h 01m	Sept. 22, 1950
C.F. Blair Jr.	Norway/Alaska	3,300	10h 29m	May 29, 1951
Canberra Bomber [11]	N. Ireland/Newfoundland	2073	04h 34m	Aug. 26, 1952
	Newfoundland/N. Ireland	2073	03h 25m	Aug. 26, 1952
3 USAF B-52 Strato-fortresses [12]	Merced, CA/CA	24,325	45h 19m	Jan. 15-18, 1957
USSR TU-114 [13]	Moscow/New York	5,092	11h 06m	June 28, 1959
Peter Gluckmann (solo)	San Francisco/San Francisco	22,800	29d	Aug. 22-Sept. 20, 1959
Sue Snyder	Chicago/Chicago	21,219	62h 59m	June 22-24, 1960
Robert & Joan Wallick	Manila/Manila	23,129	5d 06h 17m 10s	June 2-7, 1966
Trevor K. Brougham	Darwin, Australia/Darwin	24,800	5d 05h 57m	Aug. 5-10, 1972
Arnold Palmer	Denver/Denver	22,985	57h 7m 12s	May 17-19, 1976
Boeing 747[14]	San Francisco/San Francisco	26,382	57h 25m 42s	Oct. 28-31, 1977
Richard Rutan & Jeana Yeager[15]	Edwards AFB, CA	24,986	09d 03m 44s	Dec. 14-23, 1986
Concorde	New York/New York	1,114 mph	31h 27m 49s	Aug. 15-16, 1995
Col. Douglas L. Raaberg and crew, B1 bomber[16]	Dyess AFB, Abilene, TX/ Dyess AFB	6,250	36h 13m 36s	June 3, 1995
Linda Finch[17]	Oakland, CA/Oakland, CA	26,000	73d	Mar. 17-May 28, 1997
Bertrand Piccard, Brian Jones[18]	Switzerland/Egypt	29,054.6	19d 21h 55m	Mar. 1-21, 1999
Steve Fossett[19]	Australia/Australia	21,109.6	14d 20h 01m	June 19-July 4, 2002

(1) Nonstop transatlantic flight. (2) Claim of reaching N. Pole in dispute; if claim is untrue, then Amundsen-Ellsworth-Nobile were the first to fly over N. Pole. (3) Includes mileage by train and auto, 4,110; by plane, 6,300; by steamship, 8,000. (4) Solo transatlantic flight in the Ryan monoplane "Spirit of St. Louis." (5) Nonstop transpacific flight. (6) First woman's transoceanic solo flight. (7) First to fly solo around N circumference of the world and first to fly twice around the world. (8) Inception of regular commercial global air service. (9) First nonstop round-the-world flight, refueled 4 times in flight. (10) Nonstop jet transatlantic flight. (11) Transatlantic round trip on same day. (12) First nonstop global flight by jet planes; refueled in flight by KC-97 aerial tankers; average speed approx. 525 mph. (13) Nonstop between Moscow and New York. (14) Speed record around the world over both Earth's poles. (15) Circled Earth nonstop without refueling. (16) Refueled in flight 6 times. Tested B-1B bomber by bombing 3 pre-arranged target sites on 3 continents. (17) Followed the intended around-the-world flight route (1937) of Amelia Earhart. (18) First to circumnavigate the globe nonstop in a balloon. (19) First solo circumnavigation of the globe nonstop in a balloon; time, dates and distance are for complete flight, which exceeded circumnavigation because winds prevented landing.

TRADE AND TRANSPORTATION

U.S. Trade With Selected Countries and Major Areas, 2001

Source: Office of Trade and Econ. Analysis, U.S. Dept. of Commerce

(in millions of dollars; countries listed by amount of total trade with U.S.)

COUNTRY	Total Trade with U.S.	U.S. Exports to	Rank[1]	U.S. Imports from	Rank[1]	U.S. Trade Balance with	Rank[2]
Canada	$379,691.9	$163,424.1	1	$216,267.8	1	$–52,843.7	3
Mexico	232,634.4	101,296.5	2	131,337.9	2	–30,041.4	4
Japan	183,924.9	57,451.6	3	126,473.3	3	–69,021.7	2
China	121,460.6	19,182.3	9	102,278.3	4	–83,096.0	1
Germany	89,072.0	29,995.3	5	59,076.7	5	–29,081.4	5
U.K.	82,083.0	40,714.2	4	41,368.8	6	–654.6	43
Korea (South)	57,362.0	22,180.6	6	35,181.4	7	–13,000.9	8
Taiwan	51,496.1	18,121.6	10	33,374.5	8	–15,252.9	6
France	50,272.7	19,864.5	7	30,408.2	9	–10,543.7	11
Italy	33,705.5	9,915.6	16	23,789.9	10	–13,874.2	7
Singapore	32,651.7	17,651.7	11	15,000.0	14	2,651.8	225
Malaysia	31,698.0	9,357.7	18	22,340.3	11	–12,982.7	9
Brazil	30,345.9	15,879.5	12	14,466.4	16	1,413.0	223
Netherlands	29,000.0	19,484.7	8	9,515.3	25	9,969.4	230
Ireland	25,643.3	7,144.0	21	18,499.3	12	–11,355.2	10
Hong Kong	23,673.8	14,027.5	13	9,646.3	24	4,381.3	228
Belgium	23,660.7	13,502.3	14	10,158.4	20	3,343.9	227
Venezuela	20,892.6	5,642.1	25	15,250.5	13	–9,608.3	12
Thailand	20,716.6	5,989.4	22	14,727.2	15	–8,737.8	13
Switzerland	19,476.9	9,807.3	17	9,669.6	23	137.7	200
Israel	19,434.3	7,475.3	20	11,959.0	18	–4,483.7	20
Saudi Arabia	19,229.7	5,957.5	23	13,272.2	17	–7,314.7	16
Philippines	18,985.4	7,660.0	19	11,325.4	19	–3,665.4	21
Australia	17,408.4	10,930.5	15	6,477.9	28	4,452.7	229
India	13,494.2	3,757.0	28	9,737.2	22	–5,980.1	17
MAJOR AREA/GROUP							
North America	612,326.4	264,720.6	NA	347,605.8	NA	–82,885.1	NA
Western Europe	414,130.1	174,696.4	NA	239,433.7	NA	–64,737.3	NA
Euro Area	279,276.4	112,903.0	NA	166,373.4	NA	–53,470.4	NA
European Union (EU)	378,824.9	158,767.5	NA	220,057.4	NA	–61,290.0	NA
European Free Trade Association	27,203.6	11,874.5	NA	15,329.1	NA	–3,454.6	NA
Eastern Europe	21,175.4	6,832.3	NA	14,343.1	NA	–7,510.7	NA
Former Soviet Republics	12,292.6	4,084.7	NA	8,207.9	NA	–4,123.2	NA
OECD	412,215.1	173,756.3	NA	238,458.8	NA	–64,702.5	NA
Pacific Rim Countries	557,454.6	181,391.1	NA	376,063.5	NA	–194,672.4	NA
Asia/Near East	55,681.9	19,276.2	NA	36,405.7	NA	–17,129.5	NA
Asia/NICS	165,183.7	71,981.5	NA	93,202.2	NA	–21,220.7	NA
Asia/South	21,339.2	4,808.3	NA	16,530.9	NA	–11,722.6	NA
ASEAN	118,170.8	43,312.8	NA	74,858.0	NA	–31,545.1	NA
APEC	1,209,717.6	459,890.0	NA	749,827.6	NA	–289,937.7	NA
South/Central America	125,526.0	58,156.0	NA	67,370.0	NA	–9,214.1	NA
Twenty Latin American Republics	346,079.4	152,703.2	NA	193,376.2	NA	–40,672.9	NA
Central American Common Market	20,075.4	8,990.4	NA	11,085.0	NA	–2,094.5	NA
LAFTA	314,981.2	137,427.2	NA	177,554.0	NA	–40,126.8	NA
NATO	780,386.0	333,021.6	NA	447,364.4	NA	–114,342.7	NA
OPEC	79,806.5	20,052.6	NA	59,753.9	NA	–39,701.2	NA
WORLD TOTAL	**1,870,099.7**	**729,100.3**	**NA**	**1,140999.4**	**NA**	**–411,899.1**	**NA**

(1) Rank shown is for column to the left. (2) Rank is by size of U.S. trade deficit. NA= Not applicable. **Note:** Details may not equal totals because of rounding or incomplete enumeration.

Definitions of areas *as used in the table:* **North America**—Canada, Mexico. **Western Europe**—Andorra, Austria, Belgium, Bosnia and Herzegovina, Croatia, Cyprus, Denmark, Faroe Islands, Finland, France, Germany, Gibraltar, Greece, Iceland, Ireland, Italy, Liechtenstein, Luxembourg, Macedonia, Malta and Gozo, Monaco, Netherlands, Norway, Portugal, San Marino, Serbia & Montenegro, Slovenia, Spain, Svalbard/Jan Mayen Island, Sweden, Switzerland, Turkey, United Kingdom, Vatican City. **Euro Area**—Austria, Belgium, Finland, France, Germany, Ireland, Italy, Luxembourg, Netherlands, Portugal, Spain. **EU**—(European Union) Belgium, Denmark, France, Germany, Greece, Ireland, Italy, Luxembourg, Netherlands, Portugal, Spain, United Kingdom. **EFTA**—(European Free Trade Association) Austria, Finland, Iceland, Liechtenstein, Norway, Sweden, Switzerland. **Eastern Europe**—Albania, Armenia, Azerbaijan, Belarus, Bulgaria, Czech Republic, Estonia, Georgia, Hungary, Kazakhstan, Kyrgyzstan, Latvia, Lithuania, Moldova, Poland, Romania, Russia, Slovakia, Tajikistan, Turkmenistan, Ukraine, Uzbekistan. **Former Soviet Republics**—Armenia, Azerbaijan, Belarus, Estonia, Georgia, Kazakhstan, Kyrgyzstan, Latvia, Lithuania, Moldova, Russia, Tajikistan, Turkmenistan, Ukraine, Uzbekistan. **OECD**—(Organization for Economic Cooperation & Development in Europe) Austria, Belgium, Denmark, Finland, France, Germany, Greece, Iceland, Ireland, Italy, Liechtenstein, Luxembourg, Monaco, Netherlands, Norway, Portugal, San Marino, Spain, Svalbard/Jan Mayen Island, Sweden, Switzerland, Turkey, United Kingdom. **Pacific Rim Countries/Territories**—Australia, Brunei, China, Indonesia, Japan, South Korea, Macao, Malaysia, New Zealand, Papua New Guinea, Philippines, Singapore, Taiwan. **Asia/Middle East**—Bahrain, Iran, Iraq, Israel, Jordan, Kuwait, Lebanon, Oman, Qatar, Saudi Arabia, Syria, U.A.E., Yemen. **Asia/NICS**—(Newly Industrialized Countries) Hong Kong (special administrative region of China), Korea, Singapore, Taiwan. **Asia/South** —Afghanistan, Bangladesh, India, Nepal, Pakistan, Sri Lanka. **ASEAN**—(Association of Southeast Asian Nations) Brunei, Indonesia, Malaysia, Philippines, Singapore, Thailand. **APEC**—(Asia-Pacific Economic Cooperation) Australia, Brunei, Canada, Chile, China, Indonesia, Japan, Korea, Malaysia, Mexico, New Zealand, Papua New Guinea, Peru, Philippines, Russia, Singapore, Taiwan, Thailand, Vietnam. **South/Central America**—Anguilla, Antigua and Barbuda, Argentina, Aruba, Bahamas, Barbados, Belize, Bermuda, Bolivia, Brazil, British Virgin Islands, Cayman Islands, Chile, Colombia, Costa Rica, Cuba, Dominica, Dominican Republic, Ecuador, El Salvador, Falkland Islands, French Guiana, Grenada, Guadeloupe, Guatemala, Guyana, Haiti, Honduras, Jamaica, Martinique, Montserrat, Netherland Antilles, Nicaragua, Panama, Paraguay, Peru, St. Kitts and Nevis, St. Lucia, St. Vincent and the Grenadines, Suriname, Trinidad and Tobago, Turks and Caicos Islands, Uruguay, Venezuela. **20 Latin American Republics**—Argentina, Bolivia, Brazil, Chile, Colombia, Costa Rica, Cuba, Dominican Republic, Ecuador, El Salvador, Guatemala, Haiti, Honduras, Mexico, Nicaragua, Panama, Paraguay, Peru, Uruguay, Venezuela. **Central American Common Market**—Costa Rica, El Salvador, Guatemala, Honduras, Nicaragua. **LAFTA**—(Latin American Free Trade Assn.) Argentina, Bolivia, Brazil, Chile, Colombia, Ecuador, Mexico, Paraguay, Peru, Uruguay, Venezuela. **NATO**—(North Atlantic Treaty Organization) Belgium, Canada, Denmark, France, Germany, Greece, Iceland, Ireland, Italy, Liechtenstein, Luxembourg, Monaco, Netherlands, Norway, Portugal, San Marino, Spain, Svalbard/Jan Mayan Island, Sweden, Switzerland, Turkey, United Kingdom. **OPEC**—(Organization of Petroleum Exporting Countries) Algeria, Indonesia, Iran, Iraq, Kuwait, Libya, Nigeria, Qatar, Saudi Arabia, United Arab Emirates, Venezuela.

U.S. Exports and Imports by Principal Commodity Groupings, 2001

Source: Office of Trade and Economic Analysis, U.S. Dept. of Commerce

(millions of dollars)

Items	Exports	Imports
TOTAL	**$729,100**	**$1,140,999**
Agricultural commodities	**53,705**	**39,544**
Animal feeds	4,221	574
Cereal flour	1,412	1,895
Coffee	16	1,357
Corn	4,755	135
Cotton, raw and linters	2,174	27
Hides and skins	1,813	100
Live animals	890	2,238
Meat and preparations	7,231	4,254
Oils/fats, vegetable	787	999
Rice	692	168
Soybeans	5,429	31
Sugar	24,230	480
Tobacco, unmanufactured	3,217	710
Vegetables and fruits	54,347	9,517
Wheat	1,568	282
Manufactured goods	**577,714**	**950,679**
ADP equipment; office machinery	39,240	75,859
Airplane parts	15,735	6,287
Airplanes	26,961	14,884
Aluminum	3,253	6,406
Artwork/antiques	1,637	5,458
Basketware, etc.	3,579	5,591
Chemicals-cosmetics	5,825	3,750
Chemicals-dyeing	3,782	2,478
Chemicals-fertilizers	2,077	1,890
Chemicals-inorganic	5,578	6,153
Chemicals-medicinal	15,031	18,628
Chemicals[1]	12,382	5,927
Chemicals-organic	16,424	29,712
Chemicals-plastics	18,485	10,401
Clothing	6,510	63,856
Copper	1,091	4,046
Electrical machinery	72,055	84,670
Footwear	639	15,234
Furniture and bedding	4,255	18,610
Gem diamonds	1,714	10,616
General industrial machinery	32,153	33,264
Glass	2,475	2,201
Glassware	882	1,740
Gold, nonmonetary	4,872	2,079
Iron and steel mill prod.	5,482	12,449
Jewelry	$1,951	$6,275
Lighting, plumbing	1,321	4,895
Metal manufactures[1]	11,365	15,510
Metalworking machinery	4,703	6,587
Nickel	512	1,079
Optical goods	3,036	3,455
Paper and paperboard	10,042	14,815
Photographic equipment	3,281	5,596
Plastic articles[1]	7,065	8,257
Platinum	962	5,240
Pottery	96	1,642
Power generating machinery	33,577	36,118
Printed materials	4,746	3,721
Records/magnetic media	4,611	4,883
Rubber articles[1]	1,569	1,979
Rubber tires and tubes	2,287	4,209
Scientific instruments	29,123	21,356
Ships, boats	1,801	1,209
Silver and bullion	234	530
Spacecraft	201	71
Specialized industr. machinery	25,747	19,554
Television, VCR, etc.	10,074	62,836
Textile yarn, fabric	1,269	14,616
Toys/games/sporting goods	3,217	20,901
Travel goods	308	4,300
Vehicles	277	157,400
Watches/clocks/parts	277	3,048
Wood manufactures	1,568	6,998
Mineral fuels	**12,494**	**121,923**
Coal	1,915	1,022
Crude oil	187	74,293
Liquified propane/butane	338	1,880
Mineral fuels, other	3,309	1,954
Natural gas	536	15,417
Petroleum preparations	5,034	24,620
Selected commodities	**18,973**	**28,196**
Alcoholic bev., distilled	489	3,063
Cigarettes	2,118	238
Cork, wood, lumber	3,533	7,968
Crude fertilizers	1,654	1,318
Fish and preparations	3,069	9,712
Metal ores; scrap	4,420	3,237
Pulp and waste paper	3,690	2,630

(1) Those not specified elsewhere. **NOTE:** Not all products are listed in each commodity group.

Trends in U.S. Foreign Trade, 1790-2001

Source: Office of Trade and Economic Analysis, U.S. Dept. of Commerce

In 1790, U.S. exports and imports combined came to $43 million and there was a $3 million trade deficit. In 2001, U.S. exports and imports combined amounted to nearly $2 trillion, and the trade deficit, which had generally been climbing in recent years (after a century of trade surpluses), reached $412 billion, the 2nd-highest total in history.

(in millions of dollars)

Year	Exports	Imports	Trade Balance
1790	$20	$23	$–3
1795	48	70	–22
1800	71	91	–20
1805	96	121	–25
1810	67	85	–19
1815	53	113	–60
1820	70	74	–5
1825	91	90	1
1830	72	63	9
1835	115	137	–22
1840	124	98	25
1845	106	113	–7
1850	144	174	–29
1855	219	258	–39
1860	334	354	–20
1865	166	239	–73
1870	393	436	–43
1875	513	533	–20
1880	$836	$668	$168
1885	742	578	165
1890	858	789	69
1895	808	732	76
1900	1,394	850	545
1905	1,519	1,118	401
1910	1,745	1,557	188
1915	2,769	1,674	1,094
1920	8,228	5,278	2,950
1925	4,910	4,227	683
1930	3,843	3,061	782
1935	2,283	2,047	235
1940	4,021	2,625	1,396
1945	9,806	4,159	5,646
1950	9,997	8,954	1,043
1955	14,298	11,566	2,732
1960	19,659	15,073	4,586
1965	$26,742	$21,520	$5,222
1970	42,681	40,356	2,325
1975	107,652	98,503	9,149
1980	220,626	244,871	–24,245
1985	213,133	345,276	–132,143
1990	394,030	495,042	–101,012
1991	421,730	485,453	–63,723
1992	448,164	532,665	–84,501
1993	465,091	580,659	–115,568
1994	512,626	683,256	–170,630
1995	584,742	743,445	–158,703
1996	625,075	795,289	–170,214
1997	689,182	870,671	–181,489
1998	682,138	911,896	–229,758
1999	695,797	1,024,618	–328,821
2000	781,918	1,218,022	–436,104
2001	729,100	1,140,999	–411,899

WORLD ALMANAC QUICK QUIZ

With which country did the United States have the highest trade deficit in 2001, at more than $83 billion?

(a) Canada (b) United Kingdom (c) China (d) Japan

For the answer look in this chapter, or see page 1008.

The North American Free Trade Agreement (NAFTA)

NAFTA, a comprehensive plan for free trade between the U.S., Canada, and Mexico, took effect Jan. 1, 1994. Major provisions are:

Agriculture—Tariffs on all farm products are to be eliminated over 15 years. Domestic price-support systems may continue provided they do not distort trade.

Automobiles—By 2003, at least 62.5% of an automobile's value must have been produced in North America for it to qualify for duty-free status. Tariffs are to be phased out over 10 years.

Banking—U.S. and Canadian banks may acquire Mexican commercial banks accounting for as much as 8% of the industry's capital. All limits on ownership end in 2004.

Disputes—Special judges have jurisdiction to resolve disagreements within strict timetables.

Energy—Mexico continues to bar foreign ownership of its oil fields but, starting in 2004, U.S. and Canadian companies can bid on contracts offered by Mexican oil and electricity monopolies.

Environment—The trade agreement cannot be used to overrule national and state environmental, health, or safety laws.

Immigration—All 3 countries must ease restrictions on the movement of business executives and professionals.

Jobs—Barriers to limit Mexican migration to U.S. remain.

Patent and copyright protection—Mexico strengthened its laws providing protection to intellectual property.

Tariffs—Tariffs on 10,000 customs goods are to be eliminated over 15 years. One-half of U.S. exports to Mexico are to be considered duty-free within 5 years.

Textiles—A "rule of origin" provision requires most garments to be made from yarn and fabric that have been produced in North America. Most tariffs are being phased out over 5 years.

Trucking—Trucks were to have free access on crossborder routes and throughout the 3 countries by 1999, but the U.S. continued to impose restrictions on Mexican trucks. In 2001, an arbitration panel ruled that the U.S. restrictions were in violation of NAFTA. Pres. Bush pledged to work with Congress to bring the U.S. into compliance with NAFTA.

U.S. Trade With Mexico and Canada, 1993-2001

Source: Office of Trade and Economic Analysis, U.S. Dept. of Commerce

(U.S. exports to, imports from, Canada and Mexico in millions of dollars)

	MEXICO				CANADA		
Year	Exports	Imports	Trade Balance[1]	Year	Exports	Imports	Trade Balance[1]
1993	$41,581	$39,917	$1,664	1993	$100,444	$111,216	$–10,772
1994[2]	50,844	49,494	1,350	1994[2]	114,439	128,406	–13,968
1995	46,292	61,685	–15,393	1995	127,226	145,349	–18,123
1996	56,792	74,297	–17,506	1996	134,210	155,893	–21,682
1997	71,388	85,938	–14,549	1997	151,767	167,234	–15,467
1998	78,773	94,629	–15,857	1998	156,603	173,256	–16,653
1999	86,909	109,721	–22,812	1999	166,600	198,711	–32,111
2000	111,349	135,926	–24,577	2000	178,941	230,838	–51,897
2001	101,297	131,338	–30,041	2001	163,424	216,268	–52,844

(1) Totals may not add due to rounding. (2) NAFTA provisions began to take effect Jan. 1, 1994.

Foreign Exchange Rates, 1970-2001

Source: International Monetary Fund, Federal Reserve Board; Federal Reserve Board

(National currency units per dollar except as indicated; data are annual averages)

Note: As of 2002, the euro, the European Union's single currency, replaced the national currencies in the EU nations shown (Austria, Belgium, France, Gemany, Greece, Ireland, Italy, Netherlands, Portugal, and Spain), as well as in Finland and Luxembourg.

Year	Australia[1] (dollar)	Austria[1] (schilling)	Belgium[1] (franc)	Canada (dollar)	Denmark (krone)	France[1] (franc)	Germany[1, 2] (deutsche mark)	Greece (drachma)
1970	1.1136	25.880	49.680	1.0103	7.489	5.5200	3.6480	30.00
1975	1.3077	17.443	36.799	1.0175	5.748	4.2876	2.4613	32.29
1980	1.1400	12.945	29.237	1.1693	5.634	4.2250	1.8175	42.62
1985	0.7003	20.690	59.378	1.3655	10.596	8.9852	2.9440	138.12
1990	0.7813	11.370	33.418	1.1668	6.189	5.4453	1.6157	158.51
1995	0.7415	10.081	29.480	1.3724	5.602	4.9915	1.4331	231.66
1998	0.6294	12.379	36.299	1.4835	6.701	5.8995	1.7597	295.53
1999	0.6453	0.9386[3]	0.9386[3]	1.4857	6.976	0.9386[3]	0.9386[3]	305.65
2000	0.5815	0.9232[3]	0.9232[3]	1.4855	8.095	0.9232[3]	0.9232[3]	365.92
2001	0.5169	0.8952[3]	0.8952[3]	1.5487	8.3323	0.8952[3]	0.8952[3]	0.8952[3]

Year	India (rupee)	Ireland[1] (pound)	Italy[1] (lira)	Japan (yen)	Malaysia (ringgit)	Mexico (new peso)	Netherlands[1] (guilder)	Norway (krone)
1970	7.576	2.3959	623	357.60	3.0900	—	3.5970	7.1400
1975	8.409	2.2216	653	296.78	2.4030	—	2.5293	5.2282
1980	7.887	2.0577	856	226.63	2.1767	—	1.9875	4.9381
1985	12.369	1.0656	1,909	238.54	2.4830	—	3.3214	8.5972
1990	17.504	1.6585	1,198	144.79	2.7049	2.8126	1.8209	6.2597
1995	32.427	1.6038	1,628.9	94.06	2.5044	6.4194	1.6057	6.3352
1998	41.259	1.4257	1,736.2	130.91	3.9244	9.1360	1.9837	7.5451
1999	43.055	1.0668	0.9386[3]	113.91	3.8000	9.5604	0.9386[3]	7.7992
2000	45.000	0.9232[3]	0.9232[3]	107.80	3.8000	9.4590	0.9232[3]	8.8131
2001	47.22	0.8952[3]	0.8952[3]	121.57	3.8000	9.337	0.8952[3]	8.9964

Year	Portugal (escudo)	Singapore (dollar)	South Korea (won)	Spain[1] (peseta)	Sweden (krona)	Switzerland (franc)	Thailand (baht)	UK[1] (pound)
1970	28.75	3.0800	310.57	69.72	5.1700	4.3160	21.000	2.3959
1975	25.51	2.3713	484.00	57.43	4.1530	2.5839	20.379	2.2216
1980	50.08	2.1412	607.43	71.76	4.2309	1.6772	20.476	2.3243
1985	170.39	2.2002	870.02	170.04	8.6039	2.4571	27.159	1.2963
1990	142.55	1.8125	707.76	101.93	5.9188	1.3892	25.585	1.7847
1995	151.11	1.4174	771.27	124.69	7.1333	1.1825	24.915	1.5785
1998	180.10	1.6736	1,401.44	149.40	7.9499	1.4498	41.359	1.6564
1999	0.9386[3]	1.6950	1,188.82	0.9386[3]	8.2624	1.5022	37.814	1.6182
2000	0.9232[3]	1.7250	1,130.90	0.9232[3]	9.1735	1.6904	40.210	1.5156
2001	0.8952[3]	1.7930	1,292.01	0.8952[3]	10.3425	1.6891	44.532	1.4396

(1) U.S. dollars per unit of national currency. (2) West Germany before 1991. (3) Euro Area member, figures in euros per dollar. 1 EUR=13.7063 Aust. schillings, 40.3399 Bel. francs, 5.94573 Fin. markkas, 6.55957 Fr. francs, 1.95583 Ger. marks, 340.75 Gr. drachmas, .787564 Ir. pounds, 1936.27 It. lire, 40.3399 Lux. francs, 2.20371 Neth. guilders, 200.482 Port. escudos, 166.386 Sp. pesetas.

Foreign Direct Investment[1] in the U.S. by Selected Countries and Territories

Source: Bureau of Economic Analysis; U.S. Dept. of Commerce

(millions of dollars)

	1995	2000	2001
ALL COUNTRIES[2]	**$54,368**	**$1,214,254**	**$1,321,063**
Canada	**6,481**	**114,599**	**108,600**
Europe[3]	**36,654**	**835,137**	**946,758**
Austria	8	3,174	3,298
Belgium	38	14,585	14,721
Denmark	NA	4,428	2,091
Finland	0	9,107	8,762
France	1,217	131,484	147,207
Germany	14,155	124,839	152,760
Ireland	106	23,528	28,196
Italy	NA	5,994	5,916
Luxembourg	NA	53,794	40,232
Netherlands	855	146,493	158,020
Norway	14	2,241	2,277
Spain	147	5,459	5,092
Sweden	NA	22,427	23,299
Switzerland	4,198	69,240	125,521
United Kingdom	9,676	213,820	217,746
South and Central America[3]	**NA**	**13,682**	**17,040**
Brazil	5	886	570
Mexico	146	7,832	7,418
Panama	0	3,726	4,199
Venezuela	NA	802	4,722

	1995	2000	2001
Other W. Hemisphere[3]	**NA**	**$40,782**	**$41,840**
Bahamas	0	1,268	1,351
Bermuda	166	18,502	15,748
Netherlands Antilles	NA	3,940	3,923
UK islands, Caribbean	64	15,353	18,244
Africa[3]	**NA**	**2,756**	**3,264**
South Africa	NA	1,218S	1,867
Middle East[3]	**500**	**6,189**	**6,039**
Israel	NA	2,690	2,876
Kuwait	31	908	990
Lebanon	0	1	1
Saudi Arabia	NA	NA	NA
United Arab Emirates	NA	64	–23
Asia and Pacific[3]	**9,169**	**201,110**	**197,522**
Australia	2,488	20,701	23,488
Hong Kong	252	1,544	1,552
Japan	3,758	163,577	158,988
Korea, Republic of	1,257	3,287	3,121
Malaysia	57	92	21
New Zealand	NA	385	465
Singapore	863	7,751	6,502
Taiwan	286	3,131	2,551
European Union[4]	**32,436**	**760,017**	**808,301**
OPEC[5]	**504**	**4,363**	**7,968**

(1) The book value of foreign direct investors' equity in, and net outstanding loans to, their U.S. affiliates. A U.S. affiliate is a U.S. business enterprise in which a single foreign direct investor owns at least 10% of the voting securities or the equivalent. (2) Total includes sources not reflected in regional subtotals. (3) Totals include countries or territories not shown. (4) The European Union comprises Austria, Belgium, Denmark, Finland, France, Germany, Greece, Ireland, Italy, Luxembourg, the Netherlands, Portugal, Spain, Sweden, and the United Kingdom. (5) Organization of Petroleum Exporting Countries: Algeria, Indonesia, Iran, Iraq, Kuwait, Libya, Nigeria, Qatar, Saudi Arabia, the United Arab Emirates, and Venezuela. NA = Not available.

U.S. Direct Investment[1] Abroad in Selected Countries and Territories

Source: Bureau of Economic Analysis, U.S. Dept. of Commerce

(millions of dollars)

	1990	2000	2001
ALL COUNTRIES[2]	**$424,086**	**$1,293,431**	**$1,381,674**
Canada	**67,033**	**128,814**	**139,031**
Europe	**211,194**	**679,457**	**725,793**
Austria	889	2,686	3,374
Belgium	9,050	19,527	20,392
Denmark	1,597	5,363	6,537
Finland	551	1,110	1,143
France	18,874	38,752	38,457
Germany	27,259	50,963	61,437
Greece	288	637	648
Ireland	6,880	33,816	34,499
Italy	13,117	22,392	23,893
Luxembourg	1,390	25,571	30,039
Netherlands	22,658	117,557	131,884
Norway	3,815	5,833	6,660
Portugal	598	1,888	1,924
Spain	7,704	19,846	19,421
Sweden	1,600	22,676	17,968
Switzerland	25,199	55,854	62,897
Turkey	494	1,356	1,207
United Kingdom	68,224	241,663	249,201
Other	NA	11,969	14,212
South America[3]	**23,760**	**84,012**	**83,415**
Argentina	2,956	15,646	14,234
Brazil	14,918	39,033	36,317
Chile	1,368	9,451	11,674
Colombia	1,728	4,606	4,844
Ecuador	387	763	417
Peru	410	3,485	3,591
Venezuela	1,490	9,530	10,680
Central America[3]	**17,719**	**70,474**	**80,560**
Costa Rica	NA	1,655	1,614
Guatemala	NA	907	477
Honduras	NA	257	49
Mexico	9,398	37,332	52,168
Panama	7,409	29,316	25,296

	1990	2000	2001
Other Western Hemisphere[3]	**$30,113**	**$97,377**	**$105,581**
Bahamas	3,309	2,317	2,125
Barbados	NA	1,170	1,238
Bermuda	21,737	56,594	61,929
Dominican Republic	NA	813	752
Jamaica	604	2,354	2,280
Netherlands Antilles	–2,229	3,518	3,661
Trinidad and Tobago	508	1,524	1,978
UK islands, Caribbean	4,800	28,514	30,680
Africa[3]	**4,861**	**14,417**	**15,872**
Egypt	1,465	2,344	3,068
Nigeria	161	1,237	1,467
South Africa	956	3,245	2,950
Middle East[3]	**3,973**	**11,087**	**12,643**
Israel	756	3,386	4,122
Saudi Arabia	1,981	4,225	4,162
United Arab Emirates	519	737	942
Asia and Pacific[3]	**61,869**	**205,317**	**216,501**
Australia	14,846	35,364	34,041
China	NA	9,861	10,526
Hong Kong	6,187	26,621	29,389
India	513	1,431	1,739
Indonesia	3,226	8,514	8,807
Japan	20,997	59,441	64,103
Korea, Republic of	2,178	8,914	9,864
Malaysia	1,384	7,400	6,820
New Zealand	3,131	3,854	3,992
Philippines	1,629	2,735	2,776
Singapore	3,385	25,634	27,295
Taiwan	2,014	7,821	8,814
Thailand	1,585	6,635	7,337
European Union[4]	**NA**	**11,149**	**13,119**
Eastern Europe[5]	**NA**	**604,445**	**640,817**
OPEC[6]	**NA**	**28,736**	**31,362**

(1) The book value of U.S. direct investors' equity in, and net outstanding loans to, their foreign affiliates. A foreign affiliate is a foreign business enterprise in which a single U.S. investor owns at least 10% of the voting securities or the equivalent. (2) Total includes countries not reflected in regional totals. (3) Total includes countries not shown. (4) The European Union comprises Austria, Belgium, Denmark, Finland, France, Germany, Greece, Ireland, Italy, Luxembourg, the Netherlands, Portugal, Spain, Sweden, and the United Kingdom. (5) Eastern Europe consists of Albania, Armenia, Azerbaijan, Belarus, Bulgaria, Czech Rep., Estonia, Georgia, Hungary, Kazakhstan, Latvia, Lithuania, Moldova, Poland, Romania, Russia, Slovakia, Tajikstan, Turkmenistan, Ukraine, and Uzbekistan. (6) Organization of Petroleum Exporting Countries: Algeria, Indonesia, Iran, Iraq, Kuwait, Libya, Nigeria, Qatar, Saudi Arabia, the United Arab Emirates, and Venezuela. NA = not available.

U.S. International Transactions, 1965-2001

Source: Bureau of Economic Analysis, U.S. Dept. of Commerce; revised as of July 2002

(millions of dollars)

	1965	1970	1975	1980	1985	1990	1995	2000	2001
Exports of goods, services, and income[1]	$42,722	$68,387	$157,936	$344,440	$382,749	$700,455	$991,490	$1,417,236	$1,281,793
Merchandise bal. of payments basis[2]	26,461	42,469	107,088	224,250	215,915	389,307	575,871	771,994	718,762
Services	8,824	14,171	25,497	47,584	73,155	147,824	218,739	292,245	279,260
Income receipts on U.S.-owned assets abroad	7,437	11,748	25,351	72,606	93,679	163,324	196,880	350,656	281,389
Imports of goods and services and income payments	–32,708	–59,901	–132,745	–333,774	–484,037	–757,758	–1,086,539	–1,774,135	–1,625,701
Merchandise balance of payments basis[2]	–21,510	–39,866	–98,185	–249,750	–338,088	–498,337	–749,431	–1,224,417	–1,145,927
Services	–9,111	–14,520	–21,996	–41,491	–72,862	–120,019	–147,036	–218,503	–210,385
Income payments on foreign assets in the U.S.	–2,088	–5,515	–12,564	–42,532	–73,087	–139,402	–190,072	–323,005	–260,850
Unilateral transfers, net	–4,583	–6,156	–7,075	–8,349	–22,700	–34,588	–34,046	–53,442	–49,463
Capital acct. transactions, net	NA	NA	NA	NA	NA	NA	NA	837	826
U.S. assets abroad, net (increase)/capital outflow [–])	–5,716	–9,337	–39,703	–86,967	–39,889	–74,011	–307,207	–606,489	–370,962
U.S. official reserve assets, net	1,225	2,481	–849	–8,155	–3,858	–2,158	–9,742	–290	–4,911
U.S. government assets, other than official reserve assets, net	–1,605	–1,589	–3,474	–5,162	–2,821	2,307	–549	–941	–486
U.S. private assets, net	–5,336	–10,229	–35,380	–73,651	–33,211	–74,160	–296,916	–605,258	–365,565
Foreign assets in the U.S., net (increase/capital inflow [+])	742	6,359	17,170	62,612	146,383	140,992	451,234	1,015,986	752,806
Stat. discrepancy (sum of above items with sign reversed)	–457	–219	4,417	20,886	17,494	24,911	–14,931	7	10,701
Memorandum: Balance on current account	5,431	2,331	18,116	2,317	–123,987	–91,892	–129,095	–410,341	–393,371

NA = Not available. (1) Excludes transfers of goods and services under U.S. military grant programs. (2) Excludes exports of goods under U.S. military agency sales contracts identified in Census export documents, excludes imports of goods under direct defense expenditures identified in Census import documents, and reflects various other adjustments.

Merchant Fleets of the World by Flag of Registry, 2002

Source: Maritime Administration, U.S. Dept. of Commerce

Self-propelled oceangoing vessels of 1,000 gross deadweight tons and over, as of Jan. 1, 2002 (tonnage in thousands)

		All Vessels		Tanker		Dry Bulk Carrier		Container		Other[1]	
		No.	Tons	No.	Tons	No.	Tons	No.	Tons	No.	Tons
By Flag	Panama	4,727	180,170	1,131	61,285	1,448	88,779	534	16,281	1,614	13,825
	Liberia	1,509	78,490	581	42,930	343	21,240	292	9,647	293	4,673
	Greece	707	47,168	283	28,556	280	16,067	43	1,866	101	679
	Bahamas	990	44,928	247	28,206	157	9,336	70	1,893	516	5,493
	Malta	1,319	44,198	332	20,164	432	18,437	58	1,070	497	4,527
	Cyprus	1,222	35,687	162	7,179	452	20,999	119	2,700	489	4,809
	Singapore	852	32,365	407	17,017	130	9,067	164	4,106	151	2,175
	Norway (NIS)[2]	651	28,480	315	17,728	86	7,138	5	66	245	3,548
	China[3]	1,453	22,480	271	3,829	325	10,876	102	1,761	755	6,014
	Hong Kong SAR	419	22,387	48	2,899	248	15,834	68	2,504	55	1,150
	Marshall Isls.	258	18,787	116	12,352	83	4,912	43	1,142	16	382
	United States	443	14,968	130	7,529	17	707	89	3,195	207	3,537
	Japan	603	14,095	244	7,068	154	5,449	21	627	184	951
	India	298	10,271	101	5,190	113	4,502	7	143	77	435
	St. Vincent & the Grenadines	740	9,815	87	1,101	137	5,188	29	186	487	3,340
	Italy	420	9,733	214	4,013	46	3,369	28	975	132	1,376
	Isle of Man	205	9,288	88	6,637	24	1,612	19	425	74	613
	Korea (South)	485	8,907	140	1,863	99	5,148	47	832	199	1,064
	Turkey	541	8,856	99	1,486	147	5,609	26	281	269	1,480
	Bermuda	97	8,405	20	3,896	28	3,699	16	459	33	351
	All Other Flags	10,357	144,359	2,107	50,473	982	34,718	946	25,431	6,322	33,736
By Country	Greece	2,935	145,051	776	63,259	1,320	70,358	132	3,955	707	7,479
	Japan	2,703	100,361	733	37,072	859	48,727	197	5,858	914	8,705
	Norway	1,254	58,517	523	38,656	185	12,353	27	779	519	6,730
	United States	968	43,556	398	30,032	118	5,825	87	2,964	365	4,734
	China[3]	1,957	40,695	298	6,461	555	22,883	191	3,961	913	7,390
	Hong Kong SAR	538	36,157	139	15,061	241	18,054	45	1,530	113	1,512
	Germany	1,903	36,148	165	4,987	133	5,434	731	19,560	874	6,167
	Korea	771	25,415	203	7,019	193	14,211	103	2,588	272	1,598
	Taiwan	535	21,875	42	3,541	163	10,245	210	7,209	120	881
	United Kingdom	542	18,227	150	8,246	59	4,355	97	3,831	236	1,795
	Denmark	585	16,849	146	7,558	37	1,865	125	5,801	277	1,625
	Singapore	665	16,636	302	9,274	93	3,459	125	2,630	145	1,273
	Russia	1,628	13,755	340	6,587	116	1,884	33	793	1,139	4,490
	Italy	468	12,250	231	4,776	75	5,112	13	315	149	2,048
	India	298	11,311	110	5,488	122	5,279	3	87	63	457
	Saudi Arabia	96	10,115	72	9,518	1	2	3	203	20	392
	Turkey	530	9,027	90	1,223	151	5,855	29	307	260	1,642
	Sweden	297	7,795	126	6,073	10	246	—	—	161	1,476
	Belgium	122	7,067	66	4,811	17	1,996	3	19	36	241
	Brazil	138	6,605	71	3,147	37	2,994	1	18	29	447
	All Other Countries	9,363	156,424	2,142	58,613	1,246	51,552	571	13,183	5,404	33,076
TOTAL ALL SHIPS		**28,296**	**793,836**	**7,123**	**331,401**	**5,731**	**292,687**	**2,726**	**75,590**	**12,716**	**94,158**

(1) Includes roll-on/roll-off, passenger, breakbulk ships, partial container ships, refrigerated cargo ships, barge carriers, and specialized cargo ships. (2) NIS = Norwegian International Ship Registry. (3) Excluding Hong Kong.

50 Busiest U.S. Ports, 2000

Source: Corps of Engineers, Dept. of the Army, U.S. Dept. of Defense

(ports ranked by tonnage handled; all figures in tons)

Rank	Port Name	Total	Domestic	Foreign	Imports	Exports
1.	South Louisiana, LA	217,756,734	119,141,265	98,615,469	35,985,794	62,629,675
2.	Houston, TX	191,419,265	62,616,967	128,802,298	91,883,723	36,918,575
3.	New York, NY and NJ	138,669,879	72,272,507	66,397,372	58,852,576	7,544,796
4.	New Orleans, LA	90,768,449	38,316,314	52,452,135	30,274,738	22,177,397
5.	Corpus Christi, TX	83,124,950	23,988,548	59,136,402	50,223,701	8,912,701
6.	Beaumont, TX	82,652,554	16,043,113	66,609,441	61,444,343	5,165,098
7.	Huntington-Tristate, WV	76,867,987	76,867,987	0	0	0
8.	Long Beach, CA	70,149,684	17,399,570	52,750,114	36,986,787	15,763,327
9.	Baton Rouge, LA	65,631,084	42,505,495	23,125,589	13,653,589	9,472,000
10.	Texas City, TX	61,585,891	20,330,368	41,255,523	36,794,212	4,461,311
11.	Plaquemines, LA	59,910,084	38,863,773	21,046,311	12,393,761	8,652,550
12.	Lake Charles, LA	55,517,891	20,476,123	35,041,768	30,296,672	4,745,096
13.	Mobile, AL	54,156,967	24,231,755	29,925,212	17,997,481	11,927,731
14.	Pittsburgh, PA	53,922,676	53,922,676	0	0	0
15.	Los Angeles, CA	48,192,271	6,065,008	42,127,263	27,086,032	15,041,231
16.	Valdez, AK	48,080,894	46,409,056	1,671,838	0	1,671,838
17.	Tampa, FL	46,460,327	31,662,135	14,798,192	6,770,355	8,027,837
18.	Philadelphia, PA	43,854,766	14,066,391	29,788,375	29,424,177	364,198
19.	Norfolk Harbor, VA	42,376,778	10,504,788	31,871,990	8,631,350	23,240,640
20.	Duluth-Superior, MN/WI	41,677,699	28,165,480	13,512,219	637,156	12,875,063
21.	Baltimore, MD	40,831,802	14,534,986	26,296,816	17,904,000	8,392,816
22.	Portland, OR	34,333,784	16,357,090	17,976,694	4,861,346	13,115,348
23.	St. Louis, MO and IL	33,337,815	33,337,815	0	0	0
24.	Freeport, TX	30,984,736	5,598,981	25,385,755	22,646,802	2,738,953
25.	Portland, ME	29,330,407	2,337,176	26,993,231	26,835,286	157,945
26.	Pascagoula, MS	28,710,087	10,453,597	18,256,490	15,391,290	2,865,200
27.	Paulsboro, NJ	26,874,417	9,186,492	17,687,925	17,543,389	144,536
28.	Seattle, WA	24,158,942	8,717,982	15,440,960	8,421,551	7,019,409
29.	Chicago, IL	23,929,489	20,063,334	3,866,155	3,309,258	556,897
30.	Marcus Hook, PA	22,583,985	8,871,903	13,712,082	13,639,504	72,578
31.	Port Everglades, FL	22,500,201	13,287,357	9,212,844	6,867,196	2,345,648
32.	Tacoma, WA	22,286,610	8,275,037	14,011,573	4,579,736	9,431,837
33.	Port Arthur, TX	21,387,322	8,474,498	12,912,824	10,973,450	1,939,374
34.	Charleston, SC	21,081,838	4,529,778	16,552,060	9,423,270	7,128,790
35.	Boston, MA	20,750,789	8,386,804	12,363,985	11,754,702	609,283
36.	Jacksonville, FL	19,701,277	10,181,057	9,520,220	8,573,309	946,911
37.	Savannah, GA	19,670,923	2,736,542	16,934,381	10,109,181	6,825,200
38.	Richmond, CA	19,463,609	9,093,977	10,369,632	9,324,564	1,045,068
39.	Memphis, TN	18,269,265	18,269,265	0	0	0
40.	Anacortes, WA	18,034,543	15,938,545	2,095,998	1,578,325	517,673
41.	Detroit, MI	17,294,541	11,992,084	5,302,457	5,121,638	180,819
42.	Indiana Harbor, IN	16,187,079	15,508,694	678,385	651,453	26,932
43.	Honolulu, HI	15,796,807	10,942,157	4,854,650	4,272,509	582,141
44.	Cleveland, OH	14,390,802	11,914,437	2,476,365	2,262,104	214,261
45.	Cincinnati, OH	14,337,043	14,337,043	0	0	0
46.	Lorain, OH	14,180,191	13,905,629	274,562	274,562	0
47.	San Juan, PR	13,904,237	7,781,392	6,122,845	5,544,685	578,160
48.	Newport News, VA	13,803,114	7,158,769	6,644,345	1,251,636	5,392,709
49.	Toledo, OH	13,321,657	5,941,347	7,380,310	1,915,302	5,465,008
50.	Two Harbors, MN	13,060,019	13,060,019	0	0	0

World Trade Organization (WTO)

Following World War II, the major world economic powers negotiated a set of rules for reducing and limiting trade barriers and settling trade disputes. These rules were called the General Agreement on Tariffs and Trade (GATT). Headquarters to oversee administration of the GATT were established in Geneva, Switzerland. Rounds of multilateral trade negotiations under the GATT were carried out periodically. The 8th round, begun in 1986 in Punta del Este, Uruguay, and dubbed the Uruguay Round, ended Dec. 15, 1993, when 117 countries completed a new trade-liberalization agreement. The name for the GATT was changed to the World Trade Organization (WTO), which officially came into being Jan. 1, 1995.

Leading Motor Vehicle Producers, 2001[1]

Source: Automotive News Data Center and Marketing Systems GmbH

	Total	Passenger Cars	Trucks
United States	11,516,467	4,879,119	6,637,348
Japan	9,797,456	8,117,563	1,679,893
Germany	5,691,401	5,299,670	391,731
France	3,603,213	3,140,412	462,801
S. Korea	2,957,937	2,463,858	494,079
Spain	2,836,327	2,211,172	625,155
Canada	2,535,352	1,274,853	1,260,499
China	2,269,232	743,336	1,525,896
Mexico	1,827,586	1,209,029	618,557
Brazil	1,795,273	1,482,000	313,273
United Kingdom	1,677,295	1,481,903	195,392
Italy	1,579,492	1,271,780	307,712
Russia	1,262,190	1,009,580	252,610
Belgium	1,186,070	1,058,656	127,414
India	823,843	686,500	137,343
Sweden	516,503	418,312	98,191
Poland	505,766	440,510	65,256
Czech Republic	452,540	444,099	8,441
Thailand	430,410	138,700	291,710
Malaysia	411,071	355,863	55,208
South Africa	370,124	250,500	119,624
Indonesia	339,713	33,900	305,813
Australia	332,838	306,000	26,838
Turkey	270,685	175,343	95,342
Taiwan	270,536	195,109	75,427
Iran	264,922	245,000	19,922
Portugal	240,053	177,357	62,696
Netherlands	237,663	189,261	48,402
Argentina	235,577	169,580	65,997
Slovakia	164,160	164,000	160
World Total	**57,484,354**	**40,867,742**	**16,616,612**

(1) Totals include countries or territories not shown.

World Motor Vehicle Production, 1950-2001

Source: American Automobile Manufacturers Assn.; for 1998-2000: Automotive News Data Center and Marketing Systems GmbH
(in thousands)

Year	United States	Canada	Europe	Japan	Other	World total	U.S. % of world total
1950	8,006	388	1,991	32	160	10,577	75.7
1960	7,905	398	6,837	482	866	16,488	47.9
1970	8,284	1,160	13,049	5,289	1,637	29,419	28.2
1980	8,010	1,324	15,496	11,043	2,692	38,565	20.8
1985	11,653	1,933	16,113	12,271	2,939	44,909	25.9
1990	9,783	1,928	18,866	13,487	4,496	48,554	20.1
1991	8,811	1,888	17,804	13,245	5,180	46,928	18.8
1992	9,729	1,961	17,628	12,499	6,269	48,088	20.2
1993	10,898	2,246	15,208	11,228	7,205	46,785	23.3
1994	12,263	2,321	16,195	10,554	8,167	49,500	24.8
1995	11,985	2,408	17,045	10,196	8,349	49,983	24.0
1996	11,799	2,397	17,550	10,346	9,241	51,332	23.0
1997	12,119	2,571	17,773	10,975	10,024	53,463	22.7
1998	12,047	2,568	16,332	10,050	12,844	53,841	22.4
1999	13,107	3,042	17,603	9,985	14,050	57,787	22.7
2000	12,832	2,952	17,678	10,145	16,098	59,704	21.5
2001	11,516	2,535	17,733	9,797	15,902	57,484	20.0

Note: Data for 1998-2001 may not be fully comparable with earlier years because derived from different source.

New Passenger Cars Imported Into the U.S., by Country of Origin,[1] 1970-2001

Source: Bureau of the Census, Foreign Trade Division

	Japan	Germany[2]	Italy	United Kingdom	Sweden	France	South Korea	Mexico	Canada	Total[3]
1970	381,338	674,945	42,523	76,257	57,844	37,114	NA	NA	692,783	2,013,420
1971	703,672	770,807	51,469	106,710	61,925	23,316	NA	0	802,281	2,587,484
1972	697,788	676,967	64,614	72,038	64,541	14,713	NA	9	842,300	2,485,901
1973	624,805	677,465	56,102	64,140	58,626	8,219	NA	4,469	871,557	2,437,345
1974	791,791	619,757	107,071	72,512	60,817	21,331	NA	3,914	817,559	2,572,557
1975	695,573	370,012	102,344	67,106	51,993	15,647	NA	0	733,766	2,074,653
1976	1,128,936	349,804	82,500	77,190	37,466	21,916	NA	0	825,590	2,536,749
1977	1,341,530	423,492	55,437	56,889	39,370	19,215	NA	NA	849,814	2,790,144
1978	1,563,047	416,231	69,689	54,478	56,140	28,502	NA	6	833,061	3,024,982
1979	1,617,328	495,565	72,456	46,911	65,907	27,887	NA	4	677,008	3,005,523
1980	1,991,502	338,711	46,899	32,517	61,496	47,386	NA	1	594,770	3,116,448
1981	1,911,525	234,052	21,635	12,728	68,042	42,477	NA	1	563,943	2,856,286
1982	1,801,185	259,385	9,402	13,023	89,231	50,032	NA	27	702,495	2,926,407
1983	1,871,192	239,807	5,442	17,261	114,726	40,823	NA	2	835,665	3,133,836
1984	1,948,714	335,032	8,582	19,833	114,854	37,788	NA	NA	1,073,425	3,559,427
1985	2,527,467	473,110	8,689	24,474	142,640	42,882	NA	13,647	1,144,805	4,397,679
1986	2,618,711	451,699	11,829	27,506	148,700	10,869	169,309	41,983	1,162,226	4,691,297
1987	2,417,509	377,542	8,648	50,059	138,565	26,707	399,856	126,266	926,927	4,589,010
1988	2,123,051	264,249	6,053	31,636	108,006	15,990	455,741	148,065	1,191,357	4,450,213
1989	2,051,525	216,881	9,319	29,378	101,571	4,885	270,609	133,049	1,151,122	4,042,728
1990	1,867,794	245,286	11,045	27,271	93,084	1,976	201,475	215,986	1,220,221	3,944,602
1991	1,762,347	171,097	2,886	14,862	62,905	1,727	186,740	249,498	1,109,248	3,612,665
1992	1,598,919	205,248	1,791	10,997	76,832	65	130,110	266,111	1,119,223	3,447,200
1993	1,501,953	180,383	1,178	20,029	58,742	23	122,943	299,634	1,371,856	3,604,361
1994	1,488,159	178,774	1,010	28,217	63,867	58	213,962	360,367	1,525,746	3,909,079
1995	1,114,360	204,932	1,031	42,450	82,593	14	131,718	462,800	1,552,691	3,624,428
1996	1,190,896	234,909	1,365	44,373	86,619	27	225,623	550,867	1,690,733	4,069,113
1997	1,387,812	300,489	1,912	43,691	79,780	67	222,568	544,075	1,731,209	4,378,295
1998	1,456,081	373,330	2,104	49,891	84,543	56	211,650	584,795	1,837,615	4,673,418
1999	1,707,277	461,061	1,697	68,394	83,399	186	372,965	639,878	2,170,427	5,639,616
2000	1,839,093	488,323	3,125	81,196	86,707	134	568,121	934,000	2,138,811	6,324,284
2001	1,790,346	494,131	2,580	82,487	92,439	92	633,769	861,853	1,855,789	6,065,138

(1) Excludes passenger cars assembled in U.S. foreign trade zones. (2) Figures prior to 1991 are for West Germany. (3) Includes countries not shown separately.

Passenger Car Production, U.S. Plants, 2000-2001

Source: Ward's AutoInfoBank

	2000	2001
TOTAL PASSENGER CARS	**5,542,217**	**4,879,119**
Total Autoalliance[1]	**107,431**	**71,723**
Mazda 626	67,255	46,707
Mercury Cougar	40,176	25,016
Total BMW	**38,665**	**34,169**
BMW Z3	38,665	34,169
Total Chrysler Group	**432,933**	**438,141**
Total Chrysler	**80,348**	**135,707**
Cirrus	39,232	0
Prowler	0	3,002
Sebring Convertible	7,338	50,597
Sebring Sedan	33,778	82,108
Total Dodge	**298,042**	**266,476**
Neon (Dodge)	179,039	145,718
Stratus Sedan	117,272	118,871
Viper	1,731	1,887
Total Plymouth	**54,543**	**35,958**
Breeze	2,030	0
Neon (Plymouth)	49,623	35,958
Prowler	2,890	0
Total Ford Motor Co.	**1,247,333**	**989,868**
Total Ford	**965,041**	767,595
Contour	17,410	0
Focus	325,720	251,879
Mustang	180,431	160,184
Taurus	441,480	347,577
Thunderbird	0	7,955
Total Lincoln	**162,771**	**124,583**
Continental	22,589	17,923
Lincoln LS	58,791	39,081
Town Car	81,391	67,579
Total Mercury	**119,521**	**97,690**
Mystique	5,388	0
Sable	114,133	97,690
Total General Motors	**1,989,031**	**1,656,172**
Total Buick	**209,337**	**165,269**
LeSabre	163,919	135,338
Park Ave	45,418	29,931
Total Cadillac	**159,036**	**133,436**
CTS	0	1,424
Eldorado	12,043	8,171

	2000	2001
Fleetwood Deville	118,967	98,420
Seville	28,026	25,421
Total Chevrolet	**547,493**	**446,332**
Cavalier	252,028	240,830
Corvette	34,919	35,535
Malibu	260,546	169,967
Total Oldsmobile	**234,817**	**177,676**
Alero	135,012	119,752
Aurora	39,921	19,420
Intrigue	59,884	38,504
Total Pontiac	**576,338**	**458,034**
Bonneville	66,783	46,795
Grand Am	250,452	197,123
Grand Prix	166,929	131,105
Sunfire	92,174	83,011
Total Saturn	**260,899**	**275,425**
Saturn LS	85,953	103,516
Saturn S	174,946	171,909
Total American Honda Motor Corp	**677,090**	**692,377**
Total Acura	**115,333**	**93,116**
Acura CL	31,440	14,802
Acura TL	83,893	78,314
Total Honda	**561,757**	**599,261**
Accord	336,034	363,232
Civic	225,723	236,029
Total Mitsubishi	**222,036**	**193,435**
Sebring Coupe (Chrysler)	19,952	10,892
Avenger (Dodge)	1,360	0
Stratus Coupe (Dodge)	17,596	17,426
Eclipse	78,985	70,467
Galant	104,143	94,650
Total Nissan	**150,129**	**157,876**
Altima	150,129	157,876
Total NUMMI[2]	**197,737**	**188,967**
Prizm (Chevrolet)	49,996	46,020
Corolla (Toyota)	147,741	142,947
Total Subaru-Isuzu	**107,955**	**103,010**
Legacy	107,955	103,010
Total Toyota	**371,877**	**353,381**
Avalon	120,252	81,321
Camry	251,625	272,060
Cavalier (Chevrolet)	1,111	0

(1) Company is a joint venture between Ford and Mazda. (2) NUMMI (New United Motor Manufacturing, Inc.) is a joint venture between GM and Toyota.

U.S. Car Sales by Vehicle Size and Type, 1985-2001

Source: Ward's Communications

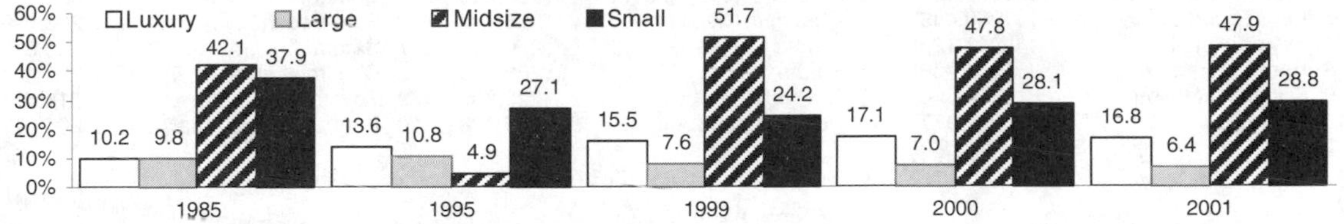

Domestic and Imported Retail Car Sales in the U.S., 1980-2001

Source: Ward's Communications

		IMPORTS					Import %	
Calendar year	Domestic[1]	From Japan	From Germany	From other countries	Total imports	Total U.S. sales	Total	Japan
1980	6,581,307	1,905,968	305,219	186,700	2,397,887	8,979,194	26.7	21.2
1981	6,208,760	1,858,896	282,881	185,502	2,327,279	8,536,039	27.3	21.8
1982	5,758,586	1,801,969	247,080	174,508	2,223,557	7,982,143	27.9	22.6
1983	6,795,295	1,915,621	279,748	191,403	2,386,772	9,182,067	26.0	20.9
1984	7,951,523	1,906,206	344,416	188,220	2,438,842	10,390,365	23.5	18.3
1985	8,204,542	2,217,837	423,983	195,925	2,837,745	11,042,287	25.7	20.1
1986	8,214,897	2,382,614	443,721	418,286	3,244,621	11,459,518	28.3	20.8
1987	7,080,858	2,190,405	347,881	657,465	3,195,751	10,276,609	31.1	21.3
1988	7,526,038	2,022,602	280,099	700,991	3,003,692	10,529,730	28.5	19.2
1989	7,072,902	1,897,143	248,561	553,660	2,699,364	9,772,266	27.6	19.4
1990	6,896,888	1,719,384	265,116	418,823	2,403,323	9,300,211	25.8	18.5
1991	6,136,757	1,500,309	192,776	344,814	2,037,899	8,174,656	24.9	18.4
1992	6,276,557	1,451,766	200,851	283,938	1,936,555	8,213,112	23.6	17.7
1993	6,741,667	1,328,445	186,177	261,570	1,776,192	8,517,859	20.9	15.6
1994	7,255,303	1,239,450	192,241	303,489	1,735,214	8,990,517	19.3	13.8
1995	7,128,712	981,462	207,555	317,269	1,506,257	8,634,964	17.4	11.4
1996	7,253,582	726,940	237,984	308,247	1,273,171	8,526,753	14.9	8.5
1997	6,916,769	726,104	297,028	332,173	1,355,305	8,272,074	16.4	8.8
1998	6,761,940	691,162	366,724	321,895	1,379,781	8,141,721	15.9	8.5
1999	6,979,357	757,568	466,870	494,489	1,718,927	8,698,284	21.1	8.7
2000	6,830,505	862,780	516,614	636,726	2,016,120	8,846,625	22.8	9.8
2001	6,487,655	920,467	522,659	724,292	2,167,418	8,655,073	25.0	10.6

(1) Includes cars manufactured in Canada and Mexico.

U.S. Light-Vehicle Fuel Efficiency, 1975-2001

Source: Environmental Protection Agency, Office of Mobile Sources

Since 1975, both light-duty trucks (SUVs, minivans, vans, and light trucks) and cars have generally become more fuel-efficient, but their fuel efficiency has declined in recent years. In addition, light-duty trucks, which are less fuel-efficient than cars, have come to occupy an increasing proportion of the total light vehicle market, rising from only 19% in 1975 to an estimated 47% by 2001. This increase has been a major factor in the recent decline in the fuel efficiency of the average light vehicle sold. The average fuel economy for all light vehicles in 2001 was 23.9 miles per gallon, the lowest it had been since 1980.

YEAR	Cars (MPG*)	Light-duty Trucks (MPG*)	All Light Vehicles (MPG*)
1975	15.8	13.7	15.3
1980	23.5	18.6	22.5
1985	27.0	20.6	25.0
1990	27.8	20.7	25.2
1994	[illegible]	20.8	24.6
1995	28.3	[illegible]	24.7
1996	28.3	20.8	24.8
1997	28.4	20.6	24.5
1998	28.5	20.9	24.5
1999	28.2	20.5	24.1
2000	28.3	20.5	24.0
2001	28.3	20.3	23.9

* MPG value represents laboratory city and highway fuel efficiency combined in a 55%/45% ratio.

Top-Selling Passenger Cars in the U.S. by Calendar Year, 1997-2001 (Domestic and Import)

Source: Ward's Communications

2001

Rank	Car	Sales
1.	Honda Accord	414,718
2.	Toyota Camry	390,449
3.	Ford Taurus	353,560
4.	Honda Civic	331,780
5.	Ford Focus	264,414
6.	Toyota Corolla	245,023
7.	Chevrolet Cavalier	233,298
8.	Chevrolet Impala	208,395
9.	Pontiac Grand Am	182,046
10.	Chevrolet Malibu	176,583
11.	Ford Mustang	169,198
12.	Saturn S	162,110
13.	Nissan Altima	148,345
14.	Buick LeSabre	145,304
15.	Volkswagen Jetta	145,221
16.	Buick Century	142,157
17.	Pontiac Grand Prix	128,935
18.	Mercury Grand Marquis	112,034
19.	Hyundai Elantra	111,293
20.	Nissan Sentra	111,082

2000

Rank	Car	Sales
1.	Toyota Camry	422,961
2.	Honda Accord	404,515
3.	Ford Taurus	382,035
4.	Honda Civic	324,528
5.	Ford Focus	286,166
6.	Chevrolet Cavalier	236,803
7.	Toyota Corolla	230,156
8.	Pontiac Grand Am	214,923
9.	Chevrolet Malibu	207,376
10.	Saturn S	177,355
11.	Chevrolet Impala	174,358
12.	Ford Mustang	173,676
13.	Buick LeSabre	148,633
14.	Pontiac Grand Prix	148,521
15.	Volkswagen Jetta	144,853
16.	Dodge Intrepid	143,840
17.	Buick Century	143,085
18.	Nissan Altima	136,971
19.	Nissan Maxima	129,235
20.	Oldsmobile Alero	122,722

1999

Rank	Car	Sales
1.	Toyota Camry	448,162
2.	Honda Accord	404,192
3.	Ford Taurus	368,327
4.	Honda Civic	318,308
5.	Chevrolet Cavalier	272,122
6.	Ford Escort	260,486
7.	Toyota Corolla	249,128
8.	Pontiac Grand Am	234,936
9.	Chevrolet Malibu	218,540
10.	Saturn S	207,977

1998

Rank	Car	Sales
1.	Toyota Camry	429,575
2.	Honda Accord	401,071
3.	Ford Taurus	371,074
4.	Honda Civic	334,562
5.	Ford Escort	291,936
6.	Chevrolet Cavalier	256,099
7.	Toyota Corolla	250,501
8.	Saturn	231,786
9.	Chevrolet Malibu	223,703
10.	Pontiac Grand Am	180,428

1997

Rank	Car	Sales
1.	Toyota Camry	397,156
2.	Honda Accord	384,609
3.	Ford Taurus	357,162
4.	Honda Civic	315,546
5.	Chevrolet Cavalier	302,161
6.	Ford Escort	283,898
7.	Saturn	250,810
8.	Chevrolet Lumina	228,451
9.	Toyota Corolla	218,461
10.	Pontiac Grand Am	204,078

Sport Utility Vehicle Sales in the U.S., 1988-2001

Source: Ward's Communications

In 1988, 960,852 sport utility vehicles (SUVs) were sold in the United States, accounting for 6.3% of all sales of light vehicles (cars, SUVs, minivans, vans, pickup trucks, and trucks under 14,000 lbs.). By 2001, sales reached 3,787,250, or 22% of light vehicle sales, an increase of 12% over the previous year.

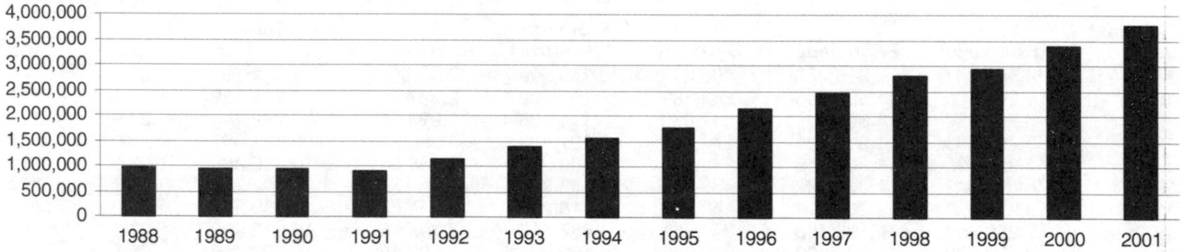

The Most Popular Colors, by Type of Vehicle, 2001 Model Year

Source: Du Pont Automotive Products

Luxury Cars		Full Size/Intermediate Cars		Compact/Sports Cars		Light Trucks	
Color	**Percent**	**Color**	**Percent**	**Color**	**Percent**	**Color**	**Percent**
Silver	18.4	Silver	24.9	Silver	25.4	White	19.6
Medium/Dark Gray	17.3	White	14.1	Black	14.5	Silver	17.8
White Pearl	14.8	Medium/Dark Green	10.0	Medium/Dark Blue	11.3	Black	11.2
Black	11.1	Black	9.8	White	9.8	Medium/Dark Blue	10.4
Medium/Dark Blue	9.4	Medium/Dark Blue	8.9	Medium Red	7.4	Medium Red	8.4
White	9.0	Light Brown	8.1	Medium/Dark Green	6.7	Medium/Dark Green	7.4
Medium Red	6.0	Gold	7.2	Light Brown	6.2	Bright Red	5.3
Gold	5.4	Dark Red	4.9	Bright Red	5.3	Light Brown	4.6
Medium/Dark Green	3.1	Medium Red	4.8	Dark Red	2.6	Gold	3.8
Dark Red	2.2	Bright Red	3.1	Medium/Dark Gray	2.0	Medium/Dark Gray	2.5
Other	3.3	Other	4.2	Other	8.8	Other	9.0

Cars Registered in the U.S., 1900-2000[1]

Source: U.S. Dept. of Transportation, Federal Highway Administration

(includes automobiles for public and private use)

Year	Cars Registered	Year	Cars Registered	Year	Cars Registered	Year	Cars Registered
1900	8,000	1940	27,465,826	1975	106,705,934	1994	127,883,469
1905	77,400	1945	25,796,985	1980	121,600,843	1995	128,386,775
1910	458,377	1950	40,339,077	1985	127,885,193	1996	129,728,311
1915	2,332,426	1955	52,144,739	1990	133,700,497	1997	129,748,704
1920	8,131,522	1960	61,671,390	1991	128,299,601	1998	131,838,538
1925	17,481,001	1965	75,257,588	1992	126,581,148	1999	132,432,044
1930	23,034,753	1970	89,243,557	1993	127,327,189	2000	133,621,420
1935	22,567,827						

(1) There were no publicly owned vehicles before 1925; statistics also exclude military vehicles for all years. Alaska and Hawaii data included since 1960.

Licensed Drivers, by Age, 1980-2000

Source: Federal Highway Administration, U.S. Dept. of Transportation

(in thousands)

AGE	1980 Male	1980 Female	1980 Total	1990 Male	1990 Female	1990 Total	2000 Male	2000 Female	2000 Total
(under 16)	52	41	93	23	20	43	14	13	27
16	1,001	822	1,823	769	674	1,443	755	715	1,470
17	1,530	1,260	2,790	1,136	996	2,132	1,201	1,130	2,331
18	1,763	1,484	3,247	1,378	1,217	2,595	1,471	1,368	2,839
19	1,900	1,643	3,542	1,608	1,429	3,037	1,589	1,488	3,077
(19 and under)	6,246	5,249	11,496	4,913	4,336	9,249	5,029	4,714	9,744
20	1,930	1,706	3,636	1,691	1,538	3,229	1,611	1,530	3,140
21	1,961	1,772	3,733	1,694	1,555	3,249	1,620	1,552	3,172
22	1,998	1,813	3,811	1,701	1,561	3,262	1,624	1,557	3,182
23	2,062	1,876	3,938	1,767	1,631	3,398	1,656	1,591	3,247
24	2,047	1,868	3,915	1,951	1,807	3,758	1,648	1,577	3,225
(20-24)	9,998	9,034	19,032	8,804	8,093	16,897	8,159	7,807	15,966
25-29	9,865	9,060	18,925	10.239	9,656	19,895	8,988	8,598	17,586
30-34	9,010	8,359	17,369	10,507	10,071	20,578	9,767	9,387	19,155
35-39	7,113	6,583	13,696	9,684	9,371	19,055	10,622	10,438	21,059
40-44	5,828	5,306	11,134	8,610	8,295	16,905	10,577	10,516	21,093
45-49	5,311	4,765	10,076	6,642	6,378	13,020	9,578	9,575	19,154
50-54	5,351	4,739	10,090	5,376	5,108	10,484	8,448	8,420	16,868
55-59	5,198	4,572	9,770	4,855	4,583	9,438	6,394	6,366	12,760
60-64	4,439	3,793	8,232	4,738	4,497	9,235	4,970	4,944	0,915
65-69	3,631	2,949	6,580	4,266	4,109	8,375	4,183	4,203	8,386
70 and over	5,195	3,699	8,894	7,159	6,726	13,885	9,079	9,861	18,940
70-74	NA	NA	NA	NA	NA	NA	3,645	3,823	7,468
75-79	NA	NA	NA	NA	NA	NA	2,820	3,091	5,911
80-84	NA	NA	NA	NA	NA	NA	1,657	1,854	3,511
85 and over	NA	NA	NA	NA	NA	NA	957	1,093	2,050
TOTAL	**77,187**	**68,108**	**145,295**	**85,792**	**81,223**	**167,015**	**95,796**	**94,829**	**190,625**

(1) Comparisons between "licensed" drivers under age 16 in 1980, 1990, and 2000 are not entirely valid because of a change in definition in 1990, which interpreted "licensed" drivers more strictly than before. NA = not available.

IT'S A FACT: The number of U.S. drivers age 70 and over holding a valid license has continued to increase. In 1980, the number of drivers 70 years and over was 8.8 million. It rose to 18.9 million in 2000. This represented a 111% increase in older drivers since 1980. The number of female drivers increased by about 39% from 1980 to 2000, whereas the number of male drivers grew by only by 24%.

Highway Speed Limits, by State

Source: Insurance Institute for Highway Safety

Under the National Highway System Designation Act, signed Nov. 28, 1995, by Pres. Bill Clinton, states were allowed to set their own highway speed limits, as of Dec. 8, 1995. Under federal legislation enacted in 1974 during the energy crisis, states had been, in effect, restricted to a National Maximum Speed Limit (NMSL) of 55 miles per hour (raised in 1987 to 65 mph on rural interstates). Maximum posted speed limits, in miles per hour, are given by state in the table below. (Speeds shown in parentheses are for commercial trucks.) Most data current as of May 15, 2002. For more information visit the Insurance Institute for Highway Safety website at www.hwysafety.org

STATE	Rural Interstate	Urban[1] Interstate	Limited[2] Access Roads	Other Roads
AL	70	70	65	65
AK	65	55	65	55
AZ	75	55	55	55
AR	70 (65)	55	60	55
CA	70 (55)	65	70	55
CO	75	65	65	55
CT	65	55	65	55
DE	65	55	65	55
FL	70	65	70	65
GA	70	65	65	65
HI	55	50	45	45
ID	75 (65)	65	65	65
IL	65 (55)	55	65	55
IN	65 (60)	55	55	55
IA	65	55	65	55
KS	70	70	70	65
KY	65	55	55	55
LA	70	55	70	65
ME	65	55	55	55
MD	65	65	65	55
MA	65	65	65	55
MI	70 (55)	65	70	55
MN	70	65	65	55
MS	70	70	70	65
MO	70	60	70	65
MT	75 (65)	65	70[3]	70[3]
NE	75	65	65	60
NV	75	65	70	70
NH	65	65	55	55
NJ	65	55	65	55
NM	75	55	65	55
NY	65	65	65	55
NC	70	65	65	55
ND	70	55	65	65[4]
OH	65 (55)	65	55	55
OK	75	70	70	70
OR	65 (55)	55	55	55
PA	65	55	65	55
RI	65	55	55	55
SC	70	70	60	55
SD	75	65	65	65
TN	70	70	70	55
TX	70	70	70	70
UT	75	65	55	55
VT	65	55	50	50
VA	65	55	65	55
WA	70 (60)	60	55	55
WV	70	55	65	55
WI	65	65	65	55
WY	75	60	65	65

(1) Urban interstates are determined from U.S. Census Bureau criteria, which may be adjusted by state and local governments to reflect planning and other issues. (2) Limited access roads are multiple-lane highways with restricted access via exit and entrance ramps rather than intersections. (3) Speed limit is 65 mph at night. (4) Speed limit is 55 mph at night. "Night" means from one-half hour after sunset to one-half hour before sunrise.

Selected Motor Vehicle Statistics

Source: Federal Highway Administration; U.S. Dept. of Transportation; Insurance Institute for Highway Safety

Driver's license age requirements, state gas tax, and safety belt laws as of August 2002; figures for 2000 where not specified.

STATE	Driver's license age requirements: Regular[1]	Learner's Permit	State gas tax cents/ gal.	Safety belt use law[11]	Licensed drivers per 1,000 resident pop.	Regist. motor vehicles per 1,000 pop.	Licensed drivers per motor vehicle[12]	Gals. of fuel used per vehicle	Miles per gal.	Annual miles driven per vehicle	Vehicle miles per licensed driver
Alabama	17y, 6m	15	18	P	792	891	1.80	808	17.67	14,276	16,406
Alaska	16	14	8	S	742	948	1.90	616	12.59	7,761	10,042
Arizona	16	15y, 7m	18	S	669	740	1.59	800	16.39	13,116	15,094
Arkansas	16	14	21.5	S	729	688	2.05	1,089	14.55	15,850	15,146
California	17[2]	15	18	P	627	818	1.23	622	17.81	11,071	14,721
Colorado	17	15	22	S	722	843	1.62	687	16.77	11,520	13,967
Connecticut	16y, 4m[2]	16	25	P	779	838	1.32	616	17.49	10,779	12,957
Delaware	16y, 10m[2]	15y, 10m	23	S	710	805	1.39	700	18.68	13,070	14,933
Dist. of Col.	18[3]	16	20	P	609	423	1.74	810	17.85	14,450	10,027
Florida	18	15	13.9	S	804	737	1.75	753	17.15	12,914	12,268
Georgia	18	15	7.5	P	678	874	1.36	854	17.18	14,676	19,194
Hawaii	16y3m[2]	15y, 6m	16	P	635	609	1.67	583	19.87	11,583	11,350
Idaho	17[4]	14y, 6m	25	S	683	910	1.71	739	15.55	11,492	15,506
Illinois	17[2]	15	19	S	641	722	1.34	711	16.12	11,464	12,980
Indiana	18	15	15	P	654	916	1.23	793	16.04	12,720	18,376
Iowa	17[2]	14	20.1	P	667	1,061	1.11	664	14.27	9,475	15,209
Kansas	16	14	23	S	710	854	2.31	751	16.32	12,251	14,864
Kentucky	16y, 6m[5]	16	15	S	667	699	1.61	1,028	16.10	16,559	17,592
Louisiana	17[6]	15	20	P	617	796	1.40	815	14.10	11,484	14,787
Maine	16y, 3m[2]	15	22	S	722	803	1.49	840	16.50	13,856	15,564
Maryland	17y, 7m[7]	15y, 9m	23.5	P	639	726	1.30	761	17.13	13,041	15,706
Massachusetts	18	16	21.5	S	707	829	1.22	603	16.64	10,027	11,942
Michigan	17[2]	14y, 9m	19	P	697	849	1.38	704	16.46	11,593	14,249
Minnesota	17[2]	15	20	S	598	941	1.12	699	16.24	11,361	18,094
Mississippi	16[8]	15	18	S[a]	706	805	1.52	916	16.94	15,522	19,873
Missouri	18	15	17	S[a]	689	818	1.42	886	16.53	14,648	17,471
Montana	15[9]	14y, 6m	27.75	S	752	1,137	1.45	669	14.39	9,629	14,969
Nebraska	17	15	24.5	S	698	946	1.40	763	14.64	11,168	15,036
Nevada	16[2]	15y, 6m	23	S	686	610	2.09	987	14.65	14,461	13,343
New Hampshire	18	15y, 6m	18	none	752	851	1.39	739	15.46	11,430	13,087
New Jersey	17y, 6m	16	14.5	P	672	759	1.27	753	14.02	10,555	12,151
New Mexico	16	15	17	P	681	840	1.70	857	17.37	14,890	18,626
New York	17[2]	16[10]	30.25	P	573	539	1.45	648	19.45	12,610	12,145
North Carolina	16y, 6m	15	22.1	P	707	773	1.52	832	17.28	14,384	16,299
North Dakota	16	14	21	S	715	1,080	1.35	730	14.24	10,401	15,761
Ohio	17[2]	15y, 6m	22	S	723	922	1.22	634	15.97	10,117	13,162
Oklahoma	16	15y, 6m	17	P	665	874	1.45	839	17.14	14,382	18,747
Oregon	17	15	24	P	729	883	1.62	648	17.89	11,587	14,222
Pennsylvania	17[2]	16	26.6	S	670	754	1.36	690	16.01	11,052	12,070
Rhode Island	17y, 6m[2]	16	30	S[a]	624	725	1.21	601	18.30	11,005	12,138
South Carolina	16y, 6m	15	16	S[a]	709	771	1.48	929	15.84	14,715	16,204
South Dakota	16	14	22	S	720	1,050	1.43	740	14.38	10,640	15,512
Tennessee	17	15	20	S	747	847	1.49	792	17.22	13,638	15,741
Texas	16y, 6[2]	15	20	P	646	675	1.77	956	16.36	15,641	16,473
Utah	17[8]	15y, 9m	24.5	S[a]	655	729	1.69	833	16.66	13,884	15,697
Vermont	16y, 6m[2]	15	20	S[a]	831	846	1.71	798	16.57	13,228	13,737
Virginia	18[2]	15	17.5	S	683	854	1.25	766	16.14	12,372	15,816
Washington	17[2]	15	23	S	705	868	1.44	636	16.38	10,424	12,917
West Virginia	17	15	20.5	S	745	797	1.69	767	17.39	13,346	15,107
Wisconsin	16y, 9[2]	15y, 6m	31.1	S	703	814	1.49	717	18.30	13,118	15,340
Wyoming	16	15	14	S	751	1,186	1.72	1,049	13.16	13,813	22,258
AVERAGE					**677**	**787**	**1.43**	**746**	**16.64**	**12,416**	**14,691**

NOTE: Many states are moving toward graduated licensing systems that phase in full driving privileges. During the learner's phase, driving generally is not permitted unless there is an adult supervisor. In an intermediate phase, young licensees not yet having unrestricted licenses may be allowed to drive unsupervised under certain conditions but not others. (1) Unrestricted operation of private passenger car. (2) Applicants under age 18 (19 in VA) must have completed an approved driver education course. (3) Learner's phase mandatory for all ages. Applicants under age 21 must complete a 6-month intermediate phase. (4) Applicants under age 17 must have completed an approved driver education course. (5) License holders under age 18 must complete a 4-hour course on safe driving within 1 yr. of receiving license (6) Applicants age 17 and older must have completed an educational program, but doesn't require behind-the-wheel training. (7) Initial applicants of any age must have completed an approved driver education course. (8) Applicants age 17 and older not subject to learner's permit and intermediate license requirements. (9) Applicants under age 16 must have completed an approved driver education course. (10) Driving in New York City is prohibited for all licensees age 16 and for those age 17 without driver education. (11) P = officer may stop vehicle for a violation (primary); S = an officer may issue seat belt citation only when vehicle is stopped for another moving violation (secondary). (a) Primary enforcement for children under a specified age: MS-8; MO-16; RI-13; SC, UT-19. (12) Private and commercial automobiles (including taxicabs), excludes trucks and buses.

Road Mileage Between Selected U.S. Cities

	Atlanta	Boston	Chicago	Cincin-nati	Cleve-land	Dallas	Denver	Des Moines	Detroit	Houston
Atlanta, Ga.	...	1,037	674	440	672	795	1,398	870	699	789
Boston, Mass.	1,037	...	963	840	628	1,748	1,949	1,280	695	1,804
Chicago, Ill.	674	963	...	287	335	917	996	327	266	1,067
Cincinnati, Oh.	440	840	287	...	244	920	1,164	571	259	1,029
Cleveland, Oh.	672	628	335	244	...	1,159	1,321	652	170	1,273
Dallas Tex.	795	1,748	917	920	1,159	...	781	684	1,143	243
Denver, Col.	1,398	1,949	996	1,164	1,321	781	...	669	1,253	1,019
Detroit, Mich.	699	695	266	259	170	1,143	1,253	584	...	1,265
Houston, Tex.	789	1,804	1,067	1,029	1,273	243	1,019	905	1,265	...
Indianapolis, Ind.	493	906	181	106	294	865	1,058	465	278	987
Kansas City, Mo.	798	1,391	499	591	779	489	600	195	743	710
Los Angeles, Cal.	2,182	2,979	2,054	2,179	2,367	1,387	1,059	1,727	2,311	1,538
Memphis, Tenn.	371	1,296	530	468	712	452	1,040	599	713	561
Milwaukee, Wis.	761	1,050	87	374	422	991	1,029	361	353	1,142
Minneapolis, Minn.	1,068	1,368	405	692	740	936	841	252	671	1,157
New Orleans, La.	479	1,507	912	786	1,030	496	1,273	978	1,045	356
New York, N.Y.	841	206	802	647	473	1,552	1,771	1,119	637	1,608
Omaha, Neb.	986	1,412	459	693	784	644	537	132	716	865
Philadelphia, Pa.	741	296	738	567	413	1,452	1,691	1,051	573	1,508
Pittsburgh, Pa.	687	561	452	287	129	1,204	1,411	763	287	1,313
Portland Ore.	2,601	3,046	2,083	2,333	2,418	2,009	1,238	1,786	2,349	2,205
St. Louis, Mo.	541	1,141	289	340	529	630	857	333	513	779
San Francisco	2,496	3,095	2,142	2,362	2,467	1,753	1,235	1,815	2,399	1,912
Seattle, Wash.	2,618	2,976	2,013	2,300	2,348	2,078	1,307	1,749	2,279	2,274
Tulsa, Okla.	772	1,537	683	736	925	257	681	443	909	478
Washington, DC	608	429	671	481	346	1,319	1,616	984	506	1,375

	India-napolis	Kansas City	Los Angeles	Louis-ville	Memphis	Mil-waukee	Minne-apolis	New Orleans	New York	Omaha
Atlanta, Ga.	493	798	2,182	382	371	761	1,068	479	841	986
Boston, Mass.	906	1,391	2,979	941	1,296	1,050	1,368	1,507	206	1,412
Chicago, Ill.	181	499	2,054	292	530	87	405	912	802	459
Cincinnati, Oh.	106	591	2,179	101	468	374	692	786	647	693
Cleveland Oh.	294	779	2,367	345	712	422	740	1,030	473	784
Dallas, Tex.	865	489	1,387	819	452	991	936	496	1,552	644
Denver, Col.	1,058	600	1,059	1,120	1,040	1,029	841	1,273	1,771	537
Detroit, Mich.	278	743	2,311	360	713	353	671	1,045	637	716
Houston, Tex.	987	710	1,538	928	561	1,142	1,157	356	1,608	865
Indianapolis, Ind.	...	485	2,073	111	435	268	586	796	713	587
Kansas City, Mo.	485	...	1,589	520	451	537	447	806	1,198	201
Los Angeles, Cal.	2,073	1,589	...	2,108	1,817	2,087	1,889	1,883	2,786	1,595
Memphis, Tenn.	435	451	1,817	367	...	612	826	390	1,100	652
Milwaukee, Wis.	268	537	2,087	379	612	...	332	994	889	493
Minneapolis, Minn.	586	447	1,889	697	826	332	...	1,214	1,207	357
New Orleans, La.	796	806	1,883	685	390	994	1,214	...	1,311	1,007
New York, N.Y.	713	1,198	2,786	748	1,100	889	1,207	1,311	...	1,251
Omaha, Neb.	587	201	1,595	687	652	493	357	1,007	1,251	...
Philadelphia, Pa.	633	1,118	2,706	668	1,000	825	1,143	1,211	100	1,183
Pittsburgh, Pa.	353	838	2,426	388	752	539	857	1,070	368	895
Portland, Ore.	2,272	1,809	959	2,320	2,259	2,010	1,678	2,505	2,885	1,654
St. Louis, Mo.	235	257	1,845	263	285	363	552	673	948	449
San Francisco	2,293	1,835	379	2,349	2,125	2,175	1,940	2,249	2,934	1,683
Seattle, Wash.	2,194	1,839	1,131	2,305	2,290	1,940	1,608	2,574	2,815	1,638
Tulsa, Okla.	631	248	1,452	659	401	757	695	647	1,344	387
Washington, DC	558	1,043	2,631	582	867	758	1,076	1,078	233	1,116

	Phila-dephia	Pitts-burgh	Portland	St. Louis	Salt Lake City	San Francisco	Seattle	Toledo	Tulsa	Wash., DC
Atlanta, Ga.	741	687	2,601	541	1,878	2,496	2,618	640	772	608
Boston, Mass.	296	561	3,046	1,141	2,343	3,095	2,976	739	1,537	429
Chicago, Ill.	738	452	2,083	289	1,390	2,142	2,013	232	683	671
Cincinnati, Oh.	567	287	2,333	340	1,610	2,362	2,300	200	736	481
Cleveland Oh.	413	129	2,418	529	1,715	2,467	2,348	111	925	346
Dallas, Tex.	1,452	1,204	2,009	630	1,242	1,753	2,078	1,084	257	1,319
Denver, Col.	1,691	1,411	1,238	857	504	1,235	1,307	1,218	681	1,616
Detroit, Mich.	576	287	2,349	513	1,647	2,399	2,279	59	909	506
Houston, Tex.	1,508	1,313	2,205	779	1,438	1,912	2,274	1,206	478	1,375
Indianapolis, Ind.	633	353	2,272	235	1,504	2,293	2,194	219	631	558
Kansas City, Mo.	1,118	838	1,809	257	1,086	1,835	1,839	687	248	1,043
Los Angeles, Cal.	2,706	2,426	959	1,845	715	379	1,131	2,276	1,452	2,631
Memphis, Tenn.	1,000	752	2,259	285	1,535	2,125	2,290	654	401	867
Milwaukee, Wis.	825	539	2,010	363	1,423	2,175	1,940	319	757	758
Minneapolis, Minn.	1,143	857	1,678	552	1,186	1,940	1,608	637	695	1,076
New Orleans, La.	1,211	1,070	2,505	673	1,738	2,249	2,574	986	647	1,078
New York, N.Y.	100	368	2,885	948	2,182	2,934	2,815	578	1,344	233
Omaha, Neb.	1,183	895	1,654	449	931	1,683	1,638	681	387	1,116
Philadelphia, Pa.	...	288	2,821	868	2,114	2,866	2,751	514	1,264	133
Pittsburgh, Pa.	288	...	2,535	588	1,826	2,578	2,465	228	984	221
Portland, Ore.	2,821	2,535	...	2,060	767	636	172	2,315	1,913	2,754
St. Louis, Mo.	868	588	2,060	...	1,337	2,089	2,081	454	396	793
San Francisco	2,866	2,578	636	2,089	752	...	808	2,364	1,760	2,799
Seattle, Wash.	2,751	2,465	172	2,081	836	808	...	2,245	1,982	2,684
Tulsa, Okla.	1,264	984	1,913	396	1,172	1,760	1,982	850	...	1,189
Washington, DC	133	221	2,754	793	2,047	2,799	2,684	447	1,189	...

Air Distances Between Selected World Cities in Statute Miles

Point-to-point measurements are usually from City Hall.

	Bangkok	Beijing	Berlin	Cairo	Cape Town	Caracas	Chicago	Hong Kong	Honolulu	Lima
Bangkok	...	2,046	5,352	4,523	6,300	10,555	8,570	1,077	6,609	12,244
Beijing	2,046	...	4,584	4,698	8,044	8,950	6,604	1,217	5,077	10,349
Berlin	5,352	4,584	...	1,797	5,961	5,238	4,414	5,443	7,320	6,896
Cairo	4,523	4,698	1,797	...	4,480	6,342	6,141	5,066	8,848	7,726
Cape Town	6,300	8,044	5,961	4,480	...	6,366	8,491	7,376	11,535	6,072
Caracas	10,555	8,950	5,238	6,342	6,366	...	2,495	10,165	6,021	1,707
Chicago	8,570	6,604	4,414	6,141	8,491	2,495	...	7,797	4,256	3,775
Hong Kong	1,077	1,217	5,443	5,066	7,376	10,165	7,797	...	5,556	11,418
Honolulu	6,609	5,077	7,320	8,848	11,535	6,021	4,256	5,556	...	5,947
London	5,944	5,074	583	2,185	5,989	4,655	3,958	5,990	7,240	6,316
Los Angeles	7,637	6,250	5,782	7,520	9,969	3,632	1,745	7,240	2,557	4,171
Madrid	6,337	5,745	1,165	2,087	5,308	4,346	4,189	6,558	7,872	5,907
Melbourne	4,568	5,643	9,918	8,675	6,425	9,717	9,673	4,595	5,505	8,059
Mexico City	9,793	7,753	6,056	7,700	8,519	2,234	1,690	8,788	3,789	2,639
Montreal	8,338	6,519	3,740	5,427	7,922	2,438	745	7,736	4,918	3,970
Moscow	4,389	3,607	1,006	1,803	6,279	6,177	4,987	4,437	7,047	7,862
New York	8,669	6,844	3,979	5,619	7,803	2,120	714	8,060	4,969	3,639
Paris	5,877	5,120	548	1,998	5,786	4,732	4,143	5,990	7,449	6,370
Rio de Janeiro	9,994	10,768	6,209	6,143	3,781	2,804	5,282	11,009	8,288	2,342
Rome	5,494	5,063	737	1,326	5,231	5,195	4,824	5,774	8,040	6,750
San Francisco	7,931	5,918	5,672	7,466	10,248	3,902	1,859	6,905	2,398	4,518
Singapore	883	2,771	6,164	5,137	6,008	11,402	9,372	1,605	6,726	11,689
Stockholm	5,089	4,133	528	2,096	6,423	5,471	4,331	5,063	6,875	7,166
Tokyo	2,865	1,307	5,557	5,958	9,154	8,808	6,314	1,791	3,859	9,631
Warsaw	5,033	4,325	322	1,619	5,935	5,559	4,679	5,147	7,366	7,215
Washington, DC	8,807	6,942	4,181	5,822	7,895	2,047	596	8,155	4,838	3,509

	London	Los Angeles	Madrid	Melbourne	Mexico City	Montreal	Moscow	New Delhi	New York	Paris
Bangkok	5,944	7,637	6,337	4,568	9,793	8,338	4,389	1,813	8,669	5,877
Beijing	5,074	6,250	5,745	5,643	7,753	6,519	3,607	2,353	6,844	5,120
Berlin	583	5,782	1,165	9,918	6,056	3,740	1,006	3,598	3,979	548
Cairo	2,185	7,520	2,087	8,675	7,700	5,427	1,803	2,758	5,619	1,998
Cape Town	5,989	9,969	5,308	6,425	8,519	7,922	6,279	5,769	7,803	5,786
Caracas	4,655	3,632	4,346	9,717	2,234	2,438	6,177	8,833	2,120	4,732
Chicago	3,958	1,745	4,189	9,673	1,690	745	4,987	7,486	714	4,143
Hong Kong	5,990	7,240	6,558	4,595	8,788	7,736	4,437	2,339	8,060	5,990
Honolulu	7,240	2,557	7,872	5,505	3,789	4,918	7,047	7,412	4,969	7,449
London	...	5,439	785	10,500	5,558	3,254	1,564	4,181	3,469	214
Los Angeles	5,439	...	5,848	7,931	1,542	2,427	6,068	7,011	2,451	5,601
Madrid	785	5,848	...	10,758	5,643	3,448	2,147	4,530	3,593	655
Melbourne	10,500	7,931	10,758	...	8,426	10,395	8,950	6,329	10,359	10,430
Mexico City	5,558	1,542	5,643	8,426	...	2,317	6,676	9,120	2,090	5,725
Montreal	3,254	2,427	3,448	10,395	2,317	...	4,401	7,012	331	3,432
Moscow	1,564	6,068	2,147	8,950	6,676	4,401	...	2,698	4,683	1,554
New York	3,469	2,451	3,593	10,359	2,090	331	4,683	7,318	...	3,636
Paris	214	5,601	655	10,430	5,725	3,432	1,554	4,102	3,636	...
Rio de Janeiro	5,750	6,330	5,045	8,226	4,764	5,078	7,170	8,753	4,801	5,684
Rome	895	6,326	851	9,929	6,377	4,104	1,483	3,684	4,293	690
San Francisco	5,367	347	5,803	7,856	1,887	2,543	5,885	7,691	2,572	5,577
Singapore	6,747	8,767	7,080	3,759	10,327	9,203	5,228	2,571	9,534	6,673
Stockholm	942	5,454	1,653	9,630	6,012	3,714	716	3,414	3,986	1,003
Tokyo	5,959	5,470	6,706	5,062	7,035	6,471	4,660	3,638	6,757	6,053
Warsaw	905	5,922	1,427	9,598	6,337	4,022	721	3,277	4,270	852
Washington, DC	3,674	2,300	3,792	10,180	1,885	489	4,876	7,500	205	3,840

	Rio de Janeiro	Rome	San Francisco	Singapore	Stockholm	Tehran	Tokyo	Vienna	Warsaw	Wash., DC
Bangkok	9,994	5,494	7,931	883	5,089	3,391	2,865	5,252	5,033	8,807
Beijing	10,768	5,063	5,918	2,771	4,133	3,490	1,307	4,648	4,325	6,942
Berlin	6,209	737	5,672	6,164	528	2,185	5,557	326	322	4,181
Cairo	6,143	1,326	7,466	5,137	2,096	1,234	5,958	1,481	1,619	5,822
Cape Town	3,781	5,231	10,248	6,008	6,423	5,241	9,154	5,656	5,935	7,895
Caracas	2,804	5,195	3,902	11,402	5,471	7,320	8,808	5,372	5,559	2,047
Chicago	5,282	4,824	1,859	9,372	4,331	6,502	6,314	4,698	4,679	596
Hong Kong	11,009	5,774	6,905	1,605	5,063	3,843	1,791	5,431	5,147	8,155
Honolulu	8,288	8,040	2,398	6,726	6,875	8,070	3,859	7,632	7,366	4,838
London	5,750	895	5,367	6,747	942	2,743	5,959	771	905	3,674
Los Angeles	6,330	6,326	347	8,767	5,454	7,682	5,470	6,108	5,922	2,300
Madrid	5,045	851	5,803	7,080	1,653	2,978	6,706	1,128	1,427	3,792
Melbourne	8,226	9,929	7,856	3,759	9,630	7,826	5,062	9,790	9,598	10,180
Mexico City	4,764	6,377	1,887	10,327	6,012	8,184	7,035	6,320	6,337	1,885
Montreal	5,078	4,104	2,543	9,203	3,714	5,880	6,471	4,009	4,022	489
Moscow	7,170	1,483	5,885	5,228	716	1,532	4,660	1,043	721	4,876
New York	4,801	4,293	2,572	9,534	3,986	6,141	6,757	4,234	4,270	205
Paris	5,684	690	5,577	6,673	1,003	2,625	6,053	645	852	3,840
Rio de Janeiro	...	5,707	6,613	9,785	6,683	7,374	11,532	6,127	6,455	4,779
Rome	5,707	...	6,259	6,229	1,245	2,127	6,142	477	820	4,497
San Francisco	6,613	6,259	...	8,448	5,399	7,362	5,150	5,994	5,854	2,441
Singapore	9,785	6,229	8,448	...	5,936	4,103	3,300	6,035	5,843	9,662
Stockholm	6,683	1,245	5,399	5,936	...	2,173	5,053	780	494	4,183
Tokyo	11,532	6,142	5,150	3,300	5,053	4,775	...	5,689	5,347	6,791
Warsaw	6,455	820	5,854	5,843	494	1,879	5,689	347	...	4,472
Washington, DC	4,779	4,497	2,441	9,662	4,183	6,341	6,791	4,438	4,472	...

TELECOMMUNICATIONS

Worldwide Telecommunications: Market Data (1990-2002)

Source: © International Telecommunication Union

	1990	1991	1992	1993	1994	1995	1996	1997	1998	1999	2000	2001[3]	2002[4]
Total market revenue (billions of U.S. $)[1]	$508	$522	$580	$606	$675	$778	$885	$946	$1,015	$1,112	$1,210	$1,320	$1,445
Intl. phone traffic (billions of minutes)[2]	33	38	43	49	57	63	71	79	89	99	110	120	135
Main telephone lines (millions)	520	546	574	606	645	691	741	795	849	907	986	1,040	1,115
Mobile cellular subscribers (millions)	11	16	23	34	56	91	144	215	319	491	741	1,030	1,390

(1) Revenue from installation, subscription, and local, trunk, and international call charges. (2) From 1994 including traffic between countries of the former Soviet Union. (3) Estimate. (4) Projection.

Worldwide Use of Cellular Telephones, 2001

Source: © International Telecommunication Union; estimated; top countries or regions ranked by number of subscribers per 100 pop.

Country/Region	Number of subscribers (thousands)	per 100 pop.	Country/Region	Number of subscribers (thousands)	per 100 pop.	Country/Region	Number of subscribers (thousands)	per 100 pop.
Luxembourg	432	97	United Arab Emirates	1,909	72	Bahrain	300	42
Taiwan	21,633	97	Martinique	286	72	Slovak Republic	2,147	40
Hong Kong	5,776	85	Jersey	61	70	Croatia	1,755	38
Italy	48,698	84	Germany	56,245	68	Malta	139	35
Norway	3,737	83	Czech Republic	6,769	66	Chile	5,272	34
Iceland	235	82	Spain	26,494	60	Canada	9,924	32
Israel	5,260	81	Guadeloupe	293	64	Antigua & Barbuda	25	32
Austria	6,566	81	New Zealand	2,417	62	Puerto Rico	1,211	31
Sweden	7,042	79	Korea, South	29,045	61	Turkey	20,000	30
United Kingdom	47,026	78	France	35,922	61	Malaysia	7,128	30
Finland	4,044	78	Japan	74,819	59	Greenland	17	30
Portugal	7,977	77	Australia	11,169	58	Qatar	179	29
Slovenia	1,516	76	Seychelles	44	55	Virgin Islands (U.S.)	35	29
Greece	7,962	75	Aruba	53	50	Latvia	657	28
Belgium	7,690	75	Guernsey	31.5	50	Jamaica	700	27
Netherlands	11,900	74	Hungary	4,968	50	Venezuela	6,490	26
Denmark	3,954	74	Cyprus	314	46	Poland	10,050	26
Ireland	2,800	73	Estonia	651	46	Lithuania	932	25
Singapore	2,992	72	**United States**	**127,000**	**44**	Mauritius	300	25
Switzerland	5,226	72	Macao	194	43	**WORLD**	**946,297**	**16**

IT'S A FACT: According to the International Telecommunication Union (ITU), in 2002, the number of mobile phones in the world surpassed the number of fixed lines for the first time; nearly 1 out of 6 people worldwide had mobile phones.

U.S. Cellular Telephone Subscribership, 1985–2001

Source: The CTIA Semi-Annual Wireless Survey. Used with permission of CTIA; in thousands of subscribers in December[1]

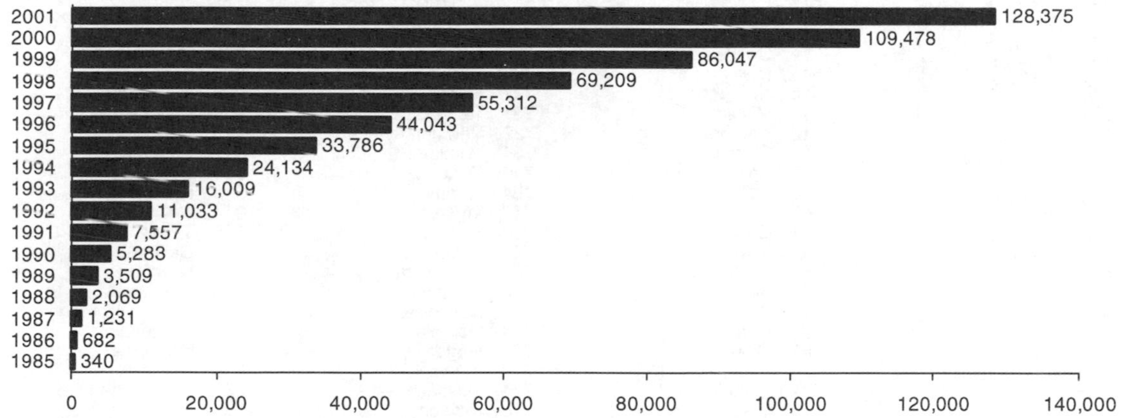

(1) Data may differ slightly from other sources.

U.S. Sales and Household Penetration, Selected Telecommunication Products[1], 1985-2001

Source: eBrain Market Research

	1985		1990		1995		2000		2001	
	Sales[2]	% of all households	Sales[2]	% of all households	Sales[2]	% of all households	Sales[2]	% of all households	Sales[2]	% of all households
Cordless telephones	$280	11	$842	28	$1,141	55	$1,307	80	$1,358	81
Pagers	—	—	118	1	300	11	750	40	790	41
Modems/fax modems	10	0	191	2.7	770	16	1,564	55	1,564	55
Telephone answering devices	325	7	827	35	1,077	57	984	75	1,062	77
Cellular phones	NA	NA	NA	NA	NA	NA	8,995	60	8,651	66

NA = Not available. (1) Data may differ slightly from other sources. (2) In millions of dollars.

Telephone Area Codes, by Number

As of Sept. 2002. For area codes listed by place, see pages 410-443.

Area Code	Location or Service
201	New Jersey
202	District of Columbia
203	Connecticut
204	Manitoba
205	Alabama
206	Washington
207	Maine
208	Idaho
209	California
210	Texas
211	Community Info.
212	New York
213	California
214	Texas
215	Pennsylvania
216	Ohio
217	Illinois
218	Minnesota
219	Indiana
224	Illinois
225	Louisiana
228	Mississippi
229	Georgia
231	Michigan
234	Ohio
239	Florida
240	Maryland
242	Bahamas
246	Barbados
248	Michigan
250	British Columbia
251	Alabama
252	North Carolina
253	Washington
254	Texas
256	Alabama
260	Indiana
262	Wisconsin
264	Anguilla
267	Pennsylvania
268	Antigua/Barbuda
269	Michigan
270	Kentucky
276	Virginia
281	Texas
284	British Virgin Islands
289	Ontario
301	Maryland
302	Delaware
303	Colorado
304	West Virginia
305	Florida
306	Saskatchewan
307	Wyoming
308	Nebraska
309	Illinois
310	California
311	Non-Emergency Access
312	Illinois
313	Michigan
314	Missouri
315	New York
316	Kansas
317	Indiana
318	Louisiana
319	Iowa
320	Minnesota
321	Florida
323	California
330	Ohio
334	Alabama
336	North Carolina
337	Louisiana
339	Massachusetts
340	U.S. Virgin Islands
345	Cayman Islands
347	New York
351	Massachusetts
352	Florida
360	Washington
361	Texas
386	Florida
401	Rhode Island
402	Nebraska
403	Alberta
404	Georgia
405	Oklahoma
406	Montana
407	Florida
408	California
409	Texas
410	Maryland
411	Directory Assistance
412	Pennsylvania
413	Massachusetts
414	Wisconsin
415	California
416	Ontario
417	Missouri
418	Quebec
419	Ohio
423	Tennessee
425	Washington
434	Virginia
435	Utah
440	Ohio
441	Bermuda
443	Maryland
450	Quebec
456	Inbound International
469	Texas
473	Grenada
478	Georgia
479	Arkansas
480	Arizona
484	Pennyslvania
500	Personal Comm. Serv.
501	Arkansas
502	Kentucky
503	Oregon
504	Louisiana
505	New Mexico
506	New Brunswick
507	Minnesota
508	Massachusetts
509	Washington
510	California
511	Traffic Info.
512	Texas
513	Ohio
514	Quebec
515	Iowa
516	New York
517	Michigan
518	New York
519	Ontario
520	Arizona
530	California
540	Virginia
541	Oregon
551	New Jersey
559	California
561	Florida
562	California
563	Iowa
567	Ohio
570	Pennsylvania
571	Virginia
573	Missouri
574	Indiana
580	Oklahoma
585	New York
586	Michigan
600	(Canadian Services)
601	Mississippi
602	Arizona
603	New Hampshire
604	British Columbia
605	South Dakota
606	Kentucky
607	New York
608	Wisconsin
609	New Jersey
610	Pennsylvania
611	Repair Service
612	Minnesota
613	Ontario
614	Ohio
615	Tennessee
616	Michigan
617	Massachusetts
618	Illinois
619	California
620	Kansas
623	Arizona
626	California
630	Illinois
631	New York
636	Missouri
641	Iowa
646	New York
647	Ontario
649	Turks & Caicos Islands
650	California
651	Minnesota
660	Missouri
661	California
662	Mississippi
664	Montserrat
670	N. Mariana Islands
671	Guam
678	Georgia
682	Texas
700	IC Services
701	North Dakota
702	Nevada
703	Virginia
704	North Carolina
705	Ontario
706	Georgia
707	California
708	Illinois
709	Newfoundland
710	U.S. Government
711	TRS Access
712	Iowa
713	Texas
714	California
715	Wisconsin
716	New York
717	Pennsylvania
718	New York
719	Colorado
720	Colorado
724	Pennsylvania
727	Florida
731	Tennessee
732	New Jersey
734	Michigan
740	Ohio
754	Florida
757	Virginia
758	St. Lucia
760	California
763	Minnesota
765	Indiana
767	Dominica
770	Georgia
772	Florida
773	Illinois
774	Massachusetts
775	Nevada
778	British Columbia
780	Alberta
781	Massachusetts
784	St. Vincent & Gren.
785	Kansas
786	Florida
787	Puerto Rico
800	Toll-Free Service
801	Utah
802	Vermont
803	South Carolina
804	Virginia
805	California
806	Texas
807	Ontario
808	Hawaii
809	Dominican Republic
810	Michigan
811	Business Office
812	Indiana
813	Florida
814	Pennsylvania
815	Illinois
816	Missouri
817	Texas
818	California
819	Quebec
828	North Carolina
830	Texas
831	California
832	Texas
843	South Carolina
845	New York
847	Illinois
848	New Jersey
850	Florida
856	New Jersey
857	Massachusetts
858	California
859	Kentucky
860	Connecticut
862	New Jersey
863	Florida
864	South Carolina
865	Tennessee
866	Toll-Free Service
867	Yukon, NW Terr., Nunavut
868	Trinidad & Tobago
869	St. Kitts & Nevis
870	Arkansas
876	Jamaica
877	Toll-Free Service
878	Pennsylvania
880	Toll-Free Service
881	Toll-Free Service
882	Toll-Free Service
888	Toll-Free Service
900	Premium Service
901	Tennessee
902	Nova Scotia
903	Texas
904	Florida
905	Ontario
906	Michigan
907	Alaska
908	New Jersey
909	California
910	North Carolina
911	Emergency
912	Georgia
913	Kansas
914	New York
915	Texas
916	California
917	New York
918	Oklahoma
919	North Carolina
920	Wisconsin
925	California
928	Arizona
931	Tennessee
936	Texas
937	Ohio
939	Puerto Rico
940	Texas
941	Florida
947	Michigan
949	California
952	Minnesota
954	Florida
956	Texas
970	Colorado
971	Oregon
972	Texas
973	New Jersey
978	Massachusetts
979	Texas
980	North Carolina
985	Louisiana
989	Michigan

Codes for International Direct Dial Calling From the U.S.

Basic station-to-station calls: 011 + country code (as shown) + city code (if required) + local number.

Person-to-person, operator-assisted, collect, credit card calls; calls billed to another number: 01 + country code (below) + city code (if required) + local number.

Selected city codes given below. For further information, contact your long distance company.

Country/Territory	Code
Afghanistan	93
Albania	355
Algeria	213
American Samoa	684
Andorra	376
Angola	244
Anguilla	264*
Antarctica (Scott Base and Casey Base)	672
Antigua & Barbuda	268*
Argentina	54
Armenia	374
Aruba	297
Ascension Island	247
Australia	61
Austria	43
Azerbaijan	994
Bahamas	242*
Bahrain	973
Bangladesh	880
Barbados	246*
Belarus	375
Belgium	32
Belize	501
Benin	229
Bermuda	441*
Bhutan	975
Bolivia	591
Bosnia & Herzegovina	387
Botswana	267
Brazil	55
British Virgin Islands	284
Brunei	673
Bulgaria	359
Burkina Faso	226
Burundi	257
Cambodia	855
Cameroon	237
Canada	1
Alberta	403*/ 780*
British Columbia	250*
British Columbia (lower mainland)	604*
Vancouver	604*
Manitoba	204*
New Brunswick	506*
Newfoundland	709*
NW Territories	867*
Nova Scotia	902*
Nunavut	867*
Ontario	
London	519*
North Bay	705*
Ottawa	613*
Thunder Bay	807*
Toronto Metro	416*
Toronto Vicinity	905*
Prince Edward Isl.	902*
Quebec	
Montreal	514*
Quebec City	418*
Sherbrooke	819*
Saskatchewan	306*
Yukon Territory	867*
Cape Verde	238
Cayman Islands	345*
Central African Rep.	236
Chad Republic	235
Chile	56
China	86
Christmas and the Cocos Islands	672
Colombia	57
Comoros	269
Congo, Dem. Rep.	243
Congo Republic	242
Cook Islands	682
Costa Rica	506
Côte d'Ivoire	225
Croatia	385
Cuba	53
Curacao	599
Cyprus	357
Czech Republic	420
Denmark	45
Diego Garcia	246
Djibouti	253
Dominica	767*
Dominican Republic	809*
East Timor	670
Ecuador	593
Egypt	20
El Salvador	503
Equatorial Guinea	240
Estonia	372
Falkland Islands	500
Faroe Islands	298
Fiji	679
Finland	358
France	33
French Antilles	596
French Guiana	594
French Polynesia	689
Gabon	241
Gambia, The	220
Georgia	995
Germany	49
Ghana	233
Gibraltar	350
Greece	30
Greenland	299
Grenada	473*
Guadeloupe	590
Guam	671*
Guantanamo Bay	53
Guatemala	502
Guinea	224
Guinea-Bissau	245
Guyana	592
Haiti	509
Honduras	504
Hong Kong	852
Hungary	36
Iceland	354
India	91
Indonesia	62
Iran	98
Iraq	964
Ireland	353
Israel	972
Italy	39
Jamaica	876*
Japan	81
Jordan	962
Kazakhstan	7
Kenya	254
Kiribati	686
Korea, North	850
Korea, South	82
Kuwait	965
Kyrgyzstan	7
Laos	856
Latvia	371
Lebanon	961
Lesotho	266
Liberia	231
Libya	218
Liechtenstein	423
Lithuania	370
Luxembourg	352
Macao	853
Macedonia	389
Madagascar	261
Malawi	265
Malaysia	60
Maldives	90
Mali	223
Malta	356
Marshall Islands	692
Mauritania	222
Mauritius	230
Mayotte Island	269
Mexico	52
Micronesia	691
Moldova	373
Monaco	33
Mongolia	976
Montserrat	473*
Morocco	212
Mozambique	258
Myanmar	95
Namibia	264
Nauru	674
Nepal	977
Netherlands	31
Netherlands Antilles	599
New Caledonia	687
New Zealand	64
Nicaragua	505
Niger	227
Nigeria	234
Nive	683
N. Mariana Isls.	670
Norway	47
Oman	968
Pakistan	92
Palau	680
Panama	507
Papua New Guinea	675
Paraguay	595
Peru	51
Philippines	63
Poland	48
Portugal	351
Puerto Rico	787*
Qatar	974
Reunion Island	262
Romania	40
Russia	7
Rwanda	250
St. Kitts & Nevis	869*
St. Lucia	758*
St. Maarten	599
St. Pierre and Miquelon	508
St. Vincent & the Grenadines	809*
Samoa (formerly Western Samoa)	685
San Marino	378
São Tomé & Príncipe	239
Saudi Arabia	966
Senegal	221
Serbia & Montenegro	381
Seychelles	248
Sierra Leone	232
Singapore	65
Slovakia	421
Slovenia	386
Solomon Islands	677
Somalia	252
South Africa	27
Spain	34
Sri Lanka	94
Sudan	249
Suriname	597
Swaziland	268
Sweden	46
Switzerland	41
Syria	963
Taiwan	886
Tajikistan	992
Tanzania	255
Thailand	66
Togo	228
Tonga	676
Trinidad & Tobago	868*
Tunisia	216
Turkey	90
Turkmenistan	7
Turks & Caicos Isls.	649*
Tuvalu	688
Uganda	256
Ukraine	380
United Arab Emirates	971
United Kingdom	44
Uruguay	598
Uzbekistan	998
Vanuatu	678
Vatican City	39
Venezuela	58
Vietnam	84
Virgin Islands, British	284*
Virgin Islands, U.S.	340*
Yemen (North)	967
Yemen (South)	969
Zambia	260
Zimbabwe	263

* These numbers are area codes. Follow Domestic Dialing instructions: dial "1" + area code + number you are calling.

Selected city codes: Beijing, 10; Brasilia, 61; Buenos Aires, 11; Dhaka, 2; Dublin, 1; Islamabad, 51; Jakarta, 21; Jerusalem, 2; Lagos, 1; London, 20; Madrid, 91; Mexico City, 55; New Delhi, 11; Paris, 1; Rome, 06; Tokyo, 3.

EDUCATION

Historical Overview of U.S. Public Elementary and Secondary Schools

Source: National Center for Education Statistics, U.S. Dept. of Education

	1899-1900	1919-20	1939-40	1959-60	1969-70	1979-80	1989-90	1998-99	1999-2000
Population statistics (thousands)									
Total U.S. population[1]	75,995	104,514	131,028	177,830	201,385	224,567	246,819	270,248	272,691
Population 5-17 years of age	21,573	27,571	30,151	43,881	52,386	48,041	44,947	50,915	51,257
Percentage 5-17 years of age	28.4	26.4	23.0	24.7	26.0	21.4	18.2	18.8	18.8
Enrollment (thousands)									
Elementary and secondary[2]	15,503	21,578	25,434	36,087	45,550	41,651	40,543	46,539	46,587
Kindergarten & grades 1-8	14,984	19,378	18,833	27,602	32,513	28,034	29,152	33,346	33,488
Grades 9-12	519	2,200	6,601	8,485	13,037	13,616	11,390	13,193	13,369
Percentage pop. 5-17 enrolled	71.9	78.3	84.4	82.2	87.0	86.7	90.2	91.4	91.4
Percentage in high schools	3.3	10.2	26.0	23.5	28.6	32.7	28.1	28.3	28.5
High school graduates (thousands)	62	231	1,143	1,627	2,589	2,748	2,320	2,489	2,546
School term; staff									
Average school term (in days)	144.3	161.9	175.0	178.0	178.9	178.5	*	*	*
Total instructional staff (thousands)	*	678	912	1,457	2,286	2,406	2,986	3,694	3,819
Teachers, librarians, and other non-supervisory instructional staff (thousands)	423	657	875	1,393	2,195	2,300	2,860	3,564	3,682
Revenue and expenditures (millions)									
Total revenue	$220	$970	$2,261	$14,747	$40,267	$96,881	$208,548	$347,330	$372,865
Total expenditures	215	1,036	2,344	15,613	40,683	95,962	212,770	355,859	381,829
Current expenditures[3]	180	861	1,942	12,329[5]	34,218[5]	86,984[5]	188,229[5]	302,874[5]	323,809[5]
Capital outlay	35	154	258	2,662	4,659	6,506	17,781	39,527	43,401
Interest on school debt	*	18	131	490	1,171	1,874	3,776	6,196	9,135
Others	*	3	13	133	636	598	2,983	5,263	5,484
Salaries and pupil cost									
Avg. annual salary of instruct. staff[4]	$325	$871	$1,441	$5,174	$9,047	$16,715	$32,638	$42,488	$43,768
Expenditure per capita total pop.	2.83	9.91	17.89	88	202	427	862	1,317	1,400
Current expenditure per pupil ADA[6]	16.67	53.32	88.09	375	816	2,272	4,980	7,013	7,392

NOTE: Because of rounding, details may not add to totals. Prior to 1959-60, data do not include Alaska and Hawaii. * = Data not collected. (1) Population data for 1899-1900 are based on total population from the decennial census. From 1919-20 to 1959-60, population data are total population, including armed forces overseas, as of July 1 preceding the school year. Data for later years are for resident population that excludes armed forces overseas. (2) Data for 1899-1900 are school year enrollment; data for later years are fall enrollment. (3) In 1899-1900, includes interest on school debt. (4) Includes supervisors, principals, teachers, and nonsupervisory instructional staff. (5) Because of changes in the definition of "current expenditures," data for 1959-60 and later years are not entirely comparable with prior years. (6) ADA means average daily attendance.

Programs for the Disabled, 1990-2001

Source: Office of Special Education Programs, U.S. Dept. of Education

(Number of children from 6 to 21 years old served annually in educational programs for the disabled; in thousands)

Type of Disability	1990-91	1992-93	1993-94	1994-95	1995-96	1996-97	1997-98	1998-99	1999-2000	2000-2001
Learning disabilities	2,144	2,366	2,428	2,510	2,602	2,674	2,754	2,817	2,834	2,848
Speech impairments	988	998	1,018	1,020	1,027	1,049	1,064	1,075	1,081	1,085
Mental retardation	551	532	554	571	586	594	603	611	600	599
Emotional disturbance	391	402	415	428	439	446	454	463	469	472
Multiple disabilities	98	103	110	90	95	99	107	108	111	121
Hearing impairments	59	61	65	65	68	69	70	71	71	70
Orthopedic impairments	49	53	57	60	63	66	67	69	71	73
Other health impairments	56	66	83	107	134	161	191	221	253	290
Visual impairments	24	24	25	25	25	26	26	26	65	25
Autism	NA	16	19	23	29	34	43	54	65	78
Deaf-blindness	2	1	1	1	1	1	1	2	2	1
Traumatic brain injury	NA	4	5	7	10	10	12	13	14	15
ALL DISABILITIES	**4,362**	**4,626**	**4,779**	**4,908**	**5,079**	**5,231**	**4,397**	**5,541**	**5,614**	**5,705**

NOTE: Counts are based on reports from the 50 states and the District of Columbia. Details may not add to totals because of rounding and/or incomplete enumeration. NA = not available or unreliable because of incomplete reporting.

Technology in U.S. Public Schools, 2002

Source: Quality Education Data, Inc., Denver, CO

(Number and percentage of schools in each category that have the technology indicated)

	Elementary[1]		Middle/Jr. High[2]		Senior High[3]		K-12[4]		Special Ed./ Adult Ed.	
TOTAL SCHOOLS	**55,186**	**100%**	**13,986**	**100%**	**18,674**	**100%**	**2,317**	**100%**	**2,405**	**100%**
Schools with Computers	51,314	93	12,696	91	16,482	88	1,917	83	1,662	69
By number of computers:										
1-10	3,021	5	276	2	670	4	80	3	487	20
11-20	4,546	8	510	4	882	5	175	8	300	12
21-50	13,418	24	2,136	15	2,692	14	466	20	425	18
51-100	16,077	29	3,496	25	3,146	17	552	24	243	10
100+	14,252	26	6,278	45	9,092	49	644	28	207	9
Schools with LANs[5]	32,109	58	9,210	66	12,783	68	1,548	67	574	24
By enrollment:										
100-299	7,053	13	1,081	8	2,961	16	747	32	396	16
300-499	12,158	22	1,964	14	2,136	11	396	17	53	2
500+	12,898	23	6,165	44	7,686	41	405	17	125	5
Schools with WANs[6]	18,369	33	5,180	37	6,286	34	539	23	282	12
By enrollment:										
100-299	2,869	5	439	3	1,086	6	212	9	202	8
300-499	7,922	14	1,275	9	1,132	6	176	8	27	1
500+	7,578	14	3,466	25	4,068	22	151	7	53	2

(1) Includes preschool and schools with grade spans of K-3, K-5, K-6, K-8, and K-12. (2) Includes schools with grade spans of 4-8, 7-8, and 7-9. (3) Includes vocational, technical, and alternative high schools and schools with grade spans of 7-12, 9-12, and 10-12. (4) K-12 also included under Elementary schools. (5) LAN=Local area computer network. (6) WAN=Wide area computer network.

Students Per Computer in U.S. Public Schools, 1983-2001

Source: Quality Education Data, Inc., Denver, CO

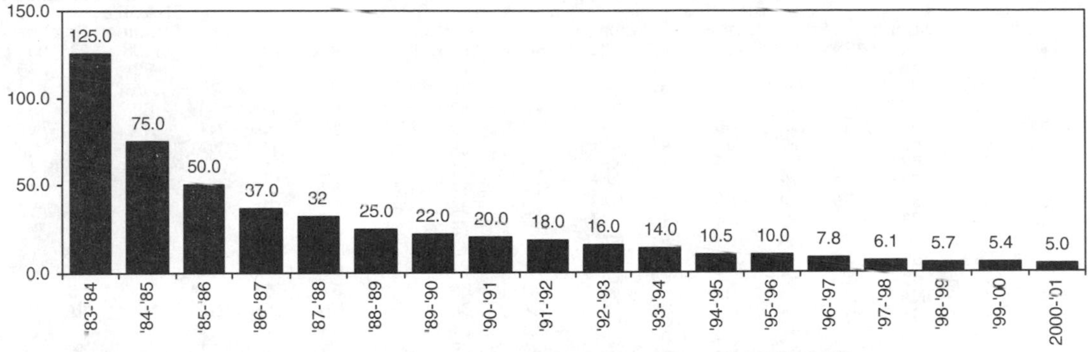

Overview of U.S. Public Schools, Fall 2000*

Source: National Center for Education Statistics, U.S. Dept. of Education; National Education Association

	Local school districts	Elementary schools[1]	Secondary schools[2]	Classroom teachers	Total enrollment	Pupils per teacher	Teacher's avg. pay[3]	Expend. per pupil[4]
Alabama	128	900	394	48,199	740,176	15.4	$37,956	$5,758
Alaska	53	193	89	7,880	133,356	16.9	46,986	9,668
Arizona	410	1,061	399	44,438	877,696	19.8	36,302	5,444
Arkansas	310	711	403	31,947	449,959	14.1	34,476	5,628
California	985	6,344	2,029	298,064	6,142,348	20.6	48,923	6,401
Colorado	176	1,165	380	41,983	724,508	17.3	39,284	6,702
Connecticut	166	832	209	41,044	562,179	13.7	52,100	10,122
Delaware	19	127	42	7,471	114,676	15.3	47,047	8,809
Dist. of Columbia	1	131	35	4,949	68,925	13.9	48,651	11,935
Florida	67	2,179	448	132,030	2,434,821	18.4	37,824	6,383
Georgia	180	1,567	339	91,044	1,444,937	15.9	42,216	6,903
Hawaii	1	196	50	10,927	184,360	16.9	41,980	7,090
Idaho	115	415	222	13,714	245,117	17.9	36,375	5,644
Illinois	894	3,174	984	127,620	2,048,792	16.1	48,053	8,084
Indiana	295	1,417	456	59,226	989,225	16.7	43,055	7,652
Iowa	374	1,055	430	34,636	495,080	14.3	36,479	6,925
Kansas	304	1,000	424	32,742	470,610	14.4	39,432	6,962
Kentucky	176	1,009	417	39,589	665,850	16.8	37,234	6,784
Louisiana	78	1,027	327	49,916	743,089	16.6	34,253	6,256
Maine	282	534	163	16,559	207,037	12.5	36,256	8,247
Maryland	24	1,083	257	52,433	852,920	16.3	44,997	8,273
Massachusetts	349	1,486	343	67,432	975,150	14.5	47,523	9,317
Michigan	734	2,687	854	97,031	1,743,337	18.0	49,975	8,886
Minnesota	415	1,237	755	53,457	854,340	16.0	40,577	7,499
Mississippi	152	581	327	31,006	497,871	16.1	32,957	5,356
Missouri	524	1,551	642	64,739	912,744	14.1	36,764	6,764
Montana	453	516	363	10,411	154,875	14.9	32,930	6,990
Nebraska	576	937	341	20,983	286,199	13.6	34,175	7,360
Nevada	17	371	124	18,294	340,706	18.6	40,172	6,148
New Hampshire	178	430	95	14,341	208,461	14.5	38,303	7,082
New Jersey	604	1,907	449	99,718	1,307,828	13.1	53,281	10,903
New Mexico	89	559	190	21,043	320,306	15.2	33,785	5,835
New York	703	3,102	935	206,961	2,882,188	13.9	50,920	10,957
North Carolina	120	1,723	372	83,680	1,293,638	15.5	41,167	6,505
North Dakota	230	336	209	8,141	109,201	13.4	30,891	6,078
Ohio	662	2,715	956	118,361	1,835,049	15.5	42,716	7,816
Oklahoma	544	1,224	586	41,318	623,110	15.1	34,434	5,770
Oregon	197	933	278	28,094	546,231	19.4	42,333	8,129
Pennsylvania	501	2,394	796	116,963	1,814,311	15.5	49,500	8,380
Rhode Island	36	260	63	10,646	157,347	14.8	48,474	9,646
South Carolina	90	832	271	45,380	677,411	14.9	37,327	6,545
South Dakota	176	468	281	9,397	128,603	13.7	30,265	6,037
Tennessee	138	1,195	353	61,233	909,388	14.9	37,074	5,837
Texas	1,040	4,965	1,737	274,826	4,059,619	14.8	38,614	6,771
Utah	40	510	254	22,008	481,687	21.9	36,049	4,692
Vermont	288	279	70	8,414	102,049	12.1	38,651	8,799
Virginia	135	1,459	372	91,560	1,144,915	12.5	40,197	6,491
Washington	296	1,401	606	51,098	1,004,770	19.7	42,101	6,914
West Virginia	55	609	203	20,930	286,367	13.7	35,764	7,637
Wisconsin	431	1,549	561	62,332	879,476	14.1	41,646	8,299
Wyoming	48	265	111	6,783	89,940	13.3	34,189	7,944
TOTAL U.S.	**14,859**	**64,601**	**21,994**	**2,952,991**	**47,222,778**	**16.0**	**$42,898**	**$7,392**

*Full-time elementary and secondary day schools only. (1) Includes schools below grade 9. (2) Includes schools with no grade lower than 7. (3) National Education Association estimate, Fall 2000. (4) Fall 1999.

IT'S A FACT: In 1959-60, $375 was spent per student in U.S. public elementary and secondary schools. Allowing for inflation, that would be about $2,100 today. The actual figure for 1999-2000 was $7,392.

Mathematics, Reading, and Science Achievement of U.S. Students

Source: National Assessment of Educational Progress, National Center for Education Statistics, U.S. Dept. of Education

Percent of students who scored at or above basic level in national tests.[1]

	GRADE 4			GRADE 8				
	Math		Reading	Math		Reading	Science	
State[2]	1996	2000	1998	1996	2000	1998	1996	2000
AL	48	57	56	45	52	66	47	51
AK	65	NA	NA	68	NA	NA	65	54
AZ	57	58	53	57	62	73	55	57
AR	54	56	55	52	52	68	55	54
CA	46	52	48	51	52	64	47	40
CO	67	NA	69	67	NA	76	68	NA
CT	75	77	78	70	72	82	68	65
DE	54	NA	57	55	NA	66	51	NA
DC	20	24	28	20	23	44	19	NA
FL	55	NA	54	54	NA	65	51	NA
GA	53	58	55	51	55	68	49	52
HI	53	55	45	51	52	60	42	40
ID	NA	71	NA	NA	71	NA	NA	73
IL	NA	66	NA	NA	68	NA	NA	62
IN	72	78	NA	68	76	NA	65	68
IA	74	78	70	78	NA	NA	71	NA
KS	NA	75	71	NA	77	81	NA	NA
KY	60	60	63	56	63	74	58	62
LA	44	57	48	38	48	64	40	45
ME	75	74	73	77	76	84	78	75
MD	59	61	61	57	65	72	55	59
MA	71	79	73	68	76	80	69	74
MI	68	72	63	67	70	NA	65	69
MN	76	78	69	75	80	81	72	73
MS	42	45	48	36	41	61	39	42
MO	66	72	63	64	67	76	64	68
MT	71	73	73	75	80	83	77	80
NE	70	67	NA	76	74	NA	71	70
NV	57	61	53	NA	58	69	NA	54
NH	NA	NA	75	NA	NA	NA	NA	NA
NJ	68	NA	NA	NA	NA	NA	NA	NA
NM	51	51	52	51	50	70	49	48
NY	64	67	62	61	68	78	57	61
NC	64	76	62	56	70	76	56	56
ND	75	75	NA	77	77	NA	78	74
OH	NA	73	NA	NA	75	NA	NA	73
OK	NA	69	66	NA	64	80	NA	62
OR	65	67	61	67	71	78	68	67
PA	68	NA	NA	NA	NA	NA	NA	NA
RI	61	67	65	60	64	74	59	61
SC	48	60	55	48	55	65	45	50
TN	58	60	58	53	53	71	53	57
TX	69	77	63	59	68	76	55	53
UT	69	70	62	70	68	77	70	68
VT	67	73	NA	72	75	NA	70	74
VA	62	73	64	58	67	78	59	63
WA	67	NA	63	67	NA	77	61	NA
WV	63	68	62	54	62	74	56	61
WI	74	NA	72	75	NA	79	73	NA
WY	64	73	65	68	70	76	71	71
U.S.[2]	**64**	**69**	**62**	**62**	**66**	**74**	60	**59**

NA = Not administered. (1) Basic level denotes a partial mastery of prerequisite knowledge and skills fundamental for proficient work at each grade. (2) Excluding South Dakota, which did not participate.

WORLD ALMANAC QUICK QUIZ

In 2000, about what percent of students attended private elementary or secondary schools?

(a) 3% (b) 7% (c) 11% (d) 18%

For the answer look in this chapter, or see page 1008.

Revenues[1] for Public Elementary and Secondary Schools, by State, 2001-2002

Source: National Education Association; estimated; in thousands

		Federal		State		Local and intermediate	
STATE	Total	Amount	%	Amount	%	Amount	%
Alabama	$4,524,478*	$469,540*	10.4*	$2,853,116*	63.1*	$1,201,822*	26.6*
Alaska	1,245,142	156,124	12.5	791,222	63.5	297,797	23.9
Arizona	5,139,973*	315,306*	6.1*	2,744,260*	53.4*	2,080,407*	40.5*
Arkansas	2,757,190	223,459	8.1	1,716,800	62.3	816,931	29.6
California	50,720,529	5,390,308	10.6	30,356,946	59.9	14,973,275	29.5
Colorado	5,688,775*	292,380*	5.1*	2,297,904*	40.4*	3,098,491*	54.5*
Connecticut	6,878,417	338,082	4.9	2,872,315	41.8	3,668,020	53.3
Delaware	1,223,009*	98,648*	8.1*	822,053*	67.2*	302,308*	24.7*
District of Columbia	773,997*	112,873	14.6*	0	0.0*	661,124	85.4*
Florida	18,429,443	1,769,884	9.6	8,599,422	46.7	8,060,137	43.7
Georgia	13,417,163*	854,469*	6.4*	6,135,650*	45.7*	6,427,045*	47.9*
Hawaii	1,710,694	143,065	8.4	1,533,987	89.7	33,642	2.0
Idaho	1,689,919*	123,729*	7.3*	1,003,153*	59.4*	563,037*	33.3*
Illinois	19,400,051*	1,654,091*	8.5*	6,143,708*	31.7*	11,602,252*	59.8*
Indiana	9,154,711*	512,020*	5.6*	4,844,333*	52.9*	3,798,358*	41.5*
Iowa	3,863,954	183,394	4.7	2,039,814	52.8	1,640,746	42.5
Kansas	3,714,818	228,880	6.2	2,324,777	62.6	1,161,161	31.3
Kentucky	5,008,017*	424,031*	8.5*	3,081,035*	61.5*	1,502,952*	30.0*
Louisiana	5,072,365	591,196	11.7	2,462,694	48.6	2,018,475	39.8
Maine	1,816,165	132,495	7.3	869,251	47.9	814,419	44.8
Maryland	7,452,405	370,832	5.0	2,693,512	36.1	4,388,061	58.9
Massachusetts	10,487,927*	561,631	5.4*	4,863,964	46.4*	5,062,332	48.3*
Michigan	13,051,839*	581,637*	4.5*	10,129,654*	77.6*	2,340,548*	17.9*
Minnesota	8,018,507*	395,976*	4.9*	4,933,737*	61.5*	2,688,794*	33.5*
Mississippi	3,083,956	443,018	14.4	1,690,334	54.8	950,604	30.8
Missouri	7,343,481*	534,419	7.3*	2,675,447*	36.4*	4,133,614*	56.3*
Montana	1,115,265*	131,147*	11.8*	488,093*	43.8*	496,025*	44.5*
Nebraska	2,013,731	110,385	5.5	819,848	40.7	1,083,498	53.8
Nevada	2,613,814	141,008	5.4	745,684	28.5	1,727,122	66.1
New Hampshire	1,550,586*	79,339*	5.1*	776,884*	50.1*	694,363*	44.8*
New Jersey	13,921,800*	399,127*	2.9*	5,129,820*	36.8*	8,392,853*	60.3*
New Mexico	2,465,843	317,114	12.9	1,828,411	74.1	320,318	13.0
New York	32,264,449*	2,253,598*	7.0*	15,172,348*	47.0*	14,838,503*	46.0*
North Carolina	9,540,783*	733,678*	7.7*	6,814,143*	71.4*	1,992,962*	20.9*
North Dakota	802,581*	92,705*	11.6*	302,525*	37.7*	407,352*	50.8*
Ohio	16,700,000	1,000,000	6.0	7,200,000	43.1	8,500,000	50.9
Oklahoma	4,136,867*	443,227*	10.7*	2,410,600*	58.3*	1,283,041*	31.0*
Oregon	4,909,655	346,345	7.1	2,870,968	58.5	1,692,342	34.5

STATE	Total	Federal Amount	Federal %	State Amount	State %	Local and intermediate Amount	Local and intermediate %
Pennsylvania	$17,437,000*	$891,003	5.1*	$7,006,147*	40.2*	$9,539,850*	54.7*
Rhode Island	1,385,189*	52,107*	3.8*	518,235*	37.4*	814,847*	58.8*
South Carolina	5,170,449*	402,882*	7.8*	2,606,204*	50.4*	2,161,362*	41.8*
South Dakota	924,957*	92,428*	10.0*	386,167*	41.7*	446,361*	48.3*
Tennessee	5,614,786	501,710	8.9	2,708,976	48.2	2,404,100	42.8
Texas	32,660,567	3,146,753	9.6	13,911,171	42.6	15,602,643	47.8
Utah	2,863,658	215,082	7.5	1,669,858	58.3	978,718	34.2
Vermont	1,064,051	63,549	6.0	768,855	72.3	231,647	21.8
Virginia	10,682,058*	606,311*	5.7*	4,769,325*	44.6*	5,306,422*	49.7*
West Virginia	2,488,577	286,689	11.5	1,496,605	60.1	705,283	28.3
Wisconsin	8,583,610	408,424	4.8	4,632,298	54.0	3,542,888	41.3
Wyoming	848,638	70,000	8.2	412,638	48.6	366,000	43.1
50 States and DC	**$401,715,022**	**$30,401,825**	**7.6**	**$201,241,829**	**50.1**	**$170,071,368**	**42.3**

*Indicates NEA estimate. (1) Included as revenue receipts are all appropriations from general funds of federal, state, county, and local governments; receipts from taxes levied for school purposes; income from permanent school funds and endowments; and income from leases of school lands and miscellaneous sources (interest on bank deposits, tuition, gifts, school lunch charges, etc.).

Enrollment in U.S. Public and Private Schools, 1899-2010*

Source: National Center for Education Statistics, U.S. Dept. of Education

School year[1]	Public school[2] enrollment	Private school[2] enrollment	% Private
1899-1900	15,503	1,352	8.7
1909-10	17,814	1,558	8.7
1919-20	21,578	1,699	7.9
1929-30	25,678	2,651	10.3
1939-40	25,434	2,611	10.3
1949-50	25,111	3,380	13.5
1959-60	35,182	5,675	16.1
1969-70	45,550	5,500[3]	12.1
1979-80	41,651	5,000[3]	12.0
1989-90	40,543	5,198	11.4
1999-2000	46,857	6,018	11.4
2001-2002[4]	47,213	5,852	11.0
2002-2003[4]	47,358	5,860	11.0
2009-2010[4]	47,178	5,836	11.0

*Private includes all nonpublic schools, including religious schools. (1) Fall enrollment. (2) In thousands. (3) Estimated. (4) Projected.

U.S. Public High School Graduation Rates, 1999-2000

Source: National Center for Education Statistics, U.S. Dept. of Education

	Rate (%)[1]	Rank
Alabama	62.9	37
Alaska	62.8	38
Arizona	59.9	45
Arkansas	79.4	7
California	68.7	33
Colorado	70.7	29
Connecticut	77.1	12
Delaware	61.5	41
District of Columbia	58.9	47
Florida	57.3	49
Georgia	56.8	50
Hawaii	65.6	35
Idaho	77.1	13
Illinois	71.1	27
Indiana	70.5	30
Iowa	83.3	6
Kansas	74.4	20
Kentucky	66.4	34
Louisiana	57.6	48
Maine	77.3	11
Maryland	74.0	22
Massachusetts	74.8	18
Michigan	65.2	36
Minnesota	83.7	5
Mississippi	60.8	41
Missouri	73.2	24
Montana	78.1	9
Nebraska	84.5	3
Nevada	72.7	26
New Hampshire	73.9	23
New Jersey	85.5	1
New Mexico	62.1	39
New York	60.9	42
North Carolina	59.4	46
North Dakota	84.1	4
Ohio	69.6	32
Oklahoma	72.8	25
Oregon	74.8	17
Pennsylvania	74.9	16
Rhode Island	69.7	31
South Carolina	54.7	51
South Dakota	74.2	21
Tennessee	60.4	44
Texas	61.9	40
Utah	84.7	2
Vermont	78.9	8
Virginia	76.0	14
Washington	70.8	28
West Virginia	74.8	19
Wisconsin	78.0	10
Wyoming	75.3	15
TOTAL U.S.	**68.1**	

NOTE: Data exclude ungraded pupils and have not been adjusted for interstate migration. (1) Graduates as percentage of fall 1996 9th-grade enrollment.

Teachers' Salaries in Upper Secondary Education, Selected Countries, 1999

Source: Organization for Economic Cooperation and Development

Annual statutory teachers' salaries in public institutions in upper secondary (senior high school) education, general programs, in equivalent U.S. dollars converted using PPPs[1]; ranked by starting salaries.

	Starting salary	Salary with 15 years' experience	Salary at top of scale
Switzerland	$46,866	$62,052	$70,548
Germany	35,546	41,745	49,445
Denmark	29,986	40,019	42,672
Belgium	29,075	41,977	50,461
Spain	29,058	33,988	43,100
Netherlands	27,133	46,148	54,720
Australia	26,658	37,138	37,577
United States	**25,405**	**36,219**	**44,394**
Austria	24,027	30,376	53,443
Korea (South)	23,613	39,265	62,135
Ireland	23,033	35,944	40,523
Norway	22,194	25,854	27,453
France	21,918	28,757	41,537
Finland	21,047	29,530	31,325
Italy	20,822	26,175	32,602
Iceland	20,775	25,795	30,954
Sweden	20,549	26,210	NA
England	19,999	33,540	33,540
Scotland	$19,765	$32,858	$32,858
Greece	19,650	23,943	28,987
Portugal	18,751	27,465	50,061
Tunisia	18,235	19,770	20,577
New Zealand	16,678	32,573	32,573
Argentina	15,789	22,266	26,759
Chile	14,644	16,214	19,597
Malaysia	13,575	21,568	29,822
Philippines	12,620	13,715	14,609
Brazil	12,598	16,103	18,556
Uruguay	10,305	12,489	15,585
Turkey	8,144	9,355	10,568
Jordan	8,096	10,652	27,347
Czech Republic	8,052	10,695	14,316
Hungary	6,908	10,355	13,217
Thailand	5,781	14,208	27,098
Peru	4,701	4,701	4,701
Indonesia	1,689	3,537	5,598

NA = Not available. (1) Purchasing power parities (PPPs) are the rates of currency conversion that equalize the purchasing power of different currencies by eliminating the differences in price levels between countries.

Percent of Population with Upper Secondary Education, Selected Countries, 1999

Source: Organization for Economic Cooperation and Development

Percentage of the population ages 25-64 having attained at least upper secondary (senior high school) education

United States	**87**	Sweden	77	Australia	57	Peru[1]	46	Zimbabwe	29
Czech Republic	86	Austria[1]	74	Belgium	57	Philippines	44	Brazil[1]	24
Norway[1]	85	New Zealand	74	Iceland	56	Chile[1]	43	Indonesia	22
Switzerland	82	Finland	72	Luxembourg	56	Italy	42	Turkey	22
Germany	81	Hungary	67	Poland[1]	54	Sri Lanka[1]	36	Portugal	21
Japan	81	Korea	66	Ireland[1]	51	Malaysia[1]	35	Mexico	20
Denmark	80	France	62	Jordan	51	Spain	35	Thailand[1]	16
Canada	79	United Kingdom	62	Greece	50	Uruguay[1]	32	Tunisia	8

(1) Year of reference 1998.

Government Expenditure Per Student, Selected Countries, 1998

Source: Organization for Economic Cooperation and Development

Expenditure per student in U.S. dollars, converted using PPPs[1], on public and private institutions, by level of education, based on full-time equivalents

	Primary[2]	Secondary[3]		Primary[2]	Secondary[3]		Primary[2]	Secondary[3]
Australia	3,981	5,830	Indonesia[5]	116	497	Philippines[4]	689	726
Austria	6,065	8,163	Ireland	2,745	3,934	Poland	1,496	1,438
Belgium	3,799	6,238	Israel	4,135	5,115	Portugal	3,121	4,636
Brazil[4]	837	1,076	Italy	5,653	6,458	Spain	3,267	4,274
Chile	1,500	1,713	Japan	5,075	5,890	Sweden	5,579	5,648
Czech Republic	1,645	3,182	Korea (South)	2,838	3,544	Switzerland	6,470	9,348
Denmark	6,713	7,200	Malaysia	919	1,469	Thailand	1,048	1,177
Finland	4,641	5,111	Mexico	863	1,586	Tunisia[5]	891	1,633
France	3,752	6,605	Netherlands	3,795	5,304	United Kingdom	3,329	5,230
Germany	3,531	6,209	Norway	5,761	7,343	**United States**	**6,043**	**7,764**
Greece	2,368	3,287	Paraguay	572	948	Uruguay	971	1,246
Hungary	2,028	2,140	Peru	479	671	Zimbabwe	768	1,179

(1) Purchasing power parities (PPPs) are the rates of currency conversion that equalize the purchasing power of different currencies by eliminating the differences in price levels between countries. (2) Primary—elementary school age. (3) Lower secondary—(junior high) and upper secondary (senior high school) combined. (4) For 1997. (5) For 1999.

Charges at U.S. Institutions of Higher Education, 1969-70 to 2000-2001

Source: National Center for Education Statistics, U.S. Dept. of Education

Figures for 1969-70 are average charges for full-time resident degree-credit students; figures for later years are average charges per full-time equivalent student. Room and board are based on full-time students. These figures are enrollment-weighted, according to the number of full-time-equivalent undergraduates, and thus vary from averages given elsewhere.

	TUITION AND FEES			BOARD RATES			DORMITORY CHARGES		
	All institutions	2-yr	4-yr	All institutions	2-yr	4-yr	All institutions	2-yr	4-yr
PUBLIC (in-state)									
1969-70	$323	$178	$427	$511	$465	$540	$369	$308	$395
1979-80	583	355	840	867	894	898	715	572	749
1989-90	1,356	756	2,035	1,635	1,581	1,728	1,513	962	1,561
1990-91	1,454	824	2,159	1,691	1,594	1,767	1,612	1,050	1,658
1991-92	1,624	937	2,410	1,780	1,612	1,852	1,731	1,074	1,789
1992-93	1,782	1,025	2,349	1,841	1,668	1,854	1,756	1,106	1,816
1993-94	1,942	1,125	2,537	1,880	1,681	1,895	1,873	1,190	1,934
1994-95	2,057	1,192	2,681	1,949	1,712	1,967	1,959	1,232	2,023
1995-96	2,179	1,239	2,848	2,020	1,681	2,045	2,057	1,297	2,121
1996-97	2,271	1,276	2,987	2,111	1,789	2,133	2,148	1,339	2,214
1997-98	2,360	1,314	3,110	2,228	1,795	2,263	2,225	1,401	2,301
1998-99	2,430	1,327	3,229	2,347	1,828	2,389	2,330	1,450	2,409
1999-2000	2,506	1,338	3,349	2,364	1,834	2,406	2,440	1,549	2,519
2000-2001	2,600	1,359	3,506	2,454	1,900	2,498	2,566	1,603	2,651
PRIVATE									
1969-70	1,533	1,034	1,809	561	546	608	436	413	503
1979-80	3,130	2,062	3,811	955	924	1,078	827	769	999
1989-90	8,147	5,196	10,348	1,948	1,811	2,339	1,923	1,663	2,411
1990-91	8,772	5,570	11,379	2,074	1,989	2,470	2,063	1,744	2,654
1991-92	9,434	5,752	12,192	2,252	2,090	2,727	2,221	1,789	2,860
1992-93	9,942	6,059	10,294	2,344	1,875	2,354	2,348	1,970	2,362
1993-94	10,572	6,370	10,952	2,434	1,970	2,445	2,490	2,067	2,506
1994-95	11,111	6,914	11,481	2,509	2,023	2,520	2,587	2,233	2,601
1995-96	11,563	7,094	12,243	2,606	2,098	2,617	2,738	2,371	2,751
1996-97	11,954	7,236	12,881	2,663	2,181	2,672	2,878	2,537	2,889
1997-98	12,921	7,464	13,344	2,762	2,785	2,761	2,954	2,672	2,964
1998-99	13,319	7,854	13,973	2,865	2,884	2,865	3,075	2,581	2,865
1999-2000	13,965	8,235	14,588	2,882	2,922	2,881	3,224	2,808	2,882
2000-2001	14,690	8,961	15,531	2,989	2,962	2,989	3,370	2,768	2,989

IT'S A FACT: More men than women received bachelor's degrees every school year until 1981-82, when women obtained 479,634 and men 473,364. In every year since then, more women received degrees than men.

Top 20 Colleges and Universities in Endowment Assets, 2001[1]

Source: National Association of College and University Business Officers (NACUBO)

College/University	Endowment assets[2]	College/University	Endowment assets[2]
1. Harvard University	$17,950,843	11. Washington University	$3,951,509
2. Yale University	10,700,000	12. University of Michigan	3,614,100
3. University of Texas System	9,363,588	13. University of Chicago	3,516,238
4. Princeton University	8,359,000	14. University of Pennsylvania	3,381,848
5. Stanford University	8,249,551	15. Northwestern University	3,256,282
6. Massachusetts Institute of Technology	6,134,712	16. Rice University	3,243,033
7. University of California	4,702,729	17. Cornell University	3,151,384
8. Emory University	4,315,998	18. Duke University	3,131,375
9. Columbia University	4,292,793	19. University of Notre Dame	2,829,914
10. The Texas A&M University System and Foundations	4,030,881	20. Dartmouth College	2,414,231

NOTE: Market value of endowment assets, excluding pledges and working capital. (1) As of June 30, 2001. (2) In thousands.

U.S. Higher Education Trends: Bachelor's Degrees Conferred

Source: National Center for Education Statistics, U.S. Dept. of Education

Figures for 2002-2003 and 2009-2010 are projected.

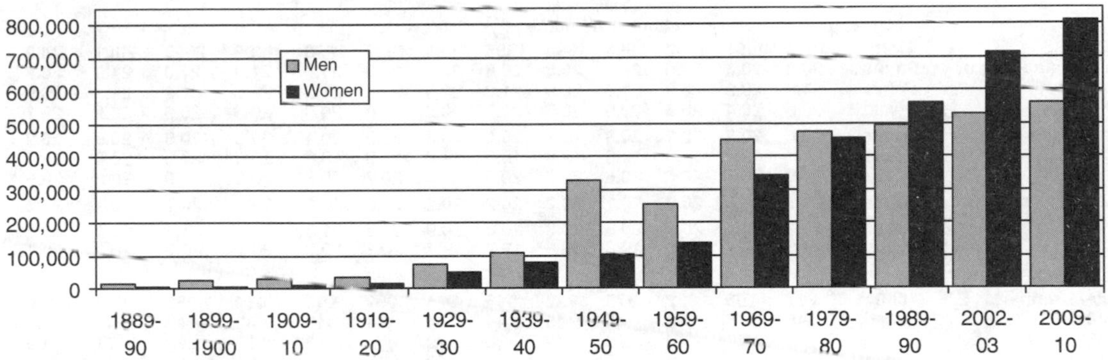

Financial Aid for College and Other Postsecondary Education

Reviewed by National Assoc. of Student Financial Aid Administrators

The cost of postsecondary education in the U.S. has increased in recent years, but financial aid, which may be in the form of grants (no repayment needed), loans, and/or work-study programs, is widely available to help families meet these expenses. Most aid is limited to family financial need as determined by standard formulas. Students interested in receiving aid are advised to apply, without making prior assumptions. Financial aid personnel at each school can provide information about programs available to students, steps to apply for them, and deadlines, all of which may vary.

First-time applicants for federal aid must file a Free Application for Federal Student Aid (FAFSA), generally as soon as possible after Jan. 1 for the academic year starting the following September. Figures provided must agree with federal income tax forms filed for the previous year. Other possible sources of aid include state governments, employers and unions, civic organizations, and the institutions themselves. There are also special federal programs that pay for postsecondary education in return for service: AmeriCorps (phone: 1-800-942-2677) and ROTC (phone: 1-800-USA-ROTC). Additional forms and certain fees may be required if a student is to be considered for institutional aid. Aid must be reapplied for annually.

A federal formula, based on information provided on the FAFSA, takes into account such factors as family after-tax income in the preceding calendar year, parental assets (excluding the parents' home) and length of time to retirement, and unusual expenses (such as very high medical expenses).

The resulting Expected Family Contribution, or EFC (which is divided among the family members—excluding parents—in college), is subtracted from the total cost of attendance for each person (including room and board or allowance for living costs) to determine financial need, and thus the maximum federal aid for which the family may be eligible. (Some institutions use a separate formula for need-based institutional aid.) Some schools guarantee to meet the full financial need of each admitted student; others try to do so but may fall short, depending on the availability of funds. Outside scholarships (even if non-need-based) are taken into account in determining need.

The aid package offered by each school may include one or more of the following resources: Federal Pell Grants, for those with greatest financial need; Federal Supplemental Educational Opportunity Grants, for those with relatively great financial need; grants from the school; Federal Work-Study or other work programs; low-interest Perkins loans; and subsidized and unsubsidized Stafford loans. For unsubsidized Stafford loans and all PLUS loans to parents, financial need is not a requirement. Loans have varying interest rates and other requirements. Repayment of Perkins and Stafford loans does not begin until after graduation; deferments are available under certain circumstances. For PLUS loans, parents must pass a credit check and begin repayment of both principal and interest while the student is still in school.

Certain federal income tax credits—dollar for dollar reductions of the amount of tax due—are available to families who meet income and other requirements; see the chapter on Taxes.

Rules for financial aid are complex and changeable. *The Student Guide*, a comprehensive resource on financial aid from the U.S. Dept. of Education, can be found at the website www.ed.gov/prog_info/SFA/StudentGuide

Further information and FAFSA forms are available from the school or from the Federal Student Aid Information Center, PO Box 84, Washington, DC 20044; phone: 1-800-4-FED-AID, Mon.-Fri., 8 AM - 8 PM Eastern Time. The Information Center also has a free booklet called *The EFC Formula Book*. FAFSA forms can be obtained online at www.fafsa.ed.gov

Average Salaries of U.S. College Professors, 2001-2002

Source: American Association of University Professors

TEACHING LEVEL		MEN Type of institution Public	Private/ Independent	Church-related	WOMEN Type of institution Public	Private/ Independent	Church-related
Doctoral level	Professor	$91,035	$114,193	$100,874	$82,626	$104,169	$93,077
	Associate	64,352	75,159	69,751	60,463	69,939	64,844
	Assistant	55,541	66,923	59,117	50,564	59,501	54,192
Master's level	Professor	73,526	78,231	75,100	70,497	74,305	68,015
	Associate	58,648	60,612	58,406	56,430	57,518	54,181
	Assistant	48,286	49,336	47,433	46,591	47,639	45,009
General 4-year	Professor	65,300	78,243	59,683	62,243	72,655	56,531
	Associate	53,384	55,886	48,889	50,941	53,752	47,168
	Assistant	44,596	46,040	41,017	42,852	44,712	40,110
2-year	Professor	62,806	54,036	45,483	58,510	49,391	45,773
	Associate	48,983	47,512	42,584	47,050	45,353	40,502
	Assistant	43,413	42,727	37,610	42,104	41,460	35,546

ACT (formerly American College Testing) Mean Scores and Characteristics of College-Bound Students, 1990-2002

Source: ACT, Inc.

(for school year ending in year shown)

SCORES[1]	Unit[1]	1990	1991	1992	1993	1994	1995	1996	1997	1998	1999	2000	2001	2002
Composite Scores	**Points**	**20.6**	**20.6**	**20.6**	**20.7**	**20.8**	**20.8**	**20.9**	**21.0**	**21.0**	**21.0**	**21.0**	**21.0**	**20.8**
Male	Points	21.0	20.9	20.9	21.0	20.9	21.0	21.0	21.1	21.2	21.1	21.2	21.1	20.9
Female	Points	20.3	20.4	20.5	20.5	20.7	20.7	20.8	20.8	20.9	20.9	20.9	20.9	20.7
English Score	**Points**	**20.5**	**20.3**	**20.2**	**20.3**	**20.3**	**20.2**	**20.3**	**20.3**	**20.4**	**20.5**	**20.5**	**20.5**	**20.2**
Male	Points	20.1	19.8	19.8	19.8	19.8	19.8	19.8	19.9	19.9	20.0	20.0	20.0	19.7
Female	Points	20.9	20.7	20.6	20.6	20.7	20.6	20.7	20.7	20.8	20.9	20.9	20.8	20.6
Math Score	**Points**	**19.9**	**20.0**	**20.0**	**20.1**	**20.2**	**20.2**	**20.2**	**20.6**	**20.8**	**20.7**	**20.7**	**20.7**	**20.6**
Male	Points	20.7	20.6	20.7	20.8	20.8	20.9	20.9	21.3	21.5	21.4	21.4	21.4	21.2
Female	Points	19.3	19.4	19.5	19.6	19.6	19.7	19.7	20.1	20.2	20.2	20.2	20.2	20.1
PARTICIPANTS														
Total Number	**(1000s)**	**817**	**796**	**832**	**875**	**892**	**945**	**925**	**959**	**995**	**1,019**	**1,065**	**1,070**	**1,116**
Male	Percent	46	45	45	45	45	44	44	44	43	43	43	43	44
White	Percent	79	79	79	79	79	80	79	74	76	72	72	71	69
Black	Percent	9	9	9	9	9	9	9	10	11	10	10	11	11
Composite Scores														
27 or above	Percent	12	11	12	12	13	13	13	14	14	14	14	14	13
18 or below	Percent	35	35	35	35	34	34	34	33	33	33	32	33	35

Note: Beginning with the Oct. 1989 test (1990 scores), an entirely new ACT Assessment was introduced. It is not possible to directly compare these data with data from earlier years. (1) Minimum point score, 1; maximum score, 36. Test scores and characteristics of college-bound students are based on the performance of all ACT-tested students who graduated in the spring of a given school year and took the ACT Assessment during junior or senior year of high school.

ACT Average Composite Scores by State, 2001-2002

Source: ACT, Inc.

STATE	Avg. Comp. Score	% Grads Taking ACT[1]	STATE	Avg. Comp. Score	% Grads Taking ACT[1]	STATE	Avg. Comp. Score	% Grads Taking ACT[1]	STATE	Avg. Comp. Score	% Grads Taking ACT[1]
Alabama	20.1	71	Illinois	20.1	99	Nebraska	21.7	72	Rhode Island	21.9	6
Alaska	21.3	31	Indiana	21.5	19	Nevada	21.3	36	South Carolina	19.2	32
Arizona	21.3	26	Iowa	22.0	66	New Hampshire	22.0	7	South Dakota	21.4	71
Arkansas	20.2	72	Kansas	21.6	76	New Jersey	20.7	5	Tennessee	20.0	79
California	21.4	13	Kentucky	20.0	72	New Mexico	20.0	63	Texas	20.1	32
Colorado	20.1	99	Louisiana	19.6	79	New York	22.2	14	Utah	21.4	66
Connecticut	21.6	5	Maine	22.5	6	North Carolina	19.9	13	Vermont	22.3	10
Delaware	21.3	4	Maryland	20.4	11	North Dakota	21.2	78	Virginia	20.6	11
District of Columbia	17.5	28	Masschusetts	21.9	8	Ohio	21.4	62	Washington	22.3	16
Florida	20.4	39	Michigan	21.3	68	Oklahoma	20.5	69	West Virginia	20.3	61
Georgia	19.8	20	Minnesota	22.1	65	Oregon	22.5	12	Wisconsin	22.2	68
Hawaii	2.02	18	Mississippi	18.6	84	Pennsylvania	21.5	7	Wyoming	21.4	64
Idaho	21.2	57	Missouri	21.5	68				**U.S. AVG.**	20.8	39
			Montana	21.7	52						

(1) Based on number of high school graduates in 2001, as projected by the Western Interstate Commission for Higher Education, and number of students in the class of 2001 who took the ACT.

SAT Mean Verbal and Math Scores of College-Bound Seniors, 1975-2002

Source: The College Board

(recentered scale; for school year ending in year shown)

	1975	1980	1985	1990	1995	1996	1997	1998	1999	2000	2001	2002
Verbal Scores	**512**	**502**	**509**	**500**	**504**	**505**	**505**	**505**	**505**	**505**	**506**	**504**
Male	515	506	514	505	505	507	507	509	509	507	509	507
Female	509	498	503	496	502	503	503	502	502	504	502	502
Math Scores	**498**	**492**	**500**	**501**	**506**	**508**	**511**	**512**	**511**	**514**	**514**	**516**
Male	518	515	522	521	525	527	530	531	531	533	533	534
Female	479	473	480	483	490	492	494	496	495	498	498	500

NOTE: In 1995, the College Board recentered the scoring scale for the SAT by reestablishing the original mean score of 500 on the 200-800 scale. Earlier scores have been adjusted to account for this recentering.

SAT Mean Scores by State, 1990 and 1998-2002

Source: The College Board

(recentered scale; for school year ending in year shown)

STATE	1990 V	1990 M	1998 V	1998 M	1999 V	1999 M	2000 V	2000 M	2001 V	2001 M	2002 V	2002 M	% Grads Taking SAT[1]
Alabama	545	534	562	558	561	555	559	555	559	554	560	559	9
Alaska	514	501	521	520	516	514	519	515	514	510	516	519	52
Arizona	521	520	525	528	524	525	521	523	523	525	520	523	36
Arkansas	545	532	568	555	563	556	563	554	562	550	560	556	5
California	494	508	497	516	497	514	497	518	498	517	496	517	52
Colorado	533	534	537	542	536	540	534	537	539	542	543	548	28
Connecticut	506	496	510	509	510	509	508	509	509	510	509	509	83
Delaware	510	496	501	493	503	497	502	496	501	499	502	500	69
District of Columbia	483	467	488	476	494	478	494	486	482	474	480	473	76
Florida	495	493	500	501	499	498	498	500	498	499	496	499	57
Georgia	478	473	486	482	487	482	488	486	491	489	489	491	65
Hawaii	480	505	483	513	482	513	488	519	486	515	488	520	53
Idaho	542	524	545	544	542	540	540	541	543	542	539	541	18
Illinois	542	547	564	581	569	585	568	586	576	589	578	596	11
Indiana	486	486	497	500	496	498	498	501	499	501	498	503	62
Iowa	584	588	593	601	594	598	589	600	593	603	591	602	5
Kansas	566	563	582	585	578	576	574	580	577	580	578	580	9
Kentucky	548	541	547	550	547	547	548	550	550	550	550	552	12
Louisiana	551	537	562	558	561	558	562	558	564	562	561	559	8
Maine	501	490	504	501	507	503	504	500	506	500	503	502	69
Maryland	506	502	506	508	507	507	507	509	508	510	507	513	67
Massachusetts	503	498	508	508	511	511	511	513	511	515	512	516	81
Michigan	529	534	558	569	557	565	557	569	561	572	558	572	11
Minnesota	552	558	585	598	586	598	581	594	580	589	581	591	10
Mississippi	552	538	562	549	563	548	562	549	566	551	559	547	4
Missouri	548	541	570	573	572	572	572	577	577	577	574	580	8
Montana	540	542	543	546	545	546	543	546	539	539	541	547	23
Nebraska	559	562	565	571	568	571	560	571	562	568	561	570	8
Nevada	511	511	510	513	512	517	510	517	509	515	509	518	34
New Hampshire	518	510	523	520	520	518	520	519	520	516	519	519	73
New Jersey	495	498	497	508	498	510	498	513	499	513	498	513	82
New Mexico	554	546	554	551	549	542	549	543	551	542	551	543	14
New York	489	496	495	503	495	502	494	506	495	505	494	506	79
North Carolina	478	470	490	492	493	493	492	496	493	499	493	505	67
North Dakota	579	578	590	599	594	605	588	609	592	599	507	610	4
Ohio	526	522	536	540	534	568	533	539	534	539	533	540	27
Oklahoma	553	542	568	564	567	560	563	560	567	561	565	562	8
Oregon	515	509	528	528	525	525	527	527	526	526	524	528	56
Pennsylvania	497	490	497	495	498	495	498	497	500	499	498	500	72
Rhode Island	498	488	501	495	504	499	505	500	501	499	504	503	73
South Carolina	475	467	478	473	479	475	484	482	486	488	488	493	59
South Dakota	580	570	584	581	585	588	587	588	577	582	576	586	5
Tennessee	558	544	564	557	559	553	563	553	562	553	562	555	14
Texas	490	489	494	501	494	499	493	500	493	499	491	500	55
Utah	566	555	572	570	570	568	570	569	575	570	563	559	6
Vermont	507	493	508	504	514	506	513	508	511	506	512	510	69
Virginia	501	496	507	499	508	499	509	500	510	501	510	506	68
Washington	513	511	524	526	525	526	526	528	527	527	525	529	54
West Virginia	520	514	525	513	527	512	526	511	527	512	525	515	18
Wisconsin	552	559	581	594	584	595	584	597	584	596	583	599	7
Wyoming	534	538	548	546	546	551	545	545	547	545	531	537	11
NATIONAL AVG.	**500**	**501**	**505**	**512**	**505**	**511**	**505**	**514**	**506**	**514**	**504**	**516**	**46**

NOTE: In 1995, the College Board recentered the scoring scale for the SAT by reestablishing the original mean score of 500 on the 200-800 scale. The College Board states that comparing states or ranking them on the basis of SAT scores alone is invalid, and the College Board discourages doing so. (1) Based on number of high school graduates in 2002, as projected by the Western Interstate Commission for Higher Education, and number of students in the class of 2002 who took the SAT.

Average SAT Scores by Parental Education, 2002

Source: The College Board

(Deviation in points from mean score shown by highest level of educational attainment of test taker's parent. Mean 2002 verbal score was 504. Mean 2002 math score was 516.)

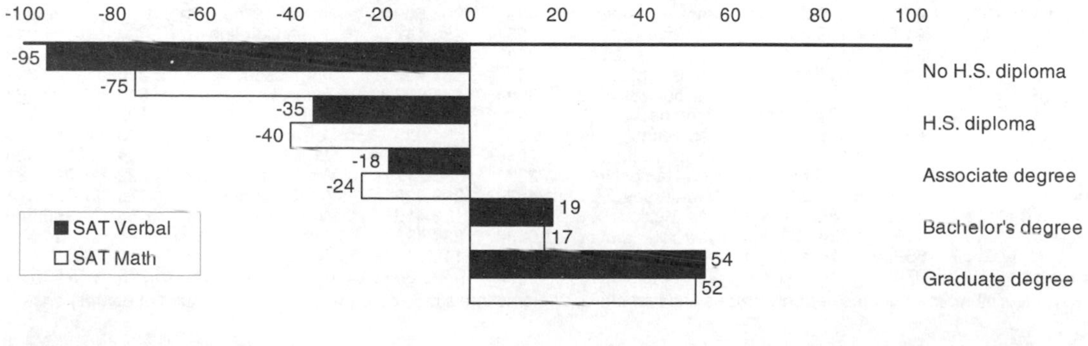

Top 50 Public Libraries in the U.S. and Canada, 2002

Source: Public Library Data Service, Statistical Report 2002, Public Library Association

Ranked at end of the 2001 fiscal year by population served.

Population served	Library name and location	No. of branches[1]	No. of holdings	Circulation	Annual acquisition expenditures
3,694,820	Los Angeles Public Library (CA)	67	6,023,257	11,727,095	$9,603,561
3,484,800	Los Angeles Public Library, County of (CA)	84	8,255,100	14,699,904	7,435,398
3,313,573	New York Public Library	84	10,608,570	13,486,215	13,233,195
2,896,016	Chicago Public Library (IL)	78	10,994,943	7,029,976	10,000,000
2,481,494	Toronto Public Library (ON)	97	8,046,502	27,697,666	8,460,432
2,465,326	Brooklyn Public Library (NY)	59	7,189,998	11,340,237	9,879,766
2,229,379	Queens Borough Public Library (NY)	62	10,357,159	16,829,291	10,170,110
1,924,770	Houston Public Library (TX)	37	4,426,737	6,060,702	6,558,555
1,896,495	Miami-Dade Public Library System (FL)	32	3,538,382	4,686,791	5,685,687
1,623,018	Broward County Libraries Division (FL)	36	2,270,000	7,894,672	7,798,575
1,517,550	Philadelphia, The Free Library of (PA)	54	6,225,098	6,668,923	7,724,599
1,462,500	San Antonio Public Library (TX)	18	1,982,577	4,586,483	3,155,312
1,350,435	Phoenix Public Library (AZ)	12	2,015,587	9,150,821	4,286,213
1,336,449	Carnegie Library of Pittsburgh (PA)	19	2,338,528	3,009,354	3,344,977
1,301,100	San Diego Public Library (CA)	34	4,999,256	6,587,877	3,904,374
1,211,537	Hawaii State Public Library System (HI)	49	3,282,457	6,748,048	3,407,950
1,188,580	Dallas Public Library (TX)	22	4,735,702	4,291,781	4,047,496
1,178,553	Harris County Public Library (TX)	25	1,885,146	5,076,955	2,830,048
1,137,943	Las Vegas-Clark County Library District (NV)	24	2,230,308	6,174,743	5,794,683
1,115,440	King County Library System (WA)	43	8,128,576	14,097,008	7,690,783
1,090,000	San Bernardino County Library (CA)	28	1,177,779	2,502,570	1,809,218
1,003,099	Fairfax County Public Library (VA)	21	2,599,280	11,492,624	6,586,510
1,001,838	Providence Public Library (RI)	9	1,073,628	815,544	1,130,371
998,948	Tampa-Hillsborough County Public Library (FL)	21	2,199,593	4,463,097	4,072,966
965,413	San Diego County Library (CA)	31	1,257,267	3,253,781	3,158,860
951,270	Detroit Public Library (MI)	24	3,088,277	1,041,468	2,290,736
950,265	Buffalo & Erie County Public Library (NY)	51	3,391,780	7,671,078	4,813,682
918,800	San Jose Public Library (CA)	17	1,888,457	9,408,793	3,006,134
876,519	Calgary Public Library (AB)	15	2,080,021	11,657,785	3,258,638
873,490	St. Louis County Library District (MO)	18	2,543,767	8,245,073	4,664,203
873,341	Montgomery County Dept. of Public Libraries (MD)	22	2,580,534	10,677,210	6,170,510
868,825	Memphis/Shelby County Public Library & Info. Ctr. (TN)	22	1,977,070	3,337,361	3,341,115
860,000	Orange County Library System (FL)	13	1,967,249	4,614,409	3,666,013
847,591	Tucson-Pima Public Library (AZ)	18	1,255,629	5,524,253	3,207,550
845,303	Cincinnati & Hamilton County, The Public Lib. of (OH)	41	9,952,009	13,808,229	8,106,419
845,000	Atlanta-Fulton Public Library (GA)	32	2,318,149	2,994,202	3,364,694
835,600	Contra Costa County Library (CA)	22	1,182,663	3,819,549	1,979,502
832,162	Indianapolis-Marion County Public Library (IN)	22	2,129,268	11,444,749	5,433,100
801,515	Prince George's County Memorial Library System (MD)	18	2,087,716	3,929,152	3,890,391
798,140	Fresno County Library (CA)	34	984,442	2,176,071	1,876,493
790,770	Columbus Metropolitan Library (OH)	20	2,940,503	14,370,089	8,129,751
790,000	Ottawa Public Library (ON)	33	2,204,614	6,954,246	2,594,257
778,979	Jacksonville Public Library (FL)	14	2,345,481	4,315,518	2,505,745
776,733	San Francisco Public Library (CA)	26	2,276,202	5,438,451	5,026,357
747,692	Palm Beach County Library System (FL)	14	1,184,413	5,326,147	4,067,670
735,343	Rochester Public Library (NY)	10	1,143,337	1,742,332	1,418,274
734,523	Baltimore County Public Library (MD)	16	1,880,922	9,561,701	5,112,034
733,415	Hennepin County Library (MN)	26	2,000,000	11,180,881	4,706,712
720,490	Charlotte & Mecklenburg County, Pub. Lib. of (NC)	22	1,714,062	6,376,531	3,319,259
693,604	Louisville Free Public Library (KY)	16	1,256,466	3,473,508	3,014,241

(1) Main branch not included.

Number of Public Libraries and Operating Income, by State, 2000

Source: Public Libraries Survey, National Center for Education Statistics, U.S. Dept. of Education

(data for fiscal year 2000; operating income in thousands)

STATE	No. of libraries[1]	Operating income[2]
Alabama	275	$64,927
Alaska	104	24,458
Arizona	170	110,803
Arkansas	209	38,531
California	1,065	830,267
Colorado	243	158,704
Connecticut	242	137,326
Delaware	35	14,513
District of Columbia	27	25,669
Florida	466	355,388
Georgia	367	143,396
Hawaii	50	22,789
Idaho	142	23,811
Illinois	786	481,279
Indiana	426	224,581
Iowa	559	70,422
Kansas	370	70,936
Kentucky	190	$72,818
Louisiana	327	112,091
Maine	278	26,059
Maryland	179	174,458
Massachusetts	489	205,569
Michigan	655	288,142
Minnesota	359	146,199
Mississippi	241	35,998
Missouri	359	146,528
Montana	107	16,021
Nebraska	255	34,635
Nevada	83	63,119
New Hampshire	237	33,217
New Jersey	452	299,426
New Mexico	99	29,416
New York	1,083	834,402
North Carolina	372	145,107
North Dakota	87	8,134
Ohio	716	$680,401
Oklahoma	210	61,141
Oregon	206	108,554
Pennsylvania	631	235,416
Rhode Island	72	33,990
South Carolina	183	71,918
South Dakota	139	13,618
Tennessee	280	73,891
Texas	816	294,967
Utah	105	54,114
Vermont	193	12,640
Virginia	334	178,385
Washington	322	218,086
West Virginia	175	NA
Wisconsin	454	156,649
Wyoming	74	14,539
U.S. TOTAL	**16,298**	**$7,702,768**

NA = Not available. (1) Includes central libraries and branches. (2) Some totals may be underestimated because of nonresponse.

American Colleges and Universities

General Information for the 2001–2002 Academic Year

Source: Peterson's, part of The Thomson Corporation, Copyright 2002

These listings **include only accredited undergraduate degree-granting institutions** in the United States and the U.S. territories **with a total enrollment of 1,000 or more.** Four-year colleges (which award a bachelor's degree as their highest undergraduate degree) are listed first, followed by two-year colleges (which generally award an associate as their highest or primary undergraduate degree). Data reported **only for institutions that provided adequate updated information** on Peterson's Annual Survey of Undergraduate Institutions for the 2001–2002 academic year.

All institutions are coeducational except those where the ZIP code is followed directly by: (1)–men only, (2)–primarily men, (3)–women only, (4)–primarily women.

The **Tuition & Fees** column shows the annual tuition and required fees for full-time students, or, where indicated, the tuition and standard fees per unit for part-time students. Where tuition costs vary according to residence, the figure is given for the most local resident and is coded: (A)–area residents, (S)–state residents; all other figures apply to all students regardless of residence. Where annual expenses are expressed as a lump sum (including full-time tuition, mandatory fees, and room and board), the figure is coded: (C)–comprehensive fee. **Rm. & Board** is the average cost for one academic year.

Control: 1–independent (nonprofit), 2–independent-religious, 3–proprietary (profit-making), 4–federal, 5–state, 6–commonweath (Puerto Rico), 7–territory (U.S. territories), 8–county, 9–district, 10–city, 11–state and local, 12–state-related, 13–private (unspecified). **Degree** means the highest degree offered (B–bachelor's, M–master's, F–first professional, D–doctorate). Where no letter is given, as for most two-year colleges, the highest degree offered is the associate degree.

Enrollment is the total number of matriculated undergraduate and (if applicable) graduate students. **Faculty** is the total number of faculty members teaching undergraduate courses and (if available) graduate courses.

NA or a **dash** indicates category is inapplicable or data not available. **NR** indicates data not reported.

Four-Year Colleges

Name, address	Year Founded	Tuition & Fees	Rm. & Board	Control, Degree	Enrollment	Faculty
Abilene Christian Univ, Abilene, TX 79699-9100	1906	$11,650	$4,650	2-D	4,673	323
Acad of Art Coll, San Francisco, CA 94105-3410	1929	$12,060	$8,400	3-M	6,282	587
Adams State Coll, Alamosa, CO 81102	1921	$2,367 (S)	$5,607	5-M	2,417	138
Adelphi Univ, Garden City, NY 11530	1896	$16,270	$7,050	1-D	6,331	565
Adrian Coll, Adrian, MI 49221-2575	1859	$14,850	$4,850	2-B	1,055	108
Alabama Agr & Mech Univ, Normal, AL 35762	1875	$2,820 (S)	$4,500	5-D	5,523	307
Alabama State Univ, Montgomery, AL 36101-0271	1867	$2,904 (S)	$3,500	5-M	5,590	356
Albany State Univ, Albany, GA 31705-2717	1903	$2,476 (S)	$3,406	5-M	3,456	190
Albertus Magnus Coll, New Haven, CT 06511-1189	1925	$15,246	$6,908	2-M	2,278	68
Albion Coll, Albion, MI 49224-1831	1835	$19,620	$5,604	2-B	1,548	125
Albright Coll, Reading, PA 19612-5234	1856	$21,300	$6,342	2-B	1,809	128
Alcorn State Univ, Alcorn State, MS 39096-7500	1871	$3,203 (S)	$3,090	5-M	3,096	196
Alfred Univ, Alfred, NY 14802-1205	1836	$10,480 (S)	$8,016	1-D	2,443	206
Allegheny Coll, Meadville, PA 16335	1815	$22,490	$5,290	2-B	1,879	161
Alliant Intl Univ, San Diego, CA 92131-1799	1952	$14,340	$6,180	1-D	1,926	118
Alma Coll, Alma, MI 48801-1599	1886	$16,602	$5,984	2-B	1,366	119
Alvernia Coll, Reading, PA 19607-1799	1958	$14,140	$6,650	2-M	1,815	184
Alverno Coll, Milwaukee, WI 53234-3922 (3)	1887	$12,150	$4,780	2-M	1,952	191
Amberton Univ, Garland, TX 75041-5595	1971	$4,050	NA	2-M	1,648	39
American Coll of Computer & Information Sci, Birmingham, AL 35205	1988	NA	NA	3-M	11,000	26
American InterContinental Univ, Atlanta, GA 30326-1016	1977	$12,600	$4,835	3-B	1,292	110
American InterContinental Univ, Atlanta, GA 30328	NR	$22,050	NA	3-M	1,248	119
American Intl Coll, Springfield, MA 01109-3189	1885	$14,800	$7,468	1-D	1,509	155
American Univ, Washington, DC 20016-8001	1893	$22,481	$9,063	2-D	10,693	NA
American Univ of Puerto Rico, Bayamón, PR 00960-2037	1963	$3,578	NA	1-B	4,537	222
Amherst Coll, Amherst, MA 01002-5000	1821	$27,258	$7,100	1-B	1,631	207
Anderson Coll, Anderson, SC 29621-4035	1911	$11,395	$5,040	2-B	1,450	109
Anderson Univ, Anderson, IN 46012-3495	1917	$15,380	$5,020	2-D	2,426	223
Andrews Univ, Berrien Springs, MI 49104	1874	$13,676	$4,420	2-D	2,721	261
Angelo State Univ, San Angelo, TX 76909	1928	$2,722 (S)	$4,810	5-M	6,262	261
Anna Maria Coll, Paxton, MA 01612	1946	$16,500	$6,300	2-M	1,264	163
Appalachian State Univ, Boone, NC 28608	1899	$2,308 (S)	$4,045	5-D	13,762	921
Aquinas Coll, Grand Rapids, MI 49506-1799	1886	$14,876	$5,176	2-M	2,571	206
Arcadia Univ, Glenside, PA 19038-3295	1853	$18,670	$7,980	2-D	2,992	289
Argosy Univ-Sarasota, Sarasota, FL 34235-8246	1974	NA	NA	3	NA	NA
Arizona State Univ, Tempe, AZ 85287	1885	$2,488 (S)	$5,416	5-D	45,693	1,814
Arizona State Univ East, Mesa, AZ 85212	1995	$2,412 (S)	$4,740	5-M	2,403	84
Arizona State Univ West, Phoenix, AZ 85069-7100	1984	$2,488 (S)	NA	5-M	5,804	311
Arkansas State Univ, State University, AR 72467	1909	$4,270 (S)	$3,210	5-D	10,568	543
Arkansas Tech Univ, Russellville, AR 72801-2222	1909	$2,976 (S)	$3,280	5-M	5,576	300
Armstrong Atlantic State Univ, Savannah, GA 31419-1997	1935	$2,314 (S)	$4,770	5-M	5,747	361
Art Ctr Coll of Design, Pasadena, CA 91103-1999	1930	$21,110	NA	1-M	1,465	409
The Art Inst of Colorado, Denver, CO 80203	1952	$19,840	$7,400	3-B	2,253	167
The Art Inst of Fort Lauderdale, Fort Lauderdale, FL 33316-3000	1968	$319	$4,480	3-B	3,500	110
The Art Inst of Phoenix, Phoenix, AZ 85021-2859 (2)	1995	$14,304	$5,324	3-B	1,122	71
Asbury Coll, Wilmore, KY 40390-1198	1890	$14,764	$3,794	2-M	1,352	153
Ashland Univ, Ashland, OH 44805-3702	1878	$16,320	$5,862	2-D	6,359	222
Assumption Coll, Worcester, MA 01609-1296	1904	$18,945	$7,375	2-M	2,422	193
Athens State Univ, Athens, AL 35611-1902	1822	$2,730 (S)	$900	5-B	2,573	117
Auburn Univ, Auburn University, AL 36849	1856	$3,380 (S)	$2,130	5-D	22,469	1,230
Auburn Univ Montgomery, Montgomery, AL 36124-4023	1967	$3,440 (S)	$4,770	5-D	4,982	318
Audrey Cohen Coll, New York, NY 10013-1919 (4)	1964	$14,505	NA	1-M	1,519	184
Augsburg Coll, Minneapolis, MN 55454-1351	1869	$17,438	$5,540	2-M	2,911	296
Augustana Coll, Rock Island, IL 61201-2296	1860	$18,720	$5,397	2-B	2,232	209
Augustana Coll, Sioux Falls, SD 57197	1860	$15,460	$4,478	2-M	1,807	170
Augusta State Univ, Augusta, GA 30904-2200	1925	$2,282 (S)	NA	5-M	5,407	282
Aurora Univ, Aurora, IL 60506-4892	1893	$13,767	$5,133	1-D	2,801	88
Austin Coll, Sherman, TX 75090-4400	1849	$16,537	$6,234	2-M	1,261	116
Austin Peay State Univ, Clarksville, TN 37044-0001	1927	$3,208 (S)	$3,670	5-M	7,033	463
Averett Univ, Danville, VA 24541-3692	1859	$14,990	$5,000	2-M	2,396	244
Avila Coll, Kansas City, MO 64145-1698	1916	$13,420	$5,150	2-M	1,644	174

Name, address	Year Founded	Tuition & Fees	Rm. & Board	Control, Degree	Enroll-ment	Faculty
Azusa Pacific Univ, Azusa, CA 91702-7000	1899	$17,495	$6,230	2-D	6,835	736
Babson Coll, Babson Park, MA 02457-0310	1919	$24,544	$8,746	1-M	3,328	201
Baker Coll of Auburn Hills, Auburn Hills, MI 48326-1586	1911	$5,580	NA	1-B	2,192	115
Baker Coll of Cadillac, Cadillac, MI 49601	1986	$5,580	NA	1-B	1,021	73
Baker Coll of Clinton Township, Clinton Township, MI 48035-4701	1990	$5,580	NA	1-B	3,091	133
Baker Coll of Flint, Flint, MI 48507-5508	1911	$5,580	$1,950	1-B	4,399	173
Baker Coll of Jackson, Jackson, MI 49202	1994	$5,580	$1,950	1-B	1,238	90
Baker Coll of Muskegon, Muskegon, MI 49442-3497	1888	$5,580	$1,950	1-B	2,924	145
Baker Coll of Owosso, Owosso, MI 48867-4400	1984	$5,580	NA	1-B	2,062	103
Baker Coll of Port Huron, Port Huron, MI 48060-2597	1990	$5,580	NA	1-B	1,301	95
Baker Univ, Baldwin City, KS 66006-0065	1858	$12,900	$4,880	2-B	1,002	109
Baldwin-Wallace Coll, Berea, OH 44017-2088	1845	$16,330	$5,680	2-M	4,884	365
Ball State Univ, Muncie, IN 47306-1099	1918	$4,034 (S)	$5,100	5-D	19,408	1,097
Bard Coll, Annandale-on-Hudson, NY 12504	1860	$26,170	$7,742	1-D	1,515	203
Barnard Coll, New York, NY 10027-6598 (3)	1889	$24,036	$9,658	1-B	2,261	293
Barry Univ, Miami Shores, FL 33161-6695	1940	$17,500	$6,600	2-D	8,691	806
Barton Coll, Wilson, NC 27893-7000	1902	$13,084	$4,754	2-B	1,229	100
Bates Coll, Lewiston, ME 04240-6028	1855	$34,100 (C)	NA	1-B	1,767	183
Bayamón Central Univ, Bayamón, PR 00960-1725	1970	$3,740	NA	2-M	3,269	203
Baylor Univ, Waco, TX 76798	1845	$17,214	$5,714	2-D	14,221	813
Becker Coll, Worcester, MA 01609	1784	$13,750	$7,180	1-B	1,298	107
Belhaven Coll, Jackson, MS 39202-1789	1883	$11,600	$4,440	2-M	1,883	193
Bellarmine Univ, Louisville, KY 40205-0671	1950	$17,010	$5,300	2-M	2,248	235
Bellevue Univ, Bellevue, NE 68005-3098	1965	$4,085	NA	1-M	3,925	140
Belmont Univ, Nashville, TN 37212-3757	1951	$13,400	$5,666	2-D	3,129	387
Beloit Coll, Beloit, WI 53511-5596	1846	$23,236	$5,268	1-B	1,273	122
Bemidji State Univ, Bemidji, MN 56601-2699	1919	$4,164 (S)	$4,158	5-M	4,660	257
Benedict Coll, Columbia, SC 29204	1870	$9,764	$5,050	2-B	2,936	169
Benedictine Coll, Atchison, KS 66002-1499	1859	$13,795	$5,300	2-M	1,348	84
Benedictine Univ, Lisle, IL 60532-0900	1887	$15,630	$5,700	2-D	2,700	218
Bentley Coll, Waltham, MA 02452-4705	1917	$20,061	$9,010	1-M	5,587	422
Berea Coll, Berea, KY 40404	1855	$205	$4,099	1-B	1,674	150
Berklee Coll of Music, Boston, MA 02215-3693	1945	$18,769	$9,790	1-B	3,415	498
Bernard M. Baruch Coll of the City Univ of New York, New York, NY 10010	1919	$3,350 (S)	NA	11-D	15,821	873
Berry Coll, Mount Berry, GA 30149-0159	1902	$13,450	$5,730	2-M	2,038	179
Bethel Coll, Mishawaka, IN 46545-5591	1947	$13,400	$4,350	2-M	1,660	106
Bethel Coll, St. Paul, MN 55112-6999	1871	$17,735	$6,200	2-M	2,991	288
Bethune-Cookman Coll, Daytona Beach, FL 32114-3099	1904	$9,617	$6,129	2-B	2,724	202
Biola Univ, La Mirada, CA 90639-0001	1908	$18,454	$5,930	2-D	4,317	315
Birmingham-Southern Coll, Birmingham, AL 35254	1856	$17,185	$5,980	2-M	1,424	131
Bloomfield Coll, Bloomfield, NJ 07003-9981	1868	$11,450	$5,550	2-B	1,785	196
Bloomsburg Univ of Pennsylvania, Bloomsburg, PA 17815-1301	1839	$4,992 (S)	$4,442	5-M	7,914	394
Bluefield State Coll, Bluefield, WV 24701-2198	1895	$2,288 (S)	NA	5-B	2,768	198
Bluffton Coll, Bluffton, OH 45817-1196	1899	$16,430	$5,636	2-M	1,020	106
Boise State Univ, Boise, ID 83725-0399	1932	$2,665 (S)	$3,869	5-D	17,100	912
Boricua Coll, New York, NY 10032-1560	1974	$7,350	NA	1-M	1,520	116
Boston Coll, Chestnut Hill, MA 02467-3800	1863	$24,470	$8,860	2-D	13,510	1,120
Boston Univ, Boston, MA 02215	1839	$26,228	$8,750	1-D	27,756	3,283
Bowdoin Coll, Brunswick, ME 04011	1794	$27,280	$7,000	1-B	1,635	186
Bowie State Univ, Bowie, MD 20715-9465	1865	$3,782 (S)	$5,440	5-D	5,181	312
Bowling Green State Univ, Bowling Green, OH 43403	1910	$5,604 (S)	$5,190	5-D	18,739	1,082
Bradley Univ, Peoria, IL 61625-0002	1897	$15,340	$5,630	1-M	5,996	516
Brandeis Univ, Waltham, MA 02454-9110	1948	$27,076	$7,405	1-D	4,882	470
Brewton-Parker Coll, Mt. Vernon, GA 30445-0197	1904	$8,000	$3,700	2-B	1,219	225
Briarcliffe Coll, Bethpage, NY 11714	1966	$11,400	NA	3-B	2,608	160
Bridgewater Coll, Bridgewater, VA 22812-1599	1880	$16,090	$7,860	2-B	1,260	97
Bridgewater State Coll, Bridgewater, MA 02325-0001	1840	$2,823 (S)	$4,996	5-M	9,038	462
Brigham Young Univ-Hawaii, Laie, HI 96762-1294	1955	$2,490	$4,400	2-B	2,278	183
Brigham Young Univ, Provo, UT 84602-1001	1875	$3,060	$4,780	2-D	32,771	2,066
Brooklyn Coll of the City Univ of New York, Brooklyn, NY 11210-2889	1930	$3,393 (S)	NA	11-M	15,137	935
Brown Univ, Providence, RI 02912	1764	$27,172	$7,578	1-D	7,774	758
Bryant Coll, Smithfield, RI 02917-1284	1863	$19,776	$7,776	1-M	3,494	208
Bryn Mawr Coll, Bryn Mawr, PA 19010-2899 (3)	1885	$24,990	$8,590	1-D	1,756	184
Bucknell Univ, Lewisburg, PA 17837	1846	$25,335	$5,761	1-M	3,587	314
Buena Vista Univ, Storm Lake, IA 50588	1891	$17,846	$4,982	2-M	1,392	115
Butler Univ, Indianapolis, IN 46208-3485	1855	$19,130	$6,450	1-F	4,264	438
Cabrini Coll, Radnor, PA 19087-3698	1957	$18,090	$7,860	2-M	2,100	198
Caldwell Coll, Caldwell, NJ 07006-6195	1939	$14,190	$6,600	2-M	2,238	190
California Baptist Univ, Riverside, CA 92504-3206	1950	$11,690	$5,046	2-M	2,090	188
California Coll for Health Sci, National City, CA 91950-6605	1978	$399	NA	3-M	7,380	19
California Coll of Arts & Crafts, San Francisco, CA 94107	1907	$20,690	$6,776	1-M	1,291	326
California Inst of Tech, Pasadena, CA 91125-0001	1891	$22,119	$6,999	1-D	2,058	322
California Inst of the Arts, Valencia, CA 91355-2340	1961	$22,535	$6,000	1-M	1,249	267
California Lutheran Univ, Thousand Oaks, CA 91360-2787	1959	$18,800	$6,656	2-M	2,857	241
California Polytechnic State Univ, San Luis Obispo, CA 93407	1901	$2,153 (S)	$6,594	5-M	18,079	1,161
California State Polytechnic Univ, Pomona, Pomona, CA 91768-2557	1938	$1,772 (S)	$6,843	5-M	19,041	1,205
California State Univ, Bakersfield, Bakersfield, CA 93311-1099	1970	$1,797 (S)	$5,400	5-M	7,050	484
California State Univ, Chico, Chico, CA 95929-0722	1887	$2,086 (S)	$6,973	5-M	16,704	1,014
California State Univ, Dominguez Hills, Carson, CA 90747-0001	1960	$1,800 (S)	$6,156	5-M	12,871	762
California State Univ, Fresno, Fresno, CA 93740-8027	1911	$1,762 (S)	$6,000	5-D	20,007	1,190
California State Univ, Fullerton, Fullerton, CA 92834-9480	1957	$1,849 (S)	$3,993	5-M	30,357	1,822
California State Univ, Hayward, Hayward, CA 94542-3000	1957	$1,767 (S)	$3,200	5-M	13,240	761
California State Univ, Long Beach, Long Beach, CA 90840	1949	$1,744 (S)	$5,800	5-M	33,259	1,924
California State Univ, Los Angeles, Los Angeles, CA 90032-8530	1947	$1,782 (S)	$6,399	5-D	20,675	1,155
California State Univ, Monterey Bay, Seaside, CA 93955-8001	1994	$928 (S)	$5,220	5-M	3,020	280
California State Univ, Northridge, Northridge, CA 91330	1958	$1,814 (S)	$6,400	5-M	31,448	1,746
California State Univ, Sacramento, Sacramento, CA 95819-6048	1947	$1,887 (S)	$5,601	5-D	26,923	1,473
California State Univ, San Bernardino, San Bernardino, CA 92407-2397	1965	$1,733 (S)	$4,783	5-M	15,985	588
California State Univ, San Marcos, San Marcos, CA 92096-0001	1990	$1,706 (S)	NA	5-M	5,676	398
California State Univ, Stanislaus, Turlock, CA 95382	1957	$1,875 (S)	$7,020	5-M	7,534	463

Name, address	Year Founded	Tuition & Fees	Rm. & Board	Control, Degree	Enroll-ment	Faculty
California Univ of Pennsylvania, California, PA 15419-1394	1852	$5,204 (S)	$5,134	5-M	5,948	334
Calvin Coll, Grand Rapids, MI 49546-4388	1876	$14,870	$5,180	2-M	4,258	353
Cambridge Coll, Cambridge, MA 02138-5304	1971	$9,150	NA	1-M	2,700	50
Cameron Univ, Lawton, OK 73505-6377	1908	$2,300 (S)	$2,830	5-M	5,262	289
Campbellsville Univ, Campbellsville, KY 42718-2799	1906	$10,070	$4,400	2-M	1,777	188
Campbell Univ, Buies Creek, NC 27506	1887	$12,849	$4,550	2-D	3,862	288
Canisius Coll, Buffalo, NY 14208-1098	1870	$17,536	$7,160	2-M	4,870	465
Capital Univ, Columbus, OH 43209-2394	1830	$17,990	$5,640	2-F	3,843	444
Cardinal Stritch Univ, Milwaukee, WI 53217-3985	1937	$12,780	$4,840	2-D	5,855	397
Caribbean Univ, Bayamón, PR 00960-0493	1969	$3,000	NA	1-M	3,352	158
Carleton Coll, Northfield, MN 55057-4001	1866	$25,530	$5,250	1-B	1,948	223
Carlow Coll, Pittsburgh, PA 15213-3165 (4)	1929	$13,876	$5,490	2-M	1,898	217
Carnegie Mellon Univ, Pittsburgh, PA 15213-3891	1900	$25,872	$7,264	1-D	8,588	874
Carroll Coll, Helena, MT 59625-0002	1909	$12,816	$5,168	2-B	1,347	125
Carroll Coll, Waukesha, WI 53186-5593	1846	$16,200	$4,970	2-M	2,921	243
Carson-Newman Coll, Jefferson City, TN 37760	1851	$12,890	$4,350	2-M	2,195	177
Carthage Coll, Kenosha, WI 53140-1994	1847	$18,205	$5,465	2-M	2,345	147
Case Western Reserve Univ, Cleveland, OH 44106	1826	$21,168	$6,250	1-D	9,216	562
Castleton State Coll, Castleton, VT 05735	1787	$5,654 (S)	$5,782	5-M	1,656	167
Catawba Coll, Salisbury, NC 28144-2488	1851	$14,540	$5,080	2-M	1,453	126
The Catholic Univ of America, Washington, DC 20064	1887	$20,950	$8,382	2-D	5,510	642
Cedar Crest Coll, Allentown, PA 18104-6196 (3)	1867	$18,680	$6,465	2-B	1,619	86
Cedarville Univ, Cedarville, OH 45314-0601	1887	$12,624	$4,929	2-M	2,951	221
Centenary Coll, Hackettstown, NJ 07840-2100	1867	$16,030	$6,400	2-M	1,645	106
Centenary Coll of Louisiana, Shreveport, LA 71134-1188	1825	$15,800	$4,800	2-M	1,049	115
Central Coll, Pella, IA 50219-1999	1853	$15,714	$5,492	2-B	1,425	135
Central Connecticut State Univ, New Britain, CT 06050-4010	1849	$4,374 (S)	$6,030	5-M	12,368	801
Central Methodist Coll, Fayette, MO 65248-1198	1854	$12,790	$4,820	2-M	1,281	97
Central Michigan Univ, Mount Pleasant, MI 48859	1892	$4,366 (S)	$5,220	5-D	27,797	1,072
Central Missouri State Univ, Warrensburg, MO 64093	1871	$3,510 (S)	$4,410	5-M	10,822	561
Central State Univ, Wilberforce, OH 45384	1887	$3,714 (S)	$5,208	5-M	1,400	127
Central Washington Univ, Ellensburg, WA 98926-7463	1891	$3,348 (S)	$5,220	5-M	8,826	507
Centre Coll, Danville, KY 40422-1394	1819	$18,000	$6,000	2-B	1,070	104
Chadron State Coll, Chadron, NE 69337	1911	$2,481 (S)	$3,828	5-M	2,804	120
Chaminade Univ of Honolulu, Honolulu, HI 96816-1578	1955	$12,705	$5,990	2-M	2,547	318
Champlain Coll, Burlington, VT 05402-0670	1878	$11,605	$8,075	1-B	2,523	193
Chapman Univ, Orange, CA 92866	1861	$23,316	$8,082	2-F	4,192	465
Charleston Southern Univ, Charleston, SC 29423-8087	1964	$12,368	$4,754	2-M	2,682	202
Charter Oak State Coll, New Britain, CT 06053-2142	1973	$125/credit (S)	NA	5-B	1,496	69
Chatham Coll, Pittsburgh, PA 15232-2826 (3)	1869	$18,960	$6,494	1-D	1,065	80
Chestnut Hill Coll, Philadelphia, PA 19118-2693	1924	$17,620	$7,170	2-D	1,645	258
Cheyney Univ of Pennsylvania, Cheyney, PA 19319	1837	$4,071 (S)	$5,322	5-M	1,514	129
Chicago State Univ, Chicago, IL 60628	1867	$3,434 (S)	$5,825	5-M	7,079	439
Christian Brothers Univ, Memphis, TN 38104-5581	1871	$15,300	$4,520	2-M	2,123	196
Christopher Newport Univ, Newport News, VA 23606-2998	1960	$3,112 (S)	$5,750	5-M	5,388	315
The Citadel, The Military Coll of South Carolina, Charleston, SC 29409 (2)	1842	$4,601 (S)	$4,525	5-M	4,001	196
City Coll of the City Univ of New York, New York, NY 10031-9198	1847	$3,200 (S)	NA	11-F	10,824	902
City Univ, Bellevue, WA 98005	1973	$7,280	NA	1-M	7,124	1,095
Claflin Univ, Orangeburg, SC 29115	1869	$8,290	$4,445	2-B	1,460	96
Claremont McKenna Coll, Claremont, CA 91711	1946	$24,540	$8,160	1-B	1,044	160
Clarion Univ of Pennsylvania, Clarion, PA 16214	1867	$4,359 (S)	$2,420	5-M	6,271	292
Clark Atlanta Univ, Atlanta, GA 30314	1865	$12,538	$6,054	2-D	4,882	328
Clarke Coll, Dubuque, IA 52001-3198	1843	$15,120	$5,505	2-M	1,201	137
Clarkson Univ, Potsdam, NY 13699	1896	$22,635	$8,398	1-D	2,949	185
Clark Univ, Worcester, MA 01610-1477	1887	$24,620	$4,550	1-D	2,955	251
Clayton Coll & State Univ, Morrow, GA 30260-0285	1969	$2,322 (S)	NA	5-B	4,675	282
Clemson Univ, Clemson, SC 29634	1889	$5,090 (S)	$4,532	5-D	17,101	1,126
Cleveland State Univ, Cleveland, OH 44115	1964	$4,728 (S)	$5,550	5-D	15,703	917
Coastal Carolina Univ, Conway, SC 29528-6054	1954	$3,770 (S)	$5,450	5-M	4,965	309
Coe Coll, Cedar Rapids, IA 52402-5070	1851	$19,340	$5,410	2-M	1,311	119
Colby Coll, Waterville, ME 04901-8840	1813	$34,290 (C)	NA	1-B	1,809	187
Coleman Coll, La Mesa, CA 91942-1532	1963	$6,000	NA	1-M	1,022	101
Colgate Univ, Hamilton, NY 13346-1386	1819	$27,025	$6,455	1-M	2,785	291
Coll for Creative Studies, Detroit, MI 48202-4034	1926	$18,598	$3,300	1-B	1,152	199
Coll Misericordia, Dallas, PA 18612-1098	1924	$17,300	$7,130	2-M	1,765	161
Coll of Aeronautics, Flushing, NY 11369-1037 (2)	1932	$9,250	NA	1-B	1,384	60
Coll of Charleston, Charleston, SC 29424-0001	1770	$3,780 (S)	$4,570	5-M	11,428	794
Coll of Mount St. Joseph, Cincinnati, OH 45233-1670	1920	$15,040	$5,520	2-M	2,273	205
Coll of Mount Saint Vincent, Riverdale, NY 10471-1093	1911	$17,030	$7,300	1-M	1,379	146
The Coll of New Jersey, Ewing, NJ 08628	1855	$6,661 (S)	$6,764	5-M	6,847	658
The Coll of New Rochelle, New Rochelle, NY 10805-2308 (3)	1904	$13,250	$6,850	1-M	2,506	160
Coll of Notre Dame of Maryland, Baltimore, MD 21210-2476 (3)	1873	$17,925	$7,400	2-M	3,187	90
Coll of Saint Benedict, Saint Joseph, MN 56374-2091	1887	$18,315	$5,606	2-B	2,100	160
Coll of St. Catherine, St. Paul, MN 55105-1789 (3)	1905	$17,402	$4,922	2-M	4,632	443
Coll of Saint Elizabeth, Morristown, NJ 07960-6989 (3)	1899	$15,310	$7,200	2-M	1,741	166
The Coll of Saint Rose, Albany, NY 12203-1419	1920	$13,918	$6,746	1-M	4,411	NA
The Coll of St. Scholastica, Duluth, MN 55811-4199	1912	$17,180	$5,198	2-M	2,231	175
Coll of Santa Fe, Santa Fe, NM 87505-7634	1947	$18,284	$5,484	1-M	1,588	255
Coll of Staten Island of the City Univ of New York, Staten Island, NY 10314	1955	$3,358 (S)	NA	11-M	11,284	719
Coll of the Holy Cross, Worcester, MA 01610-2395	1843	$26,440	$8,000	2-B	2,811	268
Coll of the Ozarks, Point Lookout, MO 65726	1906	$150	$2,500	2-B	1,395	123
The Coll of William & Mary, Williamsburg, VA 23187-8795	1693	$4,780 (S)	$5,222	5-D	7,489	743
The Coll of Wooster, Wooster, OH 44691-2363	1866	$22,430	$5,920	2-B	1,823	169
Collins Coll: A School of Design & Tech, Tempe, AZ 85281-5206	1978	$10,082	NA	3-B	1,804	70
Colorado Christian Univ, Lakewood, CO 80226-7499	1914	$12,244	$5,470	2-M	1,849	119
The Colorado Coll, Colorado Springs, CO 80903-3294	1874	$24,893	$6,632	1-M	1,952	206
Colorado School of Mines, Golden, CO 80401-1887	1874	$5,898 (S)	$5,680	5-D	3,255	327
Colorado State Univ, Fort Collins, CO 80523-0015	1870	$4,252 (S)	$5,670	5-D	23,934	934

Name, address	Year Founded	Tuition & Fees	Rm. & Board	Control, Degree	Enroll-ment	Faculty
Colorado Tech Univ, Colorado Springs, CO 80907-3896	1965	$8,982	NA	3-D	1,680	136
Columbia Coll, New York, NY 10027	1754	$26,908	$8,280	1-B	4,092	NA
Columbia Coll, Columbia, SC 29203-5998 (3)	1854	$16,620	$5,240	2-M	1,471	171
Columbia Coll Chicago, Chicago, IL 60605-1996	1890	$12,844	$5,900	1-M	9,416	1,164
Columbia Intl Univ, Columbia, SC 29230-3122	1923	$10,688	$4,940	2-D	1,025	49
Columbia Southern Univ, Orange Beach, AL 36561	NR	$125	NA	3-M	2,200	45
Columbia Union Coll, Takoma Park, MD 20912-7796	1904	$13,960	$4,849	2-M	1,073	50
Columbia Univ, School of General Studies, New York, NY 10027-6939	1754	$21,655	$7,980	1-B	1,167	632
Columbia Univ, The Fu Foundation School of Engineering & Applied Sci, New York, NY 10027	1864	$26,908	$8,280	1-D	1,264	NA
Columbus Coll of Art & Design, Columbus, OH 43215-1758	1879	$16,330	$6,200	1-B	1,737	165
Columbus State Univ, Columbus, GA 31907-5645	1958	$2,352 (S)	$4,876	5-M	5,522	350
Concord Coll, Athens, WV 24712-1000	1872	$2,724 (S)	$4,358	5-B	3,055	167
Concordia Coll, Moorhead, MN 56562	1891	$15,635	$4,310	2-M	2,766	255
Concordia Univ, Irvine, CA 92612-3299	1972	$16,480	$5,810	2-M	1,314	115
Concordia Univ, River Forest, IL 60305-1499	1864	$16,900	$5,100	2-D	1,947	225
Concordia Univ, St. Paul, MN 55104-5494	1893	$17,326	$5,530	2-M	1,773	310
Concordia Univ, Seward, NE 68434-1599	1894	$14,546	$4,388	2-M	1,369	128
Concordia Univ, Portland, OR 97211-6099	1905	$16,900	$4,400	2-M	1,054	107
Concordia Univ Wisconsin, Mequon, WI 53097-2402	1881	$13,610	$5,070	2-M	4,810	164
Connecticut Coll, New London, CT 06320-4196	1911	$33,585 (C)	NA	1-M	1,879	194
Converse Coll, Spartanburg, SC 29302-0006 (3)	1889	$16,850	$5,140	1-M	1,527	86
Coppin State Coll, Baltimore, MD 21216-3698	1900	$3,477 (S)	$5,734	5-M	4,003	202
Cornell Univ, Ithaca, NY 14853-0001	1865	$12,062 (S)	$8,552	1-D	19,420	1,777
Cornerstone Univ, Grand Rapids, MI 49525-5897	1941	$13,070	$5,022	2-B	1,937	136
Covenant Coll, Lookout Mountain, GA 30750	1955	$18,230	$5,260	2-M	1,245	72
Creighton Univ, Omaha, NE 68178-0001	1878	$17,136	$6,190	2-D	6,297	886
Crichton Coll, Memphis, TN 38175-7830	1941	$9,480	$3,200	1-B	1,043	92
The Culinary Inst of America, Hyde Park, NY 12538-1499	1946	$19,035	$3,780	1-B	2,012	120
Cumberland Coll, Williamsburg, KY 40769-1372	1889	$10,958	$4,676	2-M	1,707	100
Cumberland Univ, Lebanon, TN 37087-3554	1842	$10,950	$4,380	1-M	1,471	122
Curry Coll, Milton, MA 02186-9984	1879	$18,595	$7,210	1-M	2,399	393
Daemen Coll, Amherst, NY 14226-3592	1947	$13,620	$7,000	1-M	1,984	198
Dakota State Univ, Madison, SD 57042-1799	1881	$4,026 (S)	$2,924	5-M	2,015	100
Dallas Baptist Univ, Dallas, TX 75211-9299	1965	$9,750	$3,932	2-M	4,302	319
Dalton State Coll, Dalton, GA 30720-3797	1963	$2,160 (S)	NA	5-B	3,647	179
Daniel Webster Coll, Nashua, NH 03063-1300	1965	$17,870	$7,000	1-B	1,055	60
Dartmouth Coll, Hanover, NH 03755	1769	$26,562	$7,896	1-D	5,495	640
Davenport Univ, Lansing, MI 48933-2197	1979	$8,656	NA	1-B	1,209	79
Davenport Univ, Dearborn, MI 48126-3799	1962	$7,449	NA	1-M	3,138	190
Davenport Univ, Kalamazoo, MI 49006-2791	1866	$9,645	NA	1-B	1,063	110
Davenport Univ, Grand Rapids, MI 49503	1866	$8,691	$7,335	1-M	1,743	129
Davenport Univ, Warren, MI 48092-5209	1962	$7,449	NA	1-M	2,486	114
David N. Myers Univ, Cleveland, OH 44115-1096	1848	$9,450	NA	1-M	1,177	165
Davidson Coll, Davidson, NC 28036-1719	1837	$23,995	$6,828	2-B	1,673	164
Defiance Coll, Defiance, OH 43512-1610	1850	$15,855	$4,700	2-M	1,000	78
Delaware State Univ, Dover, DE 19901-2277	1891	$3,682 (S)	$5,362	5-M	3,343	249
Delaware Valley Coll, Doylestown, PA 18901-2697	1896	$17,374	$6,544	1-M	1,982	135
Delta State Univ, Cleveland, MS 38733-0001	1924	$3,100 (S)	$2,920	5-D	3,746	278
Denison Univ, Granville, OH 43023	1831	$23,090	$6,550	1-B	2,107	187
DePaul Univ, Chicago, IL 60604-2287	1898	$16,170	$6,960	2-D	21,363	2,205
DePauw Univ, Greencastle, IN 46135-0037	1837	$21,500	$6,500	2-B	2,219	254
DeSales Univ, Center Valley, PA 18034-9568	1964	$16,340	$6,270	2-M	2,730	124
DeVry Coll of Tech, North Brunswick, NJ 08902-3362	1969	$8,805	NA	3-B	3,912	193
DeVry Inst of Tech, Long Island City, NY 11101	1998	$9,800	NA	3-B	2,036	125
DeVry Univ, Phoenix, AZ 85021-2995	1967	$8,805	NA	3-B	3,050	112
DeVry Univ, West Hills, CA 91304	1999	$9,205	NA	3-B	1,351	84
DeVry Univ, Fremont, CA 94555	1998	$9,800	NA	3-B	2,278	88
DeVry Univ, Pomona, CA 91768-2642	1983	$9,205	NA	3-B	3,669	144
DeVry Univ, Long Beach, CA 90806	1984	$9,205	NA	3-B	2,853	129
DeVry Univ, Alpharetta, GA 30004	1997	$8,740	NA	3-B	1,548	86
DeVry Univ, Decatur, GA 30030-2198	1969	$8,805	NA	3-B	2,925	225
DeVry Univ, Chicago, IL 60618-5994	1931	$8,805	NA	3-B	4,011	189
DeVry Univ, Addison, IL 60101-6106	1982	$8,740	NA	3-B	3,543	165
DeVry Univ, Tinley Park, IL 60477	2000	$8,805	NA	3-B	1,662	83
DeVry Univ, Kansas City, MO 64131-3698	1931	$8,740	NA	3-B	2,620	143
DeVry Univ, Columbus, OH 43209-2705	1952	$8,805	NA	3-B	3,793	157
DeVry Univ, Irving, TX 75063-2439	1969	$8,740	NA	3-B	3,569	179
Dickinson Coll, Carlisle, PA 17013-2896	1773	$25,485	$6,725	1-B	2,208	203
Dickinson State Univ, Dickinson, ND 58601-4896	1918	$2,463 (S)	$3,032	5-B	2,101	146
Dillard Univ, New Orleans, LA 70122-3097	1869	$10,030	$6,296	2-B	2,137	187
Doane Coll, Crete, NE 68333-2430	1872	$13,470	$4,130	2-M	1,597	128
Dominican Coll, Orangeburg, NY 10962-1210	1952	$13,910	$7,400	1-M	1,618	154
Dominican Univ, River Forest, IL 60305-1099	1901	$15,700	$5,100	2-M	2,533	229
Dominican Univ of California, San Rafael, CA 94901-2298	1890	$20,670	$9,400	2-M	1,436	228
Dordt Coll, Sioux Center, IA 51250-1697	1955	$14,100	$4,000	2-M	1,396	117
Dowling Coll, Oakdale, NY 11769-1999	1955	$14,090	$4,800	1-D	5,580	456
Drake Univ, Des Moines, IA 50311-4516	1881	$17,790	$5,040	1-D	5,150	375
Drew Univ, Madison, NJ 07940-1493	1867	$25,122	$7,030	2-D	2,418	152
Drexel Univ, Philadelphia, PA 19104-2875	1891	$18,413	$9,090	1-D	13,546	889
Drury Univ, Springfield, MO 65802-3791	1873	$12,565	$4,460	1-M	1,777	141
Duke Univ, Durham, NC 27708-0586	1838	$26,768	$7,628	2-D	11,794	NA
Duquesne Univ, Pittsburgh, PA 15282-0001	1878	$17,478	$6,764	2-D	9,451	885
D'Youville Coll, Buffalo, NY 14201-1084	1908	$12,550	$6,154	1-M	2,486	196
Earlham Coll, Richmond, IN 47374-4095	1847	$22,308	$5,138	2-M	1,098	107
East Carolina Univ, Greenville, NC 27858-4353	1907	$2,566 (S)	$5,200	5-D	19,412	1,096
East Central Univ, Ada, OK 74820-6899	1909	$2,172 (S)	$2,452	5-M	4,195	265
Eastern Connecticut State Univ, Willimantic, CT 06226-2295	1889	$4,713 (S)	NA	5-M	5,313	351
Eastern Illinois Univ, Charleston, IL 61920-3099	1895	$4,469 (S)	$5,800	5-M	10,531	639
Eastern Kentucky Univ, Richmond, KY 40475-3102	1906	$2,928 (S)	$2,924	5-M	14,697	575

Name, address	Year Founded	Tuition & Fees	Rm. & Board	Control, Degree	Enroll-ment	Faculty
Eastern Mennonite Univ, Harrisonburg, VA 22802-2462	1917	$15,300	$5,400	2-F	1,304	141
Eastern Michigan Univ, Ypsilanti, MI 48197	1849	$4,603 (S)	$5,252	5-D	23,798	1,166
Eastern Nazarene Coll, Quincy, MA 02170-2999	1918	$15,315	$5,215	2-M	1,228	48
Eastern New Mexico Univ, Portales, NM 88130	1934	$2,088 (S)	$4,160	5-M	3,556	192
Eastern Oregon Univ, La Grande, OR 97850-2899	1929	$3,621 (S)	$5,151	5-M	3,023	129
Eastern Univ, St. Davids, PA 19087-3696	1952	$15,832	$6,784	2-M	3,054	278
Eastern Washington Univ, Cheney, WA 99004-2431	1882	$3,186 (S)	$4,786	5-M	8,932	636
East Stroudsburg Univ of Pennsylvania, East Stroudsburg, PA 18301-2999	1893	$4,984 (S)	$4,224	5-M	5,996	292
East Tennessee State Univ, Johnson City, TN 37614	1911	$3,119 (S)	$4,008	5-D	11,331	703
East Texas Baptist Univ, Marshall, TX 75670-1498	1912	$9,050	$3,299	2-B	1,509	118
East-West Univ, Chicago, IL 60605-2103	1978	$9,735	NA	1-B	1,076	78
Eckerd Coll, St. Petersburg, FL 33711	1958	$20,085	$5,415	2-B	1,582	134
Edgewood Coll, Madison, WI 53711-1997	1927	$13,300	$5,004	2-M	2,110	190
Edinboro Univ of Pennsylvania, Edinboro, PA 16444	1857	$4,944 (A)	$4,384	5-M	7,498	376
Edward Waters Coll, Jacksonville, FL 32209-6199	1866	$3,695	$2,735	2-B	1,320	49
Elizabeth City State Univ, Elizabeth City, NC 27909-7806	1891	$1,840 (S)	$4,172	5-M	2,004	183
Elizabethtown Coll, Elizabethtown, PA 17022-2298	1899	$21,350	$6,000	2-M	1,901	198
Elmhurst Coll, Elmhurst, IL 60126-3296	1871	$16,200	$5,550	2-M	2,540	267
Elmira Coll, Elmira, NY 14901	1855	$24,560	$7,850	1-B	1,584	110
Elon Univ, Elon, NC 27244-2010	1889	$14,560	$4,432	2-M	4,341	287
Embry-Riddle Aeronautical Univ, Prescott, AZ 86301-3720 (2)	1978	$18,210	$5,040	1-M	1,740	113
Embry-Riddle Aeronautical Univ, Daytona Beach, FL 32114-3900 (2)	1926	$18,400	$5,760	1-M	4,921	272
Embry-Riddle Aeronautical Univ, Extended Campus, Daytona Beach, FL 32114-3900 (2)	1970	$4,152	NA	1-M	8,999	2,947
Emerson Coll, Boston, MA 02116-4624	1880	$20,718	$9,290	1-D	4,339	356
Emmanuel Coll, Boston, MA 02115	1919	$17,100	$9,615	2-M	1,449	76
Emory & Henry Coll, Emory, VA 24327-0947	1836	$14,800	$5,550	2-M	1,079	87
Emory Univ, Atlanta, GA 30322-1100	1836	$25,552	$8,240	2-D	11,443	NA
Emporia State Univ, Emporia, KS 66801-5087	1863	$2,284 (S)	$3,914	5-D	5,823	344
Endicott Coll, Beverly, MA 01915-2096	1939	$15,704	$8,000	1-M	1,937	124
Evangel Univ, Springfield, MO 65802-2191	1955	$10,770	$4,000	2-M	1,570	141
The Evergreen State Coll, Olympia, WA 98505	1967	$3,191 (S)	$5,610	5-M	4,227	276
Excelsior Coll, Albany, NY 12203-5159	1970	$1,295	NA	1-M	19,131	NA
Fairfield Univ, Fairfield, CT 06430-5195	1942	$22,885	$8,000	2-M	5,154	476
Fairleigh Dickinson Univ, Coll at Florham, Madison, NJ 07940-1099	1942	$19,074	$7,904	1-M	3,460	245
Fairleigh Dickinson Univ, Metro Campus, Teaneck, NJ 07666-1914	1942	$19,074	$7,904	1-D	6,092	433
Fairmont State Coll, Fairmont, WV 26554	1865	$2,408 (S)	NA	5-M	6,724	517
Fashion Inst of Tech, New York, NY 10001-5992	1944	$3,366 (S)	$7,535	11-M	10,786	928
Faulkner Univ, Montgomery, AL 36109-3398	1942	$8,700	$4,300	2-F	2,640	62
Fayetteville State Univ, Fayetteville, NC 28301-4298	1867	$1,770 (S)	$3,820	5-D	5,010	231
Felician Coll, Lodi, NJ 07644-2117	1942	$12,410	$6,250	2-M	1,717	163
Ferris State Univ, Big Rapids, MI 49307	1884	$5,070 (S)	$5,628	5-F	10,930	510
Fitchburg State Coll, Fitchburg, MA 01420-2697	1894	$2,988 (S)	$4,838	5-M	5,033	328
Five Towns Coll, Dix Hills, NY 11746-6055	1972	$11,000	$7,800	1-M	1,081	87
Flagler Coll, St. Augustine, FL 32085-1027	1968	$6,870	$4,120	1-B	1,852	152
Florida Agr & Mech Univ, Tallahassee, FL 32307-3200	1887	$2,691 (S)	$4,742	5-D	12,316	NA
Florida Atlantic Univ, Boca Raton, FL 33431-0991	1961	$2,699 (S)	$6,134	5-D	23,537	1,269
Florida Gulf Coast Univ, Fort Myers, FL 33965-6565	1991	$2,524 (S)	$7,000	5-M	4,214	163
Florida Inst of Tech, Melbourne, FL 32901-6975	1958	$19,700	$5,550	1-D	4,409	242
Florida Intl Univ, Miami, FL 33199	1965	$2,562 (S)	$3,504	5-D	31,727	1,394
Florida Metro Univ-South Orlando Campus, Orlando, FL 32809	NR	$6,806	NA	3-M	1,582	77
Florida Metro Univ-Tampa Campus, Tampa, FL 33614-5899	1890	$7,638	NA	3-M	1,218	54
Florida Southern Coll, Lakeland, FL 33801-5698	1885	$13,930	$5,500	2-M	1,875	219
Florida State Univ, Tallahassee, FL 32306	1851	$2,513 (S)	$5,322	5-D	34,982	NA
Fontbonne Univ, St. Louis, MO 63105-3098	1917	$12,896	$5,500	2-M	2,192	185
Fordham Univ, New York, NY 10458	1841	$22,460	$8,745	2-D	13,843	1,125
Fort Hays State Univ, Hays, KS 67601-4099	1902	$2,217 (S)	$4,077	5-M	5,626	273
Fort Lewis Coll, Durango, CO 81301-3999	1911	$2,521 (S)	$5,424	5-B	4,441	231
Fort Valley State Univ, Fort Valley, GA 31030-4313	1895	$1,770 (S)	$1,915	5-D	2,823	174
Framingham State Coll, Framingham, MA 01701-9101	1839	$2,770 (S)	$4,403	5-M	5,912	332
Franciscan Univ of Steubenville, Steubenville, OH 43952-1763	1946	$13,900	$5,200	2-M	2,208	169
Francis Marion Univ, Florence, SC 29501-0547	1970	$3,790 (S)	$3,892	5-M	3,513	199
Franklin & Marshall Coll, Lancaster, PA 17604-3003	1787	$26,110	$6,300	1-B	1,887	185
Franklin Coll of Indiana, Franklin, IN 46131-2598	1834	$14,885	$5,020	2-B	1,028	103
Franklin Pierce Coll, Rindge, NH 03461-0060	1962	$20,525	$6,930	1-M	1,548	141
Franklin Univ, Columbus, OH 43215-5399	1902	$6,324	NA	1-M	5,537	350
Freed-Hardeman Univ, Henderson, TN 38340-2399	1869	$9,580	$4,710	2-M	1,870	143
Fresno Pacific Univ, Fresno, CA 93702-4709	1944	$16,416	$4,630	2-M	1,456	181
Friends Univ, Wichita, KS 67213	1898	$11,740	$3,540	1-M	3,190	225
Frostburg State Univ, Frostburg, MD 21532-1099	1898	$4,432 (S)	$5,424	5-M	5,283	346
Furman Univ, Greenville, SC 29613	1826	$20,076	$5,416	1-M	3,183	273
Gallaudet Univ, Washington, DC 20002-3625	1864	$8,990	$7,564	1-D	1,583	223
Gannon Univ, Erie, PA 16541-0001	1925	$15,780	$5,990	2-D	3,407	264
Gardner-Webb Univ, Boiling Springs, NC 28017	1905	$12,870	$4,880	2-D	3,564	132
Geneva Coll, Beaver Falls, PA 15010-3599	1848	$14,050	$5,940	2-M	2,174	142
George Fox Univ, Newberg, OR 97132-2697	1891	$18,325	$5,770	2-D	2,640	134
George Mason Univ, Fairfax, VA 22030-4444	1957	$3,792 (S)	$5,400	5-D	24,897	1,512
Georgetown Coll, Georgetown, KY 40324-1696	1829	$14,640	$5,050	2-M	1,703	126
Georgetown Univ, Washington, DC 20057	1789	$25,425	$9,422	2-D	12,688	922
The George Washington Univ, Washington, DC 20052	1821	$27,820	$9,110	1-D	22,184	1,626
Georgia Coll & State Univ, Milledgeville, GA 31061	1889	$3,032 (S)	$4,962	5-M	5,079	364
Georgia Inst of Tech, Atlanta, GA 30332-0001	1885	$3,454 (S)	$5,574	5-D	15,576	770
Georgian Court Coll, Lakewood, NJ 08701-2697 (3)	1908	$14,855	$5,600	2-M	2,708	213
Georgia Southern Univ, Statesboro, GA 30460	1906	$2,596 (S)	$4,382	5-D	14,371	717
Georgia Southwestern State Univ, Americus, GA 31709-4693	1906	$2,500 (S)	$3,790	5-M	2,535	185
Georgia State Univ, Atlanta, GA 30303-3083	1913	$3,292 (S)	$4,500	5-D	25,745	1,318
Gettysburg Coll, Gettysburg, PA 17325-1483	1832	$25,748	$6,322	2-B	2,258	246
Glenville State Coll, Glenville, WV 26351-1200	1872	$2,488 (S)	$4,100	5-B	2,144	175
Global Univ of the Assemblies of God, Springfield, MO 65804	1948	$1,800	NA	2-M	4,284	473

Name, address	Year Founded	Tuition & Fees	Rm. & Board	Control, Degree	Enroll-ment	Faculty
Golden Gate Univ, San Francisco, CA 94105-2968	1853	$9,192	NA	1-D	5,322	662
Goldey-Beacom Coll, Wilmington, DE 19808-1999	1886	$10,132	$3,937	1-M	1,400	49
Gonzaga Univ, Spokane, WA 99258	1887	$18,541	$5,680	2-D	5,128	501
Gordon Coll, Wenham, MA 01984-1899	1889	$18,134	$5,460	2-M	1,694	130
Goucher Coll, Baltimore, MD 21204-2794	1885	$22,300	$7,750	1-M	1,996	154
Governors State Univ, University Park, IL 60466-0975	1969	$2,632 (S)	NA	5-M	5,911	203
Grace Coll, Winona Lake, IN 46590-1294	1948	$11,720	$5,008	2-M	1,299	84
Graceland Univ, Lamoni, IA 50140	1895	$13,145	$4,305	2-M	2,523	104
Grambling State Univ, Grambling, LA 71245	1901	$2,589 (S)	$2,712	5-D	4,500	259
Grand Canyon Univ, Phoenix, AZ 85061-1097	1949	$10,500	$4,500	2-M	4,113	274
Grand Valley State Univ, Allendale, MI 49401-9403	1960	$4,660 (S)	$5,380	5-M	19,762	1,146
Grand View Coll, Des Moines, IA 50316-1599	1896	$13,430	$4,166	2-B	1,402	131
Greensboro Coll, Greensboro, NC 27401-1875	1838	$13,700	$5,380	2-B	1,139	112
Greenville Coll, Greenville, IL 62246-0159	1892	$14,000	$5,186	2-M	1,155	145
Grinnell Coll, Grinnell, IA 50112-1690	1846	$22,250	$6,050	1-B	1,338	140
Grove City Coll, Grove City, PA 16127-2104	1876	$7,870	$4,410	2-B	2,334	165
Guilford Coll, Greensboro, NC 27410-4173	1837	$18,200	$5,780	2-B	1,490	136
Gustavus Adolphus Coll, St. Peter, MN 56082-1498	1862	$19,355	$4,900	2-B	2,592	231
Gwynedd-Mercy Coll, Gwynedd Valley, PA 19437-0901	1948	$15,350	$7,000	2-M	2,177	218
Hamilton Coll, Clinton, NY 13323-1296	1812	$27,350	$6,800	1-B	1,770	198
Hamline Univ, St. Paul, MN 55104-1284	1854	$17,602	$5,887	2-D	4,123	354
Hampden-Sydney Coll, Hampden-Sydney, VA 23943 (1)	1776	$18,485	$6,386	2-B	1,026	107
Hampshire Coll, Amherst, MA 01002	1965	$26,871	$7,010	1-B	1,219	118
Hampton Univ, Hampton, VA 23668	1868	$11,666	$5,446	1-D	5,793	388
Hannibal-LaGrange Coll, Hannibal, MO 63401-1999	1858	$9,130	$3,400	2-B	1,099	87
Hanover Coll, Hanover, IN 47243-0108	1827	$12,370	$5,190	2-B	1,111	106
Harding Univ, Searcy, AR 72149-0001	1924	$9,030	$4,498	2-M	4,677	301
Hardin-Simmons Univ, Abilene, TX 79698-0001	1891	$11,250	$3,515	2-F	2,335	193
Harris-Stowe State Coll, St. Louis, MO 63103-2136	1857	$2,310 (S)	NA	5-B	1,306	61
Hartwick Coll, Oneonta, NY 13820-4020	1797	$26,040	$7,050	1-B	1,446	152
Harvard Univ, Cambridge, MA 02138	1636	$26,019	$8,250	1-D	17,850	760
Haskell Indian Nations Univ, Lawrence, KS 66046-4800	1884	$210 (S)	$70	4-B	1,028	48
Hastings Coll, Hastings, NE 68901-7696	1882	$13,666	$4,188	2-M	1,108	110
Haverford Coll, Haverford, PA 19041-1392	1833	$26,070	$8,230	1-B	1,138	111
Hawai`i Pacific Univ, Honolulu, HI 96813-2785	1965	$9,360	$8,430	1-M	8,033	600
Heidelberg Coll, Tiffin, OH 44883-2462	1850	$13,143	$5,978	2-M	1,517	122
Henderson State Univ, Arkadelphia, AR 71999-0001	1890	$2,736 (S)	NA	5-M	3,428	217
Hendrix Coll, Conway, AR 72032-3080	1876	$13,711	$4,752	2-M	1,085	91
Heritage Coll, Toppenish, WA 98948-9599	1982	$5,430	NA	1-M	1,127	130
High Point Univ, High Point, NC 27262-3598	1924	$13,900	$6,320	2-M	2,752	209
Hillsdale Coll, Hillsdale, MI 49242-1298	1844	$14,700	$5,886	1-B	1,168	130
Hiram Coll, Hiram, OH 44234-0067	1850	$19,392	$6,514	2-B	1,190	110
Hobart & William Smith Colleges, Geneva, NY 14456-3397	1822	$26,177	$7,018	1-B	1,892	166
Hofstra Univ, Hempstead, NY 11549	1935	$15,722	$7,530	1-D	13,428	1,272
Hollins Univ, Roanoke, VA 24020-1603 (3)	1842	$17,720	$6,608	1-M	1,091	100
Holy Family Coll, Philadelphia, PA 19114-2094	1954	$13,710	NA	2-M	2,665	276
Hood Coll, Frederick, MD 21701-8575 (3)	1893	$19,120	$6,900	1-M	1,607	179
Hope Coll, Holland, MI 49422-9000	1866	$17,448	$5,474	2-B	2,999	295
Houghton Coll, Houghton, NY 14744	1883	$16,290	$5,520	2-B	1,422	100
Houston Baptist Univ, Houston, TX 77074-3298	1960	$11,355	$4,443	2-M	2,829	189
Howard Payne Univ, Brownwood, TX 76801-2715	1889	$10,000	$3,834	2-B	1,526	134
Howard Univ, Washington, DC 20059-0002	1867	$10,070	$5,000	1-D	10,509	1,360
Humboldt State Univ, Arcata, CA 95521-8299	1913	$1,892 (S)	$6,690	5-M	7,382	565
Hunter Coll of the City Univ of New York, New York, NY 10021-5085	1870	$3,343 (S)	$1,890	11-M	20,398	1,298
Husson Coll, Bangor, ME 04401-2999	1898	$9,990	$5,350	1-M	1,797	90
Idaho State Univ, Pocatello, ID 83209	1901	$140/cr. hr. (S)	$4,230	5-D	13,663	633
The Illinois Inst of Art, Chicago, IL 60654	1916	$14,769	NA	3-B	1,789	108
Illinois Inst of Tech, Chicago, IL 60616-3793	1890	$19,365	$5,882	1-D	6,050	587
Illinois State Univ, Normal, IL 61790-2200	1857	$4,929 (S)	$4,932	5-D	21,240	1,149
Illinois Wesleyan Univ, Bloomington, IL 61702-2900	1850	$23,036	$5,550	1-B	2,064	182
Immaculata Coll, Immaculata, PA 19345-0500 (3)	1920	$15,200	$7,200	2-D	3,170	234
Indiana Inst of Tech, Fort Wayne, IN 46803-1297	1930	$14,560	$5,246	1-M	2,756	162
Indiana State Univ, Terre Haute, IN 47809-1401	1865	$3,722 (S)	$4,789	5-D	11,321	NA
Indiana Univ-Purdue Univ Fort Wayne, Fort Wayne, IN 46805-1499	1917	$3,166 (S)	NA	5-M	11,129	634
Indiana Univ-Purdue Univ Indianapolis, Indianapolis, IN 46202-2896	1969	$4,172 (S)	$5,302	5-D	28,339	2,630
Indiana Univ Bloomington, Bloomington, IN 47405	1820	$4,735 (S)	$5,978	5-D	37,963	1,881
Indiana Univ East, Richmond, IN 47374-1289	1971	$3,415 (S)	NA	5-B	2,469	177
Indiana Univ Kokomo, Kokomo, IN 46904-9003	1945	$3,421 (S)	NA	5-M	2,741	151
Indiana Univ Northwest, Gary, IN 46408-1197	1959	$3,447 (S)	NA	5-M	4,639	311
Indiana Univ of Pennsylvania, Indiana, PA 15705-1087	1875	$4,875 (S)	$4,258	5-D	13,457	758
Indiana Univ South Bend, South Bend, IN 46634-7111	1922	$3,515 (S)	NA	5-M	7,417	496
Indiana Univ Southeast, New Albany, IN 47150-6405	1941	$3,460 (S)	NA	5-M	6,557	410
Indiana Wesleyan Univ, Marion, IN 46953-4974	1920	$12,740	$4,940	2-M	7,933	175
Inter American Univ of Puerto Rico, Aguadilla Campus, Aguadilla, PR 00605	1957	$3,278	NA	1-B	3,800	209
Inter American Univ of Puerto Rico, Arecibo Campus, Arecibo, PR 00614-4050	1957	$2,990	NA	1-M	3,926	234
Inter American Univ of Puerto Rico, Barranquitas Campus, Barranquitas, PR 00794	1957	$3,000	NA	1-B	1,710	90
Inter American Univ of Puerto Rico, Bayamón Campus, Bayamón, PR 00957	1912	$3,236	NA	1-B	4,960	280
Inter American Univ of Puerto Rico, Fajardo Campus, Fajardo, PR 00738-7003	1965	$3,600	NA	1-B	1,971	163
Inter American Univ of Puerto Rico, Metro Campus, San Juan, PR 00919-1293	1960	$3,866	NA	1-D	10,272	713
Inter American Univ of Puerto Rico, Ponce Campus, Mercedita, PR 00715	1962	$4,200	NA	1-B	4,123	212
Inter American Univ of Puerto Rico, San Germán Campus, San Germán, PR 00683-5008	1912	$3,990	$2,400	1-D	5,742	309
Intl Acad of Design & Tech, Tampa, FL 33634-7350	1984	$14,160	NA	3-B	1,688	126

Name, address	Year Founded	Tuition & Fees	Rm. & Board	Control, Degree	Enroll-ment	Faculty
Intl Acad of Design & Tech, Chicago, IL 60602-9736	1977	$13,038	NA	3-B	2,063	178
Intl Coll, Naples, FL 34119	1990	$7,230	NA	1-M	1,227	85
Intl Fine Arts Coll, Miami, FL 33132-1121	1965	$13,025	NA	3-M	1,100	93
Iona Coll, New Rochelle, NY 10801-1890	1940	$17,040	$9,416	2-M	4,388	339
Iowa State Univ of Sci & Tech, Ames, IA 50011	1858	$3,442 (S)	$4,666	5-D	27,823	1,644
Ithaca Coll, Ithaca, NY 14850-7020	1892	$20,104	$8,615	1-M	6,483	587
Jackson State Univ, Jackson, MS 39217	1877	$3,206 (S)	$4,014	5-D	7,098	423
Jacksonville State Univ, Jacksonville, AL 36265-1602	1883	$2,940 (S)	$3,080	5-M	8,478	386
Jacksonville Univ, Jacksonville, FL 32211-3394	1934	$16,780	$5,900	1-M	2,346	221
James Madison Univ, Harrisonburg, VA 22807	1908	$4,094 (S)	$5,458	5-D	15,562	938
Jamestown Coll, Jamestown, ND 58405	1883	$8,350	$3,550	2-B	1,136	72
John Brown Univ, Siloam Springs, AR 72761-2121	1919	$13,024	$4,798	2-M	1,675	120
John Carroll Univ, University Heights, OH 44118-4581	1886	$19,192	$6,564	2-M	4,301	417
John F. Kennedy Univ, Orinda, CA 94563-2603	1964	$11,646	NA	1-D	1,525	715
John Jay Coll of Criminal Justice of the City Univ of New York, New York, NY 10019-1093	1964	$3,459 (S)	NA	11-M	11,209	628
Johns Hopkins Univ, Baltimore, MD 21218-2699	1876	$27,690	$8,870	1-D	5,832	1,104
Johnson & Wales Univ, Providence, RI 02903-3703	1914	$15,192	$6,366	1-D	9,261	440
Johnson C. Smith Univ, Charlotte, NC 28216-5398	1867	$11,971	$4,589	1-B	1,595	116
Johnson State Coll, Johnson, VT 05656-9405	1828	$5,252 (S)	$5,520	5-M	1,590	181
Jones Intl Univ, Englewood, CO 80112	1995	$4,740	NA	1-M	2,000	124
Judson Coll, Elgin, IL 60123-1498	1963	$15,150	$5,800	2-B	1,089	171
Juniata Coll, Huntingdon, PA 16652-2119	1876	$21,580	$5,930	2-B	1,302	112
Kalamazoo Coll, Kalamazoo, MI 49006-3295	1833	$20,652	$6,228	2-B	1,384	107
Kansas State Univ, Manhattan, KS 66506	1863	$2,333 (S)	$4,662	5-D	22,396	NA
Kean Univ, Union, NJ 07083	1855	$5,121 (S)	$4,840	5-M	12,094	385
Keene State Coll, Keene, NH 03435	1909	$5,554 (S)	$5,256	5-M	4,633	376
Kennesaw State Univ, Kennesaw, GA 30144-5591	1963	$2,828 (S)	NA	5-M	13,951	650
Kent State Univ, Kent, OH 44242-0001	1910	$5,954 (S)	$5,150	5-D	22,828	1,263
Kentucky State Univ, Frankfort, KY 40601	1886	$2,846 (S)	$4,214	12-M	2,254	130
Kenyon Coll, Gambier, OH 43022-9623	1824	$27,550	$4,580	1-B	1,587	165
Kettering Univ, Flint, MI 48504-4898	1919	$18,656	$4,600	1-M	3,346	162
Keuka Coll, Keuka Park, NY 14478-0098	1890	$14,290	$6,880	2-M	1,063	53
King's Coll, Wilkes-Barre, PA 18711-0801	1946	$17,450	$7,230	2-M	2,226	189
Knox Coll, Galesburg, IL 61401	1837	$22,620	$5,610	1-B	1,143	117
Kutztown Univ of Pennsylvania, Kutztown, PA 19530-0730	1866	$4,947 (S)	$4,426	5-M	8,268	384
Lafayette Coll, Easton, PA 18042-1798	1826	$24,921	$7,734	2-B	2,330	226
Lake Forest Coll, Lake Forest, IL 60045-2399	1857	$22,206	$5,254	1-M	1,277	142
Lakeland Coll, Sheboygan, WI 53082-0359	1862	$13,835	$5,358	2-M	3,588	48
Lake Superior State Univ, Sault Sainte Marie, MI 49783-1626	1946	$4,334 (S)	$5,281	5-B	3,219	221
Lamar Univ, Beaumont, TX 77710	1923	$2,756 (S)	$4,854	5-D	8,969	421
Lander Univ, Greenwood, SC 29649-2099	1872	$4,242 (S)	$4,376	5-M	2,710	175
La Roche Coll, Pittsburgh, PA 15237-5898	1963	$12,380	$6,474	2-M	1,908	207
La Salle Univ, Philadelphia, PA 19141-1199	1863	$19,890	$7,010	2-D	5,428	463
La Sierra Univ, Riverside, CA 92515-8247	1922	$15,997	$4,302	2-D	1,566	90
Lawrence Tech Univ, Southfield, MI 48075-1058	1932	$12,250	$2,475	1-M	4,117	NA
Lawrence Univ, Appleton, WI 54912-0599	1847	$22,728	$4,983	1-B	1,323	166
Lebanon Valley Coll, Annville, PA 17003-1400	1866	$19,810	$5,890	2-M	2,117	179
Lee Univ, Cleveland, TN 37320-3450	1918	$360	NA	2-M	3,511	248
Lehigh Univ, Bethlehem, PA 18015-3094	1865	$25,140	$7,150	1-D	6,479	457
Lehman Coll of the City Univ of New York, Bronx, NY 10468-1589	1931	$3,310 (S)	NA	11-M	9,027	634
Le Moyne Coll, Syracuse, NY 13214-1399	1946	$16,850	$6,990	2-M	3,166	253
Lenoir-Rhyne Coll, Hickory, NC 28603	1891	$14,994	$5,300	2-M	1,456	158
Lesley Univ, Cambridge, MA 02138-2790 (4)	1909	$18,475	$8,300	1-D	6,192	70
LeTourneau Univ, Longview, TX 75607-7001	1946	$13,410	$5,610	2-M	3,098	310
Lewis & Clark Coll, Portland, OR 97219-7899	1867	$22,810	$6,650	1-F	2,947	334
Lewis-Clark State Coll, Lewiston, ID 83501-2698	1893	$5,100 (S)	$2,970	5-B	2,953	248
Lewis Univ, Romeoville, IL 60446	1932	$14,040	$6,920	2-M	4,407	152
Liberty Univ, Lynchburg, VA 24502	1971	$10,340	$5,100	2-D	6,162	265
Lincoln Memorial Univ, Harrogate, TN 37752-1901	1897	$11,760	$4,380	1-M	1,773	135
Lincoln Univ, Jefferson City, MO 65102	1866	$3,638 (S)	$3,790	5-M	3,332	153
Lincoln Univ, Lincoln University, PA 19352	1854	$5,786 (S)	$5,412	12-M	1,871	159
Lindenwood Univ, St. Charles, MO 63301-1695	1827	$11,650	$5,600	2-M	6,446	327
Lindsey Wilson Coll, Columbia, KY 42728-1298	1903	$12,098	$5,274	2-M	1,303	87
Linfield Coll, McMinnville, OR 97128-6894	1849	$19,550	$6,290	2-B	1,602	158
Lipscomb Univ, Nashville, TN 37204-3951	1891	$10,828	$5,420	2-F	2,661	231
Lock Haven Univ of Pennsylvania, Lock Haven, PA 17745-2390	1870	$4,884 (S)	$4,776	5-M	4,252	231
Loma Linda Univ, Loma Linda, CA 92350	1905	$15,600	$2,724	2-D	3,260	2,330
Long Island Univ, Brooklyn Campus, Brooklyn, NY 11201-8423	1926	$15,938	NA	1-D	8,051	1,028
Long Island Univ, C.W. Post Campus, Brookville, NY 11548-1300	1954	$18,090	$7,290	1-D	10,133	1,139
Long Island Univ, Southampton Coll, Southampton, NY 11968-4198	1963	$18,120	$8,150	1-M	1,531	206
Longwood Coll, Farmville, VA 23909-1800	1839	$4,226 (S)	$4,724	5-M	4,114	232
Loras Coll, Dubuque, IA 52004-0178	1839	$17,069	$5,925	2-M	1,758	178
Louisiana Coll, Pineville, LA 71359-0001	1906	$8,200	$3,316	2-B	1,204	102
Louisiana State Univ & Agr & Mech Coll, Baton Rouge, LA 70803	1860	$3,468 (S)	$4,546	5-D	31,392	1,415
Louisiana State Univ Health Sci Ctr, New Orleans, LA 70112-2223	1931	$3,875 (S)	$1,975	5-D	2,755	3,000
Louisiana State Univ in Shreveport, Shreveport, LA 71115-2399	1965	$2,550 (S)	NA	5-M	4,113	230
Louisiana Tech Univ, Ruston, LA 71272	1894	$3,041 (S)	$3,465	5-D	10,694	442
Lourdes Coll, Sylvania, OH 43560-2898	1958	$13,100	NA	2-B	1,219	127
Loyola Coll in Maryland, Baltimore, MD 21210-2699	1852	$23,500	$7,400	2-D	6,144	413
Loyola Marymount Univ, Los Angeles, CA 90045-2659	1911	$20,954	$7,800	2-F	7,921	802
Loyola Univ Chicago, Chicago, IL 60611-2196	1870	$19,274	$7,266	2-D	13,019	1,979
Loyola Univ New Orleans, New Orleans, LA 70118-6195	1912	$19,212	$6,908	2-F	5,509	408
Lubbock Christian Univ, Lubbock, TX 79407-2099	1957	$10,994	$3,900	2-M	1,823	139
Luther Coll, Decorah, IA 52101-1045	1861	$19,325	$3,975	2-B	2,575	232
Luther Rice Bible Coll & Seminary, Lithonia, GA 30038-2454	1962	$2,834	NA	2-D	1,600	33
Lycoming Coll, Williamsport, PA 17701-5192	1812	$19,404	$5,376	2-B	1,429	103
Lynchburg Coll, Lynchburg, VA 24501-3199	1903	$20,165	$4,600	2-M	1,937	194
Lyndon State Coll, Lyndonville, VT 05851-0919	1911	$5,252 (S)	$5,520	5-M	1,138	122
Lynn Univ, Boca Raton, FL 33431-5598	1962	$21,750	$7,650	1-D	2,006	247

Name, address	Year Founded	Tuition & Fees	Rm. & Board	Control, Degree	Enroll-ment	Faculty
Macalester Coll, St. Paul, MN 55105-1899	1874	$22,608	$6,206	2-B	1,822	205
Macon State Coll, Macon, GA 31206-5144	1968	$1,438 (S)	NA	5-B	4,482	215
Madonna Univ, Livonia, MI 48150-1173	1947	$7,660	$5,054	2-M	3,819	266
Malone Coll, Canton, OH 44709-3897	1892	$13,550	$5,640	2-M	2,139	195
Manchester Coll, North Manchester, IN 46962-1225	1889	$16,080	$3,720	2-M	1,166	87
Manhattan Coll, Riverdale, NY 10471	1853	$19,200	$7,700	2-M	2,946	253
Manhattanville Coll, Purchase, NY 10577-2132	1841	$21,430	$8,730	1-M	2,468	201
Mansfield Univ of Pennsylvania, Mansfield, PA 16933	1857	$5,096 (S)	$4,552	5-M	3,303	191
Marian Coll, Indianapolis, IN 46222-1997	1851	$15,670	$5,390	2-M	1,260	145
Marian Coll of Fond du Lac, Fond du Lac, WI 54935-4699	1936	$13,545	$4,390	2-M	2,558	81
Marietta Coll, Marietta, OH 45750-4000	1835	$19,076	$5,504	1-M	1,278	128
Marist Coll, Poughkeepsie, NY 12601-1387	1929	$16,792	$7,964	1-M	5,553	489
Marquette Univ, Milwaukee, WI 53201-1881	1881	$19,706	$6,350	2-D	10,832	1,115
Marshall Univ, Huntington, WV 25755	1837	$3,212 (S)	$5,028	5-D	13,827	708
Martin Luther Coll, New Ulm, MN 56073	1995	$11,710	$1,850	2-B	1,060	99
Mary Baldwin Coll, Staunton, VA 24401-3610 (4)	1842	$15,990	$7,450	2-M	1,564	130
Marygrove Coll, Detroit, MI 48221-2599 (4)	1905	$10,750	$5,200	2-M	6,097	75
Maryland Inst, Coll of Art, Baltimore, MD 21217-4191	1826	$21,080	$6,640	1-M	1,333	231
Marymount Manhattan Coll, New York, NY 10021-4597	1936	$14,695	$8,500	1-B	2,707	352
Marymount Univ, Arlington, VA 22207-4299	1950	$14,970	$6,590	2-M	3,475	372
Maryville Coll, Maryville, TN 37804-5907	1819	$17,560	$5,650	2-B	1,026	97
Maryville Univ of Saint Louis, St. Louis, MO 63141-7299	1872	$13,770	$6,000	1-M	3,162	290
Mary Washington Coll, Fredericksburg, VA 22401-5358	1908	$3,340 (S)	$5,692	5-M	4,483	321
Marywood Univ, Scranton, PA 18509-1598	1915	$17,429	$7,310	2-D	2,925	302
Massachusetts Coll of Art, Boston, MA 02115-5882	1873	$4,068 (S)	$7,742	5-M	2,245	207
Massachusetts Coll of Liberal Arts, North Adams, MA 01247-4100	1894	$3,897 (S)	$5,846	5-M	1,613	121
Massachusetts Coll of Pharmacy & Health Sci, Boston, MA 02115-5896	1823	$18,221	$8,910	1-D	1,907	128
Massachusetts Inst of Tech, Cambridge, MA 02139-4307	1861	$26,960	$7,500	1-D	10,204	1,760
The Master's Coll & Seminary, Santa Clarita, CA 91321-1200	1927	$16,620	$5,780	2-F	1,522	113
McDaniel Coll, Westminster, MD 21157-4390	1867	$22,110	$5,280	1-M	3,124	153
McKendree Coll, Lebanon, IL 62254-1299	1828	$13,350	$4,950	2-B	2,107	181
McMurry Univ, Abilene, TX 79697	1923	$10,905	$4,512	2-B	1,378	110
McNeese State Univ, Lake Charles, LA 70609	1939	$2,545 (S)	$3,720	5-M	7,780	392
MCP Hahnemann Univ, Philadelphia, PA 19102-1192	1848	$10,410	$8,100	1-D	2,579	187
Medaille Coll, Buffalo, NY 14214-2695	1875	$12,520	$5,800	1-M	1,788	117
Medgar Evers Coll of the City Univ of New York, Brooklyn, NY 11225-2298	1969	$3,282 (S)	NA	11-B	4,716	424
Medical Coll of Georgia, Augusta, GA 30912	1828	$3,083 (S)	$1,302	5-D	1,939	722
Medical Univ of South Carolina, Charleston, SC 29425-0002	1824	$6,230 (S)	NA	5-D	2,297	1,209
Mercer Univ, Macon, GA 31207-0003	1833	$18,290	$5,840	2-D	7,315	554
Mercy Coll, Dobbs Ferry, NY 10522-1189	1951	$10,000	$8,000	1-M	9,752	665
Mercyhurst Coll, Erie, PA 16546	1926	$15,870	$5,979	2-M	3,375	224
Meredith Coll, Raleigh, NC 27607-5298 (3)	1891	$14,300	$4,600	1-M	2,466	282
Merrimack Coll, North Andover, MA 01845-5800	1947	$17,645	$8,080	2-M	2,593	210
Mesa State Coll, Grand Junction, CO 81501	1925	$2,288 (S)	$5,763	5-M	5,346	321
Messiah Coll, Grantham, PA 17027	1909	$17,210	$5,970	2-B	2,858	262
Methodist Coll, Fayetteville, NC 28311-1420	1956	$14,196	$5,330	2-M	2,143	211
Metro State Coll of Denver, Denver, CO 80217-3362	1963	$2,479 (S)	NA	5-B	18,445	1,000
Metro State Univ, St. Paul, MN 55106-5000	1971	$3,111 (S)	NA	5-M	6,010	587
Miami Univ, Oxford, OH 45056	1809	$6,915 (S)	$5,970	12-D	16,946	1,035
Michigan State Univ, East Lansing, MI 48824	1855	$5,627 (S)	$4,678	5-D	44,227	2,673
Michigan Tech Univ, Houghton, MI 49931-1295	1885	$5,887 (S)	$5,181	5-D	6,336	415
MidAmerica Nazarene Univ, Olathe, KS 66062-1899	1966	$12,280	$5,614	2-M	1,684	151
Middlebury Coll, Middlebury, VT 05753-6002	1800	$34,300 (C)	NA	1-D	2,307	237
Middle Tennessee State Univ, Murfreesboro, TN 37132	1911	$3,194 (S)	$3,800	5-D	20,073	963
Midwestern State Univ, Wichita Falls, TX 76308	1922	$2,576 (S)	$4,392	5-M	5,969	330
Millersville Univ of Pennsylvania, Millersville, PA 17551-0302	1855	$5,053 (S)	$5,100	5-M	7,556	447
Millikin Univ, Decatur, IL 62522-2084	1901	$18,384	$6,106	2-B	2,389	242
Millsaps Coll, Jackson, MS 39210-0001	1890	$16,546	$6,062	2-M	1,330	100
Mills Coll, Oakland, CA 94613-1000 (3)	1852	$20,622	$8,000	1-D	1,176	158
Milwaukee School of Engineering, Milwaukee, WI 53202-3109 (2)	1903	$21,855	$5,115	1-M	2,563	227
Minnesota State Univ, Mankato, Mankato, MN 56001	1868	$3,619 (S)	$3,677	5-M	13,242	600
Minnesota State Univ Moorhead, Moorhead, MN 56563-0002	1885	$3,377 (S)	$3,706	5-M	7,431	334
Minot State Univ, Minot, ND 58707-0002	1913	$2,554 (S)	$3,100	5-M	3,515	236
Mississippi Coll, Clinton, MS 39058	1826	$10,712	$4,680	2-F	3,223	247
Mississippi State Univ, Mississippi State, MS 39762	1878	$3,586 (S)	$5,704	5-D	16,878	1,065
Mississippi Univ for Women, Columbus, MS 39701-9998 (4)	1884	$3,054 (S)	$3,030	5-M	2,328	214
Mississippi Valley State Univ, Itta Bena, MS 38941-1400	1946	$3,158 (S)	$3,187	5-M	3,081	162
Missouri Baptist Coll, St. Louis, MO 63141-8660	1964	$10,682	$5,080	2-M	3,105	141
Missouri Southern State Coll, Joplin, MO 64801-1595	1937	$2,866 (S)	$3,800	5-B	5,899	294
Missouri Valley Coll, Marshall, MO 65340-3197	1889	$12,750	$5,200	2-B	1,577	92
Missouri Western State Coll, St. Joseph, MO 64507-2294	1915	$3,224 (S)	$3,636	5-B	5,102	323
Molloy Coll, Rockville Centre, NY 11571-5002	1955	$13,940	NA	1-M	2,538	324
Monmouth Coll, Monmouth, IL 61462-1998	1853	$17,760	$4,730	2-B	1,072	113
Monmouth Univ, West Long Branch, NJ 07764-1898	1933	$17,074	$7,076	1-M	5,753	463
Montana State Univ-Billings, Billings, MT 59101-0298	1927	$3,430 (S)	$3,000	5-M	4,313	249
Montana State Univ-Bozeman, Bozeman, MT 59717	1893	$3,381 (S)	$5,050	5-D	11,670	735
Montana State Univ-Northern, Havre, MT 59501-7751	1929	$3,214 (S)	$4,190	5-M	1,589	103
Montana Tech of The Univ of Montana, Butte, MT 59701-8997	1895	$3,404 (S)	$4,441	5-M	2,086	150
Montclair State Univ, Upper Montclair, NJ 07043-1624	1908	$5,741 (S)	$6,956	5-D	13,855	962
Montreat Coll, Montreat, NC 28757-1267	1916	$12,318	$4,846	2-M	1,109	57
Moody Bible Inst, Chicago, IL 60610-3284	1886	$1,382	$6,020	2-F	1,624	101
Moravian Coll, Bethlehem, PA 18018-6650	1742	$20,495	$6,570	2-F	1,834	177
Morehead State Univ, Morehead, KY 40351	1922	$2,710 (S)	$3,800	5-M	9,027	469
Morehouse Coll, Atlanta, GA 30314 (1)	1867	$12,432	$7,382	1-B	2,808	237
Morgan State Univ, Baltimore, MD 21251	1867	$4,508 (S)	$5,980	5-D	7,112	576
Morris Brown Coll, Atlanta, GA 30314-4140	1881	$10,866	$5,870	2-B	2,874	184
Mountain State Univ, Beckley, WV 25802-2830	1933	$4,560	$3,982	1-M	2,525	126
Mount Aloysius Coll, Cresson, PA 16630-1999	1939	$13,936	$5,190	2-B	1,153	123
Mount Holyoke Coll, South Hadley, MA 01075 (3)	1837	$26,408	$7,720	1-M	2,038	238

Name, address	Year Founded	Tuition & Fees	Rm. & Board	Control, Degree	Enroll-ment	Faculty
Mount Ida Coll, Newton Center, MA 02459-3310	1899	$15,830	$8,950	1-B	1,165	153
Mount Marty Coll, Yankton, SD 57078-3724	1936	$11,384	$4,272	2-M	1,168	104
Mount Mary Coll, Milwaukee, WI 53222-4597 (3)	1913	$13,394	$4,630	2-M	1,216	164
Mount Mercy Coll, Cedar Rapids, IA 52402-4797	1928	$14,560	$4,830	2-B	1,387	121
Mount Olive Coll, Mount Olive, NC 28365	1951	$10,010	$4,400	2-B	1,775	176
Mount Saint Mary Coll, Newburgh, NY 12550-3494	1960	$12,675	$6,020	1-M	2,366	178
Mount St. Mary's Coll, Los Angeles, CA 90049-1599 (4)	1925	$18,588	$7,459	2-M	1,965	269
Mount Saint Mary's Coll & Seminary, Emmitsburg, MD 21727-7799	1808	$18,680	$7,060	2-F	1,969	166
Mt. Sierra Coll, Monrovia, CA 91016	NR	$9,359	NA	3-B	1,100	50
Mount Union Coll, Alliance, OH 44601-3993	1846	$16,310	$4,810	2-B	2,368	231
Mount Vernon Nazarene Univ, Mount Vernon, OH 43050-9500	1964	$13,288	$4,527	2-M	2,232	182
Muhlenberg Coll, Allentown, PA 18104-5586	1848	$22,210	$5,960	2-B	2,629	235
Murray State Univ, Murray, KY 42071-0009	1922	$2,755 (S)	$4,150	5-M	9,635	509
Muskingum Coll, New Concord, OH 43762	1837	$14,075	$5,600	2-M	2,022	140
Naropa Univ, Boulder, CO 80302-6697	1974	$15,056	$5,810	1-M	1,127	209
Natl-Louis Univ, Evanston, IL 60201-1796	1886	$14,910	$6,013	1-D	7,879	298
Natl Univ, La Jolla, CA 92037-1011	1971	$8,025	NA	1-M	18,267	821
Nazareth Coll of Rochester, Rochester, NY 14618-3790	1924	$15,384	$6,660	1-M	3,107	204
Nebraska Wesleyan Univ, Lincoln, NE 68504-2796	1887	$14,641	$4,126	2-M	1,719	164
Neumann Coll, Aston, PA 19014-1298	1965	$15,030	$7,010	2-M	2,014	192
New Coll of California, San Francisco, CA 94102-5206	1971	$9,240	NA	1-M	1,088	90
New Jersey City Univ, Jersey City, NJ 07305-1597	1927	$5,063 (S)	$5,800	5-M	8,824	520
New Jersey Inst of Tech, Newark, NJ 07102	1881	$7,200 (S)	$7,490	5-D	8,862	651
Newman Univ, Wichita, KS 67213-2097	1933	$12,040	$4,590	2-M	2,071	181
New Mexico Highlands Univ, Las Vegas, NM 87701	1893	$2,094 (S)	$3,998	5-M	3,284	136
New Mexico Inst of Mining & Tech, Socorro, NM 87801	1000	$2,722 (S)	$4,430	5-D	1,588	127
New Mexico State Univ, Las Cruces, NM 88003-8001	1888	$3,006 (S)	$4,296	5-D	15,224	934
New Orleans Baptist Theological Seminary, New Orleans, LA 70126-4858 (2)	1917	$3,050	NA	2-D	2,712	84
New School Bachelor of Arts, New School Univ, New York, NY 10011-8603	1919	$14,558	$9,612	1-D	1,154	442
New York Inst of Tech, Old Westbury, NY 11568-8000	1955	$14,876	$7,580	1-F	8,934	784
New York Univ, New York, NY 10012-1019	1831	$25,380	$9,820	1-D	37,134	3,742
Niagara Univ, Niagara University, NY 14109	1856	$15,300	$6,950	2-M	3,278	280
Nicholls State Univ, Thibodaux, LA 70310	1948	$2,440 (S)	$3,002	5-M	7,188	275
Nichols Coll, Dudley, MA 01571-5000	1815	$15,650	$7,810	1-M	1,363	42
Norfolk State Univ, Norfolk, VA 23504	1935	$2,916 (S)	$5,466	5-D	6,721	466
North Carolina Agr & Tech State Univ, Greensboro, NC 27411	1891	$2,189 (S)	$2,595	5-D	7,748	NA
North Carolina Central Univ, Durham, NC 27707-3129	1910	$2,350 (S)	$3,284	5-F	5,753	349
North Carolina State Univ, Raleigh, NC 27695	1887	$3,452 (S)	$5,796	5-D	29,286	1,684
North Carolina Wesleyan Coll, Rocky Mount, NC 27804-8677	1956	$9,768	$5,882	2-B	1,886	192
North Central Coll, Naperville, IL 60566-7063	1861	$17,175	$5,724	2-M	2,605	226
North Central Univ, Minneapolis, MN 55404-1322	1930	$8,554	$2,270	2-B	1,163	88
North Dakota State Univ, Fargo, ND 58105-5454	1890	$3,272 (S)	$3,732	5-D	10,538	595
Northeastern Illinois Univ, Chicago, IL 60625-4699	1961	$2,898 (S)	NA	5-M	10,999	590
Northeastern State Univ, Tahlequah, OK 74464-2399	1846	$2,130 (S)	$2,724	5-F	8,603	446
Northeastern Univ, Boston, MA 02115-5096	1898	$20,733	$9,345	1-D	18,180	1,105
Northern Arizona Univ, Flagstaff, AZ 86011	1899	$2,488 (S)	$4,910	5-D	19,728	1,389
Northern Illinois Univ, De Kalb, IL 60115-2854	1895	$4,475 (S)	$5,070	5-D	23,783	1,249
Northern Kentucky Univ, Highland Heights, KY 41099	1968	$2,886 (S)	$4,460	5-F	12,529	878
Northern Michigan Univ, Marquette, MI 49855-5301	1899	$4,257 (S)	$5,436	5-M	8,577	399
Northern State Univ, Aberdeen, SD 57401-7198	1901	$3,539 (S)	$2,740	5-M	3,088	109
North Georgia Coll & State Univ, Dahlonega, GA 30597-1001	1873	$2,496 (S)	$3,826	5-M	3,864	313
North Greenville Coll, Tigerville, SC 29688-1892	1892	$8,450	$4,790	2-B	1,380	120
North Park Univ, Chicago, IL 60625-4895	1891	$17,790	$5,830	2-D	2,181	121
Northwest Coll, Kirkland, WA 98083-0579	1934	$12,853	$5,996	2-M	1,096	82
Northwestern Coll, Orange City, IA 51041-1996	1882	$13,750	$3,880	2-B	1,294	115
Northwestern Coll, St. Paul, MN 55113-1598	1902	$16,500	$5,330	2-B	2,278	182
Northwestern Oklahoma State Univ, Alva, OK 73717-2799	1897	$2,032 (S)	$2,550	5-M	2,055	149
Northwestern State Univ of Louisiana, Natchitoches, LA 71497	1884	$2,429 (S)	$3,132	5-M	9,415	256
Northwestern Univ, Evanston, IL 60208	1851	$27,228	$8,446	1-D	15,649	1,103
Northwest Missouri State Univ, Maryville, MO 64468-6001	1905	$3,600 (S)	$4,322	5-M	6,925	242
Northwest Nazarene Univ, Nampa, ID 83686-5897	1913	$15,060	$4,285	2-M	1,316	90
Northwood Univ, Midland, MI 48640-2398	1959	$12,531	$5,829	1-M	3,654	113
Northwood Univ, Texas Campus, Cedar Hill, TX 75104-1204	1966	$12,531	$5,604	1-B	1,114	25
Norwich Univ, Northfield, VT 05663	1819	$16,194	$6,068	1-M	2,707	272
Notre Dame de Namur Univ, Belmont, CA 94002-1997	1851	$19,390	$8,982	2-M	1,712	180
Nova Southeastern Univ, Fort Lauderdale, FL 33314-7721	1964	$12,180	NA	1-D	19,029	1,279
Nyack Coll, Nyack, NY 10960-3698	1882	$13,280	$6,200	2-B	1,897	192
Oakland City Univ, Oakland City, IN 47660-1099	1885	$11,808	$4,330	2-D	1,800	162
Oakland Univ, Rochester, MI 48309-4401	1957	$4,638 (S)	$4,978	5-D	15,875	803
Oakwood Coll, Huntsville, AL 35896	1896	$9,420	$5,484	2-B	1,778	161
Oberlin Coll, Oberlin, OH 44074	1833	$26,580	$6,560	1-M	2,863	273
Occidental Coll, Los Angeles, CA 90041-3314	1887	$25,420	$7,100	1-M	1,796	179
Oglethorpe Univ, Atlanta, GA 30319-2797	1835	$19,100	$6,060	1-M	1,267	122
Ohio Dominican Coll, Columbus, OH 43219-2099	1911	$12,730	$5,370	2-B	2,197	131
Ohio Northern Univ, Ada, OH 45810-1599	1871	$22,275	$5,490	2-F	3,345	315
The Ohio State Univ-Mansfield Campus, Mansfield, OH 44906-1599	1958	$3,606 (S)	NA	5-B	1,495	64
The Ohio State Univ-Newark Campus, Newark, OH 43055-1797	1957	$3,606 (S)	NA	5-B	2,079	89
The Ohio State Univ, Columbus, OH 43210	1870	$4,788 (S)	$6,031	5-D	48,477	3,526
The Ohio State Univ at Lima, Lima, OH 45804-3576	1960	$3,606 (S)	NA	5-B	1,356	91
The Ohio State Univ at Marion, Marion, OH 43302-5695	1958	$3,606 (S)	NA	5-B	1,390	95
Ohio Univ-Chillicothe, Chillicothe, OH 45601-0629	1946	$3,246 (S)	NA	5-M	1,645	101
Ohio Univ-Eastern, St. Clairsville, OH 43950-9724	1957	$3,033 (S)	NA	5-B	1,118	114
Ohio Univ-Lancaster, Lancaster, OH 43130-1097	1968	$3,246 (S)	NA	5-M	1,664	101
Ohio Univ-Southern Campus, Ironton, OH 45638-2214	1956	$2,988 (S)	NA	5-M	1,891	120
Ohio Univ-Zanesville, Zanesville, OH 43701-2695	1946	$3,246 (S)	NA	5-M	1,630	96
Ohio Univ, Athens, OH 45701-2979	1804	$5,493 (S)	$6,276	5-D	20,163	1,143
Ohio Wesleyan Univ, Delaware, OH 43015	1842	$22,860	$6,810	2-B	1,886	177
Oklahoma Baptist Univ, Shawnee, OK 74804	1910	$11,040	$3,750	2-M	1,933	153
Oklahoma Christian Univ, Oklahoma City, OK 73136-1100	1950	$12,100	$4,400	2-M	1,811	165

Name, address	Year Founded	Tuition & Fees	Rm. & Board	Control, Degree	Enroll-ment	Faculty
Oklahoma City Univ, Oklahoma City, OK 73106-1402	1904	$12,000	$5,200	2-F	3,705	304
Oklahoma Panhandle State Univ, Goodwell, OK 73939-0430	1909	$1,911 (S)	$2,580	5-B	1,226	67
Oklahoma State Univ, Stillwater, OK 74078	1890	$2,794 (S)	$4,856	5-D	21,872	1,111
Old Dominion Univ, Norfolk, VA 23529	1930	$4,022 (S)	$5,364	5-D	19,627	934
Olivet Nazarene Univ, Bourbonnais, IL 60914-2271	1907	$13,464	$4,980	2-M	3,350	108
Oral Roberts Univ, Tulsa, OK 74171-0001	1963	$12,980	$5,570	2-D	3,677	289
Oregon Health & Sci Univ, Portland, OR 97201-3098	1974	$6,005 (S)	NA	12-D	1,849	836
Oregon Inst of Tech, Klamath Falls, OR 97601-8801	1947	$3,642 (S)	$5,154	5-M	3,088	214
Oregon State Univ, Corvallis, OR 97331	1868	$3,987 (S)	$5,625	5-D	18,034	1,386
Otterbein Coll, Westerville, OH 43081	1847	$17,928	$5,511	2-M	2,985	246
Ouachita Baptist Univ, Arkadelphia, AR 71998-0001	1886	$12,010	$4,450	2-B	1,657	147
Our Lady of Holy Cross Coll, New Orleans, LA 70131-7399	1916	$5,620	NA	2-M	1,347	110
Our Lady of the Lake Univ of San Antonio, San Antonio, TX 78207-4689	1895	$12,786	$4,550	2-D	3,324	264
Pace Univ, New York, NY 10038	1906	$17,030	$7,170	1-D	13,498	1,282
Pacific Lutheran Univ, Tacoma, WA 98447	1890	$17,728	$5,590	2-M	3,425	280
Pacific Union Coll, Angwin, CA 94508-9707	1882	$16,575	$4,806	2-M	1,422	115
Pacific Univ, Forest Grove, OR 97116-1797	1849	$19,292	$5,379	1-D	2,293	259
Palm Beach Atlantic Coll, West Palm Beach, FL 33416-4708	1968	$13,170	$5,070	2-F	2,584	215
Palmer Coll of Chiropractic, Davenport, IA 52803-5287	1897	$17,550	NA	1-F	1,721	97
Park Univ, Parkville, MO 64152-3795	1875	$5,160	$5,000	1-M	9,482	651
Parsons School of Design, New School Univ, New York, NY 10011-8878	1896	$23,126	$9,612	1-M	2,733	643
Peirce Coll, Philadelphia, PA 19102-4699 (4)	1865	$10,650	NA	1-B	2,837	148
Pennsylvania Coll of Tech, Williamsport, PA 17701-5778	1965	$8,610 (S)	$5,000	12-B	5,538	411
The Pennsylvania State Univ Abington Coll, Abington, PA 19001-3918	1950	$7,258 (S)	NA	12-B	3,179	211
The Pennsylvania State Univ Altoona Coll, Altoona, PA 16601-3760	1939	$7,278 (S)	$5,300	12-B	3,823	258
The Pennsylvania State Univ at Erie, The Behrend Coll, Erie, PA 16563-0001	1948	$7,396 (S)	$5,300	12-M	3,708	255
The Pennsylvania State Univ Berks Campus of the Berks-Lehigh Valley Coll, Reading, PA 19610-6009	1924	$7,278 (S)	$5,300	12-B	2,329	150
The Pennsylvania State Univ Harrisburg Campus of the Capital Coll, Middletown, PA 17057-4898	1966	$7,376 (S)	$5,980	12-D	3,239	256
The Pennsylvania State Univ Schuylkill Campus of the Capital Coll, Schuylkill Haven, PA 17972-2208	1934	$7,154 (S)	$5,300	12-B	1,092	83
The Pennsylvania State Univ Univ Park Campus, University Park, PA 16802	1855	$7,396 (S)	$5,310	12-D	40,828	2,407
Pepperdine Univ, Malibu, CA 90263-0002	1937	$26,370	$7,930	2-D	7,383	680
Peru State Coll, Peru, NE 68421	1867	$2,546 (S)	$3,796	5-M	1,629	120
Pfeiffer Univ, Misenheimer, NC 28109-0960	1885	$12,066	$3,874	2-M	1,671	124
Philadelphia Biblical Univ, Langhorne, PA 19047-2990	1913	$11,985	$5,405	2-M	1,444	133
Philadelphia Univ, Philadelphia, PA 19144-5497	1884	$17,600	$7,122	1-M	3,204	374
Piedmont Coll, Demorest, GA 30535-0010	1897	$10,500	$4,400	2-M	1,933	169
Pikeville Coll, Pikeville, KY 41501	1889	$8,200	$3,800	2-F	1,194	92
Pittsburg State Univ, Pittsburg, KS 66762	1903	$2,338 (S)	$3,890	5-M	6,723	269
Plattsburgh State Univ of New York, Plattsburgh, NY 12901-2681	1889	$4,149 (S)	$5,580	5-M	6,236	437
Plymouth State Coll, Plymouth, NH 03264-1595	1871	$5,550 (S)	$5,474	5-M	4,418	301
Point Loma Nazarene Univ, San Diego, CA 92106-2899	1902	$15,300	$6,320	2-M	2,881	277
Point Park Coll, Pittsburgh, PA 15222-1984	1960	$13,686	$5,948	1-M	2,969	266
Polytechnic Univ, Brooklyn Campus, Brooklyn, NY 11201-2990	1854	$22,940	$5,250	1-D	3,051	333
Polytechnic Univ of Puerto Rico, Hato Rey, PR 00919	1966	$5,025	NA	1-M	5,408	279
Pomona Coll, Claremont, CA 91711	1887	$25,010	$8,950	1-B	1,577	227
Pontifical Catholic Univ of Puerto Rico, Ponce, PR 00717-0777	1948	$4,160	$2,840	2-D	7,270	248
Portland State Univ, Portland, OR 97207-0751	1946	$3,720 (S)	$7,500	5-D	20,185	998
Prairie View A&M Univ, Prairie View, TX 77446-0188	1878	$3,232 (S)	$6,461	5-D	6,747	299
Pratt Inst, Brooklyn, NY 11205-3899	1887	$21,354	$7,940	1-F	4,199	756
Presbyterian Coll, Clinton, SC 29325	1880	$18,200	$5,156	2-B	1,202	110
Prescott Coll, Prescott, AZ 86301-2990	1966	$14,055	NA	1-M	1,005	83
Princeton Univ, Princeton, NJ 08544-1019	1746	$26,160	$7,453	1-D	6,668	961
Providence Coll, Providence, RI 02918	1917	$19,695	$7,925	2-M	5,308	329
Purchase Coll, State Univ of New York, Purchase, NY 10577-1400	1967	$4,200 (S)	$6,500	5-M	4,018	341
Purdue Univ, West Lafayette, IN 47907	1869	$4,164 (S)	$6,120	5-D	38,158	1,891
Purdue Univ Calumet, Hammond, IN 46323-2094	1951	$3,339 (S)	NA	5-M	NA	480
Purdue Univ North Central, Westville, IN 46391-9542	1967	$3,589 (S)	NA	5-M	3,492	242
Queens Coll of the City Univ of New York, Flushing, NY 11367-1597	1937	$3,403 (S)	NA	11-M	15,391	1,065
Queens Univ of Charlotte, Charlotte, NC 28274-0002	1857	$12,290	$6,010	2-M	1,704	91
Quincy Univ, Quincy, IL 62301-2699	1860	$16,360	$5,320	2-M	1,319	122
Quinnipiac Univ, Hamden, CT 06518-1940	1929	$18,840	$8,530	1-F	6,675	435
Radford Univ, Radford, VA 24142	1910	$3,069 (S)	$5,233	5-M	9,142	551
Ramapo Coll of New Jersey, Mahwah, NJ 07430-1680	1969	$6,178 (S)	$7,372	5-M	5,199	339
Randolph-Macon Coll, Ashland, VA 23005-5505	1830	$19,095	$5,300	2-B	1,150	137
Reed Coll, Portland, OR 97202-8199	1908	$26,260	$7,090	1-M	1,420	124
Regis Coll, Weston, MA 02493 (3)	1927	$18,400	$8,350	2-M	1,081	117
Regis Univ, Denver, CO 80221-1099	1877	$18,570	$7,150	2-M	13,547	942
Reinhardt Coll, Waleska, GA 30183-2981	1883	$8,700	$4,885	2-B	1,083	106
Rensselaer Polytechnic Inst, Troy, NY 12180-3590	1824	$25,555	$8,308	1-D	8,106	465
Rhode Island Coll, Providence, RI 02908-1924	1854	$3,521 (S)	$5,760	5-D	8,513	646
Rhode Island School of Design, Providence, RI 02903-2784	1877	$23,397	$6,830	1-F	2,119	399
Rhodes Coll, Memphis, TN 38112-1690	1848	$20,536	$5,900	2-M	1,551	155
Rice Univ, Houston, TX 77251-1892	1912	$17,135	$7,200	1-D	4,534	741
The Richard Stockton Coll of New Jersey, Pomona, NJ 08240-0195	1969	$5,136 (S)	$5,845	5-M	6,457	359
Rider Univ, Lawrenceville, NJ 08648-3001	1865	$19,700	$7,950	1-M	5,456	438
Rivier Coll, Nashua, NH 03060-5086	1933	$15,520	$6,100	2-M	2,375	209
Roanoke Coll, Salem, VA 24153-3794	1842	$18,681	$6,008	2-B	1,790	176
Robert Morris Coll, Chicago, IL 60605	1913	$12,750	NA	1-B	5,319	391
Robert Morris Univ, Moon Township, PA 15108-1189	1921	$12,000	$6,580	1-D	4,719	312
Roberts Wesleyan Coll, Rochester, NY 14624-1997	1866	$14,916	$5,244	2-M	1,697	151
Rochester Inst of Tech, Rochester, NY 14623-5698	1829	$18,966	$7,266	1-D	14,430	1,139
Rockford Coll, Rockford, IL 61108-2393	1847	$17,450	$5,630	1-M	1,359	147
Rockhurst Univ, Kansas City, MO 64110-2561	1910	$15,140	$4,920	2-M	2,730	225
Rogers State Univ, Claremore, OK 74017-3252	1909	$1,730 (S)	$3,070	5-B	2,852	122
Roger Williams Univ, Bristol, RI 02809	1956	$20,075	$8,935	1-F	4,663	337

Name, address	Year Founded	Tuition & Fees	Rm. & Board	Control, Degree	Enroll-ment	Faculty
Rollins Coll, Winter Park, FL 32789-4499	1885	$24,958	$7,657	1-M	2,421	239
Roosevelt Univ, Chicago, IL 60605-1394	1945	$13,970	$6,270	1-D	7,490	640
Rose-Hulman Inst of Tech, Terre Haute, IN 47803-3920 (2)	1874	$21,668	$6,039	1-M	1,749	136
Rosemont Coll, Rosemont, PA 19010-1699 (3)	1921	$16,750	$7,310	2-M	1,108	167
Rowan Univ, Glassboro, NJ 08028-1701	1923	$5,779 (S)	$6,586	5-D	9,790	747
Rutgers, The State Univ of New Jersey, Camden, Camden, NJ 08102-1401	1927	$6,484 (S)	$6,776	5-F	5,097	380
Rutgers, The State Univ of New Jersey, Newark, Newark, NJ 07102	1892	$6,376 (S)	$7,208	5-D	9,592	643
Rutgers, The State Univ of New Jersey, New Brunswick, New Brunswick, NJ 08901-1281	1766	$6,620 (S)	$6,676	5-D	35,652	2,179
Sacred Heart Univ, Fairfield, CT 06432-1000	1963	$17,060	$7,998	2-M	5,959	455
Sage Coll of Albany, Albany, NY 12208-3425	1957	$14,320	$6,626	1-B	1,271	65
Saginaw Valley State Univ, University Center, MI 48710	1963	$4,340 (S)	$5,200	5-M	8,900	228
St. Ambrose Univ, Davenport, IA 52803-2898	1882	$15,750	$5,560	2-D	3,291	289
Saint Anselm Coll, Manchester, NH 03102-1310	1889	$20,125	$7,350	2-B	1,964	164
St. Augustine Coll, Chicago, IL 60640-3501	1980	$7,232	NA	1-B	1,814	131
Saint Augustine's Coll, Raleigh, NC 27610-2298	1867	$8,030	$4,960	2-B	1,360	129
St. Bonaventure Univ, St. Bonaventure, NY 14778-2284	1858	$16,156	$5,950	2-M	2,710	207
St. Cloud State Univ, St. Cloud, MN 56301-4498	1869	$3,883 (S)	$3,614	5-D	15,961	733
St. Edward's Univ, Austin, TX 78704-6489	1885	$12,728	$5,118	2-M	4,151	336
St. Francis Coll, Brooklyn Heights, NY 11201-4398	1884	$9,550	NA	2-B	2,451	227
Saint Francis Univ, Loretto, PA 15940-0600	1847	$17,512	$6,974	2-M	2,027	117
St. John Fisher Coll, Rochester, NY 14618-3597	1948	$16,450	$7,000	2-M	2,968	283
Saint John's Univ, Collegeville, MN 56321	1857	$18,325	$5,606	2-F	2,039	198
St. John's Univ, Jamaica, NY 11439	1870	$17,330	$9,330	2-D	18,623	1,167
Saint Joseph Coll, West Hartford, CT 06117-2700 (3)	1932	$18,360	$7,600	2-M	1,939	84
St. Joseph's Coll, New York, Brooklyn, NY 11205-3688	1916	$10,400	NA	1-M	1,189	139
St. Joseph's Coll, Suffolk Campus, Patchogue, NY 11772-2399	1916	$10,082	NA	1-M	3,444	318
Saint Joseph's Univ, Philadelphia, PA 19131-1395	1851	$21,270	$8,445	2-D	7,313	454
St. Lawrence Univ, Canton, NY 13617-1455	1856	$24,850	$7,755	1-M	2,097	192
Saint Leo Univ, Saint Leo, FL 33574-6665	1889	$12,770	$6,480	2-M	1,159	102
Saint Louis Univ, St. Louis, MO 63103-2097	1818	$19,830	$6,760	2-D	11,145	878
Saint Martin's Coll, Lacey, WA 98503-7500	1895	$16,860	$5,098	2-M	1,474	75
Saint Mary-of-the-Woods Coll, Saint Mary-of-the-Woods, IN 47876 (3)	1840	$15,560	$5,750	2-M	1,498	62
Saint Mary's Coll, Notre Dame, IN 46556 (3)	1844	$19,390	$6,549	2-B	1,523	181
Saint Mary's Coll of California, Moraga, CA 94556	1863	$19,525	$8,050	2-D	4,127	467
St. Mary's Coll of Maryland, St. Mary's City, MD 20686-3001	1840	$8,082 (S)	$6,613	5-B	1,688	184
Saint Mary's Univ of Minnesota, Winona, MN 55987-1399	1912	$15,195	$4,780	2-D	5,008	146
St. Mary's Univ of San Antonio, San Antonio, TX 78228-8507	1852	$14,700	$5,535	2-D	4,136	337
Saint Michael's Coll, Colchester, VT 05439	1904	$21,200	$7,255	2-M	2,630	190
St. Norbert Coll, De Pere, WI 54115-2099	1898	$18,007	$5,162	2-M	2,131	175
St. Olaf Coll, Northfield, MN 55057-1098	1874	$22,200	$4,750	2-B	3,011	322
Saint Peter's Coll, Jersey City, NJ 07306-5997	1872	$16,552	$7,053	2-M	3,225	305
St. Thomas Aquinas Coll, Sparkill, NY 10976	1952	$14,100	$7,980	1-M	2,140	150
St. Thomas Univ, Miami, FL 33054-6459	1961	$15,450	$5,040	2-F	2,403	221
Saint Vincent Coll, Latrobe, PA 15650-2690	1846	$17,380	$5,434	2-B	1,222	112
Saint Xavier Univ, Chicago, IL 60655-3105	1847	$15,130	$5,974	2-M	4,916	347
Salem Coll, Winston-Salem, NC 27108-0548 (3)	1772	$14,495	$8,570	2-M	1,074	92
Salem State Coll, Salem, MA 01970-5353	1854	$3,738 (S)	$5,428	5-M	8,349	533
Salisbury Univ, Salisbury, MD 21801-6837	1925	$4,656 (S)	$6,340	5-M	6,682	454
Salve Regina Univ, Newport, RI 02840-4192	1934	$18,360	$8,100	2-D	2,267	269
Samford Univ, Birmingham, AL 35229-0002	1841	$11,490	$4,850	2-D	4,377	409
Sam Houston State Univ, Huntsville, TX 77341	1879	$2,818 (S)	$3,672	5-D	12,996	528
San Diego State Univ, San Diego, CA 92182	1897	$1,776 (S)	$7,970	5-D	34,171	1,924
San Francisco State Univ, San Francisco, CA 94132-1722	1899	$1,826 (S)	$6,930	5-D	26,862	1,712
San Jose State Univ, San Jose, CA 95192-0001	1857	$1,912 (S)	$7,220	5-M	28,007	1,622
Santa Clara Univ, Santa Clara, CA 95053	1851	$22,572	$8,436	2-D	7,368	623
Sarah Lawrence Coll, Bronxville, NY 10708	1926	$27,982	$9,534	1-M	1,553	222
Savannah Coll of Art & Design, Savannah, GA 31402-3146	1978	$17,955	$7,620	1-M	5,338	285
Savannah State Univ, Savannah, GA 31404	1890	$2,550 (S)	$4,204	5-M	2,360	138
School of the Art Inst of Chicago, Chicago, IL 60603-3103	1866	$21,300	$6,500	1-M	2,675	455
School of the Museum of Fine Arts, Boston, MA 02115	1876	$19,676	$9,240	1-M	1,085	104
School of Visual Arts, New York, NY 10010-3994	1947	$17,000	$6,700	3-M	5,186	848
Seattle Pacific Univ, Seattle, WA 98119-1997	1891	$16,425	$6,249	2-D	3,615	267
Seattle Univ, Seattle, WA 98122	1891	$17,865	$6,318	2-D	5,981	480
Seton Hall Univ, South Orange, NJ 07079-2697	1856	$19,400	$8,060	2-D	9,604	834
Seton Hill Univ, Greensburg, PA 15601 (4)	1883	$16,425	$5,450	2-M	1,370	128
Shawnee State Univ, Portsmouth, OH 45662-4344	1986	$3,402 (S)	$5,232	5-B	3,364	257
Shaw Univ, Raleigh, NC 27601-2399	1865	$7,930	$4,880	2-F	2,523	298
Shenandoah Univ, Winchester, VA 22601-5195	1875	$17,000	$6,400	2-D	2,451	288
Shepherd Coll, Shepherdstown, WV 25443-3210	1871	$2,608 (S)	$4,454	5-B	4,391	330
Shippensburg Univ of Pennsylvania, Shippensburg, PA 17257-2299	1871	$5,004 (S)	$4,864	5-M	7,193	351
Siena Coll, Loudonville, NY 12211-1462	1937	$15,870	$6,815	2-M	3,384	272
Siena Heights Univ, Adrian, MI 49221-1796	1919	$13,630	$5,130	2-M	2,024	NA
Simmons Coll, Boston, MA 02115 (3)	1899	$21,668	$8,750	1-D	3,282	351
Simpson Coll, Indianola, IA 50125-1297	1860	$15,908	$5,292	2-B	1,816	140
Simpson Coll & Graduate School, Redding, CA 96003-8606	1921	$12,470	$5,410	2-M	1,161	75
Skidmore Coll, Saratoga Springs, NY 12866-1632	1903	$26,676	$7,525	1-M	2,544	206
Slippery Rock Univ of Pennsylvania, Slippery Rock, PA 16057	1889	$4,942 (S)	$4,210	5-D	7,197	400
Smith Coll, Northampton, MA 01063 (3)	1871	$24,550	$8,560	1-D	3,113	300
Sojourner-Douglass Coll, Baltimore, MD 21205-1814 (4)	1980	$4,984	NA	1-M	1,124	136
Sonoma State Univ, Rohnert Park, CA 94928-3609	1960	$2,032 (S)	$6,921	5-M	7,590	502
South Carolina State Univ, Orangeburg, SC 29117-0001	1896	$4,096 (S)	$1,792	5-D	4,467	271
South Dakota School of Mines & Tech, Rapid City, SD 57701-3995	1885	$3,849 (S)	$3,370	5-D	2,424	130
South Dakota State Univ, Brookings, SD 57007	1881	$3,808 (S)	$3,040	5-D	9,350	517
Southeastern Coll of the Assemblies of God, Lakeland, FL 33801-6099	1935	$8,247	$4,606	2-B	1,363	80
Southeastern Louisiana Univ, Hammond, LA 70402	1925	$2,607 (S)	$3,440	5-M	14,522	655
Southeastern Oklahoma State Univ, Durant, OK 74701-0609	1909	$2,264 (S)	$2,542	5-M	4,025	225
Southeast Missouri State Univ, Cape Girardeau, MO 63701-4799	1873	$3,525 (S)	$4,842	5-M	9,352	544
Southern Adventist Univ, Collegedale, TN 37315-0370	1892	$12,220	$4,110	2-M	2,200	161

Name, address	Year Founded	Tuition & Fees	Rm. & Board	Control, Degree	Enroll-ment	Faculty
Southern Arkansas Univ-Magnolia, Magnolia, AR 71753	1909	$2,716 (S)	$3,082	5-M	3,127	168
Southern Connecticut State Univ, New Haven, CT 06515-1355	1893	$4,026 (S)	$6,588	5-M	12,254	906
Southern Illinois Univ Carbondale, Carbondale, IL 62901-6806	1869	$4,468 (S)	$4,610	5-D	21,598	1,126
Southern Illinois Univ Edwardsville, Edwardsville, IL 62026-0001	1957	$3,573 (S)	$5,016	5-F	12,442	751
Southern Methodist Univ, Dallas, TX 75275	1911	$20,796	$7,553	2-D	10,266	732
Southern Nazarene Univ, Bethany, OK 73008	1899	$10,086	$2,314	2-M	2,086	203
Southern New Hampshire Univ, Manchester, NH 03106-1045	1932	$16,786	$7,066	1-D	5,611	265
Southern Oregon Univ, Ashland, OR 97520	1926	$3,555 (S)	$5,445	5-M	5,465	327
Southern Polytechnic State Univ, Marietta, GA 30060-2896	1948	$2,354 (S)	$4,308	5-M	3,397	207
Southern Univ & Agr & Mech Coll, Baton Rouge, LA 70813	1880	$2,682 (S)	$3,683	5-D	9,095	548
Southern Univ at New Orleans, New Orleans, LA 70126-1009	1959	NA	NA	5-M	5,000	NA
Southern Utah Univ, Cedar City, UT 84720-2498	1897	$2,194 (S)	$2,866	5-M	6,095	300
Southern Wesleyan Univ, Central, SC 29630-1020	1906	$12,800	$4,480	2-M	2,166	149
Southwest Baptist Univ, Bolivar, MO 65613-2597	1878	$10,326	$3,100	2-M	3,564	212
Southwestern Adventist Univ, Keene, TX 76059	1894	$10,020	$4,778	2-M	1,191	92
Southwestern Assemblies of God Univ, Waxahachie, TX 75165-2397	1927	$8,600	$4,470	2-M	1,738	90
Southwestern Coll, Winfield, KS 67156-2499	1885	$13,076	$4,580	2-M	1,276	100
Southwestern Oklahoma State Univ, Weatherford, OK 73096-3098	1901	$2,138 (S)	$2,550	5-F	4,468	223
Southwestern Univ, Georgetown, TX 78626	1840	$16,650	$5,900	2-B	1,320	156
Southwest Missouri State Univ, Springfield, MO 65804-0094	1905	$3,748 (S)	$4,284	5-M	18,252	979
Southwest State Univ, Marshall, MN 56258-1598	1963	$3,716 (S)	$3,934	5-M	5,056	156
Southwest Texas State Univ, San Marcos, TX 78666	1899	$3,578 (S)	$5,152	5-D	23,517	989
Spalding Univ, Louisville, KY 40203-2188	1814	$11,496	$2,930	2-D	1,481	140
Spelman Coll, Atlanta, GA 30314-4399 (3)	1881	$11,880	$7,050	1-B	2,139	204
Spring Arbor Univ, Spring Arbor, MI 49283-9799	1873	$13,136	$4,840	2-M	2,616	84
Springfield Coll, Springfield, MA 01109-3797	1885	$18,690	$6,740	1-D	2,939	346
Spring Hill Coll, Mobile, AL 36608-1791	1830	$18,092	$6,540	2-M	1,483	126
Stanford Univ, Stanford, CA 94305-9991	1891	$25,917	$8,305	1-D	17,540	1,701
State Univ of New York at Albany, Albany, NY 12222-0001	1844	$4,720 (S)	$6,635	5-D	16,831	886
State Univ of New York at Binghamton, Binghamton, NY 13902-6000	1946	$4,551 (S)	$6,102	5-D	12,820	758
State Univ of New York at Farmingdale, Farmingdale, NY 11735	1912	$4,240 (S)	$7,250	5-B	5,449	322
State Univ of New York at New Paltz, New Paltz, NY 12561	1828	$4,000 (S)	$5,600	5-M	7,868	558
State Univ of New York at Oswego, Oswego, NY 13126	1861	$4,160 (S)	$6,696	5-M	8,407	421
State Univ of New York Coll at Brockport, Brockport, NY 14420-2997	1867	$4,127 (S)	$6,140	5-M	8,634	620
State Univ of New York Coll at Buffalo, Buffalo, NY 14222-1095	1867	$4,029 (S)	$5,484	5-M	11,743	716
State Univ of New York Coll at Cortland, Cortland, NY 13045	1868	$4,174 (S)	$6,390	5-M	7,705	479
State Univ of New York Coll at Fredonia, Fredonia, NY 14063-1136	1826	$4,375 (S)	$5,900	5-M	5,305	428
State Univ of New York Coll at Geneseo, Geneseo, NY 14454-1401	1871	$4,310 (S)	$5,660	5-M	5,649	340
State Univ of New York Coll at Old Westbury, Old Westbury, NY 11568-0210	1965	$3,985 (S)	$5,769	5-B	3,076	228
State Univ of New York Coll at Oneonta, Oneonta, NY 13820-4015	1889	$4,231 (S)	$5,750	5-M	5,740	415
State Univ of New York Coll at Potsdam, Potsdam, NY 13676	1816	$4,129 (S)	$6,390	5-M	4,325	346
State Univ of New York Coll of Agriculture & Tech at Cobleskill, Cobleskill, NY 12043	1916	$4,740 (S)	$6,460	5-B	2,450	169
State Univ of New York Coll of Environmental Sci & Forestry, Syracuse, NY 13210-2779	1911	$3,776 (S)	$8,670	5-D	1,971	125
State Univ of New York Empire State Coll, Saratoga Springs, NY 12866-4391	1971	$3,555 (S)	NA	5-M	8,395	419
State Univ of New York Inst of Tech at Utica/Rome, Utica, NY 13504-3050	1966	$4,055 (S)	$6,240	5-M	2,537	172
State Univ of New York Upstate Medical Univ, Syracuse, NY 13210-2334	1950	$3,860 (S)	$6,665	5-D	1,155	695
State Univ of West Georgia, Carrollton, GA 30118	1933	$2,468 (S)	$4,100	5-D	9,040	438
Stephen F. Austin State Univ, Nacogdoches, TX 75962	1923	$2,330 (S)	$4,575	5-D	11,569	582
Stetson Univ, DeLand, FL 32720-3781	1883	$20,975	$6,650	1-F	3,255	260
Stevens Inst of Tech, Hoboken, NJ 07030	1870	$23,150	$7,730	1-D	4,263	212
Stonehill Coll, Easton, MA 02357-5510	1948	$18,360	$8,492	2-M	2,622	230
Stony Brook Univ, State Univ of New York, Stony Brook, NY 11794	1957	$4,268 (S)	$6,730	5-D	20,855	1,264
Strayer Univ, Washington, DC 20005-2603	1892	$8,789	NA	3-M	14,009	528
Suffolk Univ, Boston, MA 02108-2770	1906	$16,616	$9,990	1-D	6,897	550
Sullivan Univ, Louisville, KY 40205	1864	$11,695	$3,555	3-M	4,422	120
Sul Ross State Univ, Alpine, TX 79832	1920	$2,792 (S)	$3,790	5-M	1,992	113
Susquehanna Univ, Selinsgrove, PA 17870	1858	$21,270	$6,000	2-B	1,949	163
Swarthmore Coll, Swarthmore, PA 19081-1397	1864	$26,376	$8,162	1-B	1,473	193
Syracuse Univ, Syracuse, NY 13244-0003	1870	$23,424	$9,510	1-D	14,421	1,404
Tarleton State Univ, Stephenville, TX 76402	1899	$2,920 (S)	$4,486	5-M	8,024	428
Taylor Univ, Upland, IN 46989-1001	1846	$16,572	$4,990	2-B	1,861	172
Teikyo Post Univ, Waterbury, CT 06723-2540	1890	$15,200	$6,600	1-B	1,350	153
Temple Univ, Philadelphia, PA 19122-6096	1884	$7,324 (S)	$6,800	12-D	29,872	2,046
Tennessee State Univ, Nashville, TN 37209-1561	1912	$3,033 (S)	$3,600	5-D	8,666	517
Tennessee Tech Univ, Cookeville, TN 38505	1915	$2,822 (S)	$3,880	5-D	8,653	500
Texas A&M Intl Univ, Laredo, TX 78041-1900	1969	$2,869 (S)	$3,210	5-M	3,373	196
Texas A&M Univ-Commerce, Commerce, TX 75429-3011	1889	$2,776 (S)	$4,800	5-D	7,934	518
Texas A&M Univ-Corpus Christi, Corpus Christi, TX 78412-5503	1947	$3,038 (S)	$7,020	5-D	7,369	304
Texas A&M Univ-Kingsville, Kingsville, TX 78363	1925	$2,862 (S)	$3,584	5-D	6,150	365
Texas A&M Univ-Texarkana, Texarkana, TX 75505-5518	1971	$1,896 (S)	NA	5-M	1,233	73
Texas A&M Univ, College Station, TX 77843	1876	$3,722 (S)	$5,266	5-D	44,618	2,178
Texas A&M Univ at Galveston, Galveston, TX 77553-1675	1962	$3,243 (S)	$3,977	5-B	1,366	129
Texas Christian Univ, Fort Worth, TX 76129-0002	1873	$15,040	$4,870	2-D	8,054	593
Texas Lutheran Univ, Seguin, TX 78155-5999	1891	$13,540	$4,150	2-B	1,473	128
Texas Southern Univ, Houston, TX 77004-4584	1947	$2,078 (S)	$4,498	5-D	8,119	291
Texas Tech Univ, Lubbock, TX 79409	1923	$3,489 (S)	$5,337	5-D	25,573	1,005
Texas Wesleyan Univ, Fort Worth, TX 76105-1536	1890	$10,690	$3,990	2-F	2,939	226
Texas Woman's Univ, Denton, TX 76201 (4)	1901	$2,504 (S)	$4,427	5-D	7,928	443
Thiel Coll, Greenville, PA 16125-2181	1866	$12,445	$5,974	2-B	1,189	105
Thomas Edison State Coll, Trenton, NJ 08608-1176	1972	$2,750 (S)	NA	5-M	8,335	613
Thomas Jefferson Univ, Philadelphia, PA 19107	1824	$18,200	$6,463	1-M	2,252	152
Thomas More Coll, Crestview Hills, KY 41017-3495	1921	$13,550	$4,150	2-M	1,555	136
Tiffin Univ, Tiffin, OH 44883-2161	1888	$11,850	$5,400	1-M	1,578	98
Touro Coll, New York, NY 10010	1971	$10,250	$4,700	1-D	7,791	889

Name, address	Year Founded	Tuition & Fees	Rm. & Board	Control, Degree	Enroll-ment	Faculty
Touro Univ Intl, Los Alamitos, CA 90720	NR	$6,400	NA	1-D	1,357	19
Towson Univ, Towson, MD 21252-0001	1866	$4,984 (S)	$6,030	5-D	16,980	1,219
Transylvania Univ, Lexington, KY 40508-1797	1780	$16,010	$5,770	2-B	1,052	97
Trevecca Nazarene Univ, Nashville, TN 37210-2877	1901	$11,390	$5,150	2-D	1,819	166
Trinity Coll, Hartford, CT 06106-3100	1823	$26,786	$7,514	1-M	2,256	249
Trinity Coll, Washington, DC 20017-1094 (3)	1897	$15,600	$6,970	2-M	1,410	195
Trinity Intl Univ, Deerfield, IL 60015-1284	1897	$15,350	$5,290	2-D	2,168	82
Trinity Univ, San Antonio, TX 78212-7200	1869	$16,554	$6,560	2-M	2,592	271
Tri-State Univ, Angola, IN 46703-1764	1884	$15,950	$5,250	1-B	1,268	88
Troy State Univ, Troy, AL 36082	1887	$3,296 (S)	$4,400	5-M	6,777	380
Troy State Univ Dothan, Dothan, AL 36304-0368	1961	$3,296 (S)	NA	5-M	1,855	110
Troy State Univ Montgomery, Montgomery, AL 36103-4419	1965	$3,080 (S)	NA	5-M	NA	222
Truman State Univ, Kirksville, MO 63501-4221	1867	$4,200 (S)	$4,928	5-M	5,919	403
Tufts Univ, Medford, MA 02155	1852	$26,892	$7,987	1-D	9,031	1,103
Tulane Univ, New Orleans, LA 70118-5669	1834	$26,886	$7,128	1-D	12,373	1,105
Tusculum Coll, Greeneville, TN 37743-9997	1794	$13,400	$4,500	2-M	1,794	120
Tuskegee Univ, Tuskegee, AL 36088	1881	$10,784	$5,680	1-D	2,880	256
Union Coll, Schenectady, NY 12308-2311	1795	$26,007	$6,639	1-M	2,427	224
Union Inst & Univ, Cincinnati, OH 45206-1925	1969	$6,912	NA	1-D	1,769	222
Union Univ, Jackson, TN 38305-3697	1823	$14,580	$4,350	2-M	2,544	222
United States Air Force Acad, USAF Academy, CO 80840-5025 (2)	1954	$0 (C)	NA	4-B	4,365	531
United States Military Acad, West Point, NY 10996 (2)	1802	$0 (C)	NA	4-B	4,394	588
United States Naval Acad, Annapolis, MD 21402-5000	1845	$0 (C)	NA	4-B	4,297	554
Universidad del Turabo, Turabo, PR 00778-3030	1972	$3,324	NA	1-M	8,065	410
Universidad Metropolitana, Río Piedras, PR 00928-1150	1980	$3,324	NA	1-M	5,857	358
Univ at Buffalo, The State Univ of New York, Buffalo, NY 14260	1846	$4,790 (S)	$6,318	5-D	25,838	1,932
The Univ of Akron, Akron, OH 44325-0001	1870	$4,930 (S)	$5,600	5-D	24,358	1,634
The Univ of Alabama, Tuscaloosa, AL 35487	1831	$3,292 (S)	$4,110	5-D	10,130	1,044
The Univ of Alabama at Birmingham, Birmingham, AL 35294	1969	$3,640 (S)	$6,471	5-D	14,686	796
The Univ of Alabama in Huntsville, Huntsville, AL 35899	1950	$3,536 (S)	$4,380	5-D	6,754	446
Univ of Alaska Anchorage, Anchorage, AK 99508-8060	1954	$2,748 (S)	$5,780	5-M	15,040	1,240
Univ of Alaska Fairbanks, Fairbanks, AK 99775-7480	1917	$3,495 (S)	$4,770	5-D	7,142	592
Univ of Alaska Southeast, Juneau, AK 99801	1972	$2,062 (S)	NA	5-M	2,799	NA
The Univ of Arizona, Tucson, AZ 85721	1885	$2,490 (S)	$6,124	5-D	35,747	1,413
Univ of Arkansas, Fayetteville, AR 72701-1201	1871	$3,880 (S)	$4,454	5-D	15,752	866
Univ of Arkansas at Little Rock, Little Rock, AR 72204-1099	1927	$3,138 (S)	$2,600	5-D	11,318	793
Univ of Arkansas at Monticello, Monticello, AR 71656	1909	$2,670 (S)	$2,780	5-M	2,323	136
Univ of Arkansas at Pine Bluff, Pine Bluff, AR 71601-2799	1873	$3,209 (S)	$4,716	5-M	3,144	217
Univ of Baltimore, Baltimore, MD 21201-5779	1925	$5,324 (S)	NA	5-D	4,639	332
Univ of Bridgeport, Bridgeport, CT 06601	1927	$15,582	$7,500	1-D	3,162	302
Univ of California, Berkeley, Berkeley, CA 94720-1500	1868	$4,122 (S)	$10,047	5-D	31,276	1,804
Univ of California, Davis, Davis, CA 95616	1905	$4,594 (S)	$6,982	5-D	26,513	1,950
Univ of California, Irvine, Irvine, CA 92697	1965	$4,556 (S)	$7,098	5-D	21,885	989
Univ of California, Los Angeles, Los Angeles, CA 90095	1919	$4,236 (S)	$8,991	5-D	37,494	2,305
Univ of California, Riverside, Riverside, CA 92521-0102	1954	$4,379 (S)	$7,200	5-D	14,429	714
Univ of California, San Diego, La Jolla, CA 92093	1959	$3,863 (S)	$7,510	5-D	21,560	1,045
Univ of California, Santa Barbara, Santa Barbara, CA 93106	1909	$3,841 (S)	$7,891	5-D	20,373	963
Univ of California, Santa Cruz, Santa Cruz, CA 95064	1965	$4,300 (S)	$9,355	5-D	13,170	691
Univ of Central Arkansas, Conway, AR 72035-0001	1907	$3,738 (S)	$3,490	5-D	8,486	516
Univ of Central Florida, Orlando, FL 32816	1963	$2,582 (S)	$5,670	5-D	35,927	1,454
Univ of Central Oklahoma, Edmond, OK 73034-5209	1890	$2,067 (S)	$3,138	5-M	14,099	713
Univ of Charleston, Charleston, WV 25304-1099	1888	$14,900	$5,740	1-M	1,150	108
Univ of Chicago, Chicago, IL 60637-1513	1891	$26,475	$8,312	1-D	12,576	1,861
Univ of Cincinnati, Cincinnati, OH 45221	1819	$5,823 (S)	$6,498	5-D	27,289	1,160
Univ of Colorado at Boulder, Boulder, CO 80309	1876	$3,357 (S)	$5,898	5-D	29,609	2,121
Univ of Colorado at Colorado Springs, Colorado Springs, CO 80933-7150	1965	$4,250 (S)	$5,893	5-D	6,835	437
Univ of Colorado at Denver, Denver, CO 80217-3364	1912	$2,934 (S)	NA	5-D	15,004	933
Univ of Colorado Health Sci Ctr, Denver, CO 80262	1883	$8,980 (S)	NA	5-D	2,165	1,700
Univ of Connecticut, Storrs, CT 06269	1881	$5,824 (S)	$6,298	5-D	19,876	1,075
Univ of Dallas, Irving, TX 75062-4736	1955	$16,084	$5,950	2-D	3,518	237
Univ of Dayton, Dayton, OH 45469-1300	1850	$18,000	$5,600	2-D	10,253	815
Univ of Delaware, Newark, DE 19716	1743	$5,290 (S)	$5,534	12-D	20,373	1,295
Univ of Denver, Denver, CO 80208	1864	$22,035	$6,747	1-D	9,385	923
Univ of Detroit Mercy, Detroit, MI 48219-0900	1877	NA	NA	2-D	6,212	407
Univ of Dubuque, Dubuque, IA 52001-5099	1852	$14,910	$5,020	2-F	1,036	86
Univ of Evansville, Evansville, IN 47722-0002	1854	$17,395	$5,470	2-M	2,687	178
The Univ of Findlay, Findlay, OH 45840-3653	1882	$17,528	$6,434	2-M	4,585	350
Univ of Florida, Gainesville, FL 32611	1853	$2,444 (S)	$5,430	5-D	45,114	1,646
Univ of Georgia, Athens, GA 30602	1785	$3,418 (S)	$5,388	5-D	32,317	2,038
Univ of Guam, Mangilao, GU 96923	1952	NA	NA	7-M	3,748	230
Univ of Hartford, West Hartford, CT 06117-1599	1877	$20,810	$8,074	1-D	6,844	690
Univ of Hawaii at Hilo, Hilo, HI 96720-4091	1970	$1,658 (S)	$4,839	5-M	2,913	217
Univ of Hawaii at Manoa, Honolulu, HI 96822	1907	$3,216 (S)	NA	5-D	17,532	1,142
Univ of Houston-Clear Lake, Houston, TX 77058-1098	1974	$3,456 (S)	NA	5-M	7,738	583
Univ of Houston-Downtown, Houston, TX 77002-1001	1974	$2,414 (S)	NA	5-B	8,951	471
Univ of Houston-Victoria, Victoria, TX 77901-4450	1973	$2,304 (S)	NA	5-M	1,927	88
Univ of Houston, Houston, TX 77204	1927	$3,168 (S)	$5,242	5-D	33,007	2,039
Univ of Idaho, Moscow, ID 83844-2282	1889	$2,720 (S)	$4,306	5-D	12,067	615
Univ of Illinois at Chicago, Chicago, IL 60607-7128	1946	$4,944 (S)	$6,058	5-D	24,955	1,549
Univ of Illinois at Springfield, Springfield, IL 62794-9243	1969	$3,611 (S)	$3,060	5-M	4,288	260
Univ of Illinois at Urbana-Champaign, Champaign, IL 61820	1867	$5,794 (S)	$6,090	5-D	38,759	2,652
Univ of Indianapolis, Indianapolis, IN 46227-3697	1902	$15,350	$5,490	2-D	3,701	367
The Univ of Iowa, Iowa City, IA 52242-1316	1847	$4,191 (S)	$5,440	5-D	28,768	1,707
Univ of Kansas, Lawrence, KS 66045	1866	$2,884 (S)	$4,348	5-D	28,190	1,749
Univ of Kentucky, Lexington, KY 40506-0032	1865	$3,734 (S)	$3,980	5-D	23,901	NA
Univ of La Verne, La Verne, CA 91750-4443	1891	$18,000	$6,280	1-D	3,358	232
Univ of Louisiana at Lafayette, Lafayette, LA 70504	1898	$2,316 (S)	$2,886	5-D	15,489	672
Univ of Louisiana at Monroe, Monroe, LA 71209-0001	1931	$2,307 (S)	$5,740	5-D	8,965	NA
Univ of Louisville, Louisville, KY 40292-0001	1798	$3,794 (S)	$3,608	5-D	19,682	1,231

Name, address	Year Founded	Tuition & Fees	Rm. & Board	Control, Degree	Enroll-ment	Faculty
Univ of Maine, Orono, ME 04469	1865	$5,250 (S)	$6,014	5-D	10,648	720
The Univ of Maine at Augusta, Augusta, ME 04330-9410	1965	$3,928 (S)	NA	5-B	5,575	235
Univ of Maine at Farmington, Farmington, ME 04938-1990	1863	$4,317 (S)	$4,846	5-B	2,435	151
Univ of Maine at Machias, Machias, ME 04654-1321	1909	$3,755 (S)	$4,644	5-B	1,017	74
Univ of Maine at Presque Isle, Presque Isle, ME 04769-2888	1903	$3,700 (S)	$4,264	5-B	1,367	118
Univ of Mary, Bismarck, ND 58504-9652	1959	$9,400	$3,735	2-M	2,444	198
Univ of Mary Hardin-Baylor, Belton, TX 76513	1845	$9,890	$4,039	2-M	2,628	225
Univ of Maryland, Baltimore County, Baltimore, MD 21250-5398	1963	$5,910 (S)	$6,280	5-D	11,237	754
Univ of Maryland, Coll Park, College Park, MD 20742	1856	$5,341 (S)	$6,618	5-D	34,160	2,136
Univ of Maryland Eastern Shore, Princess Anne, MD 21853-1299	1886	$4,128 (S)	$5,130	5-D	3,426	280
Univ of Maryland Univ Coll, Adelphi, MD 20783	1947	$4,728 (S)	NA	5-D	22,233	962
Univ of Massachusetts Amherst, Amherst, MA 01003	1863	$5,880 (S)	$5,115	5-D	24,678	1,276
Univ of Massachusetts Boston, Boston, MA 02125-3393	1964	$4,222 (S)	NA	5-D	13,348	885
Univ of Massachusetts Dartmouth, North Dartmouth, MA 02747-2300	1895	$4,129 (S)	$5,723	5-D	7,460	475
Univ of Massachusetts Lowell, Lowell, MA 01854-2881	1894	$4,255 (S)	$5,095	5-D	12,397	553
The Univ of Memphis, Memphis, TN 38152	1912	$3,470 (S)	$3,801	5-D	20,332	1,268
Univ of Miami, Coral Gables, FL 33124	1925	$24,810	$8,062	1-D	14,436	1,129
Univ of Michigan-Dearborn, Dearborn, MI 48128-1491	1959	$5,095 (S)	NA	5-M	8,049	493
Univ of Michigan-Flint, Flint, MI 48502-1950	1956	$4,328 (S)	NA	5-M	6,397	392
Univ of Michigan, Ann Arbor, MI 48109	1817	$6,935 (S)	$6,068	5-D	38,248	2,678
Univ of Minnesota, Duluth, Duluth, MN 55812-2496	1947	$5,844 (S)	$4,592	5-F	9,374	445
Univ of Minnesota, Morris, Morris, MN 56267-2134	1959	$6,246 (S)	$4,470	5-B	1,924	NA
Univ of Minnesota, Twin Cities Campus, Minneapolis, MN 55455-0213	1851	$5,536 (S)	$5,582	5-D	46,597	3,079
Univ of Mississippi, University, MS 38677	1844	$3,626 (S)	$4,040	5-D	11,879	NA
Univ of Mississippi Medical Ctr, Jackson, MS 39216-4505	1955	$2,850 (S)	$1,836	5-D	1,200	2,301
Univ of Missouri-Columbia, Columbia, MO 65211	1839	$3,985 (S)	$5,043	5-D	23,667	1,761
Univ of Missouri-Kansas City, Kansas City, MO 64110-2499	1929	$5,050 (S)	$4,950	5-D	12,969	769
Univ of Missouri-Rolla, Rolla, MO 65409-0910	1870	$4,974 (S)	$5,060	5-D	4,883	385
Univ of Missouri-St. Louis, St. Louis, MO 63121-4499	1963	$4,566 (S)	$5,400	5-D	14,993	657
Univ of Mobile, Mobile, AL 36663-0220	1961	$8,770	$4,850	2-M	1,987	154
The Univ of Montana-Missoula, Missoula, MT 59812-0002	1893	$3,642 (S)	$4,890	5-D	12,646	728
The Univ of Montana-Western, Dillon, MT 59725-3598	1893	$3,016 (S)	$4,220	5-B	1,163	60
Univ of Montevallo, Montevallo, AL 35115	1896	$3,974 (S)	$3,576	5-M	2,935	199
Univ of Nebraska-Lincoln, Lincoln, NE 68588	1869	$3,759 (S)	$4,565	5-D	22,764	1,072
Univ of Nebraska at Kearney, Kearney, NE 68849-0001	1903	$3,106 (S)	$3,902	5-M	6,426	398
Univ of Nebraska at Omaha, Omaha, NE 68182	1908	$2,638 (S)	$2,439	5-D	14,143	871
Univ of Nebraska Medical Ctr, Omaha, NE 68198	1869	$4,115 (S)	NA	5-D	2,724	786
Univ of Nevada, Las Vegas, Las Vegas, NV 89154-9900	1957	$2,481 (S)	$5,800	5-D	23,314	1,270
Univ of Nevada, Reno, Reno, NV 89557	1874	$2,622 (S)	$6,190	5-D	14,316	684
Univ of New England, Biddeford, ME 04005-9526	1831	$17,260	$6,770	1-F	2,862	210
Univ of New Hampshire, Durham, NH 03824	1866	$8,130 (S)	$5,882	5-D	13,650	714
Univ of New Hampshire at Manchester, Manchester, NH 03101-1113	1967	$5,064 (S)	NA	5-B	1,086	108
Univ of New Haven, West Haven, CT 06516-1916	1920	$16,560	$7,300	1-M	4,226	464
Univ of New Mexico, Albuquerque, NM 87131-2039	1889	$3,326 (S)	$5,217	5-D	23,753	875
Univ of New Orleans, New Orleans, LA 70148	1958	$3,602 (S)	$3,900	5-D	17,014	578
Univ of North Alabama, Florence, AL 35632-0001	1830	$3,678 (S)	$3,662	5-M	5,522	NA
The Univ of North Carolina at Asheville, Asheville, NC 28804-3299	1927	$2,496 (S)	$4,400	5-M	3,247	300
The Univ of North Carolina at Chapel Hill, Chapel Hill, NC 27599	1789	$3,277 (S)	$5,570	5-D	25,494	2,690
The Univ of North Carolina at Charlotte, Charlotte, NC 28223-0001	1946	$2,460 (S)	$4,798	5-D	18,308	1,020
The Univ of North Carolina at Greensboro, Greensboro, NC 27412-5001	1891	$2,545 (S)	$4,313	5-D	13,343	886
The Univ of North Carolina at Pembroke, Pembroke, NC 28372-1510	1887	$2,069 (S)	$3,845	5-M	3,933	247
The Univ of North Carolina at Wilmington, Wilmington, NC 28403-3297	1947	$2,627 (S)	$5,142	5-M	10,599	641
Univ of North Dakota, Grand Forks, ND 58202	1883	$3,770 (S)	$3,805	5-D	11,764	593
Univ of Northern Colorado, Greeley, CO 80639	1890	$2,842 (S)	$5,240	5-D	12,301	588
Univ of Northern Iowa, Cedar Falls, IA 50614	1876	$3,440 (S)	$4,410	5-D	14,410	852
Univ of North Florida, Jacksonville, FL 32224-2645	1965	$2,669 (S)	$5,380	5-D	12,992	612
Univ of North Texas, Denton, TX 76203	1890	$3,050 (S)	$4,400	5-D	27,858	1,075
Univ of Notre Dame, Notre Dame, IN 46556	1842	$24,497	$6,210	2-D	11,054	NA
Univ of Oklahoma, Norman, OK 73019-0390	1890	$2,713 (S)	$4,903	5-D	22,646	1,171
Univ of Oklahoma Health Sci Ctr, Oklahoma City, OK 73190	1890	$2,978 (S)	NA	5-D	2,862	347
Univ of Oregon, Eugene, OR 97403	1872	$4,071 (S)	$5,898	5-D	18,956	1,078
Univ of Pennsylvania, Philadelphia, PA 19104	1740	$26,630	$7,984	1-D	20,013	1,770
Univ of Phoenix-Colorado Campus, Lone Tree, CO 80124-5453	NR	$7,950	NA	3-D	3,103	363
Univ of Phoenix-Fort Lauderdale Campus, Plantation, FL 33324-1393	NR	$8,100	NA	3-D	1,524	157
Univ of Phoenix-Hawaii Campus, Honolulu, HI 96813-4317	NR	$9,360	NA	3-D	1,311	228
Univ of Phoenix-Jacksonville Campus, Jacksonville, FL 32216-0959	1976	$8,100	NA	3-D	1,604	231
Univ of Phoenix-Louisiana Campus, Metairie, LA 70001-2082	1976	$7,350	NA	3-D	1,934	303
Univ of Phoenix-Metro Detroit Campus, Troy, MI 48098-2623	NR	$8,700	NA	3-D	3,462	424
Univ of Phoenix-Nevada Campus, Las Vegas, NV 89106-3797	1994	$8,160	NA	3-D	2,455	207
Univ of Phoenix-New Mexico Campus, Albuquerque, NM 87109-4645	NR	$7,860	NA	3-D	3,729	451
Univ of Phoenix-Northern California Campus, Pleasanton, CA 94588-3677	NR	$10,200	NA	3-D	6,379	791
Univ of Phoenix-Oregon Campus, Portland, OR 97223-8368	1976	$8,880	NA	3-D	1,333	237
Univ of Phoenix-Orlando Campus, Maitland, FL 32751	NR	$8,100	NA	3-D	1,666	181
Univ of Phoenix-Phoenix Campus, Phoenix, AZ 85040-1958	1976	$8,100	NA	3-D	7,885	1,019
Univ of Phoenix-Puerto Rico Campus, Guaynabo, PR 00970-3870	NR	$4,740	NA	3-D	1,921	166
Univ of Phoenix-Sacramento Campus, Sacramento, CA 95833-3632	NR	$10,500	NA	3-D	3,516	302
Univ of Phoenix-San Diego Campus, San Diego, CA 92130-2092	NR	$9,750	NA	3-D	4,007	920
Univ of Phoenix-Southern Arizona Campus, Tucson, AZ 85712	NR	$7,800	NA	3-D	3,155	381
Univ of Phoenix-Southern California Campus, Fountain Valley, CA 92708	NR	$10,470	NA	3-D	11,464	1,267
Univ of Phoenix-Tampa Campus, Tampa, FL 33637-1920	NR	$8,100	NA	3-D	1,368	180
Univ of Phoenix-Utah Campus, Salt Lake City, UT 84123-4617	NR	$8,220	NA	3-D	2,885	304
Univ of Phoenix-Washington Campus, Seattle, WA 98188-7500	NR	$8,940	NA	3-D	1,563	286
Univ of Pittsburgh, Pittsburgh, PA 15260	NR	$7,482 (S)	$6,110	12-D	26,710	1,828
Univ of Pittsburgh at Bradford, Bradford, PA 16701-2812	1963	$7,386 (S)	$5,310	12-B	1,465	114
Univ of Pittsburgh at Greensburg, Greensburg, PA 15601-5860	1963	$7,442 (S)	$5,930	12-B	1,758	126
Univ of Pittsburgh at Johnstown, Johnstown, PA 15904-2990	1927	$7,464 (S)	$5,510	12-B	3,096	188
Univ of Portland, Portland, OR 97203-5798	1901	$19,650	$5,872	2-M	3,087	263
Univ of Puerto Rico at Humacao, Humacao, PR 00791	1962	$1,245 (S)	NA	6-B	4,476	284
Univ of Puerto Rico at Ponce, Ponce, PR 00732-7186	1970	$2,245 (S)	NA	6-B	4,070	178
Univ of Puerto Rico at Utuado, Utuado, PR 00641-2500	1979	$1,315 (S)	NA	6-B	1,620	90

Name, address	Year Founded	Tuition & Fees	Rm. & Board	Control, Degree	Enroll-ment	Faculty
Univ of Puerto Rico, Cayey Univ Coll, Cayey, PR 00736	1967	$1,245 (A)	NA	6-B	4,019	230
Univ of Puerto Rico, Mayagüez Campus, Mayagüez, PR 00681-9000	1911	$1,160 (S)	NA	6-D	12,414	761
Univ of Puerto Rico, Medical Sci Campus, San Juan, PR 00936-5067 (4)	1950	$2,098 (S)	NA	6-D	2,732	605
Univ of Puerto Rico, Río Piedras, San Juan, PR 00931	1903	$790 (S)	$4,180	6-D	21,539	1,293
Univ of Puget Sound, Tacoma, WA 98416	1888	$22,505	$5,780	1-D	2,848	259
Univ of Redlands, Redlands, CA 92373-0999	1907	$21,406	$7,840	1-M	2,017	233
Univ of Rhode Island, Kingston, RI 02881	1892	$5,386 (S)	$7,028	5-D	14,264	682
Univ of Richmond, University of Richmond, VA 23173	1830	$22,570	$4,730	1-F	3,727	337
Univ of Rio Grande, Rio Grande, OH 45674	1876	$8,984 (A)	$5,362	1-M	2,076	146
Univ of Rochester, Rochester, NY 14627-0250	1850	$24,754	$8,585	1-D	7,355	NA
Univ of St. Francis, Joliet, IL 60435-6169	1920	$14,990	$5,580	2-M	2,630	168
Univ of Saint Francis, Fort Wayne, IN 46808-3994	1890	$13,640	$5,000	2-M	1,683	161
Univ of St. Thomas, St. Paul, MN 55105-1096	1885	$18,421	$5,623	2-D	11,473	799
Univ of St. Thomas, Houston, TX 77006-4696	1947	$13,162	$5,920	2-D	4,310	242
Univ of San Diego, San Diego, CA 92110-2492	1949	$20,458	$8,440	2-D	7,062	654
Univ of San Francisco, San Francisco, CA 94117-1080	1855	$20,310	$8,800	2-D	8,063	778
Univ of Sci & Arts of Oklahoma, Chickasha, OK 73018	1908	$2,308 (S)	$2,790	5-B	1,452	94
The Univ of Scranton, Scranton, PA 18510	1888	$19,530	$8,434	2-M	4,658	377
Univ of Sioux Falls, Sioux Falls, SD 57105-1699	1883	$13,400	$3,900	2-M	1,332	96
Univ of South Alabama, Mobile, AL 36688-0002	1963	$3,070 (S)	$3,746	5-D	12,122	917
Univ of South Carolina, Columbia, SC 29208	1801	$4,064 (S)	$4,684	5-D	23,000	1,023
Univ of South Carolina Aiken, Aiken, SC 29801-6309	1961	$3,778 (S)	$4,050	5-M	3,282	222
Univ of South Carolina Spartanburg, Spartanburg, SC 29303-4999	1967	$4,014 (S)	$3,360	5-M	3,993	268
The Univ of South Dakota, Vermillion, SD 57069-2390	1862	$3,885 (S)	$3,151	5-D	8,232	249
Univ of Southern California, Los Angeles, CA 90089	1880	$25,533	$8,114	1-D	29,813	2,103
Univ of Southern Colorado, Pueblo, CO 81001-4901	1933	$2,449 (S)	$5,372	5-M	5,531	240
Univ of Southern Indiana, Evansville, IN 47712-3590	1965	$3,143 (S)	$5,512	5-M	9,362	507
Univ of Southern Maine, Portland, ME 04104-9300	1878	$4,696 (S)	$5,873	5-D	10,066	696
Univ of Southern Mississippi, Hattiesburg, MS 39406	1910	$3,416 (S)	$4,450	5-D	15,233	757
Univ of South Florida, Tampa, FL 33620-9951	1956	$2,520 (S)	$5,600	5-D	37,221	1,973
The Univ of Tampa, Tampa, FL 33606-1490	1931	$16,542	$5,890	1-M	3,823	310
The Univ of Tennessee, Knoxville, TN 37996	1794	$4,034 (S)	$4,402	5-D	26,033	1,244
The Univ of Tennessee at Chattanooga, Chattanooga, TN 37403-2598	1886	$3,236 (S)	$2,400	5-M	8,485	608
The Univ of Tennessee at Martin, Martin, TN 38238-1000	1900	$4,442 (S)	$3,820	5-M	5,900	414
The Univ of Texas-Pan American, Edinburg, TX 78539-2999	1927	$2,704 (S)	$5,531	5-D	13,640	601
The Univ of Texas at Arlington, Arlington, TX 76019	1895	$3,068 (S)	$4,124	5-D	21,180	951
The Univ of Texas at Austin, Austin, TX 78712-1111	1883	$3,766 (S)	$5,671	5-D	50,616	2,653
The Univ of Texas at Brownsville, Brownsville, TX 78520-4991	1973	$1,682 (A)	NA	5-M	9,373	489
The Univ of Texas at Dallas, Richardson, TX 75083-0688	1969	$3,658 (S)	$5,914	5-D	12,455	537
The Univ of Texas at El Paso, El Paso, TX 79968-0001	1913	$2,556 (S)	$4,120	5-D	16,220	877
The Univ of Texas at San Antonio, San Antonio, TX 78249-0617	1969	$3,503 (S)	$6,113	5-D	19,883	963
The Univ of Texas at Tyler, Tyler, TX 75799-0001	1971	$3,062 (S)	$3,267	5-M	3,742	271
The Univ of Texas Health Sci Ctr at Houston, Houston, TX 77225-0036	1972	$0,774 (S)	NA	5-D	3,286	1,115
The Univ of Texas Medical Branch, Galveston, TX 77555	1891	$2,219 (S)	$2,400	5-D	1,927	134
The Univ of Texas of the Permian Basin, Odessa, TX 79762-0001	1969	$2,434 (S)	$1,900	5-M	2,409	146
The Univ of Texas Southwestern Medical Ctr at Dallas, Dallas, TX 75390	1943	$2,345 (S)	NA	5-D	1,554	103
The Univ of the Arts, Philadelphia, PA 19102-4944	1870	$19,230	$4,800	1-M	2,094	420
Univ of the District of Columbia, Washington, DC 20008-1175	1976	$2,070 (S)	NA	9-M	5,456	479
Univ of the Incarnate Word, San Antonio, TX 78209-6397	1881	$13,498	$5,250	2-D	4,283	418
Univ of the Pacific, Stockton, CA 95211-0197	1851	$21,525	$6,730	1-D	5,697	622
Univ of the Sacred Heart, San Juan, PR 00914-0383	1935	$5,010	$1,800	2-M	5,234	374
Univ of the Sci in Philadelphia, Philadelphia, PA 19104-4495	1821	$18,062	$7,450	1-D	2,400	236
Univ of the South, Sewanee, TN 37383-1000	1857	$21,340	$5,950	2-D	1,442	163
Univ of the Virgin Islands, Charlotte Amalie, VI 00802-9990	1962	$4,946 (S)	$5,830	7-M	2,291	246
Univ of Toledo, Toledo, OH 43606-3398	1872	$5,102 (S)	$6,104	5-D	20,313	1,049
Univ of Tulsa, Tulsa, OK 74104-3189	1894	$14,280	$4,810	2-D	4,119	410
Univ of Utah, Salt Lake City, UT 84112-1107	1850	$3,057 (S)	$4,646	5-D	27,668	1,246
Univ of Vermont, Burlington, VT 05405	1791	$8,665 (S)	$6,096	5-D	10,081	680
Univ of Virginia, Charlottesville, VA 22903	1819	$4,421 (S)	$4,970	5-D	22,739	1,265
The Univ of Virginia's Coll at Wise, Wise, VA 24293	1954	$3,470 (S)	$5,226	5-B	1,480	95
Univ of Washington, Seattle, WA 98195	1861	$3,983 (S)	$6,378	5-D	37,412	3,282
The Univ of West Alabama, Livingston, AL 35470	1835	$3,174 (S)	$2,874	5-M	1,974	97
Univ of West Florida, Pensacola, FL 32514-5750	1963	$2,528 (S)	$5,440	5-D	9,052	532
Univ of Wisconsin-Eau Claire, Eau Claire, WI 54702-4004	1916	$3,472 (S)	$3,560	5-M	10,634	487
Univ of Wisconsin-Green Bay, Green Bay, WI 54311-7001	1968	$3,648 (S)	$2,200	5-M	5,551	279
Univ of Wisconsin-La Crosse, La Crosse, WI 54601-3742	1909	$3,777 (S)	$3,766	5-M	9,105	491
Univ of Wisconsin-Madison, Madison, WI 53706-1380	1848	$4,086 (S)	$5,700	5-D	41,552	NA
Univ of Wisconsin-Milwaukee, Milwaukee, WI 53201-0413	1956	$4,057 (S)	$2,700	5-D	24,223	1,333
Univ of Wisconsin-Oshkosh, Oshkosh, WI 54901	1871	$3,228 (S)	$3,816	5-M	10,909	593
Univ of Wisconsin-Parkside, Kenosha, WI 53141-2000	1968	$3,298 (S)	$4,960	5-M	5,068	187
Univ of Wisconsin-Platteville, Platteville, WI 53818-3099	1866	$3,473 (S)	$3,799	5-M	5,540	347
Univ of Wisconsin-River Falls, River Falls, WI 54022-5001	1874	$3,990 (S)	$3,582	5-M	5,844	248
Univ of Wisconsin-Stevens Point, Stevens Point, WI 54481-3897	1894	$3,375 (S)	$3,738	5-M	8,944	430
Univ of Wisconsin-Stout, Menomonie, WI 54751	1891	$3,502 (S)	$3,690	5-M	7,780	395
Univ of Wisconsin-Superior, Superior, WI 54880-4500	1893	$3,233 (S)	$3,818	5-M	2,842	175
Univ of Wisconsin-Whitewater, Whitewater, WI 53190-1790	1868	$3,367 (S)	$3,570	5-M	10,551	494
Univ of Wyoming, Laramie, WY 82071	1886	$2,807 (S)	$4,748	5-D	12,402	643
Univ System Coll for Lifelong Learning, Concord, NH 03301	1972	$4,302 (S)	NA	11-B	2,095	498
Urbana Univ, Urbana, OH 43078-2091	1850	$12,004	$5,000	2-M	1,432	92
Ursinus Coll, Collegeville, PA 19426-1000	1869	$24,850	$6,500	2-B	1,340	147
Ursuline Coll, Pepper Pike, OH 44124-4398 (4)	1871	$14,730	$5,000	2-M	1,281	167
Utah State Univ, Logan, UT 84322	1888	$2,591 (S)	$4,180	5-D	23,001	673
Utica Coll of Syracuse Univ, Utica, NY 13502-4892	1946	$18,050	$7,070	1-M	2,286	213
Valdosta State Univ, Valdosta, GA 31698	1906	$2,526 (S)	$4,462	5-D	9,238	510
Valley City State Univ, Valley City, ND 58072	1890	$3,306 (S)	$3,010	5-B	1,005	79
Valparaiso Univ, Valparaiso, IN 46383-6493	1859	$18,700	$4,870	2-F	3,533	340
Vanderbilt Univ, Nashville, TN 37240-1001	1873	$25,847	$8,635	1-D	10,338	938
Vanguard Univ of Southern California, Costa Mesa, CA 92626-6597	1920	$14,944	$5,268	2-M	1,827	105
Vassar Coll, Poughkeepsie, NY 12604	1861	$26,290	$7,160	1-M	2,439	286
Villa Julie Coll, Stevenson, MD 21153	1952	$12,076	$3,950	1-M	2,447	264

Name, address	Year Founded	Tuition & Fees	Rm. & Board	Control, Degree	Enroll-ment	Faculty
Villanova Univ, Villanova, PA 19085-1699	1842	$23,727	$8,270	2-D	10,156	840
Virginia Coll at Birmingham, Birmingham, AL 35209	1989	$8,100	NA	3-B	1,641	159
Virginia Commonwealth Univ, Richmond, VA 23284-9005	1838	$3,675 (S)	$5,355	5-D	25,001	2,029
Virginia Military Inst, Lexington, VA 24450 (2)	1839	$5,130 (S)	$4,838	5-B	1,311	145
Virginia Polytechnic Inst & State Univ, Blacksburg, VA 24061	1872	$3,664 (S)	$4,032	5-D	26,490	1,491
Virginia State Univ, Petersburg, VA 23806-0001	1882	$3,312 (S)	$5,594	5-M	4,638	NA
Virginia Union Univ, Richmond, VA 23220-1170	1865	$10,690	$4,664	2-D	1,533	85
Virginia Wesleyan Coll, Norfolk, VA 23502-5599	1961	$16,500	$5,850	2-B	1,408	109
Viterbo Univ, La Crosse, WI 54601-4797	1890	$13,630	$4,710	2-M	2,167	160
Wagner Coll, Staten Island, NY 10301-4495	1883	$20,500	$7,000	1-M	2,124	NA
Wake Forest Univ, Winston-Salem, NC 27109	1834	$23,530	$6,760	2-D	6,216	550
Walla Walla Coll, College Place, WA 99324-1198	1892	$16,599	$4,326	2-M	1,823	203
Walsh Coll of Accountancy & Business Administration, Troy, MI 48007-7006	1922	$5,452	NA	1-M	3,214	131
Walsh Univ, North Canton, OH 44720-3396	1958	$13,870	$8,270	2-M	1,522	NA
Warner Southern Coll, Lake Wales, FL 33853-8725	1968	$10,040	$4,820	2-M	1,117	77
Wartburg Coll, Waverly, IA 50677-0903	1852	$16,565	$4,600	2-B	1,649	153
Washburn Univ of Topeka, Topeka, KS 66621	1865	$3,356 (S)	$4,300	10-F	6,118	457
Washington & Jefferson Coll, Washington, PA 15301-4801	1781	$20,550	$5,705	1-B	1,240	108
Washington & Lee Univ, Lexington, VA 24450-0303	1749	$19,345	$5,750	1-F	2,124	254
Washington Coll, Chestertown, MD 21620-1197	1782	$23,300	$5,740	1-M	1,260	126
Washington State Univ, Pullman, WA 99164	1890	$4,236 (S)	$5,152	5-D	21,078	1,255
Washington Univ in St. Louis, St. Louis, MO 63130-4899	1853	$27,619	$8,678	1-D	12,187	1,056
Waynesburg Coll, Waynesburg, PA 15370-1222	1849	$12,560	$5,050	2-M	1,787	97
Wayne State Coll, Wayne, NE 68787	1910	$2,735 (S)	$3,590	5-M	3,311	205
Wayne State Univ, Detroit, MI 48202	1868	$4,330 (S)	NA	5-D	31,040	1,754
Weber State Univ, Ogden, UT 84408-1001	1889	$2,252 (S)	$4,645	5-M	16,873	705
Webster Univ, St. Louis, MO 63119-3194	1915	$13,920	$5,889	1-D	15,402	1,862
Wellesley Coll, Wellesley, MA 02481 (3)	1870	$25,504	$7,890	1-B	2,273	315
Wentworth Inst of Tech, Boston, MA 02115-5998	1904	$13,650	$7,400	1-B	3,273	239
Wesleyan Univ, Middletown, CT 06459-0260	1831	$27,100	$6,950	1-D	3,237	336
Wesley Coll, Dover, DE 19901-3875	1873	$13,123	$5,810	2-M	1,510	92
West Chester Univ of Pennsylvania, West Chester, PA 19383	1871	$4,924 (S)	$4,990	5-M	12,244	757
Western Carolina Univ, Cullowhee, NC 28723	1889	$2,243 (S)	$3,424	5-D	6,863	513
Western Connecticut State Univ, Danbury, CT 06810-6885	1903	$4,455 (S)	$6,224	5-M	5,918	442
Western Illinois Univ, Macomb, IL 61455-1390	1899	$4,509 (S)	$5,062	5-M	13,206	684
Western Intl Univ, Phoenix, AZ 85021-2718	1978	$8,320	NA	3-M	3,504	230
Western Kentucky Univ, Bowling Green, KY 42101-3576	1906	$2,844 (S)	$3,990	5-M	16,579	1,008
Western Michigan Univ, Kalamazoo, MI 49008-5202	1903	$4,499 (S)	$5,517	5-D	28,931	1,142
Western New England Coll, Springfield, MA 01119-2654	1919	$16,494	$7,388	1-F	4,540	351
Western New Mexico Univ, Silver City, NM 88062-0680	1893	NA	NA	5-M	2,580	145
Western Oregon Univ, Monmouth, OR 97361-1394	1856	$3,660 (S)	$5,169	5-M	4,878	313
Western State Coll of Colorado, Gunnison, CO 81231	1901	$2,403 (S)	$5,690	5-B	2,302	137
Western Washington Univ, Bellingham, WA 98225-5996	1893	$3,288 (S)	$5,700	5-M	11,708	630
Westfield State Coll, Westfield, MA 01086	1838	$2,956 (S)	$4,789	5-M	5,153	262
West Liberty State Coll, West Liberty, WV 26074	1837	$2,516 (S)	$3,540	5-B	2,633	166
Westminster Coll, New Wilmington, PA 16172-0001	1852	$17,750	$5,210	2-M	1,676	138
Westminster Coll, Salt Lake City, UT 84105-3697	1875	$14,780	$4,650	1-M	2,474	257
Westmont Coll, Santa Barbara, CA 93108-1099	1937	$22,256	$7,492	2-B	1,374	142
West Texas A&M Univ, Canyon, TX 79016-0001	1909	$2,301 (S)	$3,831	5-M	6,675	315
West Virginia State Coll, Institute, WV 25112-1000	1891	$2,562 (S)	$4,300	5-B	4,836	282
West Virginia Univ, Morgantown, WV 26506	1867	$2,948 (S)	$5,326	5-D	22,774	1,766
West Virginia Univ Inst of Tech, Montgomery, WV 25136	1895	$2,836 (S)	$4,682	5-M	2,374	177
West Virginia Wesleyan Coll, Buckhannon, WV 26201	1890	$19,300	$4,820	2-M	1,592	144
Wheaton Coll, Wheaton, IL 60187-5593	1860	$16,390	$5,544	2-D	2,844	273
Wheaton Coll, Norton, MA 02766	1834	$25,790	$7,150	1-B	1,551	150
Wheeling Jesuit Univ, Wheeling, WV 26003-6295	1954	$17,240	$5,420	2-M	1,466	95
Wheelock Coll, Boston, MA 02215 (4)	1888	$18,195	$7,325	1-M	1,090	221
Whitman Coll, Walla Walla, WA 99362-2083	1859	$24,274	$6,550	1-B	1,439	165
Whittier Coll, Whittier, CA 90608-0634	1887	$21,336	$7,042	1-F	2,170	133
Whitworth Coll, Spokane, WA 99251-0001	1890	$18,038	$5,900	2-M	1,855	110
Wichita State Univ, Wichita, KS 67260	1895	$2,857 (S)	$4,260	5-D	14,854	522
Widener Univ, Chester, PA 19013-5792	1821	$19,300	$7,620	1-D	5,484	391
Wilkes Univ, Wilkes-Barre, PA 18766-0002	1933	$18,020	$7,780	1-F	3,697	NA
Willamette Univ, Salem, OR 97301-3931	1842	$23,272	$6,150	2-F	2,466	235
William Carey Coll, Hattiesburg, MS 39401-5499	1906	$6,515	$1,990	2-M	2,318	172
William Jewell Coll, Liberty, MO 64068-1843	1849	$14,750	$4,390	2-B	1,089	133
William Paterson Univ of New Jersey, Wayne, NJ 07470-8420	1855	$5,700 (S)	$6,680	5-M	10,466	844
William Penn Univ, Oskaloosa, IA 52577-1799	1873	$13,270	$4,305	2-B	1,547	65
Williams Coll, Williamstown, MA 01267	1793	$25,540	$6,930	1-M	2,048	250
William Woods Univ, Fulton, MO 65251-2388	1870	$13,790	$5,600	2-M	1,659	98
Wilmington Coll, New Castle, DE 19720-6491	1967	$6,530	NA	1-D	5,051	584
Wilmington Coll, Wilmington, OH 45177	1870	$16,514	$6,251	2-B	1,243	77
Wingate Univ, Wingate, NC 28174-0159	1896	$13,680	$5,460	2-M	1,357	119
Winona State Univ, Winona, MN 55987-5838	1858	$3,630 (S)	$3,940	5-M	9,345	357
Winston-Salem State Univ, Winston-Salem, NC 27110-0003	1892	$2,063 (S)	$3,864	5-M	2,992	263
Winthrop Univ, Rock Hill, SC 29733	1886	$4,688 (S)	$4,418	5-M	6,306	405
Wittenberg Univ, Springfield, OH 45501-0720	1845	$22,840	$5,776	2-M	2,269	NA
Wofford Coll, Spartanburg, SC 29303-3663	1854	$18,515	$5,480	2-B	1,107	109
Woodbury Univ, Burbank, CA 91504-1099	1884	$18,344	$6,454	1-M	1,404	206
Worcester Polytechnic Inst, Worcester, MA 01609-2280	1865	$24,890	$7,900	1-D	3,887	341
Worcester State Coll, Worcester, MA 01602-2597	1874	$2,430 (S)	$5,186	5-M	5,768	258
Wright State Univ, Dayton, OH 45435	1964	$4,596 (S)	$5,400	5-D	15,810	801
Xavier Univ, Cincinnati, OH 45207	1831	$16,780	$7,230	2-D	6,660	547
Xavier Univ of Louisiana, New Orleans, LA 70125-1098	1925	$10,500	$5,700	2-F	4,111	259
Yale Univ, New Haven, CT 06520	1701	$26,100	$7,930	1-D	11,136	1,298
Yeshiva Univ, New York, NY 10033-3201	1886	$19,510	$6,426	1-D	5,998	NA
York Coll of Pennsylvania, York, PA 17405-7199	1787	$7,422	$5,128	1-M	5,293	377
York Coll of the City Univ of New York, Jamaica, NY 11451-0001	1967	$3,290 (S)	NA	11-B	5,253	433
Youngstown State Univ, Youngstown, OH 44555-0001	1908	$4,588 (S)	$4,970	5-D	12,250	831

Two-Year Colleges

Figures for Room & Board are given where applicable. See other notes, page 243.

Name, address	Year Founded	Tuition & Fees	Rm. & Board	Control, Degree	Enroll-ment	Faculty
Abraham Baldwin Agr Coll, Tifton, GA 31794-2601	1933	$1,618 (S)	$3,308	5	2,857	96
Adirondack Comm Coll, Queensbury, NY 12804	1960	$2,576 (S)	—	11	3,200	244
AIBT Intl Inst of the Americas, Phoenix, AZ 85019	NA	$8,150	—	1-B	1,036	95
Aims Comm Coll, Greeley, CO 80632-0069	1967	$1,665 (A)	—	9	6,868	425
Alamance Comm Coll, Graham, NC 27253-8000	1959	$1,052 (S)	—	5	3,991	226
Albuquerque Tech Voc Inst, Albuquerque, NM 87106-4096	1965	$1,313 (S)	—	5	18,833	798
Alexandria Tech Coll, Alexandria, MN 56308-3707	1961	$3,012 (S)	—	5	2,066	100
Allan Hancock Coll, Santa Maria, CA 93454-6399	1920	$288 (S)	—	11	12,548	576
Allegany Coll of Maryland, Cumberland, MD 21502-2596	1961	$2,720 (A)	—	11	2,879	215
Allentown Business School, Allentown, PA 18103-3880	1869	$18,600	—	3	1,230	65
Alpena Comm Coll, Alpena, MI 49707-1495	1952	$2,140 (A)	—	11	1,932	123
Alvin Comm Coll, Alvin, TX 77511-4898	1949	$656 (S)	—	11	3,671	240
American River Coll, Sacramento, CA 95841-4286	1955	$332 (S)	—	9	28,747	914
Angelina Coll, Lufkin, TX 75902-1768	1968	$840 (A)	$3,710	11	4,418	292
Anne Arundel Comm Coll, Arnold, MD 21012-1895	1961	$1,600 (A)	—	11	52,088	773
Anoka-Hennepin Tech Coll, Anoka, MN 55303	1967	$3,131 (A)	—	5	3,970	112
Anoka-Ramsey Comm Coll, Coon Rapids, MN 55433-3470	1965	$2,300 (S)	—	5	4,416	250
Anoka-Ramsey Comm Coll, Cambridge Campus, Cambridge, MN 55008-5706	NA	$91/credit (S)	—	5	1,411	67
Antelope Valley Coll, Lancaster, CA 93536-5426	1929	$264 (S)	—	11	12,500	324
Arapahoe Comm Coll, Littleton, CO 80160-9002	1965	$1,400 (S)	—	5	7,076	414
Argosy Univ-Twin Cities, Bloomington, MN 55437-1003 (4)	1961	$10,700	—	3-D	1,150	89
Arizona Western Coll, Yuma, AZ 85366-0929	1962	$990 (S)	$3,680	11	6,089	373
Arkansas State Univ-Beebe, Beebe, AR 72012-1000	1927	$1,752 (S)	$2,800	5	3,302	97
Arkansas State Univ-Mountain Home, Mountain Home, AR 72650	NA	$1,392 (S)	—	5	1,238	58
The Art Inst of Atlanta, Atlanta, GA 30328	1949	$14,544	$5,490	3-B	2,137	140
The Art Inst of Dallas, Dallas, TX 75231-9959	1978	$12,870	—	3	1,532	94
The Art Inst of Houston, Houston, TX 77056-4115	1978	$14,625	$4,185	3-B	1,679	121
The Art Inst of Los Angeles, Santa Monica, CA 90405-3035	NA	$16,550	$7,688	3-B	1,429	103
The Art Inst of Philadelphia, Philadelphia, PA 19103-5198	1966	$14,625	$7,472	3-B	2,807	230
The Art Inst of Pittsburgh, Pittsburgh, PA 15219	1921	$14,670	$4,800	3-B	2,500	120
The Art Inst of Seattle, Seattle, WA 98121-1642	1982	$14,040	$8,025	3	2,480	195
Asheville-Buncombe Tech Comm Coll, Asheville, NC 28801-4897	1959	$907 (A)	—	5	5,448	567
Ashland Comm Coll, Ashland, KY 41101-3683	1937	$1,932 (S)	—	5	2,252	85
Asnuntuck Comm Coll, Enfield, CT 06082-3800	1972	$1,980 (S)	—	5	1,723	115
Athens Tech Coll, Athens, GA 30601-1500	1958	$1,217 (S)	—	5	3,200	190
Atlanta Metro Coll, Atlanta, GA 30310-4498	1974	$1,450 (S)	—	5	1,917	84
Atlantic Cape Comm Coll, Mays Landing, NJ 08330-2699	1964	$2,079 (A)	—	8	5,483	504
Augusta Tech Coll, Augusta, GA 30906	1961	$25/qtr. hr. (S)	—	5	3,711	327
Austin Comm Coll, Austin, TX 78752-4390	1972	$1,296 (A)	—	9	27,548	1,525
Bainbridge Coll, Bainbridge, GA 31717	1972	$1,401 (S)	—	5	1,736	67
Bakersfield Coll, Bakersfield, CA 93305-1299	1913	NA	—	11	15,001	NA
Baltimore City Comm Coll, Baltimore, MD 21215-7893	1947	$1,536 (S)	—	5	6,268	123
Barstow Coll, Barstow, CA 92311-6699	1959	$264 (S)	—	11	3,264	127
Barton County Comm Coll, Great Bend, KS 67530-9283	1969	$1,472 (S)	$2,904	11	4,178	203
Bates Tech Coll, Tacoma, WA 98405-4895	NA	$2,690 (S)	—	5	16,162	290
Bay de Noc Comm Coll, Escanaba, MI 49829-2511	1963	$2,184 (A)	$1,600	8	2,200	172
Beaufort County Comm Coll, Washington, NC 27889-1069	1967	$1,020 (S)	—	5	1,721	136
Bellevue Comm Coll, Bellevue, WA 98007-6484	1966	$3,050 (A)	—	5	21,700	572
Bellingham Tech Coll, Bellingham, WA 98225	NA	$2,029 (S)	—	5	3,791	162
Belmont Tech Coll, St. Clairsville, OH 43950-9735	1971	$2,790 (S)	—	5	1,623	101
Bergen Comm Coll, Paramus, NJ 07652-1595	1965	$2,049 (A)	—	8	12,145	653
Berkeley Coll, West Paterson, NJ 07424-3353	1931	$14,340	$8,100	3-B	2,144	118
Berkeley Coll, New York, NY 10017-4604	1936	$14,340	—	3-B	1,666	110
Berkshire Comm Coll, Pittsfield, MA 01201-5786	1960	$2,745 (S)	—	5	2,401	167
Bessemer State Tech Coll, Bessemer, AL 35021-0308	1966	$1,440 (S)	—	5	2,087	200
Bevill State Comm Coll, Sumiton, AL 35148	1969	$1,982 (A)	—	5	3,504	195
Big Bend Comm Coll, Moses Lake, WA 98837-3299	1962	$1,743 (S)	$4,220	5	1,912	112
Bishop State Comm Coll, Mobile, AL 36603-5898	1965	$1,248 (S)	—	5	3,393	176
Bismarck State Coll, Bismarck, ND 58506-5587	1939	$2,316 (S)	$2,998	5	3,044	193
Black Hawk Coll, Moline, IL 61265-5899	1946	$1,650 (A)	—	11	6,248	352
Blackhawk Tech Coll, Janesville, WI 53547-5009	1968	$2,111 (S)	—	9	2,300	341
Black River Tech Coll, Pocahontas, AR 72455	1972	$1,032 (A)	—	5	1,243	70
Bladen Comm Coll, Dublin, NC 28332-0266	1967	$1,030 (A)	—	11	1,033	92
Blinn Coll, Brenham, TX 77833-4049	1883	$1,080 (A)	—	11	12,025	323
Blue Ridge Comm Coll, Flat Rock, NC 28731-9624	1969	$1,019 (S)	—	11	1,907	225
Blue Ridge Comm Coll, Weyers Cave, VA 24486-0080	1967	$1,481 (S)	—	5	3,197	166
Blue River Comm Coll, Blue Springs, MO 64015	NA	$1,740 (A)	—	11	2,294	258
Borough of Manhattan Comm Coll of the City Univ of New York, New York, NY 10007-1097	1963	$2,500 (S)	—	11	16,025	1,006
Bossier Parish Comm Coll, Bossier City, LA 71111-5801	1967	$1,360 (S)	—	5	3,964	185
Bowling Green State Univ-Firelands Coll, Huron, OH 44839-9791	1968	$3,186 (S)	—	5	1,537	80
Brazosport Coll, Lake Jackson, TX 77566-3199	1968	$940 (A)	—	11	4,022	191
Brevard Comm Coll, Cocoa, FL 32922-6597	1960	$1,808 (A)	—	5	13,681	956
Brigham Young Univ -Idaho, Rexburg, ID 83460-1650	1888	$2,100	$3,668	2	9,000	437
Bristol Comm Coll, Fall River, MA 02720-7395	1965	$2,592 (S)	—	5	6,132	279
Bronx Comm Coll of the City Univ of New York, Bronx, NY 10453	1959	$2,610 (S)	—	11	6,942	662
Brookdale Comm Coll, Lincroft, NJ 07738-1597	1967	$2,246 (A)	—	8	11,876	624
Broome Comm Coll, Binghamton, NY 13902-1017	1946	$2,598 (S)	—	11	5,818	145
Broward Comm Coll, Fort Lauderdale, FL 33301-2298	1960	NA	—	5	30,333	775
Brown Coll, Mendota Heights, MN 55120	1946	$23,000	—	3	2,250	140
Bucks County Comm Coll, Newtown, PA 18940-1525	1964	$2,509 (A)	—	8	8,806	577
Bunker Hill Comm Coll, Boston, MA 02129	1973	$2,400 (S)	—	5	6,914	373
Burlington County Coll, Pemberton, NJ 08068-1599	1966	$1,800 (A)	—	8	6,467	371
Butler County Comm Coll, Butler, PA 16003-1203	1965	$1,896 (A)	—	8	3,183	198
Butte Coll, Oroville, CA 95965-8399	1966	$428 (S)	—	9	14,724	617
Cabrillo Coll, Aptos, CA 95003-3194	1959	NA	—	9	13,147	552

Name, address	Year Founded	Tuition & Fees	Rm. & Board	Control, Degree	Enroll-ment	Faculty
Caldwell Comm Coll & Tech Inst, Hudson, NC 28638-2397	1964	$1,024 (S)	—	5	3,636	401
Calhoun Comm Coll, Decatur, AL 35609-2216	1965	$4,160 (S)	—	5	8,372	421
Cambria County Area Comm Coll, Johnstown, PA 15907-0068	NA	$1,815 (A)	—	11	1,208	140
Camden County Coll, Blackwood, NJ 08012-0200	1967	$1,440 (A)	—	11	12,566	717
Cape Cod Comm Coll, West Barnstable, MA 02668-1599	1961	$2,760 (S)	—	5	4,176	331
Cape Fear Comm Coll, Wilmington, NC 28401-3993	1959	$1,030 (S)	—	5	6,051	536
Capital Comm Coll, Hartford, CT 06105-2354	1946	$2,136 (S)	—	5	3,129	222
Carl Sandburg Coll, Galesburg, IL 61401-9576	1967	$2,412 (A)	—	11	4,000	208
Carroll Comm Coll, Westminster, MD 21157	1993	$1,800 (A)	—	11	2,634	163
Carteret Comm Coll, Morehead City, NC 28557-2989	1963	$1,051 (S)	—	5	1,555	93
Cascadia Comm Coll, Bothell, WA 98011	1999	$1,322 (S)	—	5	2,011	91
Casper Coll, Casper, WY 82601-4699	1945	$1,368 (S)	$2,950	9	3,853	249
Catawba Valley Comm Coll, Hickory, NC 28602-9699	1960	$1,016 (S)	—	11	3,943	443
Cayuga County Comm Coll, Auburn, NY 13021-3099	1953	$2,978 (S)	—	11	2,739	162
Cecil Comm Coll, North East, MD 21901-1999	1968	$2,143 (A)	—	8	1,448	178
Cedar Valley Coll, Lancaster, TX 75134-3799	1977	$624 (A)	—	5	3,974	164
Central Alabama Comm Coll, Alexander City, AL 35011-0699	1965	$1,728 (S)	—	5	1,609	193
Central Caroli— Comm Coll, Sanford, NC 27330-9000	1962	$1,347 (S)	—	11	4,062	426
Central Carolina Tech Coll, Sumter, SC 29150-2499	1963	$1,700 (A)	—	5	2,963	142
Central Comm Coll-Columbus Campus, Columbus, NE 68602-1027	1968	$1,200 (S)	$3,120	11	1,794	91
Central Comm Coll-Grand Island Campus, Grand Island, NE 68802-4903	1976	$1,200 (S)	—	11	2,780	114
Central Comm Coll-Hastings Campus, Hastings, NE 68902-1024	1966	$1,200 (S)	$3,120	11	2,245	91
Central Florida Comm Coll, Ocala, FL 34478-1388	1957	$1,846 (S)	—	11	5,708	238
Central Georgia Tech Coll, Macon, GA 31206-3628	1966	$1,262 (S)	—	5	4,955	387
Centralia Coll, Centralia, WA 98531-4099	1925	$1,878 (S)	—	5	3,823	197
Central Lakes Coll, Brainerd, MN 56401-3904	1938	$1,211 (A)	—	5	2,857	140
Central Maine Tech Coll, Auburn, ME 04210-6498	1964	$2,866 (A)	$4,175	5	1,435	135
Central Ohio Tech Coll, Newark, OH 43055-1767	1971	$2,970 (S)	$1,215	5	1,973	139
Central Oregon Comm Coll, Bend, OR 97701-5998	1949	$2,093 (A)	$5,300	9	4,399	264
Central Piedmont Comm Coll, Charlotte, NC 28235-5009	1963	$1,030 (S)	—	11	15,648	1,312
Central Texas Coll, Killeen, TX 76540-1800	1967	$672 (A)	$2,742	11	15,473	675
Central Virginia Comm Coll, Lynchburg, VA 24502-2498	1966	$1,179 (S)	—	5	4,791	173
Central Wyoming Coll, Riverton, WY 82501-2273	1966	$1,636 (S)	$2,750	11	1,544	109
Century Comm & Tech Coll, White Bear Lake, MN 55110	1970	$2,596 (S)	—	5	7,396	279
Cerritos Coll, Norwalk, CA 90650-6298	1956	NA	—	11	23,000	690
Cerro Coso Comm Coll, Ridgecrest, CA 93555-9571	1973	$330 (S)	—	5	6,653	233
Chabot Coll, Hayward, CA 94545-5001	1961	$264 (S)	—	5	15,149	516
Chaffey Coll, Rancho Cucamonga, CA 91737-3002	1883	NA	—	9	18,025	893
Chattahoochee Tech Coll, Marietta, GA 30060	1961	$780 (A)	—	5	5,963	173
Chattahoochee Valley Comm Coll, Phenix City, AL 36869-7928	1974	$2,040 (S)	—	5	1,891	98
Chattanooga State Tech Comm Coll, Chattanooga, TN 37406-1097	1965	$1,649 (S)	—	5	9,600	626
Chemeketa Comm Coll, Salem, OR 97309-7070	1955	$1,755 (S)	—	11	8,718	632
Chesapeake Coll, Wye Mills, MD 21679-0008	1965	$1,890 (A)	—	11	2,186	166
Chipola Jr Coll, Marianna, FL 32446-3065	1947	$1,600 (S)	—	5	1,834	69
Chippewa Valley Tech Coll, Eau Claire, WI 54701-6162	1912	$1,680 (S)	—	9	2,600	400
Cincinnati State Tech & Comm Coll, Cincinnati, OH 45223-2690	1966	$3,575 (S)	—	5	7,184	804
Cisco Jr Coll, Cisco, TX 76437-9321	1940	$311/term (A)	—	11	2,616	95
Citrus Coll, Glendora, CA 91741-1899	1915	$386 (S)	—	11	11,159	525
City Coll of San Francisco, San Francisco, CA 94112-1821	1935	NA	—	11	100,544	890
City Colleges of Chicago, Harry S. Truman Coll, Chicago, IL 60640-5616	1956	$52/cr. hr. (A)	—	11	32,859	503
City Colleges of Chicago, Kennedy-King Coll, Chicago, IL 60621-3733	1935	$1,529 (A)	—	11	6,575	77
City Colleges of Chicago, Malcolm X Coll, Chicago, IL 60612-3145	1911	$1,690 (A)	—	11	8,791	171
City Colleges of Chicago, Olive-Harvey Coll, Chicago, IL 60628-1645	1970	$50/cr. hr. (A)	—	11	3,165	133
City Colleges of Chicago, Richard J. Daley Coll, Chicago, IL 60652-1242	1960	$1,750 (A)	—	11	5,149	180
City Colleges of Chicago, Wilbur Wright Coll, Chicago, IL 60634-1591	1934	$1,700 (A)	—	11	6,253	231
Clackamas Comm Coll, Oregon City, OR 97045-7998	1966	$1,770 (S)	—	9	6,715	582
Clarendon Coll, Clarendon, TX 79226-0968	1898	$1,024 (A)	$2,250	11	1,000	61
Clark Coll, Vancouver, WA 98663-3598	1933	$1,950 (S)	—	5	9,274	477
Clark State Comm Coll, Springfield, OH 45501-0570	1962	$3,156 (S)	—	5	2,808	251
Clatsop Comm Coll, Astoria, OR 97103-3698	1958	$1,512 (S)	—	8	1,796	198
Cleveland Comm Coll, Shelby, NC 28152	1965	$1,030 (S)	—	5	2,782	62
Cleveland Inst of Electronics, Cleveland, OH 44114-3636 (2)	1934	$1,645	—	3	3,077	5
Cleveland State Comm Coll, Cleveland, TN 37320-3570	1967	$1,782 (S)	—	5	3,177	184
Clinton Comm Coll, Clinton, IA 52732-6299	1946	$2,160 (S)	—	11	1,217	75
Clinton Comm Coll, Plattsburgh, NY 12901-9573	1969	$2,528 (S)	$2,000	11	1,852	128
Clover Park Tech Coll, Lakewood, WA 98499	1942	$2,346 (S)	—	5	7,429	239
Clovis Comm Coll, Clovis, NM 88101-8381	1990	$612 (A)	—	5	2,767	222
Coahoma Comm Coll, Clarksdale, MS 38614-9799	1949	$1,360 (S)	$2,844	11	1,400	55
Coastal Bend Coll, Beeville, TX 78102-2197	1965	$940 (A)	$1,920	8	3,259	179
Coastal Carolina Comm Coll, Jacksonville, NC 28546-6899	1964	$1,022 (S)	—	11	4,033	253
Coastal Georgia Comm Coll, Brunswick, GA 31520-3644	1961	$1,280 (S)	—	5	2,210	94
Coastline Comm Coll, Fountain Valley, CA 92708-2597	1976	$350 (S)	—	11	12,220	350
Cochise Coll, Douglas, AZ 85607-9724	1962	$1,030 (S)	$3,228	11	6,011	406
Coconino Comm Coll, Flagstaff, AZ 86003	1991	$990 (S)	—	5	3,689	205
Coffeyville Comm Coll, Coffeyville, KS 67337-5063	1923	$1,760 (A)	$3,200	11	1,499	85
Colby Comm Coll, Colby, KS 67701-4099	1964	$1,440 (S)	$3,136	11	2,166	53
Coll of Alameda, Alameda, CA 94501-2109	1970	$264 (S)	—	11	5,500	166
Coll of DuPage, Glen Ellyn, IL 60137-6599	1967	$1,961 (A)	—	11	29,423	1,573
Coll of Eastern Utah, Price, UT 84501-2699	1937	$1,529 (S)	$3,420	5	2,742	206
Coll of Lake County, Grayslake, IL 60030-1198	1967	$1,650 (A)	—	9	14,886	977
Coll of Marin, Kentfield, CA 94904	1926	$354 (S)	—	11	8,365	464
Coll of St. Catherine-Minneapolis, Minneapolis, MN 55454-1494 (4)	1964	$18,362	$5,170	2	3,610	443
Coll of San Mateo, San Mateo, CA 94402-3784	1922	$0 (S)	—	11	10,872	476
Coll of Southern Idaho, Twin Falls, ID 83303-1238	1964	$1,550 (S)	$3,200	11	5,344	141
Coll of Southern Maryland, La Plata, MD 20646-0910	1958	$2,520 (A)	—	11	6,803	389
Coll of the Canyons, Santa Clarita, CA 91355-1899	1969	NA	—	11	10,700	400
Coll of the Desert, Palm Desert, CA 92260-9305	1959	$332 (S)	—	11	9,794	279
Coll of the Mainland, Texas City, TX 77591-2499	1967	$718 (A)	—	11	3,400	459
Coll of the Redwoods, Eureka, CA 95501-9300	1964	$294 (S)	$5,310	11	7,503	413
Coll of the Sequoias, Visalia, CA 93277-2234	1925	$330 (S)	—	11	10,780	NA

Name, address	Year Founded	Tuition & Fees	Rm. & Board	Control, Degree	Enroll-ment	Faculty
Coll of the Siskiyous, Weed, CA 96094-2899	1957	$350 (S)	$4,910	11	3,127	164
Collin County Comm Coll District, Plano, TX 75093-8309	1985	$934 (A)	—	11	14,497	773
Colorado Northwestern Comm Coll, Rangely, CO 81648-3598	1962	$2,055 (S)	$4,890	5	2,109	198
Columbia Basin Coll, Pasco, WA 99301-3397	1955	$1,755 (S)	—	5	5,837	609
Columbia-Greene Comm Coll, Hudson, NY 12534-0327	1969	$2,540 (S)	—	11	1,624	106
Columbus State Comm Coll, Columbus, OH 43216-1609	1963	$2,196 (S)	—	5	19,549	966
Comm Coll of Allegheny County, Pittsburgh, PA 15233-1894	1966	$1,930 (A)	—	8	16,999	2,017
Comm Coll of Aurora, Aurora, CO 80011-9036	1983	$1,905 (S)	—	5	4,000	340
The Comm Coll of Baltimore County-Catonsville Campus, Baltimore, MD 21228-5381	1957	$2,356 (A)	—	8	18,898	965
Comm Coll of Beaver County, Monaca, PA 15061-2588	1966	$2,002 (A)	—	5	2,260	106
Comm Coll of Denver, Denver, CO 80217-3363	1970	$1,742 (S)	—	5	6,509	372
Comm Coll of Philadelphia, Philadelphia, PA 19130-3991	1964	NA	—	11	42,000	1,182
Comm Coll of Rhode Island, Warwick, RI 02886-1807	1964	$1,854 (S)	—	5	16,223	730
Comm Coll of Southern Nevada, North Las Vegas, NV 89030-4296	1971	$1,494 (S)	—	5	31,851	2,223
Comm Coll of the Air Force, Maxwell Air Force Base, AL 36112-6613 (2)	1972	$0 (C)	—	4	373,943	6,269
Comm Coll of Vermont, Waterbury, VT 05676-0120	1970	$2,932 (S)	—	5	5,000	508
Connors State Coll, Warner, OK 74469-9700	1908	$1,685 (S)	$2,340	5	1,954	109
Corning Comm Coll, Corning, NY 14830-3297	1956	$2,860 (S)	—	11	4,596	260
Cosumnes River Coll, Sacramento, CA 95823-5799	1970	NA	—	9	15,002	425
County Coll of Morris, Randolph, NJ 07869-2086	1966	$2,120 (A)	—	8	8,190	495
Cowley County Comm Coll & Area Voc-Tech School, Arkansas City, KS 67005	1922	$1,530 (S)	—	11	4,475	216
Crafton Hills Coll, Yucaipa, CA 92399-1799	1972	$264 (S)	—	11	5,200	217
Craven Comm Coll, New Bern, NC 28562-4984	1965	$524 (A)	—	5	2,555	166
Crowder Coll, Neosho, MO 64850-9160	1963	$1,560 (A)	$2,700	11	2,012	168
Cuesta Coll, San Luis Obispo, CA 93403-8106	1964	$401 (S)	—	9	10,165	401
Cumberland County Coll, Vineland, NJ 08362-1500	1963	$2,041 (A)	—	11	2,775	178
Cuyahoga Comm Coll, Cleveland, OH 44115-2878	1963	$1,857 (A)	—	11	21,278	1,036
Cuyamaca Coll, El Cajon, CA 92019-4304	1978	$298 (S)	—	5	7,423	342
Cypress Coll, Cypress, CA 90630-5897	1966	$326 (S)	—	11	15,347	590
Dakota County Tech Coll, Rosemount, MN 55068	1970	$3,106 (S)	—	5	3,103	199
Danville Area Comm Coll, Danville, IL 61832-5199	1946	$1,224 (A)	—	11	3,000	121
Danville Comm Coll, Danville, VA 24541-4088	1967	$1,362 (S)	—	5	3,879	203
Darton Coll, Albany, GA 31707-3098	1965	$1,496 (S)	—	5	3,185	317
Davenport Univ, Midland, MI 48642	1907	$6,102	—	1-B	1,500	144
Daytona Beach Comm Coll, Daytona Beach, FL 32120-2811	1958	$1,603 (S)	—	5	11,214	956
De Anza Coll, Cupertino, CA 95014-5793	1967	NA	—	11	24,984	775
Delaware County Comm Coll, Media, PA 19063-1094	1967	$1,818 (A)	—	11	9,467	629
Delaware Tech & Comm Coll, Jack F. Owens Campus, Georgetown, DE 19947	1967	$1,653 (S)	—	5	3,546	240
Delaware Tech & Comm Coll, Stanton/Wilmington Campus, Newark, DE 19713	1968	$1,770 (S)	—	5	6,667	471
Delaware Tech & Comm Coll, Terry Campus, Dover, DE 19901	1972	$1,770 (S)	—	5	2,004	170
Delgado Comm Coll, New Orleans, LA 70119-4399	1921	$1,574 (S)	—	5	13,404	643
Del Mar Coll, Corpus Christi, TX 78404-3897	1935	NA	—	11	10,256	635
Delta Coll, University Center, MI 48710	1961	$1,524 (A)	—	9	10,000	400
Denmark Tech Coll, Denmark, SC 29042-0327	1948	$1,704 (S)	$3,096	5	1,401	59
Des Moines Area Comm Coll, Ankeny, IA 50021-8995	1966	$2,202 (S)	—	11	11,886	270
Diablo Valley Coll, Pleasant Hill, CA 94523-1544	1949	$264 (S)	—	11	23,035	868
Diné Coll, Tsaile, AZ 86556	1968	$640 (S)	$3,552	4	1,725	152
Dixie State Coll of Utah, St. George, UT 84770-3876	1911	$1,544 (S)	$2,850	5-B	7,001	301
Dodge City Comm Coll, Dodge City, KS 67801-2399	1935	$1,200 (S)	—	11	1,956	163
Doña Ana Branch Comm Coll, Las Cruces, NM 88003-8001	1973	$903 (A)	—	11	4,987	324
Don Bosco Coll of Sci & Tech, Rosemead, CA 91770-4299 (2)	1955	$5,400	—	2	1,208	80
Dunwoody Coll of Tech, Minneapolis, MN 55403 (2)	1914	$7,689	—	1	1,164	63
Durham Tech Comm Coll, Durham, NC 27703-5023	1961	$904 (S)	—	5	5,283	514
Dutchess Comm Coll, Poughkeepsie, NY 12601-1595	1957	$2,420 (S)	—	11	6,981	396
Dyersburg State Comm Coll, Dyersburg, TN 38024	1969	$1,629 (S)	—	5	2,284	179
East Arkansas Comm Coll, Forrest City, AR 72335-2204	1974	$1,108 (A)	—	5	1,358	100
East Central Coll, Union, MO 63084-0529	1959	$1,404 (A)	—	9	3,462	172
East Central Comm Coll, Decatur, MS 39327-0129	1928	$1,400 (A)	$2,540	11	2,382	144
Eastern Arizona Coll, Thatcher, AZ 85552-0769	1888	$788 (S)	$3,580	11	6,492	269
Eastern Maine Tech Coll, Bangor, ME 04401-4206	1966	$2,448 (S)	$4,052	5	1,604	142
Eastern Oklahoma State Coll, Wilburton, OK 74578-4999	1908	$1,700 (S)	$2,600	5	2,026	51
Eastern Wyoming Coll, Torrington, WY 82240-1699	1948	$1,736 (S)	$2,866	11	1,278	137
Eastfield Coll, Mesquite, TX 75150-2099	1970	$780 (A)	—	11	9,210	483
East Georgia Coll, Swainsboro, GA 30401-2699	1973	$1,424 (S)	—	5	1,393	61
East Los Angeles Coll, Monterey Park, CA 91754-6001	1945	$286 (S)	—	11	17,197	450
East Mississippi Comm Coll, Scooba, MS 39358-0158	1927	$1,260 (S)	$2,210	11	3,009	188
Edgecombe Comm Coll, Tarboro, NC 27886-9399	1968	$1,016 (S)	—	11	2,032	218
Edison Comm Coll, Fort Myers, FL 33906-6210	1962	$1,221 (S)	—	11	9,390	417
Edison State Comm Coll, Piqua, OH 45356-9253	1973	$1,380 (S)	—	5	2,915	298
Edmonds Comm Coll, Lynnwood, WA 98036-5999	1967	$1,865 (S)	—	11	7,738	424
Elaine P. Nunez Comm Coll, Chalmette, LA 70043-1249	1992	$1,360 (S)	—	5	1,924	103
El Camino Coll, Torrance, CA 90506-0001	1947	NA	—	5	23,985	533
El Centro Coll, Dallas, TX 75202-3604	1966	$710 (A)	—	8	4,923	526
Elgin Comm Coll, Elgin, IL 60123-7193	1949	$1,575 (A)	—	11	10,174	664
El Paso Comm Coll, El Paso, TX 79998-0500	1969	$469 (S)	—	8	18,566	1,183
Erie Comm Coll, City Campus, Buffalo, NY 14203-2698	1971	$2,655 (A)	—	11	2,517	181
Erie Comm Coll, North Campus, Williamsville, NY 14221-7095	1946	$2,655 (A)	—	11	5,162	352
Erie Comm Coll, South Campus, Orchard Park, NY 14127-2199	1974	$2,655 (A)	—	11	3,370	223
Essex County Coll, Newark, NJ 07102-1798	1966	$2,580 (A)	—	8	9,539	514
Eugenio María de Hostos Comm Coll of the City Univ of New York, Bronx, NY 10451	1968	$2,672 (S)	—	11	3,285	304
Everett Comm Coll, Everett, WA 98201-1327	1941	$1,738 (S)	—	5	7,227	352
Evergreen Valley Coll, San Jose, CA 95135-1598	1975	$310 (A)	—	11	10,000	NA
Fashion Inst of Design & Merchandising, Los Angeles Campus, Los Angeles, CA 90015-1421	1969	$14,500	—	3	2,873	147
Fayetteville Tech Comm Coll, Fayetteville, NC 28303-0236	1961	$887 (S)	—	5	8,310	790
Feather River Comm Coll District, Quincy, CA 95971-9124	1968	$382 (S)	—	11	1,200	87

Name, address	Year Founded	Tuition & Fees	Rm. & Board	Control, Degree	Enroll-ment	Faculty
Fergus Falls Comm Coll, Fergus Falls, MN 56537-1009	1960	$3,405 (S)	$2,500	5	2,401	94
Finger Lakes Comm Coll, Canandaigua, NY 14424-8395	1965	$2,600 (S)	—	11	4,753	258
Fiorello H. LaGuardia Comm Coll of the City Univ of New York, Long Island City, NY 11101-3071	1970	$2,622 (A)	—	11	11,427	790
Flathead Valley Comm Coll, Kalispell, MT 59901-2622	1967	$1,835 (A)	—	11	1,867	168
Florence-Darlington Tech Coll, Florence, SC 29501-0548	1963	$1,882 (A)	—	5	3,632	305
Florida Comm Coll at Jacksonville, Jacksonville, FL 32202-4030	1963	$1,544 (S)	—	5	23,425	1,134
Florida Culinary Inst, West Palm Beach, FL 33407	NA	$21,600	—	3	1,500	21
Florida Natl Coll, Hialeah, FL 33012	1982	$8,010	—	3	1,248	35
Floyd Coll, Rome, GA 30162-1864	1970	$1,510 (S)	—	5	2,500	250
Foothill Coll, Los Altos Hills, CA 94022-4599	1958	$401 (S)	—	11	18,500	587
Forsyth Tech Comm Coll, Winston-Salem, NC 27103-5197	1964	$900 (S)	—	5	6,246	664
Fort Scott Comm Coll, Fort Scott, KS 66701	1919	$1,650 (S)	—	11	1,900	173
Fox Valley Tech Coll, Appleton, WI 54912-2277	1967	$1,968 (S)	—	11	6,291	1,170
Frederick Comm Coll, Frederick, MD 21702-2097	1957	$2,112 (A)	—	11	4,558	240
Fresno City Coll, Fresno, CA 93741-0002	1910	NA	—	9	30,069	1,617
Front Range Comm Coll, Westminster, CO 80031-2105	1968	$1,985 (S)	—	5	13,511	789
Fullerton Coll, Fullerton, CA 92832-2095	1913	NA	—	11	21,104	835
Full Sail Real World Education, Winter Park, FL 32792-7437	1979	$30,000	—	3	3,100	550
Fulton-Montgomery Comm Coll, Johnstown, NY 12095-3790	1964	$2,516 (S)	—	11	1,949	132
Gadsden State Comm Coll, Gadsden, AL 35902-0227	1965	$2,888 (S)	$2,350	5	4,729	324
Galveston Coll, Galveston, TX 77550-7496	1967	$560 (S)	—	11	2,255	101
Garden City Comm Coll, Garden City, KS 67846-6399	1919	$1,600 (S)	$3,800	8	2,047	157
Garland County Comm Coll, Hot Springs, AR 71913	1973	$980 (A)	—	11	2,300	105
Gaston Coll, Dallas, NC 28034-1499	1963	$790 (S)	—	11	4,250	195
GateWay Comm Coll, Phoenix, AZ 85034-1795	1968	$1,920 (A)	—	11	9,377	259
Gateway Comm Coll, New Haven, CT 06511-5918	1992	$1,980 (S)	—	5	4,724	294
Gateway Tech Coll, Kenosha, WI 53144-1690	1911	$2,245 (S)	—	11	6,247	602
Gavilan Coll, Gilroy, CA 95020-9599	1919	$308 (S)	—	11	5,925	164
Genesee Comm Coll, Batavia, NY 14020-9704	1966	$2,772 (S)	$4,750	11	4,809	333
George Corley Wallace State Comm Coll, Selma, AL 36702-2530	1966	$2,040 (S)	—	5	1,579	93
Georgia Military Coll, Milledgeville, GA 31061-3398	1879	$10,760	$3,600	11	3,465	190
Georgia Perimeter Coll, Decatur, GA 30034-3897	1964	$1,510 (S)	—	5	15,372	783
Germanna Comm Coll, Locust Grove, VA 22508-2102	1970	$1,334 (S)	—	5	5,637	255
Glendale Comm Coll, Glendale, AZ 85302-3090	1965	$1,042 (A)	—	11	19,775	914
Glendale Comm Coll, Glendale, CA 91208-2894	1927	NA	—	11	17,303	742
Glen Oaks Comm Coll, Centreville, MI 49032-9719	1965	$1,923 (A)	—	11	1,894	108
Gloucester County Coll, Sewell, NJ 08080	1967	$2,528 (A)	—	8	4,895	220
Gogebic Comm Coll, Ironwood, MI 49938	1932	$1,739 (A)	—	11	1,165	91
Golden West Coll, Huntington Beach, CA 92647-2748	1966	$312 (S)	—	11	13,091	440
Gordon Coll, Barnesville, GA 30204-1762	1852	$1,512 (S)	—	5	3,074	139
Grand Rapids Comm Coll, Grand Rapids, MI 49503-3201	1914	$1,576 (A)	—	9	13,483	511
Grayson County Coll, Denison, TX 75020-8299	1964	$792 (A)	$2,530	11	3,471	219
Great Basin Coll, Elko, NV 89801-3348	1967	$50/credit (S)	—	5-B	2,470	213
Greenfield Comm Coll, Greenfield, MA 01301-9739	1962	$2,030 (S)	—	5	2,355	185
Green River Comm Coll, Auburn, WA 98092-3699	1965	$1,920 (S)	—	5	6,566	484
Greenville Tech Coll, Greenville, SC 29606-5616	1962	$1,750 (A)	—	5	11,500	478
Griffin Tech Coll, Griffin, GA 30223	1965	$661 (S)	—	5	4,383	110
Grossmont Coll, El Cajon, CA 92020-1799	1961	$297 (S)	—	11	16,175	653
Guam Comm Coll, Barrigada, GU 96921-3069	1977	$1,310 (S)	—	7	1,754	94
Guilford Tech Comm Coll, Jamestown, NC 27282-0309	1958	$1,035 (S)	—	11	8,573	808
Gulf Coast Comm Coll, Panama City, FL 32401-1058	1957	$1,522 (S)	—	5	5,765	611
Gwinnett Tech Coll, Lawrenceville, GA 30046-1505	1984	$1,404 (S)	—	5	3,964	300
Hagerstown Comm Coll, Hagerstown, MD 21742-6590	1946	$2,440 (A)	—	8	2,679	180
Halifax Comm Coll, Weldon, NC 27890-0809	1967	$902 (S)	—	11	1,580	147
Harford Comm Coll, Bel Air, MD 21015-1698	1957	$1,950 (A)	—	11	5,256	323
Harrisburg Area Comm Coll, Harrisburg, PA 17110-2999	1964	$2,325 (A)	—	11	11,671	743
Harry M. Ayers State Tech Coll, Anniston, AL 36202-1647	1966	$1,632 (S)	—	5	1,137	94
Hawaii Comm Coll, Hilo, HI 96720-4091	1954	$1,082 (S)	—	5	2,181	149
Hawkeye Comm Coll, Waterloo, IA 50704-8015	1966	$2,580 (A)	—	11	4,456	235
Haywood Comm Coll, Clyde, NC 28721-9453	1964	$1,006 (S)	—	11	1,874	190
Hazard Comm Coll, Hazard, KY 41701-2403	1968	$1,450 (S)	—	5	3,000	160
Heald Coll, Schools of Business & Tech, Milpitas, CA 95035	1863	$2,520	—	1	1,200	50
Heald Coll, Schools of Business & Tech, San Francisco, CA 94105-2206	1863	NA	—	1	12,000	37
Heald Coll, Schools of Business & Tech, Hayward, CA 94545-1557	1863	$11,400	—	1	1,250	52
Heartland Comm Coll, Normal, IL 61761	1990	$1,440 (A)	—	11	4,558	252
Henderson Comm Coll, Henderson, KY 42420-4623	1963	$1,230 (A)	—	5	1,407	101
Hennepin Tech Coll, Brooklyn Park, MN 55445	1972	$2,816 (S)	—	5	14,733	368
Henry Ford Comm Coll, Dearborn, MI 48128-1495	1938	$1,704 (S)	—	9	12,123	770
Herkimer County Comm Coll, Herkimer, NY 13350	1966	$2,684 (S)	$5,200	11	2,873	128
Hesser Coll, Manchester, NH 03103-7245	1900	$10,210	$6,000	3-B	2,766	164
Hibbing Comm Coll, Hibbing, MN 55746-3300	1916	$2,632 (S)	—	5	1,541	82
Highland Comm Coll, Freeport, IL 61032-9341	1962	$1,540 (A)	—	11	2,541	188
Highland Comm Coll, Highland, KS 66035	1858	$1,368 (A)	$3,340	11	2,673	226
Highline Comm Coll, Des Moines, WA 98198-9800	1961	$1,743 (S)	—	5	6,372	356
Hill Coll of the Hill Jr Coll District, Hillsboro, TX 76645-0619	1923	$1,065 (A)	$2,680	9	2,421	159
Hillsborough Comm Coll, Tampa, FL 33631-3127	1968	$1,581 (S)	—	5	19,436	1,518
Hinds Comm Coll, Raymond, MS 39154-1100	1917	$1,170 (A)	$2,160	11	14,390	905
Hocking Coll, Nelsonville, OH 45764-9588	1968	$2,151 (S)	—	5	6,435	229
Holmes Comm Coll, Goodman, MS 39079-0369	1928	$1,688 (A)	$1,100	11	3,252	125
Holyoke Comm Coll, Holyoke, MA 01040-1099	1946	$1,776 (S)	—	5	5,998	300
Honolulu Comm Coll, Honolulu, HI 96817-4598	1920	$1,052 (S)	—	5	4,653	187
Hopkinsville Comm Coll, Hopkinsville, KY 42241-2100	1965	$1,450 (S)	—	5	2,849	166
Horry-Georgetown Tech Coll, Conway, SC 29528-6066	1966	$1,926 (A)	—	11	4,113	267
Housatonic Comm Coll, Bridgeport, CT 06604-4704	1965	$1,888 (S)	—	5	4,247	227
Houston Comm Coll System, Houston, TX 77002-9330	1971	$936 (A)	—	11	38,175	2,019
Howard Coll, Big Spring, TX 79720	1945	$1,130 (S)	—	11	2,135	146
Howard Comm Coll, Columbia, MD 21044-3197	1966	$2,430 (A)	—	11	5,934	369
Hudson County Comm Coll, Jersey City, NJ 07306	1974	$2,248 (A)	—	11	5,285	297
Hudson Valley Comm Coll, Troy, NY 12180-6096	1953	$2,530 (S)	—	11	8,116	511

Name, address	Year Founded	Tuition & Fees	Rm. & Board	Control, Degree	Enroll-ment	Faculty
Hutchinson Comm Coll & Area Voc School, Hutchinson, KS 67501-5894	1928	$1,568 (S)	$3,364	11	3,733	287
Illinois Central Coll, East Peoria, IL 61635-0001	1967	NA	—	11	12,341	658
Illinois Eastern Comm Colleges, Frontier Comm Coll, Fairfield, IL 62837-2601	1976	$1,428 (A)	—	11	1,913	141
Illinois Eastern Comm Colleges, Lincoln Trail Coll, Robinson, IL 62454	1969	$1,428 (A)	—	11	1,100	81
Illinois Eastern Comm Colleges, Olney Central Coll, Olney, IL 62450	1962	$1,428 (A)	—	11	1,617	83
Illinois Eastern Comm Colleges, Wabash Valley Coll, Mount Carmel, IL 62863	1960	$1,428 (A)	—	11	2,643	78
Illinois Valley Comm Coll, Oglesby, IL 61348-9692	1924	$1,717 (A)	—	9	4,582	189
Imperial Valley Coll, Imperial, CA 92251-0158	1922	$330 (S)	—	11	7,223	272
Independence Comm Coll, Independence, KS 67301-0708	1925	$44/sem. hr. (S)	$3,600	5	1,022	49
Indian Hills Comm Coll, Ottumwa, IA 52501-1398	1966	$2,070 (S)	$1,820	11	3,926	148
Indian River Comm Coll, Fort Pierce, FL 34981-5596	1960	$1,200 (S)	—	5	23,160	796
Instituto Comercial de Puerto Rico Jr Coll, San Juan, PR 00919-0304	1946	$4,470	—	3	1,562	94
Interboro Inst, New York, NY 10019-3602	1888	$7,825	—	3	1,344	59
Inver Hills Comm Coll, Inver Grove Heights, MN 55076-3224	1969	$2,885 (S)	—	5	4,943	220
Iowa Central Comm Coll, Fort Dodge, IA 50501-5798	1966	$1,614 (S)	$3,800	11	4,295	280
Iowa Lakes Comm Coll, Estherville, IA 51334-2295	1967	$2,768 (S)	$6,660	11	2,711	123
Iowa Western Comm Coll, Council Bluffs, IA 51502	1966	$2,580 (S)	$3,700	9	4,299	222
Irvine Valley Coll, Irvine, CA 92620-4399	1979	NA	—	11	10,511	344
Isothermal Comm Coll, Spindale, NC 28160-0804	1965	$1,020 (A)	—	5	1,801	92
Itasca Comm Coll, Grand Rapids, MN 55744	1922	$3,030 (S)	—	5	1,094	83
Ivy Tech State Coll-Bloomington, Bloomington, IN 47404	2001	$2,264 (S)	—	5	2,391	186
Ivy Tech State Coll-Central Indiana, Indianapolis, IN 46206-1763	1963	$2,264 (S)	—	5	7,357	386
Ivy Tech State Coll-Columbus, Columbus, IN 47203-1868	1963	$2,264 (S)	—	5	1,600	139
Ivy Tech State Coll-Eastcentral, Muncie, IN 47302-9448	1968	$2,264 (S)	—	5	4,052	276
Ivy Tech State Coll-Kokomo, Kokomo, IN 46903-1373	1968	$2,264 (S)	—	5	2,003	161
Ivy Tech State Coll-Lafayette, Lafayette, IN 47905-5266	1968	$2,264 (S)	—	5	4,143	197
Ivy Tech State Coll-North Central, South Bend, IN 46601	1968	$2,264 (S)	—	5	3,784	276
Ivy Tech State Coll-Northeast, Fort Wayne, IN 46805-1430	1969	$2,264 (S)	—	5	4,019	337
Ivy Tech State Coll-Northwest, Gary, IN 46409-1499	1963	$2,264 (S)	—	5	5,146	305
Ivy Tech State Coll-Southcentral, Sellersburg, IN 47172-1829	1968	$2,264 (S)	—	5	2,035	146
Ivy Tech State Coll-Southeast, Madison, IN 47250-1883	1963	$2,264 (S)	—	5	1,495	134
Ivy Tech State Coll-Southwest, Evansville, IN 47710-3398	1963	$2,264 (S)	—	5	4,290	223
Ivy Tech State Coll-Wabash Valley, Terre Haute, IN 47802	1966	$2,264 (S)	—	5	3,810	227
Ivy Tech State Coll-Whitewater, Richmond, IN 47374-1220	1963	$2,264 (S)	—	5	1,469	131
Jackson Comm Coll, Jackson, MI 49201-8399	1928	$1,917 (A)	—	8	6,457	363
Jackson State Comm Coll, Jackson, TN 38301-3797	1967	$1,639 (S)	—	5	3,933	221
James H. Faulkner State Comm Coll, Bay Minette, AL 36507	1965	$2,352 (S)	$2,970	5	3,500	152
James Sprunt Comm Coll, Kenansville, NC 28349-0398	1964	$1,030 (S)	—	5	1,344	163
Jamestown Comm Coll, Jamestown, NY 14701-1999	1950	$3,050 (S)	—	11	4,092	266
Jefferson Coll, Hillsboro, MO 63050-2441	1963	$1,620 (A)	—	11	3,899	228
Jefferson Comm Coll, Louisville, KY 40202-2005	1968	$768 (S)	—	5	9,227	463
Jefferson Comm Coll, Watertown, NY 13601	1961	$2,583 (S)	—	11	3,602	189
Jefferson Comm Coll, Steubenville, OH 43952-3598	1966	$1,890 (A)	—	11	1,612	124
Jefferson Davis Comm Coll, Brewton, AL 36427-0958	1965	$2,040 (S)	—	5	1,300	121
Jefferson State Comm Coll, Birmingham, AL 35215-3098	1965	$2,280 (S)	—	5	5,652	335
John A. Logan Coll, Carterville, IL 62918-9900	1967	$1,380 (A)	—	11	5,130	43
Johnson County Comm Coll, Overland Park, KS 66210-1299	1967	$1,392 (A)	—	11	17,776	797
Johnston Comm Coll, Smithfield, NC 27577-2350	1969	$906 (S)	—	5	3,296	306
John Tyler Comm Coll, Chester, VA 23831-5316	1967	$977 (S)	—	5	5,656	320
John Wood Comm Coll, Quincy, IL 62301-9147	1974	$1,980 (A)	—	9	2,111	176
Joliet Jr Coll, Joliet, IL 60431-8938	1901	$1,470 (A)	—	11	12,089	597
Jones County Jr Coll, Ellisville, MS 39437-3901	1928	$1,138 (S)	$2,472	11	5,025	175
J. Sargeant Reynolds Comm Coll, Richmond, VA 23285-5622	1972	$1,408 (S)	—	5	11,079	583
Kalamazoo Valley Comm Coll, Kalamazoo, MI 49003-4070	1966	$1,473 (A)	—	11	12,500	110
Kankakee Comm Coll, Kankakee, IL 60901-0888	1966	$1,320 (A)	—	11	3,000	162
Kansas City Kansas Comm Coll, Kansas City, KS 66112-3003	1923	$1,260 (S)	—	11	5,240	347
Kapiolani Comm Coll, Honolulu, HI 96816-4421	1957	$1,052 (S)	—	5	6,760	317
Kaskaskia Coll, Centralia, IL 62801-7878	1966	$1,536 (A)	—	11	3,097	194
Katharine Gibbs School, New York, NY 10166-0005	1918	$12,120	—	3	2,717	118
Keiser Coll, Fort Lauderdale, FL 33309	1977	$8,500	—	3	2,850	56
Kellogg Comm Coll, Battle Creek, MI 49017-3397	1956	$1,793 (A)	—	11	9,741	356
Kennebec Valley Tech Coll, Fairfield, ME 04937-1367	1970	$2,040 (S)	—	5	1,255	103
Kent State Univ, Salem Campus, Salem, OH 44460-9412	1966	$3,160 (S)	—	5	1,150	93
Kent State Univ, Trumbull Campus, Warren, OH 44483-1998	1954	$3,344 (S)	—	5	2,219	155
Kent State Univ, Tuscarawas Campus, New Philadelphia, OH 44663-9403	1962	$3,184 (S)	—	5-B	1,857	147
Keystone Coll, La Plume, PA 18440	1868	$12,621	$6,400	1-B	1,373	179
Kilgore Coll, Kilgore, TX 75662-3299	1935	$744 (A)	$2,800	11	4,194	257
Kingsborough Comm Coll of the City Univ of New York, Brooklyn, NY 11235	1963	$2,600 (S)	—	11	15,055	752
Kingwood Coll, Kingwood, TX 77339-3801	1984	$804 (A)	—	11	5,302	238
Kirkwood Comm Coll, Cedar Rapids, IA 52406-2068	1966	$2,190 (S)	—	11	12,555	669
Kirtland Comm Coll, Roscommon, MI 48653-9699	1966	$1,803 (A)	—	9	1,175	95
Kishwaukee Coll, Malta, IL 60150	1967	$1,538 (A)	—	11	4,337	210
Labette Comm Coll, Parsons, KS 67357-4299	1923	$1,560 (A)	$3,040	11	1,354	208
Lake Area Tech Inst, Watertown, SD 57201	1964	$3,024 (A)	—	5	1,057	65
Lake City Comm Coll, Lake City, FL 32025-8703	1962	$1,403 (S)	—	5	2,287	209
Lake Land Coll, Mattoon, IL 61938-9366	1966	$1,614 (A)	—	11	6,102	197
Lakeland Comm Coll, Kirtland, OH 44094-5198	1967	$2,046 (A)	—	11	8,253	611
Lake Michigan Coll, Benton Harbor, MI 49022-1899	1946	$1,488 (A)	—	9	3,478	213
Lake Region State Coll, Devils Lake, ND 58301-1598	1941	$2,242 (S)	$3,250	5	1,308	96
Lakeshore Tech Coll, Cleveland, WI 53015-1414	1967	$2,350 (S)	—	11	2,886	514
Lake-Sumter Comm Coll, Leesburg, FL 34788-8751	1962	$1,569 (S)	—	11	2,881	146
Lake Tahoe Comm Coll, South Lake Tahoe, CA 96150-4524	1975	$327 (S)	—	11	3,400	200
Lake Washington Tech Coll, Kirkland, WA 98034-8506	1949	$2,915 (A)	—	9	4,934	209
Lamar Comm Coll, Lamar, CO 81052-3999	1937	$3,411 (S)	—	5	1,021	48
Lamar State Coll-Orange, Orange, TX 77630-5899	1969	$2,104 (S)	—	5	2,020	114
Lamar State Coll-Port Arthur, Port Arthur, TX 77641-0310	1909	$2,534 (S)	—	5	2,497	135
Lane Comm Coll, Eugene, OR 97405-0640	1964	$1,426 (S)	—	11	10,626	605
Lansing Comm Coll, Lansing, MI 48901-7210	1957	$1,240 (A)	—	11	17,358	800
Laramie County Comm Coll, Cheyenne, WY 82007-3299	1968	$1,644 (S)	$4,186	8	3,863	246

Name, address	Year Founded	Tuition & Fees	Rm. & Board	Control, Degree	Enroll-ment	Faculty
Laredo Comm Coll, Laredo, TX 78040-4395	1946	$876 (A)	$3,641	11	7,493	327
Lawson State Comm Coll, Birmingham, AL 35221-1798	1949	$1,824 (A)	—	5	2,017	123
LDS Business Coll, Salt Lake City, UT 84111-1392	1886	$2,260	$3,850	2	1,025	77
Lehigh Carbon Comm Coll, Schnecksville, PA 18078-2598	1967	$2,640 (A)	—	11	4,958	314
Lenoir Comm Coll, Kinston, NC 28502-0188	1960	$763 (S)	—	5	3,033	80
Lewis & Clark Comm Coll, Godfrey, IL 62035-2466	1970	$1,740 (A)	—	9	6,985	382
Lima Tech Coll, Lima, OH 45804-3597	1971	$72/cr. hr. (S)	—	5	2,894	222
Lincoln Land Comm Coll, Springfield, IL 62794-9256	1967	$1,260 (A)	—	9	6,873	341
Linn-Benton Comm Coll, Albany, OR 97321	1966	$1,845 (S)	—	11	4,746	501
Long Beach City Coll, Long Beach, CA 90808-1780	1927	$318 (S)	—	5	28,000	1,800
Longview Comm Coll, Lee's Summit, MO 64081-2105	1969	$1,740 (A)	—	11	5,791	341
Lorain County Comm Coll, Elyria, OH 44035	1963	$2,129 (A)	—	11	7,818	538
Lord Fairfax Comm Coll, Middletown, VA 22645-0047	1969	$943 (S)	—	5	4,587	198
Los Angeles City Coll, Los Angeles, CA 90029-3590	1929	NA	—	9	24,652	625
Los Angeles Harbor Coll, Wilmington, CA 90744-2397	1949	$310 (S)	—	11	7,467	270
Los Angeles Pierce Coll, Woodland Hills, CA 91371-0001	1947	NA	—	11	18,260	800
Los Angeles Valley Coll, Valley Glen, CA 91401-4096	1949	NA	—	11	17,786	510
Louisiana State Univ at Alexandria, Alexandria, LA 71302-9121	1960	$1,438 (A)	—	5	2,715	131
Louisiana State Univ at Eunice, Eunice, LA 70535-1129	1967	$1,456 (S)	$4,200	5	2,748	108
Lower Columbia Coll, Longview, WA 98632-0310	1934	$2,098 (S)	—	5	3,651	215
Luzerne County Comm Coll, Nanticoke, PA 18634-9804	1966	$2,280 (A)	—	8	6,076	461
Macomb Comm Coll, Warren, MI 48093-3896	1954	$1,736 (A)	—	9	21,818	864
Madison Area Tech Coll, Madison, WI 53704-2599	1911	NA	—	9	13,479	1,881
Manatee Comm Coll, Bradenton, FL 34206-7046	1957	$1,600 (S)	—	5	8,369	417
Manchester Comm Coll, Manchester, CT 06045-1046	1963	$1,980 (S)	—	5	5,405	268
Maple Woods Comm Coll, Kansas City, MO 64156-1299	1969	$1,740 (A)	—	11	5,045	380
Marion Tech Coll, Marion, OH 43302-5694	1971	$2,844 (S)	—	12	2,739	105
Marshalltown Comm Coll, Marshalltown, IA 50158-4760	1927	$2,292 (S)	$2,600	9	1,188	107
Massachusetts Bay Comm Coll, Wellesley Hills, MA 02481	1961	$1,890 (S)	—	5	4,950	304
Massasoit Comm Coll, Brockton, MA 02302-3996	1966	$1,950 (S)	—	5	6,906	440
Maui Comm Coll, Kahului, HI 96732	1967	$1,068 (S)	—	5	2,657	94
Mayland Comm Coll, Spruce Pine, NC 28777-0547	1971	$772 (S)	—	11	1,350	65
Maysville Comm Coll, Maysville, KY 41056	1967	$1,450 (S)	—	5	1,393	128
McDowell Tech Comm Coll, Marion, NC 28752-9724	1964	$880 (S)	—	5	1,078	58
McHenry County Coll, Crystal Lake, IL 60012-2761	1967	$1,724 (A)	—	11	5,747	275
McIntosh Coll, Dover, NH 03820-3990	1896	$24,300	$8,400	3	1,224	66
McLennan Comm Coll, Waco, TX 76708-1499	1965	$1,410 (A)	—	8	6,133	297
Mendocino Coll, Ukiah, CA 95482-0300	1973	$342 (S)	—	11	5,200	193
Mercer County Comm Coll, Trenton, NJ 08690-1004	1966	$1,950 (A)	—	11	8,132	423
Meridian Comm Coll, Meridian, MS 39307	1937	$651 (A)	$1,575	11	3,248	250
Merritt Coll, Oakland, CA 94619-3196	1953	$268 (S)	—	11	6,000	201
Mesabi Range Comm & Tech Coll, Virginia, MN 55792-3448	1918	$2,826 (S)	$2,310	5	1,687	67
Mesa Comm Coll, Mesa, AZ 85202-4866	1965	NA	—	11	24,000	852
Metro Comm Coll, Omaha, NE 68103-0777	1974	$1,463 (S)	—	11	11,704	664
Miami-Dade Comm Coll, Miami, FL 33132-2296	1960	$51/credit (S)	—	11	53,486	2,046
Miami Univ-Hamilton Campus, Hamilton, OH 45011-3399	1968	$3,140 (S)	—	5-M	2,990	207
Miami Univ-Middletown Campus, Middletown, OH 45042-3497	1966	$3,465 (S)	—	5-B	2,061	158
Middle Georgia Coll, Cochran, GA 31014-1599	1884	$1,742 (S)	$3,454	5	2,164	125
Middlesex Comm Coll, Middletown, CT 06457-4889	1966	$1,888 (S)	—	5	2,309	120
Middlesex Comm Coll, Bedford, MA 01730-1655	1970	$2,018 (S)	—	5	7,568	468
Middlesex County Coll, Edison, NJ 08818-3050	1964	$2,040 (S)	—	8	10,500	552
Midland Coll, Midland, TX 79705-6399	1969	$1,066 (A)	$3,120	11	5,034	195
Midlands Tech Coll, Columbia, SC 29202-2408	1974	$1,800 (A)	—	11	9,874	630
Mid Michigan Comm Coll, Harrison, MI 48625-9447 (4)	1965	$1,400 (A)	—	11	2,350	80
Mid-Plains Comm Coll Area, North Platte, NE 69101	NA	$1,440 (S)	$2,900	9	2,823	193
Mid-State Tech Coll, Wisconsin Rapids, WI 54494-5599	1917	$70/credit (A)	—	11	10,737	300
Milwaukee Area Tech Coll, Milwaukee, WI 53233-1443	1912	$1,600 (S)	—	9	60,174	1,759
Mineral Area Coll, Park Hills, MO 63601-1000	1922	$1,590 (A)	$3,159	9	2,878	168
Minnesota State Coll-Southeast Tech, Winona, MN 55987	1992	$99/cr. hr. (S)	—	5	2,058	84
Minnesota West Comm & Tech Coll, Pipestone, MN 56164	1967	$2,978 (S)	—	5	2,044	127
MiraCosta Coll, Oceanside, CA 92056-3899	1934	$362 (S)	—	5	10,129	393
Mission Coll, Santa Clara, CA 95054-1897	1977	$370 (S)	—	11	10,500	382
Mississippi County Comm Coll, Blytheville, AR 72316-1109	1975	$1,052 (A)	—	5	1,840	98
Mississippi Delta Comm Coll, Moorhead, MS 38761-0668	1926	$1,250 (S)	$1,690	9	2,956	130
Mississippi Gulf Coast Comm Coll, Perkinston, MS 39573-0548	1911	$1,232 (S)	$1,960	9	8,944	348
Mitchell Comm Coll, Statesville, NC 28677-5293	1852	$1,022 (S)	—	5	2,160	135
Moberly Area Comm Coll, Moberly, MO 65270-1304	1927	$1,450 (A)	$1,400	11	3,269	210
Modesto Jr Coll, Modesto, CA 95350-5800	1921	$334 (S)	—	11	15,696	563
Mohave Comm Coll, Kingman, AZ 86401	1971	$792 (S)	—	5	5,736	349
Mohawk Valley Comm Coll, Utica, NY 13501-5394	1946	$2,640 (A)	$5,685	11	5,287	273
Monroe Coll, Bronx, NY 10468-5407	1933	$7,840	$8,800	3-B	3,449	149
Monroe Coll, New Rochelle, NY 10801	1983	$7,840	$8,800	3-B	1,156	54
Monroe Comm Coll, Rochester, NY 14623-5780	1961	$2,500 (S)	—	11	16,157	1,082
Monroe County Comm Coll, Monroe, MI 48161-9047	1964	$1,368 (A)	—	8	3,800	201
Montana State Univ-Great Falls Coll of Tech, Great Falls, MT 59405	1969	$2,386 (S)	—	5	1,251	83
Montcalm Comm Coll, Sidney, MI 48885-9723	1965	$1,687 (A)	—	11	1,520	92
Monterey Peninsula Coll, Monterey, CA 93940-4799	1947	$306 (S)	—	5	15,831	388
Montgomery Coll, Rockville, MD 20850	NA	$2,832 (A)	—	11	21,347	1,140
Montgomery Coll, Conroe, TX 77384	1995	$696 (A)	—	11	5,312	236
Montgomery County Comm Coll, Blue Bell, PA 19422-0796	1964	$2,460 (A)	—	8	9,592	552
Moorpark Coll, Moorpark, CA 93021-1695	1967	$302 (S)	—	8	14,538	422
Moraine Park Tech Coll, Fond du Lac, WI 54936-1940	1967	$2,228 (A)	—	11	24,295	555
Moraine Valley Comm Coll, Palos Hills, IL 60465-0937	1967	$1,620 (A)	—	11	14,033	786
Morgan Comm Coll, Fort Morgan, CO 80701-4399	1967	$2,098 (S)	—	5	1,781	221
Morton Coll, Cicero, IL 60804-4398	1924	$1,488 (A)	—	11	4,698	191
Motlow State Comm Coll, Lynchburg, TN 37352-8500	1969	$1,635 (S)	—	5	3,586	216
Mott Comm Coll, Flint, MI 48503-2089	1923	$2,332 (A)	—	9	9,019	437
Mountain Empire Comm Coll, Big Stone Gap, VA 24219-0700	1972	$1,436 (S)	—	5	2,900	150
Mountain View Coll, Dallas, TX 75211-6599	1970	$312 (A)	—	11	6,350	264
Mt. Hood Comm Coll, Gresham, OR 97030-3300	1966	$582 (A)	—	11	8,771	638

Name, address	Year Founded	Tuition & Fees	Rm. & Board	Control, Degree	Enroll-ment	Faculty
Mt. San Antonio Coll, Walnut, CA 91789-1399	1946	NA	$7,038	9	28,329	1,130
Mt. San Jacinto Coll, San Jacinto, CA 92583-2399	1963	NA	—	11	12,288	421
Mount Wachusett Comm Coll, Gardner, MA 01440-1000	1963	$3,030 (S)	—	5	3,711	257
Murray State Coll, Tishomingo, OK 73460-3130	1908	$46/cr. hr. (S)	—	5	1,825	73
Muscatine Comm Coll, Muscatine, IA 52761-5396	1929	$2,160 (S)	—	5	1,129	95
Muskingum Area Tech Coll, Zanesville, OH 43701-2626	1969	$2,970 (A)	—	11	2,007	116
Nash Comm Coll, Rocky Mount, NC 27804-0488	1967	$1,024 (S)	—	5	2,184	120
Nashville State Tech Inst, Nashville, TN 37209-4515	1970	$1,613 (S)	—	5	7,017	431
Nassau Comm Coll, Garden City, NY 11530-6793	1959	$2,520 (S)	—	11	19,712	1,341
Naugatuck Valley Comm Coll, Waterbury, CT 06708-3000	1992	$1,980 (S)	—	5	5,223	180
Navarro Coll, Corsicana, TX 75110-4899	1946	$776 (A)	$3,224	11	4,411	380
Neosho County Comm Coll, Chanute, KS 66720-2699	1936	$1,088 (S)	—	11	1,519	96
Newbury Coll, Brookline, MA 02445	1962	$14,300	$7,400	1-B	1,689	89
New England Inst of Tech, Warwick, RI 02886-2244	1940	$13,130	—	1-B	2,660	397
New England Inst of Tech at Palm Beach, West Palm Beach, FL 33407	1983	$18,000	—	3	1,200	46
New Hampshire Tech Inst, Concord, NH 03301-7412	1964	$131/cr. hr. (S)	$4,960	5	3,308	146
New Mexico Jr Coll, Hobbs, NM 88240-9123	1965	$332 (A)	$3,325	11	3,200	120
New Mexico State Univ-Alamogordo, Alamogordo, NM 88311-0477	1958	$912 (A)	—	5	1,839	77
New Mexico State Univ-Carlsbad, Carlsbad, NM 88220-3509	1950	$840 (A)	—	5	1,011	73
New River Comm Coll, Dublin, VA 24084-1127	1969	$1,328 (S)	—	5	3,947	192
New York City Tech Coll of the City Univ of New York, Brooklyn, NY 11201	1946	$3,438 (A)	—	11-B	11,028	989
Niagara County Comm Coll, Sanborn, NY 14132-9460	1962	$2,785 (S)	—	11	4,915	283
Nicolet Area Tech Coll, Rhinelander, WI 54501-0518	1968	$2,680 (S)	—	11	1,415	84
Northampton County Area Comm Coll, Bethlehem, PA 18020-7599	1967	$2,490 (A)	$5,084	11	6,216	329
North Arkansas Coll, Harrison, AR 72601	1974	$1,080 (A)	—	11	1,889	121
North Central Michigan Coll, Petoskey, MI 49770-8717	1958	$1,710 (A)	$2,000	8	2,248	133
North Central State Coll, Mansfield, OH 44901-0698	1961	$1,550 (S)	—	5	2,760	182
Northcentral Tech Coll, Wausau, WI 54401-1899	1912	$2,049 (S)	—	9	3,609	226
North Central Texas Coll, Gainesville, TX 76240-4699	1924	$648 (A)	$2,200	8	5,180	290
North Country Comm Coll, Saranac Lake, NY 12983-0089	1967	$2,850 (S)	—	11	1,217	107
North Dakota State Coll of Sci, Wahpeton, ND 58076	1903	$1,938 (S)	$3,765	5	2,292	140
Northeast Alabama Comm Coll, Rainsville, AL 35986-0159	1963	$1,920 (S)	—	5	1,714	50
Northeast Comm Coll, Norfolk, NE 68702-0469	1973	$1,538 (S)	$3,260	11	4,600	210
Northeastern Jr Coll, Sterling, CO 80751-2399	1941	$2,364 (S)	$5,949	5	3,633	286
Northeastern Oklahoma Agr & Mech Coll, Miami, OK 74354-6434	1919	$46/cr. hr. (S)	—	5	2,000	100
Northeast Iowa Comm Coll, Calmar, IA 52132-0480	1966	$3,520 (A)	—	11	3,615	168
Northeast State Tech Comm Coll, Blountville, TN 37617-0246	1966	$1,648 (S)	—	5	4,462	236
Northeast Texas Comm Coll, Mount Pleasant, TX 75456-1307	1985	$960 (S)	$2,900	11	2,212	134
Northern Essex Comm Coll, Haverhill, MA 01830	1960	$2,280 (S)	—	5	6,372	486
Northern New Mexico Comm Coll, Española, NM 87532	1909	$694 (S)	$2,928	5	2,116	253
Northern Oklahoma Coll, Tonkawa, OK 74653-0310	1901	$1,105 (S)	$1,060	5	2,900	80
Northern Virginia Comm Coll, Annandale, VA 22003-3796	1965	$39/cr. hr. (S)	—	5	37,073	1,508
North Florida Comm Coll, Madison, FL 32340-1602	1958	$1,560 (S)	—	5	1,012	44
North Harris Coll, Houston, TX 77073-3499	1972	$696 (A)	—	11	9,127	497
North Hennepin Comm Coll, Minneapolis, MN 55445-2231	1966	$2,324 (S)	—	5	4,452	200
North Idaho Coll, Coeur d'Alene, ID 83814-2199	1933	$1,544 (A)	$5,400	11	4,133	338
North Iowa Area Comm Coll, Mason City, IA 50401-7299	1918	$2,526 (S)	$3,450	11	2,722	231
North Lake Coll, Irving, TX 75038-3899	1977	$562 (A)	—	8	8,000	666
Northland Comm & Tech Coll, Thief River Falls, MN 56701	1965	$3,090 (S)	—	5	2,152	89
Northland Pioneer Coll, Holbrook, AZ 86025-0610	1974	$720 (S)	$1,500	11	5,374	397
North Seattle Comm Coll, Seattle, WA 98103-3599	1970	$1,901 (S)	—	5	6,340	412
North Shore Comm Coll, Danvers, MA 01923-4093	1965	$1,992 (S)	—	5	6,100	441
NorthWest Arkansas Comm Coll, Bentonville, AR 72712	1989	$1,068 (A)	—	11	4,292	235
Northwest Coll, Powell, WY 82435-1898	1946	$1,660 (S)	$3,194	11	1,576	150
Northwestern Business Coll, Chicago, IL 60630-2298	1902	$12,420	—	3	1,600	45
Northwestern Connecticut Comm Coll, Winsted, CT 06098-1798	1965	$1,888 (S)	—	5	1,609	107
Northwestern Michigan Coll, Traverse City, MI 49686-3061	1951	$1,995 (A)	$5,350	11	4,251	88
Northwestern Tech Coll, Rock Springs, GA 30739	1966	$1,360 (A)	—	5	1,500	79
Northwest Mississippi Comm Coll, Senatobia, MS 38668-1701	1927	$1,200 (A)	$2,200	11	5,000	200
Northwest-Shoals Comm Coll, Muscle Shoals, AL 35662	1963	$2,176 (S)	$1,450	5	3,922	208
Northwest State Comm Coll, Archbold, OH 43502-9542	1968	$3,000 (S)	—	5	2,931	163
Norwalk Comm Coll, Norwalk, CT 06854-1655	1961	$1,980 (S)	—	5	5,569	349
Oakland Comm Coll, Bloomfield Hills, MI 48304-2266	1964	$1,800 (A)	—	11	23,503	845
Oakton Comm Coll, Des Plaines, IL 60016-1268	1969	$1,620 (A)	—	9	10,000	659
Ocean County Coll, Toms River, NJ 08754-2001	1964	$95/credit (A)	—	8	7,441	371
Odessa Coll, Odessa, TX 79764-7127	1946	$708 (S)	$3,100	11	4,579	291
Ohlone Coll, Fremont, CA 94539-5884	1967	NA	—	11	10,500	434
Okaloosa-Walton Comm Coll, Niceville, FL 32578-1295	1963	$1,360 (S)	—	11	7,148	295
Oklahoma City Comm Coll, Oklahoma City, OK 73159-4419	1969	$1,434 (S)	—	5	10,321	427
Oklahoma State Univ, Oklahoma City, Oklahoma City, OK 73107-6120	1961	$1,900 (S)	$3,500	5	4,522	241
Oklahoma State Univ, Okmulgee, Okmulgee, OK 74447-3901	1946	$1,057 (S)	—	5	2,329	129
Olympic Coll, Bremerton, WA 98337-1699	1946	$1,923 (S)	—	5	5,613	533
Onondaga Comm Coll, Syracuse, NY 13215-2099	1962	$98/credit (A)	—	11	8,000	457
Orangeburg-Calhoun Tech Coll, Orangeburg, SC 29118-8299	1968	$1,311 (A)	—	11	2,020	112
Orange Coast Coll, Costa Mesa, CA 92628-5005	1947	$410 (S)	—	11	24,630	801
Orange County Comm Coll, Middletown, NY 10940-6437	1950	$2,445 (S)	—	11	5,532	322
Otero Jr Coll, La Junta, CO 81050-3415	1941	$1,694 (S)	$4,010	5	1,402	75
Our Lady of the Lake Coll, Baton Rouge, LA 70808	1990	$6,680 (A)	—	2-B	1,218	113
Owensboro Comm Coll, Owensboro, KY 42303-1899	1986	$1,570 (S)	—	5	3,362	138
Owens Comm Coll, Findlay, OH 45840	1983	$1,820 (S)	—	5	1,985	158
Owens Comm Coll, Toledo, OH 43699-1947	1966	$1,820 (S)	—	5	14,820	NA
Oxnard Coll, Oxnard, CA 93033-6699	1975	$286 (S)	—	5	7,594	349
Ozarks Tech Comm Coll, Springfield, MO 65801	1990	$1,680 (A)	—	9	6,343	264
Paducah Comm Coll, Paducah, KY 42002-7380	1932	$1,920 (S)	—	5	3,322	151
Palm Beach Comm Coll, Lake Worth, FL 33461-4796	1933	$1,650 (S)	$4,356	5	23,410	1,190
Palomar Coll, San Marcos, CA 92069-1487	1946	NA	—	11	29,715	1,210
Palo Verde Coll, Blythe, CA 92225-1118	1947	$264 (S)	—	11	2,903	129
Panola Coll, Carthage, TX 75633-2397	1947	$930 (A)	$2,860	11	1,424	93
Paradise Valley Comm Coll, Phoenix, AZ 85032-1200	1985	$1,290 (A)	—	11	7,349	344
Paris Jr Coll, Paris, TX 75460-6298	1924	$1,106 (A)	$2,650	11	2,850	147

Name, address	Year Founded	Tuition & Fees	Rm. & Board	Control, Degree	Enrollment	Faculty
Parkland Coll, Champaign, IL 61821-1899	1967	$1,620 (A)	—	9	8,482	485
Pasadena City Coll, Pasadena, CA 91106-2041	1924	NA	—	11	29,286	1,296
Pasco-Hernando Comm Coll, New Port Richey, FL 34654-5199	1972	$1,504 (S)	—	5	5,625	262
Passaic County Comm Coll, Paterson, NJ 07505-1179	1968	$2,432 (S)	—	8	4,633	357
Patrick Henry Comm Coll, Martinsville, VA 24115-5311	1962	$1,169 (S)	—	5	3,024	149
Paul D. Camp Comm Coll, Franklin, VA 23851-0737	1971	$1,394 (S)	—	5	1,552	74
Pellissippi State Tech Comm Coll, Knoxville, TN 37933-0990	1974	$75/credit (S)	—	5	7,833	412
Peninsula Coll, Port Angeles, WA 98362-2779	1961	$1,957 (S)	$5,403	5	4,355	296
Pennsylvania Inst of Culinary Arts, Pittsburgh, PA 15222-3500	1986	$15,200	$6,566	3	1,447	46
The Pennsylvania State Univ Delaware County Campus of the Commonwealth Coll, Media, PA 19063-5596	1966	$7,164 (S)	—	12-B	1,649	119
The Pennsylvania State Univ DuBois Campus of the Commonwealth Coll, DuBois, PA 15801-3199	1935	$7,154 (S)	—	12-B	1,003	89
The Pennsylvania State Univ Fayette Campus of the Commonwealth Coll, Uniontown, PA 15401-0519	1934	$7,154 (S)	—	12-B	1,128	93
The Pennsylvania State Univ Hazleton Campus of the Commonwealth Coll, Hazleton, PA 18201-1291	1934	$7,164 (S)	$5,300	12-B	1,353	98
The Pennsylvania State Univ Mont Alto Campus of the Commonwealth Coll, Mont Alto, PA 17237-9703	1929	$7,164 (S)	$5,300	12-B	1,164	95
The Pennsylvania State Univ Worthington Scranton Campus of the Commonwealth Coll, Dunmore, PA 18512-1699	1923	$7,154 (S)	—	12-B	1,609	117
The Pennsylvania State Univ York Campus of the Commonwealth Coll, York, PA 17403-3298	1926	$7,154 (S)	—	12-B	1,954	130
Penn Valley Comm Coll, Kansas City, MO 64111	1969	$1,740 (A)	—	11	4,376	397
Pensacola Jr Coll, Pensacola, FL 32504-8998	1948	$1,211 (S)	—	5	6,680	747
Phillips Comm Coll of the Univ of Arkansas, Helena, AR 72342-0785	1965	$984 (A)	—	11	2,100	70
Phoenix Coll, Phoenix, AZ 85013-4234	1920	$43/cr. hr. (A)	—	11	12,296	104
Piedmont Comm Coll, Roxboro, NC 27573-1197	1970	$1,062 (S)	—	5	2,029	108
Piedmont Tech Coll, Greenwood, SC 29648-1467	1966	$1,512 (A)	—	5	4,544	233
Piedmont Virginia Comm Coll, Charlottesville, VA 22902-7589	1972	$1,181 (S)	—	5	4,171	232
Pierce Coll, Lakewood, WA 98498-1999	1967	$2,324 (S)	—	5	13,294	590
Pikes Peak Comm Coll, Colorado Springs, CO 80906-5498	1968	$2,009 (S)	—	5	9,772	662
Pima Comm Coll, Tucson, AZ 85709-1010	1966	$850 (S)	—	11	28,176	1,622
Pine Tech Coll, Pine City, MN 55063	1965	$3,328 (S)	—	5	1,074	65
Pitt Comm Coll, Greenville, NC 27835-7007	1961	$1,032 (S)	—	11	5,600	406
Polk Comm Coll, Winter Haven, FL 33881-4299	1964	$1,539 (S)	—	5	6,329	322
Porterville Coll, Porterville, CA 93257-6058	1927	$382 (S)	—	5	5,418	140
Portland Comm Coll, Portland, OR 97280-0990	1961	$1,958 (S)	—	11	46,295	1,385
Potomac State Coll of West Virginia Univ, Keyser, WV 26726-2698	1901	$2,278 (S)	$4,196	5	1,109	95
Prairie State Coll, Chicago Heights, IL 60411-8226	1958	$60/cr. hr. (A)	—	11	5,188	315
Pratt Comm Coll & Area Voc School, Pratt, KS 67124-8317	1938	$1,632 (S)	$3,288	11	1,374	96
Prestonsburg Comm Coll, Prestonsburg, KY 41653-1815	1964	$1,616 (S)	—	5	2,371	129
Prince George's Comm Coll, Largo, MD 20774-2199	1958	$2,842 (A)	—	8	12,287	646
Pulaski Tech Coll, North Little Rock, AR 72118	1945	$1,860 (S)	—	5	4,966	155
Queensborough Comm Coll of the City Univ of New York, Bayside, NY 11364	1958	$2,616 (S)	—	11	10,880	756
Quinebaug Valley Comm Coll, Danielson, CT 06239-1440	1971	$1,886 (S)	—	5	1,347	82
Quinsigamond Comm Coll, Worcester, MA 01606-2092	1963	$2,250 (S)	—	5	6,137	370
Randolph Comm Coll, Asheboro, NC 27204-1009	1962	$1,168 (S)	—	5	2,007	164
Rappahannock Comm Coll, Glenns, VA 23149-2616	1970	$953 (S)	—	12	2,615	79
Raritan Valley Comm Coll, Somerville, NJ 08876-1265	1965	$2,330 (S)	—	8	5,830	356
Redlands Comm Coll, El Reno, OK 73036-5304	1938	$1,448 (S)	—	5	2,173	107
Red Rocks Comm Coll, Lakewood, CO 80228-1255	1969	$1,646 (S)	—	5	7,394	276
Reedley Coll, Reedley, CA 93654-2099	1926	$330 (S)	—	11	11,305	542
Rend Lake Coll, Ina, IL 62846-9801	1967	$1,536 (A)	—	5	3,637	147
Renton Tech Coll, Renton, WA 98056-4195	1942	$1,810 (S)	—	5	5,424	253
Richard Bland Coll of The Coll of William & Mary, Petersburg, VA 23805-7100	1961	$1,652 (S)	—	5	1,304	65
Richland Comm Coll, Decatur, IL 62521-8513	1971	$1,530 (A)	—	9	3,261	227
Richmond Comm Coll, Hamlet, NC 28345-1189	1964	$782 (S)	—	5	1,465	100
Rich Mountain Comm Coll, Mena, AR 71953	1983	$936 (A)	—	11	1,005	55
Ridgewater Coll, Willmar, MN 56201-1097	1961	$2,883 (S)	—	5	3,129	229
Rio Hondo Coll, Whittier, CA 90601-1699	1960	NA	—	11	15,000	710
Rio Salado Coll, Tempe, AZ 85281-6950	1978	$1,240 (A)	—	11	11,386	1,004
Riverland Comm Coll, Austin, MN 55912	1940	$2,794 (S)	$2,565	5	3,175	158
Riverside Comm Coll, Riverside, CA 92506-1299	1916	$350 (S)	—	11	29,865	1,436
Roane State Comm Coll, Harriman, TN 37748-5011	1971	$1,638 (S)	—	5	5,233	382
Robeson Comm Coll, Lumberton, NC 28359-1420	1965	$688 (S)	—	5	2,125	114
Rockingham Comm Coll, Wentworth, NC 27375-0038	1964	$1,029 (S)	—	5	2,085	123
Rockland Comm Coll, Suffern, NY 10901-3699	1959	$2,479 (S)	—	11	6,260	359
Rogue Comm Coll, Grants Pass, OR 97527-9298	1970	$2,401 (A)	—	11	4,496	505
Rose State Coll, Midwest City, OK 73110-2799	1968	$1,100 (S)	—	11	7,350	412
Rowan-Cabarrus Comm Coll, Salisbury, NC 28145-1595	1963	$1,024 (A)	—	5	4,705	302
Roxbury Comm Coll, Roxbury Crossing, MA 02120-3400	1973	$1,656 (S)	—	5	2,382	120
Sacramento City Coll, Sacramento, CA 95822-1386	1916	NA	—	11	20,781	554
Saint Charles Comm Coll, St. Peters, MO 63376-0975	1986	$1,590 (A)	—	5	6,171	359
St. Clair County Comm Coll, Port Huron, MI 48061-5015	1923	$2,186 (A)	—	11	4,066	276
St. Cloud Tech Coll, St. Cloud, MN 56303-1240	1948	$2,551 (S)	—	5	3,023	147
St. Johns River Comm Coll, Palatka, FL 32177-3897	1958	$1,315 (S)	—	5	3,459	157
St. Louis Comm Coll at Florissant Valley, St. Louis, MO 63135-1499	1963	$1,792 (A)	—	9	7,365	353
St. Louis Comm Coll at Forest Park, St. Louis, MO 63110-1316	1962	$1,344 (A)	—	9	6,749	314
St. Louis Comm Coll at Meramec, Kirkwood, MO 63122-5720	1963	$1,008 (A)	—	9	12,518	570
St. Paul Tech Coll, St. Paul, MN 55102-1800	1919	$2,559 (S)	—	12	5,381	287
St. Petersburg Coll, St. Petersburg, FL 33733-3489	1927	$1,582 (S)	—	11-B	20,734	1,258
St. Philip's Coll, San Antonio, TX 78203-2098	1898	$1,118 (A)	—	9	8,326	510
Salem Comm Coll, Carneys Point, NJ 08069-2799	1972	$2,236 (A)	—	8	1,229	69
Salish Kootenai Coll, Pablo, MT 59855-0117	1977	$2,775 (A)	—	1-B	1,042	92
Salt Lake Comm Coll, Salt Lake City, UT 84130-0808	1948	$1,636 (S)	—	5	21,596	1,130
Sampson Comm Coll, Clinton, NC 28329-0318	1965	$1,028 (S)	—	11	1,399	102
San Antonio Coll, San Antonio, TX 78212-4299	1925	$816 (A)	—	11	21,853	1,092
Sandhills Comm Coll, Pinehurst, NC 28374-8299	1963	$1,020 (A)	—	11	3,174	232

Name, address	Year Founded	Tuition & Fees	Rm. & Board	Control, Degree	Enroll-ment	Faculty
San Diego City Coll, San Diego, CA 92101-4787	1914	$363 (S)	—	11	14,126	485
San Diego Mesa Coll, San Diego, CA 92111-4998	1964	$290 (S)	—	11	21,700	745
San Jacinto Coll Central Campus, Pasadena, TX 77501-2007	1961	$724 (A)	—	11	10,854	387
San Jacinto Coll North Campus, Houston, TX 77049-4599	1974	$846 (A)	—	11	5,020	298
San Jacinto Coll South Campus, Houston, TX 77089-6099	1979	$724 (A)	—	11	6,269	214
San Joaquin Delta Coll, Stockton, CA 95207-6370	1935	$330 (S)	—	9	18,546	561
San Juan Coll, Farmington, NM 87402-4699	1958	$360 (S)	—	8	4,558	277
Santa Ana Coll, Santa Ana, CA 92706-3398	1915	$301 (S)	—	5	25,386	1,296
Santa Barbara City Coll, Santa Barbara, CA 93109-2394	1908	NA	—	11	14,949	639
Santa Fe Comm Coll, Gainesville, FL 32606-6200	1966	$1,514 (S)	—	11	13,225	830
Santa Fe Comm Coll, Santa Fe, NM 87505-4887	1983	$694 (A)	—	11	5,056	373
Santa Monica Coll, Santa Monica, CA 90405-1628	1929	$388 (S)	—	11	29,077	1,267
Santa Rosa Jr Coll, Santa Rosa, CA 95401-4395	1918	$264 (S)	$2,035	11	25,233	1,767
Santiago Canyon Coll, Orange, CA 92869	2000	$301 (S)	—	5	9,742	417
Sauk Valley Comm Coll, Dixon, IL 61021	1965	$1,530 (A)	—	9	2,688	152
Savannah Tech Coll, Savannah, GA 31405	1929	$1,077 (S)	—	5	3,134	201
Schenectady County Comm Coll, Schenectady, NY 12305-2294	1968	$2,455 (S)	—	11	3,526	195
Schoolcraft Coll, Livonia, MI 48152-2696	1961	$1,760 (A)	—	9	9,530	406
Scott Comm Coll, Bettendorf, IA 52722-6804	1966	$2,160 (S)	—	11	3,985	235
Scottsdale Comm Coll, Scottsdale, AZ 85256-2626	1969	$1,390 (A)	—	11	10,397	509
Seattle Central Comm Coll, Seattle, WA 98122-2400	1966	$2,036 (S)	—	5	10,500	388
Seminole Comm Coll, Sanford, FL 32773-6199	1966	$1,258 (S)	—	11	10,556	788
Seminole State Coll, Seminole, OK 74818-0351	1931	$1,557 (S)	$3,700	5	1,965	93
Seward County Comm Coll, Liberal, KS 67905-1137	1969	$1,440 (S)	$3,200	11	2,325	208
Shasta Coll, Redding, CA 96049-6006	1948	$319 (S)	—	11	10,108	491
Shelton State Comm Coll, Tuscaloosa, AL 35405	1979	$1,560 (S)	—	5	6,211	215
Sheridan Coll, Sheridan, WY 82801-1500	1948	$1,584 (S)	$3,620	11	2,730	201
Shoreline Comm Coll, Seattle, WA 98133-5696	1964	$1,908 (S)	—	5	7,000	415
Sierra Coll, Rocklin, CA 95677-3397	1936	$264 (S)	$5,790	5	19,000	530
Sinclair Comm Coll, Dayton, OH 45402-1460	1887	$1,440 (A)	—	11	18,869	974
Skagit Valley Coll, Mount Vernon, WA 98273-5899	1926	$2,100 (S)	$3,400	5	6,174	301
Skyline Coll, San Bruno, CA 94066-1698	1969	$298 (S)	—	11	8,573	300
Snead State Comm Coll, Boaz, AL 35957-0734	1898	$1,856 (S)	$1,724	5	1,679	94
Snow Coll, Ephraim, UT 84627-1203	1888	$1,522 (S)	$3,800	5	2,999	148
Solano Comm Coll, Suisun, CA 94585-3197	1945	NA	—	11	10,076	374
Somerset Comm Coll, Somerset, KY 42501-2973	1965	$1,450 (S)	—	5	2,799	193
South Arkansas Comm Coll, El Dorado, AR 71731-7010	1975	$1,354 (A)	—	5	1,173	88
Southeast Arkansas Coll, Pine Bluff, AR 71603	1991	$1,290 (S)	—	5	2,025	125
Southeast Comm Coll, Cumberland, KY 40823-1099	1960	$61/cr. hr. (S)	—	5	2,491	119
Southeast Comm Coll, Lincoln Campus, Lincoln, NE 68520-1299	1973	$1,800 (S)	—	9	5,431	548
Southeastern Baptist Theological Seminary, Wake Forest, NC 27588-1889	1950	$140/credit (S)	—	2-D	1,702	53
Southeastern Comm Coll, Whiteville, NC 28472-0151	1964	$1,056 (S)	—	5	1,950	145
Southeastern Illinois Coll, Harrisburg, IL 62946-4925	1960	$1,248 (A)	$2,600	5	3,272	208
Southeast Tech Inst, Sioux Falls, SD 57107-1301	1968	$2,987 (S)	—	5	2,246	182
Southern Maine Tech Coll, South Portland, ME 04106	1946	$2,540 (S)	$4,200	5	2,471	202
Southern State Comm Coll, Hillsboro, OH 45133-9487	1975	$2,925 (S)	—	5	2,038	109
Southern Union State Comm Coll, Wadley, AL 36276	1922	$1,440 (S)	—	5	4,500	217
Southern West Virginia Comm & Tech Coll, Mount Gay, WV 25637-2900	1971	$1,440 (S)	—	5	2,520	177
South Mountain Comm Coll, Phoenix, AZ 85040	1979	$1,032 (A)	—	11	3,406	195
South Piedmont Comm Coll, Polkton, NC 28135-0126	1962	$898 (S)	$2,175	5	1,875	146
South Plains Coll, Levelland, TX 79336-6595	1958	$1,022 (S)	$2,900	11	8,574	375
South Puget Sound Comm Coll, Olympia, WA 98512-6292	1970	$2,324 (S)	—	5	5,678	250
Southside Virginia Comm Coll, Alberta, VA 23821-9719	1970	$1,219 (S)	—	5	4,313	240
South Suburban Coll, South Holland, IL 60473-1270	1927	$1,532 (A)	—	11	5,580	329
South Texas Comm Coll, McAllen, TX 78501	1993	$1,260 (A)	—	9	12,469	592
Southwestern Coll, Chula Vista, CA 91910-7299	1961	$364 (S)	—	11	19,538	NA
Southwestern Comm Coll, Creston, IA 50801	1966	$2,848 (S)	$3,200	5	1,198	84
Southwestern Comm Coll, Sylva, NC 28779	1964	$1,024 (S)	—	5	1,802	229
Southwestern Illinois Coll, Belleville, IL 62221-5899	1946	$1,128 (A)	—	9	13,923	791
Southwestern Michigan Coll, Dowagiac, MI 49047-9793	1964	$1,891 (A)	—	11	3,172	193
Southwest Georgia Tech Coll, Thomasville, GA 31792	1963	$1,368 (S)	—	5	2,448	104
Southwest Mississippi Comm Coll, Summit, MS 39666	1918	$1,200 (A)	$1,900	11	1,772	94
Southwest Tennessee Comm Coll, Memphis, TN 38101-0780	NA	$1,788 (S)	—	5	12,736	271
Southwest Virginia Comm Coll, Richlands, VA 24641-1101	1968	$1,079 (S)	—	5	4,621	244
Southwest Wisconsin Tech Coll, Fennimore, WI 53809-9778	1967	$2,304 (S)	$2,250	11	2,993	112
Spartan School of Aeronautics, Tulsa, OK 74158-2833 (2)	1928	$9,750	—	3-B	1,625	150
Spokane Comm Coll, Spokane, WA 99217-5399	1963	$1,733 (S)	—	5	7,468	456
Spokane Falls Comm Coll, Spokane, WA 99224-5288	1967	$1,733 (S)	—	5	14,974	604
Spoon River Coll, Canton, IL 61520-9801	1959	$1,824 (A)	—	5	1,861	147
Springfield Tech Comm Coll, Springfield, MA 01105-1296	1967	$2,380 (S)	—	5	6,257	396
Stark State Coll of Tech, Canton, OH 44720-7299	1970	$3,010 (A)	—	11	4,774	340
State Fair Comm Coll, Sedalia, MO 65301-2199	1966	$1,392 (A)	$2,100	9	3,356	171
State Univ of New York Coll of Agriculture & Tech at Morrisville, Morrisville, NY 13408-0901	1908	$4,300 (S)	$6,030	5-B	3,130	174
State Univ of New York Coll of Tech at Alfred, Alfred, NY 14802	1908	$3,990 (S)	$5,358	5-B	3,041	184
State Univ of New York Coll of Tech at Canton, Canton, NY 13617	1906	$4,005 (S)	$6,490	5-B	2,223	114
State Univ of New York Coll of Tech at Delhi, Delhi, NY 13753	1913	$3,935 (S)	$5,790	5-B	2,013	140
Suffolk County Comm Coll, Selden, NY 11784-2899	1959	$2,774 (A)	—	11	19,851	1,162
Sullivan County Comm Coll, Loch Sheldrake, NY 12759	1962	$2,656 (S)	—	11	1,591	108
Sussex County Comm Coll, Newton, NJ 07860	1981	$2,438 (A)	—	11	2,479	185
Tacoma Comm Coll, Tacoma, WA 98466	1965	$61/credit (S)	—	5	7,299	320
Taft Coll, Taft, CA 93268-2317	1922	$370 (S)	$2,720	11	2,929	95
Tallahassee Comm Coll, Tallahassee, FL 32304-2895	1966	$1,340 (S)	—	11	11,606	467
Tarrant County Coll District, Fort Worth, TX 76102-6599	1967	$876 (A)	—	8	28,751	1,245
TCI-The Coll for Tech, New York, NY 10001-2705	1909	$7,555	—	3	4,319	215
Temple Coll, Temple, TX 76504-7435	1926	$1,390 (A)	—	9	3,585	181
Terra State Comm Coll, Fremont, OH 43420-9670	1968	$2,112 (S)	—	5	2,554	139
Texarkana Coll, Texarkana, TX 75599-0001	1927	$784 (A)	$1,200	11	3,875	266
Texas State Tech Coll-Harlingen, Harlingen, TX 78550-3697	1967	$2,268 (S)	$4,407	5	3,846	252

Name, address	Year Founded	Tuition & Fees	Rm. & Board	Control, Degree	Enroll-ment	Faculty
Texas State Tech Coll-Waco, Waco, TX 76705-1695	1965	$1,770 (S)	$2,352	5	4,068	280
Texas State Tech Coll-West Texas, Sweetwater, TX 79556-4108	1970	$2,330 (A)	$3,550	5	1,607	160
Three Rivers Comm Coll, Norwich, CT 06360	1963	$1,888 (S)	—	5	3,426	222
Three Rivers Comm Coll, Poplar Bluff, MO 63901-2393	1966	$1,694 (A)	—	11	2,500	67
Tidewater Comm Coll, Norfolk, VA 23510	1968	$1,171 (S)	—	5	22,091	1,206
Tomball Coll, Tomball, TX 77375-4036	1988	$852 (A)	—	11	8,357	359
Tompkins Cortland Comm Coll, Dryden, NY 13053-0139	1968	$3,000 (S)	$3,600	11	2,889	213
Trenholm State Tech Coll, Patterson Campus, Montgomery, AL 36116-2699	1962	$1,824 (A)	—	5	1,800	90
Tri-County Comm Coll, Murphy, NC 28906-7919	1964	$1,033 (A)	—	5	1,368	80
Tri-County Tech Coll, Pendleton, SC 29670-0587	1962	$1,700 (A)	—	5	3,773	400
Trident Tech Coll, Charleston, SC 29423-8067	1964	$1,750 (A)	—	11	10,461	510
Trinidad State Jr Coll, Trinidad, CO 81082-2396	1925	$2,386 (S)	$4,700	5	2,804	171
Trinity Valley Comm Coll, Athens, TX 75751-2765	1946	$300 (A)	$1,581	11	4,605	217
Triton Coll, River Grove, IL 60171-9983	1964	$1,766 (A)	—	5	10,672	579
Truckee Meadows Comm Coll, Reno, NV 89512-3901	1971	$1,152 (S)	—	5	9,697	480
Truett-McConnell Coll, Cleveland, GA 30528	1946	$7,100	$3,520	2	1,747	180
Tulsa Comm Coll, Tulsa, OK 74135-6198	1968	$1,612 (S)	—	5	20,827	1,094
Tunxis Comm Coll, Farmington, CT 06032-3026	1969	$2,096 (S)	—	5	3,720	247
Tyler Jr Coll, Tyler, TX 75711-9020	1926	$830 (A)	$2,800	11	8,451	364
Ulster County Comm Coll, Stone Ridge, NY 12484	1961	$2,735 (S)	—	11	2,913	194
Union County Coll, Cranford, NJ 07016-1528	1933	$2,686 (A)	—	11	8,950	383
Universal Tech Inst, Houston, TX 77073-5598	NA	$15,100	—	13	1,400	65
The Univ of Akron-Wayne Coll, Orrville, OH 44667-9192	1972	$1,964 (A)	—	5	1,932	155
Univ of Alaska Anchorage, Kenai Peninsula Coll, Soldotna, AK 99669-9798	1964	$92/credit (S)	—	5	1,911	150
Univ of Alaska Anchorage, Matanuska-Susitna Coll, Palmer, AK 99645-2889	1958	$2,068 (S)	—	5	1,594	106
Univ of Alaska Southeast, Sitka Campus, Sitka, AK 99835-9418	1962	$2,568 (S)	—	5	1,503	105
Univ of Arkansas at Fort Smith, Fort Smith, AR 72913-3649	1928	$1,290 (A)	—	11-B	5,746	293
Univ of Arkansas Comm Coll at Batesville, Batesville, AR 72503	NA	$1,042 (A)	—	5	1,236	99
Univ of Arkansas Comm Coll at Hope, Hope, AR 71801-0140	1966	$1,336 (A)	—	5	1,137	68
Univ of Arkansas Comm Coll at Morrilton, Morrilton, AR 72110	1961	$1,558 (A)	—	5	1,294	65
Univ of Kentucky, Lexington Comm Coll, Lexington, KY 40506-0235	1965	$1,371 (A)	—	5	7,793	393
Univ of New Mexico-Gallup, Gallup, NM 87301-5603	1968	$1,200 (S)	—	5-B	2,515	159
Univ of New Mexico-Valencia Campus, Los Lunas, NM 87031-7633	1981	$1,368 (S)	—	5	1,544	93
Univ of Northwestern Ohio, Lima, OH 45805-1498	1920	$8,880	$3,040	1-B	2,125	92
Univ of South Carolina Beaufort, Beaufort, SC 29902-4601	1959	$2,310 (S)	—	5	1,070	64
Univ of South Carolina Sumter, Sumter, SC 29150-2498	1966	$2,410 (S)	—	5	1,229	67
Univ of Wisconsin-Fox Valley, Menasha, WI 54952	1933	$2,624 (S)	—	5	1,782	57
Univ of Wisconsin-Marathon County, Wausau, WI 54401-5396	1933	$2,640 (S)	$3,300	5	1,339	79
Univ of Wisconsin-Waukesha, Waukesha, WI 53188-2799	1966	$2,280 (S)	—	5	2,253	79
Utah Valley State Coll, Orem, UT 84058-5999	1941	$2,002 (S)	—	5-B	20,946	976
Valencia Comm Coll, Orlando, FL 32802-3028	1967	$1,480 (S)	—	5	27,565	934
Vance-Granville Comm Coll, Henderson, NC 27536-0917	1969	$763 (S)	—	5	3,733	317
Ventura Coll, Ventura, CA 93003-3899	1925	NA	—	11	11,860	574
Vermont Tech Coll, Randolph Center, VT 05061-0500	1866	$5,340 (S)	$5,520	5-B	1,272	113
Vernon Coll, Vernon, TX 76384-4092	1970	$960 (A)	$2,243	11	2,270	128
Victor Valley Coll, Victorville, CA 92392-5849	1961	$330 (S)	—	5	8,111	539
Vincennes Univ, Vincennes, IN 47591-5202	1801	$2,601 (S)	$4,726	5	4,883	383
Virginia Highlands Comm Coll, Abingdon, VA 24212-0828	1967	$1,259 (S)	—	5	3,867	135
Virginia Western Comm Coll, Roanoke, VA 24038	1966	$1,300 (S)	—	5	8,311	403
Vista Comm Coll, Berkeley, CA 94704-5102	1974	$334 (S)	—	11	4,500	172
Volunteer State Comm Coll, Gallatin, TN 37066-3188	1970	$1,613 (S)	—	5	6,822	383
Wake Tech Comm Coll, Raleigh, NC 27603-5696	1958	$1,008 (S)	—	11	10,984	895
Wallace State Comm Coll, Hanceville, AL 35077-2000	1966	$52/credit (S)	$1,350	5	4,770	339
Walla Walla Comm Coll, Walla Walla, WA 99362-9267	1967	$2,103 (S)	—	5	6,775	415
Walters State Comm Coll, Morristown, TN 37813-6899	1970	$1,627 (S)	—	5	5,995	253
Warren County Comm Coll, Washington, NJ 07882-4343	1981	$1,812 (A)	—	11	1,659	81
Washington State Comm Coll, Marietta, OH 45750-9225	1971	$2,500 (S)	—	5	1,911	132
Washtenaw Comm Coll, Ann Arbor, MI 48106	1965	$1,726 (A)	—	11	11,089	654
Waubonsee Comm Coll, Sugar Grove, IL 60554-9799	1966	$1,604 (A)	—	9	7,890	692
Wayne Comm Coll, Goldsboro, NC 27533-8002	1957	$1,024 (S)	—	11	3,162	215
Wayne County Comm Coll District, Detroit, MI 48226-3010	1967	$1,770 (A)	—	11	10,000	286
Weatherford Coll, Weatherford, TX 76086-5699	1869	$1,000 (A)	$2,707	11	3,172	100
West Central Tech Coll, Carrollton, GA 30116	1968	$1,047 (S)	—	5	2,620	150
The Westchester Business Inst, White Plains, NY 10602	1915	$14,715	—	3	1,113	74
Westchester Comm Coll, Valhalla, NY 10595-1698	1946	$2,653 (S)	—	11	11,025	674
Western Dakota Tech Inst, Rapid City, SD 57703	1968	$3,198 (A)	—	5	1,052	84
Western Iowa Tech Comm Coll, Sioux City, IA 51102-5199	1966	$2,580 (S)	$2,075	5	4,920	253
Western Nebraska Comm Coll, Scottsbluff, NE 69361	1926	$1,560 (S)	$3,300	11	2,479	358
Western Nevada Comm Coll, Carson City, NV 89703-7316	1971	$1,440 (S)	—	5	5,117	354
Western Oklahoma State Coll, Altus, OK 73521-1397	1926	$1,484 (S)	$1,600	5	2,296	99
Western Piedmont Comm Coll, Morganton, NC 28655-4511	1964	$1,024 (S)	—	5	2,405	133
Western Texas Coll, Snyder, TX 79549-6105	1969	$1,253 (S)	$3,300	11	1,404	55
Western Wisconsin Tech Coll, La Crosse, WI 54602-0908	1911	$2,215 (S)	$1,900	9	5,181	426
Western Wyoming Comm Coll, Rock Springs, WY 82902-0428	1959	$1,474 (S)	$2,826	11	2,612	183
West Georgia Tech Coll, LaGrange, GA 30240	1966	$1,224 (S)	—	5	1,234	75
Westmoreland County Comm Coll, Youngwood, PA 15697-1895	1970	$1,620 (S)	—	8	5,700	410
West Shore Comm Coll, Scottville, MI 49454-0277	1967	$1,833 (S)	—	9	1,338	55
West Valley Coll, Saratoga, CA 95070-5698	1963	NA	—	11	11,000	560
West Virginia Northern Comm Coll, Wheeling, WV 26003-3699	1972	$1,680 (S)	—	5	2,994	131
West Virginia Univ at Parkersburg, Parkersburg, WV 26101-9577	1961	$1,548 (S)	—	5-B	3,340	172
Wharton County Jr Coll, Wharton, TX 77488-3298	1946	$855 (A)	$2,180	11	5,281	220
Whatcom Comm Coll, Bellingham, WA 98226-8003	1970	$1,782 (S)	—	5	3,993	212
Wilkes Comm Coll, Wilkesboro, NC 28697	1965	$1,030 (S)	—	5	2,334	305
Wilson Tech Comm Coll, Wilson, NC 27893-3310	1958	$868 (S)	—	5	1,732	99
Wisconsin Indianhead Tech Coll, Shell Lake, WI 54871	1912	$2,048 (S)	—	9	3,765	898
Wor-Wic Comm Coll, Salisbury, MD 21804	1976	$1,488 (A)	—	11	2,721	147
York Tech Coll, Rock Hill, SC 29730-3395	1961	$1,720 (A)	—	5	3,700	218
York Tech Inst, York, PA 17402-9017	NA	$11,360	—	13	1,100	52
Yuba Coll, Marysville, CA 95901-7699	1927	$672 (S)	—	11	12,348	595

ARTS AND MEDIA

Some Notable Movies, Sept. 2001 – Aug. 2002

Film	Stars	Director
Ali	Will Smith, Jamie Foxx, Jon Voight, Mario Van Peebles, Ron Silver, Jada Pinkett Smith	Michael Mann
Amelie	Audrey Tautou, Mathieu Kassovitz	Jean-Pierre Jeunet
Austin Powers in Goldmember	Mike Myers, Michael Caine, Beyoncé Knowles	Jay Roach
A Beautiful Mind	Russell Crowe, Ed Harris, Jennifer Connelly	Ron Howard
Black Hawk Down	Josh Hartnett, Tom Sizemore, Sam Shepard	Ridley Scott
Blade II	Wesley Snipes, Kris Kristofferson, Ron Perlman, Luke Goss, Thomas Kretschmann, Norman Reedus	Guillermo del Toro
The Bourne Identity	Matt Damon, Franka Potente, Chris Cooper	Doug Liman
The Fast Runner (Atanarjuat)	Natar Ungalaaq, Sylvia Ivalu, Peter-Henry Arnatsiaq	Zacharias Kunuk
Gosford Park	Maggie Smith, Michael Gambon, Helen Mirren, Kristin Scott Thomas	Robert Altman
Harry Potter and the Sorcerer's Stone	Daniel Radcliffe, Emma Watson, Rupert Grint, Richard Harris, Maggie Smith, Alan Rickman, Robbie Coltrane	Chris Columbus
I Am Sam	Sean Penn, Michelle Pfeiffer	Jessie Nelson
Ice Age	Ray Romano, John Leguizamo, Denis Leary	Chris Wedge
In the Bedroom	Tom Wilkinson, Sissy Spacek, Marisa Tomei	Todd Field
Iris	Judi Dench, Jim Broadbent, Kate Winslet	Sir Richard Eyre
Jimmy Neutron: Boy Genius	Debi Derryberry, Rob Paulsen, Jeff Garcia	John A. Davis
John Q.	Denzel Washington, Robert Duvall	Nick Cassavetes
Lilo & Stitch	Chris Sanders, Daveigh Chase, Tia Carrere, Ving Rhames	Chris Sanders, Dean DeBlois
The Lord of The Rings: The Fellowship of the Ring	Elijah Wood, Ian McKellen, Viggo Mortensen, Sean Astin, Cate Blanchett, Liv Tyler, Ian Holm	Peter Jackson
Men in Black II	Tommy Lee Jones, Will Smith	Barry Sonnenfeld
Minority Report	Tom Cruise, Colin Farrell	Steven Spielberg
Monsoon Wedding	Naseeruddin Shah, Lillete Dubey, Shefali Shetty	Mira Nair
Monster's Ball	Billy Bob Thornton, Heath Ledger, Halle Berry, Peter Boyle, Sean Combs	Marc Forster
Monsters, Inc.	Billy Crystal, John Goodman, Steve Buscemi, Mary Gibbs	Pete Docter
Mr. Deeds	Adam Sandler, Winona Ryder, John Turturro	Steven Brill
Mulholland Drive	Naomi Watts, Laura Elena Harring	David Lynch
My Big Fat Greek Wedding	Nia Vardalos, John Corbett	Joel Zwick
No Man's Land	Branko Djuric, Rene Bitorajac	Danis Tanovic
Ocean's Eleven	George Clooney, Brad Pitt, Matt Damon, Julia Roberts, Andy Garcia	Steven Soderbergh
Panic Room	Jodie Foster, Forest Whitaker, Dwight Yoakam, Jared Leto	David Fincher
The Piano Teacher	Isabelle Huppert, Benoît Magimel	Michael Haneke
Riding in Cars With Boys	Drew Barrymore, Steve Zahn, Brittany Murphy	Penny Marshall
Road to Perdition	Tom Hanks, Paul Newman, Jude Law	Sam Mendes
The Rookie	Dennis Quaid, Rachel Griffiths, Jay Hernandez	John Lee Hancock
The Royal Tenenbaums	Gene Hackman, Anjelica Huston, Ben Stiller, Gwyneth Paltrow, Luke Wilson, Owen Wilson	Wes Anderson
Scooby-Doo	Matthew Lillard, Sarah Michelle Gellar, Freddie Prinze Jr.	Raja Gosnell
The Scorpion King	The Rock, Steven Brand, Michael Clarke Duncan, Kelly Hu	Chuck Russell
Shallow Hal	Gwyneth Paltrow, Jack Black, Jason Alexander	Bobby & Peter Farrelly
Signs	Mel Gibson, Joaquin Phoenix	M. Night Shyamalan
Snow Dogs	Cuba Gooding Jr., James Coburn, Sisqo, Nichelle Nichols	Brian Levant
Spider-Man	Tobey Maguire, Kirsten Dunst, Willem Dafoe	Sam Raimi
Spirit: Stallion of the Cimarron	Matt Damon, James Cromwell, Daniel Studi	Kelly Asbury, Lorna Cook
Spy Kids 2: Island of Lost Dreams	Antonio Banderas, Alexa Vega, Daryl Sabara, Carla Gugino	Robert Rodriguez
Star Wars: Episode II—Attack of the Clones	Ewan McGregor, Natalie Portman, Hayden Christensen	George Lucas
Stuart Little 2	Geena Davis, Hugh Laurie, Jonathan Lipnicki; voices: Michael J. Fox, Nathan Lane, Melanie Griffith, James Woods	Rob Minkoff
The Sum of All Fears	Ben Affleck, Morgan Freeman, James Cromwell	Phil Alden Robinson
Training Day	Denzel Washington, Ethan Hawke, Scott Glenn, Tom Berenger	Antoine Fuqua
Vanilla Sky	Tom Cruise, Penelope Cruz, Cameron Diaz, Kurt Russell	Cameron Crowe
We Were Soldiers	Mel Gibson, Sam Elliott, Chris Klein	Randall Wallace
XXX	Vin Diesel, Samuel L. Jackson, Asia Argento	Rob Cohen
Y Tu Mamá También	Gael García Bernal, Diego Luna, Maribel Verdú	Alfonso Cuarón

50 Top-Grossing Movies, 2001

Source: Variety, box-office grosses in the U.S. and Canada during calendar year 2001

Rank	Title	Gross (millions)
1.	Harry Potter and the Sorcerer's Stone	$294.5
2.	Shrek	267.7
3.	Monsters, Inc.	240.8
4.	Rush Hour 2	226.2
5.	The Mummy Returns	202.0
6.	Pearl Harbor	198.5
7.	The Lord of the Rings: The Fellowship of the Ring	182.5
8.	Jurassic Park 3	181.2
9.	Planet of the Apes	179.8
10.	Hannibal	165.1
11.	American Pie 2	145.1
12.	The Fast and the Furious	144.5
13.	Ocean's Eleven	140.9
14.	Lara Croft: Tomb Raider	131.2
15.	Traffic	123.6
16.	Cast Away	114.2
17.	Crouching Tiger, Hidden Dragon	$113.0
18.	Dr. Dolittle 2	113.0
19.	Spy Kids	112.7
20.	The Princess Diaries	108.2
21.	The Others	96.5
22.	Legally Blonde	96.5
23.	America's Sweethearts	93.6
24.	Cats & Dogs	93.4
25.	Save the Last Dance	91.1
26.	Atlantis: The Lost Empire	84.1
27.	A.I. Artificial Intelligence	78.6
28.	Training Day	76.3
29.	Along Came a Spider	74.1
30.	Vanilla Sky	74.0
31.	Bridget Jones's Diary	71.5
32.	Scary Movie 2	71.3
33.	The Score	71.1
34.	Swordfish	$69.8
35.	Shallow Hal	68.5
36.	The Mexican	66.8
37.	Chocolat	66.6
38.	Down to Earth	64.2
39.	Spy Game	61.1
40.	What Women Want	60.5
41.	The Wedding Planner	60.4
42.	Moulin Rouge	57.1
43.	Rat Race	56.6
44.	A Knight's Tale	56.1
45.	The Animal	55.8
46.	Don't Say a Word	54.9
47.	Miss Congeniality	54.5
48.	Jimmy Neutron: Boy Genius	53.3
49.	Blow	53.0
50.	Exit Wounds	51.8

National Film Registry, 1989-2001

Source: National Film Registry, Library of Congress

"Culturally, historically, or esthetically significant" films placed on the registry. * = selected in 2001.

Abbott and Costello Meet Frankenstein (1948)*
Adam's Rib (1949)
The Adventures of Robin Hood (1938)
The African Queen (1951)
All About Eve (1950)
All That Heaven Allows (1955)
All That Jazz (1979)*
All Quiet on the Western Front (1930)
All the King's Men (1949)*
An American in Paris (1951)
America, America (1963)*
American Graffiti (1973)
A Movie (1958)
Annie Hall (1977)
The Apartment (1960)
Apocalypse Now (1979)
The Awful Truth (1937)
Badlands (1973)
The Band Wagon (1953)
The Bank Dick (1940)
The Battle of San Pietro (1945)
Ben-Hur (1926)
The Best Years of Our Lives (1946)
Big Business (1929)
The Big Parade (1925)
The Big Sleep (1946)
The Birth of a Nation (1915)
The Black Pirate (1926)
Blacksmith Scene (1893)
Blade Runner (1982)
The Blood of Jesus (1941)
Bonnie and Clyde (1967)
Bride of Frankenstein (1935)
The Bridge on the River Kwai (1957)
Bringing Up Baby (1938)
Broken Blossoms (1919)
Cabaret (1972)
Carmen Jones (1954)
Casablanca (1942)
Castro Street (1966)
Cat People (1942)
Chan Is Missing (1982)
The Cheat (1915)
Chinatown (1974)
Chulas Fronteras (1976)
Citizen Kane (1941)
The City (1939)
City Lights (1931)
Civilization (1916)
Cologne: From the Diary of Ray and Esther (1939)*
The Conversation (1974)
The Cool World (1963)
Cops (1922)
A Corner in Wheat (1909)
The Crowd (1928)
Czechoslovakia 1968 (1968)
David Holzman's Diary (1968)
The Day the Earth Stood Still (1951)
Dead Birds (1964)
The Deer Hunter (1978)
Destry Rides Again (1939)
Detour (1946)
Dodsworth (1936)
The Docks of New York (1928)
Dog Star Man (1964)
Don't Look Back (1967)
Do the Right Thing (1989)
Double Indemnity (1944)
Dracula (1931)
Dr. Strangelove (or, How I Learned to Stop Worrying and Love the Bomb)(1964)
Duck Amuck (1953)
Duck Soup (1933)
Easy Rider (1969)
Eaux D'Artifice (1953)
El Norte (1983)
The Emperor Jones (1933)
E.T.: The Extra-Terrestrial (1982)
Evidence of the Film (1913)*
The Exploits of Elaine (1914)
The Fall of the House of Usher (1928)
Fantasia (1940)
Fatty's Tintype Tangle (1915)
Five Easy Pieces (1970)
Flash Gordon serial (1936)
Footlight Parade (1933)
Force of Evil (1948)
The Forgotten Frontier (1931)
42nd Street (1933)
The Four Horsemen of the Apocalypse (1921)
Frankenstein (1931)
Frank Film (1973)
Freaks (1932)
The Freshman (1925)
From the Manger to the Cross (1912)
Fury (1936)
The General (1927)
Gerald McBoing Boing (1951)
Gertie the Dinosaur (1914)
Gigi (1958)
The Godfather (1972)
The Godfather, Part II (1974)
The Gold Rush (1925)
Gone With the Wind (1939)
GoodFellas (1990)
The Graduate (1967)
The Grapes of Wrath (1940)
Grass (1925)
The Great Dictator (1940)
The Great Train Robbery (1903)
Greed (1924)
Gun Crazy (1949)
Gunga Din (1939)
Harlan County, U.S.A. (1976)
Harold and Maude (1972)
The Heiress (1949)
Hell's Hinges (1916)
High Noon (1952)
High School (1968)
Hindenburg Disaster Newsreel Footage (1937)
His Girl Friday (1940)
The Hitch-Hiker (1953)
Hoosiers (1986)*
Hospital (1970)
The Hospital (1971)
The House in the Middle (1954)*
How Green Was My Valley (1941)
How the West Was Won (1962)
The Hustler (1961)
I Am a Fugitive From a Chain Gang (1932)
The Immigrant (1917)
In the Land of the Head-Hunters aka In the Land of the War Canoes (1914)
Intolerance (1916)
Invasion of the Body Snatchers (1956)
It (1927)*
It Happened One Night (1934)
It's a Wonderful Life (1946)
The Italian (1915)
Jammin' the Blues (1944)
Jam Session (1942)*
Jaws (1975)*
Jazz on a Summer's Day (1959)
The Jazz Singer (1927)
Killer of Sheep (1977)
King: A Filmed Record . . . Montgomery to Memphis (1970)
King Kong (1933)
The Kiss (1896)
Kiss Me Deadly (1955)
Knute Rockne, All American (1940)
Koyaanisqatsi (1983)
The Lady Eve (1941)
Lambchops (1929)
The Land Beyond the Sunset (1912)
Lassie Come Home (1943)
The Last of the Mohicans (1920)
The Last Picture Show (1972)
Laura (1944)
Lawrence of Arabia (1962)
The Learning Tree (1969)
Let's All Go to the Lobby (1957)
Letter From an Unknown Woman (1948)
The Life and Death of 9413—A Hollywood Extra (1928)
Life and Times of Rosie the Riveter (1980)
The Life of Emile Zola (1937)
Little Caesar (1930)
The Little Fugitive (1953)
Little Miss Marker (1934)
The Living Desert (1953)
The Lost World (1925)
Louisiana Story (1948)
Love Finds Andy Hardy (1938)
Love Me Tonight (1932)
Magical Maestro (1952)
The Magnificent Ambersons (1942)
The Maltese Falcon (1941)
The Manchurian Candidate (1962)
Manhattan (1921)
Manhattan (1979)*
March of Time: Inside Nazi Germany—1938 (1938)
Marian Anderson: The Lincoln Memorial Concert (1939)*
Marty (1955)
M*A*S*H (1970)
Master Hands (1936)
Mean Streets (1973)
Meet Me in St. Louis (1944)
Memphis Belle (1944)*
Meshes of the Afternoon (1943)
Midnight Cowboy (1969)
Mildred Pierce (1945)
The Miracle of Morgan's Creek (1944)*
Miss Lulu Bett (1921)*
Modern Times (1936)
Modesta (1956)
Morocco (1930)
Motion Painting No. 1 (1947)
Mr. Smith Goes to Washington (1939)
Multiple Sidosis (1970)
The Music Box (1932)
My Darling Clementine (1946)
My Man Godfrey (1936)
The Naked Spur (1953)
Nanook of the North (1922)
Nashville (1975)
National Lampoon's Animal House (1978)*
Network (1976)
A Night at the Opera (1935)
The Night of the Hunter (1955)
Night of the Living Dead (1968)
Ninotchka (1939)
North by Northwest (1959)
Nothing but a Man (1964)
One Flew Over the Cuckoo's Nest (1975)
On the Waterfront (1954)
The Outlaw Josey Wales (1976)
Out of the Past (1947)
The Ox-Bow Incident (1943)
Pass the Gravy (1928)
Paths of Glory (1957)
Peter Pan (1924)
Phantom of the Opera (1925)
The Philadelphia Story (1940)
Pinocchio (1940)
A Place in the Sun (1951)
Planet of the Apes (1968)*
The Plow That Broke the Plains (1936)
Point of Order (1964)
The Poor Little Rich Girl (1917)
Porky in Wackyland (1938)
Powers of Ten (1978)
President McKinley Inauguration Footage (1901)
Primary (1960)
The Prisoner of Zenda (1937)
The Producers (1968)
Psycho (1960)
The Public Enemy (1931)
Pull My Daisy (1959)
Raging Bull (1980)
Raiders of the Lost Ark (1981)
Rear Window (1954)
Rebel Without a Cause (1955)
Red River (1948)
Regeneration (1915)
Republic Steel Strike Riots Newsreel Footage (1937)
Return of the Secaucus 7 (1980)
Ride the High Country (1962)
Rip Van Winkle (1896)
The River (1937)
Road to Morocco (1942)
Roman Holiday (1953)
Rose Hobart (1936)*
Safety Last (1923)
Salesman (1969)
Salomé (1922)
Salt of the Earth (1954)
Scarface (1932)
The Searchers (1956)
Serene Velocity (1970)*
Seventh Heaven (1927)
Shadow of a Doubt (1943)
Shadows (1959)
Shaft (1971)
Shane (1953)
She Done Him Wrong (1933)
Sherlock, Jr. (1924)
Sherman's March (1986)
Shock Corridor (1963)
The Shop Around the Corner (1940)
Show Boat (1936)
Singin' in the Rain (1952)
Sky High (1922)
Snow White (1933)
Snow White and the Seven Dwarfs (1937)
Some Like It Hot (1959)
The Sound of Music (1965)*
Stagecoach (1939)
A Star Is Born (1954)
Star Wars (1977)
Steamboat Willie (1928)
A Streetcar Named Desire (1951)
Stormy Weather (1943)*
Sullivan's Travels (1941)
Sunrise (1927)
Sunset Boulevard (1950)
Sweet Smell of Success (1957)
Tabu (1933)
Tacoma Narrows Bridge Collapse (1940)
The Tall T (1957)
Taxi Driver (1976)
The Ten Commandments (1956)
The Tell-Tale Heart (1953)*
Tevye (1939)
The Thief of Bagdad (1924)
The Thin Blue Line (1988)*
The Thing From Another World (1951)*
The Thin Man (1934)
To Be or Not To Be (1942)

To Fly (1976)
To Kill a Mockingbird (1962)
Tootsie (1982)
Topaz (1943-45)
Top Hat (1935)
Touch of Evil (1958)
Trance and Dance in Bali (1939)
The Treasure of the Sierra Madre (1948)
Trouble in Paradise (1932)
Tulips Shall Grow (1942)
Twelve O'Clock High (1949)
2001: A Space Odyssey (1968)
Verbena Tragica (1939)
Vertigo (1958)
Westinghouse Works 1904 (1904)
West Side Story (1961)
What's Opera, Doc? (1957)
Where Are My Children? (1916)
Why We Fight (Series/1943-45)
The Wild Bunch (1969)
Will Success Spoil Rock Hunter? (1957)
The Wind (1928)
Wings (1927)
Within Our Gates (1920)
The Wizard of Oz (1939)
Woman of the Year (1942)
A Woman Under the Influence (1974)
Woodstock (1970)
Yankee Doodle Dandy (1942)
Zapruder Film (1963)

100 Best American Movies of All Time

Source: American Film Institute

Compiled in 1998 based on ballots sent to 1,500 figures, mostly from the film world. Criteria for judging included historical significance, critical recognition and awards, and popularity. The year each film was first released is in parentheses.

1. Citizen Kane (1941)
2. Casablanca (1942)
3. The Godfather (1972)
4. Gone With the Wind (1939)
5. Lawrence of Arabia (1962)
6. The Wizard of Oz (1939)
7. The Graduate (1967)
8. On the Waterfront (1954)
9. Schindler's List (1993)
10. Singin' in the Rain (1952)
11. It's a Wonderful Life (1946)
12. Sunset Boulevard (1950)
13. The Bridge on the River Kwai (1957)
14. Some Like It Hot (1959)
15. Star Wars (1977)
16. All About Eve (1950)
17. The African Queen (1951)
18. Psycho (1960)
19. Chinatown (1974)
20. One Flew Over the Cuckoo's Nest (1975)
21. The Grapes of Wrath (1940)
22. 2001: A Space Odyssey (1968)
23. The Maltese Falcon (1941)
24. Raging Bull (1980)
25. E.T.: The Extra-Terrestrial (1982)
26. Dr. Strangelove (1964)
27. Bonnie and Clyde (1967)
28. Apocalypse Now (1979)
29. Mr. Smith Goes to Washington (1939)
30. Treasure of the Sierra Madre (1948)
31. Annie Hall (1977)
32. The Godfather, Part II (1974)
33. High Noon (1952)
34. To Kill a Mockingbird (1962)
35. It Happened One Night (1934)
36. Midnight Cowboy (1969)
37. The Best Years of Our Lives (1946)
38. Double Indemnity (1944)
39. Doctor Zhivago (1965)
40. North by Northwest (1959)
41. West Side Story (1961)
42. Rear Window (1954)
43. King Kong (1933)
44. The Birth of a Nation (1915)
45. A Streetcar Named Desire (1951)
46. A Clockwork Orange (1971)
47. Taxi Driver (1976)
48. Jaws (1975)
49. Snow White and the Seven Dwarfs (1937)
50. Butch Cassidy and the Sundance Kid (1969)
51. The Philadelphia Story (1940)
52. From Here to Eternity (1953)
53. Amadeus (1984)
54. All Quiet on the Western Front (1930)
55. The Sound of Music (1965)
56. M*A*S*H (1970)
57. The Third Man (1949)
58. Fantasia (1940)
59. Rebel Without a Cause (1955)
60. Raiders of the Lost Ark (1981)
61. Vertigo (1958)
62. Tootsie (1982)
63. Stagecoach (1939)
64. Close Encounters of the Third Kind (1977)
65. The Silence of the Lambs (1991)
66. Network (1976)
67. The Manchurian Candidate (1962)
68. An American in Paris (1951)
69. Shane (1953)
70. The French Connection (1971)
71. Forrest Gump (1994)
72. Ben-Hur (1959)
73. Wuthering Heights (1939)
74. The Gold Rush (1925)
75. Dances With Wolves (1990)
76. City Lights (1931)
77. American Graffiti (1973)
78. Rocky (1976)
79. The Deer Hunter (1978)
80. The Wild Bunch (1969)
81. Modern Times (1936)
82. Giant (1956)
83. Platoon (1986)
84. Fargo (1996)
85. Duck Soup (1933)
86. Mutiny on the Bounty (1935)
87. Frankenstein (1931)
88. Easy Rider (1969)
89. Patton (1970)
90. The Jazz Singer (1927)
91. My Fair Lady (1964)
92. A Place in the Sun (1951)
93. The Apartment (1960)
94. Goodfellas (1990)
95. Pulp Fiction (1994)
96. The Searchers (1956)
97. Bringing Up Baby (1938)
98. Unforgiven (1992)
99. Guess Who's Coming to Dinner (1967)
100. Yankee Doodle Dandy (1942)

100 Greatest Love Stories

Source: American Film Institute

Compiled in 2002 based on ballots sent to 1,500 figures, mostly from the film world. Criteria for judging included historical significance, critical recognition and awards, and popularity. The year each film was first released is in parentheses.

1. Casablanca (1942)
2. Gone With the Wind (1939)
3. West Side Story (1961)
4. Roman Holiday (1953)
5. An Affair to Remember (1957)
6. The Way We Were (1973)
7. Doctor Zhivago (1965)
8. It's a Wonderful Life (1946)
9. Love Story (1970)
10. City Lights (1931)
11. Annie Hall (1977)
12. My Fair Lady (1964)
13. Out Of Africa (1985)
14. The African Queen (1951)
15. Wuthering Heights (1939)
16. Singin' in the Rain (1952)
17. Moonstruck (1987)
18. Vertigo (1958)
19. Ghost (1990)
20. From Here to Eternity (1953)
21. Pretty Woman (1990)
22. On Golden Pond (1981)
23. Now, Voyager (1942)
24. King Kong (1933)
25. When Harry Met Sally... (1989)
26. The Lady Eve (1941)
27. The Sound of Music (1965)
28. The Shop Around the Corner (1940)
29. An Officer and a Gentleman (1982)
30. Swing Time (1936)
31. The King and I (1956)
32. Dark Victory (1939)
33. Camille (1937)
34. Beauty and the Beast (1991)
35. Gigi (1958)
36. Random Harvest (1942)
37. Titanic (1997)
38. It Happened One Night (1934)
39. An American in Paris (1951)
40. Ninotchka (1939)
41. Funny Girl (1968)
42. Anna Karenina (1935)
43. A Star Is Born (1954)
44. The Philadelphia Story (1940)
45. Sleepless in Seattle (1993)
46. To Catch a Thief (1955)
47. Splendor in the Grass (1961)
48. Last Tango in Paris (1972)
49. The Postman Always Rings Twice (1946)
50. Shakespeare in Love (1998)
51. Bringing Up Baby (1938)
52. The Graduate (1967)
53. A Place in the Sun (1951)
54. Sabrina (1954)
55. Reds (1981)
56. The English Patient (1996)
57. Two for the Road (1967)
58. Guess Who's Coming to Dinner (1967)
59. Picnic (1955)
60. To Have and Have Not (1944)
61. Breakfast at Tiffany's (1961)
62. The Apartment (1960)
63. Sunrise (1927)
64. Marty (1955)
65. Bonnie and Clyde (1967)
66. Manhattan (1979)
67. A Streetcar Named Desire (1951)
68. What's Up, Doc? (1972)
69. Harold and Maude (1971)
70. Sense and Sensibility (1995)
71. Way Down East (1920)
72. Roxanne (1987)
73. The Ghost and Mrs. Muir (1947)
74. Woman of the Year (1942)
75. The American President (1995)
76. The Quiet Man (1952)
77. The Awful Truth (1937)
78. Coming Home (1978)
79. Jezebel (1939)
80. The Sheik (1921)
81. The Goodbye Girl (1977)
82. Witness (1985)
83. Morocco (1930)
84. Double Indemnity (1944)
85. Love Is a Many-Splendored Thing (1955)
86. Notorious (1946)
87. The Unbearable Lightness of Being (1988)
88. The Princess Bride (1987)
89. Who's Afraid of Virginia Woolf? (1966)
90. The Bridges of Madison County (1995)
91. Working Girl (1988)
92. Porgy and Bess (1959)
93. Dirty Dancing (1987)
94. Body Heat (1981)
95. Lady and the Tramp (1955)
96. Barefoot in the Park (1967)
97. Grease (1978)
98. The Hunchback of Notre Dame (1939)
99. Pillow Talk (1959)
100. Jerry Maguire (1996)

All-Time Top-Grossing American Movies[1]

Source: *Variety* magazine

Rank	Title (original release)	Gross[2]
1.	Titanic (1997)	$600.8
2.	Star Wars: Episode IV—A New Hope (1977)	461.0
3.	E.T.: The Extra-Terrestrial (1982)	435.0
4.	Star Wars: Episode I—The Phantom Menace (1999)	431.1
5.	Spider-Man (2002)	403.7
6.	Jurassic Park (1993)	357.1
7.	Forrest Gump (1994)	329.7
8.	Harry Potter and the Sorcerer's Stone (2001)	317.6
9.	The Lord of the Rings: The Fellowship of the Ring (2001)	313.4
10.	The Lion King (1994)	312.9
11.	Return of the Jedi (1983)	309.2
12.	Independence Day (1996)	306.2
13.	Star Wars: Episode II—Attack of the Clones (2002)	300.7
14.	The Sixth Sense (1999)	293.5
15.	The Empire Strikes Back (1980)	290.3
16.	Home Alone (1990)	285.8
17.	Shrek (2001)	267.7
18.	Dr. Seuss' How the Grinch Stole Christmas (2000)	260.0
19.	Jaws (1975)	260.0
20.	Monsters, Inc. (2001)	255.8
21.	Batman (1989)	251.2
22.	Men in Black (1997)	250.7
23.	Toy Story 2 (1999)	245.9
24.	Raiders of the Lost Ark (1981)	242.4
25.	Twister (1996)	$241.7
26.	Ghostbusters (1984)	238.6
27.	Beverly Hills Cop (1984)	234.8
28.	Cast Away (2000)	233.6
29.	The Exorcist (1973)	232.7
30.	The Lost World: Jurassic Park (1997)	229.1
31.	Rush Hour 2 (2001)	226.2
32.	Mrs. Doubtfire (1993)	219.2
33.	Ghost (1990)	217.6
34.	Aladdin (1992)	217.4
35.	Saving Private Ryan (1998)	216.2
36.	Mission: Impossible 2 (2000)	215.4
37.	Back to the Future (1985)	208.2
38.	Austin Powers: The Spy Who Shagged Me (1999)	205.4
39.	Terminator 2: Judgment Day (1991)	204.8
40.	Austin Powers in Goldmember (2002)	203.5
41.	The Mummy Returns (2001)	202.0
42.	Armageddon (1998)	201.6
43.	Pearl Harbor (2001)	198.5
44.	Indiana Jones and the Last Crusade (1989)	197.2
45.	Signs (2002)	195.6
46.	Toy Story (1995)	191.8
47.	Men in Black 2 (2002)	190.4
48.	Grease (1978)	188.4
49.	Gladiator (2000)	187.7
50.	Dances With Wolves (1990)	184.2

(1) Through Sept. 2, 2002. (2) Gross is in millions of absolute dollars based on box office sales in the U.S. and Canada. Rising ticket prices favor newer films, but older films have the advantage of reissues.

Most Popular Movie Videos/DVDs

Source: Alexander & Associates/Video Flash, New York, NY

All Time

Top Ten Rental Titles

VHS[1]

1. Pretty Woman
2. Top Gun
3. The Little Mermaid
4. Home Alone
5. Cinderella
6. Ghost
7. The Lion King
8. Beauty and the Beast
9. Aladdin
10. Terminator 2: Judgment Day

DVD[2]

1. Gladiator (2000)
2. The Matrix
3. Cast Away
4. Hannibal
5. Shrek
6. The Sixth Sense
7. The Green Mile
8. Meet the Parents
9. Gone in 60 Seconds (2001)
10. The Family Man

Top Ten Purchase Titles

VHS[3]

1. The Lion King
2. Snow White and the Seven Dwarfs
3. Forrest Gump
4. Aladdin
5. Toy Story
6. Jurassic Park
7. Pocahontas
8. Beauty and the Beast
9. The Little Mermaid
10. Cinderella

DVD[2]

1. Gladiator (2000)
2. Shrek
3. The Matrix
4. The Sixth Sense
5. A Knight's Tale
6. The Green Mile
7. Remember the Titans
8. The Mummy Returns (2001)
9. How the Grinch Stole Christmas (2000)
10. Crouching Tiger, Hidden Dragon

2001

Top Ten Rental Titles

VHS

1. Gladiator (2000)
2. Meet the Parents
3. Miss Congeniality
4. Cast Away
5. Remember the Titans
6. Gone in 60 Seconds (2001)
7. What Women Want
8. Shrek
9. Me, Myself and Irene
10. Hannibal

DVD

1. Gladiator (2000)
2. Cast Away
3. Hannibal
4. Shrek
5. Meet the Parents
6. The Family Man
7. What Women Want
8. Unbreakable
9. Gone in 60 Seconds (2001)
10. Tailor of Panama

Top Ten Purchase Titles

VHS

1. Shrek
2. How the Grinch Stole Christmas (2000)
3. Dinosaur (2000)
4. Gladiator (2000)
5. Lady and the Tramp 2
6. Emperor's New Groove
7. Remember the Titans
8. 102 Dalmatians
9. Toy Story 2
10. The Patriot (2000)

DVD

1. Shrek
2. Gladiator (2000)
3. Remember the Titans
4. The Mummy Returns (2001)
5. A Knight's Tale
6. How the Grinch Stole Christmas (2000)
7. Miss Congeniality
8. Hannibal
9. Crouching Tiger, Hidden Dragon
10. Cast Away

Note: Year given to distinguish from other films with the same title. (1) Mar. 1, 1987, to Dec. 31, 2001. (2) Jan. 1, 2000, to Dec. 31, 2001. (3) Feb. 16, 1988, to Dec. 31, 2001.

Top 50 Record Long-Run Broadway Plays[1]

Source: The League of American Theatres and Producers, Inc., New York, NY

	Title	Performances
1.	Cats	7,485
2.	*Les Miserables	6,276
3.	A Chorus Line	6,137
4.	*The Phantom of the Opera	5,979
5.	Oh! Calcutta! (revival)	5,959
6.	Miss Saigon	4,092
7.	42nd Street	3,486
8.	Grease (original)	3,388
9.	*Beauty and the Beast	3,306
10.	Fiddler on the Roof	3,242
11.	Life With Father	3,224
12.	Tobacco Road	3,182
13.	Hello Dolly	2,844
14.	My Fair Lady	2,717
15.	*Rent	2,535
16.	Annie	2,377
17.	Man of La Mancha	2,328
18.	Abie's Irish Rose	2,327
19.	*Chicago (revival)	2,306
20.	Oklahoma!	2,212
21.	Smokey Joe's Cafe	2,037
22.	Pippin	1,944
23.	South Pacific	1,925
24.	The Magic Show	1,920
25.	*The Lion King	1,896
26.	Gemini	1,819
27.	Deathtrap	1,793
28.	Harvey	1,775
29.	Dancin'	1,774
30.	La Cage aux Folles	1,761
31.	Hair	1,750
32.	*Cabaret (revival)	1,706
33.	The Wiz	1,672
34.	Born Yesterday	1,642
35.	Crazy for You	1,622
36.	Ain't Misbehavin'	1,604
37.	The Best Little Whorehouse in Texas	1,584
38.	Mary, Mary	1,572
39.	Evita	1,567
40.	The Voice of the Turtle	1,557
41.	Jekyll & Hyde	1,543
42.	Barefoot in the Park	1,530
43.	Dreamgirls	1,521
44.	Mame	1,508
45.	Grease (revival)	1,505
46.	Same Time, Next Year	1,453
47.	Arsenic and Old Lace	1,444
48.	The Sound of Music (orig.)	1,443
49.	Me and My Girl	1,420
50.	How to Succeed in Business Without Really Trying (orig.)	1,417

*Still running May 26, 2002. (1) Number of performances through May 26, 2002.

Broadway Season Statistics, 1959-2002

Source: The League of American Theatres and Producers, Inc., New York, NY

Season	Gross (mil $)	Attendance (mil)	Playing Weeks	New Productions
1959-1960	46	7.9	1,156	58
1960-1961	44	7.7	1,210	48
1961-1962	44	6.8	1,166	53
1962-1963	44	7.4	1,134	54
1963-1964	40	6.8	1,107	63
1964-1965	50	8.2	1,250	67
1965-1966	54	9.6	1,295	68
1966-1967	55	9.3	1,269	69
1967-1968	59	9.5	1,259	74
1968-1969	58	8.6	1,209	67
1969-1970	53	7.1	1,047	62
1970-1971	55	7.4	1,107	49
1971-1972	52	6.5	1,157	55
1972-1973	45	5.4	889	55
1973-1974	46	5.7	907	43
1974-1975	57	6.6	1,101	54
1975-1976	71	7.3	1,136	55
1976-1977	93	8.8	1,349	54
1977-1978	114	9.6	1,433	42
1978-1979	134	9.6	1,542	50
1979-1980	146	9.6	1,540	61
1980-1981	107	11.0	1,544	60
1981-1982	223	10.1	1,455	48
1982-1983	209	8.4	1,258	50
1983-1984	227	7.9	1,097	36
1984-1985	209	7.3	1,078	33
1985-1986	190	6.5	1,041	34
1986-1987	208	7.1	1,039	41
1987-1988	253	8.1	1,113	30
1988-1989	262	8.1	1,108	33
1989-1990	282	8.0	1,070	40
1990-1991	267	7.3	971	28
1991-1992	293	7.4	905	37
1992-1993	328	7.9	1,019	34
1993-1994	356	8.1	1,066	39
1994-1995	406	9.0	1,120	33
1995-1996	436	9.5	1,146	38
1996-1997	499	10.6	1,349	37
1997-1998	558	11.5	1,442	33
1998-1999	588	11.7	1,441	39
1999-2000	603	11.4	1,464	37
2000-2001	666	11.9	1,484	28
2001-2002	643	11.0	1,434	28

Some Notable Non-Profit Theater Companies in the U.S

Source: Theatre Communications Group, Inc.

ACT Theatre	Seattle	WA
Actors Theatre of Louisville	Louisville	KY
Alabama Shakespeare Festival	Montgomery	AL
Alley Theatre	Houston	TX
Alliance Theatre Company	Atlanta	GA
American Conservatory Theater	San Francisco	CA
American Repertory Theatre	Boston	MA
Arena Stage	Washington	DC
Arizona Theatre Company	Tucson	AZ
Berkeley Repertory Theatre	Berkeley	CA
Center Stage	Baltimore	MD
Chicago Shakespeare Theater	Chicago	IL
The Children's Theatre Company	Minneapolis	MN
Cincinnati Playhouse in the Park	Cincinnati	OH
The Cleveland Play House	Cleveland	OH
Coconut Grove Playhouse	Miami	FL
Denver Center Theatre Company	Denver	CO
The 5th Avenue Theatre Association	Seattle	WA
Ford's Theatre	Washington	DC
Geffen Playhouse	Los Angeles	CA
The Globe Theatres	San Diego	CA
Goodman Theatre	Chicago	IL
Goodspeed Musicals	East Haddam	CT
Guthrie Theater	Minneapolis	MN
Hartford Stage Company	Hartford	CT
Huntington Theatre Company	Boston	MA
Joseph Papp Public Theater	New York	NY
La Jolla Playhouse	La Jolla	CA
Lincoln Center Theater	New York	NY
Long Wharf Theatre	New Haven	CT
Manhattan Theatre Club	New York	NY
Mark Taper Forum	Los Angeles	CA
McCarter Theatre Center	Princeton	NJ
Milwaukee Repertory Theater	Milwaukee	WI
Missouri Repertory Theatre	Kansas City	MO
Oregon Shakespeare Festival	Ashland	OR
Pasadena Playhouse	Pasadena	CA
Pittsburgh Public Theatre	Pittsburgh	PA
Repertory Theatre of St. Louis	St. Louis	MO
Roundabout Theatre Company	New York	NY
San Jose Repertory Theatre	San Jose	CA
Seattle Children's Theatre	Seattle	WA
Seattle Repertory Theatre	Seattle	WA
The Shakespeare Theatre	Washington	DC
South Coast Repertory	Costa Mesa	CA
Steppenwolf Theatre Company	Chicago	IL
Theatreworks/USA	New York	NY
Trinity Repertory Company	Providence	RI
Village Theatre	Issaquah	WA

U.S. Symphony Orchestras[1]

Source: American Symphony Orchestra League, 33 West 60th St., New York, NY 10023

Symphony Orchestra[2]	Music Director[3]
Alabama Symphony (AL)	Richard Westerfield
American (NY)	Steven Sloane
Arkansas Symphony (AR)	David Itkin
Atlanta (GA)	Robert Spano
Austin (TX)	Peter Bay
Baltimore (MD)	Yuri Temirkanov
Baton Rouge Symphony (LA)	Timothy Muffitt
Boston (MA)	James Levine
Brooklyn Philharmonic (NY)	Robert Spano
Buffalo Philharmonic (NY)	JoAnne Falletta
Charlotte (NC)	Christof Perick
Chicago (IL)	Daniel Barenboim
Cincinnati (OH)	Paavo Järvi
Cleveland Orchestra (OH)	Franz Welser-Möst
Colorado (CO)	Marin Alsop
Colorado Springs (CO)	Lawrence Leighton Smith
Columbus (OH)	Alessandro Siciliani
Dallas (TX)	Andrew Litton
Dayton Philharmonic (OH)	Neal Gittleman
Delaware Symphony (DE)	Stephen Gunzenhauser
Detroit (MI)	Neeme Jarvi
Evansville Philharmonic (IN)	Alfred Savia
Florida Orchestra (Tampa)	Stefan Sanderling
Florida Philharmonic (Ft. Lauderdale)	Joseph Silverstein, act.
Florida West Coast (FL)	Leif Bjaland
Fort Wayne Philharmonic (IN)	Edvard Tchivzhel
Fort Worth (TX)	Miguel Harth-Bedoya
Grand Rapids (MI)	David Lockington
Grant Park (Chicago, IL)	Carlos Kalmar
Hartford (CT)	Edward Cumming
Honolulu (HI)	Samuel Wong
Houston (TX)	Hans Graf
Indianapolis (IN)	Mario Venzago
Jacksonville (FL)	Fabio Mechetti
Kansas City (MO)	Anne Manson
Knoxville (TN)	Kirk Trevor
Long Beach (CA)	Enrique Arturo Diemecke
Los Angeles Chamber (CA)	Jeffrey Kahane
Los Angeles Philharmonic (CA)	Esa-Pekka Salonen
Louisiana Philharmonic (New Orleans)	Klauspeter Seibel
Louisville Orchestra (KY)	Uriel Segal
Memphis (TN)	David Loebel
Milwaukee (WI)	Andreas Delfs
Minnesota (Minneapolis)	Osmo Vanska
Naples Philharmonic (FL)	Christopher Seaman
Nashville Symphony (TN)	Kenneth D. Schermerhorn
National (Washington, DC)	Leonard Slatkin
New Jersey (Newark)	Zdenek Macal
New Mexico (Albuquerque)	Guillermo Figureoa
New York Philharmonic (NYC)	Lorin Maazel
North Carolina Symphony (Raleigh)	Gerhardt Zimmermann
Oklahoma City Philharmonic (OK)	Joel A. Levine
Omaha Symphony (NE)	Victor Yampolsky
Orchestra of St. Luke's (NY)	Donald Runnicles
Oregon Symphony (Portland)	James DePreist
Pasadena Symphony Association (CA)	Jorge Mester
Philadelphia (PA)	Wolfgang Sawallisch
Phoenix Symphony (AZ)	Hermann Michael
Pittsburgh (PA)	Mariss Jansons

Symphony Orchestra[2]	Music Director[3]	Symphony Orchestra[2]	Music Director[3]
Portland (ME)	Toshiyuki Shimada	Santa Rosa Symphony (CA)	Jeffrey Kahane
Rhode Island Philharmonic (RI)	Larry Rachleff	Seattle (WA)	Gerard Schwarz
Richmond Symphony (VA)	Mark Russell Smith	Spokane (WA)	Fabio Mechetti
Rochester Philharmonic Orch. (NY)	Christopher Seaman	Syracuse (NY)	Daniel Hege
St. Louis (MO)	David Amado	Toledo (OH)	Carl Topilow
St. Paul Chamber Orchestra (MN)	Andreas Delfs	Tucson (AZ)	George Hanson
San Antonio (TX)	Christopher Wilkins	Utah (Salt Lake City)	Keith Lockhart
San Diego Symphony (CA)	Murry Sidlin	Virginia Symphony (VA)	JoAnn Falletta
San Francisco (CA)	Michael Tilson Thomas	West Virginia (Charleston)	Grant Cooper
San Jose (CA)	Leonid Grin	Youngstown Symphony Orchestra (OH)	Isaiah Jackson

(1) Includes only orchestras with annual expenses $2 mil or greater. (2) If only place name is given, add Symphony Orchestra. (3) General title; listed is highest-ranking member of conducting personnel.

U.S. Opera Companies[1]

Source: OPERA America, 1156 15th Street NW, Washington, DC 20005-1704; 1999-2000 season

Anchorage Opera (AK); Ed Bourgeois, exec. dir.
Arizona Opera (Tucson); David Speers, gen. dir.
Atlanta Opera (GA); Alfred Kennedy, exec. dir.
Austin Lyric Opera (TX); Joseph McClain, gen. dir.
Baltimore Opera Company (MD); Michael Harrison, gen. dir.
Boston Lyric Opera Company (MA); Janice Mancini Del Sesto, gen. dir.
Central City Opera (Denver, CO); Pelham Pearce, gen. dir.
Chicago Opera Theater (IL); Brian Dickie, gen. dir.
Cincinnati Opera (OH); Patricia Beggs, mng. dir.
Cleveland Opera (OH); David Bamberger, gen. dir.
Connecticut Grand Opera and Orchestra (Stamford, CT); Laurence Gilgore, gen. dir.
Connecticut Opera (Hartford); Willie Anthony Waters, gen./art. dir.
Dayton Opera (OH); Mark Light, pres.
Des Moines Metro Opera, Inc. (IA); Jerilee Mace, exec. dir.
Florentine Opera Company (Milwaukee, WI); Dennis Hanthorn, gen. dir.
Florida Grand Opera (Miami, FL); Robert Heuer, gen. dir.
Fort Worth Opera (TX); Darren Keith Woods, gen. dir.
Glimmerglass Opera (Cooperstown, NY); Esther Nelson, gen. dir.
Hawaii Opera Theatre (Honolulu); Henry Akina, gen./art. dir.
Houston Grand Opera (TX); David Gockley, gen. dir.
Indianapolis Opera (IN); John C. Pickett, exec. dir.
Knoxville Opera Company (TN); Francis Graffeo, gen. dir.
Los Angeles Opera (CA); Plácido Domingo, art. dir.
Lyric Opera of Chicago (IL); William Mason, gen. dir.
Lyric Opera of Kansas City (MO); Evan R. Luskin, gen. dir.
Metropolitan Opera (New York, NY); Joseph Volpe, gen. mgr.
Michigan Opera Theatre (Detroit); David DiChiera, gen. dir.
Minnesota Opera (Minneapolis); Kevin Smith, pres./gen. dir.
Nashville Opera Association (TN); Carol Penterman, exec. dir.
New Orleans Opera Association (LA); Robert Lyall, gen. dir.
New York City Opera (NY); Paul Kellogg, gen. art. dir.
Opera Carolina (Charlotte, NC); James Meena, gen. dir.
Opera Colorado (Denver); Peter Russell, gen. dir.
Opera/Columbus (OH); Philip M. Dobard, mng. dir.
Opera Company of Philadelphia (PA); Jack Mulroney, exec. dir.
OperaDelaware (Wilmington); Leland P. Kimball III, gen. dir.
Opera Grand Rapids (MI); John Peter Jeffries, exec. dir.
Opera Memphis (TN); Michael Ching, gen./art. dir.
Opera Omaha (NE); Joan Desens, exec. dir.
Opera Pacific (Irvine, CA); Martin G. Hubbard, exec. dir.
Opera Theatre of Saint Louis (MO); Charles MacKay, gen. dir.
Orlando Opera (FL); Robert Swedberg, gen. dir.
Palm Beach Opera (FL); Herbert P. Benn, gen. dir.
Pittsburgh Opera (PA); Mark Weinstein, gen. dir.
Portland Opera (OR); Robert Bailey, gen. dir.
San Diego Opera (CA); Ian D. Campbell, gen. dir.
San Francisco Opera (CA); Pamela Rosenberg, gen. dir.
Santa Fe Opera (NM); Richard Gaddes, gen. dir.
Sarasota Opera (FL); Susan T. Danis, exec. dir.
Seattle Opera (WA); Speight Jenkins, gen. dir.
Syracuse Opera (NY); Catherine Wolff, gen. dir.
Toledo Opera (OH); Renay Conlin, gen. dir.
Tri-Cities Opera (Binghamton, NY); Grant Best, pres.
Utah Festival Opera Company (Logan); Michael Ballam, gen. dir.
Utah Opera (Salt Lake City); Anne Ewers, gen. dir.
Virginia Opera (Norfolk); Peter Mark, gen./art. dir.
Washington Opera (DC); Plácido Domingo, art. dir.
Wolf Trap Opera Company (Vienna, VA); Kim Pensinger Witman, gen. dir.

(1) Includes only opera companies with budgets of $1 million or more.

Some Notable U.S. Dance Companies

Source: DanceUSA

Organization	City	State	Organization	City	State
Alabama Ballet	Birmingham	AL	Doug Varone & Dancers/DOVA, Inc.	New York	NY
Alvin Ailey American Dance Theater	New York	NY	EIKO & KOMA	New York	NY
American Ballet Theatre	New York	NY	Felice Lesser Dance Theater	New York	NY
American Repertory Ballet Company	New Brunswick	NJ	Flamenco Vivo Carlota Santana	New York	NY
American Repertory Dance Company	Los Angeles	CA	Fort Worth Dallas Ballet	Fort Worth	TX
Aspen Santa Fe Ballet	Aspen	CO	Garth Fagan Dance	Rochester	NY
Ballet Austin	Austin	TX	Gina Gibney Dance Inc.	New York	NY
Ballet Concierto de Puerto Rico	Santurce	PR	Houston Ballet Foundation	Houston	TX
Ballet Florida	W. Palm Beach	FL	Hubbard Street Dance Chicago	Chicago	IL
Ballet Hispanico of New York	New York	NY	James Sewell Ballet	Minneapolis	MN
Ballet Memphis	Cordova	TN	Joe Goode Performance Group	San Francisco	CA
Ballet San Jose Silicon Valley	San Jose	CA	Joffrey Ballet of Chicago	Chicago	IL
Ballet West	Salt Lake City	UT	June Watanabe in Company	San Rafael	CA
BalletMet Columbus	Columbus	OH	Kansas City Ballet	Kansas City	MO
Betty Salamun's DANCECIRCUS	Milwaukee	WI	Ko-Thi Dance Company	Milwaukee	WI
Bill T. Jones/Arnie Zane Dance Company	New York	NY	Lar Lubovitch Dance Company	New York	NY
Boston Ballet	Boston	MA	Lily Cai Chinese Dance Company	San Francisco	CA
Bowen McCauley Dance	Arlington	VA	Limón Dance Company	New York	NY
Buglisi/Foreman Dance	New York	NY	Lizz Lerman Dance Exchange	Takoma Park	MD
Carolyn Dorfman Dance Company	Union	NJ	Lori Belilove & Company	New York	NY
Chamber Dance Project	Sleepy Hollow	NY	Luna Negra Dance Theatre	Chicago	IL
Charleston Ballet Theatre	Charleston	SC	Malashock Dance & Company	San Diego	CA
Chen & Dancers	New York	NY	Margaret Jenkins Dance Company	San Francisco	CA
Cincinnati Ballet	Cincinnati	OH	Mark Morris Dance Group	Brooklyn	NY
Collage Dance Theatre	Los Angeles	CA	Meredith Monk/The House Foundation	New York	NY
Colorado Ballet Company	Denver	CO	Milwaukee Ballet	Milwaukee	WI
Contemporary Dance/Fort Worth	Fort Worth	TX	Monte/Brown Dance	New York	NY
Cunningham Dance Foundation	New York	NY	Montgomery Ballet	Montgomery	AL
Dance Alloy	Pittsburgh	PA	Moving Arts Dance Company	Walnut Creek	CA
Dance Consort: Mezzacappa-Gabrian	New York	NY	Nai-Ni Chen Dance Company	Fort Lee	NJ
Dance Institute of Washington	Washington	DC	Nancy Karp and Dancers	San Francisco	CA
Dance Theatre of Harlem	New York	NY	New York City Ballet	New York	NY
Dayton Ballet	Dayton	OH	ODC/San Francisco	San Francisco	CA
Dayton Contemporary Dance Company	Dayton	OH	Ohio Ballet	Akron	OH
Demetrius Klein Dance Company	Lake Worth	FL	Pacific Northwest Ballet	Seattle	WA
Diavolo Dance Theater	Los Angeles	CA	Parsons Dance Foundation, Inc.	New York	NY
Donald Byrd/The Group	Brooklyn	NY	Paul Taylor Dance Foundation	New York	NY

Organization	City	State
Paula Jose-Jones/Performance Works	Chilmark	MA
Pittsburgh Ballet Theatre	Pittsburgh	PA
Randy James Dance Works	Highland Park	NJ
Richmond Ballet	Richmond	VA
Rincones & Company	Washington	DC
Sandra Organ Dance Company	Houston	TX
San Francisco Ballet	San Francisco	CA
Stephen Petronio Company	New York	NY
Tennessee Children's Dance Ensemble	Knoxville	TN
Trinity Irish Dance Co.	Chicago	IL
Troika Ranch	Brooklyn	NY
Tulsa Ballet Theatre	Tulsa	OK
Urban Bush Women	Brooklyn	NY
The Washington Ballet	Washington	DC
Yu Wei Dance Collection	Philadelphia	PA

Some Notable Museums

This unofficial list of some of the largest museums in the U.S. by budget was compiled with the assistance of the American Association of Museums, a national association representing the concerns of the museum community. Association members also include zoos, aquariums, arboretums, botanical gardens, and planetariums, but these are not included in *The World Almanac* listing. See also Major U.S. Public Zoological Parks and Major Canadian Public Zoological Parks.

Museum	City	State
American Museum of Natural History	New York	NY
Amon Carter Museum of Western Art	Ft. Worth	TX
The Art Institute of Chicago	Chicago	IL
Autry Museum of Western Heritage	Los Angeles	CA
Brooklyn Museum of Art	Brooklyn	NY
Busch-Reisinger Museum	Cambridge	MA
California Academy of Science	San Francisco	CA
California Science Center	Los Angeles	CA
Carnegie Museums of Pittsburgh	Pittsburgh	PA
Chicago Historical Society	Chicago	IL
Children's Museum of Indianapolis	Indianapolis	IN
Cincinnati Art Museum	Cincinnati	OH
Cincinnati Museum Center	Cincinnati	OH
Cleveland Museum of Art	Cleveland	OH
Colonial Williamsburg	Williamsburg	VA
Corning Museum of Glass	Corning	NY
Dallas Museum of Art	Dallas	TX
Denver Art Museum	Denver	CO
Denver Museum of Nature and Science	Denver	CO
Detroit Institute of Arts	Detroit	MI
Exploratorium	San Francisco	CA
The Field Museum of Natural History	Chicago	IL
Fine Arts Museum of San Francisco	San Francisco	CA
Franklin Institute	Philadelphia	PA
The Frick Collection	New York	NY
Harvard University Art Museum	Cambridge	MA
Henry F. Dupont Winterthur Museum	Winterthur	DE
Henry Ford Museum/Greenfield Village	Dearborn	MI
High Museum of Art	Atlanta	GA
Houston Museum of Natural Science	Houston	TX
Jamestown-Yorktown Foundation	Williamsburg	VA
Jewish Museum	New York	NY
L.A. County Museum of Art	Los Angeles	CA
Liberty Science Center, Liberty State Park	Jersey City	NJ
Maryland Academy of Sciences	Baltimore	MD
Maryland Science Center	Baltimore	MD
Mashantucket Pequot Museum and Research Center	Mashantucket	CT
Metropolitan Museum of Art	New York	NY
Milwaukee Public Museum	Milwaukee	WI
Minneapolis Institute of Art	Minneapolis	MN
Museum of African American History	Detroit	MI
Museum of Contemporary Art	Los Angeles	CA
Museum of Fine Arts	Boston	MA
Museum of Fine Arts	Houston	TX
Museum of Modern Art	New York	NY
Museum of New Mexico	Santa Fe	NM
Museum of Science	Boston	MA
Mystic Seaport Museum	Mystic	CT
National Air & Space Museum	Washington	DC
National Baseball Hall of Fame and Museum, Inc.	Cooperstown	NY
National Gallery of Art	Washington	DC
National Museum of American History-Smithsonian Inst.	Washington	DC
National Museum of Natural History	Washington	DC
Nelson-Atkins Museum of Art	Kansas City	MO
New York Historical Society	New York	NY
New York State Museum	Albany	NY
The Newseum	Arlington	VA
Peabody Essex Museum	Salem	MA
Pennsylvania Historical & Museum Commission	Harrisburg	PA
Philadelphia Museum of Art	Philadelphia	PA
Public Museum of Grand Rapids	Grand Rapids	MI
Rock & Roll Hall of Fame and Museum Inc.	Cleveland	OH
San Diego Museum of Art	San Diego	CA
San Francisco Museum of Modern Art	San Francisco	CA
Science Museum of Minnesota	Saint Paul	MN
Scottsdale Museum of Contemp. Art	Scottsdale	AZ
St. Louis Science Center	St. Louis	MO
Toledo Museum of Art	Toledo	OH
U.S. Holocaust Memorial Museum	Washington	DC
Univ. of Pennsylvania Museum	Philadelphia	PA
Virginia Museum of Fine Arts	Richmond	VA
Wadsworth Atheneum	Hartford	CT
Walker Art Center	Minneapolis	MN
Whitney Museum of American Art	New York	NY

Best-Selling U.S. Magazines, 2001

Source: Audit Bureau of Circulations, Schaumburg, IL

General magazines, exclusive of groups and comics; also excluding magazines that failed to file reports to ABC by press time. Based on total average paid circulation during the 6 months ending Dec. 31, 2001.

	Publication	Total paid circ.
1.	Reader's Digest	12,212,040
2.	TV Guide	9,072,609
3.	Better Homes and Gardens	7,602,575
4.	National Geographic	6,890,852
5.	Good Housekeeping	4,708,964
6.	Family Circle	4,671,052
7.	Woman's Day	4,167,933
8.	Time	4,114,137
9.	Ladies' Home Journal	4,101,280
10.	My Generation	3,846,955
11.	People Weekly	3,617,127
12.	Rosie	3,503,993
13.	Westways	3,328,280
14.	Home and Away	3,313,966
15.	Sports Illustrated	3,252,896
16.	Newsweek	3,248,097
17.	Playboy	3,217,269
18.	Prevention	3,131,814
19.	Cosmopolitan	2,963,351
20.	Guideposts	2,747,626
21.	Via Magazine	2,655,203
22.	The American Legion Magazine	2,644,518
23.	Maxim	2,569,172
24.	Southern Living	2,546,471
25.	Glamour	2,509,566
26.	Seventeen	2,431,943
27.	Redbook	2,380,410
28.	Martha Stewart Living	2,323,129
29.	O, The Oprah Magazine	2,275,599
30.	YM	2,262,574
31.	AAA Going Places	2,191,629
32.	Parents	2,092,443
33.	Smithsonian	2,040,294
34.	Parenting Magazine	2,039,462
35.	U.S. News & World Report	2,018,621
36.	Money	1,945,265
37.	Ebony	1,884,739
38.	National Enquirer	1,801,598
39.	Country Living	1,711,449
40.	Shape	1,692,690
41.	Woman's World	1,668,482
42.	In Style	1,660,193
43.	Men's Health	1,659,594
44.	Teen People	1,651,723
45.	V.F.W. Magazine	1,645,944
46.	Entertainment Weekly	1,635,623
47.	Cooking Light	1,603,680
48.	Golf Digest	1,578,248
49.	Endless Vacation	1,541,107
50.	ESPN The Magazine	1,536,346
51.	First for Women	1,534,370
52.	American Rifleman	1,525,370
53.	Field & Stream	1,519,280
54.	Family Fun	1,482,788
55.	Popular Science	1,468,346
56.	Sunset	1,446,911
57.	Star	1,435,863
58.	Golf Magazine	1,426,304
59.	Boys' Life	1,410,198
60.	Health	1,407,660
61.	Car and Driver	1,369,848
62.	Self	1,284,604
63.	Motor Trend	1,272,053
64.	Bon Appetit	1,263,134
65.	Rolling Stone	1,254,200
66.	Vogue	1,245,490
67.	Popular Mechanics	1,239,186
68.	PC Magazine	1,232,840
69.	Scholastic Parent and Child	1,223,634
70.	Fitness	1,197,638
71.	Stuff	1,170,555
72.	The Family Handyman	1,152,187
73.	Outdoor Life	1,149,876
74.	The American Hunter	1,113,834

Publication	Total paid circ.	Publication	Total paid circ.	Publication	Total paid circ.
75. PC World	1,112,089	83. Discover	1,054,788	92. Business Week	977,128
76. Vanity Fair	1,107,802	84. Cosmo Girl!	1,054,638	93. This Old House	974,052
77. Country Home	1,101,234	85. Essence	1,052,925	94. Travel + Leisure	960,779
78. The Elks Magazine	1,078,955	86. Real Simple	1,047,796	95. Food & Wine	957,838
79. Kiplinger's Personal Finance	1,072,471	87. Soap Opera Digest	1,041,354	96. Victoria	957,638
80. Us Weekly	1,065,589	88. Michigan Living	1,037,811	97. Allure	957,276
81. Scouting	1,056,679	89. Home	1,010,623	98. Marie Claire	952,223
82. FHM (For Him Magazine)	1,056,587	90. Elle	989,728	99. Child	942,193
		91. Jet	987,121	100. Gourmet	934,778

Some Notable New Books, 2001

Source: List published by American Library Association, Chicago, IL, 2002, for books published in 2001

Fiction

True History of the Kelly Gang, Peter Carey
Among the Missing, Dan Chaon
Samuel Johnson Is Indignant: Stories, Lydia Davis
Erasure, Percival Everett
The Corrections, Jonathan Franzen
The Pickup, Nadine Gordimer
Island: The Complete Stories, Alistair MacLeod
Bucking the Tiger, Bruce Olds
Austerlitz, W.G Sebald
The Death of Vishnu, Manil Suri
Crooked River Burning, Mark Winegardner

Poetry

Sailing Alone Around the Room: New and Selected Poems, Billy Collins
What the Ice Gets: Shackleton's Antarctic Expedition 1914-1916, Melinda Mueller

Nonfiction

American Chica: Two Worlds, One Childhood, Marie Arana
Aztec Treasure House: New and Selected Essays, Evan Connell
An Unexpected Light: Travels in Afghanistan, Jason Elliot
War in a Time of Peace: Bush, Clinton and the Generals, David Halberstam
Going up the River: Travels in a Prison Nation, Joseph T. Hallinan
River Town: Two Years on the Yangtze, Peter Hessler
Seabiscuit: an American Legend, Laura Hillenbrand
The Breast Cancer Wars: Hope, Fear & the Pursuit of a Cure in Twentieth-Century America, Barron H. Lerner
Crossing Over: A Mexican Family on the Migrant Trail, Ruben Martinez
John Adams, David McCullough
Fast Food Nation: The Dark Side of the All-American Meal, Eric Schlosser
Grant, Jean Edward Smith
The Noonday Demon: An Atlas of Depression, Andrew Solomon

Young Adults

Nonfiction

Voices: Poetry and Art From Around the World, Barbara Brenner (editor)
Coup: The True Story of Basketball and Honor on the Little Big Horn, Larry Colton
Fighting for Honor: Japanese Americans and World War II, Michael Cooper
Finding Fish, Antwone Fisher with Mim Eichler Rivas
Bound for the North Star: True Stories of Fugitive Slaves, Dennis Brindell Fradin
Things I Have to Tell You: Poems and Writing by Teenage Girls, Betsy Franco (editor)
Vincent Van Gogh: Portrait of an Artist, Jan and Sandra Jordan Greenberg
Heart to Heart: New Poems Inspired by 20th Century American Art, Jan Greenberg (editor)
We Were There, Too!: Young People in U.S. History, Phillip Hoose
Failure Is Impossible: The History of American Women's Rights, Martha Kendall
Into the New Country: Eight Remarkable Women of the West, Liza Ketchum
Chess: From First Moves to Checkmate, Daniel King
Helen Keller: Rebellious Spirit, Laurie Lawlor
Bruce Lee: The Celebrated Life of the Golden Dragon, Bruce Lee (selected and edited by John Little)
George *Washington and the Founding of a Nation*, Albert Marrin
Blizzard: The Storm that Changed America, Jim Murphy
Bad Boy: A Memoir, Walter Dean Myers
The Greatest: Muhammad Ali, Walter Dean Myers
Yell-OH Girls!: Emerging Voices Explore Culture, Identity and Growing-Up Asian American, Vickie Nam (editor)
Carver: A Life in Poems, Marilyn Nelson
Shout, Sister, Shout!: Ten Girl Singers Who Shaped a Century, Roxane Orgill
Hidden Evidence: Forty True Crimes and How Forensic Science Helped Solve Them, David Owen
Words with Wings: A Treasury of African-American Poetry and Art, Belinda Rochelle (editor)

Fiction

A Matter of Profit, Hilari Bell
The Sisterhood of the Traveling Pants, Ann Brashares
All That Remains, Bruce Brooks
Shadow of the Hegemon, Orson Scott Card
Love and Sex: Ten Stories of Truth, Michael Cart (editor)
Fire Bringer, David Clement-Davies
The Rag and Bone Shop, Robert Cormier
Whale Talk, Chris Crutcher
Eight Seconds, Jean Ferris
Of Sound Mind, Jean Ferris
Seek, Paul Fleischman
Breathing Underwater, Alex Flinn
On the Fringe, Don Gallo (editor)
Troy, Adele Geras
Amandine, Adele Griffin
The Grave, James Heneghan
Boston Jane: An Adventure, Jennifer Holm
Color of Absence: Twelve Stories About Love and Hope, James Howe (editor)
Damage, A. M. Jenkins
Breaking Through, Francisco Jimenez
Secret Sacrament, Sherryl Jordan
You Don't Know Me, David Klass
Brimstone Journals, Ron Koertge
The Stones of Mourning Creek, Diane Les Becquets
Freewill, Chris Lynch
Cut, Patricia McCormick
Spellbound, Janet McDonald
Shades of Simon Gray, Joyce McDonald
Touching Spirit Bear, Ben Mikaelsen
Feeling Sorry for Celia, Jaclyn Moriarty
Zazoo, Richard Mosher
A Step from Heaven, An Na
The Other Side of Truth, Beverly Naidoo
Lirael, Garth Nix
Born Blue, Han Nolan
A Single Shard, Linda Sue Park
Fair Weather, Richard Peck
Treasure at the Heart of the Tanglewood, Meredith Ann Pierce
Protector of the Small: Squire, Tamora Pierce
The Amazing Maurice and His Educated Rodents, Terry Pratchett
The Amber Spyglass, Philip Pullman
Witch Child, Celia Rees
Crazy Loco, David Rice
Empress of the World, Sara Ryan
The Lord of the Deep, Graham Salisbury
Rainbow Boys, Alex Sanchez
Summers at Castle Auburn, Sharon Shinn
What My Mother Doesn't Know, Sonya Sones
Leslie's Journal, Allan Stratton
The Gospel According to Larry, Janet Tashjian
The Land, Mildred Taylor
The Edge on the Sword, Rebecca Tingle
Sights, Susanna Vance
Being Dead, Vivian Vande Velde
Motherland, Vineeta Vijayaraghaven
Rooster, Beth Weaver
Black Mirror, Nancy Werlin
Every Time a Rainbow Dies, Rita Williams-Garcia
Razzle, Ellen Wittlinger
True Believer, Virginia Euwer Wolff
Fighting Ruben Wolfe, Markus Zusak

Some Notable New Books for Children, 2001

Source: List published by American Library Association, Chicago, IL, 2002, for books published in 2001.

Younger Readers

Milo's Hat Trick, Jon Agee
Iguanas in the Snow, Francisco X. Alarcón
My Car, Byron Barton
Crossing, Philip Booth
Inside Freight Train, Donald Crews
Waiting for Wings, Lois Ehlert
Olivia Saves the Circus, Ian Falconer
Turtle Splash: Countdown at the Pond, Cathryn Falwell
The Hickory Chair, Lisa Rowe Fraustino
"Let's Get A Pup," Said Kate, Bob Graham
Sheila Rae's Peppermint Stick, Kevin Henkes
You Read to Me, I'll Read to You: Very Short Stories to Read Together, Mary Ann Hoberman
Kipper's A to Z: An Alphabet Adventure, Mick Inkpen
Five Creatures, Emily Jenkins
Emma's Yucky Brother, Jean Little
Harley, Star Livingston
Henry's First-Moon Birthday, Lenore Look
The Race of the Birkebeiners, Lise Lunge-Larsen
Goin' Someplace Special, Patricia C. McKissack
Gus and Grandpa at Basketball, Claudia Mills
Juan Bobo Goes to Work, Marisa Montes
The Web Files, Margie Palatini
Mice and Beans, Pam Muñoz Ryan
The Stray Dog, Marc Simont
Car Wash, Sandra and Susan Steen
And the Dish Ran Away with the Spoon, Janet Stevens and Susan Stevens Crummel
Clever Beatrice, Margaret Willey
The Other Side, Jacqueline Woodson
Lady Lollipop, Dick King-Smith

Middle Readers

Remember Pearl Harbor: American and Japanese Survivors Tell Their Stories, Thomas B. Allen
Handel: Who Knew What He Liked, M.T. Anderson
Shipwrecked!: The True Adventures of a Japanese Boy, Rhoda Blumberg
Skeleton Man, Joseph Bruchac
Storm Warriors, Elisa Carbone
Woody Guthrie: Poet of the People, Bonnie Christensen
Love That Dog, Sharon Creech
Brooklyn Bridge, Lynn Curlee
In the Days of the Vaqueros: America's First True Cowboys, Russell Freedman
Leonardo's Horse, Jean Fritz
The Hero of Ticonderoga, Gail Gauthier
The Chimpanzees I Love: Saving Their World and Ours, Jane Goodall
How I Became an American, Karin Gündisch
Runaway Radish, Jessie Haas
Everything on a Waffle, Polly Horvath
Celebrating Ramadan, Diane Hoyt-Goldsmith
The Black Bull of Norroway: A Scottish Tale, Charlotte Huck
Rocks in His Head, Carol Otis Hurst
The Dinosaurs of Waterhouse Hawkins: An Illuminating History of Mr. Waterhouse Hawkins, Artist and Lecturer, Barbara Kerley
Lady Lollipop, Dick King-Smith
Hidden Worlds: Looking Through a Scientist's Microscope, Stephen Kramer
The Cod's Tale, Mark Kurlansky
Bull's Eye: A Photobiography of Annie Oakley, Sue Macy
The Lamp, the Ice, and the Boat Called Fish, Jacqueline Martin
Judy Moody Gets Famous!, Megan McDonald
A Book of Coupons, Susie Morgenstern
A Single Shard, Linda Sue Park
Traveling Man: The Journey of Ibn Battuta, 1325-1354, James Rumford
Esperanza Rising, Pam Muñoz Ryan
Blister, Susan Shreve
Love, Ruby Lavender, Deborah Wiles
Coolies, Yin
Dinosaur Parents, Dinosaur Young: Uncovering the Mystery of Dinosaur Families, Kathleen Zoehfeld

Older Readers-Junior High School

The Gawgon and the Boy, Lloyd Alexander
Heaven Eyes, David Almond
Black Potatoes: The Story of the Great Irish Famine, 1845-1850, Susan Campbell Bartoletti
The Seeing Stone, Kevin Crossley-Holland
A Face First, Priscilla Cummings
The World at Her Fingertips: The Story of Helen Keller, Joan Dash
The Ropemaker, Peter Dickinson
Seek, Paul Fleischman
Heart to Heart: New Poems Inspired by Twentieth-Century American Art, Jan Greenberg (editor)
Vincent van Gogh: Portrait of an Artist, Jan Greenberg and Sandra Jordan
Witness, Karen Hesse
We Were There, Too!: Young People in U.S. History, Phillip Hoose
Breaking Through, Francisco Jiménez
Helen Keller: Rebellious Spirit, Laurie Lawlor
Zazoo, Richard Mosher
The Greatest: Muhammad Ali, Walter Dean Myers
A Step from Heaven, An Na
The Other Side of Truth, Beverley Naidoo
Carver: A Life in Poems, Marilyn Nelson
Slaves of the Mastery, William Nicholson
Words With Wings: A Treasury of African-American Poetry and Art, Belinda Rochelle (editor)
The Land, Mildred Taylor
Surviving Hitler: A Boy in the Nazi Death Camps, Andrea Warren
True Believer, Virginia Euwer Wolff

All Ages

A Poke in the I: A Collection of Concrete Poems, Paul Janeczko (editor)
The Midnight Ride of Paul Revere, Henry Wadsworth Longfellow
Martin's Big Words: The Life of Dr. Martin Luther King, Jr, Doreen Rappaport
The Three Pigs, David Wiesner
Amber Was Brave, Essie Was Smart, Vera B. Williams.

Best-Selling Books, 2001

Source: *Publishers Weekly*

Rankings are based on copies "shipped and billed" in 2001, minus returns through early 2002.

Fiction

1. *Desecration*, Jerry B. Jenkins and Tim LaHaye
2. *Skipping Christmas*, John Grisham
3. *A Painted House*, John Grisham
4. *Dreamcatcher*, Stephen King
5. *The Corrections*, Jonathan Franzen
6. *Black House*, Stephen King and Peter Straub
7. *The Kiss*, Danielle Steel
8. *Valhalla Rising*, Clive Cussler
9. *A Day Late and a Dollar Short*, Terry McMillan
10. *Violets Are Blue*, James Patterson
11. *P Is for Peril*, Sue Grafton
12. *He Sees You When You're Sleeping*, Mary and Carol Higgins Clark
13. *A Common Life*, Jan Karon
14. *Isle of Dogs*, Patricia Cornwell
15. *Suzanne's Diary for Nicholas*, James Patterson

Nonfiction

1. *The Prayer of Jabez*, Bruce Wilkinson
2. *Secrets of the Vine*, Bruce Wilkinson
3. *Who Moved My Cheese?*, Spencer Johnson
4. *John Adams*, David McCullough
5. *Guinness World Records 2002*, Guinness World Records Ltd.
6. *Prayer of Jabez Devotional*, Bruce Wilkinson
7. *The No Spin Zone: Confrontations with the Powerful and Famous in America*, Bill O'Reilly
8. *Body for Life: 12 Weeks to Mental and Physical Strength*, Bill Phillips
9. *How I Play Golf*, Tiger Woods
10. *Jack*, Jack Welch
11. *I Hope You Dance*, Mark D. Sanders and Tia Sillers
12. *Self Matters*, Phillip C. McGraw
13. *The Blue Day Book*, Bradley Trevor Greive
14. *The Road to Wealth*, Suze Orman
15. *America's Heroes: Inspiring Stories of Courage, Sacrifice and Patriotism*, the editors at SP LLC.

Trade Paperbacks

1. *Life Strategies*, Phillip McGraw
2. *We Were the Mulvaneys*, Joyce Carol Oates
3. *The Indwelling*, Jerry B. Jenkins and Tim LaHaye
4. *The Lord of the Rings*, J.R.R. Tolkien
5. *Icy Sparks*. Gwyn Hyman Rubio
6. *The Red Tent*, Anita Diamant
7. *Girl with a Pearl Earring*, Tracy Chevalier

8. *The Fellowship of the Ring,* J.R.R. Tolkien
9. *The Mark: The Beast Rules the World,* Jerry B. Jenkins and Tim LaHaye
10. *Left Behind,* Jerry B. Jenkins and Tim LaHaye
11. *Bridget Jones's Diary,* Helen Fielding
12. *The Hobbit,* J.R.R. Tolkien
13. *Band of Brothers,* Stephen E. Ambrose
14. *The Four Agreements,* Don Miguel Ruiz
15. *Tribulation Force,* Jerry B. Jenkins and Tim LaHaye

Almanacs, Atlases, and Annuals

1. *The World Almanac and Book of Facts 2002,* Edited by Ken Park
2. *The World Almanac and Book of Facts 2001,* Edited by Ken Park
3. *The Ernst & Young Tax Guide 2002*
4. *J.K. Lasser's Your Income Tax 2002*
5. *The Best American Short Stories 2001,* Edited by Barbara Kingsolver

Mass Market

1. *A Painted House,* John Grisham
2. *Hannibal,* Thomas Harris
3. *Dance Upon the Air,* Nora Roberts
4. *Heaven and Earth,* Nora Roberts
5. *Bear and Dragon,* Tom Clancy
6. *Carolina Moon,* Nora Roberts
7. *The Lord of the Rings: The Fellowship of the Ring,* J.R.R. Tolkien
8. *Last Precinct,* Patricia Cornwell
9. *Before I Say Goodbye,* Mary Higgins Clark
10. *Time and Again,* Nora Roberts
11. *Reflections and Dreams,* Nora Roberts
12. *Journey,* Danielle Steel
13. *Stanislaski Sisters,* Nora Roberts
14. *The Hobbit,* J.R.R. Tolkien
15. *Dreamcatcher,* Stephen King

Leading U.S. Daily Newspapers, 2001

Source: 2001 *Editor & Publisher International Yearbook*

(Circulation as of Sept. 30, 2001; m = morning, e = evening)

As of Feb. 1, 2002, the number of U.S. daily newspapers had dropped to 1,468, for a net loss of 12 since Feb. 1, 2001. Average daily circulation for the 6 months ending Sept. 30, 2001, was 55,578,801, down 194,801 from the same period in 2000, for a decrease of about 0.3%. The overall number of Sunday papers decreased by 4 to 913. Average Sunday circulation for the 6 months ending Sept. 30, 2001, fell 330,635, or about 0.6%, from 59,420,999 to 59,090,364.

Newspaper		Circulation
1. Arlington (VA) *USA Today*	(m)	2,149,933
2. New York (NY) *Wall Street Journal*	(m)	1,780,605
3. New York (NY) *Times*	(m)	1,109,371
4. Los Angeles (CA) *Times*	(m)	944,303
5. Washington (DC) *Post*	(m)	759,864
6. New York (NY) *Daily News*	(m)	734,473
7. Chicago (IL) *Tribune*	(m)	675,847
8. Long Island (NY) *Newsday*	(m)	577,354
9. Houston (TX) *Chronicle*	(m)	551,854
10. New York (NY) *Post*	(m)	533,860
11. San Francisco (CA) *Chronicle*	(all day)	512,042
12. Dallas (TX) *Morning News*	(m)	494,890
13. Chicago (IL) *Sun-Times*	(m)	480,920
14. Boston (MA) *Globe*	(m)	471,199
15. Phoenix (AZ) *Arizona Republic*	(m)	451,288
16. Newark (NJ) *Star-Ledger*	(m)	410,547
17. Atlanta (GA) *Journal-Constitution*	(m)	396,464
18. Detroit (MI) *Free Press*	(m)	371,261
19. Philadelphia (PA) *Inquirer*	(m)	365,154
20. Cleveland(OH) *Plain Dealer*	(m)	359,978
21. San Diego (CA) *Union-Tribune*	(m)	351,762
22. Portland (OR) *Oregonian*	(all day)	351,303
23. Minneapolis (MN) *Star Tribune*	(m)	340,445
24. St. Petersburg (FL) *Times*	(m)	331,903
25. Orange County (CA) *Register*	(m)	324,056
26. Miami (FL) *Herald*	(m)	317,690
27. Denver (CO) *Rocky Mountain News*	(m)	309,938
28. Baltimore (MD) *Sun*	(m)	306,341
29. Denver (CO) *Post*	(m)	305,929
30. St. Louis (MO) *Post-Dispatch*	(m)	290,615
31. Sacramento (CA) *Bee*	(m)	285,863
32. Los Angeles (CA) *Investor's Business Daily*	(m)	281,173
33. San Jose (CA) *Mercury News*	(m)	268,621
34. Kansas City (MO) *Star*	(m)	259,612
35. Boston (MA) *Herald*	(m)	259,228
36. Milwaukee (WI) *Journal Sentinel*	(m)	255,098
37. Orlando (FL) *Sentinel*	(all day)	260,802
38. New Orleans (LA) *Times-Picayune*	(m)	254,897
39. Indianapolis (IN) *Star*	(m)	252,349
40. Fort Lauderdale (FL) *Sun-Sentinel*	(m)	251,886
41. Columbus (OH) *Dispatch*	(m)	244,204
42. Detroit (MI) *News*	(e)	242,855
43. Pittsburgh (PA) *Post-Gazette*	(m)	242,141
44. Charlotte (NC) *Observer*	(m)	235,375
45. Louisville (KY) *Courier-Journal*	(m)	222,332
46. Seattle (WA) *Times*	(m)	219,941
47. Buffalo (NY) *News*	(all day)	218,781
48. Fort Worth (TX) *Star-Telegram*	(m)	213,781
49. Tampa (FL) *Tribune*	(m)	212,983
50. San Antonio (TX) *Express-News*	(m)	208,951
51. Hartford (CT) *Courant*	(m)	198,651
52. Omaha (NE) *World-Herald*	(m)	196,326
53. Norfolk (VA) *Virginian-Pilot*	(m)	195,583
54. Oklahoma City (OK) *Daily Oklahoman*	(m)	195,454
55. St. Paul (MN) *Pioneer Press*	(m)	195,042
56. Richmond (VA) *Times-Dispatch*	(m)	190,509
57. Cincinnati (OH) *Enquirer*	(m)	188,173
58. Austin (TX) *American-Statesman*	(m)	183,873
59. Nashville (TN) *Tennessean*	(m)	183,406
60. Walnut Creek (CA) *Contra Costa Times*	(m)	182,727
61. Little Rock (AR) *Democrat-Gazette*	(m)	182,609
62. Los Angeles (CA) *Daily News*	(m)	178,156
63. Bergen County (NJ) *Record*	(m)	178,029
64. Rochester (NY) *Democrat and Chronicle*	(m)	176,040
65. Jacksonville (FL) *Times-Union*	(m)	172,239
66. West Palm Beach (FL) *Post*	(m)	171,572
67. Neptune (NJ) *Asbury Park Press*	(m)	170,229
68. Seattle (WA) *Post-Intelligencer*	(m)	169,105
69. Riverside (CA) *Press-Enterprise*	(m)	168,765
70. Providence (RI) *Journal*	(m)	165,880
71. Las Vegas (NV) *Review-Journal*	(m)	165,754
72. Raleigh (NC) *News & Observer*	(m)	162,869
73. Fresno (CA) *Bee*	(m)	157,820
74. Memphis (TN) *Commercial Appeal*	(m)	155,196
75. Philadelphia (PA) *Daily News*	(m)	152,435
76. Des Moines (IA) *Register*	(m)	152,402
77. Honolulu (HI) *Advertiser*	(all day)	152,098
78. Arlington Heights (IL) *Daily Herald*	(m)	148,375
79. Birmingham (AL) *News*	(m)	145,760
80. White Plains (NY) *Journal News*	(m)	144,439
81. Akron (OH) *Beacon Journal*	(m)	141,073
82. Toledo (OH) *Blade*	(m)	140,406
83. Grand Rapids (MI) *Press*	(e)	139,800
84. Tulsa (OK) *World*	(m)	139,383
85. Dayton (OH) *Daily News*	(m)	135,818
86. Salt Lake City (UT) *Tribune*	(m)	134,712
87. Allentown (PA) *Morning Call*	(m)	128,204
88. Tacoma (WA) *News Tribune*	(m)	127,786
89. Los Angeles (CA) *La Opinion*	(m)	127,576
90. Syracuse (NY) *The Post-Standard*	(m)	126,761
91. Greensburg (PA) *Tribune-Review*	(m)	124,851
92. Wilmington (DE) *News Journal*	(all day)	121,480
93. Columbia (SC) *State*	(m)	117,423
94. Knoxville (TN) *News-Sentinel*	(m)	114,989
95. Albuquerque (NM) *Journal*	(m)	108,668
96. Lexington (KY) *Herald-Leader*	(m)	107,670
97. Sarasota (FL) *Herald-Tribune*	(m)	106,077
98. Spokane (WA) *Spokesman-Review*	(m)	105,911
99. Worcester (MA) *Telegram & Gazette*	(m)	103,565
100. Washington (DC) *Times*	(m)	103,505

Leading Canadian Daily Newspapers, 2001

Source: 2001 *Editor & Publisher International Yearbook*

(Circulation as of Sept. 30, 2001; m = morning)

Newspaper		Circulation
Toronto (ON) *Star*	(m)	460,989
Toronto (ON) *Globe and Mail*	(m)	368,857
Toronto (ON) *National Post*	(m)	320,224
Montreal (QC) *Le Journal*	(m)	259,081
Toronto (ON) *Sun*	(m)	228,596
Vancouver (BC) *Sun*	(m)	187,170
Montreal (QC) *La Presse*	(m)	183,178
Vancouver (BC) *Province*	(m)	157,896
Montreal (QC) *Gazette*	(m)	136,463
Edmonton (AB) *Journal*	(m)	136,193

Top 20 News/Information Websites, July 2002

Source: comScore Media Metrix, Inc.

Rank		Visitors[1]
1.	CNN.COM (www.cnn.com)	121,758
2.	AOL Proprietary News*	78,352
3.	Yahoo! News (news.yahoo.com)	21,717
4.	WeatherBug (www.weatherbug.com)	18,228
5.	MSNBC (www.msnbc.com)	16,114
6.	ABOUT.COM (www.about.com)	16,006
7.	The Weather Channel (www.weather.com)	15,704
8.	New York Times Digital* (www.nytimes.com)	15,310
9.	ABC News Digital* (abc.abcnews.go.com)	14,252
10.	Time.com Sites* (www.time.com)	10,597
11.	Tribune Interactive*	9,329
12.	USATODAY Sites* (www.usatoday.com)	8,912
13.	Knight Ridder Digital*	7,988
14.	CBS Sites* (www.cbs.com)	7,926
15.	AOL Newsgroup*	5,984
16.	WASHINGTONPOST.COM (www.washingtonpost.com)	4,989
17.	MSN Slate (www.slate.msn.com)	4,890
18.	Discovery.com Sites* (www.discovery.com)	4,660
19.	Hearst Newspaper Digital*	4,563
20.	BBC.CO.UK (www.bbc.co.uk)	4,552

(1) Number of unique visitors in thousands who visited website at least once in July 2002. *Represents an aggregation of commonly owned/branded domain names.

U.S. Commercial Radio Stations, by Format, 1995-2002[1]

Source: M Street Corporation, Littleton, NH © 2002; counts are for June of each year

Primary format	2002	2001	1999	1998	1997	1996	1995
1. Country	2,131	2,190	2,306	2,368	2,491	2,525	2,613
2. News/Talk	1,179	1,139	1,159	1,131	1,111	1,116	1,036
3. Oldies	813	786	766	799	755	738	710
4. Adult Contemporary (AC)	713	709	775	844	902	952	1,052
5. Spanish	603	574	536	493	474	463	427
6. Adult Standards	547	509	595	561	551	499	470
7. Top 40	474	468	401	379	358	333	318
8. Hot AC	395	369	325	281	260	283	256
9. Sports	388	338	256	251	220	156	148
10. Classic Rock	384	338	314	282	240	349	306
11. Soft AC	340	375	382	368	346	337	347
12. Religion (Teaching, Variety)	332	356	363	356	404	424	418
13. Rock	278	282	280	266	262	273	301
14. Classic Hits	258	265	222	192	172	—	—
15. Black Gospel	254	264	257	238	208	166	147
16. Southern Gospel	240	255	269	273	255	248	239
17. R&B	193	183	166	171	169	183	184
18. Contemporary Christian	164	164	167	164	159	142	132
19. Modern Rock	147	140	136	145	137	147	141
20. Urban AC	121	118	112	127	134	121	116
Off Air	110	113	96	102	143	279	308
Changing format/not available	5	3	3	3	2	4	19
TOTAL STATIONS	**10,569**	**10,516**	**10,444**	**10,292**	**10,207**	**9,991**	**9,889**

(1) Data for 2000 unavailable.

Top-Grossing North American Concert Tours, 1985-2001

Source: Pollstar, Fresno, CA

Artist (Year)	Total gross[1]	Cities/ Shows
1. The Rolling Stones (1994)	$121.2	43/60
2. U2 (2001)	109.7	56/80
3. Pink Floyd (1994)	103.5	39/59
4. The Rolling Stones (1989)	98.0	33/60
5. The Rolling Stones (1997)	89.3	26/33
6. 'N Sync (2001)	86.8	36/43
7. Backstreet Boys (2001)	82.1	73/98
8. Tina Turner (2000)	80.2	88/95
9. U2 (1997)	79.9	37/46
10. The Eagles (1994)	79.4	32/54
11. 'N Sync (2000)	76.4	64/86
12. The New Kids on the Block (1990)	$74.1	122/152
13. Dave Matthews Band (2000)	68.2	43/63
14. U2 (1992)	67.0	61/73
15. The Rolling Stones (1999)	64.7	26/34
16. The Eagles (1995)	63.3	46/58
17. KISS (2000)	62.7	120/128
18. Bruce Springsteen & The E Street Band (1999)	61.4	18/54
19. Dave Matthews Band (2001)	60.5	36/51
20. Barbra Streisand (1994)	58.9	6/22

(1) In millions. Not adjusted for inflation.

Sales of Recorded Music and Music Videos, by Genre and Format, 1996-2001

Source: Recording Industry Assn. of America, Washington, DC

Breakdown is by percentage of sales revenue for all recorded music sold, ranked for 2001.

GENRE	2001	2000	1999	1998	1997	1996
Rock	24.4	24.8	25.2	25.7	32.5	32.6
Pop	12.1	11.0	10.3	10.0	9.4	9.3
Rap/Hip-Hop[1]	11.4	12.9	10.8	9.7	10.1	8.9
R&B/Urban[2]	10.6	9.7	10.5	12.8	11.2	12.1
Country	10.5	10.7	10.8	14.1	14.4	14.7
Religious[3]	6.7	4.8	5.1	6.3	4.5	4.3
Jazz	3.4	2.9	3.0	1.9	2.8	3.3
Classical	3.2	2.7	3.5	3.3	2.8	3.4
Soundtracks	1.4	0.7	0.8	1.7	1.2	0.8
New Age	1.0	0.5	0.5	0.6	0.8	0.7
Oldies	0.8	0.9	0.7	0.7	0.8	0.8
Children's	0.5	0.6	0.4	0.4	0.9	0.7
Other[4]	7.9	8.3	9.1	7.9	5.7	5.2
FORMAT						
Compact disc (CD)	68.4	70.2	74.8	83.2	89.3	89.2
Cassette	19.3	18.2	14.8	8.0	4.9	3.4
Singles (all types)	9.3	9.3	6.8	5.4	2.5	2.4
Music Videos/ Digital video disc (DVD)[5]	1.0	0.6	1.0	0.9	0.8	1.1
LPs	0.6	0.7	0.7	0.5	0.5	0.6

(1) "Rap" includes Rap (9.1% in 2001) and Hip-Hop (2.3% in 2001). (2) "R&B" includes R&B, blues, dance, disco, funk, fusion, Motown, reggae, soul. (3) "Religious" includes Christian, Gospel, Inspirational, Religious, and Spiritual. (4) "Other" includes Ethnic, Standards, Big Band, Swing, Latin, Electronic, Instrumental, Comedy, Humor, Spoken Word, Exercise, Language, Folk and Holiday Music. (5) 2001 is the first year that music video DVD was recorded separately.

Sales of Recorded Music and Music Videos, by Units Shipped and Value, 1992-2001

Source: Recording Industry Assn. of America, Washington, DC
(in millions, net after returns)

FORMAT	1992	1993	1994	1995	1996	1997	1998	1999	2000	2001	% CHANGE 2000-2001
Compact disc (CD)											
Units shipped	407.5	495.4	662.1	722.9	778.9	753.1	847.0	938.9	942.5	881.9	–6.4%
Dollar value	5,326.5	6,511.4	8,464.5	9,377.4	9,934.7	9,915.1	11,416.0	12,816.3	13,214.5	12,909.4	–2.3%
CD single											
Units shipped	7.3	7.8	9.3	21.5	43.2	66.7	56.0	55.9	34.2	17.3	–49.4%
Dollar value	45.1	45.8	56.1	110.9	184.1	272.7	213.2	222.4	142.7	79.4	–44.4%
Cassette											
Units shipped	366.4	339.5	345.4	272.6	225.3	172.6	158.5	123.6	76.0	45.0	–40.8%
Dollar value	3,116.3	2,915.8	2,976.4	2,303.6	1,905.3	1,522.7	1,419.9	1,061.6	626.0	363.4	–41.9%
Cassette single											
Units shipped	84.6	85.6	81.1	70.7	59.9	42.2	26.4	14.2	1.3	–1.5	–215.4%
Dollar value	298.8	298.5	274.9	236.3	189.3	133.5	94.4	48.0	4.6	–5.3	–215.2%
LP/EP											
Units shipped	2.3	1.2	1.9	2.2	2.9	2.7	3.4	2.9	2.2	2.3	4.5%
Dollar value	13.5	10.6	17.8	25.1	36.8	33.3	34.0	31.8	27.7	27.4	–1.1%
Vinyl single											
Units shipped	19.8	15.1	11.7	10.2	10.1	7.5	5.4	5.3	4.8	5.5	14.6%
Dollar value	66.4	51.2	47.2	46.7	47.5	35.6	25.7	27.9	26.3	31.4	19.4%
Music video											
Units shipped	7.6	11.0	11.2	12.6	16.9	18.6	27.2	19.8	18.2	17.7	–2.7%
Dollar value	157.4	213.3	231.1	220.3	236.1	323.9	508.0	376.7	281.9	329.2	16.8%
DVD audio											
Units shipped	—	—	—	—	—	—	—	—	—	0.3	NA
Dollar value	—	—	—	—	—	—	—	—	—	6.0	NA
DVD video*											
Units shipped	—	—	—	—	—	—	0.5	2.5	3.3	7.9	139.4%
Dollar value	—	—	—	—	—	—	12.2	66.3	80.3	190.7	137.5%
TOTAL UNITS	**895.5**	**955.6**	**1,122.7**	**1,112.7**	**1,137.2**	**1,063.4**	**1,123.9**	**1,160.6**	**1,079.2**	**968.5**	**–10.3%**
TOTAL VALUE	**9,024.0**	**10,046.6**	**12,068.0**	**12,320.3**	**12,533.8**	**12,236.8**	**13,711.2**	**14,584.7**	**14,323.7**	**13,740.9**	**–4.1%**

* While broken out for this chart, DVD Video Product is included in the Music Video totals. NA = Not applicable.

Multi-Platinum and Platinum Awards for Recorded Music and Music Videos, 2001

Source: Recording Industry Assn. of America, Washington, DC

To achieve platinum status, an **album** must reach a minimum sale of 1 mil units in LPs, tapes, and CDs, with a manufacturer's dollar volume of at least $2 mil based on one-third of the suggested retail list price for each record, tape, or CD sold. To achieve multi-platinum status, an album must reach a minimum sale of at least 2 mil units in LPs, tapes, and CDs, with a manufacturer's dollar volume of at least $4 mil based on one-third of the list price.

Singles must sell 1 mil units to achieve a platinum award and 2 mil to achieve a multi-platinum award. EP singles count as 2 units. Double-CD sets count as 2 units. **Music videos** (long form) must sell 100,000 units to qualify for a platinum award and must sell more than 200,000 units for a multi-platinum award. **Video singles**, which must have a maximum running time of 15 minutes and no more than 2 songs per title, must sell 50,000 units to qualify for a platinum award and at least 100,000 units to qualify for a multi-platinum award.

Awards listed were for albums and singles released in 2001 and for music videos released at any time.

Albums, Multi-Platinum

(numbers in parentheses = millions sold)

8701, Usher (2)
All for You, Janet Jackson (2)
Break the Cycle, Staind (4)
Britney, Britney Spears (4)
Celebrity, 'N Sync (5)
Christmas Extraordinaire, Mannheim Steamroller (2)
Despreciado, Lupillo Rivera (2)
Drops of Jupiter, Train (2)
Echoes: The Best of Pink Floyd, Pink Floyd (2)
Everyday, Dave Matthews Band (2)
La Historia, Ricky Martin (2)
Marc Anthony, Marc Anthony (3)
Now That's What I Call Christmas!, various artists (4)
Now That's What I Call Music! Vol. 4, various artists (2)
Now That's What I Call Music! Vol. 6, various artists (3)
Now That's What I Call Music! Vol. 7, various artists (3)
Now That's What I Call Music! Vol. 8, various artists (3)
Scarecrow, Garth Brooks (3)
Shhh!, A.B. Quintanilla y Los Kumbia Kings (2)
Silver Side Up, Nickelback (2)
Songs in A Minor, Alicia Keys (4)
Survivor, Destiny's Child (3)
Until the End of Time, 2 Pac (3)
Weathered, Creed (4)
Wingspan: Hits and History, Paul McCartney (2)

Albums, Platinum

12 Chichicuilotazos Con Banda, El Chichicuilote
Aaliyah, Aaliyah
Acoustic Soul, India.Arie
All Killer No Filler, Sum 41
Anthology, Alien Ant Farm
Azul, Cristian
The Blueprint, Jay-Z
Christmas Memories, Barbra Streisand
Cieli di Toscana, Andrea Bocelli
Cocky, Kid Rock
Come Clean, Puddle of Mudd
The Concert for New York City, Various
Devil's Night, D12
Escape, Enrique Iglesias
Eternal, Isely Brothers
Free City, St. Lunatics
GHV2: Greatest Hits, Vol. 2, Madonna
Glitter (soundtrack), Mariah Carey
Gorillaz, Gorillaz
The Great Depression, DMX
Invincible, Michael Jackson
Iowa, Slipknot
It Was All a Dream, Dream
Jagged Little Thrill, Jagged Edge
Just Push Play, Aerosmith
Lateralus, Tool
Laundry Service, Shakira
Lenny, Lenny Kravitz
The Life, Ginuwine
Live in New York City, Bruce Springsteen
Luther Vandross, Luther Vandross
M!ssundaztood, Pink
Mas Con El Numero Uno, Vicente Fernandez
Miss E . . . So Addictive, Missy Elliot
Morning View, Incubus
Moulin Rouge (soundtrack)
No More Drama, Mary J. Blige
Now, Maxwell
Oh Aaron, Aaron Carter
Origenes, Alejandro Fernandez
O-Town, O-Town
Pain is Love, Ja Rule
Part III, 112
Pull My Chain, Toby Keith
Return of Dragon, Sisqo

Satellite, P.O.D.
Scorpion, Eve
Set this Circus Down, Tim McGraw
Shrek (soundtrack)
Sinner, Drowning Pool
Sufreiendo a Solas, Lupillo Rivera
Take Off Your Pants and Jacket, Blink 182
Thugs are Us, Trick Daddy
Totally Hits 2001, various artists
Toxicity, System of a Down
Weezer (2001), Weezer

Music Videos, Platinum

Aaron's Party...Live in Concert, Aaron Carter
Around the World, Backstreet Boys
Britney—The Videos, Britney Spears
The Hits, Backstreet Boys
Making the Tour, 'N Sync
Timeless: Live in Concert, Barbra Streisand
Touring Band 2000, Pearl Jam
The Videos: 1994-2001, Dave Matthews Band

Top-Selling Video Games, 2001

Source: The NPDFunworldSM TRSTS® Service, The NPD Group, Inc., Port Washington, NY; ranked by units sold.

Platform, Title
1. Sony PlayStation 2 , Grand Theft Auto III
2. Sony PlayStation 2, Madden NFL 2002
3. Nintendo Gameboy Color, Pokémon Crystal
4. Sony PlayStation 2, Metal Gear Solid 2: Sons of Liberty
5. Nintendo Gameboy, Super Mario Advance
6. Sony PlayStation 2, Gran Turismo 3: A-spec
7. Sony PlayStation 2, Tony Hawk's Pro Skater 3
8. Sony PlayStation, Tony Hawk's Pro Skater 2

Platform, Title
9. Nintendo Gameboy Color, Pokémon Silver
10. Sony PlayStation, Driver 2
11. Nintendo Gameboy Color, Pokémon Gold
12. Nintendo 64, Pokémon Stadium 2
13. Sony PlayStation, Gran Turismo 2
14. Microsoft Xbox, Halo
15. Sony PlayStation, Harry Potter and the Sorcerer's Stone

U.S. Television Set Owners, 2002

Source: Nielsen Media Research; March 2002

Of the 105.5 million homes (98% of U.S. households) that owned at least one TV set in 2002:

99% had color televisions
34% had 2 TV sets
40% had 3 or more TV sets
91% had a VCR
69% received basic cable
40% received premium cable

Some Television Addresses, Phone Numbers, Internet Sites

ABC—American Broadcasting Co.
77 W. 66th St.
New York, NY 10023; (212) 456-7777
Website: www.abc.com

CBS—Columbia Broadcasting System
51 W. 52nd St.
New York, NY 10019; (212) 975-4321
Website: www.cbs.com

Fox—Fox Network
Fox Entertainment Group
1211 Avenue of the Americas
New York, NY 10036; (212) 556-2500
Website: www.fox.com

NBC—National Broadcasting Co.
30 Rockefeller Plaza
New York, NY 10112; (212) 664-4444
Website: www.nbc.com

PBS—Public Broadcasting Service
1320 Braddock Place
Alexandria, VA 22314; (703) 739-5000
Website: www.pbs.org

UPN—United Paramount Network
11800 Wilshire Blvd.
Los Angeles, CA 90025; (310) 575-7000
Website: www.upn.com

WB—WB Television Network
4000 Warner Blvd.
Burbank, CA 91522; (818) 977-5000
Website: www.thewb.com

CABLE

ABCFAMILY—ABC Family Channel
10960 Wilshire Blvd.
Los Angeles, CA 90024; (310) 235-5100
Website: www.ABCfamilychannel.com

A&E—Arts & Entertainment Network
235 E 45th St.
New York, NY 10017; (212) 210-1400
Website: www.aande.com

AMC—American Movie Classics
Rainbow Media Holdings, Inc.
200 Jericho Quadrangle
Jericho, NY 11753; (516) 364-2222
Website: www.amctv.com

APL—Animal Planet
Discovery Communications
7700 Wisconsin Ave.
Bethesda, MD 20814; (301) 986-0444
Website: animal.discovery.com

BET—Black Entertainment Television
2 BET Plaza, 1900 W Place NE
Washington, DC 20018; (202) 608-2000
Website: www.bet.com

CNBC—Consumer News and Business Channel
2200 Fletcher Ave.
Fort Lee, NJ 07024; (201) 346-2100
Website: www.cnbc.com

CNN—Cable News Network
One CNN Center, Box 105366
Atlanta, GA 30348-5366; (404) 827-1500
Website: www.cnn.com

COMEDY—Comedy Central
1775 Broadway
11th Floor
New York, NY 10019; (212) 767-8600
Website: www.comedycentral.com

C-SPAN—Cable-Satellite Public Affairs Network
400 N Capitol St. NW, Suite 650
Washington, DC 20001; (202) 737-3220
Website: www.c-span.org

DISN—The Disney Channel
3800 W Alameda Ave.
Burbank, CA 91505; (818) 569-7500
Website: www.disneychannel.com

DSC—The Discovery Channel
Discovery Communications
7700 Wisconsin Ave., Suite 700
Bethesda, MD 20814; (301) 986-1999
Website: dsc.discovery.com

ESPN—ESPN, Inc.
ESPN Plaza, 935 Middle St.
Bristol, CT 06010; (860) 585-2000
Website: espn.com

FOOD—Food Network
1177 Avenue of the Americas, 31st Floor
New York, NY 10036; (212) 398-8836
Website: www.foodtv.com

HBO—Home Box Office
1100 Avenue of the Americas
New York, NY 10036; (212) 512-1000
Website: www.hbo.com

HIST—The History Channel
235 E. 45th St.
New York, NY 10017; (212) 210-1400
Website: www.historychannel.com

LIFE—Lifetime
309 W 49th St.
New York, NY 10019; (212) 424-7000
Website: www.lifetimetv.com

MSNBC—Microsoft NBC News
1 MSNBC Plaza
Secaucus, NJ 07094; (201) 583-5000
Website: www.msnbc.com

MTV—Music Television
MTV Networks, Inc.
1515 Broadway
New York, NY 10036; (212) 258-8000
Website: www.mtv.com

NICK—Nickelodeon/Nick at Nite
MTV Networks, Inc.
1515 Broadway
New York, NY 10036; (212) 258-8000
Websites: www.nick.com; www.nick-at-nite.com

TBS—Turner Broadcasting System
Turner Entertainment Group
One CNN Center, Box 105366
Atlanta, GA 30348-5366
(404) 827-1700
Website: www.tbssuperstation.com

TLC—The Learning Channel
Discovery Communications
7700 Wisconsin Avenue
Bethesda, MD 20814; (301) 986-0444
Website: tlc.discovery.com

TWC—The Weather Channel
300 Interstate North Parkway
Atlanta, GA 30339-2404; (770) 226-0000
Website: www.weather.com

USA—USA Network
USA Networks
1230 Avenue of the Americas
New York, NY 10020; (212) 408-9100
Website: www.usanetwork.com

WORLD ALMANAC QUICK QUIZ

Which is the only film to appear in the top 15 of both the American Film Institute's list of the "100 Greatest American Movies of All Time" and the "All-Time Top Grossing American Movies" list?

(a) E.T.: The Extra-Terrestrial (b) Star Wars (c) The Godfather, Part II (d) Raiders of the Lost Ark

For the answer look in this chapter, or see page 1008.

Number of Cable TV Systems,[1] 1975-2001

Source: *Television and Cable Factbook*, Warren Publishing, Inc., Washington, DC; estimates as of Jan. 1

Year	Systems	Year	Systems	Year	Systems	Year	Systems	Year	Systems	Year	Systems
1975	3,506	1980	4,225	1985	6,600	1990	9,575	1994	11,214	1998	10,845
1976	3,681	1981	4,375	1986	7,500	1991	10,704	1995	11,218	1999	10,700
1977	3,832	1982	4,825	1987	7,900	1992	11,035	1996	11,119	2000	10,400
1978	3,875	1983	5,600	1988	8,500	1993	11,108	1997	10,950 (R)	2001	9,924
1979	4,150	1984	6,200	1989	9,050						

(1) The satellite-signal-receiving hardware, cable lines, and cable boxes that provide cable programming to homes within a geographic area. (R)=revised.

Top 20 Cable TV Networks, 2002

Source: *Cable Television Developments*, Natl. Cable Television Assn., Jan.-June 2002; ranked by number of subscribers

Rank	Network[1]	Affiliates	Subscribers (mil)
1.	TBS Superstation (1976)	11,668	87.3
2.	C-SPAN (1979)	NA	86.5
3.	ESPN (1979)	NA	86.3
4.	CNN (Cable News Network) (1980)	11,528	86.2
5.	Discovery Channel (1985)	NA	86.1
6.	TNT (Turner Network Television) (1988)	10,637	86.0
7.	USA (1980)	NA	85.9
8.	Nickelodeon (1979)/Nick at Nite (1985)	11,788	85.6
9.	TNN (The National Network) (1983)	NA	85.5
10.	A&E Network (1984)	12,000[2]	85.4
11.	Lifetime Television (LIFE) (1984)	11,000+	85.2
12.	The Weather Channel (1982)	12,763	84.6
13.	ABC Family Channel[3]	13,700	84.2
14.	MTV (Music Television) (1981)	9,176	84.0
15.	TLC (The Learning Channel) (1980)	NA	84.0
16.	ESPN2 (1993)	NA	83.6
17.	QVC (1986)	7,511	83.4
18.	CNBC (1989)	5,000	83.3
19.	AMC (American Movie Classics) (1984)	NA	83.1
20.	VH1 (Music First) (1985)	5,457	82.9

NA = Not available. **Note:** Data include noncable affiliates. (1) Date in parentheses is year service began. (2) U.S. and Canada. (3) Began 1977 as the Family Channel; relaunched as FOX Family Channel, 1998; purchased by Walt Disney Co. and renamed, 2001.

U.S. Households With Cable Television, 1977-2001

Source: Nielsen Media Research

Year	Basic cable subscribers	As % of households with TVs	Year	Basic cable subscribers	As % of households with TVs	Year	Basic cable subscribers	As % of households with TVs
1977	12,168,450	16.6	1985	39,872,520	46.2	1993	58,834,440	62.5
1978	13,391,910	17.9	1986	42,237,140	48.1	1994	60,483,600	63.4
1979	14,814,380	19.4	1987	44,970,880	50.5	1995	62,956,470	65.7
1980	17,671,490	22.6	1988	48,636,520	53.8	1996	64,654,160	66.7
1981	23,219,200	28.3	1989	52,564,470	57.1	1997	65,929,420	67.3
1982	29,340,570	35.0	1990	54,871,330	59.0	1998	67,011,180	67.4
1983	34,113,790	40.5	1991	55,786,390	60.6	1999	67,592,000	68.0
1984	37,290,870	43.7	1992	57,211,600	61.5	2000	68,544,000	68.0
						2001	74,148,000	70.2

Average U.S. Television Viewing Time, October 2001

Source: Nielsen Media Research (hours: minutes per week)

Group	Age	Total per week	M-F 7-10 AM	M-F 10 AM-4:00 PM	M-SUN 8-11 PM	SAT 7 AM-1 PM	M-F 11:30 PM-1 AM	Sunday 1-7:00 PM
Women	18+	35:37	2:20	5:15	9:49	0:53	1:40	1:41
	18-24	22:11	1:07	3:32	5:41	0:32	1:11	1:08
	25-54	33:36	2:13	4:26	9:29	0:53	1:41	1:37
	55+	44:11	3:07	7:23	12:00	1:02	1:46	2:02
Men	18+	21:35	1:38	3:38	9:13	0:49	1:54	1:58
	18-24	21:00	0:50	2:35	5:27	0:30	1:18	1:21
	25-54	30:35	1:30	3:09	9:07	0:49	1:40	1:58
	55+	38:59	2:20	5:15	11:20	0:58	1:34	2:17
Teens	12-17	20:10	0:44	1:46	5:55	0:44	0:52	1:14
Children	2-11	20:50	1:46	3:07	4:53	1:10	0:29	1:06
TOTAL		**30:35**	**1:52**	**4:01**	**8:31**	**0:53**	**1:14**	**1:40**

TV Viewing Shares, Broadcast Years 1990-2001[1]

Source: *Cable TV Facts*, Cable Advertising Bureau, New York, NY

	All Television Households[2]					All Cable Households[2]					Pay Cable Households[2]				
	'90	'95	'99	'00	'01	'90	'95	'99	'00	'01	'90	'95	'99	'00	'01
Network Affiliates[3]	55	48	46	44	42	46	41	41	40	37	43	38	39	37	35
Indep. TV Stations[4]	20	22	11	12	11	16	17	8	9	8	16	17	8	9	8
Public TV Stations	3	3	3	3	3	3	3	2	2	2	2	2	2	2	2
Basic Cable[5]	21	30	44	46	49	32	42	54	55	57	30	41	55	55	57
Pay Cable	6	6	6	6	6	10	8	7	7	7	18	15	10	11	11

Note: After 1998, Fox affiliates switched from Independent classification to Network Affiliates. (1) Broadcast years represent the 12-month period October-September. (2) Share figures refer to percentage of the viewing audience for all television viewing, 24 hours/day. As a result of multiset use and rounding of numbers, share figures add to more than 100. (3) Includes CBS, NBC, ABC, and FOX. (4) Includes WB, UPN, and PAX. (5) Includes ad-supported cable and all other cable (non-pay and non-ad-supported channels).

Favorite Syndicated Programs, 2001-2002

Source: Nielsen Media Research, Aug. 27, 2001-May 12, 2002

Average audience percentages, or ratings, are estimates of the percentage of TV-owning households watching a program.

Rank	Program	Avg. audience (%)
1.	Wheel of Fortune	9.5
2.	Jeopardy!	8.0
3.	Friends	6.9
4.	Seinfeld (7:30 PM)	6.3
5.	Entertainment Tonight	6.1
6.	ESPN NFL Regular Season	5.9
7.	Judge Judy	5.8
	Oprah Winfrey Show	5.8
9.	Everybody Loves Raymond	5.6
10.	Seinfeld (weekend)	5.0
11.	Seinfeld (11:00 PM)	4.3
12.	Wheel of Fortune (weekend)	4.2
13.	Buena Vista VI	3.9
14.	ESPN NFL Regular Season	3.8
	LIVE with Regis and Kelly	3.8
16.	Buena Vista III	3.6
	Entertainment Tonight (weekend)	3.6
18.	Frasier	3.4
	Imagination VI	3.4
20.	Friends (weekend)	3.3
	Judge Joe Brown	3.3

Favorite Prime-Time Television Programs, 2001-2002

Source: Nielsen Media Research

Data are for regularly scheduled network programs in 2001-2002 season through May 22; ranked by average audience percentage. Average audience percentages, or ratings, are estimates of the percentage of all TV-owning households that are watching a particular program. Audience share percentages are estimates of the percentage of those watching TV that are tuned into a particular program. Tied programs are given the same rank.

Rank	Programs	Avg. Audience	Audience Share
1.	Friends	15.3	25
2.	CSI	14.6	22
3.	E.R.	14.4	24
4.	Everybody Loves Raymond	12.8	19
5.	Law & Order	12.6	21
6.	Friends (8:30 PM)*	12.2	19
7.	Survivor: Africa	11.8	18
	Survivor: Marquesas	11.8	19
9.	NFL Monday Night Football	11.5	19
10.	West Wing	11.4	18
11.	Will & Grace	11.1	17
12.	Leap of Faith	11.0	17
13.	Becker	10.7	16
14.	Law & Order: SVU	10.4	19
15.	60 Minutes	10.2	17
16.	Frasier	9.9	15
	JAG	9.9	16
18.	Inside Schwartz	9.8	15
	Judging Amy	9.8	16
20.	NFL Monday Showcase	9.6	15
21.	Just Shoot Me	9.5	14
22.	King of Queens	8.9	14
23.	Crossing Jordan	8.8	14
	Yes, Dear	8.8	13
25.	The Practice	8.5	14
26.	CBS Sunday Movie	8.4	13
	The Guardian	8.4	13
28.	NYPD Blue	8.3	13
29.	Dateline NBC–Friday	8.2	14
30.	Baby Bob	8.1	13
31.	Dateline NBC–Monday	8.0	12
32.	Fear Factor	7.9	12
	Fox NFL Sunday–Post Game	7.9	14
	Law & Order: Criminal Intent	7.9	12
	Providence	7.9	14
36.	60 Minutes II	7.7	13
	Family Law	7.7	13
38.	Dateline NBC–Tuesday	7.6	13
39.	20/20–Wednesday	7.4	12
	Millionaire–Monday	7.4	12
	Primetime Thursday	7.4	12
	Scrubs	7.4	11
	Third Watch	7.4	11
44.	The Bachelor	7.3	11
45.	Education of Max Bickford	7.2	11
	Malcolm in the Middle	7.2	11
47.	My Wife and Kids	7.1	12
48.	The District	7.0	13
	Simpsons	7.0	11
50.	The Agency	6.9	11
	Boston Public	6.9	11
	Philly	6.9	11
	Watching Ellie	6.9	11

* Program ran at 8:30 pm for 5 weeks.

All-Time Highest-Rated Television Programs

Source: Nielsen Media Research, Jan. 1961-Feb. 2002

Estimates exclude unsponsored or joint network telecasts or programs under 30 minutes long. Ranked by rating (percentage of TV-owning households tuned in to the program).

Rank	Program	Telecast date	Network	Rating (%)	Avg. households (in thousands)
1.	M*A*S*H (last episode)	2/28/83	CBS	60.2	50,150
2.	Dallas (Who Shot J.R.?)	11/21/80	CBS	53.3	41,470
3.	Roots-Pt. 8	1/30/77	ABC	51.1	36,380
4.	Super Bowl XVI	1/24/82	CBS	49.1	40,020
5.	Super Bowl XVII	1/30/83	NBC	48.6	40,480
6.	XVII Winter Olympics - 2nd Wed.	2/23/94	CBS	48.5	45,690
7.	Super Bowl XX	1/26/86	NBC	48.3	41,490
8.	Gone With the Wind-Pt. 1	11/7/76	NBC	47.7	33,960
9.	Gone With the Wind-Pt. 2	11/8/76	NBC	47.4	33,750
10.	Super Bowl XII	1/15/78	CBS	47.2	34,410
11.	Super Bowl XIII	1/21/79	NBC	47.1	35,090
12.	Bob Hope Christmas Show	1/15/70	NBC	46.6	27,260
13.	Super Bowl XVIII	1/22/84	CBS	46.4	38,800
	Super Bowl XIX	1/20/85	ABC	46.4	39,390
15.	Super Bowl XIV	1/20/80	CBS	46.3	35,330
16.	Super Bowl XXX	1/28/96	NBC	46.0	44,150
	ABC Theater (The Day After)	11/20/83	ABC	46.0	38,550

Rank	Program	Telecast date	Network	Rating (%)	Avg. households (in thousands)
18.	Roots-Pt. 6	1/28/77	ABC	45.9	32,680
	The Fugitive	8/29/67	ABC	45.9	25,700
20.	Super Bowl XXI	1/25/87	CBS	45.8	40,030
21.	Roots-Pt. 5	1/27/77	ABC	45.7	32,540
22.	Super Bowl XXVIII	1/30/94	NBC	45.5	42,860
	Cheers (last episode)	5/20/93	NBC	45.5	42,360
24.	Ed Sullivan	2/9/64	CBS	45.3	23,240
25.	Super Bowl XXVII	1/31/93	NBC	45.1	41,990
26.	Bob Hope Christmas Show	1/14/71	NBC	45.0	27,050
27.	Roots-Pt. 3	1/25/77	ABC	44.8	31,900
28.	Super Bowl XXXII	1/25/98	NBC	44.5	43,630
29.	Super Bowl XI	1/9/77	NBC	44.4	31,610
	Super Bowl XV	1/25/81	NBC	44.4	34,540
31.	Super Bowl VI	1/16/72	CBS	44.2	27,450
32.	XVII Winter Olympics - 2nd Fri.	2/25/94	CBS	44.1	41,540
	Roots-Pt. 2	1/24/77	ABC	44.1	31,400
34.	Beverly Hillbillies	1/8/64	CBS	44.0	22,570
35.	Roots-Pt. 4	1/26/77	ABC	43.8	31,190
	Ed Sullivan	2/16/64	CBS	43.8	22,445
37.	Super Bowl XXIII	1/22/89	NBC	43.5	39,320
38.	Academy Awards	4/7/70	ABC	43.4	25,390
39.	Super Bowl XXXI	1/26/97	FOX	43.3	42,000
	Super Bowl XXXIV	1/30/00	ABC	43.3	43,620
41.	Thorn Birds-Pt. 3	3/29/83	ABC	43.2	35,990
42.	Thorn Birds-Pt. 4	3/30/83	ABC	43.1	35,900
43.	CBS NFC Championship	1/10/82	CBS	42.9	34,960
44.	Beverly Hillbillies	1/15/64	CBS	42.8	21,960
45.	Super Bowl VII	1/14/73	NBC	42.7	27,670

IT'S A FACT: Though HBO is seen in only about 40% of U.S. homes with cable, the season premiere of the HBO series *The Sopranos*, on Sept. 15, 2002, was the most-watched non-sports program on cable TV since 1994, attracting 13.4 million viewers according to Nielsen Media Research.

Top-Rated TV Shows of Each Season, 1950-51 to 2001-2002

Source: Nielsen Media Research; regular series programs, Sept.-May season

Season	Program	Rating[1]	TV-owning households (in thousands)
1950-51	Texaco Star Theatre	61.6	10,320
1951-52	Godfrey's Talent Scouts	53.8	15,300
1952-53	I Love Lucy	67.3	20,400
1953-54	I Love Lucy	58.8	26,000
1954-55	I Love Lucy	49.3	30,700
1955-56	$64,000 Question	47.5	34,900
1956-57	I Love Lucy	43.7	38,900
1957-58	Gunsmoke	43.1	41,920
1958-59	Gunsmoke	39.6	43,950
1959-60	Gunsmoke	40.3	45,750
1960-61	Gunsmoke	37.3	47,200
1961-62	Wagon Train	32.1	48,555
1962-63	Beverly Hillbillies	36.0	50,300
1963-64	Beverly Hillbillies	39.1	51,600
1964-65	Bonanza	36.3	52,700
1965-66	Bonanza	31.8	53,850
1966-67	Bonanza	29.1	55,130
1967-68	Andy Griffith	27.6	56,670
1968-69	Rowan & Martin's Laugh-In	31.8	58,250
1969-70	Rowan & Martin's Laugh-In	26.3	58,500
1970-71	Marcus Welby, MD	29.6	60,100
1971-72	All in the Family	34.0	62,100
1972-73	All in the Family	33.3	64,800
1973-74	All in the Family	31.2	66,200
1974-75	All in the Family	30.2	68,500
1975-76	All in the Family	30.1	69,600
1976-77	Happy Days	31.5	71,200
1977-78	Laverne & Shirley	31.6	72,900
1978-79	Laverne & Shirley	30.5	74,500
1979-80	60 Minutes	28.2	76,300
1980-81	Dallas	31.2	79,900
1981-82	Dallas	28.4	81,500
1982-83	60 Minutes	25.5	83,300
1983-84	Dallas	25.7	83,800
1984-85	Dynasty	25.0	84,900
1985-86	Cosby Show	33.8	85,900
1986-87	Cosby Show	34.9	87,400
1987-88	Cosby Show	27.8	88,600
1988-89	Roseanne	25.5	90,400
1989-90	Roseanne	23.4	92,100
1990-91	Cheers	21.6	93,100
1991-92	60 Minutes	21.7	92,100
1992-93	60 Minutes	21.6	93,100
1993-94	Home Improvement	21.9	94,200
1994-95	Seinfeld	20.5	95,400
1995-96	E.R.	22.0	95,900
1996-97	E.R.	21.2	97,000
1997-98	Seinfeld	22.0	98,000
1998-99	E.R.	17.8	99,400
1999-2000	Who Wants to Be a Millionaire	18.6	100,800
2000-01	Survivor II	17.4	102,200
2001-02	Friends	15.3	105,500

(1) Rating is percent of TV-owning households tuned in to the program. Data prior to 1988-89 exclude Alaska and Hawaii.

100 Leading U.S. Advertisers, 2001

Source: Reprinted with permission from AdAge.com and the June 24, 2002, issue of *Advertising Age*, © Crain Communications Inc. 2002

(in millions of dollars)

Rank	Advertiser	Ad Spending
1.	General Motors Corp.	$3,374.4
2.	Procter & Gamble Co.	2,540.6
3.	Ford Motor Co.	2,408.2
4.	PepsiCo	2,210.4
5.	Pfizer	2,189.5
6.	DaimlerChrysler	1,985.3
7.	AOL Time Warner	$1,885.3
8.	Philip Morris Cos.	1,815.7
9.	Walt Disney Co.	1,757.3
10.	Johnson & Johnson	1,618.1
11.	Unilever	1,483.6
12.	Sears, Roebuck & Co.	1,480.1
13.	Verizon Communications	$1,461.6
14.	Toyota Motor Corp.	1,399.1
15.	AT&T Corp.	1,371.9
16.	Sony Corp.	1,310.1
17.	Viacom	1,282.8
18.	McDonald's Corp.	1,194.7

Rank	Advertiser	Ad Spending
19.	Diageo	$1,180.8
20.	Sprint Corp.	1,160.1
21.	Merck & Co.	1,136.6
22.	Honda Motor Co.	1,102.9
23.	J.C. Penney Corp.	1,085.7
24.	U.S. Government	1,056.8
25.	L'Oreal	1,040.7
26.	IBM Corp.	993.5
27.	Bristol-Myers Squibb Co.	973.8
28.	Nestle	967.1
29.	SBC Communications	943.1
30.	Target Corp.	925.7
31.	Microsoft Corp.	919.7
32.	Coca-Cola Co.	903.5
33.	Hewlett-Packard Co.	898.7
34.	AT&T Wireless	887.7
35.	General Mills	883.5
36.	GlaxoSmithKline	881.1
37.	WorldCom	840.0
38.	Sara Lee Corp.	812.1
39.	Home Depot	778.0
40.	Nissan Motor Co.	774.7
41.	Wyeth	770.8
42.	Estee Lauder Cos.	766.4
43.	Federated Department Stores	746.1
44.	Yum Brands	676.5
45.	News Corp.	670.4
46.	ConAgra	668.3
47.	General Electric Co.	$663.8
48.	Anheuser-Busch Cos.	655.6
49.	Mars Inc.	614.8
50.	Kmart Corp.	596.7
51.	Volkswagen	595.8
52.	Pharmacia Corp.	590.3
53.	Nike	576.6
54.	Wal-Mart Stores	573.4
55.	Bayer	567.1
56.	May Department Stores Co.	552.8
57.	Novartis	552.4
58.	Best Buy Co.	542.7
59.	Cendant Corp.	527.2
60.	Kroger Co.	511.6
61.	Vivendi Universal	498.5
62.	Schering-Plough Corp.	497.8
63.	S.C. Johnson & Son	478.8
64.	Gillette Co.	463.4
65.	Albertson's	457.7
66.	Mattel	448.6
67.	American Express Co.	444.5
68.	Safeway	440.5
69.	Adolph Coors Co.	430.1
70.	Limited Brands	428.3
71.	Intel Corp.	426.1
72.	Gap Inc.	425.9
73.	Kellogg Co.	421.5
74.	Aventis	421.0
75.	Circuit City Stores	$410.0
76.	Campbell Soup Co.	397.0
77.	Morgan Stanley Dean Witter & Co.	385.1
78.	Hershey Foods Corp.	365.5
79.	Colgate-Palmolive Co.	355.2
80.	Visa International	347.4
81.	Berkshire Hathaway	339.4
82.	Clorox Co.	337.6
83.	U.S. dairy producers, processors	330.4
84.	Eastman Kodak Co.	323.9
85.	Reckitt Benckiser	316.2
86.	Wendy's International	312.2
87.	Kimberly-Clark Corp.	304.3
88.	Dell Computer Corp.	302.2
89.	Hilton Hotels Corp.	296.0
90.	Saks Inc.	294.9
91.	State Farm Mutual Automobile Insurance	291.8
92.	Mitsubishi Motors Corp.	289.8
93.	Office Depot	289.6
94.	Gateway	289.0
95.	Deutsche Telekom	289.0
96.	Marriott International	288.2
97.	MasterCard International	288.1
98.	Kia Motors Corp.	286.9
99.	Doctor's Associates	285.9
100.	Dillard's	285.4

U.S. Ad Spending by Top Categories, 2001

Source: Reprinted with permission from AdAge.com and the June 24, 2002, issue of *Advertising Age*, © Crain Communications Inc. 2002

(in millions of dollars, Jan.-Dec. 2001)

							Television				Radio	
Category	Total	Mag.	Sun. Mag.	Newspaper	Nat'l Newspaper	Outdoor	Network	Spot	Syndicated	Cable	Network	Nat'l Spot
Automotive	$14,491	$1,698	$32	$4,405	$323	$282	$2,448	$3,869	$171	$952	$58	$252
Retail, & discount stores	12,938	883	132	5,704	288	276	1,802	2,350	196	703	110	496
Movies, media, & advertising	5,828	976	27	1,447	322	215	1,188	660	194	525	90	184
Food, beverages, & confectionary	5,821	1,219	55	26	9	72	1,950	831	437	1,011	91	121
Medicines & proprietary remedies	5,213	1,229	125	148	28	6	2,035	214	496	797	91	43
Financial	4,512	707	47	882	388	125	1,039	341	93	734	40	118
Telecommunications	3,805	227	3	1,085	172	115	781	664	87	430	21	220
Toiletries, cosmetics, & personal care	3,711	1,427	27	8	5	12	1,226	162	341	462	28	13
Airline travel, hotels, & resorts	3,654	750	44	1,158	281	272	257	466	26	298	38	64
Restaurants	3,474	37	3	89	8	184	1,166	1,296	183	364	24	120
Direct response companies	3,257	1,111	397	153	109	1	270	172	212	790	31	12
Home furnishings, appliances, etc.	2,739	899	53	44	16	8	829	205	172	472	27	15
Computers, software, Internet	2,668	864	5	112	257	42	623	212	57	408	18	70
Insurance & real estate	2,376	263	24	663	152	130	314	332	89	309	38	64
Apparel	1,924	1,327	32	8	19	28	303	23	27	143	4	10
Government, politics, & organizations	1,564	199	33	243	69	86	274	366	40	137	26	92
Beer, wine, & liquor	1,516	398	6	19	14	149	545	123	22	182	9	48
Sporting goods, games, toys	1,201	351	2	18	8	5	347	31	57	372	5	5
Audio & video equip. & supplies	1,101	306	24	46	22	9	332	86	34	200	19	24
Business & manufacturing equipment	888	298	5	27	72	24	236	36	15	126	18	31
Pets, pet foods, & supplies	459	108	12	2	1	1	182	24	39	88	<1	3
Cigarettes, tobacco, & accessories	358	259	11	8	3	1	41	2	22	11	0	<1
Gasoline & oil	211	35	1	4	8	4	44	28	10	51	3	26
Fitness & diet programs	167	7	<1	18	1	4	4	114	8	5	<1	7
Miscellaneous	5,959	842	56	1,413	358	330	403	1,495	164	724	47	125
TOTAL	**89,835**	**16,417**	**1,157**	**17,729**	**2,932**	**2,380**	**18,638**	**14,100**	**3,192**	**10,291**	**834**	**2,164**

AWARDS — MEDALS — PRIZES

The Alfred B. Nobel Prize Winners, 1901-2001

Alfred B. Nobel (1833-96), inventor of dynamite, bequeathed $9 mil, the interest on which was to be distributed yearly to those judged to have most benefited humankind in physics, chemistry, medicine-physiology, literature, and the promotion of peace. Prizes were first awarded in 1901. The 1st Nobel Memorial Prize in Economic Science was awarded in 1969, funded by the central bank of Sweden. Each prize is now worth about $1 million. If year is omitted, no award was given. To find the 2002 winners, see Table of Contents.

Physics

2001 Eric A. Cornell, Carl E. Wieman, U.S.; Wolfgang Ketterle, Ger.
2000 Jack S. Kilby, U.S.; Zhores I. Alferov, Russ.
1999 Gerardus 't Hooft and Martinus J. G. Veltman, Netherlands
1998 Robert B. Laughlin, Horst L. Störmer, Daniel C. Tsui, U.S.
1997 Steven Chu, William D. Phillips, U.S.; Claude Cohen-Tannoudji, Fr.
1996 David M. Lee, Douglas D. Osheroff, Robert C. Richardson, U.S.
1995 Martin Perl, Frederick Reines, U.S.
1994 Bertram N. Brockhouse, Can.; Clifford G. Shull, U.S.
1993 Joseph H. Taylor, Russell A. Hulse, U.S.
1992 Georges Charpak, Pol.-Fr.
1991 Pierre-Giles de Gennes, Fr.
1990 Richard E. Taylor, Can.; Jerome I. Friedman, Henry W. Kendall, U.S.
1989 Norman F. Ramsey, U.S.; Hans G. Dehmelt, Ger.-U.S.; Wolfgang Paul, Ger.
1988 Leon M. Lederman, Melvin Schwartz, Jack Steinberger, U.S.
1987 K. Alex Müller, Swiss; J. Georg Bednorz, Ger.
1986 Ernest Ruska, Ger.; Gerd Binnig, Ger.; Heinrich Rohrer, Swiss
1985 Klaus von Klitzing, Ger.
1984 Carlo Rubbia, It.; Simon van der Meer, Dutch
1983 Subrahmanyan Chandrasekhar, William A. Fowler, U.S.
1982 Kenneth G. Wilson, U.S.
1981 Nicolaas Bloembergen, Arthur Schaalow, U.S.; Kai M. Siegbahn, Swed.
1980 James W. Cronin, Val L. Fitch, U.S.
1979 Steven Weinberg, Sheldon L. Glashow, U.S.; Abdus Salam, Pakistani
1978 Pyotr Kapitsa, USSR; Arno Penzias, Robert Wilson, U.S.
1977 John H. Van Vleck, Philip W. Anderson, U.S.; Nevill F. Mott, Br.
1976 Burton Richter, Samuel C.C. Ting, U.S.
1975 James Rainwater, U.S.; Ben Mottelson, U.S.-Dan.; Aage Bohr, Dan.
1974 Martin Ryle, Antony Hewish, Br.
1973 Ivar Giaever, U.S.; Leo Esaki, Jpn.; Brian D. Josephson, Br.
1972 John Bardeen, Leon N. Cooper, John R. Schrieffer, U.S.
1971 Dennis Gabor, Br.
1970 Louis Neel, Fr.; Hannes Alfven, Swed.
1969 Murray Gell-Mann, U.S.
1968 Luis W. Alvarez, U.S.
1967 Hans A. Bethe, U.S.
1966 Alfred Kastler, Fr.
1965 Richard P. Feynman, Julian S. Schwinger, U.S.; Shinichiro Tomonaga, Jpn.
1964 Nikolai G. Basov, Aleksander M. Prochorov, USSR; Charles H. Townes, U.S.
1963 Maria Goeppert-Mayer, Eugene P. Wigner, U.S.; J. Hans D. Jensen, Ger.
1962 Lev. D. Landau, USSR
1961 Robert Hofstadter, U.S.; Rudolf L. Mossbauer, Ger.
1960 Donald A. Glaser, U.S.
1959 Owen Chamberlain, Emilio G. Segre, U.S.
1958 Pavel Cherenkov, Ilya Frank, Igor Y. Tamm, USSR
1957 Tsung-dao Lee, Chen Ning Yang, U.S.
1956 John Bardeen, Walter H. Brattain, William Shockley, U.S.
1955 Polykarp Kusch, Willis E. Lamb, U.S.
1954 Max Born, Br.; Walter Bothe, Ger.
1953 Frits Zernike, Dutch
1952 Felix Bloch, Edward M. Purcell, U.S.
1951 Sir John D. Cockroft, Br.; Ernest T. S. Walton, Ir.
1950 Cecil F. Powell, Br.
1949 Hideki Yukawa, Jpn.
1948 Patrick M. S. Blackett, Br.
1947 Sir Edward V. Appleton, Br.
1946 Percy W. Bridgman, U.S.
1945 Wolfgang Pauli, U.S.
1944 Isidor Isaac Rabi, U.S.
1943 Otto Stern, U.S.
1939 Ernest O. Lawrence, U.S.
1938 Enrico Fermi, It.-U.S.
1937 Clinton J. Davisson, U.S.; Sir George P. Thomson, Br.
1936 Carl D. Anderson, U.S.; Victor F. Hess, Aus.
1935 Sir James Chadwick, Br.
1933 Paul A. M. Dirac, Br.; Erwin Schrodinger, Austria
1932 Werner Heisenberg, Ger.
1930 Sir Chandrasekhara V. Raman, Indian
1929 Prince Louis-Victor de Broglie, Fr.
1928 Owen W. Richardson, Br.
1927 Arthur H. Compton, U.S.; Charles T. R. Wilson, Br.
1926 Jean B. Perrin, Fr.
1925 James Franck, Gustav Hertz, Ger.
1924 Karl M. G. Siegbahn, Swed.
1923 Robert A. Millikan, U.S.
1922 Niels Bohr, Dan.
1921 Albert Einstein, Ger.-U.S.
1920 Charles E. Guillaume, Fr.
1919 Johannes Stark, Ger.
1918 Max K. E. L. Planck, Ger.
1917 Charles G. Barkla, Br.
1915 Sir William H. Bragg, Sir William L. Bragg, Br.
1914 Max von Laue, Ger.
1913 Heike Kamerlingh-Onnes, Dutch
1912 Nils G. Dalen, Swed.
1911 Wilhelm Wien, Ger.
1910 Johannes D. van der Waals, Dutch
1909 Carl F. Braun, Ger.; Guglielmo Marconi, It.
1908 Gabriel Lippmann, Fr.
1907 Albert A. Michelson, U.S.
1906 Sir Joseph J. Thomson, Br.
1905 Philipp E. A. von Lenard, Ger.
1904 John W. Strutt, Lord Rayleigh, Br.
1903 Antoine Henri Becquerel, Pierre Curie, Fr.; Marie Curie, Pol.-Fr.
1902 Hendrik A. Lorentz, Pieter Zeeman, Dutch
1901 Wilhelm C. Roentgen, Ger.

Chemistry

2001 K. Barry Sharpless, U.S.; William S. Knowles, U.S., Ryoji Noyori, Japan
2000 Alan J. Heeger, U.S.; Alan G. MacDiarmid, NZ-U.S.; Hideki Shirakawa, Japan
1999 Ahmed H. Zewail, U.S.
1998 Walter Kohn, U.S.; John A. Pople, Br.
1997 Paul D. Boyer, U.S., & John E. Walker, Br.; Jens C. Skou, Dan.
1996 Harold W. Kroto, Br.; Robert F. Curl Jr., Richard E. Smalley, U.S.
1995 Paul Crutzen, Dutch; Mario Molina, Mex.-U.S.; Sherwood Rowland, U.S.
1994 George A. Olah, U.S.
1993 Kary B. Mullis, U.S.; Michael Smith, Br.-Can.
1992 Rudolph A. Marcus, Can.-U.S.
1991 Richard R. Ernst, Swiss
1990 Elias James Corey, U.S.
1989 Thomas R. Cech, Sidney Altman, U.S.
1988 Johann Deisenhofer, Robert Huber, Hartmut Michel, Ger.
1987 Donald J. Cram, Charles J. Pedersen, U.S.; Jean-Marie Lehn, Fr.
1986 Dudley Herschbach, Yuan T. Lee, U.S.; John C. Polanyi, Can.
1985 Herbert A. Hauptman, Jerome Karle, U.S.
1984 Bruce Merrifield, U.S.
1983 Henry Taube, Can.
1982 Aaron Klug, S. Afr.
1981 Kenichi Fukui, Jpn.; Roald Hoffmann, U.S.
1980 Paul Berg, Walter Gilbert, U.S.; Frederick Sanger, Br.
1979 Herbert C. Brown, U.S.; George Wittig, Ger.
1978 Peter Mitchell, Br.
1977 Ilya Prigogine, Belg.
1976 William N. Lipscomb, U.S.
1975 John Cornforth, Austral.-Br.; Vladimir Prelog, Yugo.-Swiss
1974 Paul J. Flory, U.S.
1973 Ernst Otto Fischer, Ger.; Geoffrey Wilkinson, Br.
1972 Christian B. Anfinsen, Stanford Moore, William H. Stein, U.S.
1971 Gerhard Herzberg, Canadian
1970 Luis F. Leloir, Arg.
1969 Derek H. R. Barton, Br.; Odd Hassel, Nor.
1968 Lars Onsager, U.S.
1967 Manfred Eigen, Ger.; Ronald G. W. Norrish, George Porter, Br.
1966 Robert S. Mulliken, U.S.
1965 Robert B. Woodward, U.S.
1964 Dorothy C. Hodgkin, Br.
1963 Giulio Natta, It.; Karl Ziegler, Ger.
1962 John C. Kendrew, Max F. Perutz, Br.
1961 Melvin Calvin, U.S.
1960 Willard F. Libby, U.S.
1959 Jaroslav Heyrovsky, Czech.
1958 Frederick Sanger, Br.
1957 Sir Alexander R. Todd, Br.
1956 Sir Cyril N. Hinshelwood, Br.; Nikolai N. Semenov, USSR
1955 Vincent du Vigneaud, U.S.
1954 Linus C. Pauling, U.S.
1953 Hermann Staudinger, Ger.
1952 Archer J. P. Martin, Richard L. M. Synge, Br.
1951 Edwin M. McMillan, Glenn T. Seaborg, U.S.
1950 Kurt Alder, Otto P. H. Diels, Ger.
1949 William F. Giauque, U.S.
1948 Arne W. K. Tiselius, Swed.
1947 Sir Robert Robinson, Br.
1946 James B. Sumner, John H. Northrop, Wendell M. Stanley, U.S.
1945 Artturi I. Virtanen, Fin.
1944 Otto Hahn, Ger.
1943 Georg de Hevesy, Hung.
1939 Adolf F. J. Butenandt, Ger.; Leopold Ruzicka, Swiss
1938 Richard Kuhn, Ger.
1937 Walter N. Haworth, Br.; Paul Karrer, Swiss

1936 Peter J. W. Debye, Dutch
1935 Frederic & Irene Joliot-Curie, Fr.
1934 Harold C. Urey, U.S.
1932 Irving Langmuir, U.S.
1931 Friedrich Bergius, Karl Bosch, Ger.
1930 Hans Fischer, Ger.
1929 Sir Arthur Harden, Br.; Hans von Euler-Chelpin, Swed.
1928 Adolf O. R. Windaus, Ger.
1927 Heinrich O. Wieland, Ger.
1926 Theodor Svedberg, Swed.
1925 Richard A. Zsigmondy, Ger.
1923 Fritz Pregl, Austrian
1922 Francis W. Aston, Br.
1921 Frederick Soddy, Br.
1920 Walther H. Nernst, Ger.
1918 Fritz Haber, Ger.
1915 Richard M. Willstatter, Ger.
1914 Theodore W. Richards, U.S.
1913 Alfred Werner, Swiss
1912 Victor Grignard, Paul Sabatier, Fr.
1911 Marie Curie, Pol.-Fr.
1910 Otto Wallach, Ger.
1909 Wilhelm Ostwald, Ger.
1908 Ernest Rutherford, Br.
1907 Eduard Buchner, Ger.
1906 Henri Moissan, Fr.
1905 Adolf von Baeyer, Ger.
1904 Sir William Ramsay, Br.
1903 Svante A. Arrhenius, Swed.
1902 Emil Fischer, Ger.
1901 Jacobus H. van't Hoff, Dutch

Physiology or Medicine

2001 Leland H. Hartwell, U.S.; R. Timothy (Tim) Hunt, Sir Paul M. Nurse, Br.
2000 Arvid Carlsson, Swed.; Paul Greengard, U.S.; Eric R. Kandel, Aus-U.S.
1999 Günter Blobel, U.S.
1998 Robert F. Furchgott, Louis J. Ignarro, Ferid Murad, U.S.
1997 Stanley B. Prusiner, U.S.
1996 Peter C. Doherty, Austral.; Rolf M. Zinkernagel, Swiss
1995 Edward B. Lewis, Eric F. Wieschaus, U.S.; Christiane Nuesslein-Volhard, Ger.
1994 Alfred G. Gilman, Martin Rodbell, U.S.
1993 Phillip A. Sharp, U.S.; Richard J. Roberts, Br.
1992 Edmond H. Fisher, Edwin G. Krebs, U.S.
1991 Edwin Neher, Bert Sakmann, Ger.
1990 Joseph E. Murray, E. Donnall Thomas, U.S.
1989 J. Michael Bishop, Harold E. Varmus, U.S.
1988 Gertrude B. Elion, George H. Hitchings, U.S; Sir James Black, Br.
1987 Susumu Tonegawa, Jpn.
1986 Rita Levi-Montalcini, It.-U.S., Stanley Cohen, U.S.
1985 Michael S. Brown, Joseph L. Goldstein, U.S.
1984 Cesar Milstein, Br.-Arg.; Georges J. F. Koehler, Ger.; Niels K. Jerne, Br.-Dan.
1983 Barbara McClintock, U.S.
1982 Sune Bergstrom, Bengt Samuelsson, Swed.; John R. Vane, Br.
1981 Roger W. Sperry, David H. Hubel, Torsten N. Wiesel, U.S.
1980 Baruj Benacerraf, George Snell, U.S.; Jean Dausset, Fr.
1979 Allan M. Cormack, U.S.; Godfrey N. Hounsfield, Br.
1978 Daniel Nathans, Hamilton O. Smith, U.S.; Werner Arber, Swiss
1977 Rosalyn S. Yalow, Roger C.L. Guillemin, Andrew V. Schally, U.S.
1976 Baruch S. Blumberg, Daniel Carleton Gajdusek, U.S.
1975 David Baltimore, Howard Temin, U.S.; Renato Dulbecco, It.-U.S.
1974 Albert Claude, Lux.-U.S.; George Emil Palade, Rom.-U.S.; Christian Rene de Duve, Belg.
1973 Karl von Frisch, Ger.; Konrad Lorenz, Ger.-Aus.; Nikolaas Tinbergen, Br.
1972 Gerald M. Edelman, U.S.; Rodney R. Porter, Br.
1971 Earl W. Sutherland Jr., U.S.
1970 Julius Axelrod, U.S.; Sir Bernard Katz, Br.; Ulf von Euler, Swed.
1969 Max Delbrück, Alfred D. Hershey, Salvador Luria, U.S.
1968 Robert W. Holley, H. Gobind Khorana, Marshall W. Nirenberg, U.S.
1967 Ragnar Granit, Swed.; Haldan Keffer Hartline, George Wald, U.S.
1966 Charles B. Huggins, Francis Peyton Rous, U.S.
1965 François Jacob, Andre Lwoff, Jacques Monod, Fr.
1964 Konrad E. Bloch, U.S.; Feodor Lynen, Ger.
1963 Sir John C. Eccles, Austral.; Alan L. Hodgkin, Andrew F. Huxley, Br.
1962 Francis H. C. Crick, Maurice H. F. Wilkins, Br.; James D. Watson, U.S.
1961 Georg von Bekesy, U.S.
1960 Sir F. MacFarlane Burnet, Austral.; Peter B. Medawar, Br.
1959 Arthur Kornberg, Severo Ochoa, U.S.
1958 George W. Beadle, Edward L. Tatum, Joshua Lederberg, U.S.
1957 Daniel Bovet, It.
1956 Andre F. Cournand, Dickinson W. Richards Jr., U.S.; Werner Forssmann, Ger.
1955 Alex H. T. Theorell, Swed.
1954 John F. Enders, Frederick C. Robbins, Thomas H. Weller, U.S.
1953 Hans A. Krebs, Br.; Fritz A. Lipmann, U.S.
1952 Selman A. Waksman, U.S.
1951 Max Theiler, U.S.
1950 Philip S. Hench, Edward C. Kendall, U.S.; Tadeus Reichstein, Swiss
1949 Walter R. Hess, Swiss; Antonio Moniz, Port.
1948 Paul H. Müller, Swiss
1947 Carl F. Cori, Gerty T. Cori, U.S.; Bernardo A. Houssay, Arg.
1946 Hermann J. Muller, U.S.
1945 Ernst B. Chain, Sir Alexander Fleming, Sir Howard W. Florey, Br.
1944 Joseph Erlanger, Herbert S. Gasser, U.S.
1943 Henrik C. P. Dam, Dan.; Edward A. Doisy, U.S.
1939 Gerhard Domagk, Ger.
1938 Corneille J. F. Heymans, Belg.
1937 Albert Szent-Gyorgyi, Hung.-U.S.
1936 Sir Henry H. Dale, Br.; Otto Loewi, U.S.
1935 Hans Spemann, Ger.
1934 George R. Minot, William P. Murphy, G. H. Whipple, U.S.
1933 Thomas H. Morgan, U.S.
1932 Edgar D. Adrian, Sir Charles S. Sherrington, Br.
1931 Otto H. Warburg, Ger.
1930 Karl Landsteiner, U.S.
1929 Christiaan Eijkman, Dutch; Sir Frederick G. Hopkins, Br.
1928 Charles J. H. Nicolle, Fr.
1927 Julius Wagner-Jauregg, Austrian
1926 Johannes A. G. Fibiger, Dan.
1924 Willem Einthoven, Dutch
1923 Frederick G. Banting, Can.; John J. R. Macleod, Scot.
1922 Archibald V. Hill, Br.; Otto F. Meyerhof, Ger.
1920 Schack A. S. Krogh, Dan.
1919 Jules Bordet, Belg.
1914 Robert Barany, Aus.
1913 Charles R. Richet, Fr.
1912 Alexis Carrel, Fr.
1911 Allvar Gullstrand, Swed.
1910 Albrecht Kossel, Ger.
1909 Emil T. Kocher, Swiss
1908 Paul Ehrlich, Ger.; Elie Metchnikoff, Fr.
1907 Charles L. A. Laveran, Fr.
1906 Camillo Golgi, It.; Santiago Ramon y Cajal, Span.
1905 Robert Koch, Ger.
1904 Ivan P. Pavlov, Russ.
1903 Niels R. Finsen, Dan.
1902 Sir Ronald Ross, Br.
1901 Emil A. von Behring, Ger.

Literature

2001 Sir V.S. Naipaul, Br.
2000 Gao Xingjian, Chin.
1999 Günter Grass, Ger.
1998 José Saramago, Por.
1997 Dario Fo, It.
1996 Wislawa Szymborska, Pol.
1995 Seamus Heaney, Ir.
1994 Kenzaburo Oe, Jpn.
1993 Toni Morrison, U.S.
1992 Derek Walcott, W. Ind.
1991 Nadine Gordimer, S. Afr.
1990 Octavio Paz, Mex.
1989 Camilo José Cela, Span.
1988 Naguib Mahfouz, Egy.
1987 Joseph Brodsky, USSR-U.S.
1986 Wole Soyinka, Nig.
1985 Claude Simon, Fr.
1984 Jaroslav Siefert, Czech.
1983 William Golding, Br.
1982 Gabriel Garcia Marquez, Colombian-Mex.
1981 Elias Canetti, Bulg.-Br.
1980 Czeslaw Milosz, Pol.-U.S.
1979 Odysseus Elytis, Gk.
1978 Isaac Bashevis Singer, U.S.
1977 Vicente Aleixandre, Span.
1976 Saul Bellow, U.S.
1975 Eugenio Montale, It.
1974 Eyvind Johnson, Harry Edmund Martinson, Swed.
1973 Patrick White, Austral.
1972 Heinrich Böll, Ger.
1971 Pablo Neruda, Chil.
1970 Aleksandr I. Solzhenitsyn, USSR
1969 Samuel Beckett, Ir.
1968 Yasunari Kawabata, Jpn.
1967 Miguel Angel Asturias, Guat.
1966 Samuel Joseph Agnon, Isr.; Nelly Sachs, Swed.
1965 Mikhail Sholokhov, USSR
1964 Jean Paul Sartre, Fr. (declined)
1963 Giorgos Seferis, Gk.
1962 John Steinbeck, U.S.
1961 Ivo Andric, Yugo.
1960 Saint-John Perse, Fr.
1959 Salvatore Quasimodo, It.
1958 Boris L. Pasternak, USSR (declined)
1957 Albert Camus, Fr.
1956 Juan Ramon Jimenez, Span.
1955 Halldor K. Laxness, Ice.
1954 Ernest Hemingway, U.S.
1953 Sir Winston Churchill, Br.
1952 Francois Mauriac, Fr.
1951 Par F. Lagerkvist, Swed.
1950 Bertrand Russell, Br.
1949 William Faulkner, U.S.
1948 T.S. Eliot, Br.
1947 Andre Gide, Fr.
1946 Hermann Hesse, Ger.-Swiss
1945 Gabriela Mistral, Chil.
1944 Johannes V. Jensen, Dan.
1939 Frans E. Sillanpaa, Fin.
1938 Pearl S. Buck, U.S.
1937 Roger Martin du Gard, Fr.
1936 Eugene O'Neill, U.S.
1934 Luigi Pirandello, It.
1933 Ivan A. Bunin, USSR
1932 John Galsworthy, Br.
1931 Erik A. Karlfeldt, Swed.
1930 Sinclair Lewis, U.S.
1929 Thomas Mann, Ger.
1928 Sigrid Undset, Nor.

1927 Henri Bergson, Fr.
1926 Grazia Deledda, It.
1925 George Bernard Shaw, Ir.-Br.
1924 Wladyslaw S. Reymont, Pol.
1923 William Butler Yeats, Ir.
1922 Jacinto Benavente, Span.
1921 Anatole France, Fr.
1920 Knut Hamsun, Nor.
1919 Carl F. G. Spitteler, Swiss
1917 Karl A. Gjellerup, Henrik Pontoppidan, Dan.
1916 Verner von Heidenstam, Swed.
1915 Romain Rolland, Fr.
1913 Rabindranath Tagore, Indian
1912 Gerhart Hauptmann, Ger.
1911 Maurice Maeterlinck, Belg.
1910 Paul J. L. Heyse, Ger.
1909 Selma Lagerlof, Swed.
1908 Rudolf C. Eucken, Ger.
1907 Rudyard Kipling, Br.
1906 Giosue Carducci, It.
1905 Henryk Sienkiewicz, Pol.
1904 Frederic Mistral, Fr.; Jose Echegaray, Span.
1903 Bjornsterne Bjornson, Nor.
1902 Theodor Mommsen, Ger.
1901 Rene F. A. Sully Prudhomme, Fr.

Peace

2001 UN; Kofi Annan, Ghana
2000 Kim Dae Jung, S. Kor.
1999 Doctors Without Borders (Médecins Sans Frontières), Fr.
1998 John Hume, David Trimble, N. Ir.
1997 Jody Williams, U.S.; International Campaign to Ban Landmines
1996 Bishop Carlos Ximenes Belo, José Ramos-Horta, Timorese
1995 Joseph Rotblat, Pol.-Br.; Pugwash Conference
1994 Yasir Arafat, Pal.; Shimon Peres, Yitzhak Rabin, Isr.
1993 Frederik W. de Klerk, Nelson Mandela, S. Afr.
1992 Rigoberta Menchú, Guat.
1991 Aung San Suu Kyi, Myanmarese
1990 Mikhail S. Gorbachev, USSR
1989 Dalai Lama, Tibet
1988 UN Peacekeeping Forces
1987 Oscar Arias Sanchez, Costa Rican
1986 Elie Wiesel, Rom.-U.S.
1985 Intl. Physicians for the Prevention of Nuclear War, U.S.
1984 Bishop Desmond Tutu, S. Afr.
1983 Lech Walesa, Pol.
1982 Alva Myrdal, Swed.; Alfonso Garcia Robles, Mex.
1981 Office of UN High Com. for Refugees
1980 Adolfo Perez Esquivel, Arg.
1979 Mother Teresa of Calcutta, Alb.-Ind.
1978 Anwar Sadat, Egy.; Menachem Begin, Isr.
1977 Amnesty International
1976 Mairead Corrigan, Betty Williams, N. Ir.
1975 Andrei Sakharov, USSR
1974 Eisaku Sato, Jpn.; Sean MacBride, Ir.
1973 Henry Kissinger, U.S.; Le Duc Tho, N. Viet. (Tho declined)
1971 Willy Brandt, Ger.
1970 Norman E. Borlaug, U.S.
1969 Intl. Labor Organization
1968 Rene Cassin, Fr.
1965 UN Children's Fund (UNICEF)
1964 Martin Luther King Jr., U.S.
1963 International Red Cross, League of Red Cross Societies
1962 Linus C. Pauling, U.S.
1961 Dag Hammarskjold, Swed.
1960 Albert J. Luthuli, S. Afr.
1959 Philip J. Noel-Baker, Br.
1958 Georges Pire, Belg.
1957 Lester B. Pearson, Can.
1954 Office of UN High Com. for Refugees
1953 George C. Marshall, U.S.
1952 Albert Schweitzer, Fr.
1951 Leon Jouhaux, Fr.
1950 Ralph J. Bunche, U.S.
1949 Lord John Boyd Orr of Brechin Mearns, Br.
1947 Friends Service Council, Br.; Amer. Friends Service Committee, U.S.
1946 Emily G. Balch, John R. Mott, U.S.
1945 Cordell Hull, U.S.
1944 International Red Cross
1938 Nansen International Office for Refugees
1937 Viscount Cecil of Chelwood, Br.
1936 Carlos de Saavedra Lamas, Arg.
1935 Carl von Ossietzky, Ger.
1934 Arthur Henderson, Br.
1933 Sir Norman Angell, Br.
1931 Jane Addams, Nicholas Murray Butler, U.S.
1930 Nathan Soderblom, Swed.
1929 Frank B. Kellogg, U.S.
1927 Ferdinand E. Buisson, Fr.; Ludwig Quidde, Ger.
1926 Aristide Briand, Fr.; Gustav Stresemann, Ger.
1925 Sir J. Austen Chamberlain, Br.; Charles G. Dawes, U.S.
1922 Fridtjof Nansen, Nor.
1921 Karl H. Branting, Swed.; Christian L. Lange, Nor.
1920 Leon V.A. Bourgeois, Fr.
1919 Woodrow Wilson, U.S.
1917 International Red Cross
1913 Henri La Fontaine, Belg.
1912 Elihu Root, U.S.
1911 Tobias M.C. Asser, Dutch; Alfred H. Fried, Austrian
1910 Permanent Intl. Peace Bureau
1909 Auguste M. F. Beernaert, Belg.; Paul H. B. B. d'Estournelles de Constant, Fr.
1908 Klas P. Arnoldson, Swed.; Fredrik Bajer, Dan.
1907 Ernesto T. Moneta, It.; Louis Renault, Fr.
1906 Theodore Roosevelt, U.S.
1905 Baroness Bertha von Suttner, Austrian
1904 Institute of International Law
1903 Sir William R. Cremer, Br.
1902 Elie Ducommun, Charles A. Gobat, Swiss
1901 Jean H. Dunant, Swiss; Frederic Passy, Fr.

Nobel Memorial Prize in Economic Science

2001 George A. Akerlof, A. Michael Spence, Joseph E. Stiglitz, U.S.
2000 James J. Heckman, Daniel L. McFadden, U.S.
1999 Robert A. Mundell, Can.
1998 Amartya Sen, Indian
1997 Robert C. Merton, U.S.; Myron S. Scholes, Can.-U.S.
1996 James A. Mirrlees, Br.; William Vickrey, Can.-U.S.
1995 Robert E. Lucas Jr., U.S.
1994 John C. Harsanyi, John F. Nash, U.S.; Reinhard Selten, Ger.
1993 Robert W. Fogel, Douglass C. North, U.S.
1992 Gary S. Becker, U.S.
1991 Ronald H. Coase, Br.-U.S.
1990 Harry M. Markowitz, William F. Sharpe, Merton H. Miller, U.S.
1989 Trygve Haavelmo, Nor.
1988 Maurice Allais, Fr.
1987 Robert M. Solow, U.S.
1986 James M. Buchanan, U.S.
1985 Franco Modigliani, It.-U.S.
1984 Richard Stone, Br.
1983 Gerard Debreu, Fr.-U.S.
1982 George J. Stigler, U.S.
1981 James Tobin, U.S.
1980 Lawrence R. Klein, U.S.
1979 Theodore W. Schultz, U.S.; Sir Arthur Lewis, Br.
1978 Herbert A. Simon, U.S.
1977 Bertil Ohlin, Swed.; James E. Meade, Br.
1976 Milton Friedman, U.S.
1975 Tjalling Koopmans, Dutch-U.S.; Leonid Kantorovich, USSR
1974 Gunnar Myrdal, Swed.; Friedrich A. von Hayek, Austrian
1973 Wassily Leontief, U.S.
1972 Kenneth J. Arrow, U.S.; John R. Hicks, Br.
1971 Simon Kuznets, U.S.
1970 Paul A. Samuelson, U.S.
1969 Ragnar Frisch, Nor.; Jan Tinbergen, Dutch

Pulitzer Prizes in Journalism, Letters, and Music

Endowed by Joseph Pulitzer (1847-1911), publisher of the *New York World*, in a bequest to Columbia Univ. and awarded annually, in years shown, for work the previous year. Prizes are now $7,500 in each category, except Public Service (in Journalism), for which a medal is given. For letters and music, prizes in past years are listed; if a year is omitted, no award was given that year.

Journalism, 2002

Public Service: *NY Times;* for "A Nation Challenged," a special section published regularly after the Sept. 11 terrorist attacks on the U.S., which "coherently and comprehensively covered the tragic events, profiled the victims, and tracked the developing story, locally and globally."

Breaking News Reporting: *Wall Street Journal* staff; for "comprehensive and insightful coverage, executed under the most difficult circumstances, of the terrorist attacks on New York City."

Investigative Reporting: Sari Horwitz, Scott Higham, and Sarah Cohen, *Wash. Post*; for a series that exposed the District of Columbia's role in the neglect and death of 229 children placed in protective care between 1993 and 2000.

Explanatory Reporting: *NY Times* staff; for "informed and detailed reporting" before and after the Sept. 11 attacks that "profiled the global terrorism network and the threats it posed."

Beat Reporting: Gretchen Morgenson, *NY Times*; for "trenchant and incisive Wall Street coverage."

National Reporting: *Wash. Post* staff; for "comprehensive coverage of America's war on terrorism, which regularly brought forth new information together with skilled analysis of unfolding developments."

Internat. Reporting: Barry Bearak, *NY Times*; for "deeply affecting and illuminating coverage of daily life in war-torn Afghanistan."

Feature Writing: Barry Siegel, *LA Times*; for "humane and haunting portrait of a man tried for negligence in the death of his son, and the judge who heard the case."

Commentary: Thomas Friedman, *NY Times*; for "his clarity of vision, based on extensive reporting, in commenting on the worldwide impact of the terrorist threat."

Criticism: Justin Davidson, *Newsday*, Long Island, NY; for "crisp coverage of classical music that captures its essence."

Editorial Writing: Alex Raksin and Bob Sipchen, *LA Times*; for "comprehensive and powerfully written editorials exploring the issues and dilemmas provoked by mentally ill people dwelling on the streets."

Editorial Cartooning: Clay Bennett, *Christian Science Monitor.*

Breaking News Photography: *NY Times* staff; for "consistently outstanding photographic coverage of the terrorist attack on New York City and its aftermath."

Feature Photography: *NY Times* staff; for "photographs chronicling the pain and the perseverance of people enduring protracted conflict in Afghanistan and Pakistan."

Letters

Fiction

1918—Ernest Poole, *His Family*
1919—Booth Tarkington, *The Magnificent Ambersons*
1921—Edith Wharton, *The Age of Innocence*
1922—Booth Tarkington, *Alice Adams*
1923—Willa Cather, *One of Ours*
1924—Margaret Wilson, *The Able McLaughlins*
1925—Edna Ferber, *So Big*
1926—Sinclair Lewis, *Arrowsmith* (refused prize)
1927—Louis Bromfield, *Early Autumn*
1928—Thornton Wilder, *Bridge of San Luis Rey*
1929—Julia M. Peterkin, *Scarlet Sister Mary*
1930—Oliver LaFarge, *Laughing Boy*
1931—Margaret Ayer Barnes, *Years of Grace*
1932—Pearl S. Buck, *The Good Earth*
1933—T. S. Stribling, *The Store*
1934—Caroline Miller, *Lamb in His Bosom*
1935—Josephine W. Johnson, *Now in November*
1936—Harold L. Davis, *Honey in the Horn*
1937—Margaret Mitchell, *Gone With the Wind*
1938—John P. Marquand, *The Late George Apley*
1939—Marjorie Kinnan Rawlings, *The Yearling*
1940—John Steinbeck, *The Grapes of Wrath*
1942—Ellen Glasgow, *In This Our Life*
1943—Upton Sinclair, *Dragon's Teeth*
1944—Martin Flavin, *Journey in the Dark*
1945—John Hersey, *A Bell for Adano*
1947—Robert Penn Warren, *All the King's Men*
1948—James A. Michener, *Tales of the South Pacific*
1949—James Gould Cozzens, *Guard of Honor*
1950—A. B. Guthrie Jr., *The Way West*
1951—Conrad Richter, *The Town*
1952—Herman Wouk, *The Caine Mutiny*
1953—Ernest Hemingway, *The Old Man and the* Sea
1955—William Faulkner, *A Fable*
1956—MacKinlay Kantor, *Andersonville*
1958—James Agee, *A Death in the Family*
1959—Robert Lewis Taylor, *The Travels of Jaimie McPheeters*
1960—Allen Drury, *Advise and Consent*
1961—Harper Lee, *To Kill a Mockingbird*
1962—Edwin O'Connor, *The Edge of Sadness*
1963—William Faulkner, *The Reivers*
1965—Shirley Ann Grau, *The Keepers of the House*
1966—Katherine Anne Porter, *Collected Stories*
1967—Bernard Malamud, *The Fixer*
1968—William Styron, *The Confessions of Nat Turner*
1969—N. Scott Momaday, *House Made of Dawn*
1970—Jean Stafford, *Collected Stories*
1972—Wallace Stegner, *Angle of Repose*
1973—Eudora Welty, *The Optimist's Daughter*
1975—Michael Shaara, *The Killer Angels*
1976—Saul Bellow, *Humboldt's Gift*
1978—James Alan McPherson, *Elbow Room*
1979—John Cheever, *The Stories of John Cheever*
1980—Norman Mailer, *The Executioner's Song*
1981—John Kennedy Toole, *A Confederacy of Dunces*
1982—John Updike, *Rabbit Is Rich*
1983—Alice Walker, *The Color Purple*
1984—William Kennedy, *Ironweed*
1985—Alison Lurie, *Foreign Affairs*
1986—Larry McMurtry, *Lonesome Dove*
1987—Peter Taylor, *A Summons to Memphis*
1988—Toni Morrison, *Beloved*
1989—Anne Tyler, *Breathing Lessons*
1990—Oscar Hijuelos, *The Mambo Kings Play Songs of Love*
1991—John Updike, *Rabbit at Rest*
1992—Jane Smiley, *A Thousand Acres*
1993—Robert Olen Butler, *A Good Scent From a Strange Mountain*
1994—E. Annie Proulx, *The Shipping News*
1995—Carol Shields, *The Stone Diaries*
1996—Richard Ford, *Independence Day*
1997—Steven Millhauser, *Martin Dressler: The Tale of an American Dreamer*
1998—Philip Roth, *American Pastoral*
1999—Michael Cunningham, *The Hours*
2000—Jhumpa Lahiri, *Interpreter of Maladies*
2001—Michael Chabon, *The Amazing Adventures of Kavalier & Clay*
2002—Richard Russo, *Empire Falls*

Drama

1918—Jesse Lynch Williams, *Why Marry?*
1920—Eugene O'Neill, *Beyond the Horizon*
1921—Zona Gale, *Miss Lulu Bett*
1922—Eugene O'Neill, *Anna Christie*
1923—Owen Davis, *Icebound*
1924—Hatcher Hughes, *Hell-Bent for Heaven*
1925—Sidney Howard, *They Knew What They Wanted*
1926—George Kelly, *Craig's Wife*
1927—Paul Green, *In Abraham's Bosom*
1928—Eugene O'Neill, *Strange Interlude*
1929—Elmer Rice, *Street Scene*
1930—Marc Connelly, *The Green Pastures*
1931—Susan Glaspell, *Alison's House*
1932—George S. Kaufman, Morrie Ryskind, and Ira Gershwin, *Of Thee I Sing*
1933—Maxwell Anderson, *Both Your Houses*
1934—Sidney Kingsley, *Men in White*
1935—Zoe Akins, *The Old Maid*
1936—Robert E. Sherwood, *Idiot's Delight*
1937—George S. Kaufman and Moss Hart, *You Can't Take It With You*
1938—Thornton Wilder, *Our Town*
1939—Robert E. Sherwood, *Abe Lincoln in Illinois*
1940—William Saroyan, *The Time of Your Life*
1941—Robert E. Sherwood, *There Shall Be No Night*
1943—Thornton Wilder, *The Skin of Our Teeth*
1945—Mary Chase, *Harvey*
1946—Russel Crouse and Howard Lindsay, *State of the Union*
1948—Tennessee Williams, *A Streetcar Named Desire*
1949—Arthur Miller, *Death of a Salesman*
1950—Richard Rodgers, Oscar Hammerstein 2d and Joshua Logan, *South Pacific*
1952—Joseph Kramm, *The Shrike*
1953—William Inge, *Picnic*
1954—John Patrick, *Teahouse of the August Moon*
1955—Tennessee Williams, *Cat on a Hot Tin Roof*
1956—Frances Goodrich and Albert Hackett, *The Diary of Anne Frank*
1957—Eugene O'Neill, *Long Day's Journey Into Night*
1958—Ketti Frings, *Look Homeward, Angel*
1959—Archibald MacLeish, *J. B.*
1960—George Abbott, Jerome Weidman, Sheldon Harnick, and Jerry Bock, *Fiorello!*
1961—Tad Mosel, *All the Way Home*
1962—Frank Loesser and Abe Burrows, *How to Succeed in Business Without Really Trying*
1965—Frank D. Gilroy, *The Subject Was Roses*
1967—Edward Albee, *A Delicate Balance*
1969—Howard Sackler, *The Great White Hope*
1970—Charles Gordone, *No Place to Be Somebody*
1971—Paul Zindel, *The Effect of Gamma Rays on Man-in-the-Moon Marigolds*
1973—Jason Miller, *That Championship Season*
1975—Edward Albee, *Seascape*
1976—Michael Bennett, James Kirkwood, Nicholas Dante, Marvin Hamlisch, and Edward Kleban, *A Chorus Line*
1977—Michael Cristofer, *The Shadow Box*
1978—Donald L. Coburn, *The Gin Game*
1979—Sam Shepard, *Buried Child*
1980—Lanford Wilson, *Talley's Folly*
1981—Beth Henley, *Crimes of the Heart*
1982—Charles Fuller, *A Soldier's Play*
1983—Marsha Norman, *'night, Mother*
1984—David Mamet, *Glengarry Glen Ross*
1985—Stephen Sondheim and James Lapine, *Sunday in the Park With George*
1987—August Wilson, *Fences*
1988—Alfred Uhry, *Driving Miss Daisy*
1989—Wendy Wasserstein, *The Heidi Chronicles*
1990—August Wilson, *The Piano Lesson*
1991—Neil Simon, *Lost in Yonkers*
1992—Robert Schenkkan, *The Kentucky Cycle*
1993—Tony Kushner, *Angels in America: Millennium Approaches*
1994—Edward Albee, *Three Tall Women*
1995—Horton Foote, *The Young Man From Atlanta*
1996—Jonathan Larson, *Rent*
1998—Paula Vogel, *How I Learned to Drive*
1999—Margaret Edson, *Wit*
2000—Donald Margulies, *Dinner With Friends*
2001—David Auburn, *Proof*
2002—Suzan-Lori Parks, *Topdog/Underdog*

History (U.S.)

1917—J. J. Jusserand, *With Americans of Past and Present Days*
1918—James Ford Rhodes, *History of the Civil War*
1920—Justin H. Smith, *The War With Mexico*
1921—William Sowden Sims, *The Victory at Sea*

1922—James Truslow Adams, *The Founding of New England*
1923—Charles Warren, *The Supreme Court in United States History*
1924—Charles Howard McIlwain, *The American Revolution: A Constitutional Interpretation*
1925—Frederick L. Paxton, *A History of the American Frontier*
1926—Edward Channing, *A History of the U.S.*
1927—Samuel Flagg Bemis, *Pinckney's Treaty*
1928—V. L Parrington, *Main Currents in American Thought*
1929—Fred A. Shannon, *The Organization and Administration of the Union Army, 1861-65*
1930—Claude H. Van Tyne, *The War of Independence*
1931—Bernadotte E. Schmitt, *The Coming of the War, 1914*
1932—Gen. John J. Pershing, *My Experiences in the World War*
1933—Frederick J. Turner, *The Significance of Sections in American History*
1934—Herbert Agar, *The People's Choice*
1935—Charles McLean Andrews, *The Colonial Period of American History*
1936—Andrew C. McLaughlin, *The Constitutional History of the United States*
1937—Van Wyck Brooks, *The Flowering of New England*
1938—Paul Herman Buck, *The Road to Reunion, 1865-1900*
1939—Frank Luther Mott, *A History of American Magazines*
1940—Carl Sandburg, *Abraham Lincoln: The War Years*
1941—Marcus Lee Hansen, *The Atlantic Migration, 1607-1860*
1942—Margaret Leech, *Reveille in Washington*
1943—Esther Forbes, *Paul Revere and the World He Lived In*
1944—Merle Curti, *The Growth of American Thought*
1945—Stephen Bonsal, *Unfinished Business*
1946—Arthur M. Schlesinger Jr., *The Age of Jackson*
1947—James Phinney Baxter 3d, *Scientists Against Time*
1948—Bernard De Voto, *Across the Wide Missouri*
1949—Roy F. Nichols, *The Disruption of American Democracy*
1950—O. W. Larkin, *Art and Life in America*
1951—R. Carlyle Buley, *The Old Northwest: Pioneer Period 1815-1840*
1952—Oscar Handlin, *The Uprooted*
1953—George Dangerfield, *The Era of Good Feelings*
1954—Bruce Catton, *A Stillness at Appomattox*
1955—Paul Horgan, *Great River: The Rio Grande in North American History*
1956—Richard Hofstadter, *The Age of Reform*
1957—George F. Kennan, *Russia Leaves the War*
1958—Bray Hammond, *Banks and Politics in America—From the Revolution to the Civil War*
1959—Leonard D. White and Jean Schneider, *The Republican Era; 1869-1901*
1960—Margaret Leech, *In the Days of McKinley*
1961—Herbert Feis, *Between War and Peace: The Potsdam Conference*
1962—Lawrence H. Gibson, *The Triumphant Empire: Thunderclouds Gather in the West*
1963—Constance McLaughlin Green, *Washington: Village and Capital, 1800-1878*
1964—Sumner Chilton Powell, *Puritan Village: The Formation of a New England Town*
1965—Irwin Unger, *The Greenback Era*
1966—Perry Miller, *Life of the Mind in America*
1967—William H. Goetzmann, *Exploration and Empire: The Explorer and Scientist in the Winning of the American West*
1968—Bernard Bailyn, *The Ideological Origins of the American Revolution*
1969—Leonard W. Levy, *Origin of the Fifth Amendment*
1970—Dean Acheson, *Present at the Creation: My Years in the State Department*
1971—James McGregor Burns, *Roosevelt: The Soldier of Freedom*
1972—Carl N. Degler, *Neither Black nor White*
1973—Michael Kammen, *People of Paradox: An Inquiry Concerning the Origins of American Civilization*
1974—Daniel J. Boorstin, *The Americans: The Democratic Experience*
1975—Dumas Malone, *Jefferson and His Time*
1976—Paul Horgan, *Lamy of Santa Fe*
1977—David M. Potter, *The Impending Crisis*
1978—Alfred D. Chandler Jr., *The Visible Hand: The Managerial Revolution in American Business*
1979—Don E. Fehrenbacher, *The Dred Scott Case: Its Significance in American Law and Politics*
1980—Leon F. Litwack, *Been in the Storm So Long*
1981—Lawrence A. Cremin, *American Education: The National Experience, 1783-1876*
1982—C. Vann Woodward, ed., *Mary Chesnut's Civil War*
1983—Rhys L. Issac, *The Transformation of Virginia, 1740-1790*
1985—Thomas K. McCraw, *Prophets of Regulation*
1986—Walter A. McDougall, *The Heavens and the Earth*
1987—Bernard Bailyn, *Voyagers to the West*
1988—Robert V. Bruce, *The Launching of Modern American Science, 1846-1876*
1989—Taylor Branch, *Parting the Waters: America in the King Years, 1954-63*; and James M. McPherson, *Battle Cry of Freedom: The Civil War Era*
1990—Stanley Karnow, *In Our Image: America's Empire in the Philippines*
1991—Laurel Thatcher Ulrich, *A Midwife's Tale: The Life of Martha Ballard,* based on her diary, 1785-1812
1992—Mark E. Neely Jr., *The Fate of Liberty: Abraham Lincoln and Civil Liberties*
1993—Gordon S. Wood, *The Radicalism of the American Revolution*
1995—Doris Kearns Goodwin, *No Ordinary Time: Franklin and Eleanor Roosevelt: The Home Front in World War II*
1996—Alan Taylor, *William Cooper's Town: Power and Persuasion on the Frontier of the Early American Republic*
1997—Jack N. Rakove, *Original Meanings: Politics and Ideas in the Making of the Constitution*
1998—Edward J. Larson, *Summer for the Gods: The Scopes Trial and America's Continuing Debate Over Science and Religion*
1999—Edwin G. Burrows and Mike Wallace, *Gotham: A History of New York City to 1898*
2000—David M. Kennedy, *Freedom From Fear: The American People in Depression and War, 1929-1945*
2001—Joseph J. Ellis, *Founding Brothers: The Revolutionary Generation*
2002—Louis Menand, *The Metaphysical Club: A Story of Ideas in America*

Biography or Autobiography

1917—Laura E. Richards and Maude Howe Elliott, assisted by Florence Howe Hall, *Julia Ward Howe*
1918—William Cabell Bruce, *Benjamin Franklin, Self-Revealed*
1919—Henry Adams, *The Education of Henry Adams*
1920—Albert J. Beveridge, *The Life of John Marshall*
1921—Edward Bok, *The Americanization of Edward Bok*
1922—Hamlin Garland, *A Daughter of the Middle Border*
1923—Burton J. Hendrick, *The Life and Letters of Walter H. Page*
1924—Michael Pupin, *From Immigrant to Inventor*
1925—M. A. DeWolfe Howe, *Barrett Wendell and His Letters*
1926—Harvey Cushing, *Life of Sir William Osler*
1927—Emory Holloway, *Whitman: An Interpretation in Narrative*
1928—Charles Edward Russell, *The American Orchestra and Theodore Thomas*
1929—Burton J. Hendrick, *The Training of an American: The Earlier Life and Letters of Walter H. Page*
1930—Marquis James, *The Raven* (Sam Houston)
1931—Henry James, *Charles W. Eliot*
1932—Henry F. Pringle, *Theodore Roosevelt*
1933—Allan Nevins, *Grover Cleveland*
1934—Tyler Dennett, *John Hay*
1935—Douglas Southall Freeman, *R. E. Lee*
1936—Ralph Barton Perry, *The Thought and Character of William James*
1937—Allan Nevins, *Hamilton Fish: The Inner History of the Grant Administration*
1938—Divided between Odell Shepard, *Pedlar's Progress* (Bronson Alcott) and Marquis James, *Andrew Jackson*
1939—Carl Van Doren, *Benjamin Franklin*
1940—Ray Stannard Baker, *Woodrow Wilson, Life and Letters*
1941—Ola Elizabeth Winslow, *Jonathan Edwards*
1942—Forrest Wilson, *Crusader in Crinoline* (Harriet Beecher Stowe)
1943—Samuel Eliot Morison, *Admiral of the Ocean Sea* (Christopher Columbus)
1944—Carleton Mabee, *The American Leonardo: The Life of Samuel F. B. Morse*
1945—Russell Blaine Nye, *George Bancroft: Brahmin Rebel.*
1946—Linny Marsh Wolfe, *Son of the Wilderness* (John Muir)
1947—William Allen White, *Autobiography of William Allen White*
1948—Margaret Clapp, *Forgotten First Citizen: John Bigelow*
1949—Robert E. Sherwood, *Roosevelt and Hopkins*
1950—Samuel Flagg Bemis, *John Quincy Adams and the Foundations of American Foreign Policy*
1951—Margaret Louise Coit, *John C. Calhoun: American Portrait*
1952—Merlo J. Pusey, *Charles Evans Hughes*
1953—David J. Mays, *Edmund Pendleton, 1721-1803*
1954—Charles A. Lindbergh, *The Spirit of St. Louis*
1955—William S. White, *The Taft Story*
1956—Talbot F. Hamlin, *Benjamin Henry Latrobe*
1957—John F. Kennedy, *Profiles in Courage*
1958—Douglas Southall Freeman (Vols. I-VI) and John Alexander Carroll and Mary Wells Ashworth (Vol. VII), *George Washington*
1959—Arthur Walworth, *Woodrow Wilson: American Prophet*
1960—Samuel Eliot Morison, *John Paul Jones*
1961—David Donald, *Charles Sumner and the Coming of the Civil War*
1963—Leon Edel, *Henry James: Vols. 2-3*
1964—Walter Jackson Bate, *John Keats*
1965—Ernest Samuels, *Henry Adams*
1966—Arthur M. Schlesinger Jr., *A Thousand Days*
1967—Justin Kaplan, *Mr. Clemens and Mark Twain*
1968—George F. Kennan, *Memoirs (1925-1950)*
1969—B. L. Reid, *The Man From New York: John Quinn and His Friends*

1970—T. Harry Williams, *Huey Long*
1971—Lawrence Thompson, *Robert Frost: The Years of Triumph, 1915-1938*
1972—Joseph P. Lash, *Eleanor and Franklin*
1973—W. A. Swanberg, *Luce and His Empire*
1974—Louis Sheaffer, *O'Neill, Son and Artist*
1975—Robert A. Caro, *The Power Broker: Robert Moses and the Fall of New York*
1976—R.W.B. Lewis, *Edith Wharton: A Biography*
1977—John E. Mack, *A Prince of Our Disorder: The Life of T. E. Lawrence*
1978—Walter Jackson Bate, *Samuel Johnson*
1979—Leonard Baker, *Days of Sorrow and Pain: Leo Baeck and the Berlin Jews*
1980—Edmund Morris, *The Rise of Theodore Roosevelt*
1981—Robert K. Massie, *Peter the Great: His Life and World*
1982—William S. McFeely, *Grant: A Biography*
1983—Russell Baker, *Growing Up*
1984—Louis R. Harlan, *Booker T. Washington*
1985—Kenneth Silverman, *The Life and Times of Cotton Mather*
1986—Elizabeth Frank, *Louise Bogan: A Portrait*
1987—David J. Garrow, *Bearing the Cross: Martin Luther King Jr. and the Southern Christian Leadership Conference*
1988—David Herbert Donald, *Look Homeward: A Life of Thomas Wolfe*
1989—Richard Ellmann, *Oscar Wilde*
1990—Sebastian de Grazia, *Machiavelli in Hell*
1991—Steven Naifeh and Gregory White Smith, *Jackson Pollock: An American Saga*
1992—Lewis B. Puller Jr., *Fortunate Son: The Healing of a Vietnam Vet*
1993—David McCullough, *Truman*
1994—David Levering Lewis, *W.E.B. DuBois: Biography of a Race, 1868-1919*
1995—Joan D. Hedrick, *Harriet Beecher Stowe: A Life*
1996—Jack Miles, *God: A Biography*
1997—Frank McCourt, *Angela's Ashes: A Memoir*
1998—Katharine Graham, *Personal History*
1999—A. Scott Berg, *Lindbergh*
2000—Stacy Schiff, *Véra (Mrs. Vladimir Nabokov)*
2001—David Levering Lewis, *W.E.B. Du Bois: The Fight for Equality and the American Century, 1919-1963*
2002—David McCullough, *John Adams*

American Poetry

Before 1922, awards were funded by the Poetry Society
1918—*Love Songs*, by Sara Teasdale;
1919—*Old Road to Paradise*, by Margaret Widdemer; *Corn Huskers*, by Carl Sandburg.
1922—Edwin Arlington Robinson, *Collected Poems*
1923—Edna St. Vincent Millay, *The Ballad of the Harp-Weaver; A Few Figs From Thistles; other works*
1924—Robert Frost, *New Hampshire: A Poem With Notes and Grace Notes*
1925—Edwin Arlington Robinson, *The Man Who Died Twice*
1926—Amy Lowell, *What's O'Clock*
1927—Leonora Speyer, *Fiddler's Farewell*
1928—Edwin Arlington Robinson, *Tristram*
1929—Stephen Vincent Benet, *John Brown's Body*
1930—Conrad Aiken, *Selected Poems*
1931—Robert Frost, *Collected Poems*
1932—George Dillon, *The Flowering Stone*
1933—Archibald MacLeish, *Conquistador*
1934—Robert Hillyer, *Collected Verse*
1935—Audrey Wurdemann, *Bright Ambush*
1936—Robert P. Tristram Coffin, *Strange Holiness*
1937—Robert Frost, *A Further Range*
1938—Marya Zaturenska, *Cold Morning Sky*
1939—John Gould Fletcher, *Selected Poems*
1940—Mark Van Doren, *Collected Poems*
1941—Leonard Bacon, *Sunderland Capture*
1942—William Rose Benet, *The Dust Which Is God*
1943—Robert Frost, *A Witness Tree*
1944—Stephen Vincent Benet, *Western Star*
1945—Karl Shapiro, *V-Letter and Other Poems*
1947—Robert Lowell, *Lord Weary's Castle*
1948—W. H. Auden, *The Age of Anxiety*
1949—Peter Viereck, *Terror and Decorum*
1950—Gwendolyn Brooks, *Annie Allen*
1951—Carl Sandburg, *Complete Poems*
1952—Marianne Moore, *Collected Poems*
1953—Archibald MacLeish, *Collected Poems*
1954—Theodore Roethke, *The Waking*
1955—Wallace Stevens, *Collected Poems*
1956—Elizabeth Bishop, *Poems, North and South*
1957—Richard Wilbur, *Things of This World*
1958—Robert Penn Warren, *Promises: Poems 1954-1956*
1959—Stanley Kunitz, *Selected Poems 1928-1958*
1960—W. D. Snodgrass, *Heart's Needle*
1961—Phyllis McGinley, *Times Three: Selected Verse From Three Decades*
1962—Alan Dugan, *Poems*
1963—William Carlos Williams, *Pictures From Breughel*
1964—Louis Simpson, *At the End of the Open Road*
1965—John Berryman, *77 Dream Songs*
1966—Richard Eberhart, *Selected Poems*
1967—Anne Sexton, *Live or Die*
1968—Anthony Hecht, *The Hard Hours*
1969—George Oppen, *Of Being Numerous*
1970—Richard Howard, *Untitled Subjects*
1971—William S. Merwin, *The Carrier of Ladders*
1972—James Wright, *Collected Poems*
1973—Maxine Winokur Kumin, *Up Country*
1974—Robert Lowell, *The Dolphin*
1975—Gary Snyder, *Turtle Island*
1976—John Ashbery, *Self-Portrait in a Convex Mirror*
1977—James Merrill, *Divine Comedies*
1978—Howard Nemerov, *Collected Poems*
1979—Robert Penn Warren, *Now and Then: Poems 1976-1978*
1980—Donald Justice, *Selected Poems*
1981—James Schuyler, *The Morning of the Poem*
1982—Sylvia Plath, *The Collected Poems*
1983—Galway Kinnell, *Selected Poems*
1984—Mary Oliver, *American Primitive*
1985—Carolyn Kizer, *Yin*
1986—Henry Taylor, *The Flying Change*
1987—Rita Dove, *Thomas and Beulah*
1988—William Meredith, *Partial Accounts: New and Selected Poems*
1989—Richard Wilbur, *New and Collected Poems*
1990—Charles Simic, *The World Doesn't End*
1991—Mona Van Duyn, *Near Changes*
1992—James Tate, *Selected Poems*
1993—Louise Glück, *The Wild Iris*
1994—Yusef Komunyakaa, *Neon Vernacular*
1995—Philip Levine, *The Simple Truth*
1996—Jorie Graham, *The Dream of the Unified Field*
1997—Lisel Mueller, *Alive Together: New and Selected Poems*
1998—Charles Wright, *Black Zodiac*
1999—Mark Strand, *Blizzard of One*
2000—C. K. Williams, *Repair*
2001—Stephen Dunn, *Different Hours*
2002—Carl Dennis, *Practical Gods*

General Nonfiction

1962—Theodore H. White, *The Making of the President 1960*
1963—Barbara W. Tuchman, *The Guns of August*
1964—Richard Hofstadter, *Anti-Intellectualism in American Life*
1965—Howard Mumford Jones, *O Strange New World*
1966—Edwin Way Teale, *Wandering Through Winter*
1967—David Brion Davis, *The Problem of Slavery in Western Culture*
1968—Will and Ariel Durant, *Rousseau and Revolution*
1969—Norman Mailer, *The Armies of the Night;* Rene Jules Dubos, *So Human an Animal: How We Are Shaped by Surroundings and Events*
1970—Eric H. Erikson, *Gandhi's Truth*
1971—John Toland, *The Rising Sun*
1972—Barbara W. Tuchman, *Stilwell and the American Experience in China, 1911-1945*
1973—Frances FitzGerald, *Fire in the Lake: The Vietnamese and the Americans in Vietnam*; Robert Coles, *Children of Crisis,* Volumes II & III
1974—Ernest Becker, *The Denial of Death*
1975—Annie Dillard, *Pilgrim at Tinker Creek*
1976—Robert N. Butler, *Why Survive? Being Old in America*
1977—William W. Warner, *Beautiful Swimmers*
1978—Carl Sagan, *The Dragons of Eden*
1979—Edward O. Wilson, *On Human Nature*
1980—Douglas R. Hofstadter, *Gödel, Escher, Bach: An Eternal Golden Braid*
1981—Carl E. Schorske, *Fin-de-Siecle Vienna: Politics and Culture*
1982—Tracy Kidder, *The Soul of a New Machine*
1983—Susan Sheehan, *Is There No Place on Earth for Me?*
1984—Paul Starr, *Social Transformation of American Medicine*
1985—Studs Terkel, *The Good War*
1986—Joseph Lelyveld, *Move Your Shadow;* J. Anthony Lukas, *Common Ground*
1987—David K. Shipler, *Arab and Jew*
1988—Richard Rhodes, *The Making of the Atomic Bomb*
1989—Neil Sheehan, *A Bright Shining Lie: John Paul Vann and America in Vietnam*
1990—Dale Maharidge and Michael Williamson, *And Their Children After Them*
1991—Bert Holldobler and Edward O. Wilson, *The Ants*
1992—Daniel Yergin, *The Prize: The Epic Quest for Oil*
1993—Garry Wills, *Lincoln at Gettysburg*
1994—David Remnick, *Lenin's Tomb: The Last Days of the Soviet Empire*
1995—Jonathan Weiner, *The Beak of the Finch: A Story of Evolution in Our Time*
1996—Tina Rosenberg, *The Haunted Land: Facing Europe's Ghosts After Communism*

1997—Richard Kluger, *Ashes to Ashes: America's Hundred-Year Cigarette War, the Public Health, and the Unabashed Triumph of Philip Morris*
1998—Jared Diamond, *Guns, Germs, and Steel: The Fates of Human Societies*
1999—John McPhee, *Annals of the Former World*
2000—John W. Dower, *Embracing Defeat: Japan in the Wake of World War II*
2001—Herbert P. Bix, *Hirohito and the Making of Modern Japan*
2002—Diane McWhorter, *Carry Me Home: Birmingham, Alabama, the Climactic Battle of the Civil Rights Revolution*

Special Citation in Letters

1944—Richard Rodgers and Oscar Hammerstein II, for *Oklahoma!*
1957—Kenneth Roberts, for his historical novels
1960—*The Armada*, by Garrett Mattingly
1961—*American Heritage Picture History of the Civil War*
1973—*George Washington, Vols. I-IV*, by James Thomas Flexner
1977—Alex Haley, for *Roots*
1978—E.B. White
1984—Theodore Seuss Geisel (Dr. Seuss)
1992—Art Spiegleman, for *Maus*

Music

1943—William Schuman, *Secular Cantata No. 2, A Free Song*
1944—Howard Hanson, *Symphony No. 4, Op. 34*
1945—Aaron Copland, *Appalachian Spring*
1946—Leo Sowerby, *The Canticle of the Sun*
1947—Charles E. Ives, *Symphony No. 3*
1948—Walter Piston, *Symphony No. 3*
1949—Virgil Thomson, *Louisiana Story*
1950—Gian-Carlo Menotti, *The Consul*
1951—Douglas Moore, *Giants in the Earth*
1952—Gail Kubik, *Symphony Concertante*
1954—Quincy Porter, *Concerto for Two Pianos and Orchestra*
1955—Gian-Carlo Menotti, *The Saint of Bleecker Street*
1956—Ernest Toch, *Symphony No. 3*
1957—Norman Dello Joio, *Meditations on Ecclesiastes*
1958—Samuel Barber, *Vanessa*
1959—John La Montaine, *Concerto for Piano and Orchestra*
1960—Elliott Carter, *Second String Quartet*
1961—Walter Piston, *Symphony No. 7*
1962—Robert Ward, *The Crucible*
1963—Samuel Barber, *Piano Concerto No. 1*
1966—Leslie Bassett, *Variations for Orchestra*
1967—Leon Kirchner, *Quartet No. 3*
1968—George Crumb, *Echoes of Time and The River*
1969—Karel Husa, *String Quartet No. 3*
1970—Charles W. Wuorinen, *Time's Encomium*
1971—Mario Davidovsky, *Synchronisms No. 6*
1972—Jacob Druckman, *Windows*
1973—Elliott Carter, *String Quartet No. 3*
1974—Donald Martino, *Notturno*
1975—Dominick Argento, *From the Diary of Virginia Woolf*
1976—Ned Rorem, *Air Music*
1977—Richard Wernick, *Visions of Terror and Wonder*
1978—Michael Colgrass, *Deja Vu for Percussion and Orchestra*
1979—Joseph Schwantner, *Aftertones of Infinity*
1980—David Del Tredici, *In Memory of a Summer Day*
1982—Roger Sessions, *Concerto for Orchestra*
1983—Ellen T. Zwilich, *Three Movements for Orchestra*
1984—Bernard Rands, *Canti del Sole*
1985—Stephen Albert, *Symphony, RiverRun*
1986—George Perle, *Wind Quintet IV*
1987—John Harbison, *The Flight Into Egypt*
1988—William Bolcom, *12 New Etudes for Piano*
1989—Roger Reynolds, *Whispers Out of Time*
1990—Mel Powell, *Duplicates: A Concerto for Two Pianos and Orchestra*
1991—Shulamit Ran, *Symphony*
1992—Wayne Peterson, *The Face of the Night, The Heart of the Dark*
1993—Christopher Rouse, *Trombone Concerto*
1994—Gunther Schuller, *Of Reminiscences and Reflections*
1995—Morton Gould, *Stringmusic*
1996—George Walker, *Lilacs*
1997—Wynton Marsalis, *Blood on the Fields*
1998—Aaron Jay Kernis, *String Quartet No. 2*
1999—Melinda Wagner, *Concerto for Flute, Strings and Percussion*
2000—Lewis Spratlan, *Life is a Dream, Opera in Three Acts: Act II, Concert Version*
2001—John Corigliano, *Symphony No. 2 for String Orchestra*
2002—Henry Brant, *Ice Field*

Special Citation in Music

1974—Roger Sessions
1976—Scott Joplin
1982—Milton Babbitt
1985—William Schuman
1998—George Gershwin
1999—Edward Kennedy "Duke" Ellington

National Book Awards, 1950-2001

The National Book Awards (known as the American Book Awards from 1980 to 1986) are administered by the National Book Foundation and have been given annually since 1950. The prizes, each valued at $10,000, are awarded to U.S. citizens for works published in the U.S. in the 12 months prior to the nominations. In some years, multiple awards were given for nonfiction in various categories; in such cases, the history and biography (if any) or biography winner is listed. Selected additional awards in nonfiction are given in footnotes. Nonfiction winners in certain separate categories may not be shown.

Fiction

Year	Author, Title
1950	Nelson Algren, *The Man With the Golden Arm*
1951	William Faulkner, *The Collected Stories*
1952	James Jones, *From Here to Eternity*
1953	Ralph Ellison, *Invisible Man*
1954	Saul Bellow, *The Adventures of Augie March*
1955	William Faulkner, *A Fable*
1956	John O'Hara, *Ten North Frederick*
1957	Wright Morris, *The Field of Vision*
1958	John Cheever, *The Wapshot Chronicle*
1959	Bernard Malamud, *The Magic Barrel*
1960	Philip Roth, *Goodbye, Columbus*
1961	Conrad Richter, *The Waters of Kronos*
1962	Walker Percy, *The Moviegoer*
1963	J.F. Powers, *Morte d'Urban*
1964	John Updike, *The Centaur*
1965	Saul Bellow, *Herzog*
1966	Katherine Anne Porter, *The Collected Stories*
1967	Bernard Malamud, *The Fixer*
1968	Thornton Wilder, *The Eighth Day*
1969	Jerzy Kosinski, *Steps*
1970	Joyce Carol Oates, *Them*
1971	Saul Bellow, *Mr. Sammler's Planet*
1972	Flannery O'Connor, *The Complete Stories*
1973	John Barth, *Chimera*
1974	Thomas Pynchon, *Gravity's Rainbow*
1974	Isaac Bashevis Singer, *A Crown of Feathers*
1975	Robert Stone, *Dog Soldiers*
1976	William Gaddis, *JR*
1977	Wallace Stegner, *The Spectator Bird*
1978	Mary Lee Settle, *Blood Ties*
1979	Tim O'Brien, *Going After Cacciato*
1980	William Styron, *Sophie's Choice*
1981	Wright Morris, *Plains Song*
1982	John Updike, *Rabbit Is Rich*
1983	Alice Walker, *The Color Purple*
1984	Ellen Gilchrist, *Victory Over Japan*
1985	Don DeLillo, *White Noise*
1986	E.L. Doctorow, *World's Fair*
1987	Larry Heinemann, *Paco's Story*
1988	Pete Dexter, *Paris Trout*
1989	John Casey, *Spartina*
1990	Charles Johnson, *Middle Passage*
1991	Norman Rush, *Mating*
1992	Cormac McCarthy, *All the Pretty Horses*
1993	E. Annie Proulx, *The Shipping News*
1994	William Gaddis, *A Frolic of His Own*
1995	Philip Roth, *Sabbath's Theater*
1996	Andrea Barrett, *Ship Fever and Other Stories*
1997	Charles Frazier, *Cold Mounatin*
1998	Alice McDermott, *Charming Billy*
1999	Ha Jin, *Waiting*
2000	Susan Sontag, *In America*
2001	Jonathan Franzen, *The Corrections*

Nonfiction

Year	Author, Title
1950	Ralph L. Rusk, *Ralph Waldo Emerson*
1951	Newton Arvin, *Herman Melville*
1952	Rachel Carson, *The Sea Around Us*
1953	Bernard A. De Voto, *The Course of an Empire*
1954	Bruce Catton, *A Stillness at Appomattox*
1955	Joseph Wood Krutch, *The Measure of Man*
1956	Herbert Kubly, *An American in Italy*
1957	George F. Kennan, *Russia Leaves the War*

Year Author, Title
1958 Catherine Drinker Bowen, *The Lion and the Throne*
1959 J. Christopher Herold, *Mistress to an Age: A Life of Madame De Stael*
1960 Richard Ellman, *James Joyce*
1961 William L. Shirer, *The Rise and Fall of the Third Reich*
1962 Lewis Mumford, *The City in History: Its Origins, Its Transformations, and Its Prospects*
1963 Leon Edel, *Henry James: Vol. II: The Conquest of London; Vol. III: The Middle Years*
1964 William H. McNeill, *The Rise of the West: A History of the Human Community*
1965 Louis Fisher, *The Life of Lenin*
1966 Arthur M. Schlesinger, Jr., *A Thousand Days: John F. Kennedy in the White House*
1967 Peter Gay, *The Enlightenment, An Interpretation Vol I: The Rise of Modern Paganism*
1968 George F. Kennan, *Memoirs: 1925–1950*[1]
1969 Winthrop D. Jordan, *White Over Black: American Attitudes Toward the Negro, 1550-1812*[2]
1970 T. Harry Williams, *Huey Long*[3]
1971 James MacGregor Burns, *Roosevelt: The Soldier of Freedom*
1972 Joseph P. Lash, *Eleanor and Franklin: The Story of Their Relationship, Based on Eleanor Roosevelt's Private Papers*
1973 James Thomas Flexner, *George Washington, Vol. IV: Anguish and Farewell, 1793-1799*[4]
1974 John Clive, *Macaulay, The Shaping of the Historian*; Douglas Day, *Malcolm Lowry: A Biography*[5]
1975 Richard B. Sewall, *The Life of Emily Dickinson*[6]
1976 David Brion Davis, *The Problem of Slavery in the Age of Revolution, 1770-1823*
1977 W.A. Swanberg, *Norman Thomas: The Last Idealist*[7]
1978 W. Jackson Bate, *Samuel Johnson*

Year Author, Title
1979 Arthur M. Schlesinger, Jr., *Robert Kennedy and His Times*
1980 Tom Wolfe, *The Right Stuff*
1981 Maxine Hong Kingston, *China Men*
1982 Tracy Kidder, *The Soul of a New Machine*
1983 Fox Butterfield, *China: Alive in the Bitter Sea*
1984 Robert V. Remini, *Andrew Jackson and the Course of American Democracy, 1833-1845*
1985 J. Anthony Lukas, *Common Ground: A Turbulent Decade in the Lives of Three American Families*
1986 Barry Lopez, *Arctic Dreams*
1987 Richard Rhodes, *The Making of the Atom Bomb*
1988 Neil Sheehan, *A Bright Shining Lie: John Paul Vann and America in Vietnam*
1989 Thomas L. Friedman, *From Beirut to Jerusalem*
1990 Ron Chernow, *The House of Morgan: An American Banking Dynasty and the Rise of Modern Finance*
1991 Orlando Patterson, *Freedom*
1992 Paul Monette, *Becoming a Man: Half a Life Story*
1993 Gore Vidal, *United States: Essays 1952-1992*
1994 Sherwin B. Nuland, *How We Die: Reflections on Life's Final Chapter*
1995 Tina Rosenberg, *The Haunted Land: Facing Europe's Ghosts After Communism*
1996 James Carroll, *An American Requiem: God, My Father, and the War That Came Between Us*
1997 Joseph J. Ellis, *American Sphinx: The Character of Thomas Jefferson*
1998 Edward Ball, *Slaves in the Family*
1999 John W. Dower, *Embracing Defeat: Japan in the Wake of World War II*
2000 Nathaniel Philbrick, *In the Heart of the Sea: The Tragedy of the Whaleship* Essex
2001 Andrew Solomon, *The Noonday Demon: An Atlas of Depression*[8]

(1) Science, Philosophy, and Religion: Jonathan Kozol, *Death at an Early Age.* (2) Arts & Letters: Norman Mailer, *The Armies of the Night: History as a Novel, The Novel as History.* (3) Arts & Letters: Lillian Hellman, *An Unfinished Woman: A Memoir.* (4) Contemp. Affairs: Frances FitzGerald, *Fire in the Lake: The Vietnamese and the Americans in Vietnam.* (5) Arts & Letters: Pauline Kael, *Deeper Into the Movies.* (6) Arts & Letters: Roger Shattuck, *Marcel Proust;* Lewis Thomas, *The Lives of a Cell: Notes of a Biology Watcher.* (7) Contemp. Thought: Bruno Bettelheim, *The Uses of Enchantment: The Meaning and Importance of Fairy Tales.* (8) **Other National Book Awards, 2001**: Poetry: Alan Dugan, *Poems Seven: New and Complete Poetry.* Young people's literature: Virginia Euwer Wolff, *True Believer.* Medal for Distinguished Contr. to American Letters: Arthur Miller.

The (Man) Booker Prize for Fiction, 1969-2001

The Booker Prize for fiction, established in 1968, is awarded annually in October for what is judged the best full-length novel written in English by a citizen of the UK, the Commonwealth, or the Irish Republic. The 2001 prize was worth £21,000, or about $33,000. In 2002 sponsorship of the award was taken over by Man Group PLC, the name was changed to the Man Booker Prize, and the amount was increased to £50,000. The new sponsors indicated the award might in 2004 be opened to writers from the U.S.

1969—P. H. Newby, *Something to Answer For*
1970—Bernice Rubens, *The Elected Member*
1971—V. S. Naipaul, *In a Free State*
1972—John Berger, *G*
1973—J. G. Farrell, *The Siege of Krishnapur*
1974—Nadine Gordimer, *The Conservationist*; Stanley Middleton, *Holiday*
1975—Ruth Prawer Jhabvala, *Heat & Dust*
1976—David Storey, *Saville*
1977—Paul Scott, *Staying On*
1978—Iris Murdoch, *The Sea, The Sea*
1979—Penelope Fitzgerald, *Offshore*
1980—William Golding, *Rites of Passage*
1981—Salman Rushdie, *Midnight's Children*
1982—Thomas Keneally, *Schindler's Ark*
1983—J. M. Coetzee, *Life and Times of Michael K*
1984—Anita Brookner, *Hotel du Lac*
1985—Keri Hulme, *The Bone People*
1986—Kingsley Amis, *The Old Devils*
1987—Penelope Lively, *Moon Tiger*
1988—Peter Carey, *Oscar and Lucinda*
1989—Kazuo Ishiguro, *The Remains of the Day*
1990—A. S. Byatt, *Possession*
1991—Ben Okri, *The Famished Road*
1992—Michael Ondaatje, *The English Patient*; Barry Unsworth, *Sacred Hunger*
1993—Roddy Doyle, *Paddy Clarke Ha Ha Ha*
1994—James Kelman, *How Late It Was, How Late*
1995—Pat Barker, *The Ghost Road*
1996—Graham Swift, *Last Orders*
1997—Arundhati Roy, *The God of Small Things*
1998—Ian McEwan, *Amsterdam*
1999—J. M. Coetzee, *Disgrace*
2000—Margaret Atwood, *The Blind Assassin*
2001—Peter Carey, *True History of the Kelly Gang*

Miscellaneous Book Awards

(Awarded in 2002)

Academy of American Poets Awards. Academy Fellowship, $35,000 stipend: Ellen Bryant Voigt. James Laughlin Award, $5,000: Karen Volkman, *Spar.* Raiziss/de Palchi Translation Award, $5,000: Stephen Sartarelli, *Songbook: The Selected Poems of Umberto Saba.* Walt Whitman Award, $5,000: Sue Kwock Kim, *Notes From the Divided Country.* Harold Morton Landon Translation Award, $1,000: David Ferry, *The Epistles of Horace.* (2001): Lenore Marshall Poetry Prize, $25,000: Fanny Howe, *Selected Poems.* Wallace Stevens Award, for mastery in the art of poetry, $150,000: John Ashbery.

American Academy of Arts and Letters. Gold Medal for History: John Hope Franklin. Academy Awards in Literature ($7,500 each): Benson Bobrick, Christoper Durang, Linda Gregerson, Tony Hoagland, Charles Johnson, Stanley Plumly, James Richardson, Alan Shapiro. Michael Braude Award for Light Verse, $5,000: Henry Taylor. Witter Bynner Prize for Poetry, $5,000: Susan Wheeler. E. M. Forster Award, $15,000: Helen Simpson. Sue Kaufman Prize for First Fiction, $2,500: Donald Lee, *Yellow.* Addison M. Metcalf Award, $10,000: Claire Messud. Katherine Anne Porter Award, $20,000: Lynn Freed. Arthur Rense Poetry Prize, $20,000: B.H. Fairchild. Richard and Hinda Rosenthal Foundation Award, $5,000: Amy Wilentz, *Martyrs' Crossing.* Harold D. Vursell Memorial Award, $10,000: Freeman House. Morton Dauwen Zabel Award for Poetry, $10,000: Ronald Sukenick. Rome Fellowships in Literature, one-year residence at the American Academy in Rome, for 2002-2003: Jennifer Clarvoe (poetry), Peter Orner (fiction).

Edgar Awards, by the Mystery Writers of America: Grand Master award: Robert B. Parker. Best novel: *Silent Joe,* T. Jefferson Parker. Best short story: "Double-Crossing Delancy," S.J. Rozan.

Golden Kite Awards, by Society of Children's Book Writers and Illustrators. Fiction: Virginia Euwer Wolff, *True Believer.* Nonfiction: Susan Campbell Bartoletti, *Black Potatoes: The Story of the Great Irish Famine.* Picture-illustration: Beth Krommes,

The Lamp, the Ice, and the Boat Called Fish (Jacqueline Briggs Martin, author). Picture book text: J. Patrick Lewis, *The Shoe Tree of Chagrin* (Chris Sheban, illus.).

Hugo Awards, by the World Science Fiction Convention. Novel: *American Gods,* Neil Gaiman. Novella: *Fast Times at Fairmont High,* Vernor Vinge. Novelette: *Hell Is the Absence of God,* Ted Chiang. Short story: "The Dog Said Bow-Wow," Michael Swanwick.

Nebula Awards, by the Science Fiction Writers of America. Novel: *The Quantum Rose,* Catherine Asaro. Novella: *The Ultimate Earth,* Jack Williamson. Novelette: *Louise's Ghost,* Kelly Link. Short story: "The Cure for Everything," Severna Park.

Coretta Scott King Award, by American Library Assn. for African American authors and illustrators of outstanding books for children and young adults. Author: Mildred D. Taylor, *The Land.* Illustrator: Jerry Pinkney, *Goin' Someplace Special* (Patricia McKissack, author).

Lincoln Prize, by Lincoln and Soldiers Institute at Gettysburg College, for contribution to Civil War studies, $50,000 and bronze bust of Lincoln; David Blight, *Race and Reunion: The Civil War in American Memory.*

National Book Critics Circle Awards. Fiction: W.G. Sebald, *Austerlitz.* Nonfiction: Nicholson Baker, *Double Fold: Libraries and the Assault on Paper.* Criticism: Martin Amis, *The War Against Cliché: Essays and Reviews, 1971-2000.* Biography and autobiography: Adam Sisman, *Boswell's Presumptuous Task: The Making of the Life of Dr. Johnson.* Poetry: Albert Goldbarth, *Saving Lives.* Nona Balakian Citation for Excellence in Reviewing: Michael Gorra. Ivan Sandrof Lifetime Achievement Award: Jason Epstein.

PEN/Faulkner Award, for fiction, $15,000, Ann Patchett, *Bel Canto.*

Whitbread Book of the Year Award, by Whitbread PLC: £25,000, to Philip Pullman for his children's fantasy novel *The Amber Spyglass.*

Newbery Medal Books, 1922-2002

The Newbery Medal is awarded annually by the Association for Library Service to Children, a division of the American Library Association, to the author of the most distinguished contribution to American literature for children.

Year Given	Book, Author
1922	*The Story of Mankind,* Hendrik Willem van Loon
1923	*The Voyages of Dr. Dolittle,* Hugh Lofting
1924	*The Dark Frigate,* Charles Boardman Hawes
1925	*Tales From Silver Lands,* Charles Joseph Finger
1926	*Shen of the Sea,* Arthur Bowie Chrisman
1927	*Smoky, the Cowhorse,* Will James
1928	*Gay-Neck,* Dhan Gopal Mukerji
1929	*The Trumpeter of Krakow,* Eric P. Kelly
1930	*Hitty, Her First Hundred Years,* Rachel Field
1931	*The Cat Who Went to Heaven,* Elizabeth Coatsworth
1932	*Waterless Mountain,* Laura Adams Armer
1933	*Young Fu of the Upper Yangtze,* Elizabeth Foreman Lewis
1934	*Invincible Louisa,* Cornelia Lynde Meigs
1935	*Dobry,* Monica Shannon
1936	*Caddie Woodlawn,* Carol Ryrie Brink
1937	*Roller Skates,* Ruth Sawyer
1938	*The White Stag,* Kate Seredy
1939	*Thimble Summer,* Elizabeth Enright
1940	*Daniel Boone,* James Daugherty
1941	*Call It Courage,* Armstrong Sperry
1942	*The Matchlock Gun,* Walter D. Edmonds
1943	*Adam of the Road,* Elizabeth Janet Gray
1944	*Johnny Tremain,* Esther Forbes
1945	*Rabbit Hill,* Robert Lawson
1946	*Strawberry Girl,* Lois Lenski
1947	*Miss Hickory,* Carolyn S. Bailey
1948	*Twenty-One Balloons,* William Pène Du Bois
1949	*King of the Wind,* Marguerite Henry
1950	*The Door in the Wall,* Marguerite de Angeli
1951	*Amos Fortune, Free Man,* Elizabeth Yates
1952	*Ginger Pye,* Eleanor Estes
1953	*Secret of the Andes,* Ann Nolan Clark
1954	*. . . And Now Miguel,* Joseph Krumgold
1955	*The Wheel on the School,* Meindert DeJong
1956	*Carry On, Mr. Bowditch,* Jean Lee Latham
1957	*Miracles on Maple Hill,* Virginia Sorensen
1958	*Rifles for Watie,* Harold Keith
1959	*The Witch of Blackbird Pond,* Elizabeth George Speare
1960	*Onion John,* Joseph Krumgold
1961	*Island of the Blue Dolphins,* Scott O'Dell
1962	*The Bronze Bow,* Elizabeth George Speare
1963	*A Wrinkle in Time,* Madeleine L'Engle
1964	*It's Like This, Cat,* Emily Cheney Neville
1965	*Shadow of a Bull,* Maja Wojciechowska
1966	*I, Juan de Pareja,* Elizabeth Borton de Trevino
1967	*Up a Road Slowly,* Irene Hunt
1968	*From the Mixed-Up Files of Mrs. Basil E. Frankweiler,* E. L. Konigsburg
1969	*The High King,* Lloyd Alexander
1970	*Sounder,* William H. Armstrong
1971	*The Summer of the Swans,* Betsy Byars
1972	*Mrs. Frisby and the Rats of NIMH,* Robert C. O'Brien
1973	*Julie of the Wolves,* Jean George
1974	*The Slave Dancer,* Paula Fox
1975	*M. C. Higgins the Great,* Virginia Hamilton
1976	*Grey King,* Susan Cooper
1977	*Roll of Thunder, Hear My Cry,* Mildred D. Taylor
1978	*Bridge to Terabithia,* Katherine Paterson
1979	*The Westing Game,* Ellen Raskin
1980	*A Gathering of Days,* Joan Blos
1981	*Jacob Have I Loved,* Katherine Paterson
1982	*A Visit to William Blake's Inn: Poems for Innocent and Experienced Travelers,* Nancy Willard
1983	*Dicey's Song,* Cynthia Voigt
1984	*Dear Mr. Henshaw,* Beverly Cleary
1985	*The Hero and the Crown,* Robin McKinley
1986	*Sarah, Plain and Tall,* Patricia MacLachlan
1987	*The Whipping Boy,* Sid Fleischman
1988	*Lincoln: A Photobiography,* Russell Freedman
1989	*Joyful Noise: Poems for Two Voices,* Paul Fleischman
1990	*Number the Stars,* Lois Lowry
1991	*Maniac Magee,* Jerry Spinelli
1992	*Shiloh,* Phyllis Reynolds Naylor
1993	*Missing May,* Cynthia Rylant
1994	*The Giver,* Lois Lowry
1995	*Walk Two Moons,* Sharon Creech
1996	*The Midwife's Apprentice,* Karen Cushman
1997	*The View From Saturday,* E. L. Konigsburg
1998	*Out of the Dust,* Karen Hesse
1999	*Holes,* Louis Sachar
2000	*Bud, Not Buddy,* Christopher Paul Curtis
2001	*A Year Down Yonder,* Richard Peck
2002	*A Single Shard,* Linda Sue Park

Caldecott Medal Books, 1938-2002

The Caldecott Medal is awarded annually by the Association for Library Service to Children, a division of the American Library Association, to the illustrator of the most distinguished American picture book for children.

Year Given	Book, Illustrator
1938	*Animals of the Bible*, Dorothy P. Lathrop
1939	*Mei Li*, Thomas Handforth
1940	*Abraham Lincoln*, Ingri & Edgar Parin d'Aulaire
1941	*They Were Strong and Good*, Robert Lawson
1942	*Make Way for Ducklings*, Robert McCloskey
1943	*The Little House*, Virginia Lee Burton
1944	*Many Moons*, Louis Slobodkin
1945	*Prayer for a Child*, Elizabeth Orton Jones
1946	*The Rooster Crows*, Maude & Miska Petersham
1947	*The Little Island*, Leonard Weisgard
1948	*White Snow, Bright Snow*, Roger Duvoisin
1949	*The Big Snow*, Berta & Elmer Hader
1950	*Song of the Swallows*, Leo Politi
1951	*The Egg Tree*, Karherine Milhous
1952	*Finders Keepers*, Nicolas, pseud. (Nicholas Mordvinoff)
1953	*The Biggest Bear*, Lynd Ward
1954	*Madeline's Rescue*, Ludwig Bemelmans
1955	*Cinderella, or the Little Glass Slipper*, Marcia Brown
1956	*Frog Went A-Courtin'*, Feodor Rojankovsky
1957	*A Tree Is Nice*, Marc Simont
1958	*Time of Wonder*, Robert McCloskey
1959	*Chanticleer and the Fox*, Barbara Cooney
1960	*Nine Days to Christmas*, Marie Hall Ets
1961	*Baboushka and the Three Kings*, Nicolas Sidjakov
1962	*Once a Mouse*, Marcia Brown
1963	*The Snowy Day*, Ezra Jack Keats
1964	*Where the Wild Things Are*, Maurice Sendak
1965	*May I Bring a Friend?*, Beni Montressor
1966	*Always Room for One More*, Nonny Hogrogian
1967	*Sam, Bang, and Moonshine*, Evaline Ness
1968	*Drummer Hoff*, Ed Emberley
1969	*The Fool of the World and the Flying Ship*, Uri Shulevitz
1970	*Sylvester and the Magic Pebble*, William Steig
1971	*A Story A Story*, Gail E. Haley

Year Given	Book, Illustrator
1972	*One Fine Day,* Nonny Hogrogian
1973	*The Funny Little Woman,* Blair Lent
1974	*Duffy and the Devil,* Margot Zemach
1975	*Arrow to the Sun,* Gerald McDermott
1976	*Why Mosquitoes Buzz in People's Ears,* Leo & Diane Dillon
1977	*Ashanti to Zulu: African Traditions,* Leo & Diane Dillon
1978	*Noah's Ark,* Peter Spier
1979	*The Girl Who Loved Wild Horses,* Paul Goble
1980	*Ox-Cart Man,* Barbara Cooney
1981	*Fables,* Arnold Lobel
1982	*Jumanji,* Chris Van Allsburg
1983	*Shadow,* Marcia Brown
1984	*The Glorious Flight: Across the Channel with Louis Bleriot,* Alice and Martin Provensen
1985	*Saint George and the Dragon,* Trina Schart Hyman
1986	*The Polar Express,* Chris Van Allsburg
1987	*Hey, Al,* Richard Egielski
1988	*Owl Moon,* John Schoenherr
1989	*Song and Dance Man,* Stephen Grammell
1990	*Lon Po Po: A Red-Riding Hood Story From China,* Ed Young
1991	*Black and White,* David Macaulay
1992	*Tuesday,* David Wiesner
1993	*Mirette on the High Wire,* Emily Arnold McCully
1994	*Grandfather's Journey,* Allen Say
1995	*Smoky Night,* David Diaz
1996	*Officer Buckle and Gloria,* Peggy Rathmann
1997	*Golem,* David Wisniewski
1998	*Rapunzel,* Paul O. Zelinsky
1999	*Snowflake Bentley,* Mary Azarian
2000	*Joseph Had a Little Overcoat,* Simms Taback
2001	*So You Want to be President?,* David Small
2002	*The Three Pigs,* David Wiesner

Journalism Awards, 2002

National Journalism Awards, by Scripps Howard Foundation, $2,500 each. Editorial writing: Kate Stanley, *Star Tribune* (Minneapolis); human interest writing: Ken Fuson, *Des Moines Register* (IA); environmental reporting (over 100,000 circ.): Julie Hauserman, *St. Petersburg Times* (FL); environmental reporting (under 100,000 circ.): Scott Streater, *Pensacola News Journal* (FL); public service reporting (over 100,000 circ.): *The Seattle Times* (Duff Wilson, David Heath); public service reporting (under 100,000 circ.). (tie) *York Daily Record* and *The York Dispatch/Sunday News* (both PA); commentary: Leonard Pitts, *The Miami Herald;* photojournalism: Aristide Economopoulos, *The Star-Ledger* (Newark, NJ); editorial cartooning: John Sherffius, *St. Louis Post-Dispatch;* college cartooning: Nate Beeler, *The Eagle,* American University (Washington, DC); distinguished service to literacy: Paul Riede, *The Post-Standard* (Syracuse, NY); distinguished service to First Amendment: *Orlando Sentinel* (FL); business/economics reporting: *The Wall Street Journal,* (Rebecca Smith, John Emshwiller); web reporting: USATODAY.com; Electronic journalism—Small market radio: KOSU-FM (Stillwater, OK); large market radio: Latino USA, National Public Radio (Los Angeles); small market TV/cable: KTUU-TV (Anchorage, AK); large market TV/cable: WFLD-TV, Chicago.

National Magazine Awards, by American Society of Magazine Editors and Columbia Univ. Graduate School of Journalism. Gen. excel., circ. over 2 mil: *Newsweek*; 1 mil-2 mil: *Entertainment Weekly;* 500,000 to 1 mil: *Vibe*; 200,000-500,000: *National Geographic Adventure*; under 200,000: *Print*; personal service: *National Geographic Adventure;* leisure interests: *Vogue*; feature writing: *The Atlantic Monthly;* fiction: *The New Yorker*, design: *Details*; photography: *Vanity Fair;* reporting: *The Atlantic Monthly;* public interest: *The Atlantic Monthly;* profiles: *The New Yorker;* essays: *The New Yorker;* criticism/reviews: *Harper's Magazine;* columns/commentary: *New York Magazine;* single-topic issue: *Time;* gen. excellence online: National Geographic Magazine Online.

George Foster Peabody Awards, by Univ. of Georgia. ABC News Coverage of Sept.11, 2001, ABC News, NY; National Public Radio Coverage of Sept. 11, 2001, NPR, Washington, DC; *CNN Presents: Beneath the Veil and Unholy War,* CNN Productions (Atlanta), Channel 4 International and Hard Cash Productions; *Third Watch: In Their Own Words,* NBC, John Wells Productions in assoc. with Warner Bros. Television; *America: A Tribute to Heroes,* Joel Gallen and the U.S. Broadcast and Cable Networks; *Anne Frank,* Touchstone Television, presented on ABC; *American Masters: F. Scott Fitzgerald: Winter Dreams,* Thirteen/WNET (NY), presented on PBS; *Jazz Profiles,* National Public Radio, Washington, DC; *The Cliburn: Playing on the Edge,* Peter Rosen Productions, Inc., and KERA-TV, Dallas/Ft. Worth, TX; *Mzima—Haunt of the Riverhorse,* Survival Anglia Ltd., U.K.; *ExxonMobil Masterpiece Theatre: Talking Heads II: Miss Fozzard Finds Her Feet,* Slow Motion Ltd. production for the BBC, presented on PBS; *The Life and Times of Hank Greenberg,* The Chiesla Foundation and Cinemax; *Still Life with Animated Dogs,* Independent Television Service (ITVS) and Paul & Sandra Fierlinger, AR&T Associates, Inc.; *The DNA Files,* SoundVision Productions, presented on National Public Radio; *Visions of Vine Street,* WCPO-TV, Cincinnati, OH; *A Murder in the Neighbourhood,* Canadian Broadcasting Corporation; *WTO Challenge,* Television Broadcasts Limited, Hong Kong, SAR, People's Republic of China; *Endgame in Ireland,* Brook Lapping Productions for BBC2 in association with WGBH/Boston, RTE (Ireland), La Sept ARTE (France and Germany), SBS (Australia), and YLE (Finland); *A Huey P. Newton Story,* 40 Acres & A Mule Filmworks, Luna Ray Films, BLACK STARZ!, PBS and African Heritage Network; *Hell in the Pacific,* a Carlton Production in assoc. with The Learning Channel for Channel Four Television; *Conspiracy,* HBO Films produced in assoc. with the British Broadcasting Corporation; *Things Behind the Sun,* Showtime, An Echo Lake Productions/Sidekick Entertainment Prod.; *Boycott,* Norman Twain Productions with Shelby Stone Productions in assoc. with HBO Films; *The First Year,* Teachers Documentary Project, presented on PBS; *My Father's Camera,* National Film Board of Canada; Youth Radio, Berkeley, CA; *Little Bill,* Nickelodeon; *Blue's Clues,* Nickelodeon; WGBH, Boston; *60 Minutes II: Memories of a Massacre,* CBS News, NY; *Wit,* Avenue Pictures in assoc. with HBO Films; *The Bernie Mac Show,* Wilmore Films, Regency Television, and 20th Century Fox; *Band of Brothers,* Band of Brothers Ltd. on behalf of DreamWorks and Playtone, presented on HBO; *Nightline,* ABC News, NY.

Reuben Award, by National Cartoonists Society. For best cartoonist of 2001: Jerry Scott

The Spingarn Medal, 1915-2002

The Spingarn Medal has been awarded annually since 1915 (except in 1938) by the National Assoc. for the Advancement of Colored People for the highest achievement by an African American in the previous year.

1915	Ernest E. Just	1939	Marian Anderson	1960	Langston Hughes	1983	Lena Horne
1916	Charles Young	1940	Louis T. Wright	1961	Kenneth B. Clark	1984	Thomas Bradley
1917	Harry T. Burleigh	1941	Richard Wright	1962	Robert C. Weaver	1985	Bill Cosby
1918	William S. Braithwaite	1942	A. Philip Randolph	1963	Medgar W. Evers	1986	Dr. Benjamin L. Hooks
1919	Archibald H. Grimké	1943	William H. Hastie	1964	Roy Wilkins	1987	Percy E. Sutton
1920	W. E. B. Du Bois	1944	Charles Drew	1965	Leontyne Price	1988	Frederick D. Patterson
1921	Charles S. Gilpin	1945	Paul Robeson	1966	John H. Johnson	1989	Jesse Jackson
1922	Mary B. Talbert	1946	Thurgood Marshall	1967	Edward W. Brooke	1990	L. Douglas Wilder
1923	George W.Carver	1947	Dr. Percy L. Julian	1968	Sammy Davis Jr.	1991	Gen. Colin L. Powell
1924	Roland Hayes	1948	Channing H. Tobias	1969	Clarence M. Mitchell Jr.	1992	Barbara Jordan
1925	James W. Johnson	1949	Ralph J. Bunche	1970	Jacob Lawrence	1993	Dorothy I. Height
1926	Carter G. Woodson	1950	Charles H. Houston	1971	Leon H. Sullivan	1994	Maya Angelou
1927	Anthony Overton	1951	Mabel K. Staupers	1972	Gordon Parks	1995	John Hope Franklin
1928	Charles W. Chesnutt	1952	Harry T. Moore	1973	Wilson C. Riles	1996	A. Leon Higginbotham
1929	Mordecai W. Johnson	1953	Paul R. Williams	1974	Damon Keith	1997	Carl T. Rowan
1930	Henry A. Hunt	1954	Theodore K. Lawless	1975	Henry (Hank) Aaron	1998	Myrlie Evers-Williams
1931	Richard B. Harrison	1955	Carl Murphy	1976	Alvin Ailey	1999	Earl G. Graves Sr.
1932	Robert R. Moton	1956	Jack R. Robinson	1977	Alex Haley	2000	Oprah Winfrey
1933	Max Yergan	1957	Martin Luther King Jr.	1978	Andrew Young	2001	Vernon E. Jordan Jr.
1934	William T. B. Williams	1958	Daisy Bates and the Little Rock Nine	1979	Rosa L. Parks	2002	John Lewis
1935	Mary McLeod Bethune	1959	Edward Kennedy (Duke) Ellington	1980	Dr. Rayford W. Logan		
1936	John Hope			1981	Coleman Young		
1937	Walter White			1982	Dr. Benjamin E. Mays		

Miscellaneous Awards, 2002

American Academy of Arts and Letters. Gold Medal for Architecture: Frank Gehry; Award for Distinguished Service to the Arts: Robert Giroux; Award of Merit for Sculpture, $10,000: Judy Pfaff; Arnold W. Brunner Memorial Prize in Architecture, $5,000: Kazuyo Sejima and Ryue Nishizawa; Academy Awards, $7,500 each, in Architecture: Rick Joy, Office dA (Mónica Ponce de León and Nader Tehrani); in Art: Polly Apfelbaum, Mel Kendrick, Lucas Samaras, Peter Saul, Stephen Westfall; in Music: Claude Baker, Daniel Becker, David Liptak, Cindy McTee; Jimmy Ernst Award in Art, $5,000: Carolee Schneemann; Walter Hinrichsen Award (Music): James Matheson; Charles Ives Fellowships in Music, $15,000: Mason Bates, Leslie Hogan; Charles Ives Scholarships in Music, $7,500 each: Kati Agocs, Nancy Kho, Nathan Michel, David Schober, Gregory Spears, Dmitri Tymoczko; Wladimir and Rhoda Lakond Award in Music, $5,000: Eric Moe; Goddard Lieberson Fellowships in Music, $12,500 each: Alla Borzova, Steven Stucky; Willard L. Metcalf Award in Art, $5,000: Hilary Harkness; Marc Blitzstein Award in Music: Arnold Weinstein; Richard Rodgers Awards for the Musical Theater, $100,000: (development) *The Fabulist,* David Spencer and Stephen Witkin; *The Tutor,* Andrew Ferle and Maryrose Wood; Richard and Hinda Rosenthal Foundation Award in Art, $5,000: Tom Burckhardt.

National Humanities Medal (formerly Charles Frankel Prize), by National Endowment for the Humanities. $5,000 each: Jose Cisneros, Robert Coles, Sharon Darling, WIlliam Manchester, National Trust for Historic Preservation, Richard Peck, Eileen Jackson Southern, Tom Wolfe.

Intel Science Talent Search (formerly given by Westinghouse). First ($100,000 schol.): Ryan Patterson, Grand Junction, CO; Second ($75,000 schol.): Jacob Licht, West Hartfort, CT; Third ($50,000 schol.): Emily Riehl, Bloomington, IL.

National Inventor of the Year Awards, by Intellectual Property Owners. Eli Lilly and Company research team (Nils U. Bang, M.D., Robert J. Beckmann, Brian W. Grinnell, Ph.D., Daniel L. Hartman, M.D., Richard Jaskunas, Ph.D., Mei-Hui T. Lai, Ph.D., Sheila Little, Ph.D., George L. Long, Ph.D., Robert F. Santerre, Ph.D., Sau-Chi Betty Yan, Ph.D.).

John F. Kennedy Center for the Performing Arts Awards. James Earl Jones, James Levine, Chita Rivera, Paul Simon, Elizabeth Taylor.

Library of the Year Award, by Gale Research, Inc., and Library Journal. Kalamazoo (MI) Public Library.

Congressional Gold Medal, by Congress. Former Pres. Ronald Reagan and Nancy Reagan.

National Medal of the Arts, by the National Endowment for the Arts and the White House. Alvin Ailey Dance Foundation, Rudolfo Anaya, Johnny Cash, Kirk Douglas, Helen Frankenthaler, Judith Jamison, Yo-Yo Ma, Mike Nichols.

Pritzker Architecture Prize, by the Hyatt Foundation, $100,000: Glenn Murcutt, Australia.

Teacher of the Year, by Council of Chief State School Officers and Scholastic, Inc.: Chauncey Veatch, Social Studies, Coachella Valley HS, Thermal, CA.

Templeton Prize for Progress Toward Research or Discoveries about Spiritual Realities, by Templeton Foundation, £700,000 (about $1 million): John C. Polkinghorne, Anglican priest, physicist, and author.

Miss America Winners, for 1921-2003

1921	Margaret Gorman, Washington, DC
1922-23	Mary Campbell, Columbus, Ohio
1924	Ruth Malcolmson, Philadelphia, Pennsylvania
1925	Fay Lamphier, Oakland, California
1926	Norma Smallwood, Tulsa, Oklahoma
1927	Lois Delander, Joliet, Illinois
1933	Marion Bergeron, West Haven, Connecticut
1935	Henrietta Leaver, Pittsburgh, Pennsylvania
1936	Rose Coyle, Philadelphia, Pennsylvania
1937	Bette Cooper, Bertrand Island, New Jersey
1938	Marilyn Meseke, Marion, Ohio
1939	Patricia Donnelly, Detroit, Michigan
1940	Frances Marie Burke, Philadelphia, Pennsylvania
1941	Rosemary LaPlanche, Los Angeles, California
1942	Jo-Caroll Dennison, Tyler, Texas
1943	Jean Bartel, Los Angeles, California
1944	Venus Ramey, Washington, D.C.
1945	Bess Myerson, New York City, New York
1946	Marilyn Buferd, Los Angeles, California
1947	Barbara Walker, Memphis, Tennessee
1948	BeBe Shopp, Hopkins, Minnesota
1949	Jacque Mercer, Litchfield, Arizona
1951	Yolande Betbeze, Mobile, Alabama
1952	Coleen Kay Hutchins, Salt Lake City, Utah
1953	Neva Jane Langley, Macon, Georgia
1954	Evelyn Margaret Ay, Ephrata, Pennsylvania
1955	Lee Meriwether, San Francisco, California
1956	Sharon Ritchie, Denver, Colorado
1957	Marian McKnight, Manning, South Carolina
1958	Marilyn Van Derbur, Denver, Colorado
1959	Mary Ann Mobley, Brandon, Mississippi
1960	Lynda Lee Mead, Natchez, Mississippi
1961	Nancy Fleming, Montague, Michigan
1962	Maria Fletcher, Asheville, North Carolina
1963	Jacquelyn Mayer, Sandusky, Ohio
1964	Donna Axum, El Dorado, Arkansas
1965	Vonda Kay Van Dyke, Phoenix, Arizona
1966	Deborah Irene Bryant, Overland Park, Kansas
1967	Jane Anne Jayroe, Laverne, Oklahoma
1968	Debra Dene Barnes, Moran, Kansas
1969	Judith Anne Ford, Belvidere, Illinois
1970	Pamela Anne Eldred, Birmingham, Michigan
1971	Phyllis Ann George, Denton, Texas
1972	Laurie Lea Schaefer, Columbus, Ohio
1973	Terry Anne Meeuwsen, DePere, Wisconsin
1974	Rebecca Ann King, Denver, Colorado
1975	Shirley Cothran, Fort Worth, Texas
1976	Tawney Elaine Godin, Yonkers, New York
1977	Dorothy Kathleen Benham, Edina, Minnesota
1978	Susan Perkins, Columbus, Ohio
1979	Kylene Barker, Galax, Virginia
1980	Cheryl Prewitt, Ackerman, Mississippi
1981	Susan Powell, Elk City, Oklahoma
1982	Elizabeth Ward, Russellville, Arkansas
1983	Debra Maffett, Anaheim, California
1984	Vanessa Williams*, Milwood, New York
	Suzette Charles, Mays Landing, New Jersey
1985	Sharlene Wells, Salt Lake City, Utah
1986	Susan Akin, Meridian, Mississippi
1987	Kellye Cash, Memphis, Tennessee
1988	Kaye Lani Rae Rafko, Monroe, Michigan
1989	Gretchen Carlson, Anoka, Minnesota
1990	Debbye Turner, Columbia, Missouri
1991	Marjorie Vincent, Oak Park, Illinois
1992	Carolyn Suzanne Sapp, Honolulu, Hawaii
1993	Leanza Cornett, Jacksonville, Florida
1994	Kimberly Aiken, Columbia, South Carolina
1995	Heather Whitestone, Birmingham, Alabama
1996	Shawntel Smith, Muldrow, Oklahoma
1997	Tara Dawn Holland, Overland Park, Kansas
1998	Kate Shindle, Evanston, Illinois
1999	Nicole Johnson, Roanoke, Virginia
2000	Heather Renee French, Maysville, Kentucky
2001	Angela Perez Baraquio, Honolulu, Hawaii
2002	Katie Harman, Gresham, Oregon
2003	Erika Harold, Urbana, Illinois

* Resigned July 23, 1984.

Entertainment Awards

Tony (Antoinette Perry) Awards, 2002

Play: *The Goat or Who Is Sylvia*?
Musical: *Thoroughly Modern Millie*
Book of a musical: Greg Kotis for *Urinetown the Musical*
Actor, play: Alan Bates, *Fortune's Fool*
Actress, play: Lindsay Duncan, *Private Lives*
Actor, musical: John Lithgow, *Sweet Smell of Success*
Actress, musical: Sutton Foster, *Thoroughly Modern Millie*
Musical score: Mark Hollman & Greg Kotis, *Urinetown the Musical*
Director, play: Mary Zimmermann, *Metamorphoses*
Director, musical: John Rando, *Urinetown the Musical*
Play revival: *Private Lives*
Musical revival: *Into the Woods*
Featured actor, play: Frank Langella, *Fortune's Fool*
Featured actress, play: Katie Finneran, *Noises Off*
Featured actor, musical: Shuler Hensley, *Oklahoma!*
Featured actress, musical: Harriet Harris, *Thoroughly Modern Millie*
Choreography: Rob Ashford, *Thoroughly Modern Millie*
Costume design: Martin Pakledinaz, *Thoroughly Modern Millie*
Scenic design: Tim Hatley, *Private Lives*
Lighting design: Brian MacDevitt, *Into the Woods*
Orchestrations: Doug Besterman & Ralph Burns, *Thoroughly Modern Mille*
Lifetime achievement: Julie Harris & Robert Whitehead
Special Theatrical Event: *Elaine Stritch at Liberty*
Regional Theater: Williamstown Theatre Festival

Tony Awards, 1948-2001

Year	Play	Musical
1948	*Mister Roberts*	No Award
1949	*Death of a Salesman*	*Kiss Me Kate*
1950	*The Cocktail Party*	*South Pacific*
1951	*The Rose Tattoo*	*Guys and Dolls*
1952	*The Fourposter*	*The King and I*
1953	*The Crucible*	*Wonderful Town*
1954	*The Teahouse of the August Moon*	*Kismet*
1955	*The Desperate Hours*	*The Pajama Game*
1956	*The Diary of Anne Frank*	*Damn Yankees*
1957	*Long Day's Journey Into Night*	*My Fair Lady*
1958	*Sunrise at Campobello*	*The Music Man*
1959	*J.B.*	*Redhead*
1960	*The Miracle Worker*	(tie) *Fiorello!, The Sound of Music*
1961	*Becket*	*Bye, Bye Birdie*
1962	*A Man for All Seasons*	*How to Succeed in Business Without Really Trying*
1963	*Who's Afraid of Virginia Woolf?*	*A Funny Thing Happened on the Way to the Forum*
1964	*Luther*	*Hello, Dolly!*
1965	*The Subject Was Roses*	*Fiddler on the Roof*
1966	*Marat/Sade*	*Man of La Mancha*
1967	*The Homecoming*	*Cabaret*
1968	*Rosencrantz and Guildenstern Are Dead*	*Hallelujah, Baby!*
1969	*The Great White Hope*	*1776*
1970	*Borstal Boy*	*Applause*
1971	*Sleuth*	*Company*
1972	*Sticks and Bones*	*Two Gentleman of Verona*
1973	*That Championship Season*	*A Little Night Music*
1974	*The River Niger*	*Raisin*
1975	*Equus*	*The Wiz*
1976	*Travesties*	*A Chorus Line*
1977	*The Shadow Box*	*Annie*
1978	*Da*	*Ain't Misbehavin'*
1979	*The Elephant Man*	Sweeney Todd
1980	*Children of a Lesser God*	*Evita*
1981	*Amadeus*	*42nd Street*
1982	*The Life and Adventures of Nicholas Nickelby*	*Nine*
1983	*Torch Song Trilogy*	*Cats*
1984	*The Real Thing*	*La Cage aux Folles*
1985	*Biloxi Blues*	*Big River*
1986	*I'm Not Rappaport*	*The Mystery of Edwin Drood*
1987	*Fences*	*Les Miserables*
1988	*M. Butterfly*	*Phantom of the Opera*
1989	*The Heidi Chronicles*	*Jerome Robbins' Broadway*
1990	*The Grapes of Wrath*	*City of Angels*
1991	*Lost in Yonkers*	*The Will Rogers Follies*
1992	*Dancing at Lughnasa*	*Crazy for You*
1993	*Angels in America: Millennium Approaches*	*Kiss of the Spider Woman*
1994	*Angels in America: Perestroika*	*Passion*
1995	*Love! Valour! Compassion!*	*Sunset Boulevard*
1996	*Master Class*	*Rent*
1997	*The Last Night of Ballyhoo*	*Titanic*
1998	*Art*	*The Lion King*
1999	*Side Man*	*Fosse*
2000	*Copenhagen*	*Contact*
2001	*Proof*	*The Producers*

2002 Selected Prime-Time Emmy Awards (for 2001-2002 season)

Drama series: *The West Wing*, NBC
Comedy series: *Friends*, NBC
Miniseries: *Band of Brothers*, HBO
Variety, music, or comedy series: *Late Show with David Letterman*, CBS
Variety, music, or comedy special: *America: A Tribute to Heroes*, various networks
Made-for-television movie: *The Gathering Storm*, HBO
Lead actor, drama series: Michael Chiklis, *The Shield*, FX
Lead actress, drama series: Allison Janney, *The West Wing*, NBC
Lead actor, comedy series: Ray Romano, *Everybody Loves Raymond*, CBS
Lead actress, comedy series: Jennifer Aniston, *Friends*, NBC
Lead actor, miniseries/movie: Albert Finney, *The Gathering Storm*, HBO
Lead actress, miniseries/movie: Laura Linney, *Wild Iris*, Showtime
Sup. actor, drama series: John Spencer, *The West Wing*, NBC
Sup. actress, drama series: Stockard Channing, *The West Wing*, NBC
Sup. actor, comedy series: Brad Garrett, *Everybody Loves Raymond*, CBS
Sup. actress, comedy series: Doris Roberts, *Everybody Loves Raymond*, CBS
Sup. actor, miniseries/movie: Michael Moriarty, *James Dean*, TNT
Sup. actress, miniseries/movie: Stockard Channing, *The Matthew Shepard Story*, NBC
Individual performance, variety series/music program: Sting, *Sting in Tuscany . . . All This Time*, A&E

2002 Selected Daytime Emmy Awards (for 2001-2002 season)

Drama series: *One Life to Live*, ABC
Actress: Susan Flannery, *The Bold and the Beautiful*, CBS
Actor: Peter Bergman, *The Young and the Restless*, CBS
Sup. actress: Crystal Chappell, *Guiding Light*, CBS
Sup. actor: Josh Duhamel, *All My Children*, ABC
Younger actress: Jennifer Finnigan, *The Bold and the Beautiful*, CBS
Younger actor: Jacob Young, *General Hospital*, ABC
Drama Series directing team: *The Young and the Restless*, CBS
Drama Series writing team: *As the World Turns*, CBS
Preschool children's series: *Sesame Street*, PBS
Performer in children's series: Levar Burton, *Reading Rainbow*, PBS
Children's special: *My Louisiana Sky*, Showtime
Performer in a children's special: Kelsey Keel, *My Louisiana Sky*, Showtime
Children's animated program: *Madeline*, Disney Channel
Performer in a children's animated program: Charles Shaughnessy, *Stanley*, Disney Channel
Game/audience participation show: *Jeopardy!*, syndicated
Game show host: Bob Barker, *The Price Is Right*, CBS
Talk Show: *The Rosie O'Donnell Show*, syndicated
Talk show host: Rosie O'Donnell, *The Rosie O'Donnell Show*, syndicated
Service show: *Wolfgang Puck*, Food Network
Service show host: Martha Stewart, *Martha Stewart Living*, syndicated

2001 Selected Prime-Time Emmy Awards (for 2000-2001 season)

Drama series: *The West Wing*, NBC
Comedy series: *Sex and the City*, HBO
Miniseries: *Anne Frank*, ABC
Variety, music, or comedy series: *Late Show with David Letterman*, CBS
Variety, music, or comedy special: *Cirque du Soleil's Dralion*, Bravo
Made-for-television movie: *Wit*, HBO
Actor, drama series: James Gandolfini, *The Sopranos*, HBO
Actress, drama series: Edie Falco, *The Sopranos*, HBO
Actor, comedy series: Eric McCormack, *Will & Grace*, NBC
Actress, comedy series: Patricia Heaton, *Everybody Loves Raymond*, NBC
Actor, miniseries/movie: Kenneth Brannagh, *Conspiracy*, HBO
Actress, miniseries/movie: Judy Davis, *Life with Judy Garland: Me and My Shadows*, ABC
Sup. actor, drama series: Bradley Whitford, *The West Wing*, NBC
Sup. actress, drama series: Allison Janney, *The West Wing*, NBC
Sup. actor, comedy series: Peter MacNicol, *Ally McBeal*, FOX
Sup. actress, comedy series: Doris Roberts, *Everybody Loves Raymond*, CBS
Sup. actor, miniseries/movie: Brian Cox, *Nuremberg*, TNT
Sup. actress, miniseries/movie: Tammy Blanchard, *Life with Judy Garland: Me and My Shadows*
Individual performance, variety series/music program: Barbra Streisand, *Barbra Streisand: Timeless*

2001 Selected Daytime Emmy Awards (for 2000-2001 season)

Drama series: *As the World Turns*, CBS
Actress: Martha Byrne, *As the World Turns*, CBS
Actor: David Canary, *All My Children*, ABC
Sup. actress: Lesli Kay, *As the World Turns*, CBS
Sup. actor: Michael E. Knight, *All My Children*, ABC
Younger actress: Adrienne Frantz, *The Bold and the Beautiful*, CBS
Younger actor: Justin Torkildsen, *The Bold and the Beautiful*, CBS
Drama series directing team: *The Young and the Restless*, CBS
Drama series writing team: *As the World Turns*, CBS
Preschool children's series: *Sesame Street*, PBS

Children's series: *Reading Rainbow,* PBS
Performer in children's series: Levar Burton, *Reading Rainbow,* PBS
Children's special: *Run the Wild Fields* and *A Storm in Summer,* Showtime
Performer in a children's special: Ossie Davis, *Finding Buck McHenry,* Showtime
Children's animated program: *Arthur,* PBS
Performer in a children's animated program: Nathan Lane, *Disney's Teacher's Pet,* ABC
Game/audience participation show: *Who Wants to Be a Millionaire?,* ABC
Game show host: Regis Philbin, *Who Wants to Be a Millionaire?,* ABC
Talk show: *The Rosie O'Donnell Show,* syndicated
Talk show host (tie): Rosie O'Donnell, *The Rosie O'Donnell Show,* syndicated; Regis Philbin, *Live with Regis,* syndicated
Service show: *Martha Stewart Living,* syndicated
Service show host: Julia Child and Jacques Pepin, *Julia & Jacques Cooking at Home,* PBS

Prime-Time Emmy Awards, 1952-2000

The National Academy of Television Arts and Science, presented the first Emmy Awards in 1949. Through the years, the number and names of award categories have changed, but since 1952, the Academy has recognized an outstanding comedy and drama each year.

Year Given	Comedy	Drama
1952	*Red Skelton Show,* NBC	*Studio One,* CBS
1953	*I Love Lucy,* CBS	*Robert Montgomery Presents,* NBC
1954	*I Love Lucy,* CBS	*The U.S. Steel Hour,* ABC
1955	*Make Room for Daddy,* ABC	*The U.S. Steel Hour,* ABC
1956	*Phil Silvers Show,* CBS	*Producer's Showcase,* NBC
1957	*Phil Silvers Show,* CBS	*Requiem for a Heavyweight,* CBS[1]
1958	*Phil Silvers Show,* CBS	*Gunsmoke,* CBS
1959[2]	*Jack Benny Show,* CBS	(3)
1960	*Art Carney Special,* NBC	*Playhouse 90,* CBS
1961	*Jack Benny Show,* CBS	*Hallmark Hall of Fame: Macbeth,* NBC
1962	*Bob Newhart Show,* CBS	*The Defenders,* CBS
1963	*Dick Van Dyke Show,* CBS	*The Defenders,* CBS
1964	*Dick Van Dyke Show,* CBS	*The Defenders,* CBS
1965	*Dick Van Dyke Show,* CBS	*Hallmark Hall of Fame: The Magnificent Yankee,* NBC
1966	*Dick Van Dyke Show,* CBS	*The Fugitive,* ABC
1967	*The Monkees,* NBC	*Mission: Impossible,* CBS
1968	*Get Smart,* NBC	*Mission: Impossible,* CBS
1969	*Get Smart,* NBC	*NET Playhouse,* NET
1970	*My World and Welcome to It,* NBC	*Marcus Welby, M.D.,* ABC
1971	*All in the Family,* CBS	*The Bold Ones: "The Senator,"* NBC
1972	*All in the Family,* CBS	*Masterpiece Theatre: Elizabeth R,* PBS
1973	*All in the Family,* CBS	*The Waltons,* CBS
1974	*M*A*S*H,* CBS	*Masterpiece Theatre: Upstairs, Downstairs;* PBS
1975	*Mary Tyler Moore Show,* CBS	*Masterpiece Theatre: Upstairs, Downstairs;* PBS
1976	*Mary Tyler Moore Show,* CBS	*Police Story,* NBC
1977	*Mary Tyler Moore Show,* CBS	*Masterpiece Theatre: Upstairs, Downstairs;* PBS
1978	*All in the Family,* CBS	*The Rockford Files,* NBC
1979	*Taxi,* ABC	*Lou Grant,* CBS
1980	*Taxi,* ABC	*Lou Grant,* CBS
1981	*Taxi,* ABC	*Hill Street Blues,* NBC
1982	*Barney Miller,* ABC	*Hill Street Blues,* NBC
1983	*Cheers,* NBC	*Hill Street Blues,* NBC
1984	*Cheers,* NBC	*Hill Street Blues,* NBC
1985	*The Cosby Show,* NBC	*Cagney & Lacey,* CBS
1986	*Golden Girls,* NBC	*Cagney & Lacey,* CBS
1987	*Golden Girls,* NBC	*L.A. Law,* NBC
1988	*The Wonder Years,* ABC	*thirtysomething,* ABC
1989	*Cheers,* NBC	*L.A. Law,* NBC
1990	*Murphy Brown,* CBS	*L.A. Law,* NBC
1991	*Cheers,* NBC	*L.A. Law,* NBC
1992	*Murphy Brown,* CBS	*Northern Exposure,* CBS
1993	*Seinfeld,* NBC	*Picket Fences,* CBS
1994	*Frasier,* NBC	*Picket Fences,* CBS
1995	*Frasier,* NBC	*NYPD Blue,* ABC
1996	*Frasier,* NBC	*ER,* NBC
1997	*Frasier,* NBC	*Law & Order,* NBC
1998	*Frasier,* NBC	*The Practice,* ABC
1999	*Ally McBeal,* Fox	*The Practice,* ABC
2000	*Will & Grace,* NBC	*The West Wing,* NBC

(1) "Best Single Program of the Year," shown on *Playhouse 90,* which was named "Best New Series." (2) Beginning in 1959, Emmys awarded for work in the season encompassing the previous and current year. (3) *Playhouse 90* (CBS) was best drama of 1 hour or longer; *Alcoa-Goodyear Theatre* (NBC) was best drama of less than 1 hour.

2002 Golden Globe Awards

(Awarded for work in 2001)

Film

Drama: *A Beautiful Mind*
Musical/comedy: *Moulin Rouge*
Actress, drama: Sissy Spacek, *In the Bedroom*
Actor, drama: Russell Crowe, *A Beautiful Mind*
Actress, musical/comedy: Nicole Kidman, *Moulin Rouge*
Actor, musical/comedy: Gene Hackman, *The Royal Tenenbaums*
Sup. actress, drama: Jennifer Connelly, *A Beautiful Mind*
Sup. actor, drama: Jim Broadbent, *Iris*
Director: Robert Altman, *Gosford Park*
Screenplay: Akiva Goldsman, *A Beautiful Mind*
Foreign-language film: *No Man's Land* (Bosnia & Herzegovina)
Original score: Craig Armstrong, *Moulin Rouge*
Original song: "Until . . .," from *Kate & Leopold,* Sting
Cecil B. De Mille award for lifetime achievement: Harrison Ford

Television

Series, drama: *Six Feet Under,* HBO
Actress, drama: Jennifer Garner, *Alias,* ABC
Actor, drama: Kiefer Sutherland, *24,* Fox
Series, musical/comedy: *Sex and the City,* HBO
Actress, musical/comedy: Sarah Jessica Parker, *Sex and the City,* HBO
Actor, musical/comedy: Charlie Sheen, *Spin City,* ABC
Miniseries, movie made for TV: *Band of Brothers,* HBO
Actress, miniseries/movie: Judy Davis, *Life with Judy Garland: Me and My Shadows,* ABC
Actor, miniseries/movie: James Franco, *James Dean,* TNT
Sup. actress, miniseries/movie: Rachel Griffiths, *Six Feet Under,* HBO
Sup. actor, miniseries/movie: Stanley Tucci, *Conspiracy,* HBO

Academy Awards (Oscars) for 1927-2001

Year	Picture	Actor	Actress	Sup. Actor[1]	Sup. Actress[1]	Director
1927-28	*Wings*	Emil Jannings, *The Way of All Flesh*	Janet Gaynor, *Seventh Heaven*			Frank Borzage, *Seventh Heaven;* Lewis Milestone, *Two Arabian Knights*
1928-29	*Broadway Melody*	Warner Baxter, *In Old Arizona*	Mary Pickford, *Coquette*			Frank Lloyd, *The Divine Lady*
1929-30	*All Quiet on the Western Front*	George Arliss *Disraeli*	Norma Shearer *The Divorcee*			Lewis Milestone *All Quiet on the Western Front*
1930-31	*Cimarron*	Lionel Barrymore *Free Soul*	Marie Dressler *Min and Bill*			Norman Taurog *Skippy*
1931-32	*Grand Hotel*	Fredric March *Dr. Jekyll and Mr. Hyde;* Wallace Beery *The Champ* (tie)	Helen Hayes *The Sin of Madelon Claudet*			Frank Borzage *Bad Girl*

Year	Picture	Actor	Actress	Sup. Actor[1]	Sup. Actress[1]	Director
1932-33	*Cavalcade*	Charles Laughton *The Private Life of Henry VIII*	Katharine Hepburn *Morning Glory*			Frank Lloyd *Cavalcade*
1934	*It Happened One Night*	Clark Gable *It Happened One Night*	Claudette Colbert *It Happened One Night*			Frank Capra *It Happened One Night*
1935	*Mutiny on the Bounty*	Victor McLaglen *The Informer*	Bette Davis *Dangerous*			John Ford *The Informer*
1936	*The Great Ziegfeld*	Paul Muni *Story of Louis Pasteur*	Luise Rainer *The Great Ziegfeld*	Walter Brennan *Come and Get It*	Gale Sondergaard *Anthony Adverse*	Frank Capra *Mr. Deeds Goes to Town*
1937	*Life of Emile Zola*	Spencer Tracy *Captains Courageous*	Luise Rainer *The Good Earth*	Joseph Schildkraut *Life of Emile Zola*	Alice Brady *In Old Chicago*	Leo McCarey *The Awful Truth*
1938	*You Can't Take It With You*	Spencer Tracy *Boys Town*	Bette Davis *Jezebel*	Walter Brennan *Kentucky*	Fay Bainter *Jezebel*	Frank Capra *You Can't Take It With You*
1939	*Gone With the Wind*	Robert Donat *Goodbye Mr. Chips*	Vivien Leigh *Gone With the Wind*	Thomas Mitchell *Stage Coach*	Hattie McDaniel *Gone With the Wind*	Victor Fleming *Gone With the Wind*
1940	*Rebecca*	James Stewart *The Philadelphia Story*	Ginger Rogers *Kitty Foyle*	Walter Brennan *The Westerner*	Jane Darwell *The Grapes of Wrath*	John Ford *The Grapes of Wrath*
1941	*How Green Was My Valley*	Gary Cooper *Sergeant York*	Joan Fontaine *Suspicion*	Donald Crisp *How Green Was My Valley*	Mary Astor *The Great Lie*	John Ford *How Green Was My Valley*
1942	*Mrs. Miniver*	James Cagney *Yankee Doodle Dandy*	Greer Garson *Mrs. Miniver*	Van Heflin *Johnny Eager*	Teresa Wright *Mrs. Miniver*	William Wyler *Mrs. Miniver*
1943	*Casablanca*	Paul Lukas *Watch on the Rhine*	Jennifer Jones *The Song of Bernadette*	Charles Coburn *The More the Merrier*	Katina Paxinou *For Whom the Bell Tolls*	Michael Curtiz *Casablanca*
1944	*Going My Way*	Bing Crosby *Going My Way*	Ingrid Bergman *Gaslight*	Barry Fitzgerald *Going My Way*	Ethel Barrymore *None But the Lonely Heart*	Leo McCarey *Going My Way*
1945	*The Lost Weekend*	Ray Milland *The Lost Weekend*	Joan Crawford *Mildred Pierce*	James Dunn *A Tree Grows in Brooklyn*	Anne Revere *National Velvet*	Billy Wilder *The Lost Weekend*
1946	*The Best Years of Our Lives*	Fredric March *The Best Years of Our Lives*	Olivia de Havilland *To Each His Own*	Harold Russell *The Best Years of Our Lives*	Anne Baxter *The Razor's Edge*	William Wyler *The Best Years of Our Lives*
1947	*Gentleman's Agreement*	Ronald Colman *A Double Life*	Loretta Young *The Farmer's Daughter*	Edmund Gwenn *Miracle on 34th Street*	Celeste Holm *Gentleman's Agreement*	Elia Kazan *Gentleman's Agreement*
1948	*Hamlet*	Laurence Olivier *Hamlet*	Jane Wyman *Johnny Belinda*	Walter Huston *Treasure of Sierra Madre*	Claire Trevor *Key Largo*	John Huston *Treasure of Sierra Madre*
1949	*All the King's Men*	Broderick Crawford *All the King's Men*	Olivia de Havilland *The Heiress*	Dean Jagger *Twelve O'Clock High*	Mercedes McCambridge *All the King's Men*	Joseph L. Mankiewicz *Letter to Three Wives*
1950	*All About Eve*	Jose Ferrer *Cyrano de Bergerac*	Judy Holliday *Born Yesterday*	George Sanders *All About Eve*	Josephine Hull *Harvey*	Joseph L. Mankiewicz *All About Eve*
1951	*An American in Paris*	Humphrey Bogart *The African Queen*	Vivien Leigh *A Streetcar Named Desire*	Karl Malden *A Streetcar Named Desire*	Kim Hunter *A Streetcar Named Desire*	George Stevens *A Place in the Sun*
1952	*The Greatest Show on Earth*	Gary Cooper *High Noon*	Shirley Booth *Come Back Little Sheba*	Anthony Quinn *Viva Zapata!*	Gloria Grahame *The Bad and the Beautiful*	John Ford *The Quiet Man*
1953	*From Here to Eternity*	William Holden *Stalag 17*	Audrey Hepburn *Roman Holiday*	Frank Sinatra *From Here to Eternity*	Donna Reed *From Here to Eternity*	Fred Zinnemann *From Here to Eternity*
1954	*On the Waterfront*	Marlon Brando *On the Waterfront*	Grace Kelly *The Country Girl*	Edmond O'Brien *The Barefoot Contessa*	Eva Marie Saint *On the Waterfront*	Elia Kazan *On the Waterfront*
1955	*Marty*	Ernest Borgnine *Marty*	Anna Magnani *The Rose Tattoo*	Jack Lemmon *Mister Roberts*	Jo Van Fleet *East of Eden*	Delbert Mann *Marty*
1956	*Around the World in 80 Days*	Yul Brynner *The King and I*	Ingrid Bergman *Anastasia*	Anthony Quinn *Lust for Life*	Dorothy Malone *Written on the Wind*	George Stevens *Giant*
1957	*The Bridge on the River Kwai*	Alec Guinness *The Bridge on the River Kwai*	Joanne Woodward *The Three Faces of Eve*	Red Buttons *Sayonara*	Miyoshi Umeki *Sayonara*	David Lean *The Bridge on the River Kwai*
1958	*Gigi*	David Niven *Separate Tables*	Susan Hayward *I Want to Live*	Burl Ives *The Big Country*	Wendy Hiller *Separate Tables*	Vincente Minnelli *Gigi*
1959	*Ben-Hur*	Charlton Heston *Ben-Hur*	Simone Signoret *Room at the Top*	Hugh Griffith *Ben-Hur*	Shelley Winters *Diary of Anne Frank*	William Wyler *Ben-Hur*
1960	*The Apartment*	Burt Lancaster *Elmer Gantry*	Elizabeth Taylor *Butterfield 8*	Peter Ustinov *Spartacus*	Shirley Jones *Elmer Gantry*	Billy Wilder *The Apartment*
1961	*West Side Story*	Maximilian Schell *Judgment at Nuremberg*	Sophia Loren *Two Women*	George Chakiris *West Side Story*	Rita Moreno *West Side Story*	Jerome Robbins, Robert Wise *West Side Story*

Year	Picture	Actor	Actress	Sup. Actor[1]	Sup. Actress[1]	Director
1962	*Lawrence of Arabia*	Gregory Peck *To Kill a Mockingbird*	Anne Bancroft *The Miracle Worker*	Ed Begley *Sweet Bird of Youth*	Patty Duke *The Miracle Worker*	David Lean *Lawrence of Arabia*
1963	*Tom Jones*	Sidney Poitier *Lilies of the Field*	Patricia Neal *Hud*	Melvyn Douglas *Hud*	Margaret Rutherford *The V.I.P.s*	Tony Richardson *Tom Jones*
1964	*My Fair Lady*	Rex Harrison *My Fair Lady*	Julie Andrews *Mary Poppins*	Peter Ustinov *Topkapi*	Lila Kedrova *Zorba the Greek*	George Cukor *My Fair Lady*
1965	*The Sound of Music*	Lee Marvin *Cat Ballou*	Julie Christie *Darling*	Martin Balsam *A Thousand Clowns*	Shelley Winters *A Patch of Blue*	Robert Wise *The Sound of Music*
1966	*A Man for All Seasons*	Paul Scofield *A Man for All Seasons*	Elizabeth Taylor *Who's Afraid of Virginia Woolf?*	Walter Matthau *The Fortune Cookie*	Sandy Dennis *Who's Afraid of Virginia Woolf?*	Fred Zinnemann *A Man for All Seasons*
1967	*In the Heat of the Night*	Rod Steiger *In the Heat of the Night*	Katharine Hepburn *Guess Who's Coming to Dinner*	George Kennedy *Cool Hand Luke*	Estelle Parsons *Bonnie and Clyde*	Mike Nichols *The Graduate*
1968	*Oliver!*	Cliff Robertson *Charly*	Katharine Hepburn *The Lion in Winter;* Barbra Streisand *Funny Girl* (tie)	Jack Albertson *The Subject Was Roses*	Ruth Gordon *Rosemary's Baby*	Sir Carol Reed *Oliver!*
1969	*Midnight Cowboy*	John Wayne *True Grit*	Maggie Smith *The Prime of Miss Jean Brodie*	Gig Young *They Shoot Horses, Don't They?*	Goldie Hawn *Cactus Flower*	John Schlesinger *Midnight Cowboy*
1970	*Patton*	George C. Scott *Patton* (refused)	Glenda Jackson *Women in Love*	John Mills *Ryan's Daughter*	Helen Hayes *Airport*	Franklin Schaffner *Patton*
1971	*The French Connection*	Gene Hackman *The French Connection*	Jane Fonda *Klute*	Ben Johnson *The Last Picture Show*	Cloris Leachman *The Last Picture Show*	William Friedkin *The French Connection*
1972	*The Godfather*	Marlon Brando *The Godfather* (refused)	Liza Minnelli *Cabaret*	Joel Grey *Cabaret*	Eileen Heckart *Butterflies Are Free*	Bob Fosse *Cabaret*
1973	*The Sting*	Jack Lemmon *Save the Tiger*	Glenda Jackson *A Touch of Class*	John Houseman *The Paper Chase*	Tatum O'Neal *Paper Moon*	George Roy Hill *The Sting*
1974	*The Godfather Part II*	Art Carney *Harry and Tonto*	Ellen Burstyn *Alice Doesn't Live Here Anymore*	Robert DeNiro *The Godfather Part II*	Ingrid Bergman *Murder on the Orient Express*	Francis Ford Coppola *The Godfather Part II*
1975	*One Flew Over the Cuckoo's Nest*	Jack Nicholson *One Flew Over the Cuckoo's Nest*	Louise Fletcher *One Flew Over the Cuckoo's Nest*	George Burns *The Sunshine Boys*	Lee Grant *Shampoo*	Milos Forman *One Flew Over the Cuckoo's Nest*
1976	*Rocky*	Peter Finch *Network*	Faye Dunaway *Network*	Jason Robards *All the President's Men*	Beatrice Straight *Network*	John G. Avildsen *Rocky*
1977	*Annie Hall*	Richard Dreyfuss *The Goodbye Girl*	Diane Keaton *Annie Hall*	Jason Robards *Julia*	Vanessa Redgrave *Julia*	Woody Allen *Annie Hall*
1978	*The Deer Hunter*	Jon Voight *Coming Home*	Jane Fonda *Coming Home*	Christopher Walken *The Deer Hunter*	Maggie Smith *California Suite*	Michael Cimino *The Deer Hunter*
1979	*Kramer vs. Kramer*	Dustin Hoffman *Kramer vs. Kramer*	Sally Field *Norma Rae*	Melvyn Douglas *Being There*	Meryl Streep *Kramer vs. Kramer*	Robert Benton *Kramer vs. Kramer*
1980	*Ordinary People*	Robert DeNiro *Raging Bull*	Sissy Spacek *Coal Miner's Daughter*	Timothy Hutton *Ordinary People*	Mary Steenburgen *Melvin & Howard*	Robert Redford *Ordinary People*
1981	*Chariots of Fire*	Henry Fonda *On Golden Pond*	Katharine Hepburn *On Golden Pond*	John Gielgud *Arthur*	Maureen Stapleton *Reds*	Warren Beatty *Reds*
1982	*Gandhi*	Ben Kingsley *Gandhi*	Meryl Streep *Sophie's Choice*	Louis Gossett Jr. *An Officer and a Gentleman*	Jessica Lange *Tootsie*	Richard Attenborough *Gandhi*
1983	*Terms of Endearment*	Robert Duvall *Tender Mercies*	Shirley MacLaine *Terms of Endearment*	Jack Nicholson *Terms of Endearment*	Linda Hunt *The Year of Living Dangerously*	James L. Brooks *Terms of Endearment*
1984	*Amadeus*	F. Murray Abraham *Amadeus*	Sally Field *Places in the Heart*	Haing S. Ngor *The Killing Fields*	Peggy Ashcroft *A Passage to India*	Milos Forman *Amadeus*
1985	*Out of Africa*	William Hurt *Kiss of the Spider Woman*	Geraldine Page *The Trip to Bountiful*	Don Ameche *Cocoon*	Anjelica Huston *Prizzi's Honor*	Sydney Pollack *Out of Africa*
1986	*Platoon*	Paul Newman *The Color of Money*	Marlee Matlin *Children of a Lesser God*	Michael Caine *Hannah and Her Sisters*	Dianne Wiest *Hannah and Her Sisters*	Oliver Stone *Platoon*
1987	*The Last Emperor*	Michael Douglas *Wall Street*	Cher *Moonstruck*	Sean Connery *The Untouchables*	Olympia Dukakis *Moonstruck*	Bernardo Bertolucci *The Last Emperor*
1988	*Rain Man*	Dustin Hoffman *Rain Man*	Jodie Foster *The Accused*	Kevin Kline *A Fish Called Wanda*	Geena Davis *The Accidental Tourist*	Barry Levinson *Rain Man*
1989	*Driving Miss Daisy*	Daniel Day-Lewis *My Left Foot*	Jessica Tandy *Driving Miss Daisy*	Denzel Washington *Glory*	Brenda Fricker *My Left Foot*	Oliver Stone *Born on the Fourth of July*
1990	*Dances With Wolves*	Jeremy Irons *Reversal of Fortune*	Kathy Bates *Misery*	Joe Pesci *Goodfellas*	Whoopi Goldberg *Ghost*	Kevin Costner *Dances With Wolves*
1991	*The Silence of the Lambs*	Anthony Hopkins *The Silence of the Lambs*	Jodie Foster *The Silence of the Lambs*	Jack Palance *City Slickers*	Mercedes Ruehl *The Fisher King*	Jonathan Demme *The Silence of the Lambs*
1992	*Unforgiven*	Al Pacino *Scent of a Woman*	Emma Thompson *Howards End*	Gene Hackman *Unforgiven*	Marisa Tomei *My Cousin Vinny*	Clint Eastwood *Unforgiven*

Year	Picture	Actor	Actress	Sup. Actor[1]	Sup. Actress[1]	Director
1993	*Schindler's List*	Tom Hanks *Philadelphia*	Holly Hunter *The Piano*	Tommy Lee Jones *The Fugitive*	Anna Paquin *The Piano*	Steven Spielberg *Schindler's List*
1994	*Forrest Gump*	Tom Hanks *Forrest Gump*	Jessica Lange *Blue Sky*	Martin Landau *Ed Wood*	Dianne Wiest *Bullets Over Broadway*	Robert Zemeckis *Forrest Gump*
1995	*Braveheart*	Nicolas Cage *Leaving Las Vegas*	Susan Sarandon *Dead Man Walking*	Kevin Spacey *The Usual Suspects*	Mira Sorvino *Mighty Aphrodite*	Mel Gibson *Braveheart*
1996	*The English Patient*	Geoffrey Rush *Shine*	Frances McDormand *Fargo*	Cuba Gooding Jr. *Jerry Maguire*	Juliette Binoche *The English Patient*	Anthony Minghella *The English Patient*
1997	*Titanic*	Jack Nicholson *As Good As It Gets*	Helen Hunt *As Good As It Gets*	Robin Williams *Good Will Hunting*	Kim Basinger *L.A. Confidential*	James Cameron *Titanic*
1998	*Shakespeare in Love*	Roberto Benigni *Life Is Beautiful*	Gwyneth Paltrow *Shakespeare in Love*	James Coburn *Affliction*	Judi Dench *Shakespeare in Love*	Steven Spielberg *Saving Private Ryan*
1999	*American Beauty*	Kevin Spacey *American Beauty*	Hilary Swank *Boys Don't Cry*	Michael Caine *The Cider House Rules*	Angelina Jolie *Girl, Interrupted*	Sam Mendes *American Beauty*
2000	*Gladiator*	Russell Crowe *Gladiator*	Julia Roberts *Erin Brockovich*	Benicio Del Toro *Traffic*	Marcia Gay Harden *Pollock*	Steven Soderbergh *Traffic*
2001	*A Beautiful Mind*	Denzel Washington *Training Day*	Halle Berry *Monster's Ball*	Jim Broadbent *Iris*	Jennifer Connelly *A Beautiful Mind*	Ron Howard *A Beautiful Mind*

(1) These awards not given until 1936.

OTHER 2001 OSCAR WINNERS: Foreign film: *No Man's Land,* Bosnia & Herzegovina. Original screenplay: Julian Fellowes, *Gosford Park.* Adapted screenplay: Akiva Goldsman, *A Beautiful Mind.* Cinematography: Andrew Lesnie, *Lord of the Rings.* Art direction: Catherine Martin (art direction) and Brigitte Broch (set direction) *Moulin Rouge.* Film editing: Pietro Scalia, *Black Hawk Down.* Original Song: "If I Didn't Have You," *Monsters, Inc.,* Randy Newman. Original score: Howard Shore, *Lord of the Rings.* Costume Design: Catherine Martin and Angus Strathie, *Moulin Rouge.* Makeup: Peter Owen and Richard Taylor, *Lord of the Rings.* Sound: Michael Minkler, Myron Nettinga, and Chris Munro, *Black Hawk Down.* Documentary feature: Jean-Xavier de Lestrade and Denis Poncet, *Murder on a Sunday Morning.* Documentary short subject: Sarah Kernochan and Lynn Appelle, *Thoth.* Short Film, live: Ray McKinnon and Lisa Blount, *The Accountant.* Short film, animated: Ralph Eggelston, *For the Birds.* Visual effects: Jim Rygiel, Randall William Cook, Richard Taylor, and Mark Stetson, *Lord of the Rings.* Sound Effects Editing: George Watters II and Christopher Boyes, *Pearl Harbor.* Jean Hersholt Humanitarian Award: Arthur Hiller. Honorary Oscar: Sidney Poitier, Robert Redford.

IT'S A FACT: Many of Hollywood's top stars never won an Oscar for acting. To name a few: Fred Astaire, Richard Burton, Charlie Chaplin, Kirk Douglas, Greta Garbo, Ava Gardner, Judy Garland, Cary Grant, Gene Kelly, Deborah Kerr, Marilyn Monroe, Robert Mitchum, Barbara Stanwyck, Orson Welles, and Natalie Wood.

Other Film Awards

Year in parentheses is year awarded.

Cannes Film Festival Awards (2002), Feature Films—Palme d'Or (Golden Palm): *The Pianist,* Roman Polanski (France-Poland); Grand prize: *Mies Vailla Menneisyytta* (*The Man Without a Past*), Aki Kaurismaki (*Finland*); Best Actress: Kati Outinen, *The Man Without a Past* (Finland); Best Actor: Olivier Gourmet, Le Fils (*The Son*) (Belgium); Best Director: (tie) Paul Thomas Anderson, *Punch-Drunk Love* (U.S.); Kwon-Taek Im, *Chihwaseon* (South Korea); Best Screenplay: Paul Laverty, *Sweet Sixteen* (Britain); Special Jury Prize: *Yadon Ilaheyya* (*Divine Intervention*), Elia Suleiman (Palestinian); Special 55th Anniversary Prize: *Bowling for Columbine,* Michael Moore (U.S.); Camera d'Or (Golden Camera, first-time director): Julie Lopes-Curval, *Bord de Mer* (France); Lifetime Achievement Award: Woody Allen. Short Films—Palme d'Or: *Eso Utan* (*After Rain*), Peter Meszaros (Hungary); Jury Prize: (tie) *A Very Very Silent Film* (India), *Manish Jha and The Stone of Folly* (Canada), Jesse Rosensweet.

Director's Guild of America Awards (2002), Feature film: Ron Howard, *A Beautiful Mind;* documentary: Chris Hedegus & Jehane Noujaim, *Startup.com.*

Sundance Film Festival Awards (2002), Grand Jury Prize: (drama) *Personal Velocity,* Rebecca Miller; (documentary) *Daughter From Danang,* Gail Dolgin and Vicente Franco. Directing Award: (drama) Gary Winick, *Tadpole;* (documentary) Rob Fruchtman & Rebecca Cammisa, *Sister Helen.* Waldo Salt Screenwriting Award: Gordy Hoffman, *Love Liza.* Freedom of Expression Award: (documentary) *Amandla! A Revolution in Four Part Harmony,* Lee Hirsch. Audience Award: (drama) *Real Women Have Curves,* Patricia Cardoso; (documentary) *Amandla! A Revolution in Four Part Harmony,* Lee Hirsch; (world) *Bloody Sunday,* Paul Greengrass, and *The Last Kiss,* Gabriele Muccino (split). Cinematography Award: (drama) Ellen Kuras, *Personal Velocity;* (documentary) Daniel B. Gold, *Blue Vinyl.* Special Jury Awards: (drama) Steven Shainberg, *Secretary;* (documentary) *How to Draw a Bunny,* John Walter, and *Señorita Extraviada,* Lourdes Portillo (split). Latin Amer. Cinema Award: (Jury Prize) *The Trespasser,* Beto Brant; Short Filmmaking: (Jury Prize) *Gasline,* Dave Silver.

2002 Academy of Country Music Awards

Entertainer of the Year: Brooks & Dunn
Album of the Year: *O Brother Where Art Thou?,* film soundtrack; T-Bone Burnett, producer; Mercury
Single of the Year: "Where Were You (When the World Stopped Turning)," Alan Jackson; Keith Stagall, producer; Arista
Top Female Vocalist: Martina McBride
Top Male Vocalist: Alan Jackson
Top Vocal Duo: Brooks & Dunn
Top Vocal Group: Lonestar
Top New Female Vocalist: Carolyn Dawn Johnson
Top New Male Vocalist: Phil Vassar
Top New Vocal Duo or Group: Trick Pony
Video of the Year: "Only in America," Brooks & Dunn; Stephanie Reeves, producer; Michael Merriman, director
Song of the Year: "Where Were You (When the World Stopped Turning)," Alan Jackson; EMI April, Tri-Angels, publisher
Vocal Event of the Year: "I Am a Man of Constant Sorrow," Soggy Bottom Boys; T-Bone Burnett, producer
Pioneer Award: Ronnie Milsap
Humanitarian Award: Reba McEntire

2002 MTV Video Music Awards

Video of the Year: Eminem, "Without Me"
Best Male Video: Eminem, "Without Me"
Best Female Video: Pink, "Get the Party Started"
Best Group Video: No Doubt, featuring Bounty Killer, "Hey Baby"
Best Rap Video: Eminem, "Without Me"
Best Dance Video: Pink, "Get the Party Started"
Best Pop Video: No Doubt, featuring Bounty Killer, "Hey Baby"
Best Rock Video: Linkin Park, "In the End"
Best Hip Hop Video: Jennifer Lopez, featuring Ja Rule, "I'm Real (Remix)"
Best New Artist: Avril Lavigne, "Complicated"
Breakthrough Video: The White Stripes, "Fell In Love with a Girl"
Best R&B Video: Mary J. Blige, "No More Drama"
Best Video From a Film: Chad Kroeger, featuring Josey Scott, "Hero" (Spider-Man)
Best MTV2 Video: Dashboard Confessional, "Screaming Infidelities"
Best Direction: Joseph Kahn for Eminem's "Without Me"
Best Choreography: Michael Rooney for Kylie Minogue's "Can't Get You Out Of My Head"
Best Art Direction: Tim Hope for Coldplay's "Trouble"
Best Editing: Samuel Denesi for The White Stripes' "Fell In Love with a Girl"
Best Cinematography: Brad Rushing for Moby's "We Are All Made of Stars"
Best Special Effects: Michel Gondry, Olivier "Twist" Gondry, and Sebastian Fau for The White Stripes' "Fell In Love with a Girl"
Viewers' Choice: Michelle Branch, "Everywhere"

Grammy Awards

Source: National Academy of Recording Arts & Sciences

Selected Grammy Awards for 2002

Record of the Year (single): "Walk On," U2
Album of the Year: *O Brother, Where Art Thou?,* various artists
Song of the Year: "Fallin'," Alicia Keys, songwriter (Alicia Keys)
New artist: Alicia Keys
Pop vocal perf., female: "I'm Like a Bird," Nelly Furtado
Pop vocal perf., male: "Don't Let Me Be Lonely Tonight," James Taylor
Pop vocal perf., duo/group: "Stuck in A Moment You Can't Get Out of," U2
Pop vocal album, traditional: *Songs I Heard,* Harry Connick Jr.
Pop instrumental album: *No Substitutions—Live in Osaka*, Larry Carlton & Steve Lukather
Pop vocal album: *Lovers Rock*, Sade
Dance recording: "All for You," Janet Jackson
Rock vocal perf., female: "Get Right With God," Lucinda Williams
Rock vocal perf., male: "Dig In," Lenny Kravitz
Rock vocal perf., duo/group: "Elevation," U2
Rock instrumental perf.: "Dirty Mind," Jeff Beck
Hard rock perf.: "Crawling," Linkin Park
Metal perf.: "Schism," Tool
Rock song: "Drops of Jupiter," Charlie Colin, Rob Hotchkiss, Pat Monahan, Jimmy Stafford, & Scott Underwood, songwriters (Train)
Rock album: *All That You Can't Leave Behind,* U2
R&B vocal perf., female: "Fallin'," Alicia Keys
R&B vocal perf., male: "U Remind Me," Usher
R&B vocal perf., duo/group: "Survivor," Destiny's Child
R&B song: "Fallin'," Alicia Keys, songwriter (Alicia Keys)
R&B vocal album, traditional: *At Last,* Gladys Knight
R&B album: *Songs in A Minor,* Alicia Keys
Rap solo perf.: "Get Ur Freak On," Missy "Misdemeanor" Elliott
Rap vocal perf., duo/group: "Ms. Jackson," Outkast
Rap album: *Stankonia,* Outkast
Country vocal perf., female: "Shine," Dolly Parton
Country vocal perf., male: "O Death," Ralph Stanley
Country perf. with vocal, duo/group: "The Lucky One," by Alison Krauss & Union Station
Country song: "The Lucky One," Robert Lee Castleman, songwriter (Alison Krauss & Union Station)
Country album: *Timeless—Hank Williams Tribute,* various artists
Bluegrass album: *New Favorite,* Alison Krauss & Union Station
Jazz album, vocal: *The Calling,* Dianne Reeves
Jazz album, instr.: *This Is What I Do,* Sonny Rollins
Jazz album, contemporary: *M²*, Marcus Miller
Blues album, contemporary: *Nothing Personal,* Delbert McClinton
Blues album, traditional: *Do You Get the Blues?,* Jimmie Vaughan
Folk album, contemporary: *Love and Theft,* Bob Dylan
Folk album, traditional: *Down From the Mountain,* various artists
Reggae album: *Halfway Tree,* Damian Marley
Latin pop album: *La Musica de Baldemar Huerta,* Freddy Fender
Producer: non-classical, T Bone Burnett
Opera recording: *Berlioz: Les Troyens*; Sir Colin Davis, London Sym. Orch; Michelle De Young, Ben Heppner, Petra Lang, Peter Mattei, Stephen Milling, Sara Mingardo, & Kenneth Tarver; James Mallinson, producer
Classical vocal perf.: *Dreams & Fables—Gluck Italian Arias,* Cecilia Bartoli (mezzo soprano)
Classical album: *Berlioz: Les Troyens*; see above.

Grammy Awards for 1958-2001

Record of the Year (single)	Year	Album of the Year
Domenico Modugno, "Nel Blu Dipinto Di Blu (Volare)"	1958	Henry Mancini, *The Music From Peter Gunn*
Bobby Darin, "Mack the Knife"	1959	Frank Sinatra, *Come Dance With Me*
Percy Faith, "Theme From a Summer Place"	1960	Bob Newhart, *Button Down Mind*
Henry Mancini, "Moon River"	1961	Judy Garland, *Judy at Carnegie Hall*
Tony Bennett, "I Left My Heart in San Francisco"	1962	Vaughn Meader, *The First Family*
Henry Mancini, "The Days of Wine and Roses"	1963	Barbra Streisand, *The Barbra Streisand Album*
Stan Getz, Astrud Gilberto, "The Girl From Ipanema"	1964	Stan Getz, Astrud Gilberto, *Getz/Gilberto*
Herb Alpert, "A Taste of Honey"	1965	Frank Sinatra, *September of My Years*
Frank Sinatra, "Strangers in the Night"	1966	Frank Sinatra, *A Man and His Music*
5th Dimension, "Up, Up and Away"	1967	The Beatles, *Sgt. Pepper's Lonely Hearts Club Band*
Simon & Garfunkel, "Mrs. Robinson"	1968	Glen Campbell, *By the Time I Get to Phoenix*
5th Dimension, "Aquarius/Let the Sunshine In"	1969	Blood Sweat and Tears, *Blood, Sweat and Tears*
Simon & Garfunkel, "Bridge Over Troubled Water"	1970	Simon & Garfunkel, *Bridge Over Troubled Water*
Carole King, "It's Too Late"	1971	Carole King, *Tapestry*
Roberta Flack, "The First Time Ever I Saw Your Face"	1972	George Harrison and friends, *The Concert for Bangla Desh*
Roberta Flack, "Killing Me Softly With His Song"	1973	Stevie Wonder, *Innervisions*
Olivia Newton-John, "I Honestly Love You"	1974	Stevie Wonder, *Fulfillingness' First Finale*
Captain & Tennille, "Love Will Keep Us Together"	1975	Paul Simon, *Still Crazy After All These Years*
George Benson, "This Masquerade"	1976	Stevie Wonder, *Songs in the Key of Life*
Eagles, "Hotel California"	1977	Fleetwood Mac, *Rumours*
Billy Joel, "Just the Way You Are"	1978	Bee Gees, *Saturday Night Fever*
The Doobie Brothers, "What a Fool Believes"	1979	Billy Joel, *52nd Street*
Christopher Cross, "Sailing"	1980	Christopher Cross, *Christopher Cross*
Kim Carnes, "Bette Davis Eyes"	1981	John Lennon, Yoko Ono, *Double Fantasy*
Toto, "Rosanna"	1982	Toto, *Toto IV*
Michael Jackson, "Beat It"	1983	Michael Jackson, *Thriller*
Tina Turner, "What's Love Got to Do With It"	1984	Lionel Richie, *Can't Slow Down*
USA for Africa, "We Are the World"	1985	Phil Collins, *No Jacket Required*
Steve Winwood, "Higher Love"	1986	Paul Simon, *Graceland*
Paul Simon, "Graceland"	1987	U2, *The Joshua Tree*
Bobby McFerrin, "Don't Worry, Be Happy"	1988	George Michael, *Faith*
Bette Midler, "Wind Beneath My Wings"	1989	Bonnie Raitt, *Nick of Time*
Phil Collins, "Another Day in Paradise"	1990	Quincy Jones, *Back on the Block*
Natalie Cole, with Nat "King" Cole, "Unforgettable"	1991	Natalie Cole, with Nat "King" Cole, *Unforgettable*
Eric Clapton, "Tears in Heaven"	1992	Eric Clapton, *Unplugged*
Whitney Houston, "I Will Always Love You"	1993	Whitney Houston, *The Bodyguard*
Sheryl Crow, "All I Wanna Do"	1994	Tony Bennett, *MTV Unplugged*
Seal, "Kiss From a Rose"	1995	Alanis Morissette, *Jagged Little Pill*
Eric Clapton, "Change the World"	1996	Celine Dion, *Falling Into You*
Shawn Colvin, "Sunny Came Home"	1997	Bob Dylan, *Time Out of Mind*
Celine Dion, "My Heart Will Go On"	1998	Lauryn Hill, *The Miseducation of Lauryn Hill*
Santana featuring Rob Thomas, "Smooth"	1999	*Santana, Supernatural*
U2, "Beautiful Day"	2000	Steely Dan, *Two Against Nature*
U2, "Walk On"	2001	Various Artists, *O Brother, Where Art Thou?*

IT'S A FACT: Aretha Franklin has won 11 Grammy Awards for best female R&B vocal performance, including a span of 8 years in a row (1968-1975, 1982, 1986, and 1988).

NOTED PERSONALITIES

This chapter contains the following sections:

Widely Known Americans of the Present

Political leaders, journalists, other widely known living persons. As of Sept. 2002. Excludes many in categories listed elsewhere in Noted Personalities, such as Writers of the Present and Entertainment Personalities of the Present, or in the Sports section.

Spencer Abraham, b 6/12/52 (East Lansing, MI), energy sec.
Roger Ailes, b 5/15/40 (Warren, OH), TV exec.
Madeleine K. Albright, b 5/15/37 (Prague, Czech.), former sec. of state.
Lamar Alexander, b 7/3/40 (Maryville, TN), former TN gov., presid. candidate.
Stephen E. Ambrose, b 1/10/36 (Decatur, IL), historian.
Walter H. Annenberg, b 3/13/08 (Milwaukee), publisher, philanthropist.
Roone Arledge, b 7/8/31 (Forest Hills, NY), TV exec.
Richard K. Armey, b 7/7/40 (Cando, ND), House majority leader.
Neil Armstrong, b 8/5/30 (Wapakoneta, OH), former astronaut.
John Ashcroft, b 5/9/42 (Chicago), attorney general.
Bruce Babbitt, b 6/27/38 (Los Angeles), former AZ gov., interior sec.
F. Lee Bailey, b 6/10/33 (Waltham, MA), attorney.
Russell Baker, b 8/14/25 (Loudoun Co., VA), columnist.
Dave Barry, b 7/3/47 (Armonk, NY), humorist.
Marion Barry, b 3/6/36 (Itta Bena, MS), former Wash., DC, mayor.
Gary Bauer, b 1956 (Covington, KY), political activist.
Lloyd Bentsen, b 2/11/21 (Mission, TX), former senator, treasury sec., vice-presid. nominee.
Samuel "Sandy" Berger, b 10/28/45 (Sharon, CT), former national security adviser.
Chris Berman, b 5/10/55 (Rye, NY), sportscaster.
Jeff Bezos, b 1/12/64 (Albuquerque, NM), founder and CEO of Amazon.com.
Joseph R. Biden Jr., b 11/20/42 (Scranton, PA), senator (DE).
James H. Billington, b 6/1/29 (Bryn Mawr, PA), librarian of Congress.
Wolf Blitzer, b 1948 (Augsburg, Germany), TV journalist.
Michael R. Bloomberg, b 2/14/42 (Boston, MA), NYC mayor; financial information/media entrepreneur.
Julian Bond, b 1/14/40 (Nashville), civil rights leader.
David Bonior, b 6/6/45 (Detroit), House minority whip.
Daniel Boorstin, b 10/1/14 (Atlanta), historian, former librarian of Congress.
Barbara Boxer, b 11/11/40 (Brooklyn, NY), senator (CA).
Bill Bradley, b 7/28/43 (Crystal City, MO), former senator (NJ), basketball player, presid. candidate.
Ed Bradley, b 6/22/41 (Philadelphia), TV journalist.
James Brady, b 9/17/44 (Grand Rapids, MI), former presid. press sec.; gun control advocate.
Jimmy Breslin, b 10/17/30 (Jamaica, NY), columnist, author.
Stephen Breyer, b 8/15/38 (San Francisco), Sup. Ct. justice.
David Brinkley, b 7/10/20 (Wilmington, NC), former TV journalist.
David Broder, b 9/11/29 (Chicago Heights, IL), journalist.
Tom Brokaw, b 2/6/40 (Webster, SD), TV journalist.
Joyce Brothers, b 9/20/28 (NYC), psychologist.
Edmund G. ("Jerry") Brown Jr., b 4/7/38 (San Francisco), Oakland mayor; former CA gov., pres. candidate.
Willie Brown, b 3/20/34 (Mineola, TX), San Francisco mayor.
Pat Buchanan, b 11/2/38 (Wash., DC), journalist, former presid. candidate.
Art Buchwald, b 10/20/25 (Mt. Vernon, NY), humorist.
William F. Buckley Jr., b 11/24/25 (NYC), columnist, author.
Warren Buffett, b 8/30/30 (Omaha), investor.
Dan Burton, b 6/21/38 (Indianapolis), U.S. representative.
Barbara Bush, b 6/8/25 (Rye, NY), former first lady.
Barbara Bush, b 11/25/81 (Dallas, TX), daughter of Pres. George W. Bush.
George H. W. Bush, b 6/12/24 (Milton, MA), former president.
George W. Bush, b 7/6/46 (New Haven, CT), U.S. president.
Jeb Bush, b 2/11/53 (Houston), FL governor.
Jenna Bush, b 11/25/81(Dallas, TX), daughter of Pres. George W. Bush.
Laura Bush, b 11/4/46 (Midland, TX), first lady.
Robert Byrd, b 11/20/17 (N. Wilkesboro, NC), senator (WV), former majority leader.
Andrew Card, b 5/10/47 (Brockton, MA), White House chief of staff.
Tucker Carlson, b 5/16/69 (San Francisco), journalist, TV commentator.
Jimmy Carter, b 10/1/24 (Plains, GA), former president.
Rosalynn Carter, b 8/18/27 (Plains, GA), former first lady.
James Carville Jr., b 10/25/44 (Fort Benning, GA), TV political commentator.
Steve Case, b 8/21/58 (Honolulu, HI), AOL Time Warner chairman.
Elaine Chao, b 3/26/53 (Taipei, Taiwan), labor sec.
Dick Cheney, b 1/30/41 (Lincoln, NE), U.S. vice president.
Lynne Cheney, b 8/14/41 (Casper, WY), political commentator, wife of Dick Cheney.
Julia Child, b 8/15/12 (Pasadena, CA), TV chef, author.
Noam Chomsky, b 12/7/28 (Philadelphia), linguist; activist.
Connie Chung, b 8/20/46 (Wash., DC), TV journalist.
Liz Claiborne, b 3/31/29 (Brussels, Belg.), fashion designer.
Wesley Clark, b 12/23/44 (Chicago), retired general, former NATO commander in Europe.
Kelly Clarkson, b 4/24/82 (Burleson, TX), winner of *American Idol* contest.
Bill Clinton, b 8/19/46 (Hope, AR), former U.S. president.
Chelsea Clinton, b 2/27/80 (Little Rock, AR), daughter of former Pres. Clinton and Hillary Rodham Clinton.
Hillary Rodham Clinton, b 10/26/47 (Chicago), senator (NY), former first lady.
Johnnie L. Cochran Jr., b 10/2/37 (Shreveport, LA), attorney.
Gary Condit, b 4/21/48 (Salina, OK), U.S. representative (CA).
Bob Costas, b 3/22/52 (NYC), TV journalist.
Katie Couric, b 1/7/57 (Wash., DC), TV journalist.
Walter Cronkite, b 11/4/16 (St. Joseph, MO), former TV journalist.
Mario Cuomo, b 6/15/32 (Queens, NY), former NY gov.
Richard M. Daley, b 4/24/42 (Chicago), Chicago mayor.
Thomas Daschle, b 12/9/47 (Aberdeen, SD), Senate majority leader.
Gray Davis, b 12/26/42 (NYC), CA governor.
Tom DeLay, b 4/8/47 (Laredo, TX), House majority whip.
Alan Dershowitz, b 9/1/38 (Brooklyn, NY), attorney.
Barry Diller, b 2/2/42 (San Francisco), TV exec.
Lou Dobbs, b 9/24/45 (Childress, TX), TV journalist.
Christopher Dodd, b 5/27/44 (Willimantic, CT), senator.
Elizabeth Hanford Dole, b 7/29/36 (Salisbury, NC), former Red Cross pres., transp. sec., labor sec., presid. contender.
Robert Dole, b 7/22/23 (Russell, KS), former Senate majority leader, presid. nominee.
Pete Domenici, b 5/7/32 (Albuquerque, NM), senator.
Sam Donaldson, b 3/11/34 (El Paso, TX), TV journalist.
Elizabeth Drew, b 11/16/35 (Cincinnati), journalist.
Michael S. Dukakis, b 11/3/33 (Boston), former MA gov., presid. nominee.
Roger Ebert, b 6/18/42 (Urbana, IL), film critic.
Marian Wright Edelman, b 6/6/39 (Bennettsville, SC), children's rights advocate.
John Edwards, b 6/10/53 (Robbins, NC), senator.
Edward Egan, Cardinal, b 4/2/32 (Oak Park, IL), Catholic archbishop of New York.
Michael Eisner, b 3/7/42 (NYC), Disney Co. exec.
John Engler, b 10/12/48 (Mount Pleasant, MI), MI gov.
Donald Evans, b 7/27/46 (Houston), commerce sec.
Rev. Jerry Falwell, b 8/11/33 (Lynchburg, VA), TV evangelist, religious educator.
Louis Farrakhan, b 5/11/33 (NYC), Nation of Islam leader.

Russell Feingold, b 3/2/53 (Janesville, WI), senator.
Dianne Feinstein, b 6/22/33 (San Francisco), senator.
Geraldine Ferraro, b 8/26/35 (Newburgh, NY), former U.S. representative, vice-presid. nominee.
Ari Fleischer b 1960, White House press secretary.
Larry Flynt, b 11/1/42 (Magoffin Co., KY), publisher.
Shelby Foote, b 11/17/16 (Greenville, MS), historian.
Malcolm "Steve" Forbes Jr., b 7/18/47 (Morristown, NJ), publisher, former presid. contender.
Betty Ford, b 4/8/18 (Chicago), former first lady.
Gerald R. Ford, b 7/14/13 (Omaha), former president.
Steve Fossett, b 1944 (California), adventurer, balloonist.
John Hope Franklin, b 1/2/15 (Rentiesville, OK), historian.
Tommy R. Franks, b 6/17/45 (Wynnewood, OK), gen., commander in chief U.S. Central Command.
Betty Friedan, b 2/4/21 (Peoria, IL), author, feminist.
Milton Friedman, b 7/31/12 (Bklyn, NY), economist.
John Kenneth Galbraith, b 10/15/08 (Iona Station, Ont.), economist.
Bill Gates, b 10/28/55 (Seattle), Microsoft exec.
Henry Louis Gates Jr., b 9/16/50 (Keyser, WV), scholar.
David Geffen, b 2/21/43 (Brooklyn, NY), entertainment exec.
Richard Gephardt, b 1/31/41 (St. Louis, MO), House minority leader.
Louis Gerstner, b 3/1/42 (Mineola, NY), retired IBM exec.
Newt Gingrich, b 6/17/43 (Harrisburg, PA), former House Speaker.
Ruth Bader Ginsburg, b 3/15/33 (Bklyn, NY), Sup. Ct. justice.
Rudolph Giuliani, b 5/28/44 (Bklyn, NY) former NYC mayor.
John Glenn, b 7/18/21 (Cambridge, OH), former senator, astronaut.
Ellen Goodman, b 4/11/41 (Newton, MA), columnist.
Doris Kearns Goodwin, b 1/4/43 (Rockville Centre, NY), historian, TV commentator.
Berry Gordy, b 11/28/29 (Detroit), Motown founder.
Al Gore Jr., b 3/31/48 (Wash., DC), former U.S. vice president, presid. candidate.
Tipper Gore, b 8/19/48 (Wash., DC), wife of Al Gore.
Rev. Billy Graham, b 11/7/18 (Charlotte, NC), evangelist.
Phil Gramm, b 7/8/42 (Ft. Benning, GA), senator (TX), former presid. contender.
Jeff Greenfield, b 6/10/43 (NYC), TV journalist.
Alan Greenspan, b 3/6/26 (NYC), Fed chairman.
Andrew Grove, b 9/2/36 (Budapest, Hungary), Intel exec.
Bryant Gumbel, b 9/29/48 (New Orleans), TV journalist.
David Halberstam, b 4/10/34 (NYC), journalist, author.
Pete Hamill, b 6/24/35 (Brooklyn, NY), journalist, author.
Paul Harvey, b 9/4/18 (Tulsa, OK), radio journalist.
J. Dennis Hastert, b 1/2/42 (Aurora, IL), House Speaker.
Orrin Hatch, b 3/22/34 (Homestead Park, PA), senator (UT).
Hugh Hefner, b 4/9/26 (Chicago), publisher.
Jesse Helms, b 10/18/21 (Monroe, NC), senator.
Leona Helmsley, b c1920 (NYC), real estate exec.
Heloise, b 4/15/51 (Waco, TX), advice columnist.
Tommy Hilfiger, b 1951 (Elmira, NY), fashion designer.
Anita Hill, b 7/10/56 (Morris, OK), legal scholar, complainant against Clarence Thomas.
Christopher Hitchens, b 4/13/49 (Portsmouth, England), journalist, author.
James P. Hoffa, b 5/19/41, (Detroit), Teamsters Union head.
Richard Holbrooke, b 4/24/41 (NYC), former U.S. rep. to UN.
David Horowitz, b 1/10/39 (NYC), columnist, author.
H. Wayne Huizenga, b 12/29/39 (Evergreen Park, IL), entrepreneur, sports exec.
Kay Bailey Hutchison, b 7/22/43 (Galveston, TX), senator.
Henry J. Hyde, b 4/18/24 (Chicago), U.S. representative.
Lee Iacocca, b 10/15/24 (Allentown, PA), former auto exec.
Carl Icahn, b 1936 (Queens, NY), financier.
Don Imus, b 7/23/40 (?) (Riverside, CA), talk-show host.
Patricia Ireland, b 10/19/45 (Oak Park, IL), feminist leader.
Molly Ivins, b 1944 (Texas), columnist.
Rev. Jesse Jackson, b 10/8/41 (Greenville, SC), civil rights leader, former presid. contender.
James Jeffords, b 5/11/34 (Rutland, VT), senator.
Steven Jobs, b 2/24/55 (San Francisco), Apple Computer exec.
Lady Bird Johnson, b 12/22/12 (Karnack, TX), former first lady.
Vernon E. Jordan Jr., b 8/15/35 (Atlanta), attorney, former presid. adviser, civil rights leader.
Donna Karan, b 10/2/48 (Forest Hills, NY), fashion designer.
John R. Kasich, b 5/13/52 (McKees Rocks, PA), U.S. representative (OH).
Jeffrey Katzenberg, b 1950 (NYC), entertainment exec.
Garrison Keillor, b 8/7/42 (Anoka, MN), author, broadcaster.
Jack Kemp, b 7/13/35 (Los Angeles), former vice-presid. nominee, HUD sec., pro football quarterback.
Anthony Kennedy, b 7/23/36 (Sacramento, CA), Sup. Ct. justice.
Caroline Kennedy Schlossberg, b 11/27/57 (Boston), author, daughter of Pres. Kennedy.
Edward M. Kennedy, b 2/22/32 (Brookline, MA), senator.
Bob (Joseph Robert) **Kerrey**, b 8/27/43 (Lincoln, NE), former senator.
John Kerry, b 12/11/43 (Denver), senator (MA).
Jack Kevorkian, b 5/26/28 (Pontiac, MI), physican, assisted-suicide activist.
Coretta Scott King, b 4/27/27 (Marion, AL), civil rights leader, widow of Martin Luther King Jr.
Larry King, b 11/19/33 (Brooklyn, NY), TV journalist.
Michael Kinsley, b 3/9/51 (Detroit), editor, political commenator.
Jeane J. Kirkpatrick, b 11/19/26 (Duncan, OK), political scientist, former ambassador to UN.
Henry Kissinger, b 5/27/23 (Fuerth, Germany), former sec. of state, national security adviser; Nobel Peace Prize winner.
Calvin Klein, b 11/19/42 (NYC), fashion designer.
Philip H. Knight, b 2/24/38 (Portland, OR), CEO of Nike.
Edward I. Koch, b 12/12/24 (NYC), former NYC mayor.
C. Everett Koop, b 10/14/16 (Brooklyn, NY), former surgeon general.
Ted Koppel, b 2/8/40 (Lancashire, England), TV journalist.
William Kristol, b 12/23/52 (NYC), editor, columnist.
Brian Lamb, b 10/9/41 (Lafayette, IN), cable TV exec., journalist.
Estee Lauder, b 9/1/08 (NYC), founder, cosmetics and fragrance firm.
Matt Lauer, b 12/30/57 (NYC), TV journalist.
Ralph Lauren, b 10/14/39 (Bronx, NY), fashion designer.
Bernard F. Law, b 11/4/31 (Torreon, Mexico), cardinal, archbishop of Boston, figure in church scandal.
Kenneth L. Lay, b 4/15/42 (Tyrone, MO), former chairman and CEO of Enron.
Patrick Leahy, b 3/31/40 (Montpelier, VT), senator.
Norman Lear, b 7/27/22 (New Haven, CT), TV producer, political activist.
Jim Lehrer, b 5/19/34 (Wichita, KS), TV journalist, author.
James Levine, b 6/23/43 (Cincinnati) conductor.
Monica Lewinsky, b 7/23/73 (San Francisco), former White House intern, key figure in White House scandal.
Joseph Lieberman, b 2/24/42 (Stamford, CT), senator, former vice presid. candidate.
Rush Limbaugh, b 1/12/51 (Cape Girardeau, MO), radio talk-show host.
Gary Locke, b 1/21/50 (Seattle), WA gov.
Trent Lott, b 10/9/41 (Grenada, MS), Senate minority leader.
Richard G. Lugar, b 4/4/32 (Indianapolis), senator.
Connie Mack, b 10/29/40 (Philadelphia), senator (FL).
John Madden, b 4/10/36 (Austin, MN), sportscaster.
Melquiades Martinez, b 10/23/46 (Sagua la Grande, Cuba), housing and urban development sec.
Janet Maslin, b 8/12/49 (NYC), film critic, author.
Mary Matalin, b 8/19/53 (Chicago), political commentator.
Chris Matthews, b 1945 (Philadelphia), TV journalist.
Terry McAuliffe, b 1947 (Syracuse, NY), Democratic national chairman.
John McCain, b 8/29/36 (Panama Canal Zone), senator (AZ); former presid. contender.
David McCullough, b 7/7/33 (Pittsburgh, PA), historian, biographer.
George McGovern, b 7/19/22 (Avon, SD), former senator, presid. nominee.
John McLaughlin, b 3/29/27 (Providence, RI), TV journalist.
Robert S. McNamara, b 6/9/16 (San Francisco), former defense sec., World Bank head.
Kweisi Mfume, b 10/24/48 (Baltimore), civil rights leader, former U.S. representative.
Kate Michelman, b 8/4/42 (New Jersey), abortion-rights activist.
Kate Millett, b 9/14/34 (St. Paul, MN), author, feminist.
Norman Mineta, b 11/12/31 (San Jose, CA), transportation sec.
George Mitchell, b 8/20/33, (Waterville, ME), former Senate majority leader, N. Ireland peace negotiator.
Walter Mondale, b 1/5/28 (Ceylon, MN), former vice pres., senator, presid. nominee.
Bill Moyers, b 6/5/34 (Hugo, OK), TV journalist, author.
Daniel P. Moynihan, b 3/16/27 (Tulsa, OK), former senator, author.
Robert S. Mueller III, b 8/7/44 (NYC), FBI director.
Rupert Murdoch, b 3/11/31 (Melbourne, Aust.), media exec.
Richard B. Myers, b 3/1/42 (Kansas City, MO) chairman of the Joint Chiefs of Staff.
Ralph Nader, b 2/27/34 (Winsted, CT), consumer advocate, former presid. candidate.
John Negroponte, b 7/21/39 (London, Eng.), U.S. representative to UN.
Don Nickles, b 12/6/48 (Ponca City, OK), Senate minority whip.
Oliver North, b 10/7/43 (San Antonio, TX), radio talk-show host, former National Security Council aide.
Eleanor Holmes Norton, b 6/13/37 (Wash., DC), U.S. House delegate.
Gale Norton, b 3/11/54 (Wichita, KS), interior sec.
Robert Novak, b 2/26/31 (Joliet, IL), journalist.

Sam Nunn, b 9/8/38 (Perry, GA), former senator.
Sandra Day O'Connor, b 3/26/30 (El Paso, TX), Sup. Ct. justice.
Paul O'Neill, b 12/4/35 (Pittsburgh), treasury sec.
Bill O'Reilly, b 1949 (NYC), TV commentator, host.
Michael Ovitz, b 12/4/46 (Encino, CA), entertainment exec.
Camille Paglia, b 1947 (Endicott, NY), scholar, author.
Roderick R. Paige, b 6/17/33 (Monticello, MS), education sec.
Leon F. Panetta, b 6/28/38 (Monterey, CA), former White House chief of staff, U.S. representative.
Rosa Parks, b 2/4/13 (Tuskegee, AL), civil rights activist.
Richard Parsons, b 4/4/48 (NYC), AOL Time-Warner CEO.
George Pataki, b 6/24/45 (Peekskill, NY), NY gov.
Jane Pauley, b 10/31/50 (Indianapolis), TV journalist.
Nancy Pelosi, b 3/26/41 (Baltimore, MD), House minority whip.
H. Ross Perot, b 6/27/30 (Texarkana, TX), entrepreneur, former presid. nominee.
George Plimpton, b 3/18/27 (NYC), author, editor.
Alvin F. Poussaint, b 5/15/34 (NYC), child psychiatrist.
Colin Powell, b 4/5/37 (NYC), sec. of state; former national security adviser, Joint Chiefs of Staff chairman.
Anthony Principi, b 4/16/44 (Bronx, NY), sec. of veterans affairs.
Dan Quayle, b 2/4/47 (Indianapolis), former U.S. vice pres., senator, presid. contender.
Anna Quindlen, b 7/8/53 (Philadelphia), author, columnist.
Marc Racicot, b 7/24/48 (Thompson Falls, MT), Republican national chairman, former (MT) gov.
Dan Rather, b 10/31/31 (Wharton, TX), TV journalist.
Nancy Reagan, b 7/6/23 (NYC), former first lady.
Ronald Reagan, b 2/6/11 (Tampico, IL), former president.
Sumner Redstone, b 5/27/23 (Boston), media exec.
Ralph Reed, b 6/24/61 (Portsmouth, VA), political adviser.
William Rehnquist, b 10/1/24 (Milwaukee), Sup. Ct. chief justice.
Robert B. Reich, b 6/24/46 (Scranton, PA), economist, former labor sec.
Harry Reid, b 12/2/39 (Searchlight, NV), Senate majority whip.
Janet Reno, b 7/21/38 (Miami, FL), former attorney general.
Condoleezza Rice, b 11/14/54 (Birmingham, AL), national security advisor.
Ann Richards, b 9/3/33 (Waco, TX), former TX gov.
Bill Richardson, b 11/15/47 (Pasadena, CA), former energy sec., UN ambassador, congressman.
Sally K. Ride, b 5/26/51 (Encino, CA), former astronaut.
Tom (Thomas Joseph) Ridge, b 8/26/45 (Munhall, PA), director, Office of Homeland Security; former PA gov.
Richard Riordan, b 1930 (Flushing, NY), Los Angeles mayor.
Cokie Roberts, b 12/27/43 (New Orleans), TV journalist.
Rev. Oral Roberts, b 1/24/18 (nr. Ada, OK), TV evangelist, educator.
Rev. Pat Robertson, b 3/22/30 (Lexington, VA), religious broadcasting exec, former presid. contender.
David Rockefeller, b 6/12/15 (NYC), banker.
John D. "Jay" Rockefeller 4th, b 6/18/37 (NYC), senator, former WV gov.
Laurance S. Rockefeller, b 5/26/10 (NYC), philanthropist.
Fred Rogers, b 3/20/28 (Latrobe, PA), children's TV personality.
Al Roker, b 1954 (Queens, NY), TV weather person.
Andy Rooney, b 1/14/19 (Albany, NY), TV commentator.
Charlie Rose, b 1/5/42 (Henderson, NC), TV journalist.
Karl Rove, b 12/25/50 (Denver) political consultant.
Louis Rukeyser, b 1/30/33 (NYC), TV journalist, financial analyst.
Donald Rumsfeld, b 7/9/32 (Chicago), defense sec.
Tim Russert, b 5/7/50 (Buffalo, NY), TV journalist.
William Safire, b 12/17/29 (NYC), columnist.
Diane Sawyer, b 12/22/45 (Glasgow, KY), TV journalist.
Antonin Scalia, b 3/11/36 (Trenton, NJ), Sup. Ct. justice.
Phyllis Schlafly, b 8/15/24 (St. Louis, MO) political activist.
Arthur Schlesinger Jr., b 10/15/17 (Columbus, OH), historian.
Patricia Schroeder, b 7/30/40 (Portland, OR), former U.S. representative.
Rev. Robert Schuller, b 9/16/26 (Alton, IA), TV evangelist.
Charles Schumer, b 11/23/50 (Brooklyn, NY), senator.
H. Norman Schwarzkopf, b 8/22/34 (Trenton, NJ), former military leader.
Willard Scott, b 3/7/34 (Alexandria, VA), TV weather person.
Allan H. ("Bud") Selig, b 7/30/34 (Milwaukee), baseball comm.
Donna E. Shalala, b 2/14/41 (Cleveland), former sec. of health and human services.
Gene Shalit, b 3/25/32 (NYC), TV film critic.
Al Sharpton, b 10/3/54 (NYC), activist, civil rights leader.
Maria Shriver, b 11/6/55 (Chicago), TV journalist.
George P. Shultz, b 12/13/20 (NYC), former sec. of state, other cabinet posts.
O. J. Simpson, b 7/9/47 (San Francisco), former football star, murder defendant.
Liz Smith, b 2/2/23 (Ft. Worth, TX), gossip columnist.
David H. Souter, b 9/17/39 (Melrose, MA), Sup. Ct. justice.
George Soros, b 8/12/30 (Budapest, Hungary), financier, philanthropist.
Arlen Specter, b 2/12/30 (Wichita, KS), senator (PA).
Kenneth Starr, b 7/21/46 (Vernon, TX), former Whitewater independent counsel.
Shelby Steele, b 1/1/46 (Chicago), scholar, critic.
George Steinbrenner, b 7/4/30 (Rocky River, OH), NY Yankees owner.
Gloria Steinem, b 3/25/34 (Toledo, OH), author, feminist.
George Stephanopoulos, b 2/10/61 (Fall River, MA), TV journalist, former presid. adviser.
David J. Stern, b 9/22/42 (NYC), basketball comm.
John Paul Stevens, b 4/20/20 (Chicago), Sup. Ct. justice.
Martha Stewart, b 8/3/41 (Nutley, NJ), homemaking adviser, entrepreneur.
Arthur Ochs Sulzberger Jr., b 9/22/51 (Mt. Kisco, NY), newspaper publisher.
John H. Sununu, b 7/2/39 (Havana, Cuba), political commentator, former White House chief of staff.
John J. Sweeney, b 5/5/34 (NYC), AFL-CIO pres.
Paul Tagliabue, b 11/24/40 (Jersey City, NJ), football comm.
George Tenet, b 1/5/53 (Queens, NY), CIA director.
Clarence Thomas, b 6/23/48 (Savannah, GA), Sup. Ct. justice.
Helen Thomas, b 8/4/20 (Winchester, KY), journalist.
Fred Thompson, b 8/19/42 (Sheffield, AL), senator.
Hunter S. Thompson, b 7/18/37 (Louisville, KY), journalist.
Tommy G. Thompson, b 11/19/41 (Elroy, WI), sec. of health and human services, former WI gov.
J. Strom Thurmond, b 12/5/02 (Edgefield, SC), senator.
Laurence Tisch, b 3/15/23 (NYC), entertainment exec.
Margaret Truman, b 2/17/24 (Independence, MO), author, daughter of Pres. Truman.
Donald Trump, b 1946 (NYC), real estate exec.
Ted Turner, b 11/19/38 (Cincinnati), TV exec, philanthropist.
Peter Ueberroth, b 9/2/37 (Chicago), sports & travel exec.
Jack Valenti, b 9/5/21 (Houston), movie industry exec.
Abigail Van Buren, b 7/4/18 (Sioux City, IA), advice columnist.
Greta Van Susteren, b 6/11/54 (Appleton, WI), lawyer, TV commentator.
Ann Veneman, b 6/29/49 (Sacramento, CA), agriculture sec.
Jesse Ventura, b 7/15/51 (Minneapolis), MN governor, former wrestler.
Paul Volcker, b 9/5/27 (Cape May, NJ), economist, former Fed chairman.
Mike Wallace, b 5/9/18 (Brookline, MA), TV journalist.
Barbara Walters, b 9/25/31 (Boston), TV journalist.
J. C. Watts Jr. b 11/18/57 (Eufaula, OK), U.S. representative, Republican Conference chair.
Andrew Weil, b 6/8/42 (Philadelphia), health adviser.
Caspar Weinberger, b 8/18/17 (San Francisco), business exec, former defense sec., other cabinet posts.
Harvey Weinstein, b 3/19/52 (NYC), movie executive.
Jack Welch, b 1935 (Salem, MA), former General Electric CEO.
Jann Wenner, b 1/7/46 (NYC), publisher.
Cornel West, b 6/23/53 (Tulsa, OK), scholar, critic.
Ruth Westheimer, b. 1928 (Germany), human sexuality expert.
Christine Todd Whitman, b 9/26/46 (NYC), EPA head, former NJ gov.
Meg Whitman, b 1957 (Cold Spring Harbor, NY), eBay pres. & CEO.
Elie Wiesel, b 9/30/28 (Sighet, Romania), scholar, author, Nobel Peace Prize winner.
L. Douglas Wilder, b 1/17/31 (Richmond, VA), former VA gov.
George Will, b 5/4/41 (Champaign, IL), journalist, author.
Jody Williams, b 10/9/50 (Brattleboro, VT), anti-landmine activist, Nobel Peace Prize winner.
Pete Wilson, b 8/23/33 (Lake Forest, IL), former CA gov.
Oprah Winfrey, b 1/29/54 (Kosciusko, MS), TV and media personality, businessperson, actress.
Paul Wolfowitz, b 12/22/43 (NYC), deputy defense secretary.
Bob Woodward, b 3/26/43 (Geneva, IL), journalist, author.
Paula Zahn, 2/24/56 (Omaha, NE), TV journalist.
Mortimer Zuckerman, b 6/4/37 (Montreal, Quebec), publisher, columnist.

WORLD ALMANAC QUICK QUIZ

Which of the following groups was not in the Rock and Roll Hall of Fame as of 2002?
(a) The Impressions (b) The Flamingos (c) The Coasters (d) Little Anthony and the Imperials

For the answer look in this chapter, or see page 1008.

African-Americans of the Past

See also other categories.

Ralph David Abernathy, 1926-90, organizer, 1957, pres., 1968, Southern Christian Leadership Conf.
Crispus Attucks, c1723-70, leader of group of colonists that clashed with British soldiers in 1770 Boston Massacre.
Benjamin Banneker, 1731-1806, inventor, astronomer, mathematician, gazetteer.
Daisy Bates, 1920?-99, Arkansas, civil rights leader who fought for school integration.
James P. Beckwourth, 1798-c1867, western fur trader, scout; Beckwourth Pass in N California named for him.
Mary McCleod Bethune, 1875-1955, adviser to FDR and Truman; founder, pres., Bethune-Cookman College.
Henry Blair, 19th cent., pioneer inventor; obtained patents for a corn-planter, 1834, and cotton-planter, 1836.
Edward Bouchet, 1852-1918, first black to earn a PhD at a U.S. university (Yale, 1876).
Tom Bradley, 1917-98, first African-American mayor of L.A.
Sterling A. Brown, 1901-89, poet, literature professor; helped establish African-American literary criticism.
William Wells Brown, 1815-84, memoirist, ex-slave; first African American to publish a novel, 1853.
Ralph Bunche, 1904-71, first black to win the Nobel Peace Prize, 1950; undersecretary of the UN, 1950.
Stokely Carmichael (Kwame Toure), 1941-98, black power activist.
George Washington Carver, 1864-1943, botanist, chemist, and educator; transformed the economy of the South.
Charles Waddell Chesnutt, 1858-1932, author known for his short stories, such as in *The Conjure Woman (1899).*
Eldridge Cleaver, 1935-98, revolutionary social critic; former "minister of information" for Black Panthers; *Soul on Ice.*
James Cleveland, 1931-91, composer, musician, singer; first black gospel artist to appear at Carnegie Hall.
Countee Cullen, 1903-46, poet, prominent in the Harlem Renaissance of the 1920s; *The Black Christ.*
Benjamin O. Davis Jr., 1912-2002, leader of World War II black aviators, first African-American general in U.S. Air Force.
Benjamin O. Davis Sr., 1877-1970, first African-American general, 1940, in U.S. Army.
William L. Dawson, 1886-1970, Illinois congressman, first black chairman of a major U.S. House committee.
Aaron Douglas, 1900-79, "father of black American art."
Frederick Douglass, 1817-95, author, editor, orator, diplomat; edited abolitionist weekly *The North Star.*
St. Clair Drake, 1911-90, black studies pioneer, *Black Metropolis* (1945), with Horace R. Cayton.
Charles Richard Drew, 1904-50, physician, pioneered in development of blood banks.
William Edward Burghardt (W.E.B.) Du Bois, 1868-1963, historian, sociologist; an NAACP founder, 1909.
Paul Laurence Dunbar, 1872-1906, poet, novelist; won fame with *Lyrics of Lowly Life,* 1896.
Jean Baptiste Point du Sable, c1750-1818, pioneer trader and first settler of Chicago, 1779.
Medgar Evers, 1925-63, Mississippi civil rights leader; campaigned to register black voters; assassinated.
James Farmer, 1920-99, civil rights leader; founded Congress of Racial Equality.
Henry O. Flipper, 1856-1940, first African-American to graduate, 1877, from West Point.
Marcus Garvey, 1887-1940, founded Universal Negro Improvement Assn., 1911.
Ewart Guinier, 1911-90, trade unionist; first chairman of Harvard Univ.'s Dept. of African American Studies.
Prince Hall, 1735-1807, activist; founded black Freemasonry; served in American Revolutionary war.
Jupiter Hammon, c1720-1800, poet; first African-American to have his works published, 1761.
Lorraine Hansberry, 1930-65, playwright; won New York Drama Critics Circle Award, 1959; *A Raisin in the Sun.*
William H. Hastie, 1904-76, first black federal judge, appointed 1937; governor of Virgin Islands, 1946-49.
Matthew A. Henson, 1866-1955, member of Peary's 1909 expedition to the North Pole; placed U.S. flag at the pole.
Chester Himes, 1909-84, novelist; *Cotton Comes to Harlem.*
William A. Hinton, 1883-1959, physician, developed tests for syphilis; first black prof., 1949, at Harvard Med. School.
Charles Hamilton Houston, 1895-1950, lawyer, Howard University instructor, champion of minority rights,
Langston Hughes, 1902-67, poet, lyric writer, author; a major influence in 1920s Harlem Renaissance.
Daniel James Jr., 1920-78, first black 4-star general, 1975; commander, North American Air Defense Command.
Henry Johnson, 1897-1929, first American decorated by France in WW1 with the Croix de Guerre.
James Weldon Johnson, 1871-1938, poet, novelist, diplomat; lyricist for *Lift Every Voice and Sing.*
Barbara Jordan, 1936-96, congresswoman, orator, educator.; first black woman to win a seat in the Texas senate, 1966.
Ernest Everett Just, 1883-1941, marine biologist; studied egg development; author, *Biology of Cell Surfaces,* 1941.
Rev. Martin Luther King Jr., 1929-68, civil rights leader; led 1956 Montgomery, AL, boycott; founder, pres., Southern Christian Leadership Conference, 1957; Nobel laureate (1964); assassinated.
Lewis H. Latimer, 1848-1928, associate of Edison; supervised installation of first electric street lighting in NYC.
Mickey Leland, 1944-89, U.S. representative from Texas, 1978 until death; chairman of Congressional Black Caucus.
Henry Lewis, 1932-1996, (U.S.) conductor; first black conductor and musical director of major American orchestra.
Malcolm X (Little), 1925-65, Black Muslim, black nationalist leader; promoted black pride; assassinated.
Thurgood Marshall, 1908-93, first black U.S. solicitor general, 1965; first black justice of U.S. Sup. Ct., 1967-91.
Jan Matzeliger, 1852-89, invented lasting machine, patented 1883, which revolutionized the shoe industry.
Benjamin Mays, 1895-1984, educator, civil rights leader; headed Morehouse College, 1940-67.
Ronald McNair, 1950-86, physicist, astronaut; killed in *Challenger* explosion.
Dorie Miller, 1919-43, Navy hero of Pearl Harbor attack.
Elijah Muhammad, 1897-1975, founded Nation of Islam, 1931.
Pedro Alonzo Niño, navigator of Columbus's Niña, 1492.
Frederick D. Patterson, 1901-88, founder of United Negro College Fund, 1944.
Harold R. Perry, 1916-91, first black American Roman Catholic bishop in the 20th cent.
Adam Clayton Powell Jr., 1908-72, early civil rights leader, congressman, 1945-69.
Joseph H. Rainey, 1832-87, first black elected to U.S. House, 1869, from South Carolina.
A. Philip Randolph, 1889-1979, organized Brotherhood of Sleeping Car Porters, 1925; an organizer of 1941 and 1963 March on Washington movements.
Hiram R. Revels, 1822-1901, first African-American U.S. senator, elected in Mississippi, served 1870-71.
Norbert Rillieux, 1806-94; invented a vacuum pan evaporator, 1846, revolutionizing sugar-refining industry.
Paul Robeson, 1898-1976, actor, singer, civil rights activist; ostracized by conservatives in the 1950s.
Jackie Robinson, 1919-72, first African-American in major league baseball, 1947, and the Baseball Hall of Fame, 1962.
Carl T. Rowan, 1925-2000, reporter, columnist, author.
Bayard Rustin, 1910-87, an organizer of the 1963 March on Washington; exec. director, A. Philip Randolph Institute.
Peter Salem, at the Battle of Bunker Hill, June 17, 1775, shot and killed British commander Maj. John Pitcairn.
Carl Stokes, 1927-1996, first black mayor of a major American city (Cleveland), 1967-72.
Willard Townsend, 1895-1957, organized the United Transport Service Employees (redcaps), 1935.
Sojourner Truth, 1797-1883, born Isabella Baumfree; preacher, abolitionist; worked for black educ. opportunity.
Harriet Tubman, 1823-1913, Underground Railroad conductor, nurse and spy for Union Army in the Civil War.
Nat Turner, 1800-31, led most significant of more than 200 slave revolts in U.S., in Southampton, VA; hanged.
Booker T. Washington, 1856-1915, founder, 1881, and first pres. of Tuskegee Institute; *Up From Slavery.*
Harold Washington, 1922-87, first black mayor of Chicago.
Robert C. Weaver, 1907-97, first African-American appointed to cabinet; secretary of HUD.
Phillis Wheatley, c1753-84, poet; 2d American woman and first black woman to be published, 1770.
Walter White, 1893-1955, exec. sec., NAACP, 1931-55.
Roy Wilkins, 1901-81, exec. director, NAACP, 1955-77.
Daniel Hale Williams, 1858-1931, surgeon; performed one of first two open-heart operations, 1893.
Granville T. Woods, 1856-1910, invented third-rail system now used in subways, and automatic air brake.
Carter G. Woodson, 1875-1950, historian; founded Assn. for the Study of Negro Life and History.
Frank Yerby, 1916-91, first best-selling African-American novelist; *The Foxes of Harrow.*
Coleman A. Young, 1918-97, first Afr.-Amer. mayor of Detroit, 1974-93.

Architects and Some of Their Achievements

Max Abramovitz, b 1908, Avery Fisher Hall, NYC; U.S. Steel Bldg. (now USX Towers), Pittsburgh, PA.
Henry Bacon, 1866-1924, Lincoln Memorial, Wash., DC.
Pietro Belluschi, 1899-1994, Juilliard School, Lincoln Center, Pan Am, now MetLife, Bldg. (with Walter Gropius), NYC.
Marcel Breuer, 1902-81, Whitney Museum of American Art (with Hamilton Smith), NYC.
Charles Bulfinch, 1763-1844, State House, Boston; Capitol (part), Wash., DC.
Gordon Bunshaft, 1909-90, Lever House, Park Ave, NYC; Hirshhorn Museum, Wash., DC.
Daniel H. Burnham, 1846-1912, Union Station, Wash. DC; Flatiron Bldg., NYC.
Irwin Chanin, 1892-1988, theaters, skyscrapers, NYC.
Lucio Costa, 1902-98, master plan for city of Brasilia, with Oscar Niemeyer.
Ralph Adams Cram, 1863-1942, Cath. of St. John the Divine, NYC; U.S. Military Acad. (part), West Point, NY.
R. Buckminster Fuller, 1895-1983, U.S. Pavilion (geodesic domes), Expo 67, Montreal.
Frank O. Gehry, b 1929, Guggenheim Museum, Bilbao, Spain; Experience Music Project, Seattle, WA.
Cass Gilbert, 1859-1934, Custom House, Woolworth Bldg., NYC; Supreme Court Bldg., Wash., DC.
Bertram G. Goodhue, 1869-1924, Capitol, Lincoln, NE; St. Thomas's Church, St. Bartholomew's Church, NYC.
Michael Graves, b 1934, Portland Bldg., Portland, OR; Humana Bldg., Lexington, KY.
Walter Gropius, 1883-1969, Pan Am Bldg. (now MetLife Bldg.) (with Pietro Belluschi), NYC.
Lawrence Halprin, b 1916, Ghirardelli Sq., San Francisco; Nicollet Mall, Minneapolis; FDR Memorial, Wash., DC.
Peter Harrison, 1716-75, Touro Synagogue, Redwood Library, Newport, RI.
Wallace K. Harrison, 1895-1981, Metropolitan Opera House, Lincoln Center, NYC.
Thomas Hastings, 1860-1929, NY Public Library (with John Carrère), Frick Mansion, NYC.
James Hoban, 1762-1831, White House, Wash., DC.
Raymond Hood, 1881-1934, Rockefeller Center (part), Daily News, NYC; Tribune, Chicago, IL.
Richard M. Hunt, 1827-95, Metropolitan Museum (part), NYC; National Observatory, Wash., DC.
Helmut Jahn, b 1940, United Airlines Terminal, O'Hare Airport, Chicago.
William Le Baron Jenney, 1832-1907, Home Insurance (demolished 1931), Chicago, IL.
Philip C. Johnson, b 1906, AT&T headquarters (now 550 Madison Ave.), NYC; Transco Tower, Houston, TX.
Albert Kahn, 1869-1942, General Motors Bldg., Detroit, MI.
Louis Kahn, 1901-74, Salk Laboratory, La Jolla, CA; Yale Art Gallery, New Haven, CT.
Christopher Grant LaFarge, 1862-1938, Roman Catholic Chapel, West Point, NY.
Benjamin H. Latrobe, 1764-1820, Capitol (part), Wash., DC; State Capitol Bldg., Richmond, VA.
Le Corbusier, (Charles-Edouard Jeanneret), 1887-1965, Salvation Army Hostel and Swiss Dormitory, both Paris; master plan for cities of Algiers and Buenos Aires.
William Lescaze, 1896-1969, Philadelphia Savings Fund Society; Borg-Warner Bldg., Chicago.
Maya Lin, b 1959, Vietnam Veterans Memorial, Wash., DC.
Charles Rennie Mackintosh, 1868-1928, Glasgow School of Art; Hill House, Helensburgh.
Bernard R. Maybeck, 1862-1957, Hearst Hall, Univ. of CA, Berkeley; First Church of Christ Scientist, Berkeley, CA.
Charles F. McKim, 1847-1909, Public Library, Boston; Columbia Univ. (part), NYC.
Charles M. McKim, b 1920, KUHT-TV Transmitter Bldg., Lutheran Church of the Redeemer, Houston, TX.
Richard Meier, b 1934, Getty Center Museum, Los Angeles, CA; High Museum of Art, Atlanta, GA.
Ludwig Mies van der Rohe, 1886-1969, Seagram Bldg., (with Philip C. Johnson), NYC; National Gallery, Berlin.
Robert Mills, 1781-1855, Washington Monument, Wash., DC.
Charles Moore, 1925-93, Sea Ranch, near San Francisco; Piazza d'Italia, New Orleans, LA.
Richard J. Neutra, 1892-1970, Mathematics Park, Princeton, NJ; Orange Co. Courthouse, Santa Ana, CA.
Oscar Niemeyer, b 1907, government buildings, Brasilia Palace Hotel, all Brasilia.
Gyo Obata, b 1923, Natl. Air & Space Museum, Smithsonian Inst., Wash., DC; Dallas-Ft. Worth Airport.
Frederick L. Olmsted, 1822-1903, Central Park, NYC; Fairmount Park, Philadelphia, PA.
I(eoh) M(ing) Pei, b 1917, East Wing, Natl. Gallery of Art, Wash., DC; Pyramid, The Louvre, Paris; Rock & Roll Hall of Fame and Museum, Cleveland, OH.
Cesar Pelli, b 1926, World Financial Center, Carnegie Hall Tower, NYC; Petronas Twin Towers, Malaysia.
William Pereira, 1909-85, Cape Canaveral; Transamerica Bldg., San Francisco, CA.
John Russell Pope, 1874-1937, National Gallery, Wash., DC.
John Portman, b 1924, Peachtree Center, Atlanta, GA.
George Browne Post, 1837-1913, NY Stock Exchange; Capitol, Madison, WI.
James Renwick Jr., 1818-95, Grace Church, St. Patrick's Cath., NYC.; Corcoran (now Renwick) Gallery, Wash., DC.
Henry H. Richardson, 1838-86, Trinity Church, Boston, MA.
Kevin Roche, b 1922, Oakland Museum, Oakland, CA; Fine Arts Center, University of Massachusetts, Amherst.
James Gamble Rogers, 1867-1947, Columbia-Presbyterian Medical Center, NYC; Northwestern Univ., Evanston, IL.
John Wellborn Root, 1887-1963, Palmolive Bldg., Chicago; Hotel Statler, Wash., DC.
Paul Rudolph, 1918-97, Jewitt Art Center, Wellesley Colllege, MA; Art & Architecture Bldg., Yale Univ., New Haven, CT.
Eero Saarinen, 1910-61, Gateway to the West Arch, St. Louis, MO; Trans World Flight Center, NYC.
Louis Skidmore, 1897-1962, Atomic Energy Commission town site, Oak Ridge, TN; Terrace Plaza Hotel, Cincinnati, OH.
Clarence S. Stein, 1882-1975, Temple Emanu-El, NYC.
Edward Durell Stone, 1902-78, U.S. Embassy, New Delhi, India; (H. Hartford) Gallery of Modern Art, NYC.
Louis H. Sullivan, 1856-1924, Auditorium Bldg., Chicago, IL.
Richard Upjohn, 1802-78, Trinity Church, NYC.
Max O. Urbahn, 1912-95, Vehicle Assembly Bldg., Cape Canaveral, FL.
Robert Venturi, b 1925, Gordon Wu Hall, Princeton, NJ; Mielparque Nikko Kirifuri Resort, Japan.
Ralph T. Walker, 1889-1973, NY Telephone Bldg. (now NYNEX); IBM Research Lab, Poughkeepsie, NY.
Roland A. Wank, 1898-1970, Cincinnati Union Terminal, OH; head architect (1933-44), Tennessee Valley Authority.
Stanford White, 1853-1906, Washington Arch in Washington Square Park, first Madison Square Garden, NYC.
Frank Lloyd Wright, 1867-1959, Imperial Hotel, Tokyo; Guggenheim Museum, NYC; Marin County Civic Center, San Rafael; Kaufmann "Fallingwater" house, Bear Run, PA.; Taliesen West, Scottsdale, AZ.
William Wurster, 1895-1973, Ghirardelli Sq., San Francisco; Cowell College, UC, Berkeley, CA.
Minoru Yamasaki, 1912-86, World Trade Center, NYC.

WORLD ALMANAC QUICK QUIZ

Can you list these famous Americans in order from oldest to youngest?

(a) George W. Bush (b) Bill Clinton
(c) Colin Powell (d) Bill Gates

For the answer look in this chapter, or see page 1008.

Artists, Photographers, and Sculptors of the Past

Artists are painters unless otherwise indicated.

Berenice Abbott, 1898-1991, (U.S.) photographer. Documentary of New York City, *Changing New York* (1939).
Ansel Easton Adams, 1902-84, (U.S.) photographer. Landscapes of the American Southwest.
Washington Allston, 1779-1843, (U.S.) landscapist. *Belshazzar's Feast.*
Albrecht Altdorfer, 1480-1538, (Ger.) landscapist.
Andrea del Sarto, 1486-1530, (It.) frescoes. *Madonna of the Harpies.*
Fra Angelico, c1400-55, (It.) Renaissance muralist. *Madonna of the Linen Drapers' Guild.*
Diane Arbus, 1923-71, (U.S.) photographer. Disturbing images.
Alexsandr Archipenko, 1887-1964, (U.S.) sculptor. *Boxing Match, Medranos.*
Eugène Atget, 1856-1927, (Fr.) photographer. Paris life.
John James Audubon, 1785-1851, (U.S.) *Birds of America.*
Hans Baldung-Grien, 1484-1545, (Ger.) *Todentanz.*
Ernst Barlach, 1870-1938, (Ger.) Expressionist sculptor. *Man Drawing a Sword.*
Frederic-Auguste Bartholdi, 1834-1904, (Fr.) *Liberty Enlightening the World, Lion of Belfort.*
Fra Bartolommeo, 1472-1517, (It.) *Vision of St. Bernard.*
Aubrey Beardsley, 1872-98, (Br.) illustrator. *Salome, Lysistrata, Morte d'Arthur, Volpone.*

Max Beckmann, 1884-1950, (Ger.) Expressionist. *The Descent From the Cross.*
Gentile Bellini, 1426-1507, (It.) Renaissance. *Procession in St. Mark's Square.*
Giovanni Bellini, 1428-1516, (It.) *St. Francis in Ecstasy.*
Jacopo Bellini, 1400-70, (It.) *Crucifixion.*
George Wesley Bellows, 1882-1925, (U.S.) sports artist, portraitist, landscapist. *Stag at Sharkey's, Edith Clavell.*
Thomas Hart Benton, 1889-1975, (U.S.) American regionalist. *Threshing Wheat, Arts of the West.*
Gianlorenzo Bernini, 1598-1680, (It.) Baroque sculpture. *The Assumption.*
Albert Bierstadt, 1830-1902, (U.S.) landscapist. *The Rocky Mountains, Mount Corcoran.*
George Caleb Bingham, 1811-79, (U.S.) *Fur Traders Descending the Missouri.*
William Blake, 1752-1827, (Br.) engraver. *Book of Job, Songs of Innocence, Songs of Experience.*
Rosa Bonheur, 1822-99, (Fr.) *The Horse Fair.*
Pierre Bonnard, 1867-1947, (Fr.) Intimist. *The Breakfast Room, Girl in a Straw Hat.*
Gutzon Borglum, 1871-1941, (U.S.) sculptor. Mt. Rushmore Memorial.
Hieronymus Bosch, 1450-1516, (Flem.) religious allegories. *The Crowning With Thorns.*
Sandro Botticelli, 1444-1510, (It.) Renaissance. *Birth of Venus, Adoration of the Magi, Guiliano de'Medici.*
Margaret Bourke-White, 1906-71, (U.S.) photographer, photojournalist. WW2, USSR, rural South during the Depression.
Mathew Brady, c1823-96, (U.S.) photographer. Official photographer of the Civil War.
Constantin Brancusi, 1876-1957, (Romanian-Fr.) Nonobjective sculptor. *Flying Turtle, The Kiss.*
Georges Braque, 1882-1963, (Fr.) Cubist. *Violin and Palette.*
Pieter Bruegel the Elder, c1525-69, (Flem.) *The Peasant Dance, Hunters in the Snow, Magpie on the Gallows.*
Pieter Bruegel the Younger, 1564-1638, (Flem.) *Village Fair, The Crucifixion.*
Edward Burne-Jones, 1833-98, (Br.) Pre-Raphaelite artist-craftsman. *The Mirror of Venus.*
Alexander Calder, 1898-1976, (U.S.) sculptor. *Lobster Trap and Fish Tail.*
Julia Cameron, 1815-79, (Br.) photographer. Considered one of the most important portraitists of the 19th cent.
Robert Capa (Andrei Friedmann), 1913-54, (Hung.-U.S.) photographer. War photojournalist; invasion of Normandy.
Michelangelo Merisi da Caravaggio, 1573-1610, (It.) Baroque. *The Supper at Emmaus.*
Emily Carr, 1871-1945, (Can.) landscapist. *Blunden Harbour, Big Raven, Rushing Sea of Undergrowth.*
Carlo Carrà, 1881-1966, (It.) Metaphysical school. *Lot's Daughters, The Enchanted Room.*
Mary Cassatt, 1844-1926, (U.S.) Impressionist. *The Cup of Tea, Woman Bathing, The Boating Party.*
George Catlin, 1796-1872, (U.S.) American Indian life. *Gallery of Indians, Buffalo Dance.*
Benvenuto Cellini, 1500-71, (It.) Mannerist sculptor, goldsmith. *Perseus and Medusa.*
Paul Cézanne, 1839-1906, (Fr.) *Card Players, Mont-Sainte-Victoire With Large Pine Trees.*
Marc Chagall, 1887-1985, (Russ.) Jewish life and folklore. *I and the Village, The Praying Jew.*
Jean Simeon Chardin, 1699-1779, (Fr.) still lifes. *The Kiss, The Grace.*
Frederick Church, 1826-1900, (U.S.) Hudson River school. *Niagara, Andes of Ecuador.*
Giovanni Cimabue, 1240-1302, (It.) Byzantine mosaicist. *Madonna Enthroned With St. Francis.*
Claude Lorrain (Claude Gellé), 1600-82, (Fr.) ideal-landscapist. *The Enchanted Castle.*
Thomas Cole, 1801-48, (U.S.) Hudson River school. *The Ox-Bow, In the Catskills.*
John Constable, 1776-1837, (Br.) landscapist. *Salisbury Cathedral From the Bishop's Grounds.*
John Singleton Copley, 1738-1815, (U.S.) portraitist. *Samuel Adams, Watson and the Shark.*
Lovis Corinth, 1858-1925, (Ger.) Expressionist. *Apocalypse.*
Jean-Baptiste-Camille Corot, 1796-1875, (Fr.) landscapist. *Souvenir de Mortefontaine, Pastorale.*
Correggio, 1494-1534, (It.) Renaissance muralist. *Mystic Marriages of St. Catherine.*
Gustave Courbet, 1819-77, (Fr.) Realist. *The Artist's Studio.*
Lucas Cranach the Elder, 1472-1553, (Ger.) Protestant Reformation portraitist. *Luther.*
Imogen Cunningham, 1883-1976, (U.S.) photographer, portraitist. Plant photography.
Nathaniel Currier, 1813-88, and **James M. Ives,** 1824-95, (both U.S.) lithographers. *A Midnight Race on the Mississippi, American Forest Scene—Maple Sugaring.*
John Steuart Curry, 1897-1946, (U.S.) Americana, murals. *Baptism in Kansas.*
Salvador Dalí, 1904-89, (Sp.) Surrealist. *Persistence of Memory, The Crucifixion.*
Honoré Daumier, 1808-79, (Fr.) caricaturist. *The Third-Class Carriage.*
Jacques-Louis David, 1748-1825, (Fr.) Neoclassicist. *The Oath of the Horatii.*
Arthur Davies, 1862-1928, (U.S.) Romantic landscapist. *Unicorns, Leda and the Dioscuri.*
Willem de Kooning, 1904-1997, (Dutch-U.S.) abstract expressionist. *Excavation, Woman I, Door to the River.*
Edgar Degas, 1834-1917, (Fr.) *The Ballet Class.*
Eugène Delacroix, 1798-1863, (Fr.) Romantic. *Massacre at Chios, Liberty Leading the People.*
Paul Delaroche, 1797-1856, (Fr.) historical themes. *Children of Edward IV.*
Luca Della Robbia, 1400-82, (It.) Renaissance terracotta artist. *Cantoria* (singing gallery), Florence cathedral.
Donatello, 1386-1466, (It.) Renaissance sculptor. *David, Gattamelata.*
Jean Dubuffet, 1902-85, (Fr.) painter, sculptor, printmaker. *Group of Four Trees.*
Marcel Duchamp, 1887-1968, (Fr.) Dada artist. *Nude Descending a Staircase, No. 2.*
Raoul Dufy, 1877-1953, (Fr.) Fauvist. *Chateau and Horses.*
Asher Brown Durand, 1796-1886, (U.S.) Hudson River school. *Kindred Spirits.*
Albrecht Dürer, 1471-1528, (Ger.) Renaissance painter, engraver, woodcuts. *St. Jerome in His Study, Melencolia I.*
Anthony van Dyck, 1599-1641, (Flem.) Baroque portraitist. *Portrait of Charles I Hunting.*
Thomas Eakins, 1844-1916, (U.S.) Realist. *The Gross Clinic.*
Alfred Eisenstaedt, 1898-1995, (Ger.-U.S.) photographer, photojournalist. Famous photo, V-J Day, Aug. 14, 1945.
Peter Henry Emerson, 1856-1936, (Br.) photographer. Promoted photography as an independent art form.
Jacob Epstein, 1880-1959, (Br.) religious and allegorical sculptor. *Genesis, Ecce Homo.*
Jan van Eyck, c1390-1441, (Flem.) naturalistic panels. *Adoration of the Lamb.*
Roger Fenton, 1819-68, (Br.) photographer. Crimean War.
Anselm Feuerbach, 1829-80, (Ger.) Romantic Classicist. *Judgment of Paris, Iphigenia.*
John Bernard Flannagan, 1895-1942, (U.S.) animal sculptor. *Triumph of the Egg.*
Jean-Honoré Fragonard, 1732-1806, (Fr.) Rococo. *The Swing.*
Daniel Chester French, 1850-1931, (U.S.) *The Minute Man of Concord;* seated *Lincoln*, Lincoln Memorial, Wash., DC.
Caspar David Friedrich, 1774-1840, (Ger.) Romantic landscapes. *Man and Woman Gazing at the Moon.*
Thomas Gainsborough, 1727-88, (Br.) portraitist. *The Blue Boy, The Watering Place, Orpin the Parish Clerk.*
Alexander Gardner, 1821-82, (U.S.) photographer. Civil War; railroad construction; Great Plains Indians.
Paul Gauguin, 1848-1903, (Fr.) Post-impressionist. *The Tahitians, Spirit of the Dead Watching.*
Lorenzo Ghiberti, 1378-1455, (It.) Renaissance sculptor. Gates of Paradise baptistery doors, Florence.
Alberto Giacometti, 1901-66, (Swiss) attenuated sculptures of solitary figures. *Man Pointing.*
Giorgione, c1477-1510, (It.) Renaissance. *The Tempest.*
Giotto di Bondone, 1267-1337, (It.) Renaissance. *Presentation of Christ in the Temple.*
François Girardon, 1628-1715, (Fr.) Baroque sculptor of classical themes. *Apollo Tended by the Nymphs.*
Vincent van Gogh, 1853-90, (Dutch) *The Starry Night, L'Arlesienne, Bedroom at Arles, Self-Portrait.*
Arshile Gorky, 1905-48, (U.S.) Surrealist. *The Liver Is the Cock's Comb.*
Francisco de Goya y Lucientes, 1746-1828, (Sp.) *The Naked Maja, The Disasters of War* (etchings).
El Greco, 1541-1614, (Sp.) *View of Toledo, Assumption of the Virgin.*
Horatio Greenough, 1805-52, (U.S.) Neo-classical sculptor.
Matthias Grünewald, 1480-1528, (Ger.) mystical religious themes. *The Resurrection.*
Frans Hals, c1580-1666, (Dutch) portraitist. *Laughing Cavalier, Gypsy Girl.*
Austin Hansen, 1910-96, (U.S.) photographer. Harlem, NY, life.
Childe Hassam, 1859-1935, (U.S.) Impressionist. *Southwest Wind, July 14 Rue Daunon.*
Edward Hicks, 1780-1849, (U.S.) folk painter. *The Peaceable Kingdom.*
Lewis Wickes Hine, 1874-1940, (U.S.) photographer. Studies of immigrants, children in industry.
Hans Hofmann, 1880-1966, (U.S.) early abstract Expressionist. *Spring, The Gate.*

William Hogarth, 1697-1764, (Br.) caricaturist. *The Rake's Progress.*
Katsushika Hokusai, 1760-1849, (Jpn.) printmaker. *Crabs.*
Hans Holbein the Elder, 1460-1524, (Ger.) late Gothic. *Presentation of Christ in the Temple.*
Hans Holbein the Younger, 1497-1543, (Ger.) portraitist. *Henry VIII, The French Ambassadors.*
Winslow Homer, 1836-1910, (U.S.) naturalist painter, marine themes. *Marine Coast, High Cliff.*
Edward Hopper, 1882-1967, (U.S.) realistic urban scenes. *Nighthawks, House by the Railroad.*
Horst P. Horst, 1906-99, (Ger.) fashion, celebrity photographer.
Jean-Auguste-Dominique Ingres, 1780-1867, (Fr.) Classicist. *Valpincon Bather.*
George Inness, 1825-94, (U.S.) luminous landscapist. *Delaware Water Gap.*
William Henry Jackson, 1843-1942, (U.S.) photographer. American West, building of Union Pacific Railroad.
Donald Judd, 1928-94, (U.S.) sculptor, major Minimalist.
Frida Kahlo, 1907-54, (Mex.) painter; *Self Portrait With Monkey.*
Vasily Kandinsky, 1866-1944, (Russ.) Abstractionist. *Capricious Forms, Improvisation 38 (second version).*
Paul Klee, 1879-1940, (Swiss) Abstractionist. *Twittering Machine, Pastoral, Death and Fire.*
Gustav Klimt, 1862-1918, (Austrian) cofounder of Vienna Secession Movement, *The Kiss.*
Oscar Kokoschka, 1886-1980, (Austrian) Expressionist. *View of Prague, Harbor of Marseilles.*
Kathe Kollwitz, 1867-1945, (Ger.) printmaker, social justice themes. *The Peasant War.*
Gaston Lachaise, 1882-1935, (U.S.) figurative sculptor. *Standing Woman.*
John La Farge, 1835-1910, (U.S.) muralist. *Red and White Peonies, The Ascension.*
Sir Edwin (Henry) Landseer, 1802-73, (Br.) painter, sculptor. *Shoeing, Rout of Comus.*
Dorothea Lange, 1895-1965, (U.S.) photographer. Depression photographs, migrant farm workers.
Fernand Léger, 1881-1955, (Fr.) machine art. *The Cyclists.*
Leonardo da Vinci, 1452-1519, (It.) *Mona Lisa, Last Supper, The Annunciation.*
Emanuel Leutze, 1816-68, (U.S.) historical themes. *Washington Crossing the Delaware.*
Roy Lichtenstein, 1923-97, (U.S.) pop artist.
Jacques Lipchitz, 1891-1973, (Fr.) Cubist sculptor. *Harpist.*
Filippino Lippi, 1457-1504, (It.) Renaissance.
Fra Filippo Lippi, 1406-69, (It.) Renaissance. *Coronation of the Virgin, Madonna and Child With Angels.*
Morris Louis, 1912-62, (U.S.) abstract Expressionist. *Signa, Stripes, Alpha-Phi.*
Rene Magritte, 1898-1967, (Belgian) Surrealist. *The Descent of Man, The Betrayal of Images.*
Aristide Maillol, 1861-1944, (Fr.) sculptor. *L'Harmonie.*
Édouard Manet, 1832-83, (Fr.) forerunner of Impressionism. *Luncheon on the Grass, Olympia.*
Andrea Mantegna, 1431-1506, (It.) Renaissance frescoes. *Triumph of Caesar.*
Franz Marc, 1880-1916, (Ger.) Expressionist. *Blue Horses.*
John Marin, 1870-1953, (U.S.) Expressionist seascapes. *Maine Island.*
Reginald Marsh, 1898-1954, (U.S.) satirical artist. *Tattoo and Haircut.*
Masaccio, 1401-28, (It.) Renaissance. *The Tribute Money.*
Henri Matisse, 1869-1954, (Fr.) Fauvist. *Woman With the Hat.*
Michelangelo Buonarroti, 1475-1564, (It.) *Pietà, David, Moses, The Last Judgment,* Sistine Chapel ceiling.
Jean-Francois Millet, 1814-75, (Fr.) painter of peasant subjects. *The Gleaners, The Man With a Hoe.*
Joan Miró, 1893-1983, (Sp.) Exuberant colors, playful images. Catalan landscape, *Dutch Interior.*
Amedeo Modigliani, 1884-1920, (It.) *Reclining Nude.*
Piet Mondrian, 1872-1944, (Dutch) Abstractionist. *Composition With Red, Yellow and Blue.*
Claude Monet, 1840-1926, (Fr.) Impressionist. *The Bridge at Argenteuil, Haystacks.*
Henry Moore, 1898-1986, (Br.) sculptor of large-scale, abstract works. *Reclining Figure* (several).
Gustave Moreau, 1826-98, (Fr.) Symbolist. *The Apparition, Dance of Salome.*
James Wilson Morrice, 1865-1924, (Can.) landscapist. *The Ferry, Quebec, Venice, Looking Over the Lagoon.*
William Morris, 1834-1896, (Br.) decorative artist, leader of the Arts and Crafts movement.
Grandma Moses, 1860-1961, (U.S.) folk painter. *Out for the Christmas Trees, Thanksgiving Turkey.*
Edvard Munch, 1863-1944, (Nor.) Expressionist. *The Cry.*
Bartolome Murillo, 1618-82, (Sp.) Baroque religious artist. *Vision of St. Anthony, The Two Trinities.*
Eadweard Muybridge, 1830-1904, (Br.-U.S.) photographer. Studies of motion, *Animal Locomotion.*
Nadar (Gaspar-Félix Tournachon), 1820-1910, (Fr.) photographer, caricaturist, portraitist. Invented photo-essay.
Barnett Newman, 1905-70, (U.S.) abstract Expressionist. *Stations of the Cross.*
Isamu Noguchi, 1904-88, (U.S.) abstract sculptor, designer. *Kouros, BirdC(MU),* sculptural gardens.
Georgia O'Keeffe, 1887-1986, (U.S.) Southwest motifs. *Cow's Skull: Red, White, and Blue, The Shelton With Sunspots.*
José Clemente Orozco, 1883-1949, (Mex.) frescoes. *House of Tears, Pre-Columbian Golden Age.*
Timothy H. O'Sullivan, 1840-82, (U.S.) Civil War photographer.
Charles Willson Peale, 1741-1827, (U.S.) Amer. Revolutionary portraitist. *The Staircase Group,* U.S. presidents.
Rembrandt Peale, 1778-1860, (U.S.) portraitist. Thomas Jefferson.
Pietro Perugino, 1446-1523, (It.) Renaissance. *Delivery of the Keys to St. Peter.*
Pablo Picasso, 1881-1973, (Sp.) painter, sculptor. *Guernica; Dove; Head of a Woman; Head of a Bull, Metamorphosis.*
Piero della Francesca, c1415-92, (It.) Renaissance. *Duke of Urbino, Flagellation of Christ.*
Camille Pissarro, 1830-1903, (Fr.) Impressionist. *Boulevard des Italiens, Morning, Sunlight; Bather in the Woods.*
Jackson Pollock, 1912-56, (U.S.) abstract Expressionist. *Autumn Rhythm.*
Nicolas Poussin, 1594-1665, (Fr.) Baroque pictorial classicism. *St. John on Patmos.*
Maurice B. Prendergast, c1860-1924, (U.S.) Post-impressionist water colorist. *Umbrellas in the Rain.*
Pierre-Paul Prud'hon, 1758-1823, (Fr.) Romanticist. *Crime Pursued by Vengeance and Justice.*
Pierre Cecile Puvis de Chavannes, 1824-98, (Fr.) muralist. *The Poor Fisherman.*
Raphael Sanzio, 1483-1520, (It.) Renaissance. *Disputa, School of Athens, Sistine Madonna.*
Man Ray, 1890-1976, (U.S.) Dada artist. *Observing Time, The Lovers, Marquis de Sade.*
Odilon Redon, 1840-1916, (Fr.) Symbolist painter, lithographer. *In the Dream, Vase of Flowers.*
Rembrandt van Rijn, 1606-69, (Dutch) *The Bridal Couple, The Night Watch.*
Frederic Remington, 1861-1909, (U.S.) painter, sculptor. Portrayer of the American West, *Bronco Buster.*
Pierre-Auguste Renoir, 1841-1919, (Fr.) Impressionist. *The Luncheon of the Boating Party, Dance in the Country.*
Joshua Reynolds, 1723-92, (Br.) portraitist. *Mrs. Siddons as the Tragic Muse.*
Diego Rivera, 1886-1957, (Mex.) frescoes. *The Fecund Earth.*
Larry Rivers, 1923-2002, (U.S.) painter, sculptor, often realistic; Dutch Masters series.
Henry Peach Robinson, 1830-1901 (Br.) photographer. A leader of "high art" photography.
Norman Rockwell, 1894-1978, (U.S.) painter, illustrator. *Saturday Evening Post* covers.
Auguste Rodin, 1840-1917, (Fr.) sculptor. *The Thinker.*
Mark Rothko, 1903-70, (U.S.) abstract Expressionist. *Light, Earth and Blue.*
Georges Rouault, 1871-1958, (Fr.) Expressionist. *Three Judges.*
Henri Rousseau, 1844-1910, (Fr.) primitive exotic themes. *The Snake Charmer.*
Theodore Rousseau, 1812-67, (Swiss-Fr.) landscapist. *Under the Birches, Evening.*
Peter Paul Rubens, 1577-1640, (Flem.) Baroque. *Mystic Marriage of St. Catherine.*
Jacob van Ruisdael, c1628-82, (Dutch) landscapist. *Jewish Cemetery.*
Charles M. Russell, 1866-1926, (U.S.) Western life.
Salomon van Ruysdael, c1600-70, (Dutch) landscapist. *River With Ferry-Boat.*
Albert Pinkham Ryder, 1847-1917, (U.S.) seascapes and allegories. *Toilers of the Sea.*
Augustus Saint-Gaudens, 1848-1907, (U.S.) memorial statues. *Farragut, Mrs. Henry Adams (Grief).*
Andrea Sansovino, 1460-1529, (It.) Renaissance sculptor. *Baptism of Christ.*
Jacopo Sansovino, 1486-1570, (It.) Renaissance sculptor. *St. John the Baptist.*

IT'S A FACT: Grandma Moses, whose real name was Anna Mary Robertson, started painting in her late 70s. She was 80 years old when her first solo public show, at a New York City gallery, launched her career as a major artist. She died at the age of 101.

John Singer Sargent, 1856-1925, (U.S.) Edwardian society portraitist. The Wyndham Sisters, Madam X.
George Segal, 1924-2000, (U.S.) sculptor of life-sized figures realistically depicting daily life.
Georges Seurat, 1859-91, (Fr.) Pointillist. *Sunday Afternoon on the Island of La Grande Jatte.*
Gino Severini, 1883-1966, (It.) Futurist and Cubist. *Dynamic Hieroglyph of the Bal Tabarin.*
Ben Shahn, 1898-1969, (U.S.) social and political themes. Sacco and Vanzetti series, *Seurat's Lunch, Handball.*
Charles Sheeler, 1883-1965, (U.S.) abstractionist.
David Alfaro Siqueiros, 1896-1974, (Mex.) political muralist. *March of Humanity.*
David Smith, 1906-65, (U.S.) welded metal sculpture. *Hudson River Landscape, Zig, Cubi* series.
Edward Steichen, 1879-1973, (U.S.) photographer. Credited with transforming photography into an art form.
Alfred Stieglitz, 1864-1946, (U.S.) photographer, editor; helped create acceptance of photography as art.
Paul Strand, 1890-1976, (U.S.) photographer. People, nature, landscapes.
Gilbert Stuart, 1755-1828, (U.S.) portraitist. George Washington, Thomas Jefferson, James Madison.
Thomas Sully, 1783-1872, (U.S.) portraitist. *Col. Thomas Handasyd Perkins, The Passage of the Delaware.*
William Henry Fox Talbot, 1800-77, (Br.) photographer. *Pencil of Nature*, early photographically illustrated book.
George Tames, 1919-94, (U.S.) photographer. Chronicled presidents, political leaders.
Yves Tanguy, 1900-55, (Fr.) Surrealist. *Rose of the Four Winds, Mama, Papa Is Wounded!*
Giovanni Battista Tiepolo, 1696-1770, (It.) Rococo frescoes. *The Crucifixion.*
Jacopo Tintoretto, 1518-94, (It.) Mannerist. *The Last Supper.*
Titian, c1485-1576, (It.) Renaissance. *Venus and the Lute Player, The Bacchanal.*
Jose Rey Toledo, 1916-94, (U.S.) Native American artist. Captured the essence of tribal dances on canvas.
Henri de Toulouse-Lautrec, 1864-1901, (Fr.) *At the Moulin Rouge.*
John Trumbull, 1756-1843, (U.S.) historical themes. *The Declaration of Independence.*
J(oseph) M(allord) W(illiam) Turner, 1775-1851, (Br.) Romantic landscapist. *Snow Storm.*
Paolo Uccello, 1397-1475, (It.) Gothic-Renaissance. *The Rout of San Romano.*
Maurice Utrillo, 1883-1955, (Fr.) Impressionist. *Sacre-Coeur de Montmartre.*
John Vanderlyn, 1775-1852, (U.S.) Neo-classicist. *Ariadne Asleep on the Island of Naxos.*
Diego Velázquez, 1599-1660, (Sp.) Baroque. *Las Meninas, Portrait of Juan de Pareja.*
Jan Vermeer, 1632-75, (Dutch) interior genre subjects. *Young Woman With a Water Jug.*
Paolo Veronese, 1528-88, (It.) devotional themes, vastly peopled canvases. *The Temptation of St. Anthony.*
Andrea del Verrocchio, 1435-88, (It.) Floren. sculptor. *Colleoni.*
Maurice de Vlaminck, 1876-1958, (Fr.) Fauvist landscapist. *Red Trees.*
Andy Warhol, 1928-87, (U.S.) Pop Art. *Campbell's Soup Cans, Marilyn Diptych.*
Antoine Watteau, 1684-1721, (Fr.) Rococo painter of "scenes of gallantry." *The Embarkation for Cythera.*
George Frederic Watts, 1817-1904, (Br.) painter and sculptor of grandiose allegorical themes. *Hope.*
Benjamin West, 1738-1820, (U.S.) realistic historical themes. *Death of General Wolfe.*
Edward Weston, 1886-1958, (U.S.) photographer. Landscapes of American West.
James Abbott McNeill Whistler, 1834-1903, (U.S.) *Arrangement in Grey and Black, No. 1: The Artist's Mother.*
Archibald M. Willard, 1836-1918, (U.S.) *The Spirit of '76.*
Grant Wood, 1891-1942, (U.S.) Midwestern regionalist. *American Gothic, Daughters of Revolution.*
Ossip Zadkine, 1890-1967, (Russ.) School of Paris sculptor. *The Destroyed City, Musicians, Christ.*

Business Leaders and Philanthropists of the Past

Elizabeth Arden (F. N. Graham), 1884-1966, (U.S.) Canadian-born founder of cosmetics empire.
Philip D. Armour, 1832-1901, (U.S.) industrialist; streamlined meatpacking.
John Jacob Astor, 1763-1848, (U.S.) German-born fur trader, banker, real estate magnate; at death, richest in U.S.
Francis W. Ayer, 1848-1923, (U.S.) ad industry pioneer.
August Belmont, 1816-90, (U.S.) German-born financier.
James B. (Diamond Jim) Brady, 1856-1917, (U.S.) financier, philanthropist, legendary bon vivant.
Adolphus Busch, 1839-1913, (U.S.) German-born businessman; established brewery empire.
Asa Candler, 1851-1929, (U.S.) founded Coca-Cola Co.
Andrew Carnegie, 1835-1919, (U.S.) Scottish-born industrialist; philanthropist; founded Carnegie Steel Co.
Tom Carvel, 1908-89, (Gr.-U.S.) founded ice cream chain.
William Colgate, 1783-1857, (Br.-U.S.) Br.-born businessman, philanthropist; founded soap-making empire.
Jay Cooke, 1821-1905, (U.S.) financier; sold $1 billion in Union bonds during Civil War.
Peter Cooper, 1791-1883, (U.S.) industrialist, inventor, philanthropist; founded Cooper Union (1859).
Ezra Cornell, 1807-74, (U.S.) businessman, philanthropist; headed Western Union, established university.
Erastus Corning, 1794-1872, (U.S.) financier; headed N.Y. Central.
Charles Crocker, 1822-88, (U.S.) railroad builder, financier.
Samuel Cunard, 1787-1865, (Can.) pioneered trans-Atlantic steam navigation.
Marcus Daly, 1841-1900, (U.S.) Irish-born copper magnate.
W. Edwards Deming, 1900-93, (U.S.) quality-control expert who revolutionized Japanese manufacturing.
Walt Disney, 1901-66, (U.S.) pioneer in cinema animation; built entertainment empire.
Herbert H. Dow, 1866-1930, (U.S.) founder of chemical co.
James Duke, 1856-1925, (U.S.) founded American Tobacco, Duke Univ.
Eleuthere I. du Pont, 1771-1834, (Fr.-U.S.) gunpowder manufacturer; founded one of the largest business empires.
Thomas C. Durant, 1820-85, (U.S.) railroad official, financier.
William C. Durant, 1861-1947, (U.S.) industrialist; formed General Motors.
George Eastman, 1854-1932, (U.S.) inventor; manufacturer of photographic equipment.
Marshall Field, 1834-1906, (U.S.) merchant; founded Chicago's largest department store.
Harvey Firestone, 1868-1938, (U.S.) founded tire company.
Avery Fisher, 1906-94, (U.S.) industrialist, philanthropist, founded Fisher electronics.
Henry M. Flagler, 1830-1913, (U.S.) financier; helped form Standard Oil; developed Florida as resort state.
Malcolm Forbes, 1919-90, (U.S.) magazine publisher.
Henry Ford, 1863-1947, (U.S.) auto maker; developed first popular low-priced car.
Henry Ford 2nd, 1917-87, (U.S.) headed auto company founded by grandfather.
Henry C. Frick, 1849-1919, (U.S.) steel and coke magnate; had prominent role in development of U.S. Steel.
Jakob Fugger (Jakob the Rich), 1459-1525, (Ger.) headed leading banking, trading house, in 16th-cent. Europe.
Alfred C. Fuller, 1885-1973, (U.S.) Canadian-born businessman; founded brush company.
Elbert H. Gary, 1846-1927, (U.S.) one of the organizers of U.S. Steel; chaired board of directors, 1903-27.
Jean Paul Getty, 1892-1976, (U.S.) founded oil empire.
Amadeo Giannini, 1870-1949, (U.S.) founded Bank of America.
Stephen Girard, 1750-1831, (U.S.) French-born financier, philanthropist; richest man in U.S. at his death.
Leonard H. Goldenson, 1905-99, (U.S.) turned ABC into major TV network.
Jay Gould, 1836-92, (U.S.) railroad magnate, financier.
Hetty Green, 1834-1916, (U.S.) financier, the "witch of Wall St."; richest woman in U.S. in her day.
William Gregg, 1800-67, (U.S.) launched textile industry in S.
Meyer Guggenheim, 1828-1905, (U.S.) Swiss-born merchant, philanthropist; built merchandising, mining empires.
Armand Hammer, 1898-1990, (U.S.) headed Occidental Petroleum; promoted U.S.-Soviet ties.
Edward H. Harriman, 1848-1909, (U.S.) railroad financier, administrator; headed Union Pacific.
Henry J. Heinz, 1844-1919, (U.S.) founded food empire.
James J. Hill, 1838-1916, (U.S.) Canadian-born railroad magnate, financier; founded Great Northern Railway.
Conrad N. Hilton, 1888-1979, (U.S.) hotel chain founder.
Howard Hughes, 1905-76, (U.S.) industrialist, aviator, movie maker.
H. L. Hunt, 1889-1974, (U.S.) oil magnate.
Collis P. Huntington, 1821-1900, (U.S.) railroad magnate.
Henry E. Huntington, 1850-1927, (U.S.) railroad builder, philanthropist.
Walter L. Jacobs, 1898-1985, (U.S.) founder of the first rental car agency, which later became Hertz.
Howard Johnson, 1896-1972, (U.S.) founded restaurants.
Henry J. Kaiser, 1882-1967, (U.S.) industrialist; built empire in steel, aluminum.

Minor C. Keith, 1848-1929, (U.S.) railroad magnate; founded United Fruit Co.
Will K. Kellogg, 1860-1951, (U.S.) businessman, philanthropist; founded breakfast food co.
Richard King, 1825-85, (U.S.) cattleman; founded half-million-acre King Ranch in Texas.
William S. Knudsen, 1879-1948, (U.S.) Danish-born auto industry executive.
Samuel H. Kress, 1863-1955, (U.S.) businessman, art collector, philanthropist; founded "dime store" chain.
Ray A. Kroc, 1902-84, (U.S.) founded McDonald's fast-food chain.
Alfred Krupp, 1812-87, (Ger.) armaments magnate.
William Levitt, 1907-94, (U.S.) industrialist, "suburb maker".
Thomas Lipton, 1850-1931, (Scot.) merchant, tea empire.
James McGill, 1744-1813, (Scot.-Can.) founded university.
Andrew W. Mellon, 1855-1937, (U.S.) financier, industrialist; benefactor of National Gallery of Art.
Charles E. Merrill, 1885-1956, (U.S.) financier; developed firm of Merrill Lynch.
John Pierpont Morgan, 1837-1913, (U.S.) most powerful figure in finance and industry at the turn of the cent.
Akio Morita, 1921-99, (Japan) co-founded Sony Corp.
Malcolm Muir, 1885-1979, (U.S.) created *Business Week* magazine; headed *Newsweek,* 1937-61.
Samuel Newhouse, 1895-1979, (U.S.) publishing and broadcasting magnate; built communications empire.
Aristotle Onassis, 1906-75, (Gr.) shipping magnate.
William S. Paley, 1901-90, (U.S.) built CBS communic. empire.
George Peabody, 1795-1869, (U.S.) merchant, financier, philanthropist.
James C. Penney, 1875-1971, (U.S.) businessman; developed department store chain.
William C. Procter, 1862-1934, (U.S.) headed soap co.
John D. Rockefeller, 1839-1937, (U.S.) industrialist; established Standard Oil.
John D. Rockefeller Jr., 1874-1960, (U.S.) philanthropist; established foundation; provided land for UN.
Meyer A. Rothschild, 1743-1812, (Ger.) founded international banking house.
Thomas Fortune Ryan, 1851-1928, (U.S.) financier; a founder of American Tobacco.
Edmond J. Safra, 1932-99, (U.S.) founded Republic National Bank of New York.
David Sarnoff, 1891-1971, (U.S.) broadcasting pioneer; established first radio network, NBC.
Richard Sears, 1863-1914, (U.S.) founded mail-order co.
Werner von Siemens, 1816-92, (Ger.) industrialist; inventor.
Alfred P. Sloan, 1875-1966, (U.S.) industrialist, philanthropist; headed General Motors.
A. Leland Stanford, 1824-93, (U.S.) railroad official, philanthropist; founded university.
Nathan Straus, 1848-1931, (U.S.) German-born merchant, philanthropist; headed Macy's.
Levi Strauss, c1829-1902, (U.S.) pants manufacturer.
Clement Studebaker, 1831-1901, (U.S.) wagon, carriage (maker).
Gustavus Swift, 1839-1903, (U.S.) pioneer meatpacker.
Gerard Swope, 1872-1957, (U.S.) industrialist, economist; headed General Electric.
Dave Thomas, 1932-2002, (U.S.) Wendy's founder.
James Walter Thompson, 1847-1928, (U.S.) ad executive.
Alice Tully, 1902-93, (U.S.) philanthropist, arts patron.
Theodore N. Vail, 1845-1920, (U.S.) organized Bell Telephone system; headed AT&T.
Cornelius Vanderbilt, 1794-1877, (U.S.) financier; established steamship, railroad empires.
Henry Villard, 1835-1900, (U.S.) German-born railroad executive, financier.
George Westinghouse, 1846-1914, (U.S) inventor, manufacturer; organized Westinghouse Electric Co., 1886.
Charles R. Walgreen, 1873-1939, (U.S.) founded drugstore chain.
DeWitt Wallace, 1889-1981, (U.S.) and **Lila Wallace,** 1889-1984, (U.S.) cofounders of *Reader's Digest* magazine.
Sam Walton, 1918-92, (U.S.) founder of Wal-Mart stores.
John Wanamaker, 1838-1922, (U.S.) pioneered department-store merchandising.
Aaron Montgomery Ward, 1843-1913, (U.S.) established first mail-order firm.
Thomas J. Watson, 1874-1956, (U.S.) IBM head, 1914-56.
John Hay Whitney, 1905-82, (U.S.) publisher, sportsman, philanthropist.
Charles E. Wilson, 1890-1961, (U.S.) auto industry exec., public official.
Frank W. Woolworth, 1852-1919, (U.S.) created 5 & 10 chain.
William Wrigley Jr., 1861-1932, (U.S.) founded Wrigley chewing gum company.

American Cartoonists

Reviewed by Lucy Shelton Caswell, Professor and Curator, Cartoon Research Library, Ohio State University

Scott Adams, b 1957, Dilbert.
Charles Addams, 1912-88, macabre cartoons.
Brad Anderson, b 1924, Marmaduke.
Sergio Aragones, b 1937, *MAD Magazine.*
Peter Arno, 1904-68, *The New Yorker.*
Tex Avery, 1908-80, animator, Bugs Bunny, Porky Pig.
George Baker, 1915-75, The Sad Sack.
Carl Barks, 1901-2000, Donald Duck comic books.
C. C. Beck, 1910-89, Captain Marvel.
Jim Berry, b 1932, Berry's World.
Herb Block (Herblock), b 1909, political cartoonist.
George Booth, b 1926, *The New Yorker.*
Berkeley Breathed, b 1957, Bloom County.
Dik Browne, 1917-89, Hi & Lois, Hagar the Horrible.
Marjorie Buell, 1904-93, Little Lulu.
Ernie Bushmiller, 1905-82, Nancy.
Milton Caniff, 1907-88, Terry & the Pirates, Steve Canyon.
Al Capp, 1909-79, Li'l Abner.
Roz Chast, b 1954, *The New Yorker.*
Paul Conrad, 1924, political cartoonist.
Roy Crane, 1901-77, Captain Easy, Buz Sawyer.
Robert Crumb, b 1943, underground cartoonist.
Shamus Culhane, 1908-96, animator.
Jay N. Darling (Ding), 1876-1962, political cartoonist.
Jack Davis, b 1926, *MAD Magazine.*
Jim Davis, b 1945, Garfield.
Billy DeBeck, 1890-1942, Barney Google.
Rudolph Dirks, 1877-1968, The Katzenjammer Kids.
Walt Disney, 1901-66, produced animated cartoons, created Mickey Mouse, Donald Duck.
Steve Ditko, b 1927, Spider-Man.
Mort Drucker, b 1929, *MAD Magazine.*
Will Eisner, b 1917, The Spirit.
Jules Feiffer, b 1929, political cartoonist.
Bud Fisher, 1884-1954, Mutt & Jeff.
Ham Fisher, 1900-55, Joe Palooka.
Max Fleischer, 1883-1972, Betty Boop.
Hal Foster, 1892-1982, Tarzan, Prince Valiant.
Fontaine Fox, 1884-1964, Toonerville Folks.
Isadore "Friz" Freleng, 1905-95, animator, Yosemite Sam, Porky Pig, Sylvester and Tweety Bird.
Rube Goldberg, 1883-1970, Boob McNutt.
Chester Gould, 1900-85, Dick Tracy.
Harold Gray, 1894-1968, Little Orphan Annie.
Matt Groening, b 1954, Life in Hell, The Simpsons.
Cathy Guisewite, b 1950, Cathy.
Bill Hanna, 1910-2001, & **Joe Barbera,** b 1911, animators, Tom & Jerry, Yogi Bear, Flintstones.
Johnny Hart, b 1931, BC, Wizard of Id.
Oliver Harrington, 1912-95, Bootsie.
Alfred Harvey, 1913-94, created Casper the Friendly Ghost.
Jimmy Hatlo, 1898-1963, Little Iodine.
John Held Jr., 1889-1958, Jazz Age.
George Herriman, 1881-1944, Krazy Kat.
Harry Hershfield, 1885-1974, Abie the Agent.
Al Hirschfeld, b 1903, *N.Y. Times* theater caricaturist.
Burne Hogarth, 1911-96, Tarzan.
Helen Hokinson, 1900-49, *The New Yorker.*
Nicole Hollander, b 1939, Sylvia.
Lynn Johnston, b 1947, For Better or For Worse.
Chuck Jones, 1912-2002, animator, Bugs Bunny, Porky Pig.
Mike Judge, b. 1962, Beavis and Butt-head, King of the Hill.
Bob Kane, b 1916-98, Batman.
Bil Keane, b 1922, The Family Circus.
Walt Kelly, 1913-73, Pogo.
Hank Ketcham, 1920-2001, Dennis the Menace.
Ted Key, b 1912, Hazel.
Frank King, 1883-1969, Gasoline Alley.
Jack Kirby, 1917-94, Fantastic Four, The Incredible Hulk.
Rollin Kirby, 1875-1952, political cartoonist.
B(ernard) Kliban, 1935-91, cat books.
Edward Koren, b 1935, *The New Yorker.*
Harvey Kurtzman, 1921-93, *MAD Magazine.*
Walter Lantz, 1900-94, Woody Woodpecker.
Gary Larson, b 1950, The Far Side.
Mell Lazarus, b 1929, Momma, Miss Peach.
Stan Lee, b 1922, Marvel Comics.
David Levine, b 1926, *N.Y. Review of Books* caricatures.
Doug Marlette, b 1949, political cartoonist, Kudzu.
Don Martin, 1931-2000, *MAD Magazine.*
Bill Mauldin, b 1921, political cartoonist.
Jeff MacNelly, 1947-2000, political cartoonist, Shoe.
Winsor McCay, 1872-1934, Little Nemo.
John T. McCutcheon, 1870-1949, political cartoonist.

George McManus, 1884-1954, Bringing Up Father.
Dale Messick, b 1906, Brenda Starr.
Norman Mingo, 1896-1980, Alfred E. Neuman.
Bob Montana, 1920-75, Archie.
Dick Moores, 1909-86, Gasoline Alley.
Willard Mullin, 1902-78, sports cartoonist; Dodgers "Bum," Mets "Kid."
Russell Myers, b 1938, Broom Hilda.
Thomas Nast, 1840-1902, political cartoonist; Republican elephant.
Pat Oliphant, b 1935, political cartoonist.
Frederick Burr Opper, 1857-1937, Happy Hooligan.
Richard Outcault, 1863-1928, Yellow Kid, Buster Brown.
Trey Parker, b 1969?, animator, co-creator of *South Park.*
Mike Peters, b 1943, cartoonist, Mother Goose & Grimm.
George Price, 1901-95, *The New Yorker.*
Antonio Prohias, 1921(?)-98, Spy vs. Spy.
Alex Raymond, 1909-56, Flash Gordon, Jungle Jim.
Forrest (Bud) Sagendorf, 1915-94, Popeye.
Art Sansom, 1920-91, The Born Loser.
Charles Schulz, 1922-2000, Peanuts.
Elzie C. Segar, 1894-1938, Popeye.
Joe Shuster, 1914-92, & **Jerry Siegel**, 1914-96, Superman.
Sidney Smith, 1887-1935, The Gumps.
Otto Soglow, 1900-75, Little King.
Art Spiegelman, b 1948, Raw, Maus.
William Steig, b 1907, *The New Yorker.*
Matt Stone, b 1971?, animator, co-creator of South Park.
Paul Szep, b 1941, political cartoonist.
James Swinnerton, 1875-1974, Little Jimmy, Canyon Kiddies.
Paul Terry, 1887-1971, animator of Mighty Mouse.
Bob Thaves, b 1924, Frank and Ernest.
James Thurber, 1894-61, *The New Yorker.*
Garry Trudeau, b 1948, Doonesbury.
Mort Walker, b 1923, Beetle Bailey.
Bill Watterson, b 1958, Calvin and Hobbes.
Russ Westover, 1887-1966, Tillie the Toiler.
Signe Wilkinson, b 1950, political cartoonist.
Frank Willard, 1893-1958, Moon Mullins.
J. R. Williams, 1888-1957, The Willets Family, Out Our Way.
Gahan Wilson, b 1930, *The New Yorker.*
Tom Wilson, b 1931, Ziggy.
Art Young, 1866-1943, political cartoonist.
Chic Young, 1901-73, Blondie.

Economists, Educators, Historians, and Social Scientists of the Past

For Psychologists see Scientists of the Past.

Brooks Adams, 1848-1927, (U.S.) historian, political theoretician; *The Law of Civilization and Decay.*
Henry Adams, 1838-1918, (U.S.) historian, autobiographer; *History of the United States of America, The Education of Henry Adams.*
Francis Bacon, 1561-1626, (Eng.) philosopher, essayist, and statesman; championed observation and induction.
George Bancroft, 1800-91, (U.S.) historian; wrote 10-volume *History of the United States.*
Jack Barbash, 1911-94, (U.S.) labor economist who helped create the AFL-CIO.
Henry Barnard, 1811-1900, (U.S.) public school reformer.
Charles A. Beard, 1874-1948, (U.S.) historian; *The Economic Basis of Politics.*
Bede (the Venerable), c673-735, (Br.) scholar, historian; *Ecclesiastical History of the English People.*
Ruth Benedict, 1887-1948, (U.S.) anthropologist; studied Indian tribes of the Southwest.
Sir Isaiah Berlin, 1909-97, (Br.) philosopher, historian; *The Age of Enlightenment.*
Louis Blanc, 1811-82, (Fr.) Socialist leader and historian.
Sarah G. Blanding, 1899-1985, (U.S.) head of Vassar College, 1946-64.
Leonard Bloomfield, 1887-1949, (U.S.) linguist; *Language.*
Franz Boas, 1858-1942, (U.S.) German-born anthropologist; studied American Indians.
Van Wyck Brooks, 1886-1963, (U.S.) historian; critic of New England culture, especially literature.
Edmund Burke, 1729-97, (Ir.) British parliamentarian and political philosopher; *Reflections on the Revolution in France.*
Nicholas Murray Butler, 1862-1947, (U.S.) educator; headed Columbia Univ., 1902-45; Nobel Peace Prize, 1931.
Joseph Campbell, 1904-87, (U.S.) author, editor, teacher; wrote books on mythology, folklore.
Thomas Carlyle, 1795-1881, (Sc.) historian, critic; *Sartor Resartus, Past and Present, The French Revolution.*
Edward Channing, 1856-1931, (U.S.) historian; wrote 6-volume *History of the United States.*
Henry Steele Commager, 1902-98, (U.S.) historian, educator; wrote *The Growth of the American Republic.*
John R. Commons, 1862-1945, (U.S.) economist, labor historian; *Legal Foundations of Capitalism.*
James B. Conant, 1893-1978, (U.S.) educator, diplomat; *The American High School Today.*
Benedetto Croce, 1866-1952, (It.) philosopher, statesman, and historian; *Philosophy of the Spirit.*
Bernard A. De Voto, 1897-1955, (U.S.) historian; wrote trilogy on American West; edited Mark Twain manuscripts.
Melvil Dewey, 1851-1931, (U.S.) devised decimal system of library-book classification.
Emile Durkheim, 1858-1917, (Fr.) a founder of modern sociology; *The Rules of Sociological Method.*
Charles Eliot, 1834-1926, (U.S.) educator, Harvard president.
Friedrich Engels, 1820-95, (Ger.) political writer; with Marx wrote the *Communist Manifesto.*
Irving Fisher, 1867-1947, (U.S.) economist; contributed to the development of modern monetary theory.
John Fiske, 1842-1901, (U.S.) historian and lecturer; popularized Darwinian theory of evolution.
Charles Fourier, 1772-1837, (Fr.) utopian socialist.
Giovanni Gentile, 1875-1944, (It.) philosopher, educator; reformed Italian educational system.
Sir James George Frazer, 1854-1941, (Br.) anthropologist; studied myth in religion; *The Golden Bough.*
Henry George, 1839-97, (U.S.) economist, reformer; led single-tax movement.
Edward Gibbon, 1737-94, (Br.) historian; *The History of the Decline and Fall of the Roman Empire.*
Francesco Guicciardini, 1483-1540, (It.) historian; *Storia d'Italia,* principal historical work of the 16th cent.
Thomas Hobbes, 1588-1679, (Eng.) philosopher, political theorist; *Leviathan.*
Richard Hofstadter, 1916-70, (U.S.) historian; *The Age of Reform.*
John Holt, 1924-85, (U.S.) educator and author.
John Maynard Keynes, 1883-1946, (Br.) economist; principal advocate of deficit spending.
Russell Kirk, 1918-94, (U.S.), social philosopher; *The Conservative Mind.*
Alfred L. Kroeber, 1876-1960, (U.S.) cultural anthropologist; studied Indians of North and South America.
Christopher Lasch, 1932-94, (U.S.) social critic, historian; *The Culture of Narcissism.*
James L. Laughlin, 1850-1933, (U.S.) economist; helped establish Federal Reserve System.
Lucien Lévy-Bruhl, 1857-1939, (Fr.) philosopher; studied the psychology of primitive societies; *Primitive Mentality.*
John Locke, 1632-1704, (Eng.) philosopher and political theorist; *Two Treatises of Government.*
Thomas B. Macaulay, 1800-59, (Br.) historian, statesman.
Niccolò Machiavelli, 1469-1527, (It.) writer, statesman. *The Prince.*
Bronislaw Malinowski, 1884-1942, (Pol.) considered the father of social anthropology.
Thomas R. Malthus, 1766-1834, (Br.) economist; famed for *Essay on the Principle of Population.*
Horace Mann, 1796-1859, (U.S.) pioneered modern public school system.
Karl Mannheim, 1893-1947, (Hung.) sociologist, historian; *Ideology and Utopia.*
Karl Marx, 1818-83, (Ger.) political theorist, proponent of Communism; *Communist Manifesto, Das Kapital.*
Giuseppe Mazzini, 1805-72, (It.) political philosopher.
William H. McGuffey, 1800-73, (U.S.) whose *Reader* was a mainstay of 19th-cent. U.S. public education.
George H. Mead, 1863-1931, (U.S.) philosopher, social psychologist.
Margaret Mead, 1901-78, (U.S.) cultural anthropologist; popularized field; *Coming of Age in Samoa.*
Alexander Meiklejohn, 1872-1964, (U.S.) Br.-born educator; championed academic freedom and experimental curricula.
James Mill, 1773-1836, (Sc.) philosopher, historian, economist; a proponent of utilitarianism.
Perry G. Miller, 1905-63, (U.S.) historian; interpreted 17th-cent. New England.
Theodor Mommsen, 1817-1903, (Ger.) historian; *The History of Rome.*
Ashley Montagu, 1905-99, (Eng.) anthropologist; *The Natural Superiority of Women.*
Charles-Louis Montesquieu, 1689-1755, (Fr.) social philosopher; *The Spirit of Laws.*
Maria Montessori, 1870-1952, (It.) educator, physician; started Montessori method of student self-motivation.

Samuel Eliot Morison, 1887-1976, (U.S.) historian; chronicled voyages of early explorers.
Lewis Mumford, 1895-1990, (U.S.) sociologist, critic; *The Culture of Cities.*
Gunnar Myrdal, 1898-1987, (Swed.) economist, social scientist; *Asian Drama: An Inquiry Into the Poverty of Nations.*
Joseph Needham, 1900-95, (Br.) scientific historian; *Science and Civilization in China.*
Allan Nevins, 1890-1971, (U.S.) historian, biographer; *The Ordeal of the Union.*
José Ortega y Gasset, 1883-1955, (Sp.) philosopher; advocated control by elite, *The Revolt of the Masses.*
Robert Owen, 1771-1858, (Br.) political philosopher, reformer; pioneer in cooperative movement.
Thomas (Tom) Paine, 1737-1809, (U.S.) political theorist, writer. *Common Sense.*
Vilfredo Pareto, 1848-1923, (It.) economist, sociologist.
Francis Parkman, 1823-93, (U.S.) historian; *France and England in North America.*
Elizabeth P. Peabody, 1804-94, (U.S.) education pioneer; founded 1st kindergarten in U.S., 1860.
William Prescott, 1796-1859, (U.S.) early American historian; *The Conquest of Peru.*
Pierre Joseph Proudhon, 1809-65, (Fr.) social theorist; father of anarchism; *The Philosophy of Property.*
François Quesnay, 1694-1774, (Fr.) economic theorist.
David Ricardo, 1772-1823, (Br.) economic theorist; advocated free international trade.
David Riesman, 1909-2002, (U.S.) sociologist, coauthor *The Lonely Crowd.*
Jean-Jacques Rousseau, 1712-78, (Fr.) social philosopher; the father of romantic sensibility; *Confessions.*
Edward Sapir, 1884-1939, (Ger.-U.S.) anthropologist; studied ethnology and linguistics of U.S. Indian groups.
Ferdinand de Saussure, 1857-1913, (Swiss) a founder of modern linguistics.
Hjalmar Schacht, 1877-1970, (Ger.) economist.
Joseph Schumpeter, 1883-1950, (Czech.-U.S.) economist, sociologist.
Elizabeth Seton, 1774-1821, (U.S.) nun; est. parochial school education in U.S.; first native born American saint.
George Simmel, 1858-1918, (Ger.) sociologist, philosopher; helped establish German sociology.
Adam Smith, 1723-90, (Br.) economist; advocated laissez-faire economy, free trade; *The Wealth of Nations.*
Jared Sparks, 1789-1866, (U.S.) historian, educator, editor; *The Library of American Biography.*
Oswald Spengler, 1880-1936, (Ger.) philosopher and historian; *The Decline of the West.*
William G. Sumner, 1840-1910, (U.S.) social scientist, economist; laissez-faire economy, Social Darwinism.
Hippolyte Taine, 1828-93, (Fr.) historian; basis of naturalistic school; *The Origins of Contemporary France.*
A(lan) J(ohn) P(ercivale) Taylor, 1906-89, (Br.) historian; *The Origins of the Second World War.*
Nikolaas Tinbergen, 1907-88, (Dutch-Br.) ethologist; pioneer in study of animal behavior.
Alexis de Tocqueville, 1805-59, (Fr.) political scientist, historian; *Democracy in America.*
Francis E. Townsend, 1867-1960, (U.S.) led old-age pension movement, 1933.
Arnold Toynbee, 1889-1975, (Br.) historian; *A Study of History,* sweeping analysis of hist. of civilizations.
George Trevelyan, 1838-1928, (Br.) historian, statesman; favored "literary" over "scientific" history; *History of England.*
Barbara Tuchman, 1912-89, (U.S.) author of popular history books, *The Guns of August, The March of Folly.*
Frederick J. Turner, 1861-1932, (U.S.) historian, educator; *The Frontier in American History.*
Thorstein B. Veblen, 1857-1929, (U.S.) economist, social philosopher; *The Theory of the Leisure Class.*
Giovanni Vico, 1668-1744, (It.) historian, philosopher; regarded by many as first modern historian; *New Science.*
Izaak Walton, 1593-1683, (Eng.) wrote biographies; political-philosophical study of fishing, *The Compleat Angler.*
Sidney J., 1859-1947, and **Beatrice,** 1858-1943, **Webb,** (Br.) leading figures in Fabian Society and Labor Party.
Max Weber, 1864-1920, (Ger.) sociologist; *The Protestant Ethic and the Spirit of Capitalism.*
Emma Hart Willard, 1787-1870, (U.S.) pioneered higher education for women.
C. Vann Woodward, 1908-99, (U.S.) historian; *The Strange Career of Jim Crow.*

American Journalists of the Past

Reviewed by Dean Mills, Dean, Missouri School of Journalism

See also African-Americans, Business Leaders, Cartoonists, Writers of the Past.

Franklin P. Adams (F.P.A.), 1881-1960, humorist; wrote column "The Conning Tower."
Martin Agronsky, 1915-99, broadcast journalist; developed Agronsky & Company.
Joseph W. Alsop, 1910-89, and **Stewart Alsop,** 1914-74, Washington-based political analysts, columnists.
Brooks Atkinson, 1894-1984, theater critic.
James Gordon Bennett, 1795-1872, editor and publisher; founded *NY Herald.*
James Gordon Bennett, 1841-1918, succeeded father, financed expeditions, founded afternoon paper.
Elias Boudinot, d 1839, founding editor of first Native American newspaper in U.S., *Cherokee Phoenix* (1828-34).
Margaret Bourke-White, 1904-71, photojournalist.
Arthur Brisbane, 1864-1936, editor; helped introduce "yellow jounalism" with sensational, simply written articles.
Heywood Broun, 1888-1939, author, columnist; founded American Newspaper Guild.
Herb Caen, 1916-97, longtime columnist for *San Francisco Chronicle* and *Examiner.*
John Campbell, 1653-1728, published *Boston News-Letter,* first continuing newspaper in the American colonies.
Jimmy Cannon, 1909-73, syndicated sports columnist.
John Chancellor, 1927-96, TV journalist; anchored *NBC Nightly News.*
Harry Chandler, 1864-1944, *Los Angeles Times* publisher, 1917-41; made it a dominant force.
Marquis Childs, 1903-90, reporter and columnist for *St. Louis Post-Dispatch* and United Feature syndicate.
Craig Claiborne, 1920-2000, *NY Times* food editor and critic; key in internationalizing American taste.
Elizabeth Cochrane (Nellie Bly), pioneer woman journalist, investig. reporter, noted for series on trip around the world.
Charles Collingwood, 1917-85, CBS news correspondent, foreign affairs reporter, documentary host.
Howard Cosell, 1920-95, TV and radio sportscaster.
Gardner Cowles, 1861-1946, founded newspaper chain.
Cyrus Curtis, 1850-1933, publisher of *Saturday Evening Post, Ladies' Home Journal, Country Gentleman.*
Charles Anderson Dana, 1819-97, editor, publisher; made *NY Sun* famous for its news reporting.
Elmer (Holmes) Davis, 1890-1958, *NY Times* editorial writer; radio commentator.
Richard Harding Davis, 1864-1916, war correspondent, travel writer, fiction writer.
Benjamin Day, 1810-89, published *NY Sun* beginning in 1833, introducing penny press to the U.S.
Frederick Douglass, 1817-95, ex-slave, social reformer, newspaper editor.
Finley Peter Dunne, 1867-1936, humorist, social critic, wrote "Mr. Dooley" columns.
Mary Baker Eddy, 1821-1910, founded Christian Science movement and *Christian Science Monitor.*
Rowland Evans Jr., 1921-2001, Washington columnist and commentator.
Marshall Field III, 1893-1956, retail magnate, *Chicago Sun* founder.
Doris Fleeson, 1901-70, war correspondent, columnist.
James Franklin, 1697-1735, printer, pioneer journalist, publisher of *New England Courant* and *Rhode Island Gazette.*
Fred W. Friendly, 1915-98, radio, TV reporter, announcer, producer, executive, collaborator with Edward R. Murrow.
Margaret Fuller, 1810-50, social reformer, transcendentalist, critic and foreign correspondent for *NY Tribune.*
Frank E. Gannett, 1876-1957, founded newspaper chain.
William Lloyd Garrison, 1805-79, abolitionist; publisher of *The Liberator.*
Elizabeth Meriwether Gilmer (Dorothy Dix), 1861-1951, reporter, pioneer of the advice column genre.
Edwin Lawrence Godkin, 1831-1902, founder of *The Nation,* editor of *N.Y. Evening Post.*
Katharine Graham,1917-2001, publisher of the *Washington Post.*
Sheilah Graham, 1904-89, Hollywood gossip columnist.
Horace Greeley, 1811-72, editor and politician; founded *NY Tribune.*
Meg Greenfield, 1930-1999, *Newsweek* columnist, editorial page editor Wash. Post.
Gilbert Hovey Grosvenor, 1875-1966, longtime editor of *National Geographic* magazine.
John Gunther, 1901-70, *Chicago Daily News* foreign correspondent, author.
Sarah Josepha Buell Hale, 1788-1879, first female magazine editor, (Ladies' Magazine, later Godey's Lady's Book)

Benjamin Harris, 1673-1716, publisher (1690) of *Publick Occurrences*, 1st newspaper in the American colonies; suppressed after one issue.
William Randolph Hearst, 1863-1951, founder of Hearst newspaper chain and one of the pioneer yellow journalists.
Gabriel Heatter, 1890-1972, radio commentator.
John Hersey, 1914-98, foreign correspondent for *Time, Life,* and *The New Yorker*; author.
Marguerite Higgins, 1920-66, reporter, war correspondent.
Hedda Hopper, 1885-1966, Hollywood gossip columnist.
Roy Howard, 1883-1964, editor, executive, Scripps-Howard papers and United Press (later United Press International).
Chet (Chester Robert) Huntley, 1911-74, co-anchor of NBC's *Huntley-Brinkley Report.*
Ralph Ingersoll, 1900-85, editor, *Fortune, Time, Life* exec.
H. V. (Hans von) Kaltenborn, 1878-1965, radio commentator, reporter.
Murray Kempton, 1917-97, reporter, columnist for magazines and newspapers, including *NY Post.*
John S. Knight, 1894-1981, editor, publisher; founded Knight newspaper group, which merged into Knight-Ridder.
Joseph Kraft, 1942-86, foreign policy columnist.
Arthur Krock, 1886-1974, *NY Times* political writer, Washington bureau chief.
Charles Kuralt, 1934-97, TV anchor and host of CBS "On the Road" feature stories about life in the U.S.
Ann Landers, real name Eppie Lederer, 1918-2002, advice columnist.
David Lawrence, 1888-1973, reporter, columnist, publisher; founded *U.S. News & World Report.*
Frank Leslie, 1821-80, engraver and publisher of newspapers and magazines, notably *Leslie's Illustrated Newspaper.*
Alexander Liberman, 1912-99, editorial director for Conde Nast magazines.
A(bbott) J(oseph) Liebling, 1904-63, foreign correspondent, critic, principally with *The New Yorker.*
Walter Lippmann, 1889-1974, political analyst, social critic, columnist, author.
Peter Lisagor, 1915-76, Washington bureau chief, *Chicago Daily News;* broadcast commentator.
David Ross Locke, 1833-88, humorist, satirist under pseudonym P.V. Nasby; owned *Toledo (Ohio) Blade.*
Elijah Parish Lovejoy, 1802-37, abolitionist editor in St. Louis and in Alton, IL; killed by proslavery mob.
Clare Booth Luce, 1903-87, war correspondent for *Life;* diplomat, playwright.
Henry R. Luce, 1898-1967, founded *Time, Fortune, Life, Sports Illustrated.*
C(harles) K(enny) McClatchy, 1858-1936 founder of McClatchy newspaper chain.
Samuel McClure, 1857-1949, founder (1893) of *McClure's Magazine*, famous for its investigative reporting.
Anne O'Hare McCormick, 1889-1954, foreign correspondent, first woman on *NY Times* editorial board.
Robert R. McCormick, 1880-1955, editor, publisher, executive of *Chicago Tribune* and *NY Daily News.*
Dwight Macdonald, 1906-1982, reporter, social critic for *The New Yorker, The Nation, Esquire.*
Ralph McGill, 1893-1969, crusading editor and publisher of *Atlanta Constitution.*
O(scar) O(dd) McIntyre, 1884-1938, feature writer, syndicated columnist concentrating on everyday life in New York City.
Don Marquis, 1878-1937, humor columnist for *NY Sun* and *N.Y. Tribune;* wrote "archy and mehitabel" stories.
Robert Maynard, 1937-97, first African-American editor and then owner of major U.S. paper, the *Oakland Tribune.*
Joseph Medill, 1823-99, longtime *editor of Chicago Tribune.*
H(enry) L(ouis) Mencken, 1880-1956, reporter, editor, columnist with *Baltimore Sun* papers; anti-establishment viewpoint.
Edwin Meredith, 1876-1928, founder of magazine company.
Frank A. Munsey, 1854-1925, owner, editor, and publisher of newspapers and magazines, including *Munsey's Magazine.*
Edward R. Murrow, 1908-65, broadcast reporter, executive; reported from Britain in WW2; hosted *See It Now, Person to Person.*
William Rockhill Nelson, 1841-1915, cofounder, editor, and publisher, *Kansas City Star.*
Adolph S. Ochs, 1858-1935, publisher; built *NY Times* into a leading newspaper.
Louella Parsons, 1881-1972, Hollywood gossip columnist.
Drew (Andrew Russell) Pearson, 1879-1969, investigative reporter and columnist.
(James) Westbrook Pegler, 1894-1969, reporter, columnist.
Shirley Povich, 1905-98, sports columnist.
Joseph Pulitzer, 1847-1911, *NY World* publisher; founded Columbia Journalism School, Pulitzer Prizes.
Joseph Pulitzer II, 1885-1955, longtime *St. Louis Post-Dispatch* editor, publisher; built it into major paper.
Ernie (Ernest Taylor) Pyle, 1900-45, reporter, war correspondent; killed in WW2.
Henry Raymond, 1820-69, cofounder, editor, *NY Times.*
Harry Reasoner, 1923-91, TV reporter, anchor.
John Reed, 1887-1920, reporter, foreign correspondent famous for coverage of Bolshevik Revolution.
Whitelaw Reid, 1837-1912, longtime editor, *NY Tribune.*
James Reston, 1909-95 *NY Times* political reporter, columnist.
Frank Reynolds, 1923-83, TV reporter, anchor.
(Henry) Grantland Rice, 1880-1954, sportswriter.
Jacob Riis, 1849-1914, reporter, photographer; exposed slum conditions in *How the Other Half Lives.*
Max Robinson, 1939-88, TV journalist, first African-American to anchor network news, 1978.
Harold Ross, 1892-1951, founder, editor, The *New Yorker.*
Mike Royko, 1932-97, columnist for *Chicago Sun-Times* and *Chicago Tribune.*
(Alfred) Damon Runyon, 1884-1946, sportswriter, columnist; stories collected in *Guys and Dolls.*
John B. Russwurm, 1799-1851, cofounded (1827) nation's first black newspaper, *Freedom's Journal,* in NYC.
Adela Rogers St. Johns, 1894-1988, reporter, sportswriter for Hearst newspapers.
Harrison Salisbury, 1908-93, reporter, foreign correspondent; a Soviet specialist.
E(dward) W(yllis) Scripps, 1854-1926, founded first large U.S. newspaper chain, pioneered syndication.
Eric Sevareid, 1912-92, war correspondent, radio newscaster, TV commentator.
William L. Shirer, 1904-93, broadcaster, foreign correspondent; wrote *The Rise and Fall of the Third Reich.*
Howard K. Smith, 1914-2002, broadcast journalist.
Red (Walter) Smith, 1905-82, sportswriter.
Edgar P. Snow, 1905-71, correspondent, expert on Chinese Communist movement.
Lawrence Spivak, 1900-94, co-creator, moderator, producer of *Meet the Press.*
(Joseph) Lincoln Steffens, 1866-1936, muckraking journalist.
I(sidor) F(einstein) Stone, 1907-89, one-man editor of *I.F. Stone's Weekly.*
Arthur Hays Sulzberger, 1891-1968, longtime publisher of *N.Y. Times.*
C(yrus) L(eo) Sulzberger, 1912-93, *N.Y. Times* foreign correspondent and columnist.
David Susskind, 1920-87, TV producer, public affairs talk-show host (*Open End*).
John Cameron Swayze, 1906-95, newscaster, anchor of *Camel News Caravan.*
Herbert Bayard Swope, 1882-1958, war correspondent and editor of *N.Y. World.*
Ida Tarbell, 1857-1944, muckraking journalist.
Isaiah Thomas, 1750-1831, printer, publisher, cofounder of revolutionary journal, *Massachusetts Spy.*
Lowell Thomas, 1892-1981, radio newscaster, world traveler.
Dorothy Thompson, 1894-1961, foreign correspondent, columnist, radio commentator.
Ida Bell Wells-Barnett, 1862-1931, African-American reporter, editor, anti-lynching crusader.
William Allen White, 1868-1944, editor, publisher; made *Emporia* (KS) *Gazette* known worldwide.
Walter Winchell, 1897-1972, reporter, columnist, broadcaster of celebrity news.
John Peter Zenger, 1697-1746, printer and journalist; acquitted in precedent-setting libel suit (1735).

Military and Naval Leaders of the Past

Reviewed by Alan C. Aimone, USMA Library

Creighton Abrams, 1914-74, (U.S.) commanded forces in Vietnam, 1968-72.
Alexander the Great, 356-323 B.C., (Maced.) conquered Persia and much of the world known to Europeans.
Harold Alexander, 1891-1969, (Br.) led Allied invasion of Italy, 1943, WW2.
Ethan Allen, 1738-89, (U.S.) headed Green Mountain Boys; captured Ft. Ticonderoga, 1775, Amer. Rev.
Edmund Allenby, 1861-1936, (Br.) in Boer War, WW1; led Egyptian expeditionary force, 1917-18.
Benedict Arnold, 1741-1801, (U.S.) victorious at Saratoga; tried to betray West Point to British, Amer. Rev.
Henry "Hap" Arnold, 1886-1950, (U.S.) commanded Army Air Force in WW2.
John Barry, 1745-1803, (U.S.) won numerous sea battles during Amer. Rev.

Belisarius, c505-565, (Byzant.) won remarkable victories for Byzantine Emperor Justinian I.
Pierre Beauregard, 1818-93, (U.S.) Confed. general, ordered bombardment of Ft. Sumter that began Civil War.
Gebhard von Blücher, 1742-1819, (Ger.) helped defeat Napoleon at Waterloo.
Napoleon Bonaparte, 1769-1821, (Fr.) defeated Russia and Austria at Austerlitz, 1805; invaded Russia, 1812; defeated at Waterloo, 1815.
Edward Braddock, 1695-1755, (Br.) commanded forces in French and Indian War.
Omar N. Bradley, 1893-1981, (U.S.) headed U.S. ground troops in Normandy invasion, 1944, WW2.
John Burgoyne, 1722-92, (Br.) defeated at Saratoga, Amer. Rev.
Julius Caesar, 100-44 BC (Rom.) general and politician; conquered N Gaul; overthrew Roman Republic.
Claire Lee Chennault, 1893-1958, (U.S.) headed Flying Tigers in WW2.
Mark W. Clark, 1896-1984, (U.S.) helped plan N African invasion in WW2; commander of UN forces, Korean War.
Karl von Clausewitz, 1780-1831, (Pruss.) military theorist.
Lucius D. Clay, 1897-1978, (U.S.) led Berlin airlift, 1948-49.
Henry Clinton, 1738-95, (Br.) commander of forces in Amer. Rev., 1778-81.
Cochise, c1815-74, (Nat. Am.) chief of Chiricahua band of Apache Indians in Southwest.
Charles Cornwallis, 1738-1805, (Br.) victorious at Brandywine, 1777; surrendered at Yorktown, Amer. Rev.
Hernan Cortes, 1485-1547, (Sp.) led Spanish conquistadors in the defeat of the Aztec empire, 1519-28.
Crazy Horse, 1849-77, (Nat. Am.) Sioux war chief victorious at battle of Little Bighorn.
George Armstrong Custer, 1839-76, (U.S.) U.S. army officer defeated and killed at battle of Little Bighorn.
Moshe Dayan, 1915-81, (Isr.) directed campaigns in the 1967, 1973 Arab-Israeli wars.
Stephen Decatur, 1779-1820, (U.S.) naval hero of Barbary wars, War of 1812.
Anton Denikin, 1872-1947, (Russ.) led White forces in Russian civil war.
George Dewey, 1837-1917, (U.S.) destroyed Spanish fleet at Manila, 1898, Span.-Amer. War.
Karl Doenitz, 1891-1980, (Ger.) submarine com. in chief and naval commander, WW2.
Jimmy Doolittle, 1896-1993, (U.S.) led 1942 air raid on Tokyo and other Japanese cities in WW2.
Hugh C. Dowding, 1883-1970, (Br.) headed RAF, 1936-40, WW2.
Jubal Early, 1816-94, (U.S.) Confed. general, led raid on Washington, 1864, Civil War.
Dwight D. Eisenhower, 1890-1969, (U.S.) commanded Allied forces in Europe, WW2.
David Farragut, 1801-70, (U.S.) Union admiral, captured New Orleans, Mobile Bay, Civil War.
Ferdinand Foch, 1851-1929, (Fr.) headed victorious Allied armies, 1918, WW1.
Nathan Bedford Forrest, 1821-77, (U.S.) Confed. general, led raids against Union supply lines, Civil War.
Frederick the Great, 1712-86, (Pruss.) led Prussia in Seven Years War.
Horatio Gates, 1728-1806, (U.S.) commanded army at Saratoga, Amer. Rev.
Genghis Khan, 1162-1227, (Mongol) unified Mongol tribes and subjugated much of Asia, 1206-21.
Geronimo, 1829-1909, (Nat. Am.) leader of Chiricahua band of Apache Indians.
Charles G. Gordon, 1833-85, (Br.) led forces in China, Crimean War; killed at Khartoum.
Ulysses S. Grant, 1822-85, (U.S.) headed Union army, Civil War, 1864-65; forced Lee's surrender, 1865.
Nathanael Greene, 1742-86, (U.S.) defeated British in Southern campaign, 1780-81.
Heinz Guderian, 1888-1953, (Ger.) tank theorist, led panzer forces in Poland, France, Russia, WW2.
Che (Ernesto) Guevara, 1928-67, (Arg.) guerrilla leader; prominent in Cuban revolution; killed in Bolivia.
Gustavus Adolphus, 1594-1632, (Swed.) King; military tactician; reformer; led forces in Thirty Years' War.
Douglas Haig, 1861-1928, (Br.) led British armies in France, 1915-18, WW1.
William F. Halsey, 1882-1959, (U.S.) defeated Japanese fleet at Leyte Gulf, 1944, WW2.
Hannibal, 247-183 B.C., (Carthag.) invaded Rome, crossing Alps, in Second Punic War, 218-201 B.C.
Sir Arthur Travers Harris, 1895-1984, (Br.) led Britain's WW2 bomber command.
Richard Howe, 1726-99, (Br.) commanded navy in Amer. Rev., 1776-78; June 1 victory against French, 1794.
William Howe, 1729-1814, (Br.) commanded forces in Amer. Rev., 1776-78.
Isaac Hull, 1773-1843, (U.S.) sunk British frigate Guerriere, War of 1812.
Thomas (Stonewall) Jackson, 1824-63, (U.S.) Confed. general, led Shenandoah Valley campaign, Civil War.
Joseph Joffre, 1852-1931, (Fr.) headed Allied armies, won Battle of the Marne, 1914, WW1.
Chief Joseph, c1840-1904, (Nat. Am.) chief of the Nez Percé, led his tribe across 3 states seeking refuge in Canada; surrendered about 30 mi from Canadian border.
John Paul Jones, 1747-92, (U.S.) commanded Bonhomme Richard in victory over Serapis, Amer. Rev., 1779.
Stephen Kearny, 1794-1848, (U.S.) headed Army of the West in Mexican War.
Albert Kesselring, 1885-1960 (Ger.) field marshal who led the defense of Italy in WW2.
Ernest J. King, 1878-1956, (U.S.) key WW2 naval strategist.
Horatio H. Kitchener, 1850-1916, (Br.) led forces in Boer War; victorious at Khartoum; organized army in WW1.
Henry Knox, 1750-1806, (U.S.) general in Amer. Rev.; first sec. of war under U.S. Constitution.
Lavrenti Kornilov, 1870-1918, (Russ.) commander-in-chief, 1917; led counter-revolutionary march on Petrograd.
Thaddeus Kosciusko, 1746-1817, (Pol.) aided Amer. Rev.
Walter Krueger, 1881-1967, (U.S.) led Sixth Army in WW2 in Southwest Pacific.
Mikhail Kutuzov, 1745-1813, (Russ.) fought French at Borodino, Napoleonic Wars, 1812; abandoned Moscow; forced French retreat.
Marquis de Lafayette, 1757-1834, (Fr.) fought in, secured French aid for Amer. Rev.
T(homas) E. Lawrence (of Arabia), 1888-1935, (Br.) organized revolt of Arabs against Turks in WW1.
Henry (Light-Horse Harry) Lee, 1756-1818, (U.S.) cavalry officer in Amer. Rev.
Robert E. Lee, 1807-70, (U.S.) Confed. general defeated at Gettysburg, Civil War; surrendered to Grant, 1865.
Curtis LeMay, 1906-90, (U.S.) Air Force commander in WW2, Korean War, and Vietnam War.
Lyman Lemnitzer, 1899-1988, (U.S.) WW2 hero, later general, chairman of Joint Chiefs of Staff.
James Longstreet, 1821-1904, (U.S.) aided Lee at Gettysburg, Civil War.
Maurice, Count of Nassau, 1567-1625, (Dutch) military innovator; led forces in Thirty Years' War.
Douglas MacArthur, 1880-1964, (U.S.) commanded forces in SW Pacific in WW2; headed occupation forces in Japan, 1945-51; UN commander in Korean War.
Erich von Manstein, 1887-1973, (Ger.) served WW1–2, planned inv. of France (1940), convicted of war crimes.
Carl Gustaf Mannerheim, 1867-1951, (Finn.) army officer and pres. of Finland 1944-46.
Francis Marion, 1733-95, (U.S.) led guerrilla actions in South Carolina during Amer. Rev.
Duke of Marlborough, 1650-1722, (Br.) led forces against Louis XIV in War of the Spanish Succession.
George C. Marshall, 1880-1959, (U.S.) chief of staff in WW2; authored Marshall Plan.
George B. McClellan, 1826-85, (U.S.) Union general, commanded Army of the Potomac, 1861-62, Civil War.
George Meade, 1815-72, (U.S.) commanded Union forces at Gettysburg, Civil War.
Billy Mitchell, 1879-1936, (U.S.) WW1 air-power advocate; court-martialed for insubordination, later vindicated.
Helmuth von Moltke, 1800-91, (Ger.) victorious in Austro-Prussian, Franco-Prussian wars.
Louis de Montcalm, 1712-59, (Fr.) headed troops in Canada, French and Indian War; defeated at Quebec, 1759.
Bernard Law Montgomery, 1887-1976, (Br.) stopped German offensive at Alamein, 1942, WW2; helped plan Normandy.
Daniel Morgan, 1736-1802, (U.S.) victorious at Cowpens, 1781, Amer. Rev.
Louis Mountbatten, 1900-79, (Br.) Supreme Allied Commander of SE Asia, 1943-46, WW2.
Joachim Murat, 1767-1815, (Fr.) led cavalry at Marengo, Austerlitz, and Jena, Napoleonic Wars.
Horatio Nelson, 1758-1805, (Br.) naval commander, destroyed French fleet at Trafalgar.
Michel Ney, 1769-1815, (Fr.) commanded forces in Switz., Aust., Russ., Napoleonic Wars; defeated at Waterloo.
Chester Nimitz, 1885-1966, (U.S.) commander of naval forces in Pacific in WW2.
George S. Patton, 1885-1945, (U.S.) led assault on Sicily, 1943, Third Army invasion of Europe, WW2.
Oliver Perry, 1785-1819, (U.S.) won Battle of Lake Erie in War of 1812.
John Pershing, 1860-1948, (U.S.) commanded Mexican border campaign, 1916, Amer. Expeditionary Force, WW1.

Henri Philippe Pétain, 1856-1951, (Fr.) defended Verdun, 1916; headed Vichy government in WW2.
George E. Pickett, 1825-75, (U.S.) Confed. general famed for "charge" at Gettysburg, Civil War.
Charles Portal, 1893-1971, (Br.) chief of staff, Royal Air Force, 1940-45, led in Battle of Britain.
Hyman Rickover, 1900-86, (U.S.) father of nuclear navy.
Matthew Bunker Ridgway, 1895-1993, (U.S.) commanded Allied ground forces in Korean War.
Erwin Rommel, 1891-1944, (Ger.) headed Afrika Korps, WW2.
Gerd von Rundstedt, 1875-1953, (Ger.) supreme commander in West, 1942-45, WW2.
Aleksandr Samsonov, 1859-1914, (Russ.) led invasion of E Prussia, WW1, defeated at Tannenberg, 1914.
Winfield Scott, 1786-1866, (U.S.) hero of War of 1812; headed forces in Mexican War, took Mexico City.
Philip Sheridan, 1831-88, (U.S.) Union cavalry officer, headed Army of the Shenandoah, 1864-65, Civil War.
William T. Sherman, 1820-91, (U.S.) Union general, sacked Atlanta during "march to the sea," 1864, Civil War.
Carl Spaatz, 1891-1974, (U.S.) directed strategic bombing against Germany, later Japan, in WW2.
Raymond Spruance, 1886-1969, (U.S.) victorious at Midway Island, 1942, WW2.
Joseph W. Stilwell, 1883-1946, (U.S.) headed forces in the China, Burma, India theater in WW2.
J.E.B. Stuart, 1833-64, (U.S.) Confed. cavalry commander, Civil War.
Aleksandr Suvorov, 1729-1800, (Rus.) commanded Allied Russian and Austrian armies against Ottoman Turks in Russo-Turkish War.
George H. Thomas, 1816-70, (U.S.) saved Union army at Chattanooga, 1863; won at Nashville, 1864, Civil War.
Semyon Timoshenko, 1895-1970, (USSR) defended Moscow, Stalingrad, WW2; led winter offensive, 1942-43.
Alfred von Tirpitz, 1849-1930, (Ger.) responsible for submarine blockade in WW1.
Sebastien Le Prestre de Vauban, 1633-1707, (Fr.) innovative military engineer and theorist.
Jonathan M. Wainwright, 1883-1953, (U.S.) forced to surrender on Corregidor, 1942, WW2.
George Washington, 1732-99, (U.S.) led Continental army, 1775-83, Amer. Rev.
Archibald Wavell, 1883-1950, (Br.) commanded forces in N and E Africa, and SE Asia in WW2.
Anthony Wayne, 1745-96, (U.S.) captured Stony Point, 1779, Amer. Rev.
Duke of Wellington, 1769-1852, (Br.) defeated Napoleon at Waterloo, 1815.
James Wolfe, 1727-59, (Br.) captured Quebec from French, 1759, French and Indian War.
Isoroku Yamamoto, 1884-1943, (Jpn.) com. in chief of Japanese fleet and naval planner before and during WW2.
Georgi Zhukov, 1895-1974, (Russ.) defended Moscow, 1941, led assault on Berlin, 1945, WW2.

Philosophers and Religious Figures of the Past

For other Greeks and Romans, see Historical Figures chapter.

Lyman Abbott, 1835-1922, (U.S.) clergyman, reformer; advocate of Christian Socialism.
Pierre Abelard, 1079-1142, (Fr.) philosopher, theologian, teacher; used dialectic method to support Christian beliefs.
Mortimer Adler, 1902-2001, (U.S.) philosopher, helped create "Great Books" program.
Felix Adler, 1851-1933, (U.S.) German-born founder of the Ethical Culture Society.
(St.) Anselm, c1033-1109, (It.) philosopher-theologian, church leader; "ontological argument" for God's existence.
(St.) Thomas Aquinas, 1225-74, (It.) preeminent medieval philosopher-theologian; *Summa Theologica.*
Aristotle, 384-322 BC, (Gr.) pioneering wide-ranging philosopher, logician, ethician, naturalist.
(St.) Augustine, 354-430, (N Africa) philosopher, theologian, bishop; *Confessions, City of God, On the Trinity.*
J. L. Austin, 1911-60, (Br.) ordinary-language philosopher.
Averroes (Ibn Rushd), 1126-98, (Sp.) Islamic philosopher, physician.
Avicenna (Ibn Sina), 980-1037, (Iran.) Islamic philosopher, scientist.
A(lfred) J(ules) Ayer, 1910-89, (Br.) philosopher; logical positivist; *Language, Truth, and Logic.*
Roger Bacon, c1214-94, (Eng.) philosopher and scientist.
Bahaullah (Mirza Husayn Ali), 1817-92, (Pers.) founder of Bahá'í faith.
Karl Barth, 1886-1968, (Swiss) theologian; a leading force in 20th-cent. Protestantism.
Thomas à Becket, 1118-70, (Eng.) archbishop of Canterbury; opposed Henry II; murdered by King's men.
(St.) Benedict, c480-547, (It.) founded the Benedictines.
Jeremy Bentham, 1748-1832, (Br.) philosopher, reformer; enunciated utilitarianism.
Henri Bergson, 1859-1941, (Fr.) philosopher of evolution.
George Berkeley, 1685-1753, (Ir.) idealist philosopher, churchman.
John Biddle, 1615-62, (Eng.) founder of English Unitarianism.
Jakob Boehme, 1575-1624, (Ger.) theosophist and mystic.
Dietrich Bonhoeffer, 1906-1945 (Ger.) Lutheran theologian, pastor; executed as opponent of Nazis.
William Brewster, 1567-1644, (Eng.) headed Pilgrims.
Emil Brunner, 1889-1966, (Swiss) Protestant theologian.
Giordano Bruno, 1548-1600, (It.) philosopher, pantheist.
Martin Buber, 1878-1965, (Ger.) Jewish philosopher, theologian; *I and Thou.*
Buddha (Siddhartha Gautama), c563-c483 BC, (Indian) philosopher; founded Buddhism.
John Calvin, 1509-64, (Fr.) theologian; a key figure in the Protestant Reformation.
Rudolph Carnap, 1891-1970, (U.S.) German-born analytic philosopher; a founder of logical positivism.
William Ellery Channing, 1780-1842, (U.S.) clergyman; early spokesman for Unitarianism.
Auguste Comte, 1798-1857, (Fr.) philosopher; originated positivism.
Confucius, 551-479 BC, (Chin.) founder of Confucianism.
John Cotton, 1584-1652, (Eng.) Puritan theologian.
Thomas Cranmer, 1489-1556, (Eng.) churchman; wrote much of *Book of Common Prayer.*
René Descartes, 1596-1650, (Fr.) philosopher, mathematician; "father of modern philosophy." *Discourse on Method, Meditations on First Philosophy.*
John Dewey, 1859-1952, (U.S.) philosopher, educator; instrumentalist theory of knowledge; helped inaugurate progressive education movement.
Denis Diderot, 1713-84, (Fr.) philosopher, encyclopedist.
John Duns Scotus, c1266-1308, (Sc.) Franciscan philosopher and theologian.
Mary Baker Eddy, 1821-1910, (U.S.) founder of Christian Science; *Science and Health.*
Jonathan Edwards, 1703-58, (U.S.) preacher, theologian; "Sinners in the Hands of an Angry God."
(Desiderius) Erasmus, c1466-1536, (Dutch) Renaissance humanist; *On the Freedom of the Will.*
Johann Fichte, 1762-1814, (Ger.) idealist philosopher.
Michel Foucault, 1926-84, (Fr.) structuralist philosopher, historian.
George Fox, 1624-91, (Br.) founder of Society of Friends.
(St.) Francis of Assisi, 1182-1226, (It.) founded Franciscans.
al-Ghazali, 1058-1111, Islamic philosopher.
Georg W. F. Hegel, 1770-1831, (Ger.) idealist philosopher; *Phenomenology of Mind.*
Martin Heidegger, 1889-1976, (Ger.) existentialist philosopher; affected many fields; *Being and Time.*
Johann G. Herder, 1744-1803, (Ger.) philosopher, cultural historian; a founder of German Romanticism.
Thomas Hobbes, 1588-1679, (Eng.) philosopher, political theorist; *Leviathan.*
David Hume, 1711-76, (Sc.) empiricist philosopher; *Enquiry Concerning Human Understanding.*
Jan Hus, 1369-1415, (Czech.) religious reformer.
Edmund Husserl, 1859-1938, (Ger.) philosopher; founded the phenomenological movement.
Thomas Huxley, 1825-95, (Br.) philosopher, educator.
William Inge, 1860-1954, (Br.) theologian; explored mystic aspects of Christianity.
William James, 1842-1910, (U.S.) philosopher, psychologist; pragmatist; studied religious experience.
Karl Jaspers, 1883-1969, (Ger.) existentialist philosopher.
Joan of Arc, 1412-1431, (Fr.) national heroine and a patron saint of France; key figure in the Hundred Years' War.
Immanuel Kant, 1724-1804, (Ger.) philosopher; founder of modern critical philosophy; *Critique of Pure Reason.*
Thomas à Kempis, c1380-1471, (Ger.) monk, devotional writer; *Imitation of Christ.* attributed to him.
Soren Kierkegaard, 1813-55, (Dan.) religious philosopher; pre-existentialist; *Either/Or, The Sickness Unto Death.*
John Knox, 1505-72, (Sc.) leader of the Protestant Reformation in Scotland.
Lao-Tzu, 604-531 BC, (Chin.) philosopher; considered the founder of the Taoist religion.
Gottfried von Leibniz, 1646-1716, (Ger.) rationalistic philosopher, logician, mathematician.
John Locke, 1632-1704, (Eng.) political theorist, empiricist philosopher; *Essay Concerning Human Understanding.*

(St.) Ignatius Loyola, 1491-1556, (Sp.) founder of the Jesuits; *Spiritual Exercises.*
Martin Luther, 1483-1546, (Ger.) leader of the Protestant Reformation, founded Lutheran church.
Jean-Francois Lyotard, 1924-98, (Fr.) postmodern philosopher, lecturer; *The Post-Modern Condition.*
Maimonides, 1135-1204, (Sp.) major Jewish philosopher.
Gabriel Marcel, 1889-1973, (Fr.) Roman Catholic existentialist philosopher, dramatist, and critic.
Jacques Maritain, 1882-1973, (Fr.) Neo-Thomist philosopher.
Cotton Mather, 1663-1728, (U.S.) defender of orthodox Puritanism; founded Yale, 1701.
Philipp Melanchthon, 1497-1560, (Ger.) theologian, humanist; an important voice in the Reformation.
Maurice Merleau-Ponty, 1908-61, (Fr.) existentialist philosopher; *Phenomenology of Perception.*
Thomas Merton, 1915-68, (U.S.) Trappist monk, spiritual writer; *The Seven Storey Mountain.*
John Stuart Mill, 1806-73, (Br.) philosopher, economist; libertarian political theorist; *Utilitarianism.*
Muhammad, c570-632, (Arab) the prophet of Islam.
Dwight Moody, 1837-99, (U.S.) evangelist.
G(eorge) E(dward) Moore, 1873-1958, (Br.) philosopher; *Principia Ethica,* "A Defense of Common Sense."
Elijah Muhammad, 1897-1975, (U.S.) leader of the Black Muslim sect.
Heinrich Muhlenberg, 1711-87, (Ger.) organized the Lutheran Church in America.
John H. Newman, 1801-90, (Br.) Roman Catholic convert, cardinal; led Oxford Movement; *Apologia pro Vita Sua.*
Reinhold Niebuhr, 1892-1971, (U.S.) Protestant theologian.
Richard Niebuhr, 1894-1962 (U.S.) Protestant theologian.
Friedrich Nietzsche, 1844-1900, (Ger.) philosopher; *The Birth of Tragedy, Beyond Good and Evil, Thus Spake Zarathustra.*
Robert Nozick, 1938-2002, (U.S.) political philosopher; *Anarchy, State, and Utopia.*
Blaise Pascal, 1623-62, (Fr.) philosopher, mathematician; *Pensées.*
(St.) Patrick, c389-c461, (Br.) brought Christianity to Ireland.
(St.) Paul, ?-c67, a key proponent of Christianity; his epistles are first Christian theological writing.
Norman Vincent Peale, 1898-1993, (U.S.) minister, author; *The Power of Positive Thinking.*
C(harles) S. Peirce, 1839-1914, (U.S.) philosopher, logician; originated concept of pragmatism, 1878.
Plato, c428-347 BC, (Gr.) philosopher; wrote classic Socratic dialogues; argued for universal truths and independent reality of ideas or forms; *Republic.*
Plotinus, 205-70, (Rom.) a founder of neo-Platonism; *Enneads.*
W(illard) V(an) O(rman) Quine, 1908-2001, (U.S.) philosopher, logician; "On What There Is."
Josiah Royce, 1855-1916, (U.S.) idealist philosopher
Bertrand Russell, 1872-1970, (Br.) philosopher, logician; one of the founders of modern logic; a prolific popular writer.
Charles T. Russell, 1852-1916, (U.S.) founder of Jehovah's Witnesses.
Gilbert Ryle, 1900-76, (Br.) analytic philosopher; *The Concept of Mind.*
George Santayana, 1863-1952, (U.S.) philosopher, writer, critic; *The Sense of Beauty, The Realms of Being.*
Jean-Paul Sartre, 1905-80, (Fr.) philosopher, novelist, playwright. *Nausea, No Exit, Being and Nothingness.*
Friedrich von Schelling, 1775-1854, (Ger.) philosopher of romantic movement.
Friedrich Schleiermacher, 1768-1834, (Ger.) theologian; a founder of modern Protestant theology.
Arthur Schopenhauer, 1788-1860, (Ger.) philosopher; *The World as Will and Idea.*
Albert Schweitzer, 1875-1965, (Ger.) theologian, social philosopher, medical missionary.
Joseph Smith, 1805-44, (U.S.) founded Latter-Day Saints (Mormon) movement, 1830.
Socrates, 469-399 BC, (Gr.) influential philosopher immortalized by Plato.
Herbert Spencer, 1820-1903, (Br.) philosopher of evolution.
Baruch de Spinoza, 1632-77, (Dutch) rationalist philosopher; *Ethics.*
Billy Sunday, 1862-1935, (U.S.) evangelist.
Pierre Teilhard de Chardin, 1881-1955, (Fr.) Jesuit priest, paleontologist, philosopher-theologian; *The Divine Milieu.*
Daisetz Teitaro Suzuki, 1870-1966, (Jpn.) Buddhist scholar.
(St.) Theresa of Lisieux, 1873-97, (Fr.) Carmelite nun revered for everyday sanctity; *The Story of a Soul.*
Emanuel Swedenborg, 1688-1772, (Swed.) philosopher, mystic.
Paul Tillich, 1886-1965, (U.S.) German-born philosopher and theologian; brought depth psychology to Protestantism.
John Wesley, 1703-91, (Br.) theologian, evangelist; founded Methodism.
Alfred North Whitehead, 1861-1947, (Br.) philosopher, mathematician; *Process and Reality.*
William of Occam, c1285-c1349 (Eng.) medieval scholastic philosopher; nominalist.
Roger Williams, c1603-83, (U.S.) clergyman; championed religious freedom and separation of church and state.
Ludwig Wittgenstein, 1889-1951, (Austrian) philosopher; major influence on contemporary language philosophy; *Tractatus Logico-Philosophicus, Philosophical Investigations.*
John Woolman, 1720-72, (U.S.) Quaker social reformer, abolitionist, writer; *The Journal.*
John Wycliffe, 1320-84, (Eng.) theologian, reformer.
(St.) Francis Xavier, 1506-52, (Sp.) Jesuit missionary, "Apostle of the Indies."
Brigham Young, 1801-77, (U.S.) Mormon leader after Smith's assassination; colonized Utah.
Huldrych Zwingli, 1484-1531, (Swiss) theologian; led Swiss Protestant Reformation.

Political Leaders of the Past

(U.S. presidents, vice presidents, Supreme Ct. justices, signers of Decl. of Indep., listed elsewhere.)

Abu Bakr, 573-634, Muslim leader, first caliph, chosen successor to Muhammad.
Dean Acheson, 1893-1971, (U.S.) sec. of state; architect of cold war foreign policy.
Samuel Adams, 1722-1803, (U.S.) patriot, Boston Tea Party firebrand.
Konrad Adenauer, 1876-1967, (Ger.) first West German chancellor.
Emilio Aguinaldo, 1869-1964, (Philip.) revolutionary; fought against Spain and the U.S.
Akbar, 1542-1605, greatest Mogul emperor of India.
Carl Albert, 1908-2000 (U.S.) House rep. from OK, Speaker, 1971-76.
Salvador Allende Gossens, 1908-1973, (Chilean) Marxist pres. 1970-73; ousted and died in coup.
Hafez al Assad, 1930-2000 (Syr.), Syrian ruler from 1970.
Herbert H. Asquith, 1852-1928, (Br.) liberal prime min.; instituted major social reform.
Atahualpa, ?-1533, Inca (ruling chief) of Peru.
Kemal Ataturk, 1881-1938, (Turk.) founded modern Turkey.
Clement Attlee, 1883-1967, (Br.) Labour party leader, prime min.; enacted natl. health, nationalized many industries.
Stephen F. Austin, 1793-1836, (U.S.) led Texas colonization.
Mikhail Bakunin, 1814-76, (Rus.) revolutionary; leading exponent of anarchism.
Arthur J. Balfour, 1848-1930, (Br.) foreign sec. under Lloyd George; issued Balfour Declaration backing Zionism.
Bernard M. Baruch, 1870-1965, (U.S.) financier, govt. adviser.
Fulgencio Batista y Zaldívar, 1901-73, (Cub.) Cuban pres. (1940-44, 1952-59), overthrown by Castro.
Lord Beaverbrook, 1879-1964, (Br.) financier, statesman, newspaper owner.
Menachem Begin, 1913-92, (Isr.) Israeli prime min., shared 1978 Nobel Peace Prize.
Eduard Benes, 1884-1948, (Czech.) pres. during interwar and post-WW2 eras.
David Ben-Gurion, 1886-1973, (Isr.) first prime min. of Israel, 1948-53, 1955-63.
Thomas Hart Benton, 1782-1858, (U.S.) Missouri senator; championed agrarian interests and westward expansion.
Aneurin Bevan, 1897-1960, (Br.) Labour party leader.
Ernest Bevin, 1881-1951, (Br.) Labour party leader, foreign minister; helped lay foundation for NATO.
Otto von Bismarck, 1815-98, (Ger.) statesman known as the Iron Chancellor; uniter of Germany, 1870.
James G. Blaine, 1830-93, (U.S.) Republican politician, diplomat; influential in Pan-American movement.
Léon Blum, 1872-1950, (Fr.) socialist leader, writer; headed first Popular Front government.
Simón Bolívar, 1783-1830, (Venez.) S. Amer. Revolutionary who liberated much of the continent from Spanish rule.
William E. Borah, 1865-1940, (U.S.) isolationist senator; helped block U.S. membership in League of Nations.
Cesare Borgia, 1476-1507, (It.) soldier, politician; an outstanding figure of the Italian Renaissance.
Willy Brandt, 1913-92, (Ger.) statesman, chancellor of West Germany, 1969-74; promoted East/West peace, *Ostpolitik.*
Leonid Brezhnev, 1906-82, (USSR) Soviet leader, 1964-82.
Aristide Briand, 1862-1932, (Fr.) foreign min.; chief architect of Locarno Pact and anti-war Kellogg-Briand Pact.
William Jennings Bryan, 1860-1925, (U.S.) Democratic, populist leader, orator; 3 times lost race for presidency.
Ralph Bunche, 1904-71, (U.S.) a founder and key diplomat of United Nations for more than 20 years.

John C. Calhoun, 1782-1850, (U.S.) political leader; champion of states' rights and a symbol of the Old South.
Robert Castlereagh, 1769-1822, (Br.) foreign sec.; guided Grand Alliance against Napoleon.
Camillo Benso Cavour, 1810-61, (It.) statesman; largely responsible for uniting Italy under the House of Savoy.
Nicolae Ceausescu, 1918-89, (Roman.) Communist leader, head of state 1967-89; executed.
Austen Chamberlain, 1863-1937, (Br.) statesman; helped finalize Locarno Treaties, both 1925.
Neville Chamberlain, 1869-1940, (Br.) Conservative prime min. whose appeasement of Hitler led to Munich Pact.
Chiang Kai-shek, 1887-1975, (Chin.) Nationalist Chinese pres. whose government was driven from mainland to Taiwan.
Winston Churchill, 1874-1965, (Br.) prime min., soldier, author; guided Britain through WW2.
Galeazzo Ciano, 1903-44, (It.) fascist foreign minister; helped create Rome-Berlin Axis, executed by Mussolini.
Henry Clay, 1777-1852, (U.S.) "The Great Compromiser," one of the most influential pre-Civil War political leaders.
Georges Clemenceau, 1841-1929, (Fr.) twice prem., Wilson's antagonist at Paris Peace Conference after WW1.
DeWitt Clinton, 1769-1828, (U.S.) political leader; responsible for promoting idea of the Erie Canal.
Robert Clive, 1725-74, (Br.) first administrator of Bengal; laid foundation for British Empire in India.
Jean Baptiste Colbert, 1619-83, (Fr.) statesman; influential under Louis XIV, created the French navy.
Bettino Craxi, 1934-2000, (It.) Italy's first post-WWII Socialist premier.
Oliver Cromwell, 1599-1658, (Br.) Lord Protector of England, led parliamentary forces during Civil War.
Curzon of Kedleston, 1859-1925, (Br.) viceroy of India, foreign sec.; major force in post-WW1 world.
Édouard Daladier, 1884-1970, (Fr.) Radical Socialist politician, arrested by Vichy, interned by Germans until 1945.
Richard J. Daley, 1902-1976, (U.S.) Chicago mayor.
Georges Danton, 1759-94, (Fr.) leading French Rev. figure.
Jefferson Davis, 1808-89, (U.S.) pres. of the Confederacy.
Charles G. Dawes, 1865-1951, (U.S.) statesman, banker; advanced plan to stabilize post-WW1 German finances.
Alcide De Gasperi, 1881-1954, (It.) prime min.; founder of Christian Democratic party.
Charles De Gaulle, 1890-1970, (Fr.) general, statesman; first pres. of the Fifth Republic.
Deng Xiaoping, 1904-97, (Chin.) "paramount leader" of China; backed economic modernization.
Eamon De Valera, 1882-1975, (Ir.-U.S.) statesman; led fight for Irish independence.
Thomas E. Dewey, 1902-71, (U.S.) NY governor; twice loser in try for presidency.
Ngo Dinh Diem, 1901-63, (Viet.) South Vietnamese pres.; assassinated in government takeover.
Everett M. Dirksen, 1896-1969, (U.S.) Senate Republican minority leader, orator.
Benjamin Disraeli, 1804-81, (Br.) prime min.; considered founder of modern Conservative party.
Engelbert Dollfuss, 1892-1934, (Austrian) chancellor; assassinated by Austrian Nazis.
Andrea Doria, 1466-1560, (It.) Genoese admiral, statesman; called "Father of Peace" and "Liberator of Genoa."
Stephen A. Douglas, 1813-61, (U.S.) Democratic leader, orator; opposed Lincoln for the presidency.
Alexander Dubcek, 1921-92, (Czech.) statesman whose attempted liberalization was crushed, 1968.
John Foster Dulles, 1888-1959, (U.S.) sec. of state under Eisenhower, cold war policy-maker.
Friedrich Ebert, 1871-1925, (Ger.) Social Democratic movement leader; 1st pres., Weimar Republic, 1919-25.
Sir Anthony Eden, 1897-1977, (Br.) foreign sec., prime min. during Suez invasion of 1956.
Ludwig Erhard, 1897-1977, (Ger.) economist, West German chancellor; led nation's economic rise after WW2.
Amintore Fanfani, 1908-99, (It.) six-time premier of Italy.
Joao Baptista de Figueiredo, 1918-99, (Braz.) president of Brazil, restored the nation's democracy.
Hamilton Fish, 1808-93, (U.S.) sec. of state, successfully mediated disputes with Great Britain, Latin America.
James V. Forrestal, 1892-1949, (U.S.) sec. of navy, first sec. of defense.
Francisco Franco, 1892-1975, (Sp.) leader of rebel forces during Spanish Civil War and longtime ruler of Spain.
Benjamin Franklin, 1706-90, (U.S.) printer, publisher, author, inventor, scientist, diplomat.
Louis de Frontenac, 1620-98, (Fr.) governor of New France (Canada); encouraged explorations, fought Iroquois.
J. William Fulbright, 1905-95, (U.S.) U.S. senator; leading figure in U.S. foreign policy during cold war years.
Hugh Gaitskell, 1906-63, (Br.) Labour party leader; major force in reversing its stand for unilateral disarmament.
Albert Gallatin, 1761-1849, (U.S.) sec. of treasury; instrumental in negotiating end of War of 1812.
Léon Gambetta, 1838-82, (Fr.) statesman, politician; one of the founders of the Third Republic.
Indira Gandhi, 1917-84, (In.) daughter of Jawaharlal Nehru, prime min. of India, 1966-77, 1980-84; assassinated.
Mohandas K. Gandhi, 1869-1948, (In.) political leader, ascetic; led movement against British rule; assassinated.
Giuseppe Garibaldi, 1807-82, (It.) patriot, soldier; a leader in the Risorgimento, Italian unification movement.
William E. Gladstone, 1809-98, (Br.) prime min. 4 times; dominant force of Liberal party from 1868 to 1894.
Paul Joseph Goebbels, 1897-1945, (Ger.) Nazi propagandist, master of mass psychology.
Barry Goldwater, 1909-98 (U.S.) conservative U.S. senator and 1964 Republican presid. nominee.
Klement Gottwald, 1896-1953, (Czech.) Communist leader; ushered Communism into his country.
Alexander Hamilton, 1755-1804, (U.S.) first treasury sec.; champion of strong central government.
Dag Hammarskjold, 1905-61, (Swed.) statesman; UN sec.-general.
Hassan II, King, 1929-99, (Moroc.), ruler of Morocco,1962-99.
John Hay, 1838-1905, (U.S.) sec. of state; primarily associated with Open Door Policy toward China.
Patrick Henry, 1736-99, (U.S.) major revolutionary figure, remarkable orator.
Édouard Herriot, 1872-1957, (Fr.) Radical Socialist leader; twice prem., pres. of National Assembly.
Theodor Herzl, 1860-1904, (Hung.) founded modern Zionism.
Heinrich Himmler, 1900-45, (Ger.) head of Nazi SS and Gestapo.
Paul von Hindenburg, 1847-1934, (Ger.) field marshal, WW1; 2d pres. of Weimar Republic, 1925-34.
Adolf Hitler, 1889-1945, (Ger.) dictator; built Nazism, launched WW2, presided over the Holocaust.
Ho Chi Minh, 1890-1969, (Viet.) N Vietnamese pres., Vietnamese Communist leader.
Harry L. Hopkins, 1890-1946, (U.S.) New Deal administrator; closest adviser to FDR during WW2.
Edward M. House, 1858-1938, (U.S.) diplomat; confidential adviser to Woodrow Wilson.
Samuel Houston, 1793-1863, (U.S.) leader of struggle to win control of Texas from Mexico.
Cordell Hull, 1871-1955, (U.S.) sec. of state, 1933-44; initiated reciprocal trade to lower tariffs, helped organize UN.
Hubert H. Humphrey, 1911-78, (U.S.) Minnesota Democrat; senator; vice pres., pres. candidate.
Hussein, King, 1935-99 (Jordan), peacemaker; ruler of Jordan, 1952-99.
Jinnah, Muhammad Ali, 1876-1948, (Pak.) founder, first governor-general of Pakistan.
Benito Juarez, 1806-72, (Mex.) rallied his country against foreign threats, sought to create democratic, federal republic.
Constantine Karamanlis, 1907-98, (Gr.) Greek prime min. (1955-63, 1974-80); restored democracy; later president.
Frank B. Kellogg, 1856-1937, (U.S.) sec. of state; negotiated Kellogg-Briand Pact to outlaw war.
Robert F. Kennedy, 1925-68, (U.S.) attorney general, senator; assassinated while seeking presidency.
Aleksandr Kerensky, 1881-1970, (Russ.) headed provisional government after Feb. 1917 revolution.
Ayatollah Ruhollah Khomeini, 1900-89, (Iranian), religious-political leader, spearheaded overthrow of shah, 1979.
Nikita Khrushchev, 1894-1971, (USSR) prem., first sec. of Communist party; initiated de-Stalinization.
Kim Il Sung, 1912-94, (Korean) N Korean dictator, 1948-94.
Lajos Kossuth, 1802-94, (Hung.) principal figure in 1848 Hungarian revolution.
Pyotr Kropotkin, 1842-1921, (Russ.) anarchist; championed the peasants but opposed Bolshevism.
Kublai Khan, c1215-94, Mongol emperor; founder of Yüan dynasty in China.
Béla Kun, 1886-c1939, (Hung.) member of 3d Communist Internat.; tried to foment worldwide revolution.
Robert M. LaFollette, 1855-1925, (U.S.) Wisconsin public official; leader of progressive movement.
Fiorello La Guardia, 1882-1947, (U.S.) colorful NYC reform mayor.
Pierre Laval, 1883-1945, (Fr.) politician, Vichy foreign min.; executed for treason.
Andrew Bonar Law, 1858-1923, (Br.) Conservative party politician; led opposition to Irish home rule.
Vladimir Ilyich Lenin (Ulyanov), 1870-1924, (Russ.) revolutionary; founded Bolshevism; Soviet leader 1917-24.
Ferdinand de Lesseps, 1805-94, (Fr.) diplomat, engineer; conceived idea of Suez Canal.
Rene Levesque, 1922-87, (Can.) prem. of Quebec, 1976-85; led unsuccessful separartist campaign.

Maxim Litvinov, 1876-1951, (Pol.-Russ.) revolutionary, commissar of foreign affairs; favored cooperation with West.
Liu Shaoqi, c1898-1974, (Chin.) Communist leader; fell from grace during Cultural Revolution.
David Lloyd George, 1863-1945, (Br.) Liberal party prime min.; laid foundations for modern welfare state.
Henry Cabot Lodge, 1850-1924, (U.S.) Republican senator; led opposition to participation in League of Nations.
Huey P. Long, 1893-1935, (U.S.) Louisiana political demagogue, governor; assassinated.
Rosa Luxemburg, 1871-1919, (Ger.) revolutionary; leader of the German Social Democratic party and Spartacus party.
J. Ramsay MacDonald, 1866-1937, (Br.) first Labour party prime min. of Great Britain.
Harold Macmillan, 1895-1986, (Br.) prime min. of Great Britain, 1957-63.
Joseph R. McCarthy, 1908-57, (U.S.) senator, extremist in searching out alleged Communists and pro-Communists.
Makarios III, 1913-77, (Cypriot) Greek Orthodox archbishop; first pres. of Cyprus.
Mao Zedong, 1893-1976, (Chin.) chief Chinese Marxist theorist, revolutionary, political leader; led Chinese revolution establishing his nation as Communist state.
Jean Paul Marat, 1743-93, (Fr.) revolutionary, politician; identified with radical Jacobins; assassinated.
José Martí, 1853-95, (Cub.) patriot, poet; leader of Cuban struggle for independence.
Jan Masaryk, 1886-1948, (Czech.) foreign min., died by mysterious alleged suicide following Communist coup.
Thomas G. Masaryk, 1850-1937, (Czech.) statesman, philosopher; first pres. of Czechoslovak Republic.
Jules Mazarin, 1602-61, (Fr.) cardinal, statesman; prime min. under Louis XIII and queen regent Anne of Austria.
Giusseppe Mazzini, 1805-72, (It.), reformer dedicated to Risorgimento movement for renewal of Italy.
Tom Mboya, 1930-69, (Kenyan) political leader; instrumental in securing independence for Kenya.
Cosimo I de' Medici, 1519-74, (It.) Duke of Florence, grand duke of Tuscany.
Lorenzo de' Medici, the Magnificent, 1449-92, (It.) merchant prince; a towering figure in Italian Renaissance.
Catherine de Médicis, 1519-89, (Fr.) queen consort of Henry II, regent of France; influential in Catholic-Huguenot wars.
Golda Meir, 1898-1978, (Isr.) a founder of the state of Israel and prime min., 1969-74.
Klemens W. N. L. Metternich, 1773-1859, (Austrian) statesman; arbiter of post-Napoleonic Europe.
François Mitterrand, 1916-96, (Fr.) pres. of France, 1981-95.
Mobutu Sese Seko, 1930-97, (Zaire) longtime ruler of Zaire (now Congo) (1965-97); exiled after rebellion.
Guy Mollet, 1905-75, (Fr.) socialist politician, resistance leader.
Henry Morgenthau Jr., 1891-1967, (U.S.) sec. of treasury; fund-raiser for New Deal and U.S. WW2 activities.
Gouverneur Morris, 1752-1816, (U.S.) statesman, diplomat. financial expert, helped plan decimal coinage.
Benito Mussolini, 1883-1945, (It.) leader of the Italian fascist state; assassinated.
Imre Nagy, c1896-1958, (Hung.) Communist prem.; assassinated after Soviets crushed 1956 uprising.
Gamal Abdel Nasser, 1918-70, (Egypt.) leader of Arab unification, 2d Egyptian pres.
Jawaharlal Nehru, 1889-1964, (In.) prime min.; guided India through its early years of independence.
Kwame Nkrumah, 1909-72, (Ghan.) 1st prime min., 1957-60, and pres., 1960-66, of Ghana.
Frederick North, 1732-92, (Br.) prime min.; his inept policies led to loss of American colonies.
Daniel O'Connell, 1775-1847, (Ir.) political leader; known as The Liberator.
Julius K. Nyerere, 1923?-99, (Tanz.) founding father, 1st pres., 1962-85, of Tanzania.
Omar, c581-644, Muslim leader; 2nd caliph, led Islam to become an imperial power.
Thomas P. (Tip) O'Neill Jr., 1912-94, (U.S.) U.S. congressman, Speaker of the House, 1977-86.
Ignace Paderewski, 1860-1941, (Pol.) statesman, pianist; composer, briefly prime min., an ardent patriot.
Viscount Palmerston, 1784-1865, (Br.) Whig-Liberal prime min., foreign min.; embodied British nationalism.
Andreas George Papandreou, 1919-1996, (Gk.) leftist politician, served 2 times as prem. (1981-89, 1993-96).
Georgios Papandreou, 1888-1968, (Gk.) Republican politician; served 3 times as prime min.
Franz von Papen, 1879-1969, (Ger.) politician; major role in overthrow of Weimar Republic and rise of Hitler.
Charles Stewart Parnell, 1846-1891, (Ir.) nationalist leader; "uncrowned king of Ireland."
Lester Pearson, 1897-1972, (Can.) diplomat, Liberal party leader, prime min.
Robert Peel, 1788-1850, (Br.) reformist prime min., founder of Conservative party.
Eva (Evita) Perón, 1919-52 (Arg.) highly influential 2nd wife of Juan Perón.
Juan Perón, 1895-1974, (Arg.) dynamic pres. of Argentina (1946-55, 1973-74).
Joseph Pilsudski, 1867-1935, (Pol.) statesman; instrumental in reestablishing Polish state in the 20th cent.
Charles Pinckney, 1757-1824, (U.S.) founding father; his Pinckney plan largely incorporated into Constitution.
Christian Pineau, 1905-95, (Fr.) leader of French Resistance during WW2; French foreign min., 1956-58.
William Pitt, the Elder, 1708-78, (Br.) statesman; the "Great Commoner," transformed Britain into imperial power.
William Pitt, the Younger, 1759-1806, (Br.) prime min. during French Revolutionary wars.
Georgi Plekhanov, 1857-1918, (Russ.) revolutionary, social philosopher; called "father of Russian Marxism."
Raymond Poincaré, 1860-1934, (Fr.) 9th pres. of the Republic; advocated harsh punishment of Germany after WW1.
Pol Pot, 1925-98, (Camb.) leader of Khmer Rouge; ruled Cambodia, 1975-79; responsible for mass deaths.
Georges Pompidou, 1911-74, (Fr.) Gaullist political leader; pres. 1969-74.
Grigori Potemkin, 1739-91, (Russ.) field marshal; favorite of Catherine II.
Yitzhak Rabin, 1922-95, (Isr.) military, political leader; prime min. of Israel, 1974-77, 1992-95; assassinated.
Edmund Randolph, 1753-1813, (U.S.) attorney; prominent in drafting, ratification of constitution.
John Randolph, 1773-1833, (U.S.) Southern planter; strong advocate of states' rights.
Jeannette Rankin, 1880-1973, (U.S.) pacifist; first woman member of U.S. Congress.
Walter Rathenau, 1867-1922, (Ger.) industrialist, statesman.
Sam Rayburn, 1882-1961, (U.S.) Democratic leader; representative for 47 years, House Speaker for 17.
Paul Reynaud, 1878-1966, (Fr.) statesman; prem. in 1940 at the time of France's defeat by Germany.
Syngman Rhee, 1875-1965, (Korean) first pres. of S Korea.
Cecil Rhodes, 1853-1902, (Br.) imperialist, industrial magnate; established Rhodes scholarships in his will.
Cardinal de Richelieu, 1585-1642, (Fr.) statesman, known as "red eminence;" chief minister to Louis XIII.
Maximilien Robespierre, 1758-94, (Fr.) leading figure in French Revolution and Reign of Terror.
Nelson Rockefeller, 1908-79, (U.S.) Republican governor of NY, 1959-73; U.S. vice pres., 1974-77.
George W. Romney, 1907-95, (U.S.) auto exec.; 3-term Republican governor of Michigan.
Eleanor Roosevelt, 1884-1962, (U.S.) influential First Lady, humanitarian, UN diplomat.
Elihu Root, 1845-1937, (U.S.) lawyer, statesman, diplomat; leading Republican supporter of the League of Nations.
Dean Rusk, 1909-95, (U.S.) statesman; sec. of state, 1961-69.
John Russell, 1792-1878, (Br.) Liberal prime min. during the Irish potato famine.
Anwar al-Sadat, 1918-81, (Egypt.) pres., 1970-1981, promoted peace with Israel; Nobel laureate; assassinated.
António de Salazar, 1889-1970, (Port.) longtime dictator.
José de San Martin, 1778-1850, S Amer. revolutionary; protector of Peru.
Eisaku Sato, 1901-75, (Jpn.) prime min.; presided over Japan's post-WW2 emergence as major world power.
Abdul Aziz Ibn Saud, c1880-1953, (Saudi Arabia) king of Saudi Arabia, 1932-53.
Robert Schuman, 1886-1963, (Fr.) statesman; founded European Coal and Steel Community.
Carl Schurz, 1829-1906, (U.S.) German-American political leader, journalist, orator, dedicated reformer.
Kurt Schuschnigg, 1897-1977, (Austrian) chancellor; unsuccessful in stopping Austria's annexation by Germany.
William H. Seward, 1801-72, (U.S.) anti-slavery activist; as U.S. sec. of state purchased Alaska.
Carlo Sforza, 1872-1952, (It.) foreign min., anti-fascist.
Sitting Bull, c1831-90, (Nat. Am.) Sioux leader in Battle of Little Bighorn over George A. Custer, 1876.
Alfred E. Smith, 1873-1944, (U.S.) NY Democratic governor; first Roman Catholic to run for presidency.
Margaret Chase Smith, 1897-1995, (U.S.) congresswoman, senator; 1st woman elected to both houses of Congress.
Jan C. Smuts, 1870-1950, (S. African) statesman, philosopher, soldier, prime min.
Paul Henri Spaak, 1899-1972, (Belg.) statesman, socialist leader.
Joseph Stalin, 1879-1953, (USSR) Soviet dictator, 1924-53; instituted forced collectivization, massive purges, and labor camps, causing millions of deaths.
Edwin M. Stanton, 1814-69, (U.S.) sec. of war, 1862-68.

Edward R. Stettinius Jr., 1900-49, (U.S.) industrialist, sec. of state who coordinated aid to WW2 allies.
Adlai E. Stevenson, 1900-65, (U.S.) Democratic leader, diplomat, Illinois governor, presidenial candidate.
Henry L. Stimson, 1867-1950, (U.S.) statesman; served in 5 administrations, foreign policy adviser in 30s and 40s.
Gustav Stresemann, 1878-1929, (Ger.) chancellor, foreign minister; strove to regain friendship for post-WW1 Germany.
Sukarno, 1901-70, (Indon.) dictatorial first pres. of the Indonesian republic.
Sun Yat-sen, 1866-1925, (Chin.) revolutionary; leader of Kuomintang, regarded as the father of modern China.
Robert A. Taft, 1889-1953, (U.S.) conservative Senate leader, called "Mr. Republican."
Charles de Talleyrand, 1754-1838, (Fr.) statesman, diplomat; the major force of the Congress of Vienna of 1814-15.
U Thant, 1909-74 (Bur.) statesman, UN sec.-general.
Norman M. Thomas, 1884-1968, (U.S.) social reformer; 6 times Socialist party presidential candidate.
Josip Broz Tito, 1892-1980, (Yug.) pres. of Yugoslavia from 1953, WW2 guerrilla chief, postwar rival of Stalin.
Palmiro Togliatti, 1893-1964, (It.) major Italian Communist leader.
Hideki Tojo, 1885-1948, (Jpn.) statesman, soldier; prime min. during most of WW2.
François Toussaint L'Ouverture, c1744-1803, (Haitian) patriot, martyr; thwarted French colonial aims.
Leon Trotsky, 1879-1940, (Russ.) revolutionary, founded Red Army, expelled from party in conflict with Stalin; assassinated.
Pierre Elliott Trudeau, 1919-2000, (Can.) longtime liberal prime minister of Canada, 1968-79, 1980-84; achieved native Canadian constitution.
Rafael L. Trujillo Molina, 1891-1961, (Dom.) dictator of Dominican Republic, 1930-61; assassinated.
Moise K. Tshombe, 1919-69, (Cong.) pres. of secessionist Katanga, prem. of Congo.
William M. Tweed, 1823-78, (U.S.) politicial boss of Tammany Hall, NYC's Democratic political machine.
Walter Ulbricht, 1893-1973, (Ger.) Communist leader of German Democratic Republic.
Arthur H. Vandenberg, 1884-1951, (U.S.) senator; proponent of bipartisan anti-Communist foreign policy.
Eleutherios Venizelos, 1864-1936, (Gk.) most prominent Greek statesman of early 20th cent.
Hendrik F. Verwoerd, 1901-66, (S. African) prime min.; rigorously applied apartheid policy despite protest.
George Wallace, 1919-98, (U.S.) former segregationist governor of Alabama and presid. candidate.
Robert Walpole, 1676-1745, (Br.) statesman; generally considered Britain's first prime min.
Daniel Webster, 1782-1852, (U.S.) orator, politician; advocate of business interests during Jacksonian agrarianism.
Chaim Weizmann, 1874-1952, (Russ.-Isr.) Zionist leader, scientist; first Israeli pres.
Wendell L. Willkie, 1892-1944, (U.S.) Republican who tried to unseat FDR when he ran for his 3d term.
Harold Wilson, 1916-95, (Br.) Labour party leader; prime min., 1964-70, 1974-76.
Emiliano Zapata, c1879-1919, (Mex.) revolutionary; major influence on modern Mexico.
Todor Zhivkov, 1911-98, (Bulg.) Communist ruler of Bulgaria from 1954 until ousted in a 1989 coup.
Zhou Enlai, 1898-1976, (Chin.) diplomat, prime min.; a leading figure of the Chinese Communist party.

Scientists of the Past

Revised by Peter Barker, Prof. & Chair, Dept. of the Hist. of Science, Univ. of Oklahoma

For pre-modern scientists see also Philosophers and Religious Figures of the Past and Historical Figures chapter.

Albertus Magnus, c1200-1280, (Ger.) theologian, philosopher; helped found medieval study of natural science.
Alhazen (Ibn al-Haytham), c965-ca.1040, mathematician, astronomer; optical theorist.
Andre-Marie Ampère, 1775-1836, (Fr.) mathematician, chemist; founder of electrodynamics.
John V. Atanasoff, 1903-95, (U.S.) physicist; co-invented Atanasoff-Berry Computer (1939-41), regarded in law as the original "automatic electronic digital computer".
Amedeo Avogadro, 1776-1856, (It.) chemist, physicist; proposed that equal volumes of gas contain equal numbers of molecules, permitting determination of molecular weights.
John Bardeen, 1908-91, (U.S.) double Nobel laureate in physics (transistor, 1956; superconductivity, 1972).
A. H. Becquerel, 1852-1908, (Fr.) physicist; discovered radioactivity in uranium (1896).
Alexander Graham Bell, 1847-1922, (U.S.) inventor; first to patent and commercially exploit the telephone (1876).
Daniel Bernoulli, 1700-82, (Swiss) mathematician; developed fluid dynamics and kinetic theory of gases.
Clifford Berry, 1918-1963, (U.S.) collaborated with Atanasoff on the ABC computer (1939-41).
Jöns Jakob Berzelius, 1779-1848, (Swed.) chemist; developed modern chemical symbols and formulas, discovered selenium and thorium.
Henry Bessemer, 1813-98, (Br.) engineer; invented Bessemer steel-making process.
Bruno Bettelheim, 1903-90, (Austrian-U.S.) psychoanalyst specializing in autistic and other disturbed children; *Uses of Enchantment* (1976).
Louis Blériot, 1872-1936, (Fr.) engineer; monoplane pioneer, first Channel flight (1909).
Franz Boas, 1858-1942, (Ger.-U.S.) founded modern anthropology; studied Pacific Coast tribes.
Niels Bohr, 1885-1962, (Dan.) atomic and nuclear physicist; founded quantum mechanics.
Max Born, 1882-1970, (Ger.) atomic and nuclear physicist; helped develop quantum mechanics.
Satyendranath Bose, 1894-1974, (Indian) physicist; forerunner of modern quantum theory for integral-spin particles.
Louis de Broglie, 1892-1987, (Fr.) physicist; proposed quantum wave-particle duality.
Robert Bunsen, 1811-99, (Ger.) chemist; pioneered spectroscopic analysis; discovered rubidium, caesium.
Luther Burbank, 1849-1926, (U.S.) naturalist; developed plant breeding into a modern science.
Vannevar Bush, 1890-1974, (U.S.) electrical engineer; developed differential analyzer, an early analogue computer; headed WWII Office of Scientific Res. and Dev.
Marvin Camras, 1916-95, (U.S.) inventor, electrical engineer; invented magnetic tape recording.
Alexis Carrel, 1873-1944, (Fr.) surgeon, biologist; developed methods of suturing blood vessels and transplanting organs.
Rachel Carson, 1907-64, (U.S.) marine biologist, environmentalist; *Silent Spring* (1962).
George Washington Carver, c1864-1943, (U.S.) agricultural scientist, nutritionist; improved and pioneered new uses for peanuts and sweet potatoes.
James Chadwick, 1891-1974, (Br.) physicist; discovered the neutron (1932); led British Manhattan Project group in U.S. (1943-45).
Albert Claude, 1898-1983, (Belg.-U.S.) a founder of modern cell biology; determined role of mitochondria.
Nicolaus Copernicus, 1473-1543, (Pol.) first modern astronomer to propose sun as center of the planets' motions.
Jacques Yves Cousteau, 1910-1997, (Fr.) oceanographer; co-inventor, with E. Gagnan, of the Aqualung (1943).
Seymour Cray, 1925-96, (U.S.) computer industry pioneer; developed supercomputers.
Marie, 1867-1934 (Pol.-Fr.) and **Pierre Curie**, 1859-1906, (Fr.) physical chemists; pioneer investigators of radioactivity, discovered radium and polonium (1898).
Gottlieb Daimler, 1834-1900, (Ger.) engineer, inventor; pioneer automobile manufacturer.
John Dalton, 1766-1844, (Br.) chemist, physicist; formulated atomic theory, made first table of atomic weights.
Charles Darwin, 1809-82, (Br.) naturalist; established theory of organic evolution; *Origin of Species* (1859).
Lee De Forest, 1873-1961, (U.S.) inventor of triode, pioneer in wireless telegraphy, sound pictures, television.
Max Delbruck, 1906-81, (Ger.-U.S.) founded molecular biology.
Rudolf Diesel, 1858-1913, (Ger.) mechanical engineer; patented Diesel engine (1892).
Theodosius Dobzhansky, 1900-75, (Russ.-U.S.) biologist; reconciled genetics and natural selection contributing to "modern synthesis" in evolution.
Christian Doppler, 1803-53, (Austrian) physicist; showed change in wave frequency caused by motion of source, now known as Doppler effect.
J. Presper Eckert Jr., 1919-95, (U.S.) co-inventor, with Mauchly, of the ENIAC computer (1943-45).
Thomas A. Edison, 1847-1931, (U.S.) inventor; held more than 1,000 patents, including incandescent electric lamp.
Paul Ehrlich, 1854-1915, (Ger.) medical researcher in immunology and bacteriology; pioneered antitoxin production.
Albert Einstein, 1879-1955, (Ger.-U.S.) theoretical physicist; founded relativity theory, replacing Newton's theories of space, time, and gravity. Proved $E=mc^2$ (1905).
John F. Enders, 1897-1985, (U.S.) virologist, helped discover vaccines against polio, measles, mumps and chicken pox.
Erik Erikson, 1902-94, (U.S.) psychoanalyst, author; theory of developmental stages of life, *Childhood and Society* (1950).

Leonhard Euler, 1707-83, (Swiss) mathematician, physicist; pioneer of calculus, revived ideas of Fermat.
Gabriel Fahrenheit, 1686-1736, (Ger.) physicist; improved thermometers and introduced Fahrenheit temperature scale.
Michael Faraday, 1791-1867, (Br.) chemist, physicist; discovered electrical induction and invented dynamo (1831).
Philo T. Farnsworth, 1906-71, (U.S.) inventor; built first television system (San Francisco, 1928).
Pierre de Fermat, 1601-65, (Fr.) mathematician; founded modern theory of numbers.
Enrico Fermi, 1901-54, (It.-U.S.) nuclear physicist; demonstrated first controlled chain reaction (Chicago, 1942).
Richard Feynman, 1918-88, (U.S.) theoretical physicist, author; founder of Quantum Electrodynamics (QED).
Alexander Fleming, 1881-1955, (Br.) bacteriologist; discovered penicillin (1928).
Jean B. J. Fourier, 1768-1830, (fr.) introduced method of analysis in math and physics known as Fourier Series.
Sigmund Freud, 1856-1939, (Austrian) psychiatrist; founder of psychoanalysis. *Interpretation of Dreams* (1901).
Erich Fromm, 1900-1980, (U.S.) psychoanalyst. *Man for Himself* (1947).
Galileo Galilei, 1564-1642, (It.) physicist; used telescope to vindicate Copernicus, founded modern science of motion.
Luigi Galvani, 1737-98, (It.) physiologist; studied electricity in living organisms.
Carl Friedrich Gauss, 1777-1855, (Ger.) math. physicist; completed work of Fermat and Euler in number theory.
Joseph Gay-Lussac, 1778-1850, (Fr.) chemist, physicist; investigated behavior of gases, discovered boron.
Josiah W. Gibbs, 1839-1903, (U.S.) theoretical physicist, chemist; founded chemical thermodynamics.
Robert H. Goddard, 1882-1945, (U.S.) physicist; invented liquid fuel rocket (1926).
George W. Goethals, 1858-1928, (U.S.) chief engineer who completed Panama Canal (1907-14).
William C. Gorgas, 1854-1920, (U.S.) physician; pioneer in prevention of yellow fever and malaria.
Stephen Jay Gould, 1941-2002, (U.S.) paleontologist, evolutionary biologist, writer.
Ernest Haeckel, 1834-1919, (Ger.) zoologist, evolutionist; early Darwinist, introduced concept of "ecology."
Otto Hahn, 1879-1968, (Ger.) chemist; with Meitner discovered nuclear fission (1938).
Edmund Halley, 1656-1742, (Br.) astronomer; predicted return of 1682 comet ("Halley's Comet") in 1759.
William Harvey, 1578-1657, (Br.) physician, anatomist; discovered circulation of the blood (1628).
Werner Heisenberg, 1901-76, (Ger.) physicist; developed matrix mechanics and uncertainty principle (1927).
Hermann von Helmholtz, 1821-94, (Ger.) physicist, physiologist; formulated principle of conservation of energy.
William Herschel, 1738-1822, (Ger.-Br.) astronomer; discovered Uranus (1781).
Heinrich Hertz, 1857-94, (Ger.) physicist; discovered radio waves and photo-electric effect (1886-7).
David Hilbert, 1862-1943, (Ger.) mathematician; contributed to algebra, calculus and foundational studies (formalism).
Edwin P. Hubble, 1889-1953, (U.S.) astronomer; discovered observational evidence of expanding universe.
Alexander von Humboldt, 1769-1859, (Ger.) naturalist, author; explored S America, created ecology.
Edward Jenner, 1749-1823, (Br.) physician; pioneered vaccination, introduced term "virus."
James Joule, 1818-89, (Br.) physicist; found relation between heat and mechanical energy (conservation of energy).
Carl Jung, 1875-1961, (Swiss) psychiatrist; founder of analytical psychology.
Sister Elizabeth Kenny, 1886-1952, (Austral.) nurse; developed treatment for polio.
Johannes Kepler, 1571-1630, (Ger.) astronomer; discovered laws of planetary motion.
Al-Khawarizmi, early 9th cent., (Arab.), mathematician; regarded as founder of algebra.
Robert Koch, 1843-1910 (Ger.) bacteriologist; isolated bacterial causes of tuberculosis and other diseases.
Georges Köhler, 1946-95, (Ger.) immunologist; with Cesar Milstein he developed monoclonal antibody technique.
Jacques Lacan, 1901-81, (Fr.) controversial influential psychoanalyst.
Joseph Lagrange, 1736-1813, (Fr.) geometer, astronomer; showed that gravity of earth and moon cancels creating stable points in space around them.
Jean B. Lamarck, 1744-1829, (Fr.) naturalist; forerunner of Darwin in evolutionary theory.
Pierre Simon de Laplace, 1749-1827, (Fr.) astronomer, physicist; proposed nebular origin for solar system.
Antoine Lavoisier, 1743-94, (Fr.) a founder of mod. chemistry.
Ernest O. Lawrence, 1901-58, (U.S.) physicist; invented the cyclotron.
Jerome Lejeune, 1927-94, (Fr.) geneticist; discovered chromosomal cause of Down syndrome (1959).
Louis 1903-72, and **Mary Leakey**, 1913-96, (Br.) early hominid paleoanthropologists; discovered remains in Africa.
Anton van Leeuwenhoek, 1632-1723, (Dutch) founder of microscopy.
Kurt Lewin, 1890-1947, (Ger.-U.S.) social psychologist; studied human motivation and group dynamics.
Justus von Liebig, 1803-73, (Ger.) founded quantitative organic chemistry.
Joseph Lister, 1827-1912, (Br.) physician; pioneered antiseptic surgery.
Konrad Lorenz, 1903-89, (Austrian) ethologist; pioneer in study of animal behavior.
Percival Lowell, 1855-1916, (U.S.) astronomer; predicted the existence of Pluto.
Louis, 1864-1948, and **Auguste Lumière**, 1862-1954, (Fr.) invented cinematograph and made first motion picture (1895).
Guglielmo Marconi, 1874-1937, (It.) physicist; developed wireless telegraphy.
John W. Mauchly, 1907-80, (U.S.) co-inventor, with Eckert, of computer ENIAC (1943-45).
James Clerk Maxwell, 1831-79, (Br.) physicist; unified electricity and magnetism; electromagnetic theory of light.
Maria Goeppert Mayer, 1906-72, (Ger.-U.S.) physicist; developed shell model of atomic nuclei.
Barbara McClintock, 1902-92, (U.S.) geneticist; showed that some genetic elements are mobile.
Lise Meitner, 1878-1968, (Austrian) co-discoverer, with Hahn, of nuclear fission (1938).
Gregor J. Mendel, 1822-84, (Austrian) botanist, monk; his experiments became the foundation of modern genetics.
Dmitri Mendeleyev, 1834-1907, (Russ.) chemist; established Periodic Table of the Elements.
Franz Mesmer, 1734-1815, (Ger.) physician; introduced hypnotherapy.
Albert A. Michelson, 1852-1931, (U.S.) physicist; invented interferometer.
Robert A. Millikan, 1868-1953, (U.S.) physicist; measured electronic charge.
Thomas Hunt Morgan, 1866-1945, (U.S.) geneticist, embryologist; established role of chromosomes in heredity.
Isaac Newton, 1642-1727, (Br.) natural philosopher; discovered laws of gravitation, motion; with Leibniz, founded calculus.
Robert N. Noyce, 1927-90, (U.S.) invented microchip.
J. Robert Oppenheimer, 1904-67, (U.S.) physicist; scientific director of Manhattan project.
Wilhelm Ostwald, 1853-1932, (Ger.) chemist, philosopher; main founder of modern physical chemistry.
Louis Pasteur, 1822-95, (Fr.) chemist; showed that germs cause disease and fermentation, originated pasteurization.
Linus C. Pauling, 1901-94, (U.S.) chemist; studied chemical bonds; campaigned for nuclear disarmament.
Jean Piaget, 1896-1980, (Swiss) psychologist; four-stage theory of intellectual development in children.
Max Planck, 1858-1947, (Ger.) physicist; introduced quantum hypothesis (1900).
Walter S. Reed, 1851-1902, (U.S.) army physician; proved mosquitoes transmit yellow fever.
Theodor Reik, 1888-1969, (Austrian-U.S.) psychoanalyst, major Freudian disciple.
Bernhard Riemann, 1826-66, (Ger.) mathematician; developed non-Euclidean geometry used by Einstein.
Wilhelm Roentgen, 1845-1923, (Ger.) physicist; discovered X-rays (1895).
Carl Rogers, 1902-87, (U.S.) psychotherapist, author; originated nondirective therapy.
Ernest Rutherford, 1871-1937, (Br.) physicist; pioneer investigator of radioactivity, identified the atomic nucleus.
Albert B. Sabin, 1906-93, (Russ.-U.S.), developed oral polio live-virus vaccine.
Carl Sagan, 1934-96, (U.S.) astronomer, author.
Jonas Salk, 1914-95, (U.S.) developed first successful polio vaccine, widely used in U.S. after 1955.
Giovanni Schiaparelli, 1835-1910, (It.) astronomer; reported canals on Mars.
Erwin Schrödinger, 1887-1961, (Austrian) physicist; developed wave equation for quantum systems.
Glenn T. Seaborg, 1912-99, (U.S.) chemist, Nobel Prize winner (1951); codiscoverer of plutonium.
Harlow Shapley, 1885-1972, (U.S.) astronomer; mapped galactic clusters and position of Sun in our own galaxy.
B(urrhus) F(rederick) Skinner, 1904-89, (U.S.) psychologist; leading advocate of behaviorism.
Roger W. Sperry, 1913-94, (U.S.) neuorobiologist; established different functions of right and left sides of brain.
Benjamin Spock, 1903-98, (U.S.) pediatrician, child care expert; *Common Sense Book of Baby and Child Care.*
Charles P. Steinmetz, 1865-1923, (Ger.-U.S.) electrical engineer; developed basic ideas on alternating current.

Leo Szilard, 1898-1964, (Hung.-U.S.) physicist; helped on Manhattan project, later opposed nuclear weapons.
Nikola Tesla, 1856-1943, (Serb.-U.S.) invented a number of electrical devices including a.c. dynamos, transformers and motors.
William Thomson (Lord Kelvin), 1824-1907, (Br.) physicist; aided in success of transatlantic telegraph cable (1865); proposed Kelvin absolute temperature scale.
Alan Turing, 1912-54, (Br.) mathematician; helped develop basis for computers.
Rudolf Virchow, 1821-1902, (Ger.) pathologist; pioneered the modern theory that diseases affect the body through cells.
Alessandro Volta, 1745-1827, (It.) physicist; electricity pioneer.
Werner von Braun, 1912-77, (Ger.-U.S.) developed rockets for warfare and space exploration.
John Von Neumann, 1903-57, (Hung.-U.S.) mathematician; originated game theory; basic design for modern computers.
Alfred Russell Wallace, 1823-1913, (Br.) naturalist; proposed concept of evolution independently of Darwin.
John B. Watson, 1878-1958, (U.S.) psychologist; a founder of behaviorism.
James E. Watt, 1736-1819, (Br.) mechanical engineer, inventor; invented modern steam engine (1765).
Alfred L. Wegener, 1880-1930, (Ger.) meteorologist, geophysicist; postulated continental drift.
Norbert Wiener, 1894-1964, (U.S.) mathematician; founder of cybernetics.
Sewall Wright, 1889-1988, (U.S.) evolutionary theorist; helped found population genetics.
Wilhelm Wundt, 1832-1920, (Ger.) founder of experimental psychology.
Ferdinand von Zeppelin, 1838-1917, (Ger.) soldier, aeronaut, airship designer.

Social Reformers, Activists, and Humanitarians of the Past

Jane Addams, 1860-1935, (U.S.) cofounder of Hull House; won Nobel Peace Prize, 1931.
Susan B. Anthony, 1820-1906, (U.S.) a leader in temperance, anti-slavery, and woman suffrage movements.
Thomas Barnardo, 1845-1905, (Br.) social reformer; pioneered in care of destitute children.
Clara Barton, 1821-1912, (U.S.) organized American Red Cross.
Henry Ward Beecher, 1813-87, (U.S.) clergyman, abolitionist.
Amelia Bloomer, 1818-94, (U.S.) suffragette, social reformer.
William Booth, 1829-1912, (Br.) founded Salvation Army.
John Brown, 1800-59, (U.S.) abolitionist who led murder of 5 pro-slavery men, was hanged.
Frances Xavier (Mother) Cabrini, 1850-1917, (It.-U.S.) Italian-born nun; founded charitable institutions; first American canonized as a saint, 1946.
Carrie Chapman Catt, 1859-1947, (U.S.) suffragette.
Cesar Chavez, 1927-93, (U.S.) labor leader; helped establish United Farm Workers of America.
Clarence Darrow, 1857-1938, (U.S.) lawyer; defender of "underdog," opponent of capital punishment.
Dorothy Day, 1897-1980, (U.S.) founder of Catholic Worker movement.
Eugene V. Debs, 1855-1926, (U.S.) labor leader; led Pullman strike, 1894; 4-time Socialist presidential candidate.
Dorothea Dix, 1802-87, (U.S.) crusader for mentally ill.
Thomas Dooley, 1927-61, (U.S.) "jungle doctor," noted for efforts to supply medical aid to developing countries.
Marjory Stoneman Douglas, 1890-1998, (U.S.) writer and environmentalist; campaigned to save Florida Everglades.
William Lloyd Garrison, 1805-79, (U.S.) abolitionist.
Emma Goldman, 1869-1940, (Russ.-U.S.) published anarchist *Mother Earth,* birth-control advocate.
Samuel Gompers, 1850-1924, (U.S.) labor leader.
Michael Harrington, 1928-89, (U.S.) exposed poverty in affluent U.S. in *The Other America,* 1963.
Sidney Hillman, 1887-1946, (U.S.) labor leader; helped organize CIO.
Samuel G. Howe, 1801-76, (U.S.) social reformer; changed public attitudes toward the handicapped.
Helen Keller, 1880-1968, (U.S.) crusader for better treatment for the handicapped; deaf and blind herself.
Maggie Kuhn, 1905-95, (U.S.) founded Gray Panthers, 1970.
William Kunstler, 1919-95, (U.S.) civil liberties attorney.
John L. Lewis, 1880-1969, (U.S.) labor leader; headed United Mine Workers, 1920-60.
Karl Menninger, 1893-1990, (U.S.) with brother William founded Menninger Clinic and Menninger Foundation.
Lucretia Mott, 1793-1880, (U.S.) reformer, pioneer feminist.
Philip Murray, 1886-1952, (U.S.) Scottish-born labor leader.
Florence Nightingale, 1820-1910, (Br.) founder of modern nursing.
Emmeline Pankhurst, 1858-1928, (Br.) woman suffragist.
Walter Reuther, 1907-70, (U.S.) labor leader; headed UAW.
Jacob Riis, 1849-1914, (U.S.) crusader for urban reforms.
Margaret Sanger, 1883-1966, (U.S.) social reformer; pioneered the birth-control movement.
Earl of Shaftesbury (A. A. Cooper), 1801-85, (Br.) social reformer.
Elizabeth Cady Stanton, 1815-1902, (U.S.) woman suffrage pioneer.
Lucy Stone, 1818-93, (U.S.) feminist, abolitionist.
Mother Teresa of Calcutta, 1910-97, (Alban.) nun; founded order to care for sick, dying poor; 1979 Nobel Peace Prize.
Philip Vera Cruz, 1905-94, (Filipino-U.S.) helped to found the United Farm Workers Union.
William Wilberforce, 1759-1833, (Br.) social reformer; prominent in struggle to abolish the slave trade.
Frances E. Willard, 1839-98, (U.S.) temperance, women's rights leader.
Mary Wollstonecraft, 1759-97, (Br.) wrote *Vindication of the Rights of Women.*

Writers of the Present

Name (Birthplace)	Birthdate
Chinua Achebe (Ogidi, Nigeria)	11/16/30
Richard Adams (Newbury, Eng.)	5/10/20
Edward Albee (Wash., DC)	3/12/28
Isabel Allende (Chile)	8/2/42
Martin Amis (Oxford, Eng.)	8/25/49
Maya Angelou (St. Louis, MO)	4/4/28
Piers Anthony (Oxford, Eng.)	8/6/34
Jeffrey Archer (Somerset, Eng.)	4/15/40
Oscar Arias Sanchez (Heredia, Costa Rica)	9/13/41
John Ashbery (Rochester, NY)	1927
Margaret Atwood (Ottawa, Ont.)	11/18/39
David Auburn (Chicago, IL)	1969
Louis Auchincloss (Lawrence, NY)	9/27/17
Paul Auster (Newark, NJ)	2/3/47
Russell Banks (Newton, MA)	3/28/40
John Barth (Cambridge, MD)	5/27/30
Ann Beattie (Wash., DC)	9/7/47
Saul Bellow (Lachine, Que.)	6/10/15
Peter Benchley (NYC)	5/8/40
John Berendt (Syracuse, NY)	12/5/39
Thomas Berger (Cincinnati, OH)	7/20/24
Judy Blume (Elizabeth, NJ)	2/12/38
T. Coraghessan Boyle (Peekskill, NY)	12/2/47
Ray Bradbury (Waukegan, IL)	8/22/20
Barbara Taylor Bradford (Leeds, Eng.)	5/10/33
Rita Mae Brown (Hanover, PA)	11/28/44
Christopher Buckley (NYC)	1952
A. S. Byatt (Sheffield, England)	8/24/36
Hortense Calisher (NYC)	12/20/11
Ethan Canin (Ann Arbor, MI)	7/19/60
Michael Chabon (Washington, DC)	1963
Sandra Cisneros (Chicago, IL)	12/20/54
Tom Clancy (Baltimore, MD)	4/12/47
Mary Higgins Clark (NYC)	12/24/31
Arthur C. Clarke (Minehead, Eng.)	12/16/17
Beverly Cleary (McMinnville, OR)	4/12/16
Billy Collins (NYC)	1941
Jackie Collins (London, Eng.)	10/4/41?
Evan S. Connell (Kansas City, MO)	8/17/24
Pat Conroy (Atlanta, GA)	10/26/45
Robin Cook (NYC)	5/4/40
Patricia Cornwell (Miami, FL)	6/9/56
Harry Crews (Alma, GA)	6/6/35
Michael Crichton (Chicago, IL)	10/23/42
Michael Cunningham (Ohio)	1952
Don DeLillo (NYC)	11/20/36
Nelson DeMille (NYC)	8/23/43
Joan Didion (Sacramento, CA)	12/5/34
E. L. Doctorow (NYC)	1/6/31
Takako Doi (Hyogo, Jap.)	11/30/28
Rita Dove (Akron, OH)	8/28/52
Roddy Doyle (Dublin, Ireland)	5/58
John Gregory Dunne (Hartford, CT)	5/25/32
Umberto Eco (Alessandria, Italy)	1/5/32
Bret Easton Ellis (Los Angeles, CA)	1964
James Ellroy (Los Angeles)	3/4/48
Louise Erdrich (Little Falls, MN)	7/6/54
Laura Esquivel (Mexico City, Mexico)	1950
Howard Fast (NYC)	11/11/14
Ken Follet (Cardiff, Wales)	6/5/49

Name (Birthplace)	Birthdate
Dario Fo (San Giano, Italy)	3/26/26
Horton Foote (Wharton, TX)	3/14/16
Richard Ford (Jackson, MS)	2/16/44
Frederick Forsyth (Ashford, Eng.)	1938
John Fowles (Leigh-on-Sea, Eng.)	3/31/26
Paula Fox (NYC)	4/22/23
Dick Francis (Lawrenny, S. Wales)	10/31/20
Jonathan Franzen (Western Springs, IL)	8/17/59
Michael Frayn (London, Eng.)	9/8/33
Marilyn French (NYC)	11/21/29
Brian Friel (Omagh, Ire.)	11/9/29
Carlos Fuentes (Mexico City, Mex.)	11/11/28
Ernest J. Gaines (Oscar, LA)	1/15/33
Gabriel Garcia Marquez (Aracata, Colombia)	3/6/28
Frank Gilroy (NYC)	10/13/25
Gail Godwin (Birmingham, AL)	6/18/37
William Goldman (Chicago, IL)	8/12/31
Nadine Gordimer (Springs, S. Africa)	11/20/23
Mary Gordon (Long Island, NY)	12/8/49
Sue Grafton (Louisville, KY)	4/24/40
Günter Grass (Danzig, Ger.)	10/16/27
Shirley Ann Grau (New Orleans, LA)	7/8/29
John Grisham (Jonesboro, AR)	2/8/55
John Guare (NYC)	2/5/38
Arthur Hailey (Luton, Eng.)	4/5/20
David Hare (St. Leonards, Sussex, Eng.)	6/5/47
Robert Hass (San Francisco, CA)	3/1/41
Vaclav Havel (Prague, Czech.)	10/5/36
Seamus Heaney (N. Ireland)	1939
Mark Helprin (NYC)	6/28/47
Tony Hillerman (Sacred Heart, OK)	5/27/25
S. E. Hinton (Tulsa, OK)	1948
Alice Hoffman (NYC)	3/16/52
John Irving (Exeter, NH)	3/2/42
John Jakes (Chicago, IL)	3/31/32
P. D. James (Oxford, Eng.)	8/3/20
Erica Jong (NYC)	3/26/42
Garrison Keillor (Anoka, MN)	8/7/42
Thomas Keneally (Sydney, Austral.)	10/7/35
William Kennedy (Albany, NY)	1/16/28
Jamaica Kincaid (St. Johns, Antigua)	5/25/39
Stephen King (Portland, ME)	9/21/47
Barbara Kingsolver (Annapolis, MD)	4/8/55
Maxine Hong Kingston (Stockton, CA)	10/27/40
Galway Kinnell (Providence, RI)	2/1/27
Kenneth Koch (Cincinnati, OH)	2/27/25
Dean Koontz (Everett, PA)	7/9/45
Judith Krantz (NYC)	1/9/28
Maxine Kumin (Philadelphia, PA)	6/6/25
Milan Kundera (Brno, Czechoslovakia)	4/21/29
Tony Kushner (NYC)	1956
John Le Carré (Poole, Eng.)	10/19/31
Ursula K. Le Guin (Berkeley, CA)	10/21/29
Madeleine L'Engle (NYC)	11/29/18
Elmore Leonard (New Orleans, LA)	10/11/25
Doris Lessing (Kermanshah, Persia)	10/22/19
Ira Levin (NYC)	8/27/29
Alison Lurie (Chicago, IL)	9/3/26
Naguib Mahfouz (Cairo, Egypt)	12/11/11
Norman Mailer (Long Branch, NJ)	1/31/23
David Mamet (Chicago, IL)	11/30/47
Bobbie Ann Mason (nr. Mayfield, KY)	5/1/40
Peter Matthiessen (NYC)	5/22/27
Ed McBain (NYC)	10/15/26
Cormac McCarthy (Providence, RI)	7/20/33
Frank McCourt (Brooklyn, NY)	1930
Colleen McCullough (Wellington, N.S.W.)	6/1/37
Alice McDermot (NYC)	6/27/53
Ian McEwan (Aldershot, England)	6/21/48
Thomas McGuane (Wyandotte, MI)	12/11/39
Terry McMillan (Port Huron, MI)	10/18/51
Larry McMurtry (Wichita Falls, TX)	6/3/36

Name (Birthplace)	Birthdate
John McPhee (Princeton, NJ)	3/8/31
Arthur Miller (NYC)	10/17/15
Czeslaw Milosz (Seteiniai, Lithuania)	6/30/11
Toni Morrison (Lorain, OH)	2/18/31
Walter Mosley (Los Angeles, CA)	1952
Alice Munro (Wingham, Ont.)	7/10/31
Haruki Murakami (Kyoto, Japan)	1/12/49
V. S. Naipaul (Port-of-Spain, Trin.)	8/17/32
Joyce Carol Oates (Lockport, NY)	6/16/38
Edna O'Brien (Tuamgraney, Ir.)	12/15/30
Tim O'Brien (Austin, MN)	10/1/46
Kenzaburo Oe (Ose, Shikoku, Japan)	1/31/35
Cynthia Ozick (NYC)	4/17/28
Grace Paley (NYC)	12/11/22
Suzan-Lori Parks (Fort Knox, KY)	1963
Marge Piercy (Detroit, MI)	3/31/36
Robert Pinsky (Long Branch, NJ)	10/20/40
Harold Pinter (London, Eng.)	10/10/30
Reynolds Price (Macon, NC)	2/1/33
Richard Price (NYC)	10/12/49
E. Annie Proulx (Norwich, CT)	8/22/35
Thomas Pynchon (Glen Cove, NY)	5/8/37
David Rabe (Dubuque, IA)	3/10/40
Ishmael Reed (Chattanooga, TN)	2/22/38
Ruth Rendell (England)	2/17/30
Anne Rice (New Orleans, LA)	10/14/41
Adrienne Rich (Baltimore, MD)	5/16/29
Nora Roberts (Washington, DC)	10/10/50
Philip Roth (Newark, NJ)	3/19/33
J.K. Rowling (Bristol, Eng.)	7/31/66
Salman Rushdie (Bombay, India)	6/19/47
Richard Russo (Johnstown, NY)	7/15/49
J. D. Salinger (NYC)	1/1/19
Jose Saramago (Azinhaga, Portugal)	1922
David Sedaris (Binghamton, NY)	12/26/56
Vikram Seth (Calcutta, India)	6/20/52
Sidney Sheldon (Chicago, IL)	2/11/17
Sam Shepard (Ft. Sheridan, IL)	11/5/43
Carol Shields (Oak Park, IL)	6/2/35
Claude Simon (Tananarive, Madagascar)	1913
Neil Simon (NYC)	7/4/27
Jane Smiley (Los Angeles, CA)	9/26/49
Aleksandr Solzhenitsyn (Kislovodsk, Russia)	12/11/18
Susan Sontag (NYC)	1/16/33
Wole Soyinka (Abeokuta, Nigeria)	7/13/34
Mickey Spillane (Brooklyn, NY)	3/9/18
Danielle Steel (NYC)	8/14/47
Richard Stern (NYC)	2/25/28
Mary Stewart (Sunderland, Eng.)	9/17/16
Tom Stoppard (Zlin, Czech.)	7/13/37
William Styron (Newport News, VA)	6/11/25
Wislawa Szymborska (Kornik, Poland)	7/2/23
Amy Tan (Oakland, CA)	2/19/52
Paul Theroux (Medford, MA)	4/10/41
Scott F. Turow (Chicago, IL)	4/2/49
Anne Tyler (Minneapolis, MN)	10/25/41
John Updike (Shillington, PA)	3/18/32
Leon Uris (Baltimore, MD)	8/3/24
Mario Vargas Llosa (Arequipa, Peru)	3/28/36
Gore Vidal (West Point, NY)	10/3/25
Paula Vogel (Wash., DC)	11/16/51
Kurt Vonnegut Jr. (Indianapolis, IN)	11/11/22
Derek Walcott (Castries, Saint Lucia)	1930
Alice Walker (Eatonton, GA)	2/9/44
Robert James Waller (Rockford, IA)	8/1/39
Joseph Wambaugh (East Pittsburgh, PA)	1/22/37
Wendy Wasserstein (NYC)	10/18/50
August Wilson (Pittsburgh, PA)	4/27/45
Lanford Wilson (Lebanon, MO)	4/13/37
Tom Wolfe (Richmond, VA)	3/2/31
Tobias Wolff (Birmingham, AL)	6/19/45
Herman Wouk (NYC)	5/27/15

Writers of the Past

See also Journalists of the Past, and Greeks and Romans in Historical Figures chapter.

Alice Adams, 1926-99, (U.S.) novelist, short-story writer. *Superior Woman.*

James Agee, 1909-55, (U.S.) novelist. *A Death in the Family.*

Conrad Aiken, 1889-1973, (U.S.) poet, critic. *Ushant.*

Louisa May Alcott, 1832-88, (U.S.) novelist. *Little Women.*

Sholom Aleichem, 1859-1916, (Russ.) Yiddish writer. *Tevye's Daughter, The Old Country.*

Vicente Aleixandre, 1898-1984, (Sp.) poet. *La destrucción o el amor, Dialogolos del conocimiento.*

Horatio Alger, 1832-1899, (U.S.) "rags-to-riches" books.

Jorge Amado, 1912-2001, (Brazil) novelist. *Dona Flor and Her Two Husbands, The Violent Land.*

Eric Ambler, 1909-98, (Br.) suspense novelist. *A Coffin for Dimitrios.*

Kingsley Amis, 1922-95, (Br.) novelist, critic. *Lucky Jim.*

Hans Christian Andersen, 1805-75, (Dan.) author of fairy tales. *The Ugly Duckling.*

Maxwell Anderson, 1888-1959, (U.S.) playwright. *What Price Glory?, High Tor, Winterset, Key Largo.*

Sherwood Anderson, 1876-1941, (U.S.) short-story writer. "Death in the Woods;" *Winesburg, Ohio.*

Reinaldo Arenas, 1943-1990, (Cuba) short-story writer, novelist. *Before Night Falls.*

Ludovico Ariosto, 1474-1533, (It.) poet. *Orlando Furioso.*

Matthew Arnold, 1822-88, (Br.) poet, critic. "Thrysis," "Dover Beach," "Culture and Anarchy."
Isaac Asimov, 1920-92, (U.S.) versatile writer, espec. of science-fiction. *I Robot.*
Miguel Angel Asturias, 1899-1974, (Guatemala) novelist. *El Señor Presidente.*
W(ystan) H(ugh) Auden, 1907-73, (Br.) poet, playwright, literary critic. "The Age of Anxiety."
Jane Austen, 1775-1817, (Br.) novelist. *Pride and Prejudice, Sense and Sensibility, Emma, Mansfield Park.*
Isaac Babel, 1894-1941, (Russ.) short-story writer, playwright. *Odessa Tales, Red Cavalry.*
James Baldwin, 1924-87, author, playwright. *The Fire Next Time, Blues for Mister Charlie.*
Honoré de Balzac, 1799-1850, (Fr.) novelist. *Le Père Goriot, Cousine Bette, Eugénie Grandet.*
James M. Barrie, 1860-1937, (Br.) playwright, novelist. *Peter Pan, Dear Brutus, What Every Woman Knows.*
Charles Baudelaire, 1821-67, (Fr.) poet. *Les Fleurs du Mal.*
L(yman) Frank Baum, 1856-1919, (U.S.) *Wizard of Oz* series.
Simone de Beauvoir, 1908-86, (Fr.) novelist, essayist. *The Second Sex, Memoirs of a Dutiful Daughter.*
Samuel Beckett, 1906-89, (Ir.) novelist, playwright. *Waiting for Godot, Endgame* (plays); *Murphy, Watt, Molloy* (novels).
Brendan Behan, 1923-64, (Ir.) playwright. *The Quare Fellow, The Hostage, Borstal Boy.*
Robert Benchley, 1889-1945, (U.S.) humorist.
Stephen Vincent Benét, 1898-1943, (U.S.) poet, novelist. *John Brown's Body.*
John Berryman, 1914-72, (U.S.) poet. *Homage to Mistress Bradstreet.*
Ambrose Bierce, 1842-1914, (U.S.) short-story writer, journalist. *In the Midst of Life, The Devil's Dictionary.*
Elizabeth Bishop, 1911-79, (U.S.) poet. *North and South—A Cold Spring.*
William Blake, 1757-1827, (Br.) poet, artist. *Songs of Innocence, Songs of Experience.*
Giovanni Boccaccio, 1313-75, (It.) poet. *Decameron.*
Heinrich Böll, 1917-85, (Ger.) novelist, short-story writer. *Group Portrait With Lady.*
Jorge Luis Borges, 1900-86, (Arg.) short-story writer, poet, essayist. *Labyrinths.*
James Boswell, 1740-95, (Sc.) biographer. *The Life of Samuel Johnson.*
Pierre Boulle, (1913-94), (Fr.) novelist. *The Bridge Over the River Kwai, Planet of the Apes.*
Paul Bowles, 1910-99, (U.S.) novelist, short-story writer. The Sheltering Sky
Anne Bradstreet, c1612-72, (U.S.) poet. *The Tenth Muse Lately Sprung Up in America.*
Bertolt Brecht, 1898-1956, (Ger.) dramatist, poet. *The Threepenny Opera, Mother Courage and Her Children.*
Charlotte Brontë, 1816-55, (Br.) novelist. *Jane Eyre.*
Emily Brontë, 1818-48, (Br.) novelist. *Wuthering Heights.*
Elizabeth Barrett Browning, 1806-61, (Br.) poet. *Sonnets From the Portuguese, Aurora Leigh.*
Joseph Brodsky, 1940-96, (Russ.-U.S.) poet. *A Part of Speech, Less Than One, To Urania.*
Robert Browning, 1812-89, (Br.) poet. "My Last Duchess," "Fra Lippo Lippi," *The Ring and The Book.*
Pearl S. Buck, 1892-1973, (U.S.) novelist. *The Good Earth.*
Mikhail Bulgakov, 1891-1940, (Russ.) novelist, playwright. *The Heart of a Dog, The Master and Margarita.*
John Bunyan, 1628-88, (Br.) writer. *Pilgrim's Progress.*
Anthony Burgess, 1917-93, (Br.) author. *A Clockwork Orange.*
Frances Hodgson Burnett, 1849-1924, (Br.-U.S.) novelist. *The Secret Garden.*
Robert Burns, 1759-96, (Sc.) poet. "Flow Gently, Sweet Afton," "My Heart's in the Highlands," "Auld Lang Syne."
Edgar Rice Burroughs, 1875-1950, (U.S.) "Tarzan" books.
William S. Burroughs, 1914-97, (U.S.) novelist. *Naked Lunch.*
George Gordon, Lord Byron, 1788-1824, (Br.) poet. *Don Juan, Childe Harold, Manfred, Cain.*
Italo Calvino, 1923-85, (It.) novelist, short-story writer. *If on a Winter's Night a Traveler.*
Luis Vaz de Camoes, 1524?-80 (Port.) poet. *The Lusiads.*
Albert Camus, 1913-60, (Fr.) writer. *The Stranger, The Fall.*
Karel Capek, 1890-1938, (Czech.) playwright, novelist, essayist. *R.U.R. (Rossum's Universal Robots).*
Truman Capote, 1924-84, (U.S.) author. *Other Voices, Other Rooms, Breakfast at Tiffany's, In Cold Blood.*
Lewis Carroll (Charles Dodgson), 1832-98, (Br.) writer, mathematician. *Alice's Adventures in Wonderland.*
Giacomo Casanova, 1725-98, (It.) adventurer, memoirist.
Willa Cather, 1873-1947, (U.S.) novelist. *O Pioneers!, My Ántonia, Death Comes for the Archbishop.*
Camilo Jose Cela, 1916-2001, (Sp.) novelist. *The Family of Pascual Duarte, The Hive.*
Miguel de Cervantes Saavedra, 1547-1616, (Sp.) novelist, dramatist, poet. *Don Quixote.*
Raymond Chandler, 1888-1959, (U.S.) writer of detective fiction. Philip Marlowe series.
Geoffrey Chaucer, c1340-1400, (Br.) poet. *The Canterbury Tales, Troilus and Criseyde.*
John Cheever, 1912-82, (U.S.) novelist, short-story writer. *The Wapshot Scandal,* "The Country Husband."
Anton Chekhov, 1860-1904, (Russ.) short-story writer, dramatist. *Uncle Vanya, The Cherry Orchard, The Three Sisters.*
G(ilbert) K(eith) Chesterton, 1874-1936, (Br.) critic, novelist, relig. apologist. Father Brown series of mysteries.
Kate Chopin, 1851-1904, (U.S.) writer. *The Awakening.*
Agatha Christie, 1890-1976, (Br.) mystery writer; created Miss Marple, Hercule Poirot; *And Then There Were None., Murder on the Orient Express, Murder of Roger Ackroyd.*
James Clavell, 1924-94, (Br.-U.S.) novelist. *Shogun, King Rat.*
Jean Cocteau, 1889-1963, (Fr.) writer, visual artist, filmmaker. *The Beauty and the Beast, Les Enfants Terribles.*
Samuel Taylor Coleridge, 1772-1834, (Br.) poet, critic. "Kubla Khan," "The Rime of the Ancient Mariner."
(Sidonie) Colette, 1873-1954, (Fr.) novelist. *Claudine, Gigi.*
Wilkie Collins, 1824-89, (Br.) Novelist. *The Moonstone.*
Joseph Conrad, 1857-1924, (Br.) novelist. *Lord Jim, Heart of Darkness, The Nigger of the Narcissus.*
James Fenimore Cooper, 1789-1851, (U.S.) novelist. *Leatherstocking Tales, The Last of the Mohicans.*
Pierre Corneille, 1606-84, (Fr.) dramatist. *Medeé, Le Cid.*
Hart Crane, 1899-1932, (U.S.) poet. "The Bridge."
Stephen Crane, 1871-1900, (U.S.) novelist, short-story writer. *The Red Badge of Courage,* "The Open Boat."
E. E. Cummings, 1894-1962, (U.S.) poet. *Tulips and Chimneys.*
Roald Dahl, 1916-90, (Br.-U.S.) writer. *Charlie and the Chocolate Factory, James and the Giant Peach.*
Gabriele D'Annunzio, 1863-1938, (It.) poet, novelist, dramatist. *The Child of Pleasure, The Intruder, The Victim.*
Dante Alighieri, 1265-1321, (It.) poet. *The Divine Comedy.*
Robertson Davies, 1913-95, (Can.) novelist, playwright, essayist. Salterton, Deptford, and Cornish trilogies.
Daniel Defoe, 1660-1731, (Br.) writer. *Robinson Crusoe, Moll Flanders, Journal of the Plague Year.*
Charles Dickens, 1812-70, (Br.) novelist. *David Copperfield, Oliver Twist, Great Expectations, A Tale of Two Cities.*
James Dickey, 1923-1997, (U.S.) poet, novelist. *Deliverance.*
Emily Dickinson, 1830-86, (U.S.) lyric poet. "Because I could not stop for Death . . .," "Success is counted sweetest . . ."
Isak Dinesen (Karen Blixen), 1885-1962, (Dan.) author. *Out of Africa, Seven Gothic Tales, Winter's Tales.*
John Donne, 1573-1631, (Br.) poet, divine. *Songs and Sonnets.*
José Donoso, 1924-96, (Chil.) surreal novelist and short-story writer. *The Obscene Bird of Night.*
John Dos Passos, 1896-1970, (U.S.) novelist. *U.S.A.*
Fyodor Dostoyevsky, 1821-81, (Russ.) novelist. *Crime and Punishment, The Brothers Karamazov, The Possessed.*
Arthur Conan Doyle, 1859-1930, (Br.) novelist. Sherlock Holmes mystery stories.
Theodore Dreiser, 1871-1945, (U.S.) novelist. *An American Tragedy, Sister Carrie.*
John Dryden, 1631-1700, (Br.) poet, dramatist, critic. *All for Love, Mac Flecknoe, Absalom and Achitophel.*
Alexandre Dumas, 1802-70, (Fr.) novelist, dramatist. *The Three Musketeers, The Count of Monte Cristo.*
Alexandre Dumas (fils), 1824-95, (Fr.) dramatist, novelist. *La Dame aux Camélias, Le Demi-Monde.*
Lawrence Durrell, 1912-90, (Br.) novelist, poet. *Alexandria Quartet.*
Ilya G. Ehrenburg, 1891-1967, (Russ.) writer. *The Thaw.*
George Eliot (Mary Ann Evans or Marian Evans), 1819-80, (Br.) novelist. *Silas Marner, Middlemarch.*
T(homas) S(tearns) Eliot, 1888-1965, (Br.) poet, critic. *The Waste Land,* "The Love Song of J. Alfred Prufrock."
Stanley Elkin, 1930-95, (U.S.) novelist, short story writer. *George Mills.*
Ralph Ellison, 1914-94, (U.S.), writer. *Invisible Man.*
Ralph Waldo Emerson, 1803-82, (U.S.) poet, essayist. "Brahma," "Nature," "The Over-Soul," "Self-Reliance."
James T. Farrell, 1904-79, (U.S.) novelist. *Studs Lonigan.*
William Faulkner, 1897-1962, (U.S.) novelist. *Sanctuary, Light in August, The Sound and the Fury, Absalom, Absalom!*
Edna Ferber, 1887-1968, (U.S.) novelist, short-story writer, playwright. *So Big, Cimarron, Show Boat.*
Henry Fielding, 1707-54, (Br.) novelist. *Tom Jones.*
F(rancis) Scott Fitzgerald, 1896-1940, (U.S.) short-story writer, novelist. *The Great Gatsby, Tender Is the Night.*
Gustave Flaubert, 1821-80, (Fr.) novelist. *Madame Bovary.*
Ian Fleming, 1908-64, (Br.) novelist; James Bond spy thrillers.
Ford Madox Ford, 1873-1939, (Br.) novelist, critic, poet. *The Good Soldier.*
C(ecil) S(cott) Forester, 1899-1966, (Br.) writer. Horatio Hornblower books.

E(dward) M(organ) Forster, 1879-1970, (Br.) novelist. *A Passage to India, Howards End.*
Anatole France, 1844-1924, (Fr.) writer. *Penguin Island, My Friend's Book, The Crime of Sylvestre Bonnard.*
Robert Frost, 1874-1963, (U.S.) poet. "Birches," "Fire and Ice," "Stopping by Woods on a Snowy Evening."
William Gaddis, 1922-98, (U.S.) novelist. *The Recognitions.*
John Galsworthy, 1867-1933, (Br.) novelist, dramatist. *The Forsyte Saga.*
Erle Stanley Gardner, 1889-1970, (U.S.) mystery writer; created Perry Mason.
Jean Genet, 1911-86, (Fr.) playwright, novelist. *The Maids.*
Kahlil Gibran, 1883-1931, (Lebanese-U.S.) mystical novelist, essayist, poet. *The Prophet.*
André Gide, 1869-1951, (Fr.) writer. *The Immoralist, The Pastoral Symphony, Strait Is the Gate.*
Allen Ginsberg, 1926-1997, (U.S.) Beat poet. "Howl."
Jean Giraudoux, 1882-1944, (Fr.) novelist, dramatist. *Electra, The Madwoman of Chaillot, Ondine, Tiger at the Gate.*
Johann Wolfgang von Goethe, 1749-1832, (Ger.) poet, dramatist, novelist. *Faust, Sorrows of Young Werther.*
Nikolai Gogol, 1809-52, (Russ.) short-story writer, dramatist, novelist. *Dead Souls, The Inspector General.*
William Golding, 1911-93, (Br.) novelist. *Lord of the Flies.*
Oliver Goldsmith, 1728-74, (Br.-Ir.) dramatist, novelist. *The Vicar of Wakefield, She Stoops to Conquer.*
Maxim Gorky, 1868-1936, (Russ.) dramatist, novelist. *The Lower Depths.*
Robert Graves, 1895-1985, (Br.) poet, classical scholar, novelist. *I, Claudius; The White Goddess.*
Thomas Gray, 1716-71, (Br.) poet. "Elegy Written in a Country Churchyard," "The Progress of Poesy."
Julien Green, 1900-98, (U.S.-Fr.) expatriate American, French novelist. *Moira, Each Man in His Darkness.*
Graham Greene, 1904-91, (Br.) novelist. *The Power and the Glory, The Heart of the Matter, The Ministry of Fear.*
Zane Grey, 1872-1939, (U.S.) writer of Western stories.
Jakob Grimm, 1785-1863, (Ger.) philologist, folklorist; with brother **Wilhelm,** 1786-1859, collected *Grimm's Fairy Tales.*
Alex Haley, 1921-92, (U.S.) author. *Roots.*
Dashiell Hammett, 1894-1961, (U.S.) detective-story writer; created Sam Spade. *The Maltese Falcon, The Thin Man.*
Knut Hamsun, 1859-1952 (Nor.) novelist. *Hunger.*
Thomas Hardy, 1840-1928, (Br.) novelist, poet. *The Return of the Native, Tess of the D'Urbervilles, Jude the Obscure.*
Joel Chandler Harris, 1848-1908, (U.S.) Uncle Remus stories.
Moss Hart, 1904-61, (U.S.) playwright. *Once in a Lifetime, You Can't Take It With You, The Man Who Came to Dinner.*
Bret Harte, 1836-1902, (U.S.) short-story writer, poet. *The Luck of Roaring Camp.*
Jaroslav Hasek, 1883-1923, (Czech.) writer, playwright. *The Good Soldier Schweik.*
John Hawkes, 1925-98, (U.S.) experimental fiction writer. *The Goose on the Grave, Blood Oranges.*
Nathaniel Hawthorne, 1804-64, (U.S.) novelist, short-story writer. *The Scarlet Letter,* "Young Goodman Brown."
Heinrich Heine, 1797-1856, (Ger.) poet. *Book of Songs.*
Joseph Heller, 1923-99, (U.S.) novelist. Catch-22.
Lillian Hellman, 1905-84, (U.S.) playwright, author of memoirs. *The Little Foxes, An Unfinished Woman, Pentimento.*
Ernest Hemingway, 1899-1961, (U.S.) novelist, short-story writer. *A Farewell to Arms, For Whom the Bell Tolls.*
O. Henry (W. S. Porter), 1862-1910, (U.S.) short-story writer. "The Gift of the Magi."
George Herbert, 1593-1633, (Br.) poet. "The Altar," "Easter Wings."
Zbigniew Herbert, 1924-98, (Pol.) poet. "Apollo and Marsyas."
Robert Herrick, 1591-1674, (Br.) poet. "To the Virgins to Make Much of Time."
James Herriot (James Alfred Wight), 1916-95, (Br.) novelist, veterinarian. *All Creatures Great and Small.*
John Hersey, 1914-93, (U.S.) novelist, journalist. *Hiroshima, A Bell for Adano.*
Hermann Hesse, 1877-1962, (Ger.) novelist, poet. *Death and the Lover, Steppenwolf, Siddhartha.*
James Hilton, 1900-54, (Br.) novelist. *Lost Horizon.*
Oliver Wendell Holmes, 1809-94, (U.S.) poet, novelist. *The Autocrat of the Breakfast-Table.*
Gerard Manley Hopkins, 1844-89, (Br.) poet. "Pied Beauty."
A(lfred) E. Housman, 1859-1936, (Br.) poet. *A Shropshire Lad.*
William Dean Howells, 1837-1920, (U.S.) novelist, critic. *The Rise of Silas Lapham.*
Langston Hughes, 1902-67, (U.S.) poet, playwright. *The Weary Blues, One-Way Ticket, Shakespeare in Harlem.*
Ted Hughes, 1930-98, (Br.) British poet laureate, 1984-98. *Crow, The Hawk in the Rain.*
Victor Hugo, 1802-85, (Fr.) poet, dramatist, novelist. *Notre Dame de Paris, Les Misérables.*
Zora Neale Hurston, 1903-60, (U.S.) novelist, folklorist. *Their Eyes Were Watching God, Mules and Men.*
Aldous Huxley, 1894-1963, (Br.) writer. *Brave New World.*
Henrik Ibsen, 1828-1906, (Nor.) dramatist, poet. *A Doll's House, Ghosts, The Wild Duck, Hedda Gabler.*
William Inge, 1913-73, (U.S.) playwright. *Picnic; Come Back, Little Sheba; Bus Stop.*
Eugene Ionesco, 1910-94, (Fr.) surrealist dramatist. *The Bald Soprano, The Chairs.*
Washington Irving, 1783-1859, (U.S.) writer. "Rip Van Winkle," "The Legend of Sleepy Hollow."
Christopher Isherwood, 1904-1986, (Br.) novelist, playwright. *The Berlin Stories.*
Shirley Jackson, 1919-65, (U.S.) writer. "The Lottery."
Henry James, 1843-1916, (U.S.) novelist, short-story writer, critic. *The Portrait of a Lady, The Ambassadors, Daisy Miller.*
Robinson Jeffers, 1887-1962, (U.S.) poet, dramatist. *Tamar and Other Poems, Medea.*
Samuel Johnson, 1709-84, (Br.) author, scholar, critic. *Dictionary of the English Language, Vanity of Human Wishes.*
Ben Jonson, 1572-1637, (Br.) dramatist, poet. *Volpone.*
James Joyce, 1882-1941, (Ir.) writer. *Ulysses, Dubliners, A Portrait of the Artist as a Young Man, Finnegans Wake.*
Ernst Junger, 1895-1998, (Ger.) novelist, essayist. *The Peace, On the Marble Cliff.*
Franz Kafka, 1883-1924, (Ger.) novelist, short-story writer. *The Trial, The Castle, The Metamorphosis.*
George S. Kaufman, 1889-1961, (U.S.) playwright. *The Man Who Came to Dinner, You Can't Take It With You, Stage Door.*
Nikos Kazantzakis, 1883-1957, (Gk.) novelist. *Zorba the Greek, A Greek Passion.*
Alfred Kazin, 1915-98 (U.S.) author, critic, teacher. *On Native Grounds.*
John Keats, 1795-1821, (Br.) poet. "Ode on a Grecian Urn," "Ode to a Nightingale," "La Belle Dame Sans Merci."
Jack Kerouac, 1922-1969, (U.S.), author, Beat poet. *On the Road, The Dharma Bums,* "Mexico City Blues."
Joyce Kilmer, 1886-1918, (U.S.) poet. "Trees."
Rudyard Kipling, 1865-1936, (Br.) author, poet. "The White Man's Burden," "Gunga Din," *The Jungle Book.*
Jean de la Fontaine, 1621-95, (Fr.) poet. *Fables choisies.*
Pär Lagerkvist, 1891-1974, (Swed.) poet, dramatist, novelist. *Barabbas, The Sybil.*
Selma Lagerlöf, 1858-1940, (Swed.) novelist. *Jerusalem, The Ring of the Lowenskolds.*
Alphonse de Lamartine, 1790-1869, (Fr.) poet, novelist, statesman. *Méditations poétiques.*
Charles Lamb, 1775-1834, (Br.) essayist. *Specimens of English Dramatic Poets, Essays of Elia.*
Giuseppe di Lampedusa, 1896-1957, (It.) novelist. *The Leopard.*
William Langland, c1332-1400, (Eng.) poet. *Piers Plowman.*
Ring Lardner, 1885-1933, (U.S.) short-story writer, humorist.
Louis L'Amour, 1908-88, (U.S.) western author, screenwriter. *Hondo, The Cherokee Trail.*
D(avid) H(erbert) Lawrence, 1885-1930, (Br.) novelist. *Sons and Lovers, Women in Love, Lady Chatterley's Lover.*
Halldor Laxness, 1902-98, (Icelandic) novelist. *Iceland's Bell.*
Mikhail Lermontov, 1814-41, (Russ.) novelist, poet. "Demon," *Hero of Our Time.*
Alain-René Lesage, 1668-1747, (Fr.) novelist. *Gil Blas de Santillane.*
Gotthold Lessing, 1729-81, (Ger.) dramatist, philosopher, critic. *Miss Sara Sampson, Minna von Barnhelm.*
C(live) S(taples) Lewis, 1898-1963, (Br.) critic, novelist, religious writer. *Allegory of Love; The Lion, the Witch and the Wardrobe; Out of the Silent Planet.*
Sinclair Lewis, 1885-1951, (U.S.) novelist. *Babbitt, Main Street, Arrowsmith, Dodsworth.*
Vachel Lindsay, 1879-1931, (U.S.) poet. *General William Booth Enters Into Heaven, The Congo.*
Hugh Lofting, 1886-1947, (Br.) writer. Dr. Doolittle series.
Jack London, 1876-1916, (U.S.) novelist, journalist. *Call of the Wild, The Sea-Wolf, White Fang.*
Henry Wadsworth Longfellow, 1807-82, (U.S.) poet. *Evangeline, The Song of Hiawatha.*
Amy Lowell, 1874-1925, (U.S.) poet, critic. "Lilacs."
James Russell Lowell, 1819-91, (U.S.) poet, editor. *Poems, The Biglow Papers.*
Robert Lowell, 1917-77, (U.S.) poet. "Lord Weary's Castle."
Archibald MacLeish, 1892-1982, (U.S.) poet. *Conquistador.*
Bernard Malamud, 1914-86, (U.S.) short-story writer, novelist. "The Magic Barrel," *The Assistant, The Fixer.*
Stéphane Mallarmé, 1842-98, (Fr.) poet. *Poésies.*
Sir Thomas Malory, ?-1471, (Br.) writer. *Morte d'Arthur.*
Andre Malraux, 1901-76, (Fr.) novelist. *Man's Fate.*
Osip Mandelstam, 1891-1938, (Russ.) poet. *Stone, Tristia.*
Thomas Mann, 1875-1955, (Ger.) novelist, essayist. *Buddenbrooks, The Magic Mountain,* "Death in Venice."
Katherine Mansfield, 1888-1923, (Br.) short-story writer. "Bliss."

Christopher Marlowe, 1564-93, (Br.) dramatist, poet. *Tamburlaine the Great,* Dr. *Faustus, The Jew of Malta.*
Andrew Marvell, 1621-78, (Br.) poet. "To His Coy Mistress."
John Masefield, 1878-1967, (Br.) poet. "Sea Fever," "Cargoes," *Salt Water Ballads.*
Edgar Lee Masters, 1869-1950, (U.S.) poet, biographer. *Spoon River Anthology.*
W(illiam) Somerset Maugham, 1874-1965, (Br.) author. *Of Human* Bondage, *The Moon and Sixpence.*
Guy de Maupassant, 1850-93, (Fr.) novelist, short-story writer. "A Life," "Bel-Ami," "The Necklace."
François Mauriac, 1885-1970, (Fr.) novelist, dramatist. *Viper's Tangle, The Kiss to the Leper.*
Vladimir Mayakovsky, 1893-1930, (Russ.) poet, dramatist. *The Cloud in Trousers.*
Mary McCarthy, 1912-89, (U.S.) critic, novelist, memoirist. *Memories of a Catholic Girlhood.*
Carson McCullers, 1917-67, (U.S.) novelist. *The Heart Is a Lonely Hunter, Member of the Wedding.*
Herman Melville, 1819-91, (U.S.) novelist, poet. *Moby-Dick, Typee, Billy Budd, Omoo.*
George Meredith, 1828-1909, (Br.) novelist, poet. *The Ordeal of Richard Feverel, The Egoist.*
Prosper Mérimée, 1803-70, (Fr.) author. *Carmen.*
James Merrill, 1926-95, (U.S.) poet. *Divine Comedies.*
James Michener, 1907-97, (U.S.) novelist. *Tales of the South Pacific.*
Edna St. Vincent Millay, 1892-1950, (U.S.) poet. *The Harp Weaver and Other Poems.*
Henry Miller, 1891-1980, (U.S.) erotic novelist. *Tropic of Cancer.*
A(lan) A(lexander) Milne, 1882-1956, (Br.) author. *Winnie-the-Pooh.*
John Milton, 1608-74, (Br.) poet, writer. *Paradise Lost, Comus, Lycidas, Areopagitica.*
Mishima Yukio (Hiraoka Kimitake), 1925-70, (Jpn.) writer. *Confessions of a Mask.*
Gabriela Mistral, 1889-1957, (Chil.) poet. *Sonnets of Death.*
Margaret Mitchell, 1900-49, (U.S.) novelist. *Gone With the Wind.*
Jean Baptiste Molière, 1622-73, (Fr.) dramatist. *Le Tartuffe, Le Misanthrope, Le Bourgeois Gentilhomme.*
Ferenc Molnár, 1878-1952, (Hung.) dramatist, novelist. *Liliom, The Guardsman, The Swan.*
Michel de Montaigne, 1533-92, (Fr.) essayist. *Essais.*
Eugenio Montale, 1896-1981, (It.) poet.
Brian Moore, 1921-99, (Ir.-U.S.) novelist. *The Lonely Passion of Judith Hearne.*
Clement C. Moore, 1779-1863, (U.S.) poet, educator. "A Visit From Saint Nicholas."
Marianne Moore, 1887-1972, (U.S.) poet.
Alberto Moravia, 1907-90, (It.) novelist, short-story writer. *The Time of Indifference.*
Sir Thomas More, 1478-1535, (Br.) writer, statesman, saint. *Utopia.*
Wright Morris, 1910-98 (U.S.) novelist. *My Uncle Dudley.*
Murasaki Shikibu, c978-1026, (Jpn.) novelist. *The Tale of Genji.*
Iris Murdoch, 1919-99 (Br.), novelist, philosopher. *The Sea, The Sea.*
Alfred de Musset, 1810-57, (Fr.) poet, dramatist. *La Confession d'un Enfant du Siècle.*
Vladimir Nabokov, 1899-1977, (Russ.-U.S.) novelist. *Lolita, Pale Fire.*
Ogden Nash, 1902-71, (U.S.) poet of light verse.
Pablo Neruda, 1904-73, (Chil.) poet. *Twenty Love Poems and One Song of Despair, Toward the Splendid City.*
Patrick O'Brian, 1914-2000, (Br.) historical novelist. *Master and Commander, Blue at the Mizzen.*
Sean O'Casey, 1884-1964, (Ir.) dramatist. *Juno and the Paycock, The Plough and the Stars.*
Frank O'Connor (Michael Donovan), 1903-66, (Ir.) short-story writer. "Guests of a Nation."
Flannery O'Connor, 1925-64, (U.S.) novelist, short-story writer. *Wise Blood,* "A Good Man Is Hard to Find."
Clifford Odets, 1906-63, (U.S.) playwright. *Waiting for Lefty, Awake and Sing, Golden Boy, The Country Girl.*
John O'Hara, 1905-70, (U.S.) novelist, short-story writer. *From the Terrace, Appointment in Samarra, Pal Joey.*
Omar Khayyam, c1028-1122, (Per.) poet. *Rubaiyat.*
Eugene O'Neill, 1888-1953, (U.S.) playwright. *Emperor Jones, Anna Christie, Long Day's Journey Into Night.*
George Orwell, 1903-50, (Br.) novelist, essayist. *Animal Farm, Nineteen Eighty-Four.*
John Osborne, 1929-95, (Br.) dramatist, novelist. *Look Back in Anger, The Entertainer.*
Wilfred Owen, 1893-1918 (Br.) poet. "Dulce et Decorum Est."
Dorothy Parker, 1893-1967, (U.S.) poet, short-story writer. *Enough Rope, Laments for the Living.*
Boris Pasternak, 1890-1960, (Russ.) poet, novelist. *Doctor Zhivago.*
Octavio Paz, 1914-98, (Mex.) poet, essayist. *The Labyrinth of Solitude, They Shall Not Pass!, The Sun Stone.*
Samuel Pepys, 1633-1703, (Br.) public official, diarist.
S(idney) J(oseph) Perelman, 1904-79, (U.S.) humorist. *The Road to Miltown, Under the Spreading Atrophy.*
Charles Perrault, 1628-1703, (Fr.) writer. *Tales From Mother Goose* (*Sleeping Beauty, Cinderella*).
Petrarch (Francesco Petrarca), 1304-74, (It.) poet. *Africa, Trionfi, Canzoniere.*
Luigi Pirandello, 1867-1936, (It.) novelist, dramatist. *Six Characters in Search of an Author.*
Sylvia Plath, 1932-63, (U.S.) author, poet. *The Bell Jar.*
Edgar Allan Poe, 1809-49, (U.S.) poet, short-story writer, critic. "Annabel Lee," "The Raven," "The Purloined Letter."
Alexander Pope, 1688-1744, (Br.) poet. *The Rape of the Lock, The Dunciad, An Essay on Man.*
Katherine Anne Porter, 1890-1980, (U.S.) novelist, short-story writer. *Ship of Fools.*
Chaim Potok, 1929-2002, (U.S.) novelist. *The Chosen.*
Ezra Pound, 1885-1972, (U.S.) poet. *Cantos.*
Anthony Powell, 1905-2000, (Br.) novelist. *A Dance to the Music of Time* series.
J(ohn) B. Priestley, 1894-1984, (Br.) novelist, dramatist. *The Good Companions.*
Marcel Proust, 1871-1922, (Fr.) novelist. *Remembrance of Things Past.*
Aleksandr Pushkin, 1799-1837, (Russ.) poet, novelist. *Boris Godunov, Eugene Onegin.*
Mario Puzo, 1920-99, (U.S.) novelist. *The Godfather.*
François Rabelais, 1495-1553, (Fr.) writer. *Gargantua.*
Jean Racine, 1639-99, (Fr.) dramatist. *Andromaque, Phèdre, Bérénice, Britannicus.*
Ayn Rand, 1905-82, (Russ.-U.S.) novelist, moral theorist. *The Fountainhead, Atlas Shrugged.*
Terence Rattigan, 1911-77, (Br.) playwright. *Separate Tables, The Browning Version.*
Erich Maria Remarque, 1898-1970, (Ger.-U.S.) novelist. *All Quiet on the Western Front.*
Samuel Richardson, 1689-1761, (Br.) novelist. *Pamela; or Virtue Rewarded.*
Rainer Maria Rilke, 1875-1926, (Ger.) poet. *Life and Songs, Duino Elegies, Poems From the Book of Hours.*
Arthur Rimbaud, 1854-91, (Fr.) poet. *A Season in Hell.*
Edwin Arlington Robinson, 1869-1935, (U.S.) poet. "Richard Cory," "Miniver Cheevy," *Merlin.*
Theodore Roethke, 1908-63, (U.S.) poet. *Open House, The Waking, The Far Field.*
Romain Rolland, 1866-1944, (Fr.) novelist, biographer. *Jean-Christophe.*
Pierre de Ronsard, 1524-85, (Fr.) poet. *Sonnets pour Hélène, La Franciade.*
Christina Rossetti, 1830-94, (Br.) poet. "When I Am Dead, My Dearest."
Dante Gabriel Rossetti, 1828-82, (Br.) poet, painter. "The Blessed Damozel."
Edmond Rostand, 1868-1918, (Fr.) poet, dramatist. *Cyrano de Bergerac.*
Damon Runyon, 1880-1946, (U.S.) short-story writer, journalist. *Guys and Dolls, Blue Plate Special.*
John Ruskin, 1819-1900, (Br.) critic, social theorist. *Modern Painters, The Seven Lamps of Architecture.*
Antoine de Saint-Exupéry, 1900-44, (Fr.) writer. *Wind, Sand and Stars, The Little Prince.*
Saki, or H(ector) H(ugh) Munro, 1870-1916, (Br.) writer. *The Chronicles of Clovis.*
George Sand (Amandine Lucie Aurore Dupin), 1804-76, (Fr.) novelist. *Indiana, Consuelo.*
Carl Sandburg, 1878-1967, (U.S.) poet. *The People, Yes; Chicago Poems, Smoke and Steel, Harvest Poems.*
William Saroyan, 1908-81, (U.S.) playwright, novelist. *The Time of Your Life, The Human Comedy.*
Nathalie Sarraute, 1900-99, (Fr.) Nouveau Roman novelist. Tropismes.
May Sarton, 1914-95, (Belg.-U.S.) poet, novelist. *Encounter in April, Anger.*
Dorothy L. Sayers, 1893-1957, (Br.) mystery writer; created Lord Peter Wimsey.
Richard Scarry, 1920-94, (U.S.) author of children's books. *Richard Scarry's Best Story Book Ever.*

IT'S A FACT: Regarded as perhaps the greatest female writer of her generation, Dorothy Parker (1893-1967) was known for acerbic wit. One of her most famous comments was made in a book review where she said, "This is not a novel to be tossed aside lightly. It should be thrown aside with great force."

Friedrich von Schiller, 1759-1805, (Ger.) dramatist, poet, historian. *Don Carlos, Maria Stuart, Wilhelm Tell.*
Sir Walter Scott, 1771-1832, (Sc.) novelist, poet. *Ivanhoe.*
Jaroslav Seifert, 1902-86, (Czech.) poet.
Dr. Seuss (Theodor Seuss Geisel), 1904-91, (U.S.) children's book author and illustrator. *The Cat in the Hat.*
William Shakespeare, 1564-1616, (Br.) dramatist, poet. *Romeo and Juliet, Hamlet, King Lear, Julius Caesar,* sonnets.
Karl Shapiro, 1913-2000, (U.S.) poet. "Elegy for a Dead Soldier".
George Bernard Shaw, 1856-1950, (Ir.-Br.) playwright, critic. *St. Joan, Pygmalion, Major Barbara, Man and Superman.*
Mary Wollstonecraft Shelley, 1797-1851, (Br.) novelist, feminist. *Frankenstein. The Last Man.*
Percy Bysshe Shelley, 1792-1822, (Br.) poet. *Prometheus Unbound, Adonais,* "Ode to the West Wind," "To a Skylark."
Richard B. Sheridan, 1751-1816, (Br.) dramatist. *The Rivals, School for Scandal.*
Robert Sherwood, 1896-1955, (U.S.) playwright, biographer. *The Petrified Forest, Abe Lincoln in Illinois.*
Mikhail Sholokhov, 1906-84, (Russ.) writer. *The Silent Don.*
Upton Sinclair, 1878-1968, (U.S.) novelist. *The Jungle.*
Isaac Bashevis Singer, 1904-91, (Pol.-U.S.) novelist, short-story writer, in Yiddish. *The Magician of Lublin.*
C(harles) P(ercy) Snow, 1905-80, (Br.) novelist, scientist. *Strangers and Brothers, Corridors of Power.*
Stephen Spender, 1909-95, (Br.) poet, critic, novelist. *Twenty Poems,* "Elegy for Margaret."
Edmund Spenser, 1552-99, (Br.) poet. *The Faerie Queen.*
Johanna Spyri, 1827-1901, (Swiss) children's author. *Heidi.*
Christina Stead, 1903-83, (Austral.) novelist, short-story writer. *The Man Who Loved Children.*
Richard Steele, 1672-1729, (Br.) essayist, playwright, began the *Tatler* and *Spectator. The Conscious Lovers.*
Gertrude Stein, 1874-1946, (U.S.) writer. *Three Lives.*
John Steinbeck, 1902-68, (U.S.) novelist. *The Grapes of Wrath, Of Mice and Men, The Winter of Our Discontent.*
Stendhal (Marie Henri Beyle), 1783-1842, (Fr.) novelist. *The Red and the Black, The Charterhouse of Parma.*
Laurence Sterne, 1713-68, (Br.) novelist. *Tristram Shandy.*
Wallace Stevens, 1879-1955, (U.S.) poet. *Harmonium, The Man With the Blue Guitar, Notes Toward a Supreme Fiction.*
Robert Louis Stevenson, 1850-94, (Br.) novelist, poet, essayist. *Treasure Island, A Child's Garden of Verses.*
Bram Stoker, 1845-1910, (Br.) writer. *Dracula.*
Rex Stout, 1886-1975, (U.S.) mystery writer; created Nero Wolfe.
Harriet Beecher Stowe, 1811-96, (U.S.) novelist. *Uncle Tom's Cabin.*
Lytton Strachey, 1880-1932, (Br.) biographer, critic. *Eminent Victorians. Queen Victoria, Elizabeth and Essex.*
August Strindberg, 1849-1912, (Swed.) dramatist, novelist. *The Father, Miss Julie, The Creditors.*
Jonathan Swift, 1667-1745, (Br.) satirist, poet. *Gulliver's Travels,* "A Modest Proposal."
Algernon C. Swinburne, 1837-1909, (Br.) poet, dramatist. *Atalanta in Calydon.*
John M. Synge, 1871-1909, (Ir.) poet, dramatist. *Riders to the Sea, The Playboy of the Western World.*
Rabindranath Tagore, 1861-1941, (In.) author, poet. *Sadhana, The Realization of Life, Gitanjali.*
Booth Tarkington, 1869-1946, (U.S.) novelist. *Seventeen.*
Peter Taylor, 1917-94, (U.S.) novelist. A *Summons to Memphis.*
Sara Teasdale, 1884-1933, (U.S.) poet. *Helen of Troy and Other Poems, Rivers to the Sea.*
Alfred, Lord Tennyson, 1809-92, (Br.) poet. *Idylls of the King, In Memoriam,* "The Charge of the Light Brigade."
William Makepeace Thackeray, 1811-63, (Br.) novelist. *Vanity Fair, Henry Esmond, Pendennis.*
Dylan Thomas, 1914-53, (Welsh) poet. *Under Milk Wood, A Child's Christmas in Wales.*
Henry David Thoreau, 1817-62, (U.S.) writer, philosopher, naturalist. *Walden,* "Civil Disobedience."
James Thurber, 1894-1961, (U.S.) humorist; "The Secret Life of Walter Mitty," *My Life and Hard Times.*
J(ohn) R(onald) R(euel) Tolkien, 1892-1973, (Br.) writer. *The Hobbit, Lord of the Rings* trilogy.
Leo Tolstoy, 1828-1910, (Russ.) novelist, short-story writer. *War and Peace, Anna Karenina,* "The Death of Ivan Ilyich."
Anthony Trollope, 1815-82, (Br.) novelist. *The Warden, Barchester Towers,* the Palliser novels.
Ivan Turgenev, 1818-83, (Russ.) novelist, short-story writer. *Fathers and Sons, First Love, A Month in the Country.*
Amos Tutuola, 1920-97, (Nigerian) novelist. *The Palm-Wine Drunkard, My Life in the Bush of Ghosts.*
Mark Twain (Samuel Clemens), 1835-1910, (U.S.) novelist, humorist. *The Adventures of Huckleberry Finn, Tom Sawyer; Life on the Mississippi.*
Sigrid Undset, 1881-1949, (Nor.) novelist, poet. *Kristin Lavransdatter.*
Paul Valéry, 1871-1945, (Fr.) poet, critic. *La Jeune Parque, The Graveyard by the Sea.*
Jules Verne, 1828-1905, (Fr.) novelist. *Twenty Thousand Leagues Under the Sea.*
François Villon, 1431-63?, (Fr.) poet. *The Lays, The Grand Testament.*
Voltaire (F.M. Arouet), 1694-1778, (Fr.) writer of "philosophical romances"; philosopher, historian; *Candide.*
Robert Penn Warren, 1905-89, (U.S.) novelist, poet, critic. *All the King's Men.*
Evelyn Waugh, 1903-66, (Br.) novelist. *The Loved One, Brideshead Revisited, A Handful of Dust.*
H(erbert) G(eorge) Wells, 1866-1946, (Br.) novelist. *The Time Machine, The Invisible Man, The War of the Worlds.*
Eudora Welty, 1909-2001, (U.S.) Southern short story writer. "Why I Live at the P.O," "The Ponder Heart."
Rebecca West, 1893-1983, (Br.) novelist, critic, journalist. *Black Lamb and Grey Falcon.*
Edith Wharton, 1862-1937, (U.S.) novelist. *The Age of Innocence, The House of Mirth, Ethan Frome.*
E(lwyn) B(rooks) White, 1899-1985, (U.S.) essayist, novelist. *Charlotte's Web, Stuart Little.*
Patrick White, 1912-90, (Austral.) novelist. *The Tree of Man.*
T(erence) H(anbury) White, 1906-64, (Br.) author. *The Once and Future King, A Book of Beasts.*
Walt Whitman, 1819-92, (U.S.) poet. *Leaves of Grass.*
John Greenleaf Whittier, 1807-92, (U.S.) poet, journalist. *Snow-Bound.*
Oscar Wilde, 1854-1900, (Ir.) novelist, playwright. *The Picture of Dorian Gray, The Importance of Being Earnest.*
Laura Ingalls Wilder, 1867-1957, (U.S.) novelist. Little House on the Prairie series of children's books.
Thornton Wilder, 1897-1975, (U.S.) playwright. *Our Town, The Skin of Our Teeth, The Matchmaker.*
Tennessee Williams, 1911-83, (U.S.) playwright. *A Streetcar Named Desire, Cat on a Hot Tin Roof, The Glass Menagerie.*
William Carlos Williams, 1883-1963, (U.S.) poet, physician. *Tempers, Al Que Quiere! Paterson,* "This Is Just to Say."
Edmund Wilson, 1895-1972, (U.S.) critic, novelist. *Axel's Castle, To the Finland Station.*
P(elham) G(renville) Wodehouse, 1881-1975, (Br.-U.S.) humorist. The "Jeeves" novels, *Anything Goes.*
Thomas Wolfe, 1900-38, (U.S.) novelist. *Look Homeward, Angel; You Can't Go Home Again.*
Virginia Woolf, 1882-1941, (Br.) novelist, essayist. *Mrs. Dalloway, To the Lighthouse, A Room of One's Own.*
William Wordsworth, 1770-1850, (Br.) poet. "Tintern Abbey," "Ode: Intimations of Immortality," *The Prelude.*
Richard Wright, 1908-60, novelist, short-story writer. *Native Son, Black Boy, Uncle Tom's Children.*
Elinor Wylie, 1885-1928, (U.S.) poet. *Nets to Catch the Wind.*
William Butler Yeats, 1865-1939, (Ir.) poet, playwright. "The Second Coming," *The Wild Swans at Coole.*
Émile Zola, 1840-1902, (Fr.) novelist. *Nana, Thérese Raquin.*

Poets Laureate

There is no record of the origin of the office of Poet Laureate of England. Henry III (1216-72) reportedly had a Versificator Regis, or King's Poet, paid 100 shillings a year. Other poets said to have filled the role include Geoffrey Chaucer (d 1400), Edmund Spenser (d 1599), Ben Jonson (d 1637), and Sir William d'Avenant (d 1668).

The first official English poet laureate was John Dryden, appointed 1668, for life (as was customary). Then came Thomas Shadwell, in 1689; Nahum Tate, 1692; Nicholas Rowe, 1715; Rev. Laurence Eusden, 1718; Colley Cibber, 1730; William Whitehead, 1757; Rev. Thomas Warton, 1785; Henry James Pye, 1790; Robert Southey, 1813; William Wordsworth, 1843; Alfred, Lord Tennyson, 1850; Alfred Austin, 1896; Robert Bridges, 1913; John Masefield, 1930; C. Day Lewis, 1968; Sir John Betjeman, 1972; Ted Hughes, 1984; Andrew Motion, 1999.

In U.S., appointment is by Librarian of Congress and is not for life: Robert Penn Warren, appointed 1986; Richard Wilbur, 1987; Howard Nemerov, 1988; Mark Strand, 1990; Joseph Brodsky, 1991; Mona Van Duyn, 1992; Rita Dove, 1993; Robert Hass, 1995; Robert Pinsky, 1997; Stanley Kunitz, 2000; Billy Collins, 2001.

Composers of Classical and Avant Garde Music

Carl Philipp Emanuel Bach, 1714-88, (Ger.) Cantatas, passions, numerous keyboard and instrumental works.
Johann Christian Bach, 1735-82, (Ger.) Concertos, operas, sonatas.
Johann Sebastian Bach, 1685-1750, (Ger.) St. Matthew Passion, The Well-Tempered Clavier.
Samuel Barber, 1910-81, (U.S.) Adagio for Strings, Vanessa.
Béla Bartók, 1881-1945, (Hung.) Concerto for Orchestra, The Miraculous Mandarin.
Amy Beach (Mrs. H. H. A. Beach), 1867-1944, (U.S.) The Year's at the Spring, Fireflies, The Chambered Nautilus.
Ludwig van Beethoven, 1770-1827, (Ger.) Concertos (Emperor), sonatas (Moonlight, Pathetique), 9 symphonies.
Vincenzo Bellini, 1801-35, (It.) I Puritani, La Sonnambula, Norma.
Alban Berg, 1885-1935, (Austrian) Wozzeck, Lulu.
Hector Berlioz, 1803-69, (Fr.) Damnation of Faust, Symphonie Fantastique, Requiem.
Leonard Bernstein, 1918-90, (U.S.) Chichester Psalms, Jeremiah Symphony, Mass.
Georges Bizet, 1838-75, (Fr.) Carmen, Pearl Fishers.
Ernest Bloch, 1880-1959, (Swiss-U.S.) Macbeth (opera), Schelomo, Voice in the Wilderness.
Luigi Boccherini, 1743-1805, (It.) Chamber music and guitar pieces.
Alexander Borodin, 1833-87, (Russ.) Prince Igor, In the Steppes of Central Asia, Polovtzian Dances.
Pierre Boulez, b 1925, (Fr.) LeVisage nuptial, Edats/Multiple, Domaines.
Johannes Brahms, 1833-97, (Ger.) Liebeslieder Waltzes, Acad. Festival Overture, chamber music, 4 symphonies.
Benjamin Britten, 1913-76, (Br.) Peter Grimes, Turn of the Screw, A Ceremony of Carols, War Requiem.
Anton Bruckner, 1824-96, (Austrian) 9 symphonies.
Dietrich Buxtehude, 1637-1707, (Dan.) Organ works, vocal music.
William Byrd, 1543-1623, (Br.) Masses, motets.
John Cage, 1912-92, (U.S.) Winter Music, Fontana Mix.
Emmanuel Chabrier, 1841-94, (Fr.) Le Roi Malgré Lui, Espana.
Gustave Charpentier, 1860-1956, (Fr.) Louise.
Frédéric Chopin, 1810-49, (Pol.) Mazurkas, waltzes, etudes, nocturnes, polonaises, sonatas.
Aaron Copland, 1900-90, (U.S.) Appalachian Spring, Fanfare for the Common Man, Lincoln Portrait.
Claude Debussy, 1862-1918, (Fr.) Pelleas et Melisande, La Mer, Prelude to the Afternoon of a Faun.
Gaetano Donizetti, 1797-1848, (It.) Elixir of Love, Lucia di Lammermoor, Daughter of the Regiment.
Paul Dukas, 1865-1935, (Fr.) Sorcerer's Apprentice.
Antonin Dvorak, 1841-1904, (Czech.) Songs My Mother Taught Me, Symphony in E Minor (From the New World).
Edward Elgar, 1857-1934, (Br.) Enigma Variations, Pomp and Circumstance.
Manuel de Falla, 1876-1946, (Sp.) El Amor Brujo, La Vida Breve, The Three-Cornered Hat.
Gabriel Faurè, 1845-1924, (Fr.) Requiem, Elègie for Cello and Piano.
Cesar Franck, 1822-90, (Belg.) Symphony in D minor, Violin Sonata.
George Gershwin, 1898-1937, (U.S.) Rhapsody in Blue, An American in Paris, Porgy and Bess.
Philip Glass, b 1937, (U.S.) Einstein on the Beach, The Voyage.
Mikhail Glinka, 1804-57, (Russ.) A Life for the Tsar, Ruslan and Ludmilla.
Christoph W. Gluck, 1714-87, (Ger.) Alceste, Iphigènie en Tauride.
Charles Gounod, 1818-93, (Fr.) Faust, Romeo and Juliet.
Edvard Grieg, 1843-1907, (Nor.) Peer Gynt Suite, Concerto in A minor for piano.
George Frideric Handel, 1685-1759, (Ger.-Br.) Messiah, Water Music.
Howard Hanson, 1896-1981, (U.S.) Symphonies No. 1 (Nordic) and No. 2 (Romantic).
Roy Harris, 1898-1979, (U.S.) Symphonies.
(Franz) Joseph Haydn, 1732-1809, (Austrian) Symphonies (Clock, London, Toy), chamber music, oratorios.
Paul Hindemith, 1895-1963, (U.S.) Mathis der Maler.
Gustav Holst, 1874-1934, (Br.) The Planets.
Arthur Honegger, 1892-1955, (Fr.) Judith, Le Roi David, Pacific 231.
Alan Hovhaness, 1911-2000, (U.S.) Symphonies, Magnificat.
Engelbert Humperdinck, 1854-1921, (Ger.) Hansel and Gretel.
Charles Ives, 1874-1954, (U.S.) Concord Sonata, symphonies.
Aram Khachaturian, 1903-78, (Russ.) Ballets, piano pieces, Sabre Dance.
Zoltán Kodaly, 1882-1967, (Hung.) Háry János, Psalmus Hungaricus.
Fritz Kreisler, 1875-1962, (Austrian) Caprice Viennois, Tambourin Chinois.
Edouard Lalo, 1823-92, (Fr.) Symphonie Espagnole.
Ruggero Leoncavallo, 1857-1919, (It.) Pagliacci.
Franz Liszt, 1811-86, (Hung.) 20 Hungarian rhapsodies, symphonic poems.
Edward MacDowell, 1861-1908, (U.S.) To a Wild Rose.
Gustav Mahler, 1860-1911, (Austrian) Das Lied von der Erde; 9 complete symphonies.
Pietro Mascagni, 1863-1945, (It.) Cavalleria Rusticana.
Jules Massenet, 1842-1912, (Fr.) Manon, Le Cid, Thaïs.
Felix Mendelssohn, 1809-47, (Ger.) A Midsummer Night's Dream, Songs Without Words, violin concerto.
Gian-Carlo Menotti, b 1911, (It.-U.S.) The Medium, The Consul, Amahl and the Night Visitors.
Claudio Monteverdi, 1567-1643, (It.) Opera, masses, madrigals.
Modest Moussorgsky, 1839-81, (Russ.) Boris Godunov, Pictures at an Exhibition.
Wolfgang Amadeus Mozart, 1756-91, (Austrian) Chamber music, concertos, operas (Magic Flute, Marriage of Figaro), 41 symphonies.
Jacques Offenbach, 1819-80, (Fr.) Tales of Hoffmann.
Carl Orff, 1895-1982, (Ger.) Carmina Burana.
Johann Pachelbel, 1653-1706, (Ger.) Canon and Fugue in D major.
Ignacy Paderewski, 1860-1941, (Pol.) Minuet in G.
Niccolò Paganini, 1782-1840, (It.) Caprices for violin solo.
Giovanni Palestrina, c1525-94, (It.) Masses, madrigals.
Krzystof Pendercki, b 1933, (Pol.) Psalmus, Polymorphia, De natura sonoris.
Francis Poulenc, 1899-1963, (Fr.) Dialogues des Carmèlites.
Mel Powell, 1923-98, (U.S.) *Duplicates: A Concerto for Two Pianos and Orchestra, Cantilena Concertante.*
Sergei Prokofiev, 1891-1953, (Russ.) Classical Symphony, Love for Three Oranges, Peter and the Wolf.
Giacomo Puccini, 1858-1924, (It.) La Boheme, Manon Lescaut, Tosca, Madama Butterfly.
Henry Purcell, 1659-95, (Eng.) Dido and Aeneas.
Sergei Rachmaninoff, 1873-1943, (Russ.) Concertos, preludes (Prelude in C sharp minor), symphonies.
Maurice Ravel, 1875-1937, (Fr.) Bolèro, Daphnis et Chloè, Piano Concerto in D for Left Hand Alone.
Nikolai Rimsky-Korsakov, 1844-1908, (Russ.) Golden Cockerel, Scheherazade, Flight of the Bumblebee.
Gioacchino Rossini, 1792-1868, (It.) Barber of Seville, Othello, William Tell.
Camille Saint-Saëns, 1835-1921, (Fr.) Carnival of Animals (The Swan), Samson and Delilah, Danse Macabre.
Alessandro Scarlatti, 1660-1725, (It.) Cantatas, oratorios, operas.
Domenico Scarlatti, 1685-1757, (It.) Harpsichord works.
Alfred Schnittke, 1934-98 (Sov.-Ger.) *Life With an Idiot.*
Arnold Schoenberg, 1874-1951, (Austrian) Pelleas and Melisande, Pierrot Lunaire, Verklärte Nacht.
Franz Schubert, 1797-1828, (Austrian) Chamber music (Trout Quintet), lieder, symphonies (Unfinished).
Robert Schumann, 1810-56, (Ger.) Die Frauenliebe und Leben, Träumerei.
Dimitri Shostakovich, 1906-75, (Russ.) Symphonies, Lady Macbeth of the District Mzensk.
Jean Sibelius, 1865-1957, (Finn.) Finlandia.
Bedrich Smetana, 1824-84, (Czech.) The Bartered Bride.
Karlheinz Stockhausen, b 1928, (Ger.) KontraPunkte, Kontakte for Electronic Instruments.
Richard Strauss, 1864-1949, (Ger.) Salome, Elektra, Der Rosenkavalier, Thus Spake Zarathustra.
Igor Stravinsky, 1882-1971, (Russ.) Noah and the Flood, The Rake's Progress, The Rite of Spring.
Toru Takemitsu, 1930-96, (Jpn.) Requiem for Strings, Dorian Horizon.
Peter I. Tchaikovsky, 1840-93, (Russ.) Nutcracker, Swan Lake, The Sleeping Beauty.
Virgil Thomson, 1896-1989, (U.S.) Opera, film music, Four Saints in Three Acts.
Dmitri Tiomkin, 1894-1979, (Russ.-U.S.) film scores, including *High Noon.*
Sir Michael Tippett, 1905-98, (Br.) *A Child of Our Time, The Midsummer Marriage, The Knot Garden.*
Ralph Vaughan Williams, 1872-1958, (Eng.) Fantasiz on a Theme by Thomas Tallis, symphonies, vocal music.
Giuseppe Verdi, 1813-1901, (It.) Aida, Rigoletto, Don Carlo, Il Trovatore, La Traviata, Falstaff, Macbeth.
Heitor Villa-Lobos, 1887-1959, (Brazil) Bachianas Brasileiras.
Antonio Vivaldi, 1678-1741, (It.) Concerto grossos (The Four Seasons).
Richard Wagner, 1813-83, (Ger.) Rienzi, Tannhäuser, Lohengrin, Tristan und Isolde.
Carl Maria von Weber, 1786-1826, (Ger.) Der Freischutz.

Composers of Operettas, Musicals, and Popular Music

Richard Adler, b 1921, (U.S.) *Pajama Game; Damn Yankees.*
Milton Ager, 1893-1979, (U.S.) I Wonder What's Become of Sally; Hard Hearted Hannah; Ain't She Sweet?
Arthur Altman, 1910-94, (U.S.) *All or Nothing at All.*
Leroy Anderson, 1908-75, (U.S.) Sleigh Ride, Blue Tango, Syncopated Clock.
Paul Anka, b 1941, (Can.) My Way; *Tonight Show* theme.
Harold Arlen, 1905-86, (U.S.) Stormy Weather; Over the Rainbow; Blues in the Night; That Old Black Magic.
Burt Bacharach, b 1928, (U.S.) Raindrops Keep Fallin' on My Head; Walk on By; What the World Needs Now Is Love.
Ernest Ball, 1878-1927, (U.S.) Mother Machree; When Irish Eyes Are Smiling.
Irving Berlin, 1888-1989, (U.S.) *Annie Get Your Gun; Call Me Madam;* God Bless America; White Christmas.
Leonard Bernstein, 1918-90, (U.S.) *On the Town; Wonderful Town; Candide; West Side Story.*
Eubie Blake, 1883-1983, (U.S.) *Shuffle Along;* I'm Just Wild About Harry.
Jerry Bock, b 1928, (U.S.) *Mr. Wonderful; Fiorello; Fiddler on the Roof; The Rothschilds.*
Carrie Jacobs Bond, 1862-1946, (U.S.) I Love You Truly.
Nacio Herb Brown, 1896-1964, (U.S.) Singing in the Rain; You Were Meant for Me; All I Do Is Dream of You.
Hoagy Carmichael, 1899-1981, (U.S.) Stardust; Georgia on My Mind; Old Buttermilk Sky.
George M. Cohan, 1878-1942, (U.S.) Give My Regards to Broadway; You're a Grand Old Flag; Over There.
Cy Coleman, b 1929, (U.S.) *Sweet Charity;* Witchcraft.
John Frederick Coots, 1895-1985, (U.S.) Santa Claus Is Coming to Town; You Go to My Head; For All We Know.
Noel Coward, 1899-1973, (Br.) *Bitter Sweet;* Mad Dogs and Englishmen; Mad About the Boy.
Neil Diamond, b 1941, (U.S.) I'm a Believer; Sweet Caroline.
Walter Donaldson, 1893-1947, (U.S.) My Buddy; Carolina in the Morning; Makin' Whoopee.
Vernon Duke, 1903-69, (U.S.) April in Paris.
Bob Dylan, b 1941, (U.S.) Blowin' in the Wind.
Gus Edwards, 1879-1945, (U.S.) School Days; By the Light of the Silvery Moon; In My Merry Oldsmobile.
Sherman Edwards, 1919-81, (U.S.) See You in September; Wonderful! Wonderful!
Duke Ellington, 1899-1974, (U.S.) Sophisticated Lady; Satin Doll; It Don't Mean a Thing; Solitude.
Sammy Fain, 1902-89, (U.S.) I'll Be Seeing You; Love Is a Many-Splendored Thing.
Fred Fisher, 1875-1942, (U.S.) Peg O' My Heart; Chicago.
Stephen Collins Foster, 1826-64, (U.S.) My Old Kentucky Home; Old Folks at Home, Beautiful Dreamer.
Rudolf Friml, 1879-1972, (Czech-U.S.) *The Firefly; Rose Marie; Vagabond King; Bird of Paradise.*
John Gay, 1685-1732, (Br.) *The Beggar's Opera.*
George Gershwin, 1898-1937, (U.S.) Someone to Watch Over Me; I've Got a Crush on You; Embraceable You.
Morton Gould, 1913-96, (U.S.) Fall River Suite, Holocaust Suite, Spirituals for Orchestra, Stringmusic.
Ferde Grofe, 1892-1972, (U.S.) Grand Canyon Suite.
Marvin Hamlisch, b 1944, (U.S.) The Way We Were; Nobody Does It Better; *A Chorus Line.*
Ray Henderson, 1896-1970, (U.S.) *George White's Scandals;* That Old Gang of Mine; Five Foot Two, Eyes of Blue.
Victor Herbert, 1859-1924, (Ir.-U.S.) *Mlle. Modiste; Babes in Toyland; The Red Mill; Naughty Marietta; Sweethearts.*
Jerry Herman, b 1933, (U.S.) *Hello Dolly; Mame.*
Brian Holland, b 1941, **Lamont Dozier,** b 1941, **Eddie Holland,** b 1939, (all U.S.) Heat Wave; Stop! In the Name of Love; Baby, I Need Your Loving.
Antonio Carlos Jobim, 1927-94, (Brazil) *The Girl From Ipanema; Desafinado; One Note Samba.*
Billy (William Martin) Joel, b 1949, (U.S.) *Just the Way You Are; Honesty;* Piano Man.
Scott Joplin, 1868-1917, (U.S.) Maple Leaf Rag; *Treemonisha.*
John Kander, b 1927, (U.S.) *Cabaret; Chicago; Funny Lady.*
Jerome Kern, 1885-1945, (U.S.) *Sally; Sunny; Show Boat.*
Carole King, b 1942, (U.S.) Will You Love Me Tomorrow?; Natural Woman; One Fine Day; Up on the Roof.
Burton Lane, 1912-1997, (U.S.) *Finian's Rainbow.*
Franz Lehar, 1870-1948, (Hung.) *Merry Widow.*
Jerry Leiber, & **Mike Stoller,** both b 1933, (both U.S.) Hound Dog; Searchin'; Yakety Yak; Love Me Tender.
Mitch Leigh, b 1928, (U.S.) *Man of La Mancha.*
John Lennon, 1940-80, & **Paul McCartney,** b 1942, (both Br.) I Want to Hold Your Hand; She Loves You.
Jay Livingston, 1915-2001 (U.S.) Mona Lisa; Que Sera, Sera.
Andrew Lloyd Webber, b 1948, (Br.) *Jesus Christ Superstar; Evita; Cats; The Phantom of the Opera.*
Frank Loesser, 1910-69, (U.S.) *Guys and Dolls; Where's Charley?; The Most Happy Fella; How to Succeed....*
Frederick Loewe, 1901-88, (Austrian-U.S.) *Brigadoon; Paint Your Wagon; My Fair Lady; Camelot.*
Henry Mancini, 1924-94, (U.S.) Moon River; Days of Wine and Roses; Pink Panther Theme.
Barry Mann, b 1939, & **Cynthia Weil,** b 1937, (both U.S.) You've Lost That Loving Feeling.
Jimmy McHugh, 1894-1969, (U.S.) Don't Blame Me; I'm in the Mood for Love; I Feel a Song Coming On.
Alan Menken, b 1949, (U.S.) *Little Shop of Horrors, Beauty and the Beast.*
Joseph Meyer, 1894-1987, (U.S.) If You Knew Susie; California, Here I Come; Crazy Rhythm.
Chauncey Olcott, 1858-1932, (U.S.) Mother Machree.
Jerome "Doc" Pomus, 1925-91, (U.S.) Save the Last Dance for Me; A Teenager in Love.
Cole Porter, 1893-1964, (U.S.) *Anything Goes; Kiss Me Kate; Can Can; Silk Stockings.*
Smokey Robinson, b 1940, (U.S.) Shop Around; My Guy; My Girl; Got Ready.
Richard Rodgers, 1902-79, (U.S.) *Oklahoma!; Carousel; South Pacific; The King and I; The Sound of Music.*
Sigmund Romberg, 1887-1951, (Hung.) *Maytime; The Student Prince; Desert Song; Blossom Time.*
Harold Rome, 1908-93, (U.S.) *Pins and Needles; Call Me Mister; Wish You Were Here; Fanny; Destry Rides Again.*
Vincent Rose, b 1880-1944, (U.S.) Avalon; Whispering; Blueberry Hill.
Harry Ruby, 1895-1974, (U.S.) Three Little Words; Who's Sorry Now?
Arthur Schwartz, 1900-84, (U.S.) *The Band Wagon;* Dancing in the Dark; By Myself; That's Entertainment.
Neil Sedaka, b 1939, (U.S.) Breaking Up Is Hard to Do.
Paul Simon, b 1942, (U.S.) Sounds of Silence; I Am a Rock; Mrs. Robinson; Bridge Over Troubled Waters.
Stephen Sondheim, b 1930, (U.S.) *A Little Night Music; Company; Sweeney Todd; Sunday in the Park With George.*
John Philip Sousa, 1854-1932, (U.S.) *El Capitan;* Stars and Stripes Forever.
Oskar Straus, 1870-1954, (Austrian) *Chocolate Soldier.*
Johann Strauss, 1825-99, (Austrian) *Gypsy Baron; Die Fledermaus;* waltzes: Blue Danube; Artist's Life.
Charles Strouse, b 1928, (U.S.) *Bye Bye, Birdie; Annie.*
Jule Styne, 1905-94, (Br.-U.S.) *Gentlemen Prefer Blondes; Bells Are Ringing; Gypsy; Funny Girl.*
Arthur S. Sullivan, 1842-1900, (Br.) *H.M.S. Pinafore; Pirates of Penzance; The Mikado.*
Deems Taylor, 1885-1966, (U.S.) *Peter Ibbetson.*
Harry Tobias, 1905-94, (U.S.) *I'll Keep the Lovelight Burning.*
Egbert van Alstyne, 1882-1951, (U.S.) In the Shade of the Old Apple Tree; Memories; Pretty Baby.
Jimmy Van Heusen, 1913-90, (U.S.) Moonlight Becomes You; Swinging on a Star; All the Way; Love and Marriage.
Albert von Tilzer, 1878-1956, (U.S.) I'll Be With You in Apple Blossom Time; Take Me Out to the Ball Game.
Harry von Tilzer, 1872-1946, (U.S.) Only a Bird in a Gilded Cage; On a Sunday Afternoon.
Fats Waller, 1904-43, (U.S.) Honeysuckle Rose; Ain't Misbehavin'.
Harry Warren, 1893-1981, (U.S.) You're My Everything; We're in the Money; I Only Have Eyes for You.
Jimmy Webb, b 1946, (U.S.) Up, Up and Away; By the Time I Get to Phoenix; Didn't We?; Wichita Lineman.
Kurt Weill, 1900-50, (Ger.-U.S.) *Threepenny Opera; Lady in the Dark; Knickerbocker Holiday; One Touch of Venus.*
Percy Wenrich, 1887-1952, (U.S.) When You Wore a Tulip; Moonlight Bay; Put On Your Old Gray Bonnet.
Richard A. Whiting, 1891-1938, (U.S.) Till We Meet Again; Sleepytime Gal; Beyond the Blue Horizon; My Ideal.
John Williams, b 1932, (U.S.) *Jaws; E.T.; Star Wars* series; *Raiders of the Lost Ark* series.
Meredith Willson, 1902-84, (U.S.) *The Music Man.*
Stevie Wonder, b 1950, (U.S.) You Are the Sunshine of My Life; Signed, Sealed, Delivered, I'm Yours.
Vincent Youmans, 1898-1946, (U.S.) *Two Little Girls in Blue; Wildflower; No, No, Nanette; Hit the Deck; Rainbow; Smiles.*

Lyricists

Howard Ashman, 1950-91, (U.S.) Little Shop of Horrors; The Little Mermaid.
Johnny Burke, 1908-84, (U.S.) Misty; Imagination.
Irving Caesar, 1895-1996, (U.S.) Swanee; Tea for Two; Just a Gigolo.
Sammy Cahn, 1913-93, (U.S.) High Hopes; Love and Marriage; The Second Time Around; It's Magic.
Leonard Cohen, b 1934, (Can.) Suzanne; Stranger Song.
Betty Comden, b 1919, (U.S.) and **Adolph Green,** b 1915, (U.S.) The Party's Over; Just in Time; New York, New York.
Hal David, b 1921, (U.S.) What the World Needs Now Is Love.
Buddy De Sylva, 1895-1950, (U.S.) When Day Is Done; Look for the Silver Lining; April Showers.
Howard Dietz, 1896-1983, (U.S.) Dancing in the Dark; You and the Night and the Music; That's Entertainment.
Al Dubin, 1891-1945, (U.S.) Tiptoe Through the Tulips; Anniversary Waltz; Lullaby of Broadway.
Fred Ebb, b 1936, (U.S.) Cabaret; Zorba; Woman of the Year.
Ray Evans, b 1915 (U.S.) Mona Lisa; Que Sera, Sera.
Dorothy Fields, 1905-74, (U.S.) On the Sunny Side of the Street; Don't Blame Me; The Way You Look Tonight.
Ira Gershwin, 1896-1983, (U.S.) The Man I Love; Fascinating Rhythm; S'Wonderful; Embraceable You.
William S. Gilbert, 1836-1911, (Br.) The Mikado; H.M.S. Pinafore; Pirates of Penzance.
Gerry Goffin, b 1939, (U.S.) Will You Love Me Tomorrow; Take Good Care of My Baby; Up on the Roof.
Mack Gordon, 1905-59, (Pol.-U.S.) You'll Never Know; The More I See You; Chattanooga Choo-Choo.
Oscar Hammerstein II, 1895-1960, (U.S.) Ol' Man River; Oklahoma; Carousel.
E. Y. (Yip) Harburg, 1898-1981, (U.S.) Brother, Can You Spare a Dime; April in Paris; Over the Rainbow.
Lorenz Hart, 1895-1943, (U.S.) Isn't It Romantic; Blue Moon; Lover; Manhattan; My Funny Valentine.
DuBose Heyward, 1885-1940, (U.S.) Summertime.
Gus Kahn, 1886-1941, (U.S.) Memories; Ain't We Got Fun.
Alan J. Lerner, 1918-86, (U.S.) Brigadoon; My Fair Lady; Camelot; Gigi; On a Clear Day You Can See Forever.
Johnny Mercer, 1909-76, (U.S.) Blues in the Night; Come Rain or Come Shine; Laura; That Old Black Magic.
Bob Merrill, 1921-98, (U.S.) People; (How Much Is That) Doggie in the Window.
Jack Norworth, 1879-1959, (U.S.) Take Me Out to the Ball Game; Shine On Harvest Moon.
Mitchell Parish, 1901-93, (U.S.) Stairway to the Stars; Stardust.
Andy Razaf, 1895-1973, (U.S.) Honeysuckle Rose; Ain't Misbehavin'; S'posin'.
Leo Robin, 1900-84, (U.S.) Thanks for the Memory; Hooray for Love; Diamonds Are a Girl's Best Friend.
Paul Francis Webster, 1907-84, (U.S.) Secret Love; The Shadow of Your Smile; Love Is a Many-Splendored Thing.
Jack Yellen, 1892-1991, (U.S.) Down by the O-Hi-O; Ain't She Sweet; Happy Days Are Here Again.

Blues and Jazz Artists of the Past

Julian "Cannonball" Adderley, 1928-75, alto sax
Nat Adderley, 1931-2000, cornet, trumpet, composer
Louis "Satchmo" Armstrong, 1900-71, trumpet, singer; "scat" vocals
Mildred Bailey, 1907-51, blues singer
Chet Baker, 1929-88, trumpet
Count Basie, 1904-84, orchestra leader, piano
Sidney Bechet, 1897-1959, early innovator, soprano sax
Bix Beiderbecke, 1903-31, cornet, piano, composer
Tex Beneke, 1914-2000, tenor sax, vocalist, band leader
Tommy Benford, 1906-94, drummer
Bunny Berigan, 1909-42, trumpet, singer
Barney Bigard, 1906-80, clarinet
Ed Blackwell, 1929-92, drummer
Jimmy Blanton, 1921-42, bass
Charles "Buddy" Bolden, 1868-1931, cornet; formed first jazz band.
Lester Bowie, 1941-99, trumpet, composer, band leader
Big Bill Broonzy, 1893-1958, blues singer, guitar
Clifford Brown, 1930-56, trumpet
Don Byas, 1912-72, tenor sax
Charlie Byrd, 1925-99, guitarist; popularized bossa nova
Cab Calloway, 1907-94, band leader
Harry Carney, 1910-74, baritone sax
Betty Carter, 1930-98, jazz singer
Sidney Catlett, 1910-51, drums
Doc Cheatham, 1905-97, trumpet
Don Cherry, 1937-95, lyrical jazz trumpet
Charlie Christian, 1919-42, guitar
Kenny Clarke, 1914-85, modern drums
Buck Clayton, 1911-91, trumpet, arranger
James Cleveland, 1931-91, gospel singer
Al Cohn, 1925-88, tenor sax, composer
Cozy Cole, 1909-81, drums
Johnny Coles, 1926-96, trumpet
John Coltrane, 1926-67, tenor sax innovator
Eddie Condon, 1904-73, guitar, band leader; Dixieland
Tadd Dameron, 1917-65, piano, composer
Eddie "Lockjaw" Davis, 1921-86, tenor sax
Miles Davis, 1926-91, trumpet; pioneer of cool jazz
Wild Bill Davison, 1906-89, cornet, early Chicago jazz
Paul Desmond, 1924-77, alto sax
Vic Dickenson, 1906-84, trombone, composer
Willie Dixon, 1915-92, songwriter, blues, "You Shook Me"
Warren "Baby" Dodds, 1898-1959, Dixieland drummer
Johnny Dodds, 1892-1940, clarinet
Jimmy Dorsey, 1904-57, clarinet, alto sax; band leader
Tommy Dorsey, 1905-56, trombone; band leader
Roy Eldridge, 1911-89, trumpet, drums, singer
Duke Ellington, 1899-1974, piano, band leader, composer
Bill Evans, 1929-80, piano
Gil Evans, 1912-88, composer, arranger, piano
Tal Farlow, 1921-98, jazz guitarist
Ella Fitzgerald, 1918-1996, jazz vocalist, "first lady of song"
"Red" Garland, 1923-84, piano
Erroll Garner, 1921-77, piano, composer, "Misty"
Stan Getz, 1927-91, tenor sax
Dizzy Gillespie, 1917-93, trumpet, composer; bop developer
Benny Goodman, 1909-86, clarinet; band, combo leader
Dexter Gordon, 1923-90, tenor sax, bop-derived style
Stéphane Grappelli, 1908-97, violin
Bobby Hackett, 1915-76, trumpet, cornet
Lionel Hampton, 1908-2002, jazz vibraphonist
W. C. Handy, 1873-1958, composer, "St. Louis Blues"
Coleman Hawkins, 1904-69, tenor sax, "Body and Soul"
Fletcher Henderson, 1898-1952, orchestra leader, arranger
Woody Herman, 1913-87, clarinet, alto sax, band leader
Jay C. Higginbotham, 1906-73, trombone
Earl "Fatha" Hines, 1905-83, piano, songwriter
Al Hirt, 1922-99, trumpet
Johnny Hodges, 1906-70, alto sax
Billie Holiday, 1915-59, blues singer, "Strange Fruit"
John Lee Hooker, 1917-2001, blues guitarist, singer
Sam "Lightnin" Hopkins, 1912-82, blues singer, guitarist
Howlin' Wolf, 1910-1976, blues singer, harmonica, guitar
Mahalia Jackson, 1911-72, gospel singer
Elmore James, 1918-63, blues songwriter, singer, guitarist
Blind Lemon Jefferson, 1897-1930, blues singer, guitar
Little Willie John, 1937-68, singer, songwriter
Bunk Johnson, 1879-1949, cornet, trumpet
J.J. Johnson, 1924-2001, modern jazz trombone
James P. Johnson, 1891-1955, piano, composer
Robert Johnson, 1912-38, blues songwriter, singer, guitarist
Jo Jones, 1911-85, drums
Philly Joe Jones, 1923-85, drums
Thad Jones, 1923-86, trumpet, cornet
Scott Joplin, 1868-1917, ragtime composer
Louis Jordan, 1908-75, singer, alto sax
Stan Kenton, 1912-79, orchestra leader, composer, piano
Albert King, 1923-92, blues guitarist
Gene Krupa, 1909-73, drums, band and combo leader
Scott LaFaro, 1936-61, bass
Huddie Ledbetter (Lead Belly), 1888-1949, blues singer, guitar
John Lewis, 1920-2001, pianist, Modern Jazz Quartet founder
Mel Lewis, 1929-90, drummer, orchestra leader
Jimmie Lunceford, 1902-47, band leader, sax
Jimmy McPartland, 1907-91, trumpet
Carmen McRae, 1920-94, jazz singer
Glenn Miller, 1904-44, trombone, dance band leader
Charles Mingus, 1922-79, bass, composer, combo leader
Thelonious Monk, 1920-82, piano, composer, combo leader; bop developer
Wes Montgomery, 1925-68, guitar
"Jelly Roll" Morton, 1885-1941, composer, piano, singer
Bennie Moten, 1894-1935, piano
Gerry Mulligan, 1927-96, baritone sax, songwriter, "cool school"
Turk Murphy, 1915-87, trombone, band leader
Theodore "Fats" Navarro, 1923-50, trumpet
Red Nichols, 1905-65, cornet, combo leader
King Oliver, 1885-1938, cornet, band leader; Louis Armstrong
Sy Oliver, 1910-88, Swing Era arranger, composer, conductor
Kid Ory, 1886-1973, trombone, "Muskrat Ramble"
Charlie "Bird" Parker, 1920-55, alto sax, noted jazz improviser
Joe Pass, 1929-94, guitarist
Art Pepper, 1925-82, alto sax

Oscar Pettiford, 1922-60, a leading bop-era bassist
Bud Powell, 1924-66, piano; modern jazz pioneer
Louis Prima, 1911-78, singer, band leader.
Tito Puente, 1923-2000, jazz percussionist, band leader
Don Pullen, 1942-95, piano; percussive pianist
Sun Ra, 1915?-93, bandleader, pianist, composer
Gertrude "Ma" Rainey, 1886-1939, blues singer
Don Redman, 1900-64, composer, arranger
Django Reinhardt, 1910-53, guitar; influenced Amer. jazz
Buddy Rich, 1917-87, drums, band leader
Red Rodney, 1928-94, trumpeter
Frank Rosollino, 1926-78, trombone
Jimmy Rowles, 1918-96, jazz composer, accompanist
Jimmy Rushing, 1903-72, blues singer
Pee Wee Russell, 1906-69, clarinet
Zoot Sims, 1925-85, tenor, alto sax, clarinet
Zutty Singleton, 1898-1975, Dixieland drummer
Bessie Smith, 1894-1937, blues singer
Clarence "Pinetop" Smith, 1904-29, piano, singer; pioneer of boogie woogie
Willie "The Lion" Smith, 1897-1973, stride style pianist
Muggsy Spanier, 1906-67, cornet, band leader
Billy Strayhorn, 1915-67, composer, piano
Sonny Stitt, 1924-82, alto, tenor sax
Art Tatum, 1910-56, piano; technical virtuoso
Art Taylor, 1929-95, jazz drummer, bandleader
Jack Teagarden, 1905-64, trombone, singer
Mel Torme, 1925-99, "Velvet Fog", singer
Dave Tough, 1908-48, drums
Lennie Tristano, 1919-78, piano, composer
Joe Turner, 1911-85, blues singer
Sarah Vaughan, 1924-90, singer
Joe Venuti, 1904-78, first great jazz violinist
T-Bone Walker, 1910-75, guitarist; electric blues guitar
Thomas "Fats" Waller, 1904-43, piano, singer, composer
Dinah Washington, 1924-63, singer
Grover Washington Jr., 1943-99, jazz sax, composer
Ethel Waters, 1896-1977, jazz and blues singer
Muddy Waters, 1915-83, blues singer, songwriter
Johnny Watson, 1935-96, rhythm and blues guitarist
Chick Webb, 1902-39, band leader, drums
Ben Webster, 1909-73, tenor sax
Junior Wells, 1934-98, blues singer, harmonica
Paul Whiteman, 1890-1967, jazz orchestra leader
Charles "Cootie" Williams, 1908-85, trumpet, band leader
Mary Lou Williams, 1914-81, piano, composer
John Lee "Sonny Boy" Williamson, 1914-48, blues singer, harmonica virtuoso
Sonny Boy Williamson ("Rice" Miller), 1900?-65, Delta bluesman, singer, songwriter, harmonica
Teddy Wilson, 1912-86, piano, composer
Kai Winding, 1922-83, trombone, composer
Jimmy Yancey, 1894-1951, piano
Lester "Pres" Young, 1909-59, tenor sax, composer

Noted Country Music Artists of the Past and Present

Roy Acuff, 1903-92, fiddler, singer, songwriter; "Wabash Cannon Ball"
Alabama (Randy Owen, 1949- ; Jeff Cook, 1949- ; Teddy Gentry, 1952- ; Mark Herndon, 1955-) "Feels So Right"
Eddy Arnold, 1918- , singer, guitarist, the "Tennessee Plowboy"
Chet Atkins, 1924-2001, guitarist, composer, producer, helped create the "Nashville sound"
Gene Autry, 1907-98, first great singing movie cowboy; "Back in the Saddle Again"
Garth Brooks, 1962- , singer, songwriter; "Friends in Low Places"
Brooks & Dunn (Kix Brooks, 1955- ; Ronnie Dunn, 1953-) "Hard Workin' Man"
Boudleaux and Felice Bryant (Boudleau, 1920-87, Felice, 1925-), songwriting team; "Hey Joe"
Glen Campbell, 1936- , singer, instrumentalist, TV host; "Gentle on My Mind," "Rhinestone Cowboy"
Mary Chapin Carpenter, 1958- , singer, songwriter; "I Feel Lucky"
Carter Family (original members, **"Mother" Maybelle** 1909-78; **A.P.**, 1891-1960, **Sara**, 1898-1979) "Wildwood Flower"
Johnny Cash, 1932- , singer, songwriter; "I Walk the Line," "Ring of Fire," "Folsom Prison Blues"
Patsy Cline, 1932-63, singer; "Walkin' After Midnight," "Crazy," "Sweet Dreams"
John Denver, 1943-97, singer, songwriter; "Rocky Mountain High"
Dixie Chicks (Natalie Maines, 1974- ; Martie Seidel, 1969- ; Emily Erwin Robison, 1972-) "Wide Open Spaces," "Fly"
Dale Evans (Lucille Wood Smith), 1912-2001, singer, actress, married Roy Rogers
Flatt & Scruggs (Lester Flatt, 1914-79; Earl Scruggs, 1924-), guitar-banjo duo and soloists; "Foggy Mountain Breakdown"
Red Foley, 1910-68, singer; "Chattanoogie Shoe Shine Boy"
Tennessee Ernie Ford, 1919-91, singer, TV host; "Sixteen Tons"
Lefty Frizzell, 1928-75, singer, guitarist; "Long Black Veil"
Vince Gill, 1957- , singer, songwriter; "When I Call Your Name"
Merle Haggard, 1937- , singer, songwriter; "Okie from Muskogee"
Emmylou Harris, 1947- , singer, songwriter, folk-country crossover artist; "If I Could Only Win Your Love"
Faith Hill, 1967-, singer, songwriter, married Tim McGraw; "Wild One," "This Kiss," "Breathe"
Waylon Jennings, 1937–2002, singer, songwriter, "outlaw country" pioneer; "Luckenbach, Texas"
George Jones, 1931- , singer, songwriter; "Why Baby Why"
The Judds (Naomi, 1946- ; Wynonna, 1964-), mother-daughter duo; Wynonna also a solo act
Alison Krauss, 1971– , bluegrass fiddler, singer, bandleader; "When You Say Nothing at All"
Kris Kristofferson, 1936- , singer, songwriter, actor; "Me and Bobby McGee"
Brenda Lee, 1944- , singer; "I'm Sorry"
Patty Loveless, 1957- , singer, songwriter; "How Can I Help You Say Goodbye"
Lyle Lovett, 1957- , singer, songwriter, bandleader, actor; "Cowboy Man"
Loretta Lynn, 1935- , singer, songwriter; "Coal Miner's Daughter"
Kathy Mattea, 1959- , singer, songwriter; "Eighteen Wheels and a Dozen Roses"
Reba McEntire, 1955- , singer, songwriter, actress; "Whoever's in New England"
Tim McGraw, 1967- , singer; "It's Your Love," with wife, Faith Hill
Roger Miller, 1936-92, singer, songwriter; "King of the Road"
Ronnie Milsap, 1944- , singer, songwriter; "There's No Gettin' Over Me"
Bill Monroe, 1911-96, singer, songwriter, mandolin player, "father of bluegrass music"; "Mule Skinner Blues"
Patsy Montana, 1908-96, yodeling/singing cowgirl; "I Want to Be a Cowboy's Sweetheart"
Willie Nelson, 1933- , singer, songwriter, actor; "On the Road Again"
Mark O'Connor, 1961- , fiddler, country-classical crossover composer
Dolly Parton, 1946- , singer, songwriter, actress; "Dollywood" theme park; "Here You Come Again," "9 to 5"
Minnie Pearl, 1912-96, comedienne, Grand Ole Opry star
Charley Pride, 1938- , singer, 1st African-American country star; "Kiss an Angel Good Mornin'"
Jim Reeves, 1923-64, singer, songwriter; "Four Walls"
Charlie Rich, 1932-95, singer, songwriter called the "Silver Fox"; "The Most Beautiful Girl"
LeAnn Rimes, 1982- , singer; "Blue"
Tex Ritter, 1905-74, singer, songwriter; "Jingle, Jangle, Jingle"
Marty Robbins, 1925-82, singer, songwriter; "A White Sport Coat and a Pink Carnation"
Jimmie Rodgers, 1897-1933, singer, songwriter; "T for Texas"
Kenny Rogers, 1938- , singer, songwriter, actor; "The Gambler"
Roy Rogers (Leonard Slye), 1911-98, singer, actor, "King of the Cowboys," sang with Sons of the Pioneers.
Fred Rose, 1898-1954, songwriter, singer, producer; "Blue Eyes Cryin' in the Rain"
Ricky Skaggs, 1954- , singer, songwriter, bandleader; "Don't Cheat in Our Hometown"
George Strait, 1952- , singer, bandleader; "Ace in the Hole"
Merle Travis, 1917-83, singer, guitarist, songwriter; "Divorce Me C.O.D."
Randy Travis, 1959- , singer, songwriter; "Forever and Ever, Amen"
Ernest Tubb, 1914-84, singer, songwriter, guitarist; "Walking the Floor Over You"
Shania Twain, 1965- , singer, songwriter; "You're Still the One"
Conway Twitty, 1933-93, singer, songwriter; "Hello Darlin' "
Dottie West, 1932-91, singer, songwriter; "Here Comes My Baby"
Hank Williams Jr., 1949- , singer, songwriter; "Bocephus"; "All My Rowdy Friends (Have Settled Down)"
Hank Williams Sr., 1923-53, singer, songwriter; "Your Cheatin' Heart"
Bob Wills, 1905-75, Western Swing fiddler, singer, bandleader, songwriter; "New San Antonio Rose"
Tammy Wynette, 1942-98, singer; "Stand By Your Man"
Trisha Yearwood, 1964- , singer, songwriter; "How Do I Live"
Dwight Yoakam, 1957- , singer, songwriter, actor; "Ain't That Lonely Yet"

Dance Figures of the Past

Source: Reviewed by Gary Parks, Reviews editor, *Dance* magazine

Alvin Ailey, 1931-89, (U.S.) modern dancer, choreographer; melded modern dance and Afro-Caribbean techniques.
Frederick Ashton, 1904-88, (Br.) ballet choreographer; director of Great Britain's Royal Ballet, 1963-70.
Fred Astaire, 1899-1987, (U.S.) dancer, actor; teamed with dancer/actress **Ginger Rogers** (1911-95) in movie musicals.
George Balanchine, 1904-83, (Russ.-U.S.) ballet choreographer, teacher; most influential exponent of the neoclassical style; founded, with Lincoln Kirstein, School of American Ballet and New York City Ballet.
Carlo Blasis, 1803-78, (It.) ballet dancer, choreographer, writer; his teaching methods are standards of classical dance.
August Bournonville, 1805-79, (Dan.) ballet dancer, choreographer, teacher; exuberant, light style.
Gisella Caccialanza, 1914-97, (U.S.) ballerina, charter member of Balanchine's American Ballet.
Enrico Cecchetti, 1850-1928, (It.) ballet dancer, leading dancer of Russia's Imperial Ballet; his technique was basis for Britain's Imperial Soc. of Teachers of Dancing.
Gower Champion, 1921-80, (U.S.) dancer, choreographer, director; with his wife **Marge,** b 1923, (U.S.) choreographed, danced in Broadway musicals and films.
John Cranko, 1927-73, (S. African) choreographer; created narrative ballets based on literary works.
Agnes de Mille, 1909-93, (U.S.) ballerina, choreographer; known for using American themes, she choreographed the ballet *Rodeo* and the musical *Oklahoma*.
Dame Ninette DeValois, 1898-2001, (Br.) choreographer, founding director London's Royal Ballet; *The Rake's Progress*.
Sergei Diaghilev, 1872-1929, (Russ.) impresario; founded Les Ballet Russes; saw ballet as an art unifying dance, drama, music, and decor.
Alexandra Danilova, 1903-97, (Russ.) ballerina; noted teacher at the School of American Ballet.
Isadora Duncan, 1877-1927, (U.S.) expressive dancer who united free movement with serious music; one of the founders of modern dance.
Fanny Elssler, 1810-84, (Austrian) ballerina of the Romantic era; known for dramatic skill, sensual style.
Michel Fokine, 1880-1942, (Russ.) ballet dancer, choreographer, teacher; rejected strict classicism in favor of dramatically expressive style.
Margot Fonteyn, 1919-91, (Br.) prima ballerina, Royal Ballet of Great Britain; famed performance partner of Rudolf Nureyev.
Bob Fosse, 1927-87, (U.S.) jazz dancer, choreographer, director; Broadway musicals and film.
Serge Golovine, 1924-98, (Fr.) ballet dancer with Grand Ballet du Marquis de Cuevas; choreographer.
Martha Graham, 1893-1991, (U.S.) modern dancer, choreographer; created and codified her own dramatic technique.
Martha Hill, 1901-95, (U.S.) educator; leading figure in modern dance; founded American Dance Festival.
Doris Humphrey, 1895-1958, (U.S.) modern dancer, choreographer, writer, teacher.
Robert Joffrey, 1930-88, (U.S.) ballet dancer, choreographer; cofounded with **Gerald Arpino,** b 1928, (U.S.), the Joffrey Ballet.
Kurt Jooss, 1901-79, (Ger.) choreographer, teacher; created expressionist works using modern and classical techniques.
Tamara Karsavina, 1885-1978, (Russ.) prima ballerina of Russia's Imperial Ballet and Diaghilev's Ballets Russes; partner of Nijinsky.
Nora Kaye, 1920-87, (U.S.) ballerina with Metropolitan Opera Ballet and Ballet Theater (now American Ballet Theatre).
Lincoln Kirstein, 1907-96 (U.S.) brought ballet as an art form to U.S.; founded, with George Balanchine, School of American Ballet and New York City Ballet.
Serge Lifar, 1905-86, (Russ.-Fr.) prem. danseur, choreographer; director of dance at Paris Opera, 1930-45, 1947-58.
José Limón, 1908-72, (Mex.-U.S.) modern dancer, choreographer, teacher; developed technique based on Humphrey.
Catherine Littlefield, 1908-51, (U.S.) ballerina, choreographer, teacher; pioneer of American ballet.
Léonide Massine, 1896-1979, (Russ.-U.S.) ballet dancer, choreographer; his "symphonic ballet" used concert music previously thought unsuitable for dance.
Kenneth MacMillan, 1929-92, (Br.) dancer, choreographer; directed Royal Ballet of Great Britain 1970-77.
Vaslav Nijinsky, 1890-50, (Russ.) prem. danseur, choreographer; leading member of Diaghilev's Ballets Russes; his ballets were revolutionary for their time.
Alwin Nikolais, 1910-93, (U.S.) modern choreographer; created dance theater utilizing mixed media effects.
Jean-George Noverre, 1727-1810, (Fr.) ballet choreographer, teacher, writer; "Shakespeare of the Dance."
Rudolf Nureyev, 1938-93, (Russ.) prem. danseur, choreographer; leading male dancer of his generation; director of dance at Paris Opera, 1983-89.
Ruth Page, 1903-91, (U.S.) ballerina, choreographer; danced and directed ballet at Chicago Lyric Opera.
Anna Pavlova, 1881-1931, (Russ.) prima ballerina; toured with her own company to world acclaim.
Marius Petipa, 1818-1910, (Fr.) ballet dancer, choreographer; ballet master of the Imperial Ballet; established Russian classicism as leading style of late 19th cent.
Pearl Primus, 1919-95, (Trinidad-U.S.) modern dancer, choreographer, scholar; combined African, Caribbean, and African-American styles.
Jerome Robbins, 1918-98, (U.S.) choreographer, director, dancer; *The King and I, West Side Story, Fiddler on the Roof; Gypsy.*
Bill (Bojangles) Robinson, 1878-1949, (U.S.) famed tap dancer; called King of Tapology on stage and screen.
Ruth St. Denis, 1877-1968, (U.S.) influential interpretive dancer, choreographer, teacher.
Ted Shawn, 1891-1972, (U.S.) modern dancer, choreographer; formed dance company and school with Ruth St. Denis; established Jacob's Pillow Dance Festival.
Marie Taglioni, 1804-84, (It.) ballerina, teacher; in title role of *La Sylphide* established image of the ethereal ballerina.
Antony Tudor, 1908-87, (Br.) choreographer, teacher; exponent of the "psychological ballet."
Galina Ulanova, 1910-98, (Russ.) revered ballerina with Bolshoi Ballet.
Agrippina Vaganova, 1879-1951, (Russ.) ballet teacher, director; codified Soviet ballet technique that developed virtuosity; called "queen of variations."
Mary Wigman, 1886-1973, (Ger.) modern dancer, choreographer, teacher; influenced European expressionist dance.

Opera Singers of the Past

Frances Alda, 1883-1952, (N.Z.) soprano
Pasquale Amato, 1878-1942, (It.) baritone
Marian Anderson, 1897-1993, (U.S.) contralto
Jussi Björling, 1911-60, (Swed.) tenor
Lucrezia Bori, 1887-1960, (It.) soprano
Maria Callas, 1923-77, (U.S.) soprano
Emma Calvé, 1858-1942, (Fr.) soprano
Enrico Caruso, 1873-1921, (It.) tenor
Feodor Chaliapin, 1873-1938, (Russ.) bass
Boris Christoff, 1914-93, (Bulg.) bass
Giuseppe De Luca, 1876-1950, (It.) baritone
Fernando De Lucia, 1860-1925, (It.) tenor
Edouard De Reszke, 1853-1917, (Pol.) bass
Jean De Reszke, 1850-1925, (Pol.) tenor
Emmy Destinn, 1878-1930, (Czech.) soprano
Emma Eames, 1865-1952, (U.S.) soprano
(Carlo Broschi) Farinelli, 1705-82, (It.) castrato
Geraldine Farrar, 1882-1967, (U.S.) soprano
Eileen Farrell, 1920-2002, (U.S.) soprano
Kathleen Ferrier, 1912-53, (Eng.) contralto
Kirsten Flagstad, 1895-1962, (Nor.) soprano
Olive Fremstad, 1871-1951, (Swed.-U.S.) soprano
Amelita Galli-Curci, 1882-1963, (It.) soprano
Mary Garden, 1874-1967, (Br.) soprano
Beniamino Gigli, 1890-1957, (It.) tenor
Tito Gobbi, 1913-84, (It.) baritone
Giulia Grisi, 1811-69, (It.) soprano
Frieda Hempel, 1885-1955, (Ger.) soprano
Maria Jeritza, 1887-1982, (Czech.) soprano
Alexander Kipnis, 1891-1978, (Russ.-U.S.) bass
Alfredo Kraus, 1927-99, (Sp.) tenor
Luigi Lablache, 1794-1858, (It.) bass
Lilli Lehmann, 1848-1929, (Ger.) soprano
Lotte Lehmann, 1888-1976, (Ger.-U.S.) soprano
Jenny Lind, 1820-87, (Swed.) soprano
Maria Malibran, 1808-36, (Sp.) mezzo-soprano
Giovanni Martinelli, 1885-1969, (It.) tenor
John McCormack, 1884-1945, (Ir.) tenor
Nellie Melba, 1861-1931, (Austral.) soprano.
Lauritz Melchior, 1890-1973, (Dan.) tenor
Zinka Milanov, 1906-89, (Yugo.) soprano
Lillian Nordica, 1857-1914, (U.S.) soprano
Giuditta Pasta, 1797-1865, (It.) soprano
Adelina Patti, 1843-1919, (It.) soprano
Peter Pears, 1910-86, (Eng.) tenor
Jan Peerce, 1904-84, (U.S.) tenor
Ezio Pinza, 1892-1957, (It.) bass
Lily Pons, 1898-1976, (Fr.) soprano

Rosa Ponselle, 1897-1981, (U.S.) soprano
Hermann Prey, 1929-98, (Ger.) baritone.
Elisabeth Rethberg, 1894-1976, (Ger.) soprano
Giovanni Battista Rubini, 1794-1854, (It.) tenor
Leonie Rysanek, 1926-1998, (Austrian) soprano
Bidú Sayão, 1902-99, (Braz.) soprano
Friedrich Schorr, 1888-1953, (Hung.) bass-baritone
Marcella Sembrich, 1858-1935, (Pol.) soprano
Eleanor Steber, 1916-90, (U.S.) soprano
Ferrucio Tagliavini, 1913-95, (It.) tenor
Luisa Tetrazzini, 1871-1940, (It.) soprano
Lawrence Tibbett, 1896-1960, (U.S.) baritone
Tatiana Troyanos, 1938-93, (U.S.) mezzo-soprano
Richard Tucker, 1913-75, (U.S.) tenor
Pauline Viardot, 1821-1910, (Fr.) mezzo-soprano
William Warfield, 1920-2002, (U.S.) bass-baritone
Leonard Warren, 1911-60, (U.S.) baritone
Ljuba Welitsch, 1913-96, (Bulg.) soprano
Wolfgang Windgassen, 1914-74, (Ger.) tenor

Rock and Roll, Rhythm and Blues, and Rap Artists

Titles in quotation marks are singles; others are albums.

AC/DC: "Back in Black"
Bryan Adams: "Cuts Like a Knife"
***Aerosmith (2001):** "Sweet Emotion"
Christina Aguilera: "What a Girl Wants"
Alice In Chains: "Heaven Beside You"
***The Allman Brothers Band (1995):** "Ramblin' Man"
***The Animals (1994):** "House of the Rising Sun"
Paul Anka: "Lonely Boy"
Fiona Apple: "Criminal"
Ashanti: "Foolish"
The Association: "Cherish"
Frankie Avalon: "Venus"
The B-52s: "Love Shack"
Bachman Turner Overdrive: "Takin' Care of Business"
Backstreet Boys: "I Want it That Way"
Bad Company: "Can't Get Enough"
Erykah Badu: "On and On"
***La Vern Baker (1991):** "I Cried a Tear"
***Hank Ballard and the Midnighters (1990):** "Work With Me, Annie"
***The Band (1994):** "The Weight"
Barenaked Ladies: "One Week"
***The Beach Boys (1988):** "Good Vibrations"
Beastie Boys: "(You Gotta) Fight for Your Right (to Party)"
***The Beatles (1988):** *Sgt. Pepper's Lonely Hearts Club Band*
Beck: "Loser"
***The Bee Gees (1997):** "Stayin' Alive"
Pat Benatar: "Hit Me With Your Best Shot"
Ben Folds Five: "Brick"
***Chuck Berry (1986):** "Johnny B. Goode"
The Big Bopper: "Chantilly Lace"
Bjork: "Human Behavior"
The Black Crowes: "Hard to Handle"
Black Sabbath: "Paranoid"
***Bobby "Blue" Bland (1992):** "Turn On Your Love Light"
Mary J. Blige: *My Life*
Blind Faith: "Can't Find My Way Home"
Blink-182: "All the Small Things"
Blondie: "Heart of Glass"
Blood, Sweat, and Tears: "Spinning Wheel"
Blues Traveler: "Run-Around"
Gary "U.S." Bonds: "Quarter to Three"
Bon Jovi: "Livin' on a Prayer"
***Booker T. and the M.G.'s (1992):** "Green Onions"
Earl Bostic: "Flamingo"
Boston: "More Than A Feeling"
***David Bowie (1996):** "Space Oddity"
Boyz II Men: "I'll Make Love to You"
Toni Braxton: "Un-Break My Heart"
***James Brown (1986):** "Papa's Got a Brand New Bag"
***Ruth Brown (1993):** "Lucky Lips"
Jackson Browne: "Doctor My Eyes"
***Buffalo Springfield (1997):** "For What It's Worth"
Jimmy Buffett: "Margaritaville"
***Solomon Burke (2001):** "Over and Over (Huggin' and Lovin')"
Bush: "Glycerine"
***The Byrds (1991):** "Turn! Turn! Turn!"
Mariah Carey: "Vision of Love"
The Cars: "Shake It Up"
***Johnny Cash (1992):** "I Walk the Line"
***Ray Charles (1986):** "Georgia on My Mind"
Cheap Trick: "Surrender"
Chicago: "Saturday in the Park"
Chubby Checker: "The Twist"
***Eric Clapton (2000):** "Layla"
The Clash: "Rock the Casbah"
***The Coasters (1987):** "Yakety Yak"
***Eddie Cochran (1987):** "Summertime Blues"
Joe Cocker: "With a Little Help From My Friends"
Collective Soul: "The World I Know"
Phil Collins: "Against All Odds"
***Sam Cooke (1986):** "You Send Me"
Coolio: "Gangsta's Paradise"
Alice Cooper: "School's Out"
Elvis Costello: "Alison"
Counting Crows: "Mr. Jones"
***Cream (1993):** "Sunshine of Your Love"
Creed: "Arms Wide Open"
***Creedence Clearwater Revival (1993):** "Proud Mary"
***Crosby, Stills, and Nash (1997):** "Suite: Judy Blue Eyes"
Sheryl Crow: "All I Want to Do"
The Cure: "Boys Don't Cry"
The Crystals: "Da Doo Ron Ron"
Cypress Hill: "Insane in the Brain"
Danny and the Juniors: "At the Hop"
***Bobby Darin (1990):** "Splish Splash"
Spencer Davis Group: "Gimme Some Lovin' "
Deep Purple: "Smoke on the Water"
Def Leppard: "Photograph"
Depeche Mode: "Strange Love"
Destiny's Child: "Survivor"
***Bo Diddley (1987):** "Who Do You Love?"
***Dion and the Belmonts (1989):** "A Teenager in Love"
Celine Dion: "Because You Loved Me"
Dire Straits: "Money for Nothing"
DMX: "What's My Name"
***Fats Domino (1986):** "Blueberry Hill"
Donovan: "Mellow Yellow"
The Doobie Brothers: "What a Fool Believes"
***The Doors (1993):** "Light My Fire"
Dr. Dre: "Nothin' But a 'G' Thang"
***The Drifters (1988):** "Save the Last Dance for Me"
Duran Duran: "Hungry Like the Wolf"
***Bob Dylan (1988):** "Like a Rolling Stone"
***The Eagles (1998):** "Hotel California"
***Earth, Wind, and Fire (2000):** "Shining Star"
***Duane Eddy (1994):** "Rebel-Rouser"
Missy Elliott: "Sock It 2 Me"
Emerson, Lake, and Palmer: "Lucky Man"
Eminem: "The Real Slim Shady"
En Vogue: "Hold On"
Enya: *Shepherd Moons*
The Eurythmics: "Sweet Dreams (Are Made of This)"
Everclear: "Father Of Mine"
***The Everly Brothers (1986):** "Wake Up, Little Susie"
The Five Satins: "In the Still of the Night"
***The Flamingos (2001):** "I Only Have Eyes for You"
***Fleetwood Mac (1998):** *Rumours*
The Foo Fighters: "I'll Stick Around"
Foreigner: "Double Vision"
***The Four Seasons (1990):** "Sherry"
***The Four Tops (1990):** "I Can't Help Myself (Sugar Pie, Honey Bunch)"
***Aretha Franklin (1987):** "Respect"
Nelly Furtado: "I'm Like a Bird"
Peter Gabriel: "Shock the Monkey"
Marvin Gaye (1987): "I Heard It Through the Grapevine"
Genesis: "No Reply at All"
Goo Goo Dolls: "Iris"
Grand Funk Railroad: "We're an American Band"
Grand Master Flash and the Furious Five: "The Message"
***The Grateful Dead (1994):** "Uncle John's Band"
Macy Gray: "I Try"
***Al Green (1995):** "Let's Stay Together"
Green Day: "Time of Your Life"
The Guess Who: "American Woman"
Guns N' Roses: "Sweet Child o' Mine"
***Bill Haley and His Comets (1987):** "Rock Around the Clock"
Hall and Oates: "Kiss on My List"
Hanson: "MMMBop"
Juliana Hatfield: "Spin the Bottle"
***Isaac Hayes (2002):** "Theme from 'Shaft'"
Heart: "Barracuda"
***Jimi Hendrix (1992):** "Purple Haze"
Lauryn Hill: "Doo-Wop (That Thing)"
Hole: "Doll Parts"
***Buddy Holly (1986):** "Peggy Sue"
***John Lee Hooker (1991):** "Boogie Chillen"
Hootie and the Blowfish: *Cracked Rear View*
Whitney Houston: "I Will Always Love You"
***The Impressions (1991):** "For Your Precious Love"
Indigo Girls: "Closer to Fine"

INXS: "Need You Tonight"
***The Isley Brothers (1992):** "It's Your Thing"
***The Jackson Five (1997):** "ABC"
Janet Jackson: *Rhythm Nation*
***Michael Jackson (2000):** *Thriller*
***Etta James (1993):** "At Last"
Tommy James & The Shondells: "Crimson and Clover"
Jane's Addiction: "Jane Says"
Ja Rule: *Venni, Vetti, Vecci*
Jay and the Americans: "This Magic Moment"
Jay-Z: "Can I Live"
***Jefferson Airplane (1996):** "White Rabbit"
Jethro Tull: *Aqualung*
Joan Jett: "I Love Rock 'n' Roll"
Jewel: "You Were Meant for Me"
***Billy Joel (1999):** "Piano Man"
***Elton John (1994):** "Candle in the Wind"
***Little Willie John (1996):** "Sleep"
***Janis Joplin (1995):** "Me and Bobby McGee"
Journey: "Don't Stop Believin'"
K.C. and the Sunshine Band: "Get Down Tonight"
R. Kelly: "I Can't Sleep Baby (If I)"
Alicia Keys: "Fallin'"
Kid Rock: "Cowboy"
***B.B. King (1987):** "The Thrill Is Gone"
Carole King: *Tapestry*
***The Kinks (1990):** "You Really Got Me"
Kiss: "Rock 'n' Roll All Night"
***Gladys Knight and the Pips (1996):** "Midnight Train to Georgia"
Korn: "Blind"
Lenny Kravitz: "Are You Gonna Go My Way?"
***Led Zeppelin (1995):** "Stairway to Heaven"
***Brenda Lee (2002):** "I'm Sorry"
***John Lennon (1994):** "Imagine"
***Jerry Lee Lewis (1986):** "Whole Lotta Shakin' Going On"
Lil' Kim: "No Matter What They Say"
Limp Bizkit: "Break Stuff"
Linkin Park: "One Step Closer"
Little Anthony and the Imperials: "Tears on My Pillow"
***Little Richard (1986):** "Tutti Frutti"
Live: "Lightning Crashes"
L. L. Cool J: "Mama Said Knock You Out"
Jennifer Lopez: "Love Don't Cost aThing"
***The Lovin' Spoonful (2000):** "Summer in the City"
***Frankie Lymon and the Teenagers (1993):** "Why Do Fools Fall in Love?"
Lynyrd Skynyrd: "Free Bird"
Madonna: "Material Girl"
***The Mamas and the Papas (1998):** "Monday, Monday"
Aimee Mann: "Save Me"
Marilyn Manson: "Beautiful People"
***Bob Marley (1994):** *Exodus*
***Martha and the Vandellas (1995):** "Dancin' in the Streets"
The Marvelettes: "Please, Mr. Postman"
Matchbox 20: "Push"
Dave Matthews Band: "Don't Drink the Water"
***Curtis Mayfield (1999):** "Superfly"
***Paul McCartney (1999):** "Band on the Run"
Don McLean: "American Pie"
***Clyde McPhatter (1987):** "A Lover's Question"
Meat Loaf: "Paradise by the Dashboard Light"
John (Cougar) Mellencamp: "Jack and Diane"
Men at Work: "Who Can It Be Now?"
Metallica: "Enter Sandman"
George Michael: "Faith"
***Joni Mitchell (1997):** "Big Yellow Taxi"
Moby: "Bodyrock"
The Monkees: "I'm a Believer"
Moody Blues: "Nights in White Satin"
***The Moonglows (2000):** "Blue Velvet"
Alanis Morissette: "Ironic"
***Van Morrison (1993):** "Brown-Eyed Girl"
Nelly: *Country Grammar*
***Ricky Nelson (1987):** "Hello, Mary Lou"
Nine Inch Nails: "Closer"
Nirvana: *Nevermind*
No Doubt: *Rock Steady*
The Notorious B.I.G.: "Mo Money Mo Problems"
'N Sync: "Bye, Bye, Bye"
Oasis: "Wonderwall"
The Offspring: "Pretty Fly (for a White Guy)"
***Roy Orbison (1987):** "Oh, Pretty Woman"
Ozzy Osbourne: "Crazy Train"
***Parliament/Funkadelic (1997):** "One Nation Under a Groove"
Pearl Jam: "Jeremy"
***Carl Perkins (1987):** "Blue Suede Shoes"
Peter, Paul, and Mary: "Leaving on a Jet Plane"
***Tom Petty and the Heartbreakers (2002):** "Refugee"
Liz Phair: *Exile in Guyville*
Phish: "Sample in a Jar"
***Wilson Pickett (1991):** "Land of 1,000 Dances"
Pink: *Missundazstood!*
***Pink Floyd (1996):** *The Wall*
***Gene Pitney (2002):** "Only Love Can Break a Heart"
***The Platters (1990):** "The Great Pretender"
Poco: "Crazy Love"
The Police: "Every Breath You Take"
Iggy Pop: "Lust for Life"
***Elvis Presley (1986):** "Love Me Tender"
The Pretenders: "Brass in Pocket"
***Lloyd Price (1998):** "Stagger Lee"
Prince (The Artist): "Purple Rain"
Procol Harum: "A Whiter Shade of Pale"
Public Enemy: "Fight the Power"
Puff Daddy and the Family: *No Way Out*
***Queen (2000):** "Bohemian Rhapsody"
Radiohead: "Creep"
Rage Against the Machine: "Bulls on Parade"
***Bonnie Raitt (2000):** "Something to Talk About"
***The Ramones (2002):** "I Wanna Be Sedated"
***Otis Redding (1989):** "(Sittin' on) the Dock of the Bay"
Red Hot Chili Peppers: "Under the Bridge"
***Jimmy Reed (1991):** "Ain't That Loving You, Baby?"
Lou Reed: "Walk on the Wild Side"
R.E.M.: "Losing My Religion"
REO Speedwagon: "Can't Fight This Feeling"
Busta Rhymes: "What's It Gonna Be?"
The Righteous Brothers: "You've Lost That Lovin' Feelin' "
Johnny Rivers: "Poor Side of Town"
***Smokey Robinson and the Miracles (1987):** "Shop Around"
***The Rolling Stones (1989):** "Satisfaction"
The Ronettes: "Be My Baby"
Linda Ronstadt: "You're No Good"
Run-D.M.C.: "Raisin' Hell"
Rush: "Tom Sawyer"
Sade: "Smooth Operator"
Salt-N-Pepa: "Shoop"
***Sam and Dave (1992):** "Soul Man"
***Santana (1998):** "Black Magic Woman"
Seal: "Kiss From a Rose"
Neil Sedaka: "Breaking Up Is Hard to Do"
Bob Seger: "Old Time Rock & Roll"
The Sex Pistols: "Anarchy in the U.K."
Shaggy: "It Wasn't Me"
Shakira: "Whenever, Wherever"
Tupac Shakur: "How Do U Want It"
***Del Shannon (1999):** "Runaway"
***The Shirelles (1996):** "Soldier Boy"
Carly Simon: "You're So Vain"
***Paul Simon (2001):** "50 Ways to Leave Your Lover"
***Simon and Garfunkel (1990):** "Bridge Over Troubled Water"
Sisqo: "Thong Song"
***Sly and the Family Stone (1993):** "Everyday People"
Smashing Pumpkins: "Today"
Patti Smith: "Because the Night"
Will Smith: "Gettin' Jiggy With It"
The Smiths: "This Charming Man"
Snoop Dogg: "Gin and Juice"
Sonic Youth: "Bull in the Heather"
Soundgarden: "Black Hole Sun"
Britney Spears: "Hit Me Baby One More Time"
Spice Girls: "Wannabe"
***Dusty Springfield (1999):** "I Only Want to Be With You"
***Bruce Springsteen (1999):** "Born to Run"
Squeeze (2001): "Tempted"
***Staple Singers (1999):** "I'll Take You There"
***Steely Dan (2001):** "Rikki Don't Lose That Number"
Steppenwolf: "Born to Be Wild"
***Rod Stewart (1994):** "Maggie Mae"
Sting: "If You Love Somebody, Set Them Free"
Styx: "Come Sail Away"
Sublime: "What I Got"
The Sugar Hill Gang: "Rapper's Delight"
Donna Summer: "Bad Girls"
***The Supremes (1988):** "Stop! In the Name of Love"
***Talking Heads (2002):** "Once in a Lifetime"
***James Taylor (2001):** "You've Got a Friend"
***The Temptations (1989):** "My Girl"
Three Dog Night: "Joy to the World"
TLC: "Waterfalls"
T. Rex: "Bang a Gong (Get It On)"
***Big Joe Turner (1987):** "Shake, Rattle & Roll"
***Ike and Tina Turner (1991):** "Proud Mary"
***Tina Turner:** "What's Love Got to Do With It?"
The Turtles: "Happy Together"
U2: "With or Without You"
Usher: "You Make Me Wanna"
***Ritchie Valens (2001):** "La Bamba"
Van Halen: "Running With the Devil"

Stevie Ray Vaughan: "Crossfire"
***The Velvet Underground (1996):** "Sweet Jane"
***Gene Vincent1 (1998):** "Be-Bop-A-Lula"
Tom Waits: "Downtown Train"
The Wallflowers: "One Headlight"
Dionne Warwick: "I Say a Little Prayer"
***Muddy Waters (1987):** "I Can't Be Satisfied"
Mary Wells: "My Guy"
***The Who (1990):** *Tommy*
Lucinda Williams: *Car Wheels on a Gravel Road*
***Jackie Wilson (1987):** "That's Why"
***Stevie Wonder (1989):** "You Are the Sunshine of My Life"
Wu-Tang Clan: "Protect Ya Neck"
***The Yardbirds (1992):** "For Your Love"
Yes: "Roundabout"
***Neil Young (1995):** "Down by the River"
***The Young Rascals/The Rascals (1997):** "Good Lovin' "
***Frank Zappa1/Mothers of Invention (1995):** *Sheik Yerbouti*
ZZ Top: "Legs"

* Inducted into Rock and Roll Hall of Fame as performer between 1986 and 2002; year is in parentheses. (1) Only individual performer is in Rock and Roll Hall of Fame.

WORLD ALMANAC QUICK QUIZ

Which of the following performers was not born in Brooklyn?
(a) Valerie Harper (b) Mary Tyler Moore (c) Barbra Streisand (d) Beverly Sills
For the answer look in this chapter, or see page 1008.

Entertainment Personalities of the Present

Living actors, musicians, dancers, singers, producers, directors, radio-TV performers.

Name	Birthplace	Birthdate
Abbado, Claudio	Milan, Italy	6/26/33
Abdul, Paula	San Fernando, CA	6/19/62
Abraham, F. Murray	Pittsburgh, PA	10/24/39
Adams, Bryan	Kingston, Ontario	11/5/59
Adams, Don	New York, NY	4/19/26
Adams, Edie	Kingston, PA	4/16/29
Adams, Mason	New York, NY	2/26/19
Adjani, Isabelle	Paris, France	6/27/55
Affleck, Ben	Berkeley, CA	8/15/72
Agar, John	Chicago, IL	1/31/21
Agutter, Jenny	London, England	12/20/52
Aiello, Danny	New York, NY	6/20/33
Aimee, Anouk	Paris, France	4/27/34
Albanese, Licia	Bari, Italy	7/22/13
Alberghetti, Anna Maria	Pesaro, Italy	5/15/36
Albert, Eddie	Rock Island, IL	4/22/08
Albert, Marv	New York, NY	6/12/43
Alda, Alan	New York, NY	1/28/36
Alexander, Jane	Boston, MA	10/28/39
Alexander, Jason	Newark, NJ	9/23/59
Allen, Debbie	Houston, TX	1/16/50
Allen, Joan	Rochelle, IL	8/20/56
Allen, Karen	Carrollton, IL	10/5/51
Allen, Tim	Denver, CO	6/13/53
Allen, Woody	Brooklyn, NY	12/1/35
Alley, Kirstie	Wichita, KS	1/12/51
Allman, Gregg	Nashville, TN	12/7/47
Allyson, June	New York, NY	10/7/17
Alonso, Maria Conchita	Cienfuegos, Cuba	6/29/57
Alpert, Herb	Los Angeles, CA	3/31/35
Altman, Robert	Kansas City, MO	2/20/25
Almodóvar, Pedro	Calzada de Calatrava, Spain	9/25/51
Ambrose, Lauren	New Haven, CT	2/20/78
Ames, Ed	Boston, MA	7/9/27
Amos, John	Newark, NJ	12/27/42
Amos, Tori	North Carolina	8/22/64
Anderson, Gillian	Chicago, IL	8/9/68
Anderson, Harry	Newport, RI	10/14/49
Anderson, Ian	Dunfermline, Scotland	8/10/47
Anderson, Kevin	Illinois	1/13/60
Anderson, Loni	St. Paul, MN	8/5/46
Anderson, Lynn	Grand Forks, ND	9/26/47
Anderson, Melissa Sue	Berkeley, CA	9/26/62
Anderson, Richard	Long Branch, NJ	8/8/26
Anderson, Richard Dean	Minneapolis, MN	1/23/50
Anderson, Wes	Houston, TX	1969
Andersson, Bibi	Stockholm, Sweden	11/11/35
Andress, Ursula	Bern, Switzerland	3/19/36
Andrews, Anthony	London, England	1/12/48
Andrews, Julie	Walton, England	10/1/35
Andrews, Patty	Minneapolis, MN	2/16/20
Aniston, Jennifer	Sherman Oaks, CA	2/11/69
Anka, Paul	Ottawa, Ontario	7/30/41
Ann-Margret	Stockholm, Sweden	4/28/41
Antonioni, Michelangelo	Ferrara, Italy	9/29/12
Apple, Fiona	New York, NY	9/13/77
Applegate, Christina	Los Angeles, CA	11/25/72
Archer, Anne	Los Angeles, CA	8/25/47
Arkin, Adam	Brooklyn, NY	8/19/56
Arkin, Alan	New York, NY	3/26/34
Arnaz, Desi, Jr.	Los Angeles, CA	1/19/53
Arnaz, Lucie	Los Angeles, CA	7/17/51
Arness, James	Minneapolis, MN	5/26/23
Arnold, Eddy	Henderson, TN	5/15/18
Arnold, Tom	Ottumwa, IA	3/6/59
Arquette, Patricia	New York, NY	4/8/68
Arquette, Rosanna	New York, NY	8/10/59
Arroyo, Martina	New York, NY	2/2/37
Arthur, Beatrice	New York, NY	5/13/23
Ashley, Elizabeth	Ocala, FL	8/30/41
Asner, Ed	Kansas City, MO	11/15/29
Assante, Armand	New York, NY	10/4/49
Astin, John	Baltimore, MD	3/30/30
Atkinson, Rowan	Newcastle-Upon-Tyne, Eng.	1/6/55
Attenborough, Richard	Cambridge, England	8/29/23
Auberjonois, Rene	New York, NY	6/1/40
Austin, Patti	New York, NY	8/10/48
Autry, Alan	Shreveport, LA	7/31/52
Avalon, Frankie	Philadelphia, PA	9/18/39
Aykroyd, Dan	Ottawa, Ontario	7/1/52
Azaria, Hank	Forest Hills, NY	4/25/64
Aznavour, Charles	Paris, France	5/22/24
Babyface	Indianapolis, IN	4/10/59
Bacall, Lauren	New York, NY	9/16/24
Bacon, Kevin	Philadelphia, PA	7/8/58
Badu, Erykah	Dallas, TX	2/26/71
Baez, Joan	Staten Island, NY	1/9/41
Bain, Conrad	Lethbridge, Alberta	2/4/23
Baio, Scott	Brooklyn, NY	9/22/61
Baker, Anita	Toledo, OH	1/26/58
Baker, Carroll	Johnstown, PA	5/28/31
Baker, Diane	Hollywood, CA	2/25/38
Baker, Joe Don	Groesbeck, TX	2/12/36
Baker, Kathy	Midland, TX	6/8/50
Baker, Kenny	Birmingham, England	8/24/34
Bakula, Scott	St. Louis, MO	10/9/55
Baldwin, Alec	Massapequa, NY	4/3/58
Baldwin, Daniel	Massapequa, NY	10/5/60
Baldwin, Stephen	Massapequa, NY	5/12/66
Baldwin, William	Massapequa, NY	2/21/63
Bale, Cristian	Pembrokeshire, Wales	1/30/74
Ballard, Kaye	Cleveland, OH	11/20/26
Bancroft, Anne	New York, NY	9/17/31
Banderas, Antonio	Málaga, Spain	8/10/60
Banks, Tyra	Los Angeles, CA	12/4/73
Bannon, Jack	Los Angeles, CA	6/14/40
Baranski, Christine	Buffalo, NY	5/2/52
Bardem, Javier	Canary Islands	5/1/69
Bardot, Brigitte	Paris, France	9/28/34
Barker, Bob	Darrington, WA	12/12/23
Barkin, Ellen	New York, NY	4/16/55
Barrie, Barbara	Chicago, IL	5/23/31
Barry, Gene	New York, NY	6/14/19
Barrymore, Drew	Los Angeles, CA	2/22/75
Bartoli, Cecilia	Rome, Italy	6/4/66
Baryshnikov, Mikhail	Riga, Latvia	1/28/48
Basinger, Kim	Athens, GA	12/8/53
Bass, Lance	Mississippi	5/4/79
Bassett, Angela	New York, NY	8/16/58
Bassey, Shirley	Cardiff, Wales	1/8/37
Bateman, Jason	Rye, NY	1/14/69
Bateman, Justine	Rye, NY	2/19/66
Bates, Alan	Allestree, England	2/17/34
Bates, Kathy	Memphis, TN	6/28/48
Battle, Kathleen	Portsmouth, OH	8/13/48
Baxter, Meredith	Los Angeles, CA	6/21/47
Bean, Orson	Burlington, VT	7/22/28
Beatty, Ned	Louisville, KY	7/6/37
Beatty, Warren	Richmond, VA	3/30/37

Name	Birthplace	Birthdate
Beck (Hansen)	Los Angeles, CA	7/8/70
Beck, Jeff	Surrey, England	6/24/44
Beck, John	Chicago, IL.	1/28/43
Beckinsale, Kate	London, England	7/26/73
Bedelia, Bonnie	New York, NY	3/25/48
Begley, Ed, Jr.	Los Angeles, CA	9/16/49
Behar, Joy	Brooklyn, NY	10/7/43
Belafonte, Harry	New York, NY	3/1/27
Bel Geddes, Barbara	New York, NY	10/31/22
Bell, Art	Pahrump, NV	6/17/45
Bell, Catherine	London, England	8/14/68
Bello, Maria	Norristown, PA	4/18/67
Belmondo, Jean-Paul	Neuilly-sur-Seine, France	4/9/33
Belushi, Jim	Chicago, IL.	6/15/54
Belzer, Richard	Bridgeport, CT	8/4/44
Benatar, Pat	Brooklyn, NY	1/10/53
Benedict, Dirk	Helena, MT.	3/1/45
Benigni, Roberto	Misericordia, Italy	10/27/52
Bening, Annette	Topeka, KS	5/29/58
Benjamin, Richard	New York, NY	5/22/38
Bennett, Tony	New York, NY	8/3/26
Benson, George	Pittsburgh, PA	3/22/43
Benson, Robby	Dallas, TX	1/21/56
Berenger, Tom	Chicago, IL.	5/31/50
Bergen, Candice	Beverly Hills, CA	5/9/46
Bergen, Polly	Knoxville, TN	7/14/30
Bergman, Ingmar	Uppsala, Sweden	7/14/18
Berlinger, Warren	Brooklyn, NY	8/31/37
Berman, Lazar	Leningrad, Russia	2/26/30
Berman, Shelley	Chicago, IL.	2/3/26
Bernard, Crystal	Dallas, TX	9/30/64
Bernhard, Sandra	Flint, MI	6/6/55
Bernsen, Corbin	N. Hollywood, CA.	9/7/54
Berry, Chuck	St. Louis, MO	10/18/26
Berry, Halle	Cleveland, OH	8/14/68
Berry, Ken	Moline, IL	11/3/33
Bertinelli, Valerie	Wilmington, DE	4/23/60
Bertolucci, Bernardo	Parma, Italy	3/16/41
Bialik, Mayim	San Diego, CA	12/12/75
Biggs, Jason	Pompton Plains, NJ	5/12/78
Bikel, Theodore	Vienna, Austria	5/2/24
Billingsley, Barbara	Los Angeles, CA	12/22/22
Binoche, Juliette	Paris, France	4/9/64
Birch, Thora	Los Angeles, CA	3/11/82
Birney, David	Washington, DC.	4/23/39
Bishop, Joey	Bronx, NY	2/3/18
Bisset, Jacqueline	Weybridge, England	9/13/44
Bissett, Josie	Seattle, WA	10/5/69
Björk (Gudmundsdottir)	Rheinberg, Iceland	11/21/65
Black, Clint	Katy, TX	2/4/62
Black, Jack	Los Angeles, CA	4/7/69
Black, Karen	Park Ridge, IL	7/1/42
Blades, Ruben	Panama City, Panama	7/16/48
Blair, Janet	Altoona, PA	4/23/21
Blair, Linda	St. Louis, MO	1/22/59
Blair, Selma	Southfield, MI	6/23/72
Blake, Robert	Nutley, NJ	9/18/33
Blanchett, Cate	Melbourne, Australia	1969
Bledsoe, Tempestt	Chicago, IL.	8/1/73
Bleeth, Yasmine	New York, NY	6/16/68
Blethyn, Brenda	Kent, England	2/20/46
Blige, Mary J.	Bronx, NY	1/11/71
Bloom, Claire	London, England	2/15/31
Bloom, Orlando	Canterbury, England	1/13/77
Blyth, Ann	Mt. Kisco, NY	8/16/28
Bochco, Steven	New York, NY	12/16/43
Bogdanovich, Peter	Kingston, NY	7/30/39
Bogosian, Eric	Boston, MA	4/24/53
Bologna, Joseph	Brooklyn, NY	12/30/38
Bolton, Michael	New Haven, CT	2/26/53
Bonet, Lisa	San Francisco, CA.	11/16/67
Bonham Carter, Helena	London, England	5/23/66
Bon Jovi, Jon	Sayreville, NJ.	3/2/62
Bono (Vox)	Dublin, Ireland	5/10/60
Boone, Debby	Hackensack, NJ	9/22/56
Boone, Pat	Jacksonville, FL	6/1/34
Boreanaz, David	Buffalo, NY	5/16/71
Borgnine, Ernest	Hamden, CT	1/24/17
Bosson, Barbara	Charleroi, PA	11/1/39
Bosco, Philip	Jersey City, NJ.	9/26/30
Bosley, Tom	Chicago, IL.	10/1/27
Bostwick, Barry	San Mateo, CA	2/24/45
Bottoms, Timothy	Santa Barbara, CA.	8/30/51
Bowen, Julie	Baltimore, MD	3/3/70
Bowie, David	London, England	1/8/47
Boxleitner, Bruce	Elgin, IL	5/12/50
Boy George	London, England	6/14/61
Boyle, Lara Flynn	Davenport, IA.	3/24/70
Boyle, Peter	Philadelphia, PA	10/18/33
Bracco, Lorraine	Brooklyn, NY	10/2/55
Bracken, Eddie	New York, NY	2/7/20
Branagh, Kenneth	Belfast, N. Ireland	12/10/60
Brandauer, Klaus Maria	Steiermark, Austria	6/22/44
Brando, Marlon	Omaha, NE.	4/3/24
Brandy (Norwood)	McComb, MS	2/11/79
Braschi, Nicoletta	Gesena, Italy	1960
Bratt, Benjamin	San Francisco, CA	12/16/63
Braugher, Andre	Chicago, Il	7/1/62
Braxton, Toni	Severn, MD.	10/7/66
Brendon, Nicholas	Los Angeles, CA.	4/12/71
Brennan, Eileen	Los Angeles, CA.	9/3/35
Brenner, David	Philadelphia, PA	2/4/45
Brewer, Teresa	Toledo, OH	5/7/31
Bridges, Beau	Hollywood, CA	12/9/41
Bridges, Jeff	Los Angeles, CA.	12/4/49
Brightman, Sarah	Berkhamstead, England	8/14/60
Brimley, Wilford	Salt Lake City, UT.	9/27/34
Brinkley, Christie	Malibu, CA	2/2/54
Broadbent, Jim	Lincolnshire, England	5/24/49
Broderick, Matthew	New York, NY.	3/21/62
Brolin, James	Los Angeles, CA.	7/18/40
Bronson, Charles	Ehrenfeld, PA	11/3/22
Brooks, Albert	Beverly Hills, CA.	7/22/47
Brooks, Foster	Louisville, KY	5/11/12
Brooks, Garth	Tulsa, OK	2/7/62
Brooks, James L	North Bergen, NJ	5/9/40
Brooks, Mel	New York, NY	6/28/26
Brosnan, Pierce	Co. Meath, Ireland	5/16/53
Brown, Blair	Washington, DC	1948
Brown, Bobby	Boston, MA.	2/5/69
Brown, Bryan	Sydney, Australia	6/23/47
Brown, James	Pulaski, TN (?)	6/17/28(?)
Browne, Jackson	Heidelberg, Germany	10/9/48
Browne, Roscoe Lee	Woodbury, NJ.	5/2/25
Brubeck, Dave	Concord, CA.	12/6/20
Bryson, Peabo	Greenville, SC	4/13/51
Buckley, Betty	Ft. Worth, TX	7/3/47
Buffett, Jimmy	Pascagoula, MS	12/25/46
Bujold, Genevieve	Montreal, Quebec	7/1/42
Bullock, Sandra	Arlington, VA	7/26/64
Bumbry, Grace	St. Louis, MO	1/4/37
Bundchen, Gisele	Horizontina, Brazil	7/20/80
Burghoff, Gary	Bristol, CT.	5/24/40
Burke, Delta	Orlando, FL	7/30/56
Burnett, Carol	San Antonio, TX	4/26/33
Burns, Edward	Valley Stream, NY	1/29/68
Burrows, Darren E.	Winfield, KS	9/12/66
Burstyn, Ellen	Detroit, MI	12/7/32
Burton, LeVar	Landstuhl, W Germany	2/16/57
Burton, Tim	Burbank, CA	8/25/58
Buscemi, Steve	Brooklyn, NY	12/13/57
Busey, Gary	Goose Creek, TX	6/29/44
Busfield, Timothy	Lansing, MI	6/12/57
Butler, Brett	Montgomery, AL	1/30/58
Buttons, Red	New York, NY	2/5/19
Buzzi, Ruth	Westerly, RI	7/24/36
Bynes, Amanda	Thousand Oaks, CA	4/3/86
Byrne, David	Dumbarton, Scotland	5/14/52
Byrne, Gabriel	Dublin, Ireland	5/12/50
Caan, James	New York, NY	3/26/39
Caballe, Montserrat	Barcelona, Spain	4/12/33
Caesar, Sid	Yonkers, NY	9/8/22
Cage, Nicolas	Long Beach, CA	1/7/64
Cain, Dean	Mt. Clemens, MI	7/31/66
Caine, Michael	London, England	3/14/33
Caldwell, Sarah	Maryville, MO	3/6/24
Caldwell, Zoe	Melbourne, Australia	9/14/33
Cameron, James	Kapuskasiny, Ontario	8/16/54
Cameron, Kirk	Panorama City, CA	10/12/70
Camp, Hamilton	London, England	10/30/34
Campanella, Joseph	New York, NY	11/21/27
Campbell, Bruce	Royal Oak, MI	6/22/58
Campbell, Glen	Billstown, AR	4/22/36
Campbell, Naomi	London, England	5/22/70
Campbell, Neve	Toronto, Ontario	10/3/73
Campion, Jane	Wellington, New Zealand	1955
Cannell, Stephen J.	Los Angeles, CA.	2/5/42
Cannon, Dyan	Tacoma, WA.	1/4/37
Capshaw, Kate	Ft. Worth, TX	11/3/53
Cardinale, Claudia	Tunis, Tunisia	4/15/39
Carey, Drew	Cleveland, OH	5/23/58
Carey, Mariah	Huntington, NY	3/27/70
Cariou, Len	Winnipeg, Canada	9/30/39
Carlin, George	New York, NY	5/12/37
Carlisle Hart, Kitty	New Orleans, LA	9/3/10
Carlyle, Robert	Glasgow, Scotland	4/14/61
Carmen, Eric	Cleveland, OH	8/11/49
Carney, Art	Mt. Vernon, NY	11/4/18
Carpenter, John	Carthage, NY	1/16/48
Carpenter, Mary Chapin	Princeton, NJ	2/21/58
Caron, Leslie	Boulogne, France	7/1/31

Name	Birthplace	Birthdate
Carr, Vikki	El Paso, TX	7/19/41
Carradine, David	Hollywood, CA	10/8/36
Carradine, Keith	San Mateo, CA	8/8/49
Carreras, Jose	Barcelona, Spain	12/5/46
Carrere, Tia	Honolulu, HI	1/2/66
Carrey, Jim	Toronto, Ontario	1/17/62
Carroll, Diahann	Bronx, NY	7/17/35
Carroll, Pat	Shreveport, LA	5/5/27
Carson, Johnny	Corning, IA	10/23/25
Carson, Lisa Nicole	Brooklyn, NY	7/12/69
Carter, Benny	New York, NY	8/8/07
Carter, Dixie	McLemoresville, TN	5/25/39
Carter, Jack	New York, NY	6/24/23
Carter, June	Maces Spring, VA	6/23/29
Carter, Lynda	Phoenix, AZ	7/24/51
Carter, Nell	Birmingham, AL	9/13/48
Carter, Ron	Royal Oak Twp, MI	5/4/37
Carter, Nick	Jamestown, NY	1/28/80
Cartwright, Nancy	Dayton, OH	10/25/59
Caruso, David	Forest Hills, NY	1/17/56
Carvey, Dana	Missoula, MT	4/2/55
Cash, Johnny	Kingsland, AR	2/26/32
Cash, Rosanne	Memphis, TN	5/24/55
Cassidy, David	New York, NY	4/12/50
Castellaneta, Dan	Chicago, IL	1958
Cates, Phoebe	New York, NY	7/16/63
Cathbert, Lacey	Purvis, MS	9/30/82
Cattrall, Kim	Liverpool, England	8/21/56
Cavanagh, Tom	Ottawa, Canada	10/26/68
Cavett, Dick	Gibbon, NE	11/19/36
Chamberlain, Richard	Beverly Hills, CA	3/31/35
Chan, Jackie	Hong Kong	4/7/54
Channing, Carol	Seattle, WA	1/31/23
Channing, Stockard	New York, NY	2/13/44
Chaplin, Geraldine	Santa Monica, CA	7/31/44
Chapman, Tracy	Cleveland, OH	3/30/64
Charisse, Cyd	Amarillo, TX	3/8/21
Charles, Ray	Albany, GA	9/23/30
Charo	Murcia, Spain	1/15/51
Chase, Chevy	New York, NY	10/8/43
Chasez, Joshua (J.C.)	Washington, DC	8/8/76
Cheadle, Don	Kansas City, MO	11/29/64
Checker, Chubby	Philadelphia, PA	10/3/41
Cher	El Centro, CA	5/20/46
Chianese, Dominic	Bronx, NY	9/2/34
Chiklis, Michael	Lowell, MA	8/30/63
Cho, Margaret	San Francisco	12/5/68
Chong, Rae Dawn	Vancouver, British Columbia	2/28/62
Chong, Thomas	Edmonton, Alberta	5/24/38
Chow Yun-Fat	Hong Kong	5/18/55
Christensen, Hayden	Vancouver, British Columbia	4/19/81
Christensen, Helena	Copenhagen, Denmark	12/25/68
Christie, Julie	Assam, India	4/14/40
Christopher, William	Evanston, IL	10/20/32
Church, Charlotte	Llandaff, Wales	2/21/86
Church, Thomas Haden	El Paso, TX	6/17/61
Clapton, Eric	Surrey, England	3/30/45
Clark, Dick	Mt. Vernon, NY	11/30/29
Clark, Petula	Ewell, Surrey, England	11/15/32
Clark, Roy	Meherrin, VA	4/15/33
Clay, Andrew Dice	Brooklyn, NY	9/29/58
Clayburgh, Jill	New York, NY	4/30/44
Cleese, John	Weston-Super-Mare, Eng.	10/27/39
Cliburn, Van	Shreveport, LA	7/12/34
Clooney, George	Lexington, KY	5/6/61
Close, Glenn	Greenwich, CT	3/19/47
Coburn, James	Laurel, NE	8/31/28
Coen, Ethan	St. Louis Park, MN	9/21/57
Coen, Joel	St. Louis Park, MN	11/29/54
Cole, Gary	Park Ridge, IL	9/20/57
Cole, Natalie	Los Angeles, CA	2/6/50
Cole, Olivia	Memphis, TN	11/26/42
Cole, Paula	Manchester, CT	4/5/68
Coleman, Dabney	Austin, TX	1/3/32
Coleman, Gary	Zion, IL	2/8/68
Coleman, Ornette	Fort Worth, TX	3/9/30
Collette, Toni	Blacktown, Australia	11/1/72
Collins, Joan	London, England	5/23/33
Collins, Judy	Seattle, WA	5/1/39
Collins, Pauline	Exmouth, England	9/3/40
Collins, Phil	London, England	1/30/51
Collins, Stephen	Des Moines, IA	10/1/47
Colvin, Shawn	Vermillion, SD	1/10/56
Combs, Sean "Puffy"	Harlem, NY	11/9/69
Comden, Betty	Brooklyn, NY	5/3/19
Connelly, Jennifer	Catskill Mountains, NY	12/12/70
Connery, Sean	Edinburgh, Scotland	8/25/30
Connick, Harry, Jr.	New Orleans, LA	9/11/67
Conniff, Ray	Attleboro, MA	11/6/16
Connors, Mike	Fresno, CA	8/15/25
Conrad, Robert	Chicago, IL	3/1/35
Conroy, Francis	Monroe, GA	11/13/53
Constantine, Michael	Reading, PA	5/22/27
Conti, Tom	Paisley, Scotland	11/22/41
Conway, Tim	Willoughby, OH	12/15/33
Cook, Barbara	Atlanta, GA	10/25/27
Cooke, Alistair	Manchester, England	11/20/08
Coolidge, Rita	Nashville, TN	5/1/45
Coolio	Los Angeles, CA	8/1/63
Cooper, Alice	Detroit, MI	2/4/48
Cooper, Jackie	Los Angeles, CA	9/15/21
Copperfield, David	Metuchen, NJ	9/16/56
Coppola, Francis Ford	Detroit, MI	4/7/39
Coppola, Sofia	New York, NY	3/12/71
Corbett, John	Wheeling, WV	5/9/61
Corbin, Barry	Lamesa, TX	10/16/40
Cord, Alex	New York, NY	8/3/31
Corea, Chick	Chelsea, MA	6/12/41
Corelli, Franco	Ancona, Italy	4/8/23
Corey, Jeff	New York, NY	8/10/14
Corley, Pat	Dallas, TX	6/1/30
Corwin, Jeff	Halifax, Nova Sotia	1967
Cosby, Bill	Philadelphia, PA	7/12/37
Costas, Bob	New York, NY	3/22/52
Costello, Elvis	London, England	8/25/54
Costner, Kevin	Compton, CA	1/18/55
Courtenay, Tom	Hull, England	2/25/37
Cowell, Simon	London, England	10/7/59
Cox, Courteney	Birmingham, AL	6/15/64
Cox, Nikki	Los Angeles, CA	6/2/78
Cox, Ronny	Cloudcroft, NM	8/23/38
Coyote, Peter	New York, NY	10/10/42
Crain, Jeanne	Barstow, CA	5/25/25
Crawford, Cindy	DeKalb, IL	2/20/66
Crawford, Michael	Salisbury, England	1/19/42
Crenna, Richard	Los Angeles, CA	11/30/26
Crespin, Regine	Marseilles, France	2/23/26
Cronyn, Hume	London, Ontario	7/18/11
Crosby, David	Los Angeles, CA	8/14/41
Cross, Ben	London, England	12/16/47
Crouse, Lindsay	New York, NY	5/12/48
Crow, Sheryl	Kennett, MO	2/11/63
Crowe, Cameron	Palm Springs, CA	7/13/57
Crowe, Russell	New Zealand	4/7/64
Crowell, Rodney	Houston, TX	8/17/50
Crudup, Billy	New York, NY	6/8/68
Cruise, Tom	Syracuse, NY	7/3/62
Cruz, Penelope	Madrid, Spain	4/28/74
Crystal, Billy	Long Beach, NY	3/14/47
Culkin, Kieran	New York, NY	9/30/82
Culkin, Macaulay	New York, NY	8/26/80
Culkin, Rory	New York, NY	1989
Cullum, John	Knoxville, TN	3/2/30
Culp, Robert	Oakland, CA	8/16/30
Cummings, Constance	Seattle, WA	5/15/10
Curry, Tim	Cheshire, England	4/19/46
Curtin, Jane	Cambridge, MA	9/6/47
Curtis, Jamie Lee	Los Angeles, CA	11/22/58
Curtis, Keene	Salt Lake City, UT	2/15/23
Curtis, Tony	New York, NY	6/3/25
Cusack, Joan	Evanston, IL	10/11/62
Cusack, John	Evanston, IL	6/28/66
Cyrus, Billy Ray	Flatwoods, KY	8/25/61
Dafoe, Willem	Appleton, WI	7/22/55
Dahl, Arlene	Minneapolis, MN	8/11/28
Dale, Jim	Rothwell, England	8/15/35
Dalton, Abby	Las Vegas, NV	8/15/32
Dalton, Timothy	Colwyn Bay, Wales	3/21/44
Daltrey, Roger	London, England	3/1/44
Daly, Carson	Santa Monica, CA	6/22/73
Daly, Timothy	Suffern, NY	3/1/56
Daly, Tyne	Madison, WI	2/21/47
Damon, Matt	Cambridge, MA	10/8/70
Damone, Vic	Brooklyn, NY	6/12/28
Danes, Claire	New York, NY	4/12/79
Daniels, Anthony	Salisbury, England	2/21/46
D'Angelo	Richmond, VA	2/11/74
D'Angelo, Beverly	Columbus, OH	11/15/54
Dangerfield, Rodney	Babylon, NY	11/22/21
Daniels, Charlie	Wilmington, NC	10/28/36
Daniels, Jeff	Georgia	2/19/55
Daniels, William	Brooklyn, NY	3/31/27
Danner, Blythe	Philadelphia, PA	2/3/44
Danson, Ted	San Diego, CA	12/29/47
Danza, Tony	New York, NY	4/21/51
Darby, Kim	Hollywood, CA	7/8/48
David, Larry	Brooklyn, NY	1947
Davidson, John	Pittsburgh, PA	12/13/41
Davis, Ann B.	Schenectady, NY	5/5/26
Davis, Clifton	Chicago, IL	10/4/45
Davis, Geena	Wareham, MA	1/21/57

Name	Birthplace	Birthdate
Davis, Judy	Perth, Australia	1955
Davis, Kristin	Boulder, CO	2/24/65
Davis, Mac	Lubbock, TX	1/21/42
Davis, Ossie	Cogdell, GA	12/18/17
Dawber, Pam	Farmington Hills, MI	10/18/51
Dawson, Richard	Hampshire, England	11/20/32
Dawson, Rosario	New York, NY	5/9/79
Day, Doris	Cincinnati, OH	4/3/24
Day, Laraine	Roosevelt, UT	10/13/20
Day-Lewis, Daniel	London, England	4/29/57
Dean, Jimmy	Plainview, TX	8/10/28
Dearie, Blossom	E. Durham, NY	4/28/26
DeCarlo, Yvonne	Vancouver, BC	9/1/22
Dee, Frances	Los Angeles, CA	11/26/07
Dee, Ruby	Cleveland, OH	10/27/23
Dee, Sandra	Bayonne, NJ	4/23/42
DeFranco, Buddy	Camden, NJ	2/17/23
DeGeneres, Ellen	Metairie, LA	1/26/58
DeHaven, Gloria	Los Angeles, CA	7/23/25
De Havilland, Olivia	Tokyo, Japan	7/1/16
Delaney, Kim	Philadelphia, PA	11/29/64
Delany, Dana	New York, NY	3/11/56
DeLaurentiis, Dino	Torre Annunziata, Italy	8/8/19
Delon, Alain	Sceaux, France	11/8/35
Del Toro, Benicio	Santurce, Puerto Rico	2/19/67
DeLuise, Dom	Brooklyn, NY	8/1/33
Demme, Jonathan	Rockville Centre, NY	2/22/44
DeMornay, Rebecca	Santa Rosa, CA	11/29/61
Dench, Judi	York, England	12/9/34
Deneuve, Catherine	Paris, France	10/22/43
De Niro, Robert	New York, NY	8/17/43
Dennehy, Brian	Bridgeport, CT	7/9/38
Denver, Bob	New Rochelle, NY	1/9/35
DePalma, Brian	Newark, NJ	9/11/40
Depardieu, Gerard	Chateauroux, France	12/27/48
Depp, Johnny	Owensboro, KY	6/9/63
Derek, Bo	Long Beach, CA	11/20/56
Dern, Bruce	Chicago, IL	6/4/36
Dern, Laura	Santa Monica, CA	2/1/67
Devane, William	Albany, NY	9/5/37
DeVito, Danny	Neptune, NJ	11/17/44
DeWitt, Joyce	Wheeling, WV	4/23/49
Dey, Susan	Pekin, IL	12/10/52
Diamond, Neil	Brooklyn, NY	1/24/41
Diaz, Cameron	San Diego, CA	8/30/72
DiCaprio, Leonardo	Los Angeles, CA	11/11/74
Dick, Andy	Charleston, SC	12/21/66
Dickinson, Angie	Kulm, ND	9/30/31
Diddley, Bo	McComb, MS	12/20/28
Diesel, Vin	New York, NY	7/18/67
Diggs, Taye	Rochester, NY	1/2/71
Diller, Phyllis	Lima, OH	7/17/17
Dillman, Bradford	San Francisco, CA	4/14/30
Dion, Celine	Charlemagne, Quebec	3/30/68
Dillon, Matt	New Rochelle, NY	2/18/64
Dobson, Kevin	New York, NY	3/18/44
Dogg, Snoop	Long Beach, CA	10/20/72
Doherty, Shannen	Memphis, TN	4/21/71
Dolenz, Mickey	Los Angeles, CA	3/8/45
Domingo, Placido	Madrid, Spain	1/21/41
Domino, Fats	New Orleans, LA	2/26/28
Donahue, Phil	Cleveland, OH	12/21/35
D'Onofrio, Vincent	Brooklyn, NY	6/30/59
Donovan (Leitch)	Glasgow, Scotland	2/10/46
Dorn, Michael	Luling, TX	12/5/52
Dorough, Howie	Orlando, FL	8/22/73
Dotrice, Roy	Guernsey, England	5/26/23
Douglas, Kirk	Amsterdam, NY	12/9/16
Douglas, Michael	New Brunswick, NJ	9/25/44
Dow, Tony	Holywood, CA	3/17/45
Down, Lesley-Ann	London, England	3/17/54
Downey, Robert, Jr.	New York, NY	4/4/65
Downey, Roma	Derry, Northern Ireland	5/6/60
Downs, Hugh	Akron, OH	2/14/21
Drescher, Fran	Queens, NY	9/30/57
Drew, Ellen	Kansas City, MO	11/23/15
Dreyfuss, Richard	Brooklyn, NY	10/29/47
Driver, Minnie	London, England	1/31/71
Dryer, Fred	Hawthorne, CA	7/6/46
Duchovny, David	New York, NY	8/7/60
Duff, Hilary	Houston, TX	9/28/87
Duffy, Julia	Minneapolis, MN	6/27/51
Duffy, Patrick	Townsend, MT	3/17/49
Dukakis, Olympia	Lowell, MA	6/20/31
Duke, Patty	New York, NY	12/14/46
Dullea, Keir	Cleveland, OH	5/30/36
Dunaway, Faye	Bascom, FL	1/14/41
Duncan, Lindsay	Edinburgh, Scotland	11/7/50
Duncan, Sandy	Henderson, TX	2/20/46
Dunham, Katherine	Joliet, IL	6/22/10
Dunne, Griffin	New York, NY	6/8/55
Dunst, Kirsten	New Jersey	4/30/82
Durbin, Deanna	Winnipeg, Manitoba	12/4/21
Durning, Charles	Highland Falls, NY	2/28/23
Dussault, Nancy	Pensacola, FL	6/30/36
Dutton, Charles S.	Baltimore, MD	1/30/51
Duvall, Robert	San Diego, CA	1/5/31
Duvall, Shelley	Houston, TX	7/7/49
Dylan, Bob	Duluth, MN	5/24/41
Dylan, Jakob	New York, NY	12/9/69
Dysart, Richard	Augusta, ME	3/30/29
Dzundza, George	Rosenheim, Germany	7/19/45
Easton, Sheena	Bellshill, Scotland	4/27/59
Eastwood, Clint	San Francisco, CA	5/31/30
Ebert, Roger	Urbana, IL	6/18/42
Ebsen, Buddy	Belleville, IL	4/2/08
Eden, Barbara	Tucson, AZ	8/23/34
Edwards, Anthony	Santa Barbara, CA	7/19/63
Edwards, Blake	Tulsa, OK	7/26/22
Edwards, Ralph	Merino, CO	6/13/13
Eichhorn, Lisa	Reading, PA	2/4/52
Eikenberry, Jill	New Haven, CT	1/21/47
Ekberg, Anita	Malmo, Sweden	9/29/31
Ekland, Britt	Stockholm, Sweden	10/6/42
Elam, Jack	Miami, AZ	11/13/16
Electra, Carmen	Cincinnati, OH	4/20/73
Elfman, Jenna	Los Angeles, CA	9/30/71
Elizabeth, Shannon	Houston, TX	9/7/73
Elizondo, Hector	New York, NY	12/22/36
Elliott, Bob	Boston, MA	3/26/23
Elliott, Chris	New York, NY	1960
Elliott, Sam	Sacramento, CA	8/9/44
Elvira	Manhattan, KS	9/17/51
Eminem	St. Joseph, MO	10/17/72
Enberg, Dick	Auburn Hills, MI	1/5/35
Englund, Robert	Hollywood, CA	6/6/48
Enya	Gweedore, Ireland	5/17/61
Ephron, Nora	New York, NY	5/19/41
Estefan, Gloria	Havana, Cuba	9/1/57
Estevez, Emilio	New York, NY	5/12/62
Estrada, Erik	New York, NY	3/16/49
Etheridge, Melissa	Leavenworth, KS	5/29/61
Evans, Linda	Hartford, CT	11/18/42
Evans, Robert	New York, NY	6/29/30
Everett, Chad	South Bend, IN	6/11/36
Everett, Rupert	Norfolk, England	5/29/59
Everly, Don	Brownie, KY	2/1/37
Everly, Phil	Chicago, IL	1/19/39
Evigan, Greg	South Amboy, NJ	10/14/53
Fabares, Shelley	Santa Monica, CA	1/19/42
Fabian (Forte)	Philadelphia, PA	2/6/43
Fabio	Milan, Italy	3/15/61
Fabray, Nanette	San Diego, CA	10/27/20
Fairchild, Morgan	Dallas, TX	2/3/50
Falana, Lola	Philadelphia, PA	9/11/46
Falco, Edie	Brooklyn, NY	1965?
Falk, Peter	New York, NY	9/16/27
Fallon, Jimmy	Brooklyn, NY	9/19/74
Farentino, James	Brooklyn, NY	2/24/38
Fargo, Donna	Mt. Airy, NC	11/10/45
Farina, Dennis	Chicago, IL	2/29/44
Farr, Jamie	Toledo, OH	7/1/34
Farrell, Mike	St. Paul, MN	2/6/39
Farrelly, Bob	Cumberland, RI	1958
Farrelly, Peter	Phoenixville, PA	12/17/56
Farrow, Mia	Los Angeles, CA	2/9/45
Fatone, Joey	New York, NY	1/29/76
Faustino, David	California	3/3/74
Fawcett, Farrah	Corpus Christi, TX	2/2/47
Feinstein, Michael	Columbus, OH	9/7/56
Feldon, Barbara	Pittsburgh, PA	3/12/41
Feliciano, Jose	Lares, Puerto Rico	9/10/45
Feldshuh, Tovah	New York, NY	12/27/53
Fenn, Sherilyn	Detroit, MI	2/1/65
Ferrell, Conchata	Charleston, WV	3/28/43
Ferrell, Will	Irvine, CA	7/16/68
Ferrer, Mel	Elberon, NJ	8/25/17
Fey, Tina	Upper Darby, PA	5/18/70
Fiedler, John	Platteville, WI	2/3/25
Field, Sally	Pasadena, CA	11/6/46
Fiennes, Joseph	Salisbury, England	5/27/70
Fiennes, Ralph	Suffolk, England	12/22/62
Fincher, David	Denver, CO	1962
Finney, Albert	Salford, England	5/9/36
Fiorentino, Linda	Philadelphia, PA	3/9/60
Firth, Colin	Grayshott, England	9/10/60
Firth, Peter	Yorkshire, England	10/27/53
Fischer-Dieskau, Dietrich	Berlin, Germany	5/28/25
Fishburne, Laurence	Augusta, GA	7/30/61
Fisher, Carrie	Beverly Hills, CA	10/21/56

Name	Birthplace	Birthdate
Fisher, Eddie	Philadelphia, PA	8/10/28
Fitzgerald, Geraldine	Dublin, Ireland	11/24/13
Flack, Roberta	Black Mountain, NC	2/10/39
Flanagan, Fionnula	Dublin, Ireland	12/10/41
Fleming, Rhonda	Hollywood, CA	8/10/23
Fletcher, Louise	Birmingham, AL	7/22/34
Flockhart, Calista	Freeport, IL	11/11/64
Florek, Dann	Flat Rock, MI	5/1/50
Foch, Nina	Leyden, Netherlands	4/20/24
Fogelberg, Dan	Peoria, IL	8/13/51
Fogerty, John	Berkeley, CA	5/28/45
Foley, Dave	Toronto, Ontario	1/4/63
Fonda, Bridget	Los Angeles, CA	1/27/64
Fonda, Jane	New York, NY	12/21/37
Fonda, Peter	New York, NY	2/23/40
Fontaine, Joan	Tokyo, Japan	10/22/17
Ford, Faith	Alexandria, LA	9/14/64
Ford, Glenn	Quebec, Canada	5/1/16
Ford, Harrison	Chicago, IL	7/13/42
Forman, Milos	Caslav, Czechoslovakia	2/18/32
Forsythe, John	Penns Grove, NJ	1/29/18
Foster, Jodie	New York, NY	11/19/62
Fox, James	London, England	5/19/39
Fox, Matthew	Crowheart, WY	7/14/66
Fox, Michael J.	Edmonton, Alberta	6/9/61
Fox, Vivica A.	Indianapolis, IN	7/30/64
Foxworth, Robert	Houston, TX	11/1/41
Foxworthy, Jeff	Atlanta, GA	9/6/57
Foxx, Jamie	Terrell, TX	12/13/67
Frampton, Peter	Kent, England	4/22/50
Franciosa, Anthony	New York, NY	10/25/28
Francis, Anne	Ossining, NY	9/16/30
Francis, Connie	Newark, NJ	12/12/38
Franken, Al	New York, NY	5/21/51
Franklin, Aretha	Memphis, TN	3/25/42
Franklin, Bonnie	Santa Monica, CA	1/6/44
Franz, Dennis	Maywood, IL	10/28/44
Fraser, Brendan	Indianapolis, IN	12/3/67
Freeman, Al, Jr.	San Antonio, TX	3/21/34
Freeman, Mona	Baltimore, MD	6/9/26
Freeman, Morgan	Memphis, TN	6/1/37
French, Dawn	Holyhead, Wales	10/11/57
Fricker, Brenda	Dublin, Ireland	2/17/45
Friedkin, William	Chicago, IL	8/29/35
Frost, David	Tenterden, England	4/7/39
Fry, Stephen	London, England	8/24/57
Fuentes, Daisy	Havana, Cuba	11/17/66
Fuller, Robert	Troy, NY	7/29/34
Funicello, Annette	Utica, NY	10/22/42
Furlong, Edward	Glendale, CA	8/2/77
Furtado, Nelly	Victoria, British Columbia	12/2/78
Gabor, Zsa Zsa	Budapest, Hungary	2/6/17
Gabriel, John	Niagara Falls, NY	5/25/31
Gabriel, Peter	London, England	2/13/50
Galway, James	Belfast, Ireland	12/8/39
Gandolfini, James	Westwood, NJ	9/18/61
Garagiola, Joe	St. Louis, MO	2/12/26
Garcia, Andy	Havana, Cuba	4/12/56
Garofalo, Janeane	New Jersey	9/28/64
Garfunkel, Art	New York, NY	11/5/41
Garland, Beverly	Santa Cruz, CA	10/17/26
Garner, James	Norman, OK	4/7/28
Garner, Jennifer	Houston, TX	4/17/72
Garr, Teri	Lakewood, OH	12/11/45
Garrett, Betty	St. Joseph, MO	5/23/19
Garrett, Brad	Woodland Hills, CA	4/14/60
Garth, Jennie	Champaign, IL	4/3/72
Gatlin, Larry	Seminole, TX	5/2/48
Gavin, John	Los Angeles, CA	4/8/28
Gayle, Crystal	Paintsville, KY	1/9/51
Gaynor, Mitzi	Chicago, IL	9/4/30
Gazzara, Ben	New York, NY	8/28/30
Geary, Anthony	Coalville, UT	5/29/47
Geary, Cynthia	Jackson, MS	3/21/66
Gedda, Nicolai	Stockholm, Sweden	7/11/25
Gellar, Sarah Michelle	New York, NY	4/14/77
Gere, Richard	Philadelphia, PA	8/31/49
Getty, Estelle	New York, NY	7/25/24
Ghostley, Alice	Eve, MO	8/14/26
Giannini, Giancarlo	Spezia, Italy	8/1/42
Gibb, Barry	Isle of Man, England	9/1/46
Gibb, Maurice	Manchester, England	12/22/49
Gibb, Robin	Manchester, England	12/22/49
Gibbons, Leeza	South Carolina	3/26/57
Gibbs, Marla	Chicago, IL	6/14/31
Gibson, Deborah	New York, NY	8/31/70
Gibson, Henry	Germantown, PA	9/21/35
Gibson, Mel	Peekskill, NY	1/3/56
Gibson, Thomas	Charleston, SC	7/3/62
Gifford, Frank	Santa Monica, CA	8/16/30
Gifford, Kathie Lee	Paris, France	8/16/53
Gilbert, Sara	Santa Monica, CA	1/29/75
Gilbert, Melissa	Los Angeles, CA	5/8/64
Gilberto, Astrud	Salvador, Brazil	3/30/40
Gill, Vince	Norman, OK	4/12/57
Gillette, Anita	Baltimore, MD	8/16/38
Gilley, Mickey	Natchez, MS	3/9/36
Gilliam, Terry	Minneapolis, MN	11/22/40
Gilpin, Peri	Waco, TX	5/27/63
Ginty, Robert	New York, NY	11/14/48
Givens, Robin	New York, NY	11/27/64
Glaser, Paul Michael	Cambridge, MA	3/25/42
Glenn, Scott	Pittsburgh, PA	1/26/42
Gless, Sharon	Los Angeles, CA	5/31/43
Glover, Crispin	New York, NY	9/20/64
Glover, Danny	San Francisco, CA	7/22/47
Glover, Savion	Newark, NJ	1973
Godard, Jean Luc	Paris, France	12/3/30
Goldberg, Whoopi	New York, NY	11/13/49
Goldblum, Jeff	Pittsburgh, PA	10/22/52
Goldthwait, Bobcat	Syracuse, NY	5/1/62
Goldwyn, Tony	Los Angeles, CA	5/20/60
Gooding, Cuba, Jr.	Bronx, NY	1/2/68
Goodman, John	St. Louis, MO	6/20/52
Gordon-Levitt, Joseph	Los Angeles, CA	2/17/81
Gorme, Eydie	Bronx, NY	8/16/32
Gorshin, Frank	Pittsburgh, PA	4/5/34
Gossett, Louis, Jr.	Brooklyn, NY	5/27/36
Gould, Elliott	Brooklyn, NY	8/29/38
Gould, Harold	Schenectady, NY	12/10/23
Goulet, Robert	Lawrence, MA	11/26/33
Gowdy, Curt	Green River, WY	7/31/19
Graham, Heather	Milwaukee, WI	1/29/70
Grammer, Kelsey	St. Thomas, Virgin Isl.	2/20/55
Granger, Farley	San Jose, CA	7/1/25
Grant, Amy	Augusta, GA	12/25/60
Grant, Hugh	London, England	9/9/60
Grant, Lee	New York, NY	10/31/29
Graves, Peter	Minneapolis, MN	3/18/26
Gray, Linda	Santa Monica, CA	9/12/40
Gray, Macy	Canton, OH	1970?
Gray, Spaulding	Barrington, RI	6/5/41
Grayson, Kathryn	Winston-Salem, NC	2/9/22
Green, Adolph	New York, NY	12/2/15
Green, Al	Forrest City, AR	4/13/46
Green, Seth	Philadelphia, PA	2/8/74
Green, Tom	Pembroke, Canada	7/30/71
Greene, Shecky	Chicago, IL	4/8/26
Greenwood, Bruce	Quebec, Canada	8/12/56
Gregory, Cynthia	Los Angeles, CA	7/8/46
Gregory, Dick	St. Louis, MO	10/12/32
Gregory, James	Bronx, NY	12/23/11
Grey, Jennifer	New York, NY	3/22/60
Grey, Joel	Cleveland, OH	4/11/32
Grier, David Alan	Detroit, MI	6/30/55
Grier, Pam	Winston-Salem, NC	5/26/49
Griffin, Merv	San Mateo, CA	7/6/25
Griffith, Andy	Mount Airy, NC	6/1/26
Griffith, Melanie	New York, NY	8/9/57
Griffiths, Rachel	New Castle, Australia	1968
Grimes, Tammy	Lynn, MA	1/30/34
Grint, Rupert	Hertfordshire, England	8/24/88
Grizzard, George	Roanoke Rapids, NC	4/1/28
Grodin, Charles	Pittsburgh, PA	4/21/35
Grosbard, Ulu	Antwerp, Belgium	1/19/29
Gross, Michael	Chicago, IL	6/21/47
Guest, Christopher	New York, NY	2/5/48
Guillaume, Robert	St. Louis, MO	11/30/37
Gumbel, Greg	New Orleans, LA	5/3/46
Guthrie, Arlo	New York, NY	7/10/47
Guttenberg, Steve	New York, NY	8/24/58
Guy, Buddy	Lettsworth, LA	7/30/36
Guy, Jasmine	Boston, MA	3/10/64
Gyllenhaal, Jake	Los Angeles, CA	12/19/80
Hackett, Buddy	Brooklyn, NY	8/31/24
Hackman, Gene	San Bernardino, CA	1/30/30
Hagen, Uta	Gottingen, Germany	6/12/19
Haggard, Merle	Bakersfield, CA	4/6/37
Hagman, Larry	Weatherford, TX	9/21/31
Haid, Charles	San Francisco, CA	6/2/44
Haines, Connie	Savannah, GA	1/20/22
Hale, Barbara	DeKalb, IL	4/18/22
Hall, Arsenio	Cleveland, OH	2/12/55
Hall, Daryl	Pottstown, PA	10/11/48
Hall, Deidre	Milwaukee, WI	10/31/48
Hall, Michael C.	Raleigh, NC	2/1/71
Hall, Monty	Winnipeg, Manitoba	8/25/25
Hall, Tom T.	Olive Hill, KY	5/25/36
Halliwell, Geri	Hertfordshire, England	8/6/72
Hamill, Mark	Oakland, CA	9/25/51

Name	Birthplace	Birthdate
Hamilton, George	Memphis, TN	8/12/39
Hamilton, Linda	Salisbury, MD	9/26/56
Hamlin, Harry	Pasadena, CA	10/30/51
Hammer	Oakland, CA	3/29/63
Hammond, Darrell	Melbourne, FL	10/8/60
Hancock, Herbie	Chicago, IL	4/12/40
Hanks, Tom	Oakland, CA	7/9/56
Hannah, Daryl	Chicago, IL	12/3/60
Hannigan, Alyson	Washington, DC	3/24/74
Hanson, Curtis	Los Angeles, CA	3/24/45
Hanson, Isaac	Tulsa, OK	11/17/80
Hanson, Taylor	Tulsa, OK	3/14/83
Hanson, Zac	Arlington, VA	10/22/85
Harden, Marcia Gay	Tokyo, Japan	8/14/59
Hardison, Kadeem	New York, NY	7/24/66
Harewood, Dorian	Dayton, OH	8/6/51
Harmon, Angie	Dallas, TX	8/10/72
Harmon, Mark	Burbank, CA	9/2/51
Harper, Jessica	Chicago, IL	10/10/49
Harper, Tess	Mammoth Springs, AR	8/15/50
Harper, Valerie	Suffern, NY	8/22/40
Harrelson, Woody	Midland, TX	7/23/61
Harrington, Pat	New York, NY	8/13/29
Harris, Barbara	Evanston, IL	7/25/35
Harris, Ed	Englewood, NJ	11/28/50
Harris, Emmylou	Birmingham, AL	4/2/47
Harris, Julie	Grosse Pte. Park, MI	12/2/25
Harris, Neil Patrick	Albuquerque, NM	6/15/73
Harris, Richard	Co. Limerick, Ireland	10/1/33
Harris, Rosemary	Ashby, England	9/19/30
Harrison, Gregory	Avalon, CA	5/31/50
Harry, Deborah	Miami, FL	7/1/45
Hart, Mary	Madison, SD	11/8/51
Hart, Melissa Joan	Sayville, NY	4/18/76
Hartley, Hal	Lindenhurst, NY	11/3/59
Hartley, Mariette	New York, NY	6/21/40
Hartman, David	Pawtucket, RI	5/19/35
Hartman, Lisa	Houston, TX	6/1/56
Hartnett, Josh	San Francisco, CA	7/21/78
Hasselhoff, David	Baltimore, MD	7/17/52
Hatcher, Teri	Sunnyvale, CA	12/8/64
Hathaway, Anne	Brooklyn, NY	11/12/82
Hauer, Rutger	Breukelen, Netherlands	1/23/44
Haver, June	Rock Island, IL	6/10/26
Havoc, June	Seattle, WA	11/8/16
Hawke, Ethan	Austin, TX	11/6/70
Hawn, Goldie	Washington, DC	11/21/45
Hayden, Melissa	Toronto, Ontario	4/25/23
Hayek, Salma	Coatzacoalcos, Mexico	9/2/68
Hayes, Isaac	Covington, TN	8/20/42
Hayes, Sean	Glen Ellyn, IL	6/26/70
Hays, Robert	Bethesda, MD	7/24/47
Head, Anthony Stewart	London, England	2/20/54
Heard, John	Washington, DC	3/7/45
Hearn, George	Memphis, TN	1935
Heaton, Patricia	Bay Village, OH	3/4/59
Heche, Anne	Aurora, OH	5/25/69
Hedren, Tippi	New Ulm, MN	1/19/35
Helfgott, David	Melbourne, Australia	5/19/47
Helgenberger, Marg	North Bend, NE	11/16/68
Helmond, Katherine	Galveston, TX	7/5/34
Hemingway, Mariel	Mill Valley, CA	11/21/61
Hemmings, David	Guildford, England	11/18/41
Hemsley, Sherman	Philadelphia, PA	2/1/38
Henderson, Florence	Dale, IN	2/14/34
Henderson, Skitch	Halstad, MN	1/27/18
Henley, Don	Gilmer, TX	7/22/47
Henner, Marilu	Chicago, IL	4/6/52
Hennessey, Jill	Edmonton, Canada	11/25/69
Henry, Buck	New York, NY	12/9/30
Hepburn, Katharine	Hartford, CT	5/12/07
Herman, Pee-Wee	Peekskill, NY	8/27/52
Herrmann, Edward	Washington, DC	7/21/43
Hershey, Barbara	Los Angeles, CA	2/5/48
Hesseman, Howard	Lebanon, OR	2/27/40
Heston, Charlton	Evanston, IL	10/4/24
Hetfield, James	Los Angeles, CA	8/3/63
Hewitt, Jennifer Love	Waco, TX	2/21/79
Hildegarde	Adell, WI	2/1/06
Hill, Arthur	Melfort, Sask	8/1/22
Hill, Dulé	Orange, NJ	5/3/74
Hill, Faith	Jackson, MS	9/21/67
Hill, George Roy	Minneapolis, MN	12/20/22
Hill, Lauryn	South Orange, NJ	5/25/75
Hill, Steven	Seattle, WA	2/24/22
Hiller, Wendy	Stockport, England	8/15/12
Hillerman, John	Denison, TX	12/30/32
Hines, Gregory	New York, NY	2/14/46
Hines, Roy	Boston, MA	3/13/26
Hines, Jerome	Hollywood, CA	11/8/21
Hingle, Pat	Miami, FL	7/19/24

Name	Birthplace	Birthdate
Hirsch, Judd	New York, NY	3/15/35
Ho, Don	Kakaako, Oahu, HI	8/13/30
Hoffman, Dustin	Los Angeles, CA	8/8/37
Hoffman, Philip Seymour	Fairport, NY	7/23/67
Hogan, Paul	New South Wales, Australia	10/8/39
Holbrook, Hal	Cleveland, OH	2/17/25
Holder, Geoffrey	Trinidad	8/1/30
Holliday, Polly	Jasper, AL	8/2/37
Holliman, Earl	Delhi, LA	9/11/28
Holly, Lauren	Bristol, PA	10/28/63
Holm, Celeste	New York, NY	4/29/19
Holm, Ian	Goodmayes, England	9/12/31
Holmes, Katie	Toledo, OH	12/18/78
Hooks, Jan	Decatur, GA	4/23/57
Hope, Bob	London, England	5/29/03
Hopkins, Anthony	Port Talbot, South Wales	12/31/37
Hopkins, Bo	Greenville, SC	2/2/42
Hopkins, Telma	Louisville, KY	10/28/48
Hopper, Dennis	Dodge City, KS	5/17/36
Horne, Lena	Brooklyn, NY	6/30/17
Horne, Marilyn	Bradford, PA	1/16/34
Hornsby, Bruce	Williamsburg, VA	11/23/54
Horsley, Lee	Muleshoe, TX	5/15/55
Horton, Robert	Los Angeles, CA	7/29/24
Hoskins, Bob	Suffolk, England	10/26/42
Houston, Whitney	E Orange, NJ	8/9/63
Howard, Ken	El Centro, CA	3/28/44
Howard, Ron	Duncan, OK	3/1/54
Howell, C. Thomas	Los Angeles, CA	12/7/66
Howes, Sally Ann	London, England	7/20/30
Hudson, Kate	Los Angeles, CA	4/19/79
Hughes, Barnard	Bedford Hills, NY	7/16/15
Hulce, Tom	Whitewater, WI	12/6/53
Humperdinck, Engelbert	Madras, India	5/3/36
Hunt, Helen	Los Angeles, CA	6/15/63
Hunt, Linda	Morristown, NJ	4/2/45
Hunter, Holly	Conyers, GA	3/20/58
Hunter, Tab	New York, NY	7/11/31
Hurley, Elizabeth	Hampshire, England	6/10/65
Hurt, John	Chesterfield, England	1/22/40
Hurt, Mary Beth	Marshalltown, IA	9/26/46
Hurt, William	Washington, DC	3/20/50
Hussey, Ruth	Providence, RI	10/30/14
Huston, Anjelica	Santa Monica, CA	7/8/51
Hutton, Betty	Battle Creek, MI	2/26/21
Hutton, Lauren	Charleston, SC	11/17/44
Hutton, Timothy	Malibu, CA	8/16/60
Hyman, Earle	Rocky Mount, NC	10/11/26
Ian, Janis	New York, NY	4/7/51
Ice Cube	Los Angeles, CA	6/15/69
Ice-T	Newark, NJ	2/16/58
Idle, Eric	Durham, England	3/29/43
Idol, Billy	London, England	11/30/55
Iglesias, Enrique	Madrid, Spain	5/8/75
Iglesias, Julio	Madrid, Spain	9/23/43
Iler, Robert	New York, NY	3/2/85
Iman	Mogadishu, Somalia	7/25/55
Imbruglia, Natalie	Australia	2/4/75
Imperioli, Michael	Mount Vernon, NY	1/1/66
Imus, Don	Riverside, CA	7/23/40
Ireland, Kathy	Santa Barbara, CA	3/8/63
Ingram, James	Akron, OH	2/16/56
Irons, Jeremy	Cowes, England	9/19/48
Irving, Amy	Palo Alto, CA	9/10/53
Irving, George S.	Springfield, MA	11/1/22
Irwin, Bill	Santa Monica, CA	4/11/50
Irwin, Steve	Victoria, Australia	2/22/62
Ivey, Judith	El Paso, TX	9/4/51
Ivory, James	Berkeley, CA	6/7/28
Jackee	Winston-Salem, NC	8/14/56
Jackman, Hugh	Sydney, Australia	10/12/68
Jackson, Anne	Allegheny, PA	9/3/25
Jackson, Glenda	Liverpool, England	5/9/36
Jackson, Janet	Gary, IN	5/16/66
Jackson, Jermaine	Gary, IN	12/11/54
Jackson, Jonathan	Orlando, FL	5/11/82
Jackson, Joshua	Vancouver, Brit. Columbia	6/11/78
Jackson, Kate	Birmingham, AL	10/29/48
Jackson, La Toya	Gary, IN	5/29/56
Jackson, Michael	Gary, IN	8/29/58
Jackson, Peter	Pukerua, New Zealand	10/31/61
Jackson, Samuel L.	Chattanooga, TN	12/21/48
Jacobi, Derek	London, England	10/22/38
Jagger, Mick	Dartford, England	7/26/43
James, Etta	Los Angeles, CA	1938
James, Kevin	Stony Brook, NY	4/26/65
Janis, Conrad	New York, NY	2/11/28
Janney, Allison	Dayton, OH	11/19/60
Janssen, Famke	Amsterdam, Netherlands	11/5/65

Name	Birthplace	Birthdate
Jardine, Al	Lima, OH	9/3/42
Jarmusch, Jim	Akron, OH	1/22/53
Jarreau, Al	Milwaukee, WI	3/12/40
Jarrette, Keith	Allentown, PA	5/8/45
Jeffreys, Anne	Goldsboro, NC	1/26/23
Jeter, Michael	Lawrenceburg, TN	8/20/52
Jett, Joan	Philadelphia, PA	9/22/60
Jewel (Kilcher)	Payson, UT	5/23/74
Jewison, Norman	Toronto, Ontario	7/21/26
Jillian, Ann	Cambridge, MA	1/29/50
Jillette, Penn	Greenfield, MA	3/5/55
Joel, Billy	Bronx, NY	5/9/49
John, Elton	Middlesex, England	3/25/47
Johns, Glynis	Durban, S Africa	10/5/23
Johnson, Arte	Benton Harbor, MI	1/20/29
Johnson, Beverly	Buffalo, NY	10/13/52
Johnson, Don	Flatt Creek, MO	12/15/49
Johnson, Van	Newport, RI	8/25/16
Johnston, Bruce	Chicago, IL	6/24/44
Johnston, Kristen	Washington, DC	9/20/67
Jolie, Angelina	Los Angeles, CA	6/4/75
Jones, Charlie	Ft. Smith, AR	11/9/30
Jones, Cherry	Paris, TN	11/21/56
Jones, Davy	Manchester, England	12/30/45
Jones, Dean	Morgan City, AL	1/25/35
Jones, Elvin	Pontiac, MI	9/9/27
Jones, Gemma	London, England	12/4/42
Jones, George	Saratoga, TX	9/12/31
Jones, Grace	Spanishtown, Jamaica	5/19/52
Jones, Jack	Hollywood, CA	1/14/38
Jones, James Earl	Tate Co., MS	1/17/31
Jones, Jennifer	Tulsa, OK	3/2/19
Jones, Quincy	Chicago, IL	3/14/33
Jones, Shirley	Smithton, PA	3/31/34
Jones, Star	Badin, NC	3/24/62
Jones, Tom	Pontypridd, Wales	6/7/40
Jones, Tommy Lee	San Saba, TX	9/15/46
Jonze, Spike	Rockville, MD	1969
Jourdan, Louis	Marseilles, France	6/19/19
Jovovich, Milla	Kiev, Ukraine	12/19/75
Judd, Ashley	Los Angeles, CA	4/19/68
Judd, Naomi	Ashland, KY	1/11/46
Judd, Wynonna	Ashland, KY	5/30/64
Jump, Gordon	Dayton, OH	4/1/32
Kanaly, Steve	Burbank, CA	3/14/46
Kane, Carol	Cleveland, OH	6/18/52
Kaplan, Gabe	Brooklyn, NY	3/31/45
Karlen, John	New York, NY	5/28/33
Karn, Richard	Seattle, WA	2/17/56
Karras, Alex	Gary, IN	7/15/35
Kasem, Casey	Detroit, MI	4/27/33
Kattan, Chris	Los Angeles, CA	10/19/70
Kavner, Julie	Los Angeles, CA	9/7/51
Kazan, Elia	Istanbul, Turkey	9/7/09
Kazan, Lainie	New York, NY	5/15/42
Keach, Stacy	Savannah, GA	6/2/41
Keaton, Diane	Santa Ana, CA	1/5/46
Keaton, Michael	Pittsburgh, PA	9/9/51
Keel, Howard	Gillespie, IL	4/13/17
Keener, Catherine	Miami FL	1961
Keeshan, Bob	Lynbrook, NY	6/27/27
Keitel, Harvey	Brooklyn, NY	5/13/39
Keith, David	Knoxville, TN	5/8/54
Keith, Penelope	Sutton, Surrey, Eng.	4/2/40
Kellerman, Sally	Long Beach, CA	6/2/37
Kelly, R(obert)	Illinois	1967?
Kennedy, George	New York, NY	2/18/25
Kennedy, Jayne	Washington, DC	11/27/51
Kenny G	Seattle, WA	6/5/56
Kent, Allegra	Los Angeles, CA	8/11/37
Kercheval, Ken	Wolcottville, IN	7/15/35
Kerns, Joanna	San Francisco, CA	2/12/53
Kerr, Deborah	Helensburgh, Scotland	9/30/21
Kessel, Barney	Muskogee, OK	10/17/23
Keys, Alicia	New York, NY	1/25/81
Khan, Chaka	Great Lakes, IL	3/23/53
Kidder, Margot	Yellowknife, N.W.T.	10/17/48
Kidman, Nicole	Honolulu, HI	6/20/67
Kilborn, Craig	Hastings, MN	8/24/62
Kilmer, Val	Los Angeles, CA	12/31/59
Kimbrough, Charles	St. Paul, MN	5/23/36
King, Alan	Brooklyn, NY	12/26/27
King, B. B.	Itta Bena, MS	9/16/25
King, Carole	Brooklyn, NY	2/9/42
King, Larry	Brooklyn, NY	11/19/33
King, Perry	Alliance, OH	4/30/48
Kingsley, Ben	Yorkshire, England	12/31/43
Kinnear, Greg	Logansport, IN	6/17/63
Kinney, Kathy	Stevens Point, WI	11/3/54
Kinski, Nastassja	Berlin, W. Germany	1/24/60

Name	Birthplace	Birthdate
Kirby, Bruno	New York, NY	4/28/49
Kirkland, Gelsey	Bethlehem, PA	12/29/53
Kirkpatrick, Chris	Pennsylvania	10/17/71
Kitt, Eartha	North, SC	1/17/27
Klein, Robert	New York, NY	2/8/42
Kline, Kevin	St. Louis, MO	10/24/47
Klugman, Jack	Philadelphia, PA	4/27/22
Knight, Gladys	Atlanta, GA	5/28/44
Knight, Shirley	Goessel, KS	7/5/36
Knight, Wayne	Cartersville, GA	8/7/55
Knotts, Don	Morgantown, WV	7/21/24
Knowles, Beyoncé	Houston, TX	9/4/80
Konitz, Lee	Chicago, IL	10/13/27
Kopell, Bernie	New York, NY	6/21/33
Korman, Harvey	Chicago, IL	2/15/27
Kotto, Yaphet	New York, NY	11/15/37
Krakowski, Jane	Parsippany, NJ	1969
Krause, Peter	Alexandria, MN	8/12/65
Kristofferson, Kris	Brownsville, TX	6/22/36
Kudrow, Lisa	Encino, CA	5/30/63
Kurtz, Swoosie	Omaha, NE	9/6/44
LaBelle, Patti	Philadelphia, PA	5/24/44
Ladd, Cheryl	Huron, SD	7/12/51
Ladd, Diane	Meridian, MS	11/29/32
Lagassé, Emeril	Fall River, MA	10/15/59(?)
Lahti, Christine	Detroit, MI	4/5/50
Laine, Cleo	Middlesex, England	10/28/27
Laine, Frankie	Chicago, IL	3/30/13
Lake, Ricki	New York, NY	9/21/68
Lamas, Lorenzo	Santa Monica, CA	1/20/58
Lambert, Christopher	New York, NY	3/29/57
Landau, Martin	New York, NY	6/20/34
Landis, John	Chicago, IL	8/3/50
Lane, Diane	New York, NY	1/22/63
Lane, Nathan	Jersey City, NJ	2/3/56
lang, k.d.	Consort, Alberta	11/2/61
Lang, Stephen	New York, NY	7/11/52
Lange, Hope	Redding Ridge, CT	11/28/31
Lange, Jessica	Cloquet, MN	4/20/49
Langella, Frank	Bayonne, NJ	1/1/40
Langford, Frances	Lakeland, FL	4/4/13
Lansbury, Angela	London, England	10/16/25
LaPaglia, Anthony	Adelaide, Australia	1/31/59
Laredo, Ruth	Detroit, MI	11/20/37
Larroquette, John	New Orleans, LA	11/25/47
LaSalle, Eriq	Hartford, CT	6/23/63
Lauper, Cyndi	New York, NY	6/20/53
Laurie, Piper	Detroit, MI	1/22/32
Lavin, Linda	Portland, ME	10/15/37
Law, Jude	London, England	12/29/72
Lawless, Lucy	Mount Albert, New Zealand	3/28/68
Lawrence, Carol	Melrose Park, IL	9/5/34
Lawrence, Joey	Montgomery, PA	4/20/76
Lawrence, Martin	Frankfurt, Germany	4/16/65
Lawrence, Steve	Brooklyn, NY	7/8/35
Lawrence, Vicki	Inglewood, CA	3/26/49
Leach, Robin	London, England	8/29/41
Leachman, Cloris	Des Moines, IA	4/4/26
Lear, Norman	New Haven, CT	7/27/22
Leary, Denis	Boston, MA	8/18/57
Learned, Michael	Washington, DC	4/9/39
LeBlanc, Matt	Newton, MA	7/25/67
LeBon, Simon	Bushey, England	10/27/58
Ledger, Heath	Perth, Australia	4/4/79
Lee, Ang	Taiwan	10/23/54
Lee, Brenda	Atlanta, GA	12/11/44
Lee, Christopher	London, England	5/27/22
Lee, Michele	Los Angeles, CA	6/24/42
Lee, Pamela Anderson	Comox, Canada	7/1/67
Lee, Spike	Atlanta, GA	3/20/57
Leeves, Jane	London, England	4/18/62
Legrand, Michel	Paris, France	2/24/32
Leguizamo, John	Bogota, Colombia	7/22/65
Leibman, Ron	New York, NY	10/11/37
Leigh, Janet	Merced, CA	7/6/27
Leigh, Jennifer Jason	Los Angeles, CA	2/5/62
Leighton, Laura	Iowa City, IA	3/14/69
Lennox, Annie	Aberdeen, Scotland	12/25/54
Leno, Jay	New Rochelle, NY	4/28/50
Leonard, Robert Sean	Westwood, NJ	2/28/69
Leoni, Tea	New York, NY	2/25/66
Leslie, Joan	Detroit, MI	1/26/25
Leto, Jared	Bossier City, LA	12/26/71
Letterman, David	Indianapolis, IN	4/12/47
Levine, James	Cincinnati, OH	6/23/43
Levinson, Barry	Baltimore, MD	6/2/32
Levy, Eugene	Hamilton, Canada	12/17/46
Lewis, Al	New York, NY	4/30/10
Lewis, Huey	New York, NY	7/5/51
Lewis, Jerry	Newark, NJ	3/16/26

Name	Birthplace	Birthdate
Lewis, Jerry Lee	Ferriday, LA	9/29/35
Lewis, John	La Grange, IL	5/30/20
Lewis, Juliette	San Fernando Valley, CA	6/21/73
Lewis, Richard	New York, NY	6/29/47
Li, Jet	Beijing, China	4/26/63
Light, Judith	Trenton, NJ	2/9/50
Lightfoot, Gordon	Orillia, Ontario	11/17/38
Lil' Kim	Brooklyn, NY	7/11/75
Linden, Hal	New York, NY	3/20/31
Ling, Lisa	Sacramento, CA	8/30/73
Linkletter, Art	Saskatchewan, Canada	7/17/12
Linn-Baker, Mark	St. Louis, MO	6/17/53
Linney, Laura	New York, NY	2/5/64
Liotta, Ray	Newark, NJ	12/18/55
Lithgow, John	Rochester, NY	10/19/45
Little, Rich	Ottawa, Ontario	11/26/38
Little Richard	Macon, GA	12/5/32
Littrell, Brian	Lexington, KY	2/20/75
Liu, Lucy	New York, NY	12/2/67
L. L. Cool J	New York, NY	1/14/68
Lloyd, Christopher	Stamford, CT	10/22/38
Lloyd, Emily	England	9/29/70
Lloyd Webber, Andrew	London, England	3/22/48
Locke, Sondra	Shelbyville, TN	5/28/47
Lockhart, June	New York, NY	6/25/25
Locklear, Heather	Los Angeles, CA	9/25/61
Loggia, Robert	New York, NY	1/3/30
Loggins, Kenny	Everett, WA	1/17/47
Lollobrigida, Gina	Subiaco, Italy	7/4/27
Lom, Herbert	Prague, Czechoslovakia	1/9/17
Lonergan, Kenneth	New York, NY	1963
Long, Nia	New York, NY	10/30/70
Long, Shelley	Ft. Wayne, IN	8/23/49
Lopez, Jennifer	Bronx, NY	7/24/70
Loren, Sophia	Rome, Italy	9/20/34
Loring, Gloria	New York, NY	12/10/46
Loudon, Dorothy	Boston, MA	9/17/33
Louis-Dreyfus, Julia	New York, NY	1/13/61
Love, Courtney	San Francisco, CA	7/9/64
Love, Mike	Los Angeles, CA	3/15/41
Lovett, Lyle	Klein, TX	11/1/57
Lovitz, Jon	Tarzana, CA	7/21/57
Loveless, Patty	Pikeville, KY	1/4/57
Lowe, Rob	Charlottesville, VA	3/17/64
Lowell, Carey	New York, NY	2/11/61
Lucas, George	Modesto, CA	5/14/44
Lucci, Susan	Scarsdale, NY	12/23/48
Luckinbill, Laurence	Ft. Smith, AR	11/21/34
Ludwig, Christa	Berlin, Germany	3/16/28
Luhrmann, Baz	New South Wales, Australia	9/17/62
Lumet, Sidney	Philadelphia, PA	6/25/24
LuPone, Patti	Northport, NY	4/21/49
Lynch, David	Missoula, MT	1/20/46
Lynley, Carol	New York, NY	2/13/42
Lynn, Loretta	Butcher Hollow, KY	4/14/35
Lynne, Shelby	Quantico, VA	10/22/68
Lyonne, Natasha	New York, NY	4/4/79
Ma, Yo-Yo	Paris, France	10/7/55
Maazel, Lorin	Paris, France	3/6/30
Mac, Bernie	Chicago, IL	1958
MacArthur, James	Los Angeles, CA	12/8/37
MacCorkindale, Simon	Cambridge, England	2/12/52
MacDowell, Andie	Gaffney, SC	4/21/58
MacGraw, Ali	Pound Ridge, NY	4/1/38
MacLachlan, Kyle	Yakima, WA	2/22/59
MacLaine, Shirley	Richmond, VA	4/24/34
MacLeod, Gavin	Mt. Kisco, NY	2/28/30
MacNee, Patrick	London, England	2/6/22
MacNeil, Cornell	Minneapolis, MN	9/24/22
MacNicol, Peter	Dallas, TX	4/10/54
MacPherson, Elle	Sydney, Australia	3/29/64
Macchio, Ralph	Long Island, NY	11/4/62
Macy, Bill	Revere, MA	5/18/22
Macy, William H.	Miami, FL	3/13/50
Madden, John	Austin, MN	4/10/36
Madigan, Amy	Chicago, IL	9/11/51
Madonna (Ciccone)	Bay City, MI	8/16/58
Maguire, Tobey	Santa Monica, CA	6/27/75
Maher, Bill	Rivervale, NJ	1/20/56
Mahoney, John	Manchester, England	6/20/40
Majors, Lee	Wyandotte, MI	4/23/40
Malden, Karl	Chicago, IL	3/22/13
Malick, Terrence	Ottawa, IL	11/30/43
Malick, Wendie	Buffalo, NY	12/13/50
Malkovich, John	Christopher, IL	12/9/53
Malone, Dorothy	Chicago, IL	1/30/25
Mamet, David	Chicago, IL	11/30/47
Manchester, Melissa	Bronx, NY	2/15/51
Mandel, Howie	Toronto, Ontario	11/29/55
Mandrell, Barbara	Houston, TX	12/25/48
Mangione, Chuck	Rochester, NY	11/29/40
Manilow, Barry	New York, NY	6/17/46
Mann, Herbie	New York, NY	4/16/30
Manoff, Dinah	New York, NY	1/25/58
Manson, Marilyn	Canton, OH	1/5/69
Mantegna, Joe	Chicago, IL	11/13/47
Marceau, Marcel	Strasbourg, France	3/22/23
Margulies, Julianna	Spring Valley, NY	6/8/66
Marin, Cheech	Los Angeles, CA	7/13/46
Marinaro, Ed	New York, NY	3/31/50
Markova, Alicia	London, England	12/1/10
Marriner, Neville	Lincoln, England	4/15/24
Marsalis, Branford	New Orleans, LA	8/26/60
Marsalis, Wynton	New Orleans, LA	10/18/61
Marsh, Jean	London, England	7/1/34
Marshall, Garry	New York, NY	11/13/34
Marshall, Penny	New York, NY	10/15/43
Marshall, Peter	Huntington, WV	3/30/27
Martin, Dick	Detroit, MI	1/30/23
Martin, Jesse L.	Rocky Mountain, VA	1/18/69
Martin, Kellie	Riverside, CA	10/16/75
Martin, Ricky	San Juan, Puerto Rico	12/24/71
Martin, Steve	Waco, TX	1945
Martin, Tony	San Francisco, CA	12/25/13
Martins, Peter	Copenhagen, Denmark	10/27/46
Mason, Jackie	Sheboygan, WI	6/9/31
Mason, Marsha	St. Louis, MO	4/3/42
Masterson, Mary Stuart	Los Angeles, CA	6/28/66
Mastrantonio, Mary Elizabeth	Lombard, IL	11/17/58
Masur, Kurt	Brieg, Germany	7/18/27
Masur, Richard	New York, NY	11/20/48
Mathers, Jerry	Sioux City, IA	6/2/48
Matheson, Tim	Glendale, CA	12/31/47
Mathis, Johnny	San Francisco, CA	9/30/35
Matlin, Marlee	Morton Grove, IL	8/24/65
Matthews, Dave	Johannesburg, South Africa	1/9/67
May, Elaine	Philadelphia, PA	4/21/32
Mayo, Virginia	St. Louis, MO	11/30/20
Mazursky, Paul	Brooklyn, NY	4/25/30
McArdle, Andrea	Philadelphia, PA	11/5/63
McBride, Patricia	Teaneck, NJ	8/23/42
McCallum, David	Glasgow, Scotland	9/19/33
McCambridge, Mercedes	Joliet, IL	3/17/18
McCarthy, Andrew	Westfield, NJ	11/29/62
McCarthy, Jenny	Chicago, IL	11/1/72
McCarthy, Kevin	Seattle, WA	2/15/14
McCartney, Paul	Liverpool, England	6/18/42
McCarver, Tim	Memphis, TN	10/16/41
McClanahan, Rue	Healdton, OK	2/21/36
McConaughey, Matthew	Uvalde, Texas	11/4/69
McCoo, Marilyn	Jersey City, NJ	9/30/43
McCormack, Eric	Toronto, Canada	4/18/63
McCormack, Mary	Plainsfield, NJ	4/8/69
McDaniel, James	Washington, DC	3/25/58
McDermott, Dylan	Waterbury, CT	10/26/62
McDiarmid, Ian	Dundee, Tayside, Scotland	4/17/47
McDonald, Audra	Berlin, Germany	1970
McDonnell, Mary	Wilkes-Barre, PA	1952
McDormand, Frances	Illinois	6/23/57
McDowell, Malcolm	Leeds, England	6/13/43
McEntire, Reba	McAlester, OK	3/28/55
McFerrin, Bobby	New York, NY	3/11/50
McGavin, Darren	Spokane, WA	5/7/22
McGillis, Kelly	Newport Beach, CA	7/9/57
McGoohan, Patrick	New York, NY	3/19/28
McGovern, Elizabeth	Evanston, IL	7/18/61
McGovern, Maureen	Youngstown, OH	7/27/49
McGraw, Tim	Delhi, LA	5/1/67
McGregor, Ewan	Crieff, Scotland	3/31/71
McGuire, Al	New York, NY	9/7/31
McKean, Michael	New York, NY	10/17/47
McKechnie, Donna	Pontiac, MI	11/16/42
McKellen, Ian	Burnley, England	5/25/39
McLachlan, Sarah	Halifax, Nova Scotia	1/28/68
McLean, A.J.	West Palm Beach, FL	1/9/78
McMahon, Ed	Detroit, MI	3/6/23
McNichol, Kristy	Los Angeles, CA	9/11/62
McPartland, Marian	Stough, England	3/20/20
McRaney, Gerald	Collins, MS	8/19/48
Meadows, Jayne	Wu Chang, China	9/27/20
Meara, Anne	New York, NY	9/20/29
Meat Loaf	Dallas, TX	9/27/47
Mehta, Zubin	Bombay, India	4/29/36
Mellencamp, John	Seymour, IN	10/7/51
Mendes, Sam	Reading, England	8/1/65
Mendes, Sergio	Niteroi, Brazil	2/11/41
Mercer, Marian	Akron, OH	11/26/35
Merchant, Natalie	Jamestown, NY	10/26/63
Merrill, Dina	New York, NY	12/9/25

Name	Birthplace	Birthdate
Merrill, Robert	Brooklyn, NY	6/4/19
Messing, Debra	Brooklyn, NY	8/15/68
Metcalf, Laurie	Carbondale, IL	6/16/55
Michael, George	Watford, England	6/25/63
Michaels, Al	New York, NY	11/12/44
Michaels, Lorne	Toronto, Canada	11/17/44
Midler, Bette	Honolulu, HI	12/1/45
Midori	Osaka, Japan	10/25/71
Milano, Alyssa	New York, NY	12/19/72
Miles, Sarah	Ingatestone, England	12/31/41
Miles, Vera	near Boise City, OK	8/23/29
Miller, Ann	Houston, TX	4/12/19
Miller, Dennis	Pittsburgh, PA	11/3/53
Miller, Mitch	Rochester, NY	7/4/11
Miller, Penelope Ann	Los Angeles, CA	1/13/64
Mills, Donna	Chicago, IL	12/11/42
Mills, John	Suffolk, England	2/22/08
Milner, Martin	Detroit, MI	12/28/27
Milnes, Sherrill	Downers Grove, IL	1/10/35
Milsap, Ronnie	Robinsville, NC	1/16/44
Minghella, Anthony	Isle of Wight, England	1/6/54
Minnelli, Liza	Los Angeles, CA	3/12/46
Minogue, Kylie	Melbourne, Australia	5/28/68
Mirren, Helen	London, England	7/2/46
Mitchell, Joni	McLeod, Alberta	11/7/43
Moby	New York, NY	9/11/65
Modine, Matthew	Loma Linda, CA	3/22/59
Moffat, Donald	Plymouth, England	12/26/30
Moffo, Anna	Wayne, PA	6/27/27
Molinaro, Al	Kenosha, WI	6/24/19
Moll, Richard	Pasadena, CA	1/13/43
Monica (Arnold)	College Park, GA	10/24/80
Montalban, Ricardo	Mexico City, Mexico	11/25/20
Moody, Ron	London, England	1/8/24
Moore, Demi	Roswell, NM	11/11/62
Moore, Julianne	Boston, MA	12/30/60
Moore, Mandy	Nashua, NH	4/10/84
Moore, Mary Tyler	Brooklyn, NY	12/29/36
Moore, Melba	New York, NY	10/29/45
Moore, Roger	London, England	10/14/27
Moore, Terry	Los Angeles, CA	1/1/29
Moranis, Rick	Toronto, Ontario	4/18/53
Moreau, Jeanne	Paris, France	1/23/28
Moreno, Rita	Humacao, PR	12/11/31
Morgan, Harry	Detroit, MI	4/10/15
Moriarty, Michael	Detroit, MI	4/5/41
Morissette, Alanis	Ottawa, Ontario	6/1/74
Morita, Pat	Isleton, CA	6/28/32
Morris, Garrett	New Orleans, LA	2/1/37
Morris, Howard	New York, NY	9/4/25
Morrison, Van	Belfast, N. Ireland	8/31/45
Morrissey	Manchester, England	5/22/59
Morrow, Rob	New Rochelle, NY	9/21/62
Morse, David	Hamilton, MA	10/11/53
Morse, Robert	Newton, MA	5/18/31
Mortensen, Viggo	New York, NY	10/20/58
Morton, Joe	New York, NY	10/18/47
Morton, Samantha	Nottingham, Enlgand	5/13/77
Moses, William	Los Angeles, CA	11/17/59
Moss, Carrie-Ann	Vancouver, British Columbia	8/21/67
Moss, Kate	London, England	1/16/74
Mr. T	Chicago, IL	5/21/52
Mueller-Stahl, Armin	Tilsit, E. Prussia	12/17/20
Muldaur, Diana	New York, NY	8/19/38
Mulgrew, Kate	Dubuque, IA	4/29/55
Mull, Martin	Chicago, IL	8/18/43
Mullally, Megan	Los Angeles, CA	11/12/58
Mulroney, Dermot	Alexandria, VA	10/31/63
Muniz, Frankie	Ridgewood, NJ	12/5/85
Munsel, Patrice	Spokane, WA	5/14/25
Murphy, Ben	Jonesboro, AR	3/6/42
Murphy, Brittany	Atlanta, GA	11/10/77
Murphy, Eddie	Brooklyn, NY	4/3/61
Murphy, Michael	Los Angeles, CA	5/5/38
Murray, Anne	Springhill, Nova Scotia	6/20/45
Murray, Bill	Evanston, IL	9/21/50
Murray, Don	Hollywood, CA	7/31/29
Musburger, Brent	Portland, OR	5/26/39
Muti, Riccardo	Naples, Italy	7/28/41
Myers, Mike	Toronto, Ontario	5/25/63
Nabors, Jim	Sylacauga, AL	6/12/33
Nash, Graham	Blackpool, England	2/2/42
Naughton, James	Middletown, CT	7/6/46
Neal, Patricia	Packard, KY	1/20/26
Nealon, Kevin	Bridgeport, CT	11/18/53
Neeson, Liam	Ballymena, N. Ireland	6/7/52
Neill, Sam	Ulster, N. Ireland	9/14/47
Nelligan, Kate	London, Ontario	3/16/51
Nelson, Craig T.	Spokane, WA	4/4/46
Nelson, Ed	New Orleans, LA	12/21/28
Nelson, Judd	Portland, ME	11/28/59
Nelson, Tracy	Santa Monica, CA	10/25/63
Nelson, Willie	Abbott, TX	4/30/33
Nero, Peter	New York, NY	5/22/34
Nesmith, Mike	Dallas, TX	12/30/42
Nettleton, Lois	Oak Park, IL	8/16/31
Neuwirth, Bebe	Princeton, NJ	12/31/58
Neville, Aaron	New Orleans, LA	1/24/41
Newhart, Bob	Oak Park, IL	9/5/29
Newman, Paul	Cleveland, OH	1/26/25
Newman, Randy	Los Angeles, CA	11/28/43
Newton, Wayne	Norfolk, VA	4/3/42
Newton-John, Olivia	Cambridge, England	9/26/47
Nicholas, Denise	Detroit, MI	7/12/44
Nicholas, Fayard	Philadelphia, PA	10/20/14
Nichols, Mike	Berlin, Germany	11/6/31
Nicholson, Jack	Neptune, NJ	4/28/37
Nicks, Stevie	Phoenix, AZ	5/26/48
Nielsen, Connie	Elling, Jutland, Denmark	7/3/65
Nielsen, Leslie	Regina, Sask	2/11/26
Nilsson, Birgit	Karup, Sweden	5/17/18
Nimoy, Leonard	Boston, MA	3/26/31
Nixon, Cynthia	New York, NY	4/9/66
Nolte, Nick	Omaha, NE	2/8/40
Noone, Peter	Manchester, England	11/5/47
Norman, Jessye	Augusta, GA	9/15/45
Norris, Chuck	Ryan, OK	3/10/40
North, Sheree	Los Angeles, CA	1/17/33
Northam, Jeremy	Cambridge, Enlgand	12/1/61
Norton, Edward	Columbia, MD	1969
Noth, Christopher	Madison, WI	11/13/57
Novak, Kim	Chicago, IL	2/13/33
Nuyen, France	Marseille, France	7/31/39
Oates, John	New York, NY	4/7/48
O'Brian, Hugh	Rochester, NY	4/19/25
O'Brien, Conan	Brookline, MA	4/18/63
O'Brien, Margaret	San Diego, CA	1/15/37
Ocean, Billy	Fyzabad, Trinidad	1/21/50
O'Connor, Donald	Chicago, IL	8/28/25
O'Connor, Frances	Oxford, England	6/12/69
O'Connor, Sinead	Dublin, Ireland	12/8/66
Odotta	Birmingham, AL	12/31/30
O'Donnell, Chris	Winnetka, IL	6/26/70
O'Donnell, Rosie	Commack, NY	3/21/62
O'Hara, Catherine	Toronto, Canada	3/4/54
O'Hara, Maureen	Dublin, Ireland	8/17/20
O'Herlihy, Dan	Wexford, Ireland	5/1/19
Oldman, Gary	London, England	3/21/58
Olin, Ken	Chicago, IL	7/30/54
Olin, Lena	Stockholm, Sweden	3/22/55
Olmos, Edward James	E. Los Angeles, CA	2/24/47
Olsen, Ashley	California	6/13/86
Olsen, Mary-Kate	California	6/13/86
Olsen, Merlin	Logan, UT	9/15/40
O'Neal, Ryan	Los Angeles, CA	4/20/41
O'Neal, Tatum	Los Angeles, CA	11/5/63
O'Neill, Ed	Youngstown, OH	4/12/46
Ontkean, Michael	Vancouver, B.C.	1/24/46
Orbach, Jerry	New York, NY	10/20/35
Orlando, Tony	New York, NY	4/3/44
Ormond, Julia	Epsom, England	1/4/65
Osbourne, Jack	London, England (?)	11/8/85
Osbourne, Kelly	London, England	10/27/84
Osbourne, Ozzy	Birmingham, England	12/3/48
Osbourne, Sharon	London, England	10/10/52
O'Shea, Milo	Dublin, Ireland	6/2/26
Oslin, K.T.	Crosset, AR	1942
Osment, Haley Joel	Los Angeles, CA	4/10/88
Osmond, Donny	Ogden, UT	12/9/57
Osmond, Marie	Ogden, UT	10/13/59
O'Toole, Annette	Houston, TX	4/1/53
O'Toole, Peter	Connemara, Ireland	8/2/32
Owens, Buck	Sherman, TX	8/12/29
Oz, Frank	Herford, England	5/25/44
Ozawa, Seiji	Shenyang, China	9/1/35
Paar, Jack	Canton, OH	5/1/18
Pacino, Al	New York, NY	4/25/40
Packer, Billy	Wellsville, NY	2/25/40
Page, Bettie	Kingsport, TN	4/22/23
Page, Jimmy	Heston, England	1/9/44
Page, Patti	Claremore, OK	11/8/27
Paget, Debra	Denver, CO	8/19/33
Paige, Janis	Tacoma, WA	9/16/22
Palance, Jack	Lattimer, PA	2/18/20
Palin, Michael	Sheffield, England	5/5/43
Palmer, Betsy	East Chicago, IN	11/1/29
Palmer, Geoffrey	London, England	6/4/27
Palmer, Robert	Bately, England	1/19/49

Name	Birthplace	Birthdate
Palminteri, Chazz	Bronx, NY	5/15/51
Paltrow, Gwyneth	Los Angeles, CA	9/28/73
Pantoliano, Joe	Hoboken, NJ	9/12/51
Papas, Irene	Chiliomedion, Greece	3/9/26
Paquin, Anna	Wellington, New Zealand	6/24/82
Parker, Alan	London, England	2/14/44
Parker, Eleanor	Cedarville, OH	6/26/22
Parker, Fess	Ft. Worth, TX	8/16/25
Parker, Jameson	Baltimore, MD	11/18/47
Parker, Jean	Deer Lodge, MT	8/11/15
Parker, Mary-Louise	Fort Jackson, SC	8/2/64
Parker, Sarah Jessica	Nelsonville, OH	3/25/65
Parsons, Estelle	Lynn, MA	11/20/27
Parton, Dolly	Sevierville, TN	1/19/46
Patinkin, Mandy	Chicago, IL	11/30/52
Patric, Jason	Queens, NY	6/17/66
Patton, Will	Charleston, SC	6/14/54
Paul, Adrian	London, England	5/29/59
Paulson, Sarah	Tampa, FL	12/17/75
Pavarotti, Luciano	Modena, Italy	10/12/35
Paxton, Bill	Fort Worth, TX	5/17/55
Paycheck, Johnny	Greenfield, OH	5/31/41
Pearce, Guy	Ely, England	10/5/67
Peck, Gregory	La Jolla, CA	4/5/16
Peet, Amanda	New York, NY	1/11/72
Pendergrass, Teddy	Philadelphia, PA	3/26/50
Penn, Arthur	Philadelphia, PA	9/27/22
Penn, Sean	Burbank, CA	8/17/60
Penny, Joe	London, England	9/14/56
Perez, Rosie	Brooklyn, NY	9/6/64
Perkins, Elizabeth	New York, NY	11/18/60
Perlman, Itzhak	Tel Aviv, Israel	8/31/45
Perlman, Rhea	Brooklyn, NY	3/31/48
Perlman, Ron	New York, NY	4/13/50
Perrine, Valerie	Galveston, TX	9/3/43
Perry, Luke	Fredericktown, OH	10/11/66
Perry, Mathew	Williamstown, MA	8/19/69
Persoff, Nehemiah	Jerusalem, Israel	8/14/20
Pesci, Joe	Newark, NJ	2/9/43
Peters, Bernadette	New York, NY	2/28/48
Peters, Brock	New York, NY	7/2/27
Peters, Roberta	New York, NY	5/4/30
Peterson, Oscar	Montreal, Quebec	8/15/25
Peterson, Wolfgang	Emden, Germany	3/14/41
Petty, Tom	Gainesville, FL	10/20/53
Pfeiffer, Michelle	Santa Ana, CA	4/29/58
Philbin, Regis	New York, NY	8/25/34
Phillippe, Ryan	New Castle, DE	9/10/75
Phillips, Lou Diamond	Philippines	2/17/62
Phillips, Mackenzie	Alexandria, VA	11/10/59
Phillips, Michelle	Long Beach, CA	6/4/44
Phoenix, Joaquin	Puerto Rico	10/28/74
Pickett, Wilson	Prattville, AL	3/18/41
Pierce, David Hyde	Albany, NY	4/3/59
Pinchot, Bronson	New York, NY	5/20/59
Pinkett Smith, Jada	Baltimore, MD	9/18/71
Pirner, David	Green Bay, WI	4/16/64
Piscopo, Joe	Passaic, NJ	6/17/51
Pitt, Brad	Shawnee, OK	12/18/64
Plant, Robert	W. Bromwich, England	8/20/48
Pleshette, Suzanne	New York, NY	1/31/37
Plowright, Joan	Brigg, England	10/28/29
Plummer, Amanda	New York, NY	3/23/57
Plummer, Christopher	Toronto, Ontario	12/13/27
Poitier, Sidney	Miami, FL	2/20/27
Polanski, Roman	Paris, France	8/18/33
Pollack, Sydney	Lafayette, IN	7/1/34
Ponti, Carlo	Milan, Italy	12/11/13
Pop, Iggy	Ann Arbor, MI	4/21/47
Portman, Natalie	Jerusalem, Israel	6/9/81
Posey, Parker	Baltimore, MD	11/8/64
Post, Markie	Palo Alto, CA	11/4/50
Poston, Tom	Columbus, OH	10/17/27
Potts, Annie	Nashville, TN	10/28/52
Povich, Maury	Washington, DC	1/17/39
Powell, Jane	Portland, OR	4/1/28
Powers, Stefanie	Hollywood, CA	11/2/42
Prentiss, Paula	San Antonio, TX	3/4/39
Presley, Priscilla	New York, NY	5/24/46
Preston, Billy	Houston, TX	9/9/46
Previn, Andre	Berlin, Germany	4/6/29
Price, Leontyne	Laurel, MS	2/10/27
Price, Ray	Perryville, TX	1/12/26
Pride, Charley	Sledge, MS	3/18/38
Priestley, Jason	Vancouver, Brit. Columbia	8/28/69
Prince (The Artist)	Minneapolis, MN	6/7/58
Principal, Victoria	Fukuoka, Japan	1/3/50
Prinze, Freddie, Jr.	Albuquerque, NM	3/8/76
Probst, Jeff	Wichita, KS	1962
Prosky, Robert	Philadelphia, PA	12/13/30
Pryce, Jonathan	Wales	6/1/47

Name	Birthplace	Birthdate
Pryor, Richard	Peoria, IL	12/1/40
Puck, Wolfgang	St. Veit, Austria	1/8/49
Pulliam, Keshia Knight	Newark, NJ	4/9/79
Pullman, Bill	Hornell, NY	12/17/54
Purcell, Sarah	Richmond, IN	10/8/48
Quaid, Dennis	Houston, TX	4/9/54
Quaid, Randy	Houston, TX	10/1/50
Queen Latifah	East Orange, NJ	3/18/70
Quinn, Aidan	Chicago, IL	3/8/59
Quinn, Colin	Brooklyn, NY	1959
Quinn, Martha	Albany, NY	5/11/59
Rachins, Alan	Cambridge, MA	10/10/47
Radcliffe, Daniel	London, England	7/23/89
Rae, Charlotte	Milwaukee, WI	4/22/26
Raffi	Cairo, Egypt	7/8/48
Rainer, Luise	Vienna, Austria	1/12/10
Raitt, Bonnie	Burbank, CA	11/8/49
Ramey, Samuel	Colby, KS	3/28/42
Ramone, Johnny	Long Island, NY	10/8/51
Ramone, Tommy	Budapest, Hungary	1/29/52
Randall, Tony	Tulsa, OK	2/26/20
Randolph, John	New York, NY	6/1/15
Randolph, Joyce	Detroit, MI	10/21/25
Raphael, Sally Jessy	Easton, PA	2/25/43
Rashad, Phylicia	Houston, TX	6/17/48
Ratzenberger, John	Bridgeport, CT	4/6/47
Rawls, Lou	Chicago, IL	12/1/36
Reagan, Ronald	Tampico, IL	2/6/11
Reddy, Helen	Melbourne, Australia	10/25/41
Redford, Robert	Santa Monica, CA	8/18/37
Redgrave, Lynn	London, England	3/8/43
Redgrave, Vanessa	London, England	1/30/37
Reed, Jerry	Atlanta, GA	3/20/37
Reed, Lou	Long Island, NY	3/2/43
Reed, Rex	Ft. Worth, TX	10/2/38
Reese, Della	Detroit, MI	7/6/31
Reeve, Christopher	New York, NY	9/25/52
Reeves, Keanu	Beirut, Lebanon	9/2/64
Regalbuto, Joe	New York, NY	8/24/49
Reid, Tara	Wyckoff, NJ	11/8/75
Reid, Tim	Norfolk, VA	12/19/44
Reilly, Charles Nelson	New York, NY	1/13/31
Reilly, John C.	Chicago, IL	5/24/65
Reiner, Carl	Bronx, NY	3/20/22
Reiner, Rob	Bronx, NY	3/6/45
Reinhold, Judge	Wilmington, DE	5/21/56
Reinking, Ann	Seattle, WA	11/10/50
Reiser, Paul	New York, NY	3/30/57
Reitman, Ivan	Czechoslovakia	10/27/46
Remini, Leah	Brooklyn, NY	6/15/70
Resnik, Regina	New York, NY	8/30/24
Reynolds, Burt	Waycross, GA	2/11/36
Reynolds, Debbie	El Paso, TX	4/1/32
Reznor, Trent	Mercer, PA	5/17/65
Rhames, Ving	New York, NY	5/12/61
Rhymes, Busta	Brooklyn, NY	5/20/72
Ribisi, Giovanni	Los Angeles, CA	12/17/74
Ricci, Christina	Santa Monica, CA	2/12/80
Richards, Denise	Downers Grove, IL	2/17/72
Richards, Keith	Kent, England	12/18/43
Richards, Michael	Culver City, CA	7/21/49
Richardson, Ian	Edinburgh, Scotland	4/7/34
Richardson, Kevin	Lexington, KY	10/3/72
Richardson, Miranda	Lancashire, England	3/3/58
Richardson, Natasha	London, England	5/11/63
Richardson, Patricia	Bethesda, MD	2/23/51
Richie, Lionel	Tuskegee, AL	6/20/50
Rickles, Don	New York, NY	5/8/26
Rickman, Alan	Hammersmith, England	2/21/46
Riegert, Peter	New York, NY	4/11/47
Rigg, Diana	Doncaster, England	7/20/38
Rimes, LeAnn	Jackson, MS	8/28/82
Ringwald, Molly	Roseville, CA	2/18/68
Ripa, Kelly	Berlin, NJ	10/2/70
Ritter, John	Burbank, CA	9/17/48
Rivera, Chita	Washington, DC	1/23/33
Rivera, Geraldo	New York, NY	7/4/43
Rivers, Joan	Brooklyn, NY	6/8/37
Roach, Max	Elizabeth City, NC	1/10/24
Robbins, Tim	W. Covina, CA	10/16/58
Roberts, Doris	St. Louis, MO	11/4/25
Roberts, Eric	Biloxi, MS	4/18/56
Roberts, Julia	Smyrna, GA	10/28/67
Roberts, Pernell	Waycross, GA	5/18/30
Roberts, Tony	New York, NY	10/22/39
Robertson, Cliff	La Jolla, CA	9/9/25
Robertson, Dale	Harrah, OK	7/14/23
Robinson, Smokey	Detroit, MI	2/19/40
Roche, Eugene	Boston, MA	9/22/28

Name	Birthplace	Birthdate
Rochon, Lela	Los Angeles, CA	4/17/64
Rock, Chris	South Carolina	2/7/66
Rock, The (Dwayne Johnson)	Hayward, CA	5/2/72
Rodgers, Jimmy	Camas, WA	9/18/33
Rodriquez, Johnny	Sabinal, TX	12/10/51
Rogers, Fred	Latrobe, PA	3/20/28
Rogers, Kenny	Houston, TX	8/21/38
Rogers, Mimi	Coral Gables, FL	1/27/56
Rogers, Wayne	Birmingham, AL	4/7/33
Rohm, Elisabeth	Dusseldorf, Germany	4/28/73
Rollins, Henry	Washington, DC	2/13/61
Rollins, Sonny	New York, NY	9/7/29
Romano, Ray	New York, NY	12/21/57
Ronstadt, Linda	Tucson, AZ	7/15/46
Rooney, Mickey	Brooklyn, NY	9/23/20
Rose, Axl	Lafayette, IN	2/6/62
Rose Marie	New York, NY	8/15/25
Roseanne	Salt Lake City, UT	11/3/52
Ross, Diana	Detroit, MI	3/26/44
Ross, Katharine	Hollywood, CA	1/29/42
Rossdale, Gavin (Bush)	London, England	10/30/67
Ross, Marion	Albert Lea, MN	10/25/28
Rossellini, Isabella	Rome, Italy	6/18/52
Rostropovich, Mstislav	Baku, Azerbaijan	3/12/27
Roth, David Lee	Bloomington, IN	10/10/55
Roth, Tim	London, England	5/14/61
Rotten, Johnny	England	1/31/56
Rourke, Mickey	Schenectady, NY	7/16/53
Routledge, Patricia	Birkenhead, England	2/17/29
Rowlands, Gena	Cambria, WI	6/19/30
Rubinstein, John	Los Angeles, CA	12/8/46
Rudner, Rita	Coconut Grove, FL	9/17/56
Ruehl, Mercedes	Queens, NY	2/28/48
Ruffalo, Mark	Kenosha, WI	1968
Rush, Barbara	Denver, CO	1/4/30
Rush, Geoffrey	Toowoomba, Australia	1951
Russell, Jane	Bemidji, MN	6/21/21
Russell, Ken	Southampton, England	7/3/27
Russell, Keri	Fountain Valley, CA	3/23/76
Russell, Kurt	Springfield, MA	3/17/51
Russell, Mark	Buffalo, NY	8/23/32
Russell, Leon	Lawton, OK	4/2/41
Russell, Nipsey	Atlanta, GA	10/13/24
Russell, Theresa	San Diego, CA	3/20/57
Russo, Rene	Burbank, CA	2/17/54
Rutherford, Ann	Toronto, Ontario	11/2/20
Ruttan, Susan	Oregon City, OR	9/16/50
Ryan, Meg	Fairfield, CT	11/19/61
Ryan, Roz	Detroit, MI	7/7/51
Rydell, Bobby	Philadelphia, PA	4/26/42
Ryder, Winona	Winona, MN	10/29/71
Sabato, Antonio, Jr.	Rome, Italy	2/29/72
Sade	Ibadan, Nigeria	1/16/59
Sagal, Katie	Los Angeles, CA	1956
Saget, Bob	Philadelphia, PA	5/17/56
Sahl, Mort	Montreal, Quebec	5/11/27
Saint, Eva Marie	Newark, NJ	7/4/24
St. James, Susan	Los Angeles, CA	8/14/46
St. John, Jill	Los Angeles, CA	8/19/40
Sajak, Pat	Chicago, IL	10/26/47
Saks, Gene	New York, NY	11/8/21
Sales, Soupy	Franklinton, NC	1/8/26
Samms, Emma	London, England	8/28/60
Sandler, Adam	Brooklyn, NY	9/9/66
Sands, Julian	Yorkshire, England	1/15/58
Sanford, Isabel	New York, NY	8/29/17
San Giacomo, Laura	Hoboken, NJ	11/14/62
Santana, Carlos	Autlan, Mexico	7/20/47
Sarandon, Susan	New York, NY	10/4/46
Sarnoff, Dorothy	New York, NY	5/25/17
Sartain, Gailard	Tulsa, OK	9/18/46
Savage, Ben	Chicago, IL	9/13/80
Savage, Fred	Highland Park, IL	7/9/76
Sawa, Devon	Vancouver, Canada	9/7/78
Saxon, John	Brooklyn, NY	8/5/35
Sayles, John	Schenectady, NY	9/28/50
Scaggs, Boz	Dallas, TX	6/8/44
Scales, Prunella	Surrey, England	1933
Scalia, Jack	Brooklyn, NY	11/10/51
Schallert, William	Los Angeles, CA	7/6/22
Scheider, Roy	Orange, NJ	11/10/32
Schell, Maria	Vienna, Austria	1/15/26
Schell, Maximilian	Vienna, Austria	12/8/30
Schenkel, Chris	Bippus, IN	8/21/23
Schiffer, Claudia	Rheinbach, Germany	8/25/70
Schneider, John	Mt. Kisco, NY	4/8/54
Schneider, Rob	San Francisco, CA	10/31/64
Schreiber, Liev	San Francisco, CA	10/4/67
Schroder, Rick	Staten Island, NY	4/13/70
Schwarzenegger, Arnold	Graz, Austria	7/30/47
Schwarzkopf, Elisabeth	Jarotschin, Poland	12/9/15
Schwimmer, David	Queens, NY	11/12/67
Sciorra, Annabella	New York, NY	3/24/64
Scofield, Paul	Hurstpierpoint, England	1/21/22
Scolari, Peter	New Rochelle, IL	9/12/54
Scorsese, Martin	New York, NY	11/17/42
Scott, Lizabeth	Scranton, PA	9/29/22
Scott, Martha	Jamesport, MO	9/22/14
Scott, Ridley	Durham, England	11/30/37
Scott-Heron, Gil	Chicago, IL	4/1/49
Scott Thomas, Kristin	Cornwall, England	1960
Scotto, Renata	Savona, Italy	2/24/35
Scully, Vin	New York, NY	11/29/27
Seagal, Steven	Lansing, MI	4/10/51
Secor, Kyle	Tacoma, WA	5/31/60
Sedaka, Neil	New York, NY	3/13/39
Seeger, Pete	New York, NY	5/3/19
Segal, George	Great Neck, NY	2/13/34
Seidelman, Susan	Philadelphia, PA	12/11/52
Seinfeld, Jerry	New York, NY	4/29/54
Sellecca, Connie	New York, NY	5/25/55
Selleck, Tom	Detroit, MI	1/29/45
Severinsen, Doc	Arlington, OR	7/7/27
Sevigny, Chloë	Springfield, MA	11/18/74
Sewell, Rufus	London, England	10/29/67
Seymour, Jane	Middlesex, England	2/15/51
Shackelford, Ted	Oklahoma City, OK	6/23/46
Shaffer, Paul	Thunder Bay, Ontario	11/28/49
Shandling, Garry	Chicago, IL	11/29/49
Shankar, Ravi	Benares, India	4/7/20
Shannon, Molly	Shaker Heights, OH	9/16/64
Sharif, Omar	Alexandria, Egypt	4/10/32
Shatner, William	Montreal, Quebec	3/22/31
Shaughnessy, Charles	London, England	2/9/55
Shaver, Helen	St. Thomas, Ontario	2/24/51
Shaw, Artie	New York, NY	5/23/10
Shea, John	N. Conway, NH	4/14/49
Shearer, Harry	Los Angeles, CA	12/23/43
Shearer, Moira	Scotland	1/17/26
Shearing, George	London, England	8/13/19
Sheedy, Ally	New York, NY	6/12/62
Sheen, Charlie	Los Angeles, CA	9/3/65
Sheen, Martin	Dayton, OH	8/3/40
Sheindlin, Judge Judy	Brooklyn, NY	1942?
Shelley, Carole	London, England	8/16/39
Shepard, Sam	Ft. Sheridan, IL	11/5/43
Shepherd, Cybill	Memphis, TN	2/18/49
Sheridan, Nicollette	Northington, England	11/21/63
Shields, Brooke	New York, NY	5/31/65
Shire, Talia	New York, NY	4/25/46
Short, Bobby	Danville, IL	9/15/24
Short, Martin	Hamilton, Ontario	3/26/50
Show, Grant	Detroit, MI	4/27/62
Shue, Andrew	South Orange, NJ	2/20/67
Shue, Elisabeth	Wilmington, DE	6/10/63
Shyamalan, M. Night	Pondicherry, India	8/6/70
Siepi, Cesare	Milan, Italy	2/10/23
Sigler, Jamie-Lynn	Jericho, NY	5/15/81
Sikking, James B.	Los Angeles, CA	3/5/34
Sills, Beverly	Brooklyn, NY	5/25/29
Silver, Ron	New York, NY	7/2/46
Silverman, Jonathan	Los Angeles, CA	8/5/66
Silverstone, Alicia	San Francisco, CA	10/4/76
Simmons, Gene	Haifa, Israel	8/25/49
Simmons, Jean	London, England	1/31/29
Simmons, Richard	New Orleans, LA	7/12/48
Simon, Carly	New York, NY	6/25/45
Simon, Paul	Newark, NJ	10/13/41
Simone, Nina	Tyron, NC	2/21/33
Sinatra, Nancy	Jersey City, NJ	6/8/40
Sinbad	Benton Harbor, MI	11/10/56
Sinise, Gary	Blue Island, IL	3/7/55
Singleton, John	Los Angeles, CA	1/6/68
Singleton, Penny	Philadelphia, PA	9/15/08
Sirico, Tony	Brooklyn, NY	7/29/42
Sizemore, Tom	Detroit, MI	9/29/64
Skerritt, Tom	Detroit, MI	8/25/33
Skye, Ione	Hertfordshire, England	9/4/70
Slater, Christian	New York, NY	8/19/69
Slater, Helen	Massapequa, NY	12/14/63
Slezak, Erika	Hollywood, CA	8/5/46
Slick, Grace	Chicago, IL	10/30/39
Smirnoff, Yakov	Odessa, Ukraine	1/24/51
Smith, Allison	New York, NY	12/9/69
Smith, Jaclyn	Houston, TX	10/26/47
Smith, Keely	Norfolk, VA	3/9/35
Smith, Kevin	Red Bank, NJ	8/2/70
Smith, Maggie	Ilford, England	12/28/34
Smith, Will	Philadelphia, PA	9/25/68
Smits, Jimmy	New York, NY	7/9/55

Name	Birthplace	Birthdate
Smothers, Dick	New York, NY	11/20/39
Smothers, Tom	New York, NY	2/2/37
Snipes, Wesley	Orlando, FL	7/31/63
Snyder, Tom	Milwaukee, WI	5/12/36
Soderbergh, Steven	Baton Rouge, LA	1/14/63
Somers, Suzanne	San Bruno, CA	10/16/46
Sommer, Elke	Berlin, Germany	11/5/41
Sorbo, Kevin	Mound, MN	9/24/58
Sorvino, Mira	Tenafly, NJ	9/28/70
Sorvino, Paul	Brooklyn, NY	4/13/39
Soul, David	Chicago, IL	8/28/43
Spacek, Sissy	Quitman, TX	12/25/49
Spacey, Kevin	S. Orange, NJ	7/26/59
Spade, David	Birmingham, MI	7/22/65
Spader, James	Boston, MA	2/7/60
Spano, Joe	San Francisco, CA	7/7/46
Spears, Britney	Kentwood, LA	12/2/81
Spector, Phil	Bronx, NY	12/25/40
Spelling, Aaron	Dallas, TX	4/22/28
Spelling, Tori	Los Angeles, CA	5/16/73
Spencer, John	New York, NY	12/20/46
Spielberg, Steven	Cincinnati, OH	12/18/47
Spiner, Brent	Houston, TX	2/2/49
Springer, Jerry	London, England	2/13/44
Springfield, Rick	Sydney, Australia	8/23/49
Springsteen, Bruce	Freehold, NJ	9/23/49
Stack, Robert	Los Angeles, CA	1/13/19
Stafford, Jo	Coalinga, CA	11/12/18
Stahl, Richard	Detroit, MI	1/4/32
Stallone, Sylvester	New York, NY	7/6/46
Stamos, John	Cypress, CA	8/19/63
Stamp, Terence	Stepney, England	7/22/39
Stang, Arnold	New York, NY	9/28/25
Stanton, Harry Dean	West Irvine, KY	7/14/26
Stapleton, Jean	New York, NY	1/19/23
Stapleton, Maureen	Troy, NY	6/21/25
Starr, Ringo	Liverpool, England	7/7/40
Steenburgen, Mary	Newport, AR	2/8/53
Stefani, Gwen	Anaheim, CA	10/3/69
Stein, Ben	Washington, DC	11/25/44
Stephens, James	Mt. Kisco, NY	5/18/51
Stern, Daniel	Stamford, CT	5/28/57
Stern, Howard	New York, NY	1/12/54
Sternhagen, Frances	Washington, DC	1/13/30
Stevens, Andrew	Memphis, TN	6/10/55
Stevens, Cat	London, England	7/21/48
Stevens, Connie	Brooklyn, NY	8/8/38
Stevens, Rise	New York, NY	6/11/13
Stevens, Stella	Yazoo City, MS	10/1/36
Stevenson, Parker	Philadelphia, PA	6/4/52
Stewart, French	Albuquerque, NM	2/20/64
Stewart, Jon	New York, NY	11/28/62
Stewart, Patrick	Mirfield, England	7/13/40
Stewart, Rod	London, England	1/10/45
Stiers, David Ogden	Peoria, IL	10/31/42
Stiles, Julia	New York, NY	3/28/81
Stiller, Ben	New York, NY	11/30/65
Stiller, Jerry	New York, NY	6/8/27
Stills, Stephen	Dallas, TX	1/3/45
Sting	Newcastle, England	10/2/51
Stipe, Michael	Decatur, GA	1/4/60
Stockwell, Dean	Hollywood, CA	3/5/36
Stoltz, Eric	American Samoa	9/30/61
Stone, Dee Wallace	Kansas City, KS	12/14/48
Stone, Oliver	New York, NY	9/15/46
Stone, Sharon	Meadville, PA	3/10/58
Stookey, Paul	Baltimore, MD	12/30/37
Storch, Larry	New York, NY	1/8/23
Storm, Gale	Bloomington, TX	4/5/22
Stowe, Madeleine	Los Angeles, CA	8/18/58
Strait, George	Pearsall, TX	5/18/52
Strasser, Robin	New York, NY	5/7/45
Stratas, Teresa	Toronto, Ontario	5/26/38
Strathairn, David	San Francisco, CA	1/26/49
Strauss, Peter	New York, NY	2/20/47
Streep, Meryl	Summit, NJ	6/22/49
Streisand, Barbra	Brooklyn, NY	4/24/42
Stringfield, Sherry	Colorado Springs, CO	6/24/67
Stritch, Elaine	Detroit, MI	2/2/26
Stroman, Susan	Wilmington, DE	10/17/54
Struthers, Sally	Portland, OR	7/28/48
Stuart, Gloria	Santa Monica, CA	7/4/10
Stuarti, Enzo	Rome, Italy	3/3/25
Sullivan, Susan	New York, NY	11/18/44
Sumac, Yma	Ichocan, Peru	9/10/27
Summer, Donna	Boston, MA	12/31/48
Sutherland, Donald	St. John, New Brunswick	7/17/34
Sutherland, Joan	Sydney, Australia	11/7/26
Sutherland, Kiefer	London, England	12/20/66
Suvari, Mena	Newport, RI	2/9/79
Swank, Hilary	Bellingham, WA	7/30/74

Name	Birthplace	Birthdate
Swayze, Patrick	Houston, TX	8/18/54
Swinton, Tilda	London, England	11/5/60
Swit, Loretta	Passaic, NJ	11/4/37
Takei, George	Los Angeles, CA	4/20/39
Tallchief, Maria	Fairfax, OK	1/24/25
Tamblyn, Russ	Los Angeles, CA	12/30/34
Tarantino, Quentin	Knoxville, TN	3/27/63
Tautou, Audrey	Beaumont, France	8/9/78
Taylor, Billy	Greenville, SC	7/24/21
Taylor, Buck	Hollywood, CA	5/13/38
Taylor, Elizabeth	London, England	2/27/32
Taylor, James	Boston, MA	3/12/48
Taylor, Rip	Washington, DC	1/13/30
Taylor, Rod	Sydney, Australia	1/11/29
Taymor, Julie	Newton, MA	12/15/52
Te Kanawa, Kiri	Gisborne, New Zealand	3/6/44
Tebaldi, Renata	Pesaro, Italy	2/1/22
Teller	Philadelphia, PA	2/14/48
Temple Black, Shirley	Santa Monica, CA	4/23/28
Tennant, Victoria	London, England	9/30/50
Tennille, Toni	Montgomery, AL	5/8/43
Tesh, John	Garden City, NY	7/9/52
Tharp, Twyla	Portland, IN	7/1/41
Thaxter, Phyllis	Portland, ME	11/20/21
Theron, Charlize	South Africa	8/7/75
Thicke, Alan	Kirkland Lake, Ontario	3/1/47
Thiessen, Tiffani-Amber	Long Beach, CA	1/23/74
Thomas, Jay	New Orleans, LA	7/12/48
Thomas, Jonathan Taylor	Bethlehem, PA	9/8/81
Thomas, Marlo	Detroit, MI	11/21/38
Thomas, Michael Tilson	Hollywood, CA	12/21/44
Thomas, Philip Michael	Columbus, OH	5/26/49
Thomas, Richard	New York, NY	6/13/51
Thompson, Emma	London, England	4/15/59
Thompson, Jack	Sydney, Australia	8/31/40
Thompson, Lea	Rochester, MN	5/31/61
Thompson, Sada	Des Moines, IA	9/27/29
Thorne-Smith, Courtney	San Francisco, CA	11/8/68
Thornton, Billy Bob	Hot Springs, AR	8/4/55
Thurman, Uma	Boston, MA	4/29/70
Tiegs, Cheryl	Minnesota	9/25/47
Tillis, Mel	Tampa, FL	8/8/32
Tilly, Jennifer	Los Angeles, CA	9/6/61
Tilly, Meg	Texada, B.C.	2/14/60
Timberlake, Justin	Memphis, TN	1/31/81
Todd, Richard	Dublin, Ireland	6/11/19
Tomei, Marisa	New York, NY	12/4/64
Tomlin, Lily	Detroit, MI	9/1/39
Tork, Peter	Washington, DC	2/13/44
Torn, Rip	Temple, TX	2/6/31
Townsend, Robert	Chicago, IL	2/6/57
Townshend, Peter	Chiswick, England	5/19/45
Travanti, Daniel J.	Kenosha, WI	3/7/40
Travers, Mary	Louisville, KY	11/9/36
Travis, Nancy	New York, NY	9/21/61
Travis, Randy	Marshville, NC	5/4/59
Travolta, John	Englewood, NJ	2/18/54
Trebek, Alex	Sudbury, Ontario	7/22/40
Tritt, Travis	Marietta, GA	2/9/63
Tucci, Stanley	Katonah, NY	1/11/60
Tucker, Chris	Atlanta, GA	8/31/72
Tucker, Michael	Baltimore, MD	2/6/44
Tucker, Tanya	Seminole, TX	10/10/58
Tune, Tommy	Wichita Falls, TX	2/28/39
Turlington, Christy	San Francisco, CA	1/2/69
Turner, Janine	Lincoln, NE	12/6/62
Turner, Kathleen	Springfield, MO	6/19/54
Turner, Tina	Brownsville, TN	11/26/39
Turturro, John	Brooklyn, NY	2/28/57
Twain, Shania	Windsor, Ontario	8/28/65
Twiggy	London, England	9/19/46
Tyler, Liv	Portland, ME	7/1/77
Tyler, Steven	Boston, MA	3/26/48
Tyson, Cicely	New York, NY	12/19/33
Uecker, Bob	Milwaukee, WI	1/26/35
Uggams, Leslie	New York, NY	5/25/43
Ullman, Tracey	Slough, England	12/30/59
Ullmann, Liv	Tokyo, Japan	12/16/38
Ulrich, Skeet	North Carolina	1/20/70
Underwood, Blair	Tacoma, WA	8/25/64
Usher (Raymond IV)	Chattanooga,TN	10/14/79
Ustinov, Peter	London, England	4/16/21
Vaccaro, Brenda	Brooklyn, NY	11/18/39
Vale, Jerry	New York, NY	7/8/31
Valente, Caterina	Paris, France	1/14/31
Valli, Frankie	Newark, NJ	5/3/37
Van Ark, Joan	New York, NY	6/16/43
Vance, Courtney B.	Detroit, MI	3/12/60

Name	Birthplace	Birthdate
Van Damme, Jean-Claude	Brussels, Belgium	10/18/60
Van Der Beek, James	Chesire, CT	3/8/77
Van Doren, Mamie	Rowena, SD.	2/6/36
Vandross, Luther	New York, NY	4/20/51
Van Dyke, Dick	West Plains, MO	12/13/25
Van Dyke, Jerry	Danville, IL.	7/27/31
Van Halen, Eddie	Nijmegen, Netherlands	1/26/57
Van Patten, Dick	New York, NY	12/9/28
Van Peebles, Mario	Mexico	1/15/57
Van Sant, Gus	Louisville, KY	7/24/52
Van Zandt, Steven	Boston, MA	11/22/50
Vaughn, Robert	New York, NY	11/22/32
Vaughn, Vince	Minneapolis, MN	3/28/70
Vedder, Eddie	Evanston, IL.	12/23/65
Vereen, Ben	Miami, FL.	10/10/46
Verrett, Shirley	New Orleans, LA	5/31/31
Vickers, Jon	Prince Albert, Sask.	10/26/26
Viera, Meredith	Providence, RI	12/30/53
Vigoda, Abe	New York, NY	2/24/21
Vincent, Jan-Michael	Denver, CO	7/15/44
Vinton, Bobby	Canonsburg, PA	4/16/35
Vitale, Dick	East Rutherford, NJ	6/9/40
Voight, Jon	Yonkers, NY.	12/29/38
Von Stade, Frederica	Somerville, NJ	6/1/45
Von Sydow, Max	Lund, Sweden	4/10/29
Von Trier, Lars	Copenhagen, Denmark	4/30/56
Wagner, Jack	Washington, MO	10/3/59
Wagner, Lindsay	Los Angeles, CA	6/22/49
Wagner, Robert	Detroit, MI	2/10/30
Wahl, Ken	Chicago, IL.	2/14/56
Wahlberg, Mark	Dorchester, MA	6/5/71
Wain, Bea	Bronx, NY	4/30/17
Waite, Ralph	White Plains, NY	6/22/29
Waits, Tom	Pomona, CA	12/7/49
Walden, Robert	New York, NY	9/25/43
Walken, Christopher	New York, NY	3/31/43
Wallace, Marcia	Creston, IA.	11/1/42
Wallach, Eli	Brooklyn, NY	12/7/15
Walter, Jessica	New York, NY	1/31/44
Ward, Fred	San Diego, CA	1943
Ward, Sela	Meridian, MS	8/11/56
Ward, Simon	London, England	10/19/41
Warden, Jack	Newark, NJ	9/18/20
Warfield, Marsha	Chicago, IL.	3/5/54
Warner, Malcolm-Jamal	Jersey City, NJ.	8/18/70
Warren, Lesley Ann	New York, NY	8/16/46
Warrick, Ruth	St. Joseph, MO	6/29/16
Warwick, Dionne	East Orange, NJ	12/12/41
Washington, Denzel	Mt. Vernon, NY	12/28/54
Waters, John	Baltimore, MD	4/22/46
Waters, Roger	Great Bookham, England	9/9/44
Waterston, Sam	Cambridge, MA	11/15/40
Watson, Emily	London, England	1/14/67
Watson, Emma	Oxford, England	4/15/90
Watts, Andre	Nuremberg, Germany	6/20/46
Watts, Naomi	Shoreham, England	9/28/68
Wayans, Damon	New York, NY	9/4/60
Wayans, Keenen Ivory	New York, NY	6/8/58
Weathers, Carl	New Orleans, LA	1/14/48
Weaver, Dennis	Joplin, MO	6/4/24
Weaver, Fritz	Pittsburgh, PA	1/19/26
Weaver, Sigourney	New York, NY	10/8/49
Weir, Peter	Sydney, Australia	8/8/44
Weisz, Rachel	London, England	3/7/71
Weitz, Bruce	Norwalk, CT	5/27/43
Welch, Raquel	Chicago, IL.	9/5/40
Weld, Tuesday	New York, NY	8/27/43
Wells, Kitty	Nashville, TN	8/30/19
Wendt, George	Chicago, IL.	10/17/48
West, Adam	Walla Walla, WA	9/19/29
West, Shane	Baton Rouge, LA	6/10/78
Wettig, Patricia	Cincinnati, OH	12/4/51
Whalley-Kilmer, Joanne	Manchester, England	8/25/64
Wheaton, Wil	Burbank, CA	7/29/72
Whitaker, Forest	Longview, TX	7/15/61
White, Barry	Galveston, TX	9/12/44
White, Betty	Oak Park, IL.	1/17/22
White, Jaleel	Los Angeles, CA	11/27/76
White, Vanna	N. Myrtle Beach, SC	2/18/57
Whitford, Bradley	Wisconsin	10/10/59
Whiting, Margaret	Detroit, MI	7/22/24
Whitman, Stuart	San Francisco, CA.	2/1/26
Whitmore, James	White Plains, NY	10/1/21
Widmark, Richard	Sunrise, MN.	12/26/14
Wiest, Dianne	Kansas City, MO	3/28/48
Wilder, Gene	Milwaukee, WI	6/11/35
Wilkinson, Tom	Leeds, Enlgand	12/12/48
Williams, Andy	Wall Lake, IA	12/3/30
Williams, Barry	Santa Monica, CA.	9/30/54
Williams, Billy Dee	New York, NY.	4/6/37
Williams, Cindy	Van Nuys, CA.	8/22/47
Williams, Esther	Los Angeles, CA.	8/8/23
Williams, Hal	Columbus, OH	12/14/38
Williams, Hank, Jr.	Shreveport, LA	5/26/49
Williams, JoBeth	Houston, TX	1949
Williams, Lucinda	Lake Charles, LA	1/26/53
Williams, Michelle	Kalispell, MT.	9/9/80
Williams, Montel	Baltimore, MD.	7/3/56
Williams, Paul	Omaha, NE.	9/19/40
Williams, Robin	Chicago, IL.	7/21/52
Williams, Treat	Rowayton, CT.	12/1/51
Williams, Vanessa	New York, NY.	3/18/63
Williamson, Kevin	Bern, NC.	3/14/65
Williamson, Nicol	Hamilton, Scotland	9/14/38
Willis, Bruce	W. Germany	3/19/55
Wilson, Brian	Hawthorne, CA.	6/20/42
Wilson, Cassandra	Jackson, MS.	12/4/55
Wilson, Demond	Valdosta, GA	10/13/46
Wilson, Elizabeth	Grand Rapids, MI	4/4/25
Wilson, Luke	Dallas, TX.	9/21/71
Wilson, Nancy	Chillicothe, OH	2/20/37
Wilson, Owen	Dallas, TX.	11/18/68
Windom, William	New York, NY.	9/28/23
Winfield, Paul	Los Angeles, CA.	5/22/41
Winfrey, Oprah	Kosciusko, MS	1/29/54
Winger, Debra	Cleveland, OH	5/16/55
Winkler, Henry	New York, NY.	10/30/45
Winningham, Mare	Phoenix, AZ	5/6/59
Winslet, Kate	Reading, England	10/5/75
Winter, Johnny	Beaumont,TX	2/23/44
Winters, Jonathan	Dayton, OH.	11/11/25
Winters, Shelley	St. Louis, MO	8/18/22
Winwood, Steve	Birmingham, England	5/12/48
Wiseman, Joseph	Montreal, Quebec.	5/15/18
Withers, Jane	Atlanta, GA.	4/12/26
Witherspoon, Reese	Nashville, TN	4/22/76
Witt, Alicia	Worcester, MA	8/21/75
Wolf, Scott	Boston, MA.	6/4/68
Wonder, Stevie	Saginaw, MI	5/13/50
Wong, Faye	Beijing, China	8/8/69
Woo, John	Guangzhou, China	5/1/46
Wood, Elijah	Cedar Rapids, IA	1/28/81
Woodard, Alfre	Tulsa, OK	11/2/53
Woods, James	Vernal, NJ.	4/18/47
Woodward, Edward	Croyden, England.	6/1/30
Woodward, Joanne	Thomasville, GA	2/27/30
Wopat, Tom	Lodi, WI	9/9/50
Wray, Fay	Alberta, Canada	9/10/07
Wright, Martha	Seattle, WA	3/23/26
Wright, Max	Detroit, MI.	8/2/43
Wright, Steven	New York, NY.	12/6/55
Wright, Teresa	New York, NY.	10/27/18
Wright Penn, Robin	Dallas, TX.	4/8/66
Wyatt, Jane	Campgaw, NJ.	8/10/11
Wyle, Noah	Hollywood, CA	6/4/71
Wyman, Bill	London, England	10/24/36
Wyman, Jane	St. Joseph, MO.	1/4/14
Yankovic, Weird Al.	Lynwood, CA	10/23/59
Yanni	Kalamata, Greece.	11/4/54
Yarborough, Glenn	Milwaukee, WI	1/12/30
Yarrow, Peter	New York, NY.	5/31/38
Yearwood, Trisha	Monticello, GA	9/19/64
Yoakam, Dwight	Pikesville, KY	10/23/56
York, Michael	Fulmer, England	3/27/42
York, Susannah	London, England	1/9/42
Young, Alan	Northumberland, England.	11/19/19
Young, Burt	New York, NY.	4/30/40
Young, Neil	Toronto, Ontario	11/12/45
Young, Sean	Louisville, KY	11/20/59
Zane, Billy	Chicago, IL	2/24/66
Zeffirelli, Franco	Florence, Italy	2/12/23
Zellweger, Renee	Katy, TX	1969
Zemeckis, Robert	Chicago, IL	5/14/51
Zerbe, Anthony	Long Beach, CA	5/20/36
Zeta-Jones, Catherine	Swansea, Wales	9/25/69
Zimbalist, Efrem, Jr.	New York, NY.	11/30/23
Zimbalist, Stephanie	Encino, CA	10/8/56
Zimmer, Kim	Grand Rapids, MI	2/2/55
Zukerman, Pinchas	Tel Aviv, Israel	7/16/48
Zuniga, Daphne	San Francisco, CA	10/28/62

Entertainment Personalities of the Past

See also other lists for some deceased entertainers not included here.

Name	Born	Died
Aaliyah	1979	2001
Abbott, Bud	1895	1974
Abbott, George	1887	1995
Acuff, Roy	1903	1992
Adams, Joey	1911	1999
Adams, Maude	1872	1953
Adler, Jacob P	1855	1926
Adler, Luther	1903	1984
Adoree, Renee	1898	1933
Agar, John	1921	2002
Aherne, Brian	1902	1986
Ailey, Alvin	1931	1989
Akins, Claude	1918	1994
Albertson, Frank	1909	1964
Albertson, Jack	1907	1981
Alda, Robert	1914	1986
Alexander, Ben	1911	1969
Allen, Fred	1894	1956
Allen, Gracie	1906	1964
Allen, Mel	1913	1996
Allen, Peter	1944	1992
Allen, Steve	1921	2000
Allgood, Sara	1883	1950
Ameche, Don	1908	1993
Ames, Leon	1903	1993
Amsterdam, Morey	1909?	1996
Anderson, Judith	1897	1992
Anderson, Marian	1902	1993
Andre the Giant	1946	1993
Andrews, Dana	1909	1992
Andrews, Laverne	1913	1967
Andrews, Maxine	1918	1995
Angeli, Pier	1933	1971
Anita Louise	1915	1970
Arbuckle, Fatty (Roscoe)	1887	1933
Arden, Eve	1908	1990
Arlen, Richard	1900	1976
Arliss, George	1868	1946
Armetta, Henry	1888	1945
Armstrong, Louis	1900	1971
Arnaz, Desi	1917	1986
Arnold, Edward	1890	1956
Arquette, Cliff	1905	1974
Arthur, Jean	1900	1991
Ashcroft, Peggy	1907	1991
Astaire, Fred	1899	1987
Astor, Mary	1906	1987
Atkins, Chet	1924	2001
Atwill, Lionel	1885	1946
Auer, Mischa	1905	1967
Aumont, Jean-Pierre	1911	2001
Austin, Gene	1900	1972
Autry, Gene	1907	1998
Axton, Hoyt	1938	1999
Ayres, Lew	1908	1996
Backus, Jim	1913	1989
Bailey, Pearl	1918	1990
Bainter, Fay	1892	1968
Baker, Josephine	1906	1975
Balanchine, George	1904	1983
Ball, Lucille	1911	1989
Balsam, Martin	1919	1996
Bancroft, George	1882	1956
Bankhead, Tallulah	1903	1968
Banks, Leslie	1890	1952
Bara, Theda	1890	1955
Barnes, Binnie	1903	1998
Barnum, Phineas T.	1810	1891
Barrymore, Ethel	1879	1959
Barrymore, John	1882	1942
Barrymore, Lionel	1878	1954
Barrymore, Maurice	1848	1905
Bartel, Paul	1938	2000
Barthelmess, Richard	1897	1963
Bartholomew, Freddie	1924	1992
Bartok, Eva	1926	1998
Barty, Billy	1924	2000
Basehart, Richard	1914	1984
Basie, Count	1904	1984
Bates, Clayton (Peg Leg)	1907	1998
Bates, Florence	1888	1954
Bavier, Francis	1902	1989
Baxter, Anne	1923	1985
Baxter, Warner	1889	1951
Beatty, Clyde	1904	1965
Beaumont, Hugh	1909	1982
Beavers, Louise	1902	1962
Beery, Noah, Sr.	1884	1946
Beery, Noah, Jr.	1913	1994
Beery, Wallace	1889	1949
Begley, Ed	1901	1970
Bellamy, Ralph	1904	1991
Belushi, John	1949	1982
Benaderet, Bea	1906	1968
Bendix, William	1906	1964
Bennett, Constance	1904	1965
Bennett, Joan	1910	1990
Bennett, Michael	1943	1987
Benny, Jack	1894	1974
Benzell, Mimi	1924	1970
Beradino, John	1917	1996
Berg, Gertrude	1899	1966
Bergen, Edgar	1903	1978
Bergman, Ingrid	1915	1982
Berkeley, Busby	1895	1976
Berle, Milton	1908	2002
Bernardi, Herschel	1923	1986
Bernhardt, Sarah	1844	1923
Bernie, Ben	1893	1943
Bessell, Ted	1939	1996
Bickford, Charles	1889	1967
Big Bopper, The	1930	1959
Bing, Rudolf	1902	1997
Bissell, Whit	1909	1996
Bixby, Bill	1934	1993
Bjoerling, Jussi	1911	1960
Blackmer, Sidney	1895	1973
Blackstone, Harry	1885	1965
Blake, Amanda	1931	1989
Blaine, Vivian	1921	1995
Blanc, Mel	1908	1989
Blocker, Dan	1928	1972
Blondell, Joan	1909	1979
Blore, Eric	1888	1959
Blue, Ben	1901	1975
Blyden, Larry	1925	1975
Bogarde, Dirk	1920	1999
Bogart, Humphrey	1899	1957
Boland, Mary	1880	1965
Boles, John	1895	1969
Bolger, Ray	1904	1987
Bond, Ward	1903	1960
Bondi, Beulah	1892	1981
Bono, Sonny	1935	1998
Boone, Richard	1917	1981
Booth, Edwin	1833	1893
Booth, Junius Brutus	1796	1852
Booth, Shirley	1898	1992
Borge, Victor	1909	2000
Bow, Clara	1905	1965
Bowes, Maj. Edward	1874	1946
Bowman, Lee	1914	1979
Brown, Les	1912	2001
Boxcar Willie	1931	1999
Boyd, Stephen	1928	1977
Boyd, William	1898	1972
Boyer, Charles	1899	1978
Brady, Alice	1893	1939
Brand, Neville	1921	1992
Brazzi, Rossano	1916	1994
Brennan, Walter	1894	1974
Brent, George	1904	1979
Brett, Jeremy	1935	1995
Brice, Fanny	1891	1951
Bridges, Lloyd	1913	1998
Broderick, Helen	1891	1959
Brown, Joe E.	1892	1973
Bruce, Lenny	1925	1966
Bruce, Nigel	1895	1953
Bruce, Virginia	1910	1982
Brynner, Yul	1915	1985
Buchanan, Edgar	1903	1979
Buñuel, Luis	1900	1983
Buono, Victor	1938	1982
Burke, Billie	1885	1970
Burnette, Smiley	1911	1967
Burns, George	1896	1996
Burr, Raymond	1917	1993
Burton, Richard	1925	1984
Busch, Mae	1897	1946
Bushman, Francis X.	1883	1966
Butterworth, Charles	1896	1946
Byington, Spring	1893	1971
Cabot, Bruce	1904	1972
Cabot, Sebastian	1918	1977
Cagney, James	1899	1986
Calhern, Louis	1895	1956
Calhoun, Rory	1923	1999
Callas, Maria	1923	1977
Calloway, Cab	1907	1994
Cambridge, Godfrey	1933	1976
Campbell, Mrs. Patrick	1865	1940
Candy, John	1950	1994
Cantinflas	1911	1993
Cantor, Eddie	1892	1964
Capra, Frank	1897	1991
Carey, Harry	1878	1947
Carey, Macdonald	1913	1994
Carle, Frankie	1903	2001
Carpenter, Karen	1950	1983
Carradine, John	1906	1988
Carrillo, Leo	1880	1961
Carroll, Leo G.	1892	1972
Carroll, Madeleine	1906	1987
Carroll, Nancy	1905	1965
Carson, Jack	1910	1963
Caruso, Enrico	1873	1921
Casadesus, Gaby	1901	1999
Casals, Pablo	1876	1973
Cass, Peggy	1924	1999
Cassidy, Jack	1927	1976
Cassavetes, John	1929	1989
Castle, Irene	1893	1969
Castle, Vernon	1887	1918
Caulfield, Joan	1922	1991
Chaliapin, Feodor	1873	1938
Champion, Gower	1919	1980
Chandler, Jeff	1918	1961
Chaney, Lon	1883	1930
Chaney, Lon, Jr.	1905	1973
Chapin, Harry	1942	1981
Chaplin, Charles	1889	1977
Chapman, Graham	1941	1989
Chase, Ilka	1905	1978
Chatterton, Ruth	1893	1961
Cherrill, Virginia	1908	1996
Chevalier, Maurice	1888	1972
Clair, René	1898	1981
Clark, Bobby	1888	1960
Clark, Dane	1913	1998
Clark, Fred	1914	1968
Clayton, Jan	1917	1983
Clift, Montgomery	1920	1966
Cline, Patsy	1932	1963
Clooney, Rosemary	1928	2002
Clyde, Andy	1892	1967
Cobain, Kurt	1967	1994
Cobb, Lee J.	1911	1976
Coburn, Charles	1877	1961
Coca, Imogene	1908	2001
Cochran, Steve	1917?	1965
Cody, Buffalo Bill	1846	1917
Cody, Iron Eyes	1907	1999
Cohan, George M.	1878	1942
Cohen, Myron	1902	1986
Colbert, Claudette	1903	1996
Cole, Nat "King"	1919	1965
Collins, Ray	1890	1965
Colman, Ronald	1891	1958
Columbo, Russ	1908	1934
Como, Perry	1912	2001
Connors, Chuck	1921	1992
Conrad, William	1920	1994
Conried, Hans	1917	1982
Conte, Richard	1911	1975
Convy, Bert	1933	1991
Conway, Tom	1904	1967
Coogan, Jackie	1914	1984
Cook, Elisha, Jr.	1904	1995
Cooke, Sam	1935	1964
Cooper, Gary	1901	1961
Cooper, Gladys	1888	1971
Cooper, Melville	1896	1973
Corby, Ellen	1913	1999
Corio, Ann	1914	1999
Cornell, Katharine	1893	1974
Correll, Charles ("Andy")	1890	1972
Costello, Dolores	1905	1979
Costello, Lou	1906	1959

Name	Born	Died
Cotten, Joseph	1905	1994
Coward, Noel	1899	1973
Cox, Wally	1924	1973
Crabbe, Buster	1908	1983
Crane, Bob	1928	1978
Crawford, Broderick	1911	1986
Crawford, Joan	1904	1977
Crews, Laura Hope	1880	1942
Crisp, Donald	1880	1974
Croce, Jim	1942	1973
Crosby, Bing	1903	1977
Crothers, Scatman	1910	1986
Cugat, Xavier	1900	1990
Cukor, George	1899	1983
Cullen, Bill	1920	1990
Cummings, Robert	1908	1990
Currie, Finlay	1878	1968
Curtis, Ken	1916	1991
Cushing, Peter	1913	1994
Dailey, Dan	1914	1978
Dandridge, Dorothy	1923	1965
Daniell, Henry	1894	1963
Daniels, Bebe	1901	1971
Darin, Bobby	1936	1973
Darnell, Linda	1921	1965
Darwell, Jane	1879	1967
Da Silva, Howard	1909	1986
Davenport, Harry	1866	1949
Davies, Marion	1897	1961
Davis, Bette	1908	1989
Davis, Joan	1907	1961
Davis, Sammy Jr.	1925	1990
Day, Dennis	1917	1988
Dean, James	1931	1955
Defore, Don	1917	1993
Dekker, Albert	1905	1968
Del Rio, Dolores	1908	1983
Demarest, William	1892	1983
DeMille, Agnes	1905	1993
DeMille, Cecil B.	1881	1959
Denison, Michael	1915	1998
Denning, Richard	1914	1998
Dennis, Sandy	1937	1992
Denny, Reginald	1891	1967
Denver, John	1943	1997
Derek, John	1926	1998
DeSica, Vittorio	1901	1974
Devine, Andy	1905	1977
Dewhurst, Colleen	1924	1991
De Wilde, Brandon	1942	1972
De Wolfe, Billy	1907	1974
Diamond, Selma	1920	1985
Dietrich, Marlene	1901	1992
Digges, Dudley	1879	1947
Disney, Walt	1901	1966
Dix, Richard	1894	1949
Dmytryk, Edward	1908	1999
Donahue, Troy	1936	2001
Donat, Robert	1905	1958
Donlevy, Brian	1901?	1972
Dors, Diana	1931	1984
Douglas, Melvyn	1901	1981
Douglas, Paul	1907	1959
Dove, Billie	1900	1998
Downey, Morton, Jr.	1933	2001
Doyle, David	1929	1997
Drake, Alfred	1914	1992
Draper, Ruth	1889	1956
Dresser, Louise	1881	1965
Dressler, Marie	1869	1934
Drew, Mrs. John	1820	1897
Dru, Joanne	1923	1996
Duchin, Eddy	1909	1951
Duff, Howard	1917	1990
Dumbrille, Douglass	1890	1974
Dumont, Margaret	1889	1965
Duncan, Isadora	1878	1927
Dunn, James	1905	1967
Dunne, Irene	1898	1990
Dunnock, Mildred	1904	1991
Durante, Jimmy	1893	1980
Duryea, Dan	1907	1968
Duse, Eleanora	1858	1924
Eagels, Jeanne	1894	1929
Eckstine, Billy	1914	1993
Eddy, Nelson	1901	1967
Edelman, Herb	1933	1996
Edwards, Cliff	1897	1971
Edwards, Gus	1879	1945

Name	Born	Died
Edwards, Vince	1928	1996
Egan, Richard	1923	1987
Ellington, Duke	1899	1974
Elliot, Cass	1941	1974
Elman, Mischa	1891	1967
Errol, Leon	1881	1951
Evans, Dale	1912	2001
Evans, Edith	1888	1976
Evans, Maurice	1901	1989
Ewell, Tom	1909	1994
Fadiman, Clifton	1904	1999
Fairbanks, Douglas	1883	1939
Fairbanks, Douglas, Jr.	1909	2000
Farley, Chris	1964	1997
Farmer, Frances	1914	1970
Farnsworth, Richard	1920	2000
Farnum, Dustin	1870	1929
Farnum, William	1876	1953
Farrar, Geraldine	1882	1967
Farrell, Charles	1901	1990
Farrell, Eileen	1920	2002
Farrell, Glenda	1904	1971
Fassbinder, Rainer Werner	1946	1982
Fay, Frank	1897	1961
Faye, Alice	1912	1998
Fazenda, Louise	1895	1962
Feld, Fritz	1900	1993
Feldman, Marty	1933	1982
Fell, Norman	1924	1998
Fellini, Federico	1920	1993
Fenneman, George	1919	1997
Ferrer, Jose	1912	1992
Fetchit, Stepin	1898	1985
Fiedler, Arthur	1894	1979
Field, Betty	1918	1973
Fields, Gracie	1898	1979
Fields, W.C.	1879	1946
Fields, Totie	1931	1978
Finch, Peter	1916	1977
Fine, Larry	1902	1975
Firkusny, Rudolf	1912	1994
Fiske, Minnie Maddern	1865	1932
Fitzgerald, Barry	1888	1961
Flagstad, Kirsten	1895	1962
Fleming, Art	1924	1995
Fleming, Eric	1925	1966
Flippen, Jay C.	1900	1971
Flynn, Errol	1909	1959
Flynn, Joe	1925	1974
Foley, Red	1910	1968
Fonda, Henry	1905	1982
Fontaine, Frank	1920	1978
Fontanne, Lynn	1887	1983
Fonteyn, Margot	1919	1991
Ford, John	1895	1973
Ford, Paul	1901	1976
Ford, Tennessee Ernie	1919	1991
Ford, Wallace	1899	1966
Forrest, Helen	1918	1999
Fosse, Bob	1927	1987
Foster, Phil	1914	1985
Foster, Preston	1901	1970
Foxx, Redd	1922	1991
Foy, Eddie	1857	1928
Franchi, Sergio	1933?	1990
Francis, Arlene	1908	2001
Francis, Kay	1903	1968
Franciscus, James	1934	1991
Frankenheimer, John	1930	2002
Frann, Mary	1943	1998
Frawley, William	1893	1966
Frederick, Pauline	1885	1938
French, Victor	1934	1989
Friganza, Trixie	1870	1955
Frisco, Joe	1890	1958
Froman, Jane	1907	1980
Fuller, Samuel	1912	1997
Funt, Allen	1914	1999
Furness, Betty	1916	1994
Gabin, Jean	1904	1976
Gable, Clark	1901	1960
Gabor, Eva	1920	1995
Garbo, Greta	1905	1990
Garcia, Jerry	1942	1995
Gardenia, Vincent	1922	1992
Gardner, Ava	1922	1990
Garfield, John	1913	1952
Garland, Judy	1922	1969
Garson, Greer	1904	1996

Name	Born	Died
Gassman, Vittorio	1922	2000
Gaye, Marvin	1939	1984
Gaynor, Janet	1906	1984
Geer, Will	1902	1978
George, Gladys	1900	1954
Gibb, Andy	1958	1988
Gibson, Hoot	1892	1962
Gielgud, John	1904	2000
Gilbert, Billy	1894	1971
Gilbert, John	1895	1936
Gilford, Jack	1907	1990
Gillette, William	1855	1937
Gingold, Hermione	1897	1987
Gish, Dorothy	1898	1968
Gish, Lillian	1893	1993
Gleason, Jackie	1916	1987
Gleason, James	1886	1959
Gluck, Alma	1884	1938
Gobel, George	1919	1991
Goddard, Paulette	1905	1990
Godfrey, Arthur	1903	1983
Godunov, Alexander	1949	1995
Goldwyn, Samuel	1882	1974
Gomez, Thomas	1905	1971
Goodman, Benny	1909	1986
Gorcey, Leo	1915	1969
Gordon, Gale	1906	1995
Gordon, Ruth	1896	1985
Gosden, Freeman ("Amos")	1899	1982
Gottschalk, Ferdinand	1869	1944
Gottschalk, Louis	1829	1869
Gould, Glenn	1932	1982
Gould, Morton	1913	1996
Grable, Betty	1916	1973
Graham, Martha	1894	1991
Graham, Virginia	1912	1998
Grahame, Gloria	1925	1981
Granger, Stewart	1913	1993
Grant, Cary	1904	1986
Granville, Bonita	1923	1988
Gray, Dolores	1924	2002
Greco, Jose	1918	2001
Greene, Lorne	1915	1987
Greenstreet, Sydney	1879	1954
Greenwood, Charlotte	1890	1978
Greer, Jane	1924	2001
Griffith, David Wark	1874	1948
Griffith, Hugh	1912	1980
Guardino, Harry	1925	1995
Guinness, Sir Alec	1914	2000
Guthrie, Woody	1912	1967
Gwenn, Edmund	1875	1959
Gwynne, Fred	1926	1993
Hale, Alan	1892	1950
Hale, Alan, Jr.	1918	1990
Haley, Bill	1925	1981
Haley, Jack	1899	1979
Hall, Huntz	1919	1999
Hamilton, Margaret	1902	1985
Hammerstein, Oscar	1847	1919
Hampton, Lionel	1908	2002
Hardwicke, Cedric	1893	1964
Hardy, Oliver	1892	1957
Harlow, Jean	1911	1937
Harris, Phil	1904	1995
Harrison, George	1943	2001
Harrison, Rex	1908	1990
Hart, William S.	1870	1946
Hartman, Phil	1948	1998
Harvey, Laurence	1928	1973
Hawkins, Jack	1910	1973
Hawkins, Screamin' Jay	1929	2000
Hawthorne, Nigel	1929	2001
Hayakawa, Sessue	1890	1973
Hayden, Sterling	1916	1986
Hayes, Gabby	1885	1969
Hayes, Helen	1900	1993
Hayes, Peter Lind	1915	1998
Hayward, Leland	1902	1971
Hayward, Louis	1909	1985
Hayward, Susan	1917	1975
Hayworth, Rita	1918	1987
Head, Edith	1907	1981
Healy, Ted	1896	1937
Heckart, Eileen	1919	2001
Heflin, Van	1910	1971
Heifetz, Jascha	1901	1987
Held, Anna	1873	1918
Hemingway, Margaux	1955	1996
Hendrix, Jimi	1942	1970

Name	Born	Died
Henie, Sonja	1912	1969
Henreid, Paul	1908	1992
Henson, Jim	1936	1990
Hepburn, Audrey	1929	1993
Hersholt, Jean	1886	1956
Hewett, Christopher	1922	2001
Hickey, William	1928	1997
Hickson, Joan	1906	1998
Hill, Benny	1925	1992
Hirt, Al	1922	1999
Hitchcock, Alfred	1899	1980
Hobson, Valerie	1917	1998
Hodiak, John	1914	1955
Holden, Fay	1894	1973
Holden, William	1918	1981
Holliday, Judy	1922	1965
Holloway, Sterling	1905	1992
Holly, Buddy	1936	1959
Holt, Jack	1888	1951
Holt, Tim	1918	1973
Homolka, Oscar	1898	1978
Hooker, John Lee	1917	2001
Hoon, Shannon	1967	1995
Hopkins, Miriam	1902	1972
Hopper, DeWolf	1858	1935
Hopper, William	1915	1970
Horowitz, Vladimir	1904	1989
Horton, Edward Everett	1886	1970
Houdini, Harry	1874	1926
Houseman, John	1902	1988
Howard (Horwitz), Curly	1903	1952
Howard, Eugene	1881	1965
Howard, Joe	1867	1961
Howard, Leslie	1890	1943
Howard (Horwitz), Moe	1897	1975
Howard (Horwitz), Shemp	1895	1955
Howard, Tom	1885	1955
Howard, Trevor	1916	1988
Howard, Willie	1885	1949
Hudson, Rock	1925	1985
Hull, Henry	1890	1977
Hull, Josephine	1886	1957
Humphrey, Doris	1895	1958
Hunter, Jeffrey	1925	1969
Hunter, Kim	1922	2002
Hunter, Ross	1921	1996
Husing, Ted	1901	1962
Huston, John	1906	1987
Huston, Walter	1884	1950
Hutchence, Michael	1960	1997
Hutton, Jim	1934	1979
Hutton, Robert	1920	1994
Hyde-White, Wilfrid	1903	1991
Ingram, Rex	1895	1969
Iturbi, Jose	1895	1980
Ireland, Jill	1936	1990
Ireland, John	1915	1992
Irving, Henry	1838	1905
Ives, Burl	1909	1995
Jack, Wolfman	1938	1995
Jackson, Joe	1875	1942
Jackson, Mahalia	1911	1972
Jackson, Milt	1922	1999
Jaeckel, Richard	1926	1997
Jaffe, Sam	1891	1984
Jagger, Dean	1903	1991
James, Dennis	1917	1997
James, Harry	1916	1983
Janis, Elsie	1889	1956
Jannings, Emil	1886	1950
Janssen, David	1930	1980
Jenkins, Allen	1900	1974
Jennings, Waylon	1937	2002
Jessel, George	1898	1981
Johnson, Ben	1918	1996
Johnson, Celia	1908	1982
Johnson, Chic	1892	1962
Johnson, J.J.	1924	2001
Jolson, Al	1886	1950
Jones, Brian	1942	1969
Jones, Buck	1889	1942
Jones, Carolyn	1933	1983
Jones, Henry	1912	1999
Jones, Spike	1911	1965
Joplin, Janis	1943	1970
Jory, Victor	1902	1982
Joslyn, Allyn	1905	1981
Julia, Raul	1940	1994
Jurado, Katy	1924	2002
Kahn, Madeline	1942	1999
Kane, Helen	1910	1966
Kanin, Garson	1912	1999
Karloff, Boris	1887	1969
Karns, Roscoe	1893	1970
Kaufman, Andy	1949	1984
Kaye, Danny	1913	1987
Kaye, Stubby	1918	1997
Kean, Charles	1811	1868
Kean, Mrs. Charles	1806	1880
Kean, Edmund	1787	1833
Keaton, Buster	1895	1966
Keeler, Ruby	1910	1993
Keith, Brian	1921	1997
Kellaway, Cecil	1894	1973
Kelley, DeForest	1920	1999
Kelly, Emmett	1898	1979
Kelly, Gene	1912	1996
Kelly, Grace	1929	1982
Kelly, Jack	1927	1992
Kelly, Nancy	1921	1985
Kelly, Patsy	1910	1981
Kelton, Pert	1907	1968
Kendall, Kay	1926	1959
Kennedy, Arthur	1914	1990
Kennedy, Edgar	1890	1948
Kibbee, Guy	1886	1956
Kilbride, Percy	1888	1964
Kiley, Richard	1922	1999
Kirby, George	1923	1995
Kirby, Durward	1912	2000
Klemperer, Werner	1919	2000
Kramer, Stanley	1913	2001
Knight, Ted	1923	1986
Kostelanetz, Andre	1901	1980
Kovacs, Ernie	1919	1962
Kramer, Stanley	1913	2001
Kruger, Otto	1885	1974
Kubrick, Stanley	1928	1999
Kulp, Nancy	1921	1991
Kurosawa, Akira	1910	1998
Ladd, Alan	1913	1964
Lahr, Bert	1895	1967
Lake, Arthur	1905	1987
Lake, Veronica	1919	1973
Lamarr, Hedy	1913	2000
Lamas, Fernando	1915	1982
Lamour, Dorothy	1914	1996
Lancaster, Burt	1913	1994
Lanchester, Elsa	1902	1986
Lane, Pricilla	1917	1995
Landis, Carole	1919	1948
Landis, Jessie Royce	1904	1972
Landon, Michael	1936	1991
Lang, Fritz	1890	1976
Langdon, Harry	1884	1944
Langtry, Lillie	1853	1929
Lanza, Mario	1921	1959
LaRue, Lash (Alfred)	1917	1996
Lauder, Harry	1870	1950
Laughton, Charles	1899	1962
Laurel, Stan	1890	1965
Lawford, Peter	1923	1984
Lawrence, Gertrude	1898	1952
Lean, David	1908	1991
Lee, Bernard	1908	1981
Lee, Bruce	1940	1973
Lee, Canada	1907	1952
Lee, Gypsy Rose	1914	1970
Lee, Peggy	1920	2002
LeGallienne, Eva	1899	1991
Lehmann, Lotte	1888	1976
Leigh, Vivien	1913	1967
Leighton, Margaret	1922	1976
Lemmon, Jack	1925	2001
Lennon, John	1940	1980
Lenya, Lotte	1898	1981
Leonard, Eddie	1870	1941
Leonard, Sheldon	1907	1997
LeRoy, Mervyn	1900	1987
Levant, Oscar	1906	1972
Levene, Sam	1905	1980
Levenson, Sam	1911	1980
Lewis, Joe E.	1902	1971
Lewis, Shari	1934	1998
Lewis, Ted	1892	1971
Liberace	1919	1987
Lillie, Beatrice	1894	1989
Lind, Jenny	1820	1887
Lindfors, Viveca	1920	1995
Lindley, Audra	1918	1997
Linville, Larry	1939	2000
Little, Cleavon	1939	1992
Llewelyn, Desmond	1914	1999
Lloyd, Harold	1893	1971
Lloyd, Marie	1870	1922
Lockhart, Gene	1891	1957
Logan, Ella	1913	1969
Lombard, Carole	1909	1942
Lombardo, Guy	1902	1977
Long, Richard	1927	1974
Lopes, Lisa	1971	2002
Lopez, Vincent	1895	1975
Lord, Jack	1920?	1998
Lorne, Marion	1888	1968
Lorre, Peter	1904	1964
Lovejoy, Frank	1912	1962
Lowe, Edmund	1890	1971
Loy, Myrna	1905	1993
Lubitsch, Ernst	1892	1947
Ludden, Allen	1918	1981
Lugosi, Bela	1882	1956
Lukas, Paul	1894	1971
Lundigan, William	1914	1975
Lunt, Alfred	1892	1977
Lupino, Ida	1918	1995
Lymon, Frankie	1942	1968
Lynde, Paul	1926	1982
Lynn, Diana	1926	1971
MacDonald, Jeanette	1903	1965
Mack, Ted	1904	1976
MacLane, Barton	1902	1969
MacMurray, Fred	1908	1991
MacRae, Gordon	1921	1986
Macready, George	1909	1973
Madison, Guy	1922	1996
Magnani, Anna	1908	1973
Mancini, Henry	1924	1994
Main, Marjorie	1890	1975
Malle, Louis	1932	1995
Mansfield, Jayne	1932	1967
Mantovani, Annunzio	1905	1980
Marais, Jean	1913	1998
March, Fredric	1897	1975
March, Hal	1920	1970
Marchand, Nancy	1928	2000
Marley, Bob	1945	1981
Marshall, Brenda	1915	1992
Marshall, E.G.	1910	1998
Marshall, Herbert	1890	1966
Martin, Dean	1917	1995
Martin, Mary	1913	1990
Martin, Ross	1920	1981
Marvin, Lee	1924	1987
Marx, Arthur (Harpo)	1888	1964
Marx, Herbert (Zeppo)	1901	1979
Marx, Julius (Groucho)	1890	1977
Marx, Leonard (Chico)	1886	1961
Marx, Milton (Gummo)	1893	1977
Mason, James	1909	1984
Massey, Daniel	1933	1998
Massey, Raymond	1896	1983
Mastroianni, Marcello	1924	1996
Matthau, Walter	1920	2000
Mature, Victor	1916	1999
Maxwell, Marilyn	1921	1972
Mayer, Louis B.	1885	1957
Mayfield, Curtis	1942	1999
Maynard, Ken	1895	1973
Mazurki, Mike	1909	1990
McCartney, Linda	1941	1998
McClure, Doug	1935	1995
McCormack, John	1884	1945
McCrea, Joel	1905	1990
McDaniel, Hattie	1895	1952
McDowall, Roddy	1928	1998
McFarland, George "Spanky"	1928	1993
McHugh, Frank	1899	1981
McIntire, John	1907	1991
McKay, Gardner	1932	2001
McKern, Leo	1920	2002
McLaglen, Victor	1883	1959
McMahon, Horace	1907	1971
McNeill, Don	1907	1979
McQueen, Butterfly	1911	1995
McQueen, Steve	1930	1980
Meadows, Audrey	1924	1996
Medford, Kay	1920	1980
Meek, Donald	1880	1946
Meeker, Ralph	1920	1989

Name	Born	Died
Melba, Nellie	1861	1931
Melchior, Lauritz	1890	1973
Menjou, Adolphe	1890	1963
Menken, Helen	1902	1966
Menuhin, Yehudi	1916	1999
Mercouri, Melina	1925	1994
Mercury, Freddie	1946	1991
Meredith, Burgess	1909	1997
Merman, Ethel	1908	1984
Merrick, David	1911	2000
Merrill, Gary	1915	1990
Mifune, Toshiro	1920	1997
Milland, Ray	1905	1986
Miller, Glenn	1904	1944
Miller, Marilyn	1898	1936
Miller, Roger	1936	1992
Mills, Harry	1913	1982
Minnevitch, Borrah	1903	1955
Mineo, Sal	1939	1976
Mingus, Charles	1922	1979
Miranda, Carmen	1913	1955
Mitchell, Cameron	1918	1994
Mitchell, Thomas	1892	1962
Mitchum, Robert	1917	1997
Mix, Tom	1880	1940
Monica, Corbett	1930	1998
Monroe, Marilyn	1926	1962
Monroe, Vaughn	1911	1973
Montand, Yves	1921	1991
Montez, Maria	1917	1951
Montgomery, Elizabeth	1933	1995
Montgomery, George	1916	2000
Montgomery, Robert	1904	1981
Moore, Clayton	1914	1999
Moore, Colleen	1900	1988
Moore, Dudley	1935	2002
Moore, Grace	1901	1947
Moore, Garry	1914	1993
Moore, Victor	1876	1962
Moorehead, Agnes	1906	1974
Morgan, Dennis	1910	1994
Morgan, Frank	1890	1949
Morgan, Helen	1900	1941
Morgan, Henry	1915	1994
Morley, Robert	1908	1992
Morris, Chester	1901	1970
Morris, Greg	1934	1996
Morris, Wayne	1914	1959
Morrison, Jim	1943	1971
Morrow, Vic	1932	1982
Mostel, Zero	1915	1977
Mowbray, Alan	1897	1969
Mulhare, Edward	1923	1997
Mulligan, Gerry	1927	1996
Mulligan, Richard	1932	2000
Muni, Paul	1895	1967
Munshin, Jules	1915	1970
Murphy, Audie	1924	1971
Murphy, George	1902	1992
Murray, Arthur	1895	1991
Murray, Kathryn	1906	1999
Murray, Mae	1885	1965
Nagel, Conrad	1896	1970
Naish, J. Carroll	1900	1973
Naldi, Nita	1898	1961
Nance, Jack	1943	1997
Natwick, Mildred	1908	1994
Negri, Pola	1897	1987
Nelson, Harriet (Hilliard)	1909	1994
Nelson, Ozzie	1906	1975
Nelson, Rick	1940	1985
Nesbit, Evelyn	1885	1967
Newley, Anthony	1931	1999
Newton, Robert	1905	1956
Nicholas, Harold	1924	2000
Nijinsky, Vaslav	1890	1950
Nilsson, Anna Q.	1893	1974
Niven, David	1909	1983
Nolan, Lloyd	1902	1985
Normand, Mabel	1894	1930
Notorious B.I.G.	1972	1997
Novarro, Ramon	1899	1968
Nureyev, Rudolf	1938	1993
Oakie, Jack	1903	1978
Oakley, Annie	1860	1926
Oates, Warren	1928	1982
Oberon, Merle	1911	1979
O'Brien, Edmond	1915	1985
O'Brien, Pat	1899	1983

Name	Born	Died
O'Connell, Arthur	1908	1981
O'Connell, Helen	1921	1993
O'Connor, Carroll	1924	2001
O'Connor, Una	1880	1959
O'Keefe, Dennis	1908	1968
Oland, Warner	1880	1938
Olcott, Chauncey	1860	1932
Oliver, Edna May	1883	1942
Olivier, Laurence	1907	1989
Olsen, Ole	1892	1963
O'Neill, James	1849	1920
Orbison, Roy	1936	1988
Ormandy, Eugene	1899	1985
O'Sullivan, Maureen	1911	1998
Ouspenskaya, Maria	1876	1949
Owen, Reginald	1887	1972
Paderewski, Ignace	1860	1941
Page, Geraldine	1924	1987
Pakula, Alan	1928	1998
Pallette, Eugene	1889	1954
Palmer, Lilli	1914	1986
Pangborn, Franklin	1894	1958
Parks, Bert	1914	1992
Parks, Larry	1914	1975
Pasternack, Josef A.	1881	1940
Pastor, Tony (vaudevillian)	1837	1908
Pastor, Tony (bandleader)	1907	1969
Patti, Adelina	1843	1919
Patti, Carlotta	1840	1889
Patrick, Gail	1911	1980
Pavlova, Anna	1885	1931
Payne, John	1912	1989
Pearl, Minnie	1912	1996
Peerce, Jan	1904	1984
Pendleton, Nat	1899	1967
Penner, Joe	1905	1941
Peppard, George	1928	1994
Perkins, Anthony	1932	1992
Perkins, Carl	1932	1998
Perkins, Marlin	1905	1986
Peters, Jean	1926	2000
Peters, Susan	1921	1952
Phillips, John	1935	2001
Phoenix, River	1970	1993
Piaf, Edith	1915	1963
Pickens, Slim	1919	1983
Pickford, Mary	1893	1979
Picon, Molly	1898	1992
Pidgeon, Walter	1897	1984
Pinza, Ezio	1892	1957
Pitts, Zasu	1898	1963
Plato, Dana	1964	1999
Pleasence, Donald	1919	1995
Pons, Lily	1904	1976
Ponselle, Rosa	1897	1981
Porter, Nyree Dawn	1940	2001
Powell, Dick	1904	1963
Powell, Eleanor	1912	1982
Powell, William	1892	1984
Power, Tyrone	1913	1958
Preminger, Otto	1905	1986
Presley, Elvis	1935	1977
Preston, Robert	1918	1987
Price, Vincent	1911	1993
Prima, Louis	1911	1978
Prinze, Freddie	1954	1977
Prowse, Juliet	1936	1996
Puente, Tito	1923	2000
Pyle, Denver	1920	1997
Quayle, Anthony	1913	1989
Questel, Mae	1908	1998
Quinn, Anthony	1915	2001
Quintero, José	1924	1999
Rabb, Ellis	1930	1998
Rabbit, Eddie	1941	1998
Radner, Gilda	1946	1989
Raft, George	1895	1980
Rains, Claude	1890	1967
Ralston, Esther	1902	1994
Ramone, Dee Dee	1952	2002
Ramone, Joey	1951	2001
Rampal, Jean-Pierre	1922	2000
Rathbone, Basil	1892	1967
Ratoff, Gregory	1897	1960
Ray, Aldo	1926	1991
Ray, Johnnie	1927	1990
Rayburn, Gene	1917	1999
Raye, Martha	1916	1994

Name	Born	Died
Raymond, Gene	1908	1998
Redding, Otis	1941	1967
Redgrave, Michael	1908	1985
Reed, Donna	1921	1986
Reed, Oliver	1938	1999
Reed, Robert	1932	1992
Reeves, George	1914	1959
Reeves, Steve	1926	2000
Reinhardt, Max	1873	1943
Remick, Lee	1935	1991
Renaldo, Duncan	1904	1980
Rennie, Michael	1909	1971
Renoir, Jean	1894	1979
Rettig, Tommy	1941	1996
Reynolds, Marjorie	1923	1997
Rich, Charlie	1932	1995
Richardson, Ralph	1902	1983
Riddle, Nelson	1921	1985
Ripperton, Minnie	1947	1979
Ritchard, Cyril	1898	1977
Ritter, Tex	1907	1974
Ritter, Thelma	1905	1969
Ritz, Al	1901	1965
Ritz, Harry	1906	1986
Ritz, Jimmy	1903	1985
Robards, Jason	1922	2000
Robbins, Jerome	1918	1998
Robbins, Marty	1925	1982
Robeson, Paul	1898	1976
Robinson, Bill	1878	1949
Robinson, Edward G.	1893	1973
Rochester (E. Anderson)	1905	1977
Roddenberry, Gene	1921	1991
Rodgers, Jimmie	1897	1933
Rogers, Buddy	1904	1999
Rogers, Ginger	1911	1995
Rogers, Roy	1911	1998
Rogers, Will	1879	1935
Roland, Gilbert	1905	1994
Rolle, Esther	1920?	1998
Rollins, Howard	1950	1996
Roman, Ruth	1924	1999
Romero, Cesar	1907	1994
Rooney, Pat	1880	1962
Rose, Billy	1899	1966
Rossellini, Roberto	1906	1977
Rowan, Dan	1922	1987
Rubinstein, Artur	1887	1982
Ruggles, Charles	1886	1970
Russell, Gail	1924	1961
Russell, Harold	1914	2002
Russell, Lillian	1861	1922
Russell, Rosalind	1911	1976
Rutherford, Margaret	1892	1972
Ryan, Irene	1903	1973
Ryan, Robert	1909	1973
Sargent, Dick	1933	1994
St. Cyr, Lili	1917	1999
St. Denis, Ruth	1877	1968
Sakall, S.Z.	1884	1955
Sale (Chic), Charles	1885	1936
Sanders, George	1906	1972
Savalas, Telly	1924	1994
Schildkraut, Joseph	1895	1964
Schipa, Tito	1889	1965
Schnabel, Artur	1882	1951
Scott, George C.	1927	1999
Scott, Hazel	1920	1981
Scott, Randolph	1898	1987
Scott, Zachary	1914	1965
Scott-Siddons, Mrs.	1843	1896
Seberg, Jean	1938	1979
Seeley, Blossom	1892	1974
Segovia, Andres	1893	1987
Selena	1971	1995
Sellers, Peter	1925	1980
Selznick, David O.	1902	1965
Sennett, Mack	1884	1960
Senor Wences	1896	1999
Serling, Rod	1924	1975
Shakur, Tupac	1971	1996
Shaw, Robert (actor)	1927	1978
Shaw, Robert (conductor)	1916	1999
Shawn, Ted	1891	1972
Shean, Al	1868	1949
Shearer, Norma	1902	1983
Sheridan, Ann	1915	1967
Shore, Dinah	1917	1994
Shubert, Lee	1875	1953
Shull, Richard B.	1929	1999

Name	Born	Died
Siddons, Mrs. Sarah	1755	1831
Sidney, Sylvia	1910	1999
Signoret, Simone	1921	1985
Silverheels, Jay	1912	1980
Silvers, Phil	1912	1985
Sim, Alastair	1900	1976
Sims, Irene	1930	2001
Sinatra, Frank	1915	1998
Sinclair, Madge	1938	1995
Siskel, Gene	1946	1999
Sitka, Emil	1914	1998
Sjostrom, Victor	1879	1960
Skelton, Red	1913	1997
Skinner, Otis	1858	1942
Smith, Alexis	1921	1992
Smith, Buffalo Bob	1917	1998
Smith, C. Aubrey	1863	1948
Smith, Kate	1907	1986
Snow, Hank	1914	1999
Solti, George	1912	1997
Sondergaard, Gale	1899	1985
Sothern, Ann	1909	2001
Sousa, John Philip	1854	1932
Sparks, Ned	1884	1957
Springfield, Dusty	1939	1999
Stander, Lionel	1908	1994
Stanley, Kim	1925	2001
Stanwyck, Barbara	1907	1990
Steiger, Rod	1925	2002
Stern, Isaac	1920	2001
Stevens, Craig	1918	2000
Stevens, Inger	1934	1970
Stevens, Mark	1916	1994
Stevenson, McLean	1929	1996
Stewart, James	1908	1997
Stickney, Dorothy	1896	1998
Stokowski, Leopold	1882	1977
Stone, Lewis	1879	1953
Stone, Milburn	1904	1980
Straight, Beatrice	1918	2001
Strasberg, Lee	1901	1999
Strasberg, Susan	1938	1999
Sturges, Preston	1898	1959
Sullavan, Margaret	1911	1960
Sullivan, Barry	1912	1994
Sullivan, Ed	1902	1974
Sullivan, Francis L.	1903	1956
Summerville, Slim	1892	1946
Swanson, Gloria	1899	1983
Swarthout, Gladys	1904	1969
Switzer, Carl "Alfalfa"	1926	1959
Talbot, Lyle	1904	1996
Talmadge, Norma	1893	1957
Tamiroff, Akim	1899	1972
Tandy, Jessica	1909	1994
Tanguay, Eva	1878	1947
Tati, Jacques	1908	1982
Taylor, Deems	1885	1966
Taylor, Dub	1907	1994
Taylor, Estelle	1899	1958
Taylor, Laurette	1887	1946
Taylor, Robert	1911	1969
Terry, Ellen	1847	1928
Thalberg, Irving	1899	1936
Thaw, John	1942	2002
Thomas, Danny	1912	1991
Thomas, John Charles	1892	1960
Thorndike, Sybil	1882	1976
Tibbett, Lawrence	1896	1960
Tierney, Gene	1920	1991
Tiny Tim	1932?	1996
Tippett, Sir Michael	1905	1998
Todd, Michael	1909	1958
Tomlinson, David	1917	2000
Tone, Franchot	1903	1968
Torme, Mel	1925	1999
Toscanini, Arturo	1867	1957
Tracy, Lee	1898	1968
Tracy, Spencer	1900	1967
Traubel, Helen	1903	1972
Travers, Henry	1874	1965
Treacher, Arthur	1894	1975
Tree, Herbert Beerbohm	1853	1917
Trevor, Claire	1909	2000
Truex, Ernest	1890	1973
Truffaut, Francois	1932	1984
Tucker, Forrest	1919	1986
Tucker, Richard	1913	1975
Tucker, Sophie	1884	1966
Turner, Lana	1920	1995
Turpin, Ben	1874	1940
Twelvetrees, Helen	1908	1959
Twitty, Conway	1933	1993
Urich, Robert	1947	2002
Valens, Ritchie	1941	1959
Valentino, Rudolph	1895	1926
Vallee, Rudy	1901	1986
Van, Bobby	1928	1980
Vance, Vivian	1912	1979
Van Fleet, Jo	1922	1996
Varney, Jim	1949	2000
Vaughan, Sarah	1924	1990
Veidt, Conrad	1893	1943
Velez, Lupe	1908	1944
Vera-Ellen	1926	1981
Verdon, Gwen	1925	2000
Vernon, Jackie	1925	1987
Villechaize, Herve	1943	1993
Vincent, Gene	1935	1971
Vicious, Sid	1958	1979
Vinson, Helen	1907	1999
Von Stroheim, Erich	1885	1957
Von Zell, Harry	1906	1981
Walker, Junior	1942	1995
Walker, Nancy	1922	1992
Walker, Robert	1918	1951
Wallenda, Karl	1905	1978
Walsh, J. T.	1943	1998
Walsh, Raoul	1887	1980
Walston, Ray	1914	2001
Walter, Bruno	1876	1962
Ward, Helen	1916	1998
Waring, Fred	1900	1984
Warner, H. B.	1876	1958
Washington, Dinah	1924	1963
Waters, Ethel	1896	1977
Waxman, Al	1935	2001
Wayne, David	1914	1995
Wayne, John	1907	1979
Webb, Clifton	1891	1966
Webb, Jack	1920	1982
Weems, Ted	1901	1963
Weissmuller, Johnny	1904	1984
Welk, Lawrence	1903	1992
Welles, Orson	1915	1985
Wellman, William	1896	1975
Werner, Oskar	1922	1984
West, Mae	1893	1980
Weston, Jack	1924	1996
Whale, James	1889	1957
Wheeler, Bert	1895	1968
White, Jesse	1919	1997
White, Pearl	1889	1938
Whiteman, Paul	1891	1967
Whitty, May	1865	1948
Wickes, Mary	1910	1995
Wilde, Cornel	1918	1989
Wilder, Billy	1906	2002
Wilding, Michael	1912	1979
Williams, Bert	1877	1922
Williams, Guy	1924	1989
Williams, Hank Sr.	1923	1953
Wills, Bob	1905	1975
Wills, Chill	1903	1978
Wilson, Carl	1946	1998
Wilson, Dennis	1944	1983
Wilson, Dooley	1894	1953
Wilson, Flip	1933	1998
Wilson, Marie	1917	1972
Windsor, Marie	1919	2000
Winninger, Charles	1884	1969
Withers, Grant	1904	1959
Wong, Anna May	1907	1961
Wood, Natalie	1938	1981
Wood, Peggy	1892	1978
Woolley, Monty	1888	1963
Worth, Irene	1916	2002
Wyler, William	1902	1981
Wynette, Tammy	1942	1998
Wynn, Ed	1886	1966
Wynn, Keenan	1916	1986
Yankovic, Frank	1915	1998
York, Dick	1929	1992
Young, Clara Kimball	1890	1960
Young, Gig	1913	1978
Young. Loretta	1913	1999
Young, Robert	1907	1998
Young, Roland	1887	1953
Youngman, Henny	1906	1998
Zanuck, Darryl F.	1902	1979
Zappa, Frank	1940	1993
Zinneman, Fred	1907	1997
Ziegfeld, Florenz	1869	1932
Zukor, Adolph	1873	1976

Original Names of Selected Entertainers

EDIE ADAMS: Elizabeth Edith Enke
EDDIE ALBERT: Edward Albert Heimberger
ALAN ALDA: Alphonso D'Abruzzo
JASON ALEXANDER: Jay Greenspan
FRED ALLEN: John Sullivan
WOODY ALLEN: Allen Konigsberg
JUNE ALLYSON: Ella Geisman
JULIE ANDREWS: Julia Wells
EVE ARDEN: Eunice Quedens
BEATRICE ARTHUR: Bernice Frankel
JEAN ARTHUR: Gladys Greene
FRED ASTAIRE: Frederick Austerlitz
BABYFACE: Kenneth Edmonds
LAUREN BACALL: Betty Joan Perske
ERYKAH BADU: Erica Wright
ANNE BANCROFT: Anna Maria Italiano
GENE BARRY: Eugene Klass
PAT BENATAR: Patricia Andrejewski
TONY BENNETT: Anthony Benedetto
IRVING BERLIN: Israel Baline
JACK BENNY: Benjamin Kubelsky
JOEY BISHOP: Joseph Gottlieb
THE BIG BOPPER: Jiles Perry "J.P." Richardson
BONO (VOX): Paul Hewson
VICTOR BORGE: Borge Rosenbaum
DAVID BOWIE: David Robert Jones
BOY GEORGE: George Alan O'Dowd
FANNY BRICE: Fanny Borach
CHARLES BRONSON: Charles Buchinski
ALBERT BROOKS: Albert Einstein
MEL BROOKS: Melvin Kaminsky
GEORGE BURNS: Nathan Birnbaum
ELLEN BURSTYN: Edna Gilhooley
RICHARD BURTON: Richard Jenkins
RED BUTTONS: Aaron Chwatt
NICOLAS CAGE: Nicholas Coppola
MICHAEL CAINE: Maurice Micklewhite
MARIA CALLAS: Maria Kalogeropoulos
DIAHANN CARROLL: Carol Diahann Johnson
JACKIE CHAN: Chan Kwong-Sung
CYD CHARISSE: Tula Finklea
RAY CHARLES: Ray Charles Robinson
CHUBBY CHECKER: Ernest Evans
CHER: Cherilyn Sarkisian
PATSY CLINE: Virginia Patterson Hensley
LEE J. COBB: Leo Jacoby
CLAUDETTE COLBERT: Lily Chauchoin
ALICE COOPER: Vincent Furnier
DAVID COPPERFIELD: David Kotkin
HOWARD COSELL: Howard Cohen
ELVIS COSTELLO: Declan McManus
LOU COSTELLO: Louis Cristillo
PETER COYOTE: Peter Cohon
MICHAEL CRAWFORD: Michael Dumble-Smith
TOM CRUISE: Thomas Mapother IV
TONY CURTIS: Bernard Schwartz
VIC DAMONE: Vito Farinola
RODNEY DANGERFIELD: Jacob Cohen
BOBBY DARIN: Walden Robert Cassotto
DORIS DAY: Doris von Kappelhoff

YVONNE DE CARLO: Peggy Middleton
SANDRA DEE: Alexandra Zuck
JOHN DENVER: Henry John Deutschendorf Jr.
BO DEREK: Mary Cathleen Collins
DANNY DEVITO: Daniel Michaeli
ANGIE DICKINSON: Angeline Brown
BO DIDDLEY: Elias Bates
PHYLLIS DILLER: Phyllis Driver
TROY DONAHUE: Merle Johnson Jr.
KIRK DOUGLAS: Issur Danielovitch
MELVYN DOUGLAS: Melvyn Hesselberg
BOB DYLAN: Robert Zimmerman
BARBARA EDEN: Barbara Huffman
ELVIRA: Cassandra Peterson
EMINEM: Marshall Mathers
ENYA: Eithne Ni Bhraonian
DALE EVANS: Frances Smith
CHAD EVERETT: Raymond Cramton
DOUGLAS FAIRBANKS: Douglas Ullman
MORGAN FAIRCHILD: Patsy McClenny
JAMIE FARR: Jameel Farah
ALICE FAYE: Alice Jeanne Leppert
STEPIN FETCHIT: Lincoln Perry
W.C. FIELDS: William Claude Dukenfield
BARRY FITZGERALD: William Shields
JOAN FONTAINE: Joan de Havilland
JODIE FOSTER: Alicia Christian Foster
REDD FOXX: John Sanford
ANTHONY FRANCIOSA: Anthony Papaleo
ARLENE FRANCIS: Arlene Kazanjian
CONNIE FRANCIS: Concetta Franconero
GRETA GARBO: Greta Gustafsson
VINCENT GARDENIA: Vincent Scognamiglio
JOHN GARFIELD: Julius Garfinkle
JUDY GARLAND: Frances Gumm
JAMES GARNER: James Bumgarner
CRYSTAL GAYLE: Brenda Gayle Webb
KATHIE LEE GIFFORD: Kathie Epstein
WHOOPI GOLDBERG: Caryn Johnson
EYDIE GORME: Edith Gormezano
STEWART GRANGER: James Stewart
CARY GRANT: Archibald Leach
LEE GRANT: Lyova Rosenthal
JOEL GREY: Joe Katz
ROBERT GUILLAUME: Robert Williams
BUDDY HACKETT: Leonard Hacker
HAMMER: Stanley Kirk Burrell
JEAN HARLOW: Harlean Carpentier
REX HARRISON: Reginald Carey
LAURENCE HARVEY: Larushka Skikne
HELEN HAYES: Helen Brown
SUSAN HAYWARD: Edythe Marriner
RITA HAYWORTH: Margarita Cansino
PEE-WEE HERMAN: Paul Reubenfeld
CHARLTON HESTON: John Charlton Carter
WILLIAM HOLDEN: William Beedle
BILLIE HOLIDAY: Eleanora Fagan
JUDY HOLLIDAY: Judith Tuvim
HARRY HOUDINI: Ehrich Weiss
LESLIE HOWARD: Leslie Stainer
HOWLIN' WOLF: Chester Burnett
ROCK HUDSON: Roy Scherer Jr. (later Fitzgerald)
ENGELBERT HUMPERDINCK: Arnold Dorsey
KIM HUNTER: Janet Cole
BETTY HUTTON: Betty Thornberg
ICE CUBE: O'Shea Jackson
ICE-T: Tracy Morrow
BILLY IDOL: William Broad
DAVID JANSSEN: David Meyer
JAY-Z: Shawn Carter
ANN JILLIAN: Anne Nauseda
ELTON JOHN: Reginald Dwight
DON JOHNSON: Donald Wayne
AL JOLSON: Asa Yoelson
JENNIFER JONES: Phylis Isley
TOM JONES: Thomas Woodward
LOUIS JOURDAN: Louis Gendre
WYNONNA JUDD: Christina Ciminella
BORIS KARLOFF: William Henry Pratt
DANNY KAYE: David Kaminsky
DIANE KEATON: Diane Hall
MICHAEL KEATON: Michael Douglas
CHAKA KHAN: Yvette Stevens
CAROLE KING: Carole Klein
LARRY KING: Larry Zeiger
BEN KINGSLEY: Krishna Banji
NASTASSJA KINSKI: Nastassja Naksyznyski
TED KNIGHT: Tadeus Wladyslaw Konopka
CHERYL LADD: Cheryl Stoppelmoor
VERONICA LAKE: Constance Ockleman
HEDY LAMARR: Hedwig Kiesler
DOROTHY LAMOUR: Mary Leta Dorothy Slaton
MICHAEL LANDON: Eugene Orowitz
MARIO LANZA: Alfredo Cocozza
QUEEN LATIFAH: Dana Owens
STAN LAUREL: Arthur Jefferson
STEVE LAWRENCE: Sidney Leibowitz
BRENDA LEE: Brenda Mae Tarpley
GYPSY ROSE LEE: Rose Louise Hovick
MICHELLE LEE: Michelle Dusiak
PEGGY LEE: Norma Egstrom
JANET LEIGH: Jeanette Morrison
VIVIEN LEIGH: Vivian Hartley
HUEY LEWIS: Hugh Cregg
JERRY LEWIS: Joseph Levitch
LIL' KIM: Kimberly Denise Jones
CAROLE LOMBARD: Jane Peters
JACK LORD: John Joseph Ryan
SOPHIA LOREN: Sophia Scicolone
PETER LORRE: Laszio Lowenstein
MYRNA LOY: Myrna Williams
BELA LUGOSI: Bela Ferenc Blasko
MOMS MABLEY: Loretta Mary Aitken
SHIRLEY MACLAINE: Shirley Beaty
ELLE MACPHERSON: Eleanor Gow
LEE MAJORS: Harvey Lee Yeary 2nd
KARL MALDEN: Mladen Sekulovich
BARRY MANILOW: Barry Alan Pincus
JAYNE MANSFIELD: Vera Jane Palmer
MARILYN MANSON: Brian Warner
FREDRIC MARCH: Frederick Bickel
PETER MARSHALL: Pierre LaCock
WALTER MATTHAU: Walter Matuschanskayasky
DEAN MARTIN: Dino Crocetti
MEAT LOAF: Marvin Lee Aday
FREDDIE MERCURY: Frederick Bulsara
ETHEL MERMAN: Ethel Zimmerman
GEORGE MICHAEL: Georgios Panayiotou
RAY MILLAND: Reginald Truscott-Jones
ANN MILLER: Lucille Collier
JONI MITCHELL: Roberta Joan Anderson
MOBY: Richard Melville Hall
MARILYN MONROE: Norma Jean Mortenson (later Baker)
YVES MONTAND: Ivo Livi
RON MOODY: Ronald Moodnick
DEMI MOORE: Demetria Guynes
GARRY MOORE: Thomas Garrison Morfit
RITA MORENO: Rosita Alverio
HARRY MORGAN: Harry Bratsburg
MR. T: Lawrence Tero
PAUL MUNI: Muni Weisenfreund
MIKE NICHOLS: Michael Igor Peschowsky
CHUCK NORRIS: Carlos Ray
NOTORIOUS B.I.G.: Christopher Wallace
HUGH O'BRIAN: Hugh Krampke
MAUREEN O'HARA: Maureen Fitzsimons
OZZY OSBOURNE: John Michael Osbourne
PATTI PAGE: Clara Ann Fowler
JACK PALANCE: Walter Palanuik
BERT PARKS: Bert Jacobson
MINNIE PEARL: Sarah Ophelia Cannon
BERNADETTE PETERS: Bernadette Lazzaro
EDITH PIAF: Edith Gassion
SLIM PICKENS: Louis Lindley
MARY PICKFORD: Gladys Smith
STEFANIE POWERS: Stefania Federkiewicz
PAULA PRENTISS: Paula Ragusa
ROBERT PRESTON: Robert Preston Meservey
PRINCE (THE ARTIST): Prince Rogers Nelson
DEE DEE RAMONE: Douglas Colvin
JOEY RAMONE: Jeffrey Hyman
JOHNNY RAMONE: John Cummings
TOMMY RAMONE: Tom Erdelyi
TONY RANDALL: Leonard Rosenberg
JOHNNIE RAY: John Alvin
MARTHA RAYE: Margaret O'Reed
DONNA REED: Donna Belle Mullenger
DELLA REESE: Delloreese Patricia Early
BUSTA RHYMES: Trevor Smith Jr.
JOAN RIVERS: Joan Sandra Molinsky
EDWARD G. ROBINSON: Emmanuel Goldenberg
THE ROCK: Dwayne Johnson
GINGER ROGERS: Virginia McMath
ROY ROGERS: Leonard Franklin Slye
MICKEY ROONEY: Joe Yule Jr.
JOHNNY ROTTEN: John Lydon
LILLIAN RUSSELL: Helen Leonard
MEG RYAN: Margaret Hyra
WINONA RYDER: Winona Horowitz
SADE: Helen Folsad Abu
SOUPY SALES: Milton Hines
SUSAN SARANDON: Susan Tomaling
SEAL: Samuel Sealhenry
RANDOLPH SCOTT: George Randolph Crane
JANE SEYMOUR: Joyce Frankenberg
OMAR SHARIF: Michael Shalhoub
CHARLIE SHEEN: Carlos Irwin Estevez
MARTIN SHEEN: Ramon Estevez
BEVERLY SILLS: Belle Silverman
TALIA SHIRE: Talia Coppola
PHIL SILVERS: Philip Silversmith
SINBAD: David Atkins
"BUFFALO BOB" SMITH: Robert Schmidt
SNOOP DOGGY DOG: Calvin Broadus
ANN SOTHERN: Harriette Lake
ROBERT STACK: Robert Modini
BARBARA STANWYCK: Ruby Stevens
JEAN STAPLETON: Jeanne Murray
RINGO STARR: Richard Starkey
CONNIE STEVENS: Concetta Ingolia
STING: Gordon Sumner
DONNA SUMMER: La Donna Gaines
RIP TAYLOR: Charles Elmer Jr.
ROBERT TAYLOR: Spangler Brugh
DANNY THOMAS: Muzyad Yakhoob, later Amos Jacobs
TINY TIM: Herbert Khaury
RIP TORN: Elmore Rual Torn Jr.
RANDY TRAVIS: Randy Traywick
SOPHIE TUCKER: Sophia Kalish
TINA TURNER: Annie Mae Bullock
TWIGGY: Leslie Hornby
CONWAY TWITTY: Harold Lloyd Jenkins
RUDOLPH VALENTINO: Rudolpho D'Antonguolla
FRANKIE VALLI: Frank Castelluccio
SID VICIOUS: John Simon Ritchie
JOHN WAYNE: Marion Morrison
CLIFTON WEBB: Webb Hollenbeck
RAQUEL WELCH: Raquel Tejada
GENE WILDER: Jerome Silberman
SHELLEY WINTERS: Shirley Schrift
STEVIE WONDER: Stevland Morris
JANE WYMAN: Sarah Jane Fulks
GIG YOUNG: Byron Barr
LORETTA YOUNG: Gretchen Michaels

CITIES OF THE U.S.

Source: Bureau of Labor Statistics: employment; Bureau of Economic Analysis: per capita personal income. All other data from Census 2000, U.S. Census Bureau.

Included here are the 100 most populous U.S. cities, based on the 2000 Census. Population rank indicated by figure in parentheses. Most data are for the city proper; employment figures are for 2001, income figures for 2000. Mayors are as of Sept. 2002. Some statistics, where noted, apply to the whole Metropolitan Statistical Area (MSA). Inc.=incorporated; est.=established.

Note: Websites are as of Sept. 2002 and subject to change.

Akron, Ohio

Population: 217,074 (81); **Pop. density:** 3,496 per sq. mi; **Pop. change (1990-2000):** –2.7%. **Area:** 62.1 sq. mi. **Employment:** 107,642 employed; 6.0% unemployed. **Per capita income (MSA):** $29,023; increase (1999-2000): 4.9%.

Mayor: Donald L. Plusquellic, Democrat

History: settled 1825; inc. as city 1865; located on Ohio-Erie Canal and is a port of entry; polymer center of the Americas.

Transportation: 1 airport; major trucking industry; Conrail, Amtrak; metro transit system. **Communications:** 7 radio stations. **Medical facilities:** 4 hosp.; specialized children's treatment center. **Educational facilities:** 4 univ. and colleges; 68 pub. schools. **Further information:** Greater Akron Chamber, One Cascade Plaza, 17th Floor, Akron, OH 44308; www.ci.akron.oh.us; www.greaterakronchamber.org

Albuquerque, New Mexico

Population: 448,607 (35); **Pop. density:** 2,484 per sq. mi; **Pop. change (1990-2000):** +16.6%. **Area:** 180.6 sq. mi. **Employment:** 234,883 employed; 3.4% unemployed. **Per capita income (MSA):** $25,894; increase (1999-2000): 5.3%.

Mayor: Martin Chavez, Democrat

History: founded 1706 by the Spanish; inc. 1890.

Transportation: 1 intl. airport; 1 railroad; 11 bus service/charters. **Communications:** 14 TV, 42 radio stations. **Medical facilities:** 6 major hosp. **Educational facilities:** 1 univ., 13 colleges. **Further information:** Albuquerque Convention & Visitors Bureau, PO Box 26866, Albuquerque, NM 87125-6866; www.ci.albuquerque.nm.us; www.abqcvb.org; www.cabq.org

Anaheim, California

Population: 328,014 (55); **Pop. density:** 6,708 per sq. mi; **Pop. change (1990-2000):** +23.1%. **Area:** 48.9 sq. mi. **Employment:** 163,746 employed; 3.5% unemployed. **Per capita income (MSA):** $34,862; increase (1999-2000): 5.8%.

Mayor: Tom Daly, Non-Partisan

History: founded 1857; inc. 1870; now known as home of The Disneyland Resort, the Mighty Ducks of Anaheim, and the Anaheim Angels.

Transportation: Amtrak, Metrolink (2 sta.), OCTA bus service, Greyhound. **Communications:** 2 TV, 2 radio stations (MSA). **Medical facilities:** 4 hosp.; 5 medical centers. **Educational facilities:** 13 univ. and colleges; 39 elem., 11 junior high, 10 high schools (MSA). **Further information:** City Hall, 200 South Anaheim Blvd., Ste. 733, Anaheim, CA 92805; www.anaheim.net

Anchorage, Alaska

Population: 260,283 (65); **Pop. density:** 153 per sq. mi; **Pop. change (1990-2000):** +15.0%. **Area:** 1,697.2 sq. mi. **Employment:** 138,686 employed; 4.3% unemployed. **Per capita income (MSA):** $34,950; increase (1999-2000): 5.4%.

Mayor: George Wuerch, Republican

History: founded 1914 as a construction camp for railroad; HQ of Alaska Defense Command, WWII; severely damaged in earthquake 1964, but now rebuilt and currently population center of Alaska.

Transportation: 1 intl. airport; 1 railroad; transit system, 1 port. **Communications:** 9 TV, 28 radio stations. **Medical facilities:** 4 hosp. **Educational facilities:** 3 univ., 1 college, 89 pub. schools. **Further information:** Anchorage Chamber of Commerce, 441 W. 5th Ave., Ste. 300, Anchorage, AK 99501-2309; www.ci.anchorage.ak.us; www.anchoragechamber.org

Arlington, Texas

Population: 332,969 (53); **Pop. density:** 3,476 per sq. mi; **Pop. change (1990-2000):** +27.2%. **Area:** 95.8 sq. mi. **Employment:** 188,417 employed; 3.6% unemployed. **Per capita income (MSA):** $29,305; increase (1999-2000): 5.6%.

Mayor: Elzie Odom, Non-Partisan

History: settled in 1840s between Dallas and Ft. Worth; inc. 1884.

Transportation: Dallas/Ft. Worth airport is 10 min. away; 11 railway lines; intercity transport system in planning stage. **Communications:** 11 TV, 44 radio stations. **Medical facilities:** 2 hosp. **Educational facilities:** 1 univ., 1 junior college; 60 pub. schools. **Further information:** Arlington Chamber of Commerce, 505 East Border, Arlington, TX 76010; www.ci.arlington.tx.us; www.arlingtontx.com

Atlanta, Georgia

Population: 416,474 (39); **Pop. density:** 3,162 per sq. mi; **Pop. change (1990-2000):** +5.7%. **Area:** 131.7 sq. mi. **Employment:** 215,987 employed; 5.8% unemployed. **Per capita income (MSA):** $33,013; increase (1999-2000): 5.0%.

Mayor: Shirley Franklin, Democrat

History: founded as "Terminus" 1837; renamed Atlanta 1845; inc. 1847; played major role in Civil War; became permanent state capital 1877; birthplace of civil rights movement; host to 1996 Centennial Olympic Games.

Transportation: 1 intl. airport; 3 railroad lines; MARTA bus and rapid rail service. **Communications:** 14 TV, 56 radio stations; 29 cable TV cos. **Medical facilities:** 61 hosp.; VA hosp.; U.S. Centers for Disease Control and Prevention; American Cancer Society. **Educational facilities:** 43 colleges, univ., seminaries, junior colleges; 813 pub. schools (metro area). **Further information:** Metro Atlanta Chamber of Commerce, 235 Andrew Young Intl. Blvd. NW, Atlanta, GA 30303; www.atlantasmartcity.com; www.metroatlantachamber.com

Augusta, Georgia

Population: 199,775 (89); **Pop. density:** 661 per sq. mi. **Pop. change (1990-2000):** +347.5%. **Area:** 302.1 sq. mi. **Employment:** 74,704 employed; 5.5% unemployed. **Per capita income (MSA):** $23,816; increase (1999-2000): 4.5%.

Mayor: Bob Young, Non-Partisan

History: founded 1736 as colonial trading post; one of the few pre-Civil War manufacturing centers in the South. Augusta National Golf Club, home of Masters Tournament, founded 1933.

Transportation: 1 regional, 1 local airport; Savannah River; 1 interstate highway. **Communications:** 4 TV, 20+ radio stations; 2 major cable TV providers. **Medical facilities:** 9 hosp., including Eisenhower Army Medical Center. **Educational facilities:** 1 univ., 1 medical univ., 1 tech. college; 36 elem., 10 middle, 9 pub. high schools. **Further information:** Augusta Metropolitan Convention and Visitors Bureau, PO Box 1331, Augusta, GA 30903; augusta.co.richmond.ga.us; www.augustagausa.com

Aurora, Colorado

Population: 276,393 (61); **Pop. density:** 1,940 per sq. mi; **Pop. change (1990-2000):** +24.4%. **Area:** 142.5 sq. mi. **Employment:** 156,829 employed; 3.5% unemployed. **Per capita income (MSA):** $37,153; increase (1999-2000): 8.4%.

Mayor: Paul E. Tauer, Non-Partisan

History: located 5 mi east of Denver; early growth stimulated by presence of military bases; fast-growing trade center.

Transportation: adjacent to Denver Intl. Airport; 1 airport; bus system. **Communications:** 1 TV station. **Medical facilities:** 2 private hosp. **Educational facilities:** 1 univ., 4 community and junior colleges, 2 technical colleges; 86 pub. schools. **Further information:** Aurora Planning Dept., 1470 S. Havana St., Rm. 134, Aurora, CO 80012; www.auroragov.org; www.aurorachamber.org

Austin, Texas

Population: 656,562 (16); **Pop. density:** 2,611 per sq. mi; **Pop. change (1990-2000):** +41.0%. **Area:** 251.5 sq. mi. **Employment:** 382,907 employed; 4.3% unemployed. **Per capita income (MSA):** $32,039; increase (1999-2000): 4.5%.

Mayor: Gus Garcia, Democrat

History: first permanent settlement 1835; capital of Rep. of Texas 1839; named after Stephen Austin; inc. 1840.

Transportation: 1 intl. airport; 4 railroads. **Communications:** 12 TV, 24 radio stations. **Medical facilities:** 12 hosp. **Educational facilities:** 7 univ. and colleges. **Further information:** Chamber of Commerce, PO Box 1967, Austin, TX 78767; www.ci.austin.tx.us; www.austinchamber.org

Bakersfield, California

Population: 247,057 (69); **Pop. density:** 2,184 per sq. mi; **Pop. change (1990-2000):** +41.3%. **Area:** 113.1 sq. mi. **Employment:** 94,350 employed; 7.7% unemployed. **Per capita income (MSA):** $20,767; increase (1999-2000): 5.3%.

Mayor: Harvey Hall, Non-Partisan

History: named after Col. Thomas Baker, an early settler; inc. 1898.

Transportation: 2 airports; 3 railroads; Amtrak; Greyhound buses; local bus system. **Communications:** 7 TV, 34 radio stations. **Medical facilities:** 8 major hosp.; 9 convalescent, 1 psychiatric, 3 physical rehab., 5 urgent care facilities; 3 clinics. **Educational facilities:** 8 univ., 1 community college, 14 vocational schools, 1 adult school, 32 elem., 8 junior high, 14 high schools (Kern County). **Further information:** Greater Bakersfield Chamber of Commerce, 1725 Eye St., PO Box 1947, Bakersfield, CA 93303; www.bakersfieldchamber.org

Baltimore, Maryland

Population: 651,154 (17); **Pop. density:** 8,058 per sq. mi; **Pop. change (1990-2000):** –11.5%. **Area:** 80.8 sq. mi. **Employment:** 272,030 employed; 7.9% unemployed. **Per capita income (MSA):** $32,265; increase (1999-2000): 5.6%.

Mayor: Martin O'Malley, Democrat

History: founded by Maryland legislature 1729; inc. 1797; bombing of Ft. McHenry (1814) inspired Francis Scott Key to write "Star-Spangled Banner"; birthplace of America's railroads 1828; rebuilt after fire 1904; site of National Aquarium 1981.

Transportation: 1 major airport; 3 railroads; bus system; subway system; light rail system; Inner Harbor water taxi system; 2 underwater tunnels. **Communications:** 6 TV, 26 radio stations. **Medical facilities:** 31 hosp.; 2 major medical centers. **Educational facilities:** over 30 univ. and colleges; 173 pub. schools. **Further information:** Greater Baltimore Committee, 111 S. Calvert St., Ste. 1700, Baltimore, MD 21202-6180; www.ci.baltimore.md.us; www.baltimore.org

Baton Rouge, Louisiana

Population: 227,818 (74); **Pop. density:** 2,966 per sq. mi; **Pop. change (1990-2000):** +3.8%. **Area:** 76.8 sq. mi. **Employment:** 113,960 employed; 5.9% unemployed. **Per capita income (MSA):** $25,117; increase (1999-2000): 3.3%.

Mayor: Bobby Simpson, Republican

History: claimed by Spain at time of Louisiana Purchase 1803; est. independence by rebellion 1810; inc. as town 1817; became state capital 1849; Union-held most of Civil War.

Transportation: 1 airport, 5 airlines; 1 bus line; 3 railroad trunk lines. **Communications:** 5 TV, 19 radio stations. **Medical facilities:** 5 hosp. **Educational facilities:** 2 univ.; 105 pub., 52 nonpublic schools. **Further information:** The Chamber of Greater Baton Rouge, PO Box 3217, Baton Rouge, LA 70821; www.baton-rouge.com/BatonRouge; www.brchamber.org

Birmingham, Alabama

Population: 242,820 (71); **Pop. density:** 1,620 per sq. mi; **Pop. change (1990-2000):** –8.7%. **Area:** 149.9 sq. mi. **Employment:** 123,272 employed; 5.5% unemployed. **Per capita income (MSA):** $29,057; increase (1999-2000): 3.9%.

Mayor: Bernard Kincaid, Democrat

History: settled 1871 at the intersection of 2 major railroads within proximity of elements required for iron and steel production.

Transportation: 1 intl. airport; 4 major rail freight lines, Amtrak; 1 bus line; 75 truck line terminals; 5 air cargo cos.; 7 barge lines; 5 interstate highways. **Communications:** 7 TV, 32 radio stations; 1 educational TV, 1 educational radio station. **Medical facilities:** 16, including the Univ. of Alabama at Birmingham Medical Center; VA hosp. **Educational facilities:** 1 pub., 2 private univ.; 4 private colleges, 1 private law school. **Further information:** Birmingham Area Chamber of Commerce, 2027 First Ave. N, Birmingham, AL 35203; www.birminghamchamber.com; www.ci.bham.al.us

Boston, Massachusetts

Population: 589,141 (20); **Pop. density:** 12,172 per sq. mi; **Pop. change (1990-2000):** +2.6%. **Area:** 48.4 sq. mi. **Employment:** 284,816 employed; 4.1% unemployed. **Per capita income (MSA):** $38,758; increase (1999-2000): 9.8%.

Mayor: Thomas M. Menino, Democrat

History: settled 1630 by John Winthrop; capital of Mass. Bay Colony; figured strongly in Am. Revolution, earning distinction as the "Cradle of Liberty"; inc. 1822.

Transportation: 1 major airport; 2 railroads; city rail and subway system; 3 underwater tunnels; port. **Communications:** 12 TV, 21 radio stations. **Medical facilities:** 31 hosp.; 8 major medical research centers. **Educational facilities:** 30 univ. and colleges. **Further information:** Greater Boston Convention and Visitors Bureau, 2 Copley Pl., Suite 105, Boston, MA 02116; www.bostonusa.com; www.gbcc.org

Buffalo, New York

Population: 292,648 (58); **Pop. density:** 7,208 per sq. mi; **Pop. change (1990-2000):** –10.8%. **Area:** 40.6 sq. mi. **Employment:** 124,368 employed; 8.6% unemployed. **Per capita income (MSA):** $26,846; increase (1999-2000): 4.4%.

Mayor: Anthony M. Masiello, Democrat

History: settled 1780 by Seneca Indians; raided twice by British, War of 1812; served as western terminus for Erie Canal, became a center for trade and manufacturing; inc. 1832; last stop on the Underground Railroad; key point for Canada-U.S. political, trade, and social relations.

Transportation: 1 intl. airport; 4 Class I railroads; Amtrak metro rail system; water service to Great Lakes-St. Lawrence Seaway system and Atlantic seaboard. **Communications:** 11 TV, 12 radio stations. **Medical facilities:** 16 hosp., 40 research centers. **Educational facilities:** 15 colleges and univ.; 400 pub. and private schools. **Further information:** Buffalo Niagara Partnership, 300 Main Place Tower, Buffalo, NY 14202-3797; www.ci.buffalo.ny.us; buffaloniagara.org

Charlotte, North Carolina

Population: 540,828 (26); **Pop. density:** 2,232 per sq. mi; **Pop. change (1990-2000):** +36.6%. **Area:** 242.3 sq. mi. **Employment:** 280,221 employed; 4.5% unemployed. **Per capita income (MSA):** $30,901; increase (1999-2000): 5.2%.

Mayor: Patrick McCrory, Republican

History: settled by Scotch-Irish immigrants 1740s; inc. 1768 and named after Queen Charlotte, George III's wife; scene of first major U.S. gold discovery 1799.

Transportation: 1 airport; 2 major railway lines; 1 bus line; 300 trucking firms. **Communications:** 7 TV, 26 radio stations. **Medical facilities:** 10 hosp., 1 medical center. **Educational facilities:** 5 univ., 8 colleges, 86 elem. schools, 28 middle schools, 14 high schools. **Further information:** Chamber of Commerce, PO Box 32785, Charlotte, NC 28232; www.charlottechamber.com

Chesapeake, Virginia

Population: 199,184 (91); **Pop. density:** 585 per sq. mi; **Pop. change (1990-2000):** +31.1%. **Area:** 340.7 sq. mi. **Employment:** 105,167 employed; 2.9% unemployed. **Per capita income (MSA):** $26,159; increase (1999-2000): 4.9%.

Mayor: William E. Ward, Non-Partisan

History: region settled in 1620s with first English colonies on banks of Elizabeth River; home to Great Dismal Swamp Canal, first envisioned by George Washington in 1763; Battle of Great Bridge fought here Dec. 1775; inc. as a city 1963.

Transportation: Amtrak, freight rail service; bus service; 2 regional airports. **Communications:** 9 TV, 48 radio stations (serving Hampton Roads community). **Medical facilities:** 1 hosp. **Educational facilities:** 9 colleges and univ.; 49 pub. schools and educational centers. **Further information:** Hampton Roads Chamber of Commerce, Chesapeake Div., 400 Volvo Pky., Chesapeake, VA 23320; www.chesapeake.va.us; www.cityofchesapeake.net

Chicago, Illinois

Population: 2,896,016 (3); **Pop. density:** 12,752 per sq. mi; **Pop. change (1990-2000):** +4.0%. **Area:** 227.1 sq. mi. **Employment:** 1,241,886 employed; 6.9% unemployed. **Per capita income (MSA):** $35,336; increase (1999-2000): 5.1%.

Mayor: Richard M. Daley, Democrat

History: site acquired from Indians 1795; significant white settlement began with opening of Erie Canal 1825; chartered as city 1837; boomed with arrival of railroads from east and canal to Mississippi R.; about one-third of city destroyed by fire 1871; major grain and livestock market.

Transportation: 3 airports; major railroad system, trucking industry. **Communications:** 9 TV, 31 radio stations. **Medical facilities:** over 123 hosp. **Educational facilities:** 95 insts. of higher learning. **Further information:** Chicagoland Chamber of Commerce, 1 IBM Plaza, Ste. 2800, Chicago, IL 60611; www.ci.chi.il.us; www.chicagolandchamber.org

Cincinnati, Ohio

Population: 331,285 (54); **Pop. density:** 4,247 per sq. mi; **Pop. change (1990-2000):** –9.0%. **Area:** 78.0 sq. mi. **Employment:** 167,098 employed; 5.2% unemployed. **Per capita income (MSA):** $30,891; increase (1999-2000): 4.5%.

Mayor: Charlie Luken, Democrat

History: founded 1788 and named after the Society of Cincinnati, an organization of Revolutionary War officers; chartered as village 1802; inc. as city 1819.

Transportation: 1 intl. airport; 3 railroads; 1 bus system. **Communications:** 7 TV, 25 radio stations. **Medical facilities:** 27 hosp.; Children's Hosp. Medical Center; VA hosp. **Educational facilities:** 4 univ., 11 colleges, 8 technical & 2-year colleges. **Further information:** Chamber of Commerce, 300 Carew Tower, 441 Vine St., Cincinnati, OH 45202; www.cincinnatichamber.com, www.cincinnatiusa.org

Cleveland, Ohio

Population: 478,403 (33); **Pop. density:** 6,165 per sq. mi; **Pop. change (1990-2000):** –5.4%. **Area:** 77.6 sq. mi. **Employment:** 187,670 employed; 8.8% unemployed. **Per capita income (MSA):** $30,909; increase (1999-2000): 4.6%.

Mayor: Jane Campbell, Democrat

History: surveyed in 1796; given recognition as village 1815, inc. as city 1836; annexed Ohio City 1854.

Transportation: 1 intl. airport; rail service; major port; rapid transit system. **Communications:** 9 TV, 21 radio stations. **Medical facilities:** 14 hosp. **Educational facilities:** 8 univ. and colleges; 127 pub. schools. **Further information:** Greater Cleveland Growth Assn., Tower City Center, 50 Pub. Square, Suite 200, Cleveland, OH 44113-2291; www.cleveland.oh.us; www.clevelandgrowth.com

Colorado Springs, Colorado

Population: 360,890 (48); **Pop. density:** 1,943 per sq. mi; **Pop. change (1990-2000):** +28.4%. **Area:** 185.7 sq. mi. **Employment:** 187,286 employed; 4.5% unemployed. **Per capita income (MSA):** $28,804; increase (1999-2000): 6.7%.

Mayor: Mary Lou Makepeace, Republican

History: city founded in 1871 at the foot of Pike's Peak; inc. 1872.

Transportation: 1 municipal airport; 1 bus line. **Communications:** 9 TV, 28 radio stations. **Medical facilities:** 5 hosp. **Educational facilities:** 11 univ., 5 colleges. **Further information:** Chamber of Commerce, PO Box B, Colorado Springs, CO 80901; www.springsgov.com; www.coloradospringschamber.org

Columbus, Ohio

Population: 711,470 (15); **Pop. density:** 3,383 per sq. mi; **Pop. change (1990-2000):** +12.4%. **Area:** 210.3 sq. mi. **Employment:** 396,089 employed; 3.2% unemployed. **Per capita income (MSA):** $30,619; increase (1999-2000): 5.2%.

Mayor: Michael B. Coleman, Democrat

History: first settlement 1797; laid out as new capital 1812 with current name; became city 1834.

Transportation: 6 airports; 2 railroads; 2 intercity bus lines. **Communications:** 8 TV, 29 radio stations. **Medical facilities:** 17 hosp. **Educational facilities:** 11 univ. and colleges; 8 technical/2-year schools; 129 pub. schools (67 elem., 21 middle, 14 high, 27 magnet). **Further information:** Greater Columbus Chamber of Commerce, 37 N. High St., Columbus, OH 43215. Greater Columbus Convention and Visitors Bureau, 90 N. High St., Columbus, OH 43215; www.columbus.org

Corpus Christi, Texas

Population: 277,454 (60); **Pop. density:** 1,795 per sq. mi; **Pop. change (1990-2000):** +7.8%. **Area:** 154.6 sq. mi. **Employment:** 122,499 employed; 5.7% unemployed. **Per capita income (MSA):** $23,323; increase (1999-2000): 5.9%.

Mayor: Samuel Loyd Neal, Non-Partisan

History: settled 1839 and inc. 1852.

Transportation: 1 intl. airport; 2 bus lines, metro bus system; 3 freight railroads. **Communications:** 6 TV, 17 radio stations. **Medical facilities:** 14 hosp. including a children's center. **Educational facilities:** 1 univ., 1 college. **Further information:** Corpus Christi Regional Economic Development Corp., PO Box 2724, Corpus Christi, TX 78403; www.ccredc.com; www.ci.corpus-christi.tx.us

Dallas, Texas

Population: 1,188,580 (8); **Pop. density:** 3,470 per sq. mi; **Pop. change (1990-2000):** +18.0%. **Area:** 342.5 sq. mi. **Employment:** 653,889 employed; 6.2% unemployed. **Per capita income (MSA):** $35,216; increase (1999-2000): 6.8%.

Mayor: Laura Miller, Democrat

History: first settled 1841; platted 1846; inc. 1871; developed as the financial and commercial center of Southwest; headquarters of regional Federal Reserve Bank; major center for distribution and high-tech manufacturing.

Transportation: 1 intl. airport, 1 regional airport; Amtrak; transit system. **Communications:** 17 TV, 51 radio stations. **Medical facilities:** 22 general hosp.; major medical center. **Educational facilities:** 218 pub. schools, 12 univ. and colleges, 3 community college campuses. **Further information:** Greater Dallas Chamber, Resource Center, 1201 Elm St., Ste. 2000, Dallas, TX 75270; www.dallaschamber.org; www.ci.dallas.tx.us

Denver, Colorado

Population: 554,636 (25); **Pop. density:** 3,616 per sq. mi; **Pop. change (1990-2000):** +18.6%. **Area:** 153.4 sq. mi. **Employment:** 266,790 employed; 4.5% unemployed. **Per capita income (MSA):** $37,153; increase (1999-2000): 8.4%.

Mayor: Wellington E. Webb, Democrat

History: settled 1858 by gold prospectors and miners; inc. 1861; became territorial capital 1867; growth spurred by gold and silver boom; became financial, industrial, cultural center of Rocky Mt. region.

Transportation: 1 intl. airport, 3 corporate reliever airports; 5 rail freight lines, Amtrak; 1 bus line. **Communications:** 14 TV, 29 radio stations. **Medical facilities:** 20 hosp. **Educational facilities:** 15 four-yr. colleges and univ.; 8 two-yr. and community colleges. **Further information:** Denver Metro Chamber of Commerce, 1445 Market St., Denver, CO 80202-1729; www.denverchamber.org

Des Moines, Iowa

Population: 198,682 (93); **Pop. density:** 2,621 per sq. mi; **Pop. change (1990-2000):** +2.8%. **Area:** 75.8 sq. mi. **Employment:** 119,152 employed; 3.3% unemployed. **Per capita income (MSA):** $31,347; increase (1999-2000): 3.1%.

Mayor: Preston Daniels, Democrat

History: Fort Des Moines built 1843; settled and inc. 1851; chartered as city 1857.

Transportation: 1 intl. airport; 7 bus lines; 4 railroads; metro bus system. **Communications:** 4 TV, 12 radio stations. **Medical facilities:** 6 hosp. **Educational facilities:** 2 univ., 6 colleges. **Further information:** Greater Des Moines Partnership, 700 Locust St., Ste. 100, Des Moines, IA 50309; www.desmoinesmetro.com; www.ci.des-moines.ia.us

Detroit, Michigan

Population: 951,270 (10); **Pop. density:** 6,854 per sq. mi; **Pop. change (1990-2000):** –7.5%. **Area:** 138.8 sq. mi. **Employment:** 364,828 employed; 9.7% unemployed. **Per capita income (MSA):** $33,259; increase (1999-2000): 5.2%.

Mayor: Kwame M. Kilpatrick, Democrat

History: founded by French 1701; controlled by British 1760; acquired by U.S. 1796; destroyed by fire 1805; inc. as city 1824; capital of state 1837-47; auto manufacturing began 1899.

Transportation: 1 intl. airport; 4 railroads; major intl. port; pub. transit system. **Communications:** 10 TV, 15 radio stations. **Medical facilities:** 23 hosp.; 2 major medical centers. **Educational facilities:** 5 univ. and colleges, 1 community college. **Further information:** Detroit Regional Chamber, One Woodward Ave., PO Box 33840, Detroit, MI 48232-0840; www.detroitchamber.com

El Paso, Texas

Population: 563,662 (23); **Pop. density:** 2,263 per sq. mi; **Pop. change (1990-2000):** +9.4%. **Area:** 249.1 sq. mi. **Employment:** 235,325 employed; 7.8% unemployed. **Per capita income (MSA):** $18,535; increase (1999-2000): 4.4%.

Mayor: Raymond C. Caballero, Non-Partisan

History: first settled 1827; inc. 1873; arrival of railroad 1881 boosted city's population and industries.

Transportation: 1 intl. airport; 3 rail providers; 2 interstate highways; 4 intl. ports of entry. **Communications:** 12 TV, 21 radio stations. **Medical facilities:** 6 hosp.; 3 rehabilitation, 11 specialty centers. **Educational facilities:** 5 univ., 2 colleges (1 grad. only). **Further information:** Greater El Paso Chamber of Commerce, 10 Civic Center Plaza, El Paso, TX 79901; www.ci.el-paso.tx.us

Fort Wayne, Indiana

Population: 205,727 (84); **Pop. density:** 2,604 per sq. mi; **Pop. Change (1990-2000):** +18.9%. **Area:** 79.0 sq. mi. **Employment:** 92,325 employed; 5.7% unemployed. **Per capita income (MSA):** $27,591; increase (1999-2000): 4.2%.

Mayor: Graham A. Richard, Democrat

History: French fort 1680; U.S. fort 1794; settled by 1832; inc. 1840 prior to Wabash-Erie canal completion 1843.

Transportation:1 airport; 3 railroads; 6 bus lines. **Communications:** 5 TV, 21 radio stations. **Medical facilities:** 5 regional hosp.; VA hosp. **Educational facilities:** 5 univ., 4 colleges, 3 bus. schools; 86 pub. schools. **Further information:** Chamber of Commerce, 826 Ewing Street, Fort Wayne, IN 46802-2182; www.ft-wayne.in.us; www.fwchamber.org

Fort Worth, Texas

Population: 534,694 (27); **Pop. density:** 1,828 per sq. mi; **Pop. change (1990-2000):** +19.5%. **Area:** 292.5 sq. mi. **Employment:** 266,499 employed; 5.5% unemployed. **Per capita income (MSA):** $29,305; increase (1999-2000): 5.6%.

Mayor: Kenneth L. Barr, Non-Partisan

History: established as military post 1849; inc. 1873; oil discovered 1917.

Transportation: 2 intl. airport; 10 major railroads, Amtrak; local bus service; 2 transcontinental, 2 intrastate bus lines. **Communications:** 14 TV, 11 local radio stations. **Medical facilities:** 25 hosp.; 1 children's hosp.; 4 government hosp. **Educational facilities:** 8 univ. and colleges. **Further information:** Chamber of Commerce, 777 Taylor St. #900, Fort Worth, TX 76102; www.ci.fort-worth.tx.us; www.fortworthchamber.com

Fremont, California

Population: 203,413 (85); **Pop. density:** 2,652 per sq. mi; **Pop. change (1990-2000):** +17.3%. **Area:** 76.7 sq. mi. **Employment:** 109,152 employed; 3.1% unemployed. **Per capita income (MSA):** $39,6111; increase (1999-2000): 10.6%.

Mayor: Gus Morrison, Non-Partisan

History: area first settled by Spanish 1769; inc. 1956 with consolidation of 5 communities.

Transportation: intracity bus line; Bay Area Rapid Transit System (southern terminal). **Communications:** 1 radio station. **Medical facilities:** 1 hosp.; 2 major medical facilities; 18 clinics. **Educational facilities:** 1 community college; 42 pub. schools. **Further information:** Chamber of Commerce, 39488 Stevenson Place, Suite 100, Fremont, CA 94539; www.fremontbusiness.com

Fresno, California

Population: 427,652 (37); **Pop. density:** 4,096 per sq. mi; **Pop. change (1990-2000):** +20.7%. **Area:** 104.4 sq. mi. **Employment:** 172,973 employed; 12.3% unemployed. **Per capita income (MSA):** $21,121; increase (1999-2000): 4.2%.

Mayor: Alan Autry, Non-Partisan

History: founded 1872; inc. as city 1885.

Transportation: 1 municipal airport; Amtrak; 1 bus line; intracity bus system. **Communications:** 13 TV, 23 radio stations. **Medical facilities:** 17 general hosp. **Educational facilities:** 9 colleges; 102 pub. schools. **Further information:** Greater Fresno Area Chamber of Commerce, PO Box 1469, Fresno, CA 93716-1469; www.fresnochamber.com; fresno-online.com/cvb

Garland, Texas

Population: 215,768 (82); **Pop. density:** 3,778 per sq. mi; **Pop. change (1990-2000):** +19.4%. **Area:** 57.1 sq. mi. **Employment:** 122,365 employed; 4.1% unemployed. **Per capita income (MSA):** $35,216; increase (1999-2000): 6.8%.

Mayor: Bob Day, Democrat

History: settled 1850s; inc. 1891.

Transportation: 30 min. from Dallas/Ft. Worth Intl. Airport; 2 railroads. **Communications:** 14 local TV (Dallas/Ft. Worth), 25+ radio stations. **Medical facilities:** 2 hosp.; 348 beds. **Educational facilities:** 3 univ., 2 community colleges; 61 pub. schools. **Further information:** Chamber of Commerce, 914 S. Garland Ave., Garland, TX 75040; www.garlandchamber.com

Glendale, Arizona

Population: 218,812 (80); **Pop. density:** 3,928 per sq. mi; **Pop. change (1990-2000):** +47.7%. **Area:** 55.7 sq. mi. **Employment:** 109,630 employed; 3.9% unemployed. **Per capita income (MSA):** $27,564; increase (1999-2000): 6.0%.

Mayor: Elaine M. Scruggs, Non-Partisan

History: est. 1892; inc. 1910.

Transportation: 1 local airport, 30 min. from Phoenix Sky Harbor Intl. Airport. **Communications:** 12 TV stations, 40 radio stations. **Medical facilities:** 3 hosp. **Educational facilities:** 12 institutes of higher education, 9 pub. school districts. **Further information:** Chamber of Commerce, PO Box 249, 7105 N. 59th Ave., Glendale, AZ 85311; www.glendaleazchamber.org

Glendale, California

Population: 194,973 (98); **Pop. density:** 6,372 per sq. mi; **Pop. change (1990-2000):** +8.3%. **Area:** 30.6 sq. mi. **Employment:** 95,286 employed, 5.4% unemployed. **Per capita income (MSA):** $29,522; increase (1999-2000): 5.0%.

Mayor: Rafi Manoukian, Non-Partisan

History: became a town in 1887; inc. 1906.

Transportation: near Los Angeles Intl. airport; 1 local airport; commuter trains, Amtrak; bus system. **Communications:** 21 TV, 70 radio stations. **Medical facilities:** 3 hosp; other facilities. **Educational facilities:** 1 community college; 26 pub. schools. **Further information:** City of Glendale Public Information Officer, 613 E. Broadway, Glendale, CA 91206; www.ci.glendale.ca.us

Grand Rapids, Michigan

Population: 197,800 (94); **Pop. density:** 4,434 per sq. mi; **Pop. change (1990-2000):** +4.6%. **Area:** 44.6 sq. mi. **Employment:** 110,593 employed, 7.0% unemployed. **Per capita income (MSA):** $27,977; increase (1999-2000): 4.2%.

Mayor: John H. Logie, Non-Partisan

History: originally site of Ottawa Indian village; trading post 1826; became lumbering center and incorporated city 1850.

Transportation: 1 intl. airport; 3 rail carriers; Amtrak, Greyhound bus line; transit bus system. **Communications:** 8 TV, 39 radio stations. **Medical facilities:** 13 hosp. **Educational facilities:** 16 colleges; 19 pub. schools, 17 charter schools. **Further information:** Grand Rapids Area Chamber of Commerce, 111 Pearl St. NW, Grand Rapids, MI 49503; www.grandrapids.org

Greensboro, North Carolina

Population: 223,891 (77); **Pop. density:** 2,138 per sq. mi; **Pop. change (1990-2000):** +22.0%. **Area:** 104.7 sq. mi. **Employment:** 109,857 employed; 5.1% unemployed. **Per capita income (MSA):** $28,522; increase (1999-2000): 4.7%.

Mayor: Keith Holliday, Non-Partisan

History: settled 1749; site of Revolutionary War conflict 1781 between Generals Nathanael Greene and Cornwallis; inc. 1807.

Transportation: 1 regional airport; 2 railroads; Trailways/Greyhound bus service. **Communications:** all cable TV stations; 11 radio stations. **Medical facilities:** 4 hosp. **Educational facilities:** 2 univ., 3 colleges; 94 pub. schools. **Further information:** Chamber of Commerce, PO Box 3246, Greensboro, NC 27402; www.ci.greensboro.nc.us; www.greensboro.org

Hialeah, Florida

Population: 226,419 (75); **Pop. density:** 11,793 per sq. mi; **Pop. change (1990-2000):** +20.4%. **Area:** 19.2 sq. mi. **Employment:** 100,107 employed; 7.2% unemployed. **Per capita income (MSA):** $25,320; increase (1999-2000): 3.4%.

Mayor: Raul L. Martinez, Republican

History: founded 1917, inc. 1925; industrial and residential city NW of Miami; Hialeah Park Horse Racing Track.

Transportation: 5 mi from Miami Intl. Airport; access to Port of Miami; Amtrak; 2 rail freight lines; Metrorail, Metrobus systems. **Communications:** 5 TV, 7 radio stations. **Medical facilities:** 4 hosp. (30 more in the area). **Educational facilities:** 8 univ. and colleges, 25 pub., 39 private schools. **Further information:** Hialeah-Dade Development, Inc., 501 Palm Ave., Hialeah, FL 33010; www.ci.hialeah.fl.us; www.hddi.org

Honolulu, Hawaii

Population: 371,657 (46); **Pop. density:** 4,336 per sq. mi; **Pop. change (1990-2000):** +1.7%. **Area:** 85.7 sq. mi. **Employment (MSA):** 411,735 employed, 4.1% unemployed. **Per capita income (MSA):** $29,960; increase (1999-2000): 4.2%.

Mayor: Jeremy Harris, Non-Partisan

History: harbor entered by Europeans 1778; declared capital of kingdom by King Kamehameha III 1850; Pearl Harbor naval base attacked by Japanese Dec. 7, 1941.

Transportation: 1 major airport; 3 commercial harbors. **Communications:** 12 TV, 36 radio stations. **Medical facilities:** 10 major medical centers. **Educational facilities:** 5 univ., 4 community colleges; 169 pub. schools, 88 private schools. **Further information:** Hawaii Visitors and Convention Bureau, 2270 Kalakaua Avenue, 8th Floor, Honolulu, HI 96815; www.co.honolulu.hi.us; www.gohawaii.com

Houston, Texas

Population: 1,953,631 (4); **Pop. density:** 3,372 per sq. mi; **Pop. change (1990-2000):** +19.8%. **Area:** 579.4 sq. mi. **Employment:** 990,597 employed; 5.3% unemployed. **Per capita income (MSA):** $33,891; increase (1999-2000): 6.8%.

Mayor: Lee P. Brown, Non-Partisan

History: founded 1836; inc. 1837; capital of Repub. of Texas 1837-39; developed rapidly after construction of channel to Gulf of Mexico 1914; world center of oil and natural gas technology.

Transportation: 3 commercial airports; 2 mainline railroads; major bus transit system; major intl. port. **Communications:** 16 TV, 63 radio stations. **Medical facilities:** 72 hosp. (Harris Co.); major medical center. **Educational facilities:** 34 univ. and colleges. **Further information:** Greater Houston Partnership, 1200 Smith St., Houston, TX 77002-4400; www.houston.org; www.cityofhouston.gov

Indianapolis, Indiana

Population: 791,926 (12); **Pop. density:** 2,191 per sq. mi; **Pop. change (1990-2000):** +6.7%. **Area:** 361.5 sq. mi. **Employment:** 409,986 employed; 3.9% unemployed. **Per capita income (MSA):** $30,906; increase (1999-2000): 4.8%.

Mayor: Bart Peterson, Democrat

History: settled 1820; became capital 1825.

Transportation: 1 intl. airport; 5 railroads; 3 interstate bus lines. **Communications:** 10 TV, 27 radio stations. **Medical facilities:** 17 hosp.; 1 major medical and research center. **Educational facilities:** 8 univ. and colleges; major pub. library system. **Further information:** Chamber of Commerce, 320 N. Meridian St., Suite 200, Indianapolis, IN 46204; www.ci.indianapolis.in.us; www.indychamber.com

Irving, Texas

Population: 191,615 (100); **Pop. density:** 2,851 per sq. mi; **Pop. change (1990-2000):** +23.6%. **Area:** 67.2 sq. mi. **Employment:** 113,788 employed, 4.4% unemployed. **Per capita income (MSA):** $35,216; increase (1999-2000): 6.8% .

Mayor: Joe Putnam, Non-Partisan

History: founded 1903; inc. 1914; remained a small city until the 1950s.

Transportation: 1 intl. airport, 1 bus system, 1 RR express (train service). **Communications:** 9 TV, 7 radio stations. **Medical facilities:** 2 hosp. **Educational facilities:** 1 univ., 2 colleges. **Further information:** Greater Irving-Las Colinas Chamber of Commerce, 3333 N. MacArthur Blvd., Ste. 100, Irving, TX 75062; Irving Convention and Visitors Bureau, 1231 Greenway Dr.. Ste. 1060, Irving, TX 75038; www.irvingchamber.com; www.ci. irving.tx.us; www.irvingtexas.com

Jacksonville, Florida

Population: 735,617 (14); **Pop. density:** 971 per sq. mi; **Pop. change (1990-2000):** +15.8%. **Area:** 757.7 sq. mi. **Employment:** 380,985 employed; 4.5% unemployed. **Per capita income (MSA):** $28,456; increase (1999-2000): 5.4%.

Mayor: John A. Delaney, Republican

History: settled 1816 as Cowford; renamed after Andrew Jackson 1822; inc. 1832; rechartered 1851; scene of conflicts in Seminole and Civil wars.

Transportation: 1 intl. airport; 3 railroads; 2 interstate bus lines; 2 seaports. **Communications:** 7 TV, 34 radio stations. **Medical facilities:** 11 hosp. **Educational facilities:** 7 univ., 5 colleges, 2 community colleges; 233 pub. schools, 155 private schools. **Further information:** Chamber of Commerce, 3 Independent Drive, Jacksonville, FL 32202; www.expandinjax.com; www.myjaxchamber.com; www.coj.net

Jersey City, New Jersey

Population: 240,055 (72); **Pop. density:** 16,111 per sq. mi; **Pop. change (1990-2000):** +5.0%. **Area:** 14.9 sq. mi. **Employment:** 102,295 employed; 7.7% unemployed. **Per capita income (MSA):** $27,522; increase (1999-2000): 6.2%.

Mayor: Glenn Cunningham, Democrat

History: site bought from Indians 1630; chartered as town by British 1668; scene of Revolutionary War conflict 1779; chartered under present name 1838; important station on Underground Railroad.

Transportation: Intercity bus and subway system; ferry service to Manhattan. **Communications:** see New York, NY. **Medical facilities:** 4 hosp. **Educational facilities:** 3 colleges. **Further information:** Hudson County Chamber of Commerce, 253 Washington St., Jersey City, NJ 07302; www.jerseycityonline.com

Kansas City, Missouri

Population: 441,545 (36); **Pop. density:** 1,408 per sq. mi; **Pop. change (1990-2000):** +1.5%. **Area:** 313.5 sq. mi. **Employment:** 256,221 employed; 5.3% unemployed. **Per capita income (MSA):** $31,765; increase (1999-2000): 5.6%.

Mayor: Kay Barnes, Non-Partisan

History: settled by 1838 at confluence of the Missouri and Kansas rivers; inc. 1850.

Transportation: 1 intl. airport; a major rail center; more than 300 motor freight carriers; 7 barge lines. **Communications:** 9 TV, 43 radio stations. **Medical facilities:** 50 hosp.; 2 VA hosp. **Educational facilities:** 22 univ. and colleges. **Further information:** Greater Kansas City Chamber of Commerce, 911 Main St., Ste. 2600, Kansas City, MO 64105; www.kansascity.com; www.kcchamber.com

Las Vegas, Nevada

Population: 478,434 (32); **Pop. density:** 4,223 per sq. mi; **Pop. change (1990-2000):** +85.2%. **Area:** 113.3 sq. mi. **Employment:** 240,423 employed; 5.5% unemployed. **Per capita income (MSA):** $27,558; increase (1999-2000): 2.1%.

Mayor: Oscar B. Goodman, Democrat

History: occupied by Mormons 1855-57; bought by railroad 1903; city of Las Vegas inc. 1911; gambling legalized 1931.

Transportation: 1 intl. airport; 1 railroad; bus system. **Communications:** 21 TV, 44 radio stations. **Medical facilities:** 11 hosp. **Educational facilities:** 3 univ., 2 state colleges; 277 pub. schools in area. **Further information:** Las Vegas Chamber of Commerce, 3720 Howard Hughes Parkway, Las Vegas, NV 89109-0937; www.lvchamber.com

Lexington, Kentucky

Population: 260,512 (64); **Pop. density:** 916 per sq. mi; **Pop. change (1990-2000):** +15.6%. **Area:** 284.5 sq. mi. **Employment:** 139,960 employed; 3.0% unemployed. **Per capita income (MSA):** $28,597; increase (1999-2000): 6.0%.

Mayor: Pam Miller, Non-Partisan

History: site was founded and named in 1775 by hunters after the site of the opening battle of the Revolutionary War at Lexington, Mass.; settled 1779; chartered 1782; inc. as a city 1832.

Transportation: 6 comm. airlines; 2 railroads; city buses. **Communications:** 5 TV, 20 radio stations. **Medical facilities:** 5 general, 5 specialized hosp. **Educational facilities:** 2 univ., 4 colleges, 53 public schools: 6 high schools, 10 middle schools, 35 elementary schools, 2 technology schools. **Further information:** Greater Lexington Chamber of Commerce, 330 E. Main St., Lexington, KY 40507; www.lexchamber.com

Lincoln, Nebraska

Population: 225,581 (76); **Pop. density:** 3,023 per sq. mi; **Pop. change (1990-2000):** +17.5%. **Area:** 74.6 sq. mi. **Employment:** 127,965 employed; 3.0% unemployed. **Per capita income (MSA):** $28,752; increase (1999-2000): 3.7%.

Mayor: Don Wesely, Non-Partisan

History: originally called Lancaster; chosen state capital 1867, renamed after Abraham Lincoln; inc. 1869.

Transportation: 1 airport; Greyhound; Amtrak, 2 railroads. **Communications:** 2 TV, 15 radio stations. **Medical facilities:** 5 hosp. including VA, rehabilitation facilities. **Educational facilities:** 3 univ., 3 voc.-tech./business colleges; 55 pub., 15 private schools, 3 focus programs. **Further information:** Chamber of Commerce, PO Box 83006, Lincoln, NE 68501-3006; www.lincoln.org; www.lcoc.com

Long Beach, California

Population: 461,522 (34); **Pop. density:** 9,157 per sq. mi; **Pop. change (1990-2000):** +7.5%. **Area:** 50.4 sq. mi. **Employment:** 215,613 employed; 5.3% unemployed. **Per capita income (MSA):** $29,522; increase (1999-2000): 5.0%.

Mayor: Beverly O'Neill, Non-Partisan

History: settled as early as 1784 by Spanish; by 1884 present site developed on harbor; inc. 1888; oil discovered 1921.

Transportation: 1 airport; 3 railroads; major intl. port; 4 bus co. with 40 bus lines, light rail service. **Communications:** 1 radio station, 1 CATV franchise. **Medical facilities:** 5 hosp. **Educational facilities:** 1 univ., 1 community college (2 campuses); 87 pub. schools in district. **Further information:** Long Beach City Hall, 333 W. Ocean Blvd., Long Beach, CA 90802; www.ci.long-beach.ca.us; www.lbchamber.com

Los Angeles, California

Population: 3,694,820 (2); **Pop. density:** 7,876 per sq. mi; **Pop. change (1990-2000):** +6.0%. **Area:** 469.1 sq. mi. **Employment:** 1,827,227 employed; 6.5% unemployed. **Per capita income (MSA):** $29,522; increase (1999-2000): 5.0%.

Mayor: James K. Hahn, Democrat

History: founded by Spanish 1781; captured by U.S. 1846; inc. 1850; grew rapidly after coming of rairoads, 1876 & 1885, Hollywood a district of L.A.

Transportation: 1 intl. airport; 3 railroads; major freeway system; intracity transit system. **Communications:** 21 TV, 70 radio stations. **Medical facilities:** 822 hosp. and clinics in metro. area. **Educational facilities:** 192 univ. and colleges (incl. junior, community, and other); 1,678 pub. schools; 1,470 private schools. **Further information:** Los Angeles Area Chamber of Commerce, 350 S. Bixel St., PO Box 513696, Los Angeles, CA 90051-1696; www.ci.la.ca.us; www.lachamber.org

Louisville, Kentucky

Population: 256,231 (66); **Pop. density:** 4,126 per sq. mi; **Pop. change (1990-2000):** –4.8%. **Area:** 62.1 sq. mi. **Employment:** 121,911 employed; 4.4% unemployed. **Per capita income (MSA):** $30,191; increase (1999-2000): 5.3%.

Mayor: David Armstrong, Democrat

History: settled 1778; named for Louis XVI of France; inc. 1828; base for Union forces in Civil War.

Transportation: 1 municipal airport, 2 private-craft airport; 1 terminal, 4 trunk-line railroads; metro bus line, Greyhound station; 5 barge lines. **Communications:** 6 TV, 21 radio stations, 2 educational. **Medical facilities:** 23 hosp. **Educational facilities:** 10 univ. and colleges, 32 business and vocational schools. **Further information:** Greater Louisville, Inc. Metro Chamber of Commerce, 614 W. Main St., Louisville, KY 40202; www.greaterlouisville.com

WORLD ALMANAC QUICK QUIZ

Which of these cities shrunk the most (lost the most population in percentage terms) between 1990 and 2000?

(a) St. Louis, MO (b) Baltimore, MD (c) Washington, DC (d) Las Vegas, NV

For the answer look in this chapter, or see page 1008.

Lubbock, Texas

Population: 199,564 (90); **Pop. density:** 1,738 per sq. mi; **Pop. change (1990-2000):** +7.2%. **Area:** 114.8 sq. mi. **Employment:** 104,352 employed; 2.6% unemployed. **Per capita income (MSA):** $24,613; increase (1999-2000): 5.9%.

Mayor: Mark McDougal, Non-Partisan

History: settled 1879; laid out 1891; inc. 1909 through merger of two towns.

Transportation: 1 intl. airport; 2 railroads, bus line. **Communications:** 9 TV, 25 radio stations. **Medical facilities:** 7 hosp. **Educational facilities:** 3 univ., 1 junior college; 51 pub. schools. **Further information:** Chamber of Commerce, 1301 Broadway, Lubbock, TX 79401; www.ci.lubbock.tx.us; www.lubbockchamber.com

Madison, Wisconsin

Population: 208,054 (83); **Pop. density:** 3,028 per sq. mi; **Pop. change (1990-2000):** +8.8%. **Area:** 68.7 sq. mi. **Employment:** 131,147 employed; 2.2% unemployed. **Per capita income (MSA):** $34,301; increase (1999-2000): 5.7%.

Mayor: Susan J.M. Bauman, Non-Partisan

History: first white settlement 1832; selected as site for state capital, named after James Madison, 1836; chartered 1856.

Transportation: 1 airport, 12 airlines; 1 intracity, 3 intercity bus systems; 3 freight rail lines. **Communications:** 8 TV, 24 radio stations, 3 cable providers. **Medical facilities:** 6 hosp., 92 clinics. **Educational facilities:** 7 colleges and univ., including main branch of Univ. of Wisconsin; 30 elem. schools, 12 middle schools, 5 high schools. **Further information:** Greater Madison Chamber of Commerce, PO Box 71, Madison, WI 53701-0071; www.ci.madison.wi.us; www.madisonchamber.com

Memphis, Tennessee

Population: 650,100 (18); **Pop. density:** 2,328 per sq. mi; **Pop. change (1990-2000):** +6.5%. **Area:** 279.3 sq. mi. **Employment:** 303,256 employed; 5.1% unemployed. **Per capita income (MSA):** $29,275; increase (1999-2000): 3.7%.

Mayor: Willie W. Herenton, Democrat

History: French, Spanish, and U.S. forts by 1797; settled by 1819; inc. as town 1826, as city 1840; surrendered charter to state 1879 after yellow fever epidemics; rechartered as city 1893.

Transportation: 1 intl. airport; 5 railroads; 1 bus system. **Communications:** 7 TV, 32 radio stations. **Medical facilities:** 20 hosp. **Educational facilities:** 17 univ. and colleges; 233 pub., 111 private schools. **Further information:** Memphis Area Chamber of Commerce, 22 N. Front St., Ste. 200, PO Box 224, Memphis, TN 38101-0224; www.ci.memphis.tn.us; www.memphischamber.com

Mesa, Arizona

Population: 396,375 (42); **Pop. density:** 3,171 per sq. mi; **Pop. change (1990-2000):** +37.6%. **Area:** 125.0 sq. mi. **Employment:** 201,851 employed; 3.3% unemployed. **Per capita income (MSA):** $27,564; increase (1999-2000): 6.0%.

Mayor: Keno Hawker, Non-Partisan

History: founded by Mormons 1878; inc. 1883; 13 mi. from Phoenix; population boomed fivefold 1960-80.

Transportation: near Sky Harbor Intl. Airport in Phoenix, 2 local airports; metro bus service. **Medical facilities:** 5 major hosp. **Educational facilities:** 1 univ., 3 colleges; 85 pub. schools. **Further information:** Convention and Visitor's Bureau and Mesa Chamber of Commerce, 120 N. Center, Mesa, AZ 85201; www.ci.mesa.az.us; www.mesacvb.com; www.mesachamber.org

Miami, Florida

Population: 362,470 (47); **Pop. density:** 10,153 per sq. mi; **Pop. change (1990-2000):** +1.1%. **Area:** 35.7 sq. mi. **Employment:** 168,908 employed; 10.0% unemployed. **Per capita income (MSA):** $25,320; increase (1999-2000): 3.4%.

Mayor: Manuel A. Diaz, Independent

History: site of fort 1836; settlement began 1870; inc. 1896, modern city developed into financial and recreation center; land speculation in 1920s added to city's growth, as did Cuban, Central and South American, and Haitian immigration since 1960.

Transportation: 1 intl. airport; seaport; Amtrak, transit rail system; 2 bus lines; 65 truck lines. **Communications:** 9 commercial, 2 educational TV stations; 48 radio stations. **Medical facilities:** 8 hosp.; VA hosp. **Educational facilities:** 6 univ. and colleges. **Further information:** Miami-Dade Dept. of Planning, Development, and Regulation, Research Div., 111 NW 1st St., Ste. 1220, Miami, FL 33128; www.ci.miami.fl.us; www.greatermiami.com

Milwaukee, Wisconsin

Population: 596,974 (19); **Pop. density:** 6,212 per sq. mi; **Pop. change (1990-2000):** –5.0%. **Area:** 96.1 sq. mi. **Employment:** 249,584 employed; 7.9% unemployed. **Per capita income (MSA):** $32,538; increase (1999-2000): 4.5%.

Mayor: John O. Norquist, Democrat

History: Indian trading post by 1674; settlement began 1835; inc. as city 1848; famous beer industry.

Transportation: 1 intl. airport; 3 railroads; major port; 4 bus lines. **Communications:** 12 TV, 37 radio stations. **Medical facilities:** 8 hosp.; major medical center. **Educational facilities:** 7 univ. and colleges, 160 pub. schools. **Further information:** Metropolitan Milwaukee Association of Commerce, 756 N. Milwaukee St., Milwaukee, WI 53202; www.ci.mil.wi.us; www.milwaukee.org; www.mmac.org

Minneapolis, Minnesota

Population: 382,618 (45); **Pop. density:** 6,969 per sq. mi; **Pop. change (1990-2000):** +3.9%. **Area:** 54.9 sq. mi. **Employment:** 204,491 employed; 3.9% unemployed. **Per capita income (MSA):** $36,666; increase (1999-2000): 6.2%.

Mayor: R.T. Rybak, Democrat

History: site visited by Hennepin 1680; included in area of military reservations 1819; inc. 1867.

Transportation: 1 intl. airport; 5 railroads. **Communications:** 7 TV, 30 radio stations. **Medical facilities:** 7 hosp., incl. leading heart hosp. at Univ. of Minnesota. **Educational facilities:** 10 univ. and colleges; 121 pub., 28 private schools. **Further information:** City of Minneapolis Office of Pub. Affairs, 323M City Hall, 350 S. 5th St., Minneapolis, MN 55415; www.ci.minneapolis.mn.us

Mobile, Alabama

Population: 198,915 (92); **Pop. density:** 1,687 per sq. mi; **Pop. change (1990-2000):** +1.3%. **Area:** 117.9 sq. mi. **Employment:** 96,494 employed; 6.6% unemployed. **Per capita income (MSA):** $22,677; increase (1999-2000): 3.4%.

Mayor: Michael C. Dow, Republican

History: settled by French 1702; occupied by U.S. 1813; inc. as city 1814; only seaport of Alabama.

Transportation: 4 rail freight lines, Amtrak; 4 airlines; 55 truck lines; leading river system. **Communications:** 8 TV, 27 radio stations. **Medical facilities:** 7 hosp. **Educational facilities:** 3 univ., 5 colleges. **Further information:** Chamber of Commerce, PO Box 2187, Mobile, AL 36652; www.ci.mobile.al.us; www.mobilechamber.com

Montgomery, Alabama

Population: 201,568 (87); **Pop. density:** 1,297 per sq. mi; **Pop. change (1990-2000):** +7.7%. **Area:** 155.4 sq. mi. **Employment:** 96,472 employed; 4.2% unemployed. **Per capita income (MSA):** $25,740; increase (1999-2000): 3.3%.

Mayor: Bobby N. Bright, Democrat

History: inc. as town 1819, as city 1837; became state capital 1846; first capital of Confederacy 1861.

Transportation: 3 airlines; 2 railroads; 2 bus lines; Alabama R. navigable to Gulf of Mexico. **Communications:** 4 TV, 2 CATV, 1 public TV, 16 radio stations. **Medical facilities:** 3 major hosp.; VA and 32 clinics. **Educational facilities:** 8 colleges and univ.; 35 pub., 35 private schools. **Further information:** Montgomery Area Chamber of Commerce, PO Box 79, Montgomery, AL 36101; www.montgomerychamber.com

Nashville, Tennessee

Population: 569,891 (22); **Pop. density:** 1,204 per sq. mi; **Pop. change (1990-2000):** +11.6%. **Area:** 473.3 sq. mi. **Employment:** 298,686 employed; 3.1% unemployed. **Per capita income (MSA):** $30,962; increase (1999-2000): 5.2%.

Mayor: Bill Purcell, Non-Partisan

History: settled 1779; first chartered 1806; became permanent state capital 1843; home of Grand Ole Opry.

Transportation: 1 airport; 1 railroad; bus line; transit system of buses and trolleys. **Communications:** 11 TV, 34 radio stations. **Medical facilities:** 14 hosp.; VA and speech-hearing center. **Educational facilities:** 17 universities and colleges, 129 pub. schools. **Further information:** Chamber of Commerce, 211 Commerce St., Ste 100, Nashville, TN 37201; www.nashvillechamber.com

Newark, New Jersey

Population: 273,546 (63); **Pop. density:** 11,494 per sq. mi; **Pop. change (1990-2000):** –0.6%. **Area:** 23.8 sq. mi. **Employment:** 99,632 employed; 9.2% unemployed. **Per capita income (MSA):** $40,061; increase (1999-2000): 7.4%.

Mayor: Sharpe James, Democrat

History: settled by Puritans 1666; used as supply base by Washington 1776; inc. as town 1833, as city 1836.

Transportation: 1 intl. airport; 1 intl. seaport, 3 railroads; bus system; subways. **Communications:** 3 TV, 3 radio stations within city limits, 1 daily newspaper, 8 weekly papers. **Medical facilities:** 5 hosp. **Educational facilities:** 5 univ. and colleges; 55 pub. elementary schools, 20 junior and senior high schools, 2 special schools, 2 vocational schools, and 40 private schools. **Further information:** Newark Public Information Office, City of Newark, 920 Broad St., Newark, NJ 07102; www.ci.newark.nj.us; www.rbp.org

New Orleans, Louisiana

Population: 484,674 (31); **Pop. density:** 2,684 per sq. mi; **Pop. change (1990-2000):** –2.5%. **Area:** 180.6 sq. mi. **Employment:** 184,182 employed; 5.9% unemployed. **Per capita income (MSA):** $26,056; increase (1999-2000): 3.5%.

Mayor: Ray Nagin, Democrat

History: founded by French 1718; became major seaport on Mississippi R.; acquired by U.S. as part of Louisiana Purchase 1803; inc. as city 1805; Battle of New Orleans was last battle of War of 1812.

Transportation: 2 airports; major railroad center; major intl. port. **Communications:** 8 TV, 26 radio stations. **Medical facilities:** 22 hosp.; 2 major research centers. **Educational facilities:** 10 univ. and 9 colleges. **Further information:** New Orleans Metropolitan Convention & Visitors Bureau, Inc., 1520 Sugar Bowl Dr., New Orleans, LA 70112; www.neworleanscvb.com

New York, New York

Population: 8,008,278 (1); **Pop. density:** 26,404 per sq. mi; **Pop. change (1990-2000):** +9.4%. **Area:** 303.3 sq. mi. **Employment:** 3,296,174 employed; 6.1% unemployed. **Per capita income (MSA):** $39,259; increase (1999-2000): 7.5%.

Mayor: Michael Bloomberg, Republican

History: trading post established 1624; British took control from Dutch 1664 and named city New York; briefly U.S. capital; Washington inaugurated as president 1789; under new charter, 1898, city expanded to include 5 boroughs: The Bronx, Brooklyn, Queens, and Staten Island, as well as Manhattan. Sept. 11, 2001, terrorist attack destroyed World Trade Center, killed about 2,800.

Transportation: 3 intl. airports serve area; 2 rail terminals; major subway network that includes 25 routes; 235 bus routes; ferry system; 4 underwater tunnels. **Communications:** 17 TV, 67 radio stations. **Medical facilities:** 79 hosp.; 6 academic medical centers. **Educational facilities:** 100 univ. and colleges; 1,198 pub. schools. **Further information:** Convention and Visitors Bureau, 810 Seventh Ave., New York, NY 10019; www.ci.nyc.ny.us; www.nycvisit.com

Norfolk, Virginia

Population: 234,403 (73); **Pop. density:** 4,365 per sq. mi; **Pop. change (1990-2000):** –10.3%. **Area:** 53.7 sq. mi. **Employment:** 80,493 employed, 5.7% unemployed. **Per capita income (MSA):** $26,159; increase (1999-2000): 4.9%.

Mayor: Paul D. Fraim, Non-Partisan.

History: founded 1682; burned by patriots to prevent capture by British during Revolutionary War; rebuilt and inc. as town 1805, as city 1845; site of world's largest naval base; major east coast commercial port.

Transportation: 1 intl. airport; 2 railroads; Amtrak; bus system. **Communications:** 13 TV, 6 city-access TV, 27 radio stations. **Medical facilities:** 6 hosp. **Educational facilities:** 3 univ., 1 college, 1 medical school; 59 pub. schools. **Further information:** Norfolk Convention and Visitors Bureau, 232 E. Main St., Norfolk, VA 23510; www.norfolk.va.us; www.norfolkcvb.com

Oakland, California

Population: 399,484 (41); **Pop. density:** 7,121 per sq. mi; **Pop. change (1990-2000):** +7.3%. **Area:** 56.1 sq. mi. **Employment:** 184,246 employed; 7.1% unemployed. **Per capita income (MSA):** $39,611; increase (1999-2000): 10.6%.

Mayor: Jerry Brown, Non-Partisan

History: area settled by Spanish 1820; inc. as city under present name 1854.

Transportation: 1 intl. airport; western terminus for 2 railroads; underground, 75-mi underwater subway. **Communications:** 1 TV, 3 radio stations in city. **Medical facilities:** 10 hosp. in MSA. **Educational facilities:** 8 East Bay colleges and univ.; 81 pub. schools. **Further information:** Oakland Metropolitan Chamber of Commerce, 475 14th St., Oakland, CA 94612-1903; www.oaklandchamber.com; www.oaklandnet.com

Oklahoma City, Oklahoma

Population: 506,132 (29); **Pop. density:** 834 per sq. mi; **Pop. change (1990-2000):** +13.8%. **Area.** 607.0 sq. mi. **Employment:** 244,059 employed; 4.2% unemployed. **Per capita income (MSA):** $25,436; increase (1999-2000): 6.1%.

Mayor: Kirk Humphreys, Non-Partisan

History: settled during land rush in Midwest 1889; inc. 1890; became capital 1910; oil discovered 1928. Bomb in 1995 destroyed federal office bldg., killed 168 people.

Transportation: 1 intl. airport; 3 railroads; pub. transit system; 2 major bus lines. **Communications:** 7 TV, 17 radio stations. **Medical facilities:** 23 hosp. **Educational facilities:** 18 univ. and colleges; 89 pub., 36 private schools. **Further information:** Chamber of Commerce, Economic Development Division, 123 Park Ave., Oklahoma City, OK 73102; www.okcchamber.com; www.okccvb.org; www.okcedis.com

Omaha, Nebraska

Population: 390,007 (44); **Pop. density:** 3,371 per sq. mi; **Pop. change (1990-2000):** +16.1%. **Area:** 115.7 sq. mi. **Employment:** 199,136 employed; 3.8% unemployed. **Per capita income (MSA):** $31,866; increase (1999-2000): 4.6%.

Mayor: Mike Fahey, Democrat

History: founded 1854; inc. 1857; large food-processing, telecommunications, information-processing center; home of more than 20 insurance companies.

Transportation: 12 major airlines; 3 major railroads; intercity bus line. **Communications:** 8 TV, 22 radio stations. **Medical facilities:** 12 hosp.; institute for cancer research. **Educational facilities:** 5 univ., 4 colleges; 243 pub., 78 private schools. **Further information:** Greater Omaha Chamber of Commerce, 1301 Harney St., Omaha, NE 68102; www.ci.omaha.ne.us; www.accessomaha.com

Philadelphia, Pennsylvania

Population: 1,517,550 (5) **Pop. density:** 11,233 per sq. mi; **Pop. change (1990-2000):** –4.3%. **Area:** 135.1 sq. mi. **Employment:** 599,072 employed; 6.4% unemployed. **Per capita income (MSA):** $33,742; increase (1999-2000): 5.5%.

Mayor: John F. Street, Democrat

History: first settled by Swedes 1638; Swedes surrendered to Dutch 1654; settled by English and Scottish Quakers 1678; named Philadelphia 1682; chartered 1701; Continental Congresses convened 1774, 1775; Declaration of Independence signed here 1776; national capital 1790-1800; state capital 1683-1799.

Transportation: 1 major airport; 3 railroads; major freshwater port; subway, el, rail commuter, bus, and streetcar system. **Communications:** 2 major daily newspapers, 12 TV, 67 radio stations. **Medical facilities:** 44 hosp. **Educational facilities:** 29 univ. and colleges. **Further information:** Greater Philadelphia Chamber of Commerce, Business Information Center, 200 South Broad St., Suite 700, Philadelphia PA 19102; www.phila.gov; www.philachamber.com

Phoenix, Arizona

Population: 1,321,045 (6); **Pop. density:** 2,782 per sq. mi; **Pop. change (1990-2000):** +34.3%. **Area:** 474.9 sq. mi. **Employment:** 716,292 employed; 4.3% unemployed. **Per capita income (MSA):** $27,564; increase (1999-2000): 6.0%.

Mayor: Skip Rimsza, Republican

History: settled 1870; inc. as city 1881; became territorial capital 1889.

Transportation: 1 intl. airport; 3 railroads; transcontinental bus line; pub. transit system. **Communications:** 12 TV, 17 radio stations. **Medical facilities:** 19 hosp., 1 medical research center. **Educational facilities:** 36 institutions of higher learning; 380 pub. schools (247 elem. and junior high schools, 35 senior high schools, 98 charter schools). **Further information:** Greater Phoenix Chamber of Commerce, 201 N. Central Ave., 27th fl., Phoenix, AZ 85073; www.phoenix.gov; www.phoenixchamber.com

Pittsburgh, Pennsylvania

Population: 334,563 (52); **Pop. density:** 6,017 per sq. mi; **Pop. change (1990-2000):** –9.5%. **Area:** 55.6 sq. mi. **Employment:** 155,501 employed; 4.0% unemployed. **Per capita income (MSA):** $30,644; increase (1999-2000): 5.3%.

Mayor: Tom J. Murphy, Democrat

History: settled around Ft. Pitt 1758; inc. as city 1816; has one of the largest inland ports; by Civil War, already a center for iron production.

Transportation: 1 intl. airport; 20 railroads; 2 bus lines; trolley/subway system. **Communications:** 6 TV, 26 radio stations. **Medical facilities:** 35 hosp.; VA installation. **Educational facilities:** 3 univ., 6 colleges; 86 pub. schools. **Further information:** Greater Pittsburgh Convention & Visitors Bureau, Regional Enterprise Tower, 30th Floor, 425 Sixth Ave., Pittsburgh, PA 15219; Pittsburgh Regional Alliance, Regional Enterprise Tower, 36th Floor, 425 Sixth Ave., Pittsburgh, PA 15219; www.visitpittsburgh.com; www.pittsburghregion.org

Plano, Texas

Population: 222,030 (78); **Pop. density:** 3,101 per sq. mi; **Pop. change (1990-2000):** +72.5%. **Area:** 71.6 sq. mi. **Employment:** 139,217 employed; 3.5% unemployed. **Per capita income (MSA):** $35,216; increase (1999-2000): 6.8%.

Mayor: Pat Evans, Non-Partisan

History: settled 1846; inc. as city 1873.

Transportation: 1 bus line; DART rail (Dec. 2002). **Communications:** 2 TV, 1 radio stations. **Medical facilities:** 6 medical facilities. **Educational facilities:** 1 institute of higher learning, 58 pub. schools. **Further information:** Plano Chamber of Commerce, PO Drawer 940287, Plano, TX 75094-0287; www.planotx.org; www.planocc.org

Portland, Oregon

Population: 529,121 (28); **Pop. density:** 3,940 per sq. mi; **Pop. change (1990-2000):** +21.0%. **Area:** 134.3 sq. mi. **Employment:** 262,616 employed; 6.7% unemployed. **Per capita income (MSA):** $31,620; increase (1999-2000): 6.6%.

Mayor: Vera Katz, Non-Partisan

History: settled by pioneers 1845; developed as trading center, aided by California Gold Rush 1849; city chartered 1851.

Transportation: 1 intl. airport; 2 major rail freight lines, Amtrak; 2 intercity bus lines; 27-mi. frontage freshwater port; mass transit bus and rail system. **Communications:** 9 TV, 27 radio stations. **Medical facilities:** 12 hosp.; VA hosp. **Educational facilities:** 25 univ. and colleges, 1 community college. **Further information:** Portland Metropolitan Chamber of Commerce, 221 N.W. 2nd Ave., Portland, OR 97209; www.pdxchamber.org

Raleigh, North Carolina

Population: 276,093 (62); **Pop. density:** 2,409 per sq. mi; **Pop. change (1990-2000):** +32.8%. **Area:** 114.6 sq. mi. **Employment:** 169,453 employed; 3.9% unemployed. **Per capita income (MSA):** $32,537; increase (1999-2000): 6.9%.

Mayor: Charles Meeker, Democrat

History: named after Sir Walter Raleigh; site chosen for capital 1788; laid out 1792; inc. 1795; occupied by Gen. Sherman 1865.

Transportation: 1 intl. airport, 14 airlines, 8 commuter airlines; 3 railroads; 2 bus lines. **Communications:** 8 TV, 31 radio stations. **Medical facilities:** 6 hosp. **Educational facilities:** 6 univ. and colleges; 1 community college; 1067 pub. schools (county). **Further information:** Chamber of Commerce, 800 S. Salisbury St., PO Box 2978, Raleigh, NC 27602; www.raleighwake.org; www.raleighchamber.org

Richmond, Virginia

Population: 197,790 (95); **Pop. density:** 3,291 per sq. mi; **Pop. change (1990-2000):** –2.6%. **Area:** 60.1 sq. mi. **Employment:** 92,531 employed, 5.0% unemployed. **Per capita income (MSA):** $31,292; increase (1999-2000): 5.2%.

Mayor: Rudolph C. McCollum Jr., Democrat

History: first settled 1607; became capital of Commonwealth of Virginia, 1779; attacked by British under Benedict Arnold 1781; inc. as city 1782; capital of Confederate States of America, 1861-65.

Transportation: 1 intl. airport; 3 railroads; 2 intracity bus lines; deepwater terminal accessible to oceangoing ships. **Communications:** 6 TV, 28 radio stations. **Medical facilities:** Virginia Commonwealth Univ. Health Systems renowned for heart and kidney transplants; 8 hosp. **Educational facilities:** 20 univ. and colleges incl. 7 branches; 173 pub., 49 private schools. **Further information:** Chamber of Commerce, PO Box 12280, Richmond, VA 23241; www.ci.richmond.va.us; www.grcc.com

Riverside, California

Population: 255,166 (67); **Pop. density:** 3,267 per sq. mi; **Pop. change (1990-2000):** +12.7%. **Area:** 78.1 sq. mi. **Employment:** 151,349 employed; 5.2% unemployed. **Per capita income (MSA):** $23,350; increase (1999-2000): 4.6%.

Mayor: Ronald O. Loveridge, Non-Partisan

History: founded 1870; inc. 1886; known for its citrus industry; home of the parent navel orange tree and the historic Mission Inn.

Transportation: municipal airport, intl. airport nearby; rail freight lines, commuter line; trolley/bus system; interstate freeways. **Communications:** 15 TV, 47 radio stations. **Medical facilities:** 3 hosp.; many clinics. **Educational facilities:** 3 univ., 1 community college. **Further information:** Chamber of Commerce, 3985 University Ave., Riverside, CA 92501; www.ci.riverside.ca.us; www.riverside-chamber.com

Rochester, New York

Population: 219,773 (79); **Pop. density:** 6,139 per sq. mi; Pop. change (1990-2000): –5.1%. **Area:** 35.8 sq. mi. **Employment:** 102,026 employed; 7.8% unemployed. **Per capita income (MSA):** 28,419; increase (1999-2000): 3.4%.

Mayor: William A. Johnson Jr., Democrat

History: first permanent settlement 1812; inc. as village 1817, as city 1834; developed as Erie Canal town.

Transportation: 1 intl. airport; Amtrak; 2 bus lines; intracity transit service; Port of Rochester. **Communications:** 6 TV, 19 radio stations. **Medical facilities:** 8 general hosp. **Educational facilities:** 11 colleges, 3 community colleges. **Further information:** Greater Rochester Metro Chamber of Commerce, 55 St. Paul St., Rochester, NY 14604-1391; www.rnychamber.com; www.ci.rochester.ny.us

Sacramento, California

Population: 407,018 (40); **Pop. density:** 4,187 per sq. mi; **Pop. change (1990-2000):** +10.2%. **Area:** 97.2 sq. mi. **Employment:** 197,499 employed; 5.1% unemployed. **Per capita income (MSA):** $30,252; increase (1999-2000): 6.1%.

Mayor: Heather Fargo, Non-Partisan

History: settled 1839; important trading center during California Gold Rush 1840s; became state capital 1854.

Transportation: international, executive, and cargo airports; 2 mainline transcontinental rail carriers; bus and light rail system; Port of Sacramento. **Communications:** 8 TV, 34 radio stations; 3 cable TV cos. **Medical facilities:** 12 major hosp. **Educational facilities:** 7 colleges and univ., 5 private colleges and univ., 5 community colleges, 81 pub. schools. **Further information:** Sacramento Metropolitan Chamber of Commerce, 917 7th St., Sacramento, CA 95814; www.ci.sacramento.ca.us; www.sacog.org; www.sacramentocvb.org

St. Louis, Missouri

Population: 348,189 (49); **Pop. density:** 5,625 per sq. mi; **Pop. change (1990-2000):** –12.2%. **Area:** 61.9 sq. mi. **Employment:** 144,819 employed; 8.2% unemployed. **Per capita income (MSA):** $31,354; increase (1999-2000): 5.0%.

Mayor: Francis Slay, Democrat

History: founded 1764 as a fur trading post by French; acquired by U.S. 1803; chartered as city 1822; became independent city 1876; lies on Mississippi R., near confluence with Missouri R.

Transportation: 2 intl. airports; 2d largest rail center, 10 trunk-line railroads; 2nd largest inland port; Amtrak; Greyhound; bus & light rail; 13 barge lines. **Communications:** 8 TV, 17 radio stations. **Medical facilities:** 9 hosp., 2 teaching hosp. **Educational facilities:** 8 univ., 11 colleges and seminaries, 69 elem., 22 middle, 16 high schools. **Further information:** St. Louis Planning & Urban Design Agency, 1015 Locust St., Ste. 1200, St. Louis, MO 63101; stlouis.missouri.org

St. Paul, Minnesota

Population: 287,151 (59); **Pop. density:** 5,438 per sq. mi; **Pop. change (1990-2000):** +5.5%. **Area:** 52.8 sq. mi. **Employment:** 138,827 employed; 4.1 unemployed. **Per capita income (MSA):** $36,666; increase (1999-2000): 6.2%.

Mayor: Randy C. Kelly, Democrat

History: founded in early 1840s as "Pig's Eye Landing"; became capital of the Minnesota territory 1849 and chartered as St. Paul 1854.

Transportation: 1 intl., 1 business airport; 6 major rail lines; 2 interstate bus lines; pub. transit system. **Communications:** 9 TV, 47 radio stations. **Medical facilities:** 6 hosp. **Educational facilities:** 5 univ., 4 colleges; 1 technical, 3 law schools, 1 art and design college; 65 public, 39 private schools. **Further information:** St. Paul Area Chamber of Commerce, 401 N. Robert St., Ste. 150, St. Paul, MN 55101; www.ci.stpaul.mn.us; www.saintpaulchamber.com; www.stpaulcvb.org

St. Petersburg, Florida

Population: 248,232 (68); **Pop. density:** 4,165 per sq. mi; **Pop. change (1990-2000):** +4.0%. **Area:** 59.6 sq. mi. **Employment:** 136,238 employed; 4.3% unemployed. **Per capita income (MSA):** $28,214; increase (1999-2000): 5.5%.

Mayor: Rick Baker, Non-Partisan

History: founded 1888; inc. 1903.

Transportation: 1 municipal, 2 intl. airports; Amtrak bus connection; county-wide public bus system; 1 marina; 1 cruise port. **Communications:** 17 TV, 41 radio stations in area. **Medical facilities:** 4 major hosp.; VA hosp. **Educational facilities:** 1 univ., 2 colleges, 1 law school; 118 pub. schools (county-wide). **Further information:** City of St. Petersburg , PO Box 2842, St. Petersburg, FL 33731; www.stpete.org

San Antonio, Texas

Population: 1,144,646 (9); **Pop. density:** 2,808 per sq. mi; **Pop. change (1990-2000):** +22.3%. **Area:** 407.6 sq. mi. **Employment:** 517,065 employed; 4.4% unemployed. **Per capita income (MSA):** $25,741; increase (1999-2000): 4.6%.

Mayor: Ed Garza, Non-Partisan

History: first Spanish garrison 1718; Battle at the Alamo fought here 1836; city subsequently captured by Texans; inc. 1837.

Transportation: 1 intl. airport; 4 railroads; 3 bus lines; pub. transit system. **Communications:** 9 TV, 42 radio stations. **Medical facilities:** 36 hosp.; major medical center. **Educational facilities:** 18 univ. and colleges; 16 pub. school districts. **Further information:** Chamber of Commerce, 602 E. Commerce, PO Box 1628, San Antonio, TX 78296; www.ci.sat.tx.us; www.sachamber.org

San Diego, California

Population: 1,223,400 (7); **Pop. density:** 3,772 per sq. mi; **Pop. change (1990-2000):** +10.2%. **Area:** 324.3 sq. mi. **Employment:** 632,025 employed; 3.3% unemployed. **Per capita income (MSA):** $32,515; increase (1999-2000): 7.3%.

Mayor: Dick Murphy, Republican

History: claimed by the Spanish 1542; first mission est. 1769; scene of conflict during Mexican-American War 1846; inc. 1850.

Transportation: 1 major airport; 1 railroad; major freeway system; bus system; trolley system. **Communications:** 9 TV, 25 radio stations, 2 cable providers. **Medical facilities:** 17 hosp. **Educational facilities:** 25 colleges and univ.; 177 pub. schools. **Further information:** San Diego Regional Chamber of Commerce, 402 W. Broadway, Ste. 1000, San Diego, CA 92101; www.sannet.gov; www.sdchamber.org

San Francisco, California

Population: 776,733 (13); **Pop. density:** 16,632 per sq. mi; **Pop. change (1990-2000):** +7.3%. **Area:** 46.7 sq. mi. **Employment:** 414,394 employed; 5.2% unemployed. **Per capita income (MSA):** $57,414; increase (1999-2000): 15.2%.

Mayor: Willie L. Brown Jr., Non-Partisan

History: nearby Farallon Islands sighted by Spanish 1542; city settled by 1776; claimed by U.S. 1846; became a major city during California Gold Rush 1849; inc. as city 1850; earthquake devastated city 1906.

Transportation: 1 major airport; intracity railway system; 2 railway transit systems; bus and railroad service; ferry system; 1 underwater tunnel. **Communications:** 10 TV; 15 radio stations. **Medical facilities:** 16 medical centers. **Educational facilities:** 16 univ. and colleges, 111 pub. schools, 5 charter schools. **Further information:** Convention & Visitors Bureau, 201 3d St., Ste. 900, San Francisco, CA 94103; www.ci.sf.ca.us; www.sfchamber.com

San Jose, California

Population: 894,943 (11); **Pop. density:** 5,117 per sq. mi; **Pop. change (1990-2000):** +14.4%. **Area:** 174.9 sq. mi. **Employment:** 489,020 employed; 5.2% unemployed. **Per capita income (MSA):** $55,157; increase (1999-2000): 20.1%

Mayor: Ron Gonzales, Democrat

History: founded by the Spanish 1777 between San Francisco and Monterey; state cap. 1849-51; inc. 1850.

Transportation: 1 intl. airport; 2 railroads; light rail system; bus system. **Communications:** 5 TV, 14 radio stations. **Medical facilities:** 6 hosp. **Educational facilities:** 3 univ. and colleges. **Further information:** Chamber of Commerce, 310 S. First St., San Jose, CA 95113; www.ci.san-jose.ca.us; www.sjchamber.com

Santa Ana, California

Population: 337,977 (51); **Pop. density:** 12,471 per sq. mi; **Pop. change (1990-2000):** +15.1%. **Area:** 27.1 sq. mi. **Employment:** 162,435 employed; 5.4% unemployed. **Per capita income (MSA):** $34,862; increase (1999-2000): 5.8%

Mayor: Miguel Pulido, Non-Partisan

History: founded 1769; inc. as city 1869.

Transportation: 1 airport; 5 major freeways including main Los Angeles-San Diego artery; Amtrak. **Communications:** 14 TV, 28 radio stations. **Medical facilities:** 4 hosp. **Educational facilities:** 1 community college. **Further information:** Santa Ana Chamber of Commerce, 2020 N. Broadway, 2nd floor, Santa Ana, CA 92706; www.santaanachamber.com

Scottsdale, Arizona

Population: 202,705 (86); **Pop. density:** 1,100 per sq. mi; **Pop. change (1990-2000):** +55.8%. **Area:** 184.2 sq. mi. **Employment:** 104,673 employed; 2.8% unemployed. **Per capita income (MSA):** $27,564; increase (1999-2000): 6.0%

Mayor: Mary Manross, Democrat

History: founded 1888 by Army Chaplain Winfield Scott; inc. June 25, 1951; Frank Lloyd Wright built winter home here (Taliesin West); slogan "West's Most Western Town," by Mayor Malcolm White adopted 1951.

Transportation: 1 intl. airport in area, 1 local airport; regional bus system; local bus system; taxi system. **Communications:** 12 TV, 45 radio stations. **Medical facilities:** 2 general hospitals; Mayo Clinic. **Educational facilities:** 1 univ. nearby, 1 community college; 3 unified school districts. **Further information:** Scottsdale Chamber of Commerce, 7343 Scottsdale Mall, Scottsdale, AZ 85251-4498; www.ci.scottsdale.az.us; www.scottsdalechamber.com

Seattle, Washington

Population: 563,374 (24); **Pop. density:** 6,715 per sq. mi; **Pop. change (1990-2000):** +9.1%. **Area:** 83.9 sq. mi. **Employment:** 329,347 employed; 6.0% unemployed. **Per capita income (MSA):** $40,686; increase (1999-2000): 4.7%.

Mayor: Greg Nickels, Democrat

History: settled 1851; inc. 1869; suffered severe fire 1889; played prominent role during Alaska Gold Rush 1897; growth followed opening of Panama Canal 1914; center of aircraft industry WWII.

Transportation: 1 intl. airport; 2 railroads; ferries serve Puget Sound, Alaska, Canada. **Communications:** 7 TV, 39 radio stations. **Medical facilities:** 40 hosp. **Educational facilities:** 7 univ., 6 colleges, 11 community colleges. **Further information:** Greater Seattle Chamber of Commerce, 1301 5th Ave., Ste. 2400, Seattle, WA 98101-2611; www.ci.seattle.wa.us; www.seattlechamber.com

Shreveport, Louisiana

Population: 200,145 (88); **Pop. density:** 1,941 per sq. mi; **Pop. change (1990-2000):** +0.8%. **Area:** 103.1 sq. mi. **Employment:** 89,625 employed; 6.6% unemployed. **Per capita income (MSA):** $23,972; increase (1999-2000): 3.9%.

Mayor: Keith Hightower, Democrat

History: founded 1836 near site of a 180-mi logjam cleared by Capt. Henry Shreve; inc. 1839; oil discovered 1905.

Transportation: 2 airports; 3 bus lines. **Communications:** 6 TV, 20 radio stations. **Medical facilities:** 16 hosp. **Educational facilities:** 4 univ., 2 colleges; 74 pub. schools. **Further information:** Chamber of Commerce, PO Box 20074, 400 Edwards St., Shreveport, LA 71120; www.shreveportchamber.org

Spokane, Washington

Population: 195,629 (97); **Pop. density:** 3,385 per sq. mi; **Pop. change (1990-2000):** +10.4%. **Area:** 57.8 sq. mi. **Employment:** 92,468 employed, 7.5% unemployed. **Per capita income (MSA):** $25,550; increase (1999-2000): 6.4%.

Mayor: John Powers, Non-Partisan

History: settled 1872; inc. as village of Spokane Falls 1881, destroyed in fire 1889; reinc. as city of Spokane 1891.

Transportation: 1 intl. airport; 2 railroads; bus system. **Communications:** 5 TV, 25 radio stations. **Medical facilities:** 6 major hosp. **Educational facilities:** 9 univ. and colleges; 14 pub. school districts, 16 high schools. **Further information:** Spokane Regional Chamber of Commerce, 801 W. Riverside Ave., Spokane, WA 99201; www.spokanechamber.org

Stockton, California

Population: 243,771 (70); **Pop. density:** 4,457 per sq. mi; **Pop. change (1990-2000):** +15.6%. **Area:** 54.7 sq. mi. **Employment:** 97,811 employed; 10.3% unemployed. **Per capita income (MSA):** $23,242; increase (1999-2000): 4.4%.

Mayor: Gary Podesto, Non-Partisan

History: site purchased 1842; settled 1849; inc. 1850; chief distributing point for agric. products of San Joaquin Valley.

Transportation: 1 airport; deepwater inland seaport; 4 railroads; 2 bus lines, county bus system. **Communications:** 5 TV stations. **Medical facilities:** 4 hosp.; regional burn, cancer, heart centers. **Educational facilities:** 9 univ. and colleges; 58 pub. schools. **Further information:** Chamber of Commerce, 445 W. Weber Ave., Ste. 220, Stockton, CA 95203; www.stocktongov.com; www.stocktonchamber.org

Tacoma, Washington

Population: 193,556 (99); **Pop. density:** 3,863 per sq. mi; **Pop. change (1990-2000):** +9.6%. **Area:** 50.1 sq. mi. **Employment:** 91,377 employed, 7.3% unemployed. **Per capita income (MSA):** $25,587; increase (1999-2000): 2.9%.

Mayor: Bill Baarsma, Non-Partisan.

History: first European explorer of area was British Capt. George Vancouver 1792; colonized by Hudson's Bay Co. at Ft. Nisqually 1833; inc. 1884.

Transportation: 1 intl. airport; 3 railroads; transit system; Port of Tacoma. **Communications:** 6 TV stations. **Medical facilities:** 7 hosp.; Army Medical Center; VA facility. **Educational facilities:** 3 univ., 4 colleges. **Further information:** Tacoma-Pierce County Chamber of Commerce, PO Box 1933, Tacoma, WA 98401; www.cityoftacoma.org; www.tacomachamber.org

Tampa, Florida

Population: 303,447 (57); **Pop. density:** 2,707 per sq. mi; **Pop. change (1990-2000):** +8.4%. **Area:** 112.1 sq. mi. **Employment:** 176,442 employed; 4.5% unemployed. **Per capita income (MSA):** $28,214; increase (1999-2000): 5.5%.

Mayor: Dick A. Greco, Non-Partisan

History: U.S. army fort on site 1824; inc. 1849; Ybor City National Historical Landmark district.

Transportation: 1 intl. airport; Port of Tampa; CSX rail, Amtrak Rail; bus system; downtown streetcar. **Communications:** 14 TV, 57 radio stations. **Medical facilities:** 21 hosp. **Educational facilities:** 6 univ. and colleges; 178 pub. schools. **Further information:** Greater Tampa Chamber of Commerce, 615 Channelside Drive, Ste. 108, P.O. Box 420, Tampa, FL 33601; www.tampachamber.com

Toledo, Ohio

Population: 313,619 (56); **Pop. density:** 3,892 per sq. mi; **Pop. change (1990-2000):** –5.8%. **Area:** 80.6 sq. mi. **Employment:** 152,070 employed; 5.8% unemployed. **Per capita income (MSA):** $27,521; increase (1999-2000): 3.2%.

Mayor: Jack Ford, Democrat

History: site of Ft. Industry 1794; Battles of Ft. Meigs and Ft. Timbers 1812; figured in "Toledo War" 1835-36 between Ohio and Michigan over borders; inc. 1837.

Transportation: 5 major airlines; 4 railroads, 53 motor freight lines; 7 interstate bus lines. **Communications:** 6 TV, 22 radio stations. **Medical facilities:** 7 major hosp. complexes. **Educational facilities:** 6 univ. and colleges. **Further information:** Toledo Area Chamber of Commerce, 300 Madison Ave., Ste. 200, Toledo, OH 43604; www.toledochamber.com

Tucson, Arizona

Population: 486,699 (30); **Pop. density:** 2,500 per sq. mi; **Pop. change (1990-2000):** +20.1%. **Area:** 194,7 sq. mi. **Employment: 234,825** employed; 3.8% unemployed. **Per capita income (MSA):** $23,705; increase (1999-2000): 3.2%.

Mayor: Robert E. Walkup, Republican

History: settled 1775 by Spanish as a presidio; acquired by U.S. in Gadsden Purchase 1853; inc. 1877.

Transportation: 1 intl. airport; 2 railroads; 1 bus sysytem, 1 trolley. **Communications:** 10 TV, 34 radio stations. **Medical facilities:** 12 hosp. **Educational facilities:** 2 univ., 1 community college; 216 pub. schools. **Further information:** Tucson Metropolitan Chamber of Commerce, PO Box 991, Tucson, AZ 85702; www.ci.tucson.az.us; www.tucsonchamber.org

Tulsa, Oklahoma

Population: 393,049 (43); **Pop. density:** 2,152 per sq. mi; **Pop. change (1990-2000):** +7.0%. **Area:** 182.6 sq. mi. **Employment:** 212,995 employed; 3.7% unemployed. **Per capita income (MSA):** $28,775; increase (1999-2000): 4.5%.

Mayor: Bill LaFortune, Republican

History: settled in 1836 by Creek Indians; modern town founded 1882 and inc. 1898; oil discovered early 20th century; emerging as telecommunications hub.

Transportation: 1 intl. airport; 5 rail lines; 5 bus lines; transit bus system. **Communications:** 130 TV, 31 radio stations. **Medical facilities:** 10 hosp. **Educational facilities:** 8 univ. and colleges; 85 pub., 39 private schools. **Further information:** Tulsa Metro Chamber, 616 S. Boston Ave., Ste. 100, Tulsa, OK 74119-1298; www.tulsachamber.com; www.cityoftulsa.org

Virginia Beach, Virginia

Population: 425,257 (38); **Pop. density:** 1,713 per sq. mi; **Pop. change (1990-2000):** +8.2%. **Area:** 248.3 sq. mi. **Employment:** 209,537 employed; 3.0% unemployed. **Per capita income (MSA):** $26,159; increase (1999-2000): 4.9%.

Mayor: Meyera E. Oberndorf, Independent

History: area founded by Capt. John Smith 1607; formed by merger with Princess Anne Co. 1963.

Transportation: 1 airport; 2 railroads; 1 bus line; pub. transit system. **Communications:** 8 TV, 44 radio stations. **Medical facilities:** 2 hosp. **Educational facilities:** 1 univ., 2 colleges; 84 pub. schools. **Further information:** Virginia Beach Dept. of Economic Development, One Columbus Center, Ste. 300, Virginia Beach, VA 23462; www.yesvirginiabeach.com

Washington, District of Columbia

Population: 572,059 (21); **Pop. density:** 9,317 per sq. mi; **Pop. change (1990-2000):** –5.7%. **Area:** 61.4 sq. mi. **Employment:** 259,744 employed, 6.5% unemployed. **Per capita income (MSA):** $40,046; increase (1999-2000): 6.5%.

Mayor: Anthony A. Williams, Democrat

History: U.S. capital; site at Potomac R. chosen by George Washington 1790 on land ceded from VA and MD (portion S of Potomac returned to VA 1846); Congress first met 1800; inc. 1802; sacked by British, War of 1812; one of the most important Civil War battles was fought at Ft. Stevens.

Transportation: 3 intl. airports in area; Amtrak, 6 other passenger & cargo rail lines; Metrobus/Metrorail transit system; bus line. **Communications:** 5 TV, 61 radio stations. **Medical facilities:** 16 hosp. **Educational facilities:** 10 univ. and colleges. **Further information:** DC Chamber of Commerce, 1213 K Street NW, Washington, DC 20005; www.dc.gov; www.dcchamber.org

Wichita, Kansas

Population: 344,284 (50); **Pop. density:** 2,535 per sq. mi; **Pop. change (1990-2000):** +13.2%. **Area:** 135.8 sq. mi. **Employment:** 166,830 employed; 4.6% unemployed. **Per capita income (MSA):** $27,904; increase (1999-2000): 3.7%.

Mayor: Bob Knight, Non-Partisan

History: founded 1864; inc. 1871.

Transportation: 2 airports; 3 major rail freight lines; 2 bus lines. **Communications:** 80 TV, 34 radio stations. **Medical facilities:** 7 hosp., 2 psychiatric rehab. centers. **Educational facilities:** 3 univ., 1 medical school; 96 pub. schools. **Further information:** Chamber of Commerce, 350 W. Douglas Ave., Wichita, KS 67202; www.wichitakansas.org; www.wichitagov.org

Yonkers, New York

Population: 196,086 (96); **Pop. density:** 10,833 per sq. mi; **Pop. change (1990-2000):** +4.3%. **Area:** 18.1 sq. mi. **Employment:** 85,911 employed; 4.7% unemployed. **Per capita income (MSA):** $39,259; increase (1999-2000): 7.5%.

Mayor: John Spencer, Republican

History: founded 1641 by the Dutch; inc. as town 1855; chartered as city 1872; directly north of NYC.

Transportation: intracity bus system; rail service. **Communications:** see New York, NY. **Medical facilities:** 3 hosp. **Educational facilities:** 3 colleges; 41 pub. schools. **Further information:** Chamber of Commerce, 20 S. Broadway, 12th fl., Yonkers, NY 10701; www.cityofyonkers.com; www.yonkerschamber.com; www.yonkersprogress.com

Fastest-Growing Big Cities*

City	2000 population	1990 population	% change
1. Las Vegas, NV	478,434	258,295	85.2
2. Plano, TX	222,030	128,713	72.5
3. Scottsdale, AZ	202,705	130,069	55.8
4. Glendale, AZ	218,812	148,134	47.7
5. Bakersfield, CA	247,057	174,820	41.3
6. Austin, TX	656,562	465,622	41.0
7. Mesa, AZ	396,375	288,091	37.6
8. Charlotte, NC	540,828	395,934	36.6
9. Phoenix, AZ	1,321,045	983,403	34.3
10. Raleigh, NC	276,093	207,951	32.8

Fastest-Shrinking Big Cities*

City	2000 population	1990 population	% change
1. St. Louis, MO	348,189	396,685	–12.2
2. Baltimore, MD	651,154	736,014	–11.5
3. Buffalo, NY	292,648	328,123	–10.8
4. Norfolk, VA	234,403	261,229	–10.3
5. Pittsburgh, PA	334,563	369,879	–9.5
6. Cincinnati, OH	331,285	364,040	–9.0
7. Birmingham, AL	242,820	265,968	–8.7
8. Detroit, MI	951,270	1,027,974	–7.5
9. Toledo, OH	313,619	332,943	–5.8
10. Washington, DC	572,059	606,900	–5.7

*Among those with populations of 200,000 or more, based on 2000 U.S. Census.

Percent of Population by Race and Hispanic Origin for the 10 Largest Cities

City	White	Black or African-Amer.	Amer. Indian, Alaska Native	Asian	Hawaiian & Other Pacific Isl.	Some other race[1]	Two or more races	Hispanic or Latino (of any race)
1. New York, NY	44.7	26.6	0.5	9.8	0.1	13.4	4.9	27.0
2. Los Angeles, CA	46.9	11.2	0.8	10.0	0.2	25.7	5.2	46.5
3. Chicago, IL	42.0	36.8	0.4	4.3	0.1	13.6	2.9	26.0
4. Houston, TX	49.3	25.3	0.4	5.3	0.1	16.5	3.1	37.4
5. Philadelphia, PA	45.0	43.2	0.3	4.5	0.0	4.8	2.2	8.5
6. Phoenix, AZ	71.1	5.1	2.0	2.0	0.1	16.4	3.3	34.1
7. San Diego, CA	60.2	7.9	0.6	13.6	0.5	12.4	4.8	25.4
8. Dallas, TX	50.8	25.9	0.5	2.7	0.0	17.2	2.7	35.6
9. San Antonio, TX	67.7	6.8	0.8	1.6	0.1	19.3	3.7	58.7
10. Detroit, MI	12.3	81.6	0.3	1.0	0.0	2.5	2.3	5.0

(1) Persons who, instead of checking off a race shown, filled in a designation under "some other race."

STATES AND OTHER AREAS OF THE U.S.

Sources: Population: U.S. Commerce Dept., Bureau of the Census—Census 2000: April 1, 2000, and July 2001 est. (including armed forces stationed in the state). Area: Bureau of the Census, Geography Division; forested land: Agriculture Dept., Forest Service. Lumber production: Bureau of the Census, Industry Division; mineral production: Dept. of Interior, Office of Mineral Information; commercial fishing: Commerce Dept., Natl. Marine Fisheries Service; value of construction: McGraw-Hill Information Systems Co., F.W. Dodge Division. Personal per capita income: Commerce Dept., Bureau of Economic Analysis; sales tax: CCH Inc.; unemployment: Labor Dept., Bureau of Labor Statistics. Tourism: Tourism Industries/ITA, Tourism Works for America Report. Lottery figures (not all states have a lottery): *La Fleur's Lottery World*. Finance: Federal Deposit Insurance Corp. Federal employees: Labor Dept., Office of Personnel Management. Energy: Energy Dept., Energy Information Administration. Other information from sources in individual states.

NOTE: Population density is for land area only. Categories under racial distribution may not add to 100% due to rounding. "Nat. American" includes American Indians and Alaska Natives (including Eskimos and Aleuts). Hispanic population may be any race and is dispersed among racial categories, besides being listed separately. Nonfuel mineral values for some states exclude small amounts to avoid disclosing proprietary data. Categories under employment distribution are not all-inclusive. Famous Persons lists may include some nonnatives associated with the state as well as persons born there. Website addresses listed may not be official state sites and are not endorsed by *The World Almanac;* all website addresses are subject to change.

Alabama

Heart of Dixie, Camellia State

People. Population (2001 est.): 4,464,356; rank: 23; **net change** (2000-2001): 0.4%. **Pop. density:** 88 per sq mi. **Racial distribution** (2000): 71.1% white; 26.0% black; 0.7% Asian; 0.5% Native American/Nat. AK; <0.1% Hawaiian/Pacific Islander; 0.7% other race; 2 or more races, 1.0%. **Hispanic pop.** (any race): 1.7%.

Geography. Total area: 52,419 sq mi; rank: 30. **Land area:** 50,744 sq mi; rank: 28. **Acres forested:** 21,974,000. **Location:** East South Central state extending N-S from Tenn. to the Gulf of Mexico; E of the Mississippi River. **Climate:** long, hot summers; mild winters; generally abundant rainfall. **Topography:** coastal plains, including Prairie Black Belt, give way to hills, broken terrain; highest elevation, 2,407 ft. **Capital:** Montgomery.

Economy. Chief industries: pulp & paper, chemicals, electronics, apparel, textiles, primary metals, lumber and wood products, food processing, fabricated metals, automotive tires, oil and gas exploration. **Chief manuf. goods:** electronics, cast iron & plastic pipe, fabricated steel products, ships, paper products, chemicals, steel, mobile homes, fabrics, poultry processing, soft drinks, furniture, tires. **Chief crops**: cotton, greenhouse & nursery, peanuts, sweet potatoes, potatoes and other vegetables. **Livestock**: (Jan. 2002) 1.4 mil cattle/calves; (Dec. 2001) 195,000 hogs/pigs; 15.9 mil chickens (excl. broilers); 1 bil broilers. **Timber/lumber** (est. 2001): 2.5 bil bd. ft.; pine, hardwoods. **Nonfuel minerals** (est. 2001): 938 mil; mostly portland cement, crushed stone, lime, sand & gravel, and masonry. **Commercial fishing** (2000): $64.1 mil. **Chief port:** Mobile. **Principal internat. airports at:** Birmingham, Huntsville. **Value of construction** (1997): $4.8 bil. **Gross state product** (2000): $119.9 bil. **Employment dist.** (May 2002): 25.4% services; 22.9% trade; 18.7% govt.; 17.3% mfg. **Per cap. pers. income** (2001): $24,426. **Sales tax** (2002): 4%. **Unemployment** (2001): 5.3%. **Tourism expends.** (1999): $5.1 bil.

Finance. FDIC-insured commercial banks (2001): 158. **Deposits:** $132.1 bil. **FDIC-insured savings institutions (2001):** 12. **Assets:** $2.3 bil.

Federal govt. Fed. civ. employees (Mar. 2001): 35,510. **Avg. salary:** $52,692. **Notable fed. facilities:** George C. Marshall NASA Space Center; Gunter Annex & Maxwell AFB; Ft. Rucker; Ft. McClellan; Natl. Fertilizer Develop. Center; Navy Station & U.S. Corps of Engineers; Redstone Arsenal.

Energy. Electricity production (est. 2001, kWh, by source): Coal: 71.5 bil; Petroleum: 263 mil; Gas: 8.1 bil; Hydroelectric: 8.4 bil; Nuclear: 30.4 bil.

State data. Motto: We dare defend our rights. **Flower:** Camellia. **Bird:** Yellowhammer. **Tree:** Southern Longleaf pine. **Song:** Alabama. **Entered union** Dec. 14, 1819; rank, 22nd. **State fair:** Regional and county fairs held in Sept. and Oct.; no state fair.

History. Alabama was inhabited by the Creek, Cherokee, Chickasaw, Alabama, and Choctaw peoples when the Europeans arrived. The first Europeans were Spanish explorers in the early 1500s. The French made the first permanent settlement on Mobile Bay, 1702. France later gave up the entire region to England under the Treaty of Paris, 1763. Spanish forces took control of the Mobile Bay area, 1780, and it remained Spanish until U.S. troops seized the area, 1813. Most of present-day Alabama was held by the Creeks until Gen. Andrew Jackson broke their power, 1814, and they were removed to Oklahoma Territory. The state seceded, 1861, and the Confederate states were organized Feb. 4, at Montgomery, the first capital; it was readmitted, 1868.

Tourist attractions. First White House of the Confederacy, Civil Rights Memorial, Alabama Shakespeare Festival, all Montgomery; Ivy Green, Helen Keller's birthplace, Tuscumbia; Civil Rights Museum, statue of Vulcan, Birmingham; Carver Museum, Tuskegee; W. C. Handy Home & Museum, Florence; Alabama Space and Rocket Center, Huntsville; Moundville State Monument, Moundville; Pike Pioneer Museum, Troy; USS *Alabama* Memorial Park, Mobile; Russell Cave Natl. Monument, near Bridgeport: a detailed record of occupancy by humans from about 10,000 BC to AD 1650.

Famous Alabamians. Hank Aaron, Tallulah Bankhead, Hugo L. Black, Paul "Bear" Bryant, George Washington Carver, Nat King Cole, William C. Handy, Bo Jackson, Helen Keller, Coretta Scott King, Harper Lee, Joe Louis, Willie Mays, John Hunt Morgan, Jim Nabors, Jesse Owens, Condoleezza Rice, George Wallace, Booker T. Washington, Hank Williams.

Tourist information. Bureau of Tourism and Travel, 401 Adams Avenue, Suite 126, Montgomery, AL 36104.

Toll-free travel information. 1-800-ALABAMA out of state.

Website. www.alabama.gov

Tourism website. www.touralabama.org

Alaska

The Last Frontier (unofficial)

People. Population (2001 est.): 634,892; rank: 47; **net change** (2000-2001): 1.3%. **Pop. density:** 1.1 per sq mi. **Racial distribution** (2000): 69.3% white; 3.5% black; 4.0% Asian; 15.6% Native American/Nat. AK; 0.5% Hawaiian/Pacific Islander; 1.6% other race; 2 or more races, 5.4%. **Hispanic pop.** (any race): 4.1%.

Geography. Total area: 663,267 sq mi; rank: 1. **Land area:** 571,951 sq mi; rank: 1. **Acres forested:** 129,131,000. **Location:** NW corner of North America, bordered on E by Canada. **Climate:** SE, SW, and central regions, moist and mild; far north extremely dry. Extended summer days, winter nights, throughout. **Topography:** includes Pacific and Arctic mountain systems, central plateau, and Arctic slope. Mt. McKinley, 20,320 ft, is the highest point in North America. **Capital:** Juneau.

Economy. Chief industries: petroleum, tourism, fishing, mining, forestry, transportation, aerospace. **Chief manuf. goods:** fish products, lumber & pulp, furs. **Agriculture: Chief crops:** greenhouse products, barley, oats, hay, potatoes, lettuce, aquaculture. **Livestock**: (Jan. 2002) 11,500 cattle/calves; (Dec. 2001) 1,000 hogs/pigs.**Timber/lumber:** (2001 est.): NA; spruce, yellow cedar, hemlock; . **Nonfuel minerals** (est. 2001): 1.1 bil; mostly zinc, lead, silver, gold, sand & gravel. **Commercial fishing** (2000): $957 mil. **Chief ports:** Anchorage, Dutch Harbor, Kodiak, Seward, Skagway, Juneau, Sitka, Valdez, Wrangell. **Principal internat. airports at:** Anchorage, Fairbanks, Juneau. **Value of construction** (1997): $1 bil. **Gross state product** (2000): $27.7 bil. **Employment distrib.** (May 2002): 25.4% services; 20.1% trade; 27.9% govt.; 3.9% mfg. **Per cap. pers. income** (2001): $30,997. **Sales tax:** (2002): none. **Unemployment** (2001): 6.3%. **Tourism expends.** (1999): $1.5 bil.

Finance. FDIC-insured commercial banks (2001): 6. **Deposits:** $4.3 bil. **FDIC-insured savings institutions** (2001): 2. **Assets:** $334 mil.

Federal govt. Fed. civ. employees (Mar. 2001): 11,223. **Avg. salary:** $49,365.

Energy. Electricity production (est. 2001, kWh, by source): Coal: 194 mil; Petroleum: 760 mil; Gas: 3 bil; Hydroelectric: 989 mil.

State data. Motto: North to the future. **Flower:** Forget-Me-Not. **Bird:** Willow ptarmigan. **Tree:** Sitka spruce. **Song:** Alaska's Flag. **Entered union** Jan. 3, 1959; rank, 49th. **State fair** at Palmer; late Aug.-early Sept.

History. Early inhabitants were the Tlingit-Haida people and tribes of the Athabascan family. The Aleut and Inuit (Eskimo), who arrived about 4,000 years ago from Siberia, lived in the coastal areas. Vitus Bering, a Danish explorer working for Russia, was the first European to land in Alaska, 1741. The first permanent Russian settlement was established on Kodiak Island, 1784. In 1799, the Russian-American Co. controlled the region, and the first chief manager, Aleksandr Baranov, set up headquarters at Archangel, near present-day Sitka. Sec. of State William H. Seward bought Alaska from Russia for $7.2 mil in 1867, a bargain some called "Seward's Folly." In 1896, gold was discovered in the Klondike region, and the famed gold rush began. Alaska became a territory in 1912.

Tourist attractions. Inside Passage; Portage Glacier; Mendenhall Glacier; Ketchikan Totems; Glacier Bay Natl. Park and Preserve; Denali Natl. Park, one of N. America's great wildlife sanctuaries, surrounding Mt. McKinley, N. America's highest peak; Mt. Roberts Tramway, Juneau; Pribilof Islands fur seal rookeries; restored St. Michael's Russian Orthodox Cathedral, Sitka; White Pass & Yukon Route railroad; Skagway; Katmai Natl. Park & Preserve.

Famous Alaskans. Tom Bodett, Susan Butcher, Ernest Gruening, Jewel (Kilcher), Gov. Tony Knowles, Sydney Laurence, Libby Riddles, Jefferson "Soapy" Smith.

Tourist information. Alaska Division of Tourism, PO Box 110801, Juneau, AK 99811-0801; 1-907-465-2012.

Website. www.state.ak.us

Tourism website. www.dced.state.ak.us/tourism

Arizona

Grand Canyon State

People. Population (2001 est.): 5,307,331; rank: 20; **net change** (2000-2001): 3.4%. **Pop. density:** 46.7 per sq mi. **Racial distribution** (2000): 75.5% white; 3.1% black; 1.8% Asian; 5.0% Native American/Nat. AK; 0.1% Hawaiian/Pacific Islander; 11.6% other race; 2 or more races, 2.9%. **Hispanic pop.** (any race): 25.3%.

Geography. Total area: 113,998 sq mi; rank: 6. **Land area:** 113,635 sq mi; rank: 6. **Acres forested:** 19,596,000. **Location:** in the southwestern U.S. **Climate:** clear and dry in the southern regions and northern plateau; high central areas have heavy winter snows. **Topography:** Colorado plateau in the N, containing the Grand Canyon; Mexican Highlands running diagonally NW to SE; Sonoran Desert in the SW. **Capital:** Phoenix.

Economy. Chief industries: manufacturing, construction, tourism, mining, agriculture. **Chief manuf. goods:** electronics, printing & publishing, foods, prim. & fabric. metals, aircraft and missiles, apparel. **Chief crops:** cotton, lettuce, cauliflower, broccoli, sorghum, barley, corn, wheat, citrus fruits. **Livestock:** (Jan. 2002) 840,000 cattle/calves; 134,000 sheep/lambs; (Dec. 2001) 133,000 hogs/pigs. **Timber/lumber** (est. 2001): 60 mil bd. ft.; pine, fir, spruce. **Nonfuel minerals** (est. 2001): 2.1 bil; mostly copper, sand & gravel, cement, molybdenum, crushed stone. **Principal internat. airports at:** Phoenix, Tucson. **Value of construction** (1997): $10 bil. **Gross state product** (2000): $156.3 bil. **Employment distrib.** (May 2002): 31.5% services; 23.9% trade; 17.3% govt.; 8.7% mfg. **Per cap. pers. income** (2001): $25,479. **Sales tax** (2002): 5.6%. **Unemployment** (2001): 4.7%. **Tourism expends.**(1999): $9.5 bil. **Lottery** (2001): total sales: $272.7 mil; net income: $77.8 mil.

Finance. FDIC-insured commercial banks (2001): 43. **Deposits:** $18.4 bil. **FDIC-insured savings institutions (2001):** 3. **Assets:** $425 mil.

Federal govt. Fed. civ. employees (Mar. 2001): 29,088. **Avg. salary:** $45,886. **Notable fed. facilities:** Luke, Davis-Monthan AF bases; Ft. Huachuca Army Base; Yuma Proving Grounds.

Energy. Electricity production (est. 2001, kWh, by source): Coal: 39.7 bil; Petroleum: 312 mil; Gas: 9.1 bil; Hydroelectric: 7.8 bil; Nuclear: 28.7 bil; Other: 34 mil.

State data. Motto: Ditat Deus (God enriches). **Flower:** Blossom of the Saguaro cactus. **Bird:** Cactus wren. **Tree:** Paloverde. **Song:** Arizona. **Entered union** Feb. 14, 1912; rank, 48th. **State fair** at Phoenix; late Oct.-early Nov.

History. Anasazi, Mogollon, and Hohokam civilizations inhabited the area c 300 BC-AD 1300, later Pueblo peoples; Navajo and Apache came c 15th cent. Marcos de Niza, a Franciscan, and Estevanico, a former black slave, explored, 1539; Spanish explorer Francisco Vásquez de Coronado visited, 1540. Eusebio Francisco Kino, a Jesuit missionary, taught Indians 1692-1711, and left missions. Tubac, a Spanish fort, became the first European settlement, 1752. Spain ceded Arizona to Mexico, 1821. The U.S. took over, 1848, after the Mexican War. The area below the Gila River was obtained from Mexico in the Gadsden Purchase, 1853. Arizona became a territory, 1863. Apache wars ended with Geronimo's surrender, 1886.

Tourist attractions. The Grand Canyon; Painted Desert; Petrified Forest Natl. Park; Canyon de Chelly; Meteor Crater; London Bridge, Lake Havasu City; Biosphere 2, Oracle; Navajo Natl. Monument; Sedona.

Famous Arizonans. Bruce Babbitt, Cochise, Alice Cooper, Geronimo, Barry Goldwater, Zane Grey, Carl Hayden, George W. P. Hunt, Helen Jacobs, Bil Keane, Percival Lowell, William H. Pickering, John J. Rhodes, Morris Udall, Stewart Udall, Frank Lloyd Wright.

Tourist information. Arizona Office of Tourism, Ste. 4015, 2702 N. 3rd St., Phoenix, AZ 85004, 1-800-520-3433.

Website. www.state.az.gov

Tourism website. www.arizonaguide.com

Arkansas

The Natural State, The Razorback State

People. Population (2001 est.): 2,692,090; rank: 33; **net change** (2000-2001): 0.7%. **Pop. density:** 51.7 per sq mi. **Racial distribution** (2000): 80.0% white; 15.7% black; 0.8% Asian; 0.8% Native American/Nat. AK; 0.1% Hawaiian/Pacific Islander; 1.5% other race; 2 or more races, 1.3%. **Hispanic pop.** (any race): 3.2%.

Geography. Total area: 53,179 sq mi; rank: 29. **Land area:** 52,068 sq mi; rank: 27. **Acres forested:** 17,864,000. **Location:** in the west south-central U.S. **Climate:** long, hot summers, mild winters; generally abundant rainfall. **Topography:** eastern delta and prairie, southern lowland forests, and the northwestern highlands, which include the Ozark Plateaus. **Capital:** Little Rock.

Economy. Chief industries: manufacturing, agriculture, tourism, forestry. **Chief manuf. goods:** food products, chemicals, lumber, paper, plastics, electric motors, furniture, auto components, airplane parts, apparel, machinery, steel. **Chief crops:** rice, soybeans, cotton, tomatoes, grapes, apples, commercial vegetables, peaches, wheat. **Livestock:** (Jan. 2002) 1.8 mil cattle/calves; (Dec. 2001) 570,000 hogs/pigs; 23.5 mil chickens (excl. broilers); 1.2 bil broilers. **Timber/lumber** (est. 2001): 2.6 bil bd. ft.; oak, hickory, gum, cypress, pine. **Nonfuel minerals** (est. 2001): 491 mil; mostly bromine, crushed stone, portland cement, sand & gravel. **Chief ports:** Little Rock, Pine Bluff, Osceola, Helena, Fort Smith, Van Buren, Camden, Dardanelle, North Little Rock, West Memphis, Crossett, McGehee, Morrilton. **Value of construction** (1997): $3 bil. **Gross state product** (2000): $67.7 bil. **Employment distrib.** (May 2002): 24.3% services; 23.1% trade; 17.2% govt.; 19.7% mfg. **Per cap. pers. income** (2001): $22,912. **Sales tax** (2002): 5.125%. **Unemployment** (2001): 5.1%. **Tourism expends.** (1999): $3.7 bil.

Finance. FDIC-insured commercial banks (2001): 178. **Deposits:** $23.5 bil. **FDIC-insured savings institutions (2001):** 9. **Assets:** $3.4 bil.

Federal govt. Fed. civ. employees (Mar. 2001): 11,052. **Avg. salary:** $44,751. **Notable fed. facilities:** Nat'l. Center for Toxicological Research, Jefferson; Pine Bluff Arsenal, Little Rock AFB.

Energy. Electricity production (est. 2001, kWh, by source): Coal: 24.4 bil; Petroleum: 846 mil; Gas: 1.9 bil; Hydroelectric: 2.6 bil; Nuclear: 14.8 bil.

State data. Motto: Regnat Populus (The people rule). **Flower:** Apple blossom. **Bird:** Mockingbird. **Tree:** Pine. **Song:** Arkansas. **Entered union** June 15, 1836; rank, 25th. **State fair** at Little Rock; late Sept.-early Oct.

History. Quapaw, Caddo, Osage, Cherokee, and Choctaw peoples lived in the area at the time of European contact. The first European explorers were de Soto, 1541; Marquette and Jolliet, 1673; and La Salle, 1682. The first settlement was by the French under Henri de Tonty, 1686, at Arkansas Post. In 1762, the area was ceded by France to Spain, then given back again, 1800, and was part of the Louisiana Purchase, 1803. It was made a territory, 1819. Arkansas seceded in 1861, only after the Civil War began; more than 10,000 Arkansans fought on the Union side.

Tourist attractions. Hot Springs Natl. Park (water ranging from 95° F-147° F); Eureka Springs; Ozark Folk Center, Blanchard Caverns, both near Mountain View; Crater of Diamonds (only U.S. diamond mine) near Murfreesboro; Toltec Mounds Archeological State Park, Little Rock; Buffalo Natl. River; Mid-America Museum, Hot Springs; Pea Ridge National Military Park, Pead Ridge; Tanyard Springs, Morrilton; Wiederkehr Wine Village, Wiederkehr Village.

Famous Arkansans. Daisy Bates, Dee Brown, Paul "Bear" Bryant, Glen Campbell, Johnny Cash, Hattie Caraway, Bill Clinton, "Dizzy" Dean, Orval Faubus, James W. Fulbright, John Grisham, John H. Johnson, Douglas MacArthur, John L. McClellan, James S. McDonnell, Scottie Pippen, Dick Powell, Brooks Robinson, Billy Bob Thornton, Winthrop Rockefeller, Mary Steenburgen, Edward Durell Stone, Sam Walton, Archibald Yell.

Tourist Information. Arkansas Dept. of Parks & Tourism, One Capitol Mall, Little Rock, AR 72201

Toll-free travel information. 1-800-NATURAL.

Website. www.state.ar.us

Tourism website. www.state.ar.us/tourism.php

California

Golden State

People. Population (2001 est.): 34,501,130; rank: 1; **net change** (2000-2001): 1.9%. **Pop. density:** 221.2 per sq mi. **Racial distribution** (2000): 59.5; white; 6.7% black; 10.9% Asian; 1.0% Native American/Nat. AK; 0.3% Hawaiian/Pacific Islander; 16.8% other race; 2 or more races, 4.7% **Hispanic pop.** (any race): 32.4%.

Geography. Total area: 163,696 sq mi; rank: 3. **Land area:** 155,959 sq mi; rank: 3. **Acres forested:** 37,263,000. **Location:** on western coast of the U.S. **Climate:** moderate temperatures and rainfall along the coast; extremes in the interior. **Topography:** long mountainous coastline; central valley; Sierra Nevada on the east; desert basins of the southern interior; rugged mountains of the north. **Capital:** Sacramento.

Economy. Chief industries: agriculture, tourism, apparel, electronics, telecommunications, entertainment. **Chief manuf. goods:** electronic and electrical equip., computers, industrial machinery, transportation equip. and instruments, food. **Chief farm products**: milk and cream, grapes, cotton, flowers, oranges, rice, nursery products, hay, tomatoes, lettuce, strawberries, almonds, asparagus. **Livestock**: (Jan. 2002) 5.2 mil cattle/calves; 800,000 sheep/lambs; (Dec. 2001) 110,000 hogs/pigs; 28 mil chickens (excl. broilers).**Timber/lumber** (est. 2001): 3.0 bil bd. ft.; fir, pine, redwood, oak. **Nonfuel minerals** (est. 2001): 3.3 bil; mostly portland cement, sand & gravel, boron, crushed stone, gold. **Commercial fishing** (2000): $140 mil. **Chief ports:** Long Beach, Los Angeles, San Diego, Oakland, San Francisco, Sacramento, Stockton. **Principal internat. airports at:** Fresno, Los Angeles, Oakland, Ontario, Sacramento, San Diego, San Francisco, San Jose. **Value of construction** (1997): $36.7 bil. **Gross state product** (2000): $1.3 tril. **Employment distrib.** (May 2002): 31.9% services; 22.8% trade; 17% govt.; 12.4% mfg. **Per cap. pers. income** (2001): $32,678. **Sales tax** (2002): 7.25%. **Unemployment** (2001): 5.3%. **Tourism expends.** (1999): $71.4 bil. **Lottery** (2001): total sales: $2.9 bil; net income: $1 bil..

Finance. FDIC-insured commercial banks (2001): 301. **Deposits:** $257.6 bil. **FDIC-insured savings institutions (2001):** 42. **Assets:** $407.3 bil.

Federal govt. Fed. civ. employees (Mar. 2001): 137,376. **Avg. salary:** $53,457. **Notable fed. facilities:** Vandenberg, Beale, Travis, McClellan AF bases; San Francisco Mint.

Energy. Electricity production(est. 2001, kWh, by source): Petroleum: 317 mil; Gas: 12 bil; Hydroelectric: 24.8 bil; Nuclear: 33.2 bil; **Other:** 191 mil..

State data. Motto: Eureka (I have found it). **Flower:** Golden poppy. **Bird:** California valley quail. **Tree:** California redwood. **Song:** I Love You, California. **Entered union** Sept. 9, 1850; rank, 31st. **State fair** at Sacramento; late Aug.-early Sept.

History. Early inhabitants included more than 100 different Native American tribes with multiple dialects. The first European explorers were Cabrillo, 1542, and Drake, 1579. The first settlement was the Spanish Alta California mission at San Diego, 1769, first in a string founded by Franciscan Father Junipero Serra. U.S. traders and settlers arrived in the 19th cent. and staged the Bear Flag revolt, 1846, in protest against Mexican rule; later that year U.S. forces occupied California. At the end of the Mexican War, Mexico ceded the territory to the U.S., 1848; that same year gold was discovered, and the famed gold rush began.

WORLD ALMANAC QUICK QUIZ

How many U.S. state capitals have the word "city" in their names?

(a) 2; (b) 3; (c) 4; (d) 5

For the answer look in this chapter, or see page 1008.

Tourist attractions. The *Queen Mary*, Long Beach; Palomar Mountain; Disneyland, Anaheim; Getty Center, Los Angeles; Tournament of Roses and Rose Bowl, Pasadena; Universal Studios, Hollywood; Long Beach Aquarium of the Pacific; Golden State Museum, Sacramento; San Diego Zoo; Yosemite Valley; Lassen and Sequoia-Kings Canyon natl. parks; Lake Tahoe; Mojave and Colorado deserts; San Francisco Bay; Napa Valley; Monterey Peninsula; oldest living things on earth believed to be a stand of Bristlecone pines in the Inyo National Forest, est. 4,700 years old; world's tallest tree, 365-ft "National Geographic Society" coast redwood, in Humboldt Redwoods State Park.

Famous Californians. Edmund G. (Pat) Brown, Jerry Brown, Luther Burbank, Julia Child, Ted Danson, Cameron Diaz, Leonardo DiCaprio, Joe DiMaggio, Dianne Feinstein, John C. Fremont, Robert Frost, Tom Hanks, Bret Harte, William Randolph Hearst, Helen Hunt, Jack Kemp, Monica Lewinsky, Jack London, George Lucas, Mark McGwire, Aimee Semple McPherson, Marilyn Monroe, John Muir, Richard M. Nixon, George S. Patton Jr., Ronald Reagan, Sally K. Ride, William Saroyan, Father Junípero Serra, O.J. Simpson, Kevin Spacey, Leland Stanford, John Steinbeck, Shirley Temple, Earl Warren, Ted Williams, Venus Williams, Tiger Woods.

California Division of Tourism. P.O. Box 1499, Sacramento, CA 95812-1499.

Toll-free travel information. 1-800-GOCALIF.

Website. www.state.ca.us

Tourism website. www.gocalif.ca.gov

Colorado

Centennial State

People. Population (2001 est.): 4,417,714; rank: 24; **net change** (2000-2001): 2.7%. **Pop. density:** 42.6 per sq mi. **Racial distribution** (2000): 82.8% white; 3.8% black; 2.2% Asian; 1.0% Native American/Nat. AK; 0.1% Hawaiian/Pacific Islander; 7.2% other race; 2 or more races, 2.8% **Hispanic pop.** (any race): 17.1%.

Geography. Total area: 104,094 sq mi; rank: 8. **Land area:** 103,718 sq mi; rank: 8. **Acres forested:** 21,338,000. **Location:** in W central U.S. **Climate:** low relative humidity, abundant sunshine, wide daily, seasonal temp. ranges; alpine conditions in the high mountains. **Topography:** eastern dry high plains; hilly to mountainous central plateau; western Rocky Mountains of high ranges, with broad valleys, deep, narrow canyons. **Capital:** Denver.

Economy. Chief industries: manufacturing, construction, government, tourism, agriculture, aerospace, electronics equipment. **Chief manuf. goods:** computer equip. & instruments, foods, machinery, aerospace products. **Chief crops:** corn, wheat, hay, sugar beets, barley, potatoes, apples, peaches, pears, dry edible beans, sorghum, onions, oats, sunflowers, vegetables. **Livestock**: (Jan. 2002) 3.1 mil cattle/calves; 370,000 sheep/lambs; (Dec. 2001) 780,000 hogs/pigs; 4.2 mil chickens (excl. broilers). **Timber/lumber** (est. 2001): 109 mil bd. ft.; oak, ponderosa pine, Douglas fir. **Nonfuel minerals** (est. 2001): 676 mil; mostly sand & gravel, portland cement, crushed stone, gold, helium. **Principal internat. airport at:** Denver. **Value of construction** (1997): $9.2 bil. **Gross state product** (2000): $167.9 bil. **Employment distrib.** (May 2002): 30.6% services; 23.5% trade; 16.6% govt.; 8.5% mfg. **Per cap. pers. income** (2001): $32,957. **Sales tax** (2002): 2.9%. **Unemployment** (2001): 3.7%. **Tourism expends.** (1999): $9.4 bil. **Lottery** (2001): total sales: $350.6 mil; net income: $79.9 mil.

Finance. FDIC-insured commercial banks (2001): 176. **Deposits:** $36.9 bil. **FDIC-insured savings institutions (2001):** 10. **Assets:** $909 mil.

Federal govt. Fed. civ. employees (Mar. 2001): 32,336. **Avg. salary:** $54,185. **Notable fed. facilities:** U.S. Air Force Academy; U.S. Mint; Ft. Carson; Natl. Renewable Energy Labs; U.S. Rail Transportation Test Center; N. American Aerospace Defense Command; Consolidated Space Operations Ctr.; Denver Federal Center; Natl. Center for Atmospheric Research; Natl. Instit. for Standards in Technology; Natl. Oceanic and Atmospheric Administration.

Energy. Electricity production (est. 2001, kWh, by source): Coal: 35.7 bil; Petroleum: 159 mil; Gas: 4.9 bil; Hydroelectric: 1.2 bil.

State data. Motto: Nil Sine Numine (Nothing Without Providence). **Flower:** Rocky Mountain columbine. **Bird:** Lark bunting. **Tree:** Colorado blue spruce. **Song:** Where the Columbines Grow. **Entered union** Aug. 1, 1876; rank 38th. **State fair** at Pueblo; mid-Aug.—early Sept.

History. Early civilization centered around the Mesa Verde c 2,000 years ago; later, Ute, Pueblo, Cheyenne, and Arapaho peoples lived in the area. The region was claimed by Spain, but passed to France. The U.S. acquired eastern Colorado in the Louisiana Purchase, 1803. Lt. Zebulon M. Pike explored the area, 1806, discovering the peak that bears his name. After the Mexican War, 1846-48, U.S. immigrants settled in the east, former Mexicans in the south. Gold was discovered in 1858, causing a population boom. Displaced Native Americans protested, resulting in the so-called Sand Creek Massacre, 1864, where more than 200 Cheyenne and Arapaho were killed. All Native Americans were later removed to Oklahoma Territory.

Tourist attractions. Rocky Mountain and Black Canyon of the Gunnison natl. parks; Aspen Ski Resort; Garden of the Gods, Colorado Springs; Great Sand Dunes, Dinosaur, and Colorado natl. monuments; Pikes Peak and Mt. Evans highways; Mesa Verde Natl. Park (ancient Anasazi Indian cliff dwellings); Grand Mesa Natl. Forest; mining towns of Central City, Silverton, Cripple Creek; Burlington's Old Town; Bent's Fort, outside La Junta; Georgetown Loop Historic Mining Railroad Park, Cumbres & Toltec Scenic Railroad; limited stakes gaming in Central City, Blackhawk, Cripple Creek, Ignacio, and Towaoe.

Famous Coloradans. Tim Allen, Frederick Bonfils, Henry Brown, Molly Brown, William N. Byers, M. Scott Carpenter, Lon Chaney, Jack Dempsey, Mamie Eisenhower, Douglas Fairbanks, Barney Ford, Scott Hamilton, Chief Ourey, "Baby Doe" Tabor, Lowell Thomas, Byron R. White, Paul Whiteman.

State Chamber of Commerce. 1776 Lincoln, Ste. 1200, Denver, CO 80203. Phone: 303-831-7411

Tourist information. Colorado Travel and Tourism Authority, P. O. Box 3524, Englewood, CO 80155.

Toll-free travel information. 1-800-COLORADO.

Website. www.colorado.gov

Tourism website. www.colorado.com

Connecticut

Constitution State, Nutmeg State

People. Population (2001 est.): 3,425,074; rank: 29; **net change** (2000-2001): 0.6%. **Pop. density:** 706.9 per sq mi. **Racial distribution** (2000): 81.6% white; 9.1% black; 2.4% Asian; 0.3% Native American/Nat. AK; <0.1% Hawaiian/Pacific Islander; 4.3% other race; 2 or more races, 2.2%. **Hispanic pop.** (any race): 9.4%.

Geography. Total area: 5,543 sq mi; rank: 48. **Land area:** 4,845 sq mi; rank: 48. **Acres forested:** 1,819,000. **Location:** New England state in NE corner of the U.S. **Climate:** moderate; winters avg. slightly below freezing; warm, humid summers. **Topography:** western upland, the Berkshires, in the NW, highest elevations; narrow central lowland N-S; hilly eastern upland drained by rivers. **Capital:** Hartford.

Economy. Chief industries: manufacturing, retail trade, government, services, finances, insurance, real estate. **Chief manuf. goods:** aircraft engines and parts, submarines, helicopters, machinery and computer equipment, electronics and electrical equipment, medical instruments, pharmaceuticals. **Chief crops:** nursery stock, Christmas trees, mushrooms, vegetables, sweet corn, tobacco, apples. **Livestock:** (Jan. 2002) 61,000 cattle/calves; (Dec. 2001) 3,500 hogs/pigs; 3.7 mil chickens (excl. broilers). **Timber/lumber** (est. 2001): 48 mil bd. ft.; oak, birch, beech, maple. **Nonfuel minerals** (est. 2001): 104 mil; mostly crushed stone, sand & gravel, dimension stone, clays, gemstones. **Commercial fishing** (2000): $31.2 mil. **Chief ports:** New Haven, Bridgeport, New London. **Principal internat. airport at:** Windsor Locks. **Value of construction** (1997): $3.8 bil. **Gross state product** (2000): $159.3 bil. **Employment distrib.** (May 2002): 32.3% services; 21.4% trade; 15% govt.; 14.4% mfg. **Per cap. pers. income** (2001): $41,930. **Sales tax** (2002): 6%. **Unemployment** (2001): 3.3%. **Tourism expends.** (1999): $5.2 bil. **Lottery** (2001): total sales: $839.7 mil; net income: $251.7 mil.

Finance. FDIC-insured commercial banks (2001): 25. **Deposits:** $3.1 bil. FDIC-insured savings institutions (2001): 44. **Assets:** $47.3 bil.

Federal govt. Fed. civ. employees (Mar. 2001): 6,756. Avg. salary: $53,146. **Notable fed. facilities:** U.S. Coast Guard Academy; U.S. Navy Submarine Base.

Energy. Electricity production (est. 2001, kWh, by source): Petroleum: 10 mil; Hydroelectric: 40 mil; Nuclear: 2.6 bil; Other: 344 mil.

State data. Motto: Qui Transtulit Sustinet (He who transplanted still sustains). **Flower:** Mountain laurel. **Bird:** American robin. **Tree:** White oak. **Song:** Yankee Doodle. **Fifth** of the 13 original states to ratify the Constitution, Jan. 9, 1788. **State Fair:** largest fair at Durham, late Sept.; no state fair.

History. At the time of European contact, inhabitants of the area were Algonquian peoples, including the Mohegan and Pequot. Dutch explorer Adriaen Block was the first European visitor, 1614. By 1634, settlers from Plymouth Bay had started colonies along the Connecticut River; in 1637 they defeated the Pequots. The Colony of Connecticut was chartered by England, 1662, adding New Haven, 1665. In the American Revolution, Connecticut Patriots fought in most major campaigns, while Connecticut privateers captured British merchant ships.

Tourist attractions. Mark Twain House, Hartford; Yale University's Art Gallery, Peabody Museum, both in New Haven; Mystic Seaport; Mystic Marine Life Aquarium; P. T. Barnum Museum, Bridgeport; Gillette Castle, Hadlyme; U.S.S. *Nautilus* Memorial, Groton (1st nuclear-powered submarine); Mashantucket Pequot Museum & Research Center, Foxwoods Resort & Casino, both in Ledyard; Mohegan Sun, Uncasville; Lake Compounce, Bristol.

Famous "Nutmeggers." Ethan Allen, Phineas T. Barnum, Samuel Colt, Jonathan Edwards, Nathan Hale, Katharine Hepburn, Isaac Hull, Robert Mitchum, J. Pierpont Morgan, Ralph Nader, Israel Putnam, Wallace Stevens, Harriet Beecher Stowe, Mark Twain, Noah Webster, Eli Whitney.

Tourist information. Dept. of Economic and Community Development, 505 Hudson St., Hartford, CT 06106.

Toll-free travel information. 1-800-CTBOUND

Website. www.state.ct.us

Tourism website. www.ctbound.org

Delaware

First State, Diamond State

People. Population (2001 est.): 796,165; rank: 45; **net change** (2000-2001): 1.6%. **Pop. density:** 407.5 per sq mi. **Racial distribution** (2000): 74.6% white; 19.2% black; 2.1% Asian; 0.3% Native American/Nat. AK; <0.1% Hawaiian/Pacific Islander; 2.0% other race; 2 or more races, 1.7%. **Hispanic pop.** (any race): 4.8%.

Geography. Total area: 2,489 sq mi; rank: 49. **Land area:** 1,954 sq mi; rank: 49. **Acres forested:** 398,000. **Location:** occupies the Delmarva Peninsula on the Atlantic coastal plain. **Climate:** moderate. **Topography:** Piedmont plateau to the N, sloping to a near sea-level plain. **Capital:** Dover.

Economy. Chief industries: chemicals, agriculture, finance, poultry, shellfish, tourism, auto assembly, food processing, transportation equipment. **Chief manuf. goods:** nylon, apparel, luggage, foods, autos, processed meats and vegetables, railroad & aircraft equipment. **Chief crops:** soybeans, potatoes, corn, mushrooms, lima beans, green peas, barley, cucumbers, wheat, corn, grain sorghum, greenhouse & nursery. **Livestock:** (Jan. 2002) 26,000 cattle/calves; (Dec. 2001) 26,000 hogs/pigs; 1.3 mil chickens (excl. broilers); 247.7 mil broilers. **Timber/lumber** (est. 2001): 14 mil bd. ft.; hardwoods and softwoods (except for southern yellow pine). **Nonfuel minerals** (est. 2001): 13.1 mil; mostly magnesium compounds, sand & gravel, gemstones. **Commercial fishing** (2000): $6.8 mil. **Chief ports:** Wilmington. **Principal internat. airport at:** Philadelphia/Wilmington. **Value of construction** (1997): $935 mil. **Gross state product** (2000): $36.3 bil. **Employment distrib.** (May 2002): 29.3% services; 21.9% trade; 13.4% govt.; 13.3% mfg. **Per cap. pers. income** (2001): $32,121. **Sales tax:** (2002): none. **Unemployment** (2001): 3.5%. **Tourism expends.** (1999): $1.1 bil. **Lottery** (2001): total sales: $601.2 mil; net income: $260 mil.

IT'S A FACT: In 1878, Alexander Graham Bell set up the world's 1st commercial telephone exchange, in New Haven, CT, and the world's 1st telephone directory was printed up. It was one page long, and had just 50 listings, most of them local businesses seeking customers.

Finance. FDIC-insured commercial banks (2001): 33. **Deposits**: $83.5 bil. FDIC-insured savings institutions (2001): 7. **Assets**: $25.3 bil.

Federal govt. Fed. civ. employees (Mar. 2001): 2,508. **Avg. salary**: $47,011. **Notable fed. facilities:** Dover Air Force Base, Federal Wildlife Refuge, Bombay Hook.

Energy. Electricity production (est. 2001, kWh, by source): Coal: 2.9 bil; Petroleum: 239 mil; Gas: 37 mil.

State data. Motto: Liberty and independence. **Flower:** Peach blossom. **Bird:** Blue hen chicken. **Tree:** American holly. **Song:** Our Delaware. **First** of original 13 states to ratify the Constitution, Dec. 7, 1787. **State fair** at Harrington; end of July.

History. The Lenni Lenape (Delaware) people lived in the region at the time of European contact. Henry Hudson located the Delaware R., 1609, and in 1610, English explorer Samuel Argall entered Delaware Bay, naming the area after Virginia's governor, Lord De La Warr. The Dutch first settled near present Lewes, 1631, but the colony was destroyed by Indians. Swedes settled at Fort Christina (now Wilmington), 1638. Dutch settled anew, 1651, near New Castle and seized the Swedish settlement, 1655, only to lose all Delaware and New Netherland to the British, 1664. After 1682, Delaware became part of Pennsylvania, and in 1704 it was granted its own assembly. In 1776, it adopted a constitution as the state of Delaware. Although it remained in the Union during the Civil War, Delaware retained slavery until abolished by the 13th Amendment in 1865.

Tourist attractions. Ft. Christina Monument, site of founding of New Sweden, Holy Trinity (Old Swedes) Church, erected 1698, the oldest Protestant church in the U.S. still in use, Wilmington; Hagley Museum, Winterthur Museum and Gardens, both near Wilmington; historic district, New Castle; John Dickinson "Penman of the Revolution" home, Dover; Rehoboth Beach, "nation's summer capital," Rehoboth; Dover Downs Intl. Speedway.

Famous Delawareans. Thomas F. Bayard, Henry Seidel Canby, E. I. du Pont, John P. Marquand, Howard Pyle, Caesar Rodney.

Chamber of Commerce. 1200 N. Orange St., Ste. 200, Wilmington, DE 19899-0671.

Toll-free travel information. 1-800-2VISITDE.

Website. www.delaware.gov

Tourism website. www.visitdelaware.net

Florida

Sunshine State

People. Population (2001 est.): 16,396,515; rank: 4; **net change** (2000-2001): 2.6%. **Pop. density:** 304.1 per sq mi. **Racial distribution** (2000): 78.0% white; 14.6% black; 1.7% Asian; 0.3% Native American/Nat. AK; 0.1% Hawaiian/Pacific Islander; 3.0% other race; 2 or more races, 2.4%. **Hispanic pop.** (any race): 16.8%.

Geography. Total area: 65,755 sq mi; rank: 22. **Land area:** 53,927 sq mi; rank: 26. **Acres forested:** 16,549,000. **Location:** peninsula jutting southward 500 mi between the Atlantic and the Gulf of Mexico. **Climate:** subtropical N of Bradenton-Lake Okeechobee-Vero Beach line; tropical S of line. **Topography:** land is flat or rolling; highest point is 345 ft in the NW. **Capital:** Tallahassee.

Economy. Chief industries: tourism, agriculture, manufacturing, construction, services, international trade. **Chief manuf. goods:** electric & electronic equipment, transportation equipment, food, printing & publishing, chemicals, instruments, industrial machinery. **Chief crops:** citrus fruits, vegetables, melons, greenhouse and nursery products, potatoes, sugarcane, strawberries. **Livestock:** (Jan. 2002) 1.8 mil cattle/calves; (Dec. 2001) 35,000 hogs/pigs; 13.1 mil chickens (excl. broilers); 119.9 mil broilers. **Timber/lumber** (est. 2001): 860 mil bd. ft.; pine, cypress, cedar; 751 mil bd. ft. **Nonfuel minerals** (est. 2001): 1.8 bil; mostly phosphate rock, crushed stone, portland and masonry cement, sand & gravel. **Commercial fishing** (2000): $217.2 mil. **Chief ports:** Pensacola, Tampa, Manatee, Miami, Port Everglades, Jacksonville, St. Petersburg, Canaveral. **Principal internat. airports at:** Daytona Beach, Ft. Lauderdale/Hollywood, Ft. Myers, Jacksonville, Key West, Melbourne, Miami, Orlando, Panama City, St. Petersburg/Clearwater, Sarasota/Bradenton, Tampa, West Palm Beach. **Value of construction** (1997): $25.2 bil. **Gross state product** (2000): $ 472 bil. **Employment distrib.** (May 2002): 37.5% services; 24.6% trade; 14.7% govt.; 6.2% mfg. **Per cap. pers. income** (2001): $28,493. **Sales tax** (2002): 6%. **Unemployment** (2001): 4.8%. **Tourism expends.** (1997): (1999): $55.8 bil. **Lottery** (2001): total sales: $2.3 bil; net income: $907.2 mil.

Finance. FDIC-insured commercial banks (2001): 260. **Deposits:** $50.7 bil. **FDIC-insured savings institutions** (2001): 45. **Assets:** $26.6 bil.

Federal govt. Fed. civ. employees (Mar. 2001): 61,372. **Avg. salary:** $50,650. **Notable fed. facilities:** John F. Kennedy Space Center, NASA-Kennedy Space Center's Spaceport USA; Eglin Air Force Base; Pensacola Naval Training Center; MacDill Air Force Base, Tampa.

Energy. Electricity production (est. 2001, kWh, by source): Coal: 63 bil; Petroleum: 39 bil; Gas: 37 bil; Hydroelectric: 148 mil; Nuclear: 31 bil; Other: 125 mil.

State data. Motto: In God we trust. **Flower:** Orange blossom. **Bird:** Mockingbird. **Tree:** Sabal palmetto palm. **Song:** Old Folks at Home. **Entered union** Mar. 3, 1845; rank, 27th. **State fair** at Tampa; early Feb.

History. The original inhabitants of Florida included the Timucua, Apalachee, and Calusa peoples. Later the Seminole migrated from Georgia to Florida, becoming dominant there in the early 18th cent. The first European to see Florida was Ponce de León, 1513. France established a colony, Fort Caroline, on the St. John River, 1564. Spain settled St. Augustine, 1565, and Spanish troops massacred most of the French. Britain's Sir Francis Drake burned St. Augustine, 1586. In 1763, Spain ceded Florida to Great Britain, which held the area briefly, 1763-83, before returning it to Spain. After Andrew Jackson led a U.S. invasion, 1818, Spain ceded Florida to the U.S., 1819. The Seminole War, 1835-42, resulted in removal of most Native Americans to Oklahoma Territory. Florida seceded from the Union, 1861, and was readmitted in 1868.

Tourist attractions. Miami Beach; St. Augustine, oldest permanent European settlement in U.S.; Castillo de San Marcos, St. Augustine; Walt Disney World's Magic Kingdom, EPCOT Center, Disney-MGM Studios, and Animal Kingdom, all near Orlando; Sea World, Universal Studios, near Orlando; Spaceport USA, Kennedy Space Center; Everglades Natl. Park; Ringling Museum of Art, Ringling Museum of the Circus, both in Sarasota; Cypress Gardens, Winter Haven; Busch Gardens, Tampa; U.S. Astronaut Hall of Fame, Mariana Caverns; Church St. Station, Orlando; Silver Springs, Ocala.

Famous Floridians. Edna Buchanan, Jeb Bush, Marjory Stoneman Douglas, Henry M. Flagler, Carl Hiaasen, James Weldon Johnson, MacKinlay Kantor, John D. MacDonald, Chief Osceola, Claude Pepper, Henry B. Plant, A. Philip Randolph, Marjorie Kinnan Rawlings, Janet Reno, Joseph W. Stilwell, Charles P. Summerall, Ben Vereen.

Tourist information. Visit Florida, P.O. Box 1100, Tallahassee, FL 32302-1100, 1-850-488-5607.

Toll-free number. 1-888-735-2872 (1-888-7FLA-USA)

Website. www.myflorida.com

Tourism website. www.flausa.com

Georgia

Empire State of the South, Peach State

People. Population (2001 est.): 8,383,915; rank: 10; **net change** (2000-2001): 2.4%. **Pop. density:** 144.8 per sq mi. **Racial distribution** (2000): 65.1% white; 28.7% black; 2.1% Asian; 0.3% Native American/Nat. AK; 0.1% Hawaiian/Pacific Islander; 2.4% other race; 2 or more races, 1.4%. **Hispanic pop.** (any race): 5.3% .

Geography. Total area: 59,425 sq mi; rank: 24. **Land area:** 57,906 sq mi; rank: 21. **Acres forested:** 24,137,000. **Location:** South Atlantic state. **Climate:** maritime tropical air masses dominate in summer; polar air masses in winter; E central area drier. **Topography:** most southerly of the Blue Ridge Mts. cover NE and N central; central Piedmont extends to the fall line of rivers; coastal plain levels to the coast flatlands. **Capital:** Atlanta.

Economy. Chief industries: services, manufacturing, retail trade. **Chief manuf. goods:** textiles, apparel, food, and kindred products, pulp & paper products. **Chief crops:** peanuts, cotton, corn, tobacco, hay, soybeans. **Livestock:** (Jan. 2002) 1.2 mil cattle/calves; (Dec. 2001) 310,000 hogs/pigs; 31.2 mil chickens (excl. broilers); 1.2 bil broilers. **Timber/lumber** (est. 2001): 2.8 bil bd. ft.; pine, hardwood; 3.2 bil bd. ft. **Nonfuel minerals** (est. 2001): 1.6 bil; crushed stone, portland cement, sand & gravel. **Commercial fishing** (2000): $21.7 mil. **Chief ports:** Savannah, Brunswick. **Principal internat. airports at:** Atlanta, Savannah. **Value of construction** (1997): $13.6 bil. **Gross state product** (2000): $296.1 bil. **Employment distrib.** (May 2002): 29.2% services; 24.3% trade; 15.8% govt.; 13.8% mfg. **Per cap. pers. income** (2001): $28,438. **Sales tax** (2002): 4%. **Unemployment** (2001): 4.0%. **Tourism expends.** (1999): $14.5 bil. **Lottery** (2001): total sales: $2.1 bil; net income: $691.7 mil.

Finance. FDIC-insured commercial banks (2001): 324. **Deposits:** $107.7 bil. **FDIC-insured savings institutions (2001):** 23. **Assets:** $8 bil.

Federal govt. Fed. civ. employees (Mar. 2001): 62,938. **Avg. salary:** $49,157. **Notable fed. facilities:** Dobbins AFB; Ft. Benning; Ft. Gordon; Ft. Gillem; Ft. Stewart; King's Bay Naval Base; Moody Air Force Base; Navy Supply Corps School; Ft. McPherson; Fed. Law Enforcement Training Ctr., Glynco, Robins AFB; Centers for Disease Control.

Energy. Electricity production (est. 2001, kWh, by source): Coal: 73.4 bil; Petroleum: 299 mil; Gas: 1.2 bil; Hydroelectric: 2.3 bil; Nuclear: 33.7 bil.

State data. Motto: Wisdom, justice and moderation. **Flower:** Cherokee rose. **Bird:** Brown thrasher. **Tree:** Live oak. **Song:** Georgia On My Mind. **Fourth** of the 13 original states to ratify the Constitution, Jan. 2, 1788. **State fair** at Macon, 3rd week in Oct.

History. Creek and Cherokee peoples were early inhabitants of the region. The earliest known European settlement was the Spanish mission of Santa Catalina, 1566, on Saint Catherines Island. Gen. James Oglethorpe established a colony at Savannah, 1733, for the poor and religiously persecuted. Oglethorpe defeated a Spanish army from Florida at Bloody Marsh, 1742. In the American Revolution, Georgians seized the Savannah armory, 1775, and sent the munitions to the Continental Army. They fought seesaw campaigns with Cornwallis's British troops, twice liberating Augusta and forcing final evacuation by the British from Savannah, 1782. The Cherokee were removed to Oklahoma Territory, 1832-38, and thousands died on the long march, known as the Trail of Tears. Georgia seceded from the Union, 1861, and was invaded by Union forces, 1864, under Gen. William T. Sherman, who took Atlanta, Sept. 2, and proceeded on his famous "march to the sea," ending in Dec., in Savannah. Georgia was readmitted, 1870.

Tourist attractions. State Capitol, Stone Mt. Park, Six Flags Over Georgia, Kennesaw Mt. Natl. Battlefield Park, Martin Luther King Jr. Natl. Historic Site, Underground Atlanta, Jimmy Carter Library & Museum, all Atlanta; Chickamauga and Chattanooga Natl. Military Park, near Dalton; Chattahoochee Natl. Forest; alpine village of Helen; Dahlonega, site of America's first gold rush; Brasstown Bald Mt.; Lake Lanier; Franklin D. Roosevelt's Little White House, Warm Springs; Callaway Gardens, Pine Mt.; Andersonville Natl. Historic Site; Okefenokee Swamp, near Waycross; Jekyll Island; St. Simons Island; Cumberland Island Natl. Seashore; historic riverfront district, Savannah.

Famous Georgians. Kim Basinger, Griffin Bell, James Bowie, James Brown, Erskine Caldwell, Jimmy Carter, Ray Charles, Lucius D. Clay, Ty Cobb, James Dickey, John C. Fremont, Newt Gingrich, Joel Chandler Harris, "Doc" Holliday, Alan Jackson, Martin Luther King Jr., Gladys Knight, Sidney Lanier, Little Richard, Juliette Gordon Low, Margaret Mitchell, Sam Nunn, Flannery O'Connor, Otis Redding, Burt Reynolds, Julia Roberts, Jackie Robinson, Clarence Thomas, Travis Tritt, Ted Turner, Carl Vinson, Alice Walker, Herschel Walker, Joseph Wheeler, Joanne Woodward, Trisha Yearwood, Andrew Young.

Chamber of Commerce. 235 International Blvd., Atlanta, GA 30303; (404) 880-9000.

Toll-free travel information. 1-800-VISITGA.

Website. www.georgia.gov

Tourism website. www.georgia.org/tourism

Hawai'i

Aloha State

People. Population (2001 est.): 1,224,398; rank: 42; **net change** (2000-2001): 1.1%. **Pop. density:** 190.6 per sq mi. **Racial distribution** (2000): 24.3% white; 1.8% black; 41.6% Asian; 0.3% Native American/Nat. AK; 9.4% Hawaiian/Pacific Islander; 1.3% other race; 2 or more races, 21.4%. **Hispanic pop.** (any race): 7.2%.

Geography. Total area: 10,931 sq mi; rank: 43. **Land area:** 6,423 sq mi; rank: 47. **Acres forested:** 1,748,000. **Location:** Hawaiian Islands lie in the North Pacific, 2,397 mi SW from San Francisco. **Climate:** subtropical, with wide variations in rainfall; Waialeale, on Kaua'i, wettest spot in U.S. (annual rainfall 460 in.) **Topography:** islands are tops of a chain of submerged volcanic mountains; active volcanoes: Mauna Loa, Kilauea. **Capital:** Honolulu.

Economy. Chief industries: tourism, defense, sugar, pineapples. **Chief manuf. goods:** processed sugar, canned pineapple, clothing, foods, printing & publishing. **Chief crops:** sugar, pineapples, macadamia nuts, fruits, coffee, vegetables, floriculture. **Livestock:** (Jan. 2002) 152,000 cattle/calves; (Dec. 2001) 27,000 hogs/pigs; 659,000 chickens (excl. broilers); 900,000 broilers. **Timber/Lumber** (est. 2001): NA; **Nonfuel minerals** (est. 2001): 69.7 mil; mostly crushed stone, portland and masonry cement, sand and gravel, gemstones. **Commercial fishing** (2000): $68.4 mil. **Chief ports:** Honolulu, Hilo, Kailua. **Principal internat. airports at:** Hilo, Honolulu, Kailua, Kahului. **Value of construction** (1997): $1.7 bil. **Gross state product** (2000): $42.4 bil. **Employment distrib.** (May 2002): 33.5% services; 23.9% trade; 22% govt.; 3.2% mfg. **Per cap. pers. income** (2001): $28,554. **Sales tax** (2002): 4%. **Unemployment** (2001): 4.6%. **Tourism expenditures** (1999): $14.2 bil.

Finance. FDIC-insured commercial banks (2001): 8. **Deposits:** $16.5 bil. **FDIC-insured savings institutions (2001):** 2. **Assets:** $6.6 bil.

Federal govt. Fed. civ. employees (Mar. 2001): 19,557. **Avg. salary:** $47,077. **Notable fed. facilities:** Pearl Harbor Naval Shipyard; Hickam AFB; Schofield Barracks; Ft. Shafter; Marine Corps Base-Kaneohe Bay; Barbers Point NAS; Wheeler AFB; Prince Kuhio Federal Building.

Energy. Electricity production (est. 2001, kWh, by source): Petroleum: 6.4 bil; Hydroelectric: 18 mil; Other: 2 mil.

State data. Motto: The life of the land is perpetuated in righteousness. **Flower:** Yellow hibiscus. **Bird:** Hawaiian goose. **Tree:** Kukui (Candlenut). **Song:** Hawai'i Pono'i. **Entered union** Aug. 21, 1959; rank, 50th. **State fair:** at O'ahu, late June.

History. Polynesians from islands 2,000 mi to the south settled the Hawaiian Islands, probably between AD 300 and AD 600. The first European visitor was British captain James Cook, 1778. Between 1790 and 1810, the islands were united politically under the leadership of a native king, Kamehameha I, whose four successors—all bearing the name Kamehameha—ruled the kingdom from his death, 1819, until the end of the dynasty, 1872. Missionaries arrived, 1820, bringing Western culture. King Kamehameha III and his chiefs created the first constitution and a legislature that set up a public school system. Sugar production began, 1835, and it became the dominant industry. In 1893, Queen Liliuokalani was deposed, and a republic was instituted, 1894, headed by Sanford B. Dole. Annexation by the U.S. came in 1898. The Japanese attack on Pearl Harbor, Dec. 7, 1941, brought the U.S. into World War II.

Tourist attractions. Hawaii Volcanoes, Haleakala natl. parks; Natl. Memorial Cemetery of the Pacific, Waikiki Beach, Diamond Head, Honolulu; U.S.S. *Arizona* Memorial, Pearl Harbor; Hanauma Bay; Polynesian Cultural Center, Laie; Nu'uanu Pali; Waimea Canyon; Wailoa and Wailuku River state parks.

Famous Islanders. Bernice Pauahi Bishop, Tia Carrere, Father Damien de Veuster, Don Ho, Duke Kahanamoku, King Kamehameha, Brook Mahealani Lee, Daniel K. Inouye, Jason Scott Lee, Queen Liliuokalani, Bette Midler, Ellison Onizuka.

Chamber of Commerce of Hawaii. 1132 Bishop St., Suite 200, Honolulu, HI 96813; phone: (808) 545-4300.

Toll-free travel information. 1-800-GOHAWAII.

Website. www.hawaii.gov

Tourism website. www.gohawaii.com

Idaho

Gem State

People. Population (2001 est.): 1,321,006; rank: 39; **net change** (2000-2001): 2.1%. **Pop. density:** 16 per sq mi. **Racial distribution** (2000): 91.0% white; 0.4% black; 0.9% Asian; 1.4% Native American/Nat. AK; 0.1% Hawaiian/Pacific Islander; 4.2% other race; 2 or more races, 2.0%. **Hispanic pop.** (any race): 7.9%.

Geography. Total area: 83,570 sq mi; rank: 14. **Land area:** 82,747 sq mi; rank: 11. **Acres forested:** 21,621,000. **Location:** northwestern Mountain state bordering on British Columbia. **Climate:** tempered by Pacific westerly winds; drier, colder, continental climate in SE; altitude an important factor. **Topography:** Snake R. plains in the S; central region of mountains, canyons, gorges (Hells Canyon, 7,900 ft, deepest in N. America); subalpine northern region. **Capital:** Boise.

Economy. Chief industries: manufacturing, agriculture, tourism, lumber, mining, electronics. **Chief manuf. goods:** electronic components, computer equipment, processed foods, lumber and wood products, chemical products, primary metals, fabricated metal products, machinery. **Chief crops:** potatoes, peas, dry beans, sugar beets, alfalfa seed, lentils, wheat, hops, barley, plums and prunes, mint, onions, corn, cherries, apples, hay. **Livestock:** (Jan. 2002) 2 mil cattle/calves; 260,000 sheep/lambs; (Dec. 2001) 24,000 hogs/pigs; 1.2 mil chickens (excl. broilers). **Timber/lumber** (est. 2001): 1.7 bil bd. ft.; **Nonfuel minerals** (est. 2001): 344 mil; mostly phosphate rock, silver, sand & gravel, molybdenum, lead. **Chief port:** Lewiston. **Value of construction** (1997) $1.8 bil. **Gross state product** (2000): $37 bil. **Employment distrib.** (May 2002): 26.9% services; 24.5% trade; 20.4% govt.; 12.3% mfg. **Per cap. pers. income** (2001): $24,257. **Sales tax** (2002): 5%. **Unemployment** (2001): 5.0%. **Tourism expenditures** (1999): $2.1 bil. **Lottery** (2001): total sales: $81.7 mil; net income: $18 mil.

Finance. FDIC-insured commercial banks (2001): 17. **Deposits:** $2.4 bil. **FDIC-insured savings institutions** (2001): 3. **Assets:** $808 mil.

Federal govt. Fed. civ. employees (Mar. 2001): 7,490. **Avg. salary:** $47,785. **Notable fed. facilities:** Idaho Natl. Engineering Lab; Mt. Home Air Force Base.

Energy. Electricity production (est. 2001, kWh, by source): Petroleum: 4 mil; Hydroelectric: 6.7 bil.

State data. Motto: Esto Perpetua (It is perpetual). **Flower:** Syringa. **Bird:** Mountain bluebird. **Tree:** White pine. **Song:** Here We Have Idaho. **Entered union** July 3, 1890; rank, 43rd. **State fair** at Boise, late Aug.; at Blackfoot, early Sept.

History. Early inhabitants were Shoshone, Northern Paiute, Bannock, and Nez Percé peoples. White exploration of the region began with Lewis and Clark, 1805-6. Next came fur traders, setting up posts, 1809-34, and missionaries, 1830s-50s. Mormons made their first permanent settlement at Franklin, 1860. Idaho's gold rush began the same year and brought thousands of permanent settlers. Most remarkable of the Indian wars was the 1,700-mi trek, 1877, of Chief Joseph and the Nez Percé, pursued by U.S. troops through 3 states and caught just short of the Canadian border. The Idaho territory was organized, 1863. Idaho adopted a progressive constitution and became a state, 1890.

Tourist attractions. Hells Canyon, deepest gorge in N. America; World Center for Birds of Prey; Craters of the Moon; Sun Valley, in Sawtooth Mts.; Crystal Falls Cave; Shoshone Falls; Lava Hot Springs; Lake Pend Oreille; Lake Coeur d'Alene; Sawtooth Natl. Recreation Area; River of No Return Wilderness Area; Redfish Lake.

Famous Idahoans. William E. Borah, Frank Church, Fred T. Dubois, Chief Joseph, Ezra Pound, Sacagawea, Picabo Street, Lana Turner.

Tourist information. Department of Commerce, 700 W. State St., Boise, ID 83720.

Toll-free travel information. 1-800-842-5858.

Website. www.state.id.us

Tourism website. www.visitid.org

Illinois

Prairie State

People. Population (2001 est.): 12,482,301; rank: 5; **net change** (2000-2001): 0.5%. **Pop. density:** 224.6 per sq mi. **Racial distribution** (2000): 73.5% white; 15.1% black; 3.4% Asian; 0.2% Native American/Nat. AK; <0.1% Hawaiian/Pacific Islander; 5.8% other race; 2 or more races, 1.9%. **Hispanic pop.** (any race): 12.3%.

Geography. Total area: 57,914 sq mi; rank: 25. **Land area:** 55,584 sq mi; rank: 24. **Acres forested:** 4,266,000. **Location:** East North Central state; western, southern, and eastern boundaries formed by Mississippi, Ohio, and Wabash rivers, respectively. **Climate:** temperate; typically cold, snowy winters, hot summers. **Topography:** prairie and fertile plains throughout; open hills in the southern region. **Capital:** Springfield.

Economy. Chief industries: services, manufacturing, travel, wholesale and retail trade, finance, insurance, real estate, construction, health care, agriculture. **Chief manuf. goods:** machinery, electric and electronic equipment, prim. & fabric. metals, chemical products, printing & publishing, food and kindred products. **Chief crops:** corn, soybeans, wheat, sorghum, hay. **Livestock**: (Jan. 2002) 1.4 mil cattle/calves; 70,000 sheep/lambs; (Dec. 2001) 4.3 mil hogs/pigs; 4.1 mil chickens (excl. broilers). **Timber/lumber** (est. 2001): 128 mil bd. ft.; oak, hickory, maple, cottonwood. **Nonfuel minerals** (est. 2001): 911 mil; ; mostly crushed stone, portland cement, sand & gravel, lime. **Commercial fishing** (2000): $35,166. **Chief ports:** Chicago. **Principal internat. airport at:** Chicago. **Value of construction** (1997): $12.5 bil. **Gross state product** (2000): $467.3 bil. **Employment distrib.** (May 2002): 31% services; 22.6% trade; 14.4% govt.; 14.9% mfg. **Per cap. pers. income** (2001): $32,755. **Sales tax** (2002): 6.25%. **Unemployment** (2001): 5.4%. **Tourism expends.** (1999): $22.1 bil. **Lottery** (2001): total sales: $1.4 bil; net income: $511.3 mil.

Finance. FDIC-insured commercial banks (2001): 692. **Deposits:** $296.4 bil. **FDIC-insured savings institutions (2001):** 114. **Assets:** $40.4 bil.

Federal govt. Fed. civ. employees (Mar. 2001): 39,996. **Avg. salary:** $55,284. **Notable fed. facilities:** Fermi Natl. Accelerator Lab; Argonne Natl. Lab; Rock Island Arsenal; Great Lakes, Naval Training Station, Scott AFB.

Energy. Electricity production (est. 2001, kWh, by source): Coal: 29.1 bil; Petroleum: 113 mil; Gas: 608 mil; Hydroelectric: 59 mil; Other: 8 mil.

State data. Motto: State sovereignty—national union. **Flower:** Native violet. **Bird:** Cardinal. **Tree:** White oak. **Song:** Illinois. **Entered union** Dec. 3, 1818; rank, 21st. **State fair** at Springfield, mid-Aug.; DuQuoin, late Aug.

History. Seminomadic Algonquian peoples, including the Peoria, Illinois, Kaskaskia, and Tamaroa, lived in the region at the time of European contact. Fur traders were the first Europeans in Illinois, followed shortly by Jolliet and Marquette, 1673, and La Salle, 1680, who built a fort near present-day Peoria. The first settlements were French, at Cahokia, near present-day St. Louis, 1699, and Kaskaskia, 1703. France ceded the area to Britain, 1763, and in 1778, American Gen. George Rogers Clark took Kaskaskia from the British without a shot. Defeat of Native American tribes in the Black Hawk War, 1832, and growth of railroads brought change to the area. In 1787, it became part of the Northwest Territory. Post-Civil War Illinois became a center for the labor movement as bitter strikes, such as the Haymarket Square riot, occurred in 1885-86.

Tourist attractions. Chicago museums and parks; Lincoln shrines at Springfield, New Salem, Sangamon County; Cahokia Mounds, Collinsville; Starved Rock State Park; Crab Orchard Wildlife Refuge; Mormon settlement at Nauvoo; Fts. Kaskaskia, Chartres, Massac (parks); Shawnee Natl. Forest, Southern Illinois; Illinois State Museum, Springfield; Dickson Mounds Museum, between Havana and Lewistown.

Famous Illinoisans. Jane Addams, John Ashcroft, Saul Bellow, Jack Benny, Ray Bradbury, Gwendolyn Brooks, William Jennings Bryan, St. Frances Xavier Cabrini, Hillary Rodham Clinton, Clarence Darrow, John Deere, Stephen A. Douglas, James T. Farrell, George W. Ferris, Marshall Field, Betty Friedan, Benny Goodman, Ulysses S. Grant, Dennis Hastert, Ernest Hemingway, Charlton Heston, Wild Bill Hickok, Henry J. Hyde, Abraham Lincoln, Vachel Lindsay, Edgar Lee Masters, Oscar Mayer, Cyrus McCormick, Ronald Reagan, Donald Rumsfeld, Carl Sandburg, Adlai Stevenson, Frank Lloyd Wright, Philip Wrigley.

Tourist information. Illinois Dept. of Commerce and Community Affairs, 620 E. Adams St., Springfield, IL 62701.

Toll-free travel information: 1-800-2-CONNECT.

Website. www.state.il.us

Tourism website. www.enjoyillinois.com

Indiana

Hoosier State

People. Population (2001 est.): 6,114,745; rank: 14; **net change** (2000-2001): 0.6%. **Pop. density:** 170.5 per sq mi. **Racial distribution** (2000): 87.5% white; 8.4% black; 1.0% Asian; 0.3% Native American/Nat. AK; <0.1% Hawaiian/Pacific Islander; 1.6% other race; 2 or more races, 1.2%. **Hispanic pop.** (any race): 3.5%.

Geography. Total area: 36,418 sq mi; rank: 38. **Land area:** 35,867 sq mi; rank: 38. **Acres forested:** 4,439,000. **Location:** East North Central state; Lake Michigan on N border. **Climate:** 4 distinct seasons with a temperate climate. **Topography:** hilly southern region; fertile rolling plains of central region; flat, heavily glaciated north; dunes along Lake Michigan shore. **Capital:** Indianapolis.

Economy: Chief industries: manufacturing, services, agriculture, government, wholesale and retail trade, transportation and public utilities. **Chief manuf. goods:** primary metals, transportation equipment, motor vehicles & equip., industrial machinery & equipment, electronic & electric equipment. **Chief crops:** corn, soybeans, wheat, nursery and greenhouse products, vegetables, popcorn, fruit, hay, tobacco, mint. **Livestock:** (Jan. 2002) 880,000 cattle/calves; 57,000 sheep/lambs; (Dec. 2001) 3.2 mil hogs/pigs; 29 mil chickens (excl. broilers). **Timber/lumber** (est. 2001): 330 mil bd. ft.; oak, tulip, beech, sycamore. **Nonfuel minerals** (est. 2001): 718 mil; mostly crushed stone, portland and masonry cement, sand & gravel, lime. **Commercial fishing** (1997): $327,000. **Chief ports:** Burns Harbor, Portage; Southwind Maritime, Mt. Vernon; Clark Maritime, Jeffersonville. **Principal internat. airports at:** Indianapolis, Ft. Wayne. **Value of construction**

(1997): $9.2 bil. **Gross state product** (2000): $192.2 bil. **Employment distrib.** (May 2002): 25.9% services; 23.5% trade; 14.6% govt.; 21.2% mfg. **Per cap. pers. income** (2001): $27,532. **Sales tax** (2002): 5%. **Unemployment** (2001): 4.4%. **Tourism expends.** (1999): $6.1 bil. **Lottery** (2001): total sales: $548.3 mil; net income: $155.6 mil.

Finance. FDIC-insured commercial banks (2001): 154. **Deposits:** $67.5 bil. **FDIC-insured savings institutions** (2001): 63. **Assets:** $14.1 bil.

Federal govt. Fed. civ. employees (Mar. 2001): 19,495. **Avg. salary:** $47,765. **Notable fed. facilities:** Naval Air Warfare Center; Ft. Benjamin Harrison; Del. Grissom AFB; Naval Surface Warfare Center.

Energy. Electricity production (est. 2001, kWh, by source): Coal: 113 bil; Petroleum: 371 mil; Gas: 589 mil; Hydroelectric: 571 mil.

State data. Motto: Crossroads of America. **Flower:** Peony. **Bird:** Cardinal. **Tree:** Tulip poplar. **Song:** On the Banks of the Wabash, Far Away. **Entered union** Dec. 11, 1816; rank, 19th. **State fair** at Indianapolis; mid-Aug.

History. When the Europeans arrived, Miami, Potawatomi, Kickapoo, Piankashaw, Wea, and Shawnee peoples inhabited the area. A French trading post was built, 1731-32, at Vincennes. La Salle visited the present South Bend area, 1679 and 1681. The first French fort was built near present-day Lafayette, 1717. France ceded the area to Britain, 1763. During the American Revolution, American Gen. George Rogers Clark captured Vincennes, 1778, and defeated British forces, 1779. At war's end, Britain ceded the area to the U.S. Miami Indians defeated U.S. troops twice, 1790, but were beaten, 1794, at Fallen Timbers by Gen. Anthony Wayne. At Tippecanoe, 1811, Gen. William H. Harrison defeated Tecumseh's Indian confederation. The Delaware, Potawatomi, and Miami were moved farther west, 1820-1850.

Tourist attractions. Lincoln Log Cabin Historic Site, near Charleston; George Rogers Clark Park, Vincennes; Wyandotte Cave; Tippecanoe Battlefield Memorial Park; Benjamin Harrison home; Indianapolis 500 raceway and museum, all Indianapolis; Indiana Dunes, near Chesterton; National College Football Hall of Fame, South Bend; Hoosier Nat'l. Forest, south-central Indiana.

Famous "Hoosiers." Larry Bird, Ambrose Burnside, Hoagy Carmichael, Jim Davis, James Dean, Eugene V. Debs, Theodore Dreiser, Paul Dresser, Jeff Gordon, Benjamin Harrison, Gil Hodges, Michael Jackson, David Letterman, John Mellencamp, Jane Pauley, Cole Porter, Gene Stratton Porter, Ernie Pyle, Dan Quayle, James Whitcomb Riley, Oscar Robertson, Red Skelton, Booth Tarkington, Kurt Vonnegut, Lew Wallace, Wendell L. Willkie, Wilbur Wright.

Chamber of Commerce. One North Capital, Suite 200, Indianapolis, IN 46204.

Toll-free travel information. 1-888-ENJOYIN.

Website. www.ai.org

Tourism website. www.in.gov/enjoyindiana

Iowa

Hawkeye State

People. Population (2001 est.): 2,923,179; rank: 30; **net change** (2000-2001): -0.1%. **Pop. density:** 52.3 per sq mi. **Racial distribution** (2000): 93.9% white; 2.1% black; 1.3% Asian; 0.3% Native American/Nat. AK; <0.1% Hawaiian/Pacific Islander; 1.3% other race; 2 or more races, 1.1%. **Hispanic pop.** (any race): 2.8%.

Geography. Total area: 56,272 sq mi; rank: 26. **Land area:** 55,869 sq mi; rank: 23. **Acres forested:** 2,050,000. **Location:** West North Central state bordered by Mississippi R. on the E and Missouri R. on the W. **Climate:** humid, continental. **Topography:** Watershed from NW to SE; soil especially rich and land level in the N central counties. **Capital:** Des Moines.

Economy. Chief industries: agriculture, communications, construction, finance, insurance, trade, services, manufacturing. **Chief manuf. goods:** processed food products, tires, farm machinery, electronic products, appliances, household furniture, chemicals, fertilizers, auto accessories. **Chief crops:** silage and grain corn, soybeans, oats, hay. **Livestock:** (Jan. 2002) 3.6 mil cattle/calves; 250,000 sheep/lambs; (Dec. 2001) 15 mil hogs/pigs; 41.8 mil chickens (excl. broilers). **Timber/lumber** (est. 2001): 81 mil bd. ft.; red cedar. **Nonfuel minerals** (est. 2001): 487 mil; mostly crushed stone, portland cement, sand & gravel, gypsum, lime. **Principal internat. airport at:** Des Moines. **Value of construction** (1997): $3.2 bil. **Gross state product** (2000): $89.6 bil. **Employment distrib.** (May 2002): 26.9% services; 23.6% trade; 17.1% govt.; 16.7% mfg. **Per cap. pers. income** (2001): $27,283. **Sales tax** (2002): 5%. **Unemployment** (2001): 3.3%. **Tourism expends.** (1999): $4.2 bil. **Lottery** (2001): total sales: $174.9 mil; net income: $44.3 mil.

Finance. FDIC-insured commercial banks (2001): 417. **Deposits:** $37.9 bil. **FDIC-insured savings institutions** (2001): 24. **Assets:** $4.9 bil.

Federal govt. Fed. civ. employees (Mar. 2001): 6,992. **Avg. salary:** $46,500

Energy. Electricity production (est. 2001, kWh, by source): Coal: 34 bil; Petroleum: 92 mil; Gas: 454 mil; Hydroelectric: 830 mil; Nuclear: 3.9 bil; Other: 45 mil.

State data. Motto: Our liberties we prize, and our rights we will maintain. **Flower:** Wild rose. **Bird:** Eastern goldfinch. **Tree:** Oak. **Rock:** Geode. **Entered union** Dec. 28, 1846; rank, 29th. **State fair** at Des Moines; mid-Aug.

History. Early inhabitants were Mound Builders who dwelt on Iowa's fertile plains. Later, Woodland tribes including the Iowa and Yankton Sioux lived in the area. The first Europeans, Marquette and Jolliet, gave France its claim to the area, 1673. In 1762, France ceded the region to Spain, but Napoleon took it back, 1800. It became part of the U.S. through the Louisiana Purchase, 1803. Native American Sauk and Fox tribes moved into the area from states farther east but relinquished their land in defeat, after the 1832 uprising led by the Sauk chieftain Black Hawk. By mid-19th cent. they were forced to move on to Kansas. Iowa became a territory in 1838, and entered as a free state, 1846, strongly supporting the Union.

Tourist attractions. Herbert Hoover birthplace and library, West Branch; Effigy Mounds Natl. Monument, prehistoric Indian burial site, Marquette; Amana Colonies; Grant Wood's paintings and memorabilia, Davenport Municipal Art Gallery; Living History Farms, Des Moines; Adventureland, Altoona; Boone & Scenic Valley Railroad, Boone; Greyhound Parks, in Dubuque and Council Bluffs; Prairie Meadows horse racing, Altoona; riverboat cruises and casino gambling, Mississippi and Missouri Rivers; Iowa Great Lakes, Okoboji.

Famous Iowans. Tom Arnold, Johnny Carson, Marquis Childs, Buffalo Bill Cody, Mamie Dowd Eisenhower, Bob Feller, George Gallup, Susan Glaspell, James Norman Hall, Harry Hansen, Herbert Hoover, Ann Landers, Glenn Miller, Lillian Russell, Billy Sunday, James A. Van Allen, Abigail Van Buren, Carl Van Vechten, Henry Wallace, John Wayne, Meredith Willson, Grant Wood.

Tourist information. Division of Tourism, Iowa Dept. of Economic Development, 200 E. Grand Ave., Des Moines, IA 50309.

Toll-free travel information. 1-800-476-6035

Website. www.state.ia.us

Tourism website. www.traveliowa.com

Kansas

Sunflower State

People. Population (2001 est.): 2,694,641; rank: 32; **net change** (2000-2001): 0.2%. **Pop. density:** 32.9 per sq mi. **Racial distribution** (2000): 86.1% white; 5.7% black; 1.7% Asian; 0.9% Native American/Nat. AK; 0.1% Hawaiian/Pacific Islander; 3.4% other race; 2 or more races, 2.1%. **Hispanic pop.** (any race): 7.0%.

Geography. Total area: 82,277 sq mi; rank: 15. **Land area:** 81,815 sq mi; rank: 13. **Acres forested:** 1,359,000. **Location:** West North Central state, with Missouri R. on E. **Climate:** temperate but continental, with great extremes between summer and winter. **Topography:** hilly Osage Plains in the E; central region level prairie and hills; high plains in the W. **Capital:** Topeka.

Economy. Chief industries: manufacturing, finance, insurance, real estate, services. **Chief manuf. goods:** transportation equipment, machinery & computer equipment, food and kindred products, printing & publishing. **Chief crops:** wheat, sorghum, corn, hay, soybeans, sunflowers. **Livestock:** (Jan. 2002) 6.6 mil cattle/calves; 100,000 sheep/lambs; (Dec. 2001) 1.6 mil hogs/pigs; 2.1 mil chickens (excl. broilers). **Timber/lumber:** (est. 2001): 13 mil bd. ft.; oak, walnut; 14 mil bd. ft. **Nonfuel minerals** (est. 2001): 640 mil; mostly portland cement, salt, crushed stone, helium, sand & gravel. **Chief ports:** Kansas City. **Principal internat. airport at:** Kansas City. **Value of construction** (1997): $3.8 bil. **Gross state product** (2000): $85.1 bil. **Employment distrib.** (May 2002): 26.8% services; 23% trade; 18.8% govt.; 14.6% mfg. **Per cap. pers. income** (2001): $28,507. **Sales tax** (2002): 4.9%. **Unemployment** (2001): 4.3%. **Tourism expends.** (1999): $3.4 bil. **Lottery** (2001): total sales: $184.7 mil; net income: $55.8 mil.

Finance. FDIC-insured commercial banks (2001): 373. **Deposits:** $29.4 bil. **FDIC-insured savings institutions** (2001): 17. **Assets:** $11.9 bil.

Federal govt. Fed. civ. employees (Mar. 2001): 14,761. **Avg. salary:** $47,655. **Notable fed. facilities:** Fts. Riley, Leavenworth; Leavenworth Federal Penitentiary; Colmery-O'Neal Veterans Hospital.

Energy. Electricity production (est. 2001, kWh, by source): Coal: 31.7 bil; Petroleum: 628 mil; Gas: 2 mil; Nuclear: 10.3 bil.

State data. Motto: Ad Astra per Aspera (To the stars through difficulties). **Flower:** Native sunflower. **Bird:** Western meadowlark. **Tree:** Cottonwood. **Song:** Home on the Range. **Entered union** Jan. 29, 1861; rank, 34th. **State fair** at Hutchinson; begins Friday after Labor Day.

History. When Coronado first explored the area, Wichita, Pawnee, Kansa, and Osage peoples lived there. These Native Americans—hunters who also farmed—were joined on the Plains by the nomadic Cheyenne, Arapaho, Comanche, and Kiowa about 1800. French explorers established trading between 1682 and 1739, and the U.S. took over most of the area in the Louisiana Purchase, 1803. After 1830, thousands of eastern Native Americans were removed to Kansas. Kansas became a territory, 1854. Violent incidents between pro- and antislavery settlers caused the territory to be known as "Bleeding Kansas." It eventually entered the Union as a free state, 1861. Railroad construction after the war made Abilene and Dodge City terminals of large cattle drives from Texas.

Tourist attractions. Eisenhower Center, Abilene; Agricultural Hall of Fame and Natl. Center, Bonner Springs; Dodge City-Boot Hill & Frontier Town; Old Cowtown Museum, Wichita; Ft. Scott and Ft. Larned, restored 1800s cavalry forts; Kansas Cosmosphere and Space Center, Hutchinson; Woodlands Racetrack, Kansas City; U.S. Cavalry Museum, Ft. Riley; NCAA Visitors Center, Shawnee; Heartland Park Raceway, Topeka.

Famous Kansans. Kirstie Alley, Roscoe "Fatty" Arbuckle, Ed Asner, Gwendolyn Brooks, John Brown, George Washington Carver, Wilt Chamberlain, Walter P. Chrysler, Glenn Cunningham, John Stuart Curry, Robert Dole, Amelia Earhart, Wyatt Earp, Dwight D. Eisenhower, Ron Evans, Maurice Greene, Wild Bill Hickok, Cyrus Holliday, Dennis Hopper, William Inge, Don Johnson, Walter Johnson, Nancy Landon Kassebaum, Buster Keaton, Emmett Kelly, Alf Landon, Edgar Lee Masters, Hattie McDaniel, Oscar Micheaux, Carry Nation, Georgia Neese-Gray, Charlie Parker, Gordon Parks, Jim Ryun, Barry Sanders, Vivian Vance, William Allen White, Jess Willard.

Tourist information. Kansas Dept. of Commerce & Housing, Travel and Tourism Div., 700 SW Harrison, Suite 1300, Topeka, KS 66601; 1-913-296-2009.

Toll-free travel information. 1-800-2KANSAS.

Website. www.accesskansas.org

Tourism website. www.travelks.com

Kentucky

Bluegrass State

People. Population (2001 est.): 4,065,556; rank: 25; **net change** (2000-2001): 0.6%. **Pop. density:** 102.3 per sq mi. **Racial distribution** (2000): 90.1% white; 7.3% black; 0.7% Asian; 0.2% Native American/Nat. AK; <0.1% Hawaiian/Pacific Islander; 0.6% other race; 2 or more races, 1.1%. **Hispanic pop.** (any race): 1.5%.

Geography. Total area: 40,409 sq mi; rank: 37. **Land area:** 39,728 sq mi; rank: 36. **Acres forested:** 12,714,000. **Location:** East South Central state, bordered on N by Illinois, Indiana, Ohio; on E by West Virginia and Virginia; on S by Tennessee; on W by Missouri. **Climate:** moderate, with plentiful rainfall. **Topography:** mountainous in E; rounded hills of the Knobs in the N; Bluegrass, heart of state; wooded rocky hillsides of the Pennyroyal; Western Coal Field; the fertile Purchase in the SW. **Capital:** Frankfort.

Economy. Chief industries: manufacturing, services, finance, insurance and real estate, retail trade, public utilities. **Chief manuf. goods:** transportation & industrial machinery, apparel, printing & publishing, food products, electric & electronic equipment. **Chief crops:** tobacco, corn, soybeans. **Livestock:** (Jan. 2002) 2.3 mil cattle/calves; (Dec. 2001) 405,000 hogs/pigs; 5.6 mil chickens (excl. broilers); 208.2 mil broilers. **Timber/lumber** (est. 2001): 722 mil bd. ft.; hardwoods, pines. **Nonfuel minerals** (est. 2001): 531 mil; mostly crushed stone, lime, portland cement, sand & gravel, clays. **Chief ports:** Paducah, Louisville, Covington, Owensboro, Ashland, Henderson County, Lyon County, Hickman-Fulton County. **Principal internat. airports at:** Covington/Cincinnati, Louisville. **Value of construction** (1997): $4.8 bil. **Gross state product** (2000): $118.5 bil. **Employment distrib.** (May 2002): 27.1% services; 23.4% trade; 17.3% govt.; 16.3% mfg. **Per cap. pers. income** (2001): $25,057. **Sales tax** (2002): 6%. **Unemployment** (2001): 5.5%. **Tourism expends. (1999):** $5.1 bil. **Lottery** (2001): total sales: $590.9 mil; net income: $159.2 mil.

Finance. FDIC-insured commercial banks (2001): 230. **Deposits:** $42.3 bil. **FDIC-insured savings institutions** (2001): 28. **Assets:** $2.9 bil.

Federal govt. Fed. civ. employees (Mar. 2001): 19,264. **Avg. Salary:** $43,102. **Notable fed. facilities:** U.S. Gold Bullion Depository, Fort Knox; Federal Correctional Institution, Lexington.

Energy. Electricity production (est. 2001, kWh, by source): Coal: 79.4 bil; Petroleum: 120 mil; Gas: 321 mil; Hydroelectric: 3.9 bil.

State data. Motto: United we stand, divided we fall. **Flower:** Goldenrod. **Bird:** Cardinal. **Tree:** Tulip Poplar. **Song:** My Old Kentucky Home. **Entered union** June 1, 1792; rank, 15th. **State fair** at Louisville, late Aug.

History. The area was predominantly hunting grounds for Shawnee, Wyandot, Delaware, and Cherokee peoples. Explored by Americans Thomas Walker and Christopher Gist, 1750-51, Kentucky was the first area west of the Alleghenies settled by American pioneers. The first permanent settlement was Harrodsburg, 1774. Daniel Boone blazed the Wilderness Trail through the Cumberland Gap and founded Ft. Boonesborough, 1775. Conflicts with Native Americans, spurred by the British, were unceasing until, during the American Revolution, Gen. George Rogers Clark captured British forts in Indiana and Illinois, 1778. In 1792, Virginia dropped its claims to the region, and it became the 15th state. Although officially a Union state, Kentuckians had divided loyalties during the Civil War and were forced to choose sides; its slaves were freed only after the adoption of the 13th Amendment to the U.S. Constitution, 1865.

Tourist attractions. Kentucky Derby; Louisville; Land Between the Lakes Natl. Recreation Area, Kentucky Lake and Lake Barkley; Mammoth Cave Natl. Park; Echo River, 360 ft below ground; Lake Cumberland; Lincoln's birthplace, Hodgenville; My Old Kentucky Home State Park, Bardstown; Cumberland Gap Natl. Historical Park, Middlesboro; Kentucky Horse Park, Lexington; Shaker Village, Pleasant Hill.

Famous Kentuckians. Muhammad Ali, John James Audubon, Alben W. Barkley, Daniel Boone, Louis D. Brandeis, John C. Breckinridge, Kit Carson, Albert B. "Happy" Chandler, Henry Clay, Jefferson Davis, D. W. Griffith, "Casey" Jones, Abraham Lincoln, Mary Todd Lincoln, Thomas Hunt Morgan, Carry Nation, Col. Harland Sanders, Diane Sawyer, Adlai Stevenson, Jesse Stuart, Zachary Taylor, Hunter S. Thompson, Robert Penn Warren, Whitney Young Jr.

Tourist Information. Kentucky Dept. of Travel, 500 Mero St., #2200, Frankfort, KY 40601.

Toll-free travel information. 1-800-225-TRIP.

Website. www.kydirect.net

Tourism website. www.kentuckytourism.com

Louisiana

Pelican State

People. Population (2001 est.): 4,465,430; rank: 22; **net change** (2000-2001): -0.1%. **Pop. density:** 102.5 per sq mi. **Racial distribution** (2000): 63.9% white; 32.5% black; 1.2% Asian; 0.6% Native American/Nat. AK; <0.1% Hawaiian/Pacific Islander; 0.7% other race; 2 or more races, 1.1%. **Hispanic pop.** (any race): 2.4%.

Geography. Total area: 51,840 sq mi; rank: 31. **Land area:** 43,562 sq mi; rank: 33. **Acres forested:** 13,864,000. **Location:** West South Central state on the Gulf Coast. **Climate:** subtropical, affected by continental weather patterns. **Topography:** lowlands of marshes and Mississippi R. flood plain; Red R. Valley lowlands; upland hills in the Florida Parishes; average elevation, 100 ft. **Capital:** Baton Rouge.

Economy. Chief industries: wholesale and retail trade, tourism, manufacturing, construction, transportation, communication, public utilities, finance, insurance, real estate, mining. **Chief manuf. goods:** chemical products, foods, transportation equipment, electronic equipment, petroleum products, lumber, wood, and paper. **Chief crops:** soybeans, sugarcane, rice, corn, cotton, sweet potatoes, pecans, sorghum, aquaculture. **Livestock:** (Jan. 2002) 850,000 cattle/calves; (Dec. 2001) 26,000 hogs/pigs; 2.7 mil chickens (excl. broilers). **Timber/lumber** (est. 2001): 1.3 bil bd. ft.; pines, hardwoods, oak. **Nonfuel minerals** (est. 2001): 274 mil; mostly salt, sulfur, sand & gravel, crushed stone, clays. **Commercial fishing** (2000): $418.9 mil. **Chief ports:** New Orleans, Baton Rouge, Lake Charles, Port of S. Louisiana (La Place), Shreveport, Plaquemine, St. Bernard, Alexandria. **Principal internat. airport at:** New Orleans. **Value of construction** (1997): $4.7 bil. **Gross state product** (2000): $137.7 bil. **Employment distrib.** (May 2002): 28.2% services; 23.4% trade; 19.7% govt.; 9.2% mfg. **Per cap. pers. income** (2001): $24,084. **Sales tax** (2002): 4%. **Unemployment** (2001): 6.0%. **Tourism expends.** (1999): $8.1 bil. **Lottery** (2001): total sales: $284.5 mil; net income: $104 mil.

Finance. FDIC-insured commercial banks (2001): 143. **Deposits:** $35 bil. **FDIC-insured savings institutions** (2001): 32. **Assets:** $4.7 bil.

Federal govt. Fed. civ. employees (Mar. 2001): 19,843. **Avg. salary:** $46,732. **Notable federal facilities:** Strategic Petroleum Reserve, Michoud Assembly Plant, Southeast U.S. Agricultural Research Ctr., U.S. Army Corps of Engineers, all New Orleans; Ft. Polk military bases, Barksdale; U.S. Public Service Hospital, Carville; Naval Air Station, Chalmette; V.A. Hospital, Pineville.

Energy. Electricity production (est. 2001, kWh, by source): Coal: 10.9 bil; Petroleum: 1.8 bil; Gas: 20.4 bil; Nuclear: 17.3 bil.

State data. Motto: Union, justice, and confidence. **Flower:** Magnolia. **Bird:** Eastern brown pelican. **Tree:** Cypress. **Song:** Give Me Louisiana. **Entered union** Apr. 30, 1812; rank, 18th. **State fair** at Shreveport; Oct.

History. Caddo, Tunica, Choctaw, Chitimacha, and Chawash peoples lived in the region at the time of European contact. Europeans Cabeza de Vaca and Panfilo de Narvaez first visited, 1530. The region was claimed for France by La Salle, 1682. The first permanent settlement was by the French at Biloxi, now in Mississippi, 1699. France ceded the region to Spain, 1762, took it back, 1800, and sold it to the U.S., 1803, in the Louisiana Purchase. During the American Revolution, Spanish Louisiana aided the Americans. Admitted as a state in 1812, Louisiana was the scene of the Battle of New Orleans, 1815.

Louisiana Creoles are descendants of early French and/or Spanish settlers. About 4,000 Acadians, French settlers in Nova Scotia, Canada, were forcibly transported by the British to Louisiana in 1755 (an event commemorated in Longfellow's "Evangeline") and settled near Bayou Teche; their descendants became known as Cajuns. Another group, the Islenos, were descendants of Canary Islanders brought to Louisiana by a Spanish governor in 1770. Traces of Spanish and French survive in local dialects.

Tourist attractions. Mardi Gras, French Quarter, Superdome, Dixieland jazz, Aquarium of the Americas, Audubon Zoo & Gardens, all New Orleans; Battle of New Orleans site; Longfellow-Evangeline Memorial Park, St. Martinville; Kent House Museum, Alexandria; Hodges Gardens, Natchitoches, USS *Kidd* Memorial, Baton Rouge.

Famous Louisianans. Louis Armstrong, Pierre Beauregard, Judah P. Benjamin, Braxton Bragg, Kate Chopin, Harry Connick Jr., Ellen DeGeneres, Lillian Hellman, Grace King, Bob Livingston, Huey Long, Wynton Marsalis, Leonidas K. Polk, Anne Rice, Henry Miller Shreve, Britney Spears, Edward D. White Jr.

Tourist information. Louisiana Office of Tourism, PO Box 94291, Baton Rouge, LA 70804-9291.

Toll-free travel information. 1-800-677-4082.

Website. www.state.la.us

Tourism website. www.louisianatravel.com

Maine

Pine Tree State

People. Population (2001 est.): 1,286,670; rank: 40; **net change** (2000-2001): 0.9%. **Pop. density:** 41.7 per sq mi. **Racial distribution** (2000): 96.9% white; 0.5% black; 0.7% Asian; 0.6% Native American/Nat. AK; <0.1% Hawaiian/Pacific Islander; 0.2% other race; 2 or more races, 1.0%. **Hispanic pop.** (any race): 0.7%.

Geography. Total area: 35,385 sq mi; rank: 39. **Land area:** 30,862 sq mi; rank: 39. **Acres forested:** 17,533,000. **Location:** New England state at northeastern tip of U.S. **Climate:** Southern interior and coastal, influenced by air masses from the S and W; northern clime harsher, avg. over 100 in. snow in winter. **Topography:** Appalachian Mts. extend through state; western borders have rugged terrain; long sand beaches on southern coast; northern coast mainly rocky promontories, peninsulas, fjords. **Capital:** Augusta.

Economy. Chief industries: manufacturing, agriculture, fishing, services, trade, government, finance, insurance, real estate, construction. **Chief manuf. goods:** paper & wood products, transportation equipment. **Chief crops:** potatoes, aquaculture products. **Livestock:** (Jan. 2002) 97,000 cattle/calves; (Dec. 2001) 6,500 hogs/pigs; 5.6 mil chickens (excl. broilers). **Timber/lumber**(est. 2001): 973 mil bd. ft.; pine, spruce, fir. **Nonfuel minerals** (est. 2001): 91 mil; mostly sand & gravel, portland and masonry cement, crushed stone, peat. **Commercial fishing** (2000): $269.2 mil. **Chief ports:** Searsport, Portland, Eastport. **Principal internat. airports at:** Bangor, Portland. **Value of construction** (1997): $1.1 bil. **Gross state product** (2000): $36 bil. **Employment distrib.** (May 2002): 30.9% services; 24.7% trade; 17.6% govt.; 12.3% mfg. **Per cap. pers. income** (2001): $26,385. **Sales tax** (2002): 5%. **Unemployment** (2001): 4.0%. **Tourism expends.** (1999): $2.1 bil. (2001): total sales: $146.6 mil; net income: $36.8 mil.

Finance. FDIC-insured commercial banks (2001): 15. **Deposits:** $5.4 bil. **FDIC-insured savings institutions** (2001): 24. **Assets:** $7.8 bil.

Federal govt. Fed. civ. employees (Mar. 2001): 8,197. **Avg. salary:** $47,323. **Notable fed. facilities:** Kittery Naval Shipyard; Brunswick Naval Air Station.

Energy. Electricity production (est. 2001, kWh, by source): Hydroelectric: 3 mil.

State data. Motto: Dirigo (I direct). **Flower:** White pine cone and tassel. **Bird:** Chickadee. **Tree:** Eastern white pine. **Song:** State of Maine Song. **Entered union** Mar. 15, 1820; rank, 23rd. **State fair:** at Bangor, late July; at Skowhegan, mid-Aug.

History. When the Europeans arrived, Maine was inhabited by Algonquian peoples including the Abnaki, Penobscot, and Passamaquoddy. Maine's rocky coast was believed to have been explored by the Cabots, 1498-99. French settlers arrived, 1604, at the St. Croix River, English, c 1607, on the Kennebec; both settlements failed. Maine was made part of Massachusetts, 1691. In the American Revolution, a Maine regiment fought at Bunker Hill. A British fleet destroyed Falmouth (now Portland), 1775, but the British ship *Margaretta* was captured near Machiasport. In 1820, Maine broke off and became a separate state.

Tourist attractions. Acadia Natl. Park, Bar Harbor, on Mt. Desert Island; Old Orchard Beach; Portland's Old Port; Kennebunkport; Common Ground Country Fair; Portland Headlight; Baxter State Pk.; Freeport/L. L. Bean.

Famous "Down Easters." Leon Leonwood (L.L.) Bean, James G. Blaine, Cyrus H. K. Curtis, Hannibal Hamlin, Sarah Jewett, Stephen King, Henry Wadsworth Longfellow, Sir Hiram and Hudson Maxim, Edna St. Vincent Millay, George Mitchell, Edmund Muskie, Judd Nelson, Edwin Arlington Robinson, Joan Benoit Samuelson, Liv Tyler, Kate Douglas Wiggin, Ben Ames Williams.

Chamber of Commerce and Industry. Maine Chamber & Business Alliance, 7 Community Dr., Augusta, ME 04330.

Toll-free travel information. 1-888-MAINE45 (from within the United States and Canada).

Website. www.state.me.us

Tourism website. www.visitmaine.com

Maryland

Old Line State, Free State

People. Population (2001 est.): 5,375,156; rank: 19; **net change** (2000-2001): 1.5%. **Pop. density:** 549.9 per sq mi. **Racial distribution** (2000): 64.0% white; 27.9% black; 4.0% Asian; 0.3% Native American/Nat. AK; <0.1% Hawaiian/Pacific Islander; 1.8% other race; 2 or more races, 2.0%. **Hispanic pop.** (any race): 4.3%.

Geography. Total area: 12,407 sq mi; rank: 42. **Land area:** 9,774 sq mi; rank: 42. **Acres forested:** 2,700,000. **Location:** South Atlantic state stretching from the Ocean to the Allegheny Mts. **Climate:** continental in the west; humid subtropical in the east. **Topography:** Eastern Shore of coastal plain and Maryland Main of coastal plain, piedmont plateau, and the Blue Ridge, separated by the Chesapeake Bay. **Capital:** Annapolis.

Economy. Chief industries: manufacturing, biotechnology and information technology, services, tourism. **Chief manuf. goods:** electric and electronic equipment; food and kindred products, chemicals and allied products, printed materials. **Chief crops:** greenhouse and nursery products, soybeans, corn. **Livestock:** (Jan. 2002) 245,000 cattle/calves; (Dec. 2001) 52,000 hogs/pigs; 4.3 mil chickens (excl. broilers); 283.3 mil broilers. **Timber/lumber:** (est. 2001): 261 mil bd. ft.; hardwoods. **Nonfuel minerals** (est. 2001): 356 mil; mostly crushed stone, portland cement, sand & gravel, masonry cement, dimension stone. **Commercial fishing** (2000): $53.9 mil. **Chief port:** Baltimore. **Principal internat. airport at:** Baltimore. **Value of construction** (1997): $5.9 bil. **Gross state product** (2000): $186.1 bil. **Employment distrib.** (May 2002): 34.9% services; 22.3% trade; 19.1% govt.; 7% mfg. **Per cap. pers. income** (2001): $34,950. **Sales tax** (2002): 5%. **Unemployment** (2001): 4.1%. **Tourism expends.** (1999): $8 bil. **Lottery** (2001): total sales: $1.2 bil; net income: $407 mil.

Finance. FDIC-insured commercial banks (2001): 74. **Deposits:** $37 bil. **FDIC-insured savings institutions (2001):** 59. **Assets:** $8 bil.

Federal govt. Fed. civ. employees (Mar. 2001): 101,461. **Avg. salary:** $62,321. **Notable fed. facilities:** U.S. Naval Academy; Natl. Agriculture Research Center; Ft. George G. Meade, Aberdeen Proving Ground; Goddard Space Flight Center; Natl. Institutes of Health; Natl. Institute of Standards & Technology; Food & Drug Administration; Bureau of the Census.

Energy. Electricity production (est. 2001, kWh, by source): Petroleum: 169 mil; Gas: 1 mil; Hydroelectric: 1.8 bil..

State data. Motto: Fatti Maschii, Parole Femine (Manly deeds, womanly words). **Flower:** Black-eyed Susan. **Bird:** Baltimore oriole. **Tree:** White oak. **Song:** Maryland, My Maryland. **Seventh** of the original 13 states to ratify Constitution, Apr. 28, 1788. **State fair** at Timonium; late Aug.-early Sept.

History. Europeans encountered Algonquian-speaking Nanticoke and Piscataway and Iroquois-speaking Susquehannock when they first visited the area. Italian explorer Verrazano visited the Chesapeake region in the early 16th cent. English Capt. John Smith explored and mapped the area, 1608. William Claiborne set up a trading post on Kent Island in Chesapeake Bay, 1631. King Charles I granted land to Cecilius Calvert, Lord Baltimore, 1632; Calvert's brother Leonard, with about 200 settlers, founded St. Marys, 1634. The bravery of Maryland troops in the American Revolution, as at the Battle of Long Island, won the state its nickname "The Old Line State." In the War of 1812, when a British fleet tried to take Ft. McHenry, Marylander Francis Scott Key wrote "The Star-Spangled Banner," 1814. Although a slave-holding state, Maryland remained with the Union during the Civil War and was the site of the battle of Antietam, 1862, which halted Gen. Robert E. Lee's march north.

Tourist attractions. The Preakness at Pimlico track, Baltimore; The Maryland Million at Laurel Race Course; Ocean City; restored Ft. McHenry, near which Francis Scott Key wrote "The Star-Spangled Banner"; Edgar Allan Poe house, Ravens Football at Memorial Stadium, Camden Yards, Natl. Aquarium, Harborplace, all Baltimore; Antietam Battlefield, near Hagerstown; South Mountain Battlefield; U.S. Naval Academy, Annapolis; Maryland State House, Annapolis, 1772, the oldest still in legislative use in the U.S.

Famous Marylanders. John Astin, Benjamin Banneker, Tom Clancy, Jonathan Demme, Francis Scott Key, H. L. Mencken, Kweisi Mfume, Ogden Nash, Charles Willson Peale, William Pinkney, Edgar Allan Poe, Cal Ripken Jr., Babe Ruth, Upton Sinclair, Roger B. Taney, John Waters, Montel Williams.

Maryland Dept. of Business & Economic Development. 217 E. Redwood St., Baltimore, MD 21202; (410) 767-6870.

Toll-free travel information. 1-800-MDISFUN.

Website. www.state.md.us

Tourism website. www.mdisfun.org

Massachusetts

Bay State, Old Colony

People. Population (2001 est.): 6,379,304; rank: 13; **net change** (2000-2001): 0.5%. **Pop. density:** 813.7 per sq mi. **Racial distribution** (2000): 84.5% white; 5.4% black; 3.8% Asian; 0.2% Native American/Nat. AK; <0.1% Hawaiian/Pacific Islander; 3.7% other race; 2 or more races, 2.3%. **Hispanic pop.** (any race): 6.8%.

Geography. Total area: 10,555 sq mi; rank: 44. **Land area:** 7,840 sq mi; rank: 45. **Acres forested:** 3,203,000. **Location:** New England state along Atlantic seaboard. **Climate:** temperate, with colder and drier clime in western region. **Topography:** jagged indented coast from Rhode Island around Cape Cod; flat land yields to stony upland pastures near central region and gentle hilly country in west; except in west, land is rocky, sandy, and not fertile. **Capital:** Boston.

Economy. Chief industries: services, trade, manufacturing. **Chief manuf. goods:** electric and electronic equipment, instruments, industrial machinery and equipment, printing and publishing, fabricated metal products. **Chief crops:** cranberries, greenhouse, nursery, vegetables. **Livestock:** (Jan. 2002) 51,000 cattle/calves; (Dec. 2001) 18,000 hogs/pigs; 349,000 chickens (excl. broilers).**Timber/lumber** (est. 2001): NA; white pine, oak, other hard woods; **Nonfuel minerals** (est. 2001): 209 mil;:mostly crushed stone, sand & gravel, dimension stone, lime, clays. **Commercial fishing** (2000): $290.9 mil. **Chief ports:** Boston, Fall River, New Bedford, Salem, Gloucester, Plymouth. **Principal internat. airport at:** Boston. **Value of construction** (1997): $10.3 bil. **Gross state product** (2000): $284.9 bil. **Employment distrib.** (May 2002): 36.9% services; 22.1% trade; 13.2% govt.; 12.2% mfg. **Per cap. pers. income** (2001): $38,845. **Sales tax** (2002): 5%. **Unemployment** (2001): 3.7%. **Tourism expends.** (1999): $12.2 bil. **Lottery** (2001): total sales: $3.9 bil; net income: $864.5 mil.

Finance. FDIC-insured commercial banks (2001): 43. **Deposits:** $74.9 bil. **FDIC-insured savings institutions (2001):** 182. **Assets:** $68.3 bil.

Federal govt. Fed. civ. employees (Mar. 2001): 24,369. **Avg. salary:** $53,644. **Notable fed. facilities:** Thomas P. O'Neill Jr. Federal Bldg., J.W. McCormack Bldg., John Fitzgerald Kennedy Federal Bldg., Q.M. Laboratory, Natick.

Energy. Electricity production (est. 2001, kWh, by source): Coal: 1.1 bil; Petroleum: 125 mil; Gas: 225 mil; Hydroelectric: 124 mil.

State data. Motto: Ense Petit Placidam Sub Libertate Quietem (By the sword we seek peace, but peace only under liberty). **Flower:** Mayflower. **Bird:** Chickadee. **Tree:** American elm. **Song:** All Hail to Massachusetts. **Sixth** of the original 13 states to ratify Constitution, Feb. 6, 1788. **State Fair** at Topsfield, early Oct.

History. Early inhabitants were the Algonquian, Nauset, Wampanoag, Massachuset, Pennacook, Nipmuc, and Pocumtuc peoples. Pilgrims settled in Plymouth, 1620, giving thanks for their survival with the first Thanksgiving Day, 1621. About 20,000 new settlers arrived, 1630-40. Native American relations with the colonists deteriorated leading to King Philip's War, 1675-76, which the colonists won, ending Native American resistance. Demonstrations against British restrictions set off the Boston Massacre, 1770, and the Boston Tea Party, 1773. The first bloodshed of American Revolution was at Lexington, 1775.

Tourist attractions. Provincetown artists' colony; Cape Cod; Plymouth Rock, Plimouth Plantation, *Mayflower II*, all Plymouth; Freedom Trail, Isabella Stewart Gardner Museum, Museum of Fine Arts, Children's Museum, Museum of Science, New England Aquarium, JFK Library, Boston Ballet, Boston Pops, Boston Symphony Orchestra, all Boston; Tanglewood, Jacob's Pillow Dance Festival, Hancock Shaker Village, Berkshire Scenic Railway Museum, all in the Berkshires; Salem; Old Sturbridge Village; Deerfield Historic District; Walden Pond; Naismith Memorial Basketball Hall of Fame, Springfield.

Famous "Bay Staters." John Adams, John Quincy Adams, Samuel Adams, Louisa May Alcott, Horatio Alger, Susan B. Anthony, Crispus Attucks, Clara Barton, Alexander Graham Bell, Stephen Breyer, George H. W. Bush, John Cheever, E. E. Cummings, Emily Dickinson, Charles Eliot, Ralph Waldo Emerson, William Lloyd Garrison, Edward Everett Hale, John Hancock, Nathaniel Hawthorne, Oliver Wendell Holmes, Winslow Homer, Elias Howe, John F. Kennedy, Jack Lemmon, James Russell Lowell, Cotton Mather, Samuel F. B. Morse, Edgar Allan Poe, Paul Revere, Dr. Seuss (Theodore Seuss Geisel), Henry David Thoreau, Barbara Walters, James McNeil Whistler, John Greenleaf Whittier.

Tourist information. Massachusetts Office of Travel & Tourism, 100 Cambridge St., 13th Floor, Boston, MA 02202.

Toll-free travel information. 1-800-227-MASS.

Website. www.mass.gov

Tourism website. www.massvacation.com

Michigan

Great Lakes State, Wolverine State

People. Population (2001 est.): 9,990,817; rank: 8; **net change** (2000-2001): 0.5%. **Pop. density:** 175.9 per sq mi. **Racial distribution** (2000): 80.2% white; 14.2% black; 1.8% Asian; 0.6% Native American/Nat. AK; <0.1% Hawaiian/Pacific Islander; 1.3% other race; 2 or more races, 1.9%. **Hispanic pop.** (any race): 3.3%.

Geography. Total area: 96,716 sq mi; rank: 11. **Land area:** 56,804 sq mi; rank: 22. **Acres forested:** 18,253,000. **Location:** East North Central state bordering on 4 of the 5 Great Lakes, divided into an Upper and Lower Peninsula by the

Straits of Mackinac, which link lakes Michigan and Huron. **Climate:** well-defined seasons tempered by the Great Lakes. **Topography:** low rolling hills give way to northern tableland of hilly belts in Lower Peninsula; Upper Peninsula is level in the east, with swampy areas; western region is higher and more rugged. **Capital:** Lansing.

Economy. Chief industries: manufacturing, services, tourism, agriculture, forestry/lumber. **Chief manuf. goods:** automobiles, transportation equipment, machinery, fabricated metals, food products, plastics, office furniture. **Chief crops:** corn, wheat, soybeans, dry beans, hay, potatoes, sweet corn, apples, cherries, sugar beets, blueberries, cucumbers, Niagra grapes. **Livestock:** (Jan. 2002) 990,000 cattle/calves; 72,000 sheep/lambs; (Dec. 2001) 960,000 hogs/pigs; 8 mil chickens (excl. broilers). **Timber/lumber** (est. 2001): 706 mil bd. ft.; maple, oak, aspen; 681 mil bd. ft. **Nonfuel minerals** (est. 2001): 1.6 bil; mostly portland cement, iron ore, sand & gravel, magnesium compounds, crushed stone. **Commercial fishing** (2000): $9 mil. **Chief ports:** Detroit, Saginaw River, Escanaba, Muskegon, Sault Ste. Marie, Port Huron, Marine City. **Principal internat. airports at:** Detroit, Flint, Grand Rapids, Kalamazoo, Lansing, Saginaw. **Value of construction** (1997): $10.7 bil. **Gross state product** (2000): $325.4 bil. **Employment distrib.** (May 2002): 28.4% services; 23.1% trade; 15.6% govt.; 19.8% mfg. **Per cap. pers. income** (2001): $29,538. **Sales tax** (2002): 6%. **Unemployment** (2001): 5.3%. **Tourism expends.** (1999): $11.5 bil. **Lottery** (2001): total sales: $1.6 bil; net income: $631.8 mil.

Finance. FDIC-insured commercial banks (2001): 162. **Deposits:** $107.9 bil. **FDIC-insured savings institutions** (2001): 19. **Assets:** $11.3 bil.

Federal govt. Fed. civ. employees (Mar. 2001): 21,006. **Avg. salary:** $54,163. **Notable fed. facilities:** Isle Royal, Sleeping Bear Dunes national parks.

Energy. Electricity production (est. 2001, kWh, by source): Coal: 66.6 bil; Petroleum: 730 mil; Gas: 2.4 bil; Hydroelectric: 369 mil; Nuclear: 26.7 bil.

State data. Motto: Si Quaeris Peninsulam Amoenam, Circumspice (If you seek a pleasant peninsula, look about you). **Flower:** Apple blossom. **Bird:** Robin. **Tree:** White pine. **Song:** Michigan, My Michigan. **Entered union** Jan. 26, 1837; rank, 26th. **State fair** at Detroit, late Aug.–early Sept.; Upper Peninsula (Escanaba), mid-Aug.

History. Early inhabitants were the Ojibwa, Ottawa, Miami, Potawatomi, and Huron. French fur traders and missionaries visited the region, 1616, set up a mission at Sault Ste. Marie, 1641, and a settlement there, 1668. French settlements were taken over, 1763, by the British, who crushed a Native American uprising led by Ottawa chieftain Pontiac that same year. Treaty of Paris ceded territory to U.S., 1783, but British remained until 1796. The British seized Ft. Mackinac and Detroit, 1812. After Oliver H. Perry's Lake Erie victory and William H. Harrison's victory near the Thames River, 1813, the British retreated to Canada. The opening of the Erie Canal, 1825, and new land laws and Native American cessions led the way for a flood of settlers.

Tourist attractions. Henry Ford Museum, Greenfield Village, both in Dearborn; Michigan Space Center, Jackson; Tahquamenon *(Hiawatha)* Falls; DeZwaan windmill and Tulip Festival, Holland; "Soo Locks," St. Mary's Falls Ship Canal, Sault Ste. Marie, Kalamazoo Aviation History Museum; Mackinac Island; Kellogg's Cereal City USA, Battle Creek; Museum of African-American History, Motown Historical Museum, both Detroit.

Famous Michiganders. Ralph Bunche, Paul de Kruif, Thomas Edison, Edna Ferber, Gerald R. Ford, Henry Ford, Aretha Franklin, Edgar Guest, Lee Iacocca, Robert Ingersoll, Magic Johnson, Casey Kasem, Will Kellogg, Ring Lardner, Elmore Leonard, Charles Lindbergh, Joe Louis, Madonna, Malcolm X, Terry McMillan, Jack Paar, Pontiac, Diana Ross, Glenn Seaborg, Tom Selleck, Sinbad (David Adkins), John Smoltz, Lily Tomlin, Stewart Edward White, Serena Williams.

State Chamber of Commerce. 600 S. Walnut, Lansing, MI 48933. Phone: 517-371-2100

Toll-free travel information. 1-888-78GREAT.

Website. www.michigan.gov

Tourism website. travel.michigan.org

Minnesota

North Star State, Gopher State

People. Population (2001 est.): 4,972,294; rank: 21; **net change** (2000-2001): 1.1%. **Pop. density:** 62.5 per sq mi. **Racial distribution** (2000): 89.4% white; 3.5% black; 2.9% Asian; 1.1% Native American/Nat. AK; <0.1% Hawaiian/Pacific Islander; 1.3% other race; 2 or more races, 1.7%. **Hispanic pop.** (any race): 2.9%.

Geography. Total area: 86,939 sq mi; rank: 12. **Land area:** 79,610 sq mi; rank: 14. **Acres forested:** 16,718,000. **Location:** West North Central state bounded on the E by Wisconsin and Lake Superior, on the N by Canada, on the W by the Dakotas, and on the S by Iowa. **Climate:** northern part of state lies in the moist Great Lakes storm belt; the western border lies at the edge of the semi-arid Great Plains. **Topography:** central hill and lake region covering approx. half the state; to the NE, rocky ridges and deep lakes; to the NW, flat plain; to the S, rolling plains and deep river valleys. **Capital:** St. Paul.

Economy. Chief industries: agribusiness, forest products, mining, manufacturing, tourism. **Chief manuf. goods:** food, chemical and paper products, industrial machinery, electric and electronic equipment, computers, printing & publishing, scientific and medical instruments, fabricated metal products, forest products. **Chief crops:** corn, soybeans, wheat, sugar beets, hay, barley, potatoes, sunflowers. **Livestock:** (Jan. 2002) 2.6 mil cattle/calves; 160,000 sheep/lambs; (Dec. 2001) 5.6 mil hogs/pigs; 15.8 mil chickens (excl. broilers); 44.2 mil broilers. **Timber/lumber** (est. 2001): 268 mil bd. ft.; needleleaves and hardwoods. **Nonfuel minerals** (est. 2001): 1.4 bil; mostly iron ore, sand & gravel, crushed stone, dimension stone. **Commercial fishing** (2000): $172,041. **Chief ports:** Duluth, St. Paul, Minneapolis. **Principal internat. airport at:** Minneapolis-St. Paul. **Value of construction** (1997): $6.2 bil. **Gross state product** (2000): $184.8 bil. **Employment distrib.** (May 2002): 29.9% services; 23.5% trade; 15.5% govt.; 15.2% mfg. **Per cap. pers. income** (2001): $32,791. **Sales tax** (2002): 6.5%. **Unemployment** (2001): 3.7%. **Tourism expends.** (1999): $6.9 bil. **Lottery** (2001): total sales: $366.2 mil; net income: $81.6 mil.

Finance. FDIC-insured commercial banks (2001): 481. **Deposits:** $76.7 bil. **FDIC-insured savings institutions (2001):** 23. **Assets:** $3.1 bil.

Federal govt. Fed. civ. employees (Mar. 2001): 12,975. **Avg. salary:** $52,284.

Energy. Electricity production (est. 2001, kWh, by source): Coal: 31 bil; Petroleum: 601 mil; Gas: 401 mil; Hydroelectric: 623 mil; Nuclear: 11.8 bil; Other: 429 mil.

State data. Motto: L'Etoile du Nord (The star of the north). **Flower:** Pink and white lady's-slipper. **Bird:** Common loon. **Tree:** Red pine. **Song:** Hail! Minnesota. **Entered union** May 11, 1858; rank, 32nd. **State fair** at St. Paul/Minneapolis; late Aug.-early Sept.

History. Dakota Sioux were early inhabitants of the area, and in the 16th cent., the Ojibwa began moving in from the east. French fur traders Médard Chouart and Pierre Esprit Radisson entered the region in the mid-17th cent. In 1679, French explorer Daniel Greysolon, sieur Duluth, claimed the entire region in the name of France. Britain took the area east of the Mississippi, 1763. The U.S. took over that portion after the American Revolution and in 1803, gained the western area in the Louisiana Purchase. The U.S. built Ft. St. Anthony (now Ft. Snelling), 1819, and in 1837, bought Native American lands, spurring an influx of settlers from the east. In 1849, the Territory of Minnesota was created. Sioux Indians staged a bloody uprising, the Battle of Woods Lake, 1862, and were driven from the state.

Tourist attractions. Minneapolis Institute of Arts, Walker Art Center, Minneapolis Sculpture Garden, Minnehaha Falls (inspiration for Longfellow's *Hiawatha),* Guthrie Theater, Minneapolis; Ordway Theater, St. Paul; Voyageurs Natl. Park; Mayo Clinic, Rochester; St. Paul Winter Carnival; North Shore (of Lake Superior).

Famous Minnesotans. Warren Burger, Ethan and Joel Coen, William O. Douglas, Bob Dylan, F. Scott Fitzgerald, Al Franken, Judy Garland, Cass Gilbert, Hubert Humphrey, Garrison Keillor, Sister Elizabeth Kenny, Jessica Lange, Sinclair Lewis, Paul Manship, Roger Maris, E. G. Marshall, William and Charles Mayo, Eugene McCarthy, Walter F. Mondale, Prince (Rodgers Nelson), Charles Schulz, Harold Stassen, Thorstein Veblen, Jesse Ventura.

Chamber of Commerce. 30 East 7th St., Suite 1700, St. Paul, MN 55101-4901.

Toll-free travel information. 1-800-657-3700.

Website. www.state.mn.us

Tourism website. www.exploreminnesota.com

Mississippi

Magnolia State

People. Population (2001 est.): 2,858,029; rank: 31; **net change** (2000-2001): 0.5%. **Pop. density:** 60.9 per sq mi. **Racial distribution** (2000): 61.4% white; 36.3% black; 0.7% Asian; 0.4% Native American/Nat. AK; <0.1% Hawaiian/Pacific Islander; 0.5% other race; 2 or more races, 0.7%. **Hispanic pop.** (any race): 1.4%.

Geography. Total area: 48,430 sq mi; rank: 32. **Land area:** 46,907 sq mi; rank: 31. **Acres forested:** 17,000,000. **Location:** East South Central state bordered on the W by the Mississippi R. and on the S by the Gulf of Mexico. **Climate:** semi-tropical, with abundant rainfall, long growing season, and extreme temperatures unusual. **Topography:** low, fertile delta between the Yazoo and Mississippi rivers; loess bluffs stretching around delta border; sandy gulf coastal terraces followed by piney woods and prairie; rugged, high sandy hills in extreme NE followed by Black Prairie Belt, Pontotoc Ridge, and flatwoods into the north central highlands. **Capital:** Jackson.

Economy. Chief industries: warehousing & distribution, services, manufacturing, government, wholesale and retail trade. **Chief manuf. goods:** chemicals & plastics, food & kindred products, furniture, lumber & wood products, electrical machinery, transportation equipment. **Chief crops:** cotton, rice, soybeans. **Livestock:** (Jan. 2002) 1.1 mil cattle/calves; (Dec. 2001) 285,000 hogs/pigs; 10.4 mil chickens (excl. broilers); 739.9 mil broilers. **Timber/lumber** (est. 2001): 2.8 bil bd. ft.; pine, oak, hardwoods. **Nonfuel minerals** (est. 2001): 177 mil; mostly sand & gravel, portland cement, clays, dimension stone. **Commercial fishing** (2000): $58.7 mil. **Chief ports:** Pascagoula, Vicksburg, Gulfport, Natchez, Greenville. **Principal internat. airport at:** Jackson. **Value of construction** (1997): $2.6 bil. **Gross state product** (2000): $67.3 bil. **Employment distrib.** (May 2002): 24.1% services; 22.3% trade; 21.4% govt.; 18.4% mfg. **Per cap. pers. income** (2001): $21,643. **Sales tax** (2002): 7%. **Unemployment** (2001): 5.5%. **Tourism expends.** (1999): $4.3 bil.

Finance. FDIC-insured commercial banks (2001): 99. **Deposits:** $28.2 bil. **FDIC-insured savings institutions** (2001): 8. **Assets:** $972 mil.

Federal govt. Fed. civ. employees (Mar. 2001): 16,725. **Avg. salary:** $46,386. **Notable fed. facilities:** Columbus, Keesler AF bases; Meridian Naval Air Station, John C. Stennis Space Center; U.S. Army Corps of Engineers Waterway Experiment Station.

Energy. Electricity production (est. 2001, kWh, by source): Coal: 17.4 bil; Petroleum: 5.1 bil; Gas: 11.5 bil; Nuclear: 9.9 bil.

State data. Motto: Virtute et Armis (By valor and arms). **Flower:** Magnolia. **Bird:** Mockingbird. **Tree:** Magnolia. **Song:** Go, Mississippi! **Entered union** Dec. 10, 1817; rank, 20th. **State fair** at Jackson; early Oct.

History. Early inhabitants of the region were Choctaw, Chickasaw, and Natchez peoples. Hernando de Soto explored the area, 1540, and sighted the Mississippi River, 1541. Robert La Salle traced the river from Illinois to its mouth and claimed the entire valley for France, 1682. The first settlement was the French Ft. Maurepas, near Ocean Springs, 1699. The area was ceded to Britain, 1763; American settlers followed. During the American Revolution, Spain seized part of the area, remaining even after the U.S. acquired title at the end of the conflict; Spain finally moved out, 1798. The Territory of Mississippi was formed, 1798. Mississippi seceded, 1861. Union forces captured Corinth and Vicksburg and destroyed Jackson and much of Meridian. Mississippi was readmitted to the Union in 1870.

Tourist attractions. Vicksburg Natl. Military Park and Cemetery, other Civil War sites; Hattiesburg; Natchez Trace; Indian mounds; Antebellum homes; pilgrimages in Natchez and some 25 other cities; The Elvis Presley Birthplace & Museum, Tupelo; Smith Robertson Museum, Mynelle Gardens, both Jackson; Mardi Gras and Shrimp Festival, both in Biloxi; Gulf Islands Natl. Seashore; Casinos on the Mississippi River; the Mississippi Coast.

Famous Mississippians. Margaret Walker Alexander, Dana Andrews, Jimmy Buffett, Hodding Carter III, Bo Diddley, William Faulkner, Brett Favre, Shelby Foote, Morgan Freeman, John Grisham, Fannie Lou Hamer, Jim Henson, Faith Hill, John Lee Hooker, Robert Johnson, James Earl Jones, B. B. King, L. Q. C. Lamar, Trent Lott, Gerald McRaney, Willie Morris, Walter Payton, Elvis Presley, Leontyne Price, Charley Pride, LeAnn Rimes, Muddy Waters, Eudora Welty, Tennessee Williams, Oprah Winfrey, Johnny Winter, Richard Wright, Tammy Wynette.

Tourist Information. Dept. of Economic & Community Development. PO Box 849, Jackson, MS 39205-0849.

Toll-free travel information. 1-800-927-6378.

Website. www.ms.gov

Tourism website. www.visitmississippi.org

Missouri

Show Me State

People. Population (2001 est.): 5,629,707; rank: 17; **net change** (2000-2001): 0.6%. **Pop. density:** 81.7 per sq mi. **Racial distribution** (2000): 84.9% white; 11.2% black; 1.1% Asian; 0.4% Native American/Nat. AK; 0.1% Hawaiian/Pacific Islander; 0.8% other race; 2 or more races, 1.5%. **Hispanic pop.** (any race): 2.1%.

Geography. Total area: 69,704 sq mi; rank: 21. **Land area:** 68,886 sq mi; rank: 18. **Acres forested:** 14,007,000. **Location:** West North Central state near the geographic center of the conterminous U.S.; bordered on the E by the Mississippi R., on the NW by the Missouri R. **Climate:** continental, susceptible to cold Canadian air, moist, warm gulf air, and drier SW air. **Topography:** rolling hills, open, fertile plains, and well-watered prairie N of the Missouri R.; south of the river land is rough and hilly with deep, narrow valleys; alluvial plain in the SE; low elevation in the west. **Capital:** Jefferson City.

Economy. Chief industries: agriculture, manufacturing, aerospace, tourism. **Chief manuf. goods:** transportation equipment, food and related products, electrical and electronic equipment, chemicals. **Chief crops:** soybeans, corn, wheat, hay. **Livestock:** (Jan. 2002) 4.4 mil cattle/calves; 70,000 sheep/lambs; (Dec. 2001) 3 mil hogs/pigs; 8.5 mil chickens (excl. broilers); 240 mil broilers. **Timber/lumber** (est. 2001): 642 mil bd. ft.; oak, hickory. **Nonfuel minerals** (est. 2001): 1.3 bil; mostly crushed stone, lead, portland cement, lime, zinc. **Chief ports:** St. Louis, Kansas City. **Principal internat. airports at:** Kansas City, St. Louis. **Value of construction** (1997): $5.9 bil. **Gross state product** (2000): $178.8 bil. **Employment distrib.** (May 2002): 29.2% services; 23.7% trade; 16.1% govt.; 13.3% mfg. **Per cap. pers. income** (2001): $28,029. **Sales tax** (2002): 4.225%. **Unemployment** (2001): 4.7%. **Tourism expends.** (1999): $9.3 bil. **Lottery** (2001): total sales: $508.3 mil; net income: $153.9 mil.

Finance. FDIC-insured commercial banks (2001): 351. **Deposits:** $57.2 bil. **FDIC-insured savings institutions** (2001): 36. **Assets:** $5.4 bil.

Federal govt. Fed. civ. employees (Mar. 2001): 31,767. **Avg. salary:** $46,763. **Notable fed. facilities:** Federal Reserve banks; Ft. Leonard Wood; Jefferson Barracks; Whiteman AFB.

Energy. Electricity production (est. 2001, kWh, by source): Coal: 66.4 bil; Petroleum: 658 mil; Gas: 3.7 bil; Hydroelectric: 745 mil; Nuclear: 8.4 bil; Other: 52 mil.

State data. Motto: Salus Populi Suprema Lex Esto (The welfare of the people shall be the supreme law). **Flower:** Hawthorn. **Bird:** Bluebird. **Tree:** Dogwood. **Song:** Missouri Waltz. **Entered union** Aug. 10, 1821; rank, 24th. **State fair** at Sedalia; 3rd week in Aug.

History. Early inhabitants of the region were Algonquian Sauk, Fox, and Illinois and Siouan Osage, Missouri, Iowa, and Kansa peoples. Hernando de Soto visited 1541. French hunters and lead miners made the first settlement c 1735, at Ste. Genevieve. The territory was ceded to Spain by the French, 1763, then returned to France, 1800. The U.S. acquired Missouri as part of the Louisiana Purchase, 1803. The influx of white settlers drove Native American tribes to the Kansas and Oklahoma territories; most were gone by 1836. The fur trade and the Santa Fe Trail provided prosperity; St. Louis became the gateway for pioneers heading West. Missouri entered the Union as a slave state, 1821. Though it remained with the Union, pro- and anti-slavery forces battled there during the Civil War.

Tourist attractions. Silver Dollar City, Branson; Mark Twain Area, Hannibal; Pony Express Museum, St. Joseph; Harry S. Truman Library, Independence; Gateway Arch, St. Louis; Worlds of Fun, Kansas City; Lake of the Ozarks; Churchill Mem., Fulton; State Capitol, Jefferson City.

Famous Missourians. Maya Angelou, Robert Altman, Burt Bacharach, Josephine Baker, Scott Bakula, Thomas Hart Benton, Tom Berenger, Yogi Berra, Chuck Berry, George Caleb Bingham, Daniel Boone, Omar Bradley, William Burroughs, Kate Capshaw, Dale Carnegie, George Washington Carver, Bob Costas, Walter Cronkite, Walt Disney, T. S. Eliot, Richard Gephardt, John Goodman, Betty Grable, Edwin Hubble, Jesse James, Rush Limbaugh, Marianne Moore, Reinhold Niebuhr, J. C. Penney, John J. Pershing, Brad Pitt,

Joseph Pulitzer, Ginger Rogers, Bess Truman, Harry S. Truman, Kathleen Turner, Tina Turner, Mark Twain, Dick Van Dyke, Tennessee Williams, Lanford Wilson, Shelley Winters, Jane Wyman.

Chamber of Commerce. 428 E. Capitol, Jefferson City, MO 65101.

Toll-free travel information. 1-888-877-1234, ext. 124.

Website. www.state.mo.us

Tourism website. www.missouritourism.com

Montana

Treasure State

People. Population (2001 est.): 904,433; rank: 44; **net change** (2000-2001): 0.2%. **Pop. density:** 6.2 per sq mi. **Racial distribution** (2000): 90.6% white; 0.3% black; 0.5% Asian; 6.2% Native American/Nat. AK; 0.1% Hawaiian/Pacific Islander; 0.6% other race; 2 or more races, 1.7%. **Hispanic pop.** (any race): 2.0%.

Geography. Total area: 147,042 sq mi; rank: 4. **Land area:** 145,552 sq mi; rank: 4. **Acres forested:** 22,512,000. **Location:** Mountain state bounded on the E by the Dakotas, on the S by Wyoming, on the SSW by Idaho, and on the N by Canada. **Climate:** colder, continental climate with low humidity. **Topography:** Rocky Mts. in western third of the state; eastern two-thirds gently rolling northern Great Plains. **Capital:** Helena.

Economy. Chief industries: agriculture, timber, mining, tourism, oil and gas. **Chief manuf. goods:** food products, wood & paper products, primary metals, printing & publishing, petroleum and coal products. **Chief crops:** wheat, barley, sugar beets, hay, oats. **Livestock:** (Jan. 2002) 2.5 mil cattle/calves; 335,000 sheep/lambs; (Dec. 2001) 170,000 hogs/pigs; 480,000 chickens (excl. broilers). **Timber/lumber** (est. 2001): 1.2 bil bd. ft.; Douglas fir, pines, larch. **Nonfuel minerals** (est. 2001): 514 mil; mostly copper, gold, portland cement, palladium, sand and gravel. **Principal internat. airports at:** Billings, Missoula. **Value of construction** (1997): $827 mil. **Gross state product** (2000): $21.8 bil. **Employment distrib.** (May 2002): 29.7% services; 25.7% trade; 22% govt.; 5.8% mfg. **Per cap. pers. income** (2001): $23,532. **Sales tax:** (2002): none. **Unemployment** (2001): 4.6%. **Tourism expends.** (1999): $1.9 bil. **Lottery** (2001): total sales: $30.4 mil; net income: $6.1 mil.

Finance. FDIC-insured commercial banks (2001): 82. **Deposits:** $11.3 bil. **FDIC-insured savings institutions** (2001): 4. **Assets:** $418 mil.

Federal govt. Fed. civ. employees (Mar. 2001): 8,009. **Avg. salary:** $46,596. **Notable fed. facilities:** Malmstrom AFB; Ft. Peck, Hungry Horse, Libby, Yellowtail dams; numerous missile silos.

Energy. Electricity production (est. 2001, kWh, by source): Coal: 311 mil; Petroleum: 1 mil; Gas: 10 mil; Hydroelectric: 4.1 bil.

State data. Motto: Oro y Plata (Gold and silver). **Flower:** Bitterroot. **Bird:** Western meadowlark. **Tree:** Ponderosa pine. **Song:** Montana. **Entered union** Nov. 8, 1889; rank, 41st. **State fair** at Great Falls; late July-early Aug.

History. Cheyenne, Blackfoot, Crow, Assiniboin, Salish (Flatheads), Kootenai, and Kalispel peoples were early inhabitants of the area. French explorers visited the region, 1742. The U.S. acquired the area partly through the Louisiana Purchase, 1803, partly through explorations of Lewis and Clark, 1805-6. Fur traders and missionaries established posts early 19th cent. Gold was discovered, 1863, and the Montana territory was established, 1864. Indian uprisings reached their peak with the Battle of Little Bighorn, 1876. Chief Joseph and the Nez Percé tribe surrendered here, 1877, after long trek across the state. Mining activity and the coming of the Northern Pacific Railway, 1883, brought population growth. Copper wealth from the Butte pits resulted in the turn of the century "War of Copper Kings" as factions fought for control of "the richest hill on earth."

Tourist attractions. Glacier Natl. Park; Yellowstone Natl. Park; Museum of the Rockies, Bozeman; Museum of the Plains Indian, Blackfeet Reservation, near Browning; Little Bighorn Battlefield Natl. Monument and Custer Natl. Cemetery; Flathead Lake; Helena; Lewis and Clark Caverns State Park, near Whitehall; Lewis and Clark Interpretive Center, Great Falls.

Famous Montanans. Dana Carvey, Gary Cooper, Marcus Daly, Chet Huntley, Will James, Myrna Loy, David Lynch, Mike Mansfield, Brent Musburger, Jeannette Rankin, Charles M. Russell, Lester Thurow.

Chamber of Commerce. 2030 11th Ave., PO Box 1730, Helena, MT 59624.

Toll-free travel information. 1-800-VISITMT.

Website. www.state.mt.us

Tourism website. www.visitmt.org

Nebraska

Cornhusker State

People. Population (2001 est.): 1,713,235; rank: 38; **net change** (2000-2001): 0.1%. **Pop. density:** 22.3 per sq mi. **Racial distribution** (2000): 89.6% white; 4.0% black; 1.3% Asian; 0.9% Native American/Nat. AK; 0.1% Hawaiian/Pacific Islander; 2.8% other race; 2 or more races, 1.4%. **Hispanic pop.** (any race): 5.5%.

Geography. Total area: 77,354 sq mi; rank: 16. **Land area:** 76,872 sq mi; rank: 15. **Acres forested:** 722,000. **Location:** West North Central state with the Missouri R. for a NE and E border. **Climate:** continental semi-arid. **Topography:** till plains of the central lowland in the eastern third rising to the Great Plains and hill country of the north central and NW. **Capital:** Lincoln.

Economy. Chief industries: agriculture, manufacturing. **Chief manuf. goods:** processed foods, industrial machinery, printed materials, electric and electronic equipment, primary and fabricated metal products, transportation equipment. **Chief crops:** corn, sorghum, soybeans, hay, wheat, dry beans, oats, potatoes, sugar beets. **Livestock:** (Jan. 2002) 6.4 mil cattle/calves; 101,000 sheep/lambs; (Dec. 2001) 2.9 mil hogs/pigs; 13.7 mil chickens (excl. broilers); 3.4 mil broilers. **Timber/lumber** (est. 2001): 33 mil bd. ft.; oak, hickory, and elm. **Nonfuel minerals** (est. 2001): 163 mil; mostly portland and masonry cement, sand & gravel, crushed stone, lime. **Chief ports:** Omaha, Sioux City, Brownville, Blair, Plattsmouth, Nebraska City. **Value of construction** (1997): $2 bil. **Gross state product** (2000): $56.1 bil. **Employment distrib.** (May 2002): 28.7% services; 23.4% trade; 17.7% govt.; 12.3% mfg. **Per cap. pers. income** (2001): $28,564. **Sales tax** (2002): 5%. **Unemployment** (2001): 3.1%. **Tourism expends.** (1999): $2.6 bil. **Lottery** (2001): total sales: $66.5 mil; net income: $16.6 mil.

Finance. FDIC-insured commercial banks (2001): 275. **Deposits:** $24.7 bil. **FDIC-insured savings institutions** (2001): 15. **Assets:** $15.7 bil.

Federal govt. Fed. civ. employees (Mar. 2001): 7,595. **Avg. salary:** $47,871. **Notable fed. facilities:** Offutt AFB.

Energy. Electricity production (est. 2001, kWh, by source): Coal: 20.2 bil; Petroleum: 29 mil; Gas: 360 mil; Hydroelectric: 1.1 bil; Nuclear: 8.7 bil.

State data. Motto: Equality before the law. **Flower:** Goldenrod. **Bird:** Western meadowlark. **Tree:** Cottonwood. **Song:** Beautiful Nebraska. **Entered union** Mar. 1, 1867; rank, 37th. **State fair** at Lincoln; Aug.- Sept.

History. When the Europeans first arrived, Pawnee, Ponca, Omaha, and Oto peoples lived in the region. Spanish and French explorers and fur traders visited the area prior to its acquisition in the Louisiana Purchase, 1803. Lewis and Clark passed through, 1804-6. The first permanent settlement was Bellevue, near Omaha, 1823. The region was gradually settled, despite the 1834 Indian Intercourse Act, which declared Nebraska Indian country and excluded white settlement. Conflicts with settlers eventually forced Native Americans to move to reservations. Many Civil War veterans settled under free land terms of the 1862 Homestead Act; as agriculture grew, struggles followed between homesteaders and ranchers.

Tourist attractions. State Museum (Elephant Hall), State Capitol, both Lincoln; Stuhr Museum of the Prairie Pioneer, Grand Island; Museum of the Fur Trade, Chadron; Henry Doorly Zoo, Joslyn Art Museum, both Omaha; Ashfall Fossil Beds, Strategic Air Command Museum, Ashland; Boys Town, west of Omaha; Arbor Lodge State Park, Nebraska City; Buffalo Bill Ranch State Hist. Park, North Platte; Pioneer Village, Minden; Oregon Trail landmarks; Scotts Bluff Natl. Monument; Chimney Rock Natl. Historic Site; Ft. Robinson; Hastings Museum, Hastings.

Famous Nebraskans. Grover Cleveland Alexander, Fred Astaire, Marlon Brando, Charles W. Bryan, William Jennings Bryan, Warren Buffett, Johnny Carson, Willa Cather, Dick Cavett, Dick Cheney, William F. "Buffalo Bill" Cody, Loren Eiseley, Rev. Edward J. Flanagan, Henry Fonda, Gerald R. Ford, Bob Gibson, Rollin Kirby, Harold Lloyd, Malcolm X, J. Sterling Morton, John Neihardt, Nick Nolte, George Norris, Tom Osborne, John J. Pershing, Roscoe Pound, Chief Red Cloud, Mari Sandoz, Robert Taylor, Darryl F. Zanuck.

Chamber of Commerce and Industry. 1320 Lincoln Mall, Ste. 201, Lincoln, NE 68508; 402-474-4422

Toll-free travel information. 1-800-228-4307.

Website. www.state.ne.us

Tourism website. www.visitnebraska.org

Nevada

Sagebrush State, Battle Born State, Silver State

People. Population (2001 est.): 2,106,074; rank: 35; **net change** (2000-2001): 5.4%. **Pop. density:** 19.2 per sq mi. **Racial distribution** (2000): 75.2% white; 6.8% black; 4.5% Asian; 1.3% Native American/Nat. AK; 0.4% Hawaiian/Pacific Islander; 8.0% other race; 2 or more races, 3.8%. **Hispanic pop.** (any race): 19.7%.

Geography. Total area: 110,561 sq mi; rank: 7. **Land area:** 109,826 sq mi; rank: 7. **Acres forested:** 8,938,000. **Location:** Mountain state bordered on N by Oregon and Idaho, on E by Utah and Arizona, on SE by Arizona, and on SW and W by California. **Climate:** semi-arid and arid. **Topography:** rugged N-S mountain ranges; highest elevation, Boundary Peak, 13,140 ft; southern area is within the Mojave Desert; lowest elevation, Colorado River at southern tip of state, 479 ft. **Capital:** Carson City.

Economy. Chief industries: gaming, tourism, mining, manufacturing, government, retailing, warehousing, trucking. **Chief manuf. goods:** food products, plastics, chemicals, aerospace products, lawn and garden irrigation equipment, seismic and machinery-monitoring devices. **Chief crops:** hay, alfalfa seed, potatoes, onions, garlic, barley, wheat. **Livestock:** (Jan. 2002) 500,000 cattle/calves; 100,000 sheep/lambs; (Dec. 2001) 7,000 hogs/pigs. **Timber/lumber:** (est. 2001): NA; piñon, juniper, other pines. **Nonfuel minerals** (est. 2001): 2.9 bil; mostly gold, lime, silver, sand & gravel, diatomite. **Principal internat. airports at:** Las Vegas, Reno. **Value of construction** (1997): $6.7 bil. **Gross state product** (2000): $74.7 bil. **Employment distrib.** (May 2002): 42.6% services; 21.1% trade; 12.4% govt.; 4.3% mfg. **Per cap. pers. income** (2001): $29,860. **Sales tax** (2002): 6.5%. **Unemployment** (2001): 5.3%.**Tourism expends.** (1999): $21 bil.

Finance. FDIC-insured commercial banks (2001): 34. **Deposits:** $16.7 bil. **FDIC-insured savings institutions** (2001): 2. **Assets:** $1.1 bil.

Federal govt. Fed. civ. employees (Mar. 2001): 7,294. **Avg. salary:** $51,529. **Notable fed. facilities:** Nevada Test Site; Hawthorne Army Ammunition Plant, Nellis Air Force Base and Gunnery Range; Fallon Naval Air Station; Palomino Valley Wild Horse and Burro Placement Center.

Energy. Electricity production (est. 2001, kWh, by source): Coal: 17.7 bil; Petroleum: 912 mil; Gas: 6.7 bil; Hydroelectric: 2.5 bil.

State data. Motto: All for our country. **Flower:** Sagebrush. **Bird:** Mountain bluebird. **Trees:** Single-leaf piñon and bristlecone pine. **Song:** Home Means Nevada. **Entered union** Oct. 31, 1864; rank, 36th. **State fair** at Reno; late Aug.

History. Shoshone, Paiute, Bannock, and Washoe peoples lived in the area at the time of European contact. Nevada was first explored by Spaniards, 1776. Hudson's Bay Co. trappers explored the north and central region, 1825; trader Jedediah Smith crossed the state, 1826-27. The area was acquired by the U.S., 1848, at the end of the Mexican War. The first settlement, Mormon Station, now Genoa, was established, 1849. Discovery of the Comstock Lode, rich in gold and silver, 1859, spurred a population boom. In the early 20th cent., Nevada adopted progressive measures such as the initiative, referendum, recall, and woman suffrage.

Tourist attractions. Legalized gambling at: Lake Tahoe, Reno, Las Vegas, Laughlin, Elko County, and elsewhere. Hoover Dam; Lake Mead; Great Basin Natl. Park; Valley of Fire State Park; Virginia City; Red Rock Canyon Natl. Conservation Area; Liberace Museum, the Las Vegas Strip, Guinness World of Records Museum, Lost City Museum, Overton, Lamoille Canyon, Pyramid Lake, all Las Vegas. Skiing near Lake Tahoe.

Famous Nevadans. Andre Agassi, Walter Van Tilburg Clark, George Ferris, Sarah Winnemucca Hopkins, Paul Laxalt, Dat So La Lee, John William Mackay, Anne Martin, Pat McCarran, Key Pittman, William Morris Stewart.

Tourist information. Commission on Tourism, 5151 S. Carson St., Carson City, NV 89701.

Toll-free travel information. 1-800-NEVADA8.

Website. www.silver.state.nv.us

Tourism website. www.travelnevada.com

New Hampshire

Granite State

People. Population (2001 est.): 1,259,181; rank: 41; **net change** (2000-2001): 1.9%. **Pop. density:** 140.4 per sq mi. **Racial distribution** (2000): 96.0% white; 0.7% black; 1.3% Asian; 0.2% Native American/Nat. AK; <0.1% Hawaiian/Pacific Islander; 0.6% other race; 2 or more races, 1.1%. **Hispanic pop.** (any race): 1.7%.

Geography. Total area: 9,350 sq mi; rank: 46. **Land area:** 8,968 sq mi; rank: 44. **Acres forested:** 4,981,000. **Location:** New England state bounded on S by Massachusetts, on W by Vermont, on N and NW by Canada, on E by Maine and the Atlantic Ocean. **Climate:** highly varied, due to its nearness to high mountains and ocean. **Topography:** low, rolling coast followed by countless hills and mountains rising out of a central plateau. **Capital:** Concord.

Economy. Chief industries: tourism, manufacturing, agriculture, trade, mining. **Chief manuf. goods:** machinery, electrical and electronic products, plastics, fabricated metal products. **Chief crops:** dairy products, nursery & greenhouse products, hay, vegetables, fruit, maple syrup & sugar products. **Livestock**: (Jan. 2002) 41,000 cattle/calves; (Dec. 2001) 3,500 hogs/pigs; 215,000 chickens (excl. broilers). **Timber/lumber** (est. 2001): 280 mil bd. ft.; white pine, hemlock, oak, birch. **Nonfuel minerals** (est. 2001): 60.3 mil; mostly sand & gravel, crushed and dimension stone, gemstones. **Commercial fishing** (2000): $14 mil. **Chief ports:** Portsmouth, Hampton, Rye. **Value of construction** (1997): $1.3 bil. **Gross state product** (2000): $47.7 bil. **Employment distrib.** (May 2002): 30.7% services; 26.4% trade; 13.7% govt.; 15.9% mfg. **Per cap. pers. income** (2001): $33,928. **Sales tax:** (2002): none. **Unemployment** (2001): 3.5%. **Tourism expends.** (1999): $2.3 bil. **Lottery** (2001): total sales: $196.4 mil; net income: $59.4 mil.

Finance. FDIC-insured commercial banks (2001): 15. **Deposits:** $19.2 bil. **FDIC-insured savings institutions** (2001): 19. **Assets:** $10.4 bil.

Federal govt. Fed. civ. employees (Mar. 2001): 3,083. **Avg. salary:** $59,476.

Energy. Electricity production(est. 2001, kWh, by source): Coal: 3.7 bil; Petroleum: 430 mil; Gas: 42 mil; Hydroelectric: 225 mil; Nuclear: 8.7 bil.

State data. Motto: Live free or die. **Flower:** Purple lilac. **Bird:** Purple finch. **Tree:** White birch. **Song:** Old New Hampshire. **Ninth** of the original 13 states to ratify the Constitution, June 21, 1788. **State Fair:** Many agricultural fairs statewide, July through Sept.; no State fair.

History. Algonquian-speaking peoples, including the Pennacook, lived in the region when the Europeans arrived. The first explorers to visit the area were England's Martin Pring, 1603, and France's Champlain, 1605. The first settlement was Odiorne's Point (now port of Rye), 1623. Native American conflicts were ended, 1759, by Robert Rogers' Rangers. Before the American Revolution, New Hampshire residents seized a British fort at Portsmouth, 1774, and drove the royal governor out, 1775. New Hampshire became the first colony to adopt its own constitution, 1776. Three regiments served in the Continental Army, and scores of privateers raided British shipping.

Tourist attractions. Mt. Washington, highest peak in Northeast; Lake Winnipesaukee; White Mt. National Forest; Crawford, Franconia—famous for the Old Man of the Mountain, described by Hawthorne as the Great Stone Face, Pinkham notches, all White Mt. region; the Flume, a spectacular gorge; the aerial tramway, Cannon Mt.; Strawbery Banke, Portsmouth; Shaker Village, Canterbury; Saint-Gaudens, Natl. Historic Site, Cornish; Mt. Monadnock.

Famous New Hampshirites. Salmon P. Chase, Ralph Adams Cram, Mary Baker Eddy, Daniel Chester French, Robert Frost, Horace Greeley, Sarah Buell Hale, Franklin Pierce, Augustus Saint-Gaudens, Adam Sandler, Alan Shepard, David H. Souter, Daniel Webster.

Tourist information. Division of Travel & Tourism Development, PO Box 1856, Concord, NH 03302-1856.

Toll-free travel information. 1-800-FUNINNH ext. 169.

Website. www.state.nh.us

Tourism website. www.visitnh.gov

New Jersey

Garden State

People. Population (2001 est.): 8,484,431; rank: 9; **net change** (2000-2001): 0.8%. **Pop. density:** 1,143.9 per sq mi. **Racial distribution** (2000): 72.6% white; 13.6% black; 5.7% Asian; 0.2% Native American/Nat. AK; <0.1% Hawaiian/Pacific Islander; 5.4% other race; 2 or more races, 2.5%. **Hispanic pop.** (any race): 13.3%.

Geography. Total area: 8,721 sq mi; rank: 47. **Land area:** 7,417 sq mi; rank: 46. **Acres forested:** 2,007,000. **Location:** Middle Atlantic state bounded on N and E by New York and

Atlantic Ocean, on S and W by Delaware and Pennsylvania. **Climate:** moderate, with marked difference bet. NW and SE extremities. **Topography:** Appalachian Valley in the NW also has highest elevation, High Pt., 1,801 ft; Appalachian Highlands, flat-topped NE-SW mountain ranges; Piedmont Plateau, low plains broken by high ridges (Palisades) rising 400-500 ft; Coastal Plain, covering three-fifths of state in SE, rises from sea level to gentle slopes. **Capital:** Trenton.

Economy. Chief industries: pharmaceuticals/drugs, telecommunications, biotechnology, printing & publishing. **Chief manuf. goods:** chemicals, electronic equipment, food. **Chief crops:** nursery/greenhouse, tomatoes, blueberries, peaches, peppers, cranberries, soybeans. **Livestock:** (Jan. 2002) 44,000 cattle/calves; (Dec. 2001) 13,000 hogs/pigs; 2.3 mil chickens (excl. broilers). **Timber/lumber:** (est. 2001): 20 mil bd. ft.; pine, cedar, mixed hardwoods. **Nonfuel minerals** (est. 2001): 348 mil; mostly crushed stone, sand & gravel, clays, peat. **Commercial fishing** (2000): $107.2 mil. **Chief ports:** Newark, Elizabeth, Hoboken, Camden. **Principal internat. airports at:** Atlantic City, Newark. **Value of construction** (1997): $8.3 bil. **Gross state product** (2000): $363.1 bil. **Employment distrib.** (May 2002): 33.6% services; 23% trade; 15.3% govt.; 10.6% mfg. **Per cap. pers. income** (2001): $38,153. **Sales tax** (2002): 6%. **Unemployment** (2001): 4.2%. **Tourism expends.** (1999): $15.1 bil. **Lottery** (2001): total sales: $1.8 bil; net income: $697.4 mil.

Finance. FDIC-insured commercial banks (2001): 81. **Deposits:** $61.6 bil. **FDIC-insured savings institutions** (2001): 71. **Assets:** $47.3 bil.

Federal govt. Fed. civ. employees (Mar. 2001): 25,411. **Avg. salary:** $58,237. **Notable fed. facilities:** McGuire AFB; Fort Dix; Fort Monmouth; Picatinny Arsenal; Lakehurst Naval Air Engineering Center.

Energy. Electricity production(est. 2001, kWh, by source): Coal: 1.4 bil; Petroleum: 228 mil; Gas: 102 mil; Hydroelectric: -142 mil.

State data. Motto: Liberty and prosperity. **Flower:** Purple violet. **Bird:** Eastern goldfinch. **Tree:** Red oak. **Third** of the original 13 states to ratify the Constitution, Dec. 18, 1787. **State fair** at Cherry Hill; late July-early Aug.

History. The Lenni Lenape (Delaware) peoples lived in the region and had mostly peaceful relations with European colonists, who arrived after the explorers Verrazano, 1524, and Hudson, 1609. The first permanent European settlement was Dutch, at Bergen (now Jersey City), 1660. When the British took New Netherland, 1664, the area between the Delaware and Hudson Rivers was given to Lord John Berkeley and Sir George Carteret. During the American Revolution, New Jersey was the scene of nearly 100 battles, large and small, including Trenton, 1776; Princeton, 1777; Monmouth, 1778.

Tourist attractions. 127 mi of beaches; Miss America Pageant, Atlantic City; Grover Cleveland birthplace, Caldwell; Cape May Historic District; Edison Natl. Historic Site, W. Orange; Six Flags Great Adventure, Jackson; Liberty State Park, Jersey City; Meadowlands Sports Complex, E. Rutherford; Pine Barrens wilderness area; Princeton University; numerous Revolutionary War historical sites; State Aquarium, Camden.

Famous New Jerseyans. Jason Alexander, Count Basie, Judy Blume, Jon Bon Jovi, Bill Bradley, Aaron Burr, Grover Cleveland, James Fenimore Cooper, Stephen Crane, Danny DeVito, Thomas Edison, Albert Einstein, James Gandolfini, Allen Ginsberg, Alexander Hamilton, Ed Harris, Whitney Houston, Buster Keaton, Joyce Kilmer, Norman Mailer, Jack Nicholson, Thomas Paine, Dorothy Parker, Joe Pesci, Molly Pitcher, Paul Robeson, Philip Roth, Antonin Scalia, Wally Schirra, H. Norman Schwarzkopf, Frank Sinatra, Bruce Springsteen, Martha Stewart, Meryl Streep, Dave Thomas, John Travolta, Walt Whitman, William Carlos Williams, Woodrow Wilson.

Chamber of Commerce. 50 W. State St., Trenton, NJ 08608.

Toll-free travel information. 1-800-VISITNJ.

Website. www.state.nj.us

Tourism website. www.visitnj.org

New Mexico

Land of Enchantment

People. Population (2001 est.): 1,829,146; rank: 36; **net change** (2000-2001): 0.6%. **Pop. density:** 15.1 per sq mi. **Racial distribution** (2000): 66.8% white; 1.9% black; 1.1% Asian; 9.5% Native American/Nat. AK; 0.1% Hawaiian/Pacific Islander; 17.0% other race; 2 or more races, 3.6%. **Hispanic pop.** (any race): 42.1%.

Geography. Total area: 121,589 sq mi; rank: 5. **Land area:** 121,356 sq mi rank: 5. **Acres forested:** 15,296,000. **Location:** southwestern state bounded by Colorado on the N, Oklahoma, Texas, and Mexico on the E and S, and Arizona on the W. **Climate:** dry, with temperatures rising or falling 5× F with every 1,000 ft elevation. **Topography:** eastern third, Great Plains; central third, Rocky Mts. (85% of the state is over 4,000-ft elevation); western third, high plateau. **Capital:** Santa Fe.

Economy. Chief industries: government, services, trade. **Chief manuf. goods:** foods, machinery, apparel, lumber, printing, transportation equipment, electronics, semiconductors. **Chief crops:** hay, onions, chiles, greenhouse nursery, pecans, cotton. **Livestock:** (Jan. 2002) 1.6 mil cattle/calves; 230,000 sheep/lambs; (Dec. 2001) 3,000 hogs/pigs. **Timber/lumber** (est. 2001): 97 mil bd. ft.; ponderosa pine, Douglas fir. **Nonfuel minerals** (est. 2001): 615 mil; mostly copper, potash, sand & gravel, portland cement, crushed stone. **Principal internat. airport at:** Albuquerque. **Value of construction** (1997): $1.9 bil. **Gross state product** (2000): $54.4 bil. **Employment distrib.** (May 2002): 29.5% services; 22.7% trade; 25.3% govt.; 5.5% mfg. **Per cap. pers. income** (2001): $23,162. **Sales tax** (2002): 5%. **Unemployment** (2001): 4.8%. **Tourism expends.** (1999): $3.5 bil. **Lottery** (2001): total sales: $115.7 mil; net income: $25.9 mil.

Finance. FDIC-insured commercial banks (2001): 53. **Deposits:** $11.6 bil. **FDIC-insured savings institutions** (2001): 10. **Assets:** $3.6 bil.

Federal govt. Fed. civ. employees (Mar. 2001): 20,962. **Avg. salary:** $48,028. **Notable fed. facilities:** Kirtland, Cannon, Holloman AF bases; Los Alamos Scientific Laboratory; White Sands Missile Range; Natl. Solar Observatory; Natl. Radio Astronomy Observatory, Sandia National Laboratories.

Energy. Electricity production (est. 2001, kWh, by source): Coal: 28.4 bil; Petroleum: 30 mil; Gas: 3.5 bil; Hydroelectric: 193 mil.

State data. Motto: Crescit Eundo (It grows as it goes). **Flower:** Yucca. **Bird:** Roadrunner. **Tree:** Piñon. **Song:** O, Fair New Mexico; Asi Es Nuevo Mexico. **Entered union** Jan. 6, 1912; rank, 47th. **State fair** at Albuquerque; mid-Sept.

History. Early inhabitants were peoples of the Mogollon and Anasazi civilizations, followed by the Pueblo peoples, Anasazi descendants. The nomadic Navajo and Apache tribes arrived c 15th cent. Franciscan Marcos de Niza and a former black slave, Estevanico, explored the area, 1539, seeking gold. First settlements were at San Juan Pueblo, 1598, and Santa Fe, 1610. Settlers alternately traded and fought with the Apache, Comanche, and Navajo. Trade on the Santa Fe Trail to Missouri started, 1821. The Mexican War was declared in May 1846; Gen. Stephen Kearny took Santa Fe without firing a shot, Aug. 18, 1846, declaring New Mexico part of the U.S. All Hispanic New Mexicans and Pueblo became U.S. citizens by terms of the 1848 treaty ending the war, but Congress denied the area statehood and created the territory of New Mexico, 1850. Pancho Villa raided Columbus, 1916, and U.S. troops were sent to the area. The world's first atomic bomb was exploded near Alamogordo, south of Santa Fe, 1945.

Tourist attractions. Carlsbad Caverns Natl. Park, with the largest natural underground chamber in the world; Santa Fe, oldest capital in U.S.; White Sands Natl. Monument, the largest gypsum deposit in the world; Chaco Culture National Historical Park; Acoma Pueblo, the "sky city," built atop a 357-ft mesa; Taos; Taos Art Colony; Taos Ski Valley; Ute Lake State Park; Shiprock.

Famous New Mexicans. Ben Abruzzo, Maxie Anderson, Jeff Bezos, Billy (the Kid) Bonney, Kit Carson, Bob Foster, Peter Hurd, Tony Hillerman, Archbishop Jean Baptiste Lamy, Nancy Lopez, Bill Mauldin, Georgia O'Keeffe, Kim Stanley, Al Unser, Bobby Unser, Lew Wallace.

Tourist information. New Mexico Dept. of Tourism, PO Box 20002, Santa Fe, NM 87503.

Toll-free travel information. 1-800-733-6396, ext. 0643

Website. www.state.nm.us

Tourism website. www.newmexico.org

IT'S A FACT: The nation's 1st "automobile theater" opened in Camden, NJ, on June 6, 1933. Known as the Camden Drive-In, it had 400 parking spaces and cost $1 per car or 25 cents per person.

WORLD ALMANAC QUICK QUIZ

Which of the 13 original colonies was the first to formally renounce allegiance to King George III of England—and the last to ratify the Constitution?

(a) Massachusetts (b) Delaware
(c) Rhode Island (d) Maine

For the answer look in this chapter, or see page 1008.

New York

Empire State

People. Population (2001 est.): 19,011,378; rank: 3; **net change** (2000-2001): 0.2%. **Pop. density:** 402.7 per sq mi. **Racial distribution** (2000): 67.9% white; 15.9% black; 5.5% Asian; 0.4% Native American/Nat. AK; 0.1% Hawaiian/Pacific Islander; 7.1% other race; 2 or more races, 3.1%. **Hispanic pop.** (any race): 15.1%.

Geography. Total area: 54,556 sq mi; rank: 27. **Land area:** 47,214 sq mi; rank: 30. **Acres forested:** 18,713,000. **Location:** Middle Atlantic state, bordered by the New England states, Atlantic Ocean, New Jersey and Pennsylvania, Lakes Ontario and Erie, and Canada. **Climate:** variable; the SE region moderated by the ocean. **Topography:** highest and most rugged mountains in the NE Adirondack upland; St. Lawrence-Champlain lowlands extend from Lake Ontario NE along the Canadian border; Hudson-Mohawk lowland follows the flows of the rivers N and W, 10-30 mi wide; Atlantic coastal plain in the SE; Appalachian Highlands, covering half the state westward from the Hudson Valley, include the Catskill Mts., Finger Lakes; plateau of Erie-Ontario lowlands. **Capital:** Albany.

Economy. Chief industries: manufacturing, finance, communications, tourism, transportation, services. **Principal manufactured goods:** books & periodicals, clothing & apparel, pharmaceuticals, machinery, instruments, toys & sporting goods, electronic equipment, automotive & aircraft components. **Chief crops:** apples, grapes, strawberries, cherries, pears, onions, potatoes, cabbage, sweet corn, green beans, cauliflower, field corn, hay, wheat, oats, dry beans. **Products:** milk, cheese, maple syrup, wine. **Livestock:** (Jan. 2002) 1.4 mil cattle/calves; 60,000 sheep/lambs; (Dec. 2001) 75,000 hogs/pigs; 4.7 mil chickens (excl. broilers); 2.1 mil broilers. **Timber/lumber** (est. 2001): 501 mil bd. ft.; birch, sugar and red maple, basswood, hemlock, pine, oak, ash. **Nonfuel minerals** (est. 2001): 1.1 bil; mostly crushed stone, portland cement, salt, sand & gravel, zinc. **Commercial fishing** (2000): $59.6 mil. **Chief ports:** New York, Buffalo, Albany. **Principal internat. airports at:** Albany, Buffalo, New York, Newburgh, Rochester, Syracuse. **Value of construction** (1997): $15.8 bil. **Gross state product** (2000): $799.2 bil. **Employment distrib.** (May 2002): 35.8% services; 20% trade; 17.6% govt.; 9.3% mfg. **Per cap. pers. income** (2001): $35,884. **Sales tax** (2002): 4%. **Unemployment** (2001): 4.9%. **Tourism expends.** (1999): $36.3 bil. **Lottery** (2001): total sales: $4.2 bil; net income: $1.4 bil.

Finance. FDIC-insured commercial banks (2001): 140. **Deposits:** $826.2 bil. **FDIC-insured savings institutions** (2001): 79. **Assets:** $145.7 bil.

Federal govt. Fed. civ. employees (Mar. 2001): 56,478. **Avg. salary:** $51,972. **Notable fed. facilities:** West Point Military Academy; Merchant Marine Academy; Ft. Drum; Rome Labs.; Watervliet Arsenal.

Energy. Electricity production (est. 2001, kWh, by source): Coal: 1.9 bil; Petroleum: 8.7 bil; Gas: 8.9 bil; Hydroelectric: 17.8 bil; Nuclear: 20.8 bil.

State data. Motto: Excelsior (Ever upward). **Flower:** Rose. **Bird:** Bluebird. **Tree:** Sugar maple. **Song:** I Love New York. **Eleventh** of the original 13 states to ratify the Constitution, July 26, 1788. **State fair** at Syracuse; late Aug.-early Sept.

History. Algonquians including the Mahican, Wappinger, and Lenni Lenape inhabited the region, as did the Iroquoian Mohawk, Oneida, Onondaga, Cayuga, and Seneca tribes, who established the League of the Five Nations. In 1609, Henry Hudson visited the river named for him, and Champlain explored the lake named for him. The first permanent settlement was Dutch, near present-day Albany, 1624. New Amsterdam was settled, 1626, at the S tip of Manhattan Island. A British fleet seized New Netherland, 1664. Ninety-two of the 300 or more engagements of the American Revolution were fought in New York, including the Battle of Bemis Heights-Saratoga, 1777, a turning point of the war. Completion of Erie Canal, 1825, established the state as a gateway to the West. The first women's rights convention was held in Seneca Falls, 1848.

Tourist attractions. New York City; Adirondack and Catskill Mts.; Finger Lakes; Great Lakes; Thousand Islands; Niagara Falls; Saratoga Springs; Philipsburg Manor, Sunnyside (Washington Irving's home), the Dutch Church of Sleepy Hollow, all in Tarrytown area; Corning Glass Center and Steuben factory, Corning; Fenimore House, Natl. Baseball Hall of Fame and Museum, both in Cooperstown; Ft. Ticonderoga overlooking Lakes George and Champlain; Empire State Plaza, Albany; Lake Placid; Franklin D. Roosevelt Natl. Historic Site, including the Roosevelt Library, Hyde Park; Long Island beaches; Theodore Roosevelt estate, Sagamore Hill, Oyster Bay; Turning Stone Casino.

Famous New Yorkers. Woody Allen, Susan B. Anthony, James Baldwin, Lucille Ball, L. Frank Baum, Milton Berle, Humphrey Bogart, Barbara Boxer, Mel Brooks, Benjamin Cardozo, De Witt Clinton, Peter Cooper, Aaron Copland, George Eastman, Millard Fillmore, Lou Gehrig, George and Ira Gershwin, Ruth Bader Ginsburg, Rudolph Giuliani, Jackie Gleason, Stephen Jay Gould, Julia Ward Howe, Charles Evans Hughes, Sarah Hughes, Washington Irving, Henry and William James, John Jay, Michael Jordan, Edward Koch, Fiorello LaGuardia, Herman Melville, J. Pierpont Morgan Jr., Eddie Murphy, Joyce Carol Oates, Carroll O'Connor, Rosie O'Donnell, Eugene O'Neill, George Pataki, Colin Powell, Nancy Reagan, John D. Rockefeller, Nelson Rockefeller, Ray Romano, Eleanor Roosevelt, Franklin D. Roosevelt, Theodore Roosevelt, Tim Russert, J. D. Salinger, Jerry Seinfeld, Paul Simon, Alfred E. Smith, Elizabeth Cady Stanton, Barbra Streisand, Donald Trump, William (Boss) Tweed, Martin Van Buren, Gore Vidal, Denzel Washington, Edith Wharton, Walt Whitman.

Tourist information. Empire State Development, Travel Information Center, 1 Commerce Plaza, Albany, NY 12245.

Toll-free travel information. 1-800-CALLNYS from U.S. states and territories and Canada; 1-518-474-4116 from other areas.

Website. www.state.ny.us

Tourism website. www.iloveny.com

North Carolina

Tar Heel State, Old North State

People. Population (2001 est.): 8,186,268; rank: 11; **net change** (2000-2001): 1.7%. **Pop. density:** 168.1 per sq mi. **Racial distribution** (2000): 72.10% white; 21.6% black; 1.4% Asian; 1.2% Native American/Nat. AK; 0.1% Hawaiian/Pacific Islander; 2.3% other race; 2 or more races, 1.3%. **Hispanic pop.** (any race): 4.7%.

Geography. Total area: 53,819 sq mi; rank: 28. **Land area:** 48,711 sq mi; rank: 29. **Acres forested:** 19,278,000. **Location:** South Atlantic state bounded by Virginia, South Carolina, Georgia, Tennessee, and the Atlantic Ocean. **Climate:** subtropical in SE, medium-continental in mountain region; tempered by the Gulf Stream and the mountains in W. **Topography:** coastal plain and tidewater, two-fifths of state, extending to the fall line of the rivers; piedmont plateau, another two-fifths, of gentle to rugged hills; southern Appalachian Mts. contains the Blue Ridge and Great Smoky Mts. **Capital:** Raleigh.

Economy. Chief industries: manufacturing, agriculture, tourism. **Chief manuf. goods:** food products, textiles, industrial machinery and equipment, electrical and electronic equipment, furniture, tobacco products, apparel. **Chief crops:** tobacco, cotton, soybeans, corn, food grains, wheat, peanuts, sweet potatoes. **Livestock:** (Jan. 2002) 950,000 cattle/calves; (Dec. 2001) 9.5 mil hogs/pigs; 18.1 mil chickens (excl. broilers); 698.4 mil broilers. **Timber/lumber** (est. 2001): 2.4 bil bd. ft.; yellow pine, oak, hickory, poplar, maple. **Nonfuel minerals** (est. 2001): 744 mil; mostly crushed stone, phosphate rock, sand & gravel, clays. **Commercial fishing** (2000): $106.5 mil. **Principal internat. airports at:** Charlotte, Greensboro, Raleigh/Durham, Wilmington. **Chief ports:** Morehead City, Wilmington. **Value of construction** (1997): $14 bil. **Gross state product** (2000): $281.7 bil. **Employment distrib.** (May 2002): 27.3% services; 22.8% trade; 16.7% govt.; 17.9% mfg. **Per cap. pers. income** (2001): $27,418. **Sales tax** (2002): 4.5%. **Unemployment** (2001): 5.5%. **Tourism expends.** (1999): $11.9 bil.

Finance. FDIC-insured commercial banks (2001): 75. **Deposits:** $651.4 bil. **FDIC-insured savings institutions** (2001): 40. **Assets:** $6.4 bil.

Federal govt. Fed. civ. employees (Mar. 2001): 30,488. **Avg. salary:** $46,340. **Notable fed. facilities:** Ft. Bragg; Camp LeJeune Marine Base; U.S. EPA Research and Development Labs, Cherry Point Marine Corps Air Station; Natl. Humanities Center; Natl. Inst. of Environmental Health Science; Natl. Center for Health Statistics Lab, Research Triangle Park.

Energy. Electricity production (est. 2001, kWh, by source): Coal: 68.8 bil; Petroleum: 412 mil; Gas: 676 mil; Hydroelectric: 1.9 bil; Nuclear: 37.8 bil.

State data. Motto: Esse Quam Videri (To be rather than to seem). **Flower:** Dogwood. **Bird:** Cardinal. **Tree:** Pine. **Song:** The Old North State. **Twelfth** of the original 13 states to ratify the Constitution, Nov. 21, 1789. **State fair** at Raleigh; mid-Oct.

History. Algonquian, Siouan, and Iroquoian peoples lived in the region at the time of European contact. The first English colony in America was the first of 2 established by Sir Walter Raleigh on Roanoke Island, 1585 and 1587. The first group returned to England; the second, the "Lost Colony," disappeared without a trace. Permanent settlers came from Virginia, c 1660. Roused by British repression, the colonists drove out the royal governor, 1775. The province's congress was the first to vote for independence; ten regiments were furnished to the Continental Army. Cornwallis's forces were defeated at Kings Mountain, 1780, and forced out after Guilford Courthouse, 1781. The state seceded in 1861, and provided more troops to the Confederacy than any other state; readmitted in 1868.

Tourist attractions. Cape Hatteras and Cape Lookout natl. seashores; Great Smoky Mts.; Guilford Courthouse and Moore's Creek parks; 66 American Revolution battle sites; Bennett Place, near Durham, where Gen. Joseph Johnston surrendered the last Confederate army to Gen. William Sherman; Ft. Raleigh, Roanoke Island, where Virginia Dare, first child of English parents in the New World, was born Aug. 18, 1587; Wright Brothers Natl. Memorial, Kitty Hawk; Battleship *North Carolina*, Wilmington; NC Zoo, Asheboro; NC Symphony, NC Museum, Raleigh; Carl Sandburg Home, Hendersonville, Biltmore House & Gardens, Asheville.

Famous North Carolinians. David Brinkley, Robert Byrd, Shirley Caesar, John Coltrane, Rick Dees, Elizabeth Dole, John Edwards, Ava Gardner, Richard J. Gatling, Billy Graham, Andy Griffith, O. Henry, Andrew Jackson, Andrew Johnson, Michael Jordan, Wm. Rufus King, Charles Kuralt, Meadowlark Lemon, Dolley Madison, Thelonious Monk, Edward R. Murrow, Arnold Palmer, Richard Petty, James K. Polk, Charlie Rose, Carl Sandburg, Enos Slaughter, Dean Smith, James Taylor, Thomas Wolfe, Orville and Wilbur Wright.

Tourist information. North Carolina Division of Tourism, Film & Sports Development, 301 N. Wilmington St., Raleigh, NC 27601.

Toll-free travel information. 1-800-VISITNC.

Website. www.ncgov.com

Tourism website. www.visitnc.com

North Dakota

Peace Garden State

People. Population (2001 est.): 634,448; rank: 48; **net change** (2000-2001): -1.2%. **Pop. density:** 9.2 per sq mi. **Racial distribution** (2000): 92.4% white; 0.6% black; 0.6% Asian; 4.9% Native American/Nat. AK; <0.1% Hawaiian/Pacific Islander; 0.4% other race; 2 or more races, 1.2%. **Hispanic pop.** (any race): 1.2%.

Geography. Total area: 70,700 sq mi; rank: 19. **Land area:** 68,976 sq mi; rank: 17. **Acres forested:** 462,000. **Location:** West North Central state, situated exactly in the middle of North America, bounded on the N by Canada, on the E by Minnesota, on the S by South Dakota, on the W by Montana. **Climate:** continental, with a wide range of temperature and moderate rainfall. **Topography:** Central Lowland in the E comprises the flat Red River Valley and the Rolling Drift Prairie; Missouri Plateau of the Great Plains on the W. **Capital:** Bismarck.

Economy. Chief industries: agriculture, mining, tourism, manufacturing, telecommunications, energy, food processing. **Chief manuf. goods:** farm equipment, processed foods, fabricated metal, high-tech. electronics. **Chief crops:** spring wheat, durum, barley, flaxseed, oats, potatoes, dry edible beans, honey, soybeans, sugar beets, sunflowers, hay. **Livestock:** (Jan. 2002) 2 mil cattle/calves; 145,000 sheep/lambs; (Dec. 2001) 154,000 hogs/pigs. **Timber/lumber:** (est. 2001): 1 mil bd. ft.; oak, ash, cottonwood, aspen; 1 mil bd. ft. **Nonfuel minerals** (est. 2001): 39.3 mil; mostly sand & gravel, lime, crushed stone, clays, gemstones. **Principal internat. airport at:** Fargo. **Value of construction** (1997): $788 mil. **Gross state product** (2000): $18.3 bil. **Employment distrib.** (May 2002): 28.3% services; 24.6% trade; 22.7% govt.; 7.6% mfg. **Per cap. pers. income** (2001): $25,538. **Sales tax** (2002): 5%. **Unemployment** (2001): 2.8%. **Tourism expends.** (1999): $1.1 bil.

Finance. FDIC-insured commercial banks (2001): 104. **Deposits:** $13.4 bil. **FDIC-insured savings institutions** (2001): 3. **Assets:** $955 mil.

Federal govt. Fed. civ. employees (Mar. 2001): 5,015. **Avg. salary:** $44,724. **Notable fed. facilities:** Strategic Air Command Base; Northern Prairie Wildlife Research Center; Garrison Dam; Theodore Roosevelt Natl. Park; Grand Forks Energy Research Center; Ft. Union Natl. Historic Site.

Energy. Electricity production (est. 2001, kWh, by source): Coal: 28.8 bil; Petroleum: 34 mil; Gas: Hydroelectric: 1.3 bil.

State data. Motto: Liberty and union, now and forever, one and inseparable. **Flower:** Wild prairie rose. **Bird:** Western meadowlark. **Tree:** American elm. **Song:** North Dakota Hymn. **Entered union** Nov. 2, 1889; rank, 39th. **State fair** at Minot; July.

History. At the time of European contact, the Ojibwa, Yanktonai and Teton Sioux, Mandan, Arikara, and Hidatsa peoples lived in the region. Pierre de Varennes was the first French fur trader in the area, 1738, followed later by the English. The U.S. acquired half the territory in the Louisiana Purchase, 1803. Lewis and Clark built Ft. Mandan, near present-day Stanton, 1804-5, and wintered there. In 1818, American ownership of the other half was confirmed by agreement with Britain. The first permanent settlement was at Pembina, 1812. Missouri River steamboats reached the area, 1832, the first railroad, 1873, bringing many homesteaders. The "bonanza farm" craze of the 1870s-80s attracted many settlers. The state was first to hold a national Presidential primary, 1912.

Tourist attractions. North Dakota Heritage Center, Bismarck; Bonanzaville, Fargo; Ft. Union Trading Post Natl. Historic Site; Lake Sakakawea; Intl. Peace Garden; Theodore Roosevelt Natl. Park, including Elkhorn Ranch, Badlands; Ft. Abraham Lincoln State Park and Museum, near Mandan; Dakota Dinosaur Museum, Dickinson; Knife River Indian Villages-National Historic Site.

Famous North Dakotans. Maxwell Anderson, Angie Dickinson, John Bernard Flannagan, Phil Jackson, Louis L'Amour, Peggy Lee, Eric Sevareid, Vilhjalmur Stefansson, Lawrence Welk.

Greater North Dakota Association (Chamber of Commerce). PO Box 2639, 2000 Schafer St., Bismarck, ND 58501.

Toll-free travel information. 1-800-HELLO-ND

Website. www.discovernd.com

Tourism website. www.ndtourism.com

Ohio

Buckeye State

People. Population (2001 est.): 11,373,541; rank: 7; **net change** (2000-2001): 0.2%. **Pop. density:** 277.8 per sq mi. **Racial distribution** (2000): 85.0% white; 11.5% black; 1.2% Asian; 0.2% Native American/Nat. AK; <0.1% Hawaiian/Pacific Islander; 0.8% other race; 2 or more races, 1.4%. **Hispanic pop.** (any race): 1.9%.

Geography. Total area: 44,825 sq mi; rank: 34. **Land area:** 40,948 sq mi; rank: 35. **Acres forested:** 7,863,000. **Location:** East North Central state bounded on the N by Michigan and Lake Erie; on the E and S by Pennsylvania, West Virginia, and Kentucky; on the W by Indiana. **Climate:** temperate but variable; weather subject to much precipitation. **Topography:** generally rolling plain; Allegheny plateau in E; Lake Erie plains extend southward; central plains in the W. **Capital:** Columbus.

Economy. Chief industries: manufacturing, trade, services. **Chief manuf. goods:** transportation equipment, machinery, primary and fabricated metal products. **Chief crops:** corn, hay, winter wheat, oats, soybeans. **Livestock:** (Jan. 2002) 1.3 mil cattle/calves; 140,000 sheep/lambs; (Dec. 2001) 1.4 mil hogs/pigs; 38 mil chickens (excl. broilers); 45.7 mil broilers. **Timber/lumber** (est. 2001): 360 mil bd. ft.; oak, ash, maple, walnut, beech. **Nonfuel minerals** (est. 2001): 1.1 bil; mostly crushed stone, sand & gravel, salt, lime, portland cement. **Commercial fishing** (2000): $2.4 mil. **Chief ports:** Toledo, Conneaut, Cleveland, Ashtabula. **Principal internat. airports at:** Akron, Cincinnati, Cleveland, Columbus, Dayton. **Value of construction** (1997): $14.7 bil. **Gross state product** (2000): $372.6 bil. **Employment distrib.** (May 2002): 29% services; 23.8% trade; 14.7% govt.; 18.1% mfg. **Per cap. pers. income** (2001): $28,619. **Sales tax** (2002): 5%. **Unemployment** (2001): 4.3%. **Tourism expends.** (1999): $12.7 bil. **Lottery** (2001): total sales: $1.9 bil; net income: $637 mil.

Finance. FDIC-insured commercial banks (2001): 202. **Deposits:** $286.8 bil. **FDIC-insured savings institutions** (2001): 122. **Assets:** $80.7 bil.

Federal govt. Fed. civ. employees (Mar. 2001): 42,000. **Avg. salary:** $54,383. **Notable fed. facilities:** Wright Patterson AFB; Defense Construction Supply Center; Lewis Research Ctr.; Portsmouth Gaseous Diffusion Plant.

Energy. Electricity production (est. 2001, kWh, by source): Coal: 118.7 bil; Petroleum: 418 mil; Gas: 347 mil; Hydroelectric: 511 mil; Nuclear: 15.5 bil.

State data. Motto: With God, all things are possible. **Flower:** Scarlet carnation. **Bird:** Cardinal. **Tree:** Buckeye. **Song:** Beautiful Ohio. **Entered union** Mar. 1, 1803; rank, 17th. **State fair** at Columbus; Aug.

History. Wyandot, Delaware, Miami, and Shawnee peoples sparsely occupied the area when the first Europeans arrived. La Salle visited the region, 1669, and France claimed the area, 1682. Around 1730, traders from Pennsylvania and Virginia entered the area; the French and their Native American allies sought to drive them out. France ceded its claim, 1763, to Britain. During the American Revolution, George Rogers Clark seized British posts and held the region, until Britain gave up its claim, 1783, in the Treaty of Paris. The region became U.S. territory after the American Revolution. First organized settlement was at Marietta, 1788. Indian warfare ended with Anthony Wayne's victory at Fallen Timbers, 1794. In the War of 1812, Oliver Hazard Perry's victory on Lake Erie and William Henry Harrison's invasion of Canada, 1813, ended British incursions.

Tourist attractions. Mound City Group, a group of 24 prehistoric Indian burial mounds in Hopewell Culture Natl. Historical Park; Neil Armstrong Air and Space Museum, Wapakoneta; Air Force Museum, Dayton; Pro Football Hall of Fame, Canton; King's Island amusement park, Mason; Lake Erie Islands, Cedar Point amusement park, both Sandusky; birthplaces, homes of, and memorials to U.S. Pres. W. H. Harrison, Grant, Garfield, Hayes, McKinley, Harding, Taft, B. Harrison; Amish Region, Tuscarawas/Holmes counties; German Village, Columbus; Sea World, Aurora; Jack Nicklaus Sports Center, Mason; Bob Evans Farm, Rio Grande; Rock and Roll Hall of Fame and Museum, Cleveland.

Famous Ohioans. Sherwood Anderson, Neil Armstrong, George Bellows, Halle Berry, Ambrose Bierce, Erma Bombeck, Drew Carey, Hart Crane, George Custer, Clarence Darrow, Paul Laurence Dunbar, Thomas Edison, Clark Gable, John Glenn, Zane Grey, Bob Hope, William Dean Howells, Toni Morrison, Jack Nicklaus, Jesse Owens, Pontiac, Eddie Rickenbacker, John D. Rockefeller Sr. and Jr., Roy Rogers, Pete Rose, Arthur Schlesinger Jr., Gen. William Sherman, Steven Spielberg, Gloria Steinem, Harriet Beecher Stowe, Charles Taft, Robert A. Taft, William H. Taft, Tecumseh, James Thurber, Ted Turner, Orville and Wilbur Wright.

Chamber of Commerce. PO Box 15159. 230 E. Town St., Columbus, OH 43215-0159.

Toll-free travel information. 1-800-BUCKEYE.

Website. www.state.oh.us

Tourism website. www.ohiotourism.com

Oklahoma

Sooner State

People. Population (2001 est.): 3,460,097; rank: 28; **net change** (2000-2001): 0.3%. **Pop. density:** 50.4 per sq mi. **Racial distribution** (2000): 76.2% white; 7.6% black; 1.4% Asian; 7.9% Native American/Nat. AK; 0.1% Hawaiian/Pacific Islander; 2.4% other race; 2 or more races, 4.5%. **Hispanic pop.** (any race): 5.2%.

Geography. Total area: 69,898 sq mi; rank: 20. **Land area:** 68,667 sq mi; rank: 19. **Acres forested:** 7,539,000. **Location:** West South Central state bounded on the N by Colorado and Kansas; on the E by Missouri and Arkansas; on the S and W by Texas and New Mexico. **Climate:** temperate; southern humid belt merging with colder northern continental; humid eastern and dry western zones. **Topography:** high plains predominate in the W, hills and small mountains in the E; the east central region is dominated by the Arkansas R. Basin, and the Red R. Plains, in the S. **Capital:** Oklahoma City.

Economy. Chief industries: manufacturing, mineral and energy exploration and production, agriculture, services. **Chief manuf. goods:** nonelectrical machinery, transportation equipment, food products, fabricated metal products. **Chief crops:** wheat, cotton, hay, peanuts, grain sorghum, soybeans, corn, pecans. **Livestock:** (Jan. 2002) 5.2 mil cattle/calves; 60,000 sheep/lambs; (Dec. 2001) 2.5 mil hogs/pigs; 5.4 mil chickens (excl. broilers); 223.1 mil broilers. **Timber/lumber:** (est. 2001): NA; pine, oak, hickory; **Nonfuel minerals** (est. 2001): 530 mil; mostly crushed stone, portland cement, sand & gravel, helium. **Chief ports:** Catoosa, Muskogee. **Principal internat. airports at:** Oklahoma City, Tulsa. **Value of construction** (1997): $3.1 bil. **Gross state product** (2000): $91.8 bil. **Employment distrib.** (May 2002): 29% services; 22.6% trade; 20.1% govt.; 11.4% mfg. **Per cap. pers. income** (2001): $24,787. **Sales tax** (2002): 4.5%. **Unemployment** (2001): 3.8%. **Tourism expends.** (1999): $3.7 bil.

Finance. FDIC-insured commercial banks (2001): 282. **Deposits:** $35.1 bil. **FDIC-insured savings institutions** (2001): 7. **Assets:** $7.1 bil.

Federal govt. Fed. civ. employees (Mar. 2001): 32,673. **Avg. salary:** $46,510. **Notable fed. facilities:** Federal Aviation Agency and Tinker AFB, Oklahoma City; Ft. Sill, Lawton; Altus AFB; Vance AFB.

Energy. Electricity production (est. 2001, kWh, by source): Coal: 32.2 bil; Petroleum: 148 mil; Gas: 15.9 bil; Hydroelectric: 2.3 bil.

State data. Motto: Labor Omnia Vincit (Labor conquers all things). **Flower:** Mistletoe. **Bird:** Scissor-tailed flycatcher. **Tree:** Redbud. **Song:** Oklahoma! **Entered union** Nov. 16, 1907; rank, 46th. **State fair** at Oklahoma City; last 2 full weeks of Sept.

History. The region was sparsely inhabited by Native American tribes when Coronado, the first European, arrived in 1541; in the 16th and 17th cent., French traders visited. Part of the Louisiana Purchase, 1803, Oklahoma was established as Indian Territory (but not given territorial government). It became home to the "Five Civilized Tribes"—Cherokee, Choctaw, Chickasaw, Creek, and Seminole—after the forced removal of Indians from the eastern U.S., 1828-46. The land was also used by Comanche, Osage, and other Plains Indians. As white settlers pressed west, land was opened for homesteading by runs and lottery, the first run on Apr. 22, 1889. The most famous run was to the Cherokee Outlet, 1893.

Tourist attractions. Cherokee Heritage Center, Tahlequah; Oklahoma City Natl. Memorial; White Water Bay and Frontier City theme pks., both Oklahoma City; Will Rogers Memorial, Claremore; Natl. Cowboy Hall of Fame and Remington Park Race Track, both Oklahoma City; Ft. Gibson Stockade, near Muskogee; Ouachita Natl. Forest; Tulsa's art deco district; Wichita Mts. Wildlife Refuge, Lawton; Woolaroc Museum & Wildlife Preserve, Bartlesville; Sequoyah's Home Site, near Sallisaw; Philbrook Museum of Art and Gilcrease Museum, both Tulsa.

Famous Oklahomans. Troy Aikman, Carl Albert, Gene Autry, Johnny Bench, William "Hopalong Cassidy" Boyd, Garth Brooks, Lon Chaney, L. Gordon Cooper, Walter Cronkite, Jerome "Dizzy" Dean, Ralph Ellison, John Hope Franklin, James Garner, Geronimo, Woody Guthrie, Paul Harvey, Ron Howard, Gen. Patrick J. Hurley, Ben Johnson, Jeane Kirkpatrick, Louis L'Amour, Shannon Lucid, Mickey Mantle, Reba McEntire, Wiley Post, Tony Randall, Oral Roberts, Will Rogers, Sam Snead, Barry Switzer, Maria Tallchief, Jim Thorpe, J.C. Watts Jr.

Chamber of Commerce. Chamber of Commerce, 330 NE 10th, Oklahoma City, OK 73104.

Tourism Dept. PO Box 60789, Oklahoma City, OK 73146-0789.

Toll-free travel information. 1-800-652-OKLA.

Website. www.state.ok.us

Tourism website. www.travelok.com

Oregon

Beaver State

People. Population (2001 est.): 3,472,867; rank: 27; **net change** (2000-2001): 1.5%. **Pop. density:** 36.2 per sq mi. **Racial distribution** (2000): 86.6% white; 1.6% black; 3.0% Asian; 1.3% Native American/Nat. AK; 0.2% Hawaiian/Pacific Islander; 4.2% other race; 2 or more races, 3.1%. **Hispanic pop.** (any race): 8.0%.

Geography. Total area: 98,381 sq mi; rank: 9. **Land area:** 95,997 sq mi; rank: 10. **Acres forested:** 27,997,000. **Location:** Pacific state, bounded on N by Washington; on E by Idaho; on S by Nevada and California; on W by the Pacific. **Climate:** coastal mild and humid climate; continental dryness and extreme temperatures in the interior. **Topography:** Coast Range of rugged mountains; fertile Willamette R. Valley to E and S; Cascade Mt. Range of volcanic peaks E of the valley; plateau E of Cascades, remaining two-thirds of state. **Capital:** Salem.

Economy. Chief industries: manufacturing, services, trade, finance, insurance, real estate, government, construction. **Chief manuf. goods:** electronics & semiconductors, lumber & wood products, metals, transportation equipment, processed food, paper. **Chief crops:** greenhouse, hay, wheat, grass seed, potatoes, onions, Christmas trees, pears, mint. **Livestock:** (Jan. 2002) 1.4 mil cattle/calves; 285,000 sheep/lambs; (Dec. 2001) 29,000 hogs/pigs; 3.7 mil chickens (excl. broilers). **Timber/lumber** (est. 2001): 6.1 bil bd. ft.; Douglas fir, hemlock, ponderosa pine. **Nonfuel minerals** (est. 2001): 326 mil; mostly sand & gravel, crushed stone, portland cement, diatomite, pumice and pumicite. **Commercial fishing** (2000): $79.6 mil. **Chief ports:** Portland, Astoria, Coos Bay. **Principal internat. airports at:** Portland, Medford. **Value of construction** (1997): $6 bil. **Gross state product** (2000): $118.6 bil. **Employment distrib.** (May 2002): 28.2% services; 24.5% trade; 17.7% govt.; 14.1% mfg. **Per cap. pers. income** (2001): $28,000. **Sales tax:** (2002): none. **Unemployment** (2001): 6.3%. **Tourism expends.** (1999): $5.5 bil. **Lottery** (2001): total sales: $785.7 mil; net income: $292.2 mil.

Finance. FDIC-insured commercial banks (2001): 33. **Deposits:** $7.1 bil. **FDIC-insured savings institutions (2001):** 5. **Assets:** $2.8 bil.

Federal govt. Fed. civ. employees (Mar. 2001): 17,270. **Avg. salary:** $50,282. **Notable fed. facilities:** Bonneville Power Administration.

Energy. Electricity production (est. 2001, kWh, by source): Coal: 4.4 bil; Petroleum: 93 mil; Gas: 5.2 bil; Hydroelectric: 28.4 bil.

State data. Motto: She flies with her own wings. **Flower:** Oregon grape. **Bird:** Western meadowlark. **Tree:** Douglas fir. **Song:** Oregon, My Oregon. **Entered union** Feb. 14, 1859; rank, 33rd. **State fair** at Salem; 12 days ending with Labor Day.

History. More than 100 Native American tribes inhabited the area at the time of European contact, including the Chinook, Yakima, Cayuse, Modoc, and Nez Percé. Capt. Robert Gray sighted and sailed into the Columbia River, 1792; Lewis and Clark, traveling overland, wintered at its mouth, 1805-6; John Jacob Astor established a trading post in the Columbia River region, 1811. Settlers arrived in the Williamette Valley, 1834. In 1843, the first large wave of settlers arrived via the Oregon Trail. Early in the 20th cent., the "Oregon System"—political reforms that included the initiative, referendum, recall, direct primary, and woman suffrage—was adopted.

Tourist attractions. John Day Fossil Beds Natl. Monument; Columbia River Gorge; Timberline Lodge, Mt. Hood Natl. Forest; Crater Lake Natl. Park; Oregon Dunes Natl. Recreation Area; Ft. Clatsop Natl. Memorial; Oregon Caves Natl. Monument; Oregon Museum of Science and Industry, Portland; Shakespearean Festival, Ashland; High Desert Museum, Bend; Multnomah Falls; Diamond Lake; "Spruce Goose," Evergreen Aviation Museum, McMinnville.

Famous Oregonians. Ernest Bloch, Ernest Haycox, Chief Joseph, Ken Kesey, Phil Knight, Ursula K. Le Guin, Edwin Markham, Tom McCall, Dr. John McLoughlin, Joaquin Miller, Bob Packwood, Linus Pauling, Steve Prefontaine, John Reed, Alberto Salazar, Mary Decker Slaney, William Simon U'Ren.

Tourist information. Economic Development Department, 775 Summer St. NE, Salem, OR 97310.

Toll-free travel information. 1-800-547-7842.

Website. www.oregon.gov

Tourism website. www.traveloregon.com

Pennsylvania

Keystone State

People. Population (2001 est.): 12,287,150; rank: 6; **net change** (2000-2001): 0.0%. **Pop. density:** 274.2 per sq mi. **Racial distribution** (2000): 85.4% white; 10.0% black; 1.8% Asian; 0.1% Native American/Nat. AK; <0.1% Hawaiian/Pacific Islander; 1.5% other race; 2 or more races, 1.2%. **Hispanic pop.** (any race): 3.2%.

Geography. Total area: 46,055 sq mi; rank: 33. **Land area:** 44,817 sq mi; rank: 32. **Acres forested:** 16,969,000. **Location:** Middle Atlantic state, bordered on the E by the Delaware R.; on the S by the Mason-Dixon Line; on the W by West Virginia and Ohio; on the N/NE by Lake Erie and New York. **Climate:** continental with wide fluctuations in seasonal temperatures. **Topography:** Allegheny Mts. run SW to NE, with Piedmont and Coast Plain in the SE triangle; Allegheny Front a diagonal spine across the state's center; N and W rugged plateau falls to Lake Erie Lowland. **Capital:** Harrisburg.

Economy. Chief industries: agribusiness, advanced manufacturing, health care, travel & tourism, depository institutions, biotechnology, printing & publishing, research & consulting, trucking & warehousing, transportation by air, engineering & management, legal services. **Chief manuf. goods:** fabricated metal products; industrial machinery & equipment, transportation equipment, rubber & plastics, electronic equipment, chemicals & pharmaceuticals, lumber & wood products, stone, clay, & glass products. **Chief crops:** corn, hay, mushrooms, apples, potatoes, winter wheat, oats, vegetables, tobacco, grapes, peaches. **Livestock:** (Jan. 2002) 1.6 mil cattle/calves; 86,000 sheep/lambs; (Dec. 2001) 1.1 mil hogs/pigs; 29.3 mil chickens (excl. broilers); 133.3 mil broilers. **Timber/lumber** (est. 2001): 1.1 bil bd. ft.;pine, oak, maple. **Nonfuel minerals** (est. 2001): 1.3 bil; mostly crushed stone, portland and masonry cement, lime, sand & gravel. **Commercial fishing:** (2000): $29,349. **Chief ports:** Philadelphia, Pittsburgh, Erie. **Principal internat. airports at:** Allentown, Harrisburg, Philadelphia, Pittsburgh, Wilkes-Barre/Scranton. **Value of construction** (1997): $10.1 bil. **Gross state product** (2000): $404 bil. **Employment distrib.** (May 2002): 33.9% services; 22.3% trade; 13.2% govt.; 14.9% mfg. **Per cap. pers. income** (2001): $30,617. **Sales tax** (2002): 6%. **Unemployment** (2001): 4.7%. **Tourism expends.** (1999): $14.8 bil. **Lottery** (2001): total sales: $1.8 bil; net income: $626.5 mil.

Finance. FDIC-insured commercial banks (2001): 181. **Deposits:** $140.7 bil. **FDIC-insured savings institutions** (2001): 113. **Assets:** $80.1 bil.

Federal govt. Fed. civ. employees (Mar. 2001): 61,134. **Avg. salary:** $48,072. **Notable fed. facilities:** Carlisle Barracks; Army War College; Naval Inventory Control Point, Phila. and Mechanicsbrg; Defense Personnel Supply Center, Phila.; Defense Distribution Center, New Cumberland; Tobyhanna Army Depot; Letterkenny Army Depot; NAS Willow Grove; 911th Air Wing, Pittsburgh; Naval Surface Warfare Center, Phila.; Charles E. Kelly Support Facility.

Energy. Electricity production (est. 2001, kWh, by source): Coal: 16.9 bil; Petroleum: 973 mil; Gas: 257 mil; Hydroelectric: 693 mil; Nuclear: 13.2 bil.

State data. Motto: Virtue, liberty and independence. **Flower:** Mountain laurel. **Bird:** Ruffed grouse. **Tree:** Hemlock. **Song:** Pennsylvania. **Second** of the original 13 states to ratify the Constitution, Dec. 12, 1787. **State fair** at Harrisburg; 2nd week in Jan. at State Farm Show Building.

History. At the time of European contact, Lenni Lenape (Delaware), Shawnee and Iroquoian Susquehannocks, Erie, and Seneca occupied the region. Swedish explorers established the first permanent settlement, 1643, on Tinicum Island. In 1655, the Dutch seized the settlement but lost it to the British, 1664. The region was given by Charles II to William Penn, 1681. Philadelphia ("brotherly love") was the capital of the colonies during most of the American Revolution, and of the U.S., 1790-1800. Philadelphia was taken by the British, 1777; Washington's troops encamped at Valley Forge in the bitter winter of 1777-78. The Declaration of Independence, 1776, and the Constitution, 1787, were signed in Philadelphia. The Civil War battle of Gettysburg, July 1-3, 1863, marked a turning point, favoring Union forces.

Tourist attractions. Independence Natl. Historic Park, Franklin Institute Science Museum, Philadelphia Museum of Art, all in Philadelphia; Valley Forge Natl. Historic Park; Gettysburg Natl. Military Park; Pennsylvania Dutch Country; Hershey; Duquesne Incline, Carnegie Institute, Heinz Hall, all in Pittsburgh; Pocono Mts.; Pennsylvania's Grand Canyon, Tioga County; Allegheny Natl. Forest; Laurel Highlands; Presque Isle State Park; Fallingwater, Ligonier; Johnstown; SteamTown U.S.A., Scranton; State Flagship Niagara, Erie; Oil Heritage Region, Northwest PA.

Famous Pennsylvanians. Marian Anderson, Maxwell Anderson, George Blanda, James Buchanan, Andrew Carnegie, Rachel Carson, Perry Como, Bill Cosby, Thomas Eakins, Stephen Foster, Benjamin Franklin, Robert Fulton, Martha Graham, Milton Hershey, Gene Kelly, Grace Kelly (Princess Grace of Monaco), Dan Marino, George C. Marshall, Chris Matthews, John J. McCloy, Margaret Mead, Andrew W. Mellon, Joe Montana, Stan Musial, Joe Namath, John O'Hara, Arnold Palmer, Robert E. Peary, Mike Piazza, Tom Ridge, Mary Roberts Rinehart, Betsy Ross, Will Smith, Jimmy Stewart, Jim Thorpe, Johnny Unitas, John Updike, Honus Wagner, Andy Warhol, Benjamin West.

Chamber of Business and Industry. 417 Walnut St., Harrisburg, PA 17120; 800-VISITPA.

Toll-free travel information. 1-800-VISITPA.

Website. www.pennsylvania.gov

Tourism website. www.experiencepa.co

IT'S A FACT: Self-service gas stations have been around since 1947, and become popular in the 1970s. They are common fixtures today, but 2 states, Oregon and New Jersey, have laws requiring that all gas be pumped by attendants.

Rhode Island

Little Rhody, Ocean State

People. Population (2001 est.): 1,058,920; rank: 43; **net change** (2000-2001): 1.0%. **Pop. density:** 1,013.3 per sq mi. **Racial distribution** (2000): 85.0% white; 4.5% black; 2.3% Asian; 0.5% Native American/Nat. AK; 0.1% Hawaiian/Pacific Islander; 5.0% other race; 2 or more races, 2.7%. **Hispanic pop.** (any race): 8.7%.

Geography. Total area: 1,545 sq mi; rank: 50. **Land area:** 1,045 sq mi; rank: 50. **Acres forested:** 401,000. **Location:** New England state. **Climate:** invigorating and changeable. **Topography:** eastern lowlands of Narragansett Basin; western uplands of flat and rolling hills. **Capital:** Providence.

Economy. Chief industries: services, manufacturing. **Chief manuf. goods:** costume jewelry, toys, machinery, textiles, electronics. **Chief crops:** nursery products, turf & vegetable production. **Livestock:** (Jan. 2002) 5,500 cattle/calves; (Dec. 2001) 2,500 hogs/pigs. **Timber/lumber:** (est. 2001): 10 mil bd. ft.; **Nonfuel minerals** (est. 2001): 28.3 mil; mostly sand & gravel, crushed stone, gemstones. **Commercial fishing** (2000): $72.5 mil. **Chief ports:** Providence, Quonset Point, Newport. **Value of construction** (1997): $773 mil. **Gross state product** (2000): $36.5 bil. **Employment distrib.** (May 2002): 35.9% services; 22.4% trade; 13.6% govt.; 14% mfg. **Per cap. pers. income** (2001): $29,984. **Sales tax** (2002): 7%. **Unemployment** (2001): 4.7%. **Tourism expends.** (1999): $1.4 bil. **Lottery** (2001): total sales: $978 mil; net income: $180.7 mil.

Finance. FDIC-insured commercial banks (2001): 8. **Deposits:** $140.4 bil. **FDIC-insured savings institutions** (2001): 7. **Assets:** $2.1 bil.

Federal govt. Fed. civ. employees (Mar. 2001): 5,728. **Avg. salary:** $57,922. **Notable fed. facilities:** Naval War College; Naval Underwater Warfare Center; Natl. Marine Fisheries Laboratory; EPA Environmental Research Laboratory.

Energy. Electricity production (est. 2001, kWh, by source): Petroleum: 12 mil.

State data. Motto: Hope. **Flower:** Violet. **Bird:** Rhode Island red. **Tree:** Red maple. **Song:** Rhode Island. **Thirteenth** of original 13 states to ratify the Constitution, May 29, 1790. **State fair** at Richmond; mid-Aug.

History. When the Europeans arrived Narragansett, Niantic, Nipmuc, and Wampanoag peoples lived in the region. Verrazano visited the area, 1524. The first permanent settlement was founded at Providence, 1636, by Roger Williams, who was exiled from the Massachusetts Bay Colony; Anne Hutchinson, also exiled, settled Portsmouth, 1638. Quaker and Jewish immigrants seeking freedom of worship began arriving, 1650s-60s. The colonists broke the power of the Narragansett in the Great Swamp Fight, 1675, the decisive battle in King Philip's War. British trade restrictions angered colonists, and they burned the British customs vessel *Gaspee*, 1772. The colony became the first to formally renounce all allegiance to King George III, May 4, 1776. Initially opposed to joining the Union, Rhode Island was the last of the 13 colonies to ratify the Constitution, 1790.

Tourist attractions. Newport mansions; yachting races including Newport to Bermuda; Block Island; Touro Synagogue, oldest in U.S., Newport; first Baptist Church in America, Providence; Slater Mill Historic Site, Pawtucket; Gilbert Stuart birthplace, Saunderstown.

Famous Rhode Islanders. Ambrose Burnside, George M. Cohan, Nelson Eddy, Jabez Gorham, Nathanael Greene, Christopher and Oliver La Farge, John McLaughlin, Matthew C. and Oliver Hazard Perry, Gilbert Stuart.

Tourist Information. Rhode Island Economic Development Corporation, One W. Exchange St., Providence, RI 02903.

Toll-free travel information. 1-800-556-2484.

Website. www.state.ri.us

Tourism website. visitrhodeisland.com

South Carolina

Palmetto State

People. Population (2001 est.): 4,063,011; rank: 26; **net change** (2000-2001): 1.3%. **Pop. density:** 134.9 per sq mi. **Racial distribution** (2000): 67.2% white; 29.5% black; 0.9% Asian; 0.3% Native American/Nat. AK; <0.1% Hawaiian/Pacific Islander; 1.0% other race; 2 or more races, 1.0%. **Hispanic pop.** (any race): 2.4%.

Geography. Total area: 32,020 sq mi; rank: 40. **Land area:** 30,109 sq mi; rank: 40. **Acres forested:** 12,257,000. **Location:** South Atlantic state, bordered by North Carolina on the N; Georgia on the SW and W; the Atlantic Ocean on the E, SE, and S. **Climate:** humid subtropical. **Topography:** Blue Ridge province in NW has highest peaks; piedmont lies between the mountains and the fall line; coastal plain covers two-thirds of the state. **Capital:** Columbia.

Economy. Chief industries: tourism, agriculture, manufacturing. **Chief manuf. goods:** textiles, chemicals and allied products, machinery and fabricated metal products, apparel and related products. **Chief crops:** tobacco, cotton, soybeans, corn, wheat, peaches, tomatoes. **Livestock:** (Jan. 2002) 430,000 cattle/calves; (Dec. 2001) 320,000 hogs/pigs; 6.9 mil chickens (excl. broilers); 196.8 mil broilers. **Timber/lumber** (est. 2001): 1.5 bil bd. ft.; pine, oak. **Nonfuel minerals** (est. 2001): 531 mil; mostly portland and masonry, cement, crushed stone, gold, sand & gravel, clays. **Commercial fishing** (2000): $30.5 mil. **Chief ports:** Charleston, Georgetown, Beaufort/ Port Royal. **Principal internat. airports at:** Charleston, Greenville/Spartanburg, Myrtle Beach. **Value of construction** (1997): $6 bil. **Gross state product** (2000): $113.4 bil. **Employment distrib.** (May 2002): 25.6% services; 24% trade; 17.3% govt.; 17.2% mfg. **Per cap. pers. income** (2001): $24,594. **Sales tax** (2002): 5%. **Unemployment** (2001): 5.4%. **Tourism expends.** (1999): $7 bil.

Finance. FDIC-insured commercial banks (2001): 77. **Deposits:** $20.2 bil. **FDIC-insured savings institutions** (2001): 26. **Assets:** $7.1 bil.

Federal govt. Fed. civ. employees (Mar. 2001): 15,707. **Avg. salary:** $46,912. **Notable fed. facilities:** Polaris Submarine Base; Barnwell Nuclear Power Plant; Ft. Jackson; Parris Island; Savannah River Plant.

Energy. Electricity production (est. 2001, kWh, by source): Coal: 36.3 bil; Petroleum: 225 mil; Gas: 194 mil; Hydroelectric: 161 mil; Nuclear: 49.9 bil.

State data. Motto: Dum Spiro Spero (While I breathe, I hope). **Flower:** Yellow jessamine. **Bird:** Carolina wren. **Tree:** Palmetto. **Song:** Carolina. **Eighth** of the original 13 states to ratify the Constitution, May 23, 1788. **State fair** at Columbia; mid-Oct.

History. At the time of European settlement, Cherokee, Catawba, and Muskogean peoples lived in the area. The first English colonists settled near the Ashley River, 1670, and moved to the site of Charleston, 1680. The colonists seized the government, 1775, and the royal governor fled. The British took Charleston, 1780, but were defeated at Kings Mountain that same year, and at Cowpens and Eutaw Springs, 1781. In the 1830s, South Carolinians, angered by federal protective tariffs, adopted the Nullification Doctrine, holding that a state can void an act of Congress. The state was the first to secede from the Union, 1860, and Confederate troops fired on and forced the surrender of U.S. troops at Ft. Sumter, in Charleston Harbor, launching the Civil War. South Carolina was readmitted,1868.

Tourist attractions. Historic Charleston; Ft. Sumter Natl. Monument, in Charleston Harbor; Charleston Museum, est. 1773, oldest museum in U.S.; Middleton Place, Magnolia Plantation, Cypress Gardens, Drayton Hall, all near Charleston; other gardens at Brookgreen, Edisto, Glencairn; Myrtle Beach; Hilton Head Island; Revolutionary War battle sites; Andrew Jackson State Park & Museum; South Carolina State Museum, Columbia; Riverbanks Zoo, Columbia.

Famous South Carolinians. Charles Bolden, James F. Byrnes, John C. Calhoun, Joe Fraizer, DuBose Heyward, Ernest F. Hollings, Andrew Jackson, Jesse Jackson, "Shoeless" Joe Jackson, James Longstreet, Francis Marion, Andie McDowell, Ronald McNair, Charles Pinckney, John Rutledge, Thomas Sumter, Strom Thurmond, John B. Watson.

Tourist information. S. Carolina Dept. of Parks, Recreation, & Tourism; 803-734-0122.

Toll-free travel information. 1-800-346-3634.

Website. www.myscgov.com

Tourism website. www.discoversouthcarolina.com

IT'S A FACT: When completed, the Crazy Horse Memorial in South Dakota—showing the famous Oglala Sioux Indian chief on horseback—will be the world's largest carving, at 563 feet tall and 641 feet long. His face alone, finished in 1998, is 90 feet tall, 30 feet taller than the faces on nearby Mt. Rushmore.

South Dakota

Coyote State, Mount Rushmore State

People. Population (2001 est.): 756,600; rank: 46; **net change** (2000-2001): 0.2%. **Pop. density:** 10 per sq mi. **Racial distribution** (2000): 88.7% white; 0.6% black; 0.6% Asian; 8.3% Native American/Nat. AK; <0.1% Hawaiian/Pacific Islander; 0.5% other race; 2 or more races, 1.3%. **Hispanic pop.** (any race): 1.4%.

Geography. Total area: 77,116 sq mi; rank: 17. **Land area:** 75,885 sq mi; rank: 16. **Acres forested:** 1,690,000. **Location:** West North Central state bounded on the N by North Dakota; on the E by Minnesota and Iowa; on the S by Nebraska; on the W by Wyoming and Montana. **Climate:** characterized by extremes of temperature, persistent winds, low precipitation and humidity. **Topography:** Prairie Plains in the E; rolling hills of the Great Plains in the W; the Black Hills, rising 3,500 ft, in the SW corner. **Capital:** Pierre.

Economy. Chief industries: agriculture, services, manufacturing. **Chief manuf. goods:** food and kindred products, machinery, electric and electronic equipment. **Chief crops:** corn, soybeans, oats, wheat, sunflowers, sorghum. **Livestock:** (Jan. 2002) 4 mil cattle/calves; 400,000 sheep/lambs; (Dec. 2001) 1.3 mil hogs/pigs; 2.8 mil chickens (excl. broilers). **Timber/lumber** (est. 2001): NA; ponderosa pine. **Nonfuel minerals** (est. 2001): 255 mil; mostly gold, portland cement, sand & gravel, crushed and dimension stone. **Value of construction** (1997): $742 mil. **Gross state product** (2000): $23.2 bil. **Employment distrib.** (May 2002): 27.3% services; 24.8% trade; 19.7% govt.; 11.3% mfg. **Per cap. pers. income** (2001): $26,301. **Sales tax** (2002): 4%. **Unemployment** (2001): 3.3%. **Tourism expends.** (1999): $1.2 bil. **Lottery** (2001): total sales: $586.8 mil; net income: $101.8 mil.

Finance. FDIC-insured commercial banks (2001): 93. **Deposits:** $14.5 bil. **FDIC-insured savings institutions** (2001): 4. **Assets:** $1.1 bil.

Federal govt. Fed. civ. employees (Mar. 2001): 6,789. **Avg. salary:** $43,774. **Notable fed. facilities:** Ellsworth AFB, Corp of Engineers, Nat'l Park Service.

Energy. Electricity production (est. 2001, kWh, by source): Coal: 3.0 bil; Petroleum: 51 mil; Gas: 303 mil; Hydroelectric: 3.4 bil.

State data. Motto: Under God, the people rule. **Flower:** Pasqueflower. **Bird:** Chinese ring-necked pheasant. **Tree:** Black Hills spruce. **Song:** Hail, South Dakota. **Entered union** Nov. 2, 1889; rank, 40th. **State fair** at Huron; late Aug.-early Sept.

History. At the time of first European contact, Mandan, Hidatsa, Arikara, and Sioux lived in the area. The French Verendrye brothers explored the region, 1742-43. The U.S. acquired the area, 1803, in the Louisiana Purchase. Lewis and Clark passed through the area, 1804-6. In 1817 a trading post was opened at Fort Pierre, which later became the site of the first European settlement in South Dakota. Gold was discovered, 1874, in the Black Hills on the great Sioux reservation; the "Great Dakota Boom" began in 1879. Conflicts with Native Americans led to the Great Sioux Agreement, 1889, which established reservations and opened up more land for white settlement. The massacre of Native American families at Wounded Knee, 1890, ended Sioux resistance.

Tourist attractions. Black Hills; Mt. Rushmore; Needles Highway; Harney Peak, tallest E. of Rockies; Deadwood, 1876 Gold Rush town; Custer State Park; Jewel Cave Natl. Monument; Badlands Natl. Park "moonscape"; "Great Lakes of S. Dakota"; Ft. Sisseton; Great Plains Zoo & Museum, Sioux Falls; Corn Palace, Mitchell; Wind Cave Natl. Park; Crazy Horse Memorial, mountain carving in progress.

Famous South Dakotans. Sparky Anderson, Black Elk, Bob Barker, Tom Brokaw, Crazy Horse, Thomas Daschle, Myron Floren, Mary Hart, Cheryl Ladd, Dr. Ernest O. Lawrence, George McGovern, Billy Mills, Allen Neuharth, Pat O'Brien, Sitting Bull.

Tourist information. Department of Tourism, Capitol Lake Plaza, 711 E. Wells Ave., c/o 500 E. Capitol Ave., Pierre, SD 57501-5070.

Toll-free travel information. 1-800-SDAKOTA.

Website. www.state.sd.us

Tourism website. www.travelsd.com

Tennessee

Volunteer State

People. Population (2001 est.): 5,740,021; rank: 16; **net change** (2000-2001): 0.9%. **Pop. density:** 139.3 per sq mi. **Racial distribution** (2000): 80.2% white; 16.4% black; 1.0% Asian; 0.3% Native American/Nat. AK; <0.1% Hawaiian/Pacific Islander; 1.0% other race; 2 or more races, 1.1%. **Hispanic pop.** (any race): 2.2%.

Geography. Total area: 42,143 sq mi; rank: 36. **Land area:** 41,217 sq mi; rank: 34. **Acres forested:** 13,612,000. **Location:** East South Central state bounded on the N by Kentucky and Virginia; on the E by North Carolina; on the S by Georgia, Alabama, and Mississippi; on the W by Arkansas and Missouri. **Climate:** humid continental to the N; humid subtropical to the S. **Topography:** rugged country in the E; the Great Smoky Mts. of the Unakas; low ridges of the Appalachian Valley; the flat Cumberland Plateau; slightly rolling terrain and knobs of the Interior Low Plateau, the largest region; Eastern Gulf Coastal Plain to the W, laced with streams; Mississippi Alluvial Plain, a narrow strip of swamp and flood plain in the extreme W. **Capital:** Nashville.

Economy. Chief industries: manufacturing, trade, services, tourism, finance, insurance, real estate. **Chief manuf. goods:** chemicals, food, transportation equipment, industrial machinery & equipment, fabricated metal products, rubber/plastic products, paper & allied products, printing & publishing. **Chief crops:** tobacco, cotton, lint, soybeans, grain, corn. **Livestock:** (Jan. 2002) 2.2 mil cattle/calves; (Dec. 2001) 225,000 hogs/pigs; 2.3 mil chickens (excl. broilers); 151.3 mil broilers. **Timber/lumber** (est. 2001): 896 mil bd. ft.; red oak, white oak, yellow poplar, hickory. **Nonfuel minerals** (est. 2001): 708 mil; mostly crushed stone, zinc, portland cement, sand & gravel, clays. **Chief ports:** Memphis, Nashville, Chattanooga, Knoxville. **Principal internat. airports at:** Memphis, Nashville. **Value of construction** (1997): $8.2 bil. **Gross state product** (2000): $178.4 bil. **Employment distrib.** (May 2002): 28.5% services; 23.4% trade; 15.1% govt.; 17.2% mfg. **Per cap. pers. income** (2001): $26,758. **Sales tax** (2002): 6%. **Unemployment** (2001): 4.5%. **Tourism expends.** (1999): $9.8 bil.

Finance. FDIC-insured commercial banks (2001): 189. **Deposits:** $72.7 bil. **FDIC-insured savings institutions** (2001): 24. **Assets:** $5.8 bil.

Federal govt. Fed. civ. employees (Mar. 2001): 33,215. **Avg. salary:** $49,084. **Notable fed. facilities:** Tennessee Valley Authority; Oak Ridge Nat'l. Laboratories; Arnold Engineering Development Center; Ft. Campbell Army Base; Millington Naval Station.

Energy. Electricity production (est. 2001, kWh, by source): Coal: 58.2 bil; Petroleum: 380 mil; Gas: 6 mil; Hydroelectric: 5.8 bil; Nuclear: 28.6 bil.

State data. Motto: Agriculture and commerce. **Flower:** Iris. **Bird:** Mockingbird. **Tree:** Tulip poplar. **Songs:** My Homeland, Tennessee; When It's Iris Time in Tennessee; My Tennessee; Tennessee Waltz; Rocky Top. **Entered union** June 1, 1796; rank, 16th. **State fair** at Nashville; mid-Sept.

History. When the first European explorers arrived, Creek and Yuchi peoples lived in the area; the Cherokee moved into the region in the early 18th cent. Spanish explorers first visited the area, 1541. English traders crossed the Great Smokies from the east while France's Marquette and Jolliet sailed down the Mississippi on the west, 1673. The first permanent settlement was by Virginians on the Watauga River, 1769. During the American Revolution, the colonists helped win the Battle of Kings Mountain (NC), 1780, and joined other eastern campaigns. The state seceded from the Union, 1861, and saw many Civil War engagements, but 30,000 soldiers fought for the Union. Tennessee was readmitted in 1866, the only former Confederate state not to have a postwar military government.

Tourist attractions. Reelfoot Lake, Lookout Mountain, Chattanooga; Fall Creek Falls; Great Smoky Mountains Natl. Park; Lost Sea, Sweetwater; Cherokee Natl. Forest; Cumberland Gap Natl. Park; Andrew Jackson's home, the Hermitage, near Nashville; homes of Pres. Polk and Andrew Johnson; American Museum of Science and Energy, Oak Ridge; Parthenon, Grand Old Opry, Opryland USA, all Nashville; Dollywood theme park, Pigeon Forge; Tennessee Aquarium, Chattanooga; Graceland, home of Elvis Presley, Memphis; Alex Haley Home and Museum, Henning; Casey Jones Home and Museum, Jackson.

IT'S A FACT: In 1784, 3 counties in a remote western pocket of what was then North Carolina seceded to form their own independent state. Named in honor of Benjamin Franklin, the renegade state of Franklin was never officially recognized by the federal government; it lasted until 1788, when it was dissolved. Eventually, the area became part of the state of Tennessee.

Famous Tennesseans. Roy Acuff, Davy Crockett, David Farragut, Ernie Ford, Aretha Franklin, Morgan Freeman, Al Gore Jr., Alex Haley, William C. Handy, Sam Houston, Cordell Hull, Andrew Jackson, Andrew Johnson, Casey Jones, Estes Kefauver, Grace Moore, Dolly Parton, Minnie Pearl, James Polk, Elvis Presley, Dinah Shore, Bessie Smith, Hank Williams Jr., Alvin York.

Tourist information. Dept. of Tourist Development, 5th Floor, Rachel Jackson Bldg., 320 6th Ave. N., Nashville, TN 37202.

Texas

Lone Star State

People. Population (2001 est.): 21,325,018; rank: 2; **net change** (2000-2001): 2.3%. **Pop. density:** 81.5 per sq mi. **Racial distribution** (2000): 71.0% white; 11.5% black; 2.7% Asian; 0.6% Native American/Nat. AK; 0.1% Hawaiian/Pacific Islander; 11.7% other race; 2 or more races, 2.5%. **Hispanic pop.** (any race): 32.0%.

Geography. Total area: 268,581 sq mi; rank: 2. **Land area:** 261,797 sq mi; rank: 2. **Acres forested:** 19,193,000. **Location:** Southwestern state, bounded on the SE by the Gulf of Mexico; on the SW by Mexico, separated by the Rio Grande; surrounding states are Louisiana, Arkansas, Oklahoma, New Mexico. **Climate:** extremely varied; driest region is the Trans-Pecos; wettest is the NE. **Topography:** Gulf Coast Plain in the S and SE; North Central Plains slope upward with some hills; the Great Plains extend over the Panhandle, are broken by low mountains; the Trans-Pecos is the southern extension of the Rockies. **Capital:** Austin.

Economy. Chief industries: manufacturing, trade, oil and gas extraction, services. **Chief manuf. goods:** industrial machinery and equipment, foods, electrical and electronic products, chemicals and allied products, apparel. **Chief crops:** cotton, grains (wheat), sorghum grain, vegetables, citrus and other fruits, greenhouse/nursery, pecans, peanuts. **Chief farm products:** milk, eggs **Livestock**: (Jan. 2002) 13.6 mil cattle/calves; 1.1 mil sheep/lambs; (Dec. 2001) 900,000 hogs/pigs; 26.1 mil chickens (excl. broilers); 551 mil. broilers. **Timber/lumber** (est. 2001): 1.5 bil bd. ft.; pine, cypress. **Nonfuel minerals** (est. 2001): 2.2 bil; mostly portland cement, crushed stone, sand & gravel, lime, salt. **Commercial fishing** (2000): $293.6 mil. **Chief ports:** Houston, Galveston, Brownsville, Beaumont, Port Arthur, Corpus Christi. **Principal internat. airports at:** Amarillo, Austin, Corpus Christi, Dallas/Ft. Worth, El Paso, Harlingen, Houston, Lubbock, Odessa, San Antonio. **Value of construction** (1997): $27.2 bil. **Gross state product** (2000): $742.3 bil. **Employment distrib.** (May 2002): 29.1% services; 23.7% trade; 17.3% govt.; 10.6% mfg. **Per cap. pers. income** (2001): $28,486. **Sales tax** (2002): 6.25%. **Unemployment** (2001): 4.9%. **Tourism expends.** (1999): $33.1 bil. **Lottery** (2001): total sales: $2.8 bil; net income: $864 mil.

Finance. FDIC-insured commercial banks (2001): 686. **Deposits:** $120.9 bil. **FDIC-insured savings institutions** (2001): 49. **Assets:** $54.7 bil.

Federal govt. Fed. civ. employees (Mar. 2001): 100,006. **Avg. salary:** $49,049. **Notable fed. facilities:** Fort Hood, Kelly AFB, and Ft. Sam Houston.

Energy. Electricity production (est. 2001, kWh, by source): Coal: 132.3 bil; Petroleum: 1.7 bil; Gas: 91.6 bil; Hydroelectric: 1.3 bil; Nuclear: 38.2 bil.

State data. Motto: Friendship. **Flower:** Bluebonnet. **Bird:** Mockingbird. **Tree:** Pecan. **Song:** Texas, Our Texas. **Entered union** Dec. 29, 1845; rank, 28th. **State fair** at Dallas; mid-Oct.

History. At the time of European contact, Native American tribes in the region were numerous and diverse in culture. Coahuiltecan, Karankawa, Caddo, Jumano, and Tonkawa peoples lived in the area, and during the 19th cent., the Apache, Comanche, Cherokee, and Wichita arrived. Spanish explorer Pineda sailed along the Texas coast, 1519; Cabeza de Vaca and Coronado visited the interior, 1541. Spaniards made the first settlement at Ysleta, near El Paso, 1682. Americans moved into the land early in the 19th cent. Mexico, of which Texas was a part, won independence from Spain, 1821; Santa Anna became dictator in 1835; Texans rebelled. Santa Anna wiped out defenders of the Alamo, 1836; Sam Houston's Texans defeated Santa Anna at San Jacinto, and independence was proclaimed that same year. The Republic of Texas, with Sam Houston as its first president, functioned as a nation until 1845, when it was admitted to the Union.

Tourist attractions. Padre Island Natl. Seashore; Big Bend, Guadalupe Mts. natl. parks; The Alamo; Ft. Davis; Six Flags Amusement Park; Sea World and Fiesta Texas, both in San Antonio; San Antonio Missions Natl. Historical Park; Cowgirl Hall of Fame, Fort Worth; Lyndon B. Johnson Natl. Historical Park, marking his birthplace, boyhood home, and ranch, near Johnson City; Lyndon B. Johnson Library and Museum, Austin; Texas State Aquarium, Corpus Christi; Kimball Art Museum, Fort Worth; George Bush Library, College Station.

Famous Texans. Lance Armstrong, Stephen F. Austin, Lloyd Bentsen, James Bowie, Carol Burnett, George H. W. Bush, George W. Bush, Joan Crawford, J. Frank Dobie, Dwight D. Eisenhower, Morgan Fairchild, Farrah Fawcett, Sam Houston, Howard Hughes, Kay Bailey Hutchinson, Molly Ivins, Lyndon B. Johnson, Tommy Lee Jones, Janis Joplin, Barbara Jordan, Mary Martin, Chester Nimitz, Sandra Day O'Connor, H. Ross Perot, Katherine Ann Porter, Dan Rather, Sam Rayburn, Ann Richards, Sissy Spacek, Kenneth Starr, George Strait.

Chamber of Commerce. 900 Congress, Suite 501, Austin, TX 78701.

Toll-free travel information. 1-800-8888TEX.

Website. www.state.tx.us

Tourism website. www.traveltex.com

Utah

Beehive State

People. Population (2001 est.): 2,269,789; rank: 34; **net change** (2000-2001): 1.6%. **Pop. density:** 27.6 per sq mi. **Racial distribution** (2000): 89.2% white; 0.8% black; 1.7% Asian; 1.3% Native American/Nat. AK; 0.7% Hawaiian/Pacific Islander; 4.2% other race; 2 or more races, 2.1%. **Hispanic pop.** (any race): 9.0%.

Geography. Total area: 84,899 sq mi; rank: 13. **Land area:** 82,144 sq mi; rank: 12. **Acres forested:** 16,234,000. **Location:** Middle Rocky Mountain state; its southeastern corner touches Colorado, New Mexico, and Arizona, and is the only spot in the U.S. where 4 states join. **Climate:** arid; ranging from warm desert in SW to alpine in NE. **Topography:** high Colorado plateau is cut by brilliantly colored canyons of the SE; broad, flat, desert-like Great Basin of the W; the Great Salt Lake and Bonneville Salt Flats to the NW; Middle Rockies in the NE run E-W; valleys and plateaus of the Wasatch Front. **Capital:** Salt Lake City.

Economy. Chief industries: services, trade, manufacturing, government, transportation, utilities. **Chief manuf. goods:** medical instruments, electronic components, food products, fabricated metals, transportation equipment, steel and copper. **Chief crops:** hay, corn, wheat, barley, apples, potatoes, cherries, onions, peaches, pears. **Livestock:** (Jan. 2002) 920,000 cattle/calves; 365,000 sheep/lambs; (Dec. 2001) 610,000 hogs/pigs; 3.8 mil chickens (excl. broilers). **Timber/lumber:** (est. 2001): 51 mil bd. ft.; aspen, spruce, pine. **Nonfuel minerals** (est. 2001): 1.3 bil; mostly copper, gold, magnesium metal, portland cement, sand & gravel. **Commercial fishing:** (2000): $7.5 mil. **Principal internat. airport at:** Salt Lake City. **Value of construction** (1997): $5.3 bil. **Gross state product** (2000): $68.5 bil. **Employment distrib.** (May 2002): 29.5% services; 23.2% trade; 18.4% govt.; 11.2% mfg. **Per cap. pers. income** (2001): $24,202. **Sales tax** (2002): 4.75%. **Unemployment** (2001): 4.4%. **Tourism expends.** (1999): $3.9 bil.

Finance. FDIC-insured commercial banks (2001): 55. **Deposits:** $96.2 bil. **FDIC-insured savings institutions** (2001): 4. **Assets:** $1.5 bil.

Federal govt. Fed. civ. employees (Mar. 2001): 25,395. **Avg. salary:** $44,616. **Notable fed. facilities:** Hill AFB; Tooele Army Depot; IRS Western Service Center.

Energy. Electricity production (est. 2001, kWh, by source): Coal: 33.2 bil; Petroleum: 59 mil; Gas: 1.1 bil; Hydroelectric: 490 mil; Nuclear: Other: 153 mil.

State data. Motto: Industry. **Flower:** Sego lily. **Bird:** Seagull. **Tree:** Blue spruce. **Song:** Utah, We Love Thee. **Entered union** Jan. 4, 1896; rank, 45th. **State fair** at Salt Lake City; Sept.

History. Ute, Gosiute, Southern Paiute, and Navajo peoples lived in the region at the time of European contact. Spanish Franciscans visited the area, 1776; American fur traders followed. Permanent settlement began with the arrival of the Mormons, 1847; they made the arid land bloom and created a prosperous economy. The State of Deseret was organized in 1849, and asked admission to the Union. In 1850, Congress established the region as the territory of Utah, and Brigham Young was appointed governor. The Union and Pacific Railroads met near Promontory, May 10, 1869, creating the first transcontinental railroad. Statehood was not achieved until 1896, after a long period of controversy over the Mormon Church's doctrine of polygamy, which it discontinued in 1890.

Tourist attractions. Temple Square, Mormon Church headquarters, Salt Lake City; Great Salt Lake; Zion National Park, Canyonlands, Bryce Canyon, Arches, and Capitol Reef natl. parks; Dinosaur, Rainbow Bridge, Timpanogos Cave, and Natural Bridges natl. monuments; Lake Powell; Flaming Gorge Natl. Recreation Area.

Famous Utahans. Maude Adams, Ezra Taft Benson, John Moses Browning, Mariner Eccles, Philo Farnsworth, James Fletcher, David M. Kennedy, J. Willard Marriott, Merlin Olsen, Osmond family, Ivy Baker Priest, George Romney, Roseanne, Wallace Stegner, Brigham Young, Loretta Young.

Tourist information. Utah Travel Council, Council Hall, Salt Lake City, UT 84114; 801-538-1030.

Toll-free travel information. 1-800-200-1160 or 1-800 UTAH-FUN.

Website. www.utah.gov

Tourism website. www.utah.com

Vermont

Green Mountain State

People. Population (2001 est.): 613,090; rank: 49; **net change** (2000-2001): 0.7%. **Pop. density:** 66.3 per sq mi. **Racial distribution** (2000): 96.8% white; 0.5% black; 0.9% Asian; 0.4% Native American/Nat. AK; <0.1% Hawaiian/Pacific Islander; 0.2% other race; 2 or more races, 1.2%. **Hispanic pop.** (any race): 0.9%.

Geography. Total area: 9,614 sq mi; rank: 45. **Land area:** 9,250 sq mi; rank: 43. **Acres forested:** 4,538,000. **Location:** northern New England state. **Climate:** temperate, with considerable temperature extremes; heavy snowfall in mountains. **Topography:** Green Mts. N-S backbone 20-36 mi wide; avg. altitude 1,000 ft. **Capital:** Montpelier.

Economy. Chief industries: manufacturing, tourism, agriculture, trade, finance, insurance, real estate, government. **Chief manuf. goods:** machine tools, furniture, scales, books, computer components, speciality foods. **Chief crops:** dairy products, apples, maple syrup, greenhouse/nursery, vegetables and small fruits. **Livestock:** (Jan. 2002) 285,000 cattle/calves; (Dec. 2001) 2,500 hogs/pigs; 207,000 chickens (excl. broilers). **Timber/lumber** (est. 2001): 218 mil bd. ft.; pine, spruce, fir, hemlock. **Nonfuel minerals** (est. 2001): 68.9 mil; mostly dimension stone, crushed stone, sand & gravel, talc & pyrophyllite, gemstones. **Principal internat. airport at:** Burlington. **Value of construction** (1997): $622 mil. **Gross state product** (2000): $18.4 bil. **Employment distrib.** (May 2002): 30.4% services; 22.8% trade; 17.7% govt.; 15.2% mfg. **Per cap. pers. income** (2001): $27,992. **Sales tax** (2002): 5%. **Unemployment** (2001): 3.6%. **Tourism expends.** (1999): $1.4 bil. (2001): total sales: $81.2 mil; net income: $17 mil.

Finance. FDIC-insured commercial banks (2001): 18. **Deposits:** $6.7 bil. **FDIC-insured savings institutions** (2001): 5. **Assets:** $1.1 bil.

Federal govt. Fed. civ. employees (Mar. 2001): 2,936. **Avg. salary:** $47,071.

Energy. Electricity production (est. 2001, kWh, by source): Petroleum: 36 mil; Gas: 11 mil; Hydroelectric: 379 mil; Nuclear: 4.2 bil; Other: 189 mil.

State data. Motto: Freedom and unity. **Flower:** Red clover. **Bird:** Hermit thrush. **Tree:** Sugar maple. **Song:** These Green Mountains. **Entered union** Mar. 4, 1791; rank, 14th. **State fair** at Rutland; early Sept.

History. Before the arrival of the Europeans, Abnaki and Mahican peoples lived in the region. Champlain explored the lake that bears his name, 1609. The first American settlement was Ft. Dummer, 1724, near Brattleboro. During the American Revolution, Ethan Allen and the Green Mountain Boys captured Ft. Ticonderoga (NY), 1775; John Stark defeated part of Burgoyne's forces near Bennington, 1777. In the War of 1812, Thomas MacDonough defeated a British fleet on Lake Champlain off Plattsburgh (NY), 1814.

Tourist attractions. Shelburne Museum; Rock of Ages Quarry, Graniteville; Vermont Marble Exhibit, Proctor; Bennington Battle Monument; Pres. Calvin Coolidge homestead, Plymouth; Maple Grove Maple Museum, St. Johnsbury; Ben & Jerry's Factory, Waterbury.

Famous Vermonters. Ethan Allen, Chester A. Arthur, Calvin Coolidge, John Deere, George Dewey, John Dewey, Stephen A. Douglas, Dorothy Canfield Fisher, James Fisk, James Jeffords, Rudy Vallee.

Chamber of Commerce. PO Box 37, Montpelier, VT 05601.

Tourist information. Vermont Dept. of Tourism and Marketing, 6 Baldwin St., Drawer 33, Montpelier, VT 05633-1301.

Toll-free travel information. 1-800-VERMONT

Website. www.state.vt.us

Tourism website. www.1-800-vermont.com

Virginia

Old Dominion

People. Population (2001 est.): 7,187,734; rank: 12; **net change** (2000-2001): 1.5%. **Pop. density:** 181.5 per sq mi. **Racial distribution** (2000): 72.3% white; 19.6% black; 3.7% Asian; 0.3% Native American/Nat. AK; 0.1% Hawaiian/Pacific Islander; 2.0% other race; 2 or more races, 2.0%. **Hispanic pop.** (any race): 4.7%.

Geography. Total area: 42,774 sq mi; rank: 35. **Land area:** 39,594 sq mi; rank: 37. **Acres forested:** 15,858,000. **Location:** South Atlantic state bounded by the Atlantic Ocean on the E and surrounded by North Carolina, Tennessee, Kentucky, West Virginia, and Maryland. **Climate:** mild and equable. **Topography:** mountain and valley region in the W, including the Blue Ridge Mts.; rolling piedmont plateau; tidewater, or coastal plain, including the eastern shore. **Capital:** Richmond.

Economy. Chief industries: services, trade, government, manufacturing, tourism, agriculture. **Chief manuf. goods:** food processing, transportation equipment, printing, textiles, electronic & electrical equipment, industrial machinery & equipment, lumber & wood products, chemicals, rubber & plastics, furniture. **Chief crops:** tobacco, grain corn, soybeans, winter wheat, peanuts, lint & seed cotton. **Livestock:** (Jan. 2002) 1.7 mil. cattle/calves; 59,000 sheep/lambs; (Dec. 2001) 410,000 hogs/pigs; 4.6 mil. chickens (excl. broilers); 264.9 mil. broilers. **Timber/lumber** (est. 2001): 1.6 bil bd. ft.; pine and hardwoods. **Nonfuel minerals** (est. 2001): 751 mil; mostly crushed stone, sand & gravel, portland cement, lime, clays. **Commercial fishing** (2000): $118.3 mil. **Chief ports:** Hampton Roads, Richmond, Alexandria. **Principal internat. airports at:** Arlington, Norfolk, Loudon, Richmond, Newport News. **Value of construction** (1997): $10.1 bil. **Gross state product** (2000): $261.4 bil. **Employment distrib.** (May 2002): 33.1% services; 21.7% trade; 18.2% govt.; 10.2% mfg. **Per cap. pers. income** (2001): $32,295. **Sales tax** (2002): 4%. **Unemployment** (2001): 3.5%. **Tourism expends.**(1999): $12.9 bil. **Lottery** (2001): total sales: $1 bil; net income: $329.6 mil.

Finance. FDIC-insured commercial banks (2001): 138. **Deposits:** $50.3 bil. **FDIC-insured savings institutions** (2001): 16. **Assets:** $36.9 bil.

Federal govt. Fed. civ. employees (Mar. 2001): 113,781. **Avg. salary:** $58,129. **Notable fed. facilities:** Pentagon; Norfolk Naval Station, Norfolk Naval Air Station; Naval Shipyard; Marine Corps Base; Langley AFB; NASA at Langley.

Energy. Electricity production (est. 2001, kWh, by source): Coal: 30.6 bil; Petroleum: 4.9 bil; Gas: 2.1 bil; Hydroelectric: -1.2 bil; Nuclear: 25.8 bil.

State data. Motto: Sic Semper Tyrannis (Thus always to tyrants). **Flower:** Dogwood. **Bird:** Cardinal. **Tree:** Dogwood. **Song Emeritus:** Carry Me Back to Old Virginia. **Tenth** of the original 13 states to ratify the Constitution, June 25, 1788. **State fair** at Richmond; late Sept.-early Oct.

History. Living in the area at the time of European contact were the Cherokee and Susquehanna and the Algonquians of the Powhatan Confederacy. English settlers founded Jamestown, 1607. Virginians took over much of the government from royal governor Dunmore, 1775, forcing him to flee. Virginians under George Rogers Clark freed the Ohio-Indiana-Illinois area of British forces. Benedict Arnold burned Richmond and Petersburg for the British, 1781. That same year, Britain's Cornwallis was trapped at Yorktown and surrendered, ending the American Revolution. Virginia seceded from the Union, 1861, and Richmond became the capital of the Confederacy. Hampton Roads, off the Virginia coast, was the site of the famous naval battle of the USS *Monitor* and CSS *Virginia* (Merrimac), 1862. Virginia was readmitted, 1870.

Tourist attractions. Colonial Williamsburg; Busch Gardens, Williamsburg; Wolf Trap Farm, near Falls Church; Arlington Natl. Cemetery; Mt. Vernon, home of George Washington; Jamestown Festival Park; Yorktown; Jefferson's Monticello, Charlottesville; Robert E. Lee's birthplace, Stratford Hall, and grave, Lexington; Appomattox; Shenandoah

Natl. Park; Blue Ridge Parkway; Virginia Beach; Paramount's King's Dominion, near Richmond.

Famous Virginians. Richard E. Byrd, James B. Cabell, Henry Clay, Jubal Early, Jerry Falwell, William Henry Harrison, Patrick Henry, A.P. Hill, Thomas Jefferson, Joseph E. Johnston, Robert E. Lee, Meriwether Lewis and William Clark, James Madison, John Marshall, George Mason, James Monroe, George Pickett, Pocahontas, Edgar Allan Poe, John Randolph, Walter Reed, Rev. Pat Robertson, John Smith, J.E.B. Stuart, William Styron, Zachary Taylor, John Tyler, Maggie Walker, Booker T. Washington, George Washington, L. Douglas Wilder, Woodrow Wilson.

Chamber of Commerce. 9 South Fifth St., Richmond, VA 23219.

Toll-free travel information. 1-800-321-3244.

Website. www.myvirginia.org

Tourism website. www.virginia.org

Washington

Evergreen State

People. Population (2001 est.): 5,987,973; rank: 15; **net change** (2000-2001): 1.6%. **Pop. density:** 90 per sq mi. **Racial distribution** (2000): 81.8% white; 3.2% black; 5.5% Asian; 1.6% Native American/Nat. AK; 0.4% Hawaiian/Pacific Islander; 3.9% other race; 2 or more races, 3.6%. **Hispanic pop.** (any race): 7.5%.

Geography. Total area: 71,300 sq mi; rank: 18. **Land area:** 66,544 sq mi; rank: 20. **Acres forested:** 20,483,000. **Location:** Pacific state bordered by Canada on the N; Idaho on the E; Oregon on the S; and the Pacific Ocean on the W. **Climate:** mild, dominated by the Pacific Ocean and protected by the Cascades. **Topography:** Olympic Mts. on NW peninsula; open land along coast to Columbia R.; flat terrain of Puget Sound Lowland; Cascade Mts. region's high peaks to the E; Columbia Basin in central portion; highlands to the NE; mountains to the SE. **Capital:** Olympia.

Economy. Chief industries: advanced technology, aerospace, biotechnology, intl. trade, forestry, tourism, recycling, agriculture & food processing. **Chief manuf. goods:** computer software, aircraft, pulp & paper, lumber and plywood, aluminum, processed fruits and vegetables, machinery, electronics. **Chief crops:** apples, potatoes, hay, farm forest products. **Livestock:** (Jan. 2002) 1.1 mil cattle/calves; 56,000 sheep/lambs; (Dec. 2001) 24,000 hogs/pigs; 6.4 mil chickens (excl. broilers). **Timber/lumber** (est. 2001): 4.7 bil bd. ft.; Douglas fir, hemlock, cedar, pine. **Nonfuel minerals** (est. 2001): 545 mil; mostly sand & gravel, magnesium metal, crushed stone, portland cement, gold. **Commercial fishing** (2000): $134.2 mil. **Chief ports:** Seattle, Tacoma, Vancouver, Kelso-Longview. **Principal internat. airports at:** Seattle/Tacoma, Spokane, Boeing Field. **Value of construction** (1997): $8.5 bil. **Gross state product** (2000): $219.9 bil. **Employment distrib.** (May 2002): 29% services; 23.5% trade; 19.8% govt.; 11.7% mfg. **Per cap. pers. income** (2001): $31,582. **Sales tax** (2002): 6.5%. **Unemployment** (2001): 6.4%. **Tourism expends.** (1999): $8.5 bil. **Lottery** (2001): total sales: $483.9 mil; net income: $130.4 mil.

Finance. FDIC-insured commercial banks (2001): 76. **Deposits:** $16.9 bil. **FDIC-insured savings institutions** (2001): 22. **Assets:** $50.7 bil.

Federal govt. Fed. civ. employees (Mar. 2001): 42,105. **Avg. salary:** $51,442. **Notable fed. facilities:** Bonneville Power Admin.; Ft. Lewis; McChord AFB; Hanford Nuclear Reservation; Bremerton Naval Shipyards.

Energy. Electricity production (est. 2001, kWh, by source): Petroleum: 179 mil; Gas: 4.4 bil; Hydroelectric: 54.7 bil; Nuclear: 8.3 bil; Other: 358 mil.

State data. Motto: Alki (By and by). **Flower:** Western rhododendron. **Bird:** Willow goldfinch. **Tree:** Western hemlock. **Song:** Washington, My Home. **Entered union** Nov. 11, 1889; rank, 42nd. **State fairs:** 5 area fairs, in Aug. and Sept.; no state fair.

History. At the time of European contact, many Native American tribes lived in the area, including the Nez Percé, Spokan, Yakima, Cayuse, Okanogan, Walla Walla, and Colville peoples, who lived in the interior region, and the Nooksak, Chinook, Nisqually, Clallam, Makah, Quinault, and Puyallup peoples, who inhabited the coastal area. Spain's Bruno Hezeta sailed the coast, 1775. In 1792, British naval officer George Vancouver mapped Puget Sound area, and that same year, American Capt. Robert Gray sailed up the Columbia River. Canadian fur traders set up Spokane House, 1810. Americans under John Jacob Astor established a post at Ft. Okanogan, 1811, and missionary Marcus Whitman settled near Walla Walla, 1836. Final agreement on the border of Washington and Canada was made with Britain, 1846, and Washington became part of the Oregon Territory, 1848. Gold was discovered, 1855.

Tourist attractions. Seattle Waterfront, Seattle Center and Space Needle, Museum of Flight, Underground Tour, all Seattle; Mt. Rainier, Olympic, and North Cascades natl. parks; Mt. St. Helens; Puget Sound; San Juan Islands; Grand Coulee Dam; Columbia R. Gorge Natl. Scenic Area; Spokane's Riverfront Park.

Famous Washingtonians. Raymond Carver, Kurt Cobain, Bing Crosby, William O. Douglas, Bill Gates, Jimi Hendrix, Henry M. Jackson, Gary Larson, Mary McCarthy, Robert Motherwell, Edward R. Murrow, Theodore Roethke, Ann Rule, Hilary Swank, Julia Sweeney, Adam West, Marcus Whitman, Minoru Yamasaki.

Tourist information. WA State Tourism Division, PO Box 42500, Olympia, WA 98504-2500; 360-725-5052

Website. access.wa.gov

Tourism website. www.tourism.wa.gov

West Virginia

Mountain State

People. Population (2001 est.): 1,801,916; rank: 37; **net change** (2000-2001): -0.4%. **Pop. density:** 74.8 per sq mi. **Racial distribution** (2000): 95.0% white; 3.2% black; 0.5% Asian; 0.2% Native American/Nat. AK; <0.1% Hawaiian/Pacific Islander; 0.2% other race; 2 or more races, 0.9%. **Hispanic pop.** (any race): 0.7%.

Geography. Total area: 24,230 sq mi; rank: 41. **Land area:** 24,078 sq mi; rank: 41. **Acres forested:** 12,128,000. **Location:** South Atlantic state bounded on the N by Ohio, Pennsylvania, Maryland; on the S and W by Virginia, Kentucky, Ohio; on the E by Maryland and Virginia. **Climate:** humid continental climate except for marine modification in the lower panhandle. **Topography:** ranging from hilly to mountainous; Allegheny Plateau in the W, covers two-thirds of the state; mountains here are the highest in the state, over 4,000 ft. **Capital:** Charleston.

Economy. Chief industries: manufacturing, services, mining, tourism. **Chief manuf. goods:** machinery, plastic & hardwood prods., fabricated metals, chemicals, aluminum, automotive parts, steel. **Chief crops:** apples, peaches, hay, tobacco, corn, wheat, oats. **Chief farm products:** dairy products, eggs. **Livestock:** (Jan. 2002) 415,000 cattle/calves; 37,000 sheep/lambs; (Dec. 2001) 11,000 hogs/pigs; 2 mil chickens (excl. broilers); 91.3 mil broilers. **Timber/lumber** (est. 2001): 718 mil bd. ft.; oak, yellow poplar, hickory, walnut, cherry. **Nonfuel minerals** (est. 2001): 185 mil; mostly crushed stone, portland cement, sand & gravel, lime, salt. **Chief port:** Huntington. **Value of construction** (1997): $1.2 bil. **Gross state product** (2000): $42.3 bil. **Employment distrib.**(May 2002): 32% services; 21.9% trade; 19.3% govt.; 10% mfg. **Per cap. pers. income** (2001): $22,725. **Sales tax** (2002): 6%. **Unemployment** (2001): 4.9%. **Tourism expends.** (1999): $1.6 bil. **Lottery** (2001): total sales: $596.9 mil; net income: $189.2 mil.

Finance. FDIC-insured commercial banks (2001): 72. **Deposits:** $14.3 bil. **FDIC-insured savings institutions** (2001): 7. **Assets:** $954 mil.

Federal govt. Fed. civ. employees (Mar. 2001): 12,119. **Avg. salary:** $47,969. **Notable fed. facilities:** National Radio Astronomy Observatory; Bureau of Public Debt Bldg.; Harpers Ferry Natl. Park; Correctional Institution for Women; FBI Identification Center.

Energy. Electricity production (est. 2001, kWh, by source): Coal: 78.4 bil; Petroleum: 256 mil; Gas: 55 mil; Hydroelectric: 237 mil; Nuclear: Other: 24 mil.

State data. Motto: Montani Semper Liberi (Mountaineers are always free). **Flower:** Big rhododendron. **Bird:** Cardinal. **Tree:** Sugar maple. **Songs:** The West Virginia Hills; This Is My West Virginia; West Virginia, My Home, Sweet Home. **Entered union** June 20, 1863; rank, 35th. **State fair** at Lewisburg (Fairlea); late Aug.

History. Sparsely inhabited at the time of European contact, the area was primarily Native American hunting grounds. British explorers Thomas Batts and Robert Fallam reached the New River, 1671. Early American explorers included George Washington, 1753, and Daniel Boone. In the fall of 1774, frontiersmen defeated an allied Indian uprising at Point Pleasant. The area was part of Virginia and often objected to rule by the eastern part of the state. When Virginia seceded in 1861, the Wheeling Convention repudiated the act and created a new state, Kanawha, later renamed West Virginia. It was admitted to the Union 1863.

Tourist attractions. Harpers Ferry Natl. Historic Park; Science and Cultural Center, Charleston; White Sulphur (in Greenbrier) and Berkeley Springs mineral water spas; New River Gorge, Fayetteville; Winter Place, Exhibition Coal Mine, both Beckley; Monongahela Natl. Forest; Fenton Glass, Williamstown; Viking Glass, New Martinsville; Blenko Glass, Milton; Sternwheel Regatta, Charleston; Mountain State Forest Festival; Snowshoe Ski Resort, Slaty Fork; Canaan State Park, Davis; Mountain State Arts & Crafts Fair, Ripley; Ogle Bay, Wheeling; White water rafting, several locations.

Famous West Virginians. Newton D. Baker, Pearl Buck, John W. Davis, Thomas "Stonewall" Jackson, Don Knotts, Dwight Whitney Morrow, Michael Owens, Mary Lou Retton, Walter Reuther, Cyrus Vance, Jerry West, Charles "Chuck" Yeager.

Tourist information. Dept. of Commerce, West Virginia Division of Tourism, State Capitol, Charleston WV 25305.

Toll-free travel information. 1-800-CALLWVA.

Website. www.state.wv.us

Tourism website. www.callwva.com

Wisconsin

Badger State

People. Population (2001 est.): 5,401,906; rank: 18; **net change** (2000-2001): 0.7%. **Pop. density:** 99.5 per sq mi. **Racial distribution** (2000): 88.9% white; 5.7% black; 1.7% Asian; 0.9% Native American/Nat. AK; <0.1% Hawaiian/Pacific Islander; 1.6% other race; 2 or more races, 1.2%. **Hispanic pop.** (any race): 3.6%.

Geography. Total area: 65,498 sq mi; rank: 23. **Land area:** 54,310 sq mi; rank: 25. **Acres forested:** 15,513,000. **Location:** East North Central state, bounded on the N by Lake Superior and Upper Michigan; on the E by Lake Michigan; on the S by Illinois; on the W by the St. Croix and Mississippi rivers. **Climate:** long, cold winters and short, warm summers tempered by the Great Lakes. **Topography:** narrow Lake Superior Lowland plain met by Northern Highland, which slopes gently to the sandy crescent Central Plain; Western Upland in the SW; 3 broad parallel limestone ridges running N-S are separated by wide and shallow lowlands in the SE. **Capital:** Madison.

Economy. Chief industries: services, manufacturing, trade, government, agriculture, tourism. **Chief manuf. goods:** food products, motor vehicles & equip., paper products, medical instruments and supplies, printing, plastics. **Chief crops:** corn, hay, soybeans, potatoes, cranberries, sweet corn, peas, oats, snap beans. **Chief products:** milk, butter, cheese, canned and frozen vegetables. **Livestock:** (Jan. 2002) 3.3 mil. cattle/calves; 80,000 sheep/lambs; (Dec. 2001) 540,000 hogs/pigs; 6.1 mil. chickens (excl. broilers); 91.3 mil. broilers. **Timber/lumber** (est. 2001): 584 mil bd. ft.; maple, birch, oak, evergreens. ft. **Nonfuel minerals** (est. 2001): 368 mil; mostly crushed and dimension stone, sand & gravel, lime. **Commercial fishing** (2000): $6.8 mil. **Chief ports:** Superior, Ashland, Milwaukee, Green Bay, Kewaunee, Pt. Washington, Manitowoc, Sheboygan, Marinette, Kenosha. **Principal internat. airports at:** Green Bay, Milwaukee. **Value of construction** (1997): $6.1 bil. **Gross state product** (2000): $173.5 bil. **Employment distrib.** (May 2002): 27.9% services; 22.7% trade; 15.1% govt.; 19.8% mfg. **Per cap. pers. income** (2001): $28,911. **Sales tax** (2002): 5%. **Unemployment** (2001): 4.6%. **Tourism expends.** (1999): $6.3 bil. **Lottery** (2001): total sales: $401.2 mil; net income: $101.8 mil.

Finance. FDIC-insured commercial banks (2001): 281. **Deposits:** $59.8 bil. **FDIC-insured savings institutions** (2001): 41. **Assets:** $20.9 bil.

Federal govt. Fed. civ. employees (Mar. 2001): 11,020. **Avg. salary:** $47,297. **Notable fed. facilities:** Ft. McCoy.

Energy. Electricity production (est. 2001, kWh, by source): Coal: 40.2 bil; Petroleum: 170 mil; Gas: 869 mil; Hydroelectric: 1.9 bil; Nuclear: 11.5 bil; Other: 319 mil.

State data. Motto: Forward. **Flower:** Wood violet. **Bird:** Robin. **Tree:** Sugar maple. **Song:** On, Wisconsin! **Entered union** May 29, 1848; rank, 30th. **State fair** at State Fair Park, West Allis; July-Aug.

History. At the time of European contact, Ojibwa, Menominee, Winnebago, Kickapoo, Sauk, Fox, and Potawatomi peoples inhabited the region. Jean Nicolet was the first European to see the Wisconsin area, arriving in Green Bay, 1634; French missionaries and fur traders followed. The British took over, 1763. The U.S. won the land after the American Revolution, but the British were not ousted until after the War of 1812. Lead miners came next, then farmers. In 1816, the U.S. government built a fort at Prairie du Chien on Wisconsin's border with Iowa. Native Americans in the area rebelled against the seizure of their tribal lands in the Black Hawk War of 1832, but treaties from 1829 to 1848, transferred all land titles in Wisconsin to the U.S. government. Railroads were started in 1851, serving growing wheat harvests and iron mines. Some 96,000 soldiers served the Union cause during the Civil War.

Tourist attractions. Old Wade House and Carriage Museum, Greenbush; Villa Louis, Prairie du Chien; Circus World Museum, Baraboo; Wisconsin Dells; Old World Wisconsin, Eagle; Door County peninsula; Chequamegon and Nicolet national forests; Lake Winnebago; House on the Rock, Dodgeville; Monona Terrace, Madison.

Famous Wisconsinites. Don Ameche, Carrie Chapman Catt, Willem Dafoe, Edna Ferber, King Camp Gillette, Harry Houdini, Robert La Follette, Alfred Lunt, Pat O'Brien, Georgia O'Keeffe, William H. Rehnquist, John Ringling, Donald K. "Deke" Slayton, Spencer Tracy, Thorstein Veblen, Orson Welles, Laura Ingalls Wilder, Thornton Wilder, Frank Lloyd Wright.

Tourist information. Wisconsin Dept. of Tourism, 201 W. Washington Ave., PO Box 7976, Madison, WI 53707-7976.

Toll-free travel information. 1-800-432-TRIP.

Website. www.wisconsin.gov

Tourism website. www.travelwisconsin.com

Wyoming

Equality State, Cowboy State

People. Population (2001 est.): 494,423; rank: 50; **net change** (2000-2001): 0.1%. **Pop. density:** 5.1 per sq mi. **Racial distribution** (2000): 92.1% white; 0.8% black; 0.6% Asian; 2.3% Native American/Nat. AK; 0.1% Hawaiian/Pacific Islander; 2.5% other race; 2 or more races, 1.8%. **Hispanic pop.** (any race): 6.4%.

Geography. Total area: 97,814 sq mi; rank: 10. **Land area:** 97,100 sq mi; rank: 9. **Acres forested:** 9,966,000. **Location:** Mountain state lying in the high western plateaus of the Great Plains. **Climate:** semi-desert conditions throughout; true desert in the Big Horn and Great Divide basins. **Topography:** the eastern Great Plains rise to the foothills of the Rocky Mts.; the Continental Divide crosses the state from the NW to the SE. **Capital:** Cheyenne.

Economy. Chief industries: mineral extraction, oil, natural gas, tourism and recreation, agriculture. **Chief manuf. goods:** refined petroleum, wood, stone, clay products, foods, electronic devices, sporting apparel, and aircraft. **Chief crops:** wheat, beans, barley, oats, sugar beets, hay. **Livestock:** (Jan. 2002) 1.5 mil cattle/calves; 480,000 sheep/lambs; (Dec. 2001) 117,000 hogs/pigs; 17,000 chickens (excl. broilers). **Timber/lumber** (est. 2001): 197 mil bd. ft.; ponderosa & lodgepole pine, Douglas fir, Engelmann spruce. **Nonfuel minerals** (est. 2001): 986 mil; mostly soda ash, clays, helium, portland cement, crushed stone. **Principal internat. airport at:** Casper. **Value of construction** (1997): $655 mil. **Gross state product** (2000): $19.3 bil. **Employment distrib.** (May 2002): 23.9% services; 22.1% trade; 25.5% govt.; 4.3% mfg. **Per cap. pers. income** (2001): $28,807. **Sales tax** (2002): 4%. **Unemployment** (2001): 3.9%. **Tourism expends.** (1999): $1.5 bil.

Finance. FDIC-insured commercial banks (2001): 45. **Deposits:** $6 bil. **FDIC-insured savings institutions** (2001): 4. **Assets:** $349 mil.

Federal govt. Fed. civ. employees (Mar. 2001): 4,421. **Avg. salary:** $45,316. **Notable fed. facilities:** Warren AFB.

Energy. Electricity production (est. 2001, kWh, by source): Coal: 42.6 bil; Petroleum: 34 mil; Gas: 274 mil; Hydroelectric: 877 mil.

State data. Motto: Equal Rights. **Flower:** Indian Paintbrush. **Bird:** Western Meadowlark. **Tree:** Plains Cottonwood. **Song:** Wyoming. **Entered union** July 10, 1890; rank, 44th. **State fair** at Douglas; late Aug.

History. Shoshone, Crow, Cheyenne, Oglala Sioux, and Arapaho peoples lived in the area at the time of European contact. France's François and Louis La Verendrye were the first Europeans to see the region, 1743. John Colter, an American, was first to traverse Yellowstone area, 1807-8. Trappers and fur traders followed in the 1820s. Forts Laramie and Bridger became important stops on the pioneer trails to the West Coast. Population grew after the Union Pacific crossed the state, 1868. Women won the vote, for the first time in the U.S., from the Territorial Legislature, 1869. Disputes between large land owners and small ranchers culminated in the Johnson County Cattle War, 1892; federal troops were called in to restore order.

Tourist attractions. Yellowstone Natl. Park, the first U.S. national park, est. 1872; Grand Teton Natl. Park; Natl. Elk Refuge; Devils Tower Natl. Monument; Fort Laramie Natl. Historic Site and nearby pioneer trail ruts; Buffalo Bill Historical Center, Cody; Cheyenne Frontier Days, Cheyenne.

Famous Wyomingites. James Bridger, William F. "Buffalo Bill" Cody, Curt Gowdy, Esther Hobart Morris, Nellie Tayloe Ross.

Tourist information. Division of Tourism & State Marketing, I-25 at College Dr., Cheyenne, WY 82002.

Toll-free travel information. 1-800-CALLWYO.

Website. www.state.wy.us

Tourism website. www.wyomingtourism.org

District of Columbia

People. Population (2001 est.): 571,822; **net change** (2000-2001): 0.0%. **Pop. density:** 9,374.1 per sq mi. **Racial distribution** (2000): 30.8% white; 60.0% black; 2.7% Asian; 0.3% Native American/Nat. AK; 0.1% Hawaiian/Pacific Islander; 3.8% other race; 2 or more races, NA. **Hispanic pop.** (any race): 7.9%.

Geography. Total area: 68 sq mi; rank: 50. **Land area:** 61 sq mi; rank: 51. **Location:** at the confluence of the Potomac and Anacostia rivers, flanked by Maryland on the N, E, and SE and by Virginia on the SW. **Climate:** hot humid summers, mild winters. **Topography:** low hills rise toward the N away from the Potomac R. and slope to the S; highest elevation, 410 ft, lowest Potomac R., 1 ft.

Economy. Chief industries: government, service, tourism. **Value of construction** (1997): $673 mil. **Gross state product** (2000): $59.4 bil. **Employment distrib.** (May 2002): 47.4% services; 7.8% trade; 33.8% govt.; 1.7% mfg. **Per cap. pers. income** (2001): $40,498. **Sales tax** (2002): 5.75%. **Unemployment** (2001): 6.5%. **Tourism expenditures** (1997): (1999): $5.7 bil. **Lottery** (2001): total sales: $223.9 mil; net income: $84 mil.

Finance. FDIC-insured commercial banks & trust companies (2001): 4. **Deposits:** $353 mil. **FDIC-insured savings institutions** (2001): 1. **Assets:** $261 mil.

Federal govt. No. of federal employees (Mar. 2001): 143,768. **Avg. salary:** $67,941.

Energy. Electricity production (2000, kWh, by source): Petroleum: 95 mil; Other: 28 mil.

District data. Motto: Justitia omnibus (Justice for all). **Flower:** American beauty rose. **Tree:** Scarlet oak. **Bird:** Wood thrush.

History. The District of Columbia, coextensive with the city of Washington, is the seat of the U.S. federal government. It lies on the west central edge of Maryland on the Potomac River, opposite Virginia. Its area was originally 100 sq mi taken from the sovereignty of Maryland and Virginia. Virginia's portion south of the Potomac was given back to that state in 1846.

The 23rd Amendment (1961) granted residents the right to vote for president and vice president for the first time since 1800 and gave them 3 members in the Electoral College. The first such votes were cast in Nov. 1964.

Congress, which has legislative authority over the District under the Constitution, established in 1874 a government of 3 commissioners appointed by the president. The Reorganization Plan of 1967 substituted a single appointive commissioner (also called mayor), assistant, and 9-member City Council. Funds were still appropriated by Congress; residents had no vote in local government, except to elect school board members. In Sept. 1970, Congress approved legislation giving the District one delegate to the House of Representatives, who can vote in committee but not on the floor. The first delegate was elected 1971.

In May 1974, voters approved a congressionally drafted charter giving them the right to elect their own mayor and a 13-member city council; the first took office Jan. 2, 1975. The district won the right to levy taxes; Congress retained power to veto council actions and approve the city budget.

Proposals for a "federal town" for the deliberations of the Continental Congress were made in 1783, 4 years before the adoption of the Constitution. Rivalry between Northern and Southern delegates over the site appeared in the First Congress, 1789. John Adams, presiding officer of the Senate, cast the deciding vote of that body for Germantown, PA. In 1790 Congress compromised by making Philadelphia the temporary capital for 10 years. The Virginia members of the House wanted a permanent capital on the eastern bank of the Potomac, while the Southerners opposed having the nation assume the war debts of the 13 original states as provided under the Assumption Bill, fathered by Alexander Hamilton. Hamilton and Jefferson arranged a compromise: the Virginia men voted for the Assumption Bill, and the Northerners conceded the capital to the Potomac. Pres. Washington chose the site in Oct. 1790 and persuaded landowners to sell their holdings to the government. The capital was named Washington.

Washington appointed Pierre Charles L'Enfant, a Frenchman, to plan the capital on an area not more than 10 mi square. The L'Enfant plan, for streets 100 to 110 ft. wide and one avenue 400 ft. wide and a mile long, seemed grandiose and foolhardy, but Washington endorsed it. When L'Enfant ordered a wealthy landowner to remove his new manor house because it obstructed a vista, and demolished it when the owner refused, Washington stepped in and dismissed the architect. Andrew Ellicott, who was working on surveying the area, finished the official map and design of the city. Ellicott was assisted by Benjamin Banneker, a distinguished black architect and astronomer.

On Sept. 18, 1793, Pres. Washington laid the cornerstone of the north wing of the Capitol. On June 3, 1800, Pres. John Adams moved to Washington, and on June 10, Philadelphia ceased to be the temporary capital. The City of Washington was incorporated in 1802; the District of Columbia was created as a municipal corporation in 1874, embracing Washington, Georgetown, and Washington County.

Tourist attractions: *See* Washington, DC, Capital of the U.S.

Tourist information. Washington, DC Convention and Visitors Association, 1212 New York Ave. NW, #600, Washington, DC 20005; phone: 202-789-7000.

Website. dc.gov

Tourism website. www.washington.org

OUTLYING U.S. AREAS

American Samoa

People. Population (2002 est.): 68,688. **Population growth rate** (2002 est.): 2.3%. **Pop. density** (2002): 892.1 per sq mi. **Major ethnic group:** Samoan (Polynesian), Caucasian, Tongan. **Languages:** Samoan, English.

Land area: 77 sq. mi. **Total area:** 90 sq mi. **Capital:** Pago Pago, Island of Tutuila. **Motto:** Samoa Muamua le Atua (In Samoa, God Is First). **Song:** Amerika Samoa. **Flower:** Paogo (Ula-fala). **Plant:** Ava.

Public education. Student-teacher ratio (1995): 20.

Boasting spectacular scenery and delightful South Seas climate, American Samoa is the most southerly of all lands under U.S. sovereignty. It is an unincorporated territory consisting of 7 small islands of the Samoan group: **Tutuila, Aunu'u, Manu'a Group (Ta'u, Olosega, Ofu), Rose,** and **Swains Island.** The islands are 2,300 mi SW of Honolulu.

Economy. Chief industries: tuna processing, trade, services, tourism. **Chief crops:** vegetables, nuts, melons and other fruits. **Livestock** (2001): 103 cattle; 10,700 hogs/pigs; 37,000 chickens. **Commercial fishing** (2000): $2 mil. **Principal airport at:** Pago Pago.

Finance. FDIC-insured commercial banks (2001): 1. **Deposits:** $56 mil.

Energy. Electricity production (1999): 130 mil. kWh.

A tripartite agreement between Great Britain, Germany, and the U.S. in 1899 gave the U.S. sovereignty over the eastern islands of the Samoan group; these islands became American Samoa. Local chiefs ceded Tutuila and Aunu'u to the U.S. in 1900, and the Manu'a group and Rose in 1904; Swains Island was annexed in 1925. Samoa (Western), comprising the larger islands of the Samoan group, was a New Zealand mandate and UN Trusteeship until it became independent Jan. 1, 1962 (now called Samoa).

Tutuila and Aunu'u have an area of 53 sq mi. Ta'u has an area of 17 sq mi, and the islets of Ofu and Olosega, 5 sq mi with a population of a few thousand. Swains Island has nearly 2 sq mi and a population of about 100.

About 70% of the land is bush and mountains. Chief exports are fish products. Taro, breadfruit, yams, coconuts, pineapples, oranges, and bananas are also produced.

From 1900 to 1951, American Samoa was under the jurisdiction of the U.S. Navy. Since 1951, it has been under the Interior Dept. On Jan. 3, 1978, the first popularly elected Samoan governor and lieutenant governor were inaugurated. Previously, the governor was appointed by the Secretary of the Interior. American Samoa has a bicameral legislature and elects a delegate to the House of Representatives, with no vote except in committees.

The American Samoans are of Polynesian origin. They are nationals of the U.S.; approximately 20,000 live in Hawaii, 65,000 in California and Washington.

Website. www.samoanet.com

Tourism website: www.amsamoa.com

Guam

Where America's Day Begins

People. Population (2002 est.): 160,796. **Population growth rate** (2002 est.): 2.0%. **Pop. density** (2002): 765.7 per sq mi. **Major ethnic groups** Chamorro, Filipino, Caucasian, Chinese, Japanese, Korean. (Native Guamanians, ethnically Chamorros, are basically of Indonesian stock, with a mixture of Spanish and Filipino; in addition to the official language, they speak the native Chamorro). **Languages:** English, Chamorro, Japanese. **Migration** (1990): About 52% of population were born elsewhere; of these, 48% in Asia, 40% in U.S.

Geography. Total area: 217 sq mi. **Land area:** 210 sq. mi. **Location:** largest and southernmost of the Mariana Islands in the West Pacific, 3,700 mi W of Hawaii. **Climate:** tropical, with temperatures from 70° to 90° F; avg. annual rainfall, about 70 in. **Topography:** coralline limestone plateau in the N; southern chain of low volcanic mountains sloping gently to the W, more steeply to coastal cliffs on the E; general elevation, 500 ft; highest point, Mt. Lamlam, 1,334 ft. **Capital:** Hagatna.

Economy. Chief industries: tourism, U.S. military, construction, banking, printing & publishing. **Chief manuf. goods:** textiles, foods. **Chief crops:** cabbages, eggplants, cucumber, long beans, tomatoes, bananas, coconuts, watermelon, yams, cantaloupe, papayas, maize, sweet potatoes. **Livestock** (2001): 100 cattle; 5,000 hogs/pigs; 20,000 chickens. **Commercial fishing** (2000): $1.3 mil. **Chief port:** Apra Harbor. **Principal internat. airport at:** Hagatna. **Construction sales** (1997): $506 mil. **Employment distrib.** (2000 est.): 26% govt.; 24% trade; 40% serv.; 10% indust. **Per capita income** (1996 est.): $19,000. **Unemployment** (2000 est.): 15%. **Tourism expends.** (1995): $4.9 bil.

Finance. FDIC-insured commercial banks (2001): 2. **Deposits:** $647 mil. **FDIC-insured savings institutions** (2001): 2. **Assets:** $256 mil.

Energy. Electricity Production (1999): 800 mil. kWh

Federal govt. Federal employees (1990): 7,200. **Notable fed. facilities:** Anderson AFB; naval, air, and port bases.

Public education. Student-teacher ratio (1995): 18.3.

Misc. data. Flower: Puti Tai Nobio (Bougainvillea). **Bird:** Toto (Fruit dove). **Tree:** Ifit (Intsiabijuga). **Song:** Stand Ye Guamanians.

History. Guam was probably settled by voyagers from the Indonesian-Philippine archipelago by 3rd cent. BC. Pottery, rice cultivation, and megalithic technology show strong East Asian cultural influence. Centralized, village clan-based communities engaged in agriculture and offshore fishing. The estimated population by the early 16th cent. was 50,000-75,000. Magellan arrived in the Marianas Mar. 6, 1521. They were colonized in 1668 by Spanish missionaries, who named them the Mariana Islands in honor of Maria Anna, queen of Spain. When Spain ceded Guam to the U.S., it sold the other Marianas to Germany. Japan obtained a League of Nations mandate over the German islands in 1919; in Dec. 1941 it seized Guam, which was retaken by the U.S. in July-August 1944.

Guam is a self-governing organized unincorporated U.S. territory. The Organic Act of 1950 provided for a governor, elected to a 4-year term, and a 21-member unicameral legislature, elected biennially by the residents, who are American citizens. In 1970, the first governor was elected. In 1972, a U.S. law gave Guam one delegate to the U.S. House of Representatives who has a voice but no vote, except in committees.

Guam's quest to change its status to a U.S. Commonwealth began in the late 1970s. The Guam Commission on Self-Determination, created in 1984, developed a draft Commonwealth Act. In 1993, legislation proposing a change of status was submitted to the U.S. Congress. In 1994, the U.S. Congress passed legislation transferring 3,200 acres of land on Guam from federal to local control.

Tourist attractions. Tropical climate, oceanic marine environment; annual mid-Aug. Merizo Water Festival; Tarzan Falls; beaches; water sports; duty-free port shopping.

Website. www.gov.gu

Tourism website. www.visitguam.org

Commonwealth of the Northern Mariana Islands

People. Population (2002 est.): 77,311. **Population growth rate** (2002 est.): 3.5%. **Pop. density** (2002): 431.9 per sq mi. **Major ethnic Groups:** Chamorro, Carolinians and other Micronesians, Caucasian, Japanese, Chinese, Korean. **Languages:** English, Chamorro, Carolinian.

Total area: 189 sq. mi. **Land area:** 179 sq. mi. Located in the perpetually warm climes between Guam and the Tropic of Cancer, the 14 islands of the Northern Marianas form a 300-mi. long archipelago. The indigenous population in 1990 was concentrated on the 3 largest of the 6 inhabited islands: **Saipan,** the seat of government and commerce (38,896), **Rota** (2,295), and **Tinian** (2,118).

Economy. Chief industries: trade, services, and tourism. **Chief manuf. goods:** apparel, stone, clay and glass products. **Chief crops:** melons, vegetables, horticulture, fruits and nuts. **Livestock**: (1998): 1,789 cattle; 831 hogs/pigs; 29,409 chickens. **Commercial fishing** (2000): $938,365. **Construction sales** (1997): $88 mil. **Employment distrib.** (1999 est.): 35% manuf.; 18% managerial; 16% serv. **Unemployment** (1999): 4.3%. **Tourism expends.** (1997): $585 mil.

Education. Pupil-teacher ratio (2000): 18

The people of the Northern Marianas are predominantly of Chamorro cultural extraction, although Carolinians and immigrants from other areas of E. Asia and Micronesia have also settled in the islands. English is among the several languages commonly spoken. Pursuant to the Covenant of 1976, which established the Northern Marianas as a commonwealth in political union with the U.S., most of the indigenous population and many domiciliaries of these islands achieved U.S. citizenship on Nov. 3, 1986, when the U.S. terminated its administration of the UN trusteeship as it affected the Northern Marianas. From July 18, 1947, the U.S. had administered the Northern Marianas under a trusteeship agreement with the UN Security Council.

The Northern Mariana Islands has been self-governing since 1978, when a constitution drafted and adopted by the people became effective and a popularly elected bicameral legislature (2-year term), with offices of governor (4-year term) and lieut. governor, was inaugurated.

Website: www.mariana-islands.gov.mp

Tourism website: www.mariana-islands.gov.mp/tourism.htm

Commonwealth of Puerto Rico

(Estado Libre Asociado de Puerto Rico)

People. Population (2002 est): 3,957,988 (about 2.7 mil more Puerto Ricans reside in the mainland U.S.); **Population growth rate:** (2002 est.): 0.5%. **net change** (1999-2000): 8.1%. **Pop. density**: (2002): 1,155.6 per sq mi. **Urban** (1990): 66.8%. **Racial distribution** (2000): 80.5% white; 8% black; 0.2% Asian; 0.4% Native American/Nat. AK; 3.8% Other. **Hispanic pop.** (any race): 98.8%. **Languages:** Spanish and English are joint official languages.

Geography. Total area: 5,324 sq. mi. **Land area:** 3,425 sq mi. **Location:** island lying between the Atlantic to the N and the Caribbean to the S; it is easternmost of the West Indies group called the Greater Antilles, of which Cuba, Hispaniola, and Jamaica are the larger islands. **Climate:** mild, with a mean temperature of 77° F. **Topography:** mountainous throughout three-fourths of its rectangular area, surrounded by a broken coastal plain; highest peak, Cerro de Punto, 4,390 ft. **Capital:** San Juan.

IT'S A FACT: On the island of Guam, brown tree snakes climbing on power lines are a major cause of outages—often more than 100 per year—costing several million dollars annually.

Economy. Chief industries: manufacturing, service. **Chief manuf. goods:** pharmaceuticals, apparel, electronics & other electric equipment, industrial machinery. **Gross domestic product:** (1999 est.) $38.1 bil. **Chief crops:** coffee, plantains, pineapples, tomatoes, sugarcane, bananas, mangos, ornamental plants. **Livestock** (2001): 390,000 cattle; 118,000 hogs/pigs; 12.5 mil. chickens. **Nonfuel minerals** (1996): $31.1 mil, mostly portland cement, crushed stone. **Commercial fishing** (2000): $6.4 mil. **Chief ports/river shipping:** San Juan, Ponce, Mayagüez. **Principal airports at:** San Juan, Ponce, Mayagüez, Aguadilla. **Construction sales** (1997): $4 bil. **Employment distrib.** (May 2002): 22.2% services; 21.6% trade; 28.1% govt.; 12.9% mfg. **Per capita income** (1999 est.): $9,800. **Unemployment** (2000): 10.1%. **Tourism expends.** (1999): $2.1 mil.**Finance. FDIC-insured commercial banks** (2001): 12. **Deposits:** $33.4 bil.

Federal govt. Fed. civ. employees (1997): 13,874. **Notable fed. facilities:** U.S. Naval Station at Roosevelt Roads; P.R. National Guard Training Area at Camp Santiago, and at Ft. Allen, Juana Diaz; Sabana SECA Communications Center (U.S. Navy); U.S. Army Station at Ft. Buchanan.

Energy. Electricity production (1999): 15.6 bil kWh

Public education. Student-teacher ratio (1995): 16. **Min. teachers' salary** (1997): $1,500 monthly.

Misc. data. Motto: Joannes Est Nomen Eius (John is his name). **Flower:** Maga. **Bird:** Reinita. **Tree:** Ceiba. **National anthem:** La Borinqueña.

History. Puerto Rico (or Borinquen, after the original Arawak Indian name, Boriquen) was visited by Columbus on his second voyage, Nov. 19, 1493. In 1508, the Spanish arrived.

Sugarcane was introduced, 1515, and slaves were imported 3 years later. Gold mining petered out, 1570. Spaniards fought off a series of British and Dutch attacks; slavery was abolished, 1873. Under the treaty of Paris, Puerto Rico was ceded to the U.S. after the Spanish-American War, 1898. In 1952 the people voted in favor of Commonwealth status.

The Commonwealth of Puerto Rico is a self-governing part of the U.S. with a primarily Hispanic culture. The island's citizens have virtually the same control over their internal affairs as do the 50 states of the U.S. However, they do not vote in national general elections, only in national primaries.

Puerto Rico is represented in the U.S. House of Representatives by a delegate who has a voice but no vote, except in committees.

No federal income tax is collected from residents on income earned from local sources in Puerto Rico. Nevertheless, as part of the U.S. legal system, Puerto Rico is subject to the provisions of the U.S. Constitution; most federal laws apply as they do in the 50 states.

Puerto Rico's famous "Operation Bootstrap," begun in the late 1940s, succeeded in changing the island from "The Poorhouse of the Caribbean" to an area with the highest per capita income in Latin America. This program encouraged manufacturing and development of the tourist trade by selective tax exemption, low-interest loans, and other incentives. Despite the marked success of Puerto Rico's development efforts over an extended period of time, per capita income in Puerto Rico is low in comparison to that of the U.S.

Tourist attractions. Ponce Museum of Art; Forts El Morro and San Cristobal; Old Walled City of San Juan; Arecibo Observatory; Cordillera Central and state parks; El Yunque Rain Forest; San Juan Cathedral; Porta Coeli Chapel and Museum of Religious Art, Interamerican Univ., San Germán; Condado Convention Center; Casa Blanca, Ponce de León family home, Puerto Rican Family Museum of 16th and 17th centuries, and Fine Arts Center all in San Juan.

Cultural facilities and events. Festival Casals classical music concerts, mid-June; Puerto Rico Symphony Orchestra at Music Conservatory; Botanical Garden and Museum of Anthropology, Art, and History at the University of Puerto Rico; Institute of Puerto Rican Culture, at the Dominican Convent; and many popular festivals.

Famous Puerto Ricans. Julia de Burgos, Marta Casals Istomin, Pablo Casals, José Celso Barbosa, Orlando Cepeda, Roberto Clemente, José de Diego, José Feliciano, Doña Felisa Rincón de Gautier, Luis A. Ferré, José Ferrer, Commodore Diégo E. Hernández, Miguel Hernández Agosto, Rafael Hernández (El Jibarito), Rafael Hernández Colón, Raúl Julía, René Marqués, Ricky Martin, Concha Meléndez, Rita Moreno, Luis Muñoz Marín, Luis Palés Matos, Adm. Horacio Rivero.

Chamber of Commerce. 100 Tetuán, PO Box S-3789, San Juan, PR 00902.

Website. fortaleza.govpr.org

Tourism website. www.gobierno.pr (site is in Spanish); www.gotopuertorico.com

Virgin Islands

St. John, St. Croix, St. Thomas

People. Population (2002 est.): 123,498. **Population growth rate** (2002 est.): 1.0%. **Pop. density** (2002): 921.6 per sq mi. **Major ethnic groups:** West Indian, French, Hispanic. **Languages:** English (official), Spanish, Creole.

Geography. Total area: 171 sq mi. **Land area:** 134 sq mi. **Location:** 3 larger and 50 smaller islands and cays in the S and W of the V.I. group (British V.I. colony to the N and E), which is situated 70 mi E of Puerto Rico, located W of the Anegada Passage, a major channel connecting the Atlantic Ocean and the Caribbean Sea. **Climate:** subtropical; the sun tempered by gentle trade winds; humidity is low; average temperature, 78° F. **Topography:** St. Thomas is mainly a ridge of hills running E and W, and has little tillable land; St. Croix rises abruptly in the N but slopes to the S to flatlands and lagoons; St. John has steep, lofty hills and valleys with little level tillable land. **Capital:** Charlotte Amalie, St. Thomas.

Economy. Chief industries: tourism, rum, alumina, petroleum refining, watches, textiles, electronics, printing & publishing. **Chief manuf. goods:** rum, textiles, pharmaceuticals, perfumes, stone, glass & clay products. **Chief crops:** vegetables, horticulture, fruits and nuts. **Livestock** (2001): 8,000 cattle; 2,600 hogs/pigs; 35,000 chickens. **Minerals:** sand, gravel. **Chief ports:** Cruz Bay, St. John; Frederiksted and Christiansted, St. Croix; Charlotte Amalie, St. Thomas. **Principal internat. airports on:** St. Thomas, St. Croix. **Construction sales** (1997): $185 mil. **Employment distrib.** (1992): 50% trade; 43% serv. **Per capita income** (1999 est.): $15,000. **Unemployment** (1999): 4.9%. **Tourism expends.** (1995): $792 mil.

Finance. FDIC-insured commercial banks (2001): 2. **Deposits:** $104 mil.

Energy. Electricity production (1999): 1 bil kWh

Public education. Student-teacher ratio (1995): 14.

Misc. data. Flower: Yellow elder or yellow trumpet, local designation Ginger Thomas. **Bird:** Yellow breast. **Song:** Virgin Islands March.

History. The islands were visited by Columbus in 1493. Spanish forces, 1555, defeated the Caribes and claimed the territory; by 1596 the native population was annihilated. First permanent settlement in the U.S. territory, 1672, by the Danes; U.S. purchased the islands, 1917, for defense purposes.

The Virgin Islands has a republican form of government, headed by a governor and lieut. governor elected, since 1970, by popular vote for 4-year terms. There is a 15-member unicameral legislature, elected by popular vote for a 2-year term. Residents of the V.I. have been U.S. citizens since 1927. Since 1973 they have elected a delegate to the U.S. House of Representatives, who has a voice but no vote, except in committees.

Tourist attractions. Magens Bay, St. Thomas; duty-free shopping; Virgin Islands Natl. Park, beaches, Indian relics, and evidence of colonial Danes.

Tourist information. Dept. of Economic Development & Agriculture: St. Thomas, PO Box 6400, St. Thomas, VI 00801; St. Croix, PO Box 4535, Christiansted, St. Croix 00820.

Website. www.usvi.net

Other Islands

Navassa lies between Jamaica and Haiti, 100 mi south of Guantanamo Bay, Cuba, in the Caribbean; it covers about 2 sq mi, is reserved by the U.S. for a lighthouse, and is uninhabited. It is administered by the U.S. Coast Guard.

Wake Atoll, and its neighboring atolls, **Wilkes** and **Peale,** lie in the Pacific Ocean on the direct route from Hawaii to Hong Kong, about 2,300 mi W of Honolulu and 1,290 mi E of Guam. The group is 4.5 mi long, 1.5 mi wide, and totals less than 3 sq mi in land area. The U.S. flag was hoisted over Wake Atoll, July 4, 1898; formal possession taken Jan. 17, 1899. Wake was administered by the U.S. Air Force, 1972-94. The population consists of about 200 persons.

Midway Atoll, acquired in 1867, consists of 2 atolls, **Sand** and **Eastern,** in N Pacific 1,150 mi. NW of Honolulu, with an area of about 2 sq mi, administered by the U.S. Navy. There is no indigenous population; total pop. is about 450. **Johnston Atoll,** 717 mi WSW of Honolulu, area 1 sq mi, is operated by the Defense Nuclear Agency, and the Fish and Wildlife Service, U.S. Dept. of the Interior; its population is about 1,200. **Kingman Reef,** 920 mi S of Hawaii, is under Navy control. **Howland, Jarvis,** and **Baker Islands,** 1,400-1,650 mi SW of Honolulu, uninhabited since World War II, are under the Interior Dept. **Palmyra** is an atoll about 1,000 mi S of Hawaii, 5 sq mi. Privately owned, it is under the Interior Dept.

WASHINGTON, DC, CAPITAL OF THE U.S.

Most attractions are free. All times are subject to change. For more details call the Washington, DC, Convention and Visitors Association at 1-800-422-8644, or check out the website at: www.washington.org

Bureau of Engraving and Printing

The **Bureau of Engraving and Printing** of the U.S. Treasury Dept. is the headquarters for the making of U.S. paper money. Free 35-minute self-guided tours (tickets required) Mon.-Fri., 9 AM-2 PM year-round; extended hours, June-Aug., 5 PM-6:45 PM. Closed federal holidays. 14th and C Sts. SW. Phone: 202-874-3019.

Website. www.moneyfactory.com

Capitol

The **United States Capitol** was originally designed by Dr. William Thornton, an amateur architect, who submitted a plan in 1793 that won him $500 and a city lot.

The south, or House, wing was completed in 1807 under the direction of Benjamin H. Latrobe.

The present Senate and House wings and the iron dome were designed and constructed by Thomas U. Walter, 4th architect of the Capitol, between 1851 and 1863.

The present cast iron dome at its greatest exterior measures 135 ft 5 in., and it is topped by the bronze Statue of Freedom that stands 19½ ft and weighs 14,985 lb. On its base are the words *E Pluribus Unum* (Out of Many, One).

The Capitol is open from 9 AM to 8 PM, March-Aug., and 9 AM to 4:30 PM, Sept.-Feb., daily. It is closed Jan. 1, Thanksgiving Day, and Dec. 25. Tours (tickets required) through the Capitol, including the House and Senate galleries, are conducted Mon.-Sat. from 9 AM to 4:30 PM.

To observe debate in the House or Senate while Congress is in session, individuals living in the U.S. may obtain tickets to the visitor's galleries from their U.S. representative or senator. Visitors from other countries may obtain passes at the Capitol. Between Constitution & Independence Ave., at Pennsylvania Ave. Phone: 202-225-6827.

Website. www.aoc.gov

Federal Bureau of Investigation

The **Federal Bureau of Investigation** offers guided one-hour tours of its headquarters, beginning with a videotape presentation. Visitors learn about the history of the FBI and see such things as the weapons confiscated from famous gangsters, photos of the most-wanted fugitives, the DNA laboratory, goods forfeited and seized in narcotics operations, and a sharpshooting demonstration.

Tours are conducted Mon.-Fri., 8:45 AM-2:30 PM, except Jan. 1, Dec. 25, and other federal holidays. Tickets may be obtained at the FBI on day of tour or through a U.S. representative or senator. J. Edgar Hoover Bldg., Pennsylvania Ave., between 9th and 10th Sts. NW. Phone: 202-324-3000.

Website. www.fbi.gov

Folger Shakespeare Library

The **Folger Shakespeare Library,** on Capitol Hill, is a research institution holding rare books and manuscripts of the Renaissance period and the largest collection of Shakespearean materials in the world, including 79 copies of the First Folio. The library's museum and performing arts programs are presented in the Elizabethan Theatre, which resembles an innyard theater of Shakespeare's day.

Exhibit may be visited Mon.-Sat., 10 AM-4 PM., 201 E. Capitol St., SE , Phone: 202-544-4600.

Website. www.folger.edu

Holocaust Memorial Museum

The **U.S. Holocaust Memorial Museum** opened on Apr. 21, 1993. The museum documents, through permanent and temporary displays, interactive videos, and special lectures, the events of the Holocaust beginning in 1933 and continuing through World War II. The permanent exhibition is not recommended for children under the age of 11.

The museum is open daily, 10 AM-5:30 PM, except Yom Kippur and Dec. 25, and extended hours (8 AM-10 PM) Apr. 3-Sept. 2. A limited number of free tickets are available on day of visit; advance tickets may be ordered for a small fee. 100 Raoul Wallenberg Pl. SW. Phone: 202-488-0400.

Website. www.ushmm.org/

Jefferson Memorial

Dedicated in 1943, the **Thomas Jefferson Memorial** stands on the south shore of the Tidal Basin in West Potomac Park. It is a circular stone structure, with Vermont marble on the exterior and Georgia white marble inside, and combines architectural elements of the dome of the Pantheon in Rome and the rotunda designed by Jefferson for the University of Virginia.

The memorial, on the south edge of the Tidal Basin, is open daily, 8 AM-midnight. An elevator and curb ramps for the handicapped are in service. Phone: 202-426-6841.

Website. www.nps.gov/thje/home.htm

John F. Kennedy Center

The **John F. Kennedy Center for the Performing Arts,** designated by Congress as the National Cultural Center and the official memorial in Washington, DC, to Pres. John F. Kennedy, opened Sept. 8, 1971. Designed by Edward Durell Stone, the center includes an opera house, a concert hall, several theaters, 2 restaurants, and a library.

Free tours are available daily, 10 AM-1 PM. 2700 F St. NW. Phone: 202-407-4100, or 1-800-444-1324.

Website. www.kennedy-center.org

Korean War Veterans Memorial

Dedicated on July 27, 1995, the **Korean War Veterans Memorial** honors all Americans who served in the Korean War. Situated at the west end of the Mall, across the reflecting pool from the Vietnam Memorial, the triangular-shaped stone and steel memorial features a multiservice formation of 19 troops clad in ponchos with the wind at their back, ready for combat. A granite wall, with images of the men and women who served, juts into a pool of water, the Pool of Remembrance, and is inscribed with the words *Freedom Is Not Free*.

The $18 mil memorial, which was funded by private donations, is open 8 AM-midnight. French Dr., SW across from Lincoln Memorial. Phone: 202-426-6841.

Website. www.nps.gov/kwvm

Library of Congress

Established by and for Congress in 1800, the **Library of Congress** has extended its services over the years to other government agencies and other libraries, to scholars, and to the general public, and it now serves as the national library. It contains more than 80 million items in 470 languages.

The library's exhibit halls are open to the public Mon.-Fri., 8:30 AM-9:30 PM; Sat., 8:30 AM-6:30 PM. The library is closed Jan. 1 and Dec. 25. 101 Independence Ave., SE. Phone: 202-707-8000.

Website. www.loc.gov

Lincoln Memorial

Designed by Henry Bacon, the **Lincoln Memorial** in West Potomac Park, on the axis of the Capitol and the Washington Monument, consists of a large marble hall enclosing a heroic statue of Abraham Lincoln in meditation sitting on a large armchair. The memorial was dedicated on May 30, 1922. The statue was designed by Daniel Chester French and sculpted by French and the Piccirilli brothers. Murals and ornamentation on the bronze ceiling beams are by Jules Guerin. The text of the Gettysburg Address is in the south chamber; that of Lincoln's Second Inaugural speech is in the north chamber. Each is engraved on a stone tablet.

The memorial is open 24 hr daily. An elevator for the handicapped is in service. W. Potomac Park at 23rd St. NW. Phone: 202-426-6841.

Website. www.nps.gov/linc/home.htm

National Archives and Records

Original copies of the Declaration of Independence, the Constitution, and the Bill of Rights are on permanent display in the **National Archives** Exhibition Hall. The National Archives also holds other valuable U.S. government records and historic maps, photographs, and manuscripts.

Central Research and Microfilm Research Rooms are also available to the public for genealogical research.

The Exhibition Hall is currently closed for renovations. It will reopen summer 2003. Research Rooms remain open but hours vary. 7th & Pennsylvania Ave. NW. Phone: 202-501-5000.

Website. www.archives.gov/index.htm

National Gallery of Art

The **National Gallery of Art**, situated on the north side of the Mall facing Constitution Avenue, was established by Congress, Mar. 24, 1937, and opened Mar. 17, 1941. The original West building was designed by John Russell Pope. The East building, opened in 1978, was designed by I. M. Pei. The National Gallery is separate from, but maintains a relationship with, the Smithsonian Institution.

Open daily, Mon.-Thurs. 10 AM-7 PM, Fri., 10 AM-9 PM, Sunday 11 AM-7 PM. Closed Jan. 1 and Dec. 25. 4th & Constitution Ave NW. Phone: 202-737-4215.

Website. www.nga.gov

Franklin Delano Roosevelt Memorial

Opened May 2, 1997, by Pres. Bill Clinton, the **FDR Memorial** features 9 bronze sculptural ensembles depicting FDR, Eleanor Roosevelt (the first First Lady to be honored in a national memorial), and events from the Great Depression and World War II. This 7.5-acre memorial is located near the Tidal Basin in a park-like setting and includes waterfalls, quiet pools, and reddish Dakota granite upon which some of Pres. Roosevelt's well-known words are carved. The monument is wheelchair accessible.

Grounds, staffed daily, 8 AM-midnight, except Dec. 25. 1850 W. Basin Dr. SW. Phone: 202-426-6841.

Website. www.nps.gov/fdrm/

Smithsonian Institution

The **Smithsonian Institution,** established in 1846, is the world's largest museum complex and consists of 14 museums and the National Zoo. It holds some 100 mil. artifacts and specimens in its trust. Nine museums are on the National Mall between the Washington Monument and the Capitol; 5 other museums and the zoo are elsewhere in Washington (the Cooper-Hewitt Museum and the National Museum of the American Indian, also administered by the Smithsonian, are in New York City). The **Smithsonian Information Center** is located in "the Castle" on the Mall. Also on the Mall are the **National Museum of American History,** the **National Museum of Natural History,** the **National Air and Space Museum,** the **Hirshhorn Museum and Sculpture Garden,** the **Arthur M. Sackler Gallery,** the **National Museum of African Art,** the **Freer Gallery of Art,** and the **Arts and Industries Building.** Near the Sackler Gallery is the **Enid A. Haupt Garden.** Located nearby are the **National Postal Museum,** the **National Museum of American Art,** the **National Portrait Gallery,** and the **Renwick Gallery.** Farther away, at 1901 Fort Place SE, is the **Anacostia Museum.**

Most museums are open daily, except Dec. 25, 10 AM-5:30 PM. Phone: 202-357-2700.

Website. www.si.edu

Vietnam Veterans Memorial

Originally dedicated on Nov. 13, 1982, the **Vietnam Veterans Memorial** is a recognition of the men and women who served in the armed forces in the Vietnam War. On a V-shaped black-granite wall, designed by Maya Ying Lin, are inscribed the names of the more than 58,000 Americans who lost their lives or remain missing.

Since 1982, 2 additions have been made to the Memorial. The 1st, dedicated on Nov. 11, 1984, is the Frederick Hart sculpture *Three Servicemen.* On Nov. 11, 1993, the Vietnam Women's Memorial was dedicated, honoring the more than 11,500 women who served in Vietnam. The bronze sculpture, portraying 3 women helping a wounded male soldier, was designed by Glenna Goodacre.

The memorial is open 8am-midnight daily. Constitution Ave. & Bacon Dr. NW. Phone: 202-426-6841.

Website. www.thevirtualwall.org

Washington Monument

The **Washington Monument,** dedicated in 1885, is a tapering shaft, or obelisk, of white marble, 555 ft, 5 1/8 inches in height and 55 ft, 1½ in. square at base. Eight small windows, 2 on each side, are located at the 500-ft level, where points of interest are indicated.

Open daily (except Dec. 25), 9 AM-4:45 PM. Free timed passes are available; passes are available in advance for a small fee. 15th & Constitution Ave. NW. Phone: 202-426-6841.

Website. www.nps.gov/wash

White House

The **White House,** the President's residence, stands on 18 acres on the south side of Pennsylvania Ave., between the Treasury and the old Executive Office Building. The walls are of sandstone, quarried at Aquia Creek, VA. The exterior walls were painted, causing the building to be termed the "White House." On Aug. 24, 1814, during Madison's administration, the house was burned by the British. James Hoban rebuilt it by Oct. 1817.

The White House is normally open for free self-guided tours Tues.-Sat., 7:45 AM-10:30 AM (passes, necessary mid-March-mid-Sept., are available at White House Visitor's Center, 8 AM-noon, located at 1450 Pennsylvania Ave., NW). Only the public rooms on the ground floor and state floor may be visited. Free reserved tickets for guided congressional tours can be obtained 8 to 10 weeks in advance from your local U.S. representative or senator. 1600 Pennsylvania Ave. Phone: 202-456-7041.

Website. www.whitehouse.gov

Attractions Near Washington, DC

Arlington National Cemetery

Arlington National Cemetery, on the former Custis-Lee estate in Arlington, VA, is the site of the **Tomb of the Unknowns** and is the final resting place of Pres. John Fitzgerald Kennedy, who was buried there on Nov. 25, 1963. His wife, Jacqueline Bouvier Kennedy Onassis, was buried at the same site on May 23, 1994. An eternal flame burns over the grave site. In an adjacent area is the grave of Pres. Kennedy's brother Sen. Robert F. Kennedy (NY), interred on June 8, 1968. Many other famous Americans are also buried at Arlington, as well as more than 200,000 American soldiers from every major war.

North of the National Cemetery, approximately 350 yd, stands the **U.S. Marine Corps War Memorial**, also known as Iwo Jima. The memorial is a bronze statue of the raising of the U.S. flag on Mt. Suribachi, Feb. 23, 1945, during World War II, executed by Felix de Weldon from the photograph by Joe Rosenthal.

On the southern side of the Memorial Bridge, near the cemetery entrance, a memorial honoring the women in the military was dedicated, Oct. 18, 1997. The **Women in Military Service for America Memorial** is a half-circle granite monument, 30 ft. high and 226 ft. in diameter, with the Great Seal of the United States in the center.

Open daily, 8 AM-5 PM (8 AM-7 PM., Apr.-Sept.), Arlington, VA. Phone: 703-607-8052.

Website. www.arlingtoncemetery.org

Mount Vernon

Mount Vernon, George Washington's estate, is on the south bank of the Potomac R., 16 mi below Washington, DC, in northern Virginia. The present house is an enlargement of one apparently built on the site by Augustine Washington, who lived there 1735-38. His son Lawrence came there in 1743, and renamed the plantation Mount Vernon in honor of Admiral Vernon, under whom he had served in the West Indies. Lawrence Washington died in 1752 and was succeeded as proprietor by his half-brother, George Washington. The estate has been restored to its 18th-century appearance and includes many original furnishings. Washington and his wife, Martha, are buried on the grounds.

Open 365 days, 8 AM-5 PM, Apr.-Aug., 9 AM-5 PM, Sept., Oct., Mar.; 9 AM-4 PM, Nov.-Feb. Phone: 703-780-2000, or 1-800-429-1520. Admission: adults $9, seniors (62+) $8.50, children (6-11) $4.50, age 5 and under free.

Website. www.mountvernon.org

The Pentagon

The **Pentagon,** headquarters of the Department of Defense, is one of the world's largest office buildings. Situated in Arlington, VA, it has housed more than 23,000 employees in offices occupying 3,707,745 sq ft. The building was, however, severely damaged when struck by a plane Sept. 11, 2001.

Tours cancelled indefinitely, due to the events of Sept. 11, 2001. Arlington, VA (I-395 South to Boundary Channel Drive exit). Phone: 703-695-1776.

Website. www.defenselink.mil/pubs/pentagon

UNITED STATES POPULATION

Census 2000: Americans Are Older, Better Educated, Wealthier, Stuck in Traffic Longer, and Less Likely to Speak English

by C. Louis Kincannon, Director, U.S. Census Bureau, Department of Commerce

Census 2000 was the most complete census of population and housing in U.S. history. In 2001, it yielded its first fruit: detailed tabulations from the 7 questions asked of every household in the United States. These tabulations painted a broad demographic picture of the nation. They revealed its racial and ethnic diversity, changing age structure (partly because baby boomers are aging), and wide range of living arrangements; they also showed a continuing shift in population southward and westward.

Spring 2002 yielded a fuller statistical harvest with the release of initial data collected by the census long form, the 52-item questionnaire that went to a sample of 1 in 6 households, or about 20 million households nationwide. These statistics fill in the rich subject detail and paint a life-like portrait of the nation. They show a population that is better educated, spending more time commuting, and more likely to have been born abroad than was the case in 1990. And that's just for starters.

More Graduates

Among the highlights of the Census 2000 long-form results released so far was the trend toward increased education. Since the Census Bureau first began measuring it in the 1940 census, the educational level of the population has risen steadily. Among adults age 25 years and older in 2000, 24% had at least a bachelor's degree, up from 20% in 1990 and 16% in 1980. Increasing proportions also had advanced degrees (such as a master's, doctorate, medical degree or law degree)—9%, versus 7% in 1990. Meanwhile, the percentage of the 25-and-older population without a high school diploma declined from 25% to 20%.

Educational attainment levels varied widely across the nation. The highest state levels were found in Massachusetts and Colorado, where 33% of adults held at least a bachelor's degree in 2000. The District of Columbia had an even higher rate of 39%. In some "college towns," such as Palo Alto, CA, and Chapel Hill, NC, the rate exceeded 70%.

Longer Commutes

It's taking somewhat longer for Americans to get to work. The average travel time to work for people 16 years and older (working outside the home) was 25.5 minutes in 2000, up by more than 3 minutes from 1990. Workers in New York, New Jersey, and Maryland faced the longest commutes, averaging 30 minutes or longer.

The climb in average commute time is evidence of the nation's increasing traffic congestion. One possible reason the roads are becoming more crowded is that more people are driving alone to work—76% in 2000, up from 73% in 1990. Carpooling is down slightly (12% in 2000, compared with 13% in 1990), as is the proportion of workers who use mass transit (5% in 2000, down about half a percentage point from 1990). About 3.8 million workers, or 3%, were able to combine their commute with physical fitness by walking or bicycling.

More Newcomers

The foreign-born population—those who were not U.S. citizens at birth—numbered 31 million in 2000, the highest total in U.S. history, and an increase of 57% over the 1990 census figure of 20 million. This continued an increase observed since 1970, when the foreign-born population totaled less than 10 million. In 2000, foreign-born residents constituted 11% of the population, the highest proportion since 1930, when 12% of U.S. residents were foreign-born. From 1860 to 1920, the proportion of foreign-born was higher; ranging from 13% to 15%. During that period of large-scale immigration, Europeans accounted for the bulk of the foreign-born population. By 2000, however, nearly 8 in 10 foreign-born residents were from either Latin America or Asia, compared with fewer than 2 in 10 from Europe.

The states of California and New York had the largest international presences. Census 2000 showed that 26% and 20%, respectively, of the residents of these states were foreign-born. Some of the largest cities had even heavier concentrations. For instance, in Los Angeles, San Francisco, and New York, approximately 4 in 10 residents were foreign-born, and 6 in 10 Miami residents were foreign born, many of them Cuban.

An Increasingly Multilingual Nation

The rise in the foreign-born population brought with it a sharp increase in the number of people 5 years old and over who spoke a language other than English at home—47 million in 2000, up from 32 million in 1990. Of these, 21 million indicated that they spoke English less than "very well," up from 14 million in 1990. Among all those who spoke a language other than English, 60% spoke Spanish in 2000, up from 54% in 1990. Multilingualism was practically the rule in California, where 40% of the people spoke a language other than English at home (compared with 18% nationally). Two other states bordering on Mexico—New Mexico and Texas—also had rates exceeding 30%. In some communities along the Mexican border, such as Laredo, TX, and Nogales, AZ, more than 90% of the population spoke Spanish at home.

A Rising Income Tide

As a nation, Americans are making more money. Median household income in the United States in 1999, (the last complete calendar year before Census Day, Apr. 1, 2000) was $42,000, up from $39,000 in 1989. (The 1989 data are in 1999 dollars to adjust for inflation.) Among U.S. households, 29% had incomes of less than $25,000 and 12%, had incomes of $100,000 or more in 1999. In Alaska, Connecticut, Maryland, Massachusetts, and New Jersey, median household income levels exceeded $50,000.

In all, 12% of Americans had incomes below the poverty line in 1999—down from 13% a decade earlier. Poverty rates were highest in the District of Columbia, Louisiana, and Mississippi, where 20% were poor in 1999. U.S. families had a lower poverty rate than individuals—9%. About half the nation's poor families were maintained by women with no husband present.

A Mobile Society

If it seems as if Americans are rolling out the proverbial "welcome wagon" more frequently for new neighbors, maybe it's because they are. Census 2000 results bear this out, showing that nearly half (46%) of those age 5 and over had changed addresses during the previous 5 years. Of those who relocated during the 1995-2000 period, just over half made a short-distance move, remaining in the same county. (The 1990 census showed similar ratios for 1985-90.) Nevada was the most mobile state; more than 6 in 10 residents there had lived in a different home in 1995. New York, Pennsylvania, and West Virginia had the least mobile populations; fewer than 4 in 10 had lived elsewhere 5 years prior to Census Day, 2000.

"Home, Sweet Home" More Valuable

For most homeowners, their home is their most valuable asset. Generally speaking, this asset became even more valuable in the 1990s. The median value of owner-occupied, one-family housing units in the United States in 2000 was $119,600, up from $100,000 in 1990. (The data for 1990 are in 2000 dollars to adjust for inflation.) Among these units, 10% were valued at less than $50,000, and another 9% at $300,000 or more. Among the states, Hawaii and California had the priciest real estate, with median home values topping $200,000. In a few extra wealthy communities around the country, such as Palm Beach, FL, and Beverly Hills, CA, median home values reached or exceeded $1 million.

Housing Costs Higher

In Census 2000, the median monthly housing costs for homeowners, including mortgages, taxes, insurance, and utilities, was $1,088 for the 70% of owner-occupied, single-family units with a mortgage, and $295 for the 30% of such homes that were not mortgaged. In 2000 constant dollars, the corresponding 1990 costs were $940 and $267, respectively. Meanwhile, median gross monthly rent totaled $602, up from $571 in 1990 (2000 dollars). Among the states, New Jersey stands out for its highest all-around housing costs. In 2000, the Garden State was among the nation's leaders in median costs for owners with a mortgage ($1,534), owners without a mortgage ($533), and renters ($751).

Building Boom Slows

Signaling a somewhat slower pace in new housing construction in the 1990s, Census 2000 found that the proportion of housing units built in the preceding decade was 17%, down from 21% in the 1990 census. One state, however, where the pace of construction was anything but slow was Nevada. More than 4 in 10 housing units enumerated there during Census 2000 did not exist at the time of the 1990 census. In the city of Henderson, NV, the ratio was nearly 7 in 10.

Most Homes Still Use Gas

From natural gas to solar power, Americans use a variety of energy sources to heat their homes. The majority were heated by gas, either utility or bottled (51% and 7%, respectively). Another 30% were heated by electricity, and 9% by fuel oil or kerosene. The remaining 3% of housing units either used some other fuel or were unheated. Since 1990 electricity has become more common as a heating fuel, while fuel oil or kerosene, coal or coke, wood, and solar energy have become less common.

The data show that the fuel most people use varies in different parts of the country. All 5 states where electricity is used to heat the most homes are located in the South or West: Arizona, Florida, South Carolina, Tennessee, and Washington. New England, meanwhile, is clearly fuel oil and kerosene country. Most states there—Connecticut, Maine, New Hampshire and Vermont—predominantly use these fuels for heating. Coal or coke, while little-used nationally, was a significant factor in Pennsylvania, home to almost half of the 143,000 homes nationwide that use this energy source.

"My Grandparents Take Care of Me!"

Census 2000 marked the first census in which a question was asked about grandparents as caregivers. At the time of the census, nearly 6 million grandparents lived with one or more of their grandchildren under 18; of these grandparents, 42% were responsible for most of the basic needs of one or more of these grandchildren. Wyoming, Oklahoma, Arkansas, and South Dakota each had rates approaching 60%.

Shifting Age Structure

One of the most interesting finds that emerged from the questions asked of all respondents is the shift in age structure. The median age (meaning half are older and half younger) of the U.S. population in 2000 was 35.3 years, the highest it has ever been. This increase in the median age—which was 32.9 years in 1990—reflects the aging of the "baby boomers" (those born from 1946 to 1964). Thus, the most rapid increase for any age group was the 49% jump in the population 45 to 54 years-old.

The oldest old also saw significant increases. The nation's centenarians (people who are 100 and older) have seen it all. They were around for the turn of 2 centuries, the Wright brothers' first flight, both world wars, and at least 18 presidential administrations. In 2000, there were 50,454 of them, representing 1 out of every 5,578 people. They have become more numerous, up from 37,306, or 1 in 6,667 people, in 1990. South Dakota, with 1 centenarian for every 3,056 people, and Iowa, with 1 in 3,110, had the highest proportion of this population. The rate of growth of the centenarian population in the U.S. was almost triple the growth rate for the population as a whole (35% versus 13%).

At the other end of the age continuum are children under 5. Census 2000 counted 19.2 million of them, up from 18.4 million in 1990. The 2000 total included 7.8 million preschool-age children (3- and 4-year-olds) and 11.4 million infants and toddlers (those age 2 and younger).

More Data Still

As you read this, more detailed data are still being released from the Census 2000 long-form questionnaire. You can check it all out on our web site, www.census.gov. As we look back at Census 2000 with one eye, we have the other eye on the 2010 census, as planning is already under way. At the Census Bureau, the job of measuring America never ends.

WORLD ALMANAC QUICK QUIZ

Not counting Alaska, what state has the fewest people per square mile of land area?
(a) South Dakota (b) Texas
(c) Wyoming (d) Montana
For the answer look in this chapter, or see page 1008.

The Census: Looking Back

The U.S. Census is conducted every 10 years as mandated by the U.S. Constitution, Article I, Section 2. The primary purpose is to apportion seats in the U.S. House of Representatives and determine state legislative district boundaries. The data are also critical for a vast array of government programs at every level, and for providing demographic information to individuals and businesses.

The first U.S. census, which counted 3.9 million people, was conducted in 1790, shortly after George Washington became president. It counted the number of free white males age 16 and over, and under 16 (to measure how many men might be available for military service), the number of free white females, all other free persons (including any American Indians who paid taxes), and slaves. It took 18 months to collect the data, often on unofficial sheets of paper supplied by U.S. marshals. In contrast to today's pledge of confidentiality, the 1790 census was displayed "at two of the most public places." The 1790 census resulted in an increase of 41 seats (65 to 106) in the House of Representatives.

As the nation expanded, so did the scope of the census data. The first inquiry on manufactures was made in 1810. Questions on agriculture, mining, and fisheries were added in 1840. In 1850, the census included inquiries on social issues—taxation, churches, pauperism, and crime.

The 1880 census contained so many questions that it took the full 10 years between censuses to publish all the results. Because of this delay, Congress limited the 1900 census to questions on population, manufactures, agriculture, and mortality. (Many of the dropped topics reappeared in later censuses.)

For many years, the undertaking of each census had to be authorized by a specific act of Congress. In 1954, Congress specified the laws under which the Census Bureau operates in Title 13 of the U.S. Code. This title delineates the basic scope of the census, the requirements for the public to provide information as well as for the Bureau to keep information confidential, and the penalties for violating any of these obligations. The secretary of commerce (and through that individual, the Census Bureau) is now directed by law to take censuses of population, housing, agriculture, irrigation, manufactures, mineral industries, other businesses (wholesale trade, retail trade, services), construction, transportation, and governments at stated intervals, and may take surveys related to any of these subjects.

U.S. marshals supervised their assistants' enumeration of the first 9 censuses and reported to the president (1790), the secretary of state (1800-1840), or the secretary of the interior (1850-1870). There was no continuity of personnel from one census to the next. However, in 1902, Congress authorized the president to set up a permanent Census Office in the Interior Dept. In 1903, the agency was transferred to the new Dept. of Commerce and Labor, and when the department split in 1913, the Bureau of the Census was placed in the Commerce Dept.

The Census Bureau began using statistical sampling techniques in the 1940s, computers in the 1950s, and mail enumeration in the 1960s, all as part of an effort to publish more data sooner and at a lower cost, and with less burden on the public.

U.S. Area and Population, 1790-2000

Source: Bureau of the Census, U.S. Dept. of Commerce

	AREA			POPULATION			
						Increase over preceding census	
Census date	Gross Area	Land Area	Water Area	Number	Per sq mi of land	Number	%
1790 (Aug. 2)	891,364	864,746	26,618	3,929,214	4.5	—	—
1800 (Aug. 4)	891,364	864,746	26,618	5,308,483	6.1	1,379,269	35.1
1810 (Aug. 6)	1,722,685	1,681,828	40,857	7,239,881	4.3	1,931,398	36.4
1820 (June 1)	1,792,552	1,749,462	43,090	9,638,453	5.5	2,398,572	33.1
1830 (June 1)	1,792,552	1,749,462	43,090	12,866,020[2]	7.4	3,227,567	33.5
1840 (June 1)	1,792,552	1,749,462	43,090	17,068,953[2]	9.8	4,203,433	32.7
1850 (June 1)	2,991,655	2,940,042	51,613	23,191,876	7.9	6,122,423	35.9
1860 (June 1)	3,021,295	2,969,640	51,655	31,443,321	10.6	8,251,445	35.6
1870 (June 1)	3,612,299	3,540,705	71,594	38,558,371	10.9	7,115,050	22.6
1880 (June 1)	3,612,299	3,540,705	71,594	50,189,209	14.2	11,630,838	30.2
1890 (June 1)	3,612,299	3,540,705	71,594	62,979,766	17.8	12,790,557	25.5
1900 (June 1)	3,618,770	3,547,314	71,456	76,212,168	21.5	13,232,402	21.0
1910 (Apr. 15)	3,618,770	3,547,045	71,725	92,228,496	26.0	16,016,328	21.0
1920 (Jan. 1)	3,618,770	3,546,931	71,839	106,021,537	29.9	13,793,041	15.0
1930 (Apr. 1)	3,618,770	3,551,608	67,162	123,202,624	34.7	17,181,087	16.2
1940 (Apr. 1)	3,618,770	3,554,608	64,162	132,164,569	37.2	8,961,945	7.3
1950 (Apr. 1)	3,618,770	3,552,206	66,564	151,325,798	42.6	19,161,229	14.5
1960 (Apr. 1)	3,618,770	3,540,911	77,859	179,323,175	50.6	27,997,377	18.5
1970 (Apr. 1)	3,618,770	3,536,855	81,915	203,302,031	57.5	23,978,856	13.4
1980 (Apr. 1)	3,618,770	3,539,289	79,481	226,542,203	64.0	23,240,172	11.4
1990 (Apr. 1)	3,717,796[1]	3,536,278	181,518[1]	248,709,873	70.3	22,167,670	9.8
2000 (Apr. 1)	3,794,085	3,537,440	256,648[1]	281,421,906	79.6	32,712,033	13.2

(1) Includes inland, coastal, and Great Lakes. Data before 1990 cover inland water only. (2) The U.S. total includes persons (5,318 in 1830 and 6,100 in 1840) on public ships in the service of the U.S. not credited to any region, division, or state. **NOTE**: Percent changes are computed on the basis of change in population since the preceding census date, so the period covered is not always exactly 10 years. Population density figures given for various years represent the area within the boundaries of the U.S. that was under the jurisdiction on the date in question—including, in some cases, considerable areas not organized or settled and not actually covered by the census. In 1870, for example, Alaska was not covered by the census. Population figures shown here may reflect corrections made to the initial tabulated census counts.

Congressional Apportionment

Source: Bureau of the Census, U.S. Dept. of Commerce

	2000	1990	1980	1970	1950	1900	1850
AL	7	7	7	7	9	9	7
AK	1	1	1	1	NA	NA	NA
AZ	8	6	5	4	2	NA	NA
AR	4	4	4	4	6	7	2
CA	53	52	45	43	30	8	2
CO	7	6	6	5	4	3	NA
CT	5	6	6	6	6	5	4
DE	1	1	1	1	1	1	1
FL	25	23	19	15	8	3	1
GA	13	11	10	10	10	11	8
HI	2	2	2	2	NA	NA	NA
ID	2	2	2	2	2	1	NA
IL	19	20	22	24	25	25	9
IN	9	10	10	11	11	13	11
IA	5	5	6	6	8	11	2
KS	4	4	5	5	6	8	NA
KY	6	6	7	7	8	11	10
LA	7	7	8	8	8	7	4
ME	2	2	2	2	3	4	6
MD	8	8	8	8	7	6	6
MA	10	10	11	12	14	14	11
MI	15	16	18	19	18	12	4
MN	8	8	8	8	9	9	2
MS	4	5	5	5	6	8	5
MO	9	9	9	10	11	16	7
MT	1	1	2	2	2	1	NA

	2000	1990	1980	1970	1950	1900	1850
NE	3	3	3	3	4	6	NA
NV	3	2	2	1	1	1	NA
NH	2	2	2	2	2	2	3
NJ	13	13	14	15	14	10	5
NM	3	3	3	2	2	NA	NA
NY	29	31	34	39	43	37	33
NC	13	12	11	11	12	10	8
ND	1	1	1	1	2	2	NA
OH	18	19	21	23	23	21	21
OK	5	6	6	6	6	5	NA
OR	5	5	5	4	4	2	1
PA	19	21	23	25	30	32	25
RI	2	2	2	2	2	2	2
SC	6	6	6	6	6	7	6
SD	1	1	1	2	2	2	NA
TN	9	9	9	9	9	10	10
TX	32	30	27	24	22	16	2
UT	3	3	3	2	2	1	NA
VT	1	1	1	1	1	2	3
VA	11	11	10	10	10	10	13
WA	9	9	8	7	7	3	NA
WV	3	3	4	4	6	5	NA
WI	8	9	9	9	10	11	3
WY	1	1	1	1	1	1	NA
TOTAL	**435**	**435**	**435**	**435**	**435**	**391**	**237**

Note: NA = Not applicable.

The Constitution, in Article 1, Section 2, provided for a census of the population every 10 years to establish a basis for apportionment of representatives among the states. This apportionment largely determines the number of electoral votes allotted to each state.

The number of representatives of each state in Congress is determined by the state's population, but each state is entitled to one representative regardless of population. A congressional apportionment has been made after each decennial census except that of 1920. (The year given above is the year of the census on which apportionment for the next election year is based.) Prior to 1870, $^3/_5$ the number of slaves were added to the total free population. Indians "not taxed" were excluded until 1940.

Under provisions of a law that became effective Nov. 15, 1941, representatives are apportioned by the method of equal proportions. In the application of this method, the apportionment is made so that the average population per representative has the least possible variation between one state and any other.

The first House of Representatives, in 1789, had 65 members, as provided by the Constitution. Of these, the largest numbers were from Virginia (19), Massachusetts (14), and Pennsylvania (13).

As the population grew, the number of representatives was increased, but the total membership has been fixed at 435 since the apportionment based on the 1910 census.

U.S. Population by Official

STATE	1790[1]	1800[1]	1810[1]	1820[1]	1830[1]	1840	1850	1860	1870	1880	1890	1900
AL	....	1	9	128	310	590,756	771,623	964,201	996,992	1,262,505	1,513,401	1,828,697
AK	....	....	....	....	....	....	....	....	....	33,426	32,052	63,592
AZ	....	....	....	....	....	....	....	....	9,658	40,440	88,243	122,931
AR	....	....	1	14	30	97,574	209,897	435,450	484,471	802,525	1,128,211	1,311,564
CA	....	....	....	....	....	....	92,597	379,994	560,247	864,694	1,213,398	1,485,053
CO	....	....	....	....	....	....	....	34,277	39,864	194,327	413,249	539,700
CT	238	251	262	275	298	309,978	370,792	460,147	537,454	622,700	746,258	908,420
DE	59	64	73	73	77	78,085	91,532	112,216	125,015	146,608	168,493	184,735
DC	....	8	16	23	30	33,745	51,687	75,080	131,700	177,624	230,392	278,718
FL	....	....	....	....	35	54,477	87,445	140,424	187,748	269,493	391,422	528,542
GA	83	163	252	341	517	691,392	906,185	1,057,286	1,184,109	1,542,180	1,837,353	2,216,331
HI	....	....	....	....	....	....	....	....	....	....	....	154,001
ID	....	....	....	....	....	....	....	....	14,999	32,610	88,548	161,772
IL	....	....	12	55	157	476,183	851,470	1,711,951	2,539,891	3,077,871	3,826,352	4,821,550
IN	....	6	25	147	343	685,866	988,416	1,350,428	1,680,637	1,978,301	2,192,404	2,516,462
IA	....	....	....	....	....	43,112	192,214	674,913	1,194,020	1,624,615	1,912,297	2,231,853
KS	....	....	....	....	....	....	....	107,206	364,399	996,096	1,428,108	1,470,495
KY	74	221	407	564	688	779,828	982,405	1,155,684	1,321,011	1,648,690	1,858,635	2,147,174
LA	....	....	77	153	216	352,411	517,762	708,002	726,915	939,946	1,118,588	1,381,625
ME	97	152	229	298	399	501,793	583,169	628,279	626,915	648,936	661,086	694,466
MD	320	342	381	407	447	470,019	583,034	687,049	780,894	934,943	1,042,390	1,188,044
MA	379	423	472	523	610	737,699	994,514	1,231,066	1,457,351	1,783,085	2,238,947	2,805,346
MI	....	....	5	9	32	212,267	397,654	749,113	1,184,059	1,636,937	2,093,890	2,420,982
MN	....	....	....	....	....	....	6,077	172,023	439,706	780,773	1,310,283	1,751,394
MS	....	8	31	75	137	375,651	606,526	791,305	827,922	1,131,597	1,289,600	1,551,270
MO	....	....	20	67	140	383,702	682,044	1,182,012	1,721,295	2,168,380	2,679,185	3,106,665
MT	....	....	....	....	....	....	....	....	20,595	39,159	142,924	243,329
NE	....	....	....	....	....	....	....	28,841	122,993	452,402	1,062,656	1,066,300
NV	....	....	....	....	....	....	....	6,857	42,491	62,266	47,355	42,335
NH	142	184	214	244	269	284,574	317,976	326,073	318,300	346,991	376,530	411,588
NJ	184	211	246	278	321	373,306	489,555	672,035	906,096	1,131,116	1,444,933	1,883,669
NM	....	....	....	....	....	....	61,547	93,516	91,874	119,565	160,282	195,310
NY	340	589	959	1,373	1,919	2,428,921	3,097,394	3,880,735	4,382,759	5,082,871	6,003,174	7,268,894
NC	394	478	556	639	736	753,419	869,039	992,622	1,071,361	1,399,750	1,617,949	1,893,810
ND	....	....	....	....	....	....	....	....	2,405[2]	36,909	190,983	319,146
OH	....	45	231	581	938	1,519,467	1,980,329	2,339,511	2,665,260	3,198,062	3,672,329	4,157,545
OK	....	....	....	....	....	....	....	....	....	....	258,657	790,391
OR	....	....	....	....	....	....	12,093	52,465	90,923	174,768	317,704	413,536
PA	434	602	810	1,049	1,348	1,724,033	2,311,786	2,906,215	3,521,951	4,282,891	5,258,113	6,302,115
RI	69	69	77	83	97	108,830	147,545	174,620	217,353	276,531	345,506	428,556
SC	249	346	415	503	581	594,398	668,507	703,708	705,606	995,577	1,151,149	1,340,316
SD	....	....	....	....	....	....	....	4,837[2]	11,776[2]	98,268	348,600	401,570
TN	36	106	262	423	682	829,210	1,002,717	1,109,801	1,258,520	1,542,359	1,767,518	2,020,616
TX	....	....	....	....	....	....	212,592	604,215	818,579	1,591,749	2,235,527	3,048,710
UT	....	....	....	....	....	....	11,380	40,273	86,786	143,963	210,779	276,749
VT	85	154	218	236	281	291,948	314,120	315,098	330,551	332,286	332,422	343,641
VA	692	808	878	938	1,044	1,025,227	1,119,348	1,219,630	1,225,163	1,512,565	1,655,980	1,854,184
WA	....	....	....	....	....	....	1,201	11,594	23,955	75,116	357,232	518,103
WV	56	79	105	137	177	224,537	302,313	376,688	442,014	618,457	762,794	958,800
WI	....	....	....	....	....	30,945	305,391	775,881	1,054,670	1,315,497	1,693,330	2,069,042
WY	....	....	....	....	....	....	....	....	9,118	20,789	62,555	92,531
U.S.	**3,929**	**5,308**	**7,240**	**9,638**	**12,866[3]**	**17,068,953[3]**	**23,191,876**	**31,443,321**	**38,558,371**	**50,189,209**	**62,979,766**	**76,212,168**

Note: Where possible, population shown is that of the 2000 area of the state. Members of the Armed Forces overseas or other U.S. nationals abroad are not included. Totals revised to include corrections of initial tabulated counts. (1) Totals for 1790 through 1830 are in thousands. (2) 1860 figure is for Dakota Territory; 1870 figures are for parts of Dakota Territory. (3) Includes persons (5,318 in 1830 and 6,100 in 1840) on public ships in the service of the U.S. not credited to any region, division, or state.

Estimated Population of American Colonies, 1630-1780

Source: Bureau of the Census, U.S. Dept. of Commerce; in thousands

Colony	1630	1650	1670	1690	1700	1720	1740	1750	1770	1780
TOTAL	**4.6**	**50.4**	**111.9**	**210.4**	**250.9**	**466.2**	**905.6**	**1,170.8**	**2,148.1**	**2,780.4**
Maine (counties)[1]	0.4	1.0	...	...	...	...	...	...	31.3	49.1
New Hampshire[2]	0.5	1.3	1.8	4.2	5.0	9.4	23.3	27.5	62.4	87.8
Vermont[3]	...	...	...	...	...	...	...	...	10.0	47.6
Plymouth and Massachusetts[1,2,4]	0.9	15.6	35.3	56.9	55.9	91.0	151.6	188.0	235.3	268.6
Rhode Island[2]	...	0.8	2.2	4.2	5.9	11.7	25.3	33.2	58.2	52.9
Connecticut[2]	...	4.1	12.6	21.6	26.0	58.8	89.6	111.3	183.9	206.7
New York[2]	0.4	4.1	5.8	13.9	19.1	36.9	63.7	76.7	162.9	210.5
New Jersey[2]	...	...	1.0	8.0	14.0	29.8	51.4	71.4	117.4	139.6
Pennsylvania[2]	...	...	...	11.4	18.0	31.0	85.6	119.7	240.1	327.3
Delaware[2]	...	0.2	0.7	1.5	2.5	5.4	19.9	28.7	35.5	45.4
Maryland[2]	...	4.5	13.2	24.0	29.6	66.1	116.1	141.1	202.6	245.5
Virginia[2]	2.5	18.7	35.3	53.0	58.6	87.8	180.4	231.0	447.0	538.0
North Carolina[2]	...	...	3.8	7.6	10.7	21.3	51.8	73.0	197.2	270.1
South Carolina[2]	...	...	0.2	3.9	5.7	17.0	45.0	64.0	124.2	180.0
Georgia[2]	...	...	...	...	...	...	2.0	5.2	23.4	56.1
Kentucky[5]	...	...	...	...	...	...	...	...	15.7	45.0
Tennessee[6]	...	...	...	...	...	...	...	...	1.0	10.0

(1) For 1660-1750, Maine counties are included with Massachusetts. Maine was part of Massachusetts until it became a separate state in 1820. (2) One of the original 13 states. (3) Admitted to statehood in 1791. (4) Plymouth became a part of the Province of Massachusetts in 1691. (5) Admitted to statehood in 1792. (6) Admitted to statehood in 1796.

Census, 1790-2000

1910	1920	1930	1940	1950	1960	1970	1980	1990	2000
2,138,093	2,348,174	2,646,248	2,832,961	3,061,743	3,266,740	3,444,354	3,894,025	4,040,587	4,447,100
64,356	55,036	59,278	72,524	128,643	226,167	302,583	401,851	550,043	626,932
204,354	334,162	435,573	499,261	749,587	1,302,161	1,775,399	2,716,546	3,665,228	5,130,632
1,574,449	1,752,204	1,854,482	1,949,387	1,909,511	1,786,272	1,923,322	2,286,357	2,350,725	2,673,400
2,377,549	3,426,861	5,677,251	6,907,387	10,586,223	15,717,204	19,971,069	23,667,764	29,760,021	33,871,648
799,024	939,629	1,035,791	1,123,296	1,325,089	1,753,947	2,209,596	2,889,735	3,294,394	4,301,261
1,114,756	1,380,631	1,606,903	1,709,242	2,007,280	2,535,234	3,032,217	3,107,564	3,287,116	3,405,565
202,322	223,003	238,380	266,505	318,085	446,292	548,104	594,338	666,168	783,600
331,069	437,571	486,869	663,091	802,178	763,956	756,668	638,432	606,900	572,059
752,619	968,470	1,468,211	1,897,414	2,771,305	4,951,560	6,791,418	9,746,961	12,937,926	15,982,378
2,609,121	2,895,832	2,908,506	3,123,723	3,444,578	3,943,116	4,587,930	5,462,982	6,478,216	8,186,453
191,874	255,881	368,300	422,770	499,794	632,772	769,913	964,691	1,108,229	1,211,537
325,594	431,866	445,032	524,873	588,637	667,191	713,015	944,127	1,006,749	1,293,953
5,638,591	6,485,280	7,630,654	7,897,241	8,712,176	10,081,158	11,110,285	11,427,409	11,430,602	12,419,293
2,700,876	2,930,390	3,238,503	3,427,796	3,934,224	4,662,498	5,195,392	5,490,214	5,544,159	6,080,485
2,224,771	2,404,021	2,470,939	2,538,268	2,621,073	2,757,537	2,825,368	2,913,808	2,776,755	2,926,324
1,690,949	1,769,257	1,880,999	1,801,028	1,905,299	2,178,611	2,249,071	2,364,236	2,477,574	2,688,418
2,289,905	2,416,630	2,614,589	2,845,627	2,944,806	3,038,156	3,220,711	3,660,324	3,685,296	4,041,769
1,656,388	1,798,509	2,101,593	2,363,880	2,683,516	3,257,022	3,644,637	4,206,116	4,219,973	4,468,976
742,371	768,014	797,423	847,226	913,774	969,265	993,722	1,125,043	1,227,928	1,274,923
1,295,346	1,449,661	1,631,526	1,821,244	2,343,001	3,100,689	3,923,897	4,216,933	4,781,468	5,296,486
3,366,416	3,852,356	4,249,614	4,316,721	4,690,514	5,148,578	5,689,170	5,737,093	6,016,425	6,349,097
2,810,173	3,668,412	4,842,325	5,256,106	6,371,766	7,823,194	8,881,826	9,262,044	9,295,297	9,938,444
2,075,708	2,387,125	2,563,953	2,792,300	2,982,483	3,413,864	3,806,103	4,075,970	4,375,099	4,919,479
1,797,114	1,790,618	2,009,821	2,183,796	2,178,914	2,178,141	2,216,994	2,520,770	2,573,216	2,844,658
3,293,335	3,404,055	3,629,367	3,784,664	3,954,653	4,319,813	4,677,623	4,916,766	5,117,073	5,595,211
376,053	548,889	537,606	559,456	591,024	674,767	694,409	786,690	799,065	902,195
1,192,214	1,296,372	1,377,963	1,315,834	1,325,510	1,411,330	1,485,333	1,569,825	1,578,385	1,711,263
81,875	77,407	91,058	110,247	160,083	285,278	488,738	800,508	1,201,833	1,998,257
430,572	443,083	465,293	491,524	533,242	606,921	737,681	920,610	1,109,252	1,235,786
2,537,167	3,155,900	4,041,334	4,160,165	4,835,329	6,066,782	7,171,112	7,365,011	7,730,188	8,414,350
327,301	360,350	423,317	531,818	681,187	951,023	1,017,055	1,303,302	1,515,069	1,819,046
9,113,614	10,385,227	12,588,066	13,479,142	14,830,192	16,782,304	18,241,391	17,558,165	17,990,455	18,976,457
2,206,287	2,559,123	3,170,276	3,571,623	4,061,929	4,556,155	5,084,411	5,880,095	6,628,637	8,049,313
577,056	646,872	680,845	641,935	619,636	632,446	617,792	652,717	638,800	642,200
4,767,121	5,759,394	6,646,697	6,907,612	7,946,627	9,706,397	10,657,423	10,797,603	10,847,115	11,353,140
1,657,155	2,028,283	2,396,040	2,336,434	2,233,351	2,328,284	2,559,463	3,025,487	3,145,585	3,450,654
672,765	783,389	953,786	1,089,684	1,521,341	1,768,687	2,091,533	2,633,156	2,842,321	3,421,399
7,665,111	8,720,017	9,631,350	9,900,180	10,498,012	11,319,366	11,800,766	11,864,720	11,881,643	12,281,054
542,610	604,397	687,497	713,346	791,896	859,488	949,723	947,154	1,003,464	1,048,319
1,515,400	1,683,724	1,738,765	1,899,804	2,117,027	2,382,594	2,590,713	3,120,729	3,486,703	4,012,012
583,888	636,547	692,849	642,961	652,740	680,514	666,257	690,768	696,004	754,844
2,184,789	2,337,885	2,616,556	2,915,841	3,291,718	3,567,089	3,926,018	4,591,023	4,877,185	5,689,283
3,896,542	4,663,228	5,824,715	6,414,824	7,711,194	9,579,677	11,198,655	14,225,513	16,986,510	20,851,820
373,351	449,396	507,847	550,310	688,862	890,627	1,059,273	1,461,037	1,722,850	2,233,169
355,956	352,428	359,611	359,231	377,747	389,881	444,732	511,456	562,758	608,827
2,061,612	2,309,187	2,421,851	2,677,773	3,318,680	3,966,949	4,651,448	5,346,797	6,187,358	7,078,515
1,141,990	1,356,621	1,563,396	1,736,191	2,378,963	2,853,214	3,413,244	4,132,353	4,866,692	5,894,121
1,221,119	1,463,701	1,729,205	1,901,974	2,005,552	1,860,421	1,744,237	1,950,186	1,793,477	1,808,344
2,333,860	2,632,067	2,939,006	3,137,587	3,434,575	3,951,777	4,417,821	4,705,642	4,891,769	5,363,675
145,965	194,402	225,565	250,742	290,529	330,066	332,416	469,557	453,588	493,782
92,228,496	**106,021,537**	**123,202,624**	**132,164,569**	**151,325,798**	**179,323,175**	**203,302,031**	**226,542,203**	**248,709,873**	**281,421,906**

U.S. Center of Population, 1790-2000

Source: Bureau of the Census, U.S. Dept. of Commerce

The U.S. Center of Population is considered here as the center of population gravity, or that point upon which the U.S. would balance if it were a rigid plane without weight and the population distributed thereon, with each individual assumed to have equal weight and to exert an influence on a central point proportional to his or her distance from that point. The 2000 center is 12.1 miles south and 32.5 miles west of the 1990 center of population, and is more than 1,000 miles from the 1790 center.

YEAR	N Lat °	′	″	W Long °	′	″	APPROXIMATE LOCATION
1790	39	16	30	76	11	12	23 miles east of Baltimore, MD
1800	39	16	6	76	56	30	18 miles west of Baltimore, MD
1810	39	11	30	77	37	12	40 miles northwest by west of Washington, DC (in VA)
1820	39	5	42	78	33	0	16 miles east of Moorefield, WV[1]
1830	38	57	54	79	16	54	19 miles west-southwest of Moorefield, WV[1]
1840	39	2	0	80	18	0	16 miles south of Clarksburg, WV[1]
1850	38	59	0	81	19	0	23 miles southeast of Parkersburg, WV[1]
1860	39	0	24	82	48	48	20 miles south by east of Chillicothe, OH
1870	39	12	0	83	35	42	48 miles east by north of Cincinnati, OH
1880	39	4	8	84	39	40	8 miles west by south of Cincinnati, OH (in KY)
1890	39	11	56	85	32	53	20 miles east of Columbus, IN
1900	39	9	36	85	48	54	6 miles southeast of Columbus, IN
1910	39	10	12	86	32	20	In the city of Bloomington, IN
1920	39	10	21	86	43	15	8 miles south-southeast of Spencer, Owen Co., IN
1930	39	3	45	87	8	6	3 miles northeast of Linton, Greene Co., IN
1940	38	56	54	87	22	35	2 miles southeast by east of Carlisle, Haddon township, Sullivan Co., IN
1950 (incl. Alaska & Hawaii)	38	48	15	88	22	8	3 miles northeast of Louisville, Clay Co., IL
1960	38	35	58	89	12	35	6½ miles northwest of Centralia, Clinton Co., IL
1970	38	27	47	89	42	22	5 miles east southeast of Mascoutah, St. Clair Co., IL
1980	38	8	13	90	34	26	¼ mile west of De Soto, Jefferson Co., MO
1990	37	52	20	91	12	55	9.7 miles northwest of Steelville, MO
2000	37	41	49	91	48	34	2.8 miles east of Edgar Springs, MO

(1) West Virginia was set off from Virginia on Dec. 31, 1862, and was admitted as a state on June 20, 1863.

Population, by Sex, Race, Residence, and Median Age, 1790-2000

Source: Bureau of the Census, U.S. Dept. of Commerce

(in thousands, except as indicated)

	SEX		RACE				RESIDENCE		MEDIAN AGE (years)		
				Black							
	Male	Female	White	Number	Percent	Other[5]	Urban	Rural	All races	White	Black
Conterminous U.S.[1]											
1790 (Aug. 2)	NA	NA	3,172	757	19.3	NA	202	3,728	NA	NA	NA
1810 (Aug. 6)	NA	NA	5,862	1,378	19.0	NA	525	6,714	NA	16.0	NA
1820 (Aug. 7)	4,897	4,742	7,867	1,772	18.4	NA	693	8,945	16.7	16.6	17.2
1840 (June 1)	8,689	8,381	14,196	2,874	16.8	NA	1,845	15,224	17.8	17.9	17.6
1860 (June 1)	16,085	15,358	26,923	4,442	14.1	79	6,217	25,227	19.4	19.7	17.5
1870 (June 1)	19,494	19,065	33,589	4,880	12.7	89	9,902	28,656	20.2	20.4	18.5
1880 (June 1)	25,519	24,637	43,403	6,581	13.1	172	14,130	36,026	20.9	21.4	18.0
1890 (June 1)	32,237	30,711	55,101	7,489	11.9	358	22,106	40,841	22.0	22.5	17.8
1900 (June 1)	38,816	37,178	66,809	8,834	11.6	351	30,160	45,835	22.9	23.4	19.4
1920 (Jan. 1)	53,900	51,810	94,821	10,463	9.9	427	54,158	51,553	25.3	25.5	22.3
1930 (Apr. 1)	62,137	60,638	110,287	11,891	9.7	597	68,955	53,820	26.5	26.9	23.5
1940 (Apr. 1)	66,062	65,608	118,215	12,866	9.8	589	74,424	57,246	29.0	29.5	25.3
United States											
1950 (Apr. 1)	74,833	75,864	135,150	15,045	9.9	1,131	96,467	54,230	30.2	30.7	26.2
1960 (Apr. 1)	88,331	90,992	158,832	18,872	10.5	1,620	125,269	54,054	29.5	30.3	23.5
1970 (Apr. 1)[2]	98,912	104,300	177,749	22,580	11.1	2,883	149,647	53,565	28.1	28.9	22.4
1980 (Apr. 1)[3]	110,053	116,493	194,713	26,683	11.8	5,150	167,051	59,495	30.0	30.9	24.9
1985 (July 1, est.)	115,730	122,194	202,031	28,569	12.0	7,324	NA	NA	31.4	32.3	26.6
1990 (Apr. 1)	121,239	127,470	199,686	29,986	12.1	9,233	187,053	61,656	32.9	34.4	28.1
1991 (July 1, est.)	122,984	129,122	210,979	31,107	12.3	10,020	NA	NA	33.1	34.1	28.1
1992 (July 1, est.)	124,506	130,496	212,885	31,670	12.4	10,446	NA	NA	33.4	34.4	28.5
1993 (July 1, est.)	125,938	131,858	214,760	32,168	12.5	10,867	NA	NA	33.7	34.7	28.7
1994 (July 1, est.)	127,216	133,076	216,413	32,653	12.5	11,227	NA	NA	34.0	35.0	29.0
1995 (July 1, est.)	128,569	134,321	218,149	33,095	12.6	11,646	NA	NA	34.3	35.3	29.2
1996 (July 1, est.)	129,746	135,434	219,686	33,514	12.6	11,979	NA	NA	34.6	35.7	29.5
1997 (July 1, est.)	131,018	136,618	221,334	33,947	12.7	12,355	NA	NA	34.9	36.0	29.7
1998 (July 1, est.)	132,263	137,766	222,932	34,370	12.7	12,727	NA	NA	35.3	36.3	29.9
1999 (July 1, est.)	133,352	139,526	224,692	34,903	12.8	13,283	NA	NA	35.5	36.6	30.1
2000 (Apr. 1)[4]	138,054	143,368	211,461	34,658	12.3	13,118	NA	NA	35.3	NA	NA

NA = Not available. **NOTE:** Urban and rural definitions may change from census to census. Figures have been adjusted to be consistent with the 1990 urban and rural definitions. (1) Excludes Alaska and Hawaii. (2) The revised 1970 resident population count is 203,302,031, which incorporates changes due to errors found after tabulations were completed. The race and sex data shown here reflect the official 1970 census count; the residence data come from the tabulated count. (3) The race data shown for Apr. 1, 1980, have been modified. (4) Race data for 2000 do not include the 2.4% of the population that reported being of more than one race. (5) "Other" consists of American Indians, Alaska Natives, Asians, and Pacific Islanders.

U.S. Population by Race and Hispanic or Latino Origin, 1990-2000

	Census 2000		1990 Census		% increase, 1990 - 2000	
	One race only	One race or more[3]	Number	% of total pop.	Using one race only for 2000	Using one race only or in combination for 2000[4]
RACE[1]						
Total U.S. population[2]	281,421,906	281,421,906	248,709,873	100.0	13.2	13.2
White	211,460,626	216,930,975	199,686,070	80.3	5.9	8.6
Black or African American	34,658,190	36,419,434	29,986,060	12.1	15.6	21.5
American Indian and Alaska Native	2,475,956	4,119,301	1,959,234	0.8	26.4	110.3
Asian	10,242,998	11,898,828	6,908,638	2.8	48.3	72.2
Native Hawaiian and other Pac. Isl.	398,835	874,414	365,024	0.1	9.3	139.5
Some other race	15,359,073	18,521,486	9,804,847	3.9	56.6	88.9
HISPANIC OR LATINO AND RACE						
Total U.S. population[2]	281,421,906	281,421,906	248,709,873	100.0	13.2	13.2
Hispanic or Latino (of any race)[2]	35,305,818	35,305,818	22,354,059	9.0	57.9	57.9
Not Hispanic or Latino[2]	246,116,088	246,116,088	226,355,814	91.0	8.7	8.7
White	194,552,774	198,177,900	188,128,296	75.6	3.4	5.3
Black or African American	33,947,837	35,383,751	29,216,293	11.7	16.2	21.1
American Indian and Alaska Native	2,068,883	3,444,700	1,793,773	0.7	15.3	92.0
Asian	10,123,169	11,579,494	6,642,481	2.7	52.4	74.3
Native Hawaiian and other Pac. Isl.	353,509	748,149	325,878	0.1	8.5	129.6
Some other race	467,770	1,770,645	249,093	0.1	87.8	610.8

(1) Because individuals could report only one race in 1990 and could report more than one race in 2000, and because of other changes in the census questionnaire, the race data for 1990 and 2000 are not directly comparable. (2) The data for total U.S. population, Hispanic or Latino population, and total Not Hispanic or Latino population are not affected by the changes cited in (1). Hispanic or Latino persons may be of any race. (3) Alone or in combination with one or more of the other five races listed. (4) Columns 5 and 6 provide, respectively, a "minimum-maximum" range for the percent increase in population for each race between 1990 and 2000.

Population by State, 1990-2000

Source: Bureau of the Census, U.S. Dept. of Commerce

Rank	State	1990 population	2000 population	Percentage change 1990-2000	Rank	State	1990 population	2000 population	Percentage change 1990-2000
1.	California	29,760,021	33,871,648	13.8	27.	Oklahoma	3,145,585	3,450,654	9.7
2.	Texas	16,986,510	20,851,820	22.8	28.	Oregon	2,842,321	3,421,399	20.4
3.	New York	17,990,455	18,976,457	5.5	29.	Connecticut	3,287,116	3,405,565	3.6
4.	Florida	12,937,926	15,982,378	23.5	30.	Iowa	2,776,755	2,926,324	5.4
5.	Illinois	11,430,602	12,419,293	8.6	31.	Mississippi	2,573,216	2,844,658	10.5
6.	Pennsylvania	11,881,643	12,281,054	3.4	32.	Kansas	2,477,574	2,688,418	8.5
7.	Ohio	10,847,115	11,353,140	4.7	33.	Arkansas	2,350,725	2,673,400	13.7
8.	Michigan	9,295,297	9,938,444	6.9	34.	Utah	1,722,850	2,233,169	29.6
9.	New Jersey	7,730,188	8,414,350	8.9	35.	Nevada	1,201,833	1,998,257	66.3
10.	Georgia	6,478,216	8,186,453	26.4	36.	New Mexico	1,515,069	1,819,046	20.1
11.	North Carolina	6,628,637	8,049,313	21.4	37.	West Virginia	1,793,477	1,808,344	0.8
12.	Virginia	6,187,358	7,078,515	14.4	38.	Nebraska	1,578,385	1,711,263	8.4
13.	Massachusetts	6,016,425	6,349,097	5.5	39.	Idaho	1,006,749	1,293,953	28.5
14.	Indiana	5,544,159	6,080,485	9.7	40.	Maine	1,227,928	1,274,923	3.8
15.	Washington	4,866,692	5,894,121	21.1	41.	New Hampshire	1,109,252	1,235,786	11.4
16.	Tennessee	4,877,185	5,689,283	16.7	42.	Hawaii	1,108,229	1,211,537	9.3
17.	Missouri	5,117,073	5,595,211	9.3	43.	Rhode Island	1,003,464	1,048,319	4.5
18.	Wisconsin	4,891,769	5,363,675	9.6	44.	Montana	799,065	902,195	12.9
19.	Maryland	4,781,468	5,296,486	10.8	45.	Delaware	666,168	783,600	17.6
20.	Arizona	3,665,228	5,130,632	40.0	46.	South Dakota	696,004	754,844	8.5
21.	Minnesota	4,375,099	4,919,479	12.4	47.	North Dakota	638,800	642,200	0.5
22.	Louisiana	4,219,973	4,468,976	5.9	48.	Alaska	550,043	626,932	14.0
23.	Alabama	4,040,587	4,447,100	10.1	49.	Vermont	562,758	608,827	8.2
24.	Colorado	3,294,394	4,301,261	30.6	50.	District of Columbia	606,900	572,059	–5.7
25.	Kentucky	3,685,296	4,041,769	9.7	51.	Wyoming	453,588	493,782	8.9
26.	South Carolina	3,486,703	4,012,012	15.1		**Total Resident Pop.**	**248,709,873**	**281,421,906**	**13.2**

Density of Population by State, 1930-2000

Source: Bureau of the Census, U.S. Dept. of Commerce

(per square mile, land area only)

STATE	1930	1960	1980	1990	2000	STATE	1930	1960	1980	1990	2000
AL	51.8	64.2	76.6	79.6	87.6	MT	3.7	4.6	5.4	5.5	6.2
AK*	.1	0.4	0.7	1.0	1.1	NE	18.0	18.4	20.5	20.5	22.3
AZ	3.8	11.5	23.9	32.3	45.2	NV	.8	2.6	7.3	10.9	18.2
AR	35.2	34.2	43.9	45.1	51.3	NH	51.6	67.2	102.4	123.7	137.8
CA	36.2	100.4	151.4	190.8	217.2	NJ	537.3	805.5	986.2	1,042.0	1,134.5
CO	10.0	16.9	27.9	31.8	41.5	NM	3.5	7.8	10.7	12.5	15.0
CT	328.0	520.6	637.8	678.4	702.9	NY	262.6	350.6	370.6	381.0	401.9
DE	120.5	225.2	307.6	340.8	401.0	NC	64.5	93.2	120.4	136.1	165.2
DC	7,981.5	12,523.9	10,132.3	9,882.8	9,378.0	ND	9.7	9.1	9.4	9.3	9.3
FL	27.1	91.5	180.0	239.6	296.4	OH	161.6	236.6	263.3	264.9	277.3
GA	49.7	67.8	94.1	111.9	141.4	OK	34.6	33.8	44.1	45.8	50.3
HI*	57.5	98.5	150.1	172.5	188.6	OR	9.9	18.4	27.4	29.6	35.6
ID	5.4	8.1	11.5	12.2	15.6	PA	213.8	251.4	264.3	265.1	274.0
IL	136.4	180.4	205.3	205.6	223.4	RI	649.8	819.3	897.8	960.3	1,003.2
IN	89.4	128.8	152.8	154.6	169.5	SC	56.8	78.7	103.4	115.8	133.2
IA	44.1	49.2	52.1	49.7	52.4	SD	9.1	9.0	9.1	9.2	9.9
KS	22.9	26.6	28.9	30.3	32.9	TN	62.4	86.2	111.6	118.3	138.0
KY	65.2	76.2	92.3	92.8	101.7	TX	22.1	36.4	54.3	64.9	79.6
LA	46.5	72.2	94.5	96.9	102.6	UT	6.2	10.8	17.8	21.0	27.2
ME	25.7	31.3	36.3	39.8	41.3	VT	38.8	42.0	55.2	60.8	65.8
MD	165.0	313.5	428.7	489.2	541.9	VA	60.7	99.6	134.7	156.3	178.8
MA	537.4	657.3	733.3	767.6	809.8	WA	23.3	42.8	62.1	73.1	88.6
MI	84.9	137.7	162.6	163.6	175.0	WV	71.8	77.2	80.8	74.5	75.1
MN	32.0	43.1	51.2	55.0	61.8	WI	53.7	72.6	86.5	90.1	98.8
MS	42.4	46.0	53.4	54.9	60.6	WY	2.3	3.4	4.9	4.7	5.1
MO	52.4	62.6	71.3	74.3	81.2	**U.S.**	**41.2**	**50.6**	**64.0**	**70.3**	**79.6**

* For purposes of comparison, Alaska and Hawaii are included in above tabulation for 1930, even though not states then.

25 Largest Counties, by Population, 1990-2000

Source: Bureau of the Census, U.S. Dept of Commerce

County	2000 Population	1990 Population	Percentage change, 1990-2000	County	2000 Population	1990 Population	Percentage change, 1990-2000
Los Angeles, CA	9,519,338	8,863,164	7.4	Santa Clara, CA	1,682,585	1,497,577	12.4
Cook, IL	5,376,741	5,105,067	5.3	Broward, FL	1,623,018	1,255,488	29.3
Harris, TX	3,400,578	2,818,199	20.7	Riverside, CA	1,545,387	1,170,413	32.0
Maricopa, AZ	3,072,149	2,122,101	44.8	New York, NY	1,537,195	1,487,536	3.3
Orange, CA	2,846,289	2,410,556	18.1	Philadelphia, PA	1,517,550	1,585,577	–4.3
San Diego, CA	2,813,833	2,498,016	12.6	Middlesex, MA	1,465,396	1,398,468	4.8
Kings, NY	2,465,326	2,300,664	7.2	Tarrant, TX	1,446,219	1,170,103	23.6
Miami-Dade, FL	2,253,362	1,937,094	16.3	Alameda, CA	1,443,741	1,279,182	12.9
Queens, NY	2,229,379	1,951,598	14.2	Suffolk, NY	1,419,369	1,321,864	7.4
Dallas, TX	2,218,899	1,852,810	19.8	Cuyahoga, OH	1,393,978	1,412,140	–1.3
Wayne, MI	2,061,162	2,111,687	–2.4	Bexar, TX	1,392,931	1,185,394	17.5
King, WA	1,737,034	1,507,319	15.2	Clark, NV	1,375,765	741,459	85.5
San Bernardino, CA	1,709,434	1,418,380	20.5				

Note on least populated counties: The following are the smallest counties by 2000 population: Loving County, TX (64); Kalawao County, HI (147); King County, TX (356); Kenedy County, TX (414); Arthur County, NE (444); Petroleum County, MT (493); McPherson County, NE (533); San Juan County, CO (558); Blaine County, NE (583); and Loup County, NE (712).

Metropolitan Areas, 1990-2000

Source: Bureau of the Census, U.S. Dept. of Commerce

(CMSAs and MSAs of more than 600,000 persons listed by Census 2000 population counts)

Metropolitan statistical areas (MSAs) are defined for federal statistical use by the Office of Management and Budget (OMB), with technical assistance from the Bureau of the Census. Most individual metropolitan areas with populations over 1 million may, under specified circumstances, be subdivided into component Primary Metropolitan Statistical Areas (PMSAs), in which case the area as a whole is designated a Consolidated Metropolitan Statistical Area (CMSA).

Effective June 30, 1999, the Office of Management and Budget designated 261 MSAs, 76 PMSAs, and 19 CMSAs for the U.S. and Puerto Rico.

CMSAs and MSAs	Population 2000	Population 1990	Percent Change 1990-2000
New York–Northern New Jersey–Long Island, NY–NJ–CT–PA CMSA	21,199,865	19,549,649	8.4
Los Angeles–Riverside–Orange County, CA CMSA	16,373,645	14,531,529	12.7
Chicago–Gary–Kenosha, IL–IN–WI CMSA	9,157,540	8,239,820	11.1
Washington–Baltimore, DC–MD–VA–WV CMSA	7,608,070	6,727,050	13.1
San Francisco–Oakland–San Jose, CA CMSA	7,039,362	6,253,311	12.6
Philadelphia–Wilmington–Atlantic City, PA–NJ–DE–MD CMSA	6,188,463	5,892,937	5.0
Boston–Worcester–Lawrence, MA–NH–ME–CT CMSA	5,819,100	5,455,403	6.7
Detroit–Ann Arbor–Flint, MI CMSA	5,456,428	5,187,171	5.2
Dallas–Fort Worth, TX CMSA	5,221,801	4,037,282	29.3
Houston–Galveston–Brazoria, TX CMSA	4,669,571	3,731,131	25.2
Atlanta, GA MSA	4,112,198	2,959,950	38.9
Miami–Fort Lauderdale, FL CMSA	3,876,380	3,192,582	21.4
Seattle–Tacoma–Bremerton, WA CMSA	3,554,760	2,970,328	19.7
Phoenix–Mesa, AZ MSA	3,251,876	2,238,480	45.3
Minneapolis–St. Paul, MN–WI MSA	2,968,806	2,538,834	16.9
Cleveland–Akron, OH CMSA	2,945,831	2,859,644	3.0
San Diego, CA MSA	2,813,833	2,498,016	12.6
St. Louis, MO–IL MSA	2,603,607	2,492,525	4.5
Denver–Boulder–Greeley, CO CMSA	2,581,506	1,980,140	30.4
San Juan–Caguas–Arecibo, PR CMSA	2,450,292	2,270,808	7.9
Tampa–St. Petersburg–Clearwater, FL MSA	2,395,997	2,067,959	15.9
Pittsburgh, PA MSA	2,358,695	2,394,811	–1.5
Portland–Salem, OR–WA CMSA	2,265,223	1,793,476	26.3
Cincinnati–Hamilton, OH–KY–IN CMSA	1,979,202	1,817,571	8.9
Sacramento–Yolo, CA CMSA	1,796,857	1,481,102	21.3
Kansas City, MO–KS MSA	1,776,062	1,582,875	12.2
Milwaukee–Racine, WI CMSA	1,689,572	1,607,183	5.1
Orlando, FL MSA	1,644,561	1,224,852	34.3
Indianapolis, IN MSA	1,607,486	1,380,491	16.4
San Antonio, TX MSA	1,592,383	1,324,749	20.2
Norfolk–Virginia Beach–Newport News, VA–NC MSA	1,569,541	1,443,244	8.8
Las Vegas, NV–AZ MSA	1,563,282	852,737	83.3
Columbus, OH MSA	1,540,157	1,345,450	14.5
Charlotte–Gastonia–Rock Hill, NC–SC MSA	1,499,293	1,162,093	29.0
New Orleans, LA MSA	1,337,726	1,285,270	4.1
Salt Lake City–Ogden, UT MSA	1,333,914	1,072,227	24.4
Greensboro–Winston-Salem–High Point, NC MSA	1,251,509	1,050,304	19.2
Austin–San Marcos, TX MSA	1,249,763	846,227	47.7
Nashville, TN MSA	1,231,311	985,026	25.0
Providence–Fall River–Warwick, RI–MA MSA	1,188,613	1,134,350	4.8
Raleigh–Durham–Chapel Hill, NC MSA	1,187,941	855,545	38.9
Hartford, CT MSA	1,183,110	1,157,585	2.2
Buffalo–Niagara Falls, NY MSA	1,170,111	1,189,288	–1.6
Memphis, TN–AR–MS MSA	1,135,614	1,007,306	12.7
West Palm Beach–Boca Raton, FL MSA	1,131,184	863,518	31.0
Jacksonville, FL MSA	1,100,491	906,727	21.4
Rochester, NY MSA	1,098,201	1,062,470	3.4
Grand Rapids–Muskegon–Holland, MI MSA	1,088,514	937,891	16.1
Oklahoma City, OK MSA	1,083,346	958,839	13.0
Louisville, KY–IN MSA	1,025,598	948,829	8.1
Richmond–Petersburg, VA MSA	996,512	865,640	15.1
Greenville–Spartanburg–Anderson, SC MSA	962,441	830,563	15.9
Dayton–Springfield, OH MSA	950,558	951,270	–0.1
Fresno, CA MSA	922,516	755,580	22.1
Birmingham, AL MSA	921,106	840,140	9.6
Honolulu, HI MSA	876,156	836,231	4.8
Albany–Schenectady–Troy, NY MSA	875,583	861,424	1.6
Tucson, AZ MSA	843,746	666,880	26.5
Tulsa, OK MSA	803,235	708,954	13.3
Syracuse, NY MSA	732,117	742,177	–1.4
Omaha, NE–IA MSA	716,998	639,580	12.1
Albuquerque, NM MSA	712,738	589,131	21.0
Knoxville, TN MSA	687,249	585,960	17.3
El Paso, TX MSA	679,622	591,610	14.9
Bakersfield, CA MSA	661,645	543,477	21.7
Allentown–Bethlehem–Easton, PA MSA	637,958	595,081	7.2
Harrisburg–Lebanon–Carlisle, PA MSA	629,401	587,986	7.0
Scranton–Wilkes-Barre–Hazleton, PA MSA	624,776	638,466	–2.1
Toledo, OH MSA	618,203	614,128	0.7
Baton Rouge, LA MSA	602,894	528,264	14.1

Final 2000 census figures showed that the nation in that year had 50 metropolitan areas of at least 1 mil people, including 9 that had reached that size since 1990. The 50 areas had 161.5 mil people, or 57.5% of the U.S. population, in 2000.

Almost 226 mil people resided in metropolitan areas in 2000, an increase of 27.6 mil (13.9%) since 1990. The population outside metropolitan areas totaled 55.4 mil in 2000, up 5.1 mil (10.2%) from 1990. The metropolitan population in 2000 was 80.3% of the U.S. total, compared with 79.8% in 1990 and 76.2% in 1980.

IT'S A FACT: According to Census 2000, renters outnumbered homeowners in the 4 largest U.S. cities. About 70% of the housing units in New York City, 61% in Los Angeles, 56% in Chicago, and 54% in Houston were rented. In the whole United States, only 34% of all housing units were rented.

Population of 100 Largest U.S. Cities, 1850-2000

Source: Bureau of the Census, U.S. Dept. of Commerce (100 most populous cities ranked by Census 2000 population counts)

Rank	City	2000	1990	1980	1970	1950	1900	1850
1.	New York, NY	8,008,278	7,322,564	7,071,639	7,895,563	7,891,957	3,437,202	696,115
2.	Los Angeles, CA	3,694,820	3,485,398	2,968,528	2,811,801	1,970,358	102,479	1,610
3.	Chicago, IL	2,896,016	2,783,726	3,005,072	3,369,357	3,620,962	1,698,575	29,963
4.	Houston, TX	1,953,631	1,630,553	1,595,138	1,233,535	596,163	44,633	2,396
5.	Philadelphia, PA	1,517,550	1,585,577	1,688,210	1,949,996	2,071,605	1,293,697	121,376
6.	Phoenix, AZ	1,321,045	983,403	789,704	584,303	106,818	5,544	...
7.	San Diego, CA	1,223,400	1,110,549	875,538	697,471	334,387	17,700	...
8.	Dallas, TX	1,188,580	1,006,877	904,599	844,401	434,462	42,638	...
9.	San Antonio, TX	1,144,646	935,933	785,940	654,153	408,442	53,321	3,488
10.	Detroit, MI	951,270	1,027,974	1,203,368	1,514,063	1,849,568	285,704	21,019
11.	San Jose, CA	894,943	782,248	629,400	459,913	95,280	21,500	...
12.	Indianapolis, IN[1]	791,926	741,952	700,807	736,856	427,173	169,164	8,091
13.	San Francisco, CA	776,733	723,959	678,974	715,674	775,357	342,782	34,776
14.	Jacksonville, FL[1]	735,617	635,230	540,920	504,265	204,517	28,429	1,045
15.	Columbus, OH	711,470	632,910	565,021	540,025	375,901	125,560	17,882
16.	Austin, TX	656,562	465,622	345,890	253,539	132,459	22,258	629
17.	Baltimore, MD	651,154	736,014	786,741	905,787	949,708	508,957	169,054
18.	Memphis, TN	650,100	610,337	646,174	623,988	396,000	102,320	8,841
19.	Milwaukee, WI	596,974	628,088	636,297	717,372	637,392	285,315	20,061
20.	Boston, MA	589,141	574,283	562,994	641,071	801,444	560,892	136,881
21.	Washington, DC	572,059	606,900	638,432	756,668	802,178	278,718	40,001
22.	Nashville, TN[1]	569,891	510,784	455,651	426,029	174,307	80,865	10,165
23.	El Paso, TX	563,662	515,342	425,259	322,261	130,485	15,906	...
24.	Seattle, WA	563,374	516,259	493,846	530,831	467,591	80,671	...
25.	Denver, CO	554,636	467,610	492,686	514,678	415,786	133,859	...
26.	Charlotte, NC	540,828	395,934	315,474	241,420	134,042	18,091	1,065
27.	Fort Worth, TX	534,694	447,619	385,164	393,455	278,778	26,688	...
28.	Portland, OR	529,121	437,319	368,148	379,967	373,628	90,426	...
29.	Oklahoma City, OK	506,132	444,719	404,014	368,164	243,504	10,037	...
30.	Tucson, AZ	486,699	405,390	330,537	262,933	45,454	7,531	...
31.	New Orleans, LA	484,674	496,938	557,927	593,471	570,445	287,104	116,375
32.	Las Vegas, NV	478,434	258,295	164,674	125,787	24,624	...	...
33.	Cleveland, OH	478,403	505,616	573,822	750,879	914,808	381,768	17,034
34.	Long Beach, CA	461,522	429,433	361,498	358,879	250,767	2,252	...
35.	Albuquerque, NM	448,607	384,736	332,920	244,501	96,815	6,238	...
36.	Kansas City, MO	441,545	435,146	448,028	507,330	456,622	163,752	...
37.	Fresno, CA	427,652	354,202	217,491	165,655	91,669	12,470	...
38.	Virginia Beach, VA	425,257	393,069	262,199	172,106	5,390	...	...
39.	Atlanta, GA	416,474	394,017	425,022	495,039	331,314	89,872	2,572
40.	Sacramento, CA	407,018	369,365	275,741	257,105	137,572	29,282	6,820
41.	Oakland, CA	399,484	372,242	339,337	361,561	384,575	66,960	...
42.	Mesa, AZ	396,375	288,091	152,404	63,049	16,790	722	...
43.	Tulsa, OK	393,049	367,302	360,919	330,350	182,740	1,390	...
44.	Omaha, NE	390,007	335,795	313,939	346,929	251,117	102,555	...
45.	Minneapolis, MN	382,618	368,383	370,951	434,400	521,718	202,718	...
46.	Honolulu, HI[2]	371,657	365,272	365,048	324,871	248,034	39,306	...
47.	Miami, FL	362,470	358,548	346,681	334,859	249,276	1,681	...
48.	Colorado Springs, CO	360,890	281,140	215,105	135,517	45,472	21,085	...
49.	St. Louis, MO	348,189	396,685	452,801	622,236	856,796	575,238	77,860
50.	Wichita, KS	344,284	304,011	279,838	276,554	168,279	24,671	...
51.	Santa Ana, CA	337,977	293,742	204,023	155,710	45,533	4,933	...
52.	Pittsburgh, PA	334,563	369,879	423,959	520,089	676,806	321,616	46,601
53.	Arlington, TX	332,969	261,721	160,113	90,229	7,692	1,079	...
54.	Cincinnati, OH	331,285	364,040	385,409	453,514	503,998	325,902	115,435
55.	Anaheim, CA	328,014	266,406	219,494	166,408	14,556	1,456	...
56.	Toledo, OH	313,619	332,943	354,635	383,062	303,616	131,822	3,829
57.	Tampa, FL	303,447	280,015	271,577	277,714	124,681	15,839	...
58.	Buffalo, NY	292,648	328,123	357,870	462,768	580,132	352,387	42,261
59.	St. Paul, MN	287,151	272,235	270,230	309,866	311,349	163,065	1,112
60.	Corpus Christi, TX	277,454	257,453	232,134	204,525	108,287	4,703	...
61.	Aurora, CO	276,393	222,103	158,588	74,974	11,421	202	...
62.	Raleigh, NC	276,093	207,951	150,255	122,830	65,679	13,643	4,518
63.	Newark, NJ	273,546	275,221	329,248	381,930	438,776	246,070	38,894
64.	Lexington, KY	260,512	225,366	204,165	108,137	55,534	26,369	8,159
65.	Anchorage, AK	260,283	226,338	174,431	48,081	11,254	...	...
66.	Louisville, KY	256,231	269,063	298,694	361,706	369,129	204,731	43,194
67.	Riverside, CA	255,166	226,505	170,591	140,089	46,764	7,973	...
68.	St. Petersburg, FL	248,232	238,629	238,647	216,159	96,738	1,575	...
69.	Bakersfield, CA	247,057	174,820	105,611	69,515	34,784	4,836	...
70.	Stockton, CA	243,771	210,943	148,283	109,963	70,853	17,506	...
71.	Birmingham, AL	242,820	265,968	284,413	300,910	326,037	38,415	...
72.	Jersey City, NJ	240,055	228,537	223,532	260,350	299,017	206,433	6,856
73.	Norfolk, VA	234,403	261,229	266,979	307,951	213,513	46,624	14,326
74.	Baton Rouge, LA	227,818	219,531	220,394	165,921	125,629	11,269	3,905
75.	Hialeah, FL	226,419	188,004	145,254	102,452	19,676	...	...
76.	Lincoln, NE	225,581	191,972	171,932	149,518	98,884	40,169	...
77.	Greensboro, NC	223,891	183,521	155,642	144,076	74,389	10,035	...
78.	Plano, TX	222,030	128,713	72,331	17,872	2,126	1,304	...
79.	Rochester, NY	219,773	231,636	241,741	295,011	332,488	162,608	36,403
80.	Glendale, AZ	218,812	148,134	96,988	36,228	8,179	...	...
81.	Akron, OH	217,074	223,019	237,177	275,425	274,605	42,728	3,266
82.	Garland, TX	215,768	180,650	138,857	81,437	10,571	819	...
83.	Madison, WI	208,054	191,262	170,616	171,809	96,056	19,164	1,525
84.	Fort Wayne, IN	205,727	173,072	172,391	178,269	133,607	45,115	4,282

Rank	City	2000	1990	1980	1970	1950	1900	1850
85.	Fremont, CA	203,413	173,339	131,945	100,869	...	...	...
86.	Scottsdale, AZ	202,705	130,069	88,364	67,823	2,032	...	...
87.	Montgomery, AL	201,568	187,106	177,857	133,386	106,525	30,346	8,728
88.	Shreveport, LA	200,145	198,525	206,989	182,064	127,206	16,013	1,728
89.	Augusta, GA[1]	199,775	44,639	47,532	59,864	71,508	39,441	9,448
90.	Lubbock, TX	199,564	186,206	174,361	149,101	71,747	...	...
91.	Chesapeake, VA	199,184	151,976	114,486	89,580	...	...	...
92.	Mobile, AL	198,915	196,278	200,452	190,026	129,009	38,469	20,515
93.	Des Moines, IA	198,682	193,187	191,003	201,404	177,965	62,139	...
94.	Grand Rapids, MI	197,800	189,126	181,843	197,649	176,515	87,565	2,686
95.	Richmond, VA	197,790	203,056	219,214	249,332	230,310	85,050	27,570
96.	Yonkers, NY	196,086	188,082	195,351	204,297	152,798	47,931	...
97.	Spokane, WA	195,629	177,196	171,300	170,516	161,721	36,848	...
98.	Glendale, CA	194,973	180,038	139,060	133,000	96,000	...	...
99.	Tacoma, WA	193,556	176,664	158,501	154,407	143,673	37,714	...
100.	Irving, TX	191,615	155,037	109,943	97,457	2,615	...	...

(1) Indianapolis, IN; Jacksonville, FL; Nashville, TN; and Augusta, GA, are parts of consolidated city-county governments. Populations of other incorporated places in the county have been excluded from the population totals shown here. For years that predate the establishment of a consolidated city-county government, city population is shown. (2) Locations in Hawaii are called "census designated places (CDPs)." Although these areas are not incorporated, they are recognized for census purposes as large urban places. Honolulu CDP is coextensive with Honolulu Judicial District within the city and county of Honolulu.

Mobility, by Selected Characteristics, 1999-2000

Source: Bureau of the Census, U.S. Dept. of Commerce
(numbers in thousands)

	Total no. of movers[1]	MOVED TO: Same county	Diff. county, same state	Diff. state	Abroad
Marital status					
Married, spouse present	13,143	6,892	2,812	2,860	580
Married, spouse absent	707	348	139	127	92
Widowed	944	521	198	200	24
Divorced	3,771	2,246	748	724	55
Separated	1,231	790	220	195	27
Never married	13,393	7,562	2,819	2,439	574
Educational attainment[2]					
Less than 9th grade	1,469	854	274	219	123
Grades 9-12, no diploma	2,164	1,347	430	329	59
High school grad.	7,152	4,079	1,413	1,455	206
Some college or AA degree	6,051	3,390	1,372	1,148	141
Bachelor's degree	4,581	2,199	1,083	1,058	241
Prof. or graduate degree	1,912	843	401	520	147

	Total no. of movers[1]	MOVED TO: Same county	Diff. county, same state	Diff. state	Abroad
Income[3]					
Under $5,000	4,107	2,144	814	883	264
$5,000-$9,999	4,142	2,420	846	738	138
$10,000-$19,999	7,308	4,365	1,448	1,316	179
$20,000-$29,999	5,292	3,129	1,099	941	124
$30,000-$39,999	3,465	1,878	824	683	78
$40,000-$49,999	1,893	973	493	392	36
$50,000-$59,999	1,143	582	266	266	29
$60,000-$74,999	1,056	576	237	210	33
$75,000-$99,999	723	331	175	188	29
$100,000 and over	713	323	152	193	45
Ownership status					
Owner	17,150	9,396	4,042	1,189	478
Renter	26,238	15,003	4,772	1,917	1,268
TOTAL[4]	**43,388**	**24,399**	**8,814**	**8,428**	**1,746**

(1) People who moved to a new residence in 12-month period ending in Mar. 2000. (2) People 25 years and older. (3) People 15 years and older. (4) People 1 year and older.

U.S. Population, by Age, Sex, and Household, 2000

Source: Bureau of the Census, U.S. Dept. of Commerce; 2000 Census

	Number	%
Total population	**281,421,906**	
AGE		
Under 5 years	19,175,798	6.8
5 to 9 years	20,549,505	7.3
10 to 14 years	20,528,072	7.3
15 to 19 years	20,219,890	7.2
20 to 24 years	18,964,001	6.7
25 to 34 years	39,891,724	14.2
35 to 44 years	45,148,527	16.0
45 to 54 years	37,677,952	13.4
55 to 59 years	13,469,237	4.8
60 to 64 years	10,805,447	3.8
65 to 74 years	18,390,986	6.5
75 to 84 years	12,361,180	4.4
85 years and over	4,239,587	1.5
18 years and over	209,128,094	74.3
Male	100,994,367	35.9
Female	108,133,727	38.4
21 years and over	196,899,193	70.0
62 years and over	41,256,029	14.7
65 years and over	34,991,753	12.4
SEX		
Male	138,053,563	49.1
Female	143,368,343	50.9
HOUSEHOLDS BY TYPES		
Total Households	105,480,101	
Family households (families)	71,787,347	68.1
Married-couple families	54,493,232	51.7
Female householder, no husband present	12,900,103	12.2
Nonfamily households	33,692,754	31.9
Householder living alone	27,230,075	25.8
Householder 65 years and over	9,722,857	9.2
Persons living in households	273,643,273	NA
Persons per household	2.59	NA
Persons living in group quarters	7,778,633	NA
Institutionalized persons	4,059,039	NA
Other persons in group quarters	3,719,594	NA

NA = Not applicable.

U.S. Population Abroad, by Selected Country, 1999

Source: U.S. Dept. of State

Area	Resident U.S. citizens[1]
Argentina	27,600
Australia	102,800
Belgium	35,330
Brazil	40,640
Canada	687,700
Costa Rica	19,800
Dominican Republic	82,000
Egypt	10,890
France	101,750
Germany	210,880
Greece	72,500
Hong Kong	48,220
Ireland	46,980
Israel	18,000
Italy	168,970
Japan	70,350
Mexico	1,036,300
Netherlands	23,707
Panama	19,700
Philippines	105,000
Portugal	2,170
Saudi Arabia	35,990
South Korea	30,000
Spain	94,510
Switzerland	12,110
United Kingdom	224,000
Venezuela	25,000
Total[2]	**3,784,690**

Note: Figures do not include U.S. military or government personnel or their dependents. (1) Estimated. (2) Includes other areas not shown separately.

U.S. Foreign-Born Population

Source: Bureau of the Census, U.S. Dept. of Commerce

Percentage of Population That Is Foreign-Born, 1900-2000

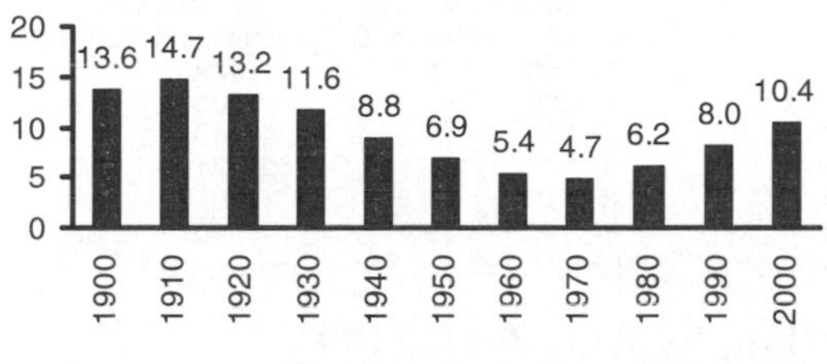

U.S. Foreign Born Population by Regional Origin, 1995-2000

Region	2000 (in thousands)	1995 (in thousands)
Europe	4,355	3,937
Under 18	250	232
Asia	7,246	6,121
Under 18	657	767
Latin America	14,477	11,777
Under 18	1,684	1,481
Other	2,301	2,658
Under 18	245	275
ALL REGIONS	28,379	24,493
Under 18	2,837	2,726

Foreign-Born Population: Top Countries of Origin, 1920, 1960, 2000

Source: Bureau of the Census, U.S. Dept. of Commerce

(in thousands)

1920

Country	Number	%
Germany	1,686	12.1
Italy	1,610	11.6
Soviet Union	1,400	10.1
Poland	1,139	8.2
Canada	1,138	8.2
Great Britain	1,135	8.2
Ireland	1,037	7.5
Sweden	625	4.5
Austria	575	4.1
Mexico	486	3.5

1960

Country	Number	%
Italy	1,256	12.9
Germany	989	10.2
Canada	953	9.8
Great Britain	764	7.9
Poland	747	7.7
Soviet Union	690	7.1
Mexico	575	5.9
Ireland	338	3.5
Austria	304	3.1
Hungary	245	2.5

2000

Country	Number	%
Mexico	7,841	27.6
Philippines	1,222	4.3
China and Hong Kong	1,066	3.8
India	1,007	3.5
Cuba	952	3.4
Vietnam	863	3.0
San Salvador	765	2.7
Korea	701	2.5
Dominican Republic	692	2.4
Canada	678	2.4

Immigrants Admitted, by Top 50 Metropolitan Areas of Intended Residence, 2000

Source: Immigration and Naturalization Service, U.S. Dept. of Justice

(fiscal year 2000)

Metropolitan Statistical Area	Number	Percentage
TOTAL immigrants admitted to U.S.	**849,807**	**100.0**
New York, NY	85,867	10.1
Los Angeles - Long Beach, CA	70,641	8.3
Miami, FL	47,404	5.6
Chicago, IL	32,300	3.8
Washington, DC-MD-VA	29,394	3.5
Orange County, CA	20,859	2.5
Houston, TX	17,429	2.1
San Jose, CA	16,874	2.0
Boston-Lawrence-Lowell-Brockton, MA	16,469	1.9
Oakland, CA	16,150	1.9
San Francisco, CA	16,143	1.9
Fort Lauderdale, FL	14,835	1.7
San Diego, CA	14,624	1.7
Dallas, TX	14,044	1.7
Riverside-San Bernardino, CA	12,994	1.5
Philadelphia, PA-NJ	12,635	1.5
Detroit, MI	11,229	1.3
Atlanta, GA	11,190	1.3
Newark, NJ	11,055	1.3
Seattle-Bellevue-Everett, WA	10,188	1.2
Nassau-Suffolk, NY	9,427	1.1
Bergen-Passaic, NJ	9,244	1.1
West Palm Beach-Boca Raton, FL	7,794	0.9
Phoenix-Mesa, AZ	7,334	0.9
Orlando, FL	7,149	0.8
Minneapolis-St. Paul, NM-WI	6,823	0.8
Middlesex-Somerset-Hunterdon, NJ	6,760	0.8
Sacramento, CA	6,653	0.8
Portland Vancouver, OR-WA	6,651	0.8
Jersey City, NJ	6,392	0.8
Tampa-St. Petersburg-Clearwater, FL	6,160	0.7
Las Vegas, NV	5,037	0.6
Denver, CO	4,934	0.6
Fresno, CA	4,899	0.6
Forth Worth-Arlington, TX	4,665	0.5
Baltimore, MD	4,452	0.5
Honolulu, HI	4,409	0.5
Bridgeport-Stamford-Norwalk-Danbury, CT	4,344	0.5
El Paso, TX	3,922	0.5
Ventura, CA	3,744	0.4
Hartford, CT	3,696	0.4
Salinas, CA	3,245	0.4
St. Louis, MO	3,186	0.4
Cleveland-Lorain-Elyria, OH	3,104	0.4
Austin - San Marcos,TX	3,060	0.4
McAllen-Edinburg-Mission, TX	2,947	0.3
Santa Cruz-Watsonville, CA	2,929	0.3
Kansas City, MO-KS	2,778	0.3
San Antonio, TX	2,777	0.3
Stockton-Lodi, CA	2,721	0.3
Other	142,864	16.8
Non-MSA	73,380	8.6

Immigrants Admitted, by State of Intended Residence, 2000

Source: Immigration and Naturalization Service, U.S. Dept. of Justice

(fiscal year 2000)

STATE	Immigrants
Alabama	1,904
Alaska	1,374
Arizona	11,980
Arkansas	1,596
California	217,753
Colorado	8,216
Connecticut	11,346
Delaware	1,570
District of Columbia	2,542
Florida	98,391
Georgia	14,778
Hawaii	6,056
Idaho	1,922
Illinois	36,180
Indiana	4,128
Iowa	3,052
Kansas	4,582
Kentucky	2,989
Louisiana	3,016
Maine	1,133
Maryland	17,705
Massachusetts	23,483
Michigan	16,773
Minnesota	8,671
Mississippi	1,083
Missouri	6,053
Montana	493
Nebraska	2,230
Nevada	7,827
New Hampshire	2,001
New Jersey	40,013
New Mexico	3,973
New York	106,061
North Carolina	9,251
North Dakota	420
Ohio	9,263
Oklahoma	4,586
Oregon	8,543
Pennsylvania	18,148
Rhode Island	2,526
South Carolina	2,267
South Dakota	465
Tennessee	4,882
Texas	63,840
Utah	3,710
Vermont	810
Virginia	20,087
Washington	18,486
West Virginia	573
Wisconsin	5,057
Wyoming	248
Guam	1,556
Northern Mariana Islands	122
Puerto Rico	2,649
U.S. Virgin Islands	1,328
Armed Services Posts	116
Total	**849,807**

IT'S A FACT: In 2000, according to the census, 10% of U.S. households consisted of 5 or more people, down from 21% in 1970. At the same time, 59% of all households in 2000 had just 1 or 2 persons, compared to 46% in 1970.

The Elderly U.S. Population, 1900-2000

Source: Bureau of the Census, U.S. Dept. of Commerce

Year[1]	65 AND OVER Number[2]	65 AND OVER Percent	85 AND OVER Number[2]	85 AND OVER Percent
1900	3,080	4.1	122	0.2
1910	3,949	4.3	167	0.2
1920	4,933	4.7	210	0.2
1930	6,634	5.4	272	0.2
1940	9,019	6.8	365	0.3
1950	12,269	8.1	577	0.4
1960	16,560	9.2	929	0.5
1970	19,980	9.8	1,409	0.7
1980	25,550	11.3	2,240	1.0
1990	31,079	12.5	3,021	1.2
1995	33,619	12.8	3,685	1.4
2000	34,992	12.4	4,240	1.5

NOTE: Figures for 1900 to 1950 exclude Alaska and Hawaii. (1) Date of Census. (2) Resident population, in thousands.

Projections of Total U.S. Population, by Age, 2010-2100

Source: Bureau of the Census, U.S. Dept. of Commerce

Age	2010 Population[1]	2010 Percentage Distribution	2025 Population[1]	2025 Percentage Distribution	2050 Population[1]	2050 Percentage Distribution	2100 Population[1]	2100 Percentage Distribution
TOTAL	299,862	**100.0**	**337,815**	**100.0**	**403,687**	**100.0**	**570,954**	**100.0**
Under 5 years	20,099	6.7	22,551	6.7	26,914	6.7	36,068	6.3
5-14 years	39,346	13.1	44,486	13.2	52,869	13.1	71,807	12.6
15-24 years	42,819	14.3	43,614	12.9	52,769	13.1	72,620	12.7
25-34 years	38,851	13.0	42,872	12.7	50,458	12.5	68,775	12.0
35-44 years	39,443	13.2	43,234	12.8	49,588	12.3	67,912	11.9
45-54 years	44,161	14.7	38,291	11.3	45,445	11.3	63,787	11.2
55-64 years	35,429	11.8	40,125	11.9	43,644	10.8	58,822	10.3
65 years and over	39,715	13.2	62,641	18.5	81,999	20.3	131,163	23.0
85 years and over	5,786	1.9	7,441	2.2	19,352	4.8	37,030	6.5
100 years and over	129	0.0	313	0.1	1,095	0.3	5,323	0.9

NOTE: Assumptions were based on July 1 estimates of U.S. population consistent with the 1990 decennial census, as enumerated. All figures shown are for July 1 of the given year, exclude Armed Forces overseas, and are middle series population projections. For the series shown, different assumptions were made regarding fertility rates (lifetime births per woman), life expectancy, and immigration in the coming decades. Yearly net immigration was assumed to be 820,000. Percentage distribution may not equal 100, because of overlapping categories shown and rounding. (1) In thousands.

U.S. Households, 1960-2000[1]

Source: Bureau of the Census, U.S. Dept. of Commerce

(as of Mar.)

YEAR	Total	Married-couple households	% of Total	Unmarried-couple households
1960	52,799	39,254	74	439
1970	63,401	44,728	71	523
1980	80,776	49,112	61	1,589
1981	82,368	49,294	60	1,808
1982	83,527	49,630	59	1,863
1983	83,918	49,908	59	1,891
1984	85,407	50,090	59	1,988
1985	86,789	50,350	58	1,983
1986	88,458	50,933	58	2,220
1987	89,479	51,537	58	2,334
1988	91,124	51,675	57	2,588
1989	92,830	52,100	56	2,764
1990	93,347	52,317	56	2,856
1991	94,312	52,147	55	3,039
1992	95,669	52,457	55	3,308
1993	96,426	53,090	55	3,510
1994	97,107	53,171	55	3,661
1995	98,990	53,858	54	3,668
1996	99,627	53,567	54	3,958
1997	101,018	53,604	53	4,130
1998	102,528	54,317	53	4,236
1999	103,874	54,770	53	4,486
2000	105,480	54,493	52	5,476

(1) All household numbers in thousands.

Young Adults Living at Home[1] in the U.S., 1960-2000

Source: Bureau of the Census, U.S. Dept. of Commerce

(numbers in thousands)

18-24 years old	Male Total	Male Percent	Female Total	Female Percent
2000	13,291	57	13,242	47
1999	12,936	58	13,031	49
1998	12,633	59	12,568	48
1997	12,534	60	12,452	48
1996	12,402	59	12,441	48
1995	12,545	58	12,613	47
1994	12,683	60	12,792	46
1993	12,049	59	12,260	47
1992	12,083	60	12,351	48
1991	12,275	60	12,627	49
1990	12,450	58	12,860	48
1985	13,695	60	14,149	48
1980	14,278	54	14,844	43
1970	10,398	54	11,959	41
1960	6,842	52	7,876	35

25-34 years old	Male Total	Male Percent	Female Total	Female Percent
2000	18,563	13	19,222	8
1999	18,924	14	19,551	9
1998	19,526	15	19,828	8
1997	20,039	15	20,217	9
1996	20,390	16	20,528	9
1995	20,589	15	20,800	8
1994	20,873	16	21,073	9
1993	20,856	16	21,007	9
1992	21,125	15	21,368	9
1991	21,319	15	21,586	9
1990	21,462	15	21,779	8
1985	20,184	13	20,673	8
1980	18,107	10	18,689	7
1970	11,929	9	12,637	7
1960	10,896	11	11,587	7

(1) Includes young adults living in their parent(s)' home and unmarried college students living in a dormitory.

Grandchildren Living in the Home of Their Grandparents, 1970-2000

Source: Bureau of the Census, U.S. Dept. of Commerce (numbers in thousands)

		Grandchildren living with grandparents				
			WITH PARENT(S) PRESENT			
YEAR	Total children under 18	Total	Both parents present	Mother only present	Father only present	Without parent(s) present
1970	69,276	2,214	363	817	78	957
1980	63,369	2,306	310	922	86	988
1990	64,137	3,155	467	1,563	191	935
1991	65,093	3,320	559	1,674	151	937
1992	65,965	3,253	502	1,740	144	867
1993	66,893	3,368	475	1,647	229	1,017
1994	69,508	3,735	436	1,764	175	1,359
1995	70,254	3,965	427	1,876	195	1,466
1996	70,908	4,060	467	1,943	220	1,431
1997	70,983	3,894	554	1,785	247	1,309
1998	71,377	3,989	503	1,827	241	1,417
1999	71,703	3,919	535	1,803	250	1,331
2000	72,012	3,842	531	1,732	220	1,359

Living Arrangements of Children, 1970-2000

Source: Bureau of the Census, U.S. Dept. of Commerce

(excludes persons under 18 years of age who maintained households or resided in group quarters)

		Percentage of children who live with—							
			MOTHER ONLY						
Race, Hispanic origin, and year	Number (1,000)	BOTH PARENTS	Total	Divorced	Married Spouse absent	Single[1]	Widowed	FATHER ONLY	NEITHER PARENT
White									
1970	58,790	90	8	3	3	Z	2	1	2
1980	52,242	83	14	7	4	1	2	2	2
1990	51,390	79	16	8	4	3	1	3	2
1997	55,868	75	18	8	4	5	1	4	3
1998	56,118	74	18	8	4	5	1	5	3
1999	56,265	74	18	NA	NA	NA	NA	4	3
2000	56,455	75	17	NA	NA	NA	NA	4	3
Black									
1970	9,422	59	30	5	16	4	4	2	10
1980	9,375	42	44	11	16	13	4	2	12
1990	10,018	38	51	10	12	27	2	4	8
1997	11,369	35	52	9	11	31	1	5	8
1998	11,407	36	51	9	9	32	1	4	9
1999	11,425	35	51	NA	NA	NA	NA	4	10
2000	11,412	38	49	NA	NA	NA	NA	4	9
Hispanic[2]									
1970	4,0063	78	NA	NA	NA	NA	NA	NA	NA
1980	5,459	75	20	6	8	4	2	2	4
1990	7,174	67	27	7	10	8	2	3	3
1997	10,525	64	27	7	7	12	1	4	5
1998	10,857	64	27	6	8	12	1	4	5
1999	11,236	63	27	NA	NA	NA	NA	5	5
2000	11,613	65	25	NA	NA	NA	NA	4	5

NA = Not available. Z = Less than 0.5%. (1) Never married. (2) Hispanic persons may be of any race. (3) All persons under 18 years old.

Block Grants for Welfare (Temporary Assistance for Needy Families), 2000-2001

Source: Admin. for Children and Families, Off. of Planning, Research, and Evaluation, U.S. Dept. of Health and Human Services

	Total Federal and State TANF	2000 Average Monthly Expenditure per		2001 Average Monthly Number of		
State	Expenditures, 2000[1]	Family	Recipient	Families	Recipients	Children
Alabama	$92,200	$402.62	$136.21	18,368	43,555	34,890
Alaska	93,427	1,059.73	326.60	5,847	16,997	11,515
Arizona	254,820	629.69	243.47	33,194	82,595	63,430
Arkansas	112,328	757.73	319.34	11,607	27,722	20,753
California	5,776,830	960.85	368.06	468,747	1,185,399	922,613
Colorado	204,624	1,528.73	591.32	10,639	27,132	20,610
Connecticut	424,587	1,259.40	532.81	25,943	59,860	42,549
Delaware	54,298	746.92	351.33	5,421	12,355	9,448
District of Columbia . .	133,869	635.20	237.90	16,241	43,013	31,546
Florida	747,633	924.99	407.98	58,849	124,586	101,431
Georgia	382,763	598.79	226.27	50,531	120,501	94,922
Hawaii	110,529	615.31	207.33	12,852	41,478	30,521
Idaho	43,706	2,855.69	1,577.73	1,290	2,246	1,872
Illinois	875,026	824.01	276.14	62,030	182,673	142,934
Indiana	310,144	720.49	260.87	41,299	115,543	82,992
Iowa	157,252	654.42	246.01	20,195	54,071	36,548
Kansas	151,184	1,001.09	398.44	13,035	32,967	23,580
Kentucky	204,951	443.13	192.45	36,127	81,809	60,129
Louisiana	126,336	378.44	121.54	25,176	65,505	51,914
Maine	91,509	701.94	270.50	9,661	26,134	18,006
Maryland	276,909	786.49	317.30	27,915	68,221	50,247
Massachusetts	585,786	1,104.71	481.17	42,570	100,300	71,437
Michigan	1,198,333	1,336.67	481.34	70,725	193,211	143,539

State	Total Federal and State TANF Expenditures, 2000[1]	2000 Average Monthly Expenditure per		2001 Average Monthly Number of		
		Family	Recipient	Families	Recipients	Children
Minnesota	$382,014	$815.43	$275.03	38,558	112,688	78,678
Mississippi	62,076	345.56	153.05	15,657	35,710	27,736
Missouri	310,512	553.20	207.38	45,556	121,364	86,975
Montana	44,270	809.99	258.90	4,934	14,004	9,264
Nebraska	72,870	636.63	252.63	9,486	23,802	17,565
Nevada	55,937	744.81	293.06	7,439	19,461	14,521
New Hampshire	73,219	1,044.66	434.74	5,659	13,501	9,301
New Jersey	309,510	499.56	197.92	45,325	113,481	84,857
New Mexico	149,090	525.23	171.74	19,322	56,105	39,580
New York	3,235,946	1,042.36	372.57	226,921	613,353	424,108
North Carolina	434,747	792.32	363.92	43,497	93,366	72,022
North Dakota	32,561	935.33	311.68	2,999	7,784	5,588
Ohio	986,714	839.31	335.50	85,005	199,352	148,603
Oklahoma	133,771	776.06	314.26	14,051	34,810	26,996
Oregon	256,047	1,261.22	509.37	16,270	36,623	27,318
Pennsylvania	891,326	826.23	310.62	82,644	216,186	159,403
Rhode Island	151,405	772.91	279.38	15,228	41,623	28,834
South Carolina	124,381	645.43	278.00	16,938	40,266	30,618
South Dakota	21,035	625.65	259.50	2,713	6,365	5,199
Tennessee	270,477	399.10	148.84	59,369	154,905	112,342
Texas	743,149	484.28	180.88	130,893	349,279	258,469
Utah	89,449	886.36	334.39	7,487	19,184	13,960
Vermont	59,035	814.09	305.20	5,524	14,604	9,344
Virginia	218,886	572.45	251.34	29,271	65,051	47,894
Washington	530,635	775.67	288.91	54,160	141,397	97,747
West Virginia	134,042	919.69	346.24	14,732	39,039	26,514
Wisconsin	417,982	2,083.42	915.29	17,680	40,030	33,817
Wyoming	14,787	2,041.56	1,041.41	524	987	819
2001 Totals[2]	**NA**	**NA**	**NA**	**2,086,103**	**5,332,195**	**3,965,497**
2000 Totals[2]	**22,614,919**	**842.54**	**319.92**	**2,229,364**	**5,838,042**	**4,303,943**
1999 Totals[2]	**18,462,703**	**575.46**	**214.06**	**2,636,485**	**7,077,115**	**5,318,722[3]**

NOTE: 2001 data are preliminary and cover the fiscal year. Under 1996 legislation, the Aid to Families with Dependent Children (AFDC) program was converted to this state block-grant program. (1) In thousands. FY 2000 represents combined spending in FY 2000 from all Federal TANF grants for Fiscal Years 1997-2000. Data provided in prior years for FYs 1997-1999 were for the specified year only. (2) Totals include territories not listed. (3) Based on sample data for some states.

Adults Receiving TANF[1] (Welfare) Funds, by Employment Status, 1998-99

Source: Admin. for Children and Families, Off. of Planning, Research, and Evaluation, U.S. Dept. of Health and Human Services

STATE	Adults	% Employed	STATE	Adults	% Employed	STATE	Adults	% Employed
AL	9,960	20.1	LA	27,438	22.4	OK	13,590	25.3
AK	8,663	37.5	ME	11,676	28.4	OR	14,048	6.9
AZ	23,030	34.1	MD	28,503	7.3	PA	87,233	27.7
AR	6,574	13.8	MA	39,484	19.7	Puerto Rico	39,254	6.9
CA	505,957	42.8	MI	68,702	44.7	RI	15,994	27.5
CO	10,345	24.0	MN	36,131	14.6	SC	10,197	23.3
CT	25,770	41.6	MS	8,656	11.0	SD	1,692	21.5
DE	4,091	30.1	MO	36,309	12.1	TN	41,590	27.5
DC	15,142	24.7	MT	4,731	14.7	TX	84,085	6.4
FL	47,222	22.8	NE	9,811	15.4	UT	7,499	27.7
GA	36,431	16.1	NV	5,216	22.5	VT	6,576	27.0
Guam	2,667	2.3	NH	5,085	21.5	VA	24,028	30.0
HI	14,629	24.4	NJ	44,944	13.3	Virgin Islands	968	1.1
ID	613	28.2	NM	26,160	22.1	WA	59,769	34.2
IL	100,384	43.1	NY	270,105	17.5	WV	11,949	9.0
IN	33,749	21.4	NC	32,513	13.2	WI	8,510	11.7
IA	18,947	31.5	ND	2,379	16.1	WY	407	15.2
KS	9,207	19.9	OH	81,195	26.9	**U.S.**	**2,068,024**	**27.6**
KY	28,219	17.5						

(1) TANF = the state block grant program known as Temporary Assistance for Needy Families.

Poverty Rate

Source: Bureau of the Census, U.S. Dept. of Commerce

The poverty rate is the proportion of the population whose income falls below the government's official poverty level, which is adjusted each year for inflation. The national poverty rate was 11.7% in 2001, an increase from the 2000 rate of 11.3%, but well below the 1990 rate of 13.5%. It was the first annual increase since 1992. The 2001 data showed 16.3% of children lived in poverty; the poverty rate among people 65 and over was 10.1%.

Poverty Level by Family Size, 1980-2001

Source: Bureau of the Census, U.S. Dept. of Commerce

	2001	2000	1990	1980
1 person	$9,039	$8,794	$6,652	$4,186
Under 65 years	9,214	8,959	6,800	4,284
65 years and over	8,494	8,259	6,268	3,950
2 persons	11,569	11,239	8,509	5,361
Householder under 65 years	11,859	11,590	8,794	5,537
Householder 65 years and over	10,705	10,419	7,905	4,982
3 persons	$14,128	$13,783	$10,419	$6,570
4 persons	18,104	17,603	13,359	8,415
5 persons	21,405	20,819	15,792	9,967
6 persons	24,195	23,528	17,839	11,272
7 persons	27,517	26,754	20,241	12,761
8 persons	30,627	29,701	22,582	14,199
9 persons or more	36,286	35,060	26,848	16,896

Persons Below Poverty Level, 1960-2001

Source: Bureau of the Census, U.S. Dept. of Commerce

	Number below poverty level (in millions)				Percentage below poverty level				Avg. income cutoffs for family of 4 at poverty level[3]
YEAR	All races[1]	White	Black	Hispanic origin[2]	All races[1]	White	Black	Hispanic origin[2]	
1960	39.9	28.3	NA	NA	22.2	17.8	NA	NA	$3,022
1970	25.4	17.5	7.5	NA	12.6	9.9	33.5	NA	3,968
1980	29.3	19.7	8.6	3.5	13.0	10.2	32.5	25.7	8,414
1990	33.6	22.3	9.8	6.0	13.5	10.7	31.9	28.1	13,359
1991	35.7	23.7	10.2	6.3	14.2	11.3	32.7	28.7	13,924
1992	38.0	25.3	10.8	7.6	14.8	11.9	33.4	29.6	14,335
1993	39.3	26.2	10.9	8.1	15.1	12.2	33.1	30.6	14,763
1994	38.1	25.4	10.2	8.4	14.5	11.7	30.6	30.7	15,141
1995	36.4	24.4	9.9	8.6	13.8	11.2	29.3	30.3	15,569
1996	36.5	24.7	9.7	8.7	13.7	11.2	28.4	29.4	16,036
1997	35.6	24.4	9.1	8.3	13.3	11.0	26.5	27.1	16,400
1998	34.5	23.5	9.1	8.1	12.7	10.5	26.1	25.6	16,660
1999	32.3	21.9	8.4	7.4	11.8	9.8	23.6	22.8	17,029
2000	31.1	21.2	7.9	7.2	11.3	9.4	22.2	21.2	17,063
2001	32.9	22.7	8.1	8.0	11.7	9.9	22.7	21.4	18,104

NA = Not available. **NOTE:** Because of a change in the definition of poverty, data prior to 1980 are not directly comparable to data since 1980. (1) Includes other races not shown separately. (2) Persons of Hispanic origin may be of any race. (3) Figures for 1960-80 represent only nonfarm families.

Poverty by Family Status, Sex, and Race, 1986-2001

Source: Bureau of the Census, U.S. Dept. of Commerce
(numbers in thousands)

	2001		2000		1995		1990		1986	
	No.	%[1]	No.	%[1]	No.	%[1]	No.	%[1]	No.	%[1]
TOTAL POOR	**32,907**	**11.7**	**31,054**	**11.3**	**36,425**	**13.8**	**33,585**	**13.5**	**32,370**	**13.6**
In families	**23,215**	**9.9**	**22,015**	**9.6**	**27,501**	**12.3**	**25,232**	**12.0**	**24,754**	**12.0**
Head of household	6,813	9.2	6,222	8.6	7,532	10.8	7,098	10.7	7,023	10.9
Related children	11,175	15.8	11,018	15.6	13,999	20.2	12,715	19.9	12,257	19.8
Unrelated individuals	**9,226**	**19.9**	**8,503**	**18.9**	**8,247**	**20.9**	**7,446**	**20.7**	**6,846**	**21.6**
In families, female householder, no husband present	**11,223**	**28.6**	**10,425**	**27.9**	**14,205**	**36.5**	**12,578**	**37.2**	**11,944**	**38.3**
Head of household	3,470	26.4	3,096	24.7	4,057	32.4	3,768	33.4	3,613	34.6
Related children	NA	NA	6,116	39.8	8,364	50.3	7,363	53.4	6,943	54.4
Unrelated female individuals	**5,393**	**22.3**	**5,071**	**21.6**	**4,865**	**23.5**	**4,589**	**24.0**	**4,311**	**25.1**
All other families	**NA**	**NA**	**NA**	**NA**	**13,296**	**7.2**	**12,654**	**7.1**	**12,811**	**7.3**
Head of household	NA	NA	NA	NA	3,475	6.1	3,330	6.0	3,410	6.3
Related children	NA	NA	NA	NA	5,635	10.7	5,352	10.7	5,313	10.8
Unrelated male individuals	**3,833**	**17.3**	**3,548**	**16.0**	**3,382**	**18.0**	**2,857**	**16.9**	**2,536**	**17.5**
TOTAL WHITE POOR	**22,739**	**9.9**	**21,242**	**9.4**	**24,423**	**11.2**	**22,326**	**10.7**	**22,183**	**11.0**
In families	**15,369**	**8.1**	**14,392**	**7.7**	**17,593**	**9.6**	**15,916**	**9.0**	**16,393**	**9.4**
Head of household	NA	NA	4,151	6.9	4,994	8.5	4,622	8.1	4,811	8.6
Related children	7,086	12.8	6,838	12.3	8,474	15.5	7,696	15.1	7,714	15.3
Female householder, no spouse present	**1,939**	**22.4**	**1,655**	**20**	**2,200**	**26.6**	**2,010**	**26.8**	**2,041**	**28.2**
Unrelated individuals	**6,996**	**18.3**	**6,402**	**17.2**	**6,336**	**19.0**	**5,739**	**18.6**	**5,198**	**19.2**
TOTAL BLACK POOR	**8,136**	**22.7**	**7,862**	**22.0**	**9,872**	**29.3**	**9,837**	**31.9**	**8,983**	**31.1**
In families	**6,389**	**21.4**	**6,108**	**20.7**	**8,189**	**28.5**	**8,160**	**31.0**	**7,410**	**29.7**
Head of household	NA	NA	1,685	19.1	2,127	26.4	2,193	29.3	1,987	28.0
Related children	3,423	30.0	3,417	30.4	4,644	41.5	4,412	44.2	4,039	42.7
Female householder, no spouse present	**1,351**	**35.2**	**1,301**	**34.6**	**1,701**	**45.1**	**1,648**	**48.1**	**1,488**	**50.1**
Unrelated individuals	**1,692**	**28.8**	**1,708**	**28.0**	**1,551**	**32.6**	**1,491**	**35.1**	**1,431**	**38.5**

NA = Not available. (1) Percentage of total U.S. population in each category who fell below poverty level and are enumerated here. For example, of all persons in families in 2001, 9.9%, or 23,215,000, were poor.

Persons in Poverty, by State, 1998-2001

Source: Bureau of the Census, U.S. Dept. of Commerce

	% 2000-01[1]	% 1998-99[1]
Alabama	14.6	14.8
Alaska	8.1	8.5
Arizona	13.2	14.3
Arkansas	17.1	14.7
California	12.6	14.6
Colorado	9.2	8.7
Connecticut	7.5	8.3
Delaware	7.6	10.3
District of Columbia	16.7	18.6
Florida	11.9	12.8
Georgia	12.5	13.2
Hawaii	10.2	10.9
Idaho	12.0	13.5
Illinois	10.4	10.0
Indiana	8.5	8.0
Iowa	7.8	8.3
Kansas	9.1	10.9
Kentucky	12.6	12.8

	% 2000-01[1]	% 1998-99[1]
Louisiana	16.7	19.1
Maine	10.2	10.5
Maryland	7.3	7.2
Massachusetts	9.4	10.2
Michigan	9.6	10.3
Minnesota	6.5	8.8
Mississippi	17.1	16.9
Missouri	9.4	10.7
Montana	13.7	16.1
Nebraska	9.0	11.6
Nevada	7.9	10.9
New Hampshire	5.5	8.8
New Jersey	7.7	8.2
New Mexico	17.7	20.5
New York	14.0	15.4
North Carolina	12.5	13.8
North Dakota	12.1	14.1
Ohio	10.3	11.6

	% 2000-01[1]	% 1998-99[1]
Oklahoma	15.0	13.4
Oregon	11.3	13.8
Pennsylvania	9.1	10.3
Rhode Island	9.9	10.7
South Carolina	13.1	12.7
South Dakota	9.6	9.3
Tennessee	13.8	12.7
Texas	15.2	15.0
Utah	9.1	7.3
Vermont	9.9	9.8
Virginia	8.1	8.4
Washington	10.8	9.2
West Virginia	15.6	16.8
Wisconsin	8.6	8.7
Wyoming	9.7	11.1
U.S. Total	**11.5**	**12.3**

(1) 2-year average.

U.S. Places of 5,000 or More Population—With ZIP and Area Codes

Source: U.S. Bureau of the Census, Dept. of Commerce; NeuStar Inc.

The following is a list of places of 5,000 or more inhabitants recognized by the Bureau of the Census, U.S. Dept. of Commerce, based on 2000 Census results. Also given are 1990 census populations. This list includes **places that are incorporated** under the laws of their respective states as cities, boroughs, towns, and villages, as well as boroughs in Alaska and towns in the 6 New England states, New York, and Wisconsin. Townships are not included.

Places that the Census Bureau designates as **"census designated places" (CDPs)** are also included; these are marked (c). CDP boundaries can change from one census to another. Hawaii is the only state that has no incorporated places recognized by the Census Bureau; all places shown for Hawaii are CDPs.

This list also includes, in *italics*, **minor civil divisions (MCDs)**, for Connecticut, Maine, Massachusetts, New Hampshire, Rhode Island, and Vermont. MCDs are not incorporated and not recognized as CDPs, but are often the primary political or administrative divisions of a county.

An **asterisk** (*) denotes that the ZIP code given is for general delivery; named streets and/or P.O. boxes within the community may differ; consult local postmaster. **Area codes** are given in parentheses. Some regions have 2 or more area codes intermixed; these are known as **overlays**. States where this occurs are noted. When 2 or more area codes are listed for one place, consult local operators for assistance. Area codes based on latest information as of Aug. 2002. For a listing in numerical order of all area codes in the U.S., Canada, and the Caribbean, see the Telecommunications chapter.

For some places listed, no area code and/or ZIP code is available. — = Not available.

Alabama

ZIP	Place	Area Code	2000	1990
35007	Alabaster	(205)	22,619	14,619
*35950	Albertville	(256)	17,247	14,507
*35010	Alexander City	(256)	15,008	14,917
36420	Andalusia	(334)	8,794	9,269
*36201	Anniston	(256)	24,276	26,638
35016	Arab	(251)	7,174	6,321
*35611	Athens	(256)	18,967	16,901
*36502	Atmore	(334)	7,676	8,046
35954	Attalla	(256)	6,592	6,859
*36830	Auburn	(251)	42,987	33,830
36507	Bay Minette	(251)	7,820	7,168
*35020	Bessemer	(205)	29,672	33,581
*35203	Birmingham	(205)	242,820	265,347
*35957	Boaz	(256)	7,411	6,928
*36426	Brewton	(251)	5,498	5,885
35243	Cahaba Heights (c)	(205)	5,203	4,778
35220	Center Point (c)	(205)	22,784	22,658
36671	Chickasaw	(251)	6,364	6,651
*35045	Clanton	(205)	7,800	7,669
*35055	Cullman	(256)	13,995	13,367
36526	Daphne	(251)	16,581	11,291
*35601	Decatur	(256)	53,929	49,917
36732	Demopolis	(334)	7,540	7,512
*36302	Dothan	(334)	57,737	54,131
*36330	Enterprise	(334)	21,178	20,119
*36027	Eufaula	(334)	13,908	13,220
35064	Fairfield	(205)	12,381	12,200
*36532	Fairhope	(251)	12,480	9,189
*35630	Florence	(256)	36,264	36,426
*36535	Foley	(251)	7,590	4,937
35214	Forestdale (c)	(205)	10,509	10,395
*35967	Fort Payne	(256)	12,938	11,838
36362	Fort Rucker (c)	(334)	6,052	7,593
35068	Fultondale	(205)	6,595	6,400
*35901	Gadsden	(256)	38,978	42,523
35071	Gardendale	(205)	11,626	9,251
35905	Glencoe	(256)	5,152	4,687
35235	Grayson Valley (c)	(205)	5,447	—
36037	Greenville	(334)	7,228	7,847
36542	Gulf Shores	(251)	5,044	3,261
*35976	Guntersville	(256)	7,395	7,038
35570	Hamilton	(205)	6,786	6,171
35640	Hartselle	(256)	12,019	11,114
35080	Helena	(205)	10,296	4,303
35259	Homewood	(205)	25,043	23,644
*35244	Hoover	(205)	62,742	39,988
35023	Hueytown	(205)	15,364	15,280
*35801	Huntsville	(256)	158,216	159,880
35210	Irondale	(205)	9,813	9,458
36545	Jackson	(251)	5,419	5,819
36265	Jacksonville	(256)	8,404	10,283
*35501	Jasper	(205)	14,052	13,553
—	Lake Purdy (c)		5,799	1,840
36863	Lanett	(334)	7,897	8,985
35094	Leeds	(205)	10,455	10,009
*35758	Madison	(256)	29,329	14,792
35228	Midfield	(205)	5,626	5,559
36054	Millbrook	(334)	10,386	6,046
*36601	Mobile	(251)	198,915	199,973
*36460	Monroeville	(251)	6,862	6,993
*36104	Montgomery	(334)	201,568	190,350
35004	Moody	(205)	8,053	4,921
—	Moores Mill (c)	(256)	5,178	3,362
35253	Mountain Brook	(205)	20,604	19,810
*35661	Muscle Shoals	(256)	11,924	9,611
*35476	Northport	(205)	19,435	17,297
35121	Oneonta	(205)	5,576	4,844
*36801	Opelika	(334)	23,498	22,122
36467	Opp	(334)	6,607	7,011
36203	Oxford	(256)	14,592	9,537
*36360	Ozark	(334)	15,119	13,030
35124	Pelham	(205)	14,369	9,356
*35125	Pell City	(205)	9,565	7,945
*36867	Phenix City	(334)	28,265	25,311
36272	Piedmont	(256)	5,120	5,347
35126	Pinson (c)	(205)	5,033	10,987
35127	Pleasant Grove	(205)	9,983	8,458
*36067	Prattville	(334)	24,303	19,816
36610	Prichard	(251)	28,633	34,320
35906	Rainbow City	(256)	8,428	7,667
36274	Roanoke	(334)	6,563	6,362
*35653	Russellville	(256)	8,971	7,812
36201	Saks (c)	(256)	10,698	11,138
36571	Saraland	(251)	12,288	11,784
36572	Satsuma	(251)	5,687	5,194
*35768	Scottsboro	(256)	14,762	13,786
*36701	Selma	(334)	20,512	23,755
35660	Sheffield	(256)	9,652	10,380
36877	Smiths (c)	(334)	21,756	3,456
35901	Southside	(256)	7,036	5,580
*36527	Spanish Fort	(251)	5,423	3,732
*35150	Sylacauga	(256)	12,616	12,520
*35160	Talladega	(256)	15,143	18,175
35217	Tarrant	(205)	7,022	8,046
*36582	Theodore (c)	(251)	6,811	6,509
36619	Tillman's Corner (c)	(251)	15,685	17,988
*36081	Troy	(334)	13,935	13,051
35173	Trussville	(205)	12,924	8,283
*35401	Tuscaloosa	(205)	77,906	77,866
35674	Tuscumbia	(256)	7,856	8,413
36083	Tuskegee	(334)	11,846	12,257
*36854	Valley	(334)	9,198	9,556
35266	Vestavia Hills	(205)	24,476	19,550
*36092	Wetumpka	(334)	5,726	4,670

Alaska (907)

ZIP	Place	2000	1990
*99501	Anchorage	260,283	226,338
99559	Bethel	5,471	4,674
*99708	College (c)	11,402	11,249
99702	Eielson AFB (c)	5,400	5,251
*99701	Fairbanks	30,224	30,843
*99801	Juneau	30,711	26,751
—	Kalifornsky (c)	5,846	285
99611	Kenai	6,942	6,327
*99901	Ketchikan	7,922	8,263
—	Knik-Fairview (c)	7,049	272
*99615	Kodiak	6,334	6,365
—	Lakes (c)	6,706	—
99835	Sitka	8,835	8,588
*99654	Wasilla	5,469	4,028

Arizona

ZIP	Place	Area Code	2000	1990
*85220	Apache Junction	(480)	31,814	18,092
85323	Avondale	(623)	35,883	17,595
85653	Avra Valley (c)	(520)	5,038	3,403
—	Big Park (c)	(928)	5,245	3,024
85603	Bisbee	(520)	6,090	6,288
85326	Buckeye	(623)	6,537	4,436
*86442	Bullhead City	(928)	33,769	21,951
86322	Camp Verde	(928)	9,451	6,243
*85222	Casa Grande	(520)	25,224	19,076
85740	Casas Adobes (c)	(520)	54,011	—
85738	Catalina (c)	(520)	7,025	4,864
—	Catalina Foothills (c)	(520)	53,794	—
*85225	Chandler	(480)	176,581	89,862
86503	Chinle (c)	(928)	5,366	5,059
86323	Chino Valley	(928)	7,835	4,837
85228	Coolidge	(520)	7,786	6,934
86326	Cottonwood	(928)	9,179	5,918
86326	Cottonwood-Verde Village (c)	(928)	10,610	7,037
86327	Dewey-Humboldt (c)	(928)	6,295	3,640
*85607	Douglas	(520)	14,312	13,908
—	Drexel Heights (c)	(520)	23,849	—
85335	El Mirage	(623)	7,609	5,001
85231	Eloy	(520)	10,375	7,211
*86004	Flagstaff	(928)	52,894	45,857
85232	Florence	(520)	17,054	7,321
85726	Flowing Wells (c)	(520)	15,050	14,013
—	Fortuna Foothills (c)	(928)	20,478	7,737

ZIP	Place	Area Code	2000	1990
*85268	Fountain Hills	(480)	20,235	10,030
*85299	Gilbert	(480)	109,697	29,149
*85301	Glendale	(623)	218,812	147,070
*85501	Globe	(928)	7,486	6,062
—	Gold Camp (c)		6,029	—
85338	Goodyear	(623)	18,911	6,258
*85622	Green Valley (c)	(520)	17,283	13,231
85283	Guadalupe	(480)	5,228	5,458
*86401	Kingman	(928)	20,069	13,208
*86403	Lake Havasu City	(928)	41,938	24,363
85653	Marana	(520)	13,556	2,565
*85201	Mesa	(480)	396,375	289,199
*86440	Mohave Valley (c)	(928)	13,694	6,962
—	New Kingman-Butler (c)	(928)	14,810	11,627
*85027	New River (c)	(602)	10,740	—
*85621	Nogales	(520)	20,878	19,489
85737	Oro Valley	(520)	29,700	9,024
86040	Page	(928)	6,809	6,598
85253	Paradise Valley	(480)	13,664	11,903
*85541	Payson	(928)	13,620	8,377
*85345	Peoria	(623)	108,364	51,080
*85034	Phoenix	(602)	1,321,045	988,015
—	Picture Rocks (c)	(520)	8,139	4,026
*86301	Prescott	(928)	33,938	26,592
*86314	Prescott Valley	(928)	23,535	8,904
*85546	Safford	(928)	9,232	7,359
85349	San Luis	(928)	15,322	4,212
*85251	Scottsdale	(480)	202,705	130,099
*86336	Sedona	(928)	10,192	7,720
*85901	Show Low	(928)	7,695	5,020
*85635	Sierra Vista	(520)	37,775	32,083
85635	Sierra Vista Southeast (c)	(520)	14,348	9,237
85350	Somerton	(928)	7,266	5,293
85713	South Tucson	(520)	5,490	5,171
*85351	Sun City (c)	(623)	38,309	38,126
*85351	Sun City West (c)	(623)	26,344	15,997
85248	Sun Lakes (c)	(480)	11,936	6,578
*85374	Surprise	(623)	30,848	7,122
—	Tanque Verde (c)	(520)	16,195	—
*85285	Tempe	(480)	158,625	141,993
—	Three Points (c)	(520)	5,273	2,175
86045	Tuba City (c)	(928)	8,225	7,323
*85726	Tucson	(520)	486,699	415,444
—	Tucson Estates (c)	(520)	9,755	2,662
85941	Whiteriver (c)	(928)	5,220	3,775
*85390	Wickenburg	(928)	5,082	4,515
86047	Winslow	(928)	9,520	9,279
*85364	Yuma	(928)	77,515	56,966

Arkansas

ZIP	Place	Area Code	2000	1990
71923	Arkadelphia	(870)	10,912	10,014
*72501	Batesville	(870)	9,445	9,187
*72714	Bella Vista (c)	(479)	16,582	9,083
*72015	Benton	(501)	21,906	18,177
72712	Bentonville	(479)	19,730	11,257
*72315	Blytheville	(870)	18,272	22,523
*72022	Bryant	(501)	9,764	5,940
72023	Cabot	(501)	15,261	8,319
*71701	Camden	(870)	13,154	14,701
72830	Clarksville	(479)	7,719	5,833
*72032	Conway	(501)	43,167	26,481
71635	Crossett	(870)	6,097	6,282
71832	De Queen	(870)	5,765	4,633
71639	Dumas	(870)	5,238	5,520
72065	East End (c)	(501)	5,623	—
*71730	El Dorado	(870)	21,530	23,146
*72701	Fayetteville	(479)	58,047	42,247
*72335	Forrest City	(870)	14,774	13,364
*72901	Fort Smith	(479)	80,268	72,798
72936	Greenwood	(479)	7,112	3,984
*72601	Harrison	(870)	12,152	9,936
72543	Heber Springs	(501)	6,432	5,628
72342	Helena	(870)	6,323	7,491
*71801	Hope	(870)	10,616	9,768
*71901	Hot Springs	(501)	35,750	33,095
*71909	Hot Springs Village (c)	(501)	8,397	6,361
*72076	Jacksonville	(501)	29,916	29,101
*72401	Jonesboro	(870)	55,515	46,535
*72201	Little Rock	(501)	183,133	175,727
72745	Lowell	(479)	5,013	1,224
*71753	Magnolia	(870)	10,858	11,151
72104	Malvern	(501)	9,021	9,236
72360	Marianna	(870)	5,181	6,033
72364	Marion	(870)	8,901	4,405
72113	Maumelle	(501)	10,557	6,714
71953	Mena	(479)	5,637	5,475
*71655	Monticello	(870)	9,146	8,119
72110	Morrilton	(501)	6,550	6,551
*72653	Mountain Home	(870)	11,012	9,027
72112	Newport	(870)	7,811	7,459
*72114	North Little Rock	(501)	60,433	61,829
72370	Osceola	(870)	8,875	9,165
*72450	Paragould	(870)	22,017	18,540
*71601	Pine Bluff	(870)	55,085	57,140
72455	Pocahontas	(870)	6,518	6,151
*72756	Rogers	(479)	38,829	24,692
*72801	Russellville	(479)	23,682	21,260
*72143	Searcy	(501)	18,928	15,180
72120	Sherwood	(501)	21,511	18,890
72761	Siloam Springs	(479)	10,843	8,151
*72764	Springdale	(479)	45,798	29,945
72160	Stuttgart	(870)	9,745	10,420
71854	Texarkana	(870)	26,448	22,631
72472	Trumann	(870)	6,889	6,346
*72956	Van Buren	(479)	18,986	14,899
71671	Warren	(870)	6,442	6,455
72390	West Helena	(870)	8,689	10,137
*72301	West Memphis	(870)	27,666	28,259
72396	Wynne	(870)	8,615	8,107

California

ZIP	Place	Area Code	2000	1990
92301	Adelanto	(760)	18,130	6,815
*91376	Agoura Hills	(818)	20,537	20,306
*94501	Alameda	(510)	72,259	73,979
94507	Alamo (c)	(925)	15,626	12,277
94706	Albany	(510)	16,444	16,327
*91802	Alhambra	(323)/(626)	85,804	82,087
92656	Aliso Viejo (c)	(949)	40,166	7,612
90249	Alondra Park (c)	(310)	8,622	12,215
*91901	Alpine (San Diego) (c)	(619)	13,143	9,695
*91003	Altadena (c)	(626)	42,610	42,658
95945	Alta Sierra (c)	(530)	6,522	5,709
95127	Alum Rock (c)	(408)	13,479	—
94589	American Canyon	(707)	9,774	7,734
*92803	Anaheim	(909)	328,014	266,406
96007	Anderson	(530)	9,022	8,299
*94509	Antioch	(925)	90,532	62,195
*92307	Apple Valley	(760)	54,239	46,079
*95003	Aptos (c)	(831)	9,396	9,061
*91006	Arcadia	(626)	53,054	48,284
*95521	Arcata	(707)	16,651	15,211
95825	Arden-Arcade (c)	(916)	96,025	92,040
*93420	Arroyo Grande	(805)	15,851	14,432
*90701	Artesia	(562)	16,380	15,464
93203	Arvin	(661)	12,956	9,286
94577	Ashland (c)	(510)	20,793	16,590
*93422	Atascadero	(805)	26,411	23,138
94027	Atherton	(650)	7,194	7,163
95301	Atwater	(209)	23,113	22,282
*95603	Auburn	(530)	12,462	10,653
95201	August (c)	(209)	7,808	6,376
93204	Avenal	(559)	14,674	9,770
91746	Avocado Heights (c)	(626)	15,148	14,232
91702	Azusa	(626)	44,712	41,203
*93302	Bakersfield	(661)	247,057	176,264
91706	Baldwin Park	(626)	75,837	69,330
92220	Banning	(909)	23,562	20,572
*92312	Barstow	(760)	21,119	21,472
94565	Bay Point (c)	(925)	21,534	17,453
—	Bayview-Montalvin (c)	(510)	5,004	3,988
93402	Baywood-Los Osos (c)	(805)	14,351	14,377
95903	Beale AFB (c)	(530)	5,115	6,912
92223	Beaumont	(909)	11,384	9,685
90201	Bell	(323)	36,664	34,365
*90706	Bellflower	(323)	72,878	61,815
90202	Bell Gardens	(213)/(323)/(562)	44,054	42,315
94002	Belmont	(650)	25,123	24,165
94510	Benicia	(707)	26,865	24,437
*94704	Berkeley	(510)	102,743	102,724
92201	Bermuda Dunes (c)	(760)	6,229	4,571
*90210	Beverly Hills	(213)/(310)/(323)	33,784	31,971
92314	Big Bear City (c)	(909)	5,779	4,920
92315	Big Bear Lake	(909)	5,438	5,351
94526	Blackhawk-Camino Tassajara (c)	(925)	10,048	6,199
92316	Bloomington (c)	(909)	19,318	15,116
*92225	Blythe	(760)	12,155	10,835
93637	Bonadelle Ranchos-Madera Ranchos (c)	(559)	7,300	5,705
*91902	Bonita (c)	(619)	12,401	12,542
92021	Bostonia (c)	(619)	15,169	13,670
95416	Boyes Hot Springs (c)	(707)	6,665	5,973
92227	Brawley	(760)	22,052	18,923
*92822	Brea	(562)/(714)	35,410	32,873
94513	Brentwood	(925)	23,302	7,563
—	Bret Harte (c)	(209)	5,161	—
*90622	Buena Park	(714)	78,282	68,784
*91510	Burbank (Los Angeles)	(818)	100,316	93,649
—	Burbank (Santa Clara) (c)	(408)	5,239	4,902
*94010	Burlingame	(650)	28,158	26,666
*91372	Calabasas	(818)	20,033	16,577
*92231	Calexico	(760)	27,109	18,633
*93504	California City	(760)	8,385	5,955
92320	Calimesa	(909)	7,139	6,654
92233	Calipatria	(760)	7,289	2,701
94515	Calistoga	(707)	5,190	4,468
*93010	Camarillo	(805)	57,077	52,297
93428	Cambria (c)	(805)	6,232	5,382
95682	Cameron Park (c)	(530)	14,549	11,897
*95008	Campbell	(408)	38,138	36,088
92055	Camp Pendleton North (c)	(949)	8,197	10,373
92055	Camp Pendleton South (c)	(949)	8,854	11,299
92587	Canyon Lake	(909)	9,952	9,991
95010	Capitola	(831)	10,033	10,171
*92008	Carlsbad	(760)	78,247	63,292
*95608	Carmichael (c)	(916)	49,742	48,702
*93013	Carpinteria	(805)	14,194	13,747

ZIP	Place	Area Code	2000	1990
*90745	Carson	(310)	89,730	83,995
92077	Casa de Oro-Mt. Helix (c)	(619)	18,874	30,727
*94546	Castro Valley (c)	(510)	57,292	48,619
95012	Castroville (c)	(831)	6,724	5,272
*92235	Cathedral City	(760)	42,647	30,085
95307	Ceres	(209)	34,609	26,413
90703	Cerritos	(562)	51,488	53,244
91724	Charter Oak (c)	(626)	9,027	8,858
94541	Cherryland (c)	(510)	13,837	11,088
92223	Cherry Valley (c)	(909)	5,891	5,945
*95926	Chico	(530)	59,954	39,970
*91708	Chino	(909)	67,168	59,682
91709	Chino Hills	(909)	66,787	37,868
93610	Chowchilla	(559)	11,127	5,930
*91910	Chula Vista	(619)	173,556	135,160
91702	Citrus (c)	(626)	10,581	9,481
*95621	Citrus Heights	(916)	85,071	107,439
91711	Claremont	(909)	33,998	32,610
94517	Clayton	(925)	10,762	7,317
95422	Clearlake	(707)	13,142	11,804
95425	Cloverdale	(707)	6,831	4,924
*93612	Clovis	(559)	68,468	50,323
92236	Coachella	(760)	22,724	16,896
93210	Coalinga	(559)	11,668	8,212
92324	Colton	(909)	47,662	40,213
95932	Colusa	(530)	5,402	4,934
90022	Commerce	(323)/(562)	12,568	12,135
*90221	Compton	(310)	93,493	90,454
*94520	Concord	(925)	121,780	111,308
93212	Corcoran	(559)	14,458	13,360
96021	Corning	(530)	6,741	5,870
*91718	Corona	(909)	124,966	75,943
*92138	Coronado	(619)	24,100	26,540
*94925	Corte Madera	(415)	9,100	8,272
*92628	Costa Mesa	(714)/(949)	108,724	96,357
94931	Cotati	(707)	6,471	5,714
92679	Coto de Caza (c)	(949)	13,057	2,853
94556	Country Club (c)	(209)	9,462	9,325
*91722	Covina	(626)	46,837	43,332
92325	Crestline (c)	(909)	10,218	8,594
90201	Cudahy	(323)	24,208	22,817
*90230	Culver City	(230)/(310)/(323)	38,816	38,793
*95014	Cupertino	(408)	50,546	39,967
90630	Cypress	(714)	46,229	42,655
*94015	Daly City	(415)/(650)	103,621	92,088
92629	Dana Point	(949)	35,110	31,896
*94526	Danville	(925)	41,715	31,306
*95616	Davis	(530)	60,308	46,322
90250	Del Aire (c)	(310)	9,012	8,040
*93215	Delano	(661)	38,824	22,762
95315	Delhi (c)	(209)	8,022	3,280
*92240	Desert Hot Springs	(760)	16,582	11,668
91765	Diamond Bar	(909)	56,287	53,672
93618	Dinuba	(559)	16,844	12,743
94514	Discovery Bay (c)	(925)	8,981	5,351
95620	Dixon	(707)	16,103	10,417
*90241	Downey	(562)	107,323	91,444
*91009	Duarte	(626)	21,486	20,716
94568	Dublin	(925)	29,973	23,229
95938	Durham (c)	(530)	5,220	4,784
93219	Earlimart (c)	(661)	6,583	5,881
90220	East Compton (c)	(310)	9,286	7,967
—	East Foothills (c)		8,133	14,898
92343	East Hemet (c)	(909)	14,823	17,611
90638	East La Mirada (c)	(562)	9,538	9,367
90022	East Los Angeles (c)	(323)/(562)	124,283	126,379
94303	East Palo Alto	(650)	29,506	23,451
91117	East Pasadena (c)		6,045	5,910
93257	East Porterville (c)	(559)	6,730	5,790
—	East San Gabriel (c)	(626)	14,512	12,736
93523	Edwards AFB (c)	(661)	5,909	7,423
*92020	El Cajon	(619)	94,869	88,918
*92244	El Centro	(760)	37,835	31,405
94530	El Cerrito	(510)	23,171	22,869
95762	El Dorado Hills (c)	(916)	18,016	6,395
94018	El Granada (c)	(650)	5,724	4,426
*95624	Elk Grove (c)	(916)	59,984	17,483
*91734	El Monte	(626)	115,965	106,162
*93446	El Paso de Robles	(805)	24,297	18,583
93030	El Rio (c)	(805)	6,193	6,419
90245	El Segundo	(310)	16,033	15,223
*94802	El Sobrante (c)	(510)	12,260	9,852
*94617	Emeryville	(510)	6,882	5,740
*92024	Encinitas	(760)	58,014	55,406
95320	Escalon	(209)	5,963	4,437
*92025	Escondido	(760)	133,559	108,648
*95501	Eureka	(707)	26,128	27,025
93221	Exeter	(559)	9,168	7,276
*94930	Fairfax	(415)	7,319	6,931
94533	Fairfield	(707)	96,178	78,650
95628	Fair Oaks (Sacramento) (c)	(916)	28,008	26,867
—	Fairview (c)		9,470	9,045
*92028	Fallbrook (c)	(760)	29,100	22,095
93223	Farmersville	(559)	8,737	6,235
*93015	Fillmore	(805)	13,643	11,992
93622	Firebaugh	(209)	5,743	4,429
90001	Florence-Graham (c)	(323)	60,197	57,147
95828	Florin (c)	(916)	27,653	24,330
*95630	Folsom	(916)	51,884	29,802
*92334	Fontana	(909)	128,929	87,535
95841	Foothill Farms (c)	(916)	17,426	17,135
92610	Foothill Ranch (c)	(949)	10,899	—
95437	Fort Bragg	(707)	7,026	6,078
95540	Fortuna	(707)	10,497	8,788
94404	Foster City	(650)	28,803	28,176
*92728	Fountain Valley	(714)	54,978	53,691
95019	Freedom(c)	(831)	6,000	8,361
*94537	Fremont	(510)	203,413	173,339
*93706	Fresno	(559)	427,652	354,091
*92834	Fullerton	(714)	126,003	114,144
95632	Galt	(209)	19,472	8,889
*90247	Gardena	(310)	57,746	51,481
95205	Garden Acres (c)	(209)	9,747	8,547
*92842	Garden Grove	(714)	165,196	142,965
*95020	Gilroy	(408)	41,464	31,487
92509	Glen Avon (c)	(909)	14,853	12,663
*91209	Glendale	(323)/(626)/(818)	194,973	180,038
*91741	Glendora	(626)	49,415	47,832
93561	Golden Hills (c)	(661)	7,434	5,423
95670	Gold River (c)	(916)	8,023	—
*93116	Goleta (c)	(805)	55,204	—
93926	Gonzales	(831)	7,525	4,660
92324	Grand Terrace	(909)	11,626	10,946
95746	Granite Bay (c)	(916)	19,388	—
*95945	Grass Valley	(530)	10,922	9,048
93927	Greenfield (Monterey)	(831)	12,583	7,464
95948	Gridley	(530)	5,382	4,631
93433	Grover Beach	(805)	13,067	11,602
93434	Guadalupe	(805)	5,659	5,479
91745	Hacienda Heights (c)	(626)	53,122	52,354
94019	Half Moon Bay	(650)	11,842	8,886
*93230	Hanford	(559)	41,686	30,463
90716	Hawaiian Gardens	(323)	14,779	13,639
*90250	Hawthorne	(213)/(310)/(323)	84,112	71,349
*94544	Hayward	(510)	140,030	114,705
95448	Healdsburg	(707)	10,722	9,469
*92546	Hemet	(909)	58,812	43,366
94547	Hercules	(510)	19,488	16,829
90254	Hermosa Beach	(310)	18,566	18,219
*92340	Hesperia	(760)	62,582	50,418
92346	Highland	(909)	44,605	34,439
94010	Hillsborough	(650)	10,825	10,667
*95023	Hollister	(831)	34,413	19,318
92250	Holtville	(760)	5,612	4,820
91720	Home Gardens (c)	(909)	9,461	7,780
*92647	Huntington Beach	(714)	189,594	181,519
90255	Huntington Park	(323)	61,348	56,129
93234	Huron	(559)	6,306	4,766
92251	Imperial	(760)	7,560	4,113
*91932	Imperial Beach	(619)	26,992	26,512
*92201	Indio	(760)	49,116	36,850
*90301	Inglewood	(213)/(310)/(323)	112,580	109,602
—	Interlaken (c)	(831)	7,328	6,404
95640	Ione	(209)	7,129	6,516
*92619	Irvine	(714)/(949)	143,072	110,330
93117	Isla Vista (c)	(805)	18,344	20,395
91935	Jamul (c)	(619)	5,920	2,258
94914	Kentfield (c)	(415)	6,351	6,030
93630	Kerman	(559)	8,551	5,448
93930	King City	(831)	11,094	7,634
93631	Kingsburg	(559)	9,199	7,245
*91011	La Canada Flintridge	(818)	20,318	19,378
*91224	La Crescenta-Montrose (c)	(818)	18,532	16,968
90045	Ladera Heights (c)	(310)	6,568	6,316
94549	Lafayette	(925)	23,908	23,366
—	Laguna (c)		34,309	9,828
*92652	Laguna Beach	(949)	23,727	23,170
*92654	Laguna Hills	(949)	31,178	22,719
*92607	Laguna Niguel	(949)	61,891	44,723
—	Laguna West-Lakeside (c)		8,414	—
*92654	Laguna Woods	(949)	16,507	—
*90631	La Habra	(562)/(949)	58,974	51,263
90631	La Habra Heights	(562)	5,712	6,226
92352	Lake Arrowhead (c)	(909)	8,934	6,539
*92531	Lake Elsinore	(909)	28,928	19,733
92630	Lake Forest	(714)	58,707	56,036
92530	Lakeland Village (c)	(909)	5,626	5,159
93535	Lake Los Angeles (c)	(661)	11,523	7,977
92040	Lakeside (c)	(619)	19,560	39,412
*90714	Lakewood	(562)	79,345	73,553
*91941	La Mesa	(619)	54,749	52,911
*90638	La Mirada	(562)/(714)	46,783	40,452
93241	Lamont (c)	(661)	13,296	11,517
*93539	Lancaster	(661)	118,718	97,300
90623	La Palma	(562)/(714)	15,408	15,392
—	La Presa (c)		32,721	—
*91747	La Puente	(626)	41,063	36,955
92253	La Quinta	(760)	23,694	11,215
95401	La Riviera (c)	(916)	10,273	10,986
95403	Larkfield-Wikiup (c)	(707)	7,479	6,779
*94939	Larkspur	(415)	12,014	11,068
92688	Las Flores (c)	(949)	5,625	—
95330	Lathrop	(209)	10,445	6,841
91750	La Verne	(909)	31,638	30,843
*90260	Lawndale	(310)	31,711	27,331
*91945	Lemon Grove	(619)	24,918	23,984
93245	Lemoore	(559)	19,712	13,622
93245	Lemoore Station (c)	(559)	5,749	0
90304	Lennox (c)	(310)	22,950	22,757
95648	Lincoln	(916)	11,205	7,248
95901	Linda (c)	(530)	13,474	13,033
93247	Lindsay	(559)	10,297	8,338

ZIP	Place	Area Code	2000	1990
95062	Live Oak (Santa Cruz) (c)	(831)	16,628	15,212
95953	Live Oak (Sutter)	(530)	6,229	4,320
*94550	Livermore	(925)	73,345	56,741
95334	Livingston	(209)	10,473	7,317
*95240	Lodi	(209)	56,999	51,874
92354	Loma Linda	(909)	18,681	18,470
90717	Lomita	(213)	20,046	19,442
*93436	Lompoc	(805)	41,103	37,649
*90801	Long Beach	(310)/(562)	461,522	429,321
95650	Loomis	(916)	6,260	5,705
*90720	Los Alamitos	(562)/(949)	11,530	11,788
*94022	Los Altos	(650)	27,693	26,599
94022	Los Altos Hills	(650)	7,902	7,514
*90086	Los Angeles	(213)/(310)/(323)/(818)	3,694,820	3,485,557
93635	Los Banos	(209)	25,869	14,519
*95030	Los Gatos	(408)	28,592	27,357
94903	Lucas Valley-Marinwood (c)	(415)	6,357	5,982
90262	Lynwood	(213)/(310)/(323)	69,845	61,945
93250	Mc Farland	(661)	9,618	7,005
95521	McKinleyville (c)	(707)	13,599	10,749
*93638	Madera	(559)	43,207	29,283
93637	Madera Acres (c)	(559)	7,741	5,245
95954	Magalia (c)	(530)	10,569	8,987
*90265	Malibu	(310)	12,575	11,730
93546	Mammoth Lakes	(760)	7,093	4,785
*90266	Manhattan Beach	(310)	33,852	32,063
*95336	Manteca	(209)	49,258	40,773
93933	Marina	(831)	25,101	26,512
*90291	Marina del Rey (c)	(310)	8,176	7,431
94553	Martinez	(925)	35,866	31,800
95901	Marysville	(530)	12,268	12,324
—	Mayflower Village (c)		5,081	4,978
90270	Maywood	(323)	28,083	27,893
92254	Mecca (c)	(619)	5,402	1,966
93640	Mendota	(559)	7,890	6,821
*94025	Menlo Park	(650)	30,785	28,403
92359	Mentone (c)	(909)	7,803	5,675
*95340	Merced	(209)	63,893	56,155
94030	Millbrae	(650)	20,718	20,414
*94941	Mill Valley	(415)	13,600	13,029
*95035	Milpitas	(408)	62,698	50,690
91752	Mira Loma (c)	(909)	17,617	15,786
93641	Mira Monte (c)	(805)	7,177	7,744
*92690	Mission Viejo	(949)	93,102	79,464
*95350	Modesto	(209)	188,856	164,746
*91017	Monrovia	(626)	36,929	35,733
91763	Montclair	(909)	33,049	28,434
90640	Montebello	(323)	62,150	59,564
*93150	Montecito	(805)	10,000	—
*93940	Monterey	(831)	29,674	31,954
*91754	Monterey Park	(323)/(626)/(818)	60,051	60,738
*93021	Moorpark	(805)	31,415	25,494
*94556	Moraga	(925)	16,290	15,987
*92552	Moreno Valley	(909)	142,381	118,779
*95037	Morgan Hill	(408)	33,556	23,928
*93442	Morro Bay	(805)	10,350	9,664
*94041	Mountain View	(650)	70,708	67,365
*92564	Murrieta	(909)	44,282	18,557
92405	Muscoy (c)	(714)	8,919	7,541
*94558	Napa	(707)	72,585	61,865
*91950	National City	(619)	54,260	54,249
94560	Newark	(510)	42,471	37,861
95360	Newman	(209)	7,093	4,158
*92658	Newport Beach	(949)	70,032	66,643
93444	Nipomo (c)	(805)	12,626	7,109
91760	Norco	(909)	24,157	23,302
95603	North Auburn (c)	(530)	11,847	10,301
94025	North Fair Oaks (c)	(650)	15,440	13,912
95660	North Highlands (c)	(916)	44,187	42,105
*90650	Norwalk	(562)	103,298	94,279
*94947	Novato	(415)	47,630	47,585
95361	Oakdale	(209)	15,503	11,978
*94617	Oakland	(510)	399,484	372,242
94561	Oakley	(925)	25,619	18,374
93445	Oceano (c)	(805)	7,260	6,169
*92056	Oceanside	(760)	161,029	128,090
93308	Oildale (c)	(661)	27,885	26,553
*93023	Ojai	(805)	7,862	7,613
95961	Olivehurst (c)	(530)	11,061	9,738
*91761	Ontario	(909)	158,007	133,179
95060	Opal Cliffs (c)	(831)	6,458	5,940
*92863	Orange	(714)	128,821	110,658
93646	Orange Cove	(559)	7,722	5,604
95662	Orangevale (c)	(916)	26,705	26,266
93457	Orcutt (c)	(805)	28,830	—
94563	Orinda	(925)	17,599	16,642
95963	Orland	(530)	6,281	5,052
93647	Orosi (c)	(559)	7,318	5,486
*95965	Oroville	(530)	13,004	11,885
95965	Oroville East (c)	(530)	8,680	8,462
*93030	Oxnard	(805)	170,358	142,560
94044	Pacifica	(650)	38,390	37,670
93950	Pacific Grove	(831)	15,522	16,117
95968	Palermo (c)	(530)	5,720	5,260
*93590	Palmdale	(661)	116,670	73,314
*92260	Palm Desert	(760)	41,155	23,252
*92262	Palm Springs	(760)	42,807	40,144
*94303	Palo Alto	(650)	58,598	55,900
90274	Palos Verdes Estates	(310)	13,340	13,512
*95969	Paradise	(530)	26,408	25,401
90723	Paramount	(562)	55,266	47,669
95823	Parkway-So. Sacramento (c)	(916)	36,468	31,903
93648	Parlier	(559)	11,145	7,938
*91109	Pasadena	(323)/(626)/(818)	133,936	131,586
	Paso Robles. *See El Paso de Robles*			
95363	Patterson	(209)	11,606	8,626
92509	Pedley (c)	(909)	11,207	8,869
*92572	Perris	(909)	36,189	21,500
*94952	Petaluma	(707)	54,548	43,166
—	Phoenix Lake-Cedar Ridge (c)		5,123	3,569
90660	Pico Rivera	(562)	63,428	59,177
94611	Piedmont	(510)	10,952	10,602
94564	Pinole	(510)	19,039	17,460
*93449	Pismo Beach	(805)	8,551	7,669
94565	Pittsburg	(925)	56,769	47,607
*92871	Placentia	(714)	46,488	41,259
95667	Placerville	(530)	9,610	8,286
94523	Pleasant Hill	(925)	32,837	31,583
*94566	Pleasanton	(925)	63,654	50,570
*91769	Pomona	(909)	149,473	131,700
*93257	Porterville	(559)	39,615	29,521
*93041	Port Hueneme	(805)	21,845	20,322
92679	Portola Hills (c)	(949)	6,391	2,677
*92064	Poway	(858)	48,044	43,396
93907	Prunedale (c)	(831)	16,432	7,393
*93551	Quartz Hill (c)	(661)	9,890	9,626
92065	Ramona (c)	(760)	15,691	13,040
*95670	Rancho Cordova (c)	(916)	55,060	48,731
*91729	Rancho Cucamonga	(909)	127,743	101,409
92270	Rancho Mirage	(760)	13,249	9,778
90275	Rancho Palos Verdes	(310)	41,145	41,667
91941	Rancho San Diego (c)	(619)	20,155	6,977
92688	Rancho Santa Margarita (c)	(949)	47,214	11,390
96080	Red Bluff	(530)	13,147	12,363
*96049	Redding	(530)	80,865	66,176
*92373	Redlands	(909)	63,591	62,667
*90277	Redondo Beach	(310)	63,261	60,167
*94063	Redwood City	(650)	75,402	66,072
93654	Reedley	(559)	20,756	15,791
*92377	Rialto	(909)	91,873	72,395
*94802	Richmond	(510)	99,216	86,019
*93556	Ridgecrest	(760)	24,927	28,295
95003	Rio del Mar (c)	(831)	9,198	8,919
95673	Rio Linda (c)	(916)	10,466	9,481
95366	Ripon	(209)	10,146	7,455
95367	Riverbank	(209)	15,826	8,591
*92502	Riverside	(909)	255,166	226,546
*95677	Rocklin	(916)	36,330	18,806
94572	Rodeo (c)	(510)	8,717	7,589
*94928	Rohnert Park	(707)	42,236	36,326
90274	Rolling Hills Estates	(310)	7,676	7,789
93560	Rosamond (c)	(661)	14,349	7,430
—	Rosedale (c)	(805)	8,445	4,673
95401	Roseland (c)	(707)	6,369	8,779
91770	Rosemead	(626)	53,505	51,638
95826	Rosemont (c)	(916)	22,904	22,851
*95678	Roseville	(916)	79,921	44,685
90720	Rossmoor (c)	(714)	10,298	9,893
91748	Rowland Heights (c)	(818)	48,553	42,647
92519	Rubidoux (c)	(909)	29,180	24,367
92382	Running Springs (c)	(909)	5,125	4,195
*95814	Sacramento	(916)	407,018	369,365
94574	Saint Helena	(707)	5,950	4,990
95368	Salida (c)	(209)	12,560	4,499
*93907	Salinas	(831)	151,060	108,777
*94960	San Anselmo	(415)	12,378	11,735
*92401	San Bernardino	(909)	185,401	170,036
94066	San Bruno	(650)	40,165	38,961
*93001	San Buenaventura (Ventura)	(805)	100,916	92,557
94070	San Carlos	(650)	27,718	26,382
*92674	San Clemente	(949)	49,936	41,100
*92138	San Diego	(619)/(858)	1,223,400	1,110,623
92065	San Diego Country Estates (c)	(760)	9,262	6,874
91773	San Dimas	(909)	34,980	32,398
*91341	San Fernando	(818)	23,564	22,580
*94142	San Francisco	(415)	776,733	723,959
*91778	San Gabriel	(626)	39,804	37,120
93657	Sanger	(559)	18,931	16,839
*92581	San Jacinto	(909)	23,779	17,614
*95113	San Jose	(408)	894,943	782,224
*92690	San Juan Capistrano	(949)	33,826	26,183
*94577	San Leandro	(510)	79,452	68,223
94580	San Lorenzo (c)	(510)	21,898	19,987
*93401	San Luis Obispo	(805)	44,174	41,958
*92069	San Marcos	(760)	54,977	38,974
*91109	San Marino	(626)	12,945	12,959
*94402	San Mateo	(650)	92,482	85,619
94806	San Pablo	(510)	30,215	25,158
*94915	San Rafael	(415)	56,063	48,410
94583	San Ramon	(925)	44,722	35,303
*92711	Santa Ana	(714)/(949)	337,977	293,827
*93102	Santa Barbara	(805)	92,325	85,571
*95050	Santa Clara	(408)	102,361	93,613
*91380	Santa Clarita	(661)	151,088	120,050
*95060	Santa Cruz	(831)	54,593	49,711
90670	Santa Fe Springs	(562)	17,438	15,520
*93454	Santa Maria	(805)	77,423	61,552
*90401	Santa Monica	(310)	84,084	86,905
*93060	Santa Paula	(805)	28,598	25,062
*95402	Santa Rosa	(707)	147,595	113,261

ZIP	Place	Area Code	2000	1990
*92071	Santee	(619)	52,975	52,902
*95070	Saratoga	(408)	29,843	28,061
*94965	Sausalito	(415)	7,330	7,152
*95066	Scotts Valley	(831)	11,385	8,667
90740	Seal Beach	(714)	24,157	25,098
93955	Seaside	(831)	31,696	38,826
*95472	Sebastopol	(707)	7,774	7,008
93662	Selma	(559)	19,444	14,757
—	Shackelford (c)		5,170	—
93263	Shafter	(661)	12,736	9,404
*96019	Shasta Lake	(916)	9,008	8,821
*91025	Sierra Madre	(626)	10,578	10,762
90806	Signal Hill	(562)	9,333	8,371
*93065	Simi Valley	(805)	111,351	100,218
92075	Solana Beach	(858)	12,979	12,956
93960	Soledad	(831)	11,263	13,426
*93463	Solvang	(805)	5,332	4,741
95476	Sonoma	(707)	9,128	8,168
95073	Soquel (c)	(831)	5,081	9,188
91733	South El Monte	(626)	21,144	20,850
90280	South Gate	(323)/(562)	96,375	86,284
*96151	South Lake Tahoe	(530)	23,609	21,586
95965	South Oroville (c)	(530)	7,695	7,463
*91030	South Pasadena	(213)/(323)/626)/(818)	24,292	23,936
*94080	South San Francisco	(650)	60,552	54,312
91770	South San Gabriel (c)	(626)	7,595	7,700
91744	South San Jose Hills (c)	(626)	20,218	17,814
90605	South Whittier (c)	(562)	55,193	49,514
95991	South Yuba City (c)	(530)	12,651	8,816
*91977	Spring Valley (c)	(619)	26,663	55,331
94309	Stanford (c)	(650)	13,315	18,097
90680	Stanton	(714)	37,403	30,491
*95208	Stockton	(209)	243,771	210,943
95375	Strawberry (c)	(209)	5,302	4,377
94585	Suisun City	(707)	26,118	22,704
*92586	Sun City (c)	(909)	17,773	14,930
*94086	Sunnyvale	(408)	131,760	117,324
*96130	Susanville	(530)	13,541	12,130
93268	Taft	(661)	6,400	5,902
94941	Tamalpais-Homestead Valley (c)	(415)	10,691	9,601
94806	Tara Hills (c)	(510)	5,332	4,998
*93581	Tehachapi	(661)	10,957	6,182
*92589	Temecula	(909)	57,716	27,177
91780	Temple City	(626)	33,377	31,153
95965	Thermalito (c)	(530)	6,045	5,646
*91359	Thousand Oaks	(805)	117,005	104,381
92276	Thousand Palms (c)	(760)	5,120	4,122
94920	Tiburon	(415)	8,666	7,554
*90503	Torrance	(310)	137,946	133,107
*95376	Tracy	(209)	56,929	33,558
*96161	Truckee	(916)	13,864	8,848
*93274	Tulare	(559)	43,994	33,249
*95380	Turlock	(209)	55,810	42,224
*92781	Tustin	(714)/(949)	67,504	50,689
92705	Tustin Foothills (c)	(714)	24,044	24,358
*92277	Twentynine Palms	(760)	14,764	11,821
92278	Twentynine Palms Base (c)	(760)	8,413	10,606
95060	Twin Lakes (c)	(831)	5,533	5,379
95482	Ukiah	(707)	15,497	14,632
94587	Union City	(510)	66,869	53,762
*91785	Upland	(909)	68,393	63,374
*95687	Vacaville	(707)	88,625	71,476
91744	Valinda (c)	(626)	21,776	18,735
*94590	Vallejo	(707)	116,760	109,199
92343	Valle Vista (c)	(909)	10,488	8,751
92082	Valley Center (c)	(760)	7,323	1,711
93437	Vandenberg AFB (c)	(805)	6,151	9,846
93436	Vandenberg Village (c)	(805)	5,802	5,971
	Ventura. *See San Buenaventura*			
*92393	Victorville	(760)	64,029	50,103
90043	View Park-Windsor Hills (c)	(310)	10,958	11,769
92861	Villa Park	(714)	5,999	6,299
—	Vincent (c)		15,097	13,713
—	Vineyard (c)		10,109	—
*93291	Visalia	(559)	91,565	75,659
*92083	Vista	(760)	89,857	71,861
—	Waldon (c)		5,133	—
*91788	Walnut	(909)	30,004	29,105
*94596	Walnut Creek	(925)	64,296	60,569
90255	Walnut Park (c)	(213)	16,180	14,722
93280	Wasco	(661)	21,263	12,412
95386	Waterford	(209)	6,924	4,771
*95076	Watsonville	(831)	44,265	31,099
90044	West Athens (c)	(310)	9,101	8,859
90502	West Carson (c)	(323)	21,138	20,143
90247	West Compton (c)	(310)	5,435	5,451
*91790	West Covina	(626)	105,080	96,226
90069	West Hollywood	(310)/(323)	35,716	36,118
*91359	Westlake Village	(805)	8,368	7,455
*92685	Westminster	(714)	88,207	78,293
—	West Modesto (c)		6,096	—
90047	Westmont (c)	(323)	31,623	31,044
91746	West Puente Valley (c)	(626)	22,589	20,254
*95691	West Sacramento	(916)	31,615	28,898
*90606	West Whittier-Los Nietos (c)	(562)	25,129	24,164
*90605	Whittier	(562)	83,680	77,671
92595	Wildomar (c)	(909)	14,064	10,411
95490	Willits	(707)	5,073	5,027
90222	Willowbrook (c)	(323)	34,138	32,772
95988	Willows	(530)	6,220	5,988
95492	Windsor	(707)	22,744	12,002
—	Winter Gardens (c)		19,771	—
95694	Winters	(530)	6,125	4,639
95388	Winton (c)	(209)	8,832	7,559
92502	Woodcrest (c)	(909)	8,342	7,796
93286	Woodlake	(559)	6,651	5,678
*95695	Woodland	(530)	49,151	40,230
94062	Woodside	(650)	5,352	5,034
*92885	Yorba Linda	(714)	58,918	52,422
96097	Yreka	(530)	7,290	6,948
*95991	Yuba City	(530)	36,758	27,385
92399	Yucaipa	(909)	41,207	32,819
*92286	Yucca Valley	(760)	16,865	16,539

Colorado

Area code (720) overlays area code (303). See introductory note.

ZIP	Place	Area Code	2000	1990
*80840	Air Force Academy (c)	(719)	7,526	9,062
81101	Alamosa	(719)	7,960	7,579
80401	Applewood (c)	(303)	7,123	11,069
*80004	Arvada	(303)	102,153	89,261
*81611	Aspen	(970)	5,914	5,049
*80017	Aurora	(303)	276,393	222,103
81620	Avon	(970)	5,561	1,798
—	Berkley (c)		10,743	—
80908	Black Forest (c)	(719)	13,247	8,143
*80302	Boulder	(303)	94,673	85,127
80601	Brighton	(303)	20,905	14,203
*80020	Broomfield	(303)	38,272	24,638
80723	Brush	(970)	5,117	4,165
*81212	Canon City	(719)	15,431	12,687
81623	Carbondale	(970)	5,196	3,004
—	Castle Pines (c)	(303)	5,958	—
80104	Castle Rock	(303)	20,224	8,710
80120	Castlewood (c)	(303)	25,567	24,392
80110	Cherry Hills Village	(303)	5,958	5,245
81220	Cimarron Hills (c)	(719)	15,194	11,160
81520	Clifton (c)	(970)	17,345	12,671
*80903	Colorado Springs	(719)	360,890	280,430
80120	Columbine (c)	(303)	24,095	23,969
*80022	Commerce City	(303)	20,991	16,466
81321	Cortez	(970)	7,977	7,284
*81625	Craig	(970)	9,189	8,091
81416	Delta	(970)	6,400	3,789
*80202	Denver	(303)	554,636	467,610
80022	Derby (c)	(303)	6,423	6,043
*81301	Durango	(970)	13,922	12,439
80214	Edgewater	(303)	5,445	4,613
81632	Edwards (c)	(970)	8,257	—
*80110	Englewood	(303)	31,727	29,396
80516	Erie	(303)	6,291	1,258
*80517	Estes Park	(970)	5,413	3,184
80620	Evans	(970)	9,514	5,876
*80439	Evergreen (c)	(303)	9,216	7,582
80221	Federal Heights	(303)	12,065	9,342
80913	Fort Carson (c)	(719)	10,566	11,309
*80525	Fort Collins	(970)	118,652	87,491
80621	Fort Lupton	(970)	6,787	5,159
80701	Fort Morgan	(970)	11,034	9,068
80817	Fountain	(719)	15,197	10,754
81521	Fruita	(970)	6,478	4,045
81504	Fruitvale (c)	(303)	6,936	5,222
*81601	Glenwood Springs	(970)	7,736	6,561
*80401	Golden	(303)	17,159	13,127
*81501	Grand Junction	(970)	41,986	32,893
*80631	Greeley	(970)	76,930	60,454
*80111	Greenwood Village	(303)	11,035	7,589
80501	Gunbarrel (c)	(303)	9,435	9,388
*81230	Gunnison	(970)	5,409	4,636
80163	Highlands Ranch (c)	(303)	70,931	10,181
80127	Ken Caryl (c)	(303)	30,887	24,391
80026	Lafayette	(303)	23,197	14,708
81050	La Junta	(719)	7,568	7,678
*80226	Lakewood	(303)	144,126	126,475
81052	Lamar	(719)	8,869	8,343
*80126	Littleton	(303)	40,340	33,711
*80501	Longmont	(303)	71,093	51,976
80027	Louisville	(303)	18,937	12,363
*80538	Loveland	(970)	50,608	37,357
*81401	Montrose	(970)	12,344	8,854
80233	Northglenn	(303)	31,575	27,195
80649	Orchard Mesa (c)	(303)	6,456	5,977
*80134	Parker	(303)	23,558	5,450
*81003	Pueblo	(719)	102,121	98,640
81007	Pueblo West (c)	(719)	16,899	4,386
81503	Redlands (c)	(970)	8,043	9,355

ZIP	Place	Area Code	2000	1990
81650	Rifle	(970)	6,784	4,858
81201	Salida	(719)	5,504	4,737
80911	Security-Widefield (c)	(719)	29,845	23,822
80110	Sheridan	(303)	5,600	4,976
80221	Sherrelwood (c)	(303)	17,657	16,636
80122	Southglenn (c)	(303)	43,520	43,087
*80477	Steamboat Springs	(970)	9,815	6,695
80751	Sterling	(970)	11,360	10,362
—	Stonegate (c)		6,284	—
80906	Stratmoor (c)	(719)	6,650	5,854
80027	Superior	(303)	9,011	255
—	The Pinery (c)	(303)	7,253	4,885
80229	Thornton	(303)	82,384	55,031
81082	Trinidad	(719)	9,078	8,580
81251	Twin Lakes (c)	(719)	6,301	—
80229	Welby (c)	(303)	12,973	10,218
80030	Westminster	(303)	100,940	74,619
*80033	Wheat Ridge	(303)	32,913	29,419
80550	Windsor	(970)	9,896	5,062
*80863	Woodland Park	(719)	6,515	4,610
80132	Woodmoor (c)	(719)	7,177	3,858

Connecticut

See introductory note.

ZIP	Place	Area Code	2000	1990
06401	Ansonia	(203)	18,554	18,403
06001	*Avon*	(860)	15,832	13,937
06403	*Beacon Falls*	(203)	5,246	5,083
06037	*Berlin*	(860)	18,215	16,787
06524	*Bethany*	(203)	5,040	—
06801	*Bethel*	(203)	18,067	17,541
06002	*Bloomfield*	(860)	19,587	19,483
06043	*Bolton*	(860)	5,017	—
06405	*Branford*	(203)	28,683	27,603
06405	Branford Center (c)	(203)	5,735	5,688
*06602	Bridgeport	(203)	139,529	141,686
*06010	Bristol	(860)	60,062	60,640
06804	*Brookfield*	(203)	15,664	14,113
06234	*Brooklyn*	(860)	7,173	6,681
06013	*Burlington*	(860)	8,190	7,026
06019	*Canton*	(860)	8,840	8,268
06040	Central Manchester (c)	(860)	30,595	30,934
06410	*Cheshire*	(203)	28,543	25,684
06410	Cheshire Village (c)	(203)	5,789	5,759
06413	*Clinton*	(860)	13,094	12,767
06415	*Colchester*	(860)	14,551	10,980
06340	Conning Towers-Nautilus Park (c)	(860)	10,241	10,013
06238	*Coventry*	(860)	11,504	10,063
06416	*Cromwell*	(860)	12,871	12,286
*06810	Danbury	(203)	74,848	65,585
06820	*Darien*	(203)	19,607	18,196
06418	Derby	(203)	12,391	12,199
06422	*Durham*	(860)	6,627	5,732
06423	*East Haddam*	(860)	8,333	6,676
06424	*East Hampton*	(860)	13,352	10,428
*06101	*East Hartford*	(860)	49,575	50,452
06512	*East Haven*	(203)	28,189	26,144
06333	*East Lyme*	(860)	18,118	15,340
06612	*Easton*	(203)	7,272	6,303
06088	*East Windsor*	(860)	9,818	10,081
06029	*Ellington*	(860)	12,921	11,197
*06082	*Enfield*	(860)	45,212	45,532
06426	*Essex*	(860)	6,505	5,904
*06430	*Fairfield*	(203)	57,340	53,418
*06032	*Farmington*	(860)	23,641	20,608
06033	*Glastonbury*	(860)	31,876	27,901
06033	Glastonbury Center (c)	(860)	7,157	7,082
06035	*Granby*	(860)	10,347	9,369
*06830	*Greenwich*	(203)	61,101	58,441
06351	*Griswold*	(860)	10,807	10,384
*06340	Groton	(860)	10,010	9,837
06340	*Groton*	(860)	39,907	45,144
06437	*Guilford*	(203)	21,398	19,848
06438	*Haddam*	(860)	7,157	6,769
*06514	*Hamden*	(203)	56,913	52,434
*06101	Hartford	(860)	124,121	139,739
06791	*Harwinton*	(860)	5,283	5,228
06248	*Hebron*	(860)	8,610	7,079
06037	Kensington (c)	(860)	8,541	8,306
06239	*Killingly*	(860)	16,472	15,889
06419	*Killingworth*	(860)	6,018	4,814
06249	*Lebanon*	(860)	6,907	6,041
06339	*Ledyard*	(860)	14,687	14,913
06759	*Litchfield*	(860)	8,316	8,365
06443	*Madison*	(203)	17,858	15,485
*06040	*Manchester*	(860)	54,740	51,618
06250	*Mansfield*	(860)	20,720	21,103
06447	*Marlborough*	(860)	5,709	5,535
*06450	Meriden	(203)	58,244	59,479
06762	*Middlebury*	(203)	6,451	6,145
06457	Middletown	(860)	43,167	42,762
06460	Milford	(203)	52,305	48,168
06468	*Monroe*	(203)	19,247	16,896
06353	*Montville*	(860)	18,546	16,673
06770	Naugatuck	(203)	30,989	30,625
*06050	New Britain	(860)	71,538	75,491
06840	*New Canaan*	(203)	19,395	17,864
06812	*New Fairfield*	(203)	13,953	12,911
06057	*New Hartford*	(860)	6,088	5,769
*06511	New Haven	(203)	123,626	130,474
*06101	*Newington*	(860)	29,306	29,208
06320	New London	(860)	25,671	28,540
06776	*New Milford*	(860)	27,121	23,629
06470	*Newtown*	(203)	25,031	20,779
06471	*North Branford*	(203)	13,906	12,996
06473	*North Haven*	(203)	23,035	22,247
*06856	Norwalk	(203)	82,951	78,331
06360	Norwich	(860)	36,117	37,391
06779	Oakville (c)	(860)	8,618	8,741
06371	*Old Lyme*	(860)	7,406	6,535
06475	*Old Saybrook*	(860)	10,367	9,552
06477	*Orange*	(203)	13,233	12,830
06478	*Oxford*	(203)	9,821	8,685
06379	Pawcatuck (c)	(860)	5,474	5,289
06374	*Plainfield*	(860)	14,619	14,363
06062	*Plainville*	(860)	17,328	17,392
06782	*Plymouth*	(860)	11,634	11,822
06480	*Portland*	(860)	8,732	8,418
06712	*Prospect*	(203)	8,707	7,775
06260	*Putnam*	(860)	9,002	9,031
06260	Putnam District (c)	(860)	6,746	6,835
06896	*Redding*	(203)	8,270	7,927
06877	Ridgefield (c)	(203)	7,212	6,363
06877	*Ridgefield*	(203)	23,643	20,919
06066	Rockville (c)	(860)	7,708	—
06067	*Rocky Hill*	(860)	17,966	16,554
06483	*Seymour*	(203)	15,454	14,288
06484	Shelton	(203)	38,101	35,418
06082	Sherwood Manor (c)	(860)	5,689	6,357
06070	*Simsbury*	(860)	23,234	22,023
06070	Simsbury Center (c)	(860)	5,603	5,577
06071	*Somers*	(860)	10,417	9,108
06488	*Southbury*	(203)	18,567	15,818
06489	*Southington*	(860)	39,728	38,518
06074	*South Windsor*	(860)	24,412	22,090
06082	Southwood Acres (c)	(860)	8,067	8,963
06075	*Stafford*	(860)	11,307	11,091
*06904	Stamford	(203)	117,083	108,056
06378	*Stonington*	(860)	17,906	16,919
06268	Storrs (c)	(860)	10,996	12,198
*06602	*Stratford*	(203)	49,976	49,389
06078	*Suffield*	(860)	13,552	11,427
06786	Terryville (c)	(860)	5,360	5,426
06787	*Thomaston*	(860)	7,503	6,947
06277	*Thompson*	(860)	8,878	8,668
06082	Thompsonville (c)	(860)	8,125	8,458
06084	*Tolland*	(860)	13,146	11,001
06790	Torrington	(860)	35,202	33,687
06611	*Trumbull*	(203)	34,243	32,016
06066	*Vernon*	(860)	28,063	29,841
06492	*Wallingford*	(203)	43,026	40,822
06492	Wallingford Center (c)	(203)	17,509	17,827
*06702	Waterbury	(203)	107,271	108,961
06385	*Waterford*	(860)	19,152	17,930
06795	*Watertown*	(860)	21,661	20,456
06498	*Westbrook*	(860)	6,292	5,414
*06101	*West Hartford*	(860)	63,589	60,110
06516	West Haven	(203)	52,360	54,021
06883	*Weston*	(203)	10,037	8,648
*06880	*Westport*	(203)	25,749	24,410
*06101	*Wethersfield*	(860)	26,271	25,651
06226	Willimantic (c)	(860)	15,823	14,746
06279	*Willington*	(860)	5,959	5,979
06897	*Wilton*	(203)	17,633	15,989
06094	*Winchester*	(860)	10,664	11,524
06280	*Windham*	(860)	22,857	22,039
06095	*Windsor*	(860)	28,237	27,817
06096	*Windsor Locks*	(860)	12,043	12,358
06098	Winsted (c)	(860)	7,321	8,254
06716	*Wolcott*	(203)	15,215	13,700
06525	*Woodbridge*	(203)	8,983	7,924
06798	*Woodbury*	(203)	9,198	8,131
06281	*Woodstock*	(860)	7,221	6,008

Delaware (302)

ZIP	Place	2000	1990
19701	Bear (c)	17,593	—
19713	Brookside (c)	14,806	15,307
19703	Claymont (c)	9,220	9,800
*19901	Dover	32,135	27,630
19809	Edgemoor (c)	5,992	5,853
19805	Elsmere	5,800	5,935
19702	Glasgow (c)	12,840	—
19707	Hockessin (c)	12,902	—
19709	Middletown	6,161	3,834
19963	Milford	6,732	6,032
*19711	Newark	28,547	26,463
—	North Star (c)	8,277	—
19800	Pike Creek (c)	19,751	10,163
19973	Seaford	6,699	5,689
19977	Smyrna	5,679	5,231
*19899	Wilmington	72,664	71,529
19720	Wilmington Manor (c)	8,262	8,568

District of Columbia (202)

ZIP	Place	2000	1990
*20090	Washington	572,059	606,900

IT'S A FACT: When a new area code was needed for the part of Florida that includes Kennedy Space Center, site of space shuttle launches, the number 321 was chosen. This was no arbitrary decision. Administrators at NANPA (North American Numbering Plan Administration) selected it because it is the end of a countdown ("3-2-1 liftoff").

Florida

Area code (321) overlays area code (407). Area code (754) overlays (954). Area code (786) overlays (305). See introductory note.

ZIP	Place	Area Code	2000	1990
*32615	Alachua	(386)	6,098	4,667
*32714	Altamonte Springs	(407)	41,200	35,167
—	Andover (c)	(305)	8,489	6,251
33572	Apollo Beach (c)	(813)	7,444	6,025
*32712	Apopka	(407)	26,642	13,611
*34266	Arcadia	(863)	6,604	6,488
32233	Atlantic Beach	(904)	13,368	11,636
33823	Auburndale	(863)	11,032	8,846
*33160	Aventura	(305)	25,267	14,914
*33825	Avon Park	(863)	8,542	8,078
32857	Azalea Park (c)	(407)	11,073	8,926
*33830	Bartow	(863)	15,340	14,716
33154	Bay Harbor Islands	(305)	5,146	4,703
—	Bay Hill (c)	(407)	5,177	5,346
34667	Bayonet Point (c)	(727)	23,577	21,860
33505	Bayshore Gardens (c)	(941)	17,350	17,062
33589	Beacon Square (c)	(727)	7,263	6,265
34233	Bee Ridge (c)	(941)	8,744	6,406
32073	Bellair-Meadowbrook Terrace (c)	(904)	16,539	15,606
33430	Belle Glade	(561)	14,906	16,177
*32802	Belle Isle	(407)	5,531	5,272
*34420	Belleview (c)	(352)	21,201	19,386
*34461	Beverly Hills (c)	(352)	8,317	6,163
33043	Big Pine Key (c)	(305)	5,032	4,206
*33509	Bloomingdale (c)	(813)	19,839	13,912
33433	Boca Del Mar (c)	(561)	21,832	17,754
*33431	Boca Raton	(561)	74,764	61,486
*34135	Bonita Springs	(239)	32,797	13,600
33547	Boyette (c)	(813)	5,895	—
*33436	Boynton Beach	(561)	60,389	46,284
*34206	Bradenton	(941)	49,504	43,769
*33509	Brandon (c)	(813)	77,895	57,985
32503	Brent (c)	(850)	22,257	21,624
33317	Broadview Park (c)	(954)	6,798	6,109
33313	Broadview-Pompano Park (c)	(954)	5,314	5,230
*34601	Brooksville	(352)	7,264	7,589
33142	Brownsville (c)	(305)	14,393	15,607
32404	Callaway	(850)	14,233	12,253
32920	Cape Canaveral	(321)	8,829	8,014
*33909	Cape Coral	(239)	102,286	74,991
33055	Carol City (c)	(305)	59,443	53,331
*32707	Casselberry	(407)	22,629	20,736
—	Cedar Grove	(850)	5,367	1,479
33401	Century Village (c)	(305)	7,616	8,363
—	Cheval (c)	(813)	7,602	—
33624	Citrus Park (c)	(813)	20,226	—
*32966	Citrus Ridge (c)	(772)	12,015	—
*33758	Clearwater	(727)	108,787	98,669
*34711	Clermont	(352)	9,333	6,910
33440	Clewiston	(863)	6,460	6,085
*32922	Cocoa	(321)	16,412	17,710
*32931	Cocoa Beach	(321)	12,482	12,123
32922	Cocoa West (c)	(321)	5,921	6,160
*33097	Coconut Creek	(954)	43,566	27,269
33064	Collier Manor-Cresthaven (c)	(954)	7,741	7,322
33801	Combee Settlement (c)	(863)	5,436	5,463
32809	Conway (c)	(407)	14,394	13,159
33328	Cooper City	(954)	27,939	21,335
*33114	Coral Gables	(305)	42,249	40,091
*33075	Coral Springs	(954)	117,549	78,864
33157	Coral Terrace (c)	(305)	24,380	23,255
33015	Country Club (c)	(305)	36,310	3,408
—	Country Walk (c)	(305)	10,653	—
*32536	Crestview	(850)	14,766	9,886
33803	Crystal Lake (c)	(863)	5,341	5,300
33157	Cutler (c)	(305)	17,390	16,201
33157	Cutler Ridge (c)	(305)	24,781	21,268
33884	Cypress Gardens (c)	(863)	8,844	9,188
33919	Cypress Lake (c)	(239)	12,072	10,491
*33525	Dade City	(352)	6,188	5,633
33004	Dania Beach	(954)	20,061	—
33329	Davie	(954)	75,720	47,143
*32114	Daytona Beach	(386)	64,112	61,991
32713	De Bary	(386)	15,559	9,327
*33441	Deerfield Beach	(954)	64,583	46,997
*32433	DeFuniak Springs	(850)	5,089	5,200
*32720	De Land	(386)	20,904	16,622
*33444	Delray Beach	(561)	60,020	47,184
*32738	Deltona	(407)	69,543	49,429
*32541	Destin	(850)	11,119	8,090
32819	Doctor Phillips (c)	(407)	9,548	7,963
33178	Doral (c)	(305)	20,438	3,126
*34698	Dunedin	(727)	35,691	34,427
33610	East Lake (c)	(813)	29,394	—
33610	East Lake-Orient Park (c)	(813)	5,703	6,171
—	East Perrine (c)	(305)	7,079	—
*32132	Edgewater	(386)	18,668	15,351
32542	Eglin AFB (c)	(850)	8,082	8,347
—	Egypt Lake-Leto (c)	(813)	32,782	—
34680	Elfers (c)	(727)	13,161	12,356
*34295	Englewood (c)	(941)	16,196	15,025
32534	Ensley (c)	(850)	18,752	16,362
33928	Estero (c)	(239)	9,503	3,177
*32726	Eustis	(352)	15,106	12,856
32804	Fairview Shores (c)	(305)	13,898	13,192
*32034	Fernandina Beach	(904)	10,549	8,765
32730	Fern Park (c)	(407)	8,318	8,294
32514	Ferry Pass (c)	(850)	27,176	26,301
33034	Florida City	(305)	7,843	5,978
32960	Florida Ridge (c)	(772)	15,217	12,218
32714	Forest City (c)	(407)	12,612	10,638
*33310	Fort Lauderdale	(954)	152,397	149,238
33841	Fort Meade	(863)	5,691	5,151
*33902	Fort Myers	(239)	48,208	44,947
*33931	Fort Myers Beach (c)	(239)	6,561	9,284
*33922	Fort Myers Shores (c)	(239)	5,793	5,460
*34981	Fort Pierce	(772)	37,516	36,830
33452	Fort Pierce North (c)	(772)	7,386	5,833
34982	Fort Pierce South (c)	(772)	5,672	5,320
*32548	Fort Walton Beach	(850)	19,973	21,407
—	Fountainbleau (c)	(305)	59,549	—
*32043	Fruit Cove (c)	(904)	16,077	5,904
34230	Fruitville (c)	(941)	12,741	9,808
33823	Fussels Corner (c)	(863)	5,313	3,840
*32602	Gainesville	(352)	95,447	91,482
33534	Gibsonton (c)	(813)	8,752	7,706
32960	Gifford (c)	(772)	7,599	6,278
33138	Gladeview (c)	(954)	14,468	15,637
33143	Glenvar Heights (c)	(305)	16,243	14,823
34116	Golden Gate (c)	(239)	20,951	14,148
33055	Golden Glades (c)	(305)	32,623	25,474
33411	Golden Lakes (c)	(561)	6,694	3,867
32733	Goldenrod (c)	(407)	12,871	12,362
32560	Gonzalez (c)	(850)	11,365	7,669
33170	Goulds (c)	(305)	7,453	7,284
—	Greater Carrollwood (c)	(813)	33,519	—
33624	Greater Northdale (c)	(813)	20,461	16,318
—	Greater Sun Center (c)	(813)	16,321	—
33454	Greenacres	(561)	27,569	18,683
32043	Green Cove Springs	(904)	5,378	4,497
*32561	Gulf Breeze	(850)	5,665	5,530
33581	Gulf Gate Estates (c)	(941)	11,647	11,622
33737	Gulfport	(727)	12,527	11,709
*33844	Haines City	(863)	13,174	11,683
*33009	Hallandale	(305)/(954)	34,282	30,997
33434	Hamptons at Boca Raton (c)	(561)	11,306	11,686
34442	Hernando (c)	(352)	8,253	2,103
*33010	Hialeah	(305)	226,419	188,008
33016	Hialeah Gardens	(305)	19,297	7,727
*33455	Hobe Sound (c)	(772)	11,376	11,507
*34689	Holiday (c)	(727)	21,904	19,360
32125	Holly Hill	(386)	12,119	11,141
*33022	Hollywood	(954)	139,357	121,720
*33030	Homestead	(305)	31,909	26,694
34447	Homosassa Springs (c)	(352)	12,458	6,271
*34668	Hudson (c)	(727)	12,765	7,344
—	Hunters Creek (c)	(407)	9,369	—
*34142	Immokalee (c)	(239)	19,763	14,120
32937	Indian Harbour Beach	(321)	8,152	6,933
32963	Indian River Estates (c)	(772)	5,793	4,858
33785	Indian Rocks Beach	(727)	5,072	3,963
34956	Indiantown (c)	(772)	5,588	4,794
*34450	Inverness	(352)	6,789	5,797
—	Inverness Highlands South (c)	(352)	5,781	—
33880	Inwood (c)	(863)	6,925	6,824
33908	Iona (c)	(239)	11,756	9,565
33036	Islamorada, Village of Islands	(305)	6,846	1,220
33162	Ives Estates (c)	(305)	17,586	13,531
*32203	Jacksonville	(904)	735,617	635,230
*32250	Jacksonville Beach	(904)	20,990	17,839
33880	Jan Phyl Village (c)	(863)	5,633	5,308
33568	Jasmine Estates (c)	(727)	18,213	17,136
*34957	Jensen Beach (c)	(772)	11,100	9,884
*33458	Jupiter	(561)	39,328	26,753
33183	Kendale Lakes (c)	(305)	56,901	48,524
33256	Kendall (c)	(305)	75,226	87,271
—	Kendall West (c)	(305)	38,034	—
33149	Key Biscayne	(305)	10,507	8,854
33037	Key Largo (c)	(305)	11,886	11,336
—	Keystone (c)	(813)	14,627	—
*33040	Key West	(305)	25,478	24,832
*33573	Kings Point (c)	(305)	12,207	12,422
*34744	Kissimmee	(407)	47,814	30,337
*32159	Lady Lake	(352)	11,828	8,071
—	Lake Butter (c)		7,062	—
*32055	Lake City	(386)	9,980	9,626
*33804	Lakeland	(863)	78,452	70,576
33801	Lakeland Highlands (c)	(863)	12,557	9,972
32569	Lake Lorraine (c)	(850)	7,106	6,779
33054	Lake Lucerne (c)	(305)	9,132	9,478
33612	Lake Magdalene (c)	(813)	28,755	15,973

ZIP	Place	Area Code	2000	1990
*32746	Lake Mary	(407)	11,458	5,929
33403	Lake Park	(561)	8,721	6,704
—	Lakes by the Bay (c)	(305)	9,055	5,615
32073	Lakeside (c)	(904)	30,927	29,137
*33853	Lake Wales	(863)	10,194	9,670
34951	Lakewood Park (c)	(772)	10,458	7,211
*33461	Lake Worth	(561)	35,133	28,564
—	Lake Worth Corridor (c)		18,663	—
34639	Land O'Lakes (c)	(813)	20,971	7,892
33465	Lantana	(561)	9,437	8,392
*33770	Largo	(727)	69,371	65,910
33313	Lauderdale Lakes	(954)	31,705	27,341
33313	Lauderhill	(954)	57,585	49,015
34272	Laurel (c)	(941)	8,393	8,245
*34461	Lecanto (c)	(352)	5,161	1,243
*34748	Leesburg	(352)	15,956	14,783
*33936	Lehigh Acres (c)	(239)	33,430	13,611
33033	Leisure City (c)	(305)	22,152	19,379
33074	Lighthouse Point	(954)	10,767	10,378
*32060	Live Oak	(386)	6,480	6,332
32860	Lockhart (c)	(407)	12,944	11,636
34228	Longboat Key	(941)	7,603	5,937
*32750	Longwood	(407)	13,745	13,316
*33549	Lutz (c)	(813)	17,081	10,552
32444	Lynn Haven	(850)	12,451	9,270
33919	McGregor (c)	(239)	7,136	6,504
*32751	Maitland	(407)	12,019	8,932
33550	Mango (c)	(813)	8,842	8,700
33050	Marathon	(305)	10,255	8,857
*34145	Marco Island	(239)	14,879	—
33003	Margate	(954)	53,909	42,985
*32446	Marianna	(850)	6,230	6,292
32824	Meadow Woods (c)	(407)	11,286	4,876
33811	Medulla (c)	(863)	6,637	3,977
*32901	Melbourne	(321)	71,382	60,034
32666	Melrose Park (c)	(954)	7,114	6,477
33561	Memphis (c)	(941)	7,264	6,760
*32953	Merritt Island (c)	(321)	36,090	32,886
*33101	Miami	(305)	362,470	358,648
*33152	Miami Beach	(305)	87,933	92,639
33014	Miami Lakes (c)	(305)	22,676	12,750
33153	Miami Shores	(305)	10,380	10,084
33266	Miami Springs	(305)	13,712	13,268
32976	Micco (c)	(772)	9,498	8,757
*32068	Middleburg (c)	(904)	10,338	6,223
*32570	Milton	(850)	7,045	7,216
32754	Mims (c)	(321)	9,147	9,412
34755	Minneola	(352)	5,435	1,515
33023	Miramar	(954)	72,739	40,663
*32757	Mount Dora	(352)	9,418	7,294
32526	Myrtle Grove (c)	(850)	17,211	17,402
*34102	Naples	(239)	20,976	19,505
34113	Naples Manor (c)	(239)	5,186	4,574
34102	Naples Park (c)	(239)	6,741	8,002
32266	Neptune Beach	(904)	7,270	6,816
*34653	New Port Richey	(727)	16,117	14,044
33552	New Port Richey East (c)	(727)	9,916	9,683
*32168	New Smyrna Beach	(386)	20,048	16,549
*32578	Niceville	(850)	11,684	10,509
33269	Norland (c)	(305)	22,995	22,109
33308	North Andrews Gardens (c)	(954)	9,656	9,002
33141	North Bay Village	(305)	6,733	5,383
33918	North Fort Myers (c)	(239)	40,214	30,027
33068	North Lauderdale	(954)	32,264	26,473
33261	North Miami	(305)	59,880	50,001
33160	North Miami Beach	(305)	40,786	35,361
33408	North Palm Beach	(561)	12,064	11,538
*34287	North Port	(941)	22,797	11,973
34234	North Sarasota (c)	(941)	6,738	6,702
33307	Oakland Park	(305)	30,966	26,326
33860	Oak Ridge (c)	(407)	22,349	15,388
*34478	Ocala	(352)	45,943	42,045
32548	Ocean City (c)	(850)	5,594	5,422
34761	Ocoee	(407)	24,391	12,778
33163	Ojus (c)	(305)	16,642	15,519
*34972	Okeechobee	(863)	5,376	4,943
34677	Oldsmar	(813)	11,910	8,361
33265	Olympia Heights (c)	(305)	13,452	37,792
*33054	Opa-Locka	(305)	14,951	15,283
33054	Opa-Locka North (c)	(305)	6,224	6,568
*32763	Orange City	(386)	6,604	5,372
*32073	Orange Park	(904)	9,081	9,488
*32802	Orlando	(407)	185,951	164,674
32861	Orlo Vista (c)	(407)	6,047	5,990
*32174	Ormond Beach	(386)	36,301	29,721
32074	Ormond By-The-Sea (c)	(386)	8,430	8,157
*32765	Oviedo	(407)	26,316	11,114
32571	Pace (c)	(850)	7,393	6,277
33476	Pahokee	(561)	5,985	6,822
*32177	Palatka	(386)	10,033	10,447
*32905	Palm Bay	(321)	79,413	62,543
33480	Palm Beach	(561)	10,468	9,814
33408	Palm Beach Gardens	(561)	35,058	24,139
*34990	Palm City (c)	(772)	20,097	3,925
*32135	Palm Coast	(386)	32,732	14,287
*34221	Palmetto	(941)	12,571	9,268
33157	Palmetto Estates (c)	(305)	13,675	12,293
*34683	Palm Harbor (c)	(727)	59,248	50,256
*33601	Palm River-Clair Mel (c)	(813)	17,589	13,691
33460	Palm Springs	(561)	11,699	9,763
33012	Palm Springs North (c)	(305)	5,460	5,300
32082	Palm Valley (c)	(904)	19,860	9,960
*32401	Panama City	(850)	36,417	34,396
32417	Panama City Beach	(850)	7,671	4,051
33060	Parkland	(954)	13,835	3,773
34108	Pelican Bay (c)		5,686	—
33021	Pembroke Park	(954)	6,299	4,933
33029	Pembroke Pines	(954)	137,427	65,566
*32502	Pensacola	(850)	56,255	59,198
*32347	Perry	(850)	6,847	7,151
32859	Pine Castle (c)	(407)	8,803	8,276
33156	Pinecrest	(305)	19,055	—
32858	Pine Hills (c)	(407)	41,764	35,322
33324	Pine Island Ridge (c)	(954)	5,199	5,244
*33781	Pinellas Park	(727)	45,658	43,571
—	Pine Ridge (c)	(352)	5,490	—
33168	Pinewood (c)	(305)	16,523	15,518
33318	Plantation	(954)	82,934	66,814
*33566	Plant City	(813)	29,915	22,754
*34758	Poinciana (c)	(407)	13,647	—
*33060	Pompano Beach	(954)	78,191	72,411
33064	Pompano Beach Highlands (c)	(954)	6,505	17,915
*33952	Port Charlotte (c)	(941)	46,451	41,535
32129	Port Orange	(904)	45,823	35,399
32927	Port St. John (c)	(321)	12,112	8,933
*34981	Port St. Lucie	(772)	88,769	55,761
34983	Port St. Lucie-River Park (c)	(772)	5,175	4,874
34992	Port Salerno (c)	(772)	10,141	7,786
*33032	Princeton (c)	(305)	10,090	7,073
*33950	Punta Gorda	(941)	14,344	10,637
*32351	Quincy	(850)	6,982	7,452
33156	Richmond Heights (c)	(305)	8,479	8,583
—	Richmond West (c)	(305)	28,082	—
34231	Ridge Wood Heights (c)	(941)	5,028	4,851
*33569	Riverview (c)	(813)	12,035	6,478
33419	Riviera Beach	(561)	29,884	27,646
*32955	Rockledge	(321)	20,170	16,023
33947	Rotonda (c)	(941)	6,574	3,576
33411	Royal Palm Beach	(561)	21,523	15,532
33570	Ruskin (c)	(813)	8,321	6,046
34695	Safety Harbor	(727)	17,203	15,120
*32084	Saint Augustine	(904)	11,592	11,695
32086	Saint Augustine South (c)	(904)	5,035	4,218
*34769	Saint Cloud	(407)	20,074	12,684
*33736	Saint Pete Beach	(727)	9,929	9,200
*33733	Saint Petersburg	(727)	248,232	240,318
33912	San Carlos Park (c)	(239)	16,317	11,785
33432	Sandalfoot Cove (c)	(305)	16,582	14,214
*32771	Sanford	(407)	38,291	32,387
33957	Sanibel	(239)	6,064	5,468
*34230	Sarasota	(941)	52,715	50,897
33577	Sarasota Springs (c)	(941)	15,875	16,088
32937	Satellite Beach	(321)	9,577	9,889
33055	Scott Lake (c)	(305)	14,401	14,588
*32958	Sebastian	(772)	16,181	10,248
*33870	Sebring	(863)	9,667	8,841
*33584	Seffner (c)	(813)	5,467	5,371
*33770	Seminole	(813)	10,890	9,251
34610	Shady Hills (c)	(727)	7,798	—
*34242	Siesta Key (c)	(941)	7,150	7,772
34472	Silver Springs Shores (c)	(352)	6,690	6,421
32809	Sky Lake (c)	(407)	5,651	6,202
32703	South Apopka (c)	(407)	5,800	6,360
33505	South Bradenton (c)	(941)	21,587	20,398
32121	South Daytona	(386)	13,177	12,488
34266	Southeast Arcadia (c)	(863)	6,064	4,145
34277	Southgate (c)	(941)	7,455	7,324
34233	South Gate Ridge (c)	(941)	5,655	5,924
—	South Highpoint (c)	(727)	8,839	—
33243	South Miami	(305)	10,741	10,404
33157	South Miami Heights (c)	(305)	33,522	30,030
33707	South Pasadena	(727)	5,778	5,644
32937	South Patrick Shores (c)	(321)	8,913	10,249
34230	South Sarasota (c)	(941)	5,314	5,298
33595	South Venice (c)	(941)	13,539	11,951
32401	Springfield	(850)	8,810	8,719
*34601	Spring Hill (c)	(352)	69,078	31,117
32091	Starke	(904)	5,593	5,226
*34994	Stuart	(772)	14,633	11,936
34446	Sugarmill Woods (c)	(352)	6,409	4,073
33160	Sunny Isles Beach	(305)	15,315	—
33345	Sunrise	(954)	85,779	65,683
33283	Sunset (c)	(305)	17,150	15,810
33144	Sweetwater	(305)	14,226	13,909
*32301	Tallahassee	(850)	150,624	124,773
33320	Tamarac	(954)	55,588	44,822
33144	Tamiami (c)	(305)	54,788	33,845
*33601	Tampa	(813)	303,447	280,015
34689	Tarpon Springs	(727)	21,003	17,874
32778	Tavares	(352)	9,700	7,488
33687	Temple Terrace	(813)	20,918	16,444
33469	Tequesta	(561)	5,273	4,499
33186	The Crossings (c)	(305)	23,557	—
—	The Hammocks (c)	(305)	47,379	—
32159	The Villages (c)	(352)	8,333	—
33592	Thonotosassa (c)	(813)	6,091	—

ZIP	Place	Area Code	2000	1990
—	Three Lakes (c)	(305)	6,955	—
33025	Timber Pines (c)	(352)	5,840	3,182
*32780	Titusville	(321)	40,670	39,394
32685	Town 'n' Country (c)	(813)	72,523	60,946
33706	Treasure Island	(727)	7,450	7,266
32867	Union Park (c)	(407)	10,191	6,890
33024	University (c)	(813)	30,736	—
—	University Park (c)	(305)	26,538	—
32401	Upper Grand Lagoon (c)	(850)	10,889	7,855
32580	Valparaiso	(850)	6,408	6,316
*33594	Valrico (c)	(813)	6,582	—
34231	Vamo (c)	(941)	5,285	3,325
*34285	Venice	(941)	17,764	17,052
33595	Venice Gardens (c)	(941)	7,466	7,701
*32960	Vero Beach	(772)	17,705	17,350
32960	Vero Beach South (c)	(772)	20,362	16,973
33901	Villas (c)	(239)	11,346	9,898
32507	Warrington (c)	(850)	15,207	16,040
32791	Wekiva Springs (c)	(407)	23,169	23,026
33414	Wellington	(561)	38,216	20,670
33543	Wesley Chapel (c)	(813)	5,691	—
—	West and East Lealman (c)	(727)	21,753	—
33626	Westchase (c)	(813)	11,116	—
33155	Westchester (c)	(305)	30,271	29,883
33409	Westgate-Belvedere Homes (c)	(561)	8,134	6,880
33138	West Little River (c)	(305)	32,498	33,575
32912	West Melbourne	(321)	9,824	8,398
33144	West Miami	(305)	5,863	5,727
33326	Weston	(954)	49,286	—
*33416	West Palm Beach	(561)	82,103	67,764
32505	West Pensacola (c)	(850)	21,939	22,107
33157	West Perrine (c)	(305)	8,600	—
34208	West Samoset (c)	(941)	5,507	3,819
—	West Vero Corridor (c)	(772)	7,695	—
33168	Westview (c)	(305)	9,692	9,668
33165	Westwood Lakes (c)	(305)	12,005	11,522
33496	Whisper Walk (c)	(561)	5,135	3,037
32821	Williamsburg (c)	(407)	6,736	3,093
33305	Wilton Manors	(954)	12,697	11,804
33803	Winston (c)	(813)	9,024	9,118
*34787	Winter Garden	(407)	14,351	9,863
*33880	Winter Haven	(863)	26,487	24,725
*32789	Winter Park	(407)	24,090	24,260
*32707	Winter Springs	(407)	31,666	22,151
32547	Wright (c)	(850)	21,697	18,945
34972	Yeehaw Junction (c)	(407)	21,778	—
*32097	Yulee (c)	(904)	8,392	6,915
*33540	Zephyrhills	(813)	10,833	8,220
33541	Zephyrhills West (c)	(813)	5,242	4,249

Georgia

Area code (678) overlays (770). See introductory note.

ZIP	Place	Area Code	2000	1990
*30101	Acworth	(770)	13,422	4,519
31620	Adel	(229)	5,307	5,093
*31706	Albany	(229)	76,939	78,804
*30004	Alpharetta	(770)	34,854	13,002
31709	Americus	(229)	17,013	16,516
*30603	Athens-Clarke County1	(706)	101,489	86,522
*30301	Atlanta	(404)	416,474	393,929
30011	Auburn	(770)	6,904	3,139
*30903	Augusta-Richmond County2	(706)	199,775	186,616
30168	Austell	(770)	5,359	4,173
*31717	Bainbridge	(229)	11,722	10,803
30204	Barnesville	(770)	5,972	4,747
30032	Belvedere Park (c)	(404)	18,945	18,089
31723	Blakely	(229)	5,696	5,595
*31520	Brunswick	(912)	15,600	16,433
*30518	Buford	(404)	10,668	8,771
31728	Cairo	(229)	9,239	9,035
*30701	Calhoun	(706)	10,667	7,135
31730	Camilla	(229)	5,669	5,124
30032	Candler-McAfee (c)	(404)	28,294	29,491
*30114	Canton	(770)	7,709	4,817
*30117	Carrollton	(770)	19,843	16,029
*30120	Cartersville	(770)	15,925	12,037
30125	Cedartown	(770)	9,470	7,976
30366	Chamblee	(404)	9,552	7,668
30021	Clarkston	(404)	7,231	5,385
30337	College Park	(404)	20,382	20,645
*31908	Columbus	(706)	186,291	178,683
30529	Commerce	(770)	5,292	4,108
30288	Conley (c)	(404)	6,188	5,528
*30013	Conyers	(404)	10,689	7,380
*31015	Cordele	(229)	11,608	10,833
—	Country Club Estates (c)		7,594	7,500
*30014	Covington	(770)	11,547	9,860
*30132	Dallas	(770)	5,056	2,810
*30720	Dalton	(706)	27,912	22,218
31742	Dawson	(229)	5,058	5,295
*30030	Decatur (DeKalb)	(404)	18,147	17,304
31520	Dock Junction (c)	(912)	6,951	7,094
30362	Doraville	(404)	9,862	7,626
*31533	Douglas	(912)	10,639	10,464
*30134	Douglasville	(404)	20,065	11,635
30333	Druid Hills (c)	(404)	12,741	12,174
*31021	Dublin	(478)	15,857	16,312
*30096	Duluth	(404)	22,122	9,821
30356	Dunwoody (c)	(404)	32,808	26,302
31023	Eastman	(478)	5,440	5,153
30364	East Point	(404)	39,595	34,595
31024	Eatonton	(706)	6,764	6,479
30809	Evans (c)	(706)	17,727	13,713
30213	Fairburn	(770)	5,464	4,013
30060	Fair Oaks (c)	(404)	8,443	6,996
30535	Fairview (c)	(706)	6,601	6,444
*30214	Fayetteville	(404)	11,148	5,827
31750	Fitzgerald	(229)	8,758	8,901
*30297	Forest Park	(404)	21,447	16,958
31905	Fort Benning South (c)	(706)	11,737	14,617
30742	Fort Oglethorpe	(706)	6,940	5,880
*31313	Fort Stewart (c)	(912)	11,205	13,774
31030	Fort Valley	(478)	8,005	8,198
*30501	Gainesville	(770)	25,578	17,885
31418	Garden City	(912)	11,289	7,410
31754	Georgetown (c)	(912)	10,599	5,554
30316	Gresham Park (c)	(404)	9,215	9,000
*30223	Griffin	(770)	23,451	21,325
30813	Grovetown	(706)	6,089	3,596
30354	Hapeville	(404)	6,180	5,483
*31313	Hinesville	(912)	30,392	21,596
—	Irondale (c)		7,727	3,352
*31546	Jesup	(912)	9,279	8,958
*30144	Kennesaw	(404)	21,675	8,936
31548	Kingsland	(912)	10,506	6,089
30728	La Fayette	(706)	6,702	6,655
*30240	LaGrange	(706)	25,998	25,574
*30045	Lawrenceville	(404)	22,397	17,250
*30047	Lilburn	(404)	11,307	9,295
30052	Loganville	(770)	5,435	3,180
30126	Mableton (c)	(404)	29,733	25,725
30253	McDonough	(770)	8,493	2,929
*31201	Macon	(478)	97,255	107,365
*30060	Marietta	(404)	58,748	44,129
30917	Martinez (c)	(706)	27,749	33,731
—	Midway-Hardwick (c)		5,135	4,910
31061	Milledgeville	(478)	18,757	17,727
*30655	Monroe	(770)	11,407	9,759
*31768	Moultrie	(229)	14,387	14,865
30087	Mountain Park (c)	(404)	11,753	11,025
*30263	Newnan	(770)	16,242	12,497
*30071	Norcross	(404)	8,410	5,947
30319	North Atlanta (c)	(404)	38,579	27,812
30033	North Decatur (c)	(404)	15,270	13,936
30033	North Druid Hills (c)	(404)	18,852	14,170
30032	Panthersville (c)	(404)	11,791	9,874
30269	Peachtree City	(404)	31,580	19,027
31069	Perry	(478)	9,602	9,452
31322	Pooler	(912)	6,239	4,649
30127	Powder Springs	(404)	12,481	6,862
30074	Redan (c)	(404)	33,841	24,376
31324	Richmond Hill	(912)	6,959	2,934
*30274	Riverdale	(404)	12,478	9,495
*30161	Rome	(706)	34,980	30,425
*30077	Roswell	(404)	79,334	47,986
31558	Saint Marys	(912)	13,761	8,204
31522	Saint Simons (c)	(912)	13,381	12,026
31082	Sandersville	(478)	6,144	6,290
30358	Sandy Springs (c)	(404)	85,781	67,842
*31402	Savannah	(912)	131,510	137,812
30079	Scottdale (c)	(404)	9,803	8,636
—	Skidaway Island (c)	(912)	6,914	4,495
*30080	Smyrna	(404)	40,999	32,453
*30078	Snellville	(404)	15,351	12,084
*30458	Statesboro	(912)	22,698	20,770
30281	Stockbridge	(404)	9,853	3,359
*30086	Stone Mountain	(404)	7,145	6,544
30518	Sugar Hill	(404)	11,399	4,519
30024	Suwanee	(770)	8,725	2,412
30401	Swainsboro	(478)	6,943	7,361
31791	Sylvester	(229)	5,990	6,023
30286	Thomaston	(706)	9,411	9,127
*31792	Thomasville	(229)	18,162	17,554
30824	Thomson	(706)	6,828	6,862
*31794	Tifton	(229)	15,060	14,215
*30577	Toccoa	(706)	9,323	8,720
*30084	Tucker (c)	(404)	26,532	25,781
30291	Union City	(404)	11,621	9,347
*31603	Valdosta	(229)	43,724	40,038
*30474	Vidalia	(912)	10,491	11,118
30339	Vinings (c)	(404)	9,677	7,417
*31088	Warner Robins	(478)	48,804	43,861
*31501	Waycross	(912)	15,333	16,410
30830	Waynesboro	(706)	5,813	5,669
—	Whitemarsh Island (c)		5,824	2,824
31410	Wilmington Island (c)	(912)	14,213	11,230
30680	Winder	(770)	10,201	7,373
*30188	Woodstock	(770)	10,050	4,361

(1) Athens merged with Clarke County in 1991. The 2000 and 1990 populations are for all of Clarke County except for Winterville and Bogart, which are part of the county but are also separate incorporated places. (2) Augusta merged with Richmond County in 1996. The 2000 and 1990 populations are for all of Richmond County except for Blythe and Hephzibah, which are part of the county but are also separate incorporated places.

Hawaii (808)

ZIP	Place	2000	1990
—	Ahuimanu (c)	8,506	8,387
96701	Aiea (c)	9,019	8,906
96706	Ewa Beach (c)	14,650	14,315
—	Haiku-Pauwela (c)	6,578	4,509
—	Halawa (c)	13,891	13,408
96778	Hawaiian Paradise Park (c)	7,051	3,389
96853	Hickam Housing (c)	5,471	6,553
*96720	Hilo (c)	40,759	37,808
96725	Holualoa (c)	6,107	3,834
*96820	Honolulu (c)	371,657	377,059
*96732	Kahului (c)	20,146	16,889
96734	Kailua (Hawaii) (c)	9,870	9,126
96863	Kailua (Honolulu) (c)	36,513	36,818
96740	Kalaoa (c)	6,794	4,490
96744	Kaneohe (c)	34,970	35,448
—	Kaneohe Station (c)	11,827	11,662
96746	Kapaa (c)	9,472	8,149
96753	Kihei (c)	16,749	11,107
*96761	Lahaina (c)	9,118	9,073
96766	Lihue (c)	5,674	5,536
96792	Maili (c)	5,943	6,059
96792	Makaha (c)	7,753	7,990
96706	Makakilo (c)	13,156	9,828
96768	Makawao (c)	6,327	5,405
96789	Mililani Town (c)	28,608	29,359
96792	Nanakuli (c)	10,814	9,575
96761	Napili-Honokowai (c)	6,788	4,332
96782	Pearl City (c)	30,976	30,993
96788	Pukalani (c)	7,380	5,879
96786	Schofield Barracks (c)	14,428	19,597
—	Village Park (c)	9,625	7,407
96786	Wahiawa (c)	16,151	17,386
96792	Waianae (c)	10,506	8,758
—	Waihee-Waiehu (c)	7,310	4,004
96753	Wailea-Makena (c)	5,671	3,799
96793	Wailuku (c)	12,296	10,688
—	Waimalu (c)	29,371	29,967
96796	Waimea (c)	7,028	5,972
96797	Waipahu (c)	33,108	31,435
96797	Waipio (c)	11,672	11,812
96786	Waipio Acres (c)	5,298	5,304

Idaho (208)

ZIP	Place	2000	1990
83401	Ammon	6,187	5,002
83221	Blackfoot	10,419	9,646
*83707	Boise	185,787	125,738
83318	Burley	9,316	8,702
*83605	Caldwell	25,967	18,586
83202	Chubbuck	9,700	7,794
*83814	Coeur d'Alene	34,514	24,561
83616	Eagle	11,085	3,327
83617	Emmett	5,490	4,601
83714	Garden City	10,624	6,369
83333	Hailey	6,200	3,575
83835	Hayden	9,159	4,888
*83402	Idaho Falls	50,730	43,973
83338	Jerome	7,780	6,529
*83654	Kuna	5,382	1,955
83501	Lewiston	30,904	28,082
*83642	Meridian	34,919	9,596
83843	Moscow	21,291	18,398
83647	Mountain Home	11,143	7,913
83648	Mountain Home AFB (c)	8,894	5,936
*83653	Nampa	51,867	28,365
83661	Payette	7,054	5,672
*83201	Pocatello	51,466	46,117
*83854	Post Falls	17,247	7,349
83440	Rexburg	17,257	14,298
83350	Rupert	5,645	5,455
83864	Sandpoint	6,835	5,561
*83301	Twin Falls	34,469	27,634
83672	Weiser	5,343	4,571

Illinois

Area code (224) overlays area code (847). See introductory note.

ZIP	Place	Area Code	2000	1990
60101	Addison	(630)	35,914	32,053
60102	Algonquin	(847)	23,276	11,764
60803	Alsip	(708)	19,725	18,227
62002	Alton	(618)	30,496	33,060
62906	Anna	(618)	5,136	4,805
60002	Antioch	(847)	8,788	6,105
*60005	Arlington Heights	(847)	76,031	75,463
*60505	Aurora	(630)	142,990	99,672
*60010	Barrington	(847)	10,168	9,538
60103	Bartlett	(630)	36,706	19,395
61607	Bartonville	(309)	6,310	6,555
60510	Batavia	(630)	23,866	17,076
60085	Beach Park	(847)	10,072	9,492
62618	Beardstown	(217)	5,766	5,270
*62220	Belleville	(618)	41,410	42,806
60104	Bellwood	(708)	20,535	20,241
61008	Belvidere	(815)	20,820	16,059
60106	Bensenville	(630)	20,703	17,767
62812	Benton	(618)	6,880	7,216
60163	Berkeley	(708)	5,245	5,137
60402	Berwyn	(708)	54,016	45,426
62010	Bethalto	(618)	9,454	9,507
60108	Bloomingdale	(630)	21,675	16,614
*61701	Bloomington	(309)	64,808	51,889
60406	Blue Island	(708)	23,463	21,203
*60440	Bolingbrook	(630)	56,321	40,843
60538	Boulder Hill (c)	(630)	8,169	8,894
60914	Bourbonnais	(815)	15,256	13,929
60915	Bradley	(815)	12,784	10,954
60408	Braidwood	(815)	5,203	3,584
60455	Bridgeview	(708)	15,335	14,402
60153	Broadview	(708)	8,264	8,538
60513	Brookfield	(708)	19,085	18,876
60089	Buffalo Grove	(847)	42,909	36,417
60459	Burbank	(708)	27,902	27,600
60521	Burr Ridge	(630)	10,408	8,247
62206	Cahokia	(618)	16,391	17,550
60409	Calumet City	(708)	39,071	37,840
60643	Calumet Park	(708)	8,516	8,418
61520	Canton	(309)	15,288	13,959
*62901	Carbondale	(618)	20,681	27,033
62626	Carlinville	(217)	5,685	5,416
62821	Carmi	(618)	5,422	5,735
*60188	Carol Stream	(630)	40,438	31,759
60110	Carpentersville	(847)	30,586	23,049
60013	Cary	(847)	15,531	10,025
62801	Centralia	(618)	14,136	14,476
62206	Centreville	(618)	5,951	7,489
*61821	Champaign	(217)	67,518	63,502
60410	Channahon	(815)	7,344	4,266
61920	Charleston	(217)	21,039	20,398
62629	Chatham	(217)	8,583	6,074
62233	Chester	(618)	5,185	8,204
*60607	Chicago	(312)/(773)	2,896,016	2,783,726
*60411	Chicago Heights	(708)	32,776	32,966
60415	Chicago Ridge	(708)	14,127	13,643
61523	Chillicothe	(309)	5,996	5,959
60804	Cicero	(708)	85,616	67,436
60514	Clarendon Hills	(630)	7,610	6,994
61727	Clinton	(217)	7,485	7,437
62234	Collinsville	(618)	24,707	22,424
61241	Colona	(309)	5,173	2,237
62236	Columbia	(618)	7,922	5,524
60478	Country Club Hills	(708)	16,169	15,431
60525	Countryside	(708)	5,991	5,961
60435	Crest Hill	(815)	13,329	10,999
60445	Crestwood	(708)	11,251	10,823
60417	Crete	(708)	7,346	6,773
61610	Creve Coeur	(309)	5,448	5,938
*60014	Crystal Lake	(815)	38,000	24,692
*61832	Danville	(217)	33,904	33,828
60561	Darien	(630)	22,860	20,556
*62525	Decatur	(217)	81,860	83,900
60015	Deerfield	(847)	18,420	17,327
60115	DeKalb	(815)	39,018	35,076
*60018	Des Plaines	(847)	58,720	53,414
61021	Dixon	(815)	15,941	15,134
60419	Dolton	(708)	25,614	23,956
*60515	Downers Grove	(630)	48,724	47,464
62832	Du Quoin	(618)	6,448	6,697
62024	East Alton	(618)	6,830	7,063
61244	East Moline	(309)	20,333	20,147
61611	East Peoria	(309)	22,638	21,378
*62201	East St. Louis	(618)	31,542	40,944
62025	Edwardsville	(618)	21,491	14,582
62401	Effingham	(217)	12,384	11,927
*60120	Elgin	(847)	94,487	77,014
*60009	Elk Grove Village	(847)	34,727	33,429
60126	Elmhurst	(630)	42,762	42,029
60707	Elmwood Park	(708)	25,405	23,206
*60201	Evanston	(847)	74,239	73,233
60805	Evergreen Park	(708)	20,821	20,874
62837	Fairfield	(618)	5,421	5,439
62208	Fairview Heights	(618)	15,034	14,768
62839	Flora	(618)	5,086	5,054
60422	Flossmoor	(708)	9,301	8,651
60130	Forest Park	(708)	15,688	14,918
60020	Fox Lake	(847)	9,178	7,539
60423	Frankfort	(815)	10,391	7,180
—	Frankfort Square (c)	(815)	7,766	6,227
60131	Franklin Park	(847)	19,434	18,485
61032	Freeport	(815)	26,443	25,840
60030	Gages Lake (c)	(847)	10,415	8,349
*61401	Galesburg	(309)	33,706	33,530
61254	Geneseo	(309)	6,480	5,990
60134	Geneva	(630)	19,515	12,625
62034	Glen Carbon	(618)	10,425	7,774
60022	Glencoe	(847)	8,762	8,499
60139	Glendale Heights	(630)	31,765	27,915
*60137	Glen Ellyn	(630)	26,999	24,919
60025	Glenview	(847)	41,847	38,436
60425	Glenwood	(708)	9,000	9,289
62035	Godfrey	(618)	16,286	15,675
—	Goodings Grove (c)	(815)	17,084	14,054
62040	Granite City	(618)	31,301	32,766
60030	Grayslake	(847)	18,506	7,388
62246	Greenville	(618)	6,955	5,108
60031	Gurnee	(847)	28,834	13,715
60103	Hanover Park	(630)	38,278	32,918
62946	Harrisburg	(618)	9,860	9,318

ZIP	Place	Area Code	2000	1990
60033	Harvard	(815)	7,996	5,975
60426	Harvey	(708)	30,000	29,771
60656	Harwood Heights	(708)	8,297	7,680
60047	Hawthorn Woods	(847)	6,002	4,423
60429	Hazel Crest	(708)	14,816	13,334
62948	Herrin	(618)	11,298	10,857
60457	Hickory Hills	(708)	13,926	13,021
62249	Highland	(618)	8,438	7,546
60035	Highland Park	(847)	31,365	30,575
60162	Hillside	(708)	8,155	7,672
*60521	Hinsdale	(630)	17,349	16,029
*60195	Hoffman Estates	(847)	49,495	46,363
60430	Homewood	(708)	19,543	19,278
60942	Hoopeston	(217)	5,965	5,871
60142	Huntley	(847)	5,730	2453
60067	Inverness	(847)	6,749	6,516
60042	Island Lake	(847)	8,153	4,449
60143	Itasca	(630)	8,302	6,947
*62650	Jacksonville	(217)	18,940	19,327
62052	Jerseyville	(618)	7,984	7,382
60050	Johnsburg	(815)	5,391	—
*60436	Joliet	(815)	106,221	77,217
60458	Justice	(708)	12,193	11,137
60901	Kankakee	(815)	27,491	27,541
61443	Kewanee	(309)	12,944	12,969
60525	La Grange	(708)	15,608	15,362
60526	La Grange Park	(708)	13,295	12,861
60044	Lake Bluff	(847)	6,056	5,486
60045	Lake Forest	(847)	20,059	17,836
60102	Lake in the Hills	(847)	23,152	5,882
60046	Lake Villa	(847)	5,864	2,857
60047	Lake Zurich	(847)	18,104	14,927
60438	Lansing	(708)	28,332	28,131
61301	La Salle	(815)	9,796	9,717
60439	Lemont	(630)	13,098	7,359
*60048	Libertyville	(847)	20,742	19,174
62656	Lincoln	(217)	15,369	15,418
60069	Lincolnshire	(847)	6,108	4,928
60645	Lincolnwood	(847)	12,359	11,365
60046	Lindenhurst	(847)	12,539	8,044
60532	Lisle	(630)	21,182	19,584
62056	Litchfield	(217)	6,815	6,883
60441	Lockport	(815)	15,191	9,401
60148	Lombard	(630)	42,322	39,408
60047	Long Grove	(847)	6,735	4,747
*61130	Loves Park	(815)	20,044	15,457
60411	Lynwood	(708)	7,377	6,535
60534	Lyons (Cook)	(708)	10,255	9,828
*60050	McHenry	(815)	21,501	16,343
61115	Machesney Park	(815)	20,759	19,042
61455	Macomb	(309)	18,558	19,952
60950	Manteno	(815)	6,414	3,709
60152	Marengo	(815)	6,355	4,768
62959	Marion	(618)	16,035	14,597
60426	Markham (Cook)	(708)	12,620	13,136
62258	Mascoutah	(618)	5,659	5,511
60443	Matteson	(708)	12,928	11,378
61938	Mattoon	(217)	18,291	18,441
60153	Maywood	(708)	26,987	27,139
*60160	Melrose Park	(708)	23,171	20,859
61342	Mendota	(815)	7,272	7,017
62960	Metropolis	(618)	6,482	6,734
60445	Midlothian	(708)	14,315	14,372
61264	Milan	(309)	5,348	5,753
60448	Mokena	(708)	14,583	6,128
*61265	Moline	(309)	43,768	43,080
61462	Monmouth	(309)	9,841	9,489
60538	Montgomery	(630)	5,471	4,487
60450	Morris	(815)	11,928	10,274
61550	Morton	(309)	15,198	13,799
60053	Morton Grove	(847)	22,451	22,373
62863	Mount Carmel	(618)	7,982	8,287
60056	Mount Prospect	(847)	56,265	53,168
62864	Mount Vernon	(618)	16,269	17,082
60060	Mundelein	(847)	30,935	21,224
62966	Murphysboro	(618)	13,295	9,176
*60540	Naperville	(630)	128,358	85,806
60451	New Lenox	(815)	17,771	9,698
60714	Niles	(847)	30,068	28,375
61761	Normal	(309)	45,386	40,023
60634	Norridge	(708)	14,582	14,459
60542	North Aurora	(630)	10,585	6,010
*60062	Northbrook	(708)	33,435	32,565
60064	North Chicago	(847)	35,918	34,978
60093	Northfield	(847)	5,389	4,924
60164	Northlake	(708)	11,878	12,505
60546	North Riverside	(708)	6,688	6,180
60521	Oak Brook	(630)	8,702	9,087
60452	Oak Forest	(708)	28,051	26,202
*60303	Oak Lawn	(708)	55,245	56,182
*60303	Oak Park	(708)	52,524	53,648
62269	O'Fallon	(618)	21,910	16,064
62450	Olney	(618)	8,631	8,873
60477	Orland Hills	(708)	6,779	5,510
*60462	Orland Park	(708)	51,077	35,720
60543	Oswego	(630)	13,326	3,949
61350	Ottawa	(815)	18,307	17,574
*60067	Palatine	(847)	65,479	41,554
60463	Palos Heights	(708)	11,260	11,478
60465	Palos Hills	(708)	17,665	17,803
62557	Pana	(217)	5,614	5,796
61944	Paris	(217)	9,077	9,105
60085	Park City	(847)	6,637	4,677
60466	Park Forest	(708)	23,462	24,656
60068	Park Ridge	(847)	37,775	37,075
61554	Pekin	(309)	33,857	32,254
*61601	Peoria	(309)	112,936	113,508
61603	Peoria Heights	(309)	6,635	6,930
61354	Peru	(815)	9,835	9,302
62274	Pinckneyville	(618)	5,464	3,372
60544	Plainfield	(815)	13,038	4,557
60545	Plano	(630)	5,633	5,104
61764	Pontiac	(815)	11,864	11,428
62040	Pontoon Beach	(618)	5,620	4,013
61356	Princeton	(815)	7,501	7,197
60070	Prospect Heights	(847)	17,081	15,236
*62301	Quincy	(217)	40,366	39,682
61866	Rantoul	(217)	12,857	17,212
60471	Richton Park	(708)	12,533	10,523
60827	Riverdale	(708)	15,055	13,671
60305	River Forest	(708)	11,635	11,669
60171	River Grove	(708)	10,668	9,961
60546	Riverside	(708)	8,895	8,774
60472	Robbins	(708)	6,635	7,498
62454	Robinson	(618)	6,822	6,740
61068	Rochelle	(815)	9,424	8,769
61071	Rock Falls	(815)	9,580	9,669
*61125	Rockford	(815)	150,115	142,815
*61201	Rock Island	(309)	39,684	40,630
61072	Rockton	(815)	5,296	2,928
60008	Rolling Meadows	(847)	24,604	22,598
60446	Romeoville	(815)	21,153	14,101
61072	Roscoe	(815)	6,244	2,079
60172	Roselle	(630)	23,115	20,803
60073	Round Lake	(847)	5,842	3,550
60073	Round Lake Beach	(847)	25,859	16,406
60073	Round Lake Park	(847)	6,038	4,045
*60174	Saint Charles	(630)	27,896	22,636
62881	Salem	(618)	7,909	7,470
60548	Sandwich	(815)	6,509	5,607
60411	Sauk Village	(708)	10,411	10,734
*60194	Schaumburg	(847)	75,386	68,586
60176	Schiller Park	(847)	11,850	11,189
*62269	Shiloh	(618)	7,643	2,655
60436	Shorewood	(815)	7,686	6,264
61282	Silvis	(309)	7,269	6,926
*60077	Skokie	(847)	63,348	59,432
61080	South Beloit	(815)	5,397	4,072
60177	South Elgin	(847)	16,100	7,474
60473	South Holland	(708)	22,147	22,105
*62703	Springfield	(217)	111,454	105,412
61362	Spring Valley	(815)	5,398	5,246
62088	Staunton	(618)	5,030	4,806
60475	Steger	(708)	9,682	9,251
61081	Sterling	(815)	15,451	15,142
60402	Stickney	(708)	6,148	5,678
60165	Stone Park	(708)	5,127	4,383
60107	Streamwood	(630)	36,407	31,197
61364	Streator	(815)	14,190	14,121
60501	Summit	(708)	10,637	9,971
62221	Swansea	(618)	10,579	8,201
60178	Sycamore	(815)	12,020	9,896
62568	Taylorville	(217)	11,427	11,133
60477	Tinley Park	(708)	48,401	37,115
62294	Troy	(618)	8,524	6,194
60466	University Park	(708)	6,662	6,204
*61801	Urbana	(217)	36,395	36,383
62471	Vandalia	(618)	6,975	6,114
60061	Vernon Hills	(847)	20,120	15,319
60181	Villa Park	(630)	22,075	22,279
60555	Warrenville	(630)	13,363	11,389
61571	Washington	(309)	10,841	10,136
62204	Washington Park	(618)	5,345	7,431
62298	Waterloo	(618)	7,614	5,030
60970	Watseka	(815)	5,670	5,424
60084	Wauconda	(847)	9,448	6,294
*60085	Waukegan	(847)	87,901	69,481
60154	Westchester	(708)	16,824	17,301
*60185	West Chicago	(630)	23,469	14,808
60118	West Dundee	(847)	5,428	3,728
60558	Western Springs	(708)	12,493	11,956
62896	West Frankfort	(618)	8,196	8,526
60559	Westmont	(630)	24,554	21,402
*60187	Wheaton	(630)	55,416	51,441
60090	Wheeling	(847)	34,496	29,911
60514	Willowbrook	(630)	8,967	8,651
60480	Willow Springs	(708)	5,027	4,509
60091	Wilmette	(847)	27,651	26,694
60481	Wilmington	(815)	5,134	4,743
60190	Winfield	(630)	8,718	7,096
60093	Winnetka	(847)	12,419	12,210
60096	Winthrop Harbor	(847)	6,670	6,240
60097	Wonder Lake (c)	(815)	7,463	6,664
60191	Wood Dale	(630)	13,535	12,394
60517	Woodridge	(630)	30,934	26,359
62095	Wood River	(618)	11,296	11,490
60098	Woodstock	(815)	20,151	14,368
60482	Worth	(708)	11,047	11,208
60560	Yorkville	(630)	6,189	3,974
60099	Zion	(847)	22,866	19,783

Indiana

ZIP	Place	Area Code	2000	1990
46001	Alexandria	(765)	6,260	5,709
*46011	Anderson	(765)	59,734	59,518
46703	Angola	(260)	7,344	5,851
46706	Auburn	(260)	12,074	9,386
46123	Avon	(317)	6,248	—
47006	Batesville	(812)	6,033	4,720
47421	Bedford	(812)	13,768	13,817
46107	Beech Grove	(317)	14,880	13,383
*47408	Bloomington	(812)	69,291	62,735
46714	Bluffton	(260)	9,536	9,104
47601	Boonville	(812)	6,834	6,686
47834	Brazil	(812)	8,188	7,640
47025	Bright (c)	(812)	5,405	3,945
46112	Brownsburg	(317)	14,520	7,751
*46032	Carmel	(317)	37,733	25,380
46303	Cedar Lake	(219)	9,279	8,885
47111	Charlestown	(812)	5,993	5,889
46304	Chesterton	(219)	10,488	9,118
47129	Clarksville (Clark)	(812)	21,400	19,838
47842	Clinton	(765)	5,126	5,040
46725	Columbia City	(260)	7,077	5,883
*47201	Columbus	(812)	39,059	33,948
47331	Connersville	(765)	15,411	15,550
47933	Crawfordsville	(765)	15,243	13,584
46307	Crown Point	(219)	19,806	17,728
46229	Cumberland	(317)	5,500	4,557
46122	Danville	(317)	6,418	4,345
46733	Decatur	(260)	9,528	8,642
46514	Dunlap (c)	(574)	5,887	5,705
46311	Dyer	(219)	13,895	10,923
46312	East Chicago	(219)	32,414	33,892
*46515	Elkhart	(574)	51,874	44,661
47429	Ellettsville	(812)	5,078	3,275
46036	Elwood	(765)	9,737	9,494
*47708	Evansville	(812)	121,582	126,272
46038	Fishers	(317)	37,835	7,189
*46802	Fort Wayne	(260)	205,727	195,680
46041	Frankfort	(765)	16,662	14,754
46131	Franklin	(317)	19,463	12,932
46738	Garrett	(260)	5,803	5,349
*46401	Gary	(219)	102,746	116,646
46933	Gas City	(765)	5,940	6,311
*46526	Goshen	(574)	29,383	23,794
46530	Granger (c)	(574)	28,284	20,241
46135	Greencastle	(765)	9,880	8,984
46140	Greenfield	(317)	14,600	11,657
47240	Greensburg	(812)	10,260	9,286
*46142	Greenwood	(317)	36,037	26,507
46319	Griffith	(219)	17,334	17,914
*46320	Hammond	(219)	83,048	84,236
47348	Hartford City	(765)	6,928	6,960
46322	Highland	(219)	23,546	23,696
46342	Hobart	(219)	25,363	24,440
47542	Huntingburg	(812)	5,598	5,236
46750	Huntington	(260)	17,450	16,389
*46206	Indianapolis	(317)	791,926	731,278
*47546	Jasper	(812)	12,100	10,030
*47130	Jeffersonville	(812)	27,362	24,016
46755	Kendallville	(260)	9,616	7,984
*46902	Kokomo	(765)	46,113	44,996
*47901	Lafayette	(765)	56,397	45,933
—	Lakes of the Four Seasons (c)	(219)	7,291	6,556
46405	Lake Station	(219)	13,948	13,899
*46350	La Porte	(219)	21,621	21,507
46226	Lawrence	(317)	38,915	26,849
46052	Lebanon	(765)	14,222	12,059
47441	Linton	(812)	5,774	5,814
46947	Logansport	(574)	19,684	16,865
46356	Lowell	(219)	7,505	6,430
47250	Madison	(812)	12,004	12,006
*46952	Marion	(765)	31,320	32,607
46151	Martinsville	(765)	11,698	11,677
*46401	Merrillville	(219)	30,560	27,257
*46360	Michigan City	(219)	32,900	33,822
*46544	Mishawaka	(574)	46,557	42,635
47960	Monticello	(574)	5,723	5,237
46158	Mooresville	(317)	9,273	5,779
47620	Mount Vernon	(812)	7,478	7,217
*47302	Muncie	(765)	67,430	71,170
46321	Munster	(219)	21,511	19,949
46550	Nappanee	(574)	6,710	5,474
*47150	New Albany	(812)	37,603	36,322
47362	New Castle	(765)	17,780	17,753
46774	New Haven	(260)	12,406	11,234
*46060	Noblesville	(317)	28,590	17,655
46962	North Manchester	(260)	6,260	6,383
47265	North Vernon	(812)	6,515	5,129
47130	Oak Park (c)	(812)	5,379	5,630
46970	Peru	(765)	12,994	12,843
46168	Plainfield	(317)	18,396	14,953
46563	Plymouth	(574)	9,840	8,291
46368	Portage	(219)	33,496	29,062
47371	Portland	(260)	6,437	6,483
47670	Princeton	(812)	8,175	8,127
47978	Rensselaer	(219)	5,294	5,045
*47374	Richmond	(765)	39,124	38,705
46975	Rochester	(574)	6,414	5,969
46173	Rushville	(765)	5,995	5,533
46373	Saint John	(219)	8,382	4,921
47167	Salem	(812)	6,172	5,619
46375	Schererville	(219)	24,851	20,155
47170	Scottsburg	(812)	6,040	5,334
47172	Sellersburg	(812)	6,071	5,936
47274	Seymour	(812)	18,101	15,605
46176	Shelbyville	(765)	17,951	15,347
*46624	South Bend	(574)	107,789	105,511
46383	South Haven (c)	(219)	5,619	6,112
46224	Speedway	(317)	12,881	13,092
47586	Tell City	(812)	7,845	8,088
*47808	Terre Haute	(812)	59,614	57,475
46072	Tipton	(765)	5,251	4,751
*46383	Valparaiso	(219)	27,428	24,414
47591	Vincennes	(812)	18,701	19,867
46992	Wabash	(260)	11,743	12,127
*46580	Warsaw	(574)	12,415	10,968
47501	Washington	(812)	11,380	10,864
46074	Westfield	(317)	9,293	3,304
*46580	West Lafayette	(765)	28,778	26,144
46394	Whiting	(219)	5,137	5,155
47394	Winchester	(765)	5,037	5,095
46077	Zionsville	(317)	8,775	6,207

Iowa

ZIP	Place	Area Code	2000	1990
50511	Algona	(515)	5,741	6,015
50009	Altoona	(515)	10,345	7,242
*50010	Ames	(515)	50,731	47,198
52205	Anamosa	(319)	5,494	5,100
50021	Ankeny	(515)	27,117	18,482
50022	Atlantic	(712)	7,257	7,432
52722	Bettendorf	(563)	31,275	28,139
*50036	Boone	(515)	12,803	12,392
52601	Burlington	(319)	26,839	27,208
51401	Carroll	(712)	10,106	9,579
50613	Cedar Falls	(319)	36,145	34,298
*52401	Cedar Rapids	(319)	120,758	108,772
52544	Centerville	(641)	5,924	5,936
50616	Charles City	(641)	7,812	7,878
51012	Cherokee	(712)	5,369	6,026
51632	Clarinda	(712)	5,690	5,104
50428	Clear Lake	(641)	8,161	8,183
*52732	Clinton	(563)	27,772	29,201
50325	Clive	(515)	12,855	7,446
52241	Coralville	(319)	15,123	10,347
*51501	Council Bluffs	(712)	58,268	54,315
50801	Creston	(641)	7,597	7,911
*52802	Davenport	(563)	98,359	95,333
52101	Decorah	(563)	8,172	8,063
51442	Denison	(712)	7,339	6,604
*50318	Des Moines	(515)	198,682	193,189
*50274	De Witt	(563)	5,049	4,514
*52001	Dubuque	(563)	57,686	57,538
51334	Estherville	(712)	6,656	6,720
52556	Fairfield	(641)	9,509	9,955
50501	Fort Dodge	(515)	25,136	26,057
52627	Fort Madison	(319)	10,715	11,614
51534	Glenwood	(712)	5,358	4,960
50111	Grimes	(515)	5,098	2,653
50112	Grinnell	(641)	9,105	8,902
*51537	Harlan	(712)	5,282	5,148
52233	Hiawatha	(319)	6,480	5,354
50644	Independence	(319)	6,014	5,972
50125	Indianola	(515)	12,998	11,340
*52240	Iowa City	(319)	62,220	59,735
50126	Iowa Falls	(641)	5,193	5,435
50131	Johnston	(515)	8,649	4,702
52632	Keokuk	(319)	11,427	12,451
50138	Knoxville	(641)	7,731	8,232
51031	Le Mars	(712)	9,237	8,454
52057	Manchester	(563)	5,257	5,137
52060	Maquoketa	(563)	6,112	6,130
52302	Marion	(319)	26,294	20,422
50158	Marshalltown	(641)	26,009	25,178
*50401	Mason City	(641)	29,172	29,040
52641	Mount Pleasant	(319)	8,751	7,959
52761	Muscatine	(563)	22,697	22,881
50201	Nevada	(515)	6,658	6,009
50208	Newton	(641)	15,579	14,799
52317	North Liberty	(319)	5,367	2,926
50211	Norwalk	(515)	6,884	5,726
50662	Oelwein	(319)	6,692	6,691
51041	Orange City	(712)	5,582	4,940
52577	Oskaloosa	(641)	10,938	10,600
52501	Ottumwa	(641)	24,998	24,488
50219	Pella	(641)	9,832	9,270
50220	Perry	(515)	7,633	6,652
*50317	Pleasant Hill	(515)	5,070	3,671
*51566	Red Oak	(712)	6,197	6,264
51601	Shenandoah	(712)	5,546	5,572
51250	Sioux Center	(712)	6,002	5,074
*51101	Sioux City	(712)	85,013	80,505
51301	Spencer	(712)	11,317	11,066
50588	Storm Lake	(712)	10,076	8,769
*50318	Urbandale	(515)	29,072	23,775
52349	Vinton	(319)	5,102	5,103
52353	Washington	(319)	7,047	7,074
*50701	Waterloo	(319)	68,747	66,467
50263	Waukee	(515)	5,126	2,512

ZIP	Place	Area Code	2000	1990
50677	Waverly	(319)	8,968	8,539
50595	Webster City	(515)	8,176	7,894
*50265	West Des Moines	(515)	46,403	31,702

Kansas

ZIP	Place	Area Code	2000	1990
67410	Abilene	(785)	6,543	6,242
67002	Andover	(316)	6,698	4,204
67005	Arkansas City	(620)	11,963	12,762
66002	Atchison	(913)	10,232	10,656
67010	Augusta	(316)	8,423	7,848
66952	Bel Aire	(316)	5,836	3,695
66012	Bonner Springs	(913)	6,768	6,413
66720	Chanute	(620)	9,411	9,488
67337	Coffeyville	(620)	11,021	12,917
67701	Colby	(785)	5,450	5,510
66901	Concordia	(785)	5,714	6,152
67037	Derby	(316)	17,807	14,691
67801	Dodge City	(620)	25,176	21,129
67042	El Dorado	(316)	12,057	11,495
66801	Emporia	(620)	26,760	25,512
66442	Fort Riley North (c)	(785)	8,114	12,848
66701	Fort Scott	(620)	8,297	8,362
67846	Garden City	(620)	28,451	24,097
66030	Gardner	(913)	9,396	4,277
67530	Great Bend	(620)	15,345	15,427
67601	Hays	(785)	20,013	18,632
67060	Haysville	(316)	8,502	8,364
*67501	Hutchinson	(620)	40,787	39,308
67301	Independence	(620)	9,846	10,030
66749	Iola	(620)	6,302	6,351
66441	Junction City	(785)	18,886	20,642
*66102	Kansas City	(913)	146,866	151,521
66043	Lansing	(913)	9,199	7,120
*66044	Lawrence	(785)	80,098	65,608
66048	Leavenworth	(913)	35,420	38,495
66209	Leawood	(913)	27,656	19,693
66214	Lenexa	(913)	40,238	34,110
*67901	Liberal	(620)	19,666	16,573
67460	McPherson	(620)	13,770	12,422
*66502	Manhattan	(785)	44,831	43,081
66202	Merriam	(913)	11,008	11,819
66203	Mission	(913)	9,727	9,504
67110	Mulvane	(316)	5,155	4,683
67114	Newton	(316)	17,190	16,700
*66061	Olathe	(913)	92,962	63,402
66067	Ottawa	(785)	11,921	10,667
66204	Overland Park	(913)	149,080	111,790
66071	Paola	(913)	5,011	4,698
67219	Park City	(316)	5,814	5,081
67357	Parsons	(620)	11,514	11,919
66762	Pittsburg	(620)	19,243	17,789
66208	Prairie Village	(913)	22,072	23,186
67124	Pratt	(620)	6,570	6,687
66205	Roeland Park	(913)	6,817	7,706
*67401	Salina	(785)	45,679	42,299
66203	Shawnee	(913)	47,996	37,962
*66601	Topeka	(785)	122,377	119,883
67880	Ulysses	(620)	5,960	5,474
67152	Wellington	(620)	8,647	8,517
*67202	Wichita	(316)	344,284	304,017
67156	Winfield	(620)	12,206	11,931

Kentucky

ZIP	Place	Area Code	2000	1990
41001	Alexandria	(859)	8,286	5,592
*41101	Ashland	(606)	21,981	23,622
40004	Bardstown	(502)	10,374	6,712
41073	Bellevue	(859)	6,480	6,997
40403	Berea	(859)	9,851	9,129
*42101	Bowling Green	(270)	49,296	41,688
40261	Buechel (c)	(502)	7,272	7,081
41005	Burlington (c)	(859)	10,779	6,070
*42718	Campbellsville	(270)	10,498	9,592
42330	Central City	(270)	5,893	4,979
*40701	Corbin	(606)	7,742	7,644
*41011	Covington	(859)	43,370	43,646
41031	Cynthiana	(859)	6,258	6,497
*40422	Danville	(859)	15,477	14,454
41074	Dayton	(859)	5,966	6,576
40243	Douglass Hills	(502)	5,718	5,431
41017	Edgewood	(859)	9,400	8,143
*42701	Elizabethtown	(270)	22,542	18,167
41018	Elsmere	(859)	8,139	6,847
41018	Erlanger	(859)	16,676	15,979
40118	Fairdale (c)	(502)	7,658	6,563
40291	Fern Creek (c)	(502)	17,870	16,406
41139	Flatwoods	(606)	7,605	7,799
*41042	Florence	(859)	23,551	18,586
42223	Fort Campbell North (c)	(270)	14,338	18,861
40121	Fort Knox (c)	(270)	12,377	21,495
41017	Fort Mitchell	(859)	8,089	7,438
41075	Fort Thomas	(859)	16,495	16,032
41011	Fort Wright	(859)	5,681	6,404
*40601	Frankfort	(502)	27,741	26,535
*42134	Franklin	(270)	7,996	7,607
40324	Georgetown	(502)	18,080	11,414
*42141	Glasgow	(270)	13,019	12,777
40330	Harrodsburg	(859)	8,014	7,335
*42420	Henderson	(270)	27,373	25,945
41076	Highland Heights	(859)	6,554	4,223
40228	Highview (c)	(502)	15,161	14,814
40229	Hillview	(502)	7,037	6,119
*42240	Hopkinsville	(270)	30,089	29,809
41051	Independence	(859)	14,982	10,444
40269	Jeffersontown	(502)	26,633	23,223
40031	La Grange	(502)	5,676	3,901
40342	Lawrenceburg	(502)	9,014	5,911
40033	Lebanon	(270)	5,718	5,695
*42754	Leitchfield	(270)	6,139	4,965
*40507	Lexington	(859)	260,512	225,366
40741	London	(606)	5,692	5,757
40232	Louisville	(502)	256,231	269,555
40252	Lyndon	(502)	9,369	8,037
42431	Madisonville	(270)	19,307	18,693
42066	Mayfield	(270)	10,349	9,935
41056	Maysville	(606)	8,993	8,113
40965	Middlesborough	(606)	10,384	11,328
40253	Middletown	(502)	5,744	5,016
42633	Monticello	(606)	5,981	5,357
40351	Morehead	(606)	5,914	8,357
40353	Mount Sterling	(859)	5,876	5,362
40047	Mount Washington	(502)	8,485	5,256
42071	Murray	(270)	14,950	14,442
40218	Newburg (c)	(502)	20,636	21,647
*41071	Newport	(859)	17,048	18,871
*40356	Nicholasville	(859)	19,680	13,603
—	Oakbrook (c)		7,726	4,113
42262	Oak Grove	(502)	7,064	2,863
40259	Okolona (c)	(502)	17,807	18,902
*42301	Owensboro	(270)	54,067	53,577
*42003	Paducah	(270)	26,307	27,256
*40361	Paris	(859)	9,183	8,730
*41501	Pikeville	(606)	6,295	6,324
40268	Pleasure Ridge Park (c)	(502)	25,776	25,131
42445	Princeton	(270)	6,536	6,940
*40160	Radcliff	(502)	21,961	19,778
*40475	Richmond	(859)	27,152	21,183
42276	Russellville	(270)	7,149	7,454
40216	Saint Dennis (c)	(502)	9,177	10,326
*40206	Saint Matthews	(502)	15,852	15,691
*40066	Shelbyville	(502)	10,085	6,155
40165	Shepherdsville	(502)	8,334	4,805
40256	Shively	(502)	15,157	15,535
*42501	Somerset	(606)	11,352	10,735
41015	Taylor Mill	(859)	6,913	5,530
40272	Valley Station (c)	(502)	22,946	22,840
40383	Versailles	(859)	7,511	7,269
41016	Villa Hills	(859)	7,948	7,370
40769	Williamsburg	(606)	5,143	5,493
40390	Wilmore	(859)	5,905	4,215
*40391	Winchester	(859)	16,724	15,799

Louisiana

ZIP	Place	Area Code	2000	1990
*70510	Abbeville	(337)	11,887	11,769
*71301	Alexandria	(318)	46,342	49,049
70032	Arabi (c)	(504)	8,093	8,787
70094	Avondale (c)	(504)	5,441	5,813
*70714	Baker	(225)	13,793	13,087
*71220	Bastrop	(318)	12,988	13,916
*70821	Baton Rouge	(225)	227,818	219,531
70360	Bayou Cane (c)	(985)	17,046	15,876
70037	Belle Chasse (c)	(504)	9,848	8,512
*70427	Bogalusa	(985)	13,365	14,280
*71111	Bossier City	(318)	56,461	52,721
70517	Breaux Bridge	(337)	7,281	6,694
70094	Bridge City (c)	(504)	8,323	8,327
70518	Broussard	(337)	5,874	3,213
70811	Brownfields (c)	(225)	5,222	5,229
71291	Brownsville-Bawcomville (c)	(318)	7,616	7,397
70520	Carencro	(337)	6,120	5,518
*70043	Chalmette (c)	(504)	32,069	31,860
71291	Claiborne (c)	(318)	9,830	8,300
*70433	Covington	(985)	8,483	7,691
*70526	Crowley	(337)	14,225	13,983
70345	Cut Off (c)	(985)	5,635	5,325
*70726	Denham Springs	(225)	8,757	8,381
70634	De Ridder	(337)	9,808	10,475
70047	Destrehan (c)	(985)	11,260	8,031
70346	Donaldsonville	(225)	7,605	7,949
—	Eden Isle (c)		6,261	3,768
70072	Estelle (c)	(504)	15,880	14,091
70535	Eunice	(337)	11,499	11,162
71459	Fort Polk South (c)	(337)	11,000	10,911
70538	Franklin	(337)	8,354	9,004
70354	Galliano (c)	(985)	7,356	4,294
70820	Gardere (c)	(225)	8,992	7,209
*70737	Gonzales	(225)	8,156	7,208
*70053	Gretna	(504)	17,423	17,208
*70401	Hammond	(985)	17,639	15,871
70123	Harahan	(504)	9,885	9,927

ZIP	Place	Area Code	2000	1990
*70058	Harvey (c)	(504)	22,226	21,222
*70360	Houma	(985)	32,393	30,495
70544	Jeanerette	(337)	5,997	6,205
70502	Jefferson (c)	(504)	11,843	14,521
70546	Jennings	(337)	10,986	11,305
70548	Kaplan	(337)	5,177	4,535
*70062	Kenner	(504)	70,517	72,033
70445	Lacombe (c)	(985)	7,518	6,523
*70501	Lafayette	(337)	110,257	101,865
*70601	Lake Charles	(337)	71,757	70,580
71254	Lake Providence	(318)	5,104	5,380
*70068	Laplace (c)	(985)	27,684	24,194
70373	Larose (c)	(985)	7,306	5,772
*71446	Leesville	(337)	6,753	7,638
70070	Luling (c)	(985)	11,512	2,803
*70471	Mandeville	(985)	10,489	7,474
71052	Mansfield	(318)	5,582	5,389
71351	Marksville	(318)	5,537	5,526
*70072	Marrero (c)	(504)	36,165	36,671
70075	Meraux (c)	(504)	10,192	8,849
70812	Merrydale (c)	(225)	10,427	10,395
*70009	Metairie (c)	(504)	146,136	149,428
*71055	Minden	(318)	13,027	13,661
*71207	Monroe	(318)	53,107	54,909
*70380	Morgan City	(985)	12,703	14,531
70612	Moss Bluff (c)	(337)	10,535	8,039
*71457	Natchitoches	(318)	17,865	16,609
*70560	New Iberia	(337)	32,623	31,828
*70140	New Orleans	(504)	484,674	496,938
71463	Oakdale	(318)	8,137	6,837
70808	Oak Hills Place (c)	(225)	7,996	5,479
—	Old Jefferson (c)		5,631	4,531
*70570	Opelousas	(337)	22,860	19,091
70392	Patterson	(985)	5,130	5,166
*71360	Pineville	(318)	13,829	15,308
*70764	Plaquemine	(225)	7,064	7,101
70454	Ponchatoula	(985)	5,180	5,499
70767	Port Allen	(225)	5,278	6,277
70601	Prien (c)	(337)	7,215	6,448
70394	Raceland (c)	(985)	10,224	5,564
70578	Rayne	(337)	8,552	8,502
71037	Red Chute (c)	(318)	5,984	5,431
70084	Reserve (c)	(985)	9,111	8,847
70123	River Ridge (c)	(504)	14,588	14,800
*71270	Ruston	(318)	20,546	20,071
70582	Saint Martinville	(337)	6,989	7,137
70087	Saint Rose (c)	(504)	6,540	6,259
70395	Schriever (c)	(985)	5,880	4,958
70583	Scott	(337)	7,870	4,912
70817	Shenandoah (c)		17,070	13,429
*71102	Shreveport	(318)	200,145	198,518
*70458	Slidell	(985)	25,695	24,124
71075	Springhill	(318)	5,439	5,668
*70663	Sulphur	(337)	20,512	20,125
*71282	Tallulah	(318)	9,189	8,526
70056	Terrytown (c)	(504)	25,430	23,787
*70301	Thibodaux	(985)	14,431	14,125
70053	Timberlane (c)	(504)	11,405	12,614
70809	Village Saint George (c)	(225)	6,993	6,242
70586	Ville Platte	(337)	8,145	9,037
70092	Violet (c)	(504)	8,555	8,574
70094	Waggaman (c)	(504)	9,435	9,405
*71291	West Monroe	(318)	13,250	14,096
*70094	Westwego	(504)	10,763	11,218
71483	Winnfield	(318)	5,749	6,138
71295	Winnsboro	(318)	5,344	5,755
—	Woodmere (c)		13,058	—
70791	Zachary	(225)	11,275	9,036

Maine (207)

See introductory note.

ZIP	Place	2000	1990
*04210	Auburn	23,203	24,309
*04330	Augusta	18,560	21,325
*04401	Bangor	31,473	33,181
04530	Bath	9,266	9,799
04915	Belfast	6,381	6,355
03901	*Berwick*	6,353	5,995
*04005	Biddeford	20,942	20,710
04412	Brewer	8,987	9,021
04011	Brunswick (c)	14,816	14,683
04011	*Brunswick*	21,172	20,906
04093	*Buxton*	7,452	6,494
04843	*Camden*	5,254	5,060
04107	*Cape Elizabeth*	9,068	8,854
04736	Caribou	8,312	9,415
04021	*Cumberland*	7,159	5,836
03903	*Eliot*	5,954	5,329
04605	Ellsworth	6,456	5,975
04937	*Fairfield*	6,573	6,718
04105	*Falmouth*	10,310	7,610
04938	*Farmington*	7,410	7,436
04032	*Freeport*	7,800	6,905
04345	Gardiner	6,198	6,746
04038	*Gorham*	14,141	11,856
04039	*Gray*	6,820	5,904
04444	*Hampden*	6,327	5,974
04079	*Harpswell*	5,239	5,012
04730	Houlton (c)	5,270	5,627
04730	*Houlton*	6,476	6,613
04043	*Kennebunk*	10,476	8,004
03904	*Kittery*	9,543	9,372
04027	*Lebanon*	5,083	—
*04240	Lewiston	35,690	39,757
04457	*Lincoln*	5,221	5,587
04250	*Lisbon*	9,077	9,457
04462	*Millinocket*	5,203	6,956
04462	Millinocket (c)	5,190	6,922
04963	*Oakland*	5,959	5,595
04064	*Old Orchard Beach*	8,856	7,789
04064	Old Orchard Beach (c)	8,856	7,789
04468	Old Town	8,130	8,317
04473	*Orono*	9,112	10,573
04473	Orono (c)	8,253	9,789
*04101	Portland	64,249	64,157
04769	Presque Isle	9,511	10,550
04841	Rockland	7,609	7,972
04276	*Rumford*	6,472	7,078
04072	Saco	16,822	15,181
04073	Sanford (c)	10,133	10,296
04073	*Sanford*	20,806	20,463
*04074	*Scarborough*	16,970	12,518
04976	Skowhegan (c)	6,696	6,990
04976	*Skowhegan*	8,824	8,725
03908	*South Berwick*	6,671	5,877
*04101	South Portland	23,324	23,163
04084	*Standish*	9,285	7,678
04086	Topsham (c)	6,271	6,147
04086	*Topsham*	9,100	8,746
04087	*Waterboro*	6,214	4,510
*04901	Waterville	15,605	17,173
04090	*Wells*	9,400	7,778
*04092	Westbrook	16,142	16,121
04062	*Windham*	14,904	13,020
04901	Winslow (c)	7,743	5,436
04901	*Winslow*	7,743	7,997
04364	*Winthrop*	6,232	5,968
04096	*Yarmouth*	8,360	7,862
03909	*York*	12,854	9,818

Maryland

Area code (240) overlays area code (301). Area code (443) overlays (410). See introductory note.

ZIP	Place	Area Code	2000	1990
21001	Aberdeen	(410)	13,842	13,087
20607	Accokeek (c)	(301)	7,349	4,477
20783	Adelphi (c)	(301)	14,998	13,524
20762	Andrews AFB (c)	(410)	7,925	10,228
*21401	Annapolis	(410)	35,838	33,195
21227	Arbutus (c)	(410)	20,116	19,750
21012	Arnold (c)	(410)	23,422	20,261
20916	Aspen Hill (c)	(301)	50,228	45,494
21220	Ballenger Creek (c)	(410)	13,518	5,546
*21203	Baltimore	(410)	651,154	736,014
*21014	Bel Air	(410)	10,080	8,942
21050	Bel Air North (c)	(410)	25,798	14,880
21014	Bel Air South (c)	(410)	39,711	26,421
*20705	Beltsville (c)	(301)	15,690	14,476
—	Bennsville (c)		7,325	—
*20814	Bethesda (c)	(301)	55,277	62,936
20710	Bladensburg	(301)	7,661	8,064
*20715	Bowie	(301)	50,269	37,642
21220	Bowleys Quarters (c)	(410)	6,314	5,595
21225	Brooklyn Park (c)	(410)	10,938	10,987
20866	Burtonsville (c)	(301)	7,305	5,853
20619	California (c)	(410)	9,307	7,626
20705	Calverton (c)	(301)	12,610	12,046
21613	Cambridge	(410)	10,911	11,514
20748	Camp Springs (c)	(301)	17,968	16,392
21401	Cape St. Clair (c)	(410)	8,022	7,878
21234	Carney (c)	(410)	28,264	25,578
21228	Catonsville (c)	(410)	39,820	35,233
20657	Chesapeake Ranch Estates-Drum Point (c)	(301)	11,503	5,423
20784	Cheverly	(301)	6,433	6,023
*20814	Chevy Chase (c)	(301)	9,381	8,559
20783	Chillum (c)	(301)	34,252	31,309
20735	Clinton (c)	(301)	26,064	19,987
20904	Cloverly (c)	(301)	7,835	7,904
21030	Cockeysville (c)	(410)	19,388	18,668
20914	Colesville (c)	(301)	19,810	18,819
*20740	College Park	(301)	24,657	23,714
*21045	Columbia (c)	(410)/(301)	88,254	75,883
20743	Coral Hills (c)	(410)	10,720	11,032
—	Cresaptown-Bel Air (c)		5,884	4,586
21114	Crofton (c)	(410)	20,091	12,781
*21502	Cumberland	(301)	21,518	23,712
20872	Damascus (c)	(301)	11,430	9,817
*20874	Darnestown (c)	(301)	6,378	—

ZIP	Place	Area Code	2000	1990
*20747	District Heights	(301)	5,958	6,711
21222	Dundalk (c)	(410)	62,306	65,800
21601	Easton	(410)	11,708	9,372
20737	East Riverdale (c)	(301)	14,961	14,187
21219	Edgemere (c)	(410)	9,248	9,226
21040	Edgewood (c)	(410)	23,378	23,903
21784	Eldersburg (c)	(410)	27,741	9,720
21227	Elkridge (c)	(410)	22,042	12,953
*21921	Elkton	(410)	11,893	9,073
*21043	Ellicott City*	(410)	56,397	41,396
21221	Essex (c)	(410)	39,078	40,872
20904	Fairland (c)	(301)	21,738	19,828
21047	Fallston (c)	(410)	8,427	5,730
21061	Ferndale (c)	(410)	16,056	16,355
—	Forest Glen (c)		7,344	—
20747	Forestville (c)	(301)	12,707	16,731
20755	Fort Meade (c)	(301)	9,882	12,509
*20744	Fort Washington (c)	(301)	23,845	24,032
*21701	Frederick	(301)	52,767	40,186
20744	Friendly (c)	(301)	10,938	9,028
21532	Frostburg	(301)	7,873	8,069
*20877	Gaithersburg	(301)	52,613	39,676
21055	Garrison (c)	(410)	7,969	5,045
*20874	Germantown (c)	(301)	55,419	41,145
20706	Glenarden	(301)	6,318	5,025
*21061	Glen Burnie (c)	(410)	38,922	37,305
20769	Glenn Dale (c)	(301)	12,609	9,689
—	Goddard (c)		5,554	4,576
—	Greater Landover (c)		22,900	—
20772	Greater Upper Marlboro (c)		18,720	11,528
*20770	Greenbelt	(301)	21,456	20,561
21122	Green Haven (c)	(410)	17,415	14,416
21771	Green Valley (c)	(301)	12,262	9,424
*21740	Hagerstown	(301)	36,687	35,306
21740	Halfway (c)	(301)	10,065	8,873
21074	Hampstead	(410)	5,060	2,608
21211	Hampton (c)		5,004	4,926
21078	Havre de Grace	(410)	11,331	8,952
20748	Hillcrest Heights (c)	(301)	16,359	17,136
*20780	Hyattsville	(301)	14,733	13,864
20794	Jessup (c)	(410)	7,865	6,537
21085	Joppatowne (c)	(410)	11,391	11,084
—	Kemp Mill (c)		9,956	—
20772	Kettering (c)	(301)	11,008	9,901
—	Lake Arbor (c)		8,533	—
21122	Lake Shore (c)	(410)	13,065	13,269
20787	Langley Park (c)	(301)	16,214	17,474
20706	Lanham-Seabrook (c)	(301)	18,190	16,792
21227	Lansdowne-Baltimore Highlands (c)		15,724	15,509
20646	La Plata	(301)	6,551	5,841
20772	Largo (c)	(301)	8,408	9,475
*20707	Laurel	(301)	19,960	19,086
20653	Lexington Park (c)	(410)	11,021	9,943
—	Linganore-Bartonsville (c)		12,529	4,079
21090	Linthicum (c)	(410)	7,539	7,547
21207	Lochearn (c)	(410)	25,269	25,240
21037	Londontowne (c)	(410)	7,595	6,992
*21093	Lutherville-Timonium (c)	(410)	15,814	16,442
20748	Marlow Heights (c)	(301)	6,059	5,885
20772	Marlton (c)	(301)	7,798	5,523
20707	Maryland City (c)	(301)	6,814	6,813
21093	Mays Chapel (c)	(410)	11,427	10,132
21220	Middle River (c)	(410)	23,958	24,616
21207	Milford Mill (c)	(410)	26,527	22,547
20717	Mitchellville (c)	(301)	9,611	12,593
20886	Montgomery Village (c)	(301)	38,051	32,315
21771	Mount Airy	(301)/(410)	6,425	3,730
20712	Mount Rainier	(301)	8,498	7,954
20784	New Carrollton	(301)	12,589	12,002
20815	North Bethesda (c)	(301)	38,610	29,656
20895	North Kensington (c)	(301)	8,940	8,607
20707	North Laurel (c)	(301)	20,468	15,008
20878	North Potomac (c)	(301)	23,044	18,456
*21842	Ocean City	(410)	7,173	5,146
21811	Ocean Pines (c)	(410)	10,496	4,251
21113	Odenton (c)	(410)	20,534	12,833
*20832	Olney (c)	(301)	31,438	23,019
21206	Overlea (c)	(410)	12,148	12,137
21117	Owings Mills (c)	(410)	20,193	9,474
*20750	Oxon Hill-Glassmanor (c)	(301)	35,355	35,794
21234	Parkville (c)	(410)	31,118	31,617
21401	Parole (c)	(410)	14,031	10,054
*21122	Pasadena (c)	(410)	12,093	10,012
21128	Perry Hall (c)	(410)	28,705	22,723
21282	Pikesville (c)	(410)	29,123	24,815
20837	Poolesville	(301)	5,151	3,796
*20850	Potomac (c)	(301)	44,822	45,634
21227	Pumphrey (c)	(410)	5,317	5,483
21133	Randallstown (c)	(301)	30,870	26,277
—	Redland (c)	(301)	16,998	16,145
21136	Reisterstown (c)	(410)	22,438	19,314
*20737	Riverdale Park	(301)	6,690	4,843
21017	Riverside (c)		6,128	—
21122	Riviera Beach (c)	(410)	12,695	11,376
*20850	Rockville	(301)	47,388	44,830
20772	Rosaryville (c)	(301)	12,322	8,976
21237	Rosedale (c)	(410)	19,199	18,703
—	Rossmoor (c)		7,569	6,182
21221	Rossville (c)	(410)	11,515	9,492
20602	Saint Charles (c)	(301)	33,379	28,717
*21801	Salisbury	(410)	23,743	20,592
20763	Savage-Guilford (c)	(410)	12,918	9,669
21144	Severn (c)	(410)	35,076	24,499
21146	Severna Park (c)	(410)	28,507	25,879
20764	Shady Side (c)	(301)	5,559	4,107
*20907	Silver Spring (c)	(301)	76,540	76,046
21061	South Gate (c)	(410)	28,672	27,564
20895	South Kensington (c)	(301)	7,887	8,777
20707	South Laurel (c)	(301)	20,479	18,591
21666	Stevensville (c)	(410)	5,880	1,862
*20752	Suitland-Silver Hills (c)	(301)	33,515	35,111
*20913	Takoma Park	(301)	17,299	16,724
21787	Taneytown	(410)	5,128	3,695
*20748	Temple Hills (c)	(301)	7,792	6,865
21788	Thurmont	(301)	5,588	3,398
*21202	Towson (c)	(410)	51,793	49,445
—	Travilah (c)	(301)	7,442	—
*20602	Waldorf (c)	(301)	22,312	15,058
20743	Walker Mill (c)	(301)	11,104	10,920
21793	Walkersville	(301)	5,192	4,145
*21157	Westminster	(410)	16,731	13,060
20902	Wheaton-Glenmont (c)	(301)	57,694	53,720
21162	White Marsh (c)	(410)	8,485	8,183
20903	White Oak (c)	(301)	20,973	18,671
21207	Woodlawn (c) (Baltimore)	(410)	36,079	32,907
21284	Woodlawn (c) (Prince George's)	(410)	6,251	5,329
—	Woodmore (c)	(240)/(301)	6,077	2,874

Massachusetts

Area code (339) overlays area code (781). Area code (351) overlays (978). Area code (774) overlays (508). Area code (857) overlays (617). See introductory note.

ZIP	Place	Area Code	2000	1990
02351	*Abington*	(781)	14,605	13,817
01720	*Acton*	(978)	20,331	17,872
02743	*Acushnet*	(508)	10,161	9,554
01220	*Adams*	(413)	8,809	9,445
01220	Adams (c)	(413)	5,784	6,356
01001	Agawam	(413)	28,144	27,323
01913	*Amesbury*	(978)	16,450	14,997
01913	Amesbury (c)	(978)	12,327	12,109
*01002	*Amherst*	(413)	34,874	35,228
*01002	Amherst Center (c)	(413)	17,050	17,824
01810	Andover (c)	(978)	7,900	8,242
01810	*Andover*	(978)	31,247	29,151
*02205	*Arlington*	(781)	42,389	44,630
01430	*Ashburnham*	(978)	5,546	5,433
01721	*Ashland*	(508)	14,674	12,066
01331	*Athol*	(978)	11,299	11,451
01331	Athol (c)	(978)	8,370	8,732
02703	Attleboro	(508)	42,068	38,383
01501	*Auburn*	(508)	15,901	15,005
01432	*Ayer*	(978)	7,287	6,871
02630	Barnstable Town	(508)	47,821	40,949
01005	*Barre*	(978)	5,113	1,094
01730	*Bedford*	(781)	12,595	12,996
01007	*Belchertown*	(413)	12,968	10,579
02019	*Bellingham*	(508)	15,314	14,877
02478	*Belmont*	(781)	24,194	24,720
02779	*Berkley*	(508)	5,749	4,237
01915	Beverly	(978)	39,862	38,195
*01821	*Billerica*	(978)	38,981	37,609
01504	*Blackstone*	(508)	8,804	8,023
—	Bliss Corner (c)		5,466	4,908
*02205	Boston	(617)	589,141	574,283
02532	*Bourne*	(508)	18,721	16,064
01921	*Boxford*	(978)	7,921	6,266
*02205	*Braintree*	(781)	33,828	33,836
02631	*Brewster*	(508)	10,094	8,440
*02324	Bridgewater (c)	(508)	6,664	7,242
02324	*Bridgewater*	(508)	25,185	21,249
*02303	Brockton	(508)	94,304	92,788
*02446	*Brookline*	(617)	57,107	54,718
01803	*Burlington*	(781)	22,876	23,302
*02139	Cambridge	(617)	101,355	95,802
02021	*Canton*	(781)	20,775	18,530
02330	*Carver*	(508)	11,163	10,590
01507	*Charlton*	(508)	11,263	9,576
02633	*Chatham*	(508)	6,625	6,579
01824	*Chelmsford*	(978)	33,858	32,383
02150	Chelsea	(617)	35,080	28,710
*01020	Chicopee	(413)	54,653	56,632
01510	*Clinton*	(978)	13,435	13,222
01510	Clinton (c)	(978)	7,884	7,943
01778	Cochituate (c)	(508)	6,768	6,046
02025	*Cohasset*	(781)	7,261	7,075
01742	*Concord*	(978)	16,993	17,076
*01226	*Dalton*	(413)	6,892	7,155
01923	*Danvers*	(978)	25,212	24,174
02714	*Dartmouth*	(508)	30,666	27,244

ZIP	Place	Area Code	2000	1990
*02026	*Dedham*	(781)	23,464	23,782
02638	*Dennis*	(508)	15,973	13,864
02715	*Dighton*	(508)	6,175	5,631
01516	*Douglas*	(508)	7,045	5,438
02030	*Dover*	(508)	5,558	4,915
01826	*Dracut*	(978)	28,562	25,594
01571	*Dudley*	(508)	10,036	9,540
*02332	*Duxbury*	(781)	14,248	13,895
02333	*East Bridgewater*	(508)	12,974	11,104
02536	East Falmouth (c)	(508)	6,615	5,577
02642	*Eastham*	(508)	5,453	4,462
01027	*Easthampton*	(413)	15,994	15,537
01028	*East Longmeadow*	(413)	14,100	13,367
02334	*Easton*	(508)	22,299	19,807
02149	Everett	(617)	38,037	35,701
02719	*Fairhaven*	(508)	16,159	16,132
*02722	Fall River	(508)	91,938	92,703
*02540	*Falmouth*	(508)	32,660	27,960
01420	Fitchburg	(978)	39,102	41,194
02035	*Foxborough*	(508)	16,246	14,637
02035	Foxborough (c)	(508)	5,509	5,706
*01701	*Framingham*	(508)	66,910	64,989
02038	Franklin	(508)	29,560	22,095
02702	*Freetown*	(508)	8,472	8,522
01440	Gardner	(978)	20,770	20,125
01833	*Georgetown*	(978)	7,377	6,384
*01930	Gloucester	(978)	30,273	28,716
01519	*Grafton*	(508)	14,894	13,035
01033	*Granby*	(413)	6,132	5,565
01230	*Great Barrington*	(413)	7,527	7,725
01301	*Greenfield*	(413)	18,168	18,666
01301	Greenfield (c)	(413)	13,716	14,016
01450	*Groton*	(978)	9,547	7,511
01834	*Groveland*	(978)	6,038	5,214
02338	*Halifax*	(781)	7,500	6,526
01936	*Hamilton*	(978)	8,315	7,280
01036	*Hampden*	(413)	5,171	—
02339	*Hanover*	(781)	13,164	11,912
02341	*Hanson*	(781)	9,495	9,028
01451	*Harvard*	(978)	5,981	12,329
02645	*Harwich*	(508)	12,386	10,275
*01830	Haverhill	(978)	58,969	51,418
*02018	Hingham (c)	(781)	5,352	5,454
02043	*Hingham*	(781)	19,882	19,821
02343	*Holbrook*	(781)	10,785	11,041
01520	*Holden*	(508)	15,621	14,628
01746	*Holliston*	(508)	13,801	12,926
*01040	Holyoke	(413)	39,838	43,704
01747	*Hopedale*	(508)	5,907	5,666
01748	*Hopkinton*	(508)	13,346	9,191
01749	*Hudson*	(978)	18,113	17,233
01749	Hudson (c)	(978)	14,388	14,267
02045	*Hull*	(781)	11,050	10,466
02601	Hyannis (c)	(508)	11,050	14,120
01938	*Ipswich*	(978)	12,987	11,873
02364	Kingston (c)	(781)	5,380	4,774
02364	*Kingston*	(781)	11,780	9,045
02347	*Lakeville*	(508)	9,821	7,785
01523	*Lancaster*	(978)	7,380	6,661
*01842	Lawrence	(978)	72,043	70,207
01238	*Lee*	(413)	5,985	5,849
01524	*Leicester*	(508)	10,471	10,191
01240	*Lenox*	(413)	5,077	5,069
01453	Leominster	(978)	41,303	38,145
*02205	*Lexington*	(781)	30,355	28,974
01773	*Lincoln*	(781)	8,056	7,666
01460	*Littleton*	(978)	8,184	7,051
*01028	*Longmeadow*	(413)	15,633	15,467
*01853	Lowell	(978)	105,167	103,439
01056	*Ludlow*	(413)	21,209	18,820
01462	*Lunenburg*	(978)	9,401	9,117
*01901	Lynn	(781)	89,050	81,245
01940	*Lynnfield*	(781)	11,542	11,049
02148	Malden	(781)	56,340	53,884
01944	*Manchester-by-the-Sea*	(978)	5,228	5,286
*02048	*Mansfield*	(508)	22,414	16,568
02048	Mansfield Center (c)	(508)	7,320	7,170
01945	*Marblehead*	(781)	20,377	19,971
02738	*Marion*	(508)	5,123	4,496
01752	Marlborough	(508)	36,255	31,813
02050	*Marshfield*	(781)	24,324	21,531
02649	*Mashpee*	(508)	12,946	7,884
02739	*Mattapoisett*	(508)	6,268	5,850
01754	*Maynard*	(978)	10,433	10,325
02052	Medfield (c)	(508)	6,670	5,985
02052	*Medfield*	(508)	12,273	10,531
*02155	Medford	(781)	55,765	57,407
02053	*Medway*	(508)	12,448	9,931
02176	Melrose	(781)	27,134	28,150
01756	*Mendon*	(508)	5,286	—
01860	*Merrimac*	(978)	6,138	5,166
01844	Methuen	(978)	43,789	39,990
02346	*Middleborough*	(508)	19,941	17,867
02346	Middleborough Center (c)	(508)	6,913	6,837
01949	*Middleton*	(978)	7,744	4,921
01757	*Milford*	(508)	26,799	25,355
01757	Milford (c)	(508)	24,230	23,339
01527	*Millbury*	(508)	12,784	12,228
02054	*Millis*	(508)	7,902	7,613
02186	*Milton*	(617)	26,062	25,725
01057	*Monson*	(413)	8,359	7,776
01351	*Montague*	(413)	8,489	8,316
*02584	*Nantucket*	(508)	9,520	6,012
01760	*Natick*	(508)	32,170	30,510
*02205	*Needham*	(781)	28,911	27,557
*02740	New Bedford	(508)	93,768	99,922
01951	*Newbury*	(978)	6,717	5,623
01950	Newburyport	(978)	17,189	16,317
*02205	Newton	(617)	83,829	82,585
02056	*Norfolk*	(508)	10,460	9,259
01247	North Adams	(413)	14,681	16,797
01059	North Amherst (c)	(413)	6,019	6,239
*01060	Northampton	(413)	28,978	11,929
01845	*North Andover*	(978)	27,202	29,289
*02760	*North Attleborough*	(508)	27,143	22,792
02760	North Attleborough Center (c)	(508)	16,796	16,178
01532	Northborough (c)	(508)	6,257	5,761
01532	*Northborough*	(508)	14,013	13,371
01534	*Northbridge*	(508)	13,182	12,002
01864	*North Reading*	(978)	13,837	25,038
02060	North Scituate (c)	(781)	5,065	4,891
02766	*Norton*	(508)	18,036	14,265
02061	*Norwell*	(781)	9,765	9,279
02062	*Norwood*	(781)	28,587	28,700
02065	Ocean Bluff-Brant Rock (c)	(781)	5,100	4,541
01364	*Orange*	(978)	7,518	7,312
02653	*Orleans*	(508)	6,341	5,838
01540	Oxford (c)	(508)	5,899	5,969
01540	*Oxford*	(508)	13,352	12,588
01069	*Palmer*	(413)	12,497	12,054
*01960	Peabody	(978)	48,129	47,264
02359	*Pembroke*	(781)	16,927	14,544
01463	*Pepperell*	(978)	11,142	10,098
01866	Pinehurst (c)	(978)	6,941	6,614
*01201	Pittsfield	(413)	45,793	48,622
02762	*Plainville*	(508)	7,683	6,871
*02360	Plymouth (c)	(508)	7,658	7,258
*02360	*Plymouth*	(508)	51,701	45,608
*02205	Quincy	(617)	88,025	84,985
02368	*Randolph*	(781)	30,963	30,093
02767	*Raynham*	(508)	11,739	9,867
01867	*Reading*	(781)	23,708	22,539
02769	*Rehoboth*	(508)	10,172	8,656
02151	Revere	(781)	47,283	42,786
02370	*Rockland*	(781)	17,670	16,123
01966	Rockport (c)	(978)	5,606	5,448
01966	*Rockport*	(978)	7,767	7,482
01969	*Rowley*	(978)	5,500	4,452
01543	*Rutland*	(508)	6,353	4,936
*01970	Salem	(978)	40,407	38,091
01952	*Salisbury*	(978)	7,827	6,882
02563	*Sandwich*	(508)	20,136	15,489
01906	*Saugus*	(781)	26,078	25,549
02066	Scituate (c)	(781)	5,069	5,180
02066	*Scituate*	(781)	17,863	16,786
02771	*Seekonk*	(508)	13,425	13,046
02067	*Sharon*	(781)	17,408	15,517
02067	Sharon (c)	(781)	5,941	5,893
01464	*Shirley*	(978)	6,373	6,118
01545	*Shrewsbury*	(508)	31,640	24,146
*02722	*Somerset*	(508)	18,234	17,655
*02205	Somerville	(617)	77,478	76,210
01002	South Amherst (c)	(413)	5,039	5,053
01073	*Southampton*	(413)	5,387	—
01772	*Southborough*	(508)	8,781	6,628
01550	*Southbridge*	(508)	17,214	17,816
01550	Southbridge (c)	(508)	12,878	13,631
01075	*South Hadley*	(413)	17,196	16,685
01077	*Southwick*	(413)	8,835	7,667
02664	South Yarmouth (c)	(508)	11,603	10,358
01562	Spencer (c)	(508)	6,032	6,306
01562	*Spencer*	(508)	11,691	11,645
*01101	Springfield	(413)	152,082	156,983
01564	*Sterling*	(978)	7,257	6,481
02180	*Stoneham*	(781)	22,219	22,203
02072	*Stoughton*	(781)	27,149	26,777
01775	*Stow*	(978)	5,902	5,328
01566	*Sturbridge*	(508)	7,837	7,775
01776	*Sudbury*	(978)	16,841	14,358
01590	*Sutton*	(508)	8,250	6,824
01907	*Swampscott*	(781)	14,412	13,650
02777	*Swansea*	(508)	15,901	15,411
02780	Taunton	(508)	55,976	49,832
01468	*Templeton*	(978)	6,799	6,438
01876	*Tewksbury*	(978)	28,851	27,266
01983	*Topsfield*	(978)	6,141	5,754
01469	*Townsend*	(978)	9,198	8,496
01879	*Tyngsborough*	(978)	11,081	8,642
01568	*Upton*	(508)	5,642	4,677
01569	*Uxbridge*	(508)	11,156	10,415

ZIP	Place	Area Code	2000	1990
01880	*Wakefield*	(781)	24,804	24,825
*02081	Walpole (c)	(508)	5,867	5,495
02081	*Walpole*	(508)	22,824	20,223
*02205	Waltham	(781)	59,226	57,878
01082	Ware (c)	(413)	6,174	6,533
01082	*Ware*	(413)	9,707	9,808
02571	*Wareham*	(508)	20,335	19,232
*02205	Watertown	(781)	32,986	33,284
01778	*Wayland*	(508)	13,100	11,874
01570	*Webster*	(508)	16,415	16,196
01570	Webster (c)	(508)	11,600	11,849
*02205	*Wellesley*	(781)	26,613	26,615
01581	*Westborough*	(508)	17,997	14,133
01583	*West Boylston*	(508)	7,481	6,611
02379	*West Bridgewater*	(508)	6,634	6,389
01742	West Concord (c)	(978)	5,632	5,761
*01085	Westfield	(413)	40,072	38,372
01886	*Westford*	(978)	20,754	16,392
01473	*Westminster*	(978)	6,907	6,191
02493	*Weston*	(781)	11,469	10,200
02790	*Westport*	(508)	14,183	13,852
*01089	*West Springfield*	(413)	27,899	27,537
02090	*Westwood*	(781)	14,117	12,557
02673	West Yarmouth (c)	(508)	6,460	5,409
*02205	*Weymouth*	(781)	53,988	54,063
01588	Whitinsville (c)	(508)	6,340	5,639
02382	*Whitman*	(781)	13,882	13,240
01095	*Wilbraham*	(413)	13,473	12,635
01267	*Williamstown*	(413)	8,424	8,220
01887	*Wilmington*	(978)	21,363	17,651
01475	*Winchendon*	(978)	9,611	8,805
01890	*Winchester*	(781)	20,810	20,267
02152	*Winthrop*	(617)	18,303	18,127
*01801	Woburn	(781)	37,258	35,943
*01613	Worcester	(508)	172,648	169,759
02093	*Wrentham*	(508)	10,554	9,006
02675	*Yarmouth*	(508)	24,807	21,174
02675	Yarmouth Port (c)	(508)	5,395	4,271

Michigan

Area code (947) overlays area code (248). See introductory note.

ZIP	Place	Area Code	2000	1990
49221	Adrian	(517)	21,574	22,097
49224	Albion	(517)	9,144	10,066
49401	Allendale (c)	(616)	11,555	6,950
48101	Allen Park	(313)	29,376	31,092
48801	Alma	(989)	9,275	9,034
49707	Alpena	(989)	11,304	11,354
*48106	Ann Arbor	(734)	114,024	109,608
*48321	Auburn Hills	(248)	19,837	17,076
*49016	Battle Creek	(269)	53,364	53,516
*48707	Bay City	(989)	36,817	38,936
48505	Beecher (c)	(810)	12,793	14,465
48809	Belding	(616)	5,877	5,969
*49022	Benton Harbor	(269)	11,182	12,818
49022	Benton Heights (c)	(269)	5,458	5,465
48072	Berkley	(248)	15,531	16,960
48025	Beverly Hills	(248)	10,437	10,610
49307	Big Rapids	(231)	10,849	12,603
*48012	Birmingham	(248)	19,291	19,997
48301	Bloomfield (c)	(248)	43,021	42,137
48722	Bridgeport (c)	(989)	7,849	8,569
*48116	Brighton	(810)	6,701	5,686
48601	Buena Vista (c)	(989)	7,845	8,196
*48501	Burton	(810)	30,308	27,437
49601	Cadillac	(231)	10,000	10,104
*48185	Canton (c)	(734)	76,366	57,047
48724	Carrollton (c)	(989)	6,602	6,521
48015	Center Line	(586)	8,531	9,026
48813	Charlotte	(517)	8,389	8,083
49721	Cheboygan	(231)	5,295	4,997
48017	Clawson	(248)	12,732	13,874
*48046	Clinton (c)	(517)	95,648	85,866
49036	Coldwater	(517)	12,697	9,607
49321	Comstock Park (c)	(616)	10,674	6,530
49508	Cutlerville (c)	(616)	15,114	11,228
48423	Davison	(810)	5,536	5,693
*48120	Dearborn	(313)	97,775	89,286
*48127	Dearborn Heights	(313)	58,264	60,838
*48231	Detroit	(313)	951,270	1,027,974
49047	Dowagiac	(269)	6,147	6,418
49506	East Grand Rapids	(616)	10,764	10,807
*48826	East Lansing	(517)	46,525	50,677
48021	Eastpointe	(586)	34,077	35,283
49001	Eastwood (c)	(269)	6,265	6,340
48827	Eaton Rapids	(517)	5,330	4,695
48229	Ecorse	(313)	11,229	12,180
49829	Escanaba	(906)	13,140	13,659
49022	Fair Plain (c)	(269)	7,828	8,051
*48333	Farmington	(248)	10,423	10,170
48333	Farmington Hills	(248)	82,111	74,614
48430	Fenton	(810)	10,582	8,434
48220	Ferndale	(248)	22,105	25,084
48134	Flat Rock	(734)	8,488	7,290
*48501	Flint	(810)	124,943	140,925
48433	Flushing	(810)	8,348	8,542
49506	Forest Hills (c)	(616)	20,942	16,690
48026	Fraser	(586)	15,297	13,899
48623	Freeland (c)	(989)	5,147	1,421
*48135	Garden City	(734)	30,047	31,846
49837	Gladstone	(906)	5,032	4,565
48439	Grand Blanc	(810)	8,242	7,760
49417	Grand Haven	(616)	11,168	11,951
48837	Grand Ledge	(517)	7,813	7,562
*49501	Grand Rapids	(616)	197,800	189,126
*49418	Grandville	(616)	16,263	15,624
48838	Greenville	(616)	7,935	8,101
48138	Grosse Ile (c)	(734)	10,894	9,781
*48231	Grosse Pointe	(313)	5,670	5,681
48230	Grosse Pointe Farms	(313)	9,764	10,092
48230	Grosse Pointe Park	(313)	12,443	12,857
48230	Grosse Pointe Woods	(313)	17,080	17,715
48212	Hamtramck	(313)	22,976	18,372
48225	Harper Woods	(313)	14,254	14,903
48625	Harrison (c)	(989)	24,461	24,685
48840	Haslett (c)	(517)	11,283	10,230
49058	Hastings	(269)	7,095	6,549
48030	Hazel Park	(248)	18,963	20,051
48203	Highland Park	(313)	16,746	20,121
49242	Hillsdale	(517)	8,233	8,175
*49423	Holland	(616)	35,048	30,745
48442	Holly	(248)	6,135	5,595
48842	Holt (c)	(517)	11,315	11,744
49931	Houghton	(906)	7,010	7,498
*48844	Howell	(517)	9,232	8,147
49426	Hudsonville	(616)	7,160	6,170
48070	Huntington Woods	(248)	6,151	6,419
48141	Inkster	(313)/(734)	30,115	30,772
48846	Ionia	(616)	10,569	10,349
49801	Iron Mountain	(906)	8,154	8,525
49938	Ironwood	(906)	6,293	6,849
49849	Ishpeming	(906)	6,686	7,200
*49204	Jackson	(517)	36,316	37,425
*49428	Jenison (c)	(616)	17,211	17,882
*49001	Kalamazoo	(269)	77,145	80,277
49518	Kentwood	(616)	45,255	37,826
49802	Kingsford	(906)	5,549	5,480
48144	Lambertville (c)	(734)	9,299	7,860
*48901	Lansing	(517)	119,128	127,321
48446	Lapeer	(810)	9,072	7,759
48146	Lincoln Park	(313)	40,008	41,832
*48150	Livonia	(734)	100,545	100,850
49431	Ludington	(231)	8,357	8,507
48071	Madison Heights	(248)	31,101	32,196
49660	Manistee	(231)	6,586	6,734
49855	Marquette	(906)	19,661	21,977
49068	Marshall	(269)	7,459	6,941
48040	Marysville	(810)	9,684	8,515
48854	Mason	(517)	6,714	6,768
48122	Melvindale	(313)	10,735	11,216
49858	Menominee	(906)	9,131	9,398
*48640	Midland	(989)	41,685	38,053
*48381	Milford	(248)	6,272	5,500
*48161	Monroe	(734)	22,076	22,902
*48046	Mount Clemens	(586)	17,312	18,405
*48804	Mount Pleasant	(989)	25,946	23,299
*49440	Muskegon	(231)	40,105	39,809
49444	Muskegon Heights	(231)	12,049	13,176
*48047	New Baltimore	(586)	7,405	5,798
49120	Niles	(269)	12,204	12,458
49505	Northview (c)	(616)	14,730	13,712
48167	Northville	(248)	6,459	6,226
49441	Norton Shores	(231)	22,527	21,755
*48376	Novi	(248)	47,386	32,998
48237	Oak Park	(248)	29,793	30,468
*48805	Okemos (c)	(517)	22,805	20,216
48867	Owosso	(989)	15,713	16,322
49770	Petoskey	(231)	6,080	6,056
48170	Plymouth	(734)	9,022	9,560
48170	Plymouth Township (c)	(734)	27,798	23,646
*48343	Pontiac	(248)	66,337	71,136
*49081	Portage	(269)	44,897	41,042
*48061	Port Huron	(810)	32,338	33,694
*48231	Redford (c)	(313)	51,622	54,387
48218	River Rouge	(313)	9,917	11,314
48192	Riverview	(734)	13,272	13,894
*48308	Rochester	(248)	10,467	7,130
48306	Rochester Hills	(248)	68,825	61,766
48174	Romulus	(313)/(734)	22,979	22,897
48066	Roseville	(586)	48,129	51,412
*48068	Royal Oak	(248)	60,062	65,410
*48605	Saginaw	(989)	61,799	69,512
48604	Saginaw Township North (c)	(989)	24,994	23,018
48603	Saginaw Township South (c)	(989)	13,801	13,987
48079	Saint Clair	(810)	5,802	5,116
*48080	Saint Clair Shores	(313)	63,096	68,107
48879	Saint Johns	(989)	7,485	7,392
49085	Saint Joseph	(269)	8,789	9,214
48176	Saline	(734)	8,034	6,663
49783	Sault Sainte Marie	(906)	16,542	14,689
49455	Shelby (c)	(231)	65,159	48,655
48609	Shields (c)	(989)	6,590	6,634
*48037	Southfield	(248)	78,296	75,727
48195	Southgate	(734)	30,136	30,771

ZIP	Place	Area Code	2000	1990
49090	South Haven	(269)	5,021	5,563
48178	South Lyon	(248)	10,036	6,479
48161	South Monroe (c)	(734)	6,370	5,266
49015	Springfield	(269)	5,189	5,582
*48311	Sterling Heights	(586)	124,471	117,810
49091	Sturgis	(269)	11,285	10,130
48473	Swartz Creek	(810)	5,102	4,851
48180	Taylor	(313)/(734)	65,868	70,811
49286	Tecumseh	(517)	8,574	7,462
48182	Temperance (c)	(734)	7,757	6,542
49093	Three Rivers	(269)	7,328	7,464
*49684	Traverse City	(231)	14,532	15,155
48183	Trenton	(734)	19,584	20,586
*48099	Troy	(248)	80,959	72,884
49504	Walker	(616)	21,842	17,279
*48390	Walled Lake	(248)	6,713	6,278
*48090	Warren	(586)	138,247	144,864
*48329	Waterford (c)	(248)	73,150	66,692
48917	Waverly (c)	(517)	16,194	15,614
48184	Wayne	(734)	19,051	19,899
*48325	West Bloomfield Township (c)	(248)	64,862	54,843
*48185	Westland	(313)/(734)	86,602	84,724
49019	Westwood (c)	(269)	9,122	8,957
48189	Whitmore Lake (c)	(734)	6,574	3,251
48393	Wixom	(248)	13,263	8,550
48183	Woodhaven	(734)	12,530	11,631
48192	Wyandotte	(734)	28,006	30,938
49509	Wyoming	(616)	69,368	63,891
*48197	Ypsilanti	(734)	22,362	24,846
49464	Zeeland	(616)	5,805	5,417

Minnesota

ZIP	Place	Area Code	2000	1990
56007	Albert Lea	(507)	18,356	18,310
56308	Alexandria	(320)	8,820	8,029
55304	Andover	(763)	26,588	15,216
*55303	Anoka	(612)/(763)	18,076	17,192
55124	Apple Valley	(952)	45,527	34,598
55112	Arden Hills	(651)	9,652	9,199
55912	Austin	(507)	23,314	21,926
56425	Baxter	(218)	5,555	3,695
*56601	Bemidji	(218)	11,917	11,165
55309	Big Lake	(763)	6,063	3,113
55014	Blaine	(651)/(763)	44,942	38,975
*55420	Bloomington	(952)	85,172	86,335
56401	Brainerd	(218)	13,178	12,353
55429	Brooklyn Center	(763)	29,172	28,887
55443	Brooklyn Park	(763)	67,388	56,381
55313	Buffalo	(763)	10,097	7,302
*55337	Burnsville	(651)/(952)	60,220	51,288
55008	Cambridge	(763)	5,520	5,094
55316	Champlin	(763)	22,193	16,849
55317	Chanhassen	(952)	20,321	11,736
55318	Chaska	(952)	17,449	11,339
55720	Cloquet	(218)	11,201	10,885
55421	Columbia Heights	(612)/(763)	18,520	18,910
55433	Coon Rapids	(763)	61,607	52,978
55340	Corcoran	(763)	5,630	5,199
55016	Cottage Grove	(651)	30,582	22,935
56716	Crookston	(218)	8,192	8,119
55428	Crystal	(763)	22,698	23,788
*56501	Detroit Lakes	(218)	7,348	7,141
*55806	Duluth	(218)	86,918	85,493
*55121	Eagan	(651)/(952)	63,557	47,409
55005	East Bethel	(763)	10,941	8,050
56721	East Grand Forks	(218)	7,501	8,658
*55344	Eden Prairie	(612)/(952)	54,901	39,311
55424	Edina	(952)	47,425	46,075
55330	Elk River	(763)	16,447	11,143
56031	Fairmont	(507)	10,889	11,265
55113	Falcon Heights	(651)	5,572	5,380
55021	Faribault	(507)	20,818	17,085
55024	Farmington	(651)/(952)	12,365	5,940
*56537	Fergus Falls	(218)	13,471	12,362
55025	Forest Lake	(651)	6,798	5,833
55432	Fridley	(763)	27,449	28,335
55336	Glencoe	(320)	5,453	4,648
55427	Golden Valley	(763)	20,281	20,971
*55744	Grand Rapids	(218)	7,764	7,976
*55304	Ham Lake	(763)	12,710	8,924
55033	Hastings	(651)	18,204	15,478
55810	Hermantown	(218)	7,448	6,761
*55746	Hibbing	(218)	17,071	18,046
*55343	Hopkins	(952)	17,145	16,529
55038	Hugo	(651)	6,363	4,417
55350	Hutchinson	(320)	13,080	11,459
56649	Internationa Falls	(218)	6,703	8,325
*55076	Inver Grove Heights	(651)	29,751	22,477
55042	Lake Elmo	(651)	6,863	5,900
55044	Lakeville	(952)	43,128	24,854
55014	Lino Lakes	(651)	16,791	8,807
55355	Litchfield	(320)	6,562	6,041
55117	Little Canada	(651)	9,771	8,971
56345	Little Falls	(320)	7,719	7,371
—	Lower Red Lake UT	(218)	5,057	—
55115	Mahtomedi	(651)	7,563	5,633
*56001	Mankato	(507)	32,427	31,459
55311	Maple Grove	(763)	50,365	38,736
55109	Maplewood	(651)	34,947	30,954
56258	Marshall	(507)	12,735	12,023
55118	Mendota Heights	(651)	11,434	9,388
*55440	Minneapolis	(612)/(763)/(952)	382,618	368,383
55345	Minnetonka	(952)	51,301	48,370
56265	Montevideo	(320)	5,346	5,499
*55362	Monticello	(763)	7,868	5,045
*56560	Moorhead	(218)	32,177	32,295
56267	Morris	(320)	5,068	5,613
55364	Mound	(952)	9,435	9,634
55112	Mounds View	(763)	12,738	12,541
55112	New Brighton	(651)	22,206	22,207
54427	New Hope	(763)	20,873	21,853
56073	New Ulm	(507)	13,594	13,132
55056	North Branch	(651)/(763)	8,023	4,267
55057	Northfield	(507)	17,147	14,684
56001	North Mankato	(507)	11,798	10,662
55109	North Saint Paul	(651)	11,929	12,376
55128	Oakdale	(651)	26,653	18,377
*55011	Oak Grove	(763)	6,903	5,488
55323	Orono	(952)	7,538	7,285
*55330	Otsego	(763)	6,389	5,219
55060	Owatonna	(507)	22,434	19,386
*55446	Plymouth	(763)	65,894	50,889
55372	Prior Lake	(952)	15,917	11,482
55303	Ramsey	(763)	18,510	12,408
55066	Red Wing	(651)	16,116	15,134
56283	Redwood Falls	(507)	5,459	4,859
55423	Richfield	(612)	34,439	35,710
55422	Robbinsdale	(763)	14,123	14,396
*55901	Rochester	(507)	85,806	70,729
55068	Rosemount	(651)/(952)	14,619	8,622
55113	Roseville	(651)	33,690	33,485
55418	Saint Anthony	(612)	8,012	7,727
*56301	Saint Cloud	(320)	59,107	48,812
55426	Saint Louis Park	(952)	44,126	43,787
*55374	Saint Michael	(763)	9,099	2,506
*55101	Saint Paul	(651)	287,151	272,235
55071	Saint Paul Park	(651)	5,070	4,965
56082	Saint Peter	(507)	9,747	9,481
56377	Sartell	(320)	9,641	5,409
56379	Sauk Rapids	(320)	10,213	7,823
56378	Savage	(952)	21,115	9,906
55379	Shakopee	(612)	20,568	11,739
55126	Shoreview	(651)	25,924	24,587
55331	Shorewood	(952)	7,400	5,917
55075	South Saint Paul	(651)	20,167	20,197
55432	Spring Lake Park	(763)	6,772	6,532
55976	Stewartville	(507)	5,411	4,520
*55082	Stillwater	(651)	15,143	13,882
56701	Thief River Falls	(218)	8,410	8,010
55127	Vadnais Heights	(651)	13,069	11,041
*55792	Virginia	(218)	9,157	9,432
55387	Waconia	(952)	6,814	3,498
56387	Waite Park	(320)	6,568	5,020
56093	Waseca	(507)	8,493	8,385
—	West Crow Wing UT		5,144	—
55118	West Saint Paul	(651)	19,405	19,248
*55110	White Bear Lake	(651)	24,325	24,622
56201	Willmar	(320)	18,351	17,531
55987	Winona	(507)	27,069	25,435
55125	Woodbury	(651)	46,463	20,075
56187	Worthington	(507)	11,283	9,977

Mississippi

ZIP	Place	Area Code	2000	1990
39730	Aberdeen	(662)	6,415	6,837
38821	Amory	(662)	6,956	7,093
38606	Batesville	(662)	7,113	6,403
*39520	Bay Saint Louis	(228)	8,209	8,063
*39530	Biloxi	(228)	50,644	46,319
38829	Booneville	(662)	8,625	7,955
*39042	Brandon	(601)	16,436	11,089
*39601	Brookhaven	(601)	9,861	10,243
39272	Byram (c)	(601)	7,386	—
39046	Canton	(601)	12,911	11,723
38614	Clarksdale	(662)	20,645	21,180
*38732	Cleveland	(662)	13,841	15,384
*39056	Clinton	(601)	23,347	21,847
39429	Columbia	(601)	6,603	6,815
*39701	Columbus	(662)	25,944	23,799
*38834	Corinth	(662)	14,054	11,820
39059	Crystal Springs	(601)	5,873	5,643
39525	Diamondhead (c)	(228)	5,912	2,661
39532	D'Iberville	(228)	7,608	6,566
39074	Forest	(601)	5,987	5,062
39553	Gautier	(228)	11,681	10,088
*38701	Greenville	(662)	41,633	45,226
*38930	Greenwood	(662)	18,425	18,906
*38901	Grenada	(662)	14,879	10,864
39564	Gulf Hills (c)	(228)	5,900	5,004
*39501	Gulfport	(228)	71,127	64,045
*39401	Hattiesburg	(601)	44,779	45,325
38632	Hernando		6,812	3,125
*38635	Holly Springs	(662)	7,957	7,261
38637	Horn Lake	(662)	14,099	9,069

ZIP	Place	Area Code	2000	1990
38751	Indianola	(662)	12,066	11,809
*39205	Jackson	(601)	184,256	202,062
39090	Kosciusko	(662)	7,372	6,986
*39440	Laurel	(601)	18,393	18,827
38756	Leland	(662)	5,502	6,366
39560	Long Beach	(228)	17,320	15,804
39339	Louisville	(662)	7,006	7,165
*39648	McComb	(601)	13,337	11,797
*39110	Madison	(601)	14,692	7,471
*39302	Meridian	(601)	39,968	41,036
*39563	Moss Point	(228)	15,851	17,837
*39120	Natchez	(601)	18,464	19,460
38652	New Albany	(662)	7,607	6,775
*39564	Ocean Springs	(228)	17,225	15,221
38654	Olive Branch	(662)	21,054	3,567
38655	Oxford	(662)	11,756	10,026
*39567	Pascagoula	(228)	26,200	25,899
39571	Pass Christian	(228)	6,579	5,557
39288	Pearl	(601)	21,961	19,588
39465	Petal	(601)	7,579	7,883
39350	Philadelphia	(601)	7,303	6,758
39466	Picayune	(601)	10,535	10,633
38863	Pontotoc	(662)	5,253	4,570
39218	Richland	(601)	6,027	4,014
*39157	Ridgeland	(601)	20,173	11,714
38663	Ripley	(662)	5,478	5,371
39533	Saint Martin (c)	(228)	6,676	6,349
38668	Senatobia	(601)	6,682	4,772
38671	Southaven	(662)	28,977	18,705
*39759	Starkville	(662)	21,869	18,458
*38801	Tupelo	(662)	34,211	30,685
*39180	Vicksburg	(601)	26,407	26,886
39576	Waveland	(228)	6,674	5,369
39367	Waynesboro	(601)	5,197	5,143
—	West Hattiesburg (c)	(601)	6,305	5,450
39773	West Point	(662)	12,145	8,489
38967	Winona	(662)	5,482	5,965
39194	Yazoo City	(662)	14,550	12,427

Missouri

ZIP	Place	Area Code	2000	1990
63123	Affton (c)	(314)	20,535	21,106
63010	Arnold	(636)	19,965	18,828
65605	Aurora	(417)	7,014	6,459
*63011	Ballwin	(636)	31,283	27,054
63012	Barnhart (c)	(314)	6,108	4,911
63137	Bellefontaine Neighbors	(314)	11,271	10,918
64012	Belton	(816)	21,730	18,145
63134	Berkeley	(314)	10,063	12,250
63031	Black Jack	(314)	6,792	6,131
*64015	Blue Springs	(816)	48,080	40,103
65613	Bolivar	(417)	9,143	6,845
65233	Boonville	(660)	8,202	7,095
*65615	Branson	(417)	6,050	3,706
63144	Brentwood	(314)	7,693	8,150
63044	Bridgeton	(314)	15,550	17,732
64429	Cameron	(816)	8,312	6,782
*63701	Cape Girardeau	(573)	35,349	34,475
64834	Carl Junction	(417)	5,294	4,123
64836	Carthage	(417)	12,668	10,747
63830	Caruthersville	(573)	6,760	7,389
*63017	Chesterfield	(636)	46,802	42,325
64601	Chillicothe	(660)	8,968	8,799
63105	Clayton	(314)	12,825	13,926
64735	Clinton	(660)	9,311	8,703
*65201	Columbia	(573)	84,531	69,133
63128	Concord (c)	(314)	16,689	19,859
63126	Crestwood	(314)	11,863	11,229
63141	Creve Coeur	(314)	16,500	12,289
*63135	Dellwood	(314)	5,255	5,245
63020	De Soto	(636)	6,375	5,993
63131	Des Peres	(636)	8,592	8,395
63841	Dexter	(573)	7,356	7,506
63011	Ellisville	(636)	9,104	7,183
63025	Eureka	(636)	7,676	4,683
64024	Excelsior Springs	(816)	10,847	10,373
63640	Farmington	(573)	13,924	11,596
63135	Ferguson	(314)	22,406	22,290
63028	Festus	(636)	9,660	8,105
*63033	Florissant	(314)	50,497	51,038
65473	Fort Leonard Wood (c)	(573)	13,666	15,863
65251	Fulton	(573)	12,128	10,033
64118	Gladstone	(816)	26,365	26,243
65254	Glasgow Village (c)	(573)	5,234	5,199
63122	Glendale	(314)	5,767	5,945
64029	Grain Valley	(816)	5,160	1,898
64030	Grandview	(816)	24,881	24,973
63401	Hannibal	(573)	17,757	18,004
64701	Harrisonville	(816)	8,946	7,696
63042	Hazelwood	(314)	26,206	15,512
*64050	Independence	(816)	113,288	112,301
63755	Jackson	(573)	11,947	9,256
*65101	Jefferson City	(573)	39,636	35,517
63136	Jennings	(314)	15,469	15,841
*64801	Joplin	(417)	45,504	41,175
*64108	Kansas City	(816)	441,545	434,829
64060	Kearney	(816)	5,472	1,790
63857	Kennett	(573)	11,260	10,941
63501	Kirksville	(660)	16,988	17,152
63122	Kirkwood	(314)	27,324	28,318
63124	Ladue (St. Louis Co.)	(314)	8,645	8,795
63367	Lake Saint Louis	(636)	10,169	7,536
65536	Lebanon	(417)	12,155	9,983
*64063	Lee's Summit	(816)	70,700	46,418
63125	Lemay (c)	(314)	17,215	18,005
*64068	Liberty	(816)	26,232	20,459
63552	Macon	(660)	5,538	5,571
63011	Manchester	(636)	19,161	6,506
63143	Maplewood	(314)	9,228	9,962
65340	Marshall	(660)	12,433	12,711
65706	Marshfield	(417)	5,720	4,374
63043	Maryland Heights	(314)	25,756	25,440
64468	Maryville	(816)	10,581	10,663
63129	Mehlville (c)	(314)	28,822	27,557
65265	Mexico	(573)	11,320	11,290
65270	Moberly	(660)	11,945	12,839
65708	Monett	(417)	7,396	6,529
63026	Murphy (c)	(636)	9,048	9,342
64850	Neosho	(417)	10,505	9,254
64772	Nevada	(417)	8,607	8,597
65714	Nixa	(417)	12,124	4,893
63121	Normandy	(314)	5,153	4,480
64075	Oak Grove	(816)	5,535	4,565
63129	Oakville (c)	(314)	35,309	31,750
63366	O'Fallon	(636)	46,169	17,427
63132	Olivette	(314)	7,438	7,573
63114	Overland	(314)	16,838	17,987
65721	Ozark	(417)	9,665	4,401
63069	Pacific	(636)	5,482	4,350
63601	Park Hills	(573)	7,861	7,866
63775	Perryville	(573)	7,667	6,933
64080	Pleasant Hill	(816)	5,582	3,827
*63901	Poplar Bluff	(573)	16,651	16,841
64083	Raymore	(816)	11,146	5,592
64133	Raytown	(816)	30,388	30,601
65738	Republic	(417)	8,438	6,290
64085	Richmond	(816)	6,116	5,738
63117	Richmond Heights	(314)	9,602	10,448
*65401	Rolla	(573)	16,367	14,090
63074	Saint Ann	(314)	13,607	14,449
*63301	Saint Charles	(636)	60,321	50,634
63114	Saint John	(314)	6,871	7,502
*64501	Saint Joseph	(816)	73,990	71,852
*63166	Saint Louis	(314)	348,189	396,685
63376	Saint Peters	(636)	51,381	40,660
63126	Sappington (c)	(314)	7,287	10,917
*65301	Sedalia	(660)	20,339	19,800
63119	Shrewsbury	(314)	6,644	6,416
63801	Sikeston	(573)	16,992	17,641
64089	Smithville	(816)	5,514	2,525
63138	Spanish Lake (c)	(314)	21,337	20,322
*65801	Springfield	(417)	151,580	140,494
63080	Sullivan	(573)	6,351	5,661
63127	Sunset Hills	(314)	8,267	4,915
63006	Town and Country	(314)	10,894	10,944
64683	Trenton	(660)	6,216	6,129
63379	Troy	(314)	6,737	3,811
63084	Union	(636)	7,757	6,196
63130	University City	(314)	37,428	40,087
63088	Valley Park	(636)	6,518	4,165
64093	Warrensburg	(660)	16,340	15,244
63383	Warrenton	(636)	5,281	3,564
63090	Washington	(636)	13,243	11,367
64870	Webb City	(417)	9,812	7,538
63119	Webster Groves	(314)	23,230	22,992
63304	Weldon Spring	(636)	5,270	1,470
63385	Wentzville	(636)	6,896	4,640
65775	West Plains	(417)	10,866	9,214
*63011	Wildwood	(314)	32,884	16,742

Montana (406)

ZIP	Place	2000	1990
59711	Anaconda	9,417	10,356
59714	Belgrade	5,728	3,422
*59101	Billings	89,847	81,125
*59718	Bozeman	27,509	22,660
*59701	Butte	34,606	33,336
59901	Evergreen (c)	6,215	4,109
*59401	Great Falls	56,690	55,125
59501	Havre	9,621	10,201
*59601	Helena	25,780	24,609
—	Helena Valley Southeast (c)	7,141	4,601
—	Helena Valley West Central (c)	6,983	6,327
*59901	Kalispell	14,223	11,917
59044	Laurel	6,255	5,686
59457	Lewistown	5,813	6,097
59047	Livingston	6,851	6,701
59301	Miles City	8,487	8,461
*59801	Missoula	57,053	42,918
59801	Orchard Homes (c)	5,199	10,317
59937	Whitefish	5,032	4,368

Nebraska

ZIP	Place	Area Code	2000	1990
69301	Alliance	(308)	8,959	9,765
68310	Beatrice	(402)	12,496	12,352
*68108	Bellevue	(402)	44,382	39,240
*68008	Blair	(402)	7,512	6,860
69337	Chadron	(308)	5,634	5,588
68108	Chalco (c)	(402)	10,736	7,337
68601	Columbus	(402)	20,971	19,480
68333	Crete	(402)	6,028	4,841
68022	Elkhorn	(402)	6,062	1,398
*68025	Fremont	(402)	25,174	23,680
69341	Gering	(308)	7,751	7,946
*68802	Grand Island	(308)	42,940	39,487
*68901	Hastings	(402)	24,064	22,837
68949	Holdrege	(308)	5,636	5,671
*68847	Kearney	(308)	27,431	24,396
68128	La Vista	(402)	11,699	9,992
68850	Lexington	(308)	10,011	6,600
*68501	Lincoln	(402)	225,581	191,972
69001	McCook	(308)	7,994	8,112
68410	Nebraska City	(402)	7,228	6,547
*68701	Norfolk	(402)	23,516	21,476
*69101	North Platte	(308)	23,878	22,605
68113	Offutt AFB (c)	(402)	8,901	—
*68005	Omaha	(402)	390,007	344,463
*68046	Papillion	(402)	16,363	13,892
68048	Plattsmouth	(402)	6,887	6,415
68127	Ralston	(402)	6,314	6,236
68661	Schuyler	(402)	5,371	4,052
*69361	Scottsbluff	(308)	14,732	13,711
68434	Seward	(402)	6,319	5,641
69162	Sidney	(308)	6,282	5,959
68776	South Sioux City	(402)	11,925	9,677
68787	Wayne	(402)	5,583	5,142
68467	York	(402)	8,081	7,940

Nevada

ZIP	Place	Area Code	2000	1990
*89005	Boulder City	(702)	14,966	12,567
*89701	Carson City	(775)	52,457	40,443
89403	Dayton (c)	(775)	5,907	2,217
*89801	Elko	(775)	16,708	14,836
—	Enterprise (c)		14,676	6,412
*89406	Fallon	(775)	7,536	6,430
89408	Fernley (c)	(775)	8,543	5,164
89410	Gardnerville Ranchos (c)	(775)	11,054	7,455
*89015	Henderson	(702)	175,381	64,948
*89450	Incline Village-Crystal Bay (c)	(775)	9,952	7,119
*89125	Las Vegas	(702)	478,434	258,877
*89028	Laughlin (c)	(702)	7,076	4,791
89506	Lemmon Valley-Golden Valley (c)	(702)	6,855	—
*89024	Mesquite	(702)	9,389	1,871
89040	Moapa Valley (c)	(702)	5,784	3,444
89191	Nellis AFB (c)	(702)	8,896	8,377
*89030	North Las Vegas	(702)	115,488	47,849
*89041	Pahrump (c)	(775)	24,631	7,424
89109	Paradise (c)	(775)	186,070	124,682
*89501	Reno	(775)	180,480	134,230
89436	Spanish Springs (c)	(775)	9,018	—
*89431	Sparks	(775)	66,346	53,367
89815	Spring Creek (c)	(702)	10,548	5,866
—	Spring Valley (c)	(702)	117,390	51,726
89110	Sunrise Manor (c)	(702)	156,120	95,362
89433	Sun Valley (c)	(775)	19,461	11,391
89101	Winchester (c)	(702)	26,958	23,365
*89445	Winnemucca	(775)	7,174	6,473

New Hampshire (603)

See introductory note.

ZIP	Place	2000	1990
03031	*Amherst*	10,769	9,068
03811	*Atkinson*	6,178	5,188
03825	*Barrington*	7,475	6,164
03110	*Bedford*	18,274	12,563
03220	*Belmont*	6,716	5,796
03570	Berlin	10,331	11,824
03304	*Bow*	7,138	5,500
03743	Claremont	13,151	13,902
*03301	Concord	40,687	36,006
03818	*Conway*	8,604	7,940
03038	Derry (c)	22,661	20,446
03038	*Derry*	34,021	29,603
*03820	Dover	26,884	25,042
03824	Durham (c)	9,024	9,236
03824	*Durham*	12,664	11,818
03042	*Epping*	5,476	5,162
03833	Exeter (c)	9,759	9,556
03833	*Exeter*	14,058	12,481
03835	*Farmington*	5,774	5,739
03235	Franklin	8,405	8,304
03246	*Gilford*	6,803	5,867
03045	*Goffstown*	16,929	14,621
03841	*Hampstead*	8,297	6,732
*03842	Hampton (c)	9,126	7,989
*03842	*Hampton*	14,937	12,278
03755	Hanover Compact (c)	8,162	6,538
03755	*Hanover*	10,850	9,212
03049	*Hollis*	7,015	5,705
03106	*Hooksett*	11,721	9,002
03229	*Hopkinton*	5,399	4,806
03051	Hudson (c)	7,814	7,626
03051	*Hudson*	22,928	19,530
03452	*Jaffrey*	5,476	5,361
03431	Keene	22,563	22,430
03848	*Kingston*	5,862	5,591
*03246	Laconia	16,411	15,743
*03766	Lebanon	12,568	12,183
03052	*Litchfield*	7,360	5,516
03561	*Littleton*	5,845	5,827
03053	Londonderry (c)	11,417	10,114
03053	*Londonderry*	23,236	19,781
*03103	Manchester	107,006	99,332
03253	*Meredith*	5,943	4,837
03054	*Merrimack*	25,119	22,156
03055	Milford (c)	8,293	8,015
03055	*Milford*	13,535	11,795
*03060	Nashua	86,605	79,662
03857	Newmarket (c)	5,124	4,917
03857	*Newmarket*	8,027	7,157
03773	*Newport*	6,269	6,110
03076	*Pelham*	10,914	9,408
03275	*Pembroke*	6,897	6,561
03458	*Peterborough*	5,883	5,239
03102	Pinardville (c)	5,779	4,654
03865	*Plaistow*	7,747	7,316
03264	*Plymouth*	5,892	5,811
*03801	Portsmouth	20,784	25,925
03077	*Raymond*	9,674	8,713
03461	*Rindge*	5,451	4,941
*03867	Rochester	28,461	26,630
03870	*Rye*	5,182	—
03079	*Salem*	28,112	25,746
03873	*Sandown*	5,143	—
03874	*Seabrook*	7,934	6,503
03878	Somersworth	11,477	11,249
03106	South Hooksett (c)	5,282	3,638
03885	*Stratham*	6,355	4,955
03275	Suncook (c)	5,362	5,214
03446	*Swanzey*	6,800	6,236
03281	*Weare*	7,776	6,193
03087	*Windham*	10,709	9,000
03894	*Wolfeboro*	6,083	4,807

New Jersey

Area code (551) overlays area code (201).
Area code (848) overlays (732). Area code (862) overlays (973).
See introductory note.

ZIP	Place	Area Code	2000	1990
08201	Absecon	(609)	7,638	7,298
07401	Allendale	(201)	6,699	5,900
07712	Asbury Park	(732)	16,930	16,799
08034	Ashland (c)		8,375	—
*08401	Atlantic City	(609)	40,517	37,986
08106	Audubon	(856)	9,182	9,205
07001	Avenel (c)	(732)	17,552	15,504
—	Barclay-Kingston (c)		10,728	—
08007	Barrington	(856)	7,084	6,792
07002	Bayonne	(201)	61,842	61,464
08722	Beachwood	(732)	10,375	9,324
07109	Belleville (c)	(973)	35,928	34,213
*08031	Bellmawr	(856)	11,262	12,603
07719	Belmar	(732)	6,045	5,877
07621	Bergenfield	(201)	26,247	24,458
07922	Berkeley Heights (c)	(908)	13,407	11,980
08009	Berlin	(856)	6,149	5,672
07924	Bernardsville	(908)	7,345	6,597
07003	Bloomfield (c)	(973)	47,683	45,061
07403	Bloomingdale	(973)	7,610	7,530
07603	Bogota	(201)	8,249	7,824
07005	Boonton	(973)	8,496	8,343
08805	Bound Brook	(732)	10,155	9,487
08302	Bridgeton	(856)	22,771	18,942
08203	Brigantine	(609)	12,594	11,354
08015	Browns Mills (c)	(609)	11,257	11,429
07828	Budd Lake (c)	(973)	8,100	7,272
08016	Burlington	(609)	9,736	9,835
07405	Butler	(973)	7,420	7,392
*07006	Caldwell	(973)	7,584	7,542
*08101	Camden	(856)	79,904	87,492
07072	Carlstadt	(201)	5,917	5,510
08069	Carney's Point (c)	(856)	6,914	8,443
07008	Carteret	(732)	20,709	19,025
07009	Cedar Grove (c) (Essex)	(973)	12,300	12,053
07928	Chatham	(973)	8,460	8,007
08002	Cherry Hill Mall (c)	(856)	13,238	—
07066	Clark (c)	(732)/(908)	14,597	14,629
08312	Clayton	(856)	7,139	6,155
07010	Cliffside Park	(201)	23,007	20,393
*07015	Clifton	(973)	78,672	71,984
07624	Closter	(201)	8,383	8,094
08108	Collingswood	(856)	14,326	15,289
07067	Colonia (c)	(732)	17,811	18,238

ZIP	Place	Area Code	2000	1990
07016	Cranford (c)	(908)	22,578	22,633
07626	Cresskill	(201)	7,746	7,558
08759	Crestwood Village (c)	(732)	8,392	8,030
08810	Dayton (c)	(732)	6,235	4,321
*07801	Dover	(973)	18,188	15,115
07628	Dumont	(201)	17,503	17,187
08812	Dunellen	(732)	6,823	6,528
08816	East Brunswick (c)	(732)	46,756	43,548
*07019	East Orange	(973)	69,824	73,552
07073	East Rutherford	(201)/(973)	8,716	7,902
*07724	Eatontown	(732)	14,008	13,800
08043	Echelon (c)	(856)	10,440	—
07020	Edgewater	(201)	7,677	5,001
*08818	Edison (c)	(732)/(908)	97,687	88,680
*07207	Elizabeth	(908)	120,568	110,002
07407	Elmwood Park	(201)	18,925	17,623
07630	Emerson	(201)	7,197	6,930
07631	Englewood	(201)	26,203	24,850
07632	Englewood Cliffs	(201)	5,322	5,634
08002	Erlton-Ellisburg (c)		8,168	—
08618	Ewing (c)	(609)	35,707	34,185
07004	Fairfield (Essex) (c)	(973)	7,063	7,615
07704	Fair Haven	(732)	5,937	5,270
07410	Fair Lawn	(201)/(973)	31,637	30,548
07022	Fairview (Bergen)	(201)	13,255	10,733
07023	Fanwood	(908)	7,174	7,115
08518	Florence-Roebling (c)	(609)	8,200	8,564
07932	Florham Park	(973)	8,857	8,521
08863	Fords (c)	(732)	15,032	14,392
08640	Fort Dix (c)	(609)	7,464	10,205
07024	Fort Lee	(201)	35,461	31,997
07416	Franklin (Sussex)	(973)	5,160	4,977
07417	Franklin Lakes	(201)	10,422	9,873
07728	Freehold	(732)	10,976	10,742
07026	Garfield	(201)	29,786	26,727
08028	Glassboro	(856)	19,068	15,614
07028	Glen Ridge	(973)	7,271	7,076
07452	Glen Rock	(201)	11,546	10,883
08030	Gloucester City	(856)	11,484	12,649
—	Greentree (c)		11,536	—
07093	Guttenberg	(201)	10,807	8,268
*07602	Hackensack	(201)	42,677	37,049
07840	Hackettstown	(908)	10,403	8,120
08033	Haddonfield	(856)	11,659	11,633
08035	Haddon Heights	(856)	7,547	7,860
*07508	Haledon	(973)	8,252	6,951
08037	Hammonton	(609)	12,604	12,208
07029	Harrison	(973)	14,424	13,425
07604	Hasbrouck Heights	(201)	11,662	11,488
*07506	Hawthorne	(973)	18,218	17,084
07422	Highland Lake (c)	(973)	5,051	4,550
08904	Highland Park (Middlesex)	(732)	13,999	13,279
07732	Highlands	(732)	5,097	4,849
08520	Hightstown	(609)	5,216	5,126
07642	Hillsdale	(201)	10,087	9,750
07205	Hillside (c)	(908)/(973)	21,747	21,044
07030	Hoboken	(201)	38,577	33,397
08753	Holiday City-Berkeley (c)	(732)	13,884	14,293
07843	Hopatcong	(973)	15,888	15,586
07111	Irvington (c)	(973)	60,695	59,774
08830	Iselin (c)	(732)	16,698	16,141
08831	Jamesburg	(732)	6,025	5,294
*07303	Jersey City	(201)	240,055	228,517
07734	Keansburg	(732)	10,732	11,069
07032	Kearny	(201)/(973)	40,513	34,874
08824	Kendall Park (c)	(908)	9,006	7,127
07033	Kenilworth	(908)	7,675	7,574
07735	Keyport	(732)	7,568	7,586
07405	Kinnelon	(973)	9,365	8,470
07871	Lake Mohawk (c)	(973)	9,755	8,930
08701	Lakewood (c)	(732)	36,065	26,095
08879	Laurence Harbor (c)	(732)	6,227	6,361
*08733	Leisure Village West-Pine Lake Park (c)	(732)	11,085	10,139
07605	Leonia	(201)	8,914	8,365
07035	Lincoln Park	(973)	10,930	10,978
07738	Lincroft (c)	(732)	6,255	6,193
07036	Linden	(732)/(908)	39,394	36,701
08021	Lindenwold	(856)	17,414	18,734
08221	Linwood	(609)	7,172	6,866
07424	Little Falls (c)	(973)	10,855	11,294
07643	Little Ferry	(201)	10,800	9,989
07739	Little Silver	(732)	6,170	5,721
07039	Livingston (c)	(973)	27,391	26,609
07644	Lodi	(201)/(973)	23,971	22,355
07740	Long Branch	(732)	31,340	28,658
07071	Lyndhurst (c)	(201)	19,383	18,262
08641	McGuire AFB (c)	(609)	6,478	7,580
07940	Madison	(973)	16,530	15,850
08859	Madison Park (c)	(732)	6,929	7,490
08736	Manasquan	(732)	6,310	5,369
08835	Manville	(908)	10,343	10,567
07040	Maplewood (c)	(973)	23,868	21,756
08402	Margate City	(609)	8,193	8,431
08053	Marlton (c)	(856)	10,260	10,228
07747	Matawan	(732)	8,910	9,239
07607	Maywood	(201)	9,523	9,536
07945	Mendham	(973)	5,097	4,890
08619	Mercerville-Hamilton Sq. (c)	(609)	26,419	26,873
08840	Metuchen	(732)	12,840	12,804
08846	Middlesex	(732)	13,717	13,055
07432	Midland Park	(201)	6,947	7,047
07041	Millburn (c)	(973)	19,765	18,630
08850	Milltown (Middlesex)	(732)	7,000	6,968
08332	Millville	(856)	26,847	25,992
*07042	Montclair (c)	(973)	38,977	37,729
07645	Montvale	(201)	7,034	6,946
08057	Moorestown-Lenola (c)	(856)	13,860	13,242
07751	Morganville (c)	(732)	11,255	—
07950	Morris Plains	(973)	5,236	5,219
*07960	Morristown	(973)	18,544	16,189
07092	Mountainside	(908)	6,602	6,657
08087	Mystic Island (c)	(609)	8,694	7,400
07753	Neptune City	(732)	5,218	4,997
*07102	Newark	(973)	273,546	275,221
*08901	New Brunswick	(732)	48,573	41,711
07646	New Milford	(201)	16,400	15,990
07974	New Providence	(908)	11,907	11,439
07860	Newton	(973)	8,244	7,521
07031	North Arlington	(201)	15,181	13,790
08902	North Brunswick Twp. (c)	(732)	36,287	31,287
07006	North Caldwell	(973)	7,375	6,706
08225	Northfield	(609)	7,725	7,305
07508	North Haledon	(973)	7,920	7,987
07060	North Plainfield	(908)	21,103	18,820
07648	Norwood	(201)	5,751	4,858
07110	Nutley (c)	(973)	27,362	27,099
07436	Oakland	(201)	12,466	11,997
*08050	Ocean Acres (c)	(609)	13,155	5,587
08226	Ocean City	(609)	15,378	15,512
07757	Oceanport	(732)	5,807	6,146
08857	Old Bridge (c)	(732)	22,833	22,151
07675	Old Tappan	(201)	5,482	4,254
07649	Oradell	(201)	8,047	8,024
*07051	Orange (c)	(973)	32,868	29,925
07650	Palisades Park	(201)	17,073	14,536
08065	Palmyra	(856)	7,091	7,056
*07652	Paramus	(201)	25,737	25,004
07656	Park Ridge	(201)	8,708	8,102
07055	Passaic	(973)	67,861	58,041
*07510	Paterson	(973)	149,222	140,891
08066	Paulsboro	(856)	6,160	6,577
08110	Pennsauken (c)	(856)	35,737	34,738
08070	Pennsville (c)	(856)	11,657	12,218
*08861	Perth Amboy	(732)	47,303	41,967
08865	Phillipsburg	(908)	15,166	15,757
08021	Pine Hill	(856)	10,880	9,854
08071	Pitman	(856)	9,331	9,365
*07061	Plainfield	(908)	47,829	46,577
08232	Pleasantville	(609)	19,012	16,027
08742	Point Pleasant	(732)	19,306	18,177
08742	Point Pleasant Beach	(732)	5,314	5,112
07442	Pompton Lakes	(973)	10,640	10,539
*08540	Princeton	(609)	14,203	12,016
—	Princeton Meadows (c)	(609)	13,436	—
07508	Prospect Park	(973)	5,779	5,053
07065	Rahway	(732)	26,500	25,325
08057	Ramblewood (c)	(856)	6,003	6,181
07446	Ramsey	(201)	14,351	13,228
—	Ramtown (c)	(732)	5,932	—
08869	Raritan	(908)	6,338	5,798
07701	Red Bank	(732)	11,844	10,636
07657	Ridgefield	(201)	10,830	9,996
07660	Ridgefield Park	(201)	12,873	12,454
*07451	Ridgewood	(201)/(973)	24,936	24,152
07456	Ringwood	(973)	12,396	12,623
07661	River Edge	(201)	10,946	10,603
07675	River Vale (c)	(201)	9,449	9,410
07662	Rochelle Park (c)	(201)	5,528	5,587
07866	Rockaway	(973)	6,473	6,243
07068	Roseland	(973)	5,298	4,847
07203	Roselle	(908)	21,274	20,314
07204	Roselle Park	(908)	13,281	12,805
07760	Rumson	(732)	7,137	6,701
08078	Runnemede	(856)	8,533	9,042
07070	Rutherford	(201)	18,110	17,790
07663	Saddle Brook (c)	(201)/(973)	13,155	13,296
08079	Salem	(856)	5,857	6,883
*08872	Sayreville	(732)	40,377	34,998
07076	Scotch Plains (c)	(732)/(908)	22,732	21,150
*07094	Secaucus	(201)	15,931	14,061
08083	Somerdale	(856)	5,192	5,440
*08873	Somerset (c)	(732)	23,040	22,070
08244	Somers Point	(609)	11,614	11,216
08876	Somerville	(908)	12,423	11,632
08879	South Amboy	(732)	7,913	7,851
07079	South Orange (c)	(973)	16,964	16,390
07080	South Plainfield	(732)/(908)	21,810	20,489
08882	South River	(732)	15,322	13,692
08884	Spotswood	(732)	7,880	7,983
—	Springdale (c)		14,409	—
07081	Springfield (c)	(908)/(973)	14,429	13,420
07762	Spring Lake Heights	(732)	5,227	5,341
08084	Stratford	(856)	7,271	7,614

ZIP	Place	Area Code	2000	1990
07747	Strathmore (c)	(732)	6,740	7,060
07876	Succasunna-Kenvil (c)	(201)	12,569	11,781
*07901	Summit	(908)	21,131	19,757
07666	Teaneck (c)	(201)	39,260	37,825
07670	Tenafly	(201)	13,806	13,326
07724	Tinton Falls	(732)	15,053	12,361
*08753	Toms River (c)	(732)	86,327	7,524
*07512	Totowa	(973)	9,892	10,177
*08650	Trenton	(609)	85,403	88,675
08520	Twin Rivers (c)	(609)	7,422	7,715
07083	Union (Union) (c)	(908)	54,405	50,024
07735	Union Beach	(732)	6,649	6,156
07087	Union City	(201)	67,088	58,012
07458	Upper Saddle River	(201)	7,741	7,198
08406	Ventnor City	(609)	12,910	11,005
07044	Verona (c)	(973)	13,533	13,597
08251	Villas (c)	(609)	9,064	8,136
*08360	Vineland	(856)	56,271	54,780
07463	Waldwick	(201)	9,622	9,757
07057	Wallington	(201)/(973)	11,583	10,828
07465	Wanaque	(201)/(973)	10,266	9,711
07882	Washington	(908)	6,712	6,474
07675	Washington Twp. (Bergen) (c)	(201)	8,938	9,245
07060	Watchung	(908)	5,613	5,110
*07470	Wayne (c)	(973)	54,069	47,025
*07006	West Caldwell (c)	(973)	11,233	10,422
*07091	Westfield	(732)/(908)	29,644	28,870
07728	West Freehold (c)	(732)	12,498	11,166
07764	West Long Branch	(732)	8,258	7,690
07480	West Milford (c)	(973)	26,410	25,430
07093	West New York	(201)	45,768	38,125
07052	West Orange (c)	(973)	44,943	39,103
07424	West Paterson	(973)	10,987	10,982
07675	Westwood	(201)	10,999	10,446
07885	Wharton	(973)	6,298	5,405
08610	White Horse (c)	(609)	9,373	9,397
07886	White Meadow Lake (c)	(973)	9,052	8,002
08260	Wildwood	(609)	5,436	4,484
08094	Williamstown (c)	(856)	11,812	10,891
07095	Woodbridge (c)	(732)	18,309	17,434
08096	Woodbury	(856)	10,307	10,904
07675	Woodcliff Lake	(201)	5,745	5,303
07075	Wood-Ridge	(201)/(973)	7,644	7,506
07481	Wyckoff (c)	(201)	16,508	15,372
08620	Yardville-Groveville (c)	(609)	9,208	9,248
07726	Yorketown (c)	(600)	6,712	6,313

New Mexico

Area code (575) goes into effect June 1, 2003. Before then use area code (505). See introductory note.

ZIP	Place	Area Code	2000	1990
*88310	Alamogordo	(505)	35,582	27,596
*87101	Albuquerque	(575)	448,607	384,915
88021	Anthony (c)	(505)	7,904	5,160
*88210	Artesia	(505)	10,692	10,610
87410	Aztec	(505)	6,378	5,480
87002	Belen	(575)	6,901	6,547
87004	Bernalillo	(575)	6,611	5,864
87413	Bloomfield	(505)	6,417	5,214
*88220	Carlsbad	(505)	25,625	24,952
88021	Chaparral (c)	(505)	6,117	2,962
*88101	Clovis	(505)	32,667	30,954
87048	Corrales	(575)	7,334	5,453
*88030	Deming	(505)	14,116	11,422
—	El Cerro-Monterey Park (c)	(575)	5,483	—
—	Eldorado at Santa Fe (c)	(575)	5,799	2,260
*87532	Espanola	(505)	9,688	8,389
*87401	Farmington	(505)	37,844	33,997
*87301	Gallup	(505)	20,209	19,157
87020	Grants	(505)	8,806	8,626
*88240	Hobbs	(505)	28,657	29,121
87417	Kirtland (c)	(505)	6,190	3,552
*88001	Las Cruces	(505)	74,267	62,360
87701	Las Vegas	(505)	14,565	14,753
87544	Los Alamos (c)	(575)	11,909	11,455
87002	Los Chaves (c)	(575)	5,033	3,872
87031	Los Lunas	(575)	10,034	6,013
87107	Los Ranchos de Albuquerque	(575)	5,092	5,075
88260	Lovington	(505)	9,471	9,322
87107	North Valley (c)	(575)	11,923	12,507
88130	Portales	(505)	11,131	10,690
87740	Raton	(505)	7,282	7,372
*87124	Rio Rancho	(575)	51,765	32,512
*88201	Roswell	(505)	45,293	44,260
*88345	Ruidoso	(505)	7,698	4,600
*87501	Santa Fe	(575)	62,203	56,537
87420	Shiprock (c)	(505)	8,156	7,687
*88061	Silver City	(505)	10,545	10,683
87801	Socorro	(505)	8,877	8,159
87105	South Valley (c)	(575)	39,060	35,701
88063	Sunland Park	(505)	13,309	8,179
87901	Truth or Consequences	(505)	7,289	6,221
88401	Tucumcari	(505)	5,989	6,827
87544	White Rock (c)	(575)	6,045	6,192
87327	Zuni Pueblo (c)	(505)	6,367	5,857

New York

Area code (347) overlays area code (718). Area codes (646) and (917) overlay (212). See introductory note.

ZIP	Place	Area Code	2000	1990
10901	Airmont	(845)	7,799	7,674
*12201	Albany	(518)	95,658	100,031
11507	Albertson (c)	(516)	5,200	5,166
14411	Albion	(585)	1,438	5,863
*11701	Amityville	(516)/(631)	9,441	9,286
12010	Amsterdam	(518)	18,355	20,714
12603	Arlington (c)	(845)	12,481	11,948
*13021	Auburn	(315)	28,574	31,258
11702	Babylon	(631)	12,615	12,249
11510	Baldwin (c)	(516)	23,455	22,719
11510	Baldwin Harbor (c)	(516)	8,147	7,899
13027	Baldwinsville	(315)	7,053	6,591
12020	Ballston Spa	(518)	5,556	5,194
*14020	Batavia	(585)	16,256	16,310
14810	Bath	(607)	5,641	5,801
11705	Bayport (c)	(631)	8,662	7,702
11706	Bay Shore (c)	(631)	23,852	21,279
11709	Bayville	(516)	7,135	7,193
11751	Baywood (c)	(631)	7,571	7,351
12508	Beacon	(845)	13,808	13,243
11710	Bellmore (c)	(516)	16,441	16,438
11714	Bethpage (c)	(516)	16,543	15,761
*13902	Binghamton	(607)	47,380	53,008
10913	Blauvelt (c)	(845)	5,207	4,838
11716	Bohemia (c)	(631)	9,871	9,556
11717	Brentwood (c)	(631)	53,017	45,218
10510	Briarcliff Manor	(914)	7,696	7,070
14610	Brighton (c)	(585)	35,584	34,455
14420	Brockport	(585)	8,103	8,749
10708	Bronxville	(914)	6,543	6,028
*14240	Buffalo	(716)	292,648	328,175
11933	Calverton (c)	(631)	5,704	4,759
*14424	Canandaigua	(585)	11,264	10,725
13617	Canton	(315)	5,882	6,379
11514	Carle Place (c)	(516)	5,247	5,107
10512	Carmel Hamlet (c)	(845)	5,650	4,800
11516	Cedarhurst	(516)	6,164	5,716
11720	Centereach (c)	(631)	27,285	26,720
11934	Center Moriches (c)	(631)	6,655	5,987
11721	Centerport (Suffolk) (c)	(631)	5,446	5,333
11722	Central Islip (c)	(516)	31,950	26,028
10514	Chappaqua (c)	(914)	9,468	—
14225	Cheektowaga (c)	(716)	79,988	84,387
10977	Chestnut Ridge	(845)	7,829	7,517
12047	Cohoes	(518)	15,521	16,825
12205	Colonie	(518)	7,916	8,019
11725	Commack (c)	(631)	36,367	36,124
10920	Congers (c)	(845)	8,303	8,003
11726	Copiague (c)	(631)	21,922	20,769
11727	Coram (c)	(631)	34,923	30,111
14830	Corning	(607)	10,842	11,938
13045	Cortland	(607)	18,740	19,801
*10520	Croton-on-Hudson	(914)	7,606	7,018
11729	Deer Park (c)	(631)	28,316	28,840
12054	Delmar (c)	(518)	8,292	8,360
14043	Depew	(716)	16,629	17,673
11746	Dix Hills (c)	(631)	26,024	25,849
10522	Dobbs Ferry	(914)	10,622	9,940
14048	Dunkirk	(716)	13,131	13,989
14052	East Aurora	(585)/(716)	6,673	6,647
10709	Eastchester (c)	(914)	18,564	18,537
11735	East Farmingdale	(516)/(631)	5,400	4,510
12302	East Glenville (c)	(518)	6,064	6,518
11576	East Hills	(516)	6,842	6,746
11730	East Islip (c)	(631)	14,078	14,325
11758	East Massapequa (c)	(516)	19,565	19,550
11554	East Meadow (c)	(516)	37,461	36,909
11731	East Northport (c)	(631)	20,845	20,411
11772	East Patchogue (c)	(631)	20,824	20,195
14445	East Rochester	(585)	6,650	6,932
11518	East Rockaway	(516)	10,414	10,152
11786	East Shoreham (c)	(631)	5,809	5,461
*14901	Elmira	(607)	30,940	33,724
11003	Elmont (c)	(516)	32,657	28,612
11731	Elwood (c)	(631)	10,916	10,916
*13760	Endicott	(607)	13,038	13,531
13762	Endwell (c)	(607)	11,706	12,602
13219	Fairmount (c)	(315)	10,795	12,266
14450	Fairport	(585)	5,740	5,943
—	Fairview (c)	(845)	5,421	4,811
11735	Farmingdale	(516)	8,399	8,022
11738	Farmingville (c)	(631)	16,458	14,842
*11001	Floral Park	(516)	15,967	15,947
13603	Fort Drum (c)	(315)	12,123	11,578
11768	Fort Salonga (c)	(631)	9,634	9,176
11010	Franklin Square (Nassau) (c)	(516)	29,342	28,205
14063	Fredonia	(716)	10,706	10,436
11520	Freeport	(516)	43,783	39,894
13069	Fulton	(315)	11,855	12,929
*11530	Garden City	(516)	21,672	21,675
11040	Garden City Park (c)	(516)	7,554	7,437
14624	Gates-North Gates (c)	(585)	15,138	14,995
14454	Geneseo	(585)	7,579	7,187
14456	Geneva	(315)	13,617	14,143

ZIP	Place	Area Code	2000	1990
11542	Glen Cove	(516)	26,622	24,149
12801	Glens Falls	(518)	14,354	15,023
12801	Glens Falls North (c)	(518)	8,061	7,978
12078	Gloversville	(518)	15,413	16,656
10924	Goshen	(845)	5,676	5,255
13642	Gouverneur	(315)	7,418	4,604
*11021	Great Neck	(516)	9,538	8,745
11020	Great Neck Plaza	(516)	6,433	5,897
14616	Greece (c)	(585)	14,614	15,632
11740	Greenlawn (c)	(631)	13,286	13,208
*10583	Greenville (Westchester) (c)	(914)	8,648	9,528
14075	Hamburg	(716)	10,116	10,442
11946	Hampton Bays (c)	(631)	12,236	7,893
10528	Harrison	(914)	24,154	23,308
10530	Hartsdale (c)	(914)	9,830	9,587
10706	Hastings-on-Hudson	(914)	7,648	8,000
*11788	Hauppauge (c)	(631)	20,100	19,750
10927	Haverstraw	(845)	10,117	9,438
10532	Hawthorne (c)	(845)	5,083	4,764
*11551	Hempstead	(516)	56,554	45,982
13350	Herkimer	(315)	7,498	7,945
11557	Hewlett (c)	(516)	7,060	6,620
*11802	Hicksville (c)	(516)	41,260	40,174
12528	Highland (c)	(845)	5,060	4,492
10977	Hillcrest (c)	(845)	7,106	6,447
14468	Hilton	(585)	5,856	5,216
11741	Holbrook (c)	(631)	27,512	25,273
11742	Holtsville (c)	(631)	17,006	14,972
14843	Hornell	(607)	9,019	9,877
*14845	Horseheads	(607)	6,452	6,802
12534	Hudson	(518)	7,524	8,034
12839	Hudson Falls	(518)	6,927	7,651
11743	Huntington (c)	(631)	18,403	18,243
11746	Huntington Station (c)	(631)	29,910	28,247
13357	Ilion	(315)	8,610	8,888
11096	Inwood (c)	(516)	9,325	7,767
14617	Irondequoit (c)	(585)	52,354	52,322
10533	Irvington	(914)	6,631	6,348
11751	Islip (c)	(631)	20,575	18,924
11752	Islip Terrace (c)	(631)	5,641	5,530
*14850	Ithaca	(607)	29,287	29,541
*14702	Jamestown	(716)	31,730	34,681
10535	Jefferson Valley-Yorktown (c)	(914)	14,891	14,118
11753	Jericho (Nassau) (c)	(516)	13,045	13,141
13790	Johnson City	(607)	15,535	16,578
12095	Johnstown	(518)	8,511	9,058
14217	Kenmore	(716)	16,426	17,180
11754	Kings Park (c)	(631)	16,146	17,773
11024	Kings Point	(516)	5,076	4,843
*12401	Kingston	(845)	23,456	23,095
10950	Kiryas Joel	(845)	13,138	7,437
14218	Lackawanna	(716)	19,064	20,585
10512	Lake Carmel (c)	(845)	8,663	8,489
11755	Lake Grove	(631)	10,250	9,612
10547	Lake Mohegan (c)	(914)	5,979	—
11779	Lake Ronkonkoma (c)	(631)	19,701	18,997
11552	Lakeview (c)	(516)	5,607	5,476
14086	Lancaster	(716)	11,188	11,940
10538	Larchmont	(914)	6,485	6,181
11559	Lawrence	(516)	6,522	6,513
11756	Levittown (c)	(516)	53,067	53,286
11757	Lindenhurst	(631)	27,819	26,879
13365	Little Falls	(315)	5,188	5,829
*14094	Lockport	(716)	22,279	24,426
11561	Long Beach	(516)	35,462	33,510
11563	Lynbrook	(516)	19,911	19,208
10541	Mahopac (c)	(845)	8,478	7,755
12953	Malone	(518)	6,075	6,777
11565	Malverne	(516)	8,934	9,054
10543	Mamaroneck	(914)	18,752	17,325
11030	Manhasset (c)	(516)	8,362	7,718
11050	Manorhaven	(516)	6,138	5,672
11949	Manorville (c)	(631)	11,131	6,198
11758	Massapequa (c)	(516)	22,652	22,018
11762	Massapequa Park	(516)	17,499	18,044
13662	Massena	(315)	11,209	11,716
11950	Mastic (c)	(631)	15,436	13,778
11951	Mastic Beach (c)	(631)	11,543	10,293
13211	Mattydale (c)	(315)	6,367	6,418
—	Mechanicstown (c)	(845)	6,061	—
12118	Mechanicville	(518)	5,019	5,249
11763	Medford (c)	(631)	21,985	21,274
14103	Medina	(585)/(716)	6,415	6,686
11747	Melville (c)	(631)	14,533	12,586
11566	Merrick (c)	(516)	22,764	23,042
11953	Middle Island (c)	(631)	9,702	7,848
*10940	Middletown	(845)	25,388	24,160
11764	Miller Place (c)	(631)	10,580	9,315
11501	Mineola	(516)	19,234	19,005
10950	Monroe	(845)	7,780	6,672
10952	Monsey (c)	(845)	14,504	13,986
12701	Monticello	(845)	6,512	6,597
10970	Mount Ivy (c)	(845)	6,536	6,013
10549	Mount Kisco	(914)	9,983	9,108
11766	Mount Sinai (c)	(631)	8,734	8,023
*10551	Mount Vernon	(914)	68,381	67,153
12590	Myers Corner (c)	(845)	5,546	5,599
10954	Nanuet (c)	(845)	16,707	14,065
11767	Nesconset (c)	(631)	11,992	10,712
14513	Newark	(315)	9,682	9,849
*12550	Newburgh	(845)	28,259	26,454
11590	New Cassel (c)	(516)	13,298	10,257
10956	New City (c)	(845)	34,038	33,673
*11040	New Hyde Park	(516)	9,523	9,728
12561	New Paltz	(845)	6,034	5,470
*10802	New Rochelle	(914)	72,182	67,265
*12550	New Windsor (c)	(845)	9,077	8,898
*10001	New York	(212)/(718)	8,008,278	7,322,564
*14302	Niagara Falls	(716)	55,593	61,840
11701	North Amityville (c)	(631)	16,572	13,849
11703	North Babylon (c)	(631)	17,877	18,081
11706	North Bay Shore (c)	(631)	14,992	12,799
11710	North Bellmore (c)	(516)	20,079	19,707
11713	North Bellport (c)	(631)	9,007	8,182
11757	North Lindenhurst (c)	(631)	11,767	10,563
11758	North Massapequa (c)	(516)	19,152	19,365
11566	North Merrick (c)	(516)	11,844	12,113
11040	North New Hyde Park (c)	(516)	14,542	14,359
11772	North Patchogue (c)	(631)	7,825	7,374
11768	Northport	(631)	7,606	7,572
13212	North Syracuse	(315)	6,862	7,363
14120	North Tonawanda	(716)	33,262	34,989
11580	North Valley Stream (c)	(516)	15,789	14,574
11793	North Wantagh (c)	(516)	12,156	12,276
13815	Norwich	(607)	7,355	7,613
10960	Nyack	(845)	6,737	6,558
11769	Oakdale (c)	(631)	8,075	7,875
11572	Oceanside (c)	(516)	32,733	32,423
13669	Ogdensburg	(315)	12,364	13,521
11804	Old Bethpage (c)	(516)	5,400	5,610
14760	Olean	(585)/(716)	15,347	16,946
13421	Oneida	(315)	10,987	10,850
13820	Oneonta	(607)	13,292	13,954
12550	Orange Lake (c)	(845)	6,085	5,196
10562	Ossining	(914)	24,010	22,582
13126	Oswego	(315)	17,954	19,195
11771	Oyster Bay (c)	(516)	6,826	6,687
11772	Patchogue	(631)	11,919	11,060
10965	Pearl River (c)	(845)	15,553	15,314
10566	Peekskill	(914)	22,441	19,536
10803	Pelham	(914)	6,400	5,443
10803	Pelham Manor	(914)	5,466	6,413
14527	Penn Yan	(315)	5,219	5,248
11714	Plainedge (c)	(516)	9,195	8,739
11803	Plainview (c)	(516)	25,637	26,207
*12901	Plattsburgh	(518)	18,816	21,255
10570	Pleasantville	(914)	7,172	6,592
10573	Port Chester	(914)	27,867	24,728
11777	Port Jefferson	(631)	7,837	7,455
11776	Port Jefferson Station (c)	(631)	7,527	7,232
12771	Port Jervis	(845)	8,860	9,060
11050	Port Washington (c)	(516)	15,215	15,387
13676	Potsdam	(315)	9,425	10,251
*12601	Poughkeepsie	(845)	29,871	28,844
12144	Rensselaer	(518)	7,761	8,255
11961	Ridge (c)	(631)	13,380	11,734
11901	Riverhead (c)	(631)	10,513	8,814
*14692	Rochester	(585)	219,773	230,356
*11571	Rockville Centre	(516)	24,568	24,727
11778	Rocky Point (c)	(631)	10,185	8,596
*13440	Rome	(315)	34,950	44,350
11779	Ronkonkoma (c)	(631)	20,029	20,391
11575	Roosevelt (c)	(516)	15,854	15,030
11577	Roslyn Heights (c)	(516)	6,295	6,405
12303	Rotterdam (c)	(518)	20,536	21,228
10580	Rye	(914)	14,955	14,936
10573	Rye Brook	(914)	8,602	7,765
11780	Saint James (c)	(631)	13,268	12,703
14779	Salamanca	(716)	6,097	6,566
13454	Salisbury (c)	(315)	12,341	12,226
12983	Saranac Lake	(518)	5,041	5,377
12866	Saratoga Springs	(518)	26,186	25,001
11782	Sayville (c)	(631)	16,735	16,550
10583	Scarsdale	(914)	17,823	16,987
*12301	Schenectady	(518)	61,821	65,566
10940	Scotchtown (c)	(845)	8,954	8,765
12302	Scotia	(518)	7,957	7,359
11579	Sea Cliff	(516)	5,066	5,054
11783	Seaford (c)	(516)	15,791	15,597
11507	Searingtown (c)	(516)	5,034	5,020
11784	Selden (c)	(631)	21,861	20,608
13148	Seneca Falls	(315)	6,861	7,370
11733	Setauket-East Setauket (c)	(516)	15,931	13,634
11967	Shirley (Suffolk) (c)	(631)	25,395	22,936
10591	Sleepy Hollow[1]	(914)	9,212	8,152
11787	Smithtown (c)	(631)	26,901	25,638
13209	Solvay	(315)	6,845	6,717
11789	Sound Beach (c)	(631)	9,807	9,102
11735	South Farmingdale (c)	(516)	15,061	15,377
14850	South Hill (c)	(607)	6,003	5,423
11746	South Huntington (c)	(631)	9,465	9,624
14094	South Lockport (c)	(716)	8,552	7,112
11971	Southold (c)	(631)	5,465	5,192
14904	Southport (c)	(607)	7,396	7,753
11581	South Valley Stream (c)	(516)	5,638	5,328

ZIP	Place	Area Code	2000	1990
10977	Spring Valley	(845)	25,464	21,802
*11790	Stony Brook (c)	(631)	13,727	13,726
10980	Stony Point (c) (Rockland)	(845)	11,744	10,587
10901	Suffern	(845)	11,006	11,055
11791	Syosset (c)	(516)	18,544	18,967
*13220	Syracuse	(315)	147,306	163,860
10983	Tappan (c)	(845)	6,757	6,867
10591	Tarrytown	(914)	11,090	10,739
11776	Terryville (c)	(631)	10,589	10,275
10594	Thornwood (c)	(914)	5,980	7,025
*14150	Tonawanda	(716)	16,136	17,284
*14150	Tonawanda (c)	(716)	61,729	65,284
*12180	Troy	(518)	49,170	54,269
10707	Tuckahoe	(914)	6,211	6,302
11553	Uniondale (c)	(516)	23,011	20,328
*13504	Utica	(315)	60,651	68,637
10595	Valhalla (c)	(914)	5,379	—
10989	Valley Cottage (c)	(845)	9,269	9,007
*11582	Valley Stream	(516)	36,368	33,946
—	Viola (c)		5,931	4,504
11792	Wading River (c)	(631)	6,668	5,317
12586	Walden	(845)	6,164	5,836
11793	Wantagh (c)	(516)	18,971	18,567
10990	Warwick	(845)	6,412	5,984
10992	Washingtonville	(845)	5,851	4,906
13165	Waterloo	(315)	5,111	5,116
*13601	Watertown	(315)	26,705	29,429
12189	Watervliet	(518)	10,207	11,061
14580	Webster	(585)	5,216	5,464
14895	Wellsville	(585)	5,171	5,241
*11704	West Babylon (c)	(631)	43,452	42,410
11590	Westbury (Nassau)	(516)	14,263	13,060
14905	West Elmira (c)	(607)	5,136	5,218
12801	West Glens Falls (c)	(518)	6,721	5,964
10993	West Haverstraw	(845)	10,295	9,183
11552	West Hempstead (c)	(516)	18,713	17,689
11743	West Hills (c)	(631)	5,607	5,849
11795	West Islip (c)	(631)	28,907	28,419
12203	Westmere (c)	(518)	7,188	6,750
*10996	West Point (c)	(845)	7,138	8,024
11796	West Sayville (c)	(631)	5,003	4,680
14224	West Seneca (c)	(716)	45,943	47,866
13219	Westvale (c)	(315)	5,166	5,952
11798	Wheatley Heights (c)	(631)	5,013	5,027
*10602	White Plains	(914)	53,077	48,718
14231	Williamsville	(716)	5,573	5,583
11596	Williston Park	(516)	7,261	7,516
11797	Woodbury (c)	(516)	9,010	8,008
11598	Woodmere (c)	(516)	16,447	15,578
11798	Wyandach (c)	(631)	10,546	8,950
11980	Yaphank (c)	(631)	5,025	4,637
*10702	Yonkers	(914)	196,086	188,082
10598	Yorktown Heights (c)	(914)	7,972	7,690

(1) North Tarrytown changed its name to Sleepy Hollow on Dec. 12, 1996.

North Carolina

Area code (980) overlays area code (704). See introductory note.

ZIP	Place	Area Code	2000	1990
*28001	Albemarle	(704)	15,680	14,940
27502	Apex	(919)	20,212	4,789
27263	Archdale	(336)	9,014	6,975
*27203	Asheboro	(336)	21,672	16,362
*28802	Asheville	(828)	68,889	63,379
28012	Belmont	(704)	8,705	8,434
28016	Bessemer City	(704)	5,119	4,698
28711	Black Mountain	(828)	7,511	7,156
28607	Boone	(828)	13,472	12,949
28712	Brevard	(828)	6,789	5,452
*27215	Burlington	(336)	44,917	39,498
27509	Butner (c)	(919)	5,792	4,679
27510	Carrboro	(919)	16,782	12,134
*27511	Cary	(919)	94,536	44,394
*27514	Chapel Hill	(919)	48,715	38,711
*28204	Charlotte	(704)	540,828	419,558
28021	Cherryville	(704)	5,361	4,756
27520	Clayton	(919)	6,973	4,756
27012	Clemmons	(336)	13,827	5,982
*28328	Clinton	(910)	8,600	8,385
*28025	Concord	(704)	55,977	29,591
28613	Conover	(828)	6,604	5,311
28031	Cornelius	(704)	11,969	2,581
28036	Davidson	(704)	7,139	4,046
*28334	Dunn	(910)	9,196	9,258
*27701	Durham	(919)	187,035	138,894
*27288	Eden	(336)	15,908	15,238
27932	Edenton	(252)	5,394	5,268
*27909	Elizabeth City	(252)	17,188	16,087
27244	Elon College	(336)	6,738	4,394
*28302	Fayetteville	(910)	121,015	75,850
28043	Forest City	(828)	7,549	7,475
28307	Fort Bragg (c)	(910)	29,183	34,744
27526	Fuquay-Varina	(919)	7,898	4,447
27529	Garner	(919)	17,757	14,716
*28052	Gastonia	(704)	66,277	54,725
*27530	Goldsboro	(919)	39,043	40,736
27253	Graham	(336)	12,833	10,368
*27420	Greensboro	(336)	223,891	185,125
*27834	Greenville	(252)	60,476	46,274
28540	Half Moon (c)	(910)	6,645	6,306
28345	Hamlet	(910)	6,018	6,722
28532	Havelock	(252)	22,442	20,300
27536	Henderson	(252)	16,095	15,655
*28739	Hendersonville	(828)	10,420	7,284
*28603	Hickory	(828)	37,222	28,474
*27260	High Point	(336)	85,839	69,428
27278	Hillsborough	(919)	5,446	4,263
27540	Holly Springs	(919)	9,192	1,203
28348	Hope Mills	(910)	11,237	8,272
*28070	Huntersville	(704)	24,960	3,014
28079	Indian Trail	(704)	11,905	1,942
*28540	Jacksonville	(910)	66,715	78,031
—	James City (c)	(252)	5,420	4,279
*28081	Kannapolis	(704)	36,910	31,592
*27284	Kernersville	(336)	17,126	11,860
27948	Kill Devil Hills	(252)	5,897	4,238
27021	King	(336)	5,952	4,059
—	Kings Grant (c)		7,738	—
28086	Kings Mountain	(704)	9,693	8,768
*28502	Kinston	(252)	23,688	25,295
27545	Knightdale	(919)	5,958	1,884
*28352	Laurinburg	(910)	15,874	16,131
28645	Lenoir	(828)	16,793	16,337
27023	Lewisville	(336)	8,826	6,433
*27292	Lexington	(336)	19,953	16,583
*28092	Lincolnton	(704)	9,965	6,955
*28358	Lumberton	(910)	20,795	18,656
28403	Masonboro (c)	(910)	11,812	7,010
*28105	Matthews	(704)	22,127	13,756
27302	Mebane	(919)	7,284	4,754
28227	Mint Hill	(704)	14,922	13,637
*28110	Monroe	(704)	26,228	18,623
*28115	Mooresville	(704)	18,823	9,563
28557	Morehead City	(252)	7,691	6,473
*28655	Morganton	(828)	17,310	15,085
27560	Morrisville	(919)	5,208	1,022
27030	Mount Airy	(336)	8,484	7,156
28120	Mount Holly	(704)	9,618	7,710
—	Murraysville (c)		7,279	—
—	Myrtle Grove (c)		7,125	4,275
*28562	New Bern	(252)	23,128	20,728
28658	Newton	(828)	12,560	11,134
*28465	Oak Island	(910)	6,571	—
—	Ogden (c)		5,481	3,228
27565	Oxford	(919)	8,338	7,965
*28374	Pinehurst	(910)	9,706	5,825
28399	Piney Green (c)	(910)	11,658	8,999
*27611	Raleigh	(919)	276,093	218,859
*27320	Reidsville	(336)	14,485	14,085
27870	Roanoke Rapids	(252)	16,957	15,722
*28379	Rockingham	(910)	9,672	9,399
*27801	Rocky Mount	(252)	55,893	53,078
27573	Roxboro	(336)	8,696	7,332
28704	Royal Pines (c)		5,334	4,418
28601	Saint Stephens (c)	(828)	9,439	8,734
*28144	Salisbury	(704)	26,462	23,626
*27330	Sanford	(919)	23,220	18,881
27576	Selma	(919)	5,914	4,600
*28150	Shelby	(704)	19,477	15,460
27344	Siler City	(919)	6,966	4,808
—	Silver Lake (c)		5,788	4,071
27577	Smithfield	(919)	11,510	10,180
*28387	Southern Pines	(910)	10,918	9,213
28052	South Gastonia (c)	(704)	5,433	5,487
28390	Spring Lake	(910)	8,098	7,552
*28677	Statesville	(704)	23,320	20,647
27358	Summerfield	(336)	7,018	2,051
27886	Tarboro	(252)	11,138	11,037
*27360	Thomasville	(336)	19,788	15,915
27370	Trinity	(336)	6,690	5,469
*27587	Wake Forest	(919)	12,588	5,832
27889	Washington	(252)	9,583	9,160
28786	Waynesville	(828)	9,232	7,282
28104	Weddington	(704)	6,696	3,803
28472	Whiteville	(910)	5,148	5,340
27892	Williamston	(252)	5,843	5,870
*28402	Wilmington	(910)	75,838	55,530
*27893	Wilson	(252)	44,405	38,400
*27102	Winston-Salem	(336)	185,776	162,292

North Dakota (701)

ZIP	Place	2000	1990
*58501	Bismarck	55,532	49,272
58301	Devils Lake	7,222	7,782
*58601	Dickinson	16,010	16,097
*58102	Fargo	90,599	74,084
*58201	Grand Forks	49,321	49,417
*58401	Jamestown	15,527	15,571
58554	Mandan	16,718	15,177
*58701	Minot	36,567	34,544
*58701	Minot AFB (c)	7,599	9,095
58072	Valley City	6,826	7,163
*58075	Wahpeton	8,586	8,751
58078	West Fargo	14,940	12,287
*58801	Williston	12,512	13,136

Ohio

Area code (234) overlays area code (330). Area code (567) overlays (419). See introductory note.

ZIP	Place	Area Code	2000	1990
45810	Ada	(419)	5,582	5,428
*44309	Akron	(330)	217,074	223,019
44601	Alliance	(330)	23,253	23,376
44001	Amherst	(440)	11,797	10,332
44805	Ashland	(419)	21,249	20,079
*44004	Ashtabula	(440)	20,962	21,633
45701	Athens	(740)	21,342	21,265
44202	Aurora	(330)	13,556	9,192
44515	Austintown (c)	(330)	31,627	32,371
44011	Avon	(440)	11,446	7,337
44012	Avon Lake	(440)	18,145	15,066
44203	Barberton	(330)	27,899	27,623
44140	Bay Village	(440)	16,087	17,000
44122	Beachwood	(216)	12,186	10,644
45434	Beavercreek	(937)	37,984	33,626
—	Beckett Ridge (c)		8,663	4,505
44146	Bedford	(216)/(440)	14,214	14,822
44146	Bedford Heights	(216)/(440)	11,375	12,131
45305	Bellbrook	(937)	7,009	6,511
43311	Bellefontaine	(937)	13,069	12,126
44811	Bellevue	(419)	8,193	8,157
45714	Belpre	(740)	6,660	6,796
44017	Berea	(440)	18,970	19,051
43209	Bexley	(614)	13,203	13,088
43004	Blacklick Estates (c)	(614)	9,518	10,080
45242	Blue Ash	(513)	12,513	11,923
44513	Boardman (c)	(330)	37,215	38,596
43402	Bowling Green	(419)	29,636	28,303
44141	Brecksville	(440)	13,382	11,818
45211	Bridgetown North (c)	(513)	12,569	11,748
44147	Broadview Heights	(440)	15,967	12,219
44144	Brooklyn	(216)	11,586	11,706
44142	Brook Park	(216)/(440)	21,218	22,865
45309	Brookville	(937)	5,289	4,621
44212	Brunswick	(330)	33,388	28,218
43506	Bryan	(419)	8,333	8,348
44820	Bucyrus	(419)	13,224	13,496
43725	Cambridge	(740)	11,520	11,748
44405	Campbell	(330)	9,460	10,038
44614	Canal Fulton	(330)	5,061	4,157
44406	Canfield	(330)	7,374	5,409
*44711	Canton	(330)	80,806	84,161
45005	Carlisle	(937)	5,121	4,872
45822	Celina	(419)	10,303	9,945
*45441	Centerville (Montgomery)	(937)	23,024	21,082
44024	Chardon	(440)	5,156	4,446
45211	Cheviot	(513)	9,015	9,616
45601	Chillicothe	(740)	21,796	21,923
*45202	Cincinnati	(513)	331,285	364,114
43113	Circleville	(740)	13,485	11,666
45315	Clayton	(937)	13,347	713
*44101	Cleveland	(216)	478,403	505,616
44118	Cleveland Heights	(216)	49,958	54,052
43410	Clyde	(419)	6,064	6,087
44408	Columbiana	(330)	5,635	4,961
*43216	Columbus	(614)	711,470	632,945
44030	Conneaut	(440)	12,485	13,241
44410	Cortland	(330)	6,830	5,652
43812	Coshocton	(740)	11,682	12,193
45238	Covedale (c)	(513)	6,360	6,669
44827	Crestline	(419)	5,088	4,934
*44222	Cuyahoga Falls	(330)	49,374	48,950
*45401	Dayton	(937)	166,179	182,011
45236	Deer Park	(513)	5,982	6,181
43512	Defiance	(419)	16,465	16,787
43015	Delaware	(740)	25,243	19,966
45833	Delphos	(419)	6,944	7,093
45247	Dent (c)	(513)	7,612	6,416
44622	Dover (Tuscarawas)	(330)	12,210	11,329
45663	Dry Run (c)	(614)	6,553	5,389
*43016	Dublin	(614)/(740)	31,392	16,366
44112	East Cleveland	(216)	27,217	33,096
44094	Eastlake	(440)	20,255	21,161
43920	East Liverpool	(330)	13,089	13,654
45320	Eaton	(937)	8,133	7,396
*44035	Elyria	(440)	55,953	56,746
45322	Englewood	(937)	12,235	11,402
*44117	Euclid	(216)	52,717	54,875
45324	Fairborn	(937)	32,052	31,300
*45011	Fairfield	(513)	42,097	39,709
44334	Fairlawn	(330)	7,307	5,779
44126	Fairview Park	(440)	17,572	18,028
*45839	Findlay	(419)	38,967	35,703
45224	Finneytown (c)	(513)	13,492	13,096
45405	Forest Park	(513)	19,463	18,621
45230	Forestville (c)	(513)	10,978	9,185
44830	Fostoria	(419)	13,931	14,971
45005	Franklin	(513)	11,396	11,026
43420	Fremont	(419)	17,375	17,619
43230	Gahanna	(614)	32,636	23,898
44833	Galion	(419)	11,341	11,859
44125	Garfield Heights	(216)	30,734	31,739
44041	Geneva	(440)	6,595	6,597
44420	Girard	(330)	10,902	11,304
43212	Grandview Heights	(614)	6,695	7,010
44232	Green	(330)	22,817	19,179
45331	Greenville	(937)	13,294	12,863
45253	Groesbeck (c)	(513)	7,202	6,684
43123	Grove City	(614)	27,075	19,661
*45011	Hamilton	(513)	60,690	61,438
45030	Harrison	(513)	7,487	7,520
43056	Heath	(740)	8,527	7,231
44134	Highland Heights	(440)	8,082	6,249
43026	Hilliard	(614)/(740)	24,230	11,794
45133	Hillsboro	(937)	6,368	6,235
44484	Howland Center (c)	(330)	6,481	6,732
44425	Hubbard	(330)	8,284	8,248
45424	Huber Heights	(937)	38,212	38,696
*44236	Hudson	(330)	22,439	5,159
44839	Huron	(419)	7,958	7,067
44131	Independence (Cuyahoga)	(216)/(440)	7,109	6,500
45638	Ironton	(740)	11,211	12,751
45640	Jackson	(740)	6,184	6,167
*44240	Kent	(330)	27,906	28,835
43326	Kenton	(419)	8,336	8,356
43606	Kenwood (c)	(513)	7,423	7,469
45429	Kettering	(937)	57,502	60,569
44094	Kirtland	(440)	6,670	5,881
44107	Lakewood	(216)	56,646	59,718
43130	Lancaster	(740)	35,335	34,507
45039	Landen (c)	(513)	12,766	9,263
45036	Lebanon (Warren)	(513)	16,962	10,461
*45802	Lima	(419)	40,081	45,553
43228	Lincoln Village (c)	(614)	9,482	9,958
43138	Logan	(740)	6,704	6,725
43140	London	(614)/(740)	8,771	7,807
*44052	Lorain	(440)	68,652	71,245
44641	Louisville	(330)	8,904	8,087
45140	Loveland	(513)	11,677	10,122
44124	Lyndhurst	(216)/(440)	15,279	15,982
44056	Macedonia	(330)	9,224	7,509
—	Mack South (c)		5,837	5,767
45243	Madeira	(513)	8,923	9,141
*44901	Mansfield	(419)	49,346	50,627
44137	Maple Heights	(216)	26,156	27,089
45750	Marietta	(740)	14,515	15,026
*43302	Marion	(740)	35,318	34,075
43935	Martins Ferry	(740)	7,226	8,003
43040	Marysville	(937)	15,942	10,362
45040	Mason	(513)	22,016	11,450
*44646	Massillon	(330)	31,325	30,969
43537	Maumee	(419)	15,237	15,561
44124	Mayfield Heights	(440)	19,386	19,847
*44256	Medina	(330)	25,139	19,231
*44060	Mentor	(440)	50,278	47,491
44060	Mentor-on-the-Lake	(216)	8,127	8,271
*45343	Miamisburg	(937)	19,489	17,834
44130	Middleburg Heights	(216)/(440)	15,542	14,702
*45042	Middletown	(513)	51,605	46,758
45150	Milford	(513)	6,284	5,660
45050	Monroe	(513)	7,133	5,380
45242	Montgomery	(513)	10,163	9,733
—	Montrose-Ghent (c)		5,261	4,906
45439	Moraine	(937)	6,897	5,989
45231	Mount Healthy	(513)	7,149	7,580
43050	Mount Vernon	(740)	14,375	14,550
44262	Munroe Falls	(330)	5,314	5,359
43545	Napoleon	(419)	9,318	8,884
45764	Nelsonville	(740)	5,230	4,563
*43055	Newark	(740)	46,279	44,396
45344	New Carlisle	(937)	5,735	6,049
44663	New Philadelphia	(330)	17,056	15,698
44444	Newton Falls	(330)	5,002	4,866
44446	Niles	(330)	20,932	21,128
45239	Northbrook (c)	(513)	11,076	11,471
44720	North Canton	(330)	16,369	14,904
45239	North College Hill	(513)	10,082	11,002
45251	Northgate (c)	(513)	8,016	7,864
44057	North Madison (c)	(440)	8,451	8,699
44070	North Olmsted	(440)	34,113	34,204
45502	Northridge (c) (Clark)	(937)	6,853	5,939
45414	Northridge (c) (Montgomery)	(937)	8,487	9,448
44039	North Ridgeville	(440)	22,338	21,564
44133	North Royalton	(440)	28,648	23,197
43619	Northwood	(419)	5,471	5,506
44203	Norton	(330)	11,523	11,477
44857	Norwalk	(419)	16,238	14,731
45212	Norwood	(513)	21,675	23,674
*45873	Oakwood	(973)	9,215	8,957
44074	Oberlin	(440)	8,195	8,191
44138	Olmsted Falls	(440)	7,962	6,741
44862	Ontario	(419)	5,303	4,026
*45054	Oregon	(419)	19,355	18,334
44667	Orrville	(330)	8,551	7,955
45056	Oxford	(513)	21,943	19,013
44077	Painesville	(440)	17,503	15,769
44129	Parma	(216)/(440)	85,655	87,876
44130	Parma Heights	(216)/(440)	21,659	21,448
43062	Pataskala	(740)	10,249	3,046
44124	Pepper Pike	(216)/(440)	6,040	6,185

ZIP	Place	Area Code	2000	1990
44646	Perry Heights (c)	(330)	8,900	9,055
*43551	Perrysburg	(419)	16,945	12,551
43147	Pickerington	(614)/(740)	9,792	5,668
45356	Piqua	(937)	20,738	20,612
—	Pleasant Run (c)		5,267	4,964
44319	Portage Lakes (c)	(330)	9,870	13,373
43452	Port Clinton	(419)	6,391	7,106
45662	Portsmouth	(740)	20,909	22,676
43065	Powell	(614)	6,247	2,154
44266	Ravenna	(330)	11,771	12,069
45215	Reading	(513)	11,292	12,038
43068	Reynoldsburg	(614)/(740)	32,069	25,748
44143	Richmond Heights	(216)/(440)	10,944	9,611
44270	Rittman	(330)	6,314	6,147
45431	Riverside	(937)	23,545	1,471
44116	Rocky River	(440)	20,735	20,410
43460	Rossford	(419)	6,406	5,861
43950	Saint Clairsville	(740)	5,057	5,136
45885	Saint Marys	(419)	8,342	8,441
44460	Salem	(330)	12,197	12,233
*44870	Sandusky	(419)	27,844	29,764
44870	Sandusky South (c)	(419)	6,599	6,336
44131	Seven Hills	(216)/(440)	12,080	12,339
44122	Shaker Heights	(216)	29,405	30,955
*45241	Sharonville	(513)	13,804	13,121
44054	Sheffield Lake	(440)	9,371	9,825
44875	Shelby	(419)	9,821	9,610
44878	Shiloh (c)	(419)	11,272	11,607
45365	Sidney	(937)	20,211	18,710
45236	Silverton	(513)	5,178	5,859
44139	Solon	(440)	21,802	18,548
44121	South Euclid	(216)	23,537	23,866
45066	Springboro	(513)	12,380	6,574
45246	Springdale	(513)	10,563	10,621
*45501	Springfield	(937)	65,358	70,487
*43952	Steubenville	(740)	19,015	22,125
44224	Stow	(330)	32,139	27,998
44241	Streetsboro	(330)	12,311	9,932
44136	Strongsville	(440)	43,858	35,308
44471	Struthers	(330)	11,756	12,284
—	Summerside (c)		5,523	4,573
43560	Sylvania	(419)	18,670	17,489
44278	Tallmadge	(330)	16,390	14,870
45243	The Village of Indian Hill	(513)	5,907	5,383
44883	Tiffin	(419)	18,135	18,604
45371	Tipp City	(937)	9,221	6,483
*43601	Toledo	(419)	313,619	332,943
43964	Toronto	(740)	5,676	6,127
45067	Trenton	(513)	8,746	6,189
45426	Trotwood	(937)	27,420	29,358
45373	Troy	(937)	21,999	19,478
44087	Twinsburg	(330)	17,006	9,606
44683	Uhrichsville	(740)	5,662	5,604
45322	Union	(937)	5,574	5,531
44122	University Heights	(216)	14,146	14,787
43221	Upper Arlington	(614)	33,686	34,128
43351	Upper Sandusky	(419)	6,533	5,906
43078	Urbana	(937)	11,613	11,353
45377	Vandalia	(937)	14,603	13,872
45891	Van Wert	(419)	10,690	10,922
44089	Vermilion	(440)	10,927	11,127
*44281	Wadsworth	(330)	18,437	15,718
45895	Wapakoneta	(419)	9,474	9,214
*44481	Warren	(330)	46,832	50,793
44122	Warrensville Heights	(216)	15,109	15,884
43160	Washington	(740)	13,524	13,080
43567	Wauseon	(419)	7,091	6,322
45692	Wellston	(740)	6,078	6,049
45449	West Carrollton City	(937)	13,818	14,403
*43081	Westerville	(614)	35,318	30,269
44145	Westlake	(440)	31,719	27,018
45694	Wheelersburg (c)	(740)	6,471	5,113
43213	Whitehall	(614)	19,201	20,572
45239	White Oak (c)	(513)	13,277	12,430
44092	Wickliffe	(440)	13,484	14,558
44890	Willard	(419)	6,806	6,210
*44094	Willoughby	(440)	22,621	20,510
44094	Willoughby Hills	(440)	8,595	8,427
*44095	Willowick	(440)	14,361	15,269
45177	Wilmington	(937)	11,921	11,199
45459	Woodbourne-Hyde Park (c)	(937)	7,910	7,837
44691	Wooster	(330)	24,811	22,427
43085	Worthington	(614)	14,125	14,869
45433	Wright-Patterson AFB (c)	(937)	6,656	8,579
45215	Wyoming	(513)	8,261	8,128
45385	Xenia	(937)	24,164	24,836
*44501	Youngstown	(330)	82,026	95,732
*43701	Zanesville	(740)	25,586	26,778

Oklahoma

ZIP	Place	Area Code	2000	1990
*74820	Ada	(580)	15,691	15,765
*73521	Altus	(580)	21,447	21,910
73717	Alva	(580)	5,288	5,495
73005	Anadarko	(405)	6,645	6,586
*73401	Ardmore	(580)	23,711	23,079
*74003	Bartlesville	(918)	34,748	34,256
73008	Bethany	(405)	20,307	20,075
74008	Bixby	(918)	13,336	9,502
74631	Blackwell	(580)	7,668	7,538
*74012	Broken Arrow	(918)	74,859	58,082
74015	Catoosa	(918)	5,449	2,954
*73018	Chickasha	(405)	15,850	14,988
73020	Choctaw	(405)	9,377	8,545
*74017	Claremore	(918)	15,873	13,280
73601	Clinton	(580)	8,833	9,298
74429	Coweta	(918)	7,139	6,159
74023	Cushing	(918)	8,371	7,218
73115	Del City	(405)	22,128	23,928
*73533	Duncan	(580)	22,505	21,732
*74701	Durant	(580)	13,549	12,929
*73034	Edmond	(405)	68,315	52,310
*73644	Elk City	(580)	10,510	10,428
73036	El Reno	(405)	16,212	15,414
*73701	Enid	(580)	47,045	45,309
74033	Glenpool	(918)	8,123	6,688
*74344	Grove	(918)	5,131	4,020
73044	Guthrie	(405)	9,925	10,440
73942	Guymon	(580)	10,472	7,803
74437	Henryetta	(918)	6,096	5,872
74743	Hugo	(580)	5,536	5,978
74745	Idabel	(580)	6,952	6,957
74037	Jenks	(918)	9,557	7,484
*73501	Lawton	(580)	92,757	80,561
*74501	McAlester	(918)	17,783	16,739
*74354	Miami	(918)	13,704	13,142
73140	Midwest City	(405)	54,088	52,267
73153	Moore	(405)	41,138	40,318
*74401	Muskogee	(918)	38,310	37,708
73064	Mustang	(405)	13,156	10,434
73065	Newcastle	(405)	5,434	4,214
73068	Noble	(405)	5,260	4,710
*73069	Norman	(405)	95,694	80,071
*73125	Oklahoma City	(405)	506,132	444,724
74447	Okmulgee	(918)	13,022	13,441
74055	Owasso	(918)	18,502	11,151
73075	Pauls Valley	(405)	6,256	6,150
73077	Perry	(580)	5,230	4,978
*74601	Ponca City	(580)	25,919	26,359
74953	Poteau	(918)	7,939	7,210
74361	Pryor Creek	(918)	8,659	8,327
73080	Purcell	(405)	5,571	4,784
74955	Sallisaw	(918)	7,989	7,122
74063	Sand Springs	(918)	17,451	15,339
*74066	Sapulpa	(918)	19,166	18,074
*74868	Seminole	(405)	6,899	7,071
*74801	Shawnee	(405)	28,692	26,017
74070	Skiatook	(918)	5,396	4,910
*74074	Stillwater	(405)	39,065	36,676
*74464	Tahlequah	(918)	14,458	10,586
74873	Tecumseh	(405)	6,098	5,750
73156	The Village	(405)	10,157	10,353
*74103	Tulsa	(918)	393,049	367,302
74301	Vinita	(918)	6,472	5,804
*74467	Wagoner	(918)	7,669	6,894
73123	Warr Acres	(405)	9,735	9,288
73096	Weatherford	(580)	9,859	10,124
*73801	Woodward	(580)	11,853	12,340
*73099	Yukon	(405)	21,043	20,935

Oregon

Area code (971) overlays area code (503). See introductory note.

ZIP	Place	Area Code	2000	1990
97321	Albany	(541)	40,852	33,523
*97006	Aloha (c)	(503)	41,741	34,284
97601	Altamont (c)	(541)	19,603	18,591
97520	Ashland	(541)	19,522	16,252
97103	Astoria	(503)	9,813	10,069
97814	Baker City	(541)	9,860	9,140
*97005	Beaverton	(503)	76,129	53,307
*97701	Bend	(541)	52,029	23,740
97415	Brookings	(541)	5,447	4,400
97013	Canby	(503)	12,790	8,990
97225	Cedar Hills (c)	(503)	8,949	9,294
97291	Cedar Mill (c)	(503)	12,597	9,697
97502	Central Point	(541)	12,493	7,512
97058	City of the Dalles	(541)	12,156	11,021
97015	Clackamas (c)	(503)	5,177	2,578
97420	Coos Bay	(541)	15,374	15,076
97113	Cornelius	(503)	9,652	6,148
*97333	Corvallis	(541)	49,322	44,757
97424	Cottage Grove	(541)	8,445	7,403
97338	Dallas	(503)	12,459	9,422
*97440	Eugene	(541)	137,893	112,733
97024	Fairview	(503)	7,561	2,588
97439	Florence	(541)	7,263	5,171
97116	Forest Grove	(503)	17,708	13,559
97301	Four Corners (c)	(503)	13,922	12,156
97223	Garden Home-Whitford (c)	(503)	6,931	6,652
97027	Gladstone	(503)	11,438	10,152
*97526	Grants Pass	(541)	23,003	17,503
97470	Green (c)	(541)	6,174	5,076
*97030	Gresham	(503)	90,205	68,285

ZIP	Place	Area Code	2000	1990
97303	Hayesville (c)	(503)	18,222	14,318
97838	Hermiston	(541)	13,154	10,047
*97123	Hillsboro	(503)	70,186	37,598
97031	Hood River	(541)	5,831	4,632
97351	Independence	(503)	6,035	4,425
97222	Jennings Lodge (c)	(503)	7,036	6,530
97307	Keizer	(503)	32,203	21,884
*97601	Klamath Falls	(541)	19,462	17,737
97850	La Grande	(541)	12,327	11,766
*97034	Lake Oswego	(503)	35,278	30,576
97739	La Pine (c)	(541)	5,799	—
97355	Lebanon	(541)	12,950	10,950
97367	Lincoln City	(541)	7,437	5,903
97128	McMinnville	(503)	26,499	17,894
97741	Madras	(541)	5,078	3,443
*97501	Medford	(541)	63,154	47,021
97862	Milton-Freewater	(541)	6,470	5,533
97269	Milwaukie	(503)	20,490	18,670
97038	Molalla	(503)	5,647	3,651
97361	Monmouth	(503)	7,741	6,288
97132	Newberg	(503)	18,064	13,086
97365	Newport	(541)	9,532	8,437
97459	North Bend	(541)	9,544	9,614
97268	Oak Grove (c)	(503)	12,808	12,576
—	Oak Hills (c)		9,050	6,450
—	Oatfield (c)		15,750	15,348
97914	Ontario	(541)	10,985	9,394
97045	Oregon City	(503)	25,754	14,698
97801	Pendleton	(541)	16,354	15,142
*97208	Portland	(503)	529,121	485,975
97754	Prineville	(541)	7,356	5,355
97225	Raleigh Hills (c)	(503)	5,865	6,066
97756	Redmond	(541)	13,481	7,165
—	Redwood (c)		5,844	3,702
—	Rockcreek (c)		9,404	8,282
97470	Roseburg	(541)	20,017	18,389
97470	Roseburg North (c)	(541)	5,473	6,831
97051	Saint Helens	(503)	10,019	7,535
*97309	Salem	(503)	136,924	107,793
97055	Sandy	(503)	5,385	4,154
97138	Seaside	(503)	5,900	5,359
97140	Sherwood	(503)	11,791	3,093
97381	Silverton	(503)	7,414	5,635
*97477	Springfield	(541)	52,864	44,664
97383	Stayton	(503)	6,816	5,011
—	Sunnyside (c)	(503)	6,791	4,423
97479	Sutherlin	(541)	6,669	5,020
97386	Sweet Home	(541)	8,016	6,850
97540	Talent	(541)	5,589	3,274
97281	Tigard	(503)	41,223	29,435
97060	Troutdale	(503)	13,777	7,852
97062	Tualatin	(503)	22,791	14,664
97225	West Haven-Sylvan (c)	(503)	7,147	6,009
97068	West Linn	(503)	22,261	16,389
*97225	West Slope (c)	(503)	6,442	7,959
97503	White City (c)	(541)	5,466	5,891
97070	Wilsonville	(503)	13,991	7,510
97071	Woodburn	(503)	20,100	13,404

Pennsylvania

Area code (267) overlays area code (215). Area code (484) overlays (610). Area code (878) overlays (412). See introductory note.

ZIP	Place	Area Code	2000	1990
15001	Aliquippa	(724)	11,734	13,374
*18105	Allentown (Lehigh)	(610)	106,632	105,301
*16603	Altoona	(814)	49,523	51,881
19002	Ambler	(215)	6,426	6,609
15003	Ambridge	(724)	7,769	8,133
18403	Archbald	(570)	6,220	6,291
19003	Ardmore (c)	(610)	12,616	12,646
15210	Arlington Heights (c)	(412)	5,132	4,768
15068	Arnold	(724)	5,667	6,113
19407	Audubon (c)	(610)	6,549	6,328
15202	Avalon	(412)	5,294	5,784
—	Back Mountain (c)		26,690	—
15234	Baldwin	(412)	19,999	21,923
18013	Bangor	(610)	5,319	5,383
15010	Beaver Falls	(724)	9,920	10,687
16823	Bellefonte	(814)	6,395	6,358
15202	Bellevue	(412)	8,770	9,126
18603	Berwick	(570)	10,774	10,976
15102	Bethel Park	(412)	33,556	33,823
*18016	Bethlehem	(610)	71,329	71,427
19508	Birdsboro	(610)	5,064	4,222
18447	Blakely	(570)	7,027	7,222
17815	Bloomsburg	(570)	12,375	12,439
19422	Blue Bell (c)	(215)/(610)	6,395	6,091
19061	Boothwyn (c)	(610)	5,206	5,069
16701	Bradford	(814)	9,175	9,625
15227	Brentwood	(412)	10,466	10,823
15017	Bridgeville	(412)	5,341	5,445
19007	Bristol	(215)	9,923	10,405
19015	Brookhaven	(610)	7,985	8,570
19008	Broomall (c)	(610)	11,046	10,930
*16001	Butler	(724)	15,121	15,714
15419	California	(724)	5,274	5,748
*17011	Camp Hill	(717)	7,636	7,831
15317	Canonsburg	(724)	8,607	9,200
18407	Carbondale	(570)	9,804	10,664
17013	Carlisle	(717)	17,970	18,419
15106	Carnegie	(412)	8,389	9,278
15108	Carnot-Moon (c)	(412)	10,637	10,187
15234	Castle Shannon	(412)	8,556	9,135
18032	Catasauqua	(610)	6,588	6,662
17201	Chambersburg	(717)	17,862	16,647
*19013	Chester	(610)	36,854	41,856
15025	Clairton	(412)	8,491	9,656
16214	Clarion	(814)	6,185	6,457
18411	Clarks Summit	(570)	5,126	5,433
16830	Clearfield	(814)	6,631	6,633
19018	Clifton Heights	(610)	6,779	7,111
19320	Coatesville	(610)	10,838	11,038
19426	Collegeville	(610)	8,032	4,227
19023	Collingdale	(610)	8,664	9,175
17109	Colonial Park (c) (Dauphin)	(717)	13,259	13,777
17512	Columbia	(717)	10,311	10,701
15425	Connellsville	(724)	9,146	9,229
19428	Conshohocken	(610)	7,589	8,064
15108	Coraopolis	(412)	6,131	6,747
16407	Corry	(814)	6,834	7,216
15205	Crafton	(412)	6,706	7,188
19021	Croydon (c)	(215)	9,993	9,967
19023	Darby	(610)	10,299	11,140
19036	Darby Twp. (c)	(610)	9,622	10,955
19333	Devon-Berwyn (c)	(610)	5,067	5,019
18519	Dickson City	(570)	6,205	6,276
15033	Donora	(724)	5,653	5,928
15216	Dormont	(412)	9,305	9,772
19335	Downingtown	(610)	7,589	7,749
18901	Doylestown	(215)	8,227	8,575
19026	Drexel Hill (c)	(610)	29,364	29,744
15801	Du Bois	(814)	8,123	8,286
18512	Dunmore	(570)	14,018	15,403
15110	Duquesne	(412)	7,332	8,525
19401	East Norriton (c)	(610)	13,211	13,324
*18042	Easton	(610)	26,263	26,276
18301	East Stroudsburg	(570)	9,888	8,781
17402	East York (c)	(717)	8,782	8,487
15005	Economy	(724)	9,363	9,305
16412	Edinboro	(814)	6,950	7,736
17022	Elizabethtown	(717)	11,887	9,952
16117	Ellwood City	(724)	8,688	8,894
18049	Emmaus	(610)	11,313	11,157
17025	Enola (c)	(717)	5,627	5,961
17522	Ephrata	(717)	13,213	12,133
*16501	Erie	(814)	103,717	108,718
18643	Exeter	(570)	5,955	5,691
19030	Fairless Hills (c)	(215)	8,365	9,026
16121	Farrell	(724)	6,050	6,835
19053	Feasterville-Trevose (c)	(215)	6,525	6,696
16063	Fernway (c)	(724)	12,188	9,072
19032	Folcroft	(610)	6,978	7,506
19033	Folsom (c)	(610)	8,072	8,173
15221	Forest Hills	(412)	6,831	7,335
15238	Fox Chapel	(412)	5,436	5,319
16323	Franklin	(814)	7,212	7,329
15143	Franklin Park	(412)	11,364	10,109
18052	Fullerton (c)	(610)	14,268	13,127
17325	Gettysburg	(717)	7,490	7,025
19036	Glenolden	(610)	7,476	7,260
19038	Glenside (c)	(215)	7,914	8,704
15601	Greensburg	(724)	15,889	16,318
16125	Greenville	(724)	6,380	6,734
16127	Grove City	(412)	8,024	8,240
15101	Hampton Twp. (c) (Allegheny)	(412)	17,526	15,568
17331	Hanover	(717)	14,535	14,399
19438	Harleysville (c)	(215)	8,795	7,405
*17105	Harrisburg	(717)	48,950	52,376
15065	Harrison Twp. (c) (Allegheny)	(412)	10,934	11,763
19040	Hatboro	(215)	7,393	7,382
18201	Hazleton	(570)	23,329	24,730
18055	Hellertown	(610)	5,606	5,662
16148	Hermitage	(724)	16,157	15,260
17033	Hershey (c)	(717)	12,771	11,860
16648	Hollidaysburg	(814)	5,368	5,624
16001	Homeacre-Lyndora (c)	(724)	6,685	7,511
19044	Horsham (c)	(215)	14,779	15,051
16652	Huntingdon	(814)	6,918	6,843
15701	Indiana	(724)	14,895	15,174
15644	Jeannette	(724)	10,654	11,221
15025	Jefferson Hills	(412)	9,666	—
*15907	Johnstown	(814)	23,906	28,124
15108	Kennedy Twp. (c)	(412)	7,504	7,152
19348	Kennett Square	(610)	5,273	5,218
19406	King of Prussia (c)	(610)	18,511	18,406
18704	Kingston	(570)	13,855	14,507
19443	Kulpsville (c)	(215)	8,005	5,183
19530	Kutztown	(610)	5,067	4,704
*17604	Lancaster	(717)	56,348	55,551
19446	Lansdale	(215)	16,071	16,362
19050	Lansdowne	(610)	11,044	11,712

ZIP	Place	Area Code	2000	1990
15650	Latrobe	(724)	8,994	9,265
17540	Leacock-Leola-Bareville (c)	(717)	6,625	5,685
*17042	Lebanon	(717)	24,461	24,800
18235	Lehighton	(610)	5,537	5,914
*19055	Levittown (c)	(215)	53,966	55,362
17837	Lewisburg	(570)	5,620	5,785
17044	Lewistown (Mifflin)	(717)	8,998	9,341
17112	Linglestown (c)	(717)	6,414	5,862
19353	Lionville-Marchwood (c)	(610)	6,298	6,468
17543	Lititz	(717)	9,029	8,280
17745	Lock Haven	(570)	9,149	9,230
17011	Lower Allen (c)	(717)	6,619	6,329
15068	Lower Burrell	(724)	12,608	12,251
15237	McCandless Twp. (c)	(412)	29,022	28,781
*15134	McKeesport	(412)	24,040	26,016
15136	McKees Rocks	(412)	6,622	7,691
19002	Maple Glen (c)	(215)	7,042	5,881
16335	Meadville	(814)	13,685	14,318
17055	Mechanicsburg	(717)	9,042	9,452
*19063	Media	(610)	5,533	5,957
17057	Middletown (Dauphin)	(717)	9,242	9,254
18017	Middletown (c) (Northampton)	(610)	7,378	6,866
17551	Millersville	(717)	7,774	8,099
17847	Milton	(570)	6,650	6,746
15061	Monaca	(724)	6,286	6,739
15062	Monessen	(724)	8,669	9,901
18936	Montgomeryville (c)	(215)	12,031	9,114
18507	Moosic	(570)	5,575	5,397
19067	Morrisville (Bucks)	(215)	10,023	9,765
18707	Mountain Top (c)	(570)	15,269	—
17851	Mount Carmel	(570)	6,390	7,196
17552	Mount Joy	(717)	6,765	6,398
15228	Mount Lebanon (c)	(412)	33,017	34,414
15120	Munhall	(412)	12,264	13,158
15146	Municipality of Monroeville	(412)	29,349	29,169
15668	Municipality of Murrysville	(724)	18,872	17,240
18634	Nanticoke	(570)	10,955	12,267
18064	Nazareth	(610)	6,023	5,713
19086	Nether Providence Twp. (c)	(610)	13,456	12,730
15066	New Brighton	(724)	6,641	6,854
*16108	New Castle	(724)	26,309	28,334
17070	New Cumberland	(717)	7,349	7,665
17557	New Holland	(717)	5,092	4,484
15068	New Kensington	(724)	14,701	15,894
*19403	Norristown	(610)	31,282	30,754
18067	Northampton	(610)	9,405	8,717
15104	North Braddock	(412)	6,410	7,036
15137	North Versailles (c)	(412)	11,125	13,294
16421	Northwest Harborcreek (c)	(814)	8,658	7,485
19074	Norwood (Delaware)	(610)	5,985	6,162
15139	Oakmont (Allegheny)	(412)	6,911	6,961
15238	O'Hara Twp. (c)	(412)	8,856	9,096
16301	Oil City	(814)	11,504	11,949
18518	Old Forge	(570)	8,798	8,834
19075	Oreland (c)	(215)	5,509	5,695
18071	Palmerton	(610)	5,248	5,394
17078	Palmyra	(717)	7,096	6,910
19301	Paoli (c)	(610)	5,425	5,277
16801	Park Forest Village (c)	(814)	8,830	6,703
17331	Parkville (c)	(717)	6,593	5,009
17112	Paxtonia (c)	(570)	5,254	4,862
15235	Penn Hills (c)	(412)	46,809	57,632
19096	Penn Wynne (c)	(610)	5,382	5,807
18944	Perkasie	(215)	8,828	7,878
*19104	Philadelphia	(215)	1,517,550	1,585,577
19460	Phoenixville	(610)	14,788	15,066
*15233	Pittsburgh	(412)	334,563	369,879
*18640	Pittston	(570)	8,104	9,389
15236	Pleasant Hills	(412)	8,397	8,884
15239	Plum	(412)	26,940	25,609
18651	Plymouth	(570)	6,507	7,134
19462	Plymouth Meeting (c)	(610)	5,593	6,241
*19464	Pottstown	(610)	21,859	21,831
17901	Pottsville	(570)	15,549	16,603
17109	Progress (c)	(717)	9,647	9,654
19076	Prospect Park	(610)	6,594	6,764
15767	Punxsutawney	(814)	6,271	6,782
18951	Quakertown	(215)	8,931	8,982
19087	Radnor Twp. (c)	(610)	30,878	27,676
*19612	Reading	(610)	81,207	78,380
17356	Red Lion	(717)	6,149	6,130
18954	Richboro (c)	(215)	6,678	5,141
19078	Ridley Park	(610)	7,196	7,592
15136	Robinson Twp. (Allegheny) (c)	(412)	12,289	10,830
15237	Ross Twp. (c)	(412)	32,551	35,102
15857	Saint Marys	(814)	14,502	14,020
19464	Sanatoga (c)	(610)	7,734	3,723
18840	Sayre	(570)	5,813	5,791
17972	Schuylkill Haven	(570)	5,548	5,610
15106	Scott Twp. (c)	(412)	17,288	20,413
*18505	Scranton	(570)	76,415	81,805
17870	Selinsgrove	(570)	5,383	5,384
15116	Shaler Twp. (c)	(412)	29,757	33,694
17872	Shamokin	(570)	8,009	9,184
16146	Sharon	(724)	16,328	17,533
19079	Sharon Hill	(610)	5,468	5,771
17976	Shenandoah	(570)	5,624	6,221
19607	Shillington	(610)	5,059	5,062
17404	Shiloh (c)	(717)	10,192	5,315
17257	Shippensburg	(717)	5,586	5,331
15501	Somerset	(814)	6,762	6,454
18964	Souderton	(215)	6,730	5,957
15129	South Park Twp. (c)	(814)	14,340	14,292
17701	South Williamsport	(570)	6,412	6,496
19064	Springfield (c) (Delaware)	(610)	23,677	25,326
*16804	State College	(814)	38,420	38,981
17113	Steelton	(717)	5,858	5,152
—	Stonybrook-Wilshire (c)		5,414	4,887
15136	Stowe Twp. (c)	(412)	6,706	9,202
18360	Stroudsburg	(570)	5,756	5,312
16323	Sugarcreek	(814)	5,331	5,532
17801	Sunbury	(570)	10,610	11,591
19081	Swarthmore	(610)	6,170	6,157
15218	Swissvale	(412)	9,653	10,637
18704	Swoyersville	(570)	5,157	5,630
18252	Tamaqua	(570)	7,174	7,943
18517	Taylor	(570)	6,475	6,941
16354	Titusville	(814)	6,146	6,434
19401	Trooper (c)	(610)	6,061	7,370
15145	Turtle Creek	(412)	6,076	6,556
16686	Tyrone	(814)	5,528	5,743
15401	Uniontown (Fayette)	(724)	12,422	12,034
19063	Upper Providence Twp. (c)	(610)	10,509	9,477
15241	Upper Saint Clair (c)	(412)	20,053	19,023
15690	Vandergrift	(724)	5,455	5,904
19013	Village Green-Green Ridge (c)	(610)	8,279	9,026
16365	Warren	(814)	10,259	11,122
15301	Washington (Washington)	(724)	15,268	15,864
17268	Waynesboro	(717)	9,614	9,578
17315	Weigelstown (c)	(717)	10,117	8,665
*19380	West Chester	(610)	17,861	18,041
19380	West Goshen (c)	(610)	8,472	8,948
*15122	West Mifflin	(412)	22,464	23,644
15905	Westmont	(814)	5,523	5,789
19401	West Norriton (c)	(610)	14,901	15,209
18643	West Pittston	(570)	5,072	5,590
15229	West View	(412)	7,277	7,734
15227	Whitehall (Allegheny)	(412)	14,444	14,451
15131	White Oak	(412)	8,437	8,761
*18703	Wilkes-Barre	(570)	43,123	47,523
15221	Wilkinsburg	(412)	19,196	21,080
15145	Wilkins Twp. (c)	(412)	6,917	7,487
*17701	Williamsport	(570)	30,706	31,933
19090	Willow Grove (c) (Montgomery)	(215)	16,234	16,325
17584	Willow Street (c)	(717)	7,258	5,817
15025	Wilson	(412)	7,682	7,830
19094	Woodlyn (c)	(610)	10,036	10,151
19038	Wyndmoor (c)	(215)	5,601	5,682
19610	Wyomissing	(610)	8,587	7,332
19050	Yeadon	(610)	11,762	11,980
*17405	York	(717)	40,862	42,192

Rhode Island (401)

See introductory note.

ZIP	Place	2000	1990
02806	*Barrington*	16,819	15,849
02809	*Bristol*	22,469	21,625
02830	*Burrillville*	15,796	16,230
02863	Central Falls	18,928	17,637
02813	*Charlestown*	7,859	6,478
02816	*Coventry*	33,668	31,083
*02904	Cranston	79,269	76,060
02864	*Cumberland*	31,840	29,038
02864	Cumberland Hill (c)	7,738	6,379
02818	*East Greenwich*	12,948	11,865
02914	East Providence	48,688	50,380
02822	*Exeter*	6,045	5,461
02814	*Glocester*	9,948	9,227
02828	Greenville (c)	8,626	8,303
02833	*Hopkinton*	7,836	6,873
02835	Jamestown	5,622	4,999
02919	*Johnston*	28,195	26,542
02881	Kingston (c)	5,446	6,504
02865	*Lincoln*	20,898	18,045
02842	*Middletown*	17,334	19,460
02882	*Narragansett*	16,361	15,004
02840	Newport	26,475	28,227
02843	Newport East (c)	11,463	11,080
02852	*North Kingstown*	26,326	23,786
02908	*North Providence*	32,411	32,090
02896	*North Smithfield*	10,618	10,497
*02860	Pawtucket	72,958	72,644
02871	*Portsmouth*	17,149	16,857
*02904	Providence	173,618	160,728
02812	*Richmond*	7,222	5,351
02857	*Scituate*	10,324	9,796
02917	*Smithfield*	20,613	19,163
02879	*South Kingstown*	27,921	24,612
02878	Tiverton (c)	7,282	7,259
02878	*Tiverton*	15,260	14,312
02864	Valley Falls (c)	11,599	11,175
*02879	Wakefield-Peacedale (c)	8,468	7,134
02885	*Warren*	11,360	11,385

ZIP	Place	2000	1990
*02886	Warwick	85,808	85,427
02891	Westerly (c)	17,682	16,477
02891	*Westerly*	22,966	21,605
02817	*West Greenwich*	5,085	—
02893	*West Warwick*	29,581	29,268
02895	Woonsocket	43,224	43,877

South Carolina

ZIP	Place	Area Code	2000	1990
29620	Abbeville	(864)	5,840	5,778
*29801	Aiken	(803)	25,337	20,386
*29621	Anderson	(864)	25,514	26,385
29812	Barnwell	(803)	5,035	5,255
—	Batesburg-Leesville	(803)	5,517	6,107
*29902	Beaufort	(843)	12,950	9,576
29841	Belvedere (c)	(803)	5,631	6,133
29512	Bennettsville	(843)	9,425	10,095
29611	Berea (c)	(864)	14,158	13,535
29902	Burton (c)	(843)	7,180	6,917
29020	Camden	(803)	6,682	6,696
29033	Cayce	(803)	12,150	10,824
—	Centerville (c)	(573)	5,181	4,866
*29402	Charleston	(843)	96,650	88,256
29520	Cheraw	(843)	5,524	5,553
29706	Chester	(803)	6,476	7,158
*29631	Clemson	(864)	11,939	11,145
29325	Clinton	(864)	8,091	9,603
*29201	Columbia	(803)	116,278	110,734
*29526	Conway	(843)	11,788	9,819
*29532	Darlington	(843)	6,720	7,310
29204	Dentsville (c)	(803)	13,009	11,839
29536	Dillon	(843)	6,316	6,829
*29640	Easley	(864)	17,754	15,179
—	Five Forks (c)		8,064	—
*29501	Florence	(843)	30,248	29,913
29206	Forest Acres	(803)	10,558	7,181
*29715	Fort Mill	(803)	7,587	4,930
29644	Fountain Inn	(864)	6,017	4,388
*29341	Gaffney	(864)	12,968	13,149
29605	Gantt (c)	(864)	13,962	13,891
29576	Garden City (c)	(843)	9,357	6,305
*29442	Georgetown	(843)	8,950	9,517
29445	Goose Creek	(843)	29,208	24,692
*29602	Greenville	(864)	56,002	58,256
*29646	Greenwood	(864)	22,071	20,807
*29650	Greer	(864)	16,843	10,322
29406	Hanahan	(843)	12,937	13,176
*29550	Hartsville	(843)	7,556	8,372
*29928	Hilton Head Island	(843)	33,862	23,694
29621	Homeland Park (c)	(864)	6,337	6,569
29063	Irmo	(803)	11,039	11,284
29456	Ladson (c)	(843)	13,264	13,540
29560	Lake City	(843)	6,478	7,153
*29720	Lancaster	(803)	8,177	8,914
29902	Laurel Bay (c)	(843)	6,625	4,972
29360	Laurens	(864)	9,916	9,694
*29072	Lexington	(803)	9,793	4,046
29566	Little River (c)	(843)	7,027	3,470
29078	Lugoff (c)	(803)	6,278	3,211
29571	Marion	(843)	7,042	7,658
29662	Mauldin	(864)	15,224	11,662
29461	Moncks Corner	(843)	5,952	5,599
*29465	Mount Pleasant	(843)	47,609	30,108
29574	Mullins	(843)	5,029	5,910
29576	Murrells Inlet (c)	(843)	5,519	3,334
*29575	Myrtle Beach	(803)	22,759	24,848
29108	Newberry	(803)	10,580	10,543
*29841	North Augusta	(803)	17,574	15,684
*29410	North Charleston	(843)	79,641	70,304
*29582	North Myrtle Beach	(843)	10,974	8,731
29565	Oak Grove (c)	(803)	8,183	7,173
*29115	Orangeburg	(803)	12,765	13,772
—	Parker (c)		10,760	11,072
—	Powderville (c)		5,362	—
29072	Red Bank (c)	(803)	8,811	5,950
29020	Red Hill (c)	(843)	10,509	6,112
*29730	Rock Hill	(803)	49,765	42,112
29417	Saint Andrews (c)	(843)	21,814	25,692
29609	Sans Souci (c)	(864)	7,836	7,612
*29678	Seneca	(864)	7,652	7,726
29210	Seven Oaks (c)	(803)	15,755	15,722
*29681	Simpsonville	(864)	14,352	11,744
29577	Socastee (c)	(843)	14,295	10,426
*29306	Spartanburg	(864)	39,673	43,479
*29483	Summerville	(843)	27,752	22,519
*29150	Sumter	(803)	39,643	40,977
29687	Taylors (c)	(864)	20,125	19,619
29379	Union	(864)	8,793	9,840
29607	Wade Hampton (c)	(864)	20,458	20,014
29488	Walterboro	(843)	5,153	5,595
29611	Welcome (c)	(864)	6,390	6,560
*29169	West Columbia	(803)	13,064	10,974
29206	Woodfield (c)	(803)	9,238	8,862
29745	York	(803)	6,985	6,709

South Dakota (605)

ZIP	Place	2000	1990
*57401	Aberdeen	24,658	24,995
57005	Brandon	5,693	3,545
57006	Brookings	18,504	16,270
57350	Huron	11,893	12,448
57042	Madison	6,540	6,257
57301	Mitchell	14,558	13,798
57501	Pierre	13,876	12,906
*57701	Rapid City	59,607	54,523
57701	Rapid Valley (c)	7,043	5,968
*57101	Sioux Falls	123,975	100,836
57783	Spearfish	8,606	6,966
57785	Sturgis	6,442	5,537
57069	Vermillion	9,765	10,034
57201	Watertown	20,237	17,623
57078	Yankton	13,528	12,703

Tennessee

ZIP	Place	Area Code	2000	1990
37701	Alcoa	(865)	7,734	6,400
*37303	Athens	(423)	13,220	12,054
38184	Bartlett	(901)	40,543	27,038
37660	Bloomingdale (c)	(423)	10,350	10,953
38008	Bolivar	(731)	5,802	5,969
*37027	Brentwood	(615)	23,445	16,392
*37621	Bristol	(423)	24,821	23,421
38012	Brownsville	(731)	10,748	10,017
*37401	Chattanooga	(423)	155,554	152,393
37642	Church Hill	(423)	5,916	5,208
*37040	Clarksville	(931)	103,455	75,542
*37311	Cleveland	(423)	37,192	32,236
*37716	Clinton	(865)	9,409	8,960
37315	Collegedale	(423)	6,514	5,048
*38017	Collierville	(901)	31,872	14,501
37663	Colonial Heights (c)	(423)	7,067	6,716
*38401	Columbia	(931)	33,055	28,583
*38501	Cookeville	(931)	23,923	21,744
38019	Covington	(901)	8,463	7,487
*38555	Crossville	(931)	8,981	6,930
37321	Dayton	(423)	6,180	5,671
*37055	Dickson	(615)	12,244	10,487
*38024	Dyersburg	(731)	17,452	16,321
37411	East Brainerd (c)	(423)	14,132	11,594
37412	East Ridge	(423)	20,640	21,101
*37643	Elizabethton	(423)	13,372	13,087
37650	Erwin	(423)	5,610	5,318
37062	Fairview	(615)	5,800	4,210
37922	Farragut	(865)	17,720	12,802
37334	Fayetteville	(931)	6,994	7,158
*37064	Franklin	(615)	41,842	20,098
37066	Gallatin	(615)	23,230	18,794
*38138	Germantown	(901)	37,348	33,159
*37072	Goodlettsville	(615)	13,780	11,219
*37743	Greeneville	(423)	15,198	13,532
37215	Green Hill (c)	(615)	7,068	6,763
37748	Harriman	(865)	6,744	7,119
37341	Harrison (c)	(423)	7,630	7,191
38340	Henderson	(731)	5,670	4,760
*37075	Hendersonville	(615)	40,620	32,188
38343	Humboldt	(731)	9,467	9,651
*38301	Jackson	(731)	59,643	49,145
37760	Jefferson City	(865)	7,760	5,875
*37601	Johnson City	(423)	55,469	50,354
*37662	Kingsport	(423)	44,905	40,457
37763	Kingston	(423)	5,264	4,552
*37950	Knoxville	(865)	173,890	169,761
37766	La Follette	(423)	7,926	7,201
38002	Lakeland	(901)	6,862	1,204
37086	La Vergne	(615)	18,687	7,496
38464	Lawrenceburg	(931)	10,796	10,397
*37087	Lebanon	(615)	20,235	15,208
*37771	Lenoir City	(865)	6,819	6,147
37091	Lewisburg	(931)	10,413	9,879
38351	Lexington	(731)	7,393	5,810
37352	Lynchburg	(931)	5,740	4,721
38201	McKenzie	(731)	5,295	5,168
*37110	McMinnville	(931)	12,749	11,194
*37355	Manchester	(931)	8,294	7,709
38237	Martin	(731)	10,515	8,588
*37804	Maryville	(865)	23,120	19,208
*38101	Memphis	(901)	650,100	618,652
37343	Middle Valley (c)	(423)	11,854	12,255
38358	Milan	(731)	7,664	7,512
37072	Millersville	(615)	5,308	2,575
*38053	Millington	(901)	10,433	17,866
*37813	Morristown	(423)	24,965	22,513
*37122	Mount Juliet	(615)	12,366	5,389
*37130	Murfreesboro	(615)	68,816	44,922
*37202	Nashville	(615)	569,891	488,366
*37821	Newport	(423)	7,242	7,123
*37830	Oak Ridge	(865)	27,387	27,310
37363	Ooltewah (c)	(423)	5,681	4,903
38242	Paris	(731)	9,763	9,332
*37862	Pigeon Forge	(865)	5,083	3,027
37148	Portland	(615)	8,458	5,539
38478	Pulaski	(931)	7,871	7,916

ZIP	Place	Area Code	2000	1990
37415	Red Bank	(423)	12,418	12,320
38063	Ripley	(731)	7,844	6,634
37854	Rockwood	(865)	5,774	5,348
38372	Savannah	(731)	6,917	6,547
*37862	Sevierville	(865)	11,757	7,178
37865	Seymour (c)	(865)	8,850	7,026
*37160	Shelbyville	(931)	16,105	14,042
37377	Signal Mountain	(423)	7,429	7,034
37167	Smyrna	(615)	25,569	14,720
*37379	Soddy-Daisy	(423)	11,530	8,240
37311	South Cleveland (c)	(423)	6,216	5,372
37172	Springfield	(615)	14,329	11,227
37174	Spring Hill	(931)	7,715	1,464
37874	Sweetwater	(423)	5,586	5,066
37388	Tullahoma	(931)	17,994	16,761
*38261	Union City	(731)	10,876	10,513
37188	White House	(615)	7,220	2,987
37398	Winchester	(931)	7,329	6,305

Texas

Area codes (325) and (432) go into effect Apr. 5, 2003. Before then use (915). Area codes (281) and (832) overlay area code (713). Area code (430) overlays (903). Area code (682) overlays (817). Area codes (972) and (469) overlay (214).
See introductory note.

ZIP	Place	Area Code	2000	1990
*79604	Abilene	(325)	115,930	106,707
—	Abram-Perezville (c)		5,444	3,999
75001	Addison	(214)	14,166	8,783
78516	Alamo	(956)	14,760	8,352
78209	Alamo Heights	(210)	7,319	6,502
77039	Aldine (c)	(713)	13,979	11,133
*78332	Alice	(361)	19,010	19,788
*75002	Allen	(214)	43,554	19,315
*79830	Alpine	(432)	5,786	5,622
—	Alton North (c)		5,051	—
*77511	Alvin	(713)	21,413	19,220
*79105	Amarillo	(806)	173,627	157,571
78750	Anderson Mill (c)		8,953	9,468
79714	Andrews	(432)	9,652	10,678
*77515	Angleton	(979)	18,130	17,140
*78336	Aransas Pass	(361)	8,138	7,180
*76004	Arlington	(817)	332,969	261,717
77346	Atascocita (c)	(281)	35,757	—
75751	Athens	(000)	11,297	10,902
75551	Atlanta	(214)	5,745	6,118
*78712	Austin	(512)	656,562	472,020
*76020	Azle	(817)	9,600	8,868
77518	Bacliff (c)	(409)	6,962	5,549
75180	Balch Springs	(214)	19,375	17,406
78602	Bastrop	(512)	5,340	4,044
*77414	Bay City	(979)	18,667	18,170
*77520	Baytown	(713)	66,430	63,843
*77707	Beaumont	(409)	113,866	114,323
*76021	Bedford	(817)	47,152	43,762
*78102	Beeville	(361)	13,129	13,547
*77401	Bellaire	(713)	15,642	13,844
76715	Bellmead	(254)	9,214	8,336
76513	Belton	(254)	14,623	12,463
76126	Benbrook	(817)	20,208	19,564
*79720	Big Spring	(432)	25,233	23,093
*78006	Boerne	(830)	6,178	4,361
75418	Bonham	(903)	9,990	6,688
*79007	Borger	(806)	14,302	15,675
76230	Bowie	(940)	5,219	4,990
76825	Brady	(325)	5,523	5,946
76424	Breckenridge	(254)	5,868	5,665
*77833	Brenham	(979)	13,507	11,952
—	Briar (c)		5,350	3,899
77611	Bridge City	(409)	8,651	8,010
79316	Brownfield	(806)	9,488	9,560
*78520	Brownsville	(956)	139,722	107,027
*76801	Brownwood	(325)	18,813	18,387
78717	Brushy Creek (c)	(903)	15,371	5,833
*77801	Bryan	(979)	65,660	55,002
76354	Burkburnett	(940)	10,927	10,145
*76028	Burleson	(817)	20,976	16,113
76520	Cameron	(254)	5,634	5,635
—	Cameron Park (c)		5,961	3,802
79835	Canutillo (c)	(915)	5,129	4,442
79015	Canyon	(806)	12,875	11,365
78130	Canyon Lake (c)	(830)	16,870	9,975
78834	Carrizo Springs	(830)	5,655	5,745
*75006	Carrolton	(214)	109,576	82,169
75633	Carthage	(903)	6,664	6,496
*75104	Cedar Hill	(214)	32,093	19,988
*78613	Cedar Park	(512)	26,049	5,161
75935	Center	(936)	5,678	4,950
77530	Channelview (c)	(713)	29,685	25,564
79201	Childress	(940)	6,778	5,055
—	Cinco Ranch (c)	(281)	11,196	—
*76031	Cleburne	(817)	26,005	22,205
*77327	Cleveland	(713)	7,605	7,124
77015	Cloverleaf (c)	(713)	23,508	18,230
77531	Clute	(979)	10,424	9,467
76834	Coleman	(325)	5,127	5,410
*77840	College Station	(979)	67,890	52,443
76034	Colleyville	(817)	19,636	12,724
*75428	Commerce	(903)	7,669	6,825
*77301	Conroe	(936)	36,811	27,675
78109	Converse	(210)	11,508	8,887
75019	Coppell	(214)	35,958	16,881
76522	Copperas Cove	(254)	29,592	24,079
76205	Corinth	(940)	11,325	3,944
*78469	Corpus Christi	(361)	277,454	257,428
*75110	Corsicana	(903)	24,485	22,911
75835	Crockett	(936)	7,141	7,024
76036	Crowley	(817)	7,467	6,974
78839	Crystal City	(830)	7,190	8,263
77954	Cuero	(361)	6,571	6,700
79022	Dalhart	(806)	7,237	6,246
*75221	Dallas	(214)	1,188,580	1,007,618
77535	Dayton	(936)	5,709	5,042
76234	Decatur	(214)	5,201	4,245
77536	Deer Park	(713)	28,520	27,424
*78840	Del Rio	(830)	33,867	30,705
*75020	Denison	(903)	22,773	21,505
*76201	Denton	(940)	80,537	66,270
*75115	De Soto	(214)	37,646	30,544
75941	Diboll	(936)	5,470	4,341
77539	Dickinson	(281)	17,093	11,692
78537	Donna	(956)	14,768	12,652
79029	Dumas	(806)	13,747	12,871
*75138	Duncanville	(214)	36,081	35,008
76135	Eagle Mountain (c)	(817)	6,599	5,847
*78852	Eagle Pass	(830)	22,413	20,651
*78539	Edinburg	(956)	48,465	31,091
77957	Edna	(361)	5,899	5,436
—	Eidson Road (c)		9,348	—
77437	El Campo	(979)	10,945	10,511
78621	Elgin	(512)	5,700	4,846
*79910	El Paso	(915)	563,662	515,342
78543	Elsa	(956)	5,549	5,242
*75119	Ennis	(214)	16,045	13,869
*76039	Euless	(817)	46,005	38,149
76140	Everman	(817)	5,836	5,672
79838	Fabens (c)	(915)	8,043	5,599
78355	Falfurrias	(361)	5,297	5,788
75381	Farmers Branch	(214)	27,508	24,250
78114	Floresville	(830)	5,868	5,247
*75067	Flower Mound	(214)	50,702	15,527
76119	Forest Hill	(817)	12,949	11,482
75126	Forney	(214)	5,588	4,070
79906	Fort Bliss (c)	(915)	8,264	13,915
76544	Fort Hood (c)	(254)	33,711	35,580
79735	Fort Stockton	(432)	7,846	8,524
*76161	Fort Worth	(817)	534,694	447,619
78624	Fredericksburg	(830)	8,911	6,934
*77541	Freeport	(979)	12,708	11,389
77545	Fresno	(281)	6,603	3,182
*77546	Friendswood	(281)	29,037	22,814
*75034	Frisco	(214)	33,714	6,138
*76240	Gainesville	(940)	15,538	14,256
77547	Galena Park	(713)	10,592	10,033
*77550	Galveston	(409)	57,247	59,067
*75040	Garland	(214)	215,768	180,635
76528	Gatesville	(254)	15,591	11,492
*78626	Georgetown	(512)	28,339	14,840
78942	Giddings	(979)	5,105	4,093
75647	Gladewater	(903)	6,078	6,027
75115	Glenn Heights	(214)	7,224	4,564
78629	Gonzales	(830)	7,202	6,527
76450	Graham	(940)	8,716	8,986
*76048	Granbury	(817)	5,718	4,045
*75051	Grand Prairie	(214)	127,427	99,606
*76051	Grapevine	(817)	42,059	29,407
—	Greatwood (c)		6,640	—
*75401	Greenville	(903)	23,960	23,071
77619	Groves	(409)	15,733	16,744
75147	Gun Barrel City	(903)	5,145	3,526
76117	Haltom City	(817)	39,018	32,856
76548	Harker Heights	(254)	17,308	12,932
*78550	Harlingen	(956)	57,564	48,746
*75652	Henderson	(903)	11,273	11,139
79045	Hereford	(806)	14,597	14,745
76643	Hewitt	(254)	11,085	8,983
78557	Hidalgo	(956)	7,322	3,292
75205	Highland Park	(214)	8,842	8,739
77562	Highlands (c)	(713)	7,089	6,632
75067	Highland Village	(214)	12,173	7,027
76645	Hillsboro	(254)	8,232	7,072
77563	Hitchcock	(409)	6,386	5,868
—	Homestead Meadows South (c)		6,807	—
78861	Hondo	(830)	7,897	6,018
*79927	Horizon City	(915)	5,233	2,308
*77052	Houston	(281)/(713)/(832)	1,953,631	1,654,348
*77338	Humble	(713)	14,579	12,060
*77340	Huntsville	(936)	35,078	30,628
*76053	Hurst	(817)	36,273	33,574
78362	Ingleside	(361)	9,388	5,696
76367	Iowa Park	(940)	6,431	6,072
*75015	Irving	(214)	191,615	155,037
77029	Jacinto City	(713)	10,302	9,343

ZIP	Place	Area Code	2000	1990
75766	Jacksonville	(214)	13,868	12,765
75951	Jasper	(409)	8,247	7,160
77040	Jersey Village	(713)	6,880	4,826
78729	Jollyville (c)	(512)	15,813	15,206
*77449	Katy	(713)	11,775	8,004
75142	Kaufman	(214)	6,490	5,251
76059	Keene	(817)	5,003	3,944
*76248	Keller	(817)	27,345	13,683
76060	Kennedale	(817)	5,850	4,096
79745	Kermit	(432)	5,714	6,875
*78028	Kerrville	(830)	20,425	17,384
*75662	Kilgore	(903)	11,301	11,066
*76540	Killeen	(254)	86,911	63,535
*78363	Kingsville	(361)	25,575	25,276
78219	Kirby	(210)	8,673	8,326
78640	Kyle	(512)	5,314	2,225
78236	Lackland AFB (c)	(210)	7,123	9,352
76705	Lacy-Lakeview	(254)	5,764	3,617
78559	La Feria	(956)	6,115	4,360
—	La Homa (c)		10,433	1,403
75065	Lake Dallas	(940)	6,166	3,656
77566	Lake Jackson	(979)	26,386	22,771
78734	Lakeway	(512)	8,002	4,044
77568	La Marque	(409)	13,682	14,120
79331	Lamesa	(806)	9,952	10,809
76550	Lampasas	(512)	6,786	6,382
*75146	Lancaster	(214)	25,894	22,117
*77571	La Porte	(713)	31,880	27,923
*78041	Laredo	(956)	176,576	122,893
*77573	League City	(281)	45,444	30,159
*78641	Leander	(512)	7,596	3,354
78268	Leon Valley	(210)	9,239	9,581
*79336	Levelland	(806)	12,866	13,986
*75067	Lewisville	(214)	77,737	46,521
77575	Liberty	(936)	8,033	7,690
79339	Littlefield	(806)	6,507	6,489
78233	Live Oak	(210)	9,156	10,023
77351	Livingston	(936)	5,433	5,019
78644	Lockhart	(512)	11,615	9,205
*75606	Longview	(903)	73,344	70,311
*79408	Lubbock	(806)	199,564	186,206
*75901	Lufkin	(936)	32,709	30,210
78648	Luling	(830)	5,080	4,661
77657	Lumberton	(409)	8,731	6,640
*78501	McAllen	(956)	106,414	84,021
*75070	McKinney	(214)	54,369	21,283
76063	Mansfield	(817)	28,031	15,615
76661	Marlin	(254)	6,628	6,386
*75670	Marshall	(903)	23,935	23,682
78368	Mathis	(361)	5,034	5,423
78570	Mercedes	(956)	13,649	12,694
*75149	Mesquite	(214)	124,523	101,484
76667	Mexia	(254)	6,563	6,933
*79701	Midland	(432)	94,996	89,343
76065	Midlothian	(214)	7,480	5,040
*76067	Mineral Wells	(940)	16,946	14,935
*78572	Mission	(956)	45,408	28,653
—	Mission Bend (c)		30,831	24,945
*77489	Missouri City	(713)	52,913	36,143
79756	Monahans	(432)	6,821	8,101
*75455	Mount Pleasant	(903)	13,935	12,291
*75961	Nacogdoches	(936)	29,914	30,872
77868	Navasota	(936)	6,789	6,296
77627	Nederland	(409)	17,422	16,192
*78130	New Braunfels	(830)	36,494	27,334
—	New Territory (c)	(281)	13,861	—
*76161	North Richland Hills	(817)	55,635	45,895
—	Nurillo (c)		5,056	—
*79761	Odessa	(432)	90,943	89,699
*77630	Orange	(409)	18,643	19,370
77465	Palacios	(361)	5,153	4,418
*75801	Palestine	(903)	17,598	18,042
—	Palmview South (c)		6,219	—
*79065	Pampa	(806)	17,887	19,959
*75460	Paris	(903)	25,898	24,799
*77501	Pasadena	(713)	141,674	119,604
*77581	Pearland	(713)	37,640	18,927
78061	Pearsall	(830)	7,157	6,924
78721	Pecan Grove (c)		13,551	9,502
79772	Pecos	(432)	9,501	12,069
79070	Perryton	(806)	7,774	7,619
*78660	Pflugerville	(512)	16,335	4,444
78577	Pharr	(956)	46,660	32,921
*79072	Plainview	(806)	22,336	21,698
*75074	Plano	(214)	222,030	127,885
78064	Pleasanton	(830)	8,266	7,678
*77640	Port Arthur	(409)	57,755	58,551
78374	Portland	(361)	14,827	12,224
77979	Port Lavaca	(361)	12,035	10,886
77651	Port Neches	(409)	13,601	12,908
78580	Raymondville	(956)	9,733	8,880
76028	Rendon (c)	(817)	9,022	7,658
*75080	Richardson	(214)	91,802	74,840
76118	Richland Hills	(817)	8,132	7,978
*77469	Richmond	(713)	11,081	10,042
78043	Rio Bravo		5,553	—
78582	Rio Grande City	(956)	11,923	10,725
76219	River Oaks	(817)	6,985	6,580
76701	Robinson	(254)	7,845	7,111
78380	Robstown	(361)	12,727	12,849
76567	Rockdale	(512)	5,439	5,235
*78382	Rockport	(361)	7,385	5,619
*75087	Rockwall	(214)	17,976	10,486
78584	Roma	(956)	9,617	8,059
77471	Rosenberg	(713)	24,043	20,183
*78681	Round Rock	(512)	61,136	30,923
*75088	Rowlett	(214)	44,503	23,260
75785	Rusk	(903)	5,085	4,366
75048	Sachse	(214)	9,751	5,346
76179	Saginaw	(817)	12,374	8,551
*76902	San Angelo	(325)	88,439	84,462
*78265	San Antonio	(210)	1,144,646	976,514
78586	San Benito	(956)	23,444	20,125
79849	San Elizario (c)	(915)	11,046	4,385
78589	San Juan	(956)	26,229	12,561
*78666	San Marcos	(512)	34,733	28,738
*77510	Santa Fe	(409)	9,548	8,429
78154	Schertz	(210)	18,694	10,597
77586	Seabrook	(281)	9,443	6,685
75159	Seagoville	(214)	10,823	8,969
77474	Sealy	(979)	5,248	4,541
*78155	Seguin	(830)	22,011	18,692
79360	Seminole	(432)	5,910	6,342
—	Shady Hollow (c)		5,140	—
*75090	Sherman	(903)	35,082	31,584
77656	Silsbee	(409)	6,393	6,368
78387	Sinton	(361)	5,676	5,549
79364	Slaton	(806)	6,109	6,078
*79549	Snyder	(325)	10,783	12,195
79910	Socorro	(915)	27,152	22,995
77587	South Houston	(713)	15,833	14,207
76092	Southlake	(817)	21,519	7,082
*77373	Spring (c)	(713)	36,385	33,111
*77477	Stafford	(713)	15,681	8,395
76401	Stephenville	(254)	14,921	13,502
*77478	Sugar Land	(713)	63,328	33,712
*75482	Sulphur Springs	(903)	14,551	14,062
79556	Sweetwater	(325)	11,415	11,967
76574	Taylor	(512)	13,575	11,472
*76501	Temple	(254)	54,514	46,150
*75160	Terrell	(214)	13,606	12,490
78209	Terrell Hills	(210)	5,019	4,592
*75501	Texarkana	(903)	34,782	32,294
*77590	Texas City	(409)	41,521	40,822
75056	The Colony	(214)	26,531	22,113
77387	The Woodlands (c)	(713)	55,649	29,205
—	Timberwood Park (c)	(210)	5,889	2,578
*77375	Tomball	(713)	9,089	6,370
76262	Trophy Club	(817)	6,350	3,922
79088	Tulia	(806)	5,117	4,699
*75702	Tyler	(903)	83,650	75,450
*78148	Universal City	(830)	14,849	13,057
76308	University Park	(214)	23,324	22,259
*78801	Uvalde	(830)	14,929	14,729
*76384	Vernon	(940)	11,660	12,001
*77901	Victoria	(361)	60,603	55,076
*77662	Vidor	(409)	11,440	10,935
*76702	Waco	(254)	113,726	103,590
75501	Wake Village	(903)	5,129	4,761
76148	Watauga	(817)	21,908	20,009
*75165	Waxahachie	(214)	21,426	17,984
*76086	Weatherford	(817)	19,000	14,804
77598	Webster	(281)	9,083	4,678
78728	Wells Branch (c)		11,271	7,094
*78596	Weslaco	(956)	26,935	22,739
—	West Livingston (c)		6,612	—
79764	West Odessa (c)	(432)	17,799	16,568
77005	West University Place	(713)	14,211	12,920
77488	Wharton	(979)	9,237	9,011
75791	Whitehouse	(903)	5,346	4,018
75693	White Oak	(903)	5,624	5,136
76108	White Settlement	(817)	14,831	15,472
*76307	Wichita Falls	(940)	104,197	96,259
78239	Windcrest	(210)	5,105	5,331
—	Windemere (c)		6,868	3,207
76712	Woodway	(254)	8,733	8,695
75098	Wylie	(214)	15,132	8,716
77995	Yoakum	(361)	5,731	5,611

Utah

Area code (385) goes into effect Mar. 30, 2003. Before then use (801).

ZIP	Place	Area Code	2000	1990
84004	Alpine	(385)	7,146	3,492
84003	American Fork	(385)	21,941	15,722
*84010	Bountiful	(385)	41,301	37,544
84302	Brigham City	(435)	17,411	15,644
84109	Canyon Rim (c)	(801)	10,428	10,527
*84720	Cedar City	(435)	20,527	13,443
84014	Centerville	(385)	14,585	11,500
*84015	Clearfield	(385)	25,974	21,435
84015	Clinton	(385)	12,585	7,945
84121	Cottonwood Heights (c)	(801)	27,569	28,766
84121	Cottonwood West (c)	(801)	18,727	17,476

ZIP	Place	Area Code	2000	1990
84020	Draper	(801)	25,220	7,143
84109	East Millcreek (c)	(801)	21,385	21,184
84025	Farmington	(385)	12,081	9,049
84029	Grantsville	(435)	6,015	4,500
84032	Heber	(801)	7,291	4,782
84003	Highland	(385)	8,172	5,007
84117	Holladay	(801)	14,561	14,095
84737	Hurricane	(435)	8,250	3,915
84319	Hyrum	(435)	6,316	4,829
84037	Kaysville	(385)	20,351	13,961
84118	Kearns (c)	(801)	33,659	28,374
*84041	Layton	(385)	58,474	41,784
84043	Lehi	(385)	19,028	8,475
84042	Lindon	(385)	8,363	3,818
—	Little Cottonwood Creek Valley (c)	(801)	7,221	5,042
*84321	Logan	(435)	42,670	32,771
84044	Magna (c)	(801)	22,770	17,829
84664	Mapleton	(801)	5,809	3,572
84047	Midvale	(801)	27,029	11,886
84109	Millcreek (c)	(801)	30,377	32,230
84117	Mount Olympus (c)	(801)	7,103	7,413
84157	Murray	(801)	34,024	31,274
84341	North Logan	(435)	6,163	3,775
84404	North Ogden	(385)	15,026	11,593
84054	North Salt Lake	(801)	8,749	6,464
*84401	Ogden	(385)	77,226	63,943
—	Oquirrh (c)	(801)	10,390	7,593
*84057	Orem	(801)	84,324	67,561
*84060	Park City	(801)	7,371	4,468
84651	Payson	(385)	12,716	9,510
84062	Pleasant Grove	(385)	23,468	13,476
84404	Pleasant View	(385)	5,632	3,597
84501	Price	(435)	8,402	8,712
*84601	Provo	(385)	105,166	86,835
84701	Richfield	(435)	6,847	5,593
84403	Riverdale	(385)	7,656	6,419
84065	Riverton	(801)	25,011	11,261
84067	Roy	(385)	32,885	24,560
*84770	Saint George	(435)	49,663	28,572
*84101	Salt Lake City	(801)	181,743	159,928
*84070	Sandy	(801)	88,418	75,240
84335	Smithfield	(435)	7,261	5,566
84095	South Jordan	(801)	29,437	12,215
84403	South Ogden	(385)	14,377	12,105
84165	South Salt Lake	(801)	22,038	10,129
84660	Spanish Fork	(385)	20,246	11,272
84663	Springville	(385)	20,424	13,950
84098	Summit Park (c)		6,597	—
84015	Sunset	(385)	5,204	5,128
84075	Syracuse	(385)	9,398	4,658
84107	Taylorsville	(801)	57,439	51,550
84074	Tooele	(435)	22,502	13,887
84337	Tremonton	(435)	5,592	4,262
*84078	Vernal	(435)	7,714	6,640
84780	Washington	(435)	8,186	4,198
84403	Washington Terrace	(385)	8,551	8,189
*84084	West Jordan	(801)	68,336	42,915
84015	West Point	(385)	6,033	4,258
84170	West Valley City	(801)	108,896	86,969
84070	White City (c)	(801)	5,988	6,506
84087	Woods Cross	(385)	6,419	5,384

Vermont (802)

See introductory note.

ZIP	Place	2000	1990
05641	Barre	9,291	9,482
05641	*Barre*	7,602	7,411
05201	Bennington (c)	9,168	9,532
05201	*Bennington*	15,737	16,451
*05301	*Brattleboro*	12,005	12,241
*05301	Brattleboro (c)	8,289	8,612
*05401	Burlington	38,889	39,127
*05446	*Colchester*	16,986	14,731
05451	*Essex*	18,626	16,498
*05452	Essex Junction	8,591	8,396
05047	*Hartford*	10,367	9,404
05465	*Jericho*	5,015	1,405
05849	*Lyndon*	5,448	5,371
05753	Middlebury (c)	6,252	6,007
*05753	*Middlebury*	8,183	8,034
05468	*Milton*	9,479	8,404
*05602	Montpelier	8,035	8,247
05661	*Morristown*	5,139	4,733
05855	Newport	5,005	4,434
05663	*Northfield*	5,791	5,610
05101	*Rockingham*	5,309	5,484
*05701	Rutland	17,292	18,230
05478	Saint Albans	7,650	7,339
05478	*Saint Albans*	5,086	4,606
05819	Saint Johnsbury (c)	6,319	6,424
05819	*Saint Johnsbury*	7,571	7,608
05482	*Shelburne*	6,944	5,871
*05401	South Burlington	15,814	12,809
05156	*Springfield*	9,078	9,579
05488	*Swanton*	6,203	5,636
05495	*Williston*	7,650	4,887
05404	Winooski	6,561	6,649

Virginia

Area code (571) overlays area code (703). See introductory note.

ZIP	Place	Area Code	2000	1990
*24210	Abingdon	(276)	7,780	7,003
*22313	Alexandria	(703)	128,283	111,182
22003	Ananndale (c)	(703)	54,994	50,975
22554	Aquia Harbour (c)	(703)	7,856	6,308
*22210	Arlington (c)	(703)	189,453	170,897
23005	Ashland	(804)	6,619	5,864
*22041	Bailey's Crossroads (c)	(703)	23,166	19,507
24523	Bedford	(540)	6,299	6,177
22306	Belle Haven (c)	(757)	6,269	6,427
23234	Bellwood (c)	(804)	5,974	6,178
23234	Bensley (c)	(804)	5,435	5,093
*24060	Blacksburg	(540)	39,573	34,590
24605	Bluefield	(276)	5,078	5,363
23235	Bon Air (c)	(804)	16,213	16,413
22812	Bridgewater	(540)	5,203	3,918
*24203	Bristol	(276)	17,367	18,426
24416	BuenaVista	(540)	6,349	6,406
—	Bull Run (c)	(703)	11,337	5,525
*22150	Burke (c)	(703)	57,737	57,734
24018	Cave Spring (c)	(540)	24,941	24,053
*20120	Centreville (c)	(703)	48,661	26,585
*20151	Chantilly (c)	(703)	41,041	29,337
*22906	Charlottesville	(434)	45,049	40,475
*23320	Chesapeake	(757)	199,184	151,982
*23831	Chester (c)	(804)	17,890	14,986
*24073	Christiansburg	(540)	16,947	15,004
24078	Collinsville (c)	(276)	7,777	7,280
23834	Colonial Heights	(804)	16,897	16,064
24426	Covington	(540)	6,303	7,198
22701	Culpeper	(540)	9,664	8,581
22193	Dale City (c)	(540)	55,971	47,170
*24541	Danville	(434)	48,411	53,056
23228	Dumbarton (c)	(804)	6,674	8,526
22027	Dunn Loring (c)	(703)	7,861	6,509
23222	East Highland Park (c)	(804)	12,488	11,850
23847	Emporia	(434)	5,665	5,479
23803	Ettrick (c)	(804)	5,627	5,290
*22030	Fairfax	(703)	21,498	19,894
*22046	Falls Church	(703)	10,377	9,522
23901	Farmville	(434)	6,845	6,505
24551	Forest (c)	(434)	8,006	5,624
22060	Fort Belvoir (c)	(703)	7,176	8,590
22308	Fort Hunt (c)	(703)	12,923	12,989
23801	Fort Lee (c)	(804)	7,269	6,895
22310	Franconia (c)	(703)	31,907	19,882
23851	Franklin	(757)	8,346	7,864
*22404	Fredericksburg	(540)	19,279	19,027
22630	Front Royal	(540)	13,589	11,880
24333	Galax	(276)	6,837	6,699
*23060	Glen Allen (c)	(804)	12,562	9,010
23062	Gloucester Point (c)	(804)	9,429	8,509
22066	Great Falls (c)	(703)	8,549	6,945
22306	Groveton (c)	(703)	21,296	19,997
*23670	Hampton	(757)	146,437	133,811
*22801	Harrisonburg	(540)	40,468	30,707
*20170	Herndon	(703)	21,655	16,139
23075	Highland Springs (c)	(804)	15,137	13,823
24019	Hollins (c)	(540)	14,309	13,305
23860	Hopewell	(804)	22,354	23,101
22303	Huntington (c)	(703)	8,325	7,489
22306	Hybla Valley (c)	(703)	16,721	15,491
22043	Idylwood (c)	(703)	16,005	14,710
22042	Jefferson (c)	(703)	27,422	25,782
22041	Lake Barcroft (c)	(703)	8,906	8,686
22963	Lake Monticello (c)	(434)	6,852	2,331
22191	Lake Ridge (c)	(540)	30,404	23,862
23228	Lakeside (c)	(804)	11,157	12,081
23060	Laurel (c)	(804)	14,875	13,011
*20175	Leesburg	(703)	28,311	16,202
24450	Lexington	(540)	6,867	6,959
22312	Lincolnia (c)	(703)	15,788	13,041
—	Linton Hall (c)		8,620	—
*22079	Lorton (c)	(703)	17,786	15,385
*24506	Lynchburg	(434)	65,269	66,049
*22101	McLean (c)	(703)	38,929	38,168
24572	Madison Heights (c)	(434)	11,584	11,700
*20110	Manassas	(703)	35,135	27,957
20113	Manassas Park	(703)	10,290	6,734
22030	Mantua (c)	(703)	7,485	6,804
24354	Marion	(276)	6,349	6,630
*24112	Martinsville	(276)	15,416	16,162
*23111	Mechanicsville (c)	(804)	30,464	22,027
*22116	Merrifield (c)	(703)	11,170	8,399
—	Montclair (c)		15,728	11,399
23231	Montrose (c)	(804)	7,018	6,405
22121	Mount Vernon (c)	(703)	28,582	27,485
22122	Newington (c)	(703)	19,784	17,965
*23607	Newport News	(757)	180,150	171,439
*23501	Norfolk	(757)	234,403	261,250
22151	North Springfield (c)	(703)	9,173	8,996
22124	Oakton (c)	(703)	29,348	24,610
*23804	Petersburg	(804)	33,740	37,027
22043	Pimmit Hills (c)	(703)	6,152	6,019

ZIP	Place	Area Code	2000	1990
23662	Poquoson	(757)	11,566	11,005
*23707	Portsmouth	(757)	100,565	103,910
24301	Pulaski	(540)	9,473	9,985
22134	Quantico Station (c)	(703)	6,571	7,425
*24141	Radford	(540)	15,859	15,940
*20190	Reston (c)	(703)	56,407	48,556
*23232	Richmond	(804)	197,790	202,798
*24022	Roanoke	(540)	94,911	96,509
24281	Rose Hill (c)	(276)	15,058	12,675
24153	Salem	(540)	24,747	23,797
22044	Seven Corners (c)	(703)	8,701	7,280
*23430	Smithfield	(757)	6,324	4,686
24592	South Boston	(434)	8,491	6,997
*22150	Springfield (c)	(703)	30,417	23,706
*24402	Staunton	(540)	23,853	24,461
24477	Stuarts Draft (c)	(540)	8,367	5,087
23162	Sudley (c)	(540)	7,719	7,321
*23434	Suffolk	(757)	63,677	52,143
24502	Timberlake (c)	(434)	10,683	10,314
22172	Triangle (c)	(703)	5,500	4,740
23229	Tuckahoe (c)	(804)	43,242	42,629
22101	Tysons Corner (c)	(703)	18,540	13,124
*22180	Vienna	(703)	14,453	14,852
24179	Vinton	(540)	7,782	7,643
*23450	Virginia Beach	(757)	425,257	393,089
*20186	Warrenton	(540)	6,670	4,882
22980	Waynesboro	(540)	19,520	18,549
22110	West Gate (c)	(703)	7,493	6,565
22152	West Springfield (c)	(703)	28,378	28,126
*23185	Williamsburg	(757)	11,998	11,409
*22601	Winchester	(540)	23,585	21,947
24592	Wolf Trap (c)	(703)	14,001	13,133
*22191	Woodbridge (c)	(540)	31,941	26,401
—	Wyndham (c)		6,176	—
24382	Wytheville	(276)	7,804	8,036
22110	Yorkshire (c)	(703)	6,732	5,699

Washington

ZIP	Place	Area Code	2000	1990
98520	Aberdeen	(360)	16,461	16,565
98036	Alderwood Manor (c)	(425)	15,329	22,945
98221	Anacortes	(360)	14,557	11,451
98223	Arlington	(360)	11,713	4,037
98335	Artondale (c)	(253)	8,630	7,141
*98002	Auburn	(253)	40,314	33,650
98110	Bainbridge Island	(206)	20,308	—
98315	Bangor Trident Base (c)	(360)	7,253	3,702
98604	Battle Ground	(360)	9,296	3,758
*98009	Bellevue	(425)	109,569	95,213
*98225	Bellingham	(360)	67,171	52,179
98390	Bonney Lake	(360)	9,687	7,494
*98011	Bothell	(425)	30,150	12,575
*98337	Bremerton	(360)	37,259	38,142
98036	Brier	(425)	6,383	5,633
98178	Bryn Mawr-Skyway (c)	(206)	13,977	12,514
98166	Burien	(206)	31,881	27,507
98233	Burlington	(360)	6,757	4,349
—	Camano (c)		13,347	—
98607	Camas	(360)	12,534	6,762
98055	Cascade-Fairwood (c)	(425)	34,580	30,107
98531	Centralia	(360)	14,742	12,101
98532	Chehalis	(360)	7,057	6,527
99004	Cheney	(509)	8,832	7,723
99403	Clarkston	(509)	7,337	6,753
—	Clarkston Heights-Vineland (c)		6,117	2,832
99324	College Place	(509)	7,818	6,308
98072	Cottage Lake (c)	(206)	24,330	—
99218	Country Homes (c)	(509)	5,203	5,126
98042	Covington	(253)	13,783	—
98198	Des Moines	(206)	29,267	20,830
99213	Dishman (c)	(509)	10,031	9,671
—	East Hill-Meridian (c)		29,308	42,696
98366	East Port Orchard (c)	(360)	5,116	5,409
98056	East Renton Highlands (c)	(425)	13,264	13,218
98802	East Wenatchee	(509)	5,757	3,886
98801	East Wenatchee Bench (c)	(509)	13,658	12,539
98371	Edgewood	(253)	9,089	8,702
*98020	Edmonds	(425)	39,515	30,743
98387	Elk Plain (c)		15,697	12,197
98926	Ellensburg	(509)	15,414	12,360
98022	Enumclaw	(360)	11,116	7,243
98823	Ephrata	(509)	6,808	5,349
*98201	Everett	(425)	91,488	70,937
99218	Fairwood (c)	(509)	6,764	5,807
*98002	Federal Way	(253)	83,259	67,535
98685	Felida (c)	(360)	5,683	3,109
98248	Ferndale	(360)	8,758	5,398
99336	Finley (c)	(509)	5,770	4,897
98466	Fircrest	(253)	5,868	5,270
98597	Five Corners (c)		12,207	6,776
98433	Fort Lewis (c)	(253)	19,089	22,224
98373	Frederickson (c)	(206)	5,758	3,502
*98329	Gig Harbor	(253)	6,465	3,236
98338	Graham (c)	(253)	8,739	—
98930	Grandview	(509)	8,377	7,169
99016	Green Acres (c)	(509)	5,158	4,626
98660	Hazel Dell North (c)	(360)	9,261	6,924
98665	Hazel Dell South (c)	(360)	6,605	5,796
98025	Hobart (c)		6,251	—
—	Hockinson (c)	(360)	5,136	—
98550	Hoquiam	(360)	9,097	8,972
98011	Inglewood-Finn Hill (c)	(425)	22,661	29,132
*98027	Issaquah	(425)	11,212	7,786
98626	Kelso	(360)	11,895	11,767
98028	Kenmore	(425)	18,678	8,917
*99336	Kennewick	(509)	54,693	42,148
*98031	Kent	(253)/(425)	79,524	37,960
98033	Kingsgate (c)	(425)	12,222	14,259
*98033	Kirkland	(425)	45,054	40,059
98509	Lacey	(360)	31,226	19,279
98155	Lake Forest Park	(206)	13,142	4,031
98002	Lakeland North (c)	(253)	15,085	14,402
98002	Lakeland South (c)	(253)	11,436	9,027
—	Lake Morton-Berrydale (c)		9,659	—
98665	Lake Shore (c)	(360)	6,670	6,268
98258	Lake Stevens	(425)	6,361	3,435
98259	Lakewood	(253)	58,211	55,937
—	Lea Hill (c)		10,871	6,876
98632	Longview	(360)	34,660	31,499
98264	Lynden	(360)	9,020	5,709
*98046	Lynnwood	(425)	33,847	28,637
98290	Maltby (c)	(360)	8,267	—
98038	Maple Valley	(425)	14,209	1,211
98012	Martha Lake (c)	(425)	12,633	10,155
*98270	Marysville	(360)	25,315	12,248
98040	Mercer Island	(206)	22,036	20,816
98444	Midland (c)	(253)	7,414	5,587
98082	Mill Creek	(425)	11,525	7,180
—	Mill Plain (c)	(360)	7,400	—
98354	Milton	(253)	5,795	4,995
98661	Minnehaha (c)	(360)	7,689	9,661
98272	Monroe	(360)	13,795	4,275
98837	Moses Lake	(509)	14,953	11,235
98043	Mountlake Terrace	(425)	20,362	19,320
*98273	Mount Vernon	(360)	26,232	17,647
—	Mount Vista (c)		5,770	—
98275	Mukilteo	(425)	18,019	11,575
98059	Newcastle	(425)	7,737	4,649
98166	Normandy Park	(206)	6,392	6,794
—	North Creek (c)		25,742	23,236
98270	North Marysville (c)	(425)	21,161	18,711
98277	Oak Harbor	(360)	19,795	17,176
*98501	Olympia	(360)	42,514	33,729
99214	Opportunity (c)	(509)	25,065	22,326
98662	Orchards (c)	(360)	17,852	—
*99327	Othello	(509)	5,847	4,638
99027	Otis Orchards-East Farms (c)	(360)	6,318	5,811
98047	Pacific	(253)	5,527	4,622
—	Paine Field-Lake Stickney (c)		24,383	18,670
98444	Parkland (c)	(253)	24,053	20,882
98366	Parkwood (c)	(360)	7,213	6,853
*99301	Pasco	(509)	32,066	20,337
—	Picnic Point-North Lynnwood (c)		22,953	—
*98362	Port Angeles	(360)	18,397	17,710
*98366	Port Orchard	(360)	7,693	4,984
98368	Port Townsend	(360)	8,334	7,001
98370	Poulsbo	(360)	6,813	4,848
98390	Prairie Ridge (c)		11,688	8,278
*99163	Pullman	(509)	24,675	23,478
*98371	Puyallup	(253)	33,011	23,878
98848	Quincy	(509)	5,044	3,738
*98052	Redmond	(425)	45,256	35,800
*98058	Renton	(425)	50,052	41,688
99352	Richland	(509)	38,708	32,315
98188	Riverton-Boulevard Park (c)	(206)	11,188	15,337
98686	Salmon Creek (c)	(360)	16,767	11,989
*98074	Sammamish	(425)	34,104	—
*98148	Seatac	(206)	25,496	22,760
*98101	Seattle	(206)/(425)	563,374	516,259
—	Seattle Hill-Silver Firs (c)		35,311	—
98284	Sedro-Woolley	(360)	8,658	6,333
98942	Selah	(509)	6,310	5,113
98584	Shelton	(360)	8,442	7,241
*98133	Shoreline	(206)	53,025	46,979
*98315	Silverdale (c)	(360)	15,816	7,660
*98290	Snohomish	(360)	8,494	6,499
98373	South Hill (c)		31,623	12,963
98387	Spanaway (c)	(253)	21,588	15,001
*99210	Spokane	(509)	195,629	177,165
98388	Steilacoom	(253)	6,049	5,728
*98371	Summit (c)	(253)	8,041	6,312
98390	Sumner	(253)	8,504	7,535
98944	Sunnyside	(509)	13,905	11,238
*98402	Tacoma	(253)	193,556	176,664
98501	Tanglewilde-Thompson Place (c)	(360)	5,670	6,061
—	Terrace Heights (c)		6,447	4,223
98948	Toppenish	(509)	8,946	7,419
98138	Tukwila	(206)	17,181	14,506
98501	Tumwater	(360)	12,698	9,976
*98901	Union Gap	(509)	5,621	3,120
—	Union Hill-Novelty Hill (c)		11,265	—
98467	University Place	(253)	29,933	26,724
*98661	Vancouver	(360)	143,560	62,065
*98013	Vashon (c)	(206)	10,123	—

ZIP	Place	Area Code	2000	1990
99037	Veradale (c)	(509)	9,387	7,836
99362	Walla Walla	(509)	29,686	26,482
—	Waller (c)		9,200	6,415
—	Walnut Grove (c)		7,164	3,906
98671	Washougal	(360)	8,595	4,764
*98801	Wenatchee	(509)	27,856	21,746
—	West Lake Sammamish (c)		5,937	6,087
98258	West Lake Stevens (c)	(425)	18,071	12,453
99353	West Richland	(509)	8,385	3,962
99181	West Valley (c)		10,433	6,594
98166	White Center (c)	(206)	20,975	20,531
98072	Woodinville	(425)	9,194	7,628
*98903	Yakima	(509)	71,845	58,427

West Virginia (304)

ZIP	Place	2000	1990
*25801	Beckley	17,254	18,274
24701	Bluefield	11,451	12,756
26330	Bridgeport	7,306	6,837
26201	Buckhannon	5,725	5,909
*25301	Charleston	53,421	57,287
*26507	Cheat Lake (c)	6,396	3,992
*26301	Clarksburg	16,743	17,970
25301	Cross Lanes (c)	10,353	10,878
25064	Dunbar	8,154	8,697
26241	Elkins	7,032	7,494
*26554	Fairmont	19,097	20,210
26354	Grafton	5,489	5,524
*25704	Huntington	51,475	54,844
25526	Hurricane	5,222	4,461
26726	Keyser	5,303	5,870
*25401	Martinsburg	14,972	14,073
*26505	Morgantown	26,809	25,879
26041	Moundsville	9,998	10,753
26155	New Martinsville	5,984	6,705
25143	Nitro	6,824	6,851
25901	Oak Hill	7,589	6,812
*26101	Parkersburg	33,099	33,862
—	Pea Ridge (c)	6,363	6,535
24740	Princeton	6,347	7,043
25177	Saint Albans	11,567	12,241
25303	South Charleston	13,390	13,645
25569	Teays Valley (c)	12,704	8,436
26105	Vienna	10,861	10,862
26062	Weirton	20,411	22,124
26003	Wheeling	31,419	34,882

Wisconsin

ZIP	Place	Area Code	2000	1990
54301	Allouez	(920)	15,443	14,431
54720	Altoona	(715)	6,698	5,889
54409	Antigo	(715)	8,560	8,284
*54911	Appleton	(920)	70,087	65,695
54806	Ashland	(715)	8,620	8,695
54304	Ashwaubenon	(920)	17,634	16,376
53913	Baraboo	(608)	10,711	9,203
53916	Beaver Dam	(920)	15,169	14,196
54311	Bellevue Town (c)	(920)	11,828	7,541
*53511	Beloit	(608)	35,775	35,571
54923	Berlin	(920)	5,305	5,371
*53045	Brookfield	(262)	38,649	35,184
53209	Brown Deer	(414)	12,170	12,236
53105	Burlington	(262)	9,936	8,851
53012	Cedarburg	(262)	10,908	10,086
54729	Chippewa Falls	(715)	12,925	12,749
53110	Cudahy	(414)	18,429	18,659
53532	De Forest	(608)	7,368	4,882
53018	Delafield	(262)	6,472	5,347
53115	Delavan	(262)	7,956	6,073
54115	De Pere	(920)	20,559	16,594
*54703	Eau Claire	(715)	61,704	56,806
53121	Elkhorn	(262)	7,305	5,337
53122	Elm Grove	(262)	6,249	6,261
53714	Fitchburg	(608)	20,501	15,648
*54935	Fond du Lac	(920)	42,203	37,755
53538	Fort Atkinson	(920)	11,621	10,213
53217	Fox Point	(414)	7,012	7,238
53132	Franklin	(414)	29,494	21,855
53022	Germantown	(262)	18,260	13,658
53209	Glendale	(414)	13,367	14,088
53024	Grafton	(262)	10,312	9,340
*54303	Green Bay	(920)	102,313	96,466
53129	Greendale	(414)	14,405	15,128
53220	Greenfield	(414)	35,476	33,403
53130	Hales Corners	(414)	7,765	7,623
53027	Hartford	(262)	10,905	8,188
53029	Hartland	(262)	7,905	6,906
54636	Holmen	(608)	6,200	3,220
54303	Howard	(920)	13,546	9,874
54016	Hudson	(715)	8,775	6,378
*53545	Janesville	(608)	59,498	52,210
53549	Jefferson	(920)	7,338	6,078
54130	Kaukauna	(920)	12,983	11,982
*53140	Kenosha	(262)	90,352	80,426
54136	Kimberly	(920)	6,146	5,406
*54601	La Crosse	(608)	51,818	51,140
53147	Lake Geneva	(262)	7,148	5,979
54140	Little Chute	(920)	10,476	9,207
53558	McFarland	(608)	6,416	5,232
*53714	Madison	(608)	208,054	190,766
*54220	Manitowoc	(920)	34,053	32,521
54143	Marinette	(715)	11,749	11,843
54449	Marshfield	(715)	18,800	19,293
54952	Menasha	(920)	16,331	14,711
*53051	Menomonee Falls	(262)	32,647	26,840
54751	Menomonie	(715)	14,937	13,547
53097	Mequon	(262)	21,823	18,885
54452	Merrill	(715)	10,146	9,860
53562	Middleton	(608)	15,770	13,785
*53201	Milwaukee	(414)	596,974	628,088
53716	Monona	(608)	8,018	8,637
53566	Monroe	(608)	10,843	10,241
53572	Mount Horeb	(608)	5,860	4,182
53149	Mukwonago	(262)	6,162	4,495
53150	Muskego	(414)	21,397	16,813
*54956	Neenah	(920)	24,507	23,219
*53186	New Berlin	(262)	38,220	33,592
54961	New London	(920)	7,085	6,658
54017	New Richmond	(715)	6,310	5,106
53154	Oak Creek	(414)	28,456	19,513
53066	Oconomowoc	(262)	12,382	10,993
54650	Onalaska	(608)	14,839	12,201
53575	Oregon	(608)	7,514	4,519
*54901	Oshkosh	(920)	62,916	55,006
53072	Pewaukee	(262)	11,783	5,287
53818	Platteville	(608)	9,989	9,862
53158	Pleasant Prairie	(262)	16,136	12,037
54467	Plover	(715)	10,520	8,176
53073	Plymouth	(920)	7,781	6,769
53901	Portage	(608)	9,728	8,640
53074	Port Washington	(262)	10,467	9,338
53821	Prairie du Chien	(608)	6,018	5,657
*53401	Racine	(262)	81,855	84,298
53959	Reedsburg	(608)	7,827	5,834
54501	Rhinelander	(715)	7,735	7,382
54401	Rib Mountain (c)	(715)	6,059	4,634
54868	Rice Lake	(715)	8,320	7,998
53581	Richland Center	(608)	5,114	5,018
54971	Ripon	(920)	6,828	7,241
54022	River Falls	(715)	12,560	10,610
53235	Saint Francis	(414)	8,662	9,245
54166	Shawano	(715)	8,298	7,598
*53081	Sheboygan	(920)	50,792	49,587
53085	Sheboygan Falls	(920)	6,772	5,823
53211	Shorewood	(414)	13,763	14,116
53172	South Milwaukee	(414)	21,256	20,958
54656	Sparta	(608)	8,648	7,788
54481	Stevens Point	(715)	24,551	23,002
53589	Stoughton	(608)	12,354	8,786
54235	Sturgeon Bay	(920)	9,437	9,176
53177	Sturtevant	(262)	5,287	3,803
53590	Sun Prairie	(608)	20,369	15,352
54880	Superior	(715)	27,368	27,134
53089	Sussex	(262)	8,828	5,039
54660	Tomah	(608)	8,419	7,572
53181	Twin Lakes	(262)	5,124	3,989
54241	Two Rivers	(920)	12,639	13,030
53593	Verona	(608)	7,052	5,374
*53094	Watertown	(920)	21,598	19,142
*53186	Waukesha	(262)	64,825	56,894
53597	Waunakee	(608)	8,995	5,897
54981	Waupaca	(715)	5,676	4,946
53963	Waupun	(920)	10,718	8,844
*54403	Wausau	(715)	38,426	37,060
53213	Wauwatosa	(414)	47,271	49,366
53214	West Allis	(414)	61,254	63,221
*53095	West Bend	(262)	28,152	24,470
54476	Weston (c)	(715)	12,079	9,714
53217	Whitefish Bay	(414)	14,163	14,272
53190	Whitewater	(262)	13,437	12,636
53185	Wind Lake (c)	(262)	5,202	3,748
*54494	Wisconsin Rapids	(715)	18,435	18,245

Wyoming (307)

ZIP	Place	2000	1990
*82609	Casper	49,644	46,765
*82009	Cheyenne	53,011	50,008
82414	Cody	8,835	7,897
82633	Douglas	5,288	5,076
*82930	Evanston	11,507	10,904
*82716	Gillette	19,646	17,545
82935	Green River	11,808	12,711
*83002	Jackson	8,647	4,708
82520	Lander	6,867	7,023
*82072	Laramie	27,204	26,687
82435	Powell	5,373	5,292
82301	Rawlins	8,538	9,380
82501	Riverton	9,310	9,202
*82901	Rock Springs	18,708	19,050
82801	Sheridan	15,804	13,904
82240	Torrington	5,776	5,651
82401	Worland	5,250	5,742

Populations and Areas of Counties and States

Source: U.S. Bureau of the Census, Dept. of Commerce; World Almanac research

State population figures are estimates for July 1, 2001. For counties, July 1, 2001, population estimates and Apr. 1, 2000, decennial census figures are given. Land areas are also from the 2000 census. County areas may not add to state areas because of rounding.

Alabama

(67 counties, 50,744 sq. mi. land; pop. 4,464,356)

County	County seat or courthouse	2001 pop.	2000 Pop.	Land area sq. mi.
Autauga	Prattville	44,876	43,671	596
Baldwin	Bay Minette	145,799	140,415	1,596
Barbour	Clayton	28,947	29,038	885
Bibb	Centreville	21,108	20,826	623
Blount	Oneonta	52,239	51,024	646
Bullock	Union Springs	11,502	11,714	625
Butler	Greenville	21,147	21,399	777
Calhoun	Anniston	111,338	112,249	608
Chambers	Lafayette	36,457	36,583	597
Cherokee	Centre	24,147	23,988	553
Chilton	Clanton	39,995	39,593	694
Choctaw	Butler	15,720	15,922	914
Clarke	Grove Hill	27,776	27,867	1,238
Clay	Ashland	14,286	14,254	605
Cleburne	Heflin	14,298	14,123	553
Coffee	Elba	43,349	43,615	679
Colbert	Tuscumbia	55,106	54,984	595
Conecuh	Evergreen	13,839	14,089	851
Coosa	Rockford	12,143	12,202	652
Covington	Andalusia	37,107	37,631	1,034
Crenshaw	Luverne	13,725	13,665	610
Cullman	Cullman	77,900	77,483	738
Dale	Ozark	48,985	49,129	561
Dallas	Selma	46,029	46,365	981
De Kalb	Fort Payne	65,506	64,452	778
Elmore	Wetumpka	67,461	65,874	621
Escambia	Brewton	38,181	38,440	947
Etowah	Gadsden	103,014	103,459	535
Fayette	Fayette	18,320	18,495	628
Franklin	Russellville	30,914	31,223	636
Geneva	Geneva	25,438	25,764	576
Greene	Eutaw	9,923	9,974	646
Hale	Greensboro	17,262	17,185	644
Henry	Abbeville	16,292	16,310	562
Houston	Dothan	89,232	88,787	580
Jackson	Scottsboro	54,147	53,926	1,079
Jefferson	Birmingham	659,743	662,047	1,113
Lamar	Vernon	15,579	15,904	605
Lauderdale	Florence	87,422	87,966	669
Lawrence	Moulton	34,928	34,803	693
Lee	Opelika	116,572	115,092	609
Limestone	Athens	66,980	65,676	568
Lowndes	Hayneville	13,418	13,473	718
Macon	Tuskegee	24,006	24,105	611
Madison	Huntsville	281,931	276,700	805
Marengo	Linden	22,367	22,539	977
Marion	Hamilton	30,621	31,214	741
Marshall	Guntersville	82,329	82,231	567
Mobile	Mobile	399,773	399,843	1,233
Monroe	Monroeville	24,177	24,324	1,026
Montgomery	Montgomery	221,973	223,510	790
Morgan	Decatur	111,429	111,064	582
Perry	Marion	11,676	11,861	719
Pickens	Carrollton	20,901	20,949	881
Pike	Troy	29,273	29,605	671
Randolph	Wedowee	22,529	22,380	581
Russell	Phenix City	49,665	49,756	641
Saint Clair	Ashville & Pell City	66,402	64,742	634
Shelby	Columbiana	149,724	143,293	795
Sumter	Livingston	14,492	14,798	905
Talladega	Talladega	80,436	80,321	740
Tallapoosa	Dadeville	41,090	41,475	718
Tuscaloosa	Tuscaloosa	165,062	164,875	1,324
Walker	Jasper	70,698	70,713	794
Washington	Chatom	17,868	18,097	1,081
Wilcox	Camden	13,130	13,183	889
Winston	Double Springs	24,654	24,843	614

WORLD ALMANAC QUICK QUIZ

Los Angeles is the nation's most populous county. Which of these ranks second?

(a) Cook County, IL (b) Harris County, TX
(c) New York County, NY (d) Miami-Dade County, FL

For the answer look in this chapter, or see page 1008.

Alaska

(27 divisions, 571,951 sq. mi. land; pop. 634,892)

Census Division	2001 Pop.	2000 Pop.	Land area sq. mi.
Aleutians East Borough	2,597	2,697	6,988
Aleutians West Census Area	5,392	5,465	4,397
Anchorage Borough	264,937	260,283	1,697
Bethel Census Area	16,280	16,006	40,633
Bristol Bay Borough	1,196	1,258	505
Denali Borough	1,914	1,893	12,750
Dillingham Census Area	4,938	4,922	18,675
Fairbanks North Star Borough	83,694	82,840	7,366
Haines Borough	2,333	2,392	2,344
Juneau Borough	30,558	30,711	2,717
Kenai Peninsula Borough	50,556	49,691	16,013
Ketchikan Gateway Borough	13,782	14,070	1,233
Kodiak Island Borough	13,915	13,913	6,560
Lake and Peninsula Borough	1,675	1,823	23,782
Matanuska-Susitna Borough	62,426	59,322	24,682
Nome Census Area	9,240	9,196	23,001
North Slope Borough	7,264	7,385	88,817
Northwest Arctic Borough	7,344	7,208	35,898
Prince of Wales-Outer Ketchikan Census Area	5,864	6,146	7,411
Sitka Borough	8,716	8,835	2,874
Skagway-Hoonah-Angoon Census Area	3,449	3,436	7,896
Southeast Fairbanks Census Area	5,702	6,174	24,815
Valdez-Cordova Census Area	10,201	10,195	34,319
Wade Hampton Census Area	7,077	7,028	17,194
Wrangell-Petersburg Census Area	6,615	6,684	5,835
Yakutat Borough	791	808	7,650
Yukon-Koyukuk Census Area	6,436	6,551	145,900

Arizona

(15 counties, 113,635 sq. mi. land; pop. 5,307,331)

County	County seat or courthouse	2001 Pop.	2000 Pop.	Land area sq. mi.
Apache	Saint Johns	68,610	69,423	11,205
Cochise	Bisbee	119,281	117,755	6,169
Coconino	Flagstaff	117,916	116,320	18,617
Gila	Globe	51,419	51,335	4,768
Graham	Safford	33,390	33,489	4,629
Greenlee	Clifton	8,301	8,547	1,847
La Paz	Parker	19,759	19,715	4,500
Maricopa	Phoenix	3,194,798	3,072,149	9,203
Mohave	Kingman	161,788	155,032	13,312
Navajo	Holbrook	100,135	97,470	9,953
Pima	Tucson	863,049	843,746	9,186
Pinal	Florence	188,846	179,727	5,370
Santa Cruz	Nogales	39,590	38,381	1,238
Yavapai	Prescott	175,507	167,517	8,123
Yuma	Yuma	164,942	160,026	5,514

Arkansas

(75 counties, 52,068 sq. mi. land; pop. 2,692,090)

County	County seat or courthouse	2001 Pop.	2000 Pop.	Land area sq.mi.
Arkansas	DeWitt & Stuttgart	20,588	20,749	988
Ashley	Hamburg	23,979	24,209	921
Baxter	Mountain Home	38,590	38,386	554
Benton	Bentonville	159,838	153,406	846
Boone	Harrison	34,569	33,948	591
Bradley	Warren	12,564	12,600	651
Calhoun	Hampton	5,672	5,744	628
Carroll	Berryville & Eureka Springs	25,761	25,357	630
Chicot	Lake Village	13,943	14,117	644
Clark	Arkadelphia	23,517	23,546	865
Clay	Corning & Piggott	17,355	17,609	639
Cleburne	Heber Springs	24,233	24,046	553
Cleveland	Rison	8,609	8,571	595
Columbia	Magnolia	25,245	25,603	766
Conway	Morrilton	20,404	20,336	556
Craighead	Jonesboro & Lake City	83,008	82,148	711
Crawford	Van Buren	54,246	53,247	595
Crittenden	Marion	51,114	50,866	610
Cross	Wynne	19,596	19,526	616
Dallas	Fordyce	9,061	9,210	667
Desha	Arkansas City	15,052	15,341	765
Drew	Monticello	18,870	18,723	828
Faulkner	Conway	88,010	86,014	647
Franklin	Charleston & Ozark	17,867	17,771	610
Fulton	Salem	11,650	11,642	618
Garland	Hot Springs	89,657	88,068	677
Grant	Sheridan	16,714	16,464	632
Greene	Paragould	37,763	37,331	578
Hempstead	Hope	23,440	23,587	729
Hot Spring	Malvern	30,489	30,353	615
Howard	Nashville	14,244	14,300	587
Independence	Batesville	34,394	34,233	764
Izard	Melbourne	13,211	13,249	581
Jackson	Newport	17,814	18,418	634
Jefferson	Pine Bluff	83,565	84,278	885
Johnson	Clarksville	22,793	22,781	662

County	County seat or courthouse	2001 Pop.	2000 Pop.	Land area sq.mi.
Lafayette	Lewisville	8,339	8,559	527
Lawrence	Walnut Ridge	17,679	17,774	587
Lee	Marianna	12,361	12,580	602
Lincoln	Star City	14,325	14,492	561
Little River	Ashdown	13,484	13,628	532
Logan	Booneville & Paris	22,374	22,486	710
Lonoke	Lonoke	54,349	52,828	766
Madison	Huntsville	14,470	14,243	837
Marion	Yellville	16,268	16,140	598
Miller	Texarkana	40,718	40,443	624
Mississippi	Blytheville & Osceola	51,071	51,979	898
Monroe	Clarendon	9,966	10,254	607
Montgomery	Mount Ida	9,244	9,245	781
Nevada	Prescott	9,865	9,955	620
Newton	Jasper	8,518	8,608	823
Ouachita	Camden	28,164	28,790	732
Perry	Perryville	10,381	10,209	551
Phillips	Helena	25,751	26,445	693
Pike	Murfreesboro	11,222	11,303	603
Poinsett	Harrisburg	25,580	25,614	758
Polk	Mena	20,238	20,229	859
Pope	Russellville	54,746	54,469	812
Prairie	Des Arc & De Valls Bluff	9,529	9,539	646
Pulaski	Little Rock	361,967	361,474	771
Randolph	Pocahontas	18,253	18,195	652
Saint Francis	Forrest City	28,952	29,329	634
Saline	Benton	85,698	83,529	723
Scott	Waldron	10,977	10,996	894
Searcy	Marshall	8,189	8,261	667
Sebastian	Fort Smith & Greenwood	115,674	115,071	536
Sevier	De Queen	15,561	15,757	564
Sharp	Ash Flat	17,299	17,119	604
Stone	Mountain View	11,596	11,499	607
Union	El Dorado	45,177	45,629	1,039
Van Buren	Clinton	16,347	16,192	712
Washington	Fayetteville	162,023	157,715	950
White	Searcy	68,542	67,165	1,034
Woodruff	Augusta	8,691	8,741	587
Yell	Danville & Dardanelle	21,077	21,139	928

California

(58 counties, 155,959 sq. mi. land; pop. 34,501,130)

County	County seat or courthouse	2001 Pop.	2000 Pop.	Land area sq.mi.
Alameda	Oakland	1,458,420	1,443,741	738
Alpine	Markleeville	1,192	1,208	739
Amador	Jackson	36,269	35,100	593
Butte	Oroville	205,973	203,171	1,639
Calaveras	San Andreas	42,005	40,554	1,020
Colusa	Colusa	19,277	18,804	1,151
Contra Costa	Martinez	975,532	948,816	720
Del Norte	Crescent City	27,554	27,507	1,008
El Dorado	Placerville	162,586	156,299	1,711
Fresno	Fresno	815,734	799,407	5,963
Glenn	Willows	26,558	26,453	1,315
Humboldt	Eureka	126,468	126,518	3,572
Imperial	El Centro	145,744	142,361	4,175
Inyo	Independence	17,944	17,945	10,203
Kern	Bakersfield	676,367	661,645	8,141
Kings	Hanford	132,119	129,461	1,391
Lake	Lakeport	60,839	58,309	1,258
Lassen	Susanville	33,830	33,828	4,557
Los Angeles	Los Angeles	9,637,494	9,519,338	4,061
Madera	Madera	126,415	123,109	2,136
Marin	San Rafael	247,707	247,289	520
Mariposa	Mariposa	17,167	17,130	1,451
Mendocino	Ukiah	86,860	86,265	3,509
Merced	Merced	219,096	210,554	1,929
Modoc	Alturas	9,333	9,449	3,944
Mono	Bridgeport	12,930	12,853	3,044
Monterey	Salinas	407,629	401,762	3,322
Napa	Napa	128,145	124,279	754
Nevada	Nevada City	94,361	92,033	958
Orange	Santa Ana	2,890,444	2,846,289	789
Placer	Auburn	268,512	248,300	1,404
Plumas	Quincy	20,942	20,824	2,554
Riverside	Riverside	1,635,888	1,545,387	7,207
Sacramento	Sacramento	1,268,770	1,223,499	966
San Benito	Hollister	55,098	53,234	1,389
San Bernardino	San Bernardino	1,766,237	1,709,434	20,053
San Diego	San Diego	2,862,019	2,813,833	4,200
San Francisco	San Francisco	770,723	776,733	47
San Joaquin	Stockton	595,324	563,598	1,399
San Luis Obispo	San Luis Obispo	250,727	246,681	3,304
San Mateo	Redwood City	702,020	707,161	449
Santa Barbara	Santa Barbara	399,543	399,347	2,737
Santa Clara	San Jose	1,668,309	1,682,585	1,291
Santa Cruz	Santa Cruz	254,538	255,602	445
Shasta	Redding	168,478	163,256	3,785
Sierra	Downieville	3,485	3,555	953
Siskiyou	Yreka	44,325	44,301	6,287
Solano	Fairfield	403,946	394,542	829
Sonoma	Santa Rosa	464,024	458,614	1,576
Stanislaus	Modesto	468,566	446,997	1,494
Sutter	Yuba City	80,530	78,930	603
Tehama	Red Bluff	57,101	56,039	2,951
Trinity	Weaverville	13,116	13,022	3,179
Tulare	Visalia	374,249	368,021	4,824
Tuolumne	Sonora	55,521	54,501	2,235
Ventura	Ventura	770,630	753,197	1,845
Yolo	Woodland	174,815	168,660	1,013
Yuba	Marysville	60,902	60,219	631

Colorado

(63 counties, 103,718 sq. mi. land; pop. 4,417,714)

County	County seat or courthouse	2001 Pop.	2000 Pop.	Land area sq. mi.
Adams	Brighton	374,891	363,857	1,192
Alamosa	Alamosa	14,884	14,966	723
Arapahoe	Littleton	500,785	487,967	803
Archuleta	Pagosa Springs	10,659	9,898	1,350
Baca	Springfield	4,495	4,517	2,556
Bent	Las Animas	5,883	5,998	1,514
Boulder	Boulder	297,686	291,288	742
Chaffee	Salida	16,520	16,242	1,013
Cheyenne	Cheyenne Wells	2,204	2,231	1,781
Clear Creek	Georgetown	9,440	9,322	395
Conejos	Conejos	8,355	8,400	1,287
Costilla	San Luis	3,647	3,663	1,227
Crowley	Ordway	5,434	5,518	789
Custer	Westcliffe	3,693	3,503	739
Delta	Delta	28,421	27,834	1,142
Denver	Denver	554,446	554,636	153
Dolores	Dove Creek	1,837	1,844	1,067
Douglas	Castle Rock	199,753	175,766	840
Eagle	Eagle	43,027	41,659	1,688
Elbert	Kiowa	21,445	19,872	1,851
El Paso	Colorado Springs	533,428	516,929	2,126
Fremont	Canon City	47,209	46,145	1,533
Garfield	GlenwoodSprings	45,521	43,791	2,947
Gilpin	Central City	4,823	4,757	150
Grand	Hot Sulphur Springs	12,711	12,442	1,847
Gunnison	Gunnison	13,947	13,956	3,200
Hinsdale	Lake City	800	790	1,118
Huerfano	Walsenburg	7,845	7,862	1,591
Jackson	Walden	1,589	1,577	1,613
Jefferson	Golden	530,966	527,056	772
Kiowa	Eads	1,537	1,622	1,771
Kit Carson	Burlington	7,813	8,011	2,161
Lake	Leadville	7,679	7,812	377
La Plata	Durango	45,157	43,941	1,692
Larimer	Fort Collins	259,472	251,494	2,601
Las Animas	Trinidad	15,341	15,207	4,772
Lincoln	Hugo	5,927	6,087	2,586
Logan	Sterling	20,921	20,504	1,839
Mesa	Grand Junction	119,281	116,255	3,328
Mineral	Creede	809	831	876
Moffat	Craig	13,154	13,184	4,742
Montezuma	Cortez	24,035	23,830	2,037
Montrose	Montrose	34,572	33,432	2,241
Morgan	Fort Morgan	27,543	27,171	1,285
Otero	La Junta	19,972	20,311	1,263
Ouray	Ouray	3,882	3,742	540
Park	Fairplay	15,580	14,523	2,201
Phillips	Holyoke	4,472	4,480	688
Pitkin	Aspen	14,810	14,872	970
Prowers	Lamar	14,206	14,483	1,640
Pueblo	Pueblo	144,955	141,472	2,389
Rio Blanco	Meeker	5,945	5,986	3,221
Rio Grande	Del Norte	12,304	12,413	912
Routt	Steamboat Springs	20,255	19,690	2,362
Saguache	Saguache	6,224	5,917	3,168
San Juan	Silverton	586	558	387
San Miguel	Telluride	6,951	6,594	1,287
Sedgwick	Julesburg	2,668	2,747	548
Summit	Breckenridge	24,225	23,548	608
Teller	Cripple Creek	21,425	20,555	557
Washington	Akron	4,861	4,926	2,521
Weld	Greeley	194,949	180,936	3,992
Yuma	Wray	9,859	9,841	2,366

Connecticut

(8 counties, 4,845 sq. mi. land; pop. 3,425,074)

County	County seat or courthouse	2001 Pop.	2000 Pop.	Land area sq. mi.
Fairfield	Bridgeport	885,368	882,567	626
Hartford	Hartford	861,152	857,183	735
Litchfield	Litchfield	184,460	182,193	920
Middlesex	Middletown	157,579	155,071	369
New Haven	New Haven	828,374	824,008	606
New London	New London	259,065	259,088	666
Tolland	Rockville	138,914	136,364	410
Windham	Putnam	110,162	109,091	513

Delaware

(3 counties, 1,954 sq. mi. land; pop. 796,165)

County	County seat or courthouse	2001 Pop.	2000 Pop.	Land area sq. mi.
Kent	Dover	129,066	126,697	590
New Castle	Wilmington	505,829	500,265	426
Sussex	Georgetown	161,270	156,638	938

District of Columbia

(61 sq. mi. land; pop. 571,822)

Has no counties; coextensive with city of Washington.

Florida

(67 counties, 53,927 sq. mi. land; pop. 16,396,515)

County	County seat or courthouse	2001 Pop.	2000 Pop.	Land area sq. mi.
Alachua	Gainesville	218,795	217,955	874
Baker	Macclenny	22,707	22,259	585
Bay	Panama City	150,316	148,217	764
Bradford	Starke	26,423	26,088	293
Brevard	Titusville	489,522	476,230	1,018
Broward	Fort Lauderdale	1,668,560	1,623,018	1,205
Calhoun	Blountstown	13,020	13,017	567
Charlotte	Punta Gorda	147,009	141,627	694
Citrus	Inverness	122,470	118,085	584
Clay	Green Cove Springs	147,542	140,814	601
Collier	Naples	265,769	251,377	2,025
Columbia	Lake City	57,841	56,513	797
De Soto	Arcadia	32,438	32,209	637
Dixie	Cross City	13,992	13,827	704
Duval	Jacksonville	792,434	778,879	774
Escambia	Pensacola	293,205	294,410	662
Flagler	Bunnell	54,964	49,832	485
Franklin	Apalachicola	11,202	11,057	544
Gadsden	Quincy	45,321	45,087	516
Gilchrist	Trenton	14,829	14,437	349
Glades	Moore Haven	10,750	10,576	774
Gulf	Port Saint Joe	13,417	13,332	555
Hamilton	Jasper	13,504	13,327	515
Hardee	Wauchula	26,759	26,938	637
Hendry	La Belle	36,562	36,210	1,153
Hernando	Brooksville	135,751	130,802	478
Highlands	Sebring	88,972	87,366	1,028
Hillsborough	Tampa	1,027,318	998,948	1,051
Holmes	Bonifay	18,811	18,564	482
Indian River	Vero Beach	116,488	112,947	503
Jackson	Marianna	46,751	46,755	916
Jefferson	Monticello	12,946	12,902	598
Lafayette	Mayo	7,245	7,022	543
Lake	Tavares	227,598	210,528	953
Lee	Fort Myers	462,455	440,888	804
Leon	Tallahassee	239,376	239,452	667
Levy	Bronson	35,520	34,450	1,118
Liberty	Bristol	7,067	7,021	836
Madison	Madison	18,718	18,733	692
Manatee	Bradenton	274,523	264,002	741
Marion	Ocala	267,889	258,916	1,579
Martin	Stuart	130,313	126,731	556
Miami-Dade	Miami	2,289,683	2,253,362	1,946
Monroe	Key West	78,556	79,589	997
Nassau	Fernandina Beach	59,830	57,663	652
Okaloosa	Crestview	173,065	170,498	936
Okeechobee	Okeechobee	36,385	35,910	774
Orange	Orlando	923,311	896,344	907
Osceola	Kissimmee	181,932	172,493	1,322
Palm Beach	West Palm Beach	1,165,049	1,131,184	1,974
Pasco	Dade City	362,658	344,765	745
Pinellas	Clearwater	924,610	921,482	280
Polk	Bartow	492,751	483,924	1,874
Putnam	Palatka	70,880	70,423	722
Saint Johns	Saint Augustine	131,684	123,135	609
Saint Lucie	Fort Pierce	200,018	192,695	572
Santa Rosa	Milton	123,101	117,743	1,017
Sarasota	Sarasota	335,323	325,957	572
Seminole	Sanford	374,334	365,196	308
Sumter	Bushnell	54,504	53,345	546
Suwannee	Live Oak	35,668	34,844	688
Taylor	Perry	19,231	19,256	1,042
Union	Lake Butler	13,672	13,442	240
Volusia	De Land	454,581	443,343	1,103
Wakulla	Crawfordville	24,761	22,863	607
Walton	De Funiak Springs	42,644	40,601	1,058
Washington	Chipley	21,192	20,973	580

Georgia

(159 counties, 57,906 sq. mi. land; pop. 8,383,915)

County	County seat or courthouse	2001 Pop.	2000 Pop.	Land area sq. mi.
Appling	Baxley	17,472	17,419	509
Atkinson	Pearson	7,571	7,609	338
Bacon	Alma	9,993	10,103	285
Baker	Newton	4,102	4,074	343
Baldwin	Milledgeville	44,806	44,700	258
Banks	Homer	14,847	14,422	234
Barrow	Winder	48,946	46,144	162
Bartow	Cartersville	80,026	76,019	459
Ben Hill	Fitzgerald	17,242	17,484	252
Berrien	Nashville	16,091	16,235	452
Bibb	Macon	153,549	153,887	250
Bleckley	Cochran	11,735	11,666	217
Brantley	Nahunta	14,877	14,629	444
Brooks	Quitman	16,397	16,450	494
Bryan	Pembroke	24,552	23,417	442
Bulloch	Statesboro	56,918	55,983	682
Burke	Waynesboro	22,591	22,243	830
Butts	Jackson	20,629	19,522	187
Calhoun	Morgan	6,307	6,320	280
Camden	Woodbine	44,061	43,664	630
Candler	Metter	9,508	9,577	247
Carroll	Carrollton	91,956	87,268	499
Catoosa	Ringgold	55,197	53,282	162
Charlton	Folkston	10,393	10,282	781
Chatham	Savannah	232,064	232,048	438
Chattahoochee	Cusseta	15,134	14,882	249
Chattooga	Summerville	25,901	25,470	313
Cherokee	Canton	152,170	141,903	424
Clarke	Athens	101,800	101,489	121
Clay	Fort Gaines	3,390	3,357	195
Clayton	Jonesboro	246,779	236,517	143
Clinch	Homerville	6,833	6,878	809
Cobb	Marietta	631,767	607,751	340
Coffee	Douglas	37,815	37,413	599
Colquitt	Moultrie	42,201	42,053	552
Columbia	Appling	92,427	89,288	290
Cook	Adel	15,855	15,771	229
Coweta	Newnan	94,571	89,215	443
Crawford	Knoxville	12,559	12,495	325
Crisp	Cordele	22,133	21,996	274
Dade	Trenton	15,508	15,154	174
Dawson	Dawsonville	17,176	15,999	211
Decatur	Bainbridge	28,175	28,240	597
De Kalb	Decatur	665,133	665,865	268
Dodge	Eastman	19,143	19,171	500
Dooly	Vienna	11,651	11,525	393
Dougherty	Albany	95,723	96,065	330
Douglas	Douglasville	96,006	92,174	199
Early	Blakely	12,282	12,354	511
Echols	Statenville	3,726	3,754	404
Effingham	Springfield	39,616	37,535	479
Elbert	Elberton	20,648	20,511	369
Emanuel	Swainsboro	21,859	21,837	686
Evans	Claxton	10,738	10,495	185
Fannin	Blue Ridge	20,661	19,798	386
Fayette	Fayetteville	95,542	91,263	197
Floyd	Rome	91,183	90,565	513
Forsyth	Cumming	110,296	98,407	226
Franklin	Carnesville	20,783	20,285	263
Fulton	Atlanta	816,638	816,006	529
Gilmer	Ellijay	24,349	23,456	427
Glascock	Gibson	2,583	2,556	144
Glynn	Brunswick	68,217	67,568	422
Gordon	Calhoun	45,555	44,104	356
Grady	Cairo	23,714	23,659	458
Greene	Greensboro	14,914	14,406	388
Gwinnett	Lawrenceville	621,528	588,448	433
Habersham	Clarkesville	37,153	35,902	278
Hall	Gainesville	145,664	139,277	394
Hancock	Sparta	10,065	10,076	473
Haralson	Buchanan	26,255	25,690	282
Harris	Hamilton	24,548	23,695	464
Hart	Hartwell	23,087	22,997	232
Heard	Franklin	11,229	11,012	296
Henry	McDonough	132,581	119,341	323
Houston	Perry	113,391	110,765	377
Irwin	Ocilla	10,028	9,931	357
Jackson	Jefferson	44,010	41,589	342
Jasper	Monticello	11,904	11,426	370
Jeff Davis	Hazlehurst	12,762	12,684	333
Jefferson	Louisville	17,090	17,266	528
Jenkins	Millen	8,637	8,575	350
Johnson	Wrightsville	8,578	8,560	304
Jones	Gray	24,203	23,639	394
Lamar	Barnesville	16,260	15,912	185
Lanier	Lakeland	7,140	7,241	187
Laurens	Dublin	45,378	44,874	812
Lee	Leesburg	25,539	24,757	356
Liberty	Hinesville	60,107	61,610	519
Lincoln	Lincolnton	8,424	8,348	211
Long	Ludowici	10,548	10,304	401
Lowndes	Valdosta	92,250	92,115	504
Lumpkin	Dahlonega	21,855	21,016	284
McDuffie	Thomson	21,286	21,231	260
McIntosh	Darien	11,085	10,847	433
Macon	Oglethorpe	14,133	14,074	403
Madison	Danielsville	26,214	25,730	284
Marion	Buena Vista	7,204	7,144	367
Meriwether	Greenville	22,625	22,534	503
Miller	Colquitt	6,381	6,383	283
Mitchell	Camilla	24,053	23,932	512
Monroe	Forsyth	22,153	21,757	396
Montgomery	Mount Vernon	8,361	8,270	245
Morgan	Madison	16,153	15,457	350
Murray	Chatsworth	37,747	36,506	344
Muscogee	Columbus	184,134	186,291	216
Newton	Covington	68,047	62,001	276

County	County seat or courthouse	2001 Pop.	2000 Pop.	Land area sq. mi.
Oconee	Watkinsville	27,059	26,225	186
Oglethorpe	Lexington	12,969	12,635	441
Paulding	Dallas	89,734	81,678	313
Peach	Fort Valley	24,196	23,668	151
Pickens	Jasper	24,776	22,983	232
Pierce	Blackshear	15,698	15,636	343
Pike	Zebulon	14,253	13,688	218
Polk	Cedartown	38,843	38,127	311
Pulaski	Hawkinsville	9,598	9,588	247
Putnam	Eatonton	19,094	18,812	345
Quitman	Georgetown	2,610	2,598	152
Rabun	Clayton	15,318	15,050	371
Randolph	Cuthbert	7,644	7,791	429
Richmond	Augusta	198,366	199,775	324
Rockdale	Conyers	71,798	70,111	131
Schley	Ellaville	3,921	3,766	168
Screven	Sylvania	15,177	15,374	648
Seminole	Donalsonville	9,365	9,369	238
Spalding	Griffin	59,066	58,417	198
Stephens	Toccoa	25,651	25,435	179
Stewart	Lumpkin	5,145	5,252	459
Sumter	Americus	33,319	33,200	485
Talbot	Talbotton	6,703	6,498	393
Taliaferro	Crawfordville	2,034	2,077	195
Tattnall	Reidsville	22,385	22,305	484
Taylor	Butler	8,836	8,815	377
Telfair	McRae	11,692	11,794	441
Terrell	Dawson	10,943	10,970	335
Thomas	Thomasville	43,012	42,737	548
Tift	Tifton	38,634	38,407	265
Toombs	Lyons	26,115	26,067	367
Towns	Hiawassee	9,641	9,319	167
Treutlen	Soperton	6,787	6,854	201
Troup	La Grange	59,478	58,779	414
Turner	Ashburn	9,621	9,504	286
Twiggs	Jeffersonville	10,589	10,590	360
Union	Blairsville	17,902	17,289	323
Upson	Thomaston	27,711	27,597	325
Walker	La Fayette	61,884	61,053	447
Walton	Monroe	65,224	60,687	329
Ware	Waycross	35,540	35,483	902
Warren	Warrenton	6,274	6,336	286
Washington	Sandersville	21,042	21,176	680
Wayne	Jesup	26,945	26,565	645
Webster	Preston	2,301	2,390	210
Wheeler	Alamo	6,183	6,179	298
White	Cleveland	21,182	19,944	242
Whitfield	Dalton	85,248	83,525	290
Wilcox	Abbeville	8,709	8,577	380
Wilkes	Washington	10,688	10,687	471
Wilkinson	Irwinton	10,300	10,220	447
Worth	Sylvester	21,938	21,967	570

Hawaii

(5 counties, 6,423 sq. mi. land; pop. 1,224,398)

County	County seat or courthouse	2001 Pop.	2000 Pop.	Land area sq. mi.
Hawaii	Hilo	152,083	148,677	4,028
Honolulu	Honolulu	881,295	876,156	600
Kalawao[1]		135	147	13
Kauai	Lihue	59,223	58,463	622
Maui	Wailuku	131,662	128,094	1,159

(1) Administered by state government.

Idaho

(44 counties, 82,747 sq. mi. land; pop. 1,321,006)

County	County seat or courthouse	2001 Pop.	2000 Pop.	Land area sq. mi.
Ada	Boise	312,337	300,904	1,055
Adams	Council	3,428	3,476	1,365
Bannock	Pocatello	75,323	75,565	1,113
Bear Lake	Paris	6,345	6,411	971
Benewah	Saint Maries	8,995	9,171	776
Bingham	Blackfoot	42,335	41,735	2,095
Blaine	Hailey	19,798	18,991	2,645
Boise	Idaho City	7,011	6,670	1,902
Bonner	Sandpoint	37,479	36,835	1,738
Bonneville	Idaho Falls	83,807	82,522	1,868
Boundary	Bonners Ferry	9,926	9,871	1,269
Butte	Arco	2,856	2,899	2,233
Camas	Fairfield	1,002	991	1,075
Canyon	Caldwell	139,821	131,441	590
Caribou	Soda Springs	7,397	7,304	1,766
Cassia	Burley	21,577	21,416	2,566
Clark	Dubois	971	1,022	1,765
Clearwater	Orofino	8,544	8,930	2,461
Custer	Challis	4,292	4,342	4,925
Elmore	Mountain Home	29,157	29130	3,078
Franklin	Preston	11,590	11,329	665
Fremont	Saint Anthony	11,822	11,819	1,867
Gem	Emmett	15,482	15,181	563
Gooding	Gooding	14,207	14,155	731
Idaho	Grangeville	15,423	15,511	8,485
Jefferson	Rigby	19,578	19,155	1,095
Jerome	Jerome	18,449	18,342	600
Kootenai	Coeur d'Alene	112,297	108,685	1,245
Latah	Moscow	34,476	34,935	1,077
Lemhi	Salmon	7,606	7,806	4,564
Lewis	Nez Perce	3,625	3,747	479
Lincoln	Shoshone	4,132	4,044	1,206
Madison	Rexberg	27,327	27,467	472
Minidoka	Rupert	19,677	20,174	760
Nez Perce	Lewiston	37,095	37,410	849
Oneida	Malad City	4,210	4,125	1,200
Owyhee	Murphy	11,008	10,644	7,678
Payette	Payette	20,868	20,578	408
Power	American Falls	7,468	7,538	1,406
Shoshone	Wallace	13,443	13,771	2,634
Teton	Driggs	6,419	5,999	450
Twin Falls	Twin Falls	64,731	64,284	1,925
Valley	Cascade	7,716	7,651	3,678
Washington	Weiser	9,956	9,977	1,456

Illinois

(102 counties, 55,584 sq. mi. land; pop. 12,482,301)

County	County seat or courthouse	2001 Pop.	2000 Pop.	Land area sq. mi.
Adams	Quincy	67,937	68,277	857
Alexander	Cairo	9,544	9,590	236
Bond	Greenville	17,758	17,633	380
Boone	Belvidere	43,472	41,786	281
Brown	Mount Sterling	6,897	6,950	306
Bureau	Princeton	35,280	35,503	869
Calhoun	Hardin	5,082	5,084	254
Carroll	Mount Carroll	16,526	16,674	444
Cass	Virginia	13,508	13,695	376
Champaign	Urbana	179,643	179,669	997
Christian	Taylorville	35,350	35,372	709
Clark	Marshall	16,964	17,008	502
Clay	Louisville	14,262	14,560	469
Clinton	Carlyle	35,658	35,535	474
Coles	Charleston	52,629	53,196	508
Cook	Chicago	5,350,269	5,376,741	946
Crawford	Robinson	20,251	20,452	444
Cumberland	Toledo	11,173	11,253	346
De Kalb	Sycamore	89,743	88,969	634
De Witt	Clinton	16,708	16,798	398
Douglas	Tuscola	10,887	19,922	417
Du Page	Wheaton	912,044	904,161	334
Edgar	Paris	19,410	19,704	624
Edwards	Albion	6,848	6,971	222
Effingham	Effingham	34,352	34,264	479
Fayette	Vandalia	21,710	21,802	716
Ford	Paxton	14,159	14,241	486
Franklin	Benton	38,796	39,018	412
Fulton	Lewiston	37,875	38,250	866
Gallatin	Shawneetown	6,318	6,445	324
Greene	Carrollton	14,573	14,761	543
Grundy	Morris	38,331	37,535	420
Hamilton	McLeansboro	8,450	8,621	435
Hancock	Carthage	19,909	20,121	795
Hardin	Elizabethtown	4,824	4,800	178
Henderson	Oquawka	8,205	8,213	379
Henry	Cambridge	50,773	51,020	823
Iroquois	Watseka	30,874	31,334	1,116
Jackson	Murphysboro	58,838	59,612	588
Jasper	Newton	10,037	10,117	494
Jefferson	Mount Vernon	40,113	40,045	571
Jersey	Jerseyville	21,832	21,668	369
Jo Daviess	Galena	22,356	22,289	601
Johnson	Vienna	13,089	12,878	345
Kane	Geneva	425,545	404,119	520
Kankakee	Kankakee	104,122	103,833	677
Kendall	Yorkville	58,227	54,544	321
Knox	Galesburg	55,314	55,836	716
Lake	Waukegan	661,111	644,356	448
La Salle	Ottawa	111,580	111,509	1,135
Lawrence	Lawrenceville	15,287	15,452	372
Lee	Dixon	35,971	36,062	725
Livingston	Pontiac	39,441	39,678	1,044
Logan	Lincoln	30,805	31,183	618
McDonough	Macomb	32,575	32,913	589
McHenry	Woodstock	270,504	260,077	604
McLean	Bloomington	151,878	150,433	1,184
Macon	Decatur	112,964	114,706	581
Macoupin	Carlinville	48,924	49,019	864
Madison	Edwardsville	260,259	258,941	725
Marion	Salem	41,446	41,691	572
Marshall	Lacon	12,971	13,180	386
Mason	Havana	15,960	16,038	539
Massac	Metropolis	15,081	15,161	239
Menard	Petersburg	12,556	12,486	314
Mercer	Aledo	16,971	16,957	561
Monroe	Waterloo	28,507	27,619	388
Montgomery	Hillsboro	30,462	30,652	704
Morgan	Jacksonville	36,221	36,616	569
Moultrie	Sullivan	14,307	14,287	336
Ogle	Oregon	51,729	51,032	759
Peoria	Peoria	181,676	183,433	620

County	County seat or courthouse	2001 Pop.	2000 Pop.	Land area sq. mi.
Perry	Pinckneyville	22,972	23,094	441
Piatt	Monticello	16,315	16,365	440
Pike	Pittsfield	17,199	17,384	830
Pope	Golconda	4,341	4,413	371
Pulaski	Mound City	7,167	7,348	201
Putnam	Hennepin	6,124	6,086	160
Randolph	Chester	33,830	33,893	578
Richland	Olney	16,042	16,149	360
Rock Island	Rock Island	148,379	149,374	427
Saint Clair	Belleville	256,599	256,082	664
Saline	Harrisburg	26,325	26,733	383
Sangamon	Springfield	189,379	188,951	868
Schuyler	Rushville	7,059	7,189	437
Scott	Winchester	5,500	5,537	251
Shelby	Shelbyville	22,681	22,893	759
Stark	Toulon	6,323	6,332	288
Stephenson	Freeport	48,401	48,979	564
Tazewell	Pekin	128,315	128,485	649
Union	Jonesboro	18,263	18,293	416
Vermilion	Danville	83,300	83,919	899
Wabash	Mount Carmel	12,784	12,937	223
Warren	Monmouth	18,374	18,735	543
Washington	Nashville	15,157	15,148	563
Wayne	Fairfield	17,076	17,151	714
White	Carmi	15,264	15,371	495
Whiteside	Morrison	60,495	60,653	685
Will	Joliet	536,416	502,266	837
Williamson	Marion	61,794	61,296	423
Winnebago	Rockford	279,943	278,418	514
Woodford	Eureka	35,833	35,469	528

Indiana

(92 counties, 35,867 sq. mi. land; pop. 6,114,745)

County	County seat or courthouse	2001 Pop.	2000 Pop.	Land area sq. mi.
Adams	Decatur	33,441	33,625	339
Allen	Fort Wayne	333,628	331,849	657
Bartholomew	Columbus	71,573	71,435	407
Benton	Fowler	9,279	9,421	406
Blackford	Hartford City	13,852	14,048	165
Boone	Lebanon	47,408	46,107	423
Brown	Nashville	15,124	14,957	312
Carroll	Delphi	20,257	20,165	372
Cass	Logansport	40,927	40,930	413
Clark	Jeffersonville	97,364	96,472	375
Clay	Brazil	26,602	26,556	358
Clinton	Frankfort	33,749	33,866	405
Crawford	English	10,920	10,743	306
Daviess	Washington	29,652	29,820	431
Dearborn	Lawrenceburg	46,806	46,109	305
Decatur	Greensburg	24,493	24,555	373
De Kalb	Auburn	40,398	40,285	363
Delaware	Muncie	118,531	118,769	393
Dubois	Jasper	39,805	39,674	430
Elkhart	Goshen	184,186	182,791	464
Fayette	Connersville	25,306	25,588	215
Floyd	New Albany	71,348	70,823	148
Fountain	Covington	17,815	17,954	396
Franklin	Brookville	22,284	22,151	386
Fulton	Rochester	20,664	20,511	369
Gibson	Princeton	32,716	32,500	489
Grant	Marion	72,605	73,403	414
Greene	Bloomfield	33,171	33,157	542
Hamilton	Noblesville	197,477	182,740	398
Hancock	Greenfield	57,160	55,391	306
Harrison	Corydon	34,929	34,325	485
Hendricks	Danville	110,784	104,093	408
Henry	New Castle	48,408	48,508	393
Howard	Kokomo	84,944	84,964	293
Huntington	Huntington	38,024	38,075	383
Jackson	Brownstown	41,258	41,335	509
Jasper	Rensselaer	30,551	30,043	560
Jay	Portland	21,769	21,806	384
Jefferson	Madison	32,051	31,705	361
Jennings	Vernon	28,097	27,554	377
Johnson	Franklin	119,240	115,209	320
Knox	Vincennes	38,822	39,256	516
Kosciusko	Warsaw	74,605	74,057	538
Lagrange	Lagrange	35,309	34,909	380
Lake	Crown Point	485,448	484,564	497
La Porte	La Porte	110,585	110,106	598
Lawrence	Bedford	46,020	45,922	449
Madison	Anderson	132,352	133,358	452
Marion	Indianapolis	856,938	860,454	396
Marshall	Plymouth	45,796	45,128	444
Martin	Shoals	10,383	10,369	336
Miami	Peru	36,269	36,082	376
Monroe	Bloomington	119,880	120,563	394
Montgomery	Crawfordsville	37,840	37,629	505
Morgan	Martinsville	67,513	66,689	406
Newton	Kentland	14,436	14,566	402
Noble	Albion	46,926	46,275	411
Ohio	Rising Sun	5,726	5,623	87
Orange	Paoli	19,442	19,306	400
Owen	Spencer	22,115	21,786	385
Parke	Rockville	17,233	17,241	445
Perry	Tell City	18,878	18,899	381
Pike	Petersburg	12,928	12,837	336
Porter	Valparaiso	148,769	146,798	418
Posey	Mount Vernon	27,067	27,061	409
Pulaski	Winamac	13,988	13,755	434
Putnam	Greencastle	36,331	36,019	480
Randolph	Winchester	27,364	27,401	453
Ripley	Versailles	26,976	26,523	446
Rush	Rushville	17,980	18,261	408
Saint Joseph	South Bend	264,779	265,559	457
Scott	Scottsburg	23,247	22,960	190
Shelby	Shelbyville	43,580	43,445	413
Spencer	Rockport	20,276	20,391	399
Starke	Knox	21,805	23,556	309
Steuben	Angola	33,404	33,214	309
Sullivan	Sullivan	21,818	21,751	447
Switzerland	Vevay	9,374	9,065	221
Tippecanoe	Lafayette	149,036	148,955	500
Tipton	Tipton	16,520	16,577	260
Union	Liberty	7,313	7,349	162
Vanderburgh	Evansville	171,268	171,922	235
Vermillion	Newport	16,581	16,788	257
Vigo	Terre Haute	104,778	105,848	403
Wabash	Wabash	34,704	34,960	413
Warren	Williamsport	8,614	8,419	365
Warrick	Boonville	53,080	52,383	384
Washington	Salem	27,585	27,223	514
Wayne	Richmond	70,515	71,097	404
Wells	Bluffton	27,689	27,600	370
White	Monticello	25,165	25,267	505
Whitley	Columbia City	31,099	30,707	336

Iowa

(99 counties, 55,869 sq. mi. land; pop. 2,923,179)

County	County seat or courthouse	2001 Pop.	2000 Pop.	Land area sq. mi.
Adair	Greenfield	8,069	8,243	569
Adams	Corning	4,395	4,482	424
Allamakee	Waukon	14,426	14,675	640
Appanoose	Centerville	13,594	13,721	496
Audubon	Audubon	6,715	6,830	443
Benton	Vinton	25,931	25,308	716
Black Hawk	Waterloo	126,483	128,012	567
Boone	Boone	26,281	26,224	571
Bremer	Waverly	23,368	23,325	438
Buchanan	Independence	20,913	21,093	571
Buena Vista	Storm Lake	20,023	20,411	575
Butler	Allison	15,145	15,305	580
Calhoun	Rockwell City	10,916	11,115	570
Carroll	Carroll	21,128	21,421	569
Cass	Atlantic	14,559	14,684	564
Cedar	Tipton	18,144	18,187	580
Cerro Gordo	Mason City	45,638	46,447	568
Cherokee	Cherokee	12,885	13,035	577
Chickasaw	New Hampton	13,050	13,095	505
Clarke	Osceola	9,143	9,133	431
Clay	Spencer	17,074	17,372	569
Clayton	Elkader	18,539	18,678	779
Clinton	Clinton	49,962	50,149	695
Crawford	Denison	16,908	16,942	714
Dallas	Adel	42,914	40,750	586
Davis	Bloomfield	8,628	8,541	503
Decatur	Leon	8,645	8,689	532
Delaware	Manchester	18,325	18,404	578
Des Moines	Burlington	41,743	42,351	416
Dickinson	Spirit Lake	16,523	16,424	381
Dubuque	Dubuque	88,856	89,143	608
Emmet	Estherville	10,813	11,027	396
Fayette	West Union	21,822	22,008	731
Floyd	Charles City	16,601	16,900	501
Franklin	Hampton	10,599	10,704	582
Fremont	Sidney	7,886	8,010	511
Greene	Jefferson	10,169	10,366	568
Grundy	Grundy Center	12,305	12,369	503
Guthrie	Guthrie Center	11,323	11,353	591
Hamilton	Webster City	16,380	16,438	577
Hancock	Garner	11,858	12,100	571
Hardin	Eldora	18,537	18,812	569
Harrison	Logan	15,626	15,666	697
Henry	Mount Pleasant	20,309	20,336	434
Howard	Cresco	9,856	9,932	473
Humboldt	Dakota City	10,292	10,381	434
Ida	Ida Grove	7,651	7,837	432
Iowa	Marengo	15,901	15,671	586
Jackson	Maquoketa	20,207	20,296	636
Jasper	Newton	37,296	37,213	730
Jefferson	Fairfield	16,029	16,181	435
Johnson	Iowa City	111,230	111,006	614
Jones	Anamosa	20,065	20,221	575
Keokuk	Sigourney	11,403	11,400	579
Kossuth	Algona	16,788	17,163	973
Lee	Fort Madison & Keokuk	37,313	38,052	517
Linn	Cedar Rapids	193,165	191,701	717
Louisa	Wapello	12,245	12,183	402
Lucas	Chariton	9,470	9,422	431

County	County seat or courthouse	2001 Pop.	2000 Pop.	Land area sq. mi.
Lyon	Rock Rapids	11,750	11,763	588
Madison	Winterset	14,190	14,019	561
Mahaska	Oskaloosa	22,123	22,335	571
Marion	Knoxville	32,610	32,052	554
Marshall	Marshalltown	39,438	39,311	572
Mills	Glenwood	14,651	14,547	437
Mitchell	Osage	10,842	10,874	469
Monona	Onawa	9,882	10,020	693
Monroe	Albia	7,839	8,016	433
Montgomery	Red Oak	11,536	11,771	424
Muscatine	Muscatine	41,831	41,722	439
O'Brien	Primghar	14,954	15,102	573
Osceola	Sibley	6,935	7,003	399
Page	Clarinda	16,682	16,976	535
Palo Alto	Emmetsburg	10,015	10,147	564
Plymouth	Le Mars	24,876	24,849	864
Pocahontas	Pocahontas	8,473	8,662	578
Polk	Des Moines	379,029	374,601	569
Pottawattamie	Council Bluffs	87,854	87,704	954
Poweshiek	Montezuma	18,899	18,815	585
Ringgold	Mount Ayr	5,376	5,469	538
Sac	Sac City	11,331	11,529	576
Scott	Davenport	158,489	158,668	458
Shelby	Harlan	13,182	13,173	591
Sioux	Orange City	31,596	31,589	768
Story	Nevada	79,462	79,981	573
Tama	Toledo	18,045	18,103	721
Taylor	Bedford	6,880	6,958	534
Union	Creston	12,240	12,309	424
Van Buren	Keosauqua	7,708	7,809	485
Wapello	Ottumwa	35,794	36,051	432
Warren	Indianola	41,149	40,671	572
Washington	Washington	21,010	20,670	569
Wayne	Corydon	6,639	6,730	526
Webster	Fort Dodge	39,806	40,235	715
Winnebago	Forest City	11,565	11,723	400
Winneshiek	Decorah	21,423	21,310	690
Woodbury	Sioux City	103,033	103,877	873
Worth	Northwood	7,810	7,909	400
Wright	Clarion	14,110	14,334	581

Kansas

(105 counties, 81,815 sq. mi. land; pop. 2,694,641)

County	County seat or courthouse	2001 Pop.	2000 Pop.	Land area sq. mi.
Allen	Iola	14,193	14,385	503
Anderson	Garnett	8,190	8,110	583
Atchison	Atchison	16,687	16,774	432
Barber	Medicine Lodge	5,163	5,307	1,134
Barton	Great Bend	27,810	28,205	894
Bourbon	Fort Scott	15,371	15,379	637
Brown	Hiawatha	10,630	10,724	571
Butler	El Dorado	60,194	59,482	1,428
Chase	Cottonwood Falls	3,033	3,030	776
Chautauqua	Sedan	4,270	4,359	642
Cherokee	Columbus	22,333	22,605	587
Cheyenne	Saint Francis	3,114	3,165	1,020
Clark	Ashland	2,371	2,390	975
Clay	Clay Center	8,771	8,822	644
Cloud	Concordia	9,985	10,268	716
Coffey	Burlington	8,815	8,865	630
Comanche	Coldwater	1,961	1,967	788
Cowley	Winfield	35,929	36,291	1,126
Crawford	Girard	37,927	38,242	593
Decatur	Oberlin	3,432	3,472	894
Dickinson	Abilene	19,155	19,344	848
Doniphan	Troy	8,303	8,249	392
Douglas	Lawrence	100,005	99,962	457
Edwards	Kinsley	3,325	3,449	622
Elk	Howard	3,189	3,261	647
Ellis	Hays	27,247	27,507	900
Ellsworth	Ellsworth	6,488	6,525	716
Finney	Garden City	40,082	40,523	1,302
Ford	Dodge City	32,314	32,458	1,099
Franklin	Ottawa	24,943	24,784	574
Geary	Junction City	26,799	27,947	385
Gove	Gove	3,008	3,068	1,071
Graham	Hill City	2,845	2,946	898
Grant	Ulysses	7,790	7,909	575
Gray	Cimarron	5,946	5,904	869
Greeley	Tribune	1,503	1,534	778
Greenwood	Eureka	7,771	7,673	1,140
Hamilton	Syracuse	2,671	2,670	996
Harper	Anthony	6,335	6,536	801
Harvey	Newton	33,031	32,869	539
Haskell	Sublette	4,285	4,307	577
Hodgeman	Jetmore	2,154	2,085	860
Jackson	Holton	12,742	12,657	656
Jefferson	Oskaloosa	18,610	18,426	536
Jewell	Mankato	3,591	3,791	909
Johnson	Olathe	465,058	451,086	477
Kearny	Lakin	4,562	4,531	871
Kingman	Kingman	8,512	8,673	863
Kiowa	Greensburg	3,132	3,278	722
Labette	Oswego	22,483	22,835	649
Lane	Dighton	2,091	2,155	717
Leavenworth	Leavenworth	70,261	68,691	463
Lincoln	Lincoln	3,547	3,578	719
Linn	Mound City	9,685	9,570	599
Logan	Oakley	2,957	3,046	1,073
Lyon	Emporia	35,560	35,935	851
McPherson	McPherson	29,618	29,554	900
Marion	Marion	13,423	13,361	943
Marshall	Marysville	10,772	10,965	903
Meade	Meade	4,647	4,631	978
Miami	Paola	28,780	28,351	577
Mitchell	Beloit	6,778	6,932	700
Montgomery	Independence	35,520	36,252	645
Morris	Council Grove	6,112	6,104	697
Morton	Elkhart	3,385	3,496	730
Nemaha	Seneca	10,516	10,717	718
Neosho	Erie	16,759	16,997	572
Ness	Ness City	3,340	3,454	1,075
Norton	Norton	5,841	5,953	878
Osage	Lyndon	16,903	16,712	704
Osborne	Osborne	4,345	4,452	892
Ottawa	Minneapolis	6,190	6,163	721
Pawnee	Larned	6,979	7,233	754
Phillips	Phillipsburg	5,873	6,001	886
Pottawatomie	Westmoreland	18,336	18,209	844
Pratt	Pratt	9,544	9,647	735
Rawlins	Atwood	2,918	2,966	1,070
Reno	Hutchinson	64,237	64,790	1,254
Republic	Belleville	5,646	5,835	716
Rice	Lyons	10,588	10,761	727
Riley	Manhattan	60,368	62,843	610
Rooks	Stockton	5,614	5,685	888
Rush	LaCrosse	3,488	3,551	718
Russell	Russell	7,166	7,370	885
Saline	Salina	53,646	53,597	720
Scott	Scott City	5,002	5,120	718
Sedgwick	Wichita	455,516	452,869	999
Seward	Liberal	22,434	22,510	640
Shawnee	Topeka	170,080	169,871	550
Sheridan	Hoxie	2,726	2,813	895
Sherman	Goodland	6,528	6,760	1,056
Smith	Smith Center	4,436	4,536	895
Stafford	Saint John	4,755	4,789	792
Stanton	Johnson	2,408	2,406	680
Stevens	Hugoton	5,379	5,463	728
Sumner	Wellington	25,749	25,946	1,182
Thomas	Colby	8,080	8,180	1,075
Trego	WaKeeney	3,195	3,319	888
Wabaunsee	Alma	6,843	6,885	797
Wallace	Sharon Springs	1,706	1,749	914
Washington	Washington	6,321	6,483	898
Wichita	Leoti	2,538	2,531	719
Wilson	Fredonia	10,235	10,332	574
Woodson	Yates Center	3,758	3,788	501
Wyandotte	Kansas City	157,461	157,882	151

Kentucky

(120 counties, 39,728 sq. mi. land; pop. 4,065,556)

County	County seat or courthouse	2001 Pop.	2000 Pop.	Land area sq. mi.
Adair	Columbia	17,291	17,244	407
Allen	Scottsville	18,056	17,800	346
Anderson	Lawrenceburg	19,564	19,111	203
Ballard	Wickliffe	8,158	8,286	251
Barren	Glasgow	38,592	38,033	491
Bath	Owingsville	11,355	11,085	279
Bell	Pineville	29,873	30,060	361
Boone	Burlington	90,489	85,991	246
Bourbon	Paris	19,478	19,360	291
Boyd	Catlettsburg	49,727	49,752	160
Boyle	Danville	27,612	27,697	182
Bracken	Brooksville	8,441	8,279	203
Breathitt	Jackson	16,024	16,100	495
Breckinridge	Hardinsburg	18,871	18,648	572
Bullitt	Shepherdsville	63,043	61,236	299
Butler	Morgantown	13,131	13,010	428
Caldwell	Princeton	12,898	13,060	347
Calloway	Murray	34,206	34,177	386
Campbell	Newport	88,362	88,616	152
Carlisle	Bardwell	5,345	5,351	192
Carroll	Carrollton	10,133	10,155	130
Carter	Grayson	27,024	26,889	411
Casey	Liberty	15,726	15,447	446
Christian	Hopkinsville	71,649	72,265	721
Clark	Winchester	33,409	33,144	254
Clay	Manchester	24,506	24,556	471
Clinton	Albany	9,616	9,634	197
Crittenden	Marion	9,281	9,384	362
Cumberland	Burkesville	7,188	7,147	306
Daviess	Owensboro	91,793	91,545	462
Edmonson	Brownsville	11,775	11644	303
Elliott	Sandy Hook	6,777	6,748	234
Estill	Irvine	15,407	15,307	254
Fayette	Lexington	260,414	260,512	285
Fleming	Flemingsburg	14,140	13,792	351
Floyd	Prestonsburg	42,350	42,441	394
Franklin	Frankfort	48,210	47,687	210

County	County seat or courthouse	2001 Pop.	2000 Pop.	Land area sq. mi.
Fulton	Hickman	7,784	7,752	209
Gallatin	Warsaw	7,961	7,870	99
Garrard	Lancaster	15,260	14,792	231
Grant	Williamstown	23,237	22,384	260
Graves	Mayfield	36,900	37,028	556
Grayson	Leitchfield	24,203	24,053	504
Green	Greensburg	11,627	11,518	289
Greenup	Greenup	36,823	36,891	346
Hancock	Hawesville	8,434	8,392	189
Hardin	Elizabethtown	95,070	94,174	628
Harlan	Harlan	32,683	33,202	467
Harrison	Cynthiana	18,048	17,983	310
Hart	Munfordville	17,383	17,445	416
Henderson	Henderson	44,835	44,829	440
Henry	New Castle	15,178	15,060	289
Hickman	Clinton	5,170	5,262	244
Hopkins	Madisonville	46,327	46,519	551
Jackson	McKee	13,651	13,495	346
Jefferson	Louisville	692,910	693,604	385
Jessamine	Nicholasville	40,016	39,041	173
Johnson	Paintsville	23,471	23,445	262
Kenton	Covington	151,366	151,464	162
Knott	Hindman	17,653	17,649	352
Knox	Barbourville	31,717	31,795	388
Larue	Hodgenville	13,395	13,373	263
Laurel	London	53,691	52,715	436
Lawrence	Louisa	15,722	15,569	419
Lee	Beattyville	7,905	7,916	210
Leslie	Hyden	12,315	12,401	404
Letcher	Whitesburg	25,018	25,277	339
Lewis	Vanceburg	13,903	14,092	484
Lincoln	Stanford	23,922	23,361	336
Livingston	Smithland	9,769	9,804	316
Logan	Russellville	26,586	26,573	556
Lyon	Eddyville	8,216	8,080	216
McCracken	Paducah	64,790	65,514	251
McCreary	Whitley City	17,057	17,080	428
McLean	Calhoun	9,949	9,938	254
Madison	Richmond	72,408	70,872	441
Magoffin	Salyersville	13,219	13,332	309
Marion	Lebanon	18,401	18,212	346
Marshall	Benton	30,308	30,125	305
Martin	Inez	12,596	12,578	231
Mason	Maysville	16,844	16,800	241
Meade	Brandenburg	27,008	26,349	309
Menifee	Frenchburg	6,642	6,556	204
Mercer	Harrodsburg	20,897	20,817	251
Metcalfe	Edmonton	10,119	10,037	291
Monroe	Tompkinsville	11,745	11,756	331
Montgomery	Mount Sterling	23,042	22,554	199
Morgan	West Liberty	14,168	13,948	381
Muhlenberg	Greenville	31,813	31,839	475
Nelson	Bardstown	38,592	37,477	423
Nicholas	Carlisle	6,827	6,813	197
Ohio	Hartford	23,036	22,916	594
Oldham	La Grange	48,000	46,178	189
Owen	Owenton	10,766	10,547	352
Owsley	Booneville	4,856	4,858	198
Pendleton	Falmouth	14,611	14,390	281
Perry	Hazard	29,279	29,390	342
Pike	Pikeville	67,887	68,736	788
Powell	Stanton	13,294	13,237	180
Pulaski	Somerset	56,774	56,217	662
Robertson	Mount Olivet	2,294	2,266	100
Rockcastle	Mount Vernon	16,629	16,582	318
Rowan	Morehead	22,174	22,094	281
Russell	Jamestown	16,492	16,315	254
Scott	Georgetown	34,519	33,061	285
Shelby	Shelbyville	34,120	33,337	384
Simpson	Franklin	16,460	16,405	236
Spencer	Taylorsville	13,039	11,766	186
Taylor	Campbellsville	23,034	22,927	270
Todd	Elkton	12,048	11,971	376
Trigg	Cadiz	12,828	12,597	443
Trimble	Bedford	8,442	8,125	149
Union	Morganfield	15,488	15,637	345
Warren	Bowling Green	93,232	92,522	545
Washington	Springfield	11,032	10,916	301
Wayne	Monticello	19,950	19,923	459
Webster	Dixon	14,034	14,120	335
Whitley	Williamsburg	36,466	35,865	440
Wolfe	Campton	6,953	7,065	223
Woodford	Versailles	23,331	23,208	191

Louisiana

(64 parishes, 43,562 sq. mi. land; pop. 4,465,430)

Parish	Parish seat or courthouse	2001 Pop.	2000 Pop.	Land area sq. mi.
Acadia	Crowley	58,910	58,861	655
Allen	Oberlin	25,342	25,440	765
Ascension	Donaldsonville	79,873	76,627	292
Assumption	Napoleonville	23,257	23,388	339
Avoyelles	Marksville	41,458	41,481	832
Beauregard	De Ridder	33,192	32,986	1,160
Bienville	Arcadia	15,563	15,752	811
Bossier	Benton	99,285	98,310	839
Caddo	Shreveport	250,760	252,161	882
Calcasieu	Lake Charles	182,842	183,577	1,071
Caldwell	Columbia	10,549	10,560	529
Cameron	Cameron	9,805	9,991	1,313
Catahoula	Harrisonburg	10,847	10,920	704
Claiborne	Homer	16,629	16,851	755
Concordia	Vidalia	20,090	20,247	696
De Soto	Mansfield	25,742	25,494	877
East Baton Rouge	Baton Rouge	409,667	412,852	455
East Carroll	Lake Providence	9,224	9,421	421
East Feliciana	Clinton	21,420	21,360	453
Evangeline	Ville Platte	35,546	35,434	664
Franklin	Winnsboro	21,018	21,263	624
Grant	Colfax	18,717	18,698	645
Iberia	New Iberia	73,530	73,266	575
Iberville	Plaquemine	33,261	33,320	619
Jackson	Jonesboro	15,409	15,397	570
Jefferson	Gretna	451,459	455,466	307
Jefferson Davis	Jennings	31,275	31,435	652
Lafayette	Lafayette	190,894	190,503	270
Lafourche	Thibodaux	90,273	89,974	1,085
La Salle	Jena	14,245	14,282	624
Lincoln	Ruston	42,173	42,509	471
Livingston	Livingston	96,257	91,814	648
Madison	Tallulah	13,506	13,728	624
Morehouse	Bastrop	30,675	31,021	794
Natchitoches	Natchitoches	38,558	39,080	1,255
Orleans	New Orleans	476,492	484,674	181
Ouachita	Monroe	146,678	147,250	611
Plaquemines	Pointe a la Hache	27,004	26,757	845
Pointe Coupee	New Roads	22,619	22,763	557
Rapides	Alexandria	126,566	126,337	1,323
Red River	Coushatta	9,578	9,622	389
Richland	Rayville	20,930	20,981	558
Sabine	Many	23,460	23,459	865
Saint Bernard	Chalmette	66,486	67,229	465
Saint Charles	Hahnville	48,548	48,072	284
Saint Helena	Greensburg	10,360	10,525	408
Saint James	Convent	21,224	21,216	246
Saint John the Baptist	Edgard	43,798	43,044	219
Saint Landry	Opelousas	88,186	87,700	929
Saint Martin	Saint Martinville	49,181	48,583	740
Saint Mary	Franklin	52,833	53,500	613
Saint Tammany	Covington	197,683	191,268	854
Tangipahoa	Amite	101,930	100,588	790
Tensas	Saint Joseph	6,507	6,618	602
Terrebonne	Houma	105,123	104,503	1,255
Union	Farmerville	22,869	22,803	878
Vermilion	Abbeville	53,661	53,807	1,174
Vernon	Leesville	51,273	52,531	1,328
Washington	Franklinton	44,072	43,926	670
Webster	Minden	41,456	41,831	595
West Baton Rouge	Port Allen	21,726	21,601	191
West Carroll	Oak Grove	12,160	12,314	359
West Feliciana	Saint Francisville	15,140	15,111	406
Winn	Winnfield	16,636	16,894	950

Maine

(16 counties, 30,862 sq. mi. land; pop. 1,286,670)

County	County seat or courthouse	2001 Pop.	2000 Pop.	Land area sq. mi.
Androscoggin	Auburn	104,131	103,793	470
Aroostook	Houlton	73,140	73,938	6,672
Cumberland	Portland	266,988	265,612	836
Franklin	Farmington	29,586	29,467	1,698
Hancock	Ellsworth	52,336	51,791	1,588
Kennebec	Augusta	117,782	117,114	868
Knox	Rockland	40,147	39,618	366
Lincoln	Wiscasset	34,316	33,616	456
Oxford	South Paris	55,378	54,755	2,078
Penobscot	Bangor	145,385	144,919	3,396
Piscataquis	Dover-Foxcroft	17,177	17,235	3,966
Sagadahoc	Bath	35,761	35,214	254
Somerset	Skowhegan	51,014	50,888	3,927
Waldo	Belfast	37,252	36,280	730
Washington	Machias	33,573	33,941	2,568
York	Alfred	192,704	186,742	991

Maryland

(23 counties, 1 ind. city, 9,774 sq. mi. land; pop. 5,375,156)

County	County seat or courthouse	2001 Pop.	2000 Pop.	Land area sq. mi.
Allegany	Cumberland	74,105	74,930	425
Anne Arundel	Annapolis	497,893	489,656	416
Baltimore	Towson	762,378	754,292	599
Calvert	Prince Frederick	78,307	74,563	215
Caroline	Denton	30,049	29,772	320
Carroll	Westminster	155,654	150,897	449
Cecil	Elkton	88,850	85,951	348
Charles	La Plata	125,371	120,546	461
Dorchester	Cambridge	30,612	30,674	558
Frederick	Frederick	203,789	195,277	663
Garrett	Oakland	29,942	29,846	648

County	County seat or courthouse	2001 Pop.	2000 Pop.	Land area sq. mi.
Harford	Bel Air	224,208	218,590	440
Howard	Ellicott City	255,707	247,842	252
Kent	Chestertown	19,532	19,197	279
Montgomery	Rockville	891,347	873,341	496
Prince George's	Upper Marlboro	816,791	801,515	485
Queen Anne's	Centreville	41,895	40,563	372
Saint Mary's	Leonardtown	87,721	86,211	361
Somerset	Princess Anne	24,937	24,747	327
Talbot	Easton	34,151	33,812	269
Washington	Hagerstown	133,197	131,923	458
Wicomico	Salisbury	85,426	84,644	377
Worcester	Snow Hill	48,084	46,543	473
Independent City				
Baltimore		635,210	651,154	81

Massachusetts

(14 counties, 7,840 sq. mi. land; pop. 6,379,304)

County	County seat or courthouse	2001 Pop.	2000 Pop.	Land area sq. mi.
Barnstable	Barnstable	226,809	222,230	396
Berkshire	Pittsfield	134,137	134,953	931
Bristol	Taunton	540,360	534,678	556
Dukes	Edgartown	15,402	14,987	104
Essex	Salem	730,296	723,419	501
Franklin	Greenfield	71,610	71,535	702
Hampden	Springfield	455,862	456,228	618
Hampshire	Northampton	152,876	152,251	529
Middlesex	East Cambridge	1,463,454	1,465,396	823
Nantucket	Nantucket	9,938	9,520	48
Norfolk	Dedham	653,232	650,308	400
Plymouth	Plymouth	481,059	472,822	661
Suffolk	Boston	682,062	689,807	59
Worcester	Worcester	762,207	750,963	1,513

Michigan

(83 counties, 56,804 sq. mi. land; pop. 9,990,817)

County	County seat or courthouse	2001 Pop.	2000 Pop.	Land area sq. mi.
Alcona	Harrisville	11,651	11,719	674
Alger	Munising	9,884	9,862	918
Allegan	Allegan	108,225	105,665	827
Alpena	Alpena	31,263	31,314	574
Antrim	Bellaire	23,610	23,110	477
Arenac	Standish	17,310	17,269	367
Baraga	L'Anse	8,735	8,746	904
Barry	Hastings	57,661	56,755	556
Bay	Bay City	109,659	110,157	444
Benzie	Beulah	16,489	15,998	321
Berrien	Saint Joseph	161,820	162,453	571
Branch	Coldwater	45,726	45,787	507
Calhoun	Marshall	138,031	137,985	709
Cass	Cassopolis	51,321	51,104	492
Charlevoix	Charlevoix	26,458	26,090	417
Cheboygan	Cheboygan	26,960	26,448	716
Chippewa	Sault Sainte Marie	38,413	38,543	1,561
Clare	Harrison	31,398	31,252	567
Clinton	Saint Johns	65,883	64,753	571
Crawford	Grayling	14,626	14,273	558
Delta	Escanaba	38,477	38,520	1,170
Dickinson	Iron Mountain	27,284	27,472	766
Eaton	Charlotte	104,837	103,655	576
Emmet	Petoskey	32,217	31,437	468
Genesee	Flint	439,117	436,141	640
Gladwin	Gladwin	26,507	26,023	507
Gogebic	Bessemer	17,670	17,370	1,102
Grand Traverse	Traverse City	80,203	77,654	465
Gratiot	Ithaca	42,272	42,285	570
Hillsdale	Hillsdale	46,879	46,527	599
Houghton	Houghton	35,698	36,016	1,012
Huron	Bad Axe	35,688	36,079	837
Ingham	Mason	278,398	279,320	559
Ionia	Ionia	62,111	61,518	573
Iosco	Tawas City	27,162	27,339	549
Iron	Crystal Falls	12,915	13,138	1,166
Isabella	Mount Pleasant	63,725	63,351	574
Jackson	Jackson	159,665	158,422	707
Kalamazoo	Kalamazoo	238,544	238,603	562
Kalkaska	Kalkaska	16,827	16,571	561
Kent	Grand Rapids	580,331	574,335	856
Keweenaw	Eagle River	2,257	2,301	541
Lake	Baldwin	11,630	11,333	567
Lapeer	Lapeer	89,728	87,904	654
Leelanau	Leland	21,518	21,119	348
Lenawee	Adrian	99,605	98,890	751
Livingston	Howell	164,678	156,951	568
Luce	Newberry	6,991	7,024	903
Mackinac	Saint Ignace	11,782	11,943	1,022
Macomb	Mount Clemens	799,954	788,149	480
Manistee	Manistee	24,857	24,527	544
Marquette	Marquette	64,383	64,634	1,821
Mason	Ludington	28,508	28,274	495
Mecosta	Big Rapids	41,011	40,553	556
Menominee	Menominee	25,246	25,326	1,044
Midland	Midland	83,879	82,874	521
Missaukee	Lake City	14,672	14,478	567
Monroe	Monroe	147,946	145,945	551
Montcalm	Stanton	61,828	61,266	708
Montmorency	Atlanta	10,494	10,315	548
Muskegon	Muskegon	171,361	170,200	509
Newaygo	White Cloud	48,875	47,874	842
Oakland	Pontiac	1,198,593	1,194,156	873
Oceana	Hart	27,321	26,873	540
Ogemaw	West Branch	21,810	21,645	564
Ontonagon	Ontonagon	7,775	7,818	1,312
Osceola	Reed City	23,365	23,197	566
Oscoda	Mio	9,588	9,418	565
Otsego	Gaylord	23,818	23,301	515
Ottawa	Grand Haven	243,571	238,314	566
Presque Isle	Rogers City	14,440	14,411	660
Roscommon	Roscommon	25,784	25,469	521
Saginaw	Saginaw	209,461	210,039	809
Saint Clair	Port Huron	166,541	164,235	724
Saint Joseph	Centreville	62,144	62,422	504
Sanilac	Sandusky	44,554	44,547	964
Schoolcraft	Manistique	8,859	8,903	1,178
Shiawassee	Corunna	72,217	71,687	539
Tuscola	Caro	58,364	58,266	812
Van Buren	Paw Paw	76,880	76,263	611
Washtenaw	Ann Arbor	326,627	322,895	710
Wayne	Detroit	2,045,473	2,061,162	614
Wexford	Cadillac	30,779	30,484	565

Minnesota

(87 counties, 79,610 sq. mi. land; pop. 4,972,294)

County	County seat or courthouse	2001 Pop.	2000 Pop.	Land area sq. mi.
Aitkin	Aitkin	15,413	15,301	1,819
Anoka	Anoka	305,681	298,084	424
Becker	Detroit Lakes	30,537	30,000	1,310
Beltrami	Bemidji	40,399	39,650	2,505
Benton	Foley	35,421	34,226	408
Big Stone	Ortonville	5,737	5,820	497
Blue Earth	Mankato	55,904	55,941	752
Brown	New Ulm	26,711	26,911	611
Carlton	Carlton	32,075	31,671	860
Carver	Chaska	73,378	70,205	357
Cass	Walker	27,638	27,150	2,018
Chippewa	Montevideo	12,951	13,088	583
Chisago	Center City	43,476	41,101	418
Clay	Moorhead	51,609	51,229	1,045
Clearwater	Bagley	8,410	8,423	995
Cook	Grand Marais	5,170	5,168	1,451
Cottonwood	Windom	11,958	12,167	640
Crow Wing	Brainerd	56,318	55,099	997
Dakota	Hastings	363,866	355,904	570
Dodge	Mantorville	18,234	17,731	440
Douglas	Alexandria	33,378	32,821	634
Faribault	Blue Earth	15,987	16,181	714
Fillmore	Preston	21,296	21,122	861
Freeborn	Albert Lea	32,300	32,584	708
Goodhue	Red Wing	44,655	44,127	758
Grant	Elbow Lake	6,238	6,289	546
Hennepin	Minneapolis	1,114,977	1,116,200	557
Houston	Caledonia	19,940	19,718	558
Hubbard	Park Rapids	18,446	18,376	922
Isanti	Cambridge	32,767	31,287	439
Itasca	Grand Rapids	44,018	43,992	2,665
Jackson	Jackson	11,160	11,268	702
Kanabec	Mora	15,340	14,996	525
Kandiyohi	Willmar	41,106	41,203	796
Kittson	Hallock	5,150	5,285	1,097
Koochiching	International Falls	14,164	14,355	3,102
Lac qui Parle	Madison	7,919	8,067	765
Lake	Two Harbors	11,084	11,058	2,099
Lake of the Woods	Baudette	4,443	4,522	1,297
Le Sueur	Le Center	25,729	25,426	449
Lincoln	Ivanhoe	6,331	6,429	537
Lyon	Marshall	25,231	25,425	714
McLeod	Glencoe	35,338	34,898	492
Mahnomen	Mahnomen	5,215	5,190	556
Marshall	Warren	10,025	10,155	1,772
Martin	Fairmont	21,536	21,802	709
Meeker	Litchfield	22,842	22,644	609
Mille Lacs	Milaca	23,044	22,330	574
Morrison	Little Falls	32,216	31,712	1,125
Mower	Austin	38,631	38,603	712
Murray	Slayton	9,003	9,165	704
Nicollet	Saint Peter	30,106	29,771	452
Nobles	Worthington	20,650	20,832	715
Norman	Ada	7,358	7,442	876
Olmsted	Rochester	126,275	124,277	653
Otter Tail	Fergus Falls	57,797	57,159	1,980
Pennington	Thief River Falls	13,448	13,584	617
Pine	Pine City	27,099	26,530	1,411
Pipestone	Pipestone	9,864	9,895	466
Polk	Crookston	31,160	31,369	1,970
Pope	Glenwood	11,216	11,236	670
Ramsey	Saint Paul	508,667	511,035	156
Red Lake	Red Lake Falls	4,295	4,299	432
Redwood	Redwood Falls	16,594	16,815	880

County	County seat or courthouse	2001 Pop.	2000 Pop.	Land area sq. mi.
Renville	Olivia	16,961	17,154	983
Rice	Faribault	57,683	56,665	498
Rock	Luverne	9,698	9,721	483
Roseau	Roseau	16,172	16,338	1,663
Saint Louis	Duluth	199,460	200,528	6,225
Scott	Shakopee	98,100	89,498	357
Sherburne	Elk River	68,621	64,417	436
Sibley	Gaylord	15,384	15,356	589
Stearns	Saint Cloud	134,509	133,166	1,345
Steele	Owatonna	34,131	33,680	430
Stevens	Morris	9,845	10,053	562
Swift	Benson	11,645	11,956	744
Todd	Long Prairie	24,569	24,426	942
Traverse	Wheaton	3,999	4,134	574
Wabasha	Wabasha	21,731	21,610	525
Wadena	Wadena	13,646	13,713	535
Waseca	Waseca	19,495	19,526	423
Washington	Stillwater	207,642	201,130	392
Watonwan	Saint James	11,779	11,876	435
Wilkin	Breckenridge	7,034	7,138	751
Winona	Winona	49,588	49,985	626
Wright	Buffalo	94,789	89,986	661
Yellow Medicine	Granite Falls	10,883	11,080	758

Mississippi

(82 counties, 46,907 sq. mi. land; pop. 2,858,029)

County	County seat or courthouse	2001 Pop.	2000 Pop.	Land area sq. mi.
Adams	Natchez	33,900	34,340	460
Alcorn	Corinth	34,612	34,558	400
Amite	Liberty	13,509	13,599	730
Attala	Kosciusko	19,655	19,661	735
Benton	Ashland	7,950	8,026	407
Bolivar	Cleveland & Rosedale	40,155	40,633	876
Calhoun	Pittsboro	14,901	15,069	587
Carroll	Carrollton & Vaiden	10,741	10,769	628
Chickasaw	Houston & Okolona	19,400	19,440	502
Choctaw	Ackerman	9,663	9,758	419
Claiborne	Port Gibson	11,823	11,831	487
Clarke	Quitman	17,877	17,955	691
Clay	West Point	21,832	21,979	409
Coahoma	Clarksdale	30,108	30,622	554
Copiah	Hazlehurst	28,886	28,757	777
Covington	Collins	19,527	19,407	414
De Soto	Hernando	114,352	107,199	478
Forrest	Hattiesburg	72,890	72,604	467
Franklin	Meadville	8,377	8,448	565
George	Lucedale	19,582	19,144	478
Greene	Leakesville	13,376	13,299	713
Grenada	Grenada	22,938	23,263	422
Hancock	Bay Saint Louis	44,031	42,967	477
Harrison	Gulfport	189,409	189,601	581
Hinds	Jackson & Raymond	249,495	250,800	869
Holmes	Lexington	21,476	21,609	756
Humphreys	Belzoni	10,929	11,206	418
Issaquena	Mayersville	2,225	2,274	413
Itawamba	Fulton	23,018	22,770	532
Jackson	Pascagoula	132,823	131,420	727
Jasper	Bay Springs & Paulding	18,333	18,149	676
Jefferson	Fayette	9,695	9,740	519
Jefferson Davis	Prentiss	13,855	13,962	408
Jones	Ellisville & Laurel	64,536	64,958	694
Kemper	De Kalb	10,464	10,453	766
Lafayette	Oxford	38,834	38,744	631
Lamar	Purvis	40,482	39,070	497
Lauderdale	Meridian	77,414	78,161	704
Lawrence	Monticello	13,379	13,258	431
Leake	Carthage	21,145	20,940	583
Lee	Tupelo	76,680	75,755	450
Leflore	Greenwood	37,316	37,947	592
Lincoln	Brookhaven	33,596	33,166	586
Lowndes	Columbus	60,933	61,586	502
Madison	Canton	76,708	74,674	717
Marion	Columbia	25,344	25,595	542
Marshall	Holly Springs	35,329	34,993	706
Monroe	Aberdeen	38,064	38,014	764
Montgomery	Winona	12,056	12,189	407
Neshoba	Philadelphia	28,516	28,684	570
Newton	Decatur	22,054	21,838	578
Noxubee	Macon	12,520	12,548	695
Oktibbeha	Starkville	42,286	42,902	458
Panola	Batesville & Sardis	34,697	34,274	684
Pearl River	Poplarville	49,969	48,621	811
Perry	New Augusta	12,273	12,138	647
Pike	Magnolia	38,956	38,940	409
Pontotoc	Pontotoc	27,053	26,726	497
Prentiss	Booneville	25,480	25,556	415
Quitman	Marks	10,065	10,117	405
Rankin	Brandon	119,141	115,327	775
Scott	Forest	28,317	28,423	609
Sharkey	Rolling Fork	6,418	6,580	428
Simpson	Mendenhall	27,568	27,639	589
Smith	Raleigh	16,168	16,182	636
Stone	Wiggins	13,960	13,622	445
Sunflower	Indianola	33,930	34,369	694
Tallahatchie	Charleston & Sumner	14,640	14,903	644
Tate	Senatobia	25,617	25,370	404
Tippah	Ripley	20,928	20,826	458
Tishomingo	Iuka	19,060	19,163	424
Tunica	Tunica	9,365	9,227	455
Union	New Albany	25,782	25,362	415
Walthall	Tylertown	15,380	15,156	404
Warren	Vicksburg	49,343	49,644	587
Washington	Greenville	61,827	62,977	724
Wayne	Waynesboro	21,193	21,216	810
Webster	Walthall	10,320	10,294	422
Wilkinson	Woodville	10,334	10,312	677
Winston	Louisville	20,129	20,160	607
Yalobusha	Coffeeville & Water Valley	13,308	13,051	467
Yazoo	Yazoo City	27,809	28,149	919

Missouri

(114 counties, 1 ind. city, 68,886 sq. mi. land; pop. 5,629,707)

County	County seat or courthouse	2001 Pop.	2000 Pop.	Land area sq. mi.
Adair	Kirksville	24,795	24,977	567
Andrew	Savannah	16,694	16,492	435
Atchison	Rockport	6,414	6,430	545
Audrain	Mexico	25,455	25,853	693
Barry	Cassville	34,352	34,010	779
Barton	Lamar	12,741	12,541	594
Bates	Butler	16,754	16,653	848
Benton	Warsaw	17,493	17,180	706
Bollinger	Marble Hill	12,335	12,029	621
Boone	Columbia	136,774	135,454	685
Buchanan	Saint Joseph	85,367	85,998	410
Butler	Poplar Buff	40,643	40,867	698
Caldwell	Kingston	9,004	8,969	429
Callaway	Fulton	41,590	40,766	839
Camden	Camdenton	37,588	37,051	655
Cape Girardeau	Jackson	69,047	68,693	579
Carroll	Carrollton	10,242	10,285	695
Carter	Van Buren	5,930	5,941	508
Cass	Harrisonville	85,630	82,092	699
Cedar	Stockton	13,821	13,733	476
Chariton	Keytesville	8,297	8,438	756
Christian	Ozark	57,270	54,285	563
Clark	Kahoka	7,504	7,416	507
Clay	Liberty	188,241	184,006	396
Clinton	Plattsburg	19,530	18,979	419
Cole	Jefferson City	71,540	71,397	391
Cooper	Boonville	16,659	16,670	565
Crawford	Steelville	22,955	22,804	743
Dade	Greenfield	7,868	7,923	490
Dallas	Buffalo	15,784	15,661	542
Daviess	Gallatin	7,917	8,016	567
De Kalb	Maysville	11,550	11,597	424
Dent	Salem	14,962	14,927	754
Douglas	Ava	13,220	13,084	815
Dunklin	Kennett	33,017	33,155	546
Franklin	Union	95,187	93,807	923
Gasconade	Hermann	15,423	15,342	521
Gentry	Albany	6,763	6,861	492
Greene	Springfield	241,926	240,391	675
Grundy	Trenton	10,281	10,432	436
Harrison	Bethany	8,756	8,850	725
Henry	Clinton	22,302	21,997	702
Hickory	Hermitage	8,928	8,940	399
Holt	Oregon	5,268	5,351	462
Howard	Fayette	10,034	10,212	466
Howell	West Plains	37,209	37,238	928
Iron	Ironton	10,546	10,697	551
Jackson	Independence	655,855	654,880	605
Jasper	Carthage	105,664	104,686	640
Jefferson	Hillsboro	201,826	198,099	657
Johnson	Warrensburg	48,888	48,258	830
Knox	Edina	4,294	4,361	506
Laclede	Lebanon	32,868	32,513	766
Lafayette	Lexington	32,975	32,960	629
Lawrence	Mount Vernon	35,651	35,204	613
Lewis	Monticello	10,375	10,494	505
Lincoln	Troy	41,010	38,944	630
Linn	Linneus	13,628	13,754	620
Livingston	Chillicothe	14,500	14,558	535
McDonald	Pineville	21,632	21,681	540
Macon	Macon	15,569	15,762	804
Madison	Fredericktown	11,784	11,800	497
Maries	Vienna	8,690	8,903	528
Marion	Palmyra	28,086	28,289	438
Mercer	Princeton	3,740	3,757	454
Miller	Tuscumbia	24,092	23,564	592
Mississippi	Charleston	13,162	13,427	413
Moniteau	California	14,861	14,827	417
Monroe	Paris	9,357	9,311	646
Montgomery	Montgomery City	12,111	12,136	537

County	County seat or courthouse	2001 Pop.	2000 Pop.	Land area sq. mi.
Morgan	Versailles	19,597	19,309	597
New Madrid	New Madrid	19,421	19,760	678
Newton	Neosho	52,852	52,636	626
Nodaway	Maryville	21,714	21,912	877
Oregon	Alton	10,255	10,344	791
Osage	Linn	12,999	13,062	606
Ozark	Gainesville	9,488	9,542	742
Pemiscot	Caruthersville	19,774	20,047	493
Perry	Perryville	18,153	18,132	475
Pettis	Sedalia	39,346	39,403	685
Phelps	Rolla	40,206	39,825	673
Pike	Bowling Green	18,285	18,351	673
Platte	Platte City	76,223	73,781	420
Polk	Bolivar	27,458	26,992	637
Pulaski	Waynesville	41,470	41,165	547
Putnam	Unionville	5,233	5,223	518
Ralls	New London	9,609	9,626	471
Randolph	Huntsville	24,635	24,663	482
Ray	Richmond	23,431	23,354	569
Reynolds	Centerville	6,606	6,689	811
Ripley	Doniphan	13,504	13,509	629
Saint Charles	Saint Charles	296,679	283,883	560
Saint Clair	Osceola	9,645	9,652	677
Sainte Genevieve	Sainte Genevieve	18,005	17,842	502
Saint Francois	Farmington	56,147	55,641	449
Saint Louis	Clayton	1,015,417	1,016,315	508
Saline	Marshall	23,334	23,756	756
Schuyler	Lancaster	4,162	4,170	308
Scotland	Memphis	4,940	4,983	438
Scott	Benton	40,509	40,422	421
Shannon	Eminence	8,359	8,324	1,004
Shelby	Shelbyville	6,758	6,799	501
Stoddard	Bloomfield	29,659	29,705	827
Stone	Galena	28,919	28,658	463
Sullivan	Milan	7,168	7,219	651
Taney	Forsyth	40,224	39,703	632
Texas	Houston	23,109	23,003	1,179
Vernon	Nevada	20,304	20,454	834
Warren	Warrenton	25,452	24,525	431
Washington	Potosi	23,454	23,344	760
Wayne	Greenville	13,215	13,259	761
Webster	Marshfield	32,183	31,045	593
Worth	Grant City	2,355	2,382	267
Wright	Hartville	18,016	17,955	682
Independent City				
Saint Louis		339,211	348,189	62

Montana

(56 counties, 145,552 sq. mi. land; pop. 904,433)

County	County seat or courthouse	2001 Pop.	2000 Pop.	Land area sq. mi.
Beaverhead	Dillon	9,089	9,202	5,542
Big Horn	Hardin	12,763	12,671	4,995
Blaine	Chinook	6,870	7,009	4,226
Broadwater	Townsend	4,457	4,385	1,191
Carbon	Red Lodge	9,696	9,552	2,048
Carter	Ekalaka	1,375	1,360	3,340
Cascade	Great Falls	79,298	80,357	2,698
Chouteau	Fort Benton	5,738	5,970	3,973
Custer	Miles City	11,372	11,696	3,783
Daniels	Scobey	1,998	2,017	1,426
Dawson	Glendive	8,877	9,059	2,373
Deer Lodge	Anaconda	9,171	9,417	737
Fallon	Baker	2,761	2,837	1,620
Fergus	Lewistown	11,693	11,893	4,339
Flathead	Kalispell	76,269	74,471	5,098
Gallatin	Bozeman	69,422	67,831	2,606
Garfield	Jordan	1,243	1,279	4,668
Glacier	Cut Bank	13,125	13,247	2,995
Golden Valley	Ryegate	1,019	1,042	1,175
Granite	Philipsburg	2,899	2,830	1,727
Hill	Havre	16,467	16,673	2,896
Jefferson	Boulder	10,405	10,049	1,657
Judith Basin	Stanford	2,280	2,329	1,870
Lake	Polson	26,904	26,507	1,494
Lewis & Clark	Helena	56,094	55,716	3,461
Liberty	Chester	2,096	2,158	1,430
Lincoln	Libby	18,664	18,837	3,613
McCone	Circle	1,900	1,977	2,643
Madison	Virginia City	6,939	6,851	3,587
Meagher	White Sulphur Springs	1,938	1,932	2,392
Mineral	Superior	3,843	3,884	1,220
Missoula	Missoula	96,303	95,802	2,598
Musselshell	Roundup	4,450	4,497	1,867
Park	Livingston	15,686	15,694	2,802
Petroleum	Winnett	488	493	1,654
Phillips	Malta	4,420	4,601	5,140
Pondera	Conrad	6,345	6,424	1,625
Powder River	Broadus	1,824	1,858	3,297
Powell	Deer Lodge	7,076	7,180	2,326
Prairie	Terry	1,216	1,199	1,737
Ravalli	Hamilton	37,304	36,070	2,394
Richland	Sidney	9,343	9,667	2,084
Roosevelt	Wolf Point	10,561	10,620	2,356
Rosebud	Forsyth	9,282	9,383	5,012
Sanders	Thompson Falls	10,443	10,227	2,762
Sheridan	Plentywood	3,940	4,105	1,677
Silver Bow	Butte	33,604	34,606	718
Stillwater	Columbus	8,433	8,195	1,795
Sweet Grass	Big Timber	3,585	3,609	1,855
Teton	Choteau	6,387	6,445	2,273
Toole	Shelby	5,151	5,267	1,911
Treasure	Hysham	802	861	979
Valley	Glasgow	7,524	7,675	4,921
Wheatland	Harlowton	2,153	2,259	1,423
Wibaux	Wibaux	1,050	1,068	889
Yellowstone	Billings	130,398	129,352	2,635

Nebraska

(93 counties, 76,872 sq. mi. land; pop. 1,713,235)

County	County seat or courthouse	2001 Pop.	2000 Pop.	Land area sq. mi.
Adams	Hastings	30,917	31,151	563
Antelope	Neligh	7,271	7,452	857
Arthur	Arthur	411	444	715
Banner	Harrisburg	802	819	746
Blaine	Brewster	548	583	711
Boone	Albion	6,168	6,259	687
Box Butte	Alliance	11,844	12,158	1,075
Boyd	Butte	2,394	2,438	540
Brown	Ainsworth	3,542	3,525	1,221
Buffalo	Kearney	42,399	42,259	968
Burt	Tekamah	7,696	7,791	493
Butler	David City	8,832	8,767	584
Cass	Plattsmouth	24,646	24,334	559
Cedar	Hartington	9,472	9,615	740
Chase	Imperial	3,974	4,068	895
Cherry	Valentine	6,120	6,148	5,961
Cheyenne	Sidney	9,974	9,830	1,196
Clay	Clay Center	6,926	7,039	573
Colfax	Schuyler	10,423	10,441	413
Cuming	West Point	10,093	10,203	572
Custer	Broken Bow	11,621	11,793	2,576
Dakota	Dakota City	20,347	20,253	264
Dawes	Chadron	8,934	9,060	1,396
Dawson	Lexington	24,432	24,365	1,013
Deuel	Chappell	2,073	2,098	440
Dixon	Ponca	6,226	6,339	476
Dodge	Fremont	35,931	36,160	534
Douglas	Omaha	465,683	463,585	331
Dundy	Benkelman	2,203	2,292	920
Fillmore	Geneva	6,470	6,634	576
Franklin	Franklin	3,495	3,574	575
Frontier	Stockville	3,066	3,099	975
Furnas	Beaver City	5,182	5,324	718
Gage	Beatrice	23,053	22,993	855
Garden	Oshkosh	2,220	2,292	1,704
Garfield	Burwell	1,904	1,902	570
Gosper	Elwood	2,049	2,143	458
Grant	Hyannis	741	747	776
Greeley	Greeley	2,670	2,714	569
Hall	Grand Island	53,304	53,534	546
Hamilton	Aurora	9,448	9,403	544
Harlan	Alma	3,759	3,786	553
Hayes	Hayes Center	1,099	1,068	713
Hitchcock	Trenton	3,082	3,111	710
Holt	O'Neill	11,351	11,551	2,413
Hooker	Mullen	749	783	721
Howard	Saint Paul	6,483	6,567	569
Jefferson	Fairbury	8,305	8,333	573
Johnson	Tecumseh	4,348	4,488	376
Kearney	Minden	6,871	6,882	516
Keith	Ogallala	8,839	8,875	1,061
Keya Paha	Springview	948	983	773
Kimball	Kimball	4,023	4,089	952
Knox	Center	9,167	9,374	1,108
Lancaster	Lincoln	252,090	250,291	839
Lincoln	North Platte	34,516	34,632	2,564
Logan	Stapleton	776	774	571
Loup	Taylor	709	712	570
McPherson	Tryon	536	533	859
Madison	Madison	35,549	35,226	573
Merrick	Central City	8,092	8,204	485
Morrill	Bridgeport	5,363	5,440	1,424
Nance	Fullerton	3,969	4,038	441
Nemaha	Auburn	7,456	7,576	409
Nuckolls	Nelson	4,987	5,057	575
Otoe	Nebraska City	15,505	15,396	616
Pawnee	Pawnee City	3,015	3,087	432
Perkins	Grant	3,153	3,200	883
Phelps	Holdrege	9,704	9,747	540
Pierce	Pierce	7,818	7,857	574
Platte	Columbus	31,332	31,662	678
Polk	Osceola	5,547	5,639	439
Red Willow	McCook	11,410	11,448	717
Richardson	Falls City	9,226	9,531	553
Rock	Bassett	1,728	1,756	1,008
Saline	Wilber	13,840	13,843	575
Sarpy	Papillion	125,836	122,595	241
Saunders	Wahoo	20,096	19,830	754

County	County seat or courthouse	2001 Pop.	2000 Pop.	Land area sq. mi.
Scotts Bluff	Gering	36,617	36,951	739
Seward	Seward	16,403	16,496	575
Sheridan	Rushville	5,997	6,198	2,441
Sherman	Loup City	3,253	3,318	566
Sioux	Harrison	1,399	1,475	2,067
Stanton	Stanton	6,425	6,455	430
Thayer	Hebron	5,864	6,055	575
Thomas	Thedford	705	729	713
Thurston	Pender	7,094	7,171	394
Valley	Ord	4,594	4,647	568
Washington	Blair	19,191	18,780	390
Wayne	Wayne	9,668	9,851	443
Webster	Red Cloud	4,015	4,061	575
Wheeler	Bartlett	858	886	575
York	York	14,371	14,598	576

Nevada

(16 counties, 1 ind. city, 109,826 sq. mi. land; pop. 2,106,074)

County	County seat or courthouse	2001 Pop.	2000 Pop.	Land area sq. mi.
Churchill	Fallon	24,044	23,982	4,929
Clark	Las Vegas	1,464,653	1,375,765	7,910
Douglas	Minden	42,658	41,259	710
Elko	Elko	45,275	45,291	17,179
Esmeralda	Goldfield	978	971	3,589
Eureka	Eureka	1,632	1,651	4,176
Humboldt	Winnemucca	15,322	16,106	9,648
Lander	Battle Mountain	5,480	5,794	5,494
Lincoln	Pioche	4,198	4,165	10,634
Lyon	Yerington	36,783	34,501	1,994
Mineral	Hawthorne	4,886	5,071	3,756
Nye	Tonopah	34,075	32,485	18,147
Pershing	Lovelock	6,598	6,693	6,037
Storey	Virginia City	3,467	3,399	263
Washoe	Reno	353,336	339,486	6,342
White Pine	Ely	8,766	9,181	8,876
Independent City				
Carson City		53,923	52,457	143

New Hampshire

(10 counties, 8,968 sq. mi. land; pop. 1,259,181)

County	County seat or courthouse	2001 Pop.	2000 Pop.	Land area sq. mi.
Belknap	Laconia	58,384	56,325	401
Carroll	Ossipee	44,612	43,666	934
Cheshire	Keene	74,243	73,825	707
Coos	Lancaster	32,964	33,111	1,800
Grafton	Woodsville	82,254	81,743	1,713
Hillsborough	Nashua	387,674	380,841	876
Merrimack	Concord	139,324	136,225	934
Rockingham	Brentwood	284,061	277,359	695
Strafford	Dover	114,632	112,233	369
Sullivan	Newport	41,033	40,458	537

New Jersey

(21 counties, 7,417 sq. mi. land; pop. 8,484,431)

County	County seat or courthouse	2001 Pop.	2000 Pop.	Land area sq. mi.
Atlantic	Mays Landing	255,479	252,552	561
Bergen	Hackensack	886,680	884,118	234
Burlington	Mount Holly	432,121	423,394	805
Camden	Camden	509,350	508,932	222
Cape May	Cape May Court House	102,352	102,326	255
Cumberland	Bridgeton	146,289	146,438	489
Essex	Newark	793,133	793,633	126
Gloucester	Woodbury	259,347	254,673	325
Hudson	Jersey City	607,554	608,975	47
Hunterdon	Flemington	125,135	121,989	430
Mercer	Trenton	353,529	350,761	226
Middlesex	New Brunswick	757,191	750,162	310
Monmouth	Freehold	622,977	615,301	472
Morris	Morristown	472,859	470,212	469
Ocean	Toms River	527,207	510,916	636
Passaic	Paterson	491,077	489,049	185
Salem	Salem	64,364	64,285	338
Somerset	Somerville	301,955	297,490	305
Sussex	Newton	146,671	144,166	521
Union	Elizabeth	523,396	522,541	103
Warren	Belvidere	105,765	102,437	358

New Mexico

(33 counties, 121,356 sq. mi. land; pop. 1,829,146)

County	County seat or courthouse	2001 Pop.	2000 Pop.	Land area sq. mi.
Bernalillo	Albuquerque	562,458	556,678	1,166
Catron	Reserve	3,512	3,543	6,928
Chaves	Roswell	60,301	61,382	6,071
Cibola	Grants	25,888	25,595	4,539
Colfax	Raton	14,140	14,189	3,757
Curry	Clovis	44,229	45,044	1,406
DeBaca	Fort Sumner	2,138	2,240	2,325
Dona Ana	Las Cruces	176,790	174,682	3,807
Eddy	Carlsbad	51,067	51,658	4,182
Grant	Silver City	30,722	31,002	3,966
Guadalupe	Santa Rosa	4,602	4,680	3,030
Harding	Mosquero	772	810	2,125
Hidalgo	Lordsburg	5,612	5,932	3,446
Lea	Lovington	55,149	55,511	4,393
Lincoln	Carrizozo	19,730	19,411	4,831
Los Alamos	Los Alamos	17,798	18,343	109
Luna	Deming	25,002	25,016	2,965
McKinley	Gallup	75,032	74,798	5,449
Mora	Mora	5,236	5,180	1,931
Otero	Alamogordo	60,747	62,298	6,627
Quay	Tucumcari	9,829	10,155	2,875
Rio Arriba	Tierra Amarilla	40,772	41,190	5,858
Roosevelt	Portales	18,120	18,018	2,449
Sandoval	Bernalillo	93,883	89,908	3,709
San Juan	Aztec	115,380	113,801	5,514
San Miguel	Las Vegas	30,156	30,126	4,717
Santa Fe	Santa Fe	130,915	129,292	1,909
Sierra	Truth or Consequences	13,188	13,270	4,180
Socorro	Socorro	17,856	18,078	6,646
Taos	Taos	30,353	29,979	2,203
Torrance	Estancia	16,792	16,911	3,345
Union	Clayton	4,022	4,174	3,830
Valencia	Los Lunas	66,955	66,152	1,068

New York

(62 counties, 47,214 sq. mi. land; pop. 19,011,378)

County	County seat or courthouse	2001 Pop.	2000 Pop.	Land area sq. mi.
Albany	Albany	294,007	294,565	523
Allegany	Belmont	49,881	49,927	1,030
Bronx[1]	Bronx	1,337,928	1,332,650	42
Broome	Binghamton	199,267	200,536	707
Cattaraugus	Little Valley	83,403	83,955	1,310
Cayuga	Auburn	81,401	81,963	693
Chautauqua	Mayville	138,662	139,750	1,062
Chemung	Elmira	90,675	91,070	408
Chenango	Norwich	51,142	51,401	894
Clinton	Plattsburgh	80,085	79,894	1,039
Columbia	Hudson	63,193	63,094	636
Cortland	Cortland	48,463	48,599	500
Delaware	Delhi	47,520	48,055	1,446
Dutchess	Poughkeepsie	284,447	280,150	802
Erie	Buffalo	944,408	950,265	1,044
Essex	Elizabethtown	38,822	38,851	1,797
Franklin	Malone	50,890	51,134	1,631
Fulton	Johnstown	54,996	55,073	496
Genesee	Batavia	59,995	60,370	494
Greene	Catskill	48,347	48,195	648
Hamilton	Lake Pleasant	5,307	5,379	1,720
Herkimer	Herkimer	64,066	64,427	1,411
Jefferson	Watertown	109,535	111,738	1,272
Kings[1]	Brooklyn	2,465,286	2,465,326	71
Lewis	Lowville	26,820	26,944	1,275
Livingston	Geneseo	64,498	64,328	632
Madison	Wampsville	69,714	69,441	656
Monroe	Rochester	733,607	735,343	659
Montgomery	Fonda	49,318	49,708	405
Nassau	Mineola	1,334,648	1,334,544	287
New York[1]	New York	1,541,150	1,537,195	23
Niagara	Lockport	218,509	219,846	523
Oneida	Utica	233,659	235,469	1,213
Onondaga	Syracuse	457,866	458,336	780
Ontario	Canandaigua	100,888	100,224	644
Orange	Goshen	348,783	341,367	816
Orleans	Albion	43,853	44,171	391
Oswego	Oswego	122,271	122,377	953
Otsego	Cooperstown	61,452	61,676	1,003
Putnam	Carmel	97,163	95,745	231
Queens[1]	Jamaica	2,224,516	2,229,379	109
Rensselaer	Troy	152,582	152,538	654
Richmond[1]	Saint George	450,153	443,728	58
Rockland	New City	288,567	286,753	174
Saint Lawrence	Canton	111,173	111,931	2,686
Saratoga	Ballston Spa	204,485	200,635	812
Schenectady	Schenectady	146,014	146,555	206
Schoharie	Schoharie	31,489	31,582	622
Schuyler	Watkins Glen	19,269	19,224	329
Seneca	Waterloo	33,486	33,342	325
Steuben	Bath	99,171	98,726	1,393
Suffolk	Riverhead	1,438,973	1,419,369	912
Sullivan	Monticello	74,107	73,966	970
Tioga	Owego	51,620	51,784	519
Tompkins	Ithaca	96,500	96,501	476
Ulster	Kingston	178,028	177,749	1,126

County	County seat or courthouse	2001 Pop.	2000 Pop.	Land area sq. mi.
Warren	Lake George	63,924	63,303	869
Washington	Hudson Falls	61,072	61,042	835
Wayne	Lyons	93,900	93,765	604
Westchester	White Plains	928,888	923,459	433
Wyoming	Warsaw	42,975	43,424	593
Yates	Penn Yan	24,561	24,621	338

(1) New York City is comprised of 5 counties: Bronx, Kings (Brooklyn), New York (Manhattan), Queens, and Richmond (Staten Island).

North Carolina

(100 counties, 48,711 sq. mi. land; pop. 8,186,268)

County	County seat or courthouse	2001 Pop.	2000 Pop.	Land area sq. mi.
Alamance	Graham	133,323	130,800	430
Alexander	Taylorsville	34,034	33,603	260
Alleghany	Sparta	10,763	10,677	235
Anson	Wadesboro	25,335	25,275	532
Ashe	Jefferson	24,715	24,384	426
Avery	Newland	17,395	17,167	247
Beaufort	Washington	45,224	44,958	828
Bertie	Windsor	19,803	19,773	699
Bladen	Elizabethtown	32,491	32,278	875
Brunswick	Bolivia	77,058	73,143	855
Buncombe	Asheville	208,850	206,330	656
Burke	Morganton	89,359	89,148	507
Cabarrus	Concord	136,418	131,063	364
Caldwell	Lenoir	70,109	77,415	472
Camden	Camden	7,097	6,885	241
Carteret	Beaufort	59,901	59,383	520
Caswell	Yanceyville	23,693	23,501	425
Catawba	Newton	145,071	141,685	400
Chatham	Pittsboro	51,645	49,329	683
Cherokee	Murphy	24,643	24,298	455
Chowan	Edenton	14,554	14,526	173
Clay	Hayesville	9,086	8,775	215
Cleveland	Shelby	97,432	96,287	465
Columbus	Whiteville	54,905	54,749	935
Craven	New Bern	91,316	91,436	708
Cumberland	Fayetteville	299,203	302,963	653
Currituck	Currituck	19,018	18,190	262
Dare	Manteo	31,168	29,967	384
Davidson	Lexington	149,690	147,246	552
Davie	Mocksville	36,193	34,835	265
Duplin	Kenansville	40,440	49,003	818
Durham	Durham	227,034	223,314	290
Edgecombe	Tarboro	54,754	55,606	505
Forsyth	Winston-Salem	310,187	306,067	410
Franklin	Louisburg	49,065	47,260	492
Gaston	Gastonia	191,952	190,365	356
Gates	Gatesville	10,592	10,516	341
Graham	Robbinsville	8,017	7,993	292
Granville	Oxford	50,183	48,498	531
Greene	Snow Hill	19,193	18,974	265
Guilford	Greensboro	425,382	421,048	649
Halifax	Halifax	56,703	57,370	725
Harnett	Lillington	93,602	91,025	595
Haywood	Waynesville	54,623	54,033	554
Henderson	Hendersonville	91,267	89,173	374
Hertford	Winton	22,099	22,601	353
Hoke	Raeford	34,906	33,646	391
Hyde	Swan Quarter	5,703	5,826	613
Iredell	Statesville	127,409	122,660	576
Jackson	Sylva	33,566	33,121	491
Johnston	Smithfield	128,248	121,965	792
Jones	Trenton	10,392	10,381	472
Lee	Sanford	49,279	49,040	257
Lenoir	Kinston	59,310	59,648	400
Lincoln	Lincolnton	64,999	63,780	299
McDowell	Marion	42,796	42,151	442
Macon	Franklin	30,533	29,811	516
Madison	Marshall	19,970	19,635	449
Martin	Williamston	25,374	25,593	461
Mecklenburg	Charlotte	716,407	695,454	526
Mitchell	Bakersville	15,869	15,687	221
Montgomery	Troy	26,898	26,822	492
Moore	Carthage	77,163	74,769	698
Nash	Nashville	88,443	87,420	540
New Hanover	Wilmington	163,455	160,307	199
Northampton	Jackson	21,980	22,086	536
Onslow	Jacksonville	145,988	150,355	767
Orange	Hillsborough	119,894	118,227	400
Pamlico	Bayboro	12,929	12,934	337
Pasquotank	Elizabeth City	34,947	34,897	227
Pender	Burgaw	42,007	41,082	871
Perquimans	Hertford	11,487	11,368	247
Person	Roxboro	36,114	35,623	392
Pitt	Greenville	134,977	133,798	652
Polk	Columbus	18,741	18,324	238
Randolph	Asheboro	131,790	130,454	787
Richmond	Rockingham	46,677	46,564	474
Robeson	Lumberton	123,891	123,339	949
Rockingham	Wentworth	92,123	91,928	566
Rowan	Salisbury	132,233	130,340	511
Rutherford	Rutherfordton	63,332	62,899	564
Sampson	Clinton	60,683	60,161	945
Scotland	Laurinburg	35,889	35,998	319
Stanly	Albemarle	58,622	58,100	395
Stokes	Danbury	45,179	44,711	452
Surry	Dobson	71,600	71,219	537
Swain	Bryson City	13,061	12,968	528
Transylvania	Brevard	29,487	29,334	378
Tyrrell	Columbia	4,031	4,149	390
Union	Monroe	132,676	123,677	637
Vance	Henderson	43,622	42,954	254
Wake	Raleigh	655,642	627,846	832
Warren	Warrenton	19,904	19,972	429
Washington	Plymouth	13,597	13,723	348
Watauga	Boone	42,909	42,695	313
Wayne	Goldsboro	112,736	113,329	553
Wilkes	Wilkesboro	66,166	65,632	757
Wilson	Wilson	74,310	73,814	371
Yadkin	Yadkinville	36,859	36,348	336
Yancey	Burnsville	17,874	17,774	312

North Dakota

(53 counties, 68,976 sq. mi. land; pop. 634,448)

County	County seat or courthouse	2001 Pop.	2000 Pop.	Land area sq. mi.
Adams	Hettinger	2,523	2,593	988
Barnes	Valley City	11,463	11,775	1,492
Benson	Minnewaukan	6,879	6,964	1,381
Billings	Medora	857	888	1,151
Bottineau	Bottineau	6,975	7,149	1,669
Bowman	Bowman	3,124	3,242	1,162
Burke	Bowbells	2,191	2,242	1,104
Burleigh	Bismarck	70,069	69,416	1,633
Cass	Fargo	124,021	123,138	1,765
Cavalier	Langdon	4,655	4,831	1,488
Dickey	Ellendale	5,612	5,757	1,131
Divide	Crosby	2,203	2,283	1,260
Dunn	Manning	3,563	3,600	2,010
Eddy	New Rockford	2,691	2,757	630
Emmons	Linton	4,209	4,331	1,510
Foster	Carrington	3,624	3,759	635
Golden Valley	Beach	1,845	1,924	1,002
Grand Forks	Grand Forks	64,390	66,109	1,438
Grant	Carson	2,775	2,841	1,659
Griggs	Cooperstown	2,628	2,754	709
Hettinger	Mott	2,650	2,715	1,132
Kidder	Steele	2,666	2,753	1,351
La Moure	La Moure	4,616	4,701	1,147
Logan	Napoleon	2,221	2,308	993
McHenry	Towner	5,742	5,987	1,874
McIntosh	Ashley	3,306	3,390	975
McKenzie	Watford City	5,705	5,737	2,742
McLean	Washburn	9,144	9,311	2,110
Mercer	Stanton	8,531	8,644	1,045
Morton	Mandan	25,149	25,303	1,926
Mountrail	Stanley	6,553	6,631	1,824
Nelson	Lakota	3,563	3,715	982
Oliver	Center	1,960	2,065	724
Pembina	Cavalier	8,408	8,585	1,119
Pierce	Rugby	4,597	4,675	1,018
Ramsey	Devils Lake	11,833	12,066	1,185
Ransom	Lisbon	5,841	5,890	863
Renville	Mohall	2,542	2,610	875
Richland	Wahpeton	17,701	17,998	1,437
Rolette	Rolla	13,745	13,674	902
Sargent	Forman	4,296	4,366	859
Sheridan	McClusky	1,605	1,710	972
Sioux	Fort Yates	4,066	4,044	1,094
Slope	Amidon	754	767	1,218
Stark	Dickinson	22,213	22,636	1,338
Steele	Finley	2,191	2,258	712
Stutsman	Jamestown	21,575	21,908	2,221
Towner	Cando	2,770	2,876	1,025
Traill	Hillsboro	8,392	8,477	862
Walsh	Grafton	12,081	12,389	1,282
Ward	Minot	57,247	58,795	2,013
Wells	Fessenden	4,882	5,102	1,271
Williams	Williston	19,606	19,761	2,070

Ohio

(88 counties, 40,048 sq. mi. land; pop. 11,373,541)

County	County seat or courthouse	2001 Pop.	2000 Pop.	Land area sq. mi.
Adams	West Union	27,566	27,330	584
Allen	Lima	108,276	108,473	404
Ashland	Ashland	52,754	52,523	424
Ashtabula	Jefferson	102,514	102,728	702
Athens	Athens	62,235	62,223	507
Auglaize	Wapakoneta	46,797	46,611	401
Belmont	Saint Clairsville	69,451	70,226	537
Brown	Georgetown	42,890	42,285	492
Butler	Hamilton	337,013	332,807	467
Carroll	Carrollton	29,086	28,836	395
Champaign	Urbana	39,182	38,890	429

County	County seat or courthouse	2001 Pop.	2000 Pop.	Land area sq. mi.
Clark	Springfield	144,076	144,742	400
Clermont	Batavia	181,673	177,977	452
Clinton	Wilmington	40,987	40,543	411
Columbiana	Lisbon	111,678	112,075	532
Coshocton	Coshocton	36,779	36,655	564
Crawford	Bucyrus	46,594	46,966	402
Cuyahoga	Cleveland	1,380,421	1,393,978	458
Darke	Greenville	53,078	53,309	600
Defiance	Defiance	39,360	39,500	411
Delaware	Delaware	119,752	109,989	442
Erie	Sandusky	79,312	79,551	255
Fairfield	Lancaster	127,395	122,759	505
Fayette	Washington Court House	28,241	28,433	407
Franklin	Columbus	1,071,524	1,068,978	540
Fulton	Wauseon	42,205	42,084	407
Gallia	Gallipolis	31,183	31,069	469
Geauga	Chardon	92,180	90,895	404
Greene	Xenia	148,426	147,886	415
Guernsey	Cambridge	40,959	40,792	522
Hamilton	Cincinnati	835,362	845,303	407
Hancock	Findlay	72,046	71,295	531
Hardin	Kenton	31,762	31,945	470
Harrison	Cadiz	15,886	15,856	404
Henry	Napoleon	29,310	29,210	417
Highland	Hillsboro	41,439	40,875	553
Hocking	Logan	28,436	28,241	423
Holmes	Millersburg	39,854	38,943	423
Huron	Norwalk	59,437	59,487	493
Jackson	Jackson	32,668	32,641	420
Jefferson	Steubenville	72,855	73,894	410
Knox	Mount Vernon	55,521	54,500	527
Lake	Painesville	228,100	227,511	228
Lawrence	Ironton	62,009	62,319	455
Licking	Newark	147,723	145,491	687
Logan	Bellefontaine	46,023	46,005	458
Lorain	Elyria	286,768	284,664	493
Lucas	Toledo	453,348	455,054	340
Madison	London	40,217	40,213	465
Mahoning	Youngstown	254,958	257,555	415
Marion	Marion	66,014	66,217	404
Medina	Medina	155,698	151,095	422
Meigs	Pomeroy	22,987	23,072	429
Mercer	Celina	40,899	40,924	463
Miami	Troy	99,351	98,868	407
Monroe	Woodsfield	15,163	15,180	456
Montgomery	Dayton	554,232	559,062	462
Morgan	McConnelsville	14,891	14,897	418
Morrow	Mount Gilead	32,674	31,628	406
Muskingum	Zanesville	84,900	84,585	665
Noble	Caldwell	14,038	14,058	399
Ottawa	Port Clinton	41,029	40,985	255
Paulding	Paulding	20,081	20,293	416
Perry	New Lexington	34,380	34,078	410
Pickaway	Circleville	52,986	52,727	502
Pike	Waverly	27,841	27,695	441
Portage	Ravenna	152,743	152,061	492
Preble	Eaton	42,520	42,337	425
Putnam	Ottawa	34,808	34,726	484
Richland	Mansfield	128,051	128,852	497
Ross	Chillicothe	74,061	73,345	688
Sandusky	Fremont	61,673	61,792	409
Scioto	Portsmouth	78,435	79,195	612
Seneca	Tiffin	58,314	58,683	551
Shelby	Sidney	48,183	47,910	409
Stark	Canton	377,438	378,098	576
Summit	Akron	544,217	542,899	413
Trumbull	Warren	223,982	225,116	616
Tuscarawas	New Philadelphia	91,066	90,914	568
Union	Marysville	42,793	40,909	437
Van Wert	Van Wert	29,440	29,659	410
Vinton	McArthur	13,150	12,806	414
Warren	Lebanon	169,025	158,383	400
Washington	Marietta	62,991	63,251	635
Wayne	Wooster	112,193	111,564	555
Williams	Bryan	39,211	39,188	422
Wood	Bowling Green	122,001	121,065	617
Wyandot	Upper Sandusky	22,773	22,908	406

Oklahoma

(77 counties, 68,667 sq. mi. land; pop. 3,460,097)

County	County seat or courthouse	2001 Pop.	2000 Pop.	Land area sq. mi.
Adair	Stillwell	21,118	21,038	576
Alfalfa	Cherokee	6,005	6,105	867
Atoka	Atoka	14,011	13,879	978
Beaver	Beaver	5,640	5,857	1,814
Beckham	Sayre	19,846	19,799	902
Blaine	Watonga	11,920	11,976	928
Bryan	Durant	36,477	36,534	909
Caddo	Anadarko	29,966	30,150	1,278
Canadian	El Reno	89,978	87,697	900
Carter	Ardmore	45,909	45,621	824
Cherokee	Tahlequah	42,697	42,521	751
Choctaw	Hugo	15,169	15,342	774
Cimarron	Boise City	3,023	3,148	1,835
Cleveland	Norman	211,908	208,016	536
Coal	Coalgate	6,074	6,031	518
Comanche	Lawton	112,466	114,996	1,069
Cotton	Walters	6,528	6,614	637
Craig	Vinita	14,757	14,950	761
Creek	Sapulpa	68,488	67,367	956
Custer	Arapaho	25,358	26,142	987
Delaware	Jay	37,699	37,077	741
Dewey	Taloga	4,672	4,743	1,000
Ellis	Arnett	3,952	4,075	1,229
Garfield	Enid	57,114	57,813	1,058
Garvin	Pauls Valley	27,105	27,210	807
Grady	Chickasha	46,139	45,516	1,101
Grant	Medford	5,091	5,144	1,001
Greer	Mangum	5,883	6,061	639
Harmon	Hollis	3,155	3,283	538
Harper	Buffalo	3,464	3,562	1,039
Haskell	Stigler	11,763	11,792	577
Hughes	Holdenville	13,927	14,154	807
Jackson	Altus	27,661	28,439	803
Jefferson	Waurika	6,623	6,818	759
Johnston	Tishomingo	10,569	10,513	645
Kay	Newkirk	47,541	48,080	919
Kingfisher	Kingfisher	13,854	13,926	903
Kiowa	Hobart	9,945	10,227	1,015
Latimer	Wilburton	10,634	10,692	722
Le Flore	Poteau	48,041	48,109	1,586
Lincoln	Chandler	32,154	32,080	958
Logan	Guthrie	34,209	33,924	744
Love	Marietta	8,863	8,831	515
McClain	Purcell	27,825	27,740	570
McCurtain	Idabel	34,194	34,402	1,852
McIntosh	Eufaula	19,522	19,456	620
Major	Fairview	7,528	7,545	957
Marshall	Madill	13,433	13,184	371
Mayes	Pryor	38,697	38,369	656
Murray	Sulphur	12,721	12,623	418
Muskogee	Muskogee	69,887	69,451	814
Noble	Perry	11,388	11,411	732
Nowata	Nowata	10,634	10,569	565
Okfuskee	Okemah	11,781	11,814	625
Oklahoma	Oklahoma City	662,153	660,448	709
Okmulgee	Okmulgee	39,715	39,685	697
Osage	Pawhuska	45,034	44,437	2,251
Ottawa	Miami	33,046	33,194	471
Pawnee	Pawnee	16,845	16,612	569
Payne	Stillwater	67,830	68,190	686
Pittsburg	McAlester	43,779	43,953	1,306
Pontotoc	Ada	34,611	35,143	720
Pottawatomie	Shawnee	66,269	65,521	788
Pushmataha	Antlers	11,706	11,667	1,397
Roger Mills	Cheyenne	3,331	3,436	1,142
Rogers	Claremore	74,066	70,641	675
Seminole	Wewoka	24,652	24,894	633
Sequoyah	Sallisaw	39,262	38,972	674
Stephens	Duncan	42,970	43,182	874
Texas	Guymon	19,754	20,107	2,037
Tillman	Frederick	9,146	9,287	872
Tulsa	Tulsa	564,079	563,299	570
Wagoner	Wagoner	59,059	57,491	563
Washington	Bartlesville	49,087	48,996	417
Washita	Cordell	11,473	11,508	1,003
Woods	Alva	8,832	9,089	1,287
Woodward	Woodward	18,392	18,486	1,242

Oregon

(36 counties, 95,997 sq. mi. land; pop. 3,472,867)

County	County seat or courthouse	2001 Pop.	2000 Pop.	Land area sq. mi.
Baker	Baker City	16,743	16,741	3,068
Benton	Corvallis	77,926	78,153	676
Clackamas	Oregon City	346,558	338,391	1,868
Clatsop	Astoria	35,586	35,630	827
Columbia	Saint Helens	44,547	43,560	657
Coos	Coquille	62,459	62,779	1,600
Crook	Prineville	20,062	19,182	2,979
Curry	Gold Beach	21,118	21,137	1,627
Deschutes	Bend	121,949	115,367	3,018
Douglas	Roseburg	100,866	100,399	5,037
Gilliam	Condon	1,851	1,915	1,204
Grant	Canyon City	7,566	7,935	4,529
Harney	Burns	7,404	7,609	10,134
Hood River	Hood River	20,439	20,411	522
Jackson	Medford	184,963	181,269	2,785
Jefferson	Madras	19,425	19,009	1,781

County	County seat or courthouse	2001 Pop.	2000 Pop.	Land area sq. mi.
Josephine	Grants Pass	77,123	75,726	1,640
Klamath	Klamath Falls	64,116	63,775	5,944
Lake	Lakeview	7,470	7,422	8,136
Lane	Eugene	324,316	322,959	4,554
Lincoln	Newport	44,264	44,479	980
Linn	Albany	103,974	103,069	2,292
Malheur	Vale	31,456	31,615	9,887
Marion	Salem	288,269	284,834	1,184
Morrow	Heppner	11,339	10,995	2,032
Multnomah	Portland	665,810	660,486	435
Polk	Dallas	63,679	62,380	741
Sherman	Moro	1,827	1,934	823
Tillamook	Tillamook	24,308	24,262	1,102
Umatilla	Pendleton	70,751	70,548	3,215
Union	La Grande	24,327	24,530	2,037
Wallowa	Enterprise	7,207	7,226	3,145
Wasco	The Dalles	23,895	23,791	2,381
Washington	Hillsboro	461,119	445,342	724
Wheeler	Fossil	1,513	1,547	1,715
Yamhill	McMinnville	86,642	84,992	716

Pennsylvania

(67 counties, 44,817 sq. mi. land; pop. 12,287,150)

County	County seat or courthouse	2001 Pop.	2000 Pop.	Land area sq. mi.
Adams	Gettysburg	92,997	91,292	520
Allegheny	Pittsburgh	1,270,612	1,281,666	730
Armstrong	Kittanning	72,101	72,392	654
Beaver	Beaver	179,871	181,412	434
Bedford	Bedford	49,899	49,984	1,015
Berks	Reading	377,679	373,638	859
Blair	Hollidaysburg	128,391	129,144	526
Bradford	Towanda	62,859	62,761	1,151
Bucks	Doylestown	605,379	597,635	607
Butler	Butler	176,593	174,083	789
Cambria	Ebensburg	150,726	152,598	688
Cameron	Emporium	5,866	5,974	397
Carbon	Jim Thorpe	59,506	58,802	381
Centre	Bellefonte	135,940	135,758	1,108
Chester	West Chester	443,346	433,501	756
Clarion	Clarion	41,478	41,765	602
Clearfield	Clearfield	83,167	83,382	1,147
Clinton	Lock Haven	37,753	37,914	891
Columbia	Bloomsburg	64,152	64,151	486
Crawford	Meadville	90,046	90,366	1,013
Cumberland	Carlisle	215,695	213,674	550
Dauphin	Harrisburg	251,316	251,798	525
Delaware	Media	551,158	550,864	184
Elk	Ridgway	34,666	35,112	829
Erie	Erie	279,636	280,843	802
Fayette	Uniontown	147,367	148,644	790
Forest	Tionesta	4,910	4,946	428
Franklin	Chambersburg	130,506	129,313	772
Fulton	McConnellsburg	14,314	14,261	438
Greene	Waynesburg	40,492	40,672	576
Huntingdon	Huntingdon	45,632	45,586	874
Indiana	Indiana	89,108	89,605	829
Jefferson	Brookville	45,712	45,932	655
Juniata	Mifflintown	22,877	22,821	392
Lackawanna	Scranton	211,829	213,295	459
Lancaster	Lancaster	474,601	470,658	949
Lawrence	New Castle	94,160	94,643	360
Lebanon	Lebanon	120,963	120,327	362
Lehigh	Allentown	314,204	312,090	347
Luzerne	Wilkes-Barre	315,754	319,250	891
Lycoming	Williamsport	118,977	120,044	1,235
McKean	Smethport	45,440	45,936	982
Mercer	Mercer	119,682	120,293	672
Mifflin	Lewistown	46,554	46,486	412
Monroe	Stroudsburg	144,676	138,687	609
Montgomery	Norristown	759,953	750,097	483
Montour	Danville	18,281	18,236	131
Northampton	Easton	269,779	267,066	374
Northumberland	Sunbury	93,662	94,556	460
Perry	New Bloomfield	43,787	43,602	554
Philadelphia	Philadelphia	1,491,812	1,517,550	135
Pike	Milford	48,507	46,302	547
Potter	Coudersport	18,154	18,080	1,081
Schuylkill	Pottsville	149,176	150,336	778
Snyder	Middleburg	37,720	37,546	331
Somerset	Somerset	79,553	80,023	1,075
Sullivan	Laporte	6,532	6,556	450
Susquehanna	Montrose	42,165	42,238	823
Tioga	Wellsboro	41,621	41,373	1,134
Union	Lewisburg	41,701	41,624	317
Venango	Franklin	57,098	57,565	675
Warren	Warren	43,593	43,863	883
Washington	Washington	203,737	202,897	857
Wayne	Honesdale	48,392	47,722	729
Westmoreland	Greensburg	368,983	369,993	1,025
Wyoming	Tunkhannock	28,055	28,080	397
York	York	386,299	381,751	904

Rhode Island

(5 counties, 1,045 sq. mi. land; pop. 1,058,920)

County	County seat or courthouse	2001 Pop.	2000 Pop.	Land area sq. mi.
Bristol	Bristol	51,173	50,648	25
Kent	East Greenwich	169,224	167,090	170
Newport	Newport	85,218	85,433	104
Providence	Providence	627,314	621,602	413
Washington	West Kingston	125,991	123,546	333

South Carolina

(46 counties, 30,110 sq. mi. land; pop. 4,063,011)

County	County seat or courthouse	2001 Pop.	2000 Pop.	Land area sq. mi.
Abbeville	Abbeville	26,314	26,167	508
Aiken	Aiken	143,905	142,552	1,073
Allendale	Allendale	11,045	11,211	408
Anderson	Anderson	168,985	165,740	718
Bamberg	Bamberg	16,393	16,658	393
Barnwell	Barnwell	23,525	23,478	548
Beaufort	Beaufort	125,212	120,937	587
Berkeley	Moncks Corner	144,078	142,651	1,098
Calhoun	Saint Matthews	15,351	15,185	380
Charleston	Charleston	312,007	309,969	919
Cherokee	Gaffney	53,161	52,537	393
Chester	Chester	34,055	34,068	581
Chesterfield	Chesterfield	43,014	42,768	799
Clarendon	Manning	32,789	32,502	607
Colleton	Walterboro	38,540	38,264	1,056
Darlington	Darlington	67,812	67,394	561
Dillon	Dillon	30,927	30,722	405
Dorchester	Saint George	98,746	96,413	575
Edgefield	Edgefield	24,470	24,595	502
Fairfield	Winnsboro	23,703	23,454	687
Florence	Florence	126,607	125,761	800
Georgetown	Georgetown	57,189	55,797	815
Greenville	Greenville	386,693	379,616	790
Greenwood	Greenwood	66,746	66,271	456
Hampton	Hampton	21,411	21,386	560
Horry	Conway	202,425	196,629	1,134
Jasper	Ridgeland	20,818	20,678	656
Kershaw	Camden	53,409	52,647	726
Lancaster	Lancaster	61,509	61,351	549
Laurens	Laurens	70,138	69,567	715
Lee	Bishopville	20,090	20,119	410
Lexington	Lexington	220,240	216,014	699
McCormick	McCormick	10,121	9,958	360
Marion	Marion	35,191	35,466	489
Marlboro	Bennettsville	28,653	28,818	480
Newberry	Newberry	36,344	36,108	631
Oconee	Walhalla	67,407	66,215	625
Orangeburg	Orangeburg	91,337	91,582	1,106
Pickens	Pickens	112,112	110,757	497
Richland	Columbia	323,303	320,677	756
Saluda	Saluda	19,114	19,181	452
Spartanburg	Spartanburg	257,262	253,791	811
Sumter	Sumter	104,237	104,646	665
Union	Union	29,548	29,881	514
Williamsburg	Kingstree	36,810	37,217	934
York	York	170,259	164,614	682

South Dakota

(66 counties, 75,885 sq. mi. land; pop. 756,600)

County	County seat or courthouse	2001 Pop.	2000 Pop.	Land area sq. mi.
Aurora	Plankinton	3,015	3,058	708
Beadle	Huron	16,785	17,023	1,259
Bennett	Martin	3,554	3,574	1,185
Bon Homme	Tyndall	7,193	7,260	563
Brookings	Brookings	28,016	28,220	794
Brown	Aberdeen	35,074	35,460	1,713
Brule	Chamberlain	5,262	5,364	819
Buffalo	Gannvalley	2,014	2,032	471
Butte	Belle Fourche	9,059	9,094	2,249
Campbell	Mound City	1,761	1,782	736
Charles Mix	Lake Andes	9,202	9,350	1,098
Clark	Clark	4,120	4,143	958
Clay	Vermillion	13,266	13,537	412
Codington	Watertown	25,782	25,897	688
Corson	McIntosh	4,221	4,181	2,473
Custer	Custer	7,370	7,275	1,558
Davison	Mitchell	18,556	18,741	435
Day	Webster	6,141	6,267	1,029
Deuel	Clear Lake	4,465	4,498	624
Dewey	Timber Lake	6,049	5,972	2,303
Douglas	Armour	3,421	3,458	434
Edmunds	Ipswich	4,331	4,367	1,146
Fall River	Hot Springs	7,392	7,453	1,740
Faulk	Faulkton	2,543	2,640	1,000
Grant	Milbank	7,741	7,847	683
Gregory	Burke	4,607	4,792	1,016
Haakon	Philip	2,099	2,196	1,813
Hamlin	Hayti	5,549	5,540	507
Hand	Miller	3,665	3,741	1,437
Hanson	Alexandria	3,294	3,139	435

County	County seat or courthouse	2001 Pop.	2000 Pop.	Land area sq. mi.
Harding	Buffalo	1,292	1,353	2,671
Hughes	Pierre	16,487	16,481	741
Hutchinson	Olivet	7,995	8,075	813
Hyde	Highmore	1,600	1,671	861
Jackson	Kadoka	2,846	2,930	1,869
Jerauld	Wessington Springs	2,275	2,295	530
Jones	Murdo	1,118	1,193	971
Kingsbury	De Smet	5,695	5,815	838
Lake	Madison	11,257	11,276	563
Lawrence	Deadwood	21,638	21,802	800
Lincoln	Canton	26,322	24,131	578
Lyman	Kennebec	3,969	3,895	1,640
McCook	Salem	5,860	5,832	575
McPherson	Leola	2,805	2,904	1,137
Marshall	Britton	4,442	4,576	838
Meade	Sturgis	24,233	24,253	3,471
Mellette	White River	2,082	2,083	1,306
Miner	Howard	2,839	2,884	570
Minnehaha	Sioux Falls	150,327	148,281	810
Moody	Flandreau	6,552	6,595	520
Pennington	Rapid City	89,829	88,565	2,776
Perkins	Bison	3,284	3,363	2,872
Potter	Gettysburg	2,544	2,693	866
Roberts	Sisseton	10,010	10,016	1,101
Sanborn	Woonsocket	2,617	2,675	569
Shannon	(Attached to Fall River)	12,783	12,466	2,094
Spink	Redfield	7,178	7,454	1,504
Stanley	Fort Pierre	2,754	2,772	1,443
Sully	Onida	1,514	1,556	1,007
Todd	(Attached to Tripp)	9,269	9,050	1,388
Tripp	Winner	6,278	6,430	1,614
Turner	Parker	8,737	8,849	617
Union	Elk Point	12,713	12,584	460
Walworth	Selby	5,806	5,974	708
Yankton	Yankton	21,586	21,652	522
Ziebach	Dupree	2,517	2,519	1,962

Tennessee

(95 counties, 41,217 sq. mi. land; pop. 5,740,021)

County	County seat or courthouse	2001 Pop.	2000 Pop.	Land area sq. mi.
Anderson	Clinton	71,457	71,330	338
Bedford	Shelbyville	38,327	37,586	474
Benton	Camden	16,616	16,537	395
Bledsoe	Pikeville	12,516	12,367	406
Blount	Maryville	108,270	105,823	559
Bradley	Cleveland	88,850	87,965	329
Campbell	Jacksboro	40,048	39,854	480
Cannon	Woodbury	12,946	12,826	266
Carroll	Huntingdon	29,538	29,475	599
Carter	Elizabethton	56,927	56,742	341
Cheatham	Ashland City	36,552	35,912	303
Chester	Henderson	15,711	15,540	289
Claiborne	Tazewell	30,146	29,862	434
Clay	Celina	7,918	7,976	236
Cocke	Newport	33,884	33,565	434
Coffee	Manchester	48,667	48,014	429
Crockett	Alamo	14,547	14,532	265
Cumberland	Crossville	48,058	46,802	682
Davidson	Nashville	565,352	569,891	502
Decatur	Decaturville	11,697	11,731	334
De Kalb	Smithville	17,552	17,423	305
Dickson	Charlotte	43,843	43,156	490
Dyer	Dyersburg	37,121	37,279	511
Fayette	Somerville	30,536	28,806	705
Fentress	Jamestown	16,805	16,625	499
Franklin	Winchester	39,770	39,270	555
Gibson	Trenton	48,031	48,152	603
Giles	Pulaski	29,675	29,447	611
Grainger	Rutledge	20,934	20,659	280
Greene	Greeneville	63,388	62,909	622
Grundy	Altamont	14,288	14,332	361
Hamblen	Morristown	58,337	58,128	161
Hamilton	Chattanooga	307,377	307,896	542
Hancock	Sneedville	6,768	6,786	222
Hardeman	Bolivar	28,361	28,105	668
Hardin	Savannah	25,791	25,578	578
Hawkins	Rogersville	54,370	53,563	487
Haywood	Brownsville	19,761	19,797	533
Henderson	Lexington	25,732	25,522	520
Henry	Paris	31,083	31,115	562
Hickman	Centerville	22,740	22,295	613
Houston	Erin	7,916	8,088	200
Humphreys	Waverly	18,114	17,929	532
Jackson	Gainesboro	11,162	10,984	309
Jefferson	Dandridge	45,070	44,294	274
Johnson	Mountain City	17,638	17,499	298
Knox	Knoxville	385,572	382,032	508
Lake	Tiptonville	7,764	7,954	163
Lauderdale	Ripley	27,021	27,101	470
Lawrence	Lawrenceburg	40,003	39,926	617
Lewis	Hohenwald	11,437	11,367	282
Lincoln	Fayetteville	31,616	31,340	570
Loudon	Loudon	40,240	39,086	229
McMinn	Athens	49,857	49,015	430
McNairy	Selmer	24,644	24,653	560
Macon	Lafayette	20,873	20,386	307
Madison	Jackson	92,389	91,837	557
Marion	Jasper	27,750	27,776	498
Marshall	Lewisburg	27,106	26,767	375
Maury	Columbia	70,376	69,498	613
Meigs	Decatur	11,194	11,086	195
Monroe	Madisonville	39,846	38,961	635
Montgomery	Clarksville	135,023	134,768	539
Moore	Lynchburg	5,887	5,740	129
Morgan	Wartburg	20,003	19,757	522
Obion	Union City	32,346	32,450	545
Overton	Livingston	20,186	20,118	433
Perry	Linden	7,504	7,631	415
Pickett	Byrdstown	5,048	4,945	163
Polk	Benton	16,226	16,050	435
Putnam	Cookeville	63,188	62,315	401
Rhea	Dayton	28,608	28,400	316
Roane	Kingston	52,033	51,910	361
Robertson	Springfield	56,083	54,433	476
Rutherford	Murfreesboro	190,143	182,023	619
Scott	Huntsville	21,548	21,127	532
Sequatchie	Dunlap	11,616	11,370	266
Sevier	Sevierville	73,703	71,170	592
Shelby	Memphis	896,013	897,472	755
Smith	Carthage	17,988	17,712	314
Stewart	Dover	12,650	12,370	458
Sullivan	Blountville	152,787	153,048	413
Sumner	Gallatin	134,336	130,449	529
Tipton	Covington	52,956	51,271	459
Trousdale	Hartsville	7,345	7,259	114
Unicoi	Erwin	17,713	17,667	186
Union	Maynardville	18,414	17,808	224
Van Buren	Spencer	5,477	5,508	273
Warren	McMinnville	38,565	38,276	433
Washington	Jonesborough	108,380	107,198	326
Wayne	Waynesboro	16,845	16,842	734
Weakley	Dresden	34,644	34,895	580
White	Sparta	23,364	23,102	377
Williamson	Franklin	133,825	126,638	583
Wilson	Lebanon	91,696	88,809	571

Texas

(254 counties, 261,797 sq. mi. land; pop. 21,325,018)

County	County seat or courthouse	2001 Pop.	2000 Pop.	Land area sq. mi.
Anderson	Palestine	55,329	55,109	1,071
Andrews	Andrews	12,795	13,004	1,501
Angelina	Lufkin	80,513	80,130	802
Aransas	Rockport	22,695	22,497	252
Archer	Archer City	8,926	8,854	910
Armstrong	Claude	2,129	2,148	914
Atascosa	Jourdanton	40,264	38,628	1,232
Austin	Bellville	24,454	23,590	653
Bailey	Muleshoe	6,571	6,594	827
Bandera	Bandera	18,553	17,645	792
Bastrop	Bastrop	62,059	57,733	888
Baylor	Seymour	3,986	4,093	871
Bee	Beeville	32,314	32,359	880
Bell	Belton	239,571	237,974	1,060
Bexar	San Antonio	1,417,501	1,392,931	1,247
Blanco	Johnson City	8,767	8,418	711
Borden	Gail	677	729	899
Bosque	Meridian	17,624	17,204	989
Bowie	Boston	89,961	89,306	888
Brazoria	Angleton	249,832	241,767	1,386
Brazos	Bryan	151,660	152,415	586
Brewster	Alpine	8,859	8,866	6,193
Briscoe	Silverton	1,710	1,790	900
Brooks	Falfurrias	7,683	7,976	943
Brown	Brownwood	37,774	37,674	944
Burleson	Caldwell	16,628	16,470	666
Burnet	Burnet	36,151	34,147	996
Caldwell	Lockhart	34,193	32,194	546
Calhoun	Port Lavaca	20,600	20,647	512
Callahan	Baird	12,863	12,905	899
Cameron	Brownsville	344,782	335,227	906
Camp	Pittsburg	11,507	11,549	198
Carson	Panhandle	6,474	6,516	923
Cass	Linden	30,471	30,438	937
Castro	Dimmitt	8,129	8,285	898
Chambers	Anahuac	26,859	26,031	599
Cherokee	Rusk	47,231	46,659	1,052
Childress	Childress	7,651	7,688	710
Clay	Henrietta	11,179	11,006	1,098
Cochran	Morton	3,689	3,730	775
Coke	Robert Lee	3,873	3,864	899
Coleman	Coleman	9,033	9,235	1,260
Collin	McKinney	541,403	491,675	848
Collingsworth	Wellington	3,135	3,206	919
Colorado	Columbus	20,230	20,390	963
Comal	New Braunfels	82,563	78,021	561
Comanche	Comanche	13,751	14,026	938
Concho	Paint Rock	3,917	3,966	991

County	County seat or courthouse	2001 Pop.	2000 Pop.	Land area sq. mi.
Cooke	Gainesville	37,193	36,363	874
Coryell	Gatesville	74,426	74,978	1,052
Cottle	Paducah	1,805	1,904	901
Crane	Crane	3,919	3,996	786
Crockett	Ozona	3,919	4,099	2,807
Crosby	Crosbyton	6,899	7,072	900
Culberson	Van Horn	2,774	2,975	3,812
Dallam	Dalhart	6,157	6,222	1,505
Dallas	Dallas	2,245,398	2,218,899	880
Dawson	Lamesa	14,838	14,985	902
Deaf Smith	Hereford	18,235	18,561	1,497
Delta	Cooper	5,379	5,327	277
Denton	Denton	466,240	432,976	889
DeWitt	Cuero	20,114	20,013	909
Dickens	Dickens	2,705	2,762	904
Dimmit	Carrizo Springs	10,170	10,248	1,331
Donley	Clarendon	3,836	3,828	930
Duval	San Diego	12,996	13,120	1,793
Eastland	Eastland	18,158	18,297	926
Ector	Odessa	121,298	121,123	901
Edwards	Rocksprings	2,044	2,162	2,120
Ellis	Waxahachie	116,555	111,360	940
El Paso	El Paso	688,039	679,622	1,013
Erath	Stephenville	32,989	33,001	1,086
Falls	Marlin	18,352	18,576	769
Fannin	Bonham	31,556	31,242	891
Fayette	La Grange	22,150	21,804	950
Fisher	Roby	4,278	4,344	901
Floyd	Floydada	7,563	7,771	992
Foard	Crowell	1,621	1,622	707
Fort Bend	Richmond	381,200	354,452	875
Franklin	Mount Vernon	9,727	9,458	286
Freestone	Fairfield	18,226	17,867	877
Frio	Pearsall	16,392	16,252	1,133
Gaines	Seminole	14,368	14,467	1,502
Galveston	Galveston	255,865	250,158	398
Garza	Post	5,011	4,872	896
Gillespie	Fredericksburg	21,280	20,814	1,061
Glasscock	Garden City	1,371	1,406	901
Goliad	Goliad	7,074	6,928	854
Gonzales	Gonzales	18,745	18,628	1,068
Gray	Pampa	22,083	22,744	928
Grayson	Sherman	113,184	110,595	934
Gregg	Longview	112,397	111,379	274
Grimes	Anderson	24,308	23,552	794
Guadalupe	Seguin	92,753	89,023	711
Hale	Plainview	36,061	36,602	1,005
Hall	Memphis	3,848	3,782	903
Hamilton	Hamilton	8,029	8,229	836
Hansford	Spearman	5,278	5,369	920
Hardeman	Quanah	4,596	4,724	695
Hardin	Kountze	48,730	48,073	894
Harris	Houston	3,460,589	3,400,578	1,729
Harrison	Marshall	62,143	62,110	899
Hartley	Channing	5,481	5,537	1,462
Haskell	Haskell	5,951	6,093	903
Hays	San Marcos	105,115	97,589	678
Hemphill	Canadian	3,346	3,351	910
Henderson	Athens	74,868	73,277	874
Hidalgo	Edinburg	590,285	569,463	1,570
Hill	Hillsboro	33,077	32,321	962
Hockley	Levelland	22,661	22,716	908
Hood	Granbury	43,181	41,100	422
Hopkins	Sulphur Springs	32,191	31,960	782
Houston	Crockett	23,195	23,185	1,231
Howard	Big Spring	33,180	33,627	903
Hudspeth	Sierra Blanca	3,318	3,344	4,571
Hunt	Greenville	77,960	76,596	841
Hutchinson	Stinnett	23,332	23,857	887
Irion	Mertzon	1,751	1,771	1,051
Jack	Jacksboro	8,785	8,763	917
Jackson	Edna	14,291	14,391	829
Jasper	Jasper	35,731	35,604	937
Jeff Davis	Fort Davis	2,211	2,207	2,264
Jefferson	Beaumont	249,640	252,051	904
Jim Hogg	Hebbronville	5,161	5,281	1,136
Jim Wells	Alice	39,950	39,326	865
Johnson	Cleburne	132,247	126,811	729
Jones	Anson	20,435	20,785	931
Karnes	Karnes City	15,428	15,446	750
Kaufman	Kaufman	75,810	71,313	786
Kendall	Boerne	24,869	23,743	662
Kenedy	Sarita	413	414	1,457
Kent	Jayton	812	859	902
Kerr	Kerrville	44,558	43,653	1,106
Kimble	Junction	4,520	4,468	1,251
King	Guthrie	319	356	912
Kinney	Brackettville	3,430	3,379	1,363
Kleberg	Kingsville	31,015	31,549	871
Knox	Benjamin	4,039	4,253	849
Lamar	Paris	48,666	48,499	917
Lamb	Littlefield	14,572	14,709	1,016
Lampasas	Lampasas	18,502	17,762	712
La Salle	Cotulla	5,849	5,866	1,489
Lavaca	Hallettsville	19,061	19,210	970
Lee	Giddings	16,163	15,657	629
Leon	Centerville	15,625	15,335	1,072
Liberty	Liberty	72,620	70,154	1,160
Limestone	Groesbeck	22,229	22,051	909
Lipscomb	Lipscomb	3,034	3,057	932
Live Oak	George West	12,177	12,309	1,036
Llano	Llano	17,561	17,044	935
Loving	Mentone	70	67	673
Lubbock	Lubbock	243,999	242,628	899
Lynn	Tahoka	6,433	6,550	892
McCulloch	Brady	8,046	8,205	1,069
McLennan	Waco	215,104	213,517	1,042
McMullen	Tilden	849	851	1,113
Madison	Madisonville	12,996	12,940	470
Marion	Jefferson	11,198	10,941	381
Martin	Stanton	4,726	4,746	915
Mason	Mason	3,805	3,738	932
Matagorda	Bay City	38,157	37,957	1,114
Maverick	Eagle Pass	48,259	47,297	1,280
Medina	Hondo	40,246	39,304	1,328
Menard	Menard	2,324	2,360	902
Midland	Midland	116,318	116,009	900
Milam	Cameron	24,644	24,238	1,017
Mills	Goldthwaite	5,128	5,151	748
Mitchell	Colorado City	9,524	9,698	910
Montague	Montague	19,156	19,117	931
Montgomery	Conroe	315,418	293,768	1,044
Moore	Dumas	20,140	20,121	900
Morris	Daingerfield	13,260	13,048	255
Motley	Matador	1,338	1,426	989
Nacogdoches	Nacogdoches	58,874	59,203	947
Navarro	Corsicana	45,971	45,124	1,008
Newton	Newton	15,139	15,072	933
Nolan	Sweetwater	15,266	15,802	912
Nueces	Corpus Christi	312,470	313,645	836
Ochiltree	Perryton	9,053	9,006	918
Oldham	Vega	2,149	2,185	1,501
Orange	Orange	84,582	84,966	356
Palo Pinto	Palo Pinto	27,211	27,026	953
Panola	Carthage	22,719	22,756	801
Parker	Weatherford	92,700	88,495	904
Parmer	Farwell	9,674	10,016	882
Pecos	Fort Stockton	16,362	16,809	4,764
Polk	Livingston	43,479	41,133	1,057
Potter	Amarillo	113,705	113,546	909
Presidio	Marfa	7,466	7,304	3,856
Rains	Emory	10,006	9,139	232
Randall	Canyon	105,671	104,312	914
Reagan	Big Lake	3,214	3,326	1,175
Real	Leakey	3,083	3,047	700
Red River	Clarksville	14,185	14,314	1,050
Reeves	Pecos	12,772	13,137	2,636
Refugio	Refugio	7,729	7,828	770
Roberts	Miami	854	887	924
Robertson	Franklin	15,929	16,000	855
Rockwall	Rockwall	47,983	43,080	129
Runnels	Ballinger	11,089	11,495	1,051
Rusk	Henderson	47,384	47,372	924
Sabine	Hemphill	10,524	10,469	490
San Augustine	San Augustine	8,772	8,946	528
San Jacinto	Coldspring	22,897	22,246	571
San Patricio	Sinton	67,120	67,138	692
San Saba	San Saba	6,219	6,186	1,134
Schleicher	Eldorado	2,963	2,935	1,311
Scurry	Snyder	15,899	16,361	903
Shackelford	Albany	3,310	3,302	914
Shelby	Center	25,347	25,224	794
Sherman	Stratford	3,185	3,186	923
Smith	Tyler	178,855	174,706	928
Somervell	Glen Rose	7,080	6,809	187
Starr	Rio Grande City	54,671	53,597	1,223
Stephens	Breckenridge	9,470	9,674	895
Sterling	Sterling City	1,336	1,393	923
Stonewall	Aspermont	1,576	1,693	919
Sutton	Sonora	4,046	4,077	1,454
Swisher	Tulia	8,106	8,378	900
Tarrant	Fort Worth	1,486,392	1,446,219	863
Taylor	Abilene	124,024	126,555	916
Terrell	Sanderson	1,005	1,081	2,358
Terry	Brownfield	12,576	12,761	890
Throckmorton	Throckmorton	1,757	1,850	912
Titus	Mount Pleasant	27,995	28,118	411
Tom Green	San Angelo	103,079	104,010	1,522
Travis	Austin	833,797	812,280	989
Trinity	Groveton	13,903	13,779	693
Tyler	Woodville	20,603	20,871	923
Upshur	Gilmer	35,888	35,291	588
Upton	Rankin	3,283	3,404	1,242
Uvalde	Uvalde	26,192	25,926	1,557
Val Verde	Del Rio	45,776	44,856	3,170
Van Zandt	Canton	49,625	48,140	849
Victoria	Victoria	84,710	84,088	883
Walker	Huntsville	61,350	61,758	787
Waller	Hempstead	33,591	32,663	514

County	County seat or courthouse	2001 Pop.	2000 Pop.	Land area sq. mi.
Ward	Monahans	10,454	10,909	835
Washington	Brenham	30,621	30,373	609
Webb	Laredo	201,292	193,117	3,357
Wharton	Wharton	41,202	41,188	1,090
Wheeler	Wheeler	5,101	5,284	914
Wichita	Wichita Falls	128,461	131,664	628
Wilbarger	Vernon	14,114	14,676	971
Willacy	Raymondville	19,905	20,082	597
Williamson	Georgetown	278,067	249,967	1,123
Wilson	Floresville	33,721	32,408	807
Winkler	Kermit	7,039	7,173	841
Wise	Decatur	51,475	48,793	905
Wood	Quitman	37,646	36,752	650
Yoakum	Plains	7,285	7,322	800
Young	Graham	17,723	17,943	922
Zapata	Zapata	12,461	12,182	997
Zavala	Crystal City	11,584	11,600	1,298

Utah

(29 counties, 82,144 sq. mi. land; pop. 2,269,789)

County	County seat or courthouse	2001 Pop.	2000 Pop.	Land area sq. mi.
Beaver	Beaver	6,059	6,005	2,590
Box Elder	Brigham City	43,397	42,745	5,723
Cache	Logan	91,208	91,391	1,165
Carbon	Price	19,703	20,422	1,478
Daggett	Manila	905	921	698
Davis	Farmington	244,840	238,994	304
Duchesne	Duchesne	14,709	14,371	3,238
Emery	Castle Dale	10,609	10,860	4,452
Garfield	Panguitch	4,724	4,735	5,174
Grand	Moab	8,633	8,485	3,682
Iron	Parowan	34,448	33,779	3,298
Juab	Nephi	8,489	8,238	3,392
Kane	Kanab	6,058	6,046	3,992
Millard	Fillmore	12,424	12,405	6,589
Morgan	Morgan	7,337	7,129	609
Piute	Junction	1,387	1,435	758
Rich	Randolph	1,979	1,961	1,029
Salt Lake	Salt Lake City	904,331	898,387	737
San Juan	Monticello	13,836	14,413	7,820
Sanpete	Manti	23,376	22,763	1,588
Sevier	Richfield	18,961	18,842	1,910
Summit	Coalville	31,103	29,736	1,871
Tooele	Tooele	44,157	40,735	6,930
Uintah	Vernal	25,926	25,224	4,477
Utah	Provo	377,411	368,536	1,998
Wasatch	Heber City	16,200	15,215	1,177
Washington	Saint George	95,590	90,354	2,427
Wayne	Loa	2,554	2,509	2,460
Weber	Ogden	199,435	196,533	576

Vermont

(14 counties, 9,250 sq. mi. land; pop. 613,090)

County	County seat or courthouse	2001 Pop.	2000 Pop.	Land area sq. mi.
Addison	Middlebury	36,263	35,974	770
Bennington	Bennington	37,148	36,994	676
Caledonia	Saint Johnsbury	29,770	29,702	651
Chittenden	Burlington	147,591	146,571	539
Essex	Guildhall	6,507	6,459	665
Franklin	Saint Albans	46,184	45,417	637
Grand Isle	North Hero	7,220	6,901	83
Lamoille	Hyde Park	23,602	23,233	461
Orange	Chelsea	28,786	28,226	689
Orleans	Newport	26,536	26,277	698
Rutland	Rutland	63,250	63,400	933
Washington	Montpelier	58,503	58,039	689
Windham	Newfane	44,055	44,216	789
Windsor	Woodstock	57,675	57,418	971

Virginia

(95 counties, 40 ind. cities, 39,594 sq. mi. land; pop. 7,187,734)

County	County seat or courthouse	2001 Pop.	2000 Pop.	Land area sq. mi.
Accomack	Accomac	38,414	38,305	455
Albemarle	Charlottesville	80,413	79,236	723
Alleghany	Covington	12,840	12,926	445
Amelia	Amelia Court House	11,652	11,400	357
Amherst	Amherst	32,139	31,894	475
Appomattox	Appomattox	13,885	13,705	334
Arlington	Arlington	187,469	189,453	26
Augusta	Staunton	66,621	65,615	970
Bath	Warm Springs	5,073	5,048	532
Bedford	Bedford	61,194	60,371	755
Bland	Bland	6,844	6,871	359
Botetourt	Fincastle	30,812	30,496	543
Brunswick	Lawrenceville	18,292	18,419	566
Buchanan	Grundy	26,331	26,978	504
Buckingham	Buckingham	15,786	15,623	581
Campbell	Rustburg	51,295	51,078	504
Caroline	Bowling Green	22,463	22,121	533
Carroll	Hillsville	29,381	29,245	476
Charles City	Charles City	6,969	6,926	183
Charlotte	Charlotte Court House	12,451	12,472	475
Chesterfield	Chesterfield	266,549	259,903	426
Clarke	Berryville	13,111	12,652	177
Craig	New Castle	5,090	5,091	331
Culpeper	Culpeper	35,715	34,262	381
Cumberland	Cumberland	9,017	9,017	298
Dickenson	Clintwood	16,329	16,395	332
Dinwiddie	Dinwiddie	24,630	24,533	504
Essex	Tappahannock	10,020	9,989	258
Fairfax	Fairfax	985,161	969,749	395
Fauquier	Warrenton	57,820	55,139	650
Floyd	Floyd	14,195	13,874	381
Fluvanna	Palmyra	21,257	20,047	287
Franklin	Rocky Mount	47,927	47,286	692
Frederick	Winchester	61,315	59,209	415
Giles	Pearisburg	16,816	16,657	357
Gloucester	Gloucester	35,410	34,780	217
Goochland	Goochland	17,323	16,863	284
Grayson	Independence	17,727	17,917	443
Greene	Stanardsville	15,945	15,244	157
Greensville	Emporia	11,536	11,560	295
Halifax	Halifax	37,074	37,355	819
Hanover	Hanover	89,714	86,320	473
Henrico	Richmond	264,973	262,300	238
Henry	Collinsville	57,332	57,930	382
Highland	Monterey	2,518	2,536	416
Isle of Wight	Isle of Wight	30,659	29,728	316
James City	Williamsburg	50,249	48,102	143
King and Queen	King and Queen Court House	6,572	6,630	316
King George	King George	17,319	16,803	180
King William	King William	13,577	13,146	275
Lancaster	Lancaster	11,553	11,567	133
Lee	Jonesville	23,431	23,589	437
Loudoun	Leesburg	190,903	169,599	520
Louisa	Louisa	26,539	25,627	497
Lunenburg	Lunenburg	13,080	13,146	432
Madison	Madison	12,761	12,520	321
Mathews	Mathews	9,300	9,207	86
Mecklenburg	Boydton	32,325	32,380	624
Middlesex	Saluda	10,013	9,932	130
Montgomery	Christiansburg	83,142	83,629	388
Nelson	Lovingston	14,678	14,445	472
New Kent	New Kent	13,986	13,462	210
Northampton	Eastville	13,125	13,093	207
Northumberland	Heathsville	12,417	12,259	192
Nottoway	Nottoway	15,650	15,725	315
Orange	Orange	26,705	25,881	342
Page	Luray	23,195	23,177	311
Patrick	Stuart	19,470	19,407	483
Pittsylvania	Chatham	61,878	61,745	971
Powhatan	Powhatan	23,425	22,377	261
Prince Edward	Farmville	19,659	19,720	353
Prince George	Prince George	33,723	33,047	266
Prince William	Manassas	298,707	280,813	338
Pulaski	Pulaski	35,024	35,127	321
Rappahannock	Washington	7,218	6,983	267
Richmond	Warsaw	8,874	8,809	191
Roanoke	Salem	86,220	85,778	251
Rockbridge	Lexington	20,861	20,808	600
Rockingham	Harrisonburg	68,505	67,725	851
Russell	Lebanon	30,098	30,308	475
Scott	Gate City	23,402	23,403	537
Shenandoah	Woodstock	35,851	35,075	512
Smyth	Marion	32,888	33,081	452
Southampton	Courtland	17,412	17,482	600
Spotsylvania	Spotsylvania	97,760	90,395	401
Stafford	Stafford	99,692	92,446	270
Surry	Surry	6,848	6,829	279
Sussex	Sussex	12,373	12,504	491
Tazewell	Tazewell	44,175	44,598	520
Warren	Front Royal	32,349	31,584	214
Washington	Abingdon	51,253	51,103	563
Westmoreland	Montross	16,788	16,718	229
Wise	Wise	39,925	40,123	404
Wythe	Wytheville	27,776	27,599	463
York	Yorktown	58,293	56,297	106
Independent Cities				
Alexandria		128,773	128,283	15
Bedford		6,282	6,299	7
Bristol		17,342	17,367	13
Buena Vista		6,334	6,349	7
Charlottesville		44,372	45,049	10
Chesapeake		203,796	199,184	341
Clifton Forge		4,181	4,289	3
Colonial Heights		17,006	16,897	7
Covington		6,286	6,303	6
Danville		47,780	48,411	43
Emporia		5,621	5,665	7
Fairfax		21,674	21,498	6
Falls Church		10,612	10,377	2
Franklin		8,196	8,346	8
Fredericksburg		19,952	19,279	11

County	County seat or courthouse	2001 Pop.	2000 Pop.	Land area sq. mi.
Galax		6,650	6,837	8
Hampton		145,665	146,437	52
Harrisonburg		39,932	40,468	18
Hopewell		22,241	22,354	10
Lexington		6,864	6,867	2
Lynchburg		64,108	65,269	49
Manassas		35,814	35,135	10
Manassas Park		10,589	10,290	2
Martinsville		15,311	15,416	11
Newport News		180,305	180,150	68
Norfolk		233,147	234,403	54
Norton		3,886	3,904	8
Petersburg		33,457	33,740	23
Poquoson		11,694	11,566	16
Portsmouth		99,494	100,565	33
Radford		15,352	15,859	10
Richmond		195,966	197,790	60
Roanoke		93,889	94,911	43
Salem		24,635	24,747	15
Staunton		23,875	23,853	20
Suffolk		67,107	63,677	400
Virginia Beach		426,931	425,257	248
Waynesboro		19,918	19,520	15
Williamsburg		12,102	11,998	9
Winchester		24,141	23,585	9

Washington

(39 counties, 66,544 sq. mi. land; pop. 5,987,973)

County	County seat or courthouse	2001 Pop.	2000 Pop.	Land area sq. mi.
Adams	Ritzville	16,286	16,428	1,925
Asotin	Asotin	20,560	20,551	635
Benton	Prosser	146,634	142,475	1,703
Chelan	Wenatchee	67,133	66,616	2,921
Clallam	Port Angeles	65,759	64,525	1,739
Clark	Vancouver	360,760	345,238	628
Columbia	Dayton	4,113	4,064	869
Cowlitz	Kelso	93,716	92,948	1,139
Douglas	Waterville	32,967	32,603	1,821
Ferry	Republic	7,296	7,260	2,204
Franklin	Pasco	51,015	49,347	1,242
Garfield	Pomeroy	2,342	2,397	711
Grant	Ephrata	76,221	74,698	2,681
Grays Harbor	Montesano	68,331	67,194	1,917
Island	Coupeville	74,114	71,558	208
Jefferson	Port Townsend	26,584	25,953	1,814
King	Seattle	1,741,785	1,737,034	2,126
Kitsap	Port Orchard	233,372	231,969	396
Kittitas	Ellensburg	33,875	33,362	2,297
Klickitat	Goldendale	19,339	19,161	1,872
Lewis	Chehalis	69,273	68,600	2,408
Lincoln	Davenport	10,257	10,184	2,311
Mason	Shelton	50,425	49,405	961
Okanogan	Okanogan	39,543	39,564	5,268
Pacific	South Bend	20,844	20,984	933
Pend Oreille	Newport	11,965	11,732	1,400
Pierce	Tacoma	719,407	700,820	1,679
San Juan	Friday Harbor	14,515	14,077	175
Skagit	Mount Vernon	105,247	102,979	1,735
Skamania	Stevenson	10,027	9,872	1,656
Snohomish	Everett	622,900	606,024	2,089
Spokane	Spokane	423,261	417,939	1,764
Stevens	Colville	40,641	40,066	2,478
Thurston	Olympia	213,546	207,355	727
Wahkiakum	Cathlamet	3,787	3,824	264
Walla Walla	Walla Walla	55,519	55,180	1,271
Whatcom	Bellingham	170,849	166,814	2,120
Whitman	Colfax	39,879	40,740	2,159
Yakima	Yakima	223,886	222,581	4,296

West Virginia

(55 counties, 24,078 sq. mi. land; pop. 1,801,916)

County	County seat or courthouse	2001 Pop.	2000 Pop.	Land area sq. mi.
Barbour	Philippi	15,514	15,557	341
Berkeley	Martinsburg	79,202	75,905	321
Boone	Madison	25,427	25,535	503
Braxton	Sutton	14,747	14,702	513
Brooke	Wellsburg	25,117	25,447	89
Cabell	Huntington	95,682	96,784	282
Calhoun	Grantsville	7,392	7,582	281
Clay	Clay	10,324	10,330	342
Doddridge	West Union	7,745	7,403	320
Fayette	Fayetteville	47,089	47,579	664
Gilmer	Glenville	7,120	7,160	340
Grant	Petersburg	11,340	11,299	477
Greenbrier	Lewisburg	34,479	34,453	1,021
Hampshire	Romney	20,798	20,203	642
Hancock	New Cumberland	32,258	32,667	83
Hardy	Moorefield	12,740	12,669	583
Harrison	Clarksburg	67,989	68,652	416
Jackson	Ripley	28,099	28,000	466
Jefferson	Charles Town	43,545	42,190	210
Kanawha	Charleston	197,338	200,073	903
Lewis	Weston	16,897	16,919	382
Lincoln	Hamlin	22,316	22,108	437
Logan	Logan	36,897	37,710	454
McDowell	Welch	26,568	27,329	535
Marion	Fairmont	56,373	56,598	310
Marshall	Moundsville	35,171	35,519	307
Mason	Point Pleasant	26,175	25,957	432
Mercer	Princeton	62,355	62,980	420
Mineral	Keyser	27,059	27,078	328
Mingo	Williamson	27,714	28,253	423
Monongalia	Morgantown	81,820	81,866	361
Monroe	Union	14,610	14,583	473
Morgan	Berkeley Springs	15,275	14,943	229
Nicholas	Summersville	26,420	26,562	649
Ohio	Wheeling	46,750	47,427	106
Pendleton	Franklin	8,070	8,196	698
Pleasants	St. Marys	7,589	7,514	131
Pocahontas	Marlinton	8,996	9,131	940
Preston	Kingwood	29,443	29,334	648
Putnam	Winfield	51,680	51,589	346
Raleigh	Beckley	78,548	79,220	607
Randolph	Elkins	28,231	28,262	1,040
Ritchie	Harrisville	10,291	10,343	454
Roane	Spencer	15,364	15,446	484
Summers	Hinton	12,796	12,999	361
Taylor	Grafton	16,017	16,089	173
Tucker	Parsons	7,214	7,321	419
Tyler	Middlebourne	9,460	9,592	258
Upshur	Buckhannon	23,374	23,404	355
Wayne	Wayne	42,665	42,903	506
Webster	Webster Springs	9,642	9,719	556
Wetzel	New Martinsville	17,395	17,693	359
Wirt	Elizabeth	5,935	5,873	233
Wood	Parkersburg	87,541	87,986	367
Wyoming	Pineville	25,320	25,708	501

Wisconsin

(72 counties, 54,310 sq. mi. land; pop. 5,401,906)

County	County seat or courthouse	2001 Pop.	2000 Pop.	Land area sq. mi.
Adams	Friendship	19,164	18,643	648
Ashland	Ashland	16,881	16,866	1,044
Barron	Barron	45,365	44,963	863
Bayfield	Washburn	15,114	15,013	1,476
Brown	Green Bay	229,212	226,778	529
Buffalo	Alma	13,814	13,804	684
Burnett	Siren	15,966	15,674	822
Calumet	Chilton	41,506	40,631	320
Chippewa	Chippewa Falls	55,960	55,195	1,010
Clark	Neillsville	33,849	33,557	1,216
Columbia	Portage	53,365	52,468	774
Crawford	Prairie du Chien	17,062	17,243	573
Dane	Madison	432,654	426,526	1,202
Dodge	Juneau	86,447	85,897	882
Door	Sturgeon Bay	28,339	27,961	483
Douglas	Superior	43,468	43,287	1,309
Dunn	Menomonie	40,352	39,858	852
Eau Claire	Eau Claire	93,278	93,142	638
Florence	Florence	5,088	5,088	488
Fond du Lac	Fond du Lac	97,781	97,296	723
Forest	Crandon	10,020	10,024	1,014
Grant	Lancaster	49,270	49,597	1,148
Green	Monroe	34,022	33,647	584
Green Lake	Green Lake	19,260	19,105	354
Iowa	Dodgeville	23,073	22,780	763
Iron	Hurley	6,806	6,861	757
Jackson	Black River Falls	19,224	19,100	987
Jefferson	Jefferson	74,588	74,021	557
Juneau	Mauston	24,577	24,316	768
Kenosha	Kenosha	152,524	149,577	273
Kewaunee	Kewaunee	20,310	20,187	343
La Crosse	La Crosse	107,705	107,120	453
Lafayette	Darlington	16,155	16,137	634
Langlade	Antigo	20,744	20,740	873
Lincoln	Merrill	29,873	29,641	883
Manitowoc	Manitowoc	82,618	82,887	592
Marathon	Wausau	126,031	125,834	1,545
Marinette	Marinette	43,417	43,384	1,402
Marquette	Montello	15,900	15,832	455
Menominee	Keshena	4,621	4,562	358
Milwaukee	Milwaukee	932,012	940,164	242
Monroe	Sparta	41,258	40,899	901
Oconto	Oconto	36,320	35,634	998
Oneida	Rhinelander	37,045	36,776	1,125
Outagamie	Appleton	164,115	160,971	640
Ozaukee	Port Washington	83,555	82,317	232
Pepin	Durand	7,330	7,213	232

County	County seat or courthouse	2001 Pop.	2000 Pop.	Land area sq. mi.
Pierce	Ellsworth	37,290	36,804	576
Polk	Balsam Lake	42,285	41,319	917
Portage	Stevens Point	66,921	67,182	806
Price	Phillips	15,602	15,822	1,253
Racine	Racine	189,613	188,831	333
Richland	Richland Center	18,133	17,924	586
Rock	Janesville	153,324	152,307	720
Rusk	Ladysmith	15,331	15,347	913
Saint Croix	Hudson	66,319	63,155	722
Sauk	Baraboo	55,904	55,225	838
Sawyer	Hayward	16,433	16,196	1,256
Shawano	Shawano	40,925	40,664	893
Sheboygan	Sheboygan	113,109	112,646	514
Taylor	Medford	19,637	19,680	975
Trempealeau	Whitehall	27,062	27,010	734
Vernon	Viroqua	28,260	28,056	795
Vilas	Eagle River	21,535	21,033	874
Walworth	Elkhorn	95,605	93,759	555
Washburn	Shell Lake	16,373	16,036	810
Washington	West Bend	119,829	117,493	431
Waukesha	Waukesha	367,065	360,767	556
Waupaca	Waupaca	52,198	51,731	751
Waushara	Wautoma	23,497	23,154	626
Winnebago	Oshkosh	157,312	156,763	439
Wood	Wisconsin Rapids	75,306	75,555	793

Wyoming

(23 counties, 97,100 sq. mi. land; pop. 494,423)

County	County seat or courthouse	2001 Pop.	2000 Pop.	Land area sq. mi.
Albany	Laramie	31,313	32,014	4,273
Big Horn	Basin	11,255	11,461	3,137
Campbell	Gillette	34,853	33,698	4,797
Carbon	Rawlins	15,505	15,639	7,896
Converse	Douglas	12,186	12,052	4,255
Crook	Sundance	5,836	5,887	2,859
Fremont	Lander	35,967	35,804	9,182
Goshen	Torrington	12,389	12,538	2,225
Hot Springs	Thermopolis	4,805	4,882	2,004
Johnson	Buffalo	7,245	7,075	4,166
Laramie	Cheyenne	81,958	81,607	2,686
Lincoln	Kemmerer	14,793	14,573	4,069
Natrona	Casper	66,798	66,533	5,340
Niobrara	Lusk	2,396	2,407	2,626
Park	Cody	25,974	25,786	6,942
Platte	Wheatland	8,782	8,807	2,085
Sheridan	Sheridan	26,833	26,560	2,523
Sublette	Pinedale	6,018	5,920	4,883
Sweetwater	Green River	36,873	37,613	10,425
Teton	Jackson	18,437	18,251	4,008
Unita	Evanston	19,572	19,742	2,082
Washakie	Worland	8,102	8,289	2,240
Weston	Newcastle	6,533	6,644	2,398

Population of Outlying Areas

Source: Bureau of the Census, U.S. Dept. of Commerce; World Almanac research

Census 2000 figures are given for all populations and land areas of Puerto Rican municipios (a municipio is the governmental unit that is the primary legal subdivision of Puerto Rico; the Census Bureau treats the municipio as the statistical equivalent of a county); all other land area figures are from the 1990 census. Because only selected areas are shown, the population and land area figures may not equal the total reported. ZIP codes with an asterisk (*) are general delivery ZIP codes. Consult the local postmaster for more specific delivery information. Wake Atoll, Johnston Atoll, and Midway Atoll receive mail through APO and FPO addresses.

Commonwealth of Puerto Rico

ZIP code	Municipio	2000 Pop.	Land area sq. mi.
00601	Adjuntas	19,143	67
00602	Aguada	42,042	31
*00605	Aguadilla	64,685	37
00703	Aguas Buenas	29,032	31
00705	Aibonito	26,493	31
00610	Añasco	28,348	39
*00613	Arecibo	100,131	126
00714	Arroyo	19,117	15
00617	Barceloneta	22,322	19
00794	Barranquitas	28,909	34
*00958	Bayamón	224,044	44
00623	Cabo Rojo	46,911	70
*00726	Caguas	140,502	59
00627	Camuy	35,244	46
00729	Canóvanas	43,335	33
*00984	Carolina	186,076	45
*00963	Cataño	30,071	5
*00737	Cayey	47,370	52
00735	Ceiba	18,004	29
00638	Ciales	19,811	67
00739	Cidra	42,753	36
00769	Coamo	37,597	78
00782	Comerío	20,002	28
00783	Corozal	36,867	43
00775	Culebra	1,868	12
00646	Dorado	34,017	23
00738	Fajardo	40,712	30
00650	Florida	12,367	15
00653	Guánica	21,888	37
*00785	Guayama	44,301	65
00656	Guayanilla	23,072	42
*00970	Guaynabo	100,053	27
00778	Gurabo	36,743	28
00659	Hatillo	38,925	42
00660	Hormigüeros	16,614	11
*00791	Humacao	59,035	45
00662	Isabela	44,444	55
00664	Jayuya	17,318	45
00795	Juana Díaz	50,531	60
00777	Juncos	36,452	27
00667	Lajas	26,261	60
00669	Lares	34,415	61
00670	Las Marías	11,061	46
00771	Las Piedras	34,485	34
00772	Loíza	32,537	19
00773	Luquillo	19,817	26
00674	Manatí	45,409	45
00606	Maricao	6,449	37
00707	Maunabo	12,741	21
*00681	Mayagüez	98,434	78
00676	Moca	39,697	50
00687	Morovis	29,965	39
00718	Naguabo	23,753	52
00719	Naranjito	29,709	27
00720	Orocovis	23,844	63
00723	Patillas	20,152	47
00624	Peñuelas	26,719	44
*00732	Ponce	186,475	115
00678	Quebradillas	25,450	23
00677	Rincón	14,767	14
00745	Río Grande	52,362	61
00637	Sabana Grande	25,935	36
00751	Salinas	31,113	69
00683	San Germán	37,105	55
*00902	San Juan	434,374	48
00754	San Lorenzo	40,997	53
00685	San Sebastián	44,204	70
00757	Santa Isabel	21,665	34
*00954	Toa Alta	63,929	27
*00950	Toa Baja	94,085	23
*00976	Trujillo Alto	75,728	21
00641	Utuado	35,336	113
00692	Vega Alta	37,910	28
*00694	Vega Baja	61,929	46
00765	Vieques	9,106	51
00766	Villalba	27,913	35
00767	Yabucoa	39,246	55
00698	Yauco	46,384	68
TOTAL		**3,808,610**	**3,425**

Commonwealth of the Northern Mariana Islands

ZIP code	Municipality	2000 Pop.	Land area sq. mi.
96950	Northern Islands	6	60
96951	Rota	3,283	33
96950	Saipan	62,392	47
96952	Tinian	3,540	39
TOTAL		**69,221**	**179**

Other U.S. External Territories

ZIP code	Location	2000 Pop.	Land area sq. mi.
	American Samoa		
96799	American Samoa	57,291	77
	Guam		
96919	Agaña Hts.	3,940	1
96928	Agat	5,656	10
96922	Asan	2,090	6
*96913	Barrigada	8,652	9
96924	Chalan-Pago-Ordot	5,923	6
96912	Dededo	42,980	30
*96913	Hagatña	1,100	1
96917	Inarajan	3,052	6
96923	Mangilao	13,313	6
96916	Merizo	2,163	19
96927	Mongmong-Toto-Maite	5,845	10
96925	Piti	1,666	6
96915	Santa Rita	7,500	2
96926	Sinajana	2,853	7
96930	Talofofo	3,215	17
*96913	Tamuning	18,012	1
96918	Umatac	887	17
96929	Yigo	19,474	35
96914	Yona	6,484	20
TOTAL		**154,805**	**210**
	Virgin Islands		
00820	Saint Croix	53,234	83
*00820	Christiansted	2,637	
*00841	Frederiksted	732	
*00830	Saint John	4,197	20
*00801	Saint Thomas	51,181	31
*00801	Charlotte Amalie	11,004	
TOTAL		**108,612**	**134**

WORLD HISTORY

Chronology of World History

Prehistory: Our Ancestors Emerge

Revised by Susan Skomal, Ph.D., American Anthropological Association

The precise origins of *Homo sapiens*, the species to which all humans belong, are subject to broad speculation based on a small, but increasing, number of fossils, on genetic and anatomical studies, and on interpretation of the geological record. Most scientists agree that humans evolved from apelike primate ancestors in a process that began millions of years ago.

Current theories trace the first hominid (upright walking, humanlike primate) to Africa, where several distinct lines of hominids appeared 5 to 7 million years before the present (BP). *Australopithecus* was a social animal that lived from 5 to 2 million years BP, then died out. The line from which humans descended was the larger brained *Homo habilis*, that appeared some 2.5 million years BP, lived in semipermanent camps, had a food-gathering economy, and produced stone tools.

Homo erectus, the nearest ancestor to humans, appeared in Africa 1.8 million BP, spread into Asia by 1.5 million BP, and into Europe by 800,000 BP. It had a fairly large brain and a skeletal structure similar to modern humans. *Homo erectus* hunted, learned to control fire, and may have had some primitive language skills. Brain development to *Homo sapiens*, then to the subspecies *Homo sapiens sapiens*, occurred between 500,000 and 50,000 BP in Africa. All modern humans are members of the subspecies *Homo sapiens sapiens*.

Humans have roamed over the globe throughout their development. Migration from Asia to Australia via the Timor Straits took place as early as 100,000 BP. Evidence of hominids in Siberia dates to 300,000 BP. First confirmation for the crossing from Asia to the Americas by land bridge dates to the end of the last Ice Age, at 11,000 BP. A growing body of evidence in N and S America, however, suggests that humans sailed even earlier from Asia to the New World, either along coastal routes or directly across the Pacific, before 12,000 BP.

A variety of cultural modes—in toolmaking, diet, shelter, and possibly social arrangements and spiritual expression—arose as humans adapted to different geographic and climatic zones and the database of knowledge grew. Sites from all over the world show seasonal migration patterns and efficient exploitation of a wide range of plant and animal foods.

During the Paleolithic, or Early Stone, Age archaeologists recognize 5 basic toolmaking traditions as arising and often coexisting from more than 2.6 million years ago to the near past: (1) the *chopper tradition* known as the Oldowan produced crude chopping tools and simple flake tools; (2) the *hand-ax tradition* produced pointed hand axes chipped on both faces for cutting; (3) the *flake tradition* produced small cutting and flaking tools; (4) the *blade tradition,* a more efficient technology, produced many usable blades from a single stone; and (5) the *microlith tradition* produced specialized small tools for use as projectile points and for carving softer materials and making more complex tools.

Fire was used for heating and cooking by 465,000 BP in W France. Fire-hardened wooden spears, weighted and set with small stone blades, were fashioned by big-game hunters 400,000 years ago in Germany. Scraping tools, dated to 200,000-30,000 BP in Europe, N Africa, the Middle East, and Cent. Asia, suggest the treatment of skins for clothing. By the time Australia was settled, human ancestors had learned to navigate in boats over open water. The earliest bone tools found so far were developed 80,000 years ago in the Congo basin by fishermen, who created sophisticated fishing tackle to catch giant catfish.

About 60,000 years ago the earliest immigrants to Australia carved and painted abstract designs on rocks. Painting and decoration flourished, along with stone and ivory sculpture, from 30,000 BP in Europe, where more than 200 caves show remarkable examples of naturalistic wall painting. Proto-religious rites are suggested by these works, and by evidence of ritual burial. A variety of musical instruments, including bone flutes with precisely bored holes, have been found in sites dated to 40,000-80,000 BP.

Some time after 10,000 BC, among widely separated communities, a series of dramatic technological and social changes occurred, marking the Neolithic, or New Stone, Age. As the world climate became drier and warmer, humans learned to cultivate plants and to domesticate animals. This encouraged growth of permanent settlements. Manufacture of pottery and cloth began at this time. These techniques permitted a dramatic increase in world population and social complexity, and accelerated humankind's ability to manipulate the environment.

Sites in N, Cent., and S America, SE Europe, and the Middle East show roughly contemporaneous (10,000-8000 BC) evidence of one or more Neolithic traits. Dates near 6000-3000 BC have been given for E and S Asian, W European, and sub-Saharan African Neolithic remains. Evidence from both archaeological sites and linguistic studies document the rapid spread of farming throughout the Mediterranean, perhaps in as few as 6 generations, or 100-200 years. The variety of crops—field grains, rice, maize, and roots—and a mix of other characteristics suggest that this adaptation occurred independently in each region.

History Begins: 4000-1000 BC

Near Eastern cradle. If history began with writing, the first chapter opened in Mesopotamia, the Tigris-Euphrates river valley. The Sumerians used clay tablets with pictographs to keep records after 4000 BC. A **cuneiform** (wedge-shaped) script evolved by 3000 BC as a full syllabic alphabet. Neighboring peoples adapted the script for their own use.

Sumerian life centered, from 4000 BC, on large cities (Eridu, Ur, Uruk, Nippur, Kish, and Lagash) organized around temples and priestly bureaucracies, with surrounding plains watered by vast irrigation works and worked with traction plows. Sailboats, wheeled vehicles, potter's wheels, and kilns were used. Copper was smelted and tempered from c 4000 BC; bronze was produced not long after. Ores, as well as precious stones and metals, were obtained through long-distance ship and caravan trade. Iron was used from c 2000 BC. Improved ironworking, developed partly by the Hittites, became widespread by 1200 BC.

Sumerian political primacy passed among cities and their kingly dynasties. Semitic-speaking peoples, with cultures derived from the Sumerian, founded a succession of dynasties that ruled in Mesopotamia and neighboring areas for most of 1,800 years; among them were the **Akkadians** (first under Sargon I, c 2350 BC), the Amorites (whose laws, codified by **Hammurabi,** c 1792-1750 BC, have biblical parallels), and the Assyrians, with interludes of rule by the Hittites, Kassites, and Mitanni.

Mesopotamian learning, maintained by scribes and preserved in vast libraries, was practically oriented. Advances in mathematics related mostly to construction, commerce, and administration. Lists of astronomical phenomena, plants, animals, and stones were maintained; medical texts listed ailments and herbal cures. The Sumerians worshiped anthropomorphic gods representing natural forces. Sacrifices were made at **ziggurats**—huge stepped temples.

The Syria-Palestine area, site of some of the earliest urban remains (Jericho, 7000 BC), and of the recently uncovered **Ebla** civilization (fl 2500 BC), experienced Egyptian cultural and political influence along with Mesopotamian. The **Phoenician** coast was an active commercial center. A phonetic alphabet was invented here before 1600 BC. It became the ancestor of many other alphabets.

Egyptian hieroglyphics

Egypt. Agricultural villages along the Nile River were united by around 3300 BC into 2 kingdoms, Upper and Lower Egypt, unified (c 3100 BC) under the pharaoh Menes. A bureaucracy supervised construction of canals and monuments (**pyramids** starting 2700 BC). Control over Nubia to the S was asserted from 2600 BC. Brilliant Old Kingdom Period achievements in architecture, sculpture, and painting reached their height during the 3rd and 4th Dynasties. **Hieroglyphic writing** appeared by 3200 BC, recording a sophisticated literature that included religious writings, philosophy, history, and science. An ordered hierarchy of gods, including totemistic animal elements, was served by a powerful priesthood in Memphis. The pharaoh was identified with the falcon god Horus. Other trends included belief in an afterlife and short-lived quasi-monotheistic reforms introduced by the pharaoh **Akhenaton** (c 1379-1362 BC).

After a period of dominance by Semitic Hyksos from Asia (c 1700-1550 BC), the New Kingdom established an empire in Syria. Egypt became increasingly embroiled in Asiatic wars and diplomacy. Conquered by Persia in 525 BC, it eventually faded away as an independent culture.

India. An urban civilization with a so-far-undeciphered writing system stretched across the Indus Valley and along the Arabian Sea c 3000-1500 BC. Major sites are Harappa and **Mohenjo-Daro** in Pakistan, well-planned geometric cities with underground sewers and vast granaries. The entire region may have been ruled as a single state. Bronze was used, and arts and crafts were well developed. Religious life apparently took the form of fertility cults. Indus civilization was probably in decline when it was destroyed by **Aryans who arrived** from the NW, speaking an Indo-European language from which most languages of Pakistan, N India, and Bangladesh descend. Led by a warrior aristocracy whose legendary deeds are in the **Rig Veda**, the Aryans spread E and S, bringing their sky gods, priestly (Brahman) ritual, and the beginnings of the caste system; local customs and beliefs were assimilated by the conquerors.

Europe. On Crete, the Bronze Age **Minoan civilization** emerged c 2500 BC. A prosperous economy and richly decorative art was supported by seaborne commerce. Mycenae and other cities in mainland Greece and Asia Minor (e.g., **Troy**) preserved elements of the culture until c 1200 BC. Cretan Linear A script (c 2000-1700 BC) remains undeciphered; Linear B script (c 1300-1200 BC) records an early Greek dialect. Unclear is the possible connection between Mycenaean monumental stonework and the megalithic monuments of W Europe, Iberia, and Malta (c 4000-1500 BC).

China. Proto-Chinese neolithic cultures had long covered N and SE China when the first large political state was organized in the N by the **Shang dynasty** (c 1523 BC). Shang kings called themselves Sons of Heaven, and they presided over a cgalult of human and animal sacrifice to ancestors and nature gods. The Chou dynasty, starting c 1027 BC, expanded the area of the Son of Heaven's dominion, but feudal states exercised most temporal power. A writing system with 2,000 characters was already in use under the Shang, with **pictographs** later supplemented by phonetic characters. Many of its principles and symbols, despite changes in spoken Chinese, were preserved in later writing systems. Technical advances allowed urban specialists to create fine ceramic and jade products, and bronze casting after 1500 BC was the most advanced in the world. Bronze artifacts have recently been discovered in N Thailand dating from 3600 BC, hundreds of years before similar Middle Eastern finds.

Americas. Olmecs settled (1500 BC) on the Gulf coast of Mexico and developed the first known civilization in the western hemisphere. Temple cities and huge stone sculpture date from 1200 BC. A rudimentary calendar and writing system existed. Olmec religion, centering on a jaguar god, and Olmec art forms influenced later Meso-American cultures.

Major Gods & Goddesses of Ancient Egypt

Name	Relations	Sphere or Position	Emblem/ Attribute
Ra (Re)/Atum/Amon	Self-created	The sun, creation	Hawk
Thoth (Djeheuty)	Son of Ra	The moon, wisdom, writing	Ibis/baboon
Ptah	Creator of Atum	Creation, craftsmen	----
Osiris	Brother of Set(h) & Isis	The underworld (dead), fertility, resurrection, vegetation	Bull
Isis	Sister/consort of Osiris	The underworld (dead)	----
Set(h)	Brother of Osiris	Evil, trickery, chaos	Boar, pig
Horus	Son of Osiris & Isis/ Ra & Hathor	The earth	Falcon
Hathor	Consort of Ra	Motherhood, love	Cow
Anubis	Son of Osiris	Embalmer & judge of the dead	Jackal/dog

Classical Era of Old World Civilizations: 1000 BC-400 BC

Greece. After a period of decline during the Dorian Greek invasions (1200-1000 BC), the Aegean area developed a unique civilization. Drawing on Mycenaean traditions, Mesopotamian learning (weights and measures, lunisolar calendar, astronomy, musical scales), the Phoenician alphabet (modified for Greek), and Egyptian art, **Greek city-states** saw a rich elaboration of intellectual life. The two great epic poems attributed to Homer, the *Iliad* and the *Odyssey,* were probably composed around the 8th cent. BC. Long-range commerce was aided by metal coinage (introduced by the Lydians in Asia Minor before 700 BC); colonies were founded around the Mediterranean (Cumae in Italy in 760 BC; Massalia in France c 600 BC) and Black Sea shores.

Parthenon

Philosophy, starting with Ionian speculation on the nature of matter (Thales, c 634-546 BC), continued by other "Pre-Socratics" (e.g., Heraclitus, c 535-415 BC; Parmenides, b. c 515 BC), reached a high point in Athens in the rationalist idealism of **Plato** (c 428-347 BC), a disciple of **Socrates** (c 469-399 BC; executed for alleged impiety), and in **Aristotle** (384-322 BC), a pioneer in many fields, from natural sciences to logic, ethics, and metaphysics. The **arts** were highly valued. Architecture culminated in the **Parthenon** (438 BC) by Phidias (fl 490-430 BC). Poetry (Sappho, c 610-580 BC; Pindar, c 518-438 BC) and **drama** (Aeschylus, 525-456 BC; Sophocles, c 496-406 BC; Euripides, c 484-406 BC) thrived. Male beauty and strength, a chief artistic theme, were celebrated at the national games at Olympia.

Ruled by local tyrants or **oligarchies**, the Greeks were not politically united, but managed to resist inclusion in the Persian Empire—Persian king Darius was defeated at Marathon (490 BC), his son Xerxes at Salamis (480 BC), and the Persian army at Plataea (479 BC). Local warfare was common; the **Peloponnesian Wars** (431-404 BC) ended in Sparta's victory over Athens. Greek political power subsequently waned, but Greek cultural forms spread far and wide.

The Seven Wonders of the Ancient World

These ancient works of art and architecture were considered awe-inspiring by the Greek and Roman world of the first few centuries BC. Later classical writers disagreed as to which works belonged, but the following were usually included:

The Pyramids of Egypt: The only surviving ancient Wonder, these monumental structures of masonry, located at Giza on the W bank of the Nile R above Cairo, were built from c 2700 to 2500 BC as royal tombs. Three—Khufu (Cheops), Khafra (Chephren), and Menkaura (Mycerimus)—were often grouped as the first Wonder of the World. The largest, the Great Pyramid of Khufu, is a solid mass of limestone blocks covering 13 acres. It is estimated to contain 2.3 million blocks of stone, the stones themselves averaging 2½ tons and some weighing 30 tons. Its construction reputedly took 100,000 laborers 20 years.

The Hanging Gardens of Babylon: These gardens were laid out on a brick terrace 400 ft square and 75 ft above the ground. To irrigate the plants, screws were turned to lift water from the Euphrates R. The gardens were probably built by King Nebuchadnezzar II about 600 BC. The Walls of Babylon, long, thick, and made of colorfully glazed brick, were also considered by some among the Seven Wonders.

The Pharos (Lighthouse) of Alexandria: This structure was designed about 270 BC, during the reign of Ptolemy II, by the Greek architect Sostratos. Estimates of its height range from 200 to 600 ft.

The Colossus of Rhodes: A bronze statue of the sun god Helios, the Colossus was worked on for 12 years in the third cent. BC by the sculptor Chares. It was probably 120 ft high. A symbol of the city of Rhodes at its height, the statue stood on a promontory overlooking the harbor.

The Temple of Artemis (Diana) at Ephesus: This largest and most complex temple of ancient times was built about 550 BC and was made of marble except for its tile-covered wooden roof. It was begun in honor of a non-Hellenic goddess who later became identified with the Greek goddess of the same name. Ephesus was one of the greatest of the Ionian cities.

The Mausoleum at Halicarnassus: The source of our word *mausoleum*, this marble tomb was built in what is now SE Turkey by Artemisia for her husband Mausolus, king of Caria in Asia Minor, who died in 353 BC. About 135 ft high, the tomb was adorned with the works of 4 sculptors.

The Statue of Zeus (Jupiter) at Olympia: This statue of the king of the gods showed him seated on a throne. His flesh was made of ivory, his robe and ornaments of gold. Reputedly 40 ft high, the statue was made by Phidias and was placed in the great temple of Zeus in the sacred grove of Olympia about 457 BC.

Hebrews. Nomadic Hebrew tribes entered Canaan before 1200 BC, settling among other Semitic peoples speaking the same language. They brought from the desert a **monotheistic** faith said to have been revealed to Abraham in Canaan c 1800 BC and Moses at Mt. Sinai c 1250 BC, after the Hebrews' escape from bondage in Egypt. David (r 1000-961 BC) and Solomon (r 961-922 BC) united them in a kingdom that briefly dominated the area. **Phoenicians** to the N founded Mediterranean colonies (Carthage, c 814 BC) and sailed into the Atlantic.

A temple in Jerusalem became the national religious center, with sacrifices performed by a hereditary priesthood. Polytheistic influences, especially of the fertility cult of Baal, were opposed by **prophets** (Elijah, Amos, Isaiah).

Divided into **two kingdoms** after Solomon, the Hebrews were unable to resist the revived Assyrian empire, which conquered Israel, the N kingdom, in 722 BC. Judah, the S kingdom, was conquered in 586 BC by the Babylonians under Nebuchadnezzar II. With the fixing of most of the biblical canon by the mid-4th cent. BC and the emergence of rabbis, Judaism successfully survived the loss of Hebrew autonomy. A Jewish kingdom was revived under the Hasmoneans (168-42 BC).

China. During the **Eastern Chou** dynasty (770-256 BC), Chinese culture spread E to the sea and S to the Yangtze R. Large feudal states on the periphery of the empire contended for preeminence, but continued to recognize the Son of Heaven (king), who retained a purely ritual role enriched with courtly music and dance. In the Age of Warring States (403-221 BC), when the first sections of the **Great Wall** were built, the Ch'in state in the W gained supremacy and finally united all of China.

Iron tools entered China c 500 BC, and casting techniques were advanced, aiding agriculture. Peasants owned their land and owed civil and military service to nobles. China's cities grew in number and size; barter remained the chief trade medium.

Intellectual ferment among noble scribes and officials produced the Classical Age of Chinese literature and philosophy. **Confucius** (551-479 BC) urged a restoration of a supposedly harmonious social order of the past through proper conduct in accordance with one's station and through filial and ceremonial piety. The *Analects* attributed to him are revered throughout E Asia.

Among other thinkers of this period, Mencius (d 289 BC) added the view that the Mandate of Heaven can be removed from an unjust dynasty. The Legalists sought to curb the supposed natural wickedness of people through new institutions and harsh laws; they aided the Ch'in rise to power. The Naturalists emphasized the balance of opposites—yin, yang—in the world. **Taoists** sought mystical knowledge through meditation and disengagement.

India. The political and cultural center of India shifted from the Indus to the Ganges River Valley. Buddhism, Jainism, and mystical revisions of orthodox Vedism all developed c 500-300 BC. The *Upanishads,* last part of the *Veda*, urged escape from the physical world. Vedism remained the preserve of the Brahman caste.

In contrast, **Buddhism**, founded by Siddarta Gautama (c 563-c 483 BC)—Buddha ("Enlightened One")—appealed to merchants in the urban centers and took hold at first (and most lastingly) on the geographic fringes of Indian civilization. The classic Indian epics were composed in this era: the **Ramayana** perhaps c 300 BC, the **Mahabharata** over a period starting around 400 BC.

N India was divided into a large number of monarchies and aristocratic republics, probably derived from tribal groupings, when the Magadha kingdom was formed in Bihar c 542 BC. It soon became the dominant power. The **Maurya dynasty**, founded by Chandragupta c 321 BC, expanded the kingdom, uniting most of N India in a centralized bureaucratic empire. The third Mauryan king, **Asoka** (reigned c 274-236 BC), conquered most of the subcontinent. He converted to Buddhism and inscribed its tenets on pillars throughout India. He downplayed the caste system and tried to end expensive sacrificial rites.

Before its final decline in India, Buddhism developed into a popular worship of heavenly Bodhisattvas ("enlightened beings"), and it produced a refined architecture (the Great Stupa [shrine] at Sanchi, AD 100) and sculpture (Gandhara reliefs, AD 1-400).

Persia. Aryan peoples (Persians, Medes) dominated the area of present Iran by the beginning of the 1st millennium BC. The prophet **Zoroaster** (born c 628 BC) introduced a dualistic religion in which the forces of good (Ahura Mazda, "Lord of Wisdom") and evil (Ahriam) battle for dominance; individuals are judged by their actions and earn damnation or salvation. Zoroaster's hymns (*Gathas*) are included in the *Avesta*, the Zoroastrian scriptures. A version of this faith became the established religion of the Persian Empire and probably influenced later monotheistic religions.

Africa. Nubia, periodically occupied by Egypt since about 2600 BC, ruled Egypt c 750-661 BC and survived as an independent Egyptianized kingdom (**Kush;** capital Meroe) for 1,000 years. The Iron Age Nok culture flourished c 500 BC- AD 200 on the Benue Plateau of **Nigeria.**

Americas. The Chavin culture controlled N Peru c 900 BC to 200 BC. Its ceremonial centers, featuring the jaguar god, survived long after. Its architecture, ceramics, and textiles had influenced other Peruvian cultures. **Mayan civilization** began to develop in Central America as early as 1500 BC.

Mayan temple

Great Empires Unite the Civilized World: 400 BC-AD 400

Persia and Alexander the Great. Cyrus, ruler of a small kingdom in Persia from 559 BC, united the Persians and Medes within 10 years and conquered Asia Minor and Babylonia in another 10. His son Cambyses, followed by **Darius** (r 522-486 BC), added vast lands to the E and N as far as the Indus Valley and Central Asia, as well as Egypt and Thrace. The whole empire was ruled by an international bureaucracy and army, with Persians holding the chief positions. The resources and styles of all the subject civilizations were exploited to create a rich syncretic art.

The kingdom of Macedon, which under Philip II dominated the Greek world and Egypt, was passed on to his son **Alexander** in 336 BC. Within 13 years, Alexander had conquered all the Persian dominions. Imbued by his tutor Aristotle with Greek ideals, Alexander encouraged Greek colonization, and Greek-style cities were founded. After his death in 323 BC, wars of succession divided the empire into 3 parts—**Macedon,** Egypt (ruled by the **Ptolemies**), and the **Seleucid** Empire.

In the ensuing 300 years (the **Hellenistic Era**), a cosmopolitan Greek-oriented culture permeated the ancient world from W Europe to the borders of India, absorbing native elites everywhere.

Hellenistic philosophy stressed the private individual's search for happiness. The Cynics followed Diogenes (c 372-287 BC), who stressed self-sufficiency and restriction of desires and expressed contempt for luxury and social convention. Zeno (c 335-c 263 BC) and the **Stoics** exalted reason, identified it with virtue, and counseled an ascetic disregard for misfortune. The **Epicureans** tried to build lives of moderate pleasure without political or emotional involvement. Hellenistic arts imitated life realistically, especially in sculpture and literature (comedies of Menander, 342-292 BC).

The sciences thrived, especially at Alexandria, where the Ptolemies financed a great library and museum. Fields of study included mathematics (**Euclid's** geometry, c 300 BC); astronomy (heliocentric theory of Aristarchus, 310-230 BC; Julian calendar, 45 BC; **Ptolemy**'s *Almagest*, c AD 150); geography (world map of Eratosthenes, 276-194 BC); hydraulics (**Archimedes,** 287-212 BC); medicine (Galen, AD 130-200); and chemistry. Inventors refined uses for siphons, valves, gears, springs, screws, levers, cams, and pulleys.

A restored Persian empire under the **Parthians** (northern Iranian tribesmen) controlled the eastern Hellenistic world from 250 BC to AD 229. The Parthians and the succeeding Sassanian dynasty (c AD 224-651) fought with Rome periodically. The **Sassanians** revived Zoroastrianism as a state religion and patronized a nationalistic artistic and scholarly renaissance.

Rome. The city of Rome was founded, according to legend, by Romulus in 753 BC. Through military expansion and colonization, and by granting citizenship to conquered tribes, the city annexed all of Italy S of the Po in the 100-year period before 268 BC. The Latin and other Italic tribes were annexed first, followed by the **Etruscans** (founders of a great civilization, N of Rome) and the Greek colonies in the S. With a large standing army and reserve forces of several hundred thousand, Rome was able to defeat **Carthage** in the 3 **Punic Wars** (264-241, 218-201, 149-146 BC), despite the invasion of Italy (218 BC) by **Hannibal,** thus gaining Sicily and territory in Spain and N Africa.

Julius Caesar

Rome exploited local disputes to conquer Greece and Asia Minor in the 2nd cent. BC, and Egypt in the 1st (after the defeat and suicide of **Antony and Cleopatra**, 30 BC). All the Mediterranean civilized world up to the disputed Parthian border was now Roman and remained so for 500 years. Less civilized regions were added to the Empire: Gaul (conquered by **Julius Caesar**, 58-51 BC), Britain (AD 43), and Dacia NE of the Danube (AD 107).

The original aristocratic republican government, with democratic features added in the 5th and 4th cent. BC, deteriorated under the pressures of empire and class conflict (**Gracchus** brothers, social reformers, murdered in 133 BC and 121 BC; slave revolts in 135 BC and 73 BC). After a series of civil wars (Marius vs. Sulla 88-82 BC, Caesar vs. **Pompey** 49-45 BC, triumvirate vs. Caesar's assassins 44-43 BC, Antony vs. Octavian 32-30 BC), the empire came under the rule of a deified monarch (first emperor, **Augustus**, 27 BC-AD 14).

Provincials (nearly all granted citizenship by Caracalla, AD 212) came to dominate the army and civil service. Traditional **Roman law,** systematized and interpreted by independent jurists, and local self-rule in provincial cities were supplanted by a vast tax-collecting bureaucracy in the 3rd and 4th cent. The legal rights of women, children, and slaves were strengthened.

Roman innovations in **civil engineering** included water mills, windmills, and rotary mills and use of cement that hardened under water. Monumental architecture (baths, theaters, temples) relied on the arch and the dome. The network of roads (some still standing) stretched 53,000 mi, passing through mountain tunnels as long as 3.5 mi. Aqueducts brought water to cities; underground sewers removed waste.

Roman art and literature were to a large extent derivative of Greek models. Innovations were made in sculpture (naturalistic busts, equestrian statues), decorative wall painting (as at Pompeii), satire (**Juvenal,** AD 60-127), history (**Tacitus,** AD 56-120), prose romance (Petronius, d AD 66). Gladiatorial contests dominated public amusements, which were supported by the state.

India. The **Gupta** monarchs reunited N India c AD 320. Their peaceful and prosperous reign saw a revival of Hindu religious thought and Brahman power. The old Vedic traditions were combined with devotion to many indigenous deities (who were seen as manifestations of Vedic gods). **Caste lines** were reinforced, and Buddhism gradually disappeared. The art (often erotic), architecture, and literature of the period, patronized by the Gupta court, are considered among India's finest achievements (Kalidasa, poet and dramatist, fl. c AD 400). Mathematical innovations included use of the zero and decimal numbers. Invasions by White Huns from the NW destroyed the empire c 550.

Rich cultures also developed in S India during this period. Emotional Tamil religious poetry contributed to the Hindu revival. The Pallava kingdom controlled much of S India c 350-880 and helped to spread Indian civilization to SE Asia.

China. The Ch'in ruler Shih Huang Ti (r 221-210 BC), known as the First Emperor, centralized political authority. standardized the written language, laws, weights, measures, and coinage, and conducted a census, but tried to destroy most philosophical texts. The **Han dynasty** (202 BC-AD 220) instituted the Mandarin bureaucracy, which lasted 2,000 years. Local officials were selected by examination in Confucian classics and trained at the imperial university and provincial schools.

The invention of **paper** facilitated this bureaucratic system. Agriculture was promoted, but peasants bore most of the tax burden. Irrigation was improved, water clocks and sundials were used, astronomy and mathematics thrived, and landscape painting was perfected.

With the expansion S and W (to nearly the present borders of today's China), trade was opened with India, SE Asia, and the Middle East, over sea and caravan routes. Indian missionaries brought Mahayana Buddhism to China by the 1st cent. AD and spawned a variety of sects. Taoism was revived and merged with popular superstitions. Taoist and Buddhist monasteries and convents multiplied in the turbulent centuries after the collapse of the Han dynasty.

Monotheism Spreads: AD 1-750

Roman Empire. Polytheism was practiced in the Roman Empire, and religions indigenous to particular Middle Eastern nations became international. Roman citizens worshiped **Isis** of Egypt, **Mithras** of Persia, **Demeter** of Greece, and the great mother **Cybele** of Phrygia. Their cults centered on mysteries (secret ceremonies) and the promise of an afterlife, symbolized by the death and rebirth of the god. The Jews of the empire preserved their monotheistic religion, Judaism, the world's oldest (c 1300 BC) continuous religion. Its teachings are contained in the Bible (the Old Testament). First-cent. Judaism embraced several sects, including the **Sadducees**, mostly drawn from the Temple priesthood, who were culturally Hellenized; the **Pharisees**, who upheld the full range of traditional customs and practices as of equal weight to literal scriptural law and elaborated synagogue worship; and the **Essenes**, an ascetic, millennarian sect. Messianic fervor led to repeated, unsuccessful rebellions against Rome (66-70, 135). As a result, the Temple in Jerusalem was destroyed and the population decimated; this event marked the beginning of the Diaspora (living in exile). To preserve the faith, a program of codification of law was begun at the academy of Yavneh. The work continued for some 500 years in Palestine and in Babylonia, ending in the final redaction (c 600) of the **Talmud**, a huge collection of legal and moral debates, rulings, liturgy, biblical exegesis, and legendary materials.

Christianity, which emerged as a distinct sect by the 2nd half of the 1st cent., is based on the teachings of **Jesus**, whom believers considered the Savior (Messiah or Christ) and son of God. Missionary activities of the Apostles and such early leaders as **Paul of Tarsus** spread the faith. Intermittent persecution, as in Rome under Nero in AD 64, on grounds of suspected disloyalty, failed to disrupt the Christian communities. Each congregation, generally urban and of plebeian character, was tightly organized under a leader (bishop), elders (presbyters or priests), and assistants (deacons). The four **Gospels** (accounts of the life and teachings of Jesus) and the Acts of the Apostles were written down in the late 1st and early 2nd cent. and circulated along with letters of Paul and other Christian leaders. An authoritative canon of these writings was not fixed until the 4th cent.

A school for priests was established at Alexandria in the 2nd cent. Its teachers (**Origen** c 182-251) helped define doctrine and promote the faith in Greek-style philosophical works. Neoplatonism underwent Christian coloration in the writings of Church Fathers such as **Augustine** (354-430). Christian hermits began to associate in monasteries, first in Egypt (St. Pachomius c 290-345), then in other eastern lands, then in the W (**St. Benedict's rule**, 529). Devotion to saints, especially Mary, mother of Jesus, spread. Under **Constantine** (r 306-37), Christianity became in effect the established religion of the Empire. Pagan temples were expropriated, state funds were used to build churches and support the hierarchy, and laws were adjusted in accordance with Christian ideas. Pagan worship was banned by the end of the 4th cent., and severe restrictions were placed on Judaism.

The newly established church was rocked by doctrinal disputes, often exacerbated by regional rivalries. Chief heresies (as defined by church councils, backed by imperial authority) were **Arianism**, which denied the divinity of Jesus; **Monophysitism,** denying the human nature of Christ; **Donatism**, which regarded as invalid any sacraments administered by sinful clergy; and **Pelagianism,** which denied the necessity of unmerited divine aid (grace) for salvation.

Islam. The earliest Arab civilization emerged by the end of the 2nd millennium BC in the watered highlands of Yemen. Seaborne and caravan trade in frankincense and myrrh connected the area with the Nile and Fertile Crescent. The Minaean, Sabean (Sheba), and Himyarite states successively held sway. By Muhammad's time (7th cent. AD), the region was a province of Sassanian Persia. In the N, the Nabataean kingdom at Petra and the kingdom of Palmyra were Aramaicized, Romanized, and finally absorbed, as neighboring Judea had been, into the Roman Empire. Nomads shared the central region with a few trading towns and oases. Wars between tribes and raids on communities were common and were celebrated in a poetic tradition that by the 6th cent. helped establish a classic literary Arabic.

About 610, **Muhammad**, a 40-year-old Arab of Mecca, emerged as a prophet. He proclaimed a revelation from the one true God, calling on contemporaries to abandon idolatry and restore the faith of Abraham. He introduced his religion as "Islam," meaning "submission" to the one God, Allah, as a continuation of the biblical faith of Abraham, Moses, and Jesus, all respected as prophets in this system. His teachings, recorded in the **Koran** (al-Qur'an in Arabic), in many ways were inclusive of Abrahamic monotheistic ideas known to the Jews and Christians in Arabia. A key aspect of the Abrahamic connection was insistence on justice in society, which led to severe opposition among the aristocrats in Mecca. As conditions worsened for Muhammad and his followers, he decided in 622 to make a ***hijra*** (emigration) to Medina, 200 mi to the N. This event marks the beginning of the Muslim lunar calendar. Hostilities between Mecca and Medina increased, and in 629 Muhammad conquered Mecca. By the time her died in 632, nearly all the Arabian peninsula accepted his political and religious leadership.

After his death the majority of Muslims recognized the leadership of the **caliph** ("successor") Abu Bakr (632-34), followed by Umar (634-44), Uthman (644-56), and Ali (656-60). A minority, the **Shiites**, insisted instead on the leadership of Ali, Muhammad's cousin and son-in-law. By 644, **Muslim rule** over Arabia was confirmed. Muslim armies had threatened the Byzantine and Persian empires, which were weakened by wars and disaffection among subject peoples (including Coptic and Syriac Christians opposed to the Byzantine Orthodox establishment). Syria,

Major Gods & Goddesses of the Classical World

Greek	Roman	Relations	Sphere or Position
Aphrodite	Venus	Daughter of Zeus & Dione	Love
Apollo	——	Son of Zeus & Leto	Healing, poetry, light
Ares	Mars	Son of Zeus & Hera	War
Artemis	Diana	Daughter of Zeus & Leto	Hunting, chastity
Athena	Minerva	Daughter of Zeus & Metis	Wisdom, crafts, war
Cronus	Saturn	Father of Zeus	Titans' ruler
Demeter	Ceres	Sister of Zeus	Agriculture, fertility
Dionysus	Bacchus	Son of Zeus & Semele	Wine, fertility, ecstasy
Eros	Cupid	Son of Ares & Aphrodite	Love
Hades	Pluto	Brother of Zeus	The underworld, death
Hephaestus	Vulcan	Son of Zeus & Hera	Fire
Hera	Juno	Wife & sister of Zeus	Earth
Hermes	Mercury	Son of Zeus & Maia	Travel, commerce, gods' messenger
Hestia	Vesta	Sister of Zeus	The hearth
Pan	——	Son of Hermes & a wood nymph	Forests, flocks, shepherds
Persephone	Proserpina	Daughter of Zeus & Demeter	Grain
Poseidon	Neptune	Brother of Zeus	The sea
Rhea	Ops	Mother of Zeus	The earth
Uranus	Uranus	Father of Titans (elder gods)	The heavens
Zeus	Jupiter	Son of Cronus & Rhea	Ruler of the gods

Palestine, Egypt, Iraq, and Persia fell to Muslim armies. The new administration assimilated existing systems in the region; hence the conquered peoples participated in running of the empire. The Koran recognized the so-called Peoples of the Book, i.e., Christians, Jews, and Zoroastrians, as tolerated monotheists, and Muslim policy was relatively tolerant to minorities living as "protected" peoples. An expanded tax system, based on conquests of the Persian and Byzantine empires, provided revenue to organize campaigns against neighboring non-Muslim regions.

Disputes over succession, and pious opposition to injustices in society, led to a number of oppositional movements, which also led to the factionalization of Muslim community. The **Shiites** supported leadership candidates descended from Muhammad, believing them to be carriers of some kind of divine authority. The **Kharijites** supported an egalitarian system derived from the Koran, opposing and even engaging in battle against those who did not agree with them.

Under the **Umayyads** (661-750) and **Abbasids** (750-1256), territorial expansion led Muslim armies across N Africa and into Spain (711). Muslim armies in the W were stopped at Tours (France) in 732 by the Frankish ruler **Charles Martel**. Asia Minor, the Indus Valley, and Transoxiana were conquered in the E. The conversion of conquered peoples to Islam was gradual. In many places the official Arabic language supplanted the local tongues. But in the eastern regions the Arab rulers and their armies adopted Persian cultures and language as part of their Muslim identity.

Major Norse Gods & Goddesses

Name	Relations	Sphere or Position	Emblem/Attribute
Odin	Father of the Aesir (gods)	War and death, poetry, wisdom, magic	Spear, mead, ring/One-eyed
Thor	Son of Odin	Thunder, lightning, rain; champion of the gods	Hammer, belt
Njord	Father of Freyja & Freyr	Wind and sea, wealth and prosperity	----
Frigg	Wife of Odin	Marriage and motherhood, home	----
Freyja (Freya)	Daughter of Njord	Fertility, birth, crops	Necklace
Freyr	Son of Njord	Agriculture, sun, rain	Magic ship, golden boar
Tyr	Son of Odin ?	Justice, war	Spear/One-handed
Heimdall	Son of nine giantesses	Watchman of the gods; keen sight & hearing	Horn
Balder (Baldur)	Son of Odin	Light, purity	----
Loki	Son of giants; father of Hel (goddess of death), Jormungand (serpent encompassing the world), Fenrir (the wolf).	Malicious trickster	----

New Peoples Enter World History: 400-900

Barbarian invasions. Germanic tribes infiltrated S and E from their Baltic homeland during the 1st millennium BC, reaching S Germany by 100 BC and the Black Sea by AD 214. Organized into large federated tribes under elected kings, most resisted Roman domination and raided the empire in time of civil war (Goths took Dacia in 214, raided Thrace in 251-69). Germanic troops and commanders dominated the Roman armies by the end of the 4th cent. **Huns**, invaders from Asia, entered Europe in 372, driving more Germans into the W empire. Emperor Valens allowed Visigoths to cross the Danube in 376. Huns under Attila (d 453) raided Gaul, Italy, and the Balkans.

The W empire, weakened by overtaxation and social stagnation, was overrun in the 5th cent. Gaul was effectively lost in 406-7, Spain in 409, Britain in 410, Africa in 429-39. Rome was sacked in 410 by Visigoths under Alaric and in 455 by Vandals. The last western emperor, Romulus Augustulus, was deposed in 476 by the Germanic chief Odovacar.

Celts. Celtic cultures, which in pre-Roman times covered most of W Europe, were confined almost entirely to the British Isles after the Germanic invasions. **St. Patrick** completed (c 457-92) the conversion of Ireland. A strong monastic tradition took hold. Irish monastic missionaries in Scotland, England, and the continent (Columba c 521-97; Columban c 543-615) helped restore Christianity after the Germanic invasions. Monasteries became centers of classic and Christian learning and presided over the recording of a Christianized Celtic mythology, elaborated by secular writers and bards. An intricate decorative art style developed, especially in book illumination (Lindisfarne Gospels, c 700; Book of Kells, 8th cent.).

Successor states. The Visigothic kingdom in Spain (from 419) and much of France (to 507) saw continuation of Roman administration, language, and law (Breviary of Alaric, 506) until its destruction by the Muslims (711). The Vandal kingdom in Africa (from 429) was conquered by the Byzantines in 533. Italy was ruled successively by an Ostrogothic kingdom under Byzantine suzerainty (489-554), direct Byzantine government, and German Lombards (568-774). The Lombards divided the peninsula with the Byzantines and papacy under the dynamic reformer **Pope Gregory the Great** (590-604) and successors.

King Clovis (r 481-511) united the Franks on both sides of the Rhine and, after his conversion to Christianity, defeated the Arian heretics, Burgundians (after 500), and Visigoths (507) with the support of native clergy and the papacy. Under the **Merovingian** kings, a feudal system emerged: Power was fragmented among hierarchies of military landowners. Social stratification, which in late Roman times had acquired legal, hereditary sanction, was reinforced. The Carolingians (747-987) expanded the kingdom and restored central power. **Charlemagne** (r 768-814) conquered nearly all the Germanic lands, including Lombard Italy, and was crowned Emperor by Pope Leo III in Rome in 800. A centuries-long decline in commerce and arts was reversed under Charlemagne's patronage. He welcomed Jews to his kingdom, which became a center of Jewish learning (Rashi, 1040-1105). He sponsored the Carolingian Renaissance of learning under the Anglo-Latin scholar Alcuin (c 732-804), who reformed church liturgy.

Byzantine Empire. Under **Diocletian** (r 284-305) the empire had been divided into 2 parts to facilitate administration and defense. **Constantine** founded (330) **Constantinople** (at old Byzantium) as a fully Christian city. Commerce and taxation financed a sumptuous, orientalized court, a class of hereditary bureaucratic families, and magnificent urban construction (Hagia Sophia, 532-37). The city's fortifications and naval innovations repelled assaults by Goths, Huns, Slavs, Bulgars, Avars, Arabs, and Scandinavians. Greek replaced Latin as the official language by c 700. Byzantine art, a solemn, sacral, and stylized variation of late classical styles (mosaics at the Church of San Vitale, Ravenna, Italy 526-48), was a starting point for medieval art in E and W Europe.

Justinian (r 527-65) reconquered parts of Spain, N Africa, and Italy, codified Roman law (Codex Justinianus [529] was medieval Europe's chief legal text), closed the Platonic Academy at Athens, and ordered all pagans to convert. Lombards in Italy and Arabs in Africa retook most of his conquests. The Isaurian dynasty from Anatolia (from 717) and the Macedonian dynasty (867-1054) restored military and commercial power. The Iconoclast controversy (726-843) over the permissibility of images helped alienate the Eastern Church from the papacy.

Abbasid Empire. Baghdad (est. 762), became seat of the **Abbasid dynasty** (est 750), while Ummayads continued to rule in Spain. A brilliant cosmopolitan civilization emerged, inaugurating a Muslim-Arab golden age. Arabic was the lingua franca of the empire; intellectual sources from Persian, Sanskrit, Greek, and Syriac were rendered into Arabic.

Christians and Jews equally participated in this translation movement, which also involved interaction between Jewish legal thought and Islamic law, as much as between Christian theology and Muslim scholasticism. Persian-style court life, with art and music, flourished at the court of **Harun al-Rashid** (786-809), celebrated in the masterpiece known to English readers as *The Arabian Nights*. The sciences, medicine, and mathematics were pursued at Baghdad, Cordova, and Cairo (est. 969). The culmination of this intellectual synthesis in Islamic civilization came with the scientific and philosophical works of **Avicenna** (Ibn Sina, 980-1037), **Averroes** (Ibn Rushd, 1126-98), and **Maimonides** (1135-1204), a Jew who wrote in Arabic. This intellectual tradition was translated into Latin and opened a new period in Christian thought.

The decentralization of the Abbasid empire, from 874, led to establishment of various Muslim dynasties under different ethnic groups. Persians, Berbers, and Turks ruled different regions, retaining connection with the Abbasid caliph at the religious level. The Abbasid period also saw various religious movements against the orthodox position held by governing authorities. This situation in religion led to establishment of different legal, theological, and mystical schools of thought. The most influential mass movement was **Sufism**, which aimed at the reaching out of the average individual in quest of a spiritual path. Al-Ghazali (1058-1111) is credited with reconciling personal Sufism with orthodox Sunni tradition.

Africa. Immigrants from Saba in S Arabia helped set up the **Axum** kingdom in Ethiopia in the 1st cent. (their language, Ge'ez, is preserved by the Ethiopian Church). In the 3rd cent., when the kingdom became Christianized, it defeated Kushite Meroe and expanded its influence into Yemen. Axum was the center of a vast ivory trade and controlled the Red Sea coast until c 1100. Arab conquest in Egypt cut Axum's political and economic ties with Byzantium.

The Iron Age entered W Africa by the end of the 1st millennium BC. **Ghana**, the first known sub-Saharan state, ruled in the upper Senegal-Niger region c 400-1240, controlling the trade of gold from mines in the S to trans-Sahara caravan routes to the N. The **Bantu** peoples, probably of W African origin, began to spread E and S perhaps 2,000 years ago, displacing the Pygmies and Bushmen of central and S Africa during a 1,500-year period.

Japan. The advanced Neolithic Yayoi period, when irrigation, rice farming, and iron and bronze casting techniques were introduced from China or Korea, persisted to c AD 400. The myriad Japanese states were then united by the **Yamato** clan, under an emperor who acted as chief priest of the animistic Shinto cult. Japanese political and military intervention by the 6th cent. in Korea, then under strong Chinese influence, quickened a Chinese cultural invasion of Japan, bringing Buddhism, the Chinese language (which long remained a literary and governmental medium), Chinese ideographs, and Buddhist styles in painting, sculpture, literature, and architecture (7th cent., Horyu-ji temple at Nara). The Taika Reforms (646) tried unsuccessfully to centralize Japan according to Chinese bureaucratic and Buddhist philosophical values.

A nativist reaction against the Buddhist **Nara period** (710-94) ushered in the **Heian period** (794-1185) centered at the new capital, Kyoto. Japanese elegance and simplicity modified Chinese styles in architecture, scroll painting, and literature; the writing system was also simplified. The courtly novel *Tale of Genji* (1010-20) testifies to the enhanced role of women.

Southeast Asia. The historic peoples of SE Asia began arriving some 2,500 years ago from China and Tibet, displacing scattered aborigines. Their agriculture relied on rice and yams. Indian cultural influences were strongest; literacy and Hindu and Buddhist ideas followed the S India-China trade route. From the S tip of Indochina, the kingdom of **Funan** (1st-7th cent.) traded as far W as Persia. It was absorbed by Chenla, itself conquered by the **Khmer Empire** (600-1300). The Khmers, under Hindu god-kings (Suryavarman II, 1113-c 1150), built the monumental Angkor Wat temple center for the royal phallic cult. The **Nam-Viet** kingdom in Annam, dominated by China and Chinese culture for 1,000 years, emerged in the 10th cent., growing at the expense of the Khmers, who also lost ground in the NW to the new, highly organized **Thai** kingdom. On Sumatra, the **Srivijaya** Empire controlled vital sea lanes (7th to 10th cent.). A Buddhist dynasty, the Sailendras, ruled central **Java** (8th-9th cent.), building at Borobudur one of the largest stupas in the world.

China. The Sui dynasty (581-618) ushered in a period of commercial, artistic, and scientific achievement in China, continuing under the **Tang** dynasty (618-906). Inventions like the magnetic compass, gunpowder, the abacus, and printing were introduced or perfected. Medical innovations included cataract surgery. The state, from its cosmopolitan capital, Chang-an, supervised foreign trade, which exchanged Chinese silks, porcelains, and art for spices, ivory, etc., over Central Asian caravan routes and sea routes reaching Africa. A golden age of poetry bequeathed valuable works to later generations (Tu Fu, 712-70; Li Po, 701-62). Landscape painting flourished. Commercial and industrial expansion continued under the **Northern Sung** dynasty (960-1126), facilitated by paper money and credit notes. But commerce never achieved respectability; government monopolies expropriated successful merchants. The population, long stable at 50 million, doubled in 200 years with the introduction of early-ripening rice and the double harvest. In art, native Chinese styles were revived.

Americas. From 300 to 600 a Native American empire stretched from the Valley of Mexico to Guatemala, centering on the huge city **Teotihuacán** (founded 100 BC). To the S, in Guatemala, a high **Mayan** civilization developed (150-900) around hundreds of rural ceremonial centers. The Mayans improved on Olmec writing and the calendar and pursued astronomy and mathematics. In South America, a widespread pre-Inca culture grew from **Tiahuanacu**, Bolivia, near Lake Titicaca (Gateway of the Sun, c 700).

Christian Europe Regroups and Expands: 900-1300

Scandinavians. Pagan Danish and Norse (Viking) adventurers, traders, and pirates raided the coasts of the British Isles (Dublin, est. c 831), France, and even the Mediterranean for over 200 years beginning in the late 8th cent. Inland settlement in the W was limited to Great Britain (King Canute, 994-1035) and Normandy, settled (911) under Rollo, as a fief of France. Vikings also reached Iceland (874), Greenland (c 986), and North America (**Leif Ericson** and others, c 1000). Norse traders (**Varangians**) developed Russian river commerce from the 8th to the 11th cent. and helped set up a state at Kiev in the late 9th cent. Conversion to Christianity occurred in the 10th cent., reaching Sweden 100 years later. In the 11th cent. Norman bands conquered S Italy and Sicily, and Duke **William of Normandy** conquered (1066) England, bringing feudalism and the French language, essential elements in later English civilization.

WORLD ALMANAC QUICK QUIZ

Can you put these developments in chronological order?

(a) Scientists discovered moving sunspots, analytic geometry, and circulation of the blood;
(b) Work began on the Panama Canal;
(c) Wigs, hoops, and ruffles passed out of fashion;
(d) Impressionists began painting the world in a new light

For the answer look in this chapter, or see page 1008.

Central and East Europe. Slavs began to expand from about AD 150 in all directions in Europe, and by the 7th cent. they reached as far S as the Adriatic and Aegean seas. In the Balkan Peninsula they dislocated Romanized local populations or assimilated newcomers (Bulgarians, a Turkic people). The first Slavic states were Moravia (628) in Central Europe and the Bulgarian state (680) in the Balkans. Missions of St. Methodius and Cyril (whose Greek-based cyrillic alphabet is still used by some S and E Slavs) converted (863) Moravia.

The Eastern Slavs, part-civilized under the overlordship of the Turkish-Jewish **Khazar** trading empire (7th-10th cent.), gravitated toward Constantinople by the 9th cent. The **Kievan state** adopted (989) Eastern Christianity under Prince Vladimir. King Boleslav I (992-1025) began **Poland's** long history of eastern conquest. The Magyars (**Hungarians**), in present-day Hungary since 896, accepted (1001) Latin Christianity.

Germany. The German kingdom that emerged after the breakup of Charlemagne's W Empire remained a confederation of largely autonomous states. Otto I, a Saxon who was king from 936, established the **Holy Roman Empire**—a union of Germany and N Italy—in alliance with Pope John XII, who crowned (962) him emperor; he defeated (955) the Magyars. Imperial power was greatest under the **Hohenstaufens** (1138-1254), despite the growing opposition of the papacy, which ruled central Italy, and the Lombard League cities. Frederick II (1194-1250) improved administration and patronized the arts; after his death, German influence was removed from Italy.

Christian Spain. From its N mountain redoubts, Christian rule slowly migrated S through the 11th cent., when Muslim unity collapsed. After the capture (1085) of **Toledo**, the kingdoms of Portugal, Castile, and Aragon undertook repeated crusades of reconquest, finally completed in 1492. Elements of Islamic civilization persisted in recaptured areas, influencing all Western Europe.

Crusades. Pope Urban II called (1095) for a crusade to restore Asia Minor to Byzantium and to regain the Holy Land from the Turks. Some ten crusades (lasting until 1291) succeeded only in founding four temporary Frankish states in the Levant. The 4th crusade sacked (1204) Constantinople. In Rhineland (1096), England (1290), and France (1306), Jews were massacred or expelled, and wars were launched against Christian heretics (**Albigensian** crusade in France, 1229). Trade in eastern luxuries expanded, led by the Venetian naval empire.

Economy. The agricultural base of European life benefited from improvements in **plow design** (c 1000) and by draining of lowlands and clearing of forests, leading to a rural population increase. Towns grew in N Italy, Flanders, and N Germany (Hanseatic League). Improvements in **loom design** permitted factory textile production. **Guilds** dominated urban trades from the 12th cent. Banking (centered in Italy, 12th-15th cent.) facilitated long-distance trade.

The Church. The split between the Eastern and Western churches was formalized in 1054. Western and Central Europe was divided into 500 bishoprics under one united hierarchy, but conflicts between secular and church authorities were frequent (German **Investiture Controversy**, 1075-1122). Clerical power was first strengthened through the international monastic reform begun at Cluny in 910. Popular religious enthusiasm often expressed itself in heretical movements (Waldensians from 1173), but was channeled by the **Dominican** (1215) and **Franciscan** (1223) friars into the religious mainstream.

Chartres Cathedral

Arts. Romanesque architecture (11th-12th cent.) expanded on late Roman models, using the rounded arch and massed stone to support enlarged basilicas. Painting and sculpture followed Byzantine models. The literature of **chivalry** was exemplified by the epic (*Chanson de Roland*, c 1100) and by courtly love poems of the troubadours of Provence and minnesingers of Germany. **Gothic** architecture emerged in France (choir of St. Denis, c 1040) and spread along with French cultural influence. Rib vaulting and pointed arches were used to combine soaring heights with delicacy, and they freed walls for display of stained glass. Exteriors were covered with painted relief sculpture and embellished with elaborate architectural detail.

Learning. Law, medicine, and philosophy were advanced at independent **universities** (Bologna, late 11th cent.), originally corporations of students and masters. Twelfth-cent. translations of Greek classics, especially Aristotle, encouraged an analytic approach. Scholastic philosophy, from Anselm (1033-1109) to **Aquinas** (1225-74), attempted to understand revelation through reason.

Apogee of Central Asian Power; Islam Grows: 1250-1500

Turks. Turkic peoples, of Central Asian ancestry, were a military threat to the Byzantine and Persian Empires from the 6th cent. After several waves of invasions, during which most of the Turks adopted Islam, the **Seljuk Turks** took (1055) Baghdad. They ruled Persia, Iraq and, after 1071, Asia Minor, where massive numbers of Turks settled. The empire was divided in the 12th cent. into smaller states ruled by Seljuks, Kurds (**Saladin,** c 1137-93), and Mamluks (a military caste of former Turk, Kurd, and Circassian slaves), which governed Egypt and the Middle East until the Ottoman era (c 1290-1922).

Osman I (r c 1290-1326) and succeeding sultans united Anatolian Turkish warriors in a militaristic state that waged holy war against Byzantium and Balkan Christians. Most of the Balkans had been subdued, and Anatolia united, when Constantinople fell (1453). By the mid-16th cent., Hungary, the Middle East, and N Africa had been conquered. The Turkish advance was stopped at Vienna (1529) and at the naval battle of Lepanto (1571) by Spain, Venice, and the papacy.

The Ottoman state was governed in accordance with orthodox Muslim law. Greek, Armenian, and Jewish communities were segregated and were ruled by religious leaders responsible for taxation; they dominated trade. State offices and most army ranks were filled by slaves through a system of child conscription among Christians.

India. Mahmud of Ghazni (971-1030) led repeated Turkish raids into N India. Turkish power was consolidated in 1206 with the start of the **Sultanate at Delhi**. Centralization of state power under the early Delhi sultans went far beyond traditional Indian practice. Muslim rule of most of the subcontinent lasted until the British conquest 600 years later.

Mongols. Genghis Khan (c 1167-1227) first united the feuding Mongol tribes, and built their armies into an effective offensive force around a core of highly mobile cavalry. He and his immediate successors created the largest land empire in history; by 1279 it stretched from the E coast of Asia to the Danube, from the Siberian steppes to the Arabian Sea. East-West trade and contacts were facilitated (Marco Polo, c 1254-1324). The W Mongols were Islamized by 1295; successor states soon lost their Mongol character by assimilation. They were briefly reunited under the Turk Tamerlane (1336-1405).

Kublai Khan ruled China from his new capital Beijing (est. c 1264). Naval campaigns against Japan (1274, 1281) and Java (1293) were defeated, the latter by the Hindu-Buddhist maritime kingdom of Majapahit. The **Yuan** dynasty used Mongols and other foreigners (including Europeans) in official posts and tolerated the return of Nestorian Christianity (suppressed 841-45) and the spread of Islam in the S and W. A native reaction expelled the Mongols in 1367-68.

Russia. The Kievan state in Russia, weakened by the decline of Byzantium and the rise of the Catholic Polish-Lithuanian state, was overrun (1238-40) by the Mongols. Only the northern trading republic of Novgorod remained independent. The grand dukes of Moscow emerged as leaders of a coalition of princes that eventually (by 1481) defeated the Mongols. After the fall of Constantinople in 1453, the **Tsars** (Caesars) at Moscow (from Ivan III, r 1462-1505) set up an independent Russian Orthodox Church. Commerce failed to revive. The isolated Russian state remained agrarian, with the peasant class falling into serfdom.

Persia. A revival of Persian literature, making use of the Arab alphabet and literary forms, began in the 10th cent. (epic of Firdausi, 935-1020). An art revival, influenced by Chinese styles introduced after the Mongols came to power in Iran, began in the 13th cent. Persian cultural and political forms, and often the Persian language, were used for centuries by Turkish and Mongol elites from the Balkans to India. Persian mystics from Rumi (1207-73) to Jami (1414-92) promoted **Sufism** in their poetry.

Africa. Two militant Islamic Berber dynasties emerged from the Sahara to carve out empires from the Sahel to central Spain—the **Almoravids** (c 1050-1140) and the fanatical **Almohads** (c 1125-1269). The Ghanaian empire was replaced in the upper Niger by Mali (c 1230-1340), whose Muslim rulers imported Egyptians to help make **Timbuktu** a center of commerce (in gold, leather, and slaves) and learning. The Songhay empire (to 1590) replaced Mali. To the S, forest kingdoms produced refined artworks (Ife terra cotta, **Benin** bronzes). Other Muslim states in Nigeria (Hausas) and Chad originated in the 11th cent. and continued in some form until the 19th-cent. European conquest. Less-developed Bantu kingdoms existed across central Africa.

Some 40 Muslim Arab-Persian trading colonies and city-states were established all along the E African coast from the 10th cent. (Kilwa, Mogadishu). The interchange with Bantu peoples produced the **Swahili** language and culture. Gold, palm oil, and slaves were brought from the interior, stimulating the growth of the Monamatapa kingdom of the Zambezi (15th cent.). The Christian Ethiopian empire (from 13th cent.) continued the traditions of Axum.

Southeast Asia. Islam was introduced into Malaya and the Indonesian islands by Arab, Persian, and Indian traders. Coastal Muslim cities and states (starting before 1300) soon dominated the interior. Chief among these was the **Malacca** state (c 1400-1511), on the Malay peninsula.

Arts and Statecraft Thrive in Europe: 1350-1600

Italian Renaissance and Humanism. Distinctive Italian achievements in the arts in the late Middle Ages (**Dante,** 1265-1321; Giotto, 1276-1337) led to the vigorous new styles of the Renaissance (14th-16th cent.). Patronized by the rulers of the quarreling petty states of Italy (**Medicis** in Florence and the papacy, c 1400-1737), the plastic arts perfected realistic techniques, including **perspective** (Masaccio, 1401-28, **Leonardo,** 1452-1519). Classical motifs were used in architecture, and increased talent and expense were put into secular buildings. The Florentine dialect was refined as a national literary language (**Petrarch,** 1304-74). Greek refugees from the E strengthened the respect of humanist scholars for the classic sources. Soon an international movement aided by the spread of **printing** (Gutenberg, c 1397(?)-1468), **humanism** was optimistic about the power of human reason (Erasmus of Rotterdam, 1466-1536, **More's** *Utopia,* 1516) and valued individual effort in the arts and in politics (**Machiavelli,** 1469-1527).

France. The French monarchy, strengthened in its repeated struggles with powerful nobles (Burgundy, Flanders, Aquitaine) by alliances with the growing commercial towns, consolidated bureaucratic control under Philip IV (r 1285-1314) and extended French influence into Germany and Italy (popes at Avignon, France, 1309-1417). The **Hundred Years War** (1337-1453) ended English dynastic claims in France (battles of Crécy, 1346, and Poitiers, 1356; Joan of Arc executed, 1431). A French Renaissance, dating from royal invasions (1494, 1499) of Italy, was encouraged at the court of Francis I (r 1515-47), who centralized taxation and law. French vernacular literature consciously asserted its independence (La Pléiade, 1549).

England. The evolution of England's unique political institutions began with the **Magna Carta** (1215), by which King John guaranteed the privileges of nobles and church against the monarchy and assured jury trial. After the **Wars of the Roses** (1455-85), the **Tudor dynasty** reasserted royal prerogatives (Henry VIII, r 1509-47), but the trend toward independent departments and ministerial government also continued. English trade (wool exports from c 1340) was protected by the nation's growing maritime power (**Spanish Armada** destroyed, 1588).

English replaced French and Latin in the late 14th cent. in law and literature (**Chaucer,** c 1340-1400) and English translation of the Bible began (Wycliffe, 1380s). **Elizabeth I** (r 1558-1603) presided over a confident flowering of poetry (Spenser, 1552-99), drama (**Shakespeare**, 1564-1616), and music.

German Empire. From among a welter of minor feudal states, church lands, and independent cities, the **Habsburgs** assembled a far-flung territorial domain, based in Austria from 1276. Family members held the title of Holy Roman Emperor from 1438 to the Empire's dissolution in 1806, but failed to centralize its domains, leaving Germany disunited for centuries. Resistance to Turkish expansion brought Hungary under Austrian control from the 16th cent. The Netherlands, Luxembourg, and Burgundy were added in 1477, curbing French expansion.

The Flemish painting tradition of naturalism, technical proficiency, and bourgeois subject matter began in the 15th cent. (**Jan Van Eyck,** c 1390-1441), the earliest northern manifestation of the Renaissance. Albrecht **Dürer** (1471-1528) typified the merging of late Gothic and Italian trends in 16th-cent. German art. Imposing civic architecture flourished in the prosperous commercial cities.

Spain. Despite the unification of Castile and Aragon in 1479, the 2 countries retained separate governments, and the nobility, especially in Aragon and Catalonia, retained many privileges. Spanish lands in Italy (Naples, Sicily) and the Netherlands entangled the country in European wars through the mid-17th cent., while explorers, traders, and conquerors built up a Spanish empire in the Americas and the Philippines. From the late 15th cent., a **golden age** of literature and art produced works of social satire (plays of Lope de Vega, 1562-1635; **Cervantes,** 1547-1616), as well as spiritual intensity (**El Greco,** 1541-1614; **Velazquez,** 1599-1660).

Black Death. The bubonic plague reached Europe from the E in 1348, killing up to half the population by 1350. Labor scarcity forced wages to rise and brought greater freedom to the peasantry, making possible **peasant uprisings** (Jacquerie in France, 1358; Wat Tyler's rebellion in England, 1381).

Explorations. Organized European maritime exploration began, seeking to evade the Venice-Ottoman monopoly of E trade and to promote Christianity. Beginning in 1418, expeditions from Portugal explored the W coast of Africa, until Vasco da Gama rounded the Cape of Good Hope in 1497 and reached India. A Portuguese trading empire was consolidated by the seizure of Goa (1510) and Malacca (1551). Japan was reached in 1542. The voyages of Christopher **Columbus** (1492-1504) uncovered a world new to Europeans, which Spain hastened to subdue. Navigation schools in Spain and Portugal, the development of large sailing ships (carracks), and the invention (c 1475) of the rifle aided European penetration.

Christopher Columbus

Mughals and Safavids. E of the Ottoman Empire, 2 Muslim dynasties ruled unchallenged in the 16th and 17th cent. The Mughal dynasty of India, founded by Persianized Turkish invaders from the NW under Babur, dates from their 1526 conquest of the Delhi Sultanate. The dynasty ruled most of India for more than 200 years, surviving nominally until 1857. **Akbar** (r 1556-1605) consolidated administration at his glorious court, where the Urdu language (Persian-influenced Hindi) developed. Trade relations with Europe increased. Under Shah Jahan (1629-58), a secularized art fusing Hindu and Muslim element flourished in miniature painting and in architecture (**Taj Mahal**). **Sikhism** (founded c 1519) combined elements of both faiths. Suppression of Hindus and Shi'ite Muslims in S India in the late 17th cent. weakened the empire.

Taj Mahal

Fanatical devotion to the Shi'ite sect characterized the Safavids (1502-1736) of Persia and led to hostilities with the Sunni Ottomans for more than a century. The prosperity and the strength of the empire are evidenced by the mosques at its capital city, **Isfahan**. The Safavids enhanced Iranian national consciousness.

China. The **Ming** emperors (1368-1644), the last native dynasty in China, wielded unprecedented personal power, while the Confucian bureaucracy began to suffer from inertia. European trade (Portuguese monopoly through **Macao** from 1557) was strictly controlled. Jesuit scholars and scientists (Matteo Ricci, 1552-1610) introduced some Western science; their writings familiarized the West with China. Chinese technological inventiveness declined from this era, but the arts thrived, especially painting and ceramics.

Japan. After the decline of the first hereditary shogunate (chief generalship) at **Kamakura** (1185-1333), fragmentation of power accelerated, as did the consequent social mobility. Under Kamakura and the Ashikaga shogunate (1338-1573), the daimyos (lords) and samurai (warriors) grew more powerful and promoted a martial ideology. Japanese pirates and traders plied the China coast. Popular Buddhist movements included the nationalist Nichiren sect (from c 1250) and **Zen** (brought from China, 1191), which stressed meditation and a disciplined esthetic (tea ceremony, gardening, martial arts, No drama).

Reformed Europe Expands Overseas: 1500-1700

Reformation begun. Theological debate and protests against real and perceived clerical corruption existed in the medieval Christian world, expressed by such dissenters as John **Wycliffe** (c 1320-84) and his followers, the Lollards, in England, and **Huss** (burned as a heretic, 1415) in Bohemia.

Martin **Luther** (1483-1546) preached that faith alone leads to salvation, without the mediation of clergy or good works. He attacked the authority of the pope, rejected priestly celibacy, and recommended individual study of the Bible (which he translated c 1525). His 95 Theses (1517) led to his excommunication (1521). John **Calvin** (1509-64) said that God's elect were predestined for salvation and that good conduct and success were signs of election. Calvin in Geneva and John **Knox** (1505-72) in Scotland established theocratic states.

Henry VIII asserted English national authority and secular power by breaking away (1534) from the Catholic Church. Monastic property was confiscated, and some Protestant doctrines given official sanction.

Religious wars. A century and a half of religious wars began with a S German peasant uprising (1524), repressed with Luther's support. Radical sects—democratic, pacifist, millennarian—arose (Anabaptists ruled Münster in 1534-35) and were suppressed violently. Civil war in France from 1562 between **Huguenots** (Protestant nobles and merchants) and Catholics ended with the 1598 **Edict of Nantes,** tolerating Protestants (revoked 1685). Habsburg attempts to restore Catholicism in Germany were resisted in 25 years of fighting; the 1555 Peace of Augsburg guarantee of religious independence to local princes and cities was confirmed only after the **Thirty Years War** (1618-48), when much of Germany was devastated by local and foreign armies (Sweden, France).

A Catholic Reformation, or **Counter Reformation**, met the Protestant challenge, defining an official theology at the Council of Trent (1545-63). The **Jesuit** order (Society of Jesus), founded in 1534 by Ignatius Loyola (1491-1556), helped reconvert large areas of Poland, Hungary, and S Germany and sent missionaries to the New World, India, and China, while the **Inquisition** suppressed heresy in Catholic countries. A revival of religious fervor appeared in the devotional literature (Teresa of Avila, 1515-82) and in grandiose **Baroque** art (Bernini, 1598-1680).

Scientific Revolution. The late nominalist thinkers (Ockham, c 1300-49) of Paris and Oxford challenged Aristotelian orthodoxy, allowing for a freer scientific approach. At the same time, metaphysical values, such as the Neoplatonic faith in an orderly, mathematical cosmos, still motivated and directed inquiry. Nicolaus **Copernicus** (1473-1543) promoted the heliocentric theory, which was confirmed when Johannes **Kepler** (1571-1630) discovered the mathematical laws describing the orbits of the planets. The traditional Christian-Aristotelian belief that the heavens and the earth were fundamentally different collapsed when **Galileo** (1564-1642) discovered moving sunspots, irregular moon topography, and moons around Jupiter. He and Sir Isaac **Newton** (1642-1727) developed a mechanics that unified cosmic and earthly phenomena. Newton and Gottfried von **Leibniz** (1646-1716) invented calculus. René **Descartes** (1596-1650), best known for his influential philosophy, also invented analytic geometry.

Galileo

An explosion of **observational science** included the discovery of blood circulation (Harvey, 1578-1657) and microscopic life (Leeuwenhoek, 1632-1723) and advances in anatomy (Vesalius, 1514-64, dissected corpses) and chemistry (Boyle, 1627-91). Scientific research institutes were founded: Florence (1657), London (**Royal Society**, 1660), Paris (1666). Inventions proliferated (Savery's steam engine, 1696).

Arts. Mannerist trends of the High Renaissance (**Michelangelo**, 1475-1564) exploited virtuosity, grace, novelty, and exotic subjects and poses. The notion of artistic genius was promoted. Private connoisseurs entered the art market. These trends were elaborated in the 17th cent. **Baroque** era on a grander scale. Dynamic movement in painting and sculpture was emphasized by sharp lighting effects, rich materials (colored marble, gilt), and realistic details. Curved facades, broken lines, rich detail, and ceiling decoration characterized Baroque architecture. Monarchs, princes, and prelates, usually Catholic, used Baroque art to enhance and embellish their authority, as in royal portraits (Velazquez, 1599-1660; Van Dyck, 1599-1641).

National styles emerged. In France, a taste for rectilinear order and serenity (Poussin, 1594-1665), linked to the new rational philosophy, was expressed in classical forms. The influence of **classical values** in French literature (tragedies of **Racine**, 1639-99) gave rise to the "battle of the Ancients and Moderns." New forms included the essay (**Montaigne**, 1533-92) and novel (*Princesse de Cleves*, La Fayette, 1678).

Dutch painting of the 17th cent. was unique in its wide social distribution. The Flemish tradition of undemonstrative realism reached its peak in **Rembrandt** (1606-69) and Jan Vermeer (1632-75).

Economy. European economic expansion was stimulated by the new trade with the East, by New World gold and silver, and by a doubling of population (50 million in 1450, 100 million in 1600). New business and financial techniques were developed and refined, such as joint-stock companies, insurance, and letters of credit and exchange. The Bank of Amsterdam (1609) and the Bank of England (1694) broke the old monopoly of private banking families. The rise of a business mentality was typified by the spread of clock towers in cities in the 14th cent. By the mid-15th cent., portable clocks were available; the first watch was invented in 1502.

By 1650, most governments had adopted the **mercantile system**, in which they sought to amass metallic wealth by protecting their merchants' foreign and colonial trade monopolies. The rise in prices and the new coin-based economy undermined the craft guild and feudal manorial systems. Expanding industries (clothweaving, mining) benefited from technical advances. Coal replaced disappearing wood as the chief fuel; it was used to fuel new 16th-cent. blast furnaces making cast iron.

New World. The **Aztecs** united much of the Meso-American culture area in a militarist empire by 1519, from their capital, Tenochtitlán (pop. 300,000), which was the center of a cult requiring ritual human sacrifice. Most of the civilized areas of South America were ruled by the centralized Inca Empire (1476-1534), stretching 2,000 mi from Ecuador to NW Argentina. Lavish and sophisticated traditions in pottery, weaving, sculpture, and architecture were maintained in both regions.

Aztec ruins

These empires, beset by revolts, fell in 2 short campaigns to gold-seeking Spanish forces based in the Antilles and Panama. Hernan **Cortes** took Mexico (1519-21); Francisco **Pizarro,** Peru (1532-35). From these centers, land and sea expeditions claimed most of North and South America for Spain. The Indian high cultures did not survive the impact of Christian missionaries and the new upper class of whites and mestizos. In turn, New World silver and such Indian products as potatoes, tobacco, corn, peanuts, chocolate, and rubber exercised a major economic influence on Europe. Although the Spanish administration intermittently concerned itself with the welfare of Indians, the population remained impoverished at most levels. European diseases reduced the native population.

Brazil, which the Portuguese reached in 1500 and settled after 1530, and the Caribbean colonies of several European nations developed a plantation economy where sugarcane, tobacco, cotton, coffee, rice, indigo, and lumber were grown by slaves. From the early 16th to late 19th cent., 10 million Africans were transported to **slavery** in the New World.

Netherlands. The urban, Calvinist N provinces of the Netherlands rebelled (1568) against Habsburg Spain and founded an oligarchic mercantile republic. Their control of the Baltic grain market enabled them to exploit Mediterranean food shortages. Religious refugees—French and Belgian Protestants, Iberian Jews—added to the commercial talent pool. After Spain absorbed Portugal (1580), the Dutch seized Portuguese possessions and created a vast but short-lived commercial empire in Brazil, the Antilles, Africa, India, Ceylon, Malacca, Indonesia, and Taiwan. The Dutch also challenged or supplanted Portuguese traders in China and Japan. Revolution in 1640 restored Portuguese independence.

England. Anglicanism became firmly established under **Elizabeth I** after a brief Catholic interlude under "Bloody Mary" (1553-58). But religious and political conflicts led to a rebellion (1642) by Parliament. Roundheads (Puritans) defeated Cavaliers (Royalists); Charles I was beheaded (1649). The new Commonwealth was ruled as a military dictatorship by Oliver **Cromwell**, who also brutally crushed (1649-51) an Irish rebellion. Conflicts within the Puritan camp (democratic Levelers defeated, 1649) aided the Stuart restoration (1660), but Parliament was strengthened and the peaceful **"Glorious Revolution"** (1688) advanced political and religious liberties (writings of **Locke,** 1632-1704). British privateers (Drake, 1540-96) challenged Spanish control of the New World and penetrated Asian trade routes (Madras taken, 1639). North American colonies (Jamestown, 1607; Plymouth, 1620) provided an outlet for religious dissenters from Europe.

Elizabeth I

France. Emerging from the religious civil wars in 1628, France regained military and commercial great power status (under the ministries of **Richelieu**, Mazarin, and Colbert). Under **Louis XIV** (reigned 1643-1715), royal absolutism triumphed over nobles and local *parlements* (defeat of Fronde, 1648-53). Permanent colonies were founded in Canada (1608), the Caribbean (1626), and India (1674).

Sweden. Sweden seceded from the Scandinavian Union in 1523. The thinly populated agrarian state (with copper, iron, and timber exports) was united by the Vasa kings, whose conquests by the mid-17th cent. made Sweden the dominant Baltic power. The empire collapsed in the Great Northern War (1700-21).

Poland. After the union with Lithuania in 1447, Poland ruled vast territories from the Baltic to the Black Sea, resisting German and Turkish incursions. Catholic nobles failed to gain the loyalty of their Orthodox Christian subjects in the E; commerce and trades were practiced by German and Jewish immigrants. The bloody 1648-49 Cossack uprising began the kingdom's dismemberment.

China. A new dynasty, the **Manchus,** invaded from the NE, seized power in 1644, and expanded Chinese control to its greatest extent in Central and SE Asia. Trade and diplomatic contact with Europe grew, carefully controlled by China. New crops (sweet potato, maize, peanut) allowed an economic and population growth (pop. 300 million, in 1800). Traditional arts and literature were pursued with increased sophistication (*Dream of the Red Chamber*, novel, mid-18th cent.).

Japan. Tokugawa Ieyasu, shogun from 1603, finally unified and pacified feudal Japan. Hereditary daimyos and samurai monopolized government office and the professions. An urban merchant class grew, literacy spread, and a cultural renaissance occurred (**haiku,** a verse innovation of the poet Basho, 1644-94). Fear of European domination led to persecution of Christian converts from 1597 and to stringent isolation from outside contact from 1640.

Philosophy, Industry, and Revolution: 1700-1800

Science and Reason. Greater faith in reason and empirical observation, espoused since the Renaissance (Francis Bacon, 1561-1626), was bolstered by scientific discoveries despite theological opposition (Galileo's retraction, 1633). René **Descartes** (1596-1650) used a rationalistic approach modeled on geometry and introspection to discover "self-evident" truths as a foundation of knowledge. Sir Isaac **Newton** emphasized induction from experimental observation. Baruch de **Spinoza** (1632-77), who called for political and intellectual freedom, developed a systematic rationalistic philosophy in his classic work *Ethics*.

French philosophers assumed leadership of the **Enlightenment** in the 18th cent. Montesquieu (1689-1755) used British history to support his notions of limited government. **Voltaire's** (1694-1778) diaries and novels of exotic travel illustrated the intellectual trends toward secular ethics and relativism. Jean-Jacques **Rousseau's** (1712-1778) radical concepts of the **social contract** and of the inherent goodness of the common man gave impetus to antimonarchical republicanism. The *Encyclopedia* (1751-72, edited by Diderot and d'Alembert), designed as a monument to reason, was largely devoted to practical technology.

In England, ideals of liberty were connected with empiricist philosophy and science in the followers of John **Locke**. But British empiricism, especially as developed by the skeptical David **Hume** (1711-76), radically reduced the role of reason in philosophy, as did the evolutionary approach to law and politics of Edmund Burke (1729-97) and the utilitarian ethics of Jeremy Bentham (1748-1832). Adam Smith (1723-90) and other **physiocrats** called for a rationalization of economic activity by removing artificial barriers to a supposedly natural free exchange of goods.

German writers participated in the new philosophical trends popularized by Christian von Wolff (1679-1754). Immanuel **Kant's** (1724-1804) transcendental idealism, unifying an empirical epistemology with a priori moral and logical concepts, directed German thought away from skepticism. Italian contributions included work on electricity (Galvani, 1737-98; Volta, 1745-1827), the pioneer historiography of Vico (1668-1744), and writings on penal reform (Beccaria, 1738-94). Benjamin Franklin (1706-90) was celebrated in Europe for his varied achievements.

The growth of the **press** (*Spectator*, 1711-12) and the wide distribution of realistic but sentimental **novels** attested to the increase of a large bourgeois public.

Arts. Rococo art, characterized by extravagant decorative effects, asymmetries copied from organic models, and artificial pastoral subjects, was favored by the continental aristocracy for most of the cent. (Watteau, 1684-1721) and had musical analogies in the ornamentalized polyphony of late Baroque. The **Neoclassical** art after 1750, associated with the new scientific archaeology, was more streamlined and was infused with the supposed moral and geometric rectitude of the Roman Republic (David, 1748-1825). In England, **town planning** on a grand scale began.

Industrial Revolution in England. Agricultural improvements, such as the sowing drill (1701) and livestock breeding, were implemented on the large fields provided by enclosure of common lands by private owners. Profits from agriculture and from colonial and foreign trade (1800 volume, £54 million) were channeled through hundreds of banks and the **Stock Exchange** (est 1773) into new industrial processes.

The Newcomen steam pump (1712) aided coal mining. Coal fueled the new efficient steam engines patented by James Watt in 1769, and coke-smelting produced cheap, sturdy iron for machinery by the 1730s. The **flying shuttle** (1733) and **spinning jenny** (c 1764) were used in the large new cotton textile factories, where women and children were much of the work force. Goods were transported cheaply over **canals** (2,000 mi; built 1760-1800).

American Revolution. The British colonies in North America attracted a mass immigration of religious dissenters and poor people throughout the 17th and 18th cent., coming from the British Isles, Germany, the Netherlands, and other countries. The population reached 3 million non-natives by the 1770s. The small native population was greatly reduced by European diseases and by wars with and between the various colonies. British attempts to control colonial trade and to tax the colonists to pay for the costs of colonial administration and defense clashed with traditions of local self-government and eventually provoked the colonies to rebellion.

Central and East Europe. The monarchs of the three states that dominated E Europe—Austria, Prussia, and Russia—accepted the advice and legitimation of philosophes in creating modern, centralized institutions in their kingdoms, which were enlarged by the division (1772-95) of Poland.

Under **Frederick II** (called the Great) (r 1740-86) Prussia, with its efficient modern army, doubled in size. State monopolies and tariff protection fostered industry, and some legal reforms were introduced. Austria's heterogeneous realms were unified under **Maria Theresa** (r 1740-80) and **Joseph II** (r 1780-90). Reforms in education, law, and religion were enacted, and the Austrian serfs were freed (1781). With its defeat in the Seven Years' War in 1763, Austria failed to regain Silesia, which had been seized by Prussia, but it was compensated by expansion to the E and S (Hungary, Slavonia, 1699; Galicia, 1772).

Russia, whose borders continued to expand, adopted some Western bureaucratic and economic policies under **Peter I** (r 1682-1725) and **Catherine II** (r 1762-96). Trade and cultural contacts with the West multiplied from the new Baltic Sea capital, **St. Petersburg** (est 1703).

French Revolution. The growing French middle class lacked political power and resented aristocratic tax privileges, especially in light of the successful American Revolution. Peasants lacked adequate land and were burdened with feudal obligations to nobles. War with Britain led to the loss of French Canada and drained the treasury, finally forcing the king to call the **Estates-General** in 1789 (first time since 1614), in an atmosphere of food riots (poor crop in 1788).

Aristocratic resistance to absolutism was soon overshadowed by the reformist Third Estate (middle class), which proclaimed itself the **National Constituent Assembly** June 17 and took the "Tennis Court oath" on June 20 to secure a constitution. The storming of the **Bastille** on July 14, 1789, by Parisian artisans was followed by looting and seizure of aristocratic property throughout France. Assembly reforms included abolition of class and regional privileges, a Declaration of Rights, suffrage by taxpayers (75% of males), and the **Civil Constitution of the Clergy** providing for election and loyalty oaths for priests. A republic was declared Sept. 22, 1792, in spite of royalist pressure from Austria and Prussia, which had declared war in April (joined by Britain the next year). Louis XVI was beheaded Jan. 21, 1793, and Queen Marie Antoinette was beheaded Oct. 16, 1793.

Royalist uprisings in La Vendée and military reverses led to institution of a **reign of terror** in which tens of thousands of opponents of the Revolution and criminals were executed. Radical reforms in the **Convention** period (Sept. 1793-Oct. 1795) included the abolition of colonial slavery, economic measures to aid the poor, support of public education, and a short-lived de-Christianization.

Napoleon Bonaparte

Division among radicals (execution of Hebert, Danton, and Robespierre, 1794) aided the ascendancy of a moderate **Directory**, which consolidated military victories. **Napoleon Bonaparte** (1769-1821), a popular young general, exploited political divisions and participated in a coup Nov. 9, 1799, making himself first consul (dictator).

India. Sikh and Hindu rebels (Rajputs, Marathas) and Afghans destroyed the power of the Mughals during the 18th cent. After France's defeat (1763) in the Seven Years' War, Britain was the primary European trade power in India. Its control of inland **Bengal and Bihar** was recognized (1765) by the Mughal shah, who granted the **British East India Co.** (under Clive, 1725-74) the right to collect land revenue there. Despite objections from Parliament (1784 India Act), the company's involvement in local wars and politics led to repeated acquisitions of new territory. The company exported Indian textiles, sugar, and indigo.

Change Gathers Steam: 1800-40

French ideals and empire spread. Inspired by the ideals of the French Revolution, and supported by the expanding French armies, new republican regimes arose near France: the **Batavian** Republic in the Netherlands (1795-1806), the **Helvetic** Republic in Switzerland (1798-1803), the **Cisalpine** Republic in N Italy (1797-1805), the **Ligurian** Republic in Genoa (1797-1805), and the **Parthenopean** Republic in S Italy (1799). A Roman Republic existed briefly in 1798 after Pope Pius VI was arrested by French troops. In Italy and Germany, new nationalist sentiments were stimulated both in imitation of and in reaction to developments in France (anti-French and anti-Jacobin peasant uprisings in Italy, 1796-99).

From 1804, when Napoleon declared himself emperor, to 1812, a succession of military victories (Austerlitz, 1805; Jena, 1806) extended his control over most of Europe, through puppet states (**Confederation of the Rhine** united W German states for the first time and **Grand Duchy of Warsaw** revived Polish national hopes), expansion of the empire, and alliances.

Among the lasting reforms initiated under Napoleon's absolutist reign were: establishment of the Bank of France, centralization of tax collection, codification of law along Roman models (Code Napoléon), and reform and extension of secondary and university education. In an 1801 concordat, the papacy recognized the effective autonomy of the French Catholic Church.

Napoleon's continental successes were offset by British victory under Adm. Horatio Nelson in the **Battle of Trafalgar** (1805).

In all, some 400,000 French soldiers were killed in the Napoleonic Wars, along with about 600,000 foreign troops.

Last gasp of old regime. The disastrous 1812 invasion of Russia exposed Napoleon's overextension. After Napoleon's 1814 exile at Elba, his armies were defeated (1815) at **Waterloo**, by British and Prussian troops.

At the **Congress of Vienna**, the monarchs and princes of Europe redrew their boundaries, to the advantage of Prussia (in Saxony and the Ruhr), Austria (in Illyria and Venetia), and Russia (in Poland and Finland). British conquest of Dutch and French colonies (S Africa, Ceylon, Mauritius) was recognized, and France, under the restored Bourbons, retained its expanded 1792 borders. The settlement brought 50 years of international peace to Europe.

But the Congress was unable to check the advance of liberal ideals and of nationalism among the smaller European nations. The 1825 **Decembrist uprising** by liberal officers in Russia was easily suppressed. But an independence movement in **Greece**, stirred by commercial prosperity and a cultural revival, succeeded in expelling Ottoman rule by 1831, with the aid of Britain, France, and Russia.

A constitutional monarchy was secured in France by the **1830 Revolution**; Louis Philippe became king. The revolutionary contagion spread to **Belgium**, which gained its independence (1830) from the Dutch monarchy, to **Poland**, whose rebellion was defeated (1830-31) by Russia, and to Germany.

Romanticism. A new style in intellectual and artistic life began to replace Neoclassicism and Rococo after the mid-18th cent. By the early 19th cent., this style, Romanticism, had prevailed in the European world.

Rousseau had begun the reaction against rationalism; in education (*Émile*, 1762) he stressed subjective spontaneity over regularized instruction. German writers (Lessing, 1729-81; Herder, 1744-1803) favorably compared the German folk song to classical forms and began a cult of Shakespeare, whose passion and "natural" wisdom was a model for the romantic *Sturm und Drang* (Storm and Stress) movement. **Goethe's** *Sorrows of Young Werther* (1774) set the model for the tragic, passionate genius.

A new interest in **Gothic architecture** in England after 1760 (Walpole, 1717-97) spread through Europe, associated with an aesthetic Christian and mystic revival (**Blake,** 1757-1827). Celtic, Norse, and German mythology and folk tales were revived or imitated (Macpherson's Ossian translation, 1762; Grimm's Fairy Tales, 1812-22). The medieval revival (Scott's *Ivanhoe*, 1819) led to a new interest in history, stressing national differences and organic growth (**Carlyle,** 1795-1881; Michelet, 1798-1874), corresponding to theories of natural evolution (Lamarck's *Philosophie Zoologique*, 1809; Lyell's *Geology*, 1830-33). A reaction against classicism characterized the English **romantic poets** (beginning with **Wordsworth,** 1770-1850). Revolution and war fed an emphasis on freedom and conflict, expressed by both poets (**Byron**, 1788-1824; **Hugo**, 1802-85) and philosophers (**Hegel**, 1770-1831).

Wild gardens replaced the formal French variety, and painters favored rural, stormy, and mountainous landscapes (**Turner**, 1775-1851; **Constable**, 1776-1837). Clothing became freer, with wigs, hoops, and ruffles discarded. Originality and genius were expected in the life as well as the work of inspired artists (Murger's *Scenes from Bohemian Life*, 1847-49). Exotic locales and themes (as in Gothic horror stories) were used in art and literature (Delacroix, 1798-1863; **Poe**, 1809-49).

Music exhibited the new dramatic style and a breakdown of classical forms (**Beethoven,** 1770-1827). The use of folk melodies and modes aided the growth of distinct national traditions (Glinka in Russia, 1804-57).

Latin America. Francois **Toussaint L'Ouverture** led a successful slave revolt in Haiti, which subsequently became the first Latin American state to achieve independence (1804). The mainland Spanish colonies won their independence (1810-24), under such leaders as Simon **Bolivar** (1783-1830). Brazil became an independent empire (1822) under the Portuguese prince regent. A new class of military officers divided power with large landholders and the church.

United States. Heavy immigration and exploitation of ample natural resources fueled rapid economic growth. The spread of the franchise, public education, and antislavery sentiment were signs of a widespread democratic ethic.

China. Failure to keep pace with Western arms technology exposed China to greater European influence and hampered efforts to bar imports of opium, which had damaged Chinese society and drained wealth overseas. In the **Opium War** (1839-42), Britain forced China to expand trade opportunities and to cede Hong Kong.

Triumph of Progress: 1840-80

Idea of Progress. As a result of the cumulative scientific, economic, and political changes of the preceding eras, the idea took hold among literate people in the West that continuing growth and improvement was the usual state of human and natural life.

Charles **Darwin's** statement of the **theory of evolution** and survival of the fittest (Origin of Species, 1859), defended by intellectuals and scientists against theological objections, was taken as confirmation that progress was the natural direction of life. The controversy helped define popular ideas of the dedicated scientist and of science's increasing control over the world (Foucault's demonstration of earth's rotation, 1851; **Pasteur's** germ theory, 1861).

Charles Darwin

Liberals following Ricardo (1772-1823) in their faith that unrestrained competition would bring continuous economic expansion sought to adjust political life to the new social realities and believed that unregulated competition of ideas would yield truth (**Mill,** 1806-73). In England, successive reform bills (1832, 1867, 1884) gave representation to the new industrial towns and extended the franchise to the middle and lower classes and to Catholics, Dissenters, and Jews. On both sides of the Atlantic, reformists tried to improve conditions for the mentally ill (**Dix,** 1802-87), women (Anthony, 1820-1906), and prisoners. Slavery was barred in the British Empire (1833), the U.S. (1865), and Brazil (1888).

Socialist theories based on ideas of human perfectibility or progress were widely disseminated. Utopian socialists such as Saint-Simon (1760-1825) envisaged an orderly, just society directed by a technocratic elite. A model factory town, New Lanark, Scotland, was set up by utopian Robert Owen (1771-1858), and communal experiments were tried in the U.S. (most notably, Brook Farm, Mass., 1841-47). Bakunin's (1814-76) anarchism represented the opposite utopian extreme of total freedom. Karl **Marx** (1818-83) posited the inevitable triumph of socialism in industrial countries through a dialectical process of class conflict.

Spread of industry. The technical processes and managerial innovations of the English industrial revolution spread to Europe (especially Germany) and the U.S., causing an explosion of industrial production, demand for raw materials, and competition for markets. Inventors, both trained and self-educated, provided the means for larger-scale production (Bessemer steel, 1856; sewing machine, 1846). Many inventions were shown at the 1851 London Great Exhibition at the **Crystal Palace,** the theme of which was universal prosperity.

Local specialization and long-distance trade were aided by a revolution in transportation and communication. Railroads were first introduced in the 1820s in England and the U.S. More than 150,000 mi of track had been laid worldwide by 1880, with another 100,000 mi laid in the next decade. Steamships were improved (*Savannah* crossed Atlantic, 1819). The **telegraph**, perfected by 1844 (Morse), connected the Old and New Worlds by cable in 1866 and quickened the pace of international commerce and politics. The first commercial **telephone** exchange went into operation in the U.S. in 1878.

The new class of industrial workers, uprooted from their rural homes, lacked job security and suffered from dangerous overcrowded conditions at work and at home. Many responded by organizing **trade unions** (legalized in England, 1824; France, 1884). The U.S. Knights of Labor had 700,000 members by 1886. The First International (1864-76) tried to unite workers internationally around a Marxist program. The quasi-Socialist Paris Commune uprising (1871) was violently suppressed. Factory Acts to reduce child labor and regulate conditions were passed (1833-50 in England). Social security measures were introduced by the Bismarck regime (1883-89) in Germany.

Revolutions of 1848. Among the causes of the continent-wide revolutions were an international collapse of credit and resulting unemployment, bad harvests in 1845-47, and a cholera epidemic. The new urban proletariat and expanding bourgeoisie demanded a greater political role. Republics were proclaimed in France, Rome, and Venice. Nationalist feelings reached fever pitch in the Habsburg empire, as Hungary declared independence under Kossuth, as a Slav Congress demanded equality, and as Piedmont tried to drive Austria from Lombardy. A national liberal assembly at Frankfurt called for German unification.

But riots fueled bourgeois fears of socialism (**Marx** and **Engels**, Communist Manifesto, 1848), and peasants remained conservative. The old establishment—the Papacy, the Habsburgs with the help of the Czarist Russian army —was able to rout the revolutionaries by 1849. The French Republic succumbed to a renewed monarchy by 1852 (Emperor Napoleon III).

Great nations unified. Using the "blood and iron" tactics of Bismarck from 1862, Prussia controlled N Germany by 1867 (war with Denmark, 1864; Austria, 1866). After defeating France in 1870 (annexation of Alsace-Lorraine), it won the allegiance of S German states. A new **German Empire** was proclaimed (1871). **Italy**, inspired by Giuseppe Mazzini (1805-72) and Giuseppe Garibaldi (1807-82), was unified by the reformed Piedmont kingdom through uprisings, plebiscites, and war.

The **U.S.**, its area expanded after the 1846-48 Mexican War, defeated (1861-65) a secession attempt by slave states. in the **Civil War.** Canadian provinces were united in an autonomous **Dominion of Canada** (1867). Control in **India** was removed from the East India Co. and centralized under British administration after the 1857-58 Sepoy rebellion, laying the groundwork for the modern Indian State. Queen Victoria was named Empress of India (1876).

Europe dominates Asia. The Ottoman Empire began to collapse in the face of Balkan nationalisms and European imperial incursions in N Africa (**Suez Canal**, 1869). The Turks had lost control of most of both regions by 1882. Russia completed its expansion S by 1884 (despite the temporary setback of the **Crimean War** with Turkey, Britain, and France, 1853-56), taking Turkestan, all the Caucasus, and Chinese areas in the E and sponsoring Balkan Slavs against the Turks. A succession of reformist and reactionary regimes presided over a slow modernization (serfs freed, 1861). Persian independence suffered as Russia and British India competed for influence.

China was forced to sign a series of unequal treaties with European powers and Japan. Overpopulation and an inefficient dynasty brought misery and caused rebellions (Taiping, Muslims) leaving tens of millions dead. **Japan** was forced by the U.S. (Commodore Perry's visits, 1853-54) and Europe to end its isolation. The Meiji restoration (1868) gave power to a Westernizing oligarchy. Intensified empire-building gave Burma to Britain (1824-85) and Indochina to France (1862-95). Christian missionary activity followed imperial and trade expansion in Asia.

Respectability. The fine arts were expected to reflect and encourage the good morals and manners among the Victorians. Prudery, exaggerated delicacy, and familial piety were heralded by **Bowdler's** expurgated edition (1818) of Shakespeare. Government-supported mass education sought to inculcate a work ethic as a means to escape poverty (**Horatio Alger,** 1832-99).

The official **Beaux Arts** school in Paris set an international style of imposing public buildings (Paris Opera, 1861-74; Vienna Opera, 1861-69) and uplifting statues (Bartholdi's Statue of Liberty, 1884). Realist painting, influenced by photography (Daguerre, 1837), appealed to a new mass audience with social or historical narrative (Wilkie, 1785-1841; Poynter, 1836-1919) or with serious religious, moral, or social messages (pre-Raphaelites, Millet's *Angelus*, 1858) often drawn from ordinary life. The **Impressionists** (Monet, 1840-1926; Pissarro, 1830-1903; Renoir, 1841-1919) rejected the formalism, sentimentality, and precise techniques of academic art in favor of a spontaneous, undetailed rendering of the world through careful representation of the effect of natural light on objects.

Realistic **novelists** presented the full panorama of social classes and personalities, but retained sentimentality and moral judgment (**Dickens,** 1812-70; **Eliot,** 1819-80; **Tolstoy,** 1828-1910; **Balzac,** 1799-1850).

Veneer of Stability: 1880-1900

Imperialism triumphant. The vast **African** interior, visited by European explorers (Barth, 1821-65; Livingstone, 1813-73), was conquered by the European powers in rapid, competitive thrusts from their coastal bases after 1880, mostly for domestic political and international strategic reasons. W African Muslim kingdoms (Fulani), Arab slave traders (Zanzibar), and Bantu military confederations (Zulu) were alike subdued. Only Christian Ethiopia (defeat of Italy, 1896) and Liberia resisted successfully. France (W Africa) and Britain ("Cape to Cairo," **Boer War,** 1899-1902) were the major beneficiaries. The ideology of "the white man's burden" (Kipling, *Barrack Room Ballads*, 1892) or of a "civilizing mission" (France) justified the conquests.

W European foreign capital investment soared to nearly $40 billion by 1914, but most was in E Europe (France, Germany), the Americas (Britain), and the Europeans' colonies. The foundation of the modern interdependent world economy was laid, with cartels dominating raw material trade.

An industrious world. Industrial and technological proficiency characterized the 2 new great powers—Germany and the U.S. Coal and iron deposits enabled Germany to reach 2nd or 3rd place status in iron, steel, and shipbuilding by the 1900s. German electrical and chemical industries were world leaders. The U.S. post-Civil War boom (interrupted by "panics"—1884, 1893, 1896) was shaped by massive immigration from S and E Europe from 1880, government subsidy of railroads, and huge private monopolies (Standard Oil, 1870; U.S. Steel, 1901). The **Spanish-American War**, 1898 (Philippine Insurrection, 1899-1902), and the **Open Door policy** in China (1899) made the U.S. a world power.

IT'S A FACT: At the turn of the century in 1900, there still were 40 reigning sovereigns in Europe (counting the 89-year-old pope, Leo XIII, who was the oldest). The youngest monarch was Alfonso XIII of Spain; since he was still only 13 his (widowed) mother, Queen Maria Christina, acted as regent. The longest reigning was Britain's 80-year-old Queen Victoria, who had ascended the throne in 1837 (she died in 1901).

England led in **urbanization**, with **London** the world capital of finance, insurance, and shipping. Sewer systems (Paris, 1850s), electric subways (London, 1890), parks, and bargain department stores helped improve living standards for most of the urban population of the industrial world.

Westernization of Asia. Asian reaction to European economic, military, and religious incursions took the form of imitation of Western techniques and adoption of Western ideas of progress and freedom. The Chinese "self-strengthening" movement of the 1860s and 1870s included rail, port, and arsenal improvements and metal and textile mills. Reformers such as **K'ang Yu-wei** (1858-1927) won liberalizing reforms in 1898, right after the European and Japanese "scramble for concessions."

A universal education system in Japan and importation of foreign industrial, scientific, and military experts aided Japan's unprecedented rapid modernization after 1868, under the authoritarian Meiji regime. Japan's victory in the **Sino-Japanese War** (1894-95) put Formosa and Korea in its power.

In India, the British alliance with the remaining princely states masked reform sentiment among the Westernized urban elite; higher education had been conducted largely in English for 50 years. The **Indian National Congress**, founded in 1885, demanded a larger government role for Indians.

***Fin-de-siècle* sophistication. Naturalist** writers pushed realism to its extreme limits, adopting a quasi-scientific attitude and writing about formerly taboo subjects such as sex, crime, extreme poverty, and corruption (Flaubert, 1821-80; Zola, 1840-1902; Hardy, 1840-1928). Unseen or repressed psychological motivations were explored in the clinical and theoretical works of Sigmund **Freud** (1856-1939) and in works of fiction (**Dostoyevsky,** 1821-81; James, 1843-1916; Schnitzler, 1862-1931; others).

A contempt for bourgeois life or a desire to shock a complacent audience was shared by the French **symbolist** poets (Verlaine, 1844-96, Rimbaud, 1854-91), by neopagan English writers (Swinburne, 1837-1909), by continental dramatists (**Ibsen,** 1828-1906), and by satirists (**Wilde,** 1854-1900). The German philosopher Friedrich **Nietzsche** (1844-1900) was influential in his elitism and pessimism.

Postimpressionist art neglected long-cherished conventions of representation (Cézanne, 1839-1906) and showed a willingness to learn from primitive and non-European art (Gauguin, 1848-1903; Japanese prints).

Racism. Gobineau (1816-82) gave a pseudobiological foundation to modern racist theories, which spread in Europe in the latter 19th cent., along with **Social Darwinism**, the belief that societies are and should be organized as a struggle for survival of the fittest. The medieval period was interpreted as an era of natural Germanic rule (Chamberlain, 1855-1927), and notions of racial superiority were associated with German national aspirations (Treitschke, 1834-96). **Anti-Semitism**, with a new racist rationale, became a significant political force in Germany (Anti-Semitic Petition, 1880), Austria (Lueger, 1844-1910), and France (Dreyfus **case**, 1894-1906).

Last Respite: 1900-9

Alliances. While the peace of Europe (and its dependencies) continued to hold (1907 **Hague Conference** extended the rules of war and international arbitration procedures), imperial rivalries, protectionist trade practices (in Germany and France), and the escalating arms race (British *Dreadnought* battleship launched; Germany widens Kiel canal, 1906) exacerbated minor disputes (German-French Moroccan "crises," 1905, 1911).

Security was sought through alliances: **Triple Alliance** (Germany, Austria-Hungary, Italy; renewed in 1902 and 1907); Anglo-Japanese Alliance (1902), Franco-Russian Alliance (1899), **Entente Cordiale** (Britain, France, 1904), Anglo-Russian Treaty (1907), German-Ottoman friendship.

Ottomans decline. The inefficient, corrupt Ottoman government was unable to resist further loss of territory. Nearly all European lands were lost in 1912 to Serbia, Greece, Montenegro, and Bulgaria. Italy took Libya and the Dodecanese islands the same year, and Britain took Kuwait (1899) and the Sinai (1906). The **Young Turk** revolution in 1908 forced the sultan to restore a constitution, and it introduced some social reform, industrialization, and secularization.

British Empire. British trade and cultural influence remained dominant in the empire, but constitutional reforms presaged its eventual dissolution: The colonies of **Australia** were united in 1901 under a self-governing commonwealth. **New Zealand** acquired dominion status in 1907. The old Boer republics joined Cape Colony and Natal in the self-governing **Union of South Africa** in 1910.

The 1909 Indian Councils Act enhanced the role of elected province legislatures in **India**. The Muslim League (founded 1906) sought separate communal representation.

East Asia. Japan exploited its growing industrial power to expand its empire. Victory in the 1904-5 war against Russia (naval battle of Tsushima, 1905) assured Japan's domination of **Korea** (annexed 1910) and Manchuria (Port Arthur taken, 1905).

In China, central authority began to crumble (empress died, 1908). Reforms (Confucian exam system ended 1905, modernization of the army, building of railroads) were inadequate, and secret societies of reformers and nationalists, inspired by the Westernized **Sun Yat-sen** (1866-1925) fomented periodic uprisings in the S.

Siam, whose independence had been guaranteed by Britain and France in 1896, was split into spheres of influence by those countries in 1907.

Russia. The population of the Russian Empire approached 150 million in 1900. Reforms in education, in law, and in local institutions (*zemstvos*) and an industrial boom starting in the 1880s (oil, railroads) created the beginnings of a modern state, despite the autocratic tsarist regime. Liberals (1903 Union of Liberation), Socialists (Social Democrats founded 1898, Bolsheviks split off 1903), and populists (Social Revolutionaries founded 1901) were periodically repressed, and national minorities were persecuted (anti-Jewish pogroms, 1903, 1905-6).

An industrial crisis after 1900 and harvest failures aggravated poverty among urban workers, and the 1904-5 defeat by Japan (which checked Russia's Asian expansion) sparked **the Revolution of 1905-6.** A **Duma** (parliament) was created, and an agricultural reform (under Stolypin, prime minister 1906-11) created a large class of land-owning peasants (kulaks).

The world shrinks. Developments in transportation and communication and mass population movements helped create an awareness of an interdependent world. Early automobiles (Daimler, Benz, 1885) were experimental or were designed as luxuries. Assembly-line mass production (Ford Motor Co., 1903) made the invention practicable, and by 1910 nearly 500,000 motor vehicles were registered

1903 Wright Flyer

in the U.S. alone. Heavier-than-air flights began in 1903 in the U.S. (Wright brothers' *Flyer*), preceded by glider, balloon, and model plane advances in several countries. Trade was advanced by improvements in ship design (gyrocompass, 1910), speed (Lusitania crossed Atlantic in 5 days, 1907), and reach (Panama Canal begun, 1904).

The first transatlantic **radio** telegraphic transmission occurred in 1901, 6 years after Marconi discovered radio. Radio transmission of human speech had been made in 1900. Telegraphic transmission of photos was achieved in 1904, lending immediacy to news reports. **Phonographs**, popularized by Caruso's recordings (starting 1902), made for quick international spread of musical styles (ragtime). **Motion pic-**

tures, perfected in the 1890s (Dickson, Lumière brothers), became a popular and artistic medium after 1900; newsreels appeared in 1909.

Emigration from crowded European centers soared in the decade: 9 million migrated to the U.S., and millions more went to Siberia, Canada, Argentina, Australia, South Africa, and Algeria. Some 70 million Europeans emigrated in the cent. before 1914. Several million Chinese, Indians, and Japanese migrated to SE Asia, where their urban skills often enabled them to take a predominant economic role.

Social reform. The social and economic problems of the poor were kept in the public eye by realist fiction writers (Dreiser's *Sister Carrie*, 1900; Gorky's *Lower Depths*, 1902; Sinclair's *The Jungle*, 1906), journalists (U.S. **muckrakers**—Steffens, Tarbell), and artists (Ashcan school). Frequent labor strikes and occasional assassinations by anarchists or radicals (Empress Elizabeth of Austria, 1898; King Umberto I of Italy, 1900; U.S. Pres. McKinley, 1901; Russian Interior Minister Plehve, 1904; Portugal's King Carlos, 1908) added to social tension and fear of revolution.

But democratic reformism prevailed. In Germany, Bernstein's (1850-1932) **revisionist Marxism**, downgrading revolution, was accepted by the powerful Social Democrats and trade unions. The British Fabian Society (the Webbs, Shaw) and the Labour Party (founded 1906) worked for reforms such as Social Security and union rights (1906), while woman suffragists grew more militant. U.S. **progressives** fought big business (Pure Food and Drug Act, 1906). In France, the 10-hour work day (1904) and separation of church and state (1905) were reform victories, as was universal suffrage in Austria (1907).

Arts. An unprecedented period of experimentation, centered in France, produced several new **painting** styles: Fauvism exploited bold color areas (Matisse, *Woman With Hat*, 1905); expressionism reflected powerful inner emotions (the Brücke group, 1905); cubism combined several views of an object on one flat surface (Picasso's *Demoiselles*, 1906-7); futurism tried to depict speed and motion (Italian Futurist Manifesto, 1910). **Architects** explored new uses of steel structures, with facades either neoclassical (Adler and Sullivan in U.S.); curvilinear Art Nouveau (Gaudi's Casa Mila, 1905-10); or functionally streamlined (Wright's Robie House, 1909).

Music and dance shared the experimental spirit. Ruth St. Denis (1877-1968) and Isadora Duncan (1878-1927) pioneered modern dance, while Sergei Diaghilev in Paris revitalized classic ballet from 1909. Composers explored atonal music (Debussy, 1862-1918) and dissonance (Schoenberg, 1874-1951) or revolutionized classical forms (Stravinsky, 1882-1971), often showing jazz or folk music influences.

War and Revolution: 1910-19

War threatens. Germany under Wilhelm II sought a political and imperial role consonant with its industrial strength, challenging Britain's world supremacy and threatening France, which was still resenting the loss (1871) of Alsace-Lorraine. Austria wanted to curb an expanded Serbia (after 1912) and the threat it posed to its own Slav lands. Russia feared Austrian and German political and economic aims in the Balkans and Turkey.

An accelerated arms race resulted from these circumstances. The German standing army rose to more than 2 million men by 1914. Russia and France had more than a million each, and Austria and the British Empire nearly a million each. Dozens of enormous battleships were built by the powers after 1906.

The **assassination of Austrian Archduke Franz Ferdinand** by a Serbian, June 28, 1914, was the pretext for war. The system of alliances made the conflict Europe-wide; Germany's invasion of Belgium to outflank France forced Britain to enter the war. Patriotic fervor was nearly unanimous among all classes in most countries.

World War I. German forces were stopped in France in one month. The rival armies dug **trench networks**. Artillery and improved machine guns prevented either side from any lasting advance despite repeated assaults (600,000 dead at **Verdun**, Feb.-July 1916). Poison gas, used by Germany in 1915, proved ineffective. The entrance of more than 1 million U.S. troops tipped the balance after mid-1917, forcing Germany to sue for peace the next year. The formal armistice was signed on Nov. 11, 1918.

In the E, the Russian armies were thrown back (battle of **Tannenberg**, Aug. 20, 1914), and the war grew unpopular in Russia. An allied attempt to relieve Russia through Turkey failed (**Gallipoli,** 1915). The **Russian Revolution** (1917) abolished the monarchy. The new Bolshevik regime signed the capitulatory Brest-Litovsk peace in March 1918. Italy entered the war on the allied side in May 1915 but was pushed back by Oct. 1917. A renewed offensive with Allied aid in Oct.-Nov. 1918 forced Austria to surrender.

The British Navy successfully blockaded Germany, which responded with submarine U-boat attacks; **unrestricted submarine warfare** against neutrals after Jan. 1917 helped bring the U.S. into the war. Other battlefields included Palestine and Mesopotamia, both of which Britain wrested from the Turks in 1917, and the African and Pacific colonies of Germany, most of which fell to Britain, France, Australia, Japan, and South Africa.

Settlement. At the **Paris Peace Conference** (Jan.-June 1919), concluded by the **Treaty of Versailles**, and in subsequent negotiations and local wars (Russian-Polish War, 1920), the map of Europe was redrawn with a nod to U.S. Pres. Woodrow Wilson's principle of self-determination. Austria and Hungary were separated, and much of their land was given to Yugoslavia (formerly Serbia), Romania, Italy, and the newly independent Poland and Czechoslovakia. Germany lost territory in the W, N, and E, while Finland and the Baltic states were detached from Russia. Turkey lost nearly all its Arab lands to British-sponsored Arab states or to direct French and British rule. Belgium's sovereignty was recognized.

From 1916, the civilian populations and economies of both sides were mobilized to an unprecedented degree. Hardships intensified among fighting nations in 1917 (French mutiny crushed in May). More than 10 million soldiers died in the war.

A huge **reparations** burden and partial demilitarization were imposed on Germany. Pres. Wilson obtained approval for a League of Nations, but the U.S. Senate refused to allow the U.S. to join.

Vladmir Lenin

Russian revolution. Military defeats and high casualties caused a contagious lack of confidence in Tsar Nicholas, who was forced to abdicate Mar. 1917. A liberal provisional government failed to end the war, and massive desertions, riots, and fighting between factions followed. A moderate socialist government under Aleksandr Kerensky was overthrown (Nov. 1917) in a violent coup by the **Bolsheviks** in Petrograd under **Lenin,** who later disbanded the elected Constituent Assembly.

The Bolsheviks brutally suppressed all opposition and ended the war with Germany in Mar. 1918. **Civil war** broke out in the summer between the Red Army, including the Bolsheviks and their supporters, and monarchists, anarchists, nationalities (Ukrainians, Georgians, Poles), and others. Small U.S., British, French, and Japanese units also opposed the Bolsheviks (1918-19; Japan in Vladivostok to 1922). The civil war, anarchy, and pogroms devastated the country until the 1920 Red Army victory. The wartime total monopoly of political, economic, and police power by the Communist Party leadership was retained.

Other European revolutions. An unpopular monarchy in **Portugal** was overthrown in 1910. The new republic took severe anticlerical measures in 1911.

After a century of Home Rule agitation, during which **Ireland** was devastated by famine (1 million dead, 1846-47) and emigration, republican militants staged an unsuccessful uprising in Dublin during Easter 1916. The execution of the leaders and mass arrests by the British won popular support for the rebels. The Irish Free State, comprising all but the 6 N counties, achieved dominion status in 1922.

In the aftermath of the world war, radical revolutions were attempted in Germany (**Spartacist** uprising, Jan. 1919), **Hungary** (Kun regime, 1919), and elsewhere. All were suppressed or failed for lack of support.

Chinese revolution. The Manchu Dynasty was overthrown and a republic proclaimed in Oct. 1911. First Pres. Sun Yat-sen resigned in favor of strongman Yuan Shih-k'ai. Sun organized the parliamentarian **Kuomintang** party.

Students launched protests on May 4, 1919, against League of Nations concessions in China to Japan. Nationalist, liberal, and socialist ideas and political groups spread. The **Communist Party** was founded in 1921. A Communist regime took power in Mongolia with Soviet support in 1921.

India restive. Indian objections to British rule erupted in nationalist riots as well as in the nonviolent tactics of Mahatma **Gandhi** (1869-1948). Nearly 400 unarmed demonstrators were shot at **Amritsar** in Apr. 1919. Britain approved limited self-rule that year.

Mexican revolution. Under the long Diaz dictatorship (1877-1911) the economy advanced, but Indian and mestizo lands were confiscated, and concessions to foreigners (mostly U.S.) damaged the middle class. A **revolution in 1910** led to civil wars and U.S. intervention (1914, 1916-17). Land reform and a more democratic constitution (1917) were achieved.

The Aftermath of War: 1920-29

U.S. Easy credit, technological ingenuity, and war-related industrial decline in Europe caused a long economic boom, in which ownership of the new products—**autos, phones, radios**—became democratized. Prosperity, an increase in women workers, woman suffrage (1920), and drastic change in fashion (flappers, mannish bob for women, clean-shaven men) created a wide perception of social change, despite prohibition of alcoholic beverages (1919-33). Union membership and strikes increased. Fear of radicals led to Palmer raids (1919-20) and the Sacco/Vanzetti case (1921-27).

Europe sorts itself out. Germany's liberal **Weimar constitution** (1919) could not guarantee a stable government in the face of rightist violence (Rathenau assassinated, 1922) and Communist refusal to cooperate with Socialists. Reparations and Allied occupation of the Rhineland caused staggering inflation that destroyed middle-class savings, but economic expansion resumed after mid-decade, aided by U.S. loans. A sophisticated, **innovative culture** developed in architecture and design (Bauhaus, 1919-28), film (Lang, *M*, 1931), painting (Grosz), music (Weill, *Threepenny Opera*, 1928), theater (Brecht, *A Man's a Man*, 1926), criticism (Benjamin), philosophy (Jung), and fashion. This culture was considered decadent and socially disruptive by rightists.

England elected its first Labour governments (Jan. 1924, June 1929). A 10-day general strike in support of coal miners failed in May 1926. In **Italy**, strikes, political chaos, and violence by small Fascist bands culminated in the Oct. 1922 Fascist March on Rome, which established **Mussolini's** dictatorship. Strikes were outlawed (1926), and Italian influence was pressed in the Balkans (Albania a protectorate, 1926). A conservative dictatorship was also established in **Portugal** in a 1926 military coup.

Czechoslovakia, the only stable democracy to emerge from the war in Central or East Europe, faced opposition from Germans (in the Sudetenland), Ruthenians, and some Slovaks. As the industrial heartland of the old Habsburg empire, it remained fairly prosperous. With French backing, it formed the Little Entente with Yugoslavia (1920) and **Romania** (1921) to block Austrian or Hungarian irredentism. Hungary remained dominated by the landholding classes and expansionist feeling. Croats and Slovenes in **Yugoslavia** demanded a federal state until King Alexander I proclaimed (1929) a royal dictatorship. Poland faced nationality problems as well (Germans, Ukrainians, Jews); Pilsudski ruled as dictator from 1926. The Baltic states were threatened by traditionally dominant ethnic Germans and by Soviet-supported Communists.

An economic collapse and famine in **Russia** (1921-22) claimed 5 million lives. The New Economic Policy (1921) allowed land ownership by peasants and some private commerce and industry. Stalin was absolute ruler within 4 years of Lenin's death (1924). He inaugurated a brutal collectivization program (1929-32) and used foreign Communist parties for Soviet state advantage.

Internationalism. Revulsion against World War I led to pacifist agitation, to the Kellogg-Briand Pact renouncing aggressive war (1928), and to **naval disarmament** pacts (Washington, 1922; London, 1930). But the League of Nations was able to arbitrate only minor disputes (Greece-Bulgaria, 1925).

Middle East. Mustafa Kemal (**Ataturk**) led **Turkish** nationalists in resisting Italian, French, and Greek military advances (1919-23). The sultanate was abolished (1922), and elaborate reforms were passed, including secularization of law and adoption of the Latin alphabet. Ethnic conflict led to persecution of **Armenians** (more than 1 million dead in 1915, 1 million expelled), Greeks (forced Greek-Turk population exchange, 1923), and Kurds (1925 uprising).

With evacuation of the Turks from **Arab** lands, the puritanical Wahabi dynasty of E Arabia conquered (1919-25) what is now Saudi Arabia. British, French, and Arab dynastic and nationalist maneuvering resulted in the creation of 2 more Arab monarchies in 1921—Iraq and Transjordan (both under British control)—and 2 French mandates—Syria and Lebanon. Jewish immigration into British-mandated **Palestine**, inspired by the Zionist movement, was resisted by Arabs, at times violently (1921, 1929 massacres).

Reza Khan ruled **Persia** after his 1921 coup (shah from 1925), centralized control, and created the trappings of a modern secular state.

China. The Kuomintang under **Chiang Kai-shek** (1887-1975) subdued the warlords by 1928. The Communists were brutally suppressed after their alliance with the Kuomintang was broken in 1927. Relative peace thereafter allowed for industrial and financial improvements, with some Russian, British, and U.S. cooperation.

Arts. Nearly all bounds of subject matter, style, and attitude were broken in the arts of the period. **Abstract** art first took inspiration from natural forms or narrative themes (Kandinsky from 1911) and then worked free of any representational aims (Malevich's suprematism, 1915-19; Mondrian's geometric style from 1917). The **Dada** movement (from 1916) mocked artistic pretension with absurd collages and constructions (Arp, Tzara, from 1916). Paradox, illusion, and psychological taboos were exploited by **surrealists** by the latter 1920s (Dali, Magritte). Architectural schools celebrated industrial values, whether vigorous abstract constructivism (Tatlin, *Monument to 3rd International*, 1919) or the machined, streamlined **Bauhaus** style, which was extended to many design fields (Helvetica typeface).

Prose writers explored revolutionary narrative modes related to dreams (Kafka's *Trial*, 1925), internal monologue (Joyce's **Ulysses**, 1922), and word play (Stein's *Making of Americans*, 1925). Poets and novelists wrote of modern alienation (Eliot's ***Waste Land***, 1922) and aimlessness (Lost Generation).

Albert Einstein

Sciences. Scientific specialization prevailed by the 20th cent. Advances in knowledge and technological aptitude increased with the geometric rise in the number of practitioners. Physicists challenged common-sense views of causality, observation, and a mechanistic universe, putting science further beyond popular grasp (**Einstein's** general theory of relativity, 1916; Bohr's quantum mechanics, 1913; Heisenberg's uncertainty principle, 1927).

Rise of Totalitarians: 1930-39

Depression. A worldwide financial panic and economic depression began with the Oct. 1929 U.S. stock market crash and the May 1931 failure of the Austrian Credit-Anstalt. A credit crunch caused international bankruptcies and **unemployment**: 12 million jobless by 1932 in the U.S., 5.6 million in Germany, 2.7 million in England. Governments responded with **tariff restrictions** (Smoot-Hawley Act, 1930; Ottawa Imperial Conference, 1932), which dried up world trade. Government public works programs were vitiated by deflationary budget balancing.

Germany. Years of agitation by violent extremists were brought to a head by the Depression. Nazi leader Adolf was named chancellor in Jan. 1933 and given dictatorial power by the Reichstag in March. Opposition parties were disbanded, strikes banned, and all aspects of economic, cultural, and religious life were brought under central government and Nazi party control and manipulated by sophisticated propaganda. Severe persecution of Jews began (**Nuremberg Laws,** Sept. 1935). Many Jews, political opponents, and others were sent to concentration camps (Dachau, 1933), where thousands died or were killed. Public works, renewed conscription (1935), arms production, and a 4-year plan (1936) all but ended unemployment.

Hitler's expansionism started with reincorporation of the Saar (1935), occupation of the **Rhineland** (Mar. 1936), and annexation of Austria (Mar. 1938). At **Munich** (Sept. 1938) an indecisive Britain and France sanctioned German dismemberment of Czechoslovakia.

Russia. Urbanization and education advanced. Rapid industrialization was achieved through successive **5-year plans** starting in 1928, using severe labor discipline and mass forced labor. Industry was financed by a decline in living standards and exploitation of agriculture, which was almost totally collectivized by the early 1930s (*kolkhoz*, collective farm; *sovkhoz*, state farm, often in newly worked lands). Successive **purges** increased the role of professionals and management at the expense of workers. Millions perished in a series of manufactured disasters: extermination (1929-34) of kulaks (peasant landowners), severe famine (1932-33), party purges and show trials (Great Purge, 1936-38), suppression of nationalities, and poor conditions in labor camps.

Spain. An industrial revolution during World War I created an urban proletariat, which was attracted to socialism and anarchism; Catalan nationalists challenged central authority. The 5 years after King Alfonso left Spain in Apr. 1931 were dominated by tension between intermittent leftist and anticlerical governments and clericals, monarchists, and other rightists. Anarchist and Communist rebellions were crushed, but a July 1936 extreme right rebellion led by Gen. Francisco **Franco** and aided by Nazi Germany and Fascist Italy succeeded, after a 3-year **civil war** (more than 1 million dead in battles and atrocities). The war polarized international public opinion.

Italy. Despite propaganda for the ideal of the Corporate State, few domestic reforms were attempted. An entente with Hungary and Austria (Mar. 1934), a pact with Germany and Japan (Nov. 1937), and intervention by 50,000-75,000 troops in Spain (1936-39) sealed Italy's identification with the fascist bloc (anti-Semitic laws after Mar. 1938). Ethiopia was conquered (1935-36), and Albania annexed (Jan. 1939) in conscious imitation of ancient Rome.

East Europe. Repressive regimes fought for power against an active opposition (liberals, socialists, Communists, peasants, Nazis). Minority groups and Jews were restricted within national boundaries that did not coincide with ethnic population patterns. In the destruction of **Czechoslovakia**, Hungary occupied S Slovakia (Nov. 1938) and Ruthenia (Mar. 1939), and a pro-Nazi regime took power in the rest of Slovakia. Other boundary disputes (e.g., Poland-Lithuania, Yugoslavia-Bulgaria, Romania-Hungary) doomed attempts to build joint fronts against Germany or Russia. Economic depression was severe.

East Asia. After a period of liberalism in **Japan**, nativist militarists dominated the government with peasant support. Manchuria was seized (Sept. 1931-Feb. 1932), and a puppet state was set up (Manchukuo). Adjacent Jehol (Inner Mongolia) was occupied in 1933. China proper was invaded in July 1937; large areas were conquered by Oct. 1938. Hundreds of thousands of rapes, murders, and other atrocities were attributed to the Japanese.

In **China** Communist forces left Kuomintang-besieged strongholds in the S in a Long March (1934-35) to the N. The Kuomintang-Communist civil war was suspended in Jan. 1937 in the face of threatening Japan.

The democracies. The Roosevelt Administration, in office Mar. 1933, embarked on an extensive program of **New Deal** social reform and economic stimulation, including protection for labor unions (heavy industries organized), Social Security, public works, wage-and-hour laws, and assistance to farmers. Isolationist sentiment (1937 Neutrality Act) prevented U.S. intervention in Europe, but military expenditures were increased in 1939.

French political instability and polarization prevented resolution of economic and international security questions. The **Popular Front** government under Leon Blum (June 1936-Apr. 1938) passed social reforms (40-hr week) and raised arms spending. National coalition governments, which ruled Britain from Aug. 1931, brought economic recovery but failed to define a consistent international policy until Chamberlain's government (from May 1937), which practiced **appeasement** of Germany and Italy.

India. Twenty years of agitation for autonomy and then for independence (Gandhi's **salt march**, 1930) achieved some constitutional reform (extended provincial powers, 1935) despite Muslim-Hindu strife. Social issues assumed prominence with peasant uprisings (1921), strikes (1928), Gandhi's efforts for untouchables (1932 "fast unto death"), and social and agrarian reform by the provinces after 1937.

Arts. The streamlined, geometric design motifs of Art Deco (from 1925) prevailed through the 1930s. **Abstract art** flourished (Moore sculptures from 1931) alongside a new **realism** related to social and political concerns (Socialist Realism, the official Soviet style from 1934; Mexican muralist Rivera, 1886-1957; and Orozco, 1883-1949), which were also expressed in fiction and poetry (Steinbeck's *Grapes of Wrath*, 1939; Sandburg's *The People, Yes*, 1936). Modern architecture (International Style, 1932) was unchallenged in its use of artificial materials (concrete, glass), lack of decoration, and monumentality (Rockefeller Center, 1929-40). U.S.-made films captured a worldwide audience with their larger-than-life fantasies (*Gone With the Wind*, *The Wizard of Oz,* both 1939).

War, Hot and Cold: 1940-49

War in Europe. The Nazi-Soviet nonaggression pact (Aug. 1939) freed Germany to attack Poland (Sept.). Britain and France, which had guaranteed Polish independence, declared war on Germany. Russia seized E Poland (Sept.), attacked Finland (Nov.), and took the Baltic states (July 1940). Mobile German forces staged *blitzkrieg* attacks during Apr.-June 1940, conquering neutral Denmark, Norway, and the Low Countries and defeating France; 350,000 British and French troops were evacuated at **Dunkirk** (May). The **Battle of Britain** (June-Dec. 1940) denied Germany air superiority. German-Italian campaigns won the Balkans by Apr. 1941. Three million Axis troops **invaded Russia** in June 1941, marching through Ukraine to the Caucasus, and through White Russia and the Baltic republics to Moscow and Leningrad.

Russian winter counterthrusts (1941-42 and 1942-43) stopped the German advance (**Stalingrad,** Sept. 1942-Feb. 1943). With British and U.S. Lend-Lease aid and sustaining great casualties, the Russians drove the Axis from all E Europe and the Balkans in the next 2 years. Invasions of N Africa (Nov. 1942), Italy (Sept. 1943), and **Normandy** (launched on **D-Day**, June 6, 1944) brought U.S., British, Free French, and allied troops to Germany by spring 1945. In Feb. 1945, the 3 Allied leaders, Winston **Churchill** (Britain), Joseph **Stalin** (USSR), and Franklin D. **Roosevelt** (U.S.), met in **Yalta** to discuss strategy and resolve political issues, including the postwar Allied occupation of Germany. Germany surrendered May 7, 1945.

War in Asia-Pacific. Japan occupied Indochina in Sept. 1940, dominated Thailand in Dec. 1941, and attacked Hawaii (**Pearl Harbor**), the Philippines, Hong Kong, and Malaya on Dec. 7, 1941 (precipitating U.S. entrance into the war). Indonesia was attacked in Jan. 1942, and Burma was conquered in Mar. 1942. The Battle of **Midway** (June 1942) turned back the Japanese advance. "Island-hopping" battles (**Guadalcanal,** Aug. 1942-Jan. 1943; **Leyte Gulf,** Oct. 1944; **Iwo Jima,** Feb.-Mar. 1945; **Okinawa,** Apr. 1945) and massive bombing raids on Japan from June 1944 wore out Japanese defenses. U.S. atom bombs, dropped Aug. 6 and 9 on **Hiroshima** and Nagasaki, forced Japan to agree, on Aug. 14, to surrender; formal surrender was on Sept. 2, 1945.

Atrocities. The war brought 20th-cent. cruelty to its peak. The Nazi regime systematically killed an estimated 5-6 million Jews, including some 3 million who died in death camps (e.g., **Auschwitz**). Gypsies, political opponents, sick and retarded people, and others deemed undesirable were also murdered by the Nazis, as were vast numbers of Slavs, especially leaders.

Civilian deaths. German bombs killed 70,000 British civilians. More than 100,000 Chinese civilians were killed by Japanese forces in the capture and occupation of Nanking. Severe retaliation by the Soviet army, E European partisans, Free French, and others took a heavy toll. U.S. and British bombing of Germany killed hundreds of thousands, as did U.S. bombing of Japan (80,000-200,000 at Hiroshima alone). Some 45 million people lost their lives in the war.

Settlement. The **United Nations** charter was signed in San Francisco on June 26, 1945, by 50 nations. The International Tribunal at **Nuremberg** convicted 22 German leaders for war crimes in Sept. 1946; 23 Japanese leaders were convicted in Nov. 1948. Postwar border changes included large gains in territory for the USSR, losses for Germany, a shift to the W in Polish borders, and minor losses for Italy. Communist regimes, supported by Soviet troops, took power in most of E Europe, including Soviet-occupied Germany (GDR proclaimed Oct. 1949). Japan lost all overseas lands.

Recovery. Basic political and social changes were imposed on Japan and W Germany by the western allies (Japan constitution adopted, Nov. 1946; W German basic law, May 1949). U.S. **Marshall Plan** aid ($12 billion, 1947-51) spurred W European economic recovery after a period of severe inflation and strikes in Europe and the U.S. The British Labour Party introduced a national health service and nationalized basic industries in 1946.

Cold War. Western fears of further Soviet advances (Cominform formed in Oct. 1947; Czechoslovakia coup, Feb. 1948; Berlin blockade, Apr. 1948-Sept. 1949) led to the formation of **NATO**. Civil War in Greece and Soviet pressure on Turkey led to U.S. aid under the **Truman Doctrine** (Mar. 1947). Other anti-Communist security pacts were the Organization of American States (Apr. 1948) and the SE Asia Treaty Organization (Sept. 1954). A new wave of **Soviet purges** and repression intensified in the last years of Stalin's rule, extending to E Europe (Slansky trial in Czechoslovakia, 1951). Only Yugoslavia resisted Soviet control (expelled by Cominform, June 1948; U.S. aid, June 1949).

China, Korea. Communist forces emerged from World War II strengthened by the Soviet takeover of industrial Manchuria. In 4 years of fighting, the Kuomintang was driven from the mainland; the People's Republic was proclaimed Oct. 1, 1949. Korea was divided by USSR and U.S. occupation forces. Separate republics were proclaimed in the 2 zones in Aug.-Sept. 1948.

India. India and Pakistan became independent dominions on Aug. 15, 1947. Millions of Hindu and Muslim refugees were created by the partition; riots (1946-47) took hundreds of thousands of lives; Mahatma **Gandhi** was assassinated in Jan. 1948. Burma became completely independent in Jan. 1948; Ceylon took dominion status in Feb.

Middle East. The UN approved partition of Palestine into Jewish and Arab states. **Israel** was proclaimed a state, May 14, 1948. Arabs rejected partition, but failed to defeat Israel in war (May 1948-July 1949). Immigration from Europe and the Middle East swelled Israel's Jewish population. British and French forces left Lebanon and Syria in 1946. Transjordan occupied most of Arab Palestine.

Southeast Asia. Communists and others fought against restoration of French rule in Indochina from 1946; a non-Communist government was recognized by France in Mar. 1949, but fighting continued. Both Indonesia and the Philippines became independent; the former in 1949 after 4 years of war with Netherlands, the latter in 1946. Philippine economic and military ties with the U.S. remained strong; a Communist-led peasant rising was checked in 1948.

Arts. New York became the center of the world art market; **abstract expressionism** was the chief mode (Pollock from 1943, de Kooning from 1947). Literature and philosophy explored **existentialism** (Camus's *The Stranger*, 1942; Sartre's *Being and Nothingness*, 1943). Non-Western attempts to revive or create regional styles (Senghor's Négritude, Mishima's novels) only confirmed the emergence of a universal culture. Radio and phonograph records spread American popular music (swing, bebop) around the world.

The American Decade: 1950-59

Polite decolonization. The peaceful decline of European political and military power in Asia and Africa accelerated in the 1950s. Nearly all of **N Africa** was freed by 1956, but France fought a bitter war to retain Algeria, with its large European minority, until 1962. **Ghana**, independent in 1957, led a parade of new black African nations (more than 2 dozen by 1962), which altered the political character of the UN. Ethnic disputes often exploded in the new nations after decolonization (UN troops in Cyprus, 1964; **Nigerian civil war**, 1967-70). Leaders of the new states, mostly sharing socialist ideologies, tried to create an Afro-Asian bloc (Bandung Conference, 1955), but Western economic influence and U.S. political ties remained strong (Baghdad Pact, 1955).

Trade. World trade volume soared, in an atmosphere of monetary stability assured by international accords (**Bretton Woods,** 1944). In Europe, economic integration advanced (**European Economic Community,** 1957; European Free Trade Association, 1960). Comecon (1949) coordinated the economies of Soviet-bloc countries.

U.S. Economic growth produced an abundance of consumer goods (9.3 million motor vehicles sold, 1955). Suburban housing tracts changed life patterns for middle and working classes (Levittown, 1947-51). Pres. Dwight **Eisenhower's** landslide election victories (1952, 1956) reflected consensus politics. Senate condemnation of Senator Joseph **McCarthy** (Dec. 1954) curbed the political abuse of anti-Communism. A system of alliances and military bases bolstered U.S. influence on all continents. Trade and payments surpluses were balanced by overseas investments and foreign aid ($50 billion, 1950-59).

USSR. In the "thaw" after Stalin's death in 1953, relations with the West improved (evacuation of Vienna, Geneva summit conference, both 1955). Repression of scientific and cultural life eased, and many prisoners were freed or rehabilitated culminating in **de-Stalinization** (1956). **Nikita Khrushchev's** leadership aimed at consumer sector growth, but farm production lagged, despite the virgin lands program (from 1954). Soviet crushing of the 1956 Hungarian revolution, the 1960 U-2 spy plane episode, and other incidents renewed East-West tension and domestic curbs.

East Europe. Resentment of Russian domination and Stalinist repression combined with nationalist, economic, and religious factors to produce periodic violence. E Berlin workers rioted (1953), Polish workers rioted in Poznan (June 1956), and a broad-based **revolution** broke out in **Hungary** (Oct. 1956). All were suppressed by Soviet force or threats (at least 7,000 dead in Hungary). But Poland was allowed to restore private ownership of farms, and a degree of personal and economic freedom returned to Hungary. Yugoslavia experimented with worker self-management and a market economy.

Korea. The 1945 division of Korea along the 38th parallel left industry in the N, which was organized into a militant regime and armed by the USSR. The S was politically disunited. More than 60,000 N Korean troops invaded the S on June 25, 1950. The U.S., backed by the UN Security Council, sent troops. UN troops reached the Chinese border in Nov. Some 200,000 Chinese troops crossed the Yalu R. and drove back UN forces. By spring 1951 battle lines had become stabilized near the original 38th parallel border, but heavy fighting continued. Finally, an armistice was signed on July 27, 1953. U.S. troops remained in the S, and U.S. economic and military aid continued. The war stimulated rapid economic recovery in Japan.

China. Starting in 1952, industry, agriculture, and social institutions were forcibly collectivized. In a massive purge, as many as several million people were executed as Kuomintang supporters or as class and political enemies. The **Great Leap Forward** (1958-60) unsuccessfully tried to force the pace of development by substituting labor for investment.

Indochina. Ho Chi Minh's forces, aided by the USSR and the new Chinese Communist government, fought French and pro-French Vietnamese forces to a standstill and captured the strategic **Dienbienphu** camp in May 1954. The Geneva Agreements divided Vietnam in half pending elections (never held) and recognized Laos and Cambodia as independent. The U.S. aided the anti-Communist Republic of Vietnam in the S.

Middle East. Arab revolutions placed leftist, militantly nationalist regimes in power in Egypt (1952) and Iraq (1958). But Arab unity attempts failed (United Arab Republic joined Egypt, Syria, Yemen, 1958-61). Arab refusal to recognize Israel (Arab League economic blockade began Sept. 1951) led to a permanent state of war, with repeated incidents (Gaza, 1955). Israel occupied Sinai, and Britain and France took (Oct. 1956) the Suez Canal, but were replaced by the UN Emergency Force. The Mossadegh government in Iran nationalized (May 1951) the British-owned oil industry in May, but was overthrown (Aug. 1953) in a U.S.-aided coup.

Latin America. Argentinian dictator Juan **Perón,** in office 1946, enforced land reform, some nationalization, welfare state measures, and curbs on the Roman Catholic Church, and crushed opposition. A Sept. 1955 coup deposed Perón. The 1952 revolution in Bolivia brought land reform, nationalization of tin mines, and improvement in the status of Indians, who nevertheless remained poor. The Batista regime in Cuba was overthrown (Jan. 1959) by Fidel **Castro,** who imposed a Communist dictatorship, aligned Cuba with the USSR, but improved education and health care. A U.S.-backed anti-Castro invasion (**Bay of Pigs**, Apr. 1961) was crushed. Self-government advanced in the British Caribbean.

Technology. Large outlays on research and development in the U.S. and the USSR focused on military applications (H-bomb in U.S., 1952; USSR, 1953; Britain, 1957; intercontinental missiles, late 1950s). Soviet launching of the **Sputnik** satellite (Oct. 4, 1957) spurred increases in U.S. science education funds (National Defense Education Act).

Literature and film. Alienation from social and literary conventions reached an extreme in the theater of the absurd (Beckett's *Waiting for Godot,* 1952), the "new novel" (Robbe-Grillet's *Voyeur,* 1955), and avant-garde film (Antonioni's *L'Avventura,* 1960). U.S. beatniks (Kerouac's *On the Road,* 1957) and others rejected the supposed conformism of Americans (Riesman's *The Lonely Crowd,* 1950).

Rising Expectations: 1960-69

Economic boom. The longest sustained economic boom on record spanned almost the entire decade in the capitalist world; the closely watched GNP figure doubled (1960-70) in the U.S., fueled by Vietnam War–related budget deficits. The **General Agreement on Tariffs and Trade** (1967) stimulated W European prosperity, which spread to peripheral areas (Spain, Italy, E Germany). Japan became a top economic power. Foreign investment aided the industrialization of Brazil. There were limited Soviet economic reform attempts.

Reform and radicalization. Pres. John F. **Kennedy**, inaugurated 1961, emphasized youthful idealism and vigor; his assassination Nov. 22, 1963, was a national trauma. A series of political and social reform movements took root in the U.S., later spreading to other countries. Blacks demonstrated nonviolently and with partial success against segregation and poverty (1963 March on Washington; 1964 **Civil Rights Act**), but some urban ghettos erupted in extensive riots (Watts, 1965; Detroit, 1967; **Martin Luther King** assassination, Apr. 4, 1968). New concern for the poor (Harrington's *Other America*, 1963) helped lead to Pres. Lyndon Johnson's **"Great Society"** programs (Medicare, Water Quality Act, Higher Education Act, all 1965). Concern with the **environment** surged (Carson's *Silent Spring*, 1962).

Feminism revived as a cultural and political movement (Friedan's *Feminine Mystique*, 1963; National Organization for Women founded 1966), and a movement for homosexual rights emerged (Stonewall riot in NYC, 1969). Pope John XXIII called the **Second Vatican Council** (1962-65), which liberalized Roman Catholic liturgy and some other aspects of Catholicism.

Opposition to U.S. involvement in Vietnam, especially among university students (**Moratorium** protest, Nov. 1969), turned violent (Weatherman Chicago riots, Oct. 1969). **New Left** and Marxist theories became popular, and membership in radical groups (Students for a Democratic Society, Black Panthers) increased. Maoist groups, especially in Europe, called for total transformation of society. In France, students sparked a nationwide strike affecting 10 million workers in May-June 1968, but an electoral reaction barred revolutionary change.

China. China's revolutionary militancy under **Mao** Zedong caused disputes with the USSR under "revisionist" Khrushchev, starting in 1960. The 2 powers exchanged fire in 1969 border disputes. China used force to capture (1962) areas disputed with India. The **"Great Proletarian Cultural Revolution"** tried to impose a utopian egalitarian program in China and spread revolution abroad; political struggle, often violent, convulsed China in 1965-68.

Mao Zedong

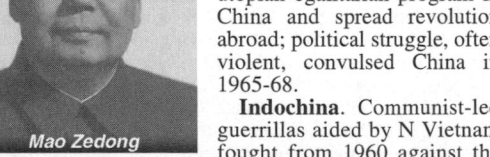

Indochina. Communist-led guerrillas aided by N Vietnam fought from 1960 against the S Vietnam government of Ngo Dinh Diem (killed 1963). The U.S. military role increased after the 1964 **Tonkin Gulf** incident. U.S. forces peaked at 543,400 in Apr. 1969. Massive numbers of N Vietnamese troops also fought. Laotian and Cambodian neutrality were threatened by Communist insurgencies, with N Vietnamese aid, and U.S. intrigues.

Third World. A bloc of authoritarian leftist regimes among the newly independent nations emerged in political opposition to the U.S.-led Western alliance and came to dominate the conference of nonaligned nations (Belgrade, 1961; Cairo, 1964; Lusaka, 1970). Soviet political ties and military bases were established in Cuba, Egypt, Algeria, Guinea, and other countries whose leaders were regarded as revolutionary heroes by opposition groups in pro-Western or colonial countries. Some leaders were ousted in coups by pro-Western groups—Zaire's Patrice Lumumba (killed 1961), Ghana's Kwame Nkrumah (exiled 1966), and Indonesia's Sukarno (effectively ousted in 1965 after a Communist coup failed).

Middle East. Arab-Israeli tension erupted into a brief war June 1967. Israel emerged from the war as a major regional power. Military shipments before and after the war brought much of the Arab world into the Soviet political sphere. Most Arab states broke U.S. diplomatic ties, while Communist countries cut their ties to Israel. Intra-Arab disputes continued: Egypt and Saudi Arabia supported rival factions in a bloody Yemen civil war 1962-70; Lebanese troops fought Palestinian commandos 1969.

East Europe. To stop the large-scale exodus of citizens, E German authorities built (Aug. 1961) a **fortified wall across Berlin.** Soviet sway in the Balkans was weakened by Albania's support of China (USSR broke ties in Dec. 1961) and Romania's assertion (1964) of industrial and foreign policy autonomy. Liberalization (spring 1968) in Czechoslovakia was crushed with massive force by troops of 5 Warsaw Pact countries. W German treaties (1970) with the USSR and Poland facilitated the transfer of German technology and confirmed postwar boundaries.

Arts and styles. The boundary between fine and popular arts was blurred to some extent by Pop Art (Warhol) and rock musicals (*Hair*, 1968). Informality and exaggeration prevailed in fashion (beards, miniskirts). A nonpolitical "counterculture" developed, rejecting traditional bourgeois life goals and personal habits, and use of marijuana and hallucinogens spread (**Woodstock** festival, Aug. 1969). Indian influence was felt in religion (Ram Dass) and fashion, and The **Beatles,** who brought unprecedented sophistication to rock music, became for many a symbol of the decade.

Buzz Aldrin on Moon, 1969

Science. Achievements in space (**humans on the moon,** July 1969) and electronics (lasers, integrated circuits) encouraged a faith in scientific solutions to problems in agriculture ("green revolution"), medicine (heart transplants, 1967), and other areas. Harmful technology, it was believed, could be controlled (1963 nuclear weapon test ban treaty, 1968 nonproliferation treaty).

Disillusionment: 1970-79

U.S.: Caution and neoconservatism. A relatively sluggish economy, energy shortages, and environmental problems contributed to a **"limits of growth"** philosophy. Suspicion of science and technology killed or delayed major projects (supersonic transport dropped, 1971; Seabrook nuclear power plant protests, 1977-78) and was fed by the Three Mile Island nuclear reactor accident (Mar. 1979).

There were signs of growing mistrust of big government and less support for new social policies. School busing and racial quotas were opposed (Bakke decision, June 1978); the proposed Equal Rights Amendment for women languished; civil rights legislation aimed at protecting homosexuals was opposed (Dade County referendum, June 1977).

Completion of Communist forces' takeover of **South Vietnam** (evacuation of U.S. civilians, Apr. 1975), revelations of Central Intelligence Agency misdeeds (Rockefeller Commission report, June 1975), and **Watergate** scandals (Nixon resigned in Aug. 1974) reduced faith in U.S. moral and material capacity to influence world affairs. Revelations of Soviet crimes (Solzhenitsyn's *Gulag Archipelago,* 1974) and Soviet intervention in Africa helped foster a revival of anti-Communist sentiment.

Economy sluggish. The 1960s boom faltered in the 1970s; a severe recession in the U.S. and Europe (1974-75) followed a huge oil price hike (Dec. 1973). Monetary instability (U.S. cut ties to gold in Aug. 1971), the decline of the dollar, and protectionist moves by industrial countries (1977-78) threatened trade. Business investment and spending for research declined. Severe inflation plagued many countries (25% in Britain, 1975; 18% in U.S., 1979).

China picks up pieces. After the 1976 deaths of Mao Zedong and Zhou Enlai, struggle for the leadership succession was won by pragmatists. A nationwide purge of orthodox Maoists was carried out, and the **Gang of Four,** led by Mao's widow, Chiang Ching, arrested. The new leaders freed more than 100,000 political prisoners and reduced public adulation of Mao. Political and trade ties were expanded with Japan, Europe, and the U.S. in the late 1970s, as relations worsened with the USSR, Cuba, and Vietnam (4-week invasion by China, 1979). Ideological guidelines in industry, science, education, and the armed forces, which the ruling faction said had caused chaos and decline, were reversed (bonuses to workers, Dec. 1977; exams for college entrance, Oct. 1977). Severe restrictions on cultural expression were eased.

Europe. European unity moves (EEC-EFTA trade accord, 1972) faltered as economic problems appeared (Britain floated pound, 1972; France floated franc, 1974). Germany and Switzerland curbed guest workers from southern Europe. Greece and Turkey quarreled over Cyprus and Aegean oil rights.

All non-Communist Europe was under democratic rule after free elections were held (June 1976) in **Spain** 7 months after the death of Franco. The conservative, colonialist regime in **Portugal** was overthrown in Apr. 1974. In **Greece** the 7-year-old military dictatorship yielded power in 1974. Northern Europe, though ruled mostly by Socialists (**Swedish** Socialists unseated in 1976 after 44 years in power), turned more conservative. The **British** Labour government imposed (1975) wage curbs and suspended nationalization schemes. Terrorism in **Germany** (1972 Munich Olympics killings) led to laws curbing some civil liberties. **French** "new philosophers" rejected leftist ideologies, and the shaky Socialist-Communist coalition lost a 1978 election bid.

Religion and politics. The improvement in **Muslim** countries' political fortunes by the 1950s (with the exception of Central Asia under Soviet and Chinese rule) and the growth of Arab oil wealth were followed by a resurgence of traditional religious fervor. Libyan dictator Muammar al-Qaddafi mixed Islamic laws with socialism and called for Muslim return to Spain and Sicily. The illegal Muslim Brotherhood in **Egypt** was accused of violence, while extreme groups bombed (1977) theaters to protest Western and secular values.

In **Turkey**, the National Salvation Party was the first Islamic group to share (1974) power since secularization in the 1920s. In **Iran, Ayatollah Ruhollah Khomeini,** led a revolution that deposed the secular shah (Jan. 1979) and created an Islamic republic there. Religiously motivated Muslims took part in an insurrection in Saudi Arabia that briefly seized (1979) the Grand Mosque in Mecca. Muslim puritan opposition to **Pakistan** Pres. Zulfikar Ali-Bhutto helped lead to his overthrow in July 1977. Muslim solidarity, however, could not prevent Pakistan's eastern province (**Bangladesh**) from declaring (Dec. 1971) independence after a bloody civil war.

Muslim and Hindu resentment of coerced sterilization in **India** helped defeat the Gandhi government, which was replaced (Mar. 1977) by a coalition including religious Hindu parties. Muslims in the S **Philippines**, aided by Libya, rebelled against central rule from 1973.

The Buddhist Soka Gakkai movement launched (1964) the Komeito party in **Japan,** which became a major opposition party in 1972 and 1976 elections.

Evangelical Protestant groups grew in the U.S. A revival of interest in Orthodox Christianity occurred among **Russian** intellectuals (Solzhenitsyn). The secularist **Israeli** Labor party, after decades of rule, was ousted in 1977 by conservatives led by Menachem Begin; religious militants founded settlements on the disputed West Bank, part of biblically promised Israel. U.S. Reform Judaism revived many previously discarded traditional practices.

Old-fashioned religious wars raged intermittently in **Northern Ireland** (Catholic vs. Protestant, 1969-) and **Lebanon** (Christian vs. Muslim, 1975-), while religious militancy complicated the Israel-Arab dispute (1973 Israel-Arab war). Despite a 1979 **peace treaty between Egypt and Israel,** increased militancy on the West Bank impeded further progress.

Latin America. Repressive conservative regimes strengthened their hold on most of the continent, with a violent coup against the elected (Sept. 1973) Allende government in **Chile**, a 1976 military coup in **Argentina**, and coups against reformist regimes in **Bolivia** (1971, 1979) and **Peru** (1976). In Central America increasing liberal and leftist militancy led to the ouster (1979) of the Somoza regime of **Nicaragua** and to civil conflict in **El Salvador**.

Indochina. Communist victories in Vietnam, Cambodia, and Laos by May 1975 led to new turmoil. The **Pol Pot regime** ordered millions of city-dwellers to resettle in rural areas, in a program of forced labor, combined with terrorism, that cost more than 1 million lives (1975-79) and caused hundreds of thousands of ethnic Chinese and others to flee Vietnam ("boat people," 1979). The Vietnamese invasion of Cambodia swelled the refugee population and contributed to widespread starvation in that devastated country.

Russian expansion. Soviet influence, checked in some countries (troops ousted by Egypt, 1972), was projected farther afield, often with the use of Cuban troops (Angola, 1975-89; Ethiopia, 1977-88) and aided by a growing navy, a merchant fleet, and international banking ability. **Détente** with the West—1972 Berlin pact, 1972 strategic arms pact (**SALT**)—gave way to a more antagonistic relationship in the late 1970s, exacerbated by the Soviet invasion (1979) of **Afghanistan.**

Africa. The last remaining European colonies were granted independence (**Spanish Sahara**, 1976; **Djibouti,** 1977) and, after 10 years of civil war and many negotiation sessions, a black government took over (1979) in Zimbabwe (Rhodesia); white domination remained in **South Africa**. Great power involvement in local wars (Russia in **Angola, Ethiopia**; France in **Chad, Zaire, Mauritania**) and the use of tens of thousands of Cuban troops were denounced by some African leaders. Ethnic or tribal clashes made Africa a locus of sustained warfare during the late 1970s.

Arts. Traditional modes of painting, architecture, and music received increased popular and critical attention in the 1970s. These more conservative styles coexisted with modernist works in an atmosphere of increased variety and tolerance.

Revitalization of Capitalism, Demand for Democracy: 1980-89

USSR, Eastern Europe. A troublesome 1980-85 for the USSR was followed by 5 years of astonishing change: the surrender of the Communist monopoly, the remaking of the Soviet state, and the beginning of the disintegration of the Soviet empire. After the deaths of Leonid **Brezhnev** (1982) and 2 successors (Andropov in 1984 and Chernenko in 1985), the harsh treatment of dissent and restriction of emigration, and the Soviet invasion (Dec. 1979) of Afghanistan, Gen. Sec. Mikhail **Gorbachev** (in office 1985-1991) promoted *glasnost* and *perestroika*—economic, political, and social reform. Supported by the Communist Party (July 1988), he signed (Dec. 1987) the INF disarmament treaty, and he pledged (1988) to cut the military budget. Military withdrawal from Afghanistan was completed in Feb. 1989, the process of democratization went ahead unhindered in Poland and Hungary, and the Soviet people chose (Mar. 1989) part of the new Congress of People's Deputies from competing candidates. By decade's end the **Cold War** appeared to be fading away.

In **Poland, Solidarity**, the labor union founded (1980) by Lech **Walesa**, was outlawed in 1982 and then legalized in 1988, after years of unrest. Poland's first free election since the Communist takeover brought Solidarity victory (June 1989); Tadeusz Mazowiecki, a Walesa adviser, became (Aug. 1989) prime minister in a government with the Communists. In the fall of 1989 the failure of Marxist economies in **Hungary**, **East Germany**, **Czechoslovakia, Bulgaria,** and **Romania** brought the collapse of the Communist monopoly and a demand for democracy. In a historic step, the **Berlin Wall** was opened in Nov. 1989.

U.S. "The Reagan Years" (1981-88) brought the **longest economic boom** yet in U.S. history via budget and tax cuts, deregulation, "junk bond" financing, leveraged buyouts, and mergers and takeovers. However, there was a stock market crash (Oct. 1987), and federal budget deficits and the trade deficit increased. Foreign policy showed a **strong anti-Communist stance**, via increased defense spending, aid to anti-Communists in Central America, invasion of Cuba-threatened Grenada, and championing of the MX missile system and "Star Wars" missile defense program. Four Reagan-Gorbachev summits (1985-88) climaxed in the INF treaty (1987), as the Cold War began to wind down. The Iran-contra affair (North's TV testimony, July 1987) was a major political scandal. Homelessness and drug abuse (especially "crack" cocaine) were growing social problems. In 1988, Vice Pres. George Bush was elected to succeed Ronald Reagan as president.

Middle East. The Middle East remained militarily unstable, with sharp divisions along economic, political, racial, and religious lines. In **Iran**, the Islamic revolution of 1979 created a strong anti-U.S. stance (hostage crisis, Nov. 1979-Jan. 1981). In Sept. 1980, **Iraq** repudiated its border agreement with Iran and began major hostilities that led to an 8-year war in which millions were killed.

Libya's support for international terrorism induced the U.S. to close (May 1981) its diplomatic mission there and embargo (Mar. 1982) Libyan oil. The U.S. accused Libyan leader Muammar al-Qaddafi of aiding (Dec. 1985) terrorists in Rome and of Vienna airport attacks, and retaliated by bombing Libya (Apr. 1986).

Israel affirmed (July 1980) all Jerusalem as its capital, destroyed (1981) an Iraqi atomic reactor, and invaded (1982) Lebanon, forcing the PLO to agree to withdraw. A **Palestinian uprising**, including women and children hurling rocks and bottles at troops, began (Dec. 1987) in Israeli-occupied Gaza and spread to the West Bank; troops responded with force, killing 300 by the end of 1988, with 6,000 more in detention camps.

Israeli withdrawal from **Lebanon** began in Feb. 1985 and ended in June 1985, as Lebanon continued torn by military and political conflict. Artillery duels (Mar.-Apr. 1989) between Christian East Beirut and Muslim West Beirut left 200 dead and 700 wounded. At decade's end, violence still dominated.

Latin America. In **Nicaragua**, the leftist Sandinista National Liberation Front, in power after the 1979 civil war, faced problems as a result of Nicaragua's military aid to leftist guerrillas in El Salvador and U.S. backing of antigovernment contras. The U.S. CIA admitted (1984) having directed the mining of Nicaraguan ports, and the U.S. sent humanitarian (1985) and military (1986) aid. Profits from secret arms sales to Iran were found (1987) diverted to contras. Cease-fire talks between the Sandinista government and contras came in 1988, and elections were held in Feb. 1990.

In **El Salvador**, a military coup (Oct. 1979) failed to halt extreme right-wing violence and left-wing terrorism. Archbishop Oscar Romero was assassinated in Mar. 1980; from Jan. to June some 4,000 civilians reportedly were killed in the civil unrest. In 1984, newly elected Pres. José Napoleon Duarte worked to stem human rights abuses, but violence continued.

In **Chile**, Gen. Augusto Pinochet yielded the presidency after a democratic election (Dec. 1989), but remained as head of the army. He had ruled the country since 1973, imposing harsh measures against leftists and dissidents; at the same time he introduced economic programs that restored prosperity to Chile.

Africa. 1980-85 marked a rapid decline in the economies of virtually all African countries, a result of accelerating desertification, the world economic recession, heavy indebtedness to overseas creditors, rapid population growth, and political instability. Some 60 million Africans faced prolonged hunger in 1981; much of Africa had one of the worst droughts ever in 1983, and by year's end **150 million faced near-famine**. "Live Aid," a marathon rock concert, was presented in July 1985, and the U.S. and Western nations sent aid in Sept. 1985. Economic hardship fueled political unrest and coups. Wars in Ethiopia and Sudan and military strife in several other nations continued. AIDS took a heavy toll.

South Africa. Anti-apartheid sentiment gathered force in South Africa as demonstrations and violent police response grew. White voters approved (Nov. 1983) the first constitution to give Coloureds and Asians a voice, while still excluding blacks (70% of the population). The U.S. imposed economic sanctions in Aug. 1985, and 11 Western nations followed in September. P. W. **Botha**, 1980s president, was succeeded by F. W. **de Klerk**, in Sept. 1989, who promised "evolutionary" change via negotiation with the black population.

China. During the 1980s the Communist government and paramount leader **Deng Xiaoping** pursued **far-reaching changes**, expanding commercial and technical ties to the industrialized world and increasing the role of market forces in stimulating urban development. Apr. 1989 brought new demands for political reforms; student demonstrators camped out in Tiananmen Sq., Beijing, in a massive peaceful protest. Some 100,000 students and workers marched, and at least 20 other cities saw protests. In response, martial law was imposed; army troops crushed the demonstration in and around Tiananmen Square on June 3-4, with death toll estimates at 500-7,000, up to 10,000 dissidents arrested, 31 people tried and executed. The conciliatory Communist Party chief was ousted; the Politburo adopted (July) reforms against official corruption.

Japan. Japan's relations with other nations, especially the U.S., were dominated by **trade imbalances favoring Japan**. In 1985 the U.S. trade deficit with Japan was $49.7 billion, one-third of the total U.S. trade deficit. After Japan was found (Apr. 1986) to sell semiconductors and computer memory chips below cost, the U.S. was assured a "fair share" of the market, but charged (Mar. 1987) Japan with failing to live up to the agreement.

European Community. With the addition of Greece, Portugal, and Spain, the EC became a common market of more than **300 million people**, the West's largest trading entity. Margaret **Thatcher** became the first British prime minister in the 20th century to win a 3rd consecutive term (1987). France elected (1981) its first socialist president, François **Mitterrand**, who was reelected in 1988. Italy elected (1983) its first socialist premier, Bettino **Craxi**.

International terrorism. With the 1979 overthrow of the shah of Iran, terrorism became a prominent tactic. It increased through the 1980s, but with fewer high-profile attacks after 1985. In 1979-81, Iranian militants held 52 U.S. hostages in Iran for 444 days; in 1983 a TNT-laden suicide terrorist blew up U.S. Marine headquarters in Beirut, killing 241 Americans, and a truck bomb blew up a French paratroop barracks, killing 58. The *Achille Lauro* cruise ship was hijacked in 1986, and an American passenger killed; the U.S. subsequently intercepted the Egyptian plane flying the terrorists to safety. Incidents rose to 700 in 1985, and to 1,000 in 1988. **Assassinated leaders** included Egypt's Pres. Anwar al-**Sadat** (1981), India's Prime Min. Indira **Gandhi** (1984), and Lebanese Premier Rashid **Karami** (1987).

Post–Cold War World: 1990-99

Soviet Empire breakup. The world community witnessed the extraordinary spectacle of a superpower's disintegration when the **Soviet Union** broke apart into 15 independent states. The 1980s had already seen internal reforms and a decline of Communist power both within the Soviet Union and in Eastern Europe. The Soviet breakup began in earnest with the declarations of independence adopted by the Baltic republics of **Lithuania, Latvia,** and **Estonia** during an abortive coup against reformist leader Mikhail **Gorbachev** (Aug. 1991). The other republics soon took the same step. In Dec. 1991, **Russia, Ukraine**, and **Belarus** declared the Soviet Union dead; Gorbachev resigned, and the Soviet Parliament went out of existence. The Warsaw Pact and the Council for Mutual Economic Assistance (Comecon) were disbanded. Most of the former republics joined in a loose confederation called the **Commonwealth of Independent States**. **Russia** remained the predominant country after the breakup, but its people soon suffered severe economic hardship as the nation, under Pres. Boris **Yeltsin,** moved to revamp the economy and to adopt a free market system. In Oct. 1993, **anti-Yeltsin forces** occupied the Parliament building and were ousted by the army; about 140 people died in the fighting.

The Muslim republic of **Chechnya** declared independence from the rest of Russia, but this was met with an invasion by Russian troops (Dec. 1994). After almost 21 months of vicious fighting, a cease-fire took hold in 1996, and the Russians withdrew. In 1999 Russia forcibly suppressed Muslim insurgents in Dagestan and entered neighboring Chechnya, again fighting to gain control over separatist rebels there. Yeltsin resigned office Dec. 31, 1999, to be replaced by Vladimir **Putin** (elected in his own right, Mar. 2000).

Europe. Yugoslavia broke apart, and hostilities ensued among the republics along ethnic and religious lines. **Croatia, Slovenia**, and **Macedonia** declared independence (1991), followed by **Bosnia-Herzegovina** (1992). **Serbia** and **Montenegro** remained as the republic of Yugoslavia. Bitter fighting followed, especially in Bosnia, where Serbs reportedly engaged in **"ethnic cleansing"** of the Muslim population; a peace plan (Dayton accord), brokered by the United States, was signed by **Bosnia, Serbia**, and **Croatia** (Dec. 1995), with **NATO** responsible for policing its implementation. In spring 1999, NATO conducted a bombing campaign aimed at stopping Yugoslavia from its campaign to drive out ethnic Albanians from the Kosovo region; a peace accord was reached in June under which NATO peacekeeping troops entered Kosovo.

The two **Germanys** were reunited after 45 years (Oct. 1990). The union was greeted with jubilation, but stresses became apparent when free market principles were applied to the aging East German industries, resulting in many plant closings and rising unemployment. German chancellor Helmut **Kohl**, a Christian Democrat, lost power after 16 years, in Sept. 1998 elections; Gerhard **Schroeder**, a Social Democrat, took over. Czechoslovakia broke apart peacefully (Jan. 1993), becoming the **Czech Republic** and **Slovakia. In Poland**, Lech **Walesa** was elected president (Dec. 1991) but was defeated in his bid for a 2nd term (Nov. 1995).

NATO approved the **Partnership for Peace** Program (Jan. 1994) coordinating the defense of **Eastern** and **Central European** countries; Russia joined the program later that year. NATO signed a pact with **Russia** (1997) providing for NATO expansion into the former Soviet-bloc countries; a similar treaty was set up with **Ukraine**. The **Czech Republic**, **Hungary**, and **Poland** became members in Jan. 1999; in that year **NATO** celebrated its 50th anniversary. Efforts toward European unity continued with adoption of a single market (Jan. 1993) and conversion of the European Community to the **European Union** as the Maestricht Treaty took effect (Nov. 1993). Agreement was reached for 11 EU members to participate in Economic and Monetary Union, adopting a common currency **(euro)** for some purposes in Jan. 1999, with the euro to go into common circulation in 2002.

An intraparty revolt forced Margaret **Thatcher** out as prime minister of **Great Britain**, to be succeeded by John **Major** (Nov. 1990); 7 years later, Major suffered an overwhelming defeat at the hands of the new Labour Party leader, Tony **Blair** (May 1997). The divorce of Prince **Charles and** Princess **Diana**, followed by the death of Diana in a car accident (Aug. 1997), made headlines around the world. Talks on **peace** in **Northern Ireland** that included participation of Sinn Fein, political arm of the IRA, led to a ground-breaking peace plan, approved in an all-Ireland vote (May 1998). In Dec. 1999, Northern Ireland was granted home rule under a power-sharing cabinet. In **Scotland** voters overwhelmingly approved establishment of a regional legislature (1997), and in **Wales** voters narrowly approved establishment of a local assembly (1997). In a historic innovation, the Church of England **ordained 32 women** as priests (Mar. 1994).

Middle East. In Aug. 1990, **Iraq's Saddam Hussein** ordered his troops to invade **Kuwait.** The UN approved military action in response (Nov. 1990), and U.S. Pres. George **Bush** put together an international military force. Allied planes bombed Iraq (Jan. 1991) and launched a land attack, crushing the invasion (Feb. 1991). After Iraq accepted a cease-fire (Apr. 1991), U.S. troops withdrew, but "no-fly" zones were set up over northern Iraq to protect the Kurds and over southern Iraq to protect Shiite Muslims. The **UN** imposed **sanctions** on Iraq for failure to abide by the cease-fire. Iraq's reported failure to cooperate with UN arms inspectors seeking to eliminate "weapons of mass destruction" led to repeated air strikes by the U.S. and Britain.

The last Western hostages were freed in **Lebanon,** June 1992. **Israel** and the **Palestine Liberation Organization** signed a peace accord (Sept. 1993) providing for Palestinian self-government in the West Bank and Gaza Strip. Prime Min. Yitzhak **Rabin** and Foreign Min. Shimon **Peres** of Israel and Yasir **Arafat** of the PLO received the Nobel Peace Prize for their efforts (1994). Six Arab nations relaxed their boycott against Israel (1994), and Israel and **Jordan** signed a peace treaty (Oct. 1994). **Rabin was assassinated** (Nov. 1995) by an Israeli opponent of the peace process. After new elections (May 1996), Benjamin Netanyahu as prime minister adopted a harder line in peace negotiations. **Arafat** was elected to the presidency of the Palestinian Authority (Jan. 1996). A long-delayed interim agreement (the Wye Memorandum) on Israel military withdrawal from part of the West Bank was reached Oct. 1998. A Labour government under Ehud **Barak** took power after May 1999 elections, but further progress in peace negotiations proved elusive.

King **Hussein** of Jordan died (Feb. 1999), to be succeeded by his son Abdullah.

Asia and the Pacific. Hong Kong was returned to **China** (July 1997) after being a British colony for 156 years. China, which emerged in the decade as a major developing economic power, had agreed to follow a policy of "one country, two systems" in Hong Kong. The territory of **Macao** reverted to Chinese sovereignty (Dec. 1999) after over 400 years of Portuguese rule; it retained its capitalist economic system. **Jiang Zemin**, general secretary of the Chinese Communist Party, assumed the additional post of president of China (Mar. 1993) and emerged as the key leader after the death of paramount leader **Deng Xiaoping** (Feb. 1997). China released from prison—and exiled—some well-known dissidents but continued to be criticized for detentions and other alleged widespread **human rights abuses**. In Nov. 1999 the U.S. and China signed a landmark pact normalizing trade relations.

After years of prosperity, **Thailand, Indonesia**, and **South Korea** in 1997 began to suffer economic reverses that had a worldwide ripple effect. These countries received billion-dollar IMF bailout packages. In **Indonesia**, protests over mismanagement led to the resignation of Pres. **Suharto** (May 1998) after 32 years of nearly autocratic rule. Abdurraham Wahid was elected (Oct. 1999) in the country's first fully democratic elections. In a referendum (Aug. 1999), **East Timor** voted overwhelmingly for independence from Indonesia; pro-Indonesian militias then rampaged through the territory, but a multinational peacekeeping force was allowed in (Sept. 1999) to help restore order. In **South Korea**, former dissident **Kim Dae Jung** was elected president (Dec. 1997). Two previous presidents, Roh Tae Woo and Chun Doo Hwan, were convicted of crimes committed in office but were given amnesty by the new president.

In Japan members of a religious cult, released the nerve gas sarin on 5 Tokyo subway cars, killing 12 people and injuring more than 5,500 (Mar. 1995). Tamil rebels continued their armed conflict in **Sri Lanka**. In **Afghanistan** the **Taliban**, an extreme Islamic fundamentalist group, gained control of Kabul (Sept. 1996) and, eventually, most of the country. In **North Korea**, longtime dictator **Kim Il Sung** died (July 1994), to be succeeded by his son, **Kim Jong Il**. In the same year the country signed an agreement with the U.S. setting a timetable for North Korea to eliminate its nuclear program. The country also suffered a severe drought, and widespread starvation was feared.

India was beset by riots following destruction of a mosque by Hindu militants (Dec. 1992); Indian army troops repeatedly clashed with pro-independence demonstrators in the disputed Muslim region of **Kashmir**, exacerbating relations with **Pakistan**. Uneasy relations between India and Pakistan reached a new level when both nations conducted nuclear tests in 1998. Conflict in Pakistan between government and the military led to a bloodless coup (Oct. 1999).

Africa. South Africa was transformed as the white-dominated government abandoned **apartheid** and the country made the transition to a nonracial democratic government. Pres. F. W. **de Klerk** released Nelson **Mandela** from prison (Feb. 1990), after he had been held by the government for 27 years, and lifted a ban on the African National Congress. The white government repealed its apartheid laws (1990, 1991). **Mandela** was elected **president** (Apr. 1994), and a new constitution became law (Dec. 1996). Thabo **Mbeki**, the ANC's candidate to succeed Mandela, was overwhelmingly elected president in June 1999. In **Nigeria**, Gen. Olusegun **Obasanjo** was elected president (Feb. 1999), to become the country's first civilian leader in 15 years.

The decades-long rule of **Mobutu** Sese Seko in **Zaire** came to an end (May 1997) at the hands of rebel forces led by Laurent **Kabila**; an ailing Mobutu fled the country and soon after died. Kabila changed the country's name back to **Democratic Republic of the Congo**; conditions remained unstable. After the presidents of **Burundi** and **Rwanda** were killed in an airplane crash (Apr. 1994), violence erupted in Rwanda between Hutu and Tutsi factions; tens of thousands were slain. The conflict spread to refugee camps in neighboring Zaire and Burundi. Factional fighting also erupted in **Somalia** after Pres. Muhammad Siad Barre was ousted (Jan. 1991). The UN sent a U.S.-led **peacekeeping force**, but it was unsuccessful in restoring order. Some soldiers of the peacekeeping force were killed, including 23 Pakistanis (June 1993) and 18 U.S. Rangers (Oct. 1993). The UN ended its mission (Mar. 1995) with no durable government in place. **Liberia** endured factional fighting that lasted almost 5 years and claimed over 150,000 lives; a cease-fire was concluded in Aug. 1995. The World Health Organization reported (1995) that Africa accounted for 70% of **AIDS** cases worldwide.

A 16-year civil war appeared to end in **Angola** (May 1991) when the government signed a peace accord with the rebel UNITA faction. But despite the inauguration of a national unity government (Apr. 1997), insurgents continued to fight and gain territory. **Namibia** officially became independent in Mar. 1990. Claimed by South Africa since 1919 and placed under UN authority in 1971, it had long been a focus of colonial rivalries. In **Algeria,** the army cancelled a 2nd round of parliamentary elections (Jan. 1992) after the Islamic party won a first round. Islamic fundamentalists then began a terrorist campaign that, along with killings by pro-government squads, eventually claimed thousands of lives. A peace plan was worked out with the militants in 1999.

North America. The **North American Free Trade Agreement** (NAFTA), liberalizing trade between the United States, Canada, and Mexico, went into effect Jan. 1, 1994. In **Canada**, the Progressive Conservative Party suffered a crushing defeat in general elections (Oct. 1993), and liberal Jean **Chrétien** became prime minister. The map of Canada was altered in Apr. 1999 to create a new territory, **Nunavut,** out of an area that had been part of Northwest Territories.

In the **United States**, in the 1992 presidential election, Democrat Bill **Clinton** defeated Pres. George Bush, but in 1994 congressional elections Republicans gained control of Congress. Congress passed legislation under which federal protection for welfare recipients was ended and funds turned over to the states for their programs. Clinton reached agreement with Congress on measures to eliminate the federal budget deficit. Clinton won reelection in 1996; the new administration was plagued by scandals but remained popular amid continued economic prosperity. In Dec. 1998 **Clinton** was **impeached** by the U.S. House on charges related to the Monica Lewinsky scandal; he was **acquitted** by the Senate in Feb. 1999.

The U.S. Army and Navy were torn by sexual scandals involving abuse of women personnel. The **United States** suffered embarrassment with the discovery of espionage by CIA agents (Aldrich Ames, Harold Nicholson).

In **Mexico,** Ernesto **Zedillo** of the ruling PRI party was elected president (July 1994) after the party's first candidate was assassinated. The country soon faced a crisis affecting the value of the peso, but recovered with the help of a bail-out package from the U.S. A peasant revolt spearheaded by the **Zapatista National Liberation Army** erupted in the state of Chiapas (Jan. 1994) and was suppressed.

Central America. In **Haiti**, Jean-Bertrand **Aristide** was elected president (Dec. 1990) but was ousted in a military coup after 9 months in office. The UN approved a U.S.-led invasion to restore the elected leader; shortly before troops arrived, a delegation headed by former U.S. Pres. Jimmy Carter arranged (Sept. 1994) for the junta to step aside for Aristide. In **Nicaragua**, Violetta Chamarro defeated Daniel **Ortega** in the presidential election (Feb. 1990), thus ousting the Sandinistas. In **Panama**, U.S. troops invaded and overthrew the government of Manuel **Noriega** (Dec. 1989), who was wanted on drug charges; Noriega was captured Jan. 1990. On Dec. 31, 1999, Panama assumed full control of the **Panama Canal**, in accord with a treaty with the U.S. In **El Salvador** (1992) and **Guatemala** (1996) the governments signed agreements with rebel factions aimed at ending long-running civil conflicts.

South America. Alberto **Fujimori** was elected president of **Peru** in June 1990 and, despite his suppression of the constitution (1992), was reelected in 1995. Peru succeeded in capturing (Sept. 1992) the leader of the **Shining Path** guerrilla movement. Leftist guerrillas took hostages at an ambassador's residence in Lima (Dec. 1996); one hostage was killed during a government assault rescuing the rest (Apr. 1997). Peronist Pres. Carlos Saúl **Menem** served as **Argentina**'s president for much of the decade (elected 1989, reelected 1995), imposing stringent economic measures; he was succeeded in 1999 by Fernando de la **Rúa**.

Former Chilean Pres. Gen. Augusto **Pinochet** continued to head the army until Mar. 1998; he was arrested in London (Oct. 1998) on human rights charges but was judged medically unfit for trial and returned to Chile (Mar. 2000).

In **Brazil**, Fernando Henrique **Cardoso** was elected president (Oct. 1994) and reelected in 1998 amid a growing economic slump; the IMF announced a $42 billion aid package (Nov. 1998). The first UN Conference on Environment and Development, or **Earth Summit**, was held (June 1992) in **Rio de Janeiro,** with delegates from 178 nations.

Terrorism and Crime. Terrorism, often linked to Mideastern sources and with the U.S. as object, continued. A terrorist bomb exploded in a garage beneath New York City's **World Trade Center**, killing 6 people (Feb. 1993). Bombings of a U.S. military training center (Nov. 1995) and a barracks holding U.S. airmen (June 1996), both in **Saudi Arabia,** killed 7 and 19, respectively. Bombs exploded outside **U.S. embassies** in Kenya and Tanzania, Aug. 1998, killing over 220 people; the U.S. retaliated with missiles fired at alleged terrorist-linked sites in Afghanistan and Sudan. The Alfred P. Murrah Federal Building in **Oklahoma City**, OK, was destroyed by a bomb that killed 168 people (Apr. 1995).

Science. The powerful **Hubble Space Telescope** was launched in Apr. 1990; flaws in its mirrors and solar panels were repaired by space-walking astronauts (Dec. 1993). The U.S. space shuttle ***Atlantis*** docked with the orbiting Russian space station ***Mir*** (June 1995) for the first time, in the first of several joint missions in a spirit of post-Cold-War cooperation. The last Russian crew of the aging *Mir* space station departed in Aug. 1999. In Nov. 1998 the first component for a new **International Space Station** was launched into space from Kazakhstan. Two U.S. unmanned space probes sent to explore **Mars** were lost (1999) before they could send back any information.

Scottish scientist Ian Wilmut announced (Feb. 1997) the **cloning** of a sheep, nicknamed Dolly—the first mammal successfully cloned from a cell from an adult animal.

Opening a New Century: 2000-2001

Middle East. Violence between Israelis and Palestinians escalated in 2000 and 2001; with **suicide bombings** by Palestinians and retaliation by Israeli armed forces, the peace process languished. Likud leader Ariel **Sharon** was **elected** prime minister of Israel (Feb. 2001). Syrian Pres. Hafez al-**Assad died** (June 2000); succeeded by his son.

Europe. In Oct. 2000, Yugoslav strongman Slobodan **Milosevic yielded** power to Vojislav Kostunica, who had declared himself president in the face of anti-Milosevic protests after a disputed election. Milosevic surrendered to Serbian authorities (Apr. 2001), to be tried for **war crimes** allegedly committed during 1990s ethnic conflicts in the Balkans. The first-ever **Concorde jet crash**, near Paris, killed 113 people (July 2000). The Russian nuclear sub ***Kursk* sank** in the Barents Sea (Aug. 2000) killing 118 crew members. By early 2002 the euro was the common currency in 12 nations.

Asia. South Korean President Kim Dae **Jung** and **North Korean** ruler Kim **Jong Il** held a **summit** meeting and agreed to seek peace and reunification (June 2000). **Nepal**'s King **Birendra** and other Nepal royals were shot to death inside the palace, apparently by Crown Prince Dipendra, who then killed himself (June 2001). **Chinese** Pres. Jiang Zemin and **Russian** Pres. Vladimir Putin signed a **friendship treaty** (July 2001).

Africa. The 13th International **AIDS Conference**, held in Durban, South Africa (July 2000), focused on ways of controlling surging AIDS rates in developing countries. **Ethiopia and Eritrea** signed a **peace treaty** (Dec. 2000). Laurent **Kabila**, president of the Democratic Republic of the **Congo**, was **shot to death** by a bodyguard (Jan. 2001).

North and South America. Vicente **Fox** of the center-right National Action Party (PAN) was elected **president of Mexico** (July 2000), in a historic defeat for the long-supreme Institutional Revolutionary Party (PRI). Peruvian Pres. Alberto **Fujimori stepped down** in the midst of his 3rd term (Nov. 2000), amid scandal, and did not run for reelection. In Jan. 2001, George W. **Bush** was inaugurated as U.S. president, after one of the tightest and most controversial elections in U.S. history.

Terrorism and Crime. In Oct. 2000, 17 American sailors were killed aboard the **USS *Cole*** in Aden, **Yemen**, when a small boat exploded alongside it in a terrorist attack. On **Sept. 11, 2001,** hijackers crashed 2 jetliners into the twin towers of the **World Trade Center** in New York City and another into the **Pentagon** outside Washington, DC; a 4th crashed in a field in **Pennsylvania**. The attacks, which destroyed both towers and damaged the Pentagon, killed an estimated 3,000 people, including all 265 aboard the planes. Pres. Bush launched a U.S.-led military campaign to root out terrorist infrastructure in **Afghanistan.**

International. Negotiators from 178 countries (not including the U.S.) agreed to adopt the **Kyoto Protocol**, calling for a reduction of greenhouse gases in developed nations (July 2001).

HISTORICAL FIGURES

Ancient Greeks and Romans

Greeks

Aeschines, orator, 389-314 BC
Aeschylus, dramatist, 525-456 BC
Aesop, fableist, c620-c560 BC
Alcibiades, politician, 450-404 BC
Anacreon, poet, c582-c485 BC
Anaxagoras, philosopher, c500-428 BC
Anaximander, philosopher, 611-546 BC
Anaximenes, philosopher, c570-500 BC
Antiphon, speechwriter, c480-411 BC
Apollonius, mathematician, c265-170 BC
Archimedes, math., 287-212 BC
Aristophanes, dramatist, c448-380 BC
Aristotle, philosopher, 384-322 BC
Athenaeus, scholar, fl. c200
Callicrates, architect, fl. 5th cent. BC
Callimachus, poet, c305-240 BC
Cratinus, comic dramatist, 520-421 BC
Democritus, philosopher, c460-370 BC
Demosthenes, orator, 384-322 BC
Diodorus, historian, fl. 20 BC
Diogenes, philosopher, 372-c287 BC
Dionysius, historian, d. c7 BC
Empedocles, philosopher, c490-430 BC
Epicharmus, dramatist, c530-440 BC
Epictetus, philosopher, c55-c135
Epicurus, philosopher, 341-270 BC
Eratosthenes, scientist, 276-194 BC
Euclid, mathematician, fl. c300 BC
Euripides, dramatist, c484-406 BC
Galen, physician, 130-200
Heraclitus, philosopher, c540-c475 BC
Herodotus, historian, c484-420 BC
Hesiod, poet, 8th cent. BC
Hippocrates, physician, c460-377 BC
Homer, poet, fl. c700 BC(?)
Isocrates, orator, 436-338 BC
Menander, dramatist, 342-292 BC
Parmenides, philosopher, b. c515 BC
Pericles, statesman, c495-429 BC
Phidias, sculptor, c500-435 BC
Pindar, poet, c518-c438 BC
Plato, philosopher, c428-347 BC
Plutarch, biographer, c46-120
Polybius, historian, c200-c118 BC
Praxiteles, sculptor, 400-330 BC
Pythagoras, phil., math., c580-c500 BC
Sappho, poet, c610-c580 BC
Simonides, poet, 556-c468 BC
Socrates, philosopher, 469-399 BC
Solon, statesman, 640-560 BC
Sophocles, dramatist, c496-406 BC
Strabo, geographer, c63 BC-AD 24
Thales, philosopher, c634-546 BC
Themistocles, politician, c524-c460 BC
Theocritus, poet, c310-250 BC
Theophrastus, phil., c372-c287 BC
Thucydides, historian, fl. 5th cent. BC
Timon, philosopher, c320-c230 BC
Xenophon, historian, c434-c355 BC
Zeno, philosopher, c335-c263 BC

Romans

Ammianus, historian, c330-395
Apuleius, satirist, c124-c170
Boethius, scholar, c480-524
Caesar, Julius, leader, 100-44 BC
Catiline, politician, c108-62 BC
Cato (Elder), statesman, 234-49 BC
Catullus, poet, c84-54 BC
Cicero, orator, 106-43 BC
Claudian, poet, c370-c404
Ennius, poet, 239-170 BC
Gellius, author, c130-c165
Horace, poet, 65-8 BC
Juvenal, satirist, 60-127
Livy, historian, 59 BC-AD 17
Lucan, poet, 39-65
Lucilius, poet, c180-c102 BC
Lucretius, poet, c99-c55 BC
Martial, epigrammatist, c38-c103
Nepos, historian, c100-c25 BC
Ovid, poet, 43 BC-AD 17
Persius, satirist, 34-62
Plautus, dramatist, c254-c184 BC
Pliny the Elder, scholar, 23-79
Pliny the Younger, author, 62-113
Quintilian, rhetorician, c35-c97
Sallust, historian, 86-34 BC
Seneca, philosopher, 4 BC-AD 65
Silius, poet, c25-101
Statius, poet, c45-c96
Suetonius, biographer, c69-c122
Tacitus, historian, 56-120
Terence, dramatist, 185-c159 BC
Tibullus, poet, c55-c19 BC
Vergil, poet, 70-19 BC
Vitruvius, architect, fl. 1st cent. BC

Rulers of England and Great Britain

ENGLAND

Name		Reign Began	Died	Death Age	Years Reigned
	Saxons and Danes				
Egbert	King of Wessex, won allegiance of all English	**829**	**839**	—	10
Ethelwulf	Son, King of Wessex, Sussex, Kent, Essex	**839**	**858**	—	19
Ethelbald	Son of Ethelwulf, displaced father in Wessex	**858**	**860**	—	2
Ethelbert	2nd son of Ethelwulf, united Kent and Wessex	**860**	**866**	—	6
Ethelred I	3rd son, King of Wessex, fought Danes	**866**	**871**	—	5
Alfred	The Great, 4th son, defeated Danes, fortified London	**871**	**899**	52	28
Edward	The Elder, Alfred's son, united English, claimed Scotland	**899**	**924**	55	25
Athelstan	The Glorious, Edward's son, King of Mercia, Wessex	**924**	**940**	45	16
Edmund	3rd son of Edward, King of Wessex, Mercia	**940**	**946**	25	6
Edred	4th son of Edward	**946**	**955**	32	9
Edwy	The Fair, eldest son of Edmund, King of Wessex	**955**	**959**	18	3
Edgar	The Peaceful, 2nd son of Edmund, ruled all English	**959**	**975**	32	17
Edward	The Martyr, eldest son of Edgar, murdered by stepmother	**975**	**978**	17	4
Ethelred II	The Unready, 2nd son of Edgar, married Emma of Normandy	**978**	**1016**	48	37
Edmund II	Ironside, son of Ethelred II, King of London	**1016**	**1016**	27	0
Canute	The Dane, gave Wessex to Edmund, married Emma	**1016**	**1035**	40	19
Harold I	Harefoot, natural son of Canute	**1035**	**1040**	—	5
Hardecanute	Son of Canute by Emma, Danish King	**1040**	**1042**	24	2
Edward	The Confessor, son of Ethelred II (canonized 1161)	**1042**	**1066**	62	24
Harold II	Edward's brother-in-law, last Saxon King	**1066**	**1066**	44	0
	House of Normandy				
William I	The Conqueror, defeated Harold at Hastings	**1066**	**1087**	60	21
William II	Rufus, 3rd son of William I, killed by arrow	**1087**	**1100**	43	13
Henry I	Beauclerc, youngest son of William I	**1100**	**1135**	67	35
	House of Blois				
Stephen	Son of Adela, daughter of William I, and Count of Blois	**1135**	**1154**	50	19
	House of Plantagenet				
Henry II	Son of Geoffrey Plantagenet (Angevin) by Matilda, daughter of Henry I	**1154**	**1189**	56	35
Richard I	Coeur de Lion, son of Henry II, crusader	**1189**	**1199**	42	10
John	Lackland, son of Henry II, signed Magna Carta, 1215	**1199**	**1216**	50	17
Henry III	Son of John, acceded at 9, under regency until 1227	**1216**	**1272**	65	56
Edward I	Son of Henry III	**1272**	**1307**	68	35
Edward II	Son of Edward I, deposed by Parliament, 1327	**1307**	**1327**	43	20
Edward III	Of Windsor, son of Edward II	**1327**	**1377**	65	50
Richard II	Grandson of Edward III, minor until 1389, deposed 1399	**1377**	**1400**	33	22
	House of Lancaster				
Henry IV	Son of John of Gaunt, Duke of Lancaster, son of Edward III	**1399**	**1413**	47	13
Henry V	Son of Henry IV, victor of Agincourt	**1413**	**1422**	34	9
Henry VI	Son of Henry V, deposed 1461, died in Tower	**1422**	**1471**	49	39
	House of York				
Edward IV	Great-great-grandson of Edward III, son of Duke of York	**1461**	**1483**	40	22
Edward V	Son of Edward IV, murdered in Tower of London	**1483**	**1483**	13	0
Richard III	Brother of Edward IV, fell at Bosworth Field	**1483**	**1485**	32	2

Name		Reign Began	Died	Death Age	Years Reigned
	House of Tudor				
Henry VII	Son of Edmund Tudor, Earl of Richmond, whose father had married the widow of Henry V; descended from Edward III through his mother, Margaret Beaufort, via John of Gaunt. By marrying daughter of Edward IV united Lancaster and York	**1485**	**1509**	53	24
Henry VIII	Son of Henry VII, by Elizabeth, daughter of Edward IV	**1509**	**1547**	56	38
Edward VI	Son of Henry VIII, by Jane Seymour, his 3rd queen. Ruled under regents. Was forced to name Lady Jane Grey his successor. Council of State proclaimed her queen July 10, 1553. Mary Tudor won Council, was proclaimed queen July 19, 1553. Mary had Lady Jane Grey beheaded for treason, Feb. 1554	**1547**	**1553**	16	6
Mary I	Daughter of Henry VIII, by Catherine of Aragon	**1553**	**1558**	43	5
Elizabeth I	Daughter of Henry VIII, by Anne Boleyn	**1558**	**1603**	69	44
	GREAT BRITAIN				
	House of Stuart				
James I	James VI of Scotland, son of Mary, Queen of Scots. *First to call himself King of Great Britain. This became official with the Act of Union, 1707*	**1603**	**1625**	59	22
Charles I	Only surviving son of James I; beheaded Jan. 30, 1649	**1625**	**1649**	48	24
	Commonwealth, 1649–1660				
	Council of State, 1649; Protectorate, 1653[1]				
The Cromwells	Oliver Cromwell, Lord Protector	**1653**	**1658**	59	5
	Richard Cromwell, son, Lord Protector, resigned May 25, 1659	**1658**	**1712**	86	1
	House of Stuart (Restored)				
Charles II	Eldest son of Charles I, died without issue	**1660**	**1685**	55	25
James II	2nd son of Charles I. Deposed 1688. Interregnum 1688-1689	**1685**	**1701**	68	3
William III	Son of William, Prince of Orange, by Mary, daughter of Charles I	**1689**	**1702**	51	13
and Mary II	Eldest daughter of James II and wife of William III	**1689**	**1694**	33	6
Anne	2nd daughter of James II	**1702**	**1714**	49	12
	House of Hanover				
George I	Son of Elector of Hanover, by Sophia, granddaughter of James I	**1714**	**1727**	67	13
George II	Only son of George I, married Caroline of Brandenburg	**1727**	**1760**	77	33
George III	Grandson of George II, married Charlotte of Mecklenburg	**1760**	**1820**	81	59
George IV	Eldest son of George III, Prince Regent, from Feb. 1811	**1820**	**1830**	67	10
William IV	3rd son of George III, married Adelaide of Saxe-Meiningen	**1830**	**1837**	71	7
Victoria	Daughter of Edward, 4th son of George III; married (1840) Prince Albert of Saxe-Coburg and Gotha, who became Prince Consort	**1837**	**1901**	81	63
	House of Saxe-Coburg and Gotha				
Edward VII	Eldest son of Victoria, married Alexandra, Princess of Denmark	**1901**	**1910**	68	9
	House of Windsor[2]				
George V	2nd son of Edward VII, married Princess Mary of Teck	**1910**	**1936**	70	25
Edward VIII	Eldest son of George V; acceded Jan. 20, 1936, abdicated Dec. 11, 1936	**1936**	**1972**	77	1
George VI	2nd son of George V; married Lady Elizabeth Bowes-Lyon	**1936**	**1952**	56	15
Elizabeth II	Elder daughter of George VI, acceded Feb. 6, 1952	**1952**			

— = age/birth date not certain. (1) The Cromwells ruled Britain following overthow of the monarchy in 1649. (2) Name adopted by proclamation of George V, July 17, 1917.

WORLD ALMANAC QUICK QUIZ

Which of these monarchs ruled the longest?
(a) Louis XIV; (b) Napoleon; (c) Queen Victoria; (d) the emperor Augustus

For the answer look in this chapter, or see page 1008.

Rulers of Scotland

Kenneth I MacAlpin was the first Scot to rule both Scots and Picts, AD 846.

Duncan I was the first general ruler, 1034. Macbeth seized the kingdom 1040, was slain by Duncan's son, Malcolm III MacDuncan (Canmore), 1057.

Malcolm married Margaret, Saxon princess who had fled from the Normans. Queen Margaret introduced English language and English monastic customs. She was canonized, 1250. Her son Edgar, 1097, moved the court to Edinburgh. His brothers Alexander I and David I succeeded. Malcolm IV, the Maiden, 1153, grandson of David I, was followed by his brother, William the Lion, 1165, whose son was Alexander II, 1214. The latter's son, Alexander III, 1249, defeated the Norse and regained the Hebrides. When he died, 1286, his granddaughter, Margaret, child of Eric of Norway and grandniece of Edward I of England, known as the Maid of Norway, was chosen ruler, but died 1290, aged 8.

John Baliol, 1292-1296. (Interregnum, 10 years.)

Robert Bruce (The Bruce), 1306-1329, victor at Bannockburn, 1314. David II, his only son, 1329-1371.

Robert II, 1371-1390, grandson of Robert Bruce, son of Walter, the Steward of Scotland, was called The Steward, first of the so-called Stuart line.

Robert III, son of Robert II, 1390-1406.

James I, son of Robert III, 1406-1437.

James II, son of James I, 1437-1460.

James III, eldest son of James II, 1460-1488.

James IV, eldest son of James III, 1488-1513.

James V, eldest son of James IV, 1513-1542.

Mary, daughter of James V, b. 1542, became queen at 1 week old; crowned 1543. Married, 1558, Francis, son of Henry II of France, who became king 1559, d. 1560. Mary ruled Scots 1561 until abdication, 1567. She also married Henry Stewart, Lord Darnley (1565), and James, Earl of Bothwell (1567). Imprisoned by Elizabeth I; beheaded 1587.

James VI, 1566-1625, son of Mary and Lord Darnley, became King of England on death of Elizabeth in 1603. Although the thrones were thus united, the legislative union of Scotland and England was not effected until the Act of Union, May 1, 1707.

IT'S A FACT: The "Stone of Destiny," which Scottish kings long ago sat on at their coronations, was stolen by English King Edward I when he invaded Scotland in 1296. Since then it has been used to crown English monarchs. Scottish nationalists heisted it from Westminster Abbey in 1950, but it was recovered after a few months (or so it seems; some think the Scots hid the original and left a copy to be recovered). In 1996, the British government finally returned the reputed Stone of Destiny to Edinburgh Castle.

Prime Ministers of Great Britain

Designations in parentheses describe each government;
W=Whig; T=Tory; Cl=Coalition; P=Peelite; Li=Liberal; C=Conservative[1]; La=Labour.

Sir Robert Walpole (W)[2]	1721-1742
Earl of Wilmington (W)	1742-1743
Henry Pelham (W)	1743-1754
Duke of Newcastle (W)	1754-1756
Duke of Devonshire (W)	1756-1757
Duke of Newcastle (W)	1757-1762
Earl of Bute (T)	1762-1763
George Grenville (W)	1763-1765
Marquess of Rockingham (W)	1765-1766
William Pitt the Elder (Earl of Chatham) (W)	1766-1768
Duke of Grafton (W)	1768-1770
Frederick North (Lord North) (T)	1770-1782
Marquess of Rockingham (W)	1782
Earl of Shelburne (W)	1782-1783
Duke of Portland (Cl)	1783
William Pitt the Younger (T)	1783-1801
Henry Addington (T)	1801-1804
William Pitt the Younger (T)	1804-1806
William Wyndham Grenville, Baron Grenville (W)	1806-1807
Duke of Portland (T)	1807-1809
Spencer Perceval (T)	1809-1812
Earl of Liverpool (T)	1812-1827
George Canning (T)	1827
Viscount Goderich (T)	1827-1828
Duke of Wellington (T)	1828-1830
Earl Grey (W)	1830-1834
Viscount Melbourne (W)	1834
Sir Robert Peel (C)	1834-1835
Viscount Melbourne (W)	1835-1841
Sir Robert Peel (C)	1841-1846
Lord (later Earl) John Russell (W)	1846-1852
Earl of Derby (C)	1852
Earl of Aberdeen (P)	1852-1855
Viscount Palmerston (Li)	1855-1858
Earl of Derby (C)	1858-1859
Viscount Palmerston (Li)	1859-1865
Earl Russell (Li)	1865-1866
Earl of Derby (C)	1866-1868
Benjamin Disraeli (C)	1868
William E. Gladstone (Li)	1868-1874
Benjamin Disraeli (C)	1874-1880
William E. Gladstone (Li)	1880-1885
Marquess of Salisbury (C)	1885-1886
William E. Gladstone (Li)	1886
Marquess of Salisbury (C)	1886-1892
William E. Gladstone (Li)	1892-1894
Earl of Rosebery (Li)	1894-1895
Marquess of Salisbury (C)	1895-1902
Arthur J. Balfour (C)	1902-1905
Sir Henry Campbell Bannerman (Li)	1905-1908
Herbert H. Asquith (Li)	1908-1915
Herbert H. Asquith (Cl)	1915-1916
David Lloyd George (Cl)	1916-1922
Andrew Bonar Law (C)	1922-1923
Stanley Baldwin (C)	1923-1924
James Ramsay MacDonald (La)	1924
Stanley Baldwin (C)	1924-1929
James Ramsay MacDonald (La)	1929-1931
James Ramsay MacDonald (Cl)	1931-1935
Stanley Baldwin (Cl)	1935-1937
Neville Chamberlain (Cl)	1937-1940
Winston Churchill (Cl)	1940-1945
Winston Churchill (C)	1945
Clement Attlee (La)	1945-1951
Sir Winston Churchill (C)	1951-1955
Sir Anthony Eden (C)	1955-1957
Harold Macmillan (C)	1957-1963
Sir Alec Douglas-Home (C)	1963-1964
Harold Wilson (La)	1964-1970
Edward Heath (C)	1970-1974
Harold Wilson (La)	1974-1976
James Callaghan (La)	1976-1979
Margaret Thatcher (C)	1979-1990
John Major (C)	1990-1997
Tony Blair (La)	1997-

(1) The Conservative Party was formed in 1834, an outgrowth and, in some respects, a continuation of the Tory party. (2) Walpole is commonly regarded as the first prime minister of Britain, though the title was not commonly used until later in the century and did not become official until 1905.

Historical Periods of Japan

Yamato	c. 300-592	Conquest of Yamato plain c. AD 300.
Asuka	592-710	Accession of Empress Suiko, 592.
Nara	710-794	Completion of Heijo (Nara), 710; the capital moves to Nagaoka, 784.
Heian	794-1185	Completion of Heian (Kyoto), 794.
Fujiwara	858-1160	Fujiwara-no-Yoshifusa becomes regent, 858.
Taira	1160-1185	Taira-no-Kiyomori assumes control, 1160; Minamoto-no-Yoritomo victor over Taira, 1185.
Kamakura	1192-1333	Yoritomo becomes shogun, 1192.
Namboku	1334-1392	Restoration of Emperor Godaigo, 1334; Southern Court established by Godaigo at Yoshino, 1336.
Ashikaga	1338-1573	Ashikaga Takauji becomes shogun, 1338.
Muromachi	1392-1573	Unification of Southern and Northern Courts, 1392.
Sengoku	1467-1600	Beginning of the Onin war, 1467.
Momoyama	1573-1603	Oda Nobunaga enters Kyoto, 1568; Nobunaga deposes last Ashikaga shogun, 1573; Tokugawa Ieyasu victor at Sekigahara, 1600.
Edo	1603-1867	Ieyasu becomes shogun, 1603.
Meiji	1868-1912	Enthronement of Emperor Mutsuhito (Meiji), 1867; Meiji Restoration and Charter Oath, 1868.
Taisho	1912-1926	Accession of Emperor Yoshihito, 1912.
Showa	1926-1989	Accession of Emperor Hirohito, 1926.
Heisei	1989-	Accession of Emperor Akihito, 1989.

Rulers of France: Kings, Queens, Presidents

Caesar to Charlemagne

Julius Caesar subdued the Gauls, native tribes of Gaul (France), 58 to 51 BC. The Romans ruled 500 years. The Franks, a Teutonic tribe, reached the Somme from the East c. AD 250. By the 5th century the Merovingian Franks ousted the Romans. In 451, with the help of Visigoths, Burgundians, and others, they defeated Attila and the Huns at Chalons-sur-Marne.

Childeric I became leader of the Merovingians 458. His son Clovis I (Chlodwig, Ludwig, Louis), crowned 481, founded the dynasty. After defeating the Alemanni (Germans) 496, he was baptized a Christian and made Paris his capital. His line ruled until Childeric III was deposed, 751.

The West Merovingians were called Neustrians, the eastern Austrasians. Pepin of Herstal (687-714), major domus, or head of the palace, of Austrasia, took over Neustria as dux (leader) of the Franks. Pepin's son, Charles, called Martel (the Hammer), defeated the Saracens at Tours-Poitiers, 732; was succeeded by his son, Pepin the Short, 741, who deposed Childeric III and ruled as king until 768.

His son, Charlemagne, or Charles the Great (742-814), became king of the Franks, 768, with his brother Carloman, who died 771. Charlemagne ruled France, Germany, parts of Italy, Spain, and Austria, and enforced Christianity. Crowned Emperor of the Romans by Pope Leo III in St. Peter's, Rome, Dec. 25, 800. Succeeded by son, Louis I the Pious, 814. At death, 840, Louis left empire to sons, Lothair (Roman emperor); Pepin I (king of Aquitaine); Louis II (of Germany); Charles the Bald (France). They quarreled and, by the peace of Verdun, 843, divided the empire.

The date preceding each entry is year of accession.

The Carolingians

843 Charles I (the Bald); Roman Emperor, 875
877 Louis II (the Stammerer), son
879 Louis III (died 882) and Carloman, brothers
885 Charles II (the Fat); Roman Emperor, 881
888 Eudes (Odo), elected by nobles
898 Charles III (the Simple), son of Louis II, defeated by
922 Robert, brother of Eudes, killed in war
923 Rudolph (Raoul), Duke of Burgundy
936 Louis IV, son of Charles III
954 Lothair, son, aged 13, defeated by Capet
986 Louis V (the Sluggard), left no heirs

The Capets

987 Hugh Capet, son of Hugh the Great
996 Robert II (the Wise), his son
1031 Henry I, son
1060 Philip I (the Fair), son
1108 Louis VI (the Fat), son
1137 Louis VII (the Younger), son
1180 Philip II (Augustus), son, crowned at Reims
1223 Louis VIII (the Lion), son
1226 Louis IX, son, crusader; Louis IX (1214-1270) reigned 44 years, arbitrated disputes with English King Henry III; led crusades, 1248 (captured in Egypt 1250) and 1270, when he died of plague in Tunis. Canonized 1297 as St. Louis.
1270 Philip III (the Hardy), son
1285 Philip IV (the Fair), son, king at 17
1314 Louis X (the Headstrong), son. His posthumous son, John I, lived only 7 days
1316 Philip V (the Tall), brother of Louis X
1322 Charles IV (the Fair), brother of Louis X

House of Valois

1328 Philip VI (of Valois), grandson of Philip III
1350 John II (the Good), his son, retired to England
1364 Charles V (the Wise), son
1380 Charles VI (the Beloved), son
1422 Charles VII (the Victorious), son. In 1429 Joan of Arc (Jeanne d'Arc) promised Charles to oust the English, who occupied northern France. Joan won at Orleans and Patay and had Charles crowned at Reims, July 17, 1429. Joan was captured May 24, 1430, and executed May 30, 1431, at Rouen for heresy. Charles ordered her rehabilitation, effected 1455.
1461 Louis XI (the Cruel), son, civil reformer
1483 Charles VIII (the Affable), son
1498 Louis XII, great-grandson of Charles V
1515 Francis I, of Angouleme, nephew, son-in-law. Francis I (1494-1547) reigned 32 years, fought 4 big wars, was patron of the arts, aided Cellini, del Sarto, Leonardo da Vinci, Rabelais, embellished Fontainebleau.
1547 Henry II, son, killed at a joust in a tournament. He was the husband of Catherine de Medicis (1519-1589) and the lover of Diane de Poitiers (1499-1566). Catherine was born in Florence, daughter of Lorenzo de Medici. By her marriage to Henry II she became the mother of Francis II, Charles IX, Henry III, and Queen Margaret (Reine Margot), wife of Henry IV. She persuaded Charles IX to order the massacre of Huguenots on the Feast of St. Bartholomew, Aug. 24, 1572, six days after her daughter was married to Henry of Navarre.
1559 Francis II, son. In 1548, Mary, Queen of Scots since infancy, was betrothed when 6 to Francis, aged 4. They were married 1558. Francis died 1560, aged 16; Mary ruled Scotland, abdicated 1567.
1560 Charles IX, brother
1574 Henry III, brother, assassinated

House of Bourbon

1589 Henry IV, of Navarre, assassinated. Henry IV made enemies when he gave tolerance to Protestants by Edict of Nantes, 1598. He was grandson of Queen Margaret of Navarre, literary patron. He married Margaret of Valois, daughter of Henry II and Catherine de Medicis; was divorced; in 1600 married Marie de Medicis, who became Regent of France, 1610-1617, for her son, Louis XIII, but was exiled by Richelieu, 1631.
1610 Louis XIII (the Just), son. Louis XIII (1601-1643) married Anne of Austria. His ministers were Cardinals Richelieu and Mazarin.
1643 Louis XIV (The Grand Monarch), son. Louis XIV was king 72 years. He exhausted a prosperous country in wars for thrones and territory. By revoking the Edict of Nantes (1685) he caused the emigration of the Huguenots. He said: "I am the state."
1715 Louis XV, great-grandson. Louis XV married a Polish princess; lost Canada to the English. His favorites, Mme. Pompadour and Mme. Du Barry, influenced policies. Noted for saying "After me, the deluge."
1774 Louis XVI, grandson; married Marie Antoinette, daughter of Empress Maria Therese of Austria. King and queen beheaded by Revolution, 1793. Their son, called Louis XVII, died in prison, never ruled.

First Republic

1792 National Convention of the French Revolution
1795 Directory, under Barras and others
1799 Consulate, Napoleon Bonaparte, first consul. Elected consul for life, 1802.

First Empire

1804 Napoleon I (Napoleon Bonaparte), emperor. Josephine (de Beauharnais), empress, 1804-1809; Marie Louise, empress, 1810-1814. Her son, Francois (1811-1832), titular King of Rome, later Duke de Reichstadt and "Napoleon II," never ruled. Napoleon abdicated 1814, died 1821.

Bourbons Restored

1814 Louis XVIII, king; brother of Louis XVI
1824 Charles X, brother; reactionary; deposed by the July Revolution, 1830

House of Orleans

1830 Louis-Philippe, the "citizen king"

Second Republic

1848 Louis Napoleon Bonaparte, president, nephew of Napoleon I.

Second Empire

1852 Napoleon III (Louis Napoleon Bonaparte), emperor; Eugenie (de Montijo), empress. Lost Franco-Prussian war, deposed 1870. Son, Prince Imperial (1856-1879), died in Zulu War. Eugenie died 1920.

Third Republic—Presidents

1871 Thiers, Louis Adolphe (1797-1877)
1873 MacMahon, Marshal Patrice M. de (1808-1893)
1879 Grevy, Paul J. (1807-1891)
1887 Sadi-Carnot, M. (1837-1894), assassinated
1894 Casimir-Perier, Jean P. P. (1847-1907)
1895 Faure, François Felix (1841-1899)
1899 Loubet, Emile (1838-1929)
1906 Fallieres, C. Armand (1841-1931)
1913 Poincare, Raymond (1860-1934)
1920 Deschanel, Paul (1856-1922)
1920 Millerand, Alexandre (1859-1943)
1924 Doumergue, Gaston (1863-1937)
1931 Doumer, Paul (1857-1932), assassinated
1932 Lebrun, Albert (1871-1950), resigned 1940
1940 Vichy govt. under German armistice: Henri Philippe Petain (1856-1951), Chief of State, 1940-1944.

Provisional govt. after liberation: Charles de Gaulle (1890-1970), Oct. 1944-Jan. 21, 1946; Felix Gouin (1884-1977), Jan. 23, 1946; Georges Bidault (1899-1983), June 24, 1946.

Fourth Republic—Presidents

1947 Auriol, Vincent (1884-1966)
1954 Coty, Rene (1882-1962)

Fifth Republic—Presidents

1959 De Gaulle, Charles Andre J. M. (1890-1970)
1969 Pompidou, Georges (1911-1974)
1974 Giscard d'Estaing, Valery (1926-)
1981 Mitterrand, François (1916-1996)
1995 Chirac, Jacques (1932-)

Rulers of Middle Europe; Rise and Fall of Dynasties; Rulers of Germany

Carolingian Dynasty

Charles the Great, or Charlemagne, ruled France, Italy, and Middle Europe; established Ostmark (later Austria); crowned Roman emperor by pope in Rome, AD 800; died 814.
Louis I (Ludwig) the Pious, son; crowned by Charlemagne 814; died 840.
Louis II, the German, son; succeeded to East Francia (Germany) 843-876.
Charles the Fat, son; inherited East Francia and West Francia (France) 876, reunited empire, crowned emperor by pope 881, deposed 887.
Arnulf, nephew, 887-899. Partition of empire.
Louis the Child, 899-911, last direct descendant of Charlemagne.
Conrad I, duke of Franconia, first elected German king, 911-918, founded House of Franconia.

Saxon Dynasty; First Reich

Henry I, the Fowler, duke of Saxony, 919-936.
Otto I, the Great, 936-973, son; crowned Holy Roman Emperor by pope, 962.
Otto II, 973-983, son; failed to oust Greeks and Arabs from Sicily.
Otto III, 983-1002, son; crowned emperor at 16.
Henry II, the Saint, duke of Bavaria, 1002-1024, great-grandson of Otto the Great.
House of Franconia
Conrad II, 1024-1039, elected king of Germany.
Henry III, the Black, 1039-1056, son; deposed 3 popes; annexed Burgundy.
Henry IV, 1056-1106, son; regency by his mother, Agnes of Poitou. Banned by Pope Gregory VII, he did penance at Canossa.
Henry V, 1106-1125, son; last of Salic House.
Lothair, duke of Saxony, 1125-1137. Crowned emperor in Rome, 1134.

House of Hohenstaufen

Conrad III, duke of Swabia, 1138-1152. In 2nd Crusade.
Frederick I, Barbarossa, 1152-1190; Conrad's nephew.
Henry VI, 1190-1196, took lower Italy from Normans. Son became king of Sicily.
Philip of Swabia, 1197-1208, brother.
Otto IV, of House of Welf, 1198-1215; deposed.
Frederick II, 1215-1250, son of Henry VI; king of Sicily; crowned king of Jerusalem in 5th Crusade.
Conrad IV, 1250-1254, son; lost lower Italy to Charles of Anjou.
Conradin, 1252-1268, son, king of Jerusalem and Sicily, beheaded. Last Hohenstaufen.
Interregnum, 1254-1273, Rise of the Electors.

Transition

Rudolph I of Hapsburg, 1273-1291, defeated King Ottocar II of Bohemia. Bequeathed duchy of Austria to eldest son, Albert.
Adolph of Nassau, 1292-1298, killed in war with Albert of Austria.
Albert I, king of Germany, 1298-1308, son of Rudolph.
Henry VII, of Luxemburg, 1308-1313, crowned emperor in Rome. Seized Bohemia, 1310.
Louis IV of Bavaria (Wittelsbach), 1314-1347. Also elected was Frederick of Austria, 1314-1330 (Hapsburg). Abolition of papal sanction for election of Holy Roman Emperor.
Charles IV, of Luxemburg, 1347-1378, grandson of Henry VII, German emperor and king of Bohemia, Lombardy, Burgundy; took Mark of Brandenburg.
Wenceslaus, 1378-1400, deposed.
Rupert, Duke of Palatine, 1400-1410.
Sigismund, 1411-1437.

Hungary

Stephen I, house of Arpad, 997-1038. Crowned king 1000; converted Magyars; canonized 1083. After several centuries of feuds Charles Robert of Anjou became Charles I, 1308-1342.
Louis I, the Great, son, 1342-1382; joint ruler of Poland with Casimir III, 1370. Defeated Turks.
Mary, daughter, 1382-1395, ruled with husband. Sigismund of Luxemburg, 1387-1437, also king of Bohemia. As brother of Wenceslaus he succeeded Rupert as Holy Roman Emperor, 1410.
Albert, 1438-1439, son-in-law of Sigismund; also Roman emperor as Albert II *(see under Hapsburg).*
Ulaszlo I of Poland, 1440-1444.
Ladislaus V, posthumous son of Albert II, 1444-1457. John Hunyadi (Hunyadi Janos), governor (1446-1452), fought Turks, Czechs; died 1456.
Matthias I (Corvinus), son of Hunyadi, 1458-1490. Shared rule of Bohemia, captured Vienna, 1485, annexed Austria, Styria, Carinthia.
Ulaszlo II (king of Bohemia), 1490-1516.
Louis II, son, aged 10, 1516-1526. Wars with Suleiman, Turk. In 1527 Hungary split between Ferdinand I, Archduke of Austria, bro.-in-law of Louis II, and John Zapolya of Transylvania. After Turkish invasion, 1547, Hungary split between Ferdinand, Prince John Sigismund (Transylvania), and the Turks.

House of Hapsburg

Albert V of Austria, Hapsburg, crowned king of Hungary, Jan. 1438, Roman emperor, March 1438, as Albert II; died 1439.
Frederick III, cousin, 1440-1493. Fought Turks.
Maximilian I, son, 1493-1519. Assumed title of Holy Roman Emperor (German), 1493.
Charles V, grandson, 1519-1556. King of Spain with mother co-regent; crowned Roman emperor at Aix, 1520. Confronted Luther at Worms; attempted church reform and religious conciliation; abdicated 1556.
Ferdinand I, king of Bohemia, 1526, of Hungary, 1527; disputed. German king, 1531. Crowned Roman emperor on abdication of brother Charles V, 1556.
Maximilian II, son, 1564-1576.
Rudolph II, son, 1576-1612.
Matthias, brother, 1612-1619, king of Bohemia and Hungary.
Ferdinand II of Styria, king of Bohemia, 1617, of Hungary, 1618, Roman emperor, 1619. Bohemian Protestants deposed him, elected Frederick V of Palatine, starting Thirty Years War.
Ferdinand III, son, king of Hungary, 1625, Bohemia, 1627, Roman emperor, 1637. Peace of Westphalia, 1648, ended war. Leopold I, 1658-1705; Joseph I, 1705-1711; Charles VI, 1711-1740.
Maria Theresa, daughter, 1740-1780, Archduchess of Austria, queen of Hungary; ousted pretender, Charles VII, crowned 1742; in 1745 obtained election of her husband Francis I as Roman emperor and co-regent (d. 1765). Fought Seven Years' War with Frederick II of Prussia. Mother of Marie Antoinette.
Joseph II, son, 1765-1790, Roman emperor, reformer; powers restricted by Empress Maria Theresa until her death, 1780. First partition of Poland. Leopold II, 1790-1792.
Francis II, son, 1792-1835. Fought Napoleon. Proclaimed first hereditary emperor of Austria, 1804. Forced to abdicate as Roman emperor, 1806; last use of title. Ferdinand I, son, 1835-1848, abdicated during revolution.

Austro-Hungarian Monarchy

Francis Joseph I, nephew, 1848-1916, emperor of Austria, king of Hungary. Dual monarchy of Austria-Hungary formed, 1867. After assassination of heir, Archduke Francis Ferdinand, June 28, 1914, Austrian diplomacy precipitated World War I.
Charles I, grand-nephew, 1916-1918, last emperor of Austria and king of Hungary. Abdicated Nov. 11-13, 1918, died 1922.

Rulers of Prussia

Nucleus of Prussia was the Mark of Brandenburg. First margrave Albert the Bear (Albrecht), 1134-1170. First Hohenzollern margrave was Frederick, burgrave of Nuremberg, 1417-1440.
Frederick William, 1640-1688, the Great Elector. Son, Frederick III, 1688-1713, crowned King Frederick of Prussia, 1701.
Frederick William I, son, 1713-1740.
Frederick II, the Great, son, 1740-1786, annexed Silesia, part of Austria.
Frederick William II, nephew, 1786-1797.
Frederick William III, son, 1797-1840. Napoleonic wars.
Frederick William IV, son, 1840-1861. Uprising of 1848 and first parliament and constitution.

Second and Third Reich

William I, 1861-1888, brother. Annexation of Schleswig and Hanover; Franco-Prussian war, 1870-1871, proclamation of German Reich, Jan. 18, 1871, at Versailles; William, German emperor (Deutscher Kaiser), Bismarck, chancellor.
Frederick III, son, 1888.
William II, son, 1888-1918. Led Germany in World War I, abdicated as German emperor and king of Prussia, Nov. 9, 1918. Died in exile in Netherlands, June 4, 1941. Minor rulers of Bavaria, Saxony, Wurttemberg also abdicated.
Germany proclaimed republic at Weimar, July 1, 1919. Presidents included: Frederick Ebert, 1919-1925; Paul von Hindenburg-Beneckendorff, 1925, reelected 1932, d. Aug. 2, 1934. Adolf Hitler, chancellor, chosen successor as Leader-Chancellor (Fuehrer-Reichskanzler) of Third Reich. Annexed Austria, Mar. 1938. Precipitated World War II, 1939-1945. Suicide Apr. 30, 1945.

Germany After 1945

Following World War II, Germany was split between democratic West and Soviet-dominated East. West German chancellors: Konrad Adenauer, 1949-1963; Ludwig Erhard, 1963-1966; Kurt Georg Kiesinger, 1966-1969; Willy Brandt, 1969-1974; Helmut Schmidt, 1974-1982; Helmut Kohl, 1982-1990. East German Communist party leaders: Walter Ulbricht, 1946-1971; Erich Honecker, 1971-1989; Egon Krenz, 1989-1990.
Germany reunited Oct. 3, 1990. Post-reunification chancellors: Helmut Kohl, 1990-1998; Gerhard Schröder, 1998- .

Rulers of Poland

House of Piasts

Miesko I, 962?-992; Poland Christianized 966. Expansion under 3 Boleslavs: I, 992-1025, son, crowned king 1024; II, 1058-1079, great-grandson, exiled after killing bishop Stanislav who became chief patron saint of Poland; III, 1106-1138, nephew, divided Poland among 4 sons, eldest suzerain.

1138-1306, feudal division. 1226 founding in Prussia of military order Teutonic Knights. 1220 invasion by Tartars/Mongols.

Vladislav I, 1306-1333, reunited most Polish territories, crowned king 1320. Casimir III the Great, 1333-1370, son, developed economic, cultural life, foreign policy.

House of Anjou

Louis I, 1370-1382, nephew/was also Louis I of Hungary.

Jadwiga, 1384-1399, daughter, married 1386 Jagiello, Grand Duke of Lithuania.

House of Jagiellonians

Vladislav II, 1386-1434, Christianized Lithuania, founded personal union between Poland and Lithuania. Defeated 1410 Teutonic Knights at Grunwald.

Vladislav III, 1434-1444, son, simultaneously king of Hungary. Fought Turks, killed 1444 in battle of Varna.

Casimir IV, 1446-1492, brother, competed with Hapsburgs, put son Vladislav on throne of Bohemia, later also of Hungary (Ulaszlo II).

Sigismund I, 1506-1548, son, patronized science and arts, his and son's reign "Golden Age."

Sigismund II, 1548-1572, son, established 1569 real union of Poland and Lithuania (lasted until 1795).

Elective Kings

Polish nobles in 1572 proclaimed Poland a republic headed by king to be elected by whole nobility.

Stephen Batory, 1576-1586, duke of Transylvania, married Ann, sister of Sigismund II August. Fought Russians.

Sigismund III Vasa, 1587-1632, nephew of Sigismund II. 1592-1598 also king of Sweden. His generals fought Russians, Turks.

Vladislav II Vasa, 1632-1648, son. Fought Russians.

John II Casimir Vasa, 1648-1668, brother. Fought Cossacks, Swedes, Russians, Turks, Tatars (the "Deluge"). Abdicated 1668.

John III Sobieski, 1674-1696. Won Vienna from besieging Turks, 1683.

Stanislav II, 1764-1795, last king. Encouraged reforms; 1791 1st modern Constitution in Europe. 1772, 1793, 1795 Poland partitioned among Russia, Prussia, Austria. Unsuccessful insurrection against foreign invasion 1794 under Kosciusko, American-Polish general.

1795-1918: Poland Under Foreign Rule

1807-1815 Grand Duchy of Warsaw created by Napoleon I, Frederick August of Saxony grand duke.

1815 Congress of Vienna proclaimed part of Poland "Kingdom" in personal union with Russia.

Polish uprisings: 1830 against Russia; 1846, 1848 against Austria; 1863 against Russia—all repressed.

1918-1939: Second Republic

1918-1922 Head of State Jozef Pilsudski. Presidents: Gabriel Narutowicz 1922, assassinated; Stanislav Wojciechowski 1922-1926, had to abdicate after Pilsudski's coup d'état; Ignacy Moscicki, 1926-1939, ruled (with Pilsudski until his death, 1935) as virtual dictator.

1939-1945: Poland Under Foreign Occupation

Nazi and Soviet invasion Sept. 1939. Polish government-in-exile, first in France, then in England. Vladislav Raczkiewicz president; Gen. Vladislav Sikorski, then Stanislav Mikolajczyk, prime ministers. Soviet-sponsored Polish Committee of National Liberation proclaimed at Lublin July 1944, transformed into government Jan. 1, 1945.

Poland After 1945

In the late 1940s, Poland came increasingly under Soviet control. Communist party ruled in Poland until Aug. 1989, when democratic Solidarity party, led by Lech Walesa, gained control of government. Walesa was elected president in 1990. Solidarity lost the presidency in 1995, but the government remained democratic.

Rulers of Denmark, Sweden, Norway

Denmark

Earliest rulers invaded Britain; King Canute, who ruled in London 1016-1035, was most famous. The Valdemars furnished kings until the 15th century. In 1282 the Danes won the first national assembly, Danehof, from King Erik V.

Most redoubtable medieval character was Margaret, daughter of Valdemar IV, born 1353, married at 10 to King Haakon VI of Norway. In 1376 she had her first infant son Olaf made king of Denmark. After his death, 1387, she was regent of Denmark and Norway. In 1388 Sweden accepted her as sovereign. In 1389 she made her grand-nephew, Duke Erik of Pomerania, titular king of Denmark, Sweden, and Norway, with herself as regent. In 1397 she effected the Union of Kalmar of the three kingdoms and had Erik VII crowned. In 1439 the three kingdoms deposed him and elected, 1440, Christopher of Bavaria king (Christopher III). On his death, 1448, the union broke up.

Succeeding rulers were unable to enforce their claims as rulers of Sweden until 1520, when Christian II conquered Sweden. He was thrown out 1522, and in 1523 Gustavus Vasa united Sweden. Denmark continued to dominate Norway until the Napoleonic wars, when Frederick VI, 1808-1839, joined the Napoleonic cause after Britain had destroyed the Danish fleet, 1807. In 1814 he was forced to cede Norway to Sweden and Helgoland to Britain, receiving Lauenburg. Successors Christian VIII, 1839; Frederick VII, 1848; Christian IX, 1863; Frederick VIII, 1906; Christian X, 1912; Frederick IX, 1947; Margrethe II, 1972.

Sweden

Early kings ruled at Uppsala, but did not dominate the country. Sverker, c1130-c1156, united the Swedes and Goths. In 1435 Sweden obtained the Riksdag, or parliament. After the Union of Kalmar, 1397, the Danes either ruled or harried the country until Christian II of Denmark conquered it anew, 1520. This led to a rising under Gustavus Vasa, who ruled Sweden 1523-1560, and established an independent kingdom. Charles IX, 1599-1611, crowned 1604, conquered Moscow. Gustavus II Adolphus, 1611-1632, was called the Lion of the North. Later rulers: Christina, 1632; Charles X Gustavus, 1654; Charles XI, 1660; Charles XII (invader of Russia and Poland, defeated at Poltava, June 28, 1709), 1697; Ulrika Eleanora, sister, elected queen 1718; Frederick I (of Hesse), her husband, 1720; Adolphus Frederick, 1751; Gustavus III, 1771; Gustavus IV Adolphus, 1792; Charles XIII, 1809. (Union with Norway began 1814.) Charles XIV John, 1818 (he was Jean Bernadotte, Napoleon's Prince of Ponte Corvo, elected 1810 to succeed Charles XIII); he founded the present dynasty: Oscar I, 1844; Charles XV, 1859; Oscar II, 1872; Gustavus V, 1907; Gustav VI Adolf, 1950; Carl XVI Gustaf, 1973.

Norway

Overcoming many rivals, Harald Haarfager, 872-930, conquered Norway, Orkneys, and Shetlands; Olaf I, great-grandson, 995-1000, brought Christianity into Norway, Iceland, and Greenland. In 1035 Magnus the Good also became king of Denmark. Haakon V, 1299-1319, had married his daughter to Erik of Sweden. Their son, Magnus, became ruler of Norway and Sweden at 6. His son, Haakon VI, married Margaret of Denmark; their son Olaf IV became king of Norway and Denmark, followed by Margaret's regency and the Union of Kalmar, 1397.

In 1450 Norway became subservient to Denmark. Christian IV, 1588-1648, founded Christiania, now Oslo. After Napoleonic wars, when Denmark ceded Norway to Sweden, a strong nationalist movement forced recognition of Norway as an independent kingdom united with Sweden under the Swedish kings, 1814-1905. In 1905 the union was dissolved and Prince Charles of Denmark became Haakon VII. He died Sept. 21, 1957; succeeded by son, Olav V. Olav V died Jan. 17, 1991; succeeded by son, Harald V.

Rulers of the Netherlands and Belgium

The Netherlands (Holland)

William Frederick, Prince of Orange, led a revolt against French rule, 1813; crowned king, 1815. Belgium seceded Oct. 4, 1830, after a revolt. The secession was ratified by the two kingdoms by treaty, Apr. 19, 1839.

Succession: William II, son, 1840; William III, son, 1849; Wilhelmina, daughter of William III and his 2nd wife Princess Emma of Waldeck, 1890; Wilhelmina abdicated, Sept. 4, 1948, in favor of daughter, Juliana. Juliana abdicated, Apr. 30, 1980, in favor of daughter, Beatrix.

Belgium

A national congress elected Prince Leopold of Saxe-Coburg as king; he took the throne July 21, 1831, as Leopold I.

Succession: Leopold II, son, 1865; Albert I, nephew of Leopold II, 1909; Leopold III, son of Albert, 1934; Prince Charles, Regent 1944; Leopold returned 1950, yielded powers to son Baudouin, Prince Royal, Aug. 6, 1950, abdicated July 16, 1951. Baudouin I took throne July 17, 1951, died July 31, 1993; succeeded by brother, Albert II.

Roman Rulers

From Romulus to the end of the Empire in the West. Rulers in the East sat in Constantinople and, for a brief period, in Nicaea, until the capture of Constantinople by the Turks in 1453, when Byzantium was succeeded by the Ottoman Empire.

The Kingdom

BC

753 Romulus (Quirinus)
716 Numa Pompilius
673 Tullus Hostilius
640 Ancus Marcius
616 L. Tarquinius Priscus
578 Servius Tullius
534 L. Tarquinius Superbus

The Republic

509 Consulate established
509 Quaestorship instituted
498 Dictatorship introduced
494 Plebeian Tribunate created
494 Plebeian Aedileship created
444 Consular Tribunate organized
435 Censorship instituted
366 Praetorship established
366 Curule Aedileship created
362 Military Tribunate elected
326 Proconsulate introduced
311 Naval Duumvirate elected
217 Dictatorship of Fabius Maximus
133 Tribunate of Tiberius Gracchus
123 Tribunate of Gaius Gracchus
82 Dictatorship of Sulla
60 First Triumvirate formed (Caesar, Pompeius, Crassus)
46 Dictatorship of Caesar
43 Second Triumvirate formed (Octavianus, Antonius, Lepidus)

The Empire

27 Augustus (Gaius Julius Caesar Octavianus)

AD

14 Tiberius I
37 Gaius Caesar (Caligula)
41 Claudius I
54 Nero
68 Galba
69 Galba; Otho, Vitellius
69 Vespasianus
79 Titus
81 Domitianus
96 Nerva
98 Trajanus
117 Hadrianus
138 Antoninus Pius
161 Marcus Aurelius and Lucius Verus
169 Marcus Aurelius (alone)
180 Commodus
193 Pertinax; Julianus I
193 Septimius Severus
211 Caracalla and Geta
212 Caracalla (alone)
217 Macrinus
218 Elagabalus (Heliogabalus)
222 Alexander Severus
235 Maximinus I (the Thracian)
238 Gordianus I and Gordianus II; Pupienus and Balbinus
238 Gordianus III
244 Philippus (the Arabian)
249 Decius
251 Gallus and Volusianus
253 Aemilianus
253 Valerianus and Gallienus
258 Gallienus (alone)
268 Claudius Gothicus
270 Quintillus
270 Aurelianus
275 Tacitus
276 Florianus
276 Probus
282 Carus
283 Carinus and Numerianus
286 Diocletianus and Maximianus
305 Galerius and Constantius I
306 Galerius, Maximinus II, Severus I
307 Galerius, Maximinus II, Constantinus I, Licinius, Maxentius
311 Maximinus II, Constantinus I, Licinius, Maxentius
314 Maximinus II, Constantinus I, Licinius
314 Constantinus I and Licinius
324 Constantinus I (the Great)
337 Constantinus II, Constans I, Constantius II
340 Constantius II and Constans I
350 Constantius II
361 Julianus II (the Apostate)
363 Jovianus

West (Rome) and East (Constantinople)

364 Valentinianus I (West) and Valens (East)
367 Valentinianus I with Gratianus (West) and Valens (East)
375 Gratianus with Valentinianus II (West) and Valens (East)
378 Gratianus with Valentinianus II (West),Theodosius I (East)
383 Valentinianus II (West) and Theodosius I (East)
394 Theodosius I (the Great)
395 Honorius (West) and Arcadius (East)
408 Honorius (West) and Theodosius II (East)
423 Valentinianus III (West) and Theodosius II (East)
450 Valentinianus III (West) and Marcianus (East)
455 Maximus (West), Avitus (West); Marcianus (East)
456 Avitus (West), Marcianus (East)
457 Majorianus (West), Leo I (East)
461 Severus II (West), Leo I (East)
467 Anthemius (West), Leo I (East)
472 Olybrius (West), Leo I (East)
473 Glycerius (West), Leo I (East)
474 Julius Nepos (West), Leo II (East)
475 Romulus Augustulus (West) and Zeno (East)
476 End of Empire in West; Odovacar, King, drops title of Emperor; murdered by King Theodoric of Ostrogoths, 493

Rulers of Modern Italy

After the fall of Napoleon in 1814, the Congress of Vienna, 1815, restored Italy as a political patchwork, comprising the Kingdom of Naples and Sicily, the Papal States, and smaller units. Piedmont and Genoa were awarded to Sardinia, ruled by King Victor Emmanuel I of Savoy.

United Italy emerged under the leadership of Camillo, Count di Cavour (1810-1861), Sardinian prime minister. Agitation was led by Giuseppe Mazzini (1805-1872) and Giuseppe Garibaldi (1807-1882), soldier; Victor Emmanuel I abdicated 1821. After a brief regency for a brother, Charles Albert was king 1831-1849, abdicating when defeated by the Austrians at Novara. Succeeded by Victor Emmanuel II, 1849-1861.

In 1859 France forced Austria to cede Lombardy to Sardinia, which gave rights to Savoy and Nice to France. In 1860 Garibaldi led 1,000 volunteers in a spectacular campaign, took Sicily and expelled the King of Naples. In 1860 the House of Savoy annexed Tuscany, Parma, Modena, Romagna, the Two Sicilys, the Marches, and Umbria. Victor Emmanuel assumed the title of King of Italy at Turin Mar. 17, 1861.

In 1866, Victor Emmanuel allied with Prussia in the Austro-Prussian War, and with Prussia's victory received Venetia. On Sept. 20, 1870, his troops under Gen. Raffaele Cadorna entered Rome and took over the Papal States, ending the temporal power of the Roman Catholic Church.

Succession: Umberto I, 1878, assassinated 1900; Victor Emmanuel III, 1900, abdicated 1946, died 1947; Humbert II, 1946, ruled a month. In 1921 Benito Mussolini (1883-1945) formed the Fascist party; he became prime minister Oct. 31, 1922. He entered World War II as an ally of Hitler. He was deposed July 25, 1943.

At a plebiscite June 2, 1946, Italy voted for a republic; Premier Alcide de Gasperi became chief of state June 13, 1946. On June 28, 1946, the Constituent Assembly elected Enrico de Nicola, Liberal, provisional president. Successive presidents: Luigi Einaudi, elected May 11, 1948; Giovanni Gronchi, Apr. 29, 1955; Antonio Segni, May 6, 1962; Giuseppe Saragat, Dec. 28, 1964; Giovanni Leone, Dec. 29, 1971; Alessandro Pertini, July 9, 1978; Francesco Cossiga, July 9, 1985; Oscar Luigi Scalfaro, May 28, 1992, Carlo Azeglio Ciampi, May 18, 1999.

Rulers of Spain

From 8th to 11th centuries Spain was dominated by the Moors (Arabs and Berbers). The Christian reconquest established small kingdoms (Asturias, Aragon, Castile, Catalonia, Leon, Navarre, and Valencia). In 1474 Isabella, b. 1451, became Queen of Castile & Leon. Her husband, Ferdinand, b. 1452, inherited Aragon 1479, with Catalonia, Valencia, and the Balearic Islands, became Ferdinand V of Castile. By Isabella's request Pope Sixtus IV established the Inquisition, 1478. Last Moorish kingdom, Granada, fell 1492. Columbus opened New World of colonies, 1492. Isabella died 1504, succeeded by her daughter, Juana "the Mad," but Ferdinand ruled until his death 1516.

Charles I, b. 1500, son of Juana, grandson of Ferdinand and Isabella, and of Maximilian I of Hapsburg; succeeded later as Holy Roman Emperor, Charles V, 1520; abdicated 1556. Philip II, son, 1556-1598, inherited only Spanish throne; conquered Portugal, fought Turks, sent Armada vs. England. Married to Mary I of England, 1554-1558. Succession: Philip III, 1598-1621; Philip IV, 1621-1665; Charles II, 1665-1700, left Spain to Philip of Anjou, grandson of Louis XIV, who as Philip V, 1700-1746, founded Bourbon dynasty; Ferdinand VI, 1746-1759; Charles III, 1759-1788; Charles IV, 1788-1808, abdicated.

Napoleon now dominated politics and made his brother Joseph King of Spain 1808, but the Spanish ousted him in 1813. Ferdinand VII, 1808, 1814-1833, lost American colonies; succeeded by daughter Isabella II, aged 3, with wife Maria Christina of Naples regent until 1843. Isabella deposed by revolution 1868. Elected king by the Cortes, Amadeo of Savoy, 1870; abdicated 1873. First republic, 1873-74. Alfonso XII, son of Isabella, 1875-85. His posthumous son was Alfonso XIII, with his mother, Queen Maria Christina regent; Spanish-American war, Spain lost Cuba, gave up Puerto Rico, Philippines, Sulu Is., Marianas. Alfonso took throne 1902, aged 16, married British Princess Victoria Eugenia of Battenberg. Dictatorship of Primo de Rivera, 1923-30, precipitated revolution of 1931. Alfonso agreed to leave without formal abdication. Monarchy abolished; the second republic established, with socialist backing. Niceto Alcala Zamora was president until 1936, when Manuel Azaña was chosen.

In July 1936, the army in Morocco revolted against the government and General Francisco Franco led the troops into Spain. The revolution succeeded by Feb. 1939, when Azaña resigned. Franco became chief of state, with provisions that if he was incapacitated, the Regency Council by two-thirds vote could propose a king to the Cortes, which needed to have a two-thirds majority to elect him.

Alfonso XIII died in Rome Feb. 28, 1941, aged 54. His property and citizenship had been restored.

A law restoring the monarchy was approved in a 1947 referendum. Prince Juan Carlos, b. 1938, grandson of Alfonso XIII, was designated by Franco and the Cortes (Parliament) in 1969 as future king and chief of state. Franco died in office, Nov. 20, 1975; Juan Carlos proclaimed king, Nov. 22.

Leaders in the South American Wars of Liberation

Simon Bolivar (1783-1830), Jose Francisco de San Martin (1778-1850), and Francisco Antonio Gabriel Miranda (1750-1816) are among the heroes of the early 19th-century struggles of South American nations to free themselves from Spain. All three, and their contemporaries, operated in periods of factional strife, during which soldiers and civilians suffered.

Miranda, a Venezuelan, who had served with the French in the American Revolution and commanded parts of the French Revolutionary armies in the Netherlands, attempted to start a revolt in Venezuela in 1806 and failed. In 1810, with British and American backing, he returned and was briefly a dictator, until the British withdrew their support. In 1812 he was overcome by the royalists in Venezuela and taken prisoner, dying in a Spanish prison in 1816.

San Martin was born in Argentina and during 1789-1811 served in campaigns of the Spanish armies in Europe and Africa. He first joined the independence movement in Argentina in 1812 and in 1817 invaded Chile with 4,000 men over the mountain passes. Here he and Gen. Bernardo O'Higgins (1778-1842) defeated the Spaniards at Chacabuco, 1817; O'Higgins was named Liberator and became first director of Chile, 1817-23. In 1821 San Martin occupied Lima and Callao, Peru, and became protector of Peru.

Bolivar, the greatest leader of South American liberation from Spain, was born in Venezuela, the son of an aristocratic family. He first served under Miranda in 1812 and in 1813 captured Caracas, where he was named Liberator. Forced out next year by civil strife, he led a campaign that captured Bogota in 1814. In 1817 he was again in control of Venezuela and was named dictator. He organized Nueva Granada with the help of General Francisco de Paula Santander (1792-1840). By joining Nueva Granada, Venezuela, and the area that is now Panama and Ecuador, the republic of Colombia was formed, with Bolivar president. After numerous setbacks he decisively defeated the Spaniards in the second battle of Carabobo, Venezuela, June 24, 1821.

In May 1822, Gen. Antonio Jose de Sucre, Bolivar's lieutenant, took Quito. Bolivar went to Guayaquil to confer with San Martin, who resigned as protector of Peru and withdrew from politics. With a new army of Colombians and Peruvians Bolivar defeated the Spaniards in a battle at Junin in 1824 and cleared Peru.

De Sucre organized Charcas (Upper Peru) as Republica Bolivar (now Bolivia) and acted as president in place of Bolivar, who wrote its constitution. De Sucre defeated the Spanish faction of Peru at Ayacucho, Dec. 19, 1824.

Continued civil strife finally caused the Colombian federation to break apart. Santander turned against Bolivar, but the latter defeated him and banished him. In 1828 Bolivar gave up the presidency he had held precariously for 14 years. He became ill from tuberculosis and died Dec. 17, 1830. He is buried in the national pantheon in Caracas.

Rulers of Russia; Leaders of the USSR and Russian Federation

First ruler to consolidate Slavic tribes was Rurik, leader of the Russians who established himself at Novgorod, AD 862. He and his immediate successors had Scandinavian affiliations. They moved to Kiev after 972 and ruled as Dukes of Kiev. In 988 Vladimir was converted and adopted the Byzantine Greek Orthodox service, later modified by Slav influences. Important as organizer and lawgiver was Yaroslav, 1019-1054, whose daughters married kings of Norway, Hungary, and France. His grandson, Vladimir II (Monomakh), 1113-1125, was progenitor of several rulers, but in 1169 Andrew Bogolubski overthrew Kiev and began the line known as Grand Dukes of Vladimir.

Of the Grand Dukes of Vladimir, Alexander Nevsky, 1246-1263, had a son, Daniel, first to be called Duke of Muscovy (Moscow), who ruled 1263-1303. His successors became Grand Dukes of Muscovy. After Dmitri III Donskoi defeated the Tatars in 1380, they also became Grand Dukes of all Russia. Tatar independence and considerable territorial expansion were achieved under Ivan III, 1462-1505.

Tsars of Muscovy—Ivan III was referred to in church ritual as Tsar. He married Sofia, niece of the last Byzantine emperor. His successor, Basil III, died in 1533 when Basil's son Ivan was only 3. He became Ivan IV, "the Terrible"; crowned 1547 as Tsar of all the Russias, ruled until 1584. Under the weak rule of his son, Feodor I, 1584-1598, Boris Godunov had control. The dynasty died, and after years of tribal strife and intervention by Polish and Swedish armies, the Russians united under 17-year-old Michael Romanov, distantly related to the first wife of Ivan IV. He ruled 1613-1645 and established the Romanov line. Fourth ruler after Michael was Peter I.

Tsars, or Emperors, of Russia (Romanovs)—Peter I, 1682-1725, known as Peter the Great, took title of Emperor in 1721. His successors and dates of accession were: Catherine, his widow, 1725; Peter II, his grandson, 1727; Anne, Duchess of Courland, 1730, daughter of Peter the Great's brother, Tsar Ivan V; Ivan VI, 1740, great-grandson of Ivan V, child, kept in prison and murdered 1764; Elizabeth, daughter of Peter I, 1741; Peter III, grandson of Peter I, 1761, deposed 1762 for his consort, Catherine II, former princess of Anhalt Zerbst (Germany) who is known as Catherine the Great; Paul I, her son, 1796, killed 1801; Alexander I, son of Paul, 1801, defeated Napoleon; Nicholas I, his brother, 1825; Alexander II, son of Nicholas, 1855, assassinated 1881 by terrorists; Alexander III, son, 1881. Nicholas II, son, 1894-1917, last Tsar of Russia, was forced to abdicate by the Revolution that followed losses to Germany in WWI. The Tsar, the Empress, the Tsarevich (Crown Prince), and the Tsar's 4 daughters were murdered by the Bolsheviks in Yekaterinburg, July 16, 1918.

Provisional Government—Prince Georgi Lvov and Alexander Kerensky, premiers, 1917.

Union of Soviet Socialist Republics

Bolshevik Revolution, Nov. 7, 1917, removed Kerensky from power; council of People's Commissars formed, Lenin (Vladimir Ilyich Ulyanov) became premier. Lenin died Jan. 21, 1924. Aleksei Rykov (executed 1938) and V. M. Molotov held the office, but actual ruler was Joseph Stalin (Joseph Vissarionovich Djugashvili), general secretary of the Central Committee of the Communist Party. Stalin became president of the Council of Ministers (premier) May 7, 1941, died Mar. 5, 1953. Succeeded by Georgi M. Malenkov, as head of the Council and premier, and Nikita S. Khrushchev, first secretary of the Central Committee. Malenkov resigned Feb. 8, 1955, became deputy premier, was dropped July 3, 1957. Marshal Nikolai A. Bulganin became premier Feb. 8, 1955; was demoted and Khrushchev became premier Mar. 27, 1958.

Khrushchev was ousted Oct. 14-15, 1964, replaced by Leonid I. Brezhnev as first secretary of the party and by Aleksei N. Kosygin as premier. On June 16, 1977, Brezhnev also took office as president. He died Nov. 10, 1982; 2 days later the Central Committee elected former KGB head Yuri V. Andropov president. Andropov died Feb. 9, 1984; on Feb. 13, Konstantin U. Chernenko chosen by Central Committee as its general secretary. Chernenko died Mar. 10, 1985; on Mar. 11, he was succeeded as general secretary by Mikhail Gorbachev, who replaced Andrei Gromyko as president on Oct. 1, 1988. Gorbachev resigned Dec. 25, 1991, and the Soviet Union officially disbanded the next day. A loose Commonwealth of Independent States, made up of most of the 15 former Soviet constituent republics, was created.

Post-Soviet Russia

After adopting a degree of sovereignty, the Russian Republic had held elections in June 1991. Boris Yeltsin was sworn in July 10, 1991, as Russia's first elected president. With the Dec. 1991 dissolution of the Soviet Union, Russia (officially Russian Federation) became a founding member of the Commonwealth of Independent States. On Dec. 31, 1999, Yeltsin stepped down as president; he named Vladimir Putin his interim successor. Putin won a presidential election Mar. 26, 2000, and was sworn in May 7.

Governments of China

(Until 221 BC and frequently thereafter, China was not a unified state. Where dynastic dates overlap, the rulers or events referred to appeared in different areas of China.)

Hsia	1994 BC – c1523 BC
Shang	c1523 BC – c1028 BC
Western Chou	c1027 BC – 770 BC
Eastern Chou	770 BC – 256 BC
Warring States	403 BC – 222 BC
Ch'in (first unified empire)	221 BC – 206 BC
Han	202 BC – AD 220
Western Han (expanded Chinese state beyond the Yellow and Yangtze River valleys)	202 BC – AD 9
Hsin (Wang Mang, usurper)	AD 9 – 23
Eastern Han (expanded Chinese state into Indochina and Turkestan)	25 – 220
Three Kingdoms (Wei, Shu, Wu)	220 – 265
Chin (western)	265 – 317
(eastern)	317 – 420
Northern Dynasties (followed several short-lived governments by Turks, Mongols, etc.)	386 – 581
Southern Dynasties (capital: Nanjing)	420 – 589
Sui (reunified China)	581 – 618
Tang (a golden age of Chinese culture; capital: Xian)	618 – 906
Five Dynasties (Yellow River basin)	902 – 960
Ten Kingdoms (southern China)	907 – 979
Liao (Khitan Mongols; capital at site of Beijing)	947 – 1125
Sung	960 – 1279
Northern Sung (reunified central and southern China)	960 – 1126
Western Hsai (non-Chinese rulers in northwest)	990 – 1227
Chin (Tatars; drove Sung out of central China)	1115 – 1234
Yuan (Mongols; Kublai Khan est. capital at site of Beijing, c. 1264)	1271 – 1368
Ming (China reunified under Chinese rule; capital: Nanjing, then Beijing in 1420)	1368 – 1644
Ch'ing (Manchus, descendents of Tatars)	1644 – 1911
Republic (disunity; provincial rulers, warlords)	1912 – 1949
People's Republic of China	1949 –

IT'S A FACT: In 221 BC the first emperor of a unified China, Shi Huang Ti, began work on the oldest part of the Great Wall of China, in an effort to keep out Mongol invaders. Work continued under the next (Han) dynasty, and the wall was massively rebuilt under the Ming dynasty. The bricks added during the Ming dynasty alone would be enough to build a wall 5 feet high and 3 feet thick circling the earth at the equator.

Leaders of China Since 1949

Mao Zedong	Chairman, Central People's Administrative Council, Communist Party (CPC), 1949-1976
Zhou Enlai	Premier, foreign minister, 1949-1976
Deng Xiaoping	Vice Premier, 1952-1966, 1973-1976, 1977-1980; "paramount leader," 1978-1997
Liu Shaoqi	President, 1959-1969
Hua Guofeng	Premier, 1976-1980; CPC Chairman, 1976-1981
Zhao Ziyang	Premier, 1980-1988; CPC General Secretary, 1987-1989
Hu Yaobang	CPC Chairman, 1981-1982; CPC General Secretary, 1982-1987
Li Xiannian	President, 1983-1988
Yang Shangkun	President, 1988-1993
Li Peng	Premier, 1988-98
Jiang Zemin	CPC General Secretary, 1989-; President, 1993-
Zhu Rongji	Premier, 1998-

AFGHANISTAN
ALBANIA
ALGERIA
ANDORRA
ANGOLA
ANTIGUA AND BARBUDA
ARGENTINA
ARMENIA
AUSTRALIA
AUSTRIA
AZERBAIJAN
THE BAHAMAS
BAHRAIN
BANGLADESH
BARBADOS
BELARUS
BELGIUM
BELIZE
BENIN
BHUTAN
BOLIVIA
BOSNIA AND HERZEGOVINA
BOTSWANA
BRAZIL
BRUNEI
BULGARIA
BURKINA FASO
BURUNDI
CAMBODIA
CAMEROON
CANADA
CAPE VERDE
CENTRAL AFRICAN REPUBLIC
CHAD
CHILE
CHINA
COLOMBIA
COMOROS
CONGO, DEM. REP. OF THE
CONGO REPUBLIC
COSTA RICA
CÔTE D'IVOIRE
CROATIA
CUBA
CYPRUS
CZECH REPUBLIC
DENMARK
DJIBOUTI
DOMINICA
DOMINICAN REPUBLIC
EAST TIMOR
ECUADOR
EGYPT
EL SALVADOR
EQUATORIAL GUINEA

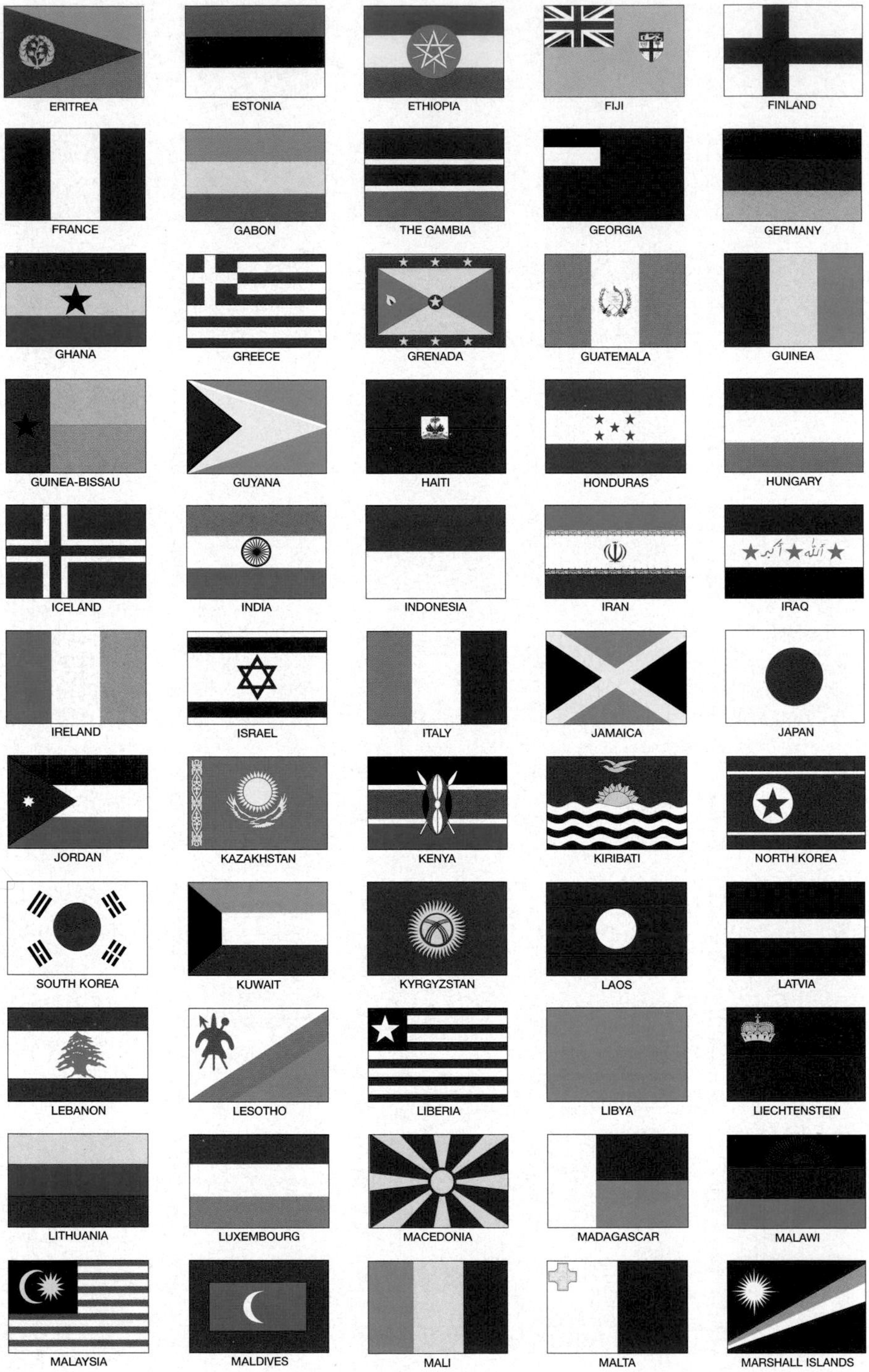
ERITREA
ESTONIA
ETHIOPIA
FIJI
FINLAND
FRANCE
GABON
THE GAMBIA
GEORGIA
GERMANY
GHANA
GREECE
GRENADA
GUATEMALA
GUINEA
GUINEA-BISSAU
GUYANA
HAITI
HONDURAS
HUNGARY
ICELAND
INDIA
INDONESIA
IRAN
الله أكبر
IRAQ
IRELAND
ISRAEL
ITALY
JAMAICA
JAPAN
JORDAN
KAZAKHSTAN
KENYA
KIRIBATI
NORTH KOREA
SOUTH KOREA
KUWAIT
KYRGYZSTAN
LAOS
LATVIA
LEBANON
LESOTHO
LIBERIA
LIBYA
LIECHTENSTEIN
LITHUANIA
LUXEMBOURG
MACEDONIA
MADAGASCAR
MALAWI
MALAYSIA
MALDIVES
MALI
MALTA
MARSHALL ISLANDS

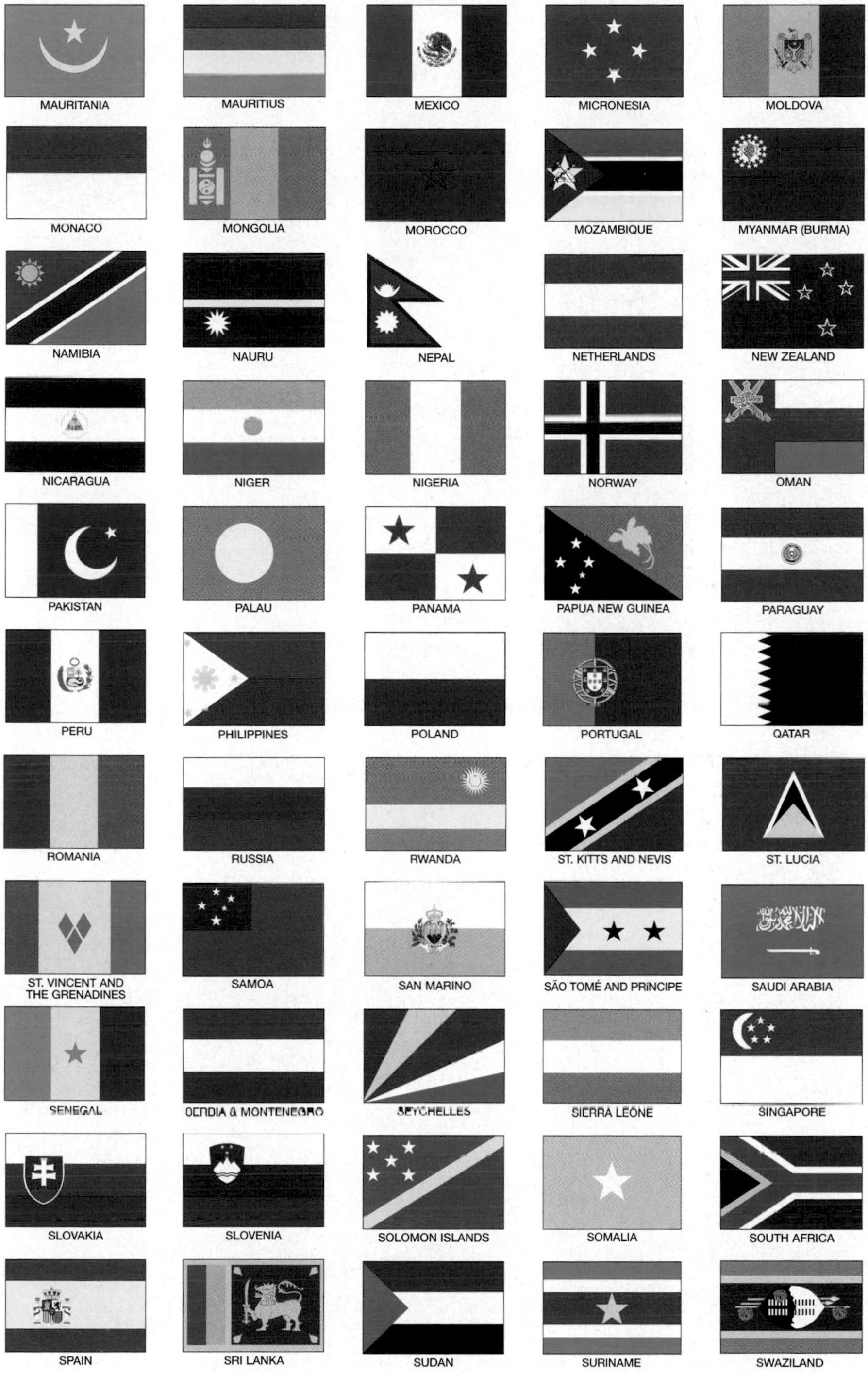
MAURITANIA
MAURITIUS
MEXICO
MICRONESIA
MOLDOVA
MONACO
MONGOLIA
MOROCCO
MOZAMBIQUE
MYANMAR (BURMA)
NAMIBIA
NAURU
NEPAL
NETHERLANDS
NEW ZEALAND
NICARAGUA
NIGER
NIGERIA
NORWAY
OMAN
PAKISTAN
PALAU
PANAMA
PAPUA NEW GUINEA
PARAGUAY
PERU
PHILIPPINES
POLAND
PORTUGAL
QATAR
ROMANIA
RUSSIA
RWANDA
ST. KITTS AND NEVIS
ST. LUCIA
ST. VINCENT AND THE GRENADINES
SAMOA
SAN MARINO
SÃO TOMÉ AND PRINCIPE
SAUDI ARABIA
SENEGAL
SERBIA & MONTENEGRO
SEYCHELLES
SIERRA LEONE
SINGAPORE
SLOVAKIA
SLOVENIA
SOLOMON ISLANDS
SOMALIA
SOUTH AFRICA
SPAIN
SRI LANKA
SUDAN
SURINAME
SWAZILAND

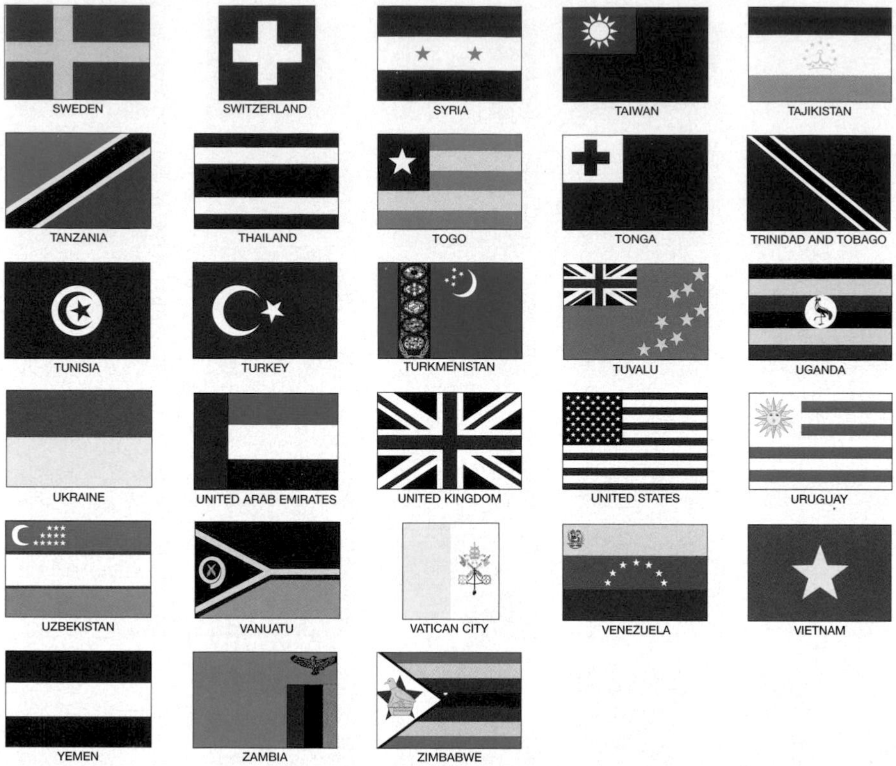

INTERNATIONAL TIME ZONES

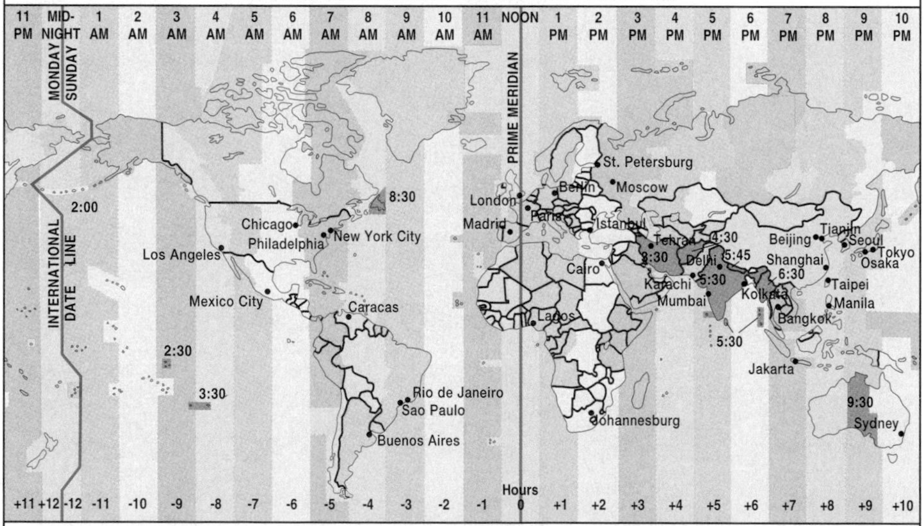

The world is divided into 24 time zones, each 15° longitude wide. The longitudinal meridian passing through Greenwich, England, is the starting point, and is called the *prime meridian.* The 12th zone is divided by the 180th meridian (International Date Line). When the line is crossed going west, the date is advanced one day; when crossed going east, the date becomes a day earlier.

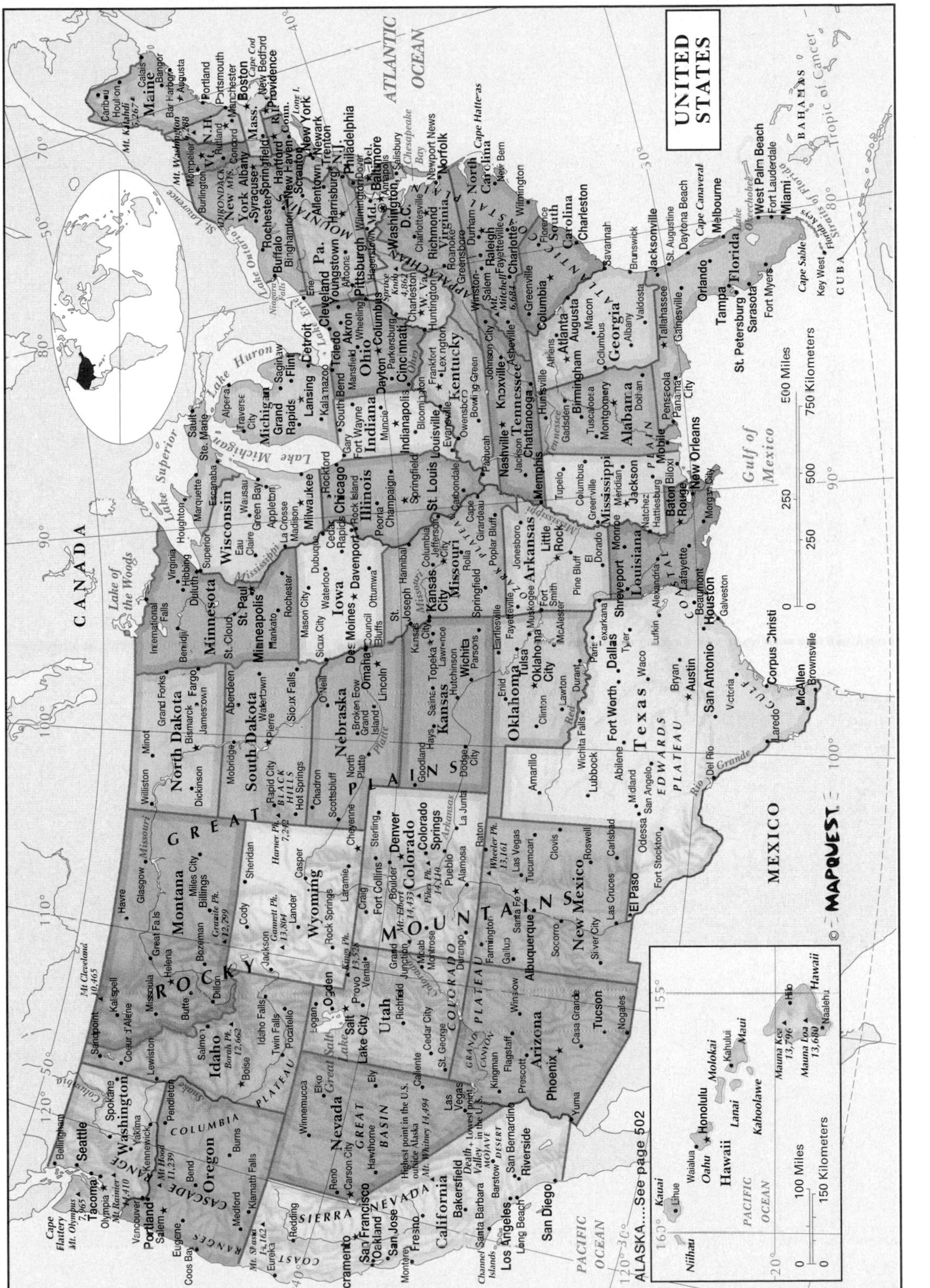
UNITED STATES
CANADA
MEXICO
CUBA
BAHAMAS
ATLANTIC OCEAN
PACIFIC OCEAN
Gulf of Mexico
Tropic of Cancer
Straits of Florida
Lake Superior
Lake Michigan
Lake Huron
Lake Erie
Lake Ontario
Lake of the Woods
Great Salt Lake
Lake Okeechobee
Chesapeake Bay
ROCKY MOUNTAINS
GREAT PLAINS
APPALACHIAN MOUNTAINS
ATLANTIC COASTAL PLAIN
GULF COASTAL PLAIN
GREAT BASIN
COLUMBIA PLATEAU
COLORADO PLATEAU
EDWARDS PLATEAU
OZARK PLATEAU
SIERRA NEVADA
CASCADE RANGE
COAST RANGES
MOJAVE DESERT
BLACK HILLS
GRAND CANYON
ADIRONDACK MTS.
Mississippi
Missouri
Columbia
Snake
Colorado
Rio Grande
Red
Arkansas
Platte
Ohio
St. Lawrence
Washington
Oregon
California
Idaho
Nevada
Utah
Arizona
Montana
Wyoming
Colorado
New Mexico
North Dakota
South Dakota
Nebraska
Kansas
Oklahoma
Texas
Minnesota
Iowa
Missouri
Arkansas
Louisiana
Wisconsin
Illinois
Michigan
Indiana
Ohio
Kentucky
Tennessee
Mississippi
Alabama
Georgia
Florida
South Carolina
North Carolina
Virginia
W. Va.
Pa.
New York
Maine
Vt.
N.H.
Mass.
Conn.
R.I.
N.J.
Del.
Md.
D.C.
Seattle
Tacoma
Portland
San Francisco
San Jose
Oakland
Los Angeles
San Diego
Sacramento
Phoenix
Tucson
Salt Lake City
Denver
Albuquerque
El Paso
Dallas
Fort Worth
Houston
San Antonio
Austin
Oklahoma City
Tulsa
Kansas City
St. Louis
Minneapolis
St. Paul
Chicago
Milwaukee
Detroit
Cleveland
Columbus
Cincinnati
Indianapolis
Louisville
Memphis
Nashville
New Orleans
Atlanta
Miami
Tampa
Jacksonville
Charlotte
Washington
Baltimore
Philadelphia
Pittsburgh
New York
Boston
Providence
Buffalo
Mt. Rainier 14,410
Mt. Whitney 14,494
Mt. Elbert 14,433
Pikes Pk. 14,110
Mt. Mitchell 6,684
Mt. Washington 6,288
Highest point in the U.S. outside Alaska
Death Valley
Lowest point in the U.S.
Cape Hatteras
Cape Cod
Cape Canaveral
Cape Sable
Hawaii
Oahu
Honolulu
Kauai
Niihau
Molokai
Lanai
Maui
Kahoolawe
Mauna Kea 13,796
Mauna Loa 13,680
Hilo
ALASKA...See page 502
0 250 500 Miles
0 250 500 750 Kilometers
0 100 Miles
0 150 Kilometers
© MAPQUEST

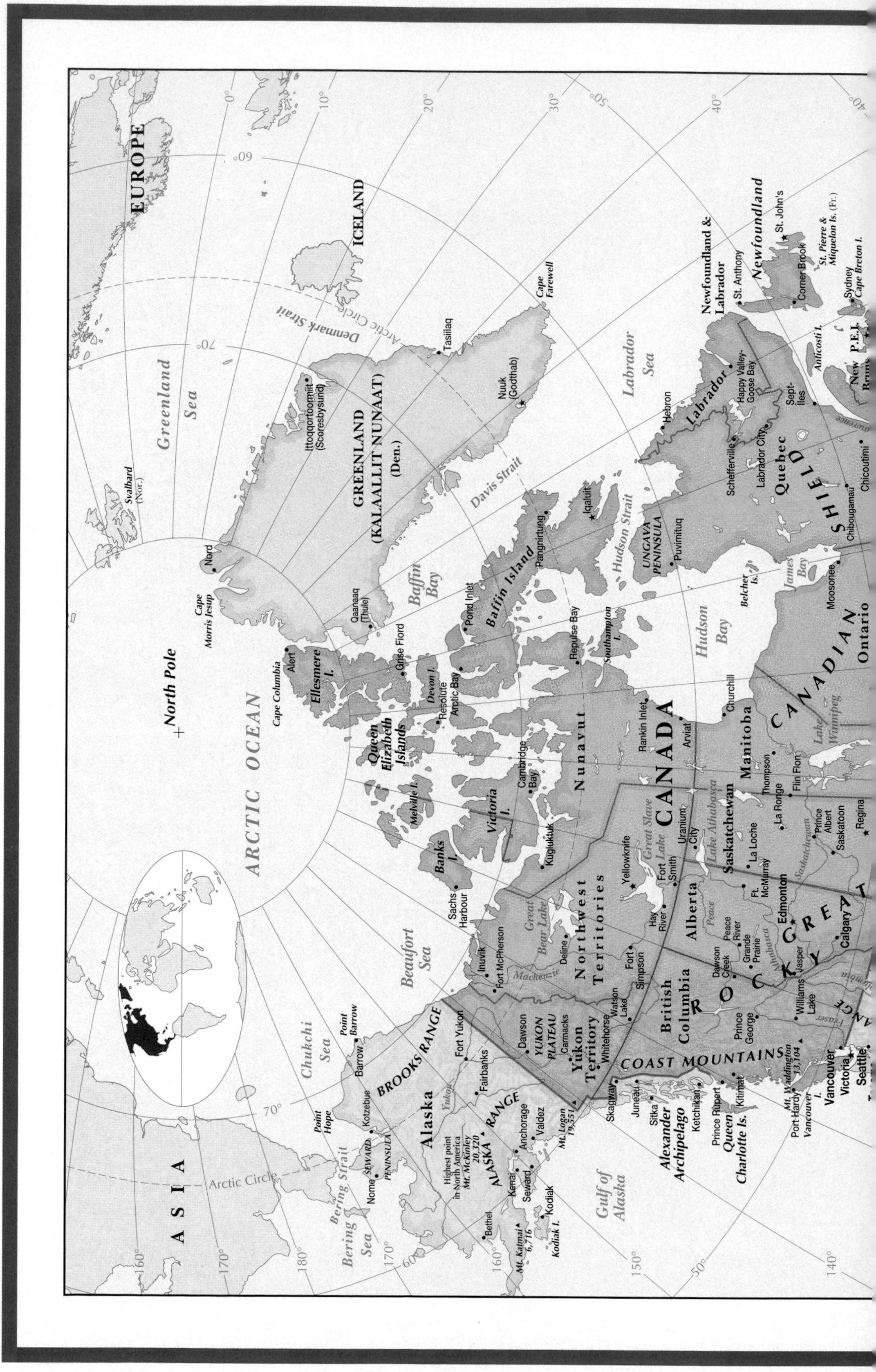
EUROPE
ASIA
ARCTIC OCEAN
North Pole
ICELAND
GREENLAND
(KALAALLIT NUNAAT)
(Den.)
Greenland Sea
Svalbard (Nor.)
Denmark Strait
Arctic Circle
Cape Farewell
Tasiilaq
Nuuk (Godthab)
Ittoqqortoormiit (Scoresbysund)
Nord
Cape Morris Jesup
Qaanaaq (Thule)
Baffin Bay
Davis Strait
Labrador Sea
Hudson Strait
Hudson Bay
James Bay
Cape Columbia
Alert
Ellesmere I.
Grise Fiord
Devon I.
Resolute
Arctic Bay
Pond Inlet
Baffin Island
Pangnirtung
Iqaluit
Repulse Bay
Southampton I.
Queen Elizabeth Islands
Melville I.
Banks I.
Victoria I.
Cambridge Bay
Kugluktuk
Sachs Harbour
Beaufort Sea
Chukchi Sea
Bering Strait
Bering Sea
Point Barrow
Barrow
Point Hope
Kotzebue
Nome
SEWARD PENINSULA
BROOKS RANGE
Alaska
Fairbanks
Fort Yukon
ALASKA RANGE
Highest point in North America
Mt. McKinley 20,320
Anchorage
Valdez
Kenai
Seward
Kodiak
Kodiak I.
Bethel
Mt. Katmai 6,716
Mt. Logan 19,551
Gulf of Alaska
Alexander Archipelago
Skagway
Juneau
Sitka
Ketchikan
Prince Rupert
Queen Charlotte Is.
Kitimat
Port Hardy
Vancouver I.
Vancouver
Victoria
Seattle
Mt. Waddington 13,104
COAST MOUNTAINS
Yukon Territory
YUKON PLATEAU
Dawson
Carmacks
Whitehorse
Watson Lake
Inuvik
Fort McPherson
Great Bear Lake
Deline
Northwest Territories
Fort Simpson
Hay River
Yellowknife
Great Slave Lake
Fort Smith
Nunavut
CANADA
Rankin Inlet
Arviat
Churchill
Uranium City
Lake Athabasca
British Columbia
Prince George
Williams Lake
Dawson Creek
Grande Prairie
Peace River
Jasper
Alberta
Edmonton
Calgary
Ft. McMurray
Saskatchewan
La Loche
La Ronge
Prince Albert
Saskatoon
Regina
Manitoba
Thompson
Flin Flon
Lake Winnipeg
ROCKY
GREAT
CANADIAN
SHIELD
Ontario
Moosonee
Belcher Is.
Quebec
UNGAVA PENINSULA
Puvirnituq
Chibougamau
Chicoutimi
Schefferville
Labrador City
Sept-Iles
Labrador
Hebron
Happy Valley-Goose Bay
Newfoundland & Labrador
St. Anthony
Newfoundland
Corner Brook
St. John's
St. Pierre & Miquelon Is. (Fr.)
Cape Breton I.
Sydney
Anticosti I.
P.E.I.
Mackenzie
Yukon
Peace
Athabasca
Saskatchewan
Fraser

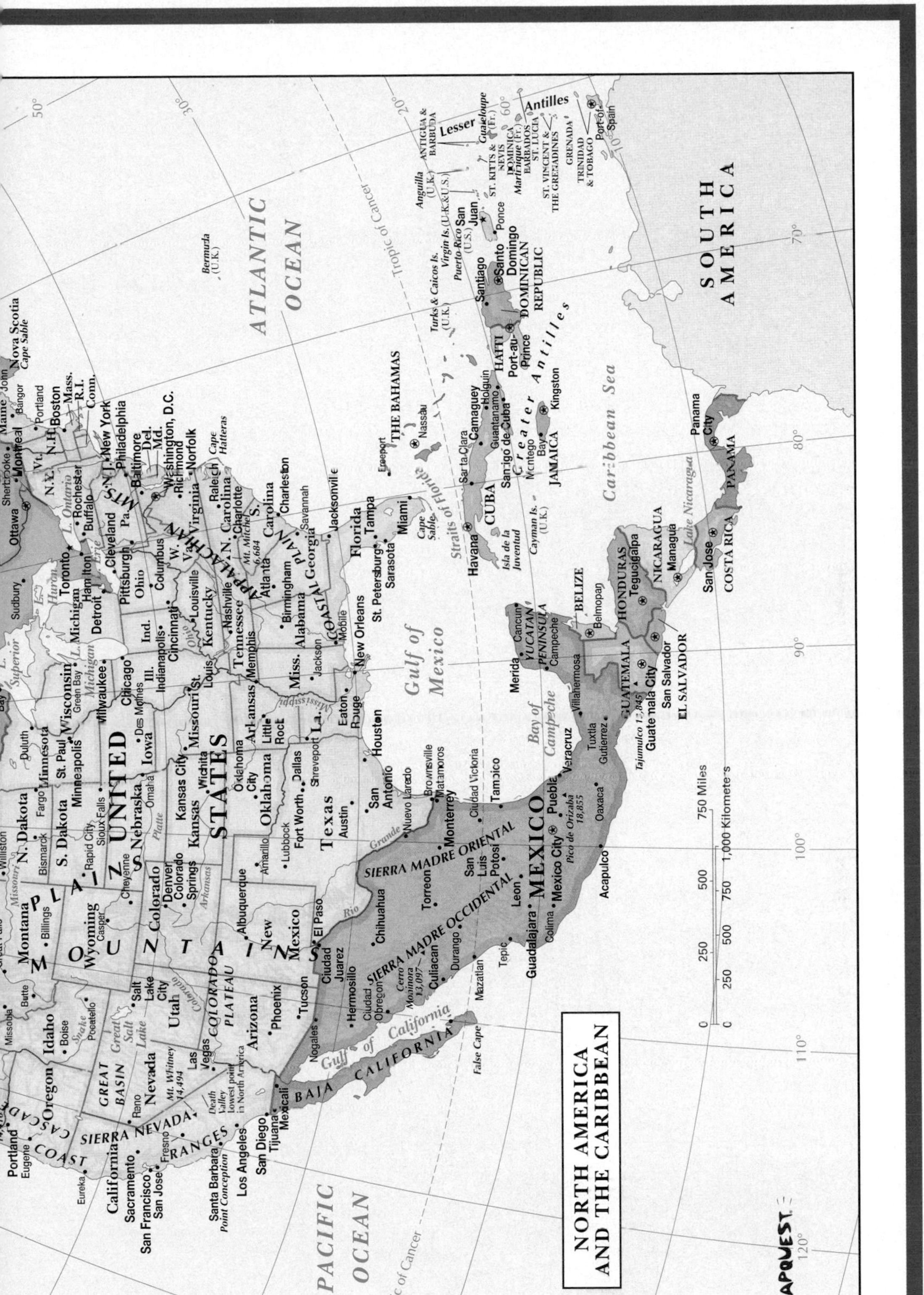
NORTH AMERICA AND THE CARIBBEAN
ATLANTIC OCEAN
PACIFIC OCEAN
Gulf of Mexico
Caribbean Sea
Bay of Campeche
Gulf of California
UNITED STATES
MEXICO
SOUTH AMERICA
ROCKY MOUNTAINS
GREAT PLAINS
COASTAL PLAIN
APPALACHIAN MTS.
SIERRA NEVADA
COAST RANGES
CASCADE
GREAT BASIN
COLORADO PLATEAU
SIERRA MADRE ORIENTAL
SIERRA MADRE OCCIDENTAL
BAJA CALIFORNIA
YUCATAN PENINSULA
THE BAHAMAS
CUBA
HAITI
DOMINICAN REPUBLIC
JAMAICA
Greater Antilles
Lesser Antilles
BELIZE
GUATEMALA
HONDURAS
EL SALVADOR
NICARAGUA
COSTA RICA
PANAMA
Tropic of Cancer
Straits of Florida
Bermuda (U.K.)
0 250 500 750 Miles
0 250 500 750 1,000 Kilometers
© MAPQUEST

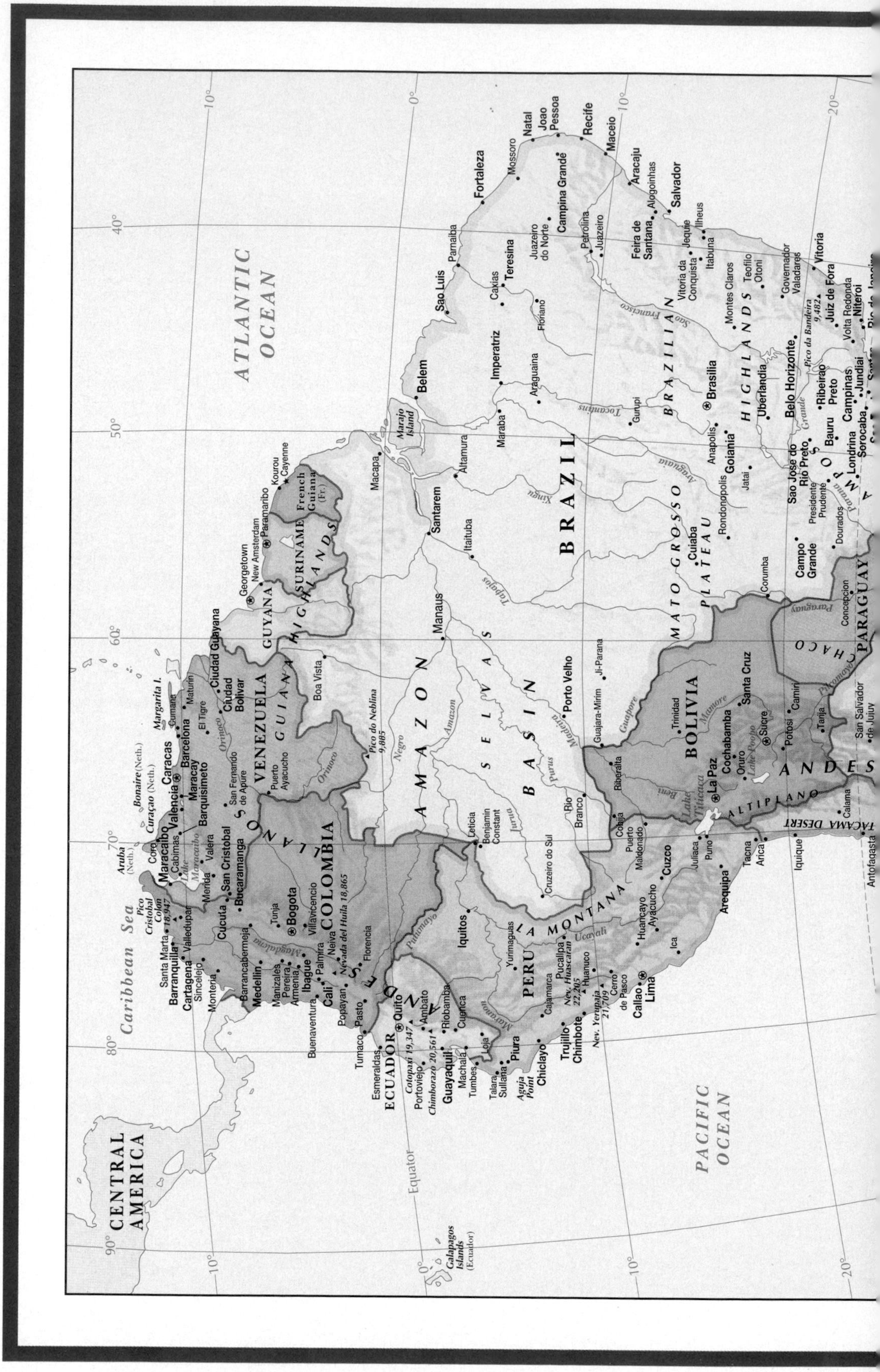

ATLANTIC OCEAN
PACIFIC OCEAN
CENTRAL AMERICA
Caribbean Sea
Equator
VENEZUELA
COLOMBIA
ECUADOR
PERU
BOLIVIA
BRAZIL
PARAGUAY
GUYANA
SURINAME
French Guiana (Fr.)
GUIANA HIGHLANDS
AMAZON BASIN
SELVAS
BRAZILIAN HIGHLANDS
MATO GROSSO PLATEAU
LLANOS
ANDES
ALTIPLANO
LA MONTANA
ATACAMA DESERT
CHACO
Galapagos Islands (Ecuador)
Aruba (Neth.)
Curaçao (Neth.)
Bonaire (Neth.)
Margarita I.
Marajo Island
Lake Titicaca
Lake Maracaibo
Lake Poopo
Pico Cristobal Colon 18,947
Nevada del Huila 18,865
Cotopaxi 19,347
Chimborazo 20,561
Nev. Huascaran 22,205
Nev. Yerupaja 21,709
Pico do Neblina 9,885
Pico da Bandeira 9,482
Aguja Point
Amazon
Negro
Orinoco
Magdalena
Putumayo
Maranon
Ucayali
Jurua
Purus
Madeira
Guapore
Mamore
Beni
Tapajos
Xingu
Tocantins
Araguaia
Sao Francisco
Paraguay
Pilcomayo
Parana
Grande
Caracas
Bogota
Quito
Lima
La Paz
Sucre
Brasilia
Georgetown
Paramaribo
Cayenne
Kourou
Maracaibo
Valencia
Maracay
Barquisimeto
Barcelona
Cumana
Maturin
El Tigre
Ciudad Guayana
Ciudad Bolivar
San Fernando de Apure
Puerto Ayacucho
Coro
Cabimas
Valera
Merida
San Cristobal
Cucuta
Bucaramanga
Barrancabermeja
Santa Marta
Barranquilla
Valledupar
Cartagena
Sincelejo
Monteria
Medellin
Manizales
Pereira
Armenia
Ibague
Tunja
Villavicencio
Neiva
Palmira
Cali
Buenaventura
Popayan
Florencia
Pasto
Tumaco
Esmeraldas
Portoviejo
Ambato
Riobamba
Guayaquil
Cuenca
Machala
Loja
Tumbes
Talara
Sullana
Piura
Chiclayo
Trujillo
Chimbote
Cajamarca
Huanuco
Cerro de Pasco
Callao
Pucallpa
Yurimaguas
Iquitos
Huancayo
Ayacucho
Ica
Cuzco
Arequipa
Juliaca
Puno
Tacna
Arica
Iquique
Calama
Antofagasta
Puerto Maldonado
Cobija
Riberalta
Trinidad
Cochabamba
Oruro
Potosi
Santa Cruz
Camiri
Tarija
San Salvador de Jujuy
Guajara-Mirim
Porto Velho
Ji-Parana
Rio Branco
Cruzeiro do Sul
Leticia
Benjamin Constant
Manaus
Boa Vista
Santarem
Itaituba
Macapa
Altamura
Belem
Maraba
Imperatriz
Araguaina
Sao Luis
Caxias
Teresina
Floriano
Parnaiba
Fortaleza
Mossoro
Natal
Joao Pessoa
Campina Grande
Recife
Maceio
Aracaju
Alagoinhas
Salvador
Feira de Santana
Jequie
Ilheus
Itabuna
Vitoria da Conquista
Petrolina
Juazeiro
Juazeiro do Norte
Teofilo Otoni
Governador Valadares
Vitoria
Montes Claros
Belo Horizonte
Juiz de Fora
Volta Redonda
Niteroi
Uberlandia
Ribeirao Preto
Campinas
Jundiai
Sorocaba
Bauru
Londrina
Sao Jose do Rio Preto
Presidente Prudente
Dourados
Campo Grande
Corumba
Cuiaba
Rondonopolis
Jatai
Goiania
Anapolis
Gurupi
Concepcion

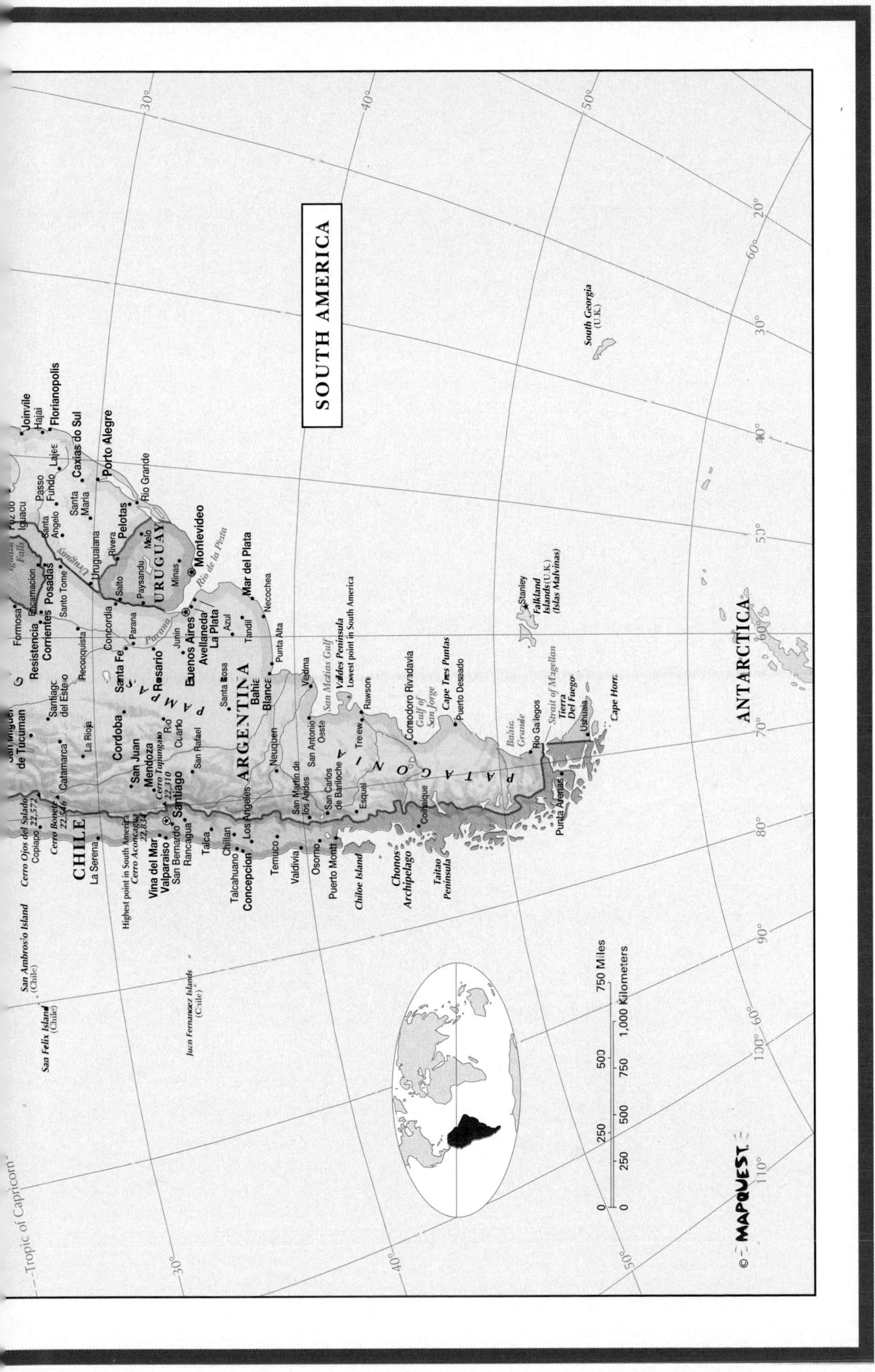
SOUTH AMERICA
ANTARCTICA
CHILE
ARGENTINA
URUGUAY
PAMPAS
PATAGONIA
Tropic of Capricorn
San Felix Island (Chile)
San Ambrosio Island (Chile)
Juan Fernandez Islands (Chile)
Cerro Ojos del Salado 22,572
Copiapo
Cerro Bonete 22,546
La Serena
Highest point in South America
Cerro Aconcagua 22,834
Cerro Tupungato 22,310
Vina del Mar
Valparaiso
Santiago
San Bernardo
Rancagua
Talca
Chillan
Talcahuano
Concepcion
Los Angeles
Temuco
Valdivia
Osorno
Puerto Montt
Chiloe Island
Chonos Archipelago
Taitao Peninsula
Coihaique
Punta Arenas
Strait of Magellan
Tierra Del Fuego
Ushuaia
Cape Horn
Rio Galegos
Bahia Grande
Puerto Deseado
Cape Tres Puntas
Gulf of San Jorge
Comodoro Rivadavia
Rawson
Trelew
Esquel
San Carlos de Bariloche
San Martin de los Andes
San Antonio Oeste
Valdes Peninsula
Lowest point in South America
San Matias Gulf
Viedma
Neuquen
Bahia Blanca
Santa Rosa
San Rafael
Rio Cuarto
Mendoza
San Juan
Cordoba
La Rioja
Catamarca
San Miguel de Tucuman
Santiago del Estero
Santa Fe
Rosario
Parana
Junin
Buenos Aires
Avellaneda
La Plata
Azul
Tandil
Mar del Plata
Necochea
Punta Alta
Reconquista
Resistencia
Corrientes
Formosa
Posadas
Encarnacion
Santo Tome
Concordia
Salto
Paysandu
Minas
Montevideo
Rio de la Plata
Uruguaiana
Rivera
Melo
Pelotas
Rio Grande
Santa Maria
Santo Angelo
Passo Fundo
Lajes
Caxias do Sul
Porto Alegre
Florianopolis
Hajai
Joinvile
Iguacu Falls
Falkland Islands (U.K.) (Islas Malvinas)
Stanley
South Georgia (U.K.)
0 250 500 750 Miles
0 250 500 750 1,000 Kilometers
© MAPQUEST

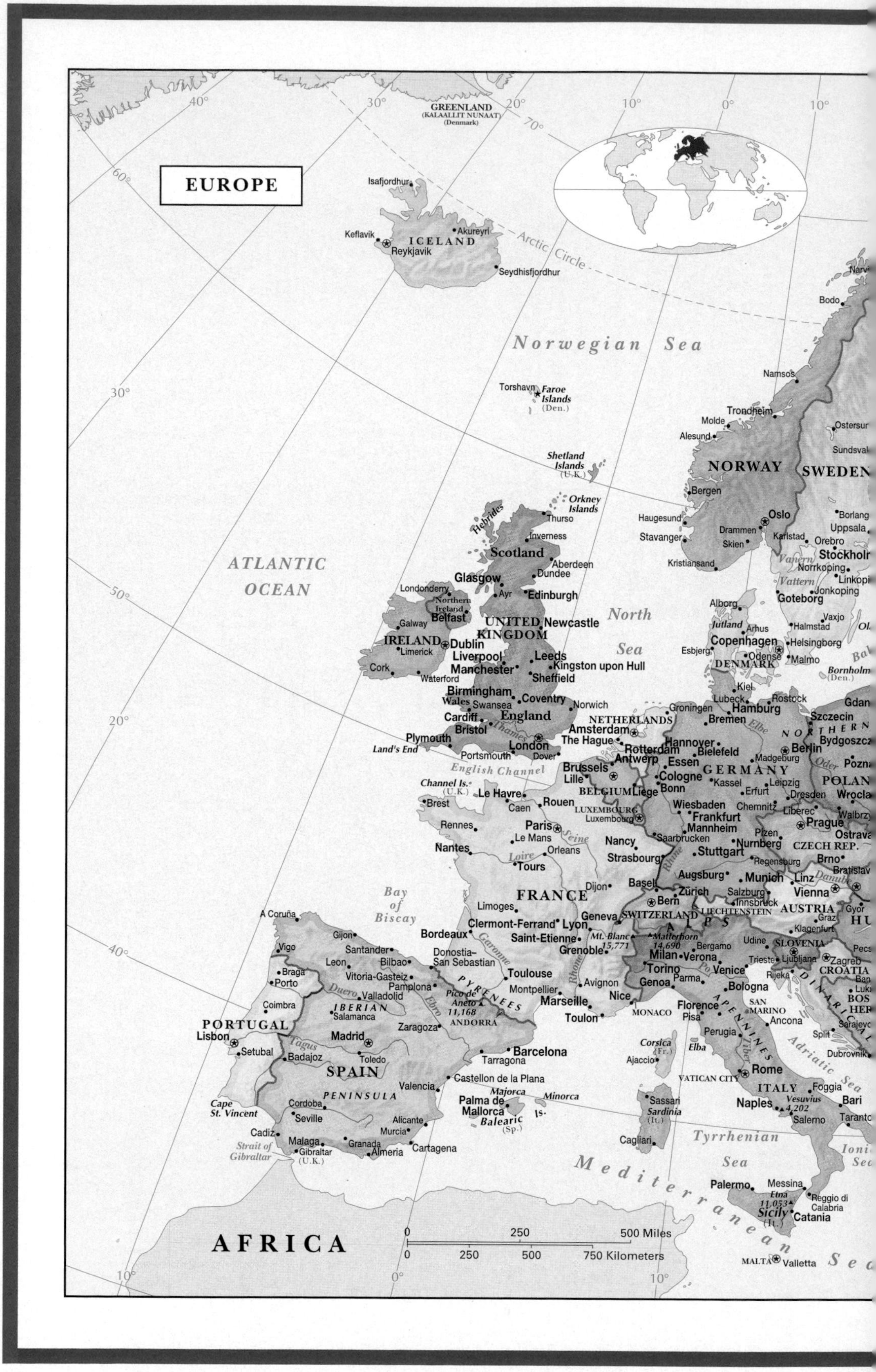
EUROPE
GREENLAND
(KALAALLIT NUNAAT)
(Denmark)
Arctic Circle
Isafjordhur
Akureyri
Keflavik
ICELAND
Reykjavik
Seydhisfjordhur
Norwegian Sea
Torshavn
Faroe Islands
(Den.)
Shetland Islands
(U.K.)
Orkney Islands
Thurso
Hebrides
Inverness
Scotland
Aberdeen
Dundee
Glasgow
Ayr
Edinburgh
ATLANTIC OCEAN
Londonderry
Northern Ireland
Belfast
Galway
IRELAND
Dublin
Limerick
Cork
Waterford
UNITED KINGDOM
Newcastle
Liverpool
Leeds
Manchester
Kingston upon Hull
Sheffield
Birmingham
Coventry
Wales
Swansea
Norwich
Cardiff
England
Bristol
Thames
Plymouth
Land's End
London
Portsmouth
Dover
English Channel
Channel Is.
(U.K.)
North Sea
Bodo
Namsos
Trondheim
Molde
Alesund
NORWAY
SWEDEN
Bergen
Haugesund
Stavanger
Oslo
Drammen
Skien
Kristiansand
Karlstad
Orebro
Borlang
Uppsala
Vanern
Norrkoping
Vattern
Jonkoping
Goteborg
Vaxjo
Halmstad
Helsingborg
Malmo
Alborg
Jutland
Arhus
Esbjerg
Copenhagen
Odense
DENMARK
Bornholm
(Den.)
Kiel
Lubeck
Rostock
Hamburg
Groningen
Bremen
Elbe
NETHERLANDS
Amsterdam
The Hague
Rotterdam
Hannover
Bielefeld
Berlin
Antwerp
Essen
Madgeburg
Brussels
Lille
Cologne
GERMANY
BELGIUM
Liege
Bonn
Kassel
Leipzig
Erfurt
Dresden
Oder
Szczecin
Bydgoszcz
Le Havre
Brest
Caen
Rouen
LUXEMBOURG
Luxembourg
Wiesbaden
Frankfurt
Chemnitz
Liberec
Prague
Mannheim
Saarbrucken
Plzen
Ostrava
CZECH REP.
Nurnberg
Regensburg
Brno
Rennes
Paris
Seine
Le Mans
Nantes
Orleans
Loire
Tours
Nancy
Strasbourg
Rhine
Stuttgart
Augsburg
Munich
Linz
Danube
Vienna
Salzburg
Innsbruck
AUSTRIA
Gyor
Graz
Klagenfurt
LIECHTENSTEIN
Basel
Zurich
Bern
SWITZERLAND
Dijon
FRANCE
Limoges
Bay of Biscay
Geneva
Lyon
Clermont-Ferrand
Bordeaux
Saint-Etienne
Mt. Blanc
15,771
Matterhorn
14,690
Grenoble
Milan
Verona
Bergamo
Udine
SLOVENIA
Ljubljana
Trieste
Pecs
Zagreb
CROATIA
Rijeka
Torino
Venice
Po
Parma
Genoa
Bologna
SAN MARINO
Ancona
Garonne
Rhone
Toulouse
Montpellier
Avignon
Nice
Marseille
Toulon
MONACO
Florence
Pisa
Perugia
Split
Sarajevo
Dubrovnik
Adriatic Sea
A Coruña
Gijon
Santander
Bilbao
Donostia-
San Sebastian
Vigo
Leon
Vitoria-Gasteiz
Pamplona
Braga
Porto
Duero
Valladolid
PYRENEES
Pico de Aneto
11,168
ANDORRA
Ebro
Coimbra
IBERIAN
Salamanca
Zaragoza
PORTUGAL
Lisbon
Madrid
Tagus
Setubal
Badajoz
Toledo
Barcelona
Tarragona
SPAIN
Castellon de la Plana
Valencia
PENINSULA
Majorca
Minorca
Palma de Mallorca
Balearic Is.
(Sp.)
Cape St. Vincent
Cordoba
Seville
Alicante
Murcia
Cadiz
Malaga
Granada
Almeria
Cartagena
Strait of Gibraltar
Gibraltar
(U.K.)
Corsica
(Fr.)
Ajaccio
Elba
VATICAN CITY
Rome
ITALY
Foggia
Sassari
Sardinia
(It.)
Naples
Vesuvius
4,202
Bari
Salerno
Cagliari
Tyrrhenian Sea
Mediterranean Sea
Palermo
Messina
Etna
11,053
Reggio di Calabria
Sicily
(It.)
Catania
MALTA
Valletta
AFRICA
0
250
500 Miles
0
250
500
750 Kilometers

Novaya Zemlya
Barents Sea
North Cape
Vardo
Naryan-Mar
Pechora
Murmansk
Ivalo
LAPLAND
Apatity
KOLA PENINSULA
Kiruna
White Sea
Ukhta
Rovaniemi
Arkhangelsk
RUSSIA
ASIA
URAL MOUNTAINS
Lulea
Oulu
Belomorsk
Syktyvkar
Berezniki
Skelleftea
Dvina
FINLAND
Kotlas
Kuopio
Vaasa
Lake Onega
Perm
Jyvaskyla
Lake Ladoga
Petrozavodsk
Kirov
Tampere
Pori
Lahti
Izhevsk
Kama
Kotka
Ufa
Turku
Helsinki
St. Petersburg
Cherepovets
Vologda
Naberezhnye Chelny
Aland Is. (Fin.)
Gulf of Finland
Rybinsk
Kostroma
Yoshkar Ola
Tallinn
Yaroslavl
Nizhniy Novgorod
Kazan
ESTONIA
Velikiy Novgorod
Cheboksary
Sterlitzmak
Tartu
Ivanovo
Pskov
Ulyanovsk
Orsk
Tver
Vladimir
Tolyatti
Orenburg
Riga
Saransk
Samara
Liepaja
LATVIA
Moscow
Ural
Daugavpils
Kaluga
Ryazan
Penza
Klaipeda
Vitsyebsk
LITHUANIA
Tula
Volga
Kaunas
Vilnius
Smolensk
Orsha
(RUSSIA)
Kaliningrad
PLAIN
Mahilyow
Tambov
Lipetsk
Saratov
EUROPEAN
Minsk
Babruysk
Bryansk
Hrodna
BELARUS
KAZAKHSTAN
Bialystok
Voronezh
Homyel
Warsaw
Brest
Pinsk
Kursk
Chernihiv
Belgorod
Lodz
Sumy
Volgograd
Radom
Kiev (Kyiv)
Kielce
Lublin
Kharkiv
Poltava
Zhytomyr
Katowice
UKRAINE
Cherkasy
Luhansk
Astrakhan
Dnieper
Lviv
Vinnytsia
Donetsk
Horlivka
Don
Krakow
Dnipropetrovsk
CARPATHIAN MOUNTAINS
SLOVAKIA
Chernivtsi
Zaporizhzhia
Rostov-na-Donu
Kosice
Kryvyi Rih
Mariupol
MOLDOVA
Budapest
Miskolc
Prut
Chisinau
Caspian Sea
Debrecen
Iasi
Mykolaiv
HUNGARY
Oradea
Odesa
Sea of Azov
Stavropol
Makhachkala
Kecskemet
Cluj-Napoca
Grozny
Szeged
CRIMEA PENINSULA
Krasnodar
Mt. Elbrus 18,510 Highest point in Europe
Nalchik
Vladikavkaz
ROMANIA
Galati
CAUCASUS MTS.
Timisoara
Simferopol
Brasov
Novi Sad
Ploiesti
Sevastopol
Belgrade
Bucharest
Constanta
Craiova
Black Sea
SERBIA & MONTENEGRO
Danube
Ruse
Pleven
Varna
Nis
BULGARIA
Burgas
Podgorica
Sofia
Stara Zagora
BALKAN
Shkoder
Skopje
Plovdiv
Istanbul
F.Y.R. MAC.
Durres
PENINSULA
Kavala
TURKEY
Tirana
ALBANIA
Thessaloniki
Vlore
Olympus 9,570
Dardanelles
Larisa
Ioannina
Volos
Aegean Sea
Corfu
GREECE
ASIA
Patras
Athens
Corinth
Peloponnese
Kalamata
Cyclades
Sparta
Rhodes (Gr.)
Sea of Crete
Crete (Gr.)
Hania
Iraklion
© MAPQUEST
30°
40°
50°
60°
70°
20°

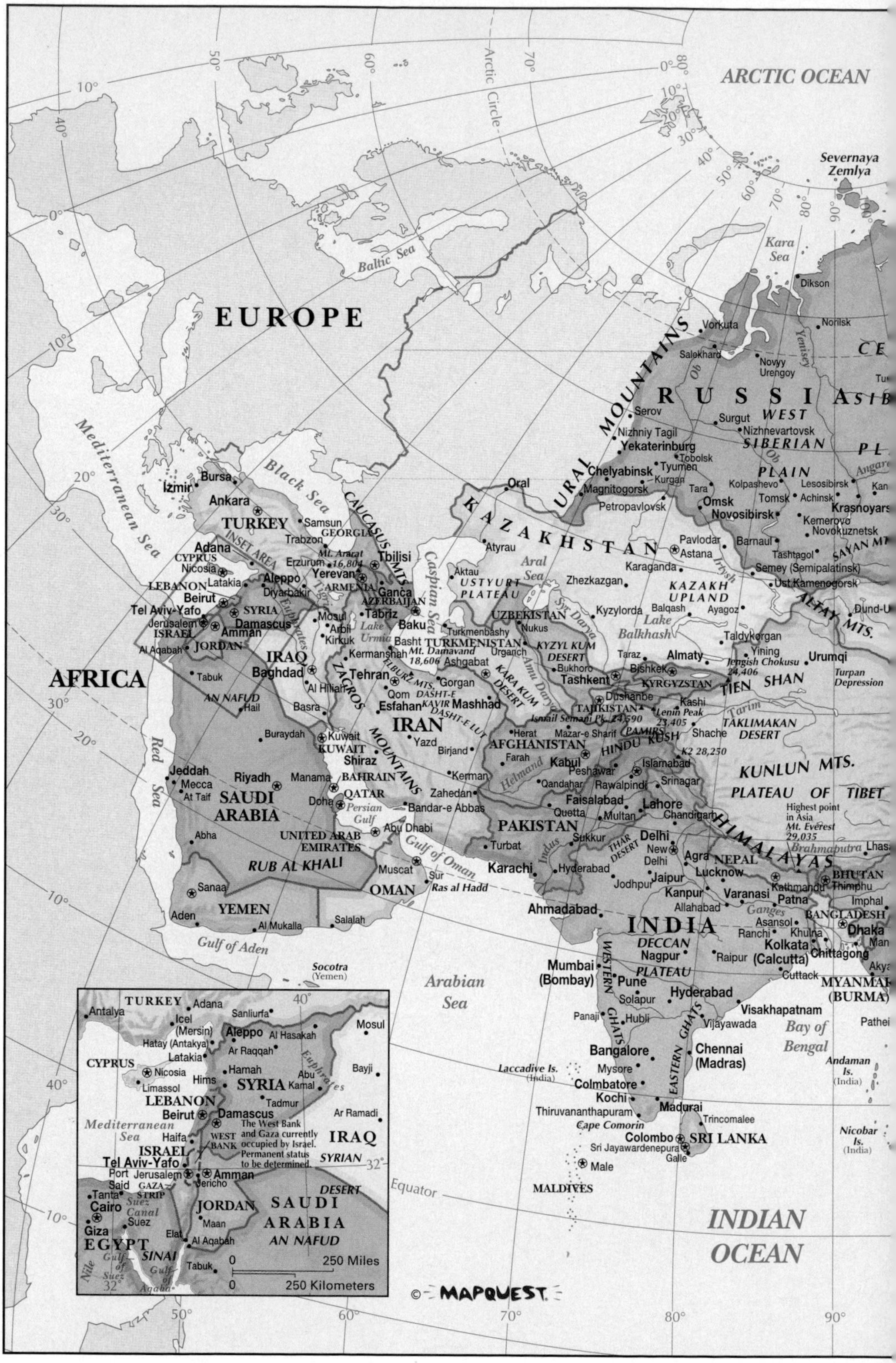
ARCTIC OCEAN
Arctic Circle
Severnaya Zemlya
Kara Sea
Dikson
Norilsk
Vorkuta
Salekhard
Novyy Urengoy
Ob
Yenisey
EUROPE
Baltic Sea
URAL MOUNTAINS
RUSSIA
ASIA
Serov
Surgut
WEST SIBERIAN PLAIN
Nizhnevartovsk
Nizhniy Tagil
Yekaterinburg
Tobolsk
Tyumen
Chelyabinsk
Kurgan
Magnitogorsk
Tara
Omsk
Kolpashevo
Lesosibirsk
Tomsk
Achinsk
Krasnoyarsk
Kemerovo
Novokuznetsk
Novosibirsk
Petropavlovsk
Oral
Pavlodar
Barnaul
Astana
Tashtagol
SAYAN MTS.
Semey (Semipalatinsk)
Ust-Kamenogorsk
ALTAY MTS.
Irtysh
KAZAKHSTAN
Atyrau
Aral Sea
Aktau
USTYURT PLATEAU
Karaganda
Zhezkazgan
KAZAKH UPLAND
Balqash
Ayagoz
Kyzylorda
Lake Balkhash
Syr Darya
UZBEKISTAN
Nukus
Turkmenbashy
TURKMENISTAN
Urganch
KYZYL KUM DESERT
Taldykorgan
Taraz
Almaty
Yining
Urumqi
Jengish Chokusu 24,406
Turpan Depression
Bishkek
KYRGYZSTAN
TIEN SHAN
Bukhoro
Tashkent
KARA KUM DESERT
Amu Darya
Dushanbe
TAJIKISTAN
Kashi
Tarim
Ismail Semani Pk. 24,590
Lenin Peak 23,405
TAKLIMAKAN DESERT
Herat
Mazar-e Sharif
PAMIRS
HINDU KUSH
Shache
AFGHANISTAN
Farah
Kabul
K2 28,250
Helmand
Peshawar
Islamabad
KUNLUN MTS.
Qandahar
Rawalpindi
Srinagar
PLATEAU OF TIBET
Faisalabad
Lahore
Quetta
Multan
Chandigarh
Highest point in Asia Mt. Everest 29,035
PAKISTAN
HIMALAYAS
Sukkur
Delhi
New Delhi
Brahmaputra
Lhasa
Turbat
THAR DESERT
Agra
NEPAL
Indus
Karachi
Hyderabad
Jaipur
Lucknow
Kathmandu
BHUTAN
Thimphu
Jodhpur
Kanpur
Varanasi
Patna
Imphal
Allahabad
Ganges
BANGLADESH
Ahmadabad
INDIA
Asansol
Dhaka
Ranchi
Khulna
Man
DECCAN
Kolkata (Calcutta)
Chittagong
Nagpur
Raipur
Akya
Mumbai (Bombay)
WESTERN GHATS
PLATEAU
Cuttack
MYANMAR (BURMA)
Pune
Hyderabad
Solapur
Visakhapatnam
Panaji
Hubli
Vijayawada
Pathei
EASTERN GHATS
Bay of Bengal
Bangalore
Chennai (Madras)
Andaman Is. (India)
Laccadive Is. (India)
Mysore
Coimbatore
Kochi
Madurai
Thiruvananthapuram
Trincomalee
Cape Comorin
Colombo
SRI LANKA
Nicobar Is. (India)
Sri Jayawardenepura
Galle
Male
MALDIVES
Equator
INDIAN OCEAN
Arabian Sea
Mediterranean Sea
Black Sea
CAUCASUS MTS.
Caspian Sea
Bursa
Izmir
Ankara
TURKEY
Samsun
GEORGIA
Trabzon
Tbilisi
Adana
INSET AREA
Mt. Ararat 16,804
Erzurum
CYPRUS
Nicosia
Yerevan
ARMENIA
Aleppo
Latakia
Diyarbakir
Ganca
LEBANON
AZERBAIJAN
Beirut
SYRIA
Baku
Tel Aviv-Yafo
Tabriz
Jerusalem
Damascus
Mosul
Lake Urmia
Arbil
ISRAEL
Amman
Kirkuk
Basht
Al Aqabah
JORDAN
Kermanshah
Mt. Damavand 18,606
Ashgabat
IRAQ
Euphrates
Tigris
Tehran
ELBURZ MTS.
Gorgan
AFRICA
Tabuk
Baghdad
Al Hillah
Qom
DASHT-E KAVIR
Mashhad
AN NAFUD
Hail
Esfahan
DASHT-E LUT
Basra
ZAGROS MOUNTAINS
IRAN
Yazd
Buraydah
Kuwait
KUWAIT
Birjand
Red Sea
Shiraz
Jeddah
Riyadh
Manama
BAHRAIN
Kerman
Mecca
At Taif
SAUDI ARABIA
Doha
QATAR
Zahedan
Persian Gulf
Bandar-e Abbas
Abha
UNITED ARAB EMIRATES
Abu Dhabi
Gulf of Oman
RUB AL KHALI
Muscat
Sur
Ras al Hadd
Sanaa
OMAN
YEMEN
Aden
Al Mukalla
Salalah
Gulf of Aden
Socotra (Yemen)
TURKEY
Adana
Antalya
Sanliurfa
Icel (Mersin)
Aleppo
Al Hasakah
Mosul
Hatay (Antakya)
Ar Raqqah
Latakia
CYPRUS
Hamah
Bayji
Nicosia
Hims
Abu Kamal
Limassol
SYRIA
LEBANON
Tadmur
Beirut
Damascus
Ar Ramadi
Mediterranean Sea
The West Bank and Gaza currently occupied by Israel. Permanent status to be determined.
IRAQ
Haifa
ISRAEL
WEST BANK
Tel Aviv-Yafo
SYRIAN DESERT
Port Said
Jerusalem
Amman
GAZA STRIP
Jericho
Tanta
Cairo
Suez Canal
JORDAN
SAUDI ARABIA
Suez
Maan
Giza
Elat
Al Aqabah
AN NAFUD
EGYPT
SINAI
Nile
Gulf of Suez
Gulf of Aqaba
Tabuk
0 250 Miles
0 250 Kilometers
© MAPQUEST

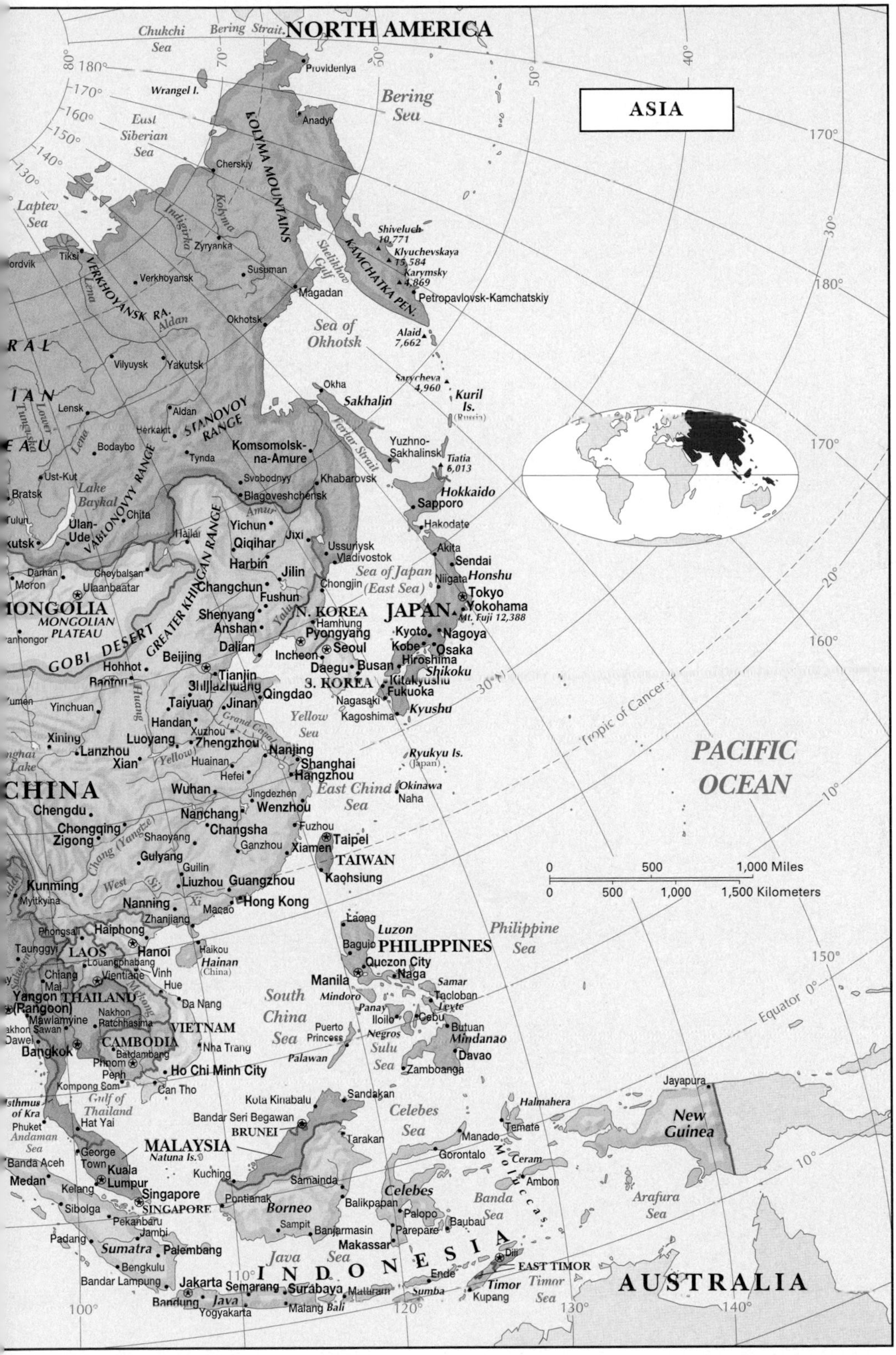
ASIA
NORTH AMERICA
Chukchi Sea
Bering Strait
Wrangel I.
Providenlya
Anadyr
Bering Sea
East Siberian Sea
Laptev Sea
Cherskiy
KOLYMA MOUNTAINS
Kolyma
Indigirka
Zyryanka
Tiksi
VERKHOYANSK RA.
Lena
Verkhoyansk
Susuman
Magadan
Shelikhov Gulf
KAMCHATKA PEN.
Shiveluch 10,771
Klyuchevskaya 15,584
Karymsky 4,869
Petropavlovsk-Kamchatskiy
Okhotsk
Aldan
Sea of Okhotsk
Alaid 7,662
Vilyuysk
Yakutsk
Sarycheva 4,960
Kuril Is. (Russia)
Okha
Sakhalin
Lensk
Aldan
Herkakit
STANOVOY RANGE
Tatar Strait
Bodaybo
Tynda
Komsomolsk-na-Amure
Yuzhno-Sakhalinsk
Tiatia 6,013
Ust-Kut
Lake Baykal
YABLONOVYY RANGE
Svobodnyy
Khabarovsk
Bratsk
Blagoveshchensk
Amur
Hokkaido
Sapporo
Hakodate
Chita
Ulan-Ude
GREATER KHINGAN RANGE
Yichun
Hailar
Jixi
Qiqihar
Harbin
Ussuriysk
Vladivostok
Akita
Sendai
Jilin
Sea of Japan (East Sea)
Niigata
Honshu
Darhan
Moron
Choybalsan
Ulaanbaatar
Changchun
Chongjin
Fushun
Tokyo
Yokohama
Mt. Fuji 12,388
MONGOLIA
MONGOLIAN PLATEAU
Shenyang
Anshan
N. KOREA
Hamhung
Pyongyang
JAPAN
GOBI DESERT
Dalian
Kyoto
Nagoya
Kobe
Osaka
Hiroshima
Shikoku
Beijing
Incheon
Seoul
Daegu
Busan
Hohhot
Baotou
Tianjin
Shijiazhuang
S. KOREA
Kitakyushu
Fukuoka
Taiyuan
Jinan
Qingdao
Nagasaki
Kagoshima
Kyushu
Yinchuan
Huang
Handan
Yellow Sea
Xuzhou
Grand Canal
Xining
Luoyang
Zhengzhou
Lanzhou
Xian
Huainan
Nanjing
Shanghai
Hangzhou
Ryukyu Is. (Japan)
Okinawa
Naha
Tropic of Cancer
PACIFIC OCEAN
Hefei
CHINA
Wuhan
Jingdezhen
Wenzhou
East China Sea
Chengdu
Nanchang
Changsha
Chongqing
Zigong
Shaoyang
Chang (Yangtze)
Fuzhou
Taipei
Ganzhou
Xiamen
TAIWAN
Guiyang
Guilin
Kaohsiung
Kunming
Liuzhou
Guangzhou
Myitkyina
Nanning
Xi
Macao
Hong Kong
Zhanjiang
0 500 1,000 Miles
0 500 1,000 1,500 Kilometers
Laoag
Luzon
Philippine Sea
Phongsali
Haiphong
Haikou
Hainan (China)
Baguio
PHILIPPINES
Taunggyi
LAOS
Hanoi
Luang Phabang
Quezon City
Chiang Mai
Vientiane
Vinh
Hue
Manila
Naga
Samar
Yangon (Rangoon)
THAILAND
Da Nang
South China Sea
Mindoro
Tacloban
Leyte
Mawlamyine
Nakhon Ratchasima
Panay
Iloilo
Cebu
VIETNAM
Puerto Princesa
Negros
Butuan
Mindanao
Bangkok
CAMBODIA
Nha Trang
Sulu Sea
Davao
Battambang
Palawan
Zamboanga
Phnom Penh
Ho Chi Minh City
Kompong Som
Can Tho
Equator 0°
Jayapura
Gulf of Thailand
Kota Kinabalu
Sandakan
Halmahera
Isthmus of Kra
Hat Yai
Bandar Seri Begawan
Celebes Sea
New Guinea
Phuket
BRUNEI
Tarakan
Manado
Ternate
Andaman Sea
MALAYSIA
Natuna Is.
Gorontalo
Banda Aceh
George Town
Kuala Lumpur
Ceram
Medan
Kuching
Samainda
Ambon
Kelang
Singapore
SINGAPORE
Pontianak
Borneo
Celebes
Balikpapan
Moluccas
Banda Sea
Arafura Sea
Sibolga
Pekanbaru
Palopo
Baubau
Jambi
Sampit
Banjarmasin
Parepare
Padang
Sumatra
Palembang
Makassar
Bengkulu
Java Sea
Dili
EAST TIMOR
Bandar Lampung
Jakarta
Semarang
INDONESIA
Ende
Timor
Timor Sea
AUSTRALIA
Bandung
Java
Surabaya
Mataram
Sumba
Kupang
Yogyakarta
Malang
Bali

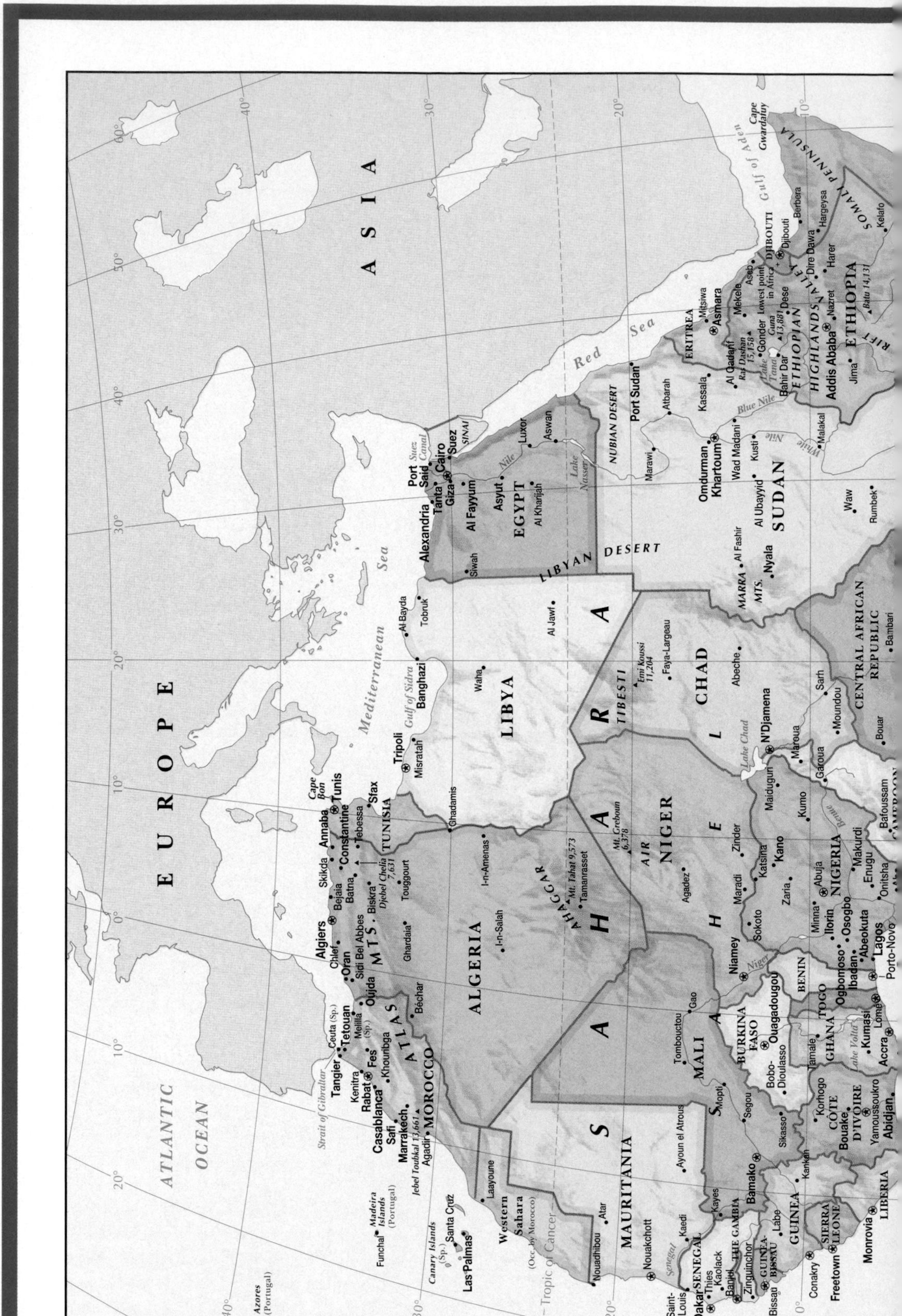

EUROPE
ASIA
ATLANTIC OCEAN
Mediterranean Sea
Red Sea
Gulf of Aden
Gulf of Sidra
Strait of Gibraltar
Tropic of Cancer
Azores (Portugal)
Madeira Islands (Portugal)
Funchal
Canary Islands (Sp.)
Santa Cruz
Las Palmas
Ceuta (Sp.)
Melilla (Sp.)
Tangier
Tetouan
Kenitra
Rabat
Fes
Khouribga
Casablanca
Safi
Marrakech
Jebel Toubkal 13,661
Agadir
MOROCCO
ATLAS MTS.
Oujda
Bechar
Oran
Sidi Bel Abbes
Chlef
Algiers
Bejaia
Batna
Biskra
Skikda
Annaba
Constantine
Tebessa
Djebel Chelia 7,631
Touggourt
Ghardaia
In-Salah
In-Amenas
ALGERIA
AHAGGAR
Mt. Tahat 9,573
Tamanrasset
Cape Bon
Tunis
Sfax
TUNISIA
Ghadamis
Tripoli
Misratah
Banghazi
Al Bayda
Tobruk
Waha
LIBYA
Al Jawf
LIBYAN DESERT
Siwah
Alexandria
Port Said
Suez Canal
Tanta
Cairo
Giza
Suez
SINAI
Al Fayyum
Asyut
EGYPT
Al Kharijah
Luxor
Aswan
Nile
Lake Nasser
NUBIAN DESERT
Port Sudan
Atbarah
Marawi
Kassala
Omdurman
Khartoum
Wad Madani
Kusti
Blue Nile
White Nile
Malakal
Al Ubayyid
SUDAN
Al Fashir
MARRA MTS.
Nyala
Waw
Rumbek
ERITREA
Mitsiwa
Asmara
Al Qadarif
Ras Dashan 15,158
Gonder
Lake Tana
Bahir Dar
Mekele
Aseb
Lowest point in Africa
Guna 13,881
Dese
DJIBOUTI
Djibouti
ETHIOPIAN HIGHLANDS
Addis Ababa
Nazret
Jima
ETHIOPIA
Batu 14,131
RIFT VALLEY
Dire Dawa
Harer
Hargeysa
Berbera
Kelafo
SOMALI PENINSULA
Cape Gwardafuy
SAHARA
TIBESTI
Emi Koussi 11,204
Faya-Largeau
CHAD
Abeche
Lake Chad
N'Djamena
Sarh
Moundou
CENTRAL AFRICAN REPUBLIC
Bouar
Bambari
AIR
Mt. Greboun 6,378
NIGER
Agadez
Zinder
Maradi
Niamey
SAHEL
Sokoto
Katsina
Kano
Zaria
Maiduguri
Maroua
Garoua
Kumo
Benue
Abuja
NIGERIA
Makurdi
Enugu
Onitsha
Minna
Ilorin
Osogbo
Ogbomoso
Ibadan
Abeokuta
Lagos
Porto-Novo
Bafoussam
BENIN
TOGO
Lome
GHANA
Tamale
Lake Volta
Kumasi
Accra
Ouagadougou
BURKINA FASO
Bobo-Dioulasso
Gao
Tombouctou
Mopti
MALI
Segou
Bamako
Sikasso
Korhogo
COTE D'IVOIRE
Bouake
Yamoussoukro
Abidjan
Kankan
GUINEA
Labe
Conakry
SIERRA LEONE
Freetown
Monrovia
LIBERIA
GUINEA-BISSAU
Bissau
Ziguinchor
THE GAMBIA
Banjul
Kaolack
Thies
Dakar
SENEGAL
Saint-Louis
Kaedi
Kayes
Senegal
Nouakchott
MAURITANIA
Nouadhibou
Atar
Ayoun el Atrous
Laayoune
Western Sahara (Occ. by Morocco)

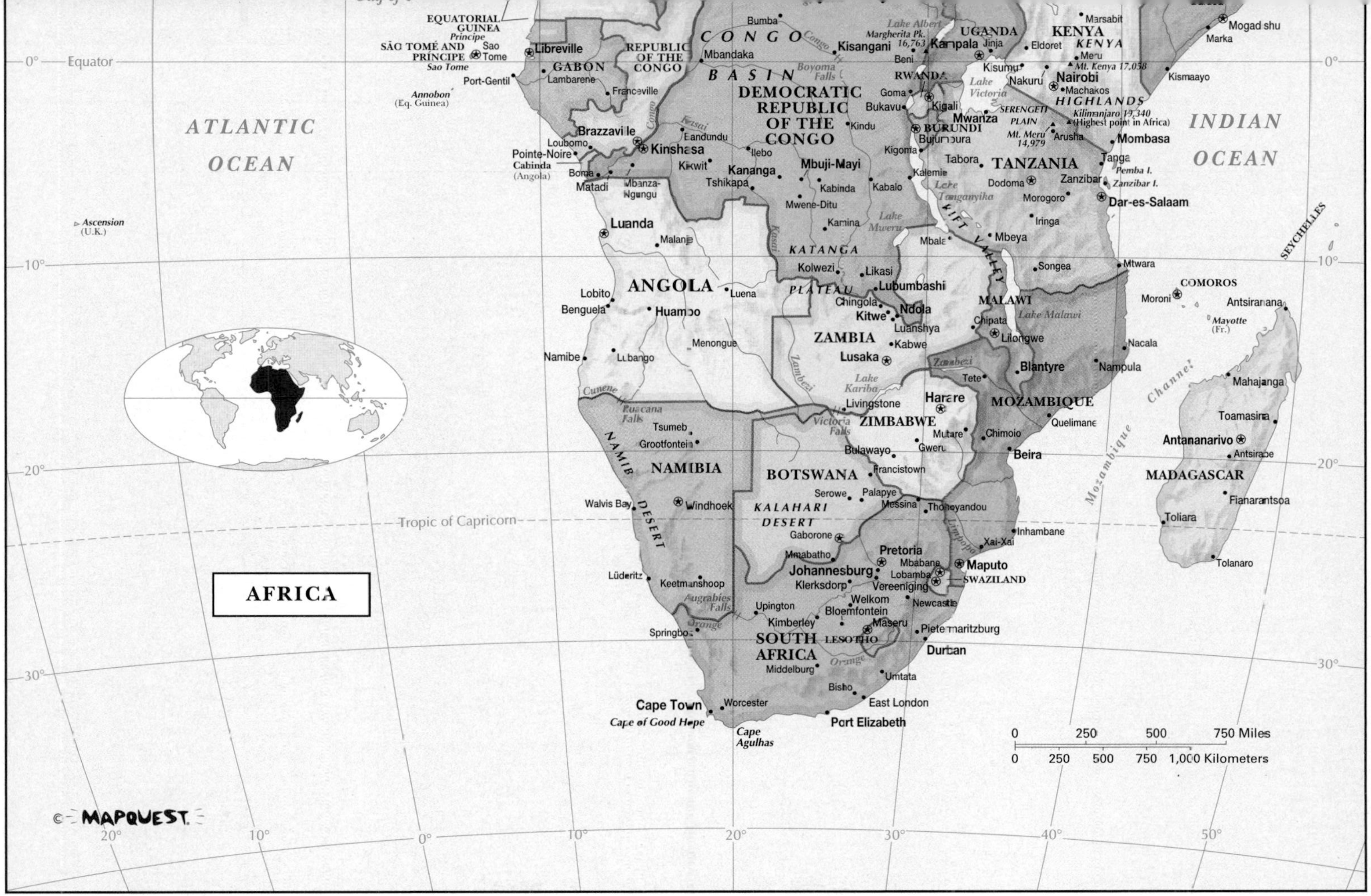

AFRICA
ATLANTIC OCEAN
INDIAN OCEAN
Equator
Tropic of Capricorn
EQUATORIAL GUINEA
Principe
SÃO TOMÉ AND PRINCIPE
Sao Tome
Annobon (Eq. Guinea)
Ascension (U.K.)
Libreville
GABON
Lambarene
Port-Gentil
Franceville
REPUBLIC OF THE CONGO
Brazzaville
Loubomo
Pointe-Noire
Cabinda (Angola)
Boma
Matadi
Kinshasa
CONGO BASIN
DEMOCRATIC REPUBLIC OF THE CONGO
Bumba
Mbandaka
Kisangani
Boyoma Falls
Kindu
Kananga
Mbuji-Mayi
Tshikapa
Kabinda
Mwene-Ditu
Kamina
Kabalo
Kalemie
KATANGA PLATEAU
Kolwezi
Likasi
Lubumbashi
Lake Albert
Margherita Pk. 16,763
UGANDA
Kampala
Jinja
KENYA
Marsabit
Eldoret
Meru
Mt. Kenya 17,058
Kisumu
Nakuru
Nairobi
Machakos
KENYA HIGHLANDS
Kilimanjaro 19,340 (Highest point in Africa)
Mombasa
Mogadishu
Marka
Kismaayo
RWANDA
Kigali
Goma
Bukavu
BURUNDI
Bujumbura
Lake Victoria
SERENGETI PLAIN
Mwanza
Mt. Meru 14,979
Arusha
TANZANIA
Tabora
Kigoma
Dodoma
Morogoro
Zanzibar
Tanga
Pemba I.
Zanzibar I.
Dar-es-Salaam
Iringa
Mbeya
Lake Tanganyika
Lake Mweru
RIFT VALLEY
Mbala
Songea
Mtwara
MALAWI
Lake Malawi
Chipata
Lilongwe
Blantyre
ANGOLA
Luanda
Malanje
Lobito
Benguela
Huambo
Luena
Menongue
Lubango
Namibe
Cunene
ZAMBIA
Chingola
Kitwe
Ndola
Luanshya
Kabwe
Lusaka
Zambezi
Lake Kariba
Livingstone
Victoria Falls
ZIMBABWE
Harare
Mutare
Gweru
Bulawayo
MOZAMBIQUE
Tete
Chimoio
Quelimane
Beira
Nampula
Nacala
Inhambane
Xai-Xai
Maputo
Mozambique Channel
COMOROS
Moroni
Mayotte (Fr.)
Antsiranana
Mahajanga
Toamasina
Antananarivo
Antsirabe
MADAGASCAR
Fianarantsoa
Toliara
Tolanaro
SEYCHELLES
NAMIBIA
Ruacana Falls
Tsumeb
Grootfontein
NAMIB DESERT
Walvis Bay
Windhoek
Lüderitz
Keetmanshoop
Augrabies Falls
Orange
Springbok
BOTSWANA
Francistown
Serowe
Palapye
KALAHARI DESERT
Gaborone
Mmabatho
Messina
Thohoyandou
Limpopo
Pretoria
Mbabane
Lobamba
SWAZILAND
Johannesburg
Klerksdorp
Vereeniging
Welkom
Newcastle
Bloemfontein
Upington
Kimberley
Maseru
LESOTHO
Pietermaritzburg
Durban
SOUTH AFRICA
Middelburg
Umtata
Bisho
East London
Port Elizabeth
Cape Town
Cape of Good Hope
Worcester
Cape Agulhas
0 250 500 750 Miles
0 250 500 750 1,000 Kilometers
0° 10° 20° 30° 40° 50°
© MAPQUEST

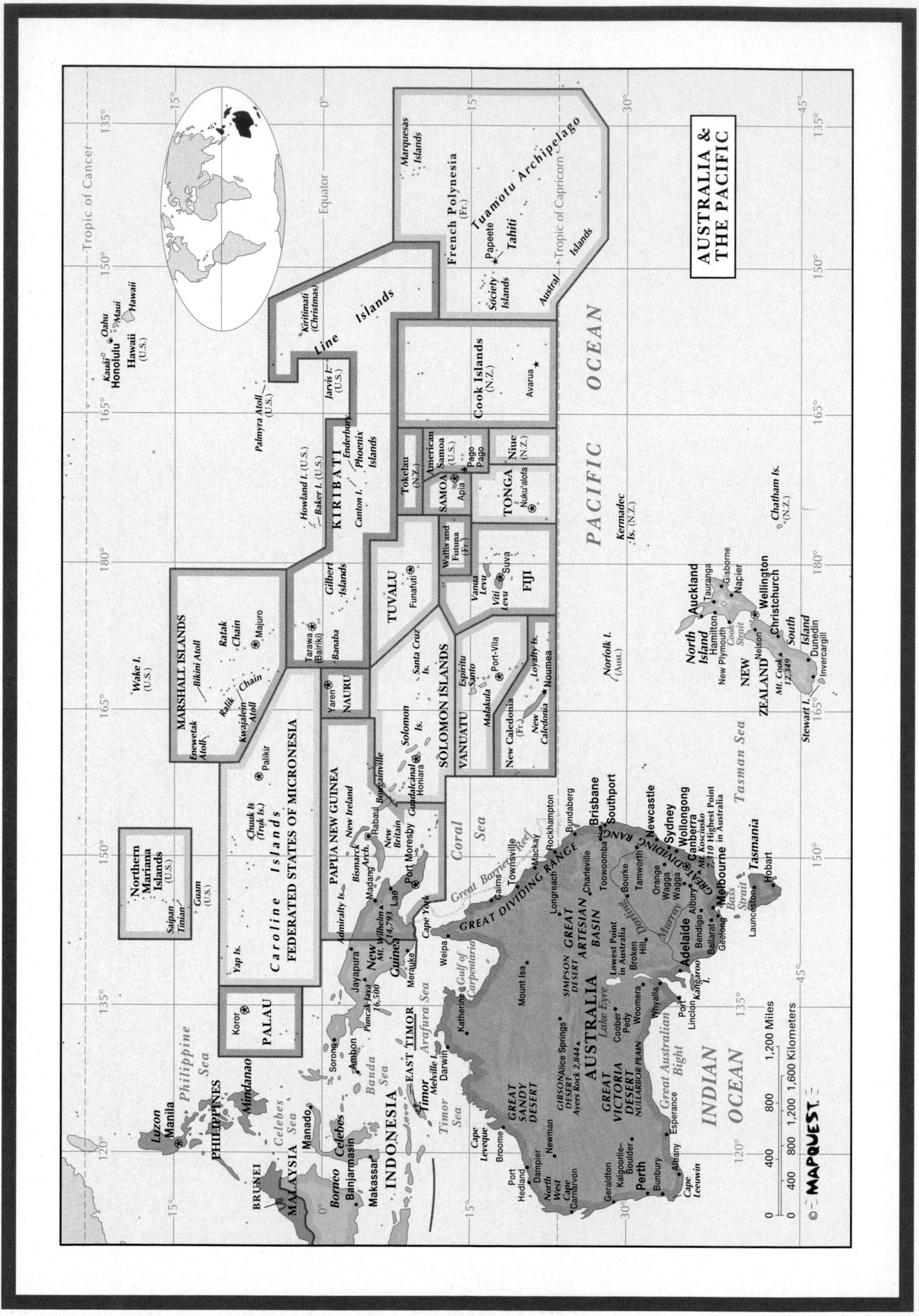
AUSTRALIA & THE PACIFIC
Tropic of Cancer
Equator
Tropic of Capricorn
PACIFIC OCEAN
INDIAN OCEAN
AUSTRALIA
Canberra
Sydney
Melbourne
Brisbane
Adelaide
Perth
Darwin
Hobart
Tasmania
NEW ZEALAND
Wellington
Auckland
Christchurch
North Island
South Island
PAPUA NEW GUINEA
Port Moresby
INDONESIA
EAST TIMOR
PHILIPPINES
Manila
MALAYSIA
BRUNEI
PALAU
Koror
FEDERATED STATES OF MICRONESIA
Palikir
MARSHALL ISLANDS
Majuro
NAURU
Yaren
KIRIBATI
Tarawa (Bairiki)
TUVALU
Funafuti
SOLOMON ISLANDS
Honiara
VANUATU
Port-Vila
New Caledonia (Fr.)
Noumea
FIJI
Suva
TONGA
Nuku'alofa
SAMOA
Apia
American Samoa (U.S.)
Pago Pago
Tokelau (N.Z.)
Niue (N.Z.)
Wallis and Futuna (Fr.)
Cook Islands (N.Z.)
Avarua
French Polynesia (Fr.)
Papeete
Tahiti
Tuamotu Archipelago
Marquesas Islands
Society Islands
Austral Islands
Line Islands
Kiritimati (Christmas)
Phoenix Islands
Gilbert Islands
Caroline Islands
Northern Mariana Islands (U.S.)
Guam (U.S.)
Wake I. (U.S.)
Hawaii (U.S.)
Honolulu
Coral Sea
Tasman Sea
Arafura Sea
Timor Sea
Great Barrier Reef
GREAT DIVIDING RANGE
GREAT SANDY DESERT
GREAT VICTORIA DESERT
GIBSON DESERT
SIMPSON DESERT
GREAT ARTESIAN BASIN
NULLARBOR PLAIN
Great Australian Bight
Mt. Kosciusko 7,310 Highest Point in Australia
Lake Eyre Lowest Point in Australia
Ayers Rock 2,844
Mt. Wilhelm 14,793
Puncak Jaya 16,500
Mt. Cook 12,349
0 400 800 1,200 Miles
0 400 800 1,200 1,600 Kilometers
© MAPQUEST

WORLD EXPLORATION AND GEOGRAPHY

Early Explorers of the Western Hemisphere

Reviewed by Susan Skomal, PhD, American Anthropological Assn., and Paul B. Frederic, PhD, prof. of geography, Univ. of Maine.

In the light of recent discoveries, theories about how the first people arrived in the western hemisphere are being reconsidered. It was once thought that humans came across a "land bridge" from Siberia to Alaska, spreading through the Americas 12,000 to 14,000 years ago. Whereas the preponderance of genetic, skeletal, and linguistic evidence indicate that current Native Americans are descended from peoples from N Asia, skeletal remains of Kennewick Man found in Washington state (dated to 9,200-9,600 BP) and "Luzia" from Brazil (11,500 BP) attest to an earlier arrival of a people with markedly different physical characteristics and uncertain origin.

Archaeologists have confirmed evidence of habitation at least 12,500 BP at Monte Verde (Chile) and 11,500 BP at Lagoa Santa (Brazil). Because a glacier covered most of N America from 20,000 to 13,000 years ago, those who settled in S America may have traveled in vessels along the west coast, sailed directly from Australia or Asia, or spread from N to S America before the ice came. There is even recent evidence from a burial site at Santana do Riacho 1 in Brazil (8,000-11,000 BP) to suggest that some of the early immigrants who crossed to the New World via the northern route may even have originated in Africa.

Norsemen (Norwegian Vikings sailing out of Iceland and Greenland), led by Leif Ericson, are credited with having been the first Europeans to reach America, with at least 5 voyages occurring about AD 1000 to areas they called Helluland, Markland, and Vinland—possibly what are known today as Labrador, Nova Scotia or Newfoundland, and New England. L'Anse aux Meadows, on the N tip of Newfoundland, is the only documented settlement.

Sustained contact between the hemispheres began with the first voyage of Christopher Columbus (born Cristoforo Colombo, c 1451, near Genoa, Italy). Columbus made trips to the New World while sailing for the Spanish.

He left Palos, Spain, Aug. 3, 1492, with 88 men and landed at San Salvador (Watling Islands, Bahamas), Oct. 12, 1492. His fleet included 3 vessels, the *Niña, Pinta,* and *Santa María*. Stops also were made on Cuba and Hispaniola. A 2nd expedition left Cadiz, Spain, Sept. 25, 1493, with 17 ships and 1,500 men, reaching the Lesser Antilles Nov. 3. His 3rd voyage brought him from Sanlucar, Spain (May 30, 1498, with 6 ships), to the N coast of S America. A 4th voyage reached the mainland of Central America, after leaving Cadiz, Spain, May 9, 1502. Columbus died in 1506 convinced he had reached Asia by sailing west.

In N America, John Cabot and Sebastian Cabot, Italian explorers sailing for the English, reached Newfoundland and possibly Nova Scotia in 1497. John's 2nd voyage (1498), seeking a new trade route to Asia, resulted in the loss of his entire fleet. During this period exploration was dominated by Spain and Portugal. In 1497 and 1499 Amerigo Vespucci (for whom the Americas are named), an Italian explorer sailing for Spain, passed along the N and E coasts of S America. He was the first to argue that the newly discovered lands were a continent other than Asia.

Year	Explorer	Nationality (sponsor, if different)	Area reached or explored
c1000	Leif Ericson	Norse	Newfoundland
1492-1502	Christopher Columbus	Italian (Spanish)	West Indies, S. and C. America
1497	John and Sebastian Cabot	Italian (English)	Atlantic Canada
1497-98	Vasco de Gama	Portuguese	Cape of Good Hope (Africa), India
1497-99	Amerigo Vespucci	Italian (Spanish)	E and N Coast of S. America
1499	Alonso de Ojeda	Spanish	N South American coast, Venezuela
1500, Feb.	Vicente Yañez Pinzon	Spanish	S. American coast, Amazon R.
1500, Apr.	Pedro Álvarez Cabral	Portuguese	Brazil
1500-02	Gaspar Corte-Real	Portuguese	Labrador
1501	Rodrigo de Bastidas	Spanish	Central America
1513	Vasco Núñez de Balboa	Spanish	Panama, Pacific Ocean
1513	Juan Ponce de Leon	Spanish	Florida, Yucatán Peninsula
1515	Juan de Solis	Spanish	Río de la Plata
1519	Alonso de Pineda	Spanish	Mouth of Mississippi R.
1519	Hernando Cortes	Spanish	Mexico
1519-20	Ferdinand Magellan	Portuguese (Spanish)	Straits of Magellan, Tierra del Fuego
1524	Giovanni da Verrazano	Italian (French)	Atlantic coast, incl. New York harbor
1528	Cabeza de Vaca	Spanish	Texas coast and interior
1532	Francisco Pizarro	Spanish	Peru
1534	Jacques Cartier	French	Canada, Gulf of St. Lawrence
1536	Pedro de Mendoza	Spanish	Buenos Aires
1539	Francisco de Ulloa	Spanish	California coast
1539-41	Hernando de Soto	Spanish	Mississippi R., near Memphis
1539	Marcos de Niza	Italian (Spanish)	SW United States
1540	Francisco de Coronado	Spanish	SW United States
1540	Hernando Alarcon	Spanish	Colorado R.
1540	Garcia de Lopez Cardenas	Spanish	Colorado, Grand Canyon
1541	Francisco de Orellana	Spanish	Amazon R.
1542	Juan Rodriguez Cabrillo	Portuguese (Spanish)	W Mexico, San Diego harbor
1565	Pedro Menéndez de Aviles	Spanish	St. Augustine, FL
1576	Sir Martin Frobisher	English	Frobisher Bay, Canada
1577-80	Sir Francis Drake	English	California coast
1582	Antonio de Espejo	Spanish	Southwest U.S. (New Mexico)
1584	Amadas & Barlow (for Raleigh)	English	Virginia
1585-87	Sir Walter Raleigh's men	English	Roanoke Isl., NC
1595	Sir Walter Raleigh	English	Orinoco R.
1603-09	Samuel de Champlain	French	Canadian interior, Lake Champlain
1607	Capt. John Smith	English	Atlantic coast
1609-10	Henry Hudson	English (Dutch)	Hudson R., Hudson Bay
1634	Jean Nicolet	French	Lake Michigan, Wisconsin
1673	Jacques Marquette, Louis Jolliet	French	Mississippi R., S to Arkansas
1682	Robert Cavelier, sieur de La Salle	French	Mississippi R., S to Gulf of Mexico
1727-29	Vitus Bering	Danish (Russian)	Bering Strait and Alaska
1789	Sir Alexander Mackenzie	Canadian	NW Canada
1804-06	Meriwether Lewis and William Clark	American	Missouri R., Rocky Mts., Columbia R.

IT'S A FACT: Ferdinand Magellan's attempt to circumnavigate the globe (in a single voyage that started from Spain in Sept. 1519) succeeded without him. He was killed in a battle between native peoples in the Philippines on Apr. 27, 1521. But one of the ships in his fleet, the *Victoria*, made it all the way around the world, reaching Spain in Sept. 1522.

Arctic Exploration

Early Explorers

1587 — John Davis (Eng.). Davis Strait to Sanderson's Hope, 72°12′ N.

1596 — Willem Barents and Jacob van Heemskerck (Holland). Discovered Bear Isl., touched NW tip of Spitsbergen, 79°49′ N, rounded Novaya Zemlya, wintered at Ice Haven.

1607 — Henry Hudson (Eng.). North along Greenland's E coast to Cape Hold-with-Hope, 73°30′, then N of Spitsbergen to 80° 23′. Explored Hudson's Touches (Jan Mayen).

1616 — William Baffin and Robert Bylot (Eng.). Baffin Bay to Smith Sound.

1728 — Vitus Bering (Russ.). Sailed through strait (Bering) proving Asia and America are separate.

1733-40 — Great Northern Expedition (Russ.). Surveyed Siberian Arctic coast.

1741 — Vitus Bering (Russ.). Sighted Alaska, named Mount St. Elias. His lieutenant, Chirikof, explored coast.

1771 — Samuel Hearne (Hudson's Bay Co.). Overland from Prince of Wales Fort (Churchill) on Hudson Bay to mouth of Coppermine R.

1778 — James Cook (Brit.). Through Bering Strait to Icy Cape, AK, and North Cape, Siberia.

1789 — Alexander Mackenzie (North West Co., Brit.). Montreal to mouth of Mackenzie River.

1806 — William Scoresby (Brit.). N of Spitsbergen to 81° 30′.

1820-23 — Ferdinand von Wrangel (Russ.). Surveyed Siberian Arctic coast. His exploration joined James Cook's at North Cape, confirming separation of the continents.

1878-79 — (Nils) Adolf Erik Nordenskjöld (Swed.). The 1st to navigate the Northeast Passage—an ocean route connecting Europe's North Sea, along the Arctic coast of Asia and through the Bering Sea, to the Pacific Ocean.

1881 — The U.S. steamer *Jeannette*, led by Lt. Cmdr. George W. DeLong, was trapped in ice and crushed, June 1881. DeLong and 11 others died; 12 survived.

1888 — Fridtjof Nansen (Nor.) crossed Greenland icecap.

1893-96 — Nansen in *Fram* drifted from New Siberian Isls. to Spitsbergen; tried polar dash in 1895, reached Franz Josef Land, 86° 14′N.

1897 — Salomon A. Andrée (Sweden) and 2 others started in balloon from Spitsbergen, July 11, to drift across pole to U.S., and disappeared. Aug. 6, 1930, their bodies were found on White Isl., 82°57′N, 29°52′E.

1903-6 — Roald Amundsen (Nor.) 1st sailed the Northwest Passage—an ocean route linking the Atlantic Ocean to the Pacific via Canada's marine waterways.

North Pole Exploration

Robert E. Peary explored Greenland's coast, 1891-92; tried for North Pole, 1893. In 1900 he reached N limit of Greenland and 83° 50′N; in 1902 he reached 8° 06′N; in 1906 he went from Ellesmere Isl. to 87°06′ N. He sailed in the *Roosevelt*, July 1908, to winter off Cape Sheridan, Grant Land. The dash for the North Pole began Mar. 1 from Cape Columbia, Ellesmere Isl. Peary reportedly reached the pole, 90° N, Apr. 6, 1909; however, later research suggests that he may have fallen short of his goal by c. 30-60 mi. Peary had several support groups carrying supplies until the last group turned back at 87° 47′N. Peary, Matthew Henson, and 4 Eskimos proceeded with dog teams and sleds. They were said to have crossed the pole several times, then built an igloo there and remained 36 hours. Started south, Apr. 7 at 4 PM, for Cape Columbia.

1914 — Donald MacMillan (U.S.). Northwest, 200 mi, from Axel Heiberg Isl. to seek Peary's Crocker Land.

1915-17 — Vihjalmur Stefansson (Can.). Discovered Borden, Brock, Meighen, and Lougheed Isls.

1918-20 — Amundsen sailed the Northeast Passage.

1925 — Amundsen and Lincoln Ellsworth (U.S.) reached 87°44′N in attempt to fly to North Pole from Spitsbergen.

1926 — Richard E. Byrd and Floyd Bennett (U.S.) reputedly flew over North Pole, May 9. (Claim to have reached the Pole is in dispute, however.)

1926 — Amundsen, Ellsworth, and Umberto Nobile (It.) flew from Spitsbergen over North Pole May 12, to Teller, AK, in dirigible *Norge*.

1928 — Nobile crossed North Pole in airship, May 24; crashed, May 25. Amundsen died attempting a rescue.

North Pole Exploration Records

On Aug. 3, 1958, the *Nautilus,* under Comdr. William R. Anderson, became the 1st ship to cross the North Pole beneath the Arctic ice.

In Aug. 1960, the nuclear-powered U.S. submarine *Seadragon* (Comdr. George P. Steele 2nd) made the 1st E-W underwater transit through the Northwest Passage. Traveling submerged for the most part, it took 6 days to make the 850-mi trek from Baffin Bay to the Beaufort Sea.

On Aug. 16, 1977, the Soviet nuclear icebreaker *Arktika* reached the North Pole, becoming the 1st surface ship to break through the Arctic ice pack.

On Apr. 30, 1978, Naomi Uemura (Jap.) became the 1st person to reach the North Pole alone, traveling by dog sled in a 54-day, 600-mi trek over the frozen Arctic.

In Apr. 1982, Sir Ranulph Fiennes and Charles Burton, Brit. explorers, reached the North Pole and became the 1st to circle the earth from pole to pole. They had reached the South Pole 16 months earlier. The 52,000-mi trek took 3 years, involved 23 people, and cost an estimated $18 mil.

On May 2, 1986, 6 explorers reached the North Pole assisted only by dogs. They became the 1st to reach the pole without aerial logistics support since at least 1909. The explorers, Amer. Will Steger, Paul Schurke, Anne Bancroft, and Geoff Carroll, and Can. Brent Boddy and Richard Weber, completed the 500-mi journey in 56 days.

On June 15, 1995, Weber and Russ. Mikhail Malakhov became the 1st pair to make it to the pole and back without any mechanical assistance. The 940-mi trip, made entirely on skis, took 121 days.

Antarctic Exploration

Antarctica has been approached since 1773-75, when Capt. James Cook (Brit.) reached 71°10′S. Many sea and landmarks bear names of early explorers. Fabian von Bellingshausen (Russ.) discovered Peter I and Alexander I Isls., 1819-21. Nathaniel Palmer (U.S.) traveled throughout Palmer Peninsula, 60° W, 1820, without realizing that this was a continent. Capt. John Davis (U.S.) made the 1st known landing on the continent on Feb. 7, 1821. Later, in 1823, James Weddell (Brit.) found Weddell Sea, 74°15′ S, the southernmost point that had been reached.

First to announce existence of the continent of Antarctica was Charles Wilkes (U.S.), who followed the coast for 1,500 mi, 1840. Adelie Coast, 140°E, was found by Dumont d'Urville (Fr.), 1840. Ross Ice Shelf was found by James Clark Ross (Brit.), 1841-42.

1895 — Leonard Kristensen (Nor.) landed a party on the coast of Victoria Land. They were the 1st ashore on the main continental mass. C. E. Borchgrevink, a member of that party, returned in 1899 with a Brit. expedition, 1st to winter on Antarctica.

1902-4 — Robert Falcon Scott (Brit.) explored Edward VII Peninsula to 82°17′S, 146°33′E from McMurdo Sound.

1908-9 — Ernest Shackleton (Brit.) 1st to use Manchurian ponies in Antarctic sledging. He reached 88°23′S, discovering a route on to the plateau by way of the Beardmore Glacier and pioneering the way to the pole.

1911 — Roald Amundsen (Nor.) with 4 men and dog teams reached the South Pole, Dec. 14.

1912 — Scott reached the pole from Ross Isl., Jan. 18, with 4 companions. None of Scott's party survived. Their bodies and expedition notes were found, Nov. 12.

1928 — 1st person to use an airplane over Antarctica was Sir George Hubert Wilkins (Austral.).

1929 — Richard E. Byrd (U.S.) established Little America on Bay of Whales. On 1,600-mi airplane flight begun Nov. 28, he crossed South Pole, Nov. 29, with 3 others.

1934-35 — Byrd led 2nd expedition to Little America, explored 450,000 sq mi, wintered alone at weather station, 80°08´S.

1934-37 — John Rymill led British Graham Land expedition; discovered Palmer Penin. is part of mainland.

1935 —Lincoln Ellsworth (U.S.) flew S along E Coast of Palmer Penin., then crossed continent to Little America, making 4 landings.

1939-41 — U.S. Navy plane flights discovered about 150,000 sq mi of new land.

1940 — Byrd charted most of coast between Ross Sea and Palmer Penin.

1946-47 — U.S. Navy undertook Operation Highjump, commanded by Byrd, included 13 ships and 4,000 men. Airplanes photomapped coastline and penetrated beyond pole.

1946-48 — Ronne Antarctic Research Expedition Comdr., Finn Ronne, USNR, determined the Antarctic to be only one continent with no strait between Weddell Sea and Ross Sea; explored 250,000 sq mi of land by flights to 79°S.

1955-57 — U.S. Navy's Operation Deep Freeze led by Adm. Byrd. Supporting U.S. scientific efforts for the International Geophysical Year (IGY), the operation was commanded by Rear Adm. George Dufek. It established 5 coastal stations fronting the Indian, Pacific, and Atlantic oceans and also 3 interior stations; explored more than 1,000,000 sq mi in Wilkes Land.

1957-58 — During the IGY, July 1957 through Dec. 1958, scientists from 12 countries conducted Antarctic research at a network of some 60 stations on Antarctica.

Dr. Vivian E. Fuchs led a 12-person Trans-Antarctic Expedition on the 1st land crossing of Antarctica. Starting from the Weddell Sea, they reached Scott Station, Mar. 2, 1958, after traveling 2,158 mi in 98 days.

1958 — A group of 5 U.S. scientists led by Edward C. Thiel, seismologist, moving by tractor from Ellsworth Station on Weddell Sea, identified a huge mountain range, 5,000 ft above the ice sheet and 9,000 ft above sea level. The range, originally seen by a Navy plane, was named the Dufek Massif, for Rear Adm. George Dufek.

1959 — Argentina, Australia, Belgium, Chile, France, Japan, New Zealand, Norway, South Africa, U.S.S.R., U.K., and U.S. signed a treaty suspending territorial claims for 30 yrs. and reserving the continent, S of 60°S, for research.

1961-62 — Scientists discovered the Bentley Trench, running from Ross Ice Shelf into Marie Byrd Land, near the end of the Ellsworth Mts., toward the Weddell Sea.

1962 — 1st nuclear power plant began operation at McMurdo Sound.

1963 — On Feb. 22, a U.S. plane made the longest nonstop flight ever in the South Pole area, covering 3,600 mi in 10 hr. The flight was from McMurdo Station S past the pole to Shackleton Mts., SE to the "Area of Inaccessibility," and back to McMurdo Station.

1964 — New Zealanders mapped the mountain area from from Cape Adare W some 400 mi to Pennell Glacier.

1985 — Igor A. Zotikov, a Russian researcher, discovered sediments in the Ross Ice Shelf that seem to support the continental drift theory. Ocean Drilling Project finds that the ice sheets of E Antarctica are 37 million yrs. old.

1989 — Victoria Murden and Shirley Metz became both the 1st women and the 1st Americans to reach the South Pole overland when they arrived with 9 others on Jan. 17, 1989. The 51-day trek on skis covered 740 mi.

1991 — 24 nations approved a protocol to the 1959 Antarctica Treaty, Oct. 4. New conservation provisions, including banning oil and other mineral exploration for 50 yrs.

1995 — On Dec. 22, a Norwegian, Borge Ousland, reached the South Pole in the fastest time on skis: 44 days.

1996-97 — Ousland became 1st person to traverse Antarctica alone; reached South Pole Dec. 19, 1996; traveled 1,675 mi in 64 days, ending Jan. 18, 1997.

Volcanoes

Sources: *Volcanoes of the World*, Geoscience Press; Global Volcanism Network, Smithsonian Institution

Roughly 540 volcanoes are known to have erupted during historical times. Nearly 75% of these historically active volcanoes lie along the so-called Ring of Fire, running along the W coast of the Americas from the southern tip of Chile to Alaska, down the E coast of Asia from Kamchatka to Indonesia, and continuing from New Guinea to New Zealand. The Ring of Fire marks the boundary between the mobile tectonic plates underlying the Pacific Ocean and those of the surrounding continents. Other active regions occur along rift zones, where plates pull apart, as in Iceland, or where molten material moves up from the mantle over local "hot spots," as in Hawaii. The vast majority of the earth's volcanism occurs at submarine rift zones. For more information on volcanoes, see the website at www.volcano.si.edu/gvp

Notable Volcanic Eruptions

Approximately 7,000 years ago, Mazama, a 9,900-ft volcano in southern Oregon, erupted violently, ejecting large amounts of ash and pumice and voluminous pyroclastic flows. The ash spread over the entire northwestern U.S. and as far away as Saskatchewan, Can. During the eruption, the top of the mountain collapsed, leaving a caldera 6 mi across and about a half mile deep, which filled with rainwater to form what is now called Crater Lake.

In AD 79, Vesuvio, or Vesuvius, a 4,190-ft volcano overlooking Naples Bay, became active after several centuries of apparent inactivity. On Aug. 24 of that year, a heated mud and ash flow swept down the mountain, engulfing the cities of Pompeii, Herculaneum, and Stabiae with debris more than 60 ft deep. About 10% of the population of the 3 towns were killed.

In 1883, an eruption similar to the Mazama eruption occurred on the island of Krakatau. At least 2,000 people died in pyroclastic flows on Aug. 26. The next day, the 2,640-ft peak of the volcano collapsed to 1,000 ft below sea level, sinking most of the island and killing over 3,000. A tsunami (tidal wave) generated by the collapse killed more than 31,000 people in Java and Sumatra, and eventually reached England. Ash from the eruption colored sunsets around the world for 2 years. A similar, even more powerful eruption had taken place 68 years earlier at Mt. Tambora on the Indonesian island of Sumbawa.

Date	Volcano	Deaths (est.)
Aug. 24, AD 79	Mt. Vesuvius, Italy	16,000
1586	Kelut, Java, Indon.	10,000
Dec. 15, 1631	Mt. Vesuvius, Italy	4,000
Aug. 12, 1772	Mt. Papandayan, Java, Indon.	3,000
June 8, 1783	Laki, Iceland	9,350
May 21, 1792	Mt. Unzen, Japan	14,500
Apr. 10-12, 1815	Mt. Tambora, Sumbawa, Indon	92,000[1]
Aug. 26-28, 1883	Krakatau, Indon.	36,000
Apr. 24, 1902	Santa María, Guatemala	1,000[2]
May 8, 1902	Mt. Pelée, Martinique	28,000
Jan. 30, 1911	Mt. Taal, Phil.	1,400
May 19, 1919	Mt. Kelut, Java, Indon.	5,000
Jan. 17-21, 1951	Mt. Lamington, New Guinea	3,000
May 18, 1980	Mt. St. Helens, U.S.	57
Mar. 28, 1982	El Chichon, Mex.	1,880
Nov. 13, 1985	Nevado del Ruiz, Colombia	23,000
Aug. 21, 1986	Lake Nyos, Cameroon	1,700
June 15, 1991	Mt. Pinatubo, Luzon, Phil.	800

(1) Of these, 10,000 were directly related to the eruption, an additional 82,000 were the result of starvation and disease brought on by the event. (2) An additional 3,000 deaths due to a malaria outbreak are sometimes attributed to the eruption.

Notable Active Volcanoes

Active volcanoes display a wide range of activity. In this table, years are given for last display of eruptive activity, as of mid-2002; list does not include submarine volcanoes. An eruption may involve explosive ejection of new or old fragmental material, escape of liquid lava, or both. Volcanoes are listed by height, which does not reflect eruptive magnitude.

Name (latest eruption)		Height (ft)
Africa		
Mt. Cameroon (2000)	Cameroon	13,435
Nyiragongo (2002)	Congo	11,384
Nyamuragira (2002)	Congo	10,033
Mt. Oku {Lake Nyos} (1986)	Cameroon	9,878
Ol Doinyo Lengai (2001)	Tanzania	9,482
Fogo (1995)	Cape Verde Isls.	9,281
Piton de la Fournaise (2001)	Réunion Isl., Indian O.	8,632
Karthala (1991)	Comoros.	7,746
Erta-Ale (2002)	Ethiopia	2,011
Antarctica		
Erebus (2002)	Ross Isl	12,447
Deception Island (1970)	S. Shetland Isl.	1,890
Asia-Oceania		
Kliuchevskoi (2000)	Kamchatka, Russia	15,863
Kerinci (2002)	Sumatra, Indon.	12,467
Fuji (1708)	Honshu, Japan	12,388
Tolbachik (1976)	Kamchatka, Russia	12,080
Semeru (2002)	Java, Indon.	12,060
Slamet (1999)	Java, Indon.	11,260
Raung (2000)	Java, Indon.	10,932
Shiveluch (2002)	Kamchatka, Russia	10,771
On-take (1980)	Honshu, Japan	10,049
Merapi (2002)	Java, Indon.	9,669
Bezymianny (2001)	Kamchatka, Russia	9,455
Peuet Sague (2000)	Sumatra, Indon.	9,190
Ruapehu (1997)	New Zealand	9,175
Heard (2001)	Indian Ocean	9,006
Baitoushan (1702)	China/Korea	9,003
Asama (1990)	Honshu, Japan	8,399
Mayon (2001)	Luzon, Phil.	8,077
Canlaon (1996)	Negros Isls., Phil.	7,989
Niigata Yake-yama (1989)	Honshu, Japan	7,874
Alaid (1996)	Kuril Isl., Russia	7,674
Ulawun (2001)	Papua New Guinea	7,657
Ngauruhoe (1977)	New Zealand	7,515
Chokai (1974)	Honshu, Japan	7,339
Galunggung (1984)	Java, Indon.	7,113
Azuma (1977)	Honshu, Japan	6,640
Sangeang Api (1988)	Lesser Sunda Isl., Indon.	6,394
Nasu (1963)	Honshu, Japan	6,289
Karkar (1979)	Papua New Guinea	6,033
Tiatia (1981)	Kuril Isl., Russia	5,968
Bandai (1888)	Honshu, Japan	5,968
Manam (2002)	Papua New Guinea	5,928
Kuju (1996)	Kyushu, Japan	5,866
Karangetang-Api Siau (2002)	Sangihe, Indon.	5,853
Soputan (2000)	Sulawesi, Indon.	5,853
Bagana (2002)	Papua New Guinea	5,741
Kelut (1990)	Java, Indon.	5,679
Adatara (1996)	Honshu, Japan	5,636
Gamalama (1994)	Halmahera, Indon.	5,627
Kirishima (1992)	Kyushu, Japan	5,577
Gamkonora (1987)	Halmahera, Indon.	5,364
Aso (1995)	Kyushu, Japan	5,223
Lokon-Empung (2002)	Sulawesi, Indon.	5,184
Bulusan (1995)	Luzon, Phil.	5,134
Karymsky (2002)	Kamchatka, Russia	5,039
Unzen (1996)	Kyushu, Japan	4,921
Akan (1998)	Hokkaido, Japan	4,917
Sarychev Peak (1989)	Kuril Isl., Russia	4,908
Pinatubo (1993)	Luzon, Phil.	4,875
Lopevi (2001)	Vanuatu	4,636
Akita-Yake-yama (1997)	Japan	4,482
Ambrym (2002)	Vanuatu	4,376
Langila (2002)	Papua New Guinea	4,363
Awu (1992)	Sangihe Isl., Indon.	4,331
Dukono (2002)	Halmahera, Indonesia	3,888
Akademia Nauk (1996)	Kamchatka, Russia	3,871
Komaga-take (2000)	Hokkaido, Japan	3,740
Sakura-jima (2002)	Kyushu, Japan	3,665
Miyake-jima (2002)	Izu Isls., Japan	2,673
Krakatau (2001)	Indonesia	2,667
Suwanose-jima (2001)	Kyushu, Japan	2,621
Gaua (1982)	Vanuatu	2,614
Oshima (1990)	Izu Isls., Japan	2,487
Usu (2001)	Hokkaido, Japan	2,398
Rabaul (2001)	Papua New Guinea	2,257
Pagan (1993)	N. Mariana Isl.	1,870
Taal (1977)	Luzon, Phil.	1,312
Yasur (2002)	Tanna Island, Vanuatu	1,184
White Island (2001)	Bay of Plenty, New Zealand	1,053
McDonald Islands (2000)	Indian Ocn., Australia	610
Central America—Caribbean		
Tacaná (1986)	Guatemala	13,320
Acatenango (1972)	Guatemala	13,044
Santa María (2002)	Guatemala	12,375
Fuego (2002)	Guatemala	12,346
Irazú (1994)	Costa Rica	11,260
Turrialba (1866)	Costa Rica	10,958
Póas (1996)	Costa Rica	8,884
Pacaya (2001)	Guatemala	8,373
San Miguel (1997)	El Salvador	6,998
Rincón de la Vieja (1999)	Costa Rica	6,286
San Cristobal (2001)	Nicaragua	5,725
Concepción (1999)	Nicaragua	5,577
Arenal (2002)	Costa Rica	5,436
Soufrière Guadeloupe (1977)	Guadeloupe	4,813
Pelée (1932)	Martinique	4,583
Momotombo (1905)	Nicaragua	4,255
Soufrière St. Vincent (1979)	St. Vincent	4,003
Soufrière Hills (2002)	Montserrat	3,001
Masaya (2001)	Nicaragua	2,083
South America		
Llullaillaco (1877)	Argentina-Chile	22,109
Guallatiri (1960)	Chile	19,918
Tupungatito (1986)	Chile	19,685
Cotopaxi (1940)	Ecuador	19,393
El Misti (1870?)	Peru	19,101
Láscar (2000)	Chile	18,346
Nevado del Ruiz (1991)	Colombia	17,457
Sangay (2002)	Ecuador	17,159
Irruputuncu (1995)	Chile	16,939
Guagua Pichincha (2001)	Ecuador	15,696
Puracé (1977)	Colombia	15,256
Tungurahua (2002)	Ecuador	14,475
Galeras (2000)	Colombia	14,029
Llaima (1998)	Chile	10,253
Villarrica (2002)	Chile	9,340
Cerro Hudson (1991)	Chile	6,250
Fernandina (1995)	Galapagos Isls., Ecuad.	4,842
Mid-Pacific		
Mauna Loa (1984)	Hawaii, HI	13,680
Kilauea (2001)	Hawaii, HI	4,009
Mid-Atlantic Ridge		
Jan Mayen (1985)	N. Atlantic Ocn., Norway	7,470
Grímsvötn (1998)	Iceland	5,659
Hekla (2000)	Iceland	4,892
Krafla (1984)	Iceland	2,133
Europe		
Etna (2002)	Italy	10,991
Vesuvius (1944)	Italy	4,203
Stromboli (2002)	Italy	3,038
Santorini (1950)	Greece	1,079
North America		
Pico de Orizaba (1687)	Mexico	18,619
Popocatépetl (2002)	Mexico	17,802
Rainier (1894?)	Washington	14,410
Wrangell (1907?)	Alaska	14,163
Shasta (1786)	California	14,162
Colima (2002)	Mexico	12,631
Lassen Peak (1917)	California	10,456
Redoubt (1990)	Alaska	10,197
Iliamna (1953)	Alaska	10,016
Shishaldin (1999)	Aleutian Isl., AK	9,373
St. Helens (1991)	Washington	8,363
Pavlof (1997)	Alaska	8,264
Veniaminof (1995)	Alaska	8,225
Novarupta [Katmai] (1912)	Alaska	6,715
Makushin (1995)	Aleutian Isl., AK	5,905
Great Sitkin (1974)	Aleutian Isl., AK	5,710
Cleveland (2001)	Aleutian Isl., AK	5,675
Gareloi (1989)	Aleutian Isl., AK	5,161
Korovin [Atka complex] (1998)	Aleutian Isl., AK	5,029
Akutan (1992)	Aleutian Isl., AK	4,275
Augustine (1986)	Alaska	4,108
Kiska (1990)	Aleutian Isl., AK	4,003
El Chichón (1982)	Mexico	3,773
Okmok (1997)	Aleutian Isl., AK	3,520
Seguam (1993)	Aleutian Isl., AK	3,458

Mountains

Height of Mount Everest

Mt. Everest, the world's highest mountain, was considered 29,002 ft when Edmund Hillary and Tenzing Norgay became the 1st climbers to scale it, in 1953. This triangulation figure had been accepted since 1850. In 1954 the Surveyor General of the Republic of India set the height at 29,028 ft, plus or minus 10 ft because of snow; this figure was also accepted by the National Geographic Society.

In 1999, a team of climbers sponsored by Boston's Museum of Science and the National Geographic Society measured the height at the summit using sophisticated satellite-based technology. This new measurement, of 29,035 ft., was accepted by the National Geographic Society and other authorities, including the U.S. National Imagery and Mapping Agency.

IT'S A FACT: A record 54 climbers reached the summit of Mt. Everest in one day, on May 16, 2002.

United States, Canada, Mexico

Name	Place	Height (ft)
McKinley	AK	20,320
Logan	Yukon	19,551
Pico de Orizaba	Mexico	18,555
St. Elias	AK-Yukon	18,008
Popocatépetl	Mexico	17,930
Foraker	AK	17,400
Iztaccihuatl	Mexico	17,343
Lucania	Yukon	17,147
King	Yukon	16,971
Steele	Yukon	16,644
Bona	AK	16,550
Blackburn	AK	16,390
Kennedy	AK	16,286
Sanford	AK	16,237
Vancouver	AK-Yukon	15,979
South Buttress	AK	15,885
Wood	Yukon	15,885
Churchill	AK	15,638
Fairweather	AK-BC	15,300
Zinantecatl (Toluca)	Mexico	15,016
Hubbard	AK-Yukon	15,015
Bear	AK	14,831
Walsh	Yukon	14,780
East Buttress	AK	14,730
Matlalcueyetl	Mexico	14,636
Hunter	AK	14,573
Alverstone	AK-Yukon	14,565
Browne Tower	AK	14,530
Whitney	CA	14,494
Elbert	CO	14,433
Massive	CO	14,421
Harvard	CO	14,420
Rainier	WA	14,410
University Peak	AK	14,410
Williamson	CA	14,375
La Plata Peak	CO	14,361
Blanca Peak	CO	14,345
Uncompahgre Peak	CO	14,309
Crestone Peak	CO	14,294
Lincoln	CO	14,286
Grays Peak	CO	14,270
Antero	CO	14,269
Torreys Peak	CO	14,267
Castle Peak	CO	14,265
Quandary Peak	CO	14,265
Evans	CO	14,264
Longs Peak	CO	14,255
McArthur	Yukon	14,253
Wilson	CO	14,246
White Mt. Peak	CA	14,246
North Palisade	CA	14,242
Cameron	CO	14,238
Shavano	CO	14,229
Belford	CO	14,197
Princeton	CO	14,197
Crestone Needle	CO	14,197
Yale	CO	14,196
Bross	CO	14,172
Kit Carson	CO	14,165
Wrangell	AK	14,163
Shasta	CA	14,162
El Diente Peak	CO	14,159
Point Success	WA	14,158
Maroon Peak	CO	14,156
Tabeguache	CO	14,155
Oxford	CO	14,153
Sill	CA	14,153
Sneffels	CO	14,150
Democrat	CO	14,148
Capitol Peak	CO	14,130
Liberty Cap	WA	14,112
Pikes Peak	CO	14,110
Snowmass	CO	14,092
Russell	CA	14,088
Eolus	CO	14,083
Windom	CO	14,082
Columbia	CO	14,073
Augusta	AK	14,070

South America

Peak, country	Height (ft)
Aconcagua, Argentina	22,834
Ojos del Salado, Arg.-Chile	22,572
Bonete, Argentina	22,546
Tupungato, Argentina-Chile	22,310
Pissis, Argentina	22,241
Mercedario, Argentina	22,211
Huascaran, Peru	22,205
Llullaillaco, Argentina-Chile	22,057
El Libertador, Argentina	22,047
Cachi, Argentina	22,047
Incahuasi, Argentina-Chile	21,720
Yerupaja, Peru	21,709
Galan, Argentina	21,654
El Muerto, Argentina-Chile	21,457
Sajama, Bolivia	21,391
Nacimiento, Argentina	21,302
Illimani, Bolivia	21,201
Coropuna, Peru	21,083
Laudo, Argentina	20,997
Ancohuma, Bolivia	20,958
Ausangate, Peru	20,945
Toro, Argentina-Chile	20,932
Illampu, Bolivia	20,873
Tres Cruces, Argentina-Chile	20,853
Huandoy, Peru	20,852
Parinacota, Bolivia-Chile	20,768
Tortolas, Argentina-Chile	20,745
Ampato, Peru	20,702
El Condor, Argentina	20,669
Salcantay, Peru	20,574
Chimborazo, Ecuador	20,561
Huancarhuas, Peru	20,531
Famatina, Argentina	20,505
Pumasillo, Peru	20,492
Solo, Argentina	20,492
Polleras, Argentina	20,456
Pular, Chile	20,423
Chani, Argentina	20,341
Aucanquilcha, Chile	20,295
Juncal, Argentina-Chile	20,276
Negro, Argentina	20,184
Quela, Argentina	20,128
Condoriri, Bolivia	20,095
Palermo, Argentina	20,079
Solimana, Peru	20,068
San Juan, Argentina-Chile	20,049
Sierra Nevada, Arg.-Chile	20,023
Antofalla, Argentina	20,013
Marmolejo, Argentina-Chile	20,013
Chachani, Peru	19,931

The highest point in the West Indies is in the Dominican Republic, Pico Duarte (10,417 ft).

Africa

Peak, country	Height (ft)
Kilimanjaro, Tanzania	19,340
Kenya, Kenya	17,058
Margherita Pk., Uganda-Congo	16,763
Ras Dashan, Ethiopia	15,158
Meru, Tanzania	14,979
Karisimbi, Congo-Rwanda	14,787
Elgon, Kenya-Uganda	14,178
Batu, Ethiopia	14,131
Guna, Ethiopia	13,881
Gughe, Ethiopia	13,780
Toubkal, Morocco	13,661
Cameroon, Cameroon	13,435

Australia, New Zealand, SE Asian Islands

Peak, country/island	Height (ft)
Jaya, New Guinea	16,500
Trikora, New Guinea	15,585
Mandala, New Guinea	15,420
Wilhelm, New Guinea	14,793
Kinabalu, Malaysia	13,455
Kerinci, Sumatra, Indon.	12,467
Cook, New Zealand	12,349
Semeru, Java, Indon.	12,060
Kosciusko, Australia	7,310

Europe

Peak, country	Height (ft)
Alps	
Mont Blanc, Fr.-It.	15,771
Monte Rosa (highest peak of group), Switz.	15,203
Dom, Switz.	14,911
Liskamm, It., Switz.	14,852
Weisshorn, Switz.	14,780
Taschhorn, Switz.	14,733
Matterhorn, It., Switz.	14,690
Dent Blanche, Switz.	14,293
Nadelhorn, Switz.	14,196
Grand Combin, Switz.	14,154
Lenzpitze, Switz.	14,088
Finsteraarhorn, Switz.	14,022
Castor, Switz.	13,865
Zinalrothorn, Switz.	13,849
Hohberghom, Switz.	13,842
Alphubel, Switz.	13,799
Rimpfischhom, Switz.	13,776
Aletschorn, Switz.	13,763
Strahlhorn, Switz.	13,747
Dent D'Herens, Switz.	13,686
Breithorn, It., Switz.	13,665
Bishorn, Switz.	13,645
Jungfrau, Switz.	13,642
Ecrins, Fr.	13,461
Monch, Switz.	13,448
Pollux, Switz.	13,422
Schreckhorn, Switz.	13,379
Ober Gabelhorn, Switz.	13,330
Gran Paradiso, It.	13,323
Bernina, It., Switz.	13,284
Fiescherhorn, Switz.	13,283
Grunhorn, Switz.	13,266
Lauteraarhorn, Switz.	13,261
Durrenhorn, Switz.	13,238
Allalinhorn, Switz.	13,213
Weissmies, Switz.	13,199
Lagginhorn, Switz.	13,156
Zupo, Switz.	13,120
Fletschhorn, Switz.	13,110
Adlerhorn, Switz.	13,081
Gletscherhorn, Switz.	13,068
Schalihorn, Switz.	13,040
Scerscen, Switz.	13,028
Eiger, Switz.	13,025
Jagerhorn, Switz.	13,024
Rottalhorn, Switz.	13,022
Pyrenees	
Aneto, Sp.	11,168
Posets, Sp.	11,073
Perdido, Sp.	11,007
Vignemale, Fr.-Sp.	10,820
Long, Sp.	10,479
Estats, Sp.	10,304
Montcalm, Sp.	10,105
Caucasus (Europe-Asia)	
Elbrus, Russia	18,510
Shkhara, Georgia	17,064
Dykh Tau, Russia	17,054
Kashtan Tau, Russia	16,877
Janqi, Georgia	16,565
Kazbek, Georgia	16,558

Asia (Mainland)

Peak	Place	Height (ft)
Everest	Nepal-Tibet	29,035
K2 (Godwin Austen)	Kashmir	28,250
Kanchenjunga	India-Nepal	28,208
Lhotse I (Everest)	Nepal-Tibet	27,923
Makalu I	Nepal-Tibet	27,824
Lhotse II (Everest)	Nepal-Tibet	27,560
Dhaulagiri	Nepal	26,810
Manaslu I	Nepal	26,760
Cho Oyu	Nepal-Tibet	26,750
Nanga Parbat	Kashmir	26,660
Annapurna I	Nepal	26,504
Gasherbrum	Kashmir	26,470
Broad	Kashmir	26,400
Gosainthan	Tibet	26,287
Annapurna II	Nepal	26,041
Gyachung Kang	Nepal-Tibet	25,910
Disteghil Sar	Kashmir	25,868
Himalchuli	Nepal	25,801
Nuptse (Everest)	Nepal-Tibet	25,726
Masherbrum	Kashmir	25,660
Nanda Devi	India	25,645
Rakaposhi	Kashmir	25,550
Kamet	India-Tibet	25,447
Namcha Barwa	Tibet	25,445
Gurla Mandhata	Tibet	25,355
Ulugh Muz Tagh	Xinjiang-Tibet	25,340
Kungur	Xinjiang	25,325
Tirich Mir	Pakistan	25,230
Makalu II	Nepal-Tibet	25,120
Minya Konka	China	24,900
Kula Gangri	Bhutan-Tibet	24,784
Changtzu (Everest)	Nepal-Tibet	24,780
Muz Tagh Ata	Xinjiang	24,757
Skyang Kangri	Kashmir	24,750
Ismail Semani Peak	Tajikistan	24,590
Jongsang Peak	India-Nepal	24,472
Jengish Chokusu	Xinjiang-Kyrgyzstan	24,406
Sia Kangri	Kashmir	24,350
Haramosh Peak	Pakistan	24,270
Istoro Nal	Pakistan	24,240
Tent Peak	India-Nepal	24,165
Chomo Lhari	Bhutan-Tibet	24,040
Chamlang	Nepal	24,012
Kabru	India-Nepal	24,002
Alung Gangri	Tibet	24,000
Baltoro Kangri	Kashmir	23,990
Mussu Shan	Xinjiang	23,890
Mana	India	23,860
Baruntse	Nepal	23,688
Nepal Peak	India-Nepal	23,500
Amne Machin	China	23,490
Gauri Sankar	Nepal-Tibet	23,440
Badrinath	India	23,420
Nunkun	Kashmir	23,410
Lenin Peak	Tajikistan	23,405
Pyramid	India-Nepal	23,400
Api	Nepal	23,399
Pauhunri	India-Tibet	23,385
Trisul	India	23,360
Kangto	India-Tibet	23,260
Nyenchhe Thanglha	Tibet	23,255
Trisuli	India	23,210
Pumori	Nepal-Tibet	23,190
Dunagiri	India	23,184
Lombo Kangra	Tibet	23,165
Saipal	Nepal	23,100
Macha Pucchare	Nepal	22,958
Numbar	Nepal	22,817
Kanjiroba	Nepal	22,580
Ama Dablam	Nepal	22,350
Cho Polu	Nepal	22,093
Lingtren	Nepal-Tibet	21,972
Khumbutse	Nepal-Tibet	21,785
Hlako Gangri	Tibet	21,266
Mt. Grosvenor	China	21,190
Thagchhab Gangri	Tibet	20,970
Damavand	Iran	18,606
Ararat	Turkey	16,804

Antarctica

Peak	Height (ft)
Vinson Massif	16,864
Tyree	16,290
Shinn	15,750
Gardner	15,375
Epperly	15,100
Kirkpatrick	14,855
Elizabeth	14,698
Markham	14,290
Bell	14,117
Mackellar	14,098
Anderson	13,957
Bentley	13,934
Kaplan	13,878
Andrew Jackson	13,750
Sidley	13,720
Ostenso	13,710
Minto	13,668
Miller	13,650
Long Gables	13,620
Dickerson	13,517
Giovinetto	13,412
Wade	13,400
Fisher	13,386
Fridtjof Nansen	13,350
Wexler	13,202
Lister	13,200
Shear	13,100
Odishaw	13,008
Donaldson	12,894
Ray	12,808
Sellery	12,779
Waterman	12,730
Anne	12,703
Press	12,566
Falla	12,549
Rucker	12,520
Goldthwait	12,510
Morris	12,500
Erebus	12,450
Campbell	12,434
Don Pedro Christophersen	12,355
Lysaght	12,326
Huggins	12,247
Sabine	12,200
Astor	12,175
Mohl	12,172
Frankes	12,064
Jones	12,040
Gjelsvik	12,008
Coman	12,000

Some Notable U.S. Mountains

Name	Place	Height (ft)
Gannett Peak	WY	13,804
Grand Teton	WY	13,766
Kings	UT	13,528
Cloud	WY	13,175
Wheeler	NM	13,161
Boundary	NV	13,140
Granite	MT	12,799
Borah	ID	12,662
Humphreys	AZ	12,633
Adams	WA	12,277
San Gorgonio	CA	11,502
Hood	OR	11,239
Lassen	CA	10,457
Granite	CA	10,321
Guadalupe	TX	8,749
Olympus	WA	7,965
Harney	SD	7,242
Mitchell	NC	6,684
Clingmans Dome	NC-TN	6,643
Washington	NH	6,288
Rogers	VA	5,729
Marcy	NY	5,344
Katahdin	ME	5,268
Spruce Knob	WV	4,861
Mansfield	VT	4,393
Black Mountain	KY	4,145

Important Islands and Their Areas

Reviewed by Laurel Duda, Marine Biological Laboratory/Woods Hole Oceanographic Inst. Library.

Figures are for total areas in square miles. Figure in parentheses shows rank among the world's 10 largest individual islands. Because some islands have not been surveyed accurately, some areas shown are estimates. Some "islands" listed are island groups. Only the largest islands in a group are listed individually. Only islands over 10 sq. miles in area are listed.

Antarctica

Adelaide	1,400
Alexander	16,700
Berkner	18,500
Roosevelt	2,900

Arctic Ocean

Akimiski, Nunavut	1,159
Amund Ringnes, Nun.	2,029
Axel Heiberg, Nun.	16,671
Baffin, Nun. **(5)**	195,928
Banks, Northwest Territories	27,038
Bathurst, Nun.	6,194
Bolshevik, Russia	4,368
Bolshoy Lyakhovsky, Russia	1,776
Borden, NWT., Nun.	1,079
Bylot, Nun.	4,273
Coats, Nun.	2,123
Cornwallis, Nun.	2,701
Devon, Nun.	21,331
Disko, Greenland	3,312
Ellef Ringnes, Nun.	4,361
Ellesmere, Nun. **(10)**	75,767
Faddayevskiy, Russia	1,930
Franz Josef Land, Russia	8,000
Iturup (Etorofu), Russia	2,596
King William, Nun.	5,062
Komsomolets, Russia	3,477
Mackenzie King, NWT	1,949
Mansel, Nun.	1,228
Melville, NWT, Nun.	16,274
Milne Land, Greenland	1,400
New Siberian Islands, Russia	14,500
Kotelnyy, Russia	4,504
Novaya Zemlya, Russia (2 isls.)	31,730
Oktyabrskoy, Russia	5,471
Prince Charles, NWT	3,676
Prince of Wales, Nun.	12,872
Prince Patrick, NWT	6,119
Somerset, Nun.	9,570
Southampton, Nun.	15,913
Svalbard (tot. group)	23,957
Nordaustlandet	5,410
Spitsbergen	15,060
Traill, Greenland	1,300
Victoria, NWT, Nun. **(9)**	83,897
Wrangel, Russia	2,800

Atlantic Ocean

Anticosti, Canada	3,068
Ascension, UK	34
Azores, Portugal (tot. group)	868
Faial	67
San Miguel	291
Bahama Isls., Bahama (tot. group)	5,382
Andros, Bahamas	2,300
Bermuda Islands, UK	20
Bioko Isl., Equatorial Guinea	785
Block Islands, RI, US	21
Canary Islands, Spain (tot. group)	2,807
Fuerteventura	688
Gran Canaria	592
Tenerife	795
Cape Breton, Canada	3,981
Cape Verde Islands	1,557
Caviana, Para, Brazil	1,918
Channel Islands, UK (tot. group)	75
Guernsey	24
Jersey	45
Faroe Islands, Denmark	540
Falkland Islands, UK (tot. group)	4,700
East Falkland	2,550
West Falkland	1,750
Great Britain, UK **(8)**	84,200
Greenland, Denmark **(1)**	840,000
Gurupa, Para, Brazil	1,878
Hebrides, Scotland	2,744
Iceland	39,699
Ireland (tot. group)	32,589
Irish Republic	27,137
Northern Ireland	5,452
Isle of Man, UK	227
Isle of Wight, England	147
Long Island, NY, US	1,320
Madeira Islands, Portugal	306
Marajo, Brazil	15,444
Martha's Vineyard, MA, US	89
Mount Desert, ME, US	104
Nantucket, MA, US	45
Newfoundland, Canada	42,031
Orkney Islands, Scotland	390
Prince Edward, Canada	2,185
St. Helena, UK	47
Shetland Islands, Scotland	587
Skye, Scotland	670
South Georgia, UK	1,450
Tierra del Fuego, Chile, Arg.	18,800
Tristan da Cunha, UK	40

Baltic Sea

Aland Islands, Finland	590
Bornholm, Denmark	227
Gotland, Sweden	1,159

Caribbean Sea

Antigua	108
Aruba, Netherlands	75
Barbados	166
Cuba	42,804
Isle of Youth	926
Cayman Islands	100
Curacao, Netherlands	171
Dominica	290
Guadeloupe, France	687
Hispaniola (Haiti and Dominican Rep).	29,389
Jamaica	4,244
Martinique, France	436
Puerto Rico, US	3,339
Tobago	116
Trinidad	1,864
Virgin Islands, UK	59
Virgin Islands, US	134

East Indies

Bali, Indonesia	2,171
Bangka, Indonesia	4,375
Borneo, Indonesia-Malaysia-Brunei **(3)**	280,100
Bougainville, Papua New Guinea	3,880
Buru, Indonesia	3,670
Celebes, Indonesia	69,000
Flores, Indonesia	5,500
Halmahera, Indonesia	6,865
Java (Jawa), Indonesia	48,900
Madura, Indonesia	2,113
Moluccas, Indonesia	32,307
New Britain, Papua New Guinea	14,093
New Guinea, Indon.-PNG **(2)**	306,000
New Ireland, PNG	3,707
Seram, Indonesia	6,621
Sumba, Indonesia	4,306
Sumbawa, Indonesia	5,965
Sumatra, Indonesia **(6)**	165,000
Timor, Indonesia	13,094
Yos Sudarsa, Indonesia	4,500

Indian Ocean

Andaman Isls., India	2,500
Kerguelen	2,247
Madagascar **(4)**	226,658
Mauritius	720
Pemba, Tanzania	380
Reunion, France	970
Seychelles	176
Sri Lanka	25,332
Zanzibar, Tanzania	640

Mediterranean Sea

Balearic Isls., Spain	1,927
Corfu, Greece	229
Corsica, France	3,369
Crete, Greece	3,189
Cyprus	3,572
Elba, Italy	86
Euboea, Greece	1,411
Malta	95
Rhodes, Greece	540
Sardinia, Italy	9,301
Sicily, Italy	9,926

Pacific Ocean

Admiralty, AK, US	1,709
Aleutian Isls., AK, US (tot. group)	6,912
Adak	275
Amchitka	116
Attu	350
Kanaga	142
Kiska	106
Tanaga	195
Umnak	686
Unalaska	1,051
Unimak	1,571
Baranof, AK, US	1,636
Chichagof, AK, US	2,062
Chiloe, Chile	3,241
Christmas, Kiribati	94
Diomede, Big, Russia	11
Easter Isl., Chile	69
Fiji (tot. group)	7,056
Vanua Levu	2,242
Viti Levu	4,109
Galapagos Isls., Ecuador	3,043
Graham Isl., British Columbia	2,456
Guadalcanal, Solomon Isls.	2,180
Guam, US	210
Hainan, China	13,000
Hawaiian Isls., HI, US (tot. group)	6,428
Hawaii	4,028
Oahu	600
Hong Kong, China	31
Hoste, Chile	1,590
Japan (tot. group)	145,850
Hokkaido	30,144
Honshu **(7)**	87,805
Kyushu	14,114
Okinawa	459
Shikoku	7,040
Kangaroo, South Australia	1,680
Kodiak, AK, US	3,485
Kupreanof, AK, US	1,084
Marquesas Isls., France	492
Marshall Isls.	70
Melville, Northern Territory, Aus.	2,240
Micronesia	271
New Caledonia, France	6,530
New Zealand (tot. group)	104,454
Chatham Isls.	372
North	44,204
South	58,384
Stewart	674
North Mariana Isls., US	179
Nunivak, AK, US	1,600
Palau	188
Philippines (tot. group)	115,860
Leyte	2,787
Luzon	40,680
Mindanao	36,775
Mindoro	3,690
Negros	4,907
Palawan	4,554
Panay	4,446
Samar	5,050
Prince of Wales, AK, US	2,770
Revillagigedo, AK, US	1,134
Riesco, Chile	1,973
St. Lawrence, AK, US	1,780
Sakhalin, Russia	29,500
Samoa Isls. (tot. group)	1,177
American Samoa, US	77
Tutuila, US	55
Savail, Samoa	659
Upolu, Samoa	432
Santa Catalina, CA, US	75
Santa Ines, Chile	1,407
Tahiti, France	402
Taiwan, China (tot. group)	13,969
Jinmen Dao (Quemoy)	56
Tasmania, Australia	26,178
Tonga Isls.	290
Vancouver Isl., Brit. Columbia	12,079
Vanuatu	4,707
Wellington, Chile	2,549

Persian Gulf

Bahrain	217

Areas and Average Depths of Oceans, Seas, and Gulfs

Geographers and mapmakers recognize 4 major bodies of water: the Pacific, the Atlantic, the Indian, and the Arctic oceans. The Atlantic and Pacific oceans are considered divided at the equator into the N and S Atlantic and the N and S Pacific. The Arctic Ocean is the name for waters N of the continental landmasses in the region of the Arctic Circle.

	Area (sq mi)	Avg. depth (ft)
Pacific Ocean	64,186,300	12,925
Atlantic Ocean	33,420,000	11,730
Indian Ocean	28,350,500	12,598
Arctic Ocean	5,105,700	3,407
South China Sea	1,148,500	4,802
Caribbean Sea	971,400	8,448
Mediterranean Sea	969,100	4,926
Bering Sea	873,000	4,893
Gulf of Mexico	582,100	5,297
Sea of Okhotsk	537,500	3,192
Sea of Japan	391,100	5,468
Hudson Bay	281,900	305
East China Sea	256,600	620
Andaman Sea	218,100	3,667
Black Sea	196,100	3,906
Red Sea	174,900	1,764
North Sea	164,900	308
Baltic Sea	147,500	180
Yellow Sea	113,500	121
Persian Gulf	88,800	328
Gulf of California	59,100	2,375

IT'S A FACT: On Jan. 23, 1960, the U.S. Navy's bathyscaphe *Trieste* descended 35,800 feet into the Challenger Deep at the southern end of the Marianas Trench, the deepest known point in any ocean.

Principal Ocean Depths

Source: National Imagery and Mapping Agency, U.S. Dept. of Defense

Name of area	Location (lat.)	Location (long.)	Depth (meters)	Depth (fathoms)	Depth (ft)
Pacific Ocean					
Marianas Trench	11° 22′ N	142° 36′ E	10,924	5,973	35,840
Tonga Trench	23° 16′ S	174° 44′ W	10,800	5,906	35,433
Philippine Trench	10° 38′ N	126° 36′ E	10,057	5,499	32,995
Kermadec Trench	31° 53′ S	177° 21′ W	10,047	5,494	32,963
Bonin Trench	24° 30′ N	143° 24′ E	9,994	5,464	32,788
Kuril Trench	44° 15′ N	150° 34′ E	9,750	5,331	31,988
Izu Trench	31° 05′ N	142° 10′ E	9,695	5,301	31,808
New Britain Trench	06° 19′ S	153° 45′ E	8,940	4,888	29,331
Yap Trench	08° 33′ N	138° 02′ E	8,527	4,663	27,976
Japan Trench	36° 08′ N	142° 43′ E	8,412	4,600	27,599
Peru-Chile Trench	23° 18′ S	71° 14′ W	8,064	4,409	26,457
Palau Trench	07° 52′ N	134° 56′ E	8,054	4,404	26,424
Aleutian Trench	50° 51′ N	177° 11′ E	7,679	4,199	25,194
New Hebrides Trench	20° 36′ S	168° 37′ E	7,570	4,139	24,836
North Ryukyu Trench	24° 00′ N	126° 48′ E	7,181	3,927	23,560
Mid. America Trench	14° 02′ N	93° 39′ W	6,662	3,643	21,857
Atlantic Ocean					
Puerto Rico Trench	19° 55′ N	65° 27′ W	8,605	4,705	28,232
S Sandwich Trench	55° 42′ S	25° 56′ W	8,325	4,552	27,313
Romanche Gap	0° 13′ S	18° 26′ W	7,728	4,226	25,354
Cayman Trench	19° 12′ N	80° 00′ W	7,535	4,120	24,721
Brazil Basin	09° 10′ S	23° 02′ W	6,119	3,346	20,076
Indian Ocean					
Java Trench	10° 19′ S	109° 58′ E	7,125	3,896	23,376
Ob' Trench	09° 45′ S	67° 18′ E	6,874	3,759	22,553
Diamantina Trench	35° 50′ S	105° 14′ E	6,602	3,610	21,660
Vema Trench	09° 08′ S	67° 15′ E	6,402	3,501	21,004
Agulhas Basin	45° 20′ S	26° 50′ E	6,195	3,387	20,325
Arctic Ocean					
Eurasia Basin	82° 23′ N	19° 31′ E	5,450	2,980	17,881
Mediterranean Sea					
Ionian Basin	36° 32′ N	21° 06′ E	5,150	2,816	16,896

Note: Greater depths have been reported in some areas but are not officially confirmed by research vessels.

Latitude, Longitude, and Altitude of World Cities

Source: National Imagery Mapping Agency, U.S. Dept. of Defense

City	Lat. °	Lat. ′	Long. °	Long. ′	Alt. (ft)
Athens, Greece	37	59 N	23	44 E	300
Bangkok, Thailand	13	45 N	100	31 E	0
Beijing, China	39	56 N	116	24 E	600
Berlin, Germany	52	31 N	13	25 E	110
Bogotá, Colombia	04	36 N	74	05 W	8,660
Bombay (Mumbai), India	18	58 N	72	50 E	27
Buenos Aires, Argentina	34	36 S	58	28 W	0
Cairo, Egypt	30	03 N	31	15 E	381
Jakarta, Indonesia	06	10 S	106	48 E	26
Jerusalem, Israel	31	46 N	35	14 E	2,500
Johannesburg, So. Afr.	26	12 S	28	05 E	5,740
Kathmandu, Nepal	27	43 N	85	19 E	4,500
Kiev, Ukraine	50	26 N	30	31 E	587
London, UK (Greenwich)	51	30 N	00	00	245
Manila, Philippines	14	35 N	121	00 E	0
Mexico City, Mexico	19	24 N	99	09 W	7,347
Moscow, Russia	55	45 N	37	35 E	394
New Delhi, India	28	36 N	77	12 E	770
Panama City, Panama	08	58 N	79	32 W	0
Paris, France	48	52 N	02	20 E	300
Quito, Ecuador	00	13 S	78	30 W	9,222
Rio de Janeiro, Brazil	22	43 S	43	13 W	30
Rome, Italy	41	53 N	12	30 E	95
Santiago, Chile	33	27 S	70	40 W	4,921
Seoul, South Korea	37	34 N	127	00 E	34
Sydney, Australia	33	53 S	151	12 E	25
Tehran, Iran	35	40 N	51	26 E	3,937
Tokyo, Japan	35	42 N	139	46 E	30
Warsaw, Poland	52	15 N	21	00 E	360
Wellington, New Zealand	41	18 S	174	47 E	0

Latitude, Longitude, and Altitude of U.S. and Canadian Cities

Source: U.S. geographic positions, U.S. altitudes provided by Geological Survey, U.S. Dept. of the Interior. Canadian geographic positions and altitudes provided by the Canada Flight Supplement, Natural Resources Canada.

City	Lat. N °	′	″	Long. W °	′	″	Elev. (ft)
Abilene, TX	32	26	55	99	43	58	1,718
Akron, OH	41	4	53	81	31	9	1,050
Albany, NY	42	39	9	73	45	24	20
Albuquerque, NM	35	5	4	106	39	2	4,955
Alert, N.W.T.	82	31	04	62	16	50	100
Allentown, PA	40	36	30	75	29	26	350
Amarillo, TX	35	13	19	101	49	51	3,685
Anchorage, AK	61	13	5	149	54	1	101
Ann Arbor, MI	42	16	15	83	43	35	880
Asheville, NC	35	36	3	82	33	15	2,134
Ashland, KY	38	28	42	82	38	17	558
Atlanta, GA	33	44	56	84	23	17	1,050
Atlantic City, NJ	39	21	51	74	25	24	8
Augusta, GA	33	28	15	81	58	30	414
Augusta, ME	44	18	38	69	46	48	45
Austin, TX	30	16	1	97	44	34	501
Bakersfield, CA	35	22	24	119	1	4	408
Baltimore, MD	39	17	25	76	36	45	100
Bangor, ME	44	48	4	68	46	42	158
Baton Rouge, LA	30	27	2	91	9	16	53
Battle Creek, MI	42	19	16	85	10	47	820
Bay City, MI	43	35	40	83	53	20	595
Beaumont, TX	30	5	9	94	6	6	20
Belleville, Ont.	44	11	32	77	18	34	320
Bellingham, WA	48	45	35	122	29	13	100
Berkeley, CA	37	52	18	122	16	18	150
Billings, MT	45	47	0	108	30	0	3,124
Biloxi, MS	30	23	45	88	53	7	25
Binghamton, NY	42	5	55	75	55	6	865
Birmingham, AL	33	31	14	86	48	9	600
Bismarck, ND	46	48	30	100	47	0	1,700
Bloomington, IL	40	29	3	88	59	37	829
Boise, ID	43	36	49	116	12	9	2,730
Boston, MA	42	21	30	71	3	37	20
Bowling Green, KY	36	59	25	86	26	37	510
Brandon, Man.	49	51	35	99	57	00	1,343
Brantford, Ont.	43	07	53	80	20	33	815
Brattleboro, VT	42	51	3	72	33	30	240
Bridgeport, CT	41	10	1	73	12	19	10
Brockton, MA	42	5	0	71	1	8	112
Buffalo, NY	42	53	11	78	52	43	585
Burlington, Ont.	43	26	33	79	51	03	640
Burlington, VT	44	28	33	73	12	45	113
Butte, MT	46	0	14	112	32	2	5,549
Calgary, Alta.	51	06	50	114	01	13	3,557
Cambridge, MA	42	22	30	71	6	22	30
Canton, OH	40	47	56	81	22	43	1,100
Carson City, NV	39	9	50	119	45	59	4,730
Cedar Rapids, IA	42	0	30	91	38	38	730
Central Islip, NY	40	47	26	73	12	8	88
Champaign, IL	40	6	59	88	14	36	740
Charleston, SC	32	46	35	79	55	52	118
Charleston, WV	38	20	59	81	37	58	606
Charlotte, NC	35	13	37	80	50	36	850
Charlottetown, P.E.I.	46	17	24	63	07	16	160
Chattanooga, TN	35	2	44	85	18	35	685
Cheyenne, WY	41	8	24	104	49	11	6,067
Chicago, IL	41	51	0	87	39	0	596
Churchill, Man.	58	44	14	94	03	26	94
Cincinnati, OH	39	9	43	84	27	25	683
Cleveland, OH	41	29	58	81	41	44	690
Colorado Springs, CO	38	50	2	104	49	15	6,008
Columbia, MO	38	57	6	92	20	2	758
Columbia, SC	34	0	2	81	2	6	314
Columbus, GA	32	27	39	84	59	16	300
Columbus, OH	39	57	40	82	59	56	800
Concord, NH	43	12	29	71	32	17	288
Corpus Christi, TX	27	48	1	97	23	46	35
Dallas, TX	32	47	0	96	48	0	463
Dawson, Yukon	64	02	35	139	07	40	1,214
Dayton, OH	39	45	32	84	11	30	750
Daytona Beach, FL	29	12	38	81	1	23	10
Decatur, IL	39	50	25	88	57	17	670
Denver, CO	39	44	21	104	59	3	5,260
Des Moines, IA	41	36	2	93	36	32	803
Detroit, MI	42	19	53	83	2	45	585
Dodge City, KS	37	45	10	100	1	0	2,550
Dubuque, IA	42	30	2	90	39	52	620
Duluth, MN	46	47	0	92	6	23	610
Durham, NC	35	59	38	78	53	56	394
Eau Claire, WI	44	48	41	91	29	54	850
Edmonton, Alta.	53	34	21	113	31	14	2,200
Elizabeth, NJ	40	39	50	74	12	40	38
El Paso, TX	31	45	31	106	29	11	3,695
Enid, OK	36	23	44	97	52	41	1,246
Erie, PA	42	7	45	80	5	7	650
Eugene, OR	44	3	8	123	5	8	419
Eureka, CA	40	48	8	124	9	45	44
Evansville, IN	37	58	29	87	33	21	388
Fairbanks, AK	64	50	16	147	42	59	440
Fall River, MA	41	42	5	71	9	20	200
Fargo, ND	46	52	38	96	47	22	900
Flagstaff, AZ	35	11	53	111	39	2	6,900
Flint, MI	43	0	45	83	41	15	750
Ft. Smith, AR	35	23	9	94	23	54	446
Ft. Wayne, IN	41	7	50	85	7	44	781
Ft. Worth, TX	32	43	31	97	19	14	670
Fredericton, N.B.	45	52	10	66	31	54	67
Fresno, CA	36	44	52	119	46	17	296
Gadsden, AL	34	0	51	86	0	24	554
Gainesville, FL	29	39	5	82	19	30	183
Gallup, NM	35	31	41	108	44	31	6,508
Galveston, TX	29	18	4	94	47	51	10
Gary, IN	41	35	36	87	20	47	600
Grand Junction, CO	39	3	50	108	33	0	4,597
Grand Rapids, MI	42	57	48	85	40	5	610
Great Falls, MT	47	30	1	111	18	0	3,334
Green Bay, WI	44	31	9	88	1	11	594
Greensboro, NC	36	4	21	79	47	32	770
Greenville, SC	34	51	9	82	23	39	966
Guelph, Ont.	43	33	0	80	16	0	1,100
Gulfport, MS	30	22	2	89	5	34	25
Halifax, N.S.	44	52	51	63	30	31	477
Hamilton, OH	39	23	58	84	33	41	600
Hamilton, Ont.	43	10	19	79	55	53	780
Harrisburg, PA	40	16	25	76	53	5	320
Hartford, CT	41	45	49	72	41	8	40
Helena, MT	46	35	34	112	2	7	4,090
Hilo, HI	19	43	47	155	5	24	38
Honolulu, HI	21	18	25	157	51	30	18
Houston, TX	29	45	47	95	21	47	40
Huntsville, AL	34	43	49	86	35	10	641
Indianapolis, IN	39	46	6	86	9	29	717
Iowa City, IA	41	39	40	91	31	48	685
Jackson, MI	42	14	45	84	24	5	940
Jackson, MS	32	17	55	90	11	5	294
Jacksonville, FL	30	19	55	81	39	21	12
Jersey City, NJ	40	43	41	74	4	41	83
Johnstown, PA	40	16	42	76	19	0	521
Joplin, MO	37	5	3	94	30	47	990
Juneau, AK	58	18	7	134	25	11	50
Kalamazoo, MI	42	17	30	85	35	14	755
Kansas City, KS	39	6	51	94	37	38	750
Kansas City, MO	39	5	59	94	34	42	740
Kenosha, WI	42	35	5	87	49	16	610
Key West, FL	24	33	19	81	46	58	8
Kingston, Ont.	44	13	31	76	35	49	305
Kitchener, Ont.	43	27	32	80	23	04	1,040
Knoxville, TN	35	57	38	83	55	15	889
Lafayette, IN	40	25	0	86	52	31	567
Lancaster, PA	40	2	16	76	18	21	368
Lansing, MI	42	43	57	84	33	20	830
Laredo, TX	27	30	22	99	30	26	414
Las Vegas, NV	36	10	30	115	8	11	2,000
Lawrence, MA	42	42	25	71	9	49	50
Lethbridge, Alta.	49	37	49	112	47	59	3,047
Lexington, KY	37	59	19	84	28	40	955
Lihue, HI	21	58	52	159	22	16	206
Lima, OH	40	44	33	84	6	19	875
Lincoln, NE	40	48	0	96	40	0	1,150
Little Rock, AR	34	44	47	92	17	22	350
London, Ont.	42	57	31	81	13	33	875
Los Angeles, CA	34	3	8	118	14	34	330
Louisville, KY	38	15	15	85	45	34	462
Lowell, MA	42	38	0	71	19	0	102
Lubbock, TX	33	34	40	101	51	17	3,195

City	Lat. N °	′	″	Long. W °	′	″	Elev. (ft)
Macon, GA	32	50	26	83	37	57	400
Madison, WI	43	4	23	89	24	4	863
Manchester, NH	42	59	44	71	27	19	175
Marshall, TX	32	32	41	94	22	2	410
Medicine Hat, Alta.	50	01	08	110	43	15	2,352
Memphis, TN	35	8	58	90	2	56	254
Meriden, CT	41	32	17	72	48	27	190
Miami, FL	25	46	26	80	11	38	11
Milwaukee, WI	43	2	20	87	54	23	634
Minneapolis, MN	44	58	48	93	15	49	815
Minot, ND	48	13	57	101	17	45	1,555
Mobile, AL	30	41	39	88	2	35	16
Moncton, N.B.	46	06	44	64	40	57	232
Montgomery, AL	32	22	0	86	18	0	250
Montpelier, VT	44	15	36	72	34	33	525
Montréal, Que.	45	41	06	73	55	52	221
Moose Jaw, Sask.	50	19	48	105	33	29	1,892
Muncie, IN	40	11	36	85	23	11	952
Nashville, TN	36	9	57	86	47	4	440
Natchez, MS	31	33	37	91	24	11	230
Newark, NJ	40	44	8	74	10	22	95
New Britain, CT	41	39	40	72	46	48	200
New Haven, CT	41	18	29	72	55	43	40
New Orleans, LA	29	57	16	90	4	30	11
New York, NY	40	42	51	74	0	23	55
Niagara Falls, Ont.	43	07	0	79	04	0	589
Nome, AK	64	30	4	165	24	23	25
Norfolk, VA	36	50	48	76	17	8	10
North Bay, Ont.	46	26	0	79	28	0	1,200
Oakland, CA	37	48	16	122	16	11	42
Ogden, UT	41	13	23	111	58	23	4,299
Oklahoma City, OK	35	28	3	97	30	58	1,195
Omaha, NE	41	15	31	95	56	15	1,040
Orlando, FL	28	32	17	81	22	46	106
Ottawa, Ont.	45	19	09	76	01	20	382
Paducah, KY	37	5	0	88	36	0	345
Pasadena, CA	34	8	52	118	8	37	865
Paterson, NJ	40	55	0	74	10	20	70
Pensacola, FL	30	25	16	87	13	1	32
Peoria, IL	40	41	37	89	35	20	470
Peterborough, Ont.	44	13	48	78	21	48	628
Philadelphia, PA	39	57	8	75	9	51	40
Phoenix, AZ	33	26	54	112	4	24	1,090
Pierre, SD	44	22	6	100	21	2	1,484
Pittsburgh, PA	40	26	26	79	59	46	770
Pittsfield, MA	42	27	0	73	14	45	1,039
Pocatello, ID	42	52	17	112	26	41	4,464
Pt. Arthur, TX	29	53	55	93	55	43	10
Portland, ME	43	39	41	70	15	21	25
Portland, OR	45	31	25	122	40	30	50
Portsmouth, NH	43	4	18	70	45	47	21
Portsmouth, VA	36	50	7	76	17	55	10
Prince Rupert, B.C.	54	17	10	130	26	41	116
Providence, RI	41	49	26	71	24	48	80
Provo, UT	40	14	2	111	39	28	4,549
Pueblo, CO	38	15	16	104	36	31	4,662
Québec City, Que.	46	47	36	71	23	29	244
Racine, WI	42	43	34	87	46	58	630
Raleigh, NC	35	46	19	78	38	20	350
Rapid City, SD	44	4	50	103	13	50	3,247
Reading, PA	40	20	8	75	55	38	266
Regina, Sask.	50	25	55	104	39	57	1,894
Reno, NV	39	31	47	119	48	46	4,498
Richmond, VA	37	33	13	77	27	38	190
Roanoke, VA	37	16	15	79	56	30	940
Rochester, MN	44	1	18	92	28	11	990
Rochester, NY	43	9	17	77	36	57	515
Rockford, IL	42	16	16	89	5	38	715
Sacramento, CA	38	34	54	121	29	36	20
Saginaw, MI	43	25	10	83	57	3	595
St. Catharines, Ont.	43	11	30	79	10	18	321
St. Cloud, MN	45	33	39	94	9	44	1,040
St. John, N.B.	45	18	58	65	53	25	357
St. John's, Nfld.	47	37	07	52	45	07	461
St. Joseph, MO	39	46	7	94	50	47	850
St. Louis, MO	38	37	38	90	11	52	455
St. Paul, MN	44	56	40	93	5	35	780
St. Petersburg, FL	27	46	14	82	40	46	44

City	Lat. N °	′	″	Long. W °	′	″	Elev. (ft)
Salem, OR	44	56	35	123	2	2	154
Salina, KS	38	50	25	97	36	40	1,225
Salt Lake City, UT	40	45	39	111	53	25	4,266
San Antonio, TX	29	25	26	98	29	36	650
San Bernardino, CA	34	6	30	117	17	20	1,200
San Diego, CA	32	42	55	117	9	23	40
San Francisco, CA	37	46	30	122	25	6	63
San Jose, CA	37	20	22	121	53	38	87
San Juan, P.R.	18	28	6	66	6	22	8
Santa Barbara, CA	34	25	15	119	41	50	50
Santa Cruz, CA	36	58	27	122	1	47	20
Santa Fe, NM	35	41	13	105	56	14	6,989
Sarasota, FL	27	20	10	82	31	51	27
Saskatoon, Sask.	52	10	15	106	41	59	1,653
Sault Ste. Marie, Ont.	46	29	06	84	30	34	630
Savannah, GA	32	5	0	81	6	0	42
Schenectady, NY	42	48	51	73	56	24	245
Seattle, WA	47	36	23	122	19	51	350
Sheboygan, WI	43	45	3	87	42	52	630
Sherbrooke, Que.	45	26	17	71	41	26	792
Sheridan, WY	44	47	50	106	57	20	3,742
Shreveport, LA	32	31	30	93	45	0	209
Sioux City, IA	42	30	0	96	24	0	1,117
Sioux Falls, SD	43	33	0	96	42	0	1,442
South Bend, IN	41	41	0	86	15	0	725
Spartanburg, SC	34	56	58	81	55	56	816
Spokane, WA	47	39	32	117	25	30	2,000
Springfield, IL	39	48	6	89	38	37	610
Springfield, MA	42	6	5	72	35	25	70
Springfield, MO	37	12	55	93	17	53	1,300
Springfield, OH	39	55	27	83	48	32	1,000
Stamford, CT	41	3	12	73	32	21	35
Steubenville, OH	40	22	11	80	38	3	1,060
Stockton, CA	37	57	28	121	17	23	15
Sudbury, Ont.	46	37	30	80	47	56	1,140
Superior, WI	46	43	15	92	6	14	642
Sydney, N.S.	46	09	41	60	02	52	203
Syracuse, NY	43	2	53	76	8	52	400
Tacoma, WA	47	15	11	122	26	35	380
Tallahassee, FL	30	26	17	84	16	51	188
Tampa, FL	27	56	50	82	27	31	48
Terre Haute, IN	39	28	0	87	24	50	501
Texarkana, TX	33	25	30	94	2	51	324
Thunder Bay, Ont.	48	22	19	89	19	26	653
Timmins, Ont.	48	34	11	81	22	36	967
Toledo, OH	41	39	50	83	33	19	615
Topeka, KS	39	2	54	95	40	40	1,000
Toronto, Ont.	43	37	39	79	23	46	251
Trenton, NJ	40	13	1	74	44	36	54
Trois-Rivières, Que.	46	21	10	72	40	46	198
Troy, NY	42	43	42	73	41	32	35
Tucson, AZ	32	13	18	110	55	33	2,390
Tulsa, OK	36	9	14	95	59	33	804
Urbana, IL	40	6	38	88	12	26	725
Utica, NY	43	6	3	75	13	59	415
Vancouver, B.C.	49	11	42	123	10	55	14
Victoria, B.C.	48	38	49	123	25	33	63
Waco, TX	31	32	57	97	8	47	405
Walla Walla, WA	46	3	53	118	20	31	1,000
Washington, DC	38	53	42	77	2	12	25
Waterloo, IA	42	29	34	92	20	34	850
West Palm Beach, FL	26	42	54	80	3	13	21
Wheeling, WV	40	3	50	80	43	16	672
Whitehorse, Yukon	60	42	36	135	04	06	2,305
White Plains, NY	41	2	2	73	45	48	220
Wichita, KS	37	41	32	97	20	14	1,305
Wilkes-Barre, PA	41	14	45	75	52	54	550
Wilmington, DE	39	44	45	75	32	49	100
Wilmington, NC	34	13	32	77	56	42	50
Windsor, Ont.	42	16	29	82	57	30	622
Winnipeg, Man.	49	54	39	97	14	36	783
Winston-Salem, NC	36	5	59	80	14	40	912
Worcester, MA	42	15	45	71	48	10	480
Yakima, WA	46	36	8	120	30	17	1,066
Yellowknife, N.W.T.	62	27	46	114	26	25	675
Youngstown, OH	41	5	59	80	38	59	861
Yuma, AZ	32	43	31	114	37	25	160
Zanesville, OH	39	56	25	82	0	48	710

Principal World Rivers

Reviewed by Laurel Duda, Marine Biological Laboratory, Woods Hole Oceanogr. Inst. Library. For N American rivers, see separate table.

River	Outflow	Length (mi)
Africa		
Chari	Lake Chad	500
Congo	Atlantic Ocean	2,900
Gambia	Atlantic Ocean	700
Kasai	Congo River	1,000
Limpopo	Indian Ocean	1,100
Lualaba	Congo River	1,100
Niger	Gulf of Guinea	2,590
Nile	Mediterranean	4,160
Okavango	Okavango Delta	1,000
Orange	Atlantic Ocean	1,300
Senegal	Atlantic Ocean	1,020
Ubangi	Congo River	660
Zambezi	Indian Ocean	1,700
Asia		
Amu Darya	Aral Sea	1,550
Amur	Tatar Strait	1,780
Angara	Yenisey River	1,151
Brahmaputra	Bay of Bengal	1,800
Chang	East China Sea	3,964
Euphrates	Shatt al-Arab	1,700
Ganges	Bay of Bengal	1,560
Godavari	Bay of Bengal	900
Hsi (see Xi)		
Huang	Yellow Sea	3,395
Indus	Arabian Sea	1,800
Irrawaddy	Andaman Sea	1,337
Jordan	Dead Sea	200
Kolyma	Arctic Ocean	1,323
Krishna	Bay of Bengal	800
Kura	Caspian Sea	848
Lena	Laptev Sea	2,734
Mekong	South China Sea	2,700
Narbada (see Narmada)		
Narmada	Arabian Sea	800
Ob	Gulf of Ob	2,268
Ob-Irtysh	Gulf of Ob	3,362
Salween	Gulf of Martaban	1,500
Songhua	Amur River	1,150
Sungari	Amur River	1,197
Sutlej	Indus River	900
Syr	Aral Sea	1,370
Tarim	Lop Nor Basin	1,261
Tigris	Shatt al-Arab	1,180
Xi	South China Sea	1,200
Yamuna	Ganges River	855
Yangtze (see Chang)		
Yellow (see Huang)		
Yenisey	Kara Seav	2,543
Australia		
Murray-Darling	Indian Ocean	2,310
Murrumbidgee	Murray River	981
Europe		
Bug, Northern	Wisla	481
Bug, Southern	Dnieper River	532
Danube	Black Sea	1,776
Don	Sea of Azov	1,224
Dnieper	Black Sea	1,420
Dniester	Black Sea	877
Drava	Danube River	447
Dvina, North.	White Sea	824
Dvina, West.	Gulf of Riga	634
Ebro	Mediterranean	565
Elbe	North Sea	724
Garonne	Bay of Biscay	357
Kama	Volga River	1,122
Loire	Bay of Biscay	634
Mame	Seine River	326
Meuse	North Sea	580
Oder	Baltic Sea	567
Oka	Volga River	932
Pechora	Barents Sea	1,124
Po	Adriatic Sea	405
Rhine	North Sea	820
Rhone	Gulf of Lions	505
Seine	English Channel	496
Shannon	Atlantic Ocean	230
Tagus	Atlantic Ocean	626
Thames	North Sea	210
Tiber	Tyrrhenian Sea	252
Tisza	Danube River	600
Ural	Caspian Sea	1,575
Volga	Caspian Sea	2,290
Weser	North Sea	454
Wisla	Gulf of Gdansk	675
South America		
Amazon	Atlantic Ocean	4,000
Araguaia	Tocantins River	1,100
Içа (see Putumayo)		
Iguaça	Parana River	808
Japura	Amazon River	1,750
Madeira	Amazon River	2,013
Magdalena	Caribbean Sea	956
Negro	Amazon River	1,400
Orinoco	Atlantic Ocean	1,600
Paraguay	Parana River	1,584
Parana	Rio de la Plata	2,485
Pilcomayo	Paraguay River	1,000
Purus	Amazon River	2,100
Putumayo	Amazon River	1,000
Rio de la Plata	Atlantic Ocean	150
Rio Roosevelt	Aripuana	400
Sao Francisco	Atlantic Ocean	1,988
Tocantins	Para River	1,677
Ucayali	Marañón River	910
Uruguay	Rio de la Plata	1,000
Xingu	Amazon River	1,300

WORLD ALMANAC QUICK QUIZ

Which one of these U.S. cities is the highest and farthest west?

(a) Detroit, MI (b) Knoxville, TN
(c) Atlanta, GA (d) Tallahassee, FL

For the answer look in this chapter, or see page 1008.

Major Rivers in North America

Reviewed by Laurel Duda, Marine Biological Laboratory, Woods Hole Oceanographic Inst. Library

River	Source or upper limit of length	Outflow	Length (mi)
Alabama	Gilmer County, GA	Mobile River	729
Albany	Lake St. Joseph, Ontario	James Bay	610
Allegheny	Potter County, PA	Ohio River	325
Altamaha-Ocmulgee	Junction of Yellow and South Rivers, Newton County, GA	Atlantic Ocean	392
Apalachicola-Chattahoochee	Towns County, GA	Gulf of Mexico	524
Arkansas	Lake County, CO	Mississippi River	1,459
Assiniboine	Eastern Saskatchewan	Red River	450
Attawapiskat	Attawapiskat, Ontario	James Bay	465
Back (NWT)	Contwoyto Lake	Chantrey Inlet, Arctic Ocean	605
Big Black (MS)	Webster County, MS	Mississippi River	330
Brazos	Junction of Salt and Double Mountain Forks, Stonewall County, TX	Gulf of Mexico	950
Canadian	Las Animas County, CO	Arkansas River	906
Cedar (IA)	Dodge County, MN	Iowa River	329
Cheyenne	Junction of Antelope Creek and Dry Fork, Converse County, WY	Missouri River	290
Churchill, Man.	Methy Lake, Saskatchewan	Hudson Bay	1,000
Cimarron	Colfax County, NM	Arkansas River	600
Colorado (AZ)	Rocky Mountain Natl. Park, CO (90 mi in Mexico)	Gulf of California	1,450
Colorado (TX)	West Texas	Matagorda Bay	862
Columbia	Columbia Lake, British Columbia	Pacific Ocean, bet. OR and WA	1,243
Columbia, Upper	Columbia Lake, British Columbia	To mouth of Snake River	890
Connecticut	Third Connecticut Lake, NH	Long Island Sound, CT	407
Coppermine (NWT)	Lac de Gras	Coronation Gulf, Arctic Ocean	525
Cumberland	Letcher County, KY	Ohio River	720
Delaware	Schoharie County, NY	Liston Point, Delaware Bay	390
Fraser	Near Mount Robson (on Continental Divide)	Strait of Georgia	850
Gila	Catron County, NM	Colorado River	649
Green (UT-WY)	Junction of Wells and Trail Creeks, Sublette County, WY	Colorado River	730
Hamilton (Lab.)	Lake Ashuanipi	Atlantic Ocean	532
Hudson	Henderson Lake, Essex County, NY	Upper NY Bay	306
Illinois	St. Joseph County, IN	Mississippi River	420
James (ND-SD)	Wells County, ND	Missouri River	710
James (VA)	Junction of Jackson and Cowpasture Rivers, Botetourt County, VA	Hampton Roads	340

River	Source or upper limit of length	Outflow	Length (mi)
Kanawha-New	Junction of North and South Forks of New River, NC	Ohio River	352
Kentucky	Junction of North and Middle Forks, Lee County, KY	Ohio River	259
Klamath	Lake Ewauna, Klamath Falls, OR	Pacific Ocean	250
Kootenay	Kootenay Lake, British Columbia	Columbia River	485
Koyukuk	Endicott Mountains, AK	Yukon River	470
Kuskokwim	Alaska Range	Kuskokwim Bay	724
Liard	Southern Yukon, AK	Mackenzie River	693
Little Missouri	Crook County, WY	Missouri River	560
Mackenzie	Great Slave Lake, N.W.T.	Arctic Ocean	1,060
Milk	Junction of North and South Forks, Alberta	Missouri River	625
Minnesota	Big Stone Lake, MN	Mississippi River	332
Mississippi	Lake Itasca, MN	Gulf of Mexico	2,340
Mississippi-Missouri-Red Rock	Source of Red Rock, Beaverhead Co., MT	Gulf of Mexico	3,710
Missouri	Junction of Jefferson, Madison, and Gallatin Rivers, Gallatin County, MT	Mississippi River	2,315
Missouri-Red Rock	Source of Red Rock, Beaverhead Co., MT	Mississippi River	2,540
Mobile-Alabama-Coosa	Gilmer County, GA	Mobile Bay	774
Nelson (Man.)	Lake Winnipeg	Hudson Bay	410
Neosho	Morris County, KS	Arkansas River, OK	460
Niobrara	Niobrara County, WY	Missouri River, NE	431
North Canadian	Union County, NM	Canadian River, OK	800
North Platte	Junction of Grizzly and Little Grizzly Creeks, Jackson County, CO	Platte River, NE	618
Ohio	Junction of Allegheny and Monongahela Rivers, Pittsburgh, PA	Mississippi River	981
Ohio-Allegheny	Potter County, PA	Mississippi River	1,310
Osage	East-central Kansas	Missouri River	500
Ottawa	Lake Capimitchigama	St. Lawrence River	790
Ouachita	Polk County, AR	Black River	605
Peace	Stikine Mountains, B.C.	Slave River	1,210
Pearl	Neshoba County, MS	Gulf of Mexico	411
Pecos	Mora County, NM	Rio Grande	926
Pee Dee-Yadkin	Watauga County, NC	Winyah Bay	435
Pend Oreille-Clark Fork	Near Butte, MT	Columbia River	531
Platte	Junction of North and South Platte Rivers, NE	Missouri River	310
Porcupine	Ogilvie Mountains, AK	Yukon River, AK	569
Potomac	Garrett County, MD	Chesapeake Bay	383
Powder	Junction of South and Middle Forks, WY	Yellowstone River	375
Red (OK-TX-LA)	Curry County, NM	Mississippi River	1,290
Red River of the North	Junction of Otter Tail and Bois de Sioux Rivers, Wilkin County, MN	Lake Winnipeg	545
Republican	Junction of North Fork and Arikaree River, NE	Kansas River	445
Rio Grande	San Juan County, CO	Gulf of Mexico	1,900
Roanoke	Junction of N and S Forks, Montgomery Co., VA	Albemarle Sound	380
Rock (IL-WI)	Dodge County, WI	Mississippi River	300
Sabine	Junction of S and Caddo Forks, Hunt County, TX	Sabine Lake	380
Sacramento	Siskiyou County, CA	Suisun Bay	377
St. Francis	Iron County, MO	Mississippi River	425
St. John	Northwestern Maine	Bay of Fundy	418
St. Lawrence	Lake Ontario	Gulf of St. Lawrence, Atlantic Ocean	800
Saguenay	Lake St. John, Quebec	St. Lawrence River	434
Salmon (ID)	Custer County, ID	Snake River	420
San Joaquin	Junction of S and Middle Forks, Madera Co., CA	Suisun Bay	350
San Juan	Silver Lake, Archuleta County, CO	Colorado River	360
Santee-Wateree-Catawba	McDowell County, NC	Atlantic Ocean	538
Saskatchewan, North	Rocky Mountains	Saskatchewan R.	800
Saskatchewan, South	Rocky Mountains	Saskatchewan R.	865
Savannah	Junction of Seneca and Tugaloo Rivers, Anderson County, SC	Atlantic Ocean, GA-SC	314
Severn (Ont.)	Sandy Lake	Hudson Bay	610
Smoky Hill	Cheyenne County, CO	Kansas River, KS	540
Snake	Teton County, WY	Columbia River, WA	1,038
South Platte	Junction of S and Middle Forks, Park County, CO	Platte River	424
Susitna	Alaska Range	Cook Inlet	313
Susquehanna	Huyden Creek, Otsego County, NY	Chesapeake Bay	447
Tallahatchie	Tippah County, MS	Yazoo River	301
Tanana	Wrangell Mountains, AK	Yukon River	659
Tennessee	Junction of French Broad and Holston Rivers	Ohio River	652
Tennessee-French Broad	Courthouse Creek, Transylvania County, NC	Ohio River	886
Tombigbee	Prentiss County, MS	Mobile River	525
Trinity	North of Dallas, TX	Galveston Bay	360
Wabash	Darke County, OH	Ohio River	512
Washita	Hemphill County, TX	Red River, OK	500
White (AR-MO)	Madison County, AR	Mississippi River	722
Willamette	Douglas County, OR	Columbia River	309
Wind-Bighorn	Junction of Wind and Little Wind Rivers, Fremont Co., WY (Source of Wind R. is Togwotee Pass, Teton Co., WY)	Yellowstone River	338
Wisconsin	Lac Vieux Desert, Vilas County, WI	Mississippi River	430
Yellowstone	Park County, WY	Missouri River	682
Yukon	McNeil R., Yukon Territory	Bering Sea	1,979

Highest and Lowest Continental Altitudes

Source: National Geographic Society

Continent	Highest point	Elev. (ft)	Lowest point	ft below sea level
Asia	Mount Everest, Nepal-Tibet	29,035	Dead Sea, Israel-Jordan	1,348
South America	Mount Aconcagua, Argentina	22,834	Valdes Peninsula, Argentina	131
North America	Mount McKinley, AK	20,320	Death Valley, California	282
Africa	Kilimanjaro, Tanzania	19,340	Lake Assal, Djibouti	512
Europe	Mount Elbrus, Russia	18,510	Caspian Sea, Russia, Azerbaijan	92
Antarctica	Vinson Massif	16,864	Bentley Subglacial Trench	8,327[1]
Australia	Mount Kosciusko, New South Wales	7,310	Lake Eyre, South Australia	52

(1) Estimated level of the continental floor. Lower points that have yet to be discovered may exist further beneath the ice.

IT'S A FACT: In 1996, scientists using radar discovered Lake Vostok beneath 12,000 feet of ice in Antarctica. Roughly 140 miles long, 30 miles wide, and 3,000 feet deep, Vostok is the largest of some 70 unfrozen lakes found under the ice sheet.

Major Natural Lakes of the World

Source: Geological Survey, U.S. Dept. of the Interior

A lake is generally defined as a body of water surrounded by land. By this definition some bodies of water that are called seas, such as the Caspian Sea and the Aral Sea, are really lakes. In the following table, the word *lake* is omitted when it is part of the name.

Name	Continent	Area (sq mi)	Length (mi)	Maximum depth (ft)	Elevation (ft)
Caspian Sea[1]	Asia-Europe	143,244	760	3,363	–92
Superior	North America	31,700	350	1,330	600
Victoria	Africa	26,828	250	270	3,720
Huron	North America	23,000	206	750	579
Michigan	North America	22,300	307	923	579
Aral Sea[1]	Asia	13,000[2]	260	220	125
Tanganyika	Africa	12,700	420	4,823	2,534
Baykal	Asia	12,162	395	5,315	1,493
Great Bear	North America	12,096	192	1,463	512
Nyasa (Malawi)	Africa	11,150	360	2,280	1,550
Great Slave	North America	11,031	298	2,015	513
Erie	North America	9,910	241	210	570
Winnipeg	North America	9,417	266	60	713
Ontario	North America	7,340	193	802	245
Balkhash[1]	Asia	7,115	376	85	1,115
Ladoga	Europe	6,835	124	738	13
Maracaibo	South America	5,217	133	115	sea level
Onega	Europe	3,710	145	328	108
Eyre[1]	Australia	3,600[3]	90	4	–52
Titicaca	South America	3,200	122	922	12,500
Nicaragua	North America	3,100	102	230	102
Athabasca	North America	3,064	208	407	700
Reindeer	North America	2,568	143	720	1,106
Tonle Sap	Asia	2,500[3]	...	45	...
Turkana (Rudolf)	Africa	2,473	154	240	1,230
Issyk Kul[1]	Asia	2,355	115	2,303	5,279
Torrens[1]	Australia	2,230[3]	130	...	92
Vanern	Europe	2,156	91	328	144
Nettilling	North America	2,140	67	...	95
Winnipegosis	North America	2,075	141	38	830
Albert	Africa	2,075	100	168	2,030
Nipigon	North America	1,872	72	540	1,050
Gairdner[1]	Australia	1,840[3]	90	...	112
Urmia[1]	Asia	1,815	90	49	4,180
Manitoba	North America	1,799	140	12	813
Chad	Africa	839[4]	175	24	787

(1) Salt lake. (2) Approximate figure, could be less. The diversion of feeder rivers since the 1960s has devastated the Aral—once the world's 4th-largest lake (26,000 sq. miles). By 2000, the Aral had effectively become three lakes, with the total area shown. (3) Approximate figure, subject to great seasonal variation. (4) Once 4th-largest lake in Africa (about 10,000 sq. miles in the 1960s), Chad had shrunk more than 90% by 2001 due to irrigation and long-term drought.

The Great Lakes

Source: National Ocean Service, U.S. Dept. of Commerce

The Great Lakes form the world's largest body of fresh water (in surface area), and with their connecting waterways are the largest inland water transportation unit. Draining the great North Central basin of the U.S., they enable shipping to reach the Atlantic via their outlet, the St. Lawrence R., and to reach the Gulf of Mexico via the Illinois Waterway, from Lake Michigan to the Mississippi R. A 3rd outlet connects with the Hudson R. and then the Atlantic via the New York State Barge Canal System. Traffic on the Illinois Waterway and the N.Y. State Barge Canal System is limited to recreational boating and small shipping vessels.

Only one of the lakes, Lake Michigan, is wholly in the U.S.; the others are shared with Canada. Ships move from the shores of Lake Superior to Whitefish Bay at the E end of the lake, then through the Soo (Sault Ste. Marie) locks, through the St. Mary's R. and into Lake Huron. To reach Gary and the Port of Indiana and South Chicago, IL, ships move W from Lake Huron to Lake Michigan through the Straits of Mackinac. Lake Superior is 601 ft above low water datum at Rimouski, Quebec, on the International Great Lakes Datum (1985). From Duluth, MN, to the E end of Lake Ontario is 1,156 mi.

	Superior	Michigan	Huron	Erie	Ontario
Length in mi	350	307	206	241	193
Breadth in mi	160	118	183	57	53
Deepest soundings in ft	1,333	923	750	210	802
Volume of water in cu mi	2,935	1,180	850	116	393
Area (sq mi) water surface—U.S.	20,600	22,300	9,100	4,980	3,460
Canada	11,100	.....	13,900	4,930	3,880
Area (sq mi) entire drainage basin—U.S.	16,900	45,600	16,200	18,000	15,200
Canada	32,400	.....	35,500	4,720	12,100
TOTAL AREA (sq mi) U.S. and Canada	**81,000**	**67,900**	**74,700**	**32,630**	**34,850**
Low water datum above mean water level at Rimouski, Quebec, avg. level in ft (1985)	601.10	577.50	577.50	569.20	243.30
Latitude, N	46° 25′	41° 37′	43° 00′	41° 23′	43° 11′
	49° 00′	46° 06′	46° 17′	42° 52′	44° 15′
Longitude, W	84° 22′	84° 45′	79° 43′	78° 51′	76° 03′
	92° 06′	88° 02′	84° 45′	83° 29′	79° 53′
National boundary line in mi	282.8	None	260.8	251.5	174.6
United States shoreline (mainland only) mi	863	1,400	580	431	300

Famous Waterfalls

Source: National Geographic Society

The earth has thousands of waterfalls, some of considerable magnitude. Their relative importance is determined not only by height but also by volume of flow, steadiness of flow, crest width, whether the water drops sheerly or over a sloping surface, and whether it descends in one leap or in a succession of leaps. A series of low falls flowing over a considerable distance is known as a **cascade**.

Estimated mean annual flow, in cubic feet per second, of major waterfalls are as follows: Niagara, 212,200; Paulo Afonso, 100,000; Urubupunga, 97,000; Iguazu, 61,000; Patos-Maribondo, 53,000; Victoria, 35,400; and Kaieteur, 23,400.

Height = total drop in feet in one or more leaps. #=falls of more than one leap; *= falls that diminish greatly seasonally; **= falls that reduce to a trickle or are dry for part of each year. If the river names are not shown, they are same as the falls. R. = river; (C) = cascade type.

Name and location	Height (ft)
Africa	
Angola	
Ruacana, Cuene R.	406
Ethiopia	
Fincha	508
Lesotho	
Maletsunyane*	630
Zimbabwe-Zambia	
Victoria, Zambezi R.*	343
South Africa	
Augrabies, Orange R.*	480
Tugela#	2,014
Tanzania-Zambia	
Kalambo*	726
Asia	
India	
Cauvery*	330
Jog (Gersoppa),Sharavathi R.*	830
Japan	
Kegon, Daiya R.*	330
Australia	
New South Wales	
Wentworth	614
Wollomombi	1,100
Queensland	
Tully	885
Wallaman, Stony Cr.#	1,137
New Zealand	
Helena	890
Sutherland, Arthur R.#	1,904
Europe	
Austria	
Gastein#	492
Krimml#	1,312
France	
Gavarnie*	1,385
Great Britain	
Scotland	
Glomach	370
Wales	
Rhaiadr	240
Italy	
Frua, Toce R. (C)	470
Norway	
Mardalsfossen (Northern)	1,535
Mardalsfossen (Southern)#	2,149
Skjeggedal, Nybuai R.#**	1,378
Skykje**	984
Vetti, Morka-Koldedola R.	900
Sweden	
Handol#	427
Switzerland	
Giessbach (C)	984
Reichenbach#	656
Simmen#	459
Staubbach	984
Trummelbach#	1,312
North America	
Canada	
Alberta	
Panther, Nigel Cr.	600
British Columbia	
Della#	1,443
Takakkaw, Daly Glacier#	1,200
Quebec	
Montmorency	274
Canada—United States	
Niagara: American	182
Horseshoe	173
United States	
California	
Feather, Fall R.*	640
Yosemite National Park	
Bridalveil*	620
Illilouette*	370
Nevada, Merced R.*	594
Ribbon**	1,612
Silver Strand, Meadow Br.**	1,170
Vernal, Merced R. *	317
Yosemite#**	2,425
Colorado	
Seven, South Cheyenne Cr.#.	300
Hawaii	
Akaka, Kolekole Str.	442
Idaho	
Shoshone, Snake R.**	212
Kentucky	
Cumberland	68
Maryland	
Great, Potomac R. (C) *	71
Minnesota	
Minnehaha**	53
New Jersey	
Passaic	70
New York	
Taughannock*	215
Oregon	
Multnomah#	620
Tennessee	
Fall Creek	256
Washington	
Mt. Rainier Natl. Park	
Sluiskin, Paradise R.	300
Snoquvalmie**	268
Wisconsin	
Big Manitou, Black R. (C)*	165
Wyoming	
Yellowstone Natl. Pk. Tower	132
Yellowstone (upper)*	109
Yellowstone (lower)*	308
Mexico	
El Salo	218
South America	
Argentina-Brazil	
Iguazu	230
Brazil	
Glass	1,325
Patos-Maribondo, Grande R.	115
Paulo Afonso, Sao Francisco R.	275
Urubupunga, Parana R.	39
Colombia	
Catarvata de Candelas, Cusiana R.	984
Tequendama, Bogota R.*	427
Ecuador	
Agoyan, Pastaza R.*	200
Guyana	
Kaieteur, Potaro R.	741
Great, Kamarang R.	1,600
Marina, Ipobe R.#	500
Venezuela	
Angel#*	3,212
Cuquenan	2,000

Notable Deserts of the World

Arabian (Eastern), 70,000 sq mi in Egypt between the Nile R. and Red Sea, extending southward into Sudan

Atacama, 600-mi-long area rich in nitrate and copper deposits in N Chile

Chihuahuan, 140,000 sq mi in TX, NM, AZ, and Mexico

Dasht-e Kauir, approx. 300 mi long by approx. 100 mi wide in N central Iran

Dasht-e Lut, 20,000 sq mi in E Iran

Death Valley, 3,300 sq mi in CA and NV

Gibson, 120,000 sq mi in the interior of W Australia

Gobi, 500,000 sq mi in Mongolia and China

Great Sandy, 150,000 sq mi in W Australia

Great Victoria, 150,000 sq mi in SW Australia

Kalahari, 225,000 sq mi in S Africa

Kara Kum, 120,000 sq mi in Turkmenistan

Kyzyl Kum, 100,000 sq mi in Kazakhstan and Uzbekistan

Libyan, 450,000 sq mi in the Sahara, extending from Libya through SW Egypt into Sudan

Mojave, 15,000 sq mi in southern CA

Namib, long narrow area (varies from 30-100 mi wide) extending 800 mi along SW coast of Africa

Nubian, 100,000 sq mi in the Sahara in NE Sudan

Painted Desert, section of high plateau in northern AZ extending 150 mi

Patagonia, 300,000 sq mi in S Argentina

Rub al-Khali (Empty Quarter), 250,000 sq mi in the S Arabian Peninsula

Sahara, 3,500,000 sq mi in N Africa, extending westward to the Atlantic. Largest desert in the world

Sonoran, 70,000 sq mi in southwestern AZ and southeastern CA extending into NW Mexico

Syrian, 100,000-sq-mi arid wasteland extending over much of N Saudi Arabia, E Jordan, S Syria, and W Iraq

Taklimakan, 140,000 sq mi in Xinjiang Prov., China

Thar (Great Indian), 100,000-sq-mi arid area extending 400 mi along India-Pakistan border

UNITED STATES HISTORY

This chapter includes the following sections:

Chronology of Events

1492

Christopher Columbus and crew sighted land **Oct. 12** in the present-day Bahamas.

1497

John Cabot explored northeast coast to Delaware.

1513

Juan Ponce de León explored Florida coast.

1524

Giovanni da Verrazano led French expedition along coast from Carolina north to Nova Scotia; entered New York harbor.

1539

Hernando de Soto landed in Florida **May 28;** crossed Mississippi River, **1541.**

1540

Francisco Vásquez de Coronado explored Southwest north of Rio Grande. Hernando de Alarcón reached Colorado River; Don Garcia Lopez de Cardenas reached Grand Canyon. Others explored California coast.

1565

St. Augustine, FL, founded **Sept. 8** by Pedro Menéndez. Razed by Francis Drake **1586.**

1579

Francis Drake entered San Francisco Bay and claimed region for Britain.

1607

Capt. John Smith and 105 cavaliers in 3 ships landed on Virginia coast, started first permanent English settlement in New World at **Jamestown** in **May.**

1609

Henry Hudson, English explorer of Northwest Passage, employed by Dutch, sailed into New York harbor in **Sept.,** and up Hudson to Albany. **Samuel de Champlain** explored Lake Champlain, just to the north.

Spaniards settled **Santa Fe, NM.**

1619

House of Burgesses, first representative assembly in New World, elected **July 30** at Jamestown, VA.

First black laborers—indentured servants—in English N. American colonies, landed by Dutch at Jamestown in **Aug.** Chattel slavery legally recognized, **1650.**

1620

Plymouth Pilgrims, Puritan separatists, left Plymouth, England, **Sept. 16** on *Mayflower*. They reached Cape Cod **Nov. 19,** explored coast; 103 passengers landed **Dec. 26** at Plymouth. **Mayflower Compact** was agreement to form a government and abide by its laws. Half of colony died during harsh winter.

1624

Dutch colonies started in Albany and in New York area, where **New Netherland** was established in **May.**

1626

Peter Minuit bought Manhattan for Dutch West India Co. from Man-a-hat-a Indians during summer for goods valued at $24; named island **New Amsterdam.**

1630

Settlement of **Boston** established by Massachusetts colonists led by John Winthrop.

1634

Maryland, founded as a Catholic colony, under a charter granted to Lord Baltimore. Religious toleration granted **1649.**

1636

Roger Williams founded Providence, RI, **June,** as a democratically ruled colony with separation of church and state. Charter granted, **1644.**

Harvard College founded **Oct. 28,** now oldest in U.S.; grammar school, compulsory education established at Boston.

1640

First book was printed in America, the so-called Bay Psalm Book.

1647

Liberal constitution drafted in Rhode Island.

1660

British Parliament passed First **Navigation Act Dec. 1,** regulating colonial commerce to suit English needs.

1664

British troops Sept. 8 seized New Netherland from Dutch. Charles II granted New Netherland and city of New Amsterdam to brother, Duke of York; both renamed **New York.** Dutch recaptured colony **1673,** but ceded it to Britain **Nov. 10, 1674.**

1673

Jacques **Marquette** and Louis **Jolliet** reached the upper **Mississippi** and traveled down it.

1676

Nathaniel Bacon led planters against autocratic British Gov. Sir William Berkeley, burned Jamestown, VA, **Sept. 19.** Rebellion collapsed when Bacon died; 23 followers executed.

Bloody **Indian war** in New England ended **Aug. 12.** King Philip, Wampanoag chief, and Narragansett Indians killed.

1682

Robert Cavelier, Sieur de La Salle, claimed lower Mississippi River country for France, called it Louisiana **Apr. 9.** Had French outposts built in Illinois and Texas, **1684.** Killed during mutiny **Mar. 19, 1687.**

William Penn arrived in **Pennsylvania.**

1683

William Penn signed treaty with Delaware Indians and made payment for Pennsylvania lands.

1692

Witchcraft delusion at Salem, MA; 20 alleged witches executed by special court.

1696

Capt. William Kidd arrested and sent to England; hanged for piracy, **1701.**

1699

French settlements made in Mississippi, Louisiana.

1704

Indians attacked Deerfield, MA, **Feb. 28-29;** killed 40, carried off 100.

Boston News Letter, **first regular newspaper,** started by John Campbell, postmaster. (An earlier paper, *Publick Occurences,* was suppressed after one issue **1690.**)

1709

British-Colonial troops captured French fort, Port Royal, Nova Scotia, in **Queen Anne's War 1701-13.** France yielded Nova Scotia by treaty **1713.**

1712

Slaves revolted in New York **Apr. 6.** Six committed suicide; 21 were executed. Second rising, **1741;** 13 slaves hanged, 13 burned, 71 deported.

1716

First theater in colonies opened in Williamsburg, VA.

1726

Poor people **rioted** in Philadelphia.

Great Awakening religious revival began.

1732

Benjamin Franklin published the first *Poor Richard's Almanack;* published annually to **1757.**

Last of the 13 colonies, **Georgia,** chartered.

1735

Editor **John Peter Zenger acquitted** in New York of libeling British governor by criticizing his conduct in office.

1740-41

Capt. Vitus Bering reached Alaska.

WORLD ALMANAC QUICK QUIZ

In what year did *The World Almanac* first appear?

(a) 1650 (b) 1868
(c) 1897 (d) 1925

For the answer look in this chapter, or see page 1008.

1744

King George's War pitted British and colonials vs. French. Colonials captured Louisburg, Cape Breton Is., **June 17, 1745.** Returned to France **1748** by Treaty of Aix-la-Chapelle.

1752

Benjamin Franklin, flying kite in thunderstorm, proved lightning is electricity **June 15;** invented lightning rod.

1754

French and Indian War began when French occupied Ft. Duquesne (Pittsburgh). British moved Acadian French from Nova Scotia to Louisiana **Oct. 8, 1755.** British captured Québec **Sept. 18, 1759,** in battles in which French Gen. Joseph de Montcalm and British Gen. James Wolfe were killed. Peace pact signed **Feb. 10, 1763.** French lost Canada and Midwest.

1764

Sugar Act placed duties on lumber, foodstuffs, molasses, and rum in colonies, to pay French and Indian War debts.

1765

Stamp Act, enacted by Parliament **Mar. 22,** required revenue stamps to help fund royal troops. Nine colonies, at **Stamp Act Congress** in New York **Oct. 7-25,** adopted Declaration of Rights. Stamp Act **repealed Mar. 17, 1766.**

1767

Townshend Acts levied taxes on glass, painter's lead, paper, and tea. In **1770** all duties except those on tea were repealed.

1770

British troops fired **Mar. 5** into Boston mob, killed 5 including **Crispus Attucks,** a black man, reportedly leader of group; later called **Boston Massacre.**

1773

East India Co. tea ships turned back at Boston, New York, and Philadelphia in **May.** Cargo ship burned at Annapolis **Oct. 14;** cargo thrown overboard at **Boston Tea Party Dec. 16,** to protest the tea tax.

1774

"Intolerable Acts" of Parliament curtailed Massachusetts self-rule; barred use of Boston harbor till tea was paid for.

First Continental Congress held in Philadelphia **Sept. 5-Oct. 26;** called for civil disobedience against British.

Rhode Island abolished slavery.

1775

Patrick Henry addressed Virginia convention, **Mar. 23,** said "Give me liberty or give me death."

Paul Revere and William Dawes on night of **Apr. 18** rode to alert Patriots that British were on their way to Concord to destroy arms. At Lexington, MA, **Apr. 19,** Minutemen lost 8. On return from Concord, British took 273 casualties.

Col. Ethan Allen (joined by Col. Benedict Arnold) captured **Ft. Ticonderoga, NY, May 10;** also Crown Point. Colonials headed for **Bunker Hill,** fortified Breed's Hill, Charlestown, MA. Repulsed British under Gen. William Howe twice before retreating **June 17;** called Battle of Bunker Hill.

Continental Congress **June 15** named **George Washington** commander in chief.

1776

France and Spain each agreed **May 2** to provide arms.

In Continental Congress **June 7,** Richard Henry Lee (VA) moved "that these united colonies are and of right ought to be free and independent states." Resolution adopted July 2. **Declaration of Independence** approved **July 4.**

Col. William Moultrie's batteries at **Charleston, SC,** repulsed British sea attack **June 28.** Washington lost **Battle of Long Island Aug. 27;** evacuated New York.

Nathan Hale executed as spy by British **Sept. 22.**

Brig. Gen. Arnold's **Lake Champlain** fleet was defeated at Valcour **Oct. 11,** but British returned to Canada. Howe failed to destroy Washington's army at **White Plains Oct. 28.** Hessians captured Ft. Washington, Manhattan, and 3,000 men **Nov. 16;** captured Ft. Lee, NJ, **Nov. 18.**

Washington, in Pennsylvania, recrossed **Delaware River Dec. 25-26,** defeated Hessians at Trenton, NJ, **Dec. 26.**

1777

Washington defeated Lord Cornwallis at **Princeton Jan. 3.** Continental Congress adopted Stars and Stripes.

Maj. Gen. John Burgoyne's force of 8,000 from Canada, captured **Ft. Ticonderoga July 6.** Americans beat back Burgoyne at Bemis Heights **Oct. 7,** cut off British escape route. Burgoyne surrendered 5,000 men at **Saratoga, NY, Oct. 17.**

Articles of Confederation adopted by Continental Congress **Nov. 15.**

1778

France signed treaty of aid with U.S. **Feb. 6.** Sent fleet; British evacuated Philadelphia in consequence **June 18.**

1779

John Paul Jones on the *Bonhomme Richard* defeated *Serapis* in British North Sea waters **Sept. 23.**

1780

Charleston, SC, fell to the British **May 12,** but a British force was defeated near **Kings Mountain, NC, Oct. 7** by militiamen.

Benedict Arnold found to be a traitor **Sept. 23.** Arnold escaped, made brigadier general in British army.

1781

Articles of Confederation took effect **Mar. 1.**

Bank of North America incorporated **May 26.**

Cornwallis retired to **Yorktown, VA.** Adm. Francois Joseph de Grasse landed 3,000 French and stopped British fleet in Hampton Roads. Washington and Jean Baptiste de Rochambeau joined forces, arrived near Williamsburg **Sept. 26.** Siege of Cornwallis began **Oct. 6; Cornwallis surrendered Oct. 19.**

1782

New **British** cabinet agreed **in March** to **recognize U.S.** independence. Preliminary agreement signed in Paris **Nov. 30.**

1783

Massachusetts Supreme Court declared **slavery** illegal in that state.

Britain, U.S. signed Paris **peace treaty Sept. 3** recognizing American independence (Congress ratified it **Jan. 14, 1784).**

Washington ordered army disbanded Nov. 3, bade farewell to his officers at Fraunces Tavern, New York City, **Dec. 4.**

Noah Webster published *American Spelling Book.*

1784

Thomas Jefferson's proposal to **ban slavery** in new territory after 1802 was narrowly defeated **Mar. 1.**

First successful daily newspaper, ***Pennsylvania Packet & General Advertiser,*** published **Sept. 21.**

1786

Delegates from 5 states at **Annapolis, MD, Sept. 11-14** asked Congress to call a constitutional convention for the 13 states.

1787

Shays's Rebellion of debt-ridden farmers in Massachusetts failed **Jan. 25.**

Northwest Ordinance adopted **July 13** by Continental Congress for Northwest Territory, N of Ohio River, W of New York; made rules for statehood. Guaranteed freedom of religion, support for schools, no slavery.

Constitutional convention opened at Philadelphia **May 25** with Washington presiding. Constitution accepted by delegates **Sept. 17;** ratification by 9th state, New Hampshire, **June 21, 1788,** meant adoption; declared in effect **Mar. 4, 1789.**

1789

George Washington chosen president by all electors voting (73 eligible, 69 voting, 4 absent); John Adams, vice president, got 34 votes. First Congress met at Federal Hall, New York City, **Mar. 4.** Washington inaugurated there **Apr. 30.** Supreme Court created by Federal Judiciary Act **Sept. 24.** Congress submitted Bill of Rights to states **Sept. 25.**

1790

Congress, **Mar. 1,** authorized decennial **U.S. census; Naturalization Act** (2-year residency) passed **Mar. 26.**

Congress met in Philadelphia, new temporary capital, **Dec. 6.**

1791

Bill of Rights went into effect **Dec. 15.**

1792

Coinage Act established **U.S. Mint** in Philadelphia **Apr. 2.**

Gen. **"Mad" Anthony Wayne** made commander in Ohio-Indiana area, trained "American Legion," established string of forts. Routed Indians at Fallen Timbers on Maumee River **Aug. 20, 1794,** checked British at Fort Miami, OH.

White House cornerstone laid **Oct. 13.**

1793

Eli Whitney invented **cotton gin,** reviving Southern slavery.

1794

Whiskey Rebellion, W Pennsylvania farmers protesting liquor tax of **1791,** was suppressed by federal militia **Sept.**

1795

U.S. bought peace from **Algerian pirates** by paying $1 mil ransom for 115 seamen **Sept. 5,** followed by annual tributes.

Gen. Wayne signed peace with Indians at Fort Greenville.

University of North Carolina became first operating state university.

1796

Washington's Farewell Address as president delivered **Sept. 19.** Gave strong warnings against permanent alliances with foreign powers, big public debt, large military establishment, and devices of "small, artful, enterprising minority."

1797

U.S. **frigate *United States*** launched at Philadelphia **July 10; *Constellation*** at Baltimore **Sept. 7; *Constitution*** (Old Ironsides) at Boston **Sept. 20.**

1798

Alien & Sedition Acts passed by Federalists **June-July**; intended to silence political opposition.

War with France threatened over French raids on U.S. shipping and rejection of U.S. diplomats. Navy (45 ships) and 365 privateers captured 84 French ships. USS *Constellation* took French warship *Insurgente* **1799.** Napoleon stopped French raids after becoming First Consul.

1800

Federal government moved to **Washington, DC.**

1801

John Marshall named Supreme Court chief justice, **Jan. 20.**

Tripoli declared war June 10 against U.S., which refused added tribute to commerce-raiding Arab corsairs. Land and naval campaigns forced Tripoli to negotiate **peace June 4, 1805.**

1803

Supreme Court, in **Marbury *v* Madison** case, for the first time overturned a U.S. law **Feb. 24.**

Napoleon sold all of **Louisiana,** stretching to Canadian border, to U.S., for $11,250,000 in bonds, plus $3,750,000 indemnities to American citizens with claims against France. U.S. took title **Dec. 20.** Purchase doubled U.S. area.

1804

Lewis and Clark expedition ordered by Pres. Thomas Jefferson to explore what is now northwest U.S. Started from St. Louis **May 14;** ended **Sept. 23, 1806.**

Vice Pres. **Aaron Burr shot Alexander Hamilton** in a duel **July 11** in Weehawken, NJ; Hamilton died the next day.

1807

Robert Fulton made first practical steamboat trip; left New York City **Aug. 17,** reached Albany, 150 mi, in 32 hr.

Embargo Act banned all trade with foreign countries, forbidding ships to set sail for foreign ports **Dec. 22.**

1808

Slave importation outlawed. Some 250,000 slaves were illegally imported **1808-60.**

1811

William Henry Harrison, governor of Indiana, defeated Indians under the Prophet, in battle of **Tippecanoe Nov. 7.**

Cumberland Road begun at Cumberland, MD; became important route to West.

1812

War of 1812 had 3 main causes: Britain seized U.S. ships trading with France; Britain seized 4,000 naturalized U.S. sailors by **1810;** Britain armed Indians who raided western border. U.S. stopped trade with Europe **1807** and **1809.** Trade with Britain only was stopped **1810.**

Unaware that Britain had raised the blockade against France 2 days before, **Congress declared war June 18.**

USS *Essex* captured *Alert* **Aug. 13;** USS *Constitution* destroyed *Guerriere* **Aug. 19;** USS *Wasp* took *Frolic* **Oct. 18;** USS *United States* defeated *Macedonian* off Azores **Oct. 25;** *Constitution* beat *Java* **Dec. 29.** British took Detroit **Aug. 16.**

1813

Oliver H. Perry defeated British fleet at Battle of Lake Erie, **Sept. 10.** U.S. won Battle of the Thames, Ontario, **Oct. 5,** but failed in Canadian invasion attempts. York (Toronto) and Buffalo were burned.

1814

British landed in Maryland in Aug., defeated U.S. force **Aug. 24, burned Capitol and White House.** Maryland militia stopped British advance **Sept. 12.** Bombardment of Ft. McHenry, Baltimore, for 25 hours, **Sept. 13-14,** by British fleet failed; Francis Scott Key wrote words to **"The Star Spangled Banner."**

U.S. won naval Battle of **Lake Champlain Sept. 11.** Peace treaty signed at Ghent **Dec. 24.**

1815

Some 5,300 British, unaware of peace treaty, attacked U.S. entrenchments near **New Orleans, Jan. 8.** British had more than 2,000 casualties; Americans lost 71.

U.S. flotilla finally ended piracy by **Algiers, Tunis, Tripoli** by **Aug. 6.**

1816

Second **Bank of the U.S.** chartered.

1817

Rush-Bagot treaty signed **Apr. 28-29;** limited U.S., British armaments on the Great Lakes.

William Cullen Bryant's poem "Thanatopsis" published.

1819

Spain ceded **Florida** to U.S. **Feb. 22.**

American steamship *Savannah* made first part-steam-powered, part-sail-powered crossing of Atlantic, Savannah, GA, to Liverpool, England, 29 days.

1820

First organized **immigration of blacks to Africa** from U.S. began with 86 free blacks sailing **Feb.** to Sierra Leone.

Henry Clay's **Missouri Compromise** bill passed by Congress **Mar. 3.** Slavery was allowed in Missouri, but not elsewhere west of the Mississippi River north of 36° 30′ latitude (the southern line of Missouri). Repealed **1854.**

1821

Emma Willard founded Troy Female Seminary, first U.S. women's college.

1823

Monroe Doctrine, opposing European intervention in the Americas, enunciated by Pres. James Monroe **Dec. 2.**

1824

Pawtucket, RI, **weavers strike,** first such action by women.

1825

After a deadlocked election, John Quincy Adams was elected president by the U.S. House, **Feb. 9.**

Erie Canal opened; first boat left Buffalo **Oct. 26,** reached New York City **Nov. 4.**

John Stevens, of Hoboken, NJ, built and operated first experimental **steam locomotive** in U.S.

1826

Thomas Jefferson and John Adams both died **July 4.**

1828

South Carolina **Dec. 19** declared the right of state **nullification of federal laws,** opposing the "Tariff of Abominations."

Noah Webster published his *American Dictionary of the English Language.*

Baltimore & Ohio, the first U.S. passenger railroad, begun **July 4.**

1829

Andrew Jackson inaugurated as president, **Mar. 4.**

1830

Mormon church organized by Joseph Smith in Fayette, NY, **Apr. 6.**

1831

William Lloyd Garrison began abolitionist newspaper *The Liberator,* **Jan. 1.**

Nat Turner, black slave in Virginia, led local slave rebellion, starting **Aug. 21;** 57 whites killed. Troops called in, 100 slaves killed, Turner captured, tried, and hanged **Nov. 11.**

1832

Black Hawk War (IL-WI) **Apr.-Sept.** pushed Sauk and Fox Indians west across Mississippi.

South Carolina convention passed **Ordinance of Nullification Nov. 24** against permanent tariff, threatening to withdraw from Union. Congress **Feb. 1833** passed compromise tariff act, whereupon South Carolina repealed its act.

1833

Oberlin College became first in U.S. to adopt coeducation.

1835

Seminole Indians in Florida under Osceola began attacks **Nov. 1,** protesting forced removal. The unpopular war ended **Aug. 14, 1842;** most of the Indians were sent to Oklahoma.

Texas proclaimed right to secede from Mexico; Sam Houston put in command of Texas army, **Nov. 2-4.**

Gold discovered on **Cherokee land** in Georgia. Indians forced to cede lands **Dec. 20** and to cross Mississippi.

1836

Texans besieged at Alamo in San Antonio by Mexicans under Santa Anna **Feb. 23-Mar. 6;** entire garrison killed. Texas independence declared, **Mar. 2.** At San Jacinto **Apr. 21,** Sam Houston and Texans defeated Mexicans.

Marcus Whitman, H. H. Spaulding, and wives reached Fort Walla Walla on Columbia River, OR. **First white women to cross plains.**

1838

Cherokee Indians made **"Trail of Tears,"** removed from Georgia to Oklahoma starting **Oct.**

1841

First emigrant **wagon train for California,** 47 persons, left Independence, MO, **May 1,** reached California **Nov. 4.**

Brook Farm commune set up by New England Transcendentalist intellectuals. Lasted to **1846.**

1842

Webster-Ashburton Treaty signed **Aug. 9,** fixing the U.S.-Canada border in Maine and Minnesota.

First use of **anesthetic** (sulfuric ether gas).

Settlement of Oregon began via **Oregon Trail.**

1843

More than 1,000 settlers left Independence, MO, for Oregon **May 22,** arrived **Oct.**

1844

First message over first **telegraph line** sent **May 24** by inventor Samuel F.B. Morse from Washington to Baltimore: "What hath God wrought!"

1845

Texas Congress **voted for annexation** by U.S. **July 4.** U.S. Congress admitted Texas to Union **Dec. 29.**

Edgar Allan Poe's poem "The Raven" published.

1846

Mexican War began after Pres. James K. Polk ordered Gen. Zachary Taylor to seize disputed Texan land settled by Mexicans. After border clash, U.S. declared war **May 13;** Mexico **May 23.**

Bear flag of Republic of California raised by American settlers at Sonoma **June 14.**

About 12,000 U.S. troops took Vera Cruz **Mar. 27, 1847,** and Mexico City **Sept. 14, 1847.** By **treaty,** signed **Feb. 2, 1848,** war was ended, and Mexico ceded claims to Texas, California, and other territory.

Treaty with Britain **June 15** set **boundary in Oregon** territory at 49th parallel (extension of existing line). Expansionists had used slogan "54° 40′ or fight."

Mormons, after violent clashes with settlers over polygamy, left Nauvoo, IL, for West under Brigham Young; settled **July 1847** at **Salt Lake City, UT.**

Elias Howe invented **sewing machine.**

1847

First **adhesive U.S. postage stamps** on sale **July 1;** Benjamin Franklin 5¢, Washington 10¢.

Ralph Waldo Emerson published first book of poems; **Henry Wadsworth Longfellow** published *Evangeline.*

1848

Gold discovered Jan. 24 in California; 80,000 prospectors emigrated in **1849.**

Lucretia Mott and Elizabeth Cady Stanton led **Seneca Falls, NY, Women's Rights Convention July 19-20.**

1850

Sen. Henry Clay's **Compromise of 1850** admitted California as 31st state **Sept. 9,** with slavery forbidden; made Utah and New Mexico territories; made Fugitive Slave Law more harsh; ended District of Columbia slave trade.

Nathaniel Hawthorne's *The Scarlet Letter* published.

1851

Herman Melville's *Moby-Dick* published.

1852

Uncle Tom's Cabin, by **Harriet Beecher Stowe,** published.

1853

Comm. Matthew C. Perry, U.S.N., received by Japan, **July 14;** negotiated **treaty to open Japan** to U.S. ships.

1854

Republican Party formed at Ripon, WI, **Feb. 28.** Opposed Kansas-Nebraska Act (became law **May 30**), which left issue of slavery to vote of settlers.

Henry David Thoreau published *Walden.*

Treaty ratified with Mexico **Apr. 25,** providing for purchase of a strip of land **(Gadsden Purchase).**

1855

Walt Whitman published *Leaves of Grass.*

First railroad train crossed Mississippi on the river's first bridge, Rock Island, IL, Davenport, IA, **Apr. 21.**

1856

Republican Party's first nominee for president, **John C. Fremont,** defeated. Abraham Lincoln made 50 speeches for him.

Lawrence, KS, sacked **May 21** by proslavery group; abolitionist **John Brown** led antislavery men against Missourians at **Osawatomie, KS, Aug. 30.**

1857

Dred Scott decision by Supreme Court **Mar. 6** held that slaves did not become free in a free state, Congress could not bar slavery from a territory, and blacks could not be citizens.

1858

First **Atlantic cable** completed, by Cyrus W. Field **Aug. 5.**

Lincoln-Douglas debates in Illinois **Aug. 21-Oct. 15.**

1859

First commercially productive **oil well,** drilled near Titusville, PA, by Edwin L. Drake **Aug. 27.**

Abolitionist **John Brown,** with 21 men, seized U.S. Armory at **Harpers Ferry Oct. 16.** U.S. Marines captured raiders, killing several. Brown was hanged for treason **Dec. 2.**

1860

Approximately 20,000 **New England shoe workers** went on strike **Feb. 22** and won higher wages.

Abraham Lincoln, Republican, elected president **Nov. 6** in 4-way race.

First **Pony Express** between Sacramento, CA, and St. Joseph, MO, started **Apr. 3;** service ended **Oct. 24, 1861,** when first transcontinental telegraph line was completed.

1861

Seven southern states set up **Confederate States of America Feb. 8,** with Jefferson Davis as president, captured federal arsenals and forts. **Civil War** began as Confederates fired on **Ft. Sumter** in Charleston, SC, **Apr. 12,** capturing it **Apr. 14.**

Pres. **Lincoln** called for 75,000 volunteers **Apr. 15.** By **May,** 11 states had seceded. Lincoln blockaded Southern ports **Apr. 19,** cutting off vital exports, aid.

Confederates repelled Union forces at first **Battle of Bull Run July 21.**

First **transcontinental telegraph** was put in operation.

1862

Homestead Act approved **May 20;** it granted free family farms to settlers.

Land Grant Act approved **July 7,** providing for public land sale to benefit agricultural education; eventually led to establishment of state university systems.

Union forces were victorious in Western campaigns, took **New Orleans May 1.** Battles in East were inconclusive.

1863

Pres. Lincoln issued **Emancipation Proclamation Jan. 1,** freeing "all slaves in areas still in rebellion."

Entire **Mississippi River** was in Union hands by **July 4.** Union forces won a major victory at **Gettysburg, PA, July 1-3.** Lincoln read his **Gettysburg Address Nov. 19.**

In **draft riots** in New York City about 1,000 were killed or wounded; some blacks were hanged by mobs **July 13-16.**

1864

Gen. William Tecumseh **Sherman marched through Georgia,** taking Atlanta **Sept. 1,** Savannah **Dec. 22.**

Sand Creek massacre of Cheyenne and Arapaho Indians **Nov. 29.** Cavalry attacked Indians awaiting surrender terms.

1865

Gen. Robert E. Lee surrendered 27,800 Confederate troops to Gen. Ulysses S. Grant at Appomattox Court House, VA, **Apr. 9.** J. E. Johnston surrendered 31,200 to Sherman at Durham Station, NC, **Apr. 18.** Last rebel troops surrendered **May 26.**

Pres. Lincoln was shot Apr. 14 by John Wilkes Booth in Ford's Theater, Washington, DC; died the following morning.

Vice Pres. **Andrew Johnson** was sworn in as president. Booth was hunted down; fatally wounded, perhaps by his own hand, **Apr. 26.** Four co-conspirators were hanged **July 7.**

13th Amendment, abolishing slavery, ratified **Dec. 6.**

1866

Ku Klux Klan formed secretly in South to terrorize blacks who voted. Disbanded **1869-71.** A 2nd Klan organized **1915.**

Congress took control of Southern Reconstruction, backed freedmen's rights.

1867

Alaska sold to U.S. by Russia for $7.2 mil **Mar. 30** through efforts of Sec. of State William H. Seward.

Horatio Alger published first book, *Ragged Dick.*

The **Grange** was organized **Dec. 4,** to protect farmer interests.

1868

The World Almanac, a publication of the *New York World,* appeared for the first time.

Pres. **Johnson** tried to remove Edwin M. Stanton, secretary of war; was impeached by House **Feb. 24** for violation of Tenure of Office Act; acquitted by Senate Mar.-May.

1869

Financial **"Black Friday"** in New York **Sept. 24;** caused by attempt to "corner" gold.

Transcontinental railroad completed; golden spike driven at Promontory, UT, **May 10,** marking the junction of Central Pacific and Union Pacific.

Knights of Labor formed in Philadelphia. By **1886,** this labor union had 700,000 members nationally.

Woman suffrage law passed in Wyoming Territory **Dec. 10.**

1871

Great fire destroyed **Chicago Oct. 8-11.**

1872

Amnesty Act restored civil rights to citizens of the South **May 22** except for 500 Confederate leaders.

Congress established first national park—**Yellowstone.**

1873

First U.S. **postal card** issued **May 1.**

Banks failed, panic began in **Sept.** Depression lasted 5 years.

"Boss" William Tweed of New York City convicted **Nov. 19** of stealing public funds. He died in jail in **1878.**

New York's Bellevue Hospital started **first nursing school.**

1875

Congress passed **Civil Rights Act Mar. 1,** giving equal rights to blacks in public accommodations and jury duty. Act invalidated in **1883** by Supreme Court.

First **Kentucky Derby** held **May 17.**

1876

Samuel J. Tilden, Democrat, received majority of popular votes for president over **Rutherford B. Hayes,** Republican, but 22 electoral votes were in dispute; issue left to Congress. Hayes won the presidency in **Feb. 1877** after Republicans agreed to end Reconstruction of South.

Col. **George A. Custer** and 264 soldiers of the 7th Cavalry killed **June 25** in "last stand," Battle of the Little Big Horn, MT, in Sioux Indian War.

1877

Molly Maguires, Irish terrorist society in Scranton, PA, mining areas, was broken up by the hanging, **June 21,** of 11 leaders for murders of mine officials and police.

Pres. Rutherford B. Hayes sent troops in violent national **railroad strike.**

1878

First commercial **telephone** exchange opened, New Haven, CT, **Jan. 28.**

Thomas A. Edison founded **Edison Electric Light Co.** on **Oct. 15.**

1879

F. W. Woolworth opened his first five-and-ten store, in Utica, NY, **Feb. 22.**

Henry George published *Progress & Poverty,* advocating single tax on land.

1881

Pres. **James A. Garfield shot** in Washington, DC, **July 2;** died **Sept. 19.**

Booker T. Washington founded Tuskegee Institute for blacks.

Helen Hunt Jackson published *A Century of Dishonor,* about mistreatment of Indians.

1883

Pendleton Act passed **Jan. 16,** reformed civil service.

Brooklyn Bridge opened **May 24.**

1884

Mark Twain's masterpiece, *The Adventures of Huckleberry Finn,* appeared.

1886

Haymarket riot and bombing, **May 4,** followed bitter labor battles for 8-hour day in Chicago; 7 police and 4 workers died. Eight anarchists found guilty **Aug. 20,** 4 hanged **Nov. 11.**

Geronimo, Apache Indian, finally surrendered **Sept. 4.**

Statue of Liberty dedicated **Oct. 28.**

American Federation of Labor (AFL) formed **Dec. 8** by 25 craft unions.

1888

Great blizzard struck eastern U.S. **Mar. 11-14,** causing about 400 deaths.

1889

U.S. opened Oklahoma to white settlement **Apr. 22;** within 24 hours **claims for 2 mil acres** were staked by 50,000 settlers.

Johnstown, PA, flood May 31; 2,200 lives lost.

1890

Battle of **Wounded Knee, SD, Dec. 29,** the last major conflict between Indians and U.S. troops. About 200 Indian men, women, and children and 29 soldiers were killed.

Sherman Antitrust Act passed **July 2,** began federal effort to curb monopolies.

Jacob Riis published *How the Other Half Lives,* about city slums.

Poems of **Emily Dickinson** published posthumously.

1891

Forest Reserve Act Mar. 3 let president close public forest land to settlement for establishment of national parks.

1892

Ellis Island, in New York Bay, opened **Jan. 1** to receive immigrants.

Homestead, PA, strike at Carnegie steel mills; 7 guards and 11 strikers and spectators shot to death **July 6.**

1893

Financial panic began, led to 4-year depression.

1894

Thomas A. Edison's kinetoscope (motion pictures) (invented **1887**) given first public showing **Apr. 14.**

The **Pullman strike** began **May 11** at a railroad car plant in Chicago.

Jacob S. Coxey led army of unemployed from the Midwest, reaching Washington, DC, **Apr. 30.** Coxey arrested **May 1** for trespassing on Capitol grounds; his army disbanded.

1896

William Jennings Bryan delivered "Cross of Gold" speech **July 8;** won Democratic Party nomination.

Supreme Court, in **Plessy *v.* Ferguson,** approved racial segregation under the "separate but equal" doctrine.

1898

U.S. **battleship *Maine*** blown up **Feb. 15** at Havana; 260 killed.

U.S. blockaded Cuba Apr. 22 in aid of independence forces. U.S. declared war on Spain, **Apr. 24,** destroyed Spanish fleet in Philippines **May 1,** took Guam **June 20.**

Puerto Rico taken by U.S. **July 25-Aug. 12.** Spain agreed **Dec. 10** to cede Philippines, Puerto Rico, and Guam, and approved independence for Cuba.

Annexation of **Hawaii** signed by Pres. William McKinley, **July 7.**

1899

Filipino insurgents, unable to get recognition of independence from U.S., started guerrilla war **Feb. 4.** Their leader, Emilio Aguinaldo, captured **May 23, 1901.** Philippine Insurrection ended **1902.**

U.S. declared **Open Door Policy** to make China an open international market and to preserve its integrity as a nation.

John Dewey published *The School and Society,* advocating "progressive education."

1900

Carry Nation, Kansas antisaloon agitator, began raiding with hatchet.

U.S. helped suppress **"Boxers"** in Beijing.

International Ladies' Garment Workers Union was founded in New York City **June 3.**

1901

Texas had first significant **oil strike, Jan. 10.**

Pres. **McKinley was shot Sept. 6** in Buffalo, NY, by an anarchist, Leon Czolgosz; died **Sept. 14.**

1903

Treaty between U.S. and Colombia to have U.S. dig **Panama Canal** signed **Jan. 22,** rejected by Colombia. Panama declared independence from Colombia with U.S. support **Nov. 3;** recognized by Pres. Theodore Roosevelt **Nov. 6.** U.S., Panama signed canal treaty **Nov. 18.**

Wisconsin set first **direct primary** voting system **May 23.**

First successful flight in heavier-than-air mechanically propelled airplane by **Orville Wright, Dec. 17** near Kitty Hawk, NC, 120 ft in 12 secs. Fourth flight same day by **Wilbur Wright,** 852 ft in 59 secs. Improved plane patented, **1906.**

Great Train Robbery, pioneering film, produced.

1904

Ida Tarbell published muckraking *The History of the Standard Oil Company.*

1905

First **Rotary Club** founded in Chicago.

1906

San Francisco earthquake and fire **Apr. 18-19** left 503 dead, $350 mil damages.

Pure Food and Drug Act and Meat Inspection Act both passed **June 30.**

1907

Financial panic and depression started **Mar. 13.**

First round-world cruise of U.S. **"Great White Fleet";** 16 battleships, 12,000 men.

1908

Henry Ford introduced **Model T** car, priced at $850, **Oct. 1.**

1909

Adm. Robert E. Peary claimed to have reached **North Pole Apr. 6** on 6th attempt, accompanied by Matthew Henson, a black man, and 4 Eskimos; may have fallen short.

National Conference on the Negro convened **May 30,** leading to founding of National Association for the Advancement of Colored People.

1910

Boy Scouts of America founded **Feb. 8.**

1911

Supreme Court dissolved **Standard Oil Co. May 15.**

Building holding New York City's **Triangle Shirtwaist Co.** factory caught fire **Mar. 25;** 146 died.

First **transcontinental airplane flight** (with numerous stops) by C. P. Rodgers, New York to Pasadena, CA, **Sept. 17-Nov. 5;** time in air 82 hr, 4 min.

1912

American Girl Guides founded **Mar. 12;** name changed in **1913** to **Girl Scouts.**

U.S. sent Marines **Aug. 14** to **Nicaragua,** which was in default of loans to U.S. and Europe.

1913

NY Armory Show brought modern art to U.S. **Feb. 17.**

U.S. blockaded Mexico in support of revolutionaries.

Charles Beard published his *Economic Interpretation of the Constitution.*

Federal Reserve System was authorized **Dec. 23,** in a major reform of U.S. banking and finance.

1914

Ford Motor Co. raised basic wage rates from $2.40 for 9-hr day to $5 for 8-hr day **Jan. 5.**

When U.S. sailors were arrested at Tampico, Mexico, **Apr. 9,** Atlantic fleet was sent to **Veracruz,** occupied city.

Pres. Woodrow Wilson proclaimed **U.S. neutrality** in the European war **Aug. 4.**

Panama Canal was officially opened **Aug. 15.**

The **Clayton Antitrust Act** was passed **Oct. 15,** strengthening federal antimonopoly powers.

1915

First transcontinental **telephone call,** New York to San Francisco, completed **Jan. 25,** by Alexander Graham Bell and Thomas A. Watson.

British ship ***Lusitania*** sunk **May 7** by German submarine; 128 American passengers lost (Germany had warned passengers in advance). As a result of U.S. campaign, Germany issued apology and promise of payments **Oct. 5.** Pres. Wilson asked for a military fund increase **Dec. 7.**

U.S. troops landed in **Haiti July 28.** Haiti became a virtual U.S. protectorate under **Sept. 16** treaty.

1916

Gen. John J. **Pershing entered Mexico** to pursue Francisco (Pancho) Villa, who had raided U.S. border areas. Forces withdrawn **Feb. 5, 1917.**

Rural Credits Act passed **July 17,** followed by Warehouse Act **Aug. 11;** both provided financial aid to farmers.

Bomb exploded during **San Francisco** Preparedness Day parade **July 22,** killed 10. Thomas J. Mooney, labor organizer, and Warren K. Billings, shoe worker, were convicted **1917;** both later pardoned.

U.S. bought **Virgin Islands** from Denmark **Aug. 4.**

Jeannette Rankin (R, MT) elected as **first-ever female** member of U.S. **House.**

U.S. established military government in the **Dominican Republic Nov. 29.**

Trade and loans to **European allies** soared during the year.

1917

Germany, suffering from British blockade, declared almost unrestricted **submarine warfare Jan. 31.** U.S. cut diplomatic ties with Germany **Feb. 3,** and formally declared war **Apr. 6.**

Conscription law was passed **May 18.** First U.S. troops arrived in Europe **June 26.**

18th **(Prohibition)** Amendment to the Constitution was submitted to the states by Congress **Dec. 18.** On **Jan. 16, 1919,** the 36th state (Nevada) ratified it.

1918

Pres. Wilson set out his **14 Points** as basis for peace **Jan. 8.**

More than 1 mil **American troops** were in Europe by **July.** Allied counteroffensive launched at Château-Thierry **July 18.** War ended with signing of armistice **Nov. 11.**

Influenza epidemic killed an estimated 20 mil worldwide, 548,000 in U.S.

1919

First **transatlantic flight,** by U.S. Navy seaplane, left Rockaway, NY, **May 8,** stopped at Newfoundland, Azores, Lisbon **May 27.**

Boston police strike Sept. 9; National Guard breaks strike.

Sherwood Anderson published *Winesburg, Ohio.*

About 250 **alien radicals** were deported **Dec. 22.**

1920

In national **Red Scare,** some 2,700 Communists, anarchists, and other radicals were arrested **Jan.-May.**

Senate refused **Mar. 19** to ratify the **League of Nations Covenant.**

Radicals Nicola **Sacco** and Bartolomeo **Vanzetti** accused of killing 2 men in Massachusetts payroll holdup **Apr. 15.** Found guilty **1921.** A 6-year campaign for their release failed, and both were executed **Aug. 23, 1927.** Verdict repudiated **1977,** by proclamation of Massachusetts Gov. Michael Dukakis.

First regular licensed **radio broadcasting** begun **Aug. 20.**

19th Amendment ratified **Aug. 18,** giving women the vote.

League of Women Voters founded.

Wall St., New York City, **bomb** explosion killed 30, injured 100, did $2 mil damage **Sept. 16.**

Sinclair Lewis's *Main Street,* **F. Scott Fitzgerald's** *This Side of Paradise* published.

1921

Congress sharply curbed **immigration,** set national quota system **May 19.**

Joint congressional resolution declaring **peace with Germany, Austria,** and **Hungary** signed **July 2** by Pres. Warren G. Harding; treaties were signed in **Aug.**

Limitation of Armaments Conference met in Washington, DC, **Nov. 12-Feb. 6, 1922.** Major powers agreed to curtail naval construction, outlaw poison gas, restrict submarine attacks on merchant vessels, respect integrity of China.

Ku Klux Klan began revival with violence against Catholics in North, South, and Midwest.

1922

Violence during **coal-mine strike** at Herrin, IL, **June 22-23** cost 36 lives, including those of 21 nonunion miners.

Reader's Digest founded.

1923

First **sound-on-film motion picture,** *Phonofilm,* shown at Rivoli Theater, New York City, beginning in **April.**

IT'S A FACT: Between 1854 and 1929, more than 100,000 poor, homeless urban children were sent on so-called orphan trains to live with new families in rural America, where there was a growing need for farm labor.

1924

Law approved by Congress **June 15** making all **Indians citizens.**

Nellie Tayloe Ross elected governor of Wyoming **Nov. 9** as nation's first woman governor. **Miriam (Ma) Ferguson** elected governor of Texas **Nov. 9; installed Jan. 20, 1925.**

George Gershwin wrote *Rhapsody in Blue.*

1925

John T. Scopes found guilty of having taught **evolution** in Dayton, TN, high school, fined $100 and costs **July 24.**

1926

Dr. Robert H. Goddard demonstrated practicality of **rockets Mar. 16** at Auburn, MA, with first liquid-fuel rocket; rocket traveled 184 ft in 2.5 sec.

Congress established **Army Air Corps July 2.**

Air Commerce Act passed **Nov. 2,** providing federal aid for airlines and airports.

Ernest Hemingway's *The Sun Also Rises* published.

1927

About 1,000 **marines landed in China Mar. 5** to protect property in civil war.

Capt. **Charles A. Lindbergh** left Roosevelt Field, NY, **May 20** alone in plane *Spirit of St. Louis* on first New York-Paris nonstop flight. Reached Le Bourget airfield **May 21,** 3,610 mi in 33½ hours.

The Jazz Singer, with **Al Jolson,** demonstrated part-talking pictures in New York City **Oct. 6.**

Show Boat opened in New York **Dec. 27.**

O. E. Rolvaag published *Giants in the Earth.*

1928

Herbert Hoover elected president, defeating New York Gov. **Alfred E. Smith,** a Catholic.

Amelia Earhart became first woman to fly the Atlantic, **June 17.**

1929

"St. Valentine's Day massacre" in Chicago **Feb. 14;** gangsters killed 7 rivals.

Farm price stability aided by **Agricultural Marketing Act,** passed **June 15.**

Albert B. Fall, former secretary of the interior, was convicted of accepting bribe of $100,000 in the leasing of the **Elk Hills (Teapot Dome)** naval oil reserve; sentenced **Nov. 1** to a year in prison and fined $100,000.

Stock market crash Oct. 29 marked end of past prosperity as stock prices plummeted. Stock losses for 1929-31 estimated at $50 bil; worst American depression began.

Thomas Wolfe published *Look Homeward, Angel.* **William Faulkner** published *The Sound and the Fury.*

1930

London **Naval Reduction Treaty** signed by U.S., Britain, Italy, France, and Japan **Apr. 22;** in effect **Jan. 1, 1931;** expired **Dec. 31, 1936.**

Hawley-Smoot Tariff signed; rate hikes slash world trade.

1931

Empire State Building opened in New York City **May 1.**

Al Capone was convicted of tax evasion **Oct. 17.**

1932

Reconstruction Finance Corp. established **Jan. 22** to stimulate banking and business. Unemployment at 12 mil.

19-month-old **Charles Lindbergh Jr. was kidnapped Mar. 1;** found dead **May 12.** Bruno Hauptmann found guilty in trial **Jan.-Feb. 1935;** executed **Apr. 3, 1936.**

Bonus March on Washington, DC, launched **May 29** by World War I veterans demanding Congress pay their bonus in full.

Franklin D. Roosevelt elected president for the first time.

1933

Pres. Roosevelt named **Frances Perkins** U.S. secretary of labor; first woman in U.S. cabinet.

All **banks in the U.S. were ordered closed** by Pres. Roosevelt **Mar. 6.**

In a "100 days" special session, **Mar. 9-June 16,** Congress passed **New Deal** social and economic measures, including measures to regulate banks, distribute funds to the jobless, create jobs, raise agricultural prices, and set wage and production standards for industry.

Tennessee Valley Authority created by act of Congress, **May 18.**

Gold standard dropped by U.S.; announced by Pres. Roosevelt **Apr. 19,** ratified by Congress **June 5.**

Prohibition ended in the U.S. as 36th state ratified 21st Amendment **Dec. 5.**

U.S. foreswore armed intervention in **western hemisphere** nations **Dec. 26.**

1934

U.S. troops pulled out of **Haiti Aug. 6.**

1935

Works Progress Administration **(WPA)** instituted **May 6.** Rural Electrification Administration created **May 11.** National Industrial Recovery Act struck down by Supreme Court **May 27.**

Comedian **Will Rogers** and aviator **Wiley Post killed Aug. 15** in Alaska plane crash.

Social Security Act passed by Congress **Aug. 14.**

Huey Long, senator from Louisiana and national political leader, **assassinated Sept. 8.**

Porgy and Bess opened **Oct. 10** in New York.

Committee for Industrial Organization (CIO; later Congress of Industrial Organizations) formed to expand industrial unionism **Nov. 9.**

1936

Boulder Dam completed.

Margaret Mitchell published *Gone With the Wind.*

1937

Joe Louis knocked out James J. Braddock, became world heavyweight champ **June 22.**

Amelia Earhart, aviator, and copilot Fred Noonan lost **July 2** near Howland Island, in the Pacific.

Pres. Roosevelt asked for 6 additional Supreme Court justices; **"packing" plan** defeated.

1938

Naval Expansion Act passed **May 17.**

National minimum wage enacted **June 25.**

Orson Welles radio dramatization of **Martian invasion,** *War of the Worlds,* caused nationwide scare **Oct. 30.**

1939

Pres. Roosevelt asked for **defense budget hike Jan. 5, 12.**

New York World's Fair opened **Apr. 30,** closed **Oct. 31;** reopened **May 11, 1940,** and finally closed **Oct. 21.**

Albert Einstein alerted Pres. Roosevelt to **A-bomb** opportunity in **Aug. 2** letter.

U.S. declared its neutrality in European war **Sept. 5.**

Roosevelt proclaimed a limited **national emergency Sept. 8,** an unlimited emergency **May 27, 1941.** Both ended by Pres. Harry Truman **Apr. 28, 1952.**

John Steinbeck published *Grapes of Wrath.*

Gone With the Wind and *The Wizard of Oz* films released.

1940

U.S. okayed sale of **surplus war materiel** to Britain **June 3;** announced transfer of 50 overaged destroyers **Sept. 3.**

First **peacetime draft** approved **Sept. 14.**

Richard Wright published *Native Son.*

1941

Four Freedoms termed essential by Pres. Roosevelt in speech to Congress **Jan. 6:** freedom of speech and religion, freedom from want and fear.

Lend-Lease Act signed **Mar. 11** provided $7 bil in military credits for Britain. Lend-Lease for USSR approved in **Nov.**

U.S. occupied **Iceland July 7.**

The **Atlantic Charter,** 8-point declaration of principles, issued by Roosevelt and British Prime Min. Winston Churchill **Aug. 14.**

Japan attacked **Pearl Harbor,** Hawaii, 7:55 AM Hawaiian time, **Dec. 7;** 19 ships sunk or damaged, 2,300 dead. U.S. declared war on Japan **Dec. 8,** on Germany and Italy **Dec. 11.**

1942

Japanese troops took Bataan peninsula **Apr. 8,** Corregidor **May 6.**

Federal government forcibly moved 110,000 **Japanese-Americans** from West Coast to detention camps. Exclusion lasted 3 years.

Battle of **Midway June 4-7** was Japan's first major defeat.

Marines landed on **Guadalcanal Aug. 7;** last Japanese not expelled until **Feb. 9, 1943.**

U.S., Britain invaded North Africa **Nov. 8.**

1943

Oklahoma! opened **Mar. 31** on Broadway.

War contractors barred from **racial discrimination, May 27.**

Pres. Roosevelt signed **June 10** pay-as-you-go income tax bill. Starting **July 1** wage and salary earners were subject to a **paycheck withholding** tax.

Pearl Buck published *The Good Earth.*

Auto, steel labor unions won first big contracts.

First **nuclear chain reaction** (fission of uranium isotope U-235) produced at University of Chicago, under physicists Arthur Compton, Enrico Fermi, others **Dec. 2.**

Race riot in Detroit June 21; 34 dead, 700 injured. Riot in Harlem section of New York City; 6 killed.

U.S., Britain invaded **Sicily July 9,** Italian **mainland Sept. 3.**

Marines recaptured the **Gilbert Islands,** captured by Japan in 1941 and 1942, in Nov.

1944

U.S., Allied forces invaded Europe at **Normandy June 6** in greatest amphibious landing in history.

GI Bill of Rights signed **June 22,** providing benefits for veterans.

U.S. forces landed on **Leyte,** Philippines, **Oct. 20.**

1945

Yalta Conference met in the Crimea, USSR, **Feb. 4-11.** Roosevelt, Churchill, and Soviet leader Joseph Stalin agreed that their 3 countries, plus France, would occupy Germany and that the Soviet Union would enter war against Japan.

Marines landed on **Iwo Jima Feb. 19,** won control of Iwo Jima **Mar. 16** after heavy casualties. U.S. forces invaded **Okinawa Apr. 1,** captured Okinawa **June 21.**

Pres. Roosevelt, 63, died in Warm Springs, GA, **Apr. 12;** Vice Pres. **Harry S. Truman** became president.

Germany surrendered May 7; May 8 proclaimed V-E Day.

First **atomic bomb,** produced at Los Alamos, NM, exploded at Alamogordo, NM, **July 16.** Bomb dropped on **Hiroshima Aug. 6,** with about 75,000 people killed; bomb dropped on **Nagasaki Aug. 9,** killing about 40,000. Japan agreed to surrender, **Aug. 14;** formally surrendered **Sept. 2.**

At **Potsdam Conference, July 17-Aug. 2,** leaders of U.S., USSR, and Britain agreed on disarmament of Germany, occupation zones, war crimes trials.

U.S. forces entered **Korea** south of 38th parallel to displace Japanese **Sept. 8.**

Gen. Douglas MacArthur took over supervision of Japan **Sept. 9.**

1946

Strike by 400,000 **mine workers** began **Apr. 1;** other industries followed.

Philippines given independence by U.S. **July 4.**

1947

Pres. Truman asked Congress to aid Greece and Turkey to combat Communist terrorism (**Truman Doctrine**), **Mar. 12.** Approved **May 15.**

UN Security Council voted **Apr. 2** to place under **U.S. trusteeship** the Pacific islands formerly mandated to Japan.

Jackie Robinson joined the Brooklyn Dodgers **Apr. 11,** breaking the color barrier in major league baseball.

Taft-Hartley Labor Act curbing strikes was vetoed by Truman **June 20;** Congress overrode the veto.

The **Marshall Plan,** for U.S. aid to European countries, was proposed by Sec. of State George C. Marshall **June 5.** Congress authorized some $12 bil in next 4 years.

1948

USSR halted all surface traffic into W. Berlin, **June 23;** in response, U.S. and British troops launched an airlift. Soviet blockade halted **May 12, 1949;** airlift ended **Sept. 30.**

Organization of American States founded **Apr. 30.**

Alger Hiss indicted **Dec. 15** for perjury, after denying he had passed secret documents to Whittaker Chambers for transmission to a Communist spy ring. Convicted **Jan. 21, 1950.**

Pres. Truman elected Nov. 2, defeating Gov. Thomas E. Dewey in a historic upset.

Kinsey Report on sexuality in the human male published.

1949

NATO established **Aug. 24** by U.S., Canada, and 10 Western European nations, agreeing that an armed attack against one or more would be considered an attack against all.

Mrs. I. Toguri D'Aquino (**Tokyo Rose** of Japanese wartime broadcasts) was sentenced **Oct. 7** to 10 years in prison for treason. Paroled **1956,** pardoned **1977.**

Eleven leaders of **U.S. Communist Party** convicted **Oct. 14** of advocating violent overthrow of U.S. government; sentenced to prison. Supreme Court upheld convictions **1951.**

1950

Masked bandits robbed **Brink's, Inc.,** Boston express office, **Jan. 17** of $2.8 mil. Case solved **1956;** 8 sentenced to life.

Pres. Truman authorized production of the **H-bomb Jan. 31.**

North Korea forces invaded **South Korea June 25.** UN asked for troops to restore peace.

Truman ordered Air Force and Navy to Korea **June 27.** Truman approved ground forces, air strikes against North Korea **June 30.**

U.S. sent 35 military advisers to **South Vietnam June 27,** and agreed to aid anti-Communist government.

Army seized all railroads Aug. 27 on Truman's order to prevent a general strike; returned to owners in **1952.**

U.S. forces landed at Inchon Sept. 15; UN force took Pyongyang **Oct. 20,** reached China border **Nov. 20;** China sent troops across border **Nov. 26.**

Two members of **Puerto Rican nationalist** movement tried to kill Pres. Truman **Nov. 1.**

U.S. **Dec. 8** banned shipments to **Communist China** and to Asiatic ports trading with it.

1951

Sen. Estes Kefauver led Senate probe into organized crime.

Julius Rosenberg, his wife, **Ethel**, and Morton Sobell found guilty **Mar. 29** of conspiracy to commit wartime **espionage**. Rosenbergs executed **June 19, 1953.** Sobell sentenced to 30 years; released **1969.**

Gen. Douglas MacArthur removed from Korea command **Apr. 11** by Pres. Truman, for unauthorized policy statements.

Korea cease-fire talks began in July; lasted 2 years. **Fighting ended July 27, 1953.**

Tariff concessions by the U.S. to the Soviet Union, Communist China, and all Communist-dominated lands were suspended **Aug. 1.**

The **U.S., Australia,** and **New Zealand** signed a mutual security pact **Sept. 1.**

Transcontinental TV begun **Sept. 4** with Pres. Truman's address at Japanese Peace Treaty Conference in San Francisco.

Japanese peace treaty signed in San Francisco **Sept. 8** by U.S., Japan, and 47 other nations.

J. D. Salinger published *Catcher in the Rye.*

1952

U.S. **seizure of nation's steel mills** was ordered by Pres. Truman **Apr. 8** to avert a strike. Ruled illegal by Supreme Court **June 2.**

Peace contract between West Germany, U.S., Great Britain, and France was signed **May 26.**

The last racial and ethnic barriers to naturalization removed, **June 26-27,** with passage of **Immigration and Naturalization Act of 1952.**

First **hydrogen device** explosion **Nov. 1** in Pacific.

1953

Pres. Dwight D. Eisenhower announced **May 8** that U.S. had given France $60 mil for **Indochina War.** More aid was announced in **Sept.**

Korean War armistice signed **July 27.**

1954

Nautilus, first atomic-powered submarine, was launched at Groton, CT, **Jan. 21.**

Five members of Congress were **wounded** in the House **Mar. 1** by 4 **Puerto Rican independence supporters** who fired at random from a spectators' gallery.

Sen. Joseph McCarthy (R, WI) led televised hearings **Apr. 22-June 17** into alleged Communist influence in the Army.

Racial segregation in public schools unanimously ruled unconstitutional by Supreme Court **May 17,** in *Brown* v. *Board of Education of Topeka.*

Southeast Asia Treaty Organization (**SEATO**) formed by defense pact signed in Manila **Sept. 8** by U.S., Britain, France, Australia, New Zealand, Philippines, Pakistan, and Thailand.

Condemnation of **Sen. McCarthy** voted by Senate, 67-22, **Dec. 2** for contempt of Senate subcommittee, abuse of its members, insults to Senate during Army investigation hearings.

IT'S A FACT: In 1957, Massachusetts formally apologized for its role in the Salem witch trials. In 1692, William Phipps, governor of Massachusetts Bay Colony, commissioned a special court to examine persons accused of witchcraft in Salem. The court hanged 19 people and pressed a 20th to death with stones.

1955

U.S. agreed **Feb. 12** to help train **South Vietnamese** army.

Supreme Court ordered **"all deliberate speed"** in integration of public schools **May 31.**

A **summit meeting** of leaders of U.S., Britain, France, and USSR took place **July 18-23** in Geneva, Switzerland.

Rosa Parks refused **Dec. 1** to give her seat to a white man on a **bus in Montgomery, AL.** Bus segregation ordinance declared unconstitutional by a federal court following boycott and NAACP protest.

America's 2 largest labor organizations merged **Dec. 5,** creating the **AFL-CIO**.

1956

Massive resistance to Supreme Court desegregation rulings was called for **Mar. 12** by 101 Southern congressmen.

Federal-Aid **Highway Act** signed **June 29,** inaugurating interstate highway system.

First transatlantic **telephone cable** activated **Sept. 25.**

1957

Congress approved first **civil rights bill** for blacks since Reconstruction, **Apr. 29,** to protect voting rights.

National Guardsmen, called out by Arkansas Gov. Orval Faubus **Sept. 4,** barred 9 black students from entering all-white high school in **Little Rock.** Faubus complied **Sept. 21** with federal court order to remove Guardsmen, but the blacks were ordered to withdraw by local authorities. Pres. Eisenhower sent federal troops **Sept. 24** to enforce court order.

Jack Kerouac published *On the Road.*

1958

First U.S. **earth satellite** to go into orbit, **Explorer I,** launched by Army **Jan. 31** at Cape Canaveral, FL; discovered Van Allen radiation belt.

U.S. Marines sent to **Lebanon** to protect elected government from threatened overthrow **July-Oct.**

First domestic **jet airline** passenger service in U.S. opened by National Airlines **Dec. 10** between New York and Miami.

1959

Alaska admitted as 49th state **Jan. 3; Hawaii** admitted as 50th **Aug. 21.**

St. Lawrence Seaway opened **Apr. 25.**

Soviet **Premier Nikita Khrushchev** paid unprecedented visit to U.S. **Sept. 15-27;** made transcontinental tour.

1960

Sit-ins began **Feb. 1** when 4 black college students in Greensboro, NC, refused to move from a Woolworth lunch counter when denied service. By **Sept. 1961** more than 70,000 students, whites and blacks, had participated in sit-ins.

Congress approved a strong **voting rights act Apr. 21.**

A U.S. **U-2 reconnaissance plane** was shot down in the Soviet Union **May 1**; pilot Gary Powers captured. The incident led to cancellation of an imminent Paris summit conference.

Vice Pres. Richard Nixon and Sen. John F. Kennedy faced each other, **Sept. 26,** in the first in a series of televised **debates. Kennedy defeated Nixon** to win presidency, **Nov. 8.**

U.S. announced **Dec. 15** it backed rightist group in **Laos,** which took power the next day.

1961

U.S. severed diplomatic and consular relations with **Cuba Jan. 3,** after disputes over nationalizations of U.S. firms, U.S. military presence at Guantanamo base.

Invasion of Cuba's **"Bay of Pigs" Apr. 17** by Cuban exiles trained, armed, and directed by U.S. attempted to overthrow the regime of Premier Fidel Castro, unsuccessfully.

Peace Corps created by executive order, **Mar. 1.**

Commander Alan B. Shepard Jr. was rocketed from Cape Canaveral, FL, 116.5 mi above the earth in a Mercury capsule **May 5,** in first U.S.-crewed suborbital space flight.

"Freedom Rides" from Washington, DC, across deep South were launched **May 20** to **protest segregation** in interstate transportation.

1962

Lt. Col. John H. Glenn Jr. became first American in orbit **Feb. 20** when he circled the earth 3 times in the Mercury capsule ***Friendship 7***.

Pres. John F. Kennedy said **Feb. 14** U.S. military advisers in Vietnam would fire if fired upon.

Supreme Court **Mar. 26** backed **"one-man one-vote"** apportionment of seats in state legislatures.

James Meredith became first black student at University of Mississippi **Oct. 1** after 3,000 troops put down riots.

A Soviet **offensive missile buildup in Cuba** was revealed **Oct. 22** by Pres. Kennedy, who ordered a naval and air quarantine on shipment of offensive military equipment to the island. He and Soviet Premier Khrushchev agreed **Oct. 28** on a formula to end the crisis. Kennedy announced **Nov. 2** that Soviet missile bases in Cuba were being dismantled.

Rachel Carson's *Silent Spring* launched environmentalist movement.

1963

Supreme Court ruled **Mar. 18** that all **criminal defendants** must have counsel and that illegally acquired evidence was inadmissible in state as well as federal courts.

University of Alabama **desegregated** after Gov. **George Wallace** stepped aside when confronted by federally deployed National Guard troops, **June 11.**

Civil rights leader **Medgar Evers** was assassinated **June 12.**

Supreme Court ruled, 8-1, **June 17** that laws requiring **recitation of the Lord's Prayer** or Bible verses in public schools were unconstitutional.

President **Kennedy**, on Europe trip, addressed huge crowd in **West Berlin, June 23.**

A limited **nuclear test-ban treaty** was agreed upon **July 25** by the U.S., the Soviet Union, and Britain.

Birmingham, AL, rocked in Apr. and May by civil rights **demonstrations**, led by **Rev. Martin Luther King Jr.;** 200,000 joined in.

March on Washington Aug. 28 in support of **black demands** for equal rights. Highlight was "I have a dream" speech by **Dr. King.**

Baptist church in Birmingham, AL, bombed **Sept. 15** in racial violence, 4 black girls killed.

South Vietnam Pres. **Ngo Dinh Diem assassinated Nov. 2;** U.S. had earlier withdrawn support.

Pres. Kennedy shot and fatally wounded Nov. 22 as he rode in a motorcade through downtown Dallas, TX. Vice Pres. **Lyndon B. Johnson sworn in** as president. **Lee Harvey Oswald arrested** and charged with the murder; he was shot and fatally wounded **Nov. 24. Jack Ruby,** a nightclub owner, was convicted of Oswald's murder; he died in **1967,** while awaiting retrial following reversal of his conviction.

Betty Friedan's *Feminine Mystique* was published.

1964

Panama suspended relations with U.S. **Jan. 9** after riots. U.S. offered **Dec. 18** to negotiate a new canal treaty.

Supreme Court ordered **Feb. 17** that **congressional districts** have equal populations.

U.S. reported **May 27** it was sending military planes to **Laos.**

Omnibus **civil rights bill** cleared by Congress **July 2,** signed same day by Pres. Johnson, banning discrimination in voting, jobs, public accommodations.

Three **civil rights workers** were reported missing in Mississippi **June 22;** found buried **Aug. 4.** Twenty-one white men were arrested. On **Oct. 20, 1967,** an all-white federal jury convicted 7 of conspiracy in the slayings.

Bill establishing **Medicare,** government health insurance program for persons over 65, signed **July 30.**

U.S. Congress **Aug. 7** passed the **Tonkin Gulf Resolution,** authorizing presidential action in Vietnam, after N Vietnamese boats reportedly attacked 2 U.S. destroyers **Aug. 2.**

Congress approved **War on Poverty** bill **Aug. 11,** providing for a domestic Peace Corps **(VISTA)**, a **Job Corps,** and antipoverty funding.

The **Warren Commission** released **Sept. 27** a report concluding that Lee Harvey Oswald was solely responsible for the Kennedy assassination.

Pres. Johnson was elected to a full term, **Nov. 3,** defeating Republican **Sen. Barry Goldwater** (AZ) in a landslide.

1965

Pres. Johnson in **Feb.** ordered continuous **bombing of North Vietnam** below 20th parallel.

Malcolm X assassinated **Feb. 21** at New York City rally.

Some 14,000 U.S. troops sent to **Dominican Republic** during civil war **Apr. 28.** All troops withdrawn by next year.

March from Selma to Montgomery, AL, **begun Mar. 21** by Rev. Martin Luther King Jr. to demand federal protection of **blacks' voting rights.** New **Voting Rights Act** signed **Aug. 6.**

Los Angeles riot by blacks living in **Watts** area resulted in 34 deaths and $200 mil in property damage **Aug. 11-16.**

National **immigration** quota system abolished **Oct. 3.**

Electric power failure blacked out most of northeastern U.S., parts of 2 Canadian provinces the night of **Nov. 9-10.**

1966

U.S. forces began firing into **Cambodia May 1.**

Bombing of Hanoi area of N Vietnam by U.S. planes began **June 29.** By **Dec. 31,** 385,300 U.S. troops were stationed in S Vietnam, plus 60,000 offshore and 33,000 in Thailand.

Medicare began **July 1.**

Edward Brooke (R, MA) elected **Nov. 8** as first black U.S. senator in 85 years.

1967

Black U.S. Rep. **Adam Clayton Powell** (D, NY) was denied his seat **Mar. 1** because of charges he misused government funds. Reelected in **1968,** he was seated, but fined $25,000 and stripped of his seniority.

Pres. Johnson and Soviet Premier Aleksei Kosygin met **June 23 and 25** at **Glassboro State College** in NJ; agreed not to let any crisis push them into war.

The **25th Amendment,** providing for **presidential succession,** was ratified **Feb. 10.**

USS *Liberty,* an intelligence ship, was torpedoed by Israel in the Mediterranean, apparently by accident **June 8;** 34 killed.

Riots by blacks in **Newark, NJ, July 12-17** killed 26, injured 1,500; more than 1,000 arrested. In **Detroit, MI, July 23-30,** 43 died; 2,000 injured, 5,000 left homeless by rioting, looting, burning in city's black ghetto.

An **antiwar march** on Washington, **Oct. 21-22,** drew 50,000 participants.

Thurgood Marshall was sworn in **Oct. 2** as first black U.S. Supreme Court Justice. **Carl B. Stokes** (D, Cleveland) and **Richard G. Hatcher** (D, Gary, IN) were elected first black mayors of major U.S. cities **Nov. 7.**

1968

USS *Pueblo* and 83-man crew seized in Sea of Japan **Jan. 23** by North Koreans; 82 men released **Dec. 22.**

"Tet offensive": Communist troops attacked Saigon, 30 province capitals **Jan. 30,** suffered heavy casualties.

Pres. Johnson **curbed bombing** of North Vietnam **Mar. 31.** Peace talks began in Paris **May 10.** All bombing of North halted **Oct. 31.**

Martin Luther King Jr., 39, assassinated Apr. 4 in Memphis, TN. **James Earl Ray,** an escaped convict, pleaded guilty to the slaying, was sentenced to 99 years.

Sen. Robert F. Kennedy (D, NY), 42, **shot June 5** in Hotel Ambassador, Los Angeles, after celebrating presidential primary victories. Died **June 6.** Sirhan Bishara Sirhan, convicted of murder, **1969;** death sentence commuted to life in prison, **1972.**

Vice Pres. **Hubert Humphrey nominated** for president by Democrats **at national convention in Chicago,** marked by clash between police and **antiwar protesters, Aug. 26-29.**

The Republican nominee, **Richard Nixon, won** the **presidency,** defeating Hubert Humphrey in a close race **Nov. 5.**

Rep. Shirley Chisholm (D, NY) became the first black woman elected to Congress.

1969

Expanded 4-party **Vietnam peace talks** began **Jan. 18.** U.S. force peaked at 543,400 in April. Withdrawal started **July 8.** Pres. Nixon set Vietnamization policy **Nov. 3.**

U.S. astronaut **Neil Armstrong,** commander of the *Apollo 11* mission, became the first person to **set foot on the moon, July 20;** followed by astronaut **Edwin Aldrin;** astronaut **Michael Collins** remained aboard command module.

Woodstock music festival near Bethel, NY, drew 300,000-500,000 people, **Aug. 15-18.**

Anti-Vietnam War **demonstrations peaked** in U.S.; some 250,000 marched in Washington, DC, **Nov. 15.**

Massacre of hundreds of civilians at **My Lai, South Vietnam,** in 1968 incident reported **Nov. 16.**

1970

United Mine Workers official **Joseph A. Yablonski,** his wife, and their daughter found shot to death **Jan. 5;** UMW chief W. A. (Tony) Boyle later convicted of the killing.

A federal jury **Feb. 18** found the **"Chicago 7"** antiwar activists innocent of conspiring to incite riots during the 1968 **Democratic National Convention.** However, 5 were convicted of crossing state lines with intent to incite riots.

Millions of Americans participated in antipollution demonstrations **Apr. 22** to mark the **first Earth Day.**

U.S. and South Vietnamese forces crossed **Cambodian** borders **Apr. 30** to get at enemy bases. Four students were killed **May 4** at **Kent State** University in Ohio by National Guardsmen during a protest against the war.

Two **women generals,** the first in U.S. history, were named by Pres. Nixon **May 15.**

A **postal reform** measure was signed **Aug. 12,** creating an independent U.S. Postal Service.

1971

Charles Manson and 3 of his cult followers were found guilty **Jan. 25** of first-degree murder in **1969** slaying of actress Sharon Tate and 6 others.

The 26th Amendment, lowering the **voting age to 18** in all elections, was ratified **June 30.**

A court-martial jury **Mar. 29** convicted **Lt. William L. Calley Jr.** of premeditated murder of 22 South Vietnamese at My Lai on **Mar. 16, 1968.** He was sentenced to life imprisonment **Mar. 31.** Sentence was reduced to 20 years **Aug. 20.**

Publication of classified **Pentagon papers** on U.S. involvement in Vietnam was begun **June 13** by the *New York Times*. In a 6-3 vote, U.S. Supreme Court **June 30** upheld the right of the *Times* and the *Washington Post* to publish the documents.

U.S. bombers struck massively in North Vietnam for 5 days starting **Dec. 26** in retaliation for alleged violations of agreements reached prior to the 1968 bombing halt.

1972

Pres. Nixon arrived in **Beijing Feb. 21** for an 8-day visit to China, in what he called a "journey for peace."

By a vote of 84 to 8, the Senate, **Mar. 22,** approved banning **discrimination** on the basis of sex, and sent the measure to the states for ratification.

North Vietnamese forces launched the biggest attacks in 4 years across the demilitarized zone **Mar. 30.** The U.S. responded **Apr. 15** by resumption of bombing of Hanoi and Haiphong after a 4-year lull.

Pres. Nixon announced **May 8** the mining of **North Vietnam ports.** Last U.S. combat troops left **Aug. 11.**

Gov. George C. Wallace (AL), campaigning for the presidency at a Laurel, MD, shopping center **May 15, was shot** and seriously wounded. Arthur H. Bremer **convicted Aug. 4,** sentenced to 63 years for shooting Wallace and 3 bystanders.

In **first visit of a U.S. president to Moscow,** Pres. Nixon arrived **May 22** for a week of summit talks with Kremlin leaders that culminated in a landmark **strategic arms pact.**

Five men were arrested **June 17** for breaking into the offices of the Democratic National Committee in the **Watergate** office complex in Washington, DC.

Pres. **Nixon** was **reelected Nov. 7** in a landslide, carrying 49 states to defeat Democratic Sen. George McGovern (SD); he won 61% of the popular vote.

The **Dow Jones** Industrial Average closed above 1,000 for the first time, **Nov. 14.**

Full-scale **bombing of North Vietnam** resumed after Paris peace negotiations reached an impasse **Dec. 18.**

1973

Five of 7 defendants in **Watergate** break-in trial pleaded guilty **Jan. 11 and 15;** the other 2 were convicted **Jan. 30.**

In ***Roe* v. *Wade,*** Supreme Court ruled, 7-2, **Jan. 22,** that states may not ban **abortions** during **first 3 months of pregnancy** and may regulate, but may not ban, abortions during 2nd trimester.

Four-party **Vietnam peace pacts** were signed in Paris **Jan. 27,** and North Vietnam released some 590 U.S. prisoners by **Apr. 1.** Last U.S. troops left **Mar. 29.**

End of the military **draft** announced **Jan. 27.**

Top **Nixon aides** H. R. Haldeman, John D. Ehrlichman, and John Dean and Attorney Gen. Richard Kleindienst **resigned Apr. 30,** amid charges of White House efforts to obstruct justice in the Watergate case.

John Dean, former Nixon counsel, told Senate hearings **June 25** that Nixon, his staff and campaign aides, and the Justice Department had conspired to cover up Watergate facts.

The U.S. officially ceased bombing in **Cambodia** at midnight **Aug. 14** in accord with a June congressional action.

Vice Pres. Spiro T. Agnew Oct. 10 resigned and pleaded no contest to a charge of tax evasion on payments made to him by contractors when he was governor of Maryland. **Gerald R. Ford Oct. 12** became **first appointed vice president** under the 25th Amendment; sworn in **Dec. 6.**

A total ban on **oil exports** to the U.S. was imposed by Arab oil-producing nations **Oct. 19-21** after the outbreak of an Arab-Israeli war. The ban was lifted **Mar. 18, 1974.**

Attorney Gen. Elliot Richardson resigned, and his deputy William D. Ruckelshaus and **Watergate Special Prosecutor Archibald Cox** were **fired** by Pres. Nixon **Oct. 20,** when Cox threatened to secure a judicial ruling that Nixon was violating a court order to give tapes to Judge John Sirica. **Leon Jaworski** named **Nov. 1** by the Nixon administration to succeed Cox.

Congress overrode **Nov. 7** Pres. Nixon's veto of the **war powers** bill, which curbed president's power to commit armed forces to hostilities abroad without congressional approval.

1974

Impeachment hearings opened **May 9** against Pres. Nixon by the House Judiciary Committee.

John D. Ehrlichman and 3 **White House "plumbers"** found guilty **July 12** of conspiring to violate the civil rights of Pentagon Papers leaker Daniel Ellsberg's psychiatrist by breaking into his office.

U.S. Supreme Court ruled, 8-0, **July 24** that Nixon had to turn over **64 tapes** of White House conversations.

House Judiciary Committee, in televised hearings **July 24-30,** recommended 3 **articles of impeachment** against Pres. Nixon. The first, voted 27-11 **July 27,** charged conspiracy to obstruct justice in the Watergate cover-up. The 2nd, voted 28-10 **July 29,** charged abuses of power. The 3rd, voted 21-17 **July 30,** charged defiance of committee subpoenas. The House voted **Aug. 20,** 412-3, to accept the committee report, which included the impeachment articles.

Pres. Nixon announced his resignation, **Aug. 8,** and **resigned Aug. 9;** his support in Congress had begun to collapse **Aug. 5,** after release of tapes implicating him in Watergate cover-up. **Vice Pres. Gerald R. Ford** was **sworn in Aug. 9** as 38th U.S. president.

A **pardon** to ex-Pres. Nixon for any federal crimes he committed while president issued by Pres. Ford **Sept. 8.**

1975

Found guilty of Watergate cover-up charges Jan. 1 were ex-Atty. Gen. John Mitchell and ex-presidential advisers H. R. Haldeman and John Ehrlichman.

U.S. launched **evacuation** of American and some South Vietnamese **from Saigon Apr. 29** as Communist forces completed takeover of South Vietnam; **South Vietnamese** government officially **surrendered Apr. 30.**

U.S. merchant ship ***Mayaguez*** and its crew of 39 were seized by Cambodian forces in Gulf of Siam **May 12.** In rescue operation, U.S. Marines attacked Tang Island, planes bombed air base; Cambodia surrendered ship and crew.

Congress voted $405 mil for **South Vietnam refugees May 16;** 140,000 were flown to the U.S.

Illegal CIA operations described by panel headed by Vice Pres. **Nelson Rockefeller June 10.**

Publishing heiress **Patricia (Patty) Hearst,** kidnapped **Feb. 5, 1974,** by "Symbionese Liberation Army" militants, was captured, in San Francisco **Sept. 18** with others. She was convicted **Mar. 20, 1976,** of bank robbery.

1976

U.S. celebrated **200th anniversary of independence July 4,** with festivals, parades, and New York City's Operation Sail, a gathering of tall ships from around the world.

"Legionnaire's disease" killed 29 persons who attended an American Legion convention **July 21-24** in Philadelphia.

Viking II set down on **Mars'** Utopia Plains **Sept. 3,** following the successful landing by *Viking I* **July 20.**

1977

Pres. Jimmy Carter **Jan. 21** pardoned most Vietnam War **draft evaders.**

Convicted murderer **Gary Gilmore executed** by a Utah firing squad **Jan. 17,** in the first exercise of capital punishment in the U.S. since **1967.**

Pres. Carter signed an act **Aug. 4** creating a new cabinet-level **Energy Department.**

1978

U.S. Senate voted **Apr. 18** to turn over **Panama Canal** to Panama Dec. 31, 1999; **Mar. 16** vote had given approval to a treaty guaranteeing the area's neutrality after the year 2000.

Californians, **June 6,** approved **Proposition 13,** a state constitutional amendment slashing property taxes.

U.S. Supreme Court, **June 28,** ruled against **racial quotas** in *Bakke* v. *University of California.*

1979

Partial meltdown released radioactive material **Mar. 28,** at nuclear reactor on **Three Mile Island** near Middletown, PA.

Federal government announced, **Nov. 1,** a $1.5 bil loan-guarantee plan to aid the ailing **Chrysler Corp.**

Some 90 people, including 63 Americans, **taken hostage, Nov. 4,** at **American embassy in Tehran,** Iran, by militant followers of **Ayatollah Khomeini.** He demanded return of former Shah Muhammad Reza Pahlavi, who was undergoing medical treatment in New York City.

1980

Pres. Carter announced, **Jan. 4, economic sanctions against the USSR,** in retaliation for Soviet invasion of Afghanistan. At Carter's request, **U.S. Olympic Committee** voted, **Apr. 12,** against U.S. participation in Moscow Summer Olympics.

Eight Americans killed and 5 wounded, **Apr. 24, in ill-fated** attempt to **rescue hostages** held by Iranian militants.

Mt. St. Helens, in Washington state, **erupted, May 18.** The blast, with others **May 25** and **June 12,** left 57 dead.

In a sweeping victory, **Nov. 4, Ronald Reagan** (R) was elected 40th president, defeating incumbent Pres. Carter. Republicans gained control of the Senate.

Former Beatle **John Lennon** was shot and **killed, Dec. 8,** in New York City.

1981

Minutes after Reagan's inauguration **Jan. 20,** the **52 Americans** held **hostage in Iran** for 444 days were **freed.**

Pres. Reagan was **shot and seriously wounded, Mar. 30,** in Washington, DC; also seriously wounded were a Secret Service agent, a policeman, and Press Sec. **James Brady. John W. Hinckley Jr.** arrested, found not guilty by reason of insanity in **1982,** and committed to mental institution.

World's first reusable spacecraft, the **space shuttle *Columbia,*** was sent into space, **Apr. 12.**

Congress, **July 29,** passed Pres. Reagan's **tax-cut legislation,** expected to save taxpayers $750 bil over 5 years.

Federal air traffic controllers, Aug. 3, began an illegal **nationwide strike.** Most defied a back-to-work order and were dismissed by Pres. Reagan **Aug. 5.**

In a 99-0 vote, the Senate confirmed, **Sept. 21,** appointment of **Sandra Day O'Connor** as **first woman justice** of U.S. Supreme Court.

1982

The 13-year-old lawsuit against **AT&T** by the **Justice Dept.** was settled **Jan. 8.** AT&T agreed to give up the 22 Bell System companies and was allowed to expand.

The Equal Rights Amendment was **defeated** after a 10-year struggle for ratification.

A retired dentist, **Dr. Barney B. Clark,** 61, became first recipient of a **permanent artificial heart, Dec. 2.**

1983

On **Apr. 20, Pres. Reagan** signed a compromise bipartisan bill designed to save **Social Security** from bankruptcy.

Sally Ride became the first American **woman** to travel in **space, June 18,** when the **space shuttle *Challenger*** was launched from Cape Canaveral, FL.

On **Sept. 1, a South Korean passenger jet** infringing on Soviet air space was **shot down;** 269 people were killed.

On **Oct. 23,** 241 **U.S. Marines and sailors** were killed in Lebanon when a TNT-laden suicide bomb blew up Marine headquarters at **Beirut** International Airport.

U.S. troops, with a small force from 6 **Caribbean** nations, invaded **Grenada Oct. 25.** After a few days, Grenadian militia and Cuban "construction workers" were overcome, U.S. citizens evacuated, and the **Marxist regime deposed.**

1984

The space shuttle *Challenger* was launched on its 4th trip into space, **Feb. 3.** On **Feb. 7,** Navy Capt. Bruce McCandless, followed by Army Lt. Colonel Robert Stewart, became **first humans to fly free of a spacecraft.**

On **May 7,** American **Vietnam war** veterans reached an out-of-court **settlement with 7 chemical companies** in a class-action suit over the herbicide **Agent Orange.**

Former Vice Pres. **Walter Mondale** won the **Democratic presidential nomination, June 6;** he chose **Rep. Geraldine Ferraro** (D, NY), as candidate for **vice president.**

Pres. **Reagan** was **reelected Nov. 6** in a Republican **landslide,** carrying 49 states for a record 525 electoral votes.

1985

"Live Aid," a rock concert broadcast around the world **July 13,** raised $70 mil for starving peoples of Africa.

On **June 14** a **TWA jet was seized** by terrorists after takeoff from Athens; 153 passengers and crew held hostage for 17 days; 1 U.S. serviceman killed.

On **Oct. 7, 4 Palestinian hijackers seized** Italian cruise ship ***Achille Lauro*** in the Mediterranean and held it hostage for 2 days; one American, Leon Klinghoffer, was killed.

1986

On **Jan. 20,** for the first time, the U.S. officially observed **Martin Luther King Jr. Day.**

Seventy-three seconds after liftoff, **Jan. 28,** the space shuttle ***Challenger*** **exploded, killing 6 astronauts and Christa McAuliffe,** a New Hampshire teacher, on board.

Congress, overriding Pres. Reagan's veto in **Sept.,** imposed **economic sanctions on South Africa.**

U.S. Senate confirmed, **Sept. 17,** Reagan's nomination of **William Rehnquist** as chief justice and **Antonin Scalia** as associate justice of the Supreme Court.

Press reports in early **Nov.** broke first news of the **Iran-contra scandal,** involving secret U.S. sale of arms to Iran.

Ivan Boesky, accused of insider trading, agreed, **Nov. 14,** to plead guilty to an unspecified criminal count.

1987

Pres. Reagan produced the nation's first **trillion-dollar budget, Jan. 5.**

Dow Jones closed above 2,000 for first time, **Jan. 8.**

An **Iraqi missile killed 37 sailors** on the frigate USS *Stark* in the Persian Gulf, **May 17.** Iraq called it an accident.

Public hearings by Senate and House committees investigating the **Iran-contra affair** were held **May-Aug.** Lt. Col. **Oliver North** said he had believed all his activities were authorized by his superiors. Pres. Reagan, **Aug. 12,** denied knowing of a diversion of funds to the contras.

Wall Street crashed, Oct. 19, with the Dow Jones plummeting a record 508 points.

Pres. Reagan and Soviet leader **Mikhail Gorbachev, Dec. 8,** signed a **pact to dismantle** all 1,752 **U.S. and** 859 **Soviet missiles** with a 300- to 3,400-mi. range.

1988

Nearly **1.4 mil illegal aliens** met **May 4** deadline for applying for **amnesty** under a new federal policy.

A missile, fired from **U.S. Navy warship *Vincennes,*** in the Persian Gulf, mistakenly struck and **destroyed** a commercial **Iranian airliner, July 3,** killing all 290.

George H. W. Bush, vice president under Reagan, was **elected** 41st U.S. **president, Nov. 8.** Bush decisively defeated the Democratic nominee, Gov. **Michael Dukakis** (MA).

Pan Am Flight 103 exploded and crashed into the town of **Lockerbie, Scotland, Dec. 21,** killing all 259 people aboard, as well as 11 people on the ground. British investigators said, **Dec. 28,** a powerful plastic explosive had destroyed the plane.

Drexel Burnham Lambert agreed, **Dec. 21, to plead guilty** to 6 violations of federal law, including insider trading, and **pay penalties of $650 mil,** the largest such settlement ever.

1989

Major oil spill occurred when the ***Exxon Valdez*** struck Bligh Reef in Alaska's Prince William Sound, **Mar. 24.**

Former National Security Council staff member **Oliver North** was convicted, **May 4,** on charges related to **Iran-contra** scandal. Conviction thrown out on appeal in **1991.**

A measure to **rescue the savings and loan industry** was signed into law, **Aug. 9,** by Pres. Bush.

Army Gen. Colin Powell was nominated **Aug. 10** by Pres. Bush, as **chairman of the Joint Chiefs of Staff;** he became the first black to hold the post.

Just before a World Series game, **Oct. 17,** an **earthquake struck the San Francisco Bay area,** causing 62 deaths.

L. Douglas Wilder (D) elected governor of Virginia, the **first U.S. black governor** since Reconstruction.

U.S. troops invaded Panama, Dec. 20, overthrowing the government of **Manuel Noriega.** Noriega, wanted by U.S. authorities on drug charges, surrendered **Jan. 3, 1990.**

1990

Pres. Bush signed **Americans With Disabilities Act** on **July 26,** barring discrimination against handicapped.

Justice William Brennan announced, **July 20,** his resignation from the U.S. Supreme Court; his replacement, **Judge David Souter,** was confirmed **Sept. 27.**

Operation Desert Shield forces left for **Saudi Arabia, Aug. 7,** to defend that country following the **invasion** of its neighbor **Kuwait by Iraq, Aug. 2.**

Pres. Bush signed, **Nov. 5,** a bill to **reduce budget deficits** $500 bil over 5 years, by spending curbs and tax hikes.

1991

The **U.S. and its allies defeated Iraq** in the **Persian Gulf War** and liberated Kuwait, which Iraq had overrun in Aug. **1990.** On **Jan. 17,** the allies launched a devastating **attack on Iraq from the air.** In a **ground war** starting **Feb. 24,** which lasted just 100 hours, the U.S.-led forces killed or captured many thousands of Iraqi soldiers and sent the rest into retreat before Pres. Bush ordered a cease-fire **Feb. 27.**

U.S. **House bank** ordered closed **Oct. 3** after revelations House members had written 8,331 bad checks.

The **Senate approved, Oct. 15, nomination of Clarence Thomas** to the Supreme Court, despite allegations of sexual harassment against him by **Anita Hill,** a former aide. He became the 2nd African-American to serve on the Court, replacing retiring Justice **Thurgood Marshall,** the 1st black.

Charles Keating convicted of securities fraud **Dec. 4.**

1992

Riots swept South-Central **Los Angeles Apr. 29,** after **jury acquitted 4 white policemen** on all but one count in videotaped 1991 beating of black motorist **Rodney King.** Death toll in the L.A. violence was put at 52.

Bill Clinton (D) was **elected** 42nd president, **Nov. 3,** defeating **Pres. Bush** (R) and independent **Ross Perot.**

A UN-sanctioned military force, led by U.S. troops, arrived in **Somalia Dec. 9.**

1993

A bomb exploded in a parking garage beneath the **World Trade Center** in New York City, **Feb. 26,** killing 6 people. Two Islamic militants were convicted in the bombing, **Nov. 12, 1997.** Four men were found guilty, **Mar. 4, 1994.**

Janet Reno became the first woman U.S. attorney general **Mar. 12.**

Four federal agents were killed, Feb. 28, during an unsuccessful raid on the **Branch Davidian compound near Waco, TX.** A 51-day siege of the compound by federal agents ended **Apr. 19,** when the compound **burned down,** leaving more than 70 cult members dead. 11 **cult** members were acquitted **Feb. 26, 1994** of charges in the deaths of the federal agents.

A federal jury, **Apr. 17,** found **2 Los Angeles police officers guilty** and 2 not guilty of violating the civil rights of motorist **Rodney King** in 1991 beating incident.

"The Great Flood of 1993" inundated 8 mil acres in 9 Midwestern states in summer, leaving 50 dead.

Pres. Clinton, **July 19,** announced a "don't ask, don't tell, don't pursue" policy for **homosexuals** in the U.S. military.

Vincent Foster, deputy White House counsel, found shot to death **July 20** in a N Virginia park, an apparent suicide.

Judge Ruth Bader Ginsburg was sworn in, **Aug. 10,** as 107th justice of the Supreme Court.

Pres. Clinton, **Aug. 10,** signed a measure designed to **cut federal budget deficits** $496 bil over 5 years, through spending cuts and new taxes.

The **"Brady Bill,"** a major gun-control measure, was signed into law by Pres. Clinton **Nov. 30.**

1994

North American Free Trade Agreement took effect **Jan. 1.**

Attorney Gen. Janet Reno **Jan. 20** appointed Robert Fiske independent counsel to probe **Whitewater affair;** under a court ruling he was replaced **Aug. 5** by **Kenneth Starr**. Congressional committees, **late July,** began Whitewater hearings.

Byron De La Beckwith convicted Feb. 5 of the 1963 murder of civil rights leader **Medgar Evers.**

Longtime CIA officer **Aldrich Ames** and his wife were **charged Feb. 21 with spying.** Under a plea bargain, he received life in prison, while she drew 63 months.

Major league **baseball players went on strike,** following **Aug. 11** games; strike ended **Apr. 25, 1995.**

Senate Majority Leader George Mitchell (D, ME), **Sept. 26,** dropped efforts to pass Clinton's **health-care reform** package.

1995

When the 104th Congress opened, **Jan. 4, Sen. Bob Dole** (R, KS) became **Senate majority leader** and **Rep. Newt Gingrich** (R, GA) was elected **House Speaker.** A bill to end Congress's exemption from federal labor laws, first in a series of measures in Republicans' **"Contract With America,"** cleared Congress **Jan. 17;** signed into law **Jan. 23.**

Clinton invoked emergency powers, **Jan. 31,** to extend a **$20 bil loan to** help **Mexico** avert financial collapse.

The last UN peacekeeping troops withdrew from **Somalia Feb. 28-Mar. 3,** with the aid of U.S. Marines. In **Haiti,** peacekeeping responsibilities were transferred from U.S. to UN forces **Mar. 31,** with the U.S. providing 2,400 soldiers.

A truck **bomb** exploded outside **a federal office building in Oklahoma City Apr. 19, killing 168** people in all.

The U.S. space shuttle *Atlantis* made the first in a series of **dockings with** the Russian space station ***Mir,* June 29-July 4.**

A U.S. **F-16 fighter jet** piloted by Air Force Capt. **Scott O'Grady** was **shot down over Bosnia and Herzegovina June 2**; O'Grady was **rescued** by U.S. Marines 6 days later.

The U.S. announced on **July 11** that it was reestablishing diplomatic **relations with Vietnam.**

Former football star **O. J. Simpson** was found **not guilty Oct. 3** of the **June 1994** murders of his former wife, Nicole Brown Simpson, and her friend Ronald Goldman.

Hundreds of thousands of African-American men participated in **"Million Man March"** and rally in Washington, DC, **Oct. 16,** organized by Rev. Louis Farrakhan.

The federal **55-mile-per-hour speed limit** was **repealed** by a measure signed **Nov. 28.**

After talks outside Dayton, OH, **warring parties in Bosnia and Herzegovina reached agreement Nov. 21** to end their conflict; treaty was signed **Dec. 14,** after which first of some 20,000 **U.S. peacekeeping troops** arrived in Bosnia.

Five Americans were among 7 **killed, Nov. 13,** when **2 bombs exploded** at a military post in **Riyadh, Saudi Arabia.**

A budget impasse between Congress and Pres. Clinton led to a partial **government shutdown** beginning **Nov. 14.** Operations resumed Nov. 20 under continuing resolutions.

1996

Long-sought records released by White House **Jan. 5** showed **Hillary Rodham Clinton** did 60 hours of work for an S&L linked to **Whitewater** scandal. Responding to a subpoena, she testified **Jan. 26** before a grand jury.

Senate, **Jan. 26,** approved, 87–4, the Second Strategic Arms Reduction Treaty.

On **Feb. 24 Cuban jets shot down** 2 unarmed planes owned by a Cuban exile organization; 4 persons presumed killed.

John Salvi found guilty, **Mar. 18,** in the **1994 murder** of receptionists **at 2 abortion clinics** in Brookline, MA.

Congress, in late **Mar.,** approved a **"line item veto"** bill; struck down by the Supreme Court, **June 25, 1998.**

U.S. Commerce Sec. **Ron Brown** was killed **Apr. 3** in a plane crash in Croatia.

James and Susan McDougal were convicted **May 28** of fraud and conspiracy. Arkansas Gov. **Jim Guy Tucker** was convicted of similar charges by the same jury.

The antitax **Freemen** surrendered to federal authorities **June 13** after an 81-day standoff at a ranch near Jordan, MT. Four were convicted, **July 8, 1998,** of conspiring to defraud banks.

Republicans **June 12** chose Sen. **Trent Lott** (MS) as new majority leader to replace Sen. **Robert Dole,** who resigned, **June 11,** to focus on his presidential campaign.

A **bomb** exploded at a military complex near Dhahran, **Saudi Arabia, June 25,** killing 19 American servicemen.

On **July 27 a bomb exploded** in Atlanta, GA, near the **Olympics;** one person was directly killed.

A **welfare reform bill** was signed into law **Aug. 22.**

Shannon Lucid, Sept. 26, completed a space voyage of 188 days, a record for women and for U.S. astronauts.

Pres. Clinton was reelected to 2nd term, **Nov. 5.**

1997

Bombs were detonated at **2 abortion clinics** in Tulsa, OK, **Jan. 1**, in Atlanta on **Jan. 16,** and again at the first site in Tulsa on **Jan. 19.** Six people were injured.

Newt Gingrich (R, GA) was reelected Speaker of the U.S. House, **Jan. 7;** he was fined and reprimanded by colleagues for alleged misuse of tax-exempt donations.

Madeleine Albright was sworn in as secretary of state **Jan. 23,** becoming the first woman to head State Dept.

Harold Nicholson, a former CIA official, pleaded guilty, **Mar. 3,** to spying for Russia.

Thirty-nine members of the **Heaven's Gate religious cult** were found dead in a large house in Rancho Santa Fe, CA, **Mar. 26,** in an apparent mass suicide.

James McDougal, former partner with then-Gov. Bill Clinton in the Whitewater Development Corp., was sentenced **Apr. 14** to 3 years in prison for seeking to enrich himself with fraudulent loans. He died in prison, **Mar. 8, 1998.**

Timothy McVeigh was convicted of conspiracy and murder, **June 2,** in 1995 Oklahoma City bombing.

On **Oct. 27,** the **Dow Jones** fell 554.26 points, the largest 1-day point decline yet. On **Oct. 28,** the Dow rebounded, surging 337.17 points, the largest-yet single-day point advance.

Islamic militants **Ramzi Ahmed Yousef** and **Eyad Ismoil Yousef** were convicted, **Nov. 12,** in the 1993 bombing of the World Trade Center in New York City.

On **Nov. 19, Bobbi McCaughey,** 29, in Des Moines, IA, delivered the first set of live septuplets (4 boys, 3 girls) to survive more than a month.

Terry Nichols was convicted **Dec. 23** on some charges related to the 1995 **Oklahoma City bombing**.

1998

It was reported **Jan. 21** that Kenneth Starr, the independent counsel investigating the **Whitewater** scandal, had evidence of a sexual relationship between Pres. Clinton and onetime White House intern Monica Lewinsky. Clinton denied any affair.

Theodore Kaczynski, the so-called **Unabomber**, pleaded guilty **Jan. 22** in connection with California and New Jersey bombings that killed 3 people and injured 2.

The state of Texas, **Feb. 3,** executed its first female convict in 135 years—**Karla Faye Tucker**.

Mitchell Johnson, 13, and **Andrew Golden, 11,** were arrested, **Mar. 24,** for allegedly killing 4 schoolgirls and a teacher outside a **Jonesboro, AR,** middle school. They were later committed to a juvenile detention center.

A federal judge, **Apr. 1,** dismissed the sexual harassment suit brought against **Pres. Clinton** by **Paula Corbin Jones.**

On **Apr. 25,** First Lady **Hillary Rodham Clinton** provided videotaped testimony at the White House for the Little Rock, AR, grand jury in the **Whitewater** case.

The TV show ***Seinfeld*** aired its last episode **May 14.**

Kipland Kinkel, 15, was arrested in Springfield, OR, **May 21,** and charged with the shotgun **murder** of his parents and 2 students at his high school. He was sentenced **Nov. 10** to life in prison without parole.

Monica Lewinsky, July 28, agreed to testify before a Whitewater grand jury in return for immunity. On **Aug. 6,** she testified to having had a sexual relationship with **Pres. Clinton,** but said she was never asked to lie. In testimony for a grand jury, and in an address to the nation on **Aug. 17, Clinton** acknowledged having had an inappropriate relationship with Lewinsky. On **Sept. 9,** independent counsel **Kenneth Starr** sent to the House what he called "substantial and credible information that may constitute grounds" for impeaching Clinton.

Mark McGwire, Sept. 8, hit his 62nd **home run** of the season, breaking **Roger Maris**'s season record.

On **Sept. 30,** Pres. Clinton announced a **budget surplus** of $70 billion for fiscal year 1998, the first since 1969.

Terrorist **bombs** in **U.S. embassies** in Nairobi, Kenya, and Dar es Salaam, Tanzania, killed as least 257, **Aug. 7.** The U.S. launched **retaliatory strikes, Aug. 20**, against alleged terrorist-related targets in Afghanistan and Sudan.

The House Judiciary Committee, **Oct. 5,** voted 21-16 along party lines to recommend that the Clinton **impeachment** investigation proceed. The House concurred **Oct. 8,** voting 258-176; 31 Democrats voted yes.

Dr. Barnett Slepian, an obstetrician who performed abortions, was shot dead near Buffalo, NY, **Oct. 23,** by a sniper.

John Glenn, the first U.S. astronaut to orbit Earth, returned to space **Oct. 29-Nov. 7,** aboard the shuttle *Discovery*.

Pres. Clinton, Nov. 13, settled a suit by agreeing to pay $850,000 to **Paula Corbin Jones.** She alleged that he had made an unwanted sexual advance to her in 1991.

The country's 4 largest **tobacco** companies, in a settlement, **Nov. 23,** with 46 states, the District of Columbia, and 4 territories, agreed to pay $206 billion over 25 years to cover public health costs related to smoking.

The U.S. House of Representatives gave its approval, **Dec. 19,** to 2 articles of **impeachment** charging **Pres. Clinton** with grand jury perjury (228-206) and obstruction of justice (221-212) in connection with a coverup of his sexual relationship with former White House intern **Monica Lewinsky**. Two other impeachment articles failed. Clinton became only the 2nd president in U.S. history to be impeached.

1999

J. Dennis Hastert (IL) was elected Speaker of the House for the 106th Congress, **Jan. 6.**

Pres. Clinton's impeachment trial—the 2nd such trial in U.S. history—began in the GOP-controlled Senate **Jan. 7**. He was acquitted, **Feb. 12.** The grand jury perjury article failed, with 45 votes; the obstruction of justice article drew a 50-50 vote, with a two-thirds vote needed for conviction.

Dr. Jack Kevorkian, who claimed he had helped 130 people kill themselves, was convicted of 2nd-degree murder **Mar. 26** in one death. On **Apr. 13,** sentenced to 10 to 25 years in prison.

Russell Henderson, 21, pleaded guilty **Apr. 5** in the 1998 beating death of **Matthew Shepard,** an openly homosexual student at the Univ. of Wyoming. Aaron McKinney was also convicted **Nov. 3**.

Eric Harris, 18, and Dylan Klebold, 17, killed 12 fellow students and a teacher **Apr. 20** at **Columbine** High School in Littleton, CO, then shot themselves fatally. More than 30 people were wounded, some critically.

One NYC police officer pleaded guilty on 6 charges, **May 25,** and another was convicted on an assault charge, **June 8,** in connection with the 1997 torture and sodomizing of Haitian immigrant **Abner Louima** in a police station.

John F. Kennedy Jr., son of the former president, died in a plane crash **July 16** along with his wife, Carolyn Bessette **Kennedy,** and his sister-in-law, Lauren Bessette.

On **July 23,** with the launch of the space shuttle *Columbia*, Air Force Col. **Eileen M. Collins** became the first woman to command a shuttle flight.

The **Dow Jones** Industrial Average closed the year at a **record** level of 11,497.12—25.2% above the 1998 close.

2000

Across the U.S., midnight **celebrations** marked the changeover to the year 2000 on **Jan. 1**.

America Online Inc. announced **Jan. 10** that it would buy **Time Warner Inc.**, in the largest merger to date. The FTC approved it **Dec. 14**.

Pres. Clinton submitted his last federal budget—for the 2001 fiscal year—on **Feb. 7**, projecting a surplus of $184 billion, the 3rd consecutive surplus and the highest ever.

Gasoline prices rose across the U.S.; in the Midwest the price of a gallon reached $2.13 by early June.

A team of scientists from the U.S. and another from Great Britain announced jointly, **June 26**, that they had determined the structure of the **human genome.**

Following a bitter legal controversy, 6-year-old Cuban **Elián González** returned to Cuba **June 28**, 7 months after he was rescued from a boatwreck off the coast of Florida.

The Justice Dept., **July 21**, cleared U.S. agents of any wrongdoing in a 1993 assault on the compound of the Branch Davidian religious sect in **Waco,** TX.

Bridgestone/Firestone, Inc. announced **Aug. 9** it was recalling 6.5 million tires after widespread reports of blowouts.

The government dropped 58 of 59 felony counts against imprisoned scientist **Wen Ho Lee**, **Sept. 10**. He had been suspected of removing classified data from the **Los Alamos** National Laboratory.

17 U.S. sailors were killed **Oct. 12** in terrorist bombing of the **USS *Cole*,** refueling in Aden, Yemen.

Independent counsel Robert Ray said **Sept. 20** that there was **insufficient evidence** to establish criminal wrongdoing by Pres. Clinton or First Lady Hillary Rodham Clinton (who was elected to the Senate, **Nov. 7**).

The U.S. Food and Drug Administration announced, **Sept. 28**, approval of **RU-486,** a pill that induces abortions.

On **Election night, Nov. 7**, the winner of Florida's 25 deciding electoral votes remained uncertain. The Florida Supreme Court, **Dec. 8**, ordered a manual recount of all ballots that did not have a vote for president recorded by machine. On **Dec. 12**, the U.S. Supreme Court reversed that decision. Vice Pres. Gore conceded the presidential election to Gov. **George W. Bush** (TX) in a televised address, **Dec. 13**.

2001

Congress, **Jan. 6**, certified **George W. Bush** as winner of the presidency by an electoral vote of 271 to 266, with 1 Gore elector abstaining.

AOL-Time Warner merger completed, **Jan. 11.**

Outgoing Pres. Clinton issued 176 pardons and commutations, **Jan. 20**, including that of **Marc Rich**, a commodities trader and fugitive whose ex-wife, Denise, was a big campaign donor.

George Walker Bush, was sworn in as the 43rd president **Jan. 20.**

Senior FBI agent **Robert Hanssen** was arrested **Feb. 20** and charged 2 days later with spying for the Soviet Union and Russia.

9 people on a **Japanese fishing boat** were killed **Feb. 9** when it collided with a U.S. Navy submarine 9 miles from Pearl Harbor in Hawaii.

Riots flared in **Cincinnati** after a white policeman shot and killed an unarmed black youth **Apr. 7**.

A **U.S. Navy spy plane** collided with a Chinese fighter plane over the South China Sea **Apr. 1**, killing the fighter pilot. The 24 U.S. crew members were detained in Hainan until U.S. officials expressed apology, **Apr. 12**.

Sen. James Jeffords (VT) announced **May 24** that he was leaving the Republican party to become an Independent. His defection gave Democrats control of the Senate.

Congress approved, **May 26**, a $1.35 trillion **tax cut** spread over 10 years.

Oklahoma City bomber **Timothy McVeigh** was executed **June 11** by lethal injection in Terre Haute, IN.

Andrea Yates, was arrested in Houston, TX, **June 20**, in the drowning deaths of her 5 children.

Rep. **Gary Condit** (D, CA) denied in a TV interview **Aug. 23** having had anything to do with the **Apr. 30** disappearance of 24-year-old intern **Chandra Levy,** with whom he had been having an affair. Skeletal remains proved to be Levy's found in a DC park **May 22, 2002**.

Pres. Bush announced **Aug. 9** he would allow federal funding of limited **stem-cell research** utilizing human embryos.

On the morning of **Sept. 11**, 2 hijacked commercial airliners struck and destroyed the twin towers of the World Trade Center in New York City, in the worst-ever **terrorist attack** on American soil. A 3rd hijacked plane destroyed a portion of the Pentagon and a 4th crashed in Pennsylvania after passengers stormed the cockpit. Some 3,000 people were killed, including about 2,800 at the World Trade Center. U.S. observed a national day of mourning, **Sept. 14.**

Congress, **Sept. 21**, approved a $15 billion bailout package for the **airline industry** after a week of massive layoffs by major airlines in the wake of the terrorist attack.

Barry Bonds, left fielder for the San Francisco Giants, hit his 71st home run **Oct. 5**, a record, and went on to hit 73.

The **U.S.** and **Britain Oct. 7** launched a sustained air strike campaign against Afghan-based terrorist organization al-Qaeda and the country's ruling Taliban militia.

Pres. Bush **created** a new **Office of Homeland Security, Oct. 8,** and **signed** a broad federal **antiterrorism bill Oct. 26**.

An **American Airlines plane crashed Nov. 12** in the New York City borough of Queens, killing 265.

5 people died and 14 took ill from exposure to **anthrax** traveling through the U.S. mail, **Oct. 5-Nov. 21**. Letters laced with the deadly bacteria reached offices of Senate Majority Leader Tom Daschle in late Sept. and NBC News anchor Tom Brokaw **Oct. 15**.

The **Taliban** surrendered Kabul, the Afghan capital, **Nov. 13,** and fled from Kandahar, their military and spiritual stronghold, **Dec. 7**.

A Mass. company announced **Nov. 25** it had created the first-ever human embryos by **cloning**.

Leading energy-trading company **Enron** became the largest firm thus far to file for bankruptcy, **Dec. 2**.

The U.S. government, **Dec. 11,** indicted Zacarias Moussaoui as an alleged conspirator in the Sept. 11 attacks.

Pres. Bush announced **Dec. 13** that the United States would withdraw from the 1972 **Antiballistic Missile Treaty**.

Richard Reid was arrested **Dec. 22,** after allegedly trying to ignite **explosives** in his sneakers aboard a Miami-Paris **jetliner**.

Pres. Bush, **Dec. 28**, formally granted permanent normal trade status to **China**, as of Jan. 1, 2002.

Taliban member **John Walker Lindh**, a U.S. citizen, was captured **Dec. 2** by U.S. forces in Afghanistan.

How the Declaration of Independence Was Adopted

On June 7, 1776, Richard Henry Lee, who had issued the first call for a congress of the colonies, introduced in the Continental Congress at Philadelphia a resolution declaring "that these United Colonies are, and of right ought to be, free and independent states, that they are absolved from all allegiance to the British Crown, and that all political connection between them and the state of Great Britain is, and ought to be, totally dissolved."

The resolution, seconded by John Adams on behalf of the Massachusetts delegation, came up again on June 10 when a committee of 5, headed by Thomas Jefferson, was appointed to express the purpose of the resolution in a declaration of independence. The others on the committee were John Adams, Benjamin Franklin, Robert R. Livingston, and Roger Sherman.

Drafting the Declaration was assigned to Jefferson, who worked on a portable desk of his own construction in a room at Market and 7th Sts. The committee reported the result on June 28, 1776. The members of the Congress suggested a number of changes, which Jefferson called "deplorable." They didn't approve Jefferson's arraignment of the British people and King George III for encouraging and fostering the slave trade, which Jefferson called "an execrable commerce." They made 86 changes, eliminating 480 words and leaving 1,337. In the final form, capitalization was erratic. Jefferson had written that men were endowed with "inalienable" rights; in the final copy it came out as "unalienable" and has been thus ever since.

The Lee-Adams resolution of independence was adopted by 12 yeas on July 2—the actual date of the act of independence. The Declaration, which explains the act, was adopted July 4, in the evening.

After the Declaration was adopted, July 4, 1776, it was turned over to John Dunlap, printer, to be printed on broadsides. The original copy was lost and one of his broadsides was attached to a page in the journal of the Congress. It was read aloud July 8 in Philadelphia, PA, Easton, PA, and Trenton, NJ. On July 9 at 6 PM it was read by order of Gen. George Washington to the troops assembled on the Common in New York City (City Hall Park).

The Continental Congress of July 19, 1776, adopted the following resolution:

"Resolved, That the Declaration passed on the 4th, be fairly engrossed on parchment with the title and stile of 'The Unanimous Declaration of the thirteen United States of America' and that the same, when engrossed, be signed by every member of Congress."

Not all delegates who signed the engrossed Declaration were present on July 4. Robert Morris (PA), William Williams (CT), and Samuel Chase (MD) signed on Aug. 2; Oliver Wolcott (CT), George Wythe (VA), Richard Henry Lee (VA), and Elbridge Gerry (MA) signed in August and September; Matthew Thornton (NH) joined the Congress Nov. 4 and signed later. Thomas McKean (DE) rejoined Washington's army before signing and said later that he signed in 1781.

Charles Carroll of Carrollton was appointed a delegate by Maryland on July 4, 1776, presented his credentials July 18, and signed the engrossed Declaration on Aug. 2. Born Sept. 19, 1737, he was 95 years old and the last surviving signer when he died on Nov. 14, 1832.

Two Pennsylvania delegates who did not support the Declaration on July 4 were replaced.

The 4 New York delegates did not have authority from their state to vote on July 4. On July 9, the New York state convention authorized its delegates to approve the Declaration, and the Congress was so notified on July 15, 1776. The 4 signed the Declaration on Aug. 2.

The original engrossed Declaration is preserved in the National Archives Building in Washington, DC.

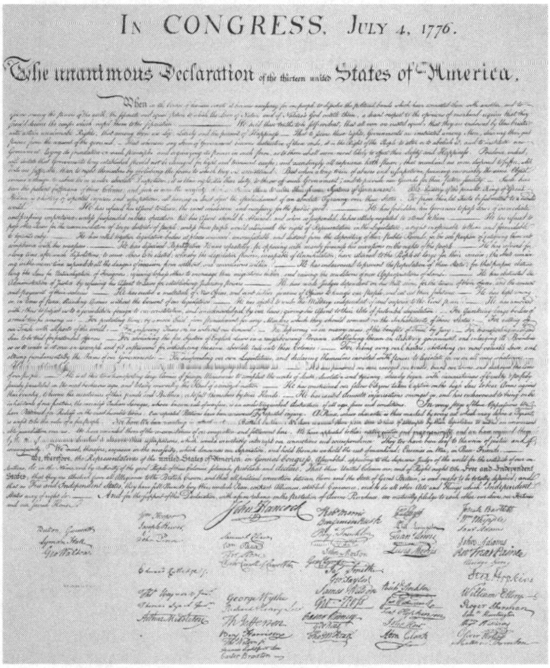
IN CONGRESS, July 4, 1776.
The unanimous Declaration of the thirteen united States of America,

Declaration of Independence

The Declaration of Independence was adopted by the Continental Congress in Philadelphia on July 4, 1776. John Hancock was president of the Congress, and Charles Thomson was secretary. A copy of the Declaration, engrossed on parchment, was signed by members of Congress on and after Aug. 2, 1776. On Jan. 18, 1777, Congress ordered that "an authenticated copy, with the names of the members of Congress subscribing the same, be sent to each of the United States, and that they be desired to have the same put upon record." Authenticated copies were printed in broadside form in Baltimore, where the Continental Congress was then in session. The following text is that of the original printed by John Dunlap at Philadelphia for the Continental Congress. The original is on display at the National Archives in Washington, DC.

IN CONGRESS, July 4, 1776.
A DECLARATION
By the REPRESENTATIVES of the
UNITED STATES OF AMERICA,
In GENERAL CONGRESS assembled

When in the Course of human Events, it becomes necessary for one People to dissolve the Political Bands which have connected them with another, and to assume among the Powers of the Earth, the separate and equal Station to which the Laws of Nature and of Nature's God entitle them, a decent Respect to the Opinions of Mankind requires that they should declare the causes which impel them to the Separation.

We hold these Truths to be self-evident, that all Men are created equal, that they are endowed by their Creator with certain unalienable Rights, that among these are Life, Liberty, and the Pursuit of Happiness—That to secure these Rights, Governments are instituted among Men, deriving their just Powers from the Consent of the Governed, that whenever any Form of Government becomes destructive of these Ends, it is the Right of the People to alter or to abolish it, and to institute new Government, laying its Foundation on such Principles, and organizing its Powers in such Form, as to them shall seem most likely to effect their Safety and Happiness. Prudence, indeed, will dictate that Governments long established should not be changed for light and transient Causes; and accordingly all Experience hath shewn, that Mankind are more disposed to suffer, while Evils are sufferable, than to right themselves by abolishing the Forms to which they are accustomed. But when a long Train of Abuses and Usurpations, pursuing invariably the same Object, evinces a Design to reduce them under absolute Despotism, it is their Right, it is their Duty, to throw off such Government, and to provide new Guards for their future Security. Such has been the patient Sufferance of these Colonies; and such is now the Necessity which constrains them to alter their former Systems of Government. The History of the present King of Great-Britain is a History of repeated Injuries and Usurpations, all having in direct Object the Establishment of an absolute Tyranny over these States. To prove this, let Facts be submitted to a candid World.

He has refused his Assent to Laws, the most wholesome and necessary for the public Good.

He has forbidden his Governors to pass Laws of immediate and pressing Importance, unless suspended in their Operation till his Assent should be obtained; and when so suspended, he has utterly neglected to attend to them.

He has refused to pass other Laws for the Accommodation of large Districts of People, unless those People would relinquish the Right of Representation in the Legislature, a Right inestimable to them, and formidable to Tyrants only.

He has called together Legislative Bodies at Places unusual, uncomfortable, and distant from the Depository of their Public Records, for the sole Purpose of fatiguing them into Compliance with his Measures.

He has dissolved Representative Houses repeatedly, for opposing with manly Firmness his Invasions on the Rights of the People.

He has refused for a long Time, after such Dissolutions, to cause others to be elected; whereby the Legislative Powers, incapable of Annihilation, have returned to the People at large for their exercise; the State remaining in the mean time exposed to all the Dangers of Invasion from without, and Convulsions within.

He has endeavoured to prevent the Population of these States; for that Purpose obstructing the Laws for Naturalization of Foreigners; refusing to pass others to encourage their Migrations hither, and raising the Conditions of new Appropriations of Lands.

He has obstructed the Administration of Justice, by refusing his Assent to Laws for establishing Judiciary Powers.

He has made Judges dependent on his Will alone, for the Tenure of their Offices, and the Amount and payment of their Salaries.

He has erected a Multitude of new Offices, and sent hither Swarms of Officers to harrass our People, and eat out their Substance.

He has kept among us, in Times of Peace, Standing Armies, without the consent of our Legislatures.

He has affected to render the Military independent of, and superior to the Civil Power.

He has combined with others to subject us to a Jurisdiction foreign to our Constitution, and unacknowledged by our Laws; giving his Assent to their Acts of pretended Legislation:

For quartering large Bodies of Armed Troops among us:

For protecting them, by a mock Trial, from Punishment for any Murders which they should commit on the Inhabitants of these States:

For cutting off our Trade with all Parts of the World:

For imposing Taxes on us without our Consent:

For depriving us, in many Cases, of the Benefits of Trial by Jury:

For transporting us beyond Seas to be tried for pretended Offences:

For abolishing the free System of English Laws in a neighbouring Province, establishing therein an arbitrary Government, and enlarging its Boundaries, so as to render it at once an Example and fit Instrument for introducing the same absolute Rule into these Colonies:

For taking away our Charters, abolishing our most valuable Laws, and altering fundamentally the Forms of our Governments:

For suspending our own Legislatures, and declaring themselves invested with Power to legislate for us in all Cases whatsoever.

He has abdicated Government here, by declaring us out of his Protection and waging War against us.

He has plundered our Seas, ravaged our Coasts, burnt our towns, and destroyed the Lives of our People.

He is, at this Time, transporting large Armies of foreign Mercenaries to complete the works of Death, Desolation, and Tyranny, already begun with circumstances of Cruelty and Perfidy, scarcely paralleled in the most barbarous Ages, and totally unworthy the Head of a civilized Nation.

He has constrained our fellow Citizens taken Captive on the high Seas to bear Arms against their Country, to become the Executioners of their Friends and Brethren, or to fall themselves by their Hands.

He has excited domestic Insurrections amongst us, and has endeavoured to bring on the Inhabitants of our Frontiers, the merciless Indian Savages, whose known Rule of Warfare, is an undistinguished Destruction, of all Ages, Sexes and Conditions.

In every stage of these Oppressions we have Petitioned for Redress in the most humble Terms: Our repeated Petitions have been answered only by repeated Injury. A Prince, whose Character is thus marked by every act which may define a Tyrant, is unfit to be the Ruler of a free People.

Nor have we been wanting in Attentions to our British Brethren. We have warned them from Time to Time of Attempts by their Legislature to extend an unwarrantable Jurisdiction over us. We have reminded them of the Circumstances of our Emigration and Settlement here. We have appealed to their native Justice and Magnanimity, and we have conjured them by the Ties of our common Kindred to disavow these Usurpations, which, would inevitably interrupt our Connections and Correspondence. They too have been deaf to the Voice of Justice and of Consanguinity. We must, therefore, acquiesce in the Necessity, which denounces our Separation, and hold them, as we hold the rest of Mankind, Enemies in War, in Peace, Friends.

We, therefore, the Representatives of the UNITED STATES OF AMERICA, in General Congress, Assembled, appealing to the Supreme Judge of the World for the Rectitude of our Intentions, do, in the Name, and by Authority of the good People of these Colonies, solemnly Publish and Declare, That these United Colonies are, and of Right ought to be, Free and Independent States; that they are absolved from all Allegiance to the British Crown, and that all political Connection between them and the State of Great-Britain, is and ought to be totally dissolved; and that as Free and Independent States, they have full Power to levy War, conclude Peace, contract Alliances, establish Commerce, and to do all other Acts and Things which Independent States may of right do. And for the support of this declaration, with a firm Reliance on the Protection of Divine Providence, we mutually pledge to each other our lives, our Fortunes, and our sacred Honor.

JOHN HANCOCK, President

Attest.

CHARLES THOMSON, Secretary.

Signers of the Declaration of Independence

Delegate (state)	Occupation	Birthplace	Born	Died
Adams, John (MA)	Lawyer	Braintree (Quincy), MA	Oct. 30, 1735	July 4, 1826
Adams, Samuel (MA)	Political leader	Boston, MA	Sept. 27, 1722	Oct. 2, 1803
Bartlett, Josiah (NH)	Physician, judge	Amesbury, MA	Nov. 21, 1729	May 19, 1795
Braxton, Carter (VA)	Farmer	Newington Plantation, VA	Sept. 10, 1736	Oct. 10, 1797
Carroll, Chas. of Carrollton (MD)	Lawyer	Annapolis, MD	Sept. 19, 1737	Nov. 14, 1832
Chase, Samuel (MD)	Judge	Princess Anne, MD	Apr. 17, 1741	June 19, 1811
Clark, Abraham (NJ)	Surveyor	Roselle, NJ	Feb. 15, 1726	Sept. 15, 1794
Clymer, George (PA)	Merchant	Philadelphia, PA	Mar. 16, 1739	Jan. 23, 1813
Ellery, William (RI)	Lawyer	Newport, RI	Dec. 22, 1727	Feb. 15, 1820
Floyd, William (NY)	Soldier	Brookhaven, NY	Dec. 17, 1734	Aug. 4, 1821
Franklin, Benjamin (PA)	Printer, publisher	Boston, MA	Jan. 17, 1706	Apr. 17, 1790
Gerry, Elbridge (MA)	Merchant	Marblehead, MA	July 17, 1744	Nov. 23, 1814
Gwinnett, Button (GA)	Merchant	Down Hatherly, England	c. 1735	May 19, 1777
Hall, Lyman (GA)	Physician	Wallingford, CT	Apr. 12, 1724	Oct. 19, 1790

Delegate (state)	Occupation	Birthplace	Born	Died
Hancock, John (MA)	Merchant	Braintree (Quincy), MA	Jan. 12, 1737	Oct. 8, 1793
Harrison, Benjamin (VA)	Farmer	Berkeley, VA	Apr. 5, 1726	Apr. 24, 1791
Hart, John (NJ)	Farmer	Stonington, CT	c. 1711	May 11, 1779
Hewes, Joseph (NC)	Merchant	Princeton, NJ	Jan. 23, 1730	Nov. 10, 1779
Heyward, Thos. Jr. (SC)	Lawyer, farmer	St. Luke's Parish, SC	July 28, 1746	Mar. 6, 1809
Hooper, William (NC)	Lawyer	Boston, MA	June 28, 1742	Oct. 14, 1790
Hopkins, Stephen (RI)	Judge, educator	Providence, RI	Mar. 7, 1707	July 13, 1785
Hopkinson, Francis (NJ)	Judge, author	Philadelphia, PA	Sept. 21, 1737	May 9, 1791
Huntington, Samuel (CT)	Judge	Windham County, CT	July 3, 1731	Jan. 5, 1796
Jefferson, Thomas (VA)	Lawyer	Shadwell, VA	Apr. 13, 1743	July 4, 1826
Lee, Francis Lightfoot (VA)	Farmer	Westmoreland County, VA	Oct. 14, 1734	Jan. 11, 1797
Lee, Richard Henry (VA)	Farmer	Westmoreland County, VA	Jan. 20, 1732	June 19, 1794
Lewis, Francis (NY)	Merchant	Llandaff, Wales	Mar., 1713	Dec. 31, 1802
Livingston, Philip (NY)	Merchant	Albany, NY	Jan. 15, 1716	June 12, 1778
Lynch, Thomas Jr. (SC)	Farmer	Winyah, SC	Aug. 5, 1749	(at sea) 1779
McKean, Thomas (DE)	Lawyer	New London, PA	Mar. 19, 1734	June 24, 1817
Middleton, Arthur (SC)	Farmer	Charleston, SC	June 26, 1742	Jan. 1, 1787
Morris, Lewis (NY)	Farmer	Morrisania (Bronx County), NY	Apr. 8, 1726	Jan. 22, 1798
Morris, Robert (PA)	Merchant	Liverpool, England	Jan. 20, 1734	May 9, 1806
Morton, John (PA)	Judge	Ridley, PA	1724	Apr., 1777
Nelson, Thos. Jr. (VA)	Farmer	Yorktown, VA	Dec. 26, 1738	Jan. 4, 1789
Paca, William (MD)	Judge	Abingdon, MD	Oct. 31, 1740	Oct. 23, 1799
Paine, Robert Treat (MA)	Judge	Boston, MA	Mar. 11, 1731	May 12, 1814
Penn, John (NC)	Lawyer	Near Port Royal, VA	May 17, 1741	Sept. 14, 1788
Read, George (DE)	Judge	Near North East, MD	Sept. 18, 1733	Sept. 21, 1798
Rodney, Caesar (DE)	Judge	Dover, DE	Oct. 7, 1728	June 29, 1784
Ross, George (PA)	Judge	New Castle, DE	May 10, 1730	July 14, 1779
Rush, Benjamin (PA)	Physician	Byberry, PA (Philadelphia)	Dec. 24, 1745	Apr. 19, 1813
Rutledge, Edward (SC)	Lawyer	Charleston, SC	Nov. 23, 1749	Jan. 23, 1800
Sherman, Roger (CT)	Lawyer	Newton, MA	Apr. 19, 1721	July 23, 1793
Smith, James (PA)	Lawyer	Dublin, Ireland	c. 1719	July 11, 1806
Stockton, Richard (NJ)	Lawyer	Near Princeton, NJ	Oct. 1, 1730	Feb. 28, 1781
Stone, Thomas (MD)	Lawyer	Charles County, MD	1743	Oct. 5, 1787
Taylor, George (PA)	Ironmaster	Ireland	1716	Feb. 23, 1781
Thornton, Matthew (NH)	Physician	Ireland	1714	June 24, 1803
Walton, George (GA)	Judge	Prince Edward County, VA	1741	Feb. 2, 1804
Whipple, William (NH)	Merchant, judge	Kittery, ME	Jan. 14, 1730	Nov. 28, 1785
Williams, William (CT)	Merchant	Lebanon, CT	Apr. 23, 1731	Aug. 2, 1811
Wilson, James (PA)	Judge	Carskerdo, Scotland	Sept. 14, 1742	Aug. 28, 1798
Witherspoon, John (NJ)	Clergyman, educator	Gifford, Scotland	Feb. 5, 1723	Nov. 15, 1794
Wolcott, Oliver (CT)	Judge	Windsor, CT	Dec. 1, 1726	Dec. 1, 1797
Wythe, George (VA)	Lawyer	Elizabeth City Co. (Hampton), VA	1726	June 8, 1806

Origin of the Constitution

The War of Independence was conducted by delegates from the original 13 states, called the Congress of the United States of America and known as the Continental Congress. In 1777 the Congress submitted to the legislatures of the states the Articles of Confederation and Perpetual Union, which were ratified by New Hampshire, Massachusetts, Rhode Island, Connecticut, New York, New Jersey, Pennsylvania, Delaware, Virginia, North Carolina, South Carolina, and Georgia and finally, in 1781, by Maryland.

The first article read: "The stile of this confederacy shall be the United States of America." This did not signify a sovereign nation, because the states delegated only those powers they could not handle individually, such as to wage war, make treaties, and contract debts for general expenses (e.g. paying the army). Taxes for payment of such debts were levied by the individual states. The president signed himself "President of the United States in Congress assembled," but here the United States were considered in the plural, a cooperating group.

When the war was won, it became evident that a stronger federal union was needed. The Congress left the initiative to the legislatures. Virginia in Jan. 1786 appointed commissioners to meet with representatives of other states; delegates from Virginia, Delaware, New York, New Jersey, and Pennsylvania met at Annapolis. Alexander Hamilton prepared their call asking delegates from all states to meet in Philadelphia in May 1787 "to render the Constitution of the federal government adequate to the exigencies of the union." Congress endorsed the plan on Feb. 21, 1787. Delegates were appointed by all states except Rhode Island.

The convention met on May 14, 1787. George Washington was chosen president (presiding officer). The states certified 65 delegates, but 10 did not attend. The work was done by 55, not all of whom were present at all sessions. Of the 55 attending delegates, 16 failed to sign, and 39 actually signed Sept. 17, 1787, some with reservations. Some historians have said 74 delegates (9 more than the 65 actually certified) were named and 19 failed to attend. These 9 additional persons refused the appointment, were never delegates, and were never counted as absentees. Washington sent the Constitution to Congress, and that body, Sept. 28, 1787, ordered it sent to the legislatures, "in order to be submitted to a convention of delegates chosen in each state by the people thereof."

The Constitution was ratified by votes of state conventions as follows: Delaware, Dec. 7, 1787, unanimous; Pennsylvania, Dec. 12, 1787, 43 to 23; New Jersey, Dec. 18, 1787, unanimous; Georgia, Jan. 2, 1788, unanimous; Connecticut, Jan. 9, 1788, 128 to 40; Massachusetts, Feb. 6, 1788, 187 to 168; Maryland, Apr. 28, 1788, 63 to 11; South Carolina, May 23, 1788, 149 to 73; New Hampshire, June 21, 1788, 57 to 46; Virginia, June 25, 1788, 89 to 79; New York, July 26, 1788, 30 to 27. Nine states were needed to establish the operation of the Constitution "between the states so ratifying the same," and New Hampshire was the 9th state. The government did not declare the Constitution in effect until the first Wednesday in Mar. 1789, which was Mar. 4. After that, North Carolina ratified it on Nov. 21, 1789, 194 to 77; and Rhode Island, May 29, 1790, 34 to 32. Vermont in convention ratified it on Jan. 10, 1791, and by act of Congress approved on Feb. 18, 1791, was admitted into the Union as the 14th state, Mar. 4, 1791.

IT'S A FACT: Hugh Williamson, a delegate to the Constitutional Convention from North Carolina, was quite the renaissance man. He developed an innoculation program for troops in the War of Independence, published articles on snakes and climatology, studied comets as a sidelight, and believed that every planet in the solar system was inhabited.

Constitution of the United States

The Original 7 Articles

The text of the Constitution given here (exception for Amendment XXVII) is taken from the pocket-size edition of the Constitution published by the U.S. Government Printing Office as a result of a U.S. House and Senate resolution to print the Constitution in its original form as amended through July 5, 1971. *Text in brackets* indicates that an item has been superseded or amended, or provides background information. **Boldface text preceding** each article, section, or amendment is a brief summary, added by *The World Almanac*.

PREAMBLE

We, the People of the United States, in Order to form a more perfect Union, establish Justice, insure domestic Tranquility, provide for the common defence, promote the general Welfare, and secure the Blessings of Liberty to ourselves and our Posterity, do ordain and establish this Constitution for the United States of America.

ARTICLE I.

Section 1—Legislative powers; in whom vested:

All legislative Powers herein granted shall be vested in a Congress of the United States, which shall consist of a Senate and House of Representatives.

Section 2—House of Representatives, how and by whom chosen. Qualifications of a Representative. Representatives and direct taxes, how apportioned. Enumeration. Vacancies to be filled. Power of choosing officers, and of impeachment.

The House of Representatives shall be composed of Members chosen every second Year by the People of the several States, and the Electors in each State shall have the Qualifications requisite for Electors of the most numerous Branch of the State Legislature.

No person shall be a Representative who shall not have attained to the Age of twenty-five Years, and been seven Years a Citizen of the United States, and who shall not, when elected, be an Inhabitant of that State in which he shall be chosen.

[Representatives and direct taxes shall be apportioned among the several States which may be included within this Union, according to their respective Numbers, which shall be determined by adding to the whole Number of free Persons, including those bound to Service for a Term of Years, and excluding Indians not taxed, three-fifths of all other persons.] [The previous sentence was superseded by Amendment XIV, section 2.] The actual Enumeration shall be made within three Years after the first Meeting of the Congress of the United States, and within every subsequent Term of ten Years, in such Manner as they shall by Law direct. The Number of Representatives shall not exceed one for every thirty Thousand, but each State shall have at Least one Representative; and until such enumeration shall be made, the State of New Hampshire shall be entitled to chuse three, Massachusetts eight, Rhode-Island and Providence Plantations one, Connecticut five, New-York six, New Jersey four, Pennsylvania eight, Delaware one, Maryland six, Virginia ten, North Carolina five, South Carolina five, and Georgia three.

When vacancies happen in the Representation from any State, the Executive Authority thereof shall issue Writs of Election to fill such Vacancies.

The House of Representatives shall chuse their Speaker and other Officers; and shall have the sole Power of Impeachment.

Section 3—Senators, how and by whom chosen. How classified. Qualifications of a Senator. President of the Senate, his right to vote. President pro tem., and other officers of the Senate, how chosen. Power to try impeachments. When President is tried, Chief Justice to preside. Sentence.

The Senate of the United States shall be composed of two Senators from each State, *[chosen by the Legislature thereof] [the preceding five words were superseded by Amendment XVII, section 1]* for six Years; and each Senator shall have one Vote.

Immediately after they shall be assembled in Consequence of the first Election, they shall be divided as equally as may be into three Classes. The Seats of the Senators of the first Class shall be vacated at the Expiration of the second Year, of the second Class at the Expiration of the fourth Year, and of the third Class at the Expiration of the Sixth year, so that one-third may be chosen every second Year; *[and if Vacancies happen by Resignation, or otherwise, during the Recess of the Legislature of any State, the Executive thereof may make temporary Appointments until the next Meeting of the Legislature, which shall then fill such Vacancies.] [The words in parentheses were superseded by Amendment XVII, section 2.]*

No person shall be a Senator who shall not have attained to the Age of thirty Years, and been nine Years a Citizen of the United States, and who shall not, when elected, be an Inhabitant of that State for which he shall be chosen.

The Vice President of the United States shall be President of the Senate, but shall have no Vote, unless they be equally divided.

The Senate shall chuse their other Officers, and also a President pro tempore, in the absence of the Vice President, or when he shall exercise the Office of President of the United States.

The Senate shall have the sole Power to try all Impeachments. When sitting for that Purpose, they shall be on Oath or Affirmation. When the President of the United States is tried, the Chief Justice shall preside: And no Person shall be convicted without the Concurrence of two thirds of the Members present.

Judgment in Cases of Impeachment shall not extend further than to removal from Office, and disqualification to hold and enjoy any Office of honor, Trust or Profit under the United States: but the Party convicted shall nevertheless be liable and subject to Indictment, Trial, Judgment and Punishment, according to Law.

Section 4—Times, etc., of holding elections, how prescribed. One session each year.

The Times, Places and Manner of holding Elections for Senators and Representatives, shall be prescribed in each State by the Legislature thereof; but the Congress may at any time by Law make or alter such Regulations, except as to the Place of Chusing Senators.

The Congress shall assemble at least once in every Year, and such Meeting shall *[be on the first Monday in December,] [The words in parentheses were superseded by Amendment XX, section 2.]* unless they shall by Law appoint a different Day.

Section 5—Membership, quorum, adjournments, rules. Power to punish or expel. Journal. Time of adjournments, how limited, etc.

Each House shall be the Judge of the Elections, Returns and Qualifications of its own Members, and a Majority of each shall constitute a Quorum to do Business; but a smaller number may adjourn from day to day, and may be authorized to compel the Attendance of absent Members, in such manner, and under such Penalties as each House may provide.

Each House may determine the Rules of its Proceedings, punish its members for disorderly Behavior, and, with the Concurrence of two thirds, expel a Member.

Each House shall keep a Journal of its Proceedings, and from time to time publish the same, excepting such Parts as may in their Judgment require Secrecy; and the Yeas and Nays of the Members of either House on any question shall, at the Desire of one fifth of those Present, be entered on the Journal.

Neither House, during the Session of Congress, shall, without the Consent of the other, adjourn for more than three days, nor to any other Place than that in which the two Houses shall be sitting.

Section 6—Compensation, privileges, disqualifications in certain cases.

The Senators and Representatives shall receive a Compensation for their Services, to be ascertained by Law, and paid out of the Treasury of the United States. They shall in all Cases, except Treason, Felony and Breach of the Peace, be privileged from Arrest during their Attendance at the Session of their respective Houses, and in going to and returning from the same; and for any Speech or Debate in either House, they shall not be questioned in any other Place.

No Senator or Representative shall, during the Time for which he was elected, be appointed to any civil Office under the Authority of the United States, which shall have been created, or the Emoluments whereof shall have been encreased during such time; and no Person holding any Office under the United States, shall be a Member of either House during his Continuance in Office.

Section 7—House to originate all revenue bills. Veto. Bill may be passed by two-thirds of each House, notwithstanding, etc. Bill, not returned in ten days, to become a law. Provisions as to orders, concurrent resolutions, etc.

All bills for raising Revenue shall originate in the House of Representatives; but the Senate may propose or concur with Amendments as on other Bills.

Every Bill which shall have passed the House of Representatives and the Senate, shall, before it become a Law, be presented to the President of the United States; If he approve he shall sign it, but if not he shall return it, with his Objections to that House in which it shall have originated, who shall enter the Objections at large on their Journal, and proceed to reconsider it. If after such Reconsideration two thirds of that House shall agree to pass the Bill, it shall be sent, together with the Objections, to the other House, by which it shall likewise be reconsidered, and if approved by two thirds of that House, it shall become a Law. But in all such Cases the Votes of both Houses shall be determined by Yeas and Nays, and the Names of the Persons voting for and against the Bill shall be entered on the Journal of each House respectively. If any Bill shall not be returned by the President within ten Days (Sundays excepted) after it shall have been presented to him, the Same shall be a Law, in like Manner as if he had signed it, unless the Congress by their Adjournment prevent its Return, in which Case it shall not be a Law.

Every order, Resolution, or Vote to which the Concurrence of the Senate and House of Representatives may be necessary (except on a question of Adjournment) shall be presented to the President of the United States; and before the Same shall take Effect, shall be approved by him, or being disapproved by him, shall be repassed by two thirds of the Senate and House of Representatives, according to the Rules and Limitations prescribed in the Case of a Bill.

Section 8—Powers of Congress.

The Congress shall have Power To lay and collect Taxes, Duties, Imposts and Excises, to pay the Debts and provide for the common Defence and general Welfare of the United States; but all Duties, Imposts and Excises shall be uniform throughout the United States;

To borrow money on the credit of the United States;

To regulate Commerce with foreign Nations, and among the several States, and with the Indian Tribes;

To establish an uniform Rule of Naturalization, and uniform Laws on the subject of Bankruptcies throughout the United States;

To coin Money, regulate the Value thereof, and of foreign Coin, and fix the Standard of Weights and Measures;

To provide for the Punishment of counterfeiting the Securities and current Coin of the United States;

To establish Post Offices and post Roads;

To promote the Progress of Science and useful Arts, by securing for limited Times to Authors and Inventors the exclusive Right to their respective Writings and Discoveries;

To constitute Tribunals inferior to the supreme Court;

To define and punish Piracies and Felonies committed on the high Seas, and Offenses against the Law of Nations;

To declare War, grant Letters of Marque and Reprisal, and make Rules concerning Captures on Land and Water;

To raise and support Armies, but no Appropriation of Money to that Use shall be for a longer Term than two Years;

To provide and maintain a Navy;

To make Rules for the Government and Regulation of the land and naval Forces;

To provide for calling forth the Militia to execute the Laws of the Union, suppress Insurrections and repel Invasions;

To provide for organizing, arming, and disciplining the Militia, and for governing such Part of them as may be employed in the Service of the United States, reserving to the States respectively, the Appointment of the Officers, and the Authority of training the Militia according to the discipline prescribed by Congress;

To exercise exclusive Legislation in all Cases whatsoever, over such District (not exceeding ten Miles square) as may, by Cession of particular States, and the acceptance of Congress, become the Seat of the Government of the United States, and to exercise like Authority over all Places purchased by the Consent of the Legislature of the State in which the Same shall be, for the Erection of Forts, Magazines, Arsenals, dock-Yards, and other needful Buildings;—And

To make all Laws which shall be necessary and proper for carrying into Execution the foregoing Powers, and all other Powers vested by this Constitution in the Government of the United States, or in any Department or Officer thereof.

Section 9—Provision as to migration or importation of certain persons. Habeas corpus, bills of attainder, etc. Taxes, how apportioned. No export duty. No commercial preference. Money, how drawn from Treasury, etc. No titular nobility. Officers not to receive presents, etc.

The Migration or Importation of such Persons as any of the States now existing shall think proper to admit, shall not be prohibited by the Congress prior to the Year one thousand eight hundred and eight, but a tax or duty may be imposed on such Importation, not exceeding ten dollars for each Person.

The privilege of the Writ of Habeas Corpus shall not be suspended, unless when in Cases of Rebellion or Invasion the public Safety may require it.

No Bill of Attainder or ex post facto Law shall be passed.

No capitation, or other direct, Tax shall be laid, unless in Proportion to the Census or Enumeration herein before directed to be taken. *[Modified by Amendment XVI.]*

No Tax or Duty shall be laid on Articles exported from any State.

No Preference shall be given by any Regulation of Commerce or Revenue to the Ports of one State over those of another: nor shall Vessels bound to, or from, one State, be obliged to enter, clear, or pay Duties in another.

No Money shall be drawn from the Treasury, but in Consequence of Appropriations made by Law; and a regular Statement and Account of the Receipts and Expenditures of all public Money shall be published from time to time.

No Title of Nobility shall be granted by the United States: and no Person holding any Office of Profit or Trust under them, shall, without the Consent of the Congress, accept of any present, Emolument, Office, or Title, of any kind whatever, from any King, Prince, or foreign State.

Section 10—States prohibited from the exercise of certain powers.

No State shall enter into any Treaty, Alliance, or Confederation; grant Letters of Marque and Reprisal; coin Money; emit Bills of Credit; make any Thing but gold and silver Coin a Tender in Payment of Debts; pass any Bill of Attainder, ex post facto Law, or Law impairing the Obligation of Contracts, or grant any Title of Nobility.

No State shall, without the Consent of the Congress, lay any Imposts or Duties on Imports or Exports, except what may be absolutely necessary for executing its inspection Laws: and the net Produce of all Duties and Imposts, laid by any State on Imports or Exports, shall be for the Use of the Treasury of the United States; and all such Laws shall be subject to the Revision and Control of the Congress.

No State shall, without the Consent of Congress, lay any duty of Tonnage, keep Troops, or Ships of War in time of Peace, enter into any Agreement or Compact with another State, or with a foreign Power, or engage in War, unless actually invaded, or in such imminent Danger as will not admit of delay.

ARTICLE II.

Section 1—President: his term of office. Electors of President; number and how appointed. Electors to vote on same day. Qualification of President. On whom his duties devolve in case of his removal, death, etc. President's compensation. His oath of office.

The executive Power shall be vested in a President of the United States of America. He shall hold his Office during the Term of four Years, and, together with the Vice President, chosen for the same Term, be elected, as follows.

Each State shall appoint, in such Manner as the Legislature thereof may direct, a Number of Electors, equal to the whole Number of Senators and Representatives to which the State may be entitled in the Congress: but no Senator or Representative, or Person holding an Office of Trust or Profit under the United States, shall be appointed an Elector.

[The Electors shall meet in their respective States, and vote by Ballot for two persons, of whom one at least shall not be an Inhabitant of the same State with themselves. And they shall make a List of all the Persons voted for, and of the Number of Votes for each; which List they shall sign and certify, and transmit sealed to the Seat of the Government of the United States, directed to the President of the Senate. The President of the Senate shall, in the Presence of the Senate and House of Representatives, open all the Certificates, and the Votes shall then be counted. The Person having the greatest Number of Votes shall be the President, if such Number be a Majority of the whole Number of Electors appointed; and if there be more than one who have such Majority, and have an equal Number of Votes, then the House of Representatives shall immediately chuse by Ballot one of them for President; and if no Person have a Majority, then from the five highest on the List the said House shall in like Manner chuse the President. But in chusing the President, the Votes shall be taken by States, the Representation from each State having one Vote; a quorum for this Purpose shall consist of a Member or Members from two thirds of the States, and a Majority of all the States shall be necessary to a Choice. In every Case, after the Choice of the President, the Person having the greatest Number of Votes of the Electors shall be the Vice President. But if there should remain two or more who have equal Votes, the Senate shall chuse from them by Ballot the Vice-President.]

[This clause was superseded by Amendment XII.]

The Congress may detemine the Time of chusing the Electors, and the Day on which they shall give their Votes; which Day shall be the same throughout the United States.

No person except a natural born Citizen, or a Citizen of the United States, at the time of the Adoption of this Constitution, shall be eligible to the Office of President; neither shall any Person be eligible to that Office who shall not have attained to the Age of thirty-five Years, and been fourteen Years a Resident within the United States.

[For qualification of the Vice President, see Amendment XII.]

In Case of the Removal of the President from Office, or of his Death, Resignation, or Inability to discharge the Powers and Duties of the said Office, the same shall devolve on the Vice President, and the Congress may by Law, provide for the Case of Removal, Death, Resignation or Inability, both of the President and Vice President, declaring what Officer shall then act as President, and such Officer shall act accordingly, until the Disability be removed, or a President shall be elected.

[This clause has been modified by Amendments XX and XXV.]

The President shall, at stated Times, receive for his Services, a Compensation, which shall neither be encreased nor diminished during the Period for which he shall have been elected, and he shall not receive within that Period any other Emolument from the United States, or any of them.

Before he enter on the Execution of his Office, he shall take the following Oath or Affirmation:–"I do solemnly swear (or affirm) that I will faithfully execute the Office of President of the United States, and will to the best of my Ability, preserve, protect and defend the Constitution of the United States."

Section 2—President to be Commander-in-Chief. He may require opinions of cabinet officers, etc., may pardon. Treaty-making power. Nomination of certain officers. When President may fill vacancies.

The President shall be Commander in Chief of the Army and Navy of the United States, and of the Militia of the several States, when called into the actual Service of the United States; he may require the Opinion in writing, of the principal Officer in each of the executive Departments, upon any subject relating to the Duties of their respective Offices, and he shall have Power to Grant Reprieves and Pardons for Offenses against the United States, except in Cases of Impeachment.

He shall have Power, by and with the Advice and Consent of the Senate, to make Treaties, provided two-thirds of the Senators present concur; and he shall nominate, and by and with the Advice and Consent of the Senate, shall appoint Ambassadors, other public Ministers and Consuls, Judges of the supreme Court, and all other Officers of the United States, whose Appointments are not herein otherwise provided for, and which shall be established by Law: but the Congress may by Law vest the Appointment of such inferior Officers, as they think proper, in the President alone, in the Courts of Law, or in the Heads of Departments.

The President shall have Power to fill up all Vacancies that may happen during the Recess of the Senate, by granting Commissions which shall expire at the End of their next Session.

Section 3—President shall communicate to Congress. He may convene and adjourn Congress, in case of disagreement, etc. Shall receive ambassadors, execute laws, and commission officers.

He shall from time to time give to the Congress Information of the State of the Union, and recommend to their Consideration such Measures as he shall judge necessary and expedient; he may, on extraordinary Occasions, convene both Houses, or either of them, and in Case of Disagreement between them, with Respect to the Time of Adjournment, he may adjourn them to such Time as he shall think proper; he shall receive Ambassadors and other public Ministers; he shall take Care that the Laws be faithfully executed, and shall Commission all the Officers of the United States.

Section 4—All civil offices forfeited for certain crimes.

The President, Vice President and all civil Officers of the United States, shall be removed from Office on Impeachment for, and Conviction of, Treason, Bribery, or other high Crimes and Misdemeanors.

ARTICLE III.

Section 1—Judicial powers, Tenure. Compensation.

The judicial Power of the United States, shall be vested in one supreme Court, and in such inferior Courts as the Congress may from time to time ordain and establish. The Judges, both of the supreme and inferior Courts, shall hold their Offices during good Behaviour, and shall, at stated Times, receive for their Services, a Compensation, which shall not be diminished during their Continuance in Office.

Section 2—Judicial power; to what cases it extends. Original jurisdiction of Supreme Court; appellate jurisdiction. Trial by jury, etc. Trial, where.

The judicial Power shall extend to all Cases, in Law and Equity, arising under this Constitution, the Laws of the United States, and Treaties made, or which shall be made, under their Authority;–to all Cases affecting Ambassadors, other public Ministers and Consuls;–to all Cases of admiralty and maritime Jurisdiction;–to Controversies to which the United States shall be a Party;–to Controversies between two or more States;–between a State and Citizens of another State;–between Citizens of different States;–between Citizens of the same State claiming Lands under Grants of different States, and between a State, or the Citizens thereof, and foreign States, Citizens or Subjects.

[This section is modified by Amendment XI.]

In all Cases affecting Ambassadors, other public Ministers and Consuls, and those in which a State shall be Party, the supreme Court shall have original Jurisdiction. In all the other Cases before mentioned, the supreme Court shall have appellate Jurisdiction, both as to Law and Fact, with such Exceptions, and under such Regulations as the Congress shall make.

The trial of all Crimes, except in Cases of Impeachment, shall be by Jury; and such Trial shall be held in the State where the said Crimes shall have been committed; but when not committed within any State, the Trial shall be at such Place or Places as the Congress may by Law have directed.

Section 3—Treason Defined, Proof of, Punishment of.

Treason against the United States, shall consist only in levying War against them, or in adhering to their Enemies, giving them Aid and Comfort. No Person shall be convicted of Treason unless on the Testimony of two Witnesses to the same overt Act, or on Confession in open Court.

The Congress shall have Power to declare the Punishment of Treason, but no Attainder of Treason shall work Corruption of Blood, or Forfeiture except during the Life of the Person attainted.

ARTICLE IV.

Section 1—Each State to give credit to the public acts, etc., of every other State.

Full Faith and Credit shall be given in each State to the public Acts, Records, and judicial Proceedings of every other State. And the Congress may by general Laws prescribe the Manner in which such Acts, Records and Proceedings shall be proved, and the Effect thereof.

Section 2—Privileges of citizens of each State. Fugitives from justice to be delivered up. Persons held to service having escaped, to be delivered up.

The Citizens of each State shall be entitled to all Privileges and Immunities of Citizens in the several States.

A Person charged in any State with Treason, Felony, or other Crime, who shall flee from Justice, and be found in another State, shall on demand of the executive Authority of the State from which he fled, be delivered up, to be removed to the State having Jurisdiction of the Crime.

[No Person held to Service or Labour in one State, under the Laws thereof, escaping into another, shall, in Consequence of any Law or Regulation therein, be discharged from such Service or Labour, but shall be delivered up on Claim of the Party to whom such Service or Labour may be due.] [This clause was superseded by Amendment XIII.]

Section 3—Admission of new States. Power of Congress over territory and other property.

New States may be admitted by the Congress into this Union; but no new State shall be formed or erected within the Jurisdiction of any other State; nor any State be formed by the Junction of two or more States, or parts of States, without the Consent of the Legislatures of the States concerned as well as of the Congress.

The Congress shall have Power to dispose of and make all needful Rules and Regulations respecting the Territory or other Property belonging to the United States; and nothing in this Constitution shall be so construed as to Prejudice any Claims of the United States, or of any particular State.

Section 4—Republican form of government guaranteed. Each state to be protected.

The United States shall guarantee to every State in this Union a Republican Form of Government, and shall protect each of them against Invasion; and on Application of the Legislature, or of the Executive (when the Legislature cannot be convened) against domestic Violence.

ARTICLE V.

Constitution: how amended; proviso.

The Congress, whenever two-thirds of both Houses shall deem it necessary, shall propose Amendments to this Constitution, or, on the Application of the Legislatures of two-thirds of the several States, shall call a Convention for proposing Amendments, which, in either Case, shall be valid to all Intents and Purposes, as part of this Constitution, when ratified by the Legislatures of three-fourths of the several States, or by Conventions in three-fourths thereof, as the one or the other Mode of Ratification may be proposed by the Congress: Provided that no Amendment which may be made prior to the Year One thousand eight hundred and eight shall in any Manner affect the first and fourth Clauses in the Ninth Section of the first Article; and that no State, without its Consent, shall be deprived of its equal Suffrage in the Senate.

ARTICLE VI.

Certain debts, etc., declared valid. Supremacy of Constitution, treaties, and laws of the United States. Oath to support Constitution, by whom taken. No religious test.

All Debts contracted and Engagements entered into, before the Adoption of this Constitution, shall be as valid against the United States under this Constitution, as under the Confederation.

This Constitution, and the Laws of the United States which shall be made in Pursuance thereof; and all Treaties made, or which shall be made, under the Authority of the United States, shall be the supreme Law of the Land; and the Judges in every State shall be bound thereby, any Thing in the Constitution or Laws of any State to the Contrary notwithstanding.

The Senators and Representatives before mentioned, and the Members of the several State Legislatures, and all executive and judicial Officers, both of the United States and of the several States, shall be bound by Oath or Affirmation, to support this Constitution; but no religious Test shall ever be required as a Qualification to any Office or public Trust under the United States.

ARTICLE VII.

What ratification shall establish Constitution.

The Ratification of the Conventions of nine States shall be sufficient for the Establishment of this Constitution between the States so ratifying the Same.

Done in Convention by the Unanimous Consent of the States present the Seventeenth Day of September in the Year of our Lord one thousand seven hundred and Eighty seven and of the Independence of the United States of America the Twelfth.

In Witness whereof We have hereunto subscribed our Names.

Go WASHINGTON, Presidt and deputy from Virginia

New Hampshire—John Langdon, Nicholas Gilman

Massachusetts—Nathaniel Gorham, Rufus King

Connecticut—Wm. Saml. Johnson, Roger Sherman

New York—Alexander Hamilton

New Jersey—Wil: Livingston, David Brearley, Wm. Paterson, Jona: Dayton

Pennsylvania—B Franklin, Thomas Mifflin, Robt Morris, Geo. Clymer, Thos. FitzSimons, Jared Ingersoll, James Wilson, Gouv Morris

Delaware—Geo: Read, Gunning Bedford jun, John Dickinson, Richard Bassett, Jaco: Broom

Maryland—James McHenry, Dan of St Thos. Jenifer, Danl Carroll

Virginia—John Blair, James Madison Jr.

North Carolina—Wm. Blount, Rich'd Dobbs Spaight, Hu Williamson

South Carolina—J. Rutledge, Charles Cotesworth Pinckney, Charles Pinckney, Pierce Butler

Georgia—William Few, Abr Baldwin

Attest: William Jackson, Secretary.

Ten Original Amendments: The Bill of Rights

In force Dec. 15, 1791

[The First Congress, at its first session in the City of New York, Sept. 25, 1789, submitted to the states 12 amendments to clarify certain individual and state rights not named in the Constitution. They are generally called the Bill of Rights.

Influential in framing these amendments was the Declaration of Rights of Virginia, written by George Mason (1725-1792) in 1776. Mason, a Virginia delegate to the Constitutional Convention, did not sign the Constitution and opposed its ratification on the ground that it did not sufficiently oppose slavery or safeguard individual rights.

In the preamble to the resolution offering the proposed amendments, Congress said: "The conventions of a number of the States having at the time of their adopting the Constitution, expressed a desire, in order to prevent misconstruction or abuse of its powers, that further declaratory and restrictive clauses should be added, and as extending the ground of public confidence in the government will best insure the beneficent ends of its institution, be it resolved," etc.

Ten of these amendments, now commonly known as one to 10 inclusive, but originally 3 to 12 inclusive, were ratified by the states as follows: New Jersey, Nov. 20, 1789; Maryland, Dec. 19, 1789; North Carolina, Dec. 22, 1789; South Carolina, Jan. 19, 1790; New Hampshire, Jan. 25, 1790; Delaware, Jan. 28, 1790; New York, Feb. 27, 1790; Pennsylvania, Mar. 10, 1790; Rhode Island, June 7, 1790; Vermont, Nov. 3, 1791; Virginia, Dec. 15, 1791; Massachusetts, Mar. 2, 1939; Georgia, Mar. 18, 1939; Connecticut, Apr. 19, 1939. These original 10 ratified amendments follow as Amendments I to X inclusive.

Of the two original proposed amendments that were not ratified promptly by the necessary number of states, the first related to apportionment of Representatives; the second, relating to compensation of members of Congress, was ratified in 1992 and became Amendment 27.]

AMENDMENT I.

Religious establishment prohibited. Freedom of speech, of press, right to assemble and to petition.

Congress shall make no law respecting an establishment of religion, or prohibiting the free exercise thereof; or abridging the freedom of speech, or of the press; or the right of the people peaceably to assemble, and to petition the Government for a redress of grievances.

AMENDMENT II.

Right to keep and bear arms.

A well regulated Militia, being necessary to the security of a free State, the right of the people to keep and bear Arms, shall not be infringed.

AMENDMENT III.

Conditions for quarters for soldiers.

No Soldier shall, in time of peace be quartered in any house, without the consent of the Owner, nor in time of war, but in a manner to be prescribed by law.

AMENDMENT IV.

Protection from unreasonable search and seizure.

The right of the people to be secure in their persons, houses, papers, and effects, against unreasonable searches and seizures, shall not be violated, and no Warrants shall issue, but upon probable cause, supported by Oath or affirmation, and particularly describing the place to be searched, and the persons or things to be seized.

AMENDMENT V.

Provisions concerning prosecution and due process of law. Double jeopardy restriction. Private property not to be taken without compensation.

No person shall be held to answer for a capital, or otherwise infamous crime, unless on a presentment or indictment of a Grand Jury, except in cases arising in the land or naval forces, or in the Militia, when in actual service in time of War or public danger; nor shall any person be subject for the same offence to be twice put in jeopardy of life or limb; nor shall be compelled in any criminal case to be a witness against himself, nor be deprived of life, liberty, or property, without due process of law; nor shall private property be taken for public use, without just compensation.

AMENDMENT VI.

Right to speedy trial, witnesses, etc.

In all criminal prosecutions, the accused shall enjoy the right to a speedy and public trial, by an impartial jury of the State and district wherein the crime shall have been committed, which district shall have been previously ascertained by law, and to be informed of the nature and cause of the accusation; to be confronted with the witnesses against him; to have compulsory process for obtaining witnesses in his favor, and to have the Assistance of Counsel for his defence.

AMENDMENT VII.

Right of trial by jury.

In suits at common law, where the value in controversy shall exceed twenty dollars, the right of trial by jury shall be preserved, and no fact tried by a jury, shall be otherwise reexamined in any Court of the United States, than according to the rules of the common law.

AMENDMENT VIII.

Excessive bail or fines; cruel and unusual punishment.

Excessive bail shall not be required, nor excessive fines imposed, nor cruel and unusual punishments inflicted.

AMENDMENT IX.

Rule of construction of Constitution.

The enumeration in the Constitution, of certain rights, shall not be construed to deny or disparage others retained by the people.

AMENDMENT X.

Rights of States under Constitution.

The powers not delegated to the United States by the Constitution, nor prohibited by it to the States, are reserved to the States respectively, or to the people.

IT'S A FACT: Of the amendments that make up The Bill of Rights, the one least often litigated is the third amendment, which bars the quartering of soldiers in private homes in peacetime without the consent of the owner.

Amendments Since the Bill of Rights

AMENDMENT XI.

Judicial powers construed.

The Judicial power of the United States shall not be construed to extend to any suit in law or equity, commenced or prosecuted against one of the United States by Citizens of another State, or by Citizens or Subjects of any Foreign State.

[This amendment was proposed to the Legislatures of the several States by the Third Congress on March. 4, 1794, and was declared to have been ratified in a message from the President to Congress, dated Jan. 8, 1798.

[It was on Jan. 5, 1798, that Secretary of State Pickering received from 12 of the States authenticated ratifications, and informed President John Adams of that fact.

[As a result of later research in the Department of State, it is now established that Amendment XI became part of the Constitution on Feb. 7, 1795, for on that date it had been ratified by 12 States as follows:

[1. New York, Mar. 27, 1794. 2. Rhode Island, Mar. 31, 1794. 3. Connecticut, May 8, 1794. 4. New Hampshire, June 16, 1794. 5. Massachusetts, June 26, 1794. 6. Vermont, between Oct. 9, 1794, and Nov. 9, 1794. 7. Virginia, Nov. 18, 1794. 8. Georgia, Nov. 29, 1794. 9. Kentucky, Dec. 7, 1794. 10. Maryland, Dec. 26, 1794. 11. Delaware, Jan. 23, 1795. 12. North Carolina, Feb. 7, 1795.

[On June 1, 1796, more than a year after Amendment XI had become a part of the Constitution—but before anyone was officially aware of this—Tennessee had been admitted as a State; but not until Oct. 16, 1797, was a certified copy of the resolution of Congress proposing the amendment sent to the Governor of Tennessee, John Sevier, by Secretary of State

Pickering, whose office was then at Trenton, New Jersey, because of the epidemic of yellow fever at Philadelphia; it seems, however, that the Legislature of Tennessee took no action on Amendment XI, owing doubtless to the fact that public announcement of its adoption was made soon thereafter.

[Besides the necessary 12 States, one other, South Carolina, ratified Amendment XI, but this action was not taken until Dec. 4, 1797; the two remaining States, New Jersey and Pennsylvania, failed to ratify.]

AMENDMENT XII.

Manner of choosing President and Vice-President.

[Proposed by Congress Dec. 9, 1803; ratified June 15, 1804.]

The Electors shall meet in their respective states and vote by ballot for President and Vice-President, one of whom, at least, shall not be an inhabitant of the same state with themselves; they shall name in their ballots the person voted for as President, and in distinct ballots the person voted for as Vice-President, and they shall make distinct lists of all persons voted for as President, and of all persons voted for as Vice-President, and of the number of votes for each, which lists they shall sign and certify, and transmit sealed to the seat of the government of the United States, directed to the President of the Senate;–The President of the Senate shall, in presence of the Senate and House of Representatives, open all the certificates and the votes shall then be counted;—The person having the greatest number of votes for President, shall be the President, if such number be a majority of the whole number of Electors appointed; and if no person have such majority, then from the persons having the highest numbers not exceeding three on the list of those voted for as President, the House of Representatives shall choose immediately, by ballot, the President. But in choosing the President, the votes shall be taken by states, the representation from each state having one vote; a quorum for this purpose shall consist of a member or members from two-thirds of the states, and a majority of all the states shall be necessary to a choice. *[And if the House of Representatives shall not choose a President whenever the right of choice shall devolve upon them, before the fourth day of March next following, then the Vice-President shall act as President, as in the case of the death or other constitutional disability of the President.] [The words in parentheses were superseded by Amendment XX, section 3.]* The person having the greatest number of votes as Vice-President, shall be the Vice-President, if such number be a majority of the whole number of Electors appointed, and if no person have a majority, then from the two highest numbers on the list, the Senate shall choose the Vice-President; a quorum for the purpose shall consist of two-thirds of the whole number of Senators, and a majority of the whole number shall be necessary to a choice. But no person constitutionally ineligible to the office of President shall be eligible to that of Vice-President of the United States.

THE RECONSTRUCTION AMENDMENTS

[Amendments XIII, XIV, and XV are commonly known as the Reconstruction Amendments, inasmuch as they followed the Civil War, and were drafted by Republicans who were bent on imposing their own policy of reconstruction on the South. Post-bellum legislatures there—Mississippi, South Carolina, Georgia, for example—had set up laws which, it was charged, were contrived to perpetuate Negro slavery under other names.]

AMENDMENT XIII.

Slavery abolished.

[Proposed by Congress Jan. 31, 1865; ratified Dec. 6, 1865. The amendment, when first proposed by a resolution in Congress, was passed by the Senate, 38 to 6, on Apr. 8, 1864, but was defeated in the House, 95 to 66 on June 15, 1864. On reconsideration by the House, on Jan. 31, 1865, the resolution passed, 119 to 56. It was approved by President Lincoln on Feb. 1, 1865, although the Supreme Court had decided in 1798 that the President has nothing to do with the proposing of amendments to the Constitution, or their adoption.]

1. Neither slavery nor involuntary servitude, except as a punishment for crime whereof the party shall have been duly convicted, shall exist within the United States, or any place subject to their jurisdiction.

2. Congress shall have power to enforce this article by appropriate legislation.

AMENDMENT XIV.

Citizenship rights not to be abridged.

[The following amendment was proposed to the Legislatures of the several states by the 39th Congress, June 13, 1866, ratified July 9, 1868, and declared to have been ratified in a proclamation by the Secretary of State, July 28, 1868.]

[The 14th amendment was adopted only by virtue of ratification subsequent to earlier rejections. Newly constituted legislatures in both North Carolina and South Carolina (respectively July 4 and 9, 1868), ratified the proposed amendment, although earlier legislatures had rejected the proposal. The Secretary of State issued a proclamation, which, though doubtful as to the effect of attempted withdrawals by Ohio and New Jersey, entertained no doubt as to the validity of the ratification by North and South Carolina. The following day (July 21, 1868), Congress passed a resolution which declared the 14th Amendment to be a part of the Constitution and directed the Secretary of State so to promulgate it. The Secretary waited, however, until the newly constituted Legislature of Georgia had ratified the amendment, subsequent to an earlier rejection, before the promulgation of the ratification of the new amendment.]

1. All persons born or naturalized in the United States, and subject to the jurisdiction thereof, are citizens of the United States and of the State wherein they reside. No State shall make or enforce any law which shall abridge the privileges or immunities of citizens of the United States; nor shall any State deprive any person of life, liberty, or property, without due process of law; nor deny to any person within its jurisdiction the equal protection of the laws.

2. Representatives shall be apportioned among the several States according to their respective numbers, counting the whole number of persons in each State, excluding Indians not taxed. But when the right to vote at any election for the choice of electors for President and Vice-President of the United States, Representatives in Congress, the Executive and Judicial officers of a State, or the members of the Legislature thereof, is denied to any of the male inhabitants of such State, being twenty-one years of age, and citizens of the United States, or in any way abridged, except for participation in rebellion, or other crime, the basis of representation therein shall be reduced in the proportion which the number of such male citizens shall bear to the whole number of male citizens twenty-one years of age in such State.

3. No person shall be a Senator or Representative in Congress, or elector of President and Vice-President, or hold any office, civil or military, under the United States, or under any State, who, having previously taken an oath, as a member of Congress, or as an officer of the United States, or as a member of any State legislature, or as an executive or judicial officer of any State, to support the Constitution of the United States, shall have engaged in insurrection or rebellion against the same, or given aid or comfort to the enemies thereof. But Congress may by a vote of two-thirds of each House, remove such disability.

4. The validity of the public debt of the United States, authorized by law, including debts incurred for payment of pensions and bounties for services in suppressing insurrection or rebellion, shall not be questioned. But neither the United States nor any State shall assume or pay any debt or obligation incurred in aid of insurrection or rebellion against the United States, or any claim for the loss or emancipation of any slave; but all such debts, obligations and claims shall be held illegal and void.

The Congress shall have power to enforce, by appropriate legislation, the provisions of this article.

AMENDMENT XV.

Race no bar to voting rights.

[The following amendment was proposed to the legislatures of the several States by the 40th Congress, Feb. 26, 1869, and ratified Feb. 8, 1870.]

1. The right of citizens of the United States to vote shall not be denied or abridged by the United States or by any State on account of race, color, or previous condition of servitude–

2. The Congress shall have power to enforce this article by appropriate legislation.

AMENDMENT XVI.
Income taxes authorized.

[Proposed by Congress July 12, 1909; ratified Feb. 3, 1913.]

The Congress shall have power to lay and collect taxes on incomes, from whatever source derived, without apportionment among the several States, and without regard to any census or enumeration.

AMENDMENT XVII.
United States Senators to be elected by direct popular vote.

[Proposed by Congress May 13, 1912; ratified Apr. 8, 1913.]

The Senate of the United States shall be composed of two Senators from each State, elected by the people thereof, for six years; and each Senator shall have one vote. The electors in each State shall have the qualifications requisite for electors of the most numerous branch of the State legislatures.

When vacancies happen in the representation of any State in the Senate, the executive authority of such State shall issue writs of election to fill such vacancies: *Provided,* That the legislature of any State may empower the executive thereof to make temporary appointments until the people fill the vacancies by election as the legislature may direct.

This amendment shall not be so construed as to affect the election or term of any Senator chosen before it becomes valid as part of the Constitution.

AMENDMENT XVIII.
Liquor prohibition amendment.

[Proposed by Congress Dec. 18, 1917; ratified Jan. 16, 1919. Repealed by Amendment XXI, effective Dec. 5, 1933.]

1. After one year from the ratification of this article the manufacture, sale, or transportation of intoxicating liquors within, the importation thereof into, or the exportation thereof from the United States and all territory subject to the jurisdiction thereof for beverage purposes is hereby prohibited.

2. The Congress and the several States shall have concurrent power to enforce this article by appropriate legislation.

3. This article shall be inoperative unless it shall have been ratified as an amendment to the Constitution by the legislatures of the several States as provided in the Constitution, within seven years from the date of the submission hereof to the States by the Congress.

[The total vote in the Senates of the various States was 1,310 for, 237 against—84.6% dry. In the lower houses of the States the vote was 3,782 for, 1,035 against—78.5% dry.

[The amendment ultimately was adopted by all the States except Connecticut and Rhode Island.]

AMENDMENT XIX.
Giving nationwide suffrage to women.

[Proposed by Congress June 4, 1919; ratified Aug. 18, 1920.]

The right of citizens of the United States to vote shall not be denied or abridged by the United States or by any State on account of sex.

Congress shall have power to enforce this Article by appropriate legislation.

AMENDMENT XX.
Terms of President and Vice President to begin on Jan. 20; those of Senators, Representatives, Jan. 3.

[Proposed by Congress Mar. 2, 1932; ratified Jan. 23, 1933.]

1. The terms of the President and Vice President shall end at noon on the 20th day of January, and the terms of Senators and Representatives at noon on the 3d day of January, of the years in which such terms would have ended if this article had not been ratified; and the terms of their successors shall then begin.

2. The Congress shall assemble at least once in every year, and such meeting shall begin at noon on the 3d day of January, unless they shall by law appoint a different day.

3. If, at the time fixed for the beginning of the term of the President, the President elect shall have died, the Vice President elect shall become President. If a President shall not have been chosen before the time fixed for the beginning of his term, or if the President elect shall have failed to qualify, then the Vice President elect shall act as President until a President shall have qualified; and the Congress may by law provide for the case wherein neither a President elect nor a Vice President elect shall have qualified, declaring who shall then act as President, or the manner in which one who is to act shall be selected, and such person shall act accordingly until a President or Vice President shall have qualified.

4. The Congress may by law provide for the case of the death of any of the persons from whom the House of Representatives may choose a President whenever the right of choice shall have devolved upon them, and for the case of the death of any of the persons from whom the Senate may choose a Vice President whenever the right of choice shall have devolved upon them.

5. Sections 1 and 2 shall take effect on the 15th day of October following the ratification of this article (Oct. 1933).

6. This article shall be inoperative unless it shall have been ratified as an amendment to the Constitution by the legislatures of three-fourths of the several States within seven years from the date of its submission.

AMENDMENT XXI.
Repeal of Amendment XVIII.

[Proposed by Congress Feb. 20, 1933; ratified Dec. 5, 1933.]

1. The eighteenth article of amendment to the Constitution of the United States is hereby repealed.

2. The transportation or importation into any State, Territory, or possession of the United States for delivery or use therein of intoxicating liquors, in violation of the laws thereof, is hereby prohibited.

3. This article shall be inoperative unless it shall have been ratified as an amendment to the Constitution by conventions in the several States, as provided in the Constitution, within seven years from the date of the submission hereof to the States by the Congress.

AMENDMENT XXII.
Limiting Presidential terms of office.

[Proposed by Congress Mar. 24, 1947; ratified Feb. 27, 1951.]

1. No person shall be elected to the office of the President more than twice, and no person who has held the office of President, or acted as President, for more than two years of a term to which some other person was elected President shall be elected to the office of the President more than once. But this Article shall not apply to any person holding the office of President when this Article was proposed by the Congress, and shall not prevent any person who may be holding the office of President, or acting as President, during the term within which this Article becomes operative from holding the office of President or acting as President during the remainder of such term.

2. This article shall be inoperative unless it shall have been ratified as an amendment to the Constitution by the legislatures of three-fourths of the several States within seven years from the date of its submission to the States by the Congress.

AMENDMENT XXIII.
Presidential vote for District of Columbia.

[Proposed by Congress June 16, 1960; ratified Mar. 29, 1961.]

1. The District constituting the seat of Government of the United States shall appoint in such manner as the Congress may direct:

A number of electors of President and Vice President equal to the whole number of Senators and Representatives in Congress to which the District would be entitled if it were a State, but in no event more than the least populous State; they shall be in addition to those appointed by the States, but they shall be considered, for the purposes of the election of President and Vice President, to be electors appointed by a State; and they shall meet in the District and perform such duties as provided by the twelfth article of amendment.

2. The Congress shall have power to enforce this article by appropriate legislation.

AMENDMENT XXIV.
Barring poll tax in federal elections.

[Proposed by Congress Aug. 27, 1962; ratified Jan. 23, 1964.]

1. The right of citizens of the United States to vote in any primary or other election for President or Vice President, for electors for President or Vice President, or for Senator or Representative in Congress, shall not be denied or abridged by the United States or any State by reason of failure to pay any poll tax or other tax.

2. The Congress shall have power to enforce this article by appropriate legislation.

AMENDMENT XXV.
Presidential disability and succession.

[Proposed by Congress July 6, 1965; ratified Feb. 10, 1967.]

1. In case of the removal of the President from office or of his death or resignation, the Vice President shall become President.

2. Whenever there is a vacancy in the office of the Vice President, the President shall nominate a Vice President who shall take office upon confirmation by a majority vote of both houses of Congress.

3. Whenever the President transmits to the President pro tempore of the Senate and the Speaker of the House of Representatives his written declaration that he is unable to discharge the powers and duties of his office, and until he transmits to them a written declaration to the contrary, such powers and duties shall be discharged by the Vice President as Acting President.

4. Whenever the Vice President and a majority of either the principal officers of the executive departments or of such other body as Congress may by law provide, transmit to the President pro tempore of the Senate and the Speaker of the House of Representatives their written declaration that the President is unable to discharge the powers and duties of his office, the Vice President shall immediately assume the powers and duties of the office as Acting President.

Thereafter, when the President transmits to the President pro tempore of the Senate and the Speaker of the House of Representatives his written declaration that no inability exists, he shall resume the powers and duties of his office unless the Vice President and a majority of either the principal officers of the executive department or of such other body as Congress may by law provide, transmit within four days to the President pro tempore of the Senate and the Speaker of the House of Representatives their written declaration that the President is unable to discharge the powers and duties of his office. Thereupon Congress shall decide the issue, assembling within forty-eight hours for that purpose if not in session. If the Congress, within twenty-one days after receipt of the latter written declaration, or, if Congress is not in session, within twenty-one days after Congress is required to assemble, determines by two-thirds vote of both Houses that the President is unable to discharge the powers and duties of his office, the Vice President shall continue to discharge the same as Acting President; otherwise, the President shall resume the powers and duties of his office.

AMENDMENT XXVI.
Lowering voting age to 18 years.

[Proposed by Congress Mar. 23, 1971; ratified June 30, 1971.]

1. The right of citizens of the United States, who are eighteen years of age or older, to vote shall not be denied or abridged by the United States or by any State on account of age.

2. The Congress shall have the power to enforce this article by appropriate legislation.

AMENDMENT XXVII.
Congressional pay.

[Proposed by Congress Sept. 25, 1789; ratified May 7, 1992.]

No law, varying the compensation for the services of the Senators and Representatives, shall take effect, until an election of Representatives shall have intervened.

How a Bill Becomes a Law

A senator or representative introduces a bill in Congress by sending it to the clerk of the House or the Senate, who assigns it a number and title. This procedure is termed the first reading. The clerk then refers the bill to the appropriate committee of the Senate or House.

If the committee opposes the bill, it will table, or kill, it. Otherwise, the committee holds hearings to listen to opinions and facts offered by members and other interested people. The committee then debates the bill and possibly offers amendments. A vote is taken, and if favorable, the bill is sent back to the clerk of the House or Senate.

The clerk reads the bill to the house—the second reading. Members may then debate the bill and suggest amendments.

After debate and possibly amendment, the bill is given a third reading, simply of the title, and put to a voice or roll-call vote.

If passed, the bill goes to the other house, where it may be defeated or passed, with or without amendments. If defeated, the bill dies. If passed with amendments, a conference committee made up of members of both houses works out the differences and arrives at a compromise.

After passage of the final version by both houses, the bill is sent to the president. If the president signs it, the bill becomes a law. The president may, however, veto the bill by refusing to sign it and sending it back to the house where it originated, with reasons for the veto.

The president's objections are then read and debated, and a roll-call vote is taken. If the bill receives less than a two-thirds majority, it is defeated. If it receives at least two-thirds, it is sent to the other house. If that house also passes it by at least a two-thirds majority, the veto is overridden, and the bill becomes a law.

The Capitol

If the president neither signs nor vetoes the bill within 10 days—not including Sundays—it automatically becomes a law even without the president's signature. However, if Congress has adjourned within those 10 days, the bill is automatically killed; this indirect rejection is termed a pocket veto.

Note: Under "line-item veto" legislation effective Jan. 1, 1997, the president was authorized, under certain circumstances, to veto a bill in part, but the legislation was found unconstitutional by the Supreme Court, June 25, 1998.

Confederate States and Secession

The American Civil War (1861-65) grew out of sectional disputes over the continued existence of slavery in the South and the contention of Southern legislators that the states retained many rights, including the right to secede.

The war was not fought by state against state but by one federal regime against another, the Confederate government in Richmond assuming control over the economic, political, and military life of the South, under protest from Georgia and South Carolina.

South Carolina voted an ordinance of secession from the Union, repealing its 1788 ratification of the U.S. Constitution on Dec. 20, 1860, to take effect on Dec. 24. Other states seceded in 1861. Their votes in conventions were: Mississippi, Jan. 9, 84-15; Florida, Jan. 10, 62-7; Alabama, Jan. 11, 61-39; Georgia, Jan. 19, 208-89; Louisiana, Jan. 26, 113-17; Texas, Feb. 1, 166-7, ratified by popular vote on Feb. 23 (for 34,794, against 11,325); Virginia, Apr. 17, 88-55, ratified by popular vote on May 23 (for 128,884; against 32,134); Arkansas, May 6, 69-1; Tennessee, May 7, ratified by popular vote on June 8 (for 104,019, against 47,238); North Carolina, May 21.

Missouri Unionists stopped secession in conventions Feb. 28 and Mar. 9. The legislature condemned secession Mar. 7. Under the protection of Confederate troops, secessionist members of the legislature adopted a resolution of secession at Neosho, Oct. 31. The Confederate Congress seated the secessionists' representatives.

Kentucky did not secede, and its government remained Unionist. In a part of the state occupied by Confederate troops, Kentuckians approved secession, and the Confederate Congress admitted their representatives.

The Maryland legislature voted against secession Apr. 27, 53-13. Delaware did not secede. Western Virginia held conventions at Wheeling, named a pro-Union governor on June 11, 1861, and was admitted to the Union as West Virginia on June 20, 1863. Its constitution provided for gradual abolition of slavery.

Confederate Government

Forty-two delegates from South Carolina, Georgia, Alabama, Mississippi, Louisiana, and Florida met in convention at Montgomery, AL, on Feb. 4, 1861. They adopted a provisional constitution of the Confederate States of America and elected Jefferson Davis (MS) as provisional president and Alexander H. Stephens (GA) as provisional vice president.

A permanent constitution was adopted Mar. 11. It abolished the African slave trade, but it did not bar interstate commerce in slaves. On July 20 the Congress moved to Richmond, VA. Davis was elected president in October and was inaugurated on Feb. 22, 1862.

The Congress adopted a flag, consisting of a red field with a white stripe, and a blue jack with a circle of white stars. Later the more popular flag was the red field with blue diagonal crossbars that held 13 white stars, for the 11 states in the Confederacy plus Kentucky and Missouri.

Lincoln's Address at Gettysburg, 1863

Fourscore and seven years ago our fathers brought forth on this continent a new nation, conceived in liberty and dedicated to the proposition that all men are created equal.

Now we are engaged in a great civil war, testing whether that nation or any nation so conceived and so dedicated can long endure. We are met on a great battle field of that war. We have come to dedicate a portion of that field, as a final resting-place for those who here gave their lives that that nation might live. It is altogether fitting and proper that we should do this.

But, in a larger sense, we can not dedicate—we can not consecrate—we can not hallow—this ground. The brave men, living and dead, who struggled here, have consecrated it, far above our poor power to add or detract. The world will little note, nor long remember, what we say here, but it can never forget what they did here. It is for us the living, rather, to be dedicated here to the unfinished work which they who fought here have thus far so nobly advanced. It is rather for us to be here dedicated to the great task remaining before us—that from these honored dead we take increased devotion to that cause for which they gave the last full measure of devotion—that we here highly resolve that these dead shall not have died in vain—that this nation, under God, shall have a new birth of freedom—and that government of the people, by the people, for the people, shall not perish from the earth.

Selected Landmark Decisions of the U.S. Supreme Court

1803: Marbury v. Madison. The Court ruled that Congress exceeded its power in the Judiciary Act of 1789; the Court thus established its power to review acts of Congress and declare invalid those it found in conflict with the Constitution.

1819: McCulloch v. Maryland. The Court ruled that Congress had the authority to charter a national bank, under the Constitution's granting of the power to enact all laws "necessary and proper" to responsibilities of government.

1819: Trustees of Dartmouth College v. Woodward. The Court ruled that a state could not arbitrarily alter the terms of a college's contract. (The Court later used a similar principle to limit the states' ability to interfere with business contracts.)

1857: Dred Scott v. Sanford. The Court declared unconstitutional the already-repealed Missouri Compromise of 1820 because it deprived a person of his or her property—a slave—without due process of law. The Court also ruled that slaves were not citizens of any state nor of the U.S. (The latter part of the decision was overturned by ratification of the 14th Amendment in 1868.)

1896: Plessy v. Ferguson. The Court ruled that a state law requiring federal railroad trains to provide separate but equal facilities for black and white passengers neither infringed upon federal authority to regulate interstate commerce nor violated the 13th and 14th Amendments. (The "separate but equal" doctrine remained effective until the 1954 **Brown v. Board of Education** decision.)

1904: Northern Securities Co. v. U.S. The Court ruled that a holding company formed solely to eliminate competition between two railroad lines was a combination in restraint of trade, violating the federal antitrust act.

1908: Muller v. Oregon. The Court upheld a state law limiting the working hours of women. (Louis D. Brandeis, counsel for the state, cited evidence from social workers, physicians, and factory inspectors that the number of hours women worked affected their health and morals.)

1911: Standard Oil Co. of New Jersey et al. v. U.S. The Court ruled that the Standard Oil Trust must be dissolved because of its unreasonable restraint of trade.

1919: Schenck v. U.S. The Court sustained the Espionage Act of 1917, maintaining that freedom of speech and press could be constrained if "the words used . . . create a clear and present danger. . ."

1925: Gitlow v. New York. The Court ruled that the First Amendment prohibition against government abridgment of the freedom of speech applied to the states as well as to the federal government. The decision was the first of a number of rulings holding that the 14th Amendment extended the guarantees of the Bill of Rights to state action.

1935: Schechter Poultry Corp. v. U.S. The Court ruled that Congress exceeded its authority to delegate legislative powers and to regulate interstate commerce when it enacted the National Industrial Recovery Act, which afforded the U.S. president too much discretionary power.

1951: Dennis et al. v. U.S. The Court upheld convictions under the Smith Act of 1940 for invoking Communist theory that advocated the forcible overthrow of the government. (In the **1957 Yates v. U.S.** decision, the Court moderated this ruling by allowing such advocacy in the abstract, if not connected to action to achieve the goal.)

1954: Brown v. Board of Education of Topeka. The Court ruled that separate public schools for black and white students were inherently unequal, so that state-sanctioned segregation in public schools violated the equal protection guarantee of the 14th Amendment. And in **Bolling v. Sharpe** the Court ruled that the congressionally mandated segregated public school system in the District of Columbia violated the 5th Amendment's due process guarantee of personal liberty. (The Brown ruling also led to abolition of state-sponsored segregation in other public facilities.)

1957: Roth v. U.S., Alberts v. California. The Court ruled obscene material was not protected by First Amendment guarantees of freedom of speech and press, defining obscene as "utterly without redeeming social value" and appealing to "prurient interests" in the view of the average person. This definition was modified in later decisions, and the "average person" standard was replaced by the "local community" standard in **Miller v. California (1973).**

1961: Mapp v. Ohio. The Court ruled that evidence obtained in violation of the 4th Amendment guarantee against unreasonable search and seizure must be excluded from use at state as well as federal trials.

1962: Engel v. Vitale. The Court held that public school officials could not require pupils to recite a state-composed prayer, even if it was nondenominational and voluntary, because this would be an unconstitutional attempt to establish religion.

1962: Baker v. Carr. The Court held that the constitutional challenges to the unequal distribution of voters among legislative districts could be resolved by federal courts.

1963: Gideon v. Wainwright. The Court ruled that state and federal defendants who are charged with serious crimes must have access to an attorney, at state expense if necessary.

1964: New York Times Co. v. Sullivan. The Court ruled that the First Amendment protected the press from libel suits for defamatory reports about public officials unless an injured party could prove that a defamatory report was made out of malice or "reckless disregard" for the truth.

1965: Griswold v. Conn. The Court ruled that a state unconstitutionally interfered with personal privacy in the marriage relationship when it prohibited anyone, including married couples, from using contraceptives.

1966: Miranda v. Arizona. The Court ruled that, under the guarantee of due process, suspects in custody, before being questioned, must be informed that they have the right to remain silent, that anything they say may be used against them, and that they have the right to counsel.

1973: Roe v. Wade, Doe v. Bolton. The Court ruled that the fetus was not a "person" with constitutional rights and that a right to privacy inherent in the 14th Amendment's due process guarantee of personal liberty protected a woman's decision to have an abortion. During the first trimester of pregnancy, the Court maintained, the decision should be left entirely to a woman and her physician. Some regulation of abortion procedures was allowed in the 2d trimester, and some restriction of abortion in the 3d.

1974: U.S. v. Nixon. The Court ruled that neither the separation of powers nor the need to preserve the confidentiality of presidential communications could alone justify an absolute executive privilege of immunity from judicial demands for evidence to be used in a criminal trial.

1976: Gregg v. Georgia, Profitt v. Fla., Jurek v. Texas. The Court held that death, as a punishment for persons convicted of first degree murder, was not in and of itself cruel and unusual punishment in violation of the 8th Amendment. But the Court ruled that the sentencing judge and jury must consider the individual character of the offender and the circumstances of the particular crime.

1978: Regents of Univ. of Calif. v. Bakke. The Court ruled that a special admissions program for a state medical school, under which a set number of places were reserved for minorities, violated the 1964 Civil Rights Act, which forbids excluding anyone, because of race, from a federally funded program. However, the Court ruled that race could be considered as one of a complex of factors.

1986: Bowers v. Hardwick. The Court refused to extend any constitutional right of privacy to homosexual activity, upholding a Georgia law that in effect made such activity a crime. (Although the Georgia law made no distinction between heterosexual or homosexual sodomy, enforcement had been confined to homosexuals; the statute was invalidated by the state supreme court in 1998.) In **Romer v. Evans (1996),** the Court struck down a Colorado constitutional provision that barred legislation protecting homosexuals from discrimination.

1990: Cruzan v. Missouri. The Court ruled that a person had the right to refuse life-sustaining medical treatment. However, the Court also ruled that, before treatment could be withheld from a comatose patient, a state could require "clear and convincing evidence" that the patient would not have wanted to live. And in 2 **1997** rulings, **Washington v. Glucksberg** and **Vacco v. Quill,** the Court ruled that states could ban doctor-assisted suicide.

1995: Adarand Constructors v. Peña. The Court held that federal programs that classify people by race, unless "narrowly tailored" to accomplish a "compelling governmental interest," may deny individuals the right to equal protection.

1995: U.S. Term Limits Inc. v. Thornton. The Court ruled that neither states nor Congress could limit terms of members of Congress, since the Constitution reserves to the people the right to choose federal lawmakers.

1997: Clinton v. Jones. Rejecting an appeal by Pres. Clinton in a sexual harassment suit, the Court ruled that a sitting president did not have temporary immunity from a lawsuit for actions outside the realm of official duties.

1997: City of Boerne v. Flores. The Court overturned a 1993 law that banned enforcement of laws that "substantially burden" religious practice unless there is a "compelling need" to do so. The Court held that the act was an unwarranted intrusion by Congress on states' prerogatives and an infringement of the judiciary's role.

1997: Reno v. ACLU. Citing the right to free expression, the Court overturned a provision making it a crime to display or distribute "indecent" or "patently offensive" material on the Internet. In **1998**, however, the Court ruled in **NEA v. Finley** that "general standards of decency" may be used as a criterion in federal arts funding.

1998: Clinton v. City of New York. The Court struck down the Line-Item Veto Act (1996), holding that it unconstitutionally gave the president "the unilateral power to change the text of duly enacted statutes."

1998: Faragher v. City of Boca Raton, Burlington Industries, Inc. v. Ellerth. The Court issued new guidelines for workplace sexual harassment suits, holding employers responsible for misconduct by supervisory employees. And in **Oncale v. Sundowner Offshore Services,** the Court ruled that the law against sexual harassment applies regardless of whether harasser and victim are the same sex.

1999: Dept. of Commerce v. U.S. House. Upholding a challenge to plans for the 2000 census, the Court required an actual head count for apportioning the U.S. House of Representatives, but allowed the use of statistical sampling methods for other purposes, such as the allocation of federal funds.

1999: Alden v. Maine, Florida Prepaid v. College Savings Bank, College Savings Bank v. Florida. In a series of rulings, the Court applied the principle of "sovereign immunity" to shield states in large part from being sued under federal law.

2000: Troxel v. Granville. The justices found that a Washington state law allowing grandparents visitation rights, as broadly applied, interfered with parents' right to determine the best care for their children.

2000: Boy Scouts of America v. Dale. The Court ruled that the Boy Scouts of America could dismiss a troop leader after learning he was gay, holding that the right to freedom of association outweighed a New Jersey anti-discrimination statute.

2000: Stenberg v. Carhart. The Court struck down a Nebraska law that banned so-called partial-birth abortion. It argued that the law could be interpreted as banning other abortion procedures and that it should have made exception for reasons of health. (See 1973: *Roe* v. *Wade*.)

2000: Bush v. Gore. The Court ruled that manual recounts of presidential ballots in the Nov. 2000 election could not proceed because inconsistent evaluation standards in different counties violated the equal protection clause. In effect, the ruling meant existing official results leaving George W. Bush as narrow winner of the election would prevail.

2001: Easley v. Cromartie. The Court ruled that North Carolina's 12th Congressional District, whose irregular shape had been challenged as an unconstitutional racial gerrymander, was the permissible result of attempts to create a majority-Democrat district.

2001: Kyllo v. U.S. The Court held that police needed a warrant to scan the outside of a home with a thermal imaging device to detect heat lamps used to grow marijuana. The justices held that the thermal imaging was equivalent to a physical intrusion into the home.

2001: Good News Club v. Milford Central School. The justices found that religious and secular organizations were entitled to equal access to public elementary school grounds for after-school meetings. The justices held that a school district's rule banning religious groups violated the First Amendment.

Presidential Oath of Office

The Constitution (Article II) directs that the president-elect shall take the following oath or affirmation to be inaugurated as president: "I do solemnly swear [affirm] that I will faithfully execute the office of President of the United States, and will, to the best of my ability, preserve, protect, and defend the Constitution of the United States." (Custom decrees the addition of the words "So help me God" at the end of the oath when taken by the president-elect, with the left hand on the Bible for the duration of the oath, and the right hand slightly raised.)

IT'S A FACT: Franklin Pierce is the only president to have substituted a different word ("promise") for "swear" (for religious reasons) when he took the presidential oath of office in March 1853.

Law on Succession to the Presidency

If by reason of death, resignation, removal from office, inability, or failure to qualify there is neither a president nor vice president to discharge the powers and duties of the office of president, then the speaker of the House of Representatives shall upon his resignation as speaker and as representative, act as president. The same rule shall apply in the case of the death, resignation, removal from office, or inability of an individual acting as president.

If at the time when a speaker is to begin the discharge of the powers and duties of the office of president there is no speaker, or the speaker fails to qualify as acting president, then the president pro tempore of the Senate, upon his resignation as president pro tempore and as senator, shall act as president.

An individual acting as president shall continue to act until the expiration of the then current presidential term, except that (1) if his discharge of the powers and duties of the office is founded in whole or in part in the failure of both the president-elect and the vice president-elect to qualify, then he shall act only until a president or vice president qualifies, and (2) if his discharge of the powers and duties of the office is founded in whole or in part on the inability of the president or vice president, then he shall act only until the removal of the disability of one of such individuals.

If, by reason of death, resignation, removal from office, or failure to qualify, there is no president pro tempore to act as president, then the officer of the United States who is highest on the following list, and who is not under any disability to discharge the powers and duties of president shall act as president; the secretaries of state, treasury, defense, attorney general; secretaries of interior, agriculture, commerce, labor, health and human services, housing and urban development, transportation, energy, education, veterans affairs.

(Legislation approved July 18, 1947; amended Sept. 9, 1965, Oct. 15, 1966, Aug. 4, 1977, and Sept. 27, 1979. See also Constitutional Amendment XXV.)

Origin of the United States National Motto

In God We Trust, designated as the U.S. National Motto by Congress in 1956, originated during the Civil War as an inscription for U. S. coins, although it was used by Francis Scott Key in a slightly different form when he wrote "The Star-Spangled Banner" in 1814. On Nov. 13, 1861, when Union morale had been shaken by battlefield defeats, the Rev. M. R. Watkinson, of Ridleyville, PA, wrote to Secy. of the Treasury Salmon P. Chase. "From my heart I have felt our national shame in disowning God as not the least of our present national disasters," the minister wrote, suggesting "recognition of the Almighty God in some form on our coins." Secy. Chase ordered designs prepared with the inscription *In God We Trust* and backed coinage legislation that authorized use of this slogan. The motto first appeared on some U.S. coins in 1864, and disappeared and reappeared on various coins until 1955, when Congress ordered it placed on all paper money and all coins.

The American's Creed

William Tyler Page, Clerk of the U.S. House of Representatives, wrote "The American's Creed" in 1917. It was accepted by the House on behalf of the American people on April 3, 1918.

"I believe in the United States of America as a government of the people, by the people, for the people; whose just powers are derived from the consent of the governed; a democracy in a republic; a sovereign Nation of many sovereign States; a perfect union, one and inseparable; established upon those principles of freedom, equality, justice, and humanity for which American patriots sacrificed their lives and fortunes.

"I therefore believe it is my duty to my country to love it, to support its Constitution, to obey its laws, to respect its flag, and to defend it against all enemies."

The Great Seal of the U.S.

On July 4, 1776, the Continental Congress appointed a committee consisting of Benjamin Franklin, John Adams, and Thomas Jefferson "to bring in a device for a seal of the United States of America." The designs submitted by this and a subsequent committee were considered unacceptable. After many delays, a third committee, appointed early in 1782, presented a design prepared by William Barton. Charles Thomson, the secretary of Congress, suggested certain changes, and Congress finally approved the design on June 20, 1782. The obverse side of the seal shows an American bald eagle. In its mouth is a ribbon bearing the motto *e pluribus unum* (one out of many). In the eagle's talons are the arrows of war and an olive branch of peace. The reverse side shows an unfinished pyramid with an eye (the eye of Providence) above it.

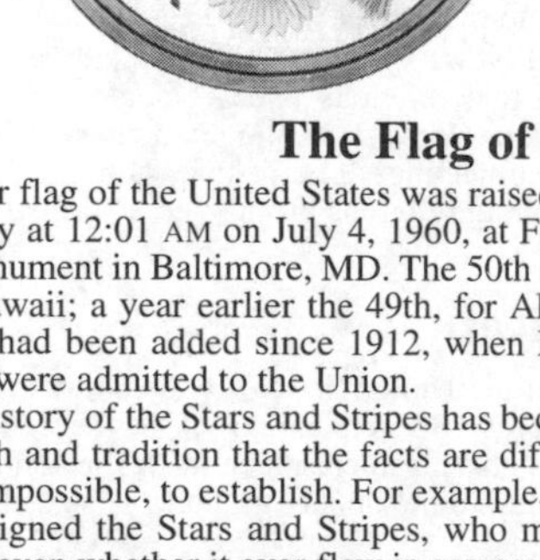

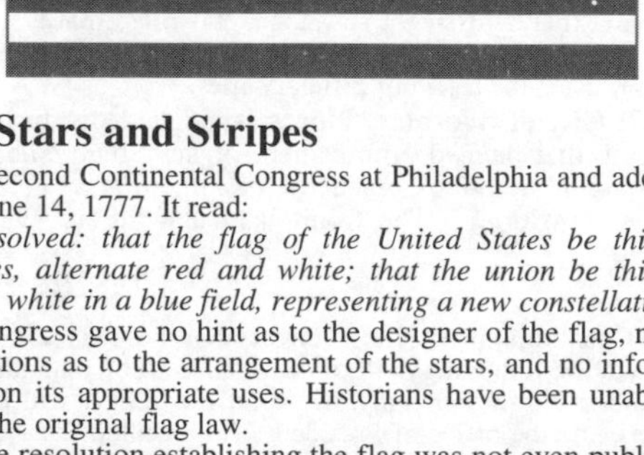

The Flag of the U.S.—The Stars and Stripes

The 50-star flag of the United States was raised for the first time officially at 12:01 AM on July 4, 1960, at Fort McHenry National Monument in Baltimore, MD. The 50th star had been added for Hawaii; a year earlier the 49th, for Alaska. Before that, no star had been added since 1912, when New Mexico and Arizona were admitted to the Union.

The true history of the Stars and Stripes has become so cluttered by myth and tradition that the facts are difficult, and in some cases impossible, to establish. For example, it is not certain who designed the Stars and Stripes, who made the first such flag, or even whether it ever flew in any sea fight or land battle of the American Revolution.

All agree, however, that the Stars and Stripes originated as the result of a resolution offered by the Marine Committee of the Second Continental Congress at Philadelphia and adopted on June 14, 1777. It read:

Resolved: that the flag of the United States be thirteen stripes, alternate red and white; that the union be thirteen stars, white in a blue field, representing a new constellation.

Congress gave no hint as to the designer of the flag, no instructions as to the arrangement of the stars, and no information on its appropriate uses. Historians have been unable to find the original flag law.

The resolution establishing the flag was not even published until Sept. 2, 1777. Despite repeated requests, Washington did not get the flags until 1783, after the American Revolution was over. And there is no certainty that they were the Stars and Stripes.

Early Flags

Many historians consider the first flag of the U.S. to have been the Grand Union (sometimes called Great Union) flag, although the Continental Congress never officially adopted it. This flag was a modification of the British Meteor flag, which had the red cross of St. George and the white cross of St. Andrew combined in the blue canton. For the Grand Union flag, 6 horizontal stripes were imposed on the red field, dividing it into 13 alternating red and white stripes. On Jan. 1, 1776, when the Continental Army came into formal existence, this flag was unfurled on Prospect Hill, Somerville, MA. Washington wrote that "we hoisted the Union Flag in compliment to the United Colonies."

One of several flags about which controversy has raged for years is at Easton, PA. Containing the devices of the national flag in reversed order, this flag has been in the public library at Easton for more than 150 years. Some contend that this flag was actually the first Stars and Stripes, first displayed on July 8, 1776. This flag has 13 red and white stripes in the canton, 13 white stars centered in a blue field.

A flag was hastily improvised from garments by the defenders of Fort Schuyler at Rome, NY, Aug. 3-22, 1777. Historians believe it was the Grand Union Flag.

The Sons of Liberty had a flag of 9 red and white stripes, to signify 9 colonies, when they met in New York in 1765 to oppose the Stamp Tax. By 1775, the flag had grown to 13 red and white stripes, with a rattlesnake on it.

At Concord, Apr. 19, 1775, the minutemen from Bedford, MA, are said to have carried a flag having a silver arm with sword on a red field. At Cambridge, MA, the Sons of Liberty used a plain red flag with a green pine tree on it.

In June 1775, Washington went from Philadelphia to Boston to take command of the army, escorted to New York by the Philadelphia Light Horse Troop. It carried a yellow flag that had an elaborate coat of arms—the shield charged with 13 knots, the motto "For These We Strive"—and a canton of 13 blue and silver stripes.

In Feb. 1776, Col. Christopher Gadsden, a member of the Continental Congress, gave the South Carolina Provincial Congress a flag "such as is to be used by the commander-in-chief of the American Navy." It had a yellow field, with a rattlesnake about to strike and the words "Don't Tread on Me."

At the Battle of Bennington, Aug. 16, 1777, patriots used a flag of 7 white and 6 red stripes with a blue canton extending down 9 stripes and showing an arch of 11 white stars over the figure 76 and a star in each of the upper corners. The stars are 7-pointed. This flag is preserved in the Historical Museum at Bennington, VT.

At the Battle of Cowpens, Jan. 17, 1781, the 3d Maryland Regiment is said to have carried a flag of 13 red and white stripes, with a blue canton containing 12 stars in a circle around one star.

Who Designed the Flag? No one knows for certain. Francis Hopkinson, designer of a naval flag, declared he also had designed the flag and in 1781 asked Congress to reimburse him for his services. Congress did not do so. Dumas Malone of Columbia University wrote: "This talented man . . . designed the American flag."

Who Called the Flag "Old Glory"? The flag is said to have been named Old Glory by William Driver, a sea captain of Salem, MA. One legend has it that when he raised the flag on his brig, the *Charles Doggett*, in 1824, he said: "I name thee Old Glory." But his daughter, who presented the flag to the Smithsonian Institution, said he named it at his 21st birthday celebration on Mar. 17, 1824, when his mother presented the homemade flag to him.

The Betsy Ross Legend. The widely publicized legend that Mrs. Betsy Ross made the first Stars and Stripes in June 1776, at the request of a committee composed of George Washington, Robert Morris, and George Ross, an uncle, was first made public in 1870, by a grandson of Mrs. Ross. Historians have been unable to find a historical record of such a meeting or committee.

Adding New Stars

The flag of 1777 was used until 1795. Then, on the admission of Vermont and Kentucky to the Union, Congress passed and Pres. Washington signed an act that after May 1, 1795, the flag should have 15 stripes, alternating red and white, and 15 white stars on a blue field.

When new states were admitted, it became evident that the flag would become burdened with stripes. Congress thereupon ordered that after July 4, 1818, the flag should have 13 stripes, symbolizing the 13 original states; that the union have 20 stars, and that whenever a new state was admitted a new star should be added on the July 4 following admission. No law designates the permanent arrangement of the stars. However, since 1912, when a new state has been admitted, the new design has been announced by executive order. No star is specifically identified with any state.

Code of Etiquette for Display and Use of the U.S. Flag

Reviewed by National Flag Foundation

Although the Stars and Stripes originated in 1777, it was not until 146 years later that there was a serious attempt to establish a uniform code of etiquette for the U.S. flag. On Feb. 15, 1923, the War Department issued a circular on the rules of flag usage. These rules were adopted almost in their entirety June 14, 1923, by a conference of 68 patriotic organizations in Washington, D.C. Finally, on June 22, 1942, a joint resolution of Congress, amended by Public Law 94-344, July 7, 1976, codified "existing rules and customs pertaining to the display and use of the flag . . ."

When to Display the Flag—The flag should be displayed on all days, especially on legal holidays and other special occasions, on official buildings when in use, in or near polling places on election days, and in or near schools when in session. Citizens may fly the flag at any time. It is customary to display it only from sunrise to sunset on buildings and on stationary flagstaffs in the open. It may be displayed at night, however, on special occasions, preferably lighted. The flag now flies over the White House both day and night. It flies over the Senate wing of the Capitol when the Senate is in session and over the House wing when that body is in session. It flies day and night over the east and west fronts of the Capitol, without floodlights at night but receiving illumination from the Capitol Dome. It flies 24 hours a day at several other places, including the Fort McHenry National Monument in Baltimore, where it inspired Francis Scott Key to write "The Star Spangled Banner." The flag also flies 24 hours a day, properly illuminated, at U.S. Customs ports of entry.

Flying the Flag at Half-Staff—Flying the flag at half-staff, that is, halfway up the staff, is a signal of mourning. The flag should be hoisted to the top of the staff for an instant before being lowered to half-staff. It should be hoisted to the peak again before being lowered for the day or night.

As provided by presidential proclamation, the flag should fly at half-staff for 30 days from the day of death of a president or former president; for 10 days from the day of death of a vice president, chief justice or retired chief justice of the U.S., or speaker of the House of Representatives; from day of death until burial of an associate justice of the Supreme Court, cabinet member, former vice president, Senate president pro tempore, or majority or minority Senate or House leader; for a U.S. senator, representative, territorial delegate, or the resident commissioner of Puerto Rico, on day of death and the following day within the metropolitan area of the District of Columbia and from day of death until burial within the decedent's state, congressional district, territory or commonwealth; and for the death of the governor of a state, territory, or possession of the U.S., from day of death until burial.

On Memorial Day, the flag should fly at half-staff until noon and then be raised to the peak. The flag should also fly at half-staff on Korean War Veterans Armistice Day (July 27), National Pearl Harbor Remembrance Day (Dec. 7), and Peace Officers Memorial Day (May 15).

How to Fly the Flag—The flag should be hoisted briskly and lowered ceremoniously and should never be allowed to touch the ground or the floor. When the flag is hung over a sidewalk from a rope extending from a building to a pole, the union should be away from the building. When the flag is hung over the center of a street the union should be to the north in an east-west street and to the east in a north-south street. No other flag may be flown above or, if on the same level, to the right of the U.S. flag, except that at the United Nations Headquarters the UN flag may be placed above flags of all member nations and other national flags may be flown with equal prominence or honor with the flag of the U.S. At services by Navy chaplains at sea, the church pennant may be flown above the flag.

When 2 flags are placed against a wall with crossed staffs, the U.S. flag should be at right—its own right, and its staff should be in front of the staff of the other flag; when a number of flags are grouped and displayed from staffs, it should be at the center and highest point of the group.

Church and Platform Use—In an auditorium, the flag may be displayed flat, above and behind the speaker. When displayed from a staff in a church or in a public auditorium, the flag should hold the position of superior prominence, in advance of the audience, and in the position of honor at the speaker's right as she or he faces the audience. Any other flag so displayed should be placed on the left of the speaker or to the right of the audience.

When the flag is displayed horizontally or vertically against a wall, the stars should be uppermost and at the observer's left.

When used to cover a casket, the flag should be placed so that the union is at the head and over the left shoulder. It should not be lowered into the grave nor touch the ground.

How to Dispose of Worn Flags—When the flag is in such condition that it is no longer a fitting emblem for display, it should be destroyed in a dignified way, preferably by burning.

When to Salute the Flag—All persons present should face the flag, stand at attention, and salute on the following occasions: (1) when the flag is passing in a parade or in a review, (2) during the ceremony of hoisting or lowering, (3) when the national anthem is played, and (4) during the Pledge of Allegiance. Those present in uniform should render the military salute. Those not in uniform should place the right hand over the heart. A man wearing a hat should remove it with his right hand and hold it to his left shoulder during the salute.

Prohibited Uses of the Flag—The flag should not be dipped to any person or thing. (An exception—customarily, ships salute by dipping their colors.) It should never be displayed with the union down save as a distress signal. It should never be carried flat or horizontally, but always aloft and free.

It should not be displayed on a float, an automobile, or a boat except from a staff. It should never be used as a covering for a ceiling, nor have placed on it any word, design, or drawing. It should never be used as a receptacle for carrying anything. It should not be used to cover a statue or a monument.

The flag should never be used for advertising purposes, nor be embroidered on such articles as cushions or handkerchiefs, printed or otherwise impressed on boxes or anything that is designed for temporary use and discard; or used as a costume or athletic uniform. Advertising signs should not be fastened to its staff or halyard.

The flag should never be used as drapery of any sort, never festooned, drawn back, nor up, in folds, but always allowed to fall free. Bunting of blue, white, and red, always arranged with the blue above and the white in the middle, should be used for covering a speaker's desk, draping the front of a platform, and for decoration in general.

An act of Congress approved on Feb. 8, 1917, provided certain penalties for the desecration, mutilation, or improper use of the flag within the District of Columbia. A 1968 federal law provided penalties of as much as a year's imprisonment or a $1,000 fine or both for publicly burning or otherwise desecrating any U.S. flag. In addition, many states have laws against flag desecration. In 1989, the Supreme Court ruled that no laws could prohibit political protesters from burning the flag. The decision had the effect of declaring unconstitutional the flag desecration laws of 48 states, as well as a similar federal statute, in cases of peaceful political expression.

The Supreme Court, in June 1990, declared that a new federal law making it a crime to burn or deface the American flag violated the free-speech guarantee of the First Amendment. The 5-4 decision led to renewed calls in Congress for a constitutional amendment to make it possible to prosecute flag burners.

Pledge of Allegiance to the Flag

I pledge allegiance to the flag of the United States of America and to the republic for which it stands, one nation under God, indivisible, with liberty and justice for all.

This, the current official version of the Pledge of Allegiance, has developed from the original pledge, which was first published in the Sept. 8, 1892, issue of *Youth's Companion*, a weekly magazine then published in Boston. The original pledge contained the phrase "my flag," which was changed more than 30 years later to "flag of the United States of America." A 1954 act of Congress added the words "under God." (In June 2002 a 3-judge panel of the 9th Circuit U.S. Court of Appeals ruled, 2-1, that recitation of the pledge in public schools could not include that phrase; the decision was being appealed.)

The authorship of the pledge was in dispute for many years. The *Youth's Companion* stated in 1917 that the original draft was written by James B. Upham, an executive of the magazine who died in 1910. A leaflet circulated by the magazine later named Upham as the originator of the draft "afterwards condensed and perfected by him and his associates of the Companion force."

Francis Bellamy, a former member of *Youth's Companion* editorial staff, publicly claimed authorship of the pledge in 1923. In 1939, the United States Flag Association, acting on the advice of a committee named to study the controversy, upheld the claim of Bellamy, who had died 8 years earlier. In 1957 the Library of Congress issued a report attributing the authorship to Bellamy.

The History of the National Anthem

"The Star-Spangled Banner" was ordered played by the military and naval services by Pres. Woodrow Wilson in 1916. It was designated the national anthem by Act of Congress, Mar. 3, 1931. The words were written by Francis Scott Key, of Georgetown, MD, during the bombardment of Fort McHenry, Baltimore, Sept. 13-14, 1814. Key was a lawyer, a graduate of St. John's College, Annapolis, and a volunteer in a light artillery company. When a friend, Dr. Beanes, a Maryland physician, was taken aboard Admiral Cockburn's British squadron for interfering with ground troops, Key and J. S. Skinner, carrying a note from Pres. Madison, went to the fleet under a flag of truce on a cartel ship to ask Beanes's release. Cockburn consented, but as the fleet was about to sail up the Patapsco to bombard Fort McHenry, he detained them, first on HMS *Surprise* and then on a supply ship.

Key witnessed the bombardment from his own vessel. It began at 7 AM, Sept. 13, 1814, and lasted, with intermissions, for 25 hr. The British fired more than 1,500 shells, each weighing as much as 220 lb. They were unable to approach closely because the U.S. had sunk 22 vessels. Only 4 Americans were killed and 24 wounded. A British bomb-ship was disabled.

During the event, Key wrote a stanza on the back of an envelope. Next day at Indian Queen Inn, Baltimore, he wrote out the poem and gave it to his brother-in-law, Judge J. H. Nicholson. Nicholson suggested use of the tune, "Anacreon in Heaven" (attributed to a British composer named John Stafford Smith), and had the poem printed on broadsides, of which 2 survive. On Sept. 20 it appeared in the *Baltimore American*. Later Key made 3 copies; one is in the Library of Congress, and one in the Pennsylvania Historical Society. The copy Key wrote on Sept. 14 remained in the Nicholson family for 93 years. In 1907 it was sold to Henry Walters of Baltimore. In 1934 it was bought at auction by the Walters Art Gallery, Baltimore, for $26,400. In 1953 it was sold to the Maryland Historical Society for the same price.

The flag that Key saw during the bombardment is preserved in the Smithsonian Institution, Washington, DC. It is 30 by 42 ft and has 15 alternating red and white stripes and 15 stars, for the original 13 states plus Kentucky and Vermont. It was made by Mary Young Pickersgill. The Baltimore Flag House, a museum, occupies her premises, which were restored in 1953.

The Star-Spangled Banner

I

Oh, say can you see by the dawn's early light
What so proudly we hailed at the twilight's last gleaming?
Whose broad stripes and bright stars thru the perilous fight,
O'er the ramparts we watched were so gallantly streaming?
And the rocket's red glare, the bombs bursting in air,
Gave proof through the night that our flag was still there.
Oh, say does that star-spangled banner yet wave
O'er the land of the free and the home of the brave?

II

On the shore, dimly seen through the mists of the deep,
Where the foe's haughty host in dread silence reposes,
What is that which the breeze, o'er the towering steep,
As it fitfully blows, half conceals, half discloses?
Now it catches the gleam of the morning's first beam,
In full glory reflected now shines in the stream:
'Tis the star-spangled banner! Oh long may it wave
O'er the land of the free and the home of the brave!

III

And where is that band who so vauntingly swore
That the havoc of war and the battle's confusion,
A home and a country should leave us no more!
Their blood has washed out their foul footsteps' pollution.
No refuge could save the hireling and slave
From the terror of flight, or the gloom of the grave:
And the star-spangled banner in triumph doth wave
O'er the land of the free and the home of the brave!

IV

Oh! thus be it ever, when freemen shall stand
Between their loved home and the war's desolation!
Blest with victory and peace, may the heav'n rescued land
Praise the Power that hath made and preserved us a nation.
Then conquer we must, when our cause it is just,
And this be our motto: "In God is our trust."
And the star-spangled banner in triumph shall wave
O'er the land of the free and the home of the brave!

America (My Country 'Tis of Thee)

First sung in public on July 4, 1831, at a service in the Park Street Church, Boston, the words were written by Rev. Samuel Francis Smith, a Baptist clergyman, who set them to a melody he found in a German songbook, unaware that it was the tune for the British anthem, "God Save the King/Queen."

My country, 'tis of thee,
Sweet land of liberty,
Of thee I sing.
Land where my fathers died!
Land of the Pilgrims' pride!
From ev'ry mountainside,
Let freedom ring!

My native country, thee,
Land of the noble free,
Thy name I love.
I love thy rocks and rills,
Thy woods and templed hills;
My heart with rapture thrills
Like that above.

Let music swell the breeze,
And ring from all the trees
Sweet freedom's song.
Let mortal tongues awake;
Let all that breathe partake;
Let rocks their silence break,
The sound prolong.

Our fathers' God, to Thee,
Author of liberty,
To Thee we sing.
Long may our land be bright
With freedom's holy light;
Protect us by Thy might,
Great God, our King!

America, the Beautiful

Words composed by Katharine Lee Bates, a Massachusetts educator and author, in 1893, inspired by the view she experienced atop Pikes Peak. The final form was established in 1911, and it is set to the music of Samuel A. Ward's "Materna."

O beautiful for spacious skies.
For amber waves of grain,
For purple mountain majesties
Above the fruited plain.
America! America!
God shed His grace on thee,
And crown thy good with brotherhood
From sea to shining sea.

O beautiful for pilgrim feet
Whose stern impassion'd stress
A thorough-fare for freedom beat
Across the wilderness.
America! America!
God mend thine ev'ry flaw,
Confirm thy soul in self control,
Thy liberty in law.

O beautiful for heroes prov'd
In liberating strife,
Who more than self their country lov'd
And mercy more than life.
America! America!
May God thy gold refine
Till all success be nobleness,
And ev'ry gain divine.

O beautiful for patriot dream
That sees beyond the years,
Thine alabaster cities gleam,
Undimmed by human tears.
America! America!
God shed His grace on thee,
And crown thy good with brotherhood
From sea to shining sea.

The Liberty Bell: Its History and Significance

The Liberty Bell is housed in Independence National Historical Park, Philadelphia.

The original bell was ordered by Assembly Speaker and Chairman of the State House Superintendents Isaac Norris and was ordered from Thomas Lester, Whitechapel Foundry, London. It reached Philadelphia at the end of August 1752. It bore an inscription from Leviticus 25:10: "PROCLAIM LIBERTY THROUGHOUT ALL THE LAND UNTO ALL THE INHABITANTS THEREOF."

The bell was cracked by a stroke of its clapper in Sept. 1752 while it hung on a truss in the State House yard for testing. Pass & Stow, Philadelphia founders, recast the bell, adding 1 ½ ounces of copper to a pound of the original "Whitechapel" metal to reduce its high tone and brittleness. It was found that the bell contained too much copper, injuring its tone, so Pass & Stow recast it again, this time successfully.

In June 1753 the bell was hung in the old wooden steeple of the State House. In use while the Continental Congress was in session in the State House, it rang out in defiance of British tax and trade restrictions, and it proclaimed the Boston Tea Party and the first public reading of the Declaration of Independence.

On Sept. 18, 1777, when the British Army was about to occupy Philadelphia, the Liberty Bell was moved in a baggage train of the American Army to Allentown, PA, where it was hidden until June 27, 1778. The bell was moved back to Philadelphia after the British left the city.

In July 1781 the wooden steeple became insecure and had to be taken down. The bell was lowered into the brick section of the tower, where it remained until 1828. Between 1828 and 1844 the old State House bell continued to ring during special occasions. It rang for the last time on Feb. 23, 1846. In 1852 it was placed on exhibition in the Declaration Chamber of Independence Hall.

In 1876, when many thousands of Americans visited Philadelphia for the Centennial Exposition, the bell was placed in its old wooden support in the tower hallway. In 1877 it was hung from the ceiling of the tower by a chain of 13 links. It was returned again to the Declaration Chamber and in 1896 taken back to the tower hall, where it occupied a glass case. In 1915 the case was removed so that the public might touch it. On Jan. 1, 1976, just after midnight to mark the opening of the Bicentennial Year, the bell was moved to a new glass and steel pavilion behind Independence Hall for easier viewing.

The measurements of the bell are: circumference around the lip, 12 ft ½ in; circumference around the crown, 6 ft 11 ¼ in; lip to the crown, 3 ft; height over the crown, 2 ft 3 in; thickness at lip, 3 in; thickness at crown, 1 ¼ in; weight, 2,080 lb; length of clapper, 3 ft 2 in.

The specific source of the crack in the bell is unknown.

Statue of Liberty National Monument

Since 1886, the Statue of Liberty Enlightening the World has stood as a symbol of freedom in New York harbor. It also commemorates French-American friendship, for it was given by the people of France and designed by French sculptor Frederic Auguste Bartholdi (1834-1904).

Edouard de Laboulaye, French historian, suggested the French present a monument to the U.S., the latter to provide pedestal and site. Bartholdi visualized a colossal statue at the entrance of New York harbor, welcoming the peoples of the world with the torch of liberty.

On Washington's Birthday, Feb. 22, 1877, Congress approved the use of a site on Bedloe's Island suggested by Bartholdi. This island of 12 acres had been owned in the 17th century by a Walloon named Isaac Bedloe. It was called Bedloe's until Aug. 3, 1956, when Pres. Eisenhower approved a resolution of Congress changing the name to Liberty Island.

The statue was finished on May 21, 1884, and formally presented to the U.S. minister to France, Levi Parsons Morton, July 4, 1884, by Ferdinand de Lesseps, head of the Franco-American Union, promoter of the Panama Canal, and builder of the Suez Canal.

On Aug. 5, 1884, the Americans laid the cornerstone for the pedestal. This was to be built on the foundations of Fort Wood, which had been erected by the government in 1811. The American committee had raised $125,000, but this was found to be inadequate. Joseph Pulitzer, owner of the *New York World,* appealed on Mar. 16, 1885, for general donations. By Aug. 11, 1885, he had raised $100,000.

The statue arrived dismantled, in 214 packing cases, from Rouen, France, in June 1885. The last rivet of the statue was driven on Oct. 28, 1886, when Pres. Grover Cleveland dedicated the monument.

The Statue of Liberty National Monument was designated as such in 1924. It is administered by the National Park Service. A $2.5 million building housing the American Museum of Immigration was opened by Pres. Richard Nixon on Sept. 26, 1972, at the base of the statue. It houses a permanent exhibition of photos, posters, and artifacts tracing the history of American immigration.

Four years of restoration work was completed before the statue's centennial celebration on July 4, 1986. Among other repairs, the $87 million dollar project included replacing the 1,600 wrought iron bands that hold the statue's copper skin to its frame, replacing its torch, and installing an elevator.

A 4-day extravaganza of concerts, tall ships, ethnic festivals, and fireworks, July 3-6, 1986, celebrated the 100th anniversary. The festivities included Chief Justice Warren E. Burger's swearing-in of 5,000 new citizens on Ellis Island, while 20,000 others across the country were simultaneously sworn in through a satellite telecast.

The ceremonies were followed by others on Oct. 28, 1986, to mark the statue's exact 100th birthday.

Statue Statistics

The statue weighs 450,000 lb, or 225 tons. The copper sheeting weighs 200,000 lb. There are 167 steps from the land level to the top of the pedestal, 168 steps inside the statue to the head, and 54 rungs on the ladder leading to the arm that holds the torch.

	Ft.	In.		Ft.	In.
Height from base to torch (45.3 meters)	151	1	Length of nose	4	6
Foundation of pedestal to torch (91.5 meters)	305	1	Right arm, length	42	0
Heel to top of head	111	1	Right arm, greatest thickness	12	0
Length of hand	16	5	Thickness of waist	35	0
Index finger	8	0	Width of mouth	3	0
Size of finger nail, 13x10 in.			Tablet, length	23	7
Head from chin to cranium	17	3	Tablet, width	13	7
Head thickness from ear to ear	10	0	Tablet, thickness	2	0

Emma Lazarus's Famous Poem

Engraved on pedestal below the statue.

The New Colossus

Not like the brazen giant of Greek fame,
With conquering limbs astride from land to land;
Here at our sea-washed, sunset gates shall stand
A mighty woman with a torch, whose flame
Is the imprisoned lightning, and her name
Mother of Exiles. From her beacon-hand
Glows world-wide welcome; her mild eyes command
The air-bridged harbor that twin cities frame.
"Keep ancient lands, your storied pomp!" cries she
With silent lips. "Give me your tired, your poor,
Your huddled masses yearning to breathe free,
The wretched refuse of your teeming shore.
Send these, the homeless, tempest-tost to me,
I lift my lamp beside the golden door!"

Ellis Island

Ellis Island was the gateway to America for more than 12 million immigrants between 1892 and 1924. In the late 18th century, Samuel Ellis, a New York City merchant, purchased the island and gave it his name. From Ellis, it passed to New York State, and the U.S. government bought it in 1808. On Jan. 1, 1892, the government opened the first federal immigration center in the U.S. on the island. The 27½-acre site eventually supported more than 35 buildings, including the Main Building with its Great Hall, in which as many as 5,000 people a day were processed.

Closed as an immigration station in 1954, Ellis Island was proclaimed part of the Statue of Liberty National Monument in 1965 by Pres. Lyndon B. Johnson. After a 6-year, $170 million restoration project funded by The Ellis Island Fdn. Inc., Ellis Island was reopened as a museum in 1990. Artifacts, historic photographs and documents, oral histories, and ethnic music depicting 400 years of American immigration are housed in the museum. The museum also includes The American Immigrant Wall of Honor® (www.wallofhonor.com). With its new edition open since late 2001, it holds more than 600,000 names. Another edition was set to open in 2003.

The American Family Immigration History Center, a genealogical center, opened in April 2001. It contains an electronic database of ship arrivals through New York harbor from 1892 to 1924 with over 22 million names, as well as an interactive database which features a Living Family Archive and multimedia presentations on various immigration groups and patterns (www.ellisisland.org).

In 1998, the Supreme Court ruled that nearly 90% of the island (the 24.2 acres which are landfill) lies in New Jersey, while the original 3.3 acres are in New York.

PRESIDENTS OF THE UNITED STATES

U.S. Presidents

No.	Name	Politics	Born	in	Inaug.	at age	Died	at age
1.	George Washington	Fed.	1732, Feb. 22	VA	1789	57	1799, Dec. 14	67
2.	John Adams	Fed.	1735, Oct. 30	MA	1797	61	1826, July 4	90
3.	Thomas Jefferson	Dem.-Rep.	1743, Apr. 13	VA	1801	57	1826, July 4	83
4.	James Madison	Dem.-Rep.	1751, Mar. 16	VA	1809	57	1836, June 28	85
5.	James Monroe	Dem.-Rep.	1758, Apr. 28	VA	1817	58	1831, July 4	73
6.	John Quincy Adams	Dem.-Rep.	1767, July 11	MA	1825	57	1848, Feb. 23	80
7.	Andrew Jackson	Dem.	1767, Mar. 15	SC	1829	61	1845, June 8	78
8.	Martin Van Buren	Dem.	1782, Dec. 5	NY	1837	54	1862, July 24	79
9.	William Henry Harrison	Whig	1773, Feb. 9	VA	1841	68	1841, Apr. 4	68
10.	John Tyler	Whig	1790, Mar. 29	VA	1841	51	1862, Jan. 18	71
11.	James Knox Polk	Dem.	1795, Nov. 2	NC	1845	49	1849, June 15	53
12.	Zachary Taylor	Whig	1784, Nov. 24	VA	1849	64	1850, July 9	65
13.	Millard Fillmore	Whig	1800, Jan. 7	NY	1850	50	1874, Mar. 8	74
14.	Franklin Pierce	Dem.	1804, Nov. 23	NH	1853	48	1869, Oct. 8	64
15.	James Buchanan	Dem.	1791, Apr. 23	PA	1857	65	1868, June 1	77
16.	Abraham Lincoln	Rep.	1809, Feb. 12	KY	1861	52	1865, Apr. 15	56
17.	Andrew Johnson	(1)	1808, Dec. 29	NC	1865	56	1875, July 31	66
18.	Ulysses Simpson Grant	Rep.	1822, Apr. 27	OH	1869	46	1885, July 23	63
19.	Rutherford Birchard Hayes	Rep.	1822, Oct. 4	OH	1877	54	1893, Jan. 17	70
20.	James Abram Garfield	Rep.	1831, Nov. 19	OH	1881	49	1881, Sept. 19	49
21.	Chester Alan Arthur	Rep.	1829, Oct. 5	VT	1881	50	1886, Nov. 18	57
22.	Grover Cleveland	Dem.	1837, Mar. 18	NJ	1885	47	1908, June 24	71
23.	Benjamin Harrison	Rep.	1833, Aug. 20	OH	1889	55	1901, Mar. 13	67
24.	Grover Cleveland	Dem.	1837, Mar. 18	NJ	1893	55	1908, June 24	71
25.	William McKinley	Rep.	1843, Jan. 29	OH	1897	54	1901, Sept. 14	58
26.	Theodore Roosevelt	Rep.	1858, Oct. 27	NY	1901	42	1919, Jan. 6	60
27.	William Howard Taft	Rep.	1857, Sept. 15	OH	1909	51	1930, Mar. 8	72
28.	Woodrow Wilson	Dem.	1856, Dec. 28	VA	1913	56	1924, Feb. 3	67
29.	Warren Gamaliel Harding	Rep.	1865, Nov. 2	OH	1921	55	1923, Aug. 2	57
30.	Calvin Coolidge	Rep.	1872, July 4	VT	1923	51	1933, Jan. 5	60
31.	Herbert Clark Hoover	Rep.	1874, Aug. 10	IA	1929	54	1964, Oct. 20	90
32.	Franklin Delano Roosevelt	Dem.	1882, Jan. 30	NY	1933	51	1945, Apr. 12	63
33.	Harry S. Truman	Dem.	1884, May 8	MO	1945	60	1972, Dec. 26	88
34.	Dwight David Eisenhower	Rep.	1890, Oct. 14	TX	1953	62	1969, Mar. 28	78
35.	John Fitzgerald Kennedy	Dem.	1917, May 29	MA	1961	43	1963, Nov. 22	46
36.	Lyndon Baines Johnson	Dem.	1908, Aug. 27	TX	1963	55	1973, Jan. 22	64
37.	Richard Milhous Nixon (2)	Rep.	1913, Jan. 9	CA	1969	56	1994, Apr. 22	81
38.	Gerald Rudolph Ford	Rep.	1913, July 14	NE	1974	61		
39.	Jimmy Carter	Dem.	1924, Oct. 1	GA	1977	52		
40.	Ronald Reagan	Rep.	1911, Feb. 6	IL	1981	69		
41.	George H. W. Bush	Rep.	1924, June 12	MA	1989	64		
42.	Bill Clinton	Dem.	1946, Aug. 19	AR	1993	46		
43.	George W. Bush	Rep.	1946, July 6	CT	2001	54		

(1) Andrew Johnson was a Democrat, nominated vice president by Republicans, and elected with Lincoln on National Union ticket.
(2) Resigned Aug. 9, 1974.

U.S. Presidents, Vice Presidents, Congresses

President	Service	Vice President	Congresses
1. George Washington	Apr. 30, 1789—Mar. 3, 1797	1. John Adams	1, 2, 3, 4
2. John Adams	Mar. 4, 1797—Mar. 3, 1801	2. Thomas Jefferson	5, 6
3. Thomas Jefferson	Mar. 4, 1801—Mar. 3, 1805	3. Aaron Burr	7, 8
"	Mar. 4, 1805—Mar. 3, 1809	4. George Clinton	9, 10
4. James Madison	Mar. 4, 1809—Mar. 3, 1813	" (1)	11, 12
"	Mar. 4, 1813—Mar. 3, 1817	5. Elbridge Gerry (2)	13, 14
5. James Monroe	Mar. 4, 1817—Mar. 3, 1825	6. Daniel D. Tompkins	15, 16, 17, 18
6. John Quincy Adams	Mar. 4, 1825—Mar. 3, 1829	7. John C. Calhoun	19, 20
7. Andrew Jackson	Mar. 4, 1829—Mar. 3, 1833	" (3)	21, 22
"	Mar. 4, 1833—Mar. 3, 1837	8. Martin Van Buren	23, 24
8. Martin Van Buren	Mar. 4, 1837—Mar. 3, 1841	9. Richard M. Johnson	25, 26
9. William Henry Harrison (4)	Mar. 4, 1841—Apr. 4, 1841	10. John Tyler	27
10. John Tyler	Apr. 6, 1841—Mar. 3, 1845		27, 28
11. James K. Polk	Mar. 4, 1845—Mar. 3, 1849	11. George M. Dallas	29, 30
12. Zachary Taylor (4)	Mar. 5, 1849—July 9, 1850	12. Millard Fillmore	31
13. Millard Fillmore	July 10, 1850—Mar. 3, 1853		31, 32
14. Franklin Pierce	Mar. 4, 1853—Mar. 3, 1857	13. William R. King (5)	33, 34
15. James Buchanan	Mar. 4, 1857—Mar. 3, 1861	14. John C. Breckinridge	35, 36
16. Abraham Lincoln	Mar. 4, 1861—Mar. 3, 1865	15. Hannibal Hamlin	37, 38
" (4)	Mar. 4, 1865—Apr. 15, 1865	16. Andrew Johnson	39
17. Andrew Johnson	Apr. 15, 1865—Mar. 3, 1869		39, 40
18. Ulysses S. Grant	Mar. 4, 1869—Mar. 3, 1873	17. Schuyler Colfax	41, 42
	Mar. 4, 1873—Mar. 3, 1877	18. Henry Wilson (6)	43, 44
19. Rutherford B. Hayes	Mar. 4, 1877—Mar. 3, 1881	19. William A. Wheeler	45, 46
20. James A. Garfield (4)	Mar. 4, 1881—Sept. 19, 1881	20. Chester A. Arthur	47
21. Chester A. Arthur	Sept. 20, 1881—Mar. 3, 1885		47, 48
22. Grover Cleveland (7)	Mar. 4, 1885—Mar. 3, 1889	21. Thomas A. Hendricks (8)	49, 50
23. Benjamin Harrison	Mar. 4, 1889—Mar. 3, 1893	22. Levi P. Morton	51, 52
24. Grover Cleveland (7)	Mar. 4, 1893—Mar. 3, 1897	23. Adlai E. Stevenson	53, 54
25. William McKinley	Mar. 4, 1897—Mar. 3, 1901	24. Garret A. Hobart (9)	55, 56
" (4)	Mar. 4, 1901—Sept. 14, 1901	25. Theodore Roosevelt	57
26. Theodore Roosevelt	Sept. 14, 1901—Mar. 3, 1905		57, 58
	Mar. 4, 1905—Mar. 3, 1909	26. Charles W. Fairbanks	59, 60
27. William H. Taft	Mar. 4, 1909—Mar. 3, 1913	27. James S. Sherman (10)	61, 62
28. Woodrow Wilson	Mar. 4, 1913—Mar. 3, 1921	28. Thomas R. Marshall	63, 64, 65, 66

President	Service	Vice President	Congresses
29. Warren G. Harding (4)	Mar. 4, 1921—Aug. 2, 1923	29. Calvin Coolidge	67
30. Calvin Coolidge	Aug. 3, 1923—Mar. 3, 1925		68
"	Mar. 4, 1925—Mar. 3, 1929	30. Charles G. Dawes	69, 70
31. Herbert C. Hoover	Mar. 4, 1929—Mar. 3, 1933	31. Charles Curtis	71, 72
32. Franklin D. Roosevelt (11)	Mar. 4, 1933—Jan. 20, 1941	32. John N. Garner	73, 74, 75, 76
"	Jan. 20, 1941—Jan. 20, 1945	33. Henry A. Wallace	77, 78
" (4)	Jan. 20, 1945—Apr. 12, 1945	34. Harry S. Truman	79
33. Harry S. Truman	Apr. 12, 1945—Jan. 20, 1949		79, 80
"	Jan. 20, 1949—Jan. 20, 1953	35. Alben W. Barkley	81, 82
34. Dwight D. Eisenhower	Jan. 20, 1953—Jan. 20, 1961	36. Richard M. Nixon	83, 84, 85, 86
35. John F. Kennedy (4)	Jan. 20, 1961—Nov. 22, 1963	37. Lyndon B. Johnson	87, 88
36. Lyndon B. Johnson	Nov. 22, 1963—Jan. 20, 1965		88
"	Jan. 20, 1965—Jan. 20, 1969	38. Hubert H. Humphrey	89, 90
37. Richard M. Nixon	Jan. 20, 1969—Jan. 20, 1973	39. Spiro T. Agnew (12)	91, 92, 93
" (13)	Jan. 20, 1973—Aug. 9, 1974	40. Gerald R. Ford (14)	93
38. Gerald R. Ford (15)	Aug. 9, 1974—Jan. 20, 1977	41. Nelson A. Rockefeller (16)	93, 94
39. Jimmy (James Earl) Carter	Jan. 20, 1977—Jan. 20, 1981	42. Walter F. Mondale	95, 96
40. Ronald Reagan	Jan. 20, 1981—Jan. 20, 1989	43. George H. W. Bush	97, 98, 99, 100
41. George H. W. Bush	Jan. 20, 1989—Jan. 20, 1993	44. Dan Quayle	101, 102
42. Bill Clinton	Jan. 20, 1993—Jan. 20, 2001	45. Al Gore	103, 104, 105, 106
43. George W. Bush	Jan. 20, 2001—	46. Richard Cheney	107

(1) Died Apr. 20, 1812. (2) Died Nov. 23, 1814. (3) Resigned Dec. 28, 1832, to become U.S. senator. (4) Died in office. (5) Died Apr. 18, 1853. (6) Died Nov. 22, 1875. (7) Terms not consecutive. (8) Died Nov. 25, 1885. (9) Died Nov. 21, 1899. (10) Died Oct. 30, 1912. (11) First president to be inaugurated under 20th Amendment, Jan. 20, 1937. (12) Resigned Oct. 10, 1973. (13) Resigned Aug. 9, 1974. (14) First nonelected vice president, chosen under 25th Amendment procedure. (15) First president never elected president or vice president. (16) Second nonelected vice president, chosen under 25th Amendment.

Vice Presidents of the U.S.

The numerals given vice presidents do not coincide with those given presidents, because some presidents had none and some had more than one.

	Name	Birthplace	Year	Home	Inaug.	Politics	Place of death	Year	Age
1.	John Adams	Quincy, MA	1735	MA	1789	Fed.	Quincy, MA	1826	90
2.	Thomas Jefferson	Shadwell, VA	1743	VA	1797	Dem.-Rep.	Monticello, VA	1826	83
3.	Aaron Burr	Newark, NJ	1756	NY	1801	Dem.-Rep.	Staten Island, NY	1836	80
4.	George Clinton	Ulster Co., NY	1739	NY	1805	Dem.-Rep.	Washington, DC	1812	73
5.	Elbridge Gerry	Marblehead, MA	1744	MA	1813	Dem.-Rep.	Washington, DC	1814	70
6.	Daniel D. Tompkins	Scarsdale, NY	1774	NY	1817	Dem.-Rep.	Staten Island, NY	1825	51
7.	John C. Calhoun (1)	Abbeville, SC	1782	SC	1825	Dem.-Rep.	Washington, DC	1850	68
8.	Martin Van Buren	Kinderhook, NY	1782	NY	1833	Dem.	Kinderhook, NY	1862	79
9.	Richard M. Johnson (2)	Louisville, KY	1780	KY	1837	Dem.	Frankfort, KY	1850	70
10.	John Tyler	Greenway, VA	1790	VA	1841	Whig	Richmond, VA	1862	71
11.	George M. Dallas	Philadelphia, PA	1792	PA	1845	Dem.	Philadelphia, PA	1864	72
12.	Millard Fillmore	Summerhill, NY	1800	NY	1849	Whig	Buffalo, NY	1874	74
13.	William R. King	Sampson Co., NC	1786	AL	1853	Dem.	Dallas Co., AL	1853	67
14.	John C. Breckinridge	Lexington, KY	1821	KY	1857	Dem.	Lexington, KY	1875	54
15.	Hannibal Hamlin	Paris, ME	1809	ME	1861	Rep.	Bangor, ME	1891	81
16.	Andrew Johnson	Raleigh, NC	1808	TN	1865	(3)	Carter Co., TN	1875	66
17.	Schuyler Colfax	New York, NY	1823	IN	1869	Rep.	Mankato, MN	1885	62
18.	Henry Wilson	Farmington, NH	1812	MA	1873	Rep.	Washington, DC	1875	63
19.	William A. Wheeler	Malone, NY	1819	NY	1877	Rep.	Malone, NY	1887	68
20.	Chester A. Arthur	Fairfield, VT	1829	NY	1881	Rep.	New York, NY	1886	57
21.	Thomas A. Hendricks	Muskingum Co., OH	1819	IN	1885	Dem.	Indianapolis, IN	1885	66
22.	Levi P. Morton	Shoreham, VT	1824	NY	1889	Rep.	Rhinebeck, NY	1920	96
23.	Adlai E. Stevenson (4)	Christian Co., KY	1835	IL	1893	Dem.	Chicago, IL	1914	78
24.	Garret A. Hobart	Long Branch, NJ	1844	NJ	1897	Rep.	Paterson, NJ	1899	55
25.	Theodore Roosevelt	New York, NY	1858	NY	1901	Rep.	Oyster Bay, NY	1919	60
26.	Charles W. Fairbanks	Unionville Centre, OH	1852	IN	1905	Rep.	Indianapolis, IN	1918	66
27.	James S. Sherman	Utica, NY	1855	NY	1909	Rep.	Utica, NY	1912	57
28.	Thomas R. Marshall	N. Manchester, IN	1854	IN	1913	Dem.	Washington, DC	1925	71
29.	Calvin Coolidge	Plymouth, VT	1872	MA	1921	Rep.	Northampton, MA	1933	60
30.	Charles G. Dawes	Marietta, OH	1865	IL	1925	Rep.	Evanston, IL	1951	85
31.	Charles Curtis	Topeka, KS	1860	KS	1929	Rep.	Washington, DC	1936	76
32.	John Nance Garner	Red River Co., TX	1868	TX	1933	Dem.	Uvalde, TX	1967	98
33.	Henry Agard Wallace	Adair County, IA	1888	IA	1941	Dem.	Danbury, CT	1965	77
34.	Harry S. Truman	Lamar, MO	1884	MO	1945	Dem.	Kansas City, MO	1972	88
35.	Alben W. Barkley	Graves County, KY	1877	KY	1949	Dem.	Lexington, VA	1956	78
36.	Richard M. Nixon	Yorba Linda, CA	1913	CA	1953	Rep.	New York, NY	1994	81
37.	Lyndon B. Johnson	Johnson City, TX	1908	TX	1961	Dem.	San Antonio, TX	1973	64
38.	Hubert H. Humphrey	Wallace, SD	1911	MN	1965	Dem.	Waverly, MN	1978	66
39.	Spiro T. Agnew (5)	Baltimore, MD	1918	MD	1969	Rep.	Berlin, MD	1996	77
40.	Gerald R. Ford (6)	Omaha, NE	1913	MI	1973	Rep.			
41.	Nelson A. Rockefeller (7)	Bar Harbor, ME	1908	NY	1974	Rep.	New York, NY	1979	70
42.	Walter F. Mondale	Ceylon, MN	1928	MN	1977	Dem.			
43.	George H. W. Bush	Milton, MA	1924	TX	1981	Rep.			
44.	Dan Quayle	Indianapolis, IN	1947	IN	1989	Rep.			
45.	Al Gore	Washington, DC	1948	TN	1993	Dem.			
46.	Richard Cheney	Lincoln, NE	1941	WY	2001	Rep.			

(1) John C. Calhoun resigned Dec. 28, 1832, having been elected to the Senate to fill a vacancy. (2) Richard M. Johnson was the only vice president to be chosen by the Senate because of a tied vote in the Electoral College. (3) Andrew Johnson was a Democrat, nominated vice president by Republicans, and elected with Lincoln on the National Union Ticket. (4) Adlai E. Stevenson, 23rd vice president, was grandfather of Democratic candidate for president in 1952 and 1956. (5) Resigned Oct. 10, 1973. (6) First nonelected vice president, chosen under 25th Amendment procedure. (7) Second nonelected vice president, chosen under 25th Amendment procedure.

Biographies of the Presidents

GEORGE WASHINGTON (1789-97), first president, Federalist, was born on Feb. 22, 1732, in Wakefield on Pope's Creek, Westmoreland Co., VA, the son of Augustine and Mary Ball Washington. He spent his early childhood on a farm near Fredericksburg. His father died when George was 11. He studied mathematics and surveying, and at 16, he went to live with his elder half brother, Lawrence, who built and named Mount Vernon. George surveyed the lands of Thomas Fairfax in the Shenandoah Valley, keeping a diary. He accompanied Lawrence to Barbados, West Indies, where he contracted smallpox and was deeply scarred. Lawrence died in 1752, and George inherited his property. He valued land, and when he died, he owned 70,000 acres in Virginia and 40,000 acres in what is now West Virginia.Washington's military service began in 1753, when Lt. Gov. Robert Dinwiddie of Virginia sent him on missions deep into Ohio country. He clashed with the French and had to surrender Fort Necessity on July 3, 1754. He was an aide to the British general Edward Braddock and was at his side when the army was ambushed and defeated (July 9, 1755) on a march to Fort Duquesne. He helped take Fort Duquesne from the French in 1758.

After Washington's marriage to Martha Dandridge Custis, a widow, in 1759, he managed his family estate at Mount Vernon. Although not at first for independence, he opposed the repressive measures of the British crown and took charge of the Virginia troops before war broke out. He was made commander of the newly created Continental Army by the Continental Congress on June 15, 1775.

The American victory was due largely to Washington's leadership. He was resourceful, a stern disciplinarian, and the one strong, dependable force for unity. Washington favored a federal government. He became chairman of the Constitutional Convention of 1787 and helped get the Constitution ratified. Unanimously elected president by the Electoral College, he was inaugurated Apr. 30, 1789, on the balcony of New York's Federal Hall. He was reelected in 1792. Washington made an effort to avoid partisan politics as president.

Refusing to consider a 3d term, Washington retired to Mount Vernon in March 1797. He suffered acute laryngitis after a ride in snow and rain around his estate, was bled profusely, and died Dec. 14, 1799.

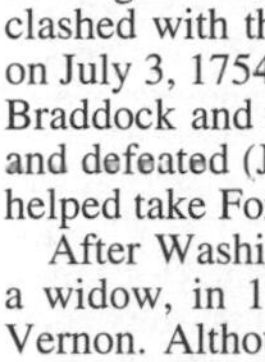

JOHN ADAMS (1797-1801), 2nd president, Federalist, was born on Oct. 30, 1735, in Braintree (now Quincy), MA, the son of John and Susanna Boylston Adams. He was a great-grandson of Henry Adams, who came from England in 1636. He graduated from Harvard in 1755 and then taught school and studied law. He married Abigail Smith in 1764. In 1765 he argued against taxation without representation before the royal governor. In 1770 he successfully defended in court the British soldiers who fired on civilians in the Boston Massacre. He was a delegate to the Continental Congress and a signer of the Declaration of Independence. In 1778, Congress sent Adams and John Jay to join Benjamin Franklin as diplomatic representatives in Europe. Because he ran second to Washington in Electoral College balloting in February 1789, Adams became the nation's first vice president, a post he characterized as highly insignificant; he was reelected in 1792.

In 1796 Adams was chosen president by the electors. His administration was marked by growing conflict with fellow Federalist Alexander Hamilton and with others in his own cabinet who supported Hamilton's strongly anti-French position. Adams avoided full-scale war with France, but became unpopular, especially after securing passage of the Alien and Sedition Acts in 1798. His foreign policy contributed significantly to the election of Thomas Jefferson in 1800.

Adams lived for a quarter century after he left office, during which time he wrote extensively. He died July 4, 1826, on the same day as Jefferson (the 50th anniversary of the Declaration of Independence).

THOMAS JEFFERSON (1801-9), 3rd president, Democratic-Republican, was born on Apr. 13, 1743, in Shadwell in Goochland (now Albemarle) Co., VA, the son of Peter and Jane Randolph Jefferson. Peter died when Thomas was 14, leaving him 2,750 acres and his slaves. Jefferson attended (1760-62) the College of William and Mary, read Greek and Latin classics, and played the violin. In 1769 he was elected to the Virginia House of Burgesses. In 1770 he began building his home, Monticello, and in 1772 he married Martha Wayles Skelton, a wealthy widow. Jefferson helped establish the Virginia Committee of Correspondence. As a member of the Second Continental Congress he drafted the Declaration of Independence. He also was a member of the Virginia House of Delegates (1776-79) and was elected governor of Virginia in 1779, succeeding Patrick Henry. He was reelected in 1780 but resigned in 1781 after British troops invaded Virginia. During his term he wrote the statute on religious freedom. After his wife's death in 1782, Jefferson again became a delegate to the Congress, and in 1784 he drafted the report that was the basis for the Ordinances of 1784, 1785, and 1787. He was minister to France from 1785 to 1789, when George Washington appointed him secretary of state.

Jefferson's strong faith in the consent of the governed conflicted with the emphasis on executive control, favored by Alexander Hamilton, secretary of the Treasury, and Jefferson resigned on Dec. 31, 1793. In the 1796 election Jefferson was the Democratic-Republican candidate for president; John Adams won the election, and Jefferson became vice president. In 1800, Jefferson and Aaron Burr received equal Electoral College votes; the House of Representatives elected Jefferson president. Jefferson was a strong advocate of westward expansion, major events of his first term were the Louisiana Purchase (1803) and the Lewis and Clark Expedition. An important development during his second term was passage of the Embargo Act, barring U.S. ships from setting sail to foreign ports. Jefferson established the University of Virginia and designed its buildings. He died July 4, 1826, on the same day as John Adams (the 50th anniversary of the Declaration of Independence).

Following analysis of DNA taken from descendants of Jefferson and Sally Hemings, one of his slaves, it has been widely acknowledged that Jefferson fathered at least one, perhaps all, of her six known children.

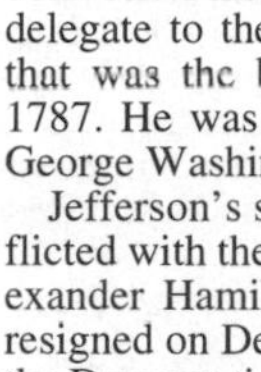

JAMES MADISON (1809-17), 4th president Democratic-Republican, was born on Mar. 16, 1751, in Port Conway, King George Co., VA, the son of James and Eleanor Rose Conway Madison. Madison graduated from Princeton in 1771. He served in the Virginia Constitutional Convention (1776), and, in 1780, became a delegate to the Second Continental Congress. He was chief recorder at the Constitutional Convention in 1787 and supported ratification in the *Federalist Papers*, written with Alexander Hamilton and John Jay. In 1789, Madison was elected to the House of Representatives, where he helped frame the Bill of Rights and fought against passage of the Alien and Sedition Acts. In the 1790s, he helped found the Democratic-Republican Party, which ultimately became the Democratic Party. He became Jefferson's secretary of state in 1801.

Madison was elected president in 1808. His first term was marked by tensions with Great Britain, and his conduct of foreign policy was criticized by the Federalists and by his own party. Nevertheless, he was reelected in 1812, the year war was declared on Great Britain. The war that many considered a second American revolution ended with a treaty that settled none of the issues. Madison's most important action after the war was demilitarizing the U.S.-Canadian border.

In 1817, Madison retired to his estate, Montpelier, where he served as an elder statesman. He edited his famous papers on the Constitutional Convention and helped found the University of Virginia, of which he became rector in 1826. He died June 28, 1836.

JAMES MONROE (1817-25), 5th president, Democratic-Republican, was born on Apr. 28, 1758, in Westmoreland Co., VA, the son of Spence and Eliza Jones Monroe. He entered the College of William and Mary in 1774 but left to serve in the 3d Virginia Regiment during the American Revolution. After the war, he studied law with Thomas Jefferson. In 1782 he was elected to the Virginia House of Delegates, and he served (1783-86) as a delegate to the Confederation Congress. He opposed ratification of the Constitution because it lacked a bill of rights. Monroe was elected to the U.S. Senate in 1790. In 1794 President George Washington appointed Monroe minister to France. He served twice as governor of Virginia (1799-1802, 1811). President Jefferson also sent him to France as minister (1803), and from 1803 to 1807 he served as minister to Great Britain.

In 1816 Monroe was elected president; he was reelected in 1820 with all but one Electoral College vote. His administration became known as the Era of Good Feeling. He obtained Florida from Spain, settled boundary disputes with Britain over Canada, and eliminated border forts. He supported the antislavery position that led to the Missouri Compromise. His most significant contribution was the Monroe Doctrine, which opposed European intervention in the Western Hemisphere and became a cornerstone of U.S. foreign policy.

Although Monroe retired to Oak Hill, VA, financial problems forced him to sell his property and move to New York City. He died there on July 4, 1831.

JOHN QUINCY ADAMS (1825-29), 6th president, independent Federalist, later Democratic-Republican, was born on July 11, 1767, in Braintree (now Quincy), MA, the son of John and Abigail Adams. His father was the 2nd president. He studied abroad and at Harvard University, from which he graduated in 1787. In 1803, he was elected to the U.S. Senate. President Monroe chose him as his secretary of state in 1817. In this capacity he negotiated the cession of the Floridas from Spain, supported exclusion of slavery in the Missouri Compromise, and helped formulate the Monroe Doctrine. In 1824 Adams was elected president by the House of Representatives after he failed to win an Electoral College majority. His expansion of executive powers was strongly opposed, and in the 1828 election he lost to Andrew Jackson. In 1831 he entered the House of Representatives and served 17 years with distinction. He opposed slavery, the annexation of Texas, and the Mexican War. He helped establish the Smithsonian Institution.

Adams suffered a stroke in the House and died in the Speaker's Room on Feb. 23, 1848.

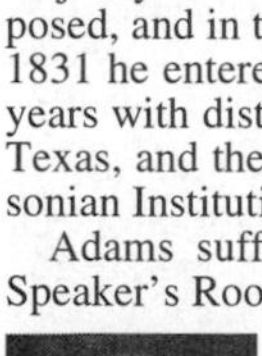

ANDREW JACKSON (1829-37), 7th president, Democratic-Republican, later a Democrat, was born on Mar. 15, 1767, in the Waxhaw district, on the border of North Carolina and South Carolina, the son of Andrew and Elizabeth Hutchinson Jackson. At the age of 13, he joined the militia to fight in the American Revolution and was captured. Orphaned at the age of 14, Jackson was brought up by a well-to-do uncle. By age 20, he was practicing law, and he later served as prosecuting attorney in Nashville, TN. In 1796 he helped draft the constitution of Tennessee, and for a year he occupied its one seat in the House of Representatives. The next year he served in the U.S. Senate.

In the War of 1812, Jackson crushed (1814) the Creek Indians at Horseshoe Bend, AL, and, with an army consisting chiefly of backwoodsmen, defeated (1815) General Edward Pakenham's British troops at the Battle of New Orleans. In 1818 he briefly invaded Spanish Florida to quell Seminoles and outlaws who harassed frontier settlements. In 1824 he ran for president against John Quincy Adams. Although he won the most popular and electoral votes, he did not have a majority. The House of Representatives decided the election and chose Adams. In the 1828 election, however, Jackson defeated Adams, carrying the West and the South.

As president, Jackson introduced what became known as the spoils system—rewarding party members with government posts. Perhaps his most controversial act, however, was depositing federal funds in so-called pet banks, those directed by Democratic bankers, rather than in the Bank of the United States. "Let the people rule" was his slogan. In 1832, Jackson killed the congressional caucus for nominating presidential candidates and substituted the national convention. When South Carolina refused to collect imports under his protective tariff, he ordered army and naval forces to Charleston. After leaving office in 1837, he retired to the Hermitage, outside Nashville, where he died on June 8, 1845.

MARTIN VAN BUREN (1837-41), 8th president, Democrat, was born on Dec. 5, 1782, in Kinderhook, NY, the son of Abraham and Maria Hoes Van Buren. After attending local schools, he studied law and became a lawyer at the age of 20. A consummate politician, Van Buren began his career in the New York state senate and then served as state attorney general from 1816 to 1819. He was elected to the U.S. Senate in 1821. He helped swing eastern support to Andrew Jackson in the 1828 election and then served as Jackson's secretary of state from 1829 to 1831. In 1832 he was elected vice president. Known as the Little Magician, Van Buren was extremely influential in Jackson's administration.

In 1836, Van Buren defeated William Henry Harrison for president and took office as the financial panic of 1837 initiated a nationwide depression. Although he instituted the independent treasury system, his refusal to spend land revenues led to his defeat by William Henry Harrison in 1840. In 1844 he lost the Democratic nomination to James Knox Polk. In 1848 he again ran for president on the Free Soil ticket but lost. He died in Kinderhook on July 24, 1862.

WILLIAM HENRY HARRISON (1841), 9th president, Whig, who served only 31 days, was born on Feb. 9, 1773, in Berkeley, Charles City Co., VA, the son of Benjamin Harrison, a signer of the Declaration of Independence, and of Elizabeth Bassett Harrison. He attended Hampden-Sydney College. Harrison served as secretary of the Northwest Territory in 1798 and was its delegate to the House of Representatives in 1799. He was the first governor of the Indiana Territory and served as superintendent of Indian affairs. With 900 men he put down a Shawnee uprising at Tippecanoe, IN, on Nov. 7, 1811. A generation later, in 1840, he waged a rousing presidential campaign, using the slogan "Tippecanoe and Tyler too." The Tyler of the slogan was his running mate, John Tyler.

Although born to one of the wealthiest, most prestigious, and most influential families in Virginia, Harrison was elected president with a "log cabin and hard cider" slogan. He caught pneumonia during the inauguration and died Apr. 4, 1841, after only one month in office.

JOHN TYLER (1841-45), 10th president, independent Whig, was born on Mar. 29, 1790, in Greenway, Charles City Co., VA, the son of John and Mary Armistead Tyler. His father was governor of Virginia (1808-11). Tyler graduated from the College of William and Mary in 1807 and in 1811 was elected to the Virginia legislature. In 1816 he was chosen for the U.S. House of Representatives. He served in the Virginia legislature again from 1823 to 1825, when he was elected governor of Virginia. After a stint in the U.S. Senate (1827-36), he was elected vice president (1840).

When William Henry Harrison died only a month after taking office, Tyler succeeded him. Because he was the first person to occupy the presidency without having been elected to that office, he was referred to as "His Accidency." He gained passage of the Preemption Act of 1841, which gave squatters on government land the right to buy 160 acres at the minimum auction price. His last act as president was to sign a resolution annexing Texas. Tyler accepted renomination in 1844 from some Democrats but withdrew in favor of the official party candidate, James K. Polk. He died in Richmond, VA, on Jan. 18, 1862.

IT'S A FACT: Zachary Taylor's death was attributed to gastroenteritis, but some historians have suspected arsenic poisoning. Most human bodies contain traces of arsenic, but elevated levels can indicate foul play. In 1991 Taylor's remains were exhumed and tested; arsenic levels were several hundred times lower than would have been expected had he been poisoned with arsenic.

JAMES KNOX POLK (1845-49), 11th president, Democrat, was born on Nov. 2, 1795, in Mecklenburg Co., NC, the son of Samuel and Jane Knox Polk. He graduated from the University of North Carolina in 1818 and served in the Tennessee state legislature from 1823 to 1825. He served in the U.S. House of Representatives from 1825 to 1839, the last 4 years as Speaker. He was governor of Tennessee from 1839 to 1841. In 1844, after the Democratic National Convention became deadlocked, it nominated Polk, who became the first "dark horse" candidate for president. He was nominated primarily because he favored annexation of Texas.

As president, Polk reestablished the independent treasury system originated by Van Buren. He was so intent on acquiring California from Mexico that he sent troops to the Mexican border and, when Mexicans attacked, declared that a state of war existed. The Mexican War ended with the annexation of California and much of the Southwest as part of America's "manifest destiny." Polk compromised on the Oregon boundary ("54-40 or fight!") by accepting the 49th parallel and yielding Vancouver Island to the British. A few weeks after leaving office, Polk died in Nashville, TN, on June 15, 1849.

ZACHARY TAYLOR (1849-50), 12th president, Whig, who served only 16 months, was born on Nov. 24, 1784, in Orange Co., VA, the son of Richard and Sarah Strother Taylor. He grew up on his father's plantation near Louisville, KY, where he was educated by private tutors. In 1808 Taylor joined the regular army and was commissioned first lieutenant. He fought in the War of 1812, the Black Hawk War (1832), and the second Seminole War (beginning in 1837). He was called "Old Rough and Ready." In 1846 President Polk sent him with an army to the Rio Grande. When the Mexicans attacked him, Polk declared war. Outnumbered 4-1, Taylor defeated (1847) Santa Anna at Buena Vista.

A national hero, Taylor received the Whig nomination in 1848 and was elected president, even though he had never bothered to vote. He resumed the spoils system and, though a slaveholder, worked to admit California as a free state. He fell ill and died in office on July 9, 1850.

MILLARD FILLMORE (1850-53), 13th president, Whig, was born on Jan. 7, 1800, in Cayuga Co., NY, the son of Nathaniel and Phoebe Millard Fillmore. Although he had little schooling, he became a law clerk at the age of 22 and a year later was admitted to the bar. He was elected to the New York state assembly in 1828 and served until 1831. From 1833 until 1835 and again from 1837 to 1843, he represented his district in the U.S. House of Representatives. He opposed the entrance of Texas as a slave territory and voted for a protective tariff. In 1844 he was defeated for governor of New York.

In 1848 he was elected vice president, and he succeeded as president after Taylor's death. Fillmore favored the Compromise of 1850 and signed the Fugitive Slave Law. His policies pleased neither expansionists nor slaveholders, and he was not renominated in 1852. In 1856 he was nominated by the American (Know-Nothing) Party, but despite the support of the Whigs, he was defeated by James Buchanan. He died in Buffalo, NY, on Mar. 8, 1874.

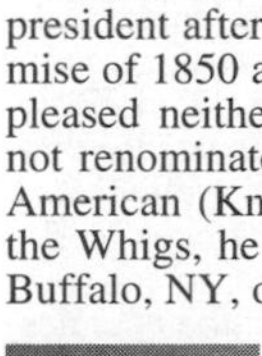

FRANKLIN PIERCE (1853-57), 14th president, Democrat, was born on Nov. 23, 1804, in Hillsboro, NH, the son of Benjamin Pierce, Revolutionary War general and governor of New Hampshire, and Anna Kendrick. He graduated from Bowdoin College in 1824 and was admitted to the bar in 1827. He was elected to the New Hampshire state legislature in 1829 and was chosen Speaker in 1831. He went to the U.S. House in 1833 and was elected a U.S. senator in 1837. He enlisted in the Mexican War and became brigadier general under Gen. Winfield Scott.

In 1852 Pierce was nominated as the Democratic presidential candidate on the 49th ballot. He decisively defeated Gen. Scott, his Whig opponent, in the election. Although against slavery, Pierce was influenced by pro-slavery Southerners. He supported the controversial Kansas-Nebraska Act, which left the question of slavery in the new territories of Kansas and Nebraska to popular vote. Pierce signed a reciprocity treaty with Canada and approved the Gadsden Purchase of a border area on a proposed railroad route, from Mexico. Denied renomination, he spent most of his remaining years in Concord, NH, where he died on Oct. 8, 1869.

JAMES BUCHANAN (1857-61), 15th president, Federalist, later Democrat, was born on Apr. 23, 1791, near Mercersburg, PA, the son of James and Elizabeth Speer Buchanan. He graduated from Dickinson College in 1809 and was admitted to the bar in 1812. He fought in the War of 1812 as a volunteer. He was twice elected to the Pennsylvania general assembly, and in 1821 he entered the U.S. House of Representatives. After briefly serving (1832-33) as minister to Russia, he was elected U.S. senator from Pennsylvania. As Polk's secretary of state (1845-49), he ended the Oregon dispute with Britain and supported the Mexican War and annexation of Texas. As minister to Great Britain, he signed the Ostend Manifesto (1854), declaring a U.S. right to take Cuba by force should efforts to purchase it fail.

Nominated by Democrats, Buchanan was elected president in 1856. On slavery he favored popular sovereignty and choice by state constitutions but did not consistently uphold this position. He denied the right of states to secede but opposed coercion and attempted to keep peace by not provoking secessionists. Buchanan left office having failed to deal decisively with the situation. He died at Wheatland, his estate, near Lancaster, PA, on June 1, 1868.

ABRAHAM LINCOLN (1861-65), 16th president, Republican, was born on Feb. 12, 1809, in a log cabin on a farm then in Hardin Co., KY, now in Larue, the son of Thomas and Nancy Hanks Lincoln. The Lincolns moved to Spencer Co., IN, near Gentryville, when Abe was 7. After Abe's mother died, his father married (1819) Mrs. Sarah Bush Johnston. In 1830 the family moved to Macon Co., IL.

Defeated in 1832 in a race for the state legislature, Lincoln was elected on the Whig ticket 2 years later and served in the lower house from 1834 to 1842. In 1837 Lincoln was admitted to the bar and became partner in a Springfield, IL, law office. He soon won recognition as an effective and resourceful attorney. In 1846, he was elected to the House of Representatives, where he attracted attention during a single term for his opposition to the Mexican War and his position on slavery. In 1856 he campaigned for the newly founded Republican Party, and in 1858 he became its senatorial candidate against Stephen A. Douglas. Although he lost the election, Lincoln gained national recognition from his debates with Douglas.

In 1860, Lincoln was nominated for president by the Republican Party on a platform of restricting slavery. He ran against Douglas, a northern Democrat; John C. Breckinridge, a Southern proslavery Democrat; and John Bell, of the Constitutional Union Party. As a result of Lincoln's winning the election, South Carolina seceded from the Union on Dec. 20, 1860, followed in 1861 by 10 other Southern states.

The Civil War erupted when Fort Sumter, which Lincoln decided to resupply, was attacked by Confederate forces on Apr. 12, 1861. Lincoln called successfully for recruits from the North. On Sept. 22, 1862, 5 days after the Battle of Antietam, Lincoln announced that slaves in territory then in rebellion would be free Jan. 1, 1863, the date of the Emancipation Proclamation. His speeches, including his Gettysburg and Inaugural addresses, are remembered for their eloquence.

Lincoln was reelected, in 1864, over Gen. George B. McClellan, Democrat. Lee surrendered on Apr. 9, 1865. On Apr. 14, Lincoln was shot by actor John Wilkes Booth in Ford's Theater, in Washington, DC. He died the next day.

ANDREW JOHNSON (1865-69), 17th president, Democrat, was born on Dec. 29, 1808, in Raleigh, NC, the son of Jacob and Mary McDonough Johnson. He was apprenticed to a tailor as a youth, but ran away after two years and eventually settled in Greenville, TN. He became popular with the townspeople and in 1829 was elected councilman and later mayor. In 1835 he was sent to the state general assembly. In 1843 he was elected to the U.S. House of Representatives, where he served for 10 years. Johnson was governor of Tennessee from 1853 to 1857, when he was elected to the U.S. Senate. He supported John C. Breckinridge against Lincoln in the 1860 election. Although Johnson had held slaves, he opposed secession and tried to prevent Tennessee from seceding. In Mar. 1862, Lincoln appointed him military governor of occupied Tennessee.

In 1864, in order to balance Lincoln's ticket with a Southern Democrat, the Republicans nominated Johnson for vice president. He was elected vice president with Lincoln and then succeeded to the presidency upon Lincoln's death. Soon afterward, in a controversy with Congress over the president's power over the South, he proclaimed an amnesty to all Confederates, except certain leaders, if they would ratify the 13th Amendment abolishing slavery. States doing so added anti-Negro provisions that enraged Congress, which restored military control over the South. When Johnson removed Edwin M. Stanton, secretary of war, without notifying the Senate, the House, in Feb. 1868, impeached him. Charging him with thereby having violated the Tenure of Office Act, the House was actually responding to his opposition to harsh congressional Reconstruction, expressed in repeated vetoes. He was tried by the Senate, and in May, in two separate votes on different counts, was acquitted, both times by only one vote.

Johnson was denied renomination but remained politically active. He was reelected to the Senate in 1874. Johnson died July 31, 1875, at Carter Station, TN.

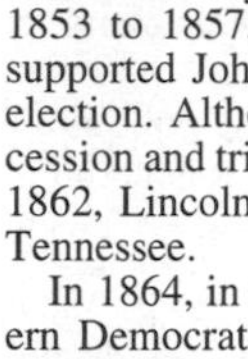

ULYSSES SIMPSON GRANT (1869-77), 18th president, Republican, was born on Apr. 27, 1822, in Point Pleasant, OH, the son of Jesse R. and Hannah Simpson Grant. The next year the family moved to Georgetown, OH. Grant was named Hiram Ulysses, but on entering West Point in 1839, his name was put down as Ulysses Simpson, and he adopted it. He graduated in 1843. During the Mexican War, Grant served under both Gen. Zachary Taylor and Gen. Winfield Scott. In 1854, he resigned his commission because of loneliness and drinking problems, and in the following years he engaged in generally unsuccessful farming and business ventures. With the start of the Civil War, he was named colonel and then brigadier general of the Illinois Volunteers. He took Forts Henry and Donelson and fought at Shiloh. His brilliant campaign against Vicksburg and his victory at Chattanooga made him so prominent that Lincoln placed him in command of all Union armies. Grant accepted Lee's surrender at Appomattox Court House on Apr. 9, 1865. President Johnson appointed Grant secretary of war when he suspended Stanton, but Grant was not confirmed.

Grant was nominated for president by the Republicans in 1868 and elected over Horatio Seymour, Democrat. The 15th Amendment, the amnesty bill, and peaceful settlement of disputes with Great Britain were events of his administration. The Liberal Republicans and Democrats opposed him with Horace Greeley in the 1872 election, but Grant was reelected. His second administration was marked by scandals, including widespread corruption in the Treasury Department and the Indian Service. An attempt by the Stalwarts (Old Guard Republicans) to nominate him in 1880 failed. In 1884 the collapse of an investment firm in which he was a partner left him penniless. He wrote his personal memoirs while ill with cancer and completed them shortly before his death at Mt. McGregor, NY, on July 23, 1885.

RUTHERFORD BIRCHARD HAYES (1877-81), 19th president, Republican, was born on Oct. 4, 1822, in Delaware, OH, the son of Rutherford and Sophia Birchard Hayes. He was reared by his uncle, Sardis Birchard. Hayes graduated from Kenyon College in 1842 and from Harvard Law School in 1845. He practiced law in Lower Sandusky (now Fremont), OH, and was city solicitor of Cincinnati from 1858 to 1861. During the Civil War, he was major of the 23rd Ohio Volunteers. He was wounded several times, and by the end of the war he had risen to the rank of brevet major general. While serving (1865-67) in the U.S. House of Representatives, Hayes supported Reconstruction and Johnson's impeachment. He was twice elected governor of Ohio (1867, 1869). After losing a race for the U.S. House in 1872, he was reelected governor of Ohio in 1875.

In 1876, Hayes was nominated for president and believed he had lost the election to Samuel J. Tilden, Democrat. But a few Southern states submitted 2 sets of electoral votes, and the result was in dispute. An electoral commission, consisting of 8 Republicans and 7 Democrats, awarded all disputed votes to Hayes, allowing him to become president by one electoral vote. Hayes, keeping a promise to southerners, withdrew troops from areas still occupied in the South, ending the era of Reconstruction. He proposed civil service reforms, alienating those favoring the spoils system, and advocated repeal of the Tenure of Office Act restricting presidential power to dismiss officials. He supported sound money and specie payments.

Hayes died in Fremont, OH, on Jan. 17, 1893.

JAMES ABRAM GARFIELD (1881), 20th president, Republican, was born on Nov. 19, 1831, in Orange, Cuyahoga Co., OH, the son of Abram and Eliza Ballou Garfield. His father died in 1833, and he was reared in poverty by his mother. He worked as a canal bargeman, a farmer, and a carpenter and managed to secure a college education. He taught at Hiram College and later became principal. In 1859 he was elected to the Ohio legislature. Antislavery and antisecession, he volunteered for military service in the Civil War, becoming colonel of the 42nd Ohio Infantry and brigadier in 1862. He fought at Shiloh, was chief of staff for Gen. William Starke Rosecrans, and was made major general for gallantry at Chickamauga. He entered Congress as a radical Republican in 1863, calling for execution or exile of Confederate leaders, but he moderated his views after the Civil War. On the electoral commission in 1877 he voted for Hayes against Tilden on strict party lines.

Garfield was a senator-elect in 1880 when he became the Republican nominee for president. He was chosen as a compromise over Gen. Grant, James G. Blaine, and John Sherman, and won election despite some bitterness among Grant's supporters. Much of his brief tenure as president was concerned with a fight with New York Sen. Roscoe Conkling, who opposed two major appointments made by Garfield. On July 2, 1881, Garfield was shot and seriously wounded by a mentally disturbed office-seeker, Charles J. Guiteau, while entering a railroad station in Washington, DC. He died on Sept. 19, 1881, in Elberon, NJ.

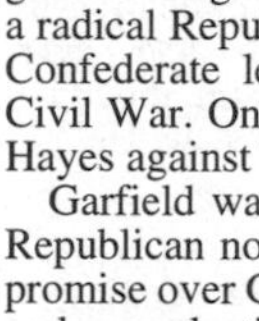

CHESTER ALAN ARTHUR (1881-85), 21st president, Republican, was born on Oct. 5, 1829, in Fairfield, VT, to William and Malvina Stone Arthur. He graduated from Union College in 1848, taught school in Vermont, then studied law and practiced in New York City. In 1853 he argued in a fugitive slave case that slaves transported through New York state were thereby freed. In 1871, he was appointed collector of the Port of New York. President Hayes, an opponent of the spoils system, forced him to resign in 1878. This made the New York machine enemies of Hayes. Arthur and the Stalwarts (Old Guard Republicans) tried to nominate Grant for a 3rd term as president in 1880. When Garfield was nominated, Arthur was nominated for vice president in the interests of harmony.

Upon Garfield's assassination, Arthur became president. Despite his past connections, he signed major civil service reform legislation. Arthur tried to dissuade Congress from enacting the high protective tariff of 1883. He was defeated for renomination in 1884 by James G. Blaine. He died in New York City on Nov. 18, 1886.

GROVER CLEVELAND (1885-89; 1893-97) *(According to a ruling of the State Dept., Grover Cleveland should be counted as both the 22nd and the 24th president, because his 2 terms were not consecutive.)*
Grover Cleveland, Democrat, was born Stephen Grover Cleveland on Mar. 18, 1837, in Caldwell, NJ, the son of Richard F. and Ann Neal Cleveland. When he was a small boy, his family moved to New York. Prevented by his father's death from attending college, he studied by himself and was admitted to the bar in Buffalo, NY, in 1859. In succession he became assistant district attorney (1863), sheriff (1871), mayor (1881), and governor of New York (1882). He was an independent, honest administrator who hated corruption. Cleveland was nominated for president over Tammany Hall opposition in 1884 and defeated Republican James G. Blaine.

As president, he enlarged the civil service and vetoed many pension raids on the Treasury. In the 1888 election he was defeated by Benjamin Harrison, although his popular vote was larger. Reelected over Harrison in 1892, he faced a money crisis brought about by a lowered gold reserve, circulation of paper, and exorbitant silver purchases under the Sherman Silver Purchase Act. He obtained a repeal of the Sherman Act, but was unable to secure effective tariff reform. A severe economic depression and labor troubles racked his administration, but he refused to interfere in business matters and rejected Jacob Coxey's demand for unemployment relief. In 1894, he broke the Pullman strike. Cleveland was not renominated in 1896. He died in Princeton, NJ, on June 24, 1908.

BENJAMIN HARRISON (1889-93), 23rd president, Republican, was born on Aug. 20, 1833, in North Bend, OH, the son of John Scott and Elizabeth Irwin Harrison. His great-grandfather, Benjamin Harrison, was a signer of the Declaration of Independence; his grandfather, William Henry Harrison, was 9th president; his father was a member of Congress. He attended school on his father's farm and graduated from Miami University in Oxford, OH, in 1852. He was admitted to the bar in 1854 and practiced in Indianapolis. During the Civil War, he rose to the rank of brevet brigadier general and fought at Kennesaw Mountain, at Peachtree Creek, at Nashville, and in the Atlanta campaign. He lost the 1876 gubernatorial election in Indiana but succeeded in becoming a U.S. senator in 1881.

In 1888 he defeated Cleveland for president despite receiving fewer popular votes. As president, he expanded the pension list and signed the McKinley high tariff bill, the Sherman Antitrust Act, and the Sherman Silver Purchase Act. During his administration, 6 states were admitted to the Union. He was defeated for reelection in 1892. He died in Indianapolis on Mar. 13, 1901.

WILLIAM MCKINLEY (1897-1901), 25th president, Republican, was born on Jan. 29, 1843, in Niles, OH, the son of William and Nancy Allison McKinley. McKinley briefly attended Allegheny College. When the Civil War broke out in 1861, he enlisted and served for the duration. He rose to captain and in 1865 was made brevet major. After studying law in Albany, NY, he opened (1867) a law office in Canton, OH. He served twice in the U.S. House (1877-83; 1885-91) and led the fight there for the McKinley Tariff, passed in 1890; he was not reelected to the House as a result. He served two terms (1892-96) as governor of Ohio.

In 1896 he was elected president as a proponent of a protective tariff and sound money (gold standard), over William Jennings Bryan, the Democrat and a proponent of free silver. McKinley was reluctant to intervene in Cuba, but the loss of the battleship *Maine* at Havana crystallized opinion. He demanded Spain's withdrawal from Cuba; Spain made some concessions, but Congress announced a state of war as of Apr. 21, 1898. He was reelected in the 1900 campaign, defeating Bryan's anti-imperialist arguments with the promise of a "full dinner pail." McKinley was respected for his conciliatory nature and for his conservative stance on business issues. On Sept. 6, 1901, while welcoming citizens at the Pan-American Exposition, in Buffalo, NY, he was shot by Leon Czolgosz, an anarchist. He died Sept. 14.

THEODORE ROOSEVELT (1901-9), 26th president, Republican, was born on Oct. 27, 1858, in New York City, the son of Theodore and Martha Bulloch Roosevelt. He was a 5th cousin of Franklin D. Roosevelt and an uncle of Eleanor Roosevelt. Roosevelt graduated from Harvard University in 1880. He attended Columbia Law School briefly but abandoned law to enter politics. He was elected to the New York state assembly in 1881 and served until 1884. He spent the next 2 years ranching and hunting in the Dakota Territory. In 1886, he ran unsuccessfully for mayor of New York City. He was Civil Service commissioner in Washington, DC, from 1889 to 1895. From 1895 to 1897, he served as New York City's police commissioner. He was assistant secretary of the navy under McKinley. The Spanish-American War made him nationally known. He organized the 1st U.S. Volunteer Cavalry (Rough Riders) and, as lieutenant colonel, led the charge up Kettle Hill in San Juan. Elected New York governor in 1898, he fought the spoils system and achieved taxation of corporation franchises.

Nominated for vice president in 1900, he became the nation's youngest president when McKinley was assassinated. He was reelected in 1904. As president he fought corruption of politics by big business, dissolved the Northern Securities Co. and others for violating antitrust laws, intervened in the 1902 coal strike on behalf of the public, obtained the Elkins Law (1903) forbidding rebates to favored corporations, and helped pass the Hepburn Railway Rate Act of 1906 (extending jurisdiction of the Interstate Commerce Commission). He helped obtain passage of the Pure Food and Drug Act (1906), and of employers' liability laws. Roosevelt vigorously organized conservation efforts. He mediated (1905) the peace between Japan and Russia, for which he won the Nobel Peace Prize. He abetted the 1903 revolution in Panama that led to U.S. acquisition of territory for the Panama Canal.

In 1908 Roosevelt obtained the nomination of William H. Taft, who was elected. Feeling that Taft had abandoned his policies, he unsuccessfully sought the nomination in 1912. He then ran on the Progressive "Bull Moose" ticket against Taft and Woodrow Wilson, splitting the Republicans and ensuring Wilson's election. He was shot during the campaign but recovered. In 1916, after unsuccessfully seeking the presidential nomination, he supported the Republican candidate, Charles E. Hughes. A strong friend of Britain, he fought for U.S. intervention in World War I. He wrote some 40 books, of which *The Winning of the West* is perhaps best known. He died Jan. 6, 1919, at Sagamore Hill, Oyster Bay, NY.

IT'S A FACT: William Howard Taft was the last president to keep a cow on the White House lawn for fresh milk.

WILLIAM HOWARD TAFT (1909-13), 27th president, Republican, and 10th chief justice of the U.S., was born on Sept. 15, 1857, in Cincinnati, OH, the son of Alphonso and Louisa Maria Torrey Taft. His father was secretary of war and attorney general in Grant's cabinet and minister to Austria and Russia under Arthur. Taft graduated from Yale in 1878 and from Cincinnati Law School in 1880. After working as a law reporter for Cincinnati newspapers, he served as assistant prosecuting attorney (1881-82), assistant county solicitor (1885), judge, superior court (1887), U.S. solicitor-general (1890), and federal circuit judge (1892). In 1900 he became head of the U.S. Philippines Commission and was the first civil governor of the Philippines (1901-4). In 1904 he served as secretary of war, and in 1906 he was sent to Cuba to help avert a threatened revolution.

Taft was groomed for the presidency by Theodore Roosevelt and elected over William Jennings Bryan in 1908. Taft vigorously continued Roosevelt's trust-busting, instituted the Department of Labor, and drafted the amendments calling for direct election of senators and the income tax. His tariff and conservation policies angered progressives. Although renominated in 1912, he was opposed by Roosevelt, who ran on the Progressive Party ticket; the result was Democrat Woodrow Wilson's election.

Taft, with some reservations, supported the League of Nations. After leaving office, he was professor of constitutional law at Yale (1913-21) and chief justice of the U.S. (1921-30). Taft was the only person in U.S. history to have been both president and chief justice. He died in Washington, DC, on Mar. 8, 1930.

(THOMAS) WOODROW WILSON (1913-21), 28th president, Democrat, was born on Dec. 28, 1856, in Staunton, VA, the son of Joseph Ruggles and Janet (Jessie) Woodrow Wilson. He grew up in Georgia and South Carolina. He attended Davidson College in North Carolina before graduating from Princeton University in 1879. He studied law at the University of Virginia and political science at Johns Hopkins University, where he received his PhD in 1886. He taught at Bryn Mawr (1885-88) and then at Wesleyan (1888-90) before joining the faculty at Princeton. He was president of Princeton from 1902 until 1910, when he was elected governor of New Jersey. In 1912 he was nominated for president with the aid of William Jennings Bryan, who sought to block James "Champ" Clark and Tammany Hall. Wilson won because the Republican vote for Taft was split by the Progressives.

As president, Wilson protected American interests in revolutionary Mexico and fought for American rights on the high seas. He oversaw the creation of the Federal Reserve system, cut the tariff, and developed a reputation as a reformer. His sharp warnings to Germany led to the resignation of his secretary of state, Bryan, a pacifist. In 1916 he was reelected by a slim margin with the slogan, "He kept us out of war," although his attempts to mediate in the war failed. After several American ships had been sunk by the Germans, he secured a declaration of war against Germany on Apr. 6, 1917.

Wilson outlined his peace program on Jan. 8, 1918, in the Fourteen Points, a state paper that had worldwide influence. He enunciated a doctrine of self-determination for the settlement of territorial disputes. The Germans accepted his terms and an armistice on Nov. 11, 1918.

Wilson went to Paris to help negotiate the peace treaty, the crux of which he considered the League of Nations. The Senate demanded reservations that would not make the U.S. subordinate to the votes of other nations in case of war. Wilson refused and toured the country to get support. He suffered a stroke in Oct. 1919. An invalid, he clung to his office while his wife and doctors effectively functioned as president.

Wilson was awarded the 1919 Nobel Peace Prize, but the treaty embodying the League of Nations was ultimately rejected by the Senate in 1920. He left the White House in Mar. 1921. He died in Washington, DC, on Feb. 3, 1924.

WARREN GAMALIEL HARDING (1921-23), 29th president, Republican, was born on Nov. 2, 1865, near Corsica (now Blooming Grove), OH, the son of George Tyron and Phoebe Elizabeth Dickerson Harding. He attended Ohio Central College, studied law, and became editor and publisher of a county newspaper. He entered the political arena as state senator (1901-4) and then served as lieutenant governor (1904-6). In 1910 he ran unsuccessfully for governor of Ohio; then in 1914 he was elected to the U.S. Senate. In the Senate he voted for antistrike legislation, woman suffrage, and the Volstead Prohibition Enforcement Act over President Wilson's veto. He opposed the League of Nations. In 1920 he was nominated for president and defeated James M. Cox in the election. The Republicans capitalized on war weariness and fear that Wilson's League of Nations would curtail U.S. sovereignty.

Harding stressed a return to "normalcy" and worked for tariff revision and the repeal of excess profits law and high income taxes. His secretary of interior, Albert B. Fall, became involved in the Teapot Dome scandal. As rumors began to circulate about the corruption in his administration, Harding became ill while returning from a trip to Alaska, and he died in San Francisco on Aug. 2, 1923.

(JOHN) CALVIN COOLIDGE (1923-29), 30th president, Republican, was born on July 4, 1872, in Plymouth, VT, the son of John Calvin and Victoria J. Moor Coolidge. Coolidge graduated from Amherst College in 1895. He entered Republican state politics and served as mayor of Northampton, MA, as state senator, as lieutenant governor, and, in 1919, as governor. In Sept. 1919, Coolidge attained national prominence by calling out the state guard in the Boston police strike. He declared: "There is no right to strike against the public safety by anybody, anywhere, anytime." This brought his name before the Republican convention of 1920, where he was nominated for vice president.

Coolige succeeded to the presidency on Harding's death. As president, he opposed the League of Nations and the soldiers' bonus bill, which was passed over his veto. In 1924 he was elected to the presidency by a huge majority. He substantially reduced the national debt. He twice vetoed the McNary-Haugen farm bill, which would have provided relief to financially hard-pressed farmers.

With Republicans eager to renominate him, Coolidge simply announced, Aug. 2, 1927: "I do not choose to run for president in 1928." He died in Northa5mpton, MA, on Jan. 5, 1933.

HERBERT CLARK HOOVER (1929-33), 31st president, Republican, was born on Aug. 10, 1874, in West Branch, IA, the son of Jesse Clark and Hulda Randall Minthorn Hoover. Hoover grew up in Indian Territory (now Oklahoma) and Oregon and graduated from Stanford University with a degree in engineering in 1895. He worked briefly with the U.S. Geological Survey and then managed mines in Australia, Asia, Europe, and Africa. While chief engineer of imperial mines in China, he directed food relief for victims of the Boxer Rebellion. He gained a reputation not only as an engineer but as a humanitarian as he directed the American Relief Committee, London (1914-15) and the U.S. Commission for Relief in Belgium (1915-19). He was U.S. Food Administrator (1917-19), American Relief Administrator (1918-23), and in charge of Russian Relief (1918-23). He served as secretary of commerce under both Harding and Coolidge. Some historians believe that he was the most effective secretary of commerce ever to hold that office.

In 1928 Hoover was elected president over Alfred E. Smith. In 1929 the stock market crashed, and the economy collapsed. During the Great Depression, Hoover inaugurated some government assistance programs, but he was opposed to administration of aid through a federal bureaucracy. As the effects of the depression continued, he was defeated in the 1932 election by Franklin D. Roosevelt. Hoover remained active after leaving office. President Truman named him coordinator of the European Food Program (1946) and chairman of the Commission on Organization of the Executive Branch (1947-49; 1953-55). Hoover died in New York City on Oct. 20, 1964.

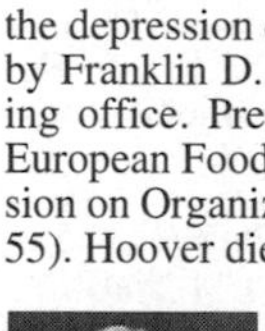

FRANKLIN DELANO ROOSEVELT (1933-45), 32nd president, Democrat, was born on Jan. 30, 1882, near Hyde Park, NY, the son of James and Sara Delano Roosevelt. He graduated from Harvard University in 1904. He attended Columbia University Law School without taking a degree and was admitted to the New York state bar in 1907. His political career began when he was elected to the New York state senate in 1910. In 1913 President Wilson appointed him assistant secretary of the navy, a post he held during World War I.

In 1920 Roosevelt ran for vice president with James Cox and was defeated. From 1921 to 1928 he worked in his New York law office and was also vice president of a bank. In Aug. 1921, he was stricken with poliomyelitis, which left his legs paralyzed. As a result of therapy he was able to stand, or walk a few steps, with the aid of leg braces.

Roosevelt served 2 terms as governor of New York (1929-33). In 1932, W. G. McAdoo, pledged to John N. Garner, threw his votes to Roosevelt, who was nominated for president. The Depression and the promise to repeal Prohibition ensured his election. He asked for emergency powers, proclaimed the New Deal, and put into effect a vast number of administrative changes. Foremost was the use of public funds for relief and public works, resulting in deficit financing. He greatly expanded the federal government's regulation of business and by an excess profits tax and progressive income taxes produced a redistribution of earnings on an unprecedented scale. He also promoted legislation establishing the Social Security system. He was the last president inaugurated on Mar. 4 (1933) and the first inaugurated on Jan. 20 (1937).

Roosevelt was the first president to use radio for "fireside chats." When the Supreme Court nullified some New Deal laws, he sought power to "pack" the Court with additional justices, but Congress refused to give him the authority. He was the first president to break the "no 3rd term" tradition (1940) and was elected to a 4th term in 1944, despite failing health. Roosevelt was openly hostile to fascist governments before World War II and launched a lend-lease program on behalf of the Allies. With British Prime Min. Winston Churchill he wrote a declaration of principles to be followed after Nazi defeat (the Atlantic Charter of Aug. 14, 1941) and urged the Four Freedoms (freedom of speech, of worship, from want, from fear) Jan. 6, 1941. When Japan attacked Pearl Harbor on Dec. 7, 1941, the U.S. entered the war. Roosevelt conferred with allied heads of state at Casablanca (Jan. 1943), Quebec (Aug. 1943), Tehran (Nov.-Dec. 1943), Cairo (Nov. and Dec. 1943), and Yalta (Feb. 1945).

Roosevelt did not, however, live to see the end of the war. He died of a cerebral hemorrhage in Warm Springs, GA, on Apr. 12, 1945.

HARRY S. TRUMAN (1945-53), 33rd president, Democrat, was born on May 8, 1884, in Lamar, MO, the son of John Anderson and Martha Ellen Young Truman. A family disagreement on whether his middle name should be Shippe or Solomon, after names of 2 grandfathers, resulted in his using only the middle initial S. After graduating from high school in Independence, MO, he worked (1901) for the *Kansas City Star,* as a railroad timekeeper, and as a clerk in Kansas City banks until about 1905. He ran his family's farm from 1906 to 1917. He served in France during World War I. After the war he opened a haberdashery shop, was a judge on the Jackson Co. Court (1922-24), and attended Kansas City School of Law (1923-25).

Truman was elected to the U.S. Senate in 1934 and reelected in 1940. In 1944, with Roosevelt's backing, he was nominated for vice president and elected. On Roosevelt's death in 1945, Truman became president. In 1948, in a famous upset victory, he defeated Republican Thomas E. Dewey to win election to a new term.

Truman authorized the first uses of the atomic bomb (Hiroshima and Nagasaki, Aug. 6 and 9, 1945), bringing World War II to a rapid end. He was responsible for what came to be called the Truman Doctrine (to aid nations such as Greece and Turkey, threatened by Communist takeover), and his strong commitment to NATO and to the Marshall Plan helped bring them about. In 1948-49, he broke a Soviet blockade of West Berlin with a massive airlift. When Communist North Korea invaded South Korea (June 1950), he won UN approval for a "police action" and sent in forces under Gen. Douglas MacArthur. When MacArthur opposed his policy of limited objectives, Truman removed him.

He died in Kansas City, MO, on Dec. 26, 1972.

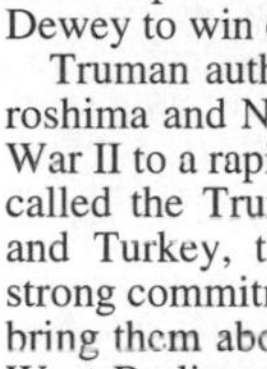

DWIGHT DAVID EISENHOWER (1953-61), 34th president, Republican, was born on Oct. 14, 1890, in Denison, TX, the son of David Jacob and Ida Elizabeth Stover Eisenhower. He grew up on a small farm in Abilene, KS, and graduated from West Point in 1915. He was on the staff of Gen. Douglas MacArthur in the Philippines from 1935 to 1939. In 1942, he was made commander of Allied forces landing in North Africa; the next year he was made full general. He became supreme Allied commander in Europe that same year and as such led the Normandy invasion (June 6, 1944). He was given the rank of general of the army on Dec. 20, 1944, which was made permanent in 1946. On May 7, 1945, Eisenhower received the surrender of Germany at Rheims. He returned to the U.S. to serve as chief of staff (1945-48). His war memoir, *Crusade in Europe* (1948), was a best-seller. In 1948 he became president of Columbia University; in 1950 he became Commander of NATO forces.

Eisenhower resigned from the army and was nominated for president by the Republicans in 1952. He defeated Adlai E. Stevenson in the 1952 election and again in 1956. Eisenhower called himself a moderate, favored the "free market system" vs. government price and wage controls, kept government out of labor disputes, reorganized the defense establishment, and promoted missile programs. He continued foreign aid, sped the end of the Korean War, endorsed Taiwan and SE Asia defense treaties, backed the UN in condemning the Anglo-French raid on Egypt, and advocated the "open skies" policy of mutual inspection with the USSR. He sent U.S. troops into Little Rock, AR, in Sept. 1957, during the segregation crisis.

Eisenhower died on Mar. 28, 1969, in Washington, DC.

JOHN FITZGERALD KENNEDY (1961-63), 35th president, Democrat, was born on May 29, 1917, in Brookline, MA, the son of Joseph P. and Rose Fitzgerald Kennedy. He graduated from Harvard University in 1940. While serving in the navy (1941-45), he commanded a PT boat in the Solomons and won the Navy and Marine Corps Medal. In 1956, while recovering from spinal surgery, he wrote *Profiles in Courage,* which won a Pulitzer Prize in 1957. He served in the House of Representatives from 1947 to 1953 and was elected to the Senate in 1952 and 1958. In 1960, he won the Democratic nomination for president and narrowly defeated Republican Vice Pres. Richard M. Nixon. Kennedy was the youngest president ever elected to the office and the first Catholic.

Kennedy also defied Soviet attempts to force the Allies out of Berlin. He started the Peace Corps, and he backed civil rights and expanded medical care for the aged. Space exploration was greatly developed during his administration. In Apr. 1961, the new Kennedy administration suffered a severe setback when an invasion force of anti-Castro Cubans, trained and directed by the CIA, failed to establish a beach head at the Bay of Pigs in Cuba. By the same token, one of Kennedy's most important acts as president was his successful demand on Oct. 22, 1962, that the Soviet Union dismantle its missile bases in Cuba.

On Nov. 22, 1963, Kennedy was assassinated while riding in a motorcade in Dallas, TX.

LYNDON BAINES JOHNSON (1963-69), 36th president, Democrat, was born on Aug. 27, 1908, near Stonewall, TX, the son of Sam Ealy and Rebekah Baines Johnson. He graduated from Southwest Texas State Teachers College in 1930 and attended Georgetown University Law School. He taught public speaking in Houston (1930-31) and then served as secretary to Rep. R. M. Kleberg (1931-35). In 1937 Johnson won an election to fill the vacancy caused by the death of a U.S. representative and in 1938 was elected to the full term, after which he returned for 4 terms. During 1941 and 1942 he also served in the Navy in the Pacific, earning a Silver Star for bravery. He was elected U.S. senator in 1948 and reelected in 1954. He became Democratic leader of the Senate in 1953. Johnson had strong support for the Democratic presidential nomination at the 1960 convention, where the nominee, John F. Kennedy, asked him to run for vice president. His campaigning helped overcome religious bias against Kennedy in the South.

Johnson became president when Kennedy was assassinated. He was elected to a full term in 1964. Johnson's domestic program was of considerable importance. He won passage of major civil rights, anti-poverty, aid to education, and health-care (Medicare, Medicaid) legislation—the "Great Society" program. However, his escalation of the war in Vietnam came to overshadow the achievements of his administration. In the face of increasing division in the nation and in his own party over his handling of the war, Johnson declined to seek another term.

Johnson died on Jan. 22, 1973, in San Antonio, TX.

RICHARD MILHOUS NIXON (1969-74), 37th president, Republican, was born on Jan. 9, 1913, in Yorba Linda, CA, the son of Francis Anthony and Hannah Milhous Nixon. He graduated from Whittier College in 1934 and from Duke University Law School in 1937. After practicing law in Whittier and serving briefly in the Office of Price Administration in 1942, he entered the Navy and served in the South Pacific. Nixon was elected to the House of Representatives in 1946 and 1948. He achieved prominence as the House Un-American Activities Committee member who forced the showdown leading to the Alger Hiss perjury conviction. In 1950 he was elected to the Senate.

Nixon was elected vice president in the Eisenhower landslides of 1952 and 1956. He won the Republican nomination for president in 1960 but was narrowly defeated by John F. Kennedy. He ran unsuccessfully for governor of California in 1962. In 1968 he again won the GOP presidential nomination, then defeated Hubert Humphrey for the presidency.

Nixon's 2nd term was cut short by scandal, after disclosures relating to a June 1972 burglary of Democratic Party headquarters in the Watergate office complex. The courts and Congress sought tapes of Nixon's office conversations and calls for criminal proceedings against former White House aides and for a House inquiry into possible impeachment. Nixon claimed executive privilege, but the Supreme Court ruled against him. In July the House Judiciary Committee recommended adoption of 3 impeachment articles charging him with obstruction of justice, abuse of power, and contempt of Congress. On Aug. 5, he released transcripts of conversations that linked him to cover-up activities. He resigned on Aug. 9, becoming the first president ever to do so. In later years, Nixon emerged as an elder statesman.

As president, Nixon appointed 4 Supreme Court justices, including the chief justice, moving the court to the right, and as a "new federalist" sought to shift responsibility to state and local governments. He dramatically altered relations with China, which he visited in 1972—the first president to do so. With foreign affairs adviser Henry Kissinger he pursued détente with the Soviet Union. He began a gradual withdrawal from Vietnam, but U.S. troops remained there through his first term. He ordered an incursion into Cambodia (1970) and the bombing of Hanoi and mining of Haiphong Harbor (1972). Reelected by a large majority in Nov. 1972, he secured a Vietnam cease-fire in Jan. 1973.

Nixon died Apr. 22, 1994, in New York City.

GERALD RUDOLPH FORD (1974-77), 38th president, Republican, was born on July 14, 1913, in Omaha, NE, the son of Leslie and Dorothy Gardner King, and was named Leslie Jr. When he was 2, his parents were divorced, and his mother moved with the boy to Grand Rapids, MI. There she met and married Gerald R. Ford, who formally adopted him and gave him his own name. Ford graduated from the University of Michigan in 1935 and from Yale Law School in 1941. He began practicing law in Grand Rapids, but in 1942 joined the navy and served in the Pacific, leaving the service in 1946 as a lieutenant commander. He entered the House of Representatives in 1949 and spent 25 years in the House, 8 of them as Republican leader.

On Oct. 12, 1973, after Vice President Spiro T. Agnew resigned, Ford was nominated by President Nixon to replace him. It was the first use of the procedures set out in the 25th Amendment. When Nixon resigned, Aug. 9, 1974, because of the Watergate scandal, Ford became president; he was the only president who was never elected either to the presidency or to the vice presidency. On Sept. 8, in a controversial move, he pardoned Nixon for any federal crimes he might have committed as president. Ford vetoed 48 bills in his first 21 months in office, mostly in the interest of fighting high inflation; he was less successful in curbing high unemployment. In foreign policy, Ford continued to pursue détente.

Ford was narrowly defeated in the 1976 election.

JIMMY (JAMES EARL) CARTER (1977-81), 39th president, Democrat, was the first president from the Deep South since before the Civil War. He was born on Oct. 1, 1924, in Plains, GA, the son of James and Lillian Gordy Carter. Carter graduated from the U.S. Naval Academy in 1946 and in 1952 entered the navy's nuclear submarine program as an aide to Capt. (later Adm.) Hyman Rickover. He studied nuclear physics at Union College. Carter's father died in 1953, and he left the navy to take over the family peanut farming businesses. He served in the Georgia state senate (1963-67) and as governor of Georgia (1971-75). In 1976, Carter won the Democratic nomination and defeated President Gerald R. Ford.

On his first full day in office, Carter pardoned all Vietnam draft evaders. He played a major role in the negotiations leading to the 1979 peace treaty between Israel and Egypt, and he won passage of new treaties with Panama providing for U.S. control of the Panama Canal to end in 2000. However, Carter was widely criticized for the poor state of the economy and was viewed by some as weak in his handling of foreign policy. In Nov. 1979, Iranian student militants attacked the U.S. embassy in Tehran and held members of the embassy staff hostage. Efforts to obtain release of the hostages were a major preoccupation during the rest of his term. He reacted to the Soviet invasion of Afghanistan by imposing a grain embargo and boycotting the Moscow Olympic Games.

Carter was defeated by Ronald Reagan in the 1980 election. Carter administration efforts led to the release of the American hostages, but not until Inauguration Day, 1981, just after Reagan officially became president. After leaving office, Carter was hailed for his humanitarian efforts and took a prominent role in mediating international disputes.

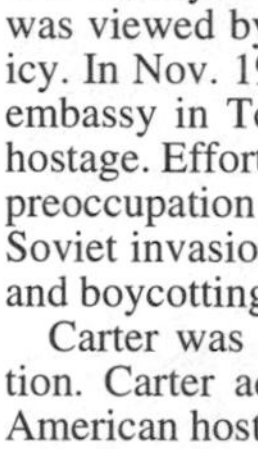

RONALD WILSON REAGAN (1981-89), 40th president, Republican, was born on Feb. 6, 1911, in Tampico, IL, the son of John Edward and Nellie Wilson Reagan. Reagan graduated from Eureka College in 1932, after which he worked as a sports announcer in Des Moines, IA. He began a successful career as an actor in 1937, starring in numerous movies, and later in television, until the 1960s. He served as president of the Screen Actors Guild from 1947 to 1952 and in 1959-60. Reagan was elected governor of California in 1966 and reelected in 1970.

In 1980, Reagan gained the Republican presidential nomination and won a landslide victory over Jimmy Carter. He was easily reelected in 1984. Reagan successfully forged a bipartisan coalition in Congress, which led to enactment of his program of large-scale tax cuts, cutbacks in many government programs, and a major defense buildup. He signed a Social Security reform bill designed to provide for the long-term solvency of the system. In 1986, he signed into law a major tax-reform bill. He was shot and wounded in an assassination attempt in 1981.

In 1982, the U.S. joined France and Italy in maintaining a peacekeeping force in Beirut, Lebanon, and the next year Reagan sent a task force to invade the island of Grenada after 2 Marxist coups there. Reagan's opposition to international terrorism led to the U.S. bombing of Libyan military installations in 1986. He strongly supported El Salvador, the Nicaraguan contras, and other anti-communist governments and forces throughout the world. He also held 4 summit meetings with Soviet leader Mikhail Gorbachev. At the 1987 meeting in Washington, DC, a historic treaty eliminating short- and medium-range missiles from Europe was signed.

Reagan faced a crisis in 1986-87, when it was revealed that the U.S. had sold weapons through Israeli brokers to Iran in exchange for release of U.S. hostages being held in Lebanon and that subsequently some of the money was diverted to the Nicaraguan contras (Congress had barred U.S. aid to the contras). The scandal led to the resignation of leading White House aides. As Reagan left office in Jan. 1989, the nation was experiencing its 6th consecutive year of economic prosperity. Over the same period, however, the federal government consistently recorded large budget deficits. In 1994, in a letter to the American people, Reagan revealed that he was suffering from Alzheimer's disease.

GEORGE HERBERT WALKER BUSH (1989-93), 41st president, Republican, was born on June 12, 1924, in Milton, MA, the son of Prescott and Dorothy Walker Bush. He served as a U.S. Navy pilot in World War II. After graduating from Yale University in 1948, he settled in Texas, where, in 1953, he helped found an oil company. After losing a bid for a U.S. Senate seat in Texas in 1964, he was elected to the House of Representatives in 1966 and 1968. He lost a 2nd U.S. Senate race in 1970. Subsequently he served as U.S. ambassador to the United Nations (1971-73), headed the U.S. Liaison Office in Beijing (1974-75), and was director of central intelligence (1976-77).

Following an unsuccessful bid for the 1980 Republican presidential nomination, Bush was chosen by Ronald Reagan as his vice presidential running mate. He served as U.S. vice president from 1981 to 1989.

In 1988, Bush gained the GOP presidential nomination and defeated Michael Dukakis in the November election. Bush took office faced with U.S. budget and trade deficits as well as the rescue of insolvent U.S. savings and loan institutions. He faced a severe budget deficit annually, struggled with military cutbacks in light of reduced cold war tensions, and vetoed abortion-rights legislation. In 1990 he agreed to a budget deficit-reduction plan that included tax hikes.

Bush supported Soviet reforms, Eastern Europe democratization, and good relations with Beijing. In Dec. 1989, Bush sent troops to Panama; they overthrew the government and captured strongman Gen. Manuel Noriega.

Bush reacted to Iraq's Aug. 1990 invasion of Kuwait by sending U.S. forces to the Persian Gulf area and assembling a UN-backed coalition, including NATO and Arab League members. After a month-long air war, in Feb. 1991, Allied forces retook Kuwait in a 4-day ground assault. The quick victory, with extremely light casualties on the U.S. side, gave Bush at the time one of the highest presidential approval ratings in history. His popularity plummeted by the end of 1991, however, as the economy slipped into recession. He was defeated by Bill Clinton in the 1992 election.

BILL (WILLIAM JEFFERSON) CLINTON (1993-2001), 42nd president, Democrat, was born on Aug. 19, 1946, in Hope, AR, son of William Blythe and Virginia Cassidy Blythe, and was named William Jefferson Blythe IV. Blythe died in an automobile accident before his son was born. His widow married Roger Clinton, and at the age of 16, William Jefferson Blythe IV changed his last name to Clinton. Clinton graduated from Georgetown University in 1968, attended Oxford University as a Rhodes scholar, and earned a degree from Yale Law School in 1973.

Clinton worked on George McGovern's 1972 presidential campaign. He taught at the University of Arkansas from 1973 to 1976, when he was elected state attorney general. In 1978, he was elected governor, becoming the nation's youngest. Defeated for reelection in 1980, he was returned to office in several times thereafter. He married Hillary Rodham in 1975.

Despite questions about his character, Clinton won most of the 1992 presidential primaries, moving his party toward the center as he tried to broaden his appeal; as the party's presidential nominee he defeated Pres. George Bush and Reform Party candidate Ross Perot in the November election. In 1993, Clinton won passage of a measure to reduce the federal budget deficit and won congressional approval of the North American Free Trade Agreement. His administration's plan for major health-care reform legislation died in Congress. After 1994 midterm elections, Clinton faced Republican majorities in both houses of Congress. He followed a centrist course at home, sent troops to Bosnia to help implement a peace settlement, and cultivated relations with Russia and China.

Though accused of improprieties in his involvement in an Arkansas real estate venture (Whitewater) and in other matters, Clinton easily won reelection in 1996. In 1997 he reached agreement with Congress on legislation to balance the federal budget by 2002. In 1998, Clinton became only the 2nd U.S. president ever to be impeached by the House of Representatives. Charged with perjury and obstruction of justice in connection with an attempted cover-up of a sexual relationship with a former White House intern, he was acquitted by the Senate in 1999. Despite the scandal he retained wide popularity, aided by a strong economy.

In 1999, the United States, under Clinton, joined other NATO nations in an aerial bombing campaign that ultimately induced Serbia to withdraw troops from the Kosovo region, where they had been terrorizing ethnic Albanians.

Shortly after leaving office, Clinton attracted headlines over a series of sometimes controversial pardons he had issued in the waning days of his presidency.

GEORGE WALKER BUSH (2001-), 43rd president, Republican, was born on July 6, 1946, in New Haven, CT. He was the first of six children born to George Herbert Walker Bush and his wife, the former Barbara Pierce, a descendant of Pres. Franklin Pierce. (His brother Jeb won the Florida governorship in 1998.) Bush was the first son of a former president to win the White House since John Quincy Adams.

Fun-loving, athletic, and popular, the young George Bush grew up in Midland and Houston, TX. In 1961 he was sent to the Phillips Academy in Andover, MA, the same prep school his father had attended. In 1964 he entered Yale University, his father's alma mater, where he majored in history. Eligible for the draft upon graduation, he signed on with the Texas Air National Guard. After earning a master's degree from the Harvard Business School, he returned to Midland in 1975 and went into the oil business. Two years later he married Laura Welch, a schoolteacher and librarian; in 1981 she gave birth to twin daughters.

Bush, who had lost a race for Congress in 1978, returned to the oil business, but success proved elusive. Realizing that he had a drinking problem, he swore off alcohol and renewed commitment to Christian faith. After aiding in his father's successful 1988 presidential campaign, he put together a group of investors to buy the Texas Rangers baseball club and took a hands-on role as managing partner. Bush ran for governor in 1994, defeating a popular incumbent, Ann Richards. He won reelection by a landslide in 1998.

As governor, he concentrated on building personal bonds with Democratic leaders. He backed education reforms, won passage of measures designed to curb so-called "junk lawsuits," and cut property taxes for homeowners.

After defeating Sen. John McCain of Arizona and several other rivals in the Republican party primaries, Bush chose Dick Cheney, a former U.S. representative and defense secretary, as his running mate. The Nov. 2000 presidential election was one of the closest in history. While Bush came out behind in the nationwide popular vote, by about 540,000 out of more than 100 million cast, the decisive electoral vote total hinged on the outcome in Florida, where official totals, challenged by Democrats, gave him a razor-thin lead. In December the Supreme Court in effect ended a controversial attempt to recount the vote there, and Florida's 25 electoral votes decided the election in Bush's favor.

Among the issues Bush had campaigned on was that of lowering federal taxes, and in May 2001 he won approval from Congress for a large tax cut package.

WORLD ALMANAC QUICK QUIZ

Which president was given at birth the same full name (shown below) that he had when he got to the White House?

(a) Ulysses Simpson Grant; (b) Warren Gamaliel Harding;
(c) Gerald Rudolph Ford; (d) William Jefferson Clinton

For the answer look in this chapter, or see page 1008.

On Sept. 11, 2001, Bush was faced with a crisis that would redefine his presidency. In a terrorist attack on U.S. soil, 2 hijacked jetliners crashed into the twin towers of the World Trade Center in New York City, which were destroyed; another jet struck the Pentagon near Washington, DC, with a 4th crashing in rural Pennsylvania. Some 3,000 people were killed in the attacks. In a televised speech, the president vowed to punish those responsible, and in a "war against terrorism," the U.S. attacked and deposed the Taliban regime in Afghanistan, which was sheltering key elements of the al-Qaeda terrorist network, held responsible by the U.S. for the attacks. Bush and administration officials warned that the struggle against terrorism by Islamic extremists would be protracted and that, despite precautions, more terrorist acts against the U.S. could be expected. In June 2002, Bush proposed a major government reorganization to create a cabinet-level department for homeland security, consolidating activities of existing agencies. Later in the year the Bush administration sought support for possible preemptive military action against the regime of Saddam Hussein in Iraq. (See also the front-of-the-book feature section.)

Bush met in May 2002 with Russian Pres. Vladimir Putin in Moscow, where they signed a pact cutting nuclear armaments in each country by two-thirds over 10 years. In July, with corporate scandals and a slumping stock market fueling demands for tighter government regulation of business, Congress cleared and Bush signed a major accounting, corporate governance, and securities fraud law, aimed at curbing abuses. The following month, Bush won approval from Congress for fast-track trade legislation.

Wives and Children of the Presidents

Name (Born–died; married)	State	Sons/ Daughters
Martha Dandridge Custis Washington (1731-1802; 1759)	VA	None
Abigail Smith Adams (1744-1818; 1764)	MA	3/2
Martha Wayles Skelton Jefferson (1748-82; 1772)	VA	1/5
Dorothea "Dolley" Payne Todd Madison (1768-1849; 1794)	NC	None
Elizabeth Kortright Monroe (1768-1830; 1786)	NY	0/2 (A)
Louisa Catherine Johnson Adams (1775-1852; 1797)	MD (B)	3/1
Rachel Donelson Robards Jackson (1767-1828; 1791)	VA	None
Hannah Hoes Van Buren (1783-1819; 1807)	NY	4/0
Anna Tuthill Symmes Harrison (1775-1864; 1795)	NJ	6/4
Letitia Christian Tyler (1790-1842; 1813)	VA	3/4(A)
Julia Gardiner Tyler (1820-89; 1844)	NY	5/2
Sarah Childress Polk (1803-91; 1824)	TN	None
Margaret Mackall Smith Taylor (1788-1852; 1810)	MD	1/5
Abigail Powers Fillmore (1798-1853; 1826)	NY	1/1
Caroline Carmichael McIntosh Fillmore (1813-81; 1858)	NJ	None
Jane Means Appleton Pierce (1806-63; 1834)	NH	3/0
Mary Todd Lincoln (1818-82; 1842)	KY	4/0
Eliza McCardle Johnson (1810-76; 1827)	TN	3/2
Julia Boggs Dent Grant (1826-1902; 1848)	MO	3/1
Lucy Ware Webb Hayes (1831-89; 1852)	OH	7/1
Lucretia Randolph Garfield (1832-1918; 1858)	OH	4/1
Ellen Lewis Herndon Arthur (1837-80; 1859)	VA	2/1
Frances Folsom Cleveland (1864-1947; 1886)	NY	2/3
Caroline Lavinia Scott Harrison 1832-92; 1853)	OH	1/1
Mary Scott Lord Dimmick Harrison (1858-1948; 1896)	PA	0/1
Ida Saxton McKinley (1847-1907; 1871)	OH	0/2
Alice Hathaway Lee Roosevelt (1861-84; 1880)	MA	0/1
Edith Kermit Carow Roosevelt (1861-1948; 1886)	CT	4/1
Helen Herron Taft (1861-1943; 1886)	OH	2/1
Ellen Louise Axson Wilson (1860-1914; 1885)	GA	0/3
Edith Bolling Galt Wilson (1872-1961; 1915)	VA	None
Florence Kling De Wolfe Harding (1860-1924; 1891)	OH	None
Grace Anna Goodhue Coolidge (1879-1957; 1905)	VT	2/0
Lou Henry Hoover (1875-1944; 1899)	IA	2/0
Anna Eleanor Roosevelt Roosevelt (1884-1962; 1905)	NY	4/1(A)
Elizabeth Virginia "Bess" Wallace Truman (1885-1982; 1919)	MO	0/1
Mamie Geneva Doud Eisenhower (1896-1979; 1916)	IA	1/0(A)
Jacqueline Lee Bouvier Kennedy (1929-94; 1953)	NY	1/1(A)
Claudia "Lady Bird" Alta Taylor Johnson (1912; 1934)	TX	0/2
Thelma Catherine Patricia Ryan Nixon (1912-1993; 1940)	NV	0/2
Elizabeth Bloomer Warren Ford (1918; 1948)	IL	3/1
Rosalynn Smith Carter (1927; 1946)	GA	3/1
Anne Frances "Nancy" Robbins Davis Reagan (1921; 1952)	NY	1/1(C)
Barbara Pierce Bush (1925; 1945)	NY	4/2
Hillary Rodham Clinton (1947; 1975)	IL	0/1
Laura Welch Bush (1946; 1977)	TX	0/2

NOTE: James Buchanan, 15th president, was unmarried. (A) plus one infant, deceased. (B) Born in London, father a MD citizen. (C) Pres. Reagan married and divorced Jane Wyman; they had a daughter who died in infancy, a son and daughter who lived past infancy.

IT'S A FACT: On the advice of her doctor, First Lady Eleanor Roosevelt ate three chocolate-covered garlic balls every morning for most of her adult life. Her doctor suggested this regimen to improve her memory.

First Lady Laura Welch Bush

Laura Welch Bush was born in Midland, TX, Nov. 4, 1946. She graduated from Southern Methodist University, earned a master's in library science at the Univ. of Texas at Austin, and became a librarian and teacher in Texas public schools. She and George W. Bush were married in 1977; in 1981, their twin daughters, Jenna and Barbara, were born.

As First Lady of Texas from 1995 to 2001, Laura Bush stressed advocacy of educational reform and literacy programs. In 1998, she launched an early childhood development initiative that included a family literacy project for Texas. She also worked to promote breast cancer awareness and other women's health issues.

Her first solo appearance as U.S. First Lady came at the launch of D.C. Teaching Fellows, a program encouraging professionals to become teachers. In Nov. 2001 she became the first First Lady to give a speech of her own in place of the president's weekly radio address; in her speech she condemned the treatment of women by the Taliban in Afghanistan.

Burial Places of the Presidents

President	Burial Place	President	Burial Place	President	Burial Place
Washington	Mt. Vernon, VA	Fillmore	Buffalo, NY	T. Roosevelt	Oyster Bay, NY
J. Adams	Quincy, MA	Pierce	Concord, NH	Taft	Arlington Natl. Cemetery
Jefferson	Charlottesville, VA	Buchanan	Lancaster, PA	Wilson	Wash. Natl. Cathedral
Madison	Montpelier Station, VA	Lincoln	Springfield, IL	Harding	Marion, OH
Monroe	Richmond, VA	A. Johnson	Greeneville, TN	Coolidge	Plymouth, VT
J. Q. Adams	Quincy, MA	Grant	New York, NY	Hoover	West Branch, IA
Jackson	Nashville, TN	Hayes	Fremont, OH	F. Roosevelt	Hyde Park, NY
Van Buren	Kinderhook, NY	Garfield	Cleveland, OH	Truman	Independence, MO
W. H. Harrison	North Bend, OH	Arthur	Albany, NY	Eisenhower	Abilene, KS
Tyler	Richmond, VA	Cleveland	Princeton, NJ	Kennedy	Arlington Natl. Cemetery
Polk	Nashville, TN	B. Harrison	Indianapolis, IN	L. B. Johnson	Johnson City, TX
Taylor	Louisville, KY	McKinley	Canton, OH	Nixon	Yorba Linda, CA

Presidential Facts

First president to have a telephone in the White House: Rutherford B. Hayes, in 1879

First president to use electricity in the White House: Benjamin Harrison, in 1891; but he and his wife were afraid to touch the switches for fear of getting a shock

First president to leave the continental U.S. while in office: Theodore Roosevelt, in 1906, on a visit to inspect construction work on the Panama Canal

First president to ride in an airplane: Theodore Roosevelt, in 1910, a year after leaving office, when he took a 4-minute ride in a Wright brothers' plane

First president to have air transport: Franklin D. Roosevelt, in a C-44 plane put into service in 1944, named "the Sacred Cow"

First president to address the nation on radio: Warren G. Harding, in 1922

First president to appear on TV: Franklin D. Roosevelt, at opening ceremonies for the 1939 World's Fair

First president to speak from the White House on TV: Harry S. Truman, in 1947

First president born a U.S. citizen: Martin Van Buren

First president of all 50 states: Dwight D. Eisenhower

Only president elected unanimously: George Washington, by 63 electoral votes

Only president to also serve as chief justice of the U.S.: William Howard Taft

Only president to have been head of a labor union: Ronald Reagan

State where the greatest number of presidents were born: Virginia (8)

Presidents who died on July 4: John Adams and Thomas Jefferson (both 1826) and James Monroe (1831)

Presidents who died in office: Eight presidents have died in office. Of these, 4 were assassinated: Abraham Lincoln, James Garfield, William McKinley, and John F. Kennedy. The other 4 were William Henry Harrison, Zachary Taylor, Warren G. Harding, and Franklin D. Roosevelt

Presidential Libraries

The libraries listed here, except for that of Richard Nixon (which is private), are coordinated by the National Archives and Records Administration (Website: www.nara.gov/nara/president/overview.html). NARA also has custody of the Nixon presidential historical materials and those of Bill Clinton. The William J. Clinton Library was under construction in 2002. NARA will release Clinton presidential records to the public at the Clinton Library beginning Jan. 20, 2006. Materials for presidents before Herbert Hoover are held by private institutions.

Herbert Hoover Library
210 Parkside Dr., Box 488
West Branch, IA 52358-0488
PHONE: 319-643-5301
FAX: 319-643-5825
E-MAIL: hoover.library@nara.gov

Franklin D. Roosevelt Library
4079 Albany Post Rd.
Hyde Park, NY 12538-1999
PHONE: 845-229-8114
FAX: 845-229-0872
E-MAIL: roosevelt.library@nara.gov

Harry S. Truman Library
500 West U.S. Hwy. 24
Independence, MO 64050-1798
PHONE: 816-833-1400
FAX: 816-833-4368
E-MAIL: truman.library@nara.gov

Dwight D. Eisenhower Library
200 S.E. 4th St.
Abilene, KS 67410-2900
PHONE: 785-263-4751
FAX: 785-263-4218
E-MAIL: eisenhower.library@nara.gov

John Fitzgerald Kennedy Library
Columbia Pt.
Boston, MA 02125-3398
PHONE: 617-929-4500
FAX: 617-929-4538
E-MAIL: kennedy.library@nara.gov

Lyndon Baines Johnson Library
2313 Red River St.
Austin, TX 78705-5702
PHONE: 512-916-5137
FAX: 512-478-9104
E-MAIL: johnson.library@nara.gov

Richard Nixon Library & Birthplace
18001 Yorba Linda Blvd.
Yorba Linda, CA 92886-3949
PHONE: 714-993-5075
FAX: 714-528-0544
WEBSITE: www.nixonfoundation.org

Gerald R. Ford Library
1000 Beal Ave.
Ann Arbor, MI 48109-2114
PHONE: 734-741-2218
FAX: 734-741-2341
E-MAIL: ford.library@nara.gov

Jimmy Carter Library
441 Freedom Pkwy.
Atlanta, GA 30307-1498
PHONE: 404-331-3942
FAX: 404-730-2215
E-MAIL: carter.library@nara.gov

Ronald Reagan Library
40 Presidential Dr.
Simi Valley, CA 93065-0666
PHONE: 805-522-8444
FAX: 805-522-9621
E-MAIL: reagan.library@nara.gov

George H. W. Bush Library
1000 George Bush Dr. West
College Station, TX 77845
PHONE: 979-260-9552
FAX: 979-260-9557
E-MAIL: library.bush@nara.gov

William J. Clinton Library
1000 La Harpe Blvd.
Little Rock, AR 72201
PHONE: 501-244-9756
FAX: 501-244-9764
E-MAIL: clinton.library@nara.gov

Impeachment in U.S. History

The U.S. Constitution provides for impeachment and, upon conviction, removal from office of federal officials on grounds of "Treason, Bribery, or other high Crimes and Misdemeanors" (Article II, Sect. 4). Impeachment is the bringing of charges by the House of Representatives. It is followed by a Senate trial; a two-thirds vote in the Senate is needed for conviction and removal from office, which does not preclude criminal indictment and trial.

In 1868, Andrew Johnson became the first president impeached by the House; he was tried but not convicted by the Senate. In 1974, impeachment articles against Pres. Richard Nixon, in connection with the Watergate scandal, were voted by the House Judiciary Committee; he resigned Aug. 9, before the full House could vote on impeaching him. In 1998, Pres. Bill Clinton was impeached by the House in connection with covering up a relationship with a former White House intern; he was tried in the Senate in 1999 and acquitted.

PRESIDENTIAL ELECTIONS

Popular and Electoral Vote, 1996 and 2000

Source: Voter News Service; Federal Election Commission; totals are official.

	2000								1996					
	Electoral Vote				Democrat	Republican	Green[1]	Reform[2]	Electoral Vote			Democrat	Republican	Reform[2]
State	Gore	Bush	Nader	Buchanan	Gore	Bush	Nader	Buchanan	Clinton	Dole	Perot	Clinton	Dole	Perot
AL	0	9	0	0	692,611	941,173	18,323	6,351	0	9	0	662,165	769,044	92,149
AK	0	3	0	0	79,004	167,398	28,747	5,192	0	3	0	80,380	122,746	26,333
AZ	0	8	0	0	685,341	781,652	45,645	12,373	8	0	0	653,288	622,073	112,072
AR	0	6	0	0	422,768	472,940	13,421	7,358	6	0	0	475,171	325,416	69,884
CA	54	0	0	0	5,861,203	4,567,429	418,707	44,987	54	0	0	5,119,835	3,828,380	697,847
CO	0	8	0	0	738,227	883,748	91,434	10,465	0	8	0	671,152	691,848	99,629
CT	8	0	0	0	816,015	561,094	64,452	4,731	8	0	0	735,740	483,109	139,523
DE	3	0	0	0	180,068	137,288	8,307	777	3	0	0	140,355	99,062	28,719
DC	2[3]	0	0	—	171,923	18,073	10,576	—	3	0	0	158,220	17,339	3,611
FL	0	25	0	0	2,912,253	2,912,790	97,488	17,484	25	0	0	2,545,968	2,243,324	483,776
GA	0	13	—	0	1,116,230	1,419,720	—	10,926	0	13	0	1,053,849	1,080,843	146,337
HI	4	0	0	0	205,286	137,845	21,623	1,071	4	0	0	205,012	113,943	27,358
ID	0	4	—	0	138,637	336,937	—	7,615	0	4	0	165,443	256,595	62,518
IL	22	0	0	0	2,589,026	2,019,421	103,759	16,106	22	0	0	2,341,744	1,587,021	346,408
IN	0	12	0	0	901,980	1,245,836	—	16,959	0	12	0	887,424	1,006,693	224,299
IA	7	0	0	0	638,517	634,373	29,374	5,731	7	0	0	620,258	492,644	105,159
KS	0	6	0	0	399,276	622,332	36,086	7,370	0	6	0	387,659	583,245	92,639
KY	0	8	0	0	638,923	872,520	23,118	4,152	8	0	0	636,614	623,283	120,396
LA	0	9	0	0	792,344	927,871	20,473	14,356	9	0	0	927,837	712,586	123,293
ME	4	0	0	0	319,951	286,616	37,127	4,443	4	0	0	312,788	186,378	85,970
MD	10	0	0	0	1,144,008	813,827	53,768	4,248	10	0	0	966,207	681,530	115,812
MA	12	0	0	0	1,616,487	878,502	173,564	11,149	12	0	0	1,571,509	718,058	227,206
MI	18	0	0	—	2,170,418	1,953,139	84,165	—	18	0	0	1,989,653	1,481,212	336,670
MN	10	0	0	0	1,168,266	1,109,659	126,696	22,166	10	0	0	1,120,438	766,476	257,704
MS	0	7	0	0	404,614	572,844	8,122	2,265	0	7	0	394,022	439,838	52,222
MO	0	11	0	0	1,111,138	1,189,924	38,515	9,818	11	0	0	1,025,935	890,016	217,188
MT	0	3	0	0	137,126	240,178	24,437	5,697	0	3	0	167,922	179,652	55,229
NE	0	5	0	0	231,780	433,862	24,540	3,646	0	5	0	236,761	363,467	71,278
NV	0	4	0	0	279,978	301,575	15,008	4,747	4	0	0	203,974	199,244	43,986
NH	0	4	0	0	266,348	273,559	22,198	2,615	4	0	0	246,166	196,486	48,387
NJ	15	0	0	0	1,788,850	1,284,173	94,554	6,989	15	0	0	1,652,361	1,103,099	262,134
NM	5	0	0	0	286,783	286,417	21,251	1,392	5	0	0	273,495	232,751	32,257
NY	33	0	0	0	4,112,965	2,405,570	244,360	31,554	33	0	0	3,756,177	1,933,492	503,458
NC	0	14	—	0	1,257,692	1,631,163	—	8,874	0	14	0	1,107,849	1,225,938	168,059
ND	0	3	0	0	95,284	174,852	9,486	7,288	0	3	0	106,905	125,050	32,515
OH	0	21	0	0	2,186,190	2,351,209	117,857	26,724	21	0	0	2,148,222	1,859,883	483,207
OK	0	8	—	0	474,276	744,337	—	9,014	0	8	0	488,105	582,315	130,788
OR	7	0	0	0	720,342	713,577	77,357	7,063	7	0	0	649,641	538,152	121,221
PA	23	0	0	0	2,485,967	2,281,127	103,392	16,023	23	0	0	2,215,819	1,801,169	430,984
RI	4	0	0	0	249,508	130,555	25,052	2,273	4	0	0	233,050	104,683	43,723
SC	0	8	0	0	566,039	786,892	20,279	3,309	0	8	0	506,283	573,458	64,386
SD	0	3	—	0	118,804	190,700	—	3,322	0	3	0	139,333	150,543	31,250
TN	0	11	0	0	981,720	1,061,949	19,781	4,250	11	0	0	909,146	863,530	105,918
TX	0	32	0	0	2,433,746	3,799,639	137,994	12,394	0	32	0	2,459,683	2,736,167	378,537
UT	0	5	0	0	203,053	515,096	35,850	9,319	0	5	0	221,633	361,911	66,461
VT	3	0	0	0	149,022	119,775	20,374	2,192	3	0	0	137,894	80,352	31,024
VA	0	13	0	0	1,217,290	1,437,490	59,398	5,455	0	13	0	1,091,060	1,138,350	159,861
WA	11	0	0	0	1,247,652	1,108,864	103,002	7,171	11	0	0	1,123,323	840,712	201,003
WV	0	5	0	0	295,497	336,475	10,680	3,169	5	0	0	327,812	233,946	71,639
WI	11	0	0	0	1,242,987	1,237,279	94,070	11,446	11	0	0	1,071,971	845,029	227,339
WY	0	3	—	0	60,481	147,947	—	2,724	0	3	0	77,934	105,388	25,928
Total	**266[3]**	**271**	**0**	**0**	**51,003,894**	**50,459,211**	**2,834,410**	**446,743**	**379**	**159**	**0**	**47,401,185**	**39,197,469**	**8,085,294**

(—) = Not listed on state's ballot. (1) Listed on the ballot in some states as party other than Green. (2) Listed on the ballot in some states as party other than Reform. (3) One Washington, DC, elector abstained.

2000 Official Presidential General Election Results

Source: Voter News Service; Federal Election Commission

Candidate (Party)	Popular Vote	Percent of Popular Vote
Al Gore (Democrat)	51,003,894	48.41
George W. Bush (Republican)	50,459,211	47.89
Ralph Nader (Green)	2,834,410	2.69
Patrick J. Buchanan (Reform)	446,743	0.42
Harry Browne (Libertarian)	386,041	0.37
Howard Phillips (Constitution)	96,919	0.09
John S. Hagelin (Natural Law)	83,117	0.08
James E. Harris Jr. (Socialist Workers)	7,354	0.01
L. Neil Smith (Libertarian)	5,775	0.01
Monica Moorehead (Workers World)	4,795	0.00
David McReynolds (Socialist)	4,194	0.00
Cathy Gordon Brown (Independent)	1,606	0.00
Denny Lane (Vermont Grassroots)	1,044	0.00
Randall Venson (Independent)	535	0.00
Earl F. Dodge (Prohibition)	208	0.00
Louie G. Youngkeit (Unaffiliated)	161	0.00
Write-in	20,938	0.02
None of These Candidates (Nevada)	3,315	0.00
Total	**105,360,260**	**100.00**

Note: Party designations may vary from one state to another

PRESIDENTIAL ELECTION RETURNS BY COUNTIES

All results official. Results for New England states are for selected cities or towns. All totals statewide. D-Democrat; R-Republican; RF-Reform; I-Independent. (In 1996, Ross Perot was listed on the ballot in some states as "Independent.")

Source: Voter News Service; Federal Election Commission; Alaska Division of Elections

Alabama

County	2000 Gore (D)	2000 Bush (R)	1996 Clinton (D)	1996 Dole (R)	1996 Perot (RF)
Autauga	4,942	11,993	5,015	9,509	813
Baldwin	13,997	40,872	12,776	29,487	4,520
Barbour	2,197	1,860	4,787	3,627	515
Bibb	2,710	4,273	2,775	3,037	455
Blount	4,977	12,667	5,061	9,056	985
Bullock	3,395	1,433	3,078	1,154	111
Butler	3,606	4,127	3,828	3,352	538
Calhoun	15,781	22,306	15,725	18,088	2,613
Chambers	5,616	6,037	5,515	4,707	812
Cherokee	3,497	4,154	4,399	3,048	899
Chilton	4,806	10,066	5,354	7,910	929
Choctaw	3,707	3,600	4,074	2,623	413
Clarke	4,679	5,988	4,831	4,785	478
Clay	2,045	3,719	2,306	2,694	538
Cleburne	1,664	3,333	1,737	2,063	385
Coffee	5,220	9,938	5,168	7,805	1,042
Colbert	10,543	10,518	10,226	8,305	1,696
Conecuh	2,783	2,699	2,903	2,093	445
Coosa	2,104	2,382	2,121	1,721	262
Covington	4,440	8,961	4,543	6,035	1,098
Crenshaw	1,934	2,793	2,172	1,939	317
Cullman	9,758	19,157	9,544	14,308	2,440
Dale	4,906	10,593	4,732	8,288	1,216
Dallas	10,967	7,360	10,507	6,612	477
DeKalb	7,056	12,827	6,544	9,823	1,609
Elmore	6,652	16,777	6,530	12,937	1,368
Escambia	4,523	6,975	4,651	5,214	867
Etowah	17,433	21,087	17,976	16,835	2,529
Fayette	3,064	4,582	3,381	3,191	590
Franklin	4,793	6,119	5,028	4,449	966
Geneva	2,769	6,588	3,174	4,725	857
Greene	3,504	850	3,526	796	55
Hale	4,652	2,981	3,372	1,803	100
Henry	2,782	4,054	3,019	3,082	515
Houston	9,412	22,150	8,791	17,476	1,653
Jackson	9,066	8,475	8,204	5,650	1,573
Jefferson	129,889	138,491	120,208	130,980	7,997
Lamar	2,653	4,470	2,843	2,955	597
Lauderdale	13,875	17,478	13,619	14,058	2,574
Lawrence	6,296	5,671	5,254	3,893	964
Lee	14,574	22,433	12,919	17,985	1,949
Limestone	8,992	14,204	8,045	10,862	1,659
Lowndes	4,557	1,638	3,970	1,369	72
Macon	7,665	1,091	7,018	987	150
Madison	48,199	62,151	42,259	50,390	7,437
Marengo	4,841	4,690	4,899	4,013	337
Marion	4,600	6,910	5,049	4,742	979
Marshall	10,381	17,084	8,722	12,323	2,150
Mobile	58,640	78,162	54,749	66,775	7,555
Monroe	3,741	5,153	3,815	4,382	486
Montgomery	40,371	38,827	38,382	37,784	2,036
Morgan	16,060	25,774	14,616	21,765	3,348
Perry	4,020	1,732	4,053	1,703	119
Pickens	4,143	4,306	4,018	3,322	403
Pike	4,357	6,058	4,514	5,281	503
Randolph	3,094	4,666	3,023	3,304	603
Russell	8,396	6,198	7,834	5,025	792
St. Clair	6,485	17,117	6,187	12,762	1,417
Shelby	13,183	47,651	11,280	37,090	2,035
Sumter	4,415	1,629	4,706	1,561	172
Talladega	11,264	13,807	10,385	10,931	1,335
Tallapoosa	6,183	9,805	6,071	7,627	1,038
Tuscaloosa	24,614	34,003	23,067	27,939	3,048
Walker	11,621	13,486	12,929	9,837	2,012
Washington	3,386	4,117	3,935	2,900	819
Wilcox	3,444	1,661	3,303	1,454	71
Winston	2,692	6,413	3,120	4,728	723
Totals	**692,611**	**941,173**	**662,165**	**769,044**	**92,149**

Alabama Vote Since 1952

1952, Eisenhower, Rep., 149,231; Stevenson, Dem., 275,075; Hamblen, Proh., 1,814.

1956, Stevenson, Dem., 290,844; Eisenhower, Rep., 195,694; Independent electors, 20,323.

1960, Kennedy, Dem., 324,050; Nixon, Rep., 237,981; Faubus, States' Rights, 4,367; Decker, Proh., 2,106; King, Afro-Americans, 1,485; scattering, 236.

1964, Dem. (electors unpledged), 209,848; Goldwater, Rep., 479,085; scattering, 105.

1968, Nixon, Rep., 146,923; Humphrey, Dem., 196,579; Wallace, 3d Party, 691,425; Munn, Proh., 4,022.

1972, Nixon, Rep., 728,701; McGovern, Dem., 219,108 plus 37,815 Natl. Dem. Party of Alabama; Schmitz, Conservative, 11,918; Munn., Proh., 8,551.

1976, Carter, Dem., 659,170; Ford, Rep., 504,070; Maddox, Amer. Ind., 9,198; Bubar, Proh., 6,669; Hall, Com., 1,954; MacBride, Libertarian, 1,481.

1980, Reagan, Rep., 654,192; Carter, Dem., 636,730; Anderson, Independent, 16,481; Rarick, Amer. Ind., 15,010; Clark, Libertarian, 13,318; Bubar, Statesman, 1,743; Hall, Com., 1,629; DeBerry, Soc. Workers, 1,303; McReynolds, Socialist, 1,006; Commoner, Citizens, 517.

1984, Reagan, Rep., 872,849; Mondale, Dem., 551,899; Bergland, Libertarian, 9,504.

1988, Bush, Rep., 815,576; Dukakis, Dem., 549,506; Paul, Lib., 8,460; Fulani, Ind., 3,311.

1992, Bush, Rep., 804,283; Clinton, Dem., 690,080; Perot, Ind., 183,109; Marrou, Libertarian, 5,737; Fulani, New Alliance, 2,161.

1996, Dole, Rep., 769,044; Clinton, Dem., 662,165; Perot, Ind. (Ref.), 92,149; Browne, Libertarian, 5,290; Phillips, Ind., 2,365; Hagelin, Natural Law, 1,697; Harris, Ind., 516.

2000, Bush, Rep., 941,173; Gore, Dem., 692,611; Nader, Ind., 18,323; Buchanan, Ind., 6,351; Browne, Libertarian, 5,893; Phillips, Ind., 775 Hagelin, Ind., 447.

Alaska

Election District	2000 Gore (D)	2000 Bush (R)	1996 Clinton (D)	1996 Dole (R)	1996 Perot (RF)
No. 1	1,284	4,681	1,480	4,209	696
No. 2	2,081	4,235	2,563	3,247	912
No. 3	3,693	3,135	3,724	2,671	654
No. 4	2,715	4,127	3,037	3,336	694
No. 5	1,931	3,545	2,148	2,564	826
No. 6	1,542	3,862	1,576	2,707	557
No. 7	1,893	4,868	2,177	3,517	907
No. 8	1,498	5,371	1,643	3,624	826
No. 9	1,203	4,789	1,334	3,459	727
No. 10	2,194	5,673	2,203	4,184	642
No. 11	2,043	3,960	1,946	3,073	603
No. 12	2,051	4,626	1,825	3,568	543
No. 13	2,661	3,853	2,780	3,270	608
No. 14	1,626	3,750	1,471	3,005	458
No. 15	2,106	2,453	2,178	1,974	552
No. 16	1,969	1,980	1,629	1,328	414
No. 17	2,230	4,564	1,868	3,284	633
No. 18	2,739	5,421	2,708	4,245	694
No. 19	2,350	4,619	2,014	3,159	636
No. 20	2,259	3,648	2,144	3,025	545
No. 21	2,309	3,263	2,228	2,553	557
No. 22	2,656	4,910	2,511	3,887	624
No. 23	1,282	2,961	1,071	2,127	388
No. 24	1,985	5,063	1,914	3,653	548
No. 25	1,697	5,489	1,629	4,099	691
No. 26	1,608	5,869	1,519	3,913	883
No. 27	2,199	6,714	1,887	4,384	1,122
No. 28	2,116	7,113	1,645	4,202	1,333
No. 29	2,806	4,054	3,023	3,012	658
No. 30	1,698	3,622	1,794	2,785	601
No. 31	1,831	3,326	1,903	2,721	684
No. 32	1,389	4,178	1,275	2,736	675
No. 33	1,765	5,804	1,852	4,089	759
No. 34	1,300	5,243	1,388	3,677	734
No. 35	1,208	4,278	1,447	3,016	875
No. 36	1,945	3,007	2,321	1,992	453
No. 37	1,821	2,725	2,134	1,835	456
No. 38	2.015	2,467	2,436	1,716	393
No. 39	2,282	2,321	2,692	1,618	404
No. 40	1,024	1,831	1,260	1,280	368
Totals	**79,004**	**167,398**	**80,377**	**122,744**	**26,333**

Alaska Vote Since 1960

1960, Kennedy, Dem., 29,809; Nixon, Rep., 30,953.

1964, Johnson, Dem., 44,329; Goldwater, Rep., 22,930.

1968, Nixon, Rep., 37,600; Humphrey, Dem., 35,411; Wallace, 3d Party, 10,024.

1972, Nixon, Rep., 55,349; McGovern, Dem., 32,967; Schmitz, Amer., 6,903.

1976, Carter, Dem., 44,058; Ford, Rep., 71,555; MacBride, Libertarian, 6,785.

1980, Reagan, Rep., 86,112; Carter, Dem., 41,842; Clark, Libertarian, 18,479; Anderson, Ind., 11,155; write-in, 857.
1984, Reagan, Rep., 138,377; Mondale, Dem., 62,007; Bergland, Libertarian, 6,378.
1988, Bush, Rep., 119,251; Dukakis, Dem., 72,584; Paul, Lib., 5,484; Fulani, New Alliance, 1,024.
1992, Bush, Rep., 102,000; Clinton, Dem., 78,294; Perot, Ind., 73,481; Gritz, Populist/America First, 1,379; Marrou, Libertarian, 1,378.
1996, Dole, Rep., 122,746; Clinton, Dem., 80,380; Perot, Ref., 26,333; Nader, Green, 7,597; Browne, Libertarian, 2,276; Phillips, Taxpayers, 925; Hagelin, Natural Law, 729.
2000, Bush, Rep., 167,398; Gore, Dem., 79,004; Nader, Green, 28,747; Buchanan, Reform, 5,192; Browne, Libertarian, 2,636; Hagelin, Natural Law, 919; Phillips, Constitution, 596.

Arizona

	2000		1996		
County	Gore (D)	Bush (R)	Clinton (D)	Dole (R)	Perot (RF)
Apache	13,025	5,947	12,394	4,761	1,296
Cochise	13,360	18,180	13,782	14,365	3,346
Coconino	20,280	17,562	20,475	13,638	3,666
Gila	7,700	9,158	8,577	6,407	2,211
Graham	3,355	6,007	3,938	4,222	1,034
Greenlee	1,216	1,619	1,755	1,159	426
La Paz	1,769	2,543	1,964	1,902	597
Maricopa	386,683	479,967	363,991	386,015	58,479
Mohave	17,470	24,386	16,629	17,997	6,369
Navajo	11,794	12,386	12,912	9,262	2,461
Pima	147,688	124,579	137,983	104,121	18,809
Pinal	19,650	20,122	19,579	13,034	3,972
Santa Cruz	5,233	3,344	5,241	2,256	600
Yavapai	24,063	40,144	21,801	29,921	6,649
Yuma	12,055	15,708	12,267	13,013	2,157
Totals	**685,341**	**781,652**	**653,288**	**622,073**	**112,072**

Arizona Vote Since 1952

1952, Eisenhower, Rep., 152,042; Stevenson, Dem., 108,528.
1956, Eisenhower, Rep., 176,990; Stevenson, Dem., 112,880; Andrews, Ind. 303.
1960, Kennedy, Dem., 176,781; Nixon, Rep., 221,241; Hass, Soc. Labor, 469.
1964, Johnson, Dem., 237,753; Goldwater, Rep., 242,535; Hass, Soc. Labor, 482.
1968, Nixon, Rep., 266,721; Humphrey, Dem., 170,514; Wallace, 3d Party, 46,573; McCarthy, New Party, 2,751; Halstead, Soc. Workers, 85; Cleaver, Peace and Freedom, 217; Blomen, Soc. Labor, 75.
1972, Nixon, Rep., 402,812; McGovern, Dem., 198,540; Schmitz, Amer., 21,208; Soc. Workers, 30,945. Because of ballot peculiarities in 3 counties (particularly Pima), thousands of voters cast ballots for the Soc. Workers Party *and* one of the major candidates. Court ordered both votes counted as official.
1976, Carter, Dem., 295,602; Ford, Rep., 418,642; McCarthy, Ind., 19,229; MacBride, Libertarian, 7,647; Camejo, Soc. Workers, 928; Anderson, Amer., 564; Maddox, Amer. Ind., 85.
1980, Reagan, Rep., 529,688; Carter, Dem., 246,843; Anderson, Ind., 76,952; Clark, Libertarian, 18,784; De Berry, Soc. Workers, 1,100; Commoner, Citizens, 551; Hall, Com., 25; Griswold, Workers World, 2.
1984, Reagan, Rep., 681,416; Mondale, Dem., 333,854; Bergland, Libertarian, 10,585.
1988, Bush, Rep., 702,541; Dukakis, Dem., 454,029; Paul, Lib., 13,351; Fulani, New Alliance, 1,662.
1992, Bush, Rep., 572,086; Clinton, Dem., 543,050; Perot, Ind., 353,741; Gritz, Populist/America First, 8,141; Marrou, Libertarian, 6,759; Hagelin, Natural Law, 2,267.
1996, Clinton, Dem., 653,288; Dole, Rep., 622,073; Perot, Ref., 112,072; Browne, Libertarian, 14,358.
2000, Gore, Bush, Rep., 781,652; Dem., 685,341; Nader, Green, 45,645; Buchanan, Rep., 12,373; Smith, Libertarian, 5,775; Hagelin, Natural Law, 1,120.

Arkansas

	2000		1996		
County	Gore (D)	Bush (R)	Clinton (D)	Dole (R)	Perot (RF)
Arkansas	2,877	3,353	4,220	1,910	463
Ashley	4,253	3,876	5,011	2,428	704
Baxter	6,516	9,538	6,703	6,877	1,572
Benton	17,277	34,838	17,205	23,748	4,147
Boone	4,493	8,569	5,745	6,093	1,132
Bradley	2,122	1,793	2,566	1,146	221
Calhoun	1,017	1,128	1,306	727	237
Carroll	3,595	5,556	3,689	3,957	986
Chicot	2,820	1,564	3,090	1,056	233
Clark	4,661	3,776	5,281	2,112	567
Clay	3,527	2,254	3,848	1,512	464
Cleburne	4,120	5,730	4,475	3,807	1,021
Cleveland	1,414	1,678	1,741	990	268
Columbia	4,003	5,018	4,730	3,376	678
Conway	3,496	3,545	4,055	2,307	746
Craighead	12,376	12,158	13,284	9,210	1,778
Crawford	6,288	10,804	6,749	7,182	1,683
Crittenden	7,224	5,857	8,415	4,673	554
Cross	3,096	3,033	3,631	2,000	466
Dallas	1,710	1,571	2,118	1,041	236
Desha	2,776	1,603	3,230	978	247
Drew	3,060	2,756	3,570	1,657	395
Faulkner	11,950	16,055	12,032	10,178	1,528
Franklin	2,674	3,277	3,269	2,246	626
Fulton	1,976	2,036	2,361	1,351	455
Garland	15,840	19,098	19,211	13,662	2,769
Grant	2,535	3,285	2,948	1,925	557
Greene	6,319	5,831	6,622	3,757	1,014
Hempstead	3,937	3,257	4,983	2,021	501
Hot Spring	5,527	5,042	6,002	2,864	1,123
Howard	2,063	2,326	2,741	1,478	369
Independence	5,146	6,145	6,240	4,021	1,126
Izard	2,587	2,301	2,818	1,678	541
Jackson	3,651	2,280	4,304	1,525	611
Jefferson	17,716	8,765	19,701	6,330	1,284
Johnson	3,270	3,657	3,585	2,367	757
Lafayette	1,806	1,538	2,466	971	374
Lawrence	3,255	2,626	3,652	1,823	609
Lee	2,727	1,351	3,267	1,013	257
Lincoln	1,957	1,526	2,517	907	221
Little River	2,883	2,283	3,183	1,409	480
Logan	3,283	4,487	3,832	2,966	1,048
Lonoke	6,851	10,606	8,049	6,414	1,369
Madison	2,055	3,387	2,504	2,303	461
Marion	2,233	3,402	2,735	2,312	764
Miller	6,278	7,276	6,469	4,874	1,043
Mississippi	7,107	5,199	8,301	3,919	1,016
Monroe	1,910	1,329	2,247	973	202
Montgomery	1,438	2,128	1,830	1,137	427
Nevada	1,867	1,796	2,279	976	345
Newton	1,205	2,529	1,631	1,927	498
Ouachita	5,464	4,739	6,635	3,136	733
Perry	1,648	2,114	1,873	1,143	395
Phillips	6,018	3,154	5,715	2,205	461
Pike	1,604	2,275	2,362	1,401	441
Poinsett	4,102	2,988	4,686	2,034	647
Polk	2,315	4,600	2,824	2,852	876
Pope	6,669	11,244	8,433	8,243	1,891
Prairie	1,563	1,862	2,211	1,025	305
Pulaski	68,320	55,866	75,084	44,780	6,014
Randolph	3,019	2,673	3,213	1,789	561
St. Francis	4,986	3,414	5,562	2,523	506
Saline	12,700	18,617	14,027	11,695	2,612
Scott	1,444	2,399	2,259	1,426	513
Searcy	1,229	2,610	1,669	1,786	381
Sebastian	15,555	23,483	15,514	16,482	2,899
Sevier	2,095	2,111	2,553	1,379	446
Sharp	3,236	3,698	3,573	2,635	687
Stone	2,043	2,623	2,227	1,526	579
Union	6,261	8,647	8,373	6,053	1,073
Van Buren	3,202	3,485	3,521	2,345	830
Washington	21,425	28,231	20,419	19,476	3,133
White	8,342	13,170	10,204	8,659	1,828
Woodruff	1,699	898	2,044	598	186
Yell	3,062	3,223	3,749	2,111	714
Totals	**422,768**	**472,940**	**475,171**	**325,416**	**69,884**

Arkansas Vote Since 1952

1952, Eisenhower, Rep., 177,155; Stevenson, Dem., 226,300; Hamblen, Proh., 886; MacArthur, Christian Nationalist, 458; Hass, Soc. Labor, 1.
1956, Stevenson, Dem., 213,277; Eisenhower, Rep., 186,287; Andrews, Ind., 7,008.
1960, Kennedy, Dem., 215,049; Nixon, Rep., 184,508; Natl. States' Rights, 28,952.
1964, Johnson, Dem., 314,197; Goldwater, Rep., 243,264; Kasper, Natl. States' Rights, 2,965.
1968, Nixon, Rep., 189,062; Humphrey, Dem., 184,901; Wallace, 3d Party, 235,627.
1972, Nixon, Rep., 445,751; McGovern, Dem., 198,899; Schmitz, Amer., 3,016.
1976, Carter, Dem., 498,604; Ford, Rep., 267,903; McCarthy, Ind., 639; Anderson, Amer., 389.
1980, Reagan, Rep., 403,164; Carter, Dem., 398,041; Anderson, Ind., 22,468; Clark, Libertarian, 8,970; Commoner, Citizens, 2,345; Bubar, Statesman, 1,350; Hall, Com., 1,244.
1984, Reagan, Rep., 534,774; Mondale, Dem., 338,646; Bergland, Libertarian, 2,220.
1988, Bush, Rep., 466,578; Dukakis, Dem., 349,237; Duke, Chr. Pop., 5,146; Paul, Lib., 3,297.

1992, Clinton, Dem., 505,823; Bush, Rep., 337,324; Perot, Ind., 99,132; Phillips, U.S. Taxpayers, 1,437; Marrou, Libertarian, 1,261; Fulani, New Alliance, 1,022.
1996, Clinton, Dem., 475,171; Dole, Rep., 325,416; Perot, Ref., 69,884; Nader, Ind., 3,649; Browne, Ind., 3,076; Phillips, Ind., 2,065; Forbes, Ind., 932; Collins, Ind., 823; Masters, Ind., 749; Hagelin, Ind., 729; Moorehead, Ind., 747; Hollis, Ind., 538; Dodge, Ind., 483.
2000, Bush, Rep., 472,940; Gore, Dem., 422,768; Nader, Green, 13,421; Buchanan, Reform, 7,358; Browne, Libertarian, 2,781; Phillips, Constitution, 1,415; Hagelin, Natural Law, 1,098.

California

	2000		1996		
County	Gore (D)	Bush (R)	Clinton (D)	Dole (R)	Perot (RF)
Alameda . . .	342,889	119,279	303,903	106,581	24,270
Alpine	265	281	258	264	63
Amador	5,906	8,766	5,868	6,870	1,267
Butte	31,338	45,584	30,651	38,961	6,393
Calaveras . .	7,093	10,599	6,646	8,279	1,612
Colusa	1,745	3,629	2,054	3,047	404
Contra Costa	224,338	141,373	196,512	123,954	20,416
Del Norte . . .	3,117	4,526	3,652	3,670	1,225
El Dorado . .	26,220	42,045	22,957	32,759	5,077
Fresno	95,059	117,342	94,448	98,813	10,962
Glenn	2,498	5,795	2,841	5,041	788
Humboldt . . .	24,851	23,219	24,628	19,803	5,811
Imperial	15,489	12,524	14,591	9,705	1,778
Inyo	2,652	4,713	2,601	3,924	811
Kern	66,003	110,663	62,658	92,151	13,452
Kings	11,041	16,377	11,254	12,368	1,745
Lake	10,717	8,699	10,432	7,458	2,539
Lassen	2,982	7,080	3,318	5,194	1,080
Los Angeles	1,710,505	871,930	1,430,629	746,544	157,752
Madera	11,650	20,283	11,254	16,510	2,192
Marin	79,135	34,872	67,406	32,714	6,559
Mariposa . . .	2,816	4,727	2,920	3,976	729
Mendocino . .	16,634	12,272	14,952	9,765	3,685
Merced	22,726	26,102	21,786	20,847	3,427
Modoc	945	2,969	1,368	2,285	528
Mono	1,788	2,296	1,580	1,882	447
Monterey . . .	67,618	43,761	57,700	39,794	7,240
Napa	28,097	20,633	24,588	17,439	4,254
Nevada	17,670	25,998	15,369	21,784	3,330
Orange	391,819	541,299	327,485	446,717	66,195
Placer	42,449	69,835	34,981	49,808	6,542
Plumas	3,458	6,343	3,540	4,905	919
Riverside . . .	202,576	231,955	168,579	178,611	35,481
Sacramento.	212,792	195,619	203,019	166,049	23,856
San Benito . .	9,131	7,015	7,030	5,384	1,044
San Bernardino	214,749	221,757	183,372	180,135	39,330
San Diego . .	437,666	475,736	389,964	402,876	63,037
San Francisco .	241,578	51,496	209,777	45,479	9,659
San Joaquin	79,776	81,773	67,253	65,131	9,692
San Luis Obispo . . .	44,526	56,859	40,395	46,733	8,204
San Mateo . .	166,757	80,296	152,304	73,508	15,047
Santa Barbara . .	73,411	71,493	70,650	63,915	9,457
Santa Clara	332,490	188,750	297,639	168,291	34,908
Santa Cruz .	66,618	29,627	58,250	27,766	6,555
Shasta	20,127	43,278	20,848	34,736	5,875
Sierra	540	1,172	573	877	170
Siskiyou	6,323	12,198	7,022	8,653	1,879
Solano	75,116	51,604	64,644	40,742	8,682
Sonoma	117,295	63,529	100,738	53,555	13,862
Stanislaus . .	56,448	67,188	53,738	52,403	8,360
Sutter	8,416	17,350	8,504	14,264	1,533
Tehama	6,507	13,270	7,290	10,292	2,325
Trinity	1,932	3,340	2,203	2,530	856
Tulare	33,006	54,070	32,669	46,272	5,106
Tuolumne . . .	9,359	13,172	8,950	10,386	1,925
Ventura	133,258	136,173	110,772	109,202	23,054
Yolo	33,747	23,057	33,033	18,807	3,150
Yuba	5,546	9,838	5,789	7,971	1,308
Totals	**5,861,203**	**4,567,429**	**5,119,835**	**3,828,380**	**697,847**

California Vote Since 1952

1952, Eisenhower, Rep., 2,897,310; Stevenson, Dem., 2,197,548; Hallinan, Prog., 24,106; Hamblen, Proh., 15,653; MacArthur, (Tenny Ticket), 3,326; (Kellems Ticket) 178; Hass, Soc. Labor, 273; Hoopes, Soc., 206; scattered, 3,249.
1956, Eisenhower, Rep., 3,027,668; Stevenson, Dem., 2,420,136; Holtwick, Proh., 11,119; Andrews, Constitution, 6,087; Hass, Soc. Labor, 300; Hoopes, Soc., 123; Dobbs, Soc. Workers, 96; Smith, Christian Natl., 8.
1960, Kennedy, Dem., 3,224,099; Nixon, Rep., 3,259,722; Decker, Proh., 21,706; Hass, Soc. Labor, 1,051.
1964, Johnson, Dem., 4,171,877; Goldwater, Rep., 2,879,108; Hass, Soc. Labor, 489; DeBerry, Soc. Workers, 378; Munn, Proh., 305; Hensley, Universal, 19.
1968, Nixon, Rep., 3,467,664; Humphrey, Dem., 3,244,318; Wallace, 3d Party, 487,270; Peace and Freedom, 27,707; McCarthy, Alternative, 20,721; Gregory, write-in, 3,230; Mitchell, Com., 260; Munn, Proh., 59; Blomen, Soc. Labor, 341; Soeters, Defense, 17.
1972, Nixon, Rep., 4,602,096; McGovern, Dem., 3,475,847; Schmitz, Amer., 232,554; Spock, Peace and Freedom, 55,167; Hall, Com., 373; Hospers, Libertarian, 980; Munn, Proh., 53; Fisher, Soc. Labor, 197; Jenness, Soc. Workers, 574; Green, Universal, 21.
1976, Carter, Dem., 3,742,284; Ford, Rep., 3,882,244; MacBride, Libertarian, 56,388; Maddox, Amer. Ind., 51,098; Wright, People's, 41,731; Camejo, Soc. Workers, 17,259; Hall, Com., 12,766; write-in, McCarthy, 58,412; other write-in, 4,935.
1980, Reagan, Rep. 4,524,858; Carter, Dem., 3,083,661; Anderson, Ind., 739,833; Clark, Libertarian, 148,434; Commoner, Ind., 61,063; Smith, Peace and Freedom, 18,116; Rarick, Amer. Ind., 9,856.
1984, Reagan, Rep. 5,305,410; Mondale, Dem., 3,815,947; Bergland, Libertarian, 48,400.
1988, Bush, Rep., 5,054,917; Dukakis, Dem., 4,702,233; Paul, Lib., 70,105; Fulani, Ind., 31,181.
1992, Clinton, Dem., 5,121,325; Bush, Rep., 3,630,575; Perot, Ind., 2,296,006; Marrou, Libertarian, 48,139; Daniels, Ind., 18,597; Phillips, U.S. Taxpayers, 12,711.
1996, Clinton, Dem., 5,119,835; Dole, Rep., 3,828,380; Perot, Ref., 697,847; Nader, Green, 237,016; Browne, Libertarian, 73,600; Feinland, Peace & Freedom, 25,332; Phillips, Amer. Ind., 21,202; Hagelin, Natural Law, 15,403.
2000, Gore, Dem., 5,861,203; Bush, Rep., 4,567,429; Nader, Green, 418,707; Browne, Libertarian, 45,520; Buchanan, Reform, 44,987; Phillips, Amer. Ind., 17,042; Hagelin, Natural Law, 10,934.

Colorado

	2000		1996		
County	Gore (D)	Bush (R)	Clinton (D)	Dole (R)	Perot (RF)
Adams	54,132	47,561	48,314	36,666	7,206
Alamosa	2,455	2,857	2,330	2,038	437
Arapahoe	82,614	97,768	68,306	82,778	8,476
Archuleta	1,432	2,988	997	1,963	360
Baca	531	1,663	659	1,321	203
Bent	783	1,096	1,046	917	209
Boulder	69,983	50,873	63,316	41,922	6,840
Chaffee	2,768	4,300	2,768	3,052	538
Cheyenne	209	957	328	739	91
Clear Creek . . .	2,188	2,247	1,863	1,746	365
Conejos	1,749	1,772	1,726	1,149	245
Costilla	1,054	504	1,168	333	112
Crowley	511	855	559	680	114
Custer	507	1,451	412	920	164
Delta	3,264	8,372	3,584	6,047	1,060
Denver	122,693	61,224	120,312	58,529	8,777
Dolores	293	741	276	417	95
Douglas	27,076	56,007	16,232	32,120	2,662
Eagle	6,772	7,165	5,094	4,637	1,193
Elbert	2,326	6,151	1,894	4,125	507
El Paso	61,799	128,294	55,822	102,403	11,175
Fremont	5,293	9,914	5,344	7,437	1,438
Garfield	6,087	9,103	5,722	6,281	1,562
Gilpin	1,099	1,006	799	682	184
Grand	2,308	3,570	2,012	2,264	473
Gunnison	3,059	3,128	2,812	2,230	570
Hinsdale	188	316	185	289	56
Huerfano	1,495	1,466	1,483	996	210
Jackson	173	682	222	486	107
Jefferson	100,970	120,138	89,494	101,517	12,967
Kiowa	211	728	246	549	74
Kit Carson	809	2,542	1,073	2,068	235
Lake	1,296	1,056	1,338	728	274
La Plata	7,864	9,993	6,509	8,057	1,403
Larimer	46,055	62,429	40,965	45,935	6,823
Las Animas	3,243	2,569	3,611	1,905	427
Lincoln	510	1,630	729	1,272	164
Logan	2,296	5,531	2,765	4,032	609
Mesa	15,465	32,396	17,114	24,761	3,707
Mineral	168	294	192	179	69
Moffat	1,223	3,840	1,635	2,466	649
Montezuma	2,556	6,158	2,578	4,175	827
Montrose	4,041	9,266	4,019	6,730	1,187
Morgan	2,885	5,722	3,347	4,557	687
Otero	2,963	4,002	3,386	3,356	581
Ouray	705	1,279	569	984	167

	2000		1996		
	Gore	Bush	Clinton	Dole	Perot
County	(D)	(R)	(D)	(R)	(RF)
Park	2,393	3,677	1,844	2,661	534
Philips	564	1,576	706	1,284	156
Pitkin	4,137	2,565	3,949	1,969	535
Prowers	1,361	3,026	1,745	2,504	342
Pueblo	28,888	22,827	28,791	17,402	3,374
Rio Blanco	543	2,185	731	1,697	243
Rio Grande	1,707	3,111	1,720	2,129	379
Routt	4,208	4,472	3,660	3,019	859
Saguache	1,145	1,078	969	712	160
San Juan	149	210	133	153	50
San Miguel	1,598	1,043	1,535	773	231
Sedgwick	384	877	519	715	101
Summit	5,304	4,497	3,970	3,261	823
Teller	2,750	6,477	2,312	4,458	707
Washington	477	1,878	649	1,566	190
Weld	23,436	37,409	21,325	26,518	4,347
Yuma	1,082	3,156	1,439	2,589	319
Totals	**738,227**	**883,748**	**671,152**	**691,848**	**99,629**

Colorado Vote Since 1952

1952, Eisenhower, Rep., 379,782; Stevenson, Dem., 245,504; MacArthur, Constitution, 2,181; Hallinan, Prog., 1,919; Hoopes, Soc., 365; Hass, Soc. Labor, 352.

1956, Eisenhower, Rep., 394,479; Stevenson, Dem., 263,997; Hass, Soc. Lab., 3,308; Andrews, Ind., 759; Hoopes, Soc., 531.

1960, Kennedy, Dem., 330,629; Nixon, Rep., 402,242; Hass, Soc. Labor, 2,803; Dobbs, Soc. Workers, 572.

1964, Johnson, Dem., 476,024; Goldwater, Rep., 296,767; Hass, Soc. Labor, 302; DeBerry, Soc. Workers, 2,537; Munn, Proh., 1,356.

1968, Nixon, Rep., 409,345; Humphrey, Dem., 335,174; Wallace, 3d Party, 60,813; Blomen, Soc. Labor, 3,016; Gregory, New-party, 1,393; Munn, Proh., 275; Halstead, Soc. Workers, 235.

1972, Nixon, Rep., 597,189; McGovern, Dem., 329,980; Fisher, Soc. Labor, 4,361; Hospers, Libertarian, 1,111; Hall, Com., 432; Jenness, Soc. Workers, 555; Munn, Proh., 467; Schmitz, Amer., 17,269; Spock, Peoples, 2,403.

1976, Carter, Dem., 460,353; Ford, Rep., 584,367; McCarthy, Ind., 26,107; MacBride, Libertarian, 5,330; Bubar, Proh., 2,882.

1980, Reagan, Rep., 652,264; Carter, Dem., 367,973; Anderson, Ind., 130,633; Clark, Libertarian, 25,744; Commoner, Citizens, 5,614; Bubar, Statesman, 1,180; Pulley, Socialist, 520; Hall, Com., 487.

1984, Reagan, Rep., 821,817; Mondale, Dem., 454,975; Bergland, Libertarian, 11,257.

1988, Bush, Rep., 728,177; Dukakis, Dem., 621,453; Paul, Lib., 15,482; Dodge, Proh., 4,604.

1992, Clinton, Dem., 629,681; Bush, Rep., 562,850; Perot, Ind., 366,010; Marrou, Libertarian, 8,669; Fulani, New Alliance, 1,608.

1996, Dole, Rep., 691,848; Clinton, Dem., 671,152; Perot, Ref., 99,629; Nader, Green, 25,070; Browne, Libertarian, 12,392; Collins, Ind., 2,809; Phillips, Amer. Constitution, 2,813; Hagelin, Natural Law, 2,547; Hollis, Soc., 669; Moorehead, Workers World, 599; Templin, Amer., 557; Dodge, Proh., 375; Harris, Soc. Workers, 244.

2000, Bush, Rep., 883,748; Gore, Dem, 738,227; Nader, Green, 91,434; Browne, Libertarian, 12,799; Buchanan, Reform, 10,465; Hagelin, Reform, 2,240; Phillips, Amer. Constitution, 1,319; McReynolds, Soc., 712; Harris, Soc. Workers, 216; Dodge, Proh., 208.

Connecticut

	2000		1996		
	Gore	Bush	Clinton	Dole	Perot
City	(D)	(R)	(D)	(R)	(RF)
Bridgeport	24,303	7,406	22,883	6,785	2,367
Bristol	14,665	7,948	13,616	6,560	3,049
Danbury	12,987	9,371	12,102	7,965	2,158
Fairfield	14,210	13,042	12,639	12,314	2,092
Greenwich	12,780	14,905	11,622	14,308	1,437
Hartford	21,445	3,095	22,929	3,082	1,010
New Britain	13,913	5,059	14,322	4,911	1,717
New Haven	28,145	5,160	26,161	4,822	1,555
Norwalk	19,293	11,519	17,354	10,800	2,237
Stamford	27,430	15,159	25,005	14,696	2,595
Waterbury	18,069	12,415	18,901	12,075	3,169
West Hartford	21,069	10,447	19,037	10,781	1,890
Other	587,706	445,568	519,169	374,010	114,247
Totals	**816,015**	**561,094**	**735,740**	**483,109**	**139,523**

Connecticut Vote Since 1952

1952, Eisenhower, Rep., 611,012; Stevenson, Dem., 481,649; Hoopes, Soc., 2,244; Hallinan, Peoples, 1,466; Hass, Soc. Labor, 535; write-in, 5.

1956, Eisenhower, Rep., 711,837; Stevenson, Dem., 405,079; scattered, 205.

1960, Kennedy, Dem., 657,055; Nixon, Rep., 565,813.

1964, Johnson, Dem., 826,269; Goldwater, Rep., 390,996; scattered, 1,313.

1968, Nixon, Rep., 556,721; Humphrey, Dem., 621,561; Wallace, 3d Party, 76,650; scattered, 1,300.

1972, Nixon, Rep., 810,763; McGovern, Dem., 555,498; Schmitz, Amer., 17,239; scattered, 777.

1976, Carter, Dem., 647,895; Ford, Rep., 719,261; Maddox, George Wallace Party, 7,101; LaRouche, U.S. Labor, 1,789.

1980, Reagan, Rep., 677,210; Carter, Dem., 541,732; Anderson, Ind., 171,807; Clark, Libertarian, 8,570; Commoner, Citizens, 6,130; scattered, 836.

1984, Reagan, Rep., 890,877; Mondale, Dem., 569,597.

1988, Bush, Rep., 750,241; Dukakis, Dem., 676,584; Paul, Lib., 14,071; Fulani, New Alliance, 2,491.

1992, Clinton, Dem., 682,318; Bush, Rep., 578,313; Perot, Ind., 348,771; Marrou, Libertarian, 5,391; Fulani, New Alliance, 1,363.

1996, Clinton, Dem., 735,740; Dole, Rep., 483,109; Perot, Ref., 139,523; Nader, Green, 24,321; Browne, Libertarian, 5,788; Phillips, Concerned Citizens, 2,425; Hagelin, Natural Law, 1,703.

2000, Gore, Dem., 816,015; Bush, Rep., 561,094; Nader, Green, 64,452; Phillips, Concerned Citizens, 9,695; Buchanan, Reform, 4,731; Browne, Libertarian, 3,484.

Delaware

	2000		1996		
	Gore				
	Gore	Bush	Clinton	Dole	Perot
County	(D)	(R)	(D)	(R)	(RF)
Kent	22,790	24,081	18,327	15,932	4,705
New Castle	127,539	78,587	98,837	60,943	17,748
Sussex	29,739	34,620	23,191	22,187	6,266
Totals	**180,068**	**137,288**	**140,355**	**99,062**	**28,719**

Delaware Vote Since 1952

1952, Eisenhower, Rep., 90,059; Stevenson, Dem., 83,315; Hass, Soc. Labor, 242; Hamblen, Proh., 234; Hallinan, Prog., 155; Hoopes, Soc., 20.

1956, Eisenhower, Rep., 98,057; Stevenson, Dem., 79,421; Oltwick, Proh., 400; Hass, Soc. Labor, 110.

1960, Kennedy, Dem., 99,590; Nixon, Rep., 96,373; Faubus, States' Rights, 354; Decker, Proh., 284; Hass, Soc. Labor, 82.

1964, Johnson, Dem., 122,704; Goldwater, Rep., 78,078; Hass, Soc. Labor, 113; Munn, Proh., 425.

1968, Nixon, Rep., 96,714; Humphrey, Dem., 89,194; Wallace, 3d Party, 28,459.

1972, Nixon, Rep., 140,357; McGovern, Dem., 92,283; Schmitz, Amer., 2,638; Munn, Proh., 238.

1976, Carter, Dem., 122,596; Ford, Rep., 109,831; McCarthy, non-partisan, 2,437; Anderson, Amer., 645; LaRouche, U.S. Labor, 136; Bubar, Proh., 103; Levin, Soc. Labor, 86.

1980, Reagan, Rep., 111,252; Carter, Dem., 105,754; Anderson, Ind., 16,288; Clark, Libertarian, 1,974; Greaves, Amer., 400.

1984, Reagan, Rep., 152,190; Mondale, Dem., 101,656; Bergland, Libertarian, 268.

1988, Bush, Rep., 139,639; Dukakis, Dem., 108,647; Paul, Lib., 1,162; Fulani, New Alliance, 443.

1992, Clinton, Dem., 126,054; Bush, Rep., 102,313; Perot, Ind., 59,213; Fulani, New Alliance, 1,105.

1996, Clinton, Dem., 140,355; Dole, Rep., 99,062; Perot, Ind. (Ref.), 28,719; Browne, Libertarian, 2,052; Phillips, Taxpayers, 348; Hagelin, Natural Law, 274.

2000, Gore, Dem., 180,068; Bush, Rep., 137,288; Nader, Green, 8,307; Buchanan, Reform, 777; Browne, Libertarian, 774; Phillips, Constitution, 208; Hagelin, Natural Law, 107.

District of Columbia

	2000		1996		
	Gore	Bush	Clinton	Dole	Perot
	(D)	(R)	(D)	(R)	(RF)
Totals	171,923	18,073	158,220	17,339	3,611

District of Columbia Vote Since 1964

1964, Johnson, Dem., 169,796; Goldwater, Rep., 28,801.

1968, Nixon, Rep., 31,012; Humphrey, Dem., 139, 566.

1972, Nixon, Rep., 35,226; McGovern, Dem., 127,627; Reed, Soc. Workers, 316; Hall, Com., 252.

1976, Carter, Dem., 137,818; Ford, Rep., 27,873; Camejo, Soc. Workers, 545; MacBride, Libertarian, 274; Hall, Com., 219; LaRouche, U.S. Labor, 157.

1980, Reagan, Rep., 23,313; Carter, Dem., 130,231; Anderson, Ind., 16,131; Commoner, Citizens, 1,826; Clark, Libertarian, 1,104; Hall, Com., 369; DeBerry, Soc. Workers, 173; Griswold, Workers World, 52; write-ins, 690.

1984, Mondale, Dem., 180,408; Reagan, Rep., 29,009; Bergland, Libertarian, 279.

1988, Bush, Rep., 27,590; Dukakis, Dem., 159,407; Fulani, New Alliance, 2,901; Paul, Lib., 554.
1992, Clinton, Dem., 192,619; Bush, Rep., 20,698; Perot, Ind., 9,681; Fulani, New Alliance, 1,459; Daniels, Ind., 1,186.
1996, Clinton, Dem., 158,220; Dole, Rep., 17,339; Perot, Ref., 3,611; Nader, Green, 4,780; Browne, Libertarian, 588; Hagelin, Natural Law, 283; Harris, Soc. Workers, 257.
2000, Gore, Dem., 171,923; Bush, Rep., 18,073; Nader, Green, 10,576; Browne, Libertarian, 669; Harris, Soc. Workers, 114.

Florida

	2000		1996		
County	Gore (D)	Bush (R)	Clinton (D)	Dole (R)	Perot (RF)
Alachua	47,380	34,135	40,144	25,303	8,072
Baker	2,392	5,611	2,273	3,684	667
Bay	18,873	38,682	17,020	28,290	5,922
Bradford	3,075	5,416	3,356	4,038	819
Brevard	97,341	115,253	80,416	87,980	25,249
Broward	387,760	177,939	320,736	142,834	38,964
Calhoun	2,156	2,873	1,794	1,717	630
Charlotte	29,646	35,428	27,121	27,836	7,783
Citrus	25,531	29,801	22,042	20,114	7,244
Clay	14,668	41,903	13,246	30,332	3,281
Collier	29,939	60,467	23,182	42,590	6,320
Columbia	7,049	10,968	6,691	7,588	1,970
Dade[1]	328,867	289,574	317,378	209,634	24,722
De Soto	3,321	4,256	3,219	3,272	965
Dixie	1,827	2,697	1,731	1,398	652
Duval	108,039	152,460	112,258	126,857	13,844
Escambia	40,990	73,171	37,768	60,839	8,587
Flagler	13,897	12,618	9,583	8,232	2,185
Franklin	2,047	2,454	2,095	1,563	878
Gadsden	9,736	4,770	9,405	3,813	938
Gilchrist	1,910	3,300	1,985	1,939	841
Glades	1,442	1,841	1,530	1,361	521
Gulf	2,398	3,553	2,480	2,424	1,054
Hamilton	1,723	2,147	1,734	1,518	406
Hardee	2,342	3,765	2,417	2,926	851
Hendry	3,240	4,747	3,882	3,855	1,135
Hernando	32,648	30,658	28,520	22,039	7,272
Highlands	14,169	20,207	14,244	15,608	3,739
Hillsborough	169,576	180,794	144,223	136,621	25,154
Holmes	2,177	5,012	2,310	3,248	1,208
Indian River	19,769	28,639	16,373	22,709	4,635
Jackson	6,870	9,139	6,665	7,187	1,602
Jefferson	3,041	2,478	2,543	1,851	393
Lafayette	789	1,670	829	1,166	316
Lake	36,571	50,010	29,750	35,089	8,813
Lee	73,571	106,151	65,692	80,882	18,389
Leon	61,444	39,073	50,058	33,914	6,672
Levy	5,398	6,863	4,938	4,299	1,774
Liberty	1,017	1,317	868	913	376
Madison	3,015	3,038	2,791	2,195	578
Manatee	49,226	58,023	41,835	44,059	10,360
Marion	44,674	55,146	37,033	41,397	11,340
Martin	26,621	33,972	20,851	28,516	5,005
Monroe	16,487	16,063	15,219	12,021	4,817
Nassau	6,955	16,408	7,276	12,134	1,657
Okaloosa	16,989	52,186	16,434	40,631	5,432
Okeechobee	4,589	5,057	4,824	3,415	1,666
Orange	140,236	134,531	105,513	106,026	18,191
Osceola	28,187	26,237	21,870	18,335	6,091
Palm Beach	269,754	152,964	230,621	133,762	30,739
Pasco	69,576	68,607	66,472	48,346	18,011
Pinellas	200,657	184,849	184,728	152,125	36,990
Polk	75,207	90,310	66,735	67,943	14,991
Putnam	12,107	13,457	12,008	9,781	3,272
St. Johns	19,509	39,564	16,713	27,311	4,205
St. Lucie	41,560	34,705	36,168	28,892	8,482
Santa Rosa	12,818	36,339	10,923	26,244	4,957
Sarasota	72,869	83,117	63,648	69,198	14,939
Seminole	59,227	75,790	45,051	59,778	9,357
Sumter	9,637	12,127	7,014	5,960	2,375
Suwannee	4,076	8,009	4,479	5,742	1,874
Taylor	2,649	4,058	3,583	3,188	1,140
Union	1,407	2,332	1,388	1,636	425
Volusia	97,313	82,368	78,905	63,067	17,319
Wakulla	3,838	4,512	3,054	2,931	1,091
Walton	5,643	12,186	5,341	7,706	2,342
Washington	2,798	4,995	2,992	3,522	1,287
Totals	**2,912,253**	**2,912,790**	**2,545,968**	**2,243,324**	**483,776**

(1) In 1997, Dade County changed its name to Miami-Dade County.

Florida Vote Since 1952

1952, Eisenhower, Rep., 544,036; Stevenson, Dem., 444,950; scattered, 351.
1956, Eisenhower, Rep., 643,849; Stevenson, Dem., 480,371.
1960, Kennedy, Dem., 748,700; Nixon, Rep., 795,476.
1964, Johnson, Dem., 948,540; Goldwater, Rep., 905,941.
1968, Nixon, Rep., 886,804; Humphrey, Dem., 676,794; Wallace, 3d Party, 624,207.
1972, Nixon, Rep., 1,857,759; McGovern, Dem., 718,117; scattered, 7,407.
1976, Carter, Dem., 1,636,000; Ford, Rep., 1,469,531; McCarthy, Ind., 23,643; Anderson, Amer., 21,325.
1980, Reagan, Rep., 2,046,951; Carter, Dem., 1,419,475; Anderson, Ind., 189,692; Clark, Libertarian, 30,524; write-ins, 285.
1984, Reagan, Rep., 2,728,775, Mondale, Dem., 1,448,344.
1988, Bush, Rep., 2,616,597; Dukakis, Dem., 1,655,851; Paul, Lib., 19,796, Fulani, New Alliance, 6,655.
1992, Bush, Rep., 2,171,781; Clinton, Dem., 2,071,651; Perot, Ind., 1,052,481; Marrou, Libertarian, 15,068.
1996, Clinton, Dem., 2,545,968; Dole, Rep., 2,243,324; Perot, Ref., 483,776; Browne, Libertarian, 23,312.
2000, Bush, Rep., 2,912,790; Gore, Dem., 2,912,253; Nader, Green, 97,488; Buchanan, Reform, 17,484; Browne, Libertarian, 16,415; Hagelin, Natural Law, 2,281; Moorehead, Workers World, 1,804; Phillips, Constitution, 1,371; McReynolds, Soc., 622; Harris, Soc. Workers, 562.

Georgia

	2000		1996		
County	Gore (D)	Bush (R)	Clinton (D)	Dole (R)	Perot (RF)
Appling	2,093	3,940	2,070	2,572	446
Atkinson	821	1,228	823	784	215
Bacon	956	2,010	1,360	1,580	402
Baker	893	615	955	408	105
Baldwin	5,893	6,041	5,740	4,570	849
Banks	1,220	3,202	1,536	1,925	595
Barrow	3,657	7,925	3,928	5,342	942
Bartow	7,508	14,720	6,853	9,250	1,770
Ben Hill	2,234	2,381	2,198	1,516	358
Berrien	1,640	2,718	2,066	1,950	525
Bibb	24,996	24,071	26,727	20,778	2,268
Bleckley	1,273	2,436	1,365	1,632	300
Brantley	1,372	3,118	1,494	1,738	386
Brooks	2,096	2,406	1,977	1,738	314
Bryan	2,172	4,835	2,152	3,577	513
Bulloch	5,561	8,990	5,396	6,646	939
Burke	3,720	3,381	3,915	2,590	389
Butts	2,281	3,108	2,271	2,027	410
Calhoun	1,107	768	1,217	541	106
Camden	3,636	6,371	3,644	4,222	572
Candler	1,053	1,643	1,097	1,131	264
Carroll	8,752	16,326	8,438	11,157	2,002
Catoosa	5,470	12,033	5,185	8,237	1,257
Charlton	1,015	1,770	1,368	1,374	280
Chatham	37,590	37,847	35,781	31,987	3,028
Chattahoochee	600	590	565	398	115
Chattooga	2,729	3,640	3,003	2,513	796
Cherokee	12,295	38,033	10,802	24,527	2,872
Clarke	15,167	11,850	15,206	10,504	1,201
Clay	821	448	787	293	62
Clayton	40,042	19,966	30,687	20,625	3,494
Clinch	816	1,091	973	789	182
Cobb	86,676	140,494	73,750	114,188	10,438
Coffee	3,593	5,756	3,407	3,934	711
Colquitt	3,297	6,589	4,135	4,847	977
Columbia	8,969	26,660	8,601	21,291	1,709
Cook	1,639	2,279	1,780	1,354	267
Coweta	9,056	21,327	7,794	13,058	1,949
Crawford	1,513	1,987	1,534	1,290	270
Crisp	2,268	3,285	2,504	2,321	445
Dade	1,628	3,333	1,737	2,295	618
Dawson	1,458	4,210	1,434	2,343	473
Decatur	3,398	4,187	3,245	3,035	497
DeKalb	154,509	58,807	137,903	60,255	6,742
Dodge	2,326	3,472	2,696	2,478	587
Dooly	1,901	1,588	1,951	990	207
Dougherty	16,650	12,248	15,600	11,144	1,072
Douglas	11,162	18,893	9,631	14,495	2,109
Early	1,622	1,938	1,648	1,374	246
Echols	272	614	308	335	97
Effingham	3,232	7,326	3,031	5,022	769
Elbert	2,527	3,262	2,900	2,393	552
Emanuel	2,835	3,343	2,947	2,451	450
Evans	1,217	1,841	1,117	1,206	204
Fannin	2,736	5,463	2,741	3,373	782
Fayette	11,912	29,338	9,875	21,005	2,016
Floyd	10,282	16,194	10,464	12,426	2,345
Forsyth	6,694	27,769	5,957	15,013	1,889
Franklin	2,040	3,659	2,338	2,364	665
Fulton	152,039	104,870	143,306	89,809	7,720
Gilmer	2,230	4,941	2,464	3,121	725
Glascock	249	763	348	532	128
Glynn	7,778	14,346	8,058	12,305	1,137
Gordon	4,032	7,944	4,239	5,232	1,284
Grady	2,721	3,894	2,862	2,674	633

County	2000 Gore (D)	2000 Bush (R)	1996 Clinton (D)	1996 Dole (R)	1996 Perot (RF)
Greene	2,137	2,980	2,115	1,702	173
Gwinnett	61,434	121,756	53,819	96,610	10,236
Habersham	2,530	6,964	3,170	4,730	1,149
Hall	10,259	26,841	10,362	19,280	2,321
Hancock	2,414	662	2,135	438	71
Haralson	2,869	5,153	2,850	3,260	808
Harris	2,912	5,554	2,779	3,829	489
Hart	3,192	4,242	3,486	2,884	767
Heard	1,178	1,947	1,248	1,170	406
Henry	11,971	25,815	9,498	16,968	2,320
Houston	13,301	23,174	12,760	17,050	2,730
Irwin	1,105	1,720	1,225	1,085	224
Jackson	3,420	7,878	3,746	4,782	899
Jasper	1,558	2,298	1,553	1,423	243
Jeff Davis	1,379	2,797	1,576	1,796	428
Jefferson	2,973	2,559	3,404	2,077	298
Jenkins	1,250	1,317	1,336	955	166
Johnson	1,065	1,797	1,194	815	242
Jones	3,102	4,850	3,195	3,272	497
Lamar	2,194	2,912	2,125	1,988	409
Lanier	832	1,048	818	519	160
Laurens	5,724	8,133	5,792	6,118	818
Lee	1,936	5,872	2,005	3,983	506
Liberty	5,347	4,455	4,462	3,042	580
Lincoln	1,275	1,807	1,334	1,391	208
Long	975	1,320	936	791	236
Lowndes	10,616	14,462	9,470	10,578	1,518
Lumpkin	2,121	4,427	1,949	2,576	588
McDuffie	2,580	3,926	2,725	3,254	395
McIntosh	2,047	1,766	1,927	1,219	293
Macon	2,757	1,566	2,618	1,006	159
Madison	2,285	5,529	2,571	3,992	868
Marion	982	1,187	977	678	159
Meriwether	3,441	3,162	3,492	2,259	480
Miller	783	1,349	909	847	235
Mitchell	2,971	2,790	3,165	2,033	372
Monroe	2,839	4,561	2,768	3,054	488
Montgomery	1,013	1,465	1,233	1,163	284
Morgan	2,238	3,524	2,111	2,118	364
Murray	2,684	5,539	2,861	3,289	938
Muscogee	28,193	23,479	24,867	19,360	1,891
Newton	6,703	11,127	6,759	7,274	1,258
Oconee	3,184	7,611	2,992	5,116	615
Oglethorpe	1,519	2,706	1,570	1,826	369
Paulding	6,743	16,881	5,699	10,152	1,603
Peach	3,540	3,525	3,582	2,676	471
Pickens	2,489	5,488	2,693	3,041	783
Pierce	1,300	3,348	1,420	2,319	333
Pike	1,413	3,358	1,474	2,054	357
Polk	4,112	5,841	4,298	4,130	1,076
Pulaski	1,390	1,922	1,554	1,196	268
Putnam	2,612	3,596	2,340	2,306	474
Quitman	542	348	514	224	59
Rabun	1,776	3,451	1,943	2,213	585
Randolph	1,381	1,174	1,438	816	126
Richmond	31,413	25,485	30,738	23,670	2,310
Rockdale	8,295	15,440	7,656	13,006	1,750
Schley	460	706	576	470	123
Screven	2,233	2,461	2,087	1,862	263
Seminole	1,313	1,537	1,265	1,003	250
Spalding	5,831	9,271	6,017	7,376	1,059
Stephens	2,869	5,370	3,072	3,890	979
Stewart	1,267	675	1,537	525	152
Sumter	4,748	4,847	4,239	3,358	451
Talbot	1,662	844	1,579	652	111
Taliaferro	556	271	615	235	36
Tattnall	1,963	3,597	2,369	2,518	541
Taylor	1,340	1,412	1,450	1,002	195
Telfair	1,777	1,693	1,856	1,143	322
Terrell	1,584	1,504	1,509	1,111	129
Thomas	4,862	7,093	5,183	5,649	667
Tift	3,547	6,678	4,198	5,613	728
Toombs	2,643	4,487	2,763	3,646	602
Towns	1,495	2,902	1,664	2,030	459
Treutlen	879	1,062	912	723	122
Troup	6,379	11,198	5,940	8,716	1,090
Turner	1,169	1,258	1,272	924	246
Twiggs	1,977	1,570	1,927	958	210
Union	2,230	4,567	2,175	2,685	622
Upson	3,158	5,019	3,491	3,783	731
Walker	6,341	12,326	6,743	8,817	1,969
Walton	5,484	12,966	5,618	7,934	1,323
Ware	3,480	6,099	4,171	4,746	636
Warren	1,196	933	1,230	735	83
Washington	3,476	3,162	4,057	2,348	488
Wayne	2,736	5,219	2,734	3,709	665
Webster	541	359	529	235	59
Wheeler	752	813	751	460	141
White	2,014	4,857	1,864	2,959	556
Whitfield	7,034	15,852	7,720	12,368	1,637
Wilcox	962	1,381	1,067	882	171
Wilkes	1,940	2,044	1,971	1,417	184
Wilkinson	1,884	1,800	2,278	1,332	287
Worth	2,214	3,792	2,300	2,752	521
Totals	**1,116,230**	**1,419,720**	**1,053,849**	**1,080,843**	**146,337**

Georgia Vote Since 1952

1952, Eisenhower, Rep., 198,979; Stevenson, Dem., 456,823; Liberty Party, 1.

1956, Stevenson, Dem., 444,388; Eisenhower, Rep., 222,778; Andrews, Ind., write-in, 1,754.

1960, Kennedy, Dem., 458,638; Nixon, Rep., 274,472; write-in, 239.

1964, Johnson, Dem., 522,557; Goldwater, Rep., 616,600.

1968, Nixon, Rep., 380,111; Humphrey, Dem., 334,440; Wallace, 3d Party, 535,550; write-in, 162.

1972, Nixon, Rep., 881,496; McGovern, Dem., 289,529; scattered, 2,935; Schmitz, Amer., 812.

1976, Carter, Dem., 979,409; Ford, Rep., 483,743; write-in, 4,306.

1980, Reagan, Rep., 654,168; Carter, Dem., 890,955; Anderson, Ind., 36,055; Clark, Libertarian, 15,627.

1984, Reagan, Rep., 1,068,722; Mondale, Dem., 706,628.

1988, Bush, Rep., 1,081,331; Dukakis, Dem., 714,792; Paul, Lib., 8,435; Fulani, New Alliance, 5,099.

1992, Clinton, Dem., 1,008,966; Bush, Rep., 995,252; Perot, Ind., 309,657; Marrou, Libertarian, 7,110.

1996, Dole, Rep., 1,080,843; Clinton, Dem., 1,053,849; Perot, Ref., 146,337; Browne, Libertarian, 17,870.

2000, Bush, Rep., 1,419,720; Gore, Dem., 1,116,230; Browne, Libertarian, 36,332; Buchanan, Independent, 10,926.

Hawaii

County	2000 Gore (D)	2000 Bush (R)	1996 Clinton (D)	1996 Dole (R)	1996 Perot (RF)
Hawaii	28,670	17,050	27,262	13,516	5,137
Honolulu	139,662	101,336	143,793	85,779	17,389
Kauai	13,470	6,583	13,357	5,325	1,568
Maui	23,484	12,876	20,600	9,323	3,264
Totals	**205,286**	**137,845**	**205,012**	**113,943**	**27,358**

Hawaii Vote Since 1960

1960, Kennedy, Dem., 92,410; Nixon, Rep., 92,295.

1964, Johnson, Dem., 163,249; Goldwater, Rep., 44,022.

1968, Nixon, Rep., 91,425; Humphrey, Dem., 141,324; Wallace, 3d Party, 3,469.

1972, Nixon, Rep., 168,865; McGovern, Dem., 101,409.

1976, Carter, Dem., 147,375; Ford, Rep., 140,003; MacBride, Libertarian, 3,923.

1980, Reagan, Rep., 130,112; Carter, Dem., 135,879; Anderson, Ind., 32,021; Clark, Libertarian, 3,269; Commoner, Citizens, 1,548; Hall, Com., 458.

1984, Reagan, Rep., 184,934; Mondale, Dem., 147,098; Bergland, Libertarian, 2,167.

1988, Bush, Rep., 158,625; Dukakis, Dem., 192,364; Paul, Lib., 1,999; Fulani, New Alliance, 1,003.

1992, Clinton, Dem., 179,310; Bush, Rep., 136,822; Perot, Ind., 53,003; Gritz, Populist/America First, 1,452; Marrou, Libertarian, 1,119.

1996, Clinton, Dem., 205,012; Dole, Rep., 113,943; Perot, Ref., 27,358; Nader, Green, 10,386; Browne, Libertarian, 2,493; Hagelin, Natural Law, 570; Phillips, Taxpayers, 358.

2000, Gore, Dem., 205,286; Bush, Rep., 137,845; Nader, Green, 21,623; Browne, Libertarian, 1,477; Buchanan, Reform, 1,071; Phillips, Constitution, 343; Hagelin, Natural Law, 306.

Idaho

County	2000 Gore (D)	2000 Bush (R)	1996 Clinton (D)	1996 Dole (R)	1996 Perot (RF)
Ada	40,650	75,050	43,040	61,811	11,171
Adams	336	1,476	537	1,053	311
Bannock	10,892	18,223	12,806	14,058	4,158
Bear Lake	517	2,296	805	1,583	396
Benewah	895	2,606	1,488	1,667	701
Bingham	3,310	10,628	4,304	8,391	2,021
Blaine	3,748	3,528	3,840	3,003	1,193
Boise	745	2,019	879	1,576	440
Bonner	4,318	8,945	5,294	6,207	2,669
Bonneville	7,235	24,988	9,013	19,977	3,921
Boundary	832	2,797	1,194	1,937	626
Butte	354	1,054	507	741	233
Camas	113	359	156	283	95
Canyon	10,588	30,560	11,800	23,988	3,956
Caribou	475	2,601	841	1,740	501
Cassia	1,087	5,983	1,596	4,663	976
Clark	63	311	117	266	45
Clearwater	841	2,885	1,507	1,658	650

County	2000 Gore (D)	2000 Bush (R)	1996 Clinton (D)	1996 Dole (R)	1996 Perot (RF)
Custer	416	1,794	635	1,249	400
Elmore	1,840	4,891	2,324	3,668	845
Franklin	513	3,594	807	2,435	589
Fremont	699	4,242	1,114	3,042	630
Gem	1,346	4,376	1,968	3,362	833
Gooding	1,282	3,502	1,503	2,637	980
Idaho	1,187	5,806	1,979	3,871	1,083
Jefferson	1,100	6,480	1,427	4,925	994
Jerome	1,360	4,418	1,679	3,358	1,014
Kootenai	13,488	28,162	13,627	18,740	6,083
Latah	5,661	8,161	7,741	6,311	1,828
Lemhi	660	2,859	1,015	2,334	461
Lewis	335	1,295	674	861	316
Lincoln	437	1,049	478	744	319
Madison	816	7,941	1,216	5,706	744
Minidoka	1,344	4,907	1,977	4,008	977
Nez Perce	4,995	10,577	7,491	6,675	2,385
Oneida	307	1,426	429	993	285
Owyhee	623	2,450	895	2,033	354
Payette	1,643	4,961	2,119	3,901	906
Power	755	1,872	1,070	1,501	344
Shoshone	2,225	2,879	2,981	1,588	1,283
Teton	720	1,745	866	1,251	326
Twin Falls	5,777	15,794	6,826	12,393	3,383
Valley	1,129	2,548	1,564	2,089	568
Washington	980	2,899	1,314	2,318	525
Totals	**138,637**	**336,937**	**164,443**	**256,595**	**62,518**

Idaho Vote Since 1952

1952, Eisenhower, Rep., 180,707; Stevenson, Dem., 95,081; Hallinan, Prog., 443; write-in, 23.

1956, Eisenhower, Rep., 166,979; Stevenson, Dem., 105,868; Andrews, Ind., 126; write-in, 16.

1960, Kennedy, Dem., 138,853; Nixon, Rep., 161,597.

1964, Johnson, Dem., 148,920; Goldwater, Rep., 143,557.

1968, Nixon, Rep., 165,369; Humphrey, Dem., 89,273; Wallace, 3d Party, 36,541.

1972, Nixon, Rep., 199,384; McGovern, Dem., 80,826; Schmitz, Amer., 28,869; Spock, Peoples, 903.

1976, Carter, Dem., 126,549; Ford, Rep., 204,151; Maddox, Amer., 5,935; MacBride, Libertarian, 3,558; LaRouche, U.S. Labor, 739.

1980, Reagan, Rep., 290,699; Carter, Dem., 110,192; Anderson, Ind., 27,058; Clark, Libertarian, 8,425; Rarick, Amer., 1,057.

1984, Reagan, Rep., 297,523; Mondale, Dem., 108,510; Bergland, Libertarian, 2,823.

1988, Bush, Rep., 253,881; Dukakis, Dem., 147,272; Paul, Lib., 5,313; Fulani, Ind., 2,502.

1992, Clinton, Dem., 137,013; Bush, Rep., 202,645; Perot, Ind., 130,395; Gritz, Populist/America First, 10,281; Marrou, Libertarian, 1,167.

1996, Dole, Rep., 256,595; Clinton, Dem., 165,443; Perot, Ref., 62,518; Browne, Libertarian, 3,325; Phillips, Taxpayers, 2,230; Hagelin, Natural Law, 1,600.

2000, Bush, Rep., 336,937; Gore, Dem., 138,637; Buchanan, Reform, 7,615; Browne, Libertarian, 3,488; Phillips, Constitution, 1,469; Hagelin, Natural Law, 1,177.

Illinois

County	2000 Gore (D)	2000 Bush (R)	1996 Clinton (D)	1996 Dole (R)	1996 Perot (RF)
Adams	12,197	17,331	11,336	13,836	3,069
Alexander	2,357	1,588	2,753	1,212	321
Bond	3,060	3,804	3,213	3,018	685
Boone	6,481	8,617	5,345	6,181	1,377
Brown	1,077	1,529	997	1,053	237
Bureau	7,754	8,526	7,651	6,528	1,798
Calhoun	1,310	1,229	1,676	941	363
Carroll	3,113	3,835	2,926	3,029	792
Cass	2,789	2,968	2,834	2,214	589
Champaign	35,515	34,645	32,454	28,232	4,806
Christian	6,799	7,537	7,431	5,563	1,727
Clark	2,932	4,398	2,995	3,409	781
Clay	2,212	3,789	2,750	2,703	719
Clinton	6,436	8,588	6,104	6,065	1,580
Coles	8,904	10,495	8,950	8,038	2,137
Cook	1,280,547	534,542	1,153,289	461,557	96,633
Crawford	3,333	4,974	3,627	3,965	1,057
Cumberland	1,870	2,964	1,776	2,002	657
DeKalb	14,798	17,139	12,715	12,380	3,009
DeWitt	2,870	3,968	2,878	2,978	694
Douglas	3,215	4,734	2,955	3,272	740
DuPage	152,550	201,037	129,709	164,630	27,419
Edgar	3,216	4,833	3,552	3,746	935
Edwards	978	2,212	1,089	1,613	384
Effingham	4,225	9,855	4,825	7,696	1,555
Fayette	3,886	5,200	3,887	3,881	964
Ford	2,090	3,889	2,065	3,077	590
Franklin	10,201	8,490	9,814	5,354	2,096
Fulton	8,940	6,936	8,857	5,155	1,610
Gallatin	1,878	1,591	2,113	856	527
Greene	2,490	3,129	2,734	2,245	903
Grundy	7,516	8,709	6,759	6,177	1,860
Hamilton	1,943	2,519	2,242	1,677	560
Hancock	4,256	5,134	4,001	3,961	1,148
Hardin	1,184	1,366	1,323	790	485
Henderson	2,030	1,708	1,953	1,233	408
Henry	11,921	10,896	11,201	8,393	2,194
Iroquois	4,397	8,685	4,559	6,564	1,522
Jackson	11,773	9,823	12,214	7,422	2,082
Jasper	1,815	3,119	2,038	2,234	641
Jefferson	6,685	8,362	7,263	5,937	1,647
Jersey	4,355	4,699	4,275	3,211	1,186
Jo Daviess	4,585	5,304	4,171	3,915	1,131
Johnson	1,928	3,285	2,009	2,241	640
Kane	60,127	76,996	47,902	54,375	11,270
Kankakee	19,180	20,049	16,820	14,595	3,574
Kendall	8,444	13,688	6,499	8,958	2,055
Knox	12,572	9,912	12,487	7,822	2,096
Lake	115,058	120,988	93,315	93,149	16,640
LaSalle	23,355	21,276	21,643	15,299	5,259
Lawrence	2,822	3,594	2,871	2,568	916
Lee	6,111	8,069	5,895	6,677	1,520
Livingston	5,829	9,187	5,641	7,653	1,409
Logan	4,600	8,141	4,618	6,518	1,141
McDonough	6,080	6,465	5,632	5,049	1,217
McHenry	40,698	62,112	31,240	41,136	10,082
McLean	24,936	34,008	22,708	26,428	3,816
Macon	24,262	23,830	24,256	18,161	4,540
Macoupin	11,015	9,749	11,107	7,235	2,532
Madison	59,077	48,821	53,568	35,758	10,121
Marion	8,068	8,240	7,792	5,999	1,825
Marshall	2,570	3,145	2,640	2,453	586
Mason	3,192	3,411	3,385	2,430	600
Massac	2,912	3,676	2,841	2,507	675
Menard	2,164	3,862	2,204	3,106	534
Mercer	4,400	3,688	4,278	2,688	889
Monroe	5,797	7,632	4,798	5,350	1,276
Montgomery	6,542	6,226	6,338	4,770	1,436
Morgan	5,899	8,058	6,150	6,352	1,633
Moultrie	2,529	3,058	2,629	2,199	596
Ogle	7,673	12,325	6,765	9,558	1,876
Peoria	38,604	36,398	37,383	30,990	5,220
Perry	4,862	4,802	5,347	3,237	1,262
Piatt	3,488	4,619	3,274	3,265	818
Pike	3,198	4,706	3,604	3,225	1,039
Pope	927	1,346	915	850	277
Pulaski	1,518	1,430	1,524	1,036	235
Putnam	1,657	1,437	1,425	987	322
Randolph	6,794	7,127	7,419	5,422	1,698
Richland	2,491	4,718	2,679	3,137	927
Rock Island	37,957	25,194	34,822	20,626	5,135
St. Clair	55,961	42,299	53,405	33,066	7,027
Saline	5,427	5,933	6,156	3,693	1,752
Sangamon	38,414	50,374	38,902	42,174	6,446
Schuyler	1,587	2,077	1,636	1,597	483
Scott	954	1,458	1,012	1,112	396
Shelby	4,018	5,851	4,249	4,215	1,262
Stark	1,211	1,694	1,262	1,278	312
Stephenson	8,062	10,715	7,145	8,871	1,940
Tazewell	25,379	31,537	24,139	24,395	4,814
Union	3,982	4,397	4,252	3,147	832
Vermilion	15,406	15,783	15,525	12,015	3,577
Wabash	1,987	3,406	2,177	2,381	683
Warren	3,524	3,899	3,500	2,974	742
Washington	2,638	4,353	2,744	3,339	790
Wayne	2,209	5,347	3,054	4,029	999
White	2,958	4,521	3,553	2,878	888
Whiteside	12,886	11,252	11,913	8,859	2,436
Will	90,902	95,828	69,354	62,506	15,485
Williamson	12,192	14,012	12,510	9,734	2,877
Winnebago	51,981	53,816	46,264	44,479	8,192
Woodford	5,529	10,905	5,270	8,527	1,170
Totals	**2,589,026**	**2,019,421**	**2,341,744**	**1,587,021**	**346,408**

Illinois Vote Since 1952

1952, Eisenhower, Rep., 2,457,327; Stevenson, Dem., 2,013,920; Hass, Soc. Labor, 9,363; write-in, 448.

1956, Eisenhower, Rep., 2,623,327; Stevenson, Dem., 1,775,682; Hass, Soc. Labor, 8,342; write-in, 56.

1960, Kennedy, Dem., 2,377,846; Nixon, Rep., 2,368,988; Hass, Soc. Labor, 10,560; write-in, 15.

1964, Johnson, Dem., 2,796,833; Goldwater, Rep., 1,905,946; write-in, 62.

1968, Nixon, Rep., 2,174,774; Humphrey, Dem., 2,039,814; Wallace, 3d Party, 390,958; Blomen, Soc. Labor, 13,878; write-in, 325.

1972, Nixon, Rep. 2,788,179; McGovern, Dem., 1,913,472; Fisher, Soc. Labor, 12,344; Schmitz, Amer., 2,471; Hall, Com., 4,541; others, 2,229.
1976, Carter, Dem., 2,271,295; Ford, Rep., 2,364,269; McCarthy, Ind., 55,939; Hall, Com., 9,250; MacBride, Libertarian, 8,057; Camejo, Soc. Workers, 3,615; Levin, Soc. Labor, 2,422; LaRouche, U.S. Labor, 2,018; write-in, 1,968.
1980, Reagan, Rep., 2,358,049; Carter, Dem., 1,981,413; Anderson, Ind., 346,754; Clark, Libertarian, 38,939; Commoner, Citizens, 10,692; Hall, Com., 9,711; Griswold, Workers World, 2,257; DeBerry, Soc. Workers, 1,302; write-ins, 604.
1984, Reagan, Rep., 2,707,103; Mondale, Dem., 2,086,499; Bergland, Libertarian, 10,086.
1988, Bush, Rep., 2,310,939; Dukakis, Dem., 2,215,940; Paul, Lib., 14,944; Fulani, Solid., 10,276.
1992, Clinton, Dem., 2,453,350; Bush, Rep., 1,734,096; Perot, Ind., 840,515; Marrou, Libertarian, 9,218; Fulani, New Alliance, 5,267; Gritz, Populist/America First, 3,577; Hagelin, Natural Law, 2,751; Warren, Soc. Workers, 1,361.
1996, Clinton, Dem., 2,341,744; Dole, Rep., 1,587,021; Perot, Ref., 346,408; Browne, Libertarian, 22,548; Phillips, Taxpayers, 7,606; Hagelin, Natural Law, 4,606.
2000, Gore, Dem., 2,589,026; Bush, Rep., 2,019,421; Nader, Green, 103,759; Buchanan, Ind., 16,106; Browne, Libertarian, 11,623; Hagelin, Reform, 2,127.

Indiana

	2000		1996		
County	Gore (D)	Bush (R)	Clinton (D)	Dole (R)	Perot (RF)
Adams	3,775	8,555	4,247	6,960	1,346
Allen	41,636	70,426	41,450	59,255	8,808
Bartholomew	9,015	16,200	9,301	13,188	2,815
Benton	1,328	2,441	1,311	1,947	609
Blackford	2,103	2,699	2,335	2,070	681
Boone	4,763	13,161	4,625	11,338	1,498
Brown	2,608	3,871	2,413	2,988	802
Carroll	2,965	5,102	2,747	4,062	1,171
Cass	5,412	9,305	5,419	8,020	2,029
Clark	17,360	19,417	17,799	14,396	3,578
Clay	3,605	6,393	3,605	4,858	1,406
Clinton	3,643	7,141	3,949	6,156	1,355
Crawford	1,817	2,327	2,324	1,759	700
Daviess	2,697	6,872	3,230	5,531	994
Dearborn	6,020	11,452	6,269	8,318	1,731
Decatur	2,889	6,115	3,190	4,782	1,389
Dekalb	4,776	8,701	4,840	6,851	1,534
Delaware	20,876	22,105	20,385	18,126	6,042
Dubois	5,090	10,134	6,499	6,840	1,777
Elkhart	16,402	36,756	16,598	28,770	5,133
Fayette	3,415	5,060	3,822	4,091	1,137
Floyd	13,209	16,486	13,814	12,473	2,609
Fountain	2,717	4,408	2,327	3,984	1,033
Franklin	2,591	5,587	2,808	4,167	943
Fulton	2,960	5,218	2,956	3,934	1,143
Gibson	5,802	7,734	6,488	5,392	1,585
Grant	9,712	16,153	9,818	13,443	3,008
Greene	4,898	7,452	5,277	5,746	1,690
Hamilton	18,002	56,372	14,153	42,792	4,234
Hancock	6,503	15,943	6,123	12,907	2,258
Harrison	5,870	8,711	5,900	6,073	1,839
Hendricks	10,786	28,651	9,392	22,293	3,405
Henry	7,647	10,321	7,667	8,537	2,381
Howard	12,899	20,331	11,999	16,771	4,172
Huntington	4,119	10,113	4,287	8,275	1,400
Jackson	5,330	9,054	5,150	5,883	1,590
Jasper	3,744	7,212	3,554	5,173	1,271
Jay	3,167	4,687	3,356	3,584	1,022
Jefferson	5,117	6,582	5,441	4,827	1,438
Jennings	3,549	5,732	4,223	4,461	1,629
Johnson	11,952	29,404	11,278	23,733	3,975
Knox	6,300	8,485	7,003	6,395	2,022
Kosciusko	5,785	19,040	6,166	15,084	2,531
LaGrange	2,733	5,437	2,704	4,033	949
Lake	109,078	63,389	100,198	47,873	15,051
LaPorte	19,736	18,994	19,879	14,106	5,133
Lawrence	5,071	10,677	5,703	8,107	2,063
Madison	23,403	27,956	23,772	23,151	6,447
Marion	134,189	137,810	124,448	133,329	21,358
Marshall	5,541	10,266	5,486	8,158	1,698
Martin	1,518	3,008	1,848	2,281	485
Miami	4,155	8,401	4,260	6,719	1,657
Monroe	17,523	19,147	18,531	16,744	3,179
Montgomery	3,899	8,891	3,825	7,705	1,766
Morgan	6,228	15,286	5,812	12,872	2,755
Newton	2,101	3,250	1,897	2,075	801
Noble	4,822	9,103	5,101	6,782	1,521
Ohio	951	1,515	1,083	1,098	281
Orange	2,601	4,687	3,016	3,355	938
Owen	2,253	4,019	2,244	3,056	874
Parke	2,481	3,841	2,453	3,151	981
Perry	3,823	3,461	4,427	2,554	913
Pike	2,605	3,566	2,780	2,174	884
Porter	26,790	31,157	24,044	22,931	7,169
Posey	4,430	6,498	4,965	4,638	1,304
Pulaski	1,919	3,497	2,010	2,693	634
Putnam	4,123	7,352	3,962	5,958	1,619
Randolph	3,906	6,020	4,087	4,708	1,557
Ripley	3,498	6,988	4,097	5,303	1,216
Rush	2,370	4,749	2,578	3,827	973
St. Joseph	47,703	47,581	45,704	38,281	8,379
Scott	3,915	3,761	3,798	2,620	760
Shelby	5,374	9,590	5,374	7,778	1,874
Spencer	3,752	5,096	4,058	3,770	739
Starke	4,136	4,349	3,854	3,108	1,096
Steuben	4,103	6,953	4,124	5,513	1,390
Sullivan	3,833	4,319	4,076	3,207	1,178
Switzerland	1,336	1,831	1,496	1,266	403
Tippecanoe	18,220	26,106	17,232	22,556	5,394
Tipton	2,392	4,784	2,478	3,980	861
Union	927	1,838	1,019	1,334	364
Vanderburgh	29,222	35,846	30,934	28,509	6,132
Vermillion	3,370	3,130	3,251	2,334	1,029
Vigo	17,570	18,021	17,974	15,751	4,508
Wabash	4,277	8,321	4,577	6,990	1,294
Warren	1,471	2,218	1,394	1,678	560
Warrick	8,749	13,205	9,285	9,221	2,471
Washington	3,675	5,868	3,819	4,066	1,264
Wayne	10,273	14,273	10,905	12,188	2,525
Wells	3,319	7,755	3,752	6,322	1,157
White	3,655	6,037	3,396	4,642	1,610
Whitley	4,107	8,080	4,176	5,965	1,392
Totals	**901,980**	1,245,836	**887,424**	**1,006,693**	**224,299**

Indiana Vote Since 1952

1952, Eisenhower, Rep., 1,136,259; Stevenson, Dem., 801,530; Hamblen, Proh., 15,335; Hallinan, Prog., 1,222; Hass, Soc. Labor, 979.
1956, Eisenhower, Rep., 1,182,811; Stevenson, Dem., 783,908; Holtwick, Proh., 6,554; Hass, Soc. Labor, 1,334.
1960, Kennedy, Dem., 952,358; Nixon, Rep., 1,175,120; Decker, Proh., 6,746; Hass, Soc. Labor, 1,136.
1964, Johnson, Dem., 1,170,848; Goldwater, Rep., 911,118; Munn, Proh., 8,266; Hass, Soc. Labor, 1,374.
1968, Nixon, Rep., 1,067,885; Humphrey, Dem., 806,659; Wallace, 3d Party, 243,108; Munn, Proh., 4,616; Halstead, Soc. Workers, 1,293; Gregory, write-in, 36.
1972, Nixon, Rep., 1,405,154; McGovern, Dem., 708,568; Reed, Soc. Workers, 5,575; Fisher, Soc. Labor, 1,688; Spock, Peace and Freedom, 4,544.
1976, Carter, Dem., 1,014,714; Ford, Rep., 1,185,958; Anderson, Amer., 14,048; Camejo, Soc. Workers, 5,695; LaRouche, U.S. Labor, 1,947.
1980, Reagan, Rep., 1,255,656; Carter, Dem., 844,197; Anderson, Ind., 111,639; Clark, Libertarian, 19,627; Commoner, Citizens, 4,852; Greaves, Amer., 4,750; Hall, Com., 702; DeBerry, Soc., 610.
1984, Reagan, Rep., 1,377,230; Mondale, Dem., 841,481; Bergland, Libertarian, 6,741.
1988, Bush, Rep., 1,297,763; Dukakis, Dem., 860,643; Fulani, New Alliance, 10,215.
1992, Bush, Rep., 989,375; Clinton, Dem., 848,420; Perot, Ind., 455,934; Marrou, Libertarian, 7,936; Fulani, New Alliance, 2,583.
1996, Dole, Rep., 1,006,693; Clinton, Dem., 887,424; Perot, Ref., 224,299; Browne, Libertarian, 15,632.
2000, Bush, Rep., 1,245,836; Gore, Dem., 901,980; Buchanan, Ind., 16,959; Browne, Libertarian, 15,530.

Iowa

	2000		1996		
County	Gore (D)	Bush (R)	Clinton (D)	Dole (R)	Perot (RF)
Adair	1,753	2,275	1,802	1,655	458
Adams	897	1,170	1,070	920	320
Allamakee	2,883	3,277	2,551	2,457	680
Appanoose	2,560	2,992	2,747	2,233	554
Audubon	1,780	1,909	1,827	1,314	314
Benton	5,915	5,468	5,546	3,835	846
Black Hawk	30,112	23,468	29,651	19,322	3,623
Boone	6,270	5,625	6,446	4,293	987
Bremer	5,169	5,675	5,023	4,213	862
Buchanan	5,045	4,092	4,997	3,043	836
Buena Vista	3,297	4,354	3,420	3,636	831
Butler	2,735	3,837	3,061	3,036	489
Calhoun	2,132	2,776	2,193	2,077	462
Carroll	4,463	4,879	4,333	3,392	998
Cass	2,481	4,206	2,616	3,384	809

	2000		1996		
County	Gore (D)	Bush (R)	Clinton (D)	Dole (R)	Perot (RF)
Cedar	4,033	4,031	3,856	2,966	756
Cerro Gordo .	12,185	9,397	11,943	7,427	1,689
Cherokee. . . .	2,845	3,463	2,853	2,629	834
Chickasaw. . .	3,435	2,936	3,355	2,191	759
Clarke	2,081	1,984	2,053	1,401	440
Clay.	3,294	3,992	3,659	3,129	802
Clayton	4,238	4,034	4,284	2,944	912
Clinton.	12,276	9,229	11,481	7,624	2,300
Crawford	2,838	3,482	3,140	2,686	847
Dallas	8,561	10,306	8,017	6,647	1,198
Davis.	1,691	1,956	1,894	1,445	382
Decatur	1,674	1,903	1,846	1,287	452
Delaware. . . .	3,808	4,273	3,704	3,065	679
Des Moines. .	11,351	7,385	10,761	5,778	1,792
Dickinson. . . .	3,660	4,225	3,562	3,129	901
Dubuque	22,341	16,462	20,839	13,391	3,304
Emmet.	2,165	2,331	2,270	1,641	470
Fayette	4,640	4,747	4,832	3,848	890
Floyd	3,830	3,191	3,769	2,379	689
Franklin	2,122	2,657	2,232	2,054	417
Fremont.	1,459	2,069	1,481	1,576	480
Greene	2,301	2,282	2,519	1,861	396
Grundy	2,139	3,851	2,322	2,928	401
Guthrie	2,493	2,840	2,552	2,034	515
Hamilton	3,407	3,968	3,455	3,109	661
Hancock	2,281	2,988	2,399	2,353	529
Hardin	3,734	4,486	4,053	3,505	713
Harrison	2,551	3,802	2,576	3,070	820
Henry	3,907	4,476	3,798	3,478	914
Howard	2,426	1,922	2,303	1,528	555
Humboldt. . . .	1,949	2,846	2,080	2,236	590
Ida	1,411	1,968	1,589	1,684	436
Iowa.	3,230	3,894	3,354	3,042	575
Jackson	4,945	3,769	4,609	2,827	936
Jasper	8,699	8,729	8,776	6,414	1,263
Jefferson	2,863	3,248	2,597	2,541	571
Johnson.	31,174	17,899	27,888	13,402	2,313
Jones.	4,690	4,201	4,668	3,083	765
Keokuk	2,181	2,571	2,545	2,080	432
Kossuth	3,960	4,612	4,031	3,477	932
Lee	9,632	6,339	8,831	4,932	1,734
Linn	48,897	40,417	45,497	30,958	5,607
Louisa	2,294	2,207	2,081	1,565	590
Lucas.	1,934	2,262	2,168	1,586	433
Lyon.	1,313	3,918	1,489	3,396	422
Madison.	3,093	3,662	3,070	2,550	654
Mahaska	3,370	5,971	3,737	4,473	656
Marion	5,741	8,358	5,978	6,100	871
Marshall.	8,322	8,785	8,669	7,017	1,455
Mills.	2,039	3,684	2,068	2,958	683
Mitchell	2,650	2,388	2,596	1,877	563
Monona	2,086	2,304	1,952	1,674	580
Monroe	1,699	1,858	1,884	1,272	329
Montgomery .	1,838	3,417	1,912	2,583	663
Muscatine . . .	8,058	7,483	7,674	5,858	1,705
O'Brien	2,170	4,674	2,236	3,877	578
Osceola.	913	2,064	1,010	1,736	274
Page	2,293	4,588	2,220	4,032	753
Palo Alto	2,326	2,341	2,371	1,817	477
Plymouth	3,499	6,189	3,745	5,117	997
Pocahontas . .	1,736	2,242	1,981	1,707	478
Polk	89,715	79,927	83,877	60,884	9,516
Pottawattamie	14,726	18,783	13,276	15,648	3,534
Poweshiek. . .	4,222	4,396	4,183	3,221	681
Ringgold	1,246	1,369	1,439	967	310
Sac	2,099	2,776	2,170	2,209	579
Scott	35,857	32,801	32,694	26,751	4,991
Shelby	2,179	3,655	2,176	3,056	652
Sioux.	2,148	12,241	2,392	10,864	718
Story	17,478	16,228	17,234	12,468	2,091
Tama	4,045	4,034	3,994	2,986	713
Taylor.	1,247	1,770	1,458	1,419	379
Union.	2,540	3,003	2,787	2,156	660
Van Buren . . .	1,440	2,016	1,536	1,460	347
Wapello	8,355	6,313	8,437	4,828	1,376
Warren	9,521	9,621	9,120	6,905	1,267
Washington . .	3,932	4,827	3,828	3,600	636
Wayne	1,300	1,666	1,650	1,295	310
Webster.	8,479	8,172	8,380	6,275	1,580
Winnebago . .	2,691	2,662	2,679	2,211	590
Winneshiek . .	4,339	4,647	4,122	3,532	973
Woodbury . . .	17,691	18,864	17,224	16,368	3,436
Worth	2,208	1,659	2,293	1,284	403
Wright	2,796	3,384	2,912	2,473	536
Totals	**638,517**	**634,373**	**620,258**	**492,644**	**105,159**

Iowa Vote Since 1952

1952, Eisenhower, Rep., 808,906; Stevenson, Dem., 451,513; Hallinan, Prog., 5,085; Hamblen, Proh., 2,882; Hoopes, Soc., 219; Hass, Soc. Labor, 139; scattering, 29.

1956, Eisenhower, Rep., 729,187; Stevenson, Dem., 501,858; Andrews (A.C.P. of Iowa), 3,202; Hoopes, Soc., 192; Hass, Soc. Labor, 125.

1960, Kennedy, Dem., 550,565; Nixon, Rep., 722,381; Hass, Soc. Labor, 230; write-in, 634.

1964, Johnson, Dem., 733,030; Goldwater, Rep., 449,148; Hass, Soc. Labor, 182; DeBerry, Soc. Workers, 159; Munn, Proh., 1,902.

1968, Nixon, Rep., 619,106; Humphrey, Dem., 476,699; Wallace, 3d Party, 66,422; Munn, Proh., 362; Halstead, Soc. Workers, 3,377; Cleaver, Peace and Freedom, 1,332; Blomen, Soc. Labor, 241.

1972, Nixon, Rep., 706,207; McGovern, Dem., 496,206; Schmitz, Amer., 22,056; Jenness, Soc. Workers, 488; Fisher, Soc. Labor, 195; Hall, Com., 272; Green, Universal, 199; scattered, 321.

1976, Carter, Dem., 619,931; Ford, Rep., 632,863; McCarthy, Ind., 20,051; Anderson, Amer., 3,040; MacBride, Libertarian, 1,452.

1980, Reagan, Rep., 676,026; Carter, Dem., 508,672; Anderson, Ind., 115,633; Clark, Libertarian, 13,123; Commoner, Citizens, 2,273; McReynolds, Socialist, 534; Hall, Com., 298; DeBerry, Soc. Workers, 244; Greaves, Amer., 189; Bubar, Statesman, 150; scattering, 519.

1984, Reagan, Rep., 703,088; Mondale, Dem., 605,620; Bergland, Libertarian, 1,844.

1988, Bush, Rep., 545,355; Dukakis, Dem., 670,557; LaRouche, Ind., 3,526; Paul, Lib., 2,494.

1992, Clinton, Dem., 586,353; Bush, Rep., 504,891; Perot, Ind., 253,468; Hagelin, Natural Law, 3,079; Gritz, Populist/America First, 1,177; Marrou, Libertarian, 1,076.

1996, Clinton, Dem., 620,258; Dole, Rep., 492,644; Perot, Ref., 105,159; Nader, Green, 6,550; Hagelin, Natural Law, 3,349; Browne, Libertarian, 2,315; Phillips, Taxpayers, 2,229; Harris, Soc. Workers, 331.

2000, Gore, Dem., 638,517; Bush, Rep., 634,373; Nader, Green, 29,374; Buchanan, Reform, 5,731; Browne, Libertarian, 3,209; Hagelin, Ind., 2,281; Phillips, Constitution, 613; Harris, Soc. Workers, 190; McReynolds, Soc., 107.

Kansas

	2000		1996		
County	Gore (D)	Bush (R)	Clinton (D)	Dole (R)	Perot (RF)
Allen.	2,132	3,379	2,299	2,797	793
Anderson	1,327	1,984	1,367	1,636	449
Atchison	3,171	3,378	2,926	2,828	727
Barber	637	1,755	730	1,696	279
Barton	3,238	7,302	3,121	7,855	1,004
Bourbon	2,211	3,852	2,491	3,318	760
Brown.	1,512	2,985	1,529	2,688	497
Butler	6,755	13,377	7,294	13,979	2,274
Chase.	391	848	496	778	259
Chautauqua	443	1,347	568	1,142	222
Cherokee	3,783	5,014	3,771	4,138	1,072
Cheyenne.	350	1,312	422	1,211	174
Clark.	292	926	334	855	109
Clay	951	2,998	963	2,793	389
Cloud	1,314	2,918	1,615	2,743	609
Coffey.	1,196	2,700	1,118	2,369	572
Comanche	211	760	298	691	133
Cowley	5,535	8,080	5,588	7,872	1,904
Crawford.	7,076	7,160	7,504	6,447	1,785
Decatur	424	1,255	417	1,255	156
Dickinson	2,413	5,243	2,423	5,174	888
Doniphan	1,134	2,350	1,050	1,962	0
Douglas	18,249	17,062	18,116	16,116	2,630
Edwards	447	1,062	539	1,088	180
Elk	402	1,080	488	933	206
Ellis	3,926	6,516	4,142	6,809	894
Ellsworth.	825	1,845	899	2,078	245
Finney	2,431	6,442	2,420	6,188	805
Ford	2,566	6,050	2,628	5,681	914
Franklin	3,321	5,925	3,552	5,007	1,184
Geary	2,660	3,977	2,444	3,686	618
Gove.	296	1,122	351	1,123	141
Graham	346	1,058	432	1,031	152
Grant	683	2,126	633	1,772	250
Gray	482	1,631	404	1,457	164
Greeley.	143	628	161	567	47
Greenwood.	1,027	2,392	1,108	1,932	552
Hamilton.	264	901	342	811	84
Harper	869	2,076	836	1,941	355
Harvey	4,591	8,271	4,918	8,382	1,023
Haskell	263	1,323	304	1,143	96
Hodgeman	217	835	251	808	99
Jackson	1,990	3,001	1,983	2,682	735

	2000		1996		
County	Gore (D)	Bush (R)	Clinton (D)	Dole (R)	Perot (RF)
Jefferson	3,000	4,423	2,757	3,781	1,030
Jewell	380	1,400	417	1,374	188
Johnson	79,118	129,965	68,129	110,368	10,425
Kearny	320	1,084	335	1,041	106
Kingman	991	2,672	1,006	2,659	409
Kiowa	294	1,262	331	1,264	170
Labette	3,745	4,475	3,931	4,283	1,091
Lane	252	846	271	865	86
Leavenworth	9,733	12,583	9,098	10,778	2,419
Lincoln	469	1,295	528	1,372	212
Linn	1,587	2,513	1,590	2,077	535
Logan	231	1,088	296	1,155	112
Lyon	5,190	6,652	4,884	6,612	1,584
McPherson	3,272	8,501	3,536	8,142	1,115
Marion	1,475	4,156	1,673	4,173	492
Marshall	1,831	3,066	1,932	2,811	713
Meade	400	1,604	426	1,443	173
Miami	4,554	6,611	4,237	5,256	1,339
Mitchell	751	2,350	833	2,435	246
Montgomery	4,770	8,496	5,269	7,428	1,528
Morris	882	1,599	965	1,553	451
Morton	321	1,203	376	1,073	124
Nemaha	1,494	3,578	1,648	3,014	676
Neosho	2,588	4,014	2,527	3,409	907
Ness	383	1,420	428	1,336	186
Norton	598	1,744	640	1,814	265
Osage	2,530	3,770	2,502	3,487	1,101
Osborne	484	1,432	608	1,582	191
Ottawa	631	1,977	752	1,846	261
Pawnee	968	1,850	932	1,927	275
Phillips	611	2,057	758	2,005	242
Pottawatomie	2,037	4,985	1,997	4,504	1,035
Pratt	1,314	2,885	1,367	2,591	408
Rawlins	306	1,349	335	1,393	146
Reno	9,025	15,179	9,108	14,275	2,661
Republic	604	2,239	688	2,283	268
Rice	1,422	2,903	1,434	2,842	482
Riley	6,188	10,672	6,746	11,113	1,478
Rooks	597	2,016	650	1,864	251
Rush	505	1,235	547	1,239	185
Russell	886	2,434	705	3,347	164
Saline	7,487	12,412	7,728	12,475	2,192
Scott	418	1,811	458	1,750	160
Sedgwick	62,561	93,724	59,643	93,397	11,875
Seward	1,126	3,869	1,309	3,812	396
Shawnee	34,818	35,894	32,803	34,845	7,304
Sheridan	281	1,132	264	1,053	95
Sherman	681	1,894	736	2,110	220
Smith	534	1,534	638	1,628	213
Stafford	567	1,546	651	1,604	276
Stanton	215	785	189	628	60
Stevens	345	1,714	405	1,548	213
Sumner	3,549	6,176	3,638	5,952	1,260
Thomas	807	2,822	866	2,725	295
Trego	516	1,220	548	1,205	209
Wabaunsee	1,025	2,182	966	1,884	479
Wallace	103	737	160	738	65
Washington	687	2,446	804	2,397	326
Wichita	207	859	239	796	80
Wilson	1,186	2,748	1,297	2,458	562
Woodson	521	974	598	953	269
Wyandotte	32,411	14,024	31,252	14,011	3,931
Totals	**399,276**	**622,332**	**387,659**	**583,245**	**92,639**

Kansas Vote Since 1952

1952, Eisenhower, Rep., 616,302; Stevenson, Dem., 273,296; Hamblen, Proh., 6,038; Hoopes, Soc., 530.

1956, Eisenhower, Rep., 566,878; Stevenson, Dem., 296,317; Holtwick, Proh., 3,048.

1960, Kennedy, Dem., 363,213; Nixon, Rep., 561,474; Decker, Proh., 4,138.

1964, Johnson, Dem., 464,028; Goldwater, Rep., 386,579; Munn, Proh., 5,393; Hass, Soc. Labor, 1,901.

1968, Nixon, Rep., 478,674; Humphrey, Dem., 302,996; Wallace, 3d Party, 88,921; Munn, Proh., 2,192.

1972, Nixon, Rep., 619,812; McGovern, Dem., 270,287; Schmitz, Conservative, 21,808; Munn, Proh., 4,188.

1976, Carter, Dem., 430,421; Ford, Rep., 502,752; McCarthy, Ind., 13,185; Anderson, Amer., 4,724; MacBride, Libertarian, 3,242; Maddox, Conservative, 2,118; Bubar, Proh., 1,403.

1980, Reagan, Rep., 566,812; Carter, Dem., 326,150; Anderson, Ind., 68,231; Clark, Libertarian, 14,470; Shelton, Amer., 1,555; Hall, Com., 967; Bubar, Statesman, 821; Rarick, Conservative, 789.

1984, Reagan, Rep., 674,646; Mondale, Dem., 332,471; Bergland, Libertarian, 3,585.

1988, Bush, Rep., 554,049; Dukakis, Dem., 422,636; Paul, Ind., 12,553; Fulani, Ind., 3,806.

1992, Clinton, Dem., 390,434; Bush, Rep., 449,951; Perot, Ind., 312,358; Marrou, Libertarian, 4,314.

1996, Dole, Rep., 583,245; Clinton, Dem., 387,659; Perot, Ref., 92,639; Browne, Libertarian, 4,557; Phillips, Ind., 3,519; Hagelin, Ind., 1,655.

2000, Bush, Rep., 622,332; Gore, Dem., 399,276; Nader, Ind., 36,086; Buchanan, Reform, 7,370; Browne, Libertarian, 4,525; Hagelin, Ind., 1,373; Phillips, Constitution, 1,254.

Kentucky

	2000		1996		
County	Gore (D)	Bush (R)	Clinton (D)	Dole (R)	Perot (RF)
Adair	1,779	5,460	1,821	3,876	790
Allen	1,950	4,415	1,781	3,032	393
Anderson	2,902	4,909	2,898	2,972	751
Ballard	1,880	1,824	2,255	1,064	411
Barren	4,930	8,741	5,044	5,700	1,065
Bath	2,087	2,303	1,886	1,229	428
Bell	4,787	5,585	5,058	3,917	940
Boone	9,248	22,016	8,379	15,085	1,900
Bourbon	3,048	3,881	3,030	2,592	603
Boyd	9,541	9,247	9,668	7,054	2,070
Boyle	3,963	6,126	3,877	4,157	709
Bracken	888	2,065	1,055	1,371	271
Breathitt	2,902	2,084	3,106	1,058	397
Breckinridge	2,595	4,763	2,956	3,151	670
Bullitt	8,195	14,054	7,651	8,697	1,973
Butler	1,299	3,654	1,260	2,531	348
Caldwell	2,223	3,161	2,434	2,067	637
Calloway	5,635	7,705	5,281	4,989	1,223
Campbell	12,040	20,789	11,957	16,640	2,312
Carlisle	1,149	1,405	1,355	816	245
Carroll	1,601	1,818	1,689	1,170	351
Carter	4,182	4,617	3,728	3,240	781
Casey	1,122	4,284	1,106	3,187	525
Christian	6,778	10,787	6,843	8,285	1,064
Clark	4,918	7,297	4,987	4,739	1,095
Clay	1,723	4,926	2,135	3,716	478
Clinton	1,032	3,224	1,072	2,521	350
Crittenden	1,610	2,469	1,480	1,509	400
Cumberland	736	2,220	753	1,654	227
Daviess	14,126	21,361	15,366	15,844	3,344
Edmonson	1,710	3,250	1,595	2,619	298
Elliott	1,525	827	1,298	421	284
Estill	1,591	3,033	1,724	2,220	479
Fayette	47,277	54,495	43,632	42,930	5,345
Fleming	1,813	3,282	1,913	2,313	522
Floyd	10,088	5,068	9,655	3,139	1,518
Franklin	10,853	10,209	11,251	7,132	1,873
Fulton	1,452	1,293	1,614	863	223
Gallatin	1,049	1,345	1,189	838	299
Garrard	1,713	4,043	1,486	2,540	337
Grant	2,568	4,405	2,541	2,697	661
Graves	6,097	7,849	6,991	5,130	1,596
Grayson	2,604	5,843	2,716	4,249	677
Green	1,085	3,615	1,285	2,763	475
Greenup	7,164	7,233	6,883	5,370	1,627
Hancock	1,508	2,032	1,547	1,356	418
Hardin	11,095	18,964	11,031	12,642	2,815
Harlan	5,365	4,980	5,874	3,337	884
Harrison	2,658	3,793	2,934	2,433	801
Hart	2,201	3,725	2,527	2,701	501
Henderson	8,054	7,698	8,051	5,092	1,556
Henry	2,117	3,244	2,324	2,110	564
Hickman	940	1,151	1,220	695	247
Hopkins	6,734	9,490	7,239	6,363	1,512
Jackson	701	4,079	960	3,045	299
Jefferson	149,901	145,052	144,207	114,860	19,413
Jessamine	4,633	10,074	4,428	6,686	1,040
Johnson	3,276	4,811	3,348	3,262	1,010
Kenton	19,100	35,363	19,407	28,579	3,680
Knott	4,349	2,029	4,842	1,201	517
Knox	3,690	6,058	3,736	4,502	811
Larue	1,727	3,384	2,040	2,140	469
Laurel	4,856	13,029	4,306	9,454	1,211
Lawrence	2,258	2,969	2,195	1,812	481
Lee	836	1,893	1,023	1,302	181
Leslie	1,210	3,159	1,466	2,296	304
Letcher	4,698	4,092	4,160	2,222	782
Lewis	1,293	3,217	1,415	2,365	561
Lincoln	2,678	4,795	2,550	3,006	526
Livingston	2,022	2,118	2,228	1,258	449
Logan	3,885	5,344	4,181	3,888	704
Lyon	1,680	1,688	1,641	999	284
McCracken	11,412	14,745	12,670	10,221	2,268
McCreary	1,418	3,321	1,710	2,527	488
McLean	1,747	2,219	1,834	1,368	385
Madison	9,309	13,682	8,142	9,212	1,613
Magoffin	2,603	2,785	2,249	1,434	337

County	2000 Gore (D)	2000 Bush (R)	1996 Clinton (D)	1996 Dole (R)	1996 Perot (RF)
Marion	2,778	3,259	2,922	2,013	757
Marshall.	6,203	7,294	6,054	4,579	1,391
Martin	1,714	2,667	1,807	1,612	401
Mason	2,178	3,572	2,444	2,588	484
Meade	3,596	5,319	3,653	2,855	912
Menifee	1,038	1,170	979	608	179
Mercer	3,092	5,362	3,179	3,264	738
Metcalfe.	1,318	2,476	1,349	1,651	355
Monroe	1,158	4,377	1,114	3,300	415
Montgomery . .	3,833	4,534	3,372	2,681	705
Morgan	1,875	2,295	1,843	1,439	380
Muhlenberg . . .	6,295	5,518	6,564	3,569	1,218
Nelson	5,481	7,714	5,392	4,645	1,067
Nicholas	994	1,613	1,092	950	265
Ohio.	3,303	5,413	3,487	3,475	1,076
Oldham	6,236	13,580	6,202	10,477	1,521
Owen.	1,394	2,582	1,603	1,709	454
Owsley	339	1,466	647	920	153
Pendleton	1,670	3,044	1,926	2,177	462
Perry	5,514	5,300	6,015	3,382	894
Pike	13,611	11,005	14,126	7,160	2,148
Powell	2,008	2,258	2,156	1,526	523
Pulaski.	5,415	15,845	5,340	11,945	1,420
Robertson	341	630	360	368	117
Rockcastle. . . .	1,174	3,992	1,160	3,106	338
Rowan	3,505	3,548	3,215	2,309	724
Russell	1,710	5,268	1,582	4,017	837
Scott	5,472	7,952	4,258	4,349	977
Shelby	4,435	8,068	4,629	5,307	780
Simpson	2,583	3,169	2,749	2,186	401
Spencer.	1,554	3,150	1,404	1,614	341
Taylor.	2,790	6,151	2,897	4,573	829
Todd	1,496	2,646	1,744	1,912	424
Trigg	2,110	3,130	2,087	1,975	394
Trimble.	1,181	1,837	1,245	999	308
Union.	2,547	2,749	2,913	1,554	598
Warren	12,180	20,235	11,642	15,784	1,835
Washington . . .	1,458	3,044	1,639	2,116	383
Wayne	2,312	4,069	2,422	3,122	481
Webster.	2,388	2,599	2,852	1,568	660
Whitley	4,101	7,502	4,174	5,402	1,027
Wolfe	1,136	1,267	1,297	772	202
Woodford.	3,995	5,890	3,910	4,270	746
Totals	**638,923**	**872,520**	**636,614**	**623,283**	**120,396**

Kentucky Vote Since 1952

1952, Eisenhower, Rep., 495,029; Stevenson, Dem., 495,729; Hamblen, Proh., 1,161; Hass, Soc. Labor, 893; Hallinan, Proh., 336.

1956, Eisenhower, Rep., 572,192; Stevenson, Dem., 476,453; Byrd, States' Rights, 2,657; Holtwick, Proh., 2,145; Hass, Soc. Labor, 358.

1960, Kennedy, Dem., 521,855; Nixon, Rep., 602,607.

1964, Johnson, Dem., 669,659; Goldwater, Rep., 372,977; Kasper, Natl. States Rights, 3,469.

1968, Nixon, Rep., 462,411; Humphrey, Dem., 397,547; Wallace, 3d Party, 193,098; Halstead, Soc. Workers, 2,843.

1972, Nixon, Rep., 676,446; McGovern, Dem., 371,159; Schmitz, Amer., 17,627; Spock, Peoples, 1,118; Jenness, Soc. Workers, 685; Hall, Com., 464.

1976, Carter, Dem., 615,717; Ford, Rep., 531,852; Anderson, Amer., 8,308; McCarthy, Ind., 6,837; Maddox, Amer. Ind., 2,328; MacBride, Libertarian, 814.

1980, Reagan, Rep., 635,274; Carter, Dem., 616,417; Anderson, Ind., 31,127; Clark, Libertarian, 5,531; McCormack, Respect For Life, 4,233; Commoner, Citizens, 1,304; Pulley, Socialist, 393; Hall, Com., 348.

1984, Reagan, Rep., 815,345; Mondale, Dem., 536,756.

1988, Bush, Rep., 734,281; Dukakis, Dem., 580,368; Duke, Pop., 4,494; Paul, Lib., 2,118.

1992, Clinton, Dem., 665,104; Bush, Rep., 617,178; Perot, Ind., 203,944; Marrou, Libertarian, 4,513.

1996, Clinton, Dem., 636,614; Dole, Rep., 623,283; Perot, Ref., 120,396; Browne, Libertarian, 4,009; Phillips, Taxpayers, 2,204; Hagelin, Natural Law, 1,493.

2000, Bush, Rep., 872,520; Gore, Dem., 638,923; Nader, Green, 23,118; Buchanan, Reform, 4,152; Browne, Libertarian, 2,885; Hagelin, Natural Law, 1,513; Phillips, Constitution, 915.

Louisiana

Parish	2000 Gore (D)	2000 Bush (R)	1996 Clinton (D)	1996 Dole (R)	1996 Perot (RF)
Acadia	8,892	13,814	12,300	9,246	2,234
Allen	3,914	4,035	4,930	2,589	1,187
Ascension	13,385	16,818	15,263	10,885	3,027
Assumption	5,222	4,388	6,416	2,698	904
Avoyelles	6,701	7,329	9,689	4,433	1,937
Beauregard	3,958	7,862	4,925	5,526	1,834
Bienville	3,413	3,269	4,335	2,402	457
Bossier.	11,933	23,224	15,504	16,852	2,660
Caddo	47,530	46,807	55,543	38,445	4,821
Calcasieu	33,919	38,086	38,238	26,494	8,281
Caldwell	1,359	2,817	2,117	1,842	514
Cameron	1,435	2,593	2,103	1,365	594
Catahoula.	1,718	2,912	2,692	1,770	615
Claiborne	2,721	3,384	3,609	2,500	530
Concordia.	3,569	4,627	4,565	3,134	855
DeSoto	5,036	5,260	6,221	3,526	646
E. Baton Rouge .	76,516	89,128	83,493	77,811	7,990
East Carroll	1,876	1,280	2,149	1,008	186
East Feliciana. . .	3,870	4,051	4,714	2,949	660
Evangeline	5,763	7,290	7,847	5,278	1,447
Franklin	2,792	5,363	4,076	3,961	814
Grant	2,099	4,784	2,980	3,117	1,055
Iberia	11,762	17,236	15,087	12,014	2,448
Iberville.	8,355	5,573	9,553	4,031	1,076
Jackson	2,582	4,347	3,368	3,030	571
Jefferson	70,411	105,003	80,407	92,820	9,667
Jefferson Davis .	5,162	6,945	6,897	4,311	1,543
Lafayette.	27,190	48,491	32,504	36,419	4,631
Lafourche	14,627	18,575	18,810	12,105	2,984
LaSalle	1,397	4,564	2,543	2,925	947
Lincoln	0,051	9,240	7,903	0,973	701
Livingston.	11,008	24,889	13,276	16,159	4,150
Madison	2,489	2,127	3,085	1,591	315
Morehouse	5,289	6,641	6,160	5,193	963
Natchitoches . . .	6,924	7,332	8,296	5,471	1,053
Orleans	137,630	39,404	144,720	39,576	3,805
Ouachita.	21,457	35,107	24,525	28,559	3,586
Plaquemines . . .	4,425	6,302	5,348	4,493	856
Pointe Coupee . .	5,813	4,710	6,835	3,545	845
Rapides	18,898	28,831	23,004	21,548	4,670
Red River	2,177	2,200	2,641	1,344	268
Richland	3,282	4,895	4,143	3,765	645
Sabine	2,846	5,754	4,263	3,543	1,043
St. Bernard.	11,682	16,255	14,312	13,549	2,664
St. Charles	8,918	11,981	10,612	9,316	1,307
St. Helena	3,059	1,965	3,692	1,455	417
St. James	6,523	3,813	7,247	2,832	608
St. John the Baptist. . . .	9,745	7,423	9,937	6,025	966
St. Landry.	18,067	15,449	20,636	12,273	2,311
St. Martin	9,853	9,961	12,492	6,296	1,607
St. Mary	9,851	11,325	12,402	8,018	1,850
St. Tammany . . .	22,722	59,193	24,281	44,761	4,741
Tangipahoa.	15,843	20,421	18,617	15,517	3,144
Tensas	1,580	1,330	1,882	1,000	176
Terrebonne.	14,414	21,314	18,550	13,944	3,359
Union	3,205	5,772	4,260	4,418	696
Vermilion	8,704	12,495	12,609	7,653	1,954
Vernon	4,655	8,794	6,195	5,449	2,068
Washington	7,399	8,983	9,603	6,642	1,643
Webster	7,197	9,420	9,688	6,153	1,324
W. Baton Rouge .	5,058	4,924	5,697	3,254	799
West Carroll	1,319	3,220	1,853	2,366	461
W. Feliciana	2,187	2,512	2,416	1,616	388
Winn.	2,167	4,028	3,779	2,803	735
Totals.	**792,344**	**927,871**	**927,837**	**712,586**	**123,293**

Louisiana Vote Since 1952

1952, Eisenhower, Rep., 306,925; Stevenson, Dem., 345,027.

1956, Eisenhower, Rep., 329,047; Stevenson, Dem., 243,977; Andrews, States' Rights, 44,520.

1960, Kennedy, Dem., 407,339; Nixon, Rep., 230,890; States' Rights (unpledged), 169,572.

1964, Johnson, Dem., 387,068; Goldwater, Rep., 509,225.

1968, Nixon, Rep., 257,535; Humphrey, Dem., 309,615; Wallace, 3d Party, 530,300.

1972, Nixon, Rep., 686,852; McGovern, Dem., 298,142; Schmitz, Amer., 52,099; Jenness, Soc. Workers, 14,398.

1976, Carter, Dem., 661,365; Ford, Rep., 587,446; Maddox, Amer., 10,058; Hall, Com., 7,417; McCarthy, Ind., 6,588; MacBride, Libertarian, 3,325.

1980, Reagan, Rep., 792,853; Carter, Dem., 708,453; Anderson, Ind., 26,345; Rarick, Amer. Ind., 10,333; Clark, Libertarian, 8,240; Commoner, Citizens, 1,584; DeBerry, Soc. Work., 783.

1984, Reagan, Rep., 1,037,299; Mondale, Dem., 651,586; Bergland, Libertarian, 1,876.

1988, Bush, Rep., 883,702; Dukakis, Dem., 717,460; Duke, Pop., 18,612; Paul, Lib., 4,115.

1992, Clinton, Dem., 815,971; Bush, Rep., 733,386; Perot, Ind., 211,478; Gritz, Populist/America First, 18,545; Marrou, Libertarian, 3,155; Daniels, Ind., 1,663; Phillips, U.S. Taxpayers, 1,552; Fulani, New Alliance, 1,434; LaRouche, Ind., 1,136.

1996, Clinton, Dem., 927,837; Dole, Rep., 712,586; Perot, Ref., 123,293; Browne, Libertarian, 7,499; Nader, Liberty, Ecology, Community, 4,719; Phillips, Taxpayers, 3,366; Hagelin, Natural Law, 2,981; Moorehead, Workers World, 1,678.

2000, Bush, Rep., 927,871; Gore, Dem., 792,344; Nader, Green, 20,473; Buchanan, Reform, 14,356; Phillips, Constitution, 5,483; Browne, Libertarian, 2,951; Harris, Soc. Workers, 1,103; Hagelin, Natural Law, 1,075.

Maine

	2000		1996		
City	Gore (D)	Bush (R)	Clinton (D)	Dole (R)	Perot (RF)
Auburn	6,014	4,568	5,750	3,060	1,484
Augusta	5,116	3,344	5,307	2,353	1,100
Bangor	7,311	6,131	7,609	4,476	1,399
Biddeford	5,383	3,126	5,653	1,768	1,019
Brunswick	5,547	3,767	5,258	2,850	841
Gorham	3,394	3,353	2,990	2,269	710
Lewiston	9,663	5,255	10,275	3,182	2,113
Orono	2,701	1,506	2,748	1,106	369
Portland	20,506	8,838	19,755	7,178	2,255
Presque Isle	2,004	2,231	2,015	1,491	594
Saco	4,783	3,402	4,506	2,140	834
Sanford	4,653	3,871	4,368	2,239	1,524
Scarborough	4,278	4,964	3,906	3,214	805
S. Portland	7,267	4,390	6,777	3,241	906
Waterville	4,279	2,115	4,219	1,478	750
Westbrook	4,316	3,258	4,373	2,186	864
Windham	3,550	3,754	3,251	2,396	898
York	3,708	3,462	2,970	2,525	649
Other	215,478	215,281	211,058	137,226	66,856
Totals	**319,951**	**286,616**	**312,788**	**186,378**	**85,970**

Maine Vote Since 1952

1952, Eisenhower, Rep., 232,353; Stevenson, Dem., 118,806; Hallinan, Prog., 332; Hass, Soc. Labor, 156; Hoopes, Soc., 138; scattered, 1.

1956, Eisenhower, Rep., 249,238; Stevenson, Dem., 102,468.

1960, Kennedy, Dem., 181,159; Nixon, Rep., 240,608.

1964, Johnson, Dem., 262,264; Goldwater, Rep., 118,701.

1968, Nixon, Rep., 169,254; Humphrey, Dem., 217,312; Wallace, 3d Party, 6,370.

1972, Nixon, Rep., 256,458; McGovern, Dem., 160,584; scattered, 229.

1976, Carter, Dem., 232,279; Ford, Rep., 236,320; McCarthy, Ind., 10,874; Bubar, Proh., 3,495.

1980, Reagan, Rep., 238,522; Carter, Dem., 220,974; Anderson, Ind., 53,327; Clark, Libertarian, 5,119; Commoner, Citizens, 4,394; Hall, Com., 591; write-ins, 84.

1984, Reagan, Rep., 336,500; Mondale, Dem., 214,515.

1988, Bush, Rep., 307,131; Dukakis, Dem., 243,569; Paul, Lib., 2,700; Fulani, New Alliance, 1,405.

1992, Clinton, Dem., 263,420; Perot, Ind., 206,820; Bush, Rep., 206,504; Marrou, Libertarian, 1,681.

1996, Clinton, Dem., 312,788; Dole, Rep., 186,378; Perot, Ref., 85,970; Nader, Green, 15,279; Browne, Libertarian, 2,996; Phillips, Taxpayers, 1,517; Hagelin, Natural Law, 825.

2000, Gore, Dem., 319,951; Bush, Rep., 286,616; Nader, Green, 37,127; Buchanan, Reform, 4,443; Browne, Libertarian, 3,074; Phillips, Constitution, 579.

Maryland

	2000		1996		
County	Gore (D)	Bush (R)	Clinton (D)	Dole (R)	Perot (RF)
Allegany	10,894	14,656	11,025	12,136	2,652
Anne Arundel	89,624	104,209	72,147	83,574	14,287
Baltimore	160,635	133,033	132,599	114,449	20,393
Calvert	12,986	16,004	10,008	11,509	1,932
Caroline	3,396	5,300	3,251	3,874	947
Carroll	20,146	41,742	17,122	30,316	4,873
Cecil	12,327	15,494	10,144	10,885	3,124
Charles	21,873	21,768	15,890	17,432	2,333
Dorchester	5,232	5,847	4,613	4,337	1,008
Frederick	30,725	45,350	25,081	34,494	4,989
Garrett	2,872	7,514	3,121	5,400	1,200
Harford	35,665	52,862	29,779	39,686	7,939
Howard	58,556	49,809	47,569	40,849	6,011
Kent	3,627	4,155	3,207	3,055	676
Montgomery	232,453	124,580	198,807	117,730	14,450
Prince George's	214,345	50,017	176,612	52,697	9,153
Queen Anne's	6,257	9,970	5,054	7,147	1,312
St. Mary's	11,912	16,856	9,988	11,835	1,827
Somerset	3,785	3,609	3,557	2,919	613
Talbot	5,854	8,874	4,821	6,997	914
Washington	18,221	27,948	16,481	21,434	3,934
Wicomico	14,469	16,338	12,303	12,687	2,160
Worcester	9,389	10,742	7,587	7,621	1,612
City					
Baltimore	158,765	27,150	145,441	28,467	7,473
Totals	**1,144,008**	**813,827**	**966,207**	**681,530**	**115,812**

Maryland Vote Since 1952

1952, Eisenhower, Rep., 499,424; Stevenson, Dem., 395,337; Hallinan, Prog., 7,313.

1956, Eisenhower, Rep., 559,738; Stevenson, Dem., 372,613.

1960, Kennedy, Dem., 565,800; Nixon, Rep., 489,538.

1964, Johnson, Dem., 730,912; Goldwater, Rep., 385,495; write-in, 50.

1968, Nixon, Rep., 517,995; Humphrey, Dem., 538,310; Wallace, 3d Party, 178,734.

1972, Nixon, Rep., 829,305; McGovern, Dem., 505,781; Schmitz, Amer., 18,726.

1976, Carter, Dem., 759,612; Ford, Rep., 672,661.

1980, Reagan, Rep., 680,606; Carter, Dem., 726,161; Anderson, Ind., 119,537; Clark, Libertarian, 14,192.

1984, Reagan, Rep., 879,918; Mondale, Dem., 787,935; Bergland, Libertarian, 5,721.

1988, Bush, Rep., 876,167; Dukakis, Dem., 826,304; Paul, Lib., 6,748; Fulani, New Alliance, 5,115.

1992, Clinton, Dem., 988,571; Bush, Rep., 707,094; Perot, Ind., 281,414; Marrou, Libertarian, 4,715; Fulani, New Alliance, 2,786.

1996, Clinton, Dem., 966,207; Dole, Rep., 681,530; Perot, Ref., 115,812; Browne, Libertarian, 8,765; Phillips, Taxpayers, 3,402; Hagelin, Natural Law, 2,517.

2000, Gore, Dem., 1,144,008; Bush, Rep., 813,827; Nader, Green, 53,768; Browne, Libertarian, 5,310; Buchanan, Reform., 4,248; Phillips, Constitution, 918.

Massachusetts

	2000		1996		
City	Gore (D)	Bush (R)	Clinton (D)	Dole (R)	Perot (RF)
Boston	132,393	36,389	125,529	33,366	8,428
Brockton	18,563	8,288	16,361	6,972	2,738
Brookline	19,384	4,350	18,812	4,579	799
Cambridge	28,846	5,166	29,913	4,976	1,415
Chicopee	13,236	6,512	14,203	5,188	2,495
Fall River	22,051	5,621	22,796	4,287	2,612
Framingham	17,308	7,347	16,836	6,669	1,700
Lawrence	10,048	3,700	8,615	2,804	1,096
Lowell	17,554	7,790	16,912	5,896	2,911
Lynn	18,836	6,776	18,370	5,634	2,726
Medford	16,776	6,353	16,639	5,844	1,741
New Bedford	23,880	5,473	23,620	4,151	2,547
Newton	29,918	8,132	30,005	8,499	1,674
Quincy	23,117	11,282	23,182	9,824	3,066
Somerville	19,984	4,468	20,206	3,983	1,455
Springfield	29,728	10,288	31,266	9,110	3,407
Waltham	13,736	6,700	13,607	5,830	1,663
Weymouth	15,570	8,884	13,536	6,904	2,181
Worcester	35,231	14,402	35,607	12,879	3,925
Other	1,110,328	710,581	1,075,494	570,663	178,627
Totals	**1,616,487**	**878,502**	**1,571,509**	**718,058**	**227,206**

Massachusetts Vote Since 1952

1952, Eisenhower, Rep., 1,292,325; Stevenson, Dem., 1,083,525; Hallinan, Prog., 4,636; Hass, Soc. Labor, 1,957; Hamblen, Proh., 886; scattered, 69; blanks, 41,150.

1956, Eisenhower, Rep., 1,393,197; Stevenson, Dem., 948,190; Hass, Soc. Labor, 5,573; Holtwick, Proh., 1,205; others, 341.

1960, Kennedy, Dem., 1,487,174; Nixon, Rep., 976,750; Hass, Soc. Labor, 3,892; Decker, Proh., 1,633; others, 31; blank and void, 26,024.

1964, Johnson, Dem., 1,786,422; Goldwater, Rep., 549,727; Hass, Soc. Labor, 4,755; Munn, Proh., 3,735; scattered, 159; blank, 48,104.

1968, Nixon, Rep., 766,844; Humphrey, Dem., 1,469,218; Wallace, 3d Party, 87,088; Blomen, Soc. Labor, 6,180; Munn, Proh., 2,369; scattered, 53; blanks, 25,394.

1972, Nixon, Rep., 1,112,078; McGovern, Dem., 1,332,540; Jenness, Soc. Workers, 10,600; Fisher, Soc. Labor, 129; Schmitz, Amer., 2,877; Spock, Peoples, 101; Hall, Com., 46; Hospers, Libertarian, 43; scattered, 342.

1976, Carter, Dem., 1,429,475; Ford, Rep., 1,030,276; McCarthy, Ind., 65,637; Camejo, Soc. Workers, 8,138; Anderson, Amer., 7,555; La Rouche, U.S. Labor, 4,922; MacBride, Libertarian, 135.

1980, Reagan, Rep., 1,057,631; Carter, Dem., 1,053,802; Anderson, Ind., 382,539; Clark, Libertarian, 22,038; DeBerry, Soc. Workers, 3,735; Commoner, Citizens, 2,056; McReynolds, Soc., 62; Bubar, Statesman, 34; Griswold, Workers World, 19; scattered, 2,382.

1984, Reagan, Rep., 1,310,936; Mondale, Dem., 1,239,606.

1988, Bush, Rep., 1,194,635; Dukakis, Dem., 1,401,415; Paul, Lib., 24,251; Fulani, New Alliance, 9,561.

1992, Clinton, Dem., 1,318,639; Bush, Rep., 805,039; Perot, Ind., 630,731; Marrou, Libertarian, 9,021; Fulani, New Alliance, 3,172; Phillips, U.S. Taxpayers, 2,218; Hagelin, Natural Law, 1,812; LaRouche, Ind., 1,027.

1996, Clinton, Dem., 1,571,509; Dole, Rep., 718,058; Perot, Ref., 227,206; Browne, Libertarian, 20,424; Hagelin, Natural Law, 5,183; Moorehead, Workers World, 3,276.

2000, Gore, Dem., 1,616,487; Bush, Rep., 878,502; Nader, Green, 173,564; Browne, Libertarian, 16,366; Buchanan, Reform, 11,149; Hagelin, Natural Law, 2,884.

Michigan

	2000		1996		
County	Gore (D)	Bush (R)	Clinton (D)	Dole (R)	Perot (RF)
Alcona	2,696	3,152	2,619	2,227	669
Alger	2,071	2,142	2,229	1,429	537
Allegan	15,495	28,197	14,361	20,859	3,269
Alpena	7,053	6,769	7,114	4,525	1,730
Antrim	4,329	6,780	4,226	4,630	1,129
Arenac	3,685	3,421	3,472	2,247	844
Baraga	1,400	1,836	1,601	1,209	460
Barry	9,769	15,716	9,467	11,139	2,282
Bay	28,251	22,150	27,835	16,038	5,410
Benzie	3,546	4,172	3,081	2,856	763
Berrien	28,152	35,689	24,614	28,254	5,958
Branch	6,691	8,743	6,567	6,321	1,779
Calhoun	27,312	26,291	26,287	20,953	4,765
Cass	8,808	10,545	8,207	7,373	2,241
Charlevoix	4,958	7,018	4,689	4,864	1,303
Cheboygan	5,484	6,815	5,018	4,244	1,462
Chippewa	6,370	7,526	6,532	5,137	1,453
Clare	6,287	5,937	6,311	3,742	1,531
Clinton	13,394	18,054	11,945	13,694	2,698
Crawford	2,790	3,345	2,666	2,157	840
Delta	7,970	9,071	8,501	5,925	1,540
Dickinson	5,533	6,932	5,614	4,408	1,478
Eaton	23,211	24,803	19,781	20,092	4,378
Emmet	5,451	8,602	4,892	6,002	1,512
Genesee	119,833	66,641	106,065	49,332	17,671
Gladwin	5,573	5,743	5,494	3,670	1,466
Gogebic	4,066	3,929	4,436	2,769	917
Grand Traverse	14,371	22,358	12,987	16,355	3,527
Gratiot	6,538	8,312	6,793	6,214	1,762
Hillsdale	6,495	10,483	5,955	7,947	2,262
Houghton	5,688	7,895	5,957	5,941	1,584
Huron	6,899	8,911	6,827	6,126	1,811
Ingham	69,231	47,314	63,584	43,096	8,640
Ionia	9,481	13,915	9,261	9,574	2,354
Iosco	6,505	6,345	6,240	4,410	1,710
Iron	3,014	2,967	3,232	2,014	755
Isabella	10,228	10,053	9,635	7,460	2,069
Jackson	28,160	32,066	24,633	24,987	5,968
Kalamazoo	48,807	48,254	45,644	40,703	5,867
Kalkaska	2,774	3,842	2,666	2,455	922
Kent	95,442	148,602	85,912	121,335	14,120
Keweenaw	540	740	572	491	169
Lake	2,584	1,961	2,606	1,213	552
Lapeer	15,749	20,351	14,308	13,369	4,793
Leelanau	4,635	6,840	4,019	5,155	924
Lenawee	18,365	20,681	16,924	14,168	4,167
Livingston	28,780	44,637	22,517	30,598	6,337
Luce	956	1,480	1,107	964	366
Mackinac	2,533	3,272	2,700	2,281	742
Macomb	172,625	164,265	151,430	120,616	29,859
Manistee	5,639	5,401	5,383	3,807	1,230
Marquette	15,503	12,577	15,168	8,805	2,492
Mason	5,579	7,066	5,597	5,066	1,525
Mecosta	6,300	8,072	6,370	5,289	1,373
Menominee	4,597	5,529	4,880	4,038	1,205
Midland	15,959	21,887	15,177	16,547	3,964
Missaukee	2,062	4,274	2,256	3,012	719
Monroe	31,555	28,940	26,072	19,678	6,315
Montcalm	9,627	12,696	10,053	8,679	2,530
Montmorency	2,139	2,750	2,120	1,760	682
Muskegon	37,865	30,028	35,328	21,873	5,794
Newaygo	7,677	11,399	7,614	7,868	2,047
Oakland	281,201	274,319	241,884	219,855	36,709
Oceana	4,597	5,913	4,419	3,947	1,286
Ogemaw	4,896	4,706	4,725	2,904	1,369
Ontonagon	1,514	2,472	2,080	1,523	604
Osceola	4,006	5,680	4,085	3,855	1,068
Oscoda	1,677	2,207	1,652	1,545	503
Otsego	4,034	6,108	3,351	3,638	1,280
Ottawa	29,600	78,703	27,024	61,436	6,275
Presque Isle	3,242	3,660	3,449	2,463	932
Roscommon	6,433	6,190	6,092	4,135	1,539
Saginaw	50,825	41,152	47,579	31,577	8,081
St. Clair	33,002	33,571	28,881	22,495	8,134
St. Joseph	8,574	12,906	8,529	9,764	2,319
Sanilac	7,153	10,966	7,092	7,821	2,265
Schoolcraft	2,036	2,088	2,187	1,200	460
Shiawassee	15,520	15,816	14,662	11,714	3,703
Tuscola	10,845	13,213	10,314	9,154	3,013
Van Buren	13,796	14,792	13,355	11,347	2,946
Washtenaw	86,647	52,459	73,106	40,097	8,020
Wayne	530,414	223,021	504,466	175,886	43,554
Wexford	5,326	7,215	5,510	4,866	1,386
Totals	**2,170,418**	**1,953,139**	**1,989,653**	**1,481,212**	**336,670**

Michigan Vote Since 1952

1952, Eisenhower, Rep., 1,551,529; Stevenson, Dem., 1,230,657; Hamblen, Proh., 10,331; Hallinan, Prog., 3,922; Hass, Soc. Labor, 1,495; Dobbs, Soc. Workers, 655; scattered, 3.

1956, Eisenhower, Rep., 1,713,647; Stevenson, Dem., 1,359,898; Holtwick, Proh., 6,923.

1960, Kennedy, Dem., 1,687,269; Nixon, Rep., 1,620,428; Dobbs, Soc. Workers, 4,347; Decker, Proh., 2,029; Daly, Tax Cut, 1,767; Hass, Soc. Labor, 1,718; Ind. Amer., 539.

1964, Johnson, Dem., 2,136,615; Goldwater, Rep., 1,060,152; DeBerry, Soc. Workers, 3,817; Hass, Soc. Labor, 1,704; Proh. (no candidate listed), 699; scattering, 145.

1968, Nixon, Rep., 1,370,665; Humphrey, Dem., 1,593,082; Wallace, 3d Party, 331,968; Halstead, Soc. Workers, 4,099; Blomen, Soc. Labor, 1,762; Cleaver, New Politics, 4,585; Munn, Proh., 60; scattering, 29.

1972, Nixon, Rep., 1,961,721; McGovern, Dem., 1,459,435; Schmitz, Amer., 63,321; Fisher, Soc. Labor, 2,437; Jenness, Soc. Workers, 1,603; Hall, Com., 1,210.

1976, Carter, Dem., 1,696,714; Ford, Rep., 1,893,742; McCarthy, Ind., 47,905; MacBride, Libertarian, 5,406; Wright, People's, 3,504; Camejo, Soc. Workers, 1,804; LaRouche, U.S. Labor, 1,366; Levin, Soc. Labor, 1,148; scattering, 2,160.

1980, Reagan, Rep., 1,915,225; Carter, Dem., 1,661,532; Anderson, Ind., 275,223; Clark, Libertarian, 41,597; Commoner, Citizens, 11,930; Hall, Com., 3,262; Griswold, Workers World, 30; Greaves, Amer., 21; Bubar, Statesman, 9.

1984, Reagan, Rep., 2,251,571; Mondale, Dem., 1,529,638; Bergland, Libertarian, 10,055.

1988, Bush, Rep., 1,965,486; Dukakis, Dem., 1,675,783; Paul, Lib., 18,336; Fulani, Ind., 2,513.

1992, Clinton, Dem., 1,871,182; Bush, Rep., 1,554,940; Perot, Ind., 824,813; Marrou, Libertarian, 10,175; Phillips, U.S. Taxpayers, 8,263; Hagelin, Natural Law, 2,954.

1996, Clinton, Dem., 1,989,653; Dole, Rep., 1,481,212; Perot, Ref., 336,670; Browne, Libertarian, 27,670; Hagelin, Natural Law, 4,254; Moorehead, Workers World, 3,153; White, Soc. Equality, 1,554.

2000, Gore, Dem., 2,170,418; Bush, Rep., 1,953,139; Nader, Green, 84,165; Browne, Libertarian, 16,711; Phillips, U.S. Taxpayers, 3,791; Hagelin, Natural Law, 2,426.

Minnesota

	2000		1996		
County	Gore (D)	Bush (R)	Clinton (D)	Dole (R)	Perot (RF)
Aitkin	3,830	3,755	3,810	2,327	1,155
Anoka	68,008	69,256	63,756	41,745	16,448
Becker	5,253	8,152	5,911	5,461	1,813
Beltrami	7,301	8,346	8,006	5,806	1,635
Benton	6,009	7,663	6,006	4,835	2,133
Big Stone	1,430	1,370	1,619	990	368
Blue Earth	12,329	12,942	12,420	9,082	3,324
Brown	4,650	7,370	4,864	5,580	1,786
Carlton	8,620	5,578	8,052	4,034	1,591
Carver	12,462	20,790	11,554	12,380	3,781
Cass	5,534	7,134	5,437	4,791	1,620
Chippewa	2,952	2,977	3,178	2,119	782
Chisago	9,593	10,937	8,611	5,984	2,812
Clay	10,128	11,712	10,476	8,764	1,733
Clearwater	1,466	2,137	1,578	1,423	471
Cook	1,171	1,295	1,169	1,010	246
Cottonwood	2,503	3,369	2,737	2,633	741
Crow Wing	11,255	15,035	11,156	10,095	3,423
Dakota	85,446	87,250	77,297	57,244	17,095
Dodge	3,370	4,213	3,233	2,888	1,223
Douglas	6,352	9,811	6,450	6,747	2,093
Faribault	3,624	4,336	3,817	3,272	1,103
Fillmore	5,020	4,646	4,732	3,466	1,575
Freeborn	8,514	6,843	8,458	5,166	2,226
Goodhue	9,981	10,852	9,931	7,293	2,806
Grant	1,507	1,804	1,806	1,284	434
Hennepin	307,599	225,657	285,126	173,887	47,663
Houston	4,502	5,077	4,153	3,674	1,439
Hubbard	3,632	5,307	3,802	3,593	1,141
Isanti	6,247	7,668	6,041	4,450	2,242
Itasca	10,583	9,545	10,706	6,506	2,889
Jackson	2,364	2,773	2,727	2,153	908
Kanabec	2,831	3,480	2,927	1,924	996
Kandiyohi	8,220	10,026	9,009	7,119	2,229
Kittson	1,107	1,353	1,394	1,055	270
Koochiching	2,903	3,523	3,472	2,080	1,098
LacQuiParle	2,244	1,941	2,420	1,447	561
Lake	3,579	2,465	3,388	1,684	752

County	2000 Gore (D)	2000 Bush (R)	1996 Clinton (D)	1996 Dole (R)	1996 Perot (RF)
Lake of the Woods	848	1,216	888	814	287
Le Sueur	5,361	6,138	5,457	3,902	1,699
Lincoln	1,590	1,513	1,641	1,199	504
Lyon	4,737	6,087	5,062	4,932	1,351
McLeod	5,609	8,782	6,027	5,474	2,402
Mahnomen	921	1,122	1,026	877	270
Marshall	1,910	2,912	2,333	2,068	710
Martin	4,166	5,686	4,718	4,303	1,405
Meeker	4,402	5,520	4,531	3,428	1,571
Mille Lacs	4,376	5,223	4,336	2,948	1,467
Morrison	5,274	8,197	5,728	5,054	2,310
Mower	10,693	6,873	10,413	4,994	2,464
Murray	2,093	2,407	2,173	1,907	753
Nicollet	7,041	7,221	6,772	5,057	1,737
Nobles	3,760	4,766	4,106	3,769	1,132
Norman	1,575	1,808	1,875	1,392	425
Olmsted	25,822	30,641	22,857	22,860	5,640
Otter Tail	9,844	16,963	10,519	11,808	3,191
Pennington	2,458	3,380	2,814	2,129	910
Pine	6,148	5,854	5,432	3,080	1,597
Pipestone	1,970	2,693	1,999	2,096	599
Polk	5,764	7,609	6,369	5,563	1,502
Pope	2,771	2,808	2,803	1,992	665
Ramsey	138,470	87,669	133,878	66,954	20,351
Red Lake	830	1,090	1,053	695	334
Redwood	2,681	4,589	2,997	3,700	1,053
Renville	3,533	4,036	3,956	2,887	1,311
Rice	13,140	10,876	12,821	7,016	2,872
Rock	2,081	2,772	2,142	2,169	554
Roseau	2,128	4,695	2,759	2,988	1,081
St. Louis	64,237	35,420	60,736	25,553	11,308
Scott	17,503	23,954	14,657	12,734	4,886
Sherburne	12,109	16,813	10,551	8,699	3,665
Sibley	2,687	4,087	2,769	2,590	1,226
Stearns	24,800	32,402	24,238	21,474	8,150
Steele	6,900	8,223	6,974	5,617	2,197
Stevens	2,434	2,831	2,741	2,141	467
Swift	2,698	2,376	3,054	1,541	690
Todd	4,132	6,031	4,520	4,078	1,958
Traverse	884	1,074	1,135	775	295
Wabasha	4,522	5,245	4,523	3,452	1,474
Wadena	2,251	3,733	2,480	2,696	801
Waseca	3,694	4,608	3,819	3,171	1,385
Washington	49,637	51,502	45,119	31,219	10,106
Watonwan	2,258	2,562	2,534	1,997	711
Wilkin	1,046	2,032	1,319	1,508	358
Winona	11,069	10,773	10,272	7,955	2,907
Wright	16,762	23,861	15,542	13,224	5,550
Yellow Medicine	2,528	2,598	2,741	2,006	818
Totals	**1,168,266**	**1,109,659**	**1,120,438**	**766,476**	**257,704**

Minnesota Vote Since 1952

1952, Eisenhower, Rep., 763,211; Stevenson, Dem., 608,458; Hallinan, Prog., 2,666; Hass, Soc. Labor, 2,383; Hamblen, Proh., 2,147; Dobbs, Soc. Workers, 618.

1956, Eisenhower, Rep., 719,302; Stevenson, Dem., 617,525; Hass, Soc. Labor (Ind. Gov.), 2,080; Dobbs, Soc. Workers, 1,098.

1960, Kennedy, Dem., 779,933; Nixon, Rep., 757,915; Dobbs, Soc. Workers, 3,077; Industrial Gov., 962.

1964, Johnson, Dem., 991,117; Goldwater, Rep., 559,624; DeBerry, Soc. Workers, 1,177; Hass, Industrial Gov., 2,544.

1968, Nixon, Rep., 658,643; Humphrey, Dem., 857,738; Wallace, 3d Party, 68,931; scattered, 2,443; Halstead, Soc. Workers, 808; Blomen, Ind. Gov't., 285; Mitchell, Com., 415; Cleaver, Peace, 935; McCarthy, write-in, 585; scattered, 170.

1972, Nixon, Rep., 898,269; McGovern, Dem., 802,346; Schmitz, Amer., 31,407; Spock, Peoples, 2,805; Fisher, Soc. Labor, 4,261; Jenness, Soc. Workers, 940; Hall, Com., 662; scattered, 962.

1976, Carter, Dem., 1,070,440; Ford, Rep., 819,395; McCarthy, Ind., 35,490; Anderson, Amer., 13,592; Camejo, Soc. Workers, 4,149; MacBride, Libertarian, 3,529; Hall, Com., 1,092.

1980, Reagan, Rep., 873,268; Carter, Dem., 954,173; Anderson, Ind., 174,997; Clark, Libertarian, 31,593; Commoner, Citizens, 8,406; Hall, Com., 1,117; DeBerry, Soc. Workers, 711; Griswold, Workers World, 698; McReynolds, Soc., 536; write-ins, 281.

1984, Reagan, Rep., 1,032,603; Mondale, Dem., 1,036,364; Bergland, Libertarian, 2,996.

1988, Bush, Rep., 962,337; Dukakis, Dem., 1,109,471; McCarthy, Minn. Prog., 5,403; Paul, Lib., 5,109.

1992, Clinton, Dem., 1,020,997; Bush, Rep., 747,841; Perot, Ind., 562,506; Marrou, Libertarian, 3,373; Gritz, Populist/America First, 3,363; Hagelin, Natural Law, 1,406.

1996, Clinton, Dem., 1,120,438; Dole, Rep., 766,476; Perot, Ref., 257,704; Nader, Green, 24,908; Browne, Libertarian, 8,271; Peron, Grass Roots, 4,898; Phillips, Taxpayers, 3,416; Hagelin, Natural Law, 1,808; Birrenbach, Ind. Grass Roots, 787; Harris, Soc. Workers, 684; White, Soc. Equality, 347.

2000, Gore, Dem., 1,168,266; Bush, Rep., 1,109,659; Nader, Green, 126,696; Buchanan, Reform Minnesota, 22,166; Browne, Libertarian, 5,282; Phillips, Constitution, 3,272; Hagelin, Reform, 2,294; Harris, Soc. Workers, 1,022.

Mississippi

County	2000 Gore (D)	2000 Bush (R)	1996 Clinton (D)	1996 Dole (R)	1996 Perot (RF)
Adams	8,065	6,691	8,218	5,378	779
Alcorn	5,059	7,254	4,964	4,960	929
Amite	2,673	3,677	2,824	2,521	351
Attala	2,922	4,206	3,092	3,130	383
Benton	1,886	1,561	1,944	993	209
Bolivar	8,436	4,847	8,670	4,027	320
Calhoun	2,251	3,448	2,178	2,470	351
Carroll	1,726	3,165	2,041	2,629	245
Chickasaw	3,519	3,549	2,971	2,535	401
Choctaw	1,278	2,398	1,247	1,715	247
Claiborne	3,670	883	3,739	784	103
Clarke	2,368	4,503	2,337	3,470	366
Clay	4,515	3,570	4,267	2,948	337
Coahoma	5,662	3,695	5,776	3,441	256
Copiah	4,845	5,643	4,415	4,138	375
Covington	2,623	4,180	2,628	3,219	417
DeSoto	9,586	24,879	10,282	18,135	2,399
Forrest	8,500	13,281	7,965	11,278	1,094
Franklin	1,486	2,427	1,381	1,586	329
George	1,977	5,143	1,888	3,311	710
Greene	1,317	3,082	1,347	1,947	322
Grenada	3,813	4,743	4,402	4,527	470
Hancock	4,801	9,326	4,303	5,820	1,143
Harrison	19,142	32,256	18,775	25,486	3,726
Hinds	46,789	37,753	45,410	35,653	2,929
Holmes	5,447	1,937	4,720	1,536	140
Humphreys	2,288	1,628	2,305	1,382	110
Issaquena	555	366	546	269	42
Itawamba	2,994	5,424	2,987	3,490	732
Jackson	14,193	30,068	13,598	24,918	2,947
Jasper	3,104	3,294	3,170	2,615	353
Jefferson	2,786	600	2,531	489	89
Jefferson Davis	2,835	2,437	2,663	1,890	264
Jones	7,713	16,341	7,360	13,020	1,362
Kemper	2,311	1,915	2,048	1,439	188
Lafayette	5,139	7,081	4,646	4,753	580
Lamar	3,478	12,795	3,169	8,609	925
Lauderdale	8,412	17,315	8,668	15,055	1,036
Lawrence	2,841	3,674	2,481	2,392	471
Leake	2,793	4,114	2,902	3,017	406
Lee	9,142	15,551	8,438	11,815	1,361
Leflore	6,401	4,626	6,853	4,456	240
Lincoln	4,358	8,540	4,294	5,960	778
Lowndes	7,537	11,404	6,220	9,169	750
Madison	10,416	19,109	9,354	14,467	759
Marion	4,114	6,796	4,334	5,023	585
Marshall	7,735	4,723	7,521	3,272	482
Monroe	5,783	7,397	5,184	5,206	889
Montgomery	2,187	2,630	1,970	1,943	197
Neshoba	2,563	6,409	2,646	4,545	560
Newton	2,147	5,540	2,163	4,223	464
Noxubee	3,383	1,530	2,801	1,287	119
Oktibbeha	6,443	7,959	5,923	6,142	395
Panola	5,880	5,424	5,408	3,701	513
Pearl River	4,611	11,575	4,892	8,212	1,190
Perry	1,285	3,026	1,413	2,178	450
Pike	6,544	7,464	6,302	5,403	683
Pontotoc	2,771	6,601	2,597	4,289	774
Prentiss	3,287	5,101	3,053	3,473	574
Quitman	2,103	1,280	2,186	1,121	126
Rankin	8,050	32,983	8,614	24,585	2,093
Scott	3,548	5,601	3,163	4,018	466
Sharkey	1,706	1,074	1,566	906	70
Simpson	3,227	6,254	2,851	4,455	525
Smith	1,620	4,838	1,858	3,371	522
Stone	1,677	3,702	1,551	2,288	417
Sunflower	4,981	3,369	4,960	2,926	290
Tallahatchie	3,041	2,428	2,990	1,676	251
Tate	3,441	5,148	3,195	3,694	406
Tippah	2,908	5,381	2,992	3,249	661
Tishomingo	2,747	4,122	2,709	2,766	609
Tunica	1,539	792	1,263	557	55
Union	3,094	6,087	3,316	4,375	788
Walthall	2,356	3,476	2,240	2,239	444
Warren	7,485	10,892	8,774	9,261	1,259
Washington	10,405	7,367	10,053	6,762	437
Wayne	2,981	4,635	2,652	3,219	595
Webster	1,426	3,069	1,379	2,254	255
Wilkinson	2,551	1,423	2,807	1,016	226
Winston	3,672	4,645	3,488	3,498	434
Yalobusha	2,674	2,470	2,437	1,711	332
Yazoo	4,997	5,254	4,754	4,152	362
Totals	**404,614**	**572,844**	**394,022**	**439,838**	**52,222**

Mississippi Vote Since 1952

1952, Eisenhower, Ind. vote pledged to Rep. candidate, 112,966; Stevenson, Dem., 172,566.
1956, Eisenhower, Rep., 56,372; Stevenson, Dem., 144,498; Black and Tan Grand Old Party, 4,313; total, 60,685; Byrd, Ind., 42,966.
1960, Kennedy, Dem., 108,362; Democratic unpledged electors, 116,248; Nixon, Rep., 73,561. Mississippi's victorious slate of 8 unpledged Democratic electors cast their votes for Sen. Harry F. Byrd (D, VA).
1964, Johnson, Dem., 52,618; Goldwater, Rep., 356,528.
1968, Nixon, Rep., 88,516; Humphrey, Dem., 150,644; Wallace, 3d Party, 415,349.
1972, Nixon, Rep., 505,125; McGovern, Dem., 126,782; Schmitz, Amer., 11,598; Jenness, Soc. Workers, 2,458.
1976, Carter, Dem., 381,309; Ford, Rep., 366,846; Anderson, Amer., 6,678; McCarthy, Ind., 4,074; Maddox, Ind., 4,049; Camejo, Soc. Workers, 2,805; MacBride, Libertarian, 2,609.
1980, Reagan, Rep., 441,089; Carter, Dem., 429,281; Anderson, Ind., 12,036; Clark, Libertarian, 5,465; Griswold, Workers World, 2,402; Pulley, Soc. Workers, 2,347.
1984, Reagan, Rep., 582,377; Mondale, Dem., 352,192; Bergland, Libertarian, 2,336.
1988, Bush, Rep., 557,890; Dukakis, Dem., 363,921; Duke, Ind., 4,232; Paul, Lib., 3,329.
1992, Bush, Rep., 487,793; Clinton, Dem., 400,258; Perot, Ind., 85,626; Fulani, New Alliance, 2,625; Marrou, Libertarian, 2,154; Phillips, U.S. Taxpayers, 1,652, Hagelin, Natural Law, 1,140.
1996, Dole, Rep., 439,838; Clinton, Dem., 394,022; Perot, Ind. (Ref.), 52,222; Browne, Libertarian, 2,809; Phillips, Taxpayers, 2,314; Hagelin, Natural Law, 1,447; Collins, Ind., 1,205.
2000, Bush, Rep., 572,844; Gore, Dem., 404,614; Nader, Ind., 8,122; Phillips, Constitution, 3,267; Buchanan, Reform, 2,265; Browne, Libertarian, 2,009; Harris, Ind., 613; Hagelin, Natural Law, 450.

Missouri

	2000		1996		
County	Gore (D)	Bush (R)	Clinton (D)	Dole (R)	Perot (RF)
Adair	4,101	6,050	4,441	4,656	1,170
Andrew	2,795	4,257	2,807	3,281	964
Atchison	1,013	1,798	1,266	1,327	367
Audrain	4,551	5,256	4,600	3,055	1,046
Barry	4,135	7,885	4,352	5,855	1,494
Barton	1,424	3,836	1,625	2,812	563
Bates	3,386	4,245	3,224	2,904	949
Benton	3,150	4,218	2,996	2,095	764
Bollinger	1,692	3,487	2,044	2,420	506
Boone	28,811	28,426	24,984	22,047	4,083
Buchanan	17,085	16,423	15,848	12,610	4,248
Butler	4,996	9,111	5,780	6,996	1,414
Caldwell	1,488	2,220	1,487	1,464	468
Callaway	6,708	8,238	5,880	5,567	1,530
Camden	6,323	10,358	5,566	7,190	1,809
Cape Girardeau	9,334	19,832	9,957	15,557	1,861
Carroll	1,620	2,880	2,080	1,839	580
Carter	997	1,730	1,172	1,180	301
Cass	14,921	20,113	11,743	13,495	3,474
Cedar	1,979	3,530	2,027	2,484	658
Chariton	1,792	2,300	2,072	1,508	423
Christian	7,896	14,824	6,627	9,477	2,301
Clark	1,812	1,899	1,749	1,081	458
Clay	39,084	39,083	32,603	28,935	7,048
Clinton	3,994	4,323	3,445	2,780	848
Cole	12,056	20,167	10,857	16,140	2,121
Cooper	2,567	4,072	2,753	2,900	891
Crawford	3,350	4,754	3,349	2,990	1,223
Dade	1,193	2,468	1,243	1,822	447
Dallas	2,311	3,723	2,277	2,554	787
Daviess	1,367	2,011	1,534	1,321	466
DeKalb	1,562	2,363	1,679	1,627	492
Dent	1,839	3,996	2,234	2,542	693
Douglas	1,546	3,599	1,744	2,601	775
Dunklin	4,947	5,426	5,428	3,766	934
Franklin	16,172	21,863	13,908	13,715	5,517
Gasconade	2,257	4,190	2,104	2,997	820
Gentry	1,271	1,771	1,493	1,361	416
Greene	41,091	59,178	39,300	48,193	8,569
Grundy	1,563	2,976	2,073	1,883	631
Harrison	1,328	2,552	1,628	1,737	484
Henry	4,459	5,120	4,579	3,260	1,231
Hickory	1,961	2,172	1,858	1,491	531
Holt	871	1,738	1,144	1,323	314
Howard	1,944	2,414	2,014	1,545	568
Howell	4,641	9,018	5,261	5,991	2,066
Iron	2,044	2,237	2,221	1,328	568
Jackson	160,419	104,418	140,317	85,534	21,047
Jasper	11,737	24,899	11,462	18,361	3,545
Jefferson	38,616	36,766	32,073	23,877	8,893
Johnson	6,926	9,339	6,220	6,276	1,911
Knox	787	1,226	891	862	254
Laclede	4,183	8,556	4,047	5,887	1,459
Lafayette	6,343	7,849	6,118	5,489	1,516
Lawrence	4,235	8,305	4,465	6,099	1,613
Lewis	2,023	2,388	2,050	1,453	644
Lincoln	6,961	8,549	5,644	4,897	1,881
Linn	2,646	3,246	2,967	2,097	781
Livingston	2,425	3,709	2,913	2,384	777
McDonald	1,866	4,460	1,980	3,008	923
Macon	2,817	4,232	2,937	2,634	848
Madison	1,828	2,460	2,351	1,595	625
Maries	1,554	2,216	1,540	1,560	516
Marion	4,993	6,550	4,924	4,653	1,082
Mercer	555	1,250	700	660	208
Miller	3,217	5,945	3,110	4,387	1,185
Mississippi	2,756	2,395	3,235	1,595	380
Moniteau	2,176	3,764	2,129	2,603	693
Monroe	1,860	2,175	1,938	1,333	532
Montgomery	2,092	3,106	2,277	2,124	772
Morgan	3,235	4,460	3,006	3,059	1,006
New Madrid	3,738	3,416	4,451	2,417	663
Newton	6,447	14,232	5,840	10,067	1,995
Nodaway	3,553	5,161	3,966	3,362	1,043
Oregon	1,568	2,521	1,795	1,502	475
Osage	1,938	4,154	2,045	2,890	608
Ozark	1,432	2,663	1,445	1,882	595
Pemiscot	3,245	2,750	3,371	1,820	458
Perry	2,085	4,667	2,517	3,427	777
Pettis	5,866	9,533	6,057	7,336	1,716
Phelps	6,262	9,444	6,405	6,990	1,703
Pike	3,557	3,648	3,495	2,209	916
Platte	15,325	17,785	12,705	13,332	3,035
Polk	3,606	6,430	3,307	4,521	1,169
Pulaski	3,800	6,531	3,783	4,089	1,141
Putnam	708	1,593	857	1,091	276
Ralls	2,033	2,446	1,998	1,513	520
Randolph	4,116	4,844	4,502	3,274	1,130
Ray	4,970	4,517	4,714	2,884	1,113
Reynolds	1,298	1,762	1,631	903	386
Ripley	1,820	3,121	2,081	1,988	530
St. Charles	53,806	72,114	41,369	47,705	11,591
St. Clair	1,866	2,731	1,974	1,815	650
St. Francois	9,075	9,327	9,034	6,200	2,266
St. Louis	250,631	224,689	225,524	196,096	34,850
Ste. Genevieve	3,600	3,505	3,597	2,078	942
Saline	4,585	4,572	4,765	2,931	1,090
Schuyler	808	1,159	857	777	287
Scotland	790	1,335	990	773	326
Scott	6,452	8,999	7,011	6,641	1,483
Shannon	1,430	2,245	1,882	1,339	524
Shelby	1,262	1,936	1,410	1,213	413
Stoddard	4,476	7,727	4,883	5,020	1,185
Stone	4,055	7,793	3,497	5,223	1,353
Sullivan	1,127	1,877	1,402	1,275	340
Taney	5,092	9,647	4,623	6,844	1,580
Texas	3,486	6,136	3,897	4,065	1,335
Vernon	3,156	4,985	3,363	3,123	1,135
Warren	4,524	5,979	3,443	3,768	1,254
Washington	4,047	4,020	4,315	2,259	1,169
Wayne	2,387	3,346	2,754	2,172	674
Webster	4,174	7,350	3,855	4,958	1,214
Worth	469	651	572	540	150
Wright	2,250	5,391	2,280	3,754	890
City					
St. Louis	96,557	24,799	91,233	22,121	7,276
Totals	**1,111,138**	**1,189,924**	**1,025,935**	**890,016**	**217,188**

Missouri Vote Since 1952

1952, Eisenhower, Rep., 959,429; Stevenson, Dem., 929,830; Hallinan, Prog., 987; Hamblen, Proh., 885; MacArthur, Christian Nationalist, 302; America First, 233; Hoopes, Soc., 227; Hass, Soc. Labor, 169.
1956, Stevenson, Dem., 918,273; Eisenhower, Rep., 914,299.
1960, Kennedy, Dem., 972,201; Nixon, Rep., 962,221.
1964, Johnson, Dem., 1,164,344; Goldwater, Rep., 653,535.
1968, Nixon, Rep., 811,932; Humphrey, Dem., 791,444; Wallace, 3d Party, 206,126.
1972, Nixon, Rep., 1,154,058; McGovern, Dem., 698,531.
1976, Carter, Dem., 999,163; Ford, Rep., 928,808; McCarthy, Ind., 24,329.
1980, Reagan, Rep., 1,074,181; Carter, Dem., 931,182; Anderson, Ind., 77,920; Clark, Libertarian, 14,422; DeBerry, Soc. Workers, 1,515; Commoner, Citizens, 573; write-ins, 31.
1984, Reagan, Rep., 1,274,188; Mondale, Dem., 848,583.
1988, Bush, Rep., 1,084,953; Dukakis, Dem., 1,001,619; Fulani, New Alliance, 6,656; Paul, write-in, 434.
1992, Clinton, Dem., 1,053,873; Bush, Rep., 811,159; Perot, Ind., 518,741; Marrou, Libertarian, 7,497.
1996, Clinton, Dem., 1,025,935; Dole, Rep., 890,016; Perot, Ref., 217,188; Phillips, Taxpayers, 11,521; Browne, Libertarian, 10,522; Hagelin, Natural Law, 2,287.
2000, Bush, Rep., 1,189,924; Gore, Dem., 1,111,138; Nader, Green, 38,515; Buchanan, Reform, 9,818; Browne, Libertarian, 7,436; Phillips, Constitution, 1,957; Hagelin, Natural Law, 1,104.

Montana

County	2000 Gore (D)	2000 Bush (R)	1996 Clinton (D)	1996 Dole (R)	1996 Perot (RF)
Beaverhead...	799	3,113	1,164	2,414	412
Big Horn.....	2,345	1,651	2,453	1,336	424
Blaine.......	1,246	1,410	1,316	1,127	435
Broadwater...	462	1,488	603	1,029	318
Carbon......	1,434	3,008	1,854	2,147	713
Carter.......	53	573	150	522	89
Cascade.....	13,137	18,164	15,707	14,291	4,749
Chouteau.....	686	2,039	1,039	1,660	434
Custer.......	1,501	3,156	2,115	2,467	695
Daniels......	303	750	510	558	240
Dawson......	1,364	2,723	1,903	1,890	842
Deer Lodge...	2,672	1,493	3,331	883	772
Fallon........	256	1,061	452	778	276
Fergus.......	1,352	4,353	1,866	3,671	605
Flathead.....	8,329	22,519	10,452	16,542	4,786
Gallatin......	10,009	18,833	10,972	14,559	3,146
Garfield......	61	651	107	562	69
Glacier.......	2,211	1,709	2,292	1,270	491
Golden Valley.	88	405	128	284	73
Granite......	295	1,181	429	733	228
Hill.........	2,760	3,392	3,517	2,601	950
Jefferson.....	1,513	3,308	1,775	2,248	729
Judith Basin...	278	1,057	452	753	126
Lake........	3,884	6,441	4,195	4,723	1,804
Lewis & Clark.	9,982	15,091	11,535	11,665	3,140
Liberty.......	243	752	379	634	144
Lincoln.......	1,629	5,578	2,705	3,552	1,425
McCone.......	267	827	390	615	244
Madison......	758	2,656	955	1,984	516
Meagher.....	176	698	281	505	142
Mineral......	382	1,078	658	549	383
Missoula.....	17,241	21,474	21,874	16,034	5,586
Musselshell...	512	1,582	652	1,121	291
Park.........	2,154	4,523	2,564	3,837	959
Petroleum....	36	254	62	186	36
Phillips.......	423	1,727	705	1,392	401
Pondera......	792	1,948	1,123	1,438	383
Powder River..	115	860	236	663	137
Powell.......	638	1,971	952	1,274	531
Prairie.......	164	541	259	417	99
Ravalli.......	4,451	11,241	5,200	8,138	2,731
Richland.....	1,018	2,858	1,614	2,021	906
Roosevelt....	2,059	1,605	2,118	1,209	645
Rosebud.....	1,394	1,826	1,681	1,413	547
Sanders......	1,165	3,144	1,573	2,043	990
Sheridan.....	702	1,176	1,187	832	408
Silver Bow....	8,967	6,299	11,199	3,909	2,447
Stillwater.....	925	2,765	1,282	1,871	618
Sweet Grass..	305	1,450	469	1,109	186
Teton........	847	2,294	1,188	1,701	416
Toole........	630	1,639	874	1,203	386
Treasure.....	106	344	171	237	87
Valley........	1,273	2,500	1,674	1,838	645
Wheatland....	243	708	391	563	127
Wibaux......	121	369	197	284	128
Yellowstone...	20,370	33,922	22,992	26,367	6,139
Totals.......	**137,126**	**240,178**	**167,922**	**179,652**	**55,229**

Montana Vote Since 1952

1952, Eisenhower, Rep., 157,394; Stevenson, Dem., 106,213; Hallinan, Prog., 723; Hamblen, Proh., 548; Hoopes, Soc., 159.

1956, Eisenhower, Rep., 154,933; Stevenson, Dem., 116,238.

1960, Kennedy, Dem., 134,891; Nixon, Rep., 141,841; Decker, Proh., 456; Dobbs, Soc. Workers, 391.

1964, Johnson, Dem., 164,246; Goldwater, Rep., 113,032; Kasper, Natl. States' Rights, 519; Munn, Proh., 499; DeBerry, Soc. Workers, 332.

1968, Nixon, Rep., 138,835; Humphrey, Dem., 114,117; Wallace, 3d Party, 20,015; Halstead, Soc. Workers, 457; Munn, Proh., 510; Caton, New Reform, 470.

1972, Nixon, Rep., 183,976; McGovern, Dem., 120,197; Schmitz, Amer., 13,430.

1976, Carter, Dem., 149,259; Ford, Rep., 173,703; Anderson, Amer., 5,772.

1980, Reagan, Rep., 206,814; Carter, Dem., 118,032; Anderson, Ind., 29,281; Clark, Libertarian, 9,825.

1984, Reagan, Rep., 232,450; Mondale, Dem., 146,742; Bergland, Libertarian, 5,185.

1988, Bush, Rep., 190,412; Dukakis, Dem., 168,936; Paul, Lib., 5,047; Fulani, New Alliance, 1,279.

1992, Clinton, Dem., 154,507; Bush, Rep., 144,207; Perot, Ind., 107,225; Gritz, Populist/America First, 3,658.

1996, Dole, Rep., 179,652; Clinton, Dem., 167,922; Perot, Ref., 55,229; Browne, Libertarian, 2,526; Hagelin, Natural Law, 1,754.

2000, Bush, Rep, 240,178; Gore, Dem., 137,126; Nader, Green, 24,437; Buchanan, Reform, 5,697; Browne, Libertarian, 1,718; Phillips, Constitution, 1,155; Hagelin, Natural Law, 675.

Nebraska

County	2000 Gore (D)	2000 Bush (R)	1996 Clinton (D)	1996 Dole (R)	1996 Perot (RF)
Adams.......	3,686	8,162	3,935	6,924	1,513
Antelope.....	678	2,562	884	2,005	457
Arthur........	26	235	25	187	46
Banner.......	65	390	62	309	30
Blaine........	43	299	53	284	39
Boone........	575	2,196	806	1,695	424
Box Butte.....	1,614	3,208	1,782	2,458	695
Boyd.........	265	931	372	778	181
Brown........	250	1,375	359	1,105	289
Buffalo.......	3,927	11,931	4,277	10,004	1,484
Burt.........	1,223	2,056	1,237	1,707	497
Butler........	1,028	2,638	1,099	2,042	512
Cass.........	3,656	6,144	3,477	4,878	1,239
Cedar........	1,062	2,989	1,218	2,171	739
Chase........	306	1,505	365	1,277	197
Cherry.......	446	2,322	551	1,905	332
Cheyenne.....	844	3,207	1,059	2,571	287
Clay.........	774	2,326	880	1,982	425
Colfax........	863	2,338	1,065	1,954	492
Cuming.......	857	3,232	1,033	2,520	503
Custer.......	976	4,245	1,293	3,453	615
Dakota.......	2,695	3,119	2,632	2,592	721
Dawes.......	823	2,549	1,108	1,991	442
Dawson......	1,740	5,511	2,180	4,794	1,044
Deuel........	213	783	245	629	111
Dixon........	820	1,834	931	1,478	414
Dodge.......	5,021	8,871	5,181	7,484	1,894
Douglas......	73,347	101,025	70,708	92,334	14,863
Dundy........	179	801	224	752	112
Fillmore......	848	2,024	1,058	1,696	321
Franklin......	420	1,196	483	1,013	215
Frontier.......	244	1,102	310	901	169
Furnas.......	534	1,849	663	1,475	207
Gage........	3,516	5,538	4,008	4,413	1,346
Garden.......	203	963	279	851	155
Garfield......	202	718	249	625	111
Gosper.......	228	757	275	609	150
Grant........	49	324	84	258	55
Greeley.......	416	839	472	642	155
Hall.........	5,952	11,803	6,708	10,183	2,403
Hamilton......	1,066	3,251	1,172	2,623	457
Harlan.......	438	1,358	520	1,120	203
Hayes........	66	486	87	439	39
Hitchcock.....	312	1,126	409	977	173
Holt.........	846	3,954	1,107	3,436	677
Hooker.......	74	317	115	308	83
Howard.......	955	1,760	853	1,294	417
Jefferson.....	1,361	2,351	1,520	1,979	495
Johnson......	794	1,210	770	1,009	309
Kearney......	680	2,333	782	1,953	296
Keith........	778	2,953	830	2,504	460
Keya Paha....	78	422	94	385	47
Kimball.......	379	1,379	527	1,011	212
Knox........	1,037	2,784	1,266	2,123	531
Lancaster.....	44,650	55,514	43,339	44,812	8,595
Lincoln......	5,205	9,220	5,165	7,482	2,043
Logan........	60	336	79	294	72
Loup........	84	284	74	229	28
McPherson....	48	244	50	233	33
Madison......	2,772	9,636	3,047	7,965	1,554
Merrick.......	848	2,380	997	2,084	449
Morrill.......	460	1,597	620	1,296	262
Nance........	497	1,105	585	892	238
Nemaha......	1,063	2,177	1,232	1,888	485
Nuckolls......	644	1,701	757	1,383	306
Otoe........	2,208	4,178	2,279	3,290	877
Pawnee......	522	937	580	766	207
Perkins.......	243	1,170	352	1,018	163
Phelps.......	934	3,575	1,071	3,015	465
Pierce.......	570	2,534	697	1,923	446
Platte........	2,612	9,861	3,010	7,948	1,353
Polk.........	610	1,925	750	1,504	268
Red Willow....	1,188	3,680	1,365	3,112	499
Richardson....	1,382	2,623	1,517	2,089	633
Rock........	141	725	180	564	135
Saline........	2,321	2,581	2,523	1,945	689
Sarpy........	14,637	28,979	12,806	23,023	3,722
Saunders.....	2,852	5,688	2,777	4,514	1,223
Scotts Bluff....	3,937	9,397	4,547	7,641	1,251
Seward.......	2,250	4,457	2,432	3,479	745
Sheridan......	392	2,105	573	1,834	289
Sherman.....	564	1,072	567	822	266
Sioux........	98	629	138	551	75
Stanton.......	500	1,895	577	1,457	386
Thayer.......	821	2,096	933	1,698	334
Thomas.......	55	329	64	303	62
Thurston......	924	1,040	962	835	293
Valley........	583	1,610	758	1,346	274
Washington...	2,550	5,758	2,248	4,391	971
Wayne.......	1,001	2,774	1,048	2,150	440

	2000		1996		
County	Gore (D)	Bush (R)	Clinton (D)	Dole (R)	Perot (RF)
Webster	584	1,302	621	1,094	236
Wheeler	85	351	106	241	69
York	1,407	4,816	1,653	4,266	559
Totals	**231,780**	**433,862**	**236,761**	**363,467**	**71,278**

Nebraska Vote Since 1952

1952, Eisenhower, Rep., 421,603; Stevenson, Dem., 188,057.
1956, Eisenhower, Rep., 378,108; Stevenson, Dem., 199,029.
1960, Kennedy, Dem., 232,542; Nixon, Rep., 380,553.
1964, Johnson, Dem., 307,307; Goldwater, Rep., 276,847.
1968, Nixon, Rep., 321,163; Humphrey, Dem., 170,784; Wallace, 3d Party, 44,904.
1972, Nixon, Rep., 406,298; McGovern, Dem., 169,991; scattered, 817.
1976, Carter, Dem., 233,287; Ford, Rep., 359,219; McCarthy, Ind., 9,383; Maddox, Amer. Ind., 3,378; MacBride, Libertarian, 1,476.
1980, Reagan, Rep., 419,214; Carter, Dem., 166,424; Anderson, Ind., 44,854; Clark, Libertarian, 9,041.
1984, Reagan, Rep., 459,135; Mondale, Dem., 187,475; Bergland, Libertarian, 2,075.
1988, Bush, Rep., 397,956; Dukakis, Dem., 259,235; Paul, Lib., 2,534; Fulani, New Alliance, 1,740.
1992, Bush, Rep., 343,678; Clinton, Dem., 216,864; Perot, Ind., 174,104; Marrou, Libertarian, 1,340.
1996, Dole, Rep., 363,467; Clinton, Dem., 236,761; Perot, Ref., 71,278; Browne, Libertarian, 2,792; Phillips, Ind., 1,928; Hagelin, Natural Law, 1,189.
2000, Bush, Rep., 433,862; Gore, Dem., 231,780; Nader, Green, 24,540; Buchanan, Ind., 3,646; Browne, Libertarian, 2,245; Hagelin, Natural Law, 478; Phillips, Ind., 468.

Nevada

	2000		1996		
County	Gore (D)	Bush (R)	Clinton (D)	Dole (R)	Perot (RF)
Churchill	2,191	6,237	2,282	4,369	821
Clark	196,100	170,932	127,963	103,431	23,177
Douglas	5,837	11,193	5,109	8,828	1,486
Elko	2,542	11,025	3,149	6,512	1,539
Esmeralda	116	333	140	277	91
Eureka	150	632	158	412	90
Humboldt	1,128	3,638	1,467	2,334	603
Lander	395	1,619	660	1,107	361
Lincoln	461	1,372	499	936	255
Lyon	3,955	7,270	3,419	4,753	1,104
Mineral	916	1,227	1,068	814	361
Nye	4,525	6,904	3,300	3,979	1,544
Pershing	476	1,221	565	743	203
Storey	666	1,014	614	705	244
Washoe	52,097	63,640	44,915	49,477	9,970
White Pine	1,069	2,234	1,397	1,399	546
City					
Carson City	7,354	11,084	7,269	9,168	1,591
Totals	**279,978**	**301,575**	**203,974**	**199,244**	**43,986**

Nevada Vote Since 1952

1952, Eisenhower, Rep., 50,502; Stevenson, Dem., 31,688.
1956, Eisenhower, Rep., 56,049; Stevenson, Dem., 40,640.
1960, Kennedy, Dem., 54,880; Nixon, Rep., 52,387.
1964, Johnson, Dem., 79,339; Goldwater, Rep., 56,094.
1968, Nixon, Rep., 73,188; Humphrey, Dem., 60,598; Wallace, 3d Party, 20,432.
1972, Nixon, Rep., 115,750; McGovern, Dem., 66,016.
1976, Carter, Dem., 92,479; Ford, Rep., 101,273; MacBride, Libertarian, 1,519; Maddox, Amer. Ind., 1,497; scattered, 5,108.
1980, Reagan, Rep., 155,017; Carter, Dem., 66,666; Anderson, Ind., 17,651; Clark, Libertarian, 4,358.
1984, Reagan, Rep., 188,770; Mondale, Dem., 91,655; Bergland, Libertarian, 2,292.
1988, Bush, Rep., 206,040; Dukakis, Dem., 132,738; Paul, Lib., 3,520; Fulani, New Alliance, 835.
1992, Clinton, Dem., 189,148; Bush, Rep., 175,828; Perot, Ind., 132,580; Gritz, Populist/America First, 2,892; Marrou, Libertarian, 1,835.
1996, Clinton, Dem., 203,974; Dole, Rep., 199,244; Perot, Ref., 43,986; "None of These Candidates," 5,608; Nader, Green, 4,730; Browne, Libertarian, 4,460; Phillips, Ind. Amer., 1,732; Hagelin, Natural Law, 545.
2000, Bush, Rep., 301,575; Gore, Dem., 279,978; Nader, Green, 15,008; Buchanan, Citizens First, 4,747; "None of these candidates," 3,315; Browne, Libertarian, 3,311; Phillips, Ind. Amer., 621; Hagelin, Natural Law, 415.

New Hampshire

	2000		1996		
City	Gore (D)	Bush (R)	Clinton (D)	Dole (R)	Perot (RF)
Concord	10,025	6,981	9,719	5,082	1,164
Derry	5,530	6,093	4,814	4,503	1,083
Dover	6,812	5,008	6,332	3,752	930
Hudson	4,573	4,527	3,841	3,167	976
Keene	5,856	3,704	5,401	2,910	621
Laconia	3,015	3,814	2,865	2,842	508
Londonderry	4,348	5,463	3,666	4,076	838
Manchester	19,991	19,152	20,185	14,704	3,053
Merrimack	5,571	6,239	4,934	4,499	949
Nashua	18,398	14,803	16,584	11,479	2,858
Portsmouth	6,862	3,896	6,343	3,014	661
Rochester	5,401	5,522	5,489	3,650	1,108
Salem	5,711	5,713	5,164	4,257	1,241
Other	164,255	182,644	150,829	128,551	32,397
Totals	**266,318**	**273,559**	**246,166**	**196,486**	**48,387**

New Hampshire Vote Since 1952

1952, Eisenhower, Rep., 166,287; Stevenson, Dem., 106,663.
1956, Eisenhower, Rep., 176,519; Stevenson, Dem., 90,364; Andrews, Const., 111.
1960, Kennedy, Dem., 137,772; Nixon, Rep., 157,989.
1964, Johnson, Dem., 182,065; Goldwater, Rep., 104,029.
1968, Nixon, Rep., 154,903; Humphrey, Dem., 130,589; Wallace, 3d Party, 11,173; New Party, 421; Halstead, Soc. Workers, 104.
1972, Nixon, Rep., 213,724; McGovern, Dem., 116,435; Schmitz, Amer., 3,386; Jenness, Soc. Workers, 368; scattered, 142.
1976, Carter, Dem., 147,645; Ford, Rep., 185,935; McCarthy, Ind., 4,095; MacBride, Libertarian, 936; Reagan, write-in, 388; La Rouche, U.S. Labor, 186; Camejo, Soc. Workers, 161; Levin, Soc. Labor, 66; scattered, 215.
1980, Reagan, Rep., 221,705; Carter, Dem., 108,864; Anderson, Ind., 49,693; Clark, Libertarian, 2,067; Commoner, Citizens, 1,325; Hall, Com., 129; Griswold, Workers World, 76; DeBerry, Soc. Workers, 72; scattered, 68.
1984, Reagan, Rep., 267,051; Mondale, Dem., 120,377; Bergland, Libertarian, 735.
1988, Bush, Rep., 281,537; Dukakis, Dem., 163,696; Paul, Lib., 4,502; Fulani, New Alliance, 790.
1992, Clinton, Dem., 209,040; Bush, Rep., 202,484; Perot, Ind., 121,337; Marrou, Libertarian, 3,548.
1996, Clinton, Dem., 246,166; Dole, Rep., 196,486; Perot, Ref., 48,387; Browne, Libertarian, 4,214; Phillips, Taxpayers, 1,344.
2000, Bush, Rep., 273,559; Gore, Dem., 266,348; Nader, Green, 22,198; Browne, Libertarian, 2,757; Buchanan, Independence, 2,615; Phillips, Constitution, 328.

New Jersey

	2000		1996		
County	Gore (D)	Bush (R)	Clinton (D)	Dole (R)	Perot (RF)
Atlantic	52,880	35,593	44,434	29,538	8,261
Bergen	202,682	152,731	191,085	141,164	25,512
Burlington	99,506	72,254	85,086	57,337	18,407
Camden	127,166	62,464	114,962	52,791	17,433
Cape May	22,189	23,794	19,849	19,357	4,978
Cumberland	28,188	18,882	25,444	14,744	5,348
Essex	185,505	66,842	175,387	65,172	9,513
Gloucester	61,095	42,315	51,928	32,138	14,361
Hudson	118,206	43,804	116,121	38,288	8,965
Hunterdon	21,387	32,210	18,446	26,379	5,686
Mercer	83,256	46,670	77,641	40,559	10,536
Middlesex	154,998	93,545	145,201	82,433	24,643
Monmouth	131,476	119,291	120,414	99,975	22,754
Morris	88,039	111,066	81,092	95,830	15,299
Ocean	102,104	105,684	94,243	82,830	22,864
Passaic	90,324	61,043	85,879	53,584	10,944
Salem	13,718	12,257	12,044	9,294	4,124
Somerset	56,232	59,725	50,673	51,868	8,377
Sussex	21,353	33,277	19,525	26,746	6,705
Union	112,003	68,554	108,102	65,912	12,432
Warren	16,543	22,172	14,805	17,160	4,992
Totals	**1,788,850**	**1,284,173**	**1,652,361**	**1,103,099**	**262,134**

New Jersey Vote Since 1952

1952, Eisenhower, Rep., 1,373,613; Stevenson, Dem., 1,015,902; Hoopes, Soc., 8,593; Hass, Soc. Labor, 5,815; Hallinan, Prog., 5,589; Krajewski, Poor Man's, 4,203; Dobbs, Soc. Workers, 3,850; Hamblen, Proh., 989.
1956, Eisenhower, Rep., 1,606,942; Stevenson Dem., 850,337; Holtwick, Proh., 9,147; Hass, Soc. Labor, 6,736; Andrews, Cons., 5,317; Dobbs, Soc. Workers, 4,004; Krajewski, Amer. Third Party, 1,829.
1960, Kennedy, Dem., 1,385,415; Nixon, Rep., 1,363,324; Dobbs, Soc. Workers, 11,402; Lee, Cons., 8,708; Hass, Soc. Labor, 4,262.
1964, Johnson, Dem., 1,867,671; Goldwater, Rep., 963,843; DeBerry, Soc. Workers, 8,181; Hass, Soc. Labor, 7,075.
1968, Nixon, Rep., 1,325,467; Humphrey, Dem., 1,264,206; Wallace, 3d Party, 262,187; Halstead, Soc. Workers, 8,667; Gregory, Peace and Freedom, 8,084; Blomen, Soc. Labor, 6,784.

1972, Nixon, Rep., 1,845,502; McGovern, Dem., 1,102,211; Schmitz, Amer., 34,378; Spock, Peoples, 5,355; Fisher, Soc. Labor, 4,544; Jenness, Soc. Workers, 2,233; Mahalchik, Amer. First, 1,743; Hall, Com., 1,263.
1976, Carter, Dem., 1,444,653; Ford, Rep., 1,509,688; McCarthy, Ind., 32,717; MacBride, Libertarian, 9,449; Maddox, Amer., 7,716; Levin, Soc. Labor, 3,686; Hall, Com., 1,662; LaRouche, U.S. Labor, 1,650; Camejo, Soc. Workers, 1,184; Wright, People's, 1,044; Bubar, Proh., 554; Zeidler, Soc., 469.
1980, Reagan, Rep., 1,546,557; Carter, Dem., 1,147,364; Anderson, Ind., 234,632; Clark, Libertarian, 20,652; Commoner, Citizens, 8,203; McCormack, Right to Life, 3,927; Lynen, Middle Class, 3,694; Hall, Com., 2,555; Pulley, Soc. Workers, 2,198; McReynolds, Soc., 1,973; Gahres, Down With Lawyers, 1,718; Griswold, Workers World, 1,288; Wendelken, Ind., 923.
1984, Reagan, Rep., 1,933,630; Mondale, Dem., 1,261,323; Bergland, Libertarian, 6,416.
1988, Bush, Rep., 1,740,604; Dukakis, Dem., 1,317,541; Lewin, Peace and Freedom, 9,953; Paul, Lib., 8,421.
1992, Clinton, Dem., 1,436,206; Bush, Rep., 1,356,865; Perot, Ind., 521,829; Marrou, Libertarian, 6,822; Fulani, New Alliance, 3,513; Phillips, U.S. Taxpayers, 2,670; LaRouche, Ind., 2,095; Warren, Soc. Workers, 2,011; Daniels, Ind., 1,996; Gritz, Populist/America First, 1,867; Hagelin, Natural Law, 1,353.
1996, Clinton, Dem., 1,652,361; Dole, Rep., 1,103,099; Perot, Ref., 262,134; Nader, Green, 32,465; Browne, Libertarian, 14,763; Hagelin, Natural Law, 3,887; Phillips, Taxpayers, 3,440; Harris, Soc. Workers, 1,837; Moorehead, Workers World, 1,337; White, Soc. Equality, 537.
2000, Gore, Dem., 1,788,850; Bush, Rep., 1,284,173; Nader, Ind., 94,554; Buchanan, Ind., 6,989; Browne, Ind., 6,312; Hagelin, Ind., 2,215; McReynolds, Ind., 1,880; Phillips, Ind., 1,409; Harris, Ind., 844.

New Mexico

	2000		1996		
County	Gore (D)	Bush (R)	Clinton (D)	Dole (R)	Perot (RF)
Bernalillo	99,461	95,249	88,140	78,832	8,708
Catron	353	1,273	423	923	114
Chaves	6,340	11,378	7,014	9,991	1,271
Cibola	4,127	2,752	4,030	2,245	488
Colfax	2,653	2,600	2,659	1,975	411
Curry	3,471	8,301	4,116	7,378	842
De Baca	349	612	509	489	86
Dona Ana	23,912	21,263	22,766	17,541	2,269
Eddy	7,108	10,335	8,959	8,534	1,297
Grant	5,673	4,961	5,860	3,993	778
Guadalupe	1,076	548	1,208	436	79
Harding	214	366	264	321	28
Hidalgo	839	954	943	789	209
Lea	3,855	10,157	5,393	7,661	1,465
Lincoln	2,027	4,458	2,209	3,396	666
Los Alamos	4,149	5,623	3,983	4,999	560
Luna	2,975	3,395	3,001	2,616	598
McKinley	10,281	5,070	10,124	4,470	650
Mora	1,456	668	1,646	561	131
Otero	5,465	10,258	5,938	9,065	1,096
Quay	1,471	2,292	1,830	1,943	377
Rio Arriba	8,169	3,495	7,965	2,551	469
Roosevelt	1,762	3,762	2,097	3,245	467
Sandoval	14,899	15,423	13,081	11,015	1,482
San Juan	11,980	21,434	12,070	17,478	2,355
San Miguel	6,540	2,215	6,995	1,938	405
Santa Fe	32,017	13,974	26,349	10,857	1,846
Sierra	1,689	2,721	2,154	2,140	431
Socorro	3,294	3,173	3,374	2,315	455
Taos	7,039	2,744	6,635	2,126	545
Torrance	1,868	2,891	2,072	2,154	332
Union	452	1,269	519	995	125
Valencia	9,819	10,803	9,169	7,779	1,222
Totals	**286,783**	**286,417**	**273,495**	**232,751**	**32,257**

New Mexico Vote Since 1952

1952, Eisenhower, Rep., 132,170; Stevenson, Dem., 105,661; Hamblen, Proh., 297; Hallinan, Ind. Prog., 225; MacArthur, Christian National, 220; Hass, Soc. Labor, 35.
1956, Eisenhower, Rep., 146,788; Stevenson, Dem., 106,098; Holtwick, Proh., 607; Andrews, Ind., 364; Hass, Soc. Labor, 69.
1960, Kennedy, Dem., 156,027; Nixon, Rep., 153,733; Decker, Proh., 777; Hass, Soc. Labor, 570.
1964, Johnson, Dem., 194,017; Goldwater, Rep., 131,838; Hass, Soc. Labor, 1,217; Munn, Proh., 543.
1968, Nixon, Rep., 169,692; Humphrey, Dem., 130,081; Wallace, 3d Party, 25,737; Chavez, 1,519; Halstead, Soc. Workers, 252.
1972, Nixon, Rep., 235,606; McGovern, Dem., 141,084; Schmitz, Amer., 8,767; Jenness, Soc. Workers, 474.
1976, Carter, Dem., 201,148; Ford, Rep., 211,419; Camejo, Soc. Workers, 2,462; MacBride, Libertarian, 1,110; Zeidler, Soc., 240; Bubar, Proh., 211.
1980, Reagan, Rep., 250,779; Carter, Dem., 167,826; Anderson, Ind., 29,459; Clark, Libertarian, 4,365; Commoner, Citizens, 2,202; Bubar, Statesman, 1,281; Pulley, Soc. Workers, 325.
1984, Reagan, Rep., 307,101; Mondale, Dem., 201,769; Bergland, Libertarian, 4,459.
1988, Bush, Rep., 270,341; Dukakis, Dem., 244,497; Paul, Lib., 3,268; Fulani, New Alliance, 2,237.
1992, Clinton, Dem., 261,617; Bush, Rep., 212,824; Perot, Ind., 91,895; Marrou, Libertarian, 1,615.
1996, Clinton, Dem., 273,495; Dole, Rep., 232,751; Perot, Ref., 32,257; Nader, Green, 13,218; Browne, Libertarian, 2,996; Phillips, Taxpayers, 713; Hagelin, Natural Law, 644.
2000, Gore, Dem., 286,783; Bush, Rep., 286,417; Nader, Green, 21,251; Browne, Libertarian, 2,058; Buchanan, Reform, 1,392; Hagelin, Natural Law, 361; Phillips, Constitution, 343.

New York

	2000		1996		
County	Gore (D)	Bush (R)	Clinton (D)	Dole (R)	Perot (RF)
Albany	85,617	47,624	85,993	39,785	11,957
Allegany	6,336	11,436	6,621	8,107	2,730
Bronx	265,801	36,245	248,276	30,435	7,186
Broome	45,381	36,946	44,407	31,327	9,114
Cattaraugus	13,697	18,382	13,029	12,971	5,151
Cayuga	17,031	14,988	15,879	11,093	4,420
Chautauqua	27,016	29,064	26,831	21,261	7,484
Chemung	17,424	18,779	16,977	14,287	3,967
Chenango	9,112	10,033	8,797	7,319	2,822
Clinton	15,542	13,274	15,386	9,759	3,488
Columbia	13,489	13,153	12,910	10,324	3,466
Cortland	9,691	9,857	9,130	7,606	2,398
Delaware	8,450	10,662	8,724	7,684	2,601
Dutchess	52,390	52,669	47,339	41,929	12,294
Erie	240,174	160,176	224,554	132,343	45,679
Essex	7,927	8,822	7,893	6,379	2,363
Franklin	8,870	7,643	8,494	5,072	2,499
Fulton	9,314	11,434	9,779	7,881	3,214
Genesee	10,191	14,459	10,074	10,821	2,996
Greene	8,480	11,332	8,251	8,712	2,790
Hamilton	1,114	2,388	1,228	1,841	492
Herkimer	12,224	14,147	11,910	10,085	4,235
Jefferson	16,799	18,192	16,783	12,362	4,561
Kings	497,513	96,609	432,232	81,406	15,031
Lewis	4,333	6,103	4,402	3,965	1,669
Livingston	10,476	15,244	10,868	10,981	2,889
Madison	12,017	14,879	11,832	11,324	3,379
Monroe	161,743	141,266	164,858	115,694	23,936
Montgomery	10,249	9,765	10,485	7,172	3,253
Nassau	341,610	226,954	303,587	196,820	36,122
New York	454,523	82,113	394,131	67,839	11,144
Niagara	47,781	40,952	44,203	31,438	12,564
Oneida	43,933	47,603	44,399	37,996	11,296
Onondaga	109,896	83,678	100,190	73,771	17,602
Ontario	19,761	23,885	19,156	17,237	4,391
Orange	58,170	62,852	54,995	45,956	11,778
Orleans	5,991	9,202	6,233	6,865	1,986
Oswego	22,857	23,249	20,440	17,159	7,499
Otsego	11,460	12,219	11,470	8,774	3,217
Putnam	18,525	21,853	16,173	17,452	4,032
Queens	416,967	122,052	372,925	107,650	22,288
Rensselaer	34,808	29,562	34,273	23,482	8,405
Richmond	73,828	63,903	64,684	52,207	8,968
Rockland	69,530	48,441	63,127	40,395	6,798
St. Lawrence	21,386	16,449	21,798	10,827	5,309
Saratoga	43,359	46,623	39,832	34,337	10,141
Schenectady	35,534	27,961	35,404	22,106	7,865
Schoharie	5,390	7,459	5,902	5,353	1,796
Schuyler	3,301	4,381	3,303	3,134	1,037
Seneca	6,841	6,734	6,825	5,004	1,889
Steuben	14,600	24,200	14,481	17,710	5,496
Suffolk	306,306	240,992	261,828	182,510	52,209
Sullivan	14,348	12,703	15,052	9,321	3,453
Tioga	9,170	12,239	8,769	9,416	2,721
Tompkins	21,807	13,351	20,772	11,532	2,623
Ulster	38,162	33,447	35,852	26,212	9,246
Warren	12,193	14,993	11,603	11,152	3,623
Washington	9,641	12,596	9,572	8,954	3,648
Wayne	14,977	21,701	15,145	15,837	4,619
Westchester	218,010	139,278	196,310	123,719	18,028
Wyoming	5,935	10,809	5,735	7,477	2,411
Yates	3,962	5,565	4,066	3,925	1,190
Totals	**4,112,963**	**2,405,570**	**3,756,177**	**1,933,492**	**503,458**

New York Vote Since 1952

1952, Eisenhower, Rep., 3,952,815; Stevenson, Dem., 2,687,890; Liberal, 416,711; total, 3,104,601; Hallinan, Amer. Lab., 64,211; Hoopes, Soc., 2,664; Dobbs, Soc. Workers, 2,212; Hass, Ind. Gov't., 1,560; scattering, 178; blank and void, 87,813.
1956, Eisenhower, Rep., 4,340,340; Stevenson, Dem., 2,458,212; Liberal, 292,557; total, 2,750,769; write-in votes for Andrews, 1,027; Werdel, 492; Hass, 150; Hoopes, 82; others, 476.

1960, Kennedy, Dem., 3,423,909; Liberal, 406,176; total, 3,830,085; Nixon, Rep., 3,446,419; Dobbs, Soc. Workers, 14,319; scattering, 256; blank and void, 88,896.
1964, Johnson, Dem., 4,913,156; Goldwater, Rep., 2,243,559; Hass, Soc. Labor, 6,085; DeBerry, Soc. Workers, 3,215; scattering, 188; blank and void, 151,383.
1968, Nixon, Rep., 3,007,932; Humphrey, Dem., 3,378,470; Wallace, 3d Party, 358,864; Blomen, Soc. Labor, 8,432; Halstead, Soc. Workers, 11,851; Gregory, Freedom and Peace, 24,517; blank, void, and scattering, 171,624.
1972, Nixon, Rep., 3,824,642; Cons., 368,136; McGovern, Dem., 2,767,956; Liberal, 183,128; Reed, Soc. Workers, 7,797; Fisher, Soc. Labor, 4,530; Hall, Com., 5,641; blank, void, or scattered, 161,641.
1976, Carter, Dem., 3,389,558; Ford, Rep., 3,100,791; MacBride, Libertarian, 12,197; Hall, Com., 10,270; Camejo, Soc. Workers, 6,996; LaRouche, U.S. Labor, 5,413; blank, void, or scattered, 143,037.
1980, Reagan, Rep., 2,893,831; Carter, Dem., 2,728,372; Anderson, Ind., 467,801; Clark, Libertarian, 52,648; McCormack, Right To Life, 24,159; Commoner, Citizens, 23,186; Hall, Com., 7,414; DeBerry, Soc. Workers, 2,068; Griswold, Workers World, 1,416; scattering, 1,064.
1984, Reagan, Rep., 3,664,763; Mondale, Dem., 3,119,609; Bergland, Libertarian, 11,949.
1988, Bush, Rep., 3,081,871; Dukakis, Dem., 3,347,882; Marra, Right to Life, 20,497; Fulani, New Alliance, 15,845.
1992, Clinton, Dem., 3,444,450; Bush, Rep., 2,346,649; Perot, Ind., 1,090,721; Warren, Soc. Workers, 15,472; Marrou, Libertarian, 13,451; Fulani, New Alliance, 11,318; Hagelin, Natural Law, 4,420.
1996, Clinton, Dem., 3,756,177; Dole, Rep., 1,933,492; Perot, Ind. (Ref.), 503,458; Nader, Green, 75,956; Phillips, Right to Life, 23,580; Browne, Libertarian, 12,220; Hagelin, Natural Law, 5,011; Harris, Soc. Workers, 2,762; Moorehead, Workers World, 3,473.
2000, Gore, Dem., 4,112,965; Bush, Rep., 2,405,570; Nader, Green, 244,360; Buchanan, Reform, 31,554; Hagelin, Independence, 24,369; Browne, Libertarian, 7,664; Harris, Soc. Workers, 1,790; Phillips, Constitution, 1,503.

North Carolina

	2000		1996		
County	Gore (D)	Bush (R)	Clinton (D)	Dole (R)	Perot (RF)
Alamance	17,459	29,305	15,814	22,461	3,395
Alexander	4,166	9,242	3,955	6,748	1,004
Alleghany	1,715	2,531	1,801	1,936	458
Anson	4,792	3,161	4,890	2,193	512
Ashe	4,011	6,226	3,825	5,203	865
Avery	1,686	4,956	1,586	3,870	655
Beaufort	6,634	10,531	6,172	8,154	834
Bertie	4,660	2,488	4,202	1,745	316
Bladen	5,889	4,977	4,952	3,335	655
Brunswick	13,118	15,427	10,041	10,065	1,815
Buncombe	38,545	46,101	31,658	30,518	6,254
Burke	11,924	18,466	11,678	13,853	2,654
Cabarrus	16,284	32,704	14,447	23,035	3,626
Caldwell	8,588	17,337	8,050	12,653	2,099
Camden	1,187	1,628	1,186	1,074	293
Carteret	8,839	17,381	7,566	11,721	1,467
Caswell	4,091	4,270	4,312	3,310	510
Catawba	16,246	34,244	15,601	26,898	3,629
Chatham	10,461	10,248	9,353	7,731	1,113
Cherokee	3,239	6,305	3,129	3,883	785
Chowan	2,430	2,415	2,239	1,659	359
Clay	1,361	2,416	1,462	1,769	387
Cleveland	13,455	19,064	12,728	13,474	1,931
Columbus	9,986	8,342	9,019	6,017	1,170
Craven	12,213	19,494	10,317	13,264	1,528
Cumberland	38,626	38,129	32,739	29,804	3,776
Currituck	2,595	4,095	2,277	2,569	770
Dare	5,589	7,301	4,522	4,977	1,258
Davidson	16,199	35,387	13,593	24,797	3,698
Davie	3,651	10,184	3,525	8,141	915
Duplin	6,475	7,840	6,179	5,432	766
Durham	53,907	30,150	49,186	27,825	3,122
Edgecombe	11,315	6,836	10,568	6,010	660
Forsyth	52,457	67,700	46,543	59,160	5,747
Franklin	7,454	8,501	6,448	5,648	891
Gaston	19,281	39,453	19,458	33,149	3,921
Gates	1,944	1,480	2,155	1,072	307
Graham	1,006	2,304	1,210	1,801	270
Granville	7,733	7,364	6,747	5,498	432
Greene	2,478	3,353	2,224	2,689	280
Guilford	80,787	84,394	69,208	67,727	9,739
Halifax	10,222	6,698	9,551	5,700	816
Harnett	9,155	14,762	8,767	11,596	1,287
Haywood	9,793	12,118	9,350	7,995	2,594
Henderson	12,562	25,688	10,626	19,182	2,679
Hertford	5,484	2,382	4,856	1,823	356
Hoke	5,017	3,439	3,510	1,914	481
Hyde	1,088	1,132	1,109	782	143
Iredell	15,434	29,853	13,102	21,163	2,970
Jackson	5,722	6,237	5,211	4,244	970
Johnston	13,704	27,212	11,175	18,704	2,163
Jones	1,822	2,114	1,829	1,682	197
Lee	6,785	9,406	6,290	7,321	980
Lenoir	9,527	11,512	8,635	9,433	822
Lincoln	8,412	15,951	7,721	11,439	1,619
McDowell	4,747	9,109	4,553	6,407	1,275
Macon	4,683	8,406	4,209	5,267	1,121
Madison	3,505	4,676	3,333	3,110	538
Martin	4,929	4,420	4,500	3,590	445
Mecklenburg	126,911	134,068	103,429	97,719	10,473
Mitchell	1,535	4,984	1,496	3,874	549
Montgomery	3,979	4,946	3,856	3,379	587
Moore	11,232	19,882	9,847	14,760	1,761
Nash	12,376	17,995	11,142	15,309	1,751
New Hanover	29,292	36,503	22,839	27,889	3,615
Northampton	5,513	2,667	5,207	1,881	402
Onslow	10,269	19,657	8,685	13,396	1,857
Orange	30,921	17,930	28,674	15,053	1,534
Pamlico	2,188	2,999	2,204	2,270	297
Pasquotank	5,874	4,943	4,233	2,999	565
Pender	6,415	7,661	5,409	5,538	945
Perquimans	2,033	2,230	2,069	1,561	369
Person	5,042	6,722	4,540	4,883	591
Pitt	19,685	23,192	17,555	18,227	2,037
Polk	3,114	5,074	2,704	3,516	493
Randolph	11,366	30,959	10,783	23,030	3,593
Richmond	7,935	6,263	7,564	3,973	1,230
Robeson	17,834	11,721	17,361	8,146	2,105
Rockingham	13,260	18,979	12,096	14,255	2,528
Rowan	14,891	28,922	13,461	22,754	2,902
Rutherford	7,697	13,755	7,162	9,792	1,585
Sampson	8,768	10,410	8,150	8,241	825
Scotland	5,627	3,740	4,870	2,858	548
Stanly	7,066	15,548	7,131	11,446	1,690
Stokes	5,030	12,028	4,769	9,471	1,025
Surry	7,757	15,401	7,303	11,117	1,538
Swain	2,097	2,224	1,869	1,444	401
Transylvania	5,044	9,011	4,842	6,734	1,183
Tyrrell	849	706	908	488	112
Union	14,890	31,876	11,525	18,802	2,477
Vance	7,092	5,564	6,385	4,651	575
Wake	123,466	142,494	103,574	108,780	11,811
Warren	4,576	2,202	4,141	1,861	319
Washington	2,704	2,169	2,790	1,562	171
Watauga	7,959	10,438	7,349	8,146	1,415
Wayne	13,005	20,758	11,580	16,588	1,178
Wilkes	7,226	16,826	6,793	12,395	1,967
Wilson	11,266	13,466	9,779	10,518	1,100
Yadkin	3,127	10,435	2,927	8,439	913
Yancey	3,714	4,970	3,956	3,973	720
Totals	**1,257,692**	**1,631,163**	**1,107,849**	**1,225,938**	**168,059**

North Carolina Vote Since 1952

1952, Eisenhower, Rep., 558,107; Stevenson, Dem., 652,803.
1956, Eisenhower, Rep., 575,062; Stevenson, Dem., 590,530.
1960, Kennedy, Dem., 713,136; Nixon, Rep., 655,420.
1964, Johnson, Dem., 800,139; Goldwater, Rep., 624,844.
1968, Nixon, Rep., 627,192; Humphrey, Dem., 464,113; Wallace, 3d Party, 496,188.
1972, Nixon, Rep., 1,054,889; McGovern, Dem., 438,705; Schmitz, Amer., 25,018.
1976, Carter, Dem., 927,365; Ford, Rep., 741,960; Anderson, Amer., 5,607; MacBride, Libertarian, 2,219; LaRouche, U.S. Labor, 755.
1980, Reagan, Rep., 915,018; Carter, Dem., 875,635; Anderson, Ind., 52,800; Clark, Libertarian, 9,677; Commoner, Citizens, 2,287; DeBerry, Soc. Workers, 416.
1984, Reagan, Rep., 1,346,481; Mondale, Dem., 824,287; Bergland, Libertarian, 3,794.
1988, Bush, Rep., 1,237,258; Dukakis, Dem., 890,167; Fulani, New Alliance, 5,682; Paul, write-in, 1,263.
1992, Clinton, Dem., 1,114,042; Bush, Rep., 1,134,661; Perot, Ind., 357,864; Marrou, Libertarian, 5,171.
1996, Dole, Rep., 1,225,938; Clinton, Dem., 1,107,849; Perot, Ref., 168,059; Browne, Libertarian, 8,740; Hagelin, Natural Law, 2,771.
2000, Bush, Rep., 1,631,163; Gore, Dem., 1,257,692; Browne, Libertarian, 13,891; Buchanan, Reform, 8,874.

North Dakota

	2000		1996		
County	Gore (D)	Bush (R)	Clinton (D)	Dole (R)	Perot (RF)
Adams	286	826	366	575	200
Barnes	1,933	3,452	2,317	2,449	666
Benson	952	1,055	1,059	850	252
Billings	82	394	116	281	107

County	2000 Gore (D)	2000 Bush (R)	1996 Clinton (D)	1996 Dole (R)	1996 Perot (RF)
Bottineau	1,173	2,349	1,280	1,682	536
Bowman	330	1,080	489	710	261
Burke	296	698	416	483	176
Burleigh	9,842	22,467	10,679	15,464	3,535
Cass	21,451	33,536	21,693	24,238	4,116
Cavalier	618	1,513	941	1,188	326
Dickey	806	1,853	953	1,418	276
Divide	306	443	637	488	209
Dunn	474	1,124	587	830	304
Eddy	458	703	553	517	201
Emmons	405	1,430	544	1,148	441
Foster	474	1,172	664	801	265
Golden Valley	156	611	235	520	163
Grand Forks	10,593	15,875	11,376	11,606	2,663
Grant	235	1,077	300	760	295
Griggs	484	920	670	731	162
Hettinger	353	1,057	418	765	238
Kidder	283	837	434	691	242
La Moure	689	1,590	880	1,220	276
Logan	223	812	360	705	254
McHenry	888	1,682	1,096	1,187	453
McIntosh	350	1,178	470	1,005	295
McKenzie	653	1,634	928	1,338	428
McLean	1,465	2,891	1,759	1,988	618
Mercer	1,011	2,984	1,300	1,953	764
Morton	3,439	6,993	3,745	4,699	1,566
Mountrail	1,256	1,466	1,277	965	360
Nelson	687	1,031	827	745	206
Oliver	244	709	333	499	183
Pembina	1,093	2,430	1,191	1,678	400
Pierce	500	1,348	671	1,017	270
Ramsey	1,658	3,005	2,123	2,077	549
Ransom	1,080	1,488	1,199	920	303
Renville	443	820	562	576	210
Richland	2,490	4,999	2,890	3,345	782
Rolette	2,681	1,416	2,299	823	448
Sargent	959	1,103	1,003	814	241
Sheridan	161	707	252	566	121
Sioux	724	269	393	207	82
Slope	85	316	123	260	60
Stark	2,784	6,387	3,095	4,086	1,456
Steele	475	655	620	486	115
Stutsman	3,067	5,488	3,589	3,784	1,141
Towner	410	694	649	542	187
Traill	1,512	2,392	1,822	1,820	380
Walsh	1,743	3,099	2,082	2,222	599
Ward	7,533	13,997	8,660	10,546	2,587
Wells	661	1,610	962	1,192	373
Williams	2,330	5,187	3,018	3,590	1,174
Totals	**95,284**	**174,852**	**106,905**	**125,050**	**32,515**

North Dakota Vote Since 1952

1952, Eisenhower, Rep., 191,712; Stevenson, Dem., 76,694; MacArthur, Christian Nationalist, 1,075; Hallinan, Prog., 344; Hamblen, Proh., 302.

1956, Eisenhower, Rep., 156,766; Stevenson, Dem., 96,742; Andrews, Amer., 483.

1960, Kennedy, Dem., 123,963; Nixon, Rep., 154,310; Dobbs, Soc. Workers, 158.

1964, Johnson, Dem., 149,784; Goldwater, Rep., 108,207; DeBerry, Soc. Workers, 224; Munn, Proh., 174.

1968, Nixon, Rep., 138,669; Humphrey, Dem., 94,769; Wallace, 3d Party, 14,244; Halstead, Soc. Workers, 128; Munn, Prohibition, 38; Troxell, Ind., 34.

1972, Nixon, Rep., 174,109; McGovern, Dem., 100,384; Jenness, Soc. Workers, 288; Hall, Com., 87; Schmitz, Amer., 5,646.

1976, Carter, Dem., 136,078; Ford, Rep., 153,470; Anderson, Amer., 3,698; McCarthy, Ind., 2,952; Maddox, Amer. Ind., 269; MacBride, Libertarian, 256; scattering, 371.

1980, Reagan, Rep., 193,695; Carter, Dem., 79,189; Anderson, Ind., 23,640; Clark, Libertarian, 3,743; Commoner, Libertarian, 429; McLain, Natl. People's League, 296; Greaves, Amer., 235; Hall, Com., 93; DeBerry, Soc. Workers, 89; McReynolds, Soc., 82; Bubar, Statesman, 54.

1984, Reagan, Rep., 200,336; Mondale, Dem., 104,429; Bergland, Libertarian, 703.

1988, Bush, Rep., 166,559; Dukakis, Dem., 127,739; Paul, Lib., 1,315; LaRouche, Natl. Econ. Recovery, 905.

1992, Clinton, Dem., 99,168; Bush, Rep., 136,244; Perot, Ind., 71,084.

1996, Dole, Rep., 125,050; Clinton, Dem., 106,905; Perot, Ref., 32,515; Browne, Libertarian, 847; Phillips, Ind., 745; Hagelin, Natural Law, 349.

2000, Bush, Rep., 174,852; Gore, Dem., 95,284; Nader, Ind., 9,486; Buchanan, Reform, 7,288; Browne, Ind., 660; Phillips, Constitution, 373; Hagelin, Ind., 313.

Ohio

County	2000 Gore (D)	2000 Bush (R)	1996 Clinton (D)	1996 Dole (R)	1996 Perot (RF)
Adams	3,581	6,380	4,317	4,763	1,223
Allen	13,996	28,647	15,529	24,325	3,799
Ashland	6,685	13,533	6,573	10,402	2,630
Ashtabula	19,831	17,940	19,341	13,287	5,700
Athens	13,158	9,703	13,418	7,154	2,777
Auglaize	5,564	13,770	6,652	10,169	2,641
Belmont	15,980	12,625	17,705	8,213	4,452
Brown	5,972	10,027	6,318	6,970	1,941
Butler	46,390	86,587	43,690	67,023	10,540
Carroll	4,960	6,732	4,792	4,449	2,445
Champaign	5,955	9,220	5,990	6,568	2,219
Clark	27,984	27,660	27,890	22,297	7,083
Clermont	20,927	47,129	21,329	36,457	5,795
Clinton	4,791	9,824	5,303	7,504	1,588
Columbiana	20,657	21,804	20,716	15,386	7,127
Coshocton	5,594	8,243	6,005	6,018	2,183
Crawford	6,721	11,666	7,449	8,730	3,072
Cuyahoga	359,913	192,099	341,357	163,770	50,691
Darke	7,741	14,817	8,871	10,798	3,168
Defiance	6,175	9,540	6,343	7,469	1,929
Delaware	17,134	36,639	13,463	24,123	3,471
Erie	17,732	16,105	16,730	12,204	4,225
Fairfield	19,065	33,523	18,821	26,850	4,660
Fayette	3,363	5,685	3,665	4,831	1,047
Franklin	202,018	197,862	192,795	178,412	25,400
Fulton	6,805	11,546	6,662	8,703	2,412
Gallia	4,872	7,511	5,386	5,135	1,839
Geauga	15,327	25,417	14,143	19,662	4,848
Greene	25,059	37,946	25,082	30,677	5,246
Guernsey	6,643	8,181	6,731	5,970	2,251
Hamilton	161,578	204,175	160,458	186,493	21,335
Hancock	8,798	20,985	9,334	17,252	2,904
Hardin	4,557	7,124	4,930	5,506	1,365
Harrison	3,351	3,417	3,721	2,310	1,302
Henry	4,367	8,530	4,762	6,385	1,550
Highland	5,328	9,728	5,837	7,102	1,629
Hocking	4,474	5,702	4,646	4,017	1,564
Holmes	2,066	6,754	2,531	5,213	1,276
Huron	8,183	12,286	8,858	8,750	3,338
Jackson	5,131	6,958	5,538	4,922	1,529
Jefferson	17,488	15,038	19,402	10,212	4,748
Knox	7,133	13,393	7,562	10,159	2,138
Lake	46,497	51,747	43,186	40,974	12,507
Lawrence	11,307	12,531	11,595	8,832	3,232
Licking	23,196	37,180	22,624	28,276	6,516
Logan	5,945	11,849	6,397	8,325	2,264
Lorain	59,809	47,957	55,744	34,937	14,889
Lucas	108,344	73,342	104,911	58,120	17,282
Madison	5,287	8,892	5,072	6,871	1,386
Mahoning	69,212	40,460	72,716	31,397	13,213
Marion	10,370	13,617	10,482	11,112	2,897
Medina	26,635	37,349	23,727	26,120	8,700
Meigs	3,674	5,750	4,275	3,622	1,453
Mercer	5,212	12,485	6,300	8,832	2,361
Miami	15,584	26,037	15,540	19,509	4,599
Monroe	3,605	3,145	3,914	1,856	1,128
Montgomery	114,597	109,792	115,416	95,391	18,298
Morgan	2,261	3,451	2,385	2,566	922
Morrow	4,529	7,842	4,627	5,655	1,745
Muskingum	13,415	17,995	13,813	13,861	4,880
Noble	2,296	3,435	2,366	2,183	899
Ottawa	9,485	9,917	9,321	6,991	2,438
Paulding	3,384	5,210	3,449	3,760	1,292
Perry	5,895	6,440	5,819	4,606	1,854
Pickaway	6,598	10,717	7,042	8,666	1,702
Pike	4,923	5,333	5,542	3,759	1,402
Portage	31,446	28,271	29,441	18,939	9,178
Preble	6,375	11,176	6,611	8,139	2,235
Putnam	4,063	12,837	4,972	9,294	1,767
Richland	20,572	30,138	20,832	23,697	6,613
Ross	11,662	13,706	12,649	10,286	2,648
Sandusky	11,146	13,699	11,547	10,033	3,617
Scioto	13,997	15,022	15,041	11,679	4,418
Seneca	9,512	13,863	10,044	9,713	3,498
Shelby	6,593	12,476	6,729	8,773	2,686
Stark	75,308	78,153	73,437	60,212	23,004
Summit	119,759	96,721	112,050	73,555	27,723
Trumbull	57,643	34,654	55,604	24,811	13,563
Tuscarawas	15,879	19,549	15,244	13,388	5,682
Union	5,040	11,502	4,989	8,290	1,596
Van Wert	4,209	8,679	4,453	6,999	1,487
Vinton	2,037	2,720	2,350	1,673	728
Warren	19,142	48,318	17,089	33,210	4,689
Washington	10,383	15,342	10,945	11,965	2,832
Wayne	14,779	25,901	14,850	19,628	5,771
Williams	5,454	9,941	5,524	7,747	2,121
Wood	22,687	27,504	23,183	20,518	5,065
Wyandot	3,397	6,113	3,677	4,473	1,347
Totals	**2,186,190**	**2,351,209**	**2,148,222**	**1,859,883**	**483,207**

Ohio Vote Since 1952

1952, Eisenhower, Rep., 2,100,391; Stevenson, Dem., 1,600,367.
1956, Eisenhower, Rep., 2,262,610; Stevenson, Dem., 1,439,655.
1960, Kennedy, Dem., 1,944,248; Nixon, Rep., 2,217,611.
1964, Johnson, Dem., 2,498,331; Goldwater, Rep., 1,470,865.
1968, Nixon, Rep., 1,791,014; Humphrey, Dem., 1,700,586; Wallace, 3d Party, 467,495; Gregory, 372; Munn, Proh., 19; Blomen, Soc. Labor, 120; Halstead, Soc. Workers, 69; Mitchell, Com., 23.
1972, Nixon, Rep., 2,441,827; McGovern, Dem., 1,558,889; Fisher, Soc. Labor, 7,107; Hall, Com., 6,437; Schmitz, Amer., 80,067; Wallace, Ind., 460.
1976, Carter, Dem., 2,011,621; Ford, Rep., 2,000,505; McCarthy, Ind., 58,258; Maddox, Amer. Ind., 15,529; MacBride, Libertarian, 8,961; Hall, Com., 7,817; Camejo, Soc. Workers, 4,717; LaRouche, U.S. Labor, 4,335; scattered, 130.
1980, Reagan, Rep., 2,206,545; Carter, Dem., 1,752,414; Anderson, Ind., 254,472; Clark, Libertarian, 49,033; Commoner, Citizens, 8,564; Hall, Com., 4,729; Congress, Ind., 4,029; Griswold, Workers World, 3,790; Bubar, Statesman, 27.
1984, Reagan, Rep., 2,678,559; Mondale, Dem., 1,825,440; Bergland, Libertarian, 5,886.
1988, Bush, Rep., 2,416,549; Dukakis, Dem., 1,939,629; Fulani, Ind., 12,017; Paul, Ind., 11,926.
1992, Clinton, Dem., 1,984,942; Bush, Rep., 1,894,310; Perot, Ind., 1,036,426; Marrou, Libertarian, 7,252; Fulani, New Alliance, 6,413; Gritz, Populist/America First, 4,699; Hagelin, Natural Law, 3,437; LaRouche, Ind., 2,446.
1996, Clinton, Dem., 2,148,222; Dole, Rep., 1,859,883; Perot, Ref., 483,207; Browne, Ind., 12,851; Moorehead, Ind., 10,813; Hagelin, Natural Law, 9,120; Phillips, Ind., 7,361.
2000, Bush, Rep., 2,351,209; Gore, Dem., 2,186,190; Nader, Ind., 117,857; Buchanan, Ind., 26,724; Browne, Libertarian, 13,475; Hagelin, Natural Law, 6,169; Phillips, Ind., 3,823.

Oklahoma

	2000		1996		
County	Gore (D)	Bush (R)	Clinton (D)	Dole (R)	Perot (RF)
Adair	2,361	3,503	2,792	2,956	751
Alfalfa	583	1,886	796	1,504	348
Atoka	1,906	2,375	2,281	1,542	532
Beaver	339	2,092	515	1,893	199
Beckham	2,408	4,067	2,797	2,912	817
Blaine	1,402	2,633	1,832	2,127	563
Bryan	5,554	6,084	5,962	3,943	1,396
Caddo	4,272	4,835	4,844	3,422	1,358
Canadian	8,367	22,679	8,977	18,139	3,297
Carter	6,659	9,667	6,979	6,769	1,997
Cherokee	7,256	6,918	6,817	5,046	1,777
Choctaw	2,799	2,461	3,198	1,580	589
Cimarron	227	1,230	361	986	102
Cleveland	27,792	47,393	26,038	36,457	6,785
Coal	1,148	1,196	1,205	734	323
Comanche	11,971	17,103	12,841	14,461	2,819
Cotton	1,068	1,388	1,258	1,042	381
Craig	2,568	2,815	2,649	2,058	758
Creek	9,753	13,580	9,674	9,861	2,837
Custer	3,115	6,527	4,027	4,723	1,101
Delaware	5,514	7,618	5,094	5,230	1,573
Dewey	599	1,607	816	1,179	292
Ellis	468	1,513	619	1,090	279
Garfield	6,543	14,902	7,504	11,712	2,523
Garvin	4,189	5,536	4,639	3,745	1,345
Grady	6,037	10,040	6,256	7,228	2,048
Grant	709	1,762	867	1,382	384
Greer	839	1,287	1,240	905	361
Harmon	507	692	729	448	143
Harper	374	1,296	511	1,036	210
Haskell	2,510	2,039	2,762	1,442	590
Hughes	2,334	2,196	2,748	1,510	730
Jackson	2,515	5,591	3,245	4,422	892
Jefferson	1,245	1,320	1,430	865	337
Johnston	1,809	2,072	1,998	1,229	532
Kay	6,122	11,768	6,882	9,741	2,785
Kingfisher	1,304	4,693	1,626	3,423	621
Kiowa	1,544	2,173	1,973	1,638	510
Latimer	1,865	1,739	2,222	1,189	578
Le Flore	6,536	8,215	6,831	5,689	1,721
Lincoln	4,140	7,387	4,332	5,243	1,500
Logan	4,510	8,187	4,854	5,949	1,410
Love	1,530	1,807	1,675	1,224	385
McClain	3,670	6,750	3,753	4,363	1,280
McCurtain	3,752	6,601	4,350	3,892	1,483
McIntosh	4,206	3,444	4,219	2,400	1,044
Major	635	2,672	900	2,188	410
Marshall	2,210	2,641	2,624	1,605	663
Mayes	6,618	7,132	6,377	5,268	1,617
Murray	2,263	2,609	2,620	1,712	723
Muskogee	12,520	11,820	12,963	8,974	3,163
Noble	1,416	3,230	1,756	2,318	694
Nowata	1,703	2,069	1,788	1,457	586
Okfuskee	1,814	1,910	2,074	1,380	536
Oklahoma	81,590	139,078	80,438	120,429	18,411
Okmulgee	7,186	5,797	7,555	4,246	1,487
Osage	7,540	8,138	7,342	5,827	1,938
Ottawa	5,647	5,625	5,844	4,127	1,496
Pawnee	2,435	3,386	2,663	2,560	756
Payne	9,319	15,256	9,985	11,686	2,472
Pittsburg	7,627	8,514	8,475	5,966	2,217
Pontotoc	5,387	7,299	6,470	5,366	1,712
Pottawatomie	8,763	13,235	9,141	9,802	2,724
Pushmataha	1,969	2,331	2,270	1,458	588
Roger Mills	441	1,234	733	959	233
Rogers	10,813	17,713	9,544	12,883	3,022
Seminole	3,783	4,011	4,225	2,935	1,041
Sequoyah	5,425	6,614	5,665	4,733	1,673
Stephens	6,467	10,860	7,248	8,144	2,312
Texas	1,084	4,964	1,408	4,139	518
Tillman	1,400	1,920	1,827	1,346	471
Tulsa	81,656	134,152	76,924	111,243	18,201
Wagoner	8,244	12,981	7,749	9,392	2,357
Washington	6,644	13,788	6,732	11,605	2,255
Washita	1,564	2,850	1,913	1,994	748
Woods	1,235	2,774	1,431	2,151	497
Woodward	1,950	5,067	2,403	4,093	963
Totals	**474,276**	**744,337**	**488,105**	**582,315**	**130,788**

Oklahoma Vote Since 1952

1952, Eisenhower, Rep., 518,045; Stevenson, Dem., 430,939.
1956, Eisenhower, Rep., 473,769; Stevenson, Dem., 385,581.
1960, Kennedy, Dem., 370,111; Nixon, Rep., 533,039.
1964, Johnson, Dem., 519,834; Goldwater, Rep., 412,665.
1968, Nixon, Rep., 449,697; Humphrey, Dem., 301,658; Wallace, 3d Party, 191,731.
1972, Nixon, Rep., 759,025; McGovern, Dem., 247,147; Schmitz, Amer., 23,728.
1976, Carter, Dem., 532,442; Ford, Rep., 545,708; McCarthy, Ind., 14,101.
1980, Reagan, Rep., 695,570; Carter, Dem., 402,026; Anderson, Ind., 38,284; Clark, Libertarian, 13,828.
1984, Reagan, Rep., 861,530; Mondale, Dem., 385,080; Bergland, Libertarian, 9,066.
1988, Bush, Rep., 678,367; Dukakis, Dem., 483,423; Paul, Lib., 6,261; Fulani, New Alliance, 2,985.
1992, Clinton, Dem., 473,066; Bush, Rep., 592,929; Perot, Ind., 319,878; Marrou, Libertarian, 4,486.
1996, Dole, Rep., 582,315; Clinton, Dem., 488,105; Perot, Ref., 130,788; Browne, Libertarian, 5,505.
2000, Bush, Rep., 744,337; Gore, Dem., 474,276; Buchanan, Reform, 9,014; Browne, Libertarian, 6,602.

Oregon

	2000		1996		
County	Gore (D)	Bush (R)	Clinton (D)	Dole (R)	Perot (RF)
Baker	2,195	5,618	2,547	3,975	900
Benton	19,444	15,825	17,211	12,450	2,445
Clackamas	76,421	77,539	67,709	59,443	12,304
Clatsop	8,296	6,950	7,732	5,334	1,582
Columbia	10,331	9,369	9,275	6,205	2,330
Coos	11,610	15,626	12,171	10,886	3,460
Crook	2,474	5,363	2,607	3,250	948
Curry	4,090	6,551	4,202	4,790	1,560
Deschutes	22,061	32,132	17,151	21,135	5,306
Douglas	14,193	30,294	15,250	21,855	4,465
Gilliam	359	679	485	398	143
Grant	589	3,078	1,180	2,110	432
Harney	766	2,799	980	1,948	506
Hood River	4,072	3,721	3,654	2,794	721
Jackson	33,153	46,052	29,230	33,771	7,470
Jefferson	2,681	3,838	2,555	2,634	813
Josephine	11,864	22,186	11,113	16,048	3,546
Klamath	7,541	18,855	7,207	12,116	2,538
Lake	707	2,830	962	2,239	385
Lane	78,583	61,578	69,461	48,253	11,498
Lincoln	10,861	8,446	10,552	6,717	2,269
Linn	16,682	25,359	17,041	18,331	4,773
Malheur	2,336	7,624	2,827	6,045	844
Marion	49,430	57,443	48,637	46,415	8,802
Morrow	1,197	2,224	1,426	1,381	455
Multnomah	188,441	83,677	159,878	71,094	17,536
Polk	11,921	14,088	10,042	11,478	2,093
Sherman	326	679	444	476	126
Tillamook	5,762	5,775	5,775	3,884	1,263
Umatilla	7,809	14,140	8,774	9,703	2,500
Union	3,577	7,836	4,379	5,414	1,241
Wallowa	836	3,279	1,321	2,379	483
Wasco	4,616	5,356	4,967	3,662	1,004
Washington	90,662	86,091	76,619	65,221	11,446
Wheeler	202	584	299	418	121
Yamhill	14,254	19,193	13,078	13,900	2,913
Totals	**720,342**	**713,577**	**649,641**	**538,152**	**121,221**

Oregon Vote Since 1952

1952, Eisenhower, Rep., 420,815; Stevenson, Dem., 270,579; Hallinan, Ind., 3,665.
1956, Eisenhower, Rep., 406,393; Stevenson, Dem., 329,204.
1960, Kennedy, Dem., 367,402; Nixon, Rep., 408,060.
1964, Johnson, Dem., 501,017; Goldwater, Rep., 282,779; write-in, 2,509.
1968, Nixon, Rep., 408,433; Humphrey, Dem., 358,866; Wallace, 3d Party, 49,683; write-in, McCarthy, 1,496; N. Rockefeller, 69; others, 1,075.
1972, Nixon, Rep., 486,686; McGovern, Dem., 392,760; Schmitz, Amer., 46,211; write-in, 2,289.
1976, Carter, Dem., 490,407; Ford, Rep., 492,120; McCarthy, Ind., 40,207; write-in, 7,142.
1980, Reagan, Rep., 571,044; Carter, Dem., 456,890; Anderson, Ind., 112,389; Clark, Libertarian, 25,838; Commoner, Citizens, 13,642; scattered, 1,713.
1984, Reagan, Rep., 658,700; Mondale, Dem., 536,479.
1988, Bush, Rep., 560,126; Dukakis, Dem., 616,206; Paul, Lib., 14,811; Fulani, Ind., 6,487.
1992, Clinton, Dem., 621,314; Bush, Rep., 475,757; Perot, Ind., 354,091; Marrou, Libertarian, 4,277; Fulani, New Alliance, 3,030.
1996, Clinton, Dem., 649,641; Dole, Rep., 538,152; Perot, Ref., 121,221; Nader, Pacific, 49,415; Browne, Libertarian, 8,903; Phillips, Taxpayers, 3,379; Hagelin, Natural Law, 2,798; Hollis, Soc., 1,922.
2000, Gore, Dem., 720,342; Bush, Rep., 713,577; Nader, Green, 77,357; Browne, Libertarian, 7,447; Buchanan, Ind., 7,063; Hagelin, Reform, 2,574; Phillips, Constitution, 2,189.

Pennsylvania

	2000		1996		
County	Gore (D)	Bush (R)	Clinton (D)	Dole (R)	Perot (RF)
Adams	11,682	20,848	10,774	15,338	3,186
Allegheny	329,963	235,361	284,480	204,067	42,309
Armstrong	11,127	15,508	11,130	11,052	3,452
Beaver	38,925	32,491	39,578	26,048	8,276
Bedford	5,474	13,598	5,954	10,064	2,041
Berks	59,150	71,273	49,887	56,289	13,788
Blair	15,774	28,376	15,036	21,282	4,014
Bradford	7,911	14,660	7,736	10,393	2,712
Bucks	132,914	121,927	103,313	94,899	24,544
Butler	25,037	44,009	21,990	32,038	6,145
Cambria	30,308	28,001	30,391	20,341	7,837
Cameron	779	1,383	822	1,113	283
Carbon	10,668	9,717	9,457	7,193	2,992
Centre	21,409	26,172	21,145	20,935	4,173
Chester	82,047	100,080	64,783	77,029	14,067
Clarion	5,605	9,796	5,954	6,916	2,064
Clearfield	11,718	18,019	11,991	12,987	3,758
Clinton	5,521	6,064	5,658	4,293	1,424
Columbia	8,975	12,095	8,379	8,234	3,654
Crawford	13,250	18,858	12,943	14,659	3,519
Cumberland	31,053	54,802	28,749	43,943	5,669
Dauphin	44,390	53,631	40,936	44,417	6,967
Delaware	134,861	105,836	115,946	92,628	21,883
Elk	5,754	7,347	5,749	4,889	2,293
Erie	59,399	49,027	57,508	39,884	10,386
Fayette	28,152	20,013	26,359	14,019	5,722
Forest	843	1,371	964	902	325
Franklin	14,922	33,042	14,980	25,392	4,127
Fulton	1,425	3,753	1,620	2,665	554
Greene	7,230	5,890	7,620	4,002	2,052
Huntingdon	5,073	10,408	5,285	7,324	1,813
Indiana	13,667	16,799	13,868	12,874	3,674
Jefferson	5,566	11,473	5,846	8,156	2,322
Juniata	2,656	5,795	2,896	4,128	911
Lackawanna	57,471	35,096	46,377	26,930	8,189
Lancaster	54,968	115,900	49,120	92,875	11,601
Lawrence	20,593	18,060	18,993	13,088	4,002
Lebanon	16,093	28,534	14,187	21,885	4,235
Lehigh	56,667	55,492	48,568	45,103	10,947
Luzerne	62,199	52,328	60,174	43,577	12,424
Lycoming	14,663	27,137	13,516	21,535	3,855
McKean	5,510	9,661	5,509	6,838	2,350
Mercer	23,817	23,132	23,003	17,213	5,108
Mifflin	4,835	9,400	5,327	6,888	1,392
Monroe	21,939	23,265	16,547	17,326	4,650
Montgomery	177,990	145,623	143,664	121,047	24,392
Montour	2,356	3,960	2,183	2,785	784
Northampton	53,097	47,396	43,959	35,726	9,848
Northumberland	13,670	18,142	13,418	13,551	5,173
Perry	4,459	11,184	4,611	8,156	1,609
Philadelphia	449,182	100,959	412,988	85,345	29,329
Pike	7,330	9,339	5,509	6,697	1,873
Potter	2,037	4,858	2,146	3,714	925
Schuylkill	26,215	29,841	24,860	22,920	8,471
Snyder	3,536	8,963	3,405	6,742	1,451
Somerset	12,028	20,218	12,719	14,735	3,968
Sullivan	1,066	1,928	1,071	1,352	418
Susquehanna	6,481	10,226	5,912	7,354	2,266
Tioga	4,617	9,635	4,961	7,382	1,993
Union	4,209	8,523	3,658	6,570	1,431
Venango	8,196	11,642	8,205	8,398	2,777
Warren	7,537	9,290	7,291	7,056	2,504
Washington	44,961	37,339	40,952	27,777	8,661
Wayne	6,904	11,201	5,928	8,077	2,126
Westmoreland	71,792	80,858	63,686	62,058	16,230
Wyoming	4,363	6,922	4,049	4,888	1,414
York	51,958	87,652	49,596	65,188	11,652
Totals	**2,485,967**	**2,281,127**	**2,215,819**	**1,801,169**	**430,984**

Pennsylvania Vote Since 1952

1952, Eisenhower, Rep., 2,415,789; Stevenson, Dem., 2,146,269; Hamblen, Proh., 8,771; Hallinan, Prog., 4,200; Hoopes, Soc., 2,684; Dobbs, Militant Workers, 1,502; Hass, Ind. Gov., 1,347; scattered, 155.
1956, Eisenhower, Rep., 2,585,252; Stevenson, Dem., 1,981,769; Hass, Soc. Labor, 7,447; Dobbs, Militant Workers, 2,035.
1960, Kennedy, Dem., 2,556,282; Nixon, Rep., 2,439,956; Hass, Soc. Labor, 7,185; Dobbs, Soc. Workers, 2,678; scattering, 440.
1964, Johnson, Dem., 3,130,954; Goldwater, Rep., 1,673,657; DeBerry, Soc. Workers, 10,456; Hass, Soc. Labor, 5,092; scattering, 2,531.
1968, Nixon, Rep., 2,090,017; Humphrey, Dem., 2,259,405; Wallace, 3d Party, 378,582; Blomen, Soc. Labor, 4,977; Halstead, Soc. Workers, 4,862; Gregory, Peace and Freedom, 7,821; others, 2,264.
1972, Nixon, Rep., 2,714,521; McGovern, Dem., 1,796,951; Schmitz, Amer., 70,593; Jenness, Soc. Workers, 4,639; Hall, Com., 2,686; others, 2,715.
1976, Carter, Dem., 2,328,677; Ford, Rep., 2,205,604; McCarthy, Ind., 50,584; Maddox, Constitution, 25,344; Camejo, Soc. Workers, 3,009; LaRouche, U.S. Labor, 2,744; Hall, Com., 1,891; others, 2,934.
1980, Reagan, Rep., 2,261,872; Carter, Dem., 1,937,540; Anderson, Ind., 292,921; Clark, Libertarian, 33,263; DeBerry, Soc. Workers, 20,291; Commoner, Consumer, 10,430; Hall, Com., 5,184.
1984, Reagan, Rep., 2,584,323; Mondale, Dem., 2,228,131; Bergland, Libertarian, 6,982.
1988, Bush, Rep., 2,300,087; Dukakis, Dem., 2,194,944; McCarthy, Consumer, 19,158; Paul, Lib., 12,051.
1992, Clinton, Dem., 2,239,164; Bush, Rep., 1,791,841; Perot, Ind., 902,667; Marrou, Libertarian, 21,477; Fulani, New Alliance, 4,661.
1996, Clinton, Dem., 2,215,819; Dole, Rep., 1,801,169; Perot, Ref., 430,984; Browne, Libertarian, 28,000; Phillips, Constitutional, 19,552; Hagelin, Natural Law, 5,783.
2000, Gore, Dem., 2,485,967; Bush, Rep., 2,281,127; Nader, Green, 103,392; Buchanan, Reform, 16,023; Phillips, Constitution, 14,428; Browne, Libertarian, 11,248.

Rhode Island

	2000		1996		
City	Gore (D)	Bush (R)	Clinton (D)	Dole (R)	Perot (RF)
Cranston	21,204	10,420	20,901	9,098	3,457
East Providence	13,033	5,072	12,846	4,199	1,971
Pawtucket	15,429	4,598	14,719	3,877	2,508
Providence	31,979	7,669	29,450	7,068	2,733
Warwick	23,948	12,741	23,152	10,414	4,541
Other	143,915	90,055	131,982	70,027	28,513
Totals	**249,508**	**130,555**	**233,050**	**104,683**	**43,723**

Rhode Island Vote Since 1952

1952, Eisenhower, Rep., 210,935; Stevenson, Dem., 203,293; Hallinan, Prog., 187; Hass, Soc. Labor, 83.
1956, Eisenhower, Rep., 225,819; Stevenson, Dem., 161,790.
1960, Kennedy, Dem., 258,032; Nixon, Rep., 147,502.
1964, Johnson, Dem., 315,463; Goldwater, Rep., 74,615.
1968, Nixon, Rep., 122,359; Humphrey, Dem., 246,518; Wallace, 3d Party, 15,678; Halstead, Soc. Workers, 383.
1972, Nixon, Rep., 220,383; McGovern, Dem., 194,645; Jenness, Soc. Workers, 729.
1976, Carter, Dem., 227,636; Ford, Rep., 181,249; MacBride, Libertarian, 715; Camejo, Soc. Workers, 462; Hall, Com., 334; Levin, Soc. Labor, 188.
1980, Reagan, Rep., 154,793; Carter, Dem., 198,342; Anderson, Ind., 59,819; Clark, Libertarian, 2,458; Hall, Com., 218; McReynolds, Soc., 170; DeBerry, Soc. Workers, 90; Griswold, Workers World, 77.
1984, Reagan, Rep., 212,080; Mondale, Dem., 197,106; Bergland, Libertarian, 277.
1988, Bush, Rep., 177,761; Dukakis, Dem., 225,123; Paul, Lib., 825; Fulani, New Alliance, 280.
1992, Clinton, Dem., 213,299; Bush, Rep., 131,601; Perot, Ind., 105,045; Fulani, New Alliance, 1,878.

1996, Clinton, Dem., 233,050; Dole, Rep., 104,683; Perot, Ref., 43,723; Nader, Green, 6,040; Browne, Libertarian, 1,109; Phillips, Taxpayers, 1,021; Hagelin, Natural Law, 435; Moorehead, Workers World, 186.

2000, Gore, Dem., 249,508; Bush, Rep., 130,555; Nader, Ind., 25,052; Buchanan, Reform, 2,273; Browne, Ind., 742; Hagelin, Ind., 271; Moorehead, Ind., 199; Phillips, Ind., 97; McReynolds, Ind., 52; Harris, Ind., 34.

South Carolina

	2000		1996		
County	Gore (D)	Bush (R)	Clinton (D)	Dole (R)	Perot (RF)
Abbeville	3,766	4,450	3,493	3,054	537
Aiken	16,409	33,203	14,314	26,539	1,984
Allendale	2,338	967	2,222	941	87
Anderson	19,606	35,827	17,460	24,137	3,896
Bamberg	3,451	2,047	3,380	1,715	192
Barnwell	3,661	4,521	3,620	3,808	310
Beaufort	17,487	25,561	15,764	17,575	1,838
Berkeley	17,707	24,796	13,358	17,691	1,922
Calhoun	3,063	3,216	2,716	2,520	316
Charleston	49,520	58,229	43,571	48,675	3,514
Cherokee	6,138	9,900	5,821	6,689	1,064
Chester	5,242	4,986	5,108	3,157	758
Chesterfield	6,111	6,266	5,734	4,028	768
Clarendon	5,999	5,186	5,930	3,841	395
Colleton	6,449	6,767	5,329	4,462	550
Darlington	10,253	11,290	8,943	8,220	898
Dillon	4,930	3,975	3,992	2,774	275
Dorchester	12,168	20,734	9,931	15,283	1,591
Edgefield	3,950	4,760	3,576	3,640	244
Fairfield	5,263	3,011	4,719	2,414	284
Florence	17,157	23,678	15,804	18,490	1,563
Georgetown	9,445	10,535	8,298	7,023	950
Greenville	43,810	92,714	41,605	71,210	6,761
Greenwood	8,139	12,193	8,193	8,865	985
Hampton	4,896	2,798	4,828	2,111	344
Horry	29,113	40,300	23,722	26,159	4,446
Jasper	3,646	2,414	4,053	2,024	348
Kershaw	7,428	11,911	6,764	8,513	996
Lancaster	8,782	11,676	8,752	7,544	1,598
Laurens	7,920	12,102	7,055	8,057	1,341
Lee	3,899	2,675	3,588	1,973	320
Lexington	22,830	58,095	18,907	39,658	3,703
McCormick	1,896	1,704	1,858	1,104	148
Marion	7,358	4,687	6,359	3,595	356
Marlboro	5,060	2,699	5,348	2,148	494
Newberry	4,428	7,492	4,804	5,670	682
Oconee	7,571	15,364	7,398	10,503	1,961
Orangeburg	19,802	12,657	18,610	10,494	1,112
Pickens	8,927	24,681	8,369	17,151	2,211
Richland	63,179	50,164	52,222	39,092	3,158
Saluda	2,682	4,098	2,486	2,825	371
Spartanburg	29,559	52,114	26,814	35,972	3,885
Sumter	14,365	15,915	12,198	12,080	933
Union	4,662	6,234	5,407	3,855	749
Williamsburg	6,723	4,524	6,987	3,957	375
York	19,251	33,776	16,873	22,222	3,173
Totals	**566,039**	**786,892**	**506,283**	**573,458**	**64,386**

South Carolina Vote Since 1952

1952, Eisenhower ran on two tickets. Under state law votes cast for two Eisenhower slates of electors could not be combined. Eisenhower, Ind., 158,289; Rep., 9,793; total, 168,082; Stevenson, Dem., 173,004; Hamblen, Proh., 1.

1956, Eisenhower, Rep., 75,700; Stevenson, Dem., 136,372; Byrd, Ind., 88,509; Andrews, Ind., 2.

1960, Kennedy, Dem., 198,129; Nixon, Rep., 188,558; write-in, 1.

1964, Johnson, Dem., 215,700; Goldwater, Rep., 309,048; write-ins: Nixon, 1, Wallace, 5; Powell, 1; Thurmond, 1.

1968, Nixon, Rep., 254,062; Humphrey, Dem., 197,486; Wallace, 3d Party, 215,430.

1972, Nixon, Rep., 477,044; McGovern, Dem., 184,559; United Citizens, 2,265; Schmitz, Amer., 10,075; write-in, 17.

1976, Carter, Dem., 450,807; Ford, Rep., 346,149; Anderson, Amer., 2,996; Maddox, Amer. Ind., 1,950; write-in, 681.

1980, Reagan, Rep., 439,277; Carter, Dem., 428,220; Anderson, Ind., 13,868; Clark, Libertarian, 4,807; Rarick, Amer. Ind., 2,086.

1984, Reagan, Rep., 615,539; Mondale, Dem., 344,459; Bergland, Libertarian, 4,359.

1988, Bush, Rep., 606,443; Dukakis, Dem., 370,554; Paul, Lib., 4,935; Fulani, United Citizens, 4,077.

1992, Clinton, Dem., 479,514; Bush, Rep., 577,507; Perot, Ind., 138,872; Marrou, Libertarian, 2,719; Phillips, U.S. Taxpayers, 2,680; Fulani, New Alliance, 1,235.

1996, Dole, Rep., 573,458; Clinton, Dem., 506,283; Perot, Ref./Patriot, 64,386; Browne, Libertarian, 4,271; Phillips, Taxpayers, 2,043; Hagelin, Natural Law, 1,248.

2000, Bush, Rep., 786,892; Gore, Dem., 566,039; Nader, United Citizens, 20,279; Browne, Libertarian, 4,898; Buchanan, Reform, 3,309; Phillips, Constitution, 1,682; Hagelin, Natural Law, 943.

South Dakota

	2000		1996		
County	Gore (D)	Bush (R)	Clinton (D)	Dole (R)	Perot (RF)
Aurora	513	847	664	709	199
Beadle	3,216	4,347	3,984	3,670	842
Bennett	377	712	507	539	93
Bon Homme	1,162	1,901	1,569	1,428	391
Brookings	4,546	6,212	5,105	5,112	979
Brown	7,173	9,000	7,913	0,001	1,022
Brule	818	1,268	1,091	981	281
Buffalo	256	140	465	134	35
Butte	840	2,760	1,132	1,947	541
Campbell	147	739	202	623	140
Charles Mix	1,300	2,205	1,913	1,711	390
Clark	791	1,272	956	998	272
Clay	2,638	2,363	2,980	2,008	505
Codington	4,192	6,718	4,722	4,995	1,239
Corson	549	629	539	533	216
Custer	955	2,495	1,122	1,740	418
Davison	2,936	4,445	3,364	3,371	737
Day	1,492	1,623	1,840	1,282	395
Deuel	926	1,245	1,090	955	275
Dewey	880	761	1,114	657	195
Douglas	363	1,311	524	1,210	161
Edmunds	676	1,257	973	1,055	263
Fall River	1,133	2,185	1,357	1,636	417
Faulk	388	904	493	726	165
Grant	1,475	2,235	1,805	1,782	471
Gregory	718	1,487	923	1,208	286
Haakon	164	938	284	887	110
Hamlin	923	1,731	1,101	1,352	285
Hand	565	1,419	803	1,187	250
Hanson	457	944	541	801	170
Harding	64	650	151	537	90
Hughes	2,212	5,188	2,788	4,469	531
Hutchinson	1,052	2,497	1,285	2,177	409
Hyde	218	592	309	493	95
Jackson/ Washabaugh	319	687	423	646	88
Jerauld	468	624	656	530	151
Jones	137	509	184	463	75
Kingsbury	1,049	1,612	1,357	1,297	320
Lake	2,331	2,724	2,526	1,966	593
Lawrence	2,797	6,327	3,568	4,430	1,308
Lincoln	3,844	6,546	3,643	4,201	682
Lyman	482	875	646	726	130
McCook	965	1,610	1,166	1,292	245
McPherson	295	1,073	463	1,080	182
Marshall	939	1,097	1,185	861	189
Meade	2,267	6,870	2,960	4,984	1,133
Mellette	222	495	302	417	67
Miner	523	724	739	571	170
Minnehaha	27,042	33,428	29,790	27,432	4,425
Moody	1,318	1,361	1,443	1,024	284
Pennington	11,123	24,696	12,784	19,293	3,149
Perkins	297	1,237	460	983	225
Potter	356	1,112	534	979	181
Roberts	1,700	2,237	2,186	1,646	474
Sanborn	468	767	647	630	151
Shannon	1,667	252	1,926	253	87
Spink	1,274	1,957	1,636	1,651	360
Stanley	402	955	454	795	121
Sully	209	633	321	592	106
Todd	993	478	1,380	482	108
Tripp	799	1,909	1,088	1,680	337
Turner	1,414	2,514	1,682	1,970	385
Union	2,358	3,265	2,378	2,234	555
Walworth	721	1,758	939	1,461	366
Yankton	3,596	4,904	3,775	3,885	1,073
Ziebach	314	384	483	375	62
Totals	**118,804**	**190,700**	**139,333**	**150,543**	**31,250**

South Dakota Vote Since 1952

1952, Eisenhower, Rep., 203,857; Stevenson, Dem., 90,426.

1956, Eisenhower, Rep., 171,569; Stevenson, Dem., 122,288.

1960, Kennedy, Dem., 128,070; Nixon, Rep., 178,417.

1964, Johnson, Dem., 163,010; Goldwater, Rep., 130,108.

1968, Nixon, Rep., 149,841; Humphrey, Dem., 118,023; Wallace, 3d Party, 13,400.

1972, Nixon, Rep., 166,476; McGovern, Dem., 139,945; Jenness, Soc. Workers, 994.

1976, Carter, Dem., 147,068; Ford, Rep., 151,505; MacBride, Libertarian, 1,619; Hall, Com., 318; Camejo, Soc. Workers, 168.

1980, Reagan, Rep., 198,343; Carter, Dem., 103,855; Anderson, Ind., 21,431; Clark, Libertarian, 3,824; Pulley, Soc. Workers, 250.

1984, Reagan, Rep., 200,267; Mondale, Dem., 116,113.

1988, Bush, Rep., 165,415; Dukakis, Dem., 145,560; Paul, Lib., 1,060; Fulani, New Alliance, 730.

1992, Clinton, Dem., 124,888; Bush, Rep., 136,718; Perot, Ind., 73,295.

1996, Dole, Rep., 150,543; Clinton, Dem., 139,333; Perot, Ref., 31,250; Browne, Libertarian, 1,472; Phillips, Taxpayers, 912; Hagelin, Natural Law, 316.

2000, Bush, Rep., 190,700; Gore, Dem., 118,804; Buchanan, Reform, 3,322; Phillips, Ind., 1,781; Browne, Libertarian, 1,662.

Tennessee

	2000		1996		
County	Gore (D)	Bush (R)	Clinton (D)	Dole (R)	Perot (RF)
Anderson	13,556	14,688	13,457	11,943	1,817
Bedford	6,136	5,911	5,735	4,634	823
Benton	3,700	2,484	4,341	2,395	663
Bledsoe	1,756	2,380	1,621	1,626	251
Blount	14,688	25,273	14,687	19,310	2,556
Bradley	8,768	20,167	9,095	15,478	1,856
Campbell	6,492	5,784	6,122	4,393	785
Cannon	2,697	1,924	2,318	1,468	361
Carroll	5,239	5,465	4,912	4,206	697
Carter	6,724	12,111	6,218	10,540	1,383
Cheatham	6,062	6,356	4,883	4,283	705
Chester	2,192	3,487	1,922	2,746	203
Claiborne	3,841	5,023	3,861	4,023	727
Clay	1,931	1,468	1,559	1,108	316
Cocke	3,872	6,185	3,326	4,481	798
Coffee	8,741	8,788	7,951	7,038	1,205
Crockett	2,705	2,676	2,256	1,872	201
Cumberland	7,644	10,994	6,676	8,096	1,399
Davidson	120,508	84,117	110,805	78,453	9,018
Decatur	2,278	2,046	2,262	1,712	229
De Kalb	3,765	2,411	3,213	1,696	342
Dickson	8,332	7,016	7,458	5,283	996
Dyer	5,425	6,282	5,602	5,059	676
Fayette	5,037	6,402	4,655	4,406	416
Fentress	2,529	3,417	2,332	2,307	386
Franklin	7,828	6,560	6,929	5,296	1,057
Gibson	8,663	8,286	8,851	6,614	891
Giles	5,527	4,377	4,948	3,269	733
Grainger	2,361	3,746	2,162	2,875	382
Greene	7,909	12,540	6,885	9,779	1,604
Grundy	2,970	1,553	2,596	1,094	326
Hamblen	7,564	11,824	7,006	9,797	1,106
Hamilton	51,708	66,605	48,008	55,205	6,699
Hancock	690	1,343	760	1,259	116
Hardeman	4,953	3,729	4,859	2,961	346
Hardin	3,735	4,951	3,508	3,980	594
Hawkins	6,753	10,071	6,367	8,164	1,282
Haywood	3,887	2,554	3,565	2,293	154
Henderson	3,166	5,153	2,841	4,002	408
Henry	6,093	5,944	6,153	4,272	992
Hickman	4,239	2,914	3,917	2,002	460
Houston	2,081	993	1,868	742	182
Humphreys	4,205	2,387	3,675	1,892	423
Jackson	3,304	1,384	2,889	944	289
Jefferson	5,226	8,657	4,688	6,446	882
Johnson	1,813	3,740	1,698	3,137	489
Knox	60,969	86,851	61,158	70,761	6,402
Lake	1,419	781	1,273	589	110
Lauderdale	4,224	3,329	4,349	2,481	308
Lawrence	6,643	7,613	6,188	6,115	973
Lewis	2,281	2,037	1,971	1,298	316
Lincoln	5,060	5,435	4,361	4,551	761
Loudon	5,905	10,266	5,552	7,097	889
McMinn	6,142	10,155	5,987	7,655	1,033
McNairy	4,003	4,897	4,050	3,960	519
Macon	3,059	3,366	2,240	2,481	421
Madison	15,781	17,862	13,577	14,908	968
Marion	5,441	4,651	5,194	3,166	768
Marshall	5,107	4,105	4,447	2,781	603
Maury	11,127	11,930	10,367	8,737	1,366
Meigs	1,555	1,797	1,476	1,228	245
Monroe	5,327	7,514	4,872	5,257	713
Montgomery	18,818	19,644	16,498	15,133	1,781
Moore	1,107	1,145	935	846	177
Morgan	2,921	3,144	2,767	2,070	446
Obion	6,056	6,168	6,226	4,310	932
Overton	4,507	2,875	3,800	1,756	431
Perry	1,650	1,165	1,444	747	178
Pickett	939	1,281	901	1,046	116
Polk	2,574	2,907	2,450	1,910	377
Putnam	10,785	11,248	10,047	9,093	1,487
Rhea	3,722	5,900	3,969	4,476	694
Roane	9,575	11,345	9,744	9,044	1,438
Robertson	10,249	9,675	8,465	6,685	993
Rutherford	27,360	33,445	22,815	24,565	3,787
Scott	2,967	3,579	2,506	2,646	431
Sequatchie	1,648	2,169	1,598	1,391	288
Sevier	8,208	16,734	7,136	11,847	1,650
Shelby	190,404	141,756	179,663	136,315	8,307
Smith	4,884	2,384	3,812	1,857	346
Stewart	2,870	1,826	2,962	1,306	386
Sullivan	21,354	33,482	20,571	29,296	3,555
Sumner	22,118	27,601	19,205	20,863	2,783
Tipton	6,300	10,070	6,596	7,585	799
Trousdale	1,966	950	1,615	683	190
Unicoi	2,566	3,780	2,131	3,122	447
Union	2,564	3,199	2,421	2,253	385
Van Buren	1,255	845	1,010	504	128
Warren	7,378	5,552	6,389	4,226	917
Washington	14,769	22,579	13,259	18,960	2,237
Wayne	1,859	3,370	1,574	2,715	323
Weakley	5,570	6,106	5,657	4,622	873
White	4,135	3,525	3,592	2,498	505
Williamson	18,745	38,901	15,231	27,699	2,071
Wilson	16,561	18,844	13,655	13,817	1,841
Totals	**981,720**	**1,061,949**	**909,146**	**863,530**	**105,918**

Tennessee Vote Since 1952

1952, Eisenhower, Rep., 446,147; Stevenson, Dem., 443,710; Hamblen, Proh., 1,432; Hallinan, Prog., 885; MacArthur, Christian Nationalist, 379.

1956, Eisenhower, Rep., 462,288; Stevenson, Dem., 456,507; Andrews, Ind., 19,820; Holtwick, Proh., 789.

1960, Kennedy, Dem., 481,453; Nixon, Rep., 556,577; Faubus, States' Rights, 11,304; Decker, Proh., 2,458.

1964, Johnson, Dem., 635,047; Goldwater, Rep., 508,965; write-in, 34.

1968, Nixon, Rep., 472,592; Humphrey, Dem., 351,233; Wallace, 3d Party, 424,792.

1972, Nixon, Rep., 813,147; McGovern, Dem., 357,293; Schmitz, Amer., 30,373; write-in, 369.

1976, Carter, Dem., 825,879; Ford, Rep., 633,969; Anderson, Amer., 5,769; McCarthy, Ind., 5,004; Maddox, Amer. Ind., 2,303; MacBride, Libertarian, 1,375; Hall, Com., 547; LaRouche, U.S. Labor, 512; Bubar, Proh., 442; Miller, Ind., 316; write-in, 230.

1980, Reagan, Rep., 787,761; Carter, Dem., 783,051; Anderson, Ind., 35,991; Clark, Libertarian, 7,116; Commoner, Citizens, 1,112; Bubar, Statesman, 521; McReynolds, Soc., 519; Hall, Com., 503; DeBerry, Soc. Workers, 490; Griswold, Workers World, 400; write-ins, 152.

1984, Reagan, Rep., 990,212; Mondale, Dem., 711,714; Bergland, Libertarian, 3,072.

1988, Bush, Rep., 947,233; Dukakis, Dem., 679,794; Paul, Ind., 2,041; Duke, Ind., 1,807.

1992, Clinton, Dem., 933,521; Bush, Rep., 841,300; Perot, Ind., 199,968; Marrou, Libertarian, 1,847.

1996, Clinton, Dem., 909,146; Dole, Rep., 863,530; Perot, Ind. (Ref.), 105,918; Nader, Ind., 6,427; Browne, Ind., 5,020; Phillips, Ind., 1,818; Collins, Ind., 688; Hagelin, Ind., 636; Michael, Ind., 408; Dodge, Ind., 324.

2000, Bush, Rep., 1,061,949; Gore, Dem., 981,720; Nader, Green, 19,781; Browne, Libertarian, 4,284; Buchanan, Reform, 4,250; Brown, Ind., 1,606; Phillips, Ind., 1,015; Hagelin, Reform, 613; Venson, Ind., 535.

Texas

	2000		1996		
County	Gore (D)	Bush (R)	Clinton (D)	Dole (R)	Perot (RF)
Anderson	5,041	9,835	5,693	6,458	1,170
Andrews	876	3,091	1,181	2,360	431
Angelina	9,957	16,648	11,346	11,789	2,160
Aransas	2,637	5,390	2,964	3,769	655
Archer	993	2,951	1,235	1,974	437
Armstrong	150	772	272	582	75
Atascosa	4,322	6,231	4,259	4,102	813
Austin	2,407	6,661	2,719	4,669	577
Bailey	488	1,589	706	1,246	109
Bandera	1,426	5,613	1,383	3,700	520
Bastrop	6,973	10,310	6,773	6,323	1,342
Baylor	663	1,285	955	860	262
Bee	3,795	4,429	4,561	3,611	539
Bell	21,011	41,208	22,638	30,348	3,666
Bexar	185,158	215,613	180,308	161,619	17,822
Blanco	811	2,777	1,028	1,919	330
Borden	62	283	93	194	45
Bosque	1,930	4,745	2,427	2,840	739
Bowie	11,662	18,325	13,657	12,750	2,760
Brazoria	24,883	53,445	22,959	36,392	5,869
Brazos	12,359	32,864	13,968	22,082	2,215
Brewster	1,349	1,867	1,643	1,438	299
Briscoe	224	544	408	416	65
Brooks	1,854	556	2,945	413	108
Brown	3,138	9,609	4,138	6,524	1,081
Burleson	2,235	3,542	2,419	2,174	347
Burnet	3,557	9,286	4,123	5,744	1,108
Caldwell	3,872	5,216	3,961	3,239	545
Calhoun	2,766	3,724	2,753	2,832	507
Callahan	1,174	3,656	1,666	2,480	534
Cameron	33,214	27,800	34,891	18,434	2,760
Camp	1,625	2,121	1,912	1,488	252
Carson	480	2,216	742	1,742	227
Cass	4,618	6,295	5,691	4,066	1,038
Castro	727	1,607	1,107	1,231	144

	2000		1996		
County	Gore (D)	Bush (R)	Clinton (D)	Dole (R)	Perot (RF)
Chambers	2,888	6,769	2,876	4,101	818
Cherokee	4,755	9,599	5,185	6,483	971
Childress	602	1,506	719	1,072	165
Clay	1,460	3,112	1,690	1,997	465
Cochran	344	807	541	667	127
Coke	355	1,137	595	790	157
Coleman	853	2,687	1,488	1,703	349
Collin	42,884	128,179	37,854	83,750	10,443
Collingsworth	429	974	581	729	118
Colorado	2,229	4,913	2,795	3,381	574
Comal	7,131	24,599	7,132	16,763	1,903
Comanche	1,636	3,334	2,138	2,123	511
Concho	268	818	434	488	107
Cooke	3,153	10,128	3,782	7,320	1,150
Coryell	4,493	10,321	5,300	7,143	1,443
Cottle	241	502	404	331	77
Crane	387	1,246	616	984	201
Crockett	467	924	684	714	147
Crosby	705	1,270	1,122	968	189
Culberson	577	413	804	329	99
Dallam	341	1,385	483	970	170
Dallas	275,308	322,345	255,766	260,058	36,759
Dawson	1,463	3,337	1,612	2,319	232
Deaf Smith	1,240	3,687	1,655	3,051	310
Delta	726	1,143	849	744	146
Denton	40,144	102,171	36,138	65,313	9,294
DeWitt	1,570	4,541	2,074	3,577	483
Dickens	284	589	509	421	117
Dimmit	2,678	1,032	2,242	604	128
Donley	360	1,333	495	988	97
Duval	3,990	1,010	3,958	543	136
Eastland	1,774	4,531	2,594	3,272	705
Ector	9,425	22,893	12,017	17,746	2,511
Edwards	261	663	437	511	60
Ellis	10,629	26,091	10,832	16,046	2,750
El Paso	83,848	57,574	83,964	43,255	6,300
Erath	2,804	8,126	3,664	4,750	1,134
Falls	2,417	3,239	3,256	2,260	479
Fannin	4,102	6,074	4,276	3,495	980
Fayette	2,542	6,658	3,119	4,195	708
Fisher	884	968	1,142	537	170
Floyd	580	1,830	986	1,530	126
Foard	263	286	355	166	52
Fort Bend	47,569	73,567	38,163	49,945	4,363
Franklin	1,018	2,420	1,484	1,575	386
Freestone	2,316	4,247	2,630	2,888	568
Frio	2,317	1,774	2,593	1,225	253
Gaines	723	2,691	1,012	1,812	353
Galveston	40,020	50,397	38,458	35,251	5,897
Garza	454	1,302	703	946	103
Gillespie	1,511	8,096	1,655	5,867	542
Glasscock	39	528	70	382	30
Goliad	1,233	2,108	1,135	1,335	148
Gonzales	1,877	4,092	2,110	2,687	354
Gray	1,376	6,732	2,114	6,102	568
Grayson	13,647	25,596	14,338	17,169	3,745
Gregg	11,244	26,739	13,659	21,611	2,079
Grimes	2,450	4,197	2,584	2,564	538
Guadalupe	8,311	21,499	8,079	14,254	1,811
Hale	2,158	6,868	3,204	5,905	605
Hall	472	966	750	626	94
Hamilton	878	2,447	1,200	1,493	323
Hansford	198	1,874	343	1,493	105
Hardeman	566	976	750	610	168
Hardin	5,595	11,962	7,179	8,529	2,112
Harris	418,267	529,159	386,726	421,462	42,364
Harrison	8,878	13,834	10,307	9,835	1,427
Hartley	359	1,645	403	1,242	101
Haskell	1,401	1,488	1,374	966	225
Hays	11,387	20,170	11,580	12,865	1,990
Hemphill	251	1,203	344	986	104
Henderson	8,704	16,607	10,085	10,345	2,274
Hidalgo	61,390	38,301	56,335	24,437	3,536
Hill	3,524	7,054	3,988	4,401	1,052
Hockley	1,419	5,250	2,170	4,230	519
Hood	4,704	12,429	5,459	7,575	1,445
Hopkins	3,692	7,076	4,522	4,341	1,034
Houston	2,833	5,308	3,383	3,443	585
Howard	2,744	6,668	3,732	5,007	1,037
Hudspeth	380	514	427	367	92
Hunt	7,857	16,177	8,801	10,746	2,225
Hutchinson	1,796	7,443	2,553	6,350	864
Irion	162	624	213	386	86
Jack	822	2,107	1,019	1,162	301
Jackson	1,446	3,365	1,785	2,533	309
Jasper	4,533	7,071	5,039	4,523	1,041
Jeff Davis	283	708	370	482	99
Jefferson	45,409	40,320	45,854	32,821	5,314
Jim Hogg	1,512	623	1,437	307	64
Jim Wells	7,418	4,498	7,116	2,989	430
Johnson	11,778	26,202	12,817	16,246	3,250
Jones	1,899	4,080	2,422	2,351	614
Karnes	1,617	2,638	2,154	1,869	291
Kaufman	7,455	15,290	7,383	8,697	1,831
Kendall	1,901	8,788	2,092	5,940	620
Kenedy	119	106	133	71	4
Kent	185	346	260	187	67
Kerr	4,002	14,637	4,192	11,173	1,236
Kimble	328	1,313	521	898	131
King	14	120	46	97	29
Kinney	486	932	503	650	97
Kleberg	4,481	4,526	5,136	3,391	431
Knox	617	947	785	599	149
Lamar	5,553	9,775	6,075	6,393	1,198
Lamb	1,114	3,451	1,683	2,593	283
Lampasas	1,569	4,526	1,819	3,008	509
LaSalle	1,266	731	1,522	570	85
Lavaca	2,171	5,288	2,575	3,697	551
Lee	1,733	3,699	2,008	2,354	421
Leon	1,893	4,362	2,217	2,839	499
Liberty	7,311	12,458	6,877	7,784	2,011
Limestone	2,768	4,212	3,236	2,691	693
Lipscomb	206	1,072	357	869	115
Live Oak	1,114	2,828	1,372	1,929	292
Llano	2,143	6,295	2,633	4,290	762
Loving	29	124	14	48	15
Lubbock	18,469	56,054	22,786	47,304	3,996
Lynn	562	1,507	903	1,151	136
McCulloch	794	2,084	1,231	1,405	290
McLennan	23,462	43,955	27,050	30,666	5,131
McMullen	77	358	117	274	35
Madison	1,241	2,333	1,470	1,576	293
Marion	1,852	2,039	2,028	1,260	353
Martin	415	1,520	643	973	140
Mason	417	1,352	618	949	151
Matagorda	4,696	7,584	5,374	5,876	1,190
Maverick	5,995	3,143	5,307	1,050	202
Medina	4,025	8,590	3,880	5,710	715
Menard	334	642	490	443	102
Midland	7,534	31,514	9,513	25,382	2,079
Milam	3,429	4,706	3,869	3,019	657
Mills	548	1,738	748	1,044	230
Mitchell	837	1,708	1,213	949	232
Montague	2,256	4,951	2,718	3,029	842
Montgomery	20,200	80,600	20,722	51,011	6,065
Moore	1,040	4,201	1,358	3,353	359
Morris	2,455	2,381	2,973	1,449	402
Motley	118	514	164	380	56
Nacogdoches	6,204	13,145	7,641	10,361	1,352
Navarro	5,366	8,358	6,078	5,236	1,140
Newton	2,503	2,423	2,554	1,409	474
Nolan	1,874	3,337	2,582	2,166	613
Nueces	45,349	49,906	50,009	37,470	5,103
Ochiltree	251	2,687	467	2,448	167
Oldham	108	659	213	583	77
Orange	11,887	17,325	13,741	12,560	2,836
Palo Pinto	3,263	5,690	3,938	3,666	1,011
Panola	3,011	5,975	4,168	4,008	777
Parker	8,878	23,651	9,447	14,580	2,703
Parmer	447	2,274	676	2,042	160
Pecos	1,539	2,700	1,816	1,730	369
Polk	6,877	11,746	6,360	6,473	1,347
Potter	7,242	17,629	9,273	14,995	1,799
Presidio	1,064	618	1,205	383	111
Rains	1,225	2,049	1,265	1,123	335
Randall	7,209	33,921	9,177	28,266	1,985
Reagan	282	959	407	645	101
Real	316	1,146	414	845	178
Red River	2,219	2,941	2,339	1,783	433
Reeves	1,872	1,273	2,279	1,007	245
Refugio	1,172	1,721	1,635	1,376	222
Roberts	72	472	122	421	40
Robertson	3,283	3,007	2,912	1,944	315
Rockwall	3,642	13,666	3,289	8,319	1,121
Runnels	969	3,020	1,417	1,941	396
Rusk	4,841	11,611	5,988	8,423	1,072
Sabine	1,753	2,764	1,913	1,660	334
San Augustine	1,636	2,116	1,924	1,296	324
San Jacinto	2,946	4,623	2,771	2,878	810
San Patricio	7,840	10,599	8,132	7,678	1,085
San Saba	618	1,691	726	991	194
Schleicher	338	826	505	587	111
Scurry	1,193	4,060	2,099	2,929	813
Shackelford	264	1,066	502	792	169
Shelby	3,227	5,692	3,720	3,482	815
Sherman	144	998	243	809	89
Smith	16,470	43,320	18,265	32,171	2,933
Somervell	752	2,120	993	1,099	273
Starr	6,505	1,911	6,312	756	157
Stephens	811	2,425	1,218	1,714	336
Sterling	132	520	186	394	86
Stonewall	294	496	487	323	105
Sutton	468	1,063	508	688	102

	2000		1996		
County	Gore (D)	Bush (R)	Clinton (D)	Dole (R)	Perot (RF)
Swisher	856	1,612	1,224	1,159	195
Tarrant	173,758	286,921	170,431	208,312	28,715
Taylor	10,504	31,701	13,213	23,682	2,912
Terrell	219	243	278	185	47
Terry	1,108	2,910	1,272	2,013	269
Throckmorton	228	608	285	360	90
Titus	3,008	4,995	3,725	3,438	744
Tom Green	9,288	24,733	11,782	18,112	2,757
Travis	125,526	141,235	128,970	98,454	14,008
Trinity	2,142	3,093	2,774	2,058	460
Tyler	2,775	4,236	3,340	2,804	645
Upshur	4,180	8,448	5,032	5,174	1,086
Upton	266	982	424	685	88
Uvalde	3,436	4,855	3,397	3,494	403
Val Verde	5,056	6,223	5,623	4,357	548
Van Zandt	5,245	12,383	5,752	7,453	1,756
Victoria	8,176	18,787	8,238	14,457	1,197
Walker	4,943	9,076	6,088	7,177	1,186
Waller	5,046	5,686	4,535	3,559	499
Ward	1,256	2,534	1,644	1,620	446
Washington	2,996	8,645	3,460	6,319	601
Webb	18,120	13,076	18,997	4,712	936
Wharton	4,838	8,455	5,176	6,163	871
Wheeler	579	1,787	750	1,355	174
Wichita	14,108	27,802	15,775	20,495	3,371
Wilbarger	1,356	3,138	1,730	2,037	465
Willacy	3,218	1,789	3,789	1,332	241
Williamson	26,591	65,041	24,175	36,836	4,931
Wilson	3,997	7,509	3,713	4,530	760
Winkler	556	1,468	872	1,009	218
Wise	4,830	11,234	5,056	6,330	1,516
Wood	3,893	9,810	4,711	6,228	1,184
Yoakum	531	1,911	738	1,485	218
Young	1,843	5,022	2,394	3,647	639
Zapata	1,638	953	1,786	521	131
Zavala	2,616	751	2,629	463	91
Totals	**2,433,746**	**3,799,639**	**2,459,683**	**2,736,167**	**378,537**

Texas Vote Since 1952

1952, Eisenhower, Rep., 1,102,878; Stevenson, Dem., 969,228; Hamblen, Proh., 1,983; MacArthur, Christian Nationalist, 833; MacArthur, Constitution, 730; Hallinan, Prog., 294.

1956, Eisenhower, Rep., 1,080,619; Stevenson, Dem., 859,958; Andrews, Ind., 14,591.

1960, Kennedy, Dem., 1,167,932; Nixon, Rep., 1,121,699; Sullivan, Constitution, 18,169; Decker, Proh., 3,870; write-in, 15.

1964, Johnson, Dem., 1,663,185; Goldwater, Rep., 958,566; Lightburn, Constitution, 5,060.

1968, Nixon, Rep., 1,227,844; Humphrey, Dem., 1,266,804; Wallace, 3d Party, 584,269; write-in, 489.

1972, Nixon, Rep., 2,298,896; McGovern, Dem., 1,154,289; Schmitz, Amer., 6,039; Jenness, Soc. Workers, 8,664; others, 3,393.

1976, Carter, Dem., 2,082,319; Ford, Rep., 1,953,300; McCarthy, Ind., 20,118; Anderson, Amer., 11,442; Camejo, Soc. Workers, 1,723; write-in, 2,982.

1980, Reagan, Rep., 2,510,705; Carter, Dem., 1,881,147; Anderson, Ind., 111,613; Clark, Libertarian, 37,643; write-in, 528.

1984, Reagan, Rep., 3,433,428; Mondale, Dem., 1,949,276.

1988, Bush, Rep., 3,036,829; Dukakis, Dem., 2,352,748; Paul, Lib., 30,355; Fulani, New Alliance, 7,208.

1992, Clinton, Dem., 2,281,815; Bush, Rep., 2,496,071; Perot, Ind., 1,354,781; Marrou, Libertarian, 19,699.

1996, Dole, Rep., 2,736,167; Clinton, Dem., 2,459,683; Perot, Ind. (Ref.), 378,537; Browne, Libertarian, 20,256; Phillips, Taxpayers, 7,472; Hagelin, Natural Law, 4,422.

2000, Bush, Rep., 3,799,639; Gore, Dem., 2,433,746; Nader, Green, 137,994; Browne, Libertarian, 23,160; Buchanan, Ind., 12,394.

Utah

	2000		1996		
County	Gore (D)	Bush (R)	Clinton (D)	Dole (R)	Perot (RF)
Beaver	541	1,653	687	1,164	217
Box Elder	2,555	12,288	3,170	8,373	1,578
Cache	5,170	25,920	6,595	16,832	2,399
Carbon	3,298	3,758	4,172	2,343	952
Daggett	104	317	131	237	55
Davis	18,845	64,375	19,301	42,768	7,495
Duchesne	779	3,622	892	2,648	566
Emery	958	3,243	1,371	2,033	663
Garfield	178	1,719	283	1,330	222
Grand	1,158	1,822	1,199	1,384	432
Iron	1,789	10,106	1,887	6,550	716
Juab	619	2,023	928	1,290	353
Kane	387	2,254	304	1,682	290
Millard	696	3,850	945	2,681	505
Morgan	553	2,464	859	1,659	337
Piute	133	626	176	475	59
Rich	152	736	179	523	88
Salt Lake	107,576	171,585	117,951	127,951	27,620
San Juan	1,838	2,721	1,675	2,139	271
Sanpete	1,211	5,781	1,568	3,631	801
Sevier	1,046	5,763	1,327	4,031	670
Summit	4,601	6,168	4,177	3,867	971
Tooele	4,001	7,807	3,992	3,881	1,244
Uintah	1,387	6,733	1,714	4,743	899
Utah	16,445	98,255	18,291	69,653	8,106
Wasatch	1,476	3,819	1,374	2,222	558
Washington	5,465	25,481	4,816	17,637	2,069
Wayne	202	953	265	741	121
Weber	19,890	39,254	21,404	27,443	6,204
Totals	**203,053**	**515,096**	**221,633**	**361,911**	**66,461**

Utah Vote Since 1952

1952, Eisenhower, Rep., 194,190; Stevenson, Dem., 135,364.

1956, Eisenhower, Rep., 215,631; Stevenson, Dem., 118,364.

1960, Kennedy, Dem., 169,248; Nixon, Rep., 205,361; Dobbs, Soc. Workers, 100.

1964, Johnson, Dem., 219,628; Goldwater, Rep., 181,785.

1968, Nixon, Rep., 238,728; Humphrey, Dem., 156,665; Wallace, 3d Party, 26,906; Halstead, Soc. Workers, 89; Peace and Freedom, 180.

1972, Nixon, Rep., 323,643; McGovern, Dem., 126,284; Schmitz, Amer., 28,549.

1976, Carter, Dem., 182,110; Ford, Rep., 337,908; Anderson, Amer., 13,304; McCarthy, Ind., 3,907; MacBride, Libertarian, 2,438; Maddox, Amer. Ind., 1,162; Camejo, Soc. Workers, 268; Hall, Com., 121.

1980, Reagan, Rep., 439,687; Carter, Dem., 124,266; Anderson, Ind., 30,284; Clark, Libertarian, 7,226; Commoner, Citizens, 1,009; Greaves, Amer., 965; Rarick, Amer. Ind., 522; Hall, Com., 139; DeBerry, Soc. Workers, 124.

1984, Reagan, Rep., 469,105; Mondale, Dem., 155,369; Bergland, Libertarian, 2,447.

1988, Bush, Rep., 428,442; Dukakis, Dem., 207,352; Paul, Lib., 7,473; Dennis, Amer., 2,158.

1992, Clinton, Dem., 183,429; Bush, Rep., 322,632; Perot, Ind., 203,400; Gritz, Populist/America First, 28,602; Marrou, Libertarian, 1,900; Hagelin, Natural Law, 1,319; LaRouche, Ind., 1,089.

1996, Dole, Rep., 361,911; Clinton, Dem., 221,633; Perot, Ref., 66,461; Nader, Green, 4,615; Browne, Libertarian, 4,129; Phillips, Taxpayers, 2,601; Templin, Ind. Amer., 1,290; Crane, Ind., 1,101; Hagelin, Natural Law, 1,085; Moorehead, Workers World, 298; Harris, Soc. Workers, 235; Dodge, Proh., 111.

2000, Bush, Rep., 515,096; Gore, Dem., 203,053; Nader, Green, 35,850; Buchanan, Reform, 9,319; Browne, Libertarian, 3,616; Phillips, Ind. Amer., 2,709; Hagelin, Natural Law, 763; Harris, Soc. Workers, 186; Youngkeit, Ind., 161.

Vermont

	2000		1996		
City	Gore (D)	Bush (R)	Clinton (D)	Dole (R)	Perot (RF)
Barre City	1,895	1,676	1,890	1,107	376
Bennington	3,745	2,384	3,454	1,654	960
Brattleboro	3,128	1,486	3,016	1,195	395
Burlington	10,961	4,273	11,600	3,762	1,309
Colchester	3,876	2,989	3,314	2,035	769
Essex	4,632	4,344	4,063	2,944	796
Hartford	2,462	1,957	2,106	1,290	400
Montpelier	2,576	1,265	2,458	1,118	269
Rutland City	3,916	3,003	3,817	2,320	741
S. Burlington	4,393	2,995	3,929	2,274	548
Springfield	2,386	1,720	2,267	1,189	561
Other	105,052	191,683	95,980	59,464	23,900
Totals	**149,022**	**119,775**	**137,894**	**80,352**	**31,024**

Vermont Vote Since 1952

1952, Eisenhower, Rep., 109,717; Stevenson, Dem., 43,355; Hallinan, Prog., 282; Hoopes, Soc., 185.

1956, Eisenhower, Rep., 110,390; Stevenson, Dem., 42,549; scattered, 39.

1960, Kennedy, Dem., 69,186; Nixon, Rep., 98,131.

1964, Johnson, Dem., 107,674; Goldwater, Rep., 54,868.

1968, Nixon, Rep., 85,142; Humphrey, Dem., 70,255; Wallace, 3d Party, 5,104; Halstead, Soc. Workers, 295; Gregory, New Party, 579.

1972, Nixon, Rep., 117,149; McGovern, Dem., 68,174; Spock, Liberty Union, 1,010; Jenness, Soc. Workers, 296; scattered, 318.

1976, Carter, Dem., 77,798; Carter, Ind. Vermonter, 991; Ford, Rep., 100,387; McCarthy, Ind., 4,001; Camejo, Soc. Workers, 430; LaRouche, U.S. Labor, 196; scattered, 99.

1980, Reagan, Rep., 94,598; Carter, Dem., 81,891; Anderson, Ind., 31,760; Commoner, Citizens, 2,316; Clark, Libertarian, 1,900; McReynolds, Liberty Union, 136; Hall, Com., 118; DeBerry, Soc. Workers, 75; scattering, 413.

1984, Reagan, Rep., 135,865; Mondale, Dem., 95,730; Bergland, Libertarian, 1,002.

1988, Bush, Rep., 124,331; Dukakis, Dem., 115,775; Paul, Lib., 1,000; LaRouche, Ind., 275.

1992, Clinton, Dem., 133,590; Bush, Rep., 88,122; Perot, Ind., 65,985.

1996, Clinton, Dem., 137,894; Dole, Rep., 80,352; Perot, Ref., 31,024; Nader, Green, 5,585; Browne, Libertarian, 1,183; Hagelin, Natural Law, 498; Peron, Grass Roots, 480; Phillips, Taxpayers, 382; Hollis, Liberty Union, 292; Harris, Soc. Workers, 199.

2000, Gore, Dem., 149,022; Bush, Rep., 119,775; Nader, Green, 20,374; Buchanan, Reform, 2,192; Lane, Grass Roots, 1,044; Browne, Libertarian, 784; Hagelin, Natural Law, 219; McReynolds, Liberty Union, 161; Phillips, Constitution, 153; Harris, Soc. Workers, 70.

Virginia

County	2000 Gore (D)	2000 Bush (R)	1996 Clinton (D)	1996 Dole (R)	1996 Perot (RF)
Accomack	5,092	6,352	5,220	5,013	1,218
Albemarle	16,255	18,291	14,089	15,243	1,533
Alleghany	2,214	2,808	2,398	2,015	607
Amelia	1,754	2,947	1,625	2,119	323
Amherst	4,812	6,660	4,864	5,094	835
Appomattox	2,132	3,654	2,239	2,625	510
Arlington	50,260	28,555	45,573	26,106	2,782
Augusta	6,643	17,744	5,965	13,458	1,916
Bath	822	1,311	922	847	247
Bedford	8,160	17,224	7,786	11,955	1,976
Bland	851	1,759	939	1,167	385
Botetourt	4,627	8,867	4,576	6,404	1,138
Brunswick	3,387	2,561	3,442	2,059	340
Buchanan	5,745	3,867	6,551	2,785	858
Buckingham	2,561	2,738	2,374	1,974	392
Campbell	6,659	13,162	6,788	10,273	1,505
Caroline	4,314	3,873	3,897	2,816	521
Carroll	3,638	7,142	3,611	5,088	1,158
Charles City	1,981	1,023	1,842	729	178
Charlotte	2,017	2,855	2,007	2,103	431
Chesterfield	38,638	69,924	30,220	56,650	6,004
Clarke	2,166	2,883	1,906	2,201	379
Craig	851	1,580	895	979	262
Culpeper	4,364	7,440	3,907	5,688	787
Cumberland	1,405	1,974	1,303	1,544	275
Dickenson	3,951	3,122	3,913	2,229	660
Dinwiddie	4,001	4,959	3,871	3,503	666
Essex	1,750	1,995	1,668	1,627	188
Fairfax	196,501	202,181	170,150	176,033	16,134
Fauquier	8,296	14,456	6,759	11,063	1,287
Floyd	1,957	3,423	1,909	2,374	545
Fluvanna	3,431	4,962	2,676	3,442	457
Franklin	7,145	11,225	7,300	7,382	2,015
Frederick	7,158	14,574	5,976	10,608	1,599
Giles	3,004	3,574	3,196	2,566	841
Gloucester	4,553	8,718	4,710	6,447	1,266
Goochland	3,197	5,378	2,784	4,119	424
Grayson	2,467	4,236	2,661	3,004	675
Greene	1,774	3,375	1,440	2,351	346
Greensville	2,314	1,565	2,381	1,176	263
Halifax	5,963	7,732	5,599	6,490	876
Hanover	12,044	28,614	9,880	22,086	2,447
Henrico	48,645	62,887	41,121	54,430	5,920
Henry	8,898	11,870	9,061	9,110	2,370
Highland	453	942	446	631	134
Isle of Wight	5,162	7,587	4,952	5,416	893
James City	9,090	14,628	7,247	10,120	1,116
King and Queen	1,387	1,423	1,393	1,073	213
King George	2,070	3,590	1,875	2,597	341
King William	2,125	3,547	1,765	2,346	339
Lancaster	1,937	3,411	1,844	2,709	324
Lee	4,031	4,551	4,444	3,225	822
Loudoun	30,938	42,453	19,942	25,715	3,082
Louisa	4,309	5,461	3,761	3,768	693
Lunenburg	2,026	2,510	1,995	2,063	299
Madison	1,844	2,940	1,734	2,296	360
Mathews	1,499	2,951	1,602	2,206	403
Mecklenburg	4,797	6,600	4,408	4,933	789
Middlesex	1,671	2,844	1,704	2,141	350
Montgomery	11,720	13,991	10,867	10,517	2,594
Nelson	2,907	2,913	2,782	1,988	411
New Kent	2,055	3,934	1,859	2,852	520
Northampton	2,340	2,299	2,569	1,763	522
Northumberland	2,118	3,362	1,957	2,605	375
Nottoway	2,460	2,870	2,327	2,416	346
Orange	4,126	5,991	3,590	4,435	750
Page	2,720	5,089	2,060	3,876	640
Patrick	2,254	4,901	2,301	3,547	719
Pittsylvania	7,834	15,760	7,681	12,127	1,469
Powhatan	2,708	6,820	2,254	4,679	626
Prince Edward	2,922	3,214	2,678	2,530	403
Prince George	4,182	6,579	3,498	5,216	698
Prince William	44,745	52,788	33,462	39,292	4,881
Pulaski	5,255	7,089	5,333	5,387	1,399
Rappahannock	1,462	1,850	1,405	1,505	213
Richmond	1,076	1,784	1,101	1,424	201
Roanoke	16,141	25,740	15,387	20,700	2,934
Rockbridge	2,953	4,522	3,116	3,274	760
Rockingham	5,834	17,482	5,867	14,035	1,318
Russell	5,442	5,065	5,437	3,706	862
Scott	3,552	5,535	3,449	4,086	798
Shenandoah	4,420	9,636	4,224	7,440	1,353
Smyth	4,836	6,580	4,990	4,966	1,407
Southampton	3,359	3,293	3,454	2,275	564
Spotsylvania	13,455	20,739	10,342	13,786	1,860
Stafford	12,596	20,731	9,902	14,098	1,856
Surry	1,845	1,313	1,753	944	181
Sussex	2,006	1,745	2,089	1,378	256
Tazewell	7,227	8,655	7,500	6,131	1,554
Warren	4,313	6,335	3,814	4,657	904
Washington	7,549	12,064	6,939	9,098	1,654
Wesmoreland	2,922	2,932	2,949	2,333	427
Wise	6,412	6,504	6,712	4,660	1,478
Wythe	3,462	6,539	3,275	4,274	955
York	8,622	15,312	7,731	11,396	1,469
Cities					
Alexandria	33,633	19,043	27,968	15,554	1,472
Bedford	1,078	1,269	1,065	990	212
Bristol	2,646	3,495	2,586	2,983	429
Buena Vista	941	980	1,090	713	216
Charlottesville	7,762	4,034	7,916	4,091	565
Chesapeake	33,578	39,684	28,713	29,251	4,456
Clifton Forge	868	613	974	486	147
Colonial Heights	2,100	5,519	1,782	4,632	518
Covington	1,168	966	1,394	763	255
Danville	8,221	9,427	8,168	9,254	762
Emporia	1,116	938	1,103	835	98
Fairfax	4,361	4,762	3,909	4,319	422
Falls Church	3,109	2,131	2,375	1,644	202
Franklin	1,763	1,393	1,962	1,200	201
Fredericksburg	3,360	2,935	3,215	2,579	300
Galax	996	1,160	1,033	910	221
Hampton	27,490	19,561	24,493	16,596	2,783
Harrisonburg	3,482	5,741	3,346	4,945	434
Hopewell	3,024	3,749	2,868	3,493	550
Lexington	1,048	957	1,059	850	112
Lynchburg	10,374	12,518	10,281	11,441	1,155
Manassas	5,262	6,752	4,378	5,799	670
Manassas Park	1,048	1,460	748	916	151
Martinsville	3,048	2,560	2,941	2,446	387
Newport News	29,779	27,006	27,678	23,072	3,090
Norfolk	38,221	21,920	37,655	18,693	3,435
Norton	867	639	802	416	138
Petersburg	8,751	2,109	8,105	2,261	423
Poquoson	1,448	4,271	1,409	3,422	400
Portsmouth	22,286	12,628	22,150	10,686	2,238
Radford	2,063	2,190	2,113	1,742	381
Richmond	42,717	20,265	42,273	20,993	2,762
Roanoke	17,920	14,630	17,282	12,283	2,169
Salem	4,348	6,188	4,282	4,936	796
Staunton	3,324	4,878	3,162	4,526	605
Suffolk	12,471	11,836	10,827	8,572	1,266
Virginia Beach	62,268	83,674	52,142	63,741	9,328
Waynesboro	2,737	4,084	2,398	3,466	462
Williamsburg	1,724	1,777	1,820	1,560	162
Winchester	3,318	4,314	3,027	3,681	434
Totals	**1,217,290**	**1,437,490**	**1,091,060**	**1,138,350**	**159,861**

Virginia Vote Since 1952

1952, Eisenhower, Rep., 349,037; Stevenson, Dem., 268,677; Hass, Soc. Labor, 1,160; Hoopes, Soc. Dem., 504; Hallinan, Prog., 311.

1956, Eisenhower, Rep., 386,459; Stevenson, Dem., 267,760; Andrews, States' Rights, 42,964; Hoopes, Soc. Dem., 444; Hass, Soc. Labor, 351.

1960, Kennedy, Dem., 362,327; Nixon, Rep., 404,521; Coiner, Cons., 4,204; Hass, Soc. Labor, 397.

1964, Johnson, Dem., 558,038; Goldwater, Rep., 481,334; Hass, Soc. Labor, 2,895.

1968, Nixon, Rep., 590,319; Humphrey, Dem., 442,387; Wallace, 3d Party, *320,272; Blomen, Soc. Labor, 4,671; Munn, Proh., 601; Gregory, Peace and Freedom, 1,680.

*10,561 votes for Wallace were omitted in the count.

1972, Nixon, Rep., 988,493; McGovern, Dem., 438,887; Schmitz, Amer., 19,721; Fisher, Soc. Labor, 9,918.

1976, Carter, Dem., 813,896; Ford, Rep., 836,554; Camejo, Soc. Workers, 17,802; Anderson, Amer., 16,686; LaRouche, U.S. Labor, 7,508; MacBride, Libertarian, 4,648.

1980, Reagan, Rep., 989,609; Carter, Dem., 752,174; Anderson, Ind., 95,418; Commoner, Citizens, 14,024; Clark, Libertarian, 12,821; DeBerry, Soc. Workers, 1,986.

1984, Reagan, Rep., 1,337,078; Mondale, Dem., 796,250.

1988, Bush, Rep., 1,309,162; Dukakis, Dem., 859,799; Fulani, Ind., 14,312; Paul, Lib., 8,336.

1992, Clinton, Dem., 1,038,650; Bush, Rep., 1,150,517; Perot, Ind., 348,639; LaRouche, Ind., 11,937; Marrou, Libertarian, 5,730; Fulani, New Alliance, 3,192.
1996, Dole, Rep., 1,138,350; Clinton, Dem., 1,091,060; Perot, Ref., 159,861; Phillips, Taxpayers, 13,687; Browne, Libertarian, 9,174; Hagelin, Natural Law, 4,510.
2000, Bush, Rep., 1,437,490; Gore, Dem., 1,217,290; Nader, Green, 59,398; Browne, Libertarian, 15,198; Buchanan, Reform, 5,455; Phillips, Constitution, 1,809.

Washington

	2000		1996		
County	Gore (D)	Bush (R)	Clinton (D)	Dole (R)	Perot (RF)
Adams	1,406	3,440	1,740	2,356	448
Asotin	2,736	4,909	3,349	2,860	936
Benton	19,512	38,367	20,783	26,664	5,311
Chelan	8,412	16,980	8,595	12,363	2,332
Clallam	13,779	16,251	12,585	12,432	3,187
Clark	61,767	67,219	52,254	46,794	9,663
Columbia	515	1,523	743	948	228
Cowlitz	18,233	16,873	18,054	11,221	3,441
Douglas	3,822	8,512	3,913	5,682	1,132
Ferry	932	1,896	1,197	1,091	408
Franklin	4,653	8,594	4,961	5,946	992
Garfield	300	982	497	623	117
Grant	7,073	15,830	8,065	10,895	2,496
Grays Harbor	13,304	11,225	14,082	7,635	3,757
Island	14,778	16,408	12,157	12,387	2,787
Jefferson	8,281	6,095	7,145	4,607	1,385
King	476,700	273,171	417,846	232,811	51,309
Kitsap	50,302	46,427	44,167	35,304	8,769
Kittitas	5,516	7,727	5,707	5,224	1,214
Klickitat	3,062	4,557	3,214	2,662	875
Lewis	9,891	18,565	10,331	13,238	3,373
Lincoln	1,417	3,546	1,806	2,587	518
Mason	10,876	10,257	10,088	7,149	2,816
Okanogan	4,335	9,384	4,810	5,890	1,797
Pacific	4,895	4,042	5,095	2,598	1,131
Pend Oreille	1,973	3,076	2,126	2,012	709
Pierce	138,249	118,431	120,893	89,295	22,051
San Juan	4,426	3,005	3,663	2,523	508
Skagit	20,432	22,163	18,295	16,397	4,818
Skamania	1,753	2,151	1,724	1,387	450
Snohomish	129,612	109,615	109,624	81,885	22,731
Spokane	74,604	89,299	71,727	66,628	16,532
Stevens	5,560	11,299	5,591	7,524	2,158
Thurston	50,467	39,924	45,522	29,835	7,622
Wahkiakum	803	1,033	924	619	215
Walla Walla	7,188	13,304	8,038	9,085	1,894
Whatcom	34,033	34,287	29,074	27,153	4,854
Whitman	6,509	9,003	7,262	6,734	1,315
Yakima	25,546	39,494	25,676	27,668	4,724
Totals	**1,247,652**	**1,108,864**	**1,123,323**	**840,712**	**201,003**

Washington Vote Since 1952

1952, Eisenhower, Rep., 599,107; Stevenson, Dem., 492,845; MacArthur, Christian Nationalist, 7,290; Hallinan, Prog., 2,460; Hass, Soc. Labor, 633; Hoopes, Soc., 254; Dobbs, Soc. Workers, 119.
1956, Eisenhower, Rep., 620,430; Stevenson, Dem., 523,002; Hass, Soc. Labor, 7,457.
1960, Kennedy, Dem., 599,298; Nixon, Rep., 629,273; Hass, Soc. Labor, 10,895; Curtis, Constitution, 1,401; Dobbs, Soc. Workers, 705.
1964, Johnson, Dem., 779,699; Goldwater, Rep., 470,366; Hass, Soc. Labor, 7,772; DeBerry, Freedom Soc., 537.
1968, Nixon, Rep., 588,510; Humphrey, Dem., 616,037; Wallace, 3d Party, 96,990; Blomen, Soc. Labor, 488; Cleaver, Peace and Freedom, 1,609; Halstead, Soc. Workers, 270; Mitchell, Free Ballot, 377.
1972, Nixon, Rep., 837,135; McGovern, Dem., 568,334; Schmitz, Amer., 58,906; Spock, Ind., 2,644; Fisher, Soc. Labor, 1,102; Jenness, Soc. Workers, 623; Hall, Com., 566; Hospers, Libertarian, 1,537.
1976, Carter, Dem., 717,323; Ford, Rep., 777,732; McCarthy, Ind., 36,986; Maddox, Amer. Ind., 8,585; Anderson, Amer., 5,046; MacBride, Libertarian, 5,042; Wright, People's, 1,124; Camejo, Soc. Workers, 905; LaRouche, U.S. Labor, 903; Hall, Com., 817; Levin, Soc. Labor, 713; Zeidler, Soc., 358.
1980, Reagan, Rep., 865,244; Carter, Dem., 650,193; Anderson, Ind., 185,073; Clark, Libertarian, 29,213; Commoner, Citizens, 9,403; DeBerry, Soc. Workers, 1,137; McReynolds, Soc., 956; Hall, Com., 834; Griswold, Workers World, 341.
1984, Reagan, Rep., 1,051,670; Mondale, Dem., 798,352; Bergland, Libertarian, 8,844.
1988, Bush, Rep., 903,835; Dukakis, Dem., 933,516; Paul, Lib., 17,240; LaRouche, Ind., 4,412.
1992, Clinton, Dem., 993,037; Bush, Rep., 731,234; Perot, Ind., 541,780; Marrou, Libertarian, 7,533; Gritz, Populist/America First, 4,854; Hagelin, Natural Law, 2,456; Phillips, U.S. Taxpayers, 2,354; Fulani, New Alliance, 1,776; Daniels, Ind., 1,171.
1996, Clinton, Dem., 1,123,323; Dole, Rep., 840,712; Perot, Ref., 201,003; Nader, Ind., 60,322; Browne, Libertarian, 12,522; Hagelin, Natural Law, 6,076; Phillips, Taxpayers, 4,578; Collins, Ind., 2,374; Moorehead, Workers World, 2,189; Harris, Soc. Workers, 738.
2000, Gore, Dem., 1,247,652; Bush, Rep., 1,108,864; Nader, Green, 103,002; Browne, Libertarian, 13,135; Buchanan, Freedom, 7,171; Hagelin, Natural Law, 2,927; ; Phillips, Constitution, 1,989; Moorehead, Workers World, 1,729; McReynolds, Soc., 660; Harris, Soc. Workers, 304.

West Virginia

	2000		1996		
County	Gore (D)	Bush (R)	Clinton (D)	Dole (R)	Perot (RF)
Barbour	2,503	3,411	3,076	2,155	784
Berkeley	8,797	13,619	8,321	9,859	2,291
Boone	5,656	3,353	6,048	1,917	927
Braxton	2,719	2,529	3,001	1,441	527
Brooke	4,678	4,195	5,338	2,741	1,375
Cabell	14,896	16,440	16,277	13,179	2,968
Calhoun	1,112	1,425	1,402	1,000	307
Clay	1,617	1,887	2,074	1,137	355
Doddridge	773	1,955	865	1,335	382
Fayette	8,371	5,897	9,471	3,669	1,552
Gilmer	1,092	1,560	1,390	933	316
Grant	891	3,571	1,206	2,599	481
Greenbrier	5,627	6,866	6,286	4,434	1,418
Hampshire	2,069	3,879	2,335	2,814	605
Hancock	6,249	6,458	7,521	4,268	2,158
Hardy	1,621	2,816	1,911	1,895	438
Harrison	13,009	12,948	14,746	8,857	3,135
Jackson	4,937	6,341	4,882	4,235	1,295
Jefferson	6,860	7,045	6,361	5,287	1,307
Kanawha	38,524	36,809	40,357	29,311	6,412
Lewis	2,355	3,606	2,868	2,285	974
Lincoln	3,939	3,389	4,994	2,530	696
Logan	8,927	5,334	10,840	2,627	1,532
McDowell	4,845	2,348	5,989	1,550	655
Marion	12,315	9,972	12,994	6,160	2,881
Marshall	6,000	6,859	7,045	4,460	2,202
Mason	4,963	5,972	5,284	3,581	1,533
Mercer	8,347	10,206	8,721	7,768	2,141
Mineral	3,341	6,180	3,487	4,380	1,170
Mingo	6,049	3,866	7,584	2,229	1,020
Monongalia	12,603	13,595	13,406	10,189	3,040
Monroe	2,094	2,940	2,382	2,131	559
Morgan	1,939	3,639	1,929	2,599	513
Nicholas	4,059	4,359	4,769	2,649	1,071
Ohio	7,653	9,607	8,781	7,267	2,065
Pendleton	1,172	1,996	1,591	1,431	276
Pleasants	1,267	1,884	1,478	1,265	416
Pocahontas	1,392	1,970	1,796	1,242	426
Preston	3,515	6,607	4,237	4,257	1,760
Putnam	7,891	12,173	8,029	8,803	1,901
Raleigh	11,047	12,587	12,547	8,628	2,355
Randolph	4,028	5,248	5,469	3,348	1,184
Ritchie	1,024	2,717	1,385	1,906	522
Roane	2,332	3,172	2,572	2,069	622
Summers	2,299	2,304	2,397	1,505	438
Taylor	2,473	3,124	2,692	1,977	844
Tucker	1,319	1,935	1,649	1,217	424
Tyler	1,214	2,582	1,459	734	563
Upshur	2,770	5,165	3,052	3,325	1,031
Wayne	7,940	7,993	8,300	5,492	1,633
Webster	1,764	1,484	2,292	654	369
Wetzel	2,849	3,239	3,209	2,037	1,004
Wirt	818	1,518	906	928	280
Wood	12,664	20,428	13,261	15,502	3,694
Wyoming	4,289	3,473	5,550	2,155	812
Totals	**295,497**	**336,475**	**327,812**	**233,946**	**71,639**

West Virginia Vote Since 1952

1952, Eisenhower, Rep., 419,970; Stevenson, Dem., 453,578.
1956, Eisenhower, Rep., 449,297; Stevenson, Dem., 381,534.
1960, Kennedy, Dem., 441,786; Nixon, Rep., 395,995.
1964, Johnson, Dem., 538,087; Goldwater, Rep., 253,953.
1968, Nixon, Rep., 307,555; Humphrey, Dem., 374,091; Wallace, 3d Party, 72,560.
1972, Nixon, Rep., 484,964; McGovern, Dem., 277,435.
1976, Carter, Dem., 435,864; Ford, Rep., 314,726.
1980, Reagan, Rep., 334,206; Carter, Dem., 367,462; Anderson, Ind., 31,691; Clark, Libertarian, 4,356.
1984, Reagan, Rep., 405,483; Mondale, Dem., 328,125.
1988, Bush, Rep., 310,065; Dukakis, Dem., 341,016; Fulani, New Alliance, 2,230.
1992, Clinton, Dem., 331,001; Bush, Rep., 241,974; Perot, Ind., 108,829; Marrou, Libertarian, 1,873.

1996, Clinton, Dem., 327,812; Dole, Rep., 233,946; Perot, Ref., 71,639; Browne, Libertarian, 3,062.
2000, Bush, Rep., 336,475; Gore, Dem., 295,497; Nader, Green, 10,680; Buchanan, Reform, 3,169; Browne, Libertarian, 1,912; Hagelin, Natural Law, 367.

Wisconsin

	2000		1996		
County	Gore (D)	Bush (R)	Clinton (D)	Dole (R)	Perot (RF)
Adams	4,826	3,920	4,119	2,450	1,122
Ashland	4,356	3,038	3,808	1,863	861
Barron	8,928	9,848	8,025	6,158	2,692
Bayfield	4,427	3,266	3,895	2,250	899
Brown	49,096	54,258	42,823	38,563	8,036
Buffalo	3,237	3,038	2,681	1,800	972
Burnett	3,626	3,967	3,625	2,452	962
Calumet	8,202	10,837	6,940	7,049	2,112
Chippewa	12,102	12,835	9,647	7,520	3,567
Clark	5,931	7,461	5,540	4,622	2,486
Columbia	12,636	11,987	10,336	8,377	2,377
Crawford	4,005	3,024	3,658	2,149	1,060
Dane	142,317	75,790	109,347	59,487	12,436
Dodge	14,580	21,684	12,625	12,890	3,322
Door	6,560	7,810	5,590	4,948	1,475
Douglas	13,593	6,930	10,976	5,167	2,001
Dunn	9,172	8,911	7,536	4,917	2,555
Eau Claire	24,078	20,921	20,298	13,900	5,160
Florence	816	1,528	869	927	316
Fond du Lac	18,181	26,548	15,542	16,488	4,204
Forest	2,158	2,404	2,092	1,166	678
Grant	10,691	10,240	9,203	7,021	2,648
Green	7,863	6,790	6,136	4,697	1,534
Green Lake	3,301	5,451	3,152	3,565	1,025
Iowa	5,842	4,221	4,690	2,866	1,071
Iron	1,620	1,734	1,725	1,260	469
Jackson	4,380	3,670	3,705	2,262	1,163
Jefferson	15,203	19,204	13,188	12,681	3,177
Juneau	4,813	4,910	4,331	3,226	1,393
Kenosha	32,429	28,891	27,964	18,296	6,507
Kewaunee	4,670	4,883	4,311	3,431	1,161
La Crosse	28,455	24,327	23,647	16,482	4,844
La Fayette	3,710	3,336	3,261	2,172	944
Langlade	4,199	5,125	4,074	3,206	1,249
Lincoln	6,664	6,727	6,166	4,076	1,800
Manitowoc	17,667	19,358	16,750	13,239	3,941
Marathon	26,546	28,883	24,012	19,874	6,749
Marinette	8,676	10,535	8,413	7,231	2,367
Marquette	3,437	3,522	2,859	2,208	915
Menominee	949	225	992	230	107
Milwaukee	252,329	163,491	216,620	119,407	26,027
Monroe	7,460	8,217	6,924	5,299	2,081
Oconto	7,260	8,706	6,723	5,389	1,655
Oneida	8,339	9,512	7,619	6,339	2,604
Outagamie	32,735	39,460	28,815	27,758	7,235
Ozaukee	15,030	31,155	13,269	22,078	2,774
Pepin	1,854	1,631	1,585	1,007	456
Pierce	8,559	8,169	7,970	4,599	2,074
Polk	8,961	9,557	8,334	5,387	2,369
Portage	17,942	13,214	15,901	9,631	3,410
Price	3,413	4,136	3,523	2,545	1,218
Racine	41,563	44,014	38,567	30,107	7,611
Richland	3,837	3,994	3,502	2,642	901
Rock	40,472	27,467	32,450	20,096	6,800
Rusk	3,161	3,758	2,941	2,219	1,331
St. Croix	13,077	15,240	11,384	8,253	3,180
Sauk	13,035	11,586	9,889	7,448	2,448
Sawyer	3,333	3,972	2,773	2,603	962
Shawano	7,335	9,548	6,850	6,396	2,071
Sheboygan	23,569	29,648	22,022	20,067	4,157
Taylor	3,254	5,278	3,253	3,108	1,457
Trempealeau	6,678	5,002	5,848	3,035	1,688
Vernon	6,577	5,684	5,572	3,796	1,523
Vilas	4,706	6,958	4,226	4,496	1,548
Walworth	15,492	22,982	13,283	15,099	3,729
Washburn	3,695	3,912	3,231	2,703	920
Washington	18,115	41,162	17,154	25,829	4,786
Waukesha	64,319	133,105	57,354	91,729	13,109
Waupaca	8,787	12,980	7,800	8,679	2,464
Waushara	4,239	5,571	3,824	3,573	1,264
Winnebago	33,983	38,330	29,564	27,880	6,531
Wood	15,936	17,803	14,650	12,666	4,599
Totals	**1,242,987**	**1,237,279**	**1,071,971**	**845,029**	**227,339**

Wisconsin Vote Since 1952

1952, Eisenhower, Rep., 979,744; Stevenson, Dem., 622,175; Hallinan, Ind., 2,174; Dobbs, Ind., 1,350; Hoopes, Ind., 1,157; Hass, Ind., 770.
1956, Eisenhower, Rep., 954,844; Stevenson, Dem., 586,768; Andrews, Ind., 6,918; Hoopes, Soc., 754; Hass, Soc. Labor, 710; Dobbs, Soc. Workers, 564.
1960, Kennedy, Dem., 830,805; Nixon, Rep., 895,175; Dobbs, Soc. Workers, 1,792; Hass, Soc. Labor, 1,310.
1964, Johnson, Dem., 1,050,424; Goldwater, Rep., 638,495; DeBerry, Soc. Workers, 1,692; Hass, Soc. Labor, 1,204.
1968, Nixon, Rep., 809,997; Humphrey, Dem., 748,804; Wallace, 3d Party, 127,835; Blomen, Soc. Labor, 1,338; Halstead, Soc. Workers, 1,222; scattered, 2,342.
1972 Nixon, Rep., 989,430; McGovern, Dem., 810,174; Schmitz, Amer., 47,525; Spock, Ind., 2,701; Fisher, Soc. Labor, 998; Hall, Com., 663; Reed, Ind., 506; scattered, 893.
1976, Carter, Dem., 1,040,232; Ford, Rep., 1,004,987; McCarthy, Ind., 34,943; Maddox, Amer. Ind., 8,552; Zeidler, Soc., 4,298; MacBride, Libertarian, 3,814; Camejo, Soc. Workers, 1,691; Wright, People's, 943; Hall, Com., 749; LaRouche, U.S. Lab., 738; Levin, Soc. Labor, 389; scattered, 2,839.
1980, Reagan, Rep., 1,088,845; Carter, Dem., 981,584; Anderson, Ind., 160,657; Clark, Libertarian, 29,135; Commoner, Citizens, 7,767; Rarick, Constitution, 1,519; McReynolds, Soc., 808; Hall, Com., 772; Griswold, Workers World, 414; DeBerry, Soc. Workers, 383; scattering, 1,337.
1984, Reagan, Rep., 1,198,584; Mondale, Dem., 995,740; Bergland, Libertarian, 4,883.
1988, Bush, Rep., 1,047,499; Dukakis, Dem., 1,126,794; Paul, Lib., 5,157; Duke, Pop., 3,056.
1992, Clinton, Dem., 1,041,066; Bush, Rep., 930,855; Perot, Ind., 544,479; Marrou, Libertarian, 2,877; Gritz, Populist/America First, 2,311; Daniels, Ind., 1,883; Phillips, U.S. Taxpayers, 1,772; Hagelin, Natural Law, 1,070.
1996, Clinton, Dem., 1,071,971; Dole, Rep., 845,029; Perot, Ref., 227,339; Nader, Green, 28,723; Phillips, Taxpayers, 8,811; Browne, Libertarian, 7,929; Hagelin, Natural Law, 1,379; Moorehead, Workers World, 1,333; Hollis, Soc., 848; Harris, Soc. Workers, 483.
2000, Gore, Dem., 1,242,987; Bush, Rep., 1,237,279; Nader, Green, 94,070; Buchanan, Reform, 11,446; Browne, Libertarian, 6,640; Phillips, Constitution, 2,042; Moorehead, Workers World, 1,063; Hagelin, Reform, 878; Harris, Soc. Workers, 306.

Wyoming

	2000		1996		
County	Gore (D)	Bush (R)	Clinton (D)	Dole (R)	Perot (RF)
Albany	5,069	7,814	6,399	5,967	1,333
Big Horn	1,004	3,720	1,438	2,821	545
Campbell	1,967	10,203	3,468	6,382	1,954
Carbon	2,206	4,498	2,690	2,930	855
Converse	1,076	[illegible]	1,520	2,702	[illegible]
Crook	361	2,289	651	1,698	394
Fremont	4,172	10,560	5,445	7,554	1,840
Goshen	1,439	3,922	1,923	2,989	547
Hot Springs	544	1,733	779	1,348	287
Johnson	555	2,886	815	2,071	378
Laramie	12,162	21,797	13,676	16,924	2,958
Lincoln	1,184	5,415	1,803	3,764	906
Natrona	8,646	18,439	11,240	13,182	3,524
Niobrara	190	888	325	757	209
Park	2,424	9,884	3,240	7,430	1,318
Platte	1,249	2,925	1,631	2,155	579
Sheridan	3,330	8,424	4,594	5,892	1,414
Sublette	458	2,624	677	1,829	401
Sweetwater	5,521	9,425	7,088	5,591	2,792
Teton	4,019	5,454	4,042	3,918	839
Uinta	1,650	5,469	2,414	3,471	1,242
Washakie	806	3,138	1,205	2,250	470
Weston	449	2,521	871	1,763	504
Totals	**60,401**	**147,947**	**77,934**	**105,388**	**25,928**

Wyoming Vote Since 1952

1952, Eisenhower, Rep., 81,047; Stevenson, Dem., 47,934; Hamblen, Proh., 194; Hoopes, Soc., 40; Haas, Soc. Labor, 36.
1956, Eisenhower, Rep., 74,573; Stevenson, Dem., 49,554.
1960, Kennedy, Dem., 63,331; Nixon, Rep., 77,451.
1964, Johnson, Dem., 80,718; Goldwater, Rep., 61,998.
1968, Nixon, Rep., 70,927; Humphrey, Dem., 45,173; Wallace, 3d Party, 11,105.
1972, Nixon, Rep., 100,464; McGovern, Dem., 44,358; Schmitz, Amer., 748.
1976, Carter, Dem., 62,239; Ford, Rep., 92,717; McCarthy, Ind., 624; Reagan, Ind., 307; Anderson, Amer., 290; MacBride, Libertarian, 89; Brown, Ind., 47; Maddox, Amer. Ind., 30.
1980, Reagan, Rep., 110,700; Carter, Dem., 49,427; Anderson, Ind., 12,072; Clark, Libertarian, 4,514.
1984, Reagan, Rep., 133,241; Mondale, Dem., 53,370; Bergland, Libertarian, 2,357.
1988, Bush, Rep., 106,867; Dukakis, Dem., 67,113; Paul, Lib., 2,026; Fulani, New Alliance, 545.
1992, Clinton, Dem., 68,160; Bush, Rep., 79,347; Perot, Ind., 51,263.
1996, Dole, Rep., 105,388; Clinton, Dem., 77,934; Perot, Ind. (Ref.), 25,928; Browne, Libertarian, 1,739; Hagelin, Natural Law, 582.
2000, Bush, Rep., 147,947; Gore, Dem., 60,481; Buchanan, Reform, 2,724; Browne, Libertarian, 1,443; Phillips, Ind., 720; Hagelin, Natural Law, 411.

Voter Turnout in Presidential Elections, 1932-2000

Source: Federal Election Commission; Commission for Study of American Electorate; *Congressional Quarterly*

	Candidates	Voter Participation (% of voting-age population)		Candidates	Voter Participation (% of voting-age population)
1932	Roosevelt-Hoover	52.4	1968	Nixon-Humphrey	60.9
1936	Roosevelt-Landon	56.0	1972	Nixon-McGovern	55.2[1]
1940	Roosevelt-Willkie	58.9	1976	Carter-Ford	53.5
1944	Roosevelt-Dewey	56.0	1980	Reagan-Carter	54.0
1948	Truman-Dewey	51.1	1984	Reagan-Mondale	53.1
1952	Eisenhower-Stevenson	61.6	1988	Bush-Dukakis	50.2
1956	Eisenhower-Stevenson	59.3	1992	Clinton-Bush-Perot	55.9
1960	Kennedy-Nixon	62.8	1996	Clinton-Dole-Perot	49.0
1964	Johnson-Goldwater	61.9	2000	Bush-Gore	51.3

(1) The sharp drop in 1972 followed the expansion of eligibility with the enfranchisement of 18- to 20-year-olds.

Electoral Votes for President

(Figures in **boldface**, based on 1990 census, were in force for 1992, 1996, and 2000 elections; where figures for 2004 election will be different, based on 2000 census, these are given in parentheses.)

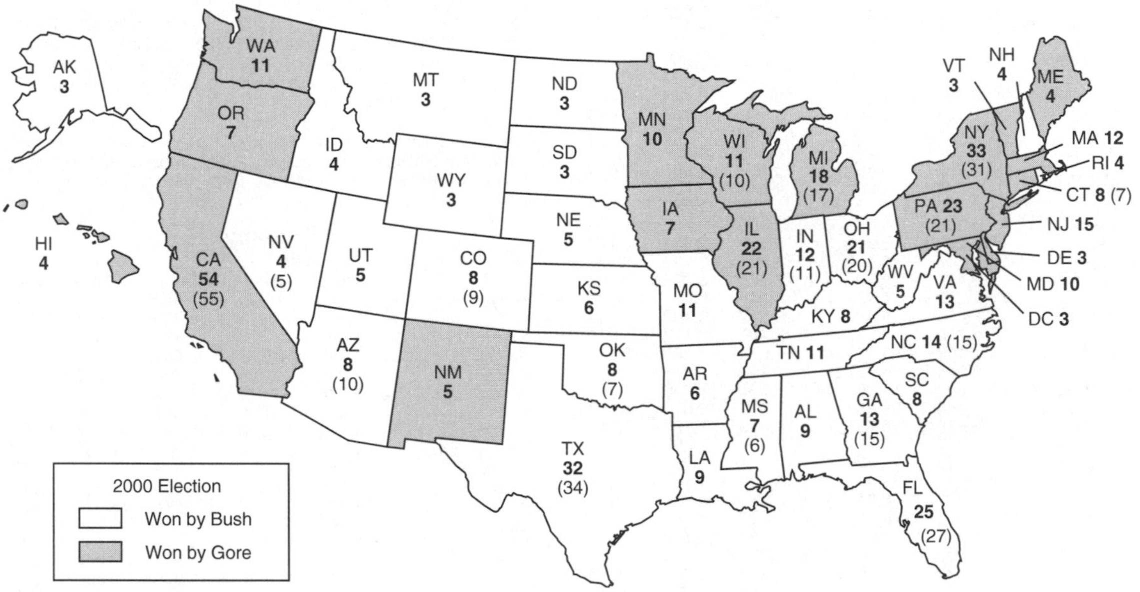

The Electoral College

The president and the vice president are the only elective federal officials not chosen by direct vote of the people. They are elected by the members of the Electoral College, an institution provided for in the U.S. Constitution.

On presidential election day, the first Tuesday after the first Monday in November of every 4th year, each state chooses as many electors as it has senators and representatives in Congress. In 1964, for the first time, as provided by the 23rd Amendment to the Constitution, the District of Columbia voted for 3 electors. Thus, with 100 senators and 435 representatives, there are 538 members of the Electoral College, with a majority of 270 electoral votes needed to elect the president and vice president.

Although political parties were not part of the original plan created by the Founding Fathers, today political parties customarily nominate their lists of electors at their respective state conventions. Some states print names of the candidates for president and vice president at the top of the Nov. ballot; others list only the electors' names. In either case, the electors of the party receiving the highest vote are elected. Two states, Maine and Nebraska, allow for proportional allocation.

The electors meet on the first Monday after the 2nd Wednesday in December in their respective state capitals or in some other place prescribed by state legislatures. By long-established custom, they vote for their party nominees, although this is not required by federal law; some states do require it.

The Constitution requires electors to cast a ballot for at least one person who is not an inhabitant of that elector's home state. This ensures that presidential and vice presidential candidates from the same party will not be from the same state. (In 2000, Republican vice presidential nominee Dick Cheney changed his voter registration to Wyoming from Gov. George W. Bush's home state of Texas.) Also, an elector cannot be a member of Congress or hold federal office.

Certified and sealed lists of the votes of the electors in each state are sent to the president of the U.S. Senate, who then opens them in the presence of the members of the Senate and House of Representatives in a joint session held in early Jan., and the electoral votes of all the states are then officially counted.

If no candidate for president has a majority, the House of Representatives chooses a president from the top 3 candidates, with all representatives from each state combining to cast one vote for that state. The House decided the outcome of the 1800 and 1824 presidential elections. If no candidate for vice president has a majority, the Senate chooses from the top 2, with the senators voting as individuals. The Senate chose the vice president following the 1836 election.

Under the electoral college system, a candidate who fails to be the top vote getter in the popular vote still may win a majority of electoral votes. This happened in the elections of 1876, 1888, and 2000.

Third-Party and Independent Presidential Candidates

Although many "third party" candidates or independents have pursued the presidency, only 10 of these have polled more than a million votes. In most elections since 1860, fewer than one vote in 20 has been cast for a third-party candidate. In only 5 presidential elections since then have all non-major-party candidates combined polled more than 10% of the vote. The major vote getters in those elections were James B. Weaver (People's Party), 1892; former President Theodore Roosevelt (Progressive Party), 1912; Robert M. La Follette (Progressive Party), 1924; George C. Wallace (American Independent Party), 1968; and H. Ross Perot, as an independent in 1992 and with the Reform Party in 1996.

Roosevelt outpolled the Republican candidate, William Howard Taft, in 1912, capturing 28% of the popular vote and 88 electoral votes. In 1948, Strom Thurmond was able to capture 39 electoral votes (from 5 Southern states); however, all third parties received only 5.75% of the popular vote in the election. Twenty years later, George Wallace's popularity in the same region allowed him to get 46 electoral votes and 13.5% of the popular vote.

In 1992 Perot captured 19% of the popular vote; however, he did not win a single state. In 1996, Perot won 8% of the popular vote; all third-party candidates combined won about 10%. Ralph Nader won about 3% of the vote in 2000.

Despite the difficulty in winning the presidency, independent and third-party candidates sometimes succeed in winning other offices and often bring to the attention of the nation their most prominent issues.

Notable Third Party and Independent Campaigns by Year

Party	Presidential nominee	Year	Issues	Strength in . . .
Anti-Masonic	William Wirt	1832	Against secret societies and oaths	PA, VT
Liberty	James G. Birney	1844	Anti-slavery	North
Free Soil	Martin Van Buren	1848	Anti-slavery	NY, OH
American (Know-Nothing)	Millard Fillmore	1856	Anti-immigrant	Northeast, South
Greenback	Peter Cooper	1876	For "cheap money," labor rights	National
Greenback	James B. Weaver	1880	For "cheap money," labor rights	National
Prohibition	John P. St. John	1884	Anti-liquor	National
People's (Populists)	James B. Weaver	1892	For "cheap money," end of national banks	South, West
Socialist	Eugene V. Debs	1900-12; 1920	For public ownership	National
Progressive (Bull Moose)	Theodore Roosevelt	1912	Against high tariffs	Midwest, West
Progressive	Robert M. La Follette	1924	Farmer and labor rights	Midwest, West
Socialist	Norman Thomas	1928-48	Liberal reforms	National
Union	William Lemke	1936	Anti-New Deal	National
States' Rights (Dixiecrats)	Strom Thurmond	1948	For states' rights	South
Progressive	Henry A. Wallace	1948	Anti-cold war	NY, CA
American Independent	George C. Wallace	1968	For states' rights	South
American	John G. Schmitz	1972	For "law and order"	Far West, OH, LA
None (Independent)	John B. Anderson	1980	A 3rd choice	National
None (Independent)	H. Ross Perot	1992	Federal budget deficit	National
Reform	H. Ross Perot	1996	Deficit; campaign finance	National
Green	Ralph Nader	2000	Corporate power	National

Major-Party Nominees for President and Vice President

Asterisk (*) denotes winning ticket

Democratic			Republican		
Year	President	Vice President	Year	President	Vice President
1856	James Buchanan*	John Breckinridge	1856	John Frémont	William Dayton
1860	Stephen A. Douglas (1)	Herschel V. Johnson	1860	Abraham Lincoln*	Hannibal Hamlin
1864	George McClellan	G.H. Pendleton	1864	Abraham Lincoln*	Andrew Johnson
1868	Horatio Seymour	Francis Blair	1868	Ulysses S. Grant*	Schuyler Colfax
1872	Horace Greeley	B. Gratz Brown	1872	Ulysses S. Grant*	Henry Wilson
1876	Samuel J. Tilden	Thomas Hendricks	1876	Rutherford B. Hayes*	William Wheeler
1880	Winfield Hancock	William English	1880	James A. Garfield*	Chester A. Arthur
1884	Grover Cleveland*	Thomas Hendricks	1884	James Blaine	John Logan
1888	Grover Cleveland	A.G. Thurman	1888	Benjamin Harrison*	Levi Morton
1892	Grover Cleveland*	Adlai Stevenson	1892	Benjamin Harrison	Whitelaw Reid
1896	William J. Bryan	Arthur Sewall	1896	William McKinley*	Garret Hobart
1900	William J. Bryan	Adlai Stevenson	1900	William McKinley*	Theodore Roosevelt
1904	Alton Parker	Henry Davis	1904	Theodore Roosevelt*	Charles Fairbanks
1908	William J. Bryan	John Kern	1908	William H. Taft*	James Sherman
1912	Woodrow Wilson*	Thomas Marshall	1912	William H. Taft	James Sherman (2)
1916	Woodrow Wilson*	Thomas Marshall	1916	Charles Hughes	Charles Fairbanks
1920	James M. Cox	Franklin D. Roosevelt	1920	Warren G. Harding*	Calvin Coolidge
1924	John W. Davis	Charles W. Bryan	1924	Calvin Coolidge*	Charles G. Dawes
1928	Alfred E. Smith	Joseph T. Robinson	1928	Herbert Hoover*	Charles Curtis
1932	Franklin D. Roosevelt*	John N. Garner	1932	Herbert Hoover	Charles Curtis
1936	Franklin D. Roosevelt*	John N. Garner	1936	Alfred M. Landon	Frank Knox
1940	Franklin D. Roosevelt*	Henry A. Wallace	1940	Wendell L. Willkie	Charles McNary
1944	Franklin D. Roosevelt*	Harry S. Truman	1944	Thomas E. Dewey	John W. Bricker
1948	Harry S. Truman*	Alben W. Barkley	1948	Thomas E. Dewey	Earl Warren
1952	Adlai E. Stevenson	John J. Sparkman	1952	Dwight D. Eisenhower*	Richard M. Nixon
1956	Adlai E. Stevenson	Estes Kefauver	1956	Dwight D. Eisenhower*	Richard M. Nixon
1960	John F. Kennedy*	Lyndon B. Johnson	1960	Richard M. Nixon	Henry Cabot Lodge
1964	Lyndon B. Johnson*	Hubert H. Humphrey	1964	Barry M. Goldwater	William E. Miller
1968	Hubert H. Humphrey	Edmund S. Muskie	1968	Richard M. Nixon*	Spiro T. Agnew
1972	George S. McGovern	R. Sargent Shriver Jr. (3)	1972	Richard M. Nixon*	Spiro T. Agnew
1976	Jimmy Carter*	Walter F. Mondale	1976	Gerald R. Ford	Bob Dole
1980	Jimmy Carter	Walter F. Mondale	1980	Ronald Reagan*	George H. W. Bush
1984	Walter F. Mondale	Geraldine Ferraro	1984	Ronald Reagan*	George H. W. Bush
1988	Michael S. Dukakis	Lloyd Bentsen	1988	George H.W. Bush*	Dan Quayle
1992	Bill Clinton*	Al Gore	1992	George H.W. Bush	Dan Quayle
1996	Bill Clinton*	Al Gore	1996	Bob Dole	Jack Kemp
2000	Al Gore	Joseph Lieberman	2000	George W. Bush*	Richard Cheney

(1) Douglas and Johnson were nominated at the Baltimore convention. An earlier convention in Charleston, SC, failed to reach a consensus and resulted in a split in the party. The Southern faction of the Democrats nominated John Breckinridge for president and Joseph Lane for vice president. (2) Died Oct. 30, replaced on ballot by Nicholas Butler. (3) Chosen by Democratic National Committee after Thomas Eagleton withdrew because of controversy over past treatments for depression.

Popular and Electoral Vote for President, 1789-2000

(D) Democrat; (DR) Democratic Republican; (F) Federalist; (LR) Liberal Republican; (NR) National Republican; (P) People's; (PR) Progressive; (R) Republican; (RF) Reform; (SR) States' Rights; (W) Whig; Asterisk (*)–See notes at bottom.

Year	President elected	Popular	Elec.	Major losing candidate(s)	Popular	Elec.
1789	George Washington (F)	Unknown	69	No opposition	—	—
1792	George Washington (F)	Unknown	132	No opposition	—	—
1796	John Adams (F)	Unknown	71	Thomas Jefferson (DR)	Unknown	68
1800*	Thomas Jefferson (DR)	Unknown	73	Aaron Burr (DR)	Unknown	73
1804	Thomas Jefferson (DR)	Unknown	162	Charles Pinckney (F)	Unknown	14
1808	James Madison (DR)	Unknown	122	Charles Pinckney (F)	Unknown	47
1812	James Madison (DR)	Unknown	128	DeWitt Clinton (F)	Unknown	89
1816	James Monroe (DR)	Unknown	183	Rufus King (F)	Unknown	34
1820	James Monroe (DR)	Unknown	231	John Quincy Adams (DR)	Unknown	1
1824*	John Quincy Adams (DR)	105,321	84	Andrew Jackson (DR)	155,872	99
				Henry Clay (DR)	46,587	37
				William H. Crawford (DR)	44,282	41
1828	Andrew Jackson (D)	647,231	178	John Quincy Adams (NR)	509,097	83
1832	Andrew Jackson (D)	687,502	219	Henry Clay (NR)	530,189	49
1836	Martin Van Buren (D)	762,678	170	William H. Harrison (W)	548,007	73
1840	William H. Harrison (W)	1,275,017	234	Martin Van Buren (D)	1,128,702	60
1844	James K. Polk (D)	1,337,243	170	Henry Clay (W)	1,299,068	105
1848	Zachary Taylor (W)	1,360,101	163	Lewis Cass (D)	1,220,544	127
				Martin Van Buren (Free Soil)	291,501	—
1852	Franklin Pierce (D)	1,601,474	254	Winfield Scott (W)	1,386,578	42
1856	James Buchanan (D)	1,927,995	174	John C. Fremont (R)	1,391,555	114
				Millard Fillmore (American)	873,053	8
1860	Abraham Lincoln (R)	1,866,352	180	Stephen A. Douglas (D)	1,375,157	12
				John C. Breckinridge (D)	845,763	72
				John Bell (Const. Union)	589,581	39
1864	Abraham Lincoln (R)	2,216,067	212	George McClellan (D)	1,808,725	21
1868	Ulysses S. Grant (R)	3,015,071	214	Horatio Seymour (D)	2,709,615	80
1872*	Ulysses S. Grant (R)	3,597,070	286	Horace Greeley (D-LR)*	2,834,079	—
1876*	Rutherford B. Hayes (R)	4,033,950	185	Samuel J. Tilden (D)	4,284,757	184
1880	James A. Garfield (R)	4,449,053	214	Winfield S. Hancock (D)	4,442,030	155
1884	Grover Cleveland (D)	4,911,017	219	James G. Blaine (R)	4,848,334	182
1888*	Benjamin Harrison (R)	5,444,337	233	Grover Cleveland (D)	5,540,050	168
1892	Grover Cleveland (D)	5,554,414	277	Benjamin Harrison (R)	5,190,802	145
				James Weaver (P)	1,027,329	22
1896	William McKinley (R)	7,035,638	271	William J. Bryan (D-P)	6,467,946	176
1900	William McKinley (R)	7,219,530	292	William J. Bryan (D)	6,358,071	155
1904	Theodore Roosevelt (R)	7,628,834	336	Alton B. Parker (D)	5,084,491	140
1908	William H. Taft (R)	7,679,006	321	William J. Bryan (D)	6,409,106	162
1912	Woodrow Wilson (D)	6,286,214	435	Theodore Roosevelt (PR)	4,216,020	88
				William H. Taft (R)	3,483,922	8
1916	Woodrow Wilson (D)	9,129,606	277	Charles E. Hughes (R)	8,538,221	254
1920	Warren G. Harding (R)	16,152,200	404	James M. Cox (D)	9,147,353	127
1924	Calvin Coolidge (R)	15,725,016	382	John W. Davis (D)	8,385,586	136
				Robert M. La Follette (PR)	4,822,856	13
1928	Herbert Hoover (R)	21,392,190	444	Alfred E. Smith (D)	15,016,443	87
1932	Franklin D. Roosevelt (D)	22,821,857	472	Herbert Hoover (R)	15,761,841	59
1936	Franklin D. Roosevelt (D)	27,751,597	523	Alfred Landon (R)	16,679,583	8
1940	Franklin D. Roosevelt (D)	27,243,466	449	Wendell Willkie (R)	22,304,755	82
1944	Franklin D. Roosevelt (D)	25,602,505	432	Thomas E. Dewey (R)	22,006,278	99
1948	Harry S. Truman (D)	24,105,812	303	Thomas E. Dewey (R)	21,970,065	189
				Strom Thurmond (SR)	1,169,021	39
				Henry A. Wallace (PR)	1,157,172	—
1952	Dwight D. Eisenhower (R)	33,936,252	442	Adlai E. Stevenson (D)	27,314,992	89
1956*	Dwight D. Eisenhower (R)	35,585,316	457	Adlai E. Stevenson (D)	26,031,322	73
1960*	John F. Kennedy (D)	34,227,096	303	Richard M. Nixon (R)	34,108,546	219
1964	Lyndon B. Johnson (D)	43,126,506	486	Barry M. Goldwater (R)	27,176,799	52
1968	Richard M. Nixon (R)	31,785,480	301	Hubert H. Humphrey (D)	31,275,166	191
				George C. Wallace (3rd party)	9,906,473	46
1972*	Richard M. Nixon (R)	47,165,234	520	George S. McGovern (D)	29,170,774	17
1976*	Jimmy Carter (D)	40,828,929	297	Gerald R. Ford (R)	39,148,940	240
1980	Ronald Reagan (R)	43,899,248	489	Jimmy Carter (D)	35,481,435	49
				John B. Anderson (independent)	5,719,437	—
1984	Ronald Reagan (R)	54,281,858	525	Walter F. Mondale (D)	37,457,215	13
1988*	George H. W. Bush (R)	48,881,221	426	Michael S. Dukakis (D)	41,805,422	111
1992	Bill Clinton (D)	44,908,254	370	George H. W. Bush (R)	39,102,343	168
				H. Ross Perot (independent)	19,741,065	—
1996	Bill Clinton (D)	47,401,185	379	Bob Dole (R)	39,197,469	159
				H. Ross Perot (RF)	8,085,294	—
2000*	George W. Bush (R)	50,459,211	271	Al Gore (D)	51,003,894	266
				Ralph Nader (Green)	2,834,410	—

***1800**—Elected by House of Representatives because of tied electoral vote. **1824**—Elected by House of Representatives because no candidate had polled a majority. By 1824, the Democratic Republicans had become a loose coalition of competing political groups. By 1828, the supporters of Jackson were known as Democrats, and the John Q. Adams and Henry Clay supporters as National Republicans. **1872**—Greeley died Nov. 29, 1872. His electoral votes were split among 4 individuals. **1876**—FL, LA, OR, and SC election returns were disputed. Congress in joint session (Mar. 2, 1877) declared Hayes and Wheeler elected president and vice president. **1888**—Cleveland had more popular votes than Harrison, but since Harrison won 233 electoral votes against 168 for Cleveland, Harrison won the presidency. **1956**—Democrats elected 74 electors, but one from Alabama refused to vote for Stevenson. **1960**—Sen. Harry F. Byrd (D, VA) received 15 electoral votes. **1972**—John Hospers of California received one vote from an elector of Virginia. **1976**—Ronald Reagan of CA received one vote from an elector of Washington. **1988**—Sen. Lloyd Bentsen (D, TX) received 1 vote from an elector of West Virginia. **2000**—One Gore elector from Washington, DC, abstained. Nader was listed as "Independent" on the ballot in some states, and was not on the ballot in all states.

UNITED STATES FACTS

Superlative U.S. Statistics[1]

Source: U.S. Geological Survey, Dept. of the Interior; U.S. Bureau of the Census, Dept. of Commerce; World Almanac research

Area for 50 states and Washington, DC	**TOTAL** Land, 3,537,440 sq mi; Water, 256,648 sq mi	3,794,085 sq mi[4]
Largest state	Alaska	663,267 sq mi[1]
Smallest state	Rhode Island	1,545 sq mi
Largest county (excluding Alaska)	San Bernardino County, CA	20,105 sq mi
Smallest county	Arlington County, VA	26 sq mi
Largest incorporated city	Sitka, AK	4,812 sq mi
Northernmost city	Barrow, AK	71° 17´ N
Northernmost point	Point Barrow, AK	71° 23´ N
Southernmost city	Hilo, HI	19° 44´ N
Southernmost settlement	Naalehu, HI	19° 03´ N
Southernmost point	Ka Lae (South Cape), Island of Hawaii	18° 55´ N (155°41´ W)
Easternmost city	Eastport, ME	66° 59´05´´ W
Easternmost settlement[2]	Amchitka Isl., AK	179° 15´ E
Easternmost point[2]	Pochnoi Point, on Semisopochnoi Isl., AK	179° 46´ E
Westernmost city	Atka, AK	174° 12´ W
Westernmost settlement	Adak Station, AK	176° 39´ W
Westernmost point	Amatignak Isl., AK	179° 06´ W
Highest settlement	Climax, CO	11,360 ft
Lowest settlement	Calipatria, CA	–184 ft
Highest point on Atlantic coast	Cadillac Mountain, Mount Desert Isl., ME	1,530 ft
Oldest national park	Yellowstone National Park (1872), WY, MT, ID	2,219,791 acres
Largest national park	Wrangell-St. Elias, AK	8,323,618 acres
Highest waterfall	Yosemite Falls—Total in 3 sections (consisting of Upper Yosemite Fall, 1,430 ft; Cascades, 675 ft; Lower Yosemite Fall, 320 ft)	2,425 ft
Longest river system	Mississippi-Missouri-Red Rock	3,710 mi
Highest mountain	Mount McKinley, AK	20,320 ft
Lowest point	Death Valley, CA	–282 ft
Deepest lake	Crater Lake, OR	1,932 ft
Rainiest spot	Mount Waialeale, HI	Annual avg rainfall 460 in
Largest gorge	Grand Canyon, Colorado River, AZ	277 mi long, 600 ft to 18 mi wide, 1 mi deep
Deepest gorge	Hells Canyon, Snake River, OR-ID	7,900 ft
Largest dam	New Cornelia Tailings, Ten Mile Wash, AZ[3]	274,026,000 cu yds material used
Tallest building	Sears Tower, Chicago, IL	1,450 ft
Largest building (volume)	Boeing Manufacturing Plant, Everett, WA	472,000,000 cu ft; covers 98 acres
Largest office building	Pentagon, Arlington, VA	77,025,000 cu ft; covers 29 acres
Tallest structure	TV tower, Blanchard, ND	2,063 ft
Longest bridge span	Verrazano-Narrows, NY	4,260 ft
Highest bridge	Royal Gorge, CO	1,053 ft above water
Deepest well	Gas well, Washita County, OK	31,441 ft

The 48 Contiguous States

Area for 48 states and Washington, DC	**TOTAL** Land, 2,959,066 sq mi; Water, 160,824 sq mi	3,119,887 sq mi[4]
Largest state	Texas	268,581 sq mi
Northernmost city	Bellingham, WA	48°46´ N
Northernmost settlement	Angle Inlet, MN	49°21´ N
Northernmost point	Northwest Angle, MN	49°23´ N
Southernmost city	Key West, FL	24°33´ N
Southernmost mainland city	Florida City, FL	25°27´ N
Southernmost point	Key West, FL	24°33´ N
Easternmost settlement	Lubec, ME	66°58´49 W
Easternmost point	West Quoddy Head, ME	66°57´ W
Westernmost town	La Push, WA	124°38´ W
Westernmost point	Cape Alava, WA	124°44´ W
Highest mountain	Mount Whitney, CA	14,494 ft

(1) All areas are total area, including water, unless otherwise noted. (2) Alaska's Aleutian Islands extend into the eastern hemisphere and thus technically contain the easternmost point and settlement in the U.S. (3) The New Cornelia Tailings Dam is a privately owned industrial dam composed of tailings, remnants of a mining process. (4) Does not add, because of rounding.

Geodetic Datum of North America

In July 1986, the National Oceanic and Atmospheric Administration's National Geodetic Survey (NGS), in cooperation with Canada and Mexico, completed readjustment and redefinition of the system of latitudes and longitudes. The resulting North American Datum of 1983 (NAD 83) replaces the North American Datum of 1927, as well as local reference systems for Hawaii and for Puerto Rico and the Virgin Islands. The change was prompted by Hawaii's increased need for accurate coordinate information. To facilitate use of satellite surveying and navigation systems, such as the Global Positioning System (GPS), the new datum was redefined using the Geodetic Reference System 1980 as the reference ellipsoid because this model more closely approximates the true size and shape of the earth. In addition, the origin of the coordinate system is referenced to the mass center of the earth to coincide with the orbital orientation of the GPS satellites. Positional changes resulting from the datum redefinition can reach 330 ft in the continental U.S., Canada, and Mexico. Changes that exceed 660 ft can be expected in Alaska, Puerto Rico, and the Virgin Islands. Hawaii's coordinates changed about 1,300 ft.

Additional Statistical Information About the U.S.

The annual *Statistical Abstract of the United States,* published by U.S. Dept. of Commerce, contains additional data. For information, write Supt. of Documents, Government Printing Office, PO Box 371954, Pittsburgh, PA 15250-7954, or call (202) 512-1800. For electronic products, write U.S. Dept. of Commerce, U.S. Census Bureau, PO Box 277943, Atlanta, GA 30384-7943, or call (301) 763-INFO (4636). Parts of *The Statistical Abstract* can be viewed on the Internet at www.census.gov/statab/www

IT'S A FACT: Maryland is the narrowest state—near the town of Hancock, the state is only about one mile wide from the border with Pennsylvania to the border with West Virginia.

Highest and Lowest Altitudes in U.S. States and Territories

Source: U.S. Geological Survey, Dept. of the Interior
(Minus sign means below sea level.)

	HIGHEST POINT			LOWEST POINT		
	Name	County	Elev. (ft)	Name	County	Elev. (ft)
Alabama	Cheaha Mountain	Cleburne	2,405	Gulf of Mexico		Sea level
Alaska	Mount McKinley	Denali	20,320	Pacific Ocean		Sea level
Arizona	Humphreys Peak	Coconino	12,633	Colorado R	Yuma	70
Arkansas	Magazine Mountain	Logan	2,753	Ouachita R	Ashley-Union	55
California	Mount Whitney	Inyo-Tulare	14,494	Death Valley	Inyo	–282
Colorado	Mount Elbert	Lake	14,433	Arikaree R	Yuma	3,315
Connecticut	Mount Frissell	Litchfield	2,380	Long Island Sound		Sea level
Delaware	On Ebright Road	New Castle	448	Atlantic Ocean		Sea level
Dist. of Columbia	Tenleytown	N W part	410	Potomac R		1
Florida	Sec. 30, T6N, R20W[1]	Walton	345	Atlantic Ocean		Sea level
Georgia	Brasstown Bald	Towns-Union	4,784	Atlantic Ocean		Sea level
Guam	Mount Lamlam	Agat District	1,332	Pacific Ocean		Sea level
Hawaii	Mauna Kea	Hawaii	13,796	Pacific Ocean		Sea level
Idaho	Borah Peak	Custer	12,662	Snake R	Nez Perce	710
Illinois	Charles Mound	Jo Daviess	1,235	Mississippi R	Alexander	279
Indiana	Franklin Township	Wayne	1,257	Ohio R	Posey	320
Iowa	Sec. 29, T100N, R41W[1]	Osceola	1,670	Mississippi R	Lee	480
Kansas	Mount Sunflower	Wallace	4,039	Verdigris R	Montgomery	679
Kentucky	Black Mountain	Harlan	4,145	Mississippi R	Fulton	257
Louisiana	Driskill Mountain	Bienville	535	New Orleans	Orleans	–8
Maine	Mount Katahdin	Piscataquis	5,267	Atlantic Ocean		Sea level
Maryland	Backbone Mountain[2]	Garrett	3,360	Atlantic Ocean		Sea level
Massachusetts	Mount Greylock	Berkshire	3,487	Atlantic Ocean		Sea level
Michigan	Mount Arvon	Baraga	1,979	Lake Erie	Monroe	571
Minnesota	Eagle Mountain	Cook	2,301	Lake Superior		602
Mississippi	Woodall Mountain	Tishomingo	806	Gulf of Mexico		Sea level
Missouri	Taum Sauk Mt.	Iron	1,772	St. Francis R	Dunklin	230
Montana	Granite Peak	Park	12,799	Kootenai R	Lincoln	1,800
Nebraska	Johnson Township	Kimball	5,424	Missouri R	Richardson	840
Nevada	Boundary Peak	Esmeralda	13,143	Colorado R	Clark	479
New Hampshire	Mt. Washington	Coos	6,288	Atlantic Ocean		Sea level
New Jersey	High Point	Sussex	1,803	Atlantic Ocean		Sea level
New Mexico	Wheeler Peak	Taos	13,161	Red Bluff Res.	Eddy	2,842
New York	Mount Marcy	Essex	5,344	Atlantic Ocean		Sea level
North Carolina	Mount Mitchell	Yancey	6,684	Atlantic Ocean		Sea level
North Dakota	White Butte	Slope	3,506	Red R	Pembina	750
Ohio	Campbell Hill	Logan	1,549	Ohio R	Hamilton	455
Oklahoma	Black Mesa	Cimarron	4,973	Little R	McCurtain	289
Oregon	Mount Hood	Clackamas-Hood R.	11,239	Pacific Ocean		Sea level
Pennsylvania	Mt. Davis	Somerset	3,213	Delaware R	Delaware	Sea level
Puerto Rico	Cerro de Punta	Ponce District	4,390	Atlantic Ocean		Sea level
Rhode Island	Jerimoth Hill	Providence	812	Atlantic Ocean		Sea level
Samoa	Lata Mountain	Tau Island	3,160	Pacific Ocean		Sea level
South Carolina	Sassafras Mountain	Pickens	3,560	Atlantic Ocean		Sea level
South Dakota	Harney Peak	Pennington	7,242	Big Stone Lake	Roberts	966
Tennessee	Clingmans Dome	Sevier	6,643	Mississippi R	Shelby	178
Texas	Guadalupe Peak	Culberson	8,749	Gulf of Mexico		Sea level
Utah	Kings Peak	Duchesne	13,528	Beaver Dam Wash	Washington	2,000
Vermont	Mount Mansfield	Lamoille	4,393	Lake Champlain		95
Virginia	Mount Rogers	Grayson-Smyth	5,729	Atlantic Ocean		Sea level
Virgin Islands	Crown Mountain	St. Thomas Island	1,556	Atlantic Ocean		Sea level
Washington	Mount Rainier West	Pierce	14,410	Pacific Ocean		Sea level
West Virginia	Spruce Knob	Pendleton	4,861	Potomac R	Jefferson	240
Wisconsin	Timms Hill	Price	1,951	Lake Michigan		579
Wyoming	Gannett Peak	Fremont	13,804	Belle Fourche R	Crook	3,099

(1) Sec.=section; T=township; R=range; N=north; W=west. (2) At the MD-WV border.

U.S. Coastline by States

Source: National Oceanic and Atmospheric Administration, U.S. Dept. of Commerce
(in statute miles)

	Coastline[1]	Shoreline[2]
ATLANTIC COAST	**2,069**	**28,673**
Connecticut	0	618
Delaware	28	381
Florida	580	3,331
Georgia	100	2,344
Maine	228	3,478
Maryland	31	3,190
Massachusetts	192	1,519
New Hampshire	13	131
New Jersey	130	1,792
New York	127	1,850
North Carolina	301	3,375
Pennsylvania	0	89
Rhode Island	40	384
South Carolina	187	2,876
Virginia	112	3,315

	Coastline[1]	Shoreline[2]
GULF COAST	**1,631**	**17,141**
Alabama	53	607
Florida	770	5,095
Louisiana	397	7,721
Mississippi	44	359
Texas	367	3,359
PACIFIC COAST	**7,623**	**40,298**
Alaska	5,580	31,383
California	840	3,427
Hawaii	750	1,052
Oregon	296	1,410
Washington	157	3,026
ARCTIC COAST	**1,060**	**2,521**
UNITED STATES	**12,383**	**88,633**

(1) Figures are lengths of general outline of seacoast. Measurements were made with a unit measure of 30 minutes of latitude on charts as near the scale of 1:1,200,000 as possible. Coastline of sounds and bays is included to a point where they narrow to width of unit measure, and includes the distance across at such point. (2) Figures obtained in 1939-40 with a recording instrument on the largest-scale charts and maps then available. Shoreline of outer coast, offshore islands, sounds, bays, rivers, and creeks is included to the head of tidewater or to a point where tidal waters narrow to a width of 100 ft.

Key Data for the 50 States

The 13 colonies that declared independence from Great Britain and fought the War of Independence (American Revolution) became the 13 original states. They were (in the order in which they ratified the Constitution): Delaware, Pennsylvania, New Jersey, Georgia, Connecticut, Massachusetts, Maryland, South Carolina, New Hampshire, Virginia, New York, North Carolina, and Rhode Island.

			Entered Union		Extent in miles		Area in sq mi			
State	Settled[1]	Capital	Date	Order	Long (approx.	Wide mean)	Land	Water	Total	Rank in area[2]
AL	1702	Montgomery	Dec. 14, 1819	22	330	190	50,744	1,675	52,419	30
AK	1784	Juneau	Jan. 3, 1959	49	1,480[3]	810	571,951	91,316	663,267	1
AZ	1776	Phoenix	Feb. 14, 1912	48	400	310	113,635	364	113,998	6
AR	1686	Little Rock	June 15, 1836	25	260	240	52,068	1,110	53,179	29
CA	1769	Sacramento	Sept. 9, 1850	31	770	250	155,959	7,736	163,696	3
CO	1858	Denver	Aug. 1, 1876	38	380	280	103,718	376	104,094	8
CT	1634	Hartford	Jan. 9, 1788	5	110	70	4,845	699	5,543	48
DE	1638	Dover	Dec. 7, 1787	1	100	30	1,954	536	2,489	49
DC	NA	NA	NA	NA	...	...	61	7	68	51
FL	1565	Tallahassee	Mar. 3, 1845	27	500	160	53,927	11,828	65,755	22
GA	1733	Atlanta	Jan. 2, 1788	4	300	230	57,906	1,519	59,425	24
HI	1820	Honolulu	Aug. 21, 1959	50	...	...	6,423	4,508	10,931	43
ID	1842	Boise	July 3, 1890	43	570	300	82,747	823	83,570	14
IL	1720	Springfield	Dec. 3, 1818	21	390	210	55,584	2,331	57,914	25
IN	1733	Indianapolis	Dec. 11, 1816	19	270	140	35,867	551	36,418	38
IA	1788	Des Moines	Dec. 28, 1846	29	310	200	55,869	402	56,272	26
KS	1727	Topeka	Jan. 29, 1861	34	400	210	81,815	462	82,277	15
KY	1774	Frankfort	June 1, 1792	15	380	140	39,728	681	40,409	37
LA	1699	Baton Rouge	Apr. 30, 1812	18	380	130	43,562	8,278	51,840	31
ME	1624	Augusta	Mar. 15, 1820	23	320	190	30,862	4,523	35,385	39
MD	1634	Annapolis	Apr. 28, 1788	7	250	90	9,774	2,633	12,407	42
MA	1620	Boston	Feb. 6, 1788	6	190	50	7,840	2,715	10,555	44
MI	1668	Lansing	Jan. 26, 1837	26	490	240	56,804	39,912	96,716	11
MN	1805	St. Paul	May 11, 1858	32	400	250	79,610	7,329	86,939	12
MS	1699	Jackson	Dec. 10, 1817	20	340	170	46,907	1,523	48,430	32
MO	1735	Jefferson City	Aug. 10, 1821	24	300	240	68,886	818	69,704	21
MT	1809	Helena	Nov. 8, 1889	41	630	280	145,552	1,490	147,042	4
NE	1823	Lincoln	Mar. 1, 1867	37	430	210	76,872	481	77,354	16
NV	1849	Carson City	Oct. 31, 1864	36	490	320	109,826	735	110,561	7
NH	1623	Concord	June 21, 1788	9	190	70	8,968	382	9,350	46
NJ	1660	Trenton	Dec. 18, 1787	3	150	70	7,417	1,304	8,721	47
NM	1610	Santa Fe	Jan. 6, 1912	47	370	343	121,356	234	121,589	5
NY	1614	Albany	July 26, 1788	11	330	283	47,214	7,342	54,556	27
NC	1660	Raleigh	Nov. 21, 1789	12	500	150	40,711	5,108	53,819	28
ND	1812	Bismarck	Nov. 2, 1889	39	340	211	68,976	1,724	70,700	19
OH	1788	Columbus	Mar. 1, 1803	17	220	220	40,948	3,877	44,825	34
OK	1889	Oklahoma City	Nov. 16, 1907	46	400	220	68,667	1,231	69,898	20
OR	1811	Salem	Feb. 14, 1859	33	360	261	95,997	2,384	98,381	9
PA	1682	Harrisburg	Dec. 12, 1787	2	283	160	44,817	1,239	46,055	33
RI	1636	Providence	May 29, 1790	13	40	30	1,045	500	1,545	50
SC	1670	Columbia	May 23, 1788	8	260	200	30,109	911	32,020	40
SD	1859	Pierre	Nov. 2, 1889	40	380	210	75,885	1,232	77,116	17
TN	1769	Nashville	June 1, 1796	16	440	120	41,217	926	42,143	36
TX	1682	Austin	Dec. 29, 1845	28	790	660	261,797	6,784	268,581	2
UT	1847	Salt Lake City	Jan. 4, 1896	45	350	270	82,144	2,755	84,899	13
VT	1724	Montpelier	Mar. 4, 1791	14	160	80	9,250	365	9,614	45
VA	1607	Richmond	June 25, 1788	10	430	200	39,594	3,180	42,774	35
WA	1811	Olympia	Nov. 11, 1889	42	360	240	66,544	4,756	71,300	18
WV	1727	Charleston	June 20, 1863	35	240	130	24,078	152	24,230	41
WI	1766	Madison	May 29, 1848	30	310	260	54,310	11,188	65,498	23
WY	1834	Cheyenne	July 10, 1890	44	360	280	97,100	713	97,814	10

Note: Land and water areas may not add to totals because of rounding. NA = Not applicable. (1) First permanent settlement by Europeans. (2) Rank is based on total area as shown. (3) Aleutian Islands and Alexander Archipelago not included.

The Continental Divide of the U.S.

The Continental Divide of the U.S., also known as the Great Divide, is located at the watershed created by the mountain ranges, or tablelands, of the Rocky Mountains. This watershed separates the waters that drain easterly into the Atlantic Ocean and its marginal seas, such as the Gulf of Mexico, from those waters that drain westerly into the Pacific Ocean. The majority of easterly flowing water in the U.S. drains into the Gulf of Mexico before reaching the Atlantic Ocean. The majority of westerly flowing water, before reaching the Pacific Ocean, drains either through the Columbia River or through the Colorado River, which flows into the Gulf of California before reaching the Pacific Ocean.

The location and route of the Continental Divide across the U.S. can briefly be described as follows:

Beginning at point of crossing the U.S.-Mexican boundary, near long. 108° 45′ W, the Divide, in a northerly direction, crosses New Mexico along the W edge of the Rio Grande drainage basin, entering Colorado near long. 106° 41′ W.

From there by a very irregular route north across Colorado along the W summits of the Rio Grande and of the Arkansas, the South Platte, and the North Platte river basins, and across Rocky Mountain National Park, entering Wyoming near long. 106° 52′ W.

From there in a northwesterly direction, forming the W rims of the North Platte, the Big Horn, and the Yellowstone river basins, crossing the SW portion of Yellowstone National Park.

From there in a westerly and then a northerly direction forming the common boundary of Idaho and Montana, to a point on said boundary near long. 114° 00′ W.

From there northeasterly and northwesterly through Montana and the Glacier National Park, entering Canada near long. 114° 04′ W.

WORLD ALMANAC QUICK QUIZ

Which state has the easternmost point in the U.S.?

(a) Florida (b) Maine
(c) Massachusetts (d) Alaska

For the answer look in this chapter, or see page 1008.

Chronological List of Territories, With State Admissions to Union

Source: National Archives and Records Service

Name of territory	Date of act creating territory	When act took effect	Admission as state	Yrs. terr.
Northwest Territory[1]	July 13, 1787	No fixed date	Mar. 1, 1803[2]	16
Territory southwest of River Ohio	May 26, 1790	No fixed date	June 1, 1796[3]	6
Mississippi	Apr. 7, 1798	When president acted	Dec. 10, 1817	19
Indiana	May 7, 1800	July 4, 1800	Dec. 11, 1816	16
Orleans	Mar. 26, 1804	Oct. 1, 1804	Apr. 30, 1812[4]	7
Michigan	Jan. 11, 1805	June 30, 1805	Jan. 26, 1837	31
Louisiana-Missouri[5]	Mar. 3, 1805	July 4, 1805	Aug. 10, 1821	16
Illinois	Feb. 3, 1809	Mar. 1, 1809	Dec. 3, 1818	9
Alabama	Mar. 3, 1817	When MS became a state	Dec. 14, 1819	2
Arkansas	Mar. 2, 1819	July 4, 1819	June 15, 1836	17
Florida	Mar. 30, 1822	No fixed date	Mar. 3, 1845	23
Wisconsin	Apr. 20, 1836	July 3, 1836	May 29, 1848	12
Iowa	June 12, 1838	July 3, 1838	Dec. 28, 1846	8
Oregon	Aug. 14, 1848	Date of act	Feb. 14, 1859	10
Minnesota	Mar. 3, 1849	Date of act	May 11, 1858	9
New Mexico	Sept. 9, 1850	On president's proclamation	Jan. 6, 1912	61
Utah	Sept. 9, 1850	Date of act	Jan. 4, 1896	46
Washington	Mar. 2, 1853	Date of act	Nov. 11, 1889	36
Nebraska	May 30, 1854	Date of act	Mar. 1, 1867	12
Kansas	May 30, 1854	Date of act	Jan. 29, 1861	6
Colorado	Feb. 28, 1861	Date of act	Aug. 1, 1876	15
Nevada	Mar. 2, 1861	Date of act	Oct. 31, 1864	3
Dakota	Mar. 2, 1861	Date of act	Nov. 2, 1889	28
Arizona	Feb. 24, 1863	Date of act	Feb. 14, 1912	49
Idaho	Mar. 3, 1863	Date of act	July 3, 1890	27
Montana	May 26, 1864	Date of act	Nov. 8, 1889	25
Wyoming	July 25, 1868	When officers were qualified	July 10, 1890	22
Alaska[6]	May 17, 1884	No fixed date	Jan. 3, 1959	75
Oklahoma	May 2, 1890	Date of act	Nov. 16, 1907	17
Hawaii	Apr. 30, 1900	June 14, 1900	Aug. 21, 1959	59

(1) Included what is now Ohio, Indiana, Illinois, Michigan, Wisconsin, E Minnesota. (2) Whole territory admitted as the state of Ohio. (3) Admitted as the state of Tennessee. (4) Admitted as the state of Louisiana. (5) The act creating Missouri Territory (June 4, 1812) became effective Dec. 7, 1812. (6) Although the May 17, 1884, act actually constituted Alaska as a district, it was often referred to as a territory, and administered as such. The Territory of Alaska was formally organized by an act of Aug. 24, 1912.

Geographic Centers, U.S. and Each State

Source: U.S. Geological Survey, Dept. of the Interior

There is no generally accepted definition of geographic center and no uniform method for determining it. Following the U.S. Geological Survey, the geographic center of an area is defined here as the center of gravity of the surface, or that point on which the surface would balance if it were a plane of uniform thickness. All locations in the following list are approximate.

No marked or monumented point has been officially established by any government agency as the geographic center of the 50 states, the conterminous U.S. (48 states), or the North American continent. A group of private citizens erected a monument in Lebanon, KS, marking it as geographic center of the conterminous U.S., and a cairn erected in Rugby, ND, asserts that location as the center of the North American continent.

Geographic centers as reported by the U.S. Geological Survey are indicated below:

United States, including Alaska and Hawaii—W of Castle Rock, Butte County, SD; lat. 44° 58′ N, long. 103° 46′ W
Conterminous U.S. (48 states)—Near Lebanon, Smith Co., Kansas, lat. 39° 50′ N, long. 98° 35′ W
North American continent—6 mi W of Balta, Pierce County, North Dakota; lat. 48° 10′ N, long. 100° 10′ W
Alabama—Chilton, 12 mi SW of Clanton
Alaska—lat. 63° 50′ N, long. 152° W; approx. 60 mi NW of Mt. McKinley
Arizona—Yavapai, 55 mi E-SE of Prescott
Arkansas—Pulaski, 12 mi NW of Little Rock
California—Madera, 38 mi E of Madera
Colorado—Park, 30 mi NW of Pikes Peak
Connecticut—Hartford, at East Berlin
Delaware—Kent, 11 mi S of Dover
District of Columbia—Near 4th and L Sts. NW
Florida—Hernando, 12 mi N-NW of Brooksville
Georgia—Twiggs, 18 mi SE of Macon
Hawaii—lat. 20° 15′ N, long. 156° 20′ W, off Maui Is.
Idaho—Custer, SW of Challis
Illinois—Logan, 28 mi NE of Springfield
Indiana—Boone, 14 mi N-NW of Indianapolis
Iowa—Story, 5 mi NE of Ames
Kansas—Barton, 15 mi NE of Great Bend
Kentucky—Marion, 3 mi N-NW of Lebanon
Louisiana—Avoyelles, 3 mi SE of Marksville
Maine—Piscataquis, 18 mi N of Dover
Maryland—Prince George's, 4.5 mi NW of Davidsonville
Massachusetts—Worcester, N part of city
Michigan—Wexford, 5 mi N-NW of Cadillac
Minnesota—Crow Wing, 10 mi SW of Brainerd
Mississippi—Leake, 9 mi W-NW of Carthage
Missouri—Miller, 20 mi SW of Jefferson City
Montana—Fergus, 11 mi W of Lewistown
Nebraska—Custer, 10 mi NW of Broken Bow
Nevada—Lander, 26 mi SE of Austin
New Hampshire—Belknap, 3 mi E of Ashland
New Jersey—Mercer, 5 mi SE of Trenton
New Mexico—Torrance, 12 mi S-SW of Willard
New York—Madison, 12 mi S of Oneida and 26 mi SW of Utica
North Carolina—Chatham, 10 mi NW of Sanford
North Dakota—Sheridan, 5 mi SW of McClusky
Ohio—Delaware, 25 mi N-NE of Columbus
Oklahoma—Oklahoma, 8 mi N of Oklahoma City
Oregon—Crook, 25 mi S-SE of Prineville
Pennsylvania—Centre, 2.5 mi SW of Bellefonte
Rhode Island—Kent, 1 mi S-SW of Crompton
South Carolina—Richland, 13 mi SE of Columbia
South Dakota—Hughes, 8 mi NE of Pierre
Tennessee—Rutherford, 5 mi NE of Murfreesboro
Texas—McCulloch, 15 mi NE of Brady
Utah—Sanpete, 3 mi N of Manti
Vermont—Washington, 3 mi E of Roxbury
Virginia—Buckingham, 5 mi SW of Buckingham
Washington—Chelan, 10 mi W-SW of Wenatchee
West Virginia—Braxton, 4 mi E of Sutton
Wisconsin—Wood, 9 mi SE of Marshfield
Wyoming—Fremont, 58 mi E-NE of Lander

International Boundary Lines of the U.S.

The length of the N boundary of the conterminous U.S.—the U.S.-Canadian border, excluding Alaska—is 3,987 mi according to the U.S. Geological Survey, Dept. of the Interior. The length of the Alaskan-Canadian border is 1,538 mi. The U.S.-Mexican border, from the Gulf of Mexico to the Pacific Ocean, is about 1,933 mi (1963 boundary agreement).

Origins of the Names of U.S. States

Source: State officials, Smithsonian Institution, and Topographic Division, U.S. Geological Survey, Dept. of the Interior

Alabama—Indian for tribal town, later a tribe (Alabamas or Alibamons) of the Creek confederacy.

Alaska—Russian version of Aleutian (Eskimo) word, *alakshak*, for "peninsula," "great lands," or "land that is not an island."

Arizona—Spanish version of Pima Indian word for "little spring place," or Aztec *arizuma*, meaning "silver-bearing."

Arkansas—Algonquin name for the Quapaw Indians, meaning "south wind."

California—Bestowed by the Spanish conquistadors (possibly by Cortez). It was the name of an imaginary island, an earthly paradise, in *Las Serges de Esplandian*, a Spanish romance written by Montalvo in 1510. *Baja California* (Lower California, in Mexico) was first visited by Spanish in 1533. The present U.S. state was called *Alta* (Upper) *California*.

Colorado—From Spanish for "red," first applied to Colorado River.

Connecticut—From Mohican and other Algonquin words meaning "long river place."

Delaware—Named for Lord De La Warr, early governor of Virginia; first applied to river, then to Indian tribe (Lenni-Lenape), and the state.

District of Columbia—For Christopher Columbus, 1791.

Florida—Named by Ponce de Leon *Pascua Florida*, "Flowery Easter," on Easter Sunday, 1513.

Georgia—For King George II of England, by James Oglethorpe, colonial administrator, 1732.

Hawaii—Possibly derived from native word for homeland, *Hawaiki* or *Owhyhee*.

Idaho—Said to be a coined name with an invented meaning: "gem of the mountains"; originally suggested for the Pikes Peak mining territory (Colorado), then applied to the new mining territory of the Pacific Northwest. Another theory suggests *Idaho* may be a Kiowa Apache term for the Comanche.

Illinois—French for *Illini* or "land of *Illini*," Algonquin word meaning "men" or "warriors."

Indiana—Means "land of the Indians."

Iowa—Indian word variously translated as "here I rest" or "beautiful land." Named for the Iowa R., which was named for the Iowa Indians.

Kansas—Sioux word for "south wind people."

Kentucky—Indian word that is variously translated as "dark and bloody ground," "meadowland," and "land of tomorrow."

Louisiana—Part of territory called Louisiana by Sieur de La Salle for French King Louis XIV.

Maine—From Maine, ancient French province. Also: descriptive, referring to the mainland as distinct from the many coastal islands.

Maryland—For Queen Henrietta Maria, wife of Charles I of England.

Massachusetts—From Indian tribe named after "large hill place" identified by Capt. John Smith as being near Milton, MA.

Michigan—From Chippewa words, *mici gama*, meaning "great water," after the lake of the same name.

Minnesota—From Dakota Sioux word meaning "cloudy water" or "sky-tinted water" of the Minnesota River.

Mississippi—Probably Chippewa; *mici zibi*, "great river" or "gathering-in of all the waters." Also: Algonquin word, *messipi*.

Missouri—An Algonquin Indian term meaning "river of the big canoes."

Montana—Latin or Spanish for "mountainous."

Nebraska—From Omaha or Otos Indian word meaning "broad water" or "flat river," describing the Platte River.

Nevada—Spanish, meaning "snow-clad."

New Hampshire—Named, 1629, by Capt. John Mason of Plymouth Council for his home county in England.

New Jersey—The Duke of York, 1664, gave a patent to John Berkeley and Sir George Carteret to be called Nova Caesaria, or New Jersey, after England's Isle of Jersey.

New Mexico—Spaniards in Mexico applied term to land north and west of Rio Grande in the 16th century.

New York—For Duke of York and Albany, who received patent to New Netherland from his brother Charles II and sent an expedition to capture it, 1664.

North Carolina—In 1619 Charles I gave a large patent to Sir Robert Heath to be called Province of Carolana, from *Carolus*, Latin name for Charles. A new patent was granted by Charles II to Earl of Clarendon and others. Divided into North and South Carolina, 1710.

North Dakota—*Dakota* is Sioux for "friend" or "ally."

Ohio—Iroquois word for "fine or good river."

Oklahoma—Choctaw word meaning "red man," proposed by Rev. Allen Wright, Choctaw-speaking Indian.

Oregon—Origin unknown. One theory holds that the name may have been derived from that of the Wisconsin River, shown on a 1715 French map as "Ouaricon-sint."

Pennsylvania—William Penn, the Quaker who was made full proprietor of this area by King Charles II in 1681, suggested "Sylvania," or "woodland," for his tract. The king's government owed Penn's father, Admiral William Penn, 16,000 pounds, and the land was granted as partial settlement. Charles II added the "Penn" to Sylvania, against the desires of the modest proprietor, in honor of the admiral.

Puerto Rico—Spanish for "rich port."

Rhode Island—Exact origin is unknown. One theory notes that Giovanni de Verrazano recorded an island about the size of Rhodes in the Mediterranean in 1524, but others believe the state was named *Roode Eylandt* by Adriaen Block, Dutch explorer, because of its red clay.

South Carolina—See North Carolina.

South Dakota—See North Dakota.

Tennessee—*Tanasi* was the name of Cherokee villages on the Little Tennessee River. From 1784 to 1788 this was the State of Franklin, or Frankland.

Texas—Variant of word used by Caddo and other Indians meaning "friends" or "allies," and applied to them by the Spanish in eastern Texas. Also written *Texias*, *Tejas*, *Teysas*.

Utah—From a Navajo word meaning "upper," or "higher up," as applied to a Shoshone tribe called Ute. Spanish form is *Yutta*. The English is *Uta* or *Utah*. Proposed name *Deseret*, "land of honeybees," from Book of Mormon, was rejected by Congress.

Vermont—From French words *vert* (green) and *mont* (mountain). The Green Mountains were said to have been named by Samuel de Champlain. When the state was formed, 1777, Dr. Thomas Young suggested combining *vert* and *mont* into Vermont.

Virginia—Named by Sir Walter Raleigh, who fitted out the expedition of 1584, in honor of Queen Elizabeth, the Virgin Queen of England.

Washington—Named after George Washington. When the bill creating the Territory of Columbia was introduced in the 32nd Congress, the name was changed to Washington because of the existence of the District of Columbia.

West Virginia—So named when western counties of Virginia refused to secede from the U.S. in 1863.

Wisconsin—An Indian name, spelled *Ouisconsin* and *Mesconsing* by early chroniclers. Believed to mean "grassy place" in Chippewa. Congress made it *Wisconsin*.

Wyoming—From the Algonquin words for "large prairie place," "at the big plains," or "on the great plain."

Territorial Sea of the U.S.

According to a Dec. 27, 1988, proclamation by Pres. Ronald Reagan: "The territorial sea of the United States henceforth extends to 12 nautical miles from the baselines of the United States determined in accordance with international law. In accordance with international law, as reflected in the applicable provisions of the 1982 United Nations Convention on the Law of the Sea, within the territorial sea of the United States, the ships of all countries enjoy the right of innocent passage and the ships and aircraft of all countries enjoy the right of transit passage through international straits."

Major Accessions of Territory by the U.S.

Source: U.S. Dept. of the Interior; Bureau of the Census, U.S. Dept. of Commerce

Not including territories such as Panama Canal Zone and the Philippines which are no longer under U.S. jurisdiction; area figures may differ from figures for current areas given elsewhere.

Territory	Acquisition date	Gross area (sq mi)
Territory in 1790[1]	NA	888,685
Louisiana Purchase	1803	827,192
Purchase of Florida	1819	58,560
Other areas from Spain	1819	13,443
Texas	1845	390,143
Oregon Territory	1846	285,580
Mexican Cession	1848	529,017
Gadsden Purchase	1853	29,640
Alaska	1867	586,412
Hawaii	1898	6,450
Puerto Rico[2]	1899	3,435
Guam[3]	1899	212
American Samoa[4]	1900	76
U.S. Virgin Islands	1917	133
Northern Mariana Islands[5]	1986	179

NA = not applicable. (1) Includes that part of a drainage basin of Red River of the North, S of 49th parallel, sometimes considered part of Louisiana Purchase. (2) Ceded by Spain in 1898, ratified in 1899, and became the Commonwealth of Puerto Rico by Act of Congress on July 25, 1952. (3) Acquired in 1898; ratified 1899. (4) Acquired in 1899; ratified 1900. (5) Formerly a part of the U.S. administered Trust Territory of the Pacific Islands; became a U.S. commonwealth, Nov. 3, 1986.

Federally Owned Land, by State

Source: Office of Governmentwide Policy, General Services Administration; as of Sept. 30, 2000

State	Federal acreage[1]	Total acreage of state[2]	Percentage of federally owned acreage[1]
AL	1,325,698.1	32,678,400	4.057
AK	220,851,882.2	365,481,600	60.428
AZ	32,379,448.9	72,688,000	44.546
AR	3,409,646.8	33,599,360	10.148
CA	47,889,218.7	100,206,720	47.790
CO	24,108,409.8	66,485,760	36.261
CT	14,150.3	3,135,360	0.451
DE	15,557.3	1,265,920	1.229
DC	9,045.0	39,040	23.169
FL	4,599,237.0	34,721,280	13.246
GA	2,027,086.9	37,295,360	5.435
HI	638,621.8	4,105,600	15.555
ID	33,106,382.4	52,933,120	62.544
IL	590,477.8	35,795,200	1.650
IN	510,316.3	23,158,400	2.204
IA	229,867.4	35,860,480	0.641
KS	674,083.8	52,510,720	1.284
KY	1,446,750.4	25,512,320	5.671
LA	1,198,765.1	28,867,840	4.153
ME	173,153.8	19,847,680	0.872
MD	166,213.0	6,319,360	2.630
MA	71,170.3	5,034,880	1.414
MI	4,075,640.0	36,492,160	11.169
MN	4,216,552.0	51,205,760	8.235
MS	1,671,595.8	30,222,720	5.531
MO	4,798,315.7	44,248,320	10.844
MT	27,427,898.6	93,271,040	29.407
NE	650,856.7	49,031,680	1.327
NV	58,319,331.6	70,264,320	83.000
NH	758,632.1	5,768,960	13.150
NJ	123,791.0	4,813,440	2.572
NM	26,572,245.8	77,766,400	34.169
NY	221,538.5	30,680,960	0.722
NC	1,988,594.7	31,402,880	6.333
ND	2,315,952.0	44,452,480	5.210
OH	441,303.3	26,222,080	1.683
OK	1,665,802.5	44,087,680	3.778
OR	32,356,070.1	61,598,720	52.527
PA	716,527.5	28,804,480	2.488
RI	3,607.2	677,120	0.533
SC	1,109,545.1	19,374,080	5.727
SD	3,120,203.3	48,881,920	6.383
TN	2,115,019.2	26,727,680	7.913
TX	2,307,171.0	168,217,600	1.372
UT	34,001,393.8	52,696,960	64.522
VT	374,667.9	5,936,640	6.311
VA	2,279,561.3	25,496,320	8.941
WA	12,176,082.0	42,693,760	28.520
WV	1,222,434.3	15,410,560	7.932
WI	1,819,189.2	35,011,200	5.196
WY	31,069,995.2	62,343,040	49.837
TOTAL	**635,354,700.5**	**2,271,343,360**	**27.973**

Note: Totals do not include inland water. (1) Excludes trust properties. (2) Bureau of the Census, U.S. Dept. of Commerce figures.

Special Recreation Areas Administered by the U.S. Forest Service, 2001

Source: U.S. Forest Service, Dept. of Agriculture

NHL=National Historic Landmark; NHS=National Historic Scenic Area; NM=National Monument; NP=National Preserve; NRA=National Recreation Area; NSA=National Scenic Area; NVM=National Volcanic Monument; SRA=Scenic Recreation Area

Area name	Location	Estab.	Acres
Admiralty Island NM	AK	1980	978,881
Allegheny NRA	PA	1984	23,063
Arapaho NRA	CO	1978	30,690
Beech Creek NS & Botanic Area	OK	1988	7,500
Cascade Head NS(-Research)A	OR	1974	6,630
Columbia River Gorge NSA	OR-WA	1986	63,150
Coosa Bald NSA	GA	1991	7,100
Ed Jenkins NRA	GA	1991	23,166
Flaming Gorge NRA	WY-UT	1968	189,825
Giant Sequoia NM	CA	2000	327,769
Grand Island NRA	MI	1990	12,961
Grey Towers NHL	PA	1963	102
Hells Canyon NRA	ID-OR	1975	536,648
Indian Nations NS & Wildlife Area	OK	1988	40,051
Jemez NRA	NM	1993	57,000
Land Between the Lakes NRA	KY-TN	1998	170,000
Misty Fiords NM	AK	1980	2,293,428
Mono Basin NSA	CA	1984	115,600
Mount Baker NRA	WA	1984	8,473
Mount Pleasant NSA	VA	1994	7,580
Mount Rogers NRA	VA	1966	114,520
Mount St. Helens NVM	WA	1989	112,593
Newberry NVM	OR	1990	54,822
North Cascades NSA	WA	1984	87,600
Opal Creek SRA	OR	1996	13,000
Oregon Dunes NRA	OR	1972	27,212
Pine Ridge NRA	NE	1986	6,600
Rattlesnake NRA	MT	1980	59,119
Santa Rosa and San Jacinto Mts. NM	CA	2000	272,000
Sawtooth NRA	ID	1972	729,322
Smith River NRA	CA	1990	305,169
Spring Mt. NRA	NV	1993	316,000
Spruce Knob-Seneca Rocks NRA	WV	1965	57,237
Valles Caldera NP	NM	2000	88,900
Whiskeytown-Shasta-Trinity NRA	CA	1965	176,367
White Rocks NRA	VT	1984	36,400
Winding Stair Mt. NRA	OK	1988	25,890

IT'S A FACT: Although Congress set aside Yellowstone National Park in 1872, there was no real system of national parks until a federal bureau, the National Park Service, was created on Aug. 25, 1916, to manage those areas then assigned to the U.S. Department of the Interior.

National Parks, Other Areas Administered by National Park Service

Dates when sites were authorized for initial protection by Congress or by presidential proclamation are given in parentheses. If different, the date the area got its current designation, or was transferred to the National Park Service, follows. Gross area in acres, as of Dec. 31, 2001, follows date(s). Over 84 mil acres of federal land are now administered by the National Park Service.

NATIONAL PARKS

Acadia, ME (1916/1929) 47,498. Includes Mount Desert Isl., half of Isle au Haut, Schoodic Peninsula on mainland. Highest elevation on Eastern seaboard.

American Samoa, AS (1988) 9,000. Features a paleotropical rain forest and a coral reef. No federal facilities.

Arches, UT (1929/1971) 76,519. Contains giant red sandstone arches and other products of erosion.

Badlands, SD (1929/1978) 242,756. Prairie with bison, bighorn, and antelope. Animal fossils 26-37 mil years old.

Big Bend, TX (1935) 801,163. Rio Grande, Chisos Mts.

Biscayne, FL (1968/1980) 172,924. Aquatic park encompassing chain of islands south of Miami.

Black Canyon of the Gunnison, CO (1933/1999) 29,927. Has a canyon 2,900 ft deep and 40 ft wide at its narrowest part.

Bryce Canyon, UT (1923/1928) 35,835. Spectacularly colorful and unusual display of erosion effects.

Canyonlands, UT (1964) 337,598. At junction of Colorado and Green rivers; extensive evidence of prehistoric Indians.

Capitol Reef, UT (1937/1971) 241,904. A 70-mi uplift of sandstone cliffs dissected by high-walled gorges.

Carlsbad Caverns, NM (1923/1930) 46,766. Largest known caverns; not yet fully explored.

Channel Islands, CA (1938/1980) 249,561. Sea lion breeding place, nesting sea birds, unique plants.

Crater Lake, OR (1902) 183,224. Extraordinary blue lake in the crater of Mt. Mazama, a volcano that erupted about 7,700 years ago; deepest U.S. lake.

Cuyahoga Valley, OH (1974/2000) 32,859. Rural landscape along Ohio and Erie Canal system between Akron and Cleveland.

Death Valley, CA-NV (1933/1994) 3,340,410. Large desert area. Includes the lowest point in the Western Hemisphere; also includes Scottys Castle.

Denali, AK (1917/1980) 4,740,912. Name changed from Mt. McKinley NP. Contains highest mountain in U.S.; wildlife.

Dry Tortugas, FL (1935/1992) 64,701. Formerly Ft. Jefferson National Monument.

Everglades, FL (1934) 1,508,355. Largest remaining subtropical wilderness in continental U.S.

Gates of the Arctic, AK (1978/1984) 7,523,898. Vast wilderness in north central region. Limited federal facilities.

Glacier, MT (1910) 1,013,572. Superb Rocky Mt. scenery, numerous glaciers and glacial lakes. Part of Waterton-Glacier Intl. Peace Park established by U.S. and Canada in 1932.

Glacier Bay, AK (1925/1986) 3,224,840. Great tidewater glaciers that move down mountainsides and break up into the sea; much wildlife.

Grand Canyon, AZ (1893/1919) 1,217,403. Most spectacular part of Colorado River's greatest canyon.

Grand Teton, WY (1929) 309,994. Most impressive part of the Teton Mts., winter feeding ground of largest American elk herd.

Great Basin, NV (1922/1986) 77,180. Includes Wheeler Pk., Lexington Arch, and Lehman Caves.

Great Smoky Mountains, NC-TN (1926/1934) 521,490. Largest Eastern mountain range, magnificent forests.

Guadalupe Mountains, TX (1966) 86,416. Extensive Permian limestone fossil reef; tremendous earth fault.

Haleakala, HI (1916/1960) 29,830. Dormant volcano on Maui with large colorful craters.

Hawaii Volcanoes, HI (1916/1961) 209,695. Contains Kilauea and Mauna Loa, active volcanoes.

Hot Springs, AR (1832/1921) 5,549. Bathhouses are furnished with thermal waters from the park's 47 hot springs; these waters are used for bathing and drinking.

Isle Royale, MI (1931) 571,790. Largest island in Lake Superior, noted for its wilderness area and wildlife.

Joshua Tree, CA (1936/1994) 1,018,123. Desert region includes Joshua trees, other plant and animal life.

Katmai, AK (1918/1980) 3,674,530. "Valley of Ten Thousand Smokes," scene of 1912 volcanic eruption.

Kenai Fjords, AK (1978/1980) 669,983. Abundant marine mammals, birdlife; the Harding Icefield, one of the 4 major icecaps in U.S.

Kings Canyon, CA (1890/1940) 461,901. Mountain wilderness, dominated by Kings River Canyons and High Sierra; contains giant sequoias.

Kobuk Valley, AK (1978/1980) 1,750,737. Contains geological and recreational sites. Limited federal facilities.

Lake Clark, AK (1978/1980) 2,619,733. Across Cook Inlet from Anchorage. A scenic wilderness rich in fish and wildlife. Limited federal facilities.

Lassen Volcanic, CA (1907/1916) 106,372. Contains Lassen Peak, recently active volcano, and other volcanic phenomena.

Mammoth Cave, KY (1926/1941) 52,830. 144 mi of surveyed underground passages, beautiful natural formations, river 300 ft below surface.

Mesa Verde, CO (1906) 52,122. Most notable and best preserved prehistoric cliff dwellings in the U.S.

Mount Rainier, WA (1899) 235,625. Greatest single-peak glacial system in the U.S.

North Cascades, WA (1968) 504,781. Spectacular mountainous region with many glaciers, lakes.

Olympic, WA (1909/1938) 922,651. Mountain wilderness containing finest remnant of Pacific Northwest rain forest, active glaciers, Pacific shoreline, rare elk.

Petrified Forest, AZ (1906/1962) 93,533. Extensive petrified wood and Indian artifacts. Contains part of Painted Desert.

Redwood, CA (1968) 112,613. 40 mi of Pacific coastline, groves of ancient redwoods and world's tallest trees.

Rocky Mountain, CO (1915) 265,769. On the Continental Divide; includes peaks over 14,000 ft.

Saguaro, AZ (1933/1994) 91,445. Part of the Sonoran Desert; includes the giant saguaro cacti, unique to the region.

Sequoia, CA (1890) 402,510. Groves of giant sequoias, highest mountain in conterminous U.S.—Mt. Whitney (14,494 ft). World's largest tree.

Shenandoah, VA (1926) 199,017. Portion of the Blue Ridge Mts.; overlooks Shenandoah Valley; Skyline Drive.

Theodore Roosevelt, ND (1947/1978) 70,447. Contains part of T.R.'s ranch and scenic badlands.

Virgin Islands, VI (1956) 14,689. Authorized to cover 75% of St. John Isl. and Hassel Isl.; lush growth, lovely beaches, Carib Indian petroglyphs, evidence of colonial Danes.

Voyageurs, MN (1971) 218,200. Abundant lakes, forests, wildlife, canoeing, boating.

Wind Cave, SD (1903) 28,295. Limestone caverns in Black Hills. Extensive wildlife includes a herd of bison.

Wrangell-St. Elias, AK (1978/1980) 8,323,147. Largest area in park system, most peaks over 16,000 ft, abundant wildlife; day's drive east of Anchorage. Limited federal facilities.

Yellowstone, ID-MT-WY (1872) 2,219,791. World's first national park. World's greatest geyser area has about 10,000 geysers and hot springs; spectacular falls and impressive canyons of the Yellowstone River; grizzly bear, moose, and bison.

Yosemite, CA (1890) 761,266. Yosemite Valley, the nation's highest waterfall, grove of sequoias, and mountains.

Zion, UT (1909/1919) 146,592. Unusual shapes and landscapes resulting from erosion and faulting; evidence of past volcanic activity; Zion Canyon has sheer walls ranging up to 2,640 ft.

NATIONAL HISTORICAL PARKS

Adams, MA (1946/1998) 24. Home of Pres. John Adams, John Quincy Adams, and celebrated descendants.

Appomattox Court House, VA (1930/1954) 1,772. Where Lee surrendered to Grant.

Boston, MA (1974) 43. Includes Faneuil Hall, Old North Church, Bunker Hill, Paul Revere House.

Cane River Creole (and heritage area), LA (1994) 207. Preserves the Creole culture as it developed along the Cane R.

Chaco Culture, NM (1907/1980) 33,974. Ruins of pueblos built by prehistoric Indians.

Chesapeake and Ohio Canal, MD-DC-WV (1938/1971) 19,551. 184-mi historic canal; DC to Cumberland, MD.

Colonial, VA (1930/1936) 9,461. Includes most of Jamestown Isl., site of first successful English colony; Yorktown, site of Cornwallis's surrender to George Washington; and the Colonial Parkway.

Cumberland Gap, KY-TN-VA (1940) 20,463. Mountain pass of the Wilderness Road, which carried the first great migration of pioneers into America's interior.

Dayton Aviation Heritage, OH (1992) 86. Commemorates the area's aviation heritage.

George Rogers Clark, Vincennes, IN (1966) 26. Commemorates American defeat of British in West during Revolution.

Harpers Ferry, MD-VA-WV (1944/1963) 2,502. At the confluence of the Shenandoah and Potomac rivers, the site of John Brown's 1859 raid on the Army arsenal.

Hopewell Culture, OH (1923/1992) 1,165. Formerly Mound City Group National Monument.

Independence, PA (1948) 45. Contains several properties associated with the American Revolution and the founding of the U.S. Includes Independence Hall.

Jean Laffite (and preserve), LA (1907/1978) 20,035. Includes Chalmette, site of 1815 Battle of New Orleans; French Quarter.

Kalaupapa, HI (1980) 10,779. Molokai's former leper colony site and other historic areas.

Kaloko-Honokohau, HI (1978) 1,161. Preserves the native culture of Hawaii. No federal facilities.

Keweenaw, MI (1992) 1,869. Site of first significant copper mine in U.S. Federal facilities are under development.

Klondike Gold Rush, AK-WA (1976) 13,191. Alaskan Trails in 1898 Gold Rush. Museum in Seattle.

Lowell, MA (1978) 141. Textile mills, canal, 19th-cent. structures; park shows planned city of Industrial Revolution.

Lyndon B. Johnson, TX (1969/1980) 1,570. President's birthplace, boyhood home, ranch.

Marsh-Billings-Rockefeller, VT (1992) 643. Boyhood home of conservationist George Perkins Marsh. No federal facilities.

Minute Man, MA (1959) 965. Where the Minute Men battled the British, Apr. 19, 1775. Also contains Hawthorne's home.

Morristown, NJ (1933) 1,706. Sites of important military encampments during the American Revolution; Washington's headquarters, 1777, 1779-80.

Natchez, MS (1988) 108. Mansions, townhouses, and villas related to history of Natchez.

New Bedford Whaling, MA (1996) 34. Preserves structures and relics associated with the city's 19th-cent. whaling industry.

New Orleans Jazz, LA (1994) 5. Preserves, educates, and interprets jazz as it has evolved in New Orleans.

Nez Perce, ID (1965) 2,134. Illustrates the history and culture of the Nez Perce Indian country (38 separate sites).

Pecos, NM (1965/1990) 6,667. Ruins of ancient Pueblo of Pecos, archaeological sites, and 2 associated Spanish colonial missions from the 17th and 18th centuries.

Pu'uhonua o Honaunau, HI (1955/1978) 182. Until 1819, a sanctuary for Hawaiians vanquished in battle and for those guilty of crimes or breaking taboos.

Rosie the Riveter WWII Home Front, CA (2000) 145. Built on site that was a shipyard employing thousands of women in WWII; commemorates women who worked in war-time industries.

Salt River Bay (and ecological preserve), St. Croix, VI (1992) 948. The only site known where, 500 years ago, members of a Columbus party landed on what is now territory of the U.S.

San Antonio Missions, TX (1978) 816. Four of finest Spanish missions in U.S., 18th-cent. irrigation system.

San Francisco Maritime, CA (1988) 50. Artifacts, photographs, and historic vessels related to the development of the Pacific Coast.

San Juan Island, WA (1966) 1,752. Commemorates peaceful relations between the U.S., Canada, and Great Britain since the 1872 boundary disputes.

Saratoga, NY (1938) 3,392. Scene of a major 1777 battle that became a turning point in the American Revolution.

Sitka, AK (1910/1972) 113. Scene of last major resistance of the Tlingit Indians to the Russians, 1804.

Tumacacori, AZ (1908/1990) 46. Historic Spanish mission building stands near site first visited by Father Kino in 1691.

Valley Forge, PA (1976) 3,462. Continental Army campsite in 1777-78 winter.

War in the Pacific, GU (1978) 2,037. Seven distinct units illustrating the Pacific theater of WWII. Limited federal facilities.

Women's Rights, NY (1980) 7. Seneca Falls site where Lucretia Mott, Elizabeth Cady Stanton began rights movement in 1848.

NATIONAL BATTLEFIELDS

Antietam, MD (1890/1978) 3,376. Battle here ended first Confederate invasion of North, Sept. 17, 1862.

Big Hole, MT (1910/1963) 656. Site of major battle with Nez Perce Indians.

Cowpens, SC (1929/1972) 842. American Revolution battlefield.

Fort Donelson, TN-KY (1928/1985) 552. Site of first major Union victory.

Fort Necessity, PA (1931/1961) 903. Site of first battle of French and Indian War.

Monocacy, MD (1934/1976) 1,647. Civil War battle in defense of Washington, DC, fought here, July 9, 1864.

Moores Creek, NC (1926/1980) 88. 1776 battle between Patriots and Loyalists commemorated here.

Petersburg, VA (1926/1962) 2,659. Scene of 10-month Union campaigns, 1864-65.

Stones River, TN (1927/1960) 714. Scene of battle that began federal offensive to trisect the Confederacy.

Tupelo, MS (1929/1961) 1. Site of crucial battle over Sherman's supply line, 1865.

Wilson's Creek, MO (1960/1970) 1,750. Scene of Civil War battle for control of Missouri.

NATIONAL BATTLEFIELD PARKS

Kennesaw Mountain, GA (1917/1935) 2,884. Site of two major battles of Atlanta campaign in Civil War.

Manassas, VA (1940) 5,067. Scene of two battles in Civil War, 1861 and 1862.

Richmond, VA (1936) 1,718. Site of battles defending Confederate capital.

NATIONAL BATTLEFIELD SITE

Brices Cross Roads, MS (1929) 1. Civil War battlefield.

NATIONAL MILITARY PARKS

Chickamauga and Chattanooga, GA-TN (1890) 8,228. Site of major Confederate victory, 1863.

Fredericksburg and Spotsylvania County, VA (1927/1933) 8,362. Sites of several major Civil War battles and campaigns.

Gettysburg, PA (1895/1933) 5,991. Site of decisive Confederate defeat in North and of Gettysburg Address.

Guilford Courthouse, NC (1917/1933) 221. American Revolution battle site.

Horseshoe Bend, AL (1956) 2,040. On Tallapoosa River, where Gen. Andrew Jackson's forces broke the power of the Upper Creek Indian Confederacy.

Kings Mountain, SC (1931/1933) 3,945. Site of American Revolution battle.

Pea Ridge, AR (1956) 4,300. Scene of Civil War battle.

Shiloh, TN (1894/1933) 4,015. Major Civil War battlesite; includes some well-preserved Indian burial mounds.

Vicksburg, MS (1899/1933) 1,738. Union victory gave North control of the Mississippi and split the Confederate forces.

NATIONAL MEMORIALS

Arkansas Post, AR (1960) 747. First permanent French settlement in the lower Mississippi River valley.

Arlington House, the Robert E. Lee Memorial, VA (1925/1972) 28. Lee's home overlooking the Potomac.

Chamizal, El Paso, TX (1966/1974) 55. Commemorates 1963 settlement of 99-year border dispute with Mexico.

Coronado, AZ (1941/1952) 4,750. Commemorates first European exploration of the Southwest.

DeSoto, FL (1948) 27. Commemorates 16th-cent. Spanish explorations.

Federal Hall, NY (1939/1955) 0.45. First seat of U.S. government under the Constitution.

Fort Caroline, FL (1950) 138. On St. Johns River, overlooks site of a French Huguenot colony.

Fort Clatsop, OR (1958) 125. Lewis and Clark encampment, 1805-6.

Franklin Delano Roosevelt, DC (1982) 8. Statues of Pres. Roosevelt and Eleanor Roosevelt; waterfalls and gardens.

General Grant, NY (1958) 0.76. Tomb of Grant and wife.

Hamilton Grange, NY (1962) 1. Home of Alexander Hamilton.

Jefferson National Expansion Memorial, St. Louis, MO (1935) 193. Commemorates westward expansion.

Johnstown Flood, PA (1964) 164. Commemorates tragic flood of 1889.

Korean War Veterans, DC (1986) 2. Dedicated in 1995; honors those who served in the Korean War.

Lincoln Boyhood, IN (1962) 200. Lincoln grew up here.

Lincoln Memorial, DC (1911/1933) 107. Marble statue of the 16th U.S. president.

Lyndon B. Johnson Memorial Grove on the Potomac, DC (1973) 17. Overlooks the Potomac R.; vista of the Capitol.

Mount Rushmore, SD (1925) 1,278. World-famous sculpture of 4 presidents.

Oklahoma City, OK (1997) 6. Commemorates site of April 19, 1995, bombing which killed 168.

Perry's Victory and International Peace Memorial, Put-in-Bay, OH (1936/1972) 25. The world's most massive Doric column, constructed 1912-15, promotes pursuit of peace through arbitration and disarmament.

Roger Williams, Providence, RI (1965) 5. Memorial to founder of Rhode Island.

Thaddeus Kosciuszko, PA (1972) 0.02. Memorial to Polish hero of American Revolution.

Theodore Roosevelt Island, DC (1932/1933) 89. Statue of Roosevelt in wooded island sanctuary.

Thomas Jefferson Memorial, DC (1934) 18. Statue of Jefferson in an inscribed circular, colonnaded structure.

USS *Arizona*, HI (1980) 11. Memorializes American losses at Pearl Harbor.

Vietnam Veterans, DC (1980) 2. Black granite wall inscribed with names of those missing or killed in action in Vietnam War.

Washington Monument, DC (1848/1933) 106. Obelisk honoring the first U.S. president.

Wright Brothers, NC (1927/1953) 428. Site of first powered flight.

NATIONAL HISTORIC SITES

Abraham Lincoln Birthplace, Hodgenville, KY (1916/1959) 117. Early 17th-cent. cabin.

Allegheny Portage Railroad, PA (1964) 1,249. Linked the Pennsylvania Canal system and the West.

Andersonville, Andersonville, GA (1970) 495. Noted Civil War prisoner-of-war camp.

Andrew Johnson, Greeneville, TN (1935/1963) 17. Two homes and the tailor shop of the 17th U.S. president.

Bent's Old Fort, CO (1960) 799. Reconstruction of S Plains outpost.

Boston African-American, MA (1980) 0.59. Pre-Civil War black history structures.

Brown v. Board of Education, KS (1992) 2. Commemorates the landmark 1954 U.S. Supreme Court decision.

Carl Sandburg Home, Flat Rock, NC (1968) 264. Poet's home.

Charles Pinckney, SC (1988) 28. Statesman's farm.

Christiansted, St. Croix, VI (1952/1961) 27. Commemorates Danish colony.

Clara Barton, MD (1974) 9. Home of founder of American Red Cross.

Edgar Allan Poe, PA (1978/1980) 0.52. Writer's home.

Edison, West Orange, NJ (1955/1962) 21. Inventor's home and laboratory.

Eisenhower, Gettysburg, PA (1967) 690. Home of 34th president.

Eleanor Roosevelt, Hyde Park, NY (1977) 181. The former first lady's personal retreat.

Eugene O'Neill, Danville, CA (1976) 13. Playwright's home.

First Ladies, Canton, OH (2000) 0.33. Library devoted to America's first ladies.

Ford's Theatre, DC (1866/1970) 0.29. Includes theater, now restored, where Lincoln was assassinated, house where he died, and Lincoln Museum.

Fort Bowie, AZ (1964) 999. Focal point of operations against Geronimo and the Apaches.

Fort Davis, TX (1961) 474. Frontier outpost in West Texas.

Fort Laramie, WY (1938/1960) 833. Military post on Oregon Trail.

Fort Larned, KS (1964/1966) 718. Military post on Santa Fe Trail.

Fort Point, San Francisco, CA (1970) 29. West Coast fortification.

Fort Raleigh, NC (1941) 513. First attempted English settlement in North America.

Fort Scott, KS (1965/1978) 17. Commemorates U.S. frontier of 1840s and '50s.

Fort Smith, AR-OK (1961) 75. Active post during 1817-90.

Fort Union Trading Post, MT-ND (1966) 444. Principal fur-trading post on upper Missouri, 1829-67.

Fort Vancouver, WA (1948/1961) 209. Headquarters for Hudson's Bay Company in 1825. Early political seat.

Frederick Douglass, DC (1962/1988) 9. Home of famous black abolitionist, writer, and orator.

Frederick Law Olmsted, MA (1979) 7. Home of famous city planner.

Friendship Hill, PA (1978) 675. Home of Albert Gallatin, Jefferson's and Madison's secretary of treasury.

Golden Spike, UT (1957) 2,735. Commemorates completion of first transcontinental railroad in 1869.

Grant-Kohrs Ranch, MT (1972) 1,618. Ranch house and part of 19th-cent. ranch.

Hampton, MD (1948) 62. 18th-cent. Georgian mansion.

Harry S. Truman, MO (1983) 7. Home of Pres. Truman after 1919.

Herbert Hoover, West Branch, IA (1965) 187. Birthplace and boyhood home of 31st president.

Home of Franklin D. Roosevelt, Hyde Park, NY (1944) 800. FDR's birthplace, home, and "summer White House."

Hopewell Furnace, PA (1938/1985) 848. 19th-cent. iron-making village.

Hubbell Trading Post, AZ (1965) 160. Still active today.

James A. Garfield, Mentor, OH (1980) 8. Home of 20th president.

Jimmy Carter, GA (1987) 71. Birthplace and home of 39th president.

John Fitzgerald Kennedy, Brookline, MA (1967) 0.09. Birthplace and childhood home of 35th president.

John Muir, Martinez, CA (1964) 345. Home of early conservationist and writer.

Knife River Indian Villages, ND (1974) 1,758. Remnants of villages last occupied by Hidatsa and Mandan Indians.

Lincoln Home, Springfield, IL (1971) 12. Lincoln's residence at the time he was elected 16th president, 1860.

Little Rock Central High School, AR (1998) 28. Commemorates 1957 desegregation during which federal troops had to be called in to protect 9 black students.

Longfellow, Cambridge, MA (1972) 2. Poet's home, 1837-82; Washington's headquarters during Boston siege, 1775-76.

Maggie L. Walker, VA (1978) 1. Richmond home of black leader and bank president, daughter of an ex-slave.

Manzanar, Lone Pine, CA (1992) 814. Commemorates Manzanar War Relocation Ctr., a Japanese-American internment camp during WWII. No federal facilities.

Martin Luther King Jr., Atlanta, GA (1980) 39. Birthplace, grave, church of the civil rights leader. Limited federal facilities.

Martin Van Buren, NY (1974) 40. Lindenwald, home of 8th president, near Kinderhook.

Mary McLeod Bethune Council House, DC (1982/1991) 0.07. Commemorates Bethune's leadership in the black women's movement.

Minuteman Missile, SD (1999) 15. Missile launch facilities dating back to the Cold War era.

Nicodemus, KS (1996) 161. Only remaining western town established by African-Americans during Reconstruction.

Ninety Six, SC (1976) 989. Colonial trading village.

Palo Alto Battlefield, TX (1978) 3,357. Scene of first battle of the Mexican War.

Pennsylvania Avenue, DC (1965) Acreage undetermined. Also includes area next to the road between Capitol and White House, encompassing Ford's Theatre and other structures.

Puukohola Heiau, HI (1972) 86. Ruins of temple built by King Kamehameha.

Sagamore Hill, Oyster Bay, NY (1962) 83. Home of Pres. Theodore Roosevelt from 1885 until his death in 1919.

Saint-Gaudens, Cornish, NH (1964) 148. Home, studio, and gardens of American sculptor Augustus Saint-Gaudens.

Saint Paul's Church, NY, NY (1943) 6. Site associated with John Peter Zenger's "freedom of press" trial.

Salem Maritime, MA (1938) 9. Only port never seized from the patriots by the British. Major fishing and whaling port.

Sand Creek Massacre, Sand Creek, CO (2000) 12,583. Site where over 100 Cheyenne and Arapaho Indians were killed by U.S. soldiers in 1864.

San Juan, PR (1949) 75. 16th-cent. Span. fortifications.

Saugus Iron Works, MA (1974) 9. Reconstructed 17th-cent. colonial ironworks.

Springfield Armory, MA (1974) 55. Small-arms manufacturing center for nearly 200 years.

Steamtown, PA (1986) 62. Railyard, roadhouse, repair shops of former Delaware, Lackawanna & Western Railroad.

Theodore Roosevelt Birthplace, New York, NY (1962) 0.11. Reconstructed brownstone.

Theodore Roosevelt Inaugural, Buffalo, NY (1966) 1. Wilcox House where he took oath of office, 1901.

Thomas Stone, MD (1978) 328. Home of signer of Declaration of Independence, built in 1771.

Tuskegee Airmen, AL (1998) 90. Airfield where pilots of all-black air corps unit of WWII received flight training.

Tuskegee Institute, AL (1974) 58. College founded by Booker T. Washington in 1881 for blacks.

Ulysses S. Grant, St. Louis Co., MO (1989) 10. Home of Grant during pre-Civil War years.

Vanderbilt Mansion, Hyde Park, NY (1940) 212. Mansion of 19th-cent. financier.

Washita Battlefield, OK (1996) 315. Scene of Nov. 27, 1868, battle between Plains tribes and the U.S. army.

Weir Farm, Wilton, CT (1990) 74. Home and studio of American impressionist painter J. Alden Weir.

Whitman Mission, WA (1936/1963) 98. Site where Dr. and Mrs. Marcus Whitman ministered to the Indians until slain by them in 1847.

William Howard Taft, Cincinnati, OH (1969) 3. Birthplace and early home of the 27th president.

NATIONAL MONUMENTS

Name	State	Year[1]	Acreage
Agate Fossil Beds	NE	1965	3,055
Alibates Flint Quarries	TX	1965	1,371
Aniakchak[2]	AK	1978	137,176
Aztec Ruins	NM	1923	318
Bandelier	NM	1916	33,677
Booker T. Washington	VA	1956	224
Buck Island Reef	VI	1961	19,015
Cabrillo	CA	1913	160
Canyon de Chelly	AZ	1931	83,840
Cape Krusenstern[3]	AK	1978	649,182
Capulin Volcano	NM	1916	793
Casa Grande Ruins	AZ	1889	473
Castillo de San Marcos	FL	1924	20
Castle Clinton	NY	1946	1
Cedar Breaks	UT	1933	6,155
Chiricahua	AZ	1924	11,985
Colorado	CO	1911	20,534
Congaree Swamp	SC	1976	21,888
Craters of the Moon	ID	1924	714,727

Name	State	Year[1]	Acreage
Devils Postpile	CA	1911	798
Devils Tower	WY	1906	1,347
Dinosaur	CO-UT	1915	210,278
Effigy Mounds	IA	1949	2,526
El Malpais	NM	1987	114,277
El Morro	NM	1906	1,279
Florissant Fossil Beds	CO	1969	5,998
Fort Frederica	GA	1936	241
Fort Matanzas	FL	1924	300
Fort McHenry National Monument and Historic Shrine	MD	1925	43
Fort Pulaski	GA	1924	5,623
Fort Stanwix	NY	1935	16
Fort Sumter	SC	1948	200
Fort Union	NM	1954	721
Fossil Butte	WY	1972	8,198
George Washington Birthplace	VA	1930	550
George Washington Carver	MO	1943	210
Gila Cliff Dwellings	NM	1907	533
Governors Island	NY	2001	20
Grand Portage	MN	1951	710
Great Sand Dunes National Monument and Preserve	CO	2000	83,958
Hagerman Fossil Beds[3]	ID	1988	4,351
Hohokam Pima[4]	AZ	1972	1,690
Homestead National Monument of America	NE	1936	195
Hovenweep	CO-UT	1923	785
Jewel Cave	SD	1908	1,274
John Day Fossil Beds	OR	1974	14,057
Lava Beds	CA	1925	46,560
Little Big Horn Battlefield	MT	1879	765
Minidoka Internment[2]	ID	2001	73
Montezuma Castle	AZ	1906	858
Muir Woods	CA	1908	554
Natural Bridges	UT	1908	7,636
Navajo	AZ	1909	360
Ocmulgee	GA	1934	702
Oregon Caves	OR	1909	488
Organ Pipe Cactus	AZ	1937	330,689
Petroglyph	NM	1990	7,232
Pinnacles	CA	1908	16,265
Pipe Spring	AZ	1923	40
Pipestone	MN	1937	282
Poverty Point[2]	LA	1988	911
Rainbow Bridge[3]	UT	1910	160
Russell Cave	AL	1961	310
Salinas Pueblo Missions	NM	1909	1,071
Scotts Bluff	NE	1919	3,003
Statue of Liberty	NJ-NY	1924	58
Sunset Crater Volcano	AZ	1930	3,040
Timpanogos Cave	UT	1922	250
Tonto	AZ	1907	1,120
Tuzigoot	AZ	1939	801
Virgin Islands Coral Reef	VI	2001	13,893
Walnut Canyon	AZ	1915	3,579
White Sands	NM	1933	143,733
Wupatki	AZ	1924	35,422
Yucca House[4]	CO	1919	34

NATIONAL PRESERVES

Aniakchak	AK	1978	465,603
Bering Land Bridge	AK	1978	2,697,406
Big Cypress	FL	1974	720,565
Big Thicket	TX	1974	97,168
Denali	AK	1917	1,334,118
Gates of the Arctic	AK	1978	948,629
Glacier Bay	AK	1925	58,406
Katmai	AK	1918	418,699
Lake Clark	AK	1978	1,410,292
Little River Canyon[2]	AL	1992	13,633
Mojave	CA	1994	1,497,665
Noatak	AK	1978	6,569,904
Tallgrass Prairie	KS	1996	10,894
Timucuan Ecological & Historic Preserve[3]	FL	1988	46,289
Wrangell-St. Elias	AK	1978	4,852,753
Yukon-Charley Rivers[3]	AK	1978	2,526,512

NATIONAL SEASHORES

Name	State	Year[1]	Acreage
Assateague Island	MD-VA	1965	39,733
Canaveral	FL	1975	57,662
Cape Cod	MA	1961	43,604
Cape Hatteras	NC	1937	30,321
Cape Lookout	NC	1966	28,243
Cumberland Island	GA	1972	36,415
Fire Island	NY	1964	19,580
Gulf Islands	FL-MS	1971	137,458
Padre Island	TX	1962	130,434
Point Reyes	CA	1962	71,068

NATIONAL PARKWAYS

Blue Ridge	NC-VA	1933	91,966
George Washington Memorial	VA-MD-DC	1930	7,248
John D. Rockefeller Jr. Mem.	WY	1972	23,777
Natchez Trace	MS-AL-TN	1938	51,980

NATIONAL LAKESHORES

Apostle Islands	WI	1970	69,372
Indiana Dunes	IN	1966	15,062
Pictured Rocks	MI	1966	73,228
Sleeping Bear Dunes	MI	1970	71,176

NATIONAL RESERVES

City of Rocks[3]	ID	1988	14,107
Ebey's Landing[3]	WA	1978	19,019

NATIONAL RIVERS

Big South Fork Natl. R and Recreation Area	KY-TN	1976	125,310
Buffalo	AR	1972	94,294
Mississippi Natl. R and Recreation Area	MN	1988	53,775
New River Gorge	WV	1978	70,075
Niobrara	NE-SD	1991	5,962
Ozark	MO	1964	80,800

NATIONAL WILD AND SCENIC RIVERS

Alagnak	AK	1980	30,665
Bluestone[2]	WV	1978	4,310
Delaware	NY-NJ-PA	1978	1,973
Great Egg Harbor	NJ	1992	43,311
Missouri	NE-SD	1991	45,350
Obed	TN	1976	5,174
Rio Grande[2]	TX	1978	9,600
Saint Croix	MN-WI	1968	92,767
Upper Delaware	NY-PA	1978	75,005

NATIONAL RECREATION AREAS

Amistad	TX	1965	58,500
Bighorn Canyon	MT-WY	1966	120,296
Boston Harbor Islands	MA	1996	1,482
Chattahoochee R.	GA	1978	9,111
Chickasaw	OK	1902	9,889
Curecanti	CO	1965	41,972
Delaware Water Gap	NJ-PA	1965	66,742
Gateway	NJ-NY	1972	26,607
Gauley R.[3]	WV	1988	11,497
Glen Canyon	AZ-UT	1958	1,254,306
Golden Gate	CA	1972	74,816
Lake Chelan	WA	1968	61,958
Lake Mead	AZ-NV	1936	1,495,666
Lake Meredith	TX	1965	44,978
Lake Roosevelt[5]	WA	1946	100,390
Ross Lake	WA	1968	117,575
Santa Monica Mts.[3]	CA	1978	153,632
Whiskeytown-Shasta-Trinity	CA	1965	42,503

NATIONAL SCENIC TRAIL

Appalachian	ME to GA	1968	222,651
Natchez Trace	MS-TN	1983	10,995
Potomac Heritage	MD-DC-VA-PA	1983	NA

PARKS (no other classification)

Catoctin Mountain	MD	1954	5,810
Constitution Gardens	DC	1974	52
Fort Washington	MD	1930	341
Greenbelt	MD	1950	1,176
National Capital	DC	1933	6,638
National Mall	DC	1933	146
Piscataway	MD	1961	4,627
Prince William Forest	VA	1948	18,729
Rock Creek	DC	1890	1,755
White House	DC	1933	18
Wolf Trap Farm Park for the Performing Arts	VA	1966	130

INTERNATIONAL HISTORIC SITE

Saint Croix Island[3]	ME	1949	45

NA=Not available. (1) Year first designated. (2) No federal facilities. (3) Limited federal facilities. (4) Not open to the public. (5) Formerly Coulee Dam National Recreation Area.

IT'S A FACT: Rainbow Bridge in Rainbow Bridge National Monument is the largest-known natural arch in the world. It is 290 feet high and spans 275 feet over the waters of Bridge Creek.

20 Most-Visited Sites in the National Park System, 2001

Source: National Park Service, Dept. of the Interior

Attendance at all areas administered by the National Park Service in 2001 totaled 279,873,926 recreation visits.

Site (location)	Recreation visits
Blue Ridge Parkway	19,969,587
Golden Gate NRA	13,457,900
Great Smoky Mountains NP	9,197,697
Lake Mead NRA	8,465,547
Gateway NRA	8,285,059
George Washington Memorial Pkwy	7,664,091
Natchez Trace Parkway	5,552,351
Delaware Water Gap NRA	4,867,273
Gulf Islands NS	4,549,900
Cape Cod NS	4,391,478
Statue of Liberty NM	4,317,998
Chesapeake & Ohio Canal NHP	4,174,048
Grand Canyon NP	4,104,809
Lincoln Memorial	3,968,357
Vietnam Veterans Memorial	3,704,008
Castle Clinton NM	3,601,635
Jefferson National Expansion Memorial	3,532,524
Olympic NP	3,416,069
Yosemite NP	3,368,731
Colonial NHP	3,282,461

U.S. States Ranked by American Indian and Alaska Native Population, 2000

Source: Bureau of the Census, U.S. Dept. of Commerce

Rank	State	One race only[1]	More than one race[2]
1	California	333,346	294,216
2	Oklahoma	273,230	118,719
3	Arizona	255,879	36,673
4	New Mexico	173,483	17,992
5	Texas	118,362	97,237
6	North Carolina	99,551	32,185
7	Alaska	98,043	21,198
8	Washington	93,301	65,639
9	New York	82,461	89,120
10	South Dakota	62,283	5,998
11	Michigan	58,479	65,933
12	Montana	56,068	10,252
13	Minnesota	54,967	26,107
14	Florida	53,541	64,339
15	Wisconsin	47,228	22,158
16	Oregon	45,211	40,456
17	Colorado	44,241	35,448
18	North Dakota	31,329	3,899
19	Illinois	31,006	42,155
20	Utah	29,684	10,761
21	Nevada	26,420	15,802
22	Louisiana	25,477	17,401
23	Missouri	25,076	35,023
24	Kansas	24,936	22,247
25	Ohio	24,486	51,589
26	Alabama	22,430	22,019
27	Georgia	21,737	31,460
28	Virginia	21,172	31,692
29	New Jersey	19,492	29,612
30	Pennsylvania	18,348	34,302
31	Arkansas	17,808	19,194
32	Idaho	17,645	9,592
33	Indiana	15,815	23,448
34	Maryland	15,423	24,014
35	Tennessee	15,152	24, 036
36	Massachusetts	15,015	23,035
37	Nebraska	14,896	7,308
38	South Carolina	13,718	13,738
39	Mississippi	11,652	7,903
40	Wyoming	11,133	0,870
41	Connecticut	9,639	14,849
42	Iowa	8,989	9,257
43	Kentucky	8,616	15,936
44	Maine	7,098	6,058
45	Rhode Island	5,121	5,604
46	West Virginia	3,606	7,038
47	Hawaii	3,535	21,347
48	New Hampshire	2,964	4,921
49	Delaware	2,731	3,338
50	Vermont	2,420	3,976
51	Washington, DC	1,713	3,062
	UNITED STATES	**2,475,956**	**1,643,345**

(1) Respondents classified themselves only under the category "American Indian and Alaska Native" on Census 2000 questionnaires. (2) Respondents classified themselves as "American Indian and Alaska Native" in combination with one or more other races.

Largest American Indian Tribes

Source: Bureau of the Census, U.S. Dept. of Commerce, as of 1990 census

Tribe	Number	Percent
ALL AMERICAN INDIANS	**1,937,391**	**100.0**
Cherokee	369,035	19.0
Navajo	225,298	11.6
Sioux[1]	107,321	5.5
Chippewa	105,988	5.5
Choctaw	86,231	4.5
Pueblo	55,330	2.9
Apache	53,330	2.8
Iroquois[2]	52,557	2.7
Lumbee	50,888	2.6
Creek	45,872	2.4
Blackfoot	37,992	2.0
Canadian and Latin American	27,179	1.4
Chickasaw	21,522	1.1
Tohono O'Odham	16,876	0.9
Potawatomi	16,719	0.9
Seminole	15,564	0.8
Pima	15,074	0.8
Tlingit	14,417	0.7
Alaskan Athabascans	14,198	0.7
Cheyenne	11,809	0.6
Comanche	11,437	0.6
Paiute	11,369	0.6
Osage	10,430	0.5
Puget Sound Salish	10,384	0.5
Yaqui	9,838	0.5

(1) Any entry from NC with the spelling "Siouan" in the 1990 census was miscoded to count as Sioux. (2) Reporting and/or processing problems in the 1990 census have affected accuracy of the data for this tribe.

WORLD ALMANAC QUICK QUIZ

At 472 million cubic feet, what is the largest building in the U.S. (and the world) by volume?

(a) The Pentagon, Arlington, VA (b) Boeing Manufacturing Plant, Everett, WA
(c) Empire State Building, NYC (d) Sears Tower, Chicago

For the answer look in this chapter, or see page 1008.

BUILDINGS, BRIDGES, AND TUNNELS

50 Tallest Buildings in the World

Source: Council on Tall Buildings and Urban Habitat, Lehigh Univ., www.lehigh.edu/%7Einctbuh/inctbuh.html

Structures under construction are denoted by asterisk *. Year is date of completion or projected completion.

Name, Year, City, Country	Ht. (ft.)	Stories
Petronas Tower I, 1998, Kuala Lumpur, Malaysia	1,483	88
Petronas Tower II, 1998, Kuala Lumpur, Malaysia	1,483	88
Sears Tower, 1974, Chicago, IL, U.S.	1,450	110
Jin Mao Bldg., 1998, Shanghai, China	1,381	88
*Two International Finance Centre, 2003, Hong Kong, China	1,352	88
CITIC Plaza, 1997, Guangzhou, China	1,283	80
Shun Hing Square, 1996, Shenzhen, China	1,260	69
Empire State Building, 1931, New York, U.S.	1,250	102
Central Plaza, 1992, Hong Kong, China	1,227	78
Bank of China, 1989, Hong Kong, China	1,209	70
Emirates Towers One, 2000, Dubai, U.A.E.	1,165	55
The Centre, 1998, Hong Kong, China	1,148	79
Tuntex & Chein-Tai Tower, 1998, Kaohsiung, Taiwan	1,140	85
Aon Center, 1973, Chicago, IL, U.S.	1,136	83
John Hancock Center, 1969, Chicago, IL, U.S.	1,127	100
Burj al Arab Hotel, 1999, Dubai, U.A.E.	1,053	60
Chrysler Bldg., 1930, New York, U.S.	1,046	77
Bank of America Plaza, 1992, Atlanta, GA, U.S.	1,023	55
Library Tower, 1990, Los Angeles, CA, U.S.	1,018	73
Telekom Malaysia Headquarters, 1999, Kuala Lumpur, Malaysia	1,017	55
Emirates Towers Two, 2000, Dubai, U.A.E.	1,014	54
AT&T Corporate Center, 1989, Chicago, IL, U.S.	1,007	60
JP Morgan Chase Tower, 1982, Houston, TX, U.S.	1,002	75
Baiyoke Tower II, 1998, Bangkok, Thailand	997	85
Two Prudential Plaza, 1990, Chicago, IL, U.S.	995	64
Ryugyong Hotel, 1995, Pyongyang, North Korea	984	105
Commerzbank Tower, 1997, Frankfurt, Germany	981	63
First Canadian Place, 1975, Toronto, Canada	978	72
Kingdom Centre, 2001, Riyadh, Saudi Arabia	972	72
Wells Fargo Plaza, 1983, Houston, TX, U.S.	972	71
Landmark Tower, 1993, Yokohama, Japan	971	70
Bank of America Tower, 1985, Seattle, WA, U.S.	967	76
311 S. Wacker Drive, 1990, Chicago, IL, U.S.	961	65
SEG Plaza, 2000, Shenzhen, China	957	72
American International Bldg., 1932, New York, U.S.	952	67
Cheung Kong Centre, 1999, Hong Kong, China	951	70
Key Tower, 1991, Cleveland, OH, U.S.	947	57
One Liberty Place, 1987, Philadelphia, PA, U.S.	945	61
Sunjoy Tomorrow Square, 1999, Shanghai, China	934	59
The Trump Bldg., 1930, New York, U.S.	927	71
Plaza 66/Nanjing Xi Lu, 2000, Shanghai, China	923	62
Bank of America Plaza, 1985, Dallas, TX, U.S.	921	72
Overseas Union Bank Centre, 1986, Singapore	919	66
United Overseas Bank Plaza One, 1992, Singapore	919	66
Republic Plaza, 1995, Singapore	919	66
Citigroup Center, 1977, New York, U.S.	915	59
Scotia Plaza, 1989, Toronto, Canada	902	68
Williams Tower, 1983, Houston, TX, U.S.	901	64
Renaissance Tower, 1974, Dallas, TX, U.S.	886	56
Trump World Tower, 2001, New York, U.S.	881	72

World Trade Center One and Two, which collapsed in the terrorist attack of Sept. 11, 2001, were each 110 stories, with heights of 1,368 and 1,362 feet, respectively. After Chicago's Sears Tower they were the tallest U.S. buildings, and ranked 5th and 6th tallest in the world.

World's 10 Tallest Free-Standing Towers

Name	City	Country	Ht. (ft.)	Year
CN Tower	Toronto	Canada	1,815	1976
Ostankino Tower	Moscow	Russia	1,772	1967
*Xi'an Broadcasting, Telephone and Television Tower	Xi'an	China	1,542	NA
Oriental Pearl Television Tower	Shanghai	China	1,535	1995
Tehran Telecommunications Tower	Tehran	Iran	1,411	2001
Manara Kuala Lumpur	Kuala Lumpur	Malaysia	1,379	1996
Beijing Radio & T.V. Tower	Beijing	China	1,369	1992
Tianjin Radio & T.V. Tower	Tianjin	China	1,362	1991
T.V. Tower	Kiev	Ukraine	1,263	1974
Tashkent Tower	Tashkent	Uzbekistan	1,230	1985

*Under construction. NA = Not available.

Tall Buildings in Selected North American Cities

Source: Marshall Gerometta and Rick Bronson, Skyscrapers.com, www.skyscrapers.com; Council on Tall Buildings and Urban Habitat, Lehigh Univ., www.lehigh.edu/%7Einctbuh/inctbuh.html

Lists include freestanding towers and other structures that do not have stories and are not technically considered "buildings." Also included are some structures still under construction (denoted by asterisk *).Year in parentheses is date of completion or projected completion. Height is generally measured from sidewalk to roof, including penthouse and tower if enclosed as integral part of structure; stories generally counted from street level. NA = not available or not applicable.

Atlanta, GA

Building	Ht. (ft.)	Stories
Bank of America Plaza, 600 Peachtree (1992)	1,023	55
SunTrust Bank Tower, 303 Peachtree (1992)	871	60
One Atlantic Center, 1201 Peachtree W (1987)	820	50
191 Peachtree Tower (1991)	770	50
Westin Peachtree Plaza, 210 Peachtree NW (1973)	723	73
Georgia Pacific Tower, 133 Peachtree NE (1981)	697	51
Promenade II/A.T.& T. (1989)	691	40
Bellsouth, 675 Peachtree NE (1980)	677	47
GLG Grand/Four Seasons Hotel, 75 14th St. (1992)	609	53
Wachovia Bank of Georgia Tower, 2 Peachtree NW (1967)	556	44
Marriott Marquis, 265 Peachtree NE (1985)	554	52
Park Avenue Condominiums, Park Avenue NE (2000)	486	42
Centennial Tower, 101 Marietta (1976)	459	36
Equitable Bldg., 100 Peachtree (1967)	453	34
One Park Tower, 34 Peachtree (1961)	439	32
Bell South Enterprises, 1100 Peachtree (1990)	428	28
Atlanta Plaza I, 950 Paces Ferry Rd. E. (1986)	425	32
Park Place, 2660 Peachtree NW (1986)	420	40
2828 Peachtree Luxury Condominiums (2002)	420	33
Oakwood Apts. (1989)	410	38
Peachtree Summit No. 1, 401 Peachtree NE (1975)	406	31
Coca-Cola Headquarters Bldg., 310 North Ave. (1979)	403	29
Tower Place, 3361 Piedmont Rd. (1974)	401	29

Baltimore, MD

Building	Ht. (ft.)	Stories
Legg Mason Building (1973)	529	40
Bank of America Building (1924)	509	37
William Donald Schaefer Tower, 6 St. Paul Pl. (1992)	493	29
Commerce Place (1992)	454	31
Marriott Baltimore Inner Harbor East (2001)	430	32
World Trade Center (1977)	405	32

Bellevue, WA

Building	Ht. (ft.)	Stories
*One Lincoln Tower, 604 Bellevue Way (2003)	450	42
*Lincoln Square, 770 Bellevue Way (2003)	412	28

Birmingham, AL

Building	Ht. (ft.)	Stories
Southtrust Tower (1986)	454	34
AmSouth/Harbert Plaza (1989)	437	32

Boston, MA

Building	Ht. (ft.)	Stories
John Hancock Tower, 200 Clarendon St. (1976)	790	60
Prudential Tower, 800 Boylston St. (1964)	750	52
Federal Reserve Bldg., 600 Atlantic Ave. (1978)	604	32
Boston Company Bldg., 1 Boston Place (1970)	601	41
One International Place, 100 Oliver St. (1987)	600	46
First National Bank of Boston, 100 Federal St. (1971)	591	37
One Financial Center (1984)	590	46
111 Huntingdon Ave, (2001)	564	36
Two International Place (1993)	538	35
One Post Office Square (1981)	525	40
1 Federal St. (1975)	520	38
Exchange Place, 53 State St. (1984)	510	39
Sixty State St. (1977)	509	38
1 Beacon St. (1972)	507	36
*1 Lincoln Place (2003)	503	36
28 State Street(1969)	500	40
Mariott's Custom House (1915)	496	32
John Hancock Bldg. (1949)	495	26
*33 Arch St. (2003)	489	31
State St. Bank (1966)	477	33
Millennium Place 1 (2001)	475	38
125 High St. (1990)	452	30
100 Summer St. (1975)	450	33
Millennium Place 2 (2001)	445	36

Building	Ht. (ft.)	Stories
McCormack Bldg.	401	22
Harbor Towers I, 85 E. India (1971)	400	40
Keystone Building (1971)	400	32

Calgary, Alberta

Building	Ht. (ft.)	Stories
Petro Canada Centre (1984)	705	53
Bankers Hall East Tower (1989)	645	50
Bankers Hall West Tower (2000)	645	50
Calgary Tower (1967)	626	NA
TransCanada Tower (2000)	608	37
Canterra Tower (1988)	580	46
First Canadian Centre (1983)	530	43
Canada Trust, Calgary Eatons Centre (1991)	530	40
Scotia Square (1975)	525	42
Western Canadian Place–N. Tower (1983)	507	41
Nexen Bldg., 801 7th Ave. SW (1982)	500	37
Petro-Canada Tower, E. Tower (1983)	469	33
Two Bow Valley Square (1974)	468	39
Dome Tower (1976)	463	34
5th & 5th Bldg. (1980)	460	35
Shell Centre (1977)	460	34
T.D. Square (1976)	449	33
Four Bow Valley Square (1982)	441	37
Fifth Avenue Place (1981)	435	34
Esso Plaza II (1981)	435	34
Cascade 300	432	31
Western Canadian Place–S. Tower (1983)	420	32
Family Life Bldg.	410	33
Pan Canadian Bldg., 150 9th Ave. SW (1982)	410	28
Serval Tower (1976)	408	33
Alberta Stock Exchange (1979)	407	33

Charlotte, NC

Building	Ht. (ft.)	Stories
Bank of America Corporate Center (1992)	871	60
Hearst Tower, 214 N. Tyron (2002)	659	50
One Wachovia Center, 301 S. College St. (1988)	588	42
Bank of America, 101 S. Tryon (1974)	503	40
Interstate Tower, 121 W. Trade St. (1990)	462	32
IJL Financial Center, 201 N. Tyron St. (1997)	447	30
Three Wachovia Center (2000)	440	29
Two Wachovia Plaza, 301 S. Tyron St. (1971)	433	32
Wachovia Center, 400 S. Tryon (1974)	420	32

Chicago, IL

Building	Ht. (ft.)	Stories
Sears Tower, 233 S. Wacker Dr. (1974)	1,450	110
Aon Center, 200 E. Randolph (1973)	1,136	83
John Hancock Center, 875 N. Michigan Ave. (1969)	1,127	100
AT&T Corporate Center, 227 W. Monroe (1989)	1,007	60
Two Prudential Plaza, 180 N. Stetson Ave. (1990)	995	64
311 S. Wacker Drive (1990)	961	65
900 N. Michigan Ave. (1989)	871	66
Water Tower Place, 845 N. Michigan Ave.(1976)	859	74
Bank One Plaza (1969)	850	60
Park Tower, 800 N. Michigan Ave. (2000)	844	67
Chicago Title & Trust Center, 161 N. Clark St. (1991)	756	50
3 First National Plaza, 70 W. Madison (1981)	753	57
Olympia Centre, 737 N. Michigan Ave. (1986)	725	63
IBM Bldg., 330 N. Wabash Ave. (1973)	695	52
Paine Webber Bldg., 181 W. Madison (1990)	680	50
One Magnificent Mile, 980 N. Michigan Ave. (1983)	673	58
R.R. Donnelley Center, 77 W. Wacker Dr. (1992)	668	50
UBS Tower, 1 N. Wacker (2001)	652	50
*55 E. Erie (2003)	650	59
Daley Center, 55 W. Washington St. (1965)	648	31
Lake Point Tower, 505 N. Lake Shore Dr. (1968)	645	70
River East Center 1, 350 E. Illinois St. (2001)	644	58
*Grand Plaza 1 (2003)	641	57
Leo Burnett, 35 W. Wacker Dr. (1989)	635	50
NBC Tower, 445 N. Cityfront Plaza Dr. (1989)	627	34
*The Heritage at Millennium Park, 130 N. Garland Ct. (2004)	621	57
Chicago Place, 700 N. Michigan Ave. (1991)	608	49
Board of Trade (incl. statue), 141 W. Jackson (1930)	605	44
CNA Plaza, 325 S. Wabash (1972)	601	45
Prudential Bldg., 130 E. Randolph (1955)	601	41
Heller International Tower, 500 W. Monroe (1992)	600	45
One Madison Plaza, 200 W. Madison (1982)	597	45
Millennium Centre, 33 W. Ontario St.(2002)	596	60
1000 Lake Shore Plaza Apts. (1964)	590	55
Marina City Apts. 1, 300 N. State (1964)	588	61
Marina City Apts. 2, 300 N. State (1964)	588	61
Citicorp Center, 500 W. Madison (1985)	588	41
Mid Continental Plaza, 55 E. Monroe (1972)	582	50
North Pier Apt. Tower, 474 N. Lake Shore Dr. (1990)	581	61
Dearborn Center, 131 S. Dearborn (2002)	580	37
Smurfit-Stone , 150 N. Michigan Ave. (1983)	575	41
*The Fordham, 25 E. Superior St. (2002)	573	50
190 S. LaSalle St. (1986)	573	42
Onterie Center, 446 E. Ontario St. (1985)	570	57
Chicago Temple, 77 W. Washington (1923)	558	21
Palmolive Bldg. 919 N. Michigan Ave. (incl. beacon) (1929)	565	37
Huron Plaza Apts., 30 E. Huron St. (1983)	560	56
Morton Intl. Tower, 100 N. Riverside Plaza (1990)	560	36
Pittsfield, 55 E. Washington (1927)	557	38
The Parkshore, 195 N. Harbor Dr. (1991)	556	56
North Harbor Tower, 175 N. Harbor Dr. (1991)	556	55
Civic Opera Bldg., 20 N. Wacker Dr. (1929)	555	45
Newberry Plaza, State & Oak (1974)	553	53
Boulevard Towers South, 205 N. Michigan Ave. (1985)	553	44
30 N. LaSalle St. (1975)	553	43
Harbor Point, 155 N. Harbor Dr. (1975)	550	54
One S. Wacker Dr. (1983)	550	42
Park Millennium, 222 Columbus Dr. (2002)	544	53
USG Building, 125 S. Franklin (1992)	538	35
LaSalle National Bank, 135 S. LaSalle St. (1934)	535	44
Park Place Tower, 655 W. Irving Park Rd. (1973)	531	56
One LaSalle St. (1930)	530	49
The Elysees, 111 E. Chestnut St. (1972)	529	56
River Plaza, Rush & Hubbard (1977)	524	56
35 E. Wacker Dr. (1926)	523	40
Unitrin, 1 E. Wacker Dr. (1962)	522	41
Chicago Mercantile Exchange, 10 S. Wacker Dr. (1987)	520	40
Chicago Merc. Exchange, 30 S. Wacker Dr. (1983)	520	40
Kluczynski Federal Bldg., 230 S. Dearborn (1976)	520	40
191 N. Wacker (2002)	516	37
401 E. Ontario (1990)	515	51
One Financial Place, 440 S. LaSalle St. (1985)	515	40
LaSalle-Wacker, 221 N. LaSalle St. (1930)	512	41
Quaker Tower, 321 N. Clark (1987)	510	35
Harris Bank III, 115 S. LaSalle St. (1977)	510	35
400 E. Ohio St. (1982)	505	50
Carbide & Carbon, 230 N. Michigan Ave. (1929)	503	37
1 Superior Place (1999)	501	52
Savings of America Tower, 120 N. LaSalle St. (1991)	501	41
Chase Plaza, 10 S. LaSalle St. (1986)	501	37
200 S. Wacker Dr. (1981)	500	38
Ontario Place, 10 E. Ontario St. (1983)	495	49
Xerox Centre, 55 W. Monroe (1980)	495	40
1 N. Franklin St. (1991)	493	38
333 Wacker Dr. (1983)	487	36
Lincoln Tower, 75 E. Wacker Dr. (1928)	484	38
American National Bank, 33 N. LaSalle St. (1930)	479	40
Park Tower Condos, 5415 N. Sheridan Rd. (1974)	476	54
Bankers Bldg., 105 W. Adams St. (1927)	476	41
Britannica Center, 310 S. Michigan Ave. (1924)	475	37
Brunswick Bldg., 69 W. Washington (1965)	475	37
American Furniture Mart, 680 N. Lake Shore Dr. (1926)	474	30
Intercontinental Hotel, 505 N. Michigan (1929)	471	42
City Place, 676 N. Michigan (1990)	470	40
Columbus Plaza, 233 E. Wacker Dr. (1980)	468	49
The Sterling, 345 N. LaSalle St. (2001)	466	50
188 Randolph Tower (1925)	465	45
The Bristol, 57 E. Delaware Pl. (2000)	465	42
200 N. Dearborn (1989)	463	47
Tribune Tower, 435 N. Michigan Ave. (1925)	462	36
The New York, 3660 N. Lake Shore Dr. (1986)	461	50
Presidential Towers, 555 W. Madison St. (1985)	461	49
Presidential Towers, 575 W. Madison St. (1985)	461	49
Presidential Towers, 605 W. Madison St. (1985)	461	49
Presidential Towers, 625 W. Madison St. (1985)	461	49
Chicago Marriott, 540 N. Michigan Ave. (1978)	460	45
Swissotel, 323 E. Wacker Dr. (1989)	457	43
Equitable Life, 401 N. Michigan Ave. (1964)	457	35
*400 N. LaSalle (2003)	454	45
*ABN-AMRO Plaza I, 550 W. Madison St. (2003)	453	37
Roanoke, 11 S. LaSalle St. (1925)	452	37
River Bend, 323 N. Canal St. (2001)	451	37
Eugenie Terrace on the Park, 1730 N. Clark St. (1987)	450	35
Gateway Center III, 222 S. Riverside Plaza (1972)	450	35

WORLD ALMANAC QUICK QUIZ

After New York and Chicago, what North American city has the tallest building (not counting towers that have no stories and are not technically buildings)?

(a) Houston, TX (b) Atlanta, GA (c) Toronto, Ont (d) Philadelphia, PA

For the answer look in this chapter, or see page 1008.

Cincinnati, OH

Building	Ht. (ft.)	Stories
Carew Tower, 441 Vine St. (1930)	574	48
PNC Tower , 1 W. 4th St. (1913)	495	28
Scripps Center, 312 Walnut St. (1990)	468	36
Atrium Two, 221 E. 4th St. (1984)	428	30
Fifth Third Center, 511 Walnut St. (1969)	423	32
Chemed Center, 255 5th St. (1990)	410	32
Cincinnati Commerce Center, 600 Vine St. (1984)	402	29

Cleveland, OH

Building	Ht. (ft.)	Stories
Key Tower, 127 Public Square (1991)	947	57
Terminal Tower, 50 Public Square (1930)	708	52
BP America, 200 Public Square (1985)	658	46
100 Erieview, 1801 E. 9th St. (1964)	529	40
One Cleveland Center, 1375 E. 9th St. (1983)	450	31
Bank One Center (1991)	446	38
Federal Courthouse, 801 W. Superior Ave. (2002)	430	23
Justice Center, 1250 Ontario (1976)	420	26
Federal Building (1967)	419	32
National City Center, 1900 E. 9th St. (1980)	410	35

Columbus, OH

Building	Ht. (ft.)	Stories
James A. Rhodes State Office Tower, 30 E. Broad (1973)	624	41
Leveque-Lincoln Tower, 50 W. Broad (1927)	555	47
William Green Building (1990)	530	33
Huntington Center, 41 S. High St. (1983)	512	37
Vern Riffe State Office Tower, 77 S. High St. (1988)	503	33
One Nationwide Plaza (1976)	485	40
Franklin County Courthouse (1991)	464	27
AEP Building, One Riverside Plaza (1983)	456	31
Borden Bldg., 180 E. Broad (1974)	438	34
Three Nationwide Plaza (1989)	408	27

Dallas, TX

Building	Ht. (ft.)	Stories
Bank of America Plaza, 901 Main St. (1985)	921	72
Renaissance Tower, 1201 Elm St. (1974)	886	56
Bank One Center, 1717 Main St. (1987)	787	60
Chase Texas Plaza, 2200 Ross Ave. (1987)	738	55
Fountain Place, 1445 Ross Ave. (1986)	720	58
Trammel Crow Tower, 2001 Ross Ave. (1984)	686	50
1700 Pacific Ave. (1983)	655	50
Thanksgiving Tower, 1600 Pacific Ave. (1982)	645	50
Energy Plaza, 1601 Bryan St. (1983)	629	49
Elm Place, 1401 Elm St. (1965)	625	52
Republic Center Tower I (1954)	602	36
Republic Center Tower II, 325 N. St. Paul (1964)	598	50
One Bell Plaza, 208 S. Akard St. (1984)	580	37
One Lincoln Plaza, 500 Akard St. (1984)	579	45
Cityplace Center East (1989)	560	42
Reunion Tower (1976)	560	NA
Southland Center, 400 Olive St. (1959)	550	42
2001 Bryan St.(1973)	512	40
Harwood Center, 1999 Bryan St. (1982)	483	36
Maxus Energy, 717 N. Harwood St. (1980)	481	34
San Jacinto Tower, 2121 San Jacinto St. (1982)	456	33
Renaissance Hotel (1983)	451	29
Adam's Mark Hotel North Tower (1980)	448	31
One Dallas Centre, 350 N. Paul St. (1979)	448	30
One Main Place, 1201 Main St. (1968)	445	34
1600 Pacific Bldg. (1964)	434	31
Mercantile National Bank Bldg. (1937)	430	31
Magnolia Bldg., 108 Akard St. (1923)	430	27
Fidelity Union Tower (1959)	400	33
Mart Hotel	400	29

Denver, CO

Building	Ht. (ft.)	Stories
Republic Plaza, 330 17th St. (1984)	714	56
1801 California (1982)	709	52
Wells Fargo Center (1983)	698	50
1999 Broadway (1985)	544	43
MCI Tower, 707 17th St. (1981)	522	42
Qwest Tower, 555 17th St. (1978)	507	40
Amoco Bldg., 1670 Broadway (1980)	448	36
17th St. Plaza, 1225 17th St. (1982)	438	32
First Interstate Tower North, 633 17th St. (1974)	434	32
Brooks Towers, 1020 15th St. (1968)	420	42
Two Denver Place, 999 18th St. (1981)	416	34
One Tabor Center, 1200 17th St. (1984)	408	32
Manville Plaza, 717 17th St. (1989)	404	29

Des Moines, IA

Building	Ht. (ft.)	Stories
801 Grand (1991)	630	44
Ruan Center (1974)	457	36

Detroit, MI

Building	Ht. (ft.)	Stories
Marriott Hotel, Renaissance Center I (1977)	725	73
Comercia Tower, 500 Woodward (1991)	619	45
Penobscot Bldg., 633 Griswold (1928)	566	46
Renaissance Center 100 Tower (1976)	534	39
Renaissance Center 200 Tower(1976)	534	39
Renaissance Center 300 Tower (1976)	534	39
Renaissance Center 400 Tower (1976)	534	39
Guardian, 500 Griswold (1928)	485	40
Book Tower, 1265 Washington (1925)	472	35
Madden Bldg., 150 W. Jefferson (1988)	470	29
Fisher Bldg., 311 W. Grand Blvd. (1928)	447	28
Cadillac Tower, 65 Cadillac Sq. (1928)	437	40
David Stott Bldg., 1150 Griswold (1928)	436	38
ANR Bldg., 1 Wood Ward (1962)	430	30

Edmonton, Alberta

Building	Ht. (ft.)	Stories
Manulife Place, 10170-101 St. (1983)	479	39
Telus Plaza, 10020-100 St. (1971)	441	34
Bell Tower (1982)	440	31
Commerce Place (1990)	409	30

Fort Worth, TX

Building	Ht. (ft.)	Stories
Burnett Plaza, 801 Cherry St. (1983)	567	40
Center Tower II, 301 Commerce St. (1984)	547	38
UPR Plaza, 777 Main St. (1982)	525	40
Landmark Tower, 200 W. 7th (1957)	481	32
Chase Texas Tower, 201 Main St. (1982)	477	33
Bank One Tower, 400 Throckmorton (1974)	454	36

Hartford, CT

Building	Ht. (ft.)	Stories
City Place (1980)	535	38
CitiGroup (1919)	527	34
Goodwin Square, 255 Asylum St. (1990)	522	30
Hartford Plaza (1967)	420	22

Honolulu, HI

Building	Ht. (ft.)	Stories
First Hawaiian Bank Bldg. (1996)	429	30
Nauru Tower (1991)	418	45
Hawaiki Tower (1999)	400	45
Waterfront Towers (1990)	400	45
Imperial Plaza (1992)	400	40
One Archer Lane (1998)	400	41

Houston, TX

Building	Ht. (ft.)	Stories
JP Morgan Chase Tower, 600 Travis (1982)	1,002	75
Wells Fargo Plaza, 1000 Louisiana (1983)	972	71
Williams Tower, 2800 Post Oak Blvd. (1983)	901	64
Bank of America Center, 700 Louisiana (1983)	780	56
Texaco Heritage Plaza, 1111 Bagby (1987)	762	53
1100 LouisianaBldg. (1980)	748	55
Houston Industries Plaza, 1111 Louisiana (1974)	741	53
1600 Smith St. (1984)	732	55
Chevron Tower, 1301 McKinney (1982)	725	52
One Shell Plaza, 900 Louisiana (1970)	714	50
Enron Bldg., 1400 Smith St. (1983)	691	50
Capital National Bank Plaza (1980)	685	50
One Houston Center, 1221 McKinney (1978)	678	47
First City Tower (1984)	662	47
San Felipe Plaza (1984)	625	45
Exxon Bldg., 800 Bell Ave. (1962)	606	44
1500 Louisiana St. (2002)	600	40
America Tower, 2929 Allen Parkway (1983)	590	42
Two Houston Center, 909 Fannin (1974)	579	40
San Jacinto Column (monument) (1983)	570	NA
Marathon Oil Tower, 5555 San Felipe (1983)	562	41
Wedge International Tower, 1415 Louisiana (1983)	550	44
Kellogg Tower, 601 Jefferson (1973)	550	40
Pennzoil Place 1, 700 Milam St. (1976)	523	36
Pennzoil Place 2, 700 Louisiana St. (1976)	523	36
Devon Energy Center, 1200 Smith St. (1978)	521	36
1201 Louisiana Bldg. (1971)	518	35
*1000 Main Street (2003)	510	36
The Huntington (1982)	503	34
El Paso Energy Bldg. (1962)	502	33
Greenway Plaza (1973)	465	31
One Allen Center, 500 Dallas (1974)	452	34
Summit Tower East (1978)	441	31
Summit Tower West (1979)	441	31
Four Leafs Towers I, 5100 San Felipe Blvd. (1982)	444	40
Four Leafs Towers II (1982)	444	40
Phoenix Tower, 3200 Southwest Fwy. (1984)	434	34
Chase Bank Bldg., 712 Main St. (1929)	428	37
The Spires (1984)	426	41
Union Texas Petroleum Tower, 4 Oaks Place (1983)	420	30
One City Center (1960)	410	32

Building	Ht. (ft.)	Stories
Bob Lanier Public Works Bldg., 611 Walker Ave. (1968)	410	27
Neils Esperson Bldg., 802 Travis St. (1927)	409	31
Hyatt Regency (1972)	401	30

Indianapolis, IN

Building	Ht. (ft.)	Stories
Bank One Tower, 11 Monument Circle (1990)	811	49
American United Life Ins. (1981)	533	37
One Indiana Square (1970)	504	36
Market Tower, 10 W. Market St. (1988)	450	32
300 N. Meridian Bldg. (1988)	408	28

Jacksonville, FL

Building	Ht. (ft.)	Stories
Bank of America Tower (1990)	617	42
Modis Tower (1975)	535	37
BellSouth Tower (1983)	435	27
Riverplace Tower (1967)	433	28

Jersey City, NJ

Building	Ht. (ft.)	Stories
*Goldman Sachs Tower (2003)	781	42
Merrill Lynch Building, 101 Hudson St. (1992)	548	42
Newport Tower, 525 Washington Blvd. (1992)	531	36
Exchange Place Centre, 10 Exchange Place (1989)	516	32
77 Hudson St. (2002)	491	32
Harborside Financial Plaza V (2002)	480	34

Kansas City, MO

Building	Ht. (ft.)	Stories
One Kansas City Place (1988)	632	42
Transamerica Tower(1986)	591	38
Hyatt Regency (1980)	504	45
Power & Light Bldg. (1931)	476	32
City Hall, 414 E. 12th St. (1937)	443	29
Federal Office Bldg. (1931)	433	35
Oak Tower, 324 E. 11th St.	430	28
1201 Walnut (1991)	427	30
Commerce Tower (1965)	407	32
City Center Square (1977)	404	30

Las Vegas, NV

Building	Ht. (ft.)	Stories
Stratosphere Tower (1996)	1,149	NA
Eiffel Tower, Paris Hotel and Casino (1998)	540	NA
New York, New York Hotel and Casino (1997)	525	48
Le Reve (2004)	514	45
Bellagio Hotel and Casino (1998)	508	36
Mandalay Resort-Bay Hotel and Casino (1999)	480	43
Venetian Resort-Hotel and Casino (1999)	480	35
Caesars Palace Hotel Tower (1998)	470	29
Treasure Island Hotel and Casino (1993)	456	38
Paris Hotel and Casino (1999)	440	34
Rio Masquerade Tower (1996)	422	42
Palms Casino Hotel (2001)	413	42
Aladdin Resort and Casino (2000)	408	38
The Mirage (1989)	400	36
Harrahs Hotel and Casino	400	35
Fitzgeralds Hotel	400	33

Little Rock, AR

Building	Ht. (ft.)	Stories
TCBY Tower (1986)	546	40
Regions Center (1975)	454	30

Los Angeles, CA

Building	Ht. (ft.)	Stories
Library Tower, 633 W. 5th St. (1990)	1,018	73
First Interstate Tower, 707 Wilshire Blvd. (1974)	858	62
Two California Plaza, 350 S. Grand Ave. (1992)	750	52
Gas Company Tower, 555 W. 5th St. (1991)	749	52
BP Plaza, 333 South Hope (1975)	735	55
777 Tower, 777 S. Figueroa St. (1990)	725	53
Wells Fargo Tower, 333 S. Grand Ave. (1983)	723	54
United California Bank Plaza, 601 S. Figueroa St. (1989)	717	52
Atlantic Richfield Tower, 515 S. Flower St. (1971)	699	52
Bank of America Tower, 555 S. Flower St. (1971)	699	52
Citibank Square, 444 S. Flower St. (1979)	625	48
611 W. 6th St. (1969)	620	42
One California Plaza, 300 S. Grand Ave. (1985)	578	42
Century Plaza Tower 1, 2029 Cent. Park E. (1973)	571	44
Century Plaza Tower 2, 2049 Cent. Park E. (1973)	571	44
KPMG Tower, 355 S. Grand Ave. (1984)	560	44
Ernst & Young, LLP Plaza, 725 S. Figueroa St. (1986)	534	41
SunAmerica Tower, 1999 Ave. of the Stars (1989)	533	39
Manulife Tower, 865 S. Figueroa St. (1990)	517	37
Union Bank Square, 445 S. Figueroa St. (1968)	516	40
10 Universal City Plaza (1984)	506	36
1100 Wilshire (1987)	496	36
Fox Plaza, 2121 Ave. of Stars (1987)	492	34
*Constellation Place, Century City (2003)	491	35
1055 W. 7th St. (1985)	462	33
Equitable Life, 3435 Wilshire Blvd. (1969)	454	34
City Hall, 200 N. Spring St. (1927)	454	28
Transamerica Center, 1150 Olive St. (1965)	452	32
Madison Complex/Pacific Bell Switching Station (1961)	448	17
Mutual Life Benefit Building (1971)	435	32
550 South Hope (1991)	423	28
Warner Center Plaza III, 21650 Oxnard St., Woodland Hills (1991)	415	25
MCI Plaza, 700 S. Flower St. (1973)	414	33

Louisville, KY

Building	Ht. (ft.)	Stories
AEGON Center, 400 W. Market St. (1992)	549	35
National City Tower, 101 S. 5th St. (1972)	512	40
PNC Bank Bldg., 5th & Jefferson (1971)	420	30
Humana Center, 5th & Main (1985)	417	28

Mexico City, Mexico

Building	Ht. (ft.)	Stories
*Torre Mayor (2002)	738	55
Torre de Pemex (1984)	702	52
Torre Altus (1999)	640	42
Torre Latino Americana (1956)	597	45
World Trade Center (1972)	565	50
Los Arcos Bosques I (1997)	529	34
*Los Arcos Bosques II (2004)	529	34
*World Trade Center Hotel (2003)	459	38
Torre Las Lomas (1993)	453	36
Hotel Nikko Mexico	446	38
Torre del Caballito	443	34
Torre Mural, Insurgentes Sur 1605 (1995)	440	33
President Inter-Continental Hotel (1976)	427	42
Torre Dahnos I (2003)	427	31
Nonoalco Tlatelolco Tower (1962)	417	25
Torre Reforma Andres Bello 45	410	28
JW Marriott Hotel, Andres Bello 29	400	27

Miami, FL

Building	Ht. (ft.)	Stories
*Four Seasons Hotel and Tower (2002)	794	64
First Union Financial Center, 200 S. Biscayne Blvd. (1983)	764	55
Bank of America Tower, 100 S. E. 2nd St. (1987)	625	47
Santa Maria, 1643 Brickell Ave. (1997)	520	51
Stephen P. Clark Center (1985)	510	28
*Jade at Brickell Bay (2003)	500	48
*Espirito Santo Plaza, 1301 Brickell Ave. (2003)	487	36
Citicorp Tower, 201 S. Biscayne Blvd. (1986)	484	35
Three Tequesta Point (2001)	480	46
One Biscayne Tower, 2 S. Biscayne Blvd. (1974)	456	30
701 Brickell Ave. (1986)	450	33
Barclay's Financial Center (2001)	435	31
Mark on Bricknell (2001)	420	36
Courthouse Center (1986)	405	30
The Palace (1982)	400	42
Two Tequesta Point, 808 Brickell Key Dr. (1999)	400	39

Miami Beach, FL

Building	Ht. (ft.)	Stories
Blue Diamond Tower (2000)	559	44
Green Diamond Tower (2000)	559	44
PortofinoTower, 100 S. Pointe Dr. (1997)	484	44
*The Continuum on South Beach, South Tower (2002)	474	43
Murano at Portofino (2001)	402	38

Milwaukee, WI

Building	Ht. (ft.)	Stories
U.S. Bank Center, 777 E. Wisconsin Ave. (1973)	601	42
100 E. Wisconsin Ave (1989)	549	37
Milwaukee Center, 111 E. Kilbourn Ave. (1987)	426	29
411 Bldg., 411 E. Wisconsin Ave. (1983)	408	30

Minneapolis, MN

Building	Ht. (ft.)	Stories
225 South Sixth, 601 2nd Ave. (1992)	776	56
IDS Center (1973)	775	57
Wells Fargo Center, 90 S. 7th St. (1988)	774	57
33 S. 6th St. (1983)	668	52
Piper Jaffray Tower, 222 S. 9th St. (1984)	579	42
Pillsbury Center, 200 S. 6th St. (1981)	561	41
Dain Rauscher Plaza, 60 S. 6th St. (1992)	539	40
Fifth Street Towers II, 150 S. 5th St. (1988)	503	36
American Express Tower, 707 2nd Ave. S. (2000)	498	30
Target Plaza South, 1020 Nicolet Mall (2001)	492	33
Plaza VII, 45 S. 7th St. (1987)	475	36
US Bankcorp Center, 800 Nicolet Mall (2000)	468	32
AT&T Tower, 901 Marquette Ave. (1991)	464	34
Accenture Tower, 333 S. 7th St. (1987)	455	33
Foshay Tower, 821 Marquette Ave. (1929)	447	32
Qwest, 224 S. 5th St. (1931)	416	26
Hennepin Co. Government Center (1973)	403	24
Dorsey & Whitney Tower, 50 S. Sixth St. (2001)	401	30

Montreal, Quebec

Building	Ht. (ft.)	Stories
1000 Rue de la Gauchetière (1991)	669	51
Marathon (IBM), 1250 Blvd. René Lévesque (1989)	640	47
Tour de la Bourse, 800 Place Victoria (1963)	624	47
Place Villa Marie (1962)	616	42
La Tour CIBC, 1155 Blvd. René Lévesque (1962)	604	43
Montreal Tower (1987)	574	NA
Place Montreal Trust (1988)	519	30
Tour McGill College (1992)	519	38
Le Complexe Desjardins Sud (1975)	498	40
Les Cooperants, 600 Maisonneuve (1987)	479	34
Le Centre Sheraton (1980)	449	38
Place Montreal Trust (1988)	440	30
Maison Royal Trust, 630 Blvd. René Lévesque (1962)	429	32
Le Complexe Desjardins Est (1975)	428	32
La Tour Laurier	425	36
Port Royal Apts. (1964)	424	33
Chateau Champlain Hotel, 1 Place du Canada (1967)	420	38
Centre Mount Royal (1976)	420	28
Tour Terminal (1966)	400	30

Nashville, TN

Building	Ht. (ft.)	Stories
BellSouth Tower (1994)	617	33
Sun Trust Bank (1986)	490	31
William R. Snodgrass Tennessee Tower (1970)	452	31
Nashville Life & Casualty	409	30
City Center (1987)	402	27

Newark, NJ

Building	Ht. (ft.)	Stories
Midatlantic National Bank, 744 Broad St. (1931)	465	36
Raymond-Commerce, 1180 Raymond Blvd. (1930)	448	34

New Orleans, LA

Building	Ht. (ft.)	Stories
One Shell Square (1972)	697	51
Bank One Center (1985)	645	53
Plaza Tower (1969)	531	45
Energy Centre (1984)	530	39
LL&E Tower, 901 Poydras (1987)	481	36
Sheraton Hotel (1985)	478	47
Marriott Hotel (1972)	450	42
Texaco Bldg. (1983)	442	33
Canal Place One (1979)	439	32
Bank of New Orleans, 1010 Common (1971)	438	31
World Trade Center (1965)	407	33
CNG Tower (1989)	406	26

New York, NY

Building	Ht. (ft.)	Stories
Empire State Bldg., 350 5th Ave. (1931)	1,250	102
Chrysler Bldg., 405 Lexington Ave. (1930)	1,046	77
American International Bldg., 70 Pine St. (1932)	952	67
The Trump Bldg., 40 Wall St. (1930)	927	71
Citigroup Center, 153 E. 53rd St. (1977)	915	59
Trump World Tower, 845 UN Plaza (2001)	881	72
G. E. Bldg., 30 Rockefeller Center (1933)	850	70
Cityspire, 150 W. 56th St. (1989)	814	75
One Chase Manhattan Plaza (1960)	813	60
Condé Nast Bldg., 4 Times Square (1999)	809	48
MetLife Bldg., 200 Park Ave. (1963)	808	59
Woolworth Bldg., 233 Broadway (1913)	792	57
1 Worldwide Plaza, 935 8th Ave. (1989)	778	47
Carnegie Hall Tower, 152 W. 57th St. (1991)	757	60
Bear Stearns World Headquarters, 383 Madison Ave. (2001)	757	47
AXA Center West, 787 7th Ave. (1985)	752	51
One Penn Plaza, 250 W. 34th St. (1972)	750	57
*Time Warner Center South Tower (2003)	750	55
*Time Warner Center North Tower (2003)	750	55
1251 Ave. of Americas (1971)	750	54
J.P. Morgan Headquarters, 60 Wall St. (1989)	745	55
1 Liberty Plaza, 165 Broadway (1973)	743	54
20 Exchange Place (1931)	741	57
American Express Tower, Three World Financial Center, 200 Vesey St. (1986)	739	51
One Astor Plaza, 1515 Broadway (1969)	730	54
Metropolitan Tower, 142 W. 57th St. (1985)	716	68
J.P. Morgan Chase World Headquarters, 270 Park Ave. (1960)	707	52
General Motors, 767 5th Ave. (1968)	705	50
Metropolitan Life Tower, 1 Madison Ave. (1909)	700	50
500 5th Ave. (1931)	697	60
*Times Square Tower (2003)	696	47
Americas Tower, 1177 Ave. of the Amer. (1992)	692	48
Solow Bldg., 9 W. 57th St. (1974)	689	49
Marine Midland Bank, 140 Broadway (1966)	688	52
55 Water St. (1972)	687	53
277 Park Ave. (1963)	687	50
1585 Broadway (1989)	685	42
*Random House Tower, 1739 Broadway (2002)	684	52
Four Seasons Hotel, 57 E. 57th St. (1993)	682	52
Bertelsmann Bldg., 1540 Broadway (1990)	676	42
McGraw Hill Bldg., 1221 Ave. of Amer. (1972)	674	51
Lincoln Bldg., 60 E. 42nd St. (1930)	673	53
Paramount Plaza, 1633 Broadway (1970)	670	48
Trump Tower, 725 5th Ave. (1982)	664	58
Citicorp, Queens (1990)	658	50
Irving Trust, 1 Wall St. (1932)	654	50
599 Lexington Ave. (1986)	653	51
712 5th Ave. (1990)	650	53
Chanin Bldg., 122 E. 42nd St. (1929)	649	56
245 Park Ave. (1967)	648	47
Sony Bldg., 550 Madison Ave. (1983)	647	37
Merrill Lynch, Two World Financial Center, 225 Liberty St. (1986)	645	44
RCA Victor Bldg., 570 Lexington Ave. (1930)	642	50
One New York Plaza (1968)	640	50
1 Dag Hammarskjold Plaza, 885 2nd Ave. (1972)	637	49
345 Park Ave. (1968)	634	44
Grace Plaza, 1114 Ave. of the Amer. (1972)	630	50
Home Insurance Co., 59 Maiden Lane (1966)	630	44
Verizon Tower, 1095 Ave. of the Amer. (1970)	630	40
Central Park Place, 301 W. 57th St. (1988)	628	56
888 7th Ave. (1971)	628	45
Alliance Capital Bldg., 1345 Ave. of the Amer. (1969)	625	50
Waldorf Astoria, 301 Park Ave. (1931)	625	47
Trump Palace, 200 E. 69th St. (1991)	623	55
Olympic Tower, 645 5th Ave. (1976)	620	51
Mercantile Bldg., 10 E. 40th St. (1929)	620	48
*425 Fifth Avenue (2003)	618	55
101 Park Ave. (1982)	618	50
919 Third Ave. (1970)	615	47
750 7th Ave. (1989)	615	35
New York Life, 51 Madison Ave. (1928)	615	33
Tower 49, 12 E. 49th St. (1985)	614	44
Credit Lyonnais Bldg., 1301 Ave. of the Amer. (1964)	609	46
Museum Tower Apts., 21 W. 53rd St. (1985)	605	58
IBM, 590 Madison Ave. (1983)	603	41
3 Lincoln Center, 160 W. 66th St. (1993)	595	60
Celanese Bldg., 1211 Ave. of the Amer. (1973)	592	45
Rihga Royal Hotel, 151 W. 54th St. (1990)	590	54
U.S. Court House, 505 Pearl St. (1927)	590	37
Millenium Hilton Hotel, 55 Church St. (1992)	588	58
Time & Life, 1271 Ave. of the Amer. (1959)	587	48
Jacob K. Javits Federal Bldg., 26 Federal Plaza (1967)	587	41
W Times Square, 1567 Broadway (2000)	584	53
Stevens Tower, 1185 Ave. of Amer. (1971)	580	42
Municipal Bldg., 1 Centre St. (1914)	580	34
Trump International Hotel & Tower (1970)	579	44
520 Madison Ave. (1981)	577	43
Oppenheimer & Co., 1 World Financial Ctr. (1985)	577	37
Merchandise Mart, 41 Madison Ave. (1973)	576	42
Park Ave. Plaza, 55 E. 52nd St. (1981)	575	44
Ernst & Young Tower, 5 Times Square (2002)	575	40
Morgan Stanley Dean Whitter Plaza (2002)	575	38
One Financial Square, 33 Old Slip (1987)	575	37
Marriott Marquis Times Square, (1985)	574	50
Westavco Bldg., 299 Park Ave. (1967)	574	42
1166 Ave. of the Americas (1974)	572	44
Socony Mobil, 150 E. 42nd Street (1956)	572	42
Wang Bldg.,780 3rd Ave. (1983)	570	49
AXA Finance Center, 1290 Ave. of the Amer. (1963)	570	43
600 3rd Ave. (1971)	570	42
450 Lexington Ave. (1991)	568	38
Paramount Tower, 240 E. 39th St. (1998)	567	51
Deutsche Bank, 130 Liberty St. (1974)	565	40
Helmsley Bldg., 230 Park Ave. (1928)	565	35
New York Palace Hotel, 455 Madison Ave. (1980)	563	51
30 Broad St. (1932)	562	48
Park Ave. Tower, 65 E. 55th St. (1986)	561	36
Nelson Tower (1931)	560	46
Sherry-Netherland, 781 5th Ave. (1927)	560	40
Swiss Bank Tower, 10 E. 50th St. (1990)	560	36
100 UN Plaza (1986)	557	52
Continental Can, 633 3rd Ave. (1962)	557	39
3 Park Ave. (1975)	556	42
Continental Corp., 180 Maiden Lane (1983)	555	41
Sperry & Hutchinson, 330 Madison Ave. (1964)	555	41
Reuters Bldg., 3 Times Square (2001)	555	30
Madison Belvedere, 14 E. 29th St. (1999)	554	48
Inmont Bldg., 1133 Ave. of the Amer. (1970)	552	45
Equitable Trust Co. Bldg. (1927)	551	42
Burroughs Bldg., 605 3rd Ave. (1963)	550	44
Bell Atlantic, 33 Thomas St. (1974)	550	29
2 Grand Central Tower, 140 E. 45th St. (1982)	550	44

IT'S A FACT: The last time before Sept. 11, 2001, that a plane crashed into a New York City skyscraper was on July 28, 1945, when an Army Air Corps B-25 bomber, headed for Newark, NJ, flew too low over Manhattan in the fog and crashed into the 79th floor of the Empire State Building. The 3 people on the plane and 11 workers in the building were killed.

Oklahoma City, OK

Building	Ht. (ft.)	Stories
Bank One Center (1971)	500	36
First National Center, 120 N. Robinson St. (1931)	493	33
City Place Tower, 204 N. Robinson St. (1931)	440	32
Oklahoma Tower (1982)	434	31

Omaha, NE

Building	Ht. (ft.)	Stories
The Tower at First National Center (2002)	634	45
Woodmen Tower (1969)	478	30

Orlando, FL

Building	Ht. (ft.)	Stories
SunTrust Center Tower (1988)	441	31
Orange County Courthouse (1997)	416	24
Bank of America Center (1988)	409	28

Philadelphia, PA

Building	Ht. (ft.)	Stories
One Liberty Place, 1650 Market St. (1987)	945	61
Two Liberty Place, 1601 Chestnut St. (1989)	848	58
Mellon Bank Center, 1735 Market St. (1990)	792	54
Verizon Tower, 18th & Arch Sts. (1991)	725	53
Blue Cross Tower, 1901 Market St. (1990)	700	50
Commerce Square #1, 2005 Market St. (1990)	572	40
Commerce Square #2, 2001 Market St. (1992)	572	40
City Hall (incl. statue) (1901)	548	9
The St. James (2003)	510	47
1818 Market St. (1974)	500	40
Lowe's Philadelphia Hotel , 12 S. 12th St. (1932)	492	39
PNC, 1600 Market St. (1983)	491	40
First Union, 1542 Market St. (1973)	490	38
5 Penn Center (1970)	488	36
1700 Market St. (1969)	482	32
Philadelphia National Bank, 1 S. Broad St. (1930)	475	25
Two Logan Square, 100 N. 18th St. (1988)	435	34
2000 Market St. (1973)	435	29
11 Penn Center, 1835 Market St. (1985)	420	29
Aramark Tower, 1101 Market St. (1984)	417	31
Centre Square, 1500 Market St. (1973)	416	32
First Union Bank, 123 S. Broad St. (1927)	405	30
Ritz-Carlton Hotel (1930)	404	30
Lewis Tower, 1419 Locust St. (1929)	400	33
One Logan Square, 130 N. 18th St. (1982)	400	32

Phoenix, AZ

Building	Ht. (ft.)	Stories
Bank One Center, 201 N. Central (1972)	486	40
101 N. Second Ave. (1976)	407	31

Pittsburgh, PA

Building	Ht. (ft.)	Stories
USX Tower, 600 Grant St. (1970)	841	64
One Mellon Bank Center, 500 Grant St. (1983)	725	54
One PPG Place (1984)	635	40
Fifth Ave. Place (1987)	616	32
One Oxford Centre, 301 Grant St. (1982)	615	46
Gulf Tower, 707 Grant St. (1932)	582	44
Univ. of Pittsburgh Cath. of Learning (1936)	535	42
3 Mellon Bank Center, 525 Wm. Penn Way (1951)	520	41
Freemarket Center, 1 Oliver Center (1968)	511	40
Grant Bldg., 330 Grant St. (1928)	485	40
Koppers, 436 7th Ave. (1929)	475	34
2 PNC Plaza (1975)	445	34
Dominion Tower (1987)	430	32
1 PNC Plaza (1972)	424	30
Regional Enterprise Tower, 425 6th Ave. (1953)	410	30

Portland, OR

Building	Ht. (ft.)	Stories
Wells Fargo Tower (1973)	546	40
U.S. Bancorp Tower (1983)	536	42
Koin Tower Plaza (1984)	509	31
Pacwest Center (1984)	418	30

Providence, RI

Building	Ht. (ft.)	Stories
Fleet Bank Bldg. (1927)	428	26
FleetBoston Tower (1973)	410	28

Richmond, VA

Building	Ht. (ft.)	Stories
James Monroe Bldg. (1981)	449	29
SunTrust Plaza, 919 E. Main St. (1984)	400	24

Sandy Springs, GA

Building	Ht. (ft.)	Stories
Concourse Tower #5 (1988)	570	34
Concourse Tower #6 (1991)	553	34

St. Louis, MO

Building	Ht. (ft.)	Stories
Gateway Arch (1965)	630	NA
Metropolitan Square Tower (1988)	593	42
One Bell Center, 900 Pine St. (1984)	588	44
Thomas F. Eagleton Fed. Courthouse (2000)	557	29
U.S. Bank Plaza, 505 N. 7th St. (1976)	484	35
Laclede Gas Bldg., 8th & Olive (1969)	400	31

St. Paul, MN

Building	Ht. (ft.)	Stories
Minnesota World Trade Center (1987)	471	36
Galtier Plaza Jackson Tower (1986)	453	46
First National Bank (1930)	417	32

Salt Lake City, UT

Building	Ht. (ft.)	Stories
Wells Fargo Center (1998)	422	24
L.D.S. Church Office Bldg. (1972)	420	28

San Antonio, TX

Building	Ht. (ft.)	Stories
Tower of the Americas (1968)	622	NA
Marriott Rivercenter, 101 Bowie St. (1988)	546	38
Weston Centre, 112 Pecan St. (1988)	444	32
Tower Life, 310 S. St. Mary's (1929)	404	30

San Diego, CA

Building	Ht. (ft.)	Stories
One American Plaza, 600 W. Broadway (1991)	500	34
Symphony Tower, 759 B St. (1989)	499	34
Hyatt Regency (1992)	497	40
Emerald Plaza, 400 W. Broadway (1991)	450	30
One and Two Harbor Drive (2 bldgs.), 100 Harbor Dr. (1992)	424	41

San Francisco, CA

Building	Ht. (ft.)	Stories
Transamerica Pyramid, 600 Montgomery St. (1972)	853	48
Bank of America, 555 California St. (1969)	779	52
345 California Center (1986)	695	48
101 California St. (1986)	600	48
50 Fremont Center (1983)	600	43
4 Embarcadero Center (1984)	570	45
1 Embarcadero Center (1970)	569	45
Spear Tower, 1 Market St. (1976)	565	42
Wells Fargo, 44 Montgomery St. (1967)	563	43
575 Market St. (1975)	551	39
One Sansome-Citicorp (1984)	550	39
Shaklee Terrace Bldg., 444 Market St. (1979)	537	38
One Post Plaza, 1 Post St. (1969)	529	38
525 Market St. (1972)	529	38
One Metro Plaza, 425 Market St. (1973)	524	38
Pacific Telesis Center (1982)	500	38
333 Bush St. (1986)	495	43
Hilton Hotel, 201 Mason St. (1971)	493	46
Pacific Gas & Electric, 77 Beale St. (1970)	492	34
50 California St. (1972)	487	37
*St. Regis Museum Tower (2003)	480	42
100 Pine Center (1972)	476	34
Bechtel Bldg., 45 Fremont St. (1979)	475	34
333 Market Bldg. (1979)	474	33
Hartford Bldg., 650 California St. (1965)	465	33
100 First Plaza (1988)	447	32
1 California St. (1969)	438	32
Marriott Hotel (1989)	436	39
Russ Bldg., 235 Montgomery St. (1927)	435	31
Pacific Bell Headquarters, 140 Montgomery St. (1925)	435	26
J.P. Morgan Chase H&Q Bldg. (2002)	421	31
Paramount (2002)	418	41
Providian Financial Bldg., 201 Mission St. (1983)	416	30
2 Embarcadero Center (1974)	412	31
3 Embarcadero Center (1976)	412	31
595 Market (1977)	410	31
123 Mission Bldg.	406	28
Embarcadero Center West, 275 Battery St. (1988)	405	33
101 Montgomery St. (1983)	405	29

IT'S A FACT: Besides the World Trade Center twin towers, New York City lost another tall building on Sept. 11, 2001, as the 47-story 7 World Trade Center building nearby caught fire from burning rubble. The Fire Dept. had to abandon efforts to control the fire, and at around 5:20 PM, after 7 hours, the building collapsed. Portions of 3 other smaller buildings in the complex suffered damage from fire, but remained standing.

Seattle, WA

Building	Ht. (ft.)	Stories
Bank of America Tower, 701 5th Ave. (1985)	967	76
Two Union Square, 600 Union St. (1989)	740	56
Washington Mutual Tower, 1201 3rd Ave. (1988)	735	55
Key Tower, 700 5th Ave. (1990)	722	62
1001 Fourth Avenue Plaza (1969)	609	50
Space Needle, 203 6th Ave. (1962)	605	NA
U.S. Bank Centre, 1420 5th Ave. (1989)	580	44
Wells Fargo Center, 999 3rd Ave. (1983)	574	47
800 Fifth Avenue Plaza (1981)	543	42
Security Pacific Bank, 900 4th Ave. (1973)	536	41
Rainier Tower, 1301 5th Ave. (1977)	514	31
*IDX Tower, 915 4th Ave. (2003)	512	40
1000 2nd Ave. (1986)	493	40
Henry M. Jackson Bldg. (1974)	487	37
Qwest Plaza, 1600 7th Ave. (1976)	466	33
Smith Tower, 506 2nd Ave. (1914)	465	38
One Union Square, 600 University Ave. (1981)	456	36
1111 3rd Ave. (1980)	454	34
Westin Hotel North Tower, 1900 5th Ave. (1982)	448	44
Westin Bldg., 2001 6th Ave. (1981)	409	34

Southfield, MI

Building	Ht. (ft.)	Stories
Prudential, 3000 Town Center (1975)	448	32
1000 Town Center (1988)	405	32

Sunny Isles Beach, FL

Building	Ht. (ft.)	Stories
The Pinnacle, 17555 Collins Ave. (1999)	476	40
*The Residences at Ocean Grande (2003)	443	38
Ocean Two (2001)	426	40
*Ocean Three (2004)	405	37

Tampa, FL

Building	Ht. (ft.)	Stories
AmSouth Bldg., 100 N. Tampa (1992)	579	42
Bank of America Plaza (1986)	577	42
Tampa City Center (1981)	537	39
Suntrust Financial Center (1992)	525	36
First Financial Tower (1973)	458	36
400 N. Ashley (1988)	454	33

Toledo, OH

Building	Ht. (ft.)	Stories
One Seagate (1982)	41132	
HyTower (1970)	40030	

Toronto, Ontario

Building	Ht. (ft.)	Stories
CN Tower, 301 Front St. W (1976)	1,815	NA
First Canadian Place (1975)	978	72
Scotia Plaza (1989)	902	68
BCE Place, Canada Trust Tower (1990)	856	53
Commerce Court West (1973)	784	57
Toronto Dominion Centre–Toronto Dominion Bank Tower (1967)	730	56
BCE Place, Bay-Wellington Tower (1991)	679	49
Toronto Dominion Centre–Royal Trust Tower (1969)	600	46
*1 King West (2003)	578	51
Royal Bank Plaza–South Tower (1976)	567	41
Manulife Centre (1974)	545	51
Toronto Dominion Centre–Canadian Pacific Tower (1985)	504	39
The 250, 250 Yonge St. (1991)	494	35
Two Bloor West (1974)	488	34
Simcoe Place (1995)	486	33
Exchange Tower (1983)	480	30
CIBC-Commerce Court North, 25 King St. (1931)	477	34
Simpson Tower, 401 Bay Street (1968)	473	33
Cadillac-Fairview (1982)	465	36
Pantages Tower (2002)	458	45
One Palace Pier Court, Etobicoke (1991)	455	46
Three Palace Pier Court, Etobicoke (1978)	453	46
Laurentian Bank, 130 Adelaide St. W (1980)	453	35
One Financial Center, 1 Adelaide Pl. (2002)	450	32
One Financial Place (1991)	450	32
Sheraton Centre, 123 Queen St. W (1972)	443	43
Two Bloor East (1974)	439	35
Royal York Hotel (1929)	439	26
TDCentre Ernst & Young Tower (1990)	437	31
Old Toronto Exchange Bldg. (1990)	436	31
Leaside Towers (2 bldgs.) (1970)	423	44
TDCentre, Maritime Life Tower, (1974)	420	32
Metro Hall, 55 John St. (1991)	420	27
Maple Leaf Mills (1977)	419	30
Marriott Hotel/Plaza 2 Apts., 90 Bloor St. E (1973)	415	41
Sun Life Financial Center East Tower, 150 King St. W (1981)	410	27
Young-Eglington Centre–Triathlon Tower (1975)	408	30

Tulsa, OK

Building	Ht. (ft.)	Stories
Williams Center (1975)	667	52
Cityplex Central Tower (1981)	648	60
First National Bank (1973)	516	41
Mid-Continent Tower (1984)	513	36
Fourth National Bank (1966)	412	33
National Bank of Tulsa, 320 South Boston (1918)	400	24

Vancouver, British Columbia

Building	Ht. (ft.)	Stories
One Wall Centre, 1000 Burrard St. (2001)	491	45
*Shaw Tower (2004)	489	40
200 Granville Square (1973)	466	32
Royal Bank Tower, 1055 W. Georgia St. (1973)	461	37
Park Place, 666 Burrard St. (1984)	459	35
Bentall IV Canada Trust, 1055 Dunsmir (1981)	454	36
Scotia Tower, 650 W. Georgia St. (1977)	452	36
Harbour Centre, 555 W. Hastings (1977)	426	28
Toronto Dominion Bank Tower, 700 W. Georgia (1970)	417	30
Bentall III, Bank of Montreal, 595 Burrard St. (1974)	400	31

Winnipeg, Manitoba

Building	Ht. (ft.)	Stories
Toronto Dominion Centre, 201 Portage Ave. (1990)	420	33
Richardson Bldg., 1 Lombard Place (1969)	406	34

Winston-Salem, NC

Building	Ht. (ft.)	Stories
Wachovia Center, 100 N. Main St. (1995)	460	34
301 N. Main St. (1965)	410	30

Other Tall Buildings in North American Cities

Building	City	Ht. (ft.)	Stories
Erastus Corning II Tower (1973)	Albany, NY	589	44
San Jacinto Monument (1936)	La Porte, TX	570	NA
Washington Monument (1884)	Washington, DC	555	NA
Dataflux Tower (2000)	Monterrey, Mexico	549	43
One HSBC Center (1970)	Buffalo, NY	529	40
Vehicle Assembly Bldg. (1965)	Cape Canaveral, FL	525	40
*Congress at Fourth (2004)	Austin, TX	520	33
Mohegan Sun Hotel (2002)	Uncasville, CT	487	34
*Borgata Hotel and Casino (2003)	Atlantic City, NJ	480	40
State Capitol (1932)	Baton Rouge, LA	460	34
Burbank Tower, 2900 W. Burbank (1988)	Burbank, CA	460	32
*Los Olas River House 1 (2004)	Ft. Lauderdale, FL	452	42
*One Lincoln Tower (2003)	Bellevue, WA	450	42
The Diplomat (2001)	Hollywood, FL	444	39
Ravinia #3 (1991)	Dunwoody, GA	444	34
Xerox Tower (1965)	Rochester, NY	443	30
One Summit Square (1981)	Fort Wayne, IN	442	27
Anadarko Tower (2002)	The Woodlands, TX	439	32
AmSouth/Harbert Plaza (1989)	Birmingham, AL	437	32
The Palisades (2001)	Fort Lee, NJ	434	42
BBT/Two Hanover Square (1991)	Raleigh, NC	431	29
Union Planters Bank, 100 N. Main (1965)	Memphis, TN	430	38
Taj Mahal, 1000 Boardwalk (1990)	Atlantic City, NJ	429	43
Torre Commercial America (1994)	Monterrey, Mexico	427	35
AmSouth Bank Bldg. (1969)	Mobile, AL	424	33
Wells Fargo Center (1991)	Sacramento, CA	423	30
Plaza Tower (1986)	Knoxville, TN	422	30
Century 21	Hamilton, Ont.	418	43
Oakbrook Terrace Tower (1985)	Oakbrook, IL	418	31
Hidden Bay 1 (2000)	Aventura, FL	417	40
Galaxie Apts. (3 bldgs.) (1976)	Guttenberg, NJ	415	44
Complexe G (1972)	Quebec City, Que.	415	33
AmSouth Bank Bldg. (1996)	Montgomery, AL	415	24
*Lincoln Square (2003)	Bellevue, WA	412	28
One Shoreline Plaza, South Tower (1988)	Corpus Christi, TX	411	28
Silver Legacy Hotel & Casino, 407 N. Virginia St. (1995)	Reno, NV	410	38
AutoNation Tower (1988)	Ft. Lauderdale, FL	410	30
Financial Center (1986)	Lexington, KY	410	30
Clark Tower (1972)	Memphis, TN	410	33
Plaza in Clayton (2002)	Clayton, MO	409	30
Kettering Tower (1970)	Dayton, OH	408	30
Wells Fargo Center (1991)	Sacramento, CA	404	30
Ordway Bldg. (1985)	Oakland, CA	404	28
Three Lakeway Center (1987)	Metairie, LA	403	34
Monarch Place (1987)	Springfield, MA	400	26
Bank of America (1990)	St. Petersburg, FL	400	26

Notable Bridges in North America

Source: Federal Highway Administration, Bridge Division, U.S. Dept. of Transportation; World Almanac research

Asterisk (*) designates railroad bridge. Year is date of completion. Span of a bridge is the distance between its supports.

Suspension

Year	Bridge	Location	Main span (ft.)
1964	Verrazano-Narrows	New York, NY	4,260
1937	Golden Gate	San Fran. Bay, CA	4,200
1957	Mackinac Straits	Sts. of Mackinac, MI	3,800
1931	Geo. Washington	Hudson R., NY-NJ	3,500
1950	Tacoma Narrows	Tacoma, WA	2,800
1950	Tacoma Narrows II	Tacoma, WA	2,800
1936	San. Fran.-Oakland Bay[1]	San Fran. Bay, CA	2,310
1939	Bronx-Whitestone	East R., NY	2,300
1970	Pierre Laporte	Quebec, Canada	2,190
1951	Del. Memorial	Wilmington, DE	2,150
1957	Walt Whitman	Philadelphia, PA	2,000
1929	Ambassador	Detroit, MI–Can.	1,850
1961	Throgs Neck	Long Is. Sound, NY	1,800
1926	Benjamin Franklin	Philadelphia, PA	1,750
1924	Bear Mt.	Hudson R., NY	1,632
1903	Williamsburg	East R., NY	1,600
1952	Wm. Preston La. Mem.[2]	Sandy Point, MD	1,600
1969	Newport	Narragansett Bay, RI	1,600
1883	Brooklyn	East R., NY	1,595
1939	Lion's Gate	Burrard Inlet, BC	1,550
1930	Mid-Hudson	Poughkeepsie, NY	1,500
1963	Vincent Thomas	L. A. Harbor, CA	1,500
1909	Manhattan	East R., NY	1,470
1955	MacDonald Bridge	Halifax, Nova Scotia	1,447
1970	A. Murray Mackay	Halifax, Nova Scotia	1,400
1936	Triborough Br., QB Mainline	East R., NY	1,380
1931	St. Johns	Portland, OR	1,207
1929	Mount Hope	RI	1,200
1960	Ogdensburg	St. Lawrence R., NY	1,150
1965	Bidwell Bar Bridge	Oroville, CA	1,108
1964	Middle Fork Feather	CA	1,105
1939	Deer Isle	ME	1,080
1931	Simon Kenton Memorial	Ohio R., Maysville, KY	1,060
1936	Ile d'Orleans	St. Lawrence R., Quebec	1,059
1867	John A. Roebling	Ohio R., KY	1,057
1971	Dent	Clearwater Co., ID	1,050
1900	Miampimi	Mexico	1,030
1849	Wheeling	Ohio R., WV	1,010

Cantilever

Year	Bridge	Location	Main span (ft.)
1917	Québec Bridge	St. Lawrence R., Quebec	1,800
1988	Greater New Orleans Bridge	Mississippi R., New Orleans, LA	1,575
1995	Gramercy Bridge	Mississippi R., Gramercy, LA	1,460
1936	Transbay	San Fran. Bay, CA	1,400
1968	Baton Rouge Bridge	Mississippi R., Baton Rouge, LA	1,235
1955	Tappan Zee	Hudson R., NY	1,212
1930	Lewis and Clark	Longview, WA–OR	1,200
1909	Queensboro	East R., NY	1,182
1927	Carquinez Strait	CA	1,100
1958	Parallel Span	CA	1,100
1930	Jacques Cartier	Montreal, Quebec	1,097
1968	Isaiah D. Hart	Jacksonville, FL	1,088
1956	Richmond[3]	San Fran. Bay, CA	1,070
1929	Grace Memorial	Charleston, SC	1,050
1980	Newburgh-Beacon	Hudson R., NY	1,000
1949	Martin Luther King	St. Louis, MO	963
1975	Caruthersville	Mississippi R., MO–TN	920
1969	Silver Memorial	Pt. Pleasant, WV–OH	900
1977	Saint Marys	Saint Marys, WV–OH	900
1981	Ravenswood	WV	900
1987	Carl Perkins	Ohio R., KY	900
1941	Mississippi R.	Natchez, MI	875
1988	Mississippi R.	Natchez, MS	875
1938	Blue Water	Pt. Huron, MI	871
1972	Mississippi R.	Vicksburg, MS	870
1972	N. Fork American R.	Auburn, CA	862
1940	*Baton Rouge	Mississippi R., LA	848
1899	*Cornwall	St. Lawrence R.	843
1940	Rte. 82	Mississippi R., AR	840
1961	Mississippi R.	Greenville, MS	840
1963	Brent Spence	KY–OH	830
1940	Mississippi R.	Vicksburg, MS	825
1963	Mississippi R.	Donaldsonville, LA	825
1931	Mississippi R.	Vicksburg, MS	824
1929	Clark Memorial	Ohio R., KY	820
1961	Campbellton-Cross Pt.	New Brunswick, Can.	815
1932	Washington Mem.	Seattle, WA	800
1935	Rip Van Winkle	Catskill, NY	800
1938	Cairo	Ohio R., IL–KY	800
1936	McCullough	Coos Bay, OR	793
1949	Memphis	Mississippi R., TN	790
1935	Huey P. Long[4]	New Orleans, LA	790
1949	Rte. 55	Mississippi R., AR–TN	790
1910	*P&LE RR Bridge	Ohio R., PA	750
1930	Coal Grove Bridge	Ashland-Coal Grove Bridge, OH	739
1922	Ohio River, N&W RR	Ironton-Russell Bridge, OH	725
1932	Bi-State Vietnam Gold Star	Henderson, KY	720
1979	I-275	Ohio R., Fort Thomas, KY	720
1926	Columbia R.	Cascade Locks, OR	706
1964	John F. Kennedy (I-65)	Ohio R., Louisville, KY	700
1928	Ohio River, B&O RR, HV RR	Pomeroy-Mason, OH	657
1943	*Pit River	Redding, CA	620
1941	Columbia R.	Kettle Falls, WA	600
1954	Columbia R.	Umatilla, OR	600
1965	Bi-State Vietnam Gold Star	Henderson, KY	600
1954	Columbia R.	The Dalles, OR	576
1968	W. 17th St.	Huntington, WV	562

Simple Truss

Year	Bridge	Location	Main span (ft.)
1976	Chester	Chester, WV	745
1929	Irvin S. Cobb	Ohio R., IL–KY	716
1922	*Tanana R.	Nenana, AK	700
1967	I-77, Ohio R.	Williamstown, WV	650
1917	MacArthur[4]	St. Louis, IL–MO	647
1992	St. Charles	Missouri R, MO	625
1933	Atchafalaya	Morgan City, LA	608
1924	*Castleton	Hudson R., NY	598
1937	Delaware R.	Easton, PA	550
1930	Swindell Bridge	Pittsburgh, PA	545
1952	Allegheny R. Tpk.	Pittsburgh, PA	534
1951	Rankin	Pittsburgh, PA	525
1914	Old Brownsville	Brownsville, PA	520
1906	Donora-Webster	Donora-Webster, PA	515
1909	Hulton	Pittsburgh, PA	505
1967	Tanana R.	AK	500

Steel Truss

Year	Bridge	Location	Main span (ft.)
1988	Glade Creek	Raleigh Co., WV	784
1973	Atchafalaya R.	Krotz Springs, LA	780
1972	Piscataqua R.	NH–ME	756
1972	Atchafalaya R.	Simmesport, LA	720
1957	SR-3, Rappahannock R.	Middlesex Co., VA	648
1978	Atchafalaya R.	Morgan City, LA	607
1959	Summit	Summit, DE	600
1969	Reedy Point	Delaware City, DE	600
1937	US-22	Delaware R., NJ	550
1955	Interstate (I-5)	Columbia R., OR–WA	531
1910	McKinley, St. Louis[4]	Mississippi R., MO	517
1972	Mississippi R.	Muscatine, IA	512
1896	Newport	Ohio R., KY	511
1989	US 190, Atchafalaya R.	Krotz Springs, LA	506
1900	Norfolk Southern RR	Cincinnati, OH	500
1931	Lucy Jefferson Lewis	Cumberland R., KY	500
1958	Lake Oahe	Gettysburg, SD	500
1958	Lake Oahe	Mobridge, SD	500
1970	Lake Koocanusa	Lincoln Co., MT	500

Continuous Truss

Year	Bridge	Location	Main span (ft.)
1966	Columbia R. (Astoria)	OR–WA	1,232
1976	Francis Scott Key	Baltimore, MD	1,200
1981	Ravenswood/Ohio R.	Ravenswood, WV	902
1995	Central	Ohio R., KY–OH	850
1943	Dubuque	Mississippi R., IA	845
1966	Charles Braga	Fall River, MA	840
1956	Earl C. Clements[5]	Ohio R., IL–KY	825
1929	U.S. 31	Ohio R., IN–KY	820
1953	John E. Mathews	Jacksonville, FL	810
1950	Maurice J. Tobin	Boston, MA	801
1940	Gov. Nice Memorial	Potomac River, MD	800
1957	Kingston-Rhinecliff	Hudson R., NY	800
1992	Mark Clark Expy. I-526	Cooper R., Charleston, SC	800
1986	Rochester-Monaca	Rochester-Monaca, PA	780
1940	U.S. 231	Ohio R., IN	750
1974	Carroll L. Cropper (I-275)	Ohio R., IN–KY	750
1981	Sewickley	Sewickley, PA	750
1984	13th St. Bridge, Ohio R.	Ashland, KY	740
1959	Monaca-E. Rochester	Monaca-E. Rochester, PA	730
1976	Betsy Ross	Philadelphia, PA	729
1929	U.S. 421	Ohio R., IN–KY	727
1967	Matthew E. Welsh (SR135)	Mauckport, IN	725
1962	U.S. 41	Ohio R., IN–KY	720
1994	6th St.	Huntington, WV	720
1970	Vanport	Vanport, PA	715
1962	Champlain	Montreal, Que.	707
1962	John F. Kennedy (I-65)	Ohio R., IN–KY	701
1973	Girard Point	Philadelphia, PA	700
1954	PA Tpk., Delaware R.	Philadelphia, PA	682
1938	Rainbow Br., Neches R.	Port Arthur-Orange, TX	680
1949	George Platt	Philadelphia, PA	680

Year	Bridge	Location	Main span (ft.)
1926	Cape Girardeau	Mississippi R., MO	677
1946	Chester	Mississippi R, IL	670
1994	Williamstown-Marietta	Williamstown, WV	650
1955	Jefferson City	Missouri R., MO	640
1930	Quincy Memorial Bridge	Mississippi R., IL	628
1959	US 181, over harbor	Corpus Christi, TX	620
1961	Shippingport	Shippingport, PA	620
1935	Bourne-Sagamore	Cape Cod Canal, MA	616
1965	Clarion R. (I-80)	Clarion, PA	612
1975	Donora-Monessen	Donora-Monessen, PA	608
1957	Blatnik	Duluth, MN	600
1965	Rio Grande Gorge	Taos, NM	600
1991	Hoffstadt Creek	Mt. St. Helens, WA	600
1991	Jefferson City	Missouri R., MO	596
1962	W. Branch Feather R.	Oroville, CA	576
1967	Glenwood	Pittsburgh, PA	567
1936	Mark Twain Mem.	Hannibal, MO	562
1932	Pulaski Skyway	Passaic R.-Hackensack R., NJ	550
1966	Emlenton	Emlenton, PA	540
1973	Gold Star Memorial	New London, CT	540
1936	Homestead High Level	Pittsburgh, PA	534
1959	Martinez	Benicia-Martinez, CA	528
1960	Brownsville High Level	Brownsville, PA	518
1971	Grandad	Elk River, ID	504
1945	Mansfield-Dravosburg	Pittsburgh, PA	500

Continuous Box and Plate Girder

Year	Bridge	Location	Main span (ft.)
1967	San Mateo-Hayward #2	San Fran. Bay, CA	750
1976	Intracoastal Canal	Forked Is., LA	750
1977	Intracoastal Canal	Gibbstown, LA	750
1969	San Diego-Coronado[8]	San Diego Bay, CA	660
1987	Umatilla, Columbia R.	OR–WA	660
1994	Acosta	Jacksonville, FL	630
1981	Douglas	Juneau, AK	620
1976	Wax L. Outlet	Calumet, LA	618
1963	Poplar St.	St. Louis, MO	600
1981	Glenn Jackson (I-205)	Columbia R., OR–WA	600
1976	Stanislaus River	Sonora, CA	580
1982	Illinois R.	Pekin, IL	550
1982	I-440	Arkansas R., AR	540
1980	US-64, Tennessee R.	Savannah, TN	525
1965	McDonald-Cartier	Ottawa, Ont.	520
1988	Mon City	Monongahela, PA	520
1984	Columbia R.	Richland, WA	450
1986	Veterans	Pittsburgh, PA	440
1987	SR 76, Cumberland R.	Dover, TN	440
1987	SR 20, Tennessee R.	Perryville, TN	440
1970	Willamette R., I-205	West Linn, OR	430
1974	I-430	Arkansas R., AR	430
1965	I-24, Tennessee R.	Marion Co., TN	420
1974	Dunbar-S. Charleston	S. Charleston, WV	420
1975	36th St.	Charleston, WV	420
1978	Snake R.	Clarkston, WA	420
1984	FAU 3456, TN R.	Chattanooga, TN	420

Continuous Plate

Year	Bridge	Location	Main span (ft.)
1973	Sidney Sherman Bridge, I-610	Houston, TX	630
1971	W. Atchafalaya	Henderson, LA	573
1992	State Route 76	Paris, TN	525
1997	SR 114, Clifton	Tennessee R., TN	525
1981	Illinois 23	Illinois R., IL	510
1968	IH-45 over Trinity R.	Dallas, TX	480
1978	San Joaquin R.	Antioch, CA	460
1977	Thomas Johnson Mem.	Solomons, MD	451
1967	Mississippi R.	La Crosse, WI	450
1975	I-129	Missouri R., IA–NE	450
1979	Lewis	St. Louis, MO	450
1992	Cuba Landing Bridge	Tennessee R., TN	450
1966	I-480	Missouri R., IA–NE	425
1972	Whiskey Bay Pilot	Ramah, LA	425
1972	I-80	Missouri R., IA–NE	425
1972	I-635, Kansas City	Missouri R., KS–MO	425
1983	US-36	Missouri R., KS–MO	425
1987	I-435	Missouri R., KS–MO	425
1978	I-24	Cumberland R., KY	420
1993	Bob Michel Bridge	Peoria, IL	360
1999	SR 53, Clear Fork River	Fentress/Morgan Co., TN	350

Cable-Stayed

Year	Bridge	Location	Main span (ft.)
1986	Annacis (Alex Fraser)	Vancouver, BC	1,526
1993	Quetzalapa Bridge	Quetzalapa, Mexico	1,391
1988	Dames Point	Jacksonville, FL	1,300
1995	Fred Hartlan Bridge, Houston Ship Channel	Baytown,TX	1,250
1983	Hale Boggs Memorial	Luling, LA	1,222
1987	Sunshine Skyway	Tampa Bay, FL	1,200
1988	Tampico/Panuco R.	Mexico	1,181
1988	ALRT Fraser River Bridge	Vancouver, BC	1,115
1990	Talmadge Mem.	Savannah, GA	1,100
1993	Mezcala	Mex. City/Acapulco Hwy.	1,024
1978	Pasco-Kennewick	Columbia R., WA	981
1984	Coatzacoalcos R.	Mexico	919
1985	E. Huntington	E. Huntington, WV	900
1987	Bayview Bridge	Quincy, IL	900
1970	Burton Bridge	New Brunswick, Canada	850
1990	Weirton-Steubenville	WV–OH	820
1969	Papineau-Leblanc	Montreal, Que.	790
1991	Cochrane	Mobile, AL	780
1994	Clark Bridge	Alton, IL	756
1995	Chesapeake & Delaware Canal Bridge	Dover-Wilmington, DE	750
2002	Leonard Zakim	Bunker Hill, Boston, MA	745
1966	Longs Creek	New Brunswick, Canada	713
1967	Hawkshaw	New Brunswick, Canada	713
1993	Quetzalapa Bridge	Quetzalapa, Mexico	699
1993	Burlington Bridge	Burlington, IA	660
1991	Vetran's Memorial Br., Neches R.	Port Arthur-Orange,TX	640
1989	James River Bridge	Richmond, VA	630

I-Beam Girder

Year	Bridge	Location	Main span (ft.)
1980	Interstate 20	Shreveport, LA	438
200?	Moore Haven Bridge	Lake Okeechobee, FL	320
1988	Route 18	Weston's Mill Pond, NJ	276

Steel Arch

Year	Bridge	Location	Main span (ft.)
1977	New River Gorge	Fayetteville, WV	1,700
1931	Bayonne (Kill Van Kull)	Bayonne, NJ	1,675
1973	Fremont	Portland, OR	1,255
1964	Port Mann	Vancouver, BC	1,200
1967	Lavioleete	Three Rivers, Canada	1,100
1967	Trois-Rivieres	St. Lawrence R., Que.	1,100
1992	Roosevelt Lake	Roosevelt Lake, AZ	1,080
1959	Glen Canyon	Page, AZ	1,028
1962	Lewiston-Queenston	Niagara R., Ont.	1,000
1976	Perrine	Twin Falls, ID	993
1941	Rainbow Bridge	Niagara Falls, NY	984
1917	*Hell Gate	East R., N.Y	977
1977	Moundsville	Ohio R., WV	912
1992	I-255, Miss. R.	St. Louis, MO	909
1972	I-40, Miss. R.[9]	AR–TN	900
1936	Henry Hudson	Harlem R., NY	840
1967	Lincoln Trail Bridge	Ohio R., IN–KY	825
1978	I-57, Miss. R.	Cairo , IL	821
1961	Sherman-Minton Bridge, I-64	IN	800
1980	I-65, Mobile R.	Mobile, AL	800
1930	West End	Pittsburgh, PA	780
1978	I-470 Bridge, Ohio R.	Wheeling, WV	780
1996	Navajo Bridge	Glen Canyon, AZ	726
1917	Cuyohoga River	Cleveland, OH	591

Concrete Arch

Year	Bridge	Location	Main span (ft.)
1995	Natchez Trace Pkwy.	Franklin, TN	582
1993	Lake Street Bridge	St. Paul, MN	556
1971	Selah Creek (twin)	Selah, WA	549
1968	Cowlitz R.	Mossyrock, WA	520
1931	Westinghouse	Pittsburgh, PA	460
1923	Cappelen	Minneapolis, MN	435
2000	Crooked River Gorge	Madras, OR	410
1930	Jack's Run	Pittsburgh, PA	400
1931	Rogue River	Gold Beach, OR	230

Segmental Concrete

Year	Bridge	Location	Main span (ft.)
1997	Confederation Bridge	Prince Edward Isl., NB	820
1978	Shubenacadie River	S. Maitland, Nova Scotia	790
1982	Jesse H, Jones Memorial	Houston, TX	750
1992	Narragansett Bay Crossing	Jamestown, RI	674
2002	SR-895, James R. & I-95	Richmond, VA	672
1986	WB I-82 (Columbia R.)	Umatilla, OR	660
1976	Stanislaus River	Parrets Ferry. CA	640
1992	Jamestown-Verrazano	Jamestown, RI	636
1981	Gastineau Channel Br.	Juneau, AK	620
1991	Veterans Memorial Centennial Bridge	Coeur d'Alene, ID	520
2001	Smart Highway	Blacksburg, VA	472
1974	Pine Valley Creek	Pine Valley, CA	450
1988	Zilwaukee Bridge (twin)	Zilwaukee, MI	392
1985	Red River Bridge	Boyce, LA	370

Twin Concrete Trestle[10]

Year	Bridge	Location	Main span (ft.)
1979	I-55/I-10	Manchac, LA	181,157
1969	L. Pontchartrain Cswy.	Mandeville, LA	126,720
1972	Atchafalaya Flwy.	Baton Rouge, LA	93,984
1963	L. Pontchartrain	Slidell, LA	28,547
1983	*Interstate 310	Kenner, LA	25,925

Concrete Slab Dam[10]

Year	Bridge	Location	Main span (ft.)
1927	Conowingo Dam	MD	4,611
1952	SR-4, Roanoke R.	Mecklenburg Co., VA	2,785
1936	Hoover Dam	Lake Mead, NV	1,324

Miscellaneous Bridges

Year	Bridge	Type	Location	Main span (ft.)
1962	International	Arch Truss	Sault Ste. Marie, MI	430
1997	Second Blue Water	Continuous Tied Arch	Pt. Huron, MI	922
1982	SR 193	Seg. Box Girder	Dauphin Is., AL	400
1958	Castleton	Through Truss	Hudson R., NY	598
1939	US 43, Tenn. R.	Through Truss	Florence, AL	420
1958	SR 117, Tenn. R.	Through Truss	Stevenson, AL	500
1936	Yaquina Bay	Steel Braced and Concrete Tied Arches	Newport, OR	600
1958	Tomibigbee R.	Steel Girder	Choctow Co., AL	400
1916	C&O RR	Steel Girder	Portsmouth, OH	775
1987	Powder Point[10]	Tropical Hardwood	Duxbury, MA	2,200
2002	Croatan Sound[10]	Continuous Postension Girder	Manteo, NC	5.2 mi

Drawbridges

Vertical Lift

Year	Bridge	Location	Main span (ft.)
1959	*Arthur Kill	NY–NJ	558
1965	Pennsylvania Railroad	Kirkwood-Mt. Pleas., DE	548
1935	*Cape Cod Canal	Cape Cod, MA	544
1961	*Delair	Delaware R., NJ	542
1931	Burlington-Bristol	Delaware R., NJ–PA	540
1937	Marine Parkway	Jamaica Bay, NY	540
1908	*Willamette R.	Portland, OR	521
1968	Second Narrows	Vancouver, B.C.	493
1912	*A-S-B Fratt	Kansas City, MO	428
1945	*Harry S Truman	Kansas City, MO	427
1955	Roosevelt Island	East R., NY	418
1980	US-17, James R.	Isle of Wight, Co., VA	415
1932	*M-K-T R.R.	Missouri R., MO	414
1969	Cape Fear Mem.	Wilmington, NC	408
1930	Aerial	Duluth, MN	386
1962	Burlington	Ontario, Can.	370
1941	Main Street	Jacksonville, FL	365
1967	SR-156, James R.	Prince George Co., VA	364
1950	Red R.	Moncla, LA	360
1957	Industrial Canal	New Orleans, LA	360
1936	Triborough	Harlem R., NY	344
1939	U.S. 1&9, Passaic R.	Newark, NJ	333
1930	*Martinez	Martinez, CA	328
1960	St. Andrews Bay	Panama City, FL	327
1929	*Penn-Lehigh	Newark Bay, PA	322
1987	Industrial Canal	New Orleans, LA	320
1920	*Chattanooga	Tennessee R., TN	310
1910	Willamette R. Hawthorne	Portland, OR	244

Steel Suspension

Year	Bridge	Location	Main span (ft.)
1931	Maumee R.	Toledo, OH	785

Bascule

Year	Bridge	Location	Main span (ft.)
1917	SR-8, Tennessee R.	Chattanooga, TN	306
2003	*SW 2nd Avenue Br	Miami, FL	302
1956	Duwamish R.	Seattle, WA	300
1955	Chehalis R.	Aberdeen, WA	288
1968	Elizabeth R.	Chesapeake, VA	280
1913	Broadway	Portland, OR	278
1936	Siuslaw River	Florence, OR	154

Swing Bridges

Year	Bridge	Location	Main span (ft.)
1927	Fort Madison[4]	Mississippi R., IA	545
1991	SW. Spokane St.	Seattle, WA	480
1930	Rigolets Pass	New Orleans, LA	400
1950	Douglass Memorial	Washington, DC	386
1945	Lord Delaware	Mattaponi R., VA	252

Swing Span

Year	Bridge	Location	Main span (ft.)
1952/1996	US-17 York R., (Coleman)	Yorktown, VA	500
1897	*Duluth	St. Louis Bay, MN	486
1899	*C.M.&N.R.R.	Chicago, IL	474
1913	Rt. 82, Conn-R.	E. Haddam, CT	465
1914	*Coos Bay RR Xing	OR	458
1936	Umpqua River	Reedsport, OR	430

Floating Pontoon

Year	Bridge	Location	Main span (ft.)
1963	Evergreen Pt.	Seattle, WA	7,578
1961	Hood Canal	Pt. Gamble, WA	6,521
1993	Lacey V. Murrow[11]	Seattle, WA	6,620
1989	Third Lake Washington	Seattle, WA	5,811

(1) Swing span bridge with 2 spans of 2,310 ft. each. (2) A second bridge in parallel was completed in 1970. (3) The Richmond Bridge has twin spans 1,070 ft. each. (4) Railroad and vehicular bridge. (5) Two spans each 825 ft. (6) Two spans each 707 ft. (7) Two spans each 700 ft. (8) Two spans each 660 ft. (9) Two spans each 900 ft. (10) Length listed is total length of bridge. (11) Replaces the original Lacey V. Murrow bridge, which opened in 1940 and sank in 1990.

Oldest U.S. Bridges in Continuous Use

Built in 1697, the stone-arch Frankford Ave. Bridge crosses Pennypack Creek in Philadelphia, PA. A 3-span bridge with a total length of 75 ft., it was constructed as part of the King's Road, which eventually connected Philadelphia to New York.

The oldest covered bridge, completed in 1827, is the double-span, 278-ft. Haverhill Bath Bridge, which spans the Ammonoosuc River, between the towns of Bath and Haverhill, NH.

Some Notable International Bridges

Span of bridge is the distance between its supports. Asterisk (*) designates under construction.

Suspension

Year	Bridge	Location	Main span (ft.)
1998	Akashi Kaikyo	Japan	6,570
2003	*Izmit Bay	Turkey	5,538
1998	Storebælt (East Bridge)	Denmark	5,328
1981	Humber	England	4,626
1999	Jiangyin Yangtze	China	4,544
1997	Tsing Ma[1]	China	4,518
1997	Hoga Kusten	Sweden	3,970
1988	Minami Bisan-Seto	Japan	3,609
1988	Bosphorus II	Turkey	3,576
1973	Bosphorus I	Turkey	3,524
1999	Kurushima III	Japan	3,379
1999	Kurushima II	Japan	3,346
1966	Tagus River[2]	Portugal	3,323
1964	Forth Road	Scotland	3,300
1988	Kita Bisan-Seto	Japan	3,248
1966	Severn	England	3,241
1988	Shimotsui Strait	Japan	3,084

Steel Arch

Year	Bridge	Location	Main span (ft.)
1932	Sydney Harbour	Australia	1,650
1967	Zdakov	Czech Republic	1,244
1962	Thatcher	Panama Canal Zone	1,128
1961	Runcorn-Widnes	England	1,082
1935	Birchenough	Zimbabwe	1,080

Concrete Arch

Year	Bridge	Location	Main span (ft.)
1980	Krk I	Croatia	1,280
1964	Gladesville	Australia	1,000
1964	Amizade	Brazil	951
1963	Arrabida	Portugal	886
1943	Sando	Sweden	866

Cantilever

Year	Bridge	Location	Main span (ft.)
1890	Forth[3] (rail)	Scotland	1,710
1974	Nanko	Japan	1,673

Steel Plate and Box Girder

Year	Bridge	Location	Main span (ft.)
1974	President Costa e Silva	Brazil	984
1956	Sava I	Serbia & Montenegro	856
1966	Zoobrüke	Germany	850

Cable-Stayed

Year	Bridge	Location	Main span (ft.)
1999	Tatara	Japan	2,920
1995	Pont de Normandie	France	2,808
1996	Quingzhou Minjang	China	1,985
1993	Yangpu	China	1,975
1997	Xupu	China	1,936
1998	Meiko Chuo	Japan	1,936
1991	Skarnsundet	Norway	1,739
1999	Queshi	China	1,700
1995	Tsurumi Tsubasa	Japan	1,673
2000	Oresund	Denmark/Sweden	1,614
1991	Ikuchi	Japan	1,608
1994	Higashi Kobe	Japan	1,591
1998	Zhanjiang	China	1,575
1997	Ting Kau	China	1,558
1999	Seo Hae Grand	South Korea	1,542
1989	Yokohama Bay	Japan	1,509
1993	Second Hooghly River	India	1,499
1995	Second Severn Crossing	England/Wales	1,496

(1) Double-decked road and rail bridge. (2) Railroad and highway bridge. (3) Two spans of 1,710 ft. each.

Underwater Vehicular Tunnels in North America

(more than 5,000 ft. in length; year in parentheses is year of completion)

Name	Location	Waterway	Feet
Brooklyn-Battery (1950) (twin)	New York, NY	East River	9,117
Holland Tunnel (1927) (twin)	New York, NY	Hudson River	8,557
Ted Williams Tunnel (1995)	Boston, MA	Boston Harbor	8,448
Lincoln Tunnel (1937, 1945, 1957) (3 tubes)	New York, NY	Hudson River	8,216
Thimble Shoal Channel (1964)	Northampton Co., VA	Chesapeake Bay	8,187
Chesapeake Channel (1964)	Northampton Co., VA	Chesapeake Bay	7,941
Fort McHenry Tunnel (1985) (twin)	Baltimore, MD	Baltimore Harbor	7,920
Hampton Roads (1957) (twin)	Hampton, VA	Hampton Roads	7,479
Baltimore Harbor Tunnel (1957) (twin)	Baltimore, MD	Patapsco River	7,392
Queens Midtown (1940) (twin)	New York, NY	East River	6,414
Sumner Tunnel (1934)	Boston, MA	Boston Harbor	5,653
Louis-Hippolyte Lafontaine Tunnel	Montreal, Que.	St. Lawrence River	5,280
Detroit-Windsor (1930)	Detroit, MI	Detroit River	5,160
Callahan Tunnel (1961)	Boston, MA	Boston Harbor	5,070

Land Vehicular Tunnels in the U.S.

Source: Federal Highway Administration

(more than 3,000 ft. in length)

Name	Location	Feet
Anton Anderson Mem. Tunnel[1]	Whittier, AK	13,300
E. Johnson Memorial	I-70, CO	8,959
Eisenhower Memorial	I-70, CO	8,941
Allegheny (twin)	PA Turnpike	6,072
Liberty Tubes	Pittsburgh, PA	5,920
Zion Natl. Park	Rte. 9, UT	5,766
East River Mt.	Mercer Co., WV/ Bland Co., VA	5,654
East River Mt. (twin)	VA–WV	5,412
Tuscarora (twin)	PA Turnpike	5,400
Tetsuo Harano (twin)	H-3, HI	5,165
Kittatinny (twin)	PA Turnpike	4,660
Cumberland Gap (twin)	KY–TN	4,600
Blue Mountain (twin)	PA Turnpike	4,435
Lehigh (twin)	PA Turnpike	4,379
Wawona	Yosemite Natl. Pk., CA	4,233
Big Walker Mt. (twin)	Bland Co., VA	4,229
Squirrel Hill	Pittsburgh, PA	4,225
Hanging Lake (twin)	Glenwood Canyon, CO	4,000
Caldecott (3 tubes)	Oakland, CA	3,616
Fort Pitt (twin)	Pittsburgh, PA	3,560
Mount Baker Ridge	Seattle, WA	3,456
Devil's Side Tunnel	U.S. 101 CA	3,400
Dingess Tunnel	Mingo Co., WV	3,400
Mall Tunnel	Dist. of Columbia	3,400
Cody No. 1	U.S. 14, 16, 20, WY	3,202

(1) Tunnel is used for vehicular and railroad traffic.

World's Longest Railway Tunnels

Source: Railway Directory & Year Book

Tunnel	Date	Miles	Operating railway	Country
Seikan	1985	33.50	Japanese Railway	Japan
English Channel Tunnel	1994	31.04	Eurotunnel	United Kingdom-France
Dai-shimizu	1979	14.00	Japanese Railway	Japan
Simplon No. 1 and 2	1906, 1922	12.00	Swiss Fed. & Italian St.	Switzerland-Italy
Kanmon	1975	12.00	Japanese Railway	Japan
Apennine	1934	11.00	Italian State	Italy
Rokko	1972	10.00	Japanese Railway	Japan
Mt. MacDonald	1989	9.10	Canadian Pacific	Canada
Gotthard	1882	9.00	Swiss Federal	Switzerland
Lotschberg	1913	9.00	Bern-Lotschberg-Simplon	Switzerland
Hokuriku	1962	9.00	Japanese Railway	Japan
Mont Cenis (Frejus)	1871	8.00	Italian State	France-Italy
Cascade	1929	8.00	Burlington Northern	United States
Shin-Shimizu	1961	8.00	Japanese Railway	Japan
Flathead	1970	8.00	Burlington Northern	United States
Aki	1975	8.00	Japanese Railway	Japan

World's Largest-Capacity Hydro Plants

Source: U.S. Committee on Large Dams of the Intl. Commission on Large Dams

Rank[1]	Name	Country	Rated capacity now (MW)	Rated capacity planned (MW)
1.	Turukhansk (Lower Tungu-ska)*	Russia	—	20,000
2.	Three Gorges Dam*	China	—	18,200
3.	Itaipu	Brazil/Paraguay	7,400	13,320
4.	Grand Coulee	U.S.	6,495	10,830
5.	Guri (Raúl Leoni)	Venezuela	10,300	10,300
6.	Tucuruí	Brazil	2,640	7,260
7.	Sayano-Shushensk*	Russia	—	6,400
8.	Corpus Posadas	Argentina /Paraguay	4,700	6,000
8.	Krasnoyarsk	Russia	6,000	6,000
10.	La Grande 2	Canada	5,328	5,328
11.	Churchill Falls	Canada	5,225	5,225
12.	Xingo	Brazil	3,012	5,020
13.	Tarbela	Pakistan	1,750	4,678
14.	Bratsk	Russia	4,500	4,500
14.	Ust-Ilim	Russia	3,675	4,500
16.	Cabora Bassa	Mozambique	2,425	4,150
17.	Boguchany*	Russia	—	4,000
18.	Oak Creek	U.S.	3,600	3,600
19.	Paulo Afonso I	Brazil	1,524	3,409
20.	Pati*	Argentina	—	3,300
21.	Ilha Solteira	Brazil	3,200	3,200
22.	Chapetón*	Argentina	—	3,000
23.	Gezhouba	China	2,715	2,715

(1) Ranked by rated capacity planned. *Planned or under construction.

World's Largest-Capacity Reservoirs

Source: U.S. Committee on Large Dams of the Intl. Commission on Large Dams, 2002

Rank order	Name	Country	Capacity cubic meters × 1,000,000
1.	Kariba	Zimbabwe/Zambia	180,600
2.	Bratsk	Russia	169,000
3.	High Aswan	Egypt	162,000
4.	Akosombo	Ghana	147,960
5.	Daniel Johnson	Canada	141,851
6.	Xinfeng	China	138,960
7.	Guri	Venezuela	135,000
8.	W A C Bennett	Canada	74,300
9.	Krasnoyarsk	Russia	73,300
10.	Zeya	Russia	68,400
11.	La Grande 2	Canada	61,715
12.	La Grande 3	Canada	60,020
13.	Ust-Ilim	Russia	59,300
14.	Kuibyshev	Russia	58,000
15.	Serra da Mesa	Brazil	54,400

Major Dams of the World

Source: U.S. Committee on Large Dams of the Intl. Commission on Large Dams

World's Highest Dams

Rank order	Name	Country	Height above lowest formation (m)
1.	Nurek	Tajikistan	300
2.	Grand Dixence	Switzerland	285
3.	Inguri	Georgia	272
4.	Vajont	Italy	262
5.	Manuel M. Torres	Mexico	261
6.	Alvaro Obregon	Mexico	260
7.	Mauvoisin	Switzerland	250
8.	Mica	Canada	243
9.	Alberto Lleras C	Colombia	243
10.	Sayano-Shushensk	Russia	242
11.	Ertan	China	240
12.	La Esmeralda	Colombia	237
13.	Oroville	U.S.	235
14.	El Cajón	Honduras	234
15.	Chirkey	Russia	233
16.	Bhakra	India	226
17.	Luzzone	Switzerland	225
18.	Hoover	U.S.	223
19.	Contra	Switzerland	220
20.	Mratinje	Serbia & Montenegro	220

World's Largest-Volume Embankment Dams

Rank order	Name	Country	Volume cubic meters × 1000
1.	Tarbela	Pakistan	148,500
2.	Fort Peck	U.S.	96,050
3.	Tucurui	Brazil	85,200
4.	Ataturk*	Turkey	85,000
5.	Yacireta*	Argentina	81,000
6.	Rogun*	Tajikistan	75,500
7.	Oahe	U.S.	70,339
8.	Guri	Venezuela	70,000
9.	Parambikulam	India	69,165
10.	High Island West	China	67,000
11.	Gardiner	Canada	65,000
12.	Afsluitdijk	Netherlands	63,400
13.	Mangla	Pakistan	63,379
14.	Oroville	U.S.	59,635
15.	San Luis	U.S.	59,559
16.	Nurek	Tajikistan	58,000
17.	Tanda	Pakistan	57,250
18.	Garrison	U.S.	50,843
19.	Cochiti	U.S.	50,228
20.	Oosterschelde	Netherlands	50,000

*Under construction.

Major U.S. Dams and Reservoirs

Source: Committee on Register of Dams, Corps of Engineers, U.S. Army, Sept. 2002

Highest U.S. Dams

Rank Order	Dam name	River	State	Type	Height Feet	Height Meters	Year completed
1.	Oroville	Feather	California	E	754	230	1968
2.	Hoover	Colorado	Nevada-Arizona	A	725	221	1936
3.	Dworshak	N. Fork Clearwater	Idaho	G	718	219	1973
4.	Glen Canyon	Colorado	Arizona	A	708	216	1966
5.	New Bullards Bar	North Yuba	California	A	636	194	1970
6.	Seven Oaks	Santa Ana	California	E	632	193	1999
7.	New Melones	Stanislaus	California	R	626	191	1979
8.	Swift	Lewis	Washington	E	610	186	1958
9.	Mossyrock	Cowlitz	Washington	A	607	185	1968
10.	Shasta	Sacramento	California	G	600	183	1945

E = Embankment, Earthfill; R = Embankment, Rockfill; G = Gravity; A = Arch.

Largest U.S. Embankment Dams

Rank Order	Dam name	River	State	Type	Volume Cubic yards × 1000	Volume Cubic meters × 1000	Year completed
1.	Fort Peck	Missouri	Montana	E	125,624	96,050	1937
2.	Oahe	Missouri	South Dakota	E	91,996	70,339	1958
3.	Oroville	Feather	California	E	77,997	59,635	1968
4.	San Luis	San Luis Creek	California	E	77,897	59,559	1967
5.	Garrison	Missouri	North Dakota	E	66,498	50,843	1953
6.	Cochiti	Rio Grande	New Mexico	E	65,693	50,228	1975
7.	Fort Randall	Missouri	South Dakota	E	49,962	38,200	1952
8.	Castaic	Castaic Creek	California	E	43,998	33,640	1973
9.	Ludington P/S	Lake Michigan	Michigan	E	37,699	28,824	1973
10.	Kingsley	N. Platte	Nebraska	E	31,999	24,466	1941

E = Earthfill.

Largest U.S. Reservoirs

Rank Order	Dam name, location	Reservoir name	Location	Reservoir capacity Acre-Feet	Reservoir capacity Cubic meters × 1000	Year completed
1.	Hoover, NV/AZ	Lake Mead	AZ/NV	28,255,000	34,850,000	1936
2.	Glen Canyon, AZ	Lake Powell	AZ/UT	27,000,000	33,300,000	1966
3.	Oahe, SD	Lake Oahe	ND/SD	19,300,000	27,430,000	1958
4.	Garrison, ND	Lake Sakakawea	ND	18,500,000	27,920,000	1953
5.	Fort Peck, MT	Fort Peck Lake	MT	15,400,000	22,120,000	1937
6.	Grand Coulee, WA	F. D. Roosevelt Lake	WA	9,562,000	11,790,000	1942
7.	Libby, MT	Lake Koocanusa	MT/B.C.	5,809,000	7,170,000	1973
8.	Shasta, CA	Lake Shasta	CA	4,552,000	5,610,000	1945
9.	Toledo Bend, LA	Toledo Bend Lake	LA/TX	4,477,000	5,520,000	1968
10.	Fort Randall, SD	Lake Francis Case	SD	3,800,000	5,700,000	1952

1 acre-foot = 1 acre of water, 1 foot deep

LANGUAGE

New Words in English

The following words and definitions were provided by Merriam-Webster Inc., publishers of *Merriam-Webster's Collegiate Dictionary, Tenth Edition*. The words or meanings are among those that the Merriam-Webster editors decided had achieved enough currency in English to be added in recent copyright revisions of the dictionary. (See also the glossary in the Science and Technology and Computers and the Internet chapters for some other words.)

anime a style of animation originating in Japan that is characterized by stark colorful graphics depicting vibrant characters in action-filled plots often with fantastic or futuristic themes
biomimetics the study of the formation, structure, or function of biologically produced substances and materials and biological mechanisms and processes especially for the purpose of synthesizing similar products by artificial mechanisms which mimic natural ones
blunt a cigar that has been hollowed out and filled with marijuana
booty, also **bootie** *slang* buttocks
chipotle a smoked and usually dried jalapeño
cred credibility: *specifically:* the quality of being deserving of acceptance as a member of a particular group or class
day trader a speculator who seeks profit from the intraday fluctuation in the price of a security or commodity by completing double trades of buying and selling or selling and covering during a single session of the market
dollarization the adoption of the U.S. dollar as a country's official national currency
duh 1: used to express actual or feigned ignorance or stupidity; **2** used derisively to indicate that something just stated is all too obvious or self-evident
e-book a book composed in or converted to digital format for display on a computer screen or handheld device
electronica dance music featuring extensive use of synthesizers, electronic percussion, and samples of recorded music or sound
e-tail retail business conducted on-line via the World Wide Web
eye candy something superficially attractive to look at
fashionista a designer, promoter, or follower of the latest fashions
flatline 1a: to register on an electronic monitor as having no brain waves or heartbeat; **b:** die; **2a:** to be in a state of no progress or advancement; **b:** to come to an end
gearhead a person who engages in technical or technological pursuits
hottie a physically attractive person
netiquette etiquette governing communication on the Internet
noogie the act of rubbing one's knuckles on a person's head so as to produce a mildly painful sensation
nutraceutical a foodstuff (as a fortified food or dietary supplement) that provides health benefits
road rage a motorist's uncontrolled anger that is usually incited by an irritating act of another motorist and is expressed in aggressive or violent behavior
sick building syndrome a set of symptoms (as headache, fatigue, and eye irritation) typically affecting workers in modern airtight office buildings that is believed to be caused by indoor pollutants (as formaldehyde fumes or microorganisms)
sophomore (adjective) being the second in a series
stent a short narrow metal or plastic tube that is inserted into the lumen of an anatomical vessel (as an artery or a bile duct) especially to keep a formerly blocked passageway open
toolbar a strip of icons on a computer display providing quick access to certain functions
tree hugger an environmentalist; *especially:* an advocate for the preservation of woodlands
urban legend an often lurid story or anecdote that is based on hearsay and widely circulated as true
webcam a camera used in transmitting live images over the World Wide Web

National Spelling Bee

The Scripps Howard National Spelling Bee, conducted by Scripps Howard Newspapers and other leading newspapers since 1939, was instituted by the Louisville (KY) *Courier-Journal* in 1925. Children under 16 years old and not beyond 8th grade are eligible to compete for cash prizes at the finals, held annually in Washington, DC. The 2002 winners were: 1st place, Pratyush Buddiga, Colorado Springs, CO; 2nd place, Steven Nalley, Starkville, MS.

Here are the last words given, and spelled correctly, in each of the years 1980-2002 at the national spelling bee.

1980	elucubrate	1985	milieu	1990	fibranne	1995	xanthosis	1999	logorrhea
1981	sarcophagus	1986	odontalgia	1991	antipyretic	1996	vivisepulture	2000	demarche
1982	psoriasis	1987	staphylococci	1992	lyceum	1997	euonym	2001	succedaneum
1983	purim	1988	elegiacal	1993	kamikaze	1998	chiaroscurist	2002	prospicience
1984	luge	1989	spoliator	1994	antediluvian				

IT'S A FACT: The playwright George Bernard Shaw was an ardent advocate of spelling reform. To show how variable and unreasonable English spelling can be, he cited the non-word *ghoti* as an alternative spelling for *fish* (it sounds the same as "fish" if you take the "gh" sound in "rough," the "o" sound in "women," and the "ti" sound in "nation").

Foreign Words and Phrases

(F=French; Ger=German; Gk=Greek; I=Italian; L=Latin; S=Spanish; Y=Yiddish)

Achtung (Ger; AHKH-toong): attention!; look out!
ad absurdum (L; ad ahb-SUR-dum): to the point of absurdity
ad hoc (L; ad HOK): for the end or purpose at hand
aloha (Hawaiian; ah-LOH-hah): love to you: greetings; farewell
antebellum (L; AHN-teh-BEL-lum): pre-war
au contraire (F; oh kon-TRAIR): on the contrary
bête noire (F; BET NWAHR): a thing or person viewed with particular dislike or fear
bona fide (L; BOH nuh-fid): genuine; in good faith
bourgeois (F; boo-ZHWAH): middle-class; conventional; materialistic
carte blanche (F; kahrt BLANSH): full discretionary power
cause célèbre (F; kawz suh-LEB-ruh): a notorious incident
chutzpah (Y; HUT-spuh): nerve bordering on arrogance
cognoscenti (I; koh-nyoh-SHEN-tee): experts; connoissuers
coup de grâce (F; kooh duh GRAHS): the final blow
crème de la crème (F; KREM duh luh KREM): best of the best
cum laude/magna cum laude/summa cum laude (L; kuhm LOUD-ay; MAGN-a ...; SOO-ma ...): with praise or honor/with great praise or honor/with the highest praise or honor
de facto (L; day FAK-toh): in fact, if not by law
de jure (L; dee JOOR-ee, day YOOR-ay): in accordance with right or law; officially
de rigueur (F; duh ree-GUR): necessary according to convention or etiquette
détente (F; day-TAHNT): an easing of strained relations
double entendre (F; DOO-blahn-TAHN-druh): expression with with double meaning, one meaning of which is often risqué
éminence grise (F; ay-meh-NAHN-suh GREEZ): one who wields power behind the scenes
enfant terrible (F; ahn-FAHN te-REE-bluh): one who is noteworthy for embarrassing or unconventional behavior
en route (F; ahn ROOT): on or along the way
esprit de corps (F; es-PREE duh KAWR): group spirit; feeling of camaraderie
eureka (Gk; yoor-EE-kuh): I have found it!; hurrah!
ex post facto (L; eks pohst FAK-toh): retroactive(ly)
fait accompli (F; fayt uh-kom-PLEE): an accomplished fact
Gesundheit (Ger; guh-ZOONT-hyt): health; Bless you!
habeas corpus (L; HAY-bee-ahs KOR-pus): an order for an accused person to be brought to court
hoi polloi (Gk; hoy puh-LOY): the masses
in loco parentis (L; in LOH-koh puh-REN-tis): in place of parent
in omnibus (L; in OHM-nee-bus): in all things; in all ways
insouciance (F; en-SOO-see-ahnce): indifference; unconcern
je ne sais quoi (F; zhuh nuh say KWAH): I don't know what; the little something that eludes description
joie de vivre (F; zhwah duh VEEV-ruh): zest for life
kudos (G; KOO-dohs): praise, honors, approval
mano a mano (S; MAH-noh ah MAH-noh): hand to hand; in direct combat
mea culpa (L; MAY-uh CUL-puh): through my fault

modus operandi (L; MOH-duhs op-uh-RAN-dee): method of operation
noblesse oblige (F; noh-BLES oh-BLEEZH): the obligation of nobility to help the less fortunate
non compos mentis (L; non KOM-puhs MEN-tis): not of sound mind
nouveau riche (F; noo-voh REESH): a person newly rich, perhaps one who spends money conspicuously
par excellence (F; par ek-seh-LANS): best of all; incomparable.
persona non grata (L; per-SOH-nah non GRAH-tah): unwelcome person
prima donna (I; pree-muh DAH-nuh): a principal female opera singer; temperamental person
pro bono (L; proh BOH-noh): (legal work) donated for the public good
qua (L; kwah): in the capacity or character of
qué será será (S; keh sair-AH sair-AH): what will be will be
quid pro quo (L; kwid proh KWOH): something given or received for something else
raison d'être (F; RAY-zohnn DET-ruh): reason for being
sans souci (F; SAHNN sooh-SEE): without worry

WORLD ALMANAC QUICK QUIZ

Which of the following names was the most common for girls born in the U.S. in 2001?
(a) Emily (b) Michelle
(c) Jennifer (d) Lisa

For the answer look in this chapter, or see page 1008.

savoir faire (F; sav-wahr-FAIR): dexterity in social affairs
schlemiel (Y; shleh-MEEL): an unlucky, bungling person
semper fidelis (L; SEM-puhr fee-DAY-lis): always faithful
status quo (L; STAH-tus QWOH): the existing order of things
terra firma (L; TER-uh FUR-muh): solid ground
tour de force (F; TOOR duh FAWRS): feat accomplished through great skill
verbatim (L; ver-BAY-tuhm): word for word
vis-à-vis (F; vee-zuh-VEE): compared with; with regard to
zeitgeist (Ger; ZITE-gyste): the general intellectual, moral, and cultural climate of an era

Some Common Abbreviations and Acronyms

Acronyms are pronounceable words formed from first letters (or syllables) of other words. Some abbreviations below (e.g., AIDS, NATO) are thus acronyms. Some acronyms are words coined as abbreviations and written in lower case (e.g., "radar," "yuppie"). Acronyms do not have periods; usage for other abbreviations varies, but periods have become less common. Capitalization usage may vary from what is shown here. Italicized words preceding parenthetical definitions below are Latin unless otherwise noted. See also other chapters, including Computers and Internet; Weights and Measures.

AA=Alcoholics Anonymous
AAA=American Automobile Association
AC=alternating current
AD=*anno Domini* (in the year of the Lord)
AFL-CIO=American Federation of Labor and Congress of Industrial Organizations
AIDS=acquired immune deficiency syndrome
AM=*ante meridiem* (before noon)
AMA=American Medical Association
anon=anonymous
APO=army post office
ASAP=as soon as possible
ASCAP=American Society of Composers, Authors, and Publishers
ASPCA=American Society for Prevention of Cruelty to Animals
ATM=automated teller machine
AWOL=absent without leave
BA=Bachelor of Arts
bbl=barrel(s)
BC=before Christ
BCE=before Common Era
bpd=barrels per day
BS=Bachelor of Science
Btu=British thermal unit(s)
bu=bushel(s)
C= Celsius, centigrade
c=*circa* (about), copyright
CE=Common Era
CEO=chief executive officer
CFO=chief financial officer
cm=centimeter(s)
COD=cash (or collect) on delivery
Col.=Colonel
COLA=cost of living allowance
CPA=certified public accountant
Cpl.=Corporal
CPR=cardiopulmonary resuscitation
DA=district attorney
DAR=Daughters of the American Revolution
DC=direct current
DD=Doctor of Divinity
DDS=Doctor of Dental Science (or Surgery)
DNA=deoxyribonucleic acid
DNR=do not resuscitate
DOA=dead on arrival
DWI=driving while intoxicated
ed.=edited, edition, editor
e.g.=*exempli gratia* (for example)
EKG=electrocardiogram
EPA=Environmental Protection Agency
ESP=extrasensory perception
et al.=*et alii* (and others)
etc.=*et cetera* (and so forth)
EU=European Union
F=Fahrenheit
FBI=Federal Bureau of Investigation
FICA=Federal Insurance Contributions Act (Social Security)
FOB=free on board
FY=fiscal year
FYI=for your information
GB=gigabyte(s)
GDP=gross domestic product
GIGO=garbage in, garbage out
GNP=gross national product
GOP=Grand Old Party (Republican Party)
Hon.=the Honorable
HOV=high-occupancy vehicle
ht=height
HVAC=heating, ventilating, and air-conditioning
i.e.=*id est* (that is)
IMF=International Monetary Fund
IQ=intelligence quotient
IRA=individual retirement account; Irish Republican Army
IRS=Internal Revenue Service
ISBN=International Standard Book Number
JD=*Juris Doctor* (doctor of laws)
K=Kelvin
k=karat
KB=kilobyte(s); kg=kilogram(s); km=kilometer(s); kw=kilowatt(s)
kwh=kilowatt-hour(s)
l=liter(s)
lb=*libra* (pound or pounds)
Lieut. or Lt.=Lieutenant
LLB=*Legum Baccalaureus* (bachelor of laws)
m=meter(s)
MA=Master of Arts
MB=megabyte(s)
MD=*Medicinae Doctor* (doctor of medicine)
MFN=most favored nation
MIA=missing in action
ml=milliliter(s); mm=millimeter(s)
mph=miles per hour
MS=Master of Science
MSG=monosodium glutamate
Msgr.=Monsignor
MVP=most valuable player
NAACP=National Association for the Advancement of Colored People
NASA=National Aeronautics and Space Administration
NAFTA=North American Free Trade Agreement
NATO=North Atlantic Treaty Organization
NB=*nota bene* (note carefully)
NCAA=National Collegiate Athletic Association
NOW=National Organization for Women
op=*opus* (work)
OPEC=Organization of Petroleum Exporting Countries
p, pp=page(s)
PAC=political action committee
PC=personal computer
PhD=*Philosophiae Doctor* (doctor of philosophy)
PIN=Personal Identification Number
PM=*post meridiem* (afternoon)
PO=post office
POW=prisoner of war
PS=*post scriptum* (postscript)
pt=part(s), pint(s), point(s)
Pvt.=Private
q.v.=*quod vide* (which see)
radar=radio detecting and ranging
REM=rapid eye movement
Rev.=Reverend
RFD=rural free delivery
RIP=*requiescat in pace* (May he/she rest in peace)
RN=registered nurse
RNA=ribonucleic acid
ROTC=Reserve Officers' Training Corps
rpm=revolutions per minute
RR=railroad
RSVP=*répondez s'il vous plaît* (Fr.) (Please reply)
SASE=self-addressed stamped envelope
Sgt.=Sergeant
SIDS=sudden infant death syndrome
S.J.=Society of Jesus (Jesuits)
SRO=standing room only
St.=Saint, Street
TGIF=Thank God It's Friday
UFO=unidentified flying object
UHF=ultrahigh frequency
UNESCO=United Nations Educational, Social, and Cultural Organization
UNICEF=United Nations (International) Children's (Emergency) Fund
UPC=Universal Product Code
USS=United States ship
v (or vs)=*versus* (against)
VCR=videocassette recorder
VHF=very high frequency
VISTA=Volunteers in Service to America
W=watt(s)
wasp=white Anglo-Saxon Protestant
WHO=World Health Organization
yd=yard(s)
yuppie=young urban professional
ZIP=zone improvement plan (U.S. Postal Service)

Names of the Days

ENGLISH	RUSSIAN	HEBREW	FRENCH	ITALIAN	SPANISH	GERMAN	JAPANESE
Sunday	Voskresenye	Yom rishon	Dimanche	Domenica	Domingo	Sonntag	Nichiyo\bi
Monday	Ponedelnik	Yom sheni	Lundi	Lunedì	Lunes	Montag	Getsuyo\bi
Tuesday	Vtornik	Yom shlishi	Mardi	Martedì	Martes	Dienstag	Kayo\bi
Wednesday	Sreda	Yom ravii	Mercredi	Mercoledì	Miércoles	Mittwoch	Suiyo\bi
Thursday	Chetverg	Yom hamishi	Jeudi	Giovedì	Jueves	Donnerstag	Mokuyo\bi
Friday	Pyatnitsa	Yom shishi	Vendredi	Venerdì	Viernes	Freitag	Kin-yo\bi
Saturday	Subbota	Shabbat	Samedi	Sabato	Sábado	Samstag	Doyo\bi

Names for Animal Young

bunny: rabbit
calf: cattle, elephant, antelope, rhino, hippo, whale, others
cheeper: grouse, partridge, quail
chick, chicken: fowl
cockerel: rooster
codling, sprag: codfish
colt: horse (male)
cub: lion, bear, shark, fox, others
cygnet: swan
duckling: duck
eaglet: eagle
elver: eel
eyas: hawk, others
fawn: deer
filly: horse (female)
fingerling: fish generally
flapper: wild fowl
fledgling: birds generally
foal: horse, zebra, others
fry: fish generally
gosling: goose
heifer: cow
joey: kangaroo, others
kid: goat
kit: fox, beaver, rabbit, cat
kitten, kitty, catling: cats, other small mammals
lamb, lambkin, cosset, hog: sheep
leveret: hare
nestling: birds generally
owlet: owl
parr, smolt, grilse: salmon
piglet, shoat, farrow, suckling: pig
polliwog, tadpole: frog
poult: turkey
pullet: hen
pup: dog, seal, sea lion, fox
puss, pussy: cat
spike, blinker, tinker: mackerel
squab: pigeon
squeaker: pigeon, others
whelp: dog, tiger, beasts of prey
yearling: cattle, sheep, horse, others

Names for Animal Collectives

ants: colony
badgers: cete
bears: sleuth
bees: grist or swarm
birds: flight or volery
boars/swine: sounder
cats: clowder or clutter
cattle/sheep: drove
chicks: brood or clutch
clams/oysters: bevy
cranes: sedge or siege
crows: murder
ducks: brace
ducks/horses: team
elephants: herd
elks: gang
fish: school or shoal
foxes: skulk
foxes/greyhounds: leash
geese: gaggle or skein
geese/sheep: flock
gnats: cloud or horde
goats: tribe or trip
goldfinches: charm
gorillas: band
hares: down or husk
hawks: cast
horses: pair
hounds: cry or mute
hounds/wolves: pack
kangaroos: mob
kangaroos/monkeys: troop
kittens: kindle or kindle
larks: exaltation
leopards: leap
lions: pride
mules: span
nightingales: watch
oxen: yoke
partridge/quail: covey
peacocks: muster
pheasants: nest or nide
pigs: litter
plovers: congregation or wing
rhinoceri: crash
seals/whales: pod
swans/partridge: bevy
swine: drift
teals: spring
toads: knot
turtles: bale
vipers: nest
whales: gam

Top 10 First Names of Americans Born in 2001

Source: Social Security Administration; World Almanac research

Boys: Jacob, Michael, Matthew, Nicholas, Joshua, Christopher, Andrew, Joseph, Daniel, William

Girls: Emily, Hannah, Madison, Sarah, Brianna, Kaitlyn, Ashley, Alexis, Hailey, Samantha

Note: These rankings are for all spellings of each name that do not affect pronunciation, e.g., Jacob and Jakob, Ashley and Ashly, Elizabeth and Elisabeth. However, only the most popular spelling of each is shown.

Top 10 First Names of Americans by Decade of Birth

Source: Compiled by Dr. Cleveland Kent Evans, Bellevue University, Bellevue, NE; based on Social Security Administration records

Dr. Evans, a noted onomastician, or expert in name forms and origins, prepared these lists with data from his own research, as well as data supplied to him by the Social Security Administration.

BOYS:

1880-1889 . . . . John, William, Charles, George, James, Frank, Joseph, Harry, Henry, Edward
1890-1899 . . . . John, William, George, James, Charles, Joseph, Frank, Robert, Harry, Henry
1900-1909 . . . . John, William, James, George, Joseph, Charles, Robert, Frank, Edward, Henry
1910-1919 . . . . John, William, James, Robert, Joseph, Charles, George, Edward, Frank, Walter
1920-1929 . . . . John, Robert, James, William, Charles, George, Joseph, Richard, Edward, Donald
1930-1939 . . . . Robert, James, John, William, Richard, Charles, Donald, George, Thomas, Joseph
1940-1949 . . . . James, Robert, John, William, Richard, David, Charles, Thomas, Michael, Ronald
1950-1959 . . . . Michael, James, Robert, John, David, William, Steven, Richard, Thomas, Mark
1960-1969 . . . . Michael, John, David, James, Robert, Mark, Steven, William, Jeffrey, Richard
1970-1979 . . . . Michael, Christopher, Jason, David, James, John, Brian, Robert, Steven, William
1980-1989 . . . . Michael, Christopher, Matthew, Joshua, David, Daniel, James, John, Robert, Brian
1990-1999 . . . . Michael, Christopher, Matthew, Joshua, Nicholas, Jacob, Andrew, Daniel, Brandon, Tyler

GIRLS:

1880-1889 . . . . Mary, Anna, Elizabeth, Catherine, Margaret, Emma, Bertha, Minnie, Florence, Clara
1890-1899 . . . . Mary, Anna, Margaret, Helen, Catherine, Elizabeth, Florence, Ruth, Rose, Ethel
1900-1909 . . . . Mary, Helen, Margaret, Anna, Ruth, Catherine, Elizabeth, Dorothy, Marie, Mildred
1910-1919 . . . . Mary, Helen, Dorothy, Margaret, Ruth, Catherine, Mildred, Anna, Elizabeth, Frances
1920-1929 . . . . Mary, Dorothy, Betty, Helen, Margaret, Ruth, Virginia, Catherine, Doris, Frances
1930-1939 . . . . Mary, Betty, Barbara, Shirley, Patricia, Dorothy, Joan, Margaret, Carol, Nancy
1940-1949 . . . . Mary, Linda, Barbara, Patricia, Carol, Sandra, Nancy, Sharon, Judith, Susan
1950-1959 . . . . Deborah, Mary, Linda, Patricia, Susan, Barbara, Karen, Nancy, Donna, Catherine
1960-1969 . . . . Lisa, Deborah, Mary, Karen, Michelle, Susan, Kimberly, Lori, Teresa, Linda
1970-1979 . . . . Jennifer, Michelle, Amy, Melissa, Kimberly, Lisa, Angela, Heather, Kelly, Sarah
1980-1989 . . . . Jessica, Jennifer, Ashley, Sarah, Amanda, Stephanie, Nicole, Melissa, Katherine, Megan
1990-1999 . . . . Ashley, Jessica, Sarah, Brittany, Emily, Kaitlyn, Samantha, Megan, Brianna, Katherine

Origins of Popular American Given Names

Source: Dr. Cleveland Kent Evans, Bellevue University, Bellevue, NE

Boys

Andrew: Gr. *andreios*, "man, manly"
Brandon: Eng. place name, "gorse-covered hill"
Brian: Irish, perhaps Celtic *Brigonos*, "high, noble"
Charles: Ger. *ceorl*, "free man"
Christopher: Gr. *Khristophoros*, "bearing Christ [in one's heart]"
Daniel: Heb. "God is my judge"
David: Heb. *Dodavehu*, perhaps "darling"
Donald: Scots Gaelic *Domhnall*, "world rule"
Edward: Old Eng. *Eadweard*, "wealth-guard"
Frank: Ger. "Frenchman"
George: Gr. *georgos*, "soil tiller, farmer"
Harry: Middle Eng. form of Henry
Henry: Ger. *Haimric*, "home-power"
Jacob: Heb. *Yaakov*, "God protects" or "supplanter"
James: Late Lat. *Iacomus*, form of Jacob
Jason: Gr. *Iason*, "healer"
Jeffrey: Norman Fr. , from Ger. *Gaufrid*, "land-peace," or *Gisfrid*, "pledge-peace"
John: Heb. *Yohanan*, "God is gracious"
Joseph: Heb. *Yosef*, "[God] shall add"
Joshua: Heb. *Yoshua*, "God saves"
Mark: Lat. *Marcus*, perhaps "of Mars, the war god"
Matthew: Heb. *Mattathia*, "gift of God"
Michael: Heb. "Who could ever be like God?"
Nicholas: Gr. *Nikolaos*, "victory-people"
Richard: Ger. "power-hardy"
Robert: Ger. *Hrodberht*, "fame-bright"
Steven: Gr. *stephanos*, "crown, garland"
Thomas: Aramaic "twin"
Tyler: Old Eng. *tigeler*, "tile layer"
Walter: Ger. *Waldheri*, "rule-army"
William: Ger. *Wilhelm*, "will-helmet"

Girls

Amanda: 17th-cent. invention from Lat., "lovable"
Amy: Old Fr. *Amee*, "beloved"
Angela: Gr. *angelos*, "messenger [of God]"
Anna: Lat. and Gr. form of Hannah
Ashley: Eng. place name, "ash grove"
Barbara: Gr. *barbarus*, "foreign"
Bertha, Ger. *behrt*, "bright"
Betty: 18th-cent. pet form of Elizabeth
Brianna: modern fem. form of Brian
Brittany: place name, Fr. province settled by Britons
Carol: form of Charles
Clara: Lat. *clarus*, "famous"
Deborah: Heb. "bee"
Donna: Ital. "lady"
Doris: Gr. "woman of the Dorian tribe," name of a sea nymph
Dorothy: Gr. *Dorothea*, "gift of God"
Elizabeth: Heb. *Elisheba*, perhaps "God is my oath" or "God is good fortune"
Emily: Roman *Aemilia*, possibly from Lat. *aemulus*, "rival"
Emma: Ger. *ermen*, "whole, entire"
Ethel: Old Eng. *aethel*, "noble"
Florence: Lat. *florens*, "flourishing"
Frances: fem. form of Francis, "a Frenchman"
Haley: Eng. place name, "hay clearing"
Hannah: Heb. "He has favored me"
Heather: Middle Eng. *hathir*, "heather"
Helen: Gr. *Helene*, possibly "sunbeam"
Jennifer: Cornish form of Welsh *Gwenhwyfar*, "fair-smooth"
Jessica: Shakespearean invention, probably fem. form of Jesse, Heb. "God exists"
Joan: Middle Eng. fem. form of John
Judith: Hebrew "Jewish woman"
Kaitlyn: American spelling of Caitlin, the Irish form of Katherine
Karen: Danish form of Katherine
Katherine: from *Aikaterine*, Egyptian name later modified to resemble Gr. *katharos*, "pure"
Kelly: Irish Gaelic *Ceallagh*, perhaps "churchgoer" or "bright-headed"
Kimberly: Eng. place name, "Cyneburgh's clearing"
Linda: Sp. "pretty" or Ger. "tender"
Lisa: pet form of Elizabeth
Lori: pet form of either Lorraine (French "land of Lothar's people") or Laura (Latin "laurel")
Madison: Middle Eng. surname, "son of Madeline or Maud"
Margaret: Gr. *margaron*, "pearl"
Maria: Lat. form of Mary
Marie: Fr. form of Mary
Mary: Eng. form of Heb. *Maryam*, perhaps "seeress" or "wished-for child"
Megan: Welsh form of Margaret
Melissa: Gr. "bee"
Michelle: Fr. fem. form of Michael
Mildred: Old Eng. *Mildthryth*, "mild-strength"
Minnie: Pet form of Wilhelminia, fem. form of William
Nancy: medieval Eng. pet form of Agnes, Gr. *hagnos*, "holy"; later also used as pet form for Ann
Nicole: Fr. fem. form of Nicholas
Patricia: Lat. *Patricius*, "belonging to the noble class"
Rose: Ger. *hros*, "horse," or Lat. *rosa*, "rose"
Ruth: Heb., perhaps "companion"
Samantha: colonial American invention, probably combining Sam from Samuel [Heb. "name of God"] with -antha from Gr. *anthos*, "flower"
Sandra: short form of Alessandra, Ital. fem. of Alexander, Gr. "defend-man"
Sarah: Heb., "princess"
Sharon: Biblical place name, Hebrew "plain"
Shirley: Eng. place name, "bright clearing" or "shire meadow"
Stephanie: Fr. fem. form of Steven
Susan: Eng. form of Heb. *Shoshana*, "lily"
Teresa: Spanish, perhaps "woman from Therasia"
Virginia: Lat., "virgin-like"

Pen Names

Shalom Aleichem (Solomon J. Rabinowitz)
Woody Allen (Allen Stewart Konigsberg)
Currer, Ellis, and Acton Bell (Charlotte, Emily, and Anne Brontë)
John le Carré (David John Moore Cornwell)
Lewis Carroll (Charles Lutwidge Dodgson)
Colette (Sidonie Gabrielle Colette)
Isak Dinesen (Karen Blixen)
Elia (Charles Lamb)
George Eliot (Mary Ann or Marian Evans)
Maksim Gorky (Aleksey Maksimovich Peshkov)
O. Henry (William Sydney Porter)
James Herriot (James Alfred Wight)
P. D. James (Phyllis Dorothy James White)
[John] Ross Macdonald (Kenneth Millar)
André Maurois (Émile Herzog)
Molière (Jean Baptiste Poquelin)
Toni Morrison (Chloe Anthony Wofford)
Frank O'Connor (Michael Donovan)
George Orwell (Eric Arthur Blair)
Mary Renault (Mary Challans)
Ellery Queen (Frederic Dannay and Manfred B. Lee)
Françoise Sagan (Françoise Quoirez)
Saki (Hector Hugh Munro)
George Sand (Amandine Lucie Aurore Dupin)
Dr. Seuss (Theodor Seuss Geisel)
Stendhal (Marie Henri Beyle)
Mark Twain (Samuel Clemens)
Voltaire (François Marie Arouet)
Tom Wolfe (Thomas Kennerly Jr.)

Ma Is a Nun as I Am.

The phrase above is a **palindrome.** A palindrome, from Greek words for "run back again," reads the same backward as forward. Famous palindromes range from Adam's possible introduction to his wife ("Madam, I'm Adam") to a slogan that could have applied to Theodore Roosevelt ("A man, a plan, a canal, Panama!"). Some are one word only (e.g., "kayak") or simple phrases (e.g. "senile felines," "no lemons, no melon"). Some are more involved (e.g., "Straw? No, too stupid a fad. I put soot on warts.").

Forms of Address

	Address	Salutation
GOVERNMENT		
President of the U.S.	The President, The White House, Washington, DC 20500; also, The President and Mrs. ____ or The President and Mr. ____	Dear Sir or Madam; Mr. President or Madam President; Dear Mr. President or Dear Madam President
U.S. Vice President	The Vice President, The White House, Washington, DC 20500; also, The Vice President and Mrs. ____ or The Vice President and Mr. ____	Dear Sir or Madam; Mr. Vice President or Madam Vice President; Dear Mr. Vice President or Dear Madam Vice President
Chief Justice	The Hon. *Firstname Surname*, Chief Justice of the U.S., The Supreme Court, Washington, DC 20543	Dear Sir or Madam; Dear Mr. or Madam Chief Justice
Associate Justice	The Hon. Justice *Firstname Surname,* The Supreme Court, Washington, DC 20543	Dear Sir or Madam; Dear Justice *Surname*
Judge	The Hon. *Firstname Surname*, Associate Judge, U.S. District Court	Dear Judge *Surname*
Attorney General	The Hon. *Firstname Surname,* Attorney General, Dept. of Justice, Constitution Ave. & 10th St. NW, Washington, DC 20530	Dear Sir or Madam; Dear Mr. or Ms. Attorney General
Cabinet Officer	The Hon. *Firstname Surname*, Secretary of ____	Dear Mr. or Madam Secretary; or Dear Mr. or Ms. *Surname*
Senator	The Hon. or Sen. *Firstname Surname*, U.S. Senate, Washington, DC 20510	Dear Mr. or Madam Senator, or Dear Mr. or Ms. *Surname*
Representative	The Hon. or Rep. *Firstname Surname*, House of Representatives, Washington, DC 20515	Dear Mr. or Madam *Surname*
Speaker of the House	The Hon. Speaker of the House of Representatives, House of Representatives, Washington, DC 20515	Dear Mr. or Madam Speaker
Ambassador, U.S.	The Hon. *Firstname Surname*, American Ambassador[1]	Sir or Madam; Dear Mr. or Madam Ambassador
Ambassador, Foreign	His or Her Excellency[2] *Firstname Surname*, Ambassador of ______	Excellency[2] ; Dear Mr. or Madam Ambassador
Governor	The Hon. *Firstname Surname*, Governor of *State*; or in some states, His or Her Excellency, the Governor of *State*	Sir or Madam; Dear Governor *Surname*
Mayor	The Hon. *Firstname Surname*, Mayor of *City*	Sir or Madam; Dear Mayor *Surname*
MILITARY PERSONNEL		
All Titles	Full or abbreviated rank + full name + comma + abbreviation for branch of service. *Example*: Adm. John Smith, USN	Dear *Rank Surname*
RELIGIOUS		
Clergy, Protestant	The Reverend *Firstname Surname*[3]	Dear Ms. or Mr. *Surname*
Pope	His Holiness Pope *Name* or His Holiness the Pope	Your Holiness or Most Holy Father
Priest	The Reverend *Firstname Surname* or The Reverend Father *Surname*	Reverend Father, Dear Father *Surname*, or Dear Father
Rabbi	Rabbi *Firstname Surname*	Dear Rabbi *Surname*
ROYALTY AND NOBILITY		
King/Queen	His or Her Majesty, King or Queen of *Country*	Sir or Madam, or May it please Your Majesty

(1) If in Canada or Latin America, The Ambassador of the United States of America. (2) An American ambassador is not properly addressed as His or Her Excellency. (3) A member of the Protestant clergy who has a doctorate may be so addressed; for example, The Reverend Firstname Surname, DD, and Dear Dr. Surname.

Commonly Misspelled English Words

accidentally	committee	environment	incidentally	miniature	privilege
accommodate	conscientious	existence	independent	misspelled	receive
acknowledgment	conscious	fascinating	indispensable	mysterious	receipt
acquainted	convenience	February	inoculate	necessary	rhythm
all right	deceive	finally	irresistible	noticeable	ridiculous
already	defendant	fluorine	judgment	occasionally	separate
amateur	describe	foreign	laboratory	occurrence	seize
appearance	description	forty	license	opportunity	similar
appropriate	desirable	government	lightning	optimistic	sincerely
bureau	despair	grammar	liquefy	parallel	supersede
business	desperate	harass	maintenance	performance	transferred
character	eliminate	humorous	marriage	permanent	Wednesday
commitment	embarrass	hurrying	millennium	perseverance	weird

Commonly Confused English Words

adverse: unfavorable
averse: opposed

affect: to influence
effect: to bring about

allusion: an indirect reference
illusion: an unreal impression

appraise: to set a value on
apprise: to inform

capital: the seat of government
capitol: building where a legislature meets

complement: to make complete; something that completes
compliment: to praise; praise

counselor: one who gives advice or counsel
councilor: a member of a council

denote: to mean
connote: to suggest beyond the explicit meaning

discreet: prudent
discrete: separate, distinct

disinterested: impartial
uninterested: without interest

elicit: to draw or bring out
illicit: illegal

emigrate: to leave for another place of residence
immigrate: to come to another place of residence

grisly: inspiring horror or great fear
grizzly: sprinkled or streaked with gray

historic: important in history
historical: relating to history

hoard: a supply stored up and often hidden
horde: a teeming croud or throng

imminent: ready to take place
eminent: standing out

imply: to suggest but not explicitly; to entail
infer: to assume or understand information not relayed explicitly

include: used when the items following are part of a whole
comprise: used when the items following are all of a whole

ingenious: clever
ingenuous: innocent

oral: spoken, as opposed to written
verbal: relating to language

prostrate: stretched out face down
prostate: relating to prostate gland

set: to place; to cause someone or something to sit
sit: to rest on the buttocks or haunches

IT'S A FACT: The word "set" has over 430 differnet senses as defined in the 2nd edition of the *Oxford English Dictionary* (1989)—more than any other word. The 20-volume edition has 231,100 main entries, covers 21,730 pages, and weighs 137.72 pounds.

The Principal Languages of the World

Source: From *Ethnologue Volume 1, Languages of the World,* 14th edition, Edited by Barbara F. Grimes, © 2000 by SIL International. Used by permission.

The following tables count only "first language" speakers. All figures are estimates, as of 2000.

Languages Spoken by the Most People

Language	Speakers (millions)	Language	Speakers (millions)	Language	Speakers (millions)	Language	Speakers (millions)
Chinese, Mandarin	874	Bengali	207	German, Standard	100	Javanese	75
Hindi	366	Portuguese	176	Korean	78	Chinese, Yue	71
English	341	Russian	167	French	77	Telugu	69
Spanish	322-358	Japanese	125	Chinese, Wu	77		

Languages Spoken by at Least 2 Million People

A "Hub" country is the country of origin, not necessarily the country where the most speakers reside (e.g., Portugal is the "hub" country of Portuguese, although more Portuguese speakers live in Brazil).

Language	Hub	Countries	Speakers (millions)
Chinese, Mandarin	China	16	874
Hindi	India	17	366
English	United Kingdom	104	341
Spanish	Spain	43	322-358
Bengali	Bangladesh	9	207
Portuguese	Portugal	33	176
Russian	Russia	30	167
Japanese	Japan	26	125
German, standard	Germany	40	100
Korean	Korea, South	31	78
French	France	53	77
Chinese, Wu	China	1	77
Javanese	Indonesia	4	75
Chinese, Yue	China	20	71
Telugu	India	7	69
Marathi	India	3	68
Vietnamese	Vietnam	20	68
Tamil	India	15	66
Italian	Italy	29	62
Turkish	Turkey	35	61
Urdu	Pakistan	21	60
Ukrainian	Ukraine	25	47
Gujarati	India	17	46
Arabic, Egyptian, spoken	Egypt	9	46
Chinese, Jinyu	China	1	45
Chinese, Min Nan	China	9	45
Polish	Poland	21	44
Chinese, Xiang	China	1	36
Malayalam	India	9	35
Kannada	India	1	35
Chinese, Hakka	China	16	33
Oriya	India	2	32
Burmese	Myanmar	5	32
Panjabi, Western	Pakistan	7	30-45
Sunda	Indonesia	1	27
Panjabi, Eastern	India	11	27
Romanian	Romania	17	26
Bhojpuri	India	3	26
Azerbaijani, South	Iran	8	24
Farsi, Western	Iran	26	24
Hausa	Nigeria	13	24
Maithili	India	2	24
Arabic, Algerian, spoken	Algeria	6	22
Serbo-Croatian	Serbia & Montenegro	23	21
Thai	Thailand	5	20-25
Yoruba	Nigeria	5	20
Dutch	Netherlands	14	20
Awadhi	India	2	20
Chinese, Gan	China	1	20
Sindhi	Pakistan	7	19
Arabic, Moroccan, spoken	Morocco	8	19
Arabic, Saidi, spoken	Egypt	1	18
Igbo	Nigeria	1	18
Uzbek, Northern	Uzbekistan	12	18
Malay	Malaysia	8	18
Indonesian	Indonesia	6	17-30
Tagalog	Philippines	8	17
Amharic	Ethiopia	4	17
Nepali	Nepal	4	16
Arabic, Sudanese, spoken	Sudan	5	16-19
Arabic, N. Levantine, spoken	Syria	15	15
Saraiki	Pakistan	3	15-30
Cebuano	Philippines	2	15
Assamese	India	3	15
Thai, Northeastern	Thailand	1	15-23
Hungarian	Hungary	11	14
Chittagonian	Bangladesh	2	14
Haryanvi	India	1	13
Sinhala	Sri Lanka	7	13
Madura	Indonesia	2	13
Arabic, Mesop., spoken	Iraq	5	13
Greek	Greece	35	12
Marwari	India	2	12
Czech	Czech Republic	9	12
Magahi	India	1	11
Chhattisgarhi	India	1	11
Zhuang, Northern	China	1	10
Belarusan	Belarus	16	10
Deccan	India	1	10
Chinese, Min Bei	China	2	10
Arabic, Najdi, spoken	Saudi Arabia	7	9
Zulu	South Africa	6	9
Pashto, Southern	Afghanistan	6	9
Somali	Somalia	12	9-10
Arabic, Tunisian, spoken	Tunisia	5	9
Swedish	Sweden	7	9
Malagasy	Madagascar	3	9
Bulgarian	Bulgaria	11	9
Pashto, Northern	Pakistan	5	9
Lombard	Italy	3	8
Ilocano	Philippines	2	8
Oromo, West-Central	Ethiopia	2	8
Kazakh	Kazakhstan	13	8
Tatar	Russia	19	7
Haitian-Creole French	Haiti	8	7
Fulfulde, Nigerian	Nigeria	3	7
Hiligaynon	Philippines	2	7
Uyghur	China	16	7
Shona	Zimbabwe	4	7
Khmer, Central	Cambodia	6	7
Kurmanji	Turkey	25	7-8
Akan	Ghana	1	7
Azerbaijani, North	Azerbaijan	9	7
Arabic, Sanaani, spoken	Yemen	1	7
Napoletano-Calabrese	Italy	1	7
Farsi, Eastern	Afghanistan	2	7
Rwanda	Rwanda	5	7
Arabic, Hijazi spoken	Saudi Arabia	2	6
Luba-Kasai	Dem. Rep. of Congo	1	6
Thai, Northern	Thailand	2	6
Finnish	Finland	7	6
Arabic, N. Mesopotamian, spoken	Iraq	4	6
Afrikaans	South Africa	10	6
Arabic, S. Levantine, spoken	Jordan	8	6
Armenian	Armenia	29	6
Rundi	Burundi	4	6
Santali	India	4	6
Alemannisch	Switzerland	5	6
Catalan-Valencian-Balear	Spain	18	6
Turkmen	Turkmenistan	13	6
Xhosa	South Africa	3	6
Kanauji	India	1	6
Arabic, Taizzi-Adeni, spoken	Yemen	5	6
Minangkabau	Indonesia	1	6
Kurdi	Iraq	3	6

Language	Hub	Countries	Speakers (millions)
Sylhetti	Bangladesh	2	5
Slovak	Slovakia	8	5
Swahili	Tanzania	12	5
Thai, Southern	Thailand	1	5
Tigrigna	Ethiopia	3	5
Hebrew	Israel	8	5
Nyanja	Malawi	6	5
Danish	Denmark	8	5
Guarani, Paraguayan	Paraguay	2	5
Gikuyu	Kenya	1	5
Moore	Burkina Faso	6	5
Sukuma	Tanzania	1	5
Norwegian, Bokmaal	Norway	6	5
Lithuanian	Lithuania	19	4
Oromo, Eastern	Ethiopia	1	4
Tswana	Botswana	4	4
Arabic, Libyan, spoken	Libya	3	4
Sotho, Southern	Lesotho	3	4
Umbundu	Angola	2	4
Kashmiri	India	3	4
Konkani	India	1	4
Galician	Spain	2	4
Georgian	Georgia	13	4
Luri	Iran	3	4
Tajiki	Tajikistan	7	4
Sicilian	Italy	1	4
Kituba	Dem. Rep. of Congo	1	4
Zhuang, Southern	China	1	4
Bali	Indonesia	1	3
Kabyle	Algeria	3	3
Gilaki	Iran	1	3
Aceh	Indonesia	1	3
Kanuri, Central	Nigeria	6	3
Emiliano-Romagnolo	Italy	2	3
Mazanderani	Iran	1	3
Wolof	Senegal	7	3
Yiddish, Eastern	Israel	20	3
Shan	Myanmar	3	3
Luo	Kenya	2	3
Luyia	Kenya	2	3
Tachelhit	Morocco	3	3
Malay, Pattani	Thailand	1	3
Tamazight, Central Atlas	Morocco	3	3
Quechua, South Bolivian	Bolivia	2	3
Balochi, Southern	Pakistan	4	3
Ganda	Uganda	2	3
Albanian, Tosk	Albania	9	3
Kongo	Dem. Rep. of Congo	3	3
Oromo, Borana-Arsi-Guji	Ethiopia	3	3
Bugis	Indonesia	2	3
Lao	Laos	5	3
Banjar	Indonesia	2	3

Language	Hub	Countries	Speakers (millions)
Mbundu, Loanda	Angola	1	3
Piedmontese	Italy	3	3
Tsonga	South Africa	4	3
Mongolian, Peripheral	China	2	3
Sotho, Northern	South Africa	2	3
Kamba	Kenya	1	2
Garhwali	India	1	2
Dogri-Kangri	India	1	2
Mundari	India	3	2
Venetian	Italy	3	2
Lambadi	India	1	2
Bemba	Zambia	5	2
Sasak	Indonesia	1	2
Aymara, Central	Bolivia	4	2
Karen, Sgaw	Myanmar	2	2
Albanian, Gheg	Serbia & Montenegro	7	2
Kirghiz	Kyrgyzstan	7	2
SW-Caribbean-Creole English	Jamaica	7	2
Betawi	Indonesia	1	2
Macedonian	Macedonia	7	2
Tumbuka	Malawi	3	2
Rajbangsi	India	3	2
Batak Toba	Indonesia	1	2
Arabic, Gulf, spoken	Iraq	9	2
Waray-Waray	Philippines	1	2
Mongolian, Halh	Mongolia	4	2
Malagasy, Southern	Madagascar	1	2
Konkani, Goanese	India	3	2
Kalenjin	Kenya	1	2
Bicolano, Central	Philippines	1	2
Bagri	India	2	2
Zarma	Niger	5	2
Baoule	Côte d'Ivoire	1	2
Kumauni	India	2	2
Lomwe	Mozambique	2	2
Tarifit	Morocco	4	2
Saxon, Upper	Germany	1	2
Kurux	India	2	2
Makhuwa	Mozambique	2	2
Maninka, Kankan	Guinea	3	2
Tiv	Nigeria	2	2
Bamanankan	Mali	7	2
Ewe	Ghana	2	2
Pulaar	Senegal	6	2
Hassaniyya	Mauritania	6	2
Arakanese	Myanmar	3	2
Slovenian	Slovenia	10	2
Jula	Burkina Faso	3	2
Bouyei	China	2	2
Brahui	Pakistan	4	2
Fuuta Jalon	Guinea	6	2

American Manual Alphabet

In the American Manual Alphabet, each letter of the alphabet is represented by a position of the fingers. This system was originally developed in France by Abbe Charles Michel De I'Epee in the late 1700s. It was brought to the United States by Laurent Clerce (1785-1869), a Frenchman who taught deaf or hearing-impaired people.

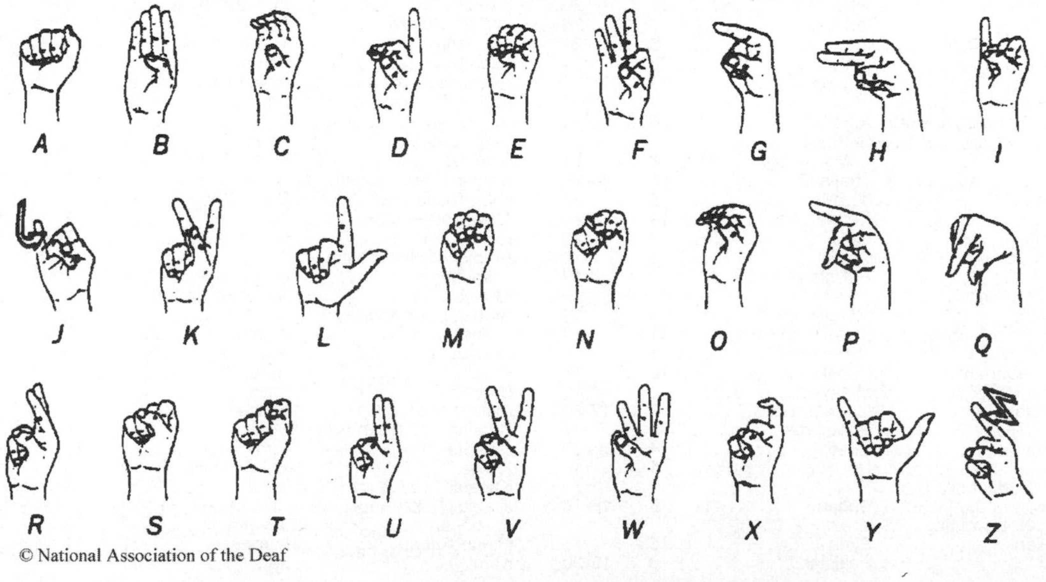

RELIGION

Membership of Religious Groups in the U.S.

Sources: *2002 Yearbook of American & Canadian Churches*, © National Council of the Churches of Christ in the USA; *World Almanac* research

These membership figures generally are based on reports made by officials of each group, and not on any religious census. Figures from other sources may vary. Many groups keep careful records; others only estimate. Not all groups report annually. Church membership figures reported in this table are generally inclusive and do not refer simply to full communicants or confirmed members. Specific definitions of "member" vary from one denomination to another.

The number of houses of worship appears in parentheses. * Indicates that the group declines to make membership figures public. Groups reporting fewer than 5,000 members are not included; where membership numbers are not available, only those groups with 50 or more houses of worship are listed.

Religious Group	Members
Adventist churches:	
Advent Christian Ch. (303)	26,264
Seventh-day Adventist Ch. (4,486)	880,921
American Catholic Church (100)	**25,000**
Apostolic Christian Churches of America (86)	**12,900**
Bahá'í Faith (173[1] centers)	**147,473[1]**
Baptist churches:	
American Baptist Assn. (1,760)	275,000
American Baptist Chs. in the U.S.A. (5,756)	1,436,909
Baptist Bible Fellowship Intl. (4,500)	1,200,000
Baptist General Conference (880)	143,200
Baptist Missionary Assn. of America (1,334)	234,732
Conservative Baptist Assn. of America (1,200)	200,000
Free Will Baptists, Natl. Assn. of (2,472)	199,134
General Assn. of General Baptists (587)	55,549
General Assn. of Regular Baptist Chs. (1,398)	92,129
Natl. Baptist Convention, U.S.A., Inc. (2,500)	3,500,000
Natl. Missionary Baptist Convention of America	2,500,000
North American Baptist Conference (270)	47,097
Progressive National Baptist Convention (2,000)	2,500,000
Separate Baptists in Christ (100)	8,000
Southern Baptist Convention (41,588)	15,960,308
Brethren in Christ (229)	**20,587**
Brethren (German Baptists):	
Brethren Ch. (Ashland, OH) (119)	13,098
Church of the Brethren (1,071)	135,879
Grace Brethren Chs., Fellowship of (260)	30,371
Old German Baptist Brethren (54)	6,084
Buddhist Churches of America (60)	**15,750[1]**
Christian Brethren (Plymouth Brethren) (1,125)	**95,000**
Christian Church (Disciples of Christ) (3,781)	**820,286**
Christian Ch. of N.A., Gen. Council (96)	**7,200**
Christian Congregation, Inc. (1,439)	**119,391**
Christian and Missionary Alliance (1,959)	**364,949**
Christian Union, Churches of Christ in (216)	**10,104**
Church of Christ (Holiness) U.S.A. (163)	**10,475**
Church of Christ, Scientist (2,200)	*
Church of the United Brethren in Christ (228)	**23,585**
Churches of Christ (15,000)	**1,500,000**
Churches of God:	
Chs. of God, General Conference (342)	32,380
Ch. of God (Anderson, IN) (2,353)	234,311
Ch. of God (Seventh Day), Denver, CO (200)	8,998
Ch. of God by Faith, Inc. (149)	35,000
Ch. of God, Mountain Assembly (118)	6,140
Church of the Nazarene (5,070)	**636,564**
Community Churches, Intl. Council of (217)	**200,263**
Congreg. Christian Chs., Nat'l Assoc. of (430)	**65,569**
Conservative Congregational Christian Conference (242)	**40,414**
Eastern Orthodox churches:	
American Carpatho-Russian Orthodox Greek Catholic Ch. (80)	13,480
Antiochian Orthodox Christian Archdiocese of N.A. (227)	70,000
Apostolic Catholic Assyrian Ch. of the East, N.A. Dioceses (22)	120,000
Armenian Apostolic Ch. of America (36)	360,000
Dioceses of America, Armenian Apostolic Church (72)	414,000
Coptic Orthodox Ch. (100)	300,000
Greek Orthodox Archdiocese of America (508)	1,500,000
Mar Thoma Syrian Church of India (68)	32,000
Orthodox Ch. in America (721)	1,000,000
Patriarchal Parishes of the Russian Orthodox Ch. in the USA (32)	20,000
Romanian Orthodox Episcopate of N. America (56)	25,000
Russian Orthodox Church Outside of Russia (177)	*
Syrian Orthodox Ch. of Antioch (22)	32,500
Episcopal Church (7,359)	**2,300,461**
Apostolic Episcopal Church (250)	14,000
Evangelical Church (133)	**12,475**
Evangelical Congregational Church (145)	**21,939**
Evangelical Covenant Church (800)	**101,003**
Evangelical Free Church of America (1,224)	**242,619**
Friends:	
Evangelical Friends Intl.-N.A. Region (284)	36,814
Friends General Conference (650)	34,577
Friends United Meeting (487)	34,863
Religious Society of Friends (Conservative) (1,200)	104,000
Full Gospel Fellowship of Churches and Ministers Intl. (896)	**325,000**
General Church of the New Jerusalem (33)	**5,791**
Grace Gospel Fellowship (128)	**60,000**
Hindu	**1,285,000[1]**
Independent Fundamental Churches of America (659)	**61,655**
Islam	**2,800,000[1]**
Jehovah's Witnesses (11,636)	**998,166**
Jewish organizations:	
Union of American Hebrew Congregations (Reform) (896)	1,500,000
Union of Orthodox Jewish Congregations of America (800)	1,075,000
United Synagogue of Conservative Judaism, The (762)	1,500,000
Jewish Reconstructionist Federation (100)	65,000
Latter-day Saints:	
Ch. of Jesus Christ of Latter-day Saints (Mormon) (11,562)	5,208,827
Reorganized Ch. of Jesus Christ of Latter-day Saints (1,236)	137,038
Liberal Catholic Church—Province of the U.S.A. (23)	**6,500**
Lutheran churches:	
Apostolic Lutheran Ch. of America (58)	*
Ch. of the Lutheran Brethren of America (115)	13,920
Ch. of the Lutheran Confession (75)	8,671
Evangelical Lutheran Ch. in America (10,816)	5,125,919
Evangelical Lutheran Synod (138)	21,729
Free Lutheran Congregations, Assn. of (245)	36,400
Latvian Evangelical Lutheran Church in America (71)	14,528
Lutheran Ch.—Missouri Synod (6,150)	2,554,088
Lutheran Chs., American Assn. of (101)	18,252
Wisconsin Evangelical Lutheran Synod (1,241)	721,665
Mennonite churches:	
Beachy Amish Mennonite Chs. (153)	9,205
Church of God in Christ (Mennonite) (106)	12,479
Hutterian Brethren (444)	43,000
Mennonite Brethren Chs., Gen. Conf. (368)	82,130
Mennonite Church (1,063)	120,381
Old Order Amish Ch. (898)	80,820
Methodist churches:	
African Methodist Episcopal Ch. (6,200)	2,500,000
African Methodist Episcopal Zion Ch. (3,218)	1,296,662
Evangelical Methodist Ch. (123)	8,615
Free Methodist Ch. of North America (971)	70,556
Primitive Methodist Ch. in the U.S.A. (77)	6,031
Southern Methodist Ch. (117)	7,686
United Methodist Ch. (35,469)	8,340,954
The Wesleyan Church (1,602)	123,181
Metropolitan Community Churches, Universal Fellowship of (300)	**44,000**
Missionary Church (368)	**29,948**
Moravian Ch. in America, Northern Province (93)	**25,872**
Natl. Organization of the New Apostolic Ch. of North America (380)	**36,438**

Religious Group	Members
Pentecostal churches:	
Apostolic Faith Mission Ch. of God (18)	10,661
Assemblies of God (12,084)	2,577,560
Bible Church of Christ (6)	6,850
Bible Fellowship Church (57)	7,258
Church of God (Cleveland, TN) (6,426)	895,536
Church of God in Christ (15,300)	5,499,875
Church of God of Prophecy (1,865)	72,899
Elim Fellowship (98)	*
Intl. Ch. of the Foursquare Gospel (1,793)	277,616
Intl. Pentecostal Church of Christ (71)	5,408
Intl. Pentecostal Holiness Church (1,868)	197,972
Open Bible Standard Chs. (357)	35,700
Pentecostal Assemblies of the World Inc. (1,750)	1,500,000
Pentecostal Church of God (1,212)	102,000
Pentecostal Free Will Baptist Ch. (150)	28,000
United Pentecostal Ch. Intl. (3,790)	*
Presbyterian churches:	
Associate Reformed Presbyterian Ch. (General Synod) (255)	41,500
Cumberland Presbyterian Ch. (779)	86,519
Cumberland Presbyterian Ch. in America (152)	15,142
Evangelical Presbyterian Ch. (189)	64,939
Genl. Assembly of the Korean Presbyterian Church in America (310)	50,221
Orthodox Presbyterian Ch. (216)	26,008
Presbyterian Ch. in America (1,458)	247,010
Presbyterian Ch. (U.S.A.) (11,178)	3,485,332
Reformed Presbyterian Ch. of N. America (86)	6,105
Reformed churches:	
Christian Reformed Ch. in N. America (739)	196,604
Hungarian Reformed Ch. in America (27)	6,000
Netherlands Reformed Congregations (25)	9,320
Protestant Reformed Churches in America (28)	6,713
Reformed Ch. in America (898)	289,329
United Church of Christ (5,923)	1,377,320
Reformed Episcopal Church (125)	**6,400**
Roman Catholic Church (19,544)	**63,683,030**
Salvation Army (1,410)	**472,871**
Unitarian Universalist Assn. of Congregations (1,051)	**220,000**

(1) Estimate; figures from other sources may vary.

WORLD ALMANAC QUICK QUIZ

Not counting John, which name has been the most common for popes?

(a) Pius (b) Gregory (c) Leo (d) Paul

For the answer look in this chapter, or see page 1008.

Headquarters of Selected Religious Groups in the U.S.

Sources: *2002 Yearbook of American & Canadian Churches*, © National Council of the Churches of Christ in the USA; *World Almanac* research

(Year organized in parentheses)

African Methodist Episcopal Church (1787), 3801 Market St., Suite 300, Philadelphia, PA 29204; Senior Bishop, Bishop John Hurst Adams

African Methodist Episcopal Zion Church (1796), 3225 West Sugar Creek Rd., Charlotte, NC 28269; Pres. Joseph Johnson (Note: Presidency rotates every 6 mos. according to seniority.)

American Baptist Churches in the U.S.A. (1907), PO Box 851, Valley Forge, PA 19482; www.abc-usa.org; Pres., David Hunt

American Hebrew Congregations, Union of, 633 3rd Ave., New York, NY 10017; www.uahc.org; Pres., Rabbi Eric Yoffie

American Rescue Workers (1890), 25 Ross St., Williamsport, PA 17701; www.arwus.com; Commander-in-Chief & Pres., Gen. Claude S. Astin Jr., Rev.

Antiochian Orthodox Christian Archdiocese of North America (1895), 358 Mountain Rd., Englewood, NJ 07631; www.antiochian.org; Primate, Metropolitan Philip Saliba

Armenian Apostolic Church of America (1887), **Eastern Prelacy**: 138 E. 39th St., New York, NY 10016; www.armprelacy.org; Prelate, Bishop Oshagan Choloyan; **Western Prelacy**: 4401 Russel Ave., Los Angeles, CA 90027; Prelate, Bishop Moushegh Mardirossian

Assemblies of God (1914), 1445 Boonville Ave., Springfield, MO 65802; www.agifellowship.org; Gen. Supt., Thomas E. Trask

Bahá'í Faith, National Spiritual Assembly of the Bahá'í's of the U.S., 536 Sheridan Rd., Wilmette, IL 60091; www.bahai.org; Secy. Gen., Dr. Robert Henderson

Baptist Bible Fellowship Intl. (1950), Baptist Bible Fellowship Missions Bldg., 720 E. Kearney St., Springfield, MO 65803; www.bbfi.org; Pres., Ken Gillming Sr.

Baptist Convention, Southern (1845), 901 Commerce St., Ste. 750, Nashville, TN 37203; www.sbc.net; Pres., Morris H. Chapman

Baptist Convention, U.S.A., Inc., National 1700 Baptist World Center Dr., Nashville, TN 37207; www.nationalbaptist.com; Pres., Dr. William J. Shaw

Baptist Convention of America, Inc., National (1880), 777 S. R.L. Thornton Freeway, Ste. 205, Dallas, TX 75203; members.aol.com/nbyc1/nbca.html; Pres., Dr. E. Edward Jones

Baptist Convention of America, Natl. Missionary (1988), 1404 E. Firestone, Los Angeles, CA 90001; www.natl-missionarybaptist.com; Pres., Dr. W. T. Snead Sr.

Baptist General Conference (1852), 2002 S. Arlington Heights Rd., Arlington Heights, IL 60005; www.bgc.bethel.edu; Pres., Dr. Robert S. Ricker

Brethren in Christ Church (1778), PO Box A, Grantham, PA 17027; www.bic-church.org/index.htm; Moderator, Dr. Warren L. Hoffman

Buddhist Churches of America (1899), 1710 Octavia St., San Francisco, CA 94109; Presiding Bishop, Hakubun Watanabe

Christian and Missionary Alliance (1897), PO Box 35000, Colorado Springs, CO 80935; www.cmalliance.org; Pres., Rev. Peter N. Nanfelt, D.D.

Christian Church (Disciples of Christ) (1832), 130 E. Washington St., PO Box 1986, Indianapolis, IN 46206; www.disciples.org; Gen. Minister and Pres., Richard L. Hamm

Christian Churches and Churches of Christ, 4210 Bridgetown Rd., Box 11326, Cincinnati, OH 45211

Christian Congregation, Inc., The (1887), 812 W. Hemlock St., LaFollette, TN 37766; www.netministries.org/see/churches.exe/ch10619; Gen. Supt., Rev. Ora W. Eads, D.D.

Christian Methodist Episcopal Church (1870), 4466 Elvis Presley Blvd., Memphis, TN 38116; www.c-m-e.org; Executive Secretary, Attorney Juanita Bryant

Christian Reformed Church in North America (1857), 2850 Kalamazoo Ave. SE, Grand Rapids, MI 49560; www.crcna.org; Gen. Secy., Dr. David H. Engelhard

Church of the Brethren (1708), 1451 Dundee Ave., Elgin, IL 60120; www.brethren.org; Moderator, Paul E. Grout

Church of Christ (1830), PO Box 472, Independence, MO 64051; www.church-of-christ.com; Council of Apostles, Secy., Apostle Smith N. Brickhouse

Church of God (Anderson, IN) (1881), Box 2420, Anderson, IN 46018; www.chog.org; Comm. Coord., Don Taylor

Church of God (Cleveland, TN) (1886), PO Box 2430, Cleveland, TN 37320; www.churchofgod.cc/default_nav40.asp; Gen. Overseer, R. Lamar Vest

Church of God in Christ (1907), Mason Temple, 938 Mason St., Memphis, TN 38126; www.cogic.org; Presiding Bishop, Bishop Gilbert E. Patterson

Church of Jesus Christ (Bickertonites) (1862), 6th & Lincoln Sts., Monongahela, PA 15063; Pres., Dominic Thomas

Church of Jesus Christ of Latter-day Saints (Mormon), The (1830), 47 E. South Temple St., Salt Lake City, UT 84150; www.lds.org; Pres., Gordon B. Hinckley

Church of the Nazarene (1907), 6401 The Paseo, Kansas City, MO 64131; www.nazarene.org; Gen. Secy., Jack Stone

Community Churches, International Council of (1950), 21116 Washington Pkwy., Frankfort, IL 60423; Pres., Rev. Albert Wright

Conservative Judaism, United Synagogue of, 155 5th Ave., New York, NY 10010; www.uscj.org; Exec. Vice Pres., Rabbi Jerome M. Epstein

Coptic Orthodox Church, 5 Woodstone Dr., Cedar Grove, NJ 07009; www.coptic.org; Fr. Abraam D. Sleman

Cumberland Presbyterian Church (1810), 1978 Union Ave., Memphis, TN 38104; www.cumberland.org; Moderator, Randy Jacob

Episcopal Church (1789), 815 Second Ave., New York, NY 10017; www.ecusa.anglican.org; Presiding Bishop and Primate, Most Rev. Frank Tracy Griswold III

Evangelical Free Church of America (1884), 901 E. 78th St., Minneapolis, MN 55420; www.efca.org; Acting Pres., Rev. William Hamel

Evangelical Lutheran Church in America (1987), 8765 W. Higgins Rd., Chicago, IL 60631; www.elca.org; Presiding Bishop, Rev. Mark Hanson

Fellowship of Grace Brethren Churches (1882), PO Box 386, Winona Lake, IN 46590; www.fgbc.org; Moderator, Dr. Galen Wiley

First Church of Christ, Scientist, The (1879), 175 Huntington Ave., Boston, MA 02115; www.tfccs.com; Pres., Christiane West Little

Free Methodist Church of North America (1860), World Ministries Center, 770 N. High School Rd., Indianapolis, IN 46214; www.freemethodistchurch.org

Friends General Conference (1900), 1216 Arch St. 2B, Philadelphia, PA 19107; www.fgcquaker.org; Gen. Secy., Bruce Birchard

Greek Orthodox Archdiocese of America (1922), 8-10 E. 79th St., New York, NY 10021; www.goarch.org; Primate of Greek Orthodox Church in America, Archbishop Demetrios

International Church of the Foursquare Gospel (1927), 1910 W. Sunset Blvd., Ste. 200, PO Box 26902, Los Angeles, CA 90026; www.foursquare.org; Pres., Dr. Paul C. Risser

Islamic Society of North America, P.O. Box 38, Plainfield, IN 46168; www.isna.net; Genl. Secy., Dr. Sayyid M. Syeed

Jehovah's Witnesses, 25 Columbia Heights, Brooklyn, NY 11201; www.watchtower.org; Pres., Don Adams

Jewish Reconstructionist Federation (1922), Beit Devora, 7804 Montgomery Ave., Suite 9, Elkins Park, PA 19027; www.jrf.org; Dir., Lani Moss

Lutheran Church—Missouri Synod (1847), 1333 S. Kirkwood Rd., St. Louis, MO 63122; www.lcms.org; Pres., Dr. Gerald B. Kieschnick

Mennonite Brethren Churches, General Conference of (1860), 4812 E. Butler Ave., Fresno CA 93727; Moderator, Ed Boschman

Mennonite Church USA (2001), 421 S. Second St., Ste. 600, Elkhart, IN 46516; www.MennoniteChurchUSA.org; Moderator, Ervin Stutzman

Mennonite Church, The General Conference (1860), 722 Main, P.O. Box 347, Newton, KS 67114; http://www2.southwind.net/~gcmc; Moderator, Lee Snyder

Moravian Church in America (1735), **Northern Prov.:** 1021 Center St., PO Box 1245, Bethlehem, PA 18016; www.moravian.org; Pres., Rev. R. Burke Johnson; **Southern Prov.:** 459 S. Church St., Winston-Salem, NC 27101; Pres., Rev. Dr. Robert E. Sawyer; **Alaska Prov.:** PO Box 545, Bethel, AK 99559; Pres., Rev. Isaac Amik

National Baptist Convention, Inc. Progressive (1961), 601 50th St., NE, Washington, DC 20019; www.pribc.org; Pres., Dr. Bennett W. Smith Sr.

Orthodox Church in America (1794), PO Box 675, Syosset, NY 11791; www.oca.org; Primate, Most Blessed Theodosius

Orthodox Jewish Congregations in America, Union of, 11 Broadway, New York, NY 10004; www.ou.org; Exec. Vice Pres., Rabbi Dr. Tzvi Hersh Weinreb

Pentecostal Assemblies of the World, Inc., 3939 Meadows Dr., Indianapolis, IN 46205; Presiding Bishop, Norman L. Wagner

Presbyterian Church (U.S.A.), (1983), 100 Witherspoon St., Louisville, KY 40202; www.pcusa.org; Moderator, Jack Rogers

Presbyterian Church in America (1973), 1700 N. Brown Rd., Lawrenceville, GA 30043 www.pcanet.org; Moderator, Mr. Steve Fox

Reformed Church in America (1628), 475 Riverside Dr., New York, NY 10115; www.rca.org; Pres., Rev. Steven Brooks

Roman Catholic Church (1634), National Conference of Catholic Bishops, 3211 Fourth St., Washington, DC 20017; www.nccbuscc.org; Pres., Bishop Joseph A. Fiorenza

Romanian Orthodox Episcopate of America (1929), PO Box 309, Grass Lake, MI 49240; www.roea.org; Ruling Bishop, His Eminence Archbishop Nathaniel Popp

Salvation Army (1865), 615 Slaters Lane, Alexandria, VA 22313; www.salvationarmy.org; National Comdr., Commissioner John A. Busby

Seventh-day Adventist Church (1863), 12501 Old Columbia Pike, Silver Spring, MD 20904; Pres., Jan Paulsen

Swedenborgian Church (1792), 11 Highland Ave., Newtonville, MA 02460, www.swedenborg.org; Pres., Rev. Ronald P. Brugler

Unitarian Universalist Association of Congregations (1961), 25 Beacon St., Boston, MA 02108; www.uua.org; Pres., The Rev. William Sinkford

United Church of Christ (1957), 700 Prospect Ave., Cleveland, OH 44115; www.ucc.org; Pres., Rev. John H. Thomas

United Methodist Church (1968), 1204 Freedom Rd., Cranberry Twp., PA 16066; www.umc.org; Pres. Council of Bishops, Bishop Elias G. Galvan

United Pentecostal Church Intl. (1925), 8855 Dunn Rd., Hazelwood, MO 63042; www.upci.org; Gen. Superintendent, Rev. Nathaniel A. Urshan

Volunteers of America (1896), 1660 Duke St., Alexandria, VA 22314; www.voa.org; Chairperson, Walt Patterson

Wesleyan Church (1968), PO Box 50434, Indianapolis, IN 46250; www.wesleyan.org; Gen. Supts., Dr. Earle L. Wilson, Dr. David H. Holdren, Dr. Thomas E. Armiger

Membership of Religious Groups in Canada

Sources: *2002 Yearbook of American & Canadian Churches*, © National Council of the Churches of Christ in the USA; *World Almanac* research

Figures are generally based on reports by officials of each group. The numbers are generally inclusive and not restricted to full communicants or the like. Specific definitions of "member" may vary, however. Some groups keep careful records; others only estimate. Not all groups report annually. The number of houses of worship appears in parentheses. *Indicates membership figures were not reported. Groups reporting fewer than 5,000 members are not included. Where membership numbers are not available, only groups with 50 or more houses of worship are listed.

Religious Group	Members
Anglican Church of Canada (2,346)	717,708
Antiochian Orthodox Christian Archdiocese of North America (215)	350,000
Apostolic Church of Pentecost of Canada, Inc. (143)	24,000
Armenian Holy Apostolic Church (Canadian Diocese) (15)	85,000
Associated Gospel Churches (139)	10,293
Bahá'í Faith (1,480)	31,396[1]
Baptist Conference, North American (124)	17,486
Baptist Convention of Ontario and Quebec (373)	58,507
Baptist Ministries, Canadian (1,133)	129,055
Baptist Union of Western Canada (155)	20,427
Christian and Missionary Alliance in Canada (418)	112,207
Christian Brethren (also known as Plymouth Brethren) (600)	50,000
Christian Reformed Church in North America (242)	82,572
Church of God (Cleveland, TN) (130)	10,914
Church of Jesus Christ of Latter-day Saints in Canada (433)	157,000
Church of the Nazarene Canada (165)	12,199
Churches of Christ in Canada (140)	8,000
Estonian Evangelical Lutheran Church (11)	5,089
Evangelical Baptist Churches in Canada, Fellowship of (506)	*
Evangelical Christian Churches, Canadian (50)	10,000
Evangelical Free Church of Canada (151)	7,690
Evangelical Lutheran Church in Canada (631)	193,915
Evangelical Mennonite Conference of Canada (53)	7,000
Evangelical Missionary Church of Canada (145)	12,217
Free Methodist Church in Canada (136)	6,930
Greek Orthodox Metropolis of Toronto (Canada) (76)	350,000
Hindu	90,000[1]
Independent Assemblies of God Intl. (Canada) (310)	*
Islam	150,000[1]
Jehovah's Witnesses (1,383)	184,787
Jewish congregations (270+)	70,000[1]
Lutheran Church–Canada (324)	79,909
Mennonite Brethren Churches, Canadian Conference of (234)	34,288
Mennonite Church (Canada) (123)	35,995
Open Bible Faith Fellowship of Canada (90)	10,000
Orthodox Church in America (Canada Section) (606)	1,000,000
Pentecostal Assemblies of Canada (1,100)	218,782
Pentecostal Assemblies of Newfoundland (140)	29,361
Presbyterian Church in Canada (992)	200,811
Reformed Church in Canada (41)	6,267
Reformed Churches, Canadian and American (49)	15,429
Reorganized Church of Jesus Christ of Latter Day Saints (75)	11,264
Roman Catholic Church in Canada (5,716)	12,498,605
Salvation Army in Canada (376)	80,180
Serbian Orthodox Church in the U.S.A. and Canada, Diocese of Canada (23)	230,000
Seventh-Day Adventist Church in Canada (327)	49,632
Southern Baptists, Canadian Convention of (152)	9,626
United Baptist Convention of the Atlantic Provinces (555)	62,276
United Church of Canada (3,764)	1,589,886
United Pentecostal Church in Canada (199)	*
Wesleyan Church of Canada (75)	5,992

(1) Estimate; figures from other sources may vary.

Headquarters of Selected Religious Groups in Canada

Sources: *2002 Yearbook of American & Canadian Churches*, © National Council of the Churches of Christ in the USA; *World Almanac* research
(Year organized in parentheses)

Anglican Church of Canada (1700), Church House, 600 Jarvis St., Toronto, ON M4Y 2J6; www.anglican.ca; Primate, Most Rev. Michael G. Peers

Bahá'í National Centre of Canada, 7200 Leslie St., Thornhill, ON L3T 6L8; Gen'l.-Secy., Judy Filson

Baptist Ministries, Canadian, 7185 Millcreek Dr., Mississauga, ON L5N 5R4; www.cbmin.org; Pres., Doug Coomas

Christian and Missionary Alliance in Canada (1887), 30 Carrier Dr, Suite 100, Toronto, ON M9W 5T7; www.cmacan.org; Pres., Dr. Franklin Pyles

Church of Jesus Christ of Latter-day Saints (Mormon), The (1830), 50 E. North Temple St., Salt Lake City, UT 84150

Church of the Nazarene in Canada (1902), 20 Regan Rd. Unit 9, Brampton, ON L7A 1C3; web.1-888.com.nazarene/national; Natl. Dir., Dr. William E. Stewart

Evangelical Baptist Churches in Canada, Fellowship of (1953), 679 Southgate Dr., Guelph, ON N1G 4S2; Pres., Rev. Terry D. Cuthbert

Evangelical Lutheran Church in Canada (1985), 302-393 Portage Ave., Winnipeg, MB R3B 3H6; www.elcic.ca; Bishop, Rev. Telmor G. Sartison

Evangelical Missionary Church of Canada (1993), 4031 Brentwood Rd., NW, Calgary, AB T2L 1L1; Pres., Rev. Mark Bolender

Greek Orthodox Metropolis of Toronto, 86 Overlea Blvd., Toronto, ON M4H 1C6; www.gocanada.org; His Eminence Metropolitan Archbishop Sotirios

Jehovah's Witnesses (1879), Canadian office: Box 4100, Halton Hills, ON L7G 4Y4; Pres., Don Adams

Jewish Congress, Canadian (1919), 100 Sparks St., Ste. 650, Ottawa, Ont. K1P 5B7; www.cjc.ca; Pres., Keith M. Landy (Nonreligious umbrella organization of Jewish groups)

Lutheran Church—Canada (1959), 3074 Portage Ave., Winnipeg, MB R3K OY2; www.lutheranchurch-canada.ca; Pres., Rev. Ralph Mayan

Mennonite Church in Canada (1902), 600 Shaftesbury Blvd., Winnipeg, MB R3P 0M4; www.mennonitechurch.ca; Chairperson, Ron Sawatsky

Muslim Communities in Canada, Council of, 1250 Ramsey View Court, Suite. 504, Sudbury, ON P3E 2E7; Director, Mir Iqbal Ali

North American Shi'a Muslim Communities Organization (NASIMCO), 300 John St., PO Box 87629, Dawnhill, ON L3T 7R3; www.nasimco.org; Pres. Ghulamabbas Sajan

Pentecostal Assemblies of Canada (1919), 6745 Century Ave., Mississauga, ON L5N 6P7; www.paoc.org; Gen. Supt., Rev. William D. Morrow

Presbyterian Church in Canada (1925), 50 Wynford Dr., Toronto, ON M3C 1J7; www.presbycan.ca; Principal Clerk: Rev. Stephen Kendall

Roman Catholic Church (1618), Canadian Conference of Catholic Bishops, 90 Parent Ave., Ottawa, ON K1N 7B1; www.cccb.ca; Pres., Most Rev. Gerald Weisner, OMI

Salvation Army (1909), 2 Overlea Blvd., Toronto, ON M4H 1P4; www.salvationarmy.ca; Territorial Cmdr., Commissioner Norman Howe

Seventh-Day Adventist Church (1901), 1148 King St. E., Oshawa, ON L1H 1H8; Pres., Orville Parchment

Ukrainian Orthodox Church (1918), Office of the Consistory, 9 St. John's Ave., Winnipeg, MB R2W 1G8; www.uocc.ca; Primate, Most Rev. Metropolitan Wasyly Fedak

United Brethren Church (1767) 302 Lake St., Huntington, IN 46750; Pres., Rev. Brian Magnus

United Church of Canada (1925), The United Church House, 3250 Bloor St. W., Ste. 300, Etobicoke, ON M8X 2Y4; www.ucan.org; Mod., Marion Pardy

Wesleyan Church (1968), The Wesleyan Church Intl. Center, PO Box 50434, Indianapolis, IN 46250; Dist. Supt., Rev. Donald E. Hodgins

Adherents of All Religions by Six Continental Areas, Mid-2001

Source: *2002 Encyclopædia Britannica Book of the Year*

	Africa	Asia	Europe	Latin America	Northern America	Oceania	World
Baha'is	1,779,000	3,538,000	132,000	893,000	799,000	113,000	7,254,000
Buddhists	139,000	356,533,000	1,570,000	660,000	2,777,000	307,000	361,985,000
Chinese folk religionists	33,100	385,758,000	258,000	197,000	857,000	64,200	387,167,000
Christians	368,244,000	317,759,000	559,359,000	486,591,000	261,752,000	25,343,000	2,019,052,000
Anglicans	43,524,000	735,000	26,628,000	1,098,000	3,231,000	5,428,000	80,644,000
Independents	85,476,000	157,605,000	25,850,000	40,357,000	81,032,000	1,536,000	391,856,000
Orthodox	36,038,000	14,219,000	158,375,000	564,000	6,400,000	718,000	216,314,000
Protestants	90,989,000	50,718,000	77,497,000	49,008,000	70,164,000	7,478,000	345,855,000
Roman Catholics	123,467,000	112,086,000	285,554,000	466,226,000	71,391,000	8,327,000	1,067,053,000
Confucianists	250	6,277,000	10,800	450	0	24,000	6,313,000
Ethnic religionists	97,762,000	129,005,000	1,258,000	1,288,000	446,000	267,000	230,026,000
Hindus	2,384,000	813,396,000	1,425,000	775,000	1,350,000	359,000	819,689,000
Jains	66,900	4,207,000	0	0	7,000	0	4,281,000
Jews	215,000	4,476,000	2,506,000	1,145,000	6,045,000	97,600	14,484,000
Muslims	323,556,000	845,341,000	31,724,000	1,702,000	4,518,000	307,000	1,207,148,000
New-Religionists	28,900	101,065,000	160,000	633,000	847,000	66,900	102,801,000
Shintoists	0	2,669,000	0	6,900	56,700	0	2,732,000
Sikhs	54,400	22,689,000	241,000	0	535,000	18,500	23,538,000
Spiritists	2,600	2,000	134,000	12,169,000	152,000	7,100	12,466,000
Taoists	0	2,658,000	0	0	11,200		2,670,000
Zoroastrians	910	2,519,000	670	0	79,100	1,400	2,601,000
Other religionists	67,300	63,100	238,000	99,600	605,000	9,500	1,082,000
Nonreligious	5,170,000	611,876,000	105,742,000	16,214,000	28,994,000	3,349,000	771,345,000
Atheists	432,000	122,408,000	22,555,000	2,787,000	1,700,000	369,000	150,252,000

Adherents. As defined in the 1948 Universal Declaration of Human Rights, a person's religion is what he or she says it is. Totals are enumerated following the methodology of the *World Christian Encyclopedia*, 2nd ed. (2001), using recent censuses, polls, literature, and other data. As a result of the varieties of sources used, totals may differ from standard estimates for total populations.

Buddhists. 56% Mahayana, 38% Theravada (Hinayana), 6% Tantrayana (Lamaism).

Chinese folk religionists. Followers of traditional Chinese religion (local deities, ancestor veneration, Confucian ethics, Taoism, universism, divination, some Buddhist elements).

Christians. Total Christians include those affiliated with churches not shown, plus other persons professing in censuses or polls to be Christians but not affiliated with any church. Figures for the subgroups of Christians do not add up to the totals because all subgroups are not shown and some Christians adhere to more than one denomination.

Confucianists. Non-Chinese followers of Confucius and Confucianism, mostly Koreans in Korea.

Ethnic religionists. Followers of local, tribal, animistic, or shamanistic religions, with members restricted to one ethnic group.

Hindus. 70% Vaishnavites, 25% Shaivites, 2% neo-Hindus and reform Hindus.

Independents. Members of churches and networks that regard themselves as postdenominationalist and neo-apostolic and thus independent of historic, organized, institutionalized denominationalist Christianity.

Jews. Adherents of Judaism.

Muslims. 83% Sunni Muslims, 16% Shia Muslims (Shi'ites), 1% other schools.

New-Religionists. Followers of Asian 20th-cent. New Religions, New Religious movements, radical new crisis religions, and non-Christian syncretistic mass religions, all founded since 1800 and most since 1945.

Other religionists. Including a handful of religions, quasi-religions, pseudo religions, parareligions, religious or mystic systems, and religious and semireligious brotherhoods of numerous varieties.

Nonreligious. Persons professing no religion, nonbelievers, agnostics, freethinkers, uninterested, dereligionized secularists indifferent to all religion.

Atheists. Persons professing atheism, skepticism, disbelief, or irreligion, including antireligious (opposed to all religion).

Episcopal Church Liturgical Colors and Calendar

Source: Church Publishing Incorporated, New York

The liturgical colors in the Episcopal Church are as follows: **White**—from Christmas Day through the First Sunday after Epiphany; Maundy Thursday (as an alternative to crimson at the Eucharist); from the Vigil of Easter to the Day of Pentecost (Whitsunday); Trinity Sunday; Feasts of the Lord (except Holy Cross Day); the Confession of St. Peter; the Conversion of St. Paul; St. Joseph; St. Mary Magdalene; St. Mary the Virgin; St. Michael and All Angels; All Saints' Day; St. John the Evangelist; memorials of other saints who were not martyred; Independence Day and Thanksgiving Day; weddings and funerals. **Red**—the Day of Pentecost; Holy Cross Day; feasts of apostles and evangelists (except those listed above); feasts and memorials of martyrs (including Holy Innocents' Day). **Violet**—Advent and Lent. **Crimson** or oxblood (dark red)—Holy Week. **Green**—the seasons after Epiphany and after Pentecost. **Black**—optional alternative for funerals and Good Friday. Alternative colors used in some churches: **Blue**—Advent; **Lenten White (unbleached linen)**—Ash Wednesday to Palm Sunday.

In the Episcopal Church the days of fasting are Ash Wednesday and Good Friday. Other days of special devotion (penitence) are the 40 days of Lent and all Fridays of the year, except those in Christmas and Easter seasons and any Feasts of the Lord that occur on a Friday or during Lent. Ember Days (optional) are days of prayer for the church's ministry. They fall on the Wednesday, Friday, and Saturday after the first Sunday in Lent, the Day of Pentecost, Holy Cross Day, and December 13. Rogation Days (also optional), the 3 days before Ascension Day, are days of prayer for God's blessing on the crops, on commerce and industry, and for conservation of the earth's resources.

Days, etc.	2002	2003	2004	2005	2006
Golden Number	8	9	10	11	12
Sunday Letter	F	E	D & C	B	A
Sundays after Epiphany	5	8	7	5	8
Ash Wednesday	Feb. 13	Mar. 5	Feb. 25	Feb. 9	Mar. 1
First Sunday in Lent	Feb. 17	Mar. 9	Feb. 29	Feb. 13	Mar. 5
Passion/Palm Sunday	Mar. 24	Apr. 13	Apr. 4	Mar. 20	Apr. 9
Good Friday	Mar. 29	Apr. 18	Apr. 9	Mar. 25	Apr. 14
Easter Day	Mar. 31	Apr. 20	Apr. 11	Mar. 27	Apr. 16
Ascension Day	May 9	May 29	May 20	May 5	May 25
The Day of Pentecost	May 19	June 8	May 30	May 15	June 4
Trinity Sunday	May 26	June 15	June 6	May 22	June 11
Numbered Proper of 2 Pentecost	#4	#7	#6	#4	#6
First Sunday of Advent	Dec. 1	Nov. 30	Nov. 28	Nov. 27	Dec. 3

Greek Orthodox Movable Ecclesiastical Dates, 2002-2006

This 5-year chart has the dates of feast days and fasting days, which are determined annually on the basis of the date of Holy Pascha (Easter). This ecclesiastical cycle begins with the first day of the Triodion and ends with the Sunday of All Saints, a total of 18 weeks.

	2002	2003	2004	2005	2006
Triodion begins	Feb. 24	Feb. 16	Feb. 1	Feb. 20	Feb. 12
Sat. of Souls	Mar. 9	Mar. 1	Feb. 14	Mar. 5	Feb. 25
Meat Fare	Mar. 10	Mar. 2	Feb. 15	Mar. 6	Feb. 26
2nd Sat. of Souls	Mar. 16	Mar. 8	Feb. 21	Mar. 12	Mar. 4
Lent Begins	Mar. 18	Mar. 10	Feb. 23	Mar. 14	Mar. 6
St. Theodore—3rd Sat. of Souls	Mar. 23	Mar. 15	Feb. 28	Mar. 19	Mar. 11
Sunday of Orthodoxy	Mar. 24	Mar. 16	Feb. 29	Mar. 20	Mar. 12
Sat. of Lazarus	Apr. 27	Apr. 19	Apr. 3	Apr. 23	Apr. 15
Palm Sunday	Apr. 28	Apr. 20	Apr. 4	Apr. 24	Apr. 16
Holy (Good) Friday	May 3	Apr. 25	Apr. 9	Apr. 29	Apr. 21
Western Easter	Mar. 31	Apr. 20	Apr. 11	Mar. 27	Apr. 16
Orthodox Easter	May 5	Apr. 27	Apr. 11	May 1	Apr. 23
Ascension	June 13	June 5	May 20	June 9	June 1
Sat. of Souls	June 22	June 14	May 29	June 18	June 10
Pentecost	June 23	June 15	May 30	June 19	June 11
All Saints	June 30	June 22	June 7	June 26	June 18

Important Islamic Dates, 1423-27 (2002-2007)

Source: Imad-ad-Dean, Inc., Bethesda, MD 20814

The Islamic calendar is a strict lunar calendar reckoned from the year of the Hijra (Muhammad's flight from Mecca to Medina). Each year consists of 12 lunar months of 29 or 30 days beginning and ending with each new moon's visible crescent. Common years have 354 days; leap years have 355 days. Some Muslim countries employ a conventionalized calendar with the leap day added to the last month, Dhûl Hijah, but for religious purposes the leap date is taken into account by tracking each new moon sighting. The dates given below are based on the convention that the first new moon must be seen before the following dawn on the East Coast of the Americas. Actual (local) Western Hemisphere sightings may occur a day later, but never a day earlier, than these dates reflect.

	(1423) 2002-03	(1424) 2003-04	(1425) 2004-05	(1426) 2005-06	(1427) 2006-07
New Year's Day (Muharram 1)	Mar. 15, 2002	Mar. 4, 2003	Feb. 21, 2004	Feb. 10, 2005	Jan. 30, 2006
Ashura (Muharram 10)	Mar. 24, 2002	Mar. 13, 2003	Mar. 1, 2004	Feb. 19, 2005	Feb. 8, 2006
Mawlid (Rabi'l 12)	May 24, 2002	May 13, 2003	May 1, 2004	April 21, 2005	Apr. 10, 2006
Ramadan 1	Nov. 6, 2002	Oct. 26, 2003	Oct. 15, 2004	Oct. 4, 2005	Sept. 23, 2006
Eid al-Fitr (Shawwal)	Dec. 5, 2002	Nov. 25, 2003	Nov. 13, 2004	Nov. 3, 2005	Oct. 23, 2006
Eid al-Adha (Dhûl-Hijjah 10)	Feb. 11, 2003	Feb. 1, 2004	Jan. 20, 2005	Jan. 10, 2006	Dec. 30, 2006

IT'S A FACT: During the Hindu "spring fever" festival of Holi in early March, it is customary for people to run around spraying each other with brightly colored water or powder until everyone is thoroughly "decorated."

Jewish Holy Days, Festivals, and Fasts 5762-5767 (2002-2006)

	(5762-63) 2002-03		(5763-64) 2003-04		(5764-65) 2004		(5765-66) 2005-06		(5766-67) 2006	
Tu B'Shvat	Jan. 28	Mon.	Jan. 18	Sat.	Feb. 7	Sat.	Jan. 25	Tue.	Feb. 13	Mon.
Ta'anis Esther (Fast of Esther)	Feb. 25	Mon.	Mar. 17	Mon.	Mar. 4	Thu.*	Mar. 24	Thu.	Mar. 13	Mon.
Purim	Feb. 26	Tue.	Mar. 18	Tue.	Mar. 7	Sun.	Mar. 25	Fri.	Mar. 14	Tue.
Pesach (Passover)	Mar. 28	Thu.	Apr. 17	Thu.	Apr. 6	Tue.	Apr. 24	Sun.	Apr. 13	Thu.
	Apr. 4	Thu.	Apr. 24	Thu.	Apr. 13	Tue.	May 1	Sun.	Apr. 20	Thu.
Lag B'Omer	Apr. 30	Tue.	May. 20	Tue.	May 9	Sun.	May 27	Fri.	May 16	Tue.
Shavuot (Pentecost)	May 17	Fri.	June 6	Fri.	May 26	Wed.	June 13	Mon.	June 2	Fri.
	May 18	Sat.	June 7	Sat.	May 27	Thu.	June 14	Tue.	June 3	Sat.
Fast of the 17th Day of Tammuz	June 27	Thu.	July 17	Thu.	July 6	Tue.	July 24	Sun.	July 13	Thu.
Fast of the 9th Day of Av	July 18	Thu.	Aug. 7	Thu.	July 27	Tue.	Aug. 14	Sun.	Aug. 3	Thu.
Rosh Hashanah (Jewish New Year)	Sept. 7	Sat.	Sept. 27	Sat.	Sept. 16	Thu.	Oct. 4	Tue.	Sept. 23	Sat.
	Sept. 8	Sun.	Sept. 28	Sun.	Sept. 17	Fri.	Oct. 5	Wed.	Sept. 24	Sun
Fast of Gedalya	Sept. 9	Mon.	Sept. 29	Mon.	Sept. 19	Sun.*	Oct. 6	Thu.	Sept. 25	Mon.
Yom Kippur (Day of Atonement)	Sept. 16	Mon.	Oct. 6	Mon.	Sept. 25	Sat.	Oct. 13	Thu.	Oct. 2	Mon.
Sukkot	Sept. 21	Sat.	Oct. 11	Sat.	Sept. 30	Thu.	Oct. 18	Tue.	Oct. 7	Sat.
	Sept. 27	Fri.	Oct. 17	Fri.	Oct. 1	Wed.	Oct. 24	Mon.	Oct. 13	Fri.
Shmini Atzeret	Sept. 28	Sat.	Oct. 18	Sat.	Oct. 7	Thu.	Oct. 25	Tue.	Oct. 14	Sat.
	Sept. 29	Sun.	Oct. 19	Sun.	Oct. 8	Fri.	Oct. 26	Wed.	Oct. 15	Sun.
Hanukkah	Nov. 30	Sat.	Dec. 20	Sat.	Dec. 8	Wed.	Dec. 26	Mon.	Dec. 16	Sat.
	Dec. 7	Sat.	Dec. 27	Sat.	Dec. 15	Wed.	Jan. 2, 2006	Mon.	Dec. 23	Sat.
Fast of the 10th of Tevet	Jan. 15, 2003	Sun.	Jan. 4, 2004	Sun.	Dec. 22	Wed.	Jan. 10, 2006	Tue.	Dec. 31	Sun.

The months of the Jewish year are: 1) Tishri; 2) Cheshvan (also Marcheshvan); 3) Kislev; 4) Tevet (also Tebeth); 5) Shebat (also Shebhat); 6) Adar; 6a) Adar Sheni (II) added in leap years; 7) Nisan; 8) Iyar; 9) Sivan; 10) Tammuz; 11) Av (also Abh); 12) Elul. All Jewish holy days, etc., begin at sunset on the previous day.

*Date changed to avoid Sabbath.

Ash Wednesday and Easter Sunday (Western churches), 1901-2100

Year	Ash Wed.	Easter Sunday	Year	Ash Wed.	Easter Sunday	Year	Ash Wed.	Easter Sunday	Year	Ash Wed.	Easter Sunday
1901	Feb. 20	Apr. 7	1951	Feb. 7	Mar. 25	2001	Feb. 28	Apr. 15	2051	Feb. 15	Apr. 2
1902	Feb. 12	Mar. 30	1952	Feb. 27	Apr. 13	2002	Feb. 13	Mar. 31	2052	Mar. 6	Apr. 21
1903	Feb. 25	Apr. 12	1953	Feb. 18	Apr. 5	2003	Mar. 5	Apr. 20	2053	Feb. 19	Apr. 6
1904	Feb. 17	Apr. 3	1954	Mar. 3	Apr. 18	2004	Feb. 25	Apr. 11	2054	Feb. 11	Mar. 29
1905	Mar. 8	Apr. 23	1955	Feb. 23	Apr. 10	2005	Feb. 9	Mar. 27	2055	Mar. 3	Apr. 18
1906	Feb. 28	Apr. 15	1956	Feb. 15	Apr. 1	2006	Mar. 1	Apr. 16	2056	Feb. 16	Apr. 2
1907	Feb. 13	Mar. 31	1957	Mar. 6	Apr. 21	2007	Feb. 21	Apr. 8	2057	Mar. 7	Apr. 22
1908	Mar. 4	Apr. 19	1958	Feb. 19	Apr. 6	2008	Feb. 6	Mar. 23	2058	Feb. 27	Apr. 14
1909	Feb. 24	Apr. 11	1959	Feb. 11	Mar. 29	2009	Feb. 25	Apr. 12	2059	Feb. 12	Mar. 30
1910	Feb. 9	Mar. 27	1960	Mar. 2	Apr. 17	2010	Feb. 17	Apr. 4	2060	Mar. 3	Apr. 18
1911	Mar. 1	Apr. 16	1961	Feb. 15	Apr. 2	2011	Mar. 9	Apr. 24	2061	Feb. 23	Apr. 10
1912	Feb. 21	Apr. 7	1962	Mar. 7	Apr. 22	2012	Feb. 22	Apr. 8	2062	Feb. 8	Mar. 26
1913	Feb. 5	Mar. 23	1963	Feb. 27	Apr. 14	2013	Feb. 13	Mar. 31	2063	Feb. 28	Apr. 15
1914	Feb. 25	Apr. 12	1964	Feb. 12	Mar. 29	2014	Mar. 5	Apr. 20	2064	Feb. 20	Apr. 6
1915	Feb. 17	Apr. 4	1965	Mar. 3	Apr. 18	2015	Feb. 18	Apr. 5	2065	Feb. 11	Mar. 29
1916	Mar. 8	Apr. 23	1966	Feb. 23	Apr. 10	2016	Feb. 10	Mar. 27	2066	Feb. 24	Apr. 11
1917	Feb. 21	Apr. 8	1967	Feb. 8	Mar. 26	2017	Mar. 1	Apr. 16	2067	Feb. 16	Apr. 3
1918	Feb. 13	Mar. 31	1968	Feb. 28	Apr. 14	2018	Feb. 14	Apr. 1	2068	Mar. 7	Apr. 22
1919	Mar. 5	Apr. 20	1969	Feb. 19	Apr. 6	2019	Mar. 6	Apr. 21	2069	Feb. 27	Apr. 14
1920	Feb. 18	Apr. 4	1970	Feb. 11	Mar. 29	2020	Feb. 26	Apr. 12	2070	Feb. 12	Mar. 30
1921	Feb. 9	Mar. 27	1971	Feb. 24	Apr. 11	2021	Feb. 17	Apr. 4	2071	Mar. 4	Apr. 19
1922	Mar. 1	Apr. 16	1972	Feb. 16	Apr. 2	2022	Mar. 2	Apr. 17	2072	Feb. 24	Apr. 10
1923	Feb. 14	Apr. 1	1973	Mar. 7	Apr. 22	2023	Feb. 22	Apr. 9	2073	Feb. 8	Mar. 26
1924	Mar. 5	Apr. 20	1974	Feb. 27	Apr. 14	2024	Feb. 14	Mar. 31	2074	Feb. 28	Apr. 15
1925	Feb. 25	Apr. 12	1975	Feb. 12	Mar. 30	2025	Mar. 5	Apr. 20	2075	Feb. 20	Apr. 7
1926	Feb. 17	Apr. 4	1976	Mar. 3	Apr. 18	2026	Feb. 18	Apr. 5	2076	Mar. 4	Apr. 19
1927	Mar. 2	Apr. 17	1977	Feb. 23	Apr. 10	2027	Feb. 10	Mar. 28	2077	Feb. 24	Apr. 11
1928	Feb. 22	Apr. 8	1978	Feb. 8	Mar.. 26	2028	Mar. 1	Apr. 16	2078	Feb. 16	Apr. 3
1929	Feb. 13	Mar. 31	1979	Feb. 28	Apr. 15	2029	Feb. 14	Apr. 1	2079	Mar. 8	Apr. 23
1930	Mar. 5	Apr. 20	1980	Feb. 20	Apr. 6	2030	Mar. 6	Apr. 21	2080	Feb. 21	Apr. 7
1931	Feb. 18	Apr. 5	1981	Mar. 4	Apr. 19	2031	Feb. 26	Apr. 13	2081	Feb. 12	Mar. 30
1932	Feb. 10	Mar. 27	1982	Feb. 24	Apr. 11	2032	Feb. 11	Mar. 28	2082	Mar. 4	Apr. 19
1933	Mar. 1	Apr. 16	1983	Feb. 16	Apr. 3	2033	Mar. 2	Apr. 17	2083	Feb. 17	Apr. 4
1934	Feb. 14	Apr. 1	1984	Mar. 7	Apr. 22	2034	Feb. 22	Apr. 9	2084	Feb. 9	Mar. 26
1935	Mar. 6	Apr. 21	1985	Feb. 20	Apr. 7	2035	Feb. 7	Mar. 25	2085	Feb. 28	Apr. 15
1936	Feb. 26	Apr. 12	1986	Feb. 12	Mar. 30	2036	Feb. 27	Apr. 13	2086	Feb. 13	Mar. 31
1937	Feb. 10	Mar. 28	1987	Mar. 4	Apr. 19	2037	Feb. 18	Apr. 5	2087	Mar. 5	Apr. 20
1938	Mar. 2	Apr. 17	1988	Feb. 17	Apr. 3	2038	Mar. 10	Apr. 25	2088	Feb. 25	Apr. 11
1939	Feb. 22	Apr. 9	1989	Feb. 8	Mar. 26	2039	Feb. 23	Apr. 10	2089	Feb. 16	Apr. 3
1940	Feb. 7	Mar. 24	1990	Feb. 28	Apr. 15	2040	Feb. 15	Apr. 1	2090	Mar. 1	Apr. 16
1941	Feb. 26	Apr. 13	1991	Feb. 13	Mar. 31	2041	Mar. 6	Apr. 21	2091	Feb. 21	Apr. 8
1942	Feb. 18	Apr. 5	1992	Mar. 4	Apr. 19	2042	Feb. 19	Apr. 6	2092	Feb. 13	Mar. 30
1943	Mar. 10	Apr. 25	1993	Feb. 24	Apr. 11	2043	Feb. 11	Mar. 29	2093	Feb. 25	Apr. 12
1944	Feb. 23	Apr. 9	1994	Feb. 16	Apr. 3	2044	Mar. 2	Apr. 17	2094	Feb. 17	Apr. 4
1945	Feb. 14	Apr. 1	1995	Mar. 1	Apr. 16	2045	Feb. 22	Apr. 9	2095	Mar. 9	Apr. 24
1946	Mar. 6	Apr. 21	1996	Feb. 21	Apr. 7	2046	Feb. 7	Mar. 25	2096	Feb. 29	Apr. 15
1947	Feb. 19	Apr. 6	1997	Feb. 12	Mar. 30	2047	Feb. 27	Apr. 14	2097	Feb. 13	Mar. 31
1948	Feb. 11	Mar. 28	1998	Feb. 25	Apr. 12	2048	Feb. 19	Apr. 5	2098	Mar. 5	Apr. 20
1949	Mar. 2	Apr. 17	1999	Feb. 17	Apr. 4	2049	Mar. 3	Apr. 18	2099	Feb. 25	Apr. 12
1950	Feb. 22	Apr. 9	2000	Mar. 8	Apr. 23	2050	Feb. 23	Apr. 10	2100	Feb. 10	Mar. 28

The Ten Commandments

According to Judeo-Christian tradition, as related in the Bible, the Ten Commandments were revealed by God to Moses and form the basic moral component of God's covenant with Israel. The Ten Commandments appear in 2 places in the Old Testament—Exodus 20:1-17 and Deuteronomy 5:6-21.

Following is the text of the Ten Commandments as it appears in Exodus 20:1-17, in the King James version of the Bible.

I. I am the LORD thy God, which have brought thee out of the land of Egypt, out of the house of bondage. Thou shalt have no other gods before me.

II. Thou shalt not make unto thee any graven image, or any likeness of any thing that is in heaven above, or that is in the earth beneath, or that is in the water under the earth. Thou shalt not bow down thyself to them, nor serve them: for I the LORD thy God am a jealous God, visiting the iniquity of the fathers upon the children unto the third and fourth generation of them that hate me.

III. Thou shalt not take the name of the LORD thy God in vain; for the LORD will not hold him guiltless that taketh his name in vain.

IV. Remember the sabbath day, to keep it holy.

V. Honour thy father and thy mother: that thy days may be long upon the land which the LORD thy God giveth thee.

VI. Thou shalt not kill.

VII. Thou shalt not commit adultery.

VIII. Thou shalt not steal.

IX. Thou shalt not bear false witness against thy neighbour.

X. Thou shalt not covet thy neighbour's house, thou shalt not covet thy neighbour's wife, nor his manservant, nor his maidservant, nor his ox, nor his ass, nor any thing that is thy neighbour's.

Most Protestant, Anglican, and Orthodox Christians follow Jewish tradition, which considers the introduction ("I am the Lord . . .") the first commandment and makes the prohibition against idolatry the second. Roman Catholic and Lutheran traditions combine I and II and split the last commandment into 2 that separately prohibit coveting of a neighbor's wife and a neighbor's goods. This arrangement alters the numbering of the other commandments by one.

Books of the Bible

Old Testament—Standard Protestant List

Genesis	I Kings	Ecclesiastes	Obadiah
Exodus	II Kings	Song of Solomon	Jonah
Leviticus	I Chronicles	Isaiah	Micah
Numbers	II Chronicles	Jeremiah	Nahum
Deuteronomy	Ezra	Lamentations	Habakkuk
Joshua	Nehemiah	Ezekiel	Zephaniah
Judges	Esther	Daniel	Haggai
Ruth	Job	Hosea	Zechariah
I Samuel	Psalms	Joel	Malachi
II Samuel	Proverbs	Amos	

New Testament List

Matthew	Ephesians	Hebrews
Mark	Phillippians	James
Luke	Colossians	I Peter
John	I Thessalonians	II Peter
Acts	II Thessalonians	I John
Romans	I Timothy	II John
I Corinthians	II Timothy	III John
II Corinthians	Titus	Jude
Galatians	Philemon	Revelation

The standard Protestant Old Testament consists of the same 39 books as in the Bible of Judaism, but the latter is organized differently. The Old Testament used by Roman Catholics has 7 additional "deuterocanonical" books, plus some additional parts of books. The 7 are: **Tobit, Judith, Wisdom, Sirach (Ecclesiasticus), Baruch, I Maccabees,** and **II Maccabees**. Both Catholic and Protestant versions of the New Testament have 27 books, with the same names.

Roman Catholic Hierarchy

Source: U.S. Catholic Conference

Supreme Pontiff

At the head of the Roman Catholic Church is the supreme pontiff, Pope John Paul II, Karol Wojtyla, born at Wadowice (Kraków), Poland, May 18, 1920; ordained priest Nov. 1, 1946; appointed bishop July 4, 1958; named archbishop of Kraków Jan. 13, 1964; proclaimed cardinal June 26, 1967; elected pope Oct. 16, 1978; installed Oct. 22, 1978.

College of Cardinals

Members of the Sacred College of Cardinals are chosen by the pope to be his chief assistants and advisers in the administration of the church. Among their duties is the election of the pope when the Holy See becomes vacant.

In its present form, the College of Cardinals dates from the 12th century. The first cardinals, from about the 6th century, were deacons and priests of the leading churches of Rome and were bishops of neighboring dioceses. The title of cardinal was limited to members of the college in 1567. The number of cardinals was set at 70 in 1586 by Pope Sixtus V. From 1959 Pope John XXIII began to increase the number; however, the number eligible to participate in papal elections was limited to 120. In Feb. 2001, Pope John Paul II waived the limit on number of electors when he created 44 new cardinals. As of Sept. 2002, there were 176 members of the College, of whom 118 were electors. In 1918 the Code of Canon Law specified that all cardinals must be priests. Pope John XXIII in 1962 established that all cardinals must be bishops. In 1971 Pope Paul VI decreed that at age 80 cardinals must retire from curial departments and offices and from participation in papal elections.

North American Cardinals

Name	Office	Born	Named Cardinal
Aloysius M. Ambrozic	Archbishop of Toronto	1930	1998
William W. Baum	Major Penitentiary of Apostolic Penitentiary, the Vatican	1926	1976
Anthony J. Bevilacqua	Archbishop of Philadelphia	1923	1991
G. Emmett Carter[1]	Archbishop emeritus of Toronto	1912	1979
Ernesto Corripio Ahumada[1]	Archbishop emeritus of Mexico	1919	1979
Avery Robert Dulles[1]	Professor, Fordham University	1918	2001
Edward M. Egan	Archbishop of New York	1932	2001
Edouard Gagnon[1]	Pres. of Pontifical Commission of Intl. Eucharistic Congresses	1918	1985
Francis E. George	Archbishop of Chicago	1937	1998
James A. Hickey[1]	Archbishop emeritus of Washington, DC	1920	1988
William Henry Keeler	Archbishop of Baltimore	1931	1994
Bernard F. Law	Archbishop of Boston	1931	1985
Roger Mahony	Archbishop of Los Angeles	1936	1991
Adam Joseph Maida	Archbishop of Detroit	1930	1994
Theodore E. McCarrick	Archbishop of Washington, DC	1930	2001
Norberto Rivera Carrera	Archbishop of Mexico City	1942	1998
Juan Sandoval Iniguez	Archbishop of Guadalajara	1933	1994
James F. Stafford	President of the Pontifical Council for the Laity	1932	1998
Adolfo Antonio Suarez Rivera	Archbishop of Monterrey	1927	1994
Edmund C. Szoka	Pres. of Prefecture of Economic Affairs of Holy See, the Vatican	1927	1988
Jean-Claude Turcotte	Archbishop of Montreal	1936	1994
Louis-Albert Vachon[1]	Archbishop emeritus of Quebec	1912	1985

(1) Ineligible to take part in papal elections (as of Sept. 2002).

Chronological List of Popes

Source: Annuario Pontificio. Table lists year of accession of each pope.

The Roman Catholic Church named the Apostle Peter as founder of the church in Rome and the first pope. He arrived there c 42, was martyred there c 67, and was ultimately canonized as a saint. **The pope's temporal title is:** Sovereign of the State of Vatican City. **The pope's spiritual titles are:** Bishop of Rome, Vicar of Jesus Christ, Successor of St. Peter, Prince of the Apostles, Supreme Pontiff of the Universal Church, Patriarch of the West, Primate of Italy, Archbishop and Metropolitan of the Roman Province.

The names of antipopes are *in italics* and followed by an *. Antipopes were illegitimate claimants to the papal throne.

Year	Pope
	St. Peter
67	St. Linus
76	St. Anacletus or Cletus
88	St. Clement I
97	St. Evaristus
105	St. Alexander I
115	St. Sixtus I
125	St. Telesphorus
136	St. Hyginus
140	St. Pius I
155	St. Anicetus
166	St. Soter
175	St. Eleutherius
189	St. Victor I
199	St. Zephyrinus
217	St. Callistus I
217	*St. Hippolytus**
222	St. Urban I
230	St. Pontian
235	St. Anterus
236	St. Fabian
251	St. Cornelius
251	*Novatian**
253	St. Lucius I
254	St. Stephen I
257	St. Sixtus II
259	St. Dionysius
269	St. Felix I
275	St. Eutychian
283	St. Caius
296	St. Marcellinus
308	St. Marcellus I
309	St. Eusebius
311	St. Melchiades
314	St. Sylvester I
336	St. Marcus
337	St. Julius I
352	Liberius
355	*Felix II**
366	St. Damasus I
366	*Ursinus**
384	St. Siricius
399	St. Anastasius I
401	St. Innocent I
417	St. Zosimus
418	St. Boniface I
418	*Eulabus**
422	St. Celestine I
432	St. Sixtus III
440	St. Leo I
461	St. Hilary
468	St. Simplicius
483	St. Felix III (II)
492	St. Gelasius I
496	Anastasius II
498	St. Symmachus
498	*Lawrence** (501-505)
514	St. Hormisdas
523	St. John I, Martyr
526	St. Felix IV (III)
530	Boniface II
530	*Dioscorus**
533	John II
535	St. Agapitus I
536	St. Silverius, Martyr
537	Vigilius
556	Pelagius I
561	John III
575	Benedict I
579	Pelagius II
590	St. Gregory I
604	Sabinian
607	Boniface III
608	St. Boniface IV
615	St. Deusdedit or Adeodatus
619	Boniface V
625	Honorius I
640	Severinus
640	John IV
642	Theodore I
649	St. Martin I, Martyr
654	St. Eugene I
657	St. Vitalian
672	Adeodatus II
676	Donus
678	St. Agatho
682	St. Leo II
684	St. Benedict II
685	John V
686	Conon
687	*Theodore**
687	*Paschal**
687	St. Sergius I
701	John VI
705	John VII
708	Sisinnius
708	Constantine
715	St. Gregory II
731	St. Gregory III
741	St. Zachary
752	Stephen II (III)
757	St. Paul I
767	*Constantine**
768	*Philip**
768	Stephen III (IV)
772	Adrian I
795	St. Leo III
816	Stephen IV (V)
817	St. Paschal I
824	Eugene II
827	Valentine
827	Gregory IV
844	*John**
844	Sergius II
847	St. Leo IV
855	Benedict III
855	*Anastasius**
858	St. Nicholas I
867	Adrian II
872	John VIII
882	Marinus I
884	St. Adrian III
885	Stephen V (VI)
891	Formosus
896	Boniface VI
896	Stephen VI (VII)
897	Romanus
897	Theodore II
898	John IX
900	Benedict IV
903	Leo V
903	*Christopher**
904	Sergius III
911	Anastasius III
913	Landus
914	John X
928	Leo VI
928	Stephen VII(VIII)
931	John XI
936	Leo VII
939	Stephen VIII(IX)
942	Marinus II
946	Agapitus II
955	John XII
963	Leo VIII
964	Benedict V
965	John XIII
973	Benedict VI
974	*Boniface VII**
974	Benedict VII
983	John XIV
985	John XV
996	Gregory V
997	*John XVI**
999	Sylvester II
1003	John VII
1004	John XVIII
1009	Sergius IV
1012	Benedict VIII
1012	*Gregory**
1024	John XIX
1032	Benedict IX
1045	Sylvester III
1045	Benedict IX
1045	Gregory VI
1046	Clement II
1047	Benedict IX
1048	Damasus II
1049	St. Leo IX
1055	Victor II
1057	Stephen IX (X)
1058	*Benedict X**
1059	Nicholas II
1061	Alexander II
1061	*Honorius II**
1073	St. Gregory VII
1080	*Clement III**
1086	Bl. Victor III
1088	Bl. Urban II
1099	Paschal II
1100	*Theodoric**
1102	*Albert**
1105	*Sylvester IV**
1118	Gelasius II
1118	*Gregory VIII**
1119	Callistus II
1124	Honorius II
1124	*Celestine II**
1130	Innocent II
1130	*Anacletus II**
1138	*Victor IV**
1143	Celestine II
1144	Lucius II
1145	Bl. Eugene III
1153	Anastasius IV
1154	Adrian IV
1159	Alexander III
1159	*Victor IV**
1164	*Paschal III**
1168	*Callistus III**
1179	*Innocent III**
1181	Lucius III
1185	Urban III
1187	Clement III
1187	Gregory VIII
1191	Celestine III
1198	Innocent III
1216	Honorius III
1227	Gregory IX
1241	Celestine IV
1243	Innocent IV
1254	Alexander IV
1261	Urban IV
1265	Clement IV
1271	Bl. Gregory X
1276	Bl. Innocent V
1276	Adrian V
1276	John XXI
1277	Nicholas III
1281	Martin IV
1285	Honorius IV
1288	Nicholas IV
1294	St. Celestine V
1294	Boniface VIII
1303	Bl. Benedict XI
1305	Clement V
1316	John XXII
1328	*Nicholas V**
1334	Benedict XII
1342	Clement VI
1352	Innocent VI
1362	Bl. Urban V
1370	Gregory XI
1378	Urban VI
1378	*Clement VII**
1389	Boniface IX
1394	*Benedict XIII**
1404	Innocent VII
1406	Gregory XII
1409	*Alexander V**
1410	*John XXIII**
1417	Martin V
1431	Eugene IV
1439	*Felix V**
1447	Nicholas V
1455	Callistus III
1458	Pius II
1464	Paul II
1471	Sixtus IV
1484	Innocent VIII
1492	Alexander VI
1503	Pius III
1503	Julius II
1513	Leo X
1522	Adrian VI
1523	Clement VII
1534	Paul III
1550	Julius III
1555	Marcellus II
1555	Paul IV
1559	Pius IV
1566	St. Pius V
1572	Gregory XIII
1585	Sixtus V
1590	Urban VII
1590	Gregory XIV
1591	Innocent IX
1592	Clement VIII
1605	Leo XI
1605	Paul V
1621	Gregory XV
1623	Urban VIII
1644	Innocent X
1655	Alexander VII
1667	Clement IX
1670	Clement X
1676	Bl. Innocent XI
1689	Alexander VIII
1691	Innocent XII
1700	Clement XI
1721	Innocent XIII
1724	Benedict XIII
1730	Clement XII
1740	Benedict XIV
1758	Clement XIII
1769	Clement XIV
1775	Pius VI
1800	Pius VII
1823	Leo XII
1829	Pius VIII
1831	Gregory XVI
1846	Pius IX
1878	Leo XIII
1903	St. Pius X
1914	Benedict XV
1922	Pius XI
1939	Pius XII
1958	John XXIII
1963	Paul VI
1978	John Paul I
1978	John Paul II

Major Non-Christian World Religions

Sources: Reviewed by Anthony Padovano, PhD, STD, prof. of literature & relig. studies, Ramapo College, NJ, adj. prof. of theol., Fordham U., NYC; Islam reviewed by Abdulaziz Sachedina, PhD, prof. of Islamic studies, Univ. of Virginia

Buddhism

Founded: About 525 BC, reportedly near Benares, India.

Founder: Gautama Siddhartha (c 563-483 BC), the Buddha, who achieved enlightenment through intense meditation.

Sacred Texts: The *Tripitaka*, a collection of the Buddha's teachings, rules of monastic life, and philosophical commentaries on the teachings; also a vast body of Buddhist teachings and commentaries, many of which are called *sutras.*

Organization: The basic institution is the *sangha*, or monastic order, through which the traditions are passed to from generation to generation. Monastic life tends to be democratic and anti-authoritarian. Large lay organizations have developed in some sects.

Practice: Varies widely according to the sect, and ranges from austere meditation to magical chanting and elaborate temple rites. Many practices, such as exorcism of devils, reflect pre-Buddhist beliefs.

Divisions: A variety of sects grouped into 3 primary branches: Theravada (sole survivor of the ancient Hinayana schools), which emphasizes the importance of pure thought and deed; Mahayana (includes Zen and Soka-gakkai), which ranges from philosophical schools to belief in the saving grace of higher beings or ritual practices and to practical meditative disciplines; and Tantrism, a combination of belief in ritual magic and sophisticated philosophy.

Location: Throughout Asia, from Sri Lanka to Japan. Zen and Soka-gakkai have some 15,000 adherents in the U.S.

Beliefs: Life is misery and decay, and there is no ultimate reality in it or behind it. The cycle of endless birth and rebirth continues because of desire and attachment to the unreal "self." Right meditation and deeds will end the cycle and achieve Nirvana, the Void, nothingness.

Hinduism

Founded: About 1500 BC by Aryans who migrated to India, where their Vedic religion intermixed with the practices and beliefs of the natives.

Sacred texts: The *Veda*, including the *Upanishads*, a collection of rituals and mythological and philosophical commentaries; a vast number of epic stories about gods, heroes, and saints, including the *Bhagavadgita,* a part of the *Mahabharata,* and the *Ramayana;* and a great variety of other literature.

Organization: None, strictly speaking. Generally, rituals should be performed or assisted by Brahmins, the priestly caste, but in practice, simpler rituals can be performed by anyone. Brahmins are the final judges of ritual purity, the vital element in Hindu life. Temples and religious organizations are usually presided over by Brahmins.

Practice: A variety of private rituals, primarily passage rites (e.g., initiation, marriage, death, etc.) and daily devotions, and a similar variety of public rites in temples. Of the public rites, the *puja,* a ceremonial dinner for a god, is the most common.

Divisions: There is no concept of orthodoxy in Hinduism, which presents a variety of sects, most of them devoted to the worship of one of the many gods. The 3 major living traditions are those devoted to the gods Vishnu and Shiva and to the goddess Shakti; each is divided into further subsects. Numerous folk beliefs and practices, often in amalgamation with the above groups, exist side by side with sophisticated philosophical schools and exotic cults.

Location: Mainly India, Nepal, Malaysia, Guyana, Suriname, and Sri Lanka.

Beliefs: There is only one divine principle; the many gods are only aspects of that unity. Life in all its forms is an aspect of the divine, but it appears as a separation from the divine, a meaningless cycle of birth and rebirth (*samsara*) determined by the purity or impurity of past deeds (*karma*). To improve one's *karma* or escape *samsara* by pure acts, thought, and/or devotion is the aim of every Hindu.

Islam

Founded: About AD 622 in Mecca, Arabian Peninsula.

Founder: Muhammad (c 570-632), the Prophet.

Sacred texts: The *Koran* (al-Qur'an), the Word of God; *Sunna*, collections of *adth*, describing what Muhammad said or did.

Organization: Since the founder was both a prophet and a statesman, Muslim leadership has combined the civil and moral function of a state. Within the larger community, there are cultural and national groups, held together by a common religious law, the *Shari'a*, enforced uniformly in matters of religion only. In social transactions the community has often departed from traditional formulations. Although Islam is basically egalitarian and suspicious of authoritarianism, Muslim culture tends to be dominated by the conservative spirit of its religious establishment, the *ulema.*

Practice: Besides the general moral guidance that determines everyday life, there are "Five Pillars of Islam": profession of faith (oneness of God and prophethood of Muhammad); prayer 5 times a day; alms *(zakat)* from one's savings and estate; dawn-to-dusk fasting in the month of Ramadan; and once in a lifetime, pilgrimage to Mecca, if possible.

Divisions: There are 2 major groups: the majority known as Sunni and the minority Shiites. Shiites believe in Twelve Imams (perfect teachers) after the Prophet, of whom the last Imam has lived an invisible existence since 874, continuing to guide his community. Sunni Muslims believe in God's overpowering will over their affairs and tend to be predestinarian; Shiites believe in free will and give a substantial role to human reason in daily life. Sufism (mystical dimension of Islam) is prevalent among both Sunni and Shiites. Sufis emphasize personal relation to God and obedience informed by love of God.

Location: W Africa to Philippines, across band including E Africa, Central Asia and W China, India, Malaysia, Indonesia. Islam has several million adherents in North America.

Beliefs: Strictly monotheistic. God is creator of the universe, omnipotent, omniscient, just, forgiving, and merciful. The human is God's highest creation, but weak and egocentric, prone to forget the goal of life, constantly tempted by the Satan, an evil being. God revealed the Koran to Muhammad to guide hu manity to truth and justice. Those who repent and sincerely "submit" (literal meaning of "islam") to God attain salvation. The forgiven enter the Paradise, and the wicked burn in Hell.

Judaism

Founded: About 1300 BC.

Founder: Abraham is regarded as the founding patriarch, but the Torah of Moses is the basic source of the teachings.

Sacred Texts: The 5 books of Moses constitute the written Torah. Special sanctity is also assigned other writings of the Hebrew Bible—the teachings of oral Torah are recorded in the Talmud, in the Midrash, and in various commentaries.

Organization: Originally theocratic, Judaism has evolved a congregational polity. The basic institution is the local synagogue, operated by the congregation and led by a rabbi of their choice. Chief rabbis in France and Great Britain have authority only over those who accept it; in Israel, the 2 chief rabbis have civil authority in family law.

Practice: Among traditional practicioners, almost all areas of life are governed by strict religious discipline. Sabbath and holidays are marked by special observances, and attendance at public worship is considered especially important then. Chief annual observances are Passover, celebrating liberation of the Israelites from Egypt and marked by the Seder meal in homes, and the 10 days from Rosh Hashanah (New Year) to Yom Kippur (Day of Atonement), a period of fasting and penitence.

Divisions: Judaism is an unbroken spectrum from ultraconservative to ultraliberal, largely reflecting different points of view regarding the binding character of the prohibitions and duties—particularly the dietary and Sabbath observations—traditionally prescribed for the daily life of the Jew.

Location: Almost worldwide, with concentrations in Israel and the U.S.

Beliefs: Strictly monotheistic. God is the creator and absolute ruler of the universe. Men and women are free to choose to rebel against God's rule. God established a particular relationship with the Hebrew people: by obeying a divine law God gave them, they would be a special witness to God's mercy and justice. Judaism stresses ethical behavior (and, among the traditional, careful ritual obedience) as true worship of God.

Major Christian Denominations:

Brackets indicate some features that tend to

Denomination	Origins	Organization	Authority	Special rites
Baptists	In radical Reformation, objections to infant baptism, demands for church and state separation; John Smyth, English Separatist, in 1609; Roger Williams, 1638, Providence, RI.	Congregational; each local church is autonomous.	Scripture; some Baptists, particularly in the South, interpret the Bible literally.	*[Baptism, usually early teen years and after, by total immersion;]* Lord's Supper.
Church of Christ (Disciples)	Among evangelical Presbyterians in KY (1804) and PA (1809), in distress over Protestant factionalism and decline of fervor; organized in 1832.	Congregational.	*["Where the Scriptures speak, we speak; where the Scriptures are silent, we are silent."]*	Adult baptism; Lord's Supper (weekly).
Episcopalians	Henry VIII separated English Catholic Church from Rome, 1534, for political reasons; Protestant Episcopal Church in U.S. founded in 1789.	*[Diocesan bishops, in apostolic succession, are elected by parish representatives; the national Church is headed by General Convention and Presiding Bishop; part of the Anglican Communion.]*	Scripture as interpreted by tradition, especially *39 Articles* (1563); triannual convention of bishops, priests, and lay people.	Infant baptism, Eucharist, and other sacraments; sacrament taken to be symbolic, but as having real spiritual effect.
Jehovah's Witnesses	Founded in 1870 in PA by Charles Taze Russell; incorporated as Watch Tower Bible and Tract Society of PA, 1884; name Jehovah's Witnesses adopted in 1931.	A governing body located in NY coordinates worldwide activities; each congregation cared for by a body of elders; each Witness considered a minister.	The Bible.	Baptism by immersion; annual Lord's Meal ceremony.
Latter-day Saints (Mormons)	In a vision of the Father and the Son reported by Joseph Smith (1820s) in NY. Smith also reported receiving new scripture on golden tablets: The Book of Mormon.	Theocratic; 1st Presidency (church president, 2 counselors), 12 Apostles preside over international church. Local congregations headed by lay priesthood leaders.	Revelation to living prophet (church president). The Bible, Book of Mormon, and other revelations to Smith and his successors.	Baptism, at age 8; laying on of hands (which confers the gift of the Holy Ghost); Lord's Supper; temple rites: baptism for the dead, marriage for eternity, others.
Lutherans	Begun by Martin Luther in Wittenberg, Germany, in 1517; objection to Catholic doctrine of salvation and sale of indulgences; break complete, 1519.	Varies from congregational to episcopal; in U.S., a combination of regional synods and congregational polities is most common.	Scripture alone. *The Book of Concord* (1580), which includes the three Ecumenical Creeds, is subscribed to as a correct exposition of Scripture.	Infant baptism; Lord's Supper; Christ's true body and blood present "in, with, and under the bread and wine."
Methodists	Rev. John Wesley began movement in 1738, within Church of England; first U.S. denomination, Baltimore (1784).	Conference and superintendent system*; [in United Methodist Church, general superintendents are bishops—not a priestly order, only an office—who are elected for life.]*	Scripture as interpreted by tradition, reason, and experience.	Baptism of infants or adults; Lord's Supper ommanded; other rites include marriage, ordination, solemnization of personal commitments.
Orthodox	Developed in original Christian proselytizing; broke with Rome in 1054, after centuries of doctrinal disputes and diverging traditions	Synods of bishops in autonomous, usually national, churches elect a patriarch, archbishop, or metropolitan; these men, as a group, are the heads of the church.	Scripture, tradition, and the first 7 church councils up to Nicaea II in 787; bishops in council have authority in doctrine and policy.	Seven sacraments: infant baptism and anointing, Eucharist, ordination, penance, marriage, and anointing of the sick.
Pentecostal	In Topeka, KS (1901) and Los Angeles (1906), in reaction to perceived loss of evangelical fervor among Methodists and others.	Originally a movement, not a formal organization, Pentecostalism now has a variety of organized forms and continues also as a movement.	Scripture; individual charismatic leaders, the teachings of the Holy Spirit.	*[Spirit baptism, especially as shown in "speaking in tongues"; healing and sometimes exorcism;]* adult baptism; Lord's Supper.
Presbyterians	In 16th-cent. Calvinist reformation; differed with Lutherans over sacraments, church government; John Knox founded Scotch Presbyerian church about 1560.	*[Highly structured representational system of ministers and lay persons (presbyters) in local, regional, and national bodies (synods).]*	Scripture.	Infant baptism; Lord's Supper; bread and wine symbolize Christ's spiritual presence.
Roman Catholics	Traditionally, founded by Jesus who named St. Peter the 1st vicar; developed in early Christian proselytizing, especially after the conversion of imperial Rome in the 4th cent.	*[Hierarchy with supreme power vested in pope elected by cardinals;]* councils of bishops advise on matters of doctrine and policy.	*[The pope, when speaking for the whole church in matters of faith and morals; and tradition (which is expressed in church councils and in part contained in Scripture).]*	Mass; 7 sacraments: baptism, reconciliation, Eucharist, confirmation, marriage, ordination, and anointing of the sick (unction).
United Church of Christ	*[By ecumenical union, in 1957, of Congregationalists and Evangelical & Reformed, representing both Calvinist and Lutheran traditions.]*	Congregational; a General Synod, representative of all congregations, sets general policy.	Scripture.	Infant baptism; Lord's Supper.

How Do They Differ?

distinguish a denomination sharply from others.

Practice	Ethics	Doctrine	Other	Denomination
Worship style varies from staid to evangelistic; extensive missionary activity.	Usually opposed to alcohol and tobacco; some tendency toward a perfectionist ethical standard.	*[No creed; true church is of believers only, who are all equal.]*	Believing no authority can stand between the believer and God, the Baptists are strong supporters of church and state separation.	**Baptists**
Tries to avoid any rite not considered part of the 1st-century church; some congregations may reject instrumental music.	Some tendency toward perfectionism; increasing interest in social action programs.	Simple New Testament faith; avoids any elaboration not firmly based on Scripture.	Highly tolerant in doctrinal and religious matters; strongly supportive of scholarly education.	**Church of Christ (Disciples)**
Formal, based on "Book of Common Prayer," updated 1979; services range from austerely simple to highly liturgical.	Tolerant, sometimes permissive; some social action programs.	Scripture; the "historic creeds," which include the Apostles, Nicene, and Athanasian, and the "Book of Common Prayer"; ranges from Anglo-Catholic to low church, with Calvinist influences.	Strongly ecumenical, holding talks with many branches of Christendom.	**Episcopalians**
Meetings are held in Kingdom Halls and members' homes for study and worship; *[extensive door-to-door visitations.]*	High moral code; stress on marital fidelity and family values; avoidance of tobacco and blood transfusions.	*[God, by his first creation, Christ, will soon destroy all wickedness; 144,000 faithful ones will rule in heaven with Christ over others on a paradise earth.]*	Total allegiance proclaimed only to God's kingdom or heavenly government by Christ; main periodical, *The Watchtower*, is printed in 115 languages.	**Jehovah's Witnesses**
Simple service with prayers, hymns, sermon; private temple ceremonies may be more elaborate.	Temperance; strict moral code; *[tithing]*; a strong work ethic with communal self-reliance; *[strong missionary activity]*; family emphasis.	Jesus Christ is the Son of God, the Eternal Father. Jesus' atonement saves all humans; those who are obedient to God's laws may become joint-heirs with Christ in God's kingdom.	Mormons believe theirs is the true church of Jesus Christ, restored by God through Joseph Smith. Official name: The Church of Jesus Christ of Latter-day Saints.	**Latter-day Saints (Mormons)**
Relatively simple, formal liturgy with emphasis on the sermon.	Generally conservative in personal and social ethics; doctrine of "2 kingdoms" (worldly and holy) supports conservatism in secular affairs.	Salvation by grace alone through faith; Lutheranism has made major contributions to Protestant theology.	Though still somewhat divided along ethnic lines (German, Swedish, etc.), main divisions are between fundamentalists and liberals.	**Lutherans**
Worship style varies widely by denomination, local church, geography.	Originally pietist and perfectionist; always strong social activist elements.	No distinctive theological development; 25 Articles abridged from Church of England's 39, not binding.	In 1968, The United Methodist Church was formed by the union of The Methodist Church and The Evangelical United Brethren Church.	**Methodists**
[Elaborate liturgy, usually in the vernacular, though extremely traditional; the liturgy is the essence of Orthodoxy; veneration of icons.]	Tolerant; little stress on social action; divorce, remarriage permitted in some cases; bishops are celibate; priests need not be.	Emphasis on Christ's resurrection, rather than crucifixion; the Holy Spirit proceeds from God the Father only.	Orthodox Church in America originally under Patriarch of Moscow, was granted autonomy in 1970; Greek Orthodox do not recognize this autonomy.	**Orthodox**
Loosely structured service with rousing hymns and sermons, culminating in spirit baptism.	Usually, emphasis on perfectionism, with varying degrees of tolerance.	Simple traditional beliefs, usually Protestant, with emphasis on the immediate presence of God in the Holy Spirit.	Once confined to lower-class "holy rollers," Pentecostalism now appears in mainline churches and has established middle-class congregations.	**Pentecostal**
A simple, sober service in which the sermon is central.	Traditionally, a tendency toward strictness, with firm church- and self-discipline; otherwise tolerant.	Emphasizes the sovereignty and justice of God; no longer dogmatic.	Although traces of belief in predestination (that God has foreordained salvation for the "elect") remain, this idea is no longer a central element in Presbyterianism.	**Presbyterians**
Relatively elaborate ritual centered on the Mass; also rosary recitation, novenas, etc.	Traditionally strict, but increasingly tolerant in practice; divorce and remarriage not accepted, but annulments sometimes granted; celibate clergy, except in Eastern rite.	Highly elaborated; salvation by merit gained through grace; dogmatic; special veneration of Mary, the mother of Jesus.	Relatively rapid change followed Vatican Council II; Mass now in vernacular; more stress on social action, tolerance, ecumenism.	**Roman Catholics**
Usually simple services with emphasis on the sermon.	Tolerant; some social action emphasis.	Standard Protestant; "Statement of Faith" (1959) is not binding.	The 2 main churches in the 1957 union represented earlier unions with small groups of almost every Protestant denomination.	**United Church of Christ**

CALENDAR

Julian and Gregorian Calendars; Leap Year; Century

The **Julian calendar**, under which all Western nations measured time until AD 1582, was authorized by Julius Caesar in 46 BC. It called for a year of 365¼ days, starting in January, with every 4th year being a **leap year** of 366 days. St. Bede the Venerable, an Anglo-Saxon monk, announced in AD 730 that the Julian year was 11 min, 14 sec too long, a cumulative error of about a day every 128 years, but nothing was done about this for centuries.

By 1582 the accumulated error was estimated at 10 days. In that year Pope Gregory XIII decreed that the day following Oct. 4, 1582, should be called Oct. 15, thus dropping 10 days and initiating the **Gregorian calendar**.

The Gregorian calendar continued a system devised by the monk Dionysius Exiguus (6th century), starting from the first year following the birth of Jesus Christ, which was inaccurately taken to be year 753 in the Roman calendar. Leap years were continued but, to prevent further displacements, centesimal years (years ending in 00) were made common years, not leap years, unless divisible by 400. Under this plan, 1600 and 2000 are leap years; 1700, 1800, and 1900 are not.

The Gregorian calendar was adopted at once by France, Italy, Spain, Portugal, and Luxembourg. Within 2 years most German Catholic states, Belgium, and parts of Switzerland and the Netherlands were brought under the new calendar, and Hungary followed in 1587. The rest of the Netherlands, along with Denmark and the German Protestant states, made the change in 1699-1700.

The British government adopted the Gregorian calendar and imposed it on all its possessions, including the American colonies, in 1752, decreeing that the day following Sept. 2, 1752, should be called Sept. 14, a loss of 11 days. All dates preceding were marked OS, for Old Style. In addition, New Year's Day was moved to Jan. 1 from Mar. 25 (under the old reckoning, for example, Mar. 24, 1700, had been followed by Mar. 25, 1701). Thus George Washington's birthdate, which was Feb. 11, 1731, OS, became Feb. 22, 1732, NS (New Style). In 1753 Sweden also went Gregorian.

In 1793 the French revolutionary government adopted a calendar of 12 months of 30 days with 5 extra days in September of each common year and a 6th every 4th year. Napoleon reinstated the Gregorian calendar in 1806.

The Gregorian system later spread to non-European regions, replacing traditional calendars at least for official purposes. Japan in 1873, Egypt in 1875, China in 1912, and Turkey in 1925 made the change, usually in conjunction with political upheaval. In China, the republican government began reckoning years from its 1911 founding. After 1949, the People's Republic adopted the Common, or Christian Era, year count, even for the traditional lunar calendar, which is also retained. In 1918 the Soviet Union decreed that the day after Jan. 31, 1918, OS, would be Feb. 14, 1918, NS. Greece changed over in 1923. For the first time in history, all major nations had one calendar. The Russian Orthodox church and some other Christian sects retained the Julian calendar.

To convert from the Julian to the Gregorian calendar, add 10 days to dates Oct. 5, 1582, through Feb. 28, 1700; after that date add 11 days through Feb. 28, 1800; 12 days through Feb. 28, 1900; and 13 days through Feb. 28, 2100.

A **century** consists of 100 consecutive years. The 1st century AD may be said to have run from the years 1 through 100. The 20th century by this reckoning consisted of the years 1901 through 2000 and technically ended Dec. 31, 2000, as did the 2nd millennium AD. The 21st century thus technically began Jan. 1, 2001.

For a **Perpetual Calendar,** see pages 648-649.

Julian Calendar

To find which of the 14 calendars of the Perpetual Calendar (pages 648-649) applies to any year, starting Jan. 1, under the Julian system, find the century for the desired year in the 3 leftmost columns below. Read across and find the year in the 4 top rows. Then read down. The number in the intersection is the calendar designation for that year.

Year (last 2 figures of desired year)

				01	**02**	**03**	**04**	**05**	**06**	**07**	**08**	**09**	**10**	**11**	**12**	**13**	**14**	**15**	**16**	**17**	**18**	**19**	**20**	**21**	**22**	**23**	**24**	**25**	**26**	**27**	**28**
				29	**30**	**31**	**32**	**33**	**34**	**35**	**36**	**37**	**38**	**39**	**40**	**41**	**42**	**43**	**44**	**45**	**46**	**47**	**48**	**49**	**50**	**51**	**52**	**53**	**54**	**55**	**56**
				57	**58**	**59**	**60**	**61**	**62**	**63**	**64**	**65**	**66**	**67**	**68**	**69**	**70**	**71**	**72**	**73**	**74**	**75**	**76**	**77**	**78**	**79**	**80**	**81**	**82**	**83**	**84**
Century			**00**	**85**	**86**	**87**	**88**	**89**	**90**	**91**	**92**	**93**	**94**	**95**	**96**	**97**	**98**	**99**													
0	**700**	**1400**	12	7	1	2	10	5	6	7	8	3	4	5	13	1	2	3	11	6	7	1	9	4	5	6	14	2	3	4	12
100	**800**	**1500**	11	6	7	1	9	4	5	6	14	2	3	4	12	7	1	2	10	5	6	7	8	3	4	5	13	1	2	3	11
200	**900**	**1600**	10	5	6	7	8	3	4	5	13	1	2	3	11	6	7	1	9	4	5	6	14	2	3	4	12	7	1	2	10
300	**1000**	**1700**	9	4	5	6	14	2	3	4	12	7	1	2	10	5	6	7	8	3	4	5	13	1	2	3	11	6	7	1	9
400	**1100**	**1800**	8	3	4	5	13	1	2	3	11	6	7	1	9	4	5	6	14	2	3	4	12	7	1	2	10	5	6	7	8
500	**1200**	**1900**	14	2	3	4	12	7	1	2	10	5	6	7	8	3	4	5	13	1	2	3	11	6	7	1	9	4	5	6	14
600	**1300**	**2000**	13	1	2	3	11	6	7	1	9	4	5	6	14	2	3	4	12	7	1	2	10	5	6	7	8	3	4	5	13

Gregorian Calendar

Choose the desired year from the table below or from the Perpetual Calendar (for years 1803 to 2080). The number after each year designates which calendar to use for that year, as shown in the Perpetual Calendar—see pages 648-649. (The Gregorian calendar was inaugurated Oct. 15, 1582. From that date to Dec. 31, 1582, use calendar 6.)

1583-1802

1583	7	1603	4	1623	1	1643	5	1663	2	1683	6	1703	2	1723	6	1743	3	1763	7	1783	4
1584	8	1604	12	1624	9	1644	13	1664	10	1684	14	1704	10	1724	14	1744	11	1764	8	1784	12
1585	3	1605	7	1625	4	1645	1	1665	5	1685	2	1705	5	1725	2	1745	6	1765	3	1785	7
1586	4	1606	1	1626	5	1646	2	1666	6	1686	3	1706	6	1726	3	1746	7	1766	4	1786	1
1587	5	1607	2	1627	6	1647	3	1667	7	1687	4	1707	7	1727	4	1747	1	1767	5	1787	2
1588	13	1608	10	1628	14	1648	11	1668	8	1688	12	1708	8	1728	12	1748	9	1768	13	1788	10
1589	1	1609	5	1629	2	1649	6	1669	3	1689	7	1709	3	1729	7	1749	4	1769	1	1789	5
1590	2	1610	6	1630	3	1650	7	1670	4	1690	1	1710	4	1730	1	1750	5	1770	2	1790	6
1591	3	1611	7	1631	4	1651	1	1671	5	1691	2	1711	5	1731	2	1751	6	1771	3	1791	7
1592	11	1612	8	1632	12	1652	9	1672	13	1692	10	1712	13	1732	10	1752	14	1772	11	1792	8
1593	6	1613	3	1633	7	1653	4	1673	1	1693	5	1713	1	1733	5	1753	2	1773	6	1793	3
1594	7	1614	4	1634	1	1654	5	1674	2	1694	6	1714	2	1734	6	1754	3	1774	7	1794	4
1595	1	1615	5	1635	2	1655	6	1675	3	1695	7	1715	3	1735	7	1755	4	1775	1	1795	5
1596	9	1616	13	1636	10	1656	14	1676	11	1696	8	1716	11	1736	8	1756	12	1776	9	1796	13
1597	4	1617	1	1637	5	1657	2	1677	6	1697	3	1717	6	1737	3	1757	7	1777	4	1797	1
1598	5	1618	2	1638	6	1658	3	1678	7	1698	4	1718	7	1738	4	1758	1	1778	5	1798	2
1599	6	1619	3	1639	7	1659	4	1679	1	1699	5	1719	1	1739	5	1759	2	1779	6	1799	3
1600	14	1620	11	1640	8	1660	12	1680	9	1700	6	1720	9	1740	13	1760	10	1780	14	1800	4
1601	2	1621	6	1641	3	1661	7	1681	4	1701	7	1721	4	1741	1	1761	5	1781	2	1801	5
1602	3	1622	7	1642	4	1662	1	1682	5	1702	1	1722	5	1742	2	1762	6	1782	3	1802	6

Chronological Eras

Era	Year	Begins in 2003
Byzantine	7512	Sept. 14
Jewish	5764	Sept. 26[1]
Roman (Ab Urbe Condita)	2756	Jan. 14
Nabonassar (Babylonian)	2752	Apr. 23
Japanese	2663	Jan. 1
Grecian (Seleucidae)	2315	Sept. 14 or Oct. 14
Diocletian	1720	Sept. 12
Indian (Saka)	1925	Mar. 22
Islamic/Muslim (Hijra)	1424	Mar. 4[1]

(1) Year begins at sunset.

Chronological Cycles, 2003

Dominical Letter	E	Roman Indiction	11	Solar Cycle	24
Golden Number (Lunar Cycle)	IX	Epact	27	Julian Period (year of)	6716

How Far Apart Are Two Dates?

This table covers a period of 2 years. To use, find the **number** for each date and subtract the smaller from the larger. Example—for days from Feb. 10, 2002, to Dec. 15, 2003, subtract 41 from 714; the result is 673. For leap years, such as 2004, one day must be added; thus Feb. 4, 2003, and Mar. 13, 2004, are 403 days apart.

First Year

Date	Jan.	Feb.	Mar.	April	May	June	July	Aug.	Sept.	Oct.	Nov.	Dec.
1	1	32	60	91	121	152	182	213	244	274	305	335
2	2	33	61	92	122	153	183	214	245	275	306	336
3	3	34	62	93	123	154	184	215	246	276	307	337
4	4	35	63	94	124	155	185	216	247	277	308	338
5	5	36	64	95	125	156	186	217	248	278	309	339
6	6	37	65	96	126	157	187	218	249	279	310	340
7	7	38	66	97	127	158	188	219	250	280	311	341
8	8	39	67	98	128	159	189	220	251	281	312	342
9	9	40	68	99	129	160	190	221	252	282	313	343
10	10	41	69	100	130	161	191	222	253	283	314	344
11	11	42	70	101	131	162	192	223	254	284	315	345
12	12	43	71	102	132	163	193	224	255	285	316	346
13	13	44	72	103	133	164	194	225	256	286	317	347
14	14	45	73	104	134	165	195	226	257	287	318	348
15	15	46	74	105	135	166	196	227	258	288	319	349
16	16	47	75	106	136	167	197	228	259	289	320	350
17	17	48	76	107	137	168	198	229	260	290	321	351
18	18	49	77	108	138	169	199	230	261	291	322	352
19	19	50	78	109	139	170	200	231	262	292	323	353
20	20	51	79	110	140	171	201	232	263	293	324	354
21	21	52	80	111	141	172	202	233	264	294	325	355
22	22	53	81	112	142	173	203	234	265	295	326	356
23	23	54	82	113	143	174	204	235	266	296	327	357
24	24	55	83	114	144	175	205	236	267	297	328	358
25	25	56	84	115	145	176	206	237	268	298	329	359
26	26	57	85	116	146	177	207	238	269	299	330	360
27	27	58	86	117	147	178	208	239	270	300	331	361
28	28	59	87	118	148	179	209	240	271	301	332	362
29	29	—	88	119	149	180	210	241	272	302	333	363
30	30	—	89	120	150	181	211	242	273	303	334	364
31	31	—	90	—	151	—	212	243	—	304	—	365

Second Year

Date	Jan.	Feb.	Mar.	April	May	June	July	Aug.	Sept.	Oct.	Nov.	Dec.
1	366	397	425	456	486	517	547	578	609	639	670	700
2	367	398	426	457	487	518	548	579	610	640	671	701
3	368	399	427	458	488	519	549	580	611	641	672	702
4	369	400	428	459	489	520	550	581	612	642	673	703
5	370	401	429	460	490	521	551	582	613	643	674	704
6	371	402	430	461	491	522	552	583	614	644	675	705
7	372	403	431	462	492	523	553	584	615	645	676	706
8	373	404	432	463	493	524	554	585	616	646	677	707
9	374	405	433	464	494	525	555	586	617	647	678	708
10	375	406	434	465	495	526	556	587	618	648	679	709
11	376	407	435	466	496	527	557	588	619	649	680	710
12	377	408	436	467	497	528	558	589	620	650	681	711
13	378	409	437	468	498	529	559	590	621	651	682	712
14	379	410	438	469	499	530	560	591	622	652	683	713
15	380	411	439	470	500	531	561	592	623	653	684	714
16	381	412	440	471	501	532	562	593	624	654	685	715
17	382	413	441	472	502	533	563	594	625	655	686	716
18	383	414	442	473	503	534	564	595	626	656	687	717
19	384	415	443	474	504	535	565	596	627	657	688	718
20	385	416	444	475	505	536	566	597	628	658	689	719
21	386	417	445	476	506	537	567	598	629	659	690	720
22	387	418	446	477	507	538	568	599	630	660	691	721
23	388	419	447	478	508	539	569	600	631	661	692	722
24	389	420	448	479	509	540	570	601	632	662	693	723
25	390	421	449	480	510	541	571	602	633	663	694	724
26	391	422	450	481	511	542	572	603	634	664	695	725
27	392	423	451	482	512	543	573	604	635	665	696	726
28	393	424	452	483	513	544	574	605	636	666	697	727
29	394	—	453	484	514	545	575	606	637	667	698	728
30	395	—	454	485	515	546	576	607	638	668	699	729
31	396	—	455	—	516	—	577	608	—	669	—	730

Chinese Calendar, Asian Festivals

Source: Chinese Information and Culture Center, New York, NY

The Chinese calendar (like the Islamic calendar; see the Religion chapter) is a lunar calendar. It is divided into 12 months of 29 or 30 days (compensating for the lunar month's mean duration of 29 days, 12 hr, 44.05 min). This calendar is synchronized with the solar year by the addition of extra months at fixed intervals.

The Chinese calendar runs on a 60-year cycle. The cycles 1876-1935 and 1936-95, with the years grouped under their 12 animal designations, are printed below, along with the first 24 years of the current cycle. It began in 1996 and will last until 2055. The year 2003 (Lunar Year 4700) is found in the 8th column, under Sheep (Goat), and is known as a Year of the Sheep (Goat). Readers can find the animal name for the year of their birth in the same chart. (Note: The first 3-7 weeks of each Western year belong to the previous Chinese year and animal designation.)

Both the Western (Gregorian) and traditional lunar calendars are used publicly in China and in North and South Korea, and 2 New Year's celebrations are held. In Taiwan, in overseas Chinese communities, and in Vietnam, the lunar calendar is used only to set the dates for traditional festivals, with the Gregorian system in general use.

The 4-day Chinese New Year, Hsin Nien, the 3-day Vietnamese New Year festival, Tet, and the 3-to-4-day Korean festival, Suhl, begin at the 2nd new moon after the winter solstice. The new moon in the Far East, which is west of the International Date Line, may be a day later than the new moon in the U.S. The festivals may start, therefore, anywhere between Jan. 21 and Feb. 19 of the Gregorian calendar. Feb. 1 marks the start of the new Chinese year in 2003.

Rat	Ox	Tiger	Hare (Rabbit)	Dragon	Snake	Horse	Sheep (Goat)	Monkey	Rooster	Dog	Pig
1876	1877	1878	1879	1880	1881	1882	1883	1884	1885	1886	1887
1888	1889	1890	1891	1892	1893	1894	1895	1896	1897	1898	1899
1900	1901	1902	1903	1904	1905	1906	1907	1908	1909	1910	1911
1912	1913	1914	1915	1916	1917	1918	1919	1920	1921	1922	1923
1924	1925	1926	1927	1928	1929	1930	1931	1932	1933	1934	1935
1936	1937	1938	1939	1940	1941	1942	1943	1944	1945	1946	1947
1948	1949	1950	1951	1952	1953	1954	1955	1956	1957	1958	1959
1960	1961	1962	1963	1964	1965	1966	1967	1968	1969	1970	1971
1972	1973	1974	1975	1976	1977	1978	1979	1980	1981	1982	1983
1984	1985	1986	1987	1988	1989	1990	1991	1992	1993	1994	1995
1996	1997	1998	1999	2000	2001	2002	2003	2004	2005	2006	2007
2008	2009	2010	2011	2012	2013	2014	2015	2016	2017	2018	2019

Perpetual Calendar

The number shown for each year indicates which Gregorian calendar to use. For 1583-1802, see "Gregorian Calendar" on page 646. For 1803-20, use numbers for 1983-2000, respectively. For Julian Calendar, see "Julian Calendar" on page 646.

1821 2	1847 6	1873 4	1899 1	1925 5	1951 2	1977 7	2003 4	2029 2	2055 6
1822 3	1848 . . .14	1874 5	1900 2	1926 6	1952 . . .10	1978 1	2004 . . .12	2030 3	2056 . . .14
1823 4	1849 2	1875 6	1901 3	1927 7	1953 5	1979 2	2005 7	2031 4	2057 2
1824 . . .12	1850 3	1876 . . .14	1902 4	1928 8	1954 6	1980 . . .10	2006 1	2032 . . .12	2058 3
1825 7	1851 4	1877 2	1903 5	1929 3	1955 7	1981 5	2007 2	2033 7	2059 4
1826 1	1852 . . .12	1878 3	1904 . . .13	1930 4	1956 8	1982 6	2008 . . .10	2034 1	2060 . . .12
1827 2	1853 7	1879 4	1905 1	1931 5	1957 3	1983 7	2009 5	2035 2	2061 7
1828 . . .10	1854 1	1880 . . .12	1906 2	1932 . . .13	1958 4	1984 8	2010 6	2036 . . .10	2062 1
1829 5	1855 2	1881 7	1907 3	1933 1	1959 5	1985 3	2011 7	2037 5	2063 2
1830 6	1856 . . .10	1882 1	1908 . . .11	1934 2	1960 . . .13	1986 4	2012 8	2038 6	2064 . . .10
1831 7	1857 5	1883 2	1909 6	1935 3	1961 1	1987 5	2013 3	2039 7	2065 5
1832 8	1858 6	1884 . . .10	1910 7	1936 . . .11	1962 2	1988 . . .13	2014 4	2040 8	2066 6
1833 3	1859 7	1885 5	1911 1	1937 6	1963 3	1989 1	2015 5	2041 3	2067 7
1834 4	1860 8	1886 6	1912 9	1938 7	1964 . . .11	1990 2	2016 . . .13	2042 4	2068 8
1835 5	1861 3	1887 7	1913 4	1939 1	1965 6	1991 3	2017 1	2043 5	2069 3
1836 . . .13	1862 4	1888 8	1914 5	1940 9	1966 7	1992 . . .11	2018 2	2044 . . .13	2070 4
1837 1	1863 5	1889 3	1915 6	1941 4	1967 1	1993 6	2019 3	2045 1	2071 5
1838 2	1864 . . .13	1890 4	1916 . . .14	1942 5	1968 9	1994 7	2020 . . .11	2046 2	2072 . . .13
1839 3	1865 1	1891 5	1917 2	1943 6	1969 4	1995 1	2021 6	2047 3	2073 1
1840 . . .11	1866 2	1892 . . .13	1918 3	1944 . . .14	1970 5	1996 9	2022 7	2048 . . .11	2074 2
1841 6	1867 3	1893 1	1919 4	1945 2	1971 6	1997 4	2023 1	2049 6	2075 3
1842 7	1868 . . .11	1894 2	1920 . . .12	1946 3	1972 . . .14	1998 5	2024 9	2050 7	2076 . . .11
1843 1	1869 6	1895 3	1921 7	1947 4	1973 2	1999 6	2025 4	2051 1	2077 6
1844 9	1870 7	1896 . . .11	1922 1	1948 . . .12	1974 3	2000 . . .14	2026 5	2052 9	2078 7
1845 4	1871 1	1897 6	1923 2	1949 7	1975 4	2001 2	2027 6	2053 4	2079 1
1846 5	1872 9	1898 7	1924 . . .10	1950 1	1976 . . .12	2002 3	2028 . . .14	2054 5	2080 9

1

JANUARY

S	M	T	W	T	F	S
1	2	3	4	5	6	7
8	9	10	11	12	13	14
15	16	17	18	19	20	21
22	23	24	25	26	27	28
29	30	31				

FEBRUARY

S	M	T	W	T	F	S
			1	2	3	4
5	6	7	8	9	10	11
12	13	14	15	16	17	18
19	20	21	22	23	24	25
26	27	28				

MARCH

S	M	T	W	T	F	S
			1	2	3	4
5	6	7	8	9	10	11
12	13	14	15	16	17	18
19	20	21	22	23	24	25
26	27	28	29	30	31	

APRIL

S	M	T	W	T	F	S
						1
2	3	4	5	6	7	8
9	10	11	12	13	14	15
16	17	18	19	20	21	22
23	24	25	26	27	28	29
30						

MAY

S	M	T	W	T	F	S
	1	2	3	4	5	6
7	8	9	10	11	12	13
14	15	16	17	18	19	20
21	22	23	24	25	26	27
28	29	30	31			

JUNE

S	M	T	W	T	F	S
				1	2	3
4	5	6	7	8	9	10
11	12	13	14	15	16	17
18	19	20	21	22	23	24
25	26	27	28	29	30	

JULY

S	M	T	W	T	F	S
						1
2	3	4	5	6	7	8
9	10	11	12	13	14	15
16	17	18	19	20	21	22
23	24	25	26	27	28	29
30	31					

AUGUST

S	M	T	W	T	F	S
		1	2	3	4	5
6	7	8	9	10	11	12
13	14	15	16	17	18	19
20	21	22	23	24	25	26
27	28	29	30	31		

SEPTEMBER

S	M	T	W	T	F	S
					1	2
3	4	5	6	7	8	9
10	11	12	13	14	15	16
17	18	19	20	21	22	23
24	25	26	27	28	29	30

OCTOBER

S	M	T	W	T	F	S
1	2	3	4	5	6	7
8	9	10	11	12	13	14
15	16	17	18	19	20	21
22	23	24	25	26	27	28
29	30	31				

NOVEMBER

S	M	T	W	T	F	S
			1	2	3	4
5	6	7	8	9	10	11
12	13	14	15	16	17	18
19	20	21	22	23	24	25
26	27	28	29	30		

DECEMBER

S	M	T	W	T	F	S
					1	2
3	4	5	6	7	8	9
10	11	12	13	14	15	16
17	18	19	20	21	22	23
24	25	26	27	28	29	30
31						

2 2001

JANUARY

S	M	T	W	T	F	S
	1	2	3	4	5	6
7	8	9	10	11	12	13
14	15	16	17	18	19	20
21	22	23	24	25	26	27
28	29	30	31			

FEBRUARY

S	M	T	W	T	F	S
				1	2	3
4	5	6	7	8	9	10
11	12	13	14	15	16	17
18	19	20	21	22	23	24
25	26	27	28			

MARCH

S	M	T	W	T	F	S
				1	2	3
4	5	6	7	8	9	10
11	12	13	14	15	16	17
18	19	20	21	22	23	24
25	26	27	28	29	30	31

APRIL

S	M	T	W	T	F	S
1	2	3	4	5	6	7
8	9	10	11	12	13	14
15	16	17	18	19	20	21
22	23	24	25	26	27	28
29	30					

MAY

S	M	T	W	T	F	S
		1	2	3	4	5
6	7	8	9	10	11	12
13	14	15	16	17	18	19
20	21	22	23	24	25	26
27	28	29	30	31		

JUNE

S	M	T	W	T	F	S
					1	2
3	4	5	6	7	8	9
10	11	12	13	14	15	16
17	18	19	20	21	22	23
24	25	26	27	28	29	30

JULY

S	M	T	W	T	F	S
1	2	3	4	5	6	7
8	9	10	11	12	13	14
15	16	17	18	19	20	21
22	23	24	25	26	27	28
29	30	31				

AUGUST

S	M	T	W	T	F	S
			1	2	3	4
5	6	7	8	9	10	11
12	13	14	15	16	17	18
19	20	21	22	23	24	25
26	27	28	29	30	31	

SEPTEMBER

S	M	T	W	T	F	S
						1
2	3	4	5	6	7	8
9	10	11	12	13	14	15
16	17	18	19	20	21	22
23	24	25	26	27	28	29
30						

OCTOBER

S	M	T	W	T	F	S
	1	2	3	4	5	6
7	8	9	10	11	12	13
14	15	16	17	18	19	20
21	22	23	24	25	26	27
28	29	30	31			

NOVEMBER

S	M	T	W	T	F	S
				1	2	3
4	5	6	7	8	9	10
11	12	13	14	15	16	17
18	19	20	21	22	23	24
25	26	27	28	29	30	

DECEMBER

S	M	T	W	T	F	S
						1
2	3	4	5	6	7	8
9	10	11	12	13	14	15
16	17	18	19	20	21	22
23	24	25	26	27	28	29
30	31					

3 2002

JANUARY

S	M	T	W	T	F	S
		1	2	3	4	5
6	7	8	9	10	11	12
13	14	15	16	17	18	19
20	21	22	23	24	25	26
27	28	29	30	31		

FEBRUARY

S	M	T	W	T	F	S
					1	2
3	4	5	6	7	8	9
10	11	12	13	14	15	16
17	18	19	20	21	22	23
24	25	26	27	28		

MARCH

S	M	T	W	T	F	S
					1	2
3	4	5	6	7	8	9
10	11	12	13	14	15	16
17	18	19	20	21	22	23
24	25	26	27	28	29	30
31						

APRIL

S	M	T	W	T	F	S
	1	2	3	4	5	6
7	8	9	10	11	12	13
14	15	16	17	18	19	20
21	22	23	24	25	26	27
28	29	30				

MAY

S	M	T	W	T	F	S
			1	2	3	4
5	6	7	8	9	10	11
12	13	14	15	16	17	18
19	20	21	22	23	24	25
26	27	28	29	30	31	

JUNE

S	M	T	W	T	F	S
						1
2	3	4	5	6	7	8
9	10	11	12	13	14	15
16	17	18	19	20	21	22
23	24	25	26	27	28	29
30						

JULY

S	M	T	W	T	F	S
	1	2	3	4	5	6
7	8	9	10	11	12	13
14	15	16	17	18	19	20
21	22	23	24	25	26	27
28	29	30	31			

AUGUST

S	M	T	W	T	F	S
				1	2	3
4	5	6	7	8	9	10
11	12	13	14	15	16	17
18	19	20	21	22	23	24
25	26	27	28	29	30	31

SEPTEMBER

S	M	T	W	T	F	S
1	2	3	4	5	6	7
8	9	10	11	12	13	14
15	16	17	18	19	20	21
22	23	24	25	26	27	28
29	30					

OCTOBER

S	M	T	W	T	F	S
		1	2	3	4	5
6	7	8	9	10	11	12
13	14	15	16	17	18	19
20	21	22	23	24	25	26
27	28	29	30	31		

NOVEMBER

S	M	T	W	T	F	S
					1	2
3	4	5	6	7	8	9
10	11	12	13	14	15	16
17	18	19	20	21	22	23
24	25	26	27	28	29	30

DECEMBER

S	M	T	W	T	F	S
1	2	3	4	5	6	7
8	9	10	11	12	13	14
15	16	17	18	19	20	21
22	23	24	25	26	27	28
29	30	31				

4 2003

JANUARY

S	M	T	W	T	F	S
			1	2	3	4
5	6	7	8	9	10	11
12	13	14	15	16	17	18
19	20	21	22	23	24	25
26	27	28	29	30	31	

FEBRUARY

S	M	T	W	T	F	S
						1
2	3	4	5	6	7	8
9	10	11	12	13	14	15
16	17	18	19	20	21	22
23	24	25	26	27	28	

MARCH

S	M	T	W	T	F	S
						1
2	3	4	5	6	7	8
9	10	11	12	13	14	15
16	17	18	19	20	21	22
23	24	25	26	27	28	29
30	31					

APRIL

S	M	T	W	T	F	S
		1	2	3	4	5
6	7	8	9	10	11	12
13	14	15	16	17	18	19
20	21	22	23	24	25	26
27	28	29	30			

MAY

S	M	T	W	T	F	S
				1	2	3
4	5	6	7	8	9	10
11	12	13	14	15	16	17
18	19	20	21	22	23	24
25	26	27	28	29	30	31

JUNE

S	M	T	W	T	F	S
1	2	3	4	5	6	7
8	9	10	11	12	13	14
15	16	17	18	19	20	21
22	23	24	25	26	27	28
29	30					

JULY

S	M	T	W	T	F	S
		1	2	3	4	5
6	7	8	9	10	11	12
13	14	15	16	17	18	19
20	21	22	23	24	25	26
27	28	29	30	31		

AUGUST

S	M	T	W	T	F	S
					1	2
3	4	5	6	7	8	9
10	11	12	13	14	15	16
17	18	19	20	21	22	23
24	25	26	27	28	29	30
31						

SEPTEMBER

S	M	T	W	T	F	S
	1	2	3	4	5	6
7	8	9	10	11	12	13
14	15	16	17	18	19	20
21	22	23	24	25	26	27
28	29	30				

OCTOBER

S	M	T	W	T	F	S
			1	2	3	4
5	6	7	8	9	10	11
12	13	14	15	16	17	18
19	20	21	22	23	24	25
26	27	28	29	30	31	

NOVEMBER

S	M	T	W	T	F	S
						1
2	3	4	5	6	7	8
9	10	11	12	13	14	15
16	17	18	19	20	21	22
23	24	25	26	27	28	29
30						

DECEMBER

S	M	T	W	T	F	S
	1	2	3	4	5	6
7	8	9	10	11	12	13
14	15	16	17	18	19	20
21	22	23	24	25	26	27
28	29	30	31			

5

JANUARY

S	M	T	W	T	F	S
				1	2	3
4	5	6	7	8	9	10
11	12	13	14	15	16	17
18	19	20	21	22	23	24
25	26	27	28	29	30	31

FEBRUARY

S	M	T	W	T	F	S
1	2	3	4	5	6	7
8	9	10	11	12	13	14
15	16	17	18	19	20	21
22	23	24	25	26	27	28

MARCH

S	M	T	W	T	F	S
1	2	3	4	5	6	7
8	9	10	11	12	13	14
15	16	17	18	19	20	21
22	23	24	25	26	27	28
29	30	31				

APRIL

S	M	T	W	T	F	S
			1	2	3	4
5	6	7	8	9	10	11
12	13	14	15	16	17	18
19	20	21	22	23	24	25
26	27	28	29	30		

MAY

S	M	T	W	T	F	S
					1	2
3	4	5	6	7	8	9
10	11	12	13	14	15	16
17	18	19	20	21	22	23
24	25	26	27	28	29	30
31						

JUNE

S	M	T	W	T	F	S
	1	2	3	4	5	6
7	8	9	10	11	12	13
14	15	16	17	18	19	20
21	22	23	24	25	26	27
28	29	30				

JULY

S	M	T	W	T	F	S
			1	2	3	4
5	6	7	8	9	10	11
12	13	14	15	16	17	18
19	20	21	22	23	24	25
26	27	28	29	30	31	

AUGUST

S	M	T	W	T	F	S
						1
2	3	4	5	6	7	8
9	10	11	12	13	14	15
16	17	18	19	20	21	22
23	24	25	26	27	28	29
30	31					

SEPTEMBER

S	M	T	W	T	F	S
		1	2	3	4	5
6	7	8	9	10	11	12
13	14	15	16	17	18	19
20	21	22	23	24	25	26
27	28	29	30			

OCTOBER

S	M	T	W	T	F	S
				1	2	3
4	5	6	7	8	9	10
11	12	13	14	15	16	17
18	19	20	21	22	23	24
25	26	27	28	29	30	31

NOVEMBER

S	M	T	W	T	F	S
1	2	3	4	5	6	7
8	9	10	11	12	13	14
15	16	17	18	19	20	21
22	23	24	25	26	27	28
29	30					

DECEMBER

S	M	T	W	T	F	S
		1	2	3	4	5
6	7	8	9	10	11	12
13	14	15	16	17	18	19
20	21	22	23	24	25	26
27	28	29	30	31		

6

JANUARY

S	M	T	W	T	F	S
					1	2
3	4	5	6	7	8	9
10	11	12	13	14	15	16
17	18	19	20	21	22	23
24	25	26	27	28	29	30
31						

FEBRUARY

S	M	T	W	T	F	S
	1	2	3	4	5	6
7	8	9	10	11	12	13
14	15	16	17	18	19	20
21	22	23	24	25	26	27
28						

MARCH

S	M	T	W	T	F	S
	1	2	3	4	5	6
7	8	9	10	11	12	13
14	15	16	17	18	19	20
21	22	23	24	25	26	27
28	29	30	31			

APRIL

S	M	T	W	T	F	S
				1	2	3
4	5	6	7	8	9	10
11	12	13	14	15	16	17
18	19	20	21	22	23	24
25	26	27	28	29	30	

MAY

S	M	T	W	T	F	S
						1
2	3	4	5	6	7	8
9	10	11	12	13	14	15
16	17	18	19	20	21	22
23	24	25	26	27	28	29
30	31					

JUNE

S	M	T	W	T	F	S
		1	2	3	4	5
6	7	8	9	10	11	12
13	14	15	16	17	18	19
20	21	22	23	24	25	26
27	28	29	30			

JULY

S	M	T	W	T	F	S
				1	2	3
4	5	6	7	8	9	10
11	12	13	14	15	16	17
18	19	20	21	22	23	24
25	26	27	28	29	30	31

AUGUST

S	M	T	W	T	F	S
1	2	3	4	5	6	7
8	9	10	11	12	13	14
15	16	17	18	19	20	21
22	23	24	25	26	27	28
29	30	31				

SEPTEMBER

S	M	T	W	T	F	S
			1	2	3	4
5	6	7	8	9	10	11
12	13	14	15	16	17	18
19	20	21	22	23	24	25
26	27	28	29	30		

OCTOBER

S	M	T	W	T	F	S
					1	2
3	4	5	6	7	8	9
10	11	12	13	14	15	16
17	18	19	20	21	22	23
24	25	26	27	28	29	30
31						

NOVEMBER

S	M	T	W	T	F	S
	1	2	3	4	5	6
7	8	9	10	11	12	13
14	15	16	17	18	19	20
21	22	23	24	25	26	27
28	29	30				

DECEMBER

S	M	T	W	T	F	S
			1	2	3	4
5	6	7	8	9	10	11
12	13	14	15	16	17	18
19	20	21	22	23	24	25
26	27	28	29	30	31	

72 2005

JANUARY
S	M	T	W	T	F	S
						1
2	3	4	5	6	7	8
9	10	11	12	13	14	15
16	17	18	19	20	21	22
23	24	25	26	27	28	29
30	31					

FEBRUARY
S	M	T	W	T	F	S
		1	2	3	4	5
6	7	8	9	10	11	12
13	14	15	16	17	18	19
20	21	22	23	24	25	26
27	28					

MARCH
S	M	T	W	T	F	S
		1	2	3	4	5
6	7	8	9	10	11	12
13	14	15	16	17	18	19
20	21	22	23	24	25	26
27	28	29	30	31		

APRIL
S	M	T	W	T	F	S
					1	2
3	4	5	6	7	8	9
10	11	12	13	14	15	16
17	18	19	20	21	22	23
24	25	26	27	28	29	30

MAY
S	M	T	W	T	F	S
1	2	3	4	5	6	7
8	9	10	11	12	13	14
15	16	17	18	19	20	21
22	23	24	25	26	27	28
29	30	31				

JUNE
S	M	T	W	T	F	S
			1	2	3	4
5	6	7	8	9	10	11
12	13	14	15	16	17	18
19	20	21	22	23	24	25
26	27	28	29	30		

JULY
S	M	T	W	T	F	S
					1	2
3	4	5	6	7	8	9
10	11	12	13	14	15	16
17	18	19	20	21	22	23
24	25	26	27	28	29	30
31						

AUGUST
S	M	T	W	T	F	S
	1	2	3	4	5	6
7	8	9	10	11	12	13
14	15	16	17	18	19	20
21	22	23	24	25	26	27
28	29	30	31			

SEPTEMBER
S	M	T	W	T	F	S
				1	2	3
4	5	6	7	8	9	10
11	12	13	14	15	16	17
18	19	20	21	22	23	24
25	26	27	28	29	30	

OCTOBER
S	M	T	W	T	F	S
						1
2	3	4	5	6	7	8
9	10	11	12	13	14	15
16	17	18	19	20	21	22
23	24	25	26	27	28	29
30	31					

NOVEMBER
S	M	T	W	T	F	S
		1	2	3	4	5
6	7	8	9	10	11	12
13	14	15	16	17	18	19
20	21	22	23	24	25	26
27	28	29	30			

DECEMBER
S	M	T	W	T	F	S
				1	2	3
4	5	6	7	8	9	10
11	12	13	14	15	16	17
18	19	20	21	22	23	24
25	26	27	28	29	30	31

8

JANUARY
S	M	T	W	T	F	S
1	2	3	4	5	6	7
8	9	10	11	12	13	14
15	16	17	18	19	20	21
22	23	24	25	26	27	28
29	30	31				

FEBRUARY
S	M	T	W	T	F	S
			1	2	3	4
5	6	7	8	9	10	11
12	13	14	15	16	17	18
19	20	21	22	23	24	25
26	27	28	29			

MARCH
S	M	T	W	T	F	S
				1	2	3
4	5	6	7	8	9	10
11	12	13	14	15	16	17
18	19	20	21	22	23	24
25	26	27	28	29	30	31

APRIL
S	M	T	W	T	F	S
1	2	3	4	5	6	7
8	9	10	11	12	13	14
15	16	17	18	19	20	21
22	23	24	25	26	27	28
29	30					

MAY
S	M	T	W	T	F	S
		1	2	3	4	5
6	7	8	9	10	11	12
13	14	15	16	17	18	19
20	21	22	23	24	25	26
27	28	29	30	31		

JUNE
S	M	T	W	T	F	S
					1	2
3	4	5	6	7	8	9
10	11	12	13	14	15	16
17	18	19	20	21	22	23
24	25	26	27	28	29	30

JULY
S	M	T	W	T	F	S
1	2	3	4	5	6	7
8	9	10	11	12	13	14
15	16	17	18	19	20	21
22	23	24	25	26	27	28
29	30	31				

AUGUST
S	M	T	W	T	F	S
			1	2	3	4
5	6	7	8	9	10	11
12	13	14	15	16	17	18
19	20	21	22	23	24	25
26	27	28	29	30	31	

SEPTEMBER
S	M	T	W	T	F	S
						1
2	3	4	5	6	7	8
9	10	11	12	13	14	15
16	17	18	19	20	21	22
23	24	25	26	27	28	29
30						

OCTOBER
S	M	T	W	T	F	S
	1	2	3	4	5	6
7	8	9	10	11	12	13
14	15	16	17	18	19	20
21	22	23	24	25	26	27
28	29	30	31			

NOVEMBER
S	M	T	W	T	F	S
				1	2	3
4	5	6	7	8	9	10
11	12	13	14	15	16	17
18	19	20	21	22	23	24
25	26	27	28	29	30	

DECEMBER
S	M	T	W	T	F	S
						1
2	3	4	5	6	7	8
9	10	11	12	13	14	15
16	17	18	19	20	21	22
23	24	25	26	27	28	29
30	31					

9

JANUARY
S	M	T	W	T	F	S
	1	2	3	4	5	6
7	8	9	10	11	12	13
14	15	16	17	18	19	20
21	22	23	24	25	26	27
28	29	30	31			

FEBRUARY
S	M	T	W	T	F	S
				1	2	3
4	5	6	7	8	9	10
11	12	13	14	15	16	17
18	19	20	21	22	23	24
25	26	27	28	29		

MARCH
S	M	T	W	T	F	S
					1	2
3	4	5	6	7	8	9
10	11	12	13	14	15	16
17	18	19	20	21	22	23
24	25	26	27	28	29	30
31						

APRIL
S	M	T	W	T	F	S
	1	2	3	4	5	6
7	8	9	10	11	12	13
14	15	16	17	18	19	20
21	22	23	24	25	26	27
28	29	30				

MAY
S	M	T	W	T	F	S
			1	2	3	4
5	6	7	8	9	10	11
12	13	14	15	16	17	18
19	20	21	22	23	24	25
26	27	28	29	30	31	

JUNE
S	M	T	W	T	F	S
						1
2	3	4	5	6	7	8
9	10	11	12	13	14	15
16	17	18	19	20	21	22
23	24	25	26	27	28	29
30						

JULY
S	M	T	W	T	F	S
	1	2	3	4	5	6
7	8	9	10	11	12	13
14	15	16	17	18	19	20
21	22	23	24	25	26	27
28	29	30	31			

AUGUST
S	M	T	W	T	F	S
				1	2	3
4	5	6	7	8	9	10
11	12	13	14	15	16	17
18	19	20	21	22	23	24
25	26	27	28	29	30	31

SEPTEMBER
S	M	T	W	T	F	S
1	2	3	4	5	6	7
8	9	10	11	12	13	14
15	16	17	18	19	20	21
22	23	24	25	26	27	28
29	30					

OCTOBER
S	M	T	W	T	F	S
		1	2	3	4	5
6	7	8	9	10	11	12
13	14	15	16	17	18	19
20	21	22	23	24	25	26
27	28	29	30	31		

NOVEMBER
S	M	T	W	T	F	S
					1	2
3	4	5	6	7	8	9
10	11	12	13	14	15	16
17	18	19	20	21	22	23
24	25	26	27	28	29	30

DECEMBER
S	M	T	W	T	F	S
1	2	3	4	5	6	7
8	9	10	11	12	13	14
15	16	17	18	19	20	21
22	23	24	25	26	27	28
29	30	31				

10

JANUARY
S	M	T	W	T	F	S
		1	2	3	4	5
6	7	8	9	10	11	12
13	14	15	16	17	18	19
20	21	22	23	24	25	26
27	28	29	30	31		

FEBRUARY
S	M	T	W	T	F	S
					1	2
3	4	5	6	7	8	9
10	11	12	13	14	15	16
17	18	19	20	21	22	23
24	25	26	27	28	29	

MARCH
S	M	T	W	T	F	S
						1
2	3	4	5	6	7	8
9	10	11	12	13	14	15
16	17	18	19	20	21	22
23	24	25	26	27	28	29
30	31					

APRIL
S	M	T	W	T	F	S
		1	2	3	4	5
6	7	8	9	10	11	12
13	14	15	16	17	18	19
20	21	22	23	24	25	26
27	28	29	30			

MAY
S	M	T	W	T	F	S
				1	2	3
4	5	6	7	8	9	10
11	12	13	14	15	16	17
18	19	20	21	22	23	24
25	26	27	28	29	30	31

JUNE
S	M	T	W	T	F	S
1	2	3	4	5	6	7
8	9	10	11	12	13	14
15	16	17	18	19	20	21
22	23	24	25	26	27	28
29	30					

JULY
S	M	T	W	T	F	S
		1	2	3	4	5
6	7	8	9	10	11	12
13	14	15	16	17	18	19
20	21	22	23	24	25	26
27	28	29	30	31		

AUGUST
S	M	T	W	T	F	S
					1	2
3	4	5	6	7	8	9
10	11	12	13	14	15	16
17	18	19	20	21	22	23
24	25	26	27	28	29	30
31						

SEPTEMBER
S	M	T	W	T	F	S
	1	2	3	4	5	6
7	8	9	10	11	12	13
14	15	16	17	18	19	20
21	22	23	24	25	26	27
28	29	30				

OCTOBER
S	M	T	W	T	F	S
			1	2	3	4
5	6	7	8	9	10	11
12	13	14	15	16	17	18
19	20	21	22	23	24	25
26	27	28	29	30	31	

NOVEMBER
S	M	T	W	T	F	S
						1
2	3	4	5	6	7	8
9	10	11	12	13	14	15
16	17	18	19	20	21	22
23	24	25	26	27	28	29
30						

DECEMBER
S	M	T	W	T	F	S
	1	2	3	4	5	6
7	8	9	10	11	12	13
14	15	16	17	18	19	20
21	22	23	24	25	26	27
28	29	30	31			

11

JANUARY
S	M	T	W	T	F	S
			1	2	3	4
5	6	7	8	9	10	11
12	13	14	15	16	17	18
19	20	21	22	23	24	25
26	27	28	29	30	31	

FEBRUARY
S	M	T	W	T	F	S
						1
2	3	4	5	6	7	8
9	10	11	12	13	14	15
16	17	18	19	20	21	22
23	24	25	26	27	28	29

MARCH
S	M	T	W	T	F	S
1	2	3	4	5	6	7
8	9	10	11	12	13	14
15	16	17	18	19	20	21
22	23	24	25	26	27	28
29	30	31				

APRIL
S	M	T	W	T	F	S
			1	2	3	4
5	6	7	8	9	10	11
12	13	14	15	16	17	18
19	20	21	22	23	24	25
26	27	28	29	30		

MAY
S	M	T	W	T	F	S
					1	2
3	4	5	6	7	8	9
10	11	12	13	14	15	16
17	18	19	20	21	22	23
24	25	26	27	28	29	30
31						

JUNE
S	M	T	W	T	F	S
	1	2	3	4	5	6
7	8	9	10	11	12	13
14	15	16	17	18	19	20
21	22	23	24	25	26	27
28	29	30				

JULY
S	M	T	W	T	F	S
			1	2	3	4
5	6	7	8	9	10	11
12	13	14	15	16	17	18
19	20	21	22	23	24	25
26	27	28	29	30	31	

AUGUST
S	M	T	W	T	F	S
						1
2	3	4	5	6	7	8
9	10	11	12	13	14	15
16	17	18	19	20	21	22
23	24	25	26	27	28	29
30	31					

SEPTEMBER
S	M	T	W	T	F	S
		1	2	3	4	5
6	7	8	9	10	11	12
13	14	15	16	17	18	19
20	21	22	23	24	25	26
27	28	29	30			

OCTOBER
S	M	T	W	T	F	S
				1	2	3
4	5	6	7	8	9	10
11	12	13	14	15	16	17
18	19	20	21	22	23	24
25	26	27	28	29	30	31

NOVEMBER
S	M	T	W	T	F	S
1	2	3	4	5	6	7
8	9	10	11	12	13	14
15	16	17	18	19	20	21
22	23	24	25	26	27	28
29	30					

DECEMBER
S	M	T	W	T	F	S
		1	2	3	4	5
6	7	8	9	10	11	12
13	14	15	16	17	18	19
20	21	22	23	24	25	26
27	28	29	30	31		

12 2004

JANUARY
S	M	T	W	T	F	S
				1	2	3
4	5	6	7	8	9	10
11	12	13	14	15	16	17
18	19	20	21	22	23	24
25	26	27	28	29	30	31

FEBRUARY
S	M	T	W	T	F	S
1	2	3	4	5	6	7
8	9	10	11	12	13	14
15	16	17	18	19	20	21
22	23	24	25	26	27	28
29						

MARCH
S	M	T	W	T	F	S
	1	2	3	4	5	6
7	8	9	10	11	12	13
14	15	16	17	18	19	20
21	22	23	24	25	26	27
28	29	30	31			

APRIL
S	M	T	W	T	F	S
				1	2	3
4	5	6	7	8	9	10
11	12	13	14	15	16	17
18	19	20	21	22	23	24
25	26	27	28	29	30	

MAY
S	M	T	W	T	F	S
						1
2	3	4	5	6	7	8
9	10	11	12	13	14	15
16	17	18	19	20	21	22
23	24	25	26	27	28	29
30	31					

JUNE
S	M	T	W	T	F	S
		1	2	3	4	5
6	7	8	9	10	11	12
13	14	15	16	17	18	19
20	21	22	23	24	25	26
27	28	29	30			

JULY
S	M	T	W	T	F	S
				1	2	3
4	5	6	7	8	9	10
11	12	13	14	15	16	17
18	19	20	21	22	23	24
25	26	27	28	29	30	31

AUGUST
S	M	T	W	T	F	S
1	2	3	4	5	6	7
8	9	10	11	12	13	14
15	16	17	18	19	20	21
22	23	24	25	26	27	28
29	30	31				

SEPTEMBER
S	M	T	W	T	F	S
			1	2	3	4
5	6	7	8	9	10	11
12	13	14	15	16	17	18
19	20	21	22	23	24	25
26	27	28	29	30		

OCTOBER
S	M	T	W	T	F	S
					1	2
3	4	5	6	7	8	9
10	11	12	13	14	15	16
17	18	19	20	21	22	23
24	25	26	27	28	29	30
31						

NOVEMBER
S	M	T	W	T	F	S
	1	2	3	4	5	6
7	8	9	10	11	12	13
14	15	16	17	18	19	20
21	22	23	24	25	26	27
28	29	30				

DECEMBER
S	M	T	W	T	F	S
			1	2	3	4
5	6	7	8	9	10	11
12	13	14	15	16	17	18
19	20	21	22	23	24	25
26	27	28	29	30	31	

13

JANUARY
S	M	T	W	T	F	S
					1	2
3	4	5	6	7	8	9
10	11	12	13	14	15	16
17	18	19	20	21	22	23
24	25	26	27	28	29	30
31						

FEBRUARY
S	M	T	W	T	F	S
	1	2	3	4	5	6
7	8	9	10	11	12	13
14	15	16	17	18	19	20
21	22	23	24	25	26	27
28	29					

MARCH
S	M	T	W	T	F	S
		1	2	3	4	5
6	7	8	9	10	11	12
13	14	15	16	17	18	19
20	21	22	23	24	25	26
27	28	29	30	31		

APRIL
S	M	T	W	T	F	S
					1	2
3	4	5	6	7	8	9
10	11	12	13	14	15	16
17	18	19	20	21	22	23
24	25	26	27	28	29	30

MAY
S	M	T	W	T	F	S
1	2	3	4	5	6	7
8	9	10	11	12	13	14
15	16	17	18	19	20	21
22	23	24	25	26	27	28
29	30	31				

JUNE
S	M	T	W	T	F	S
			1	2	3	4
5	6	7	8	9	10	11
12	13	14	15	16	17	18
19	20	21	22	23	24	25
26	27	28	29	30		

JULY
S	M	T	W	T	F	S
					1	2
3	4	5	6	7	8	9
10	11	12	13	14	15	16
17	18	19	20	21	22	23
24	25	26	27	28	29	30
31						

AUGUST
S	M	T	W	T	F	S
	1	2	3	4	5	6
7	8	9	10	11	12	13
14	15	16	17	18	19	20
21	22	23	24	25	26	27
28	29	30	31			

SEPTEMBER
S	M	T	W	T	F	S
				1	2	3
4	5	6	7	8	9	10
11	12	13	14	15	16	17
18	19	20	21	22	23	24
25	26	27	28	29	30	

OCTOBER
S	M	T	W	T	F	S
						1
2	3	4	5	6	7	8
9	10	11	12	13	14	15
16	17	18	19	20	21	22
23	24	25	26	27	28	29
30	31					

NOVEMBER
S	M	T	W	T	F	S
		1	2	3	4	5
6	7	8	9	10	11	12
13	14	15	16	17	18	19
20	21	22	23	24	25	26
27	28	29	30			

DECEMBER
S	M	T	W	T	F	S
				1	2	3
4	5	6	7	8	9	10
11	12	13	14	15	16	17
18	19	20	21	22	23	24
25	26	27	28	29	30	31

14 2000

JANUARY
S	M	T	W	T	F	S
						1
2	3	4	5	6	7	8
9	10	11	12	13	14	15
16	17	18	19	20	21	22
23	24	25	26	27	28	29
30	31					

FEBRUARY
S	M	T	W	T	F	S
		1	2	3	4	5
6	7	8	9	10	11	12
13	14	15	16	17	18	19
20	21	22	23	24	25	26
27	28	29				

MARCH
S	M	T	W	T	F	S
			1	2	3	4
5	6	7	8	9	10	11
12	13	14	15	16	17	18
19	20	21	22	23	24	25
26	27	28	29	30	31	

APRIL
S	M	T	W	T	F	S
						1
2	3	4	5	6	7	8
9	10	11	12	13	14	15
16	17	18	19	20	21	22
23	24	25	26	27	28	29
30						

MAY
S	M	T	W	T	F	S
	1	2	3	4	5	6
7	8	9	10	11	12	13
14	15	16	17	18	19	20
21	22	23	24	25	26	27
28	29	30	31			

JUNE
S	M	T	W	T	F	S
				1	2	3
4	5	6	7	8	9	10
11	12	13	14	15	16	17
18	19	20	21	22	23	24
25	26	27	28	29	30	

JULY
S	M	T	W	T	F	S
						1
2	3	4	5	6	7	8
9	10	11	12	13	14	15
16	17	18	19	20	21	22
23	24	25	26	27	28	29
30	31					

AUGUST
S	M	T	W	T	F	S
		1	2	3	4	5
6	7	8	9	10	11	12
13	14	15	16	17	18	19
20	21	22	23	24	25	26
27	28	29	30	31		

SEPTEMBER
S	M	T	W	T	F	S
					1	2
3	4	5	6	7	8	9
10	11	12	13	14	15	16
17	18	19	20	21	22	23
24	25	26	27	28	29	30

OCTOBER
S	M	T	W	T	F	S
1	2	3	4	5	6	7
8	9	10	11	12	13	14
15	16	17	18	19	20	21
22	23	24	25	26	27	28
29	30	31				

NOVEMBER
S	M	T	W	T	F	S
			1	2	3	4
5	6	7	8	9	10	11
12	13	14	15	16	17	18
19	20	21	22	23	24	25
26	27	28	29	30		

DECEMBER
S	M	T	W	T	F	S
					1	2
3	4	5	6	7	8	9
10	11	12	13	14	15	16
17	18	19	20	21	22	23
24	25	26	27	28	29	30
31						

Calendar for the Year 2003

JANUARY

S	M	T	W	T	F	S
			1	2	3	4
5	6	7	8	9	10	11
12	13	14	15	16	17	18
19	20	21	22	23	24	25
26	27	28	29	30	31	

FEBRUARY

S	M	T	W	T	F	S
						1
2	3	4	5	6	7	8
9	10	11	12	13	14	15
16	17	18	19	20	21	22
23	24	25	26	27	28	

MARCH

S	M	T	W	T	F	S
						1
2	3	4	5	6	7	8
9	10	11	12	13	14	15
16	17	18	19	20	21	22
23	24	25	26	27	28	29
30	31					

APRIL

S	M	T	W	T	F	S
		1	2	3	4	5
6	7	8	9	10	11	12
13	14	15	16	17	18	19
20	21	22	23	24	25	26
27	28	29	30			

MAY

S	M	T	W	T	F	S
				1	2	3
4	5	6	7	8	9	10
11	12	13	14	15	16	17
18	19	20	21	22	23	24
25	26	27	28	29	30	31

JUNE

S	M	T	W	T	F	S
1	2	3	4	5	6	7
8	9	10	11	12	13	14
15	16	17	18	19	20	21
22	23	24	25	26	27	28
29	30					

JULY

S	M	T	W	T	F	S
		1	2	3	4	5
6	7	8	9	10	11	12
13	14	15	16	17	18	19
20	21	22	23	24	25	26
27	28	29	30	31		

AUGUST

S	M	T	W	T	F	S
					1	2
3	4	5	6	7	8	9
10	11	12	13	14	15	16
17	18	19	20	21	22	23
24	25	26	27	28	29	30
31						

SEPTEMBER

S	M	T	W	T	F	S
	1	2	3	4	5	6
7	8	9	10	11	12	13
14	15	16	17	18	19	20
21	22	23	24	25	26	27
28	29	30				

OCTOBER

S	M	T	W	T	F	S
			1	2	3	4
5	6	7	8	9	10	11
12	13	14	15	16	17	18
19	20	21	22	23	24	25
26	27	28	29	30	31	

NOVEMBER

S	M	T	W	T	F	S
						1
2	3	4	5	6	7	8
9	10	11	12	13	14	15
16	17	18	19	20	21	22
23	24	25	26	27	28	29
30						

DECEMBER

S	M	T	W	T	F	S
	1	2	3	4	5	6
7	8	9	10	11	12	13
14	15	16	17	18	19	20
21	22	23	24	25	26	27
28	29	30	31			

Federal Holidays and Other Notable Dates, 2003

Some dates may be subject to change.

The days marked on the calendar above and shown below *in italics* are U.S. federal holidays, designated by the president or Congress and applicable to federal employees and the District of Columbia. Most U.S. states also observe these holidays, and many states observe others; practices vary from state to state. In most states the secretary of states's office can provide details.

January

1 *New Year's Day;* Cotton, Orange, Fiesta, Sugar, and Rose Bowls
7 Congress convenes
13-26 Australian Open tennis tournament
19 Golden Globe Awards
20 *Martin Luther King Jr. Day* (3rd Mon. in Jan.)
26 Super Bowl XXXVII (San Diego); Australia Day, Australia

February

1 Chinese New Year
2 Groundhog Day
5 Constitution Day, Mexico
9 NBA All-Star Game; NFL Pro Bowl
10-11 Westminster Dog Show
12 Lincoln's Birthday
14 Valentine's Day
16 Daytona 500
17 *Washington's Birthday, or Presidents' Day, or Washington-Lincoln Day* (3rd Mon. in Feb.)
23 Grammy Awards
26 Mardi Gras
28–Mar. 4 Carnival, Brazil

March

1 Iditarod Trail Sled Dog Race begins
5 Ash Wednesday
10 Commonwealth Day, Canada, UK
17 St. Patrick's Day
20 First day of Spring (North America)
21 Benito Juarez's Birthday, Mexico
23 Academy Awards

April

1 April Fool's Day
6 Daylight Savings Time begins in U.S.
7 Pulitzer Prizes announced; NCAA men's basketball championship
7-13 Masters golf tournament
8 NCAA women's basketball championship
17 Passover (1st full day)
18 Good Friday (observed in some states, in some cases only part of the day)
20 Easter
21 Patriots' Day; Boston Marathon
22 Earth Day
23 Administrative Professionals Day
24 Take Our Daughters & Sons to Work Day
25 Arbor Day, U.S.
27 Orthodox Easter

May

1 May Day
3 Kentucky Derby
5 Cinco de Mayo (Battle of Puebla Day), Mexico
6 National Teacher Day, U.S.
8 Buddha's Birthday, Korea, Hong Kong
11 Mother's Day
17 Armed Forces Day; Preakness Stakes
19 Victoria Day, Canada
26 *Memorial Day or Decoration Day* (last Mon. in May); Spring Bank Holiday, UK
26-June 8 French Open tennis tournament

June

4 Dragon Boat Festival, China
7 Belmont Stakes
14 Flag Day, U.S.
15 Father's Day
21 First day of Summer (Northern Hemisphere)
23-July 6 Wimbledon tennis tournament

July

1 Canada Day
4 *Independence Day*
7-14 Running of the Bulls (Pamplona, Spain)
14 Bastille Day, France
17-20 British Open golf tournament

August

30 St. Rose of Lima, Peru

September

1 *Labor Day, U.S.* (1st Mon. in Sept.); Labor Day, Canada
7 Grandparents' Day, U.S.
16 Independence Day, Mexico
17 Citizenship Day, U.S.
19 St. Gennaro, Italy
23 First day of Autumn
27 Rosh Hashanah (1st full day)

IT'S A FACT: Groundhog Day is celebrated on Feb. 2, or Candlemas Day, which is about halfway through winter (in the northern hemisphere). Candlemas is a Christian feast day on which candles are traditionally blessed. In European tradition clear skies that day mean 6 more weeks of winter. Groundhog Day follows the same idea. If the groundhog emerging from his hole gets scared by his shadow (because it's a sunny day), there'll be more winter; if there's no shadow (because of cloudy skies), spring is around the corner. The yearly festival in Punxsutawney, PA, involving Punxsutawney Phil, is only the most famous of many Groundhog Day festivals.

October

- **3** German Unification Day, Germany
- **6** Yom Kippur
- **7** U.S. Supreme Court session begins
- **12** Día de la Raza, Mexico
- **13** *Columbus Day, or Discoverer's Day, or Pioneers' Day* (observed in some states; 2nd Mon. in Oct.); Thanksgiving Day, Canada
- **24** United Nations Day
- **26** Daylight Savings Time ends in U.S.
- **27** Ramadan (1st full day)
- **31** Halloween

November

- **1** All Saints' Day
- **2** New York City Marathon; Day of the Dead, Mexico
- **4** Election Day (observed in some states; 1st Tues. after 1st Mon. in Nov.)
- **5** Guy Fawkes Day, UK
- **11** *Veterans Day;* Remembrance Day, Canada, UK
- **15** Shichi-Go-San (Seven-Five-Three), Japan
- **27** *Thanksgiving Day, U.S.* (4th Thurs. in Nov.)

December

- **10** Nobel Prizes awarded (announced in Oct.)
- **12** Virgin of Guadalupe Day, Mexico
- **14** Heisman Trophy awarded
- **20** Hanukkah (1st full day)
- **22** First day of Winter (Northern Hemisphere)
- **25** *Christmas Day*
- **26** Kwanzaa begins; Boxing Day, Australia, Canada, New Zealand, UK

Special Months

Every year there are many thousands of special months, days, and weeks as a result of anniversaries, official proclamations, and promotional events, both trivial and serious. Here are a few of the special months:

January: Bread Machine Baking Month, National Hot Tea Month, National Clean Up Your Computer Month
February: Black History Month, American Heart Month, Library Lovers Month
March: Women's History Month, American Red Cross Month, Optimism Month
April: National Child Abuse Prevention Month, National Poetry Month, National Pecan Month
May: Older Americans Month, Asian Pacific American Heritage Month, National Salsa Month
June: Children's Awareness Month, National Rose Month, National Safety Month
July: Cell Phone Courtesy Month, National Hot Dog Month, Anti-Borodom Month
August: National Back to School Month, National Inventors' Month, Admit You're Happy Month
September: Hispanic Heritage Month (actually runs Sept. 15-Oct. 15), National Potato Month, National Chicken Month
October: National Domestic Violence Awareness Month, National Breast Cancer Awareness Month, Go Hog Wild—Eat Country Ham Month
November: National American Indian Heritage Month, National Adoption Month, American Diabetes Month
December: Universal Human Rights Month, National Drunk and Drugged Driving Prevention Month, Safe Toys and Gifts Month

Signs of the Zodiac

The **zodiac** is the apparent yearly path of the sun among the stars as viewed from earth, and was divided by the ancients into 12 equal sections or signs, each named for the constellation situated within its limits in ancient times. Astrologers claim that the temperament and destiny of each individual depend on the zodiac sign under which the person was born and the relationships between the planets at that time and throughout life.

Below are the 12 traditional signs and the traditional range of dates pertaining to each:

- ♈ **Aries** (Ram), March 21–April 19
- ♉ **Taurus** (Bull), April 20–May 20
- ♊ **Gemini** (Twins), May 21–June 21
- ♋ **Cancer** (Crab), June 22–July 22
- ♌ **Leo** (Lion), July 23–August 22
- ♍ **Virgo** (Maiden), August 23–September 22
- ♎ **Libra** (Balance), September 23–October 23
- ♏ **Scorpio** (Scorpion), October 24–November 21
- ♐ **Sagittarius** (Archer), November 22–December 21
- ♑ **Capricorn** (Goat), December 22–January 19
- ♒ **Aquarius** (Water Bearer), January 20–February 18
- ♓ **Pisces** (Fishes), February 19–March 20

The Julian Period

How many days have you lived? To determine this, multiply your age by 365, add the number of days since your last birthday, and account for all leap years. Chances are your calculations will go wrong somewhere. Astronomers, however, find it convenient to express dates and time intervals in days rather than in years, months, and days. This is done by placing events within the Julian period.

The Julian period was devised in 1582 by the French classical scholar Joseph Scaliger (1540-1609), and it was named after his father, Julius Caesar Scaliger, not after the Julian calendar as might be supposed.

Scaliger began Julian Day (JD) #1 at noon, Jan. 1, 4713 BC, the most recent time that 3 major chronological cycles began on the same day: (1) the 28-year solar cycle, after which dates in the Julian calendar (e.g., Feb. 11) return to the same days of the week (e.g., Monday); (2) the 19-year lunar cycle, after which the phases of the moon return to the same dates of the year; and (3) the 15-year indiction cycle, used in ancient Rome to regulate taxes. It will take 7,980 years to complete the period, the product of 28, 19, and 15.

Noon of Dec. 31, 2002, marks the beginning of JD 2,452,640; that many days will have passed since the start of the Julian period. The JD at noon of any date in 2003 may be found by adding to this figure the day of the year for that date, which can be obtained from the left half of the "How Far Apart Are Two Dates?" chart on page 647.

Wedding Anniversaries

The traditional names for wedding anniversaries go back many years in social usage and have been used to suggest types of appropriate anniversary gifts. Traditional products for gifts are listed here in capital letters, with a few allowable revisions in parentheses, followed by common modern gifts in each category.

- **1st** PAPER, clocks
- **2nd** COTTON, china
- **3rd** LEATHER, crystal, glass
- **4th** LINEN (SILK), appliances
- **5th** WOOD, silverware
- **6th** IRON, wood objects
- **7th** WOOL (COPPER), desk sets
- **8th** BRONZE, linens, lace
- **9th** POTTERY (CHINA), leather goods
- **10th** TIN, ALUMINUM, diamond
- **11th** STEEL, fashion jewelry
- **12th** SILK, pearls, colored gems
- **13th** LACE, textiles, furs
- **14th** IVORY, gold jewelry
- **15th** CRYSTAL, watches
- **20th** CHINA, platinum
- **25th** SILVER, sterling silver
- **30th** PEARL, diamond
- **35th** CORAL (JADE), jade
- **40th** RUBY, ruby
- **45th** SAPPHIRE, sapphire
- **50th** GOLD, gold
- **55th** EMERALD, emerald
- **60th** DIAMOND, diamond

IT'S A FACT: On Red Nose Day, which occurs every 2 years on a Friday in March, devotees in Britain don red plastic noses and hold or participate in numerous fund-raising events for Comic Relief, an organization supporting charitable works in Britain and in Africa. A Red Nose Day was scheduled for Mar. 14 in 2003.

Birthstones

Source: Jewelry Industry Council

MONTH	Ancient	Modern
January	Garnet	Garnet
February	Amethyst	Amethyst
March	Jasper	Bloodstone or Aquamarine
April	Sapphire	Diamond
May	Agate	Emerald
June	Emerald	Pearl, Moonstone, or Alexandrite
July	Onyx	Ruby
August	Carnelian	Sardonyx or Peridot
September	Chrysolite	Sapphire
October	Aquamarine	Opal or Tourmaline
November	Topaz	Topaz
December	Ruby	Turquoise or Zircon

Standard Time, Daylight Saving Time, and Others

Source: National Imagery and Mapping Agency; U.S. Dept. of Transportation

See also Time Zone map, page 500.

Standard Time

Standard Time is reckoned from the Prime Meridian of Longitude in Greenwich, England. The world is divided into 24 zones, each 15 deg of arc, or one hour in time apart. The Greenwich meridian (0 deg) extends through the center of the initial zone, and the zones to the east are numbered from 1 to 12, with the prefix "minus" indicating the number of hours to be subtracted to obtain Greenwich Time. Each zone extends 7.5 deg on either side of its central meridian.

Westward zones are similarly numbered, but prefixed "plus," showing the number of hours that must be added to get Greenwich Time. Although these zones apply generally to sea areas, the Standard Time maintained in many countries does not coincide with zone time. A graphical representation of the zones is shown on the Standard Time Zone Chart of the World (WOBZC76) published by the National Imagery and Mapping Agency. This chart is available from the Federal Aviation Administration (FAA), 6501 Lafayette Avenue, Riverdale, MD 20737-1199; telephone: (800) 638-8972.

The U.S. and possessions are divided into 10 Standard Time zones. Each zone is approximately 15 deg of longitude in width. All places in each zone use, instead of their own local time, the time counted from the transit of the "mean sun" across the Standard Time meridian that passes near the middle of that zone. These time zones are designated as Atlantic, Eastern, Central, Mountain, Pacific, Alaska, Hawaii-Aleutian, Samoa, Wake Island, and Guam; the time in these zones is reckoned from the 60th, 75th, 90th, 105th, 120th, 135th, 150th, and 165th meridians west of Greenwich and the 165th and 150th meridians east of Greenwich. The time zone line wanders to conform to local geographical regions. The time in the various zones in the U.S. and U.S. territories west of Greenwich is earlier than Greenwich Time by 4, 5, 6, 7, 8, 9, 10, and 11 hours, respectively. However, Wake Island and Guam cross the International Date Line and are 12 and 10 hours later than Greenwich Time, respectively.

24-Hour Time

Twenty-four-hour time is widely used in scientific work throughout the world. In the U.S. it is also used in operations of the armed forces. In Europe it is frequently used by the transportation networks in preference to the 12-hour AM and PM system. With the 24-hour system the day begins at midnight, and times are designated 00:00 through 23:59.

International Date Line

The Date Line, approximately coinciding with the 180th meridian, separates the calendar dates. The date must be advanced one day when crossing in a westerly direction and set back one day when crossing in an easterly direction. The Date Line frequently deviates from the 180th meridian because of decisions made by individual nations affected. The line is deflected eastward through the Bering Strait and westward of the Aleutians to prevent separating these areas by date. The line is deflected eastward of the Tonga and New Zealand Islands in the South Pacific for the same reason. More recently it was deflected much farther eastward to include all of Kiribati. The line is established by international custom; there is no international authority prescribing its exact course.

Daylight Saving Time

Daylight Saving Time is achieved by advancing the clock one hour. Daylight Saving Time in the U.S. begins each year at 2 AM on the first Sunday in Apr. and ends at 2 AM on the last Sunday in Oct.

Daylight Saving Time was first observed in the U.S. during World War I, and then again during World War II. In the intervening years, some states and communities observed Daylight Saving Time, using whatever beginning and ending dates they chose. In 1966, Congress passed the Uniform Time Act, which provided that any state or territory that chooses to observe Daylight Saving Time must begin and end on the federal dates. Any state could, by law, exempt itself; a 1972 amendment to the act authorized states split by time zones to observe Daylight Saving Time in one time zone and standard time in the other time zone. Currently, Arizona, Hawaii, the eastern time zone portion of Indiana, Puerto Rico, the U.S. Virgin Islands, and American Samoa do not observe Daylight Saving Time.

Congress and the secretary of transportation both have authority to change time zone boundaries. Since 1966 there have been a number of changes to U.S. time zone boundaries. In addition, efforts to conserve energy have prompted various changes in the times that Daylight Saving Time is observed.

International Usage

Adjusting clock time so as to gain the added daylight on summer evenings is common throughout the world.

Canada, which extends over 6 time zones, generally observes Daylight Saving Time from the first Sunday of Apr. until the last Sunday of Oct. Saskatchewan remains on standard time all year. Communities elsewhere in Canada also may exempt themselves from Daylight Saving Time. Mexico, which occupies 3 time zones, observes Daylight Saving Time during the same period as most of Canada.

Member nations of the European Union (EU) observe a "summer-time period," the EU's version of Daylight Saving Time, from the last Sunday of Mar. until the last Sunday in Oct.

Russia, which extends over 11 time zones, maintains its Standard Time 1 hour fast for its zone designation. Additionally, it proclaims Daylight Saving Time from the last Sunday in Mar. until the 4th Sunday in Oct.

China, which extends across 5 time zones, has decreed that the entire country be placed on Greenwich Time plus 8 hours. Daylight Saving Time is not observed. Japan, which lies within one time zone, also does not modify its legal time during the summer months.

Many countries in the Southern Hemisphere maintain Daylight Saving Time, generally from Oct. to Mar.; however, most countries near the equator do not deviate from Standard Time.

WORLD ALMANAC QUICK QUIZ

Which of the following years is not a leap year?

(a) 1600 (b) 1800
(c) 2000 (d) 2004

For the answer look in this chapter, or see page 1008.

Standard Time Differences—World Cities

The time indicated in the table is fixed by law and is called the legal time or, more generally, Standard Time. Use of Daylight Saving Time varies widely. * Indicates morning of the following day. At 12:00 noon, Eastern Standard Time, the Standard Time (in 24-hour time) in selected cities is as follows:

Addis Ababa	20 00	Caracas	13 00	Lima	12 00	St. Petersburg	20 00
Amsterdam	18 00	Casablanca	17 00	Lisbon	17 00	Santiago	13 00
Ankara	19 00	Copenhagen	18 00	London	17 00	Sarajevo	18 00
Athens	19 00	Dhaka	23 00	Madrid	18 00	Seoul	2 00*
Auckland	5 00*	Dublin	17 00	Manila	1 00*	Shanghai	1 00*
Baghdad	20 00	Edinburgh	17 00	Mecca	20 00	Singapore	1 00*
Bangkok	0 00*	Geneva	18 00	Melbourne	3 00*	Stockholm	18 00
Beijing	1 00*	Helsinki	19 00	Montevideo	14 00	Sydney	3 00*
Belfast	17 00	Ho Chi Minh City	0 00*	Moscow	20 00	Taipei	1 00*
Belgrade	18 00	Hong Kong	1 00*	Munich	18 00	Tashkent	22 00
Berlin	18 00	Islamabad	22 00	Nagasaki	2 00*	Tehran	20 30
Bogotá	12 00	Istanbul	19 00	Nairobi	20 00	Tel Aviv	19 00
Bombay (Mumbai)	22 30	Jakarta	0 00*	New Delhi	22 30	Tokyo	2 00*
Brussels	18 00	Jerusalem	19 00	Oslo	18 00	Vladivostok	3 00*
Bucharest	19 00	Johannesburg	19 00	Paris	18 00	Vienna	18 00
Budapest	18 00	Kabul	21 50	Prague	18 00	Warsaw	18 00
Buenos Aires	14 00	Karachi	22 00	Quito	12 00	Wellington	5 00*
Cairo	19 00	Kathmandu	22 45	Rio de Janeiro	14 00	Yangon (Rangoon)	23 30
Calcutta (Kolkata)	22 30	Kiev	19 00	Riyadh	20 00	Yokohama	2 00*
Cape Town	19 00	Lagos	18 00	Rome	18 00	Zurich	18 00

Standard Time Differences—North American Cities

At 12:00 noon, Eastern Standard Time, the Standard Time in selected North American cities is as follows:

Akron, OH	12 00 Noon	*Fort Wayne, IN	12 00 Noon	Peoria, IL	11 00 AM
Albuquerque, NM	10 00 AM	Frankfort, KY	12 00 Noon	*Phoenix, AZ	10 00 AM
Anchorage, AK	8 00 AM	Havana, Cuba	12 00 Noon	Pierre, SD	11 00 AM
Atlanta, GA	12 00 Noon	Helena, MT	10 00 AM	Pittsburgh, PA	12 00 Noon
Austin, TX	11 00 AM	*Honolulu, HI	7 00 AM	*Regina, Sask.	11 00 AM
Baltimore, MD	12 00 Noon	Houston, TX	11 00 AM	Reno, NV	9 00 AM
Birmingham, AL	11 00 AM	*Indianapolis, IN	12 00 Noon	Richmond, VA	12 00 Noon
Bismarck, ND	11 00 AM	Jacksonville, FL	12 00 Noon	Rochester, NY	12 00 Noon
Boise, ID	10 00 AM	Juneau, AK	8 00 AM	Sacramento, CA	9 00 AM
Boston, MA	12 00 Noon	Kansas City, MO	11 00 AM	St. John's, Nfld.	1 30 PM
Buffalo, NY	12 00 Noon	*Kingston, Jamaica	12 00 Noon	St. Louis, MO	11 00 AM
Butte, MT	10 00 AM	Knoxville, TN	12 00 Noon	St. Paul, MN	11 00 AM
Calgary, Alta.	10 00 AM	Las Vegas, NV	9 00 AM	Salt Lake City, UT	10 00 AM
Charleston, SC	12 00 Noon	Lexington, KY	12 00 Noon	San Antonio, TX	11 00 AM
Charleston, WV	12 00 Noon	Lincoln, NE	11 00 AM	San Diego, CA	9 00 AM
Charlotte, NC	12 00 Noon	Little Rock, AR	11 00 AM	San Francisco, CA	9 00 AM
Charlottetown, PEI	1 00 PM	Los Angeles, CA	9 00 AM	San Jose, CA	9 00 AM
Chattanooga, TN	12 00 Noon	Louisville, KY	12 00 Noon	*San Juan, PR	1 00 PM
Cheyenne, WY	10 00 AM	Mexico City, Mexico	11 00 AM	Santa Fe, NM	10 00 AM
Chicago, IL	11 00 AM	Memphis, TN	11 00 AM	Savannah, GA	12 00 Noon
Cleveland, OH	12 00 Noon	Miami, FL	12 00 Noon	Seattle, WA	9 00 AM
Colorado Spr., CO	10 00 AM	Milwaukee, WI	11 00 AM	Shreveport, LA	11 00 AM
Columbus, OH	12 00 Noon	Minneapolis, MN	11 00 AM	Sioux Falls, SD	11 00 AM
Dallas, TX	11 00 AM	Mobile, AL	11 00 AM	Spokane, WA	9 00 AM
*Dawson, Yuk.	9 00 AM	Montreal, Que	12 00 Noon	Tampa, FL	12 00 Noon
Dayton, OH	12 00 Noon	Nashville, TN	11 00 AM	Toledo, OH	12 00 Noon
Denver, CO	10 00 AM	Nassau, Bahamas	12 00 Noon	Topeka, KS	11 00 AM
Des Moines, IA	11 00 AM	New Haven, CT	12 00 Noon	Toronto, Ont	12 00 Noon
Detroit, MI	12 00 Noon	New Orleans, LA	11 00 AM	*Tucson, AZ	10 00 AM
Duluth, MN	11 00 AM	New York, NY	12 00 Noon	Tulsa, OK	11 00 AM
Edmonton, Alta.	10 00 AM	Nome, AK	8 00 AM	Vancouver, BC	9 00 AM
El Paso, TX	10 00 AM	Norfolk, VA	12 00 Noon	Washington, DC	12 00 Noon
Erie, PA	12 00 Noon	Oklahoma City, OK	11 00 AM	Wichita, KS	11 00 AM
Evansville, IN	11 00 AM	Omaha, NE	11 00 AM	Wilmington, DE	12 00 Noon
Fairbanks, AK	8 00 AM	Ottawa, Ont	12 00 Noon	Winnipeg, Man.	11 00 AM
Flint, MI	12 00 Noon	*Panama City, Panama	12 00 Noon		

Note: This same table can be used for Daylight Saving Time when it is in effect, but allowance must be made for cities that do not observe it; they are marked with an asterisk (*). Daylight Saving Time is one hour later than Standard Time.

IT'S A FACT: In 1793, during the Revolution, France adopted a whole new calendar. The months were all 30 days and had rhyming names that fit each season. The year began with the autumnal equinox, and the months went: Vendémiaire (Vintage), Brumaire (Mist), Frimaire (Frost), Nivôse (Snow), Pluviôse (Rain), Ventôse (Wind), Germinal (Seed), Floréal (Blossom), Prairial (Meadow), Messidor (Harvest), Thermidor (Heat), and Fructidor (Fruits). Another 5 or 6 days were added at the end of the year to make a full 365 or 366. Unlike the metric system, a more lasting Revolutionary innovation, the calendar was dropped after only 12 years.

ASTRONOMY

Edited by Lee T. Shapiro, Ph. D., Head of Education and Public Outreach, National Radio Astronomy Observatory

Celestial Events Summary, 2003

There will be 4 eclipses in 2003, 1 total solar, 1 annular solar (in which a thin outer ring of the sun is not covered), and 2 total lunar. The center path of the annular solar eclipse in May starts in Scotland, crosses Iceland and Greenland, and can be seen as partial over most of Europe and parts of the Middle East and Asia. The path of the total solar eclipse in November starts in the S Indian Ocean and crosses Antarctica. It can be seen as partial in Australia, most of New Zealand, the rest of Antarctica, and the southern tip of S America. The total lunar eclipse in May will be seen best in S America, Central America, and eastern N America, though much of the rest of N America, Africa, the Middle East, and most of Europe will see portions of the eclipse. The total lunar eclipse in November will be seen in its entirety in eastern S America, the NE portion of N America, western Africa, and most of Europe, while the rest of the western hemisphere, the rest of Africa, and most of Asia will see only part of the eclipse. In May there is also a transit of the Sun by Mercury. The entire event will be visible in most of Asia, Europe, and all but the western portion of Africa. The most likely viewing successes for meteor showers will be the Quadrantids in January, the Eta Aquarids in May, and the Orionids in October.

At the start of the year, Jupiter and Saturn are up most of the night, while Venus is prominent in the early evening and Mars rises in the early morning. Venus, Saturn, and Jupiter remain visible in the early evening sky through May, while Mars remains in the morning sky. Mercury is in the morning sky through all of February and in the evening sky through most of April. May is an exciting month with both Saturn and Venus getting very low at sunset, soon to disappear in the next month or 2. There is both a total lunar eclipse and an annular solar eclipse this month, as well as a transit of the Sun by Mercury. Summer will provide less opportunity for viewing planets, with Saturn hidden during June and July, Venus gone during July and August, and Jupiter gone during August. Mercury may be found in the evening sky during August. In September, Saturn, Venus, and Jupiter are all in the morning sky, while Mars is up most of the night. Saturn, Venus, and Jupiter stay in the morning sky through October and November, while in December Saturn is up the whole night and Mars is up mainly in the first half of the night.

The crescent Moon with its light not overpowering makes pretty pairings with the 2 brightest planets, Venus and Jupiter. Waxing crescent pairings are visible in the early evening soon after sunset, while waning crescent pairings are visible in the early morning rising shortly before sunrise. The waxing crescent Moon pairs with Jupiter in early June and early July, and pairs with Venus in late October, late November, and late December. The waning crescent Moon pairs with Venus in late January, late February, late March, late April, and late May and pairs with Jupiter in late September. Of special interest are the very close pairing of Venus with Uranus in late March, the triple grouping of the Moon, Venus, and Mercury in late May, and the very close pairing of the Moon with Venus in late October.

Astronomical Positions Defined

Two celestial bodies are in **conjunction** when they are due N and S of each other, either in **right ascension** (with respect to the N celestial pole) or in **celestial longitude** (with respect to the N ecliptic pole). If the bodies are seen near each other, they will rise and set at nearly the same time. For the inner planets—Mercury and Venus—**inferior conjunction** occurs when either planet passes between Earth and the Sun, while **superior conjunction** occurs when either Mercury or Venus is on the far side of the Sun. Celestial bodies are in **opposition** when their Right Ascensions differ by exactly 12 hours, or when their Celestial Longitudes differ by 180°. One of the 2 objects in opposition will rise while the other is setting. **Quadrature** refers to the arrangement where the coordinates of 2 bodies differ by exactly 90°. These terms may refer to the relative positions of any 2 bodies as seen from Earth, but one of the bodies is so frequently the Sun that mention of the Sun is omitted in that case; otherwise, both bodies are named.

When objects are in conjunction, the alignment is not perfect, and one is usually passing above or below the other. The geocentric angular separation between the Sun and an object is termed **elongation**. Elongation is limited only for Mercury and Venus; the greatest elongation for each of these bodies is noted in the appropriate table and is approximately the time for longest observation. **Perihelion** is the point in an orbit that is nearest to the Sun, and **aphelion,** the point farthest from the Sun. **Perigee** is the point in an orbit that is nearest Earth, **apogee** the point that is farthest from Earth. An **occultation** of a planet or a star is an **eclipse** of it by some other body, usually the Moon. A transit of the Sun occurs when Mercury or Venus passes directly between Earth and the Sun, appearing to cross the disk of the Sun.

Astronomical Constants; Speed of Light

The following were adopted as part of the International Astronomical Union System of Astronomical Constants (1976): **Speed of light,** 299,792.458 km per sec., or about 186,282 statute mi per sec.; **solar parallax,** 8".794148; **Astronomical Unit,** 149,597,870 km, or 92,955,807 mi; **constant of nutation,** 9".2025; and **constant of aberration,** 20".49552.

Celestial Events Highlights, 2003

(in Coordinated Universal Time, or UTC—the standard time of the prime meridian)

January

Mercury, hidden in the Sun's glare, emerges in the morning sky during the last third of the month.

Venus, low in the SE before sunrise, passes the star Antares in the constellation Scorpius on the 15th.

Mars, rising in the SE a few hours before sunrise, passes its "rival," the star Antares in the constellation Scorpius, at the end of the month. Note the orange-reddish color of both planet and star.

Jupiter, rising shortly after sunset, is up most of the night.

Saturn, just past opposition, is up most of the night, setting a couple of hours before sunrise.

Moon passes Mercury on the 3rd and the 30th, Saturn on the 15th, Jupiter on the 19th, Mars on the 27th, and Venus on the 28th. Watch for the early morning groupings of the waning crescent Moon, on the 27th and the 28th, with Mars and Venus.

Jan. 1—Pluto in Ophiuchus. Neptune in Capricornus, stays there all year. Uranus in Capricornus. Saturn in Taurus. Jupiter in Cancer. Mars in Libra. Venus in Libra. Sun in Sagittarius.

Jan. 2—Mercury stationary, begins retrograde motion.

Jan. 4—Quadrantid meteor shower early in the morning before sunrise. Moon passes 5° south of Mercury. Earth at perihelion, closest approach to Sun. Moon passes 5° south of Neptune.

Jan. 6—Moon passes 5° south of Uranus. Mercury at perihelion.

Jan. 9—Venus enters Scorpius.

Jan. 11—Venus at greatest western elongation of 47° (W of Sun and rising before the Sun). Mercury at inferior conjunction, passing between Earth and Sun.

Jan. 14—Venus enters Ophiuchus.

Jan. 15—Moon passes 3° north of Saturn. Venus passes 8° north of Antares.

Jan. 19—Moon passes 4° north of Jupiter.

Jan. 20—Sun enters Capricornus.

Jan. 21—Mars enters Scorpius.

Jan. 22—Mercury stationary, resumes direct motion.

Jan. 27—Moon passes 0.4° south of Mars.

Jan. 28—Moon passes 4° south of Venus. Mars enters Ophiuchus.

Jan. 30—Moon passes 5° south of Mercury. Neptune at conjunction.

Jan. 31—Mars passes 5° north of Antares.

February

Mercury, very low in the SE in the early morning, is hard to see throughout the month.

Venus is low in the SE before sunrise.

Mars is low in the SSE before sunrise.

Jupiter, already up in the ENE at sunset, is prominent for much of the night.

Saturn is very high in the SE after sunset.

Moon passes Saturn on the 12th, Jupiter on the 15th, Mars on the 25th, and Venus on the 27th. Watch for the early morning groupings of the waning crescent Moon, from the 25th to the 27th, with Mars and Venus.

Feb. 1—Venus enters Sagittarius.

Feb. 2—Jupiter at opposition.

Feb. 4—Mercury at greatest western elongation of 25°degrees.

Feb. 8—Pluto enters Serpens Cauda.

Feb. 12—Moon passes 3° north of Saturn.

Feb. 15—Moon passes 4° north of Jupiter.

Feb. 16—Sun enters Aquarius.

Feb. 17—Uranus at conjunction.

Feb. 19—Mercury at aphelion.

Feb. 12—Mercury passes 1.6° south of Neptune.

Feb. 22—Saturn stationary, resumes direct motion.

Feb. 25—Moon passes 1.9° south of Mars.

Feb. 27—Moon passes 5° south of Venus. Mars enters Sagittarius.

Feb. 28—Moon passes 5° south of Neptune.

March

Mercury disappears from the morning sky into the glare of the Sun.

Venus, low in the ESE before sunrise, passes close to Uranus on the 28th—look in binoculars.

Mars is low in the SSE before sunrise.

Jupiter is high in the E after sunset.

Saturn is very high in the W after sunset.

Moon passes Mercury on the 1st, Saturn on the 11th, Jupiter on the 14th, Mars on the 25th, and Venus on the 29th. Watch for the waning crescent Moon paired with Venus on the 29th.

Mar. 1—Moon passes 3° south of Mercury.

Mar. 2—Venus enters Capricornus.

Mar. 4—Mercury passes 1.5° south of Uranus.

Mar. 11—Moon passes 3° north of Saturn.

Mar. 12—Venus passes 0.2° north of Neptune. Sun enters Pisces.

Mar. 14—Moon passes 4° north of Jupiter.

Mar. 20—Vernal Equinox at 8:00 PM EST (01:00 UTC Mar. 21); spring begins in the northern hemisphere, autumn in the southern hemisphere. Mercury, at superior conjunction, passes behind the Sun.

Mar. 23—Pluto stationary, begins retrograde motion.

Mar. 25—Moon passes 3° south of Mars. Venus enters Aquarius.

Mar. 27—Moon passes 5° south of Neptune.

Mar. 28—Venus passes 0.05° north of Uranus. Sun barely touches constellation of Cetus.

Mar. 29—Moon passes 5° south of Uranus and Venus.

WORLD ALMANAC QUICK QUIZ

How long is a (synodic) day on Mercury, compared to a 24-hour Earth day?

(a) a little shorter than an Earth day (b) a little longer than an Earth day

(c) about 1 Earth hour (d) about 175 Earth days

For the answer look in this chapter, or see page 1008.

April

Mercury is now low in the W after sunset.

Venus is low in the ESE before sunrise.

Mars continues low in the SSE before sunrise.

Jupiter is high in the S after sunset.

Saturn is high in the W after sunset.

Moon passes Saturn on the 7th, Jupiter on the 11th, Mars on the 23rd, and Venus on the 28th. Watch for the waning crescent Moon paired with Venus on the 28th.

Apr. 4—Jupiter stationary, resumes direct motion. Mercury at perihelion.

Apr. 7—Moon passes 3° north of Saturn.

Apr. 11—Moon passes 4° north of Jupiter.

Apr. 16—Mercury at greatest eastern elongation of 16°, setting after the Sun.

Apr. 17—Venus enters Pisces.

Apr. 19—Venus at aphelion. Sun enters Aries

Apr. 21—Mars enters Capricornus.

Apr. 23—Moon passes 3° south of Mars.

Apr. 24—Moon passes 5° south of Neptune.

Apr. 25—Moon passes 5° south of Uranus.

Apr. 26—Mercury stationary, begins retrograde motion

Apr. 27—Venus enters Cetus.

Apr. 28—Moon passes 3° south of Venus.

Apr. 30—Venus enters Pisces.

May

Mercury becomes visible low in the west during 2nd half of the month, passing Venus on the 27th.

Venus is very low in the E before sunrise.

Mars, rising after midnight, is low in the SSW before sunrise.

Jupiter is high in the WSW after sunset.

Saturn is low in the WNW after sunset.

Moon passes Saturn on the 5th, Jupiter on the 8th, Mars on the 21st, and Venus and Mercury on the 29th. Very thin, waning crescent Moon very low in the E triples with Venus and Mercury just before sunrise on the 29th. Total lunar eclipse on the 16th, commences about 10 PM EDT on the 15th. Moon's angular size too small to totally block the Sun; produces an annular solar eclipse on the 31st in the northern hemisphere.

May 6—Eta Aquarids meteor shower in the morning from midnight to dawn. Moon passes 3° north of Saturn.

May 7—Mercury at inferior conjunction.

May 8—Moon passes 4° north of Jupiter.

May 10—Pluto enters Ophiuchus.

May 13—Mars passes 2° south of Neptune.

May 14—Sun enters Taurus.

May 15—Saturn enters Orion.

May 16—Neptune stationary, begins retrograde motion. Total lunar eclipse; see details under Eclipses on page 663.

May 17—Venus enters Aries.

May 18—Mercury at aphelion.

May 19—Mercury stationary, resumes direct motion.

May 21—Moon passes 4° south of Neptune and 3° south of Mars.

May 22—Moon passes 5° south of Uranus.

May 27—Mercury passes 2° south of Venus.

May 29—Moon passes 2° north of Mercury and 0.1° north of Venus.

May 31—Annular solar eclipse; see details under Eclipses on page 663.

June

Mercury, low in the E before sunrise most of the month, passes close to Venus on the 21st.

Venus is very low in the ENE just before sunrise.

Mars, rising after midnight, is low in the SSW before sunrise.

Jupiter is low in the W after sunset.

Saturn is paired with very thin waxing crescent Moon low in WSW on the 1st, but soon disappears into the glare of the Sun.

Moon passes Saturn on the 1st, Jupiter on the 5th, and Mars on the 19th. Watch for waxing crescent Moon paired with Jupiter on the 4th and 5th.

June 1—Moon passes 4° north of Saturn.

June 3—Mercury at greatest western elongation of 24°.

June 4—Saturn enters Gemini. Venus enters Taurus.

June 5—Moon passes 4° north of Jupiter.

June 7—Uranus stationary, begins retrograde motion.

June 9—Mars enters Aquarius. Pluto at opposition.

June 17—Moon passes 5° south of Neptune.

June 18—Venus passes 5° north of Aldebaran.

June 19—Moon passes 1.7° south of Mars and 5° south of Uranus. Mercury passes 4° north of Aldebaran.

June 20—Mars passes 3° south of Uranus.

June 21—Mercury passes 0.4° south of Venus. Northern solstice at 3:10 PM EDT (19:10 UTC); summer begins in the northern hemisphere, winter in the southern hemisphere. Sun enters Gemini.

June 24—Saturn at conjunction.

June 30—Jupiter enters Leo.

July

Mercury, very low in the WNW before sunset, disappears into the glare of the Sun by mid-month.

Venus disappears from the morning sky after mid-month, lost in the glare of the Sun.

Mars is now rising a couple of hours before midnight and is in the SW by sunrise.

Jupiter is low in the W at sunset.

Saturn reappears in the morning sky low in the E during the 2nd half of the month.

Moon passes Jupiter on the 2nd and 30th, Mars on the 17th, Saturn on the 26th, and Mercury on 31st. Watch for the thin waxing crescent Moon paired with Jupiter on the 2nd and tripled with Jupiter and Mercury on the 30th.

July 1—Mercury at perihelion.

July 2—Moon passes 4° north of Jupiter.

July 4—Earth at aphelion. Venus enters Gemini.

July 5—Mercury at superior conjunction.

July 8—Venus passes 0.8° north of Saturn.

July 15—Moon passes 5° south of Neptune.

July 16—Moon passes 5° south of Uranus.

July 17—Moon passes 0.3° north of Mars.

July 21—Sun enters Cancer.

July 26—Mercury passes 0.4° north of Jupiter. Moon passes 4° north of Saturn. Saturn at perihelion.

July 27—Venus enters Cancer.

July 30—Mercury passes 0.2° north of Regulus. Moon passes 4° north of Jupiter. Mars stationary, begins retrograde motion.

July 31—Moon passes 5° north of Mercury.

August

Mercury is low in the western sky.

Venus is gone from view as it passes behind the Sun.

Mars is up all night long, but does not get very high even at the meridian.

Jupiter disappears from the early evening sky into the glow of sunset.

Saturn is the E at sunrise, gradually getting higher.

Moon passes Mars on the 12th, Saturn on the 23rd, and Mercury on the 29th.

Aug. 4—Neptune at opposition.

Aug. 10—Venus at perihelion.

Aug. 11—Moon passes 5° south of Neptune. Sun enters Leo.

Aug. 12—Moon passes 5° south of Uranus and 1.9° north of Mars. Venus enters Leo.

Aug. 14—Mercury at greatest eastern elongation of 27°. Mercury at aphelion.

Aug. 18—Venus at superior conjunction, passing behind the Sun.

Aug. 22—Jupiter at conjunction.

Aug. 23—Moon passes 4° north of Saturn.

Aug. 24—Uranus at opposition.

Aug. 27—Mercury stationary, begins retrograde motion.

Aug. 28—Mars at opposition.

Aug. 29—Moon passes 9° north of Mercury.

Aug. 30—Pluto stationary, resumes direct motion. Mars at perihelion.

September

Mercury is very low in the E from mid-month through the end of the month.

Venus reappears very low in the W after sunset by the end of the month.

Mars is low in the ESE after sunset and remains visible most of the night.

Jupiter reappears very low in the E before sunrise.

Saturn is high in the E before sunrise.

Moon passes Mars on the 9th, Saturn on the 20th, and both Jupiter and Mercury on the 24th. Watch for the waning crescent Moon paired with Jupiter on the 24th with Mercury lower just before sunrise.

Sept. 7—Moon passes 5° south of Neptune.

Sept. 9—Moon passes 5° south of Uranus and 1.2° north of Mars.

Sept. 10—Venus enters Virgo.

Sept. 11—Mercury at inferior conjunction.

Sept. 17—Sun enters Virgo.

Sept. 19—Mercury stationary, resumes direct motion.

Sept. 20—Moon passes 5° north of Saturn.

Sept. 23—Autumnal Equinox at 6:47 AM EDT (10:47 UTC); autumn begins in the northern hemisphere, spring begins in the southern hemisphere.

Sept. 24—Moon passes 4° north of Jupiter and 5° north of Mercury.

Sept. 26—Mercury at greatest western elongation of 18°.

Sept. 27—Mercury at perihelion.

Sept. 29—Mars stationary, resumes direct motion.

October

Mercury is very low in the E before sunrise during the first half of the month.

Venus is low in the SW after sunset, passes Spica on the 3rd.

Mars is in the SE after sunset.

Jupiter is higher in the E before sunrise.

Saturn, rising about midnight, is high in the S before sunrise.

Moon passes Mars on the 6th, Saturn on the 17th, Jupiter on the 19th, and Venus on the 26th. Watch for the waxing crescent Moon and Venus as a very close pair, very low in the SW, on the 26th just after sunset.

Oct. 3—Venus passes 3° north of Spica.

Oct. 4—Moon passes 5° south of Neptune.

Oct. 6—Moon passes 5° south of Uranus and 1.1° south of Mars.

Oct. 15—Venus enters Libra.

Oct. 17—Moon passes 5° north of Saturn.

Oct. 19—Moon passes 5° north of Jupiter.

Oct. 21—Orionid meteor shower in the morning from midnight to a couple of hours before dawn.

Oct. 22—Neptune stationary, resumes direct motion.

Oct. 25—Mercury at superior conjunction. Saturn stationary, begins retrograde motion.

Oct. 26—Moon passes 0.08° south of Venus.

Oct. 31—Sun enters Libra.

November

Mercury is very low in the SW after sunset during the 2nd half of the month.

Venus, low in the SW after sunset, passes Antares on the 10th.

Mars continues in the SE after sunset.

Jupiter, rising about an hour after midnight, is high in the south by sunrise.

Saturn rises about 3 hours before midnight in the ENE.

Moon passes Mars on the 3rd, Saturn on the 13th, Jupiter on the 13th, and both Mercury and Venus on the 25th. Watch for the Moon paired with Venus on the 25th with Mercury lower in the sky. Total lunar eclipse on the 8th-9th commences about 6:30 PM EST. Total solar eclipse on the 23rd-24th is visible in the far southern hemisphere.

Nov. 1—Moon passes 5° south of Neptune.

Nov. 2—Moon passes 5° south of Uranus. Venus enters Scorpius.

Nov. 3—Moon passes 3° south of Mars.

Nov. 8—Uranus stationary, resumes direct motion.

Nov. 8-9—Total lunar eclipse; see details under Eclipses on page 663.

Nov. 9—Venus enters Ophiuchus.

Nov. 10—Venus passes 4° north of Antares. Mercury at aphelion.

Nov. 13—Moon passes 5° north of Saturn.

Nov. 18—Mercury passes 3° north of Antares. Moon passes 4° north of Jupiter.

Nov. 23-24—Total solar eclipse; see details under Eclipses on page 663.

Nov. 23—Sun enters Scorpius.

Nov. 24—Venus enters Sagittarius.

Nov. 25—Moon passes 0.3° south of Mercury and 2° south of Venus.

Nov. 28—Moon passes 5° south of Neptune.

Nov. 29—Moon passes 5° south of Uranus.

Nov. 30—Venus at aphelion. Sun enters Ophiuchus.

December

Mercury, low in the SW after sunset, disappears into the glow of sunset during the 2nd half of the month.

Venus, low in the SW after sunset, passes Neptune on the 30th.

Mars is higher in the SE after sunset.

Jupiter, rising about midnight, is high in the S before sunrise.

Saturn, reaching opposition, is up all night long.

Moon passes Mars on the 1st and the 30th, Saturn on the 10th, Jupiter on the 16th, and Venus on the 25th. Watch for waxing crescent Moon paired with Venus on the 25th.

Dec. 1—Moon passes 4° south of Mars.

Dec. 4—Mars enters Pisces.

Dec. 5—Pluto enters Serpens Cauda.

Dec. 9—Mercury at greatest eastern elongation of 21°.

Dec. 10—Moon passes 5° north of Saturn.

Dec. 12—Pluto at conjunction.

Dec. 16—Moon passes 4° north of Jupiter.

Dec. 17—Mercury stationary, begins retrograde motion.

Dec. 18—Sun enters Sagittarius.

Dec. 20—Venus enters Capricornus.

Dec. 22—Southern Solstice at 2:04 AM EST (7:04 UTC); winter begins in the northern hemisphere, summer begins in the southern hemisphere.

Dec. 24—Mercury at perihelion.

Dec. 25—Moon passes 3° south of Venus.

Dec. 26—Moon passes 5° south of Neptune.

Dec. 27—Mercury at inferior conjunction. Moon passes 5° south of Uranus.

Dec. 30—Moon passes 4° south of Mars. Venus passes 1.9° south of Neptune.

Dec. 31—Saturn at opposition.

Meteorites and Meteor Showers

When a chunk of material, ice or rock, plunges into Earth's atmosphere and burns up in a fiery display, the event is a **meteor**. While the chunk of material is still in space, it is a **meteoroid**. If part of the material gets through the atmosphere and reaches the ground, the remnant on the ground is a **meteorite**.

Meteorites found on Earth are classified into types, depending on their composition: **irons**, those composed chiefly of iron, a small percentage of nickel, and traces of other metals such as cobalt; **stones**, stony meteors consisting of silicates; and **stony irons**, containing varying proportions of both iron and stone.

Serious study of meteorites as non-earth objects began in the 20th century. Scientists now use sophisticated chemical analysis, X rays, and mass spectrography in determining their origin and composition. In 1996, the results of a study of a Mars rock recovered 12 years earlier from the Allan Hills region of Antarctica suggested that life once existed on that planet. Although most meteorites are now believed to be fragments of **asteroids** or **comets**, geochemical studies have shown that a few Antarctic stones came from the Moon or Mars, from which they presumably were ejected by the explosive impact of asteroids.

The **largest known meteorite**, estimated to weigh about 55 metric tons, is situated at Hoba West near Grootfontein, Namibia. The Manicouagan impact crater in Quebec, Canada, is one of the largest crater structures still visible on the surface of the Earth. Other large impact craters include the Chicxulub crater off the coast of Mexico, estimated at 185 mi across, the Sudbury crater in Ontario, Canada, estimated at 125 mi across, and the Acraman crater in Australia, estimated at 100 mi across.

Sporadic meteors, which enter the atmosphere throughout the year, seem to originate from the asteroid belt. Other meteors that come in groups and tend to occur at the same time each year create what are called **meteor showers**; these are the meteors associated with comets. As a comet orbits the Sun, the Sun slowly boils away some of the comet's material, and the comet leaves a trail of tiny particles which are dispersed along the comet's path. If Earth's orbit and this path intersect, then once a year, as Earth reaches that particular point in its orbit, there will be a meteor shower.

Meteor showers vary in strength, but usually the 3 best meteor showers of the year are the **Perseids**, which occur around Aug. 12, the **Orionids**, which take place around Oct. 21, and the **Geminids**, which occur around Dec. 13. These showers feature meteors at the rate of about 60 per hour. Best observing conditions coincide with the absence of moonlight, usually when the Moon's phase is between waning crescent Moon and waxing quarter Moon. Meteor showers are also usually seen better after the middle of the night.

For most meteor showers the cometary debris is relatively uniformly scattered along the comet's orbit. However, in the case of the **Leonid** meteor shower, which occurs every year around Nov. 17-18, the cometary debris, from Comet Temple-Tuttle, seems to be bunched up in one stretch. That means that most years when Earth crosses the orbit of this comet, the meteor shower produced is relatively weak. However, approximately every 33 years Earth encounters the bunched-up debris. Sometimes the storm is a disappointment, as it was in 1899 and 1933; at other times it is a roaring success, as in 1833 and 1866. In 2001, the Leonids stormed again, producing 1,000-3,000 meteors per hour in the United States and across the Pacific to China. It was predicted that the Leonids would probably storm again in 2002, but moonlight from the nearly full Moon was expected to interfere with observing. In 2003, look for success in observing meteor showers with the Quadrantids (around Jan. 3), the Eta Aquarids (around May 5), and the Orionids.

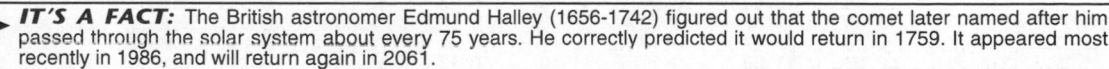

IT'S A FACT: The British astronomer Edmund Halley (1656-1742) figured out that the comet later named after him passed through the solar system about every 75 years. He correctly predicted it would return in 1759. It appeared most recently in 1986, and will return again in 2061.

Rising and Setting of Planets, 2003

In Coordinated Universal Time (0 in the *h* col. designates midnight)

Venus, 2003

	20° N Latitude		30° N Latitude		40° N Latitude		50° N Latitude		60° N Latitude	
Date	Rise h m	Set h m	Rise h m	Set h m	Rise h m	Set h m	Rise h m	Set h m	Rise h m	Set h m
Jan. 1	3 08	14 27	3 21	14 14	3 38	13 58	4 00	13 35	4 36	12 59
11	3 12	14 25	3 27	14 09	3 46	13 50	4 12	13 24	4 54	12 42
21	3 19	14 26	3 36	14 09	3 57	13 47	4 27	13 18	5 15	12 29
31	3 28	14 31	3 46	14 12	4 09	13 49	4 41	13 17	5 35	12 23
Feb. 10	3 38	14 39	3 57	14 20	4 20	13 56	4 53	13 23	5 49	12 27
20	3 47	14 49	4 05	14 31	4 28	14 08	5 01	13 36	5 55	12 41
Mar. 2	3 55	15 02	4 12	14 45	4 33	14 23	5 03	13 54	5 52	13 05
12	4 01	15 15	4 16	15 00	4 34	14 42	5 00	14 16	5 41	13 35
22	4 04	15 28	4 17	15 16	4 31	15 01	4 52	14 41	5 24	14 10
Apr. 1	4 06	15 41	4 15	15 32	4 26	15 22	4 40	15 08	5 02	14 46
11	4 06	15 53	4 11	15 49	4 17	15 43	4 25	15 35	4 38	15 23
21	4 05	16 05	4 06	16 04	4 07	16 03	4 09	16 02	4 12	16 00
May 1	4 03	16 18	4 01	16 21	3 57	16 24	3 52	16 29	3 45	16 38
11	4 02	16 30	3 55	16 37	3 47	16 46	3 35	16 57	3 18	17 16
21	4 02	16 43	3 51	16 54	3 38	17 07	3 20	17 26	2 51	17 56
31	4 04	16 57	3 50	17 12	3 32	17 30	3 07	17 55	2 27	18 36
June 10	4 08	17 12	3 51	17 30	3 29	17 52	2 58	18 23	2 06	19 16
20	4 16	17 28	3 56	17 48	3 31	18 14	2 55	18 50	1 52	19 53
30	4 26	17 44	4 05	18 05	3 37	18 33	2 58	19 12	1 47	20 23
July 10	4 39	17 58	4 18	18 20	3 50	18 48	3 10	19 28	1 57	20 41
20	4 55	18 10	4 34	18 31	4 07	18 58	3 29	19 36	2 20	20 44
30	5 11	18 20	4 52	18 39	4 28	19 03	3 54	19 36	2 55	20 34
Aug. 9	5 27	18 26	5 11	18 42	4 51	19 02	4 22	19 30	3 35	20 16
19	5 43	18 30	5 30	18 42	5 14	18 58	4 52	19 19	4 17	19 53
29	5 57	18 31	5 49	18 39	5 38	18 50	5 23	19 04	5 00	19 27
Sept. 8	6 11	18 30	6 07	18 35	6 01	18 40	5 54	18 47	5 42	18 58
18	6 25	18 29	6 24	18 29	6 24	18 29	6 24	18 29	6 23	18 29
28	6 38	18 28	6 42	18 23	6 47	18 18	6 54	18 11	7 05	18 00
Oct. 8	6 52	18 27	7 01	18 18	7 11	18 08	7 25	17 53	7 47	17 31
18	7 07	18 28	7 20	18 16	7 35	18 00	7 57	17 38	8 30	17 04
28	7 23	18 32	7 40	18 16	8 00	17 55	8 28	17 27	9 15	16 40
Nov. 7	7 40	18 39	8 00	18 20	8 24	17 55	8 59	17 20	9 58	16 21
17	7 58	18 50	8 19	18 28	8 47	18 00	9 26	17 21	10 35	16 12
27	8 14	19 03	8 37	18 40	9 06	18 11	9 47	17 30	11 02	16 15
Dec. 7	8 29	19 19	8 51	18 56	9 19	18 28	10 00	17 48	11 13	16 35
17	8 40	19 36	9 01	19 15	9 27	18 49	10 04	18 13	11 08	17 09
27	8 48	19 53	9 06	19 35	9 28	19 13	10 00	18 42	10 52	17 50

Mars, 2003

	20° N Latitude		30° N Latitude		40° N Latitude		50° N Latitude		60° N Latitude	
Date	Rise h m	Set h m	Rise h m	Set h m	Rise h m	Set h m	Rise h m	Set h m	Rise h m	Set h m
Jan. 1	2 51	14 04	3 06	13 49	3 24	13 31	3 50	13 06	4 30	12 25
11	2 41	13 48	2 57	13 32	3 18	13 11	3 46	12 43	4 33	11 56
21	2 30	13 33	2 48	13 15	3 11	12 53	3 42	12 21	4 34	11 29
31	2 20	13 19	2 39	13 00	3 03	12 36	3 37	12 02	4 34	11 04
Feb. 10	2 10	13 05	2 30	12 45	2 55	12 20	3 31	11 44	4 33	10 42
20	1 59	12 52	2 20	12 31	2 46	12 05	3 23	11 28	4 29	10 22
Mar. 2	1 48	12 40	2 09	12 19	2 36	11 52	3 14	11 14	4 22	10 06
12	1 37	12 28	1 58	12 07	2 25	11 40	3 04	11 01	4 12	9 53
22	1 25	12 17	1 46	11 55	2 13	11 29	2 51	10 51	3 58	9 44
Apr. 1	1 12	12 05	1 32	11 45	1 59	11 18	2 36	10 41	3 40	9 37
11	0 58	11 54	1 18	11 34	1 43	11 08	2 19	10 33	3 20	9 32
21	0 43	11 42	1 02	11 23	1 26	10 59	2 00	10 25	2 57	9 28
May 1	0 27	11 29	0 45	11 11	1 08	10 49	1 39	10 17	2 32	9 24
11	0 10	11 16	0 27	10 59	0 48	10 38	1 17	10 09	2 05	9 20
21	23 49	11 01	0 07	10 46	0 26	10 26	0 53	9 59	1 37	9 15
31	23 29	10 45	23 44	10 31	0 04	10 13	0 29	9 48	1 08	9 08
June 10	23 08	10 27	23 21	10 14	23 37	9 57	0 02	9 35	0 39	8 59
20	22 44	10 07	22 56	9 55	23 12	9 39	23 32	9 19	0 08	8 45
30	22 18	9 44	22 30	9 32	22 44	9 18	23 04	8 58	23 34	8 27
July 10	21 49	9 17	22 01	9 06	22 14	8 52	22 33	8 33	23 03	8 04
20	21 17	8 45	21 29	8 34	21 42	8 21	22 01	8 02	22 30	7 33
30	20 41	8 08	20 53	7 57	21 07	7 43	21 26	7 24	21 56	6 54
Aug. 9	20 00	7 26	20 13	7 14	20 27	6 59	20 48	6 39	21 20	6 07
19	19 15	6 38	19 28	6 25	19 44	6 09	20 06	5 48	20 41	5 13
29	18 27	5 48	18 41	5 34	18 58	5 17	19 22	4 54	19 59	4 17
Sept. 8	17 39	4 57	17 53	4 43	18 11	4 25	18 35	4 01	19 14	3 23
18	16 52	4 10	17 06	3 56	17 24	3 38	17 48	3 14	18 27	2 35
28	16 09	3 29	16 23	3 15	16 40	2 58	17 03	2 34	17 40	1 57
Oct. 8	15 30	2 53	15 43	2 40	15 59	2 24	16 20	2 02	16 54	1 28
18	14 55	2 22	15 07	2 10	15 21	1 56	15 40	1 37	16 10	1 06
28	14 24	1 56	14 34	1 46	14 46	1 33	15 02	1 17	15 28	0 51
Nov. 7	13 55	1 33	14 03	1 25	14 13	1 15	14 27	1 01	14 47	0 40
17	13 29	1 13	13 35	1 06	13 42	0 59	13 53	0 49	14 08	0 33
27	13 04	0 55	13 08	0 50	13 13	0 45	13 20	0 38	13 30	0 28
Dec. 7	12 40	0 38	12 42	0 36	12 45	0 33	12 48	0 30	12 52	0 25
17	12 17	0 23	12 17	0 23	12 17	0 23	12 17	0 23	12 16	0 24
27	11 55	0 08	11 53	0 11	11 50	0 13	11 46	0 17	11 40	0 24

Jupiter, 2003

	20° N Latitude		30° N Latitude		40° N Latitude		50° N Latitude		60° N Latitude	
	Rise	Set	Rise	Set	Rise	Set	Rise	Set	Rise	Set
Date	h m	h m	h m	h m	h m	h m	h m	h m	h m	h m
Jan. 1	20 06	9 03	19 52	9 18	19 33	9 37	19 07	10 02	18 25	10 45
11	19 23	8 20	19 07	8 36	18 48	8 55	18 22	9 21	17 39	10 05
21	18 38	7 37	18 22	7 53	18 03	8 12	17 36	8 39	16 51	9 24
31	17 53	6 53	17 37	7 09	17 17	7 29	16 49	7 57	16 03	8 43
Feb. 10	17 08	6 09	16 51	6 26	16 31	6 46	16 02	7 15	15 15	8 02
20	16 23	5 26	16 06	5 42	15 45	6 03	15 16	6 32	14 27	7 21
Mar. 2	15 39	4 42	15 22	4 59	15 00	5 21	14 31	5 50	13 40	6 40
12	14 56	4 00	14 38	4 17	14 17	4 39	13 47	5 09	12 56	6 00
22	14 14	3 19	13 56	3 36	13 35	3 58	13 04	4 28	12 13	5 20
Apr. 1	13 33	2 38	13 16	2 56	12 54	3 17	12 23	3 48	11 32	4 40
11	12 54	1 59	12 37	2 17	12 15	2 38	11 45	3 09	10 53	4 01
21	12 17	1 21	12 00	1 38	11 38	2 00	11 08	2 30	10 16	3 22
May 1	11 41	0 44	11 23	1 01	11 02	1 23	10 32	1 53	9 42	2 43
11	11 05	0 08	10 49	0 25	10 28	0 46	9 58	1 16	9 09	2 05
21	10 31	23 30	10 15	23 46	9 54	0 10	9 25	0 39	8 37	1 27
31	9 58	22 55	9 42	23 11	9 22	23 31	8 54	0 03	8 07	0 50
June 10	9 26	22 21	9 10	22 37	8 51	22 57	8 23	23 24	7 38	0 13
20	8 54	21 48	8 39	22 03	8 20	22 22	7 54	22 48	7 10	23 32
30	8 23	21 15	8 09	21 30	7 50	21 48	7 25	22 13	6 43	22 55
July 10	7 53	20 43	7 38	20 57	7 21	21 14	6 57	21 38	6 17	22 18
20	7 22	20 10	7 09	20 24	6 52	20 40	6 29	21 03	5 51	21 41
30	6 52	19 38	6 39	19 51	6 23	20 07	6 01	20 20	5 26	21 04
Aug. 9	6 22	19 06	6 10	19 18	5 55	19 33	5 34	19 54	5 01	20 27
19	5 52	18 34	5 41	18 45	5 27	18 59	5 07	19 19	4 36	19 50
29	5 23	18 02	5 12	18 12	4 59	18 26	4 40	18 44	4 11	19 13
Sept. 8	4 53	17 29	4 43	17 40	4 30	17 52	4 13	18 09	3 46	18 36
18	4 23	16 57	4 13	17 06	4 02	17 18	3 46	17 34	3 20	17 59
28	3 52	16 24	3 44	16 33	3 33	16 44	3 18	16 59	2 55	17 22
Oct. 8	3 22	15 52	3 14	16 00	3 03	16 10	2 50	16 23	2 28	16 45
18	2 50	15 18	2 43	15 26	2 34	15 35	2 21	15 48	2 01	16 07
28	2 19	14 45	2 12	14 52	2 03	15 00	1 52	15 12	1 33	15 30
Nov. 7	1 46	14 10	1 40	14 17	1 32	14 25	1 21	14 36	1 04	14 52
17	1 13	13 36	1 07	13 42	1 00	13 49	0 50	13 59	0 34	14 15
27	0 39	13 00	0 34	13 06	0 27	13 13	0 17	13 22	0 02	13 37
Dec. 7	0 04	12 24	23 55	12 29	23 49	12 36	23 40	12 45	23 26	12 59
17	23 24	11 47	20 10	11 52	23 13	11 58	23 04	12 07	22 51	12 20
27	22 46	11 09	22 41	11 14	22 35	11 20	22 27	11 29	22 14	11 42

Saturn, 2003

	20° N Latitude		30° N Latitude		40° N Latitude		50° N Latitude		60° N Latitude	
	Rise	Set	Rise	Set	Rise	Set	Rise	Set	Rise	Set
Date	h m	h m	h m	h m	h m	h m	h m	h m	h m	h m
Jan. 1	16 16	5 31	15 55	5 51	15 29	6 17	14 53	6 54	13 48	7 59
11	15 33	4 48	15 13	5 09	14 47	5 34	14 10	6 11	13 05	7 16
21	14 51	4 06	14 31	4 27	14 05	4 52	13 28	5 29	12 23	6 34
31	14 10	3 25	13 49	3 45	13 24	4 11	12 47	4 48	11 42	5 53
Feb. 10	13 29	2 44	13 09	3 05	12 43	3 30	12 06	4 07	11 01	5 12
20	12 49	2 04	12 29	2 25	12 03	2 51	11 26	3 27	10 21	4 33
Mar. 2	12 10	1 25	11 50	1 46	11 24	2 12	10 47	2 49	9 41	3 54
12	11 32	0 47	11 11	1 08	10 45	1 34	10 08	2 11	9 02	3 16
22	10 54	0 10	10 34	0 30	10 08	0 56	9 30	1 33	8 24	2 40
Apr. 1	10 17	23 29	9 57	23 50	9 30	0 20	8 53	0 57	7 47	2 04
11	9 41	22 53	9 20	23 14	8 54	23 40	8 17	0 21	7 10	1 28
21	9 05	22 18	8 45	22 39	8 18	23 05	7 41	23 43	6 33	0 53
May 1	8 30	21 43	8 09	22 04	7 43	22 30	7 05	23 08	5 58	0 19
11	7 55	21 08	7 35	21 29	7 08	21 56	6 30	22 34	5 22	23 42
21	7 21	20 34	7 00	20 55	6 34	21 22	5 56	22 00	4 48	23 08
31	6 47	20 00	6 26	20 21	5 59	20 48	5 21	21 26	4 13	22 34
June 10	6 13	19 26	5 52	19 47	5 25	20 14	4 47	20 52	3 39	22 00
20	5 39	18 53	5 18	19 14	4 52	19 40	4 14	20 18	3 05	21 27
30	5 06	18 19	4 45	18 40	4 18	19 06	3 40	19 45	2 32	20 53
July 10	4 32	17 45	4 11	18 06	3 44	18 33	3 06	19 11	1 58	20 19
20	3 58	17 11	3 37	17 32	3 11	17 59	2 33	18 36	1 25	19 44
30	3 24	16 37	3 03	16 58	2 37	17 24	1 59	18 02	0 51	19 10
Aug. 9	2 50	16 02	2 29	16 23	2 03	16 50	1 25	17 27	0 18	18 34
19	2 15	15 28	1 55	15 48	1 28	16 15	0 51	16 52	23 41	17 59
29	1 40	14 52	1 20	15 13	0 54	15 39	0 16	16 17	23 06	17 23
30	1 37	14 49	1 16	15 09	0 50	15 36	0 13	16 13	23 03	17 19
Sept. 8	1 05	14 17	0 44	14 37	0 18	15 03	23 37	15 40	22 31	16 47
18	0 29	13 40	0 08	14 01	23 39	14 27	23 02	15 04	21 56	16 10
28	23 48	13 03	23 28	13 24	23 02	13 50	22 25	14 27	21 19	15 32
Oct. 8	23 11	12 26	22 50	12 46	22 25	13 12	21 48	13 49	20 42	14 54
18	22 32	11 47	22 12	12 08	21 46	12 34	21 09	13 10	20 04	14 16
28	21 53	11 08	21 33	11 29	21 07	11 54	20 30	12 31	19 25	13 37
Nov. 7	21 13	10 28	20 53	10 49	20 27	11 15	19 50	11 51	18 45	12 57
17	20 33	9 48	20 12	10 08	19 46	10 34	19 09	11 11	18 04	12 17
27	19 51	9 06	19 31	9 27	19 05	9 53	18 27	10 30	17 22	11 36
Dec. 7	19 09	8 25	18 48	8 45	18 22	9 11	17 45	9 48	16 39	10 55
17	18 26	7 42	18 06	8 03	17 40	8 29	17 02	9 06	15 56	10 13
27	17 43	7 00	17 23	7 20	16 56	7 47	16 19	8 24	15 12	9 31

Brightest Stars

This table lists stars of greatest visual magnitude as seen in the night sky (the lower the number, the brighter the star). The common name of the star is in parentheses. Stars of variable magnitude are designated by v. Coordinates are for mid-2003. Greek letters in the star names indicate perceived degree of brightness within the constellation, alpha being the brightest.

To find the time when the star is on the meridian, subtract Right Ascension of Mean Sun (see the table Greenwich Sidereal Time for 0^h UTC) from the star's Right Ascension, first adding 24h to the latter if necessary. Mark this result PM if less than 12h; if greater than 12h, subtract 12h and mark the remainder AM.

Star	Magnitude	Parallax "	Light-yrs	Right ascen. h m	Declination ° '
α Canis Majoris (Sirius)	−1.44v	0.379	8.6	6 45.3	−16 43
α Carinae (Canopus)	−0.62v	0.010	313	6 24.0	−52 42
α Bootis (Arcturus)	−0.05v	0.089	37	14 15.8	+19 10
α Centauri (Rigel Kentaurus)	−0.01	0.742	4.4	14 39.8	−60 51
α Lyrae (Vega)	0.03v	0.129	25.3	18 37.1	+38 47
α Aurigae (Capella)	0.08v	0.077	42	5 16.9	+46 00
β Orionis (Rigel)	0.18v	0.004	770	5 14.7	− 8 12
α Canis Minoris (Procyon)	0.40	0.286	11.4	7 39.4	+ 5 13
α Eridani (Achernar)	0.45v	0.023	144	1 37.8	−57 13
α Orionis (Betelgeuse)	0.45v	0.008	427	5 55.3	+ 7 24
β Centauri (Hadar)	0.61v	0.006	525	14 04.1	−60 24
α Aquilae (Altair)	0.76v	0.194	16.8	19 51.0	+ 8 53
α Crucis (Acrux)	0.77	0.010	321	12 26.8	−63 07
α Tauri (Aldebaran)	0.87v	0.050	65	4 36.1	+16 31
α Virginis (Spica)	0.98v	0.012	262	13 25.4	−11 11
α Scorpii (Antares)	1.06v	0.005	600	16 29.6	−26 26
β Geminorum (Pollux)	1.16v	0.097	34	7 45.5	+28 01
α Piscis Austrinis (Fomalhaut)	1.17	0.130	25.1	22 57.8	−29 36
β Crucis (Becrux)	1.25v	0.009	353	12 47.9	−59 43
α Cygni (Deneb)	1.25v	0.001	3200	20 41.6	+45 17
α Leonis (Regulus)	1.36	0.042	77	10 08.5	+11 57
ε Canis Majoris (Adhara)	1.50v	0.008	431	6 58.7	−28 59
α Geminorum (Castor)	1.58	0.063	52	7 34.8	+31 53
γ Crucis (Gacrux)	1.59v	0.037	88	12 31.3	−57 08
λ Scorpii (Shaula)	1.62v	0.005	700	17 33.9	−37 06
γ Orionis (Bellatrix)	1.64v	0.013	243	5 25.3	+ 6 21
β Tauri (Elnath)	1.65	0.025	131	5 26.5	+28 37
β Carinae (Miaplacidus)	1.67v	0.029	111	9 13.2	−69 44
ε Orionis (Alnilam)	1.69v	0.002	1300	5 36.2	− 1 12
α Gruis (Al Nair)	1.73v	0.032	101	22 08.5	−46 57
ζ Orionis (Alnitak)	1.74	0.004	820	5 40.9	− 1 56
γ Velorum (Al Suhail)	1.75v	0.004	840	8 09.6	−47 21
ε Ursae Majoris (Alioth)	1.76v	0.040	81	12 54.2	+55 57
ε Sagittarii (Kaus Australis)	1.79	0.023	145	18 24.4	−34 23
α Persei (Mirfak)	1.79v	0.006	590	3 24.5	+49 52
α Ursae Majoris (Dubhe)	1.81	0.026	124	11 03.9	+61 44
δ Canis Majoris (Wezen)	1.83v	0.002	1800	7 08.5	−26 24
η Ursae Majoris (Alkaid)	1.85v	0.032	101	13 47.7	+49 18
θ Scorpii	1.86	0.012	272	17 37.6	−43 00
ε Carinae (Avior)	1.86v	0.005	630	8 22.5	−59 31
β Aurigae (Menkalinan)	1.90v	0.040	82	5 59.7	+44 57
α Trianguli Australis (Atria)	1.91v	0.008	415	16 49.1	−69 02
γ Geminorum (Alhena)	1.93	0.031	105	6 37.9	+16 24
δ Velorum	1.93	0.041	80	8 44.7	−54 43
α Pavonis (Peacock)	1.94v	0.018	183	20 25.9	−56 43
α Ursae Minoris (Polaris)	1.97v	0.008	431	2 34.3	+89 16
β Canis Majoris (Mirzam)	1.98v	0.007	499	6 22.8	−17 57
α Hydrae (Alphard)	1.99v	0.018	177	9 27.7	− 8 40
α Arietis (Hamal)	2.01	0.049	66	2 07.3	+23 29
γ Leonis (Algieba)	2.01v	0.026	126	10 20.1	+19 50
β Ceti (Deneb Kaitos)	2.04v	0.034	96	0 43.8	−17 58
σ Sagittarii (Nunki)	2.05v	0.015	224	18 55.5	−26 18
θ Centauri (Menkent)	2.06	0.054	61	14 06.9	−36 23
α Andromedae (Alpheratz)	2.07v	0.034	97	0 08.6	+29 06
β Andromedae (Mirach)	2.07v	0.016	199	1 09.9	+35 38
β Gruis	2.07v	0.019	170	22 42.9	−46 52
κ Orionis (Saiph)	2.07v	0.005	720	5 47.9	− 9 40
β Ursae Minoris (Kochab)	2.07v	0.026	126	14 50.8	+74 09
α Ophiuchi (Rasalhague)	2.08	0.070	47	17 35.1	+12 33
β Persei (Algol)	2.09v	0.035	93	3 08.4	+40 58
γ Andromedae (Almaak)	2.10	0.009	355	2 04.1	+42 21
β Leonis (Denebola)	2.14	0.090	36	11 49.2	+14 33
γ Cassiopeiae	2.15v	0.005	610	0 56.9	+60 44
γ Centauri	2.20	0.025	130	12 41.6	-48 58
ι Carinae (Tureis)	2.21	0.005	690	9 17.1	−59 17
ζ Puppis (Naos)	2.21v	0.002	1400	8 03.7	−40 01
α Coronae Borealis (Alphecca)	2.22v	0.044	75	15 34.8	+26 42
ζ Ursae Majoris (Mizar)	2.23	0.042	78	13 24.1	+54 55
γ Cygni (Sadr)	2.23v	0.002	1500	20 22.4	+40 16
λ Velorum (Suhail)	2.23v	0.006	573	9 08.1	−43 27
γ Draconis (Eltanin)	2.24v	0.022	148	17 56.7	+51 29
δ Orionis (Mintaka)	2.25v	0.004	920	5 32.1	− 0 18
β Cassiopeiae (Caph)	2.28v	0.060	54	0 09.3	+59 10
ε Scorpii	2.29	0.050	65	16 50.4	−34 18
ε Centauri	2.29v	0.009	376	13 40.1	−53 29
δ Scorpii (Dschubba)	2.29v	0.008	402	16 00.5	−22 38
α Lupi	2.30v	0.006	548	14 42.2	−47 24
η Centauri	2.33v	0.011	308	14 35.7	−42 11
β Ursae Majoris (Merak)	2.34	0.041	79	11 02.0	+56 22
ε Boo (Izar)	2.35	0.016	210	14 45.1	+27 04
κ Scorpii	2.39v	0.007	464	17 42.7	−39 02

Morning and Evening Stars, 2003

(in Coordinated Universal Time)

	Morning	Evening
Jan.	Mercury from Jan. 11 Venus Mars Jupiter Neptune from Jan. 30 Pluto	Mercury to Jan. 11 Saturn Uranus Neptune to Jan. 30
Feb.	Mercury Venus Mars Jupiter to Feb. 2 Uranus from Feb. 17 Neptune Pluto	Jupiter from Feb. 2 Saturn Uranus to Feb. 17
Mar.	Mercury to Mar. 21 Venus Mars Uranus Neptune Pluto	Mercury from Mar. 22 Jupiter Saturn
Apr.	Venus Mars Uranus Neptune Pluto	Mercury Jupiter Saturn

Month	Morning	Evening
May	Mercury from May 7	Mercury to May 7
	Venus	Jupiter
	Mars	Saturn
	Uranus	
	Neptune	
	Pluto	
June	Mercury	Jupiter
	Venus	Saturn to June 24
	Mars	
	Saturn from June 24	
	Uranus	
	Neptune	
	Pluto to June 9	Pluto from June 9
July	Mercury to July 5	Mercury from July 5
	Venus	Jupiter
	Mars	Pluto
	Saturn	
	Uranus	
	Neptune	
Aug.	Venus to Aug. 18	Mercury
	Mars to Aug. 28	Venus from Aug. 18
	Jupiter from Aug. 22	Mars from Aug. 28
	Saturn	Jupiter to Aug. 22
	Uranus to Aug. 24	Uranus from Aug. 24
	Neptune to Aug. 4	Neptune from Aug. 4
		Pluto
Sept.	Mercury from Sept. 11	Mercury to Sept. 11
	Jupiter	Venus
	Saturn	Mars
		Uranus
		Neptune
		Pluto
Oct.	Mercury to Oct. 25	Mercury from Oct. 25
	Jupiter	Venus
	Saturn	Mars
		Uranus
		Neptune
		Pluto
Nov.	Jupiter	Mercury
	Saturn	Venus
		Mars
		Uranus
		Neptune
		Pluto
Dec.	Mercury from Dec. 27	Mercury to Dec. 27
	Jupiter	Venus
	Saturn to Dec. 31	Mars
		Saturn from Dec. 31
		Uranus
		Neptune
	Pluto from Dec. 12	Pluto to Dec. 12

Greenwich Sidereal Time for 0^h UTC, 2003

(Add 12 hours to obtain Right Ascension of Mean Sun)

Date	d	h	m	Date	d	h	m	Date	d	h	m
Jan.	1	6	40.9	**May**	1	14	34.1	**Sept.**	8	23	06.6
	11	7	20.4		11	15	13.5		18	23	46.0
	21	7	59.8		21	15	52.9		28	0	25.4
	31	8	39.2		31	16	32.3				
Feb.	10	9	18.7	**June**	10	17	11.8	**Oct.**	8	1	04.9
	20	9	58.1		20	17	51.2		18	1	44.3
					30	18	30.6		28	2	23.7
Mar.	2	10	37.5	**July**	10	19	10.0	**Nov.**	7	3	03.2
	12	11	16.9		20	19	49.5		17	3	42.6
	22	11	56.4		30	20	28.9		27	4	22.0
Apr.	1	12	35.8	**Aug.**	9	21	08.3	**Dec.**	7	5	01.4
	11	13	15.2		19	21	47.7		17	5	40.9
	21	13	54.6		29	22	27.2		27	6	20.3

Aurora Borealis and Aurora Australis

The **Aurora Borealis,** also called the **Northern Lights,** is a broad display of rather faint light in the northern skies at night. The **Aurora Australis,** a similar phenomenon, appears at the same time in southern skies. The aurora appears in a wide variety of forms. Sometimes it is seen as a quiet glow, almost foglike in character; sometimes as vertical streamers in which there may be considerable motion; sometimes as a series of luminous expanding arcs. There are many colors, with white, yellow, and red predominating.

The auroras are most vivid and most frequently seen at about 20° from the magnetic poles, along the northern coast of the N American continent and the eastern part of the northern coast of Europe. The Aurora Borealis has been seen as far south as Key West, and the Aurora Australis has been seen as far north as Australia and New Zealand. Such occurrences are rare, however.

The Sun produces a stream of charged particles, called the **solar wind**. These particles, mainly electrons and protons, approach Earth at speeds on the order of 300 mi per second. Coronal mass ejections are large-scale, high-speed releases of as much as 10 billion tons of coronal material. Some of these particles are trapped by Earth's magnetic field, forming the **Van Allen belts**—2 donut-shaped radiation bands around Earth. Excess amounts of these charged particles, often produced by solar flares, follow Earth's magnetic lines of force toward Earth's magnetic poles. High in the atmosphere, collisions between solar and terrestrial atoms result in the glow in the upper atmosphere called the aurora. The glow may be vivid where the lines of magnetic force converge near the magnetic poles.

The auroral displays appear at heights ranging from 50 to about 600 mi and have given us a means of estimating the extent of Earth's atmosphere.

The auroras are often accompanied by magnetic storms whose forces, also guided by the lines of force of Earth's magnetic field, disrupt electrical communication. In February 2001, the Sun's magnetic field reversed, a strong indication that the Sun had reached its peak of the current solar cycle (#23). Sunspot activity then began a slow decline, though strong coronal mass ejections in late 2001 triggered displays on Nov. 5-6, 2001, as far south as Arkansas and Texas of the northern lights and as far north as Australia and New Zealand of the southern lights.

Constellations

Culturally, constellations are imagined patterns among the stars that, in some cases, have been recognized through millennia. Knowledge of constellations was once necessary in order to function as an astronomer. For today's astronomers, constellations are simply areas on the entire sky in which interesting objects await observation and interpretation.

Because Western culture has prevailed in establishing modern science, equally viable and interesting constellations and celestial traditions of other cultures are not well known outside their regions of origin. Even the patterns with which we are most familiar today have undergone considerable change over the centuries.

Today, 88 constellations are officially recognized. Although many have ancient origins, some are "modern," devised out of unclaimed stars by astronomers a few centuries ago. Unclaimed stars were those too faint or inconveniently placed to be included in the more prominent constellations. Stars in a constellation are not necessarily near each other; they are just located in the same direction on the celestial sphere.

When astronomers began to travel to S Africa in the 16th and 17th centuries, they found an unfamiliar sky that showed numerous brilliant stars. Thus, we find constellations in the southern hemisphere that depict technological marvels of the time, as well as some arguably traditional forms, such as the "fly."

Many of the commonly recognized constellations had their origins in ancient Asia Minor. These were adopted by the Greeks and Romans, who translated their names and stories into their own languages, modifying some details in the process. After the declines of these cultures, most such knowledge entered oral tradition or remained hidden in monastic libraries. From the 8th century, the Muslim explosion spread through the Mediterranean world. Wherever possible, everything was translated into Arabic to be taught in the universities the Muslims established all over their new-found world.

In the 13th century, Alfonso X of Castile, an avid student of astronomy, had Ptolemy's *Almagest* translated into Latin. It thus became widely available to European scholars. In the process, the constellation names were translated, but the star names were retained in their Arabic forms. Transliterating Arabic into the Roman alphabet has never been an exact art, so many of the star names we use today seem Arabic only to those who are not scholars.

Until the 1920s, astronomers used curved boundaries for the constellation areas. As these were rather arbitrary at best, the International Astronomical Union adopted new constellation boundaries that ran due north-south and east-west, filling the sky much as the contiguous states fill up the area of the "lower 48" United States.

Common names of stars often referred to parts of the traditional figures they represented: Deneb, the tail of the swan; Betelgeuse, the armpit of the giant. Avoiding traditional names, astronomers may label stars by using Greek letters, generally to denote order of brightness. Thus, the "alpha star" would generally be the brightest star of that constellation. The "of" implies possession, so the genitive (possessive) form of the constellation name is used, as in Alpha Orionis, the first star of Orion (Betelgeuse). Astronomers usually use a 3-letter abbreviation for the constellation name, as indicated here.

Within these boundaries, and occasionally crossing them, popular "asterisms" are recognized: the so-called Big Dipper is a small part of the constellation Ursa Major, the big bear; the Sickle is the traditional head and mane of Leo, the lion; the three stars of the Summer Triangle are each in a different constellation, with Vega in Lyra the lyre, Deneb in Cynus the swan, and Altair in Aquila the eagle; the northeast star of the Great Square of Pegasus is Alpha Andromedae.

Name	Genitive Case	Abbr.	Meaning
Andromeda	Andromedae	And	Chained Maiden
Antlia	Antliae	Ant	Air Pump
Apus	Apodis	Aps	Bird of Paradise
Aquarius	Aquarii	Aqr	Water Bearer
Aquila	Aquilae	Aql	Eagle
Ara	Arae	Ara	Altar
Aries	Arietis	Ari	Ram
Auriga	Aurigae	Aur	Charioteer
Boötes	Boötis	Boo	Herdsmen
Caelum	Caeli	Cae	Chisel
Camelopardalis	Camelopardalis	Cam	Giraffe
Cancer	Cancri	Cnc	Crab
Canes Venatici	Canum Venaticorum	CVn	Hunting Dogs
Canis Major	Canis Majoris	CMa	Greater Dog
Canis Minor	Canis Minoris	CMi	Littler Dog
Capricornus	Capricorni	Cap	Sea-goat
Carina	Carinae	Car	Keel
Cassiopeia	Cassiopeiae	Cas	Queen
Centaurus	Centauri	Cen	Centaur
Cepheus	Cephei	Cep	King
Cetus	Ceti	Cet	Whale
Chamaeleon	Chamaeleontis	Cha	Chameleon
Circinus	Circini	Cir	Compasses (art)
Columba	Columbae	Col	Dove
Coma Berenices	Comae Berenices	Com	Berenice's Hair
Corona Australis	Coronae Australis	CrA	Southern Crown
Corona Borealis	Coronae Borealis	CrB	Northern Crown
Corvus	Corvi	Crv	Crow
Crater	Crateris	Crt	Cup
Crux	Crucis	Cru	Cross (southern)
Cygnus	Cygni	Cyg	Swan
Delphinus	Delphini	Del	Dolphin
Dorado	Doradus	Dor	Goldfish
Draco	Draconis	Dra	Dragon
Equuleus	Equulei	Equ	Little Horse
Eridanus	Eridani	Eri	River
Fornax	Fornacis	For	Furnace
Gemini	Geminorum	Gem	Twins
Grus	Gruis	Gru	Crane (bird)
Hercules	Herculis	Her	Hercules
Horologium	Horologii	Hor	Clock
Hydra	Hydrae	Hya	Water Snake (female)
Hydrus	Hydri	Hyi	Water Snake (male)
Indus	Indi	Ind	Indian
Lacerta	Lacertae	Lac	Lizard
Leo	Leonis	Leo	Lion
Leo Minor	Leonis Minoris	LMi	Littler Lion
Lepus	Leporis	Lep	Hare
Libra	Librae	Lib	Balance
Lupus	Lupi	Lup	Wolf
Lynx	Lyncis	Lyn	Lynx
Lyra	Lyrae	Lyr	Lyre
Mensa	Mensae	Men	Table Mountain
Microscopium	Microscopii	Mic	Microscope
Monoceros	Monocerotis	Mon	Unicorn
Musca	Muscae	Mus	Fly
Norma	Normae	Nor	Square (rule)
Octans	Octantis	Oct	Octant
Ophiuchus	Ophiuchi	Oph	Serpent Bearer
Orion	Orionis	Ori	Hunter
Pavo	Pavonis	Pav	Peacock
Pegasus	Pegasi	Peg	Flying Horse
Perseus	Persei	Per	Hero
Phoenix	Phoenicis	Phe	Phoenix
Pictor	Pictoris	Pic	Painter
Pisces	Piscium	Psc	Fishes
Piscis Austrinus	Piscis Austrini	PsA	Southern Fish
Puppis	Puppis	Pup	Stern (deck)
Pyxis	Pyxidis	Pyx	Compass (sea)
Reticulum	Reticuli	Ret	Reticle
Sagitta	Sagittae	Sge	Arrow
Sagittarius	Sagittarii	Sgr	Archer
Scorpius	Scorpii	Sco	Scorpion
Sculptor	Sculptoris	Scl	Sculptor
Scutum	Scuti	Sct	Shield
Serpens	Serpentis	Ser	Serpent
Sextans	Sextantis	Sex	Sextant
Taurus	Tauri	Tau	Bull
Telescopium	Telescopii	Tel	Telescope
Triangulum	Trianguli	Tri	Triangle
Triangulum Australe	Trianguli Australis	TrA	Southern Triangle
Tucana	Tucanae	Tuc	Toucan
Ursa Major	Ursae Majoris	UMa	Greater Bear
Ursa Minor	Ursae Minoris	UMi	Littler Bear
Vela	Velorum	Vel	Sail
Virgo	Virginis	Vir	Maiden
Volans	Volantis	Vol	Flying Fish
Vulpecula	Vulpeculae	Vul	Fox

Eclipses, 2003

(in Coordinated Universal Time, standard time of the prime meridian)

There will be 4 eclipses in 2003, a total eclipse of the Sun, an annular eclipse of the Sun, and 2 total eclipses of the Moon. There is also a transit of the Sun by Mercury.

I. Total eclipse of the Moon, May 16

The beginning of the eclipse will be visible in Europe, eastern N America, Central America, South America, Africa, the western Middle East, the Atlantic Ocean, the southeastern Pacific Ocean, the western Indian Ocean, Greenland, and Antarctica. The end of the eclipse will be visible in most of N America, Central America, South America, part of New Zealand, most of Antarctica, western Africa, most of the Atlantic Ocean, and the eastern Pacific Ocean.

Circumstances of the Eclipse

Event	Date	h	m
Partial Eclipse begins	May 16	2	2.7
Total eclipse begins	16	3	13.7
Middle of eclipse	16	3	40.1
Total eclipse end	16	4	6.4
Partial eclipse ends	16	5	17.4

II. Annular eclipse of the Sun, May 31

The path of annularity starts in Scotland and crosses Iceland and Greenland. It can be seen as partial over most of Europe and parts of the Middle East and Asia.

Circumstances of the Eclipse

Event	Date	h	m
Partial eclipse begins	May 31	1	46.2
Annular eclipse begins	31	3	44.9
Central eclipse at midday	31	4	8.3
Annular eclipse ends	31	4	31.2
Partial eclipse ends	31	6	30.0

III. Total eclipse of the Moon, Nov. 8-9

The beginning of the eclipse will be visible in Europe, Africa, W and central Asia, Greenland, eastern N America, Central America, most of S America, the western Indian Ocean, and the Atlantic Ocean. The end of the eclipse will be visible in most of Africa, Europe, N America, Greenland, the Arctic, Antarctic Peninsula, Central America, S America, NW Asia, western Middle East, the Atlantic Ocean, and the E Pacific Ocean.

Circumstances of the Eclipse

Event	Date	h	m
Partial eclipse begins	Nov. 8	23	32.4
Total eclipse begins	9	1	6.3
Middle of eclipse	9	1	18.5
Total eclipse end	9	1	30.7
Partial eclipse ends	9	3	4.5

IV. Total eclipse of the Sun, Nov. 23-24

The path of totality begins in the S Indian Ocean and crosses over Antarctica. It can be seen as partial in Australia, most of New Zealand, the rest of Antarctica, and the southern tip of S America.

Circumstances of the Eclipse

Event	Date	h	m
Partial eclipse begins	Nov. 23	20	46.0
Total eclipse begins	23	22	19.3
Greatest eclipse	23	22	49.3
Total eclipse ends	23	23	18.8
Partial eclipse ends	24	0	52.2

V. Transit of the Sun by Mercury, May 7

Since Mercury does not block the Sun, it is dangerous to observe this event directly or with optical aids. The whole transit is visible in most of Asia, most of Africa, Europe except Portugal and Spain, most of Greenland, and most of the Indian Ocean.

Circumstances of the Transit

Event	Date	h	m
Ingress begins	May 7	5	12.9
Least angular distance	7	7	52.3
Egress ends	7	10	31.7

Total Solar Eclipses in the U.S. in the 21st Century

During the 21st century Halley's Comet will return (2061-62), and there will be 8 total solar eclipses that are visible somewhere in the continental United States. The first comes after a long gap; the last one to be seen there was on Feb. 26, 1979, in the northwestern U.S.

Date	Path of Totality	Date	Path of Totality
Aug. 21, 2017	Oregon to South Carolina	Mar. 30, 2052	Florida to Georgia
Apr. 8, 2024	Mexico to Texas and up through Maine	May 11, 2078	Louisiana to North Carolina
Aug. 23, 2044	Montana to North Dakota	May 1, 2079	New Jersey to the lower edge of New England
Aug. 12, 2045	N California to Florida	Sept. 14, 2099	North Dakota to Virginia

Total Solar Eclipses, 1961-2025

Total solar eclipses actually take place nearly as often as total lunar eclipses; they occur at a rate of about 3 every 4 years, while total lunar eclipses come at a rate of about 5 every 6 years. However, total lunar eclipses are visible over at least half of the Earth, while total solar eclipses can be seen only along a very narrow path up to a few hundred miles wide and a few thousand miles long. Observing a total solar eclipse is thus a rarity for most people. Unlike lunar eclipses, solar eclipses can be dangerous to observe. This is not because the Sun emits more potent rays during a solar eclipse, but because the Sun is always dangerous to observe directly and people are particularly likely to stare at it during a solar eclipse.

Date	Duration[1] m	s	Width (mi)	Path of Totality
1961, Feb. 15	2	45	160	Europe, Soviet Union
1962, Feb. 5	4	8	91	Borneo, New Guinea, Pacific Ocean
1963, July 20	1	39	63	Pacific Ocean, Alaska, Canada, Maine
1965, May 30	5	15	123	New Zealand, Pacific Ocean
1966, Nov. 12	1	57	52	Pacific Ocean, S America, Atlantic Ocean
1968, Sept. 22	0	39	64	Soviet Union, China
1970, Mar. 7	3	27	95	Pacific Ocean, Mexico, Eastern U.S., Canada
1972, July 10	2	35	109	Siberia, Alaska, Canada
1973, June 30	7	3	159	Atlantic Ocean, Central Africa, Indian Ocean
1974, June 20	5	8	214	Indian Ocean, Australia
1976, Oct. 23	4	46	123	Africa, Indian Ocean, Australia
1977, Oct. 12	2	37	61	Pacific Ocean, Colombia, Venezuela
1979, Feb. 26	2	49	185	NW U.S., Canada, Greenland
1980, Feb. 16	4	8	92	Africa, Indian Ocean, India, Burma, China
1981, July 31	2	2	67	Soviet Union, Pacific Ocean
1983, June 11	5	10	123	Indian Ocean, Indonesia, New Guinea
1984, Nov. 22	1	59	53	New Guinea, Pacific Ocean
1985, Nov. 12	1	58	430	Antarctica
1986, Oct. 3[h]	0	1	1	N Atlantic Ocean
1987, Mar. 29[h]	0	7	3	S Atlantic Ocean, Africa
1988, Mar. 18	3	46	104	Sumatra, Borneo, Philippines, Pacific Ocean

Date	Duration[1] m	s	Width (mi)	Path of Totality
1990, July 22	2	32	125	Finland, Soviet Union, Aleutian Islands
1991, July 11	6	53	160	Hawaii, Mexico, Central America, Colombia, Brazil
1992, June 30	5	20	182	S Atlantic Ocean
1994, Nov. 3	4	23	117	Peru, Bolivia, Paraguay, Brazil
1995, Oct. 24	2	9	48	Iran, India, SE Asia
1997, Mar. 9	2	50	221	Mongolia, Siberia
1998, Feb. 26	4	8	94	Galapagos Islands, Panama, Colombia, Venezuela
1999, Aug. 11	2	22	69	Europe, Middle East, India
2001, June 21	4	56	125	Atlantic Ocean, Africa, Madagascar
2002, Dec. 4	2	4	54	S Africa, Indian Ocean, Australia
2003, Nov. 23	1	57	338	Antarctica
2005, Apr. 8[h]	0	42	17	Pacific Ocean, northwestern S America
2006, Mar. 29	4	7	118	Atlantic Ocean, Africa, Asia
2008, Aug. 1	2	27	157	Arctic Ocean, Asia
2009, July 22	6	39	160	Asia, Pacific Ocean
2010, July 11	5	20	164	Pacific Ocean, southern S America
2012, Nov. 13	4	2	112	N Australia, Pacific Ocean
2013, Nov. 3[h]	1	40	36	Atlantic Ocean, Africa
2015, Mar. 20	2	47	304	N Atlantic Ocean, Arctic Ocean
2016, Mar. 9	4	10	96	Indonesia, Pacific Ocean
2017, Aug. 21	2	40	71	Pacific Ocean, U.S., Atlantic Ocean
2019, July 2	4	33	125	S Pacific Ocean, S America
2020, Dec. 14	2	10	56	S Pacific Ocean, S America, S Atlantic Ocean
2021, Dec. 4	1	55	282	Antarctica, S Atlantic Ocean
2023, Apr. 20[h]	1	16	31	Indian Ocean, New Guinea, Pacific Ocean
2024, Apr. 8	4	28	127	Pacific Ocean, Mexico, N America, Atlantic Ocean

h = indicates annular-total hybrid eclipse. (1) Duration refers to length of time at optimal viewing area.

Mercury and Venus Cross the Sun

Transits of Mercury across the face of the Sun occur in May or November and happen about 13 or 14 times a century. Transits of Venus are much rarer, occurring only once or twice a century, but when it is twice, the two transits are approximately 8 years apart. Since either planet covers only a miniscule part of the Sun's face, it is dangerous to observe such events directly.

Date	Event	Duration
May 7, 2003	Transit of Mercury	5.3 hours
June 8, 2004	Transit of Venus	6.2 hours
Nov. 8, 2006	Transit of Mercury	5.0 hours
June 6, 2012	Transit of Venus	6.7 hours
May 9, 2016	Transit of Mercury	7.5 hours
Nov. 11, 2019	Transit of Mercury	5.5 hours
Nov. 13, 2032	Transit of Mercury	4.4 hours
Nov. 7, 2039	Transit of Mercury	3.0 hours
May 7, 2049	Transit of Mercury	6.7 hours
Nov. 9, 2052	Transit of Mercury	5.2 hours
May 10, 2062	Transit of Mercury	6.7 hours
Nov. 11, 2065	Transit of Mercury	5.4 hours
Nov. 14, 2078	Transit of Mercury	4.0 hours
Nov. 7, 2085	Transit of Mercury	3.7 hours
May 8, 2095	Transit of Mercury	7.5 hours
Nov. 10, 2098	Transit of Mercury	5.4 hours

Largest Telescopes

Astronomers indicate the size of telescopes not by length or magnification, but by the diameter of the primary light-gathering component of the system—such as the lens or mirror. This measurement is a direct indication of the telescope's light-gathering power. The bigger the diameter, the fainter the objects you are enabled to see. For larger telescopes, the Earth's atmosphere limits the resolution of what you see. That is why the Hubble Space Telescope, which is outside the atmosphere, can have better resolution than larger telescopes on the Earth. Large mirror telescopes can be made less expensively than large **lens telescopes,** so all modern large optical telescopes are made with mirrors rather than lenses. **Radio telescopes** view at wavelengths not visible to optical telescopes, which are limited to the wavelengths detectable by the human eye. Radio telescopes have to be made larger than optical telescopes because resolving power requires larger diameters at longer wavelengths such as radio wavelengths.

Largest Refracting (lens) Optical Telescope: Yerkes Observatory—1 m (40 in), at Williams Bay, WI

Largest Reflecting (mirror) Optical Telescope: Keck—10 m (394 in), on Mauna Kea in Hawaii (segmented mirror; 2 equal-size telescopes)

Largest Space Telescope: Hubble Space Telescope—2.4 m (94 in), in orbit around Earth

Largest Fully Steerable Radio Dish: Robert C. Byrd Green Bank Telescope—100 m (328 ft), in West Virginia

Largest Single Radio Dish: Arecibo Observatory—305 m (1,000 ft), in Puerto Rico

Largest Radio Interferometer: 10 telescopes of the Very Long Baseline Array (VLBA), scattered from Hawaii to the Virgin Islands with a resolution equal to a radio dish of 8,600 km (5,000 mi)

Beginnings of the Universe

One of the dominating astronomical discoveries of the 20th century was the realization that the galaxies of the universe all seem to be moving away from us. It turned out that they are moving away not just from us but from one another—that is, the universe seems to be expanding. Scientists conclude that the universe must once, very long ago, have been extremely compact and dense. Although there are alternatives to this theory, much of the observational evidence currently available supports the idea that the universe began its existence between 12 and 15 billion years ago as an explosion of a super-dense, super-small concentration of matter.

This explosion of matter giving birth to the universe is called the **Big Bang.** On the subatomic level, according to this theory, there were vast changes of energy and matter and the way physical laws operated during the first 5 minutes. After those minutes the percentages of the basic matter of the universe—hydrogen, helium, and lithium—were set. Everything was so compact and so hot that radiation dominated the early universe and there were no stable, un-ionized atoms. At first, the universe was opaque, in the sense that any energy emitted was quickly absorbed and then re-emitted by free electrons. As the universe expanded, the density and the temperature continued to drop. A few hundred thousand years after the initial Big Bang, the temperature had dropped far enough that electrons and nuclei could combine to form stable atoms as the universe became transparent. Once that had occurred, the radiation which had been trapped was free to escape.

In the 1940s, George Gamov and others predicted that astronomers should be able to see remnants of this escaped radiation. Astronomers continued to refine the theories and were preparing to build equipment to search for this background radiation when physicists Arno Penzias and Robert

Wilson of the Bell Telephone Laboratories, using a radio telescope, inadvertently beat them to the punch (the 2 were later awarded a Nobel Prize). Despite the Big Bang's success at predicting the existence of **cosmic background radiation,** there are still many unresolved questions, and astronomers are still working on modifications of the theory.

A related mystery is that evidence suggests there is hidden matter and hidden energy that cannot be directly observed. This **dark matter** may be composed of gas, large numbers of cool, small objects, or even sub-atomic particles. The presence of dark matter is indicated by the rotation curves of galaxies and the dynamics of clusters of galaxies. Evidence for **dark energy** is derived from studies of distant Type Ia supernovae in far galaxies indicating that expansion of the universe is accelerating. The visible matter we see seems to constitute only about 10% of the total mass of the universe, while the rest of the mass of the universe is in the form of dark matter and dark energy.

The Solar System

The planets of the solar system, in order of mean distance from the Sun, are Mercury, Venus, Earth, Mars, Jupiter, Saturn, Uranus, Neptune, and Pluto (Pluto sometimes nearer than Neptune). Both Uranus and Neptune are visible through good binoculars, but Pluto is so distant and so small that only large telescopes or long-exposure photographs can make it visible. All the planets orbit or revolve counterclockwise around the Sun.

Because Mercury and Venus are nearer to the Sun than is Earth, their motions about the Sun are seen from Earth as wide swings first to one side of the Sun then to the other, though both planets move continuously around the Sun in almost circular orbits. When their passage takes them either between Earth and the Sun or beyond the Sun as seen from Earth, they are invisible to us. Because of the geometry of the planetary orbits, Mercury and Venus require much less time to pass between Earth and the Sun than around the far side of the Sun; so their periods of visibility and invisibility are unequal.

The planets that lie farther from the Sun than does Earth may be seen for longer periods and are invisible only when so located in our sky that they rise and set at about the same time as the Sun—and thus become overwhelmed by the Sun's great brilliance. Although several of the giant planets emit their own energy, they are observed from Earth as a result of sunlight reflecting from their surfaces or cloud layers. However, on occasion, radio emissions from Jupiter exceed even those emitted by the Sun in intensity. Mercury and Venus, because they are between Earth and the Sun, show phases very much as the Moon does. The planets farther from the Sun are always seen as full, although Mars does occasionally present a slightly gibbous phase—like the Moon when not quite full.

The planets appear to move rapidly among the stars because of being closer. The stars are also in motion, some at tremendous speeds, but they are so far away that their motion does not change their apparent positions in the heavens sufficiently to be perceived. The nearest star is about 7,000 times farther away than the most distant planet in our solar system.

Planets and the Sun, by Selected Characteristics

Sun and Planets	Radius: at unit distance[1] "	Radius: at mean least distance[2] "	Radius: in mi mean radius	Volume[3]	Mass[3]	Density[3]	Sidereal period d	h	m	s	Gravity at surface[3]	Reflecting power Pct°	Daytime surface temp. ° F
Sun	959.6	976	432,474	1,304,000	332,950	0.26	25	9	7	12	28.0		+9,941
Mercury	3.36	6.51	1,516	0.056	0.0553	0.98	58	15	36		0.38	0.11	846
Venus	8.34	33	3,760	0.857	0.815	0.95	243	12	R		0.91	0.65	867
Earth	8.8		3,959	1.000	1.000	1.00		23	56	4.2	1.00	0.37	64
Moon	2.39	986.0	1,079	0.0203	0.0123	0.61	27	7	43	41	0.17	0.12	260
Mars	4.67	12.85	2,106	0.151	0.107	0.71		24	37	22	0.38	0.15	–24
Jupiter	96.39	24.52	43,441	1,321	317.83	0.24		9	55	30	2.36	0.52	–162
Saturn	80.29	10.01	36,184	764	95.16	0.12		10	39	22	0.92	0.47	–218
Uranus	34.97	2.02	15,759	63	14.54	0.23		17	14	24R	0.89	0.51	–323
Neptune	33.95	1.182	15,301	58	17.15	0.30		16	6	36	1.12	0.41	–330
Pluto	1.65	0.06	743	0.007	0.0021	0.32	6	9	17	34R	0.06	0.3	–369

(1) Angular radius, in seconds of arc, if object were seen at a distance of one astronomical unit. (2) Angular radius, in seconds of arc, when object is closest to Earth. (3) Earth = 1. R = Retrograde rotation.

Planet Superlatives

Largest, most massive planet	Jupiter	Smallest, least massive planet	Pluto
Fastest orbiting planet	Mercury	Slowest orbiting planet	Pluto
Most eccentric orbit	Pluto	Most circular orbit	Venus
Longest (synodic) day	Mercury	Shortest (synodic) day	Jupiter
Coldest planet	Pluto	Hottest planet	Venus
Most moons	Jupiter (39)	No moons	Mercury, Venus
Planet with largest moon	Jupiter	Planet with moon with most eccentric orbit	Neptune
Greatest average density	Earth	Lowest average density	Saturn
Tallest mountain	Mars	Deepest oceans	Jupiter
Strongest magnetic fields	Jupiter	Greatest amount of liquid, surface water	Earth

The Planets: Motion, Distance, and Brightness

Planet	Mean daily motion[1]	Orbital velocity mi per sec.[2]	Sidereal revolution days[3]	Synodic revolution days[4]	Distance from Sun in millions of mi Max.	Distance from Sun Min.	Distance from Earth in millions of mi Max.	Distance from Earth Min.	Light at[5] perihelion	Light at aphelion
Mercury	14,732	29.75	88.0	115.9	43.4	28.6	138	48	10.56	4.59
Venus	5,768	21.76	224.7	583.9	67.7	66.8	162	24	1.94	1.89
Earth	3,548	18.50	365.3	—	94.5	91.4	—	—	1.03	0.97
Mars	1,887	14.99	687.0	779.9	154.9	128.4	249	34	0.52	0.36
Jupiter	299	8.12	4,332.6	398.9	507.4	460.1	602	366	0.041	0.034
Saturn	120	6.02	10,759.2	378.1	941.1	840.4	1,031	743	0.012	0.0098
Uranus	42	4.23	30,685.4	369.7	1,866.4	1,703.4	1,962	1,604	0.0030	0.0025
Neptune	22	3.37	60,189.0	367.5	2,824.5	2,761.6	2,913	2,676	0.0011	0.0011
Pluto	14	2.93	90,465.0	366.7	4,538.7	2,755.8	4,681	2,668	0.0011	0.00041

(1) Average angular motion measured in seconds of arc per day. (2) Speed of revolution around Sun. (3) Number of Earth days to orbit Sun with respect to background stars. (4) Number of Earth days to get back to the same position in its orbit around Sun, relative to Earth. (5) Light at perihelion and aphelion is solar illumination measured in units of mean illumination at Earth.

Planets of the Solar System

Note: AU = astronomical unit (92.96 mil mi, mean distance of Earth from the Sun); **d** = 1 Earth synodic (solar) day (24 hrs); **synodic day** = rotation period of a planet measured with respect to the Sun (the "true" day, i.e. the time from midday to midday, or from sunrise to sunrise); **sidereal day** = the rotation period of a planet with respect to the stars

Mercury

Distance from Sun	
Perihelion	28.6 mil mi
Semi-major axis	0.387 AU
Aphelion	43.4 mil mi
Period of revolution around Sun	87.97 d
Orbital eccentricity	0.2056
Orbital inclination	7.00°
Synodic day (midday to midday)	175.94 d
Sidereal day	58.65 d
Rotational inclination	0.01°
Mass (Earth = 1)	0.0553
Mean radius	1,516 mi
Mean density (Earth = 1)	0.984
Natural satellites	0
Average surface temperature	333° F

Mercury, the nearest planet to the Sun, is the 2nd-smallest of the 9 known planets. Its diameter is 3,032 mi; its mean distance from the Sun is 35,980,000 mi.

Mercury moves with great speed around the Sun, averaging about 30 mi per second to complete its circuit in about 88 Earth days. Mercury rotates upon its axis over a period of nearly 59 days, thus exposing all its surface periodically to the Sun. Because its orbital period is only about 50% longer than its sidereal rotation, the solar (synodic) day on Mercury, or the time from one sunrise to the next, is about 176 days, twice as long as a Mercurian year. It is believed that the surface passing before the Sun may reach a temperature of about 845° F, while the temperature on the nighttime side may fall as low as –300° F.

Uncertainty about conditions on Mercury and its motion arises from its short angular distance from the Sun as seen from Earth. Mercury is too much in line with the Sun to be observed against a dark sky, but is always seen during either morning or evening twilight.

Mariner 10 passed Mercury 3 times in 1974 and 1975. Less than half of the surface was photographed, revealing a degree of cratering similar to that of the Moon. The most imposing feature on Mercury, the Caloris Basin, is a huge impact crater more than 800 mi in diameter. Mercury also has a higher percentage of iron than any other planet. A very thin atmosphere of hydrogen and helium may be made up of gases of the solar wind temporarily concentrated by the presence of Mercury. The discovery of a weak but permanent magnetic field was a surprise to scientists. It has been held that both a fluid core and rapid rotation are necessary for the generation of a planetary magnetic field. Mercury may demonstrate the contrary; the field may reveal something about the history of Mercury. In 1991 and 1994, radar mapping of Mercury using the 230-foot Goldstone dish antenna as the transmitter and the 27-dish Very Large Array (VLA) as the receiver revealed evidence of possible water ice near its north and south poles.

Venus

Distance from Sun	
Perihelion	66.8 mil mi
Semi-major axis	0.723 AU
Aphelion	67.7 mil mi
Period of revolution around Sun	224.70 d
Orbital eccentricity	0.0067
Orbital inclination	3.39°
Synodic day (midday to midday)	116.75 d (retrograde)
Sidereal day	243.02 d (retrograde)
Rotational inclination	177.4°
Mass (Earth = 1)	0.815
Mean radius	3,760 mi
Mean density (Earth = 1)	0.951
Natural satellites	0
Average surface temperature	867° F

Venus, slightly smaller than Earth, moves about the Sun at a mean distance of 67,240,000 mi in 225 Earth days. Its synodical revolution—its return to the same relationship with Earth and the Sun, which is a result of the combination of its own motion with that of Earth—is 584 days. As a result, every 19 months Venus is nearer to Earth than any other planet. Venus is covered with a dense, white, cloudy atmosphere that conceals whatever is below it. This same cloud reflects sunlight efficiently so that Venus is the 3rd-brightest object in the sky, exceeded only by the Sun and the Moon.

Spectral analysis of sunlight reflected from Venus's cloud tops has shown features that can best be explained by identifying material of the clouds as sulfuric acid. In 1956, radio astronomers at the Naval Research Laboratories in Washington, DC, found a temperature for Venus of about 600° F. Subsequent data from the *Mariner 2* space probe in 1962 confirmed a high temperature. *Mariner 2* was unable to detect the existence of a magnetic field even as weak as 1/100,000 of Earth's magnetic field.

In 1967, a Soviet space probe, *Venera 4*, and the American *Mariner 5* arrived at Venus within a few hours of each other. *Venera 4* was designed to allow an instrument package to land gently on the surface, but it ceased to transmit information when its temperature reading went above 500° F, when it was still about 20 mi above the surface. The orbiting *Mariner 5*'s radio signals passed to Earth through Venus's atmosphere twice (once on the night side and once on the day side). The results were startling. Venus's atmosphere is nearly all carbon dioxide (96.5%), with 3.5% nitrogen and trace amounts of sulfur dioxide, carbon monoxide, argon, water, helium, and neon. It exerts a pressure at the planet's surface more than 90 times Earth's normal sea-level pressure of one atmosphere.

Because Earth and Venus are about the same size and were presumably formed at the same time by the same general process and from the same mixture of chemical elements, one is faced with the question: Why the difference? Recent measurements indicate that Venus has a surface temperature of over 865° F as a result of an extreme greenhouse effect. Because of the thick atmosphere, the temperature is essentially the same both day and night.

Radio astronomers determined the rotation period of Venus to be 243 days clockwise—in other words, contrary to the spin of the other planets and contrary to its own motion around the Sun. If it were exactly 243.16 days, Venus would present the same face toward Earth at every inferior conjunction. This rate and sense of rotation allows a solar day (sunrise to sunrise) on Venus of 116.8 Earth days. Any part of Venus will receive sunlight on its clouds for more than 58 days and then return to darkness for 58 days.

Mariner 10 passed Venus before traveling on to Mercury in 1974. The carbon dioxide found in abundance in the atmosphere is rather opaque to certain ultraviolet wavelengths, enabling sensitive cameras to photograph the cloud cover. Soviet spacecraft discovered that the clouds are confined in a 12-mi layer 30 to 42 mi above the surface.

In 1978, two U.S. *Pioneer* probes confirmed expected high surface temperatures and high winds aloft. Winds of about 200 mi per hour there may account for the transfer of heat into the night side despite the low rotation speed of the planet. However, at the surface, the winds are very slow. Soviet scientists obtained, in 1975 and later in 1982, 4 photos of surface rocks. Sulfur seems to play a large role in the chemistry of Venus, and reactions involving sulfur may be responsible for the glow. The *Pioneer* orbiter confirmed the cloud pattern and its circulation shown by *Mariner 10*. Radar produced maps of the entire planet showing large craters, continent-size highlands, and extensive dry lowlands.

The Venus orbiter *Magellan* launched in 1989 used sophisticated radar techniques to observe Venus and map more than 99% of the surface. The spacecraft observed over 1,600 volcanoes and volcanic features, enabling creation of a 3-dimensional map of the Venusian surface. *Magellan* has shown that more than 85% of the surface is covered by volcanic flows. Additionally, there are highly deformed mountain belts.

Craters more than 20 mi wide are believed to have been caused by impacting bodies. Theia Mons, a huge shield volcano, has a diameter of over 600 mi and a height of over 3.5 mi. (Compare this to the largest Hawaiian volcano, which is only about 125 mi in diameter, but with a height of nearly 5.5 mi from the ocean floor.)

Erosion is a very slow process on Venus due to the extreme lack of water, and features persist for long periods of time. There are indications of only restricted wind movement of dust and sand.

Tectonic actions on Venus are distinctly different from such actions on Earth. No activity on Venus has been found to be similar to Earth's moving tectonic plates, but a system of global rift zones and numerous broad, low dome-like structures, which are called coronae, may be produced by the upwelling and subsidence of magma from the mantle. Volcanic surface features, such as vast lava plains, fields of small lava domes, and large shield volcanoes, are common. The few impact craters on Venus suggest that the surface is generally geologically young—less than 800 million years old. A channel about 4,200 mi long, due to lava flows, has been mapped.

The orbit of *Magellan* was adjusted to a nearly circular shape about 300 mi from the planet's surface in 1993. In this mode, variation in *Magellan*'s orbital speed revealed information on irregularities in the gravitational field, presumably due to details in the internal structure of the planet. In 2001, the Arecibo radio telescope and the Green Bank radio telescope were partnered to produce even more detailed images of Maxwell Montes, a Venusian mountain taller than Mt. Everest. A number of spacecraft missions to other planets have flown by Venus en route to their final destinations, including *Galileo* to Jupiter in 1989 and *Cassini* to Saturn in 1997. *MESSENGER* to Mercury is scheduled to fly by in 2005.

Mars

Distance from Sun	
Perihelion	128.4 mil mi
Semi-major axis	1.524 AU
Aphelion	154.9 mil mi
Period of revolution around Sun	686.98 d (1.88 y)
Orbital eccentricity	0.0935
Orbital inclination	1.85°
Synodic day (midday to midday)	24h 39m 35s
Sidereal day	24h 37m 22s
Rotational inclination	25.19°
Mass (Earth = 1)	0.107
Mean radius	2,106 mi
Mean density (Earth = 1)	0.713
Natural satellites	2
Average surface temperature	–81° F

Mars is the first planet beyond Earth, away from the Sun. Mars's diameter is about 4,213 mi. Although Mars's orbit is nearly circular, it is somewhat more eccentric than the orbits of many of the other planets, and Mars is more than 26 mil mi farther from the Sun at its most distant point compared to its closest approach. Mars takes 687 Earth days to make one circuit of the Sun, traveling at about 15 mi a second. The planet rotates upon its axis in almost the same period of time as Earth—24 hours and 37 minutes. Mars's mean distance from the Sun is 142 mil mi, so its temperature would be lower than that on Earth even if its atmosphere were not so thin. In 1965, *Mariner 4* became the first spacecraft to fly by Mars, reporting that atmospheric pressure on Mars is between 1% and 2% of Earth's atmospheric pressure. As is the case with Venus, the atmosphere is composed largely of carbon dioxide. The planet is exposed to an influx of cosmic radiation about 100 times as intense as that on Earth.

Mars's position in its orbit and its speed around that orbit in relation to Earth's position and speed bring the planet fairly close to Earth on occasions about 2 years apart, then move Mars and Earth too far apart for favorable observation. Every 15-17 years the close approaches are especially favorable for observation.

Although early Earth telescopic observations led some to believe the colors they saw were indications of some sort of vegetation, this would only be possible if Mars had water and oxygen at that time.

Mars's axis of rotation is inclined from a vertical to the plane of its orbit about the Sun by about 25°, and therefore Mars has seasons as does Earth. White caps form about the poles of Mars, growing in the winter and shrinking in the summer. These polar caps are now believed to be both water ice and carbon dioxide ice. It is the carbon dioxide that is seen to come and go with the seasons. The water ice is apparently in many layers with dust between them, indicating climatic cycles.

Mariners 6 and *7* in 1969 sent back many photographs of higher quality showing cratering similar to the earlier views, but also other types of terrain. Some regions seemed featureless over large areas; others were chaotic, showing high relief without apparent organization into mountain chains or craters. *Mariner 9,* the first spacecraft to orbit Mars (1971), transmitted photos and other data showing that Mars resembles no other planet we know, yet there were features clearly of volcanic origin. One of these is Olympus Mons, a shield volcano whose caldera is more than 40 mi wide and whose outer slopes are 300 mi in diameter; it stands 15 mi above the surrounding plain—the tallest known mountain in the solar system. Some features may have been produced by cracking (faulting) and stretching of the surface. Valles Marineris, extending nearly 2,500 mi, is an example on a colossal scale. Many craters seem to have been produced by impacting bodies that may have come from the nearby asteroid belt. Features near the S pole may have been produced by glaciers no longer present.

In 1976, the U.S. landed 2 *Viking* spacecraft on the Martian surface. The landers had devices aboard to perform chemical analyses of the soil in search of evidence of life; results were inconclusive. The 2 *Viking* orbiters returned pictures of Martian topographic features that scientists believe can be explained only if Mars once had large quantities of flowing water.

Two U.S. spacecraft—the *Mars Pathfinder* and the *Mars Global Surveyor*—were launched toward Mars in 1996. On July 4, 1997, using a unique array of balloons, *Pathfinder*, with its small movable robot named Sojourner, bounced to a safe landing on Mars. It actually bounded about 40 feet high after striking the ground at 40 mph and bounced 15 more times before coming to a halt. Sojourner spent 3 months examining rocks near *Pathfinder*. Geological results from the *Pathfinder* indicate that in its beginning stages Mars melted to a sufficient extent to separate into dense and lighter layers. It also appears that there was an era when the planet had large amounts of flooding waters on its surface.

The *Surveyor* did extensive mapping of the planet and reported the presence of a very weak magnetic field that may have been stronger in the distant past. *Surveyor* results support a view of the southern hemisphere of Mars covered with ancient craters like Earth's Moon. Interestingly, there is a significant difference in the northern hemisphere, which consists mainly of plains that are much younger and lower in elevation. The *Surveyor* has produced a dramatic 3-D map that clearly shows this dramatic contrast.

Mars has 2 satellites, discovered in 1877 by Asaph Hall. The outer satellite, Deimos, revolves around the planet in about 31 hours. The inner satellite, Phobos, whips around Mars in a little more than 7 hours, making 3 trips around the planet each Martian day. Since it orbits Mars faster than the planet rotates, Phobos rises in the W and sets in the E, opposite to what other bodies appear to do in the Martian sky. *Mariner* and *Viking* photos show these satellites to be irregularly shaped and pitted with numerous craters. Phobos also exhibits a system of linear grooves, each about 1/3 mi across and roughly parallel. Phobos measures about 8 by 12 mi and Deimos about 5 by 7.5 mi.

IT'S A FACT: In 1877 the Italian astronomer Giovanni Schiaparelli described a network of about 100 "channels" on Mars; some astronomers came to believe these markings were bands of vegetation bordering canals, dug by Martians to carry water from polar ice caps for irrigation. Pictures taken from *Mariner* spacecraft in 1969 confirmed what many other astronomers believed: that these markings were only optical illusions.

Of the tens of thousands of meteorites found on Earth, approximately a dozen may have originated on Mars. In 1996, a NASA research team concluded that a meteorite found in 1984 on an Antarctic ice field not only might be a rock blasted from the surface of Mars but also might contain evidence that life existed on Mars more than 3.5 bil years ago. The meteorite has been age-dated to about 4.5 bil years. The scientists theorize that 3.5 bil years ago, Mars may have been warmer and wetter, and microscopic life may have formed and left evidence in the rock, including possible fossilized microscopic organisms. Then, 16 mil years ago, it is believed that a huge asteroid or comet struck Mars, blasting material, including this rock, into space. The rock may have entered Earth's atmosphere about 13,000 years ago, landing in Antarctica. The evidence is intriguing, but not conclusive, in suggesting that Mars may have had microscopic life, at least far in the past.

In 2000, pictures from the *Mars Global Surveyor* showed evidence for the presence of liquid water on Mars in recent times. Accessible water supplies would make future human exploration and settlement of Mars much easier. The *Mars Odyssey* spacecraft, launched in 2001, is currently in orbit around Mars doing science studies and will also serve as a communications link for landers scheduled to arrive in 2004.

Jupiter

Distance from Sun	
Perihelion	460.1 mil mi
Semi-major axis	5.204 AU
Aphelion	507.4 mil mi
Period of revolution around Sun	11.86 y
Orbital eccentricity	0.0489
Orbital inclination	1.304°
Synodic day (midday to midday)	9h 55m 33s
Sidereal day	9h 55m 30s
Rotational inclination	3.13°
Mass (Earth = 1)	317.8
Mean radius	43,441 mi
Mean density (Earth = 1)	0.24
Natural satellites	39
Average temperature*	–162° F

*i.e., temperature where atmosphere pressure equals 1 Earth atmosphere.

Jupiter, largest of the planets, has an equatorial diameter of nearly 89,000 mi, 11 times the diameter of Earth. Its polar diameter is more than 5,700 mi shorter. This noticeable oblateness is a result of the liquidity of the planet and its extremely rapid rate of rotation; a day is less than 10 Earth hours long. For a planet this size, this rotational speed is amazing. A point on Jupiter's equator moves at a speed of 22,000 mph, as compared with 1,000 mph for a point on Earth's equator. Jupiter is at an average distance of 484 mil mi from the Sun and takes almost 12 Earth years to make one complete circuit of the Sun.

The major chemical constituents of Jupiter's atmosphere are molecular hydrogen (H_2—90%) and helium (He—10%). Minor constituents include methane (CH_4), ammonia (NH_3), hydrogen deuteride (HD), ethane (C_2H_6), and water (H_2O).

The temperature at the tops of clouds may be about –280° F. The gases become denser with depth, until they may turn into a slush or slurry. There is no sharp interface between the gaseous atmosphere and the hydrogen ocean that accounts for most of Jupiter's volume. *Pioneer 10* and *11*, passing Jupiter in 1973 and 1974, provided evidence for considering Jupiter almost entirely liquid hydrogen. Jupiter apparently has a liquid hydrogen ocean more than 35,000 mi deep. It likely has a rocky core about the size of Earth, but 13 times more massive.

Jupiter's magnetic field is by far the strongest of any planet. Electrical activity caused by this field is so strong that it discharges billions of watts into Earth's magnetic field daily. At lower layers, under enormous pressure, the liquid hydrogen takes on the properties of a metal. It is likely that this liquid metallic hydrogen is the source for both Jupiter's persistent radio noise and its improbably strong magnetic field. Radio astronomy and information from the spacecraft passing in Jupiter's vicinity have revealed details of the overall structure of the huge magnetosphere surrounding Jupiter.

Fourteen of Jupiter's known satellites were found through Earth-based observations. Four of the moons, Io, Europa, Ganymede, and Callisto—all discovered by Galileo in 1610—are large and bright, rivaling Earth's Moon and Mercury in diameter, and may be seen through binoculars. They move rapidly around Jupiter, and it is easy to observe their change of position from night to night. The other satellites are much smaller, in all but one instance much farther from Jupiter, and cannot be seen except through powerful telescopes. Eleven additional moons were reported in 2002, all of which are in retrograde orbits. The 25 outermost satellites revolve around Jupiter clockwise as seen from the north, contrary to the motions of most satellites in the solar system and to the direction of revolution of planets around the Sun. These moons may be captured asteroids. Jupiter's mass is more than twice the mass of all the other planets, moons, and asteroids put together.

Photographs from *Pioneer 10* and *11* were far surpassed by those of *Voyager 1* and *2*, both of which rendezvoused with Jupiter in 1979. The Great Red Spot exhibited internal counterclockwise rotation. Much turbulence was seen in adjacent material passing N or S of it. The satellites Amalthea, Io, Europa, Ganymede, and Callisto were photographed, some in great detail. Io has active volcanoes that probably have ejected material into a doughnut-shaped ring, or torus, enveloping its orbit about Jupiter. This is not to be confused with Jupiter's rings which were the surprise of the *Voyager I* mission. Since then, ground-based telescopes have imaged Jupiter's rings in the infrared.

In 1994, 21 large fragments of Comet Shoemaker-Levy 9 collided with Jupiter in a dramatic barrage. Moving at 134,000 mph, stretched out like a 21-car freight train, the fragments impacted one after another against Jupiter. Massive plumes of gas erupted from the impact sites, forming brilliant fireballs and leaving dark blotches and smears behind. One of the largest chunks, labeled the G fragment, impacted with the force of 6 mil megatons of TNT, 100,000 times the power of the largest nuclear bomb ever detonated. It produced a plume 1,200-1,600 mi high and 5,000 mi wide and left a dark discoloration larger than Earth.

The *Galileo* spacecraft went into orbit around Jupiter and released an atmospheric probe into the Jovian atmosphere in Dec. 1995. The probe, traveling at a speed of over 100,000 mph, plunged into Jupiter's atmosphere relaying information about it for 57.6 minutes. The probe revealed a relatively dry atmosphere, with the upper part warmer and denser than expected. It also gave evidence of wind speeds of more than 400 mph and a relative absence of lightning. The probe found the atmosphere to be quite turbulent, driven by Jupiter's own internal heat. *Galileo* continued an extended mission to study the 4 large moons. *Galileo* observations show extensive ongoing volcanic eruptions on Io. Europa may have a 30-mi-deep liquid ocean beneath its icy crust, perhaps a small metallic core, and a very tenuous atmosphere. Ganymede, with a magnetosphere and a thin oxygen atmosphere, seems to be differentiated into 3 levels—a small metallic core and a rocky silicate mantle topped by an icy shell. Callisto has the oldest, most heavily cratered surface in the solar system, a very thin atmophere of carbon dioxide, and possibly also a subsurface liquid ocean.

Saturn

Distance from Sun	
Perihelion	840.4 mil mi
Semi-major axis	9.582 AU
Aphelion	941.1 mil mi
Period of revolution around Sun	29.46 y
Orbital eccentricity	0.0565
Orbital inclination	2.485°
Synodic day (midday to midday)	10h 39m 23s
Sidereal day	10h 39m 22s
Rotational Inclination	26.73°
Mass (Earth = 1)	95.16
Mean radius	36,184 mi
Mean density (Earth = 1)	0.125
Natural satellites	30
Average temperature*	–218° F

*i.e., temperature where atmosphere pressure equals 1 Earth atmosphere.

Saturn, last of the planets visible to the unaided eye, is almost twice as far from the Sun as Jupiter. It is 2nd in size to Jupiter, but its mass is much smaller. Saturn's specific gravity is less than that of water. Its diameter is almost 74,900 mi at the equator while its polar diameter is almost 7,300 mi shorter—even more extreme than Jupiter. This noticeable oblateness is a result of the liquidity of the planet and its extremely rapid rate of rotation; a day is little more than 10 Earth hours long. Saturn's atmosphere is much like that of Jupiter, except that the temperature at the top of its cloud layer is at least 50° F colder. At about 300° F below zero, the ammonia would be frozen out of Saturn's clouds. The theoretical construction of Saturn resembles that of Jupiter; it likely has a small dense center surrounded by a layer of liquid and a deep atmosphere.

Until *Pioneer 11* passed Saturn in 1979, only 10 satellites of the planet were known from ground-based observations. *Pioneer 11* discovered 2 more, and the other 6 were found in the *Voyager 1* and *2* flybys, which also yielded more information about Saturn's icy satellites. 12 more moons were reported in 2000. Like Jupiter, Saturn is composed of about 75% hydrogen, 25% helium, and traces of water, ammonia, methane, and rock.

Saturn's ring system begins about 4,000 mi above the visible disk of Saturn, lying above its equator and extending about 260,000 mi into space. The diameter of the ring system visible from Earth is about 170,000 mi; the rings are estimated to be about 700 feet thick. In 1973, radar observation showed the ring particles to be large chunks of material averaging a meter on a side.

Voyager 1 and *2* observations showed the rings to be considerably more complex than had been believed. To the untrained eye, the *Voyager* photographs could be mistaken for pictures of a colorful phonograph record. Launched in Oct. 1997, the *Cassini* spacecraft is scheduled to reach Saturn on July 1, 2004, to study the planet, its rings, and its satellites.

Uranus

Distance from Sun	
Perihelion	1,703 mil mi
Semi-major axis	19.201 AU
Aphelion	1,866 mil mi
Period of revolution around Sun	84.01 y
Orbital eccentricity	0.0457
Orbital inclination	0.772°
Synodic day (midday to midday)	17h 14m 23s (retrograde)
Sidereal day	17h 14m 24s (retrograde)
Rotational inclination	97.77°
Mass (Earth = 1)	14.54
Mean radius	15,759 mi
Mean density (Earth = 1)	0.230
Natural satellites	21
Average temperature*	–323° F

*i.e., temperature where atmosphere pressure equals 1 Earth atmosphere.

Voyager 2, after passing Saturn in 1981, headed for a rendezvous with Uranus, culminating in a flyby in 1986.

Uranus, discovered by Sir William Herschel on Mar. 13, 1781, lies 1.8 bil mi from the Sun, taking 84 years to make its circuit around our star. Uranus has a diameter of over 31,000 mi and spins once in some 17.4 hours, according to flyby magnetic data.

One of the most fascinating features of Uranus is how far over it is tipped. Its N pole lies 98° from being directly up and down to its orbit plane. Thus, its seasons are extreme. When the Sun rises at the N pole, it stays up for 42 Earth years; then it sets, and the N pole is in darkness (and winter) for 42 Earth years.

Uranus has 21 known moons, which have orbits lying in the plane of the planet's equator. 5 moons are relatively large, while 16 are very small and more recently discovered. In that plane there is also a complex of 10 rings, 9 of which were discovered in 1978. Invisible from Earth, the 9 original rings were found by observers watching Uranus pass before a star. As they waited, they saw their photoelectric equipment register several short eclipses of the star; then the planet occulted the star as expected. After the star came out from behind Uranus, the star winked out several more times. Subsequent observations and analyses indicated the 9 narrow, nearly opaque rings circling Uranus. Evidence from the *Voyager 2* flyby showed the ring particles to be predominantly a yard or so in diameter.

In addition to photos of the 11 new, very small satellites, *Voyager 2* returned detailed photos of the 5 large satellites. As in the case of other satellites newly observed in the *Voyager* program, these bodies proved to be quite different from one another and from any others. Miranda has grooved markings, reminiscent of Jupiter's Ganymede, but often arranged in a chevron pattern. Ariel shows rifts and channels. Umbriel is extremely dark, prompting some observers to regard its surface as among the oldest in the system. Titania has rifts and fractures, but not the evidence of flow found on Ariel. Oberon's main feature is its surface saturated with craters, unrelieved by other formations.

Uranus likely does not have a rocky core, but rather a mixture of rocks and assorted ices with less than 20% hydrogen and little helium. The atmosphere is about 83% hydrogen, 15% helium, and 2% methane. In addition to its rotational tilt, Uranus's magnetic field axis is tipped an incredible 58.6° from its rotational axis and is displaced about 30% of its radius away from the planet's center.

Neptune

Distance from Sun	
Perihelion	2,762 mil mi
Semi-major axis	30.05 AU
Aphelion	2,824 mil mi
Period of revolution around Sun	164.79 y
Orbital eccentricity	0.0113
Orbital inclination	1.769°
Synodic day (midday to midday)	16h 6m 37s
Sidereal day	16h 6m 36s
Rotational inclination	28.32°
Mass (Earth = 1)	17.15
Mean radius	15,301 mi
Mean density (Earth = 1)	0.297
Natural satellites	8
Average temperature*	–330° F

*i.e., temperature where atmosphere pressure equals 1 Earth atmosphere.

Neptune lies at an average distance of 2.8 bil mi. It was the last planet visited in *Voyager 2*'s epic 12-year trek (1977-89) from Earth.

As with other giant planets, Neptune may have no solid surface, or exact diameter. However, a mean value of 30,600 mi may be assigned to a diameter between atmosphere levels where the pressure is about the same as sea level on Earth. Without a solid surface to view, it is challenging to determine a "true" rotation rate for a giant planet.

Astronomers use a determination of the rotation rate of the planet's magnetic field to indicate the internal rotation rate, which in the case of Neptune is 16.1 hours. Neptune orbits the Sun in 164.8 years in a nearly circular orbit. Neptune was discovered in 1846; not until 2010 will it have completed one full trip around the Sun since its discovery.

Voyager 2, which passed 3,000 mi from Neptune's N pole, found a magnetic field that is considerably asymmetric to the planet's structure, similar to, but not so extreme as, that found at Uranus. Neptune's magnetic field axis is tipped 46.9° from its rotational axis and is displaced more than 55% of its radius away from the planet's center.

Neptune's atmosphere was seen to be quite blue, with quickly changing white clouds often suspended high above an apparent surface. There is a Great Dark Spot, reminiscent of the Great Red Spot of Jupiter. Observations with the Hubble Space Telescope have shown that the Great Dark Spot originally seen by *Voyager* has apparently dissipated, but a new dark spot has since appeared.

Neptune's atmosphere is about 80% hydrogen, 19% helium, and 1% methane. Although lightning and auroras have been found on other giant planets, only the aurora phenomenon has been seen on Neptune.

Six new satellites were definitively discerned around Neptune by *Voyager 2*. Five of them orbit Neptune in a half day or less. Of the 8 satellites of Neptune in all, the largest, Triton, is the only large moon in a retrograde orbit, suggesting that it was captured rather than being there from the beginning. Triton's large size, sufficient to raise significant tides on the planet, may one day, billions of years from now, cause Triton to come close enough to Neptune for it to be torn apart. Nereid was found in 1949 and has the highest orbital eccentricity (0.75) of any moon. Its long looping orbit suggests that it, too, was captured.

Each of the satellites that has been photographed by the 2 *Voyagers* in the planetary encounters has been different from any of the other satellites, and certainly different from any of the planets. Only about half of Triton has been observed, but its terrain shows cratering and a strange regional feature described as resembling the skin of a cantaloupe. Triton has a tenuous atmosphere of nitrogen with a trace of hydrocarbons and evidence of active geysers injecting material into it. At −390° F, the wintertime parts of Triton are the coldest regions yet found in the solar system.

Voyager 2 also confirmed the existence of 6 rings composed of very fine particles. There may be some clumpiness in the rings' structure. It is not known whether Neptune's satellites influence the formation or maintenance of the rings.

As with the other giant planets, Neptune is emitting more energy than it receives from the Sun. *Voyager* found the excess to be 2.7 times the solar contribution. Cooling from internal heat sources and from the heat of formation of the planets is thought to be responsible.

Pluto

Distance from Sun	
Perihelion	2,756 mil mi
Semi-major axis	39.24 AU
Aphelion	4,539 mil mi
Period of revolution around Sun	247.68 y
Orbital eccentricity	0.2444
Orbital inclination	17.16°
Synodic day (midday to midday)	6d 9h 17m (retrograde)
Sidereal day	6d 9h 18m (retrograde)
Rotational inclination	122.53°
Mass (Earth = 1)	0.0021
Mean radius	743 mi
Mean density (Earth = 1)	0.317
Natural satellites	1
Average surface temperature	−369° F

Although Pluto on the average stays about 3.6 bil mi from the Sun, its orbit is so eccentric that its minimum distance of 2.76 bil mi is less than Neptune's distance from the Sun.

Pluto is currently the most distant planet, but for about 20 years of its orbit, Pluto is closer to the Sun than Neptune. Pluto takes 247.7 years to circumnavigate the Sun, a 3/2 resonance with Neptune.

About a century ago, a hypothetical planet was believed to lie beyond Neptune and Uranus because neither planet followed paths predicted by astronomers when all known gravitational influences were considered. In little more than a guess, a mass of 1 Earth was assigned to the mysterious body, and mathematical searches were begun. Amid some controversy about the validity of the predictive process, Pluto was discovered nearly where it had been predicted to lie, by Clyde Tombaugh at the Lowell Observatory in Flagstaff, AZ, in 1930.

At the U.S. Naval Observatory in Flagstaff, in 1978, James Christy obtained a photograph of Pluto that was distinctly elongated. Repeated observations of this shape and its variation were convincing evidence of the discovery of a satellite of Pluto, now named Charon. Later observations showed its diameter to be 737 mi across, over 12,100 mi from Pluto, and taking 6.4 days to move around Pluto. In this same length of time, Pluto and Charon both rotate once around their axes. The Pluto-Charon system thus appears to rotate as virtually a rigid body. Gravitational laws allow these interactions to give the mass of Pluto as 0.0021 of Earth. This mass, together with a new diameter for Pluto of mi, make the density about twice that of water. Theorists predict that Pluto has a rocky core, surrounded by a thick mantle of ice.

It is now clear that Pluto could not have influenced Neptune and Uranus to go astray. Besides being the smallest planet, Pluto is actually smaller than 7 of the Solar System's moons. Although a 10th planet might be out there somewhere, theorists no longer believe there are unexplained perturbations in the orbit of Uranus or Neptune that might be caused by it. Astronomers have found over 500 asteroid-size objects, somewhat beyond Pluto, in a region called the Kuiper Belt, where some comets are believed to originate.

Because the rotational axis of the system is tipped more than 120°, there is only a few-years interval every 125 years when Pluto and Charon alternately eclipse each other. Both worlds are roughly spherical and have comparable densities. Large regions on Pluto are dark, others light; Pluto has spots and perhaps polar caps. Although extremely cold, Pluto appears to have a thin nitrogen–carbon dioxide–methane atmosphere, at least while it is closer to the Sun. When Pluto occulted a star, the star's light faded in such a way as to have passed through a haze layer lying above the planet's surface, indicating an inversion of temperatures, suggesting Pluto has primitive weather.

A recent controversy raised the issue of Pluto's planet status. Pluto is clearly different from both the rocky terrestrial planets and the giant planets. Although some astronomers think Pluto most closely resembles the Kuiper Belt Objects and should be grouped with them, most still classify Pluto as a planet. By way of comparison, Mercury, the 2nd-smallest planet, is about 2 times the radius of Pluto, while Pluto is about twice as large as the largest known Kuiper Belt Object, an icy body beyond Pluto that was discovered in July 2001. Closest in size to Pluto is Neptune's largest moon, Triton, which is 1.13 times the radius of Pluto.

The Sun

The Sun, the controlling body of Earth's solar system, is a star often described as average. Yet, the Sun's mass and luminosity are greater than that of 80% of the stars in our Milky Way galaxy. On the other hand, most of the stars that can be easily seen on any clear night are bigger and brighter than the Sun. It is the Sun's proximity to Earth that makes it appear tremendously large and bright. The Sun is 400,000 times as bright as the full moon and gives Earth 6 mil times as much light as do all the other stars put together. A series of nuclear fusion reactions where hydrogen nuclei are converted to helium nuclei produce the heat and light that make life possible on Earth.

The Sun has a diameter of 865,000 mi and, on average, is 92,956,000 mi from Earth. It is 1.41 times as dense as water. The light of the Sun reaches Earth in 499 seconds, or in slightly more than 8 minutes. The average solar surface temperature has been measured at a value of 5,778 K, or about 9,941° F. The interior temperature of the Sun is theorized to be about 28,000,000° F.

When sunlight is analyzed with a spectroscope, it is found to consist of a continuous spectrum composed of all the colors of the rainbow in order, crossed by many dark lines. The dark "absorption lines" are produced by gaseous materials in the outer layers of the Sun. More than 60 of the natural terrestrial elements have been identified in the Sun, all in gaseous form because of the Sun's intense heat.

Spheres and Corona

The radiating surface of the Sun is called the **photosphere;** just above it is the **chromosphere.** The chromosphere is visible to the naked eye only at total solar eclipses, appearing then to be a pinkish-violet layer with occasional great prominences projecting above its general level. With proper instruments, the chromosphere can be seen or photographed whenever the Sun is visible without waiting for a total eclipse. Above the chromosphere is the **corona,** also visible to the naked eye only at times of total eclipse. Instruments also permit the brighter portions of the corona to be studied whenever conditions are favorable. The pearly light of the corona surges mil of mi from the Sun. Iron, nickel, and calcium are believed to be principal contributors to the composition of the corona, all in a state of extreme attenuation and high ionization that indicates temperatures of nearly 2 mil degrees Fahrenheit.

Sunspots

There is an intimate connection between sunspots and the corona. At times of low sunspot activity, the fine streamers of the corona are longer above the Sun's equator than over the polar regions of the Sun; during periods of high sunspot activity, the corona extends fairly evenly outward from all regions of the Sun, but to a much greater distance in space. Sunspots are dark, irregularly shaped regions whose diameters may reach tens of thousands of mi. The average life of a sunspot group is 2 months, but some have lasted for more than a year.

Sunspots reach a low point, on average, every 11.3 years, with a peak of activity occurring irregularly between 2 successive minima. Launched in Dec. 1995, the SOHO spacecraft was designed to provide several years of study of the Sun from an orbit around the Sun. We are just past the maximum of the current sunspot cycle, for which SOHO has provided extraordinary views of the Sun's activity. Observations from SOHO show that magnetic arches, called prominences, extending tens of thousands of mi into the corona may release enormous amounts of energy heating the corona. SOHO has also highlighted enormous releases of solar energy called coronal mass ejections. Coronal holes are regions where the corona appears dark in X rays. These are regions associated with open magnetic field lines, where the magnetic field lines project out into space instead of back towards the Sun. It is in these regions where the high-speed solar wind originates.

The Moon

Distance from Earth	
Perigee	225,744 mi
Semi-major axis	238,855 mi
Apogee	251,966 mi
Period of revolution	27.322 d
Synodic orbital period (period of phases)	29.53 d
Orbital eccentricity	0.0549
Orbital inclination	5.145°
Sidereal day (rotation period	27.322 d
Rotational inclination	6.68°
Mass (Earth = 1)	0.0123
Mean radius	1,080 mi
Mean density (Earth = 1)	0.605
Average surface temperature	–10° F

The Moon completes a circuit around Earth in a period whose mean or average duration is 27 days, 7 hours, 43.2 minutes. This is the Moon's **sidereal period**. Because of the motion of the Moon in common with Earth around the Sun, the mean duration of the lunar month—the period from one New Moon to the next New Moon—is 29 days, 12 hours, 44.05 minutes. This is the Moon's **synodic period.**

The mean distance of the Moon from Earth is 238,855 mi. Because the orbit of the Moon about Earth is not circular but elliptical, however, the actual distance varies considerably. The maximum distance from Earth that the Moon may reach is 251,966 mi and the least distance is 225,744 mi. (All distances given here are from the center of one body to the center of the other.)

The Moon rotates on its axis in a period of time that is exactly equal to its sidereal revolution about Earth: 27.322 days. Thus the backside or farside of the Moon always faces away from Earth. This does not mean that the backside is always dark, since the Sun is the main source of light in the Solar System. The farside of the Moon gets just as much direct sunlight as the nearside. At New Moon phase, the farside of the Moon is fully lit. With its long day and night, the daytime temperature can reach 260° F, while the coldest nighttime temperature may reach –280° F. This day-to-night contrast is exceeded only by that on Mercury.

The Moon's revolution about Earth is irregular because of its elliptical orbit. The Moon's rotation, however, is regular, and this, together with the irregular revolution, produces what is called "libration in longitude," which permits the observer on Earth to see first farther around the E side and then farther around the W side of the Moon. The Moon's variation N or S of the ecliptic permits one to see farther over first one pole and then the other of the Moon; this is called "libration in latitude." These two libration effects permit observers on Earth to see a total of about 60% of the Moon's surface over a period of time.

The hidden side of the Moon was first photographed in 1959 by the Soviet space vehicle *Lunik III*. The moon's farside does appear noticeably different from the nearside, in that the farside has practically none of the large lava plains, called maria, so prominent on the nearside.

From 1969 through 1972, 6 American spacecraft brought 12 astronauts to walk on the surface of the Moon. In 1998 NASA's *Lunar Prospector* spacecraft provided evidence for the presence of 300 million metric tons of water ice at the lunar poles. *Lunar Prospector* results also indicate that the Moon has a small core, supporting the idea that most of the mass of the Moon was ripped away from the early Earth when a Mars-size object collided with Earth.

Tides on Earth are caused mainly by the Moon, because of its proximity to Earth. The ratio of the tide-raising power of the Moon to that of the Sun is 11 to 5.

Harvest Moon and Hunter's Moon

The Harvest Moon, the full Moon nearest the autumnal equinox, ushers in a period of several successive days when the Moon rises soon after sunset. This phenomenon gives farmers in temperate latitudes extra hours of light in which to harvest their crops before frost and winter. The 2003 Harvest Moon falls on Sept. 10 UTC. Harvest Moon in the southern hemisphere temperate latitudes falls on Mar. 18.

The next full Moon after Harvest Moon is called the Hunter's Moon; it is accompanied by a similar but less marked phenomenon. In 2003, the Hunter's Moon occurs on Oct. 10 in the northern hemisphere and on Apr. 16 in the southern hemisphere.

IT'S A FACT: The following message was inscribed on a plaque left on the Moon by Neil Armstrong and Buzz Aldrin: "Here Men From Planet Earth First Set Foot Upon the Moon. July 1969 A.D. We Came In Peace For All Mankind."

Moon Phases, 2003

(Coordinated Universal Time, standard time of the prime meridian)

New Moon				Waxing Quarter				Full Moon				Waning Quarter			
Month	d	h	m	Month	d	h	m	Month	d	h	m	Month	d	h	m
Jan.	2	20	23	Jan.	10	13	15	Jan.	18	10	48	Jan.	25	8	33
Feb.	1	10	48	Feb.	9	11	11	Feb.	16	23	51	Feb.	23	16	46
Mar.	3	2	35	Mar.	11	7	15	Mar.	18	10	34	Mar.	25	1	51
Apr.	1	19	19	Apr.	9	23	40	Apr.	16	19	36	Apr.	23	12	18
May	1	12	15	May	9	11	53	May	16	3	36	May	23	00	31
May	31	4	20	June	7	20	28	June	14	11	16	June	21	14	45
June	29	18	39	July	7	2	32	July	13	19	21	July	21	7	1
July	29	6	53	Aug.	5	7	28	Aug.	12	4	48	Aug.	20	00	48
Aug.	27	17	26	Sept.	3	12	34	Sept.	10	16	36	Sept.	18	19	3
Sept.	26	3	9	Oct.	2	19	9	Oct.	10	7	27	Oct.	18	12	31
Oct.	25	12	50	Nov.	1	4	25	Nov.	9	1	13	Nov.	17	4	15
Nov.	23	22	59	Nov.	30	17	16	Dec.	8	20	37	Dec.	16	17	42
Dec.	23	9	43	Dec.	30	10	3								

Moon's Perigee and Apogee, 2003

(Coordinated Universal Time, standard time of the prime meridian)

Perigee				Apogee			
Date	Hour	Date	Hour	Date	Hour	Date	Hour
Jan. 23	22	Aug. 6	14	Jan. 11	1	July 22	20
Feb. 19	16	Aug. 31	19	Feb. 7	22	Aug. 19	14
Mar. 19	19	Sept. 28	6	Mar. 7	17	Sept. 16	9
Apr. 17	5	Oct. 26	12	Apr. 4	4	Oct. 14	2
May 15	16	Nov. 23	23	May 1	8	Nov. 10	12
June 12	23	Dec. 22	12	May 28	13	Dec. 7	12
July 10	22			June 25	2		

Searching for Planets

People have known of the existence of the planets in the Solar System that are closest to the Sun (Mercury, Venus, Mars, Jupiter, and Saturn) since ancient times because they could be seen with the naked eye. However, the 3 farthest (Uranus, Neptune, and Pluto) were discovered only since the invention of the telescope. The first, Uranus, was discovered in 1781 by the English astronomer William Herschel. Next, Neptune's existence and location were predicted through its action upon Uranus, by both John Couch Adams of England and Urbain Jean Joseph Le Verrier of France in 1845, leading to its discovery the following year. Finally, Pluto was discovered in 1930 by the American astronomer Clyde Tombaugh.

The fact that our Sun has planets suggests that others of the more than 200 bil stars in the Milky Way galaxy may have planets as well. During the last 10 years of the 20th century astronomers began to detect the presence of such planets. As of yet, they are not actually seeing them, but merely inferring their existence by their effect on the parent star.

Using the Doppler Effect to detect radial velocity changes in the motions of individual stars, astronomers are more likely to find high-mass planets in close and eccentric orbits around stars, because that situation produces larger and more noticeable changes. Close to 100 star systems have been found that apparently have at least one planet with a mass less than 13 times the mass of Jupiter. Some 2 dozen may have planets less massive than Jupiter. In 2 cases planets may have been detected in orbit around pulsars.

The star Upsilon Andromedae seems to have 3 planets, with masses 0.71, 2.11, and 4.61 times the mass of Jupiter, yet 2 of the planets are closer to their star than Earth is to the Sun. Astronomers are puzzled as to how planets the size of Jupiter or larger can exist so close to a star. In June 2002, a planet with a mass approximately 40% that of Saturn was detected (the smallest extra-solar planet yet detected). A NASA study group has concluded that a space mission to detect, not visit, planets with masses comparable to that of the Earth could be launched within a decade.

Earth: Size, Computation of Time, Seasons

Distance from the Sun	
Perihelion	91.4 mil mi
Semi-major axis	1.0000 AU
Aphelion	94.5 mil mi
Period of revolution	365.256 d
Orbital eccentricity	0.0167
Orbital inclination	0.0°
Sidereal day (Rotation period)	23h 56m 4.1s
Synodic day (midday to midday)	24h 0m 0s
Rotational inclination	23.45°
Mass (Earth = 1)	1.00
Mean radius	3,959 mi
Mean density (Earth = 1)	1.00
Natural satellites	1
Average surface temperature	59° F

Earth is the 5th-largest planet and the 3rd from the Sun. Its mass is 6,580,000,000,000,000,000,000 tons. Earth's equatorial diameter is 7,926 mi while its polar diameter is only 7,900 mi.

Size and Dimensions

Earth is considered a solid mass, yet it has a large, liquid iron, **magnetic core** with a radius of about 2,155 mi. Surprisingly, it has a solid **inner core** that may be a large iron crystal, with a radius of 760 mi. Around the core is a thick shell, or **mantle,** of dense rock. This mantle is composed of materials rich in iron and magnesium. It is somewhat plastic-like and under slow steady pressure can flow like a liquid. The mantle, in turn, is covered by a thin **crust** forming the solid granite and basalt base of the continents and ocean basins. Over broad areas of Earth's surface, the crust has a thin cover of sedimentary rock such as sandstone, shale, and limestone formed by weathering of Earth's surface and deposits of sands, clays, and plant and animal remains.

The **temperature** inside the Earth increases about 1° F with every 100 to 200 feet in depth, in the upper 100 km of Earth, and reaches nearly 8,000-9,000° F at the center. The heat is believed to be derived from radioactivity in the rocks, pressures developed within Earth, and the original heat of formation.

Atmosphere of Earth

Earth's atmosphere is a blanket composed of nitrogen, oxygen, and argon, in amounts of about 78%, 21%, and 1% by volume. Also present in minute quantities are carbon dioxide, hydrogen, neon, helium, krypton, and xenon. Water vapor displaces other gases and varies from nearly zero to about 4% by volume. The atmosphere rests on Earth's surface with the weight equivalent to a layer of water 34 ft deep. For about 300,000 ft upward, the gases remain in the proportions stated. Gravity holds the gases to Earth. The weight of the air compresses it at the bottom so that the greatest density is at Earth's surface. Pressure and density decrease as height increases because the weight pressing upon any layer is always less than that pressing upon the layers below.

The lowest layer of the atmosphere extending up about 7.5 mi is the **troposphere**, which contains 90% of the air and the tallest mountains. This is also where most weather phenomena occur. The temperature drops with increasing height throughout this layer. The atmosphere for about 23 mi above the troposphere is the **stratosphere**, where the temperature generally increases with height. The stratosphere contains ozone, which prevents ultraviolet rays from reaching Earth's surface. Since there is very little convection in the stratosphere, jets regularly cruise in the lower parts to provide a smoother ride for passengers.

Above the stratosphere is the **mesosphere**, where the temperature again decreases with height for another 19 mi. Extending above the mesosphere to the outer fringes of the atmosphere is the **thermosphere**, a region where temperature once more increases with height to a value measured in thousands of degrees Fahrenheit. The lower portion of this region, extending from 50 to about 400 mi in altitude, is characterized by a high ion density and is thus called the **ionosphere**. Most meteors are in the lower thermosphere or the mesosphere at the time they are observed.

Longitude, Latitude

Position on the globe is measured by meridians and parallels. Meridians, which are imaginary lines drawn around Earth through the poles, determine **longitude**. The meridian running through Greenwich, England, is the **prime meridian** of longitude, and all others are either E or W. Parallels, which are imaginary circles parallel with the equator, determine **latitude**. The length of a degree of longitude varies as the cosine of the latitude. At the equator a degree of longitude is 69.171 statute mi; this is gradually reduced toward the poles. Value of a longitude degree at the poles is zero.

Latitude is reckoned by the number of degrees N or S of the **equator**, an imaginary circle on Earth's surface everywhere equidistant between the two poles. According to the International Astronomical Union ellipsoid of 1964, the length of a degree of latitude is 68.708 statute mi at the equator and varies slightly N and S because of the oblate form of the globe; at the poles it is 69.403 statute mi.

Definitions of Time

Earth rotates on its axis and follows an elliptical orbit around the Sun. The rotation makes the Sun appear to move across the sky from E to W. This rotation determines day and night, and the complete rotation, in relation to the Sun, is called the **apparent** or **true solar day**. A sundial thus measures **apparent solar time**. This length of time varies, but an average determines the mean solar day of 24 hours.

The mean solar day and mean solar time are in universal use for civil purposes. Mean solar time may be obtained from apparent solar time by correcting observations of the Sun for the **equation of time**. Mean solar time may be as much as 16 minutes behind or 14 minutes ahead of apparent solar time.

Sidereal time is the measure of time defined by the diurnal motion of the vernal equinox and is determined from observation of the meridian transits of stars. One complete rotation of Earth relative to the equinox is called the **sidereal day**. The **mean sidereal day** is 23 hours, 56 minutes, 4.091 seconds of mean solar time.

The interval required for Earth to make one absolute revolution around the Sun is a **sidereal** year; it consisted of 365 days, 6 hours, 9 minutes, and 9.5 seconds of mean solar time (approximately 24 hours per day) in 1900 and has been increasing at the rate of 0.0001 second annually.

The **tropical year**, upon which our calendar is based, is the interval between 2 consecutive returns of the Sun to the vernal equinox. The tropical year consisted of 365 days, 5 hours, 48 minutes, and 46 seconds in 1900. It has been decreasing at the rate of 0.530 second per century. The **calendar year** begins at 12 o'clock midnight precisely, local clock time, on the night of Dec. 31-Jan. 1. The day and the calendar month also begin at midnight by the clock.

On Jan. 1, 1972, the Bureau International des Poids et Mesures in Paris introduced **International Atomic Time** (TAI) as the most precisely determined time scale for astronomical usage. The fundamental unit of TAI in the international system of units is the second, defined as the duration of 9,192,631,770 periods of the radiation corresponding to the transition between 2 hyperfine levels of the ground state of the cesium 133 atom. **Coordinated Universal Time** (UTC), which serves as the basis for civil timekeeping and is the standard time of the prime meridian, is officially defined by a formula which relates UTC to mean sidereal time in Greenwich, England. (UTC has replaced GMT as the basis for standard time for the world.)

The Zones and Seasons

The 5 zones of Earth's surface are the Torrid, lying between the Tropics of Cancer and Capricorn; the N Temperate, between Cancer and the Arctic Circle; the S Temperate, between Capricorn and the Antarctic Circle; and the 2 Frigid Zones, between the Polar Circles and the Poles.

The inclination, or **tilt**, of Earth's axis, 23° 27′ away from a perpendicular to Earth's orbit of the Sun, determines the seasons. These are commonly marked in the N Temperate Zone, where spring begins at the vernal equinox, summer at the summer solstice, autumn at the autumnal equinox, and winter at the winter solstice.

In the S Temperate Zone, the seasons are reversed. Spring begins at the autumnal equinox, summer at the winter solstice, etc.

The points at which the Sun crosses the equator are the **equinoxes**, when day and night are most nearly equal. The points at which the Sun is at a maximum distance from the equator are the **solstices**. Days and nights are then most unequal. However, at the equator, day and night are equal throughout the year.

In June, the North Pole is tilted 23° 27′ toward the Sun, and the days in the northern hemisphere are longer than the nights, while the days in the southern hemisphere are shorter than the nights. In Dec., the North Pole is tilted 23° 27′ away from the Sun, and the situation is reversed.

The Seasons in 2003

In 2003 the 4 seasons begin in the northern hemisphere as shown. (Add 1 hour to Eastern Standard Time for Atlantic Time; subtract 1 hour for Central, 2 for Mountain, 3 for Pacific, 4 for Alaska, 5 for Hawaii-Aleutian. Also shown is Coordinated Universal Time.)

Seasons	Date	EST	UTC
Vernal Equinox (spring)	Mar. 21	20:00*	01:00
Northern Solstice (summer)	June 21	14:10	19:10
Autumnal Equinox (autumn)	Sept. 23	5:47	10:47
Southern Solstice (winter)	Dec. 22	2:04	7:04

* previous day

Poles of Earth

The geographic (rotation) poles, or points where Earth's axis of rotation cuts the surface, are not absolutely fixed in the body of Earth. The pole of rotation describes an irregular curve about its mean position.

Two periods have been detected in this motion: (1) an annual period due to seasonal changes in barometric pressure, to load of ice and snow on the surface, and to other phenomena of seasonal character; (2) a period of about 14 months due to the shape and constitution of Earth.

In addition, there are small but as yet unpredictable irregularities. The whole motion is so small that the actual pole at any time remains within a circle of 30 or 40 feet in radius centered at the mean position of the pole.

The pole of rotation for the time being is of course the pole having a latitude of 90° and an indeterminate longitude.

Magnetic Poles

Although Earth's magnetic field resembles that of an ordinary bar magnet, this magnetic field is probably produced by electric currents in the liquid currents of the Earth's outer core. The **north magnetic pole** of Earth is that region where the magnetic force is vertically downward, and the **south magnetic pole** is that region where the magnetic force is vertically upward. A compass placed at the magnetic poles experiences no directive force in azimuth (i.e., direction).

There are slow changes in the distribution of Earth's magnetic field. This slow temporal change is referred to as the Secular change of the main magnetic field and the magnetic poles shift due this. The location of the N magnetic pole was first measured in 1831 at Cape Adelaide on the west coast of Boothia Peninsula in Canada's Northwest Territories (about latitude 70° N and longitude 96° W). Since then it has moved over 500 miles. In 1994, the N magnetic pole was located at Ellef Ringnes Island in northern Canada; it is now northwest of that island. Measurement for the past several decades by Canadian scientists indicate the NW motion of the pole continues, averaging about 9 mi per year.

The direction of the horizontal components of the magnetic field at any point is known as magnetic N at that point, and the angle by which it deviates E or W of true N is known as the magnetic declination.

A compass without error points in the direction of magnetic north. (In general, this is not the direction of the true rotational north pole.) If one follows the direction indicated by the N end of the compass, he or she will travel along a rather irregular curve that eventually reaches the north magnetic pole (though not usually by a great-circle route). However, the action of the compass should not be thought of as due to any influence of the distant pole, but simply as an indication of the distribution of Earth's magnetism at the place of observation.

Rotation of Earth

The speed of rotation of Earth about its axis has been found to be slightly variable. The variations may be classified as:

(A) **Secular**. Tidal friction acts as a brake on the rotation and causes a slow secular increase in the length of the day, about 1 millisecond per century.

(B) **Irregular**. The speed of rotation may increase for a number of years, about 5 to 10, and then start decreasing. The maximum difference from the mean in the length of the day during a century is about 5 milliseconds. The accumulated difference in time has amounted to approximately 44 seconds since 1900. The cause is probably motion in the interior of Earth.

(C) **Periodic**. Seasonal variations exist with periods of 1 year and 6 months. The cumulative effect is such that each year, Earth is late about 30 milliseconds near June 1 and is ahead about 30 milliseconds near Oct. 1. The maximum seasonal variation in the length of the day is about 0.5 millisecond. It is believed that the principal cause of the annual variation is the seasonal change in the wind patterns of the northern and southern hemispheres. The semiannual variation is due chiefly to tidal action of the Sun, which distorts the shape of Earth slightly.

The secular and irregular variations were discovered by comparing time based on the rotation of Earth with time based on the orbital motion of the Moon about Earth and of the planets about the Sun. The periodic variation was determined largely with the aid of quartz-crystal clocks. The introduction of the cesium-beam atomic clock in 1955 made it possible to determine in greater detail than before the nature of the irregular and periodic variations.

Calculation of Rise Times

The Daily Calendar on pages 675-686 contain rise and set times for the Sun and Moon for the Greenwich Meridian at N latitudes 20°, 30°, 40°, 50°, and 60°. From day to day, the values for the Sun at any particular latitude do not change very much. This means that whatever time the Sun rises or sets at the 0° meridian, it will rise or set at the same time at the Standard Time meridian of your time zone. Standard Time meridians occur every 15° of longitude (15° E and W, 30° E and W, etc.). The corrections necessary to observe that event from your location will be to account for your distance from the Standard Time meridian and for your latitude. Thus, if your latitude is about 45°, sunrise on Jan. 1, 2003, is roughly halfway between 7:22 and 7:59 AM on the Standard Time meridian for your time zone. If you are 7.5° west of your Standard Time meridian, sunrise will be about ½ hour later than this; if 7.5° east, about ½ hour earlier.

The Moon, however, moves its own diameter, about one-half degree, in an hour, or about 13.2° in one complete turn of Earth—one day. Most of this is eastward against the background stars of the sky, but some is also N or S movement. All this motion considerably affects the times of rise or set, as you can see from the adjacent entries in the table. Thus, it is necessary to take your longitude into account in addition to your latitude. If you have no need for total accuracy, simply note that the time will be between the 4 values (see example below) you find surrounding your location and the dates of interest.

The process of finding more accurate corrections is called interpolation. In the example, linear interpolation involving simple differences is used. In extreme cases, higher order interpolation should be used. If such cases are important to you, it is suggested that you plot the times, draw smooth curves through the plots, and interpolate by eye between the relevant curves. Some people find this exercise fun.

Let's find the times of the moonrise for the August Full Moon and sunset the same day at Utica, NY.

First, where is Utica, NY? Find Utica's latitude and longitude in the "Latitude, Longitude, and Altitude of U.S. and Canadian Cities" table found in the World Exploration and Geography section of The World Almanac. You must also know the time zone in which the city is located, which you can estimate from the "International Time Zones" map in the map section of *The World Almanac.*

I. Utica, NY: 43° 6′ 3′′ N
75° 13′ 59′′ W

IA. Convert these values to decimals:
3/60 = 0.05
6 + 0.05 = 6.05
6.05/60 = 0.10
43 + 0.10 = 43.10 N
59/60 = 0.98
13 + 0.98 = 13.98
13.98/60 = 0.23
75 + 0.23 = 75.23 W

IB. Fraction Utica lies between 40° and 50°:
43.10 – 40 = 3.10; 3.10/10 = 0.310

IC. Fraction world must turn between Greenwich and Utica:
75.23/360 = 0.209

ID. Utica is in the Eastern Standard Time zone and the EST meridian is 75°; thus 75.23 is 75.23 – 75 = 0.23° W of the Eastern Standard Meridian. In 24 hours, there are 24 x 60 = 1,440 minutes; 1,440/360 = 4 minutes for every degree around Earth. So events happen 4 x 0.23 = 0.9 minutes later in Utica than at the 75° meridian. (If the location is E of the Standard Meridian, events happen earlier.)

IE. The values IB and IC are interpolates for Utica; ID is the time correction from local to Standard time for Utica. These values need never be calculated again for Utica.

IIA. To find the time of moonrise we start from the table of Moon Phases, 2003. We see that August's Full Moon occurs on August 12. We need the Greenwich times for moonrise at latitudes 40° and 50°, and for August 12 and 13, the day of the Full Moon and the next day. These values are found in the Astronomy Daily Calendar 2003; we then compute the difference between the two latitudes.

	40°	Diff.	50°
Aug. 12	19:43	0:27	20:10
Aug. 13	20:11	0:18	20:29

IIB. We want IB and the August 12 time difference:
0.310 x 27 = 8.4
Add this to the August 12, 40° rise time:
19:43 + 8.4= 19:51.4
And for August 13:
0.310 x 18 = 5.6
Add this to the August 13, 40° rise time:
20:11 + 5.6 = 20:16.6
These 2 times are for the latitude of Utica, but for the Greenwich meridian.

IIC. To get the time for the Utica meridian, take the difference between these 2 times just determined,
20:16.6 - 19:51.4 = 25.2 minutes,
and calculate what fraction of this 24-hour change took place while Earth turned between Greenwich and Utica (See IC).
25.2 x 0.209 = 5.3 minutes after 19:51.4
Thus 19:51.4 + 5.3 = 19:56.7 is the time the Full Moon will rise in the local time of Utica.

IID. But this happens 0.9 minutes (See ID) later by EST clock time at Utica, thus
19:56.7 + 0.9 = 19:57.6 EST
But this is summer, and daylight time is in effect;
19:58 + 1:00 = 20:58 EDT is the rise time for the Full Moon at Utica the evening of Aug. 12, 2003.

IIIA. To find the time of sunset we need the Greenwich times for sunset at latitudes 40° and 50°. These values are found in the Astronomy Daily Calendar 2003; we then compute the difference between the two latitudes.

	40°	Diff.	50°
Aug. 12	19:01	0:24	19:25

IIIB. We want IB and the August 12 time difference:
0.310 x 24 = 7.4
Add this to the Aug. 12, 40° set time:
19:01 + 7.4 = 19:08.4
This is the local time for the latitude of Utica.

IIIC. But this happens 0.9 minutes (See ID) later by EST clock time at Utica, thus
19:08.4 + 0.9 = 19:09.3
But daylight time is in effect;
19:09 + 1:00 = 20:09 is sunset at Utica on Aug. 12, 2003.

JANUARY 2003

1st Month **31 days**

Coordinated Universal Time (Greenwich Mean Time)

NOTE: For rising and setting each day, numbers on first line indicate Sun; numbers on second line indicate Moon.
Degrees are North Latitude.

Moon Phases: FM = Full Moon; LQ = Last (Waning) Quarter; NM = New Moon; FQ = First (Waxing) Quarter

Sun's distance is in Astronomical Units

CAUTION: Must be converted to local time. For instructions see "Calculation of Rise Times," page 674.

Day of month, of week, of year	Sun on Meridian / Moon Phase	Sun's Declination ° ′ / Distance	20° Rise Sun / Moon	20° Set Sun / Moon	30° Rise Sun / Moon	30° Set Sun / Moon	40° Rise Sun / Moon	40° Set Sun / Moon	50° Rise Sun / Moon	50° Set Sun / Moon	60° Rise Sun / Moon	60° Set Sun / Moon
	h m s		h m	h m	h m	h m	h m	h m	h m	h m	h m	h m
1 WE	12 03 25	- 23 03	6 35	17 32	6 56	17 11	7 22	16 45	7 59	16 08	9 02	15 05
1		.9833	5 08	16 18	5 32	15 53	6 01	15 23	6 44	14 38	8 04	13 17
2 TH	12 03 53	- 22 58	6 35	17 33	6 56	17 12	7 22	16 46	7 58	16 09	9 02	15 06
2	20 22 NM	.9833	6 12	17 16	6 37	16 51	7 09	16 19	7 56	15 32	9 27	14 00
3 FR	12 04 21	- 22 53	6 36	17 33	6 56	17 13	7 22	16 47	7 58	16 11	9 01	15 08
3		.9833	7 12	18 17	7 37	17 53	8 08	17 22	8 54	16 37	10 21	15 11
4 SA	12 04 48	- 22 47	6 36	17 34	6 56	17 13	7 22	16 48	7 58	16 12	9 01	15 09
4		.9833	8 06	19 10	8 20	18 56	8 57	18 29	9 38	17 50	10 51	16 39
5 SU	12 05 16	- 22 41	6 36	17 34	6 57	17 14	7 22	16 49	7 58	16 13	9 00	15 11
5		.9833	8 54	20 16	9 13	19 58	9 37	19 36	10 11	19 04	11 07	18 11
6 MO	12 05 42	- 22 34	6 36	17 35	6 57	17 15	7 22	16 50	7 58	16 14	8 59	15 13
6		.9833	9 36	21 11	9 51	20 57	10 10	20 41	10 35	20 18	11 16	19 41
7 TU	12 06 09	- 22 27	6 37	17 36	6 57	17 16	7 22	16 50	7 57	16 15	8 58	15 14
7		.9833	10 14	22 02	10 24	21 54	10 37	21 44	10 55	21 29	11 22	21 06
8 WE	12 06 34	- 22 19	6 37	17 36	6 57	17 16	7 22	16 51	7 57	16 16	8 57	15 16
8		.9833	10 48	22 52	10 54	22 48	11 01	22 44	11 11	22 38	11 26	22 28
9 TH	12 07 00	- 22 11	6 37	17 37	6 57	17 17	7 22	16 52	7 57	16 18	8 56	15 18
9		.9834	11 21	23 40	11 22	23 41	11 24	23 43	11 26	23 44	11 29	23 47
10 FR	12 07 24	- 22 03	6 37	17 38	6 57	17 18	7 22	16 53	7 56	16 19	8 55	15 20
10	13 14 FQ	.9834	11 53	none	11 50	none	11 46	none	11 40	none	11 32	none
11 SA	12 07 48	- 21 54	6 37	17 38	6 57	17 19	7 21	16 54	7 56	16 20	8 54	15 22
11		.9834	12 26	0 28	12 18	0 34	12 08	0 41	11 55	0 51	11 36	1 06
12 SU	12 08 12	- 21 45	6 38	17 39	6 57	17 20	7 21	16 55	7 55	16 22	8 53	15 24
12		.9834	13 00	1 17	12 48	1 27	12 33	1 40	12 12	1 58	11 40	2 26
13 MO	12 08 35	- 21 35	6 38	17 40	6 57	17 20	7 21	16 57	7 54	16 23	8 51	15 26
13		.9835	13 37	2 07	13 21	2 22	13 00	2 40	12 32	3 06	11 47	3 48
14 TU	12 08 57	- 21 25	6 38	17 40	6 57	17 21	7 21	16 58	7 54	16 25	8 50	15 29
14		.9835	14 18	3 00	13 58	3 18	13 33	3 42	12 57	4 16	11 57	5 13
15 WE	12 09 19	- 21 14	6 38	17 41	6 57	17 22	7 20	16 59	7 53	16 26	8 48	15 31
15		.9836	15 05	3 54	14 42	4 17	14 12	4 45	13 30	5 25	12 15	6 39
16 TH	12 09 39	- 21 03	6 38	17 42	6 57	17 23	7 20	17 00	7 52	16 27	8 47	15 33
16		.9836	15 57	4 51	15 32	5 15	15 00	5 47	14 14	6 32	12 47	7 58
17 FR	12 10 00	- 20 52	6 38	17 42	6 56	17 24	7 19	17 01	7 51	16 29	8 45	15 35
17		.9837	16 53	5 47	16 28	6 13	15 57	6 44	15 11	7 31	13 43	8 59
18 SA	12 10 19	- 20 40	6 38	17 43	6 56	17 25	7 19	17 02	7 51	16 31	8 43	15 38
18	10 47 FM	.9838	17 54	6 42	17 31	7 06	17 02	7 36	16 20	8 19	15 03	9 38
19 SU	12 10 38	- 20 28	6 38	17 44	6 56	17 26	7 18	17 03	7 50	16 32	8 42	15 40
19		.9838	18 55	7 34	18 36	7 55	18 12	8 21	17 37	8 58	16 38	10 00
20 MO	12 10 56	- 20 15	6 38	17 44	6 56	17 26	7 18	17 04	7 49	16 34	8 40	15 43
20		.9839	19 57	8 22	19 42	8 39	19 24	8 59	18 58	9 27	18 17	10 13
21 TU	12 11 13	- 20 02	6 38	17 45	6 55	17 27	7 17	17 05	7 48	16 35	8 38	15 45
21		.9840	20 57	9 06	20 48	9 18	20 36	9 32	20 20	9 51	19 55	10 21
22 WE	12 11 30	- 19 49	6 38	17 45	6 55	17 28	7 17	17 07	7 47	16 37	8 36	15 47
22		.9841	21 56	9 47	21 52	9 53	21 48	10 01	21 42	10 11	21 32	10 26
23 TH	12 11 46	- 19 35	6 38	17 46	6 55	17 29	7 16	17 08	7 46	16 38	8 34	15 50
23		.9842	22 54	10 27	22 56	10 27	22 59	10 28	23 03	10 29	23 08	10 31
24 FR	12 12 00	- 19 21	6 37	17 47	6 54	17 30	7 15	17 09	7 44	16 40	8 32	15 52
24		.9843	23 53	11 06	none	11 01	none	10 55	none	10 47	none	10 35
25 SA	12 12 15	- 19 07	6 37	17 47	6 54	17 31	7 15	17 10	7 43	16 42	8 30	15 55
25	08 33 LQ	.9844	none	11 46	0 01	11 36	0 10	11 24	0 24	11 07	0 45	10 41
26 SU	12 12 28	- 18 52	6 37	17 48	6 54	17 32	7 14	17 11	7 42	16 43	8 28	15 57
26		.9845	0 53	12 30	1 06	12 14	1 23	11 55	1 46	11 29	2 23	10 47
27 MO	12 12 41	- 18 37	6 37	17 49	6 53	17 32	7 13	17 13	7 41	16 45	8 26	16 00
27		.9846	1 54	13 17	2 13	12 57	2 36	12 32	3 08	11 57	4 04	10 58
28 TU	12 12 53	- 18 22	6 37	17 49	6 53	17 33	7 12	17 14	7 40	16 47	8 24	16 03
28		.9848	2 57	14 08	3 19	13 45	3 48	13 15	4 28	12 33	5 43	11 17
29 WE	12 13 04	- 18 06	6 36	17 50	6 52	17 34	7 12	17 15	7 38	16 48	8 22	16 05
29		.9849	3 59	15 04	4 24	14 39	4 56	14 07	5 42	13 20	7 10	11 51
30 TH	12 13 14	- 17 50	6 36	17 50	6 52	17 35	7 11	17 16	7 37	16 50	8 19	16 08
30		.9850	4 59	16 03	5 25	15 38	5 57	15 06	6 44	14 20	8 15	12 50
31 FR	12 13 24	- 17 33	6 36	17 51	6 51	17 36	7 10	17 17	7 36	16 52	8 17	16 10
31		.9852	5 55	17 03	6 19	16 40	6 49	16 11	7 33	15 29	8 52	14 11

FEBRUARY 2003

2nd Month **28 days**

Coordinated Universal Time (Greenwich Mean Time)

NOTE: For rising and setting each day, numbers on first line indicate Sun; numbers on second line indicate Moon.

Degrees are North Latitude.

Moon Phases: FM = Full Moon; LQ = Last (Waning) Quarter; NM = New Moon; FQ = First (Waxing) Quarter

Sun's distance is in Astronomical Units

CAUTION: Must be converted to local time. For instructions see "Calculation of Rise Times," page 674.

Day of month, of week, of year	Sun on Meridian / Moon Phase	Sun's Declination ° ′ / Distance	20° Rise Sun / Moon	20° Set Sun / Moon	30° Rise Sun / Moon	30° Set Sun / Moon	40° Rise Sun / Moon	40° Set Sun / Moon	50° Rise Sun / Moon	50° Set Sun / Moon	60° Rise Sun / Moon	60° Set Sun / Moon
	h m s		h m	h m	h m	h m	h m	h m	h m	h m	h m	h m
1 SA	12 13 33	- 17 17	6 36	17 52	6 51	17 37	7 09	17 19	7 34	16 53	8 15	16 13
32	10 48 NM	.9853	6 45	18 02	7 06	17 43	7 32	17 18	8 09	16 43	9 12	15 42
2 SU	12 13 40	- 17 00	6 35	17 52	6 50	17 38	7 08	17 20	7 33	16 55	8 13	16 16
33		.9854	7 29	18 58	7 46	18 43	8 07	18 24	8 36	17 58	9 24	17 14
3 MO	12 13 48	- 16 42	6 35	17 53	6 49	17 39	7 07	17 21	7 31	16 57	8 10	16 18
34		.9856	8 09	19 52	8 22	19 42	8 37	19 29	8 58	19 11	9 30	18 42
4 TU	12 13 54	- 16 25	6 35	17 53	6 49	17 39	7 06	17 22	7 30	16 59	8 08	16 21
35		.9857	8 45	20 43	8 53	20 37	9 02	20 30	9 15	20 21	9 35	20 06
5 WE	12 13 59	- 16 07	6 34	17 54	6 48	17 40	7 05	17 23	7 28	17 00	8 05	16 24
36		.9859	9 19	21 32	9 22	21 31	9 26	21 30	9 31	21 29	9 38	21 27
6 TH	12 14 04	- 15 49	6 34	17 54	6 47	17 41	7 04	17 25	7 27	17 02	8 03	16 26
37		.9860	9 51	22 20	9 50	22 24	9 48	22 29	9 45	22 36	9 41	22 46
7 FR	12 14 08	- 15 30	6 33	17 55	6 47	17 42	7 03	17 26	7 25	17 04	8 00	16 29
38		.9862	10 23	23 09	10 17	23 17	10 10	23 28	10 00	23 43	9 44	none
8 SA	12 14 10	- 15 11	6 33	17 56	6 46	17 43	7 02	17 27	7 24	17 06	7 58	16 32
39		.9864	10 57	23 58	10 46	none	10 33	none	10 15	none	9 48	0 06
9 SU	12 14 13	- 14 52	6 33	17 56	6 45	17 44	7 01	17 28	7 22	17 07	7 55	16 34
40	11 11 FQ	.9865	11 32	none	11 17	0 11	10 59	0 28	10 34	0 50	9 53	1 27
10 MO	12 14 14	- 14 33	6 32	17 57	6 44	17 44	7 00	17 29	7 20	17 09	7 53	16 37
41		.9867	12 11	0 49	11 52	1 06	11 29	1 28	10 56	1 59	10 02	2 51
11 TU	12 14 15	- 14 14	6 32	17 57	6 44	17 45	6 58	17 31	7 18	17 11	7 50	16 39
42		.9869	12 55	1 42	12 33	2 03	12 05	2 30	11 25	3 08	10 15	4 16
12 WE	12 14 14	- 13 54	6 31	17 58	6 43	17 46	6 57	17 32	7 17	17 12	7 47	16 42
43		.9870	13 44	2 37	13 19	3 01	12 48	3 31	12 03	4 15	10 40	5 38
13 TH	12 14 13	- 13 34	6 31	17 58	6 42	17 47	6 56	17 33	7 15	17 14	7 45	16 45
44		.9872	14 38	3 33	14 12	3 58	13 40	4 31	12 53	5 17	11 23	6 47
14 FR	12 14 12	- 13 14	6 30	17 59	6 41	17 48	6 55	17 34	7 13	17 16	7 42	16 47
45		.9874	15 37	4 29	15 12	4 54	14 42	5 25	13 57	6 10	12 33	7 35
15 SA	12 14 09	- 12 54	6 29	17 59	6 40	17 48	6 54	17 35	7 11	17 18	7 39	16 50
46		.9876	16 38	5 22	16 17	5 45	15 50	6 13	15 12	6 53	14 04	8 03
16 SU	12 14 06	- 12 33	6 29	18 00	6 39	17 49	6 52	17 36	7 10	17 19	7 37	16 53
47	23 51 FM	.9878	17 41	6 12	17 24	6 31	17 03	6 54	16 34	7 26	15 44	8 19
17 MO	12 14 02	- 12 12	6 28	18 00	6 39	17 50	6 51	17 38	7 08	17 21	7 34	16 55
48		.9880	18 44	6 59	18 32	7 13	18 18	7 30	17 58	7 53	17 26	8 29
18 TU	12 13 57	- 11 51	6 28	18 00	6 38	17 51	6 50	17 39	7 06	17 23	7 31	16 58
49		.9882	19 45	7 42	19 39	7 51	19 32	8 01	19 22	8 15	19 07	8 35
19 WE	12 13 52	- 11 30	6 27	18 01	6 37	17 51	6 48	17 40	7 04	17 24	7 28	17 00
50		.9884	20 46	8 24	20 46	8 26	20 46	8 30	20 46	8 34	20 47	8 40
20 TH	12 13 46	- 11 09	6 26	18 01	6 36	17 52	6 47	17 41	7 02	17 26	7 26	17 03
51		.9886	21 46	9 04	21 52	9 01	22 00	8 57	22 10	8 52	22 27	8 44
21 FR	12 13 39	- 10 47	6 26	18 02	6 35	17 53	6 46	17 42	7 00	17 28	7 23	17 06
52		.9888	22 47	9 45	22 59	9 36	23 13	9 26	23 34	9 11	none	8 49
22 SA	12 13 32	- 10 26	6 25	18 02	6 34	17 54	6 44	17 43	6 58	17 30	7 20	17 08
53		.9891	23 49	10 28	none	10 14	none	9 57	none	9 33	0 07	8 55
23 SU	12 13 24	- 10 04	6 24	18 03	6 33	17 54	6 43	17 45	6 56	17 31	7 17	17 11
54	16 45 LQ	.9893	none	11 14	0 06	10 55	0 27	10 32	0 58	9 59	1 49	9 04
24 MO	12 13 16	-9 42	6 24	18 03	6 32	17 55	6 41	17 46	6 54	17 33	7 14	17 13
55		.9895	0 51	12 04	1 13	11 42	1 40	11 13	2 19	10 32	3 29	9 20
25 TU	12 13 07	-9 20	6 23	18 03	6 31	17 56	6 40	17 47	6 52	17 35	7 11	17 16
56		.9898	1 53	12 59	2 18	12 34	2 49	12 02	3 35	11 15	5 01	9 47
26 WE	12 12 57	-8 57	6 22	18 04	6 30	17 57	6 39	17 48	6 50	17 36	7 09	17 19
57		.9900	2 53	13 56	3 19	13 31	3 52	12 58	4 39	12 10	6 13	10 37
27 TH	12 12 47	-8 35	6 22	18 04	6 29	17 57	6 37	17 49	6 48	17 38	7 06	17 21
58		.9902	3 49	14 55	4 14	14 31	4 46	14 00	5 31	13 16	6 56	11 52
28 FR	12 12 36	-8 12	6 21	18 05	6 28	17 58	6 36	17 50	6 46	17 40	7 03	17 24
59		.9905	4 40	15 53	5 03	15 32	5 30	15 06	6 10	14 28	7 20	13 20

MARCH 2003

3rd Month **31 days**

Coordinated Universal Time (Greenwich Mean Time)

NOTE: For rising and setting each day, numbers on first line indicate Sun; numbers on second line indicate Moon.

Degrees are North Latitude.

Moon Phases: FM = Full Moon; LQ = Last (Waning) Quarter; NM = New Moon; FQ = First (Waxing) Quarter

Sun's distance is in Astronomical Units

CAUTION: Must be converted to local time. For instructions see "Calculation of Rise Times," page 674.

Day of month, of week, of year	Sun on Meridian / Moon Phase (h m s)	Sun's Declination (° ′) / Distance	20° Rise Sun / Moon (h m)	20° Set Sun / Moon (h m)	30° Rise Sun / Moon (h m)	30° Set Sun / Moon (h m)	40° Rise Sun / Moon (h m)	40° Set Sun / Moon (h m)	50° Rise Sun / Moon (h m)	50° Set Sun / Moon (h m)	60° Rise Sun / Moon (h m)	60° Set Sun / Moon (h m)
1 SA	12 12 25	-7 50	6 20	18 05	6 27	17 59	6 34	17 51	6 44	17 41	7 00	17 26
60		.9907	5 26	16 50	5 44	16 33	6 07	16 12	6 39	15 42	7 33	14 52
2 SU	12 12 13	-7 27	6 19	18 05	6 25	17 59	6 33	17 52	6 42	17 43	6 57	17 29
61		.9910	6 06	17 44	6 21	17 31	6 38	17 16	7 02	16 55	7 40	16 21
3 MO	12 12 01	-7 04	6 19	18 06	6 24	18 00	6 31	17 53	6 40	17 45	6 54	17 31
62	02 35 NM	.9912	6 43	18 35	6 53	18 28	7 05	18 18	7 20	18 06	7 45	17 46
4 TU	12 11 48	-6 41	6 18	18 06	6 23	18 01	6 30	17 55	6 38	17 46	6 51	17 34
63		.9915	7 18	19 25	7 22	19 22	7 28	19 19	7 36	19 15	7 48	19 08
5 WE	12 11 35	-6 18	6 17	18 06	6 22	18 01	6 28	17 56	6 36	17 48	6 48	17 36
64		.9917	7 50	20 13	7 50	20 16	7 50	20 19	7 51	20 22	7 51	20 28
6 TH	12 11 22	-5 55	6 16	18 07	6 21	18 02	6 27	17 57	6 34	17 50	6 45	17 39
65		.9920	8 22	21 02	8 18	21 09	8 12	21 18	8 05	21 29	7 54	21 48
7 FR	12 11 08	-5 31	6 16	18 07	6 20	18 03	6 25	17 58	6 32	17 51	6 42	17 41
66		.9922	8 55	21 51	8 46	22 02	8 35	22 17	8 20	22 37	7 57	23 09
8 SA	12 10 53	-5 08	6 15	18 07	6 19	18 03	6 24	17 59	6 30	17 53	6 39	17 44
67		.9925	9 30	22 41	9 16	22 57	8 59	23 17	8 37	23 45	8 01	none
9 SU	12 10 38	-4 45	6 14	18 08	6 18	18 04	6 22	18 00	6 28	17 54	6 36	17 46
68		.9927	10 07	23 33	9 49	23 53	9 27	none	8 57	none	8 07	0 32
10 MO	12 10 23	-4 21	6 13	18 08	6 16	18 05	6 20	18 01	6 26	17 56	6 33	17 49
69		.9930	10 48	none	10 26	none	10 00	0 18	9 22	0 54	8 18	1 56
11 TU	12 10 08	-3 58	6 12	18 08	6 15	18 05	6 19	18 02	6 23	17 58	6 30	17 51
70	07 15 FQ	.9932	11 33	0 26	11 09	0 49	10 39	1 19	9 55	2 01	8 36	3 19
12 WE	12 09 52	-3 34	6 11	18 09	6 14	18 06	6 17	18 03	6 21	17 59	6 27	17 54
71		.9935	12 24	1 21	11 59	1 46	11 26	2 18	10 39	3 05	9 08	4 35
13 TH	12 09 36	-3 11	6 11	18 09	6 13	18 07	6 16	18 04	6 19	18 01	6 24	17 56
72		.9938	13 20	2 16	12 55	2 41	12 22	3 13	11 36	4 01	10 05	5 32
14 FR	12 09 19	-2 47	6 10	18 09	6 12	18 07	6 14	18 05	6 17	18 03	6 21	17 59
73		.9940	14 19	3 09	13 56	3 33	13 27	4 03	12 45	4 47	11 27	6 06
15 SA	12 09 03	-2 23	6 09	18 09	6 11	18 08	6 12	18 06	6 15	18 04	6 18	18 01
74		.9943	15 21	4 00	15 02	4 21	14 37	4 47	14 03	5 24	13 03	6 26
16 SU	12 08 46	-2 00	6 08	18 10	6 09	18 09	6 11	18 07	6 13	18 06	6 15	18 04
75		.9946	16 23	4 48	16 09	5 04	15 51	5 24	15 26	5 52	14 45	6 37
17 MO	12 08 28	-1 36	6 07	18 10	6 08	18 09	6 09	18 08	6 10	18 07	6 12	18 06
76		.9948	17 26	5 32	17 17	5 44	17 06	5 57	16 52	6 16	16 29	6 44
18 TU	12 08 11	-1 12	6 06	18 10	6 07	18 10	6 08	18 09	6 08	18 09	6 09	18 09
77	10 34 FM	.9951	18 28	6 15	18 26	6 20	18 22	6 27	18 18	6 36	18 11	6 49
19 WE	12 07 53	-0 48	6 05	18 11	6 06	18 10	6 06	18 10	6 06	18 11	6 06	18 11
78		.9954	19 30	6 57	19 34	6 56	19 38	6 56	19 45	6 55	19 54	6 53
20 TH	12 07 36	-0 25	6 05	18 11	6 05	18 11	6 04	18 11	6 04	18 12	6 03	18 13
79		.9957	20 33	7 38	20 43	7 32	20 55	7 24	21 12	7 14	21 38	6 58
21 FR	12 07 18	-0 01	6 04	18 11	6 03	18 12	6 03	18 13	6 02	18 14	6 00	18 16
80		.9959	21 37	8 22	21 53	8 10	22 12	7 55	22 39	7 35	23 24	7 03
22 SA	12 07 00	+0 23	6 03	18 11	6 02	18 12	6 01	18 14	6 00	18 15	5 57	18 18
81		.9962	22 42	9 09	23 03	8 51	23 28	8 29	none	7 59	none	7 10
23 SU	12 06 42	+0 46	6 02	18 12	6 01	18 13	6 00	18 15	5 57	18 17	5 54	18 21
82		.9965	23 47	9 59	none	9 37	none	9 09	0 05	8 31	1 10	7 23
24 MO	12 06 24	+1 10	6 01	18 12	6 00	18 14	5 58	18 16	5 55	18 18	5 51	18 23
83		.9968	none	10 53	0 11	10 28	0 41	9 57	1 26	9 11	2 50	7 45
25 TU	12 06 06	+1 34	6 00	18 12	5 58	18 14	5 56	18 17	5 53	18 20	5 48	18 26
84	01 51 LQ	.9971	0 49	11 51	1 14	11 25	1 47	10 52	2 36	10 03	4 11	8 28
26 WE	12 05 48	+1 57	5 59	18 13	5 57	18 15	5 55	18 18	5 51	18 22	5 45	18 28
85		.9974	1 46	12 50	2 12	12 25	2 44	11 53	3 31	11 07	5 02	9 37
27 TH	12 05 29	+2 21	5 58	18 13	5 56	18 15	5 53	18 19	5 49	18 23	5 42	18 30
86		.9977	2 39	13 48	3 02	13 26	3 32	12 58	4 14	12 17	5 30	11 03
28 FR	12 05 11	+2 44	5 58	18 13	5 55	18 16	5 51	18 20	5 47	18 25	5 39	18 33
87		.9980	3 25	14 45	3 45	14 26	4 10	14 03	4 45	13 30	5 44	12 34
29 SA	12 04 53	+3 08	5 57	18 13	5 54	18 17	5 50	18 21	5 44	18 26	5 36	18 35
88		.9983	4 07	15 39	4 22	15 25	4 42	15 08	5 09	14 43	5 52	14 04
30 SU	12 04 35	+3 31	5 56	18 14	5 52	18 17	5 48	18 22	5 42	18 28	5 33	18 38
89		.9985	4 44	16 30	4 55	16 21	5 09	16 10	5 28	15 54	5 57	15 30
31 MO	12 04 17	+3 54	5 55	18 14	5 51	18 18	5 47	18 23	5 40	18 30	5 30	18 40
90		.9988	5 19	17 20	5 25	17 16	5 33	17 11	5 44	17 04	6 00	16 52

APRIL 2003

4th Month **30 days**

Coordinated Universal Time (Greenwich Mean Time)

NOTE: For rising and setting each day, numbers on first line indicate Sun; numbers on second line indicate Moon.
Degrees are North Latitude.

Moon Phases: FM = Full Moon; LQ = Last (Waning) Quarter; NM = New Moon; FQ = First (Waxing) Quarter

Sun's distance is in Astronomical Units

CAUTION: Must be converted to local time. For instructions see "Calculation of Rise Times," page 674.

Day of month, of week, of year	Sun on Meridian / Moon Phase (h m s)	Sun's Declination (° ′) / Distance	20° Rise Sun / Moon (h m)	20° Set Sun / Moon (h m)	30° Rise Sun / Moon (h m)	30° Set Sun / Moon (h m)	40° Rise Sun / Moon (h m)	40° Set Sun / Moon (h m)	50° Rise Sun / Moon (h m)	50° Set Sun / Moon (h m)	60° Rise Sun / Moon (h m)	60° Set Sun / Moon (h m)
1 TU	12 03 59	+4 18	5 54	18 14	5 50	18 18	5 45	18 24	5 38	18 31	5 27	18 43
91	19 18 NM	.9991	5 51	18 09	5 53	18 09	5 55	18 10	5 58	18 11	6 02	18 13
2 WE	12 03 42	+4 41	5 53	18 14	5 49	18 19	5 43	18 25	5 36	18 33	5 24	18 45
92		.9994	6 23	18 57	6 20	19 02	6 17	19 09	6 12	19 18	6 05	19 33
3 TH	12 03 24	+5 04	5 52	18 15	5 48	18 20	5 42	18 26	5 34	18 34	5 21	18 48
93		.9997	6 55	19 46	6 48	19 56	6 39	20 08	6 26	20 26	6 07	20 53
4 FR	12 03 06	+5 27	5 52	18 15	5 46	18 20	5 40	18 27	5 31	18 36	5 18	18 50
94		1.0000	7 29	20 35	7 17	20 50	7 02	21 08	6 42	21 34	6 10	22 16
5 SA	12 02 49	+5 50	5 51	18 15	5 45	18 21	5 39	18 28	5 29	18 37	5 15	18 52
95		1.0003	8 05	21 27	7 49	21 45	7 28	22 09	7 00	22 43	6 15	23 40
6 SU	12 02 32	+6 13	5 50	18 16	5 44	18 21	5 37	18 29	5 27	18 39	5 12	18 55
96		1.0006	8 44	22 19	8 24	22 42	7 59	23 10	7 23	23 51	6 23	none
7 MO	12 02 15	+6 35	5 49	18 16	5 43	18 22	5 35	18 30	5 25	18 41	5 09	18 57
97		1.0008	9 28	23 13	9 04	23 38	8 35	none	7 53	none	6 37	1 05
8 TU	12 01 58	+6 58	5 48	18 16	5 42	18 23	5 34	18 31	5 23	18 42	5 06	19 00
98		1.0011	10 16	none	9 51	none	9 18	0 09	8 32	0 55	7 02	2 24
9 WE	12 01 42	+7 20	5 47	18 16	5 41	18 23	5 32	18 32	5 21	18 44	5 03	19 02
99	23 40 FQ	1.0014	11 08	0 07	10 43	0 33	10 10	1 06	9 22	1 54	7 48	3 28
10 TH	12 01 25	+7 43	5 46	18 17	5 39	18 24	5 31	18 33	5 19	18 45	5 00	19 05
100		1.0017	12 05	1 00	11 40	1 25	11 09	1 56	10 24	2 43	8 58	4 10
11 FR	12 01 09	+8 05	5 46	18 17	5 38	18 24	5 29	18 34	5 17	18 47	4 57	19 07
101		1.0020	13 04	1 50	12 43	2 13	12 16	2 41	11 37	3 22	10 28	4 33
12 SA	12 00 54	+8 27	5 45	18 17	5 37	18 25	5 28	18 35	5 14	18 48	4 54	19 10
102		1.0022	14 05	2 38	13 47	2 57	13 26	3 20	12 56	3 53	12 06	4 46
13 SU	12 00 38	+8 49	5 44	18 18	5 36	18 26	5 26	18 36	5 12	18 50	4 51	19 12
103		1.0025	15 06	3 22	14 54	3 36	14 39	3 54	14 19	4 17	13 47	4 54
14 MO	12 00 23	+9 11	5 43	18 18	5 35	18 26	5 25	18 37	5 10	18 51	4 48	19 15
104		1.0028	16 07	4 05	16 01	4 14	15 54	4 24	15 44	4 38	15 28	4 59
15 TU	12 00 08	+9 32	5 42	18 18	5 34	18 27	5 23	18 38	5 08	18 53	4 45	19 17
105		1.0031	17 09	4 46	17 09	4 49	17 10	4 52	17 10	4 57	17 11	5 03
16 WE	11 59 53	+9 54	5 42	18 18	5 33	18 28	5 22	18 39	5 06	18 55	4 42	19 19
106	19 35 FM	1.0034	18 12	5 28	18 19	5 25	18 27	5 21	18 38	5 15	18 56	5 07
17 TH	11 59 39	+ 10 15	5 41	18 19	5 32	18 28	5 20	18 40	5 04	18 56	4 39	19 22
107		1.0036	19 17	6 11	19 30	6 02	19 46	5 50	20 08	5 35	20 44	5 11
18 FR	11 59 26	+ 10 36	5 40	18 19	5 31	18 29	5 19	18 41	5 02	18 58	4 36	19 24
108		1.0039	20 24	6 57	20 42	6 42	21 05	6 23	21 38	5 58	22 35	5 17
19 SA	11 59 12	+ 10 57	5 39	18 19	5 29	18 29	5 17	18 42	5 00	18 59	4 33	19 27
109		1.0042	21 31	7 47	21 54	7 27	22 23	7 02	23 05	6 26	none	5 26
20 SU	11 58 59	+ 11 18	5 39	18 20	5 28	18 30	5 16	18 43	4 58	19 01	4 30	19 29
110		1.0045	22 37	8 42	23 03	8 18	23 36	7 47	none	7 04	0 23	5 44
21 MO	11 58 47	+ 11 39	5 38	18 20	5 27	18 31	5 14	18 44	4 56	19 02	4 27	19 32
111		1.0048	23 39	9 41	none	9 15	none	8 41	0 24	7 53	1 58	6 17
22 TU	11 58 34	+ 11 59	5 37	18 20	5 26	18 31	5 13	18 45	4 54	19 04	4 25	19 34
112		1.0050	none	10 41	0 05	10 16	0 38	9 43	1 27	8 54	3 03	7 19
23 WE	11 58 23	+ 12 19	5 36	18 21	5 25	18 32	5 11	18 46	4 52	19 06	4 22	19 37
113	12 18 LQ	1.0053	0 35	11 42	0 59	11 18	1 30	10 48	2 15	10 05	3 38	8 44
24 TH	11 58 12	+ 12 39	5 36	18 21	5 24	18 33	5 10	18 47	4 50	19 07	4 19	19 39
114		1.0056	1 24	12 40	1 46	12 20	2 12	11 55	2 50	11 19	3 55	10 17
25 FR	11 58 01	+ 12 59	5 35	18 21	5 23	18 33	5 09	18 48	4 48	19 09	4 16	19 42
115		1.0059	2 08	13 35	2 25	13 20	2 46	13 00	3 16	12 33	4 04	11 48
26 SA	11 57 51	+ 13 19	5 34	18 22	5 22	18 34	5 07	18 49	4 47	19 10	4 13	19 44
116		1.0061	2 46	14 27	2 59	14 17	3 14	14 03	3 36	13 45	4 09	13 15
27 SU	11 57 41	+ 13 38	5 34	18 22	5 21	18 34	5 06	18 50	4 45	19 12	4 10	19 47
117		1.0064	3 21	15 17	3 29	15 11	3 39	15 04	3 52	14 54	4 12	14 39
28 MO	11 57 32	+ 13 57	5 33	18 22	5 20	18 35	5 05	18 51	4 43	19 13	4 08	19 49
118		1.0067	3 54	16 06	3 57	16 05	4 01	16 04	4 06	16 02	4 15	15 59
29 TU	11 57 24	+ 14 16	5 32	18 23	5 19	18 36	5 03	18 52	4 41	19 15	4 05	19 52
119		1.0069	4 26	16 54	4 24	16 58	4 22	17 02	4 20	17 09	4 17	17 19
30 WE	11 57 16	+ 14 35	5 32	18 23	5 19	18 36	5 02	18 53	4 39	19 16	4 02	19 54
120		1.0072	4 57	17 42	4 51	17 51	4 44	18 01	4 34	18 16	4 19	18 39

MAY 2003

5th Month **31 days**

Coordinated Universal Time (Greenwich Mean Time)

NOTE: For rising and setting each day, numbers on first line indicate Sun; numbers on second line indicate Moon.

Degrees are North Latitude.

Moon Phases: FM = Full Moon; LQ = Last (Waning) Quarter; NM = New Moon; FQ = First (Waxing) Quarter

Sun's distance is in Astronomical Units

CAUTION: Must be converted to local time. For instructions see "Calculation of Rise Times," page 674.

Day of month, of week, of year	Sun on Meridian / Moon Phase	Sun's Declination ° ′ / Distance	20° Rise Sun/Moon	20° Set Sun/Moon	30° Rise Sun/Moon	30° Set Sun/Moon	40° Rise Sun/Moon	40° Set Sun/Moon	50° Rise Sun/Moon	50° Set Sun/Moon	60° Rise Sun/Moon	60° Set Sun/Moon
	h m s		h m	h m	h m	h m	h m	h m	h m	h m	h m	h m
1 TH	11 57 08	+ 14 53	5 31	18 23	5 18	18 37	5 01	18 54	4 37	19 18	3 59	19 57
121	12 14 NM	1.0075	5 30	18 31	5 20	18 45	5 07	19 01	4 49	19 24	4 22	20 01
2 FR	11 57 01	+ 15 11	5 31	18 24	5 17	18 38	5 00	18 55	4 36	19 19	3 57	19 59
122		1.0077	6 05	19 22	5 50	19 40	5 32	20 02	5 06	20 33	4 26	21 25
3 SA	11 56 54	+ 15 29	5 30	18 24	5 16	18 38	4 58	18 56	4 34	19 21	3 54	20 02
123		1.0080	6 44	20 15	6 24	20 36	6 01	21 03	5 27	21 42	4 32	22 51
4 SU	11 56 48	+ 15 47	5 29	18 24	5 15	18 39	4 57	18 57	4 32	19 23	3 51	20 04
124		1.0002	7 26	21 08	7 03	21 32	6 35	22 03	5 54	22 48	4 43	none
5 MO	11 56 43	+ 16 04	5 29	18 25	5 14	18 40	4 56	18 58	4 30	19 24	3 49	20 07
125		1.0084	8 12	22 02	7 47	22 28	7 15	23 01	6 30	23 49	5 03	0 13
6 TU	11 56 38	+ 16 21	5 28	18 25	5 13	18 40	4 55	18 59	4 29	19 26	3 46	20 09
126		1.0087	9 03	22 55	8 37	23 20	8 04	23 53	7 15	none	5 40	1 24
7 WE	11 56 34	+ 16 38	5 28	18 26	5 13	18 41	4 54	19 00	4 27	19 27	3 43	20 12
127		1.0089	9 57	23 45	9 32	none	9 00	none	8 13	0 40	6 42	2 12
8 TH	11 56 30	+ 16 55	5 27	18 26	5 12	18 42	4 52	19 01	4 25	19 29	3 41	20 14
128		1.0091	10 54	none	10 31	0 09	10 02	0 39	9 21	1 22	8 04	2 40
9 FR	11 56 27	+ 17 11	5 27	18 26	5 11	18 42	4 51	19 02	4 24	19 30	3 38	20 16
129	11 53 FQ	1.0094	11 53	0 32	11 34	0 53	11 10	1 19	10 36	1 55	9 38	2 56
10 SA	11 56 24	+ 17 27	5 26	18 27	5 10	18 43	4 50	19 03	4 22	19 32	3 36	20 19
130		1.0096	12 51	1 17	12 37	1 33	12 19	1 53	11 55	2 21	11 15	3 05
11 SU	11 56 22	+ 17 43	5 26	18 27	5 10	18 44	4 49	19 04	4 21	19 33	3 33	20 21
131		1.0099	13 50	1 58	13 42	2 10	13 31	2 23	13 16	2 42	12 53	3 10
12 MO	11 56 21	+ 17 59	5 25	18 28	5 09	18 44	4 48	19 05	4 19	19 34	3 31	20 24
132		1.0101	14 50	2 39	14 47	2 44	14 44	2 51	14 39	3 00	14 31	3 14
13 TU	11 56 20	+ 18 14	5 25	18 28	5 08	18 45	4 47	19 06	4 18	19 36	3 28	20 26
133		1.0103	15 51	3 19	15 58	3 18	16 04	3 18	16 04	3 18	16 12	3 17
14 WE	11 56 19	+ 18 28	5 25	18 28	5 08	18 45	4 46	19 07	4 16	19 37	3 26	20 28
134		1.0105	16 54	4 00	17 03	3 54	17 15	3 46	17 31	3 36	17 57	3 21
15 TH	11 56 20	+ 18 43	5 24	18 29	5 07	18 46	4 45	19 08	4 15	19 39	3 24	20 31
135		1.0107	18 00	4 44	18 15	4 32	18 35	4 17	19 02	3 57	19 47	3 25
16 FR	11 56 20	+ 18 57	5 24	18 29	5 06	18 47	4 44	19 09	4 13	19 40	3 21	20 33
136	03 36 FM	1.0109	19 08	5 32	19 29	5 14	19 55	4 52	20 33	4 22	21 40	3 32
17 SA	11 56 22	+ 19 11	5 23	18 30	5 06	18 47	4 43	19 10	4 12	19 41	3 19	20 35
137		1.0112	20 17	6 25	20 41	6 03	21 13	5 35	21 59	4 55	23 27	3 45
18 SU	11 56 23	+ 19 25	5 23	18 30	5 05	18 48	4 43	19 11	4 11	19 43	3 17	20 38
138		1.0114	21 23	7 24	21 49	6 58	22 23	6 26	23 12	5 39	none	4 09
19 MO	11 56 26	+ 19 38	5 23	18 30	5 05	18 49	4 42	19 12	4 09	19 44	3 14	20 40
139		1.0116	22 24	8 26	22 49	7 59	23 22	7 26	none	6 37	0 51	4 58
20 TU	11 56 29	+ 19 51	5 22	18 31	5 04	18 49	4 41	19 13	4 08	19 46	3 12	20 42
140		1.0118	23 18	9 29	23 41	9 04	none	8 32	0 09	7 46	1 39	6 17
21 WE	11 56 32	+ 20 03	5 22	18 31	5 04	18 50	4 40	19 13	4 07	19 47	3 10	20 45
141		1.0120	none	10 30	none	10 08	0 09	9 41	0 50	9 02	2 03	7 52
22 TH	11 56 36	+ 20 16	5 22	18 32	5 03	18 50	4 39	19 14	4 06	19 48	3 08	20 47
142		1.0122	0 05	11 28	0 24	11 11	0 47	10 49	1 20	10 19	2 14	9 27
23 FR	11 56 41	+ 20 27	5 22	18 32	5 03	18 51	4 39	19 15	4 05	19 49	3 06	20 49
143	00 30 LQ	1.0124	0 46	12 22	1 00	12 10	1 18	11 54	1 42	11 33	2 21	10 58
24 SA	11 56 46	+ 20 39	5 21	18 32	5 02	18 52	4 38	19 16	4 04	19 51	3 04	20 51
144		1.0126	1 22	13 13	1 32	13 06	1 44	12 57	2 00	12 44	2 24	12 24
25 SU	11 56 52	+ 20 50	5 21	18 33	5 02	18 52	4 37	19 17	4 03	19 52	3 02	20 53
145		1.0128	1 56	14 03	2 01	14 00	2 07	13 57	2 15	13 52	2 27	13 46
26 MO	11 56 58	+ 21 01	5 21	18 33	5 01	18 53	4 37	19 18	4 02	19 53	3 00	20 55
146		1.0130	2 28	14 51	2 28	14 53	2 28	14 56	2 28	15 00	2 29	15 05
27 TU	11 57 05	+ 21 11	5 21	18 34	5 01	18 53	4 36	19 19	4 01	19 54	2 58	20 57
147		1.0132	2 59	15 39	2 55	15 46	2 49	15 55	2 42	16 06	2 31	16 25
28 WE	11 57 12	+ 21 21	5 21	18 34	5 01	18 54	4 35	19 19	4 00	19 55	2 57	20 59
148		1.0133	3 32	16 28	3 23	16 39	3 11	16 54	2 56	17 14	2 33	17 46
29 TH	11 57 19	+ 21 31	5 20	18 34	5 00	18 55	4 35	19 20	3 59	19 57	2 55	21 01
149		1.0135	4 06	17 18	3 52	17 34	3 36	17 54	3 13	18 23	2 37	19 10
30 FR	11 57 28	+ 21 40	5 20	18 35	5 00	18 55	4 34	19 21	3 58	19 58	2 53	21 03
150		1.0137	4 43	18 10	4 25	18 30	4 03	18 56	3 33	19 32	2 42	20 36
31 SA	11 57 36	+ 21 49	5 20	18 35	5 00	18 56	4 34	19 22	3 57	19 59	2 52	21 05
151	04 19 NM	1.0138	5 24	19 03	5 03	19 27	4 36	19 57	3 57	20 40	2 51	22 00

JUNE 2003

6th Month **30 days**

Coordinated Universal Time (Greenwich Mean Time)

NOTE: For rising and setting each day, numbers on first line indicate Sun; numbers on second line indicate Moon.

Degrees are North Latitude.

Moon Phases: FM = Full Moon; LQ = Last (Waning) Quarter; NM = New Moon; FQ = First (Waxing) Quarter

Sun's distance is in Astronomical Units

CAUTION: Must be converted to local time. For instructions see "Calculation of Rise Times," page 674.

Day of month, of week, of year	Sun on Meridian / Moon Phase (h m s)	Sun's Declination (° ′) / Distance	20° Rise Sun/Moon (h m)	20° Set Sun/Moon (h m)	30° Rise Sun/Moon (h m)	30° Set Sun/Moon (h m)	40° Rise Sun/Moon (h m)	40° Set Sun/Moon (h m)	50° Rise Sun/Moon (h m)	50° Set Sun/Moon (h m)	60° Rise Sun/Moon (h m)	60° Set Sun/Moon (h m)
1 SU	11 57 45	+ 21 58	5 20	18 36	5 00	18 56	4 33	19 22	3 56	20 00	2 50	21 07
152		1.0140	6 09	19 58	5 45	20 23	5 14	20 56	4 30	21 43	3 08	23 16
2 MO	11 57 54	+ 22 06	5 20	18 36	4 59	18 57	4 33	19 23	3 56	20 01	2 49	21 08
153		1.0141	6 59	20 51	6 33	21 17	6 00	21 50	5 13	22 38	3 39	none
3 TU	11 58 04	+ 22 14	5 20	18 36	4 59	18 57	4 33	19 24	3 55	20 02	2 47	21 10
154		1.0143	7 53	21 42	7 27	22 07	6 54	22 38	6 07	23 23	4 33	0 12
4 WE	11 58 14	+ 22 21	5 20	18 37	4 59	18 58	4 32	19 24	3 54	20 03	2 46	21 12
155		1.0144	8 49	22 30	8 25	22 52	7 55	23 19	7 11	23 58	5 50	0 46
5 TH	11 58 24	+ 22 29	5 20	18 37	4 59	18 58	4 32	19 25	3 54	20 04	2 45	21 13
156		1.0146	9 46	23 15	9 26	23 33	9 00	23 55	8 24	none	7 20	1 04
6 FR	11 58 35	+ 22 35	5 20	18 37	4 59	18 59	4 32	19 26	3 53	20 05	2 43	21 15
157		1.0147	10 44	23 57	10 28	none	10 08	none	9 41	0 25	8 55	1 15
7 SA	11 58 46	+ 22 41	5 20	18 38	4 59	18 59	4 31	19 26	3 53	20 05	2 42	21 16
158	20 27 FQ	1.0148	11 42	none	11 31	0 10	11 17	0 26	10 59	0 47	10 30	1 21
8 SU	11 58 58	+ 22 47	5 20	18 38	4 58	19 00	4 31	19 27	3 52	20 06	2 41	21 18
159		1.0149	12 39	0 36	12 34	0 44	12 27	0 53	12 19	1 06	12 05	1 25
9 MO	11 59 09	+ 22 53	5 20	18 39	4 58	19 00	4 31	19 27	3 52	20 07	2 40	21 19
160		1.0151	13 37	1 15	13 38	1 17	13 38	1 19	13 39	1 23	13 41	1 28
10 TU	11 59 21	+ 22 58	5 20	18 39	4 58	19 01	4 31	19 28	3 51	20 08	2 39	21 20
161		1.0152	14 37	1 53	14 43	1 50	14 51	1 46	15 03	1 40	15 21	1 31
11 WE	11 59 33	+ 23 02	5 20	18 39	4 58	19 01	4 31	19 29	3 51	20 08	2 39	21 21
162		1.0153	15 39	2 34	15 52	2 25	16 07	2 14	16 29	1 59	17 05	1 35
12 TH	11 59 45	+ 23 07	5 20	18 40	4 58	19 01	4 31	19 29	3 51	20 09	2 38	21 22
163		1.0154	16 45	3 19	17 03	3 04	17 26	2 46	17 58	2 20	18 54	1 40
13 FR	11 59 57	+ 23 10	5 20	18 40	4 58	19 02	4 31	19 29	3 51	20 10	2 37	21 23
164		1.0155	17 53	4 09	18 16	3 49	18 45	3 23	19 27	2 48	20 45	1 49
14 SA	12 00 10	+ 23 14	5 20	18 40	4 58	19 02	4 31	19 30	3 50	20 10	2 37	21 24
165	11 15 FM	1.0156	19 01	5 04	19 27	4 40	20 00	4 10	20 48	3 26	22 23	2 06
15 SU	12 00 22	+ 23 17	5 20	18 40	4 58	19 02	4 31	19 30	3 50	20 11	2 36	21 25
166		1.0157	20 06	6 05	20 32	5 39	21 05	5 06	21 54	4 17	23 31	2 41
16 MO	12 00 35	+ 23 19	5 21	18 41	4 59	19 03	4 31	19 31	3 50	20 11	2 36	21 25
167		1.0158	21 05	7 09	21 29	6 44	22 00	6 11	22 44	5 23	none	3 47
17 TU	12 00 48	+ 23 22	5 21	18 41	4 59	19 03	4 31	19 31	3 50	20 12	2 36	21 26
168		1.0159	21 56	8 13	22 17	7 50	22 43	7 21	23 19	6 38	0 05	5 19
18 WE	12 01 01	+ 23 23	5 21	18 41	4 59	19 03	4 31	19 31	3 50	20 12	2 36	21 27
169		1.0160	22 41	9 15	22 57	8 56	23 17	8 32	23 45	7 57	0 22	6 58
19 TH	12 01 14	+ 23 25	5 21	18 41	4 59	19 04	4 31	19 32	3 50	20 12	2 36	21 27
170		1.0161	23 20	10 12	23 32	9 58	23 46	9 40	none	9 15	0 30	8 34
20 FR	12 01 27	+ 23 26	5 21	18 42	4 59	19 04	4 31	19 32	3 50	20 13	2 36	21 27
171		1.0161	23 55	11 06	none	10 57	none	10 45	0 05	10 29	0 35	10 03
21 SA	12 01 40	+ 23 26	5 21	18 42	4 59	19 04	4 31	19 32	3 51	20 13	2 36	21 28
172	14 45 LQ	1.0162	none	11 57	0 02	11 52	0 10	11 47	0 21	11 40	0 38	11 28
22 SU	12 01 53	+ 23 26	5 22	18 42	5 00	19 04	4 31	19 32	3 51	20 13	2 36	21 28
173		1.0163	0 28	12 46	0 30	12 46	0 32	12 47	0 35	12 48	0 40	12 49
23 MO	12 02 06	+ 23 26	5 22	18 42	5 00	19 04	4 32	19 33	3 51	20 13	2 36	21 28
174		1.0164	1 00	13 34	0 57	13 39	0 54	13 46	0 49	13 55	0 42	14 09
24 TU	12 02 19	+ 23 25	5 22	18 43	5 00	19 05	4 32	19 33	3 51	20 13	2 37	21 28
175		1.0164	1 33	14 23	1 25	14 33	1 16	14 45	1 03	15 03	0 44	15 30
25 WE	12 02 32	+ 23 24	5 22	18 43	5 00	19 05	4 32	19 33	3 52	20 13	2 37	21 28
176		1.0165	2 06	15 12	1 54	15 27	1 39	15 45	1 19	16 11	0 47	16 53
26 TH	12 02 45	+ 23 23	5 23	18 43	5 01	19 05	4 33	19 33	3 52	20 13	2 38	21 28
177		1.0165	2 42	16 04	2 26	16 23	2 05	16 46	1 37	17 20	0 52	18 18
27 FR	12 02 57	+ 23 21	5 23	18 43	5 01	19 05	4 33	19 33	3 53	20 13	2 38	21 27
178		1.0166	3 22	16 57	3 01	17 19	2 36	17 48	2 00	18 29	1 00	19 44
28 SA	12 03 10	+ 23 19	5 23	18 43	5 01	19 05	4 33	19 33	3 53	20 13	2 39	21 27
179		1.0166	4 06	17 51	3 42	18 16	3 12	18 48	2 30	19 34	1 14	21 04
29 SU	12 03 22	+ 23 16	5 23	18 43	5 02	19 05	4 34	19 33	3 54	20 13	2 40	21 26
180	18 38 NM	1.0166	4 54	18 46	4 29	19 12	3 56	19 45	3 09	20 33	1 39	22 08
30 MO	12 03 34	+ 23 13	5 24	18 43	5 02	19 05	4 34	19 33	3 54	20 13	2 41	21 26
181		1.0167	5 47	19 38	5 21	20 04	4 48	20 35	4 00	21 22	2 25	22 49

JULY 2003

7th Month **31 days**

Coordinated Universal Time (Greenwich Mean Time)

NOTE: For rising and setting each day, numbers on first line indicate Sun; numbers on second line indicate Moon. Degrees are North Latitude.

Moon Phases: FM = Full Moon; LQ = Last (Waning) Quarter; NM = New Moon; FQ = First (Waxing) Quarter

Sun's distance is in Astronomical Units

CAUTION: Must be converted to local time. For instructions see "Calculation of Rise Times," page 674.

			20°		30°		40°		50°		60°	
Day of month, of week, of year	Sun on Meridian / Moon Phase h m s	Sun's Declination ° ′ / Distance	Rise Sun / Moon h m	Set Sun / Moon h m	Rise Sun / Moon h m	Set Sun / Moon h m	Rise Sun / Moon h m	Set Sun / Moon h m	Rise Sun / Moon h m	Set Sun / Moon h m	Rise Sun / Moon h m	Set Sun / Moon h m
1 TU	12 03 46	+ 23 09	5 24	18 43	5 02	19 05	4 35	19 33	3 55	20 13	2 42	21 25
182		1.0167	6 43	20 28	6 19	20 51	5 48	21 19	5 03	22 00	3 37	23 11
2 WE	12 03 58	+ 23 05	5 24	18 43	5 03	19 05	4 35	19 33	3 55	20 12	2 43	21 24
183		1.0167	7 41	21 14	7 20	21 33	6 53	21 57	6 14	22 29	5 05	23 24
3 TH	12 04 09	+ 23 01	5 25	18 44	5 03	19 05	4 36	19 32	3 56	20 12	2 44	21 24
184		1.0167	8 39	21 57	8 22	22 11	8 01	22 29	7 30	22 53	6 39	23 31
4 FR	12 04 20	+ 22 56	5 25	18 44	5 03	19 05	4 36	19 32	3 57	20 12	2 45	21 23
185		1.0167	9 07	22 36	9 25	22 46	9 09	22 57	8 48	23 12	8 15	23 36
5 SA	12 04 31	+ 22 51	5 25	18 44	5 04	19 05	4 37	19 32	3 58	20 11	2 46	21 22
186		1.0167	10 34	23 15	10 27	23 18	10 18	23 23	10 07	23 29	9 49	23 39
6 SU	12 04 41	+ 22 45	5 26	18 44	5 04	19 05	4 37	19 32	3 58	20 11	2 48	21 21
187		1.0167	11 30	23 52	11 29	23 51	11 28	23 49	11 26	23 46	11 23	23 42
7 MO	12 04 51	+ 22 39	5 26	18 44	5 05	19 05	4 38	19 32	3 59	20 10	2 49	21 20
188	02 32 FQ	1.0167	12 28	none	12 32	none	12 38	none	12 46	none	12 58	23 45
8 TU	12 05 00	+ 22 33	5 26	18 44	5 05	19 05	4 38	19 31	4 00	20 10	2 51	21 18
189		1.0167	13 27	0 31	13 38	0 24	13 51	0 15	14 09	0 03	14 37	23 49
9 WE	12 05 10	+ 22 26	5 27	18 43	5 06	19 04	4 39	19 31	4 01	20 09	2 52	21 17
190		1.0167	14 30	1 13	14 46	1 00	15 06	0 44	15 34	0 23	16 21	23 56
10 TH	12 05 18	+ 22 19	5 27	18 43	5 06	19 04	4 40	19 30	4 02	20 08	2 54	21 16
191		1.0166	15 35	1 59	15 56	1 41	16 22	1 18	17 00	0 47	18 08	none
11 FR	12 05 26	+ 22 11	5 27	18 43	5 07	19 04	4 40	19 30	4 03	20 07	2 55	21 14
192		1.0166	16 41	2 50	17 06	2 28	17 37	1 59	18 20	1 10	19 52	0 08
12 SA	12 05 34	+ 22 03	5 28	18 43	5 07	19 04	4 41	19 30	4 04	20 07	2 57	21 13
193		1.0166	17 47	3 48	18 13	3 22	18 47	2 50	19 36	2 03	21 14	0 33
13 SU	12 05 42	+ 21 55	5 28	18 43	5 08	19 03	4 42	19 29	4 05	20 06	2 59	21 11
194	19 21 FM	1.0165	18 48	4 50	19 14	4 24	19 46	3 50	20 33	3 01	22 03	1 23
14 MO	12 05 48	+ 21 46	5 29	18 43	5 08	19 03	4 43	19 29	4 06	20 05	3 01	21 09
195		1.0165	19 44	5 54	20 06	5 30	20 35	4 58	21 15	4 13	22 26	2 44
15 TU	12 05 55	+ 21 37	5 29	18 43	5 09	19 03	4 43	19 28	4 07	20 04	3 03	21 08
196		1.0165	20 32	6 58	20 50	6 36	21 13	6 10	21 45	5 31	22 37	4 23
16 WE	12 06 01	+ 21 28	5 29	18 43	5 09	19 02	4 44	19 27	4 08	20 03	3 05	21 06
197		1.0164	21 14	7 58	21 28	7 41	21 45	7 21	22 08	6 51	22 44	6 02
17 TH	12 06 06	+ 21 18	5 30	18 42	5 10	19 02	4 45	19 27	4 09	20 02	3 07	21 04
198		1.0164	21 52	8 54	22 01	8 43	22 11	8 29	22 25	8 09	22 48	7 37
18 FR	12 06 11	+ 21 08	5 30	18 42	5 10	19 02	4 46	19 26	4 10	20 01	3 09	21 02
199		1.0163	22 26	9 47	22 30	9 41	22 35	9 33	22 41	9 22	22 50	9 05
19 SA	12 06 15	+ 20 58	5 30	18 42	5 11	19 01	4 46	19 26	4 12	20 00	3 11	21 00
200		1.0163	22 59	10 38	22 58	10 37	22 57	10 35	22 55	10 33	22 52	10 29
20 SU	12 06 19	+ 20 47	5 31	18 42	5 12	19 01	4 47	19 25	4 13	19 59	3 13	20 58
201		1.0162	23 32	11 27	23 26	11 31	23 18	11 35	23 09	11 41	22 54	11 51
21 MO	12 06 22	+ 20 36	5 31	18 41	5 12	19 00	4 48	19 24	4 14	19 58	3 15	20 56
202	07 01 LQ	1.0161	none	12 16	23 54	12 24	23 41	12 35	23 24	12 49	22 57	13 12
22 TU	12 06 25	+ 20 24	5 32	18 41	5 13	19 00	4 49	19 23	4 15	19 57	3 17	20 54
203		1.0161	0 05	13 05	none	13 18	none	13 35	23 41	13 58	23 01	14 34
23 WE	12 06 27	+ 20 12	5 32	18 41	5 13	18 59	4 50	19 23	4 16	19 56	3 19	20 52
204		1.0160	0 40	13 56	0 25	14 14	0 06	14 36	none	15 06	23 07	15 59
24 TH	12 06 29	+ 20 00	5 32	18 40	5 14	18 59	4 51	19 22	4 18	19 54	3 21	20 50
205		1.0159	1 18	14 49	0 59	15 10	0 35	15 37	0 02	16 15	23 18	17 24
25 FR	12 06 30	+ 19 47	5 33	18 40	5 15	18 58	4 52	19 21	4 19	19 53	3 23	20 48
206		1.0158	2 00	15 43	1 37	16 07	1 09	16 38	0 29	17 22	23 38	18 47
26 SA	12 06 30	+ 19 34	5 33	18 40	5 15	18 58	4 52	19 20	4 20	19 52	3 26	20 46
207		1.0157	2 47	16 37	2 22	17 03	1 50	17 36	1 04	18 24	none	19 59
27 SU	12 06 30	+ 19 21	5 33	18 39	5 16	18 57	4 53	19 19	4 22	19 50	3 28	20 43
208		1.0156	3 39	17 31	3 13	17 57	2 40	18 29	1 51	19 17	0 16	20 48
28 MO	12 06 29	+ 19 08	5 34	18 39	5 16	18 56	4 54	19 18	4 23	19 49	3 30	20 41
209		1.0155	4 34	18 22	4 09	18 46	3 37	19 16	2 50	19 59	1 19	21 16
29 TU	12 06 28	+ 18 54	5 34	18 39	5 17	18 56	4 55	19 17	4 24	19 48	3 33	20 39
210	06 52 NM	1.0154	5 33	19 10	5 10	19 31	4 41	19 56	4 00	20 32	2 45	21 32
30 WE	12 06 26	+ 18 40	5 35	18 38	5 17	18 55	4 56	19 16	4 26	19 46	3 35	20 36
211		1.0153	6 32	19 55	6 13	20 11	5 50	20 30	5 16	20 57	4 20	21 40
31 TH	12 06 24	+ 18 25	5 35	18 38	5 18	18 54	4 57	19 15	4 27	19 45	3 37	20 34
212		1.0153	7 31	20 36	7 17	20 47	7 00	21 00	6 36	21 18	5 57	21 45

AUGUST 2003

8th Month **31 days**

Coordinated Universal Time (Greenwich Mean Time)

NOTE: For rising and setting each day, numbers on first line indicate Sun; numbers on second line indicate Moon. Degrees are North Latitude.

Moon Phases: FM = Full Moon; LQ = Last (Waning) Quarter; NM = New Moon; FQ = First (Waxing) Quarter

Sun's distance is in Astronomical Units

CAUTION: Must be converted to local time. For instructions see "Calculation of Rise Times," page 674.

Day of month, of week, of year	Sun on Meridian / Moon Phase h m s	Sun's Declination ° ′ / Distance	20° Rise Sun / Moon h m	20° Set Sun / Moon h m	30° Rise Sun / Moon h m	30° Set Sun / Moon h m	40° Rise Sun / Moon h m	40° Set Sun / Moon h m	50° Rise Sun / Moon h m	50° Set Sun / Moon h m	60° Rise Sun / Moon h m	60° Set Sun / Moon h m
1 FR	12 06 20	+ 18 10	5 35	18 37	5 19	18 54	4 58	19 14	4 29	19 43	3 40	20 31
213		1.0151	8 29	21 15	8 20	21 21	8 10	21 27	7 56	21 36	7 33	21 49
2 SA	12 06 17	+ 17 55	5 36	18 37	5 19	18 53	4 59	19 13	4 30	19 42	3 42	20 29
214		1.0149	9 26	21 53	9 23	21 53	9 20	21 53	9 15	21 52	9 08	21 52
3 SU	12 06 12	+ 17 40	5 36	18 36	5 20	18 52	5 00	19 12	4 31	19 40	3 44	20 26
215		1.0148	10 23	22 31	10 26	22 26	10 30	22 19	10 35	22 09	10 43	21 55
4 MO	12 06 07	+ 17 24	5 36	18 36	5 21	18 51	5 01	19 11	4 33	19 38	3 47	20 24
216		1.0147	11 22	23 12	11 31	23 00	11 41	22 46	11 57	22 28	12 21	21 58
5 TU	12 06 02	+ 17 09	5 37	18 35	5 21	18 51	5 02	19 10	4 34	19 37	3 49	20 21
217	07 27 FQ	1.0145	12 22	23 55	12 37	23 39	12 55	23 18	13 20	22 50	14 02	22 04
6 WE	12 05 55	+ 16 52	5 37	18 35	5 22	18 50	5 03	19 09	4 36	19 35	3 51	20 19
218		1.0144	13 25	none	13 44	none	14 09	23 56	14 44	23 18	15 46	22 13
7 TH	12 05 48	+ 16 36	5 37	18 34	5 22	18 49	5 03	19 08	4 37	19 33	3 54	20 16
219		1.0142	14 29	0 43	14 53	0 22	15 23	none	16 07	23 56	17 29	22 32
8 FR	12 05 41	+ 16 19	5 38	18 33	5 23	18 48	5 04	19 06	4 39	19 32	3 56	20 13
220		1.0141	15 34	1 37	16 00	1 13	16 33	0 41	17 22	none	18 59	23 09
9 SA	12 05 33	+ 16 02	5 38	18 33	5 24	18 47	5 05	19 05	4 40	19 30	3 59	20 11
221		1.0139	16 36	2 36	17 02	2 10	17 35	1 37	18 24	0 47	19 59	none
10 SU	12 05 24	+ 15 45	5 38	18 32	5 24	18 46	5 06	19 04	4 42	19 28	4 01	20 08
222		1.0137	17 32	3 39	17 56	3 13	18 27	2 41	19 10	1 53	20 30	0 18
11 MO	12 05 15	+ 15 27	5 39	18 32	5 25	18 45	5 07	19 03	4 43	19 27	4 03	20 05
223		1.0136	18 23	4 42	18 43	4 19	19 09	3 50	19 44	3 08	20 45	1 51
12 TU	12 05 05	+ 15 10	5 39	18 31	5 25	18 44	5 08	19 01	4 44	19 25	4 06	20 03
224	04 48 FM	1.0134	19 08	5 43	19 23	5 24	19 43	5 01	20 10	4 28	20 52	3 30
13 WE	12 04 54	+ 14 52	5 39	18 30	5 26	18 44	5 09	19 00	4 46	19 23	4 08	20 00
225		1.0132	19 47	6 41	19 58	6 28	20 11	6 10	20 29	5 47	20 57	5 08
14 TH	12 04 44	+ 14 33	5 40	18 30	5 26	18 43	5 10	18 59	4 47	19 21	4 11	19 57
226		1.0131	20 23	7 36	20 29	7 28	20 36	7 17	20 45	7 02	21 00	6 39
15 FR	12 04 32	+ 14 15	5 40	18 29	5 27	18 42	5 11	18 57	4 49	19 19	4 13	19 54
227		1.0129	20 57	8 28	20 58	8 25	20 58	8 21	21 00	8 15	21 02	8 06
16 SA	12 04 20	+ 13 56	5 40	18 28	5 28	18 41	5 12	18 56	4 50	19 17	4 15	19 52
228		1.0127	21 30	9 18	21 25	9 20	21 20	9 22	21 14	9 25	21 04	9 30
17 SU	12 04 08	+ 13 37	5 40	18 28	5 28	18 40	5 13	18 55	4 52	19 15	4 18	19 49
229		1.0125	22 02	10 08	21 54	10 15	21 43	10 23	21 28	10 34	21 06	10 52
18 MO	12 03 54	+ 13 18	5 41	18 27	5 29	18 39	5 14	18 53	4 53	19 13	4 20	19 46
230		1.0123	22 37	10 57	22 23	11 09	22 07	11 23	21 44	11 43	21 09	12 14
19 TU	12 03 41	+ 12 59	5 41	18 26	5 29	18 38	5 15	18 52	4 55	19 12	4 23	19 43
231		1.0121	23 14	11 48	22 56	12 04	22 34	12 24	22 03	12 52	21 14	13 38
20 WE	12 03 27	+ 12 39	5 41	18 25	5 30	18 37	5 16	18 50	4 56	19 10	4 25	19 40
232	00 48 LQ	1.0120	23 54	12 39	23 32	12 59	23 05	13 25	22 28	14 01	21 22	15 04
21 TH	12 03 13	+ 12 20	5 42	18 25	5 31	18 35	5 17	18 49	4 58	19 08	4 27	19 37
233		1.0118	none	13 33	none	13 56	23 43	14 26	22 59	15 09	21 37	16 29
22 FR	12 02 58	+ 12 00	5 42	18 24	5 31	18 34	5 18	18 48	4 59	19 06	4 30	19 34
234		1.0116	0 38	14 27	0 14	14 52	none	15 25	23 41	16 13	22 06	17 46
23 SA	12 02 42	+ 11 39	5 42	18 23	5 32	18 33	5 19	18 46	5 01	19 04	4 32	19 32
235		1.0114	1 28	15 21	1 02	15 47	0 29	16 20	none	17 09	22 59	18 45
24 SU	12 02 27	+ 11 19	5 42	18 22	5 32	18 32	5 20	18 45	5 02	19 02	4 35	19 29
236		1.0112	2 22	16 13	1 56	16 38	1 23	17 09	0 35	17 55	none	19 20
25 MO	12 02 11	+ 10 59	5 43	18 21	5 33	18 31	5 21	18 43	5 04	19 00	4 37	19 26
237		1.0110	3 19	17 03	2 55	17 25	2 25	17 52	1 41	18 31	0 17	19 39
26 TU	12 01 54	+ 10 38	5 43	18 21	5 33	18 30	5 22	18 42	5 05	18 58	4 39	19 23
238		1.0107	4 19	17 49	3 58	18 07	3 32	18 29	2 55	18 59	1 50	19 49
27 WE	12 01 37	+ 10 17	5 43	18 20	5 34	18 29	5 22	18 40	5 07	18 55	4 42	19 20
239	17 26 NM	1.0105	5 19	18 32	5 03	18 45	4 43	19 01	4 15	19 22	3 29	19 55
28 TH	12 01 20	+9 56	5 43	18 19	5 34	18 28	5 23	18 39	5 08	18 53	4 44	19 17
240		1.0103	6 18	19 12	6 08	19 20	5 55	19 29	5 37	19 41	5 08	19 59
29 FR	12 01 02	+9 35	5 44	18 18	5 35	18 27	5 24	18 37	5 10	18 51	4 47	19 14
241		1.0101	7 17	19 51	7 12	19 53	7 07	19 55	6 59	19 58	6 46	20 02
30 SA	12 00 44	+9 14	5 44	18 17	5 36	18 25	5 25	18 35	5 11	18 49	4 49	19 11
242		1.0098	8 16	20 30	8 17	20 26	8 19	20 21	8 21	20 15	8 24	20 05
31 SU	12 00 26	+8 52	5 44	18 17	5 36	18 24	5 26	18 34	5 13	18 47	4 51	19 08
243		1.0096	9 15	21 11	9 23	21 01	9 31	20 49	9 44	20 33	10 03	20 08

SEPTEMBER 2003

9th Month **30 days**

Coordinated Universal Time (Greenwich Mean Time)

NOTE: For rising and setting each day, numbers on first line indicate Sun; numbers on second line indicate Moon. Degrees are North Latitude.

Moon Phases: FM = Full Moon; LQ = Last (Waning) Quarter; NM = New Moon; FQ = First (Waxing) Quarter

Sun's distance is in Astronomical Units

CAUTION: Must be converted to local time. For instructions see "Calculation of Rise Times," page 674.

Day of month, of week, of year	Sun on Meridian / Moon Phase h m s	Sun's Declination ° ′ / Distance	20° Rise Sun / Moon h m	20° Set Sun / Moon h m	30° Rise Sun / Moon h m	30° Set Sun / Moon h m	40° Rise Sun / Moon h m	40° Set Sun / Moon h m	50° Rise Sun / Moon h m	50° Set Sun / Moon h m	60° Rise Sun / Moon h m	60° Set Sun / Moon h m
1 MO	12 00 07	+8 31	5 44	18 16	5 37	18 23	5 27	18 32	5 14	18 45	4 54	19 05
244		1.0094	10 16	21 54	10 29	21 38	10 45	21 19	11 08	20 54	11 45	20 12
2 TU	11 59 48	+8 09	5 44	18 15	5 37	18 22	5 28	18 31	5 16	18 43	4 56	19 02
245		1.0091	11 19	22 41	11 37	22 20	12 00	21 55	12 33	21 20	13 30	20 20
3 WE	11 59 28	+7 47	5 45	18 14	5 38	18 21	5 29	18 29	5 17	18 41	4 58	18 59
246	12 34 FQ	1.0089	12 23	23 32	12 46	23 08	13 15	22 38	13 57	21 54	15 15	20 34
4 TH	11 59 09	+7 25	5 45	18 13	5 38	18 20	5 30	18 28	5 19	18 39	5 01	18 56
247		1.0086	13 27	none	13 53	none	14 26	23 30	15 14	22 40	16 50	21 03
5 FR	11 58 49	+7 03	5 45	18 12	5 39	18 18	5 31	18 26	5 20	18 36	5 03	18 53
248		1.0084	14 29	0 29	14 55	0 03	15 29	none	16 19	23 40	17 59	22 01
6 SA	11 58 29	+6 41	5 45	18 11	5 39	18 17	5 32	18 24	5 22	18 34	5 06	18 50
249		1.0081	15 26	1 30	15 51	1 03	16 23	0 30	17 09	none	18 36	23 26
7 SU	11 58 08	+6 18	5 46	18 10	5 40	18 16	5 33	18 23	5 23	18 32	5 08	18 47
250		1.0079	16 18	2 32	16 39	2 07	17 07	1 37	17 46	0 52	18 54	none
8 MO	11 57 48	+5 56	5 46	18 10	5 40	18 15	5 34	18 21	5 25	18 30	5 10	18 44
251		1.0076	17 03	3 32	17 21	3 12	17 43	2 46	18 13	2 09	19 03	1 04
9 TU	11 57 27	+5 33	5 46	18 09	5 41	18 13	5 35	18 19	5 26	18 28	5 13	18 41
252		1.0074	17 44	4 31	17 57	4 15	18 12	3 55	18 34	3 28	19 07	2 42
10 WE	11 57 06	+5 11	5 46	18 08	5 42	18 12	5 36	18 18	5 28	18 26	5 15	18 38
253	16 36 FM	1.0071	18 21	5 26	18 28	5 16	18 38	5 02	18 51	4 44	19 10	4 15
11 TH	11 56 45	+4 48	5 46	18 07	5 42	18 11	5 37	10 10	5 20	18 23	5 17	18 35
254		1.0068	18 55	6 19	18 58	6 14	19 01	6 07	19 05	5 58	19 12	5 43
12 FR	11 56 24	4 25	5 47	18 06	5 43	18 10	5 38	18 15	5 31	18 21	5 20	18 32
255		1.0066	19 28	7 10	19 26	7 10	19 23	7 10	19 19	7 09	19 14	7 08
13 SA	11 56 02	+4 02	5 47	18 05	5 43	18 08	5 39	18 13	5 32	18 19	5 22	18 29
256		1.0063	20 01	8 00	19 53	8 05	19 45	8 11	19 33	8 19	19 16	8 31
14 SU	11 55 41	+3 39	5 47	18 04	5 44	18 07	5 39	18 11	5 34	18 17	5 24	18 26
257		1.0061	20 34	8 49	20 22	8 59	20 08	9 11	19 48	9 28	19 18	9 54
15 MO	11 55 20	+3 16	5 47	18 03	5 44	18 06	5 40	18 10	5 35	18 15	5 27	18 23
258		1.0058	21 10	9 40	20 54	9 54	20 34	10 12	20 06	10 37	19 21	11 18
16 TU	11 54 58	+2 53	5 47	18 02	5 45	18 05	5 41	18 08	5 37	18 12	5 29	18 20
259		1.0055	21 49	10 31	21 28	10 50	21 03	11 13	20 28	11 47	19 28	12 44
17 WE	11 54 37	+2 30	5 48	18 01	5 45	18 03	5 42	18 06	5 38	18 10	5 31	18 17
260		1.0053	22 31	11 23	22 08	11 46	21 38	12 14	20 55	12 55	19 39	14 10
18 TH	11 54 16	+2 07	5 48	18 00	5 46	18 02	5 43	18 05	5 40	18 08	5 34	18 13
261	19 02 LQ	1.0050	23 18	12 17	22 52	12 42	22 20	13 14	21 32	14 01	20 00	15 32
19 FR	11 53 54	+1 44	5 48	17 59	5 46	18 01	5 44	18 03	5 41	18 06	5 36	18 10
262		1.0047	none	13 10	23 43	13 37	23 10	14 10	22 20	15 00	20 41	16 39
20 SA	11 53 33	+1 20	5 48	17 59	5 47	18 00	5 45	18 01	5 43	18 04	5 38	18 07
263		1.0045	+0 10	14 03	none	14 29	none	15 01	23 20	15 49	21 48	17 23
21 SU	11 53 12	+0 57	5 48	17 58	5 47	17 58	5 46	18 00	5 44	18 01	5 41	18 04
264		1.0042	1 05	14 53	0 40	15 16	0 07	15 46	none	16 29	23 16	17 46
22 MO	11 52 50	+0 34	5 49	17 57	5 48	17 57	5 47	17 58	5 46	17 59	5 43	18 01
265		1.0039	2 03	15 40	1 40	16 00	1 12	16 25	0 31	17 00	none	17 59
23 TU	11 52 29	+0 11	5 49	17 56	5 49	17 56	5 48	17 56	5 47	17 57	5 45	17 58
266		1.0036	3 02	16 24	2 44	16 39	2 21	16 58	1 48	17 24	0 53	18 05
24 WE	11 52 08	-0 13	5 49	17 55	5 49	17 55	5 49	17 55	5 49	17 55	5 48	17 55
267		1.0034	4 02	17 06	3 49	17 16	3 32	17 28	3 10	17 44	2 33	18 10
25 TH	11 51 48	-0 36	5 49	17 54	5 50	17 53	5 50	17 53	5 50	17 53	5 50	17 52
268		1.0031	5 02	17 46	4 54	17 50	4 45	17 55	4 32	18 02	4 13	18 12
26 FR	11 51 27	-1 00	5 50	17 53	5 50	17 52	5 51	17 51	5 52	17 50	5 52	17 49
269	03 09 NM	1.0028	6 02	18 25	6 00	18 24	5 58	18 22	5 56	18 19	5 53	18 15
27 SA	11 51 07	-1 23	5 50	17 52	5 51	17 51	5 52	17 50	5 53	17 48	5 55	17 46
270		1.0025	7 02	19 06	7 07	18 58	7 13	18 49	7 21	18 37	7 34	18 17
28 SU	11 50 46	-1 46	5 50	17 51	5 51	17 50	5 53	17 48	5 55	17 46	5 57	17 43
271		1.0022	8 04	19 49	8 15	19 35	8 29	19 19	8 48	18 56	9 18	18 21
29 MO	11 50 26	-2 10	5 50	17 50	5 52	17 49	5 54	17 46	5 56	17 44	6 00	17 40
272		1.0019	9 09	20 36	9 25	20 17	9 46	19 53	10 16	19 21	11 06	18 27
30 TU	11 50 07	-2 33	5 51	17 49	5 52	17 47	5 55	17 45	5 58	17 42	6 02	17 37
273		1.0017	10 14	21 27	10 36	21 04	11 04	20 35	11 43	19 53	12 56	18 38

OCTOBER 2003

10th Month **31 days**

Coordinated Universal Time (Greenwich Mean Time)

NOTE: For rising and setting each day, numbers on first line indicate Sun; numbers on second line indicate Moon.

Degrees are North Latitude.

Moon Phases: FM = Full Moon; LQ = Last (Waning) Quarter; NM = New Moon; FQ = First (Waxing) Quarter

Sun's distance is in Astronomical Units

CAUTION: Must be converted to local time. For instructions see "Calculation of Rise Times," page 674.

Day of month, of week, of year	Sun on Meridian / Moon Phase h m s	Sun's Declination ° ′ / Distance	20° Rise Sun / Moon h m	20° Set Sun / Moon h m	30° Rise Sun / Moon h m	30° Set Sun / Moon h m	40° Rise Sun / Moon h m	40° Set Sun / Moon h m	50° Rise Sun / Moon h m	50° Set Sun / Moon h m	60° Rise Sun / Moon h m	60° Set Sun / Moon h m
1 WE	11 49 47	-2 56	5 51	17 49	5 53	17 46	5 56	17 43	5 59	17 39	6 04	17 34
274		1.0014	11 20	22 24	11 45	21 58	12 18	21 24	13 05	20 36	14 39	19 01
2 TH	11 49 28	-3 20	5 51	17 48	5 54	17 45	5 57	17 42	6 01	17 37	6 07	17 31
275	19 09 FQ	1.0011	12 24	23 24	12 50	22 57	13 25	22 23	14 15	21 32	15 59	19 49
3 FR	11 49 09	-3 43	5 51	17 47	5 54	17 44	5 58	17 40	6 02	17 35	6 09	17 28
276		1.0008	13 23	none	13 49	none	14 22	23 28	15 10	22 41	16 44	21 08
4 SA	11 48 50	-4 06	5 51	17 46	5 55	17 42	5 59	17 38	6 04	17 33	6 11	17 25
277		1.0005	14 16	0 25	14 39	0 00	15 08	none	15 50	23 57	17 05	22 44
5 SU	11 48 32	-4 29	5 52	17 45	5 55	17 41	6 00	17 37	6 05	17 31	6 14	17 22
278		1.0002	15 02	1 26	15 21	1 04	15 45	0 37	16 19	none	17 14	none
6 MO	11 48 14	-4 52	5 52	17 44	5 56	17 40	6 01	17 35	6 07	17 29	6 16	17 19
279		.9999	15 44	2 25	15 58	2 07	16 16	1 45	16 41	1 14	17 20	0 22
7 TU	11 47 56	-5 15	5 52	17 43	5 57	17 39	6 02	17 34	6 08	17 27	6 19	17 16
280		.9996	16 21	3 20	16 30	3 08	16 42	2 52	16 58	2 31	17 22	1 56
8 WE	11 47 39	-5 38	5 53	17 42	5 57	17 38	6 03	17 32	6 10	17 24	6 21	17 13
281		.9993	16 55	4 13	17 00	4 06	17 05	3 57	17 13	3 44	17 24	3 25
9 TH	11 47 22	-6 01	5 53	17 42	5 58	17 37	6 04	17 30	6 12	17 22	6 23	17 10
282		.9990	17 28	5 04	17 28	5 02	17 27	4 59	17 26	4 56	17 25	4 50
10 FR	11 47 06	-6 24	5 53	17 41	5 58	17 35	6 05	17 29	6 13	17 20	6 26	17 07
283	07 27 FM	.9987	18 00	5 54	17 55	5 57	17 49	6 00	17 40	6 05	17 27	6 13
11 SA	11 46 50	-6 47	5 53	17 40	5 59	17 34	6 06	17 27	6 15	17 18	6 28	17 04
284		.9985	18 34	6 43	18 23	6 51	18 11	7 01	17 54	7 15	17 28	7 36
12 SU	11 46 35	-7 09	5 54	17 39	6 00	17 33	6 07	17 26	6 16	17 16	6 31	17 01
285		.9982	19 08	7 33	18 54	7 46	18 35	8 02	18 11	8 24	17 31	9 00
13 MO	11 46 20	-7 32	5 54	17 38	6 00	17 32	6 08	17 24	6 18	17 14	6 33	16 58
286		.9979	19 46	8 24	19 27	8 41	19 03	9 03	18 30	9 34	17 36	10 25
14 TU	11 46 05	-7 54	5 54	17 38	6 01	17 31	6 09	17 23	6 19	17 12	6 36	16 55
287		.9976	20 27	9 16	20 04	9 37	19 36	10 04	18 55	10 43	17 44	11 52
15 WE	11 45 51	-8 17	5 55	17 37	6 02	17 30	6 10	17 21	6 21	17 10	6 38	16 52
288		.9973	21 12	10 09	20 46	10 33	20 14	11 05	19 28	11 50	18 00	13 17
16 TH	11 45 38	-8 39	5 55	17 36	6 02	17 29	6 11	17 20	6 23	17 08	6 41	16 50
289		.9970	22 01	11 02	21 34	11 28	21 00	12 02	20 11	12 51	18 31	14 31
17 FR	11 45 26	-9 01	5 55	17 35	6 03	17 28	6 12	17 18	6 24	17 06	6 43	16 47
290		.9968	22 54	11 54	22 27	12 21	21 54	12 55	21 05	13 44	19 26	15 24
18 SA	11 45 14	-9 23	5 56	17 35	6 03	17 27	6 13	17 17	6 26	17 04	6 46	16 44
291	12 31 LQ	.9965	23 49	12 44	23 25	13 09	22 55	13 41	22 10	14 27	20 46	15 53
19 SU	11 45 02	9 45	5 56	17 34	6 04	17 26	6 14	17 15	6 27	17 02	6 48	16 41
292		.9962	none	13 32	none	13 54	none	14 21	23 23	15 00	22 18	16 08
20 MO	11 44 51	- 10 06	5 56	17 33	6 05	17 24	6 15	17 14	6 29	17 00	6 51	16 38
293		.9959	0 47	14 16	0 26	14 34	0 00	14 56	none	15 26	23 55	16 16
21 TU	11 44 41	- 10 28	5 57	17 32	6 06	17 23	6 16	17 13	6 31	16 58	6 53	16 35
294		.9957	1 45	14 57	1 29	15 10	1 09	15 26	0 41	15 47	none	16 21
22 WE	11 44 32	- 10 49	5 57	17 32	6 06	17 22	6 17	17 11	6 32	16 56	6 56	16 32
295		.9954	2 43	15 37	2 33	15 45	2 20	15 54	2 02	16 06	1 34	16 24
23 TH	11 44 23	- 11 11	5 57	17 31	6 07	17 21	6 18	17 10	6 34	16 54	6 58	16 30
296		.9951	3 42	16 17	3 38	16 18	3 32	16 20	3 24	16 22	3 12	16 26
24 FR	11 44 15	- 11 32	5 58	17 30	6 08	17 21	6 20	17 08	6 36	16 52	7 01	16 27
297		.9949	4 43	16 57	4 44	16 52	4 46	16 47	4 49	16 39	4 53	16 28
25 SA	11 44 07	- 11 53	5 58	17 30	6 08	17 20	6 21	17 07	6 37	16 50	7 03	16 24
298	12 50 NM	.9946	5 45	17 39	5 52	17 28	6 02	17 15	6 16	16 58	6 37	16 31
26 SU	11 44 01	- 12 13	5 59	17 29	6 09	17 19	6 22	17 06	6 39	16 48	7 06	16 21
299		.9943	6 49	18 25	7 03	18 08	7 21	17 48	7 46	17 20	8 26	16 35
27 MO	11 43 55	- 12 34	5 59	17 29	6 10	17 18	6 23	17 04	6 41	16 47	7 08	16 19
300		.9940	7 57	19 16	8 16	18 54	8 41	18 27	9 17	17 49	10 20	16 43
28 TU	11 43 50	- 12 54	5 59	17 28	6 10	17 17	6 24	17 03	6 42	16 45	7 11	16 16
301		.9938	9 05	20 13	9 30	19 47	10 00	19 15	10 46	18 28	12 12	17 00
29 WE	11 43 45	- 13 14	6 00	17 27	6 11	17 16	6 25	17 02	6 44	16 43	7 13	16 13
302		.9935	10 13	21 14	10 39	20 47	11 14	20 12	12 04	19 21	13 48	17 37
30 TH	11 43 41	- 13 34	6 00	17 27	6 12	17 15	6 26	17 01	6 46	16 41	7 16	16 11
303		.9932	11 16	22 17	11 42	21 51	12 16	21 17	13 06	20 28	14 47	18 48
31 FR	11 43 38	- 13 54	6 01	17 26	6 13	17 14	6 27	16 59	6 47	16 39	7 18	16 08
304		.9930	12 12	23 20	12 37	22 56	13 07	22 27	13 52	21 44	15 14	20 24

NOVEMBER 2003

11th Month **30 days**

Coordinated Universal Time (Greenwich Mean Time)

NOTE: For rising and setting each day, numbers on first line indicate Sun; numbers on second line indicate Moon.

Degrees are North Latitude.

Moon Phases: FM = Full Moon; LQ = Last (Waning) Quarter; NM = New Moon; FQ = First (Waxing) Quarter

Sun's distance is in Astronomical Units

CAUTION: Must be converted to local time. For instructions see "Calculation of Rise Times," page 674.

Day of month, of week, of year	Sun on Meridian / Moon Phase (h m s)	Sun's Declination (° ´) / Distance	20° Rise Sun / Moon (h m)	20° Set Sun / Moon (h m)	30° Rise Sun / Moon (h m)	30° Set Sun / Moon (h m)	40° Rise Sun / Moon (h m)	40° Set Sun / Moon (h m)	50° Rise Sun / Moon (h m)	50° Set Sun / Moon (h m)	60° Rise Sun / Moon (h m)	60° Set Sun / Moon (h m)
1 SA	11 43 36	- 14 13	6 01	17 26	6 13	17 13	6 28	16 58	6 49	16 38	7 21	16 05
305	04 24 FQ	.9927	13 01	none	13 22	none	13 48	23 37	14 24	23 03	15 26	22 04
2 SU	11 43 35	- 14 33	6 02	17 25	6 14	17 13	6 30	16 57	6 50	16 36	7 24	16 03
306		.9924	13 44	0 20	14 01	0 01	14 20	none	14 48	none	15 32	23 40
3 MO	11 43 34	- 14 52	6 02	17 25	6 15	17 12	6 31	16 56	6 52	16 34	7 26	16 00
307		.9922	14 23	1 16	14 34	1 02	14 48	0 44	15 06	0 20	15 35	none
4 TU	11 43 34	- 15 10	6 03	17 24	6 16	17 11	6 32	16 55	6 54	16 33	7 29	15 58
308		.9919	14 57	2 09	15 04	2 01	15 11	1 49	15 21	1 34	15 37	1 10
5 WE	11 43 35	- 15 29	6 03	17 24	6 17	17 10	6 33	16 54	6 55	16 31	7 31	15 55
309		.9916	15 30	3 00	15 31	2 57	15 33	2 52	15 35	2 45	15 38	2 35
6 TH	11 43 37	- 15 47	6 04	17 23	6 17	17 10	6 34	16 53	6 57	16 29	7 34	15 53
310		.9914	16 02	3 50	15 58	3 51	15 54	3 53	15 48	3 55	15 39	3 58
7 FR	11 43 40	- 16 05	6 04	17 23	6 18	17 09	6 35	16 52	6 59	16 28	7 36	15 50
311		.9911	16 35	4 39	16 26	4 45	16 16	4 53	16 02	5 04	15 40	5 20
8 SA	11 43 43	- 16 23	6 05	17 23	6 19	17 08	6 36	16 51	7 00	16 26	7 39	15 48
312		.9909	17 09	5 28	16 55	5 39	16 39	5 53	16 17	6 13	15 42	6 43
9 SU	11 43 48	- 16 40	6 05	17 22	6 20	17 08	6 38	16 50	7 02	16 25	7 42	15 45
313	01 13 FM	.9906	17 45	6 19	17 27	6 35	17 05	6 54	16 35	7 22	15 46	8 08
10 MO	11 43 53	- 16 58	6 06	17 22	6 21	17 07	6 39	16 49	7 04	16 23	7 44	15 43
314		.9904	18 24	7 10	18 03	7 31	17 36	7 56	16 58	8 32	15 53	9 35
11 TU	11 43 59	- 17 15	6 06	17 21	6 21	17 06	6 40	16 48	7 05	16 22	7 47	15 41
315		.9902	19 08	8 03	18 43	8 27	18 12	8 57	17 28	9 40	16 05	11 01
12 WE	11 44 05	- 17 31	6 07	17 21	6 22	17 06	6 41	16 47	7 07	16 21	7 49	15 38
316		.9899	19 56	8 56	19 29	9 22	18 56	9 55	18 07	10 44	16 29	12 21
13 TH	11 44 13	- 17 47	6 07	17 21	6 23	17 05	6 42	16 46	7 09	16 19	7 52	15 36
317		.9897	20 47	9 49	20 20	10 16	19 47	10 50	18 57	11 40	17 15	13 22
14 FR	11 44 22	- 18 03	6 08	17 21	6 24	17 05	6 43	16 45	7 10	16 18	7 54	15 34
318		.9895	21 41	10 39	21 16	11 05	20 44	11 38	19 57	12 26	18 26	13 58
15 SA	11 44 31	- 18 19	6 09	17 20	6 25	17 04	6 45	16 44	7 12	16 17	7 57	15 32
319		.9893	22 37	11 27	22 15	11 50	21 47	12 20	21 06	13 01	19 54	14 17
16 SU	11 44 42	- 18 34	6 09	17 20	6 25	17 04	6 46	16 43	7 14	16 15	7 59	15 29
320		.9891	23 33	12 11	23 15	12 31	22 53	12 55	22 21	13 29	21 27	14 26
17 MO	11 44 53	- 18 49	6 10	17 20	6 26	17 03	6 47	16 43	7 15	16 14	8 02	15 27
321	04 14 LQ	.9888	none	12 52	none	13 07	none	13 26	23 38	13 51	23 02	14 32
18 TU	11 45 05	- 19 04	6 10	17 20	6 27	17 03	6 48	16 42	7 17	16 13	8 04	15 25
322		.9886	0 29	13 31	0 16	13 41	0 00	13 53	none	14 10	none	14 35
19 WE	11 45 18	- 19 19	6 11	17 20	6 28	17 02	6 49	16 41	7 18	16 12	8 07	15 23
323		.9884	1 26	14 09	1 19	14 14	1 09	14 19	0 57	14 26	0 37	14 37
20 TH	11 45 31	- 19 33	6 11	17 19	6 29	17 02	6 50	16 40	7 20	16 11	8 09	15 21
324		.9882	2 24	14 47	2 22	14 46	2 20	14 44	2 17	14 42	2 13	14 39
21 FR	11 45 46	- 19 46	6 12	17 19	6 30	17 02	6 51	16 40	7 22	16 10	8 12	15 19
325		.9880	3 23	15 27	3 27	15 20	3 33	15 11	3 41	14 59	3 53	14 41
22 SA	11 46 01	- 19 59	6 13	17 19	6 30	17 01	6 52	16 39	7 23	16 09	8 14	15 17
326		.9878	4 25	16 11	4 36	15 57	4 49	15 41	5 08	15 19	5 37	14 44
23 SU	11 46 17	- 20 12	6 13	17 19	6 31	17 01	6 54	16 39	7 25	16 08	8 16	15 16
327	22 59 NM	.9876	5 31	16 59	5 48	16 40	6 09	16 17	6 39	15 44	7 29	14 50
24 MO	11 46 34	- 20 25	6 14	17 19	6 32	17 01	6 55	16 38	7 26	16 07	8 19	15 14
328		.9874	6 41	17 54	7 03	17 30	7 31	17 01	8 11	16 18	9 26	15 01
25 TU	11 46 52	- 20 37	6 15	17 19	6 33	17 01	6 56	16 38	7 28	16 06	8 21	15 12
329		.9873	7 51	18 55	8 17	18 29	8 50	17 55	9 38	17 05	11 16	15 26
26 WE	11 47 10	- 20 49	6 15	17 19	6 34	17 00	6 57	16 37	7 29	16 05	8 23	15 11
330		.9871	8 59	20 00	9 26	19 33	10 01	18 59	10 52	18 08	12 37	16 23
27 TH	11 47 30	- 21 00	6 16	17 19	6 35	17 00	6 58	16 37	7 31	16 04	8 25	15 09
331		.9869	10 01	21 06	10 27	20 41	10 59	20 10	11 47	19 24	13 18	17 55
28 FR	11 47 50	- 21 11	6 16	17 19	6 35	17 00	6 59	16 36	7 32	16 03	8 28	15 07
332		.9867	10 55	22 10	11 17	21 49	11 45	21 23	12 25	20 45	13 35	19 38
29 SA	11 48 10	- 21 22	6 17	17 19	6 36	17 00	7 00	16 36	7 33	16 03	8 30	15 06
333		.9865	11 42	23 09	12 00	22 53	12 22	22 33	12 53	22 05	13 43	21 19
30 SU	11 48 31	- 21 32	6 18	17 19	6 37	17 00	7 01	16 36	7 35	16 02	8 32	15 05
334	17 16 FQ	.9863	12 23	none	12 35	23 54	12 51	23 41	13 13	23 22	13 47	22 53

DECEMBER 2003

12th Month **31 days**

Coordinated Universal Time (Greenwich Mean Time)

NOTE: For rising and setting each day, numbers on first line indicate Sun; numbers on second line indicate Moon. Degrees are North Latitude.

Moon Phases: FM = Full Moon; LQ = Last (Waning) Quarter; NM = New Moon; FQ = First (Waxing) Quarter

Sun's distance is in Astronomical Units

CAUTION: Must be converted to local time. For instructions see "Calculation of Rise Times," page 674.

Day of month, of week, of year	Sun on Meridian Moon Phase h m s	Sun's Declination ° ′ Distance	20° Rise Sun Moon h m	20° Set Sun Moon h m	30° Rise Sun Moon h m	30° Set Sun Moon h m	40° Rise Sun Moon h m	40° Set Sun Moon h m	50° Rise Sun Moon h m	50° Set Sun Moon h m	60° Rise Sun Moon h m	60° Set Sun Moon h m
1 MO	11 48 53	- 21 42	6 18	17 19	6 38	17 00	7 02	16 35	7 36	16 01	8 34	15 03
335		.9862	12 59	0 05	13 07	none	13 16	none	13 29	none	13 49	none
2 TU	11 49 16	- 21 51	6 19	17 19	6 39	17 00	7 03	16 35	7 37	16 01	8 36	15 02
336		.9860	13 32	0 57	13 35	0 51	13 39	0 45	13 43	0 35	13 50	0 21
3 WE	11 49 39	- 22 00	6 20	17 20	6 39	17 00	7 04	16 35	7 39	16 00	8 38	15 01
337		.9858	14 04	1 47	14 02	1 46	14 00	1 46	13 56	1 45	13 51	1 44
4 TH	11 50 03	- 22 09	6 20	17 20	6 40	17 00	7 05	16 35	7 40	16 00	8 40	15 00
338		.9857	14 37	2 36	14 30	2 40	14 21	2 46	14 10	2 54	13 52	3 06
5 FR	11 50 27	- 22 17	6 21	17 20	6 41	17 00	7 06	16 35	7 41	15 59	8 42	14 59
339		.9855	15 10	3 25	14 58	3 34	14 44	3 46	14 24	4 03	13 54	4 29
6 SA	11 50 52	- 22 25	6 21	17 20	6 42	17 00	7 07	16 35	7 42	15 59	8 44	14 58
340		.9854	15 45	4 14	15 29	4 29	15 09	4 47	14 41	5 12	13 57	5 52
7 SU	11 51 17	- 22 32	6 22	17 20	6 42	17 00	7 08	16 35	7 44	15 59	8 45	14 57
341		.9852	16 23	5 06	16 03	5 24	15 38	5 48	15 02	6 21	14 03	7 18
8 MO	11 51 43	- 22 39	6 23	17 21	6 43	17 00	7 09	16 35	7 45	15 59	8 47	14 56
342	20 36 FM	.9851	17 06	5 58	16 42	6 21	16 12	6 49	15 30	7 30	14 13	8 45
9 TU	11 52 10	- 22 45	6 23	17 21	6 44	17 00	7 10	16 35	7 46	15 58	8 49	14 55
343		.9850	17 52	6 52	17 26	7 17	16 54	7 49	16 06	8 36	14 32	10 08
10 WE	11 52 36	- 22 51	6 24	17 21	6 45	17 00	7 10	16 35	7 47	15 58	8 50	14 55
344		.9848	18 43	7 45	18 16	8 11	17 42	8 45	16 52	9 35	15 11	11 16
11 TH	11 53 04	- 22 57	6 25	17 22	6 45	17 01	7 11	16 35	7 48	15 58	8 52	14 54
345		.9847	19 36	8 36	19 11	9 02	18 38	9 36	17 50	10 24	16 15	12 00
12 FR	11 53 31	- 23 02	6 25	17 22	6 46	17 01	7 12	16 35	7 49	15 58	8 53	14 54
346		.9846	20 31	9 24	20 08	9 49	19 39	10 19	18 57	11 03	17 38	12 23
13 SA	11 53 59	- 23 06	6 26	17 22	6 47	17 01	7 13	16 35	7 50	15 58	8 54	14 54
347		.9845	21 27	10 09	21 08	10 30	20 43	10 56	20 09	11 33	19 09	12 35
14 SU	11 54 28	- 23 10	6 26	17 23	6 47	17 02	7 14	16 35	7 51	15 58	8 55	14 53
348		.9844	22 22	10 51	22 08	11 07	21 49	11 28	21 24	11 56	20 42	12 42
15 MO	11 54 56	- 23 14	6 27	17 23	6 48	17 02	7 14	16 35	7 52	15 58	8 57	14 53
349		.9843	23 17	11 30	23 08	11 41	22 56	11 56	22 40	12 15	22 14	12 45
16 TU	11 55 25	- 23 17	6 27	17 23	6 49	17 02	7 15	16 36	7 52	15 58	8 58	14 53
350	17 42 LQ	.9842	none	12 06	none	12 13	none	12 21	23 57	12 32	23 46	12 48
17 WE	11 55 54	- 23 20	6 28	17 24	6 49	17 03	7 16	16 36	7 53	15 59	8 59	14 53
351		.9841	0 12	12 43	0 08	12 44	0 03	12 45	none	12 47	none	12 49
18 TH	11 56 24	- 23 22	6 29	17 24	6 50	17 03	7 16	16 36	7 54	15 59	9 00	14 53
352		.9840	1 08	13 20	1 10	13 16	1 12	13 10	1 15	13 03	1 20	12 51
19 FR	11 56 53	- 23 24	6 29	17 25	6 50	17 03	7 17	16 37	7 54	15 59	9 00	14 53
353		.9840	2 07	14 00	2 14	13 50	2 24	13 37	2 37	13 20	2 58	12 54
20 SA	11 57 23	- 23 25	6 30	17 25	6 51	17 04	7 17	16 37	7 55	16 00	9 01	14 54
354		.9839	3 09	14 45	3 22	14 29	3 39	14 09	4 03	13 41	4 43	12 58
21 SU	11 57 53	- 23 26	6 30	17 26	6 51	17 04	7 18	16 38	7 56	16 00	9 02	14 54
355		.9838	4 15	15 35	4 34	15 14	4 58	14 47	5 33	14 10	6 34	13 05
22 MO	11 58 23	- 23 26	6 31	17 26	6 52	17 05	7 19	16 38	7 56	16 01	9 02	14 54
356		.9838	5 24	16 32	5 48	16 07	6 18	15 35	7 03	14 49	8 28	13 21
23 TU	11 58 53	- 23 26	6 31	17 27	6 52	17 05	7 19	16 39	7 57	16 01	9 03	14 55
357	09 43 NM	.9837	6 34	17 36	7 00	17 09	7 34	16 35	8 25	15 44	10 09	14 00
24 WE	11 59 23	- 23 26	6 32	17 27	6 53	17 06	7 19	16 39	7 57	16 02	9 03	14 56
358		.9836	7 40	18 44	8 07	18 18	8 41	17 44	9 31	16 55	11 11	15 16
25 TH	11 59 53	- 23 25	6 32	17 28	6 53	17 06	7 20	16 40	7 57	16 02	9 03	14 56
359		.9836	8 40	19 51	9 04	19 28	9 35	18 59	10 19	18 17	11 39	16 59
26 FR	12 00 23	- 23 23	6 33	17 28	6 54	17 07	7 20	16 41	7 58	16 03	9 04	14 57
360		.9835	9 32	20 54	9 52	20 36	10 17	20 14	10 52	19 41	11 51	18 46
27 SA	12 00 52	- 23 21	6 33	17 29	6 54	17 08	7 21	16 41	7 58	16 04	9 04	14 58
361		.9835	10 17	21 54	10 32	21 41	10 51	21 25	11 16	21 03	11 56	20 27
28 SU	12 01 22	- 23 19	6 33	17 29	6 55	17 08	7 21	16 42	7 58	16 05	9 04	14 59
362		.9834	10 56	22 49	11 06	22 41	11 18	22 32	11 34	22 20	11 59	22 00
29 MO	12 01 51	- 23 16	6 34	17 30	6 55	17 09	7 21	16 43	7 58	16 05	9 03	15 00
363		.9834	11 32	23 41	11 36	23 39	11 42	23 36	11 49	23 32	12 01	23 27
30 TU	12 02 20	- 23 12	6 34	17 31	6 55	17 10	7 21	16 43	7 59	16 06	9 03	15 02
364	10 03 FQ	.9834	12 05	none	12 04	none	12 04	none	12 03	none	12 02	none
31 WE	12 02 49	- 23 09	6 35	17 31	6 55	17 10	7 22	16 44	7 59	16 07	9 03	15 03
365		.9833	12 37	0 31	12 32	0 34	12 25	0 38	12 16	0 43	12 03	0 51

SCIENCE AND TECHNOLOGY

Science News of 2002

Life Sciences news and glossary entries reviewed by Prof. Maura C. Flannery, St. John's Univ., NYC; Physical Sciences news and glossary entries reviewed by Prof. F. Paul Esposito, Univ. of Cincinnati.

The following were some of the more newsworthy developments in Science in the past year. (See also the chapters on Astronomy and Computers and the Internet.)

Life Sciences

• A skull discovered in the African desert in Chad dated back 6-7 million years, making it what some scientists termed **the most important anthropological discovery in 75 years.** The skull, described in the July 11 issue of the journal *Nature*, was found in 2001 by a team of French scientists led by Michel Brunet; only recently had its full importance been realized thanks to the determination of its age by an analysis of other fossils found in the same layers at the site. The nearly complete skull has a braincase similar to a chimpanzee's, but its flat face and fairly small teeth are like those of humans. The skull was nicknamed *Toumai* in the local Goran language, or "hope of life." Scientists noted that besides being much older than other key fossils of human precursors, the skull was also found in a part of Africa quite distant from the region—stretching from southern Africa to the Great Rift Valley—that supplied previous finds. The age and location of the fossil, as well as its combination of ape and human characteristics, lent support to the idea that human evolution did not proceed in a linear fashion, but took many divergent paths. Anthropologist Bernard Wood said this new view "predicts that because of the independent acquisition of similar shared characters, key hominid adaptations such as bipedalism, manual dexterity and a large brain are likely to have evolved more than once." Henry Gee, an editor at *Nature*, observed that paleoanthropology was about to enter "a period of chaos... [in which researchers will] discover all sorts of weird fossils from places we've never looked at before."

• Scientists in the U.S., Canada, and England **mapped** almost all of the genetic material, or **genome, of the mouse.** Describing their work in the Aug. 4 online edition of *Nature*, they claimed to have sequenced about 98% of the genome. Simon Gregory, one of the scientists leading the effort at the Wellcome Trust Sanger Institute in England, said it could benefit attempts to understand the human genome, which is about the same size and contains many of the same genes as the mouse genome. The function of many genes—in both mice and humans—is unknown; to determine what these genes do scientists could create so-called "knockout mice," in which a given gene is either activated or prevented from acting. Since in many cases the mice and human genes act in the same way, the experiments on mice could yield valuable insights for understanding human biology.

• **A gene linked to language ability was found to be alike in humans and chimpanzees,** except for just 2 subunits out of 715, according to a study described in the Aug. 14 online edition of *Nature*. The scientists, led by Svante Paabo of the Max Planck Institute for Evolutionary Anthropology in Leipzig, Germany, focused on FOXP2, which in 2001 had been identified as playing a role in language, the 1st gene to be so recognized. (Scientists had been led to FOXP2 by studying a large family in London, many members of which suffered from profound speech defects although not from other problems.) Paabo's team of researchers looked at the FOXP2 gene in humans, chimpanzees, mice and several other species of mammals. (The gene differs in only 3 subunits between mice and humans. Genetic research, however, has frequently shown that apparently small differences have major consequences.) The change in 2 subunits between the human version and the chimpanzee version apparently resulted in humans having a much finer degree of control over muscles in the face, throat and voice box. The report in *Nature* said evidence indicated that the mutations giving rise to the human variant of the gene probably had occurred fairly recently—within the last 200,000 years—and then spread throughout the human species in some 500 to 1,000 human generations (about 10,000 to 20,000 years). In evolutionary terms this meant the mutated gene became fixed quickly in the population, indicating it offered considerable evolutionary advantages to those born with it. The scientists noted that many other genes probably also played an important role in language ability.

• Separate teams of scientists in the U.S. and China published **maps of the genome of the rice plant** in the Apr. 5 issue of *Science,* revealing that rice has more genes than humans—perhaps 50,000 or more, compared with only 30,000 to 40,000 for humans. The U.S. researchers—led by Steven Briggs and Stephen Goff—were associated with an agricultural company called Syngenta International Inc., while the Chinese researchers, based in an institute in Beijing, were headed by Huanming Yang. It was hoped that the research would lead to the development of new rice varieties that produce higher yields without exhausting the soil. The map of rice's genome might also aid in improving other cereal grains, scientists believed.

• Scientists at the Australian Museum in Sydney said May 28 they had **re-created genes of the Tasmanian Tiger, a now-extinct marsupial** that had stripes like a tiger but ran like a wolf. The animal is also known as a thylacine. Mike Archer, director of the museum, said the scientists used DNA taken from a female pup preserved in alcohol 130 years ago. He described the achievement as a major step on the way to the goal of cloning the thylacine. "What was once an impossible dream has taken a giant step closer to becoming biological reality," Archer said, contending that a clone could be implanted in a Tasmanian Devil, a close relative of the tiger, within a decade. The last known Tasmanian Tiger died in a zoo in 1936.

• A combination of **childhood abuse and low activity of a certain gene** affecting brain chemistry apparently **increases the likelihood that men will engage in violent criminal activity**, according to a study that appeared in the Aug. 2 issue of *Science*. The study traced 442 New Zealand males over 26 years. The gene provides instructions for the assembly of a protein called monoamine oxidase A (MAOA); earlier research had indicated that MAOA breaks down brain chemicals (neurotransmitters) associated with aggressive behavior. Of the men studied, 279 had normally active MAOA while 163 had low levels of activity. Some 36% of the men were considered to have suffered either "severe" or "probable" maltreatment as children, including rejection by the mother or frequent changes in primary caregivers as well as physical or sexual abuse. Out of the 442 men, 12% had both low levels of MAOA activity and childhood maltreatment, and these 12% accounted for 44% of the convictions for violent crime in the group. Terrie Moffit, a psychologist at the Univ. of Wisconsin, Madison, and co-author of the study, said 85% of the men who both suffered severe childhood abuse and had low MAOA activity "developed anti-social outcomes, such as violent criminal behavior," while men abused as children with normal MAOA activity were not more likely to engage in violence than men who had not been abused.

• Scientists **created a synthetic virus from scratch in a lab,** using the genome sequence for polio, according to research published July 11 in the online version of *Science*. The researchers obtained the genetic sequence of polio's DNA from a public site on the Internet, and then pieced it together using chemicals obtained from a science mail-order house. Small changes were introduced into the synthetic virus as a signature to mark it as distinct from the natural form of polio, and these changes had the unexpected effect of making it less potent. Still, the lab-created polio paralyzed and killed the mice it was injected into for test purposes, although larger doses were required than with natural polio. Eckard Wimmer, leader of the team of researchers at the Stony Brook campus of the State Univ. of New York, said "the reason we did it was to prove that it can be done and is now a reality." One motive behind the work was to dramatize the potential for terrorists to create deadly viruses using new technology, he said. But he added that at present very few people have the necessary technical know-how. Still, the research called into question the efficacy of destroying remaining stockpiles of deadly viruses such as smallpox, since the virus could be re-created using the published knowledge of its genetic sequence. (The smallpox virus was considerably more complicated than polio, and so would be correspondingly more difficult to recreate.) Some scientists questioned whether the research should have been done or published, voicing concern that it might aid terrorists.

• Using electrodes implanted in the pleasure center and other parts of the brains of rats, scientists at the State Univ. of New York were able to train the rodents to follow "virtual" cues delivered by radio signals, so that in effect the **rodents could be guided by remote control,** according to research published May 2 in *Nature*. After training, the rats were able to successfully negotiate a laboratory obstacle course under their controllers' guidance; then they carried out similar maneuvers outdoors. The so-called "robo-rats," which were equipped with tiny video cameras, might be used for search-and-rescue missions in places too cramped or dangerous for humans or dogs, the scientists said; espionage and other exotic uses were also possible. Rats have advantages over tiny robots, being more agile and possessing a native intelligence that often outstrips the artificial intelligence of robots.

• Catherine Verfaillie and colleagues at the Univ. of Minnesota **isolated cells from adults that apparently had** many of the **qualities of embryonic stem cells.** The cells, which they termed MAPCs—for mesenchymal adult progenitor cells—were able to multiply in a culture medium, according to research published in *Nature*'s online version June 20. Verfaillie said that her lab had isolated MAPCs from the bone marrow of adult animals. When implanted in a mouse embryo, the cells could transform into most, if not all, of the different kinds of cells in the body, including cell types found in the spine, brain, kidney, guts, uterus, and skin. Verfaillie's lab injected into early-stage mouse embryos MAPCs tagged with blue dye (so the MAPCs-descended cells could be identified), and found that some of the embryos grew into animals that were 40% derived from the adult stem cells. Given the debate over the use of embryonic stem cells, many observers were excited by the thought that adult cells might offer similar therapeutic possibilities. Verfaillie herself endorsed continued research on embryonic stem cells, as well as on the adult cells.

Physical Sciences

• Physicists in Grenoble, France, found **evidence of quantum gravitational states,** according to a report in the journal *Nature* Jan. 17. The scientists, led by Valery Nesvizhevsky of the Institut Laue-Langevin, shot a beam of ultracold neutrons through an apparatus designed to isolate the neutrons from forces other than gravity. The beam of slowed neutrons was allowed to bounce upward off a mirror. Neutron absorbers placed above the mirror found that the neutrons existed only at certain discrete heights—wherever the upward energy of motion (kinetic energy) the neutrons got from bouncing off the mirror was precisely balanced by the downward force of gravity. If gravity did not exhibit quantum behavior, the experimenters would have observed neutrons at all different heights between the mirror and a maximum level, not just at a few discrete levels. The energies involved were minute, and this was what made the effect difficult to observe.

• The **mystery of missing solar neutrinos has been put to rest,** according to an announcement Apr. 20 by researchers using data collected by the Sudbury Neutrino Observatory in Ontario, Canada. Neutrinos are subatomic particles with no electric charge. They were also originally considered to have no mass, though the latest theory ascribes a very small amount of mass to them. The lack of charge and virtual lack of mass have made neutrinos very difficult to detect. The Sudbury facility employed a tank of heavy water (water in which the hydrogen atoms have an extra neutron) placed in a cave deep underground, so as to be isolated from contaminating influences. Theories of how the Sun produces its energy through fusion reactions indicate that it should produce so-called electron neutrinos, but efforts on Earth to detect these solar neutrinos had found fewer than the predicted number. Consequently, scientists wondered if their understanding of fusion in the Sun was wrong. Alternatively, it was theorized that some of these neutrinos changed their "flavor" en route to the Earth, electron neutrinos turning into muon- or tau-neutrinos. Earlier research had supported this hypothesis of a flavor change, and the data gathered by the Sudbury researchers afforded conclusive confirmation. The Sudbury facility detected all 3 flavors of neutrinos in the predicted amounts.

• Scientists at the Australian National Univ. **"teleported" a beam of laser light,** physically disassembling it in one part of their laboratory and recreating it in another place about a meter away, according to reports June 17. The accomplishment, evoking thoughts of *Star Trek* characters getting "beamed up," relied on a phenomenon known as quantum entanglement. A radio signal, encoded in the beam of light that was destroyed, was preserved in the "teleported" beam. Ping Koy Lam, who led the team of researchers, said the experiment demonstrated "that we can take billions of photons, destroy them simultaneously, and then recreate them in another place." Lam said the accomplishment could provide a way of ensuring secure transmission of data by computers. But he conceded that any idea of teleporting humans still appeared impossible, given the astronomical amount of information that would be involved.

• Scientists at CERN, Center for European Nuclear Research, in Geneva, Switzerland, claimed Sept. 18 to have **produced significant quantities of anti-hydrogen atoms.** Antimatter particles are the predicted mirror images of normal particles, having opposite electric charge and spin to their normal counterparts (e.g., a positron, the antimatter equivalent of an electron, has positive electric charge). Isolated antimatter particles had been produced in the past, but the Athena group at CERN said they have produced more than 50,000 anti-hydrogen atoms. Sufficient amounts of antimatter would allow physicists to conduct experiments to test some of the basic predictions of the current reigning "Standard Model" and possibly resolve some of the most enigmatic problems of cosmology.

• Experiments at the Stanford (CA) Linear Accelerator Center and at the KEK laboratory in Japan, described at a physics conference in the Netherlands July 25, offered insight into a question physicists have sought to answer for years: **why does matter predominate over antimatter in the universe?** The so-called Standard Model in physics explains this through an effect called Charge Parity (CP) violation, involving B-meson particles and their antimatter counterparts. The "violation" refers to a departure from perfect symmetry, and it was this lack of symmetry that allowed matter, originally created in the same amount as antimatter, to win out over its opposite a tiny fraction of a second after the Big Bang. Experiments at the Stanford Lab had by 2001 offered strong evidence for the existence of CP violation; the new data gave physicists a much better read on a fundamental parameter—called sine 2 beta—that related to the asymmetry between matter and antimatter. The new data, while confirming beyond doubt the reality of CP violation, also indicated that the effect could not on its own explain the excess of matter over antimatter. "Something else happened in addition to CP violation to create the excess of matter that became stars, planets, and living creatures," said Hassan Jawahery, physics coordinator of the Stanford experiments.

• Experimenters at the Australian National Univ. in Canberra and Griffith Univ. in Brisbane established that, **over a short time period, nano-machines can violate the 2nd law of thermodynamics.** They came to this conclusion in a paper published in the July 29 issue of *Physical Review Letters*. The 2nd law says that, for an enclosed system, disorder increases; for example, it is impossible to use the heat energy in a glass of water—that is, the energy of the molecules of water jiggling around—to run a machine and leave behind a cooler glass of water, or perhaps just ice. That would clearly violate the 2nd law. The 2nd law is admittedly regarded as a statistical law, which applies with perfect accuracy only when vast numbers of atoms are involved (objects on a human scale involve trillions of particles). The Australian experiment involved the movement of a tiny bead (micron-sized, or about 1/4000 inch wide) through water. A laser was used to position the bead—in effect, pulling the bead. But even though the bead was tiny, millions of atoms were still involved. In the experiment, friction—the 2nd law in effect—would usually resist the movement of the bead, but sometimes (although not for more than 2 seconds at a time) the water would push the bead in the direction it was being pulled, in effect extracting heat from the water to do work, in apparent violation of the second law. Scientists voiced surprise at the result. Researchers said it meant the new field of nano-technology might have to take into account unusual phenomena that could make nano-machines run backwards for brief periods. Denis Evans, one of the researchers, indicated there might also be implications for biology, since many life processes involve systems on similar size scales as those in the experiment.

• Scientists at Rice Univ. in Houston ***produced solitons in a Bose-Einstein condensate (BEC),*** according to a paper published in *Nature* May 9. The researchers, led by Randall Hulet, created a BEC out of lithium atoms cooled to near absolute zero by a process using lasers and evaporation. In a BEC, many atoms occupy the same quantum state, forming a sort of "super-atom." A BEC thus can be considered as a single atom wave. Solitons are groups of waves combining to form a single composite wave that can travel a long way without losing its shape; solitons can be found in all kinds of waves—not just quantum atom waves—and in fact were first observed on a canal in Scotland. The atom wave of the BEC usually spreads out or "disperses" soon after the BEC is released from its magnetic trap (a magnetic field which confines the atoms of the BEC in a given area), but the solitons the Rice researchers created maintained their shape for several seconds—a relative eternity for quantum phenomena! Scientists think the new techniques being developed with BECs may someday allow the creation of measuring instruments more precise than those now existing.

Science Glossary

This glossary covers some basic concepts, and others that come up frequently in the news, in biology, chemistry, geology, and physics. *See also* Astronomy, Computers and Internet, Environment, Health, Meteorology, Weights and Measures.

Biology

For classification terms such as *kingdom, phylum,* etc., see Environment chapter.

Amino acid: one of about 20 similar small molecules that are the building blocks of proteins.

Antibiotic: a drug made from a substance produced by a bacterium, fungus, or other organism that battles bacterial infections and diseases, killing the bacteria or halting their growth.

Autoimmunity: a condition in which an individual's immune system reacts against his or her own tissues; leads to diseases such as lupus, diabetes, inflammatory bowel disease, rheumatoid arthritis.

Bacterium (plural, bacteria): one of a large, varied class of microscopic and simple, single-celled organisms, bacteria live almost everywhere—some forms cause disease, while others are useful in digestion and other natural processes.

Biodiversity: richness of variety of life forms—both plant and animal—in a given environment.

Cell: the smallest unit of life capable of living independently, or with other cells; usually bounded by a membrane; may include a nucleus and other specialized parts.

Cholesterol: a fatty substance in animal tissues; it is produced by the liver in humans, and is found in foods such as butter, eggs, and meat, and is an essential body constituent.

Chromosome: one of the rod-like structures in the nuclei of cells that carry genetic material (DNA); humans have 46 chromosomes.

Cloning: the process of copying a particular piece of DNA to allow it to be sequenced, studied, or used in some other way; can also refer to producing a genetic copy of an organism.

DNA (deoxyribonucleic acid): the chemical substance that carries genetic information, which determines the form and functioning of all living things.

Ecosystem: an interdependent community of living organisms and their climatic and geographical habitat.

Enzyme: a protein that promotes a particular chemical reaction in the body.

Estrogen: one of a group of hormones that promote development of female secondary sex characteristics and the growth and health of the female reproductive system; males also produce small amounts of estrogen.

Evolution: the process of gradual change that may occur as a species adapts to its environment; natural selection is the process by which evolution occurs.

Fight-or-flight response: the physical response that occurs in all animals when they encounter a threat; bodies release hormones, such as cortisol and epinephrine, that speed up the heart rate and increase blood flow to the muscles, allowing animals to fight enemies or run away.

Gene: a portion of a DNA molecule that provides the blueprint for the assembly of a protein.

Gene pool: the collection and total diversity of genes in an interbreeding population.

Gene therapy: a treatment in which scientists try to implant functioning genes into a person's cells so the genes can produce proteins that the person lacks or that help the person fight disease.

Genetic sequencing: the process of determining the order of subunits within a gene or even the order of all genes for an organism.

Genome: the complete set of an organism's genetic material.

Hormone: a substance secreted in one part of an organism that regulates the functioning of other tissues or organs.

Metabolism: the sum total of the body's chemical processes providing energy for vital functions, and enabling new material to be synthesized.

Neuron: a nerve cell, of the type found in the brain or spinal cord, that sends electrical and chemical messages to other cells.

Nucleus (plural: nuclei): the center of an atom; or the portion of a cell containing the chemical directions for functioning.

Organism: a living being.

Phenotype: the observable properties and characteristics of an organism arising at least in part from its genetic makeup.

Pheromone: a chemical secreted by an animal to influence the behavior of other members of its own species.

Placebo effect: a phenomenon in which patients show improvements even though they have taken a medically inactive substance, called a placebo.

Protein: a complex molecule made up of one or more chains of amino acids; essential to the structure and function of all cells.

RNA (ribonucleic acid): a complex molecule similar to the genetic material DNA, but usually single-stranded; several forms of RNA translate the genetic code of DNA and use that code to assemble proteins for structural and biological functions in the body.

Species: a population of organisms that breed with each other in nature and produce fertile offspring; other definitions of species exist to accommodate the diversity of life on Earth.

Stem cell: a cell that can give rise to other types of cells; for instance, bone marrow stem cells divide and produce different types of blood cells.

Steroid: type of hormone that freely enters cells (other hormones bind to cell surfaces); different varieties can suppress immune response or influence stress reaction, blood pressure, or sexual development; includes testosterone- and estrogen-related compounds.

Testosterone: a hormone that stimulates the development and maintenance of male sexual characteristics and the production of sperm; women also produce small amounts of testosterone.

Virus: a microscopic, often disease-causing, organism made of genetic material surrounded by a protein shell; can only reproduce inside a living cell.

Chemistry

Acid: a class of compound that contrasts with bases. Acids taste sour, turn litmus red/pink, and often produce hydrogen gas in contact with some metals. Acids donate protons (hydrogen atoms minus the electron) in chemical reactions.

Base: a substance that yields hydroxyl ions (OH-) when dissolved in water; any of a class of compounds whose aqueous solutions taste bitter, feel slippery, turn litmus blue, and react with acids to form salts; also known as **alkaline.**

Carbon fiber: an extremely strong, thin fiber made by pyrolyzing (decomposing by heat) synthetic fibers, such as rayon, until charred; used to make high-strength composites

Chlorofluorocarbon (CFC): one of a group of industrial chemicals that contain chlorine, fluorine, and carbon and have been found to damage Earth's ozone layer.

Element: a substance that cannot be chemically decomposed into simpler substances; the atoms of an element all have the same number of protons and electrons.

Isotope: an atom of a chemical element with the same number of protons in its nucleus as other atoms of that element, but with a different number of neutrons.

Molecule: the basic unit of a chemical compound, composed of two or more atoms bound together.

Osmosis: the transfer of a fluid from an area of higher concentration to an area of lower concentration, usually through a membrane.

Phase: any of the possible states of matter—solid, liquid, gas, or plasma—that change according to temperature and pressure.

Polymer: a huge molecule containing hundreds or thousands of smaller molecules arranged in repeating units.

Salt: a neutral compound produced by the reaction of an acid and a base.

Geology

Fault, tectonic: a crack or break in Earth's crust, often due to the slippage of tectonic plates past or over one another; usually geologically unstable.

Igneous: a type of rock formed by solidification from a molten state, especially from molten magma.

Magma: hot liquid rock material under Earth's crust, from which igneous rock is formed by cooling.

Metamorphic: in geology, the name given to sedimentary rocks or minerals that have recrystallized under the influence of heat and pressure since their original deposition.

Pangaea: a single super-continent that scientists believe broke apart about 170 million years ago to form the current continents.

Plate tectonics: theory that Earth's crust is made up of many separate rigid plates of rock that float on top of hot semi-liquid rock.

Sedimentary rock: rock formed by the buildup of material at the bottoms of bodies of water.

Physics

Absolute zero: the theoretical temperature at which all motion within a molecule stops, corresponding to –273.15° Celsius (–459.67° Fahrenheit).

Antimatter: matter that consists of antiparticles, such as antiprotons, that have an opposite charge from normal particles; when matter meets antimatter, both are destroyed and their combined mass is converted to energy. Antimatter is created in certain radioactive decay processes, but appears to be present in only small amounts in the universe.

Atom: the basic unit of a chemical element.

Atomic mass: the total mass of an atom of a given element; atoms of the same element with different atomic masses (different numbers of neutrons, not protons) are called isotopes.

Atomic number: the number of protons in an atom of a given element of the periodic table; the characteristic that sets atoms of different elements apart.

Bose-Einstein condensate: a "super-atom" comprised of thousands of atoms super-cooled to within a few billionths of a degree of absolute zero and thus condensed into the lowest energy state; atoms bound in the BEC behave synchronously, giving the BEC wavelike properties.

Boson: force-carrying particles including photons, gluons, and the W and Z particles; one of the two primary categories of particles in the Standard Model, the other being fermions.

Dark energy: a mysterious, undefined energy leading to a repulsive force pervading all of space-time; proposed by cosmologists as counteracting gravity and accelerating the expansion of the universe; predicted to make up 65% of the universe's composition.

Dark matter: hypothetical, invisible matter that some scientists believe makes up 90% of the matter in the universe; its existence was proposed to account for otherwise inexplicable gravitational forces observed in space.

Doppler effect: a change in the frequency of sound, light, or radio waves caused by the motion of the source emitting the waves or the motion of the person or instrument perceiving the waves.

Electron: negatively charged particle that is the least massive electrically charged fundamental particle; the most common charged lepton in the Standard Model.

Energy: capacity to perform work. Energy can take various forms, such as potential energy, kinetic energy, chemical energy, etc.

Entropy: A measure of disorder in a system. According to the Second Law of Thermodynamics, disorder or entropy can only increase in a closed system.

Fermion: any one of a number of matter particles including electrons, protons, neutrons, and quarks; one of the two primary categories of particles in the Standard Model, the other being bosons.

Field: the effects of forces (gravitational, electric, etc.) are visualized and described mathematically by physicists in terms of fields, which show the strength and direction of a force at a given position.

Fission: a nuclear reaction that occurs when the nuclei of large, unstable atoms break apart, releasing large amounts of energy.

Force: In classical physics, a force is something that causes acceleration in a body, and can be thought of as a push or pull.

Fusion: a nuclear reaction occurring when atomic nuclei collide at high temperatures and combine to form one heavier atomic nucleus, releasing enormous energy in the process.

Gravity: an attractive force between any 2 objects or particles, proportional to the mass (or energy) of the objects; strength of the force decreases with greater distance; the only fundamental force still unaccounted for by the Standard Model.

Half-life: the time it takes for half of a given amount of a radioactive element to decay.

Hertz: a measure of frequency, or how many times a given event occurs per second; applied to sound waves, electrical current, microchip clock speeds; abbreviated as Hz.

Inertia: the tendency of an object to resist a change in its state of motion (i.e., to stay at rest if it is at rest, or to continue moving at a constant speed if it is moving at a constant speed). Inertia is proportional to mass, so a heavier object has more inertia.

Laser: light consisting of a cascade of photons all having the same wavelength; *laser* stands for Light Amplification by Stimulated Emission of Radiation.

Neutrino: a tiny fundamental particle with no electrical charge and very small mass that moves very quickly through the universe; in sum, predicted to make up about 5% of the mass of the universe; comes in three varieties, or flavors, called electron, muon, and tau.

Neutron: a neutral particle found in the nuclei of atoms.

Photon: the elementary unit, or quantum, of light or electromagnetic radiation, having no mass or electrical charge; one of the fundamental force-carrying particles, or bosons, described by the Standard Model.

Plasma: a high-energy state of matter different from solid, liquid or gas in which atomic nuclei and the electrons orbiting them separate from each other.

Proton: a positively charged subatomic particle found in the nuclei of atoms.

Quantum: a natural unit of some physically measurable property, such as energy or electrical charge.

Quark: a fermion and a fundamental matter particle that makes up neutrons and protons, forming atomic nuclei; there are 6 different "flavors" of quarks grouped in pairs; up and down, charm and strange, top and bottom.

Radiation: energy emitted as rays or particles; radiation includes heat, light, ultraviolet rays, gamma rays, X rays, cosmic rays, alpha particles, beta particles, and the protons, neutrons, and electrons of radioactive atoms.

Relativity, general theory of: a theory of space-time proposed by Albert Einstein in 1915; gravitational and other forces are transmitted through the effects of the curvature of space-time.

Relativity, special theory of: Einstein's theory of space and time: all laws of physics are valid in all uniformly moving frames of reference and the speed of light in a vacuum is always the same, so long as the source and the observer are moving uniformly (not accelerating).

Standard Model: prevailing theory of fundamental particles and forces of matter; matter particles are fermions: either leptons or quarks; force-carrying particles are bosons: either gluons, W or Z bosons or photons; gravity has not yet been worked into the model.

String theory: a theory that seeks to unify quantum mechanics and general relativity, positing that the basic constituents of matter can best be understood not as point objects but as tiny closed loops ("strings").

Subatomic particle: one of the small particles, such as electrons, neutrons, and protons, which make up an atom.

Superconductivity: the property of certain materials, usually metals and chemically complex ceramics, to conduct electricity without resistance, generally at very cold temperatures.

Thermodynamics: the branch of physics that describes how energy, heat, and temperature flow in physical systems.

Ultraviolet radiation: a form of light, invisible to the human eye, that has a shorter wavelength and greater energy than visible light but a longer wavelength and less energy than X rays.

Uncertainty principle: the theory that certain pairs of observable quantities—like energy and time, or position and momentum—cannot be measured with complete accuracy simultaneously; presented in 1927 by German physicist Werner Heisenberg; also known as indeterminacy principle.

Virtual particle: subatomic particles that rapidly pop into and out of existence and can exert real forces; usually occur in particle-antiparticle pairs and are rapidly annihilated.

Chemical Elements, Atomic Numbers, Year Discovered

Reviewed by Darleane C. Hoffman, Ph.D., Lawrence Berkeley National Laboratory and Department of Chemistry, University of California, Berkeley

See Periodic Table of the Elements on page 692 for atomic weights.

Element	Symbol	Atomic number	Year discov.
Actinium	Ac	89	1899
Aluminum	Al	13	1825
Americium	Am	95	1944
Antimony	Sb	51	1450
Argon	Ar	18	1894
Arsenic	As	33	13th c.
Astatine	At	85	1940
Barium	Ba	56	1808
Berkelium	Bk	97	1949
Beryllium	Be	4	1798
Bismuth	Bi	83	15th c.
Bohrium	Bh	107	1981
Boron	B	5	1808
Bromine	Br	35	1826
Cadmium	Cd	48	1817
Calcium	Ca	20	1808
Californium	Cf	98	1950
Carbon	C	6	BC
Cerium	Ce	58	1803
Cesium	Cs	55	1860
Chlorine	Cl	17	1774
Chromium	Cr	24	1797
Cobalt	Co	27	1735
Copper	Cu	29	BC
Curium	Cm	96	1944
Dysprosium	Dy	66	1886
Einsteinium	Es	99	1952
Erbium	Er	68	1843
Europium	Eu	63	1901
Fermium	Fm	100	1953
Fluorine	F	9	1771
Francium	Fr	87	1939
Gadolinium	Gd	64	1880
Gallium	Ga	31	1875
Germanium	Ge	32	1886
Gold	Au	79	BC
Hafnium	Hf	72	1923
Hahnium/ Dubnium[1]	Ha/Db	105	1970
Hassium	Hs	108	1984
Helium	He	2	1868
Holmium	Ho	67	1878
Hydrogen	H	1	1766
Indium	In	49	1863
Iodine	I	53	1811
Iridium	Ir	77	1804
Iron	Fe	26	BC
Krypton	Kr	36	1898
Lanthanum	La	57	1839
Lawrencium	Lr	103	1961
Lead	Pb	82	BC
Lithium	Li	3	1817
Lutetium	Lu	71	1907
Magnesium	Mg	12	1829
Manganese	Mn	25	1774
Meitnerium	Mt	109	1982
Mendelevium	Md	101	1955
Mercury	Hg	80	BC
Molybdenum	Mo	42	1782
Neodymium	Nd	60	1885
Neon	Ne	10	1898
Neptunium	Np	93	1940
Nickel	Ni	28	1751
Niobium[2]	Nb	41	1801
Nitrogen	N	7	1772
Nobelium	No	102	1958
Osmium	Os	76	1804
Oxygen	O	8	1774
Palladium	Pd	46	1803
Phosphorus	P	15	1669
Platinum	Pt	78	1735
Plutonium	Pu	94	1941
Polonium	Po	84	1898
Potassium	K	19	1807
Praseodymium	Pr	59	1885
Promethium	Pm	61	1945
Protactinium	Pa	91	1917
Radium	Ra	88	1898
Radon	Rn	86	1900
Rhenium	Re	75	1925
Rhodium	Rh	45	1803
Rubidium	Rb	37	1861
Ruthenium	Ru	44	1845
Rutherfordium	Rf	104	1969
Samarium	Sm	62	1879
Scandium	Sc	21	1879
Seaborgium	Sg	106	1974
Selenium	Se	34	1817
Silicon	Si	14	1823
Silver	Ag	47	BC
Sodium	Na	11	1807
Strontium	Sr	38	1790
Sulfur	S	16	BC
Tantalum	Ta	73	1802
Technetium	Tc	43	1937
Tellurium	Te	52	1782
Terbium	Tb	65	1843
Thallium	Tl	81	1861
Thorium	Th	90	1828
Thulium	Tm	69	1879
Tin	Sn	50	BC
Titanium	Ti	22	1791
Tungsten (Wolfram)	W	74	1783
Uranium	U	92	1789
Vanadium	V	23	1830
Xenon	Xe	54	1898
Ytterbium	Yb	70	1878
Yttrium	Y	39	1794
Zinc	Zn	30	BC
Zirconium	Zr	40	1789

Note: 109 elements are listed here. In addition, discovery of elements 110-112 has been reported. Discovery of element 110 was reported by 3 different groups between 1994 and 1996, but since each reported evidence for different isotopes, none can be considered confirmation of the others. A. Ghiorso, et al. at the Lawrence Berkeley National Laboratory (LBNL) in Berkeley, CA, reported evidence for element 110 with mass number 267; S. Hofmann, et al. at the Gesellschaft für Schwerionenforschung (GSI) at Darmstadt, Germany, reported element 110 with mass numbers 269, 270, and 271; Yu. Lazarev, et al. at the Flerov Laboratory for Nuclear Reactions, Dubna, Russia, reported element 110 with mass 273. The group of S. Hofmann has the most convincing data for the discovery of 110, but the half-lives and cross sections of all groups appear reasonable. In 1995-96, Hofmann, et al. also reported discovery of elements 111 and 112 at GSI with mass numbers of 272 and 277, respectively. These elements have not yet been named. In July 1999, a multinational group working at Dubna, Russia, published evidence for observation of element 114 with mass number 287. A Dubna/Lawrence Livermore National Laboratory group published their evidence in Oct. 1999 for element 114 with mass number 289 (first announced in Jan. 1999) and reported observation of element 114 with mass number 288 in Sept. 2000 and element 116 with mass number 292 in Dec. 2000. These reports await confirmation by other groups.

(1) The name Dubnium (Db) has been approved by IUPAC for element 105, but the name Hahnium (Ha) is used for element 105 in most of the scientific literature before 1998 and is still sometimes used in the U.S. (2) Formerly Columbium.

IT'S A FACT: Sir Isaac Newton made a number of his most significant discoveries in the period (1665-66) he spent at home while Cambridge University was closed because of the plague. He later recalled, "In those days I was in my prime of age for invention [he was 22 or 23], and minded mathematics and philosophy more than at any time since."

Periodic Table of the Elements

Source: © 1996 Lawrence Berkeley National Laboratory

Parentheses indicate undiscovered elements.

Key: atomic number (14), atomic weight (28.09), symbol (Si), name (Silicon)

Groups: alkali metals (column 1); alkaline earth metals (column 2); transitional metals (columns 3–12); other metals (Al, Ga, Ge, In, Sn, Sb, Tl, Pb, Bi, Po, and (113)–(116)); nonmetals (B–F, Si–Cl, As–Br, Te–I, At); noble gases (column 18)

1 1.01 H Hydrogen																	2 4.003 He Helium
3 6.94 Li Lithium	4 9.01 Be Beryllium											5 10.81 B Boron	6 12.01 C Carbon	7 14.01 N Nitrogen	8 15.999 O Oxygen	9 18.998 F Fluorine	10 20.18 Ne Neon
11 22.99 Na Sodium	12 24.31 Mg Magnesium											13 26.98 Al Aluminum	14 28.09 Si Silicon	15 30.97 P Phosphorus	16 32.06 S Sulfur	17 35.45 Cl Chlorine	18 39.95 Ar Argon
19 39.10 K Potassium	20 40.08 Ca Calcium	21 44.96 Sc Scandium	22 47.90 Ti Titanium	23 50.94 V Vanadium	24 51.996 Cr Chromium	25 54.94 Mn Manganese	26 55.85 Fe Iron	27 58.93 Co Cobalt	28 58.70 Ni Nickel	29 63.55 Cu Copper	30 65.37 Zn Zinc	31 69.72 Ga Gallium	32 72.59 Ge Germanium	33 74.92 As Arsenic	34 78.96 Se Selenium	35 79.90 Br Bromine	36 83.80 Kr Krypton
37 85.47 Rb Rubidium	38 87.62 Sr Strontium	39 88.91 Y Yttrium	40 91.22 Zr Zirconium	41 92.91 Nb Niobium	42 95.94 Mo Molybdenum	43 98 Tc Technetium	44 101.07 Ru Ruthenium	45 102.91 Rh Rhodium	46 106.40 Pd Palladium	47 107.87 Ag Silver	48 112.41 Cd Cadmium	49 114.82 In Indium	50 118.69 Sn Tin	51 121.75 Sb Antimony	52 127.60 Te Tellurium	53 126.90 I Iodine	54 131.30 Xe Xenon
55 132.91 Cs Cesium	56 137.33 Ba Barium	57 138.91 La Lanthanum	72 178.49 Hf Hafnium	73 180.95 Ta Tantalum	74 183.85 W Tungsten	75 186.21 Re Rhenium	76 190.20 Os Osmium	77 192.22 Ir Iridium	78 195.09 Pt Platinum	79 196.97 Au Gold	80 200.59 Hg Mercury	81 204.37 Tl Thallium	82 207.19 Pb Lead	83 208.98 Bi Bismuth	84 209 Po Polonium	85 210 At Astatine	86 222 Rn Radon
87 223 Fr Francium	88 226.03 Ra Radium	89 227.03 Ac Actinium	104 261 Rf Rutherfordium	105 262 Ha/Db Hahnium/ Dubnium	106 266 Sg Seaborgium	107 267 Bh Bohrium	108 269 Hs Hassium	109 268 Mt Meitnerium	110 273	111 272	112 277	(113)	(114)	(115)	(116)	(117)	(118)

Lanthanide series	58 140.12 Ce Cerium	59 140.91 Pr Praseodymium	60 144.24 Nd Neodymium	61 145 Pm Promethium	62 150.35 Sm Samarium	63 151.96 Eu Europium	64 157.25 Gd Gadolinium	65 158.93 Tb Terbium	66 162.50 Dy Dysprosium	67 164.93 Ho Holmium	68 167.26 Er Erbium	69 168.93 Tm Thulium	70 173.04 Yb Ytterbium	71 174.97 Lu Lutetium
Actinide series	90 232.04 Th Thorium	91 231.04 Pa Protactinium	92 238.03 U Uranium	93 237.05 Np Neptunium	94 244 Pu Plutonium	95 243 Am Americium	96 247 Cm Curium	97 247 Bk Berkelium	98 251 Cf Californium	99 252 Es Einsteinium	100 257 Fm Fermium	101 258 Md Mendelevium	102 259 No Nobelium	103 262 Lr Lawrencium

Discoveries and Innovations: Chemistry, Physics, Biology, Medicine

	Date	Discoverer	Nationality
Acetylene gas	**1862**	Berthelot	French
ACTH	**1927**	Evans, Long	U.S.
Adrenalin	**1901**	Takamine	Japan
Aluminum, electrolytic process	**1886**	Hall	U.S.
Aluminum, isolated	**1825**	Oersted	Danish
Anesthesia, ether	**1842**	Long	U.S.
Anesthesia, local	**1885**	Koller	Austrian
Anesthesia, spinal	**1898**	Bier	German
Aniline dye	**1856**	Perkin	English
Anti-rabies	**1885**	Pasteur	French
Antiseptic surgery	**1867**	Lister	English
Antitoxin, diphtheria	**1891**	Von Behring	German
Argyrol	**1897**	Bayer	German
Arsphenamine	**1910**	Ehrlich	German
Aspirin	**1853**	Gerhardt	French
Atabrine	**1932**	Mietzsch, et al.	German
Atomic numbers	**1913**	Moseley	English
Atomic theory	**1803**	Dalton	English
Atomic time clock	**1948**	Lyons	U.S.
Atomic time clock, cesium beam	**1948**	Essen	English
Atom-smashing theory	**1919**	Rutherford	English
Bacitracin	**1943**	Johnson, Meleneyl	U.S.
Bacteria, description	**1676**	Leeuwenhoek	Dutch
Bleaching powder	**1798**	Tennant	English
Blood, circulation	**1628**	Harvey	English
Blood plasma storage (blood banks)	**1940**	Drew	U.S.
Bordeaux mixture	**1885**	Millardet	French
Bromine from the sea	**1826**	Balard	French
Calcium carbide	**1888**	Wilson	U.S.
Calculus	**1670**	Newton	English
Camphor synthetic	**1896**	Haller	French
Canning (food)	**1804**	Appert	French
Carbon oxides	**1925**	Fisher	German
Chemotherapy	**1909**	Ehrlich	German
Chloamphenicol	**1947**	Burkholder	U.S.
Chlorine	**1774**	Scheele	Swedish
Chloroform	**1831**	Guthrie, S.	U.S.
Chlortetracycline	**1948**	Duggen	U.S.
Classification of plants and animals	**1735**	Linnaeus	Swedish
Cloning, DNA	**1973**	Boyer, Cohen	U.S.
Cloning, mammal	**1996**	Wilmut, et al.	Scottish
Cocaine	**1860**	Niermann	German
Combustion explained	**1777**	Lavoisier	French
Conditioned reflex	**1914**	Pavlov	Russian
Cortisone	**1936**	Kendall	U.S.
Cortisone, synthesis	**1946**	Sarett	U.S.
Cosmic rays	**1910**	Gockel	Swiss
Cyanamide	**1905**	Frank, Caro	German
Cyclotron	**1930**	Lawrence	U.S.
DDT (not applied as insecticide until 1939)	**1874**	Zeidler	German
Deuterium	**1932**	Urey, Brickwedde, Murphy	U.S.
DNA (structure)	**1951**	Crick	English
		Watson	U.S.
		Wilkins	English
Electric resistance, law of	**1827**	Ohm	German
Electric waves	**1888**	Hertz	German
Electrolysis	**1852**	Faraday	English
Electromagnetism	**1819**	Oersted	Danish
Electron	**1897**	Thomson, J.	English
Electron diffraction	**1936**	Thomson,	English
		G.Davisson	U.S.
Electroshock treatment	**1938**	Cerletti, Bini	Italian
Erythromycin	**1952**	McGuire	U.S.
Evolution, natural selection	**1858**	Darwin	English
Falling bodies, law of	**1590**	Galileo	Italian
Gases, law of combining volumes	**1808**	Gay-Lussac	French
Geometry, analytic	**1619**	Descartes	French
Gold, cyanide process for extraction	**1887**	MacArthur, Forest	British
Gravitation, law	**1687**	Newton	English
HIV (human immuno-deficiency virus)	**1984**	Mortagnier	French
		Gallo	U.S.
Holograph	**1948**	Gabor	British
Human heart transplant	**1967**	Barnard	S. African
Indigo, synthesis of	**1880**	Baeyer	German
Induction, electric	**1830**	Henry	U.S.
Insulin	**1922**	Banting, Best,	Canadian,
		Macleod	Scottish
Intelligence testing	**1905**	Binet, Simon	French
In vitro fertilization	**1978**	Steptoe, Edwards	English
Isoniazid	**1952**	Hoffmann-LaRoche	U.S.
		Domagk	German
Isotopes, theory	**1912**	Soddy	English
Laser	**1957**	Gould	U.S.
Light, velocity	**1675**	Roemer	Danish

	Date	Discoverer	Nationality
Light, wave theory	**1690**	Huygens	Dutch
Lithography	**1796**	Senefelder	Bohemian
Logarithms	**1614**	Napier	Scottish
LSD-25	**1943**	Hoffman	Swiss
Mendelian laws	**1866**	Mendel	Austrian
Mercator projection (map)	**1568**	Mercator (Kremer)	Flemish
Methanol	**1661**	Boyle	Irish
Milk condensation	**1853**	Borden	U.S.
Molecular hypothesis	**1811**	Avogadro	Italian
Motion, laws of	**1687**	Newton	English
Neomycin	**1949**	Waksman, Lechevalier	U.S.
Neutron	**1932**	Chadwick	English
Nitric acid	**1648**	Glauber	German
Nitric oxide	**1772**	Priestley	English
Nitroglycerin	**1846**	Sobrero	Italian
Oil cracking process	**1891**	Dewar	U.S.
Oxygen	**1774**	Priestley	English
Oxytetracycline	**1950**	Finlay, et al.	U.S.
Ozone	**1840**	Schonbein	German
Paper, sulfite process	**1867**	Tilghman	U.S.
Paper, wood pulp, sulfate process	**1884**	Dahl	German
Penicillin	**1928**	Fleming	Scottish
practical use	**1941**	Florey, Chain	English
Periodic law and table of elements	**1869**	Mendeleyev	Russian
Physostigmine synthesis	**1935**	Julian	U.S.
Pill, birth-control	**1954**	Pincus, Rock	U.S.
Planetary motion, laws	**1609**	Kepler	German
Plutonium fission	**1940**	Kennedy, Wahl, Seaborg, Segre	U.S.
Polymyxin	**1947**	Ainsworth	English
Positron	**1932**	Anderson	U.S.
Proton	**1919**	Rutherford	N. Zealand
Psychoanalysis	**1900**	Freud	Austrian
Quantum theory	**1900**	Planck	German
Quasars	**1963**	Matthews, Sandage	U.S.
Quinine synthetic	**1946**	Woodward, Doering	U.S.
Radioactivity	**1896**	Becquerel	French
Radiocarbon dating	**1947**	Libby	U.S.
Radium	**1898**	Curie, Pierre	French
		Curie, Marie	Pol.-Fr.
Relativity theory	**1905**	Einstein	German
Reserpine	**1949**	Jal Vaikl	Indian
Schick test	**1913**	Schick	U.S.
Silicon	**1823**	Berzelius	Swedish
Smallpox eradication	**1979**	World Health Org.	UN
Streptomycin	**1944**	Waksman, et al	U.S.
Sulfanilamide	**1935**	Bovet, Trefouel	French
Sulfanilamide theory	**1908**	Gelmo	German
Sulfapyridine	**1938**	Ewins, Phelps	English
Sulfathiazole	**1939**	Fosbinder, Walter	U.S.
Sulfuric acid	**1831**	Phillips	English
Sulfuric acid, lead	**1746**	Roebuck	English
Syphilis test	**1906**	Wassermann	German
Thiacetazone	**1950**	Belmisch, Mietzsch, Domagk	German
Tuberculin	**1890**	Koch	German
Uranium fission theory	**1939**	Hahn, Meitner, Strassmann	German
		Bohr	Danish
		Fermi	Italian
		Einstein, Pegram, Wheeler	U.S.
Uranium fission, atomic reactor	**1942**	Fermi, Szilard	U.S.
Vaccine, measles	**1963**	Enders	U.S.
Vaccine, meningitis (first conjugate)	**1987**	Gordon, et al., Connaught Lab.	U.S.
Vaccine, polio	**1954**	Salk	U.S.
Vaccine, polio, oral	**1960**	Sabin	U.S.
Vaccine, rabies	**1885**	Pasteur	French
Vaccine, smallpox	**1796**	Jenner	English
Vaccine, typhus	**1909**	Nicolle	French
Vaccine, varicella	**1974**	Takahashi	Japan
Van Allen belts, radiation	**1958**	Van Allen	U.S.
Vitamin A	**1913**	McCollum, Davis	U.S.
Vitamin B	**1916**	McCollum	U.S.
Vitamin C	**1928**	Szent-Gyorgyi, King	U.S.
Vitamin D	**1922**	McCollum	U.S.
Vitamin K	**1935**	Dam, Doisy	U.S.
Xerography	**1938**	Carlson	U.S.
X ray	**1895**	Roentgen	German

WORLD ALMANAC QUICK QUIZ

Which of the following was invented before 1900?

(a) Scotch tape (b) ballpoint pen
(c) cellophane (d) bubble gum

For the answer look in this chapter, or see page 1008.

Inventions

Invention	Date	Inventor	Nationality
Adding machine	**1642**	Pascal	French
Adding machine	**1885**	Burroughs	U.S.
Aerosol spray	**1926**	Rotheim	Norwegian
Airbag	**1952**	Hetrick	U.S.
Air brake	**1868**	Westinghouse	U.S.
Air conditioning	**1902**	Carrier	U.S.
Air pump	**1654**	Guericke	German
Airplane, automatic pilot	**1912**	Sperry	U.S.
Airplane, experimental	**1896**	Langley	U.S.
Airplane, hydro	**1911**	Curtiss	U.S.
Airplane jet engine	**1939**	Ohain	German
Airplane with motor	**1903**	Wright Bros.	U.S.
Airship	**1852**	Giffard	French
Arc welder	**1919**	Thomson	U.S.
Aspartame	**1965**	Schlatter	U.S.
Autogyro	**1920**	de la Cierva	Spanish
Automobile, differential gear	**1885**	Benz	German
Automobile, electric	**1892**	Morrison	U.S.
Automobile, exp'mtl	**1864**	Marcus	Austrian
Automobile, gasoline	**1889**	Daimler	German
Automobile, gasoline	**1892**	Duryea	U.S.
Automobile magneto	**1897**	Bosch	German
Automobile muffler	**1904**	Pope	U.S.
Automobile self-starter	**1911**	Kettering	U.S.
Bakelite	**1907**	Baekeland	Belgium, U.S.
Balloon	**1783**	Montgolfier	French
Barometer	**1643**	Torricelli	Italian
Bicycle, modern	**1885**	Starley	English
Bifocal lens	**1780**	Franklin	U.S.
Bottle machine	**1895**	Owens	U.S.
Braille printing	**1829**	Braille	French
Bubble gum	**1928**	Diemer	U.S.
Burner, gas	**1855**	Bunsen	German
Calculating machine	**1833**	Babbage	English
Calculator, electronic pocket	**1972**	Merryman, Van	U.S.
Camera, Kodak	**1888**	Eastman, Walker	U.S
Camera, Polaroid Land	**1948**	Land	U.S.
Car coupler	**1873**	Janney	U.S.
Carburetor, gasoline	**1893**	Maybach	German
Carding machine	**1797**	Whittemore	U.S.
Carpet sweeper	**1876**	Bissell	U.S.
Cash register	**1879**	Ritty	U.S.
Cassette, audio	**1963**	Philips Co.	Dutch
Cassette, videotape	**1969**	Sony	Japanese
Cathode-ray tube	**1897**	Braun	German
CAT, or CT, scan	**1973**	Hounsfield	English
Cellophane	**1908**	Brandenberger	Swiss
Celluloid	**1870**	Hyatt	U.S.
Cement, Portland	**1824**	Aspdin	English
Chronometer	**1735**	Harrison	English
Circuit breaker	**1925**	Hilliard	U.S.
Circuit, integrated	**1959**	Kilby, Noyce, Texas Instr.	U.S.
Clock, pendulum	**1657**	Huygens	Dutch
Coaxial cable system	**1929**	Affel, Espenschied	U.S.
Compressed air rock drill	**1871**	Ingersoll	U.S.
Comptometer	**1887**	Felt	U.S.
Computer, automatic sequence	**1944**	Aiken, et al.	U.S.
Computer, electronic	**1942**	Atanasoff, Berry	U.S.
Computer, laptop	**1987**	Sinclair	English
Computer, mini	**1960**	Digital Corp	U.S.
Condenser microphone (telephone)	**1916**	Wente	U.S.
Contact lens, corneal	**1948**	Tuohy	U.S.
Contraceptive, oral	**1954**	Pincus, Rock	U.S.
Corn, hybrid	**1917**	Jones	U.S.
Cotton gin	**1793**	Whitney	U.S.
Cream separator	**1878**	DeLaval	Swedish
Cultivator, disc	**1878**	Mallon	U.S.
Cystoscope	**1878**	Nitze	German
Diesel engine	**1895**	Diesel	German
Disc, compact	**1972**	RCA	U.S.
Disc player, compact	**1979**	Sony, Philips Co.	Japan, Dutch
Disk, floppy	**1970**	IBM	U.S.
Disk, video	**1972**	Philips Co.	Dutch
Dynamite	**1866**	Nobel	Swedish
Dynamo, contin. current	**1871**	Gramme	Belgian
Electric battery	**1800**	Volta	Italian
Electric fan	**1882**	Wheeler	U.S.
Electrocardiograph	**1903**	Einthoven	Dutch
Electroencephalograph	**1929**	Berger	German
Electromagnet	**1824**	Sturgeon	English
Electron spectrometer	**1944**	Deutsch, Elliott, Evans	U.S.
Electron tube multigrid	**1913**	Langmuir	U.S.
Electroplating	**1805**	Brugnatelli	Italian
Electrostatic generator	**1929**	Van de Graaff	U.S.
Elevator brake	**1852**	Otis	U.S.
Elevator, push button	**1922**	Larson	U.S.
Engine, automatic transmission	**1910**	Fottinger	German
Engine, coal-gas 4-cycle	**1876**	Otto	German
Engine, compression ignition	**1883**	Daimler	German
Engine, electric ignition	**1883**	Benz	German
Engine, gas, compound	**1926**	Eickemeyer	U.S.
Engine, gasoline	**1872**	Brayton, Geo.	U.S.
Engine, gasoline	**1889**	Daimler	German
Engine, jet	**1930**	Whittle	English
Engine, steam, piston	**1705**	Newcomen	English
Engine, steam, piston	**1769**	Watt	Scottish
Engraving, half-tone	**1852**	Talbot	U.S.
Fiberglass	**1938**	Owens-Corning	U.S.
Fiber optics	**1955**	Kapany	English
Fiber optic wire	**1970**	Keck, Maurer, Schulz	U.S.
Filament, tungsten	**1913**	Coolidge	U.S.
Flanged rail	**1831**	Stevens	U.S.
Flatiron, electric	**1882**	Seely	U.S.
Food, frozen	**1923**	Birdseye	U.S.
Freon	**1930**	Midgley, et al.	U.S.
Furnace (for steel)	**1858**	Siemens	German
Galvanometer	**1820**	Sweigger	German
Gas discharge tube	**1922**	Hull	U.S.
Gas lighting	**1792**	Murdoch	Scottish
Gas mantle	**1885**	Welsbach	Austrian
Gasoline (lead ethyl)	**1922**	Midgley	U.S.
Gasoline, cracked	**1913**	Burton	U.S.
Gasoline, high octane	**1930**	Ipatieff	Russian
Geiger counter	**1913**	Geiger	German
Glass, laminated safety	**1909**	Benedictus	French
Glider	**1853**	Cayley	English
Gun, breechloader	**1811**	Thornton	U.S.
Gun, Browning	**1897**	Browning	U.S.
Gun, magazine	**1875**	Hotchkiss	U.S.
Gun, silencer	**1908**	Maxim, H.P.	U.S.
Guncotton	**1847**	Schoenbein	German
Gyrocompass	**1911**	Sperry	U.S.
Gyroscope	**1852**	Foucault	French
Harvester-thresher	**1818**	Lane	U.S.
Heart, artificial	**1982**	Jarvik	U.S.
Helicopter	**1939**	Sikorsky	U.S.
Hydrometer	**1768**	Baume	French
Iron lung	**1928**	Drinker, Slaw	U.S.
Kaleidoscope	**1817**	Brewster	Scottish
Kevlar	**1965**	Kwolek, Blades	U.S.
Kinetoscope	**1889**	Edison	U.S.
Lamp, arc	**1847**	Staite	English
Lamp, fluorescent	**1938**	General Electric, Westinghouse	U.S.
Lamp, incandescent	**1879**	Edison	U.S.
Lamp, incand., gas	**1913**	Langmuir	U.S.
Lamp, klieg	**1911**	Kliegl, A. & J.	U.S.
Lamp, mercury vapor	**1912**	Hewitt	U.S.
Lamp, miner's safety	**1816**	Davy	English
Lamp, neon	**1909**	Claude	French
Lathe, turret	**1845**	Fitch	U.S.
Launderette	**1934**	Cantrell	U.S.
Lens, achromatic	**1758**	Dollond	English
Lens, fused bifocal	**1908**	Borsch	U.S.
Leyden jar (condenser)	**1745**	von Kleist	German
Lightning rod	**1752**	Franklin	U.S.
Linoleum	**1860**	Walton	English
Linotype	**1884**	Mergenthaler	U.S.
Liquid Paper	**c.1951**	Graham	U.S.
Lock, cylinder	**1851**	Yale	U.S.
Locomotive, electric	**1851**	Vail	U.S.
Locomotive, exp'mtl	**1802**	Trevithick	English
Locomotive, exp'mtl	**1812**	Fenton, et al.	English
Locomotive, exp'mtl	**1814**	Stephenson	English
Locomotive, practical	**1829**	Stephenson	English
Locomotive, 1st U.S.	**1830**	Cooper, P.	U.S.
Loom, power	**1785**	Cartwright	English
Loudspeaker, dynamic	**1924**	Rice, Kellogg	U.S.
Machine gun	**1862**	Gatling	U.S.
Machine gun, improved	**1872**	Hotchkiss	U.S.
Machine gun (Maxim)	**1883**	Maxim, H.S.	U.S., Eng.
Magnet, electro	**1828**	Henry	U.S.
Magnetic Resonance Imaging (MRI)	**1971**	Damadian	U.S.
Mantle, gas	**1885**	Welsbach	Austrian
Mason jar	**1858**	Mason, J.	U.S.
Match, friction	**1827**	Walker, J.	English
Mercerized textiles	**1843**	Mercer, J.	English
Meter, induction	**1888**	Shallenberger	U.S.
Metronome	**1816**	Malezel	German
Microcomputer	**1973**	Truong, et al.	French
Micrometer	**1636**	Gascoigne	English
Microphone	**1877**	Berliner	U.S.
Microprocessor	**1971**	Intel Corp.	U.S.
Microscope, compound	**1590**	Janssen	Dutch
Microscope, electronic	**1931**	Knoll, Ruska	German

Invention	Date	Inventor	Nationality
Microscope, field ion	1951	Mueller	German
Microwave oven	1947	Spencer	U.S.
Minivan	1983	Chrysler	U.S.
Monitor, warship	1861	Ericsson	U.S.
Monotype	1887	Lanston	U.S.
Motor, AC	1892	Tesla	U.S.
Motor, DC	1837	Davenport	U.S.
Motor, induction	1887	Tesla	U.S.
Motorcycle	1885	Daimler	German
Movie machine	1894	Jenkins	U.S.
Movie, panoramic	1952	Waller	U.S.
Movie, talking	1927	Warner Bros.	U.S.
Mower, lawn	1831	Budding, Ferrabee	English
Mowing machine	1822	Bailey	U.S.
Neoprene	1930	Carothers	U.S.
Nylon	1937	Du Pont lab	U.S.
Nylon synthetic	1930	Carothers	U.S.
Oil cracking furnace	1891	Gavrilov	Russian
Oil filled power cable	1921	Emanueli	Italian
Oleomargarine	1869	Mege-Mouries	French
Ophthalmoscope	1851	Helmholtz	German
Pacemaker	1952	Zoll	U.S.
Paper	105	Ts'ai	Chinese
Paper clip	1900	Waaler	Norwegian
Paper machine	1809	Dickinson	U.S.
Parachute	1785	Blanchard	French
Pen, ballpoint	1888	Loud	U.S.
Pen, fountain	1884	Waterman	U.S.
Pen, steel	1780	Harrison	English
Pendulum	1583	Galileo	Italian
Percussion cap	1807	Forsythe	Scottish
Phonograph	1877	Edison	U.S.
Photo, color	1892	Ives	U.S.
Photo film, celluloid	1893	Reichenbach	U.S.
Photo film, transparent	1884	Eastman, Goodwin	U.S.
Photoelectric cell	1895	Elster	German
Photocopier	1938	Carlson	U.S.
Photographic paper	1835	Talbot	English
Photography	1816	Niepce	French
Photography	1835	Talbot	English
Photography	1835	Daguerre	French
Photophone	1880	Bell	U.S.-Scot.
Phototelegraphy	1925	Bell Labs	U.S.
Piano	1709	Cristofori	Italian
Piano, player	1863	Fourneaux	French
Pin, safety	1849	Hunt	U.S.
Pistol (revolver)	1836	Colt	U.S.
Plow, cast iron	1785	Ransome	English
Plow, disc	1896	Hardy	U.S.
Pneumatic hammer	1890	King	U.S.
Post-it note	1980	3M	U.S.
Powder, smokeless	1884	Vieille	French
Printing press, rotary	1845	Hoe	U.S.
Printing press, web	1865	Bullock	U.S.
Propeller, screw	1804	Stevens	U.S.
Propeller, screw	1837	Ericsson	Swedish
Pulsars	1967	Bell	English
Punch card accounting	1889	Hollerith	U.S.
Quasars	1963	Schmidt	U.S.
Radar	1940	Watson-Watt	Scottish
Radio, magnetic detector	1902	Marconi	Italian
Radio, signals	1895	Marconi	Italian
Radio amplifier	1906	De Forest	U.S.
Radio beacon	1928	Donovan	U.S.
Radio crystal oscillator	1918	Nicolson	U.S.
Radio receiver, cascade tuning	1913	Alexanderson	U.S.
Radio receiver, heterodyne	1913	Fessenden	U.S.
Radio transmitter triode modulation	1914	Alexanderson	U.S.
Radio tube diode	1905	Fleming	English
Radio tube oscillator	1915	De Forest	U.S.
Radio tube triode	1906	De Forest	U.S.
Radio FM, 2-path	1933	Armstrong	U.S.
Rayon (acetate)	1895	Cross	English
Rayon (cuprammonium)	1890	Despeissis	French
Rayon (nitrocellulose)	1884	Chardonnet	French
Razor, electric	1917	Schick	U.S.
Razor, safety	1895	Gillette	U.S.
Reaper	1834	McCormick	U.S.
Record, cylinder	1887	Bell, Tainter	U.S.
Record, disc	1887	Berliner	U.S.
Record, long playing	1947	Goldmark	U.S.
Record, wax cylinder	1888	Edison	U.S.
Refrigerator car	1868	David	U.S.
Resin, synthetic	1931	Hill	English
Richter scale	1935	Richter	U.S.
Rifle, repeating	1860	Henry	U.S.
Rocket engine	1926	Goddard	U.S.
Rollerblades	1980	Olson	U.S.
Rubber, vulcanized	1839	Goodyear	U.S.
Saccharin	1879	Remsen, Fahlberg	U.S.
Saw, circular	1777	Miller	English
Scotch tape	1930	Drew	U.S.
Seat belt	1959	Volvo	Swedish
Sewing machine	1846	Howe	U.S.
Shoe-lasting machine	1883	Matzeliger	U.S.
Shoe-sewing machine	1860	McKay	U.S.
Shrapnel shell	1784	Shrapnel	English
Shuttle, flying	1733	Kay	English
Sleeping-car	1865	Pullman	U.S.
Slide rule	1620	Oughtred	English
Soap, hardwater	1928	Bertsch	German
Spectroscope	1859	Kirchoff, Bunsen	German
Spectroscope (mass)	1918	Dempster	U.S.
Spinning jenny	c.1764	Hargreaves	English
Spinning mule	1779	Crompton	English
Steamboat, exp'mtl	1778	Jouffroy	French
Steamboat, exp'mtl	1785	Fitch	U.S.
Steamboat, exp'mtl	1787	Rumsey	U.S.
Steamboat, exp'mtl	1803	Fulton	U.S.
Steamboat, exp'mtl	1804	Stevens	U.S.
Steamboat, practical	1802	Symington	Scottish
Steamboat, practical	1807	Fulton	U.S.
Steam car	1770	Cugnot	French
Steam turbine	1884	Parsons	English
Steel (converter)	1856	Bessemer	English
Steel alloy	1891	Harvey	U.S.
Steel alloy, high-speed	1901	Taylor, White	U.S.
Steel, manganese	1884	Hadfield	English
Steel, stainless	1916	Brearley	English
Stereoscope	1838	Wheatstone	English
Stethoscope	1819	Laennec	French
Stethoscope, binaural	1840	Cammann	U.S.
Stock ticker	1870	Edison	U.S.
Storage battery, rechargeable	1859	Plante	French
Stove, electric	1896	Hadaway	U.S.
Submarine	1891	Holland	U.S.
Submarine, even keel	1894	Lake	U.S.
Submarine, torpedo	1776	Bushnell	U.S.
Superconductivity	1957	Bardeen, Cooper, Schreiffer	U.S.
Superconductivity in ceramics at high temp	1986	Bednorz	German
		Muller	Swiss
Synthesizer	1964	Moog	U.S.
Tank, military	1914	Swinton	English
Tape recorder, magnetic	1899	Poulsen	Danish
Teflon	1938	Du Pont	U.S.
Telegraph, magnetic	1837	Morse	U.S.
Telegraph, quadruplex	1864	Edison	U.S.
Telegraph, railroad	1887	Woods	U.S.
Telegraph, wireless high frequency	1895	Marconi	Italian
Telephone	1876	Bell	U.S.-Scot.
Telephone, automatic	1891	Strowger	U.S.
Telephone, cellular	1947	Bell Labs	U.S.
Telephone, radio	1900	Poulsen, Fessenden	Danish
Telephone, radio	1906	De Forest	U.S.
Telephone, radio, long dist.	1915	AT&T	U.S.
Telephone, recording	1898	Poulsen	Danish
Telephone, wireless	1899	Collins	U.S.
Telephone amplifier	1912	De Forest	U.S.
Telescope	1608	Lippershey	Neth.
Telescope	1609	Galileo	Italian
Telescope, astronomical	1611	Kepler	German
Teletype	1928	Morkrum, Kleinschmidt	U.S.
Television, color	1928	Baird	Scottish
Television, electronic	1927	Farnsworth	U.S.
Television, iconoscope	1923	Zworykin	U.S.
Television, mech. scanner	1923	Baird	Scottish
Thermometer	1593	Galileo	Italian
Thermometer	1730	Reaumur	French
Thermometer, mercury	1714	Fahrenheit	German
Time recorder	1890	Bundy	U.S.
Tire, double-tube	1845	Thomson	Scottish
Tire, pneumatic	1888	Dunlop	Scottish
Toaster, automatic	1918	Strite	U.S.
Toilet, flush	1589	Harington	English
Tool, pneumatic	1865	Law	English
Torpedo, marine	1804	Fulton	U.S.
Tractor, crawler	1904	Holt	U.S.
Transformer, AC	1885	Stanley	U.S.
Transistor	1947	Shockley, Brattain, Bardeen	U.S.
Trolley car, electric	1884-87	Van DePoele, Sprague	U.S.
Tungsten, ductile	1912	Coolidge	U.S.
Tupperware	1945	Tupper	U.S.
Turbine, gas	1849	Bourdin	French
Turbine, hydraulic	1849	Francis	U.S.
Turbine, steam	1884	Parsons	English
Type, movable	1447	Gutenberg	German

Invention	Date	Inventor	Nationality
Typewriter	1867	Sholes, Soule, Glidden	U.S.
Vacuum cleaner, electric	1907	Spangler	U.S.
Vacuum evaporating pan	1846	Rillieux	U.S.
Velcro	1948	de Mestral	Swiss
Video game ("Pong")	1972	Bushnell	U.S.
Video home system (VHS)	1975	Matsushita, JVC	Japan
Washer, electric	1901	Fisher	U.S.
Welding, atomic hydrogen	1924	Langmuir, Palmer	U.S.
Welding, electric	1877	Thomson	U.S.
Windshield wiper	1903	Anderson	U.S.
Wind tunnel	1912	Eiffel	French
Wire, barbed	1874	Glidden	U.S.
Wrench, double-acting	1913	Owen	U.S.
X-ray tube	1913	Coolidge	U.S.
Zeppelin	1900	Zeppelin	German
Zipper, early model	1893	Judson	U.S.
Zipper, improved	1913	Sundback	Canadian

IT'S A FACT: In the early 1950s, Bette Graham, a secretary working in Dallas, had the idea of correcting her typing mistakes by painting over them with white liquid. Soon her co-workers were asking for bottles of "Mistake Out," as Graham called her invention. In 1956 she started the Mistake Out Company—later renamed Liquid Paper—and 20 years later her company was turning out 25 million bottles a year of the time-saver.

Top 20 Corporations Receiving U.S. Patents in 2001

Source: *Technology Assessment and Forecast Report,* U.S. Patent and Trademark Office, U.S. Department of Commerce

Rank	Company	Number of patents
1.	International Business Machines Corporation	3,411
2.	NEC Corporation	1,953
3.	Canon Kabushiki Kaisha	1,877
4.	Micron Technology, Inc.	1,643
5.	Samsung Electronics Co., Ltd.	1,450
6.	Matsushita Electric Industrial Co., Ltd.	1,440
7.	Sony Corporation	1,363
8.	Hitachi, Ltd	1,271
9.	Mitsubishi Denki Kabushiki Kaisha	1,184
10.	Fujitsu Limited	1,166
11.	Toshiba Corporation	1,149
12.	Lucent Technologies Inc.	1,109
13.	General Electric Company	1,107
14.	Advanced Micro Devices, Inc.	1,086
15.	Hewlett-Packard Company	978
16.	Intel Corporation	809
17.	Texas Instruments, Incorporated	799
18.	Siemens Aktiengesellschaft	793
19.	Motorola, Inc.	778
20.	Eastman Kodak Company	719

Breaking the Sound Barrier; Speed of Sound

The prefix **Mach** is used to describe supersonic speed. It was named for Ernst Mach (1838-1916), a Czech-born Austrian physicist, who contributed to the study of sound. When a plane moves at the speed of sound, it is Mach 1. When the plane is moving at twice the speed of sound, it is Mach 2. When it is moving below the speed of sound, the speed can be designated accordingly—for example, Mach 0.90. Mach may be defined as the ratio of the velocity of a rocket or a jet to the velocity of sound in the medium being considered.

When a plane passes the sound barrier—flying faster than sound travels—listeners in the area hear thunderclaps, but the pilot of the plane does not hear them.

Sound is produced by vibrations of an object and is transmitted by alternate increase and decrease in pressures that radiate outward through a material media of molecules—somewhat like waves spreading out on a pond after a rock has been tossed into it.

The **frequency of sound** is determined by the number of times the vibrating waves undulate per second and is measured in cycles per second. The slower the cycle of waves, the lower the frequency. As frequencies increase, the sound is higher in pitch.

Sound is audible to human beings only if the frequency falls within a certain range. The human ear is usually not sensitive to frequencies of fewer than 20 vibrations per second or greater than about 20,000 vibrations per second—although this range varies among individuals.

Intensity, or loudness, is the strength of the pressure of these radiating waves and is measured in decibels. The human ear responds to intensity in a range from zero to 120 decibels. Any sound with a pressure of more than 120 decibels is painful to the human ear.

The **speed of sound** is generally defined as 1,088 feet per second at sea level at 32° F. It varies in other temperatures and in different media. Sound travels faster in water than in air, and even faster in iron and steel. Here are the speeds of sound in feet per second, for various media: ice-cold water, 4,938; granite, 12,960; hardwood, 12,620; brick, 11,960; glass, 16,410 to 19,690; silver, 8,658; gold, 5,717.

Light; Colors of the Spectrum

Light, a form of electromagnetic radiation similar to radiant heat, radio waves, and X rays, is emitted from a source in straight lines and spreads out over a larger and larger area as it travels; the light per unit area diminishes as the square of the distance.

The English mathematician and physicist Sir Isaac Newton (1642-1727) described light as an **emission of particles**; the Dutch astronomer, mathematician, and physicist Christiaan Huygens (1629-95) developed the theory that light travels by a **wave motion**. It is now believed that these 2 theories are essentially complementary, and the development of quantum theory has led to results where light acts like a series of particles in some experiments and like a wave in others.

The **speed of light** was first measured in a laboratory experiment by the French physicist Armand Hippolyte Louis Fizeau (1819-96). Today the speed of light is known very precisely as 299,792.458 km per sec (or 186,282.396 mi per sec) in a vacuum; in water the speed of light is about 25% less, and in glass, 33% less.

Color sensations are produced through the excitation of the retina of the eye by light vibrating at different frequencies. The different colors of the spectrum may be produced by viewing a light beam that is refracted by passage through a prism, which breaks the light into its wavelengths.

Customarily, the **primary colors** of the spectrum are taken to be the 6 monochromatic colors that occupy relatively large areas of the spectrum: red, orange, yellow, green, blue, and violet. Scientists have differed, however, in how many primary colors they recognized, and which specific ones they were.

The color sensation of **black** is due to complete lack of stimulation of the retina, that of **white** to complete stimulation. The **infrared and ultraviolet rays**, below the red (long) end of the spectrum and above the violet (short) end respectively, are invisible to the naked eye. Heat is the principal effect of the infrared rays, and chemical action that of the ultraviolet rays.

Weight or Mass of Water

Weight, at 20° C

1	cubic inch	0.0360 pound
1	cubic foot	62.4 pounds
1	cubic foot	7.48052 U.S. gal
1	U.S. gallon	8.33 pounds
269.0	U.S. gallons	2240.0 pounds (20 gross, or 1 long ton)

Mass, at 4° C (Maximum Density)

1 cubic centimeter	1 gram
1 liter	1 kilogram
1 cubic meter	1 metric ton

WEIGHTS AND MEASURES

Source: National Institute of Standards and Technology, U.S. Dept. of Commerce

The International System of Units (SI)

Two systems of weights and measures coexist in the U.S. today: the **U.S. Customary System** and the **International System of Units** (SI, after the initials of Système International). SI, **commonly identified with the metric system,** is actually a more complete, coherent version of it. Throughout U.S. history, the Customary System (inherited from, but now different from, the British Imperial System) has been generally used; federal and state legislation has given it, through implication, standing as the primary weights and measures system. The metric system, however, is the only system that Congress has ever specifically sanctioned. An 1866 law reads:

It shall be lawful throughout the United States of America to employ the weights and measures of the metric system; and no contract or dealing, or pleading in any court, shall be deemed invalid or liable to objection because the weights or measures expressed or referred to therein are weights or measures of the metric system.

Since that time, use of the metric system in the U.S. has slowly and steadily increased, particularly in the scientific community, in the pharmaceutical industry, and in the manufacturing sector—the last motivated by the practice in international commerce, in which the metric system is now predominantly used.

On Feb. 10, 1964, the National Bureau of Standards (now known as the National Institute of Standards and Technology) issued the following statement:

Henceforth it shall be the policy of the National Bureau of Standards to use the units of the International System (SI), as adopted by the 11th General Conference on Weights and Measures (October 1960), except when the use of these units would obviously impair communication or reduce the usefulness of a report.

On Dec. 23, 1975, Pres. Gerald R. Ford signed the Metric Conversion Act of 1975. It defines the metric system as being the International System of Units as interpreted in the U.S. by the secretary of commerce. The Trade Act of 1988 and other legislation declare the metric system the preferred system of weights and measures for U.S. trade and commerce, call for the federal government to adopt metric specifications, and mandate the Commerce Dept. to oversee the program. However, the metric system has still not become the system of choice for most Americans' daily use.

The following 7 units serve as the base units for the system: **length**—meter; **mass**—kilogram; **time**—second; **electric current**—ampere; **thermodynamic temperature**—kelvin; **amount of substance**—mole; and **luminous intensity**—candela.

Frequently Used Conversions

Boldface indicates exact values. For greater accuracy, use the "multiply by" number in parentheses. For more detailed tables, see pages 699-702.

U.S. Customary to Metric

	If you have:	Multiply by:		To get:
Length	inches	**25.4**		millimeters
	inches	**2.54**		centimeters
	inches	**0.0254**		meters
	feet	0.3	(**0.3048**)	meters
	yards	0.9	(**0.9144**)	meters
	miles[1]	1.6	(**1.609344**)	kilometers
Area	sq. inches	6.5	(**6.4516**)	sq. cm.
	sq. feet	0.09	(0.09290341)	sq. meters
	sq. yards	0.84	(0.83612736)	sq. meters
	acres	0.4	(0.4046873)	hectares
	sq. miles	2.6	(2.58998811)	sq. kilometers
Weight	ounces (avdp)	28	(**28.349523125**)	grams
	pounds (avdp)	454	(**453.59237**)	grams
	pounds (avdp)	0.45	(**0.45359237**)	kilograms
	short tons[2]	0.91	(**0.90718474**)	metric tons
	long tons[3]	1	(**1.0160469088**)	metric tons
Liquid meas.	ounces	0.03	(0.02957353)	liters
	cups	0.24	(0.23658824)	liters
	pints	0.47	(0.473176473)	liters
	quarts	0.95	(0.946352946)	liters
	gallons	3.79	(3.785411784)	liters

Metric to U.S. Customary

	If you have:	Multiply by:		To get:
Length	millimeters	0.04	(0.03937)	inches
	centimeters	0.4	(0.3937)	inches
	meters	39	(39.37)	inches
	meters	3.3	(3.280840)	feet
	meters	1.1	(1.093613)	yards
	kilometers	0.6	(0.621371)	miles
Area	sq. cm.	0.16	(0.15500)	sq. inches
	sq. meters	10.8	(10.76391)	sq. feet
	sq. meters	1.2	(1.195990)	sq. yards
	hectares	2.5	(2.471044)	acres
	sq. kilometers	0.39	(0.386102)	sq. miles
Weight	grams	0.035	(0.03527396)	ounces (avdp)
	grams	0.002	(0.00220462)	pounds (avdp)
	kilograms	2.2	(2.204623)	pounds (avdp)
	metric tons	1.1	(1.102311)	short tons[2]
	metric tons	0.98	(0.9842065)	long tons[3]
Liquid meas.	liters	33.8	(33.81402)	ounces
	liters	4.2	(4.226752)	cups
	liters	2.1	(2.113376)	pints
	liters	1.1	(1.056688)	quarts
	liters	0.26	(0.264172)	gallons

(1) Statute mile. (2) A short ton is 2,000 pounds. (3) A long ton is 2,240 pounds.

Temperature Conversions

The left-hand column below gives a temperature according to the **Celsius** scale, and the right-hand gives the same temperature according to the **Fahrenheit** scale. The lowest number for each scale refers to what scientists call absolute zero, the temperature at which all molecular motion would be at its lowest level.

For temperatures not shown: To convert Fahrenheit to Celsius by formula, subtract 32 degrees and divide by 1.8; to convert Celsius to Fahrenheit, multiply by 1.8 and add 32 degrees.

Note: Although the term *centigrade* is still frequently used, the International Committee on Weights and Measures and the National Institute of Standards and Technology have recommended since 1948 that this scale be called *Celsius*.

Celsius	Fahrenheit	Celsius	Fahrenheit	Celsius	Fahrenheit	Celsius	Fahrenheit	Celsius	Fahrenheit
−273.15	−459.67	−45.6	−50	−1.1	30	30	86	66	150
−250	−418	−40	−40	0	32	32.2	90	70	158
−200	−328	−34.4	−30	4.4	40	35	95	80	176
−184	−300	−30	−22	10	50	37	98.6	90	194
−157	−250	−28.9	−20	15.6	60	37.8	100	93	200
−150	−238	−23.3	−10	20	68	40	104	100	212
−129	−200	−20	−4	21.1	70	43	110	121	250
−101	−150	−17.8	0	23.9	75	49	120	149	300
−100	−148	−12.2	10	25	77	50	122	150	302
− 73.3	−100	−10	14	26.7	80	54	130	200	392
− 50	− 58	− 6.7	20	29.4	85	60	140	300	572

Boiling and Freezing Points

Water boils at 212° F (100° C) at sea level. For every 550 feet above sea level, boiling point of water is lower by about 1° F. Methyl alcohol boils at 148° F. Average human oral temperature, 98.6° F. **Water freezes** at 32° F (0° C).

Mathematical Formulas

Note: The value of π (the Greek letter pi) is approximately 3.14159265 (equal to the ratio of the circumference of a circle to the diameter). The equivalence is typically rounded further to 3.1416 or 3.14.

To find the CIRCUMFERENCE of a:

Circle — Multiply the diameter by π.

To find the AREA of a:

Circle — Multiply the square of the radius (equal to ½ the diameter) by π.
Rectangle — Multiply the length of the base by the height.
Sphere (surface) — Multiply the square of the radius by π and multiply by 4.
Square — Square the length of one side.
Trapezoid — Add the 2 parallel sides, multiply by the height, and divide by 2.
Triangle — Multiply the base by the height, divide by 2.

To find the VOLUME of a:

Cone — Multiply the square of the radius of the base by π, multiply by the height, and divide by 3.
Cube — Cube the length of one edge.
Cylinder — Multiply the square of the radius of the base by π and multiply by the height.
Pyramid — Multiply the area of the base by the height and divide by 3.
Rectangular Prism — Multiply the length by the width by the height.
Sphere — Multiply the cube of the radius by π, multiply by 4, and divide by 3.

Playing Cards and Dice Chances

5-Card Poker Hands

Hand	Number possible	Odds against
Royal flush	4	649,739 to 1
Other straight flush	36	72,192 to 1
Four of a kind	624	4,164 to 1
Full house	3,744	693 to 1
Flush	5,108	508 to 1
Straight	10,200	254 to 1
Three of a kind	54,912	46 to 1
Two pairs	123,552	20 to 1
One pair	1,098,240	4 to 3 (1.37 to 1)
Nothing	1,302,540	1 to 1
TOTAL	**2,598,960**	

Note: Although there are only 13 4-of-a-kind combinations, the above numbers take into account the total possibilities when a 5th card is figured in to make a 5-card hand.

Bridge

The odds—against suit distribution in a hand of 4-4-3-2 are about 4 to 1, against 5-4-2-2 about 8 to 1, against 6-4-2-1 about 20 to 1, against 7-4-1-1 about 254 to 1, against 8-4-1-0 about 2,211 to 1, and against 13-0-0-0 about 158,753,389,899 to 1.

Dice

(probabilities of consecutive winning plays)

No. consecutive wins	By 7, 11, or point	No. consecutive wins	By 7, 11, or point
1	244 in 495	6	1 in 70
2	6 in 25	7	1 in 141
3	3 in 25	8	1 in 287
4	1 in 17	9	1 in 582
5	1 in 34		

Dice

(probabilities on 2 dice)

Total	Odds against (single toss)	Total	Odds against (single toss)
2	35 to 1	8	31 to 5
3	17 to 1	9	8 to 1
4	11 to 1	10	11 to 1
5	8 to 1	11	17 to 1
6	31 to 5	12	35 to 1
7	5 to 1		

Large Numbers

U.S.	Number of zeros	British[1], French, German
million	6	million
billion	9	milliard
trillion	12	billion
quadrillion	15	1,000 billion
quintillion	18	trillion
sextillion	21	1,000 trillion
septillion	24	quadrillion
octillion	27	1,000 quadrillion
nonillion	30	quintillion
decillion	33	1,000 quintillion
undecillion	36	sextillion
duodecillion	39	1,000 sextillion
tredecillion	42	septillion
quattuordecillion	45	1,000 septillion
quindecillion	48	octillion
sexdecillion	51	1,000 octillion
septendecillion	54	nonillion
octodecillion	57	1,000 nonillion
novemdecillion	60	decillion
vigintillion	63	1,000 decillion
googol	100	googol
centillion	303	—
—	600	centillion
googolplex	googol	googolplex

(1) In recent years, it has become more common in Britain to use American terminology for large numbers.

Prime Numbers

A prime number is an integer other than zero or ±1 that is divisible only by ±1 and itself.

Prime Numbers between 1 and 1,000

	2	3	5	7	11	13	17	19	23
29	31	37	41	43	47	53	59	61	67
71	73	79	83	89	97	101	103	107	109
113	127	131	137	139	149	151	157	163	167
173	179	181	191	193	197	199	211	223	227
229	233	239	241	251	257	263	269	271	277
281	283	293	307	311	313	317	331	337	347
349	353	359	367	373	379	383	389	397	401
409	419	421	431	433	439	443	449	457	461
463	467	479	487	491	499	503	509	521	523
541	547	557	563	569	571	577	587	593	599
601	607	613	617	619	631	641	643	647	653
659	661	673	677	683	691	701	709	719	727
733	739	743	751	757	761	769	773	787	797
809	811	821	823	827	829	839	853	857	859
863	877	881	883	887	907	911	919	929	937
941	947	953	967	971	977	983	991	997	(1,009)

Roman Numerals

I — 1	V — 5	IX — 9	XX — 20	LX — 60	CD — 400
II — 2	VI — 6	X — 10	XXX— 30	XC — 90	D — 500
III — 3	VII — 7	XI — 11	XL — 40	C — 100	CM — 900
IV — 4	VIII — 8	XIX — 19	L — 50	CC — 200	M — 1,000

Note: The numerals V, X, L, C, D, or M shown with a horizontal line on top denote 1,000 times the original value.

Common Fractions Reduced to Decimals

8ths	16ths	32nds	64ths		8ths	16ths	32nds	64ths		8ths	16ths	32nds	64ths	
			1	= 0.015625				23	= 0.359375		11	22	44	= 0.6875
		1	2	= 0.03125	3	6	12	24	= 0.375				45	= 0.703125
			3	= 0.046875				25	= 0.390625			23	46	= 0.71875
	1	2	4	= 0.0625			13	26	= 0.40625				47	= 0.734375
			5	= 0.078125				27	= 0.421875	6	12	24	48	= 0.75
		3	6	= 0.09375		7	14	28	= 0.4375				49	= 0.765625
			7	= 0.109375				29	= 0.453125			25	50	= 0.78125
1	2	4	8	= 0.125			15	30	= 0.46875				51	= 0.796875
			9	= 0.140625				31	= 0.484375		13	26	52	= 0.8125
		5	10	= 0.15625	4	8	16	32	= 0.5				53	= 0.828125
			11	= 0.171875				33	= 0.515625			27	54	= 0.84375
	3	6	12	= 0.1875			17	34	= 0.53125				55	= 0.859375
			13	= 0.203125				35	= 0.546875	7	14	28	56	= 0.875
		7	14	= 0.21875			18	36	= 0.5625				57	= 0.890625
			15	= 0.234375				37	= 0.578125			29	58	= 0.90625
2	4	8	16	= 0.25			19	38	= 0.59375				59	= 0.921875
			17	= 0.265625				39	= 0.609375		15	30	60	= 0.9375
		9	18	= 0.28125	5	10	20	40	= 0.625				61	= 0.953125
			19	= 0.296875				41	= 0.640625			31	62	= 0.96875
	5	10	20	= 0.3125			21	42	= 0.65625				63	= 0.984375
			21	= 0.328125				43	= 0.671875	8	16	32	64	= 1.0
		11	22	= 0.34375										

Metric System Prefixes

The following prefixes, in combination with the basic unit names, provide the multiples and submultiples in thes metric system. For example, the unit name *meter,* with the prefix *kilo* added, produces *kilometer,* meaning "1,000 meters."

Prefix	Symbol	Multiples	Equivalent
yotta	Y	10^{24}	septillionfold
zetta	Z	10^{21}	sextillionfold
exa	E	10^{18}	quintillionfold
peta	P	10^{15}	quadrillionfold
tera	T	10^{12}	trillionfold
giga	G	10^{9}	billionfold
mega	M	10^{6}	millionfold
kilo	k	10^{3}	thousandfold
hecto	h	10^{2}	hundredfold
deka	da	10	tenfold
deci	d	10^{-1}	tenth part
centi	c	10^{-2}	hundredth part
milli	m	10^{-3}	thousandth part
micro	µ	10^{-6}	millionth part
nano	n	10^{-9}	billionth part
pico	p	10^{-12}	trillionth part
femto	f	10^{-15}	quadrillionth part
atto	a	10^{-18}	quintillionth part
zepto	z	10^{-21}	sextillionth part
yocto	y	10^{-24}	septillionth part

WORLD ALMANAC QUICK QUIZ

Can you rank these units of measure from shortest to longest?

(a) foot (b) furlong
(c) fathom (d) angstrom

For the answer look in this chapter, or see page 1008.

Tables of Metric Weights and Measures

(**Note:** The metric system generally uses the term *mass* instead of *weight.* Mass is a measure of an object's inertial property, or the amount of matter it contains. Weight is a measure of the force exerted on an object by gravity or the force needed to support it. Also, the metric system does not make a distinction between "dry volume" and "liquid volume.")

Length

10 millimeters (mm) . . . .= 1 centimeter (cm)
10 centimeters . . . .= 1 decimeter (dm)
= 100 millimeters
10 decimeters. . . . .= 1 meter (m)
= 1,000 millimeters
10 meters . . . .= 1 dekameter (dam)
10 dekameters . . . .= 1 hectometer (hm)
= 100 meters
10 hectometers . . . .= 1 kilometer (km)
= 1,000 meters

Area

100 square millimeters (mm^2) .= 1 square centimeter (cm^2)
10,000 square centimeters. . . .= 1 square meter (m^2)
= 1,000,000 square millimeters
100 square meters . . . .= 1 are (a)
100 ares . . . .= 1 hectare (ha)
= 10,000 square meters
100 hectares . . . .= 1 square kilometer (km^2)
= 1,000,000 square meters

Volume

10 milliliters (mL) . . . .= 1 centiliter (cL)
10 centiliters. . . . .= 1 deciliter (dL)
= 100 milliliters
10 deciliters . . . .= 1 liter (L)
= 1,000 milliliters
10 liters . . . . = 1 dekaliter (daL)
10 dekaliters . . . . = 1 hectoliter (hL)
= 100 liters
10 hectoliters. . . . . = 1 kiloliter (kL)
= 1,000 liters

Volume (Cubic Measure)

1,000 cubic millimeters (mm^3). = 1 cubic centimeter (cm^3)
1,000 cubic centimeters . . . . . = 1 cubic decimeter (dm^3)
= 1,000,000 cubic millimeters
1,000 cubic decimeters . . . . . . = 1 cubic meter (m^3)
= 1 stere
= 1,000,000 cubic centimeters
= 1,000,000,000 cubic millimeters

Weight (Mass)

10 milligrams (mg). . . . . = 1 centigram (cg)
10 centigrams . . . . = 1 decigram (dg)
= 100 milligrams
10 decigrams. . . . . = 1 gram (g)
= 1,000 milligrams
10 grams . . . . = 1 dekagram (dag)
10 dekagrams . . . . = 1 hectogram (hg)
= 100 grams
10 hectograms. . . . . = 1 kilogram (kg)
= 1,000 grams
1,000 kilograms. . . . . = 1 metric ton (t)

Table of U.S. Customary Weights and Measures

Length

12 inches (in)	= 1 foot (ft)
3 feet	= 1 yard (yd)
5½ yards	= 1 rod (rd), pole, or perch (16½ feet)
40 rods	= 1 furlong (fur)
	= 220 yards
	= 660 feet
8 furlongs	= 1 statute mile (mi)
	= 1,760 yards
	= 5,280 feet
3 miles	= 1 league
	= 5,280 yards
	= 15,840 feet
6076.11549 feet	= 1 international nautical mile

Volume (Liquid Measure)

When necessary to distinguish the liquid pint or quart from the dry pint or quart, the word *liquid* or the abbreviation *liq* is used in combination with the name or abbreviation of the liquid unit.

4 gills (gi)	= 1 pint (pt)
	= 28.875 cubic inches
2 pints	= 1 quart (qt)
	= 57.75 cubic inches
4 quarts	= 1 gallon (gal)
	= 231 cubic inches
	= 8 pints
	= 32 gills

Volume (Dry Measure)

When necessary to distinguish the dry pint or quart from the liquid pint or quart, the word *dry* is used in combination with the name or abbreviation of the dry unit.

2 pints (pt)	= 1 quart (qt)
	= 67.2006 cubic inches
8 quarts	= 1 peck (pk)
	= 537.605 cubic inches
	= 16 pints
4 pecks	= 1 bushel (bu)
	= 2,150.42 cubic inches
	= 32 quarts

Area

Squares and cubes of units are sometimes abbreviated by using superscripts. For example, ft^2 means square foot, and ft^3 means cubic foot.

144 square inches	= 1 square foot (ft^2)
9 square feet	= 1 square yard (yd^2)
	= 1,296 square inches
30 ¼ square yards	= 1 square rod (rd^2)
	= 272¼ square feet
160 square rods	= 1 acre
	= 4,840 square yards
	= 43,560 square feet
640 acres	= 1 square mile (mi^2)
1 mile square	= 1 section (of land)
6 miles square	= 1 township
	= 36 sections
	= 36 square miles

Cubic Measure

1 cubic foot (ft^3)	= 1,728 cubic inches (in^3)
27 cubic feet	= 1 cubic yard (yd^3)

Gunter's, or Surveyor's, Chain Measure

7.92 inches (in)	= 1 link
100 links	= 1 chain (ch)
	= 4 rods
	= 66 feet
80 chains	= 1 statute mile (mi)
	= 320 rods
	= 5,280 feet

Avoirdupois Weight

When necessary to distinguish the avoirdupois ounce or pound from the troy ounce or pound, the word *avoirdupois* or the abbreviation *avdp* is used in combination with the name or abbreviation of the avoirdupois unit. The *grain* is the same in avoirdupois and troy weight.

27 $^{11}/_{32}$ grains	= 1 dram (dr)
16 drams	= 1 ounce (oz)
	= 437 ½ grains
16 ounces	= 1 pound (lb)
	= 256 drams
	= 7,000 grains
100 pounds	= 1 hundredweight (cwt)*
20 hundredweights	= 1 ton
	= 2,000 pounds*

In *gross* or *long* measure, the following values are recognized.

112 pounds	= 1 gross or long hundredweight*
20 gross or long hundredweights	= 1 gross or long ton
	= 2,240 pounds*

*When the terms *hundredweight* and *ton* are used unmodified, they are commonly understood to mean the 100-pound hundredweight and the 2,000-pound ton, respectively; these units may be designated *net* or *short* when necessary to distinguish them from the corresponding units in gross or long measure.

Troy Weight

24 grains	= 1 pennyweight (dwt)
20 pennyweights	= 1 ounce troy (oz t)
	= 480 grains
12 ounces troy	= 1 pound troy (lb t)
	= 240 pennyweights
	= 5,760 grains

Tables of Equivalents

In this table it is necessary to distinguish between the *international* and the *survey* foot. The international foot, defined in 1959 as exactly equal to 0.3048 meter, is shorter than the old survey foot by exactly 2 parts in 1 million. The survey foot is still used in data expressed in feet in geodetic surveys within the U.S. In this table the survey foot is indicated with capital letters.

When the name of a unit is enclosed in brackets, e.g., [1 hand], either (1) the unit is not in general current use in the U.S. or (2) the unit is believed to be based on custom and usage rather than on formal definition.

Equivalents involving decimals are, in most instances, rounded to the 3rd decimal place; exact equivalents are so designated.

Lengths

1 angstrom (Å)	= 0.1 nanometer (exactly)
	= 0.000 1 micrometer (exactly)
	= 0.000 000 1 millimeter (exactly)
	= 0.000 000 004 inch
1 cable's length	= 120 fathoms (exactly)
	= 720 FEET (exactly)
	= 219 meters
1 centimeter (cm)	= 0.3937 inch
1 chain (ch) (Gunter's or surveyor's)	= 66 FEET (exactly)
	= 20.1168 meters
	= 100 feet
1 chain (engineer's)	= 30.48 meters (exactly)
1 decimeter (dm)	= 3.937 inches
1 degree (geographical)	= 364,566.929 feet
	= 69.047 miles (avg.)
	= 111.123 kilometers (avg.)
of latitude	= 68.708 miles at equator
	= 69.403 miles at poles
of longitude	= 69.171 miles at equator
1 dekameter (dam)	= 32.808 feet
1 fathom	= 6 FEET (exactly)
	= 1.8288 meters
1 foot (ft)	= 0.3048 meters (exactly)
	= 10 chains (surveyors) (exactly)
1 furlong (fur)	= 660 FEET (exactly)
	= $^1/_8$ statute mile (exactly)
	= 201.168 meters
[1 hand] (height measure for horses from ground to top of shoulders)	= 4 inches
1 inch (in)	= 2.54 centimeters (exactly)
1 kilometer (km)	= 0.621371 mile
	= 3,280.8 feet
1 league (land)	= 3 statute miles (exactly)
	= 4.828 kilometers
1 link (Gunter's or surveyor's)	= 7.92 inches (exactly)
	= 0.201 meter
1 link (engineer's)	= 1 foot
	= 0.305 meter
1 meter (m)	= 39.37 inches
	= 1.09361 yards
1 micrometer (µm)	= 0.001 millimeter (exactly)
	= 0.00003937 inch

1 mil	= 0.001 inch (exactly)
	= 0.0254 millimeter (exactly)
1 mile (mi) (statute or land)	= 5,280 FEET (exactly)
	= 1.609344 kilometers (exactly)
1 international nautical mile (nmi)	= 1.852 kilometers (exactly)
	= 1.150779 statute miles
	= 6,076.11549 feet
1 millimeter (mm)	= 0.03937 inch
1 nanometer (nm)	= 0.001 micrometer (exactly)
	= 0.00000003937 inch
1 pica (typography)	= 12 points
1 point (typography)	= 0.013 837 inch (exactly)
	= 0.351 millimeter
1 rod (rd), pole, or perch	= 16½ FEET (exactly)
	= 5.029 meters
1 yard (yd)	= 0.9144 meter (exactly)

Areas or Surfaces

1 acre	= 43,560 square FEET (exactly)
	= 4,840 square yards
	= 0.405 hectare
1 are (a)	= 119.599 square yards
	= 0.025 acre
1 bolt (cloth measure):	
length	= 100 yards (on modern looms)
width	= 45 or 60 inches
1 hectare (ha)	= 2.471 acres
[1 square (building)]	= 100 square feet
1 square centimeter (cm^2)	= 0.155 square inch
1 square decimeter (dm^2)	= 15.500 square inches
1 square foot (ft^2)	= 929.030 square centimeters
1 square inch (in^2)	= 6.4516 square centimeters (exactly)
1 square kilometer (km^2)	= 247.104 acres
	= 0.386102 square mile
1 square meter (m^2)	= 1.196 square yards
	= 10.764 square feet
1 square mile (mi^2)	= 258.999 hectares
1 square millimeter (mm^2)	= 0.002 square inch
1 square rod (rd^2), sq. pole, or sq. perch	= 25.293 square meters
1 square yard (yd^2)	= 0.836127 square meter

Capacities or Volumes

1 barrel (bbl), liquid	= 31 to 42 gallons*

*There are a variety of "barrels" established by law or usage. For example: federal taxes on fermented liquors are based on a barrel of 31 gallons; many state laws fix the "barrel for liquids" as 31½ gallons; one state fixes a 36-gallon barrel for cistern measurement; federal law recognizes a 40-gallon barrel for "proof spirits"; by custom, 42 gallons constitute a barrel of crude oil or petroleum products for statistical purposes, and this equivalent is recognized "for liquids" by 4 states.

1 barrel (bbl), standard for fruits, vegetables, and other dry commodities except dry cranberries	= 7,056 cubic inches
	= 1 barrel (bbl), standard for fruits
1 barrel (bbl), standard, cranberry	= $86\frac{45}{64}$ dry quarts
	= 2.709 bushels, struck measure
	= 5,826 cubic inches
1 board foot (lumber measure)	= a foot-square board 1 inch thick
1 bushel (bu) (U.S.) (struck measure)	= 2,150.42 cubic inches (exactly)
	= 35.239 liters
[1 bushel, heaped (U.S.)]	= 2,747.715 cubic inches
	= 1.278 bushels, struck measure*

*Frequently recognized as 1¼ bushels, struck measure.

[1 bushel (bu) (British Imperial) (struck measure)]	= 1.032 U.S. bushels, struck measure
	= 2,219.36 cubic inches
1 cord (cd) firewood	= 128 cubic feet (exactly)
1 cubic centimeter (cm^3)	= 0.061 cubic inch
1 cubic decimeter (dm^3)	= 61.024 cubic inches
1 cubic inch (in^3)	= 0.554 fluid ounce
	= 4.433 fluid drams
	= 16.387 cubic centimeters
1 cubic foot (ft^3)	= 7.481 gallons
	= 28.317 cubic decimeters
1 cubic meter (m^3)	= 1.308 cubic yards
1 cubic yard (yd^3)	= 0.765 cubic meter
1 cup, measuring	= 8 fluid ounces (exactly)
	= ½ liquid pint (exactly)
[1 dram, fluid (fl dr) (British)]	= 0.961 U.S. fluid dram
	= 0.217 cubic inch
	= 3.552 milliliters
1 dekaliter (daL)	= 2.642 gallons
	= 1.135 pecks
1 gallon (gal) (U.S.)	= 231 cubic inches (exactly)
	= 3.785 liters
	= 0.833 British gallon
	= 128 U.S. fluid ounces (exactly)
[1 gallon (gal) British Imperial]	= 277.42 cubic inches
	= 1.201 U.S. gallons
	= 4.546 liters
	= 160 British fluid ounces (exactly)
1 gill (gi)	= 7.219 cubic inches
	= 4 fluid ounces (exactly)
	= 0.118 liter
1 hectoliter (hL)	= 26.418 gallons
	= 2.838 bushels
1 liter (L) (1 cubic decimeter exactly)	= 1.057 liquid quarts
	= 0.908 dry quart
	= 61.024 cubic inches
1 milliliter (mL) (1 cu cm exactly)	= 0.271 fluid dram
	= 16.231 minims
	= 0.061 cubic inch
1 ounce, liquid (U.S.)	= 1.805 cubic inches
	= 29.574 milliliters
	= 1.041 British fluid ounces
[1 ounce, fluid (fl oz) (British)]	= 0.961 U.S. fluid ounce
	= 1.734 cubic inches
	= 28.412 milliliters
1 peck (pk)	= 8.810 liters
1 pint (pt), dry	= 33.600 cubic inches
	= 0.551 liter
1 pint (pt), liquid	= 28.875 cubic inches (exactly)
	= 0.473 liter
1 quart (qt), dry (U.S.)	= 67.201 cubic inches
	= 1.101 liters
	= 0.969 British quart
1 quart (qt), liquid (U.S.)	= 57.75 cubic in (exactly)
	= 0.946 liter
	= 0.833 British quart
[1 quart (qt) (British)]	= 69.354 cubic inches
	= 1.032 U.S. dry quarts
	= 1.201 U.S. liquid quarts
1 tablespoon	= 3 teaspoons*(exactly)
	= 4 fluid drams
	= ½ fluid ounce (exactly)
1 teaspoon	= $\frac{1}{3}$ tablespoon*(exactly)
	= $1\frac{1}{3}$ fluid drams*

*The equivalent "1 teaspoon = $1\frac{1}{3}$ fluid drams" has been found to correspond more closely with the actual capacities of teaspoons in use than the equivalent "1 teaspoon = 1 fluid dram" which is given by many dictionaries.

Weights or Masses

1 assay ton** (AT)	= 29.167 grams

** Used in assaying. The assay ton bears the same relation to the milligram that a ton of 2,000 pounds avoirdupois bears to the ounce troy; hence, the weight in milligrams of precious metal obtained from one assay ton of ore gives directly the number of troy ounces to the net ton.

1 bale (cotton measure)	= 500 pounds in U.S.
	= 750 pounds in Egypt
1 carat (c)	= 200 milligrams (exactly)
	= 3.086 grains
1 dram avoirdupois (dr avdp)	= $27\frac{11}{32}$ (= 27.344) grains
	= 1.772 grams
1 gamma (g)	= 1 microgram (exactly), see below
1 grain	= 64.7989 milligrams
1 gram	= 15.432 grains
	= 0.035 ounce, avoirdupois
1 hundredweight, gross or long*** (gross cwt)	= 112 pounds (exactly)
	= 50.802 kilograms
1 hundredweight, net or short (cwt or net cwt)	= 100 pounds (exactly)
	= 45.359 kilograms
1 kilogram (kg)	= 2.20462 pounds
1 microgram (µg)	= 0.000001 gram (exactly)
1 milligram (mg)	= 0.015 grain
1 ounce, avoirdupois (oz avdp)	= 437.5 grains (exactly)
	= 0.911 troy ounce
	= 28.3495 grams

1 ounce, troy (oz t) .... = 480 grains (exactly)
= 1.097 avoirdupois ounces
= 31.103 grams
1 pennyweight (dwt) .... = 1.555 grams
1 pound, avoirdupois (lb avdp) = 7,000 grains (exactly)
= 1.215 troy pounds
= 453.59237 grams (exactly)
1 pound, troy (lb t) .... = 5,760 grains (exactly)
= 0.823 pound, avoirdupois
= 373.242 grams
1 stone, (avdp) .... = 14 pounds avdp (exactly)
= 6.350 kilograms

1 ton, gross or long***
(gross ton)............... = 2,240 pounds (exactly)
= 1.12 net tons (exactly)
= 1.016 metric tons

***The gross or long ton and hundredweight are used commercially in the U.S. to only a limited extent, usually in restricted industrial fields. These units are the same as the British ton and hundredweight.

1 ton, metric (t) .... = 2,204.623 pounds
= 0.984 gross ton
= 1.102 net tons
1 ton, net or short (sh ton) .... = 2,000 pounds (exactly)
= 0.893 gross ton
= 0.907 metric ton

Electrical Units

The **watt** is the unit of power (electrical, mechanical, thermal, etc.). Electrical power is given by the product of the voltage and the current.

Energy is sold by the **joule,** but in common practice the billing of electrical energy is expressed in terms of the **kilowatt-hour,** which is 3,600,000 joules or 3.6 megajoules.

The **horsepower** is a nonmetric unit sometimes used in mechanics. It is equal to 746 watts.

The **ohm** is the unit of electrical resistance and represents the physical property of a conductor that offers a resistance to the flow of electricity, permitting just 1 ampere to flow at 1 volt of pressure.

Measures of Force and Pressure

Dyne = force necessary to accelerate a 1-gram mass 1 centimeter per second squared = 0.000072 poundal

Poundal = force necessary to accelerate a 1-pound mass 1 foot per second squared = 13,825.5 dynes = 0.138255 newtons

Newton = force needed to accelerate a 1-kilogram mass 1 meter per second squared

Pascal (pressure) = 1 newton per square meter = 0.020885 pound per square foot

Atmosphere (air pressure at sea level) = 2,116.102 pounds per square foot = 14.6952 pounds per square inch = 1.0332 kilograms per square centimeter = 101,323 newtons per square meter

Spirits Measures

Pony .... = 0.5 jigger
Shot .... = 0.666 jigger
= 1.0 ounce
Jigger .... = 1.5 shots
Pint .... = 16 shots
= 0.625 fifth
Fifth .... = 25.6 shots
= 1.6 pints
= 0.8 quart
= 0.75706 liter

Quart .... = 32 shots
= 1.25 fifths
Magnum............ = 2 quarts
= 2.49797 bottles (wine)

For champagne and brandy only:
Jeroboam .... = 6.4 pints
= 1.6 magnum
= 0.8 gallon

For champagne only:
Rehoboam .... = 3 magnums
Methuselah........ = 4 magnums
Salmanazar .... = 6 magnums
Balthazar .... = 8 magnums
Nebuchadnezzar ... = 10 magnums
Wine bottle (standard). = 0.800633 quart
= 0.7576778 liter

Miscellaneous Modern Measures

Caliber—the diameter of a gun bore. In the U.S., caliber is traditionally expressed in hundredths of inches, e.g., .22. In Britain, caliber is often expressed in thousandths of inches, e.g., .270. Now it is commonly expressed in millimeters, e.g., the 5.56 mm M16 rifle. Heavier weapons' caliber has long been expressed in millimeters, e.g., the 155 mm howitzer. Naval guns' caliber refers to the barrel length as a multiple of the bore diameter. A 5-inch, 50-caliber naval gun has a 5-inch bore and a barrel length of 250 inches.

Decibel (dB)—a measure of the relative loudness or intensity of sound. A 20-decibel sound is 10 times louder than a 10-decibel sound; 30 decibels is 100 times louder; 40 decibels is 1,000 times louder, etc.

One decibel is the smallest difference between sounds detectable by the human ear. A 120-decibel sound is painful.

10 decibels – a light whisper
20 – quiet conversation
30 – normal conversation
40 – light traffic
50 – typewriter, loud conversation
60 – noisy office
70 – normal traffic, quiet train
80 – rock music, subway
90 – heavy traffic, thunder
100 – jet plane at takeoff

Em—a printer's measure designating the square width of any given type size. Thus, an em of 10-point type is 10 points. An en is half an em.

Gauge—a measure of shotgun bore diameter. Gauge numbers originally referred to the number of lead balls just fitting the gun barrel diameter required to make a pound. Thus, a 16-gauge shotgun's bore was smaller than a 12-gauge shotgun's. Today, an international agreement assigns millimeter measures to each gauge, e.g.:

Gauge	Bore diameter (in mm)
6	23.34
10	19.67
12	18.52
14	17.60
16	16.81
20	15.90

Horsepower—the power needed to lift 550 pounds 1 foot in 1 second or to lift 33,000 pounds 1 foot in 1 minute. Equivalent to 746 watts or 2,546.0756 Btu/h.

Karat or carat—a measure of fineness for gold equal to $^1/_{24}$ part of pure gold in an alloy. Thus 24-karat gold is pure; 18-karat gold is ¼ alloy. The *carat* is also used as a unit of weight for precious stones; it is equal to 200 milligrams or 3.086 grains troy.

Knot—a measure of the speed of ships. A knot equals 1 nautical mile per hour.

Quire—25 sheets of paper

Ream—500 sheets of paper

Ancient Measures

Biblical

Cubit...... = 21.8 inches
Omer ...... = 0.45 peck
= 3.964 liters
Ephah...... = 10 omers
Shekel .... = 0.497 ounce
= 14.1 grams

Greek

Cubit ..... = 18.3 inches
Stadion ... = 607.2 or 622 feet
Obolos .... = 715.38 milligrams
Drachma .. = 4.2923 grams
Mina...... = 0.9463 pound
Talent .... = 60 mina

Roman

Cubit ..... = 17.5 inches
Stadium... = 202 yards
As, libra, pondus . = 325.971 grams
= 0.71864 pound

COMPUTERS AND THE INTERNET

About Personal Computers

A personal computer, or PC, is a relatively small computer used by one person at a time. Portable PCs compact enough to fit on a person's lap are known as **laptops** or (in the case of lighter models) **notebooks**. Special software called the **operating system** enables you to operate the computer system's physical parts, or hardware. The most common operating systems used on PCs are Microsoft Windows, the Macintosh OS, and Linux.

(The term "personal computer" is also sometimes used more narrowly to refer just to machines conforming to the standard developed by IBM for personal computers, which uses a microprocessor made by Intel, or a compatible processor, and an operating system such as Windows or Linux that can work with that processor.)

The heart of a PC is its microprocessor, or **central processing unit**, contained on a chip of silicon. The microprocessor carries out arithmetic and logical operations specified by computer programs. PCs have several places where data and instructions are kept, among them:

• **ROM** (Read Only Memory), a type of memory in which once information is written, it cannot be changed, but only read. ROM may be used to keep information that always needs to be available, such as the instructions for loading the operating system when you turn your computer on.

• **RAM** (Random Access Memory), computer memory where data and programs are temporarily kept when they are being worked on; its contents are lost when the computer is turned off.

• **Hard drive**, a hardware device containing one or more disks for long-term storage of data and programs; information placed on a hard disk will remain there until erased or deleted. Information on a hard drive is accessed more slowly than information in RAM.

A PC usually offers several ways to put information into them and get information out. **Input devices** generally include a keyboard and a mouse (or its equivalent for a laptop, such as a trackball, pointing stick, or touch pad). There may also be a microphone and some sort of device for connecting the PC to other computers on a local network or to distant computers via, say, the Internet. A modem is a common device for connecting to the Internet via a telephone line. These days, most computers also have a CD-ROM drive, for reading information from CD-ROM discs. Some systems may include a scanner, for capturing the content of printed materials. **Output devices** typically include a video monitor, a printer, speakers, and, again, a connection to the Internet or to a local network. Many computers have one or more additional devices from which information may be input and to which information may be output, such as a floppy drive, a special type of CD-ROM drive that permits the computer to write information to the disk as well as read from it, and/or a DVD drive. All such devices connected to the computer proper (basically the microprocessor and associated circuitry and memory) are called **peripherals**.

Commonly used measures for the **capacity or power** of a PC include the speed of the microprocessor, expressed in megahertz (MHz), millions of cycles per second, or in gigahertz (GHz), billions of cycles per second; the size of the RAM, expressed in megabytes, or millions of bytes; and the size of the hard drive, expressed in gigabytes, or billions of bytes. Generally speaking, the bigger these numbers are, the more capable the machine. In mid-2002, average-priced desktop PCs (i.e., in the $700-$1,500 range) usually offered 128 or 256 megabytes of RAM, processor speeds of 1 to 2 gigahertz, and hard drives with 20 to 40 gigabytes storage capacity. (A caveat: technological improvements mean these numbers will be outdated fairly quickly.)

Computer Milestones

Devices for performing calculations are nothing new—the abacus, a frame with wires on which beads are moved back and forth (still used today in some parts of the world), traces its origins back to ancient times. But the marvels of electronic miniaturization that are modern PCs are a relatively recent development. They are the descendents of vacuum-tube devices introduced in the early 20th century.

Among early **landmark events in computer history** are:

• In 1623 the **1st mechanical calculator**, capable of adding, subtracting, multiplying, and dividing was developed by the German mathematician Wilhelm Schikard; the only 2 models Schikard made, however, were destroyed in a fire.

• In 1642 French mathematician Blaise Pascal built the 1st of more than 4 dozen copies of an adding and subtracting machine that he invented.

• In 1790, French inventor Joseph Marie Jacquard devised a new control system for looms. He "programmed" the loom, communicating desired weaving operations to the machine via patterns of holes in paper cards.

• The British mathematician and scientist Charles Babbage used the Jacquard punch-card system in his design for a sophisticated, programmable **"Analytical Engine"** that contained some of the basic features of today's computers. Babbage's conception was beyond the capabilities of the technology of his time, and the machine remained unfinished at his death in 1871.

• The **1890 U.S. census** was expedited by the rapid processing of huge amounts of data with an electrical punch-card tabulating machine developed by American inventor Herman Hollerith, whose company in 1924 became International Business Machines (IBM).

• On the eve of World War II researchers experimented with ways to speed up computation, since calculators using solely mechanical components were too slow. One approach was to use **electromechanical relays**, which basically are electrically controlled switches.

• In 1940, Bell Laboratories mathematician George Stibitz completed the 1st electromechanical relay-based calculator. In the same year Stibitz provided the 1st demonstration of remote operation of a computer, using a teletype to transmit problems to his machine and to receive the results.

• In 1941, German engineer Konrad Zuse completed the relay-based Z3, the 1st fully functional digital computer to be controlled by a program. In 1944, the **1st large-scale automatic digital computer**, the Mark I, built by IBM and Harvard Professor Howard Aiken, went into operation; this relay-based machine was 55 feet long and 8 feet high.

Efforts were also under way to develop **fully electronic machines**, using vacuum tubes, which can operate much more quickly than relays.

• Between 1937 and 1942 the 1st rudimentary vacuum-tube calculator was built by the physicist John Vincent Atanasoff and his assistant Clifford Berry at Iowa State College (now University).

• More substantial electronic machines were the Colossus, developed by the British in 1943 to break German codes, and the **Eniac** (for Electronic Numerical Integrator and Computer), a 30-ton room-sized computer with over 18,000 vacuum tubes, built by physicist John Mauchly and engineer J. Presper Eckert at the University of Pennsylvania for the U.S. Army and completed in 1946. The Colossus was a special-purpose machine; its capabilities were powerful (for its time) but limited. Eniac was a general-purpose machine and could be programmed to do different tasks, although programming could take a couple of days, since cables had to be plugged in and switches set by hand.

• In 1951, Eckert and Mauchly's **Univac** ("Universal Automatic Computer") became the 1st computer commercially available in the U.S.; the 1st customer: the Census Bureau. CBS-TV used a Univac in 1952 to predict the results of the presidential election.

The invention of the **transistor** in 1947 and the **integrated circuit** in 1958 paved the way for the development of the **microprocessor** (an entire computer processing unit on a chip), the 1st commercial example of which was the Intel 4004 in 1971. These advances allowed computers to become smaller, speedier, more reliable, and more powerful. In fact, a prediction made in 1965 by engineer and Intel cofounder Gordon Moore that the number of transistors that could be put on a computer chip would double every year (revised in 1975 to every 18 months) has largely held true, coming to be known as "Moore's Law."

• In 1975 the **1st widely marketed personal computer**, the MITS Altair 8800, was introduced in kit form, with no keyboard and no video display, for under $400. In the same year Microsoft was founded by Bill Gates and Paul Allen.

• In 1976 the **1st PC word-processing program**, the Electric Pencil, was written.

• In 1977 the **Apple II** was introduced by Apple Computer, which had been formed the previous year by Steven Jobs and Stephen Wozniak. Capable of displaying text and graphics in color, the machine enjoyed phenomenal success.

• In 1981, **IBM** unveiled its "Personal Computer," which used Microsoft's DOS (disk operating system).

• In 1984, Apple Computer introduced the 1st **Macintosh**. The easy-to-use Macintosh came with a proprietary operating system and was the 1st popular computer to have a GUI (graphical user interface) and a mouse—features originally developed by the Xerox Corporation.

• In 1990, Microsoft released **Windows** 3.0, the 1st workable version of its own GUI.

• In 1991, **Linux**, based on the Unix operating system used in high-power computers, was invented for the PC by Helsinki Univ. student Linus Torvalds and made available for free.

In 1996 the **Palm Pilot**, 1st widely successful handheld computer and personal information manager, arrived.

• In 1997 the IBM computer Deep Blue beat world chess champion Garry Kasparov in a 6-game match, 3.5-2.5.

• In 2001, Apple introduced a new Unix-based operating system called OS X for the Macintosh.

• In Mar. 2002, *The Sims*, involving a community of simulated people, became the best-selling computer game of all time, according to game maker Electronic Arts, which said more than 6.3 million copies had been shipped worldwide since its introduction in Feb. 2000.

By Apr. 2002, according to computer industry research firm Gartner Dataquest, **1 billion personal computers** (PCs), including desktop and laptop machines of all types, had been shipped by manufacturers since 1975, when the 1st commercially successful PC went on sale. The next billion were expected to ship within 5 or 6 years. Apple had less than 5% of the U.S. personal computer market as of early 2002, with machines using the Microsoft Windows operating system accounting for almost all the rest.

About the Internet

The **Internet** is a vast computer network of computer networks. In 1994, a total of 3 million people (most of them in the U.S.) made use of it. As of early 2002, according to Nielsen//NetRatings, 166 million Americans had access to the Internet from their homes, the largest number of any country in the world. China, with more than 56 million, was in 2nd place. In terms of percentage of households with Internet access, Canada, at more than 60%, was number 1. According to estimates by Global Reach in early 2002, English was the native language of 2/5 of the roughly 560 million people online; the 2nd-most-common language was Chinese, with nearly 10%

According to Nielsen//NetRatings data, as of early 2002 the U.S. and Canada were the only Internet markets where females online outnumbered males, although in New Zealand the split between the sexes was almost 50-50. A Digital Marketing Services survey found that American mothers averaged about 1/3 more time online per week than American teenagers.

As of June 2002, the search engine company FAST claimed that its AllTheWeb.com engine had indexed the most Web pages—2.1 billion, slightly more than runner-up Google. The total size of the Web, according to search engine developer BrightPlanet, lies in the hundreds of billions of pages.

By Dec. 1996, about 627,000 Internet domain names had been registered. By mid-2002, more than 30 million had been registered.

The Internet is not owned or funded by any one institution, organization, or government. It has no CEO and is not a commercial service. Its development is guided by the Internet Society (ISOC), composed of volunteers. The ISOC appoints the Internet Architecture Board (IAB), which works out issues of standards, network resources, etc. Other volunteer groups are the Internet Engineering Task Force (IETF), which handles day-to-day issues, and the Internet Research Task Force (IRTF), which carries out research on the Internet's long-term future.

Internet Milestones

The Internet grew out of a series of developments in the academic, governmental, and information technology communities. Here are some **major historical highlights**:

• In 1969, ARPANET, an experimental 4-computer network, was established by the Advanced Research Projects Agency (ARPA) of the U.S. Defense Dept. so that research scientists could communicate.

• By 1971, ARPANET linked about 2 dozen computers ("hosts") at 15 sites, including MIT and Harvard. By 1981, there were over 200 hosts.

• During the 1980s, more and more computers using different operating systems were connected. In 1983, the military portion of ARPANET was moved onto the MILNET, and ARPANET was disbanded in 1990.

• In the late 1980s, the National Science Foundation's NSFNET began its own network and allowed everyone to access it. It was, however, mainly the domain of "techies," computer-science graduates, and professors.

• In 1988, Internet Relay Chat (IRC) was developed by Finnish student Jarkko Oikarinen, enabling people to communicate via the Internet in "real time." It 1st drew world attention as a source of up-to-date information in the 1991 Persian Gulf War.

• In 1989 the 1st commercial ISP supplying dial-up Internet access appeared, known as The World.

• In 1989-90 the **World Wide Web** was invented by Tim Berners-Lee as an environment in which scientists at the European Center for Nuclear Research in Switzerland could share information. It gradually evolved into a medium with text, graphics, audio, animation, and video.

• Legislation in the early 1990s expanded NSFNET, renamed it NREN (National Research and Education Network), and encouraged development of commercial transmission and network services. The mass commercialization of today's Internet is largely a result of such legislation.

• 1991 saw release of the 1st **browser**, or software for accessing the World Wide Web. In 1993, the U.S. National Center for Supercomputing Applications released versions of Mosaic, the 1st graphical Web browser, for Microsoft Windows, Unix systems running the X Window GUI, and the Apple Macintosh.

• In 1994, **Netscape** Communications released the Netscape Navigator browser. **Microsoft** released its Internet Explorer browser the following year but initially failed to make a significant dent in Netscape's dominance of the browser market.

• By 1998, Netscape Navigator's share of the browser market had fallen below 50%, while Internet Explorer's exceeded 25%. Meanwhile, in 1998, the U.S. Justice Dept. and attorneys general from several states filed suit against Microsoft, claiming that the inclusion of Internet Explorer in Windows 98 violated antitrust guidelines.

• In Apr. 2000 a federal district judge found Microsoft guilty of antitrust violations; 2 months later he ordered the company split into 2 parts, but implementation of the penalty was stayed while Microsoft appealed. In June 2001 a federal appeals court issued an opinion skeptical of the breakup remedy, and in Sept. the Bush administration decided not to pursue a breakup.

• In Nov. 2001 the U.S. Justice Dept., Microsoft, and several states announced a settlement under which Microsoft would, among other things, make portions of its Windows operating system code available to competitors so they could ensure their software will work with it, and also permit computer makers to decide on their own which Microsoft products to include with their machines, without fear of Microsoft retaliation. Nine states plus the District of Columbia, however, continued to press for tougher restrictions.

• In June 2002, the trial portion of the Microsoft antitrust case concluded, and the judge proceeded to consider what restrictions should be imposed on the company.

• By mid-2002, according to market researchers, Internet Explorer browser was used by about 95% of people online; Netscape by over 3%, and the No. 3 browser, Opera, by less than 1%.

How the Internet Works

The 2 most popular aspects of the Internet are electronic mail, or e-mail, and the World Wide Web, which may be thought of as a graphical environment that can be navigated through **hyperlinks**—from one site you click on hyperlinks to go to related sites. The Internet in general involves 3 basic elements: server, client, and network. A **server** is a computer program that makes data available to other programs on the same or other computers—it "serves" them. A **client** is a computer that requests data from a server. A **network** is an interconnected system in which multiple computers can communicate, via copper wire, coaxial cable, fiber-optic cable, satellite transmission, etc. When you use a **browser** to go to a site on the World Wide Web, you access the site's files.

Here are the steps in opening and accessing a file:

• In the browser, specify the address, or **URL**, of the website.

• The browser sends your request to the server of your **Internet service provider** (ISP), the company that supplies your connection to the Internet.

• That server sends the request to the server at the URL.

• The file is sent to the ISP's server, which sends the file back to the browser, which displays the file.

Internet Resources

Domains. A domain is the fundamental part of an address on the Internet, such as a website address or an e-mail address. Since 1998 the system of domain names has been overseen by a nonprofit corporation called the Internet Corporation for Assigned Names and Numbers (ICANN). Dozens of companies offer domain registration services; examples include VeriSign, Register.com, and BulkRegister.com.

The final part of a domain name, known as the **top-level domain**, is its most basic part. For example, in The World Almanac's e-mail address—Walmanac@waegroup.com—the .com part is the top-level domain. ("Walmanac" is *The World Almanac*'s "username.") The top-level domains include:

Domain	What It Is
.aero	an organization in the air-transport industry
.biz	a business
.com	generally a commercial organization, business, or company
.coop	a nonprofit business cooperative, such as a rural electric coop
.edu	a 4-year higher-educational institution
.gov	a nonmilitary U.S. federal governmental entity, usually federal
.info	an informational site for an individual or organization, without restriction
.int	an international organization
.mil	a U.S. military organization
.museum	a museum
.name	an individual
.net	suggested for a network administration, but actually used by a wide variety of sites
.org	suggested for a nonprofit organization, but actually used by a wide variety of sites
.pro	a professional, such as an accountant, lawyer, or physician

The top-level domain .us is also available to persons, organizations, and entities in the U.S. Generally speaking, country codes are used for most top-level domains outside the U.S.—for example, .jp in Japan, .uk in the United Kingdom, and .ru in Russia.

FAQs. Frequently Asked Questions documents contain answers to common questions. A huge collection of FAQs can be found at the site www.faqs.org/faqs.

FTP. File Transfer Protocol is a simple method of transferring files on the Internet. Using FTP, you log on to a remote site, find files, and copy them to your computer. Sites that offer FTP capability can be accessed with special programs and also with most browsers. The address for such a site when accessed through a browser typically begins with ftp://.

HTTP. Hypertext Transfer Protocol is the file-exchange method underlying the World Wide Web. A website address begins with http:// (or https:// for "secure" sites that protect the confidentiality of information you may transmit over the Web).

Newsgroups. Newsgroups, a classic institution of the Internet, are found on the part of the Internet called Usenet. In a newsgroup, messages concerning a particular topic are posted in a public forum. You can simply read the postings, or you can post something yourself.

Online Activities

Communication via e-mail or online chat is the most widely used application of the Internet. The Net is also a major source of reference information. Health, for example, is currently a topic of particularly active interest to Internet users. As of early 2002, according to a Harris Interactive survey, about 110 million people in the U.S. were using the Internet to find information about health topics, up from 54 million in 1998. The Internet is also a vehicle for such activities as distributing music, broadcasting radio, and doing business. A Jan. 2002 analysis by Nielsen//NetRatings found that the "stickiest" websites—those with the highest online time per visitor—concerned finance and investment. They beat such other broad categories as news, search engines and portals, and travel.

Spending by U.S. consumers online reached a record $17.5 billion in the 2nd quarter of 2002, according to comScore Media Metrix, up 41% from the previous year; travel was reported to be the top spending category, at $7.8 billion.

Safety and Security on the Internet

Common sense dictates some basic security rules:

• Do not give out your phone number, address, or other personal information, unless needed for a transaction at a site you trust.

• Be careful about giving out credit card numbers.

• If you feel someone is being threatening or dangerous, inform your Internet service provider.

Viruses. There is always a risk of acquiring a computer **virus**. In a general sense, a virus is chunk of computer code designed to produce an unexpected event. Some viruses may merely display a whimsical message on your screen. Some may wreak havoc in your system. Your system can pick up a virus from a program downloaded from the Internet or elsewhere via modem (or received on a disk); a virus can also be communicated via e-mail, as was the case with Klez-H, the most common virus as of mid-2002.

You should have antivirus software installed on your computer, keep it up to date, and try to keep abreast of reports of new viruses. Be careful about opening e-mail from unknown correspondents, and if you have programs with a macro capability (macros are bits of auxiliary coding that are meant to play a helpful role but can be taken advantage of by some viruses), make sure the programs' macro virus protection (if any) is turned on. Keep macros disabled if you do not know what you might want to use them for. If you have a high-speed Internet connection that is always on, you should use protective "firewall" software to guard your system against attacks by hackers.

Some viruses propagate with the help of a carrier program. Others, such as worms, do not. A **worm** ordinarily does not damage files but reproduces itself with the help of the infected computer's resources. The term **Trojan horse** is used for malicious computer code that is concealed within harmless code or data and is capable of taking control at some point and causing damage.

Filtering. Such browsers as Internet Explorer, Netscape Navigator, and Opera, as well as some search engines, contain features that let you filter the content that can be viewed on your computer. Special filtering software is also available, and some ISPs, such as AOL and MSN, make it possible for you to restrict the type of content seen on screen.

Parents can find more information on protecting their children while online at the websites of several U.S. government agencies, such as the FBI (www.fbi.gov/publications/pguide/pguide.htm). Another helpful site is www.safekids.com.

Portals and Search Engines

Many people have a favorite site that they go to 1st when logging on to the World Wide Web. A convenient choice for such a site is a **portal,** a gateway site typically offering a search engine but also a variety of other features, which may include free e-mail (sometimes free voice mail as well), chat, instant messaging, news services, stock updates, weather reports, real estate listings, yellow pages, people finders, TV and movie listings, shopping, tools to create and post your own Web page, and perhaps even a language translation service. Many portals permit you to customize the opening screen. Another common feature is a personal calendar to help you schedule activities.

Leading portals include:

AltaVista . . . . . . www.altavista.com
AOL . . . . www.aol.com
Excite . . . . www.excite.com
Go.com . . . . www.go.com
Lycos . . . . www.lycos.com
MSN . . . . www.msn.com
Netscape.com . . . www.netscape.com
Yahoo! . . . . www.yahoo.com

By using the portal's **search engine** you can locate information and, in some cases, images on sites throughout a large part of the Internet. No search engine covers the entire Web completely, and some portals offer a list of search engines to choose from. Search engines typically allow you to find occurrences of a particular key word or words. Search engines use different methods for finding, indexing, and retrieving information. Some store only the title and URL of sites; others index every word of a site's content. Some give extra weight to words in titles or other key positions, or to sites for which more hyperlinks exist on the Web. Many search engines work with the help of a program called a "spider," "crawler," or "bot." This visits sites across the Web and extracts information that can be used to create the search engine's index.

In addition to a search engine that requires you to submit key words, some portals also offer a subject guide—a menu-like "directory," generally compiled by humans. You drill down through the directory to find a subcategory with websites of interest. Yahoo! is a popular example.

Among other search engines and directories:

AllTheWeb.com (www.alltheweb.com) is very up-to-date; it claims to completely refresh its index every 7 to 11 days and as of mid-2002 had the largest number of Web pages indexed, some 2.1 billion.

Ask Jeeves (www.askjeeves.com) provides a directory but also responds to questions entered in plain English.

Google (www.google.com) is also available via the Netscape.com and Yahoo! portals. It relies largely on link popularity in ranking the sites it retrieves and competes with AllTheWeb.com for the most Web pages covered.

HotBot (hotbot.lycos.com), owned by Lycos, offers useful advanced options.

Open Directory (dmoz.org) aims to cope with the vast size of the Web and produce the most comprehensive directory by using volunteer editors. Its information is used by such services as AOL, Netscape, Lycos, and HotBot.

Teoma (www.teoma.com) groups search results into topics and also supplies links to related resources.

A **meta-search engine** submits your request to several different search engines at the same time. However, meta-search engines typically do not exhaust each of the search engines' databases, and they may be unable to transmit complicated search requests. Among the better-known meta-search engines are **Dogpile** (www.dogpile.com); **Ixquick** (www.ixquick.com); **Queryserver** (www.queryserver.com); and **Vivísimo** (www.vivisimo.com).

Large segments of the Web are not readily searchable by general-purpose search engines. Special search tools include those available via the Direct Search site (www.freepint. com/gary/direct.htm). Another helpful site is Invisibleweb.com (www.invisibleweb.com).

If you would like more information about search engines, including links to specialized search tools, go to **Search Engine Watch,** at www.searchenginewatch.com.

WORLD ALMANAC QUICK QUIZ

What percent of Americans age 3 and up used the Internet in 2001?

(a) 31.5% (b) 53.9% (c) 73.2% (d) 86.6%

For the answer look in this chapter, or see page 1008.

Internet Lingo

The following abbreviations are sometimes used on the Internet documents and in e-mail.

BTW	By the way	**GTG**	Got to go	**OTOH**	On the other hand
F2F	Face to face; a personal meeting	**HHOK**	Ha, ha—only kidding	**PLS**	Please
FCOL	For crying out loud	**IMHO**	In my humble opinion	**ROTFL**	Rolling on the floor laughing
FWIW	For what it's worth	**IMO**	In my opinion	**TAFN**	That's all for now
GOK	God only knows	**LOL**	Laughing out loud	**TTFN**	Ta-ta for now

Emoticons, or **smileys**, are a series of typed characters that, when turned sideways, resemble a face and express an emotion. Here are some smileys often encountered on the Internet.

:-)	Smile	:-D	Laugh	:-(	Unhappy	:-b..	Drooling
;-)	Wink	:-*	Kiss	:-o	Shouting	{*}	A hug and a kiss

Internet Directory to Selected Sites

The Websites listed are but a sampling of what is available. For some others, see the following *World Almanac* features: the Where to Get Help directory (Health), the Business Directory and Tracing Your Roots (Consumer Information), the Sports Directory, Travel and Tourism, Associations and Societies, Cities of the U.S., States of the U.S., U.S. Government, and Nations of the World. You may also find suggested websites of interest in the free monthly World Almanac E-Newsletter, available at www.worldalmanac.com. (The addresses are subject to change, and sites or products are not endorsed by *The World Almanac*.)

You must type an address exactly as written. You may be unable to connect to a site because (1) you have mistyped the address, (2) the site is busy, or (3) it has moved or no longer exists.

Online Service Providers

America Online
www.aol.com

AT&T WorldNet Service
www.att.net

CompuServe
www.compuserve.com

EarthLink
www.earthlink.net

Microsoft Network
www.msn.com

Juno
www.juno.com

Prodigy
www.prodigy.com

Directories

Bigfoot (e-mail addresses and white page listings)
www.bigfoot.com

InfoSpace, the Ultimate Directory
www.infospace.com

People Search
people.yahoo.com

Switchboard, the People and Business Directory
www.switchboard.com

WhoWhere?
www.whowhere.lycos.com

Security and Screening

The National Fraud Information Center
www.fraud.org
SET Secure Electronic Transaction
www.setco.org

What's New on the Internet

Internet Scout Project (latest resources for researchers)
scout.cs.wisc.edu/index.html
Nerd World: Media (what's new in computer world)
www.nerdworld.com/whatsnew.html
Yahoo! What's New (listing of every new site each day; sometimes thousands)
www.yahoo.com/new

Auctions

eBay
www.ebay.com
uBid Online Auction
www.ubid.com
Yahoo! Auctions
auctions.yahoo.com

Audio/Video

LiveUpdate
www.liveupdate.com
MP3.com
www.mp3.com
Real Networks
www.real.com

Bookstores

Amazon.com Inc.
www.amazon.com
Barnes and Noble
www.barnesandnoble.com
Borders.Com
www.borders.com
The Complete Guide to Online Bookstores
www.bookarea.com

Chat Sites

America Online
www.aim.com/community/chats/adp
Excite
www.excite.com/communities
IVILLAGE: The Women's Network
www.ivillage.com
Lycos
chat.lycos.com
Yahoo
chat.yahoo.com

Children's Sites

(*See also Family Resources*)

Children's Television Workshop
www.sesameworkshop.org
Judy Blume's Home Base
www.judyblume.com/index.html
The Newbery Medal
www.ala.org/alsc/newbery.html
Peace Corps Kids World
www.peacecorps.gov/kids
Rock and Roll Hall of Fame and Museum
www.rockhall.com
Seussville
www.randomhouse.com/seussville
SuperSite for Kids
www.bonus.com
Weekly Reader
www.weeklyreader.com
White House for Kids
www.whitehouse.gov/kids
World Almanac for Kids
www.worldalmanacforkids.com
Yahooligans (for homework help sites)
www.yahooligans.com

Economic Data

Bureau of Economic Analysis
www.bea.doc.gov
Bureau of Labor Statistics
www.bls.gov
Economics Statistics Briefing Room
www.whitehouse.gov/fsbr/esbr.html
Economy at a Glance
stats.bls.gov/eag/
Office of Management and Budget
www.access.gpo.gov/usbudget
Statistical Abstract of the United States (a sampling)
www.census.gov/statab/www
STAT-USA/Internet (a subscription-based government service)
www.stat-usa.gov/stat-usa.html

Entertainment

Eonline
www.eonline.com
The Internet Movie Database
www.imdb.com
Movies.com
www.movies.go.com
The Movie Times
www.the-movie-times.com
Variety
www.variety.com

Family Resources

(*See also Children's Sites*)

Babies Online
www.babiesonline.com
BabyCenter
www.babycenter.com
Family.Com
family.go.com
KidsHealth.org
www.kidshealth.org
KidSource Online
www.kidsource.com
ParenthoodWeb
www.parenthoodweb.com
Parent Soup
www.parentsoup.com
ParentsPlace.com
www.parentsplace.com
Screen It! Entertainment Reviews for Parents
www.screenit.com
Zero to Three
www.zerotothree.org

Greeting Cards, Electronic

Blue Mountain Arts
www.bluemountain.com
Egreetings Network
www.egreetings.com
Micro-Images Multimedia Greeting Cards
www.microimg.com/postcards
Netcards.com
www.electronicpostcards.com
1001 Postcards
www.postcards.org
123 Greetings
www.123greetings.com

Health

CenterWatch Clinical Trials Listing Service
www.centerwatch.com
drkoop.com
www.drkoop.com
Drugstore.com
www.drugstore.com
Healthfinder
www.healthfinder.gov
Mayo Clinic Health Oasis
www.mayohealth.org
Medscape
www.medscape.com
The Merck Manual
www.merck.com
National Institutes of Health
www.nih.gov/health
U.S. National Library of Medicine
www.nlm.nih.gov
WebMD
www.webmd.com

Job Search Sites

CareerBuilder
www.careerbuilder.com
Headhunter.net
www.Headhunter.net
Monster.com
www.monster.com

Money Management

Internal Revenue Service
www.irs.gov
Wall Street Journal
www.wsj.com
American Stock Exchange
www.amex.com
E*TRADE
www.etrade.com
MarketWatch
www.marketwatch.com
NASDAQ
www.nasdaq.com
New York Stock Exchange
www.nyse.com
Priceline
www.priceline.com
Mortgage Calculator
www.weichert.com
Retirement Calculator
www.worldi.com/index.htm

News

The Associated Press
www.ap.org
BBC Online
www.bbc.co.uk/home/today
Cable News Network
www.cnn.com
The Los Angeles Times
www.latimes.com
MSNBC
www.msnbc.com
The New York Times on the Web
www.nytimes.com
Reuters
www.reuters.com
USA Today
www.usatoday.com
Washington Post
www.washingtonpost.com

Reference

About.com
www.about.com
BookWire
www.bookwire.com
CIA Publications and Reports
www.odci.gov/cia/publications/pubs.html
Explore the Internet; The Library of Congress
lcweb.loc.gov/
Libweb—Library Servers via WWW
sunsite.berkeley.edu/Libweb
Merriam-Webster Network Editions
www.m-w.com
yourDictionary.com
www.yourdictionary.com
Refdesk
www.refdesk.com
Roget's Thesaurus
www.thesaurus.com

Sports

ESPN
www.espn.go.com
Sporting News
www.sportingnews.com
Sports illustrated
www.sportsillustrated.com
Sports Network
www.sportsnetwork.com

Weather

National Weather Service Home Page
www.nws.noaa.gov
National Center for Environmental Prediction (includes links to Storm Prediction Center and other sites)
www.ncep.noaa.gov
Weather Channel
www.weather.com

Most-Visited Websites, July 2002

Source: comScore Media Metrix, Inc.

Rank	Website*	Visitors[1]	Rank	Website*	Visitors[1]
1.	AOL Time Warner Network—Proprietary & WWW	97,995	11.	InfoSpace Network	22,471
2.	MSN—Microsoft Sites	89,819	12.	Walt Disney Internet Group (WDIG)	22,261
3.	Yahoo! Sites	83,433	13.	Viacom Online	21,089
4.	Google Sites	37,460	14.	AT&T Properties	20,073
5.	Terra Lycos	36,173	15.	Gator Network	19,609
6.	About/Primedia	35,297	16.	Ticketmaster Sites	18,173
7.	eBay	33,370	17.	Real.com Network	17,932
8.	Amazon Sites	27,753	18.	Excite Network	17,514
9.	Classmates.com Sites	24,163	19.	iVillage.com: The Women's Network	17,191
10.	CNET Networks	22,762	20.	eUniverse Network	16,962

*In some cases, represents an aggregation of commonly owned domain names. (1) Number of visitors who visited website at least once in July 2002, according to a comScore Media Metrix sample.

Percent of People in the U.S. Using the Internet, 1998-2001*

Source: National Telecommunications and Information Administration, U.S. Dept. of Commerce

		Dec. 1998	Sept. 2001	% increase
Gender	Male	34.2	53.9	57.6
	Female	31.4	53.8	71.3
Race/Origin	White	37.6	59.9	59.3
	Black	19.0	39.8	109.5
	Asian Amer. & Pac. Isl.	35.8	60.4	68.7
	Hispanic	16.6	31.6	90.4
Educational attainment	Less than high school	4.2	12.8	204.8
	High school diploma / GED	19.2	39.8	107.3
	Some college	38.6	62.4	61.7
	Bachelors degree	58.4	80.8	38.4
	Beyond bachelors degree	66.4	83.7	26.1
Age group (and labor force)	Age 3–8	11.0	27.9	153.6
	Age 9–17	43.0	68.6	59.5
	Age 18–24	44.3	65.0	46.7
	Age 25–49	40.9	63.9	56.2
	Age 50+	19.3	37.1	92.2
Family income	Less than $15,000	13.7	25.0	82.5
	$15,000–$24,999	18.4	33.4	81.5
	$25,000–$34,999	25.3	44.1	74.3
	$35,000–$49,999	34.7	57.1	64.6
	$50,000–$74,999	45.5	67.3	47.9
	$75,000 & above	58.9	78.9	34.0
Total population		**32.7**	**53.9**	**64.8**

* Percentages measure Internet use from any location by individuals age 3 and older.

Percent of People in the U.S. Using Computers, 1997, 2001*

Source: National Telecommunications and Information Administration, U.S. Dept. of Commerce

		Oct. 1997	Sept. 2001	% increase
Gender	Male	53.8	65.5	21.7
	Female	53.3	65.8	23.5
Race/Origin	White	57.5	70.0	21.7
	Black	43.6	55.7	27.8
	Asian Amer. & Pac. Isl.	57.5	71.2	23.8
	Hispanic	38.0	48.8	28.4
Educational attainment	Less than high school	7.9	17.0	115.2
	High school diploma / GED	33.5	47.3	41.2
	Some college	57.8	69.5	20.2
	Bachelors degree	74.3	84.9	14.3
	Beyond bachelors degree	79.1	86.9	9.9
Age group (and labor force)	Age 3–8	59.0	71.0	20.3
	Age 9–7	85.1	92.6	8.8
	Age 18–24	58.2	71.3	22.5
	Age 25–49	57.7	70.2	21.7
	Age 50+	27.6	42.5	54.0
Family income	Less than $15,000	29.8	37.3	25.2
	$15,000–$24,999	37.4	46.8	25.1
	$25,000–$34,999	49.3	57.7	17.0
	$35,000–$49,999	60.4	70.0	15.9
	$50,000–$74,999	71.7	79.4	10.7
	$75,000 & above	80.8	88.0	8.9
Total population		**53.5**	**65.6**	**22.6**

* Percentages measure computer use from any location by individuals age 3 and older.

IT'S A FACT: About 8% of Americans who go online at home use Macintosh computers. They tend to be more educated, richer, and more Net savvy than those who use Microsoft Windows systems—or so said a mid-2002 study by Nielsen//NetRatings. More than 70% of the Mac users, for example, have a college or postgraduate degree, compared to just under 55% of surfers in general. Also, more of the Mac users—over 52%—have been online for at least 5 years, and Mac users are more likely than the average online population to create Web pages.

Top-Selling Software, 2002

Source: NPD Techworld Data, Reston, VA

(based on unit U.S. sales, Jan.-June 2002[1])

All Software

1. Norton Antivirus 2002 8.0, Symantec
2. The Sims: Vacation Expansion Pack, Electronic Arts
3. VirusScan 6.0, Network Associates
4. The Sims, Electronic Arts
5. MS Windows XP Home Ed Upgr, Microsoft
6. Medal Of Honor: Allied Assault, Electronic Arts
7. Norton System Works 2002 5.0, Symantec
8. Star Wars: Jedi Knight II: Jedi Outcast, LucasArts
9. Symantec Antivirus 8.0 Entpr Ed VLP Mnt Lic, Symantec
10. Quicken Basic 2002, Intuit

Games

1. The Sims: Vacation Expansion Pack, Electronic Arts
2. The Sims, Electronic Arts
3. Medal Of Honor: Allied Assault, Electronic Arts
4. The Sims: Hot Date Expansion Pack, Electronic Arts
5. Harry Potter & The Sorcerer's Stone, Electronic Arts
6. Star Wars: Jedi Knight II: Jedi Outcast, LucasArts
7. Dungeon Siege, Microsoft
8. Roller Coaster Tycoon, Infogrames Entertainment
9. MS Zoo Tycoon, Microsoft
10. Warcraft III: Reign Of Chaos, Vivendi Universal Publishing

Reference Software

1. MS Encarta Reference Library 2002, Microsoft
2. MS Encarta Encyclopedia 2002 Deluxe, Microsoft
3. World Book Millennium 2002 Premier Ed, Topics Entertainment
4. Dictionary & Thesaurus JC, Topics Entertainment
5. 3D Atlas JC, Topics Entertainment

Home Education Software

1. Mavis Beacon Teaches Typing 12.0, Broderbund
2. Adventure Workshop 1st-3rd Grade, The Learning Company
3. Adventure Workshop Preschool-1st Grade, The Learning Company
4. Adventure Workshop 4th-6th Grade, The Learning Company
5. Instant Immersion Spanish JC, Topics Entertainment
6. Instant Immersion Spanish, Topics Entertainment
7. Oregon Trail 5, The Learning Company
8. Blue's ABC Time Activities JC, Infogrames Entertainment
9. Mavis Beacon Teaches Typing 8.0 JC, Broderbund
10. Excelerator Math & Science Grade 3-6, Topics Entertainment

Personal Productivity Software

1. Easy CD Creator 5.0 Platinum, Roxio
2. MS Streets & Trips 2002, Microsoft
3. Print Shop 12.0 Deluxe, Broderbund
4. 3D Home Architect 4.0 Deluxe, Broderbund
5. Print Perfect Gold JC, Cosmi
6. Street Maps & Vacation Planner, Cosmi
7. MS Picture It Photo 2002, Microsoft
8. MS Works Suite 2002, Microsoft
9. Print Workshop 2002, Valusoft
10. MS Picture It Publishing 2002 Platinum, Microsoft

Business Software

1. Norton Antivirus 2002 8.0, Symantec
2. VirusScan 6.0, Network Associates
3. MS Windows XP Home Ed Upgr, Microsoft
4. Norton System Works 2002 5.0, Symantec
5. Symantec Antivirus 8.0 Entpr Ed VLP Mnt Lic, Symantec
6. Norton Antivirus 7.6 Corp Ed VLP Mnt Lic , Symantec
7. MS Windows 2000 Svr Clnt Acc OPEN Lic, Microsoft
8. MS Windows 2000 Svr Clnt Acc OPEN Mnt Lic, Microsoft
9. MS Campus Agreement 3.0 Lic, Microsoft
10. Norton Internet Security 2002 4.0, Symantec

Finance Software

1. TurboTax 2001 Deluxe, Intuit
2. TurboTax 2001, Intuit
3. TurboTax 2001 Multi State 45, Intuit
4. Taxcut 2001 Deluxe, Block Financial
5. Taxcut 2001, Block Financial
6. Taxcut 2001 State, Block Financial
7. Quicken Basic 2002, Intuit
8. TurboTax 2001 CA State, Intuit
9. Quicken Deluxe 2002, Intuit
10. QuickBooks 2002 Pro, Intuit

(1) Some widely used software is often bundled with computers when sold; these are not included in sales figures above.

Glossary of Computer and Internet Terms

Source: *Microsoft Press® Computer Dictionary, Third Edition* with updates.

application A program designed to assist in the performance of a specific task, such as word processing, accounting, or inventory management.

artificial intelligence (AI) The branch of computer science concerned with enabling computers to simulate such aspects of human intelligence as speech recognition, deduction, inference, creative response, and the ability to learn from experience.

ASCII Pronounced "askee." An acronym for American Standard Code for Information Interchange, a coding scheme using 7 or 8 bits that assigns numeric values to up to 256 characters, including letters, numerals, punctuation marks, control characters, and other symbols.

backup (noun); back up (verb) As a noun, a duplicate copy of a program, a disk, or data. As a verb, to make a duplicate copy of a program, a disk, or data.

bandwidth Data transfer capacity of a digital communications system.

baud rate Speed at which a modem can transmit data.

BBS An abbreviation for bulletin board system, a computer system equipped with one or more modems or other means of network access that serves as an information and message-passing center for remote users.

binary The binary number system has 2 as its base, so values are expressed as combinations of 2 digits, 0 and 1. These 2 digits can represent the logical values true and false as well as numerals, and they can be represented in an electronic device by the 2 states on and off, recognized as 2 voltage levels. Therefore, the binary number system is at the heart of digital computing.

bit Short for binary digit; the smallest unit of information handled by a computer. One bit expresses a 1 or a 0 in a binary numeral, or a true or a false logical condition, and is represented physically by an element such as a high or low voltage at one point in a circuit or a small spot on a disk magnetized one way or the other.

boot The process of starting or resetting a computer.

browser *See* **Web browser.**

bug An error in coding or logic that causes a program to malfunction or to produce incorrect results. Also, a recurring physical problem that prevents a system or set of components from working together properly.

bulletin board system *See* **BBS.**

byte A unit of data, today almost always consisting of 8 bits. A byte can represent a single character, such as a letter, a digit, or a punctuation mark.

CD-ROM Acronym for compact disc read-only memory, a form of storage characterized by high capacity (roughly 650 megabytes) and the use of laser optics rather than magnetic means for reading data.

central processing unit (CPU) The computational and control unit of a computer; the device that interprets and executes instructions.

chat room The informal term for a data communication channel that links computers and permits users to "converse", often about a particular subject that interests them, by sending text messages to one another in real time.

chip *See* **integrated circuit.**

client On a local area network, a computer that accesses shared network resources provided by another computer (called a server). *See also* **server.**

computer Any machine that does three things: accepts structured input, processes it according to prescribed rules, and produces the results as output.

cookie A block of data that a Web server stores on a client system. When a user returns to the same Web site, the browser sends a copy of the cookie back to the server. Cookies are used to identify users, to instruct the server to send a customized version of the requested Web page, to submit account information for the user, and for other administrative purposes.

CPU *See* **central processing unit.**

crash The failure of either a program or a disk drive. A program crash results in the loss of all unsaved data and can leave the operating system unstable enough to require restarting the computer.

cursor A special on-screen indicator, such as a blinking underline or rectangle, that marks the place of which keystrokes will appear when typed.

cyberspace The universe of environments, such as the Internet, in which persons interact by means of connected computers.

cyberspeak Terminology and language (often jargon, slang, and acronyms) relating to the Internet—computer-connected—environment, that is, cyberspace..

database A file composed of records, each of which contains fields, together with a set of operations for searching, sorting, recombining, and other functions.

data compression A means of reducing the space or bandwidth needed to store or transmit a block of data.

debug To detect, locate, and correct logical or syntactical errors in a program or malfunctions in hardware.

defragger A software utility for reuniting parts of a file that have become fragmented through rewriting and updating.

desktop publishing The use of a computer and specialized software to combine text and graphics to create a document that can be printed on either a laser printer or a typesetting machine.

dial-up access Connection to a data communications network through the public switched telecommunication network.

digital certificate 1. An assurance that software downloaded from the Internet comes from a reputable source. 2. A user identity card or "driver's license" for cyberspace. Issued by a certificate authority.

digital subscriber line Any of a family of high-bandwidth data communications technologies that can achieve high transmission speeds over standard twisted-pair copper wires originating from telephone companies. Envisioned as a means of enabling high-speed networking and Internet access, DSL, or xDSL, is the collective term for a number of technologies including ADSL, RADSL, IDSL, SDSL, HDSL, and VDSL.

digital video disc The next generation of optical disc storage technology. With digital video disc technology video, audio, and computer data can be encoded onto a compact disc (CD). A digital video disc can store greater amounts of data than traditional CDs.

directory service A service on a network that returns mail addresses of other users or enables a user to locate hosts and services.

disk A round, flat piece of flexible plastic (floppy disk) or inflexible metal (hard disk) coated with a magnetic material that can be electrically influenced to hold information recorded in digital (binary) format.

disk drive An electromechanical device that reads from and writes to disks.

disk operating system Abbreviated DOS. A generic term describing any operating system that is loaded from disk devices when the system is started or rebooted.

distance learning Broadly, any educational or learning process or system in which the teacher/instructor is separated geographically or in time from his or her students; or in which students are separated from other students or educational resources.

DOS *See* **disk operating system.**

download In communications, to transfer a copy of a file from a remote computer to the requesting computer by means of a modem or network. *See also* **upload.**

DVD *See* **digital video disc.**

dynamic HTML A technology designed to add richness, interactivity, and graphical interest to Web pages by providing those pages with the ability to change and update themselves in response to user actions, without the need for repeated downloads from a server.

encryption The process of encoding data to prevent unauthorized access, especially during transmission. The U.S. National Bureau of Standards created a complex encryption standard, DES (Data Encryption Standard), that provides almost unlimited ways to encrypt documents.

FAQ An abbreviation for Frequently Asked Questions, a document listing common questions and answers on a particular subject. FAQs are often posted on Internet newsgroups where new participants ask the same questions that regular readers have answered many times.

fatal exception error A Windows message signaling that an unrecoverable error, one that causes the system to halt, has occurred. Data being processed when the error occurs is usually lost, and the computer must be rebooted.

field A location in a record in which a particular type of data is stored.

file A complete, named collection of information, such as a program, a set of data used by a program, or a user-created document.

firewall A security system intended to protect an organization's network against external threats, such as hackers, from another network. *See also* **proxy server.**

flame An abusive or personally insulting e-mail message or newsgroup posting.

format In general, the structure or appearance of a unit of data. As a verb, to change the appearance of selected text or the contents of a selected cell in a spreadsheet.

forum A medium provided by an online service or BBS for users to carry on written discussions of a topic by posting messages and replying to them.

FTP An abbreviation for File Transfer Protocol, the protocol used for copying files to and from remote computer systems on a network using TCP/IP such as the Internet.

gigabyte Abbreviated GB; 1024 megabytes. *See* **megabyte.**

graphical user interface Abbreviated GUI (pronounced "gooey"). A type of environment that represents programs, files, and options by means of icons, menus, and dialog boxes on the screen. The user can select and activate these options by pointing and clicking with a mouse or, often, with the keyboard. *See also* **icon.**

hacker A computerphile—a person who is engrossed in computer technology and programming or who likes to examine the code of operating systems and other programs to see how they work. Also, a person who uses computer expertise for illicit ends, such as for gaining access to computer systems without permission and tampering with programs and data.

hard copy Printed output on paper, film, or other permanent medium.

hit Retrieval of a document, such as a home page, from a website.

home page A document intended to serve as a starting point in a hypertext system, especially the World Wide Web. Also, an entry page for a set of Web pages and other files in a website.

host The main computer in a system of computers or terminals connected by communications links.

HTML An abbreviation for HyperText Markup Language, the markup language used for documents on the World Wide Web.

HTTP An abbreviation for HyperText Transfer Protocol, the client/server protocol used to access information on the Web.

hyperlink A connection between an element in a hypertext document, such as a word, phrase, symbol, or image, and a different element in the document, another hypertext document, a file, or a script. The user activates the link by clicking on the linked element, which is usually highlighted.

hypermedia The integration of any combination of text, graphics, sound, and video into a primarily associative system of information storage and retrieval in which users jump from subject to related subject.

hypertext Text linked together in a complex, nonsequential web of associations in which the user can browse through related topics.

icon A small image displayed on the screen to represent an object that can be manipulated by the user.

import To bring information from one system or program into another.

instant messaging A service that alerts users when friends or colleagues are on line and allows them to communicate with each other in real time through private online chat areas.

integrated circuit Also called a chip. A device consisting of a number of connected circuit elements, such as transistors and resistors, fabricated on a single chip of silicon crystal or other semiconductor material.

interactive Characterized by conversational exchange of input and output, as when a user enters a question or command the system immediately responds.

intranet A TCP/IP network designed for information processing within a company or organization. It usually employs Web pages for information dissemination and Internet applications, such as Web browsers.

IP address Short for Internet Protocol address, a 32-bit (4-byte) binary number that uniquely identifies a host (computer) connected to the Internet to other Internet hosts, for communication through the transfer of packets.

Java A programming language, developed by Sun Microsystems, Inc., that can be run on any platform.

kilobyte Abbreviated K, KB, or Kbyte; 1,024 bytes.

LAN Rhymes with "can." Acronym for local area network, a group of computers and other devices dispersed over a limited area and connected by a link that enables any device to interact with any other on the network.

laptop A small, portable computer that runs on either batteries or AC power, designed for use during travel. Laptops have flat screens and small keyboards.

legacy system A computer, software program, network, or other computer equipment that remains in use after a business or organization installs new systems.

link *See* **hyperlink.**

local area network *See* **LAN.**

logon The process of identifying oneself to a computer after connecting to it over a communications line. Also called *login.*

lurk To receive and read articles or messages in a newsgroup or other online conference without contributing anything to the ongoing conversation.

mailing list A list of names and e-mail addresses that are grouped under a single name. When a user places the name of the mailing list in a mail client's To: field, the client automatically sends the same message to the machine where the mailing list resides, and that machine sends the message to all the addresses on the list.

mainframe computer A high-level computer designed for the most intensive computational tasks.

markup language A set of codes in a text file that instruct a printer or video display how to format, index, and link the contents of the file. Examples of markup languages are HTML (HyperText Markup Language), which is used in Web pages, and SGML (Standard Generalized Markup Language), which is used for typesetting and desktop publishing purposes and in electronic documents.

megabyte Abbreviated MB. Usually 1,048,576 bytes (2^{20}); sometimes interpreted as 1 million bytes.

memory Circuitry that allows information to be stored and retrieved. In common usage it refers to the fast semiconductor storage (RAM) directly connected to the processor. *See also* **RAM.**

menu A list of options from which a program user can make a selection in order to perform a desired action, such as choosing a command or applying a format.

microcomputer A computer built around a single-chip microprocessor.

microprocessor A central processing unit (CPU) on a single chip. *See also* **integrated circuit.**

minicomputer A mid-level computer built to perform complex computations while dealing efficiently with input and output from users connected via terminals.

modem A communications device that enables a computer to transmit information over a standard telephone line.

monitor The device on which images generated by the computer's video adapter are displayed.

motherboard The main circuit board containing the primary components of a computer system.

mouse A common pointing device. It has a flat-bottomed casing designed to be gripped by one hand.

multimedia The combination of sound, graphics, animation, and video.

multitasking A mode of operation offered by an operating system in which a computer works on more than one task at a time.

Net Short for Internet.

network A group of computers and associated devices that are connected by communications facilities.

newsgroup A forum on the Internet for threaded discussions on a specified range of subjects. A newsgroup consists of articles and follow-up posts. *See* **post, thread.**

online Activated and ready for operating; capable of communicating with or being controlled by a computer.

operating system The software that controls the allocation and usage of hardware resources such as memory, CPU time, disk space, and peripheral devices.
optical scanner An input device that uses light-sensing equipment to scan paper or another medium, translating the pattern of light and dark or color into a digital signal that can be manipulated by either optical character recognition software or graphics software.
packet A unit of information transmitted as a whole from one device to another on a network.
palmtop A portable personal computer whose size enables it to be held in one hand while it is operated with the other hand. A major difference between palmtop computers and laptop computers is that palmtops are usually powered by off-the-shelf batteries such as AA cells.
password A unique string of characters that a user types in as an identification code.
PC Abbreviation for personal computer, a microcomputer that conforms to the standard developed by IBM for personal computers, which uses an Intel microprocessor (or one that is compatible); also used as a general term for any microcomputer.
PDA Acronym for Personal Digital Assistant. A lightweight palmtop computer designed to provide specific functions like personal organization (calendar, note taking, database, calculator, and so on) as well as communications. More advanced models also offer multimedia features.
PDF Acronym for Portable Document Format. The Adobe specification for electronic documents that use the Adobe Acrobat family of servers and readers.
peripheral A device, such as a disk drive, printer, modem, or joystick, that is connected to a computer and is controlled by the computer's microprocessor.
personal computer *See* **PC.**
pixel Short for picture element; also called *pel.* One spot in a rectilinear grid of thousands of such spots that are individually "painted" to form an image produced on the screen by a computer or on paper by a printer.
portal A website that serves as a gateway to the Internet. A portal is a collection of links, content, and services designed to guide users to information they are likely to find interesting—news, weather, entertainment, commerce sites, chat rooms, and so on.
post To submit an article in a newsgroup or other online conference. *See* **thread.**
program A sequence of instructions that can be executed by a computer.
protocol A set of rules or standards designed to enable computers to communicate with one another and to exchange information with as little error as possible.
proxy server A firewall component that manages Internet traffic to and from a local area network and can provide other features, e.g., document caching and access control.
RAM Pronounced "ram." An acronym for random access memory. Semiconductor-based memory that can be read and written by the CPU or other hardware devices.
ROM 1. Acronym for read-only-memory. A semiconductor circuit into which code or data is permanently installed by the manufacturing process. 2. Any semiconductor circuit serving as a memory that contains instructions or data that can be read but not modified.
routing table In data communications, a table of information that provides network hardware (bridges and routers) with the directions needed to forward packets of data to locations on other networks.
RTF An acronym for rich text format. RTF is used for transferring formatted documents between applications, even those applications running on different platforms, such as between IBM and compatibles and Apple Macintoshes.
search engine On the Internet, a program that searches for keywords in files and documents.
server On a local area network (LAN), a computer running software that controls access to the network and its resources, such as printers and disk drives. On the Internet or other network, a computer or program that responds to commands from a client. *See* **client, LAN.**
SGML Acronym for Standard Generalized Markup Language. An information-management standard adopted by the International Organization for Standardization (ISO) in 1986 as a means of providing platform- and application-independent documents that retain formatting, indexing, and linked information. SGML provides a grammar-like mechanism for users to define the structure of their documents, and the tags they will use to denote the structure in individual documents.
sleep mode A power management mode that shuts down all unnecessary computer operations to save energy; also known as suspend mode.
snail mail A phrase popular on the Internet for referring to mail services provided by the United States Postal Service and similar agencies in other countries.
software Computer programs; instructions that make hardware work.
spam An unsolicited e-mail message sent to many recipients at one time, or a news article posted simultaneously to many newsgroups. Electronic junk mail.
spreadsheet program An application commonly used for budgets, forecasting, and other finance-related tasks that organizes data values using cells, where the relationships between cells are defined by formulas.
stream To transfer data continuously, beginning to end, in a steady flow. Many aspects of computing rely on the ability to stream data; file input and output, for example, and communications. On the Internet, streaming enables users to begin accessing and using a file before it has been transmitted in its entirety.
supercomputer A large, extremely fast, and expensive computer used for complex or sophisticated calculations.
surf To browse among collections of information on the Internet, in newsgroups, and especially the World Wide Web.
system administrator The person responsible for administering use of a multiuser computer system, communications system, or both.
TCP/IP An abbreviation for Transmission Control Protocol/Internet Protocol, a protocol developed by the Department of Defense for communications between computers. It has become the de facto standard for data transmission over networks, including the Internet.
telecommute To work in one location (often, at home) and communicate with a main office at a different location through a personal computer.
thread In electronic mail and Internet newsgroups, a series of messages and replies related to a specific topic.
upload In communications, the process of transferring a copy of a file from a local computer to a remote computer by means of a modem or network.
URL An abbreviation for Uniform Resource Locator, an address for a resource on the Internet.
Usenet A worldwide network of Unix systems that has a decentralized administration and is used as a bulletin board system by special-interest discussion groups.
user interface The portion of a program with which a user interacts.
user-friendly Easy to learn and easy to use.
virus An intrusive program that infects computer files by inserting in those files copies of itself.
voice recognition The capability of a computer to understand the spoken word for the purpose of receiving commands and data input from the speaker.
WAN *See* **wide area network**
Web *See* **World Wide Web.**
Web browser A client application that enables a user to view HTML documents, follow the hyperlinks among them, transfer files, and execute some programs.
webcasting Popular term for broadcasting information via the World Wide Web, using push and pull technologies to move selected information from a server to a client.
webmaster The person or persons responsible for creating and maintaining a site on the World Wide Web.
website A group of related HTML documents and associated files, scripts, and databases that is served up by an HTTP server on the World Wide Web.
WebTV® Trademark name for technology from Microsoft and WebTV Networks that provide consumers with the ability to access the Internet on a television by means of a set-top box equipped with a modem.
wide area network (WAN) A communications network that connects geographically separated areas.
window In applications and graphical interfaces, a portion of the screen that can contain its own document or message.
word processor A program for manipulating text-based documents; the electronic equivalent of paper, pen, typewriter, eraser, and, most likely, dictionary and thesaurus.
workstation A combination of input, output, and computing hardware used for work by an individual.
World Wide Web (WWW) The total set of interlinked hypertext documents residing on Web, or HTTP, servers all around the world.
WYSIWYG Pronounced "wizzywig." An acronym for "What you see is what you get." A display method that shows documents and graphics characters on the screen as they will appear when printed.
XML Acronym for eXtensible Markup Language. A condensed form of SGML, the Standard Generalized markup Language. XML lets Web developers and designers create customized tags that offer greater flexibility in organizing and presenting information than is possible with the older HTML document coding system.
Zip drive A disk drive developed by Iomega that uses 3.5-inch removable disks (Zip disks) capable of storing 100 megabytes of data apiece. *See also* **disk drive.**

CONSUMER INFORMATION

Business Directory

Listed below are major U.S. corporations offering products and services to consumers. Information as of Aug. 2002. Alphabetization is by first key word. Listings generally include examples of products offered.

COMPANY NAME; ADDRESS; TELEPHONE NUMBER; WEBSITE; TOP EXECUTIVE; BUSINESS, PRODUCTS, OR SERVICES.

Abbott Laboratories; One Abbott Park Rd., N. Chicago, IL 60064; (847) 937-6100; www.abbott.com; Miles D. White; develops, manufactures, and sells broad line of health care prods., including pharmaceutical, nutritional, and hospital prods.

Aetna, Inc.; 151 Farmington Ave., Hartford, CT 06156; (203) 273-0123; www.aetna.com; John W, Rowe; health insurance, financial services.

Alberto-Culver; 2525 Armitage Ave., Melrose Park, IL 60160; (708) 450-3000; www.alberto.com; Leonard H. Lavin; hair care (VO5), consumer prods. (Mrs. Dash, Sugar Twin), personal care prods. (St. Ives), Sally Beauty Supply stores.

Albertson's, Inc.; 250 Parkcenter Blvd., Boise, ID 83726; (208) 395-6200; www.albertsons.com; Lawrence Johnston; supermarkets; largest retail food and drug co. in the U.S.

Allegheny Technologies, Inc.; 1000 Six PPG Place, Pittsburgh, PA 15222-5479; (412) 394-2800; www.alleghenytechnologies.com; James L. Murdy; electronics, aerospace, industrial; specialty metals.

Allstate Corp.; Allstate Plaza, Northbrook, IL 60062; (847) 402-5000; www.allstate.com; Edward Liddy; property/casualty, life insurance.

Aluminum Co. of America (Alcoa); 201 Isabella St., Pittsburgh, PA 15212; (412) 553-4545; www.alcoa.com; Alain Belda; world's largest aluminum producer.

Amazon.com Inc.; 1200 12th Ave. S., Suite 1200 Seattle, WA 98144; (206) 266-1000; www.amazon.com; Jeff Bezos; on-line books, electronics, camera/photo, and home and garden seller.

Amerada Hess Corp.; 1185 Ave. of the Americas, NY, NY 10036; (212) 997-8500; www.hess.com; J. B. Hess; integrated international oil co.

American Express Co.; 200 Vesey St., NY, NY 10285; (212) 640-2000; www.americanexpress.com; Kenneth Chenault; travel, financial, and information services.

American Greetings Corp.; 1 American Rd., Cleveland, OH 44144; (216) 252-7300; www.americangreetings.com; Morry Weiss; greeting cards, stationery, party goods, gift items.

American Home Products: *see* Wyeth.

American Intl. Group; 70 Pine St., NY, NY 10270; (212) 770-7000; www.aig.com; Maurice R. Greenberg; insurance, financial services.

AMR Corp.; PO Box 619616, Dallas/Ft. Worth Airport, TX 75261; (817) 963-1234; www.amrcorp.com; Donald J. Carty; air transportation (American Airlines, American Eagle, TWA).

Anheuser-Busch Cos., Inc.; 1 Busch Pl., St. Louis, MO 63118; (314) 577-2000; www.anheuser-busch.com; August A. Busch 3rd; world's largest brewer (Budweiser, Michelob, BudLight, Natural Light, Busch, O'Doul's), aluminum can manuf. and recycling, theme parks.

AOL Time Warner Inc.; 75 Rockefeller Plaza, New York, NY 10019; (212) 484-8000; www.aoltimewarner.com; Stephen M. Case; world's largest Internet online service; magazine publishing (*Time, Sports Illustrated, Fortune, Money, People,* DC Comics), TV and CATV (WB Network, HBO, Cinemax, CNN, TBS, TNT), book publishing (Little, Brown; Warner Books), motion pictures (Warner Bros., New Line Cinema), recordings, sports teams (Atlanta Braves, Atlanta Hawks), retailing (Warner Bros. stores). (America Online and Time Warner completed the largest corporate merger in history in 2001, becoming the largest media company in the U.S.)

Apple Computer, Inc.; 1 Infinite Loop, Cupertino, CA 95014-2084; (408) 996-1010; www.apple.com; Steve Jobs; manuf. of personal computers, software, peripherals.

Aramark Corp.; Aramark Tower, 1101 Market St., Philadelphia, PA 19107; (215) 238-3000; www.aramark.com; Joseph Neubauer; food and support services, uniforms and career apparel, child care and early education.

Archer Daniels Midland Co.; 4666 Faries Pkwy., Box 1470, Decatur, IL 62525; (217) 424-5200; www.admworld.com; G. Allen Andreas; agricultural commodities and prods.

Armstrong World Industries, Inc.; 2500 Columbia Ave., Lancaster, PA 17603; (717) 397-0611; www.armstrong.com; Michael D. Lockhart; interior furnishings, specialty prods.

Arvinmeritor Industries, Inc.; 2135 West Maple Road, Troy, MI 48084; (248) 435-1000; www.arvinmeritor.com; Larry Yost; auto emission and ride control systems.

Ashland Inc.; 50 E. River Center, PO Box 391, Covington, KY 41012; (859) 815-3333; www.ashland.com; Tim O'Brien; petroleum producer and refiner (Valvoline), chemicals, road construction.

AT&T Corp.; 32 Ave. of the Americas, NY, NY 10013-2412; (212) 387-5400; www.att.com; C. Michael Armstrong; communications, global information management.

Avon Prods., Inc.; 1345 Ave. of Americas, NY, NY 10105; (212) 282-5000; www.avon.com; Andrea Jung; cosmetics, fragrances, toiletries, fashion jewelry, gift items, casual apparel, lingerie.

Bank of America Corp.; Bank of America Corporate Center, Charlotte, NC 28255; (704) 386-5000; www.bankofamerica.com; K.D. Lewis; major U.S. bank.

Bausch & Lomb Inc.; One Bausch & Lomb Place, Rochester, NY 14604; (716) 338-6000; www.bausch.com; Ronald L. Zarrella; vision and health-care prods., accessories.

Baxter International Inc.; 1 Baxter Pkwy., Deerfield, IL 60015; (847) 948-2000; www.baxter.com; H. M. Kraemer Jr; health care prods. & services.

Bear Stearns Cos. Inc.; 383 Madison Ave., NY, NY 10179; (212) 272-2000; www.bearstearns.com; James E. Cayne; investment banking, securities trading, brokerage.

Becton, Dickinson & Co.; 1 Becton Dr., Franklin Lakes, NJ 07417; (201) 847-6800; www.bd.com; E.J. Ludwig; medical, laboratory, diagnostic prods.

BellSouth Corp.; 1155 Peachtree St. NE, Atlanta, GA 30309; (404) 249-2000; www.bellsouth.com; F. Duane Ackerman; telephone service in southern U.S.

Berkshire Hathaway Inc.; 1440 Krewit Plaza, Omaha, NE 68131; www.berkshirehathaway.com; Warren E. Buffett; subsidiaries include GEICO Direct insurance, Johns Manville building materials, Fruit of the Loom underwear, International Dairy Queen restaurants/desserts; Shaw carpets, Benjamin Moore paints.

Best Buy Co., Inc.; 7075 Flying Cloud Dr., Eden Prairie, MN 55344; (612) 947-2000; www.bestbuy.com; Richard Schulze; retailer of software, appliances, electronics, cameras, home office equipment.

Bethlehem Steel Corp.; 1170 8th Ave., Bethlehem, PA 18016; (610) 694-2424; www.bethsteel.com; Robert S. Miller Jr.; steel & steel prods.

Black & Decker Corp.; 701 E. Joppa Rd., Towson, MD 21204; (410) 716-3900; www.blackanddecker.com; Nolan D. Archibald; manuf. power tools, household prods. (Kwikset, Price Pfister), small appliances (Black & Decker).

H & R Block, Inc.; 4410 Main St., Kansas City, MO 64111; (816) 753-6900; www.hrblock.com; Mark A. Ernst; tax return preparation.

Boeing Co.; 100 N. Riverside, Chicago, IL 60606; (312) 544-2140; www.boeing.com; Philip M. Condit; leading manufacturer of commercial, jet aircraft.

Boise Cascade Corp.; 1111 W. Jefferson St., Boise, ID 83728; (208) 384-6161; www.bc.com; George J. Harad; distributor of office products & building materials; paper, wood prods.

Borden, Inc.; 180 E. Broad St., Columbus OH 43215-3707; (614) 225-4000; C. Robert Kidder; snacks (Wise, Cheez Doodles), adhesives (Elmer's, Krazy Glue), pasta (Prince, Creamette, Goodman's), pasta sauce (Aunt Millie's, Classico), Wyler's bouillon, Soup Starter, Corning Consumer Prods. (Corningware, Corelle, Pyrex, Revere); chemicals; consumer adhesives (Elmer's). Owned by KKR Investments, Inc. (www.kkr.com).

Bristol-Myers Squibb Co.; 345 Park Ave., NY, NY 10154; (212) 546-4000; www.bms.com; Charles A. Heimbold; drugs (Bufferin, Comtrex, Excedrin, Pravachol, TAXOL), nutritionals (Enfamil infant formula, Boost energy drink).

Brown-Forman Corp.; PO Box 1080, Louisville, KY 40201-1080; (502) 585-1100; www.brown-forman.com; Owsley Brown 2nd; distilled spirits (Jack Daniel's, Southern Comfort), wines (Bolla, Fetzer, Korbel), china and crystal (Dansk, Lenox), Gorham, Kirk Steiff silver prods., Hartmann luggage.

Brown Shoe Co., Inc.; 8300 Maryland Ave., P.O. Box 29, St. Louis, MO 63166; (314) 854-4000; www.brownshoe.com; Ronald A. Fromm; manuf. and retailer (Famous Footwear) of women's, men's, and children's shoes (Buster Brown, Naturalizer, Dr. Scholl's).

Brunswick Corp.; 1 N. Field Ct., Lake Forest, IL 60045; (847) 735-4700; www.brunswickcorp.com; George Buckley; largest U.S. maker of leisure and recreation prods., marine, camping, fitness and fishing equip., bowling centers and equip.

Burlington Northern Santa Fe Inc.; 2650 Lou Menk Dr., Ft. Worth, TX 76131-2830; (817) 333-2000; www.bnsf.com; Matthew Rose; one of the largest U.S. rail transportation cos.

Campbell Soup Co.; Campbell Pl., Camden, NJ 08103; (609) 342-4800; www.campbellsoup.com; Douglas R. Conant; soups, Franco-American spaghetti, V8 vegetable juice, Godiva chocolates, Prego spaghetti sauce, Pepperidge Farm, Pace sauces.

Caterpillar Inc.; 100 N.E. Adams St., Peoria, IL 61629; (309) 675-1000; www.cat.com; Glen A. Barton; world's largest producer of earth moving equip.

Chase Manhattan Corp.: *see* JPMorgan Chase & Co. Inc.

ChevronTexaco Corp.; 575 Market St., San Francisco, CA 94105; (415) 894-7700; www.chevron.com; David J. O'Reilly; integrated oil co. (Chevron and Texaco officially merged, 10/9/01, creating the 2nd-largest U.S.-based oil co.)

Chiquita Brands International, Inc.; 250 E. 5th St., Cincinnati, OH 45202; (513) 784-8000; www.chiquita.com; Cyrus F. Friedham Jr.; bananas, fruits, vegetables.

Church & Dwight Co., Inc.; 469 N. Harrison St., Princeton, NJ 08543; (609) 683-5900; www.armhammer.com; R.A. Davies 3rd; world's largest producer of sodium bicarbonate (Arm & Hammer); household products (Brillo, Fresh'n Soft, other Arm & Hammer products); personal care products (Arrid antiperspirant, Pearl Drops, Nair, Trojan condoms, First Response pregnancy test).

CIGNA Corp.; 1 Liberty Pl., Philadelphia, PA 19103; (215) 761-1000; www.cigna.com; H. Edward Hanway; insurance holding co.

Circuit City Stores, Inc.; 9950 Mayland Dr., Richmond, VA 23233-1464; (804) 527-4000; www.circuitcity.com; Alan McCollough; retailer of electronic, audio/video equip., consumer appliances; new and used-car stores (CarMax).

Citigroup; 153 E. 53rd St., NY, NY 10043; (212) 559-1000; www.citigroup.com; Sanford I. Weill; diversified financial services.

Liz Claiborne, Inc.; 1441 Broadway, New York, NY 10018; (212) 354-4900; www.lizclaiborne.com; P. Charron; apparel, accessories.

Clorox Co.; 1221 Broadway, Oakland, CA 94612; (510) 271-7000; www.clorox.com; G. Craig Sullivan; retail consumer prods. (Clorox, Formula 409, Pine-Sol, S.O.S., Soft Scrub cleansers; Armor All, STP, Rain Dance automotive prods.; Jonny Cat, Fresh Step cat litters; Kingsford charcoal briquets; Combat and Black Flag insecticides; Hidden Valley dressing; K.C. Masterpiece barbecue sauce; Brita water systems).

Coca-Cola Co.; 1 Coca-Cola Plaza, Atlanta, GA 30313; (404) 676-2121; www.cocacola.com; Douglas N. Daft; world's largest soft drink co. (Coca-Cola, Sprite, Nestea), world's largest dist. of juice prods. (Minute Maid, Five Alive, Hi-C, Fruitopia).

Colgate-Palmolive Co.; 300 Park Ave., NY, NY 10022; (212) 310-2000; www.colgate.com; Reuben Mark; soap (Palmolive, Irish Spring), detergent (Fab, Ajax, Suavitel), toothpaste (Colgate, Ultra Brite), Hill's pet food.

Compaq Computer Corp.: *see* Hewlett-Packard Co.

CompUSA Inc.; 14951 N. Dallas Pkwy., Dallas, TX 75254; (972) 982-4000; www.compusa.com; Hal Compton; largest U.S. superstore retailer of microcomputers and peripherals.

Computer Sciences Corp.; 2100 E. Grand Ave., El Segundo, CA 90245; (310) 615-0311; www.csc.com; Van B. Honeycutt; technology services.

ConAgra; 1 ConAgra Dr., Omaha, NE 68102; (402) 595-4000; www.conagra.com; Bruce Rohde; 2nd-largest U.S. food processor (Armour, Bumble Bee, Butterball, Chef Boyardee, Healthy Choice frozen dinners, Egg Beaters, Reddi-Wip).

Continental Airlines, Inc.; 1600 Smith St. HQS11, Houston, TX 77002; (713) 324-5242; www.continental.com; Gordon M. Bethune; air transportation.

Adolph Coors Co.; Golden, CO 80401; (303) 279-6565; www.coors.com; Peter Coors; brewer (Coors, Killian's, Zima).

Corning Inc.; 1 Riverfront Plaza, Corning, NY 14831; (607) 974-9000; www.corning.com; R. G. Ackerman; telecommunications, specialty materials, optical fiber and cable.

Costco Wholesale Corp.; 999 Lake Dr., Issaquah, WA 98027; (425) 313-8100; www.costco.com; James D. Sinegal; wholesale-membership warehouses.

Crane Co.; 100 First Stamford Place, Stamford, CT 06902; (203) 363-7300; www.craneco.com; R. S. Evans; manuf. fluid control devices, vending machines, fiberglass panels, aircraft brakes.

A. T. Cross Co.; 1 Albion Rd., Lincoln, RI 02865; (401) 333-1200; www.cross.com; David Whalen; writing instruments.

Crown Cork & Seal Co.; 1 Crown Way, Philadelphia, PA 19154-4599; (215) 698-5100; www.crowncork.com; William J. Avery; world's leading supplier of packaging prods.

CSX Corp.; 901 E. Cary St., Richmond, VA 23219; (804) 782-1400; www.csx.com; John W. Snow; rail, ocean, barge freight transport.

CVS Corp.; 1 CVS Dr., Woonsocket, RI 02895; (401) 765-1500; www.CVS.com; Thomas M. Ryan; drugstore chain.

Dana Corp.; 4500 Dorr St., Toledo, OH 43615; (419) 535-4500; www.dana.com; Joseph M. Magliochetti; truck and auto parts, supplies.

Deere & Co.; John Deere Rd., Moline, IL 61265; (309) 765-8000; www.deere.com; Robert W. Lane; world's largest manuf. of farm equip.; industrial equip.; lawn and garden tractors.

Dell Computer Corp.; 1 Dell Way, Round Rock, TX 78682; (512) 338-4400; www.dell.com; Michael S. Dell; laptop and desktop computers.

Delta Air Lines, Inc.; Hartsfield Atlanta Intl. Airport, Atlanta, GA 30320; (404) 715-2600; www.delta-air.com; Leo F. Mullin; air transportation.

Dial Corp.; 15501 N. Dial Blvd., Scottsdale, AZ 85260-1619; (602) 754-3425; www.dialcorp.com; Herbert Baum; consumer prods. (Dial, Coast soap, Purex detergent, Armour Star meats, Renuzit air fresheners).

Diebold, Inc.; PO Box 8230, Canton, OH 44711; (330) 490-4000; www.diebold.com; Walden W. O'Dell; manuf. ATMs, security systems and prods.

Dillard's; 1600 Cantrell Rd., Little Rock, AR 72201; (501) 376-5200; www.dillards.com; William Dillard 2nd; 2nd-largest dept. store chain in U.S.

Walt Disney Co.; 500 S. Buena Vista St., Burbank, CA 91521-7320; (818) 560-1000; www.disney.com; Michael D. Eisner; motion pictures, television (ESPN, ABC, SoapNet, Disney Channel, Lifetime), radio stations, theme parks (Walt Disney World, Disneyland) and resorts, publishing, recordings, retailing (Disney Stores).

Dole Food Co., Inc.; One Dole Drive, Westlake Village, CA 91362; (818) 874-4000; www.dole.com; David H. Murdock; food prods., fresh fruits and vegetables.

R. R. Donnelley & Sons Co.; 77 W. Wacker Dr., Chicago, IL 60601-1696; (312) 326-8000; www.rrdonnelley.com; William L. Davis; commercial printer, digital media.

Dow Chemical Co.; 2030 Dow Center, Midland, MI 48674; (517) 636-1000; www.dow.com; William S. Stavropoulos; chemicals, plastics (world's 2nd-largest chemical co. after merger, 2/7/01, with Union Carbide).

Dow Jones & Co., Inc.; 200 Liberty St., NY, NY 10281; (212) 416-2000; www.dowjones.com; Peter R. Kann; financial news service, publishing (*Wall Street Journal*, *Barron's*, Ottaway Newspapers).

Dun & Bradstreet Corp.; 1 Diamond Hill Rd., Murray Hill, NJ 07974; (908) 665-5000; www.dnb.com; Allen Z. Loren.; business information, publishing ("Yellow Pages" phone books).

E. I. du Pont de Nemours & Co. (Dupont); 1007 Market St., Wilmington, DE 19898; (302) 774-1000; www.dupont.com; Charles Holliday; largest U.S. chemical co.; petroleum, consumer prods.

Eastman Kodak Co.; 343 State St., Rochester, NY 14650-0205; (585) 724-5492; www.kodak.com; D. Carp; world's largest producer of photographic prods.

Eaton Corp.; 1111 Superior Ave., Cleveland, OH 44114; (216) 523-5000; www.eaton.com; Alexander Cutler; manuf. of vehicle powertrain components, controls.

El Paso Corp.; 1001 Louisiana Street, Houston, TX 77002; (713) 420-2600; www.elpaso.com; William A. Wise; diversified energy company primarily engaged in interstate transmission of natural gas.

Emerson Electric Co.; 8000 West Florissant Avenue, St. Louis, MO 63136; (314) 553-2000; www. gotoemerson.com; C. F. Knight; electrical, electronics prods. & systems.

Exxon Mobil Corp.; 5959 Las Colinas Blvd., Irving, TX 75039-2298; (972) 444-1000; www.exxonmobil.com; Lee Raymond; world's largest publicly owned integrated oil co.; Exxon merged with Mobil 12/1/99.

Fannie Mae; 3900 Wisconsin Ave. NW, Washington, DC 20016; (202) 752-7115; www.fanniemae.com; Franklin Raines; largest U.S. provider of residential mortgage funds.

Fedders Corp.; 505 Martinsville Road, PO Box 813, Liberty Corner, NJ 07938; (908) 604-8686; www.fedders.com; Salvatore Giordano Jr; manuf. of room air conditioners (Fedders, Airtemp), dehumidifiers.

Federated Dept. Stores; 7 W. 7th St., Cincinnati, OH 45202; (513) 579-7000; www.Federated-fds.com; James Zimmerman; full-line dept. stores Macy's, Bloomingdale's, Burdines.

FedEx Corp.; 942 S. Shady Grove Rd., Memphis, TN 38120; (901) 369-3600; www.fedex.com; F. W. Smith; express delivery service.

First Data Corp.; 6200 S. Quebec St., Greenwood Village, CO, 30328; (303) 967-8000; www.firstdatacorp.com; Henry C. Duques; info. retrieval, data processing.

Fleetwood Enterprises, Inc.; 3125 Myers St., Riverside, CA 92503; (909) 351-3500; www.fleetwood.com; David S. Engelman; manufactured homes, recreational vehicles.

Fleming Cos. Inc.; P.O. Box 299013, Lewisville, TX 75029; (972) 906-8000; www.fleming.com; Mark S. Hansen; one of largest U.S. wholesale food distrib.

Fluor Corp.; One Enterprise Dr., Aliso Viejo, CA 92646; (949) 349-2000; www.fluor.com; Alan L. Boeckmann; largest international engineering and construction co. in U.S.

Foot Locker, Inc.; formerly Venator Group, 112 West 34th St., NY, NY 10120; (212) 720-3700; www.footlocker-inc.com; Matthew D. Serra; operates retail stores: shoes (Kinney), apparel (Eastbay), athletic footwear (Foot Locker), athletic merchandise (Champs).

Ford Motor Co.; American Rd., Dearborn, MI 48121; (313) 845-8540; www.ford.com; William Clay Ford Jr.; 2nd-largest auto manufacturer, motor vehicle sales (Ford, Lincoln-Mercury, Volvo), rentals (Hertz).

Fortune Brands, Inc.; 300 Tower Parkway, Lincolnshire, IL 60069; (847) 484-4400; www.fortunebrands.com; Norman H. Wesley; spirits and wine (Jim Beam), hardware, office prods. (Swingline), golf and leisure prods. (Titleist, Cobra, FootJoy).

Freddie Mac; 8200 Jones Branch Dr., McLean, VA 22102; (703) 903-2000; www.freddiemac.com; Leland C. Brendsel; residential mortgage provider.

Fruit of the Loom, Inc.; 1 Fruit of the Loom Dr., Bowling Green, KY 42102-9015; (270) 781-6400; www.fruit.com; Dennis Bookshester; manuf. of underwear, activewear. A subsidiary of Berkshire Hathaway, acquired 4/30/02.

Gannett Co., Inc.; 1100 Wilson Blvd., Arlington, VA 22234; (703) 284-6000; www.gannett.com; D.H. McCorkindale; newspaper publishing (*USA Today*), network and cable TV.

The Gap, Inc.; One Harrison St., San Francisco, CA 94105; (415) 952-4400; www.gap.com; Donald G. Fisher; casual and activewear retailer (Gap, Banana Republic, Old Navy).

General Dynamics; 3190 Fairview Park Drive, Falls Church, VA 22042; (703) 876-3000; www.generaldynamics.com; Nicholas D. Chabraja; nuclear submarines (Trident, Seawolf), armored vehicles, combat systems, computing devices, defense systems.

General Electric Co.; 3135 Easton Tpke., Fairfield, CT 06431; (203) 373-2211; www.ge.com; Jeffrey Immelt; electrical, electronic equip., radio and television broadcasting (NBC), aircraft engines, power generation, appliances.

General Mills, Inc.; PO Box 1113, Minneapolis, MN 55440; (612) 540-2311; www.generalmills.com; S. W. Sanger; foods (Total, Wheaties, Cheerios, Chex, Hamburger Helper, Betty Crocker, Bisquick).

General Motors; 100 Renaissance Center, Detroit, MI 48243; (313) 556-5000; www.gm.com; John F. Smith Jr; world's largest auto manuf. (Chevrolet, Pontiac, Cadillac, Buick).

Genuine Parts Co.; 2999 Circle 75 Pkwy., Atlanta, GA 30339; (770) 953-1700; www.genpt.com; Larry L. Prince; distributes auto replacement parts (NAPA).

Georgia-Pacific Corp.; 133 Peachtree St. NE, Atlanta, GA 30303; (404) 652-4000; www.gp.com; A. D. Correll; manuf. of paper and wood prods.

Gillette; Prudential Tower Bldg., Boston, MA 02199; (617) 463-3000; www.gillette.com; James M. Kilts; personal care prods. (Sensor, Atra razors, Right Guard, Soft and Dri), appliances (Braun), batteries (Duracell).

The Goodyear Tire & Rubber Co.; 1144 E. Market St., Akron, OH 44316; (330) 796-2121; www.goodyear.com; Samir F. Gibara; world's largest rubber manuf.; tires and other auto prods.

W. R. Grace & Co.; 7500 Grace Dr., Columbia, MD 21044; (410) 531-4000; www.grace.com; Paul J. Norris; chemicals, construction prods.

Great Atlantic & Pacific Tea Co. (A&P); 2 Paragon Dr., Montvale, NJ 07645; (201) 573-9700; www.aptea.com; Christian Haub; supermarkets (A&P, Waldbaum's, Kohl's, Dominion).

Halliburton Co.; 500 N. Akard St., Dallas, TX 75201; (214) 978-2600; www.halliburton.com; Dave Lesar; energy, engineering, and construction services.

Harley-Davidson, Inc.; 3700 W. Juneau Avenue, Milwaukee, WI 53208; (414) 343-4680; www.harley-davidson.com; Jeffrey Bleustein; manuf. of motorcycles, parts and accessories.

Harrah's Entertainment, Inc.; 5100 W. Sahara Ave., Las Vegas, NV 89146; (901) 762-8600; www.harrahs.com; Philip G. Satre; casino-hotels and riverboats.

Hartford Financial Services Group, Inc.; Hartford Plaza, Hartford, CT 06115; (860) 547-5000; www.thehartford.com; Ramani Ayer; insurance, finl. svces.

Hartmarx; 101 N. Wacker Dr., Chicago, IL 60606; (312) 372-6300; www.hartmarx.com; Elbert O. Hand; apparel manuf. (Hart Schaffner & Marx, Hickey Freeman, Claiborne, Tommy Hilfiger, Pierre Cardin, Perry Ellis).

Hasbro, Inc.; 1027 Newport Ave., Pawtucket, RI 02862; (401) 431-8697; www.hasbro.com; Alan G. Hassenfeld; toy and game manuf. (Milton Bradley, Playskool, G. I. Joe, Parker Bros., Tiger Electronics, Play-Doh).

HCA Inc.; 1 Park Plaza, Nashville, TN 37203; (615) 344-9551; www.hcahealthcare.com; Jack O. Bovender Jr.; largest hospital mgmt. co. in the U.S.

H. J. Heinz Co.; PO Box 57, Pittsburgh, PA 15230; (412) 456-6014; www.heinz.com; William R. Johnson; foods (StarKist, Ore-Ida, 57 Varieties), pet food (Kibbles 'n Bits, 9 Lives), Weight Watchers.

Hershey Foods Corp.; 100 Crystal A Dr., Hershey, PA 17033; (717) 534-4000; www.hersheys.com; Richard H. Lenny; largest U.S. producer of chocolate and confectionery prods. (Reese's, Kit Kat, Mounds, Almond Joy, Cadbury, Jolly Rancher, Twizzler, Milk Duds, Good & Plenty).

Hewlett-Packard Co.; 3000 Hanover St., Palo Alto, CA 94304; (650) 857-1501; www.hp.com; Carly Fiorina; manuf. computers, electronic prods. and systems. (On 5/3/02 Hewlett-Packard acquired Compaq Computer Co.)

Hillenbrand Industries, Inc.; 700 State Rte. 46 E, Batesville, IN 47006; (812) 934-7000; www.hillenbrand.com; R.J. Hillenbrand; manuf. caskets, adjustable hospital beds.

Hilton Hotels Corp.; 9336 Civic Center Dr., Beverly Hills, CA 90210; (310) 205-4545; www.hilton.com; Stephen F. Bollenbach; hotels, casinos.

Home Depot, Inc.; 2455 Paces Ferry Rd. NW, Atlanta, GA 30339; (770) 433-8211; www.homedepot.com; Robert L. Nardelli; retail building supply, home improvement warehouse stores.

Honeywell Inc.; 101 Columbia Road, Morristown, NJ 07962; (973) 455-2000; www.honeywell.com; Lawrence A. Bossidy; merger in 12/99 with AlliedSignal Corp. industrial and home control systems, aerospace guidance systems.

Hormel Foods Corp.; 1 Hormel Pl., Austin, MN 55912-3680; (507) 437-5611; www.hormel.com; Joel W. Johnson; meat processor, pork and beef prods. (SPAM, Dinty Moore, Little Sizzlers).

Houghton Mifflin Co.; 222 Berkeley St., Boston, MA 02116; (617) 351-5000; www.hmco.com; Hans Gieskes; publisher of textbooks, reference, general interest books; a subsidiary of Vivendi Universal Publishing.

Huffy Corp.; 225 Byers Rd., Miamisburg, OH 45342; (937) 866-6251; www.huffy.com; Don R. Graber; largest U.S. bicycle manuf., sports and hardware equip.

Humana, Inc.; 500 W. Main Street, PO Box 1438, Louisville, KY 40201-1438; (502) 580-1000; www. humana.com; David A. Jones; managed healthcare service provider, related specialty products.

IBP, Inc.; 800 Stevens Port Dr., Dakota Dunes, SD 57049; (605) 235-2061; www.ibpinc.com; Robert L. Peterson; world's largest processor of fresh beef and pork.

Illinois Toolworks; 3600 West Lake Ave., Glenview, IL 60025; (847) 724-7500; www.itwinc.com; W. James Farrell; food equip. (Hobart), home appliances and cookware (West Bend).

Ingersoll-Rand; 200 Chestnut Ridge Road, Woodcliff Lake, NJ 07675; (201) 573-0123; www.ingersoll-rand.com; H. Henkel; industrial machinery.

Intel Corp.; 2200 Mission College Blvd., Santa Clara, CA 95052-8119; (408) 765-8080; www.intel.com; A. S. Grove; manuf. integrated circuits (Pentium).

International Business Machines Corp. (IBM); New Orchard Rd., Armonk, NY 10504; (914) 766-1900; www.ibm.com; Louis V. Gerstner Jr; world's largest supplier of advanced information processing technology equip., services.

International Paper Co.; 400 Atlantic St., Stamford, CT 06921; (203) 541-8000; www.internationalpaper.com; John T. Dillon; world's largest paper/forest prods. co., chemicals, packaging.

Interstate Bakeries Corp.; 12 E. Armour Blvd., Kansas City, MO 64111; (816) 502-4000; www.irin.com/ibc; Charles A. Sullivan; baked goods wholesaler, distributor (Wonder, Hostess, Dolly Madison, Beefsteak, Home Pride).

Jo-Ann Stores, Inc.; 5555 Darrow Rd., Hudson, OH 44236; (330) 656-2600; www.joann.com; Alan Rosskamm; nation's largest specialty fabric and craft stores (Jo-Ann Fabric and Crafts, Jo-Ann etc.).

Johnson Controls, Inc.; 5757 N. Green Bay Avenue, Milwaukee, WI 53201; (414) 228-1200; www. johnsoncontrols.com; James H. Keyes; fire protection services, auto seats and batteries.

Johnson & Johnson; 1 Johnson & Johnson Plaza, New Brunswick, NJ 08933; (732) 524-0400; www.jnj.com; R.S. Larsen; surgical dressings (Band-Aid), pharmaceuticals (Tylenol), toiletries (Neutrogena).

S.C. Johnson & Son, Inc.; 1525 Howe St., Racine, WI 53403; (800) 494-4855; www.scjohnson.com; William D. Perez; cleaning and other household prods. (Johnson's Wax, Windex, pledge, Fantastik, Raid, OFF!, Shout, Glade, Scrubbing Bubbles, Ziploc bags).

Jostens Inc.; 5501 Norman Center Dr., Minneapolis, MN 55437; (612) 830-3300; www.jostens.com; Bob Buhrmaster; school rings, yearbooks, plaques.

JPMorgan Chase & Co. Inc.; 270 Park Ave., NY, NY 10017; (212) 270-6000; www.jpmorganchase.com; Douglas A. Warner 3rd; global financial firm; (JPMorgan & Co. and Chase Manhattan Corp. merged 12/31/00).

Kellogg Co.; One Kellogg Sq., Battle Creek, MI 49016; (616) 961-2000; www.kelloggs.com; Carlos Gutierrez; world's largest mfgr. of ready-to-eat cereals, other food prods. (Frosted Flakes, Rice Krispies, Froot Loops, Pop-Tarts, Nutri-Grain, Eggo).

Kimberly-Clark Corp.; PO Box 619100, Dallas, TX 75261-9100; (972) 281-1200; www.kimberly-clark.com; Wayne R. Sanders; personal care prods. (Kleenex, Scott, Cottonelle, Huggies, Viva, Kotex).

King World Productions, Inc.; 1700 Broadway, 33rd Floor, NY, NY 10019; (212) 315-4000; www. kingworld.com; Roger King; distributor of TV programs (*Oprah Winfrey Show, Wheel of Fortune, Jeopardy!, Inside Edition*).

Kmart Corp.; 3100 W. Big Beaver Rd., Troy, MI 48084; (248) 643-1000; www.kmart.com; James B. Adamson; discount stores.

Knight Ridder, Inc.; 50 W. San Fernando Street, San Jose, CA 95113-2413; (408) 938-7700; www.Knightridder.com; P.A. Ridder; newspaper publishing.

Kraft Foods, Inc.: *see* Philip Morris Cos. Inc

Kroger Co.; 1014 Vine St., Cincinnati, OH 45202; (513) 762-4000; www.kroger.com; Joseph A. Pichler; largest U.S. retail grocery chain, convenience stores, mall jewelry stores.

(Estee) Lauder Cos.; 767 5th Ave., NY, NY 10153; (212) 572-4200; www.esteelauder.com; Leonard A. Lauder; cosmetics (Clinique), fragrance prods. (Aramis, Aveda, Tommy Hilfiger).

La-Z-Boy Inc.; 1284 N. Telegraph Rd., Monroe, MI 48162; (734) 242-1444; www.lazboy.com; Patrick H. Norton; reclining chairs, other furniture.

Leggett & Platt, Inc.; No. 1 Leggett Rd., Carthage, MO 64836; (417) 358-8131; www.leggett.com; Felix E. Wright; furniture and furniture components, industrial materials, automotive seating suspension, train and cable control systems.

Lehman Bros. Holdings, Inc.; 745 7th Ave., NY, NY 10019; (212) 526-7000; www.lehman.com; Richard S. Fuld Jr; investment bank.

Levi Strauss & Co.; 1155 Battery St., San Francisco, CA 94111; (415) 501-6000; www.levistrauss.com; Robert D. Haas; blue jeans, casual sportswear.

Eli Lilly and Company; Lilly Corporate Center, Indianapolis, IN 46285; (317) 276-2000; www.lilly.com; Sidney Taurel; pharmaceuticals (Axid, Ceclor, Prozac) and animal health prods.

The Limited, Inc.; 3 Limited Pkwy., P.O. Box 16000, Columbus, OH 43216; (614) 479-7000; www.limited.com; Leslie H. Wexner; apparel stores (Lane Bryant, Lerner, Limited, Express, Victoria's Secret, Henri Bendel), home decor (White Barn Candle Co., Bath & Body Works).

Lockheed Martin Corp.; 6801 Rockledge Dr., Bethesda, MD 20817; (301) 897-6000; www.lockheedmartin.com; Vance Coffman; commercial and military aircraft, electronics, missiles.

Loews Corp.; 667 Madison Ave., NY, NY 10021; (212) 521-2000; www.loews.com; James S. Tisch; tobacco prods. (Kent, True, Newport), watches (Bulova), hotels, insurance (CNA Financial), offshore drilling (Diamond).

Longs Drug Stores, Inc.; 141 N. Civic Dr., P.O. Box 5222, Walnut Creek, CA 94596; (925) 937-1170; www.longs.com; Robert M. Long; drug store chain.

Lowe's Cos., Inc.; Box 1111, N. Wilkesboro, NC 28656; (336) 658-4000; www.lowes.com; Robert L. Tillman; building materials and home improvement superstores.

Luby's, Inc.; 2211 NE Loop 410, PO Box 33069, San Antonio, TX 78265; (210) 654-9000; www.lubys.com; Harris Pappas; operates cafeterias in S and SW.

Lucent Technologies, Inc.; 600 Mountain Ave., Murray Hill, NJ 07974; (888)4LU-CENT; www.lucent.com; Henry B. Schacht; leading developer, designer, and manuf. of telecommunications systems, software, and prods.

Mandalay Resort Group; 3950 Las Vegas Boulevard South, Las Vegas, NV 89109; (702) 632-6700; www.mandalayresortgroup.org; Michael Ensign; casino-resort operator (Excalibur, Luxor).

Manpower Inc.; 5301 N. Ironwood Rd., Milwaukee, WI 53201; (414) 961-1000; www.manpower.com; Jeffrey A. Joerres; second largest non-gov't. employment services co. in the world.

Marathon Oil Corp.; 555 San Felipe Rd., Houston, TX 77056; (713) 629-6600; www.marathon.com; Clarence P. Cazalot Jr.; integrated oil co. (Became independent co. 1/1/02 after being separated from USX-Marathon Group; United States Steel Corp. created as a result of a spin-off from USX.)

Marriott International, Inc.; Marriott Drive, Washington, DC 20058; (301) 380-3000; www.marriott.com; John Willard Marriott Jr; hotels, retirement communities, food service dist.

Masco Corp.; 21001 Van Born Rd., Taylor, MI 48180; (313) 274-7400; www.masco.com; Richard A. Manoogian; manuf. kitchen, bathroom prods. (Delta, Peerless faucets; Fieldstone, Merillat cabinets).

Mattel, Inc.; 333 Continental Blvd., El Segundo, CA 90245; (310) 252-2000; www.mattel.com; Robert A. Eckert; largest U.S. toymaker (Barbie, Fisher-Price, Hot Wheels, Matchbox, American Girls).

May Department Stores Co.; 611 Olive St., St. Louis, MO 63101; (314) 342-6300; www.maycompany.com; Eugene S. Kahn; department stores (Hecht's, Lord & Taylor, Filene's, Foley's).

Maytag Corp.; 403 W. Fourth St. N., Newton, IA 50208; (641) 792-7000; www.maytagcorp.com; Ralph F. Hake; major appliance mfgr. (Magic Chef, Admiral, Jenn-Air), Hoover vacuum cleaners, floor care systems.

McDonald's Corp.; 1 McDonald's Plaza, Oak Brook, IL 60523; (630) 623-3000; www.mcdonalds.com; Jack M. Greenberg; fast-food restaurants.

McGraw-Hill Cos.; 1221 Ave. of the Americas, NY, NY 10020; (212) 512-2000; www.mcgraw-hill.com; Harold (Terry) McGraw 3rd; book, textbooks, magazine publishing (*Business Week*), information and financial services (Standard and Poor's), TV stations.

McKesson Corp.; 1 Post St., San Francisco, CA 94104; (415) 983-8300; www.mckesson.com; John Hammergren; distributor of drugs and toiletries and provides software and services in U.S.; bottled water.

Mead Westvaco Corp.; One High Ridge Park, Stamford, CT 06905; (203) 461-7400; www.meadwestvaco.com; Jerome F. Tatar; printing and writing paper, paperboard, packaging, shipping containers.

Medtronic, Inc.; 7000 Central Ave. NE, Minneapolis, MN 55432; (612) 514-4000; www.medtronic.com; W. W. George; world's largest manuf. of implantable biomedical devices.

Merck & Co., Inc.; PO Box 100, Whitehouse Station, NJ 08889-0100; (908) 423-1000; www.merck.com; Raymond V. Gilmartin; pharmaceuticals (Pepcid, Zocor), animal health care prods.

Meredith Corp.; 1716 Locust St., Des Moines, IA 50336; (515) 284-3000; www.meredith.com; William T. Kerr; magazine publishing (*Better Homes and Gardens, Ladies' Home Journal*), book publishing, broadcasting.

Merrill Lynch & Co., Inc.; 4 World Financial Ctr., NY, NY 10080; (212) 449-1000; www.ml.com; David H. Komansky; securities broker, financial services.

Metropolitan Life Ins. Co.; One Madison Ave., NY, NY 10010; (212) 578-2211; www.metlife.com; Bob H. Benmosche; insurance, financial services.

MGM Mirage Resorts, Inc.; 3799 Las Vegas Blvd. S., Las Vegas, NV 89109; (702) 891-3333; www.mirage.com; J. Terrence Lanni; hotel-casino operator (Mirage, Treasure Island, Golden Nugget).

Microsoft Corp.; One Microsoft Way, Redmond, WA 98052-6399; (425) 882-8080; www.microsoft.com; William H. Gates; largest independent software maker (Windows, Word, Excel).

Mobil Corp.: *see* Exxon Mobil Corp.

Morgan Stanley Dean Witter & Co.; 1585 Broadway, NY, NY 10036; (212) 761-4000; www.msdw.com; Phillip J. Purcell; diversified financial services, major U.S. credit-card issuer.

Motorola, Inc.; 1303 E. Algonquin Rd., Schaumburg, IL 60196; (847) 576-5000; www.motorola.com; G. L. Tooker; electronic equipment and components; integrated communication devices.

Nabisco: *see* Philip Morris Cos. Inc.

National Semiconductor Corp.; 2900 Semiconductor Dr., P.O. Box 58090; Santa Clara, CA 95052-8090; (408) 721-5000; www.national.com; Brian L. Halla; manuf. of semiconductors, integrated circuits.

Navistar Intl. Corp.; 4201 Winfield Rd., PO Box 1488, Warrenville, IL 60555; (630) 735-5000; www.navistar.com; John R. Horne; manuf. heavy-duty trucks, parts, school buses.

Nestlé Purina PetCare; formerly Ralston Purina; Checkerboard Sq., St. Louis, MO 63164; (314) 982-2161; www.purina.com; W. P. Stiritz; world's largest producer of dog and cat food (Purina), and dry-cell batteries (Eveready, Energizer). Acquired by Swiss-based Nestlé SA, 12/12/01.

Newell Rubbermaid Inc.; Newell Center, 29 E. Stephenson Street, Freeport, IL 61032; (815) 235-4171; www.newellco.com; Joseph Galli; cookware (Calphalon, WearEver); hair accessories (Goody); glassware (Anchor Hocking); kitchen products (Rubbermaid); window treatments (Levelor, Kirsch, Newell); home storage (Lee Ravan); writing instruments (Eberhard Faber, Sanford); address card files (Rolodex); infant and juvenile prods (Little Tykes, Graco, Century).

WORLD ALMANAC QUICK QUIZ

What was the most popular cookie (most purchased) from August 2001 to August 2002?
(a) Mallomars (b) Oreos (c) Chips Ahoy! (d) Fig Newtons
For the answer look in this chapter, or see page 1008.

New York Times Co.; 229 W. 43rd St., NY, NY 10036; (212) 556-1234; www.nytco.com; A. O. Sulzberger Jr; newspapers (*Boston Globe*), radio and TV stations, magazines (*Golf Digest*).

Nike, Inc.; 1 Bowerman Dr., Beaverton, OR 97005; (503) 671-6453; www.NikeBiz.com; Philip H. Knight; athletic and leisure footware, apparel.

Nordstrom, Inc.; 1501 5th Ave., Seattle, WA 98101; (206) 628-2111; www.nordstrom.com; Blake W. Nordstrom; upscale dept. store chain.

Norfolk Southern Corp.; Three Commercial Pl., Norfolk, VA 23510; (757) 629-2600; www.nscorp.com; David R. Goode; operates railway, freight carrier.

Northrop Grumman Corp.; 1840 Century Park East, Los Angeles, CA 90067; (310) 553-6262; www.northgrum.com; Kent Kresa; aircraft, electronics, data systems, information systems, missiles.

Northwest Airlines Corp.; 2700 Lone Oak Pkwy., Eagan, MN 55121; (612) 726-2111; www.nwa.com; Richard H. Anderson; air transportation.

Occidental Petroleum Corp.; 10889 Wilshire Blvd., Los Angeles, CA 90024; (310) 208-8800; www.oxy.com; Ray R. Irani; oil, natural gas, chemicals, plastics, fertilizers.

Office Depot.; 2200 Old Germantown Rd., Delray Beach, FL 33445; (561) 278-4800; www.officedepot.com; Bruce Nelson; retail office supply stores.

Owens Corning; 1 Owens Corning Parkway, Toledo, OH 43659; (419) 248-8000; www.owenscorning.com; David T. Brown; world leader in advanced glass, composite materials.

Owens-Illinois; 1 SeaGate, Toledo, OH 43666; (419) 247-5000; J. H. Lemieux; www.o-i.com; one of the world's largest producer of glass and plastic packaging.

Pacific Gas & Electric Corp. (PG&E); 77 Beale St., San Francisco, CA 94106; (800) 367-7731; www.pgecorp.com; Robert D. Glynn Jr.; energy supplier.

PaineWebber Group, Inc.: *see* UBS PaineWebber Group, Inc.

J.C. Penney Co.; 6501 Legacy Dr., Plano, TX 75024; (972) 431-4757; www.jcpenney.com; Allen Questrom; dept. stores, catalog sales, drug stores (Eckerd, Fay's), insurance.

Pennzoil-Quaker State Co.; Pennzoil Pl., PO Box 2967, Houston, TX 77252; (713) 546-4000; www.pennzoil-quakerstate.com; James J. Postl; automotive consumer products co., franchises Jiffy Lube and Q-Lube service centers.

PepsiCo, Inc.; 700 Anderson Hill Rd., Purchase, NY 10577; (914) 253-2000; www.pepsico.com; Steven S. Reinemund; soft drinks (Pepsi-Cola, Mountain Dew), fruit juice (Tropicana), FritoLay snacks (Ruffles, Lay's, Fritos, Doritos, Rold Gold), Quaker Oats.

Pfizer, Inc.; 235 E. 42nd St., NY, NY 10017; (212) 573-2323; www.pfizer.com; Henry McKinnell; pharmaceuticals (Celebrex, Diflucan, Viagra, Zithromax), hospital, agricultural, chemical prods., consumer prods. (Visine, Barbasol, Halls, Desitin, Benadryl, Listerine, Lubriderm, Schick, Zantac 75, Ben-Gay). (Co. merged with Warner-Lambert 6/19/01, making it the largest pharmaceutical co. in the world in sales, and the 5th largest co. in the world; plans announced 7/02 for acquisition of Pharmacia Corp.)

Pharmacia Corp.; 100 Route 206 N., Peapack, NJ 07977; (908) 901-8853; www.pharmacia.com; Fred Hassan; pharmaceuticals (Motrin, Rogaine, Halcion, Xanax), chemicals, health-care prods., consumer prods. (Equal, NutraSweet). (Created from merger of Pharmacia & Upjohn and Monsanto, an agrochemical company, 3/00; completed spin-off of Monsanto, 8/14/02; plans announced 7/02 for Pharmacia to be acquired by Pfizer).

Philip Morris Cos. Inc.; 120 Park Ave., NY, NY 10017; (212) 880-5000; www.philipmorris.com; www.kraft.com. Louis C. Camilleri; cigarettes (largest U.S. tobacco company; Marlboro, Merit, Virginia Slims), beer (Miller, Molson, Red Dog), Kraft Foods products (Jell-O, Maxwell House coffee, Kool-Aid, Oscar Mayer, Tang, Cheez Whiz and Velveeta cheese prods., Post cereals, Tombstone Pizza, and Toblerone chocolate); Nabisco products (Oreo, Chips Ahoy! cookies, Ritz, Triscuit crackers, Mallomars).

Phillips Petroleum Co.; 4th and Keeler Ave., Bartlesville, OK 74004; (918) 661-6600; www.phillips66.com; J. J. Mulva; integrated oil and petrochemical co. Merger with Conoco conditionally approved by FTC, 8/30/02, Conoco-Phillips would be 3rd-largest U.S. integrated energy company.

Pillowtex Corp.; 1 Lake Circle Dr., Kannopolis, NC 28081; (704) 939-2000; www.pillowtex.com; David Perdue; household textile prods.

Pitney Bowes, Inc.; Walter H. Wheeler Jr. Dr., Stamford, CT 06926; (203) 356-5000; www.pb.com; Michael J. Critelli; world's largest mfgr. of postage meters, and mailing equip.

Polaroid Corp.; 784 Memorial Drive, Cambridge, MA 02139; (781) 386-2000; www.polaroid.com; Gary T. DiCamillo; photographic equip. and supplies, optical goods.

PPG Industries, Inc.; 1 PPG Place, Pittsburgh, PA 15272; (412) 434-3131; www.ppg.com; Raymond W. LeBoeuf; glass prods., silicas, fiberglass, chemicals; world's leading supplier of automobile/industrial coatings.

Procter & Gamble Co.; 1 Procter & Gamble Plaza, Cincinnati, OH 45202; (513) 983-1100; www.pg.com; Alan Lafley; soaps and detergents (Ivory, Cheer, Tide, Mr. Clean, Comet, Zest); toiletries (Crest, Scope, Head & Shoulders, Noxzema, Oil of Olay, Old Spice); pharmaceuticals (NyQuil, Pepto-Bismol, Vicks cough medicines); foods (Folgers coffee, Pringles); paper prods. (Charmin toilet tissues, Bounty towels, Tampax tampons, Pampers & Luvs disposable diapers); Cover Girl and Max Factor cosmetics, Clairol haircare.

Prudential Financial, Inc.; 751 Broad St., Newark, NJ 07102; (973) 802-6000; www.prudential.com; Arthur F. Ryan; insurance, financial services.

Quaker Oats Co.; 321 N. Clark St., Chicago, IL 60610; (312) 222-7111; www.quakeroats.com; Robert S. Morrison; cereal (Life, Cap'n Crunch), foods (Aunt Jemima, Rice-A-Roni), beverages (Gatorade). A subsidiary of PepsiCo, merged 8/2/01.

Radio Shack, formerly Tandy Corp.; 100 Throckmorton St., Suite 1800, Fort Worth, TX 76102; (817) 415-3700; www.radioshack.com; Leonard H. Roberts; consumer electronics retailer (Computer City, Radio Shack).

Ralcorp Holdings, Inc.; 800 Market St., St. Louis, MO 63101; (314) 877-7000; www.ralcorp.com; Joe R. Micheletto; private-label breakfast cereals, snack foods, baby food (Beech-Nut).

Raytheon Co.; 141 Spring St., Lexington, MA 02421; (781) 862-6600; www.raytheon.com; Daniel P. Burnham; defense systems, electronics.

Reader's Digest Assn., Inc.; Reader's Digest Road, Pleasantville, NY 10570; (914) 238-1000; www.rd.com; Thomas Ryder; direct-mail marketer of magazines, books, music and video prods.

Reebok Intl., Ltd.; 1895 J.W. Foster Blvd., Canton, MA 02021; (781) 401-5000; www.reebok.com; Paul Fireman; athletic and leisure footwear, apparel.

Revlon, Inc.; 625 Madison Ave., NY, NY 10022; (212) 527-4000; www.revlon.com; Ronald O. Perelman; cosmetics, beauty aids, skin care.

Rite Aid Corp.; 30 Hunter Lane, Camp Hill, PA 17011-2404; (717) 761-2633; www.riteaid.com; Robert G. Miller and Mary F. Sammons; discount drug stores.

RJ Reynolds Tobacco; 401 N. Main St., Winston-Salem, NC 27102; (336) 741-5000; www.rjrt.com; Andrew J. Schindler; 2nd-largest U.S. producer of cigarettes (Winston, Salem, Camel).

Rockwell Auto; 777 E. Wisconsin Ave., Suite 1400, Milwaukee, WI 53202; (414) 212-5200; www.rockwell.com; Don H. Davis; diversified high-tech. co. (world leader in electronic controls)

Ryder System, Inc.; 3600 NW 82nd Ave., Miami, FL 33166; (305) 593-3726; www.ryder.com; Gregory T. Swienton; truck-leasing service.

Safeway Inc.; 5918 Stoneridge Mall Rd., Pleasanton, CA 94588-3229; (925) 467-3000; www.safeway.com; Steven A. Burd; supermarkets.

Sara Lee Corp.; Three First National Plaza, Chicago, IL 60602; (312) 726-2600; www.saralee.com; C. Steven McMillan; baked goods, fresh and processed meats (Ball Park, Jimmy Dean, Hillshire Farms, Kahn's), hosiery, intimate apparel and knitwear (Hanes, L'eggs, Playtex, Champion).

SBC Communications, Inc.; 175 E. Houston, San Antonio, TX 78205; (210) 821-4105; www.sbc.com; Edward Whitacre Jr; telephone services (Ameritech, Southwestern Bell, Pacific Bell).

Schering-Plough Corp.; One Giralda Farms, Madison, NJ 07940; (973) 822-7000; www.sch-plough.com; R.J. Kogan; pharmaceuticals (Claritin, Proventil), consumer prods. (Afrin, Coppertone), animal health prods.

Seagate Technology; 920 Disc Dr., Scotts Valley, CA 95066; (405) 936-1234; www.seagate.com; Stephen J. Luczo; manuf. disk drives.

Sears, Roebuck and Co.; 3333 Beverly Rd., Hoffman Estates, IL 60179; (847) 286-2500; www.sears.com; Alan J. Lacey; 2nd largest U.S. retailer, department, specialty stores.

Shaw Industries, Inc.; P.O. Box 2128, 616 E. Walnut Ave., Dalton, GA 30722; (706) 278-3812; www.shawinc.com; Robert E. Shaw; world's largest carpet mfgr. (Sutton, Tuftex, Cabin Crafts). Since 1/01 a subsidiary of Berkshire Hathaway, Inc.

Sherwin-Williams Co.; 101 Prospect Ave. NW, Cleveland, OH 44115-1075; (216) 566-2000; www.sherwin.com; Christopher M. Connor; largest North American paint and varnish producer (Dutch Boy, Pratt & Lambert, Martha Stewart, Minwax).

J. M. Smucker Co.; Strawberry Lane, Orrville, OH 44667; (330) 682-3000; www.smuckers.com; Timothy P. Smucker; preserves, jams, jellies (Dickinson's), toppings (Magic Shell), syrups, juices, Jif peanut butter, Crisco oil

Smurfit-Stone Container Corp.; 150 N. Michigan Ave., Chicago, IL 60601; (312) 346-6600; www.smurfit-stone.net; Patrick J. Moore; industry leader for corrugated containers, paper bags and sacks.

Sprint Corp.; PO Box 11315, Kansas City, MO 64112; (913) 624-3000; www.sprint.com; William T. Esrey; long-distance and local telecommunications.

Staples, Inc.; 500 Staples Dr., Framingham, MA 01702; (508) 253-5000; www.staples.com; Ron Sargent; office-supply superstores.

Starwood Hotels and Resorts Worldwide; 777 Westchester Ave., White Plains, NY 10604; (914) 640-8100; www.starwood.com; Barry S. Sternlicht; hotels and leisure company (Westin, Sheraton, W Hotels).

State Farm Mutual Automobile Ins. Co.; 1 State Farm Plaza, Bloomington, IL 61701; (309) 766-2311; www.statefarm.com; Edward B. Rust Jr.; major insurance co.

Stride Rite Corp.; 191 Spring St., P.O. Box 9191, Lexington, MA 02420; (617) 824-6000; www.striderite. com; David Chamberlain; high-quality children's footwear (Keds, Sperry Top-Sider) and eyewear.

Sun Microsystems, Inc.; 2550 Garcia Ave., Mountain View, CA 94043; (650) 960-1300; www.sun.com; Scott G. McNealy; supplier of network-based distributed computer systems (Java programming language).

Sunoco, Inc.; 1801 Market St., Philadelphia, PA 19103-1699; (215) 977-3000; www.sunocoinc.com; J.D. Drosdick; energy resources co., markets Sunoco gasoline.

SUPERVALU Inc.; 11840 Valley View Rd., Eden Prairie, MN 55340; (952) 828-4000; www.supervalu.com; Jeff Noddle; food wholesaler, retailer.

Sysco Corp.; 1390 Enclave Pkwy, Houston, TX 77077-2099; (281) 584-1390; www.sysco.com; Charles H. Cotros; leading U.S. food distributor.

Target Corp.; 777 Nicollet Mall, Minneapolis, MN 55402; (612) 370-6948; www.targetcorp.com; Robert J. Ulrich; department, specialty stores (Target, Marshall Field's, Mervyn's California).

Tenneco Automotive, Inc.; 500 N. Field Drive, Lake Forest, IL 60045; (847) 482-5000; www.tenneco- automotive.com; Mark P. Frissora; automotive parts (Monroe, Walker).

Texaco Inc.: *see* ChevronTexaco Corp.

Texas Instruments Inc.; 12500 TI Blvd., Dallas, TX 75243-4136; (972) 995-3773; www.ti.com; T. J. Engibous; electronics, semiconductors, software

Textron, Inc.; 40 Westminster St., Providence, RI 02903; (401) 421-2800; www.textron.com; Lewis B. Campbell; aerospace, industrial, automotive prods., financial services.

3M Company; 3M Center, St. Paul, MN 55144-1000; (612) 733-1110; www.3m.com; W. James McNerney Jr.; abrasives, adhesives, electrical, health care, cleaning (Scotch-Brite, O-Cel-O sponges), printing, consumer prods. (Scotch Tape, Post-it).

Time Warner Inc.: *see* AOL Time Warner, Inc.

The TJX Cos., Inc.; 770 Cochituate Rd., Framingham, MA 01701; (508) 390-1000; www.tjx.com; Edmond English; world's largest off-price apparel retailer (T.J. Maxx, Marshalls).

Tootsie Roll Industries, Inc.; 7401 S. Cicero Ave., Chicago, IL 60629; (773) 838-3400; www.tootsie.com; Ellen and Melvin Gordon; candy (Tootsie Roll, Mason Dots, Charms, Sugar Daddy, Charleston Chew, Junior Mints).

Toro Co.; 8111 Lyndale Ave. S, Bloomington, MN 55420; (952) 888-8801; www.toro.com; Kendrick B. Melrose; lawn and turf maintenance (Lawn-Boy), snow removal equipment, lighting and irrigation systems.

Toys "R" Us; 461 From Rd., Paramus, NJ 07652; (201) 262-7800; www.toysrus.com; John J. Eyler Jr.; world's largest children's specialty retailer (Toys "R" Us, Kids "R" Us, Babies "R" Us, Imaginarium).

Transamerica Corp.; 1150 South Olive St. Los Angeles, CA 90015; (213) 742-2111; www.transamerica.com; Ron F. Wagley; insurance, financial services; wholly owned subsidiary of Netherlands-based AEGON.

Triarc Cos., Inc.; 280 Park Ave., NY, NY 10017; (212) 451-3000; www.triarc.com; Nelson Peltz; fast-food restaurants (Arby's), beverages (Royal Crown, Mystic, Nehi, Stewart's).

Tribune Co.; 435 N. Michigan Ave., Chicago, IL 60611; (312) 222-9100; www.tribune.com; J. W. Madigan; newspapers (*Los Angeles Times, Chicago Tribune, Newsday*), magazines (*Field & Stream, Popular Science*), broadcasting (incl. WGN-TV and 23 other stations), Chicago Cubs baseball team.

Trinity Industries, Inc.; PO Box 568887, 2525 Stemmons Freeway, Dallas, TX 75207; (214) 631-4420; www.trin.net; Timothy R. Wallace; manufactures metal prods., rail and freight prods.

TRW Inc.; 1900 Richmond Rd., Cleveland, OH 44124; (216) 291-7000; www.trw.com; Philip A. Odeen; car and truck operations, electronics, space and defense systems.

TWA: *see* AMR Corp.

Tyco Intl., Ltd.; One Tyco Pk., Exeter, NH 03833; (603) 778-9700; www.tyco.com; Edward Breen; fire protection systems, pipes, power cables, medical supplies, packaging.

Tyson Foods, Inc.; 2210 West Oaklawn, Springdale, AR 72764; (501) 290-4000; www.tysonfoodsinc.com; John Tyson; fresh and processed poultry and beef, pork, and seafood prods. (Holly Farms, Weaver, Louis Kemp, IBP).

UAL Corp.; 1200 E. Algonquin Rd., Elk Grove Twp., IL 60007; (847) 700-4000; www.ual.com; John W. Creighton; air transportation (United Airlines).

UBS PaineWebber Group, Inc.; 1285 Ave. of the Americas, NY, NY 10019; (212) 713-2000; www.ubspainewebber.com; Joseph J. Grano Jr.; financial services.

Unilever Bestfoods; 700 Sylvan Ave., Englewood Cliffs, NJ 07632; (201) 894-4000; www.bestfoods.com; Neil Beckerman; food (Hellmann's, Best Foods mayonnaise, Knorr soups, Ragu pasta sauce, Wish-Bone salad dressing, Lipton Tea, Skippy Peanut Butter).

Union Carbide Corp.: *see* Dow Chemical Co.

Union Pacific Corp.; 1416 Dodge St., Omaha, NE, 68179; (402) 271-5000; www.up.com; Richard Davidson; largest railroad, trucking co. in U.S.; Fenix, telecommunications, software.

Unisys Corp.; Unisys Way, Blue Bell, PA 19424-0001; (215) 986-4011; www.unisys.com; Lawrence A. Weinbach; designs, manuf. computer information systems and related prods..

UnitedHealth Group Corp.; 9900 Bren Rd. East, Minnetonka, MN 55343; (612) 936-1300; www.unitedhealthgroup.com; William W. McGuire; owns, manages health maintenance organizations.

United Parcel Service of America, Corp.; 55 Glenlake Pkwy. NE, Atlanta, GA 30328; (404) 828-6000; www.ups.com; Michael L. Eskew; courier services.

United States Steel Corp.; 600 Grant St., Pittsburgh, PA 15219-2800; (412) 433-1121; www.ussteel.com; Thomas J. Usher; steel, tin prods. (Became separate co. 1/1/02 as a result of a spin-off from USX-Marathon Group; rest of corp. became Marathon Oil Corp.)

United Technologies Corp.; One Financial Plaza, Hartford, CT 06101; (860) 728-7000; www.utc.com; George David; aerospace, industrial prods. and services (Otis Elevator, Pratt & Whitney, Sikorsky Aircraft).

Unocal Corp.; 2141 Rosecrans Ave., Ste. 4000, El Segundo, CA 90245; (310) 726-7731; www.unocal.com; Charles R. Williamson; integrated oil co.

US Airways Group, Inc.; 2345 Crystal Dr., Arlington, VA 22227; (703) 872-7000; www.usairways.com; David N. Siegel; air transportation.

UST Inc.; 100 W. Putnam Ave., Greenwich, CT 06830; (203) 661-1100; www.ustinc.com; Vincent A. Gierer Jr.; smokeless tobacco (Copenhagen, Skoal), pipe tobacco, wine (Chateau St. Michelle, Conn Creek, Columbia Crest).

Verizon Communications; 1095 Avenue of the Americas, New York, NY 10036; (212) 395-1525; www.verizon.com; Charles R. Lee, Ivan Seidenberg; largest U.S. wireline and wireless provider; world's lgst. provider of print and on-line directory info. (co. formed from merger of Bell Atlantic and GTE, 6/30/00.)

V.F. Corp.; 105 Corporate Center Blvd., Greensboro, NC 27408; (336) 547-6000; www.vfc.com; Mackey J. McDonald; apparel (Lee, Wrangler jeans, Vanity Fair, Healthtex, Jantzen).

Viacom, Inc.; 1515 Broadway, NY, NY 10036; (212) 258-6000; www.viacom.com; Mel Karmazin; TV broadcast stations and cable systems, channels (CBS, UPN, TNN, BET, Comedy Central, Showtime, MTV, VH1, Nickelodeon); book publishing (Simon & Schuster); produces, distributes movies, TV shows (Paramount); video stores (Blockbuster), theme parks.

Walgreen Co.; 200 Wilmot Rd., Deerfield, IL 60015; (847) 940-2500; www.walgreens.com; David W. Bernauer; nation's largest drugstore chain.

Wal-Mart Stores, Inc.; 702 SW 8th St., Bentonville, AR 72716; (479) 273-4000; www.walmart.com; S. Robson Walton; world's largest retailer; discount stores, wholesale clubs.

Washington Post Co.; 1150 15th St. NW, Washington, DC 20071; (202) 334-6000; www.washpostco.com; Donald E. Graham; newspapers, *Newsweek* magazine, TV and CATV stations, Stanley H. Kaplan Educational Centers.

Waste Management; 1001 Fannin, Suite 4000, Houston, TX 77002; (713) 512-6200; www.wm.com; Maurice Myers; N. America's largest solid waste collection and disposal co.

Wells Fargo & Co.; 420 Montgomery St., San Francisco, CA 94163; (800) 411-4932; www.wellsfargo.com; R. Kovacevich; bank holding co.

Wendy's Intl., Inc.; 4288 W. Dublin-Granville Rd., Dublin, OH 43017; (614) 764-3100; www.wendys.com; John T. Schuessler; quick-service restaurants.

Weyerhaeuser Co.; 33663 Weyerhauser Way, Federal Way, WA 98063; (253) 924-2345; www.weyerhaeuser.com; Steven R. Rogel; world's largest private owner of softwood timber, distrib. paper and wood prods.

Whirlpool Corp.; 2000 N. M-63, Benton Harbor, MI 49022; (616) 923-5000; www.whirlpoolcorp.com; David Whitwam; world's largest manuf. of major home appliances (KitchenAid, Kenmore, Roper).

Whitman Corp.; 3501 Algonquin Road, Rolling Meadows, IL 60008; (847) 818-5000; www.whitmancorp.com; Robert C. Pohlad; beverage bottler and distributor (Pepsi-Cola).

Winn-Dixie Stores, Inc.; 5050 Edgewood Ct., Jacksonville, FL 32254; (904) 783-5000; www.winn-dixie.com; Al Rowland; supermarkets (Winn Dixie, Save RIte, Thrift Way).

Winnebago Industries, Inc.; PO Box 152, Forest City, IA 50436; (641) 585-3535; www.winnebagoind.com; Bruce D. Hertzke; manuf. and financing of motor homes, recreational vehicles.

WorldCom, Inc.; 500 Clinton Ctr. Dr., Clinton, MS 39056; (877) 624-9266; www.wcom.com; John Sidgmore (temporary); long-distance telephone service; filed for bankruptcy, 7/21/02.

WRC Media Inc.; 512 Seventh Ave., New York, NY 10018; (212) 768-0455; www.wrcmedia.com; Martin E. Kenney Jr.; publisher of educational and reference media; World Almanac, Facts On File News Services, Funk & Wagnalls, Gareth Stevens Publishing, CompassLearning, Weekly Reader, American Guidance, ChildU.

Wm. Wrigley Jr. Co.; 410 N. Michigan Ave., Chicago, IL 60611; (312) 644-2121; www.wrigley.com; William Wrigley Jr.; world's largest mfgr. of chewing gum.

Wyeth, formerly American Home Products; 5 Giralda Farms, Madison, NJ 07940; (973) 660-5000; www.wyeth.com; John R. Stafford; prescription and over-the-counter drugs (Advil, Anacin, Chap Stick, Robitussin).

Xerox Corp.; 800 Long Ridge Road, Stamford, CT 06904; (203) 968-3000; www.xerox.com; Anne Mulcahy; copiers, printers, document publishing equip.

Yahoo! Inc.; 701 First Ave. Sunnyvale, CA 94089; (408) 349-3300; www.yahoo.com; Terry Semel; global internet media company.

Yum! Brands, Inc.; 1441 Gardiner Lane, Louisville, KY 40213; (502) 874-8300; www.yum.com; David C. Novack; fast food (Pizza Hut, KFC, Taco Bell).

IT'S A FACT: Wal-Mart, the world's largest retailer, had $220 million in revenues in 2001, making it bigger than the next 10 retailers (Sears, Target, Kmart, etc.) combined. Heirs of founder Sam Walton own about 38% of the company.

Who Owns What: Familiar Consumer Products and Services

Listed here are some consumer brands and their (U.S.) parent companies. Excluded are many brands whose parent companies have the same or a similar name (e.g., Colgate is Colgate-Palmolive Co.). For company contact information, see Business Directory on previous pages.

ABC broadcasting: Walt Disney
Admiral appliances: Maytag
Advil: Wyeth
Ajax cleanser: Colgate-Palmolive
Almond Joy candy bar: Hershey
American Girl: Mattel
Anacin: Wyeth
Arm & Hammer: Church & Dwight
Arrid antiperspirant: Church & Dwight
Aunt Jemima Pancake mix: Quaker Oats (PepsiCo)
Aunt Millie's pasta sauce: Borden
Banana Republic stores: The Gap
Band-Aids: Johnson & Johnson
Barbie dolls: Mattel
Beech-Nut baby food: Ralcorp
Ben-Gay: Pfizer
Betty Crocker prods.: General Mills
Black Flag insecticides: Clorox
Blockbuster video stores: Viacom
Bounty paper towels: Procter & Gamble
Brillo soap pads: Church & Dwight
Brita water systems: Clorox
Budweiser beer: Anheuser-Busch
Bufferin: Bristol-Myers Squibb
Bulova watches: Loews
Business Week magazine: McGraw-Hill
Buster Brown shoes: Brown Shoe
Cadbury: Hershey
Cap'n Crunch cereal: Quaker Oats (PepsiCo)
Calphalon cookware: Newell Rubbermaid
CBS Broadcasting: Viacom
Charmin toilet tissue: Procter & Gamble
Cheer detergent: Procter & Gamble
Cheerios cereal: General Mills
Cheez Whiz: Philip Morris (Kraft)
Chips Ahoy!: Philip Morris (Nabisco)
Cinemax: AOL Time Warner
Clairol hair prods.: Procter & Gamble
CNN: AOL Time Warner
Combat insecticides: Clorox
Comet cleanser: Procter & Gamble
Coppertone sun care prods.: Schering-Plough
Crest toothpaste: Procter & Gamble
Crisco shortening: J.M. Smucker
DC Comics: AOL Time Warner
Desitin Ointment: Pfizer
Doritos chips: PepsiCo
Dristan: Wyeth
Duracell batteries: Gillette
Dutch Boy paints: Sherwin-Williams
Efferdent dental cleanser: Warner-Lambert (Pfizer)
Elmer's glue: Borden
ESPN: Walt Disney
Eveready batteries: Nestlé Purina PetCare
Excedrin: Bristol-Myers Squibb
Fab detergent: Colgate-Palmolive
Fantastik: S.C. Johnson
Field & Stream: Tribune Co.
Fisher Price Toys: Mattel
Foamy shaving cream: Gillette
Folger's coffee: Procter & Gamble
Formula 409 spray cleaner: Clorox
Franco-American spaghetti: Campbell Soup
Frito-Lays snacks: PepsiCo
Fruitopia drinks: Coca-Cola
Gatorade: Quaker Oats (PepsiCo)
Godiva chocolate: Campbell Soup
Halcion: Pharmacia
Halls coughdrops: Pfizer
Hamburger Helper: General Mills
Hanes hosiery: Sara Lee
HBO: AOL Time Warner
Head and Shoulders shampoo: Procter & Gamble
Healthtex: V.F. Corp.
Hellmann's mayonnaise: Unilever Bestfoods
Hertz car rental: Ford
Hi-C fruit drinks: Coca-Cola
Hidden Valley prods.: Clorox
Hillshire Farms meats: Sara Lee
Holly Farms: Tyson Foods

Hostess cakes: Interstate Bakeries
Huggies diapers: Kimberly-Clark
Ivory soap: Procter & Gamble
Jack Daniel's Whiskey: Brown-Forman
Java programming language: Sun Microsystems
Jell-O: Philip Morris (Kraft)
Jenn-Air stoves: Maytag
Jif peanut butter: J.M. Smucker
Jim Beam bourbon: Fortune Brands
Keds footwear: Stride Rite
Kent cigarettes: Loews
KFC restaurants: Yum! Brands
Kibbles 'n Bits pet foods: H. J. Heinz
Kinney shoe stores: Foot Locker
KitchenAid appliances: Whirlpool
Kit Kat candy: Hershey
Kleenex: Kimberly-Clark
Knorr soups: Unilever Bestfoods
Kool-Aid: Philip Morris (Kraft)
Krazy Glue: Borden
Kwikset doorknobs: Black & Decker
Ladies Home Journal magazine: Meredith
Lee jeans: V.F. Corp.
L'eggs hosiery: Sara Lee
Lenox china: Brown-Forman
Lerner stores: The Limited
LifeSavers candy: Philip Morris (Kraft)
Lipton tea: Unilever Bestfoods
Listerine mouthwash: Pfizer
Lord & Taylor: May Dept. Stores
Marlboro cigarettes: Philip Morris
Max Factor beauty products: Procter & Gamble
Maxwell House coffee: Philip Morris (Kraft)
Metamucil: Procter & Gamble
Michelob beer: Anheuser-Busch
Miller beer: Philip Morris
Milton Bradley games: Hasbro
Minute Maid juices: Coca-Cola
Monroe automotive parts: Tenneco Automotive
MTV: Viacom
Nature Valley granola bars: General Mills
NBC broadcasting: General Electric
Neutrogena soap: Johnson & Johnson
Newsweek magazine: Washington Post
Nickelodeon TV: Viacom
9 Lives cat food: H.J. Heinz
Oil of Olay: Procter & Gamble
Old Navy Clothing: The Gap
Oreo cookies: Philip Morris (Nabisco)
Oscar Mayer meats: Philip Morris (Kraft)
Pampers: Procter & Gamble
Parker Bros. games: Hasbro
People magazine: AOL Time Warner
Pepperidge Farm prods.: Campbell Soup
Pepto-Bismol: Procter & Gamble
Philadelphia Cream Cheese: Philip Morris (Kraft)
Pine-Sol cleaner: Clorox
Pizza Hut restaurants: Yum! Brands
Planters nuts: Philip Morris (Kraft)
Playskool toys: Hasbro
Playtex apparel: Sara Lee
Post cereals: Philip Morris (Kraft)
Post-it notes: 3M
Prego pasta sauce: Campbell Soup
Prozac: Eli Lilly
Ragu sauce: Unilever Bestfoods
Red Dog beer: Philip Morris
Reese's candy: Hershey
Rice-A-Roni: Quaker Oats (PepsiCo)
Rice Krispies: Kellogg
Right Guard deodorant: Gillette
Ritz crackers: Philip Morris (Nabisco)
Robitussin: Wyeth
Rogaine hair growth aide: Pharmacia
Ruffles chips: PepsiCo
Schick razors: Warner-Lambert (Pfizer)
Scope mouthwash: Procter & Gamble
Scotch tape: 3M
Scott tissue: Kimberly-Clark
Simon & Schuster publishing: Viacom
Skippy peanut butter: Unilever Bestfoods
SnackWell's cookies: Philip Morris (Nabisco)
S.O.S. cleanser: Clorox
Southern Comfort liquor: Brown-Forman
SPAM meat: Hormel Foods
Sports Illustrated magazine: AOL Time Warner
Sprite soda: Coca-Cola
StarKist tuna: H.J. Heinz
Sugar Twin: Alberto-Culver
Swanson broth: Campbell Soup
Taco Bell restaurants: Yum! Brands
Tampax tampons: Procter & Gamble
Thomas' English muffins: Unilever Bestfoods
Tide detergent: Procter & Gamble
Time magazine: AOL Time Warner
Titleist: Fortune Brands
Tombstone pizza: Philip Morris (Kraft)
Triscuits: Philip Morris (Nabisco)
Trojan condoms: Church & Dwight
Tropicana juice: PepsiCo
Tylenol: Johnson & Johnson
Ultra Brite toothpaste: Colgate-Palmolive
USA Today newspaper: Gannett
V8 vegetable juice: Campbell Soup
Vanity Fair apparel: V.F. Corp.
Velveeta cheese prods.: Philip Morris (Kraft)
Viagra: Pfizer
Vicks cough medicines: Procter & Gamble
Victoria's Secret stores: The Limited
Visine eye drops: Pfizer
Wall Street Journal: Dow Jones
Weekly Reader: WRC Media
Weight Watchers: H.J. Heinz
Wheaties cereal: General Mills
Windex: S.C. Johnson
Windows software applications: Microsoft
Wise snacks: Borden
Wonder bread: Interstate Bakeries
The World Almanac: WRC Media
Zest soap: Procter & Gamble
Ziploc storage bags: S.C. Johnson

Top Brands in Selected Categories, 2001-2002

Source: Information Resources, Inc., a Chicago-based marketing research company; figures for 12-month period ending 8/11/02.

Ready-to-Eat Cold Cereals

	Sales	Market Share (%)
Private Label	$544,039,808	7.9
General Mills Cheerios	333,025,248	4.9
Kelloggs Frosted Flakes	281,109,824	4.1
General Mills Honey Nut Cheerios	229,125,408	3.3
Cinnamon Toast Crunch	189,967,904	2.8

Ground Coffee (excluding Decaf)

	Sales	Market Share (%)
Folgers	$349,179,584	21.6
Maxwell House	273,306,848	16.9
Private Label	129,805,656	8.0
Maxwell House Master Blend	128,839,048	8.0
Starbucks	113,367,488	7.0

(1) Excludes Wal-Mart Sales.

Toothpaste[1]

	Sales	Market Share (%)
Crest	$277,630,784	22.2
Colgate	170,529,680	13.6
Colgate Total	103,354,072	8.2
Aquafresh	89,731,256	7.2
Crest Multicare	64,826,536	5.2

Cookies[1]

	Sales	Market Share (%)
Nabisco Oreos	$524,557,312	13.4
Nabisco Chips Ahoy!	352,624,672	9.0
Private Label	334,307,040	8.5
Keebler Chips Deluxe	158,515,680	4.0
Nabisco Newtons	136,476,848	3.5

Top 10 Shopping Websites

Source: comScore Media Metrix, Inc.

Rank	Website address	Visitors[1]
1.	www.eBay.com[2]	33,370,000
2.	www.Amazon.com[2]	27,753,000
3.	www.shopping.yahoo.com[2]	23,972,000
4.	www.AmericanGreetings.com[2]	13,201,000
5.	www.BeMusic.de[2]	10,331,000
6.	www.barnesandnoble.com	9,497,000
7.	www.columbiahouse.com	9,247,000
8.	www.Dell.com	9,185,000
9.	www.bizrate.com	8,822,000
10.	www.hewlettpackard.com	8,751,000

(1) Number of visitors who visited website at least once in July 2002, according to a Media Metrix sample. (2) Represents an aggregation of commonly owned domain names.

The Cost of Raising a Child Born in 2001

Source: Center for Nutrition Policy and Promotion, U.S. Dept. of Agriculture

Estimated annual expenditures in 2001 dollars for a child born in 2001, by income group, for each year to age 17. Estimates are for the younger child in a 2-parent family with 2 children, for the overall U.S.

Year	Income group[1] Lowest	Middle	Highest
2001	$6,490	$9,030	$13,430
2002	6,710	9,340	13,890
2003	6,940	9,650	14,360
2004	7,330	10,240	15,170
2005	7,580	10,590	15,680
2006	7,840	10,940	16,220
2007	8,200	11,320	16,580
2008	$8,480	$11,700	$17,150
2009	8,770	12,100	17,730
2010	9,090	12,420	18,120
2011	9,400	12,840	18,730
2012	9,720	13,280	19,370
2013	11,290	14,850	21,300
2014	$11,680	$15,350	$22,020
2015	12,070	15,870	22,770
2016	12,350	16,740	24,220
2017	12,770	17,310	25,050
2018	13,210	17,900	25,900
TOTAL	**$169,920**	**$231,470**	**$337,690**

(1) In 2001, lowest annual income is less than $39,100 (average in this range = $24,400); middle income is $39,100-$65,800 (average = $52,100); highest income is $65,800 or more (average = $98,600).

Median Price of Existing Single-Family Homes, by Metropolitan Area, 2000-2002

Source: National Association of REALTORS®

Metropolitan Area	2000	2001	2nd Qtr 2002
Akron, OH	$110,100	$113,600	$117,400
Albany/Schenectady/Troy, NY	111,100	121,600	126,400
Albuquerque, NM	130,400	133,300	134,300
Amarillo, TX	86,300	90,200	94,500
Anaheim/Santa Ana, CA	318,000	355,600	411,100
Appleton/Oshkosh/Neenah, WI	100,500	105,100	114,300
Atlanta, GA	131,200	138,800	146,900
Atlantic City, NJ	121,500	125,700	139,100
Aurora/Elgin, IL	163,000	178,200	191,800
Austin/San Marcos, TX	142,800	152,000	160,900
Baltimore, MD	153,000	158,200	175,900
Baton Rouge, LA	109,100	114,000	117,100
Beaumont/Port Arthur, TX	80,800	84,000	86,200
Biloxi/Gulfport, MS	NA	105,700	NA
Birmingham, AL	125,500	133,600	139,000
Boise City, ID	126,000	130,000	139,600
Boston, MA	314,200	356,600	397,700
Bradenton, FL	127,300	137,800	147,600
Buffalo/Niagara Falls, NY	79,800	84,100	85,600
Canton, OH	NA	107,800	NA
Cedar Rapids, IA	112,900	115,700	120,900
Champaign/Urbana/Rantoul, IL	98,800	100,400	106,900
Charleston, SC	137,900	150,800	157,000
Charleston, WV	99,400	104,700	111,000
Charlotte/Gas./Rock Hill, NC/SC	140,300	145,300	150,500
Chattanooga, TN/GA	101,100	107,300	111,600
Chicago, IL	171,800	198,500	223,700
Cincinnati, OH/KY/IN	126,700	130,200	136,100
Cleveland, OH	NA	NA	NA
Colorado Springs, CO	154,100	173,300	185,500
Columbia, SC	112,800	115,800	119,700
Columbus, OH	129,100	135,700	142,200
Corpus Christi, TX	87,900	91,600	94,200
Dallas, TX	122,500	131,100	136,300
Davenport/Moline/Rock Isl., IA/IL	86,300	89,600	93,800
Dayton/Springfield, OH	105,100	106,900	114,000
Daytona Beach, FL	85,300	92,700	105,500
Denver, CO	196,800	218,300	227,700
Des Moines, IA	116,400	125,300	128,500
Detroit, MI	NA	NA	NA
El Paso, TX	80,200	85,800	87,800
Eugene/Springfield, OR	132,800	134,600	143,900
Fargo/Moorhead, ND/MN	97,100	99,500	105,600
Ft. Lauderdale/Hollywood/Pompano Beach, FL	148,700	168,100	195,400
Ft. Myers/Cape Coral, FL	97,600	115,700	148,300
Ft. Wayne, IN	91,600	93,900	95,700
Ft. Worth/Arlington, TX	NA	NA	NA
Gainesville, FL	113,100	118,000	128,000
Gary/Hammond, IN	107,000	114,100	113,400
Grand Rapids, MI	114,900	121,100	125,800
Green Bay, WI	118,100	123,800	130,000
Greensboro/Winston-Salem/High Point, NC	$129,300	$132,700	$134,400
Greenville/Spartanburg, SC	118,100	124,500	123,200
Hartford, CT	159,900	167,300	174,700
Honolulu, HI	295,000	299,900	330,000
Houston, TX	116,100	122,400	131,600
Indianapolis, IN	112,300	116,900	117,200
Jackson, MS	99,500	NA	NA
Jacksonville, FL	100,000	109,900	117,500
Kalamazoo, MI	109,900	112,300	119,300
Kansas City, MO/KS	127,400	135,700	137,700
Knoxville, TN	110,800	117,200	119,000
Lake County, IL	169,400	178,900	196,100
Lansing/East Lansing, MI	111,200	119,500	128,200
Las Vegas, NV	137,400	149,100	155,800
Lexington/Fayette, KY	118,200	121,700	128,100
Lincoln, NE	109,300	117,400	123,400
Little Rock-N. Little Rock, AR	87,800	95,100	NA
Los Angeles Area, CA	215,900	241,400	276,600
Louisville, KY/IN	116,700	NA	NA
Madison, WI	153,600	162,500	168,300
Melb./Titusville/Palm Bay, FL	96,900	98,400	NA
Memphis, TN/AR/MS	115,600	125,100	128,400
Miami/Hialeah, FL	144,600	162,700	186,800
Milwaukee, WI	140,700	149,400	174,500
Minneapolis/St. Paul, MN/WI	151,400	167,400	183,000
Mobile, AL	97,600	106,900	113,500
Montgomery, AL	NA	NA	110,400
Nashville, TN	147,500	130,000	NA
New Haven/Meriden, CT	151,600	168,000	191,000
New Orleans, LA	112,000	117,400	125,900
New York metropolitan area, NY/NJ/CT	230,200	258,200	303,800
Norfolk/Virginia Bch/Newport News, VA	112,300	NA	NA
Ocala, FL	70,900	NA	NA
Oklahoma City, OK	85,400	95,000	94,400
Omaha, NE/IA	116,900	117,100	122,000
Orlando, FL	111,200	124,100	139,700
Pensacola, FL	101,100	105,000	110,100
Peoria, IL	87,200	88,600	89,600
Philadelphia, PA/NJ	125,200	134,800	147,400
Phoenix, AZ	134,400	139,400	152,400
Pittsburgh, PA	93,600	97,800	102,100
Portland, ME	131,100	158,000	177,000
Portland, OR	170,100	172,300	181,200
Providence, RI	137,800	158,000	185,800
Raleigh/Durham, NC	158,400	168,200	172,900
Reno, NV	157,300	165,100	181,300
Richland/Kennewick/Pasco, WA	119,600	NA	134,000
Richmond/Petersburg, VA	129,800	133,300	143,900
Riverside/San Bernardino, CA	138,600	157,200	172,200
Rochester, NY	87,600	92,200	92,000

Metropolitan Area	2000	2001	2nd Qtr 2002
Rockford, IL	$95,900	$101,500	$106,900
Sacramento, CA	146,500	174,200	202,100
Saginaw/Bay City/Midland, MI	80,200	84,700	NA
Saint Louis, MO/IL	108,400	116,200	NA
Salt Lake City/Ogden, UT	141,500	147,600	150,400
San Antonio, TX	96,000	103,800	111,300
San Diego, CA	269,400	298,600	361,900
San Francisco Bay Area, CA	454,600	475,900	540,500
Sarasota, FL	132,000	NA	180,000
Seattle, WA	230,100	245,400	260,500
Shreveport, LA	83,800	88,000	92,000
Sioux Falls, SD	106,500	113,900	114,500
South Bend/Mishawaka, IN	82,200	92,800	90,200
Spokane, WA	104,200	108,000	106,900
Springfield, IL	85,000	87,300	93,900
Springfield, MA	120,400	127,400	140,200
Springfield, MO	86,000	92,300	92,300
Syracuse, NY	81,000	86,100	84,700
Tacoma, WA	$151,100	$159,500	$170,000
Tallahassee, FL	122,500	129,700	134,500
Tampa/St. Pete./Clearwater, FL	110,800	123,600	128,000
Toledo, OH	104,000	111,100	NA
Topeka, KS	80,600	88,700	83,800
Trenton, NJ	150,900	165,300	184,200
Tucson, AZ	120,500	128,800	149,100
Tulsa, OK	100,000	110,000	105,600
Washington, DC/MD/VA	182,600	213,900	249,700
Waterloo/Cedar Falls, IA	80,200	84,500	87,000
W. Palm Beach/Boca Raton/ Delray Beach, FL	138,400	149,500	NA
Wichita, KS	90,800	94,900	96,100
Wilmington, DE/NJ/MD	127,600	136,500	149,500
Worcester, MA	131,800	152,600	NA
Youngstown/Warren, OH	74,100	NA	NA
United States	**$139,000**	**$147,800**	**$157,700**

NA = Not available.

Housing Affordability, U.S., 1990-2002

Source: National Association of REALTORS®

Year	Median priced existing home	Average mortgage rate[1]	Monthly principal & interest payment	Payment as percentage of median income
1990	$92,000	10.04%	$648	22.0%
1991	97,100	9.30	642	21.4
1992	99,700	8.11	591	19.3
1993	103,100	7.16	558	18.1
1994	107,200	7.47	598	18.5
1995	110,500	7.85	639	18.9
1996	115,800	7.71	661	18.8
1997	$121,800	7.68%	$693	18.7%
1998	128,400	7.10	690	17.4
1999	133,300	7.33	733	18.0
2000	139,000	8.03	818	19.0
2001	147,800	7.03	789	18.2
2002[2]	162,800	6.55	827	18.9

(1) Based on effective rate on loans closed on existing homes for the period shown. (2) Preliminary.

U.S. Home Ownership Rates, by Selected Characteristics, 1997, 2002[1]

Source: Bureau of the Census, U.S. Dept. of Commerce

Region	1997	2002
Northeast	62.4%	63.9%
Midwest	70.3	72.8
South	68.1	69.3
West	59.9	62.4

Age	1997	2002
Under 35	38.6%	40.8%
35-44	66.3	68.3
45-54	75.6	76.3
55-64	80.3	80.7
65+	79.1	80.1

Race/Ethnicity	1997	2002
White, non-Hispanic	72.1%	71.4%
Black	44.4	74.2
Hispanic	43.3	46.3
Other	52.7	55.4

Income	1997	2002
Median family income or more	80.8%	82.3%
Below median family income	50.0	51.5
TOT. U.S. RATE	**65.7%**	**67.6%**

(1) For 2nd quarter of the year.

Mortgage Loan Calculator

Source: Joyce E. Boulanger, Mortgage Access Corp.

To determine monthly payments, divide loan amount by 1,000 and then multiply the resulting figure by the appropriate factor from this table. To find the appropriate factor use the mortgage term in years and the interest rate percentage. More information on calculating mortgages can be found at www.interest.com/calculators

EXAMPLE: For a 30-year mortgage at 7.25%, the factor would be 6.82. If the mortgage amount is $220,000, divide by 1,000, which comes to 220. 220 x 6.82 (factor) = $1,500.40 monthly mortgage payment of principal and interest only (there will also be property taxes, home insurance, and other possible costs).

INTEREST	MORTGAGE TERM IN YEARS							
RATE	5	10	15	20	25	30	35	40
5.00	18.88	10.61	7.91	6.60	5.85	5.37	5.05	4.83
5.25	18.99	10.73	8.04	6.74	6.00	5.53	5.21	4.99
5.50	19.11	10.86	8.18	6.88	6.15	5.68	5.38	5.16
5.75	19.22	10.98	8.31	7.03	6.30	5.84	5.54	5.33
6.00	19.33	11.10	8.44	7.16	6.44	6.00	5.70	5.50
6.25	19.45	11.23	8.57	7.31	6.60	6.16	5.87	5.68
6.50	19.57	11.35	8.71	7.46	6.75	6.32	6.04	5.85
6.75	19.68	11.48	8.85	7.60	6.91	6.49	6.21	6.03
7.00	19.80	11.61	8.99	7.75	7.07	6.65	6.39	6.21
7.25	19.92	11.74	9.13	7.90	7.23	6.82	6.56	6.40
7.50	20.04	11.87	9.27	8.06	7.39	6.99	6.74	6.58
7.75	20.16	12.00	9.41	8.21	7.55	7.16	6.92	6.77
8.00	20.28	12.13	9.56	8.36	7.72	7.34	7.10	6.95
8.25	20.40	12.27	9.70	8.52	7.88	7.51	7.28	7.14
8.50	20.52	12.40	9.85	8.68	8.06	7.69	7.47	7.34
8.75	20.64	12.54	10.00	8.84	8.23	7.87	7.66	7.53
9.00	20.76	12.67	10.15	9.00	8.40	8.05	7.84	7.72
9.25	20.88	12.81	10.30	9.16	8.57	8.23	8.03	7.91
9.50	21.01	12.94	10.45	9.33	8.74	8.41	8.22	8.11
9.75	21.13	13.08	10.60	9.49	8.92	8.60	8.41	8.30
10.00	21.25	13.22	10.75	9.66	9.09	8.78	8.60	8.50
10.25	21.38	13.36	10.90	9.82	9.27	8.97	8.79	8.69
10.50	21.50	13.50	11.06	9.99	9.45	9.15	8.99	8.89
10.75	21.62	13.64	11.21	10.16	9.63	9.34	9.18	9.09
11.00	21.75	13.78	11.37	10.33	9.81	9.53	9.37	9.29
11.25	21.87	13.92	11.53	10.50	9.99	9.72	9.57	9.49
11.50	22.00	14.06	11.69	10.67	10.17	9.91	9.77	9.69
11.75	22.12	14.21	11.85	10.84	10.35	10.10	9.96	9.89
12.00	22.25	14.35	12.01	11.02	10.54	10.29	10.16	10.09

Tracing Your Roots

By Richard Hantula

Richard Hantula is a freelance editor and writer whose interests include genealogy.

Family history is one of Americans' favorite pastimes. The fruits of their labors run the gamut from a simple listing of one's lineage (or "pedigree"); to a more wide-ranging annotated family tree that records names, marriages, births, deaths, dates, places, and the like; to an elaborate narrative that delves as far back as is possible and runs up to the present day and that may be illustrated with photos and even audio and video clips.

Getting Started

Genealogy is detective work. In some cases you may need to apply a deft combination of ingenuity and patience to get the information you want. And sometimes you may find that the answers you are looking for simply cannot be found, because records are inaccessible or do not exist. Getting started, however, is easy. To cut the job down to a manageable size, you will probably want to focus your research, at least in the beginning, on a particular branch of your family. It also makes things easier to proceed step-by-step and to search for data on one person at a time. A few pointers:

- Set up a system for organizing the information you will accumulate. Note cards and loose-leaf binders are common tools of the trade. A computer can be a big labor saver.
- Start your data collection by writing down what you already know about your family.
- Gather together the documents in your home that may contain relevant data, such as birth, marriage, and death certificates; land deeds; school records; medical records; and military papers. Helpful information may be found written in old letters and diaries or inscribed in Bibles or on dishware. Old photos can prove invaluable as well.
- Ask your relatives to write down what they know of the family history. You may want to interview them, especially those who knew relatives who are now dead.
- Record names, dates, and places accurately. Where feasible, make photocopies of papers that document such facts.
- Consider videotaping or tape-recording your interviews.

Be aware that your family may be documented under different names at different times and in different places. Adoptions, divorces, and illegitimate births all complicate the issue, as does the fact that unfamiliar-sounding names are sometimes transcribed incorrectly in official records. The names of many immigrants to the U.S. were arbitrarily anglicized by officials at ports of entry, and some immigrants altered their names themselves, hoping to improve their chances of assimilating to American life.

You can get detailed advice on how to go about tracing your roots from numerous books and videos, as well as from a Public Broadcasting Service (PBS) television series, *Ancestors*, available to local stations from mid-2000 to mid-2004. There are also genealogy websites, local genealogical clubs, and courses offered by schools and universities (some of them available online via the Internet).

Filling in the Holes

To flesh out your family history, you may want to do a little travel. Possible sources of data in the U.S. and abroad include churches, cemeteries, archives of old newspapers, public libraries, historical societies, and national, regional, and local government depositories of records. The U.S. National Archives and Records Administration, for example, contains a wealth of material such as passport applications, ships' passenger lists, Bureau of Indian Affairs documents, and census, federal court, and military records. The Family History Library of the Church of Jesus Christ of Latter Day Saints (Mormons) in Salt Lake City, UT, houses a huge collection of information on billions of individuals, some of it copied from archives in other countries (more than 3,700 branches of the library, called Family History Centers, are located around the globe, and much of the data can be accessed via the Internet). The availability of records outside the U.S. varies from country to country. In China, for example, genealogies were recorded for some families for hundreds or even thousands of years, but many documents were destroyed in the Cultural Revolution of the mid-1960s to mid-1970s.

Computer Software

Scores of genealogical computer programs are available, some for free. The typical family tree program organizes the data you collect (and, if you have access to the Internet, even helps you collect it), prints it out in attractive chart and report formats, and saves it in standard GEDCOM (for "Genealogical Data Communications") genealogy files. Some programs store electronic versions of photos, videos, and sound clips. Commercial family tree software often comes packaged with batches of CD-ROMs containing genealogical resource data, although more and more data are becoming available on the Internet for free or for a small fee.

If you are considering buying a program, check the computer requirements listed on the package. Beginners may prefer more elaborate tutorials and easier-to-use interfaces. Among the more popular commercial programs for PCs using Microsoft Windows are Ancestral Quest (Incline Software), Family Origins (FormalSoft), Family Tree Maker (Broderbund), Generations Family Tree (Broderbund), and Legacy Family Tree (Millennia). Master Genealogist (Wholly Genes Software) is a favorite of many genealogy buffs, but it can be daunting for beginners. The leading software for Macintosh computers is Reunion (Leister Productions). The most popular free software for PCs with Windows is the Mormons' Personal Ancestral File, or PAF, which can be downloaded free from the Internet (a Macintosh version can be purchased on disks). PAF lacks some of the bells and whistles of major commercial products, but is logically constructed and easy to use. An interesting free option for users of Windows, Linux, or Macintosh's OS X is GeneWeb, available on the Internet.

The Burgeoning Internet

Sites on the World Wide Web have traditionally been valuable sources of indexes and other references to records located in "offline" archives. More and more genealogical resource data, however, is becoming directly available on the Web. Information pertaining to the millions of people who entered the U.S. through Ellis Island and the Port of New York in 1892-1924, for instance, is available from the American Family Immigration History Center (www.ellisisland.org). Also, websites and e-mail offer ways to exchange information with other family history researchers.

Some of the most popular genealogy programs are associated with websites that provide how-to advice, along with access to search engines and resource databases. The Mormons' FamilySearch site (www.familysearch.org) performs this role for PAF, and the program can be downloaded from it. GeneWeb is associated with GeneaNet (www.geneanet.org), which aims to establish "a universal register of all the world's genealogical resources" (the program can be downloaded directly from cristal.inria.fr/~ddr/GeneWeb). General-purpose genealogy websites of note include Cyndi's List (www.cyndislist.com) and RootsWeb (www.rootsweb.com), which claims to be the oldest and largest free genealogy site. Also helpful are About.com (genealogy.about.com) and the website associated with the PBS Ancestors show (www.ancestors.com). Wide-ranging sites like Ancestry.com (www.ancestry.com) and Genealogy.com (www.genealogy.com) offer access to numerous databases, some of them on a subscription basis. Many sites focus on individual ethnic groups, among them JewishGen (www.jewishgen.org) for researchers of Jewish genealogy and AfriGeneas (www.afrigeneas.com) and Christine's Genealogy Website (www.ccharity.com) for African-Americans.

How to Obtain Birth, Marriage, Death Records

The pamphlet "Where to Write for Vital Records: Births, Deaths, Marriages, and Divorces" (Stock # 017-022-01196-4) is available from the Superintendent of Documents, PO Box 371954, Pittsburgh, PA 15250-7954; advance payment of $3.25 is required. Orders can also be placed by calling (866) 512-1800, via fax at (202) 512-2250, or on the website bookstore.gpo.gov. The complete pamphlet can also be accessed online at usembassy.state.gov/seoul/wwwfvitl.pdf.

POSTAL INFORMATION

Basic U.S. Postal Service

The Postal Reorganization Act, creating a government-owned postal service under the executive branch and replacing the old Post Office Department, was signed into law by Pres. Richard Nixon, Aug. 12, 1970. The service officially came into being on July 1, 1971.

The U.S. Postal Service is governed by an 11-person Board of Governors. Nine of the members are appointed by the president with Senate approval. These 9 choose a postmaster general. The board and the postmaster general choose the 11th member, who serves as deputy postmaster general. An independent Postal Rate Commission of 5 members, appointed by the president, reviews and rules on proposed postal rate increases submitted by the Board of Governors.

IT'S A FACT: According to the U.S. Postal Service, it has no official motto. The famous inscription "Neither snow nor rain nor heat nor gloom of night stays these couriers from the swift completion of their appointed rounds" (from the Greek historian Herodotus, c. 484-420 BC) was put on on the General Post Office in New York City (1914) by the architects.

U.S. Domestic Rates

(Domestic rates apply to the U.S., to its territories and possessions, and to APOs and FPOs. **Many changes** in domestic postal rates, fees, services, and terminology **took effect June 30, 2002**.)

First Class Mail

First Class Mail includes written matter such as letters, postal cards, and postcards (private mailing cards), plus all other matter wholly or partly in writing, whether sealed or unsealed, except book manuscripts, periodical articles and music, manuscript copy accompanying proofsheets or corrected proofsheets of the same, and the writing authorized by law on matter of other classes. Also included: matter sealed or closed against inspection, bills, and statements of accounts.

Written letters and matter sealed against inspection cost **37¢** for first ounce or fraction, 23¢ for each additional ounce or fraction up to and including 13 ounces. U.S. Postal Service cards and private postcards alike cost **23¢**. Presort and automation-compatible mail can qualify for lower rates if certain piece minimums, mailing permits, and other requirements are met.

Express Mail

Express mail provides guaranteed expedited service for any mailable article (up to 70 lbs and not over 108 in. in combined length and girth). Offers next day delivery by noon to most destinations; no extra charge for Saturday, Sunday, or holiday delivery. Second-day service is available to locations not on the Next Day Delivery Network. The basic rate for Express Mail weighing up to 8 oz is $13.65. All rates include insurance up to $100, shipment receipt, and record of delivery at the destination post office. Express Mail tracking is available on the USPS Web site (www.usps.com).

Express Mail Flat Rate: $13.65, regardless of weight, if matter fits into a special Postal Service flat-rate envelope.

Pickup service is available for $12.50 per stop, regardless of the number of pieces or service used (e.g., Express Mail, Priority Mail, or Parcel Post can be picked up together).

Contact your local post office for further information.

Standard Mail

Standard Mail is limited to items less than 16 ounces such as solicitations, newsletters, advertising materials, books, and cassettes. A minimum volume of 200 pieces or 50 lbs of such items is necessary, and specific bulk mail preparation and sortation requirements apply.

The minimum rate per piece for pieces 3.3 ounces or less is $0.268 for basic letters and $0.344 for basic nonletters. Contact your post office for the discounts offered for automation, presorted, carrier route, destination entry, and other discounts. Separate rates are available for some nonprofit organizations.

Any mailer who uses a permit imprint is required to pay a one-time $150 fee plus an annual (calendar year) fee of $150. Additional standards apply to mailings of nonidentical-weight pieces.

Priority Mail

Due to expeditious handling and transportation, "Priority Mail" is delivered in an average of 2-3 days. Priority Mail may include packages up to 70 lbs and not over 108 in. in length and girth combined, whether sealed or unsealed, including written and other First Class material.

Parcels weighing less than 15 lb and measuring over 84 in., but less than 108 in., in length and girth combined cost the same as a 15-lb parcel mailed to the same zone. Pickup service costs an additional $12.50 per stop.

Priority Mail Flat Rate: $3.85, regardless of weight, if matter fits into a special Postal Service flat-rate envelope.

Priority Mail Rates

(single-piece zone rate)

Weight not over (lbs)	ZONES 1-3	4	5	6	7	8
1	$3.85	$3.85	$3.85	$3.85	$3.85	$3.85
2	3.95	4.55	4.90	5.05	5.40	5.75
3	4.75	6.05	6.85	7.15	7.85	8.55
4	5.30	7.05	8.05	8.50	9.45	10.35
5	5.85	8.00	9.30	9.85	11.00	12.15
6	6.30	8.85	9.90	10.05	11.30	12.30
7	6.80	9.80	10.65	11.00	12.55	14.05
8	7.35	10.75	11.45	11.95	13.80	15.75
9	7.90	11.70	12.20	12.90	15.05	17.50
10	8.40	12.60	13.00	14.00	16.30	19.20
11	8.95	13.35	13.75	15.15	17.55	20.90
12	9.50	14.05	14.50	16.30	18.80	22.65
13	10.00	14.75	15.30	17.50	20.05	24.35
14	10.55	15.45	16.05	18.60	21.25	26.05
15[1]	11.05	16.20	16.85	19.75	22.50	27.80

(1) See postmaster for pieces greater than 15 lbs.

Periodicals

Periodicals include newspapers and magazines.

For the general public, the applicable Package Services or First-Class postage is paid for periodicals.

For publishers, rates vary according to (1) whether item is sent to same county, (2) percentage of editorial and advertising matter, (3) whether the publishing org. is nonprofit or produces educational material for use in classrooms, (4) weight, (5) distance, (6) level of presort, (7) automation compatibility.

Package Services

Package Services, formerly "Standard Mail (B)," is any mailable matter that is not included in First Class or Periodicals (unless permitted or required by regulations). There are currently four subclasses of Package Services: Parcel Post, Bound Printed Matter, Media Mail (formerly "Special Standard Mail"), and Library Mail.

The post office determines charges for Package Services according to the weight of the package in pounds and the zone distance shipped (Media Mail and Library Mail rates are determined by weight alone). There is no minimum weight; see separate headings for maximum weight. Presort and automation-compatible mail for all Package Services can qualify for lower rates if certain piece minimums, mailing permits, and other requirements are met. Contact your local post office for further information. Package Services is not sealed against postal inspection.

Parcel Post

Parcel Post is any Package Services not mailed as Bound Print Matter, Media Mail, or Library Mail. Any Package Services matter may be mailed at the Parcel Post rates, subject to these basic standards: not to exceed 70 lbs or 108 in. in combined length and girth (packages over 108 in., but not more than 130 in. in combined length and girth are subject to oversize rates). All fractions of a pound are counted as a full pound.

Parcel Post Basic Rate Schedule

(Inter BMC/ASF ZIP codes only, machinable[1] parcels, no discount, no surcharge)

Weight not over (lbs)	ZONES 1 & 2	3	4	5	6	7	8
1	$3.69	$3.75	$3.75	$3.75	$3.75	$3.75	$3.75
2	3.85	3.85	4.14	4.14	4.49	4.49	4.49
3	4.65	4.65	5.55	5.65	5.71	5.77	6.32
4	4.86	5.20	6.29	6.93	7.14	7.20	7.87
5	5.03	5.71	6.94	7.75	8.58	8.64	9.43
6	5.63	6.01	7.44	8.50	9.52	9.90	11.49
7	5.80	6.28	7.91	9.20	10.35	11.39	12.83
8	5.98	6.53	8.30	9.84	11.11	12.54	15.04
9	6.11	6.76	8.74	10.45	11.83	13.38	17.04
10	6.28	7.57	9.10	11.01	12.50	14.17	18.14
11	6.41	7.80	9.47	11.54	13.13	14.92	19.15
12	6.54	8.01	9.80	12.04	13.72	15.62	20.10
13	6.67	8.19	10.12	12.51	14.28	16.27	20.99
14	6.80	8.42	10.43	12.95	14.81	16.90	21.84
15	6.92	8.61	10.73	13.38	15.31	17.49	22.64
16	7.02	8.79	11.00	13.78	15.79	18.05	23.41
17	7.15	8.94	11.28	14.16	16.24	18.59	24.13
18	7.25	9.11	11.52	14.52	16.68	19.09	24.82
19	7.37	9.28	11.77	14.87	17.09	19.58	25.48
20[2]	7.46	9.43	11.98	15.20	17.48	20.05	26.12

(1) Machinable parcels must be: not less than 6 in. long, 3 in. high, and .25 in. thick or more than 34 in. long, 17 in. high, and 17 in. thick; at least 6 oz. but not more than 35 lbs. (2) Consult postmaster for pieces greater than 20 lbs.

Bound Printed Matter

(minimum weight: none; maximum weight: 15 lbs)

Applies to advertising, promotional, directory, or editorial material that is bound by permanent fastening and consists of sheets of which at least 90% are imprinted by any process other than handwriting or typewriting. Does not include stationery (or pads of blank forms) or personal correspondence. Packages may not exceed 108 in. in combined length and girth, marked "Bound Printed Matter" or "BPM."

Bound Printed Matter Rates

(zone rate for flat single pieces)

Weight not over (lbs)	ZONES 1&2	3	4	5	6	7	8
1.0	$1.79	$1.84	$1.88	$1.96	$2.03	$2.12	$2.29
1.5	1.79	1.84	1.88	1.96	2.03	2.12	2.29
2.0	1.86	1.92	1.98	2.08	2.18	2.30	2.52
2.5	1.93	2.01	2.08	2.21	2.33	2.48	2.76
3.0	2.00	2.09	2.18	2.33	2.48	2.66	2.99
3.5	2.07	2.18	2.28	2.46	2.63	2.84	3.23
4.0	2.14	2.26	2.38	2.58	2.78	3.02	3.46
4.5	2.21	2.35	2.48	2.71	2.93	3.20	3.70
5.0	2.28	2.43	2.58	2.83	3.08	3.38	3.93
6.0	2.42	2.60	2.78	3.08	3.38	3.74	4.40
7.0	2.56	2.77	2.98	3.33	3.68	4.10	4.87
8.0	2.70	2.94	3.18	3.58	3.98	4.46	5.34
9.0	2.84	3.11	3.38	3.83	4.28	4.82	5.81
10.0	2.98	3.28	3.58	4.08	4.58	5.18	6.28
11.0	3.12	3.45	3.78	4.33	4.88	5.54	6.75
12.0	3.26	3.62	3.98	4.58	5.18	5.90	7.22
13.0	3.40	3.79	4.18	4.83	5.48	6.26	7.69
14.0	3.54	3.96	4.38	5.08	5.78	6.62	8.16
15.0	3.68	4.13	4.58	5.33	6.08	6.98	8.63

Media Mail

(minimum weight: none; maximum weight: 70 lbs)

Formerly "Special Standard Mail." Applies to books of at least 8 printed pages; 16-mm or narrower-width films; printed music; printed test materials; sound recordings, playscripts, and manuscripts for books; printed educational charts; loose-leaf pages and binders consisting of medical information; computer-readable media. Advertising restrictions apply. Packages must be marked "Media Mail" and may not exceed 108 in. in combined length and girth. Contact your local post office for further information.

Rates are calculated by weight only. Single-piece rates are: $1.42, up to 1 lb; 42¢ for each additional pound or fraction, to 7 lbs; additional pounds thereafter, 30¢ each.

Library Mail

(minimum weight: none; maximum weight: 70 lbs)

Applies to books, printed music, bound academic theses, periodicals, sound recordings, museum materials, and other library materials mailed between schools, colleges, universities, public libraries, museums, veteran and fraternal organizations, and nonprofit religious, educational, scientific, and labor organizations or associations. Advertising restrictions apply. All packages must be marked "Library Mail," and may not exceed 108 in. in combined length and girth. Contact your local post office for further information.

Rates are calculated by weight only. Single-piece rates are: $1.35, up to 1 lb; 40¢ for each additional pound or fraction, to 7 lbs; additional pounds thereafter, 29¢ each.

Domestic Mail Special Services

Special Handling

Provides preferential handling, but not preferential delivery, to the extent practicable in dispatch and transportation. Available for First-Class Mail, Priority Mail, and Package Services for the following surcharge: up to 10 lb, $5.95; over 10 lb, $8.25 Pieces must be marked "Special Handling."

Registered Mail

Provides sender with mailing receipt, and a delivery record is maintained. Only matter prepaid with postage at First Class postage rates may be registered. Stamps or meter stamps must be attached. The face of the article must be at least 5″ long, 3½″ high. The mailer is required to declare the value of mail presented for registration.

Declared Value	Registration Fee[1]
$0.00	$7.50
$0.01 to $100.00	8.00
$100.01 to $500.00	8.85
$500.01 to $1,000.00	9.70
$1,000.01 to $2,000.00	10.55
$2,000.01 to $3,000.00	11.40
$3,000.01 to $4,000.00	$12.25
$4,000.01 to $5,000.00	13.10
$5,000.01 to $6,000.00	13.95
$6,000.01 to $7,000.00	14.80
$7,000.01 to $8,000.00	15.65
$8,000.01 to $9,000.00	16.50
$9,000.01 to $10,000.00	17.35

(1) Fee for articles with declared value over $0.00 includes insurance; fee is in addition to postage.

C.O.D.: Unregistered: Applicable to First Class, Priority Mail, Express Mail, and Package Services. Items must be sent as bona fide orders or be in conformity with agreements between senders and addressees. Maximum amount collectible is $1,000. **Registered:** For details, consult postmaster.

Certified mail: Available for any matter having no intrinsic value on which First Class or Priority Mail postage is paid. A receipt is furnished at the time of mailing, and evidence of delivery is obtained. Basic fee is $2.30 in addition to regular postage. Return receipt and restricted delivery available upon payment of additional fees. No indemnity.

Insured Mail

Applicable to Standard Mail, Package Services, and First-Class or Priority Mail items eligible to be mailed as Package Services. Matter for sale addressed to prospective purchasers who have not ordered it or authorized its sending cannot be insured. Note: for Express Mail, insurance is included up to $100. Add $1.00 per $100 or fraction thereof over $100 up to $5,000.

Declared Value	Insured Mail Fee[1]
$0.01 to $50.00	$1.30
$50.01 to $100.00	2.20
$100.01 to $200.00	3.20
$200.01 to $300.00	4.20
$300.01 to $400.00	5.20
$400.01 to $500.00	6.20
$500.01 to $600.00	7.20
$600.01 to $700.00	8.20
$700.01 to $800.00	9.20
$800.01 to $900.00	10.20
$900.01 to $1,000.00	11.20
$1,000.01 to $5,000.00	11.20 plus $1.00 per $100 or fraction thereof over $1,000 in desired coverage

(1) In addition to postage. (Maximum liability is $5,000.) See postmaster for further details on bulk discounts.

Delivery Confirmation

Applies to First-Class Mail parcels, Priority Mail and Package Services. Available for purchase at the time of mailing only. Provides mailer with the date and time an article was delivered and, if delivery was attempted but not successful, the date and time of the attempt. Electronic confirmation is available for barcoded matter.

Manual confirmation is available for retail purchasers on the Internet (www.usps.com) or toll-free by phone (800-222-1811).

Priority Mail fee: manual, 45¢; electronic, free. First-Class Mail parcels: 55¢, 13¢. Package Services fee: 55¢ and 13¢.

Forwarding Addresses

To obtain a forwarding address, the mailer must write on the envelope or cover the words "Address Correction Requested." The destination post office then will check for a forwarding address on file and provide it for 70¢ per manual correction, 20¢ per automated correction.

International Mail Special Services

Registration: Available to practically all countries for letter-post items only. Fee $7.25. The maximum indemnity payable—generally only in case of complete loss (of both contents and wrapper)—is $40.45. To Canada only, the fee is $7.50, providing indemnity for loss up to $100, $8.25 for loss up to $500, and $9.00 for loss up to $1,000. Contact your post office for more details.

Return Receipt: Shows to whom and when delivered; Fee: $1.50 (must be purchased at time of mailing).

Special Delivery: Not available as of June 1997.

Air Mail: Available daily to practically all countries.

Aerogrammes — Aerogrammes are letter sheets that can be folded into the form of an envelope and sealed. Intended for personal communication only and may not include enclosures. Fee: 70¢ from U.S. to all countries.

Air mail postcards (single) — 50¢ to Canada and Mexico; 70¢ to all other countries.

International Reply Coupons (IRC): Provide foreign addressees with a prepaid means of responding to communications initiated by a U.S. sender. Each IRC is equivalent to the destination country's minimum postage rate for an unregistered airmail letter. Fee: $1.75 per coupon.

Restricted Delivery: Available to many countries for registered mail; some limitations. Fee: $3.20.

Insurance: Available to many countries for loss of or damage to items paid at parcel post rate. Consult postmaster for indemnity limits for individual countries.

Limit of indemnity Not over	Fees Canada[1]	All other countries[1]
$ 50	$1.10	$1.85
100	2.00	2.60
200	3.00	3.60
300	4.00	4.60
400	5.00	5.60
500	6.00	6.60
600	7.00	7.60
700	8.00	8.60
800		9.60
900		10.60
1,000[2]		11.60

(1) Not all countries insure items up to the amounts listed in the table. Canada does not insure items for more than $675.
(2) For amounts more than $1,000, add $1.00 for each $100 or fraction.

Post Office-Authorized 2-Letter State Abbreviations

The abbreviations below are approved by the U.S. Postal Service for use in addresses.

Alabama	AL
Alaska	AK
American Samoa	AS
Arizona	AZ
Arkansas	AR
California	CA
Colorado	CO
Connecticut	CT
Delaware	DE
District of Columbia	DC
Federated States of Micronesia[1]	FM
Florida	FL
Georgia	GA
Guam	GU
Hawaii	HI
Idaho	ID
Illinois	IL
Indiana	IN
Iowa	IA
Kansas	KS
Kentucky	KY
Louisiana	LA
Maine	ME
Marshall Islands[1]	MH
Maryland	MD
Massachusetts	MA
Michigan	MI
Minnesota	MN
Mississippi	MS
Missouri	MO
Montana	MT
Nebraska	NE
Nevada	NV
New Hampshire	NH
New Jersey	NJ
New Mexico	NM
New York	NY
North Carolina	NC
North Dakota	ND
Northern Mariana Is.	MP
Ohio	OH
Oklahoma	OK
Oregon	OR
Palau[1]	PW
Pennsylvania	PA
Puerto Rico	PR
Rhode Island	RI
South Carolina	SC
South Dakota	SD
Tennessee	TN
Texas	TX
Utah	UT
Vermont	VT
Virgin Islands	VI
Virginia	VA
Washington	WA
West Virginia	WV
Wisconsin	WI
Wyoming	WY

(1) Although an independent nation, this country is currently subject to domestic rates and fees.

Canadian Province and Territory Postal Abbreviations

Source: Canada Post

Alberta	AB
British Columbia	BC
Manitoba	MB
New Brunswick	NB
Newfoundland and Labrador	NF
Northwest Territories	NT
Nova Scotia	NS
Nunavut	NU
Ontario	ON
Prince Edward Island	PE
Quebec	QC[1]
Saskatchewan	SK
Yukon Territory	YT

(1) PQ is also acceptable.

International Postal Rates

Letter-post—Encompasses all classes of international mail formerly categorized as LC (Letters and Cards) and AO (Other Articles), including letters, letter packages, postcards and postal cards, small packets, etc. Airmail and Economy (surface) rates are available. Maximum weight: 4 lbs (64 oz). Minimum dimensions for envelopes and packages is 5.5 in. x 3.5 in. (0.007 in. thick) and a max. of 36 in. combined length and girth (max. length: 24 in.). Consult your local post office regarding rolls (tubes), printed matter, and nonstandard sized items.

Parcel Post—Airmail or Economy (surface) rates available. Weight limits range from 22 lbs to 70 lbs, see Country Rate Group table for specific standards. Most countries require: min. length and width, 5.5 in. x 3.5 in.; max. length, 42 in.; max. length and girth combined, 79 in. Exceptions: Belgium, Canada, Germany, Great Britain, Hong Kong, Ireland, Japan, Liechtenstein, Macao, Sweden, and Switzerland. Consult your local post office for countries with exceptional size limits.

Global Priority Mail (GPM) Flat-Rate: If matter weighs 4 lbs or less, and fits into a special Postal Service flat-rate envelope, the rates are as follows: small envelope (6 in. x 10 in.), $4.00 to Canada or Mexico and $5.00 to all other countries; large envelope (9.5 in. x 12.5 in.), $7.00 to Canada or Mexico and $9.00 to all other countries. Variable-weight option available.

The U.S. Postal Service also offers expedited delivery services (**Global Express Guaranteed** and **Global Express Mail**) to many international destinations. Consult your local post office for details.

Letter-Post Rates

Not over	AIR MAIL RATE GROUPS[1]					ECONOMY (SURFACE) RATE GROUPS[1]				
(oz.)	1	2	3	4	5	1	2	3	4	5
1	$0.60	$0.60	$0.80	$0.80	$0.80	$2.70	$4.35	$3.80	$4.05	$4.95
2	0.85	0.85	1.60	1.70	1.55	—	—	—	—	—
3	1.10	1.25	2.40	2.60	2.30	—	—	—	—	—
4	1.35	1.65	3.20	3.50	3.05	—	—	—	—	—
5	1.60	2.05	4.00	4.40	3.80	—	—	—	—	—
6	1.85	2.45	4.80	5.30	4.55	—	—	—	—	—
7	2.10	2.85	5.60	6.20	5.30	—	—	—	—	—
8	2.35	3.25	6.40	7.10	6.05	—	—	—	—	—
12	3.10	4.00	7.55	8.40	7.65	—	—	—	—	—
16	3.75	5.15	8.70	9.70	9.25	2.70	4.35	3.80	4.05	4.95
20	4.40	6.30	9.85	11.00	10.85	4.05	5.15	4.45	4.70	5.70
24	5.05	7.45	11.00	12.30	12.45	4.55	5.95	5.10	5.35	6.50
28	5.70	8.60	12.15	13.60	14.05	5.05	6.70	5.70	6.00	7.30
32	6.35	9.75	13.30	14.90	15.65	5.60	7.50	6.30	6.65	8.10
36	7.00	10.95	14.50	16.25	17.35	6.00	8.15	6.90	7.25	8.75
40	7.65	12.15	15.70	17.60	19.05	6.40	8.80	7.50	7.85	9.40
44	8.30	13.35	16.90	18.95	20.75	6.80	9.45	8.10	8.45	10.05
48	8.95	14.55	18.10	20.30	22.45	7.20	10.10	8.70	9.05	10.70
52	9.65	15.80	19.35	21.70	24.20	7.60	10.75	9.30	9.65	11.35
56	10.35	17.05	20.60	23.10	25.95	8.00	11.40	9.90	10.25	12.00
60	11.05	18.30	21.85	24.50	27.70	8.40	12.05	10.50	10.85	12.65
64	11.75	19.55	23.10	25.90	29.45	8.80	12.70	11.10	11.45	13.30

(1) Rate Groups: Canada-1, Mexico-2, Australia, Japan, New Zealand-4; for other countries, see "Letter-post rate group" in Country Rate Groups table, page 727.

Air Mail Parcel Post Rates

Not Over	RATE GROUPS[1]												
	1[2]	2	3	4	5	6	7	8	9	10	11	12	13
1 lb.	$13.25	$13.00	$16.00	$16.25	$15.25	$14.00	$16.50	$12.50	$14.50	$16.00	$18.00	$14.00	$17.00
2	13.25	15.50	20.00	20.50	19.75	15.50	19.00	19.00	18.75	18.50	22.00	15.50	19.00
3	14.25	17.75	24.00	24.50	24.50	17.50	21.75	20.00	23.25	21.50	26.00	17.25	22.00
4	15.50	20.25	28.00	29.00	29.75	20.25	24.50	24.25	26.75	24.00	30.00	19.25	25.00
5	16.75	23.00	32.00	33.50	35.00	22.75	27.25	28.75	32.75	26.50	34.00	21.25	28.00
6	17.85	25.00	35.00	36.80	39.25	25.65	30.25	32.65	36.50	29.50	37.50	23.75	31.25
7	18.95	27.00	38.00	40.10	43.50	28.55	33.25	36.55	40.40	32.50	41.00	26.25	34.50
8	20.05	29.00	41.00	43.40	47.75	31.45	36.25	40.45	44.30	35.50	44.50	28.75	37.75
9	21.15	31.00	44.00	46.70	52.00	34.35	39.25	44.35	48.20	38.50	48.00	34.25	41.00
10	22.25	33.00	47.00	50.00	56.25	37.25	42.25	48.25	52.10	41.50	51.50	33.75	44.25
Add'l[3]	1.10	2.00	3.00	2.30	4.25	2.90	3.00	3.90	3.90	3.00	3.50	2.50	3.25

(1) Rate Groups: Canada-1, Mexico-2, Great Britain, Northern Ireland-3, Japan-4, China-5; for other countries, see "Parcel Post rate group" in Country Rate Groups table page 727. (2) Canada: minimum 1 lb; maximum 66 lbs, 22 lbs limit to members of the Canadian Armed Forces based outside Canada (CFPOs). (3) Price of each additional pound or fraction.

Economy (Surface) Parcel Post Rates

Not Over	RATE GROUPS[1]											
	1[2]	2	3	4	5	6	7	8	9	10	11	12
5 lbs[3]	$15.25	$19.50	$23.00	$23.25	$21.25	$18.25	$22.00	$21.50	$28.75	$21.75	$26.25	$20.25
6	15.75	20.75	25.00	25.00	22.75	19.35	24.00	22.80	30.95	23.50	28.75	22.00
7	16.50	22.00	27.00	26.25	24.25	20.45	26.00	24.10	33.15	25.00	31.00	23.75
8	17.25	23.00	29.00	27.75	25.75	21.55	28.00	25.40	35.35	26.75	33.25	25.50
9	17.75	24.00	31.00	29.00	27.25	22.65	30.00	26.70	37.55	29.00	35.50	27.25
10	18.25	24.75	32.75	30.25	28.75	23.75	32.00	28.10	39.75	32.00	37.75	28.90
11	18.70	25.50	34.45	31.30	30.00	24.70	33.60	29.40	41.65	33.40	39.80	30.55
12	19.15	26.25	36.15	32.35	31.25	25.65	35.20	30.70	43.55	34.80	41.85	32.20
13	19.60	27.00	37.85	33.40	32.50	26.60	36.80	32.00	45.45	36.20	43.90	33.85
14	20.05	27.75	39.55	34.45	33.75	27.55	38.40	33.30	47.35	37.60	45.95	35.50
15	20.50	28.50	41.25	35.50	35.00	28.50	40.00	34.60	49.25	39.00	48.00	37.15
16	20.95	29.25	42.95	36.55	36.25	29.45	41.60	35.90	51.15	40.40	50.05	38.80
17	21.40	30.00	44.65	37.60	37.50	30.40	43.20	37.20	53.05	41.80	52.10	40.45
18	21.85	30.75	46.35	38.65	38.75	31.35	44.80	38.50	54.95	43.20	54.15	42.10
19	22.30	31.50	48.05	39.70	40.00	32.30	46.40	39.80	56.85	44.60	56.20	43.75
20[4]	22.75	32.25	49.75	40.75	41.25	33.25	48.00	41.10	58.75	46.00	58.25	45.40

(1) Rate Groups: Canada-1, Mexico-2, Great Britain, Northern Ireland-3, Japan-4, China-5; for other countries, see "Parcel Post rate group" in Country Rate Groups table page 727. (2) Canada: minimum 1 lb; maximum 66 lbs, 22 lbs limit to members of the Canadian Armed Forces based outside Canada (CFPOs). (3) 5-lb rate is the minimum, even if parcel weighs less. (4) Consult postmaster for pieces greater than 20 lbs.

Country Rate Groups

(For further information, consult your local post office.)

Country or territory	Letter-post	Parcel Post: Airmail	Parcel Post: Surface	Parcel Post: Max. Wt. (lbs)
Afghanistan[1]	5	7	7	44
Albania	5	7	7	44
Algeria	5	10	11	44
Andorra	3	7	6	44*
Angola	5	10	11	22
Anguilla	5	12	12	22
Antigua & Barbuda	5	12	12	22
Argentina	5	13	12	44
Armenia	5	7	7	44
Aruba	5	12	12	44
Ascension	5	—	11	44s
Australia	4	9	8	44
Austria	5	7	6	70
Azerbaijan	5	7	7	70
Bahamas	5	12	12	44
Bahrain	5	10	10	44
Bangladesh	5	8	8	66
Barbados	5	12	12	44
Belarus	5	6	7	70
Belgium	3	6	6	70
Belize	5	12	12	44
Benin	5	10	10	66
Bermuda	5	13	12	44
Bhutan	5	9	9	22
Bolivia	5	13	12	70
Bosnia & Herzegovina	5	6	6	44
Botswana	5	11	11	70
Brazil	5	13	12	66
British Virgin Isl.	5	12	12	44
Brunei	5	8	8	44
Bulgaria	5	6	7	70
Burkina Faso	5	10	11	66
Burma	see Myanmar			
Burundi	5	11	11	66
Cambodia	5	8	—	66a
Cameroon	5	11	11	66
Cape Verde	5	10	11	66
Cayman Islands	5	12	12	44
Central African Republic	5	11	11	44
Chad	5	10	—	44a
Chile	5	13	12	44
China	5	5	5	70
Colombia	5	12	12	44
Comoros	5	10	10	44
Congo, Dem. Rep. of the	5	11	11	66
Congo, Rep. of the	5	10	10	44
Costa Rica	5	12	12	66
Côte d'Ivoire	5	11	11	70
Croatia	5	6	6	70
Cuba[1]	5	no parcel post		
Cyprus	5	6	6	70
Czech Republic	5	6	7	66
Denmark	3	6	6	70
Djibouti	5	10	10	44
Dominica	5	12	12	44
Dominican Republic	5	12	12	44
East Timor	5	8	8	44
Ecuador	5	13	12	70
Egypt	5	11	11	66
El Salvador	5	12	12	44
Equatorial Guinea	5	10	10	**
Eritrea	5	11	11	66
Estonia	5	7	7	66
Ethiopia	5	10	10	66
Falkland Islands	5	—	12	66s
Faroe Islands	3	6	6	70
Fiji	5	8	8	44
Finland	3	6	6	70
France[2]	3	6	6	66*
French Guiana	5	13	12	66
French Polynesia	5	9	9	66
Gabon	5	10	11	44
Gambia, The	5	11	11	22

Country or territory	Letter-post	Parcel Post: Airmail	Parcel Post: Surface	Parcel Post: Max. Wt. (lbs)
Georgia, Republic of	5	7	7	44
Germany	3	6	6	70
Ghana	5	11	11	70
Gibraltar	3	6	6	44*
Great Britain & N. Ireland	3	3	3	66
Greece	3	6	6	44*
Greenland	3	6	6	66
Grenada	5	12	12	44
Guadeloupe	5	13	12	66
Guatemala	5	12	12	44
Guinea	5	10	10	70
Guinea-Bissau[1]	5	11	11	22
Guyana	5	12	12	44
Haiti	5	12	12	55
Honduras	5	13	12	44
Hong Kong, China	5	9	8	44
Hungary	5	6	6	66
Iceland	3	6	6	70
India	5	9	8	44
Indonesia	5	8	8	44
Iran	5	11	11	44
Iraq[1]	5	11	11	44
Ireland	3	6	6	66*
Israel[3]	3	10	10	44
Italy	3	6	6	44*
Ivory Coast	see Côte d'Ivoire			
Jamaica	5	12	12	22
Japan	4	4	4	44
Jordan	5	10	10	70
Kazakhstan	5	6	7	44
Kenya	5	10	10	70
Kiribati	5	8	8	44
Korea, Dem. People's Rep. of (North)[1]		no parcel post		
Korea, Republic of (South)	5	9	8	44
Kuwait	5	10	10	66
Kyrgyzstan	5	6	7	70
Laos	5	9	9	44
Latvia	5	6	6	70
Lebanon[1]	5	10	—	22a
Lesotho	5	11	11	44
Liberia[1]	5	10	10	44
Libya	5	7	7	44
Liechtenstein	3	6	6	66*
Lithuania	5	6	7	70
Luxembourg	3	6	6	70
Macao	5	9	9	44
Macedonia	5	6	7	66
Madagascar	5	11	11	66
Malawi	5	11	11	44
Malaysia	5	8	8	44
Maldives	5	9	9	70
Mali	5	10	11	44
Malta	5	7	7	44*
Martinique	5	13	12	66
Mauritania	5	10	11	44
Mauritius	5	10	10	44
Moldova	5	7	7	66
Mongolia	5	9	9	**
Montserrat	5	8	8	44
Morocco	5	10	11	70
Mozambique	5	11	11	44
Myanmar	5	6	6	44
Namibia	5	11	11	44
Nauru	5	8	8	44
Nepal	5	9	9	44
Netherlands	3	6	6	44*
Netherlands Antilles	5	12	12	44
New Caledonia	5	9	9	66
New Zealand	4	8	8	66
Nicaragua	5	12	12	66
Niger	5	10	10	66

Country or territory	Letter-post	Parcel Post: Airmail	Parcel Post: Surface	Parcel Post: Max. Wt. (lbs)
Nigeria	5	10	10	66
Norway	3	6	6	55*
Oman	5	10	10	44
Pakistan	5	9	8	66
Panama	5	12	12	70
Papua New Guinea	5	9	9	44
Paraguay	5	13	12	70
Peru	5	13	12	70
Philippines	5	9	8	44
Pitcairn Island	5	8	8	22
Poland	5	6	6	44
Portugal[4]	3	7	7	66*
Qatar	5	10	10	70
Reunion	5	13	12	66
Romania	5	7	7	70
Russia	5	7	7	44
Rwanda	5	10	11	66
Saint Helena	5	11	11	44
Saint Kitts & Nevis	5	12	12	44
Saint Lucia	5	12	12	44
Saint Pierre & Miquelon	5	6	6	66
Saint Vincent & Grenadines	5	13	12	22
Samoa	5	8	8	44
San Marino	3	9	8	44*
São Tomé & Príncipe	5	10	10	44
Saudi Arabia	5	10	10	44
Senegal	5	10	10	44
Serbia-Montenegro[1]	5	7	7	33
Seychelles	5	10	11	70
Sierra Leone	5	10	10	44
Singapore	5	8	8	66
Slovakia	5	6	6	66
Slovenia	5	6	7	33
Solomon Islands	5	8	8	44
Somalia[1]	5	10	10	44
South Africa	5	11	10	66
Spain	3	7	6	44*
Sri Lanka	5	9	8	66
Sudan	5	11	11	44
Suriname	5	12	12	44
Swaziland	5	10	10	44
Sweden	3	7	7	44*
Switzerland	3	6	6	66*
Syria	5	10	10	66
Taiwan	5	9	8	44
Tajikistan	5	6	6	66
Tanzania	5	10	10	44
Thailand	5	8	8	44
Togo	5	10	10	44
Tonga	5	8	8	44
Trinidad & Tobago	5	12	12	22
Tristan da Cuñha	5	10	11	22
Tunisia	5	10	10	44
Turkey	5	10	10	70
Turkmenistan	5	7	7	22
Turks & Caicos Isl.	5	12	12	22
Tuvalu	5	8	8	55
Uganda	5	10	11	44
Ukraine	5	7	7	22
United Arab Emirates	5	10	10	70
United Kingdom	5	7	7	66
Uruguay	5	13	12	44
Uzbekistan	5	7	7	44
Vanuatu	5	8	8	44
Vatican City	3	6	6	44*
Venezuela	5	12	12	44
Vietnam	5	9	8	44
Wallis & Futuna Isl.	5	9	9	66
Yemen	5	10	11	44
Zambia	5	10	11	66
Zimbabwe	5	11	11	44

(a) Air only. (s) Surface only. *Air, 70 lbs. ** Surface, 44 lbs; air, 22 lbs. (1) Mailing restrictions currently apply. Consult local post office for details. (2) Includes Monaco and Corsica. (3) West Bank and Gaza Strip are same rate group as Israel. (4) Includes Azores and Madeira Isls.

ASSOCIATIONS AND SOCIETIES

Source: World Almanac questionnaire; World Almanac research

Selected list, by first distinctive key word in each title. (Listed by acronym when that is the official name.) Founding year in parentheses; figure after ZIP code = membership as reported. Information, especially website addresses, subject to change. For other organizations, see Directory of Sports Organizations; Where to Get Help directory in Health chapter; Labor Union Directory in Employment chapter; Membership of Religious Groups in the U.S.; Major International Organizations in Nations chapter.

AACSB-The Intl. Assoc. for Management Education (1916), 600 Emerson Rd., Ste. 300, St. Louis, MO 63141; 850 institutions; www.aacsb.edu

Abortion Federation, National (1977), 1755 Massachusetts Ave. NW, Ste. 600, Wash., DC 20036; 450 institutions; www.prochoice.org

Academic Assistance Program, Intl. (1994), 5904 Snaffle Bit Place, Ste. 17-057, Bonita, CA 91902; www.iaap.org.mx

Academies, Natl. (1863), 2101 Constitution Ave. NW, Wash., DC 20418; 2,276; www.nationalacademies.org

Accountants, American Institute of Certified Public (1887), 1211 Ave. of the Americas, New York, NY 10036; 330,000+; www.aicpa.org

Acoustical Society of America (1929), Ste. 1NO1, 2 Huntington Quad., Melville, NY 11747; 7,000; asa.aip.org

Actuaries, Society of (1949), 475 N. Martingale Rd., Ste. 800, Schaumburg, IL 60173; 17,000; www.soa.org

Administrative Professionals, Intl. Assn. of (1942), 10502 NW Ambassador Dr., Kansas City, MO 64195-0404; 40,000; www.iaap-hq.org

Advancement and Support of Education, Council for (1974); 1307 New York Ave. NW, Ste. 1000, Wash., DC 20005; 3000 member schools; www.case.org

Advertisers, Assn. of Natl. (1910), 708 Third Ave., New York, NY 10017; 312 cos.; www.ana.net

Aeronautic Assn., Natl. (1905), 1815 N. Fort Myer Dr., Ste. 500, Arlington, VA 22209; 6,000; www.naa-usa.org

Aerospace Industries Assn. of America Inc. (1919), 1250 Eye St. NW, Wash., DC 20005-3924; 63 cos.; www.aia-aerospace.org

Aerospace Medical Assn. (1929), 320 S. Henry St., Alexandria, VA 22314; 3,400; www.asma.org

AFCEA (Armed Forces Communications and Electronics Assn.) (1946), 4400 Fair Lakes Ct., Fairfax, VA 22033; 33,000 indiv., 12,000 corp.; www.afcea.org

African-American Life and History, Assn. for the Study of (1915), 7961 Eastern Ave., Ste. 301, Silver Spring, MD 20910; 2,200; www.asalh.org

African Violet Soc. of America Inc. (1946), 2375 North St., Beaumont, TX 77702; 9,000; www.avsa.org

AFS Intercultural Programs USA (1947), 198 Madison Ave., 8th Fl., New York, NY 10016; www.afs.org/usa

Agricultural Economics Assn., American (1910), 415 S. Duff Ave., Ste. C, Ames, IA 50010; 3,500; www.aaea.org

Agricultural Engineers, American Soc. of (ASAE) (1907), 2950 Niles Road, St. Joseph, MI 49085; 9,000; www.asae.org

Agronomy, American Society of (1907), 677 S. Segoe Rd., Madison, WI 53711; 11,500; www.agronomy.org

Air & Waste Management Assn. (1907), One Gateway Center, 3rd Fl., Pittsburgh, PA 15222; 8,000+; www.awma.org

Aircraft Owners and Pilots Assn. (1939), 421 Aviation Way, Frederick, MD 21701; 360,000+; www.aopa.org

Air Force Assn. (1946), 1501 Lee Hwy., Arlington, VA 22209; 150,000; www.afa.org

Al-Anon Family Group Headquarters, Inc. (1951), 1600 Corporate Landing Pkwy., Virginia Beach, VA 23454; 350,000+ worldwide; www.al-anon.alateen.org

Alcoholics Anonymous (1935), 475 Riverside Dr., New York, NY 10115; 2,000,000+; www.aa.org

Alcoholism and Drug Dependence, Inc., Natl. Council on (1944), 20 Exchange Pl., Ste. 2902, New York, NY 10005; 100 affil.; www.ncadd.org

Alexander Graham Bell Assn. for the Deaf & Hard of Hearing (1890), 3417 Volta Pl. NW, Wash., DC 20007; 5,000; www.agbell.org

Allergy, Asthma, and Immunology, American Academy of (1943), 611 E. Wells St., Milwaukee, WI 53202; 6,000+; www.aaaai.org

Alpha Delta Kappa Sorority Inc. (1947), 1615 West 92nd St., Kansas City, MO 64114; 49,560; www.alphadeltakappa.org

Alpha Lambda Delta, Natl. (1924), P.O. Box 4403, Macon, GA 31208-4403; 650,000; www.mercer.edu/ald

Alpine Club, American (1902), 710 Tenth St., Ste. 100, Golden, CO 80401; 6,000+; www.americanalpineclub.org

Alzheimer's Assn. (1980), 919 N. Michigan Ave., Ste. 1100, Chicago, IL 60611; www.alz.org

Amateur Chamber Music Players, Inc. (1969), 1123 Broadway, Rm. 304, New York, NY 10010-2007; 5,300; www.acmp.net

Amateur Radio Union, Intl. (IARU) (1925), P.O. Box 310905, Newington, CT 06131; 150 org.; www.iaru.org

Amateur Racquetball Assn., U.S. (1969), 1685 W. Vintah, Colorado Springs, CO 80904-2906; 40,000; www.usra.org

Amateur Speedskating Union of the U.S. (1927), O S 651 Forest, Winfield, IL 60190; 2,000; www.speedskating.org

AMBUCS, Inc., Natl. (1922), P.O. Box 5127, High Point, NC 27262; 5,400; www.ambucs.com

American Indians, Natl. Congress of (1944), 1301 Connecticut Ave. NW, Ste. 200, Wash., DC 20036; 250+ member tribes; www.ncai.org

American-Islamic Relations, Council on, 453 New Jersey Ave. SE, Wash., DC 20003; www.cair-net.org

American Legion (1919), P.O. Box 1055, 700 N. Pennsylvania St., Indianapolis, IN 46206; 3 mil.+; www.legion.org

American Legion Auxiliary (1919), 777 N. Meridian St., 3rd Floor, Indianapolis, IN 46204; 910,000+; www.legion-aux.org

Americares Foundation (1982), 161 Cherry St., New Canaan, CT 06840; www.americares.org

AMIDEAST (formerly American Mideast Educational & Training Services) (1951), 1730 M St. NW, Ste. 1100, Wash., DC 20036; www.amideast.org

Amnesty Intl. USA (1965), 322 8th Ave., New York, NY 10001; 320,000+; www.amnesty.org

Amputation Foundation, Inc., Natl. (1919), 40 Church St., Malverne, NY 11565; 1,100; www.nationalamputation.org

AMVETS (American Veterans) (1943); **AMVETS Natl. Auxiliary** (1946), 4647 Forbes Blvd., Lanham, MD 20706; 250,000; www.amvets.org

Amusement Parks and Attractions, Intl. Assn. of (IAAPA) (1918), 1448 Duke St., Alexandria, VA 22314; 5,000; www.iaapa.org

Animals, American Society for Prevention of Cruelty to (ASPCA) (1866), 424 E. 92nd St., New York, NY 10128; 678,000+; www.aspca.org

Animal Protection Institute (1968), 1122 S St., Sacramento, CA 95820; 80,000; www.api4animals.org

Animal Welfare Institute (1951), P.O. Box 3650, Wash., DC 20007; approx. 25,000; www.awionline.org

Anthropological Assn., American (1902), 4350 N. Fairfax Dr., Ste. 640, Arlington, VA 22203; 11,500; www.aaanet.org

Antiquarian Society, American (1812), 185 Salisbury St., Worcester, MA 01609; 675; www.americanantiquarian.org

Anti-Vivisection Society, American (AAVS), (1883), 801 Old York Road, #204, Jenkintown, PA 19046; 10,000; www.aavs.org

APICS (1957), 5301 Shawnee Rd., Alexandria, VA 22312-2317; 70,000; www.apics.org

Appalachian Mountain Club (1876), 5 Joy St., Boston, MA 02108; 90,000+; www.outdoors.org

Appalachian Trail Conference (1925), P.O. Box 807, Harpers Ferry, WV 25425; 33,250; www.appalachiantrail.org

Appraisers, American Society of (1936), 555 Herndon Parkway, Ste. 125, Herndon, VA 20170; 6,500; www.appraisers.org

Arbitration Assn., American (1926), 335 Madison Ave., Fl. 10, New York, NY 10017; 7,000; www.adr.org

Arc of the United States, The (1950), 1010 Wayne Avenue, Ste. 650, Silver Spring, MD 20910; 140,000+; www.thearc.org

Archaeological Institute of America (1879), 656 Beacon St., 4th Fl., Boston, MA 02215; 11,000+; www.archaeological.org

Archery Assn. of the United States, Natl. (1879), One Olympic Plaza, Colorado Springs, CO 80909; 6,000; www.USArchery.org

Architects, American Institute of (1857), 1735 New York Ave. NW, Wash., DC 20006; 63,000; www.e-architect.com

Architectural Historians, Society of (1940), 1365 N. Astor St., Chicago, IL 60610; 3,500; www.sah.org

ARMA Intl. (formerly Assn. of Records Managers & Administrators) (1955), 13725 W. 109th St., Lenexa, KS 66215; 10,000; www.arma.org

Army, Assn. of the United States (1950), 2425 Wilson Blvd., Arlington, VA 22201; 117,000; www.ausa.org

Arthritis Foundation (1948), 1330 W. Peachtree St., Atlanta, GA 30309; www.arthritis.org

Arts, Americans for the (1996), 1000 Vermont Ave. NW, Ste. 1200, Wash., D.C. 20005; 1,500; www.artsusa.org

Arts and Letters, Natl. Society of (1944), 4227 46th St. NW, Wash., DC 20016; 1,450+; www.arts-nsal.org

Arts and Sciences, American Academy of (1780), Norton's Woods, 136 Irving St., Cambridge, MA 02138; 4,300 fellows; www.amacad.org

ASPRS, The Imaging and Geospatial Information Society (1934), 5410 Grosvenor Ln., Ste. 210, Bethesda, MD 20814; 7,000; www.asprs.org

Associated Press (1848), 50 Rockefeller Plaza, New York, NY 10020; 1,700 newspapers, 5,000 U.S. broadcast stations, 8,500 intl. subscribers; www.ap.org

Association Executives, American Society of (1920), 1575 I St. NW, Wash., DC 20005; 25,000; www.asaenet.org
Association Managers Inc., Intl. (1974), 1224 N. Nokomis NE, Alexandria, MN 56308; 20,000; www.iami.org
Astrologers, Inc., American Federation of (AFA, Inc.) (1938), St. 6535 S. Rural Rd., Tempe, AZ 85283; 5,000+; www.astrologers.com
Astronautical Society, American (1954), 6352 Rolling Mill Pl., Springfield, VA 22152; 1,400; www.astronautical.org
Astronomical Society, American (1899), 2000 Florida Ave. NW, #400, Wash., DC 20009; 6,500; www.aas.org
Ataxia Foundation, Natl. (1957), 2600 Fernbrook Ln., Ste. 119, Minneapolis, MN 55447-4752; 10,000; www.ataxia.org
Atheists, American (1967), P.O. Box 5733, Parsippany, NJ 07054; 2,300; www.atheists.org
Auctioneers Assn., Natl. (1948), 8880 Ballentine St., Overland Park, KS 66214; approx. 6,000; www.auctioneers.org
Audubon Soc., Natl. (1905), 700 Broadway, New York, NY 10003; 600,000; www.audubon.org
Authors Guild, The (1912), 31 E. 28th St., New York, NY 10016; 8,200; www.authorsguild.org
Authors Registry, The (1995), 31 E. 28th St., New York, NY 10016; 30,000; www.authorsregistry.org
Autism Soc. of America (1965), 7910 Woodmont Ave., Ste. 300, Bethesda, MD 20814; 24,000; www.autism-society.org
Autograph Collectors Club, Universal (1965), P.O. Box 6181, Wash., DC 20044-6181; 1,700; www.uacc.org
Automobile Assn., American (AAA) (1902), 1000 AAA Dr., Heathrow, FL 32746; 45 mil.; www.aaa.com
Automobile Club of America, Antique (1935), 501 W. Governor Road, P.O. Box 417, Hershey, PA 17033; 60,000; www.aaca.org
Automobile Dealers Assn., Natl. (1917), 8400 Westpark Dr., McLean, VA 22102; 19,600; www.nada.org
Automobile License Plate Collectors Assn. (1953), 7365 Main. St., #214, Stratford, CT 06614; 3,200; www.alpca.org
Automotive Hall of Fame (1939), 21400 Oakwood Blvd., Dearborn, MI 48124; www.automotivehalloffame.org

Badminton, USA (1938), One Olympic Plaza, Colorado Springs, CO 80909; 4,000; www.usabadminton.org
Bald-Headed Men of America (1973), 102 Bald Dr., Morehead City, NC 28557; approx. 22,000; members.aol.com/baldusa
Bankers Assn., American (1875), 1120 Connecticut Ave. NW, Wash., DC 20036; www.aba.com
Bar Assn., American (1878), 541 N. Fairbanks Ct., Chicago, IL 60611; 400,000+; www.abanet.org
Bar Assn., Federal (1920), 2215 M Street NW, Wash., DC 20037; 15,002; www.fedbar.org
Barber Shop Quartet Singing in America, Inc., Soc. for the Preservation & Encouragement of (1938), 6315 Harmony Lane, Kenosha, WI 53143; 33,000+; www.spebsqsa.org
Baseball Congress, American Amateur (1935), 118-119 Redfield Plaza, P.O. Box 467, Marshall, MI 49068; 14,500 teams; www.aabc.us
Baseball Congress, Natl. (1931), 300 S. Sycamore, P.O. Box 1420, Wichita, KS 67201; 7,500; www.nbcbaseball.com
Baseball Research, Inc., Society for American (1971), 812 Huron Road E #719, Cleveland, OH 44115; 7,000+; www.sabr.org
Battleship Assn., American (1964), P.O. Box 711247, San Diego, CA 92171; 1,800
Beer Can Collectors of America (1970), 747 Merus Ct., Fenton, MO 63026; 4,200; www.bcca.com
Beta Gamma Sigma, Inc. (1913), 11701 Borman Dr., Ste. 295, St. Louis, MO 63146-4199; 430,000; www.betagamasigma.org
Beta Sigma Phi (1931), 1800 W. 91st Pl., Kansas City, MO 64114; 157,446; www.betasigmaphi.org
Better Business Bureaus, Council of (1970), 4200 Wilson Blvd., Suite 800, Arlington, VA 22203; 150 bureaus; www.bbb.org
Bible Society, American (1816), 1865 Broadway, New York, NY 10023; 650,000; www.americanbible.org
Biblical Literature, Society of (1880), 825 Houston Mill Rd., Ste. 350, Atlanta, GA 30329; 8,000; www.sbl-site.org
Bibliographical Society of America (1904), P.O. Box 1537, Lenox Hill Station, New York, NY 10021; 1,200; www.bibsoamer.org
Big Brothers/Big Sisters of America (1904), 230 N. 13th St., Philadelphia, PA 19107; 494 agencies; bbbsa.org
Biochemistry and Molecular Biology, American Society for (1906), 9650 Rockville Pike, Bethesda, MD 20814; 10,500; www.asbmb.org
Biological Sciences, American Institute of (1947), 1444 I St. NW, Ste. 200, Wash., DC 20005; 6,000; www.aibs.org
Blind, American Council of the (1961), 1155 15th St. NW, Ste. 1004, Wash., DC 20005; 25,000; www.acb.org
Blind, Natl. Federation of the (1940), 1800 Johnson St., Baltimore, MD 21230; 50,000; www.nfb.org
Blinded Veterans Assn. (1958), 477 H St. NW, Wash., DC 20001; 9,970; www.bva.org
Blindness America, Prevent (1908), 500 E. Remington Rd., Schaumburg, IL 60173; 35,000;
Blueberry Council, North American (1965) P.O. Box 1736, Folsom, CA 95763; www.blueberry.org
B'nai B'rith Intl. (1843), 2020 K St. NW, 7th Fl., Wash., DC 20006; 250,000; www.bbinet.org
Boat Owners Assn. of the U.S. (1966), 880 S. Pickett St., Alexandria, VA 22304; 500,000+; www.boats.com
Bookplate Collectors and Designers, American Soc. of (1922), P.O. Box 380340, Cambridge, MA 02238-0340; 175; www.bookplate.org
Booksellers Assn., American (1900), 828 S. Broadway, Tarrytown, NY 10591; 8,000; www.bookweb.org/aba
Boy Scouts of America (1910), 1325 Walnut Hill Lane, Irving, TX 75015; 5 mil+; www.bsa.scouting.org
Boys & Girls Clubs of America (1906), 1230 W. Peachtree St. NW, Atlanta, GA 30309; 3.3 mil; www.bgca.org
Bread for the World (1974), 50 F St. NW, Ste. 500, Washington, DC 20001; 44,000; www.bread.org
Brewing Chemists, American Society for (1934), 3340 Pilot Knob Road, St. Paul, MN 55121-2097; approx. 1,000; www.asbcnet.org
Broadcasters, Natl. Assn. of (1923), 1771 N St. NW, Wash., DC 20036; www.nab.org
Burroughs Bibliophiles, The (1960), 454 Elaine Dr., Pittsburgh, PA 15236-2417; 865
Business Communicators, Intl. Assn. of (1970), 1 Hallidie Plaza, Ste. 600, San Francisco, CA 94102; 13,700; www.iabc.com
Business Education Assn., Natl. (1946), 1914 Association Drive, Reston, VA 20191; 12,000; www.nbea.org
Business Women's Assn., American (1949), 9100 Ward Pkwy., P.O. Box 8728, Kansas City, MO 64114; 60,000; www.abwa.org
Button Society, Natl. (1938), c/o Lois Pool, 2733 Juno Pl., Akron, OH 44333-4137; 4,500

Camp Fire USA (formerly Camp Fire Boys & Girls) (1910), 4601 Madison Ave., Kansas City, MO 64112; 650,000; www.campfireusa.org
Camping Assn., American (1951), 5000 State Rd. 67 N., Martinsville, IN 46151; 6,000+; www.acacamps.org
Cancer Society, American (1913), 2200 Lake Blvd., Atlanta, GA 30319; 2 mil.; www.cancer.org
Cartoonists Society, Natl. (1946), PO Box 713, Suffield, CT 06078; 500+; www.reuben.org
Cat Fanciers' Assn., The (1906), 1805 Atlantic Ave., P.O. Box 1005, Manasquan, NJ 08736-0805; www.cfainc.org
Catholic Bishops, Natl. Conference of (1634), 3211 4th St. NE, Wash., DC 20017; 402 members, 350 staff; www.nccbuscc.org
Catholic Church Extension Society of the USA (1905), 150 S. Wacker Dr., Chicago, IL 60606; 54 staff; www.catholic-extension.org
Catholic Daughters of the Americas (1903), 10 West 71st Street, New York, NY 10023; 103,000; www.catholicdaughters.org
Catholic Educational Assn., Natl. (1904), 1077 30th St. NW, Ste. 100, Wash., DC 20007; 26,000; www.ncea.org
Catholic Historical Soc., American (1886), 263 S. Fourth St., Philadelphia, PA 19106-3819; 500; www.AMCHS.org
Catholic Library Association (1921), 100 North St., Ste. 224, Pittsfield, MA 01201-5109; 1,000; www.cathla.org
Catholic War Veterans, USA Inc. (1935), 441 N. Lee St., Alexandria, VA 22314-2301; 25,000; cwv.org
Cemetery and Funeral Assn., Intl. (1887), 1895 Preston White Dr., #220, Reston, VA 22091; 6,000; www.icfa.org
Ceramic Society, The American (1899), 735 Ceramic Pl., Westerville, OH 43081; 8,830; www.ceramics.org
Cereal Chemists, American Society of (1915), 3340 Pilot Knob Road, St. Paul, MN 55121-2097; 3,500; www.scisoc.org/aacc
Cerebral Palsy Assns., Inc., United (1949), 1660 L St. NW, Ste. 700, Wash., DC 20036; 150; www.ucpa.org
Certification of Computing Professionals, Institute for (1973), 2350 E. Devon Ave., Ste. 115, Des Plaines, IL 60018-4610; www.iccp.org
Chamber of Commerce of the U.S.A. (1912), 1615 H St. NW, Wash., DC 20062; 215,000; uschamber.com
Chamber Music Players, Inc., Amateur (1947), 1123 Broadway, New York, NY 10010; 4,200; www.acmp.net
Checker Federation, American (1949), P.O.Box 241, Petal, MS 39465; 1,000; www.acfcheckers.com
Chemical Engineers, American Inst. of (1908), 3 Park Ave., New York, NY 10016; 50,000+; www.aiche.org
Chemical Society, American (1876), 1155 16th St. NW, Wash., DC 20036; 163,000; www.acs.org

Chemistry Council, American (1872), 11300 Wilson Blvd., Arlington, VA 22209; 170; www.americanchemistry.com
Chess Federation, U.S. (1939), 3054 NYS Rt. 9W, New Windsor, NY 12553; 88,000+; www.uschess.org
Chess League of America, Correspondence (1897), P.O. Box 59625, Schaumburg, IL 60159; 1,000; www.chessbymail.com
Chiefs of Police, Intl. Assn. of (1893), 515 N. Washington St., Alexandria, VA 22314; 19,000; www.theiacp.org
Childhood Education Intl., Assn. for (1892), 17904 Georgia Ave., Ste. 215, Olney, MD 20832; 12,000; www.udel.edu/bateman/acei
Children's Aid Society (1912), 181 West Valley Ave., Ste. 300, Homewood, AL 35209; www.childrensaid.org
Children's Book Council, The (1956), 12 W. 37th St., 2nd Fl., New York, NY 10018; 78 publishers; www.cbcbooks.org
Child Welfare League of America (1920), 440 First St. NW, Wash., DC 20001; 1,100 agencies; www.cwla.org
Chiropractic Assn., American (1963), 1701 Clarendon Blvd., Arlington, VA 22209; 19,000; www.amerchiro.org
Chris-Craft Antique Boat Club (1973), 217 S. Adams St., Tallahassee, FL 32301-1708; 3,000; www.chris-craft.org
Christian Children's Fund (1938), 2821 Emerywood Pkwy., Richmond, VA 23294-3725; 160; www.christianchildrensfund.org
Cities, Natl. League of (1924), 1301 Pennsylvania Ave. NW, Ste. 550, Wash., DC 20004; 1,780; www.nlc.org
Civil Air Patrol (1941), 105 S. Hansell St., Maxwell AFB, AL 36112; 60,000; www.capnhq.gov
Civil Engineers, American Society of (1852), 1801 Alexander Bell Dr., Reston, VA 20191; 123,000+; www.asce.org
Civil Liberties Union, American (ACLU) (1920), 125 Broad St., 18 Fl., New York, NY 10004; 275,000; www.aclu.org
Civitan International, Inc. (1917), P.O. Box 130744, Birmingham, AL 35213-0744; 30,000; www.civitan.org
Clean Energy Research Inst. (1974), Univ. of Miami, Coral Gables, FL 33124; 500
Clinical Pathologists, American Society of (1922), 2100 W. Harrison St., Chicago, IL 60612; 79,000; www.ascp.org
Coaster Enthusiasts, American (1978), 5800 Foxridge Dr., Ste. 115, Mission, KS 26202-2333; 8,420; www.aceonline.org
Coast Guard Combat Veterans Assn. (1985), 295 Shalimar Dr., Shalimar, FL 32579; 1,800; www.aug.edu/~libwrw/cgcva/cgcva.htm
Co-dependents Anonymous (1986), PO Box 33577; Phoenix, AZ 85067; www.codependents.org
College Admission Counseling, Natl. Assn. for (1937), 1631 Prince Street, Alexandria, VA 22314; 8,000; www.nacac.com
College Board, The (1900), 45 Columbus Ave., New York, NY 10023; 2,900 institutions; www.collegeboard.org
College English Assn. (1939), English Dept., Winthrop Univ., Rock Hill, SC 29733; 1,000; www.winthrop.edu/cea
College Music Society, The (1958), 202 W. Spruce St., Missoula, MT 59802; 8,000; www.music.org
Colleges and Employers, Natl. Assn. of (1956), 62 Highland Ave., Bethlehem, PA 18017; 3,700; www.jobweb.org
Colleges and Universities, Assn. of American (1915), 1818 R St. NW, Wash., DC 20009; 750 institutions; www.aacu.org
Collegiate Schools of Business, Assn. to Advance (1916), 600 Emerson Rd., Ste. 300, St. Louis, MO 63141; approx. 900 org; www.aacsb.edu
Colonial Dames XVII Century, Natl. Soc. (1915), 1300 New Hampshire Ave. NW, Wash., DC 20036; 13,240; www.execpc.com/~sril/ilcd17.html
Commercial Collectors, Inc., Int'l. Assn. of (1970), 4040 W. 70th Street, Minneapolis, MN 55435; 360; www.commercialcollector.com
Commercial Law League of America (1895), 150 N. Michigan Avenue, # 600, Chicago, IL 60601; approx. 4,000; www.clla.org
Common Cause (1970), 1250 Connecticut Ave. NW, Ste. 600, Wash., DC 20036; 215,000; www.commoncause.org
Communication Assn., Natl. (1918), 1765 N St. NW, Wash., DC, 20036; 5,600; www.natcom.org
Community and Justice, National Conference for (1927), 475 Park Ave. S.; New York, NY 10016; 3,500; www.nccj.org
Community Colleges, American Assn. of (1920), One Dupont Circle NW, Ste. 410, Wash., DC 20036; 1,113 inst; www.aacc.nche.edu
Composers, Authors & Publishers, American Soc. of (ASCAP) (1914), One Lincoln Plaza, New York, NY 10023; 120,000+; www.ascap.com
Composers/USA, Natl. Assn. of (1932), Box 49256, Barrington Station, Los Angeles, CA 90049; 600; www.music-usa.org/nacusa
Computing Machinery, Assn. for (1947), 1515 Broadway, 17th Fl., New York, NY 10036; 80,000+; www.acm.org
Concerned Women for America (1979), 1015 Fifteenth St. NW, Ste. 1100, Wash., DC 20005; 500,000; www.cwfa.org
Concrete Institute, American (1904), P.O. Box 9094, Farmington Hills, MI 48333; 17,000; www.aci-int.org
Congress of Racial Equality (CORE) (1942), 817 Broadway, 3rd Floor, New York, NY 10003; 100,000; www.core-online.org
Conscientious Objectors, Central Committee for (1948), 630 20th St., #302, Oakland, CA 94612; 4,500; www.objector.org
Constantian Society, The (1970), PO Box 534, Shrewsbury, MA 01545; 750; members.tripod.com/~constantian/index.html
Construction Inspectors, Assn. of (1972), 1224 N. Nokomis NE, Alexandria, MN 56308; 2,812; www.iami.org
Construction Specifications Institute (1948); 99 Canal Center Plaza, Ste. 300, Alexandria, VA 22301; 18,000; www.csinet.org
Consumer Federation of America (1968), 1424 16th St. NW, Ste. 604, Wash., DC 20036; 300 nonprofit organizations; www.consumerfed.org
Consumer Information Center, Federal (1979), Pueblo, CO 81009; www.pueblo.gsa.gov
Consumer Interests, American Council on (ACCI) (1953), 240 Stanley Hall, Univ. of Missouri, Columbia, MO 65211-0001; 1,100; www.consumerinterests.org
Consumers Union of the U.S. (1936), 101 Truman Ave., Yonkers, NY 10703; 405,990; www.consumersunion.org
Contract Bridge League, American (1938), 2990 Airways Blvd., Memphis, TN 38116; 170,000; www.acbl.org
Co-op America (1983), 1612 K St. NW, Ste. 600, Wash., DC 20006; 50,000 individuals, 2,000 businesses; www.coopamerica.org
Correctional Assn., American (1870), 4380 Forbes Blvd., Lanham, MD 20706; 22,000; www.aca.org
Cosmetology Assn., Natl. (1921); 401 N. Michigan Ave., Chicago, IL 60611; 30,000; www.salonprofessionals.org
Cotton Council of America, Natl. (1938), 1918 N. Pkwy., Memphis, TN 38112; www.cotton.org
Counseling Assn., American (1952), 5999 Stevenson Ave., Alexandria, VA 22304; 55,424; www.counseling.org
Country Music Assn. (1958), One Music Circle S, Nashville, TN 37203; 6,700; www.CMAworld.com
Crafts & Creative Industries, Assn. of (ACCI) (1976), 1100-H Brandywine Blvd., P.O. Box 3388, Zanesville, OH 43702; 6,327; www.creative-industries.com
Credit Union Natl. Assn. & Affiliates (1934), P.O. Box 431, Madison, WI 53701; 51 credit union leagues; www.cuna.org
Crime and Delinquency, Natl. Council on (1907), 1970 Broadway, Ste. 500, Oakland, CA 94612; 300+; www.nccd-crc.org
Criminology, American Society of (1941), 1314 Kinnear Rd., Ste. 212, Columbus, OH 43212; 2,600; www.asc41.com
Croplife America (1933), 1156 15th St. NW, Ste. 400, Wash., DC 20005; 80 cos.; www.croplifeamerica.org
Crop Science Society of America (1955), 677 S. Segoe Rd., Madison, WI 53711; 4,700; www.crops.org
Cryogenic Soc. of America, Inc. (1964), 1033 South Blvd., Ste. 13, Oak Park, IL 60302; 600; www.cryogenicsociety.org
Customs Brokers and Forwarders Assn. of America, Inc., Natl. (1897), 1200 18th St. NW, Ste. 901, Wash., DC 20036; 700; www.ncbfaa.org
Cystic Fibrosis Foundation (1955), 6931 Arlington Rd., Bethesda, MD 20814; 30,000; www.cff.org

Dairy Management Inc. (1995), 10255 W. Higgins Rd., Ste. 900, Rosemont, IL 60018-5616; www.dairyinfo.com
Dark-Sky Association, Intl. (1988), 3225 N. First Ave., Tucson, AZ 85719-2103; 9,000; www.darksky.org
Daughters of the American Revolution, Natl. Society (1890), 1776 D Street NW, Wash., DC 20006; 170,000; www.dar.org
Daughters of the British Empire, Natl. Society (1909), P.O. Box 872, Ambler, PA 19002; 5,000; www.mindspring.com/~dbesociety
Daughters of the Confederacy, United (1894), 328 North Blvd., Richmond, VA 23220; 25,000; www.hqudc.org
Deaf, Natl. Assn. of the (1880), 814 Thayer Ave., Ste. 250, Silver Spring, MD 20910; 5,500; www.nad.org
Defenders of Wildlife (1947), 1101 14th St. NW, Ste. 1400, Wash., DC 20005; 480,000; www.defenders.org
Delta Kappa Gamma Society Intl. (1929), P.O. Box 1589., Austin, TX 78767; 165,000; deltakappagamma.org
Delta Mu Delta Honor Soc. (1913), P.O. Box 46935, St. Louis, MO 63146-6935; 100,000; www.deltamudelta.org
Democratic Natl. Committee (1848), 430 S. Capitol Street, SE, Wash., DC 20003; 432 elected members; www.democrats.org/index.html
DeMolay International (1919), 10200 N. Ambassador Dr., Kansas City, MO 64153; 30,000; www.demolay.org
Dental Assn., American (1859), 211 E. Chicago Ave., Chicago, IL 60611; 141,000; www.ada.org
Diabetes Assn., American (1940), 1701 North Beauregard St., Alexandria, VA 22311; 380,000+; www.diabetes.org
Dialect Society, American (1889), c/o Allan Metcalf, English Dept., MacMurray College, Jacksonville, IL 62650; 500; www.americandialect.org

Digital Printing & Imaging Assn. (1992), 10015 Main St., Fairfax, VA 22031; 900 firms; www.dpia.org
Directors Guild of America (1936), 7920 Sunset Blvd., Los Angeles, CA 90046; 12,000+; dga.org
Disabled American Veterans (1920), P.O. Box 14301, Cincinnati, OH 45250; 1,050,000; www.dav.org
Disabled Sports USA (1967), 451 Hungerford Dr., Ste. 100, Rockville, MD 20850; 60,000+; www.dsusa.org
Dogs on Stamps Study Unit (1979), 202A Newport Rd., Monroe Twp., NJ 08531-3920; 400; www.dossu.org
Down Syndrome Society, Natl. (1979), 666 Broadway, New York, NY 10012; 50,000; www.ndss.org
Dozenal Society of America (1944), Math Dept., Nassau Community College, Garden City, NY 11530-6793; 144; www.dozens.org
Ducks Unlimited (1937), One Waterfowl Way, Memphis, TN 38120; 620,000; www.ducks.org

Eagles, Fraternal Order of (1898), 1623 Gateway Circle South, Grove City, OH 43123; 1.1 mil; www.foe.com
Easter Seals (1919), 230 W. Monroe St., Ste. 1800, Chicago, IL 60606; www.easter-seals.org
Eastern Star, General Grand Chapter, Order of the (1876), 1618 New Hampshire Ave. NW, Wash., DC 20009; 1.5 mil.; www.easternstar.org
Edsel Club (1967), 19296 Tuckaway Ct., N. Fort Myers, FL 33903; 300; www.edselworld.com
Education, American Council on (1918), One Dupont Circle NW, Wash., DC 20036; 1,700 org.; www.acenet.edu
Education, Council for Advancement & Support of (1974), 1307 New York Ave. NW, Wash., DC 20005; 2,950 schools; www.case.org
Education of Young Children, Natl. Assn. for the (1926), 2021 21st Ave. S., Ste. 108, Nashville, TN 37212; 103,000; www.naeyc.org
Educators for World Peace, Intl. Assn. of (1969), P.O. Box 3282, Mastin Lake Station, Huntsville, AL 35810; 35,000; www.earthportals.com/portal_messenger/mercieca.html
Egalitarian Communities, Federation of (1976), HC-3 Box 3370, Tecumseh, MO, 65760; 250; www.thefec.org
8th Air Force Historical Society (1975), P.O. Box 7215, St. Paul, MN 55107; 18,000; www.visi.com/~mbacklund/8thaf.htm
88th Infantry Division Assn. (1946), 11 Lovett Ave., Brockton, MA 02301-1750; 4,200; www.88infdiv.org
84th Infantry Div. Railsplitters Soc., The, (1945), P.O. Box 827, Sioux Falls, SD 57101-0827; 2,400
82nd Airborne Division Assn., Inc. (1946), P.O. Box 9308, Fayetteville, NC 28311-9308; 28,000+; www.fayettevillenc.com/airborne82dassn
Electrical and Electronics Engineers, Institute of (1963), 445 Hoes Lane, Piscataway, NJ 08854; 356,000; www.ieee.org
Electrical Manufacturers Assn., Natl. (1926), 1300 N. 17th St., Ste. 1847, Rosslyn, VA 22209; 560 cos.; www.nema.org
Electrochemical Society, Inc.,The (ECS, Inc.) (1902), 65 South Main St., Bldg. D, Pennington, NJ 08534-2839; 8,000+; www.electrochem.org
Electronic Industries Assn. (1924), 2500 Wislon Blvd., Arlington, VA 22201; 1,058 cos.; www.eia.org
Electronics Technicians, Intl. Society of Certified (1970), 3608 Pershing Ave., Ft. Worth, TX 76107; 1,800; www.iscet.org
Elks of the U.S.A., Benevolent and Protective Order of (1868), 2750 N. Lakeview Ave., Chicago, IL 60614; 1.2 mil.; www.elks.org
Energy Engineers, Assn. of (1977), 4025 Pleasantdale Rd., Ste. 420, Atlanta, GA 30340; 8,500; www.aeecenter.org
Engineers, Natl. Society of Professional (1934), 1420 King St., Alexandria, VA 22314; 54,000; www.nspe.org
English Inc., U.S. (1985), 1747 Pennsylvania Ave. NW, Ste. 1050, Wash., DC 20006; 1.7 mil; www.us-english.org
English-Speaking Union of the U.S. (1920), 144 E. 39th St., New York, NY 10036; 18,000; www.english-speakingunion.org
Entomological Society of America (1889), 9301 Annapolis Rd., Lanham, MD 20706-3115; 6,700; www.entsoc.org
Environmental Health Assn., Natl. (1937), 720 S. Colorado Blvd., Ste. 970-S, Denver, CO 80246-1925; 5,000; www.neha.org
Environmental Medicine, American Academy of (1969), 7701 E. Kellogg, Ste. 625, Wichita, KS 67207; 400; www.aaem.com
Equipment Manufacturers, Assn. of (1911), 111 E. Wisconsin Ave., Milwaukee, WI 53202; 550+ cos.; www.aem.org
Esperanto League for North America Inc. (1952), P.O. Box 1129, El Cerrito, CA 94530; 725; www.esperanto-usa.org
Evangelism Crusades, Inc., Intl. (1959) 14617 Victory Blvd., Van Nuys, CA 91411
Exchange Club, Natl. (1911), 3050 Central Ave., Toledo, OH 43606; 33,000; www.nationalexchangeclub.com
Experimental Aircraft Assn. (1953), 3000 Poberezeny, Rd., Oshkosh, WI 54902; 171,000; www.eaa.org
Exploration Geophysicists, Society of (1930), 8801 South Yale, Tulsa, OK 74137; 18,000; www.seg.org
Ex-Prisoners of War, American (1942), 3201 E. Pioneer Pkwy., Arlington, TX 76010; 30,000; www.axpow.org

Fairs & Expositions, Intl. Assn. of (1919), P.O. Box 985, Springfield, MO 65809; 2,600; www.fairsandexpos.com
Family, Career and Community Leaders of America (1945), 1910 Association Dr., Reston, VA 20191; 25,500; www.fcclainc.org
Family Physicians, American Academy of (1947), 11400 Tomahawk Creek Parkway, Leawood, KS 66211; 93,100; www.aafp.org
Family Relations, Natl. Council on (1938), 3989 Central Avenue NE, Suite 550, Minneapolis, MN 55421; 4,000; www.ncfr.org
Farm Bureau Federation, American (1919), 225 Touhy Ave., Park Ridge, IL 60068; 5 mil+ families; www.fb.com
Farmers of America Org., Natl. Future (1928), P.O. Box 68960, 6060 FFA Drive, Indianapolis, IN 4626; 452,000; www.ffa.org
Farmers Union, Natl. (1902), 11900 E. Cornell Ave., Denver, CO 80014; 300,000; www.nfu.org
Fat Acceptance, Inc., Natl. Assn. to Advance (NAAFA) (1969), P.O. Box 188620, Sacramento, CA 95818; 5,000; www.naafa.org
Fellowship of Reconciliation, The (1914), P.O. Box 271, Nyack, NY 10960; 26,000; www.forusa.org
Feminists for Life of America (1972), 733 15th St. NW, Ste. 1100, Wash., DC 20005; approx. 5,000 www.feministsforlife.org
Financial Executives Institute (1938), 10 Madison Ave., Morristown, NJ 5,000; 07962; 15,000; www.fei.org
Financial Professionals, Assn. for (formerly Treasury Management Assn.) (1979), 7315 Wisconsin Ave., Ste. 600W, Bethesda, MD 20814; 14,000; www.AFPonline.org
Financial Service Professionals, Soc. of (formerly American Society of CLU & ChFC) (1928), 270 S. Bryn Mawr Ave., Bryn Mawr, PA 19010; 32,000; www.financialpro.org
Financial Women Intl. (1921 as the National Assoc. of Bank Women), 200 N. Glebe Rd., Ste. 820, Arlington, VA 22203; 2,800; www.fwi.org
Financiers, Inc., Intl. Society of (1979), P.O. Box 398, Naples, NC 28760; www.insofin.com
Fire Chiefs, Intl. Assn. of (1873), 4025 Fair Ridge Dr., Ste. 300, Fairfax, VA 22033; 12,000; www.iafc.org
Fire Protection Assn., Natl.(NFPA) (1896), 1 Batterymarch Park, Quincy, MA 02269-9101; 69,700; www.nfpa.org
Fire Protection Engineers, Soc. of (1950), 7315 Wisconsin Avenue, Ste. 1225W, Bethesda, MD 20814; 3,500; www.sfpe.org
First Amendment Studies, Inc., Institute for (1984), P.O. Box 589, Great Barrington, MA 01230; 10,000; www.ifas.org
Fisheries Soc., American (1870), 5410 Grosvenor Ln., Bethesda, MD 20814; 10,000; www.fisheries.org
Food Industry Suppliers (1911), 1451 Dolley Madison Blvd., McLean, VA 22101; 700 cos.; www.iafis.org
Food Technologists, Institute of (1939), 525 W. Van Buren, Ste. 1000, Chicago, IL 60601; 28,000; www.ift.org
Foreign Study, American Institute for, The (1964), River Plaza, 9 W. Broad St., Stamford, CT 06902; 1 mil+; www.aifs.com
Foreign Trade Council, Inc., Natl. (1914), 1625 K St. NW, Wash., DC 20006; 400 cos.; www.nftc.org
Forensic Sciences, American Academy of (1948), 410 N.21st St., Colorado Springs, CO 80904; 5,300; www.aafs.org
Foresters, Society of American (1900), 5400 Grosvenor La., Bethesda, MD 20814; 17,500; www.safnet.org
Forest History Society (1946), 701 Wm. Vickers Ave., Durham, NC 27701-3162; 2,000; www.foresthistory.org
Forest & Paper Assn., American (1993), 1111 19th St. NW, Wash., DC 20036; 400 cos.; www.afandpa.org
Forests, American (1875), 910 17th St. NW, Ste. 600, Wash., DC 20001; 50,000; www.americanforests.org
Fortean Org., Intl. (1965), P.O. Box N, Dept. W, College Park, MD 20740; 1,000; www.research.umbc.edu/~frizzell/info
Foundrymen's Society, American (1896), 505 State St., Des Plaines, IL 60016; 13,000; www.afsinc.org
4-H Clubs (1914), 1400 Independence Ave., U.S. Dept of Agriculture, Wash., DC 20250; 6.5 mil; www.4h-usa.org
Frederick A. Cook Society, (1940), P.O. Box 247, Hurleyville, NY 12747; 254; www.cookpolar.org
Freedom From Religion Foundation (1978), P.O. Box 750, Madison, WI 53701; 4,450; www.ffrf.org
Freedom of Information Center (1958), 133 Neff Annex, Univ. of Missouri, Columbia, MO 65211-0012; foi.missouri.edu

Freemasonry, Supreme Council Ancient and Accepted Scottish Rite of, Northern Masonic Jurisdiction (1872), P.O. Box 519, Lexington, MA 02420; 300,000; supremecouncil.org
Free Men, Natl. Coalition of (1977), P.O. Box 582023, Minneapolis, MN 55458; 2,000; www.ncfm.org
French Institute/Alliance Française (1972), 22 E. 60th St., New York, NY 10022; 6,500; www.fiaf.org
Frozen Food Institute, American (1942), 2000 Corporate Ridge, Suite 1000, McLean, VA 22102; 550; www.affi.com
Funeral Consumers Alliance (FAMSA) (1964), P.O. Box 10, Hinesburg, VT 05461; 500,000; www.funerals.org/famsa
Future Business Leaders of America/Phi Beta Lambda, Inc. (1942), 1912 Association Drive, Reston, VA 20191; 240,000; www.fbla-pbl.org

Gamblers Anonymous (1957), 3255 Wilshire Blvd., Los Angeles, CA 90010; approx. 30,000; www.gamblersanonymous.org
Garden Club of America (1913), 14 E. 60th St., 3rd Floor, New York, NY 10022; 195 clubs; www.gcamerica.org
Garden Clubs, Inc., National Council of State (1929), 4401 Magnolia Ave., St. Louis, MO 63110; 253,316; www.gardenclub.org
Gas Assn., American (1918), 400 North Capitol St. NW, Wash., DC 20001; 187 cos.; www.aga.org
Gay and Lesbian Task Force, Natl. (1973), 1700 Kalorama Rd. NW, Wash., DC 20009; 30,000; www.ngltf.org
Genealogical Society, Natl. (1903), 4527 17th St. N, Arlington, VA 22207; 17,000; www.ngsgenealogy.org
General Contractors of America, The Associated (1918), 333 John Carlyle St., Ste. 200, Alexandria, VA 22314; 36,000+ cos.; www.agc.org
Genetic Association, American (1903), P.O. Box 257, Buckeystown, MD 21717; lsvl.la.asu.edu/aga
Geographers, Assn. of American (1904), 1710 16th St. NW, Wash., DC 20009; 6,700; www.aag.org
Geographic Education, Natl. Council for (1915), 16A Leonard Hall, IUP, Indiana, PA 15705; 2,400; www.ncge.org
Geographic Society, Natl. (1888), 1145 17th St. NW, Wash., DC 20036; 10 mil.; www.nationalgeographic.com
Geographical Society, The American (1851), 120 Wall St., New York, NY 10005; 1,000 amergeog.org
Geological Society of America (1888), 3300 Penrose Pl., Boulder, CO 80301; 17,000; www.geosociety.org
Geriatrics Society, American (1942), 350 5th Ave., Ste. 801, New York, NY 10118; 6,000; www.americangeriatrics.org
Gideons Intl. (1899), 2900 Lebanon Rd., Nashville, TN 37214; 131,000; www.gideons.org
Gifted Children, Natl. Assn. for (1954), 1707 L Street NW, Suite 550, Washington, DC 20036; 8,000; www.nagc.org
Girl Scouts of the U.S.A. (1912), 420 5th Ave., New York, NY 10018; 3.8 mil; www.girlscouts.org
Golden Key National Honor Society (1977), 1189 Ponce de Leon Ave., Atlanta, GA 30306; 1 mil.+; gknhs.gsu.edu
Gold Star Mothers of America, Inc. (1928), 2128 Leroy Place NW, Wash., DC 20008; 1,500; www.goldstarmoms.com.
Golf Assn., U.S. (1894), Golf House, P.O. Box 708, Far Hills, NJ 07931; 800,000; www.usga.org
Gospel Music Assn. (1964), 1205 Division St., Nashville, TN 37203; 5,000; www.gospelmusic.org
Governors' Assn., Natl. (1908), Hall of the States, 444 N. Capitol, Wash., DC 20001; 55 govs.; www.nga.org
Graduate Schools, Council of (1960), One Dupont Circle NW, #430 Wash., DC 20036; 415 instits.; www.cgsnet.org
Grange of the Order of Patrons of Husbandry, Natl. (1867), 1616 H Street NW, Wash., DC 20006; 300,000; www.nationalgrange.org
Graphic Arts, American Institute of (1914), 164 5th Ave., New York, NY 10010; 15,000; www.aiga.org
Gray Panthers (1970), 733 15th St. NW, Ste 437, Wash., DC 20005; approx. 17,000; www.graypanthers.org
Green Mountain Club, The (1910), 4711 Waterbury-Stowe Rd., Waterbury Ctr., VT 05677; 9,000; www.greenmountainclub.org
Green Party (1984), P.O. Box 1406, 202 S. State St., Chicago, IL 60690; 1,500+; www.greenparty.org
Greenpeace U.S.A. (1971), 702 H St. NW, Wash., DC 20001; 250,000; www.greenpeaceusa.org.
Grocery Manufacturers of America (1908), 1010 Wisconsin Avenue., 9th Floor., Wash., DC 20007; 140 cos.; www.gmabrands.com
Ground Water Assn., Natl. (1948), 601 Dempsey Rd., Westerville, OH 43081; 16,500; www.ngwa.org
Group Against Smokers' Pollution, Inc. (GASP) (1971), P.O. Box 632, College Park, MD 20741; 10,000+
Guide Dog Foundation for the Blind, Inc. (1946), 371 E. Jericho Turnpike, Smithtown, NY 11787; 162,500; www.guidedog.org

Hadassah, the Women's Zionist Organization of America (1912), 50 W. 58th St., New York, NY 10019; 385,000; www.hadassah.org
Handball Assn., U.S. (1951), 2333 N. Tucson Blvd., Tucson, AZ 85716; 8,000; www.ushandball.org
Health Council, Natl. (1920), 1730 M St. NW, Ste. 500, Wash., DC 20036; www.nationalhealthcouncil.org
Health Info. Management Assn., American (AHIMA) (1928), 233 N. Michigan Ave., Ste. 2150, Chicago, IL 60601; 39,000; www.ahima.org
Hearing Society, Intl. (1951), 16880 Middlebelt Rd., Ste. 4, Livonia, MI 48154; 3,000; www.ihsinfo.org
Heart Assn., American (1924), 7272 Greenville Ave., Dallas, TX 75231; 22.5 mil.; www.americanheart.org
Heating, Refrigerating & Air-Conditioning Engineers, Inc., American Soc. of (1894), 1791 Tullie Cir. NE, Atlanta, GA 30329; 55,000; www.ashrae.org
Hebrew Immigrant Aid Society (1881), 333 Seventh Ave., 17th Fl., New York, NY 10001; approx. 9,000; www.hias.org
Helicopter Society, American (1943), 217 N. Washington St., Alexandria, VA 22314; 6,140; www.vtol.org
Hemispheric Affairs, Council on (1975), 1444 I St. NW, Ste. 211, Wash., DC 20005; 1,875; www.coha.org
Hibernians in America, Ancient Order of (1836), 1301 S.W. 26th Avenue, Ft. Lauderdale, FL 33312; 200,000; www.aoh.com
Highpointers Club (1987), P.O. Box 1496, Golden, CO 80402; 2,500; www.highpointers.org
High School Band Directors Hall of Fame, Natl. (1978), 519 N. Halifax Ave., Daytona Beach, FL 32118; www.banddirectorshalloffame.homestead.com
Hiking Society, American (1976), 1422 Fenwick Lane, Silver Spring, MD 20910; 5,000; www.americanhiking.org
Historians, Organization of American (1907), 112 N. Bryan St., Bloomington, IN 47408; 9,000; www.oah.org
Historic Preservation, Natl. Trust for (1949), 1785 Massachusetts Avenue NW, Wash., DC 20036; 250,000; www.nationaltrust.org
Historical Assn., American (1884), 400 A St. SE, Wash., DC 20003; 15,000; www.theaha.org
Historical Society Doll Collection, United States (1971), 1st and Main Sts., Richmond, VA 23219; 250,000; www.ushsdolls.com
Hockey, U.S.A. (1936), 1775 Bob Johnson Dr., Colorado Springs, CO 80906; 585,000; www.usahockey.com.
Home Builders, Natl. Assn. of (1942), 1201 15th St. NW, Wash., DC 20005; 203,000; www.nahb.com
Home Energy Research Organization (H.E.R.O) (2001), 10799 Sherman Grove Ave.,#18, Sunland, CA, 91040-2364; 5,600
Homeless, Natl. Coalition for the (1984), 1012 14th St., Ste. 600, Wash., DC 20005; 10,000; www.nationalhomeless.org
Honor Society, Natl. (1921), 1904 Association Dr., Reston, VA 20191; app. 750,000; dsa.principals.org
Horatio Alger Soc. (1965), P.O. Box 70361, Richmond, VA 23255; 250; www.ihot.com/~has
Horse Council, American (1969), 1616 H St., NW, 7th Fl., Wash., DC 20006; 175 org.,1,800 ind.; www.horsecouncil.org
Hospital Assn., American (1899), 1 N. Franklin, Chicago, IL 60606; 5,100 hospitals; www.aha.org
Hostelling Intl.-American Youth Hostels (1934), 733 15th Street NW, Suite 840, Wash., DC 20005; 120,000; www.hiayh.org
Hotel & Motel Assn., American (1910), 1201 New York Ave., NW, #600, Wash., DC 20005; 10,000+; www.ahma.com
Hot Rod Assn., Natl. (1951), 2035 Financial Way, Glendora, CA 91741; 85,000; www.nhra.com
Housing Inspection Foundation (1979), 1224 N. Nokomis NE, Alexandria, MN 56308; 4,114; www.iami.org
Huguenot Society, Natl. (1951), 9033 Lyndale Ave. S, #108, Bloomington, MN 55420; 5,000; www.huguenot.netnation.com
Humane Society of the U.S. (1954), 2100 L St. NW, Wash., DC 20037; 650,000; www.hsus.org
Human Resource Management, Society for (SHRM) (1948), 1800 Duke St., Alexandria, VA 22314; 115,000; www.shrm.org
Hydrogen Energy, Intl. Assn. for (1974), P.O. Box 248266, Coral Gables, FL 33124; 2,500; www.iahe.org

Identification, Intl. Assn. for (1915), 2535 Pilot Knob Road, Ste. 117, Mondota Heights, MN 55120; 5,000; www.theiai.org
Illuminating Engineering Society of N. America (1906), 120 Wall Street, 17th Floor, New York, NY 10005; 9,000; www.iesna.org
Illustrators, Inc., Society of (1901), 128 E. 63rd St., New York, NY 10021; 1,000; www.societyillustrators.org
Independent Community Bankers of America (1930), One Thomas Circle, Ste. 400, Wash., DC 20005; 5,000; www.icba.org

Industrial and Applied Mathematics, Society for (1952), 3600 Univ. City Science Ctr., Philadelphia, PA 19104; 9,000; www.siam.org
Industrial Designers Society of America (1965), 1142 Walker Rd., Ste. E, Great Falls, VA 22066; 3,200; www.idsa.org
Industrial Security, American Soc. for (1955), 1625 Prince St., Alexandria, VA 22313; 32,000; www.asisonline.org
Insurance Assn., American (1964), 1130 Connecticut Avenue NW, Suite 1000, Wash., DC 20036; 410; www.aiadc.org
Integrative and Comparative Biology, Society for (1890), 1313 Dolley Madison Blvd., Ste. 402, McClean, VA 22101; 2,400; www.sicb.org
Intellectual Property Owners Assoc. (1973), 1255 23rd St. NW, Ste. 200, Wash., DC 20037; 362; www.ipo.org
Intelligence Officers, Assoc. of Former (1976), 6723 Whittier Ave., Ste. 303A, McLean, VA 22101-4533; 3,100+; www.afio.com
Intercollegiate Athletics, Natl. Assn. of (1937), 23500 W. 105th St. P.O. Box 1325, Olathe, KS 66051-1325; 331 member colleges/universities; www.naia.org
Interior Designers, American Society of (1975), 608 Massachusetts Avenue NE, Wash., DC 20008; 30,000; www.asid.org
Intl. Education, Institute of (1919), 809 United Nations Plaza, New York, NY 10017; 650 U.S. colleges and universities; www.iie.org
Intl. Educational Exchange, Council on (1947), 633 3rd Ave., 20th Fl., New York, NY 10017; 240 organizations; www.ciee.org
Intl. Educators, Assn. of (NAFSA) (1948), 1307 New York Ave., 8th Fl.,Wash., DC 20005; 7,500; www.nafsa.org
Intl. Law, American Society of (1906), 2223 Massachusetts Ave. NW, Wash., DC 20008; 4,500; www.asil.org
Inventors, American Soc. of (1953), P.O. Box 58426, Philadelphia, PA 19102; 150; www.asoi.org
Investigative Pathology, American Soc. for (1902), 9650 Rockville Pike, Bethesda, MD 20814; 1,753; www.asip.org
Investment Management and Research, Assn. for (AIMR) (1990), 560 Ray C. Hunt Dr., Charlottesville, VA 22903-0668; 49,000; www.aimr.org
Investors Corp., Natl. Assn. of (1951), 711 W. Thirteen Mile Rd., Madison Heights, MI 48701; 700,000; www.better-investing.org
IPC-Association Connecting Electronics Industries (formerly The Institute for Interconnecting & Packaging Electronic Circults) (1957), 2215 Sanders Rd., Northbrook, IL 60062; 2,800; www.ipc.org
Irish American Cultural Inst. (1962), 1 Lackawanna Pl., Morristown, NJ 07960; 4,500; www.irishaci.org
Irish Historical Society, American (1897), 991 5th Ave., New York, NY 10028; 650; www.aihs.org
Iron and Steel Engineers, Assn. of (1907), Three Gateway Center, Ste. 1900, Pittsburgh, PA 15222; 11,650; www.aise.org

Jail Assn., American (1981), 2053 Day Rd., Ste. 100, Hagerstown, MD 21740; 4,800+; www.corrections.com/aja
Japanese-American Citizens League (1929), 1765 Sutter St., San Francisco, CA 94115; 22,000; www.jacl.org
Jewish Committee, American (1906), 165 E. 56th St., New York, NY 10022; 110,000; www.ajc.org
Jewish Community Centers Assn. of North America (1917), 15 E. 26th St., New York, NY 10014; 1,000,000+; www.jcca.org
Jewish Congress, American (1918), 15 E. 84th St., New York, NY 10028; 50,000; www.ajcongress.org
Jewish Historical Society, American (1892), 15 West 16th St. New York, NY 10011; 4,000; www.ajhs.org
Jewish War Veterans of the U.S.A. (1896), 1811 R St. NW, Wash., DC 20009; 100,000; jwv.org
Jewish Women, Natl. Council of (1893), 53 W. 23rd St., 6th Fl., New York, NY 10010; 90,000; www.ncjw.org
John Birch Society (1958), 770 Westhill Blvd, P.O. Box 8040, Appleton, WI 54912; www.jbs.org
Joint Action in Community Service (JACS) (1967), 5225 Wisconsin Ave. NW, Ste. 404, Wash., DC 20015; www.jacsinc.org
Joseph Diseases Foundation, Inc., Intl. (1977), P.O. Box 2550, Livermore, CA 94551; 1,550; www.ijdf.net
Journalists, Society of Professional (1909), 3909 N. Meridian St., Indianapolis, IN 46200-4505; 10,000+; spj.org
Journalists and Authors, American Society of (1948), 1501 Broadway, Ste. 302, New York, NY 10036; 1,012; www.asja.org
Judicature Society, American (1913), 180 N. Michigan Ave., Ste. 600, Chicago, IL 60601; 6,000; www.ajs.org
Jugglers Assn., Intl. (1947), P.O. Box 218, Montague, MA 01351; 2,500; www.juggle.org
Junior Achievement, Inc. (1919), One Education Way, Colorado Springs, CO 80906; www.ja.org
Junior Auxiliaries, Natl. Assn. of (1941), 845 South Main St., Greenville, MS 38701; 12,876; www.najanet.org
Junior Chamber of Commerce, U.S. (1920), P.O. Box 7, 4 W. 21st St., Tulsa, OK 74114; 200,000; www.usjaycees.org
Junior College Athletic Assn., Natl. (1937), P.O. Box 7305, Colorado Springs, CO 80933; 520; www.njcaa.org
Junior Honor Society, Natl. (1929), 1904 Association Dr., Reston, VA 20191; approx. 250,000; dsa.principals.org
Junior Leagues, Assn. of (1901), 132 West 31st St., New York, NY 10016; 193,000; www.ajli.org

Kidney Fund, The American (1971), 6110 Executive Blvd., Ste. 1010, Rockville, MD 20876; www.kidneyfund.org
Kiwanis International (1915), 3636 Woodview Trace, Indianapolis, IN 46268; 543,041; www.kiwanis.org
Knights of Columbus (1882), One Columbus Plaza, New Haven, CT 06510; 1,632,439; www.kofc.org
Knights of Pythias (1864), 59 Coddington Street, #202, Quincy, MA 02169; approx. 70,000; www.pythias.org
Krishna Consciousness, Intl. Soc. for (ISKON, Inc.) (1966), 3764 Watseka Ave., Los Angeles, CA 90034; approx. 20,000; www.harekrishna.com

La Leche League Intl. (1956), 1400 N. Meacham Rd., P.O. Box 4079, Schaumburg, IL 60168; www.lalecheleague.org
Lady Bird Johnson Wildflower Center (1982), 4801 La Crosse Avenue, Austin, TX 78739; 22,000; www.wildflower.org
Landscape Architects, American Society of (1899), 636 I St. NW, Wash., DC 20001-3736; 12,500; www.asla.org
Law Libraries, American Assn. of (1906), 53 W. Jackson Blvd., #940, Chicago, IL 60604; 5,150; www.aallnet.org
Learned Societies, American Council of (1919), 228 E. 45th St., New York, NY 10017; 64 societies; www.acls.org
Lefthanders Intl. (1975), P.O. Box 8249, Topeka, KS 66608; 25,000.
Legal Administrators, Assn. of (1971), 175 E. Hawthorn Parkway, Suite 325, Vernon Hills, IL 60061-1428; 9,000; www.alanet.org
Legal Secretaries, Natl. Assn. of (NALS) (1942), 314 E 3rd St., Ste. 210, Tulsa, OK 74120; 8,500; www.nals.org
Legion of Valor of the U.S.A., Inc. (1890), c/o Legion of Valor Museum, 2425 Fresno St., Ste. 103, Fresno, CA 93721; 600; www.legionofvalor.com
Leprosy Missions, Inc., American (1906), One Alm Way, Greenville, SC 29601; www.leprosy.org
Leukemia and Lymphoma Society (1949), 1311 Mamaroneck Ave., White Plains, NY 10605; 58 chapters nationwide; www.leukemia-lymphoma.org
Lewis and Clark Trail Heritage Foundation. (1969), P.O. Box 3434, Great Falls, MT 59403; 3,285; www.lewisandclark.org
Libertarian Party (1971), 2600 Virginia Ave. NW, Ste. 100, Wash., DC 20037; 224,000; www.lp.org
Liberty Lobby (1955), 300 Independence Ave. SE, Wash., DC 20003; 90,000; www.spotlight.org
Libraries Assn., Special (1909), 1700 18th St. NW, Wash., DC 20009; 15,000; www.sla.org
Library Assn., American (1876), 50 E. Huron St., Chicago, IL 60611; 64,000+; www.ala.org
Lifesaving Assn., U.S. (1964), PO Box 366, Huntington Beach, CA 92648; 100+ chapters; www.usla.org
Lighter-Than-Air Society (1952), 526 S. Main St., Ste.232, Akron, OH 44306; 850; www.blimpinfo.com.
Linguistic Society of America (1924), 1325 18th St. NW, Ste. 211, Wash., DC 20036-6401; 4,000 indiv., 2,200 inst.; www.lsadc.org
Lions Clubs, Intl., Assn. of (1917), 300 W. 22nd St., Oak Brook, IL 60523; 1,400,000; www.lionsclubs.org
Literacy Volunteers of America, Inc. (1962), P.O. Box 6506., Syracuse, NY 13217; 4,000 indiv., 2,200 Inst.; www.literacyvolunteers.org
Little League Baseball, Inc. (1939), P.O. Box 3485, S. Williamsport, PA 17701; approx. 3 mil; www.littleleague.org
Little People of America, Inc. (1961), Box 65030, Lubbock, TX 79464; 8,000; www.lpaonline.org
Logistics, International Society of (SOLE) (1966), 8100 Professional Place, Ste. 211, Hyattsville, MD 20785; 3,500; www.sole.org
London Club (1975), 214 North 2100 Rd., Lecompton, KS 66050; 100+.
Lung Assn., American (1904), 61 Broadway, 6th Fl., New York, NY 10006; www.lungusa.org

Magazine Publishers of America (1919), 919 Third Ave., New York, NY 10022; 320; www.magazine.org
Magicians, Intl. Brotherhood of (1922), 11155 S. Towne Sq., Ste. C, St. Louis, MO 63123-7813; 14,000; www.magician.org
Management Accountants, Institute of (1919), 10 Paragon Dr., Montvale, NJ 07645-1760; 75,000; www.imanet.org
Management Assn., American (1923), 1601 Broadway, New York, NY 10019; 70,000+; www.amanet.org

Management Consulting Firms, Assn. of (1929), 380 Lexington Ave., Ste. 1700, New York, NY 10168; 55 cos; www.amcf.org
Manufacturing Engineers, Soc. of (1932), One SME Dr., Dearborn, MI 48121-0930; 55,000+; www.sme.org
Manufacturers, Natl. Assn. of (1895), 1331 Pennsylvania Ave. NW, Suite 1500 N. Tower, Wash., DC 20004; 14,000 cos.; www.nam.org
March of Dimes Birth Defects Foundation (1938), 1275 Mamaroneck Avenue, White Plains, NY 10605; 3 mil; www.modimes.org
Marine Corps League (1937), P.O. Box 3070, Merrifield, VA 22116; 42,000; www.mcleague.org
Market Technicians Assn., Inc. (1973), 74 Main Street, 3rd Floor, Woodbridge, NJ, 07095; 1,800; www.mta.org
Marketing Assn., Am. (1915), 311 S. Wacker Dr., Ste. 5800, Chicago, IL 60606; 38,000; www.marketingpower.com
Materials and Process Engineering, Soc. for the Advancement of (1944), 1161 Parkview Drive, Covina, CA 91724-3748; 4,700; www.sampe.org
Mathematical Society, American (1888), 201 Charles St., Providence, RI 02904; 30,000; www.ams.org
Mayflower Descendants, General Society of (1897), 4 Winslow St., Plymouth, MA 02361; 27,000; www.mayflower.org
Mayors, U.S. Conference of (1932), 1620 Eye St. NW, Wash., DC 20006; www.usmayors.org
Mechanical Engineers, American Soc. of (1880), 3 Park Ave., New York, NY 10016; 125,000; www.asme.org
Medical Assn., American (1847), 515 N. State St., Chicago, IL 60610; 300,000; www.ama-assn.org
Medical Corps, International (1984), 11500 W. Olympic Blvd., Ste. 506, Los Angeles, CA 90064; www.imc-la.org
Medical Library Assn. (1898), 65 E. Wacker Pl., Ste. 1900, Chicago, IL 60602; 5,000; www.mlanet.org
Medieval Academy of America (1925), 1430 Massachusetts Avenue, Suite 313, Cambridge, MA 02138; 4,500; www.medievalacademy.org
Meeting Planners, Intl. Society of (1985) 1224 N. Nokomis NE, Alexandria, MN 56308; 6,000; www.iami.org
MENC: The Natl. Assn. for Music Education (formerly Music Educators Natl. Conference) (1907), 1806 Robert Fulton Dr., Reston, VA 20191; 95,000; www.menc.org
Mended Hearts, Inc. (1950), 7272 Greenville Ave., Dallas, TX 75231; 24,000; www.mendedhearts.org
Mensa, Ltd., American (1960), 1229 Corporate Dr. W, Arlington, TX 76006; 49,837; www.us.mensa.org
Mental Health Assn., Natl. (1909), 1021 Prince St., Alexandria, VA 22314; www.nmha.org
Mentally Ill, Natl. Alliance for the (1979), Colonial Place Three, 2107 Wilson Blvd. Ste. 300, Arlington, VA 22201; 220,000; www.nami.org
Merrill's Marauders Assn. (1982), 11244 N. 33rd St., Phoenix, AZ 85028-2723; 1,739; www.marauder.org
Meteorological Society, American (1919), 45 Beacon St., Boston, MA 02108; 10,000; www.ametsoc.org/AMS
Metric Assn., Inc., U.S. (1916), 10245 Andasol Ave., Northridge, CA 91325; 1,200; www.metric.org
Microbiology, American Society for (1899), 1752 N. St. NW, Wash., DC 20036; 42,000; www.asmusa.org
Military Order of the Purple Heart of the USA (1958), 5413-B Backlick Road, Springfield, VA 22151; 30,000; www.purpleheart.org
Military Order of the World Wars (1919), 435 N. Lee St., Alexandria, VA 22314; 11,250; www.militaryorder.org
Military Surgeons of the U.S., Assn. of (1898), 9320 Old Georgetown Road, Bethesda, MD 20814; 11,000; www.amsus.org
Mining, Metallurgy and Exploration, Inc., Society for (1871), 8307 Shaffer Pkwy., Littleton, CO 80127; 13,000; www.smenet.org
Mining, Metallurgical and Petroleum Engineers, American Institute of (1871), 3 Park Ave., New York, NY 10016; 90,000; www.aimeny.org
Missing and Exploited Children, Natl. Center for (1984), The Charles B. Wang International Children's Building, Alexandria, VA 22314; www.missingkids.com
Model A Ford Club of America, Inc. (1955), 250 S Cypress St., La Habra, CA 90631; 15,500; www.mafca.com
Model Railroad Assn., Natl. (1935), 4121 Cromwell Rd., Chattanooga, TN 37421-2119; 24,000; www.nmra.org
Modern Language Assn. of America (1883), 26 Bdwy., 3rd Fl., New York, NY 10014-1789; 30,000; www.mla.org
Moose Intl., Inc. (1888), Rte. 31, Mooseheart, IL 60539; 1.5 mil; www.mooseintl.org
Mothers, Inc.®, American (1938), 15 DuPont Circle N.W., Wash., DC 20036; 3,700; www.americanmothers.org
Mothers of Twins Clubs, Natl. Organization of (1963), P.O. Box 438, Thompson Station, TN 37179-0438; 24,000; www.nomotc.org
Motion Picture Arts & Sciences, Academy of (1927), 8949 Wilshire Blvd., Beverly Hills, CA 90211; 6,300; www.oscars.org
Motion Picture & Television Engineers, Soc. of (1916), 595 W. Hartsdale Ave., White Plains, NY 10607; 10,000; www.smpte.org
Motorcyclist Assn., American (1924), 13515 Yarmouth Dr., Pickerington, OH 43147; 265,000; www.amadirectlink.com
Motorists Association, Natl. (1982), 402 W. 2nd St., Waunakee, WI 53597; 7,000; www.motorists.org
Multiple Sclerosis Society, Natl. (1946), 733 Third Ave., New York, NY 10017; 518,567; www.nmss.org
Muscular Dystrophy Assn., Inc. (1950), 3300 E. Sunrise Dr., Tucson, AZ 85718; 2 mil. volunteers; www.mdausa.org
Museums, American Assn. of (1906), 1575 Eye St. NW, Ste. 400, Wash., DC 20005; 16,000; www.aam-us.org
Music Center, American (1939), 30 W. 26th St., #1001, New York, NY 10010; 2,500; www.amc.net
Music Teachers Natl. Assn. (1876), 441 Vine St., Ste. 505, Cincinnati, OH 45202; 24,000; www.mtna.org
Musicological Society, American (1934), 201 S. 34th St., Philadelphia, PA 19104-6313; 4,600; www.ams-net.org
Muzzle Loading Rifle Assn., Natl. (1933), P.O. Box 67, Friendship, IN 47021; 20,000; www.nmlra.org
Myasthenia Gravis Foundation of America (1952), 5841 Cedar Lake Rd., Ste. 204, Minneapolis, MN 55416; 47,200; www.myasthenia.org
Mystery Writers of America, Inc. (1945), 17 E. 47th St., 6th Fl., New York, NY 10017; 2,235; www.mysterywriters.org

NA'AMAT USA (1925), 350 Fifth Ave., Ste. 4700, New York, NY 10118; 50,000, U.S.; 900,000 worldwide; www.naamat.org
Name Society, American (1951), Dept. of Modern Languages, Baruch College, 17 Lexington Ave., New York, NY 10010; 750
Narcotics Anonymous World Services (1953), P.O Box 9999, Van Nuys, CA 94109; 250,000; www.na.org
Natl. Assn. for the Advancement of Colored People (NAACP) (1909), 4805 Mt. Hope Dr., Baltimore, MD 21215; www.naacp.org
National Guard Assn. of the U.S. (1878), One Massachusetts Ave. NW, Wash., DC 20001; 56,000; www.ngaus.org
National Press Club (1908), 529 14th St., 13th Fl., NW, Wash., DC 20045; 4,000+; www.press.org
Nature Conservancy, The (1951), 4245 N. Fairfax Drive, Ste. 100, Arlington, VA 22203; 1 mil+; nature.org
Naturist Society LLC (1980), P.O. Box 132, 627 Bayshore Dr., Ste. 200, Oshkosh, WI 54903; 25,000; www.naturistsociety.com
Naval Engineers, American Society of (1888), 1452 Duke St., Alexandria, VA 22314; 5,000; www.navalengineers.org
Naval Institute, U.S. (1873), 291 Wood Rd., Annapolis, MD 21402; 70,000; www.usni.org
Naval Reserve Assn. (1954), 1619 King St., Alexandria, VA 22314; 23,000; www.navy-reserve.org
Navigation, The Institute of (1945), 3975 University Dr., Ste. 390, Fairfax, VA 22030; 3,200; www.ion.org
Navy League of the United States (1902), 2300 Wilson Blvd., Arlington,VA 22201-3308; 74,000; www.navyleague.org
Navy Vets, Sampson WW2 (1987) Sampson Navy Museum, 6096 Rt. 96A, Romulus, NY 14541; 7,000
Negro College Fund, United (1944), 8260 Willow Oaks Corporate Drive, Fairfax, VA 22031; 39 institutions; www.uncf.org
Neurofibromatosis Foundation, Natl. (1978), 95 Pine St., 16th Fl., New York, NY 10005; 9,433; 30,000; www.nf.org
Newspaper Assn. of America (NAA) (1887), 1921 Gallows Rd., Ste. 600, Vienna, VA 22182-3900; 2,000+; www.naa.org
NGA, Inc. (1896), 820 Newton Rd., Walminster, PA 18974; www.nga-inc.org
Ninety-Nines (Intl. Organization of Women Pilots) (1929), 7100 Terminal Dr., Oklahoma City, OK 73159; 6,000; www.ninety-nines.org
Non-Commissioned Officers Assn. (1960), 10635 IH 35 North, San Antonio, TX 78233; 160,000; www.ncoausa.org
Northern Cross Society (1983), 214 N. 2100 Rd., Lecompton, KS 66050; 100+
NOT-SAFE: Nat'l Organization Taunting Safety and Fairness Everywhere (1984), P.O. Box 5743-WS, Montecito, CA 93150; 6,600+; www.notsafe.org
Notaries, American Society of (1965), P.O. Box 5707, Tallahassee, FL 32314; approx. 20,000; www.notaries.org
NSAC (Natl. Soc. of Accountants for Cooperatives) (1936), 6320 Augusta Dr., Ste. 800, Springfield, VA 22150; 2,000; www.nsacoop.org
Nuclear Society, American (1954), 555 N. Kensington Ave., La Grange Park, IL 60526; 11,000; www.ans.org
Nude Recreation Inc., American Assn. for (1931), 1703 N. Main Street, Suite E, Kissimmee, FL 34744; 50,000; www.aanr.com

Numismatic Assn., American (1891), 818 N. Cascade Ave., Colorado Springs, CO 80903; 30,000; www.money.org
Numismatic Society, The American (1858), Broadway at 155th St., New York, NY 10032; www.amnumsoc.org
Nursing, Natl. League for (1952), 61 Broadway, New York, NY 10006; 5,000; www.nln.org
Nutritional Sciences, American Society for (1928), 9650 Rockville Pike, Ste. 4500, Bethesda, MD 20814; 2,849; www.asns.org/asns

Ocean Conservancy (1972), 1725 DeSales St. NW, #600, Wash.,DC 20036; 200,000; www.oceanconservancy.org
Odd Fellows, Independent Order of (1819), 422 Trade St., Winston-Salem, NC 27101; 295,077; www.ioof.org
Old Crows, Assn. of (1964), 1000 N. Payne St., Alexandria, VA 22314; 16,485; www.crows.org
Ophthalmology, American Academy of (1979), P.O. Box 7424, San Francisco, CA 94120; 21,000; www.eyenet.org
Optimist Intl. (1919), 4494 Lindell Blvd., St. Louis, MO 63108; 155,000; www.optimist.org
Optometric Assn., American (1898), 243 N. Lindbergh Blvd., St. Louis, MO 63141; 32,000; www.aoanet.org
Organ Sharing, United Network for (1977), 1100 Boulders Parkway, Ste. 500, P.O. Box 13770, Richmond, VA 23225; 434; www.unos.org
Organists, American Guild of (1896), 475 Riverside Dr., Ste. 1260, New York, NY 10115; 23,200; www.agohq.org
Oriental Society, American (1842), Univ. of Michigan, Hatcher Graduate Library, 110D, Ann Arbor, MI 48109; 1,350; www.umich.edu/~aos
ORT Inc., American (Org. for Rehabilitation Through Training) (1922), 817 Broadway, 10th Fl., New York, NY 10003; 8,000; www.aort.org.
Ornithologists' Union, American (1883), c/o Division of Birds, MRC-116, Smithsonian Institution, Wash., DC 20560-0116; 4,200; www.aou.org
Osteopathic Assn., American (1897), 142 E. Ontario, Chicago, IL 60611; 28,974; www.aoa-net.org
Ostomy Assn., Inc., United (1962), 19772 MacArthur Blvd., Ste. 200, Irvine, CA 92612, 25,000; www.uoa.org
Outlaw and Lawman History, Inc., Natl. Assn. for (NOLA) (1974), 1917 Sutton Place Trail , Harker Heights, TX 76548-6043; approx. 450; www.outlawlawman.com
Overeaters Anonymous (1960) 6075 Zenith Court NE, Rio Rancho, NM 87124-4020; www.overeatersanonymous.org
Oxfam America (1970) 26 West St., Boston, MA 02111; 100,000; www.oxfamamerica.org

Paralyzed Veterans of America (1947), 801 18th St. NW, Wash., DC 20006; 18,000; www.pva.org
Parapsychology Institute of America (1972), P.O. Box 5442, Babylon, NY, 11707; 450
Parents Without Partners, Inc. (1958), 1650 S. Dixie Highway, Suite 510, Boca Raton, FL 33432; 35,000; www.parentswithoutpartners.org
Parkinson's Disease Foundation, Inc. (1957), William Black Medical Bldg., Columbia-Presbyterian Medical Center, 710 W. 168th St., New York, NY 10032; 95,000; www.pdf.org
Parliamentarians, Natl. Assn. of (1930), 213 S. Main St., Independence, MO 64050; 4,000; www.parliamentarians.org
Patton, George S. Jr. Society (1970), 3116 Thorn St., San Diego, CA 92104; 350; www.pattonhq.com/homehq.html
PBY Catalina International Association (1988), 1510 Kabel Dr., New Orleans, LA 70131; 750; www.pbycia.org
Peace Corps (1961), 111 20th St., NW, Wash., DC 20526; 8,500; www.peacecorps.gov
Pearl Harbor History Associates, Inc. (1985), P.O. Box 1007, Stratford, CT 06615; approx. 275; www.ibilio.org/phha
PEN American Center, Inc. (1922), 568 Broadway, Rm. 401, New York, NY 10012; 2,300; www.pen.org
Pen Friends, Intl. (1967), 758 Kapahulu Ave. #101, Honolulu, HI 96816; 300,000; www.pen-pals.net
Pension Plan, Committee for a Natl. (1979), P.O. Box 27851, Las Vegas, NV 89126; 340
Pen Women, Natl. League of American (1897), 1300 17th St. NW, Wash., DC 20036-1973; 4,100
People for the Ethical Treatment of Animals (PETA) (1980), 501 Front St., Norfolk, VA 23510; 600,000; www.peta-online.org
Performance Improvement, Intl. Society for (1962), 1400 Spring St., Ste. 260, Silver Spring, MD 20910; 6,100; www.ispi.org
Petroleum Institute, American (1919), 1220 L St. NW, Wash., DC 20005; 400 companies; www.api.org
Pharmaceutical Assn., American (1852), 2215 Constitution Ave. NW, Wash., DC 20037; 50,000; www.aphanet.org
Phi Beta Kappa Society (1776), 1785 Massachusetts Ave., N.W., 4th Fl., Wash., DC 20036; approx. 500,000; www.pbk.org
Phi Delta Kappa Intl., Inc. (1906), 408 N. Union, Bloomington, IN 47408; 95,223; www.pdkintl.org
Phi Kappa Phi (1897), P.O. Box 16000-Louisiana State University, Baton Rouge, LA 70893; 1,000,000+; www.phikappaphi.org
Phi Theta Kappa Int'l. Honor Society (1918), 1625 Eastover Drive, Jackson, MS 39211; 800,000; www.pk.org
Philatelic Society, American (1886), 100 Oakwood Ave., State College, PA 16803; 50,200; www.stamps.org
Philatelic Golf Society, Intl. (1987), P.O. Box 2183, Norfolk, VA 23501-2183; 250; www.ipgsonline.org
Philological Association, American (1869), 291 Logan Hall, Univ. of Penn., 249 S. 36th St., Philadelphia, PA, 19104-6304; 3,000; www.apaclassics.org
Philosophical Assn., American (1901), Univ. of Delaware, Newark, DE 19716; 10,800; www.udel.edu/apa
Photographers of America, Inc., Professional (1880) 3125 Skyway Circle N., Irving, TX 75038-3526; 14,000; www.ppa.org
Photographic Society of America, Inc. (1934), 3000 United Founders Blvd., Ste. 103, Oklahoma City, OK 73112; 6,200; www.psa-photo.org
Physical Therapy Assn., American (1921), 1111 N. Fairfax St., Alexandria, VA 22314; 63,000; www.apta.org
Physically Handicapped, Inc., Natl. Assn. of the (1958), Scarlet Oaks, 440 Lafayette Ave., #GA4, Cincinnati, OH 45220-1022; approx. 400; www.naph.net
Physics, American Inst. of (1931), One Physics Ellipse, College Park, MD 20740; 123,500; www.aip.org
Physiological Society, American (1887), 9650 Rockville Pike, Bethesda, MD 20814-3991; 11,000; www.the-aps.org
Phytopathological Society, American (1908), 3340 Pilot Knob Rd., St. Paul, MN 55121; 5,000; www.apsnet.org
Pilgrims Natl. Soc., Sons and Daughters of (1909), 3917 Heritage Dr., #104, Bloomington, MN 55437-2633; 2,000
Pilot Intl. & Pilot Intl. Foundation (1921), 244 College St., Macon, GA 31201; 14,557; www.pilotinternational.org
Planetary Society (1980), 65 N. Catalina Ave., Pasadena, CA 91106; approx. 100,000; www.planetary.org
Planned Parenthood Federation of America, Inc. (1916), 810 Seventh Avenue, New York, NY 10019; www.plannedparenthood.org
Plastic Modelers Society, Intl. (1964), P.O. Box 2475, North Canton, OH 44720; 4,750; www.ipmsusa.org
Plastics Engineers, Society of (1942), 14 Fairfield Dr., P.O. Box 403, Brookfield, CT 06804; 33,000; www.4spe.org
Plastics Industry, Inc., Society of the (1937), 1801 K Street, NW, Ste. 600K, Wash., DC 20006; 2,000+ companies; www.socplas.org
Platform Association, Intl. (1831), 101 N. Center St., Westminster, MD, 21157; 2,000; www.internationalplatform.com
Poetry Society of America (1910), 15 Gramercy Park, New York, NY 10003; approx. 3,000; www.poetrysociety.org
Poets, The Academy of American (1934), 588 Broadway, Ste. 1203, New York, NY 10012; 8,000; www.poets.org
Police Assn., Intl. (1950 in UK, 1961 in U.S.), 100 Chase Ave., Yonkers, NY 10703; 291,000+; www.ipa-usa.org
Polish Army Veterans Assn. of America, Inc. (1921), 119 E. 15th St., Ste. 1, New York, NY 10003; 3,000
Political Items Collectors, American (1945), P.O. Box 1149, Cibolo, TX 78108; 2,500; apic.ws
Political Science Assn., American (1903), 1527 New Hampshire Ave. NW, Wash., DC 20036; 16,200; www.apsanet.org
Political Science Assn., Southern (1928), PO Box 8101, Georgia Southern Univ., Statesboro, GA 30460; www2.gasou.edu/spsa
Political Science, Academy of (1880), 475 Riverside Drive, Ste. 1274, New York, NY 10115; 6,000; www.psqonline.org
Political & Social Science, American Academy of (1891), 3814 Walnut St., Univ. of Penn., Philadelphia, PA 19104; 5,000; www.1891.org
Polo Assn., U.S. (1890), 771 Corporate Dr., Ste. 505, Lexington, KY 40503; 3,545; www.uspolo.org
Population Assn. of America (1931), 8630 Fenton St., Ste. 722, Silver Spring, MD 20910; 2,900; www.popassoc.org
Portuguese-American Federation, Inc., (1974), P.O. Box 694, Bristol, RI 02809; 250; www.portuguese-american.net

IT'S A FACT: Founded in 1776, Phi Beta Kappa is the oldest American Greek letter society. Membership is based on high academic standing. Some famous members include George H. W. Bush, Bill Clinton, Condoleezza Rice, William H. Rehnquist, James Billington, Gloria Steinem, John Updike, Michael Crichton, Meg Greenfield, Hugh Downs, Jeff Bezos, Peyton Manning, Stephen Sondheim, Francis Ford Coppola, Kris Kristofferson, and Erika Harold (the 2003 Miss America winner).

Portuguese Continental Union of the U.S.A. (1925), 30 Cummings Park, Woburn, MA 01801; 5,488; members.aol.com/upceua

Postal Stationery Society, United (1945) P.O. Box 1792, Norfolk, VA 23501-1792; 1,100; www.upss.org

Postcard Dealers, Inc., International Federation of (1979), P.O. Box 1765, Manassas, VA 20108; 273; www.members.tripod.com/~IFPD

Postmasters of the U.S., Natl. League of (1887), 1023 N. Royal St., Alexandria, VA 22314; 25,000; www.postmasters.org

Postmasters of the U.S., Natl. Assn. of (1898), 8 Herbert St., Arlington, VA 22305; 43,000, www.napus.org

Powder Metallurgy Institute, American (formerly APMI International) (1959), 105 College Rd. E, Princeton, NJ 08540; approx. 2,700; www.mpif.org

Power Boat Assn., American (1903), 17640 E. Nine Mile Rd., Eastpointe, MI 48021; 6,000; www.apba.org

Printing Industries of America, Inc. (1887), 100 Daingerfield Rd., Alexandria, VA 22314; 14,000; www.gain.org

Procrastinators Club of America (1956), P.O. Box 712, Bryn Athyn, PA 19006; 14,100; www.geocities.com/PROCRASTINATORS_CLUB_OF_AMERICA

Professional Ball Players of America, Assn. of (1924), 1820 W. Orangewood Ave., Ste. 206, Orange, CA 92868; 9,918; www.apbpa.org

Protection of Old Fishes, Soc. for the (1967), NOAA HAZMAT, 7600 Sand Point Way, N.E., Seattle, WA 98115; 150.

Psoriasis Foundation, Natl. (1968), 6600 SW 92nd Ave., Ste. 300, Portland, OR 97223; 40,000; www.psoriasis.org

Psychiatric Assn., American (1844), 1400 K St. NW, Wash., DC 20005; 40,453; www.psych.org

Psychical Research, American Society for (1885), 5 W. 73rd St., New York, NY 10023; www.aspr.com

Psychoanalytic Assn., American (1911), 309 E. 49th St., New York, NY 10017; 3,500; apsa.org

Psychological Assn., American (1892), 750 1st St. NE, Wash., DC 20002; 159,000; www.apa.org

PTA, Natl. (1897), 330 N. Wabash Ave., Ste. 2100, Chicago, IL 60611; approx. 6.5 mil; www.pta.org

Public Administration, American Soc. for (1939), 1120 G St. NW, Wash., DC 20005; 11,000+; www.aspanet.org

Public Health Assn., American (1872), 800 I St. NW, Wash., DC 20001; www.apha.org

Public Relations Soc. of America, Inc. (1947), 33 Irving Pl., 3rd Fl., New York, NY 10003; 17,383; www.prsa.org

Publishers, Assn. of American (1970), 71 5th Ave., New York, NY 10003; 300 cos; www.publishers.org

Pulp and Paper Industries, Technical Assn. of the (TAPPI) (1915), 15 Technology Pkwy. S, Norcross, GA 30092; 34,000; www.tappi.org

Quill and Scroll Society (1926), School of Journalism, The University of Iowa, Iowa City, IA 52242; www.uiowa.edu/~quill.sc

Quota International, Inc. (1919), 1420 21st St. NW, Wash., DC 20036; 11,000+; www.quota.org

Rabbis, Central Conference of American (1889), 355 Lexington Ave., New York, NY 10017; 1,800; ccarnet.org

Racquetball Assn., U.S. (1968), 1685 W. Uintah, Colorado Springs, CO 80904; 20,000; www.usra.org

Radio Relay League, American (1914), 225 Main St., Newington, CT 06111; 163,582; www.arrl.org

Radio and Television Society Foundation, Intl. (1939), 420 Lexington Ave., Ste. 1601, New York, NY 10170; 1,787; www.irts.org

Railway Historical Society, Natl. (1936), P.O. Box 58547, Philadelphia, PA 19102; app. 15,000; www.nhrs.com

Railway Progress Institute (1908), 700 N. Fairfax St., #601, Alexandria, VA 22314-2098; 83 cos.; www.rpi.org

Range Management, Society for (1948), 445 Union Blvd., Ste. 230, Lakewood, CO 80228; 3,700; www.srm.org

Reading Assn., Intl. (1956), 800 Barksdale Rd., P.O. Box 8139, Newark, DE 19714; 90,000; www.reading.org

Real Estate Institute, Intl. (1978), 1224 N. Nokomis, Alexandria, MN 56302; 2,112; www.iami.org

Real Estate Appraisers, Natl. Assn. of (1962) 1224 N. Nokomis NE, Alexandria, MN 56308; 3,717; www.iami.org

Rebekah Assemblies, Intl. Assn. of (1922), 422 Trade St., Winston-Salem, NC 27101; 84,247

Recreation and Park Assn., Natl. (1965), 22377 Belmont Ridge Road, Ashburn, VA 20148; 23,425; www.activeparks.org

Recycling Coalition, Natl. (1979), 1325 G St., NW, Wash., DC, 20005; 3,500; www.nrc-recycle.org

Red Cross, American (1881), 430 17th St., NW, Wash., DC 20006; 1.3 mil volunteers; www.redcross.org

Reform Party of the U.S.A(1996), 3281 N. Meadow Mine Place, Tucson, AZ 85745; 500,000; www.reformparty.org

Refugee Committee, American (1978), 430 Oak St., Ste. 204, Minneapolis, MN 55403; www.archq.org

Rehabilitation Assn., Natl. (1927), 633 S. Washington St., Alexandria, VA 22314; approx. 11,000; www.nationalrehab.org

Religion, American Academy of (1964), 825 Houston Mill Rd., NE, Atlanta, GA 30329; 10,000; www.aarweb.org

Renaissance Society of America (1954), 365 5th. Ave., Rm. 5400, New York, NY 10016; 2,500; www.r-s-a.org

Republican National Committee (1856), 310 1st St. SE, Wash., DC 20003; www.rnc.org

Reserve Officers Assn. of the U.S. (1922), One Constitution Ave. NE, Wash., DC 20002; 95,000; www.roa.org

Restaurant Assn., Natl. (1919), 1200 17th St. NW, Wash., DC 20036; 33,000; www.restaurant.org

Retail Federation, Natl. (1908), 325 7th St. NW, Ste. 1100, Wash., DC 20004; 50,000; www.nrf.com

Retired Federal Employees, Natl. Assn. of (1921), 606 N. Washington St., Alexandria, VA 22314; 422,000; www.narfe.org

Retired Officers Assn. (1940), 201 N. Washington St., Alexandria, VA 22314; 391,000; www.troa.org

Retired Persons, American Assn. of (1958), 601 E St. NW, Wash., DC 20049; 32 mil.; www.aarp.org

Review Appraisers/Mortgage Underwriters, Natl. Assn. of (1970) 1224 N. Nokomis NE, Alexandria, MN 56308; 2,606; www.iami.org

Reye's Syndrome Foundation, Natl. (1974), 426 N. Lewis, Bryan, OH 43506-0829; 4,760; www.reyessyndrome.org

Richard III Society, Inc. (1961),P.O. Box 13786, New Orleans, LA 70185; 800; www.r3.org

Rifle Assn., Natl. (1871), 11250 Waples Mill Rd., Fairfax, VA 22030; approx 3 mil; www.nra.org

Road & Transportation Builders Assn., American (1902), The ARTBA Building, 1010 Massachusetts Ave. NW, Wash., DC 20001; 5,000+; www.artba.org

Roller Sports, U.S.A. (1937), 4730 South St., Lincoln, NE 68506; 30,000; www.usarollersports.net

Rose Society, American (1892), 8877 Jefferson Page Rd, Shreveport, LA 71119; 22,000; www.ars.org

Rotary Intl. (1905), 1560 Sherman Ave., Evanston, IL 60201; 1,203,726; www.rotary.org

Running and Fitness Assn., American (1968), 4405 East West Highway, Ste. 405, Bethesda, MD 20814; approx. 16,500; www.americanrunning.org

Ruritan Natl., Inc. (1928), P.O. Box 487, Dublin, VA 24084; 33,447; www.ruritan.org

Safety Council, Natl. (1913), 1121 Spring Lake Dr., Itasca, IL 60143; 16,000; www.nsc.org

Safety Engineers, American Soc. of (1911), 1800 E. Oakton St., Des Plaines, IL 60018; 32,000; www.asse.org

Salt Institute (1914), 700 N. Fairfax St., Ste. 600, Alexandria, VA, 22314; 7 U.S., 37 Int'l.; www.saltinstitute.org

Sand Castle Builders, Intl. Assn. of (1988), 172 N. Pershing Ave., Akron, OH 44313; 200

Save-the-Redwoods League (1918), 114 Sansome St., Ste. 1200, San Francisco, CA 94104; 50,000; www.savetheredwoods.org

School Administrators, American Assn. of (1865), 1801 N. Moore St., Arlington, VA 22209; 14,000+; www.aasa.org

School Boards Assn., Natl. (1940), 1680 Duke St., Alexandria, VA 22314; www.nsba.org

School Counselor Assn., American (1952), 801 N. Fairfax Street, Suite 310, Alexandria, VA 22314; 12,000; www.schoolcounselor.org

Science, American Assn. for the Advancement of (1848), 1200 New York Ave. NW, Wash., DC 20005; 138,000+; www.aaas.org

Science Fiction Society, World (1939), P.O. Box 426159, Kendall Square Station, Cambridge, MA 02142; 10,000; www.wsfs.org

Science Service Inc. (1921), 1719 N St. NW, Wash., DC 20036; www.sciserv.org

Sciences, Natl. Academy of (1863), 500 5th St. NW, Wash., DC 20001; 4,000+; www.nas.edu

Science Teachers Assn., Natl. (1944), 1840 Wilson Blvd., Arlington, VA 22201; 53,000; www.nsta.org

Science Writers, Natl. Assn. of (1934), P.O. Box 890, Hedgeville, WV 25427; 2,380; www.nasw.org

Scrabble® Assn., Natl. (1980), P.O. Box 700, 403 Front St., Greenport, NY 11946; 10,000+; www.scrabble-assoc.com

Screen Actors Guild (1933), 5757 Wilshire Blvd., Los Angeles, CA 90036; 90,000; www.sag.com

Screenprinting & Graphic Imaging Assn., Intl. (1948), 10015 Main St., Fairfax, VA 22031; 4,000 ; www.sgia.org

2nd Air Division Assn. of the 8th Air Force (1948), P.O. Box 484, Elkhorn, WI 53121; 6,500

Secondary School Principals, Natl. Assn. of (1916), 1904 Association Drive, Reston, VA 20191; 36,000; www.principals.org

Secular Humanism, Council for (1980), P.O. Box 664, Amherst, NY 14226; 24,000; www.secularhumanism.org

Securities Industry Assn. (1912), 120 Broadway, 35th Fl., New York, NY 10271; 620 firms; www.sia.com
Separation of Church & State, Americans United for (1947), 518 C St. NE, Wash., DC 20002; 70,000; www.au.org
Sertoma International (1912), 1912 E. Meyer Blvd., Kansas City, MO 64132; 24,992; www.sertoma.org
Sharkhunters Intl. (1983), P.O. Box 1539, Hernando, FL 34442; 6,600; www.sharkhunters.com
Shipbuilders Council of America (1920), 1455 F St., NW, Ste. 225, Wahington, DC 20005; 37 member cos; www.shipbuilders.org
Ships in Bottles Assn. of America (1983), P.O. Box 180550, Coronado, CA 92178; 250; www.shipsinbottles.org
Shrine of North America, The (1872), 2900 N. Rocky Point Dr., Tampa, FL 33607; approx 600,000+; shrinershq.org
Sierra Club (1892), 85 2nd St., 2nd Fl., San Francisco, CA 94105; 600,000+; www.sierraclub.org
Sigma Beta Delta (1994), Univ. of MO-St. Louis, 801 Natural Bridge Rd., 346 Woods Hall, St. Louis, MO 63121-0570; 20,000; www.sigmabetadelta.org
Skeet Shooting Assn., Natl. (1946), 5931 Roft Rd., San Antonio, TX 78253; 11,875; nssa-nsca.com
Small Business United, Natl. (1937), 1156 15th St. NW, Ste. 1100, Wash., DC 20005; 65,000+; www.nsbu.org
Social Work Education, Council on (1952), 1725 Duke St., Ste. 500, Alexandria, VA 22314; 2,501; www.cswe.org
Sociological Assn., American (1905), 1307 New York Avenue NW, Suite 700, Wash., DC 20005; 13,000; www.asanet.org
Softball Assn./USA Softball, Amateur (1933), 2801 Northeast 50th St., Oklahoma City, OK 73111; 240,000+ teams; www.softball.org
Software and Information Industry Assn. (formerly Information Industry Assn.) (1999), 1090 Vermont Ave. NW, Wash. DC 20005; 1,400; www.siia.net
Soil Science Society of America (1936), 677 S. Segoe Rd., Madison, WI 53711; 5,714; www.soils.org
Soldiers', Sailors', Marines' and Airmen's Club (1919), 283 Lexington Avenue, New York, NY 10016; 190; www.ssmaclub.org
Songwriters Guild of America (1931), 1500 Harbor Blvd., Weehawken, NJ 07087; 5,000+; www.songwriters.org
Sons of the American Colonists, Natl. Society of (1970) 5611 N. 15th St., Arlington, VA 22205-0482; 250
Sons of the American Legion (1932), Box 1055, Indianapolis, IN 46206; 212,000; www.sal.legion.org
Sons of the American Revolution, Natl. Society of (1889), 1000 S. Fourth St., Louisville, KY 40203; 26,000; www.sar.org
Sons of Confederate Veterans (1896), 740 Mooresville Pike, Columbia, TN 3840; 31,500; www.scv.org
Sons of the Desert Laurel & Hardy Appreciation Society (1965), P.O. Box 8341, Universal City, CA 91608; 15,000; www.wayoutwest.org.
Sons of Italy in America, Order (1905), 219 E St. NE, Wash., DC 20002; 500,000; www.osia.org
Sons of Norway (1895), 1455 W. Lake St., Minneapolis, MN 55408; 65,000; www.sofn.com
Soroptimist Intl. of the Americas (1921), Two Penn Center Plaza, Ste. 1000, Philadelphia, PA 19102; 47,000; www.soroptimist.org
Southern Christian Leadership Conference (1957), 51-A Edgewood Ave. NE, Atlanta, GA 30312; 1 mil.; www.sclcnational.org
Space Society, Natl. (1974), 600 Pennsylvania Ave SE, Ste. 201, Wash., DC 20003; 22,000; www.nss.org
Speech-Language-Hearing Assn., American (1925), 10801 Rockville Pike, Rockville, MD 20852; 99,000+; www.asha.org
Speleological Society, Natl. (1941), 2813 Cave Ave., Huntsville, AL 35810; 12,000; www.caves.org
Sports Car Club of America (1944), 9033 E. Easter Pl., Englewood, CO 80112; 50,000+; www.scca.org
Sportscasters Assn., The American (1980), 225 Broadway, Ste. 2030, New York, NY 10007; 500+; www.americansportscasters.com
State & Local History, American Assn. for (1944), 1717 Church St., Nashville, TN 37203; 5,751; www.aaslh.org
State Governments, Council of (1933), 2760 Research Park Drive, P.O. Box 11910, Lexington, KY 40517; 50 states, 4 territories; www.csg.org
Statistical Assn., American (1839), 1429 Duke St., Alexandria, VA 22314; 18,000; www.amstat.org
Steamship Historical Society of America, Inc. (1935), 300 Ray Dr., Ste. 4, Providence, RI 02906; 3,500; www.sshsa.org
Stock Exchange, American (1911), 86 Trinity Pl., New York, NY 10006; 864; www.amex.com
Stock Exchange, New York (1792), 11 Wall St., New York, NY 10005; www.nyse.com
Stock Exchange, Philadelphia (1790), 1900 Market St., Philadelphia, PA 19103; 504; www.phlx.com
Student Councils, Natl. Society of (1931) 1904 Association Dr., Reston, VA 20191; approx. 1.5 mil; dsa.principals.org
Stuttering Project, Natl. (1977), 4071 E. LaPalma Ave., Ste. A, Anaheim Hills, CA 92807; 2,800; www.nsastutter.org
Sudden Infant Death Syndrome Alliance (1987), 1314 Bedford Avenue, Suite 210, Baltimore, MD 21208; www.sidsalliance.org
Supreme Council, 33°, Scottish Rite of Freemasonry, Southern Jurisdiction (1801), 1733 16th St. NW, Wash., DC 20009-3103; 413,793; www.srmason-sj.org
Surgeons, American College of (1913), 633 N. Saint Clair St., Chicago, IL 60611; 60,000; www.facs.org
Symphony Orchestra League, American (1942), 910 17th St. NW, Wash., DC 20006; 850; www.symphony.org

Table Tennis Assn., U.S. (1933), 711 North Tejon, Colorado Springs, CO 80903; 8,000; www.usatt.org
Tailhook Assn. (1956), 9696 Businesspark Ave., San Diego, CA 92131; 11,800; www.tailhook.org
Tall Buildings and Urban Habitat, Council on (1969), Lehigh Univ., 117 ATLSS Dr., Bethlehem, PA 18015; 500; www.ctbuh.org
Tau Beta Pi Association (1885), 508 Daugherty, Engineering Bldg., Univ of Tenn., Knoxville, TN 37901-2697; 400,000; www.tbp.org
Tax Administrators, Federation of (1932), 444 N. Capitol St. NW, Ste. 348, Wash., DC 20001; www.taxadmin.org
Tax Foundation (1937), 1250 H St. NW, Ste. 750, Wash., DC 20005; 50 U.S. states; www.taxfoundation.org
Taxpayers Union, Natl. (1969), 108 N. Alfred St., Alexandria, VA 22314; 335,000; www.ntu.org
Tea Assn. of the U.S.A., Inc. (1899), 420 Lexington Ave., New York, NY 10170; 150 corps; www.teausa.com
Teachers of English, Natl. Council of (1911), 1111 W. Kenyon Rd., Urbana, IL 61801; 77,000; www.ncte.org
Teachers of English to Speakers of Other Languages (1966), 700 Washington St., Ste. 200, Alexandria, VA 22314; 16,000; www.tesol.edu
Teachers of French, American Assn. of (1927), Southern Illinois University, Mailcode 4510, Carbondale, IL 62901-4510; 9,500; www.frenchteachers.org
Teachers of German, Inc., American Assn. of (AATG) (1926), 112 Haddontowne Ct. #104, Cherry Hill, NJ 08034-3668; 6,300; www.aatg.org
Teachers of Mathematics, Natl. Council of (1920), 1906 Association Drive, Reston, VA 20191-9988; 100,000; www.nctm.org
Teachers of Singing, Natl. Assn. of (1944), 6406 Merrill Road, Ste. B, Jacksonville, FL 32277; 5,443; www.nats.org
Teachers of Spanish & Portuguese, American Assn. of (1917), 423 Exton Commons, Exton, PA, 19341-2451; 11,522; www.aatsp.org
Telecommunications Pioneer Assn., Independent (1920), 1401 H St. NW, Ste. 600, Wash., DC 20005; 26,000+; www.telecom-pioneers.com
Television Arts & Sciences, Natl. Academy of (1955), 111 W. 57th St., Ste. 1020, New York, NY 10019; 11,000; www.emmyonline.org
Testing & Materials, American Society for (1898), 100 Barr Harbor Dr., P.O. Box C700, West Conshohocken, PA 19428; 32,000; www.astm.org
Theodore Roosevelt Assn. (1920), Nassau Hall, 1864 Muttontown Rd., Muttontown, NY 11791; 2,200; www.theodoreroosevelt.org
Theological Library Assn., American (1946), 250 S. Wacker Dr., Ste 1600, Chicago, IL 60606; 590; www.atla.com
Theological Schools in the U.S. and Canada, The Assn. of (1918), 10 Summit Park Dr., Pittsburgh, PA 15275-1103; 243; www.ats.edu
Theological Seminary of California, Intl. (1984) 14617 Victory Blvd., Van Nuys, CA 94411; 2,000.
Theosophical Society in America (1875), 1926 N. Main St., Wheaton, IL 60187; 5,000; www.theosophical.org
Therapy Dogs Intl., Inc (1976), 88 Bartley Rd., Flanders, NJ 07836; approx. 8,500; www.tdi-dog.org
Thoreau Society (1941), 44 Baker Farm, Lincoln, MA 01773; 1,700+; www.walden.org
Thoroughbred Racing Assns. (1942), 420 Fair Hill Dr., Ste. 1, Elkton, MD 21921; 49 racing assoc.; www.tra-online.com
318th Service Group Assn. 9th AF (1991), 2114 West 29th St., Erie, PA 16508-1066; 311
Tin Can Sailors (1976), P.O. Box 100, Somerset, MA 02726; 23,000; www.destroyers.org
Titanic Historical Society, Inc. & Museum (1963), 208 Main St., P.O. Box 51053, Indian Orchard, MA 01151-0053; 3,785; www.titanichistoricalsociety.org
Toastmasters Intl. (1924), P.O. Box 9052, Mission Viejo, CA 92690; 180,000+; www.toastmasters.org
Topical Assn., American (1949), 301 Embank St., Albuquerque, NM 87123-0820; 6,000; home.prcn.org/~pauld/ata
Totally Useless Skills, Institute of (1987), P.O. Box 181, Temple, NH 03084; 387; www.jlc.net/~useless
Toy Industry Assn., Inc. (1916), 1115 Broadway, Suite 400, New York, NY 10010; 300+ cos; www.toy-tma.com

Translators Assn., American (1959), 225 Reinekers Lane, Ste. 590, Alexandria, VA 22314; 8,500; www.atanet.org
Transportation Alternatives (1973), 115 W. 30th St., #1207, New York, NY 10001; 5,000; www.transalt.org
Transportation Assn., American Public (1882), 1666 K Street NW Suite 1100, Wash., DC 20006; 1,400 organizations; www.apta.com
Transportation Engineers, Inst. of (1930), 1099 14th St. NW, Suite 300 West, Wash., DC 20005-3438; 15,000; www.ite.org
Trapshooting Assn. of America, Amateur (1923), 601 W. National Road, Vandalia, OH 45377; 54,000; www.shootata.com
Travel Agents, American Soc. of (1931), 1101 King St., Ste. 200, Alexandria, VA 22314; 26,000; www.astanet. com
Travelers Protective Assn. of America (1890), 3755 Lindell Blvd., St. Louis, MO 63108; 155,000; www.tpapostl.org
Trilateral Commission (1973), 1156 15th St., NW, Wash., DC 20005; 365; www.trilateral.org
Truck Historical Soc., American (1971), P.O. Box 901611, Kansas City, MO 64190; 21,950; www.aths.org
Trucking Assns., American (1933), 2200 Mill Rd., Alexandria, VA 22314; 4,000 cos.; www.truckline.com
Tuberous Sclerosis Alliance (1974), 801 Roeder Rd., Ste. 750, Silver Spring, MD 20910; 9,000+; www.tsalliance.org

UFOs, Natl. Investigations Committee on (1967) P.O. Box 5, Van Nuys, CA 91411; 1,250; www.tje.net/para/organizations/nicufo.htm
Underwriters, Natl. Assn. of Life (1890), 1922 F St. NW, Wash., DC 20006; 143,000.
Underwriters (CPCU), Soc. of Chartered Property and Casualty (1944), 720 Providence Rd., P.O. Box 3009, Malvern, PA 19355; 28,500; www.cpcusociety.org
UNICEF, U.S. Fund for (1947), 333 E. 38th St., New York, NY 10016; www.unicefusa.org
Uniformed Services, Natl. Assn. for (1968), 5535 Hempstead Way, Springfield, VA 22151; 160,000+; www.naus.org
United Nations Assn. of the U.S.A. (1943), 801 2nd Ave., New York, NY 10017; 23,000; www.unausa.org
United Order True Sisters, Inc. (1846), 100 State St., Ste. 1020, Albany, NY 12207; approx. 2,000; uots.org
United Press Intl. (1907), 1510 H St. NW, Wash., DC 20005; www.upi.com
United Service Organizations (USO) (1941), Washington Navy Yard, 1008 Eberle Place SE, Ste. 301, Wash., DC 20374; 12,000+; www.uso.org
United Way of America (1918), 701 N. Fairfax St., Alexandria, VA 22314; 1,353; national.unitedway.org
Universities, Assn. of American (1900), 1200 New York Ave., NW, Ste. 550, Wash., DC 20005; 61 institutions; www.aau.edu
University Continuing Education Assn. (1915), One Dupont Circle NW, Ste. 615, Wash., DC 20036; 441 institutions; www.ucea.edu
University Women, American Assn. of (1881), 1111 16th St. NW, Wash., DC 20036; 150,000; www.aauw.org
Urban League, Natl. (1910), 120 Wall St., New York, NY 10005; 50,000; www.nul.org
USENIX Association (1975), 2560 Ninth Street, Ste. 215, Berkeley, CA 94710; 28,000; www.usenix.org
U.S. Term Limits (1992), 10 G St.; Ste. 410, Wash., DC 20002; www.termlimits.org
USO World Headquarters (1941), 1008 Eberle Place SE, Ste. 301, Wash., DC 20374-5096; www.uso.org
USS *Forrestal* CVA/CV/AVT-59 Assn., Inc. (1990), 300 Cassady Ave., Virginia Beach, VA 23452; 2,170; www.uss-forrestal.com
USS *Idaho* Assn. (1957), P.O. Box 711247, San Diego, CA 92171; 428
USS *Los Angeles CA-135* (1978) 5933 Holgate Ave., San Jose, CA 95123; 600; www.uss-la-ca135.org
USS *North Carolina BB-55* Battleship Association (1962), P.O. Box 480, Wilmington, NC 28402; 791
Utility Commissioners, Natl. Assn. of Regulatory (1898), 1101 Vermont Ave., NW, Ste. 200, Wash., DC 20005; 425; www.naruc.org

Vampire Research Center (1971), P.O. Box 5442, Babylon, NY 11707; 600
Ventriloquists, North American Assn. of (1944), P.O. Box 420, Littleton, CO 80160; 1,450
Veterans of Foreign Wars of the U.S. (1899), 406 W. 34th St., Kansas City, MO 64111; 1.8 mil+.; www.vfw.org
Veterans of Foreign Wars of the U.S., Ladies Auxiliary to the (1914), 406 W. 34th St., Kansas City, MO 64111; 713,038; www.ladiesauxvfw.com
Veterans of the Vietnam War, Inc. (1980), 805 S. Township Blvd., Pittston, PA 18640-3327; 15,000; www.vvnw.org
Veterinary Medical Assn., American (1863), 1931 N. Meacham Rd., Ste. 100, Schaumburg, IL 60173; 64,000; www.avma.org
Victorian Society in America (1966), 219 S. Sixth St., Philadelphia, PA 19106; 1,600; www.victoriansociety.org
Volleyball, USA (1928), 715 S. Circle Dr., Colorado Springs, CO 80910; 160,000; www.usavolleyball.org
Volunteers of America (1896), 1660 Duke St., Alexandria, VA 22314-3421; 11,000 staff; www.voa.org

War Mothers, American (1917), 5415 Connecticut Ave., NW, Ste. L-30, Wash., DC 20015; under 800
Watch & Clock Collectors, Inc., Natl. Assn. of (NAWCC) (1943), 514 Poplar St., Columbia, PA 17512; 30,000; www.nawcc.org
Watercolor Society, American (1866), 47 5th Ave., New York, NY 10003; 500+; www.watercolor-online.com/aws
Water Environment Federation (1928), 601 Wythe St., Alexandria, VA 22314; 40,000; www.wef.org
Water Works Assn., American (1881), 6666 W. Quincy Ave., Denver, CO 80235; 55,000; www.awwa.org
Welding Society, American (1919), 550 NW LeJeune Rd., Miami, FL 33126; 50,400; www.aws.org
Wheelchair Sports, USA (1957), 3595 E. Fountain Blvd., Ste. L-1, Colorado Springs, CO 80910; 4,000; www.wsusa.org
Wildlife Federation, Natl. (1936),11100 Wildlife Center Dr., Reston, VA, 20190; 4 mil.; www.nwf.org
Wildlife Management Institute (1911), 1101 14th St. NW, Ste. 801, Wash., DC 20005; 250; www.wildlifemanagementinstitute.org
Wireless Pioneers Inc., The Society of (1967), P.O. Box 86, Geyserville, CA 95441; 1,500; www.sowp.org
Wizard of Oz Club, Intl. (1957), 1407 A St., Ste. D, Antioch, CA 94509; app.1,300; www.ozclub.org
Women, Natl. Organization for (NOW) (1966), 733 15th St. NW, 2nd Fl., Wash., DC 20005; 500,000; www.now.org
Women and Families, Natl. Partnership for (1971), 1875 Connecticut Ave. NW, Ste. 650, Wash., DC 20009; 2,000; www.nationalpartnership.org
Women Artists, Inc., Natl. Assn. of (1889), 41 Union Sq. W, #906, New York, NY 10003; 800; www.nawanet.org
Women in Communications, The Association for (1909 as Theta Sigma Phi), 780 Ritchie Hwy., Ste. 5-28, Severna Park, MD 21146; 7,500; www.womcom.org
Women in Radio and Television Inc., Amer. (1951), 1595 Spring Hill Rd., Vienna, VA 22182; www.awrt.org
Women Engineers, Society of (1950), 230 E. Ohio St., Ste. 400, Chicago, IL 60611; 16,500; www.swe.org
Women Voters of the U.S., League of (1920), 1730 M St. NW, #1000, Wash., DC 20036; 130,000; www.lwv.org
Women's Army Corps Veterans Assn. (1946), P.O. Box 5577, Ft. McClellan, AL 36205; 3,200; www.armywomen.org
Women's Christian Temperance Union, Natl. (1874), 1730 Chicago Ave., Evanston, IL 60201-4585; www.wctu.org
Women's Clubs, General Federation of (1890), 1734 N St. NW, Wash., DC, 20036; 300,000 U.S.; www.gfwc.org
Woodmen of America, Modern (1883), 1701 1st Ave., Rock Island, IL 61204; 750,000; www.modern-woodmen.org
Workmen's Circle (1900), 45 E. 33rd St., New York, NY 10016; 35,000; www.circle.org
World Council of Churches, U.S. Office (1948), 475 Riverside Drive, Rm. 915, New York, NY 10115; 330+ denominations.
World Federalist Assn. (1947), 418 7th St. SE, Wash., DC 20003; 11,000; www.wfa.org
World Future Society (1966), 7910 Woodmont Ave., Ste. 450, Bethesda, MD 20814; 30,000; www.wfs.org
World Learning (1932), Kipling Rd., P.O. Box 676, Brattleboro, VT 05302-0676; 100,000; www.worldlearning.org
World Wildlife Fund (1961), 1250 24th St. NW, P.O. Box 97180, Wash., DC 20037; 1 mil+; www.worldwildlife.org
World's Fair Collectors Soc., Inc. (1968), P.O. Box 20806, Sarasota, FL 34216-3806; 400; members.aol.com/bbqprod/wfcs.html
Writers Guild of America, West (1933), 7000 W. Third St., Los Angeles, CA 90048; 10,500; www.wga.org

Yachting Assn., Southern California (1921), 5855 Naples Plaza, Ste. 211, Long Beach, CA 90803; 90 clubs & orgs., 21,500 families; www.scya.org
YMCA (Young Men's Christian Assns.) of the U.S.A. (1851) 101 N. Wacker Dr., Chicago, IL 60606; 17.5 mil.; www.ymca.net
YWCA (Young Women's Christian Assn.) of the U.S.A. (1907), Empire State Bldg., 350 Fifth Ave., Ste. 301, New York, NY 10118; approx. 2 mil; www.ywca.org

Zero Population Growth (1968), 1400 16th St. NW, Ste. 320, Wash., DC 20036; 72,000+; www.populationconnection.org
Zionist Organization of America (1897), 4 E. 34th St., New York, NY 10016; 50,000+; www.zoa.org
Zoo and Aquarium Assn., American (1924), 8403 Colesville Road, Suite 710, Silver Spring, MD 20910; 205 zoos & aquariums; www.aza.org

SOCIAL SECURITY

Social Security Programs

Source: Social Security Administration; World Almanac research; data as of Sept. 2002.

Old-Age, Survivors, and Disability Insurance; Medicare; Supplemental Security Income

Social Security Benefits

Social Security benefits are based on a worker's primary insurance amount (PIA), which is related by law to the average indexed monthly earnings (AIME) on which Social Security contributions have been paid. The full PIA is payable to a retired worker who becomes entitled to benefits at age 65 and to an entitled disabled worker at any age. Spouses and children of retired or disabled workers and survivors of deceased workers receive set proportions of the PIA subject to a family maximum amount. The PIA is calculated by applying varying percentages to succeeding parts of the AIME. The formula is adjusted annually to reflect changes in average annual wages.

Automatic increases in Social Security benefits are initiated for December of each year, assuming the Consumer Price Index (CPI) for the 3rd calendar quarter of the year increased relative to the base quarter, which is either the 3rd calendar quarter of the preceding year or the quarter in which an increase legislated by Congress became effective. The size of the benefit increase is determined by the percentage rise of the CPI between the quarters measured.

The average monthly benefit payable to all retired workers amounted to $874 in Dec. 2001. The average benefit for disabled workers in that month amounted to $814.

Minimum and maximum monthly retired-worker benefits payable to individuals who retired at age 65[1]

	Minimum benefit[2]		Maximum benefit[2]			
			Payable at retirement		Payable effective Dec. 2001	
Year attaining age 65	Paid at retirement	Payable as of Dec. 2001	Men	Women[3]	Men	Women[3]
1970	$64.00	$320.50	$189.80	$196.40	$968.90	$1,003.40
1980	133.90	326.50	572.00	—	1,397.80	—
1990	(4)	(4)	975.00	—	1,395.30	—
1993	(4)	(4)	1,128.80	—	1,414.50	—
1994	(4)	(4)	1,147.50	—	1,401.50	—
1995	(4)	(4)	1,199.10	—	1,424.70	—
1996	(4)	(4)	1,248.90	—	1,493.30	—
1997	(4)	(4)	1,326.60	—	1,422.20	—
1998	(4)	(4)	1,342.80	—	1,480.40	—
1999	(4)	(4)	1,373.10	—	1,494.40	—
2000	(4)	(4)	1,434.80	—	1,526.30	—
2001	(4)	(4)	1,536.70	—	1,576.60	—

(1) Assumes retirement at beginning of year. (2) The final benefit amount payable is rounded to next lower $1 (if not already a multiple of $1). (3) Benefits for women are the same as for men except where shown. (4) Minimum eliminated for workers who reached age 62 after 1981.

Amount of Work Required

To qualify for benefits, the worker generally must have worked a certain length of time in covered employment. Just how long depends on when the worker reaches age 62 or, if earlier, when he or she dies or becomes disabled.

A person is fully insured who has 1 quarter of coverage for every year after 1950 (or year age 21 is reached, if later) up to but not including the year the worker reaches 62, dies, or becomes disabled. In 2002, a person earns 1 quarter of coverage for each $870 of annual earnings in covered employment, up to 4 quarters per year.

The law permits special monthly payments under the Social Security program to certain very old persons who are not eligible for regular benefits since they had little or no opportunity to earn work credits during their working lifetime (so-called special age-72 beneficiaries).

To receive disability benefits, the worker, in addition to being fully insured, must generally have credit for 20 quarters of coverage out of the 40 calendar quarters before he or she became disabled. A disabled blind worker need meet only the fully insured requirement. Persons disabled before age 31 can qualify with a briefer period of coverage. Certain survivor benefits are payable if the deceased worker had 6 quarters of coverage in the 13 quarters preceding death.

Work credit for fully insured status for benefits

Born after 1929; die, become disabled, or reach age 62 in	Years needed	Born after 1929; die, become disabled, or reach age 62 in	Years needed
1983	8	1987	9
1984	8½	1988	9¼
1985	8½	1989	9½
1986	8¾	1990	9¾
		1991 and after	10

Contribution and benefit base

Calendar year	OASDI[1]	HI[2]
1990	$51,300	$51,300
1992	55,500	130,200
1993	57,600	135,000
1994	60,600	no limit
1995	61,200	no limit
1996	62,700	no limit
1997	65,400	no limit
1998	68,400	no limit
1999	72,600	no limit
2000	76,200	no limit
2001	80,400	no limit
2002	84,900	no limit
2003	89,100 (est.)	no limit

(1) Old-Age, Survivors, and Disability Insurance. (2) Hospital Insurance.

Tax-rate schedule

(percentage of covered earnings)

Year	Total	OASDI	HI
	(for employees and employers, each)		
1979-80	6.13	5.08	1.05
1981	6.65	5.35	1.30
1982-83	6.70	5.40	1.30
1984	7.00	5.70	1.30
1985	7.05	5.70	1.35
1986-87	7.15	5.70	1.45
1988-89	7.51	6.06	1.45
1990 and after	7.65	6.20	1.45
	For self-employed		
1979-80	8.10	7.05	1.05
1981	9.30	8.00	1.30
1982-83	9.35	8.05	1.30
1984	14.00	11.40	2.60
1985	14.10	11.40	2.70
1986-87	14.30	11.40	2.90
1988-89	15.02	12.12	2.90
1990 and after	15.30	12.40	2.90

What Aged Workers Receive

When a person has enough work in covered employment and reaches retirement age (currently age 65 for full benefit, age 62 for reduced benefit), he or she may retire and receive monthly old-age benefits. The age when unreduced benefits become payable will increase gradually from 65 to 67 over a 21-year period beginning with workers age 62 in the year 2000 (reduced benefits will still be available as early as age 62, but with a larger reduction at that age).

Beginning with year 2000, the retirement earnings test has been eliminated beginning with the month in which the beneficiary reaches full-benefit retirement age (FRA). A person at and above FRA will not have Social Security benefits reduced because of earnings. In the calendar year in which a beneficiary reaches FRA, benefits are reduced $1 for every $3 of earnings above the limit allowed by law ($25,000 in 2001, $30,000 in 2002), but this reduction is only to months prior to attainment of FRA. For years before the year when the beneficiary attains FRA, the reduction in benefits is $1 for every $2 of earnings over the annual exempt amount $11,280 for year 2002).

For workers who reached age 65 between 1982 and 1989, Social Security benefits are raised by 3% for each year for which the worker between ages 65 and 70 (72 before 1984) failed to receive benefits, whether because of earnings from work or because the worker had not applied for benefits. The delayed retirement credit is 1% per year for workers who reached age 65 before 1982. The delayed retirement credit will gradually rise to 8% per year by 2008. The rate for workers who reached age 65 in 1998-99 is 5.5%; 2000-2001 will be 6.0%; 2002-2003, 6.5%; 2004-2005, 7.0%; 2006-2007, 7.5%

For workers retiring before age 65, benefits are permanently reduced 5/9 of 1% for each month before FRA, up to 36 months. If the number of months exceeds 36, then the benefit is further reduced 5/12 of 1% per month. For example, when FRA reaches 67, for workers who retire at exactly age 62, there are a total of 60 months of reduction. The reduction for the first 36 months is 5/9 of 36%, or 20%. The reduction for the remaining 24 months is 5/12 of 24%, or 10%. Thus, when the FRA reaches 67, the amount of reduction at age 62 will be 30%. The nearer to age 65 the worker is when he or she begins collecting a benefit, the larger the benefit will be. The nearer to the FRA the worker is when he or she begins collecting a benefit, the larger the benefit will be.

Benefits for Worker's Spouse

The spouse of a worker who is getting Social Security retirement or disability payments may become entitled to an insurance benefit of one-half of the worker's PIA, when he or she reaches 65. Reduced spouse's benefits are available at age 62 and are permanently reduced 25/36 of 1% for each month before FRA, up to 36 months. If the number of months exceeds 36, then the benefit is further reduced 5/12 of 1% per month. Benefits are also payable to the aged divorced spouse of an insured worker if he or she was married to the worker for at least 10 years.

Benefits for Children of Workers

If a retired or disabled worker has a child under age 18, the child will normally get a benefit equal to half of the worker's unreduced benefit. So will the worker's spouse, even if under age 62, if he or she is caring for an entitled child of the worker who is under 16 or became disabled before age 22. However, total benefits paid on a worker's earnings record are subject to a maximum; if the total that would be paid to a family exceeds this, the dependents' benefits are adjusted downward. (Total monthly benefits paid to the family of a worker who retired in Jan. 2002 at age 65 and always had the maximum earnings creditable under Social Security cannot exceed $2,906.10.)

When entitled children reach age 18, their benefits generally stop, but a child disabled before age 22 may get a benefit as long as the disability meets the definition in the law. Benefits will be paid until age 19 to a child attending elementary or secondary school full-time.

Benefits may also be paid to a grandchild or step-grandchild of a worker or of his or her spouse, in special circumstances.

OASDI	May 2002	May 2001	May 2000	May 1999
Monthly beneficiaries, total (in thousands)[1]	**46,190**	**45,683**	**45,132**	**44,353**
Aged 65 and over, total	32,953	32,762	32,434	31,880
Retired workers	26,352	26,055	25,644	25,050
Survivors and dependents	6,601	6,707	6,790	6,830
Under age 65, total	13,236	12,921	12,697	12,473
Retired workers	2,660	2,626	2,564	2,505
Disabled workers	5,337	5,119	4,944	4,769
Survivors and dependents	5,198	5,176	5,189	5,199
Total monthly benefits (in millions)	**$36,885**	**$35,170**	**$33,212**	**$31,449**

(1) Totals may not add because of rounding or incomplete enumeration.

What Disabled Workers Receive

A worker who becomes so disabled as to be unable to work may be eligible for a monthly disability benefit. Benefits continue until it is determined that the individual is no longer disabled. When a disabled-worker beneficiary reaches age 65, the disability benefit becomes a retired-worker benefit.

Benefits generally like those for dependents of retired-worker beneficiaries may be paid to dependents of disabled beneficiaries. However, the maximum family benefit in disability cases is generally lower than in retirement cases.

Survivor Benefits

If an insured worker should die, one or more types of benefits may be payable to survivors, again subject to a maximum family benefit as described above.

1. If claiming benefits at age 65, the surviving spouse will receive a benefit equal to 100% of the deceased worker's PIA. Benefits claimed before FRA are reduced for age with a maximum reduction of 28.5 percent at age 60. However, for those whose spouses claimed their benefits before age 65, these are limited to the reduced amount the worker would be getting if alive, but not less than 82% of the worker's PIA. Remarriage after the worker's death ends the surviving spouse's benefit rights. However, if the widow(er) marries and the marriage is ended, he or she regains benefit rights. (A marriage after age 60, age 50 if disabled, is deemed not to have occurred for benefit purposes.) Survivor benefits may also be paid to a divorced spouse if the marriage lasted for at least 10 years.

Disabled widows and widowers may under certain circumstances qualify for benefits after attaining age 50 at the rate of 71.5% of the deceased worker's PIA. The widow or widower must have become totally disabled before or within 7 years after the spouse's death or the last month in which he or she received mother's or father's insurance benefits.

2. There is a benefit for each child until the child reaches age 18. The monthly benefit for each child of a deceased worker is ¾ of the amount the worker would have received if he or she had lived and drawn full retirement benefits. A child with a disability that began before age 22 may also receive benefits. Also, a child may receive benefits until reaching age 19 if he or she is in full-time attendance at an elementary or secondary school.

3. There is a mother's or father's benefit for the widow(er) if children of the worker under age 16 are in his or her care. The benefit is 75% of the PIA, and it continues until the youngest child reaches age 16, at which time payments stop even if the child's benefit continues. However, if the widow(er) has a disabled child beneficiary age 16 or over in care, benefits may continue.

4. Dependent parents may be eligible for benefits if they have been receiving at least half their support from the worker before his or her death, have reached age 62, and (except in certain circumstances) have not remarried since the worker's death. Each parent gets 75% of the worker's PIA; if only one parent survives, the benefit is 82%.

5. A lump sum cash payment of $255 is made when there is a spouse who was living with the worker or a spouse or child who is eligible for immediate monthly survivor benefits.

Self-Employed Workers

A self-employed person who has net earnings of $400 or more in a year must report such earnings for Social Security tax and credit purposes. The person reports net returns from the business. Income from real estate, savings, dividends, loans, pensions, or insurance policies are not included unless it is part of the business.

A self-employed person receives 1 quarter of coverage for each $870 (for 2002), up to a maximum of 4 quarters.

The nonfarm self-employed have the option of reporting their earnings as $^2/_3$ of their gross income from self-employment, but not more than $1,600 a year and not less than their actual net earnings. This option can be used only if actual net earnings from self-employment income are less than $1,600, and may be used only 5 times. Also, the self-employed person must have actual net earnings of $400 or more in 2 of the 3 taxable years immediately preceding the year in which he or she uses the option.

When a person has both taxable wages and earnings from self-employment, wages are credited for Social Security purposes first; only as much self-employment income as brings total earnings up to the current taxable maximum becomes subject to the self-employment tax.

Farm Owners and Workers

Self-employed farmers whose gross annual earnings from farming are $2,400 or less may report 2/3 of their gross earnings instead of net earnings for Social Security purposes. Farmers whose gross income is over $2,400 and whose net earnings are less than $1,600 can report $1,600. Cash or crop shares received from a tenant or share farmer count if the owner participated materially in production or management. The self-employed farmer pays contributions at the same rate as other self-employed persons.

Agricultural employees. A worker's earnings from farm work count toward benefits (1) if the employer pays the worker $150 or more in cash during the year; or (2) if the employer spends $2,500 or more in the year for agricultural labor. Under these rules a person gets credit for 1 calendar quarter for each $870 in cash pay in 2002 up to 4 quarters.

Foreign farm workers admitted to the U.S. on a temporary basis are not covered.

Household Workers

Anyone 18 or older employed as maid, cook, laundry worker, nurse, babysitter, chauffeur, gardener, or other worker in the house of another is covered by Social Security if paid $1,300 or more in cash in calendar year 2001 and 2002 by any one employer. Room and board do not count, but transportation costs count if paid in cash. The job need not be regular or full-time. The employee should get a Social Security card at the Social Security office and show it to the employer.

The employer deducts the amount of the employee's Social Security tax from the worker's pay, adds an identical amount as the employer's Social Security tax, and sends the total amount to the federal government.

Medicare Coverage

The Medicare health insurance program provides acute-care coverage for Social Security and Railroad Retirement beneficiaries age 65 and over, for persons entitled for 24 months to receive Social Security or Railroad Retirement disability benefits, and for certain persons with end-stage kidney disease. What follows is a basic description and may not cover all circumstances.

The basic Medicare plan, available nationwide, is a fee-for-service arrangement, where the beneficiary may use any provider accepting Medicare; some services are not covered and there are some out-of-pocket costs.

Under "Medicare + Choice," persons eligible for Medicare may have the option of getting services through a health maintenance organization (HMO) or other managed care plan. Any such plan must provide at least the same benefits, except for hospice services, and may provide added benefits—such as lower or no deductibles and coverage for some prescription drugs—but is usually subject to restrictions in choice of health care providers. In some plans services by outside providers are still covered for an extra out-of-pocket cost. Also available as options in some areas are Medicare-approved private fee-for-service plans and Medicare medical savings accounts.

Hospital insurance (Part A). The basic hospital insurance program pays covered services for hospital and posthospital care including the following:

- All necessary inpatient hospital care for the first 60 days of each benefit period, except for a deductible ($812 in 2002). For days 61-90, Medicare pays for services over and above a coinsurance amount ($203 per day in 2002). After 90 days, the beneficiary has 60 reserve days for which Medicare helps pay. The coinsurance amount for reserve days was $406 in 2002.
- Up to 100 days' care in a skilled-nursing facility in each benefit period. Hospital insura2nce pays for all covered services for the first 20 days; for the 21-100th day, the beneficiary pays coinsurance ($101.50 a day in 2002).
- Part-time home health care provided by nurses or other health workers.
- Limited coverage of hospice care for individuals certified to be terminally ill.
- There is a premium for this insurance in certain cases.

Medical insurance (Part B). Elderly persons can receive benefits under this supplementary program only if they sign up for them and agree to a monthly premium ($54 if you sign up upon being eligible in 2002). The federal government pays the rest of the cost. The medical insurance program usually pays 80% of the approved amount (after the first $100 in each calendar year) for the following services:

- Covered services received from a doctor in his or her office, in a hospital, in a skilled-nursing facility, at home, or in other locations.
- Medical and surgical services, including anesthesia.
- Diagnostic tests and procedures that are part of the patient's treatment.
- Radiology and pathology services by doctors while the individual is a hospital inpatient or outpatient.
- Other services such as X-rays, services of a doctor's office nurse, drugs and biologicals that cannot be self-administered, transfusions of blood and blood components, medical supplies, physical/occupational therapy and speech pathology services.

In addition to the above, certain other tests or preventive measures are now covered without an additional premium. These include mammograms, bone mass measurement, colo-rectal cancer screening, and flu shots. Outpatient prescription drugs are generally not covered under the basic plan, nor are routine physical exams, dental care, hearing aids, or routine eye care. There is limited coverage for non-hospital treatment of mental illness.

To get medical insurance protection, persons approaching age 65 may enroll in the 7-month period that includes 3 months before the 65th birthday, the month of the birthday, and 3 months after the birthday, but if they wish coverage to begin in the month they reach age 65, they must enroll in the 3 months before their birthday. Persons not enrolling within their first enrollment period may enroll later, during the first 3 months of each year (coverage begins July 1), but their premium may be 10% higher for each 12-month period elapsed since they first could have enrolled.

The monthly premium is deducted from the cash benefit for persons receiving Social Security, Railroad Retirement, or Civil Service retirement benefits. Income from the medical premiums and the federal matching payments are put in a Supplementary Medical Insurance Trust Fund, from which benefits and administrative expenses are paid.

Further details are available on the Internet at www.medicare.gov or by calling 1-800-638-6833.

Medicare card. Persons qualifying for hospital insurance under Social Security receive a health insurance card similar to cards now used by Blue Cross and other health insurers. The card indicates whether the individual has taken out medical insurance protection. It is to be shown to the hospital, skilled-nursing facility, home health agency, doctor, or whoever provides the covered services.

Payments are generally made only in the 50 states, Puerto Rico, Virgin Islands, Guam, and American Samoa.

Social Security Financing

Social Security is paid for by a tax on certain earnings (for 2002, on earnings up to $84,900) for Old Age, Survivors, and Disability Insurance and on all earnings (no upper limit) for Hospital Insurance with the Medicare Program; the taxable earnings base for OASDI has been adjusted annually to reflect increases in average wages. The employed worker and his or her employer share Social Security taxes equally.

Employers remit amounts withheld from employee wages for Social Security and income taxes to the Internal Revenue Service; employer Social Security taxes are also payable at the same time. (Self-employed workers pay Social Security taxes when filing their regular income tax forms.) The Social Security taxes (along with revenues arising from partial taxation of the Social Security benefits of certain high-income people) are transferred to the Social Security Trust Funds—the Federal Old-Age and Survivors Insurance (OASI) Trust Fund, the Federal Disability Insurance (DI) Trust Fund, and the Federal Hospital Insurance (HI) Trust Fund; they can be used only to pay benefits, the cost of rehabilitation services, and administrative expenses. Money not immediately needed for these purposes is by law invested in obligations of the federal government, which must pay interest on the money borrowed and must repay the principal when the obligations are redeemed or mature.

Supplemental Security Income

On Jan. 1, 1974, the Supplemental Security Income (SSI) program established by the 1972 Social Security Act amendments replaced the former federal grants to states for aid to the needy aged, blind, and disabled in the 50 states and the District of Columbia. The program provides both for federal payments, based on uniform national standards and eligibility requirements, and for state supplementary payments varying from state to state. The Social Security Administration administers the federal payments financed from general funds of the Treasury—and the state supplements as well, if the state elects to have its supplementary program federally administered. States may supplement the federal payment for all recipients and must supplement it for persons otherwise adversely affected by the transition from the former public assistance programs. In May 2002, the number of persons receiving federally administered payments was 6,732,788 and the payments totaled $2.9 billion.

The maximum monthly federal SSI payment for individuals with no other countable income, living in their own household, was $545 in 2002. For couples it was $817.

Social Security Statement

On Oct. 1, 1999, the Social Security Administration initiated the mailing of an annual *Social Security Statement* to all workers age 25 and older not already receiving benefits. Workers will automatically receive statements about 3 months before their birth month. The statement provides estimates of potential monthly Social Security retirement, disability, and survivor benefits as well as a record of lifetime earnings. The statement also provides workers an easy way to determine whether their earnings are accurately posted in Social Security records.

For further information contact the Social Security Administration toll-free at 1-800-772-1213 or visit its website at www.ssa.gov

Examples of Monthly Benefits Available

Description of benefit or beneficiary	For low earnings ($15,899 in 2002)[1]	For avg. earnings ($35,332 in 2002)[2]	For max. earnings ($84,900 in 2002)
Primary insurance amount (worker retiring at 65)	$682.70	$1,127.30	$1,660.50
Maximum family benefit (worker retiring at 65)	1,024.00	2,052.60	2,906.10
Maximum family disability benefit (worker disabled at 55; in 2000)*	1,024.20	1,800.90	2,771.40
Disabled worker (worker disabled at 55)			
Worker alone	728.90	1,200.60	1,847.60
Worker, spouse, and 1 child	1,022.00	1,800.00	2,769.00
Retired worker claiming benefits at age 62:			
Worker alone[3]	565.00	931.00	1,375.00
Worker with spouse claiming benefits at—			
Age 65 or over	939.00	1,531.00	2,262.00
Age 62[3]	829.00	1,366.00	1,944.00
Widow or widower claiming benefits at—			
Age 65 or over[4]	682.00	1,127.00	1,660.00
Age 60 (spouse died at 65 without receiving reduced benefits)	488.00	806.00	1,187.00
Disabled widow or widower claiming benefits at age 50-59[5]	488.00	806.00	1,187.00
1 surviving child	512.00	845.00	1,245.00
Widow or widower age 65 or over and 1 child[6]	1,194.00	1,972.00	2,905.00
Widowed mother or father and 1 child[6]	1,024.00	1,690.00	2,490.00
Widowed mother or father and 2 children[6]	1,023.00	2,052.00	2,904.00

Effective Jan. 2002. *Assumes work beginning at age 22. (1) 45% of average. (2) Estimate. (3) Assumes maximum reduction. (4) A widow(er)'s benefit amount is limited to the amount the spouse would have been receiving if still living, but not less than 82.5% of the Primary Insurance Amount (PIA). (5) Effective Jan. 1984, disabled widow(er)s claiming a benefit at ages 50-59 receive a benefit equal to 71.5% of the PIA. (6) Based on worker dying at age 65.

IT'S A FACT: The most misused Social Security number ever was 078-05-1120. In 1938, a sample Social Security card inserted in wallets sold in Woolworth's and other department stores used an actual number from an employee of the wallet manufacturer. More than 40,000 people used it over the years, peaking in 1943 when 5,755 reported it as their own. As late as 1977, 12 people were found to still be using the invalid number.

Social Security Trust Funds

Old-Age and Survivors Insurance Trust Fund, 1940-2001

(in millions)

	INCOME					DISBURSEMENTS					
Fiscal year[1]	Total	Net contributions[2]	Income from taxing benefits	Payments from the Treasury fund[3]	Net interest[4]	Total	Benefit payments[5]	Administrative expenses	Transfers to Railroad Retirement program	Net increase in fund	Fund at end of period
1940	$368	$325	—	—	$43	$62	$35	$26	—	$306	$2,031
1950	2,928	2,667	—	$4	257	1,022	961	61	—	1,905	13,721
1960	11,382	10,866	—	—	516	11,198	10,677	203	$318	184	20,324
1970	32,220	30,256	—	449	1,515	29,848	28,798	471	579	2,371	32,454
1980	105,841	103,456	—	540	1,845	107,678	105,083	1,154	1,442	–1,837	22,823
1990	286,653	267,530	$4,848	–2,089	16,363	227,519	222,987	1,563	2,969	59,134	214,197
1996	363,741	321,557	6,471	7	35,706	308,217	302,861	1,802	3,554	575,096	589,121
1997	397,169	349,946	7,426	2	39,795	322,073	316,257	2,128	3,688	67,916	567,395
1998	424,848	371,207	9,149	1	44,491	332,324	326,762	1,899	3,662	92,524	681,645
1999	457,040	396,352	10,899	—	49,788	339,874	334,383	1,809	3,681	117,167	798,812
2000	484,228	418,219	12,476	—	53,532	353,396	347,868	1,990	3,538	130,832	893,003
2001	513,800	440,800	11,800	—	61,200	373,000	367,000	2,100	3,300	140,800	1,033,800

(1) Fiscal years 1980 and later consist of the 12 months ending on Sept. 30 of each year. Fiscal years prior to 1977 consisted of the 12 months ending on June 30 of each year. (2) Beginning in 1983, includes transfers from general fund of Treasury representing contributions that would have been paid on deemed wage credits for military service in 1957 and later, if such credits were considered covered wages. (3) Includes payments (a) in 1947-52 and in 1967 and later, for costs of noncontributory wage credits for military service performed before 1957; (b) in 1972-83, for costs of deemed wage credits for military service performed after 1956; and (c) in 1969 and later, for costs of benefits to certain uninsured persons who attained age 72 before 1968. (4) Net interest includes net profits or losses on marketable investments. Beginning in 1967, administrative expenses were charged currently to the trust fund on an estimated basis, with a final adjustment, including interest, made in the next fiscal year. The amounts of these interest adjustments are included in net interest. For years prior to 1967, the method of accounting for administrative expenses is described in the 1970 Annual Report. Beginning in Oct. 1973, the figures shown include relatively small amounts of gifts to the fund. During 1983-91, interest paid from the trust fund to the general fund on advance tax transfers is reflected. (5) Beginning in 1967, includes payments for vocational rehabilitation services furnished to disabled persons receiving benefits because of their disabilities. Beginning in 1983, amounts are reduced by amount of reimbursement for unnegotiated benefit checks.

Disability Insurance Trust Fund, 1970-2001

(in millions)

Fiscal year[1]	INCOME Total	Net contributions[2]	Income from taxation of benefits	Payments from the Treasury fund[3]	Net interest[4]	DISBURSEMENTS Total	Benefit payments[5]	Administrative expenses	Transfers to Railroad Retirement program	Net increase in fund	Fund at end of period
1970....	$4,774	$4,481	—	$16	$277	$3,259	$3,085	$164	$10	$1,514	$5,614
1980....	13,871	13,255	—	130	485	15,872	15,515	368	–12	2,001	3,629
1990....	28,791	28,539	$144	–775	883	25,616	24,829	707	80	3,174	11,079
1996....	60,710	57,325	373	—	3,012	45,351	44,189	1,160	2	15,359	52,924
1997....	60,499	56,037	470	—	3,992	47,034	45,695	1,280	59	13,465	66,389
1998....	64,357	58,966	558	—	4,832	49,931	48,207	1,567	157	14,425	80,815
1999....	69,541	63,203	661	—	5,677	53,035	51,381	1,519	135	16,507	97,321
2000....	77,023	70,001	756	–836	6,266	56,008	54,174	1,608	159	21,014	113,752
2001....	82,100	74,600	700	—	7,600	69,900	58,200	1,800	*	22,100	135,900

* Less than $50 million. (1) Fiscal years 1977 and later consist of the 12 months ending Sept. 30 of each year. Fiscal years prior to 1977 consisted of the 12 months ending June 30 of each year. (2) Beginning in 1983, includes transfers from general fund of Treasury representing contributions that would have been paid on deemed wage credits for military service in 1957 and later, if such credits were considered to be covered wages. (3) Includes payments (a) for costs of noncontributory wage credits for military service performed before 1957; and (b) in 1972-83, for costs of deemed wage credits for military service performed after 1956. (4) Net interest includes net profits or losses on marketable investments. Administrative expenses are charged currently to the trust fund on an estimated basis, with a final adjustment, including interest, made in the following fiscal year. Figures shown include relatively small amounts of gifts to the fund. During the years 1983-91, interest paid from the trust fund to the general fund on advance tax transfers is reflected. (5) Includes payments for vocational rehabilitation services. Beginning in 1983, amounts are reduced by amount of reimbursement for unnegotiated benefit checks. **NOTE:** Totals may not add because of rounding.

Supplementary Medical Insurance Trust Fund (Medicare), 1975-2001

(in millions)

Fiscal year[1]	INCOME Premiumfrom participants	Government contributions[2]	Interest and other income[3]	Total Income	DISBURSEMENTS Benefit payments	Administrative expenses	Total disbursements	Balance in fund at end of year[4]
1975....	$1,887	$2,330	$105	$4,322	$3,765	$405	$4,170	$1,424
1980....	2,928	6,932	415	10,275	10,144	593	10,737	4,532
1990....	11,494[5]	33,210	1,434[5]	46,138[5]	41,498	1,524[5]	43,022[5]	14,527[5]
1995....	19,244	36,988	1,937	58,169	63,491	1,722	65,213	13,874
1996....	18,031	61,702	1,392	82,025	67,176	1,771	68,946	26,953
1997....	19,141	59,471	2,193	80,806	71,133	1,420	72,553	35,206
1998....	19,427	59,919	2,608	81,955	74,837[6]	1,435	76,272	40,889
1999....	20,160	62,185	2,933	85,278	79,008[6]	1,510	80,518	45,649
2000....	20,515	65,561	3,164	89,239	87,212[6]	1,780	88,992	45,896
2001....	22,307	69,838	3,191	95,336	97,466[6]	1,986	99,452	41,780

(1) Fiscal year 1975 consists of the 12 months ending on June 30, 1975; fiscal years 1980 and later consist of the 12 months ending on September 30 of each year. (2) General fund matching payments, plus certain interest-adjustment items. (3) Other income includes recoveries of amounts reimbursed from the trust fund that are not obligations of the trust fund and other miscellaneous income. (4) The financial status of the program depends on both the assets and the liabilities of the program. (5) Includes the impact of the Medicare Catastrophic Coverage Act of 1988 (PL 100-360). (6) Benefit payments less moneys transferred from the HI trust fund for home health agency costs, as provided for by PL 105-33. **NOTE:** Totals do not necessarily equal the sums of rounded components.

Hospital Insurance Trust Fund (Medicare), 1975-2001

(in millions)

Fisc. year[1]	INCOME Payroll taxes	Income from taxation of benefits	Transfers from railroad retirement acct.	Reimbursement for uninsured persons	Premiums from voluntary enrollees	Pymts. for military wage credits	Interest on investments and other income[2]	Total income	DISBURSEMENTS Benefit pymts.[3]	Administrative expense[4]	Total disbursements	Net increase in fund	Fund at end of year
1975.	$11,291	—	$132	$481	$6	$48	$609	$12,568	$10,353	$259	$10,612	$1,956	$9,870
1980.	23,244	—	244	697	17	141	1,072	25,415	23,790	497	24,288	1,127	14,490
1990.	70,655	—	367	413	113	107	7,908	79,563	65,912	774	66,687	12,876	95,631
1995.	98,053	3,913	396	462	998	61	10,963	114,847	113,583	1,300	114,883	–36	129,520
1996.	106,934	4,069	401	419	1,107	–2,293[5]	10,496	121,135	124,088	1,229	125,317	–4,182	125,338
1997.	112,725	3,558	419	481	1,279	70	10,017	128,548	136,175	1,661	137,836	–9,287	116,050
1998.	121,913	5,067	419	34	1,320	67	9,382	138,203	135,487[6]	1,653	137,140	1,063	117,113
1999.	134,385	6,552	430	652	1,401	71	9,523	153,015	129,463[6]	1,978	131,441	21,574	138,687
2000.	137,738	8,787	465	470	1,392	2	10,827	159,681	127,934[6]	2,340	130,284	29,397	168,084
2001.	151,931	4,903	470	453	1,440	–1,175[7]	12,993	171,014	139,356	2,368	141,723	29,290	197,374

(1) Fiscal year 1975 consists of the 12 months ending on June 30, 1975; fiscal years 1980 and later consist of the 12 months ending Sept. 30 of each year. (2) Other income includes recoveries of amounts reimbursed from the trust fund that are not obligations of the trust fund, receipts from the fraud and abuse control program, and a small amount of miscellaneous income. (3) Includes costs of Peer Review Organizations (beginning with the implementation of the Prospective Payment System on Oct. 1, 1983). (4) Includes costs of experiments and demonstration projects. Beginning in 1997, includes fraud and abuse control expenses, as provided for by PL 104-191. (5) Includes the lump-sum general revenue adjustment of $–2,366 mil, as provided for by PL 98-21. (6) Includes moneys transferred to the SMI trust fund for home health agency costs, as provided for by PL 105-33. (7) Includes the lump-sum general review adjustment of $–1,117 million, as provided for by sec. 151 of PL 98-21. **NOTE:** Totals do not necessarily equal the sums of rounded components.

CRIME

Measuring Crime

The U.S. Dept. of Justice administers 2 statistical programs to measure the magnitude, nature, and impact of crime in the U.S. Because of a difference in focus and methodology, their results are not strictly comparable.

The **Uniform Crime Report** program, conducted through the Federal Bureau of Investigation, was designed to provide statistics for law enforcement administration, operation, and management. It collects information on the crimes of homicide, forcible rape, robbery, aggravated assault, burglary, larceny-theft, motor vehicle theft, and arson, as they are reported to law enforcement authorities. A preliminary annual report is released each spring, and a more final report on the same period is released in the following year.

The **National Crime Victimization Survey** is conducted by the Bureau of Justice Statistics through interviews with members of a nationally representative sample of households, who report on on their experience of crime. It complements the UCR by providing alternate information about crimes, including those not reported to police. In contrast to the UCR, it does not cover murder or arson.

Further explanation of the NCVS and UCR is available at: www.ojp.usdoj.gov/bjs/abstract/ntmc.htm

National Crime Victimization Survey for 2001

Source: Bureau of Justice Statistics, U.S. Dept. of Justice

The 2002 NCVS reported that there were about 24.2 million victimizations of Americans age 12 and up in 2001, down from 25.9 million in 2000. Criminal victimizations were estimated to be at their lowest point since the NCVS was initiated in 1973. According to this survey, the violent crime rate in 2001 fell 10% from 2000, and the property crime rate went down 6%. These decreases continued trends that began in 1994; between 1993 and 2001, violent crime, as reflected in NCVS statistics, fell 50%, and property crime 48%. According to the report, only about half of all violent victimizations and 37% of property crimes in 2001 were reported to the police.

Criminal Victimization, 2000-2001

Source: National Crime Victimization Survey, U.S. Dept. of Justice

Type of Crime	Number of victimizations (thousands) 2001	Victimization rates (per 1,000 persons age 12 or older or per 1,000 households) 2000	2001	% change, 2000-2001
ALL CRIMES	**24,216**	**NA**	**NA**	**NA**
Personal Crimes	**5,932**	**29.1**	**25.9**	**–11.0**
Crimes of violence	5,744	27.9	25.1	–10.0
Rape	84	0.4	0.4	0.0
Attempted rape	63	0.2	0.3	50.0
Sexual assault	102	0.5	0.4	–20.0
Robbery	427	2.3	1.9	–17.4
With injury	174	0.7	0.8	14.3
Aggravated assault[1]	1,222	5.7	5.3	–7.0
Simple assault[2]	3,643	17.8	15.9	–10.7
Personal theft[3]	188	1.2	0.8	–33.3
Property Crimes	**18,284**	**178.1**	**166.9**	**–6.3**
Household burglary	2,687	26.9	24.5	–8.9
Motor vehicle theft	724	5.9	6.6	11.9
Theft	13,672	132.0	124.8	–5.5

NA = Not applicable (1) Attack with a weapon or involving serious injury. (2) Attack without a weapon resulting in no injury, minor injury, or undetermined injury requiring less than 2 days hospitalization. (3) Purse snatching and pocket picking.

IT'S A FACT: According to U.S. Bureau of Justice Statistics National Crime Victimization Surveys, men are victims of more violent crime (not counting murder, which is not covered in the surveys) than women (27.3 incidents per 1,000 males in 2001, compared to 23.0 per 1,000 women), Hispanics more than non-Hispanics (29.5 compared to 24.5), and blacks more than whites (31.2 compared to 24.5).

Uniform Crime Reports for 2001

Source: FBI, *Uniform Crime Reports,* 2001, preliminary

Serious crimes, including murder and arson, reported to law enforcement agencies in the U.S. increased 2% from 2000 to 2001, according to preliminary figures from the Federal Bureau of Investigation's Uniform Crime Reporting Program, released June 4, 2002. This was the first overall increase in such figures since 1991; reported crime in the U.S. had been steady between 1999 and 2000, and had gone down 7.8% in 1999, 5% in 1998, 2% in 1997, 3% in 1996, 1% in both 1994 and 1995, 2% in 1993, and 3% in 1992.

Reported serious crime is measured by the Crime Index, which includes 4 violent crimes and 3 property crimes. From 2000 to 2001, violent crime increased slightly, by 0.3%, and property crime significantly, by 2.2%.

In the violent crime category, respective increases of 3.9%, 3.1%, and 0.2% occured in robbery, murder, and forcible rape. Aggravated assault declined by 1.4%.

Reported property crimes rose across the board from 2000 numbers. Burglary increased 2.6%, motor vehicle theft was up 5.9%, and larceny-theft rose 1.4%. Reports of arson, which is not included in the crime index proper, increased by 2%.

For all parts of the country but the Northeast, overall Crime Index totals were greater in 2001 than in 2000. The increases were 0.9%, 1.9%, and 4.5% in the Midwest, Southern, and Western regions of the country, respectively. The total was down 1.2% in the Northeast.

Cities of all sizes showed an increase in reported crime in 2001. The largest jump, 3.9%, occured in cities with populations from 250,000 to 499,999. In cities with over 1 million people, the increase was 1.8%, and in those with fewer than 10,000, it was 0.8%. The Crime Index also rose 2.4% in suburban counties and increased 0.6% in rural counties.

Federal Bureau of Investigation

The Federal Bureau of Investigation was created July 26, 1908, and was referred to as Office of Chief Examiner. It became the Bureau of Investigation (Mar. 16, 1909), United States Bureau of Investigation (July 1, 1932), Division of Investigation (Aug. 10, 1933), and Federal Bureau of Investigation (July 1, 1935).

Director	Assumed office
Stanley W. Finch	July 26, 1908
A(lexander) Bruce Bielaski	Apr. 30, 1912
William E. Allen, act.	Feb. 10, 1919
William J. Flynn	July 1, 1919
William J. Burns	Aug. 22, 1921
J. Edgar Hoover, act.	May 10, 1924
J. Edgar Hoover	Dec. 10, 1924
L. Patrick Gray, act.	May 3, 1972
William D. Ruckelshaus, act.	Apr. 27, 1973
Clarence M. Kelley	July 9, 1973
William H. Webster	Feb. 23, 1978
John E. Otto, act.	May 26, 1987
William S. Sessions	Nov. 2, 1987
Floyd I. Clarke, act.	July 19, 1993
Louis J. Freeh	Sept. 1, 1993
Thomas J. Pickard, act.	June 25, 2001
Robert S. Mueller III	Sept. 4, 2001

Crime in the U.S., 1979-2000

Source: FBI, *Uniform Crime Reports*, 2000, final statistics; additional data available at www.fbi.gov/ucr/ucr.htm

Population[1]	Crime Index (total)[2]	Violent crime	Property crime[3]	Murder and non-negligent manslaughter	Forcible rape	Robbery	Burglary	Larceny-theft
Population by year				NUMBER OF REPORTED OFFENSES				
1979–220,099,000	12,249,500	1,208,030	11,041,500	21,460	76,390	480,700	3,327,700	6,601,000
1980–225,349,264	13,408,300	1,344,520	12,063,700	23,040	82,990	565,840	3,795,200	7,136,900
1981–229,146,000	13,423,800	1,361,820	12,061,900	22,520	82,500	592,910	3,779,700	7,194,400
1982–231,534,000	12,974,400	1,322,390	11,652,000	21,010	78,770	553,130	3,447,100	7,142,500
1983–233,981,000	12,108,600	1,258,090	10,850,500	19,310	78,920	506,570	3,129,900	6,712,800
1984–236,158,000	11,881,800	1,273,280	10,608,500	18,690	84,230	485,010	2,984,400	6,591,900
1985–238,740,000	12,431,400	1,328,770	11,102,600	18,980	88,670	497,870	3,073,300	6,926,400
1986–241,077,000	13,211,900	1,489,170	11,722,700	20,610	91,460	542,780	3,241,400	7,257,200
1987–243,400,000	13,508,700	1,484,000	12,024,700	20,100	91,110	517,700	3,236,200	7,499,900
1988–245,807,000	13,923,100	1,566,220	12,356,900	20,680	92,490	542,970	3,218,100	7,705,900
1989–248,239,000	14,251,400	1,646,040	12,605,400	21,500	94,500	578,330	3,168,200	7,872,400
1990–248,709,873	14,475,600	1,820,130	12,655,500	23,440	102,560	639,270	3,073,900	7,945,700
1991–252,177,000	14,872,900	1,911,770	12,961,100	24,700	106,590	687,730	3,157,200	8,142,200
1992–255,082,000	14,438,200	1,932,270	12,505,900	23,760	109,060	672,480	2,979,900	7,915,200
1993–257,908,000	14,144,800	1,926,020	12,218,800	24,530	106,010	659,870	2,834,800	7,820,900
1994–260,341,000	13,989,500	1,857,670	12,131,900	23,330	102,220	618,950	2,712,800	7,879,800
1995–262,755,000	13,862,700	1,798,790	12,063,900	21,610	97,470	580,510	2,593,800	7,997,700
1996–265,284,000	13,493,900	1,688,540	11,805,300	19,650	96,250	535,590	2,506,400	7,904,700
1997–267,637,000	13,194,600	1,636,100	11,558,500	18,210	96,150	498,530	2,460,500	7,743,800
1998–270,296,000	12,485,700	1,533,890	10,951,800	16,970	93,140	447,190	2,332,700	7,376,300
1999–272,691,000	11,635,100	1,430,690	10,204,500	15,530	89,110	409,670	2,099,700	6,957,400
2000–281,421,906	11,605,751	1,424,289	10,208,462	15,517	90,186	407,842	2,049,946	6,965,957
				PERCENT CHANGE: NUMBER OF OFFENSES				
2000/1999	–0.2	–0.4	*	*	+1.2	–0.4	–2.4	+0.1
2000/1995	–16.3	–20.8	–15.4	–28.2	–7.5	–29.8	–21.0	–12.9
2000/1990	–19.8	–21.7	–19.4	–33.8	–12.1	–36.2	–33.3	–12.3
Year				RATE PER 100,000 INHABITANTS				
1979	5,565.5	548.9	5,016.6	9.7	34.7	218.4	1,511.9	2,999.1
1980	5,950.0	596.6	5,353.3	10.2	36.8	251.1	1,684.1	3,167.0
1981	5,858.2	594.3	5,263.9	9.8	36.0	258.7	1,649.5	3,139.7
1982	5,603.6	571.1	5,032.5	9.1	34.0	238.9	1,488.8	3,084.8
1983	5,175.0	537.7	4,637.4	8.3	33.7	216.5	1,337.7	2,868.9
1984	5,031.3	539.2	4,492.1	7.9	35.7	205.4	1,263.7	2,791.3
1985	5,207.1	556.6	4,650.5	8.0	37.1	208.5	1,287.3	2,901.2
1986	5,480.4	617.7	4,862.6	8.6	37.9	225.1	1,344.6	3,010.3
1987	5,550.0	609.7	4,940.3	8.3	37.4	212.7	1,329.6	3,081.3
1988	5,664.2	637.2	5,027.1	8.4	37.6	220.9	1,309.2	3,134.9
1989	5,741.0	663.1	5,077.9	8.7	38.1	233.0	1,276.3	3,171.3
1990	5,820.3	731.8	5,088.5	9.4	41.2	257.0	1,235.9	3,194.8
1991	5,897.8	758.1	5,139.7	9.8	42.3	272.7	1,252.0	3,228.8
1992	5,660.2	757.5	4,902.7	9.3	42.8	263.6	1,168.2	3,103.0
1993	5,484.4	746.8	4,737.6	9.5	41.1	255.9	1,099.2	3,032.4
1994	5,373.5	713.6	4,660.0	9.0	39.3	237.7	1,042.0	3,026.7
1995	5,275.9	684.6	4,591.3	8.2	37.1	220.9	987.1	3,043.8
1996	5,086.6	636.5	4,450.1	7.4	36.3	201.9	944.8	2,979.7
1997	4,930.0	611.3	4,318.7	6.8	35.9	186.3	919.4	2,893.4
1998	4,619.3	567.5	4,051.8	6.3	34.5	165.4	863.0	2,729.0
1999	4,266.8	524.7	3,742.1	5.7	32.7	150.2	770.0	2,551.4
2000	4,124.0	506.1	3,617.9	5.5	32.0	144.9	728.4	2,475.3
				PERCENT CHANGE: RATE PER 100,000 INHABITANTS				
2000/1999	–3.3	–0.1	–0.3	–3.1	–2.3	–3.5	–5.4	–3.0
2000/1995	–21.9	–26.1	–21.2	–33.0	–13.7	–34.4	–26.2	–18.7
2000/1990	–29.1	–30.9	–28.9	–41.5	–22.3	–43.6	–41.4	–22.5

* = No significant change. **Note:** All rates calculated on the offenses before rounding. (1) Populations are Bureau of the Census prov. estimates as of July 1, except 1980, 1990, and 2000, which are the decennial census counts. (2) Because of rounding, violent and property crime may not add to total. Not all categories of violent and property crime appear separately. (3) Data for arson not included.

Law Enforcement Officers, 2000

Source: FBI, *Uniform Crime Reports*, 2000; later data available at www.fbi.gov/ucr/ucr.htm

The U.S. law enforcement community employed an average of 2.5 full-time officers for every 1,000 inhabitants as of Oct. 31, 2000.

Including full-time civilian employees, the overall law enforcement employee rate was 3.5 per 1,000 inhabitants, according to 13,535 city, county, and state police agencies. These agencies collectively offered law enforcement service covering a population of about 265 million, employing 654,601 officers and 271,982 civilians.

The law enforcement employee average for all cities nationwide was 3.1 per 1,000 inhabitants. The highest city law enforcement employee average was 4.8 per 1,000 inhabitants, in cities with populations of 1,000,000 or more. Averages of 4.3 were recorded in both suburban and rural counties.

Regionally, the law enforcement employee rate was 3.5 in the Northeast and in the South, 2.8 in the Midwest, and 2.5 in the West. Nationally, males constituted 89% of all sworn employees. In rural counties, 92% of the officers were males, while in suburban counties males accounted for 87.2%.

Civilians made up 29.4% of the total U.S. law enforcement employee force. They represented 22.7% of the police employees in cities, 38.5% in rural counties, and 39.4% in suburban counties. Females accounted for 62.7% of all civilian employees.

Fifty-one law enforcement officers were feloniously slain in the line of duty in 2000, nine more than in 1999. Another 84 officers were killed as a result of accidents occurring while performing official duties, 19 lower than in the previous year.

U.S. Crime Rates by Region, Geographic Division, and State, 2000

Source: FBI, *Uniform Crime Reports*, 2000; final statistics; later data available at www.fbi.gov/ucr/ucr.htm

(rate per 100,000 population)

	Total rate	Violent crime[1]	Property crime[2]	Murder	Rape	Robbery	Aggra-vated assault	Burglary	Larceny-theft	Motor vehicle theft
U.S. TOTAL	**4,124.0**	**506.1**	**3,617.9**	**5.5**	**32.0**	**144.9**	**323.6**	**728.4**	**2,475.3**	**414.2**
Northeast	**3,064.3**	**443.4**	**2,620.9**	**4.0**	**22.2**	**156.0**	**261.2**	**477.4**	**1,821.4**	**322.1**
New England	**3,019.0**	**349.5**	**2,669.5**	**2.3**	**27.1**	**81.8**	**238.4**	**502.2**	**1,823.0**	**344.2**
Connecticut	3,232.7	324.7	2,908.0	2.9	19.9	112.5	189.4	512.0	2,011.4	384.6
Maine	2,619.8	109.6	2,510.2	1.2	25.1	19.4	63.9	531.4	1,875.1	103.7
Massachusetts	3,026.1	476.1	2,550.0	2.0	26.7	91.6	355.9	482.0	1,660.5	407.6
New Hampshire	2,433.1	175.4	2,257.8	1.8	42.2	36.7	94.7	404.0	1,680.0	173.8
Rhode Island	3,476.4	297.7	3,178.7	4.3	39.3	88.0	166.2	631.5	2,102.2	445.0
Vermont	2,986.9	113.5	2,873.4	1.5	23.0	19.2	69.8	575.0	2,165.5	132.9
Middle Atlantic	**3,080.2**	**476.4**	**2,603.8**	**4.6**	**20.5**	**182.1**	**269.1**	**468.7**	**1,820.8**	**314.3**
New Jersey	3,160.5	383.8	2,776.6	3.4	16.1	161.1	203.2	522.0	1,848.8	405.9
New York	3,099.6	553.9	2,545.7	5.0	18.6	213.6	316.7	463.4	1,796.4	285.8
Pennsylvania	2,995.3	420.0	2,575.3	4.9	26.4	147.8	240.9	440.4	1,839.2	295.8
Midwest	**3,945.0**	**427.8**	**3,517.2**	**5.1**	**35.0**	**126.8**	**260.9**	**663.7**	**2,475.1**	**378.3**
East North Central	**3,986.1**	**461.9**	**3,524.1**	**5.5**	**36.1**	**145.9**	**274.4**	**679.1**	**2,431.8**	**413.3**
Illinois	4,286.2	656.8	3,629.4	7.2	32.9	207.4	409.3	659.6	2,517.8	452.1
Indiana	3,751.9	349.1	3,402.8	5.8	28.9	103.3	211.1	676.1	2,379.9	346.8
Michigan	4,109.9	555.0	3,554.9	6.7	50.6	138.0	359.7	702.2	2,291.9	560.7
Ohio	4,041.8	334.1	3,707.7	3.7	37.6	137.5	155.3	780.7	2,583.2	343.7
Wisconsin	3,209.1	236.8	2,972.3	3.2	21.7	84.6	127.3	469.5	2,229.9	272.9
West North Central	**3,848.7**	**347.7**	**3,501.0**	**4.1**	**32.2**	**81.9**	**229.4**	**627.7**	**2,577.0**	**296.3**
Iowa	3,233.7	266.4	2,967.3	1.6	23.1	36.6	205.1	558.4	2,225.2	183.6
Kansas	4,408.8	389.4	4,019.4	6.3	38.0	76.2	269.0	799.1	2,978.6	241.6
Minnesota	3,488.4	280.8	3,207.6	3.1	45.5	75.5	156.7	530.9	2,403.7	273.0
Missouri	4,527.8	490.0	4,037.7	6.2	24.1	135.8	323.9	745.0	2,851.3	441.4
Nebraska	4,095.5	327.6	3,767.9	3.7	25.5	67.0	231.4	592.0	2,870.3	305.6
North Dakota	2,288.1	81.4	2,206.6	0.6	26.3	8.7	45.8	325.9	1,727.2	153.5
South Dakota	2,319.8	166.8	2,153.0	0.9	40.4	17.4	108.1	383.7	1,663.7	105.7
South	**4,743.4**	**580.6**	**4,162.8**	**6.8**	**34.2**	**152.3**	**387.3**	**903.0**	**2,842.7**	**417.1**
South Atlantic	**4,824.8**	**627.3**	**4,197.5**	**6.7**	**32.6**	**172.1**	**415.9**	**903.8**	**2,853.7**	**440.0**
Delaware	4,478.1	684.4	3,793.6	3.2	54.1	177.9	449.2	665.6	2,725.9	402.1
District of Columbia	7,276.5	1,507.9	5,768.6	41.8	43.9	621.3	801.0	829.5	3,785.4	1,153.7
Florida	5,694.7	812.0	4,882.7	5.6	44.2	199.0	563.2	1,081.8	3,242.9	558.0
Georgia	4,751.1	504.7	4,246.4	8.0	24.0	161.9	310.9	836.6	2,937.0	472.8
Maryland	4,816.1	786.6	4,029.5	8.1	29.1	256.0	493.3	744.4	2,745.7	539.5
North Carolina	4,919.3	497.6	4,421.8	7.0	27.1	156.5	307.0	1,216.1	2,891.8	313.9
South Carolina	5,221.4	804.9	4,416.5	5.8	37.7	146.6	614.8	969.3	3,068.1	379.0
Virginia	3,028.1	281.7	2,746.4	5.7	22.8	88.9	164.3	429.9	2,064.8	251.6
West Virginia	2,602.8	316.5	2,286.3	2.5	18.3	41.4	254.2	546.9	1,556.1	183.3
East South Central	**4,193.9**	**493.6**	**3,700.3**	**7.0**	**33.9**	**124.1**	**328.6**	**874.7**	**2,493.2**	**332.4**
Alabama	4,545.9	486.2	4,059.7	7.4	33.3	128.2	317.2	906.9	2,864.8	288.0
Kentucky	2,959.7	294.5	2,665.2	4.8	27.0	80.6	182.2	626.2	1,809.6	229.5
Mississippi	4,004.4	360.9	3,643.5	9.0	35.8	95.0	221.1	946.3	2,452.2	245.0
Tennessee	4,890.2	707.2	4,183.0	7.2	38.4	166.4	495.2	990.4	2,708.8	483.9
West South Central	**4,906.9**	**550.7**	**4,356.2**	**6.8**	**37.0**	**134.9**	**372.1**	**917.1**	**3,013.9**	**425.2**
Arkansas	4,115.3	445.3	3,670.0	6.3	31.7	74.8	332.4	802.1	2,608.7	259.3
Louisiana	5,422.8	681.1	4,741.7	12.5	33.5	168.5	466.6	1,035.8	3,229.9	475.9
Oklahoma	4,558.6	497.8	4,060.8	5.3	41.2	75.8	375.5	917.5	2,785.4	357.8
Texas	4,955.5	545.1	4,410.4	5.9	37.7	145.1	356.3	906.3	3,057.4	446.8
West	**4,222.4**	**520.9**	**3,701.5**	**5.1**	**34.0**	**142.3**	**339.5**	**730.3**	**2,447.1**	**524.1**
Mountain	**4,652.3**	**431.3**	**4,221.0**	**4.6**	**37.6**	**106.6**	**282.4**	**801.2**	**2,914.9**	**504.9**
Arizona	5,829.5	531.7	5,297.8	7.0	30.7	146.3	347.7	1,011.6	3,444.1	842.1
Colorado	3,982.6	334.0	3,648.6	3.1	41.2	70.5	219.1	630.8	2,623.5	394.3
Idaho	3,186.2	252.5	2,933.7	1.2	29.7	17.2	204.3	566.5	2,206.0	161.2
Montana	3,533.4	240.6	3,292.7	1.8	33.4	27.6	177.9	437.4	2,638.6	216.8
Nevada	4,268.6	524.2	3,744.4	6.5	43.0	227.3	247.3	877.1	2,208.2	659.2
New Mexico	5,518.9	757.9	4,761.0	7.4	50.7	137.4	562.4	1,173.1	3,184.4	403.6
Utah	4,476.1	255.7	4,220.3	1.9	38.6	55.6	159.5	642.5	3,288.5	289.3
Wyoming	3,298.0	266.5	3,031.5	2.4	32.4	14.2	217.5	420.8	2,494.6	116.0
Pacific	**4,048.9**	**557.1**	**3,491.8**	**5.3**	**32.5**	**156.7**	**362.5**	**701.7**	**2,258.3**	**531.8**
Alaska	4,249.4	566.9	3,682.5	4.3	79.3	78.2	405.1	621.9	2,685.8	374.8
California	3,739.7	621.6	3,118.2	6.1	28.9	177.9	408.7	656.3	1,924.5	537.4
Hawaii	5,198.9	243.8	4,955.1	2.9	28.6	92.7	119.7	880.3	3,570.2	504.6
Oregon	4,845.4	350.7	4,494.7	2.0	37.6	84.4	226.7	748.8	3,338.7	407.2
Washington	5,105.6	369.7	4,736.0	3.3	46.4	98.6	221.3	907.3	3,234.6	594.1
Puerto Rico	**1,979.1**	**325.7**	**1,653.4**	**18.2**	**6.0**	**229.9**	**71.6**	**552.9**	**759.9**	**340.7**

Note: Offense totals are based on all reporting agencies and estimates for unreported areas. Totals may not add because of rounding. (1) Violent crimes are murder, forcible rape, robbery, and aggravated assault. (2) Property crimes are burglary, larceny-theft, and motor vehicle theft. Data not included for property crime of arson.

IT'S A FACT: According to the FBI *Uniform Crime Reports* for 2000, males accounted for 76% of all reported murder victims. Firearms were used in 66% of the murders.

State and Federal Prison Population, Death Penalty, 2000-2001[1]

Source: Bureau of Justice Statistics, U.S. Dept. of Justice

The total number of prisoners under the jurisdiction of federal or state adult correctional authorities was 1,406,031 at year-end 2001. Overall, the U.S. prison population grew 1.1%, which was less than the average annual growth of 3.8% since 1995, and the lowest since 1972. At year-end 2001, state and federal prisons housed nearly 2/3 of the incarcerated population (1,324,465 out of 2,100,146). Jails, which are locally operated and typically hold persons awaiting trial and those with sentences of a year or less, held most of the remainder; juvenile and military facilities, territorial prisons, jails in Indian country, and facilities of the U.S. Immigration and Naturalization Service held the rest. The rate of incarceration in prisons was 470 sentenced inmates per 100,000 U.S. residents, up from 411 in 1995 (1 in every 112 men and 1 in every 1,724 women were sentenced prisoners under the jurisdiction of state or federal authorities). The number of persons under sentence of death at the end of 2000 rose to 3,593 from 3,527, while 85 prisoners were executed.

	SENTENCED PRISONERS			DEATH PENALTY, 2000		
	Advance[2] 2001	Final[3] 2000	% change 2000-2001	Under sentence of death	Executions	Death penalty
U.S. TOTAL	**1,344,512**	**1,329,367**	**1.1**	**3,593**	**85**	**—**
Federal institutions	**136,509**	**125,044**	**9.2**	**18**	**0**	**Yes**
State institutions	**1,208,003**	**1,204,323**	**0.3**	**3,575**	**85**	**38**
Northeast	**163,639**	**166,632**	**–1.8**	**266**	**0**	**—**
Connecticut	13,276	13,155	0.9	7	0	Yes
Maine	1,641	1,635	0.4	—	—	No
Massachusetts	9,358	9,479	–1.3	—	—	No
New Hampshire	2,392	2,257	6.0	0	0	Yes
New Jersey[4]	28,142	29,784	–5.5	15	0	Yes
New York	67,534	70,199	–3.8	6	0	Yes
Pennsylvania	38,057	36,844	3.3	238	0	Yes
Rhode Island	1,926	1,966	–2.0	—	—	No
Vermont	1,313	1,313	0.0	—	—	No
Midwest	**239,678**	**236,458**	**1.4**	**504**	**5**	**—**
Illinois[4]	44,348	45,281	–2.1	163	0	Yes
Indiana	20,883	19,811	5.4	43	0	Yes
Iowa[4]	7,962	7,955	0.1	—	—	No
Kansas[4]	8,577	8,344	2.8	4	0	Yes
Michigan	48,849	47,718	2.4	—	—	No
Minnesota	6,606	6,238	5.9	—	—	No
Missouri	28,736	27,519	4.4	79	5	Yes
Nebraska	3,865	3,816	1.3	11	0	Yes
North Dakota	1,017	994	2.3	—	—	No
Ohio[4]	45,281	45,833	–1.2	201	0	Yes
South Dakota	2,803	2,613	7.3	3	0	Yes
Wisconsin	20,751	20,336	2.0	—	—	No
South	**539,580**	**537,086**	**0.5**	**1,924**	**76**	**—**
Alabama	26,138	24,123	—	185	4	Yes
Arkansas	12,076	11,851	1.9	40	2	Yes
Delaware	4,034	3,937	2.5	15	1	Yes
District of Columbia[4]	795	5,008	—	—	—	No
Florida	72,398	71,318	1.5	371	6	Yes
Georgia	45,904	44,141	4.0	120	0	Yes
Kentucky	15,104	14,919	1.2	40	0	Yes
Louisiana	35,710	35,207	1.4	90	1	Yes
Maryland	22,842	22,490	1.6	16	0	Yes
Mississippi	20,476	19,239	6.4	61	0	Yes
North Carolina	27,632	27,043	2.2	215	1	Yes
Oklahoma[4]	22,780	23,181	–1.7	129	11	Yes
South Carolina	21,606	21,017	2.8	66	1	Yes
Tennessee[4]	23,671	22,166	6.8	97	1	Yes
Texas[4]	153,056	158,008	–3.1	450	40	Yes
Virginia	31,194	29,643	5.2	29	8	Yes
West Virginia	4,164	3,795	9.7	—	—	No
West	**205,100**	**204,147**	**0.4**	**881**	**1**	
Alaska	1,920	2,128	–9.8	—	—	No
Arizona	26,463	25,412	4.1	119	3	Yes
California	157,295	160,412	–1.9	586	1	Yes
Colorado	17,448	16,833	3.7	5	0	Yes
Hawaii	3,670	3,553	3.3	—	—	No
Idaho	6,006	5,535	8.5	21	0	Yes
Montana	3,328	3,105	7.2	6	0	Yes
Nevada	10,201	10,063	1.4	88	0	Yes
New Mexico	5,408	4,666	15.9	5	0	Yes
Oregon	11,413	10,553	8.1	25	0	Yes
Utah	5,250	5,541	–5.3	11	0	Yes
Washington	15,020	14,666	2.4	13	0	Yes
Wyoming	1,684	1,680	0.2	2	0	Yes

(1) All information applies to Dec. 31 of the year indicated. (2) The advance estimate of prisoners is made in Jan. and may be revised. (3) Revised from previous tabulations. (4) Includes some inmates sentenced to one year or less.

Sentences vs. Time Served for Selected Crimes

Source: Bureau of Justice Statistics, *Truth in Sentencing in State Prisons,* 1999

The following is a comparison of the average maximum sentence lengths (excluding both life and death sentences) and the actual time served for selected state-court convictions.

Type of offense	Average sentence	Avg. time served[1]
All violent	7 years, 1 month	3 years, 3 months
Homicide	15 years	7 years
Rape	9 years, 8 months	5 years, 1 month
Other sexual assault	6 years, 9 months	3 years, 3 months
Robbery	7 years, 8 months	3 years, 4 months
Negligent manslaughter	8 years, 1 month	3 years, 5 months
Assault	5 years, 1 month	2 years, 4 months
Other	5 years, 7 months	2 years, 5 months

(1) Includes jail credit and prison time.

Prison Situation Among the States and in the Federal System, 2001

Source: *Prisoners in 2001,* Bureau of Justice Statistics, U.S. Dept. of Justice; July 2002

10 largest prison populations, 2001	Number of inmates	10 highest incarceration rates, 2001	Prisoners per 100,000 residents[1]	10 largest % increases in prison population: Growth 2000-2001	% annual increase	Growth since 1995	% annual increase[2]
Texas	162,070	Louisiana	800	West Virginia	9.3	North Dakota	11.0
California	159,444	Mississippi	715	Alaska	8.9	Idaho	10.3
Federal	156,933	Texas	711	Idaho	8.5	Oregon	9.8
Florida	72,406	Oklahoma	658	Oregon	8.3	West Virginia	9.0
New York	67,534	Alabama	584	Federal	8.0	Montana	8.9
Michigan	48,849	Georgia	542	Hawaii	7.9	Mississippi	8.9
Georgia	45,937	South Carolina	529	South Dakota	7.5	Federal	8.5
Ohio	45,281	Missouri	509	Montana	7.2	Colorado	7.9
Illinois	44,348	Delaware	504	Tennessee	6.8	Tennessee	7.7
Pennsylvania	38,062	Arizona	492	New Mexico	6.1	Utah	7.3

(1) Prisoners with sentences of more than 1 year. The Federal Bureau of Prisons and the District of Columbia are excluded. (2) The average annual percent change from 1995 to 2001.

Executions, by State and Method, 1977-2001

Source: Bureau of Justice Statistics, *Capital Punishment 2000,* Dec. 2001;
Death Penalty Information Center, NAACP Legal Defense and Education Fund, *Death Row, U.S.A.*

	No.	Lethal injection	Electro-cution	Lethal gas	Firing squad	Hang-ing
TOTAL U.S.	**749**	**585**	**149**	**11**	**2**	**3**
Federal govt.	2	2	0	0	0	0
Alabama	23	0	23	0	0	0
Arizona	22	20	0	2	0	0
Arkansas	24	23	1	0	0	0
California	9	7	0	2	0	0
Colorado	1	1	0	0	0	0
Delaware	13	12	0	0	0	1
Florida	51	7	44	0	0	0
Georgia	27	4	23	0	0	0
Idaho	1	1	0	0	0	0
Illinois	12	12	0	0	0	0
Indiana	9	6	3	0	0	0
Kentucky	2	1	1	0	0	0
Louisiana	26	6	20	0	0	0
Maryland	3	3	0	0	0	0
Mississippi	4	0	0	4	0	0
Missouri	53	53	0	0	0	0
Montana	2	2	0	0	0	0
Nebraska	3	0	3	0	0	0
Nevada	9	8	0	1	0	0
New Mexico	1	1	0	0	0	0
North Carolina	21	19	0	2	0	0
Ohio	2	2	0	0	0	0
Oklahoma	48	48	0	0	0	0
Oregon	2	2	0	0	0	0
Pennsylvania	3	3	0	0	0	0
South Carolina	25	20	5	0	0	0
Tennessee	1	1	0	0	0	0
Texas	256	256	0	0	0	0
Utah	6	4	0	0	2	0
Virginia	83	58	26	0	0	0
Washington	4	2	0	0	0	2
Wyoming	1	1	0	0	0	0

Note: Table shows methods used since 1977. Lethal injection was used in 78%. 13 states—Arizona, Arkansas, California, Delaware, Georgia, Indiana, Louisiana, Nevada, North Carolina, South Carolina, Utah, Virginia, and Washington—have employed 2 methods. 28 states had no executions during the period.

Total Estimated Arrests, 2000

Source: FBI, *Uniform Crime Reports*, 2000

Total[1, 2]	**13,980,297**
Murder and nonnegligent manslaughter	13,227
Forcible rape	27,469
Robbery	106,130
Aggravated assault	478,417
Burglary	289,844
Larceny-theft	1,166,362
Motor vehicle theft	148,225
Arson	16,530
Violent crime[3]	**625,132**
Property crime[4]	**1,620,928**
Crime Index total[5]	**2,246,054**
Other assaults	1,312,169
Forgery and counterfeiting	108,654
Fraud	345,732
Embezzlement	18,952
Stolen property; buying, receiving, possessing	118,641
Vandalism	281,305
Weapons; carrying, possessing, etc.	159,181
Prostitution and commercialized vice	87,620
Sex offenses (except forcible rape and prostitution)	93,399
Drug abuse violations	1,579,566
Gambling	10,842
Offenses against the family and children	147,663
Driving under the influence	1,471,289
Liquor laws	683,124
Drunkenness	637,554
Disorderly conduct	638,740
Vagrancy	32,542
All other offenses	3,710,434
Suspicion	5,682
Curfew and loitering law violations	154,711
Runaways	141,975

(1) Does not include suspicion. (2) Because of rounding, the figures may not add to total. (3) Violent crimes are offenses of murder, forcible rape, robbery, and aggravated assault. (4) Property crimes are offenses of burglary, larceny-theft, and arson. (5) Includes arson.

Historic Assassinations Since 1865

1865—Apr. 14. U.S. Pres. Abraham Lincoln shot by John Wilkes Booth, a well-known actor with Confederate sympathies, at Ford's Theater in Washington, DC; died Apr. 15.

1881—Mar. 13. Alexander II, of Russia.—July 2. U.S. Pres. James A. Garfield shot by Charles J. Guiteau, a disappointed office seeker, in Washington, DC; died Sept. 19.

1894—June 24. Pres. Sadi Carnot of France, by Italian anarchist, Sante Caserio, in Lyon.

1898—Sept. 10. Empress Elizabeth of Austria, stabbed by Italian anarchist Luigi Luccheni.

1900—July 29. Umberto I, king of Italy.

1901—Sept. 6. U.S. Pres. William McKinley in Buffalo, NY; died Sept. 14. Leon Czolgosz executed for the crime.

1908—Feb. 1. King Carlos I of Portugal and his son Luis Felipe, in Lisbon.

1913—Feb. 23. Mexican Pres. Francisco I. Madero and Vice Pres. Jose Pino Suarez.—Mar. 18. George, king of Greece.

1914—June 28. Archduke Francis Ferdinand of Austria-Hungary and his wife in Sarajevo, Bosnia (later part of Bosnia and Herzegovina), by Gavrilo Princip.

1916—Dec. 30. Grigori Rasputin, powerful Russian monk.

1918—July 12. Grand Duke Michael of Russia, at Perm.—July 16. Nicholas II, abdicated as czar of Russia; his wife, the Czarina Alexandra; their son, Czarevitch Alexis; their daughters, Grand Duchesses Olga, Tatiana, Marie, Anastasia; and 4 members of their household, executed by Bolsheviks at Ekaterinburg.

1920—May 20. Mexican Pres. Gen. Venustiano Carranza in Tlaxcalantongo.

1922—Aug. 22. Michael Collins, Irish revolutionary.—Dec. 16. Polish Pres.Gabriel Narutowicz in Warsaw.

1923—July 20. Gen. Francisco "Pancho" Villa, ex-rebel leader, in Parral, Mexico.
1928—July 17. Gen. Alvaro Obregon, president-elect of Mexico, in San Angel, Mexico.
1932—May 6. Pres. Paul Doumer of France shot by Russian émigré, Pavel Gorgulov, in Paris.
1934—July 25. In Vienna, Austrian Chancellor Engelbert Dollfuss by Nazis.
1935—Sept. 8. U.S. Sen. Huey P. Long shot in Baton Rouge, LA, by Dr. Carl Austin Weiss, who was slain by Long's bodyguards; Long died Sept. 10.
1940—Aug. 20. Leon Trotsky (Lev Bronstein), 63, exiled Russian war minister, near Mexico City, by Ramon Mercador del Rio, a Spaniard.
1948—Jan. 30. Mohandas K. Gandhi, 78, shot in New Delhi, India, by Nathuram Vinayak Godse.—Sept. 17. Count Folke Bernadotte, UN mediator for Palestine, by Jewish extremists in Jerusalem.
1951—July 20. King Abdullah ibn Hussein of Jordan.—Oct. 16. Prime Min. Liaquat Ali Khan of Pakistan shot in Rawalpindi.
1956—Sept. 21. Pres. Anastasio Somoza of Nicaragua, shot in Leon; died Sept. 29.
1957—July 26. Pres. Carlos Castillo Armas of Guatemala, in Guatemala City by one of his own guards.
1958—July 14. King Faisal of Iraq; his uncle, Crown Prince Abdullah; and July 15, Prem. Nuri as-Said, by rebels in Baghdad.
1959—Sept. 25. Prime Min. Solomon Bandaranaike of Ceylon, by Buddhist monk in Colombo.
1961—Jan. 17. Ex-Prem. Patrice Lumumba of the Congo, in Katanga Province.—May 30. Dominican dictator Rafael Leonidas Trujillo Molina, near Ciudad Trujillo.
1963—June 12. Medgar W. Evers, NAACP's Mississippi field secretary, by Byron De La Beckwith in Jackson, MS.—Nov. 2. Pres. Ngo Dinh Diem of South Vietnam and his brother, Ngo Dinh Nhu, in a military coup.—Nov. 22. U.S. Pres. John F. Kennedy shot in Dallas, TX; accused gunman Lee Harvey Oswald was murdered by Jack Ruby while awaiting trial.
1965—Jan. 21. Iranian Prem. Hassan Ali Mansour in Tehran; 4 executed.—Feb. 21. Malcolm X, black nationalist, shot in New York City.
1966—Sept. 6. Prime Min. Hendrik F. Verwoerd of South Africa stabbed to death in parliament at Cape Town.
1968—Apr. 4. Rev. Dr. Martin Luther King Jr. fatally shot in Memphis, TN; James Earl Ray convicted of crime.—June 5. Sen. Robert F. Kennedy (D, NY) shot in Los Angeles; Sirhan Sirhan, convicted of crime.
1971—Nov. 28. Prime Min. Wasfi Tal of Jordan, in Cairo, by Palestinian guerrillas.
1973—Mar. 2. U.S. Amb. Cleo A. Noel Jr., U.S. Charge d'Affaires George C. Moore, and Belgian Charge d'Affaires Guy Eid killed by Palestinian guerrillas in Khartoum, Sudan.
1974—Aug. 19. U.S. Amb. to Cyprus, Rodger P. Davies, killed by sniper's bullet in Nicosia.
1975—Feb. 11. Pres. Richard Ratsimandrava, of Madagascar, shot in Tananarive.—Mar. 25. King Faisal of Saudi Arabia shot by nephew Prince Musad Abdel Aziz, in royal palace in Riyadh.—Aug. 15. Bangladesh Pres. Sheik Mujibur Rahman killed in coup.
1976—Feb. 13. Nigerian head of state, Gen. Murtala Ramat Mohammed, by self-styled "young revolutionaries."
1977—Mar. 16. Kamal Jumblat, Lebanese Druse chieftain, shot near Beirut.—Mar. 18. Congo Pres. Marien Ngouabi shot in Brazzaville.
1978—July 9. Former Iraqi Prem. Abdul Razak Al-Naif shot in London.
1979—Feb. 14. U.S. Amb. Adolph Dubs shot by Afghan Muslim extremists in Kabul.—Aug. 27. Lord Mountbatten, World War II hero, and 2 others killed when a bomb exploded on his fishing boat off the coast of Co. Sligo, Ire. IRA claimed responsibility.—Oct. 26. South Korean Pres. Park Chung Hee and 6 bodyguards fatally shot by Kim Jae Kyu, head of South Korean CIA, and 5 aides in Seoul.
1980—Apr. 12. Liberian Pres. William R. Tolbert slain in military coup.—Sept. 17. Former Nicaraguan Pres. Anastasio Somoza Debayle shot in Paraguay.
1981—Oct. 6. Egyptian Pres. Anwar al-Sadat shot by commandos while reviewing a military parade in Cairo; 7 others killed, 28 wounded; 4 convicted as assassins and executed.
1982—Sept. 14. Lebanese Pres.-elect Bashir Gemayel killed by bomb in east Beirut.
1983—Aug. 21. Philippine opposition leader Benigno Aquino Jr. shot by gunman at Manila International Airport.
1984—Oct. 31. Indian Prime Min. Indira Gandhi shot and killed by 2 Sikh bodyguards, in New Delhi.
1986—Feb. 28. Swedish Prem. Olof Palme shot by gunman on Stockholm street.
1987—June 1. Lebanese Prem. Rashid Karami killed when bomb exploded aboard a helicopter.
1988—Apr. 16. PLO military chief Khalil Wazir (Abu Jihad) gunned down by Israeli commandos in Tunisia.
1989—Aug. 18. Colombian presidential candidate Luis Carlos Galan killed by Medellín cartel drug traffickers at campaign rally in Bogotá.—Nov. 22. Lebanese Pres. Rene Moawad killed when bomb exploded next to his motorcade.
1990—Mar. 22. Presidential candidate Bernando Jamamillo Ossa shot by gunman at an airport in Bogotá.
1991—May 21. Rajiv Gandhi, former prime min. of India, killed by bomb during election rally in Madras.
1992—June 29. Mohammed Boudiaf, pres. of Algeria, shot by gunman in Annaba.
1993—May 1. Ranasinghe Premadasa, pres. of Sri Lanka, killed by bomb in Colombo.
1994—Mar. 23. Luis Donaldo Colosio Murrieta, Mexican presidential candidate, shot by gunman Mario Aburto Martinez. — Apr. 6. Burundian Pres. Cyprien Ntaryamira and Rwandan Pres. Juvenal Habyarimana killed, with 8 others, when their plane was apparently shot down.
1995—Nov. 4. Yitzhak Rabin, prime min. of Israel, shot by gunman Yigal Amir at peace rally in Tel Aviv.
1996—Oct. 2. Andrei Lukanov, former Bulgarian prime minister, shot outside his home by an unidentified gunman.
1998—Feb. 6. Claude Erignac, prefect of Corsica, shot in the back while walking to a concert, by two unidentified gunmen.—Apr. 26. Guatemalan Rom. Catholic Bishop Juan Gerardi Conedera, human rights champion, found beaten to death in Guatemala City; 4 persons convicted, June 8, 2001.
1999—Mar. 23. Paraguayan Vice-Pres. Luis Maria Argaña, ambushed and shot to death, along with his driver, by four unidentified assailants.—Apr. 9. Niger's Pres. Ibrahim Bare Mainassara, ambushed and killed by dissident soldiers.—Oct. 27. Armenia's Prime Min. Vazgen Sarkissian, along with 7 others, was shot to death during a session of Parliament.
2000—Jan. 15. Serbian paramilitary leader Zeljko Raznjatovic (alias Arkan), with 2 others, shot and killed by unidentified gunman in Belgrade hotel lobby; 4 suspects later charged with the killing.— June 8. Brig. Gen. Stephen Saunders, Britain's senior military representative in Greece, shot and killed by 2 men on motorcycle, while driving a car in an Athens suburb.
2001—Jan. 16. Congolese Pres. Laurent Kabila, shot to death by a bodyguard at his presidential palace in the capital, Kinshasa.—June 1. Nepal's King Birendra, Queen Aiswarya, and 7 other royals fatally shot by Crown Prince Dipendra, who also fatally wounded himself.—Sept. 9. Afghan Northern Alliance (anti-Taliban) guerrilla leader Ahmed Shah Massoud, fatally injured in suicide-attack bombing in N. Afghanistan by 2 Arabs posing as journalists; died Sept. 15.—Sept. 24. Colombian culture minister Consuelo Araujo, kidnapped, later slain, by Revolutionary Armed Forces guerrillas.—Oct. 14. Abdel Rahman Hamad, a leader of Palestinian militant group Hamas, shot dead by Israeli military snipers.—Oct. 17. Israeli tourism minister Rehavam Zeevi, fatally shot; Popular Front for the Liberation of Palestine (PFLP) claimed responsibility.—Dec. 23. Nigerian Justice Min. Bola Ige, shot dead at his home in Ibadan.
2002—Feb. 14. Afghanistan's aviation and tourism minister, Abdul Rahman, beaten and stabbed to death at Kabul airport.—May 6. Dutch right-wing politician Pim Fortuyn shot dead outside a radio station in Hilversum, the Netherlands; Volkert van der Graaf, an animal rights activist, was charged with the murder.—July 6. Afghan Vice Pres. Haji Abdul Qadir, shot dead outside his office in Kabul.—July 23. Salah Sherhada, a founder of the armed wing of Hamas, killed along with 14 civilians in an assassination air strike on Gaza City by an Israeli fighter jet.

Assassination Attempts

1912—Oct. 14. Former U.S. Pres. Theodore Roosevelt shot and wounded by demented man in Milwaukee, WI.
1933—Feb. 15. In Miami, FL, Joseph Zangara, anarchist, shot at Pres.-elect Franklin D. Roosevelt, but a woman seized his arm, and the bullet fatally wounded Mayor Anton J. Cermak, of Chicago, who died Mar. 6.
1944—July 20. Adolf Hitler was injured when a bomb, planted by a German officer, exploded in Hitler's headquarters. One aide was killed and 12 were injured in the explosion.
1950—Nov. 1. In an attempt to assassinate Pres. Harry Truman, 2 members of a Puerto Rican nationalist movement—Griselio Torresola and Oscar Collazo—tried to shoot their way into Blair House. Torresola was killed, and a White House policeman, Pvt. Leslie Coffelt, was fatally shot.
1970—Nov. 27. Pope Paul VI unharmed by knife-wielding assailant who attempted to attack him in Manila airport.
1972—May 15. Alabama Gov. George Wallace shot in Laurel, MD, by Arthur Bremer; seriously crippled.

1975—Sept. 5. Pres. Gerald R. Ford unharmed when a Secret Service agent grabbed a pistol aimed at him by Lynette (Squeaky) Fromme, a Charles Manson follower, in Sacramento.—Sept. 22. Pres. Ford again unharmed when Sara Jane Moore fired a revolver at him.

1980—May 29. Civil rights leader Vernon E. Jordan Jr. shot and wounded in Ft. Wayne, IN.

1981—Jan. 16. Irish political activist Bernadette Devlin McAliskey and her husband shot and seriously wounded by 3 members of a Protestant paramilitary group in Co. Tyrone, Ire.—Mar. 30. Pres. Ronald Reagan, along with Press Sec. James Brady, Secret Service agent Timothy J. McCarthy, and Washington, DC, policeman Thomas Delahanty shot and seriously wounded by John W. Hinckley Jr. in Washington, DC.—May 13. Pope John Paul II and 2 bystanders shot and wounded by Mehmet Ali Agca, an escaped Turkish murderer, in St. Peter's Square, Rome.

1982—May 12. Pope John Paul II unharmed after guards overpowered a man with a knife, in Fatima, Portugal.

1984—Oct. 12. British Prime Min. Margaret Thatcher narrowly escaped injury when a bomb, said to have been planted by the IRA, exploded at the Grand Hotel in Brighton, England, during a Conservative Party conference. Four died, including a member of Parliament.

1986—Sept. 7. Chilean Pres. Gen. Augusto Pinochet Ugarte escaped unharmed when his motorcade was attacked by rebels using rockets, bazookas, grenades, and rifles.

1995—June 26. Egyptian Pres. Hosni Mubarak unharmed when gunmen fired on his motorcade in Addis Ababa, Ethiopia. Four died, including 2 Ethiopian police officers.

1997—Feb. 12. Colombian Pres. Ernesto Samper Pizano unharmed when a bomb exploded on a runway in Barranquilla as his plane was preparing to land.—Apr. 30. Tajik Pres. Imamali Rakhmanov injured when a grenade was thrown at him. 2 others were killed.

1998—Feb. 9. Georgian Pres. Eduard A. Shevardnadze unharmed when gunmen fired on his motorcade in Tbilisi, Georgia. Three died, including 2 bodyguards and 1 assailant.

2000—Sept. 18. Armed men attempted to assassinate Côte d'Ivoire military leader Gen. Robert Guei in a predawn raid.

2002—Apr. 8. Afghan defense minister Muhammad Qassim Fahim, unharmed after bomb exploded in a Jalalabad marketplace as his motorcade passed. 5 others were killed.—Apr. 14. Leading Colombian presidential candidate Alvaro Uribe Velez unharmed after bomb exploded under parked bus as his motorcade passed in Barranquilla; 3 bystanders were killed.—May 6. Gulbuddin Hekmatyar, an Afghan warlord opposed to Karzai's interim government, survived an attempt on his life made outside Kabul by the CIA.—July 14. French Pres. Jacques Chirac, unharmed after Maxime Brunerie, a gunman with ties to neo-Nazi groups, fired at his open-top jeep during a Bastille Day parade in Paris.—Sept. 5. Afghan Pres. Hamid Karzai, unharmed after Abdul Rahman, apparently operating in connection with the Taliban, opened fire on his car in Kandahar; 3 were killed by Karzai's U.S. guards: the gunman, a bystander who had tackled him, and an Afghan bodyguard.

Notable U.S. Kidnappings Since 1924

Robert Franks, 13, in Chicago, **May 22, 1924,** by 2 youths, Richard Loeb and Nathan Leopold, who killed boy. Demand for $10,000 ignored. Loeb died in prison; Leopold paroled 1958.

Charles A. Lindbergh Jr., 20 mos. old, in Hopewell, NJ, **Mar. 1, 1932;** found dead **May 12.** Ransom of $50,000 paid to man identified as Bruno Richard Hauptmann, 35, paroled German convict who entered U.S. illegally. Hauptmann was convicted after spectacular trial at Flemington, and electrocuted in Trenton, NJ, prison, **Apr. 3, 1936.**

William A. Hamm Jr., 39, in St. Paul, **June 15, 1933.** $100,000 paid. Alvin Karpis given life, paroled in 1969.

Charles F. Urschel, in Oklahoma City, **July 22, 1933.** Released **July 31** after $200,000 paid. George "Machine Gun" Kelly and 5 others sentenced to life.

Brooke L. Hart, 22, in San Jose, CA. Thomas Thurmond and John Holmes arrested after demanding $40,000 ransom. When Hart's body was found in San Francisco Bay, **Nov. 26, 1933,** a mob attacked the jail and lynched the 2 kidnappers.

George Weyerhaeuser, 9, in Tacoma, WA, **May 24, 1935.** Returned home **June 1** after $200,000 paid. Kidnappers given 20 to 60 years.

Charles Mattson, 10, in Tacoma, WA, **Dec. 27, 1936.** Found dead **Jan. 11, 1937.** Kidnapper asked $28,000, but failed to contact for delivery.

Arthur Fried, in White Plains, NY, **Dec. 4, 1937.** Body not found. Two kidnappers executed.

Robert C. Greenlease, 6, taken from Kansas City, MO, school **Sept. 28, 1953,** held for $600,000. Body was found Oct. 7. Bonnie Brown Heady and Carl A. Hall pleaded guilty and were executed.

Peter Weinberger, 32 days old, Westbury, NY, **July 4, 1956,** for $2,000 ransom, not paid. Child found dead. Angelo John LaMarca, 31, convicted, executed.

Lee Crary, 8, in Everett, WA, **Sept. 22, 1957;** $10,000 ransom, not paid. He escaped after 3 days, led police to George E. Collins, who was convicted.

Frank Sinatra Jr., 19, from hotel room in Lake Tahoe, CA, **Dec. 8, 1963.** Released **Dec. 11** after his father paid $240,000 ransom. Three men sentenced to prison.

Barbara Jane Mackle, 20, abducted **Dec. 17, 1968,** from Atlanta, GA, motel; found unharmed 3 days later, buried in a coffin-like box 18 inches underground, after her father had paid $500,000 ransom; Gary Steven Krist sentenced to life, Ruth Eisenmann-Schier to 7 years.

Mrs. Roy Fuchs, 35, and 3 children held hostage 2 hours, **May 14, 1969,** in Long Island, NY, released after her husband, a bank manager, paid kidnappers $129,000 in bank funds; 4 men arrested, ransom recovered.

Virginia Piper, 49, abducted **July 27, 1972,** from her home in suburban Minneapolis; found unharmed near Duluth 2 days later after husband paid $1 million ransom.

Patricia "Patty" Hearst, 19, taken from her Berkeley, CA, apartment **Feb. 4, 1974.** "Symbionese Liberation Army" captors demanded her father, publisher Randolph Hearst, give millions to the area's poor. Implicated in a San Francisco bank holdup, **Apr. 15.** The FBI, **Sept. 18, 1975,** captured her and others; they were indicted on various charges. Patricia Hearst convicted of bank robbery, **Mar. 20, 1976;** released from prison under executive clemency, **Feb. 1, 1979.** In 1978, William and Emily Harris were sentenced to 10 years to life for the kidnapping; both were paroled in 1983.

J. Reginald Murphy, 40, an editor of *Atlanta* (GA) *Constitution,* kidnapped **Feb. 20, 1974;** freed **Feb. 22** after newspaper paid $700,000 ransom. William A. H. Williams arrested; most of the money recovered.

E. B. Reville, Hepzibah, GA, banker, and wife, Jean, kidnapped **Sept. 30, 1974.** Ransom of $30,000 paid. He was found alive; Jean Reville was found dead **Oct. 2.**

Jack Teich, Kings Point, NY, steel executive, seized **Nov. 12, 1974;** released **Nov. 19** after payment of $750,000.

Adam Walsh, 6, abducted from a Hollywood, FL, department store, **July 27, 1981.** Although his severed head was found 2 weeks later, his body was never recovered. John Walsh, Adam's father, became active in raising awareness about missing children.

Sidney J. Reso, oil company executive, seized **Apr. 29, 1992**; died **May 3;** Arthur D. Seale and wife, Irene, arrested **June 19.** Arthur Seale pleaded guilty, sentenced to life in prison; Irene Seale sentenced to 20-year prison term.

Polly Klaas, 12, Petaluma, CA, abducted at knife point, **Oct. 1, 1993,** during a slumber party at her home. Police arrested Richard Allen Davis on **Nov. 30;** he led them to her body, found **Dec. 4** in wooded area of Cloverdale, CA. Davis found guilty **June 18, 1996**, and sentenced to death **Sept. 26.**

Marshall I. Wais, 79, owner of 2 San Francisco steel companies, kidnapped **Nov. 19, 1996,** from his San Francisco home. Released unharmed the same day after $500,000 ransom paid; Thomas William Taylor and Michael K. Robinson arrested the same day.

Daniel Pearl, 38, reporter for *Wall Street Journal*, disappeared **Jan. 23, 2002**, while researching story in Karachi, Pakistan. His captors **Jan. 27** sent an e-mail demanding release of suspected Taliban and al-Qaeda fighters held by the U.S. British-born militant Ahmad Omar Saeed Sheikh **Feb. 14** admitted to organizing the kidnapping and said Pearl was dead. Sheikh and 3 others were convicted **July 15** of kidnapping and murder by a judge in Hyderabad.

Danielle van Dam, 7, discovered missing from her parents' San Diego home **Feb. 2**. David Westerfield, a neighbor, arrested **Feb. 22** after DNA evidence identified van Dam's blood in his motor home; he pleaded not guilty. Van Dam's body found **Feb. 27** in rural area outside San Diego. Westerfield convicted of murder **Aug. 21**; awaited final sentencing after jury recommended the death penalty. Among other child abductions that made headlines in 2002: **Elizabeth Smart**, 14, was apparently abducted from her home in Salt Lake City, UT, **June 5**; a suspect was charged **July 22** in the kidnapping and murder of **Samantha Runnion**, 5, whose body was discovered **July 16**, about 50 miles from her home in Stanton, CA; **Erica Pratt**, 7, was abducted in Philadelphia **July 22** but escaped her kidnappers, who had demanded a $150,000 ransom from her low-income family, **July 23**.

TRAVEL AND TOURISM

Tourism Trends

After growing by an estimated 7.4% in 2000, world tourism in 2001 fell slightly, by an estimated 0.6%, according to the World Tourism Organization. The 1st decrease in international tourist arrivals since 1982 was attributed to deteriorating economic conditions across the globe and, late in the year, the effects of the September 11th terrorist attacks on the United States. Worldwide, there were 693 million international tourist arrivals in 2001, 4 million fewer than in 2000. South Asia and the Americas were the most affected regions, experiencing 6% declines for the year. Worldwide tourism receipts fell 2.6%, from $474 billion in 2000 to $462 billion in 2001. Europe earned half of all tourism receipts, the Americas 26%, East Asia and the Pacific 18%, Africa 2.5%, and South Asia 1.0%.

In 2002, according to a preliminary analysis by the World Tourism Org., the lag in volume of tourists after Sept. 11 appeared to be easing somewhat, but revenues were not picking up proportionately, because of declining prices. According to the Travel Industry Assoc. of America, average airfares charged by U.S. carriers in Aug. 2002 were down 4% from a year before, with average U.S. lodging costs down 2%. Cruise travel volume was up in early 2002, according to the Cruise Line International Assoc., with more than 3.6 million North Americans taking cruises in 1st half 2002, compared with just under 3.5 million in 1st half 2001.

World Tourism Receipts, 1990-2001

Source: World Tourism Organization

(in billions; figures rounded)

1990	$269	1992	$315	1994	$354	1996	$436	1998	$445	2000	$476
1991	278	1993	324	1995	405	1997	436	1999	455	2001	462

World's Top 10 Tourist Destinations, 2001

Source: World Tourism Organization

(number of arrivals in millions; excluding same-day visitors)

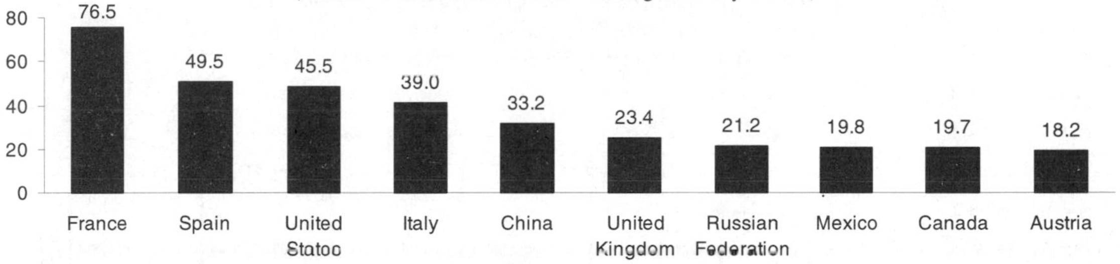

Top Countries in Tourism Earnings, 2001

Source: World Tourism Organization

International tourism receipts (excluding transportation); in billions of dollars

Rank 2001	Rank 1990	Country	Receipts 2001	Rank 2001	Rank 1990	Country	Receipts 2001	Rank 2001	Rank 1990	Country	Receipts 2001
1	1	United States	$72.3	6	6	Germany	$17.2	11	NA	Turkey	$8.9
2	4	Spain	32.9	7	5	United Kingdom	15.9	12	10	Mexico	8.4
3	2	France	29.6	8	7	Austria	12.0	13	11	Hong Kong, China	8.2
4	3	Italy	25.9	9	9	Canada	10.8*	14	15	Australia	7.6
5	25	China[1]	17.8	10	9	Greece	9.2*	15	8	Switzerland	7.6

NA = Not available. * Figures are for 2000; rank is projected. (1) Excluding Hong Kong.

Average Number of Vacation Days per Year, Selected Countries

Source: World Tourism Organization

Country	Days	Country	Days	Country	Days
Italy	42	Brazil	34	Korea	25
France	37	United Kingdom	28	Japan	25
Germany	35	Canada	26	United States	13

International Travel to the U.S., 1986-2001

Source: Tourism Industries, International Trade Administration, Dept. of Commerce

(Visitors each year are in millions; some figures are revised and may differ from other sources.)

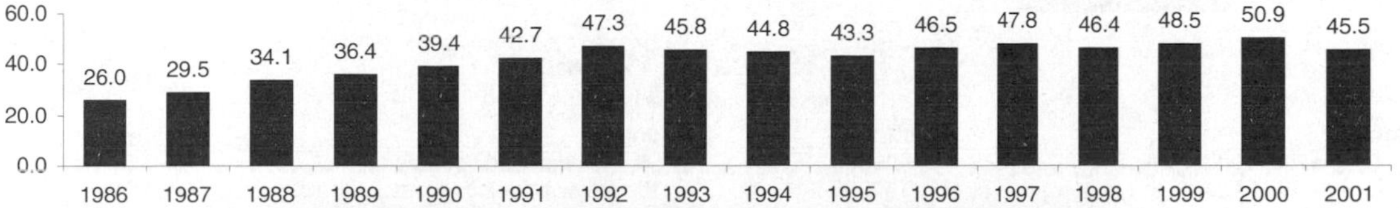

WORLD ALMANAC QUICK QUIZ

How fast can you go on the world's fastest roller coaster?

(a) 32 mph; (b) 55 mph; (c) 78 mph; (d) over 100 mph

For the answer look in this chapter, or see page 1008.

International Visitors to the U.S.[1]

Source: Tourism Industries, International Trade Administration, Dept. of Commerce

Country of origin	Visitors (thousands)[2]	Expenditures (millions)[3]	Expenditures per visitor[3]	Country of origin	Visitors (thousands)[2]	Expenditures (millions)[3]	Expenditures per visitor[3]
Canada	14,594	$6,206	$440	Brazil	737	$2,034	$3,058
Mexico	10,322	4,112	415	South Korea	662	1,251	2,507
Japan	5,061	9,711	2,012	Italy	612	1,691	2,701
United Kingdom	4,703	8,398	1,975	Venezuela	577	1,697	3,074
Germany	1,786	4,398	2,216	**All countries**	**50,891**	**$74.9 bil[4]**	**$1,472**
France	1,087	2,330	2,200				

(1) Excludes cruise travel. (2) Preliminary 2000 data. (3) Figures for expenditures and expenditures per visitor are based on 1999 data; excludes international passenger fare payments. (4) Does not include international traveler spending on U.S. carriers for transactions made outside the U.S.

Traveler Spending in the U.S., 1987-2001

Source: Tourism Industries, International Trade Administration, Dept. of Commerce

(in billions)

	Domestic Travelers	International Travelers		Domestic Travelers	International Travelers		Domestic Travelers	International Travelers
1987	$235	$31	1992	$306	$55	1997	$407	$73
1988	258	38	1993	323	58	1998	426	71
1989	273	47	1994	340	58	1999	446	75
1990	291	43	1995	360	63	2000	NA	82
1991	296	48	1996	386	70	2001	NA	73*

* Preliminary figure.

U.S. Domestic Leisure Travel Volume, 1994-2001

Source: "Tourism Works for America," 2002 edition, Travel Industry Assn. of America

(in millions of person-trips of 50 mi or more, one-way)

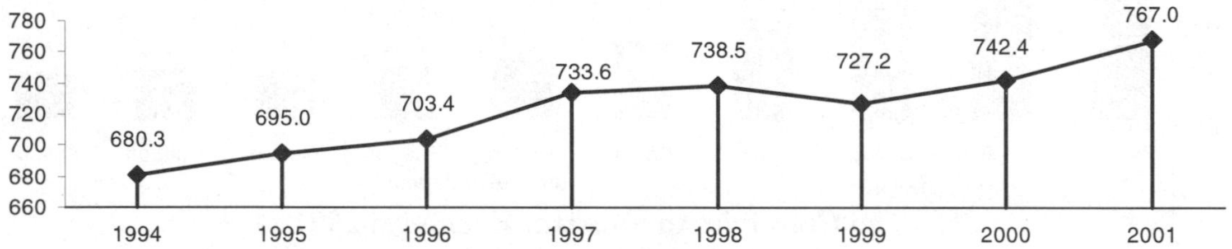

Top U.S. States by Total Traveler Spending, 2000

Source: "Tourism Works for America," 2002 edition, Travel Industry Assn. of America

(includes spending, in billions of dollars, in states by both domestic and international travelers)

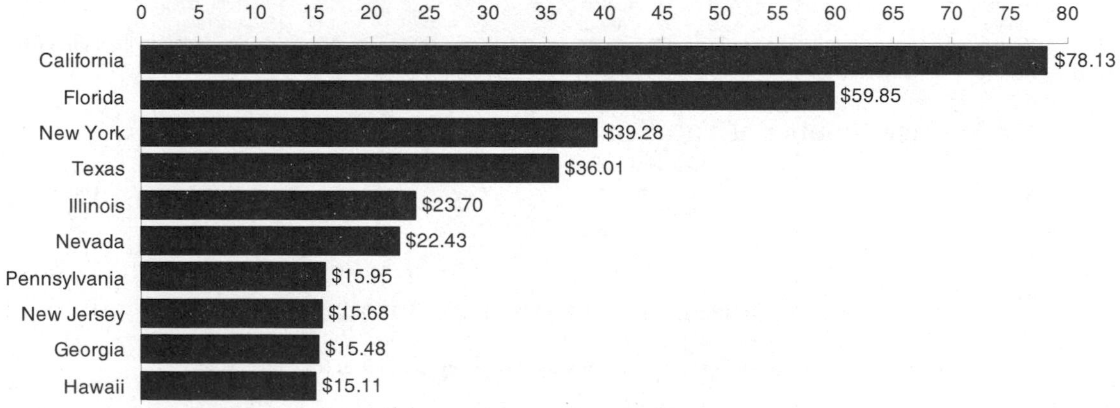

Top 15 Travel Websites

Source: comScore Media Metrix

Rank		Visitors[1]
1.	www.expedia.com	16,336,000
2.	www.orbitz.com	11,107,000
3.	www.travelocity.com	10,718,000
4.	www.priceline.com	6,367,000
5.	www.cheaptickets.com	6,091,000
6.	www.hotwire.com	5,327,000
7.	www.southwest.com	4,185,000
8.	www.trip.com	3,837,000
9.	www.hoteldiscounts.com	3,597,000
10.	www.travelnow.com	3,421,000
11.	www.aa.com	3,139,000
12.	www.sidestep.com	2,908,000
13.	www.delta.com	2,861,000
14.	www.itn.net	2,385,000
15.	www.united.com	2,140,000

(1) Number of users who visited at least once in June 2002.

Travel Websites

The following websites are among those that may be of use in planning trips and making arrangements. Websites listed under "Maps" enable the user to plot a route to a destination. Inclusion here does not represent endorsement by The World Almanac.

AIRLINES

American Airlines
www.aa.com

America West Airlines
www.americawest.com

Continental Airlines
www.flycontinental.com

Delta Air Lines
www.delta.com

Northwest Airlines
www.nwa.com

Southwest Airlines
www.iflyswa.com

United Airlines
www.ual.com

USAirways
www.usair.com

BUSES

Gray Line Worldwide
www.grayline.com

Greyhound Lines
www.greyhound.com

Peter Pan Bus Lines
www.peterpanbus.com

TRAINS

Amtrak
www.amtrak.com

BC Rail (Canada)
www.bcrail.com

Rail Europe
www.raileurope.com

CAR RENTALS

Alamo Rent A Ca
www.goalamo.com

Avis Rent-A-Car
www.avis.com

Budget Rent A Car
www.budgetrentacar.com

Dollar Rent A Car
www.dollarcar.com

Enterprise Rent-A-Car
www.enterprise.com

Hertz
www.hertz.com

National Car Rental
www.nationalcar.com

Rent-A-Wreck
www.rent-a-wreck.com

Thrifty Rent-A-Car
www.thrifty.com

CRUISE LINES

Carnival Cruise Lines
www.carnival.com

Celebrity Cruises
www.celebrity-cruises.com

Costa Cruise Lines
www.costacruises.com

Cunard Line
www.cunardline.com

Holland America Line
www.hollandamerica.com

Norwegian Cruise Line
www.ncl.com

Princess Cruises
www.princesscruises.com

Royal Caribbean Int'l.
www.rccl.com

Windjammer Barefoot Cruises
www.windjammer.com

HOTELS/RESORTS

Best Western Int'l.
www.bestwestern.com

Choice Hotels Int'l., Clarion Hotels & Resorts, Comfort Inns, Econo Lodges, MainStay Suites, Quality Inns, Rodeway Inns, Sleep Inns
www.hotelchoice.com

Days Inn of America
www.daysinn.com

Doubletree Hotels
www.doubletree.com

Embassy Suites
www.embassy-suites.com

Four Seasons Hotels
www.fshr.com

Hilton Hotels
www.hilton.com

Holiday Inn Worldwide
www.holiday-inn.com

Hyatt Hotels and Resorts
www.hyatt.com

Inter-Continental Hotels
www.interconti.com

Loews Hotels
www.loewshotels.com

Marriott Int'l.
www.marriott.com

Radisson Hotels Int'l.
www.radisson.com

Sheraton Hotels & Resorts
www.sheraton.com

Westin Hotels & Resorts
www.westin.com

Wyndham Hotels & Resorts
www.wyndham.com

TRAVEL PLANNING

www.travelocity.com
www.priceline.com
www.Expedia.com
www.itn.net
www.lowestfare.com
www.trip.com

MAPS

www.freetrip.com
www.mapquest.com
www.mapsonus.com

Some Notable Roller Coasters

Source: www.rollercoaster.com, www.rcdb.com, World Almanac research; 2001

Fastest Roller Coasters

Name	Speed	Location
Dodonpa	107 mph	Fujikyu Highland; Yamanashi, Japan
Tower of Terror	100 mph	Dreamworld; Australia
Superman The Escape	100 mph	Six Flags Magic Mountain; Valencia, CA
Steel Dragon 2000	95 mph	Nagashima Spaland; Mie, Japan
Millennium Force	93 mph	Cedar Point; Sandusky, OH

Tallest Roller Coasters

Name	Drop	Location
Superman The Escape	415 ft	Six Flags Magic Mountain; Valencia, CA
Tower of Terror	377 ft	Dreamworld; Australia
Steel Dragon 2000	318 ft	Nagashima Spaland; Mie, Japan
Millennium Force	310 ft	Cedar Point; Sandusky, OH
Fujiyama	259 ft	Fujikyu Highland; Yamanashi, Japan

Longest Roller Coasters

Name	Length	Location
Steel Dragon 2000	8,133 ft	Nagashima Spaland; Mie, Japan
Daidarasaurus	7,677 ft	Expoland, Osaka, Japan
Ultimate	7,442 ft	Lightwater Valley; Yorkshire, UK
Beast	7,400 ft	Paramount's Kings Island; Kings Island, OH
Son of Beast	7,032 ft	Paramount's Kings Island; Kings Island, OH

Roller Coasters With Longest Drop

Name	Drop	Location
Superman The Escape	328 ft	Six Flags Magic Mountain; Valencia, CA
Tower of Terror	328 ft	Dreamworld; Australia
Steel Dragon 2000	307 ft	Nagashima Spaland; Mie, Japan
Millennium Force	300 ft	Cedar Point; Sandusky, OH
Goliath	255 ft	Six Flags Magic Mountain; Valencia, CA
Titan	255 ft	Six Flags Over Texas; Dallas, TX

IT'S A FACT: The world's oldest amusement park dates back to 1583 when a young girl discovered a running spring in a deer park north of Copenhagen, Denmark. The spring quickly became a destination for the ailing, who believed its water had healing properties. Entertainment for the visitors, like traveling theater companies, dancers, bear leaders, and horse shows were soon to follow. Bakken, the hill on which the entertainers set up camp, has had a continuous history as an amusement "park" ever since, and today ranks among Europe's top ten most-visited amusement parks.

Top 50 Amusement/Theme Parks Worldwide, 2001

Source: Amusement Business, Aug. 2002, ranked by attendance

Rank	Park and Location	Country	Attendance
1.	Tokyo Disneyland	Japan	17,708,000
2.	Magic Kingdom at Walt Disney World, Lake Buena Vista, FL	United States	14,784,000*
3.	Disneyland, Anaheim, CA	United States	12,350,000*
4.	Disneyland Paris, Marne-La-Vallee	France	12,200,000
5.	Everland, Kyonggi-Do	South Korea	9,028,000
6.	Epcot at Walt Disney World, Lake Buena Vista, FL	United States	9,010,000*
7.	Universal Studios, Osaka	Japan	9,000,000*
8.	Disney-MGM Studios at Walt Disney World, Lake Buena Vista, FL	United States	8,366,000*
9.	Disney's Animal Kingdom at Walt Disney World, Lake Buena Vista, FL	United States	7,771,000*
10.	Lotte World, Seoul	South Korea	7,450,000*
11.	Universal Studios at Universal Orlando, FL	United States	7,290,000
12.	Blackpool (England) Pleasure Beach	United Kingdom	6,500,000*

Rank	Park and Location	Country	Attendance
13.	Islands of Adventure at Universal Orlando, FL	United States	5,520,000*
14.	Seaworld Florida, Orlando, FL	United States	5,100,000*
15.	Yokohama Hakkeijima Sea Paradise	Japan	5,065,400*
16.	Disney's California Adventure, Anaheim, CA	United States	5,000,000*
17.	Universal Studios Hollywood, Universal City, CA	United States	4,732,000*
18.	Busch Gardens, Tampa Bay, FL	United States	4,600,000*
19.	Seaworld California, San Diego, CA	United States	4,100,000*
20.	Tokyo Disneysea	Japan	4,000,000*
21.	Nagashima Spa Land, Kuwana	Japan	3,900,000
	Tivoli Gardens, Copenhagen	Denmark	3,900,000
23.	Knott's Berry Farm, Buena Park, CA	United States	3,589,000
24.	Six Flags Great Adventure, Jackson, NJ	United States	3,560,000*
25.	Adventuredome at Circus Circus, Las Vegas, NV	United States	3,400,000*
	Morey's Piers, Wildwood, NJ	United States	3,400,000*
27.	Paramount's Kings Island, Kings Island, OH	United States	3,350,000*
28.	Universal's Port Aventura, Salou	Spain	3,339,000*
29.	Six Flags Magic Mountain, Valencia, CA	United States	3,200,000*
30.	Seoul Land, Kyonggi-Do	South Korea	3,106,845*
31.	Cedar Point, Sandusky, OH	United States	3,100,000*
	Efteling, Kaatsheuvel	The Netherlands	3,100,000*
	Europa-Park, Rust	Germany	3,100,000*
	Liseburg, Gothenburg	Sweden	3,100,000*
35.	Ocean Park, Hong Kong	China	3,000,000
	Santa Cruz Beach Boardwalk, CA	United States	3,000,000*
	Six Flags Over Texas, Arlington, TX	United States	3,000,000*
38.	Paramount Canada's Wonderland, Maple, Ontario	Canada	2,975,000
39.	Gardaland, Castelnuovo Del Garda	Italy	2,934,378
40.	Six Flags Great America, Gurnee, IL	United States	2,900,000*
41.	Suzuka Circuit	Japan	2,889,900
42.	Six Flags Worlds of Adventure, Aurora, OH	United States	2,750,000
43.	Busch Gardens, Williamsburg, VA	United States	2,700,000*
44.	Six Flags Mexico, Mexico City	Mexico	2,670,000*
45.	La Feria De Chapultapec, Mexico City	Mexico	2,600,000
46.	Hersheypark, Hershey, PA	United States	2,560,000
47.	Bakken, Klampenborg	Denmark	2,500,000*
	Parque Espana, Shima-gun	Japan	2,500,000*
49.	Knott's Camp Snoopy, Bloomington, MN	United States	2,418,000*
50.	Six Flags Over Georgia, Atlanta, GA	United States	2,400,000*

* Figures are projected from previous year's attendance.

Passports, Health Regulations, and Travel Warnings for Foreign Travel

Source: Bureau of Consular Affairs, U.S. Dept. of State

Passports are issued by the U.S. Department of State to citizens and nationals of the U.S. for the purpose of documenting them for foreign travel and identifying them as U.S. citizens. For U.S. citizens traveling on business or as tourists, especially in Europe, a U.S. passport is often sufficient to gain admission for a limited stay. For many countries, however, a **visa** must also be obtained before entering. It is the responsibility of the traveler to check in advance and obtain any visas where required, from the appropriate embassy or nearest consulate of each country.

Each country has its own specific guidelines concerning length and purpose of visit, etc. Some may require visitors to display proof that they (1) have sufficient funds to stay for the intended time period and (2) have onward/return tickets.

Some countries, including **Canada, Mexico,** and some **Caribbean** islands, do not require a passport or a visa for limited stays. Such countries do require proof of U.S. citizenship, and may have other requirements that must be met. For further information, check with the embassy or nearest consulate of the country you plan to visit.

How to Obtain a Passport

Those who have never been issued a passport in their own name must apply in person before (1) a passport agent; (2) a clerk of any federal court or state court of record or a clerk or judge of a probate court accepting applications; (3) a postal clerk at a post office that is authorized to accept passport applications; or (4) a U.S. diplomatic or consular officer abroad.

A DSP-11 is the correct form to use for those who must apply in person. All persons are required to obtain individual passports in their own name. However, a parent or legal guardian must execute the application for children under 13.

Persons who possess their most recent passport, if it was issued within the last 12 years and after their 18th birthday, may be eligible to apply for a new passport by mail. The form DSP-82, *Application for Passport by Mail*, must be filled out and mailed to the address shown on the form, together with the previous passport, 2 recent identical photographs (see below), and a fee of $55. The DSP-82 may not be used if the most recent passport has been altered or mutilated.

Proof of citizenship—A full validity passport previously issued to the applicant or one in which he or she was included will be accepted as proof of U.S. citizenship. If the applicant has no prior passport and was born in the U.S., a certified copy of the birth certificate generally must be presented. It must generally show the given name and surname, the date and place of birth, and that the birth record was filed shortly after birth. A delayed birth certificate (filed more than 1 year after date of birth) is acceptable if it shows that acceptable secondary evidence was used for creating this record.

If a birth certificate is not obtainable, a notice from a state registrar must be submitted stating that no birth record exists. It must be accompanied by the best obtainable secondary evidence, such as a baptismal certificate or hospital birth record.

A naturalized citizen with no previous passport must present a Certificate of Naturalization. A person born abroad claiming U.S. citizenship through either a native-born or a naturalized citizen parent must normally submit a Certificate of Citizenship issued by the Immigration and Naturalization Service or a Consular Report of Birth or Certification of Birth Abroad issued by the Dept. of State. If such a document has not been obtained, evidence of citizenship of the parent(s) through whom citizenship is claimed and evidence that would establish the parent/child relationship must be submitted. Additionally, if citizenship is derived through birth to citizen parent(s), the applicant must submit parents' marriage certificate plus an affidavit from parent(s) showing periods and places of residence or presence in the U.S. and abroad, and specifying periods spent abroad in the employment of the U.S. government, including the armed forces, or with certain international organizations. If citizenship is derived through naturalization of parents, evidence of admission to the U.S. for permanent residence also is required.

It is important to apply for a passport as far in advance as possible. Passport offices are busiest between March and September. It can take several weeks to receive a passport.

Photographs—Passport applicants must submit 2 identical photographs that are recent (normally not more than 6 months old) and that are a good likeness of and satisfactorily identify the applicant. Photographs should be 2 x 2 in. in size. The image size, from bottom of chin to top of head (including hair), should not be less than 1 inch or more than 1-3/8 in. Photographs should be portrait-type prints. They must be clear, front view, full face, with a plain white or off-white background. Photos that depict the applicant as relaxed and smiling are encouraged.

Identity—Applicants must establish their identity to the satisfaction of the authorities. Generally acceptable documents of identity include a previous U.S. passport, a Certificate of Naturalization, a Certificate of Citizenship, a valid driver's license, or a government identification card. Applicants may not use a Social Security card, learner's or temporary driver's license, credit card, or expired ID card. Extremely old documents cannot be used by themselves.

Applicants unable to establish identity must present some documentation in their own name and be accompanied by a person who has known them at least 2 years and is a U.S. citizen or legal U.S. permanent resident alien. That person must sign an affidavit before the individual who executes the application, and must establish his or her own identity.

Fees—For persons under 16 years of age, the basic passport fee is $40. These passports are valid for 5 years from date of issue. The basic fee is $55 for passports issued to persons 16 and older. These passports are valid for 14 years from date of issuance. For all first-time passports, there is an additional $30 execution fee. To receive a passport within 10 days or less, a $60 expedite fee is required. There is no execution fee when using the renewal form DSP-82, *Application for Passport by Mail*. This form is available on-line at the Passport Services website. Applicants eligible to use this form pay only a $55 passport fee.

Passport loss—The loss or theft of a valid passport should be reported immediately in writing to Passport Services, Correspondence Branch, 1111 19th St., NW, Suite 500, Washington, DC 20036, telephone: (202) 955-0487, or to the nearest passport agency or nearest U.S. embassy or consulate when abroad. The DSP-64, *Statement Regarding Lost or Stolen Passport*, is available on-line at the address below.

General Information—Visit Passport Services on the internet at www.travel.state.gov/passport_services.html

Health Regulations

Under the regulations adopted by the World Health Organization, a country may require International Certificates of Vaccination against yellow fever. A cholera immunization may be required for travelers from infected areas. Check with health care providers or your records to see that other immunizations (e.g., for tetanus and polio) are up-to-date.

Prophylactic medication for malaria and certain other preventive measures are advisable for travel to some countries. No immunizations are needed to return to the U.S. An increasing number of countries have regulations regarding AIDS testing, particularly for longtime visitors. Detailed information is included in *Health Information for International Travel*, available from the U.S. Government Printing Office, Washington, DC 20402, for $24. Information may also be obtained from your local health department or physician, or by calling the Centers for Disease Control and Prevention at 1-877-FYI-TRIP (1-877-394-8747).

General information—The booklets *Passports—Applying for the Easy Way* and *Foreign Entry Requirements* are available for 50¢ each from the Consumer Information Center, Pueblo, CO 81009. For online information, as well as HIV Testing Requirements, go to the Consular Affairs website—www.travel.state.gov

Travel Warnings

Travel Warnings are issued when the State Dept. decides, based on relevant information, to recommend that Americans avoid travel to a certain country; these are subject to change. For the latest information, 24 hours a day, dial (202) 647-5225 from a touch-tone telephone. As of Oct. 1, 2002, travel warnings were in effect for: Afghanistan, Algeria, Angola, Bosnia and Herzegovina, Burundi, Central African Republic, Colombia, Congo, Côte d'Ivoire, Guinea-Bissau, Indonesia, Iran, Iraq, Israel (West Bank and Gaza), Lebanon, Liberia, Libya, Macedonia, Nigeria, Pakistan, Somalia, Sudan, Tajikistan, and Yemen.

Customs Exemptions for Travelers

Source: U.S. Dept. of the Treasury, U.S. Customs Service

U.S. residents returning after a stay abroad of at least 48 hours are usually granted customs exemptions of $800 each (this and all exemptions figured according to fair retail value). The duty-free articles must accompany the traveler at the time of return, be for personal or household use, have been acquired as an incident of the trip, and be properly declared to Customs. No more than 1 liter of alcoholic beverages or more than 100 cigars and 200 cigarettes (1 carton) may be included in the $800 exemption. The exemption for alcoholic beverages holds only if the returning resident is at least 21 years old at the time of arrival. Cuban cigars may be included only if purchased in Cuba.

If a U.S. resident arrives directly or indirectly from a U.S. island possession—American Samoa, Guam, or U.S. Virgin Islands—a customs exemption of $1,200 is allowed. Up to 1,000 cigarettes may be included, but only 200 of them may have been purchased elsewhere. If a U.S. resident returns from any one of the following places, the exemption is $600: Antigua and Barbuda, Aruba, Bahamas, Barbados, Belize, British Virgin Islands, Costa Rica, Dominica, Dominican Republic, El Salvador, Grenada, Guatemala, Guyana, Haiti, Honduras, Jamaica, Montserrat, Netherlands Antilles, Nicaragua, Panama, St. Kitts and Nevis, St. Lucia, St. Vincent and the Grenadines, Trinidad and Tobago.

The $400, $600, or $1,200 exemption may be granted only if the exemption has not been used in whole or part within the preceding 30-day period and only if the stay abroad was for at least 48 hours. The 48-hr absence requirement does not apply to travelers returning from Mexico or U.S. Virgin Islands. Travelers who cannot claim the $800, $600, or $1,200 exemption because of the 30-day or 48-hr provisions may bring in free of duty and tax articles acquired abroad for personal or household use up to a value of $25.

There are also allowances for goods when shipped. Goods shipped for personal use may be imported free of duty and tax if the total value is no more than $200. This exemption does not apply to perfume containing alcohol if it is valued at more than $5 retail, to alcoholic beverages, or to cigars and cigarettes. The $200 mail exemption does not apply to merchandise subject to absolute or tariff-rate quotas unless the item is for personal use. Tailor-made suits ordered from Hong Kong, however, are subject to quota/visa requirements even if imported for personal use.

Bona fide gifts of not more than $100 in value, when shipped, can be received in the U.S. free of duty and tax, provided that the same person does not receive more than $100 in gift shipments in one day. The limit is increased to $200 for bona fide gift items shipped from U.S. Virgin Islands, American Samoa, or Guam. (Shipping of alcoholic beverages, including wine and beer, by mail is prohibited by U.S. postal laws.) These gifts are not declared by the traveler upon return to the U.S.

The U.S. Customs Service booklet "Know Before You Go" answers frequently asked customs questions and is available free by writing U.S. Customs Services, KBYG, PO Box 7407, Washington, DC 20044, or by visiting the U.S. Customs website—www.customs.ustreas.gov

NATIONS OF THE WORLD

Initials used include: AL (Arab League), APEC (Asia-Pacific Economic Cooperation Group), ASEAN (Association of Southeast Asian Nations), AU (African Union), Benelux (Belgium, Netherlands, and Luxembourg), CARICOM (Caribbean Community and Common Market), CIS (Commonwealth of Independent States), EU (European Union), FAO (UN Food & Agriculture Org.), ILO (Intl. Labor Org.), IMF (Intl. Monetary Fund), IMO (Intl. Maritime Org.), NATO (North Atlantic Treaty Org.), OAS (Org. of American States), OECD (Org. for Economic Cooperation and Development), OECS (Org. of Eastern Caribbean States), OSCE (Org. for Security and Cooperation in Europe), UN (United Nations), WHO (World Health Org.), WTrO (World Trade Org., formerly GATT). FY = fiscal year.

Sources: American Automobile Manufacturers Assn.; (U.S.) Census Bureau: Intl. Data Base; (U.S.) Central Intelligence Agency: *The World Factbook;* (U.S.) Dept. of Commerce; (U.S.) Dept. of Energy; Intl. Institute for Strategic Studies: *The Military Balance;* Intl. Monetary Fund; (U.S.) Dept. of State; UN Demographic Yearbook; UN Food and Agriculture Organization; UN Population Division: *World Urbanization Prospects;* UN Statistical Yearbook; Ward's Communications; World Tourism Organization; Encyclopaedia Britannica Book of the Year; The Europa World Year Book; The Statesman's Yearbook. Telephone data supplied by the Intl. Telecommunication Union, from the World Telecommunication Indicators database, copyright ITU.

Note: Because of rounding or incomplete enumeration, some percentages may not add to 100%. **National population and health** figures are mid-2002 estimates, unless otherwise noted. Percentage of urban population is for 1999. **City** populations, except capitals, are 2001 estimates for the populations of **urban agglomerations,** i.e. whole metropolitan areas, in 2000. All capital populations are estimates for 2001. Where indicated, the latest available population of the city proper is also given. **Electricity production** figures are 2000. **GDP** estimates are based on purchasing power parity calculations, which involve use of intl. dollar price weights applied to quantities of goods and services produced. **Tourism** figures represent receipts from international tourism and are 1999 unless otherwise noted. **Budget** figures are for expenditures, unless otherwise noted. **Motor vehicle** statistics are for 1996 unless otherwise noted; comm. (commercial) vehicles include trucks and buses. Per-person figures in **communications** data are 1995 or later. **Telephone figures** are 2001 for total subscribers, unless otherwise noted. **Literacy** rates given generally measure the percent of population able to read and write on a lower elementary school level, not the (smaller) percent able to read instructions necessary for a job or license. **Embassy addresses** are for Wash., DC, area code (202), unless otherwise noted.

For further details and later information on developments around the world, see the front-of-the-book Feature section and the Chronology of the Year's Events. *See pages 497-512 for full-color maps and flags of all nations.*

Afghanistan

Islamic State of Afghanistan

People: Population: 27,755,775. **Age distrib.** (%): <15: 42.2; 65+: 2.8. **Pop. density:** 111 per sq. mi. **Urban:** 21%. **Ethnic groups:** Pashtun 38%, Tajik 25%, Hazara 19%, Uzbek 6%. **Principal languages:** Pashtu 35%, Afghan Persian (Dari) 50% (both official), Turkic (incl. Uzbek, Turkmen) 11%. **Chief religions:** Sunni Muslim 84%, Shi'a Muslim 15%.

Geography: Area: 250,000 sq. mi. **Location:** In SW Asia, NW of the Indian subcontinent. **Neighbors:** Pakistan on E, S; Iran on W; Turkmenistan, Tajikistan, Uzbekistan on N. The NE tip touches China. **Topography:** The country is landlocked and mountainous, much of it over 4,000 ft. above sea level. The Hindu Kush Mts. tower 16,000 ft. above Kabul and reach a height of 25,000 ft. to the E. Trade with Pakistan flows through the 35-mile-long Khyber Pass. The climate is dry, with extreme temperatures, and there are large desert regions, though mountain rivers produce intermittent fertile valleys. **Capital:** Kabul, 2,734,000.

Government: Type: Transitional administration. **Head of state and gov.:** Pres. Hamid Karzai; b Dec. 24, 1957; in office: June 19, 2002. **Local divisions:** 32 provinces. **Defense budget** (2000): $250 mil. **Active troops:** NA.

Economy: Industries: Textiles, soap, furniture, shoes. **Chief crops:** Nuts, wheat, fruits. **Minerals:** Gas, oil, copper, coal, zinc, iron. **Other resources:** Wool, karakul pelts, mutton. **Arable land:** 12%. **Livestock** (2000): cattle: 3.48 mil; chickens: 7.2 mil; goats: 7.37 mil; sheep: 18.0 mil. **Electricity prod.:** 0.38 bil. kWh. **Labor Force:** agri. 70%, ind. 15%, services 15%..

Finance: Monetary unit: Afghani (Sept. 2002: 4,750.00 = $1 U.S.). **GDP** (2000 est.): $21 bil. **Per capita GDP:** $800. **Imports** (1996 est.): $150 mil.; partners: FSU, Pakistan, Iran, Japan, Singapore, India, South Korea, Germany. **Exports** (1996 est.): $80 mil.; partners: FSU, Pakistan, Iran, Germany, India, UK, Belgium, Luxembourg, Czech Republic. **Tourism:** $1 mil. **Budget:** NA.

Transport: Railroad: Length: 16 mi. **Motor vehicles:** 35,000 pass. cars, 32,000 comm. vehicles. **Civil aviation:** 98.3 mil pass.-mi.; 3 airports.

Communications: TV sets: 10 per 1,000 pop. **Radios:** 73.7 per 1,000 pop. **Telephones**: 29,000 main lines. **Daily newspaper circ.:** 11 per 1,000 pop.

Health: Life expectancy: 47.3 male; 45.9 female. **Births** (per 1,000 pop.): 41. **Deaths** (per 1,000 pop.): 17.4. **Natural inc.:** 2.36%. **Infant mortality** (per 1,000 live births): 144.8.

Education: Compulsory: ages 7-13. **Literacy:** 31.5%.

Major Intl. Organizations: UN (FAO, IBRD, ILO, IMF, WHO).

Embassy: 2341 Wyoming Ave. NW 20008; 234-3770.

Website: www.afghanistanembassy.org

Afghanistan, occupying a favored invasion route since antiquity, has been variously known as Ariana or Bactria (in ancient times) and Khorasan (in the Middle Ages). Foreign empires alternated rule with local emirs and kings until the 18th century, when a unified kingdom was established. In 1973, a military coup ushered in a republic.

Pro-Soviet leftists took power in a bloody 1978 coup and concluded an economic and military treaty with the USSR. In Dec. 1979 the USSR began a massive airlift into Kabul and backed a new coup, leading to installation of a more pro-Soviet leader. Soviet troops fanned out over Afghanistan and waged a protracted guerrilla war with Muslim rebels, in which some 15,000 Soviet troops reportedly died.

A UN-mediated agreement was signed Apr. 14, 1988, providing for withdrawal of Soviet troops, a neutral Afghan state, and repatriation of refugees. Afghan rebels rejected the pact, vowing to continue fighting while "Soviets and their puppets" remained in Afghanistan. The Soviets completed their troop withdrawal Feb. 15, 1989; fighting between Afghan rebels and government forces ensued.

Communist Pres. Najibullah resigned Apr. 16, 1992, as competing guerrilla forces advanced on Kabul. The rebels achieved power Apr. 28, ending 14 years of Soviet-backed regimes. More than 2 million Afghans had been killed and 6 million had left the country since 1979.

Following the rebel victory there were clashes between moderates and Islamic fundamentalist forces. Burhanuddin Rabbani, a guerrilla leader, became president June 28, 1992, but fierce fighting continued around Kabul and elsewhere. The Taliban, an insurgent Islamic fundamentalist faction, gained increasing control and in Sept. 1996 captured Kabul and set up a government. The Taliban executed former President Najibullah and empowered Islamic religious police to enforce codes of dress and behavior that were especially restrictive to women. Rabbani and other ousted leaders fled to the north.

Victories in the northern cities of Mazar-e Sharif, Aug. 8, 1998, and Taloqan, Aug. 8-11, 1998, gave the Taliban control over more than 90% of the country; the killing of several Iranian diplomats during the Mazar-e Sharif takeover further heightened tensions with Iran. On Aug. 20, 1998, U.S. cruise missiles struck SE of Kabul, hitting facilities the U.S. said were terrorist training camps run by a wealthy Saudi, Osama bin Laden. The UN imposed sanctions Nov. 14, 1999, when Afghanistan refused to turn over bin Laden to the U.S. for prosecution; a UN ban on all military aid to the Taliban took effect Jan. 19, 2001. By March, aid agencies reported that drought and continued warfare had put more than 1 million people at risk of famine. Meanwhile, the Taliban launched a campaign to destroy non-Islamic antiquities.

Ahmed Shah Massoud, leader of the anti-Taliban resistance, died Sept. 9, 2001, of wounds sustained in a suicide bombing by assassins posing as journalists. After the Sept. 11 attacks on the World Trade Center and Pentagon, the U.S., blaming bin Laden, demanded that the Taliban surrender him and shut down his al-Qaeda terrorist network. When the Taliban refused, the U.S., with British assistance, began bombing Afghanistan Oct. 7. Supported by the U.S., the opposition Northern Alliance recaptured Mazar-e Sharif Nov. 9 and took Kabul 4 days later; the Taliban forces abandoned Kandahar, their last stronghold, to S tribesmen Dec. 7. A power-sharing agreement signed Dec. 5 by 4 anti-Taliban factions, including the Northern Alliance, provided for an interim government headed by Hamid Karzai, a Pashtun tribal leader; the UN authorized Dec. 20 a multinational security force. Meanwhile, U.S. and allied forces continued to hunt for bin Laden, whose fate remained unknown, and other top al-Qaeda and Taliban officials.

At a conference in Tokyo, Jan. 21-22, 2002, donor countries and agencies pledged more than $4.5 bil in aid to Afghanistan over 5 years. Meeting June 13 in Kabul, a traditional council (*loya jirga*) chose Karzai to head a new transitional government. An errant U.S. air strike on the night of June 30-July 1 apparently killed 48 people at Kakarak, N of Kandahar, while villagers were celebrating a wedding. Gunmen July 6 assassinated Vice Pres. Haji Abdul Qadir, a Pashtun. A car bomb in Kabul killed 26 people Sept. 5; in Kandahar that same day, Karzai, guarded by U.S. troops, survived an assassination attempt.

Albania

Republic of Albania

People: Population: 3,544,841. **Age distrib.** (%): <15: 29.5; 65+: 7.0. **Pop. density:** 334 per sq. mi. **Urban:** 41%. **Ethnic groups:** Albanians (Gegs in N, Tosks in S) 95%, Greeks 3%. **Principal languages:** Albanian (official; Tosk is the official dialect), Greek. **Chief religions:** Muslim 70%, Albanian Orthodox 20%, Roman Catholic 10%.

Geography: Area: 10,600 sq. mi. **Location:** SE Europe, on SE coast of Adriatic Sea. **Neighbors:** Greece on S, Yugoslavia on N, Macedonia on E. **Topography:** Apart from a narrow coastal plain, Albania consists of hills and mountains covered with scrub forest, cut by small E-W rivers. **Capital:** Tirana, 299,000.

Government: Type: Republic. **Head of state:** Pres. Alfred Moisiu; b Dec. 1, 1929; in office: July 24, 2002. **Head of gov.:** Prime Min. Fatos Nano; b 1952; in office: July 31, 2002. **Local divisions:** 36 districts, 1 municipality. **Defense budget** (1999): $43 mil. **Active troops:** 27,000.

Economy: Industries: Food processing, textiles and clothing, lumber. **Chief crops:** Corn, wheat, potatoes, watermelon, vegetables. **Minerals:** Chromium, coal, oil, gas. **Crude oil reserves** (2000): 165 mil bbls. **Other resources:** Timber. **Arable land:** 21%. **Livestock** (2001): cattle: 720,000; chickens: 4.00 mil.; goats: 1.12 mil.; pigs: 81,000; sheep: 1.94 mil . **Electricity prod.:** 4.74 bil. kWh. **Labor force:** agri. 50%, ind. and services 50%.

Finance: Monetary unit: Lek (Sept. 2002: 138.96 = $1 U.S.). **GDP** (2000 est.): $10.5 bil. **Per capita GDP:** $3,000. **Imports GDP** (2000 est.): $1 bil.; partners (2000): Italy 37%, Greece 28%. **Exports** (2000 est.): $310 mil.; partners (2000): Italy 67%, Greece 15%. **Tourism** (1998): $54 mil. **Budget** (1997 est.): $676 mil. **Intl. reserves less gold** (end 2000): $270 mil. **Gold:** 110,000 oz t. **Consumer prices** (change in 2000): 0.1%.

Transport: Railroad: Length: 419 mi. **Chief ports:** Durres, Sarande, Vlore. **Civil aviation:** 21.9 mil pass.-mi.; 1 airport.

Communications: TV sets: 89 per 1,000 pop. **Radios:** 157 per 1,000 pop. **Telephones:** 547,500. **Daily newspaper circ.:** 54 per 1,000 pop.

Health: Life expectancy: 69.3 male; 75.1 female. **Births** (per 1,000 pop.): 18.6. **Deaths** (per 1,000 pop.): 6.5. **Natural inc.:** 1.21%. **Infant mortality** (per 1,000 live births): 38.6.

Major Intl. Organizations: UN (IBRD, ILO, IMF, IMO, WHO), OSCE.

Education: Free, compulsory: ages 6-14. **Literacy** (1997): 100%.

Embassy: 2100 S St. NW 20008; 223-4942.

Website: depinf.gov.al/english/default1.htm

Ancient Illyria was conquered by Romans, Slavs, and Turks (15th century); the latter Islamized the population. Independent Albania was proclaimed in 1912, republic was formed in 1920. King Zog I ruled 1925-39, until Italy invaded.

Communist partisans took over in 1944, allied Albania with USSR, then broke with USSR in 1960 over de-Stalinization. Strong political alliance with China followed, leading to several billion dollars in aid, which was curtailed after 1974. China cut off aid in 1978 when Albania attacked its policies after the death of Chinese ruler Mao Zedong. Large-scale purges of officials occurred during the 1970s.

Enver Hoxha, the nation's ruler for 4 decades, died Apr. 11, 1985. Eventually the new regime introduced some liberalization, including measures in 1990 providing for freedom to travel abroad. Efforts were begun to improve ties with the outside world. Mar. 1991 elections left the former Communists in power, but a general strike and urban opposition led to the formation of a coalition cabinet including non-Communists.

Albania's former Communists were routed in elections Mar. 1992, amid economic collapse and social unrest. Sali Berisha was elected as the first non-Communist president since World War II. Berisha's party claimed a landslide victory in disputed parliamentary elections, May 26 and June 2, 1996. Public protests over the collapse of fraudulent investment schemes in Jan. 1997 led to armed rebellion and anarchy. The UN Security Council, Mar. 28, authorized a 7,000-member force to restore order. Socialists and their allies won parliamentary elections, June 29 and July 6, and international peacekeepers completed their pullout by Aug. 11, 1997. During NATO's air war against Yugoslavia, Mar.-June 1999, Albania hosted some 465,000 Kosovar refugees.

Algeria

Democratic and Popular Republic of Algeria

People: Population: 32,277,942. **Age distrib.** (%): <15: 34.2 65+: 4.1. **Pop. density:** 35 per sq. mi. **Urban:** 60%. **Ethnic groups:** Arab-Berber 99%. **Principal languages:** Arabic (official), French, Berber dialects. **Chief religion:** Sunni Muslim (state religion) 99%.

Geography: Area: 919,600 sq. mi. **Location:** In NW Africa, from Mediterranean Sea into Sahara Desert. **Neighbors:** Morocco on W; Mauritania, Mali, Niger on S; Libya, Tunisia on E. **Topography:** The Tell, located on the coast, comprises fertile plains 50-100 miles wide, with a moderate climate and adequate rain. Two major chains of the Atlas Mts., running roughly E-W and reaching 7,000 ft., enclose a dry plateau region. Below lies the Sahara, mostly desert with major mineral resources. **Capital:** Algiers (El Djazair), 2,861,000.

Government: Type: Republic. **Head of state:** Pres. Abdelaziz Bouteflika; b Mar. 2, 1937; in office: Apr. 27, 1999. **Head of gov.:** Prime Min. Ali Benflis; b Sept. 8, 1944; in office: Aug. 26, 2000. **Local divisions:** 48 provinces. **Defense budget:** (2000) $1.8 bil. **Active troops:** 124,000.

Economy: Industries: Petroleum, natural gas, light industries, mining. **Chief crops:** Grains, grapes, citrus, olives. **Minerals:** Iron, oil, gas, phosphates, zinc, lead. **Crude oil reserves** (2001): 12.7 bil bbls. **Arable land:** 3%. **Livestock** (2001): cattle: 1.70 mil; chickens: 110.00 mil.; goats: 3.50 mil.; pigs: 5,700; sheep: 19.30 mil. **Fish catch** (1999): 99,332 metric tons. **Electricity prod.:** 23.56 bil. kWh. **Labor force:** government 29%, agri. 25%, construction and public works 15%, ind. 11%, other 20%.

Finance: Monetary unit: Dinar (Sept. 2002: 79.14 = $1 U.S.). **GDP** (2000 est.): $171 bil. **Per capita GDP:** $5,500. **Imports** (2000 est.): $9.2 bil.; partners (1999): France 30%, Italy 9%. **Exports** (2000 est.): $19.6 bil.; partners (1999): Italy 22%, U.S. 15%. Tourism (1998): $24 mil. **Budget** (2001 est.): $16 bil. **Intl. reserves less gold** (end 2000): $9.23 bil. **Gold:** 5.58 mil. oz t. **Consumer prices** (change in 1999): 2.6%.

Transport: Railroad: Length: 2,965 mi. **Motor vehicles:** 500,000 pass. cars, 420,000 comm. vehicles. **Civil aviation:** 1.95 bil pass.-mi.; 28 airports. **Chief ports:** Algiers, Annaba, Oran.

Communications: TV sets: 71 per 1,000 pop. **Radios:** 122 per 1,000 pop. **Telephones:** 1,980,000. **Daily newspaper circ.:** 52 per 1,000 pop.

Health: Life expectancy: 68.9 male; 71.7 female. **Births** (per 1,000 pop.): 22.3. **Deaths** (per 1,000 pop.): 5.2. **Natural inc.:** 1.72%. **Infant mortality** (per 1,000 live births): 39.1.

Education: Compulsory: ages 6-15. **Literacy:** 62%.

Major Intl. Organizations: UN (FAO, IBRD, ILO, IMF, IMO, WHO), AL, AU, OPEC.

Embassy: 2118 Kalorama Rd. NW 20008; 265-2800.

Website: www.algeria-us.org

Earliest known inhabitants were ancestors of Berbers, followed by Phoenicians, Romans, Vandals, and, finally, Arabs. Turkey ruled 1518 to 1830, when France took control.

Large-scale European immigration and French cultural inroads did not prevent an Arab nationalist movement from launching guerrilla war. Peace, and French withdrawal, was negotiated with French Pres. Charles de Gaulle. One million Europeans left. Independence came July 5, 1962. Ahmed Ben Bella was the victor of infighting and ruled until 1965, when an army coup installed Col. Houari Boumedienne as leader; Boumedienne led until his death from a blood disease, 1978.

In 1967, Algeria declared war on Israel, broke ties with U.S., and moved toward eventual military and political ties with the USSR. Some 500 died in riots protesting economic hardship in 1988. In 1989, voters approved a new constitution, which cleared the way for a multiparty system.

The government canceled the Jan. 1992 elections that Islamic fundamentalists were expected to win, and banned all nonreligious activities at Algeria's 10,000 mosques. Pres. Mohammed Boudiaf was assassinated June 29, 1992. There were repeated attacks on high-ranking officials, security forces, foreigners, and others by militant Muslim fundamentalists over the next 7 years; pro-government death squads also were active.

Liamine Zeroual won the presidential election of Nov. 16, 1995. A new constitution banning Islamic political parties and increasing the president's powers passed in a referendum on Nov. 28, 1996. Pro-government parties won the parliamentary election of June 6, 1997. Abdelaziz Bouteflika, who became president after a flawed election on Apr. 15, 1999, made peace with rebels and won approval for an amnesty plan in a referendum on Sept. 16; by then, some 100,000 people had died in the civil war. Some 100 people died and thousands were injured in violent protests Apr.-June 2001, chiefly by Algeria's Berber minority. Floods in Nov. killed over 700 people.

WORLD ALMANAC QUICK QUIZ

Which animal is an Aussie?

(a) Komodo Dragon (b) Okapi

(c) Wombat (d) Great Spotted Kiwi

For the answer look in this chapter, or see page 1008.

Andorra

Principality of Andorra

People: Population: 68,403. **Age distrib.** (%): <15: 15.3; 65+: 12.6. **Pop. density:** 393 per sq. mi. **Urban:** 93%. **Ethnic groups:** Spanish 61%, Andorran 30%, French 6%. **Principal languages:** Catalan (official), French, Castilian. **Chief religion:** Predominently Roman Catholic.

Geography: Area: 174 sq. mi. **Location:** SW Europe, in Pyrenees Mts. **Neighbors:** Spain on S, France on N. **Topography:** High mountains and narrow valleys cover the country. **Capital:** Andorra la Vella, 21,000.

Government: Type: Parliamentary co-principality. **Heads of state:** President of France & Bishop of Urgel (Spain), as co-princes. **Head of gov.:** Marc Forné Molné; b Dec. 30, 1946; in office: Dec. 21, 1994. **Local divisions:** 7 parishes. **Defense budget:** Responsibility of France and Spain.

Economy: Industries: Tourism, cattle raising, timber, tobacco, banking. **Minerals:** Iron, lead. **Arable land:** 2%. **Labor force**: 78% serv., 21% ind

Finance: Monetary unit: French Franc (Sept. 2002: 6.72 = $1 U.S.). Spanish Peseta (Sept. 2001: 183.93 = $1 U.S.). **GDP** (1996 est.): $1.2 bil. **Per capita GDP:** $18,000. **Imports** (1998): $1.077 bil.; partners (1998): Spain 48%, France 35%. **Exports** (1998): $58 mil.; partners (1998): France 34%, Spain 58%. **Budget** (1997): $385 mil.

Transport: Motor vehicles: 35,358 pass. cars, 4,238 comm. vehicles.

Communications: TV sets: 315 per 1,000 pop. **Radios:** 156 per 1,000 pop. **Telephones** (2000): 57,800. **Daily newspaper circ.:** 62 per 1,000 pop.

Health: Life expectancy: 80.6 male; 86.6 female. **Births** (per 1,000 pop.): 10. **Deaths** (per 1,000 pop.): 5.6. **Natural inc.:** 0.44%. **Infant mortality** (per 1,000 live births): 4.1.

Education: Free, compulsory: ages 6-16. **Literacy** (1997): 100%.

Major Intl. Organizations: UN.

Embassy: 2 UN Plaza, 25th floor, New York, NY 10017; (212) 750-8064.

Website: www.andorra.ad/govern/governuk.html

Andorra was a co-principality, with joint sovereignty by France and the bishop of Urgel, from 1278 to 1993.

Tourism, especially skiing, is the economic mainstay. A free port, allowing for an active trading center, draws some 13 million tourists annually. Andorran voters chose to end a feudal system that had been in place for 715 years and adopt a parliamentary system of government Mar. 14, 1993.

Angola

Republic of Angola

People: Population: 10,593,171. **Age distrib.** (%): <15: 43.3; 65+: 2.7. **Pop. density:** 22 per sq. mi. **Urban:** 34%. **Ethnic groups:** Ovimbundu 37%, Kimbundu 25%, Bakongo 13%. **Principal languages:** Portuguese (official), various Bantu and other African languages. **Chief religions:** Indigenous beliefs 47%, Roman Catholic 38%, Protestant 15%.

Geography: Area: 481,400 sq. mi. **Location:** In SW Africa on Atlantic coast. **Neighbors:** Namibia on S, Zambia on E, Congo-Kinshasa (formerly Zaire) on N; Cabinda, an enclave separated from rest of country by short Atlantic coast of Congo-Kinshasa, borders Congo-Brazzaville. **Topography:** Most of Angola consists of a plateau elevated 3,000 to 5,000 feet above sea level, rising from a narrow coastal strip. There is also a temperate highland area in the west-central region, a desert in the S, and a tropical rain forest covering Cabinda. **Capital:** Luanda, 2,819,000.

Government: Type: Republic. **Head of state and gov.:** Pres. José Eduardo dos Santos; b Aug. 28, 1942; in office: Sept. 20, 1979. **Local divisions:** 18 provinces. **Defense budget:** (2000) $574 mil. **Active troops:** 130,500.

Economy: Industries: Petroleum, mining, cement; basic metal products; fish and food processing. **Chief crops:** Coffee, sugarcane, bananas. **Minerals:** Iron, diamonds (over 1 mil carats a year), gold, phosphates, oil. **Livestock** (2001): cattle: 4.04 mil; chickens: 6.80 mil.; goats: 2.15 mil.; pigs: 800,000; sheep: 350,000. **Crude oil reserves** (2001): 9.0 bil bbls. **Arable land:** 2%. **Fish catch** (1999): 72,189 metric tons. **Electricity prod.:** 1.19 bil. kWh. **Labor force:** agri. 85%, ind. and services 15%.

Finance: Monetary unit: Readjusted Kwanza (Sept. 2002: 48.15 = $1 U.S.). **GDP** (2000 est.): $10.1 bil. **Per capita GDP:** $1,000. **Imports** (2000 est.): $2.5 bil.; partners (1999): South Korea 16%, Portugal 15%. **Exports** (2000 est.): $7.8 bil.; partners (1999): U.S. 54%, South Korea 14%. **Tourism:** $13 mil. **Budget** $342 mil. **Intl. reserves less gold** (Apr. 2000): $342.52 mil. **Consumer prices** (change in 2000): 325%.

Transport: Railroad: Length: 1,739 mi. **Motor vehicles:** 197,000 pass. cars, 26,000 comm. vehicles. **Civil aviation:** 385.3 mil pass.-mi.; 17 airports. **Chief ports:** Cabinda, Lobito, Luanda.

Communications: TV sets: 48 per 1,000 pop. **Radios:** 39 per 1,000 pop. **Telephones:** 166,500. **Daily newspaper circ.:** 11 per 1,000 pop.

Health: Life expectancy: 37.6 male; 40.2 female. **Births** (per 1,000 pop.): 46.2. **Deaths** (per 1,000 pop.): 24.4. **Natural inc.:** 2.18%. **Infant mortality** (per 1,000 live births): 191.7.

Education: Free, compulsory: ages 7-15. **Literacy** (1998): 42%.

Major Intl. Organizations: UN (FAO, IBRD, ILO, IMF, IMO, WHO, WTrO), AU.

Embassy: 1615 M St. NW, Suite 900, 20036; 785-1156.

Website: www.angola.org

From the early centuries AD to 1500, Bantu tribes penetrated most of the region. Portuguese came in 1583, allied with the Bakongo kingdom in the north, and developed the slave trade. Large-scale colonization did not begin until the 20th century, when 400,000 Portuguese immigrated.

A guerrilla war begun in 1961 lasted until 1975, when Portugal granted independence. Fighting then erupted between three rival rebel groups—the National Front, based in Zaire (now Congo), the Soviet-backed Popular Movement for the Liberation of Angola (MPLA), and the National Union for the Total Independence of Angola (UNITA), aided by the U.S. and South Africa. Cuban troops and Soviet aid helped the MPLA win control of most of the country by 1976, although fighting continued through the 1980s. A peace accord between the MPLA government and UNITA was signed May 1, 1991.

Elections were held in Sept. 1992, but fighting again broke out, as UNITA rejected the results. UNITA signed a new peace treaty with the government, Nov. 20, 1994, but the rebels were slow to demobilize. The UN Security Council voted, Aug. 28, 1997, to impose sanctions on UNITA. In Aug. 1998, Angola sent thousands of troops into Congo-Kinshasa (formerly Zaire) to support Laurent Kabila's regime. The UN ended its mission in Angola in Mar. 1999, as the civil war continued.

As of 2001, the UN estimated that the war with UNITA had claimed some 1 million lives and left another 2.5 million people homeless. More than 250 died when UNITA rebels ambushed a train Aug. 10. Rebel leader Jonas Savimbi was killed by government troops Feb. 22, 2002. UNITA agreed to a truce Apr. 4.

Antigua and Barbuda

People: Population: 67,448. **Age distrib.** (%): <15: 28; 65+: 4.9. **Pop. density:** 397 per sq. mi. **Urban:** 37%. **Ethnic groups:** Primarily black. **Principal language:** English (official). **Chief religion:** Predominantly Anglican.

Geography: Area: 170 sq. mi. **Location:** Eastern Caribbean. **Neighbors:** St. Kitts & Nevis to W, Guadeloupe (Fr.) to S. **Capital:** Saint John's, (2001) 24,000.

Government: Type: Constitutional monarchy with British-style parliament. **Head of state:** Queen Elizabeth II; represented by Gov.-Gen. James Carlisle; b Aug. 5, 1937; in office: June 10, 1993. **Head of gov.:** Prime Min. Lester Bird; b Feb. 21, 1938; in office: Mar. 9, 1994. **Local divisions:** 6 parishes, 2 dependencies. **Defense budget:** (2000) $4 mil. **Active troops:** 170.

Economy: Industries: Tourism, construction, light manufacturing. **Arable land:** 18%. **Livestock** (2001): cattle: 15,700; chickens: 90,000; goats: 11,800; pigs: 2,200; sheep: 12,200. **Electricity prod.:** 0.10 bil. kWh. **Labor force:** commerce and services 82%, agri. 11%, ind. 7%.

Finance: Monetary unit: East Caribbean Dollar (Sept. 2002: 2.70 = $1 U.S.). **GDP** (1999 est.): $533 mil. **Per capita GDP:** $8,200. **Imports** (1998): $330 mil.; partners: U.S. 27%, UK 16%. **Exports** (1998): $38 mil.; partners: OECS 26%, Barbados 15%. Tourism (1998): $256 mil. **Budget** (1997 est.): $141.2 mil. **Intl. reserves less gold** (end 2000): $49 mil.

Transport: Motor vehicles: 13,250 pass. cars, 1,423 comm. vehicles. **Civil aviation:** 155.4 mil pass.-mi.; 2 airports.

Communications: TV sets: 435 per 1,000 pop. **Radios:** 776 per 1,000 pop. **Telephones:** 62,300.

Health: Life expectancy: 68.7 male; 73.5 female. **Births** (per 1,000 pop.): 18.8. **Deaths** (per 1,000 pop.): 5.8. **Natural inc.:** 1.31%. **Infant mortality** (per 1,000 live births): 21.6.

Education: Compulsory: ages 5-16. **Literacy** (1992): 90%.

Major Intl. Organizations: UN (FAO, IBRD, ILO, IMF, IMO, WHO, WTrO), Caricom, the Commonwealth, OAS, OECS.

Embassy: 3216 New Mexico Ave. NW 20016; 362-5211.

Website: www.antigua-barbuda.com

Columbus landed on Antigua in 1493. The British colonized it in 1632.

The British associated state of Antigua achieved independence as Antigua and Barbuda on Nov. 1, 1981. The government maintains close relations with the U.S., United Kingdom, and Venezuela. The country was hit hard by Hurricane Luis, Sept. 1995. About 3,000 refugees fleeing a volcanic eruption on Montserrat have settled in Antigua since 1995.

Argentina
Argentine Republic

People: Population: 37,812,817. **Age distrib.** (%): <15: 26.5; 65+: 10.4. **Pop. density:** 36 per sq. mi. **Urban:** 90%. **Ethnic groups:** White 85% (mostly Spanish, Italian); mestizo, Amerindian, other nonwhites 15%. **Principal languages:** Spanish (official), English, Italian. **Chief religion:** Nominally Roman Catholic 90%.

Geography: Area: 1,056,600 sq. mi., second largest country in South America. **Location:** Occupies most of southern South America. **Neighbors:** Chile on W; Bolivia, Paraguay on N; Brazil, Uruguay on NE. **Topography:** Mountains in the W are: the Andean, Central, Misiones, and Southern ranges. Aconcagua is the highest peak in the western hemisphere, alt. 22,834 ft. E of the Andes are heavily wooded plains, called the Gran Chaco in the N, and the fertile, treeless Pampas in the central region. Patagonia, in the S, is bleak and arid. Rio de la Plata, an estuary in the NE, 170 by 140 mi., is mostly fresh water, from 2,485-mi Parana and 1,000-mi Uruguay rivers. **Capital:** Buenos Aires (the Senate has approved moving the capital to the Patagonia Region). **Cities** (urban aggr.): Buenos Aires, 12,106,000, (2000 city proper: 2 mil.); Cordoba, 1,368,000; Rosario, 1,279,000.

Government: Type: Republic. **Head of state and gov.:** Pres. Eduardo Alberto Duhalde; b Oct. 5, 1941; in office: Jan. 2, 2002. **Local divisions:** 23 provinces, 1 federal district. **Defense budget:** (2000) $3.5 bil. **Active troops:** 70,100.

Economy: Industries: Food processing, motor vehicles, consumer durables. **Chief crops:** Sunflower seeds, lemons, grapes, peanuts, corn, soybeans. **Minerals:** Oil, lead, zinc, iron, copper, tin, uranium. **Crude oil reserves** (2001): 3.0 bil bbls. **Arable land:** 9%. **Livestock** (2001): cattle: 50.17 mil; chickens: 110.00 mil.; goats: 3.50 mil.; pigs: 4.20 mil; sheep: 13.50 mil. **Fish catch** (1999): 1.35 mil metric tons. **Electricity prod.:** 82.80 bil. kWh.

Finance: Monetary unit: Peso (Sept. 2002: 3.71 = $1 U.S.). **GDP** (2000 est.): $476 bil. **Per capita GDP:** $12,900. **Imports** (2000 est.): $25.2 bil.; partners (1999 est.): EU 28%, U.S. 22%. **Exports** (2000 est.): $26.5 bil.; partners (1999 est.): Brazil 24%, EU 21%. **Tourism:** $2.81 bil. **Budget** (2000 est.): $48 bil. **Intl. reserves less gold** (end 2000): $19.30 bil. **Gold:** 20,000 oz t. **Consumer prices** (change in 2000): –0.9%.

Transport: Railroad: Length: 21,015 mi. **Motor vehicles:** 4.78 mil pass. cars, 1.29 mil comm. vehicles. **Civil aviation:** 8.9 bil pass.-mi.; 39 airports. **Chief ports:** Buenos Aires, Bahia Blanca, La Plata.

Communications: TV sets: 289 per 1,000 pop. **Radios:** 595 per 1,000 pop. **Telephones:** 15,082,900. **Daily newspaper circ.:** 123 per 1,000 pop.

Health: Life expectancy: 72.1 male; 79 female. **Births** (per 1,000 pop.): 18.2. **Deaths** (per 1,000 pop.): 7.6. **Natural inc.:** 1.07%. **Infant mortality** (per 1,000 live births): 17.2.

Education: Free, compulsory: ages 6-14. **Literacy:** 96%.

Major Intl. Organizations: UN (FAO, IBRD, ILO, IMF, IMO, WHO, WTrO), OAS.

Embassy: 1600 New Hampshire Ave. NW 20009; 238-6400.

Websites: www.un.int/argentina/
www.congenargentinany.com

Nomadic Indians roamed the Pampas when Spaniards arrived, 1515-16, led by Juan Diaz de Solis. Nearly all the Indians were killed by the late 19th century. The colonists won independence, 1816, and a long period of disorder ended in a strong centralized government.

Large-scale Italian, German, and Spanish immigration in the decades after 1880 spurred modernization. Social reforms were enacted in the 1920s, but military coups prevailed 1930-46, until the election of Gen. Juan Perón as president.

Perón, with his wife, Eva Duarte (d 1952), effected labor reforms, but also suppressed speech and press freedoms, closed religious schools, and ran the country into debt. A 1955 coup exiled Perón, who was followed by a series of military and civilian regimes. Perón returned in 1973, and was once more elected president. He died 10 months later, succeeded by his wife Isabel, who had been elected vice president, and who became the first woman head of state in the western hemisphere.

A military junta ousted Mrs. Perón in 1976 amid charges of corruption. Under a continuing state of siege, the army battled guerrillas and leftists, killed 5,000 people, and jailed and tortured others. On Dec. 9, 1985, after a trial of 5 months and nearly 1,000 witnesses, 5 former junta members were found guilty of murder and human rights abuses.

Argentine troops seized control of the British-held Falkland Islands on Apr. 2, 1982. Both countries had claimed sovereignty over the islands, located 250 miles off the Argentine coast, since 1833. The British dispatched a task force and declared a total air and sea blockade around the Falklands. Fighting began May 1; several hundred lost their lives as the result of the destruction of a British destroyer and the sinking of an Argentine cruiser.

British troops landed on East Falkland Island May 21 and eventually surrounded Stanley, the capital city and Argentine stronghold. The Argentine troops surrendered, June 14; Argentine Pres. Leopoldo Galtieri resigned June 17.

Democratic rule returned to in 1983 as Raul Alfonsín's Radical Civic Union party gained an absolute majority in the presidential electoral college and Congress. By 1989 the nation was plagued by severe financial and political problems, as hyperinflation sparked looting and rioting in several cities. The government of Perónist Pres. Carlos Saúl Menem, installed 1989, introduced harsh economic measures to curtail inflation, control government spending, and restructure the foreign debt.

About 100 people were killed in the terrorist bombing of a Jewish cultural center in Buenos Aires, July 18, 1994. Following passage of a new constitution in Aug. 1994, Menem was reelected president on May 14, 1995. A pact restoring commercial air links between Argentina and the Falklands was signed July 14, 1999.

Buenos Aires Mayor Fernando de la Rúa won the presidential election Oct. 24, 1999. A prolonged recession and a debt of more than $130 billion left Argentina facing an economic crisis in 2001, which austerity measures and IMF aid failed to remedy. After widespread rioting and looting Dec. 19, de la Rúa resigned. A 2-week period of protests and political upheavals abated when Congress, Jan. 1, 2002, chose a Peronist, Eduardo Alberto Duhalde, to finish de la Rúa's term. Duhalde devalued the peso by cutting its ties with the U.S. dollar. Further economic decline and renewed protests led Duhalde July 2 to schedule an early presidential election for Mar. 2003.

Armenia
Republic of Armenia

People: Population: 3,330,099. **Age distrib.** (%): <15: 23.2; 65+: 9.7. **Pop. density:** 290 per sq. mi. **Urban:** 70%. **Ethnic groups:** Armenian 93%, Azeri 3%, Russian 2%, Kurd and others 2%. **Principal language:** Armenian (official). **Chief religion:** Armenian Orthodox 94%.

Geography: Area: 11,500 sq. mi. **Location:** SW Asia. **Neighbors:** Georgia on N, Azerbaijan on E, Iran on S, Turkey on W. **Topography:** Mountainous with many peaks above 10,000 ft. **Capital:** Yerevan, 1,420,000.

Government: Type: Republic. **Head of state:** Pres. Robert Kocharian; b Aug. 31, 1954; in office: Apr. 9, 1998. **Head of gov.:** Prime Min. Andranik Markarian; b June 12, 1951; in office: May 12, 2000. **Local divisions:** 10 provinces, 1 city. **Defense budget:** (2000) $75 mil. **Active troops:** 42,060.

Economy: Industries: Machine tools and machinery, electric motors, tires, knitted wear. **Chief crops:** Vegetables, grapes. **Minerals:** Copper, gold, zinc. **Arable land:** 17%. **Livestock** (2001): cattle: 485,000; chickens: 4.30 mil.; goats: 10,000; pigs: 68,900; sheep: 497,155. **Electricity prod.:** 5.69 bil. kWh. **Labor force:** agri. 55%, services 25%, ind. 20%.

Finance: Monetary unit: Dram (Sept. 2002: 558.14 = $1 U.S.). **GDP** (2000 est.): $10 bil. **Per capita GDP:** $3,000. **Imports** (2000 est.): $913 mil.; partners (1999): Russia 17%, U.S. 11%, Belgium 11%. **Exports** (2000 est.): $284 mil.; partners (1999): Belgium 36%, Iran 15%. **Tourism:** $27 mil. **Budget** (1999 est.): $566 mil. **Intl. reserves less gold** (end 2000): $244 mil. **Gold:** 40,000 oz t. **Consumer prices** (change in 2000): –0.8%.

Transport: Railroad: Length: 515 mi. **Civil aviation:** 476.6 mil pass.-mi.; 1 airport.

Communications: TV sets: 241 per 1,000 pop. **Telephones:** 554,300. **Daily newspaper circ.:** 23 per 1,000 pop.

Health: Life expectancy: 62.3 male; 71.1 female. **Births** (per 1,000 pop.): 12. **Deaths** (per 1,000 pop.): 9.9. **Natural inc.:** 0.21%. **Infant mortality** (per 1,000 live births): 41.1.

Education: Compulsory: ages 6-17. **Literacy** (1989): 99%.

Major Intl. Organizations: UN (FAO, IBRD, ILO, IMF, WHO), CIS, OSCE.

Embassy: 2225 R St. NW 20008; 319-1976.

Website: www.gov.am/en

Ancient Armenia extended into parts of what are now Turkey and Iran. Present-day Armenia was set up as a Soviet republic Apr. 2, 1921. It joined Georgian and Azerbaijan SSRs Mar. 12, 1922, to form the Transcaucasian SFSR, which became part of the USSR Dec. 30, 1922. Armenia became a constituent republic of the USSR Dec. 5, 1936. An earthquake struck Armenia Dec. 7, 1988; approximately 55,000 were killed and several cities and towns were left in ruins.

Armenia declared independence Sept. 23, 1991, and became an independent state when the USSR disbanded Dec. 26, 1991.

Fighting between mostly Christian Armenia and mostly Muslim Azerbaijan escalated in 1992 and continued through 1993. Each country claimed Nagorno-Karabakh, an enclave in Azerbaijan that has a majority population of ethnic Armenians. A temporary cease-fire was announced in May 1994, with Armenian forces in control of the enclave. Voters approved, July 5, 1995, a new constitution strengthening presidential powers. Pres. Levon Ter-Petrosian won reelection on Sept. 22, 1996, amid claims of fraud; he resigned Feb. 3, 1998, in a conflict over Nagorno-Karabakh. Robert Kocharian, a nationalist born in the disputed region, won the presidency on Mar. 30, 1998. Gunmen stormed Parliament Oct. 27, 1999, killing Prime Min. Vazgen Sarkissian and 7 others.

Australia

Commonwealth of Australia

People: Population: 19,546,792. **Age distrib.** (%): <15: 20.6; 65+: 12.5. **Pop. density:** 7 per sq. mi. **Urban:** 85%. **Ethnic groups:** Caucasian 92%, Asian 7%, aboriginal and other 1%. **Principal languages:** English (official), aboriginal languages. **Chief religions:** Anglican 26%, Roman Catholic 26%, other Christian 24%.

Geography: Area: 2,941,300 sq. mi. **Location:** SE of Asia, Indian O. is W and S, Pacific O. (Coral, Tasman seas) is E; they meet N of Australia in Timor and Arafura seas. Tasmania lies 150 mi. S of Victoria state, across Bass Strait. **Neighbors:** Nearest are Indonesia, Papua New Guinea on N; Solomons, Fiji, and New Zealand on E. **Topography:** An island continent. The Great Dividing Range along the E coast has Mt. Kosciusko, 7,310 ft. The W plateau rises to 2,000 ft., with arid areas in the Great Sandy and Great Victoria deserts. The NW part of Western Australia and Northern Terr. are arid and hot. The NE has heavy rainfall and Cape York Peninsula has jungles. **Capital:** Canberra, 387,000. **Cities** (urban aggr.): Sydney, 3,907,000; Melbourne, 3,232,000; Brisbane, 1,622,000; Perth, 1,329,000; Adelaide, 1,064,000.

Government: Type: Democratic, federal state system. **Head of state:** Queen Elizabeth II, represented by Gov.-Gen. Peter John Hollingworth; b Apr. 10, 1935; in office: June 29, 2001. **Head of gov.:** Prime Min. John Howard; b July 26, 1939; in office: Mar. 11, 1996. **Local divisions:** 6 states, 2 territories. **Defense budget** (2001): $6.6 bil. **Active troops:** 50,700.

Economy: Industries: Mining, industrial and transportation equipment, food processing, chemicals, steel. **Chief crops:** Wheat (a leading export), barley, fruit, sugarcane. **Minerals:** Bauxite, coal, copper, iron, lead, tin, uranium, zinc. **Crude oil reserves** (2001): 2.8 bil bbls. **Other resources:** Wool (world's leading producer), beef. **Arable land:** 6%. **Livestock** (2001): cattle: 27.59 mil; chickens: 96.00 mil.; goats: 200,000; pigs: 2.43 mil; sheep: 120.00 mil . **Fish catch** (1999): 214,227 metric tons. **Electricity prod.:** 202.68 bil. kWh. **Labor force:** services 73%, ind. 22%, agri. 5%.

Finance: Monetary unit: Australian Dollar (Sept. 2002: 1.84 = $1 U.S.). **GDP** (2000 est.): $445.8 bil. **Per capita GDP:** $23,200. **Imports** (2000 est.): $77 bil.; partners (1999): EU 24%, U.S. 22%. **Exports** (2000 est.): $69 bil.; partners (1999): Japan 19%, EU 14%. **Tourism:** $7.53 bil. **Budget** (1999 est.): $103 bil. **Intl. reserves less gold** (end 2000): $13.91 bil. **Gold:** 2.56 mil oz t. **Consumer prices** (change in 2000): 4.5%.

Transport: Railroad: Length: 20,567 mi. **Motor vehicles:** 8.7 mil pass. cars, 2.05 mil comm. vehicles. **Civil aviation:** 47.2 bil pass.-mi.; 400 airports. **Chief ports:** Sydney, Melbourne, Brisbane, Adelaide, Fremantle, Geelong.

Communications: TV sets: 639 per 1,000 pop. **Radios:** 1,120 per 1,000 pop. **Telephones:** 10,375,900. **Daily newspaper circ.:** 297 per 1,000 pop.

Health: Life expectancy: 77.2 male; 83 female. **Births** (per 1,000 pop.): 12.7. **Deaths** (per 1,000 pop.): 7.2. **Natural inc.:** 0.55%. **Infant mortality** (per 1,000 live births): 4.9.

Education: Free, compulsory: ages 6-15. **Literacy** (1996): 100%.

Major Intl. Organizations: UN and all of its specialized agencies, APEC, the Commonwealth, OECD.

Embassy: 1601 Massachusetts Ave. NW 20036; 797-3000.

Website: www.gov.au

Australia harbors many plant and animal species not found elsewhere, including kangaroos, koalas, platypuses, dingos (wild dogs), Tasmanian devils (raccoon-like marsupials), wombats (bear-like marsupials), and barking and frilled lizards.

Capt. James Cook explored the E coast in 1770, when the continent was inhabited by a variety of different tribes. The first settlers, beginning in 1788, were mostly convicts, soldiers, and government officials. By 1830, Britain had claimed the entire continent, and the immigration of free settlers began to accelerate. The Commonwealth was proclaimed Jan. 1, 1901. Northern Terr. was granted limited self-rule July 1, 1978.

State/Territory, Capital	Area (sq. mi.)	Population (1997)
New South Wales, Sydney	309,500	6,274,400
Victoria, Melbourne	87,900	4,605,100
Queensland, Brisbane	666,990	3,401,200
Western Australia, Perth	975,100	1,798,100
South Australia, Adelaide	379,900	1,479,800
Tasmania, Hobart	26,200	473,500
Australian Capital Terr., Canberra	900	309,800
Northern Terr., Darwin	519,800	187,100

Racially discriminatory immigration policies were abandoned in 1973, after 3 million Europeans (half British) had entered since 1945. The 50,000 aborigines and 150,000 part-aborigines are mostly detribalized, but there are several preserves in the Northern Territory. They remain economically disadvantaged.

Australia's agricultural success makes the country among the top exporters of beef, lamb, wool, and wheat. Major mineral deposits have been developed, largely for export. Industrialization has been completed. The nation endured a deep recession 1990-93 but has rebounded strongly.

The Labor Party won a majority in Feb. 1983 general elections and was reelected in 1984, 1987, 1990, and 1993. After an election that focused mainly on economic issues, conservatives swept into power in elections Mar. 2, 1996.

Prime Min. John Howard retained power, but with a reduced majority, in parliamentary elections Oct. 3, 1998. Australia led an international peacekeeping force into East Timor in Sept. 1999. In a referendum Nov. 6, voters rejected a proposal that would have made Australia a republic. Sydney hosted the Summer Olympics Sept. 15-Oct. 1, 2000. Howard won a 3rd term in the elections of Nov. 10, 2001.

Australian External Territories

Norfolk Isl., area 13.3 sq. mi., pop. (1996 est.) 2,209, was taken over, 1914. The soil is very fertile, suitable for citrus, bananas, and coffee. Many of the inhabitants are descendants of the *Bounty* mutineers, moved to Norfolk 1856 from Pitcairn Isl. Australia offered the island limited home rule in 1978.

Coral Sea Isls. Territory, area 1 sq. mi., is administered from Norfolk Isl.

Territory of Ashmore and Cartier Isls., area 2 sq. mi., in the Indian O., came under Australian authority 1934 and are administered as part of Northern Territory. **Heard Isl. and McDonald Isls.,** area 159 sq. mi., are administered by the Dept. of Science.

Cocos (Keeling) Isls., 27 small coral islands in the Indian O. 1,750 mi. NW of Australia. Pop. (1996 est.) 609; area 5.5 sq. mi. The residents voted to become part of Australia, Apr. 1984.

Christmas Isl., area 52 sq. mi., pop. (1996 est.) 813; 230 mi. S of Java, was transferred by Britain in 1958. It has phosphate deposits.

Australian Antarctic Territory was claimed by Australia in 1933, including 2,362,000 sq. mi. of territory S of 60th parallel S Lat. and between 160th-45th meridians E Long. It does not include Adelie Coast.

Austria

Republic of Austria

People: Population: 8,169,929. **Age distrib.** (%): <15: 16.6; 65+: 15.4. **Pop. density:** 256 per sq. mi. **Urban:** 65%. **Ethnic groups:** German 99%, Croatian, Slovene. **Principal language:** German (official). **Chief religions:** Roman Catholic 78%, Protestant 5%.

Geography: Area: 31,900 sq. mi. **Location:** In S Central Europe. **Neighbors:** Switzerland, Liechtenstein on W; Germany, Czech Rep. on N; Slovakia, Hungary on E; Slovenia, Italy on S. **Topography:** Austria is primarily mountainous, with the Alps and foothills covering the western and southern provinces. The eastern provinces and Vienna are located in the Danube River Basin. **Capital:** Vienna, 2,066,000.

Government: Type: Parliamentary democracy. **Head of state:** Pres. Thomas Klestil; b Nov. 4, 1932; in office: July 8, 1992. **Head of gov.:** Chancellor Wolfgang Schüssel; b June 7, 1945; in office: Feb. 4, 2000. **Local divisions:** 9 bundeslaender (states), each with a legislature. **Defense budget (2001):** $1.5 bil. **Active troops:** 34,600.

Economy: Industries: Construction, machinery, autos, food, chemicals, lumber and wood processing. **Chief crops:** Grains, fruits, potatoes, sugar beets. **Minerals:** Iron ore, oil, magnesite. **Crude oil reserves** (2001): 0.1 bil bbls. **Other resources:** Forests, hydropower. **Arable land:** 17%. **Livestock** (2001): cattle: 2.16 mil; chickens: 11.08 mil.; goats: 69,618; pigs: 3.43 mil; sheep: 357,888. **Electricity prod.:** 60.29 bil. kWh. **Labor force:** services 68%, ind. and crafts 29%, agri. and forestry 3%.

Finance: Monetary unit: Euro (Sept. 2002: 1.03 = $1 U.S.). **GDP** (2000 est.): $203 bil. **Per capita GDP:** $25,000. **Imports** (2000 est.): $65.6 bil.; partners (1999): EU 70.3%, U.S. 5.4%. **Exports** (2000 est.): $63.2 bil.; partners (1999): EU 64.2%, Switzerland 5.9%. **Tourism:** $11.09 bil. **Budget** (2000 est.): $60.5 bil. **Intl. reserves less gold** (end 2000): $10.99 bil. **Gold:** 12.14 mil oz t. **Consumer prices** (change in 2000): 2.4%.

Transport: Railroad: Length: 3,524 mi. **Motor vehicles in use (1997):** 3.78 mil pass. cars, 324,776 comm. vehicles. **Civil aviation:** 6.3 bil pass.-mi.; 6 airports. **Chief ports:** Linz, Vienna, Enns, Krems.

Communications: TV sets: 496 per 1,000 pop. **Radios:** 744 per 1,000 pop. **Telephones:** 10,375,900. **Daily newspaper circ.:** 296 per 1,000 pop.

Health: Life expectancy: 74.8 male; 81.3 female. **Births** (per 1,000 pop.): 9.6. **Deaths** (per 1,000 pop.): 9.7. **Natural inc.:** -0.01%. **Infant mortality** (per 1,000 live births): 4.4.

Education: Free, compulsory: ages 6-15. **Literacy** (1994): 100%.

Major Intl. Organizations: UN and all of its specialized agencies, EU, OECD, OSCE.

Embassy: 3524 International Ct. NW 20008; 895-6700.
Website: www.austria.gv.at/e

Rome conquered Austrian lands from Celtic tribes around 15 BC. In 788 the territory was incorporated into Charlemagne's empire. By 1300, the House of Hapsburg had gained control; they added vast territories in all parts of Europe to their realm in the next few hundred years.

Austrian dominance of Germany was undermined in the 18th century and ended by Prussia by 1866. But the Congress of Vienna, 1815, confirmed Austrian control of a large empire in southeast Europe consisting of Germans, Hungarians, Slavs, Italians, and others. The dual Austro-Hungarian monarchy was established in 1867, giving autonomy to Hungary and almost 50 years of peace.

World War I, started after the June 28, 1914, assassination of Archduke Franz Ferdinand, the Hapsburg heir, by a Serbian nationalist, destroyed the empire. By 1918 Austria was reduced to a small republic, with the borders it has today.

Nazi Germany invaded Austria Mar. 13, 1938. The republic was reestablished in 1945, under Allied occupation. Full independence and neutrality were restored in 1955. Austria joined the European Union Jan. 1, 1995. The rise of the right-wing, anti-immigrant Austrian Freedom Party challenged the dominance of the Austrian Social Democratic Party in the late 1990s. When Freedom Party members joined the cabinet, Feb. 4, 2000, the EU imposed political sanctions on Austria, Feb. 4-Sept. 12, 2000.

Azerbaijan

Azerbaijani Republic

People: Population: 7,798,497. **Age distrib.** (%): <15: 28.9; 65+: 7.1. **Pop. density:** 233 per sq. mi. **Urban:** 57%. **Ethnic groups:** Azeri 90%, Dagestani Peoples 3%, Russian 3%, Armenian 2%. **Principal languages:** Azeri (official) 89%, Russian 3%, Armenian 2%. **Chief religions:** Muslim 93%, Orthodox 5%.

Geography: Area: 33,400 sq. mi. **Location:** SW Asia. **Neighbors:** Russia, Georgia on N; Iran on S; Armenia on W; Caspian Sea on E. **Capital:** Baku, 1,964,000.

Government: Type: Republic. **Head of state:** Pres. Haydar A. Aliyev; b May 10, 1923; in office: June 30, 1993. **Head of gov.:** Prime Min. Artur Rasizade; b Feb. 26, 1935; in office: Nov. 26, 1996. **Local division:** 59 rayons, 11 cities, 1 autonomous republic. **Defense budget:** (2000) $119 mil. **Active troops:** 72,100.

Economy: Industries: Oil and gas, oil products, oilfield equipment; steel, iron ore, cement; chemicals. **Chief crops:** Grain, rice, cotton, grapes. **Minerals:** Oil, gas, iron. **Crude oil reserves** (2000): 1.2 bil bbls. **Arable land:** 18%. **Livestock** (2001): cattle: 2.00 mil; chickens: 14.50 mil.; goats: 416,000; pigs: 18,600; sheep: 5.56 mil . **Electricity prod.:** 17.56 bil. kWh. **Labor force:** agri. and forestry 32%, ind. 15%, services 53%.

Finance: Monetary unit: Manat (Sept. 2002: 4,886 = $1 U.S.). **GDP** (2000 est.): $23.5 bil. **Per capita GDP:** $3,000. **Imports** (2000 est.): $1.4 bil.; partners: Russia, Turkey, Ukraine, UAE, Iran. **Exports** (2000 est.): $1.9 bil.; partners: Italy, Turkey, Russia, Georgia, Iran. **Tourism** (1998): $125 mil. **Budget** (1999 est.): $995 mil. **Intl. reserves less gold** (end 2000): $522 mil. **Consumer prices** (change in 2000): 1.8%.

Transport: Railroad: Length: 1,305 mi. **Motor vehicles:** 289,000 pass. cars; 89,000 comm. vehicles. **Civil aviation:** 797.1 mil. pass.-mi.; 3 airports. **Chief port:** Baku.

Communications: TV sets: 212 per 1,000 pop. **Daily newspaper circ.:** 28 per 1,000 pop. **Telephones:** 1,485,500.

Health: Life expectancy: 58.8 male; 67.5 female. **Births** (per 1,000 pop.): 18.8. **Deaths** (per 1,000 pop.): 9.6. **Natural inc.:** 0.92%. **Infant mortality** (per 1,000 live births): 82.7.

Education: Compulsory: ages 6-17. **Literacy**: 100%.

Major Intl. Organizations: UN (FAO, IBRD, ILO, IMF, IMO, WHO), CIS, OSCE.

Embassy: 927 15th St. NW 20005; 842-0001.
Website: www.president.az

Azerbaijan was the home of Scythian tribes and part of the Roman Empire. Overrun by Turks in the 11th century and conquered by Russia in 1806 and 1813, it joined the USSR Dec. 30, 1922, and became a constituent republic in 1936. Azerbaijan declared independence Aug. 30, 1991, and became an independent state when the Soviet Union disbanded Dec. 26, 1991.

Fighting between mostly Muslim Azerbaijan and mostly Christian Armenia escalated in 1992 and continued in 1993 and 1994. Each country claimed Nagorno-Karabakh, an enclave in Azerbaijan with a majority population of ethnic Armenians. A temporary cease-fire was announced in May 1994, with Armenian forces in control of the enclave.

A National Council ousted Communist Pres. Mutaibov and took power May 19, 1992. Abulfez Elchibey became the nation's first democratically elected president June 7, but was ousted from office by Surat Huseynov, commander of a private militia, June 30, 1993. Huseynov became prime minister, and Haydar Aliyev, a pro-Russian former Communist, became president. Huseynov fled the country after his supporters staged an unsuccessful coup attempt Oct. 1994. Voters approved a new constitution expanding presidential powers, Nov. 12, 1995. Pres. Aliyev was reelected Oct. 11, 1998, but international monitors called the election seriously flawed. In Dec. 2001, the alphabet was officially changed from Latin to Cyrillic.

The Bahamas

Commonwealth of The Bahamas

People: Population: 300,529. **Age distrib.** (%): <15: 29.4; 65+: 6.1. **Pop. density:** 77 per sq. mi. **Urban:** 88%. **Ethnic groups:** Black 85%, white 15%. **Principal languages:** English (official), Creole. **Chief religions:** Baptist 32%, Anglican 20%, Roman Catholic 19%, other Christian 24%.

Geography: Area: 3,900 sq. mi. **Location:** In Atlantic O., E of Florida. **Neighbors:** Nearest are U.S. on W, Cuba on S. **Topography:** Nearly 700 islands (29 inhabited) and over 2,000 islets in the W Atlantic O. extend 760 mi. NW to SE. **Capital:** Nassau. **Cities** (urban aggr.): (2001 est.): Nassau, 220,000; Grand Bahama, 40,898.

Government: Type: Independent commonwealth. **Head of state:** Queen Elizabeth II, represented by Gov.-Gen. Dame Ivy Dumont; b Oct. 2, 1930; in office: Nov. 13, 2001. **Head of gov.:** Prime Min. Perry Christie; b Aug. 21,1943; in office: May 3, 2002. **Local divisions:** 21 districts. **Defense budget:** (2000) $26 mil. **Active troops:** 860.

Economy: Industries: Tourism, banking, cement, oil refining and shipment. **Chief crops:** Citrus, vegetables. **Minerals:** Salt, aragonite. **Other resources:** Lobsters, timber. **Arable land:** 1%. **Livestock** (2001): cattle: 682; chickens: 4.50 mil.; goats: 13,852; pigs: 4,873; sheep: 6,418. **Fish catch:** (1999): 10,440 metric tons. **Electricity prod.:** 1.54 bil. kWh. **Labor force:** tourism 40%, other services 50%, ind. 5%, agri. 5%.

Finance: Monetary unit: Dollar (Sept. 2002: 1.00 = $1 U.S.). **GDP** (2000 est.): $4.5 bil. **Per capita GDP:** $15,000. **Imports** (2000 est.): $1.73 bil.; partners (1998): U.S. 27.3%, Italy 26.5%. **Exports** (2000 est.): $376.8 mil.; partners (1998): U.S. 22.3%, Switzerland 15.6%. **Tourism** (1998): $1.41 bil. **Budget** (FY97/98): $845 mil. **Intl. reserves less gold** (end 2000): $268 mil. **Consumer prices** (change in 2000): 1.6%.

Transport: Motor vehicles: 69,000 pass. cars, 14,000 comm. vehicles. **Civil aviation:** 86.9 mil pass.-mi.; 22 airports. **Chief ports:** Nassau, Freeport.

Communications: TV sets: 179 per 1,000 pop. **Radios:** 282 per 1,000 pop. **Telephones:** 183,900. **Daily newspaper circ.:** 126 per 1,000 pop.

Health: Life expectancy: 66.3 male; 73.5 female. **Births** (per 1,000 pop.): 18.7. **Deaths** (per 1,000 pop.): 7.5. **Natural inc.:** 1.12%. **Infant mortality** (per 1,000 live births): 17.1.

Education: Free, compulsory: ages 5-14. **Literacy**: 98%.

Major Intl. Organizations: UN (FAO, IBRD, ILO, IMF, IMO, WHO), Caricom, the Commonwealth, OAS.

Embassy: 2220 Massachusetts Ave. NW 20008; 319-2660.
Website: www.bahamas.net

Christopher Columbus first set foot in the New World on San Salvador (Watling Isl.) in 1492, when Arawak Indians inhabited the islands. British settlement began in 1647; the islands became a British colony in 1783. Internal self-government was granted in 1964; full independence within the Commonwealth was attained July 10, 1973. International banking and investment management have become major industries alongside tourism.

Bahrain

Kingdom of Bahrain

People: Population: 656,397. **Age distrib.** (%): <15: 29.6; 65+: 3.0. **Pop. density:** 2,746 per sq. mi. **Urban:** 92%. **Ethnic groups:** Bahraini 63%, Asian 13%, other Arab 10%, Iranian 8%. **Principal languages:** Arabic (official), English, Farsi, Urdu. **Chief religions:** Shi'a Muslim 75%, Sunni Muslim 25%.

Geography: Area: 239 sq. mi. **Location:** SW Asia, in Persian Gulf. **Neighbors:** Nearest are Saudi Arabia on W, Qatar on E. **Topography:** Bahrain Island, and several adjacent, smaller islands, are flat, hot, and humid, with little rain. **Capital:** Manama, 150,000.

Government: Type: Traditional monarchy. **Head of state:** King Hamad bin Isa al-Khalifa; b Jan. 28, 1950; in office: as emir Mar. 6, 1999; as king Feb. 14, 2002. **Head of gov.:** Prime Min. Khalifa bin Sulman al-Khalifa; b 1936; in office: Jan. 19, 1970. **Local divisions:** 12 municipalities. **Defense budget:** (2001) $315 mil. **Active troops:** 11,000.

Economy: Industries: Oil refining, aluminum smelting, offshore banking. **Chief crops:** Fruits, vegetables. **Minerals:** Oil, gas. **Crude oil reserves** (2000): 148.1 mil bbls. **Arable land:** 1%. **Livestock** (2001): cattle: 11,000; chickens: 465,000; goats: 16,300; sheep: 17,500. **Fish catch:** (1999): 10,050 metric tons. **Electricity prod.:** 5.77 bil. kWh. **Labor force:** industry, commerce, and service 79%, government 20%, agri. 1%.

Finance: Monetary unit: Dinar (Sept. 2002: 0.37 = $1 U.S.). **GDP** (2000 est.): $10.1 bil. **Per capita GDP:** $15,900. **Imports** (2000): $4.2 bil.; partners (1999): France 20%, U.S. 14%. **Exports** (2000): $5.8 bil.; partners (1999): India 14%, Saudi Arabia 5%, U.S. 5%, UAE 5%. **Tourism** (1998): $366 mil. **Budget** (2001 est.): $2.2 bil. **Intl. reserves less gold** (end 2000): $1.2 bil. **Gold:** 150,000 oz t. **Consumer prices** (change in 1998): –0.4%.

Transport: Motor vehicles: 141,901 pass. cars, 30,243 comm. vehicles. **Civil aviation:** 1.6 bil pass.-mi.; 1 airport. **Chief ports:** Manama, Sitrah.

Communications: TV sets: 442 per 1,000 pop. **Radios:** 555 per 1,000 pop. **Telephones:** 473,400. **Daily newspaper circ.:** 128 per 1,000 pop.

Health: Life expectancy: 71 male; 76 female. **Births** (per 1,000 pop.): 19.5. **Deaths** (per 1,000 pop.): 4. **Natural inc.:** 1.56%. **Infant mortality** (per 1,000 live births): 19.2.

Education: Free, compulsory: ages 6-17. **Literacy:** 85%.

Major Intl. Organizations: UN (FAO, IBRD, ILO, IMF, IMO, WHO, WTrO), AL.

Embassy: 3502 International Dr. NW 20008; 342-0741.

Website: www.bahrain.gov.bh/english/index.asp

Long ruled by the Khalifa family, Bahrain was a British protectorate from 1861 to Aug. 15, 1971, when it regained independence.

Pearls, shrimp, fruits, and vegetables were the mainstays of the economy until oil was discovered in 1932. By the 1970s, oil reserves were depleted; international banking thrived.

Bahrain took part in the 1973-74 Arab oil embargo against the U.S. and other nations. The government bought controlling interest in the oil industry in 1975. Shiite dissidents have clashed with the Sunni-led government since 1996.

Emir Hamad bin Isa al-Khalifa proclaimed himself king Feb. 14, 2002. Local elections in May marked the 1st time Bahraini women were allowed to vote and run for office.

Bangladesh

People's Republic of Bangladesh

People: Population: 133,376,684. **Age distrib.** (%): <15: 35.0; 65+: 3.4 **Pop. density:** 2,580 per sq. mi. **Urban:** 24%. **Ethnic groups:** Bengali 98%, Bihari, tribals. **Principal languages:** Bangla (official), English. **Chief religions:** Muslim 88%, Hindu 11%.

Geography: Area: 51,700 sq. mi. **Location:** In S Asia, on N bend of Bay of Bengal. **Neighbors:** India nearly surrounds country on W, N, E; Myanmar on SE. **Topography:** The country is mostly a low plain cut by the Ganges and Brahmaputra rivers and their delta. The land is alluvial and marshy along the coast, with hills only in the extreme SE and NE. A tropical monsoon climate prevails, among the rainiest in the world. **Capital:** Dhaka. **Cities** (urban aggr.): Dhaka, 13,181,000; Chittagong, 3,651,000; Khulna, 1,442,000.

Government: Type: Parliamentary democracy. **Head of state:** Pres. Iajuddin Ahmed; b 1931; in office: Sept. 6, 2002. **Head of gov.:** Prime Min. Khaleda Zia; b Aug. 15,1945; in office: Oct. 10, 2001. **Local divisions:** 6 divisions. **Defense budget** (2001): $692 mil. **Active troops:** 137,000.

Economy: Industries: Cotton textiles, jute, garments, tea processing. **Chief crops:** Jute, rice, tea. **Minerals:** Natural gas. **Crude oil reserves** (2000): 56.9 mil bbls. **Arable land:** 73%. **Livestock** (2001): cattle: 23.90 mil; chickens: 140.00 mil.; goats: 34.10 mil.; sheep: 1.13 mil. **Fish catch** (1999): 1.34 mil metric tons. **Electricity prod.:** 13.49 bil. kWh. **Labor force:** agri. 63%, services 26%, ind. 11%.

Finance: Monetary unit: Taka (Sept. 2002: 57.85 = $1 U.S.). **GDP** (2000 est.): $203 bil. **Per capita GDP:** $1,570. **Imports** (2000): $8.1 bil.; partners (1999): India 12.2%, Singapore 7.8%. **Exports** (2000): $5.9 bil.; partners (1999): U.S. 31.2%, Germany 9.95%. **Tourism:** $50 mil. **Budget** (FY99/00 est.): $6.8 bil. **Intl. reserves less gold** (end 2000): $1.14 bil. **Gold:** 110,000 oz t. **Consumer prices** (change in 2000): 2.3%.

Transport: Railroad: Length: 1,681 mi. **Motor vehicles** (1997): 134,073 pass. cars, 92,133 comm. vehicles. **Civil aviation:** 2.0 bil pass.-mi.; 8 airports. **Chief ports:** Chittagong, Dhaka, Mongla Port.

Communications: TV sets: 5 per 1,000 pop. **Radios:** 63 per 1,000 pop. **Telephones: 1,034,000. Daily newspaper circ.:** 9 per 1,000 pop.

Health: Life expectancy: 61.1 male; 60.7 female. **Births** (per 1,000 pop.): 25.1. **Deaths** (per 1,000 pop.): 8.5. **Natural inc.:** 1.67%. **Infant mortality** (per 1,000 live births): 68.

Education: Free, compulsory: ages 6-11. **Literacy:** 38%.

Major Intl. Organizations: UN (FAO, IBRD, ILO, IMF, IMO, WHO, WTrO), the Commonwealth.

Embassy: 2201 Wisconsin Ave. NW 20007; 342-8372.

Website: www.bangladeshgov.com

Muslim invaders conquered the formerly Hindu area in the 12th century. British rule lasted from the 18th century to 1947, when East Bengal became part of Pakistan.

Charging West Pakistani domination, the Awami League, based in the East, won National Assembly control in 1971. Assembly sessions were postponed; riots broke out. Pakistani troops attacked Mar. 25; Bangladesh independence was proclaimed the next day. In the ensuing civil war, one million died and 10 million fled to India.

War between India and Pakistan broke out Dec. 3, 1971. Pakistan surrendered in the East on Dec. 16. Mujibur Rahman, known as Sheikh Mujib, became prime minister; he was killed in a coup Aug. 15, 1975. During the 1970s the country moved into the Indian and Soviet orbits in response to U.S. support of Pakistan, and much of the economy was nationalized.

On May 30, 1981, Pres. Ziaur Rahman was killed in an unsuccessful coup attempt by army rivals. Vice Pres. Abdus Sattar assumed the presidency but was ousted in a coup led by army chief of staff Gen. H. M. Ershad, Mar. 1982. Ershad declared Bangladesh an Islamic Republic in 1988; a parliamentary system of government was adopted in 1991.

Bangladesh is subject to devastating storms and floods that kill thousands. A cyclone struck Apr. 1991, killing over 131,000 people and causing $2.7 billion in damages. Chronic destitution in the densely crowded population has been worsened by the decline of jute as a world commodity. Pollution of surface water and naturally occurring contamination of groundwater by arsenic have caused widespread health problems.

Political turmoil led to the resignation, Mar. 30, 1996, of Prime Minister Khaleda Zia, the widow of Ziaur Rahman. Sheikh Mujib's daughter, Hasina Wazed (known as Sheikh Hasina), led the country after the June 12, 1996 election. Bangladesh and India signed a treaty, Dec. 12, resolving their long-standing dispute over the use of water from the Ganges River. A cyclone in May 1997 left an estimated 800,000 people homeless. Floods in July-Sept. 1998 inundated most of the country, killed over 1,400 people (many through disease), and stranded at least 30 million.

An interim government was installed July 2001 pending national elections. Khaleda Zia returned to power following the parliamentary elections of Oct. 1, 2001.

Barbados

People: Population: 276,607. **Age distrib.** (%): <15: 21.7; 65+: 8.9. **Pop. density:** 1,666 per sq. mi. **Urban:** 49%. **Ethnic groups:** Black 80%, white 4%, other 16%. **Principal language:** English (official). **Chief religions:** Protestant 67%, Roman Catholic 4%.

Geography: Area: 166 sq. mi. **Location:** In Atlantic O., farthest E of West Indies. **Neighbors:** Nearest are St. Lucia and St. Vincent & the Grenadines to the W. **Topography:** The island lies alone in the Atlantic almost completely surrounded by coral reefs. Highest point is Mt. Hillaby, 1,115 ft. **Capital:** Bridgetown, 136,000.

Government: Type: Parliamentary democracy. **Head of state:** Queen Elizabeth II, represented by Gov.-Gen. Sir Clifford Husbands; b Aug. 5, 1926; in office: June 1, 1996. **Head of gov.:** Prime Min. Owen Arthur; b Oct. 17, 1949; in office: Sept. 7, 1994. **Local divisions:** 11 parishes and Bridgetown. **Defense budget** (2001): $13 mil. **Active troops:** 610.

Economy: Industries: Tourism, sugar, light manufacturing. **Chief crops:** Sugar, vegetables, cotton. **Minerals:** Oil, gas. **Crude oil reserves** (2000): 3.2 mil bbls. **Other resources:** Fish. **Arable land:** 37%. **Livestock** (2001): cattle: 23,000; chickens: 3.60 mil.; goats: 4,500; pigs: 33,000; sheep: 41,000. **Electricity prod.:** 0.74 bil. kWh. **Labor force:** services 75%, ind. 15%, agri. 10%.

Finance: Monetary unit: Dollar (Sept. 2002: 1.99 = $1 U.S.). **GDP** (2000 est.): $4 bil. **Per capita GDP:** $14,500. **Imports** (2000 est.): $800.3 mil.; partners (1998): U.S. 30.7%, Trinidad and Tobago 10.2%. **Exports** (2000 est.): $260 mil.; partners (1998): UK 14.8%, U.S. 11.6%. **Tourism** (1998): $703 mil. **Budget** (FY97/98 est.): $750.6 mil. **Intl. reserves less gold** (end 2000): $363 mil. **Consumer prices** (change in 2000): 2.4%.

Transport: Motor vehicles: 45,000 pass. cars; 3,500 comm. vehicles. **Civil aviation:** 204.9 mil pass.-mi.; 1 airport. **Chief port:** Bridgetown.

Communications: TV sets: 287 per 1,000 pop. **Radios:** 1,134 per 1,000 pop. **Telephones** (2000): 152,300. **Daily newspaper circ.:** 157 per 1,000 pop.

Health: Life expectancy: 70.9 male; 76.1 female. **Births** (per 1,000 pop.): 13.3. **Deaths** (per 1,000 pop.): 8.4. **Natural inc.:** 0.49%. **Infant mortality** (per 1,000 live births): 11.7.

Education: Compulsory: ages 5-16. **Literacy:** 97%.

Major Intl. Organizations: UN (FAO, IBRD, ILO, IMF, IMO, WHO, WTrO), Caricom, the Commonwealth, OAS.

Embassy: 2144 Wyoming Ave. NW 20008; 939-9200.

Website: www.barbados.gov.bb

Barbados was probably named by Portuguese sailors in reference to bearded fig trees. An English ship visited in 1605, and British settlers arrived on the uninhabited island in 1627. Slaves worked the sugar plantations until slavery was abolished in 1834. Self-rule came gradually, with full independence proclaimed Nov. 30, 1966. British traditions have remained.

Belarus

Republic of Belarus

People: Population: 10,335,382. **Age distrib.** (%): <15: 17.9; 65+: 13.9. **Pop. density:** 129 per sq. mi. **Urban:** 71%. **Ethnic groups:** Byelorussian 78%, Russian 13%, Polish 4%. **Principal languages:** Byelorussian (official), Russian. **Chief religions:** Eastern Orthodox 80%, other 20%.

Geography: Area: 80,200 sq. mi. **Location:** E Europe. **Neighbors:** Poland on W; Latvia, Lithuania on N; Russia on E; Ukraine on S. **Capital:** Minsk, 1,664,000.

Government: Type: Republic. **Head of state:** Pres. Aleksandr Lukashenko; b Aug. 30, 1954; in office: July 20,1994. **Head of gov.:** Prime Min. Henadz Navitski; b 1949; in office, Oct. 10, 2001. **Local divisions:** 6 oblasts and 1 municipality. **Defense budget:** $125.7 mil. **Active troops:** 82,900.

Economy: Industries: Machine tools, tractors, trucks, earth movers, motorcycles. **Chief crops:** Grain, vegetables, potatoes. **Crude oil reserves** (2000): 198 mil bbls. **Arable land:** 29%. **Livestock** (2001): cattle: 4.22 mil; chickens: 32.00 mil.; goats: 61,000; pigs: 3.43 mil; sheep: 130,000. **Electricity prod.:** 24.66 bil. kWh. **Labor force:** 41% services; 40% ind. & const.; 19% agric. & forestry.

Finance: Monetary unit: Ruble (Sept. 2002: 1,867 = $1 U.S.). **GDP** (2000 est.): $78.8 bil. **Per capita GDP:** $7,500. **Imports** (2000): $8.3 bil.; partners (1998): Russia 54%, Ukraine, Germany, Poland, Lithuania. **Exports** (2000): $7.4 bil.; partners (1998): Russia 66%, Ukraine, Poland, Germany, Lithuania. **Tourism** (1998): $22 mil. **Budget** (1997 est.): $4.1 bil. **Intl. reserves less gold** (end 2000): $269 mil. **Consumer prices** (change in 2000): 168.6%.

Transport: Railroad: Length: 3,480 mi. **Motor vehicles:** 842,500 pass. cars, 10,000 comm. vehicles. **Civil aviation:** 247.9 pass.-mi.; 1 airport. **Chief port:** Mazyr.

Communications: TV sets: 265 per 1,000 pop. **Radios:** 311 per 1,000 pop. **Telephones:** 2,996,200. **Daily newspaper circ.:** 187 per 1,000 pop.

Health: Life expectancy: 62.3 male; 74.6 female. **Births** (per 1,000 pop.): 9.9. **Deaths** (per 1,000 pop.): 14. **Natural inc.:** -0.41%. **Infant mortality** (per 1,000 live births): 14.1.

Education: Compulsory: ages 6-17. **Literacy** (1994): 98%.

Major Intl. Organizations: UN (IBRD, ILO, IMF, WHO), CIS, OSCE.

Embassy: 1619 New Hampshire Ave. NW 20009; 986-1604.

Website: www.belarusembassy.org

The region was subject to Lithuanians and Poles in medieval times, and was a prize of war between Russia and Poland beginning in 1503. It became part of the USSR in 1922 although the western part of the region was controlled by Poland. Belarus was overrun by German armies in 1941; recovered by Soviet troops in 1944. Following World War II, Belarus increased in area through Soviet annexation of part of NE Poland. Belarus declared independence Aug. 25, 1991. It became an independent state when the Soviet Union disbanded Dec. 26, 1991.

A new constitution was adopted, Mar. 15, 1994, and a new president was chosen in elections concluding July 1. Russia and Belarus signed a pact Apr. 2, 1996, linking their political and economic systems. An authoritarian constitution enacted in Nov. gave Pres. Aleksandr Lukashenko vast new powers. Lukashenko's insistence on tightening ties with Russia resulted in the signing of new accords in 1997 and 1998. Opponents charged harassment and fraud in the presidential election of Sept. 9, 2001, won by Lukashenko.

Belgium

Kingdom of Belgium

People: Population: 10,274,595. **Age distrib.** (%): <15: 17.5; 65+: 16.9. **Pop. density:** 878 per sq. mi. **Urban:** 97%. **Ethnic groups:** Fleming 55%, Walloon 33%. **Principal languages:** Flemish (Dutch) 56%, French 32%, German 1% (all official). **Chief religions:** Roman Catholic 75%; Protestant, other 25%.

Geography: Area: 11,700 sq. mi. **Location:** In W Europe, on North Sea. **Neighbors:** France on W and S, Luxembourg on SE, Germany on E, Netherlands on N. **Topography:** Mostly flat, the country is trisected by the Scheldt and Meuse, major commercial rivers. The land becomes hilly and forested in the SE (Ardennes) region. **Capital:** Brussels, 1,134,000.

Government: Type: Parliamentary democracy under a constitutional monarch. **Head of state:** King Albert II; b June 6, 1934; in office: Aug. 9, 1993. **Head of gov.:** Premier Guy Verhofstadt; b Apr. 11, 1953; in office: July 12, 1999. **Local divisions:** 10 provinces and Brussels. **Defense budget** (2001): $2.2 bil. **Active troops:** 39,420.

Economy: Industries: Engineering and metal products, autos, processed food and beverages. **Chief crops:** Grain, fruits, sugar beets, vegetables. **Minerals:** Coal, gas. **Arable land:** 24%. **Livestock** (incl. Luxembourg) (2001): cattle: 3.25 mil; chickens: 38.00 mil.; goats: 14,000; pigs: 7.35 mil; sheep: 155,000. **Fish catch** (1999): 31,346 metric tons. **Electricity prod.:** 79.35 bil. kWh. **Labor force:** services 73%, ind. 25%, agri. 2%.

Finance: Monetary unit: Euro (Sept. 2002: 1.03 = $1 U.S.). **GDP** (2000 est.): $259.2 bil. **Per capita GDP:** $25,300. **Imports** (2000): $166 bil.; partners (1999): EU 71%. **Exports** (2000): $181.4 bil.; partners (1999): EU 76%. **Budget** (1999): $117 bil. **Tourism** (1998): $5.44 bil. **Intl. reserves less gold** (end 2000): $7.67 bil. **Gold:** 8.30 mil oz t. **Consumer prices** (change in 2000): 2.5%.

Transport: Railroad: Length: 2,093 mi. **Motor vehicles** (1997): 4.42 mil pass. cars, 541,422 comm. vehicles. **Civil aviation:** 7.0 bil pass.-mi.; 2 airports. **Chief ports:** Antwerp (one of the world's busiest), Zeebrugge, Ghent.

Communications: TV sets: 510 per 1,000 pop. **Radios:** 792 per 1,000 pop. **Telephones:** 12,764,000. **Daily newspaper circ.:** 161 per 1,000 pop.

Health: Life expectancy: 74.8 male; 81.6 female. **Births** (per 1,000 pop.): 10.6. **Deaths** (per 1,000 pop.): 10.1. **Natural inc.:** 0.05%. **Infant mortality** (per 1,000 live births): 4.6.

Education: Compulsory: ages 6-18. **Literacy:** 99%.

Major Intl. Organizations: UN and all of its specialized agencies, EU, NATO, OECD, OSCE.

Embassy: 3330 Garfield St. NW 20008; 333-6900.

Website: www.belgium.fgov.be

Belgium derives its name from the Belgae, the first recorded inhabitants, probably Celts. The land was conquered by Julius Caesar, and was ruled for 1800 years by conquerors, including Rome, the Franks, Burgundy, Spain, Austria, and France. After 1815, Belgium was made a part of the Netherlands, but it became an independent constitutional monarchy in 1830.

Belgian neutrality was violated by Germany in both world wars. King Leopold III surrendered to Germany, May 28, 1940. After the war, he was forced by political pressure to abdicate in favor of his son, King Baudouin. Baudouin was succeeded by his brother, Albert II, Aug. 9, 1993.

The Flemings of northern Belgium speak Dutch, while French is the language of the Walloons in the south. The language difference has been a perennial source of controversy and led to antagonism between the 2 groups. Parliament has passed measures aimed at transferring power from the central government to 3 regions—Wallonia, Flanders, and Brussels. Constitutional changes in 1993 made Belgium a federal state. Sabena, the national airline, went bankrupt Nov. 6, 2001.

Belize

People: Population: 262,999. **Age distrib.** (%): <15: 42.0; 65+: 3.5. **Pop. density:** 30 per sq. mi. **Urban:** 54%. **Ethnic groups:** Mestizo 44%, Creole 30%, Maya 11%, Garifuna 7%. **Principal languages:** English (official), Spanish, Mayan, Garifuna (Carib). **Chief religions:** Roman Catholic 62%, Protestant 30%.

Geography: Area: 8,800 sq. mi. **Location:** Eastern coast of Central America. **Neighbors:** Mexico on N, Guatemala on W and S. **Capital:** Belmopan, 9,000.

Government: Type: Parliamentary democracy. **Head of state:** Queen Elizabeth II, represented by Gov.-Gen. Sir Colville Young; b Nov. 20, 1932; in office: Nov. 17, 1993. **Head of gov.:** Prime Min. Said Musa; b Mar. 19, 1944; in office: Aug. 28, 1998. **Local divisions:** 6 districts. **Defense budget** (2001): $8 mil. **Active troops:** 700.

Economy: Industries: Garments, food processing, tourism, construction. **Chief crops:** Sugar (main export), citrus, bananas. **Arable land:** 2%. **Livestock** (2001): cattle: 45,000; chickens: 1.35 mil.; goats: 1,500; pigs: 24,000; sheep: 3,000.. **Electricity prod.:** 0.19 bil. kWh. **Labor force:** agri. 38%, ind. 32%, services 30%.

Finance: Monetary unit: Dollar (Sept. 2002: 1.97= $1 U.S.). **GDP** (2000 est.): $790 mil. **Per capita GDP:** $3,200. **Imports** (2000 est.): $413 mil.; partners (1998): U.S. 58%, Mexico 12%. **Exports** (2000 est.): $235.7 mil.; partners (1999): U.S. 42%, UK 33%. **Tourism** (1998): $99 mil. **Budget** (1999 est.): $279 mil. **Intl. reserves less gold** (end 2000): $94 mil. **Consumer prices** (change in 2000): 0.6%.

Transport: Motor vehicles: 2,300 pass. cars, 3,100 comm. vehicles. **Chief ports:** Belize City, Big Creek. **Civil aviation:** 9 airports.

Communications: TV sets: 109 per 1,000 pop. **Radios:** 133 per 1,000 pop. **Telephones:** 63,400.

Health: Life expectancy: 69.2 male; 73.9 female. **Births** (per 1,000 pop.): 31.1. **Deaths** (per 1,000 pop.): 4.6. **Natural inc.:** 2.65%. **Infant mortality** (per 1,000 live births): 24.3.

Education: Compulsory: ages 5-14. **Literacy** (1993): 93%.

Major Intl. Organizations: UN (FAO, IBRD, ILO, IMF, IMO, WHO, WTrO), Caricom, the Commonwealth, OAS.

Embassy: 2535 Massachusetts Ave. NW 20008; 332-9636.

Website: www.belize.gov.bz

Belize (formerly British Honduras) was Britain's last colony on the American mainland; independence was achieved Sept. 21, 1981. Relations with neighboring Guatemala, initially tense, have improved in recent years. Belize has become a center for drug trafficking between Colombia and the U.S.

Benin

Republic of Benin

People: Population: 6,787,625. **Age distrib.** (%): <15: 47.3; 65+: 2.3. **Pop. density:** 159 per sq. mi. **Urban:** 42%. **Ethnic groups:** African (Fon, Adja, Bariba, Yoruba, others) 99%. **Principal languages:** French (official), Fon, Yoruba, various tribal. **Chief religions:** Indigenous beliefs 70%, Muslim 15%, Christian 15%.

Geography: Area: 42,700 sq. mi. **Location:** In W Africa on Gulf of Guinea. **Neighbors:** Togo on W; Burkina Faso, Niger on N; Nigeria on E. **Topography:** Most of Benin is flat and covered with dense vegetation. The coast is hot, humid, and rainy. **Capital:** Porto-Novo 225,000. **Cities** (urban aggr., 1994 est.): Cotonou 750,000.

Government: Type: Republic. **Head of state and gov.:** Pres. Mathieu Kerekou; b Sept. 2, 1933; in office: Apr. 4, 1996. **Local divisions:** 6 departments. **Defense budget** (2001: $47 mil. **Active troops:** 4,750.

Economy: Industries: extiles, cigarettes, beverages, food, construction materials, petroleum. **Chief crops:** Palm oil, sorghum, cassava, peanuts, cotton, corn, rice. **Minerals:** Oil, limestone, marble. **Crude oil reserves** (2000): 8.2 mil bbls. **Arable land:** 13%. **Livestock** (2001): cattle: 1.50 mil; chickens: 23.00 mil.; goats: 1.18 mil.; pigs: 470,000; sheep: 644,997. **Fish catch** (1999): 43,771 metric tons. **Electricity prod.:** 0.24 bil. kWh.

Finance: Monetary unit: CFA Franc (Sept. 2002: 671.78 = $1 U.S.). **GDP** (2000 est.): $6.6 bil. **Per capita GDP:** $1,030. **Imports** (1999): $566 mil.; partners (1999): France 38%, China 16%. **Exports** (1999): $396 mil.; partners (1999): Brazil 14%, Libya 5%. **Tourism** (1998): $33 mil. **Budget** (1995 est.): $445 mil. **Intl. reserves less gold** (Apr. 2000): $352 mil. **Consumer prices** (change in 2000): 4.2%.

Transport: Railroad: Length: 359 mi. **Motor vehicles:** 35,600 pass. cars, 19,300 comm. vehicles. **Civil aviation:** 150.5 mil pass.-mi.; 1 airport. **Chief port:** Cotonou.

Communications: TV sets: 4 per 1,000 pop. **Radios:** 73 per 1,000 pop. **Telephones:** 184,300. **Daily newspaper circ.:** 2 per 1,000 pop.

Health: Life expectancy: 48.8 male; 50.6 female. **Births** (per 1,000 pop.): 43.7. **Deaths** (per 1,000 pop.): 14.5. **Natural inc.:** 2.91%. **Infant mortality** (per 1,000 live births): 88.5.

Education: Free, compulsory: ages 6-12. **Literacy:** 37%.

Major Intl. Organizations: UN (FAO, IBRD, ILO, IMF, IMO, WHO, WTrO), AU.

Embassy: 2737 Cathedral Ave. NW 20008; 232-6656.

Website: www.embassy.org/embassies/bj.html

The Kingdom of Abomey, rising to power in wars with neighboring kingdoms in the 17th century, came under French domination in the late 19th century and was incorporated into French West Africa by 1904.

Under the name Dahomey, the country gained independence Aug. 1, 1960; it became Benin in 1975. In the fifth coup since independence Col. Ahmed Kerekou took power in 1972; two years later he declared a socialist state with a "Marxist-Leninist" philosophy. In Dec. 1989, Kerekou announced Marxism-Leninism would no longer be the state ideology.

In Mar. 1991, Kerekou lost to Nicéphore Soglo in Benin's first free presidential election in 30 years. Kerekou defeated Soglo in Mar. 1996 to reclaim the presidency. He won reelection in a runoff Mar. 22, 2001.

Bhutan

Kingdom of Bhutan

People: Population: 2,094,176. **Age distrib.** (%): <15: 40.0; 65+: 4.0. **Pop. density:** 116 per sq. mi. **Urban:** 7%. **Ethnic groups:** Drukpa 50%, Nepalese 35%. **Principal languages:** Dzongkha (official), Tibetan, Nepalese dialects. **Chief religions:** Lamaistic Buddhist (state religion) 75%, Hindu 25%.

Geography: Area: 18,100 sq. mi. **Location:** S Asia, in eastern Himalayan Mts. **Neighbors:** India on W (Sikkim) and S, China on N. **Topography:** Bhutan is comprised of very high mountains in the N, fertile valleys in the center, and thick forests in the Duar Plain in the S. **Capital:** Thimphu 32,000.

Government: Type: Monarchy. **Head of state and gov.:** King Jigme Singye Wangchuk; b Nov. 11, 1955; in office: July 21, 1972. **Head of gov.:** Prime Min. Lyonpo Kinzang Dorji; b 1951; in office: Aug. 14, 2002. **Local divisions:** 18 districts. **Defense budget:** NA. **Active troops:** NA.

Economy: Industries: Cement, wood products, processed fruits. **Chief crops:** Rice, corn, citrus. **Other resources:** Timber, hydropower. **Livestock** (2001): cattle: 435,000; chickens: 310,000; goats: 42,100; pigs: 74,900; sheep: 58,500. **Arable land:** 2%. **Electricity prod.:** 1.88 bil. kWh. **Labor force:** agric. 93%.

Finance: Monetary unit: Ngultrum (Sept. 2002: 48.38 = $1 U.S.; Indian Rupee also used). **GDP** (2000 est.): $2.3 bil. **Per capita GDP:** $1,100. **Imports** (2000 est.): $269 mil.; partners: India 77%. **Exports** (2000 est.): $154 mil.; partners: India 94%, Bangladesh. **Tourism:** $9 mil. **Budget** (FY95/96 est.): $152 mil. **Intl. reserves less gold** (end 2000): $227 mil. **Consumer prices** (change in 1999): 6.8%.

Transport: Civil aviation: 30.1 mil pass.-mi.; 1 airport.

Communications: Radios: 27 per 1,000 pop. **Telephones:** 14,000.

Health: Life expectancy: 53.5 male; 52.8 female. **Births** (per 1,000 pop.): 35.3. **Deaths** (per 1,000 pop.): 13.7. **Natural inc.:** 2.15%. **Infant mortality** (per 1,000 live births): 106.8.

Education: Not compulsory. **Literacy:** 42%.

Major Intl. Organizations: UN (FAO, IBRD, IMF, WHO).

Website: www.kingdomofbhutan.com

The region came under Tibetan rule in the 16th century. British influence grew in the 19th century. A Buddhist monarchy was set up in 1907. According to a 1910 treaty, Britain guided Bhutan's external affairs, while the country remained internally self-governing. Upon independence, India assumed Britain's role in a 1949 revision of the treaty. Isolated for much of its history, Bhutan took tentative steps toward modernization in the 1990s.

Bolivia

Republic of Bolivia

People: Population: 8,445,134. **Age distrib.** (%): <15: 38.5; 65+: 4.5. **Pop. density:** 20 per sq. mi. **Urban:** 62%. **Ethnic groups:** Quechua 30%, mestizo 30%, Aymara 25%, White 15%. **Principal languages:** Spanish, Quechua, Aymara (all official). **Chief religion:** Roman Catholic 95%.

Geography: Area: 418,700 sq. mi. **Location:** In W central South America, in the Andes Mts. (one of 2 landlocked countries in South America). **Neighbors:** Peru and Chile on W, and Paraguay on S, Brazil on E and N. **Topography:** The great central plateau, at an altitude of 12,000 ft., over 500 mi. long, lies between two great cordilleras having 3 of the highest peaks in South America. Lake Titicaca, on Peruvian border, is highest lake in world on which steamboats ply (12,506 ft.). The E central region has semitropical forests; the llanos, or Amazon-Chaco lowlands are in E. **Capitals:** La Paz (administrative), Sucre (judicial). **Cities** (urban aggr.): La Paz, 1,499,000; Santa Cruz, 1,062,000, Sucre: 183,000.

Government: Type: Republic. **Head of state and gov.:** Pres. Gonzalo Sánchez de Lozada; b July 1, 1930: in office: Aug. 6, 2002. **Local divisions:** 9 departments. **Defense budget:** (2000) $130 mil. **Active troops:** 31,500.

Economy: Industries: Mining, smelting, petroleum, food and beverages. **Chief crops:** Coffee, sugarcane, potatoes, cotton, corn, coca. **Minerals:** Antimony, tin, tungsten, silver, zinc, oil, gas, iron. **Crude oil reserves** (2001): 0.2 bil bbls. **Other resources:** Timber. **Arable land:** 2%. **Livestock** (2001): cattle: 6.73 mil; chickens: 74.00 mil.; goats: 1.50 mil.; pigs: 2.80 mil; sheep: 8.75 mil. **Electricity prod.:** 3.87 bil. kWh.

Finance: Monetary unit: Boliviano (Sept. 2002: 7.34 = $1 U.S.). **GDP** (2000 est.): $20.9 bil. **Per capita GDP:** $2,600. **Imports** (2000 est.): $1.86 bil.; partners (1998): U.S. 32%, Japan 24%. **Exports** (2000 est.): $1.26 bil.; partners (1998): UK 16%, U.S. 12%. **Tourism:** $170 mil. **Budget** (1998): $2.7 bil. **Intl. reserves less gold** (end 2000): $633 mil. **Gold:** 940,000 oz t. **Consumer prices** (change in 2000): 4.6%.

Transport: Railroad: Length: 2,295 mi. **Motor vehicles:** 199,309 pass. cars, 230,245 comm. vehicles. **Civil aviation:** 1.3 bil pass.-mi.; 14 airports.

Communications: TV sets: 202 per 1,000 pop. **Radios:** 560 per 1,000 pop. **Telephones:** 1,258,800. **Daily newspaper circ.:** 69 per 1,000 pop.

Health: Life expectancy: 61.9 male; 67.1 female. **Births** (per 1,000 pop.): 26.4. **Deaths** (per 1,000 pop.): 8.1. **Natural inc.:** 1.84%. **Infant mortality** (per 1,000 live births): 57.5.

Education: Free, compulsory: ages 6-14. **Literacy:** 83%.

Major Intl. Organizations: UN (FAO, IBRD, ILO, IMF, IMO, WHO, WTrO), OAS.

Embassy: 3014 Massachusetts Ave. NW 20008; 483-4410.

The Incas conquered the region from earlier Indian inhabitants in the 13th century. Spanish rule began in the 1530s and lasted until Aug. 6, 1825. The country is named after Simon Bolivar, independence fighter.

Websites: www.embassy.org/embassies/bo.html
www.boliviaweb.com/embassies.html

In a series of wars, Bolivia lost its Pacific coast to Chile, the oil-bearing Chaco to Paraguay, and rubber-growing areas to Brazil, 1879-1935.

Economic unrest, especially among the militant mine workers, has contributed to continuing political instability. A reformist government under Victor Paz Estenssoro, 1951-64, nationalized tin mines and attempted to improve conditions for the Indian majority but was overthrown by a military junta. A long series of coups and countercoups continued until constitutional government was restored in 1982.

U.S. pressure on the government to reduce the country's coca output, the raw material for cocaine, has led to clashes between police and coca growers and increased anti-U.S. feeling among Bolivians. Gen. Hugo Banzer Suárez, who ruled as a dictator, 1971-78, became president in Aug. 1997. 105 people died in earthquakes near Aiquile May 22, 1998. Stricken with cancer, Banzer resigned and was succeeded Aug. 7, 2001, by Vice-Pres. Jorge Quiroga Ramírez. After an inconclusive presidential election June 30, 2002, Congress Aug. 4 chose Gonzalo Sánchez de Lozada, a U.S.-educated mining executive, as head of state.

Bosnia and Herzegovina

People: Population: 3,964,388. **Age distrib.** (%): <15: 20.1; 65+: 9.1. **Pop. density:** 201 per sq. mi. **Urban:** 43%. **Ethnic groups:** Serb 40%, Muslim 38%, Croat 22%. **Principal language:** Serbo-Croatian (official) 99%. **Chief religions:** Muslim 40%, Orthodox 31%, Catholic 15%.

Geography: Area: 19,700 sq. mi. **Location:** On Balkan Peninsula in SE Europe. **Neighbors:** Yugoslavia on E and SE, Croatia on N and W. **Topography:** Hilly with some mountains. About 36% of the land is forested. **Capital:** Sarajevo 552,000.

Government: Type: Republic. **Heads of state:** Collective presidency with rotating leadership. **Head of gov.:** Prime Min. Dragan Mikerevic; b Feb. 12, 1955; in office: Mar. 15, 2002. **Local divisions:** Muslim-Croat Federation, divided into 10 cantons; Republika Srpska. **Defense budget** (2001): $130 mil. Active troops: NA.

Economy: Industries: Steel, mining, vehicle assembly, textiles. **Chief crops:** Corn, wheat, fruits, vegetables. **Minerals:** Bauxite, iron, coal. **Arable land:** 14%. **Livestock** (2001): cattle: 440,000; chickens: 4.74 mil.; pigs: 330,000; sheep: 640,000. **Electricity prod.:** 2.62 bil. kWh.

Finance: Monetary unit: Conv. Mark (Sept. 2002: 2.00 = $1 U.S.). **GDP** (2000 est.): $6.5 bil. **Per capita GDP:** $1,700. **Imports** (2000 est.): $2.45 bil.; partners: Croatia, Slovenia, Germany, Italy. **Exports** (2000 est.): $950 mil.; partners: Croatia, Switzerland, Italy, Germany. **Tourism:** $13 mil. **Budget** (1999 est.): $2.2 bil.

Transport: Railroad: Length: 634 mi. **Chief port:** Bosanski Brod. **Civil aviation:** 1 airport.

Communications: TV sets: 94 per 1,000 pop. **Telephones:** 683,400. **Daily newspaper circ.:** 150 per 1,000 pop.

Health: Life expectancy: 69.3 male; 74.9 female. **Births** (per 1,000 pop.): 12.8. **Deaths** (per 1,000 pop.): 8.1. **Natural inc.:** 0.47%. **Infant mortality** (per 1,000 live births): 23.5.

Education: Free, compulsory: ages 7-15. **Literacy** (1991): 86%.

Major Intl. Organizations: UN (FAO, IBRD, ILO, IMF, IMO, WHO), OSCE.

Embassy: 2109 E St. NW, 20037; 337-1500.

Websites: www.bosnianembassy.org; www.fbihvlada.gov.ba

Bosnia was ruled by Croatian kings c. AD 958, and by Hungary 1000-1200. It became organized c. 1200 and later took control of Herzegovina. The kingdom disintegrated from 1391, with the southern part becoming the independent duchy Herzegovina. It was conquered by Turks in 1463 and made a Turkish province. The area was placed under control of Austria-Hungary in 1878, and made part of the province of **Bosnia and Herzegovina,** which was formally annexed to Austria-Hungary 1908; Bosnia became a province of Yugoslavia in 1918. It was reunited with Herzegovina as a federated republic in the 1946 Yugoslavian constitution.

Bosnia and Herzegovina declared sovereignty Oct. 15, 1991. A referendum for independence was passed Feb. 29, 1992. Ethnic Serbs' opposition to the referendum spurred violent clashes and bombings. The U.S. and EU recognized the republic Apr. 7. Fierce three-way fighting continued between Bosnia's Serbs, Muslims, and Croats. Serb forces massacred thousands of Bosnian Muslims and engaged in "ethnic cleansing" (the expulsion of Muslims and other non-Serbs from areas under Bosnian Serb control). The capital, Sarajevo, was surrounded and besieged by Bosnian Serb forces. Muslims and Croats in Bosnia reached a cease fire Feb. 23, 1994, and signed an accord, Mar. 18, to create a Muslim-Croat confederation in Bosnia. However, by mid-1994, Bosnian Serbs controlled over 70% of the country.

As fighting continued in 1995, the balance of power began to shift toward the Muslim-Croat alliance. Massive NATO air strikes at Bosnian Serb targets beginning Aug. 30 triggered a new round of peace talks, and the siege of Sarajevo was lifted Sept. 15. The new talks produced an agreement in principle to create autonomous regions within Bosnia, with the Serb region (Republika Srpska) constituting 49% of the country. A Croat-Muslim offensive in Sept. recaptured significant territory, leaving Bosnian Serbs in control of approximately half that percentage.

A peace agreement initialed in Dayton, Ohio, Nov. 21, 1995, was signed in Paris, Dec. 14, by leaders of Bosnia, Croatia, and Serbia. Some 60,000 NATO troops (about 20,000 from the U.S.) moved in to police the accord. Meanwhile, a UN tribunal began bringing charges against suspected war criminals. Elections were held Sept. 14, 1996, for a 3-person collective presidency, for seats in a federal parliament, and for regional offices. In Dec. a revamped NATO "stabilization force" (SFOR) of over 30,000 members (more than 8,000 from the U.S.) received an 18-month mandate, which was later extended.

In a landmark verdict Aug. 2, 2001, the UN tribunal found Radislav Krstic, a Bosnian Serb general, guilty of genocide for the mass killing of over 7,000 Muslims at Srebrenica in 1995. By early 2002, SFOR's troop strength in Bosnia had been reduced to 17,500.

Botswana

Republic of Botswana

People: Population: 1,591,232. **Age distrib.** (%): <15: 40.3; 65+: 4.1. **Pop. density:** 7 per sq. mi. **Urban:** 50%. **Ethnic groups:** Batswana 95%, Kalanga, Basarwa, Kgalagadi. **Principal languages:** English (official), Setswana. **Chief religions:** Indigenous beliefs 50%, Christian 50%.

Geography: Area: 226,000 sq. mi. **Location:** In southern Africa. **Neighbors:** Namibia on N and W, South Africa on S, Zimbabwe on NE; Botswana claims border with Zambia on N. **Topography:** The Kalahari Desert, supporting nomadic Bushmen and wildlife, spreads over SW; there are swamplands and farming areas in N, and rolling plains in E where livestock are grazed. **Capital:** Gaborone 225,000.

Government: Type: Parliamentary republic. **Head of state and gov.:** Pres. Festus Mogae; b Aug. 21, 1939; in office: Apr. 1, 1998. **Local divisions:** 10 districts, 4 town councils. **Defense budget** (2001): $221 mil. **Active troops:** 9,000.

Economy: Industries: Mining, livestock processing. **Chief crops:** Maize, sorghum, millet, pulses, beans. **Minerals:** Copper, coal, nickel, diamonds, salt, silver. **Arable land:** 1%. **Livestock** (2001): cattle: 2.40 mil; chickens: 4.00 mil.; goats: 2.25 mil.; pigs: 7,000; sheep: 370,000. **Electricity prod.:** 0.50 bil. kWh.

Finance: Monetary unit: Pula (Sept. 2002: 6.31 = $1 U.S.). **GDP** (2000 est.): $10.4 bil. **Per capita GDP:** $6,600. **Imports** (2000 est.): $2.2 bil.; partners (1998): Southern African Customs Union (SACU): 76%, Europe 10%. **Exports** (2000 est.): $2.6 bil.; partners (1998): EU 77%, Southern African Customs Union (SACU): 18%. **Tourism** (1998): $175 mil. **Budget** (FY96): $1.8 bil. **Intl. reserves less gold** (end 2000): $4.85 bil. **Consumer prices** (change in 2000): 8.6%.

Transport: Railroad: Length: 603 mi. **Motor vehicles:** 80,000 pass. cars, 19,869 comm. vehicles. **Civil aviation:** 34.2 mil pass.-mi.; 4 airports.

Communications: TV sets: 24 per 1,000 pop. **Radios:** 821 per 1,000 pop. **Telephones** (2000): 350,300. **Daily newspaper circ.:** 29 per 1,000 pop.

Health: Life expectancy: 35.1 male; 35.4 female. **Births** (per 1,000 pop.): 28. **Deaths** (per 1,000 pop.): 26.3. **Natural inc.:** 0.18%. **Infant mortality** (per 1,000 live births): 64.7.

Education: Not compulsory. **Literacy:** 70%.

Major Intl. Organizations: UN (FAO, IBRD, ILO, IMF, WHO, WTrO), the Commonwealth, AU.

Embassy: 1531-33 New Hampshire Ave. NW, 20036; 244-4990.

Website: www.gov.bw

First inhabited by bushmen, then Bantus, the region became the British protectorate of Bechuanaland in 1886, halting encroachment by Boers and Germans from the south and southwest. The country became fully independent Sept. 30, 1966, as Botswana. Cattle raising and mining (diamonds, copper, nickel) have contributed to economic growth; economy is closely tied to South Africa. According to UN estimates, more than one-third of the adult population has HIV/AIDS.

Brazil

Federative Republic of Brazil

People: Population: 176,029,560. **Age distrib.** (%): <15: 28.6; 65+: 5.5. **Pop. density:** 54 per sq. mi. **Urban:** 81%. **Ethnic groups:** White (incl. Portuguese, German, Italian, Spanish, Polish) 55%, mixed black and white 38%, black 6%. **Principal languages:** Portuguese (official), Spanish, English, French. **Chief religion:** Roman Catholic 70%.

Geography: Area: 3,265,100 sq. mi., largest country in South America. **Location:** Occupies E half of South America. **Neighbors:** French Guiana, Suriname, Guyana, Venezuela on N; Colombia, Peru, Bolivia, Paraguay, on W; Uruguay on S. **Topography:** Brazil's Atlantic coastline stretches 4,603 miles. In N is the heavily wooded Amazon basin covering half the country. Its network of rivers is navigable for 15,814 mi. The Amazon itself flows 2,093 miles in Brazil, all navigable. The NE region is semi-arid scrubland, heavily settled and poor. The S central region, favored by climate and resources, has almost half of the population, produces 75% of farm goods and 80% of industrial output. The narrow coastal belt includes most of the major cities. Almost the entire country has a tropical or semitropical climate. **Capital:** Brasília. **Cities** (urban aggr.): São Paulo, 17,962,000, (2001 city est.: 10.4 mil.); Rio de Janeiro, 10,652,000; Belo Horizonte, 4,224,000, Brasília, 2,073,000.

Government: Type: Federal republic. **Head of state and gov.:** Pres. Fernando Henrique Cardoso; b June 18, 1931; in office: Jan. 1, 1995. **Local divisions:** 26 states, 1 federal district (Brasília). **Defense budget** (2001): $8.8 bil. **Active troops:** 287,600.

Economy: Industries: Textiles, shoes, chemicals, cement, lumber. **Chief crops:** Coffee (leading grower), soybeans, sugarcane, cocoa, rice, corn, wheat, citrus. **Minerals:** Iron (largest producer in the world), manganese, phosphates, uranium, gold, nickel, tin, bauxite, oil. **Crude oil reserves** (2001): 8.5 bil bbls. **Arable land:** 5%. **Livestock** (2001): cattle: 171.79 mil; chickens: 1.01 bil.; goats:. 8.70 mil.; pigs: 29.42 mil; sheep: 15.00 mil. **Fish catch** (1999): 820,480 metric tons. **Electricity prod.:** 342.30 bil. kWh. **Labor force:** 53.2% services; 23.1% agric.; 23.7% industry.

Finance: Monetary unit: Real (Sept. 2002: 3.75 = $1 U.S.). **GDP** (2000 est.): $1.13 tril. **Per capita GDP:** $6,500. **Imports** (2000): $55.8 bil.; partners (1999): U.S. 24%, Argentina 12%. **Exports** (2000): $55.1 bil.; partners (1999): U.S. 23%, Argentina 11%. **Tourism:** $3.99 bil. **Budget** (1998): $149 bil. **Intl. reserves less gold** (end 2000): $24.94 bil. **Gold:** 1.89 mil oz t. **Consumer prices** (change in 2000): 7.0%.

Transport: Railroad: Length: 18,578 mi. **Motor vehicles** (1997): 14.00 mil pass. cars, 4.03 mil comm. vehicles. **Civil aviation:** 26.3 bil pass.-mi.; 139 airports. **Chief ports:** Santos, Rio de Janeiro, Vitoria, Salvador, Rio Grande, Recife.

Communications: TV sets: 317 per 1,000 pop. **Radios:** 446 per 1,000 pop. **Telephones:** 66,176,500. **Daily newspaper circ.:** 41 per 1,000 pop.

Health: Life expectancy: 59.4 male; 67.9 female. **Births** (per 1,000 pop.): 18.1. **Deaths** (per 1,000 pop.): 9.3. **Natural inc.:** 0.88%. **Infant mortality** (per 1,000 live births): 35.9.

Education: Free, compulsory: ages 7-14. **Literacy** (1996): 85%.

Major Intl. Organizations: UN and most of its specialized agencies, OAS.

Embassy: 3006 Massachusetts Ave. NW 20008; 238-2700.

Website: www.brasilemb.org

Pedro Alvares Cabral, a Portuguese navigator, is generally credited as the first European to reach Brazil, in 1500. The country was thinly settled by various Indian tribes. Only a few have survived to the present, mostly in the Amazon basin.

In the next centuries, Portuguese colonists gradually pushed inland, bringing along large numbers of African slaves. (Slavery was not abolished until 1888.) The King of Portugal, fleeing before Napoleon's army, moved the seat of government to Brazil in 1808. Brazil thereupon became a kingdom under Dom Joao VI. After his return to Portugal, his son Pedro proclaimed the independence of Brazil, Sept. 7, 1822, and was crowned emperor. The second emperor, Dom Pedro II, was deposed in 1889, and a republic proclaimed, called the United States of Brazil. In 1967 the country was renamed the Federative Republic of Brazil.

A military junta took control in 1930; dictatorial power was assumed by Getulio Vargas, until finally forced out by the military in 1945. A democratic regime prevailed 1945-64, during which time the capital was moved from Rio de Janeiro to Brasília. In 1964, Pres. Joao Belchoir Marques Goulart instituted economic policies that aggravated Brazil's inflation; he was overthrown by an army revolt. The next 5 presidents were all military leaders. Censorship was imposed, and much of the opposition was suppressed amid charges of torture.

Since 1930, successive governments have pursued industrial and agricultural growth and interior area development. Exploiting vast natural resources and a huge labor force, Brazil became the leading industrial power of Latin America by the 1970s, while agricultural output soared. By the 1990s, Brazil had one of the world's largest economies; income was poorly distributed, however, and more than one out of four Brazilians continued to survive on less than $1 a day. Despite protective environmental legislation, development has destroyed much of the Amazon ecosystem. Brazil hosted delegates from 178 countries at the Earth Summit, June 3-14, 1992.

Democratic presidential elections were held in 1985 as the nation returned to civilian rule. Fernando Collor de Mello was elected president in Dec. 1989. In Sept. 1992, Collor was impeached for corruption. He resigned on Dec. 29 as his trial was beginning, and Itamar Franco, who had been acting president, was sworn in as president. In elections held on Oct. 3, 1994, Fernando Henrique Cardoso was elected president. Reelected Oct. 4, 1998, he guided Brazil through a series of financial crises. New presidential elections were set for Oct. 2002.

A new civil code guaranteeing legal equality for women was enacted Aug. 15, 2001. The IMF approved a $30 bil. loan to Brazil Aug. 7, 2002; by then, Brazil's debt already exceeded $260 bil.

Brunei

State of Brunei Darussalam

People: Population: 350,898. **Age distrib.** (%): <15: 30.8; 65+: 2.7. **Pop. density:** 175 per sq. mi. **Urban:** 72%. **Ethnic groups:** Malay 64%, Chinese 20%. **Principal languages:** Malay (official), English, Chinese. **Chief religions:** Muslim (official) 63%, Buddhist 14%, Christian 8%.

Geography: Area: 2,000 sq. mi. **Location:** In SE Asia, on the N coast of the island of Borneo; it is surrounded on its landward side by the Malaysian state of Sarawak. **Capital:** Bandar Seri Begawan, (1999 met. area est.) 46,000.

Government: Type: Independent sultanate. **Head of state and gov.:** Sultan Sir Muda Hassanal Bolkiah Mu'izzadin Waddaulah; b July 15, 1946; in office: Jan. 1, 1984 (sultan since Oct. 5, 1967). **Local divisions:** 4 districts. **Defense budget** (2002): $267 mil. **Active troops:** 5,900.

Economy: Industries: Oil & gas, construction. **Chief crops:** Rice, bananas, cassava. **Minerals:** Oil, gas. **Crude oil reserves** (2001): 1.2 bil bbls. **Arable land:** 1%. **Livestock** (2001): cattle: 8,000; chickens: 4.70 mil.; goats: 3,500; pigs: 6,000. **Electricity prod.:** 2.22 bil. kWh. **Labor force:** government 48%, production of oil, natural gas, services and construction 42%, agri., forestry, and fishing 10%.

Finance: Monetary unit: Dollar (Sept. 2002: 1.78 = $1 U.S.). **GDP** (2000 est.): $5.9 bil. **Per capita GDP:** $17,600. **Imports** (1999 est.): $1.3 bil.; partners (1999): Singapore 34%, UK 15%, Malaysia 15%. **Exports** (1999 est.): $2.55 bil.; partners (1999): Japan 42%, U.S. 17%. **Tourism** (1998): $37 mil. **Budget** (1997 est.): $2.6 bil.

Transport: Railroad: Length: 12 mi. **Motor vehicles:** 146,000 pass. cars, 17,780 comm. vehicles. **Civil aviation:** 1.8 bil pass.-mi.; 1 airport.

Communications: TV sets: 308 per 1,000 pop. **Radios:** 417 per 1,000 pop. **Telephones** (2000): 175,500. **Daily newspaper circ.:** 70 per 1,000 pop.

Health: Life expectancy: 71.7 male; 76.6 female. **Births** (per 1,000 pop.): 20.1. **Deaths** (per 1,000 pop.): 3.4. **Natural inc.:** 1.67%. **Infant mortality** (per 1,000 live births): 13.9.

Education: Free, compulsory: ages 5-17. **Literacy:** 88%.

Major Intl. Organizations: UN and some of its specialized agencies, APEC, ASEAN, the Commonwealth.

Embassy: 2600 Virginia Ave. NW, 20037; 342-0159.

Website: www.gov.bn

The Sultanate of Brunei was a powerful state in the early 16th century, with authority over all of the island of Borneo as well as parts of the Sulu Islands and the Philippines. In 1888, a treaty placed the state under the protection of Great Britain.

Brunei became a fully sovereign and independent state on Jan. 1, 1984. Much of the country's oil wealth has been squandered in recent years by members of the royal family.

Bulgaria

Republic of Bulgaria

People: Population: 7,621,337. **Age distrib.** (%): <15: 15.1; 65+: 16.7. **Pop. density:** 178 per sq. mi. **Urban:** 69%. **Ethnic groups:** Bulgarian 85%, Turk 9%. **Principal languages:** Bulgarian (official). **Chief religions:** Bulgarian Orthodox 85%, Muslim 13%.

Geography: Area: 42,700 sq. mi. **Location:** SE Europe, in E Balkan Peninsula on Black Sea. **Neighbors:** Romania on N; Yugoslavia, Macedonia on W; Greece, Turkey on S. **Topography:** The Stara Planina (Balkan) Mts. stretch E-W across the center of the country, with the Danubian plain on N, the Rhodope Mts. on SW, and Thracian Plain on SE. **Capital:** Sofia 1,187,000.

Government: Type: Republic. **Head of state:** Pres. Georgi Parvanov; b June 28, 1957; in office: Jan. 22, 2002. **Head of gov.:** Prime Min. Simeon Sakskoburggotski (Simeon II); b June 16, 1937; in office: July 24, 2001. **Local divisions:** 9 provinces. **Defense budget (2001):** $337 mil. **Active troops:** 77,260.

Economy: Industries: Electricity, gas and water, food, beverages, tobacco **Chief crops:** Grain, fruit, oilseed, vegetables, tobacco. **Minerals:** Bauxite, copper, zinc, lead, coal. **Crude oil reserves** (2001): < 50 mil bbls. **Arable land:** 37%. **Livestock** (2001): cattle: 640,000; chickens: 14.99 mil.; goats: 970,000; pigs: 1.14 mil; sheep: 2.29 mil. **Fish catch** (1999): 16,674 metric tons. **Electricity prod.:** 38.84 bil. kWh. **Labor force:** agri. 26%, ind. 31%, services 43%.

Finance: Monetary unit: Lev (Sept. 2002: 2.00 = $1 U.S.). **GDP** (2000 est.): $48 bil. **Per capita GDP:** $6,200. **Imports** (2000 est.): $5.9 bil.; partners (2000): Russia 24%, Germany 14%. **Exports** (2000 est.): $4.8 bil.; partners (2000): Italy 14%, Turkey 10%. **Tourism:** $930 mil. **Budget** (2000 est.): $4.92 bil. **Intl. reserves less gold** (end 2000): $2.57 bil. **Gold:** 1.03 mil oz t. **Consumer prices** (change in 2000): 10.3%.

Transport: Railroad: Length: 4,043 mi. **Motor vehicles:** 1.65 mil pass. cars, 264,196 comm. vehicles. **Civil aviation:** 1.1 bil pass.-mi.; 3 airports. **Chief ports:** Burgas, Varna.

Communications: TV sets: 359 per 1,000 pop. **Telephones:** 4,463,900. **Daily newspaper circ.:** 141 per 1,000 pop.

Health: Life expectancy: 68 male; 75.2 female. **Births** (per 1,000 pop.): 8.1. **Deaths** (per 1,000 pop.): 14.4. **Natural inc.:** -0.64%. **Infant mortality** (per 1,000 live births): 14.2.

Education: Free, compulsory: ages 7-16. **Literacy:** 98%.

Major Intl. Organizations: UN (FAO, IBRD, ILO, IMF, IMO, WHO, WTrO), OSCE.

Embassy: 1621 22d St. NW 20008; 387-7969.

Website: www.government.bg/English

Bulgaria was settled by Slavs in the 6th century. Turkic Bulgars arrived in the 7th century, merged with the Slavs, became Christians by the 9th century, and set up powerful empires in the 10th and 12th centuries. The Ottomans prevailed in 1396 and remained for 500 years.

An 1876 revolt led to an independent kingdom in 1908. Bulgaria expanded after the first Balkan War but lost its Aegean coastline in World War I, when it sided with Germany. Bulgaria joined the Axis in World War II but withdrew in 1944. Communists took power with Soviet aid; monarchy was abolished Sept. 8, 1946.

On Nov. 10, 1989, Communist Party leader and head of state Todor Zhivkov, who had held power for 35 years, resigned. Zhivkov was imprisoned, Jan. 1990, and convicted, Sept. 1992, of corruption and abuse of power. In Jan. 1990, Parliament voted to revoke the constitutionally guaranteed dominant role of the Communist Party. A new constitution took effect July 13, 1991. An economic austerity program was launched in May 1996. Former Prime Min. Andrei Lukanov, a longtime Communist leader, was assassinated Oct. 2 in Sofia. Petar Stoyanov won a presidential runoff election Nov. 3.

Bulgaria's deteriorating economy provoked nationwide strikes and demonstrations in Jan. 1997. The Union of Democratic Forces, an anti-Communist group, won national elections on Apr. 19, 1997. The UDF lost the elections of June 17, 2001, to a party headed by the former king, Simeon II. Socialist opposition leader Georgi Parvanov won a presidential runoff vote Nov. 18.

Burkina Faso

People: Population: 12,603,185. **Age distrib.** (%): <15: 47.5; 65+ 2.9. **Pop. density:** 119 per sq. mi. **Urban:** 18%. **Ethnic groups:** Mossi (approx. 24%), Gurunsi, Senufo, Lobi, Bobo, Mande, Fulani. **Principal languages:** French (official), Sudanic tribal languages. **Chief religions:** Muslim 50%, indigenous beliefs 40%, Christian (mostly Roman Catholic) 10%.

Geography: Area: 105,700 sq. mi. **Location:** In W Africa, S of the Sahara. **Neighbors:** Mali on NW; Niger on NE; Benin, Togo, Ghana, Côte on S. **Topography:** Landlocked Burkina Faso is in the savanna region of W Africa. The N is arid, hot, and thinly populated. **Capital:** Ouagadougou, 862,000.

Government: Type: Republic. **Head of state:** Pres. Blaise Compaoré; b 1951; in office: Oct. 15, 1987. **Head of gov.:** Prime Min. Paramanga Ernest Yonli; b 1956; in office: Nov. 7, 2000. **Local divisions:** 45 provinces. **Defense budget** (2001): $69 mil. **Active troops:** 10,000.

Economy: Industries: Cotton lint, beverages, agricultural processing, soap. **Chief crops:** Millet, sorghum, rice, peanuts, cotton. **Minerals:** Manganese, limestone, marble. **Arable land:** 13%. **Livestock** (2001): cattle: 4.80 mil; chickens: 22.42 mil.; goats: 8.65 mil.; pigs: 622,493; sheep: 6.78 mil. **Electricity prod.:** 0.28 bil. kWh. Labor Force: agri. 90%.

Finance: Monetary unit: CFA Franc (Sept. 2002: 671.78 = $1 U.S.). **GDP** (2000 est.): $12 bil. **Per capita GDP:** $1,000. **Imports** (2000 est.): $610 mil.; partners (1999): Cote d'Ivoire 30%, France 28%. **Exports** (2000 est.): $220 mil.; partners (1999): Italy 13%, France 10%. **Tourism** (1998): $42 mil. **Budget** (1995 est.): $492 mil. **Intl. reserves less gold** (end 2000): $187 mil. **Gold:** 10,000 oz. t. **Consumer prices** (change in 2000): –0.3%.

Transport: Railroad: Length: 386 mi. **Motor vehicles:** 35,460 pass. cars, 19,473 comm. vehicles. **Civil aviation:** 154.2 mil pass.-mi.; 2 airports.

Communications: TV sets: 4.4 per 1,000 pop. **Radios:** 48.3 per 1,000 pop. **Telephones:** 132,600.

Health: Life expectancy: 45.5 male; 46.8 female. **Births** (per 1,000 pop.): 44.3. **Deaths** (per 1,000 pop.): 17.1. **Natural inc.:** 2.73%. **Infant mortality** (per 1,000 live births): 105.3.

Education: Free, compulsory: ages 7-14. **Literacy:** 19%.

Major Intl. Organizations: UN and many of its specialized agencies, AU.

Embassy: 2340 Massachusetts Ave. NW 20008; 332-5577.

Website: www.burkinaembassy–usa.org

The Mossi tribe entered the area in the 11th to 13th centuries. Their kingdoms ruled until they were defeated by the Mali and Songhai empires.

French control came by 1896, but Upper Volta (renamed Burkina Faso on Aug. 4, 1984) was not established as a separate territory until 1947. Full independence came Aug. 5, 1960, and a pro-French government was elected. The military seized power in 1980. A 1987 coup established the current regime, which instituted a multiparty democracy in the early 1990s.

Several hundred thousand farm workers migrate each year to Côte d'Ivoire and Ghana. Burkina Faso is heavily dependent on foreign aid.

Burma

(See Myanmar)

Burundi

Republic of Burundi

People: Population: 6,373,002. **Age distrib.** (%): <15: 46.8; 65+: 2.8. **Pop. density:** 644 per sq. mi. **Urban:** 9%. **Ethnic groups:** Hutu (Bantu) 85%, Tutsi 14%, Twa (Pygmy) 1%. **Principal languages:** Kirundi, French (both official), Swahili. **Chief religions:** Roman Catholic 62%, indigenous beliefs 32%, Protestant 5%.

Geography: Area: 9,900 sq. mi. **Location:** In central Africa. **Neighbors:** Rwanda on N, Dem. Rep. of the Congo (formerly Zaire) on W, Tanzania on E and S. **Topography:** Much of the country is grassy highland, with mountains reaching 8,900 ft. The southernmost source of the White Nile is located in Burundi. Lake Tanganyika is the second deepest lake in the world. **Capital:** Bujumbura 346,000.

Government: Type: In transition. **Head of state and gov.:** Pres. Pierre Buyoya; b Nov. 14, 1949; in office: July 25, 1996. **Local divisions:** 15 provinces. **Defense budget** (2001): $50 mil. **Active troops:** 45,500.

Economy: Industries: Light consumer goods, assembly. **Chief crops:** Coffee, cotton, tea. **Minerals:** Nickel, uranium. **Arable land:** 44%. **Livestock** (2001): cattle: 315,000; chickens: 4.70 mil.; goats: 600,000; pigs: 70,000; sheep: 230,000. **Fish catch:** (1999): 20,306 metric tons. **Electricity prod.:** 0.15 bil. kWh. **Labor force:** 93% agric.

Finance: Monetary unit: Franc (Sept. 2002: 1,045 = $1 U.S.). **GDP** (2000 est.): $4.4 bil. **Per capita GDP:** $720. **Imports** (2000): $110 mil.; partners (1999): Belgium 20%, Zambia 11%. **Exports** (2000): $32 mil.; partners (1999): Germany 17%, Belgium 14%. **Tourism** (1998): $1 mil. **Budget** (2000 est.): $176 mil **Intl. reserves less gold** (end 2000): $25 mil. **Gold:** 20,000 oz t. **Consumer prices** (change in 2000): 24.3%.

Transport: Motor vehicles: 8,200 pass. cars, 11,800 comm. vehicles. **Civil aviation:** 5.2 mil pass.-mi.; 1 airport. **Chief port:** Bujumbura.

Communications: TV sets: 7 per 1,000 pop. **Radios:** 50 per 1,000 pop. **Telephones:** 40,000.

Health: Life expectancy: 45.1 male; 46.8 female. **Births** (per 1,000 pop.): 39.9. **Deaths** (per 1,000 pop.): 16.3. **Natural inc.:** 2.36%. **Infant mortality** (per 1,000 live births): 70.

Education: Free, compulsory: ages 7-13. **Literacy:** 35%.

Major Intl. Organizations: UN (FAO, IBRD, ILO, IMF, WHO, WTrO), AU.

Embassy: 2233 Wisconsin Ave. NW 20007; 342-2574.

Website: www.burundi.gov.bi

The pygmy Twa were the first inhabitants, followed by Bantu Hutus, who were conquered in the 16th century by the Tutsi (Watusi), probably from Ethiopia. Under German control in 1899, the area fell to Belgium in 1916, which exercised successively a League of Nations mandate and UN trusteeship over Ruanda-Urundi (now the two countries of Rwanda and Burundi). Burundi became independent July 1, 1962.

An unsuccessful Hutu rebellion in 1972-73 left 10,000 Tutsi and 150,000 Hutu dead. Over 100,000 Hutu fled to Tanzania and Zaire (now Congo). In the 1980s, Burundi's Tutsi-dominated regime pledged itself to ethnic reconciliation and democratic reform. In the nation's first democratic presidential election, in June 1993, a Hutu, Melchior Ndadaye, was elected. He was killed in an attempted coup, Oct. 21, 1993. At least 150,000 Burundians died as a result of ethnic conflict during the next three years. Pres. Cyprien Ntaryamira, elected Jan. 1994, was killed with the president of Rwanda in a mysterious plane crash, Apr. 6. The incident sparked massive carnage in Rwanda; violence in Burundi, initially far more limited, intensified in 1995. Ethnic strife continued after a military coup, July 25, 1996. Former South African Pres. Nelson Mandela mediated peace talks from Dec. 1999; most warring groups signed a draft peace treaty in Arusha, Tanzania, Aug. 28, 2000. Coup attempts were suppressed Apr. 18 and July 23, 2001. A power-sharing government headed by Buyoya was sworn in Nov. 1, but clashes with rebels continued.

Cambodia

Kingdom of Cambodia

People: Population: 12,775,324. **Age distrib.** (%): <15: 41.3; 65+: 3.5. **Pop. density:** 187 per sq. mi. **Urban:** 16%. **Ethnic groups:** Khmer 90%, Vietnamese 5%, Chinese 1%. **Principal languages:** Khmer (official), French. **Chief religion:** Theravada Buddhism 95%.

Geography: Area: 68,200 sq. mi. **Location:** SE Asia, on Indochina Peninsula. **Neighbors:** Thailand on W and N, Laos on NE, Vietnam on E. **Topography:** The central area, formed by the Mekong R. basin and Tonle Sap lake, is level. Hills and mountains are in SE, a long escarpment separates the country from Thailand on NW. 76% of the area is forested. **Capital:** Phnom Penh 1,109,000.

Government: Type: Constitutional monarchy. **Head of state:** King Norodom Sihanouk; b Oct. 31, 1922; in office: Sept. 24, 1993. **Head of gov.:** Prime Min. Hun Sen; b Apr. 4, 1952; in office: Nov. 30, 1998. **Local divisions:** 20 provinces and 3 municipalities. **Defense budget (2001):** $128 mil. **Active troops:** 140,000.

Economy: Industries: Garments, tourism, rice milling, fishing, wood and wood products. **Chief crops:** Rice, corn, rubber, vegetables. **Minerals:** Gemstones, phosphates, manganese. **Other resources:** Timber. **Arable land:** 13%. **Livestock** (2001): cattle: 2.87 mil; chickens: 15.25 mil.; pigs: 2.12 mil. **Fish catch** (1999): 114,600 metric tons. **Electricity prod.:** 0.13 bil. kWh. **Labor force:** agri. 80%.

Finance: Monetary unit: Riel (Sept. 2002: 3,835.00 = $1 U.S.). **GDP** (2000 est.): $16.1 bil. **Per capita GDP:** $1,300. **Imports** (2000 est.): $1.3 bil.; partners (1997): Thailand 16%, Vietnam 9%. **Exports** (2000 est.): $942 mil.; partners (1997): Vietnam 18%, Thailand 15%. **Tourism:** $190 mil. **Budget** (2000 est.): $532 mil. **Intl. reserves less gold** (end 2000): $385 mil. **Consumer prices** (change in 2000): –0.8%.

Transport: Railroad: Length: 380 mi. **Motor vehicles:** 15,000 pass. cars, 15,000 comm. vehicles. **Civil aviation:** 8 airports. **Chief port:** Kampong Saom (Sihanoukville).

Communications: TV sets: 8 per 1,000 pop. **Radios:** 124 per 1,000 pop. **Telephones:** 257,000.

Health: Life expectancy: 54.8 male; 59.5 female. **Births** (per 1,000 pop.): 32.9. **Deaths** (per 1,000 pop.): 10.5. **Natural inc.:** 2.24%. **Infant mortality** (per 1,000 live births): 64.

Education: Compulsory: ages 6-12. **Literacy** (1993): 65%.

Major Intl. Organizations: UN (FAO, IBRD, ILO, IMF, IMO, WHO), ASEAN.

Embassy: 4500 16th St. NW 20011; 726-7742.

Website: www.cambodia.gov.kh

Early kingdoms dating from that of Funan in the 1st century AD culminated in the great Khmer empire that flourished from the 9th century to the 13th, encompassing present-day Thailand, Cambodia, Laos, and southern Vietnam. The peripheral areas were lost to invading Siamese and Vietnamese, and France established a protectorate in 1863. Independence came in 1953.

Prince Norodom Sihanouk, king 1941-1955 and head of state from 1960, tried to maintain neutrality. Relations with the U.S. were broken in 1965, after South Vietnam planes attacked Vietcong forces within Cambodia. Relations were restored in 1969, after Sihanouk charged Viet Communists with arming Cambodian insurgents.

In 1970, pro-U.S. Prem. Lon Nol seized power, demanding removal of 40,000 North Viet troops; the monarchy was abolished. Sihanouk formed a government-in-exile in Beijing, and open war began between the government and Communist Khmer Rouge guerrillas. The U.S. provided heavy military and economic aid.

Khmer Rouge forces captured Phnom Penh Apr. 17, 1975. The new government evacuated all cities and towns, and shuffled the rural population, sending virtually the entire population to clear jungle, forest, and scrub. Over one million people were killed in executions and enforced hardships.

Severe border fighting broke out with Vietnam in 1978 and developed into a full-fledged Vietnamese invasion. Formation of a Vietnamese-backed government was announced, Jan. 8, 1979, one day after the Vietnamese capture of Phnom Penh. Thousands of refugees flowed into Thailand, and widespread starvation was reported.

On Jan. 10, 1983, Vietnam launched an offensive against rebel forces in the west. They overran a refugee camp, Jan. 31, driving 30,000 residents into Thailand. In March, Vietnam launched a major offensive against camps on the Cambodian-Thailand border, engaged Khmer Rouge guerrillas, and crossed the border, instigating clashes with Thai troops. Vietnam withdrew nearly all its troops by Sept. 1989.

Following UN-sponsored elections in Cambodia that ended May 28, 1993, the 2 leading parties agreed to share power in an interim government until a new constitution was adopted. On Sept. 21, a constitution reestablishing a monarchy was adopted by the National Assembly. It took effect Sept. 24, with Sihanouk as king. The Khmer Rouge, which had boycotted the elections, opposed the new government, and armed violence continued in the mid-1990s. Ieng Sary, a Khmer Rouge leader, broke with the guerrillas, formed a rival group, and announced his support for the monarchy in Aug. 1996, as Khmer Rouge strength rapidly diminished.

Co-Prime Min. Hun Sen staged a coup July 5, 1997, ousting his rival, Prince Norodom Ranariddh. Pol Pot, the Khmer Rouge leader who held power during the late 1970s, was denounced by his former comrades at a show trial, July 25, and sentenced to house arrest; he died Apr. 15, 1998. Hun Sen's party won parliamentary elections on July 26. Cambodia was formally admitted to ASEAN on Apr. 30, 1999.

Cameroon

Republic of Cameroon

People: Population: 16,184,748. **Age distrib.** (%): <15: 42.4; 65+: 3.4. **Pop. density:** 89 per sq. mi. **Urban:** 48%. **Ethnic groups:** Cameroon Highlander 31%, Equatorial Bantu 19%, Kirdi 11%, Fulani 10%, NW Bantu 8%. **Principal languages:** English, French (both official), 24 African groups. **Chief religions:** Indigenous beliefs 51%, Christian 33%, Muslim 16%.

Geography: Area: 181,300 sq. mi. **Location:** Between W and central Africa. **Neighbors:** Nigeria on NW; Chad, Central African Republic on E; Congo, Gabon, Equatorial Guinea on S. **Topography:** A low coastal plain with rain forests is in S; plateaus in center lead to forested mountains in W, including Mt. Cameroon, 13,350 ft.; grasslands in N lead to marshes around Lake Chad. **Capital:** Yaoundé. **Cities** (urban agg.): Douala, 1,642,000; Yaoundé, 1,481,000.

Government: Type: Republic. **Head of state:** Pres. Paul Biya; b Feb. 13, 1933; in office: Nov. 6, 1982. **Head of gov.:** Prime Min. Peter Mafani Musonge; b Dec. 3, 1942; in office: Sept. 19, 1996. **Local divisions:** 10 provinces. **Defense budget:** (2000) $155 mil. **Active troops:** 22,100.

Economy: Industries: Oil, food processing, light consumer goods. **Chief crops:** Cocoa, coffee, cotton. **Crude oil reserves** (2000): 400 mil bbls. **Minerals:** Oil, bauxite, iron ore. **Other resources:** Timber. **Arable land:** 13%. **Livestock** (2001): cattle: 5.90 mil; chickens: 30.00 mil.; goats: 4.40 mil.; pigs: 1.35 mil; sheep: 3.80 mil. **Fish catch** (1999): 89,055 metric tons. **Electricity prod.:** 3.62 bil. kWh. **Labor force:** agric. 70%, ind. and commerce 13%, other 17%.

Finance: Monetary unit: CFA Franc (Sept. 2002: 671.78 = $1 U.S.). **GDP** (2000 est.): $26 bil. **Per capita GDP:** $1,700. **Imports** (2000 est.): $1.6 bil.; partners (2000 est.): France 29%, Germany 7%,. **Exports** (2000 est.): $2.1 bil.; partners: (2000 est.): Italy 24%, France 18%, Netherlands 10%. **Tourism** (1998): $40 mil. **Budget** (FY00/01 est.): $2.1 bil. **Intl. reserves less gold** (end 2000): $163 mil. **Consumer prices** (change in 1999): 5.3%.

Transport: Railroad: Length: 625 mi. **Motor vehicles:** 92,200 pass. cars, 60,800 comm. vehicles. **Civil aviation:** 339.9 mil pass.-mi.; 5 airports. **Chief ports:** Douala, Kribi.

Communications: TV sets: 72 per 1,000 pop. **Radios:** 325 per 1,000 pop. **Telephones:** 411,400.

Health: Life expectancy: 53.5 male; 55.2 female. **Births** (per 1,000 pop.): 35.7. **Deaths** (per 1,000 pop.): 12.1. **Natural inc.:** 2.36%. **Infant mortality** (per 1,000 live births): 68.8.

Education: Free, compulsory: ages 6-12. **Literacy:** 63%.

Major Intl. Organizations: UN (FAO, IBRD, ILO, IMF, IMO, WHO, WTrO), the Commonwealth, AU.

Embassy: 2349 Massachusetts Ave. NW 20008; 265-8790.

Website: www.cameroon.gov.cm

Portuguese sailors were the first Europeans to reach Cameroon, in the 15th century. The European and American slave trade was very active in the area. German control lasted from 1884 to 1916, when France and Britain divided the territory, later receiving League of Nations mandates and UN trusteeships. French Cameroon became independent Jan. 1, 1960; one part of British Cameroon joined Nigeria in 1961, the other part joined Cameroon. Stability has allowed for development of roads, railways, agriculture, and petroleum production.

Pres. Paul Biya retained his office in Oct. 1992 elections, but the results were widely disputed. A new constitution won legislative approval in Dec. 1995. Fraud charges accompanied legislative elections, May 17, 1997, which Biya's party won.

Canada

People: Population: 31,902,268 (2001 cen.). **Age distrib.** (%): <15: 18.9; 65+: 12.8. **Pop. density:** 9 per sq. mi. **Urban:** 77%. **Ethnic groups:** British Isles 40%, French 27%, other European 20%, Amerindian 1.5%, other (mostly Asian) 11.5%. **Principal languages:** English, French (both official). **Chief religions:** Roman Catholic 45%, United Church 12%, Anglican 8%.

Geography: Area: 3,560,200 sq. mi., the largest country in land size in the western hemisphere. **Topography:** Canada stretches 3,426 miles from east to west and extends southward from the North Pole to the U.S. border. Its seacoast includes 36,356 miles of mainland and 115,133 miles of islands, including the Arctic islands almost from Greenland to near the Alaskan border. **Climate:** While generally temperate, varies from freezing winter cold to blistering summer heat. **Capital:** Ottawa, 1,094,000. **Cities** (urban aggr.): Toronto, 4.75 mil; Montreal, 3.5 mil; Vancouver, 2.0 mil; Ottawa-Hull, 1.1 mil; Edmonton, 944,000; Calgary, 953,000.

Government: Type: Confederation with parliamentary democracy. **Head of state:** Queen Elizabeth II, represented by Gov.-Gen. Adrienne Clarkson; b Feb. 10, 1939; in office: Oct. 7, 1999. **Head of gov.:** Prime Min. Jean Chrétien; b Jan. 11, 1934; in office: Nov. 4, 1993. **Local divisions:** 10 provinces, 3 territories. **Defense budget (2002):** $7.7 bil. **Active troops:** 56,800.

Economy: Industries: Mining, food and wood products, transportation equip., chemicals, oil, gas. **Chief crops:** Grains, oilseed, tobacco, fruit, vegetables. **Minerals:** Nickel, zinc, copper, gold, lead, molybdenum, potash, silver. **Crude oil reserves** (2001): 5.6 bil bbls. **Arable land:** 5%. **Livestock** (2001): cattle: 13.00 mil; chickens: 158.00 mil.; goats: 30,000; pigs: 12.60 mil; sheep: 840,500. **Fish catch** (1999): 1.03 mil metric tons. **Electricity prod.:** 576.22 bil. kWh. **Labor force:** services 74%, manufacturing 15%, construction 5%, agri. 3%, other 3%.

Finance: Monetary unit: Dollar (Sept. 2002: 1.57 = $1 U.S.). **GDP** (2000 est.): $774.7 bil. **Per capita GDP:** $24,800. **Imports** (2000 est.): $238.2 bil.; partners (1999): U.S. 76%, Japan 3%. **Exports** (2000 est.): $272.3 bil.; partners (1999): U.S. 86%, Japan 3%. **Tourism:** $10.03 bil. **Budget** (2000): $125.3 bil. **Intl. reserves less gold** (end 2000): $24.50 bil. **Gold:** 1.18 mil oz t. **Consumer prices** (change in 2000): 2.7%.

Transport: Railroad: Length: 41,182 mi. **Motor vehicles:** 13.3 mil pass. cars, 3.52 mil comm. vehicles. **Civil aviation:** 38.4 bil pass.-mi.; 269 airports. **Chief ports:** Halifax, Montreal, Quebec, Saint John, Toronto, Vancouver.

Communications: TV sets: 708 per 1,000 pop. **Radios:** 1,078 per 1,000 pop. **Telephones:** 30,243,200. **Daily newspaper circ.:** 157 per 1,000 pop.

Health: Life expectancy: 76.3 male; 83.2 female. **Births** (per 1,000 pop.): 11.1. **Deaths** (per 1,000 pop.): 7.5. **Natural inc.:** 0.35%. **Infant mortality** (per 1,000 live births): 5.

Education: Compulsory primary education. **Literacy** (1994): 97%.

Major Intl. Organizations: UN and all of its specialized agencies, APEC, the Commonwealth, NATO, OAS, OECD, OSCE.

Embassy: 501 Pennsylvania Ave. NW 20001; 682-1740.

Websites: www.statcan.ca; canada.gc.ca

Provinces/Territories	Area (sq. mi.)	Population (2001 cen.)*
Alberta	255,287	2,974,807
British Columbia	365,948	3.907,738
Manitoba	250,947	1,119,583
New Brunswick	28,355	729,498
Newfoundland & Labrador	156,649	512,930
Nova Scotia	21,425	908.007
Ontario	412,581	11,410,046
Prince Edward Island	2,185	135,294
Quebec	594,860	7,237,479
Saskatchewan	251,866	978,933
Northwest Territories	503,951	37,360
Yukon Territory	186,661	28,674
Nunavut	818,959	26,745

*Excludes incompletely enumerated Indian reserves or settlements.

French explorer Jacques Cartier, who reached the Gulf of St. Lawrence in 1534, is generally regarded as Canada's founder. But English seaman John Cabot sighted Newfoundland in 1497, and Vikings are believed to have reached the Atlantic coast centuries before either explorer.

Canadian settlement was pioneered by the French who established Quebec City (1608) and Montreal (1642) and declared New France a colony in 1663.

Britain acquired Acadia (later Nova Scotia) in 1717 and, through military victory over French forces in Canada, captured Quebec (1759) and obtained control of the rest of New France in 1763. The French, through the Quebec Act of 1774, retained the rights to their own language, religion, and civil law. The British presence in Canada increased during the American Revolution when many colonials, proudly calling themselves United Empire Loyalists, moved north to Canada. Fur traders and explorers led Canadians westward across the continent. Sir Alexander Mackenzie reached the Pacific in 1793 and scrawled on a rock by the ocean, "from Canada by land."

In Upper and Lower Canada (later called Ontario and Quebec) and in the Maritimes, legislative assemblies appeared in the 18th century and reformers called for responsible government. But the War of 1812 intervened. The war, a conflict between Great Britain and the United States fought mainly in Upper Canada, ended in a stalemate in 1814.

In 1837 political agitation for more democratic government culminated in rebellions in Upper and Lower Canada. Britain sent Lord Durham to investigate; in a famous report (1839), he recommended union of the 2 parts into one colony called Canada. The union lasted until Confederation, July 1, 1867, when proclamation of the British North America (BNA) Act (now known as the Constitution Act, 1867) launched the Dominion of Canada, consisting of Ontario, Quebec, and the former colonies of Nova Scotia and New Brunswick.

Since 1840 the Canadian colonies had held the right to internal self-government. The BNA Act, which was the basis for the country's written constitution, established a federal system of government on the model of a British parliament and cabinet structure under the crown. Canada was proclaimed a self-governing Dominion within the British Empire in 1931. With the ratification of the Constitution Act, 1982, Canada severed its last formal legislative link with Britain by obtaining the right to amend its constitution.

The so-called Meech Lake Agreement was signed (subject to provincial ratification) June 3, 1987. The accord would have assured constitutional protection for Quebec's efforts to preserve its French language and culture. Critics charged it did not make any provision for other minority groups and it gave Quebec too much power, which might enable Quebec to override the nation's 1982 Charter of Rights and Freedoms (an integral part of the constitution). The accord died June 22, 1990.

Its failure sparked a separatist revival in Quebec, which culminated in Aug. 1992 in the Charlottetown agreement. This called for changes to the constitution, such as recognition of Quebec as a "distinct society" within the Canadian confederation. It was defeated in a national referendum Oct. 26, 1992.

Canada became the first nation to ratify the North American Free Trade Agreement between Canada, Mexico, and the U.S. June 23, 1993. It went into effect Jan. 1, 1994.

On Feb. 24, 1993, Brian Mulroney resigned as prime minister after more than 8 years in office; he was succeeded by Kim Campbell. In elections Oct. 25, 1993, the ruling Conservatives were defeated in a landslide that left them only 2 of the 295 seats in the House of Commons. Jean Chrétien became prime minister. In a Quebec referendum held Oct. 30, 1995, proponents of secession lost by a razor-thin margin. The elections of June 2, 1997, left the Liberals with a slim majority.

On Jan. 7, 1998, the government apologized to native peoples for 150 years of mistreatment and pledged to set up a "healing fund." Canada's highest court ruled, Aug. 20, that Quebec cannot secede unilaterally, even if a majority of the province approves. Nunavut ("Our Land"), carved from Northwest Territories as a homeland for the Inuit, was established Apr. 1, 1999.

Victory by the Liberals in national elections Nov. 27, 2000, made Chrétien the 1st Canadian prime minister in over 50 years to head a 3rd successive majority government. Chrétien stated Aug. 21, 2002, that he would not seek a 4th term in 2004.

Prime Ministers of Canada

Canada is a constitutional monarchy with a parliamentary system of government. It is also a federal state. Canada's official head of state, Queen Elizabeth II, is represented by a resident Governor-General. However, in practice the nation is governed by the Prime Minister, leader of the party that commands the support of a majority of the House of Commons, dominant chamber of Canada's bicameral Parliament.

Name	Party	Term
Sir John A. MacDonald	Conservative	1867-1873
Alexander Mackenzie	Liberal	1873-1878
Sir John A. MacDonald	Conservative	1878-1891
Sir John J. C. Abbott	Conservative	1891-1892
Sir John S. D. Thompson	Conservative	1892-1894
Sir Mackenzie Bowell	Conservative	1894-1896
Sir Charles Tupper	Conservative	1896[1]
Sir Wilfrid Laurier	Liberal	1896-1911
Sir Robert Laird Borden	Cons./Union.[2]	1911-1920
Arthur Meighen	Unionist	1920-1921
W. L. Mackenzie King	Liberal	1921-1926
Arthur Meighen	Conservative	1926[3]
W. L. Mackenzie King	Liberal	1926-1930
Richard Bedford Bennett	Conservative	1930-1935
W. L. Mackenzie King	Liberal	1935-1948
Louis St. Laurent	Liberal	1948-1957
John G. Diefenbaker	Prog. Cons.	1957-1963
Lester Bowles Pearson	Liberal	1963-1968
Pierre Elliott Trudeau	Liberal	1968-1979
Joe Clark	Prog. Cons.	1979-1980
Pierre Elliott Trudeau	Liberal	1980-1984
John Napier Turner	Liberal	1984[4]
Brian Mulroney	Prog. Cons.	1984-1993
Kim Campbell	Prog. Cons.	1993[5]
Jean Chrétien	Liberal	1993-

(1) May-July. (2) Conservative 1911-1917, Unionist 1917-1920. (3) June-Sept. (4) June-Sept. (5) June-Oct.

Cape Verde

Republic of Cape Verde

People: Population: 408,760. **Age distrib.** (%): <15: 42.8; 65+: 6.5. **Pop. density:** 255 per sq. mi. **Urban:** 61%. **Ethnic groups:** Creole (mulatto) 71%, African 28%, **Principal languages:** Portuguese (official), Crioulo. **Chief religion:** Roman Catholic.

Geography: Area: 1,600 sq. mi. **Location:** In Atlantic O., off W tip of Africa. **Neighbors:** Nearest are Mauritania, Senegal to E. **Topography:** Cape Verde Islands are 15 in number, volcanic in origin (active crater on Fogo). The landscape is eroded and stark, with vegetation mostly in interior valleys. **Capital:** Praia 82,000.

Government: Type: Republic. **Head of state:** Pres. Pedro Pires; b Apr. 29, 1934; in office: Mar. 22, 2001. **Head of gov.:** Prime Min. José Maria Neves; b 1959; in office: Feb. 1, 2001. **Local divisions:** 16 districts. **Defense budget (2001):** $9 mil. **Active troops:** 1,200.

Economy: Industries: Food and beverages, fish processing, shoes and garments. **Chief crops:** Bananas, coffee, sweet potatoes, corn, beans. **Minerals:** Salt. **Other resources:** Fish. **Arable land:** 11%. **Livestock** (2001): cattle: 21,500; chickens: 480,000; goats: 110,000; pigs: 200,000; sheep: 8,450. **Fish catch:** (1999): 10,039 metric tons. **Electricity prod.:** 0.04 bil. kWh.

Finance: Monetary unit: Escudo (Sept. 2002: 119.80 = $1 U.S.). **GDP** (2000 est.): $670 mil. **Per capita GDP:** $1,700. **Imports** (2000 est.): $250 mil.; partners: Portugal, Netherlands, France, UK, Spain, U.S.. **Exports** (2000 est.): $40 mil.; partners: Portugal, UK, Germany, Spain, France, Malaysia. Tourism (1998): $20 mil. **Budget** (1996) $228 mil. **Intl. reserves less gold** (end 2000): $25 mil. **Consumer prices** (change in 1999): 4.4%.

Transport: Motor vehicles: 11,000 pass. cars, 7,000 comm. vehicles. **Civil aviation:** 166.5 mil pass.-mi.; 9 airports. **Chief ports:** Mindelo, Praia.

Communications: TV sets: 2.6 per 1,000 pop. **Radios:** 146 per 1,000 pop. **Telephones:** 93,800.

Health: Life expectancy: 66.2 male; 72.9 female. **Births** (per 1,000 pop.): 27.8. **Deaths** (per 1,000 pop.): 7. **Natural inc.:** 2.08%. **Infant mortality** (per 1,000 live births): 51.9.

Education: Compulsory: ages 7-11. **Literacy:** 72%.

Major Intl. Organizations: UN (FAO, IBRD, ILO, IMF, IMO, WHO), AU.

Embassy: 3415 Massachusetts Ave. NW 20007; 965-6820.

Website: capeverdeusaembassy.org

The uninhabited Cape Verdes were discovered by the Portuguese in 1456 or 1460. The first Portuguese colonists landed in 1462; African slaves were brought soon after, and most Cape Verdeans descend from both groups. Cape Verde independence came July 5, 1975. Antonio Mascarenhas Monteiro won the nation's first free presidential election Feb. 17, 1991; he was reelected without opposition five years later. Pedro Pires won a presidential runoff election Feb. 25, 2001.

Central African Republic

People: Population: 3,642,739. **Age distrib.** (%): <15: 43.2; 65+: 3.8. **Pop. density:** 15 per sq. mi. **Urban:** 41%. **Ethnic groups:** Baya 34%, Banda 27%, Mandjia 21%, Sara 10%. **Principal languages:** French (official), Sangho (national), Arabic, Hunsa, Swahili. **Chief religions:** Protestant 25%, Roman Catholic 25%, indigenous beliefs 24%, Muslim 15%.

Geography: Area: 240,500 sq. mi. **Location:** In central Africa. **Neighbors:** Chad on N, Cameroon on W, Congo-Brazzaville and Congo-Kinshasa (formerly Zaire) on S, Sudan on E. **Topography:** Mostly rolling plateau, average altitude 2,000 ft., with rivers draining S to the Congo and N to Lake Chad. Open, well-watered savanna covers most of the area, with an arid area in NE, and tropical rain forest in SW. **Capital:** Bangui 666,000.

Government: Type: Republic. **Head of state:** Pres. Ange-Félix Patassé; b Jan. 25, 1937; in office: Oct. 22, 1993. **Head of gov.:** Prime Min. Martin Ziguéle; b Feb. 12, 1957; in office: Apr. 1, 2001. **Local divisions:** 14 prefectures, 2 economic prefectures, 1 commune. **Defense budget (2001):** $44 mil. **Active troops:** 4,150.

Economy: Industries: Diamond mining, sawmills, breweries, textiles, footwear. **Chief crops:** Cotton, coffee, corn, tobacco, yams. **Minerals:** Diamonds, uranium. **Other resources:** Timber. **Arable land:** 3%. **Livestock** (2001): cattle: 3.10 mil; chickens: 4.20 mil.; goats: 2.60 mil.; pigs: 680,000; sheep: 220,000. **Fish catch:** (1999): 12,860 metric tons. **Electricity prod.:** 0.10 bil. kWh.

Finance: Monetary unit: CFA Franc (Sept. 2002: 671.78 = $1 U.S.). **GDP** (2000 est.): $6.1 bil. **Per capita GDP:** $1,700. **Imports** (2000): $154 mil.; partners (1999): France 35%, Cameroon 13%. **Exports** (2000): $166 mil.; partners (1999): Benelux 64%. **Tourism** (1998): $6 mil. **Budget** (1994 est.): $1.9 bil. **Intl. reserves less gold** (end 2000): $102 mil. **Consumer prices** (change in 1999): –1.9%.

Transport: Motor vehicles: 11,000 pass. cars, 9,000 comm. vehicles. **Civil aviation:** 150.5 mil pass.-mi.; 1 airport. **Chief port:** Bangui.

Communications: TV sets: 5 per 1,000 pop. **Radios:** 75 per 1,000 pop. **Telephones:** 21,000.

Health: Life expectancy: 42.1 male; 45.1 female. **Births** (per 1,000 pop.): 36.6. **Deaths** (per 1,000 pop.): 18.6. **Natural inc.:** 1.8%. **Infant mortality** (per 1,000 live births): 103.8.

Education: Compulsory: ages 6-14. **Literacy:** 60%.

Major Intl. Organizations: UN (FAO, IBRD, ILO, IMF, WHO, WTrO), AU.

Embassy: 1618 22d St. NW 20008; 483-7800.

Website: embassy.org/embassies/cf.html

Various Bantu tribes migrated through the region for centuries before French control was asserted in the late 19th century, when the region was named Ubangi-Shari. Complete independence was attained Aug. 13, 1960.

All political parties were dissolved in 1960, and the country became a center for Chinese political influence in Africa. Relations with China were severed after 1965. Pres. Jean-Bedel Bokassa, who seized power in a 1965 military coup, proclaimed himself constitutional emperor of the renamed Central African Empire Dec. 1976.

Bokassa's rule was characterized by ruthless authoritarianism and human rights violations. He was ousted in a bloodless coup aided by the French government, Sept. 20, 1979. In 1981, Gen. André Kolingba became head of state in another bloodless coup. Multiparty legislative and presidential elections were held in Oct. 1992 but were canceled by the government when Kolingba was losing. New elections, held in Aug. and Sept. 1993, led to the replacement of Kolingba with a civilian government under Pres. Ange-Félix Patassé. France sent in troops to suppress army mutinies in 1996 and 1997. Patassé loyalists won a narrow majority in legislative elections on Nov. 22 and Dec. 13, 1998, and he was reelected to a 2nd 6-year term on Sept. 19, 1999. A coup attempt launched May 28, 2001, was suppressed.

Chad

Republic of Chad

People: Population: 8,997,237. **Age distrib.** (%): <15: 47.7; 65+: 2.8. **Pop. density:** 19 per sq. mi. **Urban:** 23%. **Ethnic groups:** Sara 28%, Sudanic Arab 12%, many others. **Principal languages:** French, Arabic (both official), Sara, Sango, more than 100 other languages. **Chief religions:** Muslim 50%, Christian 25%, indigenous beliefs 25%.

Geography: Area: 486,200 sq. mi. **Location:** In central N Africa. **Neighbors:** Libya on N; Niger, Nigeria, Cameroon on W; Central African Republic on S; Sudan on E. **Topography:** Wooded savanna, steppe, and desert in the S; part of the Sahara in the N. Southern rivers flow N to Lake Chad, surrounded by marshland. **Capital:** N'Djamena, 735,000.

Government: Type: Republic. **Head of state:** Pres. Idriss Déby; b 1952; in office: Dec. 4, 1990. **Head of gov.:** Prime Min. Haroun Kabadi; in office: June 12, 2002. **Local divisions:** 14 prefectures. **Defense budget (2001):** $48 mil. **Active troops:** 30,350.

Economy: Industries: Cotton textiles, meatpacking, beer brewing, sodium carbonate. **Chief crops:** Cotton, sorghum, millet. **Minerals:** Uranium. **Arable land:** 3%. **Livestock** (2001): cattle: 5.90 mil; chickens: 5.00 mil.; goats: 5.25 mil.; pigs: 22,000; sheep: 2.40 mil. **Fish catch** (1999): 85,000 metric tons. **Electricity prod.:** 0.09 bil. kWh. **Labor force:** 85% agric.

Finance: Monetary unit: CFA Franc (Sept. 2002: 671.78 = $1 U.S.). **GDP** (2000 est.): $8.1 bil. **Per capita GDP:** $1,000. **Imports** (2000 est.): $223 mil.; partners (1999): France 40%, Cameroon 13%. **Exports** (2000 est.): $172 mil.; partners (1999): Portugal 38%, Germany 12%. **Tourism** (1998): $10 mil. **Budget** (1998 est.): $218 mil. **Intl. reserves less gold** (end 2000): $85 mil. **Consumer prices** (change in 2000): 3.8%.

Transport: Motor vehicles: 9,630 pass. cars, 14,360 comm. vehicles. **Civil aviation:** 153.3 mil pass.-mi.; 1 airport.

Communications: TV sets: 8 per 1,000 pop. **Radios:** 206 per 1,000 pop. **Telephones:** 33,000.

Health: Life expectancy: 49.2 male; 53.4 female. **Births** (per 1,000 pop.): 47.7. **Deaths** (per 1,000 pop.): 15.1. **Natural inc.:** 3.27%. **Infant mortality** (per 1,000 live births): 93.5.

Education: Compulsory: ages 6-14. **Literacy:** 48%.

Major Intl. Organizations: UN (FAO, IBRD, ILO, IMF, WHO, WTrO), AU.

Embassy: 2002 R St. NW 20009; 462-4009.

Website: chadembassy.org

Chad was the site of paleolithic and neolithic cultures before the Sahara Desert formed. A succession of kingdoms and Arab slave traders dominated Chad until France took control around 1900. Independence came Aug. 11, 1960.

Northern Muslim rebels have fought animist and Christian southern government and French troops from 1966, despite numerous cease-fires and peace pacts.

Libyan troops entered the country at the request of a pro-Libyan Chad government, Dec. 1980. The troops were withdrawn from Chad in Nov. 1981. Rebel forces, led by Hissène Habré, captured the capital and forced Pres. Goukouni Oueddei to flee the country in June 1982.

In 1983, France sent some 3,000 troops to Chad to assist Pres. Habré in opposing Libyan-backed rebels. France and Libya agreed to a simultaneous withdrawal of troops from Chad in Sept. 1984, but Libyan forces remained in the north until Mar. 1987, when Chad forces drove them from their last major stronghold. In Dec. 1990, Habré was overthrown by a Libyan-supported insurgent group, the Patriotic Salvation Movement.

On Feb. 3, 1994, the World Court dismissed a long-standing territorial claim by Libya to the mineral-rich Aozou Strip, on the Libyan border. Libyan troops reportedly withdrew at the end of May. Following approval of a new constitution in March 1996, Chad's first multiparty presidential election was held in June and July. The U.S. Peace Corps withdrew from Chad in Apr. 1998 because of continuing clashes between rebels and Chad government forces.

Pres. Idriss Déby won reelection May 20, 2001, to another 5-year term.

Chile

Republic of Chile

People: Population: 15,498,930. **Age distrib.** (%): <15: 27.3; 65+: 7.4. **Pop. density:** 54 per sq. mi. **Urban:** 85%. **Ethnic groups:** White and White-Amerindian 95%, Amerindian 3%. **Principal language:** Spanish (official). **Chief religions:** Roman Catholic 89%, Protestant 11%.

Geography: Area: 289,100 sq. mi. **Location:** Occupies western coast of S South America. **Neighbors:** Peru on N, Bolivia on NE, on E. **Topography:** Andes Mts. on E border incl. some of the world's highest peaks; on W is 2,650-mile Pacific coast. Width varies between 100 and 250 miles. In N is Atacama Desert, in center are agricultural regions, in S, forests and grazing lands. **Capital:** Santiago, 5,551,000.

Government: Type: Republic. **Head of state and gov.:** Pres. Ricardo Lagos Escobar; b Mar. 2, 1938; in office: Mar. 11, 2000. **Local divisions:** 13 regions. **Defense budget (2001):** $2.1 bil. **Active troops:** 87,500.

Economy: Industries: Copper, other minerals, foodstuffs, fish processing, iron and steel. **Chief crops:** Grain, grapes, fruits, beans, potatoes, sugar beets. **Minerals:** Copper (world's largest producer and exporter), molybdenum, nitrates, iron. **Crude oil reserves** (2001): < 50 mil bbls. **Other resources:** Timber. **Arable land:** 5%. **Livestock** (2001): cattle: 4.15 mil; chickens: 78.00 mil.; goats: 750,000; pigs: 2.50 mil; sheep: 4.20 mil. **Electricity prod.:** 39.58 bil. kWh. **Labor force:** agri. 14%, ind. 27%, services 59%.

Finance: Monetary unit: Peso (Sept. 2002: 744.70 = $1 U.S.). **GDP** (2000 est.): $153.1 bil. **Per capita GDP:** $10,100. **Imports** (2000): $17 bil.; partners (1998): U.S. 24%, EU 23%, Argentina 11%. **Exports** (2000): $18 bil.; partners (1998): EU 27%, U.S. 16%. **Tourism** (1998): $1.06 bil. **Budget** (2000 est.): $17 bil. **Intl. reserves less gold** (end 2000): $11.31 bil. **Gold:** 74,000 oz. t. **Consumer prices** (change in 2000): 3.8%.

Transport: Railroad: Length: 4,084 mi. **Motor vehicles:** 900,000 pass. cars, 475,000 comm. vehicles. **Civil aviation:** 5.3 bil pass.-mi.; 23 airports. **Chief ports:** Valparaiso, Arica, Antofagasta.

Communications: TV sets: 280 per 1,000 pop. **Radios:** 305 per 1,000 pop. **Telephones:** 8,974,900. **Daily newspaper circ.:** 101 per 1,000 pop.

Health: Life expectancy: 72.8 male; 79.6 female. **Births** (per 1,000 pop.): 16.5. **Deaths** (per 1,000 pop.): 5.6. **Natural inc.:** 1.09%. **Infant mortality** (per 1,000 live births): 9.1.

Education: Free and compulsory, from age 6 or 7, for 8 years. **Literacy:** 95%.

Major Intl. Organizations: UN and all of its specialized agencies, APEC, OAS.

Embassy: 1732 Massachusetts Ave. NW 20036; 785-1746.

Website: www.chile-usa.org

Northern Chile was under Inca rule before the Spanish conquest, 1536-40. The southern Araucanian Indians resisted until the late 19th century. Independence was gained 1810-18, under José de San Martin and Bernardo O'Higgins; the latter, as supreme director 1817-23, sought social and economic reforms until deposed. Chile defeated Peru and Bolivia in 1836-39 and 1879-84, gaining mineral-rich northern land.

In 1970, Salvador Allende Gossens, a Marxist, became president with a third of the national vote. His government improved conditions for the poor, but illegal and violent actions by extremist supporters of the government, the regime's failure to attain majority support, and poorly planned socialist economic programs led to political and financial chaos.

A military junta seized power Sept. 11, 1973, and said Allende had killed himself. The junta, headed by Gen. Augusto Pinochet Ugarte, named a mostly military cabinet and announced plans to "exterminate Marxism." Repression continued during the 1980s with little sign of any political liberalization.

In a plebiscite held Oct. 5, 1988, voters rejected the incumbent president, Pinochet. He agreed to presidential elections. In Dec. 1989 voters elected a civilian president, although Pinochet continued to head the army until Mar. 10, 1998. In Mar. 1994 a Chilean human rights group estimated that human rights violations had claimed more than 3,100 lives during Pinochet's rule. Attempts to prosecute him failed when he was declared mentally unfit to stand trial by courts in Britain and Chile. Ricardo Lagos Escobar, Chile's 1st Socialist president since the 1973 coup, took office Mar. 11, 2000.

Tierra del Fuego is the largest (18,800 sq. mi.) island in the archipelago of the same name at the southern tip of South America, an area of majestic mountains, tortuous channels, and high winds. It was visited 1520 by Magellan and named Land of Fire because of its many Indian bonfires. Part of the island is in Chile, part in Argentina. Punta Arenas, on a mainland peninsula, is a center of sheep raising and the world's southernmost city (pop. about 70,000); Puerto Williams is the southernmost settlement.

China

People's Republic of China

(Statistical data do not include Hong Kong or Macao.)

People: Population: 1,284,303,705. **Age distrib.** (%): <15: 25; 65+: 7.1. **Pop. density:** 357 per sq. mi. **Urban:** 32%. **Ethnic groups:** Han Chinese 91.9%, Tibetan, Mongol, Korean, Manchu, others. **Principal languages:** Mandarin (official), Yue, Wu, Hakka, Xiang, Gan, Minbei, Minnan, others. **Chief religions:** Officially atheist; Buddhism, Taoism; some Muslims, Christians.

Geography: Area: 3,600,900 sq. mi. **Location:** Occupies most of the habitable mainland of E Asia. **Neighbors:** Mongolia on N; Russia on NE and NW; Afghanistan, Pakistan, Tajikistan, Kyrgystan, Kazakhstan on W; India, Nepal, Bhutan, Myanmar, Laos, Vietnam on S; North Korea on NE. **Topography:** Two-thirds of the vast territory is mountainous or desert; only one-tenth is cultivated. Rolling topography rises to high elevations in the N in the Daxinganlingshanmai separating Manchuria and Mongolia; the Tien Shan in Xinjiang; the Himalayan and Kunlunshanmai in the SW and in Tibet. Length is 1,860 mi. from N to S, width E to W is more than 2,000 mi. The eastern half of China is one of the world's best-watered lands. Three great river systems, the Chang (Yangtze), Huang (Yellow), and Xi, provide water for vast farmlands. **Capital:** Beijing. **Cities** (urban aggr.): Shanghai 12,887,000; Beijing 10,836,000; Tianjin 9,156,000; Chongqing 4,900,000; Shenyang 4,828,000; Guangzhou 3,893,000.

Government: Type: Communist Party-led state. **Head of state:** Pres. Jiang Zemin; b Aug. 17, 1926; in office: Mar. 27, 1993. **Head of gov.:** Premier Zhu Rongji; b Oct. 1, 1928; in office: Mar. 17, 1998. **Local divisions:** 22 provinces (not including Taiwan), 5 autonomous regions, and 4 municipalities, plus the special administrative regions of Hong Kong (as of July 1, 1997) and Macao (as of Dec. 20, 1999). **Defense budget** (2001): $17 bil. **Active troops:** 2,310 mil.

Economy: Industries: Iron and steel, coal, machinery, armaments, textiles and apparel. **Chief crops:** Grain, rice, cotton, potatoes, tea. **Minerals:** Tungsten, antimony, coal, oil, mercury, iron, lead, manganese, molybdenum, tin. **Crude oil reserves** (2000): 24 bil bbls. **Other resources:** Hydropower. **Arable land:** 10%. **Livestock** (2001): cattle: 105.69 mil; chickens: 3.77 bil.; goats:. 157.36 mil.; pigs: 454.42 mil; sheep: 133.16 mil. **Fish catch** (1999): 36.33 mil metric tons. **Electricity prod.:** 1,307.65 bil. kWh. **Labor force:** agri. 50%, ind. 24%, services 26%.

Finance: Monetary unit: Renminbi (Yuan) (Sept. 2002: 8.27 = $1 U.S.). **GDP** (2000 est.): $4.5 tril. **Per capita GDP:** $3,600. **Imports** (2000): $197 bil.; partners (2000): Japan 18%, Taiwan 11%, U.S. 10%, South Korea 10%, Germany, Hong Kong, Russia, Malaysia. **Exports** (2000): $232 bil.; partners (2000): U.S. 21%, Hong Kong 18%. **Tourism:** $14.10 bil. **Budget:** NA. **Intl. reserves less gold** (end 2000): $129.16 bil. **Gold:** 12.7 mil oz t. **Consumer prices** (change in 2000): 0.3%.

Transport: Railroad: Length: 47,672 mi. **Motor vehicles:** 4.7 mil pass. cars, 6.75 mil comm. vehicles. **Civil aviation:** 45.3 bil pass.-mi.; 113 airports. **Chief ports:** Shanghai, Qinhuangdao, Dalian, Guangzhou (Canton).

Communications: TV sets: 319 per 1,000 pop. **Radios:** 195 per 1,000 pop. **Telephones:** 323,846,000. **Daily newspaper circ.:** 23 per 1,000 pop.

Health: Life expectancy: 70 male; 73.9 female. **Births** (per 1,000 pop.): 15.8. **Deaths** (per 1,000 pop.): 6.8. **Natural inc.:** 0.91%. **Infant mortality** (per 1,000 live births): 27.2.

Education: Compulsory 7-17. **Literacy** (1996): 82%.

Major Intl. Organizations: UN (FAO, IBRD, ILO, IMF, IMO, WHO, WTrO), APEC.

Embassy: 2300 Conn. Ave. NW 20008; 328-2500.

Website: www.china-embassy.org

Remains of various humanlike creatures who lived as early as several hundred thousand years ago have been found in many parts of China. Neolithic agricultural settlements dotted the Huang (Yellow) R. basin from about 5000 BC. Their language, religion, and art were the sources of later Chinese civilization.

Bronze metallurgy reached a peak and Chinese pictographic writing, similar to today's, was in use in the more developed culture of the Shang Dynasty (c. 1500 BC-c. 1000 BC), which ruled much of North China.

A succession of dynasties and interdynastic warring kingdoms ruled China for the next 3,000 years. They expanded Chinese political and cultural domination to the south and west, and developed a brilliant technologically and a culturally advanced society. Rule by foreigners (Mongols in the Yuan Dynasty, 1271-1368, and Manchus in the Ch'ing Dynasty, 1644-1911) did not alter the underlying culture.

A period of relative stagnation left China vulnerable to internal and external pressures in the 19th century. Rebellions left tens of millions dead, and Russia, Japan, Britain, and other powers exercised political and economic control in large parts of the country. China became a republic Jan. 1, 1912, following the Wuchang Uprising inspired by Dr. Sun Yat-sen, founder of the Kuomintang (Nationalist) party. By 1928, the Kuomintang, led by Chiang Kai-shek, succeeded in nominal reunification of China. About the same time, a bloody purge of Communists from the ranks of the Kuomintang fomented hostilities between the two groups that would continue for decades.

For over 50 years, 1894-1945, China was involved in conflicts with Japan. In 1895, China ceded Korea, Taiwan, and other areas. On Sept. 18, 1931, Japan seized the Northeastern Provinces (Manchuria) and set up a puppet state called Manchukuo. The border province of Jehol was cut off as a buffer state in 1933. Taking advantage of Chinese dissension, Japan invaded China proper July 7, 1937. On Nov. 20 the retreating Nationalist government moved its capital to Chongqing (Chungking) from Nanking (Nanjing), which Japanese troops then ravaged Dec. 13.

From 1939 the Sino-Japanese War (1937-45) became part of the broader world conflict. After its defeat in World War II, Japan gave up all seized land, and internal conflicts involving the Kuomintang, Communists, and other factions resumed. China came under the domination of Communist armies, 1949-1950. The Kuomintang government moved to Taiwan, Dec. 8, 1949.

The Chinese People's Political Consultative Conference convened Sept. 21, 1949; The People's Republic of China was proclaimed in Beijing (Peking) Oct. 1, 1949, under Mao Zedong. China and the USSR signed a 30-year treaty of "friendship, alliance and mutual assistance," Feb. 15, 1950. The U.S. refused recognition of the new regime. On Nov. 26, 1950, the People's Republic sent armies into Korea against U.S. troops and forced a stalemate in the Korean War.

After an initial period of consolidation, 1949-52, industry, agriculture, and social and economic institutions were forcibly molded according to Maoist ideals. However, frequent drastic changes in policy and violent factionalism interfered with economic development. In 1957, Mao admitted an estimated 800,000 people had been executed 1949-54; opponents claimed much higher figures.

The Great Leap Forward, 1958-60, tried to force the pace of economic development through intensive labor on huge new rural communes, and through emphasis on ideological purity. The program caused resistance and was largely abandoned.

By the 1960s, relations with the USSR deteriorated, with disagreements on borders, ideology, and leadership of world Communism. The USSR canceled aid accords, and China, with Albania, launched anti-Soviet propaganda drives.

The Great Proletarian Cultural Revolution, 1965, was an attempt to oppose pragmatism and bureaucratic power and instruct a new generation in revolutionary principles. Massive purges took place. A program of forcibly relocating millions of urban teenagers into the countryside was launched. By 1968 the movement had run its course; many purged officials returned to office in subsequent years, and reforms that had placed ideology above expertise were gradually weakened.

On Oct. 25, 1971, the UN General Assembly ousted the Taiwan government from the UN and seated the People's Republic in its place. The U.S. had supported the mainland's admission but opposed Taiwan's expulsion.

U.S. Pres. Richard Nixon visited China Feb. 21-28, 1972, on invitation from Premier Zhou Enlai, ending years of antipathy between the 2 nations. China and the U.S. opened liaison offices in each other's capitals, May-June 1973. The U.S., Dec. 15, 1978, formally recognized the People's Republic of China as the sole legal government of China; diplomatic relations between the 2 nations were established, Jan. 1, 1979.

Mao died Sept. 9, 1976. By 1978, Vice Premier Deng Xiaoping had consolidated his power, succeeding Mao as "paramount leader" of China. The new ruling group modified Maoist policies in education, culture, and industry, and sought better ties with non-Communist countries. During this "reassessment" of Mao's policies his widow, Jiang Qing, and other "Gang of Four" leftists were convicted of "committing crimes during the 'Cultural Revolution,' " Jan. 25, 1981.

By the mid-1980s, China had enacted far-reaching economic reforms, deemphasizing centralized planning and incorporating market-oriented incentives. Some 100,000 students and workers staged a march in Beijing to demand political reforms, May 4, 1989. The demonstrations continued during a visit to Beijing by Soviet leader Mikhail Gorbachev May 15-18; it was the first Sino-Soviet summit since 1959. As the unrest spread, martial law was imposed, May 20. Troops entered Beijing, June 3-4, and crushed the pro-democracy protests, as tanks and armored personnel carriers rolled through Tiananmen Square. It is estimated that 5,000 died, 10,000 were injured, and hundreds of students and workers were arrested.

China had one of the world's fastest-growing economies in the 1990s. Although human rights violations have persisted, the U.S. has continued to renew China's most-favored-nation trading status. Deng died Feb. 19, 1997, leaving his chosen successor, Jiang Zemin, in firm control as president. Pres. Jiang paid a state visit to the U.S., Oct. 26-Nov. 3, and U.S. Pres. Clinton visited China, June 25-July 3, 1998. Floods in July and Aug. killed at least 3,000 and caused an estimated $20 bil. in damage.

NATO bombs hit the Chinese embassy in Belgrade, Yugoslavia, on May 7, 1999, killing 3 people and wounding 27; the U.S. agreed on July 30 to pay $4.5 million to compensate victims and their families, and on Dec. 16 to pay $28 million for damage to the embassy. The government banned a popular religious sect, the Falun Gong, July 22, after it staged the largest unauthorized demonstrations in Beijing since 1989. The U.S. and China signed a comprehensive trade agreement Nov. 15; normalization of China trade won U.S. congressional approval Sept. 19, 2000.

After a midair collision Apr. 1, 2001, a Chinese jet fighter crashed into the S China Sea and a U.S. Navy surveillance plane made an emergency landing on Hainan Is.; the 24-member U.S. crew was freed Apr. 12. Beijing was chosen, July 13, to host the 2008 Summer Olympics. China and Russia signed a 20-year friendship treaty July 16. Jiang met with Pres. Bush in Shanghai during the APEC summit Oct. 20-21. Admission to the WTrO Nov. 10 marked a milestone for the economy. China's Sept. 6, 2002, decision to begin to manufacture more generic medicines to combat HIV was a step toward fighting the country's growing AIDS problem.

By agreement with Great Britain, Hong Kong reverted to Chinese sovereignty July 1, 1997. Portugal returned Macao to China Dec. 20, 1999.

Manchuria. Home of the Manchus, rulers of China 1644-1911, Manchuria has accommodated millions of Chinese settlers in the 20th century. Under Japanese rule 1931-45, the area became industrialized. The region is divided into the 3 NE provinces of Heilongjiang, Jilin, and Liaoning.

Guangxi is in SE China, bounded on N by Guizhou and Hunan provinces, E and S by Guangdong, on SW by Vietnam, and on W by Yunnan. It produces rice in the river valleys and has valuable forest products.

Inner Mongolia was organized by the People's Republic in 1947. Its boundaries have undergone frequent changes, reaching its greatest extent in 1956 (and restored in 1979), with an area of 454,600 sq. mi., allegedly in order to dilute the minority Mongol population. Chinese settlers outnumber the Mongols more than 10 to 1. Pop. (1996 est.): 23.07 mil. Capital: Hohhot.

Xinjiang, in Central Asia, is 635,900 sq. mi., pop. (1996 est.): 16.89 mil (75% Uygurs, a Turkic Muslim group, with a heavy Chinese increase in recent years). Capital: Urumqi. It is China's richest region in strategic minerals. China has moved to crack down on Uygur separatists, whom Beijing regards as terrorists.

Tibet, 471,700 sq. mi., is a thinly populated region of high plateaus and massive mountains, the Himalayas on the S, the Kunluns on the N. High passes connect with India and Nepal; roads lead into China proper. Capital: Lhasa. Average altitude is 15,000 ft. Jiachan, 15,870 ft., is believed to be the highest inhabited town on earth. Agriculture is primitive. Pop. (1996 est.): 2.44 mil (of whom about 500,000 are Chinese). Another 4 million Tibetans form the majority of the population of vast adjacent areas that have long been incorporated into China.

China ruled all of Tibet from the 18th century, but independence came in 1911. China reasserted control in 1951, and a Communist government was installed in 1953, revising the theocratic Lamaist Buddhist rule. Serfdom was abolished, but all land remained collectivized.

A Tibetan uprising within China in 1956 spread to Tibet in 1959. The rebellion was crushed with Chinese troops, and Buddhism was almost totally suppressed. The Dalai Lama and 100,000 Tibetans fled to India.

Hong Kong

Hong Kong (Xianggang), located at the mouth of the Zhu Jiang (Pearl R.) in SE China, 90 mi. S of Canton (Guangzhou), was a British dependency from 1842 until July 1, 1997, when it became a Special Administrative Region of China. Its nucleus is Hong Kong Isl., 31 sq. mi., occupied by the British in 1841 and formally ceded to them in 1842, on which is located the seat of government. Opposite is Kowloon Peninsula, 3 sq. mi., and Stonecutters Isl., added to the territory in 1860. An additional 355 sq. mi. known as the New Territories, a mainland area and islands, were leased from China, 1898, for 99 years. Total area 422 sq. mi.; pop. (2002 est.) 7,303,334, including fewer than 20,000 British.

Hong Kong is a major center for trade and banking. Per capita GDP, $25,400 (2000 est.), is among the highest in the world. Principal industries are textiles and apparel; also tourism ($7.21 bil expenditures in 1999), electronics, shipbuilding, iron and steel, fishing, cement, and small manufactures. Hong Kong's spinning mills are among the best in the world.

Hong Kong harbor was long an important British naval station and one of the world's great transshipment ports. The colony was often a place of refuge for exiles from mainland China. It was occupied by Japan during World War II.

From 1949 to 1962 Hong Kong absorbed more than a million refugees fleeing Communist China. Starting in the 1950s, cheap labor led to a boom in light manufacturing, while liberal tax policies attracted foreign investment; Hong Kong became one of the wealthiest, most productive areas in the Far East. Poor living and working conditions and low wages for many led to political unrest in the 1960s, but legislation and public works programs raised the standard of living by the 1970s.

With the end of the 99-year lease on the New Territories drawing near, Britain and China signed an agreement, Dec. 19, 1984, under which all of Hong Kong was to be returned to China in 1997; under this agreement Hong Kong was to be allowed to keep its capitalist system for 50 years. In Dec. 1996, an electoral college appointed by China chose a shipping magnate, Tung Chee-hwa, to be Hong Kong's chief executive when it reverted to Chinese control.

The July 1 transfer of government was marked by an elaborate ceremony. In the immediate wake of the changeover, Hong Kong retained its street names and its currency, the Hong Kong dollar (HK$7.80 = $1 U.S.), but without the queen's picture. Official languages remained Chinese (Cantonese dialect) and English. The Legislative Council was disbanded, and an appointed Provisional Legislature installed in its place. The new legislature imposed limits on opposition activities and sharply cut back the number of people eligible to vote in legislative elections; despite the restrictions, pro-democracy candidates did well in May 24, 1998, balloting.

Macao

Macao, area of 6 sq. mi., is an enclave, a peninsula and 2 small islands, at the mouth of the Xi (Pearl) R. in China. It was established as a Portuguese trading colony in 1557. In 1849, Portugal claimed sovereignty over the territory; this claim was accepted by China in an 1887 treaty. Portugal granted broad autonomy in 1976. Under a 1987 agreement, Macao reverted to China Dec. 20, 1999. As in the case of Hong Kong, the Chinese government guaranteed Macao it would not interfere in its way of life and capitalist system for a period of 50 years. Pop. (2002 est.): 461,833.

Colombia

Republic of Colombia

People: Population: 41,008,227. **Age distrib.** (%): <15: 31.9; 65+: 4.8. **Pop. density:** 102 per sq. mi. **Urban:** 74%. **Ethnic groups:** Mestizo 58%, white 20%, mulatto 14%, black 4%. **Principal language:** Spanish (official). **Chief religion:** Roman Catholic 95%.

Geography: Area: 401,000 sq. mi. **Location:** At the NW corner of South America. **Neighbors:** Panama on NW, Ecuador and Peru on S, Brazil and Venezuela on E. **Topography:** Three ranges of Andes—Western, Central, and Eastern Cordilleras—run through the country from N to S. The eastern range consists mostly of high tablelands, densely populated. The Magdalena R. rises in the Andes, flows N to Caribbean, through a rich alluvial plain. Sparsely settled plains in E are drained by Orinoco and Amazon systems. **Capital:** Bogotá (Full name: Santa Fe de Bogotá.) **Cities** (urban aggr.): Bogotá 6,957,000; Medellin 2,866,000; Cali 2,233,000; Barranquilla 1,683,000.

Government: Type: Republic. **Head of state and gov.:** Pres. Álvaro Uribe Vélez; b July 4, 1952; in office: Aug. 7, 2002. **Local divisions:** 32 departments, capital district of Bogota. **Defense budget:** (2001) $2.1 bil. **Active troops:** 158,000.

Economy: Industries: Textiles, food processing, oil, clothing and footwear. **Chief crops:** Coffee, rice, bananas, oilseed, corn, sugar, tobacco, cocoa. **Minerals:** Oil, gas, emeralds, gold, copper, coal, iron, nickel. **Crude oil reserves** (2001): 2.6 bil bbls. **Other resources:** Forest products, cut flowers. **Arable land:** 4%. **Livestock** (2001): cattle: 28.33 mil; chickens: 110.00 mil.; goats: 1.20 mil.; pigs: 2.75 mil; sheep: 2.30 mil. **Fish catch** (1999): 199,227 metric tons. **Electricity prod.:** 43.34 bil. kWh. **Labor force:** services 46%, agri. 30%, ind. 24%.

Finance: Monetary unit: Peso (Sept. 2002: 2,824.8 = $1 U.S.). **GDP** (2000 est.): $250 bil. **Per capita GDP:** $6,200. **Imports** (2000 est.): $12.4 bil.; partners (2000 est.): U.S. 35%, EU 16%, Andean Community of Nations 15%. **Exports** (2000 est.): $14.5 bil.; partners (2000 est.): U.S. 50%, EU 14%, Andean Community of Nations 16%. **Tourism** (1998): $939 mil. **Budget** (2000 est.): $24 bil. **Intl. reserves less gold** (end 2000): $6.84 bil. **Gold:** 330,000 oz t. **Consumer prices** (change in 2000): 9.5%.

Transport: Railroad: Length: 2,007 mi. **Motor vehicles:** 1.15 mil pass. cars, 550,000 comm. vehicles. **Civil aviation:** 4.3 bil pass.-mi.; 43 airports. **Chief ports:** Buenaventura, Barranquilla, Cartagena.

Communications: TV sets: 188 per 1,000 pop. **Radios:** 151 per 1,000 pop. **Telephones:** 10,565,300. **Daily newspaper circ.:** 55 per 1,000 pop.

Health: Life expectancy: 67 male; 74.8 female. **Births** (per 1,000 pop.): 22. **Deaths** (per 1,000 pop.): 5.7. **Natural inc.:** 1.63%. **Infant mortality** (per 1,000 live births): 23.2.

Education: Free and compulsory for 5 years between ages 6-12. **Literacy:** 91%.

Major Intl. Organizations: UN (FAO, IBRD, ILO, IMF, IMO, WHO, WTrO), OAS.

Embassy: 2118 Leroy Pl. NW 20008; 387-8338.

Website: colombiaembassy.org

Spain subdued the local Indian kingdoms (Funza, Tunja) by the 1530s and ruled Colombia and neighboring areas as New Granada for 300 years. Independence was won by 1819. Venezuela and Ecuador broke away in 1829-30, and Panama withdrew in 1903.

Colombia is plagued by rural and urban violence. "La Violencia" of 1948-58 claimed 200,000 lives; since 1989, political violence has resulted in more than 35,000 deaths. Attempts at land and social reform and progress in industrialization have not reduced massive social problems.

The government's increased activity against local drug traffickers sparked a series of retaliation killings. On Aug. 18, 1989, Luis Carlos Galán, the ruling party's presidential hopeful for the 1990 election, was assassinated. In 1990, 2 other presidential candidates were assassinated, as drug traffickers carried on a campaign of intimidation.

Charges that Ernesto Samper Pizano's 1994 campaign received money from the Cali drug cartel engulfed his administration in scandal, although the legislature voted, June 12, 1996, not to impeach him. Andrés Pastrana Arango, son of former Pres. Misael Pastrana Borrero (in office 1970-74), won a presidential runoff election, June 21, 1998. An earthquake Jan. 25, 1999, in western Colombia killed at least 1,185 people and left 250,000 homeless. At least 5 million people in more than 700 cities took part in protests Oct. 24 against continuing violence and human rights abuses.

The U.S. authorized $1.3 billion in antidrug aid to Colombia Aug. 22, 2000. Right-wing paramilitaries launched a campaign Dec. 22 against suspected left-wing guerrillas. Legislation expanding the powers of the military was signed Aug. 13, 2001. The collapse of talks with the rebels in Feb. 2002 brought an upsurge of fighting. A hardliner, Álvaro Uribe Vélez, whose father had been killed by leftist rebels in 1983, won a presidential election May 26. A wave of guerrilla violence as he took office led Uribe to declare a "state of unrest" Aug. 12. Police powers were increased Sept. 10 as part of a new government offensive.

Comoros

Union of Comoros

People: Population: 614,382. **Age. distrib.** (%): <15: 42.8; 65+: 2.9. **Pop. density:** 838 per sq. mi. **Urban:** 33%. **Ethnic groups:** Antalote, Cafre, Makoa, Oimatsaha, Sakalava. **Principal languages:** Arabic, French, Comorian (all official). **Chief religions:** Sunni Muslim 86%, Roman Catholic 14%.

Geography: Area: 733 sq. mi. **Location:** 3 islands—Grande Comore (Njazidja), Anjouan (Nzwani), and Moheli (Mwali)—in the Mozambique Channel between NW Madagascar and SE Africa. **Neighbors:** Nearest are Mozambique on W, Madagascar on E. **Topography:** The islands are of volcanic origin, with an active volcano on Grande Comore. **Capital:** Moroni (2001 met. est.) 49,000.

Government: Type: In transition. **Head of state and gov.:** Pres. Azali Assoumani; b Jan. 1,1959; in office: May 26, 2002. **Local divisions:** 3 main islands with 4 municipalities.

Economy: Industries: Tourism, perfume, textiles. **Chief crops:** Vanilla, copra, perfume essences, cloves. **Arable land:** 35%. **Livestock** (2001): cattle: 52,000; chickens: 490,000; goats: 172,000; sheep: 21,000. **Fish catch** (1999): 12,500 metric tons. **Electricity prod.:** 0.02 bil. kWh. **Labor force:** 80% agric.

Finance: Monetary unit: Franc (Sept. 2002: 500.76 = $1 U.S.). **GDP** (2000 est.): $419 mil. **Per capita GDP:** $720. **Imports** (1999 est.): $55.1 mil.; partners (1998): France 38%, Pakistan 13%. **Exports** (1999 est.): $7.9 mil.; partners (1998): France 50%, Germany 25%. **Tourism:** $17 mil. **Budget** (1997): $53 mil. **Intl. reserves less gold** (end. 2000): $33 mil.

Transport: Civil aviation: 2.1 mil pass.-mi.; 2 airports. **Chief ports:** Fomboni, Moroni, Moutsamoudou.

Communications: Radios: 122 per 1,000 pop. **Telephones:** 8,900.

Health: Life expectancy: 58.6 male; 63.1 female. **Births** (per 1,000 pop.): 39. **Deaths** (per 1,000 pop.): 9.1. **Natural inc.:** 2.99%. **Infant mortality** (per 1,000 live births): 81.8.

Education: Compulsory: ages 7-16. **Literacy:** 57%.

Major Intl. Organizations: UN (FAO, IBRD, ILO, IMF, WHO), AL, AU.

Embassy: 336 E. 45th St., 2d Fl., New York, NY 10017; (212) 349-2030.

Website: www.presidence-rfic.com/v2/Pages/anglais/index _a.html

The islands were controlled by Muslim sultans until the French acquired them 1841-1909. They became a French overseas territory in 1947. A 1974 referendum favored independence, with only the Christian island of Mayotte preferring association with France. The French National Assembly decided to allow each of the islands to decide its own fate. The Comore Chamber of Deputies declared independence July 6, 1975, with Ahmed Abdallah as president. In a referendum in 1976, Mayotte voted to remain French.

A leftist regime that seized power from Abdallah in 1975 was deposed in a pro-French 1978 coup in which he regained the presidency. In Nov. 1989, Pres. Abdallah was assassinated; soon after, a multiparty system was instituted. A Sept. 1995 military coup, assisted by French mercenaries, ousted Pres. Said Mohamed Djohar. French troops invaded, Oct. 4, and forced coup leaders to surrender. Djohar returned from exile in Jan. 1996, and in Mar. a new presidential election was held. A hijacked Ethiopian Airlines Boeing 767 crashed offshore on Nov. 23, killing 123 of the 175 people on board.

Seeking to resume ties with France, Anjouan seceded from the Comoros, Aug. 3, 1997. Comorian troops were unable to put down the rebellion, which was joined by Moheli. Unrest on Grande Comore culminated in a military coup, Apr. 30, 1999. Anjouans endorsed secession in a disputed vote Jan. 23, 2000. A military junta took power on Anjouan Aug. 9, 2001. Irregularities marred the presidential runoff election of Apr. 14, 2002, won by Azali Assoumani, who led the 1999 coup.

Congo (formerly Zaire)

Democratic Republic of the Congo

(Congo, officially Democratic Republic of the Congo, is also known as Congo-Kinshasa. It should not be confused with Republic of the Congo, commonly called Congo Republic, and also known as Congo-Brazzaville.)

People: Population: 55,225,478. **Age distrib.** (%): <15: 48.2; 65+: 2.5. **Pop. density:** 63 per sq. mi. **Urban:** 30%. **Ethnic groups:** More than 200 tribes, mostly Bantu. **Principal languages:** French (official). **Chief religions:** Roman Catholic 50%, Protestant 20%, Muslim 10%, Kimbanguist 10%.

Geography: Area: 875,500 sq. mi. **Location:** In central Africa. **Neighbors:** Congo-Brazzaville on W; Central African Republic, Sudan on N; Uganda, Rwanda, Burundi, Tanzania on E; Zambia, Angola on S. **Topography:** Congo includes the bulk of the Congo R. basin. The vast central region is a low-lying plateau covered by rain forest. Mountainous terraces in the W, savannas in the S and SE, grasslands toward the N, and the high Ruwenzori Mts. on the E surround the central region. A short strip of territory borders the Atlantic O. The Congo R. is 2,718 mi. long. **Capital:** Kinshasa. **Cities** (urban aggr.): Kinshasa 5,064,000; Lubumbashi 965,000.

Government: Type: Republic with strong presidential authority (in transition). **Head of state and gov.:** Pres. Joseph Kabila; b June 24, 1971; in office: Jan. 26, 2001. **Local divisions:** 10 provinces, 1 city. **Defense budget (2000):** $400 mil. **Active troops:** 81,400.

Economy: Industries: Mining, mineral processing, consumer products, cement. **Chief crops:** Coffee, sugar, palm oil, rubber, tea. **Minerals:** Cobalt, copper, cadmium, oil, diamonds, gold, silver, tin, germanium, zinc, iron, manganese, uranium, radium. **Crude oil reserves** (2000): 187 mil bbls. **Other resources:** Timber. **Arable land:** 3%. **Livestock** (2001): cattle: 792,986; chickens: 20.55 mil.; goats: 4.07 mil.; pigs: 999,748; sheep: 910,793. **Electricity prod.:** 5.40 bil. kWh. **Labor force:** 65% agric., 16% ind., 19% serv.

Finance: Monetary unit: Congolese Franc (Oct. 2002: 360 = $1 U.S.). **GDP** (2000 est.): $31 bil. **Per capita GDP:** $600. **Imports** (2000 est.): $660 mil.; partners (1999): South Africa 28%, Benelux 14%. **Exports** (2000 est.): $960 mil.; partners (1999): Benelux 62%, U.S. 18%. **Tourism** (1998): $2 mil. **Budget** (1996 est.): $244 mil. **Consumer prices** (change in 1997): 176%.

Transport: Railroad: Length: 3,162 mi. **Motor vehicles:** 330,000 pass. cars, 200,000 comm. vehicles. **Civil aviation:** 189.7 mil pass.-mi.; 22 airports. **Chief ports:** Matadi, Boma, Kinshasa.

Communications: Radios: 79 per 1,000 pop. **Telephones:** 172,000. **Daily newspaper circ.:** 3 per 1,000 pop.

Health: Life expectancy: 47.2 male; 51.1 female. **Births** (per 1,000 pop.): 45.5. **Deaths** (per 1,000 pop.): 14.9. **Natural inc.:** 3.06%. **Infant mortality** (per 1,000 live births): 98.

Education: Compulsory: ages 6-12. **Literacy** 77%.

Major Intl. Organizations: UN and most of its specialized agencies, AU.

Embassy: 1800 New Hampshire Ave. NW 20009; 234-7690.

Website: www.embassy.org/embassies/ZR.html

The earliest inhabitants of Congo may have been the pygmies, followed by Bantus from the E and Nilotic tribes from the N. The large Bantu Bakongo kingdom ruled much of Congo and Angola when Portuguese explorers visited in the 15th century.

Leopold II, king of the Belgians, formed an international group to exploit the Congo region in 1876. In 1877 Henry M. Stanley explored the Congo, and in 1878 the king's group sent him back to organize the region and win over the native chiefs. The Conference of Berlin, 1884-85, organized the Congo Free State with Leopold as king and chief owner. Exploitation of native laborers on the rubber plantations caused international criticism and led to granting of a colonial charter, 1908; the colony became known as the Belgian Congo. Millions of Congolese are believed to have died between 1880 and 1920 as a result of slave labor and other causes under European rule.

Belgian and Congolese leaders agreed Jan. 27, 1960, the Congo would become independent in June. In the first general elections, May 31, the National Congolese movement of Patrice Lumumba won 35 of 137 seats in the National Assembly. He was appointed premier June 21, and formed a coalition cabinet. The Republic of the Congo was proclaimed June 30.

Widespread violence caused Europeans and others to flee. The UN Security Council, Aug. 9, 1960, called on Belgium to withdraw its troops and sent a UN contingent. Pres. Joseph Kasavubu removed Lumumba as premier in Sept.; Lumumba was murdered Jan. 17, 1961.

The last UN troops left the Congo June 30, 1964, and Moise Tshombe became president.

On Sept. 7, 1964, leftist rebels set up a "People's Republic" in Stanleyville (now Kisangani). Tshombe hired foreign mercenaries and sought to rebuild the Congolese Army. In Nov. and Dec. 1964 rebels killed scores of white hostages and thousands of Congolese; Belgian paratroopers, dropped from U.S. transport planes, rescued hundreds. By July 1965 the rebels had lost their effectiveness.

In late 1965 Gen. Joseph D. Mobutu was named president. He later changed his name to Mobutu Sese Seko. The country became the Democratic Republic of the Congo (1966) and the Republic of Zaire (1971).

Economic decline and government corruption plagued Zaire in the 1980s and worsened in the 1990s. In 1990, Pres. Mobutu announced an end to a 20-year ban on multiparty politics. He sought to retain power despite mounting international pressure and internal opposition.

During 1994, Zaire was inundated with refugees from the massive ethnic bloodshed in Rwanda. Ethnic violence spread to E Zaire in 1996. In Oct. militant Hutus, who dominated in the refugee camps, fought against rebels (mostly Tutsis) in Zaire, precipitating intervention by government troops. As a result of the fighting, Rwandan refugees abandoned the camps; hundreds of thousands returned to Rwanda, while hundreds of thousands more were dispersed throughout E Zaire. The rebels, led by Gen. Laurent Kabila—a former Marxist and longtime opponent of Mobutu—gained momentum and began to move W across Zaire. As turmoil engulfed his nation, Mobutu stayed in W Europe for most of the last 4 months of 1996, receiving treatment for prostate cancer.

With Mobutu out of the country, the Zairean army put up little resistance; rebels were aided by several of Mobutu's enemies, notably Rwanda and Uganda. Mobutu returned to Zaire in March 1997, but attempts to negotiate with Kabila were ineffectual. On May 17, Kabila's troops entered Kinshasa and Mobutu went into exile. The country again assumed the name Democratic Republic of the Congo. Mobutu died Sept. 7 in Rabat, Morocco.

Kabila, who ruled by decree, alienated UN officials, international aid donors, and former allies. Rebels assisted by Rwanda and Uganda threatened Kinshasa in Aug. 1998, but the assault was turned back with help from Angola, Namibia, and Zimbabwe. Rebel groups agreed to a cease-fire on Aug. 31, 1999, but the truce was widely violated. Kabila was assassinated Jan. 16, 2001, apparently by one of his bodyguards, and was succeeded by his son Joseph.

A volcanic eruption in E Congo near Goma, Jan. 17, 2002, engulfed much of the city in lava and left thousands homeless.

Congo and Rwanda signed a peace agreement July 30, 2002, seeking to end the Congolese civil war.

Congo Republic

Republic of the Congo

(Congo Republic, officially Republic of the Congo, is also known as Congo-Brazzaville. It should not be confused with Democratic Republic of the Congo [formerly Zaire], now commonly called Congo, and also known as Congo-Kinshasa.)

People: Population: 2,958,448. **Age distrib.** (%): <15: 42.4; 65+: 3.3. **Pop. density:** 22 per sq. mi. **Urban:** 62%. **Ethnic groups:** Kongo 48%, Sangha 20%, Teke 17%, M'Bochi 12%. **Principal languages:** French (official); Lingala, Kikongo, other African languages. **Chief religions:** Christian 50%, animist 48%, Muslim 2%.

Geography: Area: 131,900 sq. mi. **Location:** In W central Africa. **Neighbors:** Gabon and Cameroon on W, Central African Republic on N, Congo-Kinshasa (formerly Zaire) on E, Angola on SW. **Topography:** Much of the Congo is covered by thick forests. A coastal plain leads to the fertile Niari Valley. The center is a plateau; the Congo R. basin consists of flood plains in the lower and savanna in the upper portion. **Capital:** Brazzaville 1,360,000.

Government: Type: Republic. **Head of state and gov.:** Pres. Denis Sassou-Nguesso; b 1943; in office: Oct. 25, 1997. **Local divisions:** 10 regions, 6 communes. **Defense budget (2001):** $69 mil. **Active troops:** 10,000.

Economy: Industries: Oil, cement, lumber, brewing, sugar. **Chief crops:** Cassava, rice, corn, sugar, cocoa, coffee. **Minerals:** Oil, potash, lead, copper, zinc. **Crude oil reserves** (2001): 1.7 bil bbls. **Livestock** (2001): cattle: 90,000; chickens: 1.90 mil.; goats: 280,000; pigs: 46,000; sheep: 96,000. **Fish catch** (1999): 38,181 metric tons. **Electricity prod.:** 0.35 bil. kWh.

Finance: Monetary unit: CFA Franc (Sept. 2002: 671.78 = $1 U.S.). **GDP** (2000 est.): $3.1 bil. **Per capita GDP:** $1,100. **Imports** (2000): $870 mil.; partners (1997 est.): France 23%, U.S. 9%. **Exports** (2000): $2.6 bil.; partners (1998): U.S. 23%, Benelux 14%. **Tourism** (1998): $10 mil. **Budget** (1997 est.): $970 mil. **Intl. reserves less gold** (end 2000): $170.00 mil. Consumer prices (change in 2000): –0.9%.

Transport: Railroad: Length: 494 mi. **Motor vehicles:** 26,000 pass. cars, 21,100 comm. vehicles. **Civil aviation:** 10 airports. **Chief ports:** Pointe-Noire, Brazzaville.

Communications: TV sets: 17 per 1,000 pop. **Radios:** 312 per 1,000 pop. **Telephones** (1999): 22,000 main lines. **Daily newspaper circ.:** 8 per 1,000 pop.

Health: Life expectancy: 44.3 male; 51.2 female. **Births** (per 1,000 pop.): 37.9. **Deaths** (per 1,000 pop.): 16.1. **Natural inc.:** 2.18%. **Infant mortality** (per 1,000 live births): 97.9.

Education: Compulsory: ages 6-16. **Literacy:** 75%.

Major Intl. Organizations: UN (FAO, IBRD, ILO, IMF, IMO, WHO), AU.

Embassy: 4891 Colorado Ave. NW 20011; 726-5500.

Website: www.embassyofcongo.org

The Loango Kingdom flourished in the 15th century, as did the Anzico Kingdom of the Batekes; by the late 17th century they had become weakened. By 1885, France established control of the region, then called the Middle Congo. Republic of the Congo gained independence Aug. 15, 1960.

After a 1963 coup sparked by trade unions, the country adopted a Marxist-Leninist stance, with the USSR and China vying for influence. France remained a dominant trade partner and source of technical assistance, however, and French-owned private enterprise retained a major economic role. In 1970, the country was renamed People's Republic of the Congo.

In 1990, Marxism was renounced and opposition parties were legalized. In 1991 the country's name was changed back to Republic of the Congo, and a new constitution was approved. A democratically elected government came into office in 1992. Factional fighting broke out in Brazzaville, June 5, 1997, and intensified during the summer, devastating the capital. Troops loyal to former Marxist dictator Denis Sassou-Nguesso took control of the city Oct. 15. He claimed a lopsided victory in the presidential election of Mar. 10, 2002.

Costa Rica

Republic of Costa Rica

People: Population: 3,834,934. **Age distrib.** (%): <15: 31.4; 65+: 5.3. **Pop. density:** 196 per sq. mi. **Urban:** 48%. **Ethnic groups:** White and mestizo 96%. **Principal language:** Spanish (official). **Chief religion:** Roman Catholic 95%.

Geography: Area: 19,600 sq. mi. **Location:** In Central America. **Neighbors:** Nicaragua on N, Panama on S. **Topography:** Lowlands by the Caribbean are tropical. The interior plateau, with an altitude of about 4,000 ft., is temperate. **Capital:** San José, 983,000.

Government: Type: Republic. **Head of state and gov.:** Pres. Abel Pacheco; b Dec. 22, 1933; in office: May 8, 2002. **Local divisions:** 7 provinces. **Defense budget:** N/A. **Active troops:** N/A.

Economy: Industries: Computer chips, processed foods, textiles and clothing. **Chief crops:** Coffee, bananas, sugar, rice, potatoes. **Other resources:** Fish, forests, hydropower. **Arable land:** 6%. **Livestock** (2001): cattle: 1.72 mil; chickens: 17.00 mil.; goats: 1,650; pigs: 430,000; sheep: 2,500. **Fish catch** (1999): 33,613 metric tons. **Electricity prod.:** 6.89 bil. kWh. **Labor force:** agri. 20%, ind. 22%, services 58%.

Finance: Monetary unit: Colon (Sept. 2002: 368.39 = $1 U.S.). **GDP** (2000 est.): $25 bil. **Per capita GDP:** $6,700. **Imports** (2000 est.): $5.9 bil.; partners (1999): U.S. 56.4%, EU 9%. **Exports** (2000 est.): $6.1 bil.; partners (1999): U.S. 54.1%, EU 21.3%. **Tourism:** $1.00 bil. **Budget** (2000 est.): $2.4 bil. **Intl. reserves less gold** (end 2000): $1.01 bil. **Gold:** 2,000 oz t. **Consumer prices** (change in 2000): 11.0%.

Transport: Railroad: Length: 590 mi. **Motor vehicles:** 48,684 pass. cars, 70,308 comm. vehicles. **Civil aviation:** 1.2 bil pass.-mi.; 14 airports. **Chief ports:** Limon, Puntarenas, Golfito.

Communications: TV sets: 102 per 1,000 pop. **Radios:** 224 per 1,000 pop. **Telephones:** 1,256,300. **Daily newspaper circ.:** 102 per 1,000 pop.

Health: Life expectancy: 73.7 male; 78.9 female. **Births** (per 1,000 pop.): 19.8. **Deaths** (per 1,000 pop.): 4.3. **Natural inc.:** 1.55%. **Infant mortality** (per 1,000 live births): 10.9.

Education: Free, compulsory: ages 6-15. **Literacy:** 95%.

Major Intl. Organizations: UN (FAO, IBRD, ILO, IMF, IMO, WHO, WTrO), OAS.

Embassy: 2114 S St. NW 20008; 234-2945.

Websites: www.tourism–costarica.com;
embassy.org/embassies/ cr.html

Guaymi Indians inhabited the area when Spaniards arrived, 1502. Independence came in 1821. Costa Rica seceded from the Central American Federation in 1838. Since the civil war of 1948-49, there has been little violent social conflict, and free political institutions have been preserved. During 1993 there was an unusual wave of kidnappings and hostage-taking, some of it related to the international cocaine trade.

Costa Rica, though still a largely agricultural country, has achieved a relatively high standard of living, and land ownership is widespread. Tourism is growing rapidly.

Côte d'Ivoire

Republic of Ivory Coast

People: Population: 16,804,784. **Age distrib.** (%): <15: 46.2; 65+: 2.2. **Pop. density:** 137 per sq. mi. **Urban:** 46%. **Ethnic groups:** Baoule 23%, Bete 18%, Senoufou 15%, Malinke 11%, Agni, foreign Africans. **Principal languages:** French (official), Dioula and other native dialects. **Chief religions:** Muslim 60%, indigenous beliefs 18%, Christian 22%.

Geography: Area: 122,800 sq. mi. **Location:** On S coast of W Africa. **Neighbors:** Liberia, Guinea on W; Mali, Burkina Faso on N; Ghana on E. **Topography:** Forests cover the W half of the country, and range from a coastal strip to halfway to the N on the E. A sparse inland plain leads to low mountains in NW. **Capital:** Yamoussoukro (official); Abidjan (de facto). **Cities** (urban aggr.): Abidjan 3,956,000.

Government: Type: Republic. **Head of state:** Pres. Laurent Gbagbo; b May 31, 1945; in office: Oct. 26, 2000. **Head of gov.:** Prime Min. Affi N'Guessan; b 1953; in office: Oct. 27, 2000. **Local divisions:** 45 provinces. **Defense budget:** (2001) $136 mil. **Active troops:** 13,900.

Economy: Industries: Food and beverages, wood products, oil refining. **Chief crops:** Coffee, cocoa, rubber, palm kernels. **Minerals:** Oil, diamonds, manganese. **Crude oil reserves** (2000): 100 mil bbls. **Other resources:** Timber. **Arable land:** 8%. **Livestock** (2001): cattle: 1.41 mil; chickens: 29.40 mil.; goats: 1.13 mil.; pigs: 336,000; sheep: 1.45 mil. **Fish catch** (1999): 67,617 metric tons. **Electricity prod.:** 5.00 bil. kWh. **Labor force:** 51% agric.; 12% manuf. & mining.

Finance: Monetary unit: CFA Franc (Sept. 2002: 671.78 = $1 U.S.). **GDP** (2000 est.): $26.2 bil. **Per capita GDP:** $1,600. **Imports** (2000 est.): $2.5 bil.; partners (1999): France 26%, Nigeria 10%. **Exports** (2000 est.): $3.8 bil.; partners (1999): France 15%, U.S. 8%. **Tourism** (1998): $108 mil. **Budget** (2000 est.): $2.1 bil. **Intl. reserves less gold** (end 2000): $513 mil. **Gold:** 45,000 oz t. **Consumer prices** (change in 2000): 2.5%.

Transport: Railroad: Length: 405 mi. **Motor vehicles:** 160,000 pass. cars, 95,000 comm. vehicles. **Civil aviation:** 187.7 mil pass.-mi.; 5 airports. **Chief ports:** Abidjan, Dabou, San-Pédro.

Communications: TV sets: 57 per 1,000 pop. **Radios:** 112 per 1,000 pop. **Telephones:** 1,022,100. **Daily newspaper circ.:** 14 per 1,000 pop.

Health: Life expectancy: 43.5 male; 46 female. **Births** (per 1,000 pop.): 40. **Deaths** (per 1,000 pop.): 16.7. **Natural inc.:** 2.33%. **Infant mortality** (per 1,000 live births): 92.2.

Education: Free, compulsory: ages 7-13. **Literacy:** 40%.

Major Intl. Organizations: UN and all of its specialized agencies, AU.

Embassy: 2424 Massachusetts Ave. NW 20008; 797-0300.

Website: www.embassies.org/embassies/ci.html

A French protectorate from 1842, Côte d'Ivoire became independent in 1960. It is the most prosperous of all the tropical African nations, as a result of diversification of agriculture for export, close ties to France, and encouragement of foreign investment. About 20% of the population are workers from neighboring countries. Côte d'Ivoire officially changed its name from Ivory Coast in Oct. 1985.

Students and workers protested, Feb. 1990, demanding the ouster of longtime Pres. Félix Houphouët-Boigny. Côte d'Ivoire held its first multiparty presidential election Oct. 1990, and Houphouët-Boigny retained his office. He died Dec. 7, 1993. The National Assembly named a successor, Henri Konan Bédié, who was reelected Oct. 22, 1995; he was ousted in a military coup Dec. 24, 1999. The coup leader, Robert Guéi, apparently lost a presidential vote Oct. 22, 2000, but claimed victory anyway. After mass protests, he fled, and Laurent Gbagbo became president. Guéi was killed in Abidjan Sept. 19, 2002, after a mutiny broke out there and and in Bouaké and Korhogo. French troops Sept. 25 rescued 160 students (100 from the U.S.) trapped in Bouaké.

Croatia

Republic of Croatia

People: Population: 4,390,751. **Age distrib.** (%): <15: 18.2; 65+: 15.2. **Pop. density:** 201 per sq. mi. **Urban:** 57%. **Ethnic groups:** Croat 78%, Serb 12%. **Principal language:** Croatian (official) 96%. **Chief religions:** Catholic 77%, Orthodox 11%.

Geography: Area: 21,800 sq. mi. **Location:** SE Europe, on the Balkan Peninsula. **Neighbors:** Slovenia, Hungary on N; Bosnia and Herzegovina, Yugoslavia on E. **Topography:** Flat plains in NE; highlands, low mtns. along Adriatic coast. **Capital:** Zagreb 1,081,000.

Government: Type: Parliamentary democracy. **Head of state:** Pres. Stipe Mesic; b Dec. 24, 1934; in office: Feb. 18, 2000. **Head of gov.:** Prime Min. Ivica Racan; b Feb. 24, 1944; in office: Jan. 27, 2000. **Local divisions:** 21 counties. **Defense budget (2001):** $508 mil. **Active troops:** 58,300.

Economy: Industries: Chemicals, plastics, machine tools, fabricated metal, electronics. **Chief crops:** Olives, wheat, corn, sugar beets, fruits. **Minerals:** Oil, bauxite, iron, coal. **Crude oil reserves** (2001): 0.1 bil bbls. **Arable land:** 21%. **Livestock** (2001): cattle: 438,000; chickens: 10.80 mil.; goats: 80,000; pigs: 1.23 mil; sheep: 539,000. **Fish catch:** (1999): 19,885 metric tons. **Electricity prod.:** 10.58 bil. kWh. **Labor force:** 31.1% industry & mining.

Finance: Monetary unit: Kuna (Sept. 2001: 7.53 = $1 U.S.). **GDP** (2000 est.): $24.9 bil. **Per capita GDP:** $5,800. **Imports** (1999): $7.8 bil.; partners (1999): Germany 18.5%, Italy 15.9%. **Exports** (1999): $4.3 bil.; partners (1999): Italy 18%, Germany 15.7%. **Tourism:** $2.50 bil. **Budget** (1999 est.): $4.7 bil. **Intl. reserves less gold** (end 2000): $2.71 bil. **Consumer prices** (change in 2000): 5.4%.

Transport: Railroad: Length: 1,676 mi. **Motor vehicles:** 698,000 pass. cars, 54,000 comm. vehicles. **Civil aviation:** 291.4 mil pass.-mi.; 4 airports. **Chief ports:** Rijeka, Split, Dubrovnik.

Communications: TV sets: 230 per 1,000 pop. **Radios:** 230 per 1,000 pop. **Telephones:** 3,455,000. **Daily newspaper circ.:** 575 per 1,000 pop.

Health: Life expectancy: 70.5 male; 78 female. **Births** (per 1,000 pop.): 12.8. **Deaths** (per 1,000 pop.): 11.3. **Natural inc.:** 0.15%. **Infant mortality** (per 1,000 live births): 7.1.

Education: Free, compulsory: ages 7-15. **Literacy** (1993): 97%.

Major Intl. Organizations: UN (FAO, IBRD, ILO, IMF, IMO, WHO), OSCE.

Embassy: 2343 Massachusetts Ave. NW 20008; 588-5899.

Website: www.vlada.hr/english/contents.html

From the 7th century the area was inhabited by Croats, a south Slavic people. It was formed into a kingdom under Tomislav in 924, and joined with Hungary in 1102. The Croats became westernized and separated from Slavs under Austro-Hungarian influence. The Croats retained autonomy under the Hungarian crown. Slavonia was taken by Turks in the 16th century; the northern part was restored by the Treaty of Karlowitz in 1699. Croatia helped Austria put down the Hungarian revolution 1848-49 and as a result was set up with Slavonia as the separate Austrian crownland of Croatia and Slavonia, which was reunited to Hungary as part of Ausgleich in 1867. It united with other Yugoslav areas to proclaim the Kingdom of Serbs, Croats, and Slovenes in 1918. At the reorganization of Yugoslavia in 1929, Croatia and Slavonia became Savska county, which in 1939 was united with Primorje county to form the county of Croatia. A nominally independent state between 1941 and 1945, it became a constituent republic in the 1946 constitution.

On June 25, 1991, Croatia declared independence from Yugoslavia. Fighting began between ethnic Serbs and Croats, with the former gaining control of about 30% of Croatian territory. A cease-fire was declared in Jan. 1992, but new hostilities broke out in 1993. A cease-fire with Serb rebels forming a self-declared republic of Krajina was agreed to Mar. 30, 1994. Croatian government troops recaptured most of the Serb-held territory Aug. 1995. Pres. Franjo Tudjman signed a peace accord with leaders of Bosnia and Serbia in Paris, Dec. 14. Tudjman won reelection June 15, 1997; international monitors called the vote "free but not fair." The last Serb-held enclave, E Slavonia, returned to Croatian control Jan. 15, 1998.

Tudjman died Dec. 10, 1999. Stipe Mesic, a moderate, won a presidential runoff election Feb. 7, 2000.

Cuba

Republic of Cuba

People: Population: 11,224,321. **Age distrib.** (%): <15: 21; 65+: 9.9. **Pop. density:** 262 per sq. mi. **Urban:** 75%. **Ethnic groups:** Mulatto 51%, white 37%, black 11%. **Principal language:** Spanish (official). **Chief religion:** Roman Catholic 85% prior to Castro.

Geography: Area: 42,800 sq. mi. **Location:** In the Caribbean, westernmost of West Indies. **Neighbors:** Bahamas and U.S. to N, Mexico to W, Jamaica to S, Haiti to E. **Topography:** The coastline is about 2,500 miles. The N coast is steep and rocky, the S coast low and marshy. Low hills and fertile valleys cover more than half the country. Sierra Maestra, in the E, is the highest of 3 mountain ranges. **Capital:** Havana 2,268,000.

Government: Type: Communist state. **Head of state and gov.:** Pres. Fidel Castro Ruz; b Aug. 13, 1926; in office: Dec. 3, 1976 (formerly prime min. since Feb. 16, 1959). **Local divisions:** 14 provinces, 1 special municipality. **Defense budget (2001):** $33 mil. **Active troops:** 46,000.

Economy: Industries: Sugar, oil, tobacco, chemicals, construction. **Chief crops:** Sugarcane, tobacco, rice, coffee, citrus. **Minerals:** Cobalt, nickel, iron, copper, manganese, salt. **Crude oil reserves** (2001): 0.3 bil bbls. **Other resources:** Timber. **Arable land:** 24%. **Livestock** (2001): cattle: 4.40 mil; chickens: 13.30 mil.; goats: 240,000; pigs: 2.70 mil; sheep: 310,000. **Fish catch** (1999): 122,823 metric tons. **Electricity prod.:** 14.87 bil. kWh. **Labor force:** agri. 25%, ind. 24%, services 51%.

Finance: Monetary unit: Peso (Sept. 2002: 21.00 = $1 U.S.). **GDP** (2000 est.): $19.2 bil. **Per capita GDP:** $1,700. **Imports** (2000 est.): $3.4 bil.; partners (1999): Spain 18%, Venezuela 13%. **Exports** (2000 est.): $1.8 bil.; partners (1999): Russia 23%, Netherlands 23%. **Tourism:** $1.71 bil. **Budget** (2000 est.): $14.3 bil.

Transport: Railroad: Length: 2,987 mi. **Motor vehicles:** 16,500 pass. cars, 30,000 comm. vehicles. **Civil aviation:** 2.2 bil pass.-mi.; 14 airports. **Chief ports:** Havana, Matanzas, Cienfuegos, Santiago de Cuba.

Communications: TV sets: 200 per 1,000 pop. **Radios:** 327 per 1,000 pop. **Telephones:** 580,700. **Daily newspaper circ.:** 122 per 1,000 pop.

Health: Life expectancy: 74.2 male; 79.2 female. **Births** (per 1,000 pop.): 12.1. **Deaths** (per 1,000 pop.): 7.3. **Natural inc.:** 0.47%. **Infant mortality** (per 1,000 live births): 7.3.

Education: Free, compulsory: ages 6-11. **Literacy:** 96%.

Major Intl. Organizations: UN (FAO, ILO, IMO, WHO, WTrO).

Some 50,000 Indians lived in Cuba when it was reached by Columbus in 1492. Its name derives from the Indian Cubanacan. Except for British occupation of Havana, 1762-63, Cuba remained Spanish until 1898. A slave-based sugar plantation economy developed from the 18th century, aided by early mechanization of milling. Sugar remains the chief product and chief export despite government attempts to diversify.

Website: cubagob.cu/

A ten-year uprising ended in 1878 with guarantees of rights by Spain, which Spain failed to carry out. A full-scale movement under Jose Marti began Feb. 24, 1895.

The U.S. declared war on Spain in Apr. 1898, after the sinking of the USS *Maine* in Havana harbor, and defeated it in the Spanish-American War. Spain gave up all claims to Cuba. U.S. troops withdrew in 1902, but under 1903 and 1934 agreements, the U.S. leases a site at Guantánamo Bay in the SE as a naval base. U.S. and other foreign investments acquired a dominant role in the economy. In 1952, former Pres. Fulgencio Batista seized control and established a dictatorship, which grew increasingly harsh and corrupt. Fidel Castro assembled a rebel band in 1956; guerrilla fighting intensified in 1958. Batista fled Jan. 1, 1959, and in the resulting political vacuum Castro took power, becoming premier Feb. 16.

The government began a program of sweeping economic and social changes, without restoring promised liberties. Opponents were imprisoned, and some were executed. Some 700,000 Cubans emigrated in the first years after the Castro takeover, mostly to the U.S.

Cattle and tobacco lands were nationalized, while a system of cooperatives was instituted. By 1960 all banks and industrial companies had been nationalized, including over $1 billion worth of U.S.-owned properties, mostly without compensation.

Poor sugar crops resulted in farm collectivization, tight labor controls, and rationing, despite continued aid from the USSR and other Communist nations. A U.S.-imposed export embargo in 1962 severely damaged the economy.

In 1961, some 1,400 Cubans, trained and backed by the U.S. Central Intelligence Agency, unsuccessfully tried to invade and overthrow the regime. In the fall of 1962, the U.S. learned the USSR had brought nuclear missiles to Cuba. After an Oct. 22 warning from Pres. John F. Kennedy, the missiles were removed.

In 1977, Cuba and the U.S. signed agreements to exchange diplomats, without restoring full ties, and to regulate offshore fishing. In 1978 and 1980, the U.S. agreed to accept political prisoners released by Cuba, some of whom were criminals and mental patients. A 1987 agreement provided for 20,000 Cubans to emigrate to the U.S. each year; Cuba agreed to take back some 2,500 jailed in the U.S. since 1980.

In 1975-78, Cuba sent troops to aid one faction in the Angola civil war; the last Cuban troops were withdrawn by May 1991. Cuba's involvement in Central America, Africa, and the Caribbean contributed to poor relations with the U.S.

Cuba's economy, dependent on aid from other Communist countries, was severely shaken by the collapse of the Communist bloc in the late 1980s. Stiffer trade sanctions enacted by the U.S. in 1992 made things worse. Antigovernment demonstrations in Aug. 1994 prompted Castro to loosen emigration restrictions. A new U.S.-Cuba accord in Sept. ended the exodus of "boat people" after more than 30,000 had left Cuba. In another policy shift, the U.S. announced May 2, 1995, it would admit 20,000 Cuban refugees held at the Guantánamo base but would send further boat people back to Cuba.

The U.S. imposed additional sanctions after Cuba, Feb. 24, 1996, shot down 2 aircraft operated by an anti-Castro exile group based in Miami. Cuba blamed exile groups for bombings at Havana tourist hotels, July-Sept. 1997. Pope John Paul II visited Cuba, Jan. 21-25, 1998; he called for an end to U.S. trade sanctions, while pressing Castro to release political prisoners and allow political and religious freedom. U.S. restrictions on contact with Cuba were eased in 1999. On June 28, 2000, Elián González was returned to Cuba to live with his father, ending a 7-month legal battle that began when the boy was rescued off Florida from a shipwreck in which his mother was killed; the boy's Miami relatives had sought to keep him in the U.S.

The U.S., Jan. 11, 2002, began using the base at Guantánamo Bay to detain prisoners captured in Afghanistan. Visiting Havana May 12-17, former U.S. Pres. Jimmy Carter called for democratic reforms and for lifting the U.S. trade embargo.

Cyprus

Republic of Cyprus

(Figures below marked with a # do not include Turkish-held area—Turkish Republic of Northern Cyprus.)

People: Population: 767,314. **Age distrib.** (%): <15: 22.9; 65+: 10.8. **Pop. density:** 213 per sq. mi. **Urban:** 56%. **Ethnic groups:** Greek 78%, Turkish 18%. **Principal languages:** Greek, Turkish, English. **Chief religions:** Greek Orthodox 78%, Muslim 18%.

Geography: Area: 3,600 sq. mi. **Location:** In eastern Mediterranean Sea, off Turkish coast. **Neighbors:** Nearest are Turkey on N, Syria and Lebanon on E. **Topography:** Two mountain ranges run E-W, separated by a wide, fertile plain. **Capital:** Nicosia 199,000.

Government: Type: Republic. **Head of state and gov.:** Pres. Glafcos Clerides; b Apr. 24, 1919; in office: Mar. 1, 1993. **Local divisions:** 6 districts. **Defense budget (2001):** $321 mil. **Active troops#:** 10,000.

Economy: Industries: Food, beverages, textiles. **Chief crops:** Barley, grapes, vegetables, citrus, potatoes, olives. **Minerals:** Copper, pyrites, asbestos. **Arable land:** 12%. **Livestock** (2001): cattle: 54,000; chickens: 3.20 mil.; goats: 378,600; pigs: 418,500; sheep: 246,000. **Electricity prod.:** 3.13 bil. kWh. **Labor force:** services 73%, ind. 22%, agri. 5%.

Finance: Monetary unit: Pound (Sept. 2002: 0.59 = $1 U.S.). **GDP** (2000 est.): Turkish Cypriot area: purchasing power parity - $830 mil. Greek Cypriot area: $9.7 bil. Greek Cypriot area: **Per capita GDP:** $16,000. **Imports** (1999 est.); Turkish Cypriot area: $402 mil. Greek Cypriot area: $3.6 bil.; partners (1999); Turkish Cypriot area: Turkey 58.6%, UK 12.5%, other EU 13% Greek Cypriot area: UK 11.2%, U.S. 10.6%, Italy 8.8%, Greece 8.2%, Germany 6.7%. **Exports** (1999 est.): Greek Cypriot area: $1 bil.; partners (1999): Greek Cypriot area: UK 17.3%, Greece 9.7%, Russia 7.0%, Lebanon 5.2%. **Tourism:** $1.89 bil. **Budget** (2000 est.): Greek Cypriot area: $3.2 bil. **Intl. reserves less gold** (end 2000): $1.34 bil. **Gold:** 464,000 oz t. **Consumer prices** (change in 2000): 4.1%.

Transport: Motor vehicles (1997): 234,976 pass. cars, 108,452 comm. vehicles. **Civil aviation:** 1.7 bil pass.-mi.; 2 airports. **Chief ports:** Famagusta, Limassol.

Communications: Television sets: 160 per 1000 pop. **Radios:** 287 per 1,000 pop. **Telephones:** 749,300. **Daily newspaper circ.:** 135 per 1,000 pop.

Health: Life expectancy: 74.8 male; 79.5 female. **Births** (per 1,000 pop.): 12.9. **Deaths** (per 1,000 pop.): 7.6. **Natural inc.:** 0.53%. **Infant mortality** (per 1,000 live births): 7.7.

Education: Free, compulsory: ages 5½-15. **Literacy** (1994): 95%.

Major Intl. Organizations: UN (FAO, IBRD, ILO, IMF, IMO, WHO, WTrO), the Commonwealth, OSCE.

Embassy: 2211 R St. NW 20008; 462-5772.

Website: www.pio.gov.cy

Agitation for enosis (union) with Greece increased after World War II, with the Turkish minority opposed, and broke into violence in 1955-56. In 1959, Britain, Greece, Turkey, and Cypriot leaders approved a plan for an independent republic, with constitutional guarantees for the Turkish minority and permanent division of offices on an ethnic basis. Greek and Turkish Communal Chambers dealt with religion, education, and other matters.

Archbishop Makarios III, formerly the leader of the enosis movement, was elected president, and full independence became final Aug. 16, 1960. Further communal strife led the United Nations to send a peacekeeping force in 1964; its mandate has been repeatedly renewed.

The Cypriot National Guard, led by officers from the army of Greece, seized the government July 15, 1974. On July 20, Turkey invaded the island; Greece mobilized its forces but did not intervene. A cease-fire was arranged but collapsed. By Aug. 16, Turkish forces had occupied the NE 40% of the island, despite the presence of UN peacekeeping forces.

Turkish Cypriots voted overwhelmingly, June 8, 1975, to form a separate Turkish Cypriot federated state. A president and assembly were elected in 1976. Some 200,000 Greeks have been expelled from the Turkish-controlled area, replaced by thousands of Turks, some from the mainland. Face-to-face talks between the Greek and Turkish Cypriot leaders resumed Dec. 4, 2001, for the 1st time in 4 years.

Turkish Republic of Northern Cyprus

A declaration of independence was announced by Turkish-Cypriot leader Rauf Denktash, Nov. 15, 1983. The state is not internationally recognized, although it does have trade relations with some countries. Area of TRNC: 1,295 sq mi.; pop. (1995 est.): 134,000, 99% Turkish; capital: Lefkosa (Nicosia).

Czech Republic

People: Population: 10,256,760. **Age distrib.** (%): <15: 16.1; 65+: 13.9. **Pop. density:** 337 per sq. mi. **Urban:** 75%. **Ethnic groups:** Czech 94.4%, Slovak 3%. **Principal languages:** Czech, Slovak. **Chief religions:** Atheist 39.8%, Roman Catholic 39.2%, Protestant 4.6%, Orthodox 3%.

Geography: Area: 30,400 sq. mi. **Location:** In E central Europe. **Neighbors:** Poland on N, Germany on N and W, Austria on S, Slovakia on E and SE. **Topography:** Bohemia, in W, is a plateau surrounded by mountains; Moravia is hilly. **Capital:** Prague 1,202,000.

Government: Type: Republic. **Head of state:** Vaclav Havel; b Oct. 5, 1936; in office: Feb. 15, 1993. **Head of gov.:** Prime Min. Vladimir Spidla; b Apr. 22, 1951; in office: July 12, 2002. **Local divisions:** 73 districts, 4 municipalities. **Defense budget (2001):** $1.14 bil. **Active troops:** 53,600.

Economy: Industries: Metallurgy, machinery and equip., motor vehicles, glass. **Chief crops:** Wheat, sugar beets, potatoes, hops, fruit. **Minerals:** Coal, kaolin. **Arable land:** 41%. **Crude oil reserves** (2001): < 50 mil bbls. **Livestock** (2001): cattle: 1.58 mil; chickens: 14.69 mil.; goats: 28,477; pigs: 3.59 mil; sheep: 90,241 . **Fish catch:** (1999): 20,881 metric tons. **Electricity prod.:** 69.59 bil. kWh. **Labor force:** agri. 5%, ind. 40%, services 55%.

Finance: Monetary unit: Koruna (Sept. 2002: 30.91 = $1 U.S.). **GDP** (2000 est.): $132.4 bil. **Per capita GDP:** $12,900. **Imports** (2000): $31.4 bil.; partners (1999): Germany 37.5%, Slovakia 6.7%, Austria 6.2%. **Exports** (2000): $28.3 bil.; partners (1999): Germany 43%, Slovakia 8.4%. **Tourism:** $3.04 bil. **Budget** (2001 est.): $18 bil. **Intl. reserves less gold** (end 2000): $9.99 bil. **Gold:** 446,000 mil oz t. **Consumer prices** (change in 2000): 3.9%.

Transport: Railroad: Length: 5,860 mi. **Motor vehicles:** 4.41 mil pass. cars, 514,589 comm. vehicles. **Civil aviation:** 1.5 bil pass.-mi.; 2 airports. **Chief ports:** Decin, Prague, U.S.ti nad Labem.

Communications: TV sets: 446 per 1,000 pop. **Telephones:** 10,615,000. **Daily newspaper circ.:** 254 per 1,000 pop.

Health: Life expectancy: 71.5 male; 78.7 female. **Births** (per 1,000 pop.): 9.1. **Deaths** (per 1,000 pop.): 10.8. **Natural inc.:** -0.17%. **Infant mortality** (per 1,000 live births): 5.5.

Education: Compulsory: ages 6-15. **Literacy** (1998 est.): 99%.

Major Intl. Organizations: UN (FAO, IBRD, ILO, IMF, IMO, WHO, WTrO), NATO, OECD, OSCE.

Embassy: 3900 Spring of Freedom St. NW 20008; 363-6315.

Website: www.czech.cz

Bohemia and Moravia were part of the Great Moravian Empire in the 9th century and later became part of the Holy Roman Empire. Under the kings of Bohemia, Prague in the 14th century was the cultural center of Central Europe. Bohemia and Hungary became part of Austria-Hungary.

In 1914-18 Thomas G. Masaryk and Eduard Benes formed a provisional government with the support of Slovak leaders including Milan Stefanik. They proclaimed the Republic of Czechoslovakia Oct. 28, 1918.

Czechoslovakia

By 1938 Nazi Germany had worked up disaffection among German-speaking citizens in Sudetenland and demanded its cession. British Prime Min. Neville Chamberlain, with the acquiescence of France, signed with Hitler at Munich, Sept. 30, 1938, an agreement to the cession, with a guarantee of peace by Hitler and Mussolini. Germany occupied Sudetenland Oct. 1-2.

Hitler on Mar. 15, 1939, dissolved Czechoslovakia, made protectorates of Bohemia and Moravia, and supported the autonomy of Slovakia, proclaimed independent Mar. 14, 1939.

Soviet troops with some Czechoslovak contingents entered eastern Czechoslovakia in 1944 and reached Prague in May 1945; Benes returned as president. In May 1946 elections, the Communist Party won 38% of the votes, and Benes accepted Klement Gottwald, a Communist, as prime minister.

In Feb. 1948, the Communists seized power in advance of scheduled elections. In May 1948 a new constitution was approved. Benes refused to sign it. On May 30 the voters were offered a one-slate ballot and the Communists won full control. Benes resigned June 7 and Gottwald became president. The country was renamed the Czechoslovak Socialist Republic. A harsh Stalinist period followed, with complete and violent suppression of all opposition.

In Jan. 1968 a liberalization movement spread nations explosively through Czechoslovakia. Antonin Novotny, long the Stalinist ruler, was deposed as party leader and succeeded by Alexander Dubcek, a Slovak, who supported democratic reforms. On Mar. 22 Novotny resigned as president and was succeeded by Gen. Ludvik Svoboda. On Apr. 6, Prem. Joseph Lenart resigned and was succeeded by Oldrich Cernik, a reformer.

In July 1968 the USSR and 4 Warsaw Pact nations demanded an end to liberalization. On Aug. 20, the Soviet, Polish, East German, Hungarian, and Bulgarian armies invaded Czechoslovakia. Despite demonstrations and riots by students and workers, press censorship was imposed, liberal leaders were ousted from office and promises of loyalty to Soviet policies were made by some old-line Communist Party leaders.

On Apr. 17, 1969, Dubcek resigned as leader of the Communist Party and was succeeded by Gustav Husak. In Jan. 1970, Cernik was ousted. Censorship was tightened, and the Communist Party expelled a third of its members. In 1973, amnesty was offered to some of the 40,000 who fled the country after the 1968 invasion, but repressive policies continued.

More than 700 leading Czechoslovak intellectuals and former party leaders signed a human rights manifesto in 1977, called Charter 77, prompting a renewed crackdown by the regime.

The police crushed the largest antigovernment protests since 1968, when tens of thousands of demonstrators took to the streets of Prague, Nov. 17, 1989. As protesters demanded free elections, the Communist Party leadership resigned Nov. 24; millions went on strike Nov. 27.

On Dec. 10, 1989, the first cabinet in 41 years without a Communist majority took power; Vaclav Havel, playwright and human rights campaigner, was chosen president, Dec. 29. In Mar. 1990 the country was officially renamed the Czech and Slovak Federal Republic. Havel failed to win reelection July 3, 1992; his bid was blocked by a Slovak-led coalition.

Slovakia declared sovereignty, July 17. Czech and Slovak leaders agreed, July 23, on a basic plan for a peaceful division of Czechoslovakia into 2 independent states.

Czech Republic

Czechoslovakia split into 2 separate states—the Czech Republic and Slovakia—on Jan. 1, 1993. Havel was elected president of the Czech Republic on Jan. 26. Record floods in July 1997 caused more than $1.7 billion in damage. The country became a full member of NATO on Mar. 12, 1999. Floods Aug. 2002 damaged cultural treasures in Prague.

Denmark

Kingdom of Denmark

People: Population: 5,368,854. **Age distrib.** (%): <15: 18.6; 65+: 14.9. **Pop. density:** 327 per sq. mi. **Urban:** 85%. **Ethnic groups:** Scandinavian, Eskimo, Faroese, German. **Principal languages:** Danish, Faroese. **Chief religion:** Evangelical Lutheran 91%.

Geography: Area: 16,400 sq. mi. **Location:** In N Europe, separating the North and Baltic seas. **Neighbors:** Germany on S, Norway on NW, Sweden on NE. **Topography:** Denmark consists of the Jutland Peninsula and about 500 islands, 100 inhabited. The land is flat or gently rolling and is almost all in productive use. **Capital:** Copenhagen 1,332,000.

Government: Type: Constitutional monarchy. **Head of state:** Queen Margrethe II; b Apr. 16, 1940; in office: Jan. 14, 1972. **Head of gov.:** Prime Min. Anders Fogh Rasmussen; b Jan. 26, 1953; in office: Nov. 27, 2001. **Local divisions:** 14 counties, 2 kommunes. **Defense budget (2001):** $2.4 bil. **Active troops:** 21,400.

Economy: Industries: Food processing, machinery and equip., textiles, chemical products. **Chief crops:** Grains, potatoes, sugar beets. **Minerals:** Oil, gas, salt. **Crude oil reserves** (2001): 1.1 bil bbls. **Arable land:** 60%. **Livestock** (2001): cattle: 1.89 mil; chickens: 21.50 mil.; pigs: 12.13 mil; sheep: 145,000. **Fish catch** (1999): 1.87 mil metric tons. **Electricity prod.:** 35.79 bil. kWh. **Labor force:** services 79%, ind. 17%, agri. 4%.

Finance: Monetary unit: Danish Krone (Sept. 2002: 7.61 = $1 U.S.). **GDP** (2000 est.): $136.2 bil. **Per capita GDP:** $25,500. **Imports** (2000): $43.6 bil.; partners (1999): EU 72.1%, Norway 4.2%, U.S. 4.5%. **Exports** (2000): $50.8 bil.; partners (1999): EU 66.5%, Norway 5.8%, U.S. 5.4%. **Tourism:** $3.68 bil. **Budget** (2001 est.): $51.3 bil. **Intl. reserves less gold** (end 2000): $11.60 bil. **Gold:** 2.14 mil oz t. **Consumer prices** (change in 2000): 2.9%.

Transport: Railroad: Length: 1,780 mi. **Motor vehicles** (1997): 1.79 mil pass. cars, 306,403 comm. vehicles. **Civil aviation:** 3.5 bil pass.-mi.; 13 airports. **Chief ports:** Copenhagen, Alborg, Arhus, Odense.

Communications: TV sets: 569 per 1,000 pop. **Radios:** 1,145 per 1,000 pop. **Telephones:** 7,836,100. **Daily newspaper circ.:** 309 per 1,000 pop.

Health: Life expectancy: 74.3 male; 79.7 female. **Births** (per 1,000 pop.): 11.7. **Deaths** (per 1,000 pop.): 10.8. **Natural inc.:** 0.09%. **Infant mortality** (per 1,000 live births): 5.

Education: Compulsory: ages 7-15. **Literacy** (1998): 100%.

Major Intl. Organizations: UN and all of its specialized agencies, EU, NATO, OECD, OSCE.

Embassy: 3200 Whitehaven St. NW 20008; 234-4300.

Websites: www.denmarkemb.org; www.umidk/english/

The origin of Copenhagen dates back to ancient times, when the fishing and trading place named Havn (port) grew up on a cluster of islets, but Bishop Absalon (1128-1201) is regarded as the actual founder of the city.

Danes formed a large component of the Viking raiders in the early Middle Ages. The Danish kingdom was a major power until the 17th century, when it lost its land in southern Sweden. Norway was separated in 1815, and Schleswig-Holstein in 1864. Northern Schleswig was returned in 1920.

Voters ratified the Maastricht Treaty, the basic document of the European Union, in May 1993, after rejecting it in 1992. On Sept. 28, 2000, Danes voted not to join the euro currency zone.

The **Faroe Islands** in the North Atlantic, about 300 mi. NW of the Shetlands, and 850 mi. from Denmark proper, 18 inhabited, have an area of 540 sq. mi. and pop. (2002 est.) of 46,011. They are an administrative division of Denmark, self-governing in most matters. Torshavn is the capital. Fish is a primary export (345, 415 metric tons in 1999).

Greenland (Kalaallit Nunaat)

Greenland, a huge island between the North Atlantic and the Polar Sea, is separated from the North American continent by Davis Strait and Baffin Bay. Its total area is 840,000 sq. mi., 84% of which is ice-capped. Most of the island is a lofty plateau 9,000 to 10,000 ft. in altitude. The average thickness of the cap is 1,000 ft. The population (2002 est.) is 56,376. Under the 1953 Danish constitution the colony became an integral part of the realm with representatives in the Folketing (Danish legislature). The Danish parliament, 1978, approved home rule for Greenland, effective May 1, 1979. With home rule, Greenlandic place names came into official use. The technically correct name for Greenland is now Kalaallit Nunaat; the official name for its capital is Nuuk, rather than Godthab. Fish is the principal export (120,596 metric tons in 1999).

Djibouti

Republic of Djibouti

People: Population: 472,810. **Age distrib.** (%): <15: 42.6; 65+: 2.8. **Pop. density:** 56 per sq. mi. **Urban:** 83%. **Ethnic groups:** Somali 60%, Afar 35%. **Principal languages:** French, Arabic (both official); Afar, Somali. **Chief religions:** Muslim 94%, Christian 6%.

Geography: Area: 8,500 sq. mi. **Location:** On E coast of Africa, separated from Arabian Peninsula by the strategically vital strait of Bab el-Mandeb. **Neighbors:** Ethiopia on W and SW, Eritrea on NW, Somalia on SE. **Topography:** The territory, divided into a low coastal plain, mountains behind, and an interior plateau, is arid, sandy, and desolate. The climate is generally hot and dry. **Capital:** Djibouti 542,000.

Government: Type: Republic. **Head of state:** Pres. Ismail Omar Guelleh; b Nov. 27, 1947; in office: May 8, 1999. **Head of gov.:** Prime Min. Dileita Mohamed Dileita; b Mar. 12, 1958; in office: Mar. 7, 2001. **Local divisions:** 5 districts. **Defense budget (2001):** $23 mil. **Active troops:** 9,600.

Economy: Industries: Small- scale dairy production and mineral-water bottling. **Livestock** (2001): cattle: 269,000; goats: 513,000; sheep: 465,000. **Electricity prod.:** 0.18 bil. kWh. **Labor force:** agri. 75%, ind. 11%, services 14%.

Finance: Monetary unit: Djibouti Franc (Sept. 2002: 164.90 = $1 U.S.). **GDP** (2000 est.): $574 mil. **Per capita GDP:** $1,300. **Imports** (1999 est.): $440 mil.; partners (1998): France 13%, Ethiopia 12%. **Exports** (1999 est.): $260 mil.; partners (1998): Somalia 53%, Yemen 23%. **Tourism** (1998): $4 mil. **Budget** (1999 est.): $187 mil. **Intl. reserves less gold** (end 2000): $52 mil.

Transport: Railroad: Length: 66 mi. **Motor vehicles:** 13,000 pass. cars, 3,000 comm. vehicles. **Civil aviation:** 1 airport. **Chief port:** Djibouti.

Communications: TV sets: 43 per 1,000 pop. **Radios:** 80 per 1,000 pop. **Telephones:** 12,900. **Daily newspaper circ.:** 8 per 1,000 pop.

Health: Life expectancy: 49.7 male; 53.5 female. **Births** (per 1,000 pop.): 40.3. **Deaths** (per 1,000 pop.): 14.4. **Natural inc.:** 2.59%. **Infant mortality** (per 1,000 live births): 99.7.

Education: Literacy: 46%.

Major Intl. Organizations: UN (FAO, IBRD, ILO, IMF, IMO, WHO, WTrO), AL, AU.

Embassy: Suite 515, 1156 15th St. NW 20005; 331-0270.

Website: embassy.org/embassies/dj.html

France gained control of the territory in stages between 1862 and 1900. As French Somaliland it became an overseas territory of France in 1945; in 1967 it was renamed the French Territory of the Afars and the Issas.

Ethiopia and Somalia have renounced their claims to the area, but each has accused the other of trying to gain control. There were clashes between Afars (ethnically related to Ethiopians) and Issas (related to Somalis) in 1976. Immigrants from both countries continued to enter the country up to independence, which came June 27, 1977.

French aid is the mainstay of the economy, as well as assistance from Arab countries. A peace accord Dec. 1994 ended a 3-year-long uprising by Afar rebels.

Dominica

Commonwealth of Dominica

People: Population: 70,158. **Age distrib.:** (%): <15: 28.7; 65+: 7.8. **Pop. density:** 242 per sq. mi. **Urban:** 71%. **Ethnic groups:** Black, Carib Amerindian. **Principal languages:** English (official), French patois. **Chief religions:** Roman Catholic 77%, Protestant 15%.

Geography: Area: 290 sq. mi. **Location:** In Eastern Caribbean, most northerly Windward Isl. **Neighbors:** Guadeloupe to N, Martinique to S. **Topography:** Mountainous, a central ridge running from N to S, terminating in cliffs; volcanic in origin, with numerous thermal springs; rich deep topsoil on leeward side, red tropical clay on windward coast. **Capital:** Roseau 26,000.

Government: Type: Parliamentary democracy. **Head of state:** Pres. Vernon Lorden Shaw; b May 13, 1930; in office: Oct. 6, 1998. **Head of gov.:** Prime Min. Pierre Charles; b June 30,1954; in office: Oct. 3, 2000. **Local divisions:** 10 parishes.

Economy: Industries: Soap, coconut oil, tourism. **Chief crops:** Bananas, citrus, mangoes, coconuts. **Other resources:** Forests. **Arable land:** 9%. **Livestock** (2001): cattle: 13,400; chickens: 190,000; goats: 9,700; pigs: 5,000; sheep: 7,600. **Electricity prod.:** 0.07 bil. kWh. **Labor force:** ind. and commerce 32%, services 28%.

Finance: Monetary unit: East Caribbean Dollar (Sept. 2002: 2.70 = $1 U.S.). **GDP** (2000 est.): $290 mil. **Per capita GDP:** $4,000. **Imports** (2000 est.): $126 mil.; partners (1996 est.): U.S. 41%, Caricom countries 25%. **Exports** (2000 est.): $60.7 mil.; partners (1996 est.): Caricom countries 47%, UK 36%. **Tourism** (1998): $38 mil. **Budget** (FY97/98): $79.9 mil. **Intl. reserves less gold** (end 2000): $23 mil. **Consumer prices** (change in 2000): 0.8%.

Transport: Motor vehicles (1997): 7,560 pass. cars, 3,673 comm. vehicles. **Civil aviation:** 2 airports. **Chief port:** Roseau.

Communications: TV sets: 70 per 1,000 pop. **Radios:** 875 per 1,000 pop. **Telephones** (1999): 21,300 main lines.

Health: Life expectancy: 71 male; 76.9 female. **Births** (per 1,000 pop.): 17.3. **Deaths** (per 1,000 pop.): 7.1. **Natural inc.:** 1.02%. **Infant mortality** (per 1,000 live births): 15.9.

Education: Free, compulsory: ages 5-15. **Literacy** (1993): 90%.

Major Intl. Organizations: UN (FAO, IBRD, ILO, IMF, IMO, WHO, WTrO), Caricom, the Commonwealth, OAS, OECS.

Embassy: 3216 New Mexico Ave. NW 20016; 364-6781.

Website: www.ndcdominica.dm/index.htm

A British colony since 1805, Dominica was granted self-government in 1967. Independence was achieved Nov. 3, 1978.

Hurricane David struck, Aug. 30, 1979, devastating the island and destroying the banana plantations, Dominica's economic mainstay. Coups were attempted in 1980 and 1981.

Dominica participated in the 1983 U.S.-led invasion of nearby Grenada.

Dominican Republic

People: Population: 8,721,594. **Age distrib.** (%): <15: 34.1; 65+: 4.9. **Pop. density:** 466 per sq. mi. **Urban:** 64%. **Ethnic groups:** Mixed 73%, white 16%, black 11%. **Principal language:** Spanish (official). **Chief religion:** Roman Catholic 95%.

Geography: Area: 18,700 sq. mi. **Location:** In West Indies, sharing isl. of Hispaniola with Haiti. **Neighbors:** Haiti on W, Puerto Rico (U.S.) to E. **Topography:** The Cordillera Central range crosses the center of the country, rising to over 10,000 ft., highest in the Caribbean. The Cibao Valley to the N is major agricultural area. **Capital:** Santo Domingo. **Cities** (urban aggr.): Santo Domingo 2,629,000; Santiago de los Caballeros 804,000.

Government: Type: Republic. **Head of state and gov.:**Pres. Hipólito Mejía; b Feb. 22, 1941; in office: Aug. 16, 2000. **Local divisions:** 29 provinces and national district. **Defense budget (2001):** $2.5 bil. **Active troops:** 24,500.

Economy: Industries: Tourism, sugar processing, mining, textiles. **Chief crops:** Sugar, cocoa, coffee, cotton, rice. **Minerals:** Nickel, bauxite, gold, silver. **Arable land:** 21%. **Livestock** (2001): cattle: 2.11 mil; chickens: 47.38 mil.; goats: 187,425; pigs: 565,529; sheep: 105,999. **Fish catch:** (1999): 15,276 metric tons. **Electricity prod.:** 9.48 bil. kWh. **Labor force:** services and government 58.7%, ind. 24.3%, agri. 17%.

Finance: Monetary unit: Peso (Sept. 2002: 17.10 = $1 U.S.). **GDP** (2000 est.): $48.3 bil. **Per capita GDP:** $5,700. **Imports** (2000 est.): $9.6 bil.; partners (1999 est.): U.S. 25.7%, Venezuela 9.2%. **Exports** (2000): $5.8 bil.; partners (1999 est.): U.S. 66.1%, Netherlands 7.8%, Canada 7.6%, Russia 7.4%. **Tourism:** $2.52 bil. **Budget** (1999 est.): $2.9 bil. **Intl. reserves less gold** (end 2000): $480 mil. **Gold:** 18,000 oz t. **Consumer prices** (change in 1999): 6.5%.

Transport: Railroad: Length: 1,083 mi. **Motor vehicles:** 113,835 pass. cars, 92,198 comm. vehicles. **Civil aviation:** 9.8 mil pass.-mi.; 7 airports. **Chief ports:** Santo Domingo, San Pedro de Macoris, Puerto Plata.

Communications: TV sets: 97 per 1,000 pop. **Radios:** 154 per 1,000 pop. **Telephones:** 2,225,200. **Daily newspaper circ.:** 35 per 1,000 pop.

Health: Life expectancy: 71.6 male; 75.9 female. **Births** (per 1,000 pop.): 24.4. **Deaths** (per 1,000 pop.): 4.7. **Natural inc.:** 1.97%. **Infant mortality** (per 1,000 live births): 33.4.

Education: Compulsory: ages 6-14. **Literacy**: 82%.

Major Intl. Organizations: UN (FAO, IBRD, ILO, IMF, IMO, WHO, WTrO), OAS.

Embassy: 1715 22nd St. NW 20008; 332-6280.

Website: www.presidencia.gov.do/Ingles/welcome.htm

Carib and Arawak Indians inhabited the island of Hispaniola when Columbus landed in 1492. The city of Santo Domingo, founded 1496, is the oldest settlement by Europeans in the hemisphere and has the supposed ashes of Columbus in an elaborate tomb in its ancient cathedral.

The western third of the island was ceded to France in 1697. Santo Domingo itself was ceded to France in 1795. Haitian leader Toussaint L'Ouverture seized it, 1801. Spain returned intermittently 1803-21, as several native republics came and went. Haiti ruled again, 1822-44; Spanish occupation occurred 1861-63.

The country was occupied by U.S. Marines from 1916 to 1924, when a constitutionally elected government was installed.

In 1930, Gen. Rafael Leonidas Trujillo Molina was elected president. Trujillo ruled brutally until his assassination in 1961. Pres. Joaquín Balaguer, appointed by Trujillo in 1960, resigned under pressure in 1962.

Juan Bosch, elected president in the first free elections in 38 years, was overthrown in 1963. On Apr. 24, 1965, a revolt was launched by followers of Bosch and others, including a few Communists. Four days later U.S. Marines intervened against pro-Bosch forces. Token units were later sent by 5 South American countries as a peacekeeping force. A provisional government supervised a June 1966 election, in which Balaguer defeated Bosch. Balaguer remained in office for most of the next 28 years, but his May 1994 reelection was widely denounced as fraudulent. He cut short his term and on June 30, 1996, Leonel Fernández Reyna was elected.

Hurricane Georges struck Sept. 22, 1998, causing extensive property damage and claiming more than 200 lives. The leftist candidate, Hipólito Mejía, won a presidential vote May 16, 2000.

East Timor

Democratic Republic of Timor-Leste

People: Population: 825,000. **Pop. density:** 146 per sq. mi. **Urban:** 24%. **Ethnic groups:** Austronesian; Papuan. **Principal languages:** Portuguese, Tetum. **Chief religion:** Roman Catholic.

Geography: Area: 5,641 sq. mi. **Location:** E half of Timor Is. in the SW Pacific O. **Neighbors:** Indonesia (West Timor) on W. **Topography:** Terrain is rugged, rising to 9,721 ft at Mt. Ramelau. **Capital:** Dili (2002 est.): 140,000.

Government: Head of state: Pres. Xanana Gusmão; b June 20, 1946; in office: May 20, 2002. **Head of gov.:** Prime Min. Mari Alkatiri; b Nov. 26, 1949; in office: May 20, 2002.

Economy: Industries: Subsistence agriculture; oil and gas resources being developed. **Chief crops:** Coffee, coconuts, cinnamon.

Finance: Monetary unit: U.S. dollar and Indonesian Rupiah (Sept. 2002: 9,010 = $1 U.S.). **GDP:** (2000 est.): $390 mil. **Per capita GDP:** $470. **Imports** (2001 est.): $237 mil. **Exports** (2001 est.): $4 mil.

Transport: Civil aviation: 1 intl. airport. **Chief port:** Dili.

Health: Life expectancy: 57. **Infant mortality** (per 1,000 live births): 135.

Education: Literacy 48%.

Major Intl. Organizations: UN.

Website: www.un.org/peace/etimor/etimor.htm

The collapse of Portuguese rule in East Timor led to an outbreak of factional fighting in Aug. 1975 and an invasion by Indonesia in Dec. Indonesia annexed East Timor as a 27th province in 1976, despite international condemnation. In over 2 decades some 200,000 Timorese died as a result of civil war, famine, and persecution by Indonesian authorities. In a referendum held Aug. 30, 1999, under UN auspices, Timorese voted overwhelmingly for independence. Pro-Indonesian militias then went on a rampage, terrorizing the population. Under pressure, the government allowed entrance of an international peacekeeping force, which began arriving in Sept.; a UN interim administration formally took command Oct. 26, 1999.

Pro-independence forces won elections for a constituent assembly Aug. 30, 2001. Xanana Gusmão, a former guerrilla leader, won the presidential election Apr. 14, 2002. East Timor became independent May 20 and entered the UN Sept. 27.

Ecuador

Republic of Ecuador

People: Population: 13,447,494. **Age distrib.** (%): <15: 35.8; 65+: 4.4. **Pop. density:** 126 per sq. mi. **Urban:** 64%. **Ethnic groups:** Mestizo 55%, Amerindian 25%, Spanish 10%, black 10%. **Principal languages:** Spanish (official), Quechua, other Amerindian. **Chief religion:** Roman Catholic 95%.

Geography: Area: 106,900 sq. mi. **Location:** In NW South America, on Pacific coast, astride the Equator. **Neighbors:** Colombia on N, Peru on E and S. **Topography:** Two ranges of Andes run N and S, splitting the country into 3 zones: hot, humid lowlands on the coast; temperate highlands between the ranges; and rainy, tropical lowlands to the E. **Capital:** Quito. **Cities** (urban aggr.): Guayaquil: 2,118,000; Quito: 1,616,000.

Government: Type: Republic. **Head of state and gov.:** Pres. Gustavo Noboa Bejarano; b Aug. 21, 1937; in office: Jan. 22, 2000. **Local divisions:** 21 provinces. **Defense budget (2001):** $400 mil. **Active troops:** 59,500.

Economy: Industries: Oil, food processing, textiles, metal work. **Chief crops:** Bananas, cocoa, coffee, rice, sugar, potatoes, plantains. **Minerals:** Oil. **Crude oil reserves** (2001): 3.1 bil bbls. **Other resources:** Forests (leading balsawood producer), seafood (world's 2nd largest shrimp producer). **Arable land:** 6%. **Livestock** (2001): cattle: 5.57 mil; chickens: 138.43 mil.; goats: 272,560; pigs: 2.39 mil; sheep: 1.98 mil. **Fish catch** (1999): 688,297 metric tons. **Electricity prod.:** 10.40 bil. kWh. **Labor force:** agri. 30%, ind. 25%, services 45%.

Finance: Monetary unit: U.S. dollar. **GDP** (2000 est.): $37.2 bil. **Per capita GDP:** $2,900. **Imports** (2000 est.): $3.4 bil.; partners (1998): U.S. 30%, Colombia 13%. **Exports** (2000 est.): $5.6 bil.; partners (1999): U.S. 37%, Colombia 5%, Italy 5%, Chile 5%. **Tourism:** $343 mil. **Budget** (1999): $5.1 bil. **Intl. reserves less gold** (end 2000): $727 mil. **Gold:** 850,000 oz t. **Consumer prices** (change in 2000): 96.1%.

Transport: Railroad: Length: 600 mi. **Motor vehicles:** 255,640 pass. cars, 424,120 comm. vehicles. **Civil aviation:** 1.3 bil pass.-mi.; 14 airports. **Chief ports:** Guayaquil, Manta, Esmeraldas, Puerto Bolivar.

Communications: TV sets: 79 per 1,000 pop. **Radios:** 277 per 1,000 pop. **Telephones:** 2,194,900. **Daily newspaper circ.:** 72 per 1,000 pop.

Health: Life expectancy: 68.8 male; 74.6 female. **Births** (per 1,000 pop.): 25.5. **Deaths** (per 1,000 pop.): 5.4. **Natural inc.:** 2.01%. **Infant mortality** (per 1,000 live births): 33.

Education: Free and compulsory for 6 years between ages 6-14. **Literacy:** 90%.

Major Intl. Organizations: UN (FAO, IBRD, ILO, IMF, IMO, WHO, WTrO), OAS.

Embassy: 2535 15th St. NW 20009; 234-7200.

Website: mmrree.gov.ec

The region, which was the northern Inca empire, was conquered by Spain in 1533. Liberation forces defeated the Spanish May 24, 1822, near Quito. Ecuador became part of the Great Colombia Republic but seceded, May 13, 1830.

Since 1972, the economy has revolved around petroleum exports; oil revenues have declined since 1982, causing severe economic problems. Ecuador suspended interest payments for 1987 on its estimated $8.2 billion foreign debt following a Mar. 5-6 earthquake that left 20,000 homeless and destroyed a stretch of the country's main oil pipeline.

Ecuadoran Indians staged protests in the 1990s to demand greater rights. A border war with Peru flared from Jan. 26, 1995, until a truce took effect Mar. 1. Vice-Pres. Alberto Dahik resigned and fled Ecuador, Oct. 11, 1995, to avoid arrest on corruption charges. Elected president in a runoff, July 7, 1996, Abdalá Bucaram—a populist known as El Loco, or "The Crazy One"—imposed stiff price increases and other austerity measures. His rising unpopularity and erratic behavior led the National Congress, Feb. 6, 1997, to dismiss him for "mental incapacity." Bucaram went into exile, and Congress, on Feb. 11, confirmed its leader, Fabián Alarcón, as president for 18 months. Voters endorsed the actions in a referendum May 25.

Jamil Mahuad Witt, mayor of Quito, won a presidential runoff election July 12, 1998. In Sept. 1998 and Mar. 1999 he imposed emergency measures to cope with a continuing economic crisis. Opposed by Indian groups and military leaders, he was ousted Jan. 21, 2000, and succeeded by Vice-Pres. Gustavo Noboa Bejarano. Noboa went ahead with a plan introduced by Mahuad to replace the sucre with the U.S. dollar as Ecuador's currency.

The **Galápagos Islands,** pop. (2001 est.) 16,000, about 600 mi. to the W, are the home of huge tortoises and other unusual animals. The oil tanker *Jessica* ran aground Jan. 16, 2001, off San Cristóbal Is., spilling some 185,000 gallons of fuel.

Egypt

Arab Republic of Egypt

People: Population: 70,712,345. **Age distrib** (%) <15: 34.6; 65+: 3.8. **Pop. density:** 184 per sq. mi. **Urban:** 45%. **Ethnic groups:** Eastern Hamitic stock (Egyptian, Bedouin, Berber) 99%. **Principal languages:** Arabic (official), English, French. **Chief religions:** Muslim (mostly Sunni) 94%, Coptic Christian and other 6%.

Geography: Area: 384,300 sq. mi. **Location:** Northeast corner of Africa. **Neighbors:** Libya on W, Sudan on S, Israel and Gaza Strip on E. **Topography:** Almost entirely desolate and barren, with hills and mountains in E and along Nile. The Nile Valley, where most of the people live, stretches 550 miles. **Capital:** Cairo. **Cities** (urban aggr.): Cairo 9,586,000; Alexandria 3,506,000.

Government: Type: Republic. **Head of state:** Pres. Hosni Mubarak; b May 4, 1928; in office: Oct. 14, 1981. **Head of gov.:** Prime Min. Atef Obeid; b Apr. 14, 1932; in office: Oct. 5, 1999. **Local divisions:** 26 governorates. **Defense budget (2001):** $2.1 bil. **Active troops:** 443,000.

Economy: Industries: Textiles, food processing, tourism, chemicals, hydrocarbons. **Chief crops:** Cotton, rice, beans, fruits, wheat, vegetables, corn. **Minerals:** Oil, gas, phosphates, gypsum, iron, manganese, limestone. **Crude oil reserves** (2001): 3.6 bil bbls. **Arable land:** 2%. **Livestock** (2001): cattle: 3.64 mil; chickens: 88.00 mil.; goats: 3.53 mil.; pigs: 29,500; sheep: 4.55 mil. **Fish catch** (1999): 418,694 metric tons. **Electricity prod.:** 69.59 bil. kWh. **Labor force:** agri. 29%, services 49%, ind. 22%.

Finance: Monetary unit: Pound (Sept. 2002: 4.65 = $1 U.S.). **GDP** (2000 est.): $247 bil. **Per capita GDP:** $3,600. **Imports** (2000 est.): $17 bil.; partners (1999): EU 36%, U.S. 14%. **Exports** (2000 est.): $7.3 bil.; partners (1999): EU 35%, Middle East 17%. **Tourism:** $3.90 bil. **Budget** (FY99): $26.2 bil. **Intl. reserves less gold** (end 2000): $10.07 bil. **Gold:** 2.43 mil oz t. **Consumer prices** (change in 2000): 2.7%.

Transport: Railroad: Length: 2,989 mi. **Motor vehicles:** 1.28 mil pass. cars, 423,300 comm. vehicles. **Civil aviation:** 5.6 bil pass.-mi.; 11 airports. **Chief ports:** Alexandria, Port Said, Suez, Damietta.

Communications: TV sets: 127 per 1,000 pop. **Radios:** 312 per 1,000 pop. **Telephones:** 9,443,800. **Daily newspaper circ.:** 38 per 1,000 pop.

Health: Life expectancy: 62 male; 66.2 female. **Births** (per 1,000 pop.): 24.4. **Deaths** (per 1,000 pop.): 7.6. **Natural inc.:** 1.68%. **Infant mortality** (per 1,000 live births): 58.6.

Education: Compulsory for 5 years between ages 6-13. **Literacy**: 51%.

Major Intl. Organizations: UN (FAO, IBRD, ILO, IMF, IMO, WHO, WTrO), AL, AU.

Embassy: 3521 International Ct. NW 20008; 895-5400.

Website: www.sis.gov.eg

Archaeological records of ancient Egyptian civilization date back to 4000 BC. A unified kingdom arose around 3200 BC and extended its way south into Nubia and as far north as Syria. A high culture of rulers and priests was built on an economic base of serfdom, fertile soil, and annual flooding of the Nile.

Imperial decline facilitated conquest by Asian invaders (Hyksos, Assyrians). The last native dynasty fell in 341 BC to the Persians, who were in turn replaced by Greeks (Alexander and the Ptolemies), Romans, Byzantines, and Arabs, who introduced Islam and the Arabic language. The ancient Egyptian language is preserved only in Coptic Christian liturgy.

Egypt was ruled as part of larger Islamic empires for several centuries. The Mamluks, a military caste of Caucasian origin, ruled Egypt from 1250 until defeat by the Ottoman Turks in 1517. Under Turkish sultans the khedive as hereditary viceroy had wide authority. Britain intervened in 1882 and took control of administration, though nominal allegiance to the Ottoman Empire continued until 1914.

The country was a British protectorate from 1914 to 1922. A 1936 treaty strengthened Egyptian autonomy, but Britain retained bases in Egypt and a condominium over the Sudan. Britain fought German and Italian armies from Egypt, 1940-42. In 1951 Egypt abrogated the 1936 treaty; the Sudan became independent in 1956.

The uprising of July 23, 1952 was led by the Society of Free Officers, who named Maj. Gen. Mohammed Naguib commander in chief and forced King Farouk to abdicate. When the republic was proclaimed June 18, 1953, Naguib became its first president and premier. Lt. Col. Gamal Abdel Nasser removed Naguib and became premier in 1954. In 1956, he was voted president. Nasser died in 1970 and was replaced by Vice Pres. Anwar Sadat.

The Aswan High Dam, completed 1971, provides irrigation for more than a million acres of land. Artesian wells, drilled in the Western Desert, reclaimed 43,000 acres, 1960-66.

When the state of Israel was proclaimed in 1948, Egypt joined other Arab nations invading Israel and was defeated.

After terrorist raids across its border, Israel invaded Egypt's Sinai Peninsula, Oct. 29, 1956. Egypt rejected a cease-fire demand by Britain and France; on Oct. 31 the 2 nations dropped bombs and on Nov. 5-6 landed forces. Egypt and Israel accepted a UN cease-fire; fighting ended Nov. 7.

A UN Emergency Force guarded the 117-mile-long border between Egypt and Israel until May 19, 1967, when it was withdrawn at Nasser's demand. Egyptian troops entered the Gaza Strip and the heights of Sharm el Sheikh and 3 days later closed the Strait of Tiran to all Israeli shipping. Full-scale war broke out June 5; before it ended under a UN cease-fire June 10, Israel had captured Gaza and the Sinai Peninsula, controlled the east bank of the Suez Canal, and reopened the gulf. After sporadic fighting, Israel and Egypt agreed, Aug. 7, 1970, to a new cease-fire.

In a surprise attack Oct. 6, 1973, Egyptian forces crossed the Suez Canal into the Sinai. (At the same time, Syrian forces attacked Israelis on the Golan Heights.) Egypt was supplied by a USSR military airlift; the U.S. responded with an airlift to Israel. Israel counterattacked, crossed the canal, surrounded Suez City. A UN cease-fire took effect Oct. 24.

Under an agreement signed Jan. 18, 1974, Israeli forces withdrew from the canal's W bank; limited numbers of Egyptian forces occupied a strip along the E bank. A second accord was signed in 1975, with Israel yielding Sinai oil fields. Pres. Sadat's surprise visit to Jerusalem, Nov. 1977, opened the prospect of peace with Israel. On Mar. 26, 1979, Egypt and Israel signed a formal peace treaty, ending 30 years of war, and establishing diplomatic relations. Israel returned control of the Sinai to Egypt in Apr. 1982.

Tension between Muslim fundamentalists and Christians in 1981 caused street riots and culminated in a nationwide security crackdown in Sept. Pres. Sadat was assassinated on Oct. 6; he was succeeded by Hosni Mubarak.

Egypt was a political and military supporter of the Allied forces in their defeat of Iraq in the Persian Gulf War, 1991.

Egypt saw a rising tide of Islamic fundamentalist violence in the 1990s. Egyptian security forces conducted raids against Islamic militants, some of whom were executed for terrorism. Naguib Mahfouz, winner of the 1988 Nobel Prize for Literature, was stabbed by Islamic militants Oct. 14, 1994. Pres. Mubarak escaped assassination in Ethiopia, June 26, 1995; Egypt blamed Sudan for the attack. On Nov. 17, 1997, near Luxor, Muslim extremists killed 58 foreign tourists and 4 Egyptians.

Mubarak, who was grazed by a knife-wielding assailant Sept. 6, 1999, was confirmed by popular vote Sept. 26 for a 4th presidential term. An EgyptAir jetliner bound from New York to Cairo plunged into the Atlantic near Nantucket Is., Oct. 31, 1999, killing all 217 people on board. Fire on a train bound from Cairo to Luxor, Feb. 20, 2002, left more than 360 people dead.

The **Suez Canal,** 103 mi. long, links the Mediterranean and Red seas. It was built by a French corporation 1859-69, but Britain obtained controlling interest in 1875. The last British troops were removed June 13, 1956. On July 26, Egypt nationalized the canal.

El Salvador

Republic of El Salvador

People: Population: 6,353,681. **Age distrib.** (%): <15: 37.7; 65+: 5.1. **Pop. density:** 794 per sq. mi. **Urban:** 46%. **Ethnic groups:** Mestizo 94%, Amerindian 5%. **Principal language:** Spanish (official). **Chief religions:** Roman Catholic 75%, many Protestant groups.

Geography: Area: 8,000 sq. mi. **Location:** In Central America. **Neighbors:** Guatemala on W, Honduras on N. **Topography:** A hot Pacific coastal plain in the south rises to a cooler plateau and valley region, densely populated. The N is mountainous, including many volcanoes. **Capital:** San Salvador 1,381,000.

Government: Type: Republic. **Head of state and gov.:** Pres. Francisco Flores; b Oct. 17, 1959; in office: June 1, 1999. **Local divisions:** 14 departments. **Defense budget (2001):** $112 mil. **Active troops:** 16,800.

Economy: Industries: Food and beverages, oil, chemicals, fertilizer. **Chief crops:** Coffee, corn, sugar, rice. **Other resources:** Hydropower. **Arable land:** 27%. **Livestock** (2001): cattle: 1.22 mil; chickens: 8.10 mil.; goats: 15,200; pigs: 150,000; sheep: 5,100. **Fish catch:** (1999): 10,987 metric tons. **Electricity prod.:** 3.60 bil. kWh. **Labor force:** agri. 30%, ind. 15%, services 55%.

Finance: Monetary unit: Colon (Sept. 2002: 8.75 = $1 U.S.). **GDP** (2000 est.): $24 bil. **Per capita GDP:** $4,000. **Imports** (2000): $4.6 bil.; partners (1999): U.S. 52%, Guatemala 9%. **Exports** (2000): $2.8 bil.; partners (1999): U.S. 63%, Guatemala 11%. **Tourism:** $211 mil. **Budget** (1999 est.): $2.2 bil. **Intl. reserves less gold** (end 2000): $1.48 bil. **Gold:** 469,000 oz t. **Consumer prices** (change in 2000): 2.3%.

Transport: Railroad: Length: 349 mi. **Motor vehicles:** 35,300 pass. cars, 44,800 comm. vehicles. **Civil aviation:** 1.3 bil pass.-mi.; 1 airport. **Chief ports:** La Union, Acajutla, La Libertad.

Communications: TV sets: 91 per 1,000 pop. **Radios:** 373 per 1,000 pop. **Telephones:** 1,398,000. **Daily newspaper circ.:** 53 per 1,000 pop.

Health: Life expectancy: 66.7 male; 74.1 female. **Births** (per 1,000 pop.): 28.3. **Deaths** (per 1,000 pop.): 6.1. **Natural inc.:** 2.22%. **Infant mortality** (per 1,000 live births): 27.6.

Education: Free, compulsory: ages 7-16. **Literacy**: 71%.

Major Intl. Organizations: UN (FAO, IBRD, ILO, IMF, IMO, WHO, WTrO), OAS.

Embassy: 2308 California St. NW 20008; 265-9671.

Website: www.elsalvador.org (Spanish & English)

El Salvador became independent of Spain in 1821, and of the Central American Federation in 1839.

A fight with Honduras in 1969 over the presence of 300,000 Salvadoran workers left 2,000 dead.

A military coup overthrew the government of Pres. Carlos Humberto Romero in 1979, but the ruling military-civilian junta failed to quell a rebellion by leftist insurgents, armed by Cuba and Nicaragua. Extreme right-wing death squads organized to eliminate suspected leftists were blamed for thousands of deaths in the 1980s. The Reagan administration staunchly supported the government with military aid. The 12-year civil war ended Jan. 16, 1992, as the government and leftist rebels signed a formal peace treaty. The civil war had taken the lives of some 75,000 people. The treaty provided for military and political reforms.

Nine soldiers, including 3 officers, were indicted Jan. 1990 in the Nov. 1989 slaying of 6 Jesuit priests in San Salvador. Two of the officers received maximum 30-year jail sentences. They were released Mar. 20, 1993, when the National Assembly passed a sweeping amnesty.

Francisco Flores, candidate of the right-wing ARENA party, won the presidential election of Mar. 7, 1999. Earthquakes Jan. 13 and Feb. 13, 2001, left more than 1,150 people dead.

Equatorial Guinea

Republic of Equatorial Guinea

People: Population: 498,144. **Age distrib.** (%): <15: 42.6; 65+: 3.8. **Pop. density:** 46 per sq. mi. **Urban:** 47%. **Ethnic groups:** Fang 83%, Bubi 10%. **Principal languages:** Spanish, French (both official), Fang, Bubi. **Chief religion:** Predominantly Roman Catholic.

Geography: Area: 10,800 sq. mi. **Location:** Bioko Isl. off W Africa coast in Gulf of Guinea, and Rio Muni, mainland enclave. **Neighbors:** Gabon on S, Cameroon on E and N. **Topography:** Bioko Isl. consists of 2 volcanic mountains and a connecting valley. Rio Muni, with over 90% of the area, has a coastal plain and low hills beyond. **Capital:** Malabo 33,000.

Government: Type: Republic. **Head of state:** Pres. Teodoro Obiang Nguema Mbasogo; b June 5, 1942; in office: Oct. 10, 1979. **Head of gov.:** Prime Min. Cándido Muatetema Rivas; b 1961; in office: Mar. 4, 2001. **Local divisions:** 7 provinces. **Defense budget** (2001): $16 mil. **Active troops:** 1,320.

Economy: Industries: Oil, fishing, sawmilling, natural gas. **Chief crops:** Cocoa, coffee, rice, bananas, yams cassava. **Minerals:** Oil. **Other resources:** Timber. **Crude oil reserves** (2001): 0.6 bil bbls. **Arable land:** 5%. **Livestock** (2001): cattle: 5,000; chickens: 320,000; goats: 9,000; pigs: 6,100; sheep: 37,600. **Electricity prod.:** 0.02 bil. kWh.

Finance: Monetary unit: CFA Franc (Sept. 2002: 671.78 = $1 U.S.). **GDP** (2000 est.): $960 mil. **Per capita GDP:** $2,000. **Imports** (1999): $300 mil.; partners (1997): U.S. 35%, France 15%. **Exports** (2000 est.): $860 mil.; partners (1997): U.S. 62%, Spain 17%. **Tourism** (1998): $2 mil. **Budget** (1996 est.): $43 mil. **Intl. reserves less gold** (end 2000): $18 mil.

Transport: Motor vehicles: 4,000 pass. cars, 3,600 comm. vehicles. **Civil aviation:** 2.8 mil pass.-mi.; 1 airport. **Chief ports:** Malabo, Bata.

Communications: TV sets: 88 per 1,000 pop. **Radios:** 464 per 1,000 pop. **Telephones:** 21,900.

Health: Life expectancy: 52.3 male; 56.5 female. **Births** (per 1,000 pop.): 37.3. **Deaths** (per 1,000 pop.): 12.8. **Natural inc.:** 2.45%. **Infant mortality** (per 1,000 live births): 91.

Education: Free, compulsory: ages 6-11. **Literacy**: 78%.

Major Intl. Organizations: UN (FAO, IBRD, ILO, IMF, IMO, WHO), AU.

Embassy: 1712 I St. NW, Suite 410, 20005; 393-0525.

Website: www.embassy.org/embassies/gq.html

Fernando Po (now Bioko) Island was reached by Portugal in the late 15th century and ceded to Spain in 1778. Independence came Oct. 12, 1968. Riots occurred in 1969 over disputes between the island and the more backward Rio Muni province on the mainland. Masie Nguema Biyogo, a mainlander, became president for life in 1972.

Masie's reign was one of the most brutal in Africa, resulting in a bankrupted nation. Most of the nation's 7,000 Europeans emigrated. He was ousted in a military coup, Aug. 1979, and Teodoro Mbasogo, leader of the coup, became president. His regime eventually agreed to elections, held Nov. 21, 1993. These were nominally won by the ruling party, but boycotted by opposition parties that maintained the rules were rigged. Elections for president, Feb. 25, 1996, and for the legislature, Mar. 6, 1999, were similarly condemned.

Eritrea

State of Eritrea

People: Population: 4,465,651. **Age distrib.** (%): <15: 42.8; 65+: 3.3. **Pop. density:** 95 per sq. mi. **Urban:** 18%. **Ethnic groups:** Tigrinya 50%, Tigre and Kunama 40%, Afar 4%. **Principal languages:** Tigrinya, Tigre and Kunama, Afar, Amhanc, Arabic. **Chief religions:** Muslim, Coptic Christian, Roman Catholic, Protestant.

Geography: Area: 46,800 sq. mi. **Location:** In E Africa, on SW coast of Red Sea. **Neighbors:** Ethiopia on S, Djibouti on SE, Sudan on W. **Topography:** Includes many islands of the Dahlak Archipelago, low coastal plains in S, mountain range with peaks to 9,000 ft. in N. **Capital:** Asmara 503,000.

Government: Type: In transition. **Head of state and gov.:** Isaias Afwerki; b Feb. 2, 1946; in office: May 24, 1993. **Local divisions:** 8 provinces. **Defense budget** (2000): $263 mil. **Active troops:** 171,900 (est.).

Economy: Industries: Food processing, beverages, clothing and textiles. **Chief crops:** Cotton, coffee, vegetables, maize, tobacco, lentils, sorghum. **Minerals:** Gold, potash, zinc, copper. **Arable land:** 12%. **Livestock** (2001): cattle: 2.20 mil; chickens: 1.30 mil.; goats: 1.70 mil.; sheep: 1.57 mil. **Electricity prod.:** 0.21 bil. kWh. **Labor force:** agric. 80%, ind. and services 20%.

Finance: Monetary unit: Nafka (Sept. 2002: 13.65 = $1 U.S.). **GDP** (2000 est.): $2.9 bil. **Per capita GDP:** $710. **Imports** (1999): $560 mil.; partners (1998): Italy 17.4%, UAE 16.2%. **Exports** (1999): $26 mil.; partners (1998): Sudan 27.2%, Ethiopia 26.5%. **Tourism:** $28 mil. **Budget** (1997 est.): $351.6 mil.

Transport: Civil aviation: 2 airports. **Chief ports:** Mitsiwa, Aseb.

Communications: TV sets: 6 per 1,000 pop. **Telephones:** 32,000.

Health: Life expectancy: 54.1 male; 59.1 female. **Births** (per 1,000 pop.): 42.2. **Deaths** (per 1,000 pop.): 11.8. **Natural inc.:** 3.04%. **Infant mortality** (per 1,000 live births): 73.6.

Education: Free, compulsory: ages 7-13. **Literacy** (1994): 20%.

Major Intl. Organizations: UN (FAO, IBRD, ILO, IMF, IMO, WHO), AU.

Embassy: 1708 New Hampshire Ave. NW 20009; 319-1991.

Website: www.embassy.org/embassies/er.html

Eritrea was part of the Ethiopian kingdom of Aksum. It was an Italian colony from 1890 to 1941, when it was captured by the British. Following a period of British and UN supervision, Eritrea was awarded to Ethiopia as part of a federation in 1952. Ethiopia annexed Eritrea as a province in 1962. This led to a 31-year struggle for independence, which ended when Eritrea formally declared itself an independent nation May 24, 1993. A border war with Ethiopia which erupted in June 1998 intensified in May 2000, as Ethiopian troops plunged into W Eritrea; a cease-fire signed June 18 provided for UN peacekeepers to patrol a buffer zone on Eritrean territory. A peace treaty was signed Dec. 12, 2000. An international tribunal adjudicated the boundary dispute Apr. 2002.

Estonia

Republic of Estonia

People: Population: 1,415,681. **Age distrib.** (%): <15: 17.1; 65+: 14.8. **Pop. density:** 81 per sq. mi. **Urban:** 69%. **Ethnic groups:** Estonian 65%, Russian 28%. **Principal languages:** Estonian (official), Russian. **Chief religion:** Evangelical Lutheran, Russian Orthodox.

Geography: Area: 17,400 sq. mi. **Location:** E Europe, bordering the Baltic Sea and Gulf of Finland. **Neighbors:** Russia on E, Latvia on S. **Capital:** Tallinn 401,000.

Government: Type: Republic. **Head of state:** Pres. Arnold Rüütel; b May 10, 1928; in office: Oct. 8, 2001. **Head of gov.:** Prime Min. Siim Kallas; b Oct. 2, 1948; in office: Jan. 28 , 2002. **Local divisions:** 15 counties. **Defense budget** (2001): $92.4 mil . **Active troops:** 4,450.

Economy: Industries: Oil shale, shipbuilding, phosphates, electric motors. **Chief crops:** Potatoes, fruits, vegetables. **Minerals:** Shale oil, peat, phosphorite. **Other resources:** Dairy prods. **Arable land:** 25%. **Livestock** (2001): cattle: 252,800; chickens: 2.37 mil.; goats: 300,200; sheep: 29,000. **Fish catch** (1999): 123,873 metric tons. **Electricity prod.**7.06 bil. kWh. **Labor force:** ind. 20%, agri. 11%, services 69%.

Finance: Monetary unit: Kroon (Sept. 2001: 16.02 = $1 U.S.). **GDP** (2000 est.): $14.7 bil. **Per capita GDP:** $10,000. **Imports** (2000): $4 bil.; partners (1999): Finland 22.8%, Russia 13.5%. **Exports** (2000): $3.1 bil.; partners (1999): Finland 19.4%, Sweden 18.8%. **Tourism:** $560 mil. **Budget** (1997 est.): $1.37 bil. **Intl. reserves less gold** (end 2000): $707 mil. **Gold:** 8,000 oz t. **Consumer prices** (change in 2000): 4.0%.

Transport: Railroad: Length: 636 mi. **Motor vehicles:** 338,000 pass. cars, 60,000 comm. vehicles. **Civil aviation:** 83.6 mil pass.-mi.; 1 airport. **Chief port:** Tallinn.

Communications: TV sets: 411 per 1,000 pop. **Telephones:** 1,154,800. **Daily newspaper circ.:** 242 per 1,000 pop.

Health: Life expectancy: 64 male; 76.3 female. **Births** (per 1,000 pop.): 9. **Deaths** (per 1,000 pop.): 13.4. **Natural inc.:** –0.45%. **Infant mortality** (per 1,000 live births): 12.3.

Education: Compulsory: ages 7-16. **Literacy** (1994): 100%.

Major Intl. Organizations: UN (FAO, IBRD, ILO, IMF, IMO, WHO), OSCE.

Embassy: 2131 Massachusetts Ave. NW 20008; 588-0101.

Website: www.riik.ee/en/valitsus/

Estonia was a province of imperial Russia before World War I, was independent between World Wars I and II. It was conquered by the USSR in 1940 and incorporated as the Estonian SSR. Estonia declared itself an "occupied territory," and proclaimed itself a free nation Mar. 1990. During an abortive Soviet coup, Estonia declared immediate full independence, Aug. 20, 1991; the Soviet Union recognized its independence in Sept. 1991. The first free elections in over 50 years were held Sept. 20, 1992. The last occupying Russian troops were withdrawn by Aug. 31, 1994. Center-right parties won the legislative election of Mar. 7, 1999.

Ethiopia

Federal Democratic Republic of Ethiopia

People: Population: 67,673,031. **Age distrib.** (%): <15: 47.2; 65+: 2.8. **Pop. density:** 157 per sq. mi. **Urban:** 17%. **Ethnic groups:** Oromo 40%, Amhara and Tigrean 32%, Sidamo 9%. **Principal languages:** Amharic (official), Tigrinya, Orominga.

Chief religions: Muslim 45-50%, Ethiopian Orthodox 35-40%, animist 12%.

Geography: Area: 432,300 sq. mi. **Location:** In East Africa. **Neighbors:** Sudan on W, Kenya on S, Somalia and Djibouti on E, Eritrea on N. **Topography:** A high central plateau, between 6,000 and 10,000 ft. high, rises to higher mountains near the Great Rift Valley, cutting in from the SW. The Blue Nile and other rivers cross the plateau, which descends to plains on both W and SE. **Capital:** Addis Ababa 2,753,000.

Government: Type: Federal republic. **Head of state:** Pres. Girma Wolde Giorgis; b Dec, 1924; in office: Oct. 8, 2001. **Head of gov.:** Prime Min. Meles Zenawi; b May 8, 1955; in office: Aug. 23, 1995. **Local divisions:** 9 states, 2 charted cities. **Defense budget** (2000): $457 mil. **Active troops:** 252,500.

Economy: Industries: Food processing, beverages, textiles, chemicals. **Chief crops:** Coffee (60% of export earnings), cereals, sugarcane, pulses, oilseed. **Minerals:** Platinum, gold, copper. **Arable land:** 12%. **Crude oil reserves:** 428,000 bbls. **Livestock** (2001): cattle: 34.50 mil; chickens: 55.80 mil.; goats: 17.00 mil.; pigs: 25,000; sheep: 22.50 mil. **Fish catch:** (1999): 10,414 metric tons. **Electricity prod.:** 1.63 bil. kWh. **Labor force:** agri. and animal husbandry 80%, government and services 12%, ind. and construction 8%.

Finance: Monetary unit: Birr (Sept. 2002: 8.46 = $1 U.S.). **GDP** (2000 est.): $39.2 bil. **Per capita GDP:** $600. **Imports** (1999): $1.25 bil.; partners (1999 est.): Saudi Arabia 28%, Italy 10%. **Exports** (1999): $460 mil.; partners (1999 est.): Germany 16%, Japan 13%. **Tourism** (1998): $11 mil. **Budget** (FY96/97): $1.48 bil. **Intl. reserves less gold** (end 2000): $235 mil. **Gold:** 20,000 oz t. **Consumer prices** (change in 1999): 5.9%.

Transport: Railroad: Length: 486 mi. **Motor vehicles:** 45,559 pass. cars, 20,462 comm. vehicles. **Civil aviation:** 1.2 bil pass.-mi.; 31 airports.

Communications: TV sets: 4 per 1,000 pop. **Radios:** 153 per 1,000 pop. **Telephones:** 337,500.

Health: Life expectancy: 43.4 male; 45.1 female. **Births** (per 1,000 pop.): 44.3. **Deaths** (per 1,000 pop.): 18. **Natural inc.:** 2.63%. **Infant mortality** (per 1,000 live births): 98.6.

Education: Free, compulsory: ages 7-13. **Literacy:** 35%.

Major Intl. Organizations: UN (FAO, IBRD, ILO, IMF, IMO, WHO), AU.

Embassy: 2134 Kalorama Rd. NW 20008; 234-2281.

Websites: ethiospokes.net/; www.ethiiopianembassy.org

Ethiopian culture was influenced by Egypt and Greece. The ancient monarchy was invaded by Italy in 1880 but maintained its independence until another Italian invasion in 1936. British forces freed the country in 1941.

The last emperor, Haile Selassie I, established a parliament and judiciary system in 1931 but barred all political parties.

A series of droughts in the 1970s killed hundreds of thousands. An army mutiny, strikes, and student demonstrations led to the dethronement of Selassie in 1974; he died Aug. 1975, while being held by the ruling junta. The junta pledged to form a one-party socialist state and instituted a successful land reform; opposition was violently suppressed. The influence of the Coptic Church, embraced in AD 330, was curbed, and the monarchy was abolished in 1975.

The regime, torn by bloody coups, faced uprisings by tribal and political groups in part aided by Sudan and Somalia. Ties with the U.S., once a major ally, deteriorated, while cooperation accords were signed with the USSR in 1977. In 1978, Soviet advisers and Cuban troops helped defeat Somalian forces. Ethiopia and Somalia signed a peace agreement in 1988.

A worldwide relief effort began in 1984, as an extended drought threatened the country with famine; up to a million people may have died as a result of starvation and disease.

The Ethiopian People's Revolutionary Democratic Front (EPRDF), an umbrella group of 6 rebel armies, launched a major push against government forces, Feb. 1991. In May, Pres. Mengistu Haile Mariam resigned and left the country. The EPRDF took over and set up a transitional government. Ethiopia's first multiparty general elections were held in 1995.

Eritrea, a province on the Red Sea, declared its independence May 24, 1993. Fighting along the border with Eritrea, which erupted in June 1998, intensified in May 2000, as Ethiopian forces plunged into Eritrean territory; a cease-fire was signed June 18 and a peace treaty Dec. 12. The war displaced 350,000 Ethiopians and is estimated to have cost the country nearly $3 billion.

Fiji

Republic of the Fiji Islands

People: Population: 856,346. **Age distrib.** (%): <15: 32.9; 65+: 3.6. **Pop. density:** 121 per sq. mi. **Urban:** 49%. **Ethnic groups:** Fijian 51%, Indian 44%. **Principal languages:** English (official), Fijian, Hindustani. **Chief religions:** Christian 52%, Hindu 38%, Muslim 8%.

Geography: Area: 7,100 sq. mi. **Location:** In western South Pacific O. **Neighbors:** Nearest are Vanuatu to W, Tonga to E. **Topography:** 322 islands (106 inhabited), many mountainous, with tropical forests and large fertile areas. Viti Levu, the largest island, has over half the total land area. **Capital:** Suva (2001): 203,000.

Government: Type: In transition. **Head of state:** Pres. Ratu Josefa Iloilo; b Dec. 29, 1920; in office: July 18, 2000. **Head of gov.:** Laisenia Qarase; b Feb. 4, 1941; in office: Mar. 16, 2001. **Local divisions:** 4 divisions comprising 14 provinces and 1 dependency. **Defense budget** (2001): 25 mil. **Active troops:** 3,500.

Economy: Industries: Tourism, sugar, clothing, copra. **Chief crops:** Sugarcane, cassava, coconuts. **Minerals:** Gold, copper. **Other resources:** Timber, fish. **Arable land:** 10%. **Livestock** (2001): cattle: 340,000; chickens: 3.70 mil.; goats: 245,749; pigs: 137,000; sheep: 7,000. **Fish catch: (1999):** 36,374 metric tons. **Electricity prod.:** 0.52 bil. kWh. **Labor force:** subsistence agri. 67%, wage earners 18%, salary earners 15%.

Finance: Monetary unit: Dollar (Sept. 2002: 2.15 = $1.00 U.S.). **GDP** (1999 est.): $5.9 bil. **Per capita GDP:** $7,300. **Imports** (1999): $653 mil.; partners (1999): Australia 41.9%, U.S. 14%. **Exports** (1999): $537 mil.; partners (1999): Australia 33.1%, U.S. 14.8%. **Tourism** (1998): $266 mil. **Budget** (1999 est.): $501 mil. **Intl. reserves less gold** (end 2000): $314 mil. **Gold:** 1,000 oz t. **Consumer prices** (change in 2000): 1.1%.

Transport: Railroad: Length: 370 mi. **Motor vehicles:** 30,000 pass. cars, 29,000 comm. vehicles. **Civil aviation:** 1.2 bil pass.-mi.; 13 airports. **Chief ports:** Suva, Lautoka.

Communications: TV sets: 89 per 1,000 pop. **Radios:** 561 per 1,000 pop. Telephones: 166,400. **Daily newspaper circ.:** 68 per 1,000 pop.

Health: Life expectancy: 66.1 male; 71.1 female. **Births** (per 1,000 pop.): 23.2. **Deaths** (per 1,000 pop.): 5.7. **Natural inc.:** 1.75%. **Infant mortality** (per 1,000 live births): 13.7.

Education: Free: ages 6-14. **Literacy** (1996): 91%.

Major Intl. Organizations: UN (FAO, IBRD, ILO, IMF, IMO, WHO, WTrO), the Commonwealth.

Embassy: 2233 Wisconsin Ave. NW 20007; 337-8320.

Websites: www.embassy.org/embassies/fj.html
www.fiji.org.fj/

A British colony since 1874, Fiji became an independent parliamentary democracy Oct. 10, 1970. Cultural differences between the Indian community (descendants of contract laborers brought to the islands in the 19th century) and indigenous Fijians have led to political polarization.

In 1987, a military coup ousted the government; order was restored May 21 under a compromise granting Lt. Col. Sitiveni Rabuka, the coup's leader, increased power. Rabuka staged a second coup Sept. 25 and declared Fiji a republic. Civilian government was restored in Dec. A new constitution favoring indigenous Fijians was issued July 25, 1990; amendments enacted in July 1997 made the constitution more equitable.

Fiji's 1st Indian prime minister, Mahendra Chaudhry, took office May 19, 1999. He and other government officials were taken captive May 19, 2000, by indigenous Fijian gunmen led by George Speight. The hostage crisis led to a military takeover, May 29. Release of the last remaining hostages in July 2000 coincided with the installation of an interim military-backed government. Speight was charged with treason (sentenced to life in prison Feb. 18, 2002). The government was reconstituted in Mar. 2001 after an appellate court ruled it illegal. Voting ending Sept. 1, 2001, returned caretaker Prime Min. Laisenia Qarase to office.

Finland

Republic of Finland

People: Population: 5,183,545. **Age distrib.** (%): <15: 18.0; 65+: 15.0. **Pop. density:** 44 per sq. mi. **Urban:** 67%. **Ethnic groups:** Finn 93%, Swede 6%. **Principal languages:** Finnish, Swedish (both official). **Chief religion:** Evangelical Lutheran 89%.

Geography: Area: 117,900 sq. mi. **Location:** In northern Europe. **Neighbors:** Norway on N, Sweden on W, Russia on E. **Topography:** South and central Finland are generally flat areas with low hills and many lakes. The N has mountainous areas, 3,000-4,000 ft. above sea level. **Capital:** Helsinki 936,000.

Government: Type: Constitutional republic. **Head of state:** Pres. Tarja Halonen; b Dec. 24, 1943; in office: Mar. 1, 2000. **Head of gov.:** Prime Min. Paavo Lipponen; b Apr. 23, 1941; in office: Apr. 13, 1995. **Local divisions:** 6 laanit (provinces). **Defense budget (2001):** $1.4 bil. **Active troops:** 32,250.

Economy: Industries: Metal products., shipbuilding, pulp and paper, copper refining. **Chief crops:** Grains, sugar beets, potatoes. **Minerals:** Copper, iron, silver, zinc. **Other resources:** Timber, dairy prods. **Arable land:** 8%. **Livestock** (2001): cattle: 1.09 mil; chickens: 6.00 mil.; goats: 8,000; pigs: 1.30 mil; sheep: 100,000. **Fish catch** (1999): 196,513 metric tons. **Electricity prod.:** 75.36 bil. kWh. **Labor force:** public serv. 32%, ind. 22%, commerce 14%, finance, insurance, and business services 10%, agri. and forestry 8%, transport and communications 8%, construction 6%.

Finance: Monetary unit: Euro (Sept. 2002: 1.03 = $1 U.S.). **GDP** (2000 est.): $118.3 bil. **Per capita GDP:** $22,900. **Imports** (2000): $32.7 bil.; partners (1999): EU 60%, U.S. 8%. **Exports** (2000): $44.4 bil.; partners (1999): EU 58%, U.S. 8%, Russia, Japan. **Tourism:** $1.46 bil. **Budget** (2000 est.): $31 bil. **Intl. reserves less gold** (end 2000): $6.50 bil. **Gold:** 1.58 mil oz t. **Consumer prices** (change in 2000): 3.4%.

Transport: Railroad: Length: 3,641 mi. **Motor vehicles** (1997): 1.94 mil pass. cars, 291,235 comm. vehicles. **Civil aviation:** 5.9 bil pass.-mi.; 24 airports. **Chief ports:** Helsinki, Turku, Rauma, Kotka.

Communications: TV sets: 535 per 1,000 pop. **Radios:** 1,385 per 1,000 pop. **Telephones:** 6,889,000. **Daily newspaper circ.:** 455 per 1,000 pop.

Health: Life expectancy: 74.1 male; 81.5 female. **Births** (per 1,000 pop.): 10.6. **Deaths** (per 1,000 pop.): 9.8. **Natural inc.:** 0.08%. **Infant mortality** (per 1,000 live births): 3.8.

Education: Free, compulsory: ages 7-16. **Literacy** (1997): 100%.

Major Intl. Organizations: UN (FAO, IBRD, ILO, IMF, IMO, WHO, WTrO), EU, OECD, OSCE.

Embassy: 3301 Massachusetts Ave. NW 20008; 298-5800.

Website: www.president.fi/netcomm/

The early Finns probably migrated from the Ural area at about the beginning of the Christian era. Swedish settlers brought the country into Sweden, 1154 to 1809, when Finland became an autonomous grand duchy of the Russian Empire. Russian exactions created a strong national spirit; on Dec. 6, 1917, Finland declared its independence and in 1919 became a republic.

On Nov. 30, 1939, the Soviet Union invaded, and the Finns were forced to cede 16,173 sq. mi. of territory. After World War II, further cessions were exacted. In 1948, Finland signed a treaty of mutual assistance with the USSR; Finland and Russia nullified this treaty with a new pact in Jan. 1992.

Following approval by Finnish voters in an advisory referendum Oct. 16, 1994, Finland joined the European Union effective Jan. 1, 1995.

Aland or **Ahvenanmaa,** constituting an autonomous province, is a group of small islands, 590 sq. mi., in the Gulf of Bothnia, 25 mi. from Sweden, 15 mi. from Finland. Mariehamn is the principal port.

France

French Republic

People: Population: 59,765,983. **Age distrib.** (%): <15: 18.7; 65+: 16.1. **Pop. density:** 284 per sq. mi. **Urban:** 75%. **Ethnic groups:** Celtic and Latin; Teutonic, Slavic, North African, Indochinese, Basque minorities. **Principal language:** French (official). **Chief religion:** Roman Catholic 90%.

Geography: Area: 210,700 sq. mi. **Location:** In western Europe, between Atlantic O. and Mediterranean Sea. **Neighbors:** Spain on S; Italy, Switzerland, Germany on E; Luxembourg, Belgium on N. **Topography:** A wide plain covers more than half of the country, in N and W, drained to W by Seine, Loire, Garonne rivers. The Massif Central is a mountainous plateau in center. In E are Alps (Mt. Blanc is tallest in W Europe, 15,771 ft.), the lower Jura range, and the forested Vosges. The Rhone flows from Lake Geneva to Mediterranean. Pyrenees are in SW, on border with Spain. **Capital:** Paris. **Cities** (urban aggr.): Paris 9,658,000 (1997 city proper, est.: 2,152,000); Lyon 1,353,000; Marseilles 1,290,000; Lille 991,000.

Government: Type: Republic. **Head of state:** Pres. Jacques Chirac; b Nov. 29, 1932; in office: May 17, 1995. **Head of gov.:** Prime Min. Jean-Pierre Raffarin; b Aug. 3, 1948; in office: May 6, 2002. **Local divisions:** 22 administrative regions containing 96 departments. **Defense budget (2001):** $25.3 bil. **Active troops:** 273,740.

Economy: Industries: Machinery, chemicals, autos, metallurgy, aircraft, electronics, textiles, food processing, tourism. **Chief crops:** Grains, sugar beets, winegrapes, fruits, potatoes, vegetables. France is largest food producer, exporter, in W Europe. **Minerals:** Bauxite, iron, coal. **Crude oil reserves** (2001): 0.1 bil bbls. **Other resources:** Timber, dairy. **Arable land:** 33%. **Livestock** (2001): cattle: 20.50 mil; chickens: 230.00 mil.; goats: 1.20 mil.; pigs: 14.64 mil; sheep: 10.00 mil. **Fish catch** (1999): 829,914 metric tons. **Electricity prod.:** 513.92 bil. kWh. **Labor force:** services 71%, ind. 25%, agri. 4%.

Finance: Monetary unit: Euro (Sept. 2002: 1.03 = $1 U.S.). **GDP** (2000 est.): $1.448 tril. **Per capita GDP:** $24,400. **Imports** (2000 est.): $320 bil.; partners (2000 est.): EU 62%, U.S. 7%. **Exports** (2000 est.): $325 bil.; partners (1999): EU 63%,U.S. 8%. **Tourism:** $31.70 bil. **Budget** (2000 est.): $240 bil. **Intl. reserves less gold** (end 2000): $28.43 bil. **Gold:** 97.25 mil oz t. **Consumer prices** (change in 2000): 1.7%.

Transport: Railroad: Length: 19,847 mi. **Motor vehicles:** in use: 25.50 mil pass. cars, 5.26 mil comm. vehicles. **Civil aviation:** 52.6 bil pass.-mi.; 61 airports. **Chief ports:** Marseille, Le Havre, Bordeaux, Rouen.

Communications: TV sets: 606 per 1,000 pop. **Radios:** 943 per 1,000 pop. **Telephones:** 69,955,200. **Daily newspaper circ.:** 218 per 1,000 pop.

Health: Life expectancy: 75.2 male; 83.1 female. **Births** (per 1,000 pop.): 11.9. **Deaths** (per 1,000 pop.): 9. **Natural inc.:** 0.29%. **Infant mortality** (per 1,000 live births): 4.4.

Education: Free, compulsory: ages 6-16. **Literacy** (1994): 99%.

Major Intl. Organizations: UN and most of its specialized agencies, EU, NATO, OECD, OSCE.

Embassy: 4101 Reservoir Rd. NW 20007; 944-6000.

Website: www.ambafrance–us.org

Celtic Gaul was conquered by Julius Caesar 58-51 BC; Romans ruled for 500 years. Under Charlemagne, Frankish rule extended over much of Europe. After his death France emerged as one of the successor kingdoms.

The monarchy was overthrown by the French Revolution (1789-93) and succeeded by the First Republic; followed by the First Empire under Napoleon (1804-15), a monarchy (1814-48), the Second Republic (1848-52), the Second Empire (1852-70), the Third Republic (1871-1946), the Fourth Republic (1946-58), and the Fifth Republic (1958 to present).

France suffered severe losses in manpower and wealth in the First World War, when it was invaded by Germany. By the Treaty of Versailles, France exacted return of Alsace and Lorraine, provinces seized by Germany in 1871. Germany invaded France again in May 1940, and signed an armistice with a government based in Vichy. After France was liberated by the Allies in Sept. 1944, Gen. Charles de Gaulle became head of the provisional government, serving until 1946.

De Gaulle again became premier in 1958, during a crisis over Algeria, and obtained voter approval for a new constitution, U.S.hering in the Fifth Republic. He became president Jan. 1959. Using strong executive powers, he promoted French economic and technological advances in the context of the European Economic Community and guarded French foreign policy independence.

France had withdrawn from Indochina in 1954, and from Morocco and Tunisia in 1956. Most of its remaining African territories were freed 1958-62. In 1966, France withdrew all its troops from the integrated military command of NATO, though 60,000 remained stationed in Germany.

In May 1968 rebellious students in Paris and other centers rioted, battled police, and were joined by workers who launched nationwide strikes. The government awarded pay increases to the strikers May 26. De Gaulle resigned from office in Apr. 1969, after losing a nationwide referendum on constitutional reform. Georges Pompidou, who was elected to succeed him, continued De Gaulle's emphasis on French independence from the two superpowers. After Pompidou's death, in 1974, Valery Giscard d'Estaing was elected president; he continued the basically conservative policies of his predecessors.

On May 10, 1981, France elected François Mitterrand, a Socialist, president. Under Mitterrand the government nationalized 5 major industries and most private banks. After 1986, however, when rightists won a narrow victory in the National Assembly, Mitterrand chose conservative Jacques Chirac as premier. A 2-year period of "cohabitation" ensued, and France began to pursue a privatization program in which many state-owned companies were sold. After Mitterrand was elected to a 2nd 7-year term in 1988, he appointed a Socialist as premier. The center-right won a large majority in 1993 legislative elections, U.S.hering in another period of "cohabitation" with a conservative premier.

In 1993, France set tighter rules for entry into the country and made it easier for the government to expel foreigners. In 1994, France sent troops to Rwanda in an effort to help protect civilians there from ongoing massacres. The international terrorist known as Carlos the Jackal (Ilich Ramirez Sánchez) was arrested in Sudan in Aug. 1994 and extradited to France, where he had been sentenced in absentia to life imprisonment.

Former conservative Prime Min. Jacques Chirac won the presidency in a runoff May 7, 1995. A series of terrorist bombings and bombing attempts began in summer 1995; Islamic extremists, opposed to France's support of the Algerian government and its struggle with Islamic fundamentalists, were believed responsible. In Sept. 1995, France stirred widespread protests by resuming nuclear tests in the South Pacific, after a 3-year moratorium; the tests ended Jan. 1996.

Chirac cut government spending to help the French economy meet the budgetary goals set for the introduction of a common European currency. With unemployment at nearly 13%, legislative elections completed June 1, 1997, produced a decisive victory for the leftist parties. The result was a new period of "cohabitation," this time between a conservative president and a Socialist prime minister, Lionel Jospin. France contributed 7,000 troops to the NATO-led security force (KFOR) that entered Kosovo in June 1999.

French voters, disaffected by government scandals, shocked the political establishment in the 1st round of presidential voting Apr. 21, 2002, by giving Jean-Marie Le Pen, leader of the far-right National Front, a 2nd place finish with 16.9% of the vote; Chirac won only 19,9%, and Jospin was edged out of the runoff, with 16.2%.Chirac easily won the May 5 runoff, with 82%, and his center-right allies won parliamentary elections June 9 and 16.

The island of **Corsica,** in the Mediterranean W of Italy and N of Sardinia, is a territorial collectivity and region of France comprising 2 departments. It elects a total of 2 senators and 3 deputies to the French Parliament. Area: 3,369 sq. mi.; pop. (1996 est.): 258,000. The capital is Ajaccio, birthplace of Napoleon I. Violence by Corsican separatist groups has hurt tourism, a leading industry on the island.

Overseas Departments

French Guiana is on the NE coast of South America with Suriname on the W and Brazil on the E and S. Its area is 34,400 sq. mi.; pop. (2002 est.): 182,333. Guiana sends one senator and 2 deputies to the French Parliament. Guiana is administered by a prefect and has a Council General of 16 elected members; capital is Cayenne.

The famous penal colony, Devil's Island, was phased out between 1938 and 1951. The European Space Agency maintains a satellite-launching center (established by France in 1964) in the city of Kourou.

Immense forests of rich timber cover 88% of the land. Fishing (especially shrimp), forestry, and gold mining are the most important industries.

Guadeloupe, in the West Indies' Leeward Islands, consists of 2 large islands, Basse-Terre and Grande-Terre, separated by the Salt River, plus Marie Galante and the Saintes group to the S and, to the N, Desirade, St. Barthelemy, and over half of St. Martin (the Netherlands' portion is called St. Maarten). A French possession since 1635, the department is represented in the French Parliament by 2 senators and 4 deputies; administration consists of a prefect (governor) as well as an elected general and regional councils.

Area of the islands is 687 sq. mi.; pop. (2002 est.) 435,739, mainly descendants of slaves; capital is Basse-Terre on Basse-Terre Island. The land is fertile; sugar, rum, and bananas are exported. Tourism is an important industry.

Martinique, the northernmost of the Windward Islands, in the West Indies, has been a possession since 1635, and a department since Mar. 1946. It is represented in the French Parliament by 2 senators and 4 deputies. The island was the birthplace of Napoleon's Empress Josephine.

It has an area of 436 sq. mi.; pop. (2002 est.) 422,277, mostly descendants of slaves. The capital is Fort-de-France (pop. 1991: 101,000). It is a popular tourist stop. The chief exports are rum, bananas, and petroleum products.

Réunion is a volcanic island in the Indian O. about 420 mi. E of Madagascar, and has belonged to France since 1665. Area, 970 sq. mi.; pop. (2002 est.) 743,981, 30% of French extraction. Capital: Saint-Denis. The chief export is sugar. It elects 5 deputies, 3 senators to the French Parliament.

Overseas Territorial Collectivities

Mayotte, claimed by Comoros and administered by France, voted in 1976 to become a territorial collectivity of France. An island NW of Madagascar, area is 144 sq. mi., pop. (2002 est.) 170,879. The capital is Mamoutzou.

St. Pierre and Miquelon, formerly an overseas territory (1816-1976) and department (1976-85), made the transition to territorial collectivity in 1985. It consists of 2 groups of rocky islands near the SW coast of Newfoundland, inhabited by fishermen. The exports are chiefly fish products. The St. Pierre group has an area of 10 sq. mi.; Miquelon, 83 sq. mi. Total pop. (2001 est.), 6,954. The capital is St. Pierre.

Both Mayotte and St. Pierre and Miquelon elect a deputy and a senator to the French Parliament.

Overseas Territories

Territory of **French Polynesia** comprises 130 islands widely scattered among 5 archipelagos in the South Pacific; administered by a Council of Ministers (headed by a president). Territorial Assembly and the Council have headquarters at Papeete, on Tahiti, one of the **Society Islands** (which include the **Windward** and **Leeward** islands). Two deputies and a senator are elected to the French Parliament.

Other groups are the **Marquesas Islands,** the **Tuamotu Archipelago,** including the **Gambier Islands,** and the **Austral Islands.**

Total area of the islands administered from Tahiti is 1,400 sq. mi.; pop. (2002 est.), 257,847, more than half on Tahiti. Tahiti is picturesque and mountainous with a productive coastline bearing coconuts, citrus, pineapples, and vanilla. Cultured pearls are also produced.

Tahiti was visited by Capt. James Cook in 1769 and by Capt. Bligh in the *Bounty,* 1788-89. Its beauty impressed Herman Melville, Paul Gauguin, and Charles Darwin. Tahitians angered by French nuclear testing rioted Sept. 1995.

Territory of the **French Southern and Antarctic Lands** comprises **Adelie Land,** on Antarctica, and 4 island groups in the Indian O. Adelie, reached 1840, has a research station, a coastline of 185 mi., and tapers 1,240 mi. inland to the South Pole. The U.S. does not recognize national claims in Antarctica. There are 2 huge glaciers, Ninnis, 22 mi. wide, 99 mi. long, and Mentz, 11 mi. wide, 140 mi. long. The Indian O. groups are:

Kerguelen Archipelago, visited 1772, consists of one large and 300 small islands. The chief is 87 mi. long, 74 mi. wide, and has Mt. Ross, 6,429 ft. tall. Principal research station is Port-aux-Français. Seals often weigh 2 tons; there are blue whales, coal, peat, semiprecious stones. **Crozet Archipelago,** reached 1772, covers 195 sq. mi. Eastern Island rises to 6,560 ft. **Saint Paul,** in southern Indian O., has warm springs with earth at places heating to 120x to 390x F. **Amsterdam** is nearby; both produce cod and rock lobster.

Territory of **New Caledonia** and Dependencies is a group of islands in the Pacific O. about 1,115 mi. E of Australia and approx. the same distance NW of New Zealand. Dependencies are the **Loyalty Islands, Isle of Pines, Belep Archipelago,** and **Huon Islands.**

The largest island, New Caledonia, is 6,530 sq. mi. Total area of the territory is 8,548 sq. mi.; population (2002 est.) 207,858. The group was acquired by France in 1853.

The territory is administered by a High Commissioner. There is a popularly elected Territorial Congress. Two deputies and a senator are elected to the French Parliament. Capital: Noumea.

Mining is the chief industry. New Caledonia is one of the world's largest nickel producers. Other minerals found are chrome, iron, cobalt, manganese, silver, gold, lead, and copper. Agricultural products include yams, sweet potatoes, potatoes, manioc (cassava), corn, and coconuts.

In 1987, New Caledonian voters chose by referendum to remain within the French Republic. There were clashes between French and Melanesians (Kanaks) in 1988. An agreement Apr. 21, 1998, between France and rival New Caledonian factions specified a 15- to 20-year period of "shared sovereignty." The French constitution was amended, July 6, to allow the territory a gradual increase in autonomy, and New Caledonian voters approved the plan Nov. 8, 1998, by a 72% majority.

Territory of the **Wallis and Futuna Islands** comprises 2 island groups in the SW Pacific S of Tuvalu, N of Fiji, and W of Western Samoa; became an overseas territory July 29, 1961. The islands have a total area of 106 sq. mi. and population (2002 est.) of 15,585. **Alofi,** attached to Futuna, is uninhabited. Capital: Mata-Utu. Chief products are copra, yams, taro roots, bananas, and coconuts. A senator and a deputy are elected to the French Parliament.

Gabon

Gabonese Republic

People: Population: 1,223,353. **Age distrib.** (%): <15: 33.3; 65+: 5.9. **Pop. density:** 12 per sq. mi. **Urban:** 81%. **Ethnic groups:** Fang, Eshira, Bapounou, Bateke, other Bantu, other Africans, Europeans. **Principal languages:** French (official), Bantu dialects. **Chief religions:** Christian 55%-75%.

Geography: Area: 99,500 sq. mi. **Location:** On Atlantic coast of W central Africa. **Neighbors:** Equatorial Guinea and Cameroon on N, Congo on E and S. **Topography:** Heavily forested, the country consists of coastal lowlands; plateaus in N, E, and S; mountains in N, SE, and center. The Ogooue R. system covers most of Gabon. **Capital:** Libreville 573,000.

Government: Type: Republic. **Head of state:** Pres. Omar Bongo; b Dec. 30, 1935; in office: Dec. 2, 1967. **Head of gov.:** Prime Min. Jean-François Ntoutoume-Emane; b Oct. 6, 1939; in office: Jan. 23, 1999. **Local divisions:** 9 provinces. **Defense budget (2001):** $125 mil. **Active troops:** 4,700.

Economy: Industries: Food and beverage, textiles, wood products, cement. **Chief crops:** Cocoa, coffee, palm products. **Minerals:** Oil, manganese, uranium, iron, gold. **Crude oil reserves** (2001): 2.4 bil bbls. **Other resources:** Timber. **Arable land:** 1%. **Livestock** (2001): cattle: 36,000; chickens: 3.20 mil.; goats: 91,000; pigs: 213,000; sheep: 198,000. **Fish catch:** (1999): 44,772 metric tons. **Electricity prod.:** 0.85 bil. kWh. **Labor force:** agric. 60%, services and gov. 25%, ind. and commerce 15%.

Finance: Monetary unit: CFA Franc (Sept. 2002: 671.78 = $1 U.S.). **GDP** (2000 est.): $7.7 bil. **Per capita GDP:** $6,300. **Imports** (2000 est.): $1 bil.; partners (1999): France 64%, U.S. 4%. **Exports** (2000 est.): $3.4 bil.; partners (1999): U.S. 47%, France 19%. **Tourism:** $11 mil. **Budget** (1996 est.): $1.3 bil. **Intl. reserves less gold** (end 2000): $146.00 mil. **Gold:** 13,000 oz t. **Consumer prices** (change in 1997): 4.0%.

Transport: Railroad: Length: 415 mi. **Motor vehicles:** 23,800 pass. cars, 15,700 comm. vehicles. **Civil aviation:** 513.4

mil pass.-mi.; 17 airports. **Chief ports:** Port-Gentil, Owendo, Libreville.

Communications: TV sets: 35 per 1,000 pop. **Radios:** 173 per 1,000 pop. **Telephones:** 295,300. **Daily newspaper circ.:** 34 per 1,000 pop.

Health: Life expectancy: 48 male; 50.2 female. **Births** (per 1,000 pop.): 27.2. **Deaths** (per 1,000 pop.): 17.6. **Natural inc.:** 0.96%. **Infant mortality** (per 1,000 live births): 93.5.

Education: Compulsory: ages 6-16. **Literacy:** 63%.

Major Intl. Organizations: UN (FAO, IBRD, ILO, IMF, IMO, WHO, WTrO), AU.

Embassy: Suite 200, 2034 20th St. NW 20009; 797-1000.

Website: www.embassy.org/embassies/ga.html

France established control over the region in the second half of the 19th century. Gabon became independent Aug. 17, 1960. A multiparty political system was introduced in 1990, and a new constitution was enacted Mar. 14, 1991. However, the reelection of longtime Pres. Omar Bongo, on Dec. 5, 1993, prompted rioting and charges of vote fraud; another Bongo victory on Dec. 6, 1998, was likewise allegedly marred by irregularities.

Gabon is one of the most prosperous black African countries, thanks to abundant natural resources, foreign private investment, and government development programs.

The Gambia

Republic of The Gambia

People: Population: 1,455,842. **Age distrib.** (%): <15: 45.2; 65+: 2.7. **Pop. density:** 373 per sq. mi. **Urban:** 32%. **Ethnic groups:** Mandinka 42%, Fula 18%, Wolof 16%, other African. **Principal languages:** English (official), Mandinka, Wolof, Fula. **Chief religions:** Muslim 90%, Christian 9%.

Geography: Area: 3,900 sq. mi. **Location:** On Atlantic coast near W tip of Africa. **Neighbors:** Surrounded on 3 sides by Senegal. **Topography:** A narrow strip of land on each side of the lower Gambia R. **Capital:** Banjul 418,000.

Government: Type: Republic. **Head of state and gov.:** Yahya Jammeh; b May 25, 1965; in office: July 23, 1994. **Local divisions:** 5 divisions, 1 city. **Defense budget** (2001): $13 mil. **Active troops:** 800.

Economy: Industries: Processing peanuts, fish, and hides; tourism. **Chief crops:** Peanuts (main export), rice. **Arable land:** 18%. **Livestock** (2001): cattle: 365,000; chickens: 780,000; goats: 145,000; pigs: 14,000; sheep: 106,000. **Fish catch** (1999): 32,258 metric tons. **Electricity prod.:** 0.08 bil. kWh. **Labor force:** agri.75%, industry, commerce, and services 19%, government 6%.

Finance: Monetary unit: Dalasi (Sept. 2002: 22.25 = $1.00 U.S.). **GDP** (2000 est.): $1.5 bil. **Per capita GDP:** $1,100. **Imports** (1999): $202.5 mil.; partners (1997): China (including Hong Kong): 49%, UK 15%. **Exports** (1999): $125.8 mil.; partners (1999): Benelux 59%, Japan 20%. **Tourism** (1998): $33 mil. **Budget** (2001 est.): $80.9 mil. **Intl. reserves less gold** (end 2000): $84 mil. **Consumer prices** (change in 2000): 0.8%.

Transport: Motor vehicles: 8,000 pass. cars, 1,000 comm. vehicles. **Civil aviation:** 31.1 mil pass.-mi.; 1 airport. **Chief port:** Banjul.

Communications: Radios: 126 per 1,000 pop. **Telephones:** 78,000.

Health: Life expectancy: 52 male; 56 female. **Births** (per 1,000 pop.): 41.2. **Deaths** (per 1,000 pop.): 12.6. **Natural inc.:** 2.86%. **Infant mortality** (per 1,000 live births): 76.4.

Education: Free: ages 7-13. **Literacy:** 39%.

Major Intl. Organizations: UN (FAO, IBRD, ILO, IMF, IMO, WHO, WTrO), the Commonwealth, AU.

Embassy: Suite 1000, 1155 15th St. NW 20005; 785-1399.

Website: www.Gambia.com

The tribes of Gambia were at one time associated with the West African empires of Ghana, Mali, and Songhay. The area became Britain's first African possession in 1588.

Independence came Feb. 18, 1965; republic status within the Commonwealth was achieved in 1970. The country suffered from severe famine in the 1970s. After a coup attempt in 1981, The Gambia formed the confederation of Senegambia with Senegal that lasted until 1989.

On July 23, 1994, after 24 years in power, Pres. Dawda K. Jawara was deposed in a bloodless coup by a military officer, Yahya Jammeh. Jammeh barred political activity, detained potential opponents, and governed by decree. A new constitution was approved by referendum, Aug. 8, 1996. On Sept. 27 Jammeh won the presidential election. Parliamentary balloting on Jan. 2, 1997, completed the nominal return to civilian rule, but Jammeh retained a firm grip on power. He followed his reelection win on Oct. 18, 2001, with a new crackdown on dissidents.

Georgia

People: Population: 4,960,951. **Age distrib.** (%): <15: 19.6; 65+: 12.5. **Pop. density:** 184 per sq. mi. **Urban:** 60%. **Ethnic groups:** Georgian 70%, Armenian 8%, Russian 6%. **Principal languages:** Georgian (official), Russian. **Chief religions:** Georgian Orthodox 65%, Muslim 11%, Russian Orthodox 10%.

Geography: Area: 26,900 sq. mi. **Location:** SW Asia, on E coast of Black Sea. **Neighbors:** Russia on N and NE, Turkey and Armenia on S, Azerbaijan on SE. **Topography:** Separated from Russia on NE by main range of the Caucasus Mts. **Capital:** Tbilisi 1,406,000.

Government: Type: Republic. **Head of state and gov.:** Pres. Eduard A. Shevardnadze; b Jan. 25, 1928; in office: Mar. 10, 1992. **Local divisions:** 53 rayons, 9 cities, and 2 autonomous republics. **Defense budget (2001):** $22 mil. **Active troops:** 16,790.

Economy: Industries: Steel, aircraft, machine tools, electric locomotives. **Chief crops:** Citrus, potatoes, vegetables, grapes, tea. **Minerals:** Manganese, iron, copper, coal. **Other resources:** Forests. **Crude oil reserves** (2000): 35 mil bbls. **Arable land:** 9%. **Livestock** (2001): cattle: 1.18 mil; chickens: 7.83 mil.; goats: 78,000; pigs: 443,400; sheep: 545,000. **Electricity prod.:** 7.40 bil. kWh. **Labor force:** ind. 20%, agri. 40%, services 40%.

Finance: Monetary unit: Lari (Sept. 2002: 2.18 = $1 U.S.). **GDP** (2000 est.): $22.8 bil. **Per capita GDP:** $4,600. **Imports** (2000 est.): $898 mil.; partners (1999): EU 22%, Russia 19%. **Exports** (2000 est.): $372 mil.; partners (1999): Russia 19%, Turkey 16%. **Tourism:** $400 mil. **Budget** (1999): $626 mil. **Intl. reserves less gold** (June 2000): $109.97 mil. **Gold:** 2,100 oz t. **Consumer prices** (change in 1999): 19.1%.

Transport: Railroad: Length: 983 mi. **Motor vehicles:** 442,000 pass. cars, 50,000 comm. vehicles. **Civil aviation:** 128.1 mil pass.-mi.; 1 airport. **Chief ports:** Batumi, Sukhumi.

Communications: TV sets: 220 per 1,000 pop. **Telephones:** 1,162,600.

Health: Life expectancy: 61.2 male; 68.3 female. **Births** (per 1,000 pop.): 11.5. **Deaths** (per 1,000 pop.): 14.6. **Natural inc.:** -0.31%. **Infant mortality** (per 1,000 live births): 51.8.

Education: Compulsory: ages 6-14. **Literacy:** 99%.

Major Intl. Organizations: UN (FAO, IBRD, ILO, IMF, IMO, WHO), CIS, OSCE.

Embassy: Suite 300, 1615 New Hampshire Ave. NW 20009; 393-5959.

Website: www.parliament.ge

The region, which contained the ancient kingdoms of Colchis and Iberia, was Christianized in the 4th century and conquered by Arabs in the 8th century. It expanded to include an area from the Black Sea to the Caspian and parts of Armenia and Persia before its disintegration under the impact of Mongol and Turkish invasions. Annexation by Russia in 1801 led to the Russian war with Persia, 1804-1813. Georgia entered the USSR in 1922 and became a constituent republic in 1936.

Georgia declared independence Apr. 9, 1991. It became an independent state when the Soviet Union disbanded Dec. 26, 1991. There was fighting during 1991 between rebel forces and loyalists of Pres. Zviad Gamsakhurdia, who fled the capital Jan. 6, 1992. The ruling Military Council picked former Soviet Foreign Minister Eduard A. Shevardnadze to chair a newly created State Council. An attempted coup by forces loyal to Gamsakhurdia was crushed June 24, 1992. Shevardnadze was later elected president. Gamsakhurdia died Jan. 1994, reportedly by suicide.

In Abkhazia, an autonomous republic within Georgia, ethnic Abkhazis, reportedly aided by Russia, launched a bloody military campaign and, by late 1993, had gained control of much of the region. A cease-fire providing for Russian peacekeepers was signed in Moscow May 14, 1994. Intermittent clashes continued into the late 1990s.

On Feb. 3, 1994, Georgia signed agreements with Russia for economic and military cooperation. On Mar. 1, Georgia's Supreme Council ratified membership by Georgia in the Commonwealth of Independent States.

Shevardnadze was wounded by a car bomb Aug. 29, 1995, while on his way to Parliament to sign a new constitution. He was reelected president Nov. 5. Shevardnadze escaped another assassination attempt, Feb. 9, 1998, when gunmen ambushed his motorcade. A mutiny by more than 200 soldiers opposed to Shevardnadze was crushed Oct. 19. He won another 5-year presidential term Apr. 9, 2000. Chechen rebels based in Pankisi Gorge, NE of Tbilisi, have launched attacks against Russian troops in Chechnya, heightening tensions with Russia.

Germany

Federal Republic of Germany

People: Population: 83,251,851. **Age distrib.** (%): <15: 15.6; 65+: 16.6. **Pop. density:** 616 per sq. mi. **Urban:** 87%. **Ethnic groups:** German 92%, Turkish 2%. **Principal language:** German (official). **Chief religions:** Protestant 38%, Roman Catholic 34%.

Geography: Area: 135,200 sq. mi. **Location:** In central Europe. **Neighbors:** Denmark on N; Netherlands, Belgium, Luxembourg, France on W; Switzerland, Austria on S; Czech Rep., Poland on E. **Topography:** Germany is flat in N, hilly in center and W, and mountainous in Bavaria in the S. Chief rivers are Elbe, Weser, Ems, Rhine, and Main, all flowing toward North Sea, and Danube, flowing toward Black Sea. **Capital:** Berlin. **Cities** (urban aggr.): Rhein-Ruhr North (including Essen) 6.53 mil.; Rhein Main (Frankfurt am Mein) 3.68 mil.; Berlin 3.31 mil; Rhein-Ruhr Middle (Dusseldorf) 3.23 mil.; Rhein-Ruhr South (Cologne) 3.05 mil.; Stuttgart 2.67 mil.

Government: Type: Federal republic. **Head of state:** Pres. Johannes Rau; b Jan. 16, 1931; in office: July 1, 1999. **Head of gov.:** Chan. Gerhard Schröder; b Apr. 7, 1944; in office: Oct. 27, 1998. **Local divisions:** 16 laender (states). **Defense budget (2001):** $21 bil . **Active troops:** 308,400.

Economy: Industries: Iron, steel, coal, cement, chemicals, machinery, vehicles, machine tools, electronics, food and beverages. **Chief crops:** Grains, potatoes, sugar beets. **Minerals:** Coal, potash, lignite, iron, uranium. **Crude oil reserves** (2001): 0.3 bil bbls. **Other resources:** Timber. **Arable land:** 33%. **Livestock** (2001): cattle: 14.57 mil; chickens: 108.00 mil.; goats: 140,000; pigs: 25.77 mil; sheep: 2.14 mil . **Fish catch** (1999): 318,785 metric tons. **Electricity prod.:** 537.33 bil. kWh. **Labor force:** ind. 33.4%, agri. 2.8%, services 63.8%.

Finance: Monetary unit: Euro (Sept. 2002: 1.03 = $1 U.S.). **GDP** (2000 est.): $1.936 tril. **Per capita GDP:** $23,400. **Imports** (2000 est.): $505 bil.; partners (1999): EU 52.2%, U.S. 8.1%, Japan 4.9%. **Exports** (2000 est.): $578 bil.; partners (1999): EU 55.3%, U.S. 10.1%. **Tourism:** $16.83 bil. **Budget** (1999 est.): $1.036 trillion, including capital expenditures of NA. **Intl. reserves less gold** (end 2000): $43.66 bil. **Gold:** 111.52 mil oz t. **Consumer prices** (change in 2000): 1.9%.

Transport: Railroad: Length: 54,994 mi. **Motor vehicles** (1997): 41.33 mil pass. cars, 3.17 mil comm. vehicles. **Civil aviation:** 53.6 bil pass.-mi.; 35 airports. **Chief ports:** Hamburg, Bremen, Bremerhaven, Lubeck, Rostock.

Communications: TV sets: 571 per 1,000 pop. **Radios:** 946 per 1,000 pop. **Telephones:** 108,525,000. **Daily newspaper circ.:** 311 per 1,000 pop.

Health: Life expectancy: 74.6 male; 81.1 female. **Births** (per 1,000 pop.): 9. **Deaths** (per 1,000 pop.): 10.4. **Natural inc.:** –0.14%. **Infant mortality** (per 1,000 live births): 4.7.

Education: Compulsory: ages 6-15. **Literacy** (1993): 100%.

Major Intl. Organizations: UN and all of its specialized agencies, EU, NATO, OECD, OSCE.

Embassy: 4645 Reservoir Rd. NW 20007; 298-4000.

Website: www.germany–info.org

Germany is a central European nation originally composed of numerous states, with a common language and traditions, that were united in one country in 1871; Germany was split into 2 countries from the end of World War II until 1990, when it was reunified.

History and government. Germanic tribes were defeated by Julius Caesar, 55 and 53 BC, but Roman expansion N of the Rhine was stopped in AD 9. Charlemagne, ruler of the Franks, consolidated Saxon, Bavarian, Rhenish, Frankish, and other lands; after him the eastern part became the German Empire. The Thirty Years' War, 1618-1648, split Germany into small principalities and kingdoms. After Napoleon, Austria contended with Prussia for dominance, but lost the Seven Weeks' War to Prussia, 1866. Otto von Bismarck, Prussian chancellor, formed the North German Confederation, 1867.

In 1870 Bismarck maneuvered Napoleon III into declaring war. After the quick defeat of France, Bismarck formed the **German Empire** and on Jan. 18, 1871, in Versailles, proclaimed King Wilhelm I of Prussia German emperor (Deutscher kaiser).

The German Empire reached its peak before World War I in 1914, with 208,780 sq. mi., plus a colonial empire. After that war Germany ceded Alsace-Lorraine to France; West Prussia and Posen (Poznan) province to Poland; part of Schleswig to Denmark; lost all colonies and ports of Memel and Danzig.

Republic of Germany, 1919-1933, adopted the Weimar constitution; met reparation payments and elected Friedrich Ebert and Gen. Paul von Hindenburg presidents.

Third Reich, 1933-1945, Adolf Hitler led the National Socialist German Workers' (Nazi) party after World War I. In 1923 he attempted to unseat the Bavarian government and was imprisoned. Pres. von Hindenburg named Hitler chancellor Jan. 30, 1933; on Aug. 3, 1934, the day after Hindenburg's death, the cabinet joined the offices of president and chancellor and made Hitler fuehrer (leader). Hitler abolished freedom of speech and assembly, and began a long series of persecutions climaxed by the murder of millions of Jews and others.

He repudiated the Versailles treaty and reparations agreements, remilitarized the Rhineland (1936), and annexed Austria (Anschluss, 1938). At Munich he made an agreement with Neville Chamberlain, British prime minister, which permitted Germany to annex part of Czechoslovakia. He signed a nonaggression treaty with the USSR, 1939 and declared war on Poland Sept. 1, 1939, precipitating World War II. With total defeat near, Hitler committed suicide in Berlin Apr. 1945. The victorious Allies voided all acts and annexations of Hitler's Reich.

Division of Germany. Germany was sectioned into 4 zones of occupation, administered by the Allied Powers (U.S., U.S.SR, U.K., and France). The USSR took control of many E German states. The territory E of the so-called Oder-Neisse line was assigned to, and later annexed by, Poland. Northern East Prussia (now Kaliningrad) was annexed by the USSR. Administration of the remaining regions, in the W and S (which make up about two-thirds of present-day Germany), was split among the Western Allies.

There was also created the area of Greater Berlin, within but not part of the Soviet zone, administered by the 4 occupying powers under the Allied Command. In 1948 the USSR withdrew, established its single command in East Berlin, and cut off supplies. The Western Allies utilized a gigantic airlift to bring food to West Berlin, 1948-49.

In 1949, 2 separate German states were established; in May the zones administered by the Western Allies became West Germany, capital: Bonn; in Oct. the Soviet sector became East Germany, capital: East Berlin. West Berlin was considered an enclave of West Germany, although its status was disputed by the Soviet bloc.

East Germany. The German Democratic Republic (East Germany) was proclaimed in the Soviet sector of Berlin Oct. 7, 1949. It was proclaimed fully sovereign in 1954, but Soviet troops remained on grounds of security and the 4-power Potsdam agreement.

Coincident with the entrance of West Germany into the European defense community in 1952, the East German government decreed a prohibited zone 3 miles deep along its 600-mile border with West Germany and cut Berlin's telephone system in two. Berlin was further divided by erection of a fortified wall in 1961, after over 3 million East Germans had emigrated West; an exodus of refugees to the West continued, though on a smaller scale.

East Germany suffered severe economic problems at least until the mid-1960s. Then a "new economic system" was introduced, easing central planning controls and allowing factories to make profits provided they were reinvested in operations or redistributed to workers as bonuses. By the early 1970s, the economy was highly industrialized, and the nation was credited with the highest standard of living among Warsaw Pact countries. But growth slowed in the late 1970s, because of shortages of natural resources and labor, and a huge debt to lenders in the West. Comparison with the lifestyle in the West caused many young people to leave the country.

The government firmly resisted following the USSR's policy of *glasnost,* but by Oct. 1989, was faced with nationwide demonstrations demanding reform. Pres. Erich Honecker, in office since 1976, was forced to resign, Oct. 18. On Nov. 4, the border with Czechoslovakia was opened and permission granted for refugees to travel to the West. On Nov. 9, the East German government announced its decision to open the border with the West, signaling the end of the "Berlin Wall," which was the supreme emblem of the cold war. On Aug. 23, 1990, the East German parliament agreed to formal unification with West Germany; this occurred Oct. 3.

West Germany. The Federal Republic of Germany (West Germany) was proclaimed May 23, 1949, in Bonn, after a constitution had been drawn up by a consultative assembly formed by representatives of the 11 laender (states) in the French, British, and American zones. Later reorganized into 9 units, the laender numbered 10 with the addition of the Saar, 1957. Berlin also was granted land (state) status, but the 1945 occupation agreements placed restrictions on it.

The occupying powers, the U.S., Britain, and France, restored civil status, Sept. 21, 1949. The Western Allies ended the state of war with Germany in 1951 (the U.S. resumed diplomatic relations July 2), while the USSR did so in 1955. The powers lifted controls and the republic became fully independent May 5, 1955.

Dr. Konrad Adenauer, Christian Democrat, was made chancellor Sept. 15, 1949, reelected 1953, 1957, 1961. Willy Brandt, heading a coalition of Social Democrats and Free Democrats, became chancellor Oct. 21, 1969. (He resigned May 1974 because of a spy scandal.)

In 1970 Brandt signed friendship treaties with the USSR and Poland. In 1971, the U.S., Britain, France, and the USSR signed an agreement on Western access to West Berlin. In 1972 East and West Germany signed their first formal treaty, implementing the agreement easing access to West Berlin. In 1973 a West Germany-Czechoslovakia pact normalized relations and nullified the 1938 "Munich Agreement."

West Germany experienced strong economic growth starting in the 1950s. The country led Europe in provisions for worker participation in the management of industry.

In 1989 the changes in the East German government and opening of the Berlin Wall sparked talk of reunification of the 2 Germanys. In 1990, under Chancellor Kohl's leadership, West Germany moved rapidly to reunite with East Germany.

A New Era. As Communism was being rejected in East Germany, talks began concerning German reunification. At a meeting in Ottawa, Feb. 1990, the foreign ministers of the World War II "Big Four" Allied nations and of East Germany and West Germany reached agreement on a format for high-level talks on German reunification.

In May, NATO ministers adopted a package of proposals on reunification, including the inclusion of the united Germany as a full member of NATO and the barring of the new Germany from having its own nuclear, chemical, or biological weapons. In July, the USSR agreed to conditions that would allow Germany to become a member of NATO.

The 2 nations agreed to monetary unification under the West German mark beginning in July. The merger of the 2 Germanys took place Oct. 3, and the first all-German elections since 1932 were held Dec. 2. Eastern Germany received over $1 trillion in public and private funds from western Germany between 1990 and 1995. In 1991, Berlin again became the capital of Germany; the legislature, most administrative offices, and most foreign embassies had shifted from Bonn to Berlin by late 1999.

Germany's highest court ruled, July 12, 1994, that German troops could participate in international military missions abroad, when approved by Parliament. Ceremonies were held marking the final withdrawal of Russian troops from Germany, Aug. 31. Ceremonies were held the following week marking the final withdrawal of American, British, and French troops from Berlin. General elections Oct. 16 left Chancellor Helmut Kohl's governing coalition with a slim parliamentary majority. On Oct. 31, 1996, after more than 14 years in office, Kohl surpassed Adenauer as Germany's longest-serving chancellor in the 20th century.

Unemployment hit a postwar high of 12.6% in Jan. 1998. The Kohl era ended with the defeat of the Christian Democrats in parliamentary elections Sept. 27; Gerhard Schröder, of the Social Democratic Party, became chancellor. Germany contributed 8,500 troops to the NATO-led security force (KFOR) that entered Kosovo in June 1999. Kohl resigned as honorary party chairman Jan. 18, 2000, amid allegations of illegal fund-raising. Kohl reached an agreement with prosecutors Feb. 8, 2001, in which he acknowledged committing a "breach of trust" and agreed to pay a fine, but did not plead guilty to any criminal charges.

In a tight vote on Sept. 23, 2002, Schröder retained power as prime minister; he was apparently aided by his opposition to any military action against Iraq, by government response to devastating summer floods, and by the better than usual performace of the Greens, who were in coalition with Schröder's Social Democrats.

Helgoland, an island of 130 acres in the North Sea, was taken from Denmark by a British Naval Force in 1807 and later ceded to Germany to become part of Schleswig-Holstein province in return for rights in East Africa. The heavily fortified island was surrendered to UK, May 23, 1945, demilitarized in 1947, and returned to West Germany, Mar. 1, 1952. It is a free port.

Ghana

Republic of Ghana

People: Population: 20,244,154. **Age distrib.** (%): <15: 41.2; 65+: 3.5. **Pop. density:** 228 per sq. mi. **Urban:** 38%. **Ethnic groups:** Akan 44%, Moshi-Dagomba 16%, Ewe 13%, Ga 8%. **Principal languages:** English (official), Akan, Moshi-Dagomba, Ewe, Ga. **Chief religions:** Indigenous beliefs 38%, Muslim 30%, Christian 24%.

Geography: Area: 88,800 sq. mi. **Location:** On southern coast of W Africa. **Neighbors:** Côte d'Ivoire on W, Burkina Faso on N, Togo on E. **Topography:** Most of Ghana consists of low fertile plains and scrubland, cut by rivers and by the artificial Lake Volta. **Capital:** Accra 1,925,000.

Government: Type: Republic. **Head of state and gov.:** Pres. John Agyekum Kufuor; b Dec. 8, 1938; in office: Jan. 7, 2001. **Local divisions:** 10 regions. **Defense budget** (2001): $34 mil. **Active troops:** 7,000.

Economy: Industries: Mining, lumbering, light manufacturing, aluminum smelting, food processing. **Chief crops:** Cocoa, coffee, rice, cassava, peanuts, corn. **Minerals:** Gold, manganese, industrial diamonds, bauxite. **Crude oil reserves** (2000): 16.5 mil bbls. **Other resources:** Timber, rubber. **Arable land:** 12%. **Livestock** (2001): cattle: 1.30 mil; chickens: 20.47 mil.; goats: 3.08 mil.; pigs: 324,000; sheep: 2.74 mil. **Fish catch** (1999): 446,883 metric tons. **Electricity prod.:** 5.92 bil. kWh. **Labor force:** agri. 60%, ind. 15%, services 25%.

Finance: Monetary unit: Cedi (Sept. 2002: 8,175 = $1 U.S.). **GDP** (2000 est.): $37.4 bil. **Per capita GDP:** $1,900. **Imports** (2000): $2.2 bil.; partners (1998): UK, Nigeria, U.S., Germany, Italy, Spain. **Exports** (2000): $1.6 bil.; partners (1998): Togo, UK, Italy, Netherlands, Germany, U.S., France. **Tourism** (1998): $274 mil. **Budget** (1996 est.): $1.47 bil. **Intl. reserves less gold** (end 2000): $178 mil. **Gold:** 280,000 oz t. **Consumer prices** (change in 2000): 25.2%.

Transport: Railroad: Length: 592 mi. **Motor vehicles:** 90,000 pass. cars, 45,000 comm. vehicles. **Civil aviation:** 436.4 mil pass.-mi.; 1 airport. **Chief ports:** Tema, Takoradi.

Communications: TV sets: 15 per 1,000 pop. **Radios:** 249 per 1,000 pop. **Telephones:** 435,900. **Daily newspaper circ.:** 64 per 1,000 pop.

Health: Life expectancy: 55.7 male; 58.5 female. **Births** (per 1,000 pop.): 28.1. **Deaths** (per 1,000 pop.): 10.3. **Natural inc.:** 1.78%. **Infant mortality** (per 1,000 live births): 55.6.

Education: Compulsory: ages 6-16. **Literacy:** 64%.

Major Intl. Organizations: UN and all of its specialized agencies, the Commonwealth, AU.

Embassy: 3512 International Dr. NW 20008; 686-4520.

Website: www.ghana.gov.gh

Named for an African empire along the Niger River, AD 400-1240, Ghana was ruled by Britain for 113 years as the Gold Coast. The UN in 1956 approved merger with the British Togoland trust territory. Independence came Mar. 6, 1957, and republic status within the Commonwealth in 1960.

Pres. Kwame Nkrumah built hospitals and schools, promoted development projects like the Volta R. hydroelectric and aluminum plants but ran the country into debt, jailed opponents, and was accused of corruption. A 1964 referendum gave Nkrumah dictatorial powers and set up a one-party socialist state. Nkrumah was overthrown in 1966 by a police-army coup, which expelled Chinese and East German teachers and technicians. Elections were held in 1969, but 4 further coups occurred in 1972, 1978, 1979, and 1981. The 1979 and 1981 coups, led by Flight Lieut. Jerry Rawlings, were followed by suspension of the constitution and banning of political parties. A new constitution, allowing multiparty politics, was approved in April 1992.

In Feb. 1993 more than 1,000 people were killed in ethnic clashes in northern Ghana. Rawlings won the presidential election of Dec. 7, 1996. Kofi Annan, a career UN diplomat from Ghana, became UN secretary general on Jan. 1, 1997. Opposition leader John Agyekum Kufuor won a runoff vote Dec. 28, 2000, and was sworn in Jan. 7, 2001, marking Ghana's 1st peaceful transfer of power from one elected president to another.

Greece

Hellenic Republic

People: Population: 10,645,343. **Age distrib.** (%): <15: 15.0; 65+: 17.7. **Pop. density:** 211 per sq. mi. **Urban:** 60%. **Ethnic groups:** Greek 98%. (**Note:** Greek govt. states there are no ethnic divisions in Greece.) **Principal languages:** Greek (official), English, French. **Chief religion:** Greek Orthodox 98% (official).

Geography: Area: 50,500 sq. mi. **Location:** Occupies southern end of Balkan Peninsula in SE Europe. **Neighbors:** Albania, Macedonia, Bulgaria on N; Turkey on E. **Topography:** About three-quarters of Greece is nonarable, with mountains in all areas. Pindus Mts. run through the country N to S. The heavily indented coastline is 9,385 mi. long. Of over 2,000 islands, only 169 are inhabited, among them Crete, Rhodes, Milos, Kerkira (Corfu), Chios, Lesbos, Samos, Euboea, Delos, Mykonos. **Capital:** Athens 3,120,000 (1999 city proper: 748,110).

Government: Type: Parliamentary republic. **Head of state:** Pres. Konstantinos Stephanopoulos; b Aug. 15, 1926; in office: Mar. 8, 1995. **Head of gov.:** Prime Min. Costas Simitis; b June 23, 1936; in office: Jan. 18, 1996. **Local divisions:** 13 regions comprising 51 prefectures. **Defense budget** (2000): $3.3 bil. **Active troops:** 159,170.

Economy: Industries: Tourism, food and tobacco processing, textiles, chemicals, metal products. **Chief crops:** Grains, corn, sugar beets, cotton, tobacco, olives, grapes, citrus and other fruits, tomatoes. **Minerals:** Bauxite, lignite, magnesite, marble, oil. **Crude oil reserves** (2000): 10 mil bbls. **Arable land:** 19%. **Livestock** (2001): cattle: 585,000; chickens: 28.00 mil.; goats: 5.30 mil.; pigs: 905,000; sheep: 9.00 mil. **Fish catch** (1999): 214,228 metric tons. **Electricity prod.:** 49.58 bil. kWh. **Labor force:** ind. 21%, agri. 20%, services 59%.

Finance: Monetary unit: Euro (Sept. 2002: 1.03 = $1 U.S.). **GDP** (2000 est.): $181.9 bil. **Per capita GDP:** $17,200. **Imports** (2000): $33.9 bil.; partners (1999): EU 66% (Italy 15%, Germany 15%. **Exports** (2000): $15.8 bil.; partners (1999): EU 49%,U.S. 6%. **Tourism:** $8.77 bil. **Budget** (1998 est.): $47.6 bil. **Intl. reserves less gold** (end 2000): $10.30 bil. **Gold:** 4.26 mil oz t. **Consumer prices** (change in 2000): 3.2%.

Transport: Railroad: Length: 1,537 mi. **Motor vehicles:** 2.34 mil pass. cars, 939,923 comm. vehicles. **Civil aviation:** 5.8 bil pass.-mi.; 36 airports. **Chief ports:** Piraeus, Thessaloníki, Patrai.

Communications: TV sets: 466 per 1,000 pop. **Radios:** 477 per 1,000 pop. **Telephones:** 13,569,700. **Daily newspaper circ.:** 153 per 1,000 pop.

Health: Life expectancy: 76.2 male; 81.5 female. **Births** (per 1,000 pop.): 9.8. **Deaths** (per 1,000 pop.): 9.8. **Natural inc.:** 0%. **Infant mortality** (per 1,000 live births): 6.2.

Education: Free, compulsory: ages 6-15. **Literacy** (1993): 95%.

Major Intl. Organizations: UN (FAO, IBRD, ILO, IMF, IMO, WHO, WTrO), EU, NATO, OECD, OSCE.

Embassy: 2221 Massachusetts Ave. NW 20008; 939-5800.

Website: www.greekembassy.org

The achievements of ancient Greece in art, architecture, science, mathematics, philosophy, drama, literature, and democracy became legacies for succeeding ages. Greece reached the height of its glory and power, particularly in the Athenian city-state, in the 5th century BC. Greece fell under Roman rule in the 2d and 1st centuries BC. In the 4th century AD it became part of the Byzantine Empire and, after the fall of Constantinople to the Turks in 1453, part of the Ottoman Empire.

Greece won its war of independence from Turkey 1821-1829, and became a kingdom. A republic was established 1924; the monarchy was restored, 1935, and George II, King of the Hellenes, resumed the throne. In Oct. 1940, Greece rejected an ultimatum from Italy. Nazi support resulted in its defeat and occupation by Germans, Italians, and Bulgarians. By the end of 1944 the invaders withdrew. Communist resistance forces were defeated by Royalist and British troops. A plebiscite again restored the monarchy.

Communists waged guerrilla war 1947-49 against the government but were defeated with the aid of the U.S. A period of reconstruction and rapid development followed, mainly with conservative governments under Premier Constantine Karamanlis. The Center Union, led by George Papandreou, won elections in 1963 and 1964, but King Constantine, who acceded in 1964, forced Papandreou to resign. A period of political maneuvers ended in the military takeover of April 21, 1967, by Col. George Papadopoulos. King Constantine tried to reverse the consolidation of the harsh dictatorship Dec. 13, 1967, but failed and fled to Italy. Papadopoulos was ousted Nov. 25, 1973.

Greek army officers serving in the National Guard of Cyprus staged a coup on the island July 15, 1974. Turkey invaded Cyprus a week later, precipitating the collapse of the Greek junta, which was implicated in the Cyprus coup. Democratic government returned (and in 1975 the monarchy was abolished).

The 1981 electoral victory of the Panhellenic Socialist Movement (Pasok) of Andreas Papandreou brought substantial changes in Greece's internal and external policies. A scandal centered on George Kostokas, a banker and publisher, led to the arrest or investigation of leading Socialists, implicated Papandreou, and contributed to the defeat of the Socialists at the polls in 1989. However, Papandreou, who was narrowly acquitted Jan. 1992 of corruption charges, led the Socialists to a comeback victory in general elections Oct. 10, 1993.

Tensions between Greece and the Former Yugoslav Republic of Macedonia eased when the 2 countries agreed to normalize relations Sept. 13, 1995. The ailing Papandreou was replaced as prime minister by Costas Simitis, Jan. 18, 1996. Simitis led the Socialists to victory in the election of Sept. 22. The International Olympic Committee, Sept. 5, 1997, chose Athens to host the Summer Games in 2004. An earthquake that shook Athens Sept. 7, 1999, killed at least 143 people and left over 60,000 homeless. The Socialists retained power by a narrow margin in the elections of Apr. 9, 2000.

Police in 2002 cracked down on the November 17 terrorist movement, blamed for 23 killings since the mid-1970s.

Grenada

People: Population: 89,211. **Age distrib.** (%): <15: 37.0; 65+: 3.9. **Pop. density:** 682 per sq. mi. **Urban:** 37%. **Ethnic groups:** Mostly black African. **Principal languages:** English (official), French patois. **Chief religions:** Roman Catholic 53%, Protestant 33%.

Geography: Area: 131 sq. mi. **Location:** In Caribbean, 90 mi. N of Venezuela. **Neighbors:** Venezuela, Trinidid & Tobago to S; St. Vincent & the Grenadines to N. **Topography:** Main island is mountainous; country includes Carriacou and Petit Martinique islands. **Capital:** Saint George's 36,000.

Government: Type: Parliamentary democracy. **Head of state:** Queen Elizabeth II, represented by Gov.-Gen. Daniel Williams; b Nov. 4, 1935; in office: Aug. 8, 1996. **Head of gov.:** Prime Min. Keith Mitchell; b Nov. 12, 1946; in office: June 22, 1995. **Local divisions:** 6 parishes, 1 dependency.

Economy: Industries: Food and beverages, textiles, light assembly, tourism. **Chief crops:** Nutmeg, bananas, cocoa, mace. **Resources:** Timber. **Arable land:** 15%. **Livestock** (2001): cattle: 4,400; chickens: 220,000; goats: 7,100; pigs: 5,300; sheep: 13,100. **Electricity prod.:** 0.11 bil. kWh. **Labor force:** services 62%, agri. 24%, ind. 14%.

Finance: Monetary unit: East Caribbean Dollar (Sept. 2002: 2.70 = $1 U.S.). **GDP** (2000 est.): $394 mil. **Per capita GDP:** $4,400. **Imports** (2000 est.): $217.5 mil.; partners (1991): U.S. 31.2%, Caricom 23.6%. **Exports** (2000 est.): $62.3 mil.; partners (1991): Caricom 32.3%, UK 20%. **Tourism:** $63 mil. **Budget** (1997): $102.1 mil. **Intl. reserves less gold** (end 2000): $44 mil. **Consumer prices** (change in 1999): 0.2%.

Transport: Civil aviation: 2 airports. **Chief ports:** Saint George's, Grenville.

Communications: TV sets: 154 per 1,000 pop. **Radios:** 460 per 1,000 pop. **Telephones:** 39,200.

Health: Life expectancy: 62.7 male; 66.3 female. **Births** (per 1,000 pop.): 23.1. **Deaths** (per 1,000 pop.): 7.6. **Natural inc.:** 1.54%. **Infant mortality** (per 1,000 live births): 14.6.

Education: Free, compulsory: ages 5-16. **Literacy** (1994): 85%.

Major Intl. Organizations: UN (FAO, IBRD, ILO, IMF, WHO, WTrO), Caricom, the Commonwealth, OAS, OECS.

Embassy: 1701 New Hampshire Ave. NW 20009; 265-2561.

Website: www.embassy.org/embassies/gd.html

Columbus sighted Grenada in 1498. First European settlers were French, 1650. The island was held alternately by France and England until final British occupation, 1784. Grenada became fully independent Feb. 7, 1974, during a general strike. It is the smallest independent nation in the western hemisphere.

On Oct. 14, 1983, a military coup ousted Prime Minister Maurice Bishop, who was put under house arrest, later freed by supporters, rearrested, and, finally, on Oct. 19, executed. U.S. forces, with a token force from 6 area nations, invaded Grenada, Oct. 25. Resistance from the Grenadian army and Cuban advisors was quickly overcome as most people welcomed the invading forces. U.S. troops left Grenada in June 1985. Cuban Pres. Castro received an enthusiastic greeting when visiting Grenada Aug. 2-3, 1998.

Guatemala

Republic of Guatemala

People: Population: 13,314,079. **Age distrib.** (%): <15: 42.1; 65+: 3.6. **Pop. density:** 318 per sq. mi. **Urban:** 39%. **Ethnic groups:** Mestizo 56%, Amerindian 44%. **Principal languages:** Spanish (official), Mayan languages. **Religion:** Mostly Roman Catholic, some Protestant, traditional Mayan.

Geography: Area: 41,900 sq. mi. **Location:** In Central America. **Neighbors:** Mexico on N and W, El Salvador on S, Honduras and Belize on E. **Topography:** The central highland and mountain areas are bordered by the narrow Pacific coast and the lowlands and fertile river valleys on the Caribbean. There are numerous volcanoes in S, more than half a dozen over 11,000 ft. **Capital:** Guatemala City 3,366,000.

Government: Type: Republic. **Head of state and gov.:** Pres. Alfonso Portillo Cabrera; b Sept. 24, 1951; in office: Jan. 14, 2000. **Local divisions:** 22 departments. **Defense budget (2001): $108.4 mil Active troops:** 31,400.

Economy: Industries: Sugar, textiles, furniture, chemicals, oil. **Chief crops:** Coffee, sugar, bananas, corn, cardamom. **Minerals:** Oil, nickel. **Crude oil reserves** (2000): 526 mil bbls. **Other resources:** Rare woods, fish, chicle. **Arable land:** 12%. **Livestock** (2001): cattle: 2.50 mil; chickens: 35.00 mil.; goats: 111,500; pigs: 1.45 mil; sheep: 552,000. **Fish catch:** (1999): 11,303 metric tons. **Electricity prod.:** 5.93 bil. kWh. **Labor force:** agri. 50%, ind. 15%, services 35%.

Finance: Monetary unit: Quetzal (Sept. 2002: 7.82 = $1 U.S.). **GDP** (2000 est.): $46.2 bil. **Per capita GDP:** $3,700. **Imports** (2000): $4.4 bil.; partners (1998): U.S. 42.8%, Mexico 9.9%. **Exports** (2000): $2.9 bil.; partners (1998): U.S. 51.4%, El Salvador 8.7%. **Tourism:** $570 mil. **Budget** (2001 est.): $1.8 bil. **Intl. reserves less gold** (end 2000): $1.34 bil. **Gold:** 217,000 oz t. **Consumer prices** (change in 2000): 6.0%.

Transport: Railroad: Length: 549 mi. **Motor vehicles:** 102,000 pass. cars, 97,000 comm. vehicles. **Civil aviation:** 228.9 mil pass.-mi.; 2 airports. **Chief ports:** Puerto Barrios, San Jose.

Communications: TV sets: 45 per 1,000 pop. **Radios:** 52 per 1,000 pop. **Telephones:** 1,890,000. **Daily newspaper circ.:** 29 per 1,000 pop.

Health: Life expectancy: 64.2 male; 69.7 female. **Births** (per 1,000 pop.): 34.2. **Deaths** (per 1,000 pop.): 6.7. **Natural inc.:** 2.75%. **Infant mortality** (per 1,000 live births): 44.5.

Education: Free, compulsory: ages 7-14. **Literacy:** 56%.

Major Intl. Organizations: UN (FAO, IBRD, ILO, IMF, IMO, WHO, WTrO), OAS.

Embassy: 2220 R St. NW 20008; 745-4952.

Website: www.guatemala-embassy.org

The old Mayan Indian empire flourished in what is today Guatemala for over 1,000 years before the Spanish.

Guatemala was a Spanish colony 1524-1821; briefly a part of Mexico and then of the U.S. of Central America, the republic was established in 1839.

Since 1945 when a liberal government was elected to replace the long-term dictatorship of Jorge Ubico, the country has seen a variety of military and civilian governments and periods of civil war. Dissident army officers seized power Mar. 23, 1982, denouncing a presidential election as fraudulent and pledging to restore "authentic democracy" to the nation. Political violence caused large numbers of Guatemalans to seek refuge in Mexico. Another military coup occurred Oct. 8, 1983. The nation returned to civilian rule in 1986.

The crisis-ridden government of Pres. Jorge Serrano Elías was ousted by the military June 1, 1993. Ramiro de León Carpio was elected president by Congress June 6. A conservative businessman, Alvaro Arzú Irigoyen, won the presidency, Jan. 7, 1996. On Sept. 19 the Guatemalan government and leftist rebels approved a peace accord; the final agreement was signed Dec. 29. During more than 35 years of armed conflict, some 200,000 people were killed or "disappeared" (and are presumed dead); most of these casualties were attributed to the government and its paramilitary allies.

Violent episodes in 1998 included the daylight ambush of a busload of U.S. college students, Jan. 16, resulting in the rape of five young women, and the murder of Bishop Juan José Girardi, a human rights activist, Apr. 26. U.S. Pres. Bill Clinton, on a visit to Guatemala Mar. 10, 1999, apologized for aid the U.S. had given to forces which he said "engaged in violence and widespread repression." Candidates of the right-wing populist Guatemalan Republican Front won control of Congress, Nov. 7, 1999, and the presidency, Dec. 26. Drought and weak export prices during 2001-02 worsened the plight of Guatemala's poor, who make up 80% of the population.

Guinea

Republic of Guinea

People: Population: 7,775,065. **Age distrib.** (%): <15: 43.1; 65+: 2.7. **Pop. density:** 82 per sq. mi. **Urban:** 32%. **Ethnic groups:** Peuhl 40%, Malinke 30%, Soussou 20%, smaller tribes 10%. **Principal languages:** French (official), tribal languages. **Chief religions:** Muslim 85%, Christian 8%.

Geography: Area: 94,900 sq. mi. **Location:** On Atlantic coast of W Africa. **Neighbors:** Guinea-Bissau, Senegal, Mali on N; Côte d'Ivoire on E; Liberia on S. **Topography:** A narrow coastal belt leads to the mountainous middle region, the source of the Gambia, Senegal, and Niger rivers. Upper Guinea, farther inland, is a cooler upland. The SE is forested. **Capital:** Conakry 1,272,000.

Government: Type: Republic. **Head of state:** Pres. Gen. Lansana Conté; b 1934; in office: Apr. 5, 1984. **Head of gov.:** rem. Lamine Sidimé; b 1944; in office: Mar. 8, 1999. **Local divisions:** 4 administrative regions, 1 special zone. **Defense budget** (2001): $52 mil . **Active troops:** 9,700.

Economy: Industries: Mining, aluminum refining, light manufacturing, agricultural processing. **Chief crops:** Bananas, pineapples, rice, palm kernels, coffee, cassava. **Minerals:** Bauxite, iron, diamonds, gold. **Arable land:** 2%. **Livestock** (2001): cattle: 2.68 mil; chickens: 11.86 mil.; goats: 1.01 mil.; pigs: 97,835; sheep: 892,161. **Fish catch** (1999): 102,589 metric tons. **Electricity prod.:** 0.77 bil. kWh. Labor force: agri. 80%, ind. and services 20%.

Finance: Monetary unit: Franc (Sept. 2002: 1,976.50 = $1 U.S.). **GDP** (2000 est.): $10 bil. **Per capita GDP:** $1,300. **Imports** (2000 est.): $634 mil.; partners (1999): France, Belgium, U.S., Cote d'Ivoire. **Exports** (2000 est.): $820 mil.; partners (1999): U.S., Benelux, Ukraine, Ireland. **Tourism:** $7 mil. **Budget** (2000 est.): $417.7 mil. **Intl. reserves less gold** (end 2000): $114 mil.

Transport: Railroad: Length: 411 mi. **Motor vehicles:** 13,700 pass. cars, 19,300 comm. vehicles. **Civil aviation:** 33.9 mil pass.-mi.; 1 airport. **Chief port:** Conakry.

Communications: TV sets: 10 per 1,000 pop. **Radios:** 34 per 1,000 pop. **Telephones:** 81,200.

Health: Life expectancy: 43.8 male; 48.8 female. **Births** (per 1,000 pop.): 39.5. **Deaths** (per 1,000 pop.): 17.2. **Natural inc.:** 2.23%. **Infant mortality** (per 1,000 live births): 127.1.

Education: Free, compulsory: ages 7-13. **Literacy:** 36%.

Major Intl. Organizations: UN and most of its specialized agencies, AU.

Embassy: 2112 Leroy Pl. NW 20008; 483-9420.

Part of the ancient West African empires, Guinea fell under French control 1849-98. Under Sékou Touré, it opted for full independence in 1958, and France withdrew all aid.

Website: www.embassy.org/gn.html

Touré turned to Communist nations for support and set up a militant one-party state. Thousands of opponents were jailed in the 1970s, in the aftermath of an unsuccessful Portuguese invasion. Many were tortured and killed.

The military took control in a bloodless coup after the March 1984 death of Touré. A new constitution was approved in 1991, but movement toward democracy was slow. When presidential elections were finally held, in Dec. 1993, the incumbent, Gen. Lansana Conté, was the official winner; outside monitors called the elections flawed. Parliamentary elections June 11, 1995, raised similar complaints. Conté suppressed an army mutiny in Conakry, Feb. 2-3, 1996, and won reelection in Dec. 1998.

Fighting in early 2001 along the border with Liberia and Sierra Leone created a refugee crisis; as of mid-2002, more than 100,000 Liberian refugees and over 40,000 Sierra Leoneans remained in Guinea.

Guinea-Bissau

Republic of Guinea-Bissau

People: Population: 1,345,479. **Age distrib.** (%): <15: 42.1; 65+: 2.9. **Pop. density:** 125 per sq. mi. **Urban:** 23%. **Ethnic groups:** Balanta 30%, Fula 20%, Manjaca 14%, Mandinga 13%. **Principal languages:** Portuguese (official), Crioulo, tribal languages. **Chief religions:** Indigenous beliefs 50%, Muslim 45%, Christian 5%.

Geography: Area: 10,800 sq. mi. **Location:** On Atlantic coast of W Africa. **Neighbors:** Senegal on N, Guinea on E and S. **Topography:** A swampy coastal plain covers most of the country; to the east is a low savanna region. **Capital:** Bissau: 292,000.

Government: Type: Republic. **Head of state:** Pres. Kumba Yala; b 1953; in office: Feb. 17, 2000. **Head of gov.:** Prime Min. Alamara Nhassé; b June 2, 1957; in office: Dec. 9, 2001. **Local divisions:** 9 regions. **Defense budget** (2001): $3 mil. **Active troops:** 9,250.

Economy: Chief crops: Food processing, beer, soft drinks. **Minerals:** Bauxite, phosphates. **Arable land:** 11%. **Livestock** (2001): cattle: 515,000; chickens: 1.40 mil.; goats: 325,000; pigs: 350,000; sheep: 285,000. **Electricity prod.:** 0.06 bil. kWh. **Labor force:** 78% agric.

Finance: Monetary unit: CFA Franc (Sept. 2002: 671.78 = $1 U.S.). **GDP** (2000 est.): $1.1 bil. **Per capita GDP:** $850. **Imports** (2000 est.): $55.2 mil.; partners (1998): Portugal 26%, France 8%, Senegal 8%. **Exports** (2000 est.): $80 mil.; partners (1998): India 59%, Singapore 12%. **Budget:** NA. **Intl. reserves less gold** (end 2000): $51 mil. **Consumer prices** (change in 2000): 8.6%.

Transport: Motor vehicles: 3,500 pass. cars, 2,500 comm. vehicles. **Civil aviation:** 6.2 mil pass.-mi.; 2 airports. **Chief port:** Bissau. **Communications: Radios:** 42 per 1,000 pop. **Telephones:** 155,200.

Health: Life expectancy: 47.5 male; 52.2 female. **Births** (per 1,000 pop.): 39. **Deaths** (per 1,000 pop.): 15.1. **Natural inc.:** 2.39%. **Infant mortality** (per 1,000 live births): 108.5.

Education: Compulsory: ages 7-13. **Literacy**: 55%.

Major Intl. Organizations: UN (FAO, IBRD, ILO, IMF, IMO, WHO, WTrO), AU.

Embassy: 1511 K St. NW 20005; 347-3950.

Website: embassy.org/embassies/gw.html

Portuguese mariners explored the area in the mid-15th century; the slave trade flourished in the 17th and 18th centuries, and colonization began in the 19th.

Beginning in the 1960s, an independence movement waged a guerrilla war and formed a government in the interior that had international support. Independence came Sept. 10, 1974, after the Portuguese regime was overthrown.

The November 1980 coup gave Vieira absolute power. Vieira eventually initiated political liberalization; multiparty elections were held July 3, 1994. An army uprising June 7, 1998, triggered a civil war, with Senegal and Guinea aiding the Vieira regime. After a peace accord signed on Nov. 2 broke down, rebel troops ousted Vieira on May 7, 1999. Elections Nov. 28-29, 1999, and Jan. 16, 2000, brought a return of civilian rule.

Guyana

Co-operative Republic of Guyana

People: Population: 698,209. **Age distrib.** (%): <15: 28.2; 65+: 4.9. **Pop. density:** 9 per sq. mi. **Urban:** 38%. **Ethnic groups:** East Indian 49%, black 32%, mixed 12%, Amerindian 6%. **Principal languages:** English (official), Amerindian dialects. **Chief religions:** Christian 57%, Hindu 33%, Muslim 9%.

Geography: Area: 76,000 sq. mi. **Location:** On N coast of South America. **Neighbors:** Venezuela on W, Brazil on S, Suriname on E. **Topography:** Dense tropical forests cover much of the land, although a flat coastal area up to 40 mi. wide, where 90% of the population lives, provides rich alluvial soil for agriculture. A grassy savanna divides the 2 zones. **Capital:** Georgetown (2001 est.): 280,000.

Government: Type: Republic. **Head of state:** Pres. Bharrat Jagdeo; b Jan. 23, 1964; in office: Aug. 11, 1999. **Head of gov.:** Prime Min. Samuel Hinds; b Dec. 27, 1943; in office: Dec. 22, 1997. **Local divisions:** 10 regions. **Defense budget** (2001): $5 mil. **Active troops:** 1,600.

Economy: Industries: Sugar, rice milling, timber, fishing, textiles. **Chief crops:** Sugar, rice. **Minerals:** Bauxite, gold, diamonds. **Other resources:** Timber, shrimp, dairy prods. **Arable land:** 2%. **Livestock** (2001): cattle: 220,000; chickens: 12.50 mil.; goats: 79,000; pigs: 20,000; sheep: 130,000. **Fish catch:** (1999): 57,409 metric tons. **Electricity prod.:** 0.51 bil. kWh. **Labor force:** 39% agric., forestry, fishing; 24% mining, manuf., const.

Finance: Monetary unit: Dollar (Sept. 2002: 179.00 = $1 U.S.). **GDP** (2000 est.): $3.4 bil. **Per capita GDP:** $4,800. **Imports** (2000 est.): $660 mil.; partners (1999): U.S. 29%, Trinidad and Tobago 18%. **Exports** (2000 est.): $570 mil.; partners (1999): U.S. 22%, Canada 22%. **Tourism** (1998): $52 mil. **Budget** (1998): $286.4 mil. **Intl. reserves less gold** (end 2000): $234 mil. **Consumer prices** (change in 2000): 6.1%.

Transport: Motor vehicles: 24,000 pass. cars, 9,000 comm. vehicles. **Civil aviation:** 154.1 mil pass.-mi.; 1 airport. **Chief port:** Georgetown.

Communications: TV sets: 197 per 1,000 pop. **Radios:** 454 per 1,000 pop. **Telephones:** 155,200. **Daily newspaper circ.:** 585 per 1,000 pop.

Health: Life expectancy: 60 male; 65.3 female. **Births** (per 1,000 pop.): 17.9. **Deaths** (per 1,000 pop.): 9.3. **Natural inc.:** 0.86%. **Infant mortality** (per 1,000 live births): 38.4.

Education: Free, compulsory: ages 6-14. **Literacy**: 98%.

Major Intl. Organizations: UN (FAO, IBRD, ILO, IMF, IMO, WHO, WTrO), Caricom, the Commonwealth, OAS.

Embassy: 2490 Tracy Pl. NW 20008; 265-6900.

Website: guyana.org/govt/embassy.html

Guyana became a Dutch possession in the 17th century, but sovereignty passed to Britain in 1815. Indentured servants from India soon outnumbered African slaves. Ethnic tension has affected political life.

Guyana became independent May 26, 1966. A Venezuelan claim to the western half of Guyana was suspended in 1970 but renewed in 1982; an agreement was reached in 1989. The Suriname border is disputed. The government has nationalized most of the economy, which has remained severely depressed.

The Port Kaituma ambush of U.S. Rep. Leo J. Ryan and others investigating mistreatment of American followers of the Rev. Jim Jones's People's Temple cult triggered a mass suicide-execution of 911 cultists at Jonestown in the jungle, Nov. 18, 1978.

The People's National Congress, the party in power since Guyana became independent, was voted out of office with the election of Cheddi Jagan in Oct. 1992. When Pres. Jagan died Mar. 6, 1997, Prime Min. Samuel Hinds succeeded him; his widow, Janet Jagan, became prime min. Mar. 17. She won the presidency in a disputed election Dec. 15. She resigned because of ill health Aug. 11, 1999, and was succeeded by Bharrat Jagdeo, then 35, who became the youngest head of state in the Americas. He was reelected Mar. 19, 2001.

Haiti

Republic of Haiti

People: Population: 7,063,722. **Age distrib.** (%): <15: 40.3; 65+: 4.2. **Pop. density:** 666 per sq. mi. **Urban:** 35%. **Ethnic groups:** Black 95%. **Principal languages:** Haitian Creole, French (both official). **Chief religions:** Roman Catholic 80%, Protestant 16%; Voodoo widely practiced.

Geography: Area: 10,600 sq. mi. **Location:** In Caribbean, occupies western third of Isl. of Hispaniola. **Neighbors:** Dominican Republic on E, Cuba to W. **Topography:** About two-thirds of Haiti is mountainous. Much of the rest is semiarid. Coastal areas are warm and moist. **Capital:** Port-au-Prince 1,838,000.

Government: Type: Republic. **Head of state:** Pres. Jean-Baptiste Aristide; b July 15, 1953; in office Feb. 7, 2001. **Head of gov.:** Yvon Neptune; b Nov. 8, 1946; in office: Mar. 12, 2002. **Local divisions:** 9 departments. **Defense budget:** NA. **Active troops:** NA.

Economy: Industries: Sugar refining, flour milling, textiles. **Chief crops:** Coffee, sugar, mangoes, corn, rice. **Arable land:** 20%. **Livestock** (2001): cattle: 1.44 mil; chickens: 5.50 mil.; goats: 1.94 mil.; pigs: 1.00 mil; sheep: 152,000. **Electricity prod.:** 0.52 bil. kWh. **Labor force:** agri. 66%, services 25%, ind. 9%.

Finance: Monetary unit: Gourde (Sept. 2002: 28.50 = $1 U.S.). **GDP** (2000 est.): $12.7 bil. **Per capita GDP:** $1,800. **Imports** (1999): $1.2 bil.; partners (1999): U.S. 60%, EU 13%. **Exports** (1999): $186 mil.; partners (1999): U.S. 89%, EU 8%. **Tourism** (1998): $57 mil. **Budget** (FY99/00 est.): $362 mil. **Intl. reserves less gold** (end 2000): $141 mil. **Gold:** 1,000 oz t. **Consumer prices** (change in 2000): 13.7%.

Transport: Motor vehicles: 32,000 pass. cars, 21,000 comm. vehicles. **Civil aviation:** 2 airports. **Chief ports:** Port-au-Prince, Les Cayes, Cap-Haitien.

Communications: TV sets: 4 per 1,000 pop. **Radios:** 41 per 1,000 pop. **Telephones:** 171,500. **Daily newspaper circ.:** 7 per 1,000 pop.

Health: Life expectancy: 47.9 male; 51.3 female. **Births** (per 1,000 pop.): 31.4. **Deaths** (per 1,000 pop.): 14.9. **Natural inc.:** 1.65%. **Infant mortality** (per 1,000 live births): 93.3.

Education: Compulsory: ages 6-12. **Literacy**: 45%.

Major Intl. Organizations: UN and most of its specialized agencies, OAS.

Embassy: 2311 Massachusetts Ave. NW 20008; 332-4090.

Website: www.haitifocus.com/haitie/gov.html

Haiti, visited by Columbus, 1492, and a French colony from 1697, attained its independence, 1804, following the rebellion led by former slave Toussaint L'Ouverture. Following a period of political violence, the U.S. occupied the country 1915-34.

Francois Duvalier was elected president in Sept. 1957; in 1964 he was named president for life. Upon his death in 1971, he was succeeded by his son, Jean Claude. Drought in 1975-77 brought famine, and Hurricane Allen in 1980 destroyed most of the rice, bean, and coffee crops. Following several weeks of unrest, President Jean Claude Duvalier fled Haiti aboard a U.S. Air Force jet Feb. 7, 1986, ending the 28-year dictatorship by the Duvalier family.

A military-civilian council headed by Gen. Henri Namphy assumed control. In 1987, voters approved a new constitution, but the Jan. 1988 elections were marred by violence and boycotted by the opposition. Gen. Namphy seized control, June 20, but was ousted by a military coup in Sept.

Father Jean-Bertrand Aristide was elected president Dec. 1990. In Sept. 1991, Aristide was arrested by the military and expelled from the country. Some 35,000 Haitian refugees were intercepted by the U.S. Coast Guard as they tried to enter the U.S., 1991-92. Most were returned to Haiti. There was a new upsurge of refugees starting in late 1993.

The UN imposed a worldwide oil, arms, and financial embargo on Haiti June 23, 1993. The embargo was suspended when the military agreed to Aristide's return to power on Oct. 30, but the military effectively blocked his return. After renewed sanctions, the UN Security Council authorized, July 31, 1994, an invasion of Haiti by a multinational force. With U.S. troops already en route, an invasion was averted, Sept. 18, by a new agreement for military leaders to step down and Aristide to resume office. As part of the agreement, thousands of U.S. troops began arriving in Haiti, Sept. 19. Aristide returned to Haiti and was restored in office Oct. 15. A UN peacekeeping force exercised responsibility in Haiti from Mar. 31, 1995 to Nov. 30, 1997.

Aristide transferred power to his elected successor, René Préval, on Feb. 7, 1996. Prime Min. Rosny Smarth announced his resignation June 9, 1997, and quit running the government Oct. 20, but Préval and Parliament deadlocked for another 17 months until a successor was appointed by presidential decree. At least 140 people died and more than 160,000 became homeless when Hurricane Georges struck Haiti Sept. 22, 1998.

Aristide's Lavalas Family party swept parliamentary and local elections, May 21 and June 9, 2000. Aristide won the presidency Nov. 26, 2000, in an election boycotted by opposition groups. A coup attempt Dec. 17, 2001, was suppressed.

Honduras

Republic of Honduras

People: Population: 6,560,608. **Age distrib.** (%): <15: 42.2; 65+: 3.6. **Pop. density:** 152 per sq. mi. **Urban:** 52%. **Ethnic groups:** Mestizo 90%, Amerindian 7%. **Principal language:** Spanish (official). **Chief religion:** Roman Catholic 97%.

Geography: Area: 43,200 sq. mi. **Location:** In Central America. **Neighbors:** Guatemala on W, El Salvador and Nicaragua on S. **Topography:** The Caribbean coast is 500 mi. long. Pacific coast, on Gulf of Fonseca, is 40 mi. long. Honduras is mountainous, with wide fertile valleys and rich forests. **Capital:** Tegucigalpa 980,000.

Government: Type: Republic. **Head of state:** Pres. Ricardo Maduro; b Apr. 20, 1946; in office: Jan. 27, 2002. **Local divisions:** 18 departments. **Defense budget (2001):** $35 mil. **Active troops:** 8,300.

Economy: Industries: Sugar, coffee, textiles, clothing, wood products. **Chief crops:** Bananas, coffee, citrus. **Minerals:** Gold, silver, copper, lead, zinc, iron, antimony, coal. **Other resources:** Timber, fish. **Arable land:** 15%. **Livestock** (2001): cattle: 1.72 mil; chickens: 18.00 mil.; goats: 32,000; pigs: 480,000; sheep: 13,700. **Fish catch:** (1999): 23,585 metric tons. **Electricity prod.:** 3.57 bil. kWh. **Labor force:** agri. 29%, ind. 21%, services 50%.

Finance: Monetary unit: Lempira (Sept. 2002: 16.65 = $1 U.S.). **GDP** (2000 est.): $17 bil. **Per capita GDP:** $2,700. **Imports** (2000 est.): $2.8 bil.; partners (1999): U.S. 47.1%, Guatemala 7.4%. **Exports** (2000 est.): $2 bil.; partners (1999): U.S. 35.4%, Germany 7.5%. **Tourism:** $165 mil. **Budget** (1999 est.): $411.9 mil. **Intl. reserves less gold** (end 2000): $1.01 bil. **Gold:** 21,000 oz t. **Consumer prices** (change in 2000): 11.1%.

Transport: Railroad: Length: 614 mi. **Motor vehicles:** 80,000 pass. cars, 105,000 comm. vehicles. **Civil aviation:**

189.5 mil pass.-mi.; 8 airports. **Chief ports:** Puerto Cortes, La Ceiba.

Communications: TV sets: 29 per 1,000 pop. **Radios:** 337 per 1,000 pop. **Telephones:** 547,300. **Daily newspaper circ.:** 45 per 1,000 pop.

Health: Life expectancy: 67.1 male; 70.5 female. **Births** (per 1,000 pop.): 31.2. **Deaths** (per 1,000 pop.): 5.7. **Natural inc.:** 2.55%. **Infant mortality** (per 1,000 live births): 30.5.

Education: Free, compulsory: ages 7-13. **Literacy:** 73%.

Major Intl. Organizations: UN, (FAO, IBRD, ILO, IMF, IMO, WHO, WTrO), OAS.

Embassy: 3007 Tilden St. NW 20008; 966-7702.

Website: www.hondurasemb.org

Mayan civilization flourished in Honduras in the 1st millennium AD. Columbus arrived in 1502. Honduras became independent after freeing itself from Spain, 1821, and from the Fed. of Central America, 1838.

Gen. Oswaldo Lopez Arellano, president for most of the period 1963-75 by virtue of one election and 2 coups, was ousted by the army in 1975 over charges of pervasive bribery by United Brands Co. of the U.S. An elected civilian government took power in 1982. Some 3,200 U.S. troops were sent to Honduras after the Honduran border was violated by Nicaraguan forces, Mar. 1988.

Already one of the poorest countries in the western hemisphere, Honduras was devastated in late Oct. 1998 by Hurricane Mitch, which killed at least 5,600 people and caused more than $850 million in damage to crops and livestock. Ricardo Maduro, a businessman who pledged to crack down on crime, was elected president Nov. 25, 2001.

Hungary

Republic of Hungary

People: Population: 10,075,034. **Age distrib.** (%): <15: 16.6; 65+: 14.7. **Pop. density:** 282 per sq. mi. **Urban:** 64%. **Ethnic groups:** Hungarian 90%, Gypsy 4%, German 3%. **Principal language:** Hungarian (Magyar; official). **Chief religions:** Roman Catholic 68%, Calvinist 20%, Lutheran 5%.

Geography: Area: 35,700 sq. mi. **Location:** In E central Europe. **Neighbors:** Slovakia, Ukraine on N; Austria on W; Slovenia, Yugoslavia, Croatia on S; Romania on E. **Topography:** The Danube R. forms the Slovak border in the NW, then swings S to bisect the country. The eastern half of Hungary is mainly a great fertile plain, the Alfold; the W and N are hilly. **Capital:** Budapest, 1,812,000.

Government: Type: Parliamentary democracy. **Head of state:** Pres. Ferenc Mádl; b Jan. 29, 1931; in office: Aug. 4, 2000. **Head of gov.:** Prime Min. Péter Medgyessy; b Oct. 19, 1942; in office: May 27, 2002. **Local divisions:** 19 counties, 20 urban counties, 1 capital. **Defense budget** (2001): $805 mil. **Active troops:** 33,810.

Economy: Industries: Mining, metallurgy, construction materials, processed foods. **Chief crops:** Wheat, corn, sunflowers, potatoes, sugar beets. **Minerals:** Bauxite, coal, gas. **Crude oil reserves** (2001): **0.1 bil bbls. Arable land:** 51%. **Livestock** (2001): cattle: 805,000; chickens: 30.72 mil.; goats: 150,000; pigs: 4.83 mil; sheep: 1.13 mil . **Fish catch** (1999): 21,916 metric tons. **Electricity prod.:** 33.44 bil. kWh. **Labor force:** services 65%, ind. 27%, agri. 8%.

Finance: Monetary unit: Forint (Sept. 2002: 249.39 = $1 U.S.). **GDP** (2000 est.): $113.9 bil. **Per capita GDP:** $11,200. **Imports** (2000): $27.6 bil.; partners (2000): Germany 25%, Russia 8%. **Exports** (2000): $25.2 bil.; partners (2000): Germany 37%, Austria 9%. **Tourism:** $3.39 bil. **Budget** (2000 est.): $14.4 bil. **Intl. reserves less gold** (end 2000): $8.59 bil. **Gold:** 101,000 oz t. **Consumer prices** (change in 2000): 9.8%.

Transport: Railroad: Length: 8,190 mi. **Motor vehicles:** 2.28 mil pass. cars, 319,424 comm. vehicles. **Civil aviation:** 1.5 bil. pass.-mi.; 1 airport.

Communications: TV sets: 438 per 1,000 pop. **Radios:** 689 per 1,000 pop. **Telephones:** 8,698,000. **Daily newspaper circ.:** 186 per 1,000 pop.

Health: Life expectancy: 67.5 male; 76.5 female. **Births** (per 1,000 pop.): 9.3. **Deaths** (per 1,000 pop.): 13.1. **Natural inc.:** -0.38%. **Infant mortality** (per 1,000 live births): 8.8.

Education: Compulsory: ages 6-16. **Literacy** (1993): 99%.

Major Intl. Organizations: UN (FAO, IBRD, ILO, IMF, IMO, WHO, WTrO), NATO, OECD, OSCE.

Embassy: 3910 Shoemaker St. NW 20008; 966-7726.

Website: www.eKormanyzat.hu/english

Earliest settlers, chiefly Slav and Germanic, were overrun by Magyars from the E. Stephen I (997-1038) was made king by Pope Sylvester II in AD 1000. The country suffered repeated Turkish invasions in the 15th-17th centuries. After the defeats of the Turks, 1686-1697, Austria dominated, but Hungary obtained concessions until it regained internal independence in 1867, with the emperor of Austria as king of Hungary in a dual monarchy with a single diplomatic service. Defeated with the Central Powers in 1918, Hungary lost Transylvania to Romania, Croatia and Bacska to Yugoslavia, Slovakia and Carpatho-Ruthenia to Czechoslovakia, all of which had large Hungarian minorities. A republic under Michael Karolyi and a bolshevist revolt under Bela Kun were followed by a vote for a monarchy in 1920 with Admiral Nicholas Horthy as regent.

Hungary joined Germany in World War II, and was allowed to annex most of its lost territories. Russian troops captured the country, 1944-1945. By terms of an armistice with the Allied powers Hungary agreed to give up territory acquired by the 1938 dismemberment of Czechoslovakia and to return to its borders of 1937.

A republic was declared Feb. 1, 1946; Zoltan Tildy was elected president. In 1947 the Communists forced Tildy out. Premier Imre Nagy, who had been in office since mid-1953, was ousted for his moderate policy of favoring agriculture and consumer production, April 18, 1955.

In 1956, popular demands to oust Erno Gero, Communist Party secretary, and for formation of a government by Nagy, resulted in the latter's appointment Oct. 23; demonstrations against Communist rule developed into open revolt. On Nov. 4 Soviet forces launched a massive attack against Budapest with 200,000 troops, 2,500 tanks and armored cars.

About 200,000 persons fled the country. Thousands were arrested and executed, including Nagy in June 1958. In spring 1963 the regime freed many captives from the 1956 revolt.

Hungarian troops participated in the 1968 Warsaw Pact invasion of Czechoslovakia. Major economic reforms were launched early in 1968, switching from a central planning system to one based on market forces and profit.

In 1989 Parliament passed legislation legalizing freedom of assembly and association as Hungary shifted away from communism. In Oct. the Communist Party was formally dissolved. The last Soviet troops left Hungary June 19, 1991. Hungary became a full member of NATO on Mar. 12, 1999.

Iceland

Republic of Iceland

People: Population: 279,384. **Age distrib.** (%): <15: 23.2; 65+: 11.8. **Pop. density:** 7 per sq. mi. **Urban:** 92%. **Ethnic groups:** Homogeneous descendants of Norwegians, Celts. **Principal language:** Icelandic (Islenska; official). **Chief religion:** Evangelical Lutheran 96%.

Geography: Area: 38,700 sq. mi. **Location:** Isl. at N end of Atlantic O. **Neighbors:** Nearest is Greenland (Den.), to W. **Topography:** Recent volcanic origin. Three-quarters of the surface is wasteland: glaciers, lakes, a lava desert. There are geysers and hot springs, and the climate is moderated by the Gulf Stream. **Capital:** Reykjavík 175,000.

Government: Type: Constitutional republic. **Head of state:** Pres. Olafur Ragnar Grímsson; b May 14, 1943; in office: Aug. 1, 1996. **Head of gov.:** Prime Min. David Oddsson; Jan. 17, 1948; in office: Apr. 30, 1991. **Local divisions:** 23 counties, 14 independent towns. **Defense budget:** Icelandic Defense Force provided by the U.S.

Economy: Industries: Fish processing, aluminum smelting. **Chief crops:** Potatoes, turnips. **Livestock** (2001): cattle: 72,000; chickens: 180,000; goats: 400; pigs: 44,000; sheep: 465,000. **Fish catch** (1999): 2.21 mil metric tons. **Electricity prod.:** 7.55 bil. kWh. **Labor force:** agri. 5.1%, fishing and fish processing 11.8%, manufacturing 12.9%, construction 10.7%, other services 59.5%.

Finance: Monetary unit: Krona (Sept. 2002: 87.69 = $1 U.S.). Euro (Sept 2001: 1.09 = $1 U.S.). **GDP** (2000 est.): $6.85 bil. **Per capita GDP:** $24,800. **Imports** (2000): $2.2 bil.; partners (1999): EU 56%, U.S. 11%, Norway 10%. **Exports** (2000): $2 bil.; partners (1999): EU 64%,U.S. 15%. **Tourism** (1998): $207 mil. **Budget** (1999): $3.3 bil. **Intl. reserves less gold** (end 2000): $298 mil. **Gold:** 59,000 oz t. **Consumer prices** (change in 2000): 5.2%.

Transport: Motor vehicles (1997): 132,468 pass. cars, 17,511 comm. vehicles. **Civil aviation:** 2.0 bil. pass.-mi.; 24 airports. **Chief port:** Reykjavík.

Communications: TV sets: 285 per 1,000 pop. **Radios:** 733 per 1,000 pop. **Telephones:** 425,900. **Daily newspaper circ.:** 515 per 1,000 pop.

Health: Life expectancy: 77.4 male; 82.1 female. **Births** (per 1,000 pop.): 14.4. **Deaths** (per 1,000 pop.): 6.9. **Natural inc.:** 0.74%. **Infant mortality** (per 1,000 live births): 3.5.

Education: Free, compulsory: ages 7-15. **Literacy** (1997): 100%.

Major Intl. Organizations: UN (FAO, IBRD, ILO, IMF, IMO, WHO, WTrO), EFTA, NATO, OECD, OSCE.

Embassy: Suite 1200, 1156 15th St. NW 20005; 265-6653.

Website: www.brunnur.stjr.is/interpro/stjr/stjr.nsf/pages/english–index

Iceland was an independent republic from 930 to 1262, when it joined with Norway. Its language has maintained its purity for 1,000 years. Danish rule lasted from 1380-1918; the last ties with the Danish crown were severed in 1941. The Althing, or assembly, is the world's oldest surviving parliament.

India

Republic of India

People: Population: 1,045,845,226. **Age distrib.** (%): <15: 33.1; 65+: 4.7. **Pop. density:** 911 per sq. mi. **Urban:** 28%. **Ethnic groups:** Indo-Aryan 72%, Dravidian 25%. **Principal languages:** Hindi (official), English (associate official), 14 regional official languages, others. **Chief religions:** Hindu 80%, Muslim 14%.

Geography: Area: 1,148,000 sq. mi. **Location:** Occupies most of the Indian subcontinent in S Asia. **Neighbors:** Pakistan on W; China, Nepal, Bhutan on N; Myanmar, Bangladesh on E. **Topography:** The Himalaya Mts., highest in world, stretch across India's northern borders. Below, the Ganges Plain is wide, fertile, and among the most densely populated regions of the world. The area below includes the Deccan Peninsula. Close to one quarter of the area is forested. The climate varies from tropical heat in S to near-Arctic cold in N. Rajasthan Desert is in NW; NE Assam Hills get 400 in. of rain a year. **Capital:** New Delhi (2001 city est.) 300,000. **Cities** (urban aggr.): Mumbai (Bombay) 16,086,000; Kolkata (Calcutta) 13,058,000; Delhi 12,987,000; Hyderabad 5,445,000; Chennai (Madras) 6,353,000; Bangalore 5,567,000.

Government: Type: Federal republic. **Head of state:** Pres. A. P. J. Abdul Kalam; b Oct. 15, 1931; in office: July 25, 2002. **Head of gov.:** Prime Min. Atal Bihari Vajpayee; b Dec. 25, 1924; in office Mar. 19, 1998. **Local divisions:** 28 states, 6 union territories, 1 national capital territory. **Defense budget** (2001): $15.6 bil. **Active troops:** 1,263,000

Economy: Industries: Textiles, chemicals, food processing, steel, transportation equip., cement, mining. **Chief crops:** Rice, grains, sugar, spices, tea, cashews, cotton, potatoes, jute, oilseed. **Minerals:** Coal (4th largest reserves in the world), iron, manganese, mica, bauxite, titanium, chromite, diamonds, gas, oil. **Crude oil reserves** (2001): 3.3 bil bbls. **Other resources:** Timber. **Arable land:** 56%. **Livestock** (2001): cattle: 219.64 mil; chickens: 413.40 mil.; goats: 123.50 mil.; pigs: 17.50 mil; sheep: 58.20 mil. **Fish catch** (1999): 5.38 mil metric tons. **Electricity prod.:** 547.12 bil. kWh. **Labor force:** agri. 67%, services 18%, ind. 15%.

Finance: Monetary unit: Rupee (Sept. 2002: 48.38 = $1 U.S.). **GDP** (2000 est.): $2.2 tril. **Per capita GDP:** $2,200. **Imports** (2000): $60.8 bil.; partners (1999): U.S. 9%, Benelux 8%. **Exports** (2000): $43.1 bil.; partners (1999): U.S. 22%, UK 6%. **Tourism:** $3.04 bil. **Budget** (FY00/01 est.): $73.6 bil. **Intl. reserves less gold** (end 2000): $29.09 bil. **Gold:** 11.50 mil oz t. **Consumer prices** (change in 2000): 4.0%.

Transport: Railroad: Length: 38,935 mi. **Motor vehicles:** 4.25 mil pass. cars, 2.51 mil comm. vehicles. **Civil aviation:** 15.0 bil pass.-mi.; 66 airports. **Chief ports:** Kolkata (Calcutta), Mumbai (Bombay), Chennai (Madras), Vishakhapatnam, Kandla.

Communications: TV sets: 68 per 1,000 pop. **Radios:** 117 per 1,000 pop. **Telephones:** 41,162,900. **Daily newspaper circ.:** 21 per 1,000 pop.

Health: Life expectancy: 62.5 male; 63.9 female. **Births** (per 1,000 pop.): 23.8. **Deaths** (per 1,000 pop.): 8.6. **Natural inc.:** 1.52%. **Infant mortality** (per 1,000 live births): 61.5.

Education: Theoretically compulsory in 23 states to age 14. **Literacy**: 52%.

Major Intl. Organizations: UN (FAO, IBRD, ILO, IMF, IMO, WHO, WTrO), the Commonwealth.

Embassy: 2107 Massachusetts Ave. NW 20008; 939-7000.

Website: www.nic.in; www.indianembassy.org

India has one of the oldest civilizations in the world. Excavations trace the Indus Valley civilization back for at least 5,000 years. Paintings in the mountain caves of Ajanta, richly carved temples, the Taj Mahal in Agra, and the Kutab Minar in Delhi are among relics of the past.

Aryan tribes, speaking Sanskrit, invaded from the NW around 1500 BC, and merged with the earlier inhabitants to create classical Indian civilization.

Asoka ruled most of the Indian subcontinent in the 3d century BC, and established Buddhism. But Hinduism revived and eventually predominated. During the Gupta kingdom, 4th-6th century AD, science, literature, and the arts enjoyed a "golden age."

Arab invaders established a Muslim foothold in the W in the 8th century, and Turkish Muslims gained control of North India by 1200. The Mogul emperors ruled 1526-1857.

Vasco da Gama established Portuguese trading posts 1498-1503. The Dutch followed. The British East India Co. sent Capt. William Hawkins, 1609, to get concessions from the Mogul emperor for spices and textiles. Operating as the East India Co. the British gained control of most of India. The British parliament assumed political direction; under Lord Bentinck, 1828-35, rule by rajahs was curbed. After the Sepoy troops mutinied, 1857-58, the British supported the native rulers.

Nationalism grew rapidly after World War I. The Indian National Congress and the Muslim League demanded constitutional reform. A leader emerged in Mohandas K. Gandhi (called Mahatma, or Great Soul), born Oct. 2, 1869, assassinated Jan. 30, 1948. He advocated self-rule, nonviolence, and removal of the caste system of untouchability. In 1930 he launched a program of civil disobedience, including a boycott of British goods and rejection of taxes without representation.

In 1935 Britain gave India a constitution providing a bicameral federal congress. Muhammad Ali Jinnah, head of the Muslim League, sought creation of a Muslim nation, Pakistan.

The British government partitioned British India into the dominions of India and Pakistan. India became a member of the UN in 1945, a self-governing member of the Commonwealth in 1947, and a democratic republic, Jan. 26, 1950. More than 12 million Hindu and Muslim refugees crossed the India-Pakistan borders in a mass transferral of some of the 2 peoples during 1947; about 200,000 were killed in communal fighting.

After Pakistan troops began attacks on Bengali separatists in East Pakistan, Mar. 25, 1971, some 10 million refugees fled into India. India and Pakistan went to war Dec. 3, 1971, on both the East and West fronts. Pakistan troops in the east surrendered Dec. 16; Pakistan agreed to a cease-fire in the west Dec. 17.

Indira Gandhi, India's prime minister since Jan. 1966, invoked emergency powers in June 1975. Thousands of opponents were arrested and press censorship imposed. These and other actions, including enforcement of coercive birth control measures in some areas, were widely resented. Opposition parties, united in the Janata coalition, turned Gandhi's New Congress Party from power in federal and state parliamentary elections in 1977.

Gandhi became prime minister for the second time, Jan. 14, 1980. She was assassinated by 2 of her Sikh bodyguards Oct. 31, 1984, in response to the government suppression of a Sikh uprising in Punjab in June 1984, which included an assault on the Golden Temple at Amritsar, the holiest Sikh shrine. Widespread rioting followed the assassination; thousands of Sikhs were killed and some 50,000 left homeless. Rajiv, Indira Gandhi's son, replaced her as prime minister. He was swept from office in 1989 amid charges of incompetence and corruption, and assassinated May 21, 1991, while campaigning to recapture the prime ministership.

A gas leak at a Union Carbide chemical plant in Bhopal, in Dec. 1984, eventually killed an estimated 14,000 people. A lawsuit settled in 1989 provided $470 mil. in compensation to victms; in 2002 an Indian High Court upheld a culpable homicide conviction against former UC chairman Warren Anderson.

Sikhs ignited several violent clashes during the 1980s. The government's May 1987 decision to bring the state of Punjab under rule of the central government led to violence. Many died during a government siege of the Golden Temple, May 1988. In Assam in NW India, thousands were killed in ethnic violence in Feb. 1993.

Nationwide riots followed the destruction of a 16th-century mosque by Hindu militants in Dec. 1992. In the biggest wave of criminal violence in Indian history, a series of bombs jolted Bombay and Calcutta, Mar. 12-19, 1993, killing over 300.

Corruption scandals dominated Indian politics in the mid-1990s. After an inconclusive election, a Hindu nationalist party was unable to form a government, and a center-left coalition took office June 1, 1996.

India's 1st lowest-caste pres., K. R. Narayanan, took office July 25, 1997. Mother Teresa of Calcutta, renowned for her work among the poor, died Sept. 5. Parliamentary elections in Feb. 1998 resulted in a Hindu nationalist victory, and Atal Bihari Vajpayee was sworn in as prime minister Mar. 19. India conducted a series of nuclear tests in mid-May, drawing worldwide condemnation and raising tensions with Pakistan.

An alliance led by Vajpayee won a majority in legislative elections, Sept. 5-Oct. 3, 1999. A cyclone that hit the state of Orissa, E India, on Oct. 29, 1999, left some 10,000 people dead. A powerful earthquake in Gujarat state on Jan. 26, 2001, claimed more than 20,000 lives and left more than 166,00 people injured. India blamed Pakistani-sponsored terrorist groups for an Oct. 1 suicide attack on the state legislature in Jammu and Kashmir (see below), in which at least 40 people died, and a Dec. 13 assault on the Indian parliament in New Delhi Dec. 13, which left 13 people dead. Hindu-Muslim clashes in Gujarat Feb. 27-Mar. 11, 2002, claimed more than 700 lives. A. P. J. Abdul Kalam, a Muslim scientist who spearheaded India's nuclear weapons program, became president July 25.

Sikkim, bordered by Tibet, Bhutan, and Nepal, formerly British protected, became a protectorate of India in 1950. Area, 2,740 sq. mi; pop., 1994 est., 444,000; capital: Gangtok. In Sept. 1974, India's parliament voted to make Sikkim an associate Indian state, absorbing it into India.

Kashmir, a predominantly Muslim region in the NW, has been in dispute between India and Pakistan since 1947. A cease-fire was negotiated by the UN Jan. 1, 1949; it gave Pakistan control of one-third of the area, in the west and northwest, and India the remaining two-thirds, the Indian state of **Jammu and Kashmir**, which enjoys internal autonomy.

In the 1990s there were repeated clashes between Indian army troops and pro-independence demonstrators triggered by

India's decision to impose central government rule. The clashes strained relations between India and Pakistan, which India charged was aiding the Muslim separatists; the heaviest fighting in more than 2 decades took place during May-June 1999. As 2002 began, some 1 million Indian and Pakistani troops faced each other across the "line of control" that divides Kashmir. Tensions escalated when Muslin gunmen May 14 killed 34 people, many of them women and children, at an army base near Jammu, and Pakistan conducted missile tests May 25-28. U.S. mediation in June helped ease the crisis.

France, 1952-54, peacefully yielded to India its 5 colonies, former French India, comprising Pondicherry, Karikal, Mahe, Yanaon (which became **Pondicherry Union Territory**, area 190 sq. mi; pop., 1994 est., 894,000) and Chandernagor (which was incorporated into the state of **West Bengal**).

Indonesia

Republic of Indonesia

People: Population: 232,073,071. **Age distrib.** (%): <15: 30.3; 65+: 4.6. **Pop. density:** 329 per sq. mi. **Urban:** 40%. **Ethnic groups:** Javanese 45%, Sundanese 14%, Madurese 8%, Malay 8%. **Principal languages:** Bahasa Indonesian (official), English, Dutch, Javanese. **Chief religions:** Muslim 87%, Protestant 6%.

Geography: Area: 705,200 sq. mi. **Location:** Archipelago SE of Asian mainland along the Equator. **Neighbors:** Malaysia on N, Papua New Guinea on E. **Topography:** Indonesia comprises over 13,500 islands (6,000 inhabited), including Java (one of the most densely populated areas in the world with over 2,000 persons per sq. mi.), Sumatra, Kalimantan (most of Borneo), Sulawesi (Celebes), and West Irian (Irian Jaya, the W half of New Guinea). Also: Bangka, Billiton, Madura, Bali, Timor. The mountains and plateaus on the major islands have a cooler climate than the tropical lowlands. **Capital:** Jakarta. **Cities** (urban aggr.): Jakarta 11,429,000, (2000 city proper: 8.8 mil); Bandung 3,409,000; Surabaja 2,461,000.

Government: Type: Republic. **Head of state and gov.:** Megawati Sukarnoputri; b Jan. 23, 1947; in office: July 23, 2001. **Local divisions:** 30 provinces, 2 special regions, 1 capital district. **Defense budget** (2000): $1.3 bil. **Active troops:** 297,000.

Economy: Industries: Oil & gas, textiles, apparel, mining, cement. **Chief crops:** Rice, cocoa, peanuts, rubber. **Minerals:** Nickel, tin, oil, bauxite, copper, gas. **Crude oil reserves** (2001): 9.7 bil bbls. **Other resources:** Timber. **Arable land:** 10%. **Livestock** (2001): cattle: 11.19 mil; chickens: 750.95 mil.; goats: 12.46 mil.; pigs: 5.90 mil; sheep: 7.43 mil. **Fish catch** (1999): 4.40 mil metric tons. **Electricity prod.:** 92.58 bil. kWh. **Labor force:** agri. 45%, ind. 16%, services 39%.

Finance: Monetary unit: Rupiah (Sept. 2002: 9,010 = $1 U.S.). **GDP** (2000 est.): $654 bil. **Per capita GDP:** $2,900. **Imports** (2000 est.): $40.4 bil.; partners (1999 est.): Japan 12%, U.S. 12%. **Exports** (2000 est.): $64.7 bil.; partners (1999 est.): Japan 21%, U.S. 14%. **Tourism** (1998): $4.05 bil. **Budget** (2000 est.): $30 bil. **Intl. reserves less gold** (end 2000): $17.31 bil. **Gold:** 3.10 mil oz t. **Consumer prices** (change in 2000): 3.7%.

Transport: Railroad: Length: 4,090 mi. **Motor vehicles** (1997): 2.64 mil pass. cars, 2.16 mil comm. vehicles. **Civil aviation:** 14.6 bil pass.-mi.; 81 airports. **Chief ports:** Jakarta, Surabaya, Palembang, Semarang, Ujungpandang.

Communications: TV sets: 134 per 1,000 pop. **Radios:** 128 per 1,000 pop. **Telephones:** 13,252,200. **Daily newspaper circ.:** 23 per 1,000 pop.

Health: Life expectancy: 66.2 male; 71.1 female. **Births** (per 1,000 pop.): 21.9. **Deaths** (per 1,000 pop.): 6.3. **Natural inc.:** 1.56%. **Infant mortality** (per 1,000 live births): 39.6.

Education: Compulsory: ages 7-16. **Literacy**: 84%.

Major Intl. Organizations: UN and all of its specialized agencies, APEC, ASEAN, OPEC.

Embassy: 2020 Massachusetts Ave. NW 20036; 775-5200.

Websites: www.indonesiamission–ny.org/
www.embassy.org/embassy.org/embassies/id.html

Hindu and Buddhist civilization from India reached Indonesia nearly 2,000 years ago, taking root especially in Java. Islam spread along the maritime trade routes in the 15th century, and became predominant by the 16th century. The Dutch replaced the Portuguese as the area's most important European trade power in the 17th century, securing territorial control over Java by 1750. The outer islands were not finally subdued until the early 20th century, when the full area of present-day Indonesia was united under one rule for the first time.

Following Japanese occupation, 1942-45, nationalists led by Sukarno and Hatta declared independence. The Netherlands ceded sovereignty Dec. 27, 1949, after 4 years of fighting. A republic was declared, Aug. 17, 1950, with Sukarno as president. West Irian, on New Guinea, remained under Dutch control. After the Dutch in 1957 rejected proposals for new negotiations over West Irian, Indonesia stepped up the seizure of Dutch property. In 1963 the UN turned the area over to Indonesia, which promised a plebiscite. In 1969, voting by tribal chiefs favored staying with Indonesia, despite an uprising and widespread opposition.

Sukarno suspended Parliament in 1960, and was named president for life in 1963. He made close alliances with Communist governments. Russian-armed Indonesian troops staged raids in 1964 and 1965 into Malaysia, whose formation Sukarno had opposed. (In 1966 Indonesia and Malaysia signed an agreement ending hostility.)

In 1965 an attempted coup in which several military officers were murdered was successfully put down. The regime blamed the coup on the Communist Party, some of whose members were known to have been involved. In its wake more than 300,000 alleged Communists were killed in army-initiated massacres.

Parliament reelected Suharto to a 7th consecutive 5-year term Mar. 10, 1998, as a severe economic downturn focused public anger on nepotism, cronyism, and corruption in the Suharto regime. Price increases in May sparked mass protests and then mob violence in Jakarta and other cities, claiming some 500 lives. Suharto resigned May 21 and was succeeded by his vice-president, Bacharuddin Jusuf Habibie. Abdurrahman Wahid, leader of Indonesia's largest Muslim organization, was elected president Oct. 20, 1999. In Aug. 2000, under pressure from the legislature, he agreed to share power with Vice-Pres. Megawati Sukarnoputri, the daughter of the late Pres. Sukarno. Charging Wahid with incompetence and corruption, the legislature ousted him July 23, 2001, and Megawati became Indonesia's 1st woman president.

Clashes between Muslims and Christians in the Maluku (Molucca) Is. have claimed more than 2,500 lives since Jan. 1999; in addition, some 550 people, many refugees from the fighting, died when their ferry sank June 29, 2000. Ethnic violence in Kalimantan, Borneo, killed more than 400 in Feb. 2001. Separatists in Aceh, NW Sumatra, fought repeatedly against government troops during the 1980s and '90s. East Timor, a former Portuguese colony that Indonesia invaded in Dec. 1975 and controlled until Oct. 1999, became a fully independent country May 20, 2002.

Iran

Islamic Republic of Iran

People: Population: 66,622,704. **Age distrib.** (%): <15: 33.0; 65+: 4.6. **Pop. density:** 105 per sq. mi. **Urban:** 61%. **Ethnic groups:** Persian 51%, Azerbaijani 24%, Kurd 7%. **Principal languages:** Persian (Farsi; official), Turkic, Kurdish, Luri. **Chief religions:** Shi'a Muslim 89%, Sunni Muslim 10%.

Geography: Area: 631,700 sq. mi. **Location:** Between the Middle East and S Asia. **Neighbors:** Turkey, Iraq on W; Armenia, Azerbaijan, Turkmenistan on N; Afghanistan, Pakistan on E. **Topography:** Interior highlands and plains surrounded by high mountains, up to 18,000 ft. Large salt deserts cover much of area, but there are many oases and forest areas. Most of the population inhabits the N and NW. **Capital:** Tehran. **Cities** (urban aggr.): Tehran 7,038,000; Esfahan 1,381,000; Mashhad 1,990,000.

Government: Type: Islamic republic. **Religious head:** Ayatollah Sayyed Ali Khamenei; b 1939; in office: June 4, 1989. **Head of state and gov.:** Pres. Mohammad Khatami; b 1943; in office: Aug. 3, 1997. **Local divisions:** 25 provinces. **Defense budget:** (2001) $9.1 bil. **Active troops:** 513,000.

Economy: Industries: Oil, petrochemicals, textiles, cement, sugar and vegetable oil prod. **Chief crops:** Grains, rice, fruits, nuts, sugar beets, cotton. **Minerals:** Chromium, coal, oil, gas. **Crude oil reserves** (2001): 96.4 bil bbls. **Arable land:** 10%. **Livestock** (2001): cattle: 7.00 mil; chickens: 260.00 mil.; goats: 25.20 mil.; sheep: 53.00 mil. **Fish catch** (1999): 380,200 metric tons. **Electricity prod.:** 120.33 bil. kWh. **Labor force:** agri. 33%, ind. 25%, services 42%.

Finance: Monetary unit: Rial (Sept. 2002: 7,948 = $1 U.S.). **GDP** (2000 est.): $413 bil. **Per capita GDP:** $6,300. **Imports** (2000 est.): $15 bil.; partners: Germany, South Korea, Italy, UAE, France, Japan. **Exports** (2000 est.): $25 bil.; partners: Japan, Italy, UAE, South Korea, France, China. **Tourism:** $662 mil. **Budget** (1999): $27 bil. **Consumer prices** (change in 2000): 14.5%.

Transport: Railroad: Length: 4,527 mi. **Motor vehicles:** 1.63 mil pass. cars, 609,000 comm. vehicles. **Civil aviation:** 5.5 bil pass.-mi.; 19 airports. **Chief port:** Bandar-e Abbas.

Communications: TV sets: 148 per 1,000 pop. **Radios:** 273 per 1,000 pop. **Telephones:** 12,072,000. **Daily newspaper circ.:** 28 per 1,000 pop.

Health: Life expectancy: 68.9 male; 71.7 female. **Births** (per 1,000 pop.): 17.5. **Deaths** (per 1,000 pop.): 5.4. **Natural inc.:** 1.22%. **Infant mortality** (per 1,000 live births): 28.1.

Education: Free, compulsory: ages 6-10. **Literacy** (1997): 79%.

Major Intl. Organizations: UN (FAO, IBRD, ILO, IMF, IMO, WHO), OPEC.

Websites: www.daftar.org; www.un.int/iran

Iran was once called Persia. The Iranians, who supplanted an earlier agricultural civilization, came from the E during the 2d millennium BC; they were an Indo-European group related to the Aryans of India.

In 549 BC Cyrus the Great united the Medes and Persians in the Persian Empire, conquered Babylonia in 538 BC, and restored Jerusalem to the Jews. Alexander the Great conquered Persia in 333 BC, but Persians regained independence in the next century under the Parthians, themselves succeeded by Sassanian Persians in AD 226. Arabs brought Islam to Persia in the 7th century, replacing the indigenous Zoroastrian faith. After Persian political and cultural autonomy was reasserted in the 9th century, arts and sciences flourished.

Turks and Mongols ruled Persia in turn from the 11th century to 1502, when a native dynasty reasserted full independence. The British and Russian empires vied for influence in the 19th century; Afghanistan was severed from Iran by Britain in 1857.

Reza Khan abdicated as shah, 1941; succeeded by his son, Mohammad Reza Pahlavi. He brought economic and social change to Iran, but political opposition was not tolerated.

Conservative Muslim protests led to 1978 violence. Martial law was declared in 12 cities Sept. 8. A military government was appointed Nov. 6 to deal with striking oil workers. The shah, who left Iran Jan. 16, 1979, appointed Prime Min. Shahpur Bakhtiar to head a regency council in his absence.

Exiled religious leader Ayatollah Ruhollah Khomeini named a provisional government council in preparation for his return to Tehran, Feb. 1. Clashes between Khomeini's supporters and government troops culminated in a rout of Iran's elite Imperial Guard Feb. 11, leading to the fall of Bakhtiar's government.

The Iranian revolution was marked by revolts among ethnic minorities and by a continuing struggle between the clerical forces and westernized intellectuals and liberals. The Islamic Constitution established final authority to be vested in a Faghi, the Ayatollah Khomeini.

Iranian militants seized the U.S. embassy, Nov. 4, 1979, and took hostages including 62 Americans. Despite international condemnations and U.S. efforts, including an abortive Apr. 1980 rescue attempt, the crisis continued. The U.S. broke diplomatic relations with Iran, Apr. 7. The shah died in Egypt, July 27. The hostage drama ended Jan. 20, 1981, when an accord, involving the release of frozen Iranian assets, was reached.

A dispute over the Shatt al-Arab waterway that divides the two countries brought Iran and Iraq, Sept. 22, 1980, into open warfare. Iraqi troops occupied Iranian territory, including the port city of Khorramshahr in October. Iranian troops recaptured the city and drove Iraqi troops back across the border, May 1982. Iraq, and later Iran, attacked several oil tankers in the Persian Gulf during 1984.

In Nov. 1986 it became known that senior U.S. officials had secretly visited Iran and that the U.S. had provided arms in exchange for Iran's help in obtaining the release of U.S. hostages held by terrorists in Lebanon. The revelation sparked a major scandal in the Reagan administration.

A U.S. Navy warship shot down an Iranian commercial airliner, July 3, 1988, after mistaking it for an F-14 fighter jet; all 290 aboard the plane died. In Aug. 1988, Iran agreed to accept a UN resolution calling for a cease-fire with Iraq.

An earthquake struck northern Iran June 21, 1990, killing more than 45,000, injuring 100,000, and leaving 400,000 homeless. Some one million Kurdish refugees fled from Iraq to Iran following the Persian Gulf War. To curb Iran's alleged support for international terrorism, the U.S. in 1996 authorized sanctions on foreign companies that invest there.

Mohammad Khatami, a moderate Shiite Muslim cleric, was elected president on May 23, 1997, winning nearly 70% of the vote. During the next 3 years, hardline Islamists clashed repeatedly and sometimes violently with reformers, who won a majority in parliamentary elections Feb. 18 and May 5, 2000. Inviting rapprochement with Iran, the U.S. eased some sanctions Mar. 18. Reelected June 8, 2001, with a 77% majority, Khatami continued to face resistance from religious conservatives.

Iraq

Republic of Iraq

People: Population: 24,001,816. **Age distrib.** (%): <15: 41.6; 65+: 3.1. **Pop. density:** 143 per sq. mi. **Urban:** 76%. **Ethnic groups:** Arab 75-80%, Kurd 15-20%, Turkoman. **Principal languages:** Arabic (official), Kurdish. **Chief religions:** Muslim 97% (Shi'a 60-65%, Sunni 32-37%).

Geography: Area: 167,600 sq. mi. **Location:** In the Middle East, occupying most of historic Mesopotamia. **Neighbors:** Jordan and Syria on W, Turkey on N, Iran on E, Kuwait and Saudi Arabia on S. **Topography:** Mostly an alluvial plain, including the Tigris and Euphrates rivers, descending from mountains in N to desert in SW. Persian Gulf region is marshland. **Capital:** Baghdad. **Cities** (urban aggr.): Baghdad 4,958,000; Arbil 2,369,000; Basra (city est.) 1,337,000; Mosul 1,131,000.

Government: Type: Republic. **Head of state and gov.:** Pres. Saddam Hussein; b. Apr. 28, 1937; in office: July 16, 1979; also assumed post of prime minister, May 29, 1994. **Local divisions:** 18 governorates (3 in Kurdish Autonomous Region). **Defense budget** (2001): $1.4 bil. **Active troops:** 424,000.

Economy: Industries: Oil, chemicals, textiles, construction materials, food processing. **Chief crops:** Grains, dates, cotton. **Minerals:** Oil, gas. **Arable land:** 12%. **Crude oil reserves** (2001): 115.0 bil bbls. **Other resources:** Wool, hides. **Livestock** (2001): cattle: 1.35 mil; chickens: 23.00 mil.; goats: 1.60 mil.; sheep: 6.78 mil. **Fish catch:** (1999): 34,702 metric tons. **Electricity prod.:** 27.30 bil. kWh.

Finance: Monetary unit: Dinar (Sept. 2002: 0.31 = $1 U.S.). **GDP** (2000 est.): $57 bil. **Per capita GDP:** $2,500. **Imports** (2000 est.): $13.8 bil.; partners (2000): Egypt, Russia, France, Vietnam. **Exports** (2000 est.): $21.8 bil.; partners (2000): Russia, France, Switzerland, China. **Budget:** NA. **Tourism** (1998): $13 mil.

Transport: Railroad: Length: 1,263 mi. **Motor vehicles:** 672,000 pass. cars, 368,000 comm. vehicles. **Civil aviation:** 12.4 mil pass.-mi. **Chief port:** Basra.

Communications: TV sets: 48 per 1,000 pop. **Radios:** 167 per 1,000 pop. **Telephones:** 675,000 main lines. **Daily newspaper circ.:** 27 per 1,000 pop.

Health: Life expectancy: 66.3 male; 68.5 female. **Births** (per 1,000 pop.): 34.2. **Deaths** (per 1,000 pop.): 6. **Natural inc.:** 2.82%. **Infant mortality** (per 1,000 live births): 57.6.

Education: Free, compulsory: ages 6-12. **Literacy:** 58%.

Major Intl. Organizations: UN (FAO, IBRD, ILO, IMF, IMO, WHO), AL, OPEC.

Websites: www.Iraqi-mission.org;
www.uruklinkinet/iraq/e page1.htm

The Tigris-Euphrates valley, formerly called Mesopotamia, was the site of one of the earliest civilizations in the world. The Sumerian city-states of 3,000 BC originated the culture later developed by the Semitic Akkadians, Babylonians, and Assyrians.

Mesopotamia ceased to be a separate entity after the Persian, Greek, and Arab conquests. The latter founded Baghdad, from where the caliph ruled a vast empire in the 8th and 9th centuries. Mongol and Turkish conquests led to a decline in population, economy, cultural life, and the irrigation system.

Britain secured a League of Nations mandate over Iraq after World War I. Independence under a king came in 1932. A leftist, pan-Arab revolution established a republic in 1958, which oriented foreign policy toward the USSR. Most industry has been nationalized, and large land holdings broken up.

A local faction of the international Baath Arab Socialist party has ruled by decree since 1968. The USSR and Iraq signed an aid pact in 1972, and arms were sent along with several thousand advisers. The 1978 execution of 21 Communists and a shift of trade to the West signalled a more neutral policy, straining relations with the USSR. In the 1973 Arab-Israeli war Iraq sent forces to aid Syria. Within a month of assuming power, Saddam Hussein instituted a bloody purge in the wake of a reported coup attempt against the new regime.

Years of battling with the Kurdish minority resulted in total defeat for the Kurds in 1975, when Iran withdrew support. The fighting led to Iraqi bombing of Kurdish villages in Iran, causing relations with Iran to deteriorate.

After skirmishing intermittently for 10 months over the sovereignty of the disputed Shatt al-Arab waterway that divides the two countries, Iraq and Iran entered into open warfare on Sept. 22, 1980. In the following days, there was heavy ground fighting around Abadan and the port of Khorramshahr, as Iraq launched an attack on Iran's oil-rich province of Khuzistan.

Israeli planes destroyed a nuclear reactor near Baghdad June 7, 1981, claiming it could be used to produce nuclear weapons.

Iraq and Iran expanded their war to the Persian Gulf in Apr. 1984. There were several attacks on oil tankers. An Iraqi warplane launched a missile attack on the USS *Stark,* a U.S. Navy frigate on patrol in the Persian Gulf, May 17, 1987; 37 U.S. sailors died. Iraq apologized for the attack, claiming it was inadvertent. The fierce war ended Aug. 1988, when Iraq accepted a UN resolution for a cease-fire.

Iraq attacked and overran Kuwait Aug. 2, 1990, sparking an international crisis. The UN, Aug. 6, imposed a ban on all trade with Iraq and called on member countries to protect the assets of the legitimate government of Kuwait. Iraq declared Kuwait its 19th province, Aug. 28.

A U.S.-led coalition launched air and missile attacks on Iraq, Jan. 16, 1991, after the expiration of a UN Security Council deadline for Iraq to withdraw from Kuwait. Iraq retaliated by firing scud missiles at Saudi Arabia and Israel. The coalition began a ground attack to retake Kuwait Feb. 23. Iraqi forces showed little resistance and were soundly defeated in 4 days. Some 175,000 Iraqis were taken prisoner, and casualties were estimated at over 85,000. As part of the cease-fire agreement, Iraq agreed to scrap all poison gas and germ weapons and allow UN observers to inspect the sites. UN trade sanctions would remain in effect until Iraq complied with all terms.

In the aftermath of the war, there were revolts against Pres. Saddam Hussein throughout Iraq. In Feb., Iraqi troops drove Kurdish insurgents and civilians to the borders of Iran and Turkey, causing a refugee crisis. The U.S. and allies established havens inside Iraq for the Kurds. Iraqi cooperation with UN weapons inspection teams was intermittent.

The U.S. launched a missile attack aimed at Iraq's intelligence headquarters in Baghdad June 26, 1993, citing evidence that Iraq had sponsored a plot to kill former Pres. George Bush during his visit to Kuwait in Apr. 1993. In Aug. 1995, two of Saddam Hussein's sons-in-law, who held high positions in the Iraqi military, defected to Jordan; both were killed after returning to Iraq in Feb. 1996. After fighting between two Kurdish factions, one allied with Iraq, the other with Iran, erupted in the protected zone of northern Iraq, the Baghdad government intervened in the conflict by sending troops into Arbil, Aug. 31, 1996. The U.S. responded with missile strikes against air defense sites in the south. On Dec. 9 the UN allowed Baghdad to begin selling limited amounts of oil for food and medicine. Saddam Hussein's son Odai was seriously wounded in an assassination attempt in Baghdad Dec. 12.

Iraqi resistance to UN access to suspected weapons sites touched off diplomatic crises during 1997-98, culminating in intensive U.S. and British aerial bombardment of Iraqi military targets, Dec. 16-19, 1998. After 2 years of intermittent activity, U.S. and British warplanes struck harder at sites near Baghdad on Feb. 16, 2001. Hussein sought to shore up Arab support by recognizing Kuwait's sovereignty Mar. 28, 2002, and pledging not to invade that country again.

In a speech before the UN, Sept. 12, U.S. Pres. George Bush accused Iraq of repeatedly violating UN resolutions to eliminate weapons of mass destruction, refrain from supporting terrorism, and end repression. Under broad pressure, Iraq agreed Sept.16 to allow UN arms inspectors in "without preconditions"; the U.S. sought international support for strict inspections and for "regime change" if Iraq did not cooperate.

Ireland

People: Population: 3,883,159. **Age distrib.** (%): <15: 21.6; 65+: 11.4. **Pop. density:** 146 per sq. mi. **Urban:** 59%. **Ethnic groups:** Principally Celtic, English minority. **Principal languages:** English predominates, Irish (Gaelic) spoken by minority (both official). **Chief religions:** Roman Catholic 93%, Anglican 3%.

Geography: Area: 26,600 sq. mi. **Location:** In the Atlantic O. just W of Great Britain. **Neighbors:** United Kingdom (Northern Ireland) on E. **Topography:** Ireland consists of a central plateau surrounded by isolated groups of hills and mountains. The coastline is heavily indented by the Atlantic O. **Capital:** Dublin 993,000.

Government: Type: Parliamentary republic. **Head of state:** Pres. Mary McAleese; b June 27, 1951; in office: Nov. 11, 1997. **Head of gov.:** Prime Min. Bertie Ahern; b Sept. 12, 1951; in office: June 26, 1997. **Local divisions:** 26 counties. **Defense budget (2001):** $794 mil. **Active troops:** 10,460.

Economy: Industries: Food products, brewing, textiles, clothing, chemicals, pharmaceuticals. **Chief crops:** Potatoes, grains, sugar beets, turnips. **Minerals:** Zinc, lead, gas, barite, copper, gypsum. **Arable land:** 13%. **Livestock** (2001): cattle: 6.46 mil; chickens: 11.27 1.73 mil; sheep: 5.13 mil . **Fish catch** (1999): 329,496 metric tons. **Electricity prod.:** 22.28 bil. kWh. **Labor force:** services 64%, ind. 28%, agri. 8%.

Finance: Monetary unit: Euro (Sept. 2002: 1.03 = $1 U.S.). **GDP** (2000 est.): $81.9 bil. **Per capita GDP:** $21,600. **Imports** (2000 est.): $45.7 bil.; partners (2000): EU 54%, U.S. 18%. **Exports** (2000): $73.5 bil.; partners (2000): EU 59%,U.S. 20%. **Exports** (1999 est.): $66 bil; partners: UK 22%, Germany 15%. **Tourism:** $3.31 bil. **Budget** (2000): $19.2 bil. **Intl. reserves less gold** (end 2000): $4.11 bil. **Gold:** 176,000 oz t. **Consumer prices** (change in 2000): 5.6%.

Transport: Railroad: Length: 1,210 mi. **Motor vehicles:** 1.06 mil pass. cars, 161,355 comm. vehicles. **Civil aviation:** 4.5 bil pass.-mi.; 9 airports. **Chief ports:** Dublin, Cork.

Communications: TV sets: 457 per 1,000 pop. **Radios:** 580 per 1,000 pop. **Telephones:** 4,660,000. **Daily newspaper circ.:** 150 per 1,000 pop.

Health: Life expectancy: 74.4 male; 80.1 female. **Births** (per 1,000 pop.): 14.6. **Deaths** (per 1,000 pop.): 8. **Natural inc.:** 0.66%. **Infant mortality** (per 1,000 live births): 5.4.

Education: Compulsory: ages 6-15. **Literacy** (1993): 100%.

Major Intl. Organizations: UN (FAO, IBRD, ILO, IMF, IMO, WHO, WTrO), EU, OECD, OSCE.

Embassy: 2234 Massachusetts Ave. NW 20008; 462-3939.

Websites: www.irlgov.ie/; www.irelandemb.org

Celtic tribes invaded the islands about the 4th century BC; their Gaelic culture and literature flourished and spread to Scotland and elsewhere in the 5th century AD, the same century in which St. Patrick converted the Irish to Christianity. Invasions by Norsemen began in the 8th century, ended with defeat of the Danes by the Irish King Brian Boru in 1014. English invasions started in the 12th century; for over 700 years the Anglo-Irish struggle continued with bitter rebellions and savage repressions.

The Easter Monday Rebellion in 1916 failed but was followed by guerrilla warfare and harsh reprisals by British troops called the "Black and Tans." The Dail Eireann (Irish parliament) reaffirmed independence in Jan. 1919. The British offered dominion status to Ulster (6 counties) and southern Ireland (26 counties) Dec. 1921. The constitution of the Irish Free State, a British dominion, was adopted Dec. 11, 1922. Northern Ireland remained part of the United Kingdom.

A new constitution adopted by plebiscite came into operation Dec. 29, 1937. It declared the name of the state Eire in the Irish language (Ireland in the English) and declared it a sovereign democratic state. On Dec. 21, 1948, an Irish law declared the country a republic rather than a dominion and withdrew it from the Commonwealth. The British Parliament recognized both actions, 1949, but reasserted its claim to incorporate the 6 northeastern counties in the U.K. This claim has not been recognized by Ireland *(see United Kingdom—Northern Ireland)*.

Irish governments have favored peaceful unification of all Ireland and cooperated with Britain against terrorist groups. On Dec. 15, 1993, Irish and British governments agreed on outlines of a peace plan to resolve the Northern Ireland issue. On Aug. 31, 1994, the Irish Republican Army announced a cease-fire; when peace talks lagged, however, the IRA returned to its terror campaign on Feb. 9, 1996. The IRA proclaimed a new cease-fire as of July 20, 1997, and peace talks resumed Sept. 15.

Ireland's first woman president, Mary Robinson, resigned Sept. 12 to become UN high commissioner for human rights. She was succeeded by Mary McAleese, a law professor from Northern Ireland and the first northerner to hold the office. After negotiators in Northern Ireland approved a peace settlement on Good Friday, April 10, 1998, voters in the Irish Republic endorsed the accord on May 22.

Israel

State of Israel

People: Population: 6,029,529. **Age distrib.** (%): <15: 27.4; 65+: 9.9. **Pop. density:** 773 per sq. mi. **Urban:** 91%. **Ethnic groups:** Jewish 80%, non-Jewish (mostly Arab) 20%. **Principal languages:** Hebrew (official), Arabic (used officially for Arab minority), English. **Chief religions:** Judaism 80%, Muslim (mostly Sunni) 15%.

Geography: Area: 7,800 sq. mi. **Location:** Middle East, on E end of Mediterranean Sea. **Neighbors:** Lebanon on N; Syria, West Bank, and Jordan on E; Gaza Strip and Egypt on W. **Topography:** The Mediterranean coastal plain is fertile and well-watered. In the center is the Judean Plateau. A triangular-shaped semi-desert region, the Negev, extends from south of Beersheba to an apex at the head of the Gulf of Aqaba. The E border drops sharply into the Jordan Rift Valley, including Lake Tiberias (Sea of Galilee) and the Dead Sea, which is 1,312 ft. below sea level, lowest point on the earth's surface. **Capital:** Jerusalem (most countries maintain their embassy in Tel Aviv). **Cities** (urban aggr.): Jerusalem (2001 est.) 661,000; Tel Aviv-Yafo 2,001,000; Haifa (1997 est.) 255,300.

Government: Type: Republic. **Head of state:** Pres. Moshe Katsav; b 1945; in office: Aug. 1, 2000. **Head of gov.:** Prime Min. Ariel Sharon; b 1928; in office: Mar. 7, 2001. **Local divisions:** 6 districts. **Defense budget:** (2001) $9 bil. **Active troops:** 163,500.

Economy: Industries: High-tech design and manufactures, wood and paper products, food and beverages. **Chief crops:** Citrus, fruit, vegetables, cotton. **Minerals:** Copper, phosphates, bromide, potash, clay. **Crude oil reserves** (2000): 3.9 mil bbls. **Arable land:** 17%. **Livestock** (2001): cattle: 390,000; chickens: 30.00 mil.; goats: 68,000; pigs: 150,000; sheep: 389,000. **Fish catch:** (1999): 23,274 metric tons. **Electricity prod.:** 38.88 bil. kWh. **Labor force:** public services 31.2%, manufacturing 20.2%, finance and business 13.1%, commerce 12.8%, construction 7.5%, personal and other services 6.4%, transport, storage, and communications 6.2%, agri., forestry, and fishing 2.6%.

Finance: Monetary unit: New Shekel (Sept. 2002: 4.84 = $1 U.S.). **GDP** (2000 est.): $110.2 bil. **Per capita GDP:** $18,900. **Imports** (2000): $35.1 bil.; partners (1999): U.S. 20%, Benelux 11%. **Exports** (2000): $31.5 bil.; partners (1999): U.S. 36%, UK 6%, Benelux 5%. **Tourism:** $3.10 bil. **Budget** (2000 est.): $42.4 bil. **Intl. reserves less gold** (end 2000): $17.87 bil. **Consumer prices** (change in 2000): 1.1%.

Transport: Railroad: Length: 379 mi. **Motor vehicles** (1997): 1.24 mil pass. cars, 304,033 comm. vehicles. **Civil aviation:** 7.3 bil pass.-mi.; 7 airports. **Chief ports:** Haifa, Ashdod, Elat.

Communications: TV sets: 335 per 1,000 pop. **Radios:** 530 per 1,000 pop. **Telephones:** 8,360,000. **Daily newspaper circ.:** 291 per 1,000 pop.

Health: Life expectancy: 76.8 male; 81 female. **Births** (per 1,000 pop.): 18.9. **Deaths** (per 1,000 pop.): 6.2. **Natural inc.:** 1.27%. **Infant mortality** (per 1,000 live births): 7.5.

Education: Free, compulsory: ages 5-15. **Literacy**: 96%.

Major Intl. Organizations: UN (FAO, IBRD, ILO, IMF, IMO, WHO, WTrO).

Embassy: 3514 International Dr. NW 20008; 364-5500.

Websites: www.israel.org; www.israelemb.org

Occupying the SW corner of the ancient Fertile Crescent, Israel contains some of the oldest known evidence of agriculture and of primitive town life. A more advanced civilization emerged in the 3d millennium BC. The Hebrews probably arrived early in the 2d millennium BC. Under King David and his successors (c.1000 BC-597 BC), Judaism was developed and secured. After conquest by Babylonians, Persians, and Greeks, an independent Jewish kingdom was revived, 168 BC, but Rome took effective control in the next century, suppressed Jewish revolts in AD 70 and AD 135, and renamed Judea Palestine, after the earlier coastal inhabitants, the Philistines.

Arab invaders conquered Palestine in 636. The Arabic language and Islam prevailed within a few centuries, but a Jewish minority remained. The land was ruled from the 11th century as a part of non-Arab empires by Seljuks, Mamluks, and Ottomans (with a crusader interval, 1098-1291).

After 4 centuries of Ottoman rule, during which the population declined to a low of 350,000 (1785), the land was taken in 1917 by Britain, which pledged in the Balfour Declaration to support a Jewish national homeland there. In 1920 a British Palestine Mandate was recognized; in 1922 the land east of the Jordan was detached.

Jewish immigration, begun in the late 19th century, swelled in the 1930s with refugees from the Nazis; heavy Arab immigration from Syria and Lebanon also occurred. Arab opposition to Jewish immigration turned violent in 1920, 1921, 1929, and 1936. The UN General Assembly voted in 1947 to partition Palestine into an Arab and a Jewish state. Britain withdrew in May 1948.

Israel was declared an independent state May 14, 1948; the Arabs rejected partition. Egypt, Jordan, Syria, Lebanon, Iraq, and Saudi Arabia invaded, but failed to destroy the Jewish state, which gained territory. Separate armistices with the Arab nations were signed in 1949; Jordan occupied the West Bank, Egypt occupied Gaza; neither granted Palestinian autonomy.

After persistent terrorist raids, Israel invaded Egypt's Sinai, Oct. 29, 1956, aided briefly by British and French forces. A UN cease-fire was arranged Nov. 6.

An uneasy truce between Israel and the Arab countries, supervised by a UN Emergency Force, prevailed until May 19, 1967, when the UN force withdrew at Egypt's demand. Egyptian forces reoccupied the Gaza Strip and closed the Gulf of Aqaba to Israeli shipping. In a 6-day war that started June 5, the Israelis took the Gaza Strip, occupied the Sinai Peninsula to the Suez Canal, and captured East Jerusalem, Syria's Golan Heights, and Jordan's West Bank. The fighting was halted June 10 by UN-arranged cease-fire agreements.

Egypt and Syria attacked Israel, Oct. 6, 1973 (on Yom Kippur, the most solemn day on the Jewish calendar). Israel counter-attacked, driving the Syrians back, and crossed the Suez Canal. A cease-fire took effect Oct. 24 and a UN peacekeeping force went to the area. Under a disengagement agreement signed Jan. 18, 1974, Israel withdrew from the canal's west bank.

Israeli forces raided Entebbe, Uganda, July 3, 1976, and rescued 103 hostages who had been seized by Arab and German terrorists.

In 1977, the conservative opposition, led by Menachem Begin, was voted into office for the first time. Egypt's Pres. Anwar al-Sadat visited Jerusalem Nov. 1977, and on Mar. 26, 1979, Egypt and Israel signed a formal peace treaty, ending 30 years of war and establishing diplomatic relations. Israel returned the Sinai to Egypt in 1982.

Israel invaded S Lebanon, Mar. 1978, following a Lebanon-based terrorist attack in Israel. Israel withdrew in favor of a 6,000-man UN force, but continued to aid Lebanese Christian militiamen. Israel affirmed the whole of Jerusalem as its capital, July 1980, encompassing the annexed East Jerusalem.

On June 7, 1981, Israeli jets destroyed an Iraqi atomic reactor near Baghdad that, Israel claimed, would have enabled Iraq to manufacture nuclear weapons. Israeli forces invaded Lebanon, June 6, 1982, to destroy PLO strongholds there. After massive Israeli bombing of West Beirut, the PLO agreed to evacuate the city. Israeli troops entered West Beirut after newly elected Lebanese Pres. Bashir Gemayel was assassinated on Sept. 14. Israel drew widespread condemnation when Lebanese Christian forces, Sept. 16, entered two West Beirut refugee camps and slaughtered hundreds of Palestinian refugees.

In 1989, violence escalated over the Israeli military occupation of the West Bank and Gaza Strip. In a series of uprisings known as the intifada, Palestinian protesters defied Israeli troops, who forcibly retaliated. Israeli police and stone-throwing Palestinians clashed, Oct. 8, 1990, around the al-Aqsa mosque on the Temple Mount in Jerusalem; some 20 Palestinians died.

During the Persian Gulf War in early 1991, Iraq fired a series of Scud missiles at Israel. The Labor Party of Yitzhak Rabin won a clear victory in elections held June 23, 1992.

Ongoing peace talks led to historic agreements between Israel and the PLO, Sept. 1993. The PLO recognized Israel's right to exist; Israel recognized the PLO as the Palestinians' representative; the two sides then signed, Sept. 13, an agreement for limited Palestinian self-rule and the West Bank and Gaza.

Israel and Jordan signed, July 25, 1994, in Washington, DC, a declaration ending their 46-year state of war. A formal peace treaty was signed Oct. 26.

Arab and Jewish extremists repeatedly challenged the peace process. A Jewish gunman opened fire on Arab worshippers at a mosque in Hebron, Feb. 25, 1994, killing at least 29 before he himself was killed. On Nov. 4, 1995, an Orthodox Jewish Israeli assassinated Rabin as he left a peace rally in Tel Aviv.

Support for Rabin's successor, Shimon Peres, was shaken by a series of suicide bombings and rocket attacks against Israel by Islamic militants. In Apr. 1996, Israel attacked suspected guerrilla bases in southern Lebanon. Emphasizing security issues, the candidate of the conservative Likud bloc, Benjamin Netanyahu, was elected prime minister on May 29.

On Sept. 24, 1996, Israel opened a tunnel entrance near a sacred Muslim site in Jerusalem, setting off several days of violence between Israeli soldiers and Palestinian demonstrators and police. Pres. Clinton hosted a summit meeting between Netanyahu and PLO leader Yasir Arafat soon after, on Oct. 1-2, and peace talks were resumed.

Two suicide bombings in a Jerusalem market July 30, 1997, left 15 people dead and more than 170 wounded. The parliament (Knesset) reelected Ezer Weizman as president Mar. 4, 1998, despite opposition from Netanyahu.

Under an interim accord brokered by Clinton and signed by Netanyahu and Arafat at the White House, Oct. 23, 1998, Israel yielded more West Bank territory to the Palestinians, in exchange for new security guarantees. Negotiations bogged down, however, and full implementation did not begin until Sept. 1999. In the interim, Netanyahu lost by a landslide to the Labor party candidate, Ehud Barak, in the general election of May 17.

Israel pulled virtually all its troops out of S Lebanon by May 24, 2000. Marathon summit talks in the U.S. between Barak and Arafat, July 11-25, failed. A new wave of violence began in late Sept. in Israel and the Palestinian territories. Barak called new elections for prime minister but lost Feb. 6, 2001, to Ariel Sharon, a hardliner; he took office Mar. 7, heading a national unity government with Peres as foreign minister. The bloodshed intensified during the summer, as Palestinian suicide bombers hit a Tel Aviv nightclub June 1, killing 20 young Israelis, and a Jerusalem pizzeria Aug. 9, killing 15 patrons. Israel launched offensives against Palestinian-controlled territory and carried out an assassination campaign against dozens of suspected terrorists.

The assassination by Palestinian gunmen Oct. 17 of Rehavam Zeevi, an ultranationalist cabinet minister, triggered another wave of violence. After a weekend of suicide bombings Dec. 1-2 left at least 25 Israelis dead, Sharon, seeking to force Arafat to crack down on Islamic militants, unleashed military strikes against Palestinian police facilities, Arafat's own headquarters, and suspected terrorist hideouts. After West Bank gunmen killed 10 Israelis on a bus Dec. 12, Israel cut ties with Arafat. Israel launched new attacks after seizing, Jan. 4, 2002, a shipload of weapons sent from Iran for Palestinian use.

Israel launched a major West Bank offensive Mar. 29, 2002, 2 days after a suicide bomber killed 26 Israeli Jews at a Passover celebration in Netanya. Fighting was particularly fierce at the Jenin refugee camp, where 23 Israeli troops and at least 50 Palestinians were killed. Israel withdrew in early May but, after another wave of suicide bombings, reoccupied much of the West Bank June 21-27. Arafat was trapped in his Ramallah headquarters, much of which Israel leveled Sept. 20. Israeli troops withdrew from it Sept. 29.

Since Sept. 2000, the conflict has claimed the lives of more than 600 Israelis and some 1,600 Palestinians.

Gaza Strip

The Gaza Strip, also known as Gaza, extends NE from the Sinai Peninsula for 40 km (25 mi), with the Mediterranean Sea to the W and Israel to the E. The Palestinian Authority is responsible for civil government, but Israel retains control over security. Nearly all the inhabitants are Palestinian Arabs, more than 35% of whom live in refugee camps. Population (2002 est.): 1,225,911. Area: 140 sq. mi.

Israel captured Gaza from Egypt in the 1967 war. It remained under Israeli occupation until May 1994, when the Israel Defense Forces withdrew. Agreements between Israel and the PLO in 1993 and 1994 provided for interim self-rule in Gaza, pending the completion of final status negotiations.

West Bank

Located W of the Jordan R. and Dead Sea, the West Bank is bounded by Jordan on the E and by Israel on the N, W, and S. The Palestinian Authority administers several major cities, but Israel retains control over much land, including Jewish settlements. Population (2002 est.): 2,163,667. Area: 2,200 sq. mi.

Israel captured the West Bank from Jordan in the 1967 war. A 1974 Arab summit conference designated the PLO as sole representative of West Bank Arabs. In 1988 Jordan cut legal and administrative ties with the territory. Jericho was returned to Palestinian control in May 1994. An accord between Israel and the PLO expanding Palestinian self-rule in the West Bank was signed Sept. 28, 1995. Later agreements gave Palestinians full or shared control of 40% of West Bank territory.

Italy

Italian Republic

People: Population: 57,715,625. **Age distrib.** (%): <15: 14.2; 65+: 18.3. **Pop. density:** 509 per sq. mi. **Urban:** 67%. **Ethnic groups:** Italian, small minorities of German, French, Slovene, Albanian. **Principal languages:** Italian (official), German, French, Slovene. **Chief religion:** Roman Catholic 98%.

Geography: Area: 113,500 sq. mi. **Location:** In S Europe, jutting into Mediterranean Sea. **Neighbors:** France on W, Switzerland and Austria on N, Slovenia on E. **Topography:** Occupies a long boot-shaped peninsula, extending SE from the Alps into the Mediterranean, with the islands of Sicily and Sardinia offshore. The alluvial Po Valley drains most of N. The rest of the country is rugged and mountainous, except for intermittent coastal plains, like the Campania, S of Rome. Apennine Mts. run down through center of peninsula. **Capital:** Rome. **Cities** (urban aggr.): Milan 4,251,000; Naples 3,012,000; Rome 2,651,000; Turin 1,294,000.

Government: Type: Republic. **Head of state:** Pres. Carlo Azeglio Ciampi; b Dec. 9, 1920; in office: May 18, 1999. **Head of gov.:** Prime Min. Silvio Berlusconi; b Sept. 29, 1936; in office: June 11, 2001. **Local divisions:** 20 regions divided into 94 provinces. Defense budget (2001): $15.5 bil. **Active troops:** 230,350

Economy: Industries: Tourism, machinery, iron and steel, chemicals, food processing. **Chief crops:** Grapes, olives, fruits, vegetables, grain. **Minerals:** Mercury, potash, marble, sulphur. **Crude oil reserves** (2001): 0.6 bil bbls. **Arable land:** 31%. **Livestock** (2001): cattle: 7.21 mil; chickens: 100.00 mil.; goats: 1.38 mil.; pigs: 8.33 mil; sheep: 11.09 mil. **Electricity prod.:** 257.41 bil. kWh. **Labor force:** services 61.9%, ind. 32.6%, agri. 5.5%.

Finance: Monetary unit: Euro (Sept. 2002: 1.03 = $1 U.S.). **GDP** (2000 est.): $1.273 tril. **Per capita GDP:** $22,100. **Imports** (2000): $231.4 bil.; partners (1999): EU 61%, U.S. 5.0%. **Exports** (2000): $241.1 bil.; partners (1999): EU 56.8%,U.S. 9.5%. **Tourism:** $28.36 bil. **Budget** (2000 est.): $501 bil. **Intl. reserves less gold** (end 2000): $19.62 bil. **Gold:** 78.83 mil oz t. **Consumer prices** (change in 2000): 2.5%.

Transport: Railroad: Length: 9,944 mi. **Motor vehicles** (1997): 31.00 mil pass. cars, 2.99 mil comm. vehicles. **Civil aviation:** 23.6 bil pass.-mi.; 34 airports. **Chief ports:** Genoa, Venice, Trieste, Palermo, Naples, La Spezia.

Communications: TV sets: 483 per 1,000 pop. **Radios:** 874 per 1,000 pop. **Telephones:** 76,001,000. **Daily newspaper circ.:** 104 per 1,000 pop.

Health: Life expectancy: 76.1 male; 82.6 female. **Births** (per 1,000 pop.): 8.9. **Deaths** (per 1,000 pop.): 10.1. **Natural inc.:** -0.12%. **Infant mortality** (per 1,000 live births): 5.8.

Education: Free, compulsory: ages 6-13. **Literacy** (1994): 97%.

Major Intl. Organizations: UN and all of its specialized agencies, EU, NATO, OECD, OSCE.

Embassy: 1601 Fuller St. NW 20009; 328-5500.

Websites: www.italyemb.org; istat.it/homeing.html

Rome emerged as the major power in Italy after 500 BC, dominating the Etruscans to the N and Greeks to the S. Under the Empire, which lasted until the 5th century AD, Rome ruled most of Western Europe, the Balkans, the Middle East, and N Africa. In 1988, archaeologists unearthed evidence showing Rome as a dynamic society in the 6th and 7th centuries BC.

After the Germanic invasions, lasting several centuries, a high civilization arose in the city-states of the N, culminating in the Renaissance. But German, French, Spanish, and Austrian intervention prevented the unification of the country. In 1859 Lombardy came under the crown of King Victor Emmanuel II of Sardinia. By plebiscite in 1860, Parma, Modena, Romagna, and Tuscany joined, followed by Sicily and Naples, and by the Marches and Umbria. The first Italian Parliament declared Victor Emmanuel king of Italy Mar. 17, 1861. Mantua and Venetia were added in 1866 as an outcome of the Austro-Prussian war. The Papal States were taken by Italian troops Sept. 20, 1870, on the withdrawal of the French garrison. The states were annexed to the kingdom by plebiscite. Italy recognized Vatican City as independent Feb. 11, 1929.

Fascism appeared in Italy Mar. 23, 1919, led by Benito Mussolini, who took over the government at the invitation of the king Oct. 28, 1922. Mussolini acquired dictatorial powers. He made war on Ethiopia and proclaimed Victor Emmanuel III emperor, defied the sanctions of the League of Nations, sent troops to fight for Franco against the Republic of Spain, and joined Germany in World War II.

After Fascism was overthrown in 1943, Italy declared war on Germany and Japan and contributed to the Allied victory. It surrendered conquered lands and lost its colonies. Mussolini was killed by partisans Apr. 28, 1945. Victor Emmanuel III abdicated May 9, 1946; his son Humbert II was king until June 10, when Italy became a republic after a referendum, June 2-3.

Since World War II, Italy has enjoyed growth in industrial output and living standards, in part a result of membership in the European Community (now European Union). Political stability has not kept pace with economic prosperity, and organized crime and corruption have been persistent problems.

Christian Democratic leader and former Prime Min. Aldo Moro was abducted and murdered in 1978 by Red Brigade terrorists. The wave of left-wing political violence, including other kidnappings and assassinations, continued into the 1980s.

In the early 1990s, scandals implicated some of Italy's most prominent politicians. In Mar. 1994 voting, under reformed election rules, right-wing parties won a majority, dislodging Italy's long-powerful Christian Democratic Party. After a series of short-lived governments, a coalition of center-left parties won the election of Apr. 21, 1996. Italy led a 7,000-member international peacekeeping force in Albania, Apr.-Aug. 1997. Two earthquakes in central Italy Sept. 26 killed 11 people, left about 12,000 homeless, and damaged priceless frescoes in Assisi.

On Feb. 3, 1998, a low-flying U.S. military aircraft severed a gondola cable at a ski resort in N Italy, killing 20 people. Implementation of a deficit reduction plan enabled Italy to qualify in May to adopt the euro, a common European currency. Italy contributed 2,000 troops to the NATO-led security force (KFOR) that entered Kosovo in June 1999. Turin was chosen June 19 to host the Winter Olympics in 2006.

Supporters of Silvio Berlusconi, a multibillionaire media magnate, won the parliamentary elections of May 13, 2001.

Sicily, 9,926 sq. mi., pop. (1994 est.) 5,025,000, is an island 180 by 120 mi., seat of a region that embraces the island of **Pantelleria,** 32 sq. mi., and the **Lipari** group, 44 sq. mi., including 2 active volcanoes: **Vulcano,** 1,637 ft., and **Stromboli,** 3,038 ft. From prehistoric times Sicily has been settled by various peoples; a Greek state had its capital at Syracuse. Rome took Sicily from Carthage 215 BC. **Mt. Etna,** an 11,053-ft. active volcano, is its tallest peak.

Sardinia, 9,301 sq. mi., pop. (1994 est.) 1,657,000, lies in the Mediterranean, 115 mi. W of Italy and $7^{1}/_{2}$ mi. S of Corsica. It is 160 mi. long, 68 mi. wide, and mountainous, with mining of coal, zinc, lead, copper. In 1720 Sardinia was added to the possessions of the Dukes of Savoy in Piedmont and Savoy to form the Kingdom of Sardinia. Giuseppe Garibaldi is buried on the nearby isle of Caprera. **Elba,** 86 sq. mi., lies 6 mi. W of Tuscany. Napoleon I lived in exile on Elba 1814-1815.

Jamaica

People: Population: 2,680,029. **Age distrib.** (%): <15: 29.7; 65+: 6.8. **Pop. density:** 638 per sq. mi. **Urban:** 56%. **Ethnic groups:** Black 90%. **Principal languages:** English (official), Jamaican Creole. **Chief religions:** Protestant 61%, Roman Catholic 4%, spiritual cults and other 35%.

Geography: Area: 4,200 sq. mi. **Location:** In West Indies. **Neighbors:** Nearest are Cuba to N, Haiti to E. **Topography:** Four-fifths of Jamaica is covered by mountains. **Capital:** Kingston 672,000.

Government: Type: Parliamentary democracy. **Head of state:** Queen Elizabeth II, represented by Gov.-Gen. Sir Howard Cooke; b Nov. 13, 1915; in office: Aug. 1, 1991. **Head of gov.:** Prime Min. Percival J. Patterson; b Apr. 10, 1935; in office: Mar. 30, 1992. **Local divisions:** 14 parishes. **Defense budget (2001):** $48 mil . **Active troops:** 2,830.

Economy: Industries: Tourism, bauxite, textiles, food processing. **Chief crops:** Sugar, coffee, bananas, potatoes, citrus. **Minerals:** Bauxite, limestone, gypsum. **Arable land:** 14%. **Livestock** (2001): cattle: 400,000; chickens: 11.00 mil.; goats: 440,000; pigs: 180,000; sheep: 1,400. **Fish catch** (1999): 11,458 metric tons. **Electricity prod.:** 6.74 bil. kWh. **Labor force:** services 60%, agri. 21%, ind. 19%.

Finance: Monetary unit: Dollar (Sept. 2002: 48.7 = $1 U.S.). **GDP** (2000 est.): $9.7 bil. **Per capita GDP:** $3,700. **Imports** (2000 est.): $3 bil.; partners (1999): U.S. 47.8%, Caricom countries 12.4%. **Exports** (2000 est.): $1.7 bil.; partners (1999): U.S. 35.7%, EU (excluding UK): 15.8%. **Tourism:** $1.23 bil. **Budget** (FY99/00 est.): $2.56 bil. **Intl. reserves less gold** (end 2000): $809 mil. **Consumer prices** (change in 2000): 8.2%.

Transport: Railroad: Length: 129 mi. **Motor vehicles:** 43,500 pass. cars, 15,400 comm. vehicles. **Civil aviation:** 1.7 bil pass.-mi.; 4 airports. **Chief ports:** Kingston, Montego Bay.

Communications: TV sets: 306 per 1,000 pop. **Radios:** 739 per 1,000 pop. **Telephones:** 1,212,600. **Daily newspaper circ.:** 65 per 1,000 pop.

Health: Life expectancy: 73.7 male; 77.7 female. **Births** (per 1,000 pop.): 17.7. **Deaths** (per 1,000 pop.): 5.5. **Natural inc.:** 1.23%. **Infant mortality** (per 1,000 live births): 13.7.

Education: Free, compulsory: ages 6-12. **Literacy**: 85%.

Major Intl. Organizations: UN (FAO, IBRD, ILO, IMF, IMO, WHO, WTrO), Caricom, the Commonwealth, OAS.

Embassy: 1520 New Hampshire Ave. NW 20036; 452-0660.

Websites: www.cabinet.gov.jm; www.emjamusa.org

Jamaica was visited by Columbus, 1494, and ruled by Spain (under whom Arawak Indians died out) until seized by Britain, 1655. Jamaica won independence Aug. 6, 1962.

In 1974 Jamaica sought an increase in taxes paid by U.S. and Canadian bauxite mines. The socialist government acquired 50% ownership of the companies' Jamaican interests in 1976, and was reelected that year. Rudimentary welfare state measures were passed. Relations with the U.S. improved in the 1980s when Jamaican politics entered a more conservative phase. Violent clashes between government forces and West Kingston slum residents claimed at least 20 lives July 7-10, 2001.

Japan

People: Population: 126,974,628. **Age distrib.** (%): <15: 14.6; 65+: 17.5. **Pop. density:** 833 per sq. mi. **Urban:** 79%. **Ethnic groups:** Japanese 99.4%. **Principal language:** Japanese (official). **Chief religions:** Buddhism, Shintoism shared by 84%.

Geography: Area: 152,400 sq. mi. **Location:** Archipelago off E coast of Asia. **Neighbors:** Russia to N, South Korea to W. **Topography:** Japan consists of 4 main islands: Honshu ("mainland"), 87,805 sq. mi.; Hokkaido, 30,144 sq. mi.; Kyushu, 14,114 sq. mi.; and Shikoku, 7,049 sq. mi. The coast, deeply indented, measures 16,654 mi. The northern islands are a continuation of the Sakhalin Mts. The Kunlun range of China continues into southern islands, the ranges meeting in the Japanese Alps. In a vast transverse fissure crossing Honshu E-W rises a group of volcanoes, mostly extinct or inactive, including 12,388 ft. Mt. Fuji (Fujiyama) near Tokyo. **Capital:** Tokyo. **Cities** (urban aggr.): Tokyo 26,546,000 (1998 city proper: 7,854,000); Osaka 11,013,000, (1998 city proper: 2,599,642); Nagoya 3,157,000; Sapporo 1,813,000; Kyoto 1,849,000.

Government: Type: Parliamentary democracy. **Head of state:** Emp. Akihito; b Dec. 23, 1933; in office: Jan. 7, 1989. **Head of gov.:** Prime Min. Junichiro Koizumi; b Jan. 8, 1942; in office: Apr. 26, 2001. **Local divisions:** 47 prefectures. **Defense budget (2001):** $40.4 bil. **Active troops:** 239,800.

Economy: Industries: Motor vehicles, electronic equip., machine tools, steel and metallurgy, ships. **Chief crops:** Rice, sugar beets, vegetables, fruits. **Crude oil reserves** (2000): 58.6 mil bbls. **Arable land:** 11%. **Livestock** (2001): cattle: 4.53 mil; chickens: 297.00 mil.; goats: 31,000; pigs: 9.79 mil; sheep: 11,000. **Fish catch** (1999): 6.69 mil metric tons. **Electricity prod.:** 1,014.74 bil. kWh. **Labor force:** 65% services; 30 % ind.; 5% agric.

Finance: Monetary unit: Yen (Sept. 2002: 122.52 = $1 U.S.). **GDP** (2000 est.): $3.15 tril. **Per capita GDP:** $24,900. **Imports** (2000): $355 bil.; partners (2000 est.): U.S. 19%, China 14.5%. **Exports** (2000): $450 bil.; partners (2000 est.): U.S. 30%, Taiwan 7%. **Tourism:** $3.43 bil. **Budget** (FY01/02 est.): $718 bil. **Intl. reserves less gold** (end 2000): $272.39 bil. **Gold:** 24.55 mil oz t. **Consumer prices** (change in 2000): –0.6%.

Transport: Railroad: Length: 12,511 mi. **Motor vehicles** (1997): 46.64 mil pass. cars, 21.39 mil comm. vehicles. **Civil aviation:** 93.9 bil pass.-mi.; 73 airports. **Chief ports:** Tokyo, Kobe, Osaka, Nagoya, Chiba, Kawasaki, Hakodate.

Communications: TV sets: 708 per 1,000 pop. **Radios:** 957 per 1,000 pop. **Telephones:** 150,819,200. **Daily newspaper circ.:** 578 per 1,000 pop.

Health: Life expectancy: 77.7 male; 84.2 female. **Births** (per 1,000 pop.): 10. **Deaths** (per 1,000 pop.): 8.5. **Natural inc.:** 0.15%. **Infant mortality** (per 1,000 live births): 3.8.

Education: Compulsory: ages 6-15. **Literacy**: 100%.

Major Intl. Organizations: UN and all its specialized agencies, APEC, OECD.

Embassy: 2520 Massachusetts Ave. NW 20008; 238-6700.

Websites: www.us.emb-japan.go.jp; www.mofa.go.jp

According to Japanese legend, the empire was founded by Emperor Jimmu, 660 BC, but earliest records of a unified Japan date from 1,000 years later. Chinese influence was strong in the formation of Japanese civilization. Buddhism was introduced before the 6th century AD.

A feudal system, with locally powerful noble families and their samurai warrior retainers, dominated from 1192. Central power was held by successive families of shoguns (military dictators), 1192-1867, until recovered by Emperor Meiji, 1868. The Portuguese and Dutch had minor trade with Japan in the 16th and 17th centuries; U.S. Commodore Matthew C. Perry opened the country to U.S. trade in a treaty ratified 1854. Industrialization was begun in the late 19th century. Japan fought China, 1894-95, gaining Taiwan. After war with Russia, 1904-5, Russia ceded S half of Sakhalin and gave concessions in China. Japan annexed Korea 1910.

In World War I Japan ousted Germany from Shandong in China and took over German Pacific islands. Japan took Manchuria in 1931 and launched full-scale war in China in 1937. Japan launched war against the U.S. by attacking Pearl Harbor Dec. 7, 1941. The U.S. dropped atomic bombs on Hiroshima, Aug. 6, and Nagasaki, Aug. 9, 1945. Japan surrendered Aug. 14, 1945.

In a new constitution adopted May 3, 1947, Japan renounced the right to wage war; the emperor gave up claims to divinity; the Diet became the sole law-making authority. The U.S. and 48 other non-Communist nations signed a peace treaty and the U.S. a bilateral defense agreement with Japan, in San Francisco Sept. 8, 1951, restoring Japan's sovereignty as of April 28, 1952.

Rebuilding after World War II, Japan emerged as one of the most powerful economies in the world, and as a leader in technology.The U.S. and Western Europe criticized Japan for its restrictive policy on imports, which eventually allowed Japan to accumulate huge trade surpluses.

On June 26, 1968, the U.S. returned to Japanese control the Bonin Isls., Volcano Isls. (including Iwo Jima), and Marcus Isls. On May 15, 1972, Okinawa, the other Ryukyu Isls., and the Daito Isls. were returned by the U.S.; it was agreed the U.S. would continue to maintain military bases on Okinawa.

The Recruit scandal, the nation's worst political scandal since World War II, which involved illegal political donations and stock trading, led to the resignation of Premier Noboru Takeshita in May 1989. Following new political and economic scandals, the ruling Liberal Democratic Party (LDP) was denied a majority in general elections July 18, 1993. On June 29, 1994, Tomiichi Murayama became Japan's first Socialist premier since 1947-48.

An earthquake in the Kobe area in Jan. 1995 claimed more than 5,000 lives, injured nearly 35,000, and caused over $90 billion in property damage. On Mar. 20, a nerve gas attack in the Tokyo subway (blamed on a religious cult) killed 12 and injured thousands. Public anger at the rape of a 12-year-old Okinawa schoolgirl by 3 U.S. servicemen, Sept. 4, led the U.S. to begin reducing its military presence there.

Murayama resigned as prime minister, Jan. 5, 1996, and was replaced by Ryutaro Hashimoto of the LDP. Hashimoto signed a joint security declaration with U.S. Pres. Bill Clinton in Tokyo, Apr. 17, 1996. Nagano hosted the Winter Olympics, Feb. 7-22, 1998.

With Japan mired in a lengthy recession, the LDP suffered a sharp rebuke in elections for parliament's upper house, July 12, 1998. Hashimoto resigned, and on July 24, the LDP chose Keizo Obuchi as prime minister. After Obuchi had a stroke Apr. 3, 2000, an LDP stalwart, Yoshiro Mori, succeeded him on Apr. 5. Obuchi died May 14. Parliamentary elections June 25 left the LDP and its allies with a reduced majority in the lower house. The unpopular Mori was replaced as LDP leader and prime minister in Apr. 2001 by Junichiro Koizumi, a populist reformer.

Jordan

Hashemite Kingdom of Jordan

People: Population: 5,307,470. **Age distrib.** (%): <15: 37.2; 65+: 3.3. **Pop. density:** 150 per sq. mi. **Urban:** 74%. **Ethnic groups:** Arab 98%. **Principal language:** Arabic (official), English. **Chief religions:** Sunni Muslim 96%, Christian 4%.

Geography: Area: 35,300 sq. mi. **Location:** In Middle East. **Neighbors:** Israel and West Bank on W, Saudi Arabia on S, Iraq on E, Syria on N. **Topography:** About 88% of Jordan is arid. Fertile areas are in W. Only port is on short Aqaba Gulf coast. Country shares Dead Sea (1,312 ft. below sea level) with Israel. **Capital:** Amman 1,181,000.

Government: Type: Constitutional monarchy. **Head of state:** King Abdullah II; b Jan. 30, 1962; in office: Feb. 7, 1999. **Head of gov.:** Prime Min. Ali Abu al-Ragheb; b 1946; in office: June 19, 2000. **Local divisions:** 12 governorates. **Defense budget (2001):** $499 mil. **Active troops:** 100,240.

Economy: Industries: Phosphate mining, petroleum refining, cement. **Chief crops:** Grains, olives, fruits. **Minerals:** Phosphates, potash. **Crude oil reserves (2000): 900,000 bbls. Arable land:** 4%. **Livestock** (2001): cattle: 65,400; chickens: 23.70 mil.; goats: 640,000; sheep: 1.85 mil. **Electricity prod.:** 6.93 bil. kWh. **Labor force:** ind. 11.4%, commerce, restaurants, and hotels 10.5%, construction 10%, transport and communications 8.7%, agri. 7.4%, other services 52%.

Finance: Monetary unit: Dinar (Sept. 2002: 0.71 = $1 U.S.). **GDP** (2000 est.): $17.3 bil. **Per capita GDP:** $3,500. **Imports** (2000 est.): $4 bil.; partners: Iraq, Germany, U.S., Japan, UK, Italy, Turkey, Malaysia, Syria, China. **Exports** (2000 est.): $2 bil.; partners: India, Iraq, Saudi Arabia, EU, Indonesia, UAE, Lebanon, Kuwait, Syria, Ethiopia. **Tourism:** $795 mil. **Budget** (2000 est.): $3.1 bil. **Intl. reserves less gold** (end 2000): $2.56 bil. **Gold:** 399,000 oz t. **Consumer prices** (change in 2000): 0.7%.

Transport: Railroad: Length: 421 mi. **Motor vehicles:** 175,000 pass. cars, 90,000 comm. vehicles. **Civil aviation:** 3.0 bil pass.-mi.; 2 airports. **Chief port:** Al Aqabah.

Communications: TV sets: 176 per 1,000 pop. **Radios:** 224 per 1,000 pop. **Telephones:** 1,405,500. **Daily newspaper circ.:** 62 per 1,000 pop.

Health: Life expectancy: 75.3 male; 80.3 female. **Births** (per 1,000 pop.): 24.6. **Deaths** (per 1,000 pop.): 2.6. **Natural inc.:** 2.2%. **Infant mortality** (per 1,000 live births): 19.6.

Education: Free, compulsory: ages 6-16. **Literacy**: 87%.

Major Intl. Organizations: UN (FAO, IBRD, ILO, IMF, IMO, WHO), AL.

Embassy: 3504 International Dr. NW 20008; 966-2664.

Websites: www.nic.gov.jo
www.jordanembassyus.org/new/index.shtml

From ancient times to 1922 the lands to the E of the Jordan River were culturally and politically united with the lands to the W. Arabs conquered the area in the 7th century; the Ottomans took control in the 16th. Britain's 1920 Palestine Mandate covered both sides of the Jordan. In 1921, Abdullah, son of the ruler of Hejaz in Arabia, was installed by Britain as emir of an autonomous Transjordan, covering two-thirds of Palestine. An independent kingdom was proclaimed, 1946.

During the 1948 Arab-Israeli war the West Bank and East Jerusalem were added to the kingdom, which changed its name to Jordan. All these territories were lost to Israel in the 1967 war, which swelled the number of Arab refugees on the East Bank.

Some 700,000 refugees entered Jordan following Iraq's invasion of Kuwait, Aug. 1990. Jordan was viewed as supporting Iraq during the 1990-1991 Persian Gulf crisis.

Jordan and Israel officially agreed, July 25, 1994, to end their state of war; a formal peace treaty was signed Oct. 26. Following a prolonged bout with cancer, King Hussein died Feb. 7, 1999; his eldest son and designated successor immediately assumed the throne as Abdullah II.

Kazakhstan

Republic of Kazakhstan

People: Population: 16,741,519. **Age distrib.** (%): <15: 26.7; 65+: 7.2. **Pop. density:** 16 per sq. mi. **Urban:** 56%. **Ethnic groups:** Kazakh 46%, Russian 35%, Ukrainian 5%. **Principal languages:** Kazakh, Russian (both official). **Chief religions:** Muslim 47%, Russian Orthodox 44%.

Geography: Area: 1,049,200 sq. mi. **Location:** In Central Asia. **Neighbors:** Russia on N; China on E; Kyrgyzstan, Uzbekistan, Turkmenistan on S; Caspian Sea on W. **Topography:** Extends from the lower reaches of Volga in Europe to the Altay Mts. on the Chinese border. **Capital:** Astana. **Cities** (urban aggr.): Alma-Ata 1,130,000; Astana 328,000.

Government: Type: Republic. **Head of state:** Pres. Nursultan A. Nazarbayev; b July 6, 1940; in office: Apr. 1990. **Head of gov.:** Prime Min. Imangali Tasmagambetov; b Dec. 9, 1956; in office: Jan. 28, 2002. **Local divisions:** 14 oblystar, 1 city. **Defense budget (2001):** $211 mil. **Active troops:** 64,000.

Economy: Industries: Oil, mining, iron and steel, nonferrous metal, agricultural machinery. **Chief crops:** Grain, cotton. **Minerals:** Oil, gas, coal, iron, manganese, chrome ore, copper. **Crude oil reserves** (2000): 5.42 bil bbls. **Arable land:** 12%. **Livestock** (2001): cattle: 4.11 mil; chickens: 19.71 mil.; goats: 1.04 mil.; pigs: 1.08 mil; sheep: 8.94 mil. **Fish catch:** (1999): 41,367 metric tons. **Electricity prod.:** 48.69 bil. kWh. **Labor force:** ind. 27%, agri. 23%, services 50%.

Finance: Monetary unit: Tenge (Sept. 2002: 154.61 = $1 U.S.). **GDP** (2000 est.): $85.6 bil. **Per capita GDP:** $5,000. **Imports** (2000 est.): $6.9 bil.; partners (1999): Russia 37%. **Exports** (2000 est.): $8.8 bil.; partners (1999): EU 23%, Russia 20%, China 8%. **Tourism** (1998): $289 mil. **Budget** (1999 est.): $3.6 bil. **Intl. reserves less gold** (end 2000): $1.22 bil. **Gold:** 1.84 mil oz t. **Consumer prices** (change in 2000): 13.2%.

Transport: Railroad: Length: 13,422 mi. **Motor vehicles:** 1.0 mil pass. cars, 515,000 comm. vehicles. **Civil aviation:** 826.5 mil pass.-mi.; 20 airports. **Chief ports:** Aqtau, Atyrau.

Communications: TV sets: 275 per 1,000 pop. **Telephones** (2000): 2,031,500.

Health: Life expectancy: 58 male; 69 female. **Births** (per 1,000 pop.): 17.8. **Deaths** (per 1,000 pop.): 10.7. **Natural inc.:** 0.71%. **Infant mortality** (per 1,000 live births): 59.

Education: Free, compulsory: ages 7-18. **Literacy**: 98%.

Major Intl. Organizations: UN (IBRD, ILO, IMF, IMO, WHO), CIS, OSCE.

Embassy: 1401 16th St. NW 20036; 232-5488.

Websites: www.un.int/kazakhstan; www.president.kz

The region came under the Mongols' rule in the 13th century and gradually came under Russian rule, 1730-1853. It was admitted to the USSR as a constituent republic 1936. Kazakhstan declared independence Dec. 16, 1991. It became an independent state when the Soviet Union dissolved Dec. 26, 1991. The party chief, Nursultan Nazarbayev, was elected president unopposed. In legislative elections Mar. 7, 1994, criticized by international monitors, his party won a sweeping victory. Kazakhstan agreed, Feb. 14, to dismantle nuclear missiles and adhere to the 1968 Nuclear Nonproliferation Treaty; the U.S. pledged increased aid. Private land ownership was legalized Dec. 26, 1995.

Astana (formerly Akmola) was dedicated as the nation's new capital on June 9, 1998.

Pres. Nazarbayev won reelection to a 7-year term Jan. 10, 1999, after his leading opponent, former Prime Min. Akezhan Kazhegeldin, was barred on a technicality.

Kenya

Republic of Kenya

People: Population: 31,138,735. **Age distrib.** (%): <15: 41.9; 65+: 2.8. **Pop. density:** 142 per sq. mi. **Urban:** 32%. **Ethnic groups:** Kikuyu 22%, Luhya 14%, Luo 13%, Kalenjin 12%, Kamba 11%, others including Asian, Arab, European. **Principal languages:** Swahili, English (both official), numerous indigenous languages. **Chief religions:** Protestant 38%, Roman Catholic 28%, indigenous beliefs 26%.

Geography: Area: 219,800 sq. mi. **Location:** E Africa, on coast of Indian O. **Neighbors:** Uganda on W, Tanzania on S, Somalia on E, Ethiopia on N, Sudan on NW. **Topography:** The northern three-fifths of Kenya is arid. To the S, a low coastal area and a plateau varying from 3,000 to 10,000 ft. The Great Rift Valley enters the country N-S, flanked by high mountains. **Capital:** Nairobi. **Cities** (urban aggr.): Nairobi 2,343,000; Mombasa (1991 est.) 600,000.

Government: Type: Republic. **Head of state and gov.:** Pres. Daniel arap Moi; b Sept. 2, 1924; in office: Aug. 22, 1978. **Local divisions:** Nairobi and 7 provinces. **Defense budget (2000):** $235 mil. **Active troops:** 22,400.

Economy: Industries: Small-scale consumer goods, agricultural processing, oil refining, cement, tourism. **Chief crops:** Coffee, corn, tea. **Minerals:** Gold, limestone, salt, rubies, fluorspar, garnets. **Other resources:** Hides, dairy products, cut flowers (world's 4th lgst. exporter). **Arable land:** 7%. **Livestock** 2001): cattle: 12.50 mil; chickens: 32.00 mil.; goats: 9.00 mil.; pigs: 315,000; sheep: 6.50 mil. **Fish catch** (1999): 161,183 metric tons. **Electricity prod.:** 4.62 bil. kWh. **Labor force:** agri. 75-80%.

Finance: Monetary unit: Shilling (Sept. 2002: 79.00 = $1 U.S.). **GDP** (2000 est.): $45.6 bil. **Per capita GDP:** $1,500. **Imports** (2000 est.): $3 bil.; partners (1999): UK 12%, UAE 8%, Japan 8%. **Exports** (2000 est.): $1.7 bil.; partners (1999): Uganda 18%, UK 15%, Tanzania 12%, Pakistan 8%. **Tourism:** $256 mil. **Budget** (2000 est.): $2.97 bil. **Intl. reserves less gold** (end 2000): $689 mil. **Consumer prices** (change in 2000): 5.9%.

Transport: Railroad: Length: 1,885 mi. **Motor vehicles:** 271,000 pass. cars, 75,900 comm. vehicles. **Civil aviation:** 1.1 bil pass.-mi.; 11 airports. **Chief ports:** Mombasa, Kisumu, Lamu.

Communications: TV sets: 18 per 1,000 pop. **Radios:** 103 per 1,000 pop. **Telephones:** 813,100.

Health: Life expectancy: 46.2 male; 47.9 female. **Births** (per 1,000 pop.): 27.6. **Deaths** (per 1,000 pop.): 14.7. **Natural inc.:** 1.29%. **Infant mortality** (per 1,000 live births): 67.2.

Education: Free, compulsory: ages 6-14. **Literacy:** 78%.

Major Intl. Organizations: UN and all of its specialized agencies, the Commonwealth, AU.

Embassy: 2249 R St. NW 20008; 387-6101.

Websites: www.kenyaembassy.com; www.kenya.go.ke

Arab colonies exported spices and slaves from the Kenya coast as early as the 8th century. Britain obtained control in the 19th century. Kenya won independence Dec. 12, 1963, 4 years after the end of the violent Mau Mau uprising.

Kenya had steady growth in industry and agriculture under a modified private enterprise system, and enjoyed a relatively free political life. But stability was shaken in 1974-75, with opposition charges of corruption and oppression. Jomo Kenyatta, the country's leader since independence, died Aug. 22, 1978. He was succeeded by his vice president, Daniel arap Moi.

During the first half of the 1990s, Kenya suffered widespread unemployment and high inflation. Tribal clashes in the western provinces claimed thousands of lives and left tens of thousands homeless. Pres. Moi won a third term in Dec. 1992 elections, which were marred by violence and fraud. Clashes in the Mombasa region, Aug. 1997, left more than 40 people dead. Pres. Moi was reelected Dec. 29, in an election again plagued by irregularities.

A truck bomb explosion at the U.S. embassy in Nairobi, Aug. 7, 1998, killed more than 200 people and injured about 5,000. The U.S. blamed the attack and a near-simultaneous embassy bombing in Tanzania on Islamic terrorists associated with wealthy Saudi-born Osama bin Laden, believed to be sheltered in Afghanistan. After a trial in New York City, 4 conspirators were convicted May 29, 2001.

Kiribati

Republic of Kiribati

People: Population: 96,335. **Age distrib. (%): <15: 40.5; 65+: 3.2. Pop. density:** 348 per sq. mi. **Urban:** 39%. **Ethnic groups:** Micronesian. **Principal languages:** English (official), Gilbertese. **Chief religions:** Roman Catholic 53%, Protestant 41%.

Geography: Area: 277 sq. mi. **Location:** 33 Micronesian islands (the Gilbert, Line, and Phoenix groups) in the mid-Pacific scattered in a 2-mil sq. mi. chain around the point where the International Date Line formerly cut the Equator. In 1997 the Date Line was moved to follow Kiribati's E border. **Neighbors:** Nearest are Nauru to SW, Tuvalu and Tokelau Isls. to S. **Topography:** Except Banaba (Ocean) Isl., all are low-lying, with soil of coral sand and rock fragments, subject to erratic rainfall. **Capital:** South Tarawa: 32,000.

Government: Type: Republic. **Head of state and gov.:** Pres. Teburoro Tito; b Aug. 25, 1953; in office: Oct. 1, 1994. **Local divisions:** 3 units, 6 districts.

Economy: Industries: Fishing, handicrafts. **Chief crops:** Copra, taro, breadfruit, sweet potatoes, vegetables. **Livestock** chickens: 400,000; pigs: 13,000. **Fish catch:** (1999): 23,052 metric tons. **Electricity prod.:** 0.01 bil. kWh.

Finance: Monetary unit: Australian Dollar (Sept. 2002: 1.84 = $1 U.S.). **GDP** (2000 est.): supplemented by a nearly equal amount from external sources $76 mil. **Per capita GDP:** $850. **Imports** (1999): $44 mil.; partners (1999): Australia, Fiji, Japan, NZ, China. **Exports** (1998): $6 mil.; partners (1999): Bangladesh, Australia, U.S., Hong Kong. **Tourism** (1998): $1 mil. **Budget** (1996 est.): $47.7 mil.

Transport: Chief port: Tarawa. **Civil aviation:** 7.0 mil pass.-mi.; 17 airports.

Communications: Radios: 75 per 1,000 pop. **Telephones** (2000): 3,700.

Health: Life expectancy: 57.6 male; 63.6 female. **Births** (per 1,000 pop.): 31.6. **Deaths** (per 1,000 pop.): 8.8. **Natural inc.:** 2.28%. **Infant mortality** (per 1,000 live births): 52.6.

Education: Free, compulsory: ages 6-14. **Literacy**: 90%.

Major Intl. Organizations: UN (IBRD, IMF, WHO), the Commonwealth.

A British protectorate since 1892, the Gilbert and Ellice Islands colony was completed with the inclusion of the Phoenix Islands, 1937. Tarawa Atoll was the scene of some of the bloodiest fighting in the Pacific during World War II.

Self-rule was granted 1971; the Ellice Islands separated from the colony 1975 and became independent Tuvalu, 1978. Kiribati (pronounced *Kiribass)* independence was attained July 12, 1979. Under a treaty of friendship the U.S. relinquished its claims to several Line and Phoenix islands, including Christmas (Kiritimati), Canton, and Enderbury. Kiribati was admitted to the UN Sept. 14, 1999.

Korea, North

Democratic People's Republic of Korea

People: Population: 22,224,195. **Age distrib.** (%): <15: 25.5; 65+: 6.8. **Pop. density:** 478 per sq. mi. **Urban:** 60%. **Ethnic group:** Korean. **Principal language:** Korean (official). **Chief religions:** Activities almost nonexistent; traditionally Buddhism, Confucianism, Chondogyo.

Geography: Area: 46,500 sq. mi. **Location:** In northern E Asia. **Neighbors:** China and Russia on N, South Korea on S. **Topography:** Mountains and hills cover nearly all the country, with narrow valleys and small plains in between. The N and the E coasts are the most rugged areas. **Capital:** Pyongyang. **Cities** (urban aggr.): Pyongyang 3,197,000; Nampo 1,046,000.

Government: Type: Communist state. **Leader:** Kim Jong Il; b Feb. 16, 1942; officially assumed post Oct. 8, 1997. **Local divisions:** 9 provinces, 3 special cities. **Defense budget** (2001): $1.3 bil. **Active troops:** 1,082,000.

Economy: Industries: Military products, machinery, electric power, chemicals. **Chief crops:** Corn, potatoes, soybeans, rice. **Minerals:** Coal, lead, tungsten, zinc, graphite, magnesite, iron, copper, gold, salt. **Arable land:** 14%. **Livestock** (2001): cattle: 570,000; chickens: 16.89 mil.; goats: 2.57 mil.; pigs: 3.14 mil; sheep: 189,000. **Fish catch** (1999): 306,636 metric tons. **Electricity prod.:** 33.40 bil. kWh. **Labor force:** agri. 36%, nonagricultural 64%.

Finance: Monetary unit: Won (Sept. 2002: 2.20 = $1 U.S.). **GDP** (2000 est.): $22 bil. **Per capita GDP:** $1,000. **Imports** (1999 est.): $960 mil.; partners (1995): China 33%, Japan 17%. **Exports** (1999 est.): $520 mil.; partners (1995): Japan 28%, South Korea 21%. **Budget** NA.

Transport: Railroad: Length: 5,302 mi. **Civil aviation:** 177.5 mil pass.-mi.; 1 airport. **Chief ports:** Chongjin, Hamhung, Nampo.

Communications: TV sets: 85 per 1,000 pop. **Radios:** 200 per 1,000 pop. **Telephones** (1998): 1,100,000 main lines. **Daily newspaper circ.:** 213 per 1,000 pop.

Health: Life expectancy: 68.3 male; 74.4 female. **Births** (per 1,000 pop.): 17.9. **Deaths** (per 1,000 pop.): 7. **Natural inc.:** 1.1%. **Infant mortality** (per 1,000 live births): 22.8.

Education: Free, compulsory: ages 6-17. **Literacy** (1992): 95%.

Major Intl. Organizations: UN (FAO, IMO, WHO).

The Democratic People's Republic of Korea was founded May 1, 1948, in the zone occupied by Russian troops after World War II. Its armies tried to conquer the south, 1950. After 3 years of fighting, with Chinese and U.S. intervention, a cease-fire was proclaimed. For the next four decades, a hardline Communist regime headed by Kim Il Sung kept tight control over the nation's political, economic, and cultural life. The nation used its abundant mineral and hydroelectric resources to develop its military strength and heavy industry.

In Mar. 1993, North Korea became the first nation to formally withdraw from the Nuclear Nonproliferation Treaty, the international pact designed to limit the spread of nuclear weapons. The nation suspended its withdrawal in June in reaction to threats of UN economic sanctions, but was widely believed to be developing nuclear weapons. The U.S. and North Korea reached an interim agreement, Aug. 13, 1994, intended to resolve the nuclear issue, and further negotiations followed.

Kim Il Sung died July 8, 1994. He was succeeded by his son, Kim Jong Il. North Korea at this time suffered from defections by high officials, a deteriorating economy, and severe food shortages in the late 1990s.

On Sept. 17, 1999, the U.S. eased travel and trade restrictions on North Korea after Pyongyang agreed to suspend long-range missile testing. A first-ever summit conference in Pyongyang between North and South Korean leaders, June 13-15, 2000, marked an unexpected improvement in relations between the 2 Koreas, and brought an end to many U.S. sanctions. In Sept. 2002, Japanese Prime Min. Junichiro Koizumi became the 1st Japanese prime minister to visit North Korea; there, in a landmark summit, North Korea agreed to begin normalizing relations, and admitted for the 1st time that its agents had helped to kidnap 11 Japanese in the late 1970s.

Korea, South

Republic of Korea

People: Population: 48,324,000. **Age distrib.** (%): <15: 21.6; 65+: 7.3. **Pop. density:** 1,275 per sq. mi. **Urban:** 81%. **Ethnic group:** Korean. **Principal language:** Korean (official). **Chief religions:** Christianity 49%, Buddhism 47%.

Geography: Area: 37,900 sq. mi. **Location:** In northern E Asia. **Neighbors:** North Korea on N. **Topography:** The country is mountainous, with a rugged east coast. The western and southern coasts are deeply indented, with many islands and harbors. **Capital:** Seoul. **Cities** (urban aggr.): Seoul 9,862,000; Pusan 3,830,000; Inch'on 2,884,000; Taegu 2,675,000.

Government: Type: Republic, with power centralized in a strong executive. **Head of state:** Pres. Kim Dae Jung; b Dec. 3, 1925; in office: Feb. 25, 1998. **Head of gov.:** Prime Min. Kim Suk Soo; b 1932; in office: Sept.. 10, 2002 (acting). **Local divisions:** 9 provinces, 6 special cities. **Defense budget (2001):** $11.8 bil. **Active troops:** 683,000.

Economy: Industries: Electronics, autos, chemicals, shipbuilding, steel, textiles. **Chief crops:** Rice, barley, vegetables. **Minerals:** Tungsten, coal, graphite. **Arable land:** 19%. **Livestock** (2001): cattle: 1.95 mil; chickens: 102.39 mil.; goats: 430,000; pigs: 8.72 mil; sheep: 600. **Fish catch** (1999): 2.60 mil metric tons. **Electricity prod.:** 273.20 bil. kWh. **Labor force:** agri 68%, services 68%, ind. 20%, agri. 12%.

Finance: Monetary unit: Won (Sept. 2002: 1,228.70 = $1 U.S.). **GDP** (2000 est.): $764.6 bil. **Per capita GDP:** $16,100. **Imports** (2000): $160.5 bil.; partners (1999): U.S. 20.8%, Japan 20.2%. **Exports** (2000): $172.6 bil.; partners (1999): U.S. 20.5%, Japan 11%. **Tourism:** $5.62 bil. **Budget** (1999): $94.9 bil. **Intl. reserves less gold** (end 2000): $73.78 bil. **Gold:** 438,000 oz t. **Consumer prices** (change in 2000): 2.3%.

Transport: Railroad: Length: 4,072 mi. **Motor vehicles** (1997): 7.59 mil pass. cars, 2.83 mil comm. vehicles. **Civil aviation:** 34.62 bil pass.-mi.; 14 airports. **Chief ports:** Pusan, Inchon.

Communications: TV sets: 337 per 1,000 pop. **Radios:** 1,037 per 1,000 pop. **Telephones:** 51,770,300. **Daily newspaper circ.:** 394 per 1,000 pop.

Health: Life expectancy: 71.2 male; 79 female. **Births** (per 1,000 pop.): 14.6. **Deaths** (per 1,000 pop.): 6. **Natural inc.:** 0.85%. **Infant mortality** (per 1,000 live births): 7.6.

Education: Free, compulsory: ages 6-12. **Literacy**: 98%.

Major Intl. Organizations: UN (FAO, IBRD, ILO, IMF, IMO, WHO, WTrO), APEC, OECD.

Embassy: 2450 Massachusetts Ave. NW 20008; 939-5600.

Website: www.korea.net

Korea, once called the Hermit Kingdom, has a recorded history since the 1st century BC. It was united in a kingdom under the Silla Dynasty, AD 668. It was at times associated with the Chinese empire; the treaty that concluded the Sino-Japanese war of 1894-95 recognized Korea's complete independence. In 1910 Japan forcibly annexed Korea as Chosun.

At the Potsdam conference, July 1945, the 38th parallel was designated as the line dividing the Soviet and the American occupation. Russian troops entered Korea Aug. 10, 1945; U.S. troops entered Sept. 8, 1945. The Soviet military organized socialists and Communists and blocked efforts to let the Koreans unite their country.

The South Koreans formed the Republic of Korea in May 1948 with Seoul as the capital. Dr. Syngman Rhee was chosen president. A separate, Communist regime was formed in the N; its army attacked the S in June 1950, initiating the Korean War. UN troops, under U.S. command, supported the S in the war, which ended in an armistice (July 1953) leaving Korea divided by a "no-man's land" along the 38th parallel.

Rhee's authoritarian rule became increasingly unpopular, and a movement spearheaded by college students forced his resignation Apr. 26, 1960. In an army coup May 16, 1961, Gen. Park Chung Hee became chairman of a ruling junta. He was elected president, 1963; a 1972 referendum allowed him to be reelected for an unlimited series of 6-year terms. Park was assassinated by the chief of the Korean CIA, Oct. 26, 1979. In May 1980, Gen. Chun Doo Hwan, head of military intelligence, reinstated full martial law and ordered the brutal suppression of pro-democracy demonstrations in Kwangju.

In July 1972 South and North Korea agreed on a common goal of reunifying the 2 nations by peaceful means. But there was no sign of a thaw in relations between the two regimes until 1985, when they agreed to discuss economic issues.

On June 10, 1987, middle-class office workers, shopkeepers, and business executives joined with students in antigovernment protests in Seoul calling for democratic reforms. Following weeks of rioting and violence, Chun, July 1, agreed to permit election of the next president by direct popular vote and other reforms. In Dec., Roh Tae Woo was elected president. In 1990, the nation's 3 largest political parties merged; some 100,000 students protested the merger as undemocratic.

Kim Young Sam took office in 1993 as the first civilian president since 1961. Convicted of mutiny, treason, and corruption, Chun was sentenced to death by a Seoul court, Aug. 26, 1996, for his role in the 1979 coup and 1980 Kwangju massacre; Roh received a 22-1/2 year prison sentence. On Dec. 16, Chun's term was reduced to life in prison, and Roh's to 17 years.

The collapse in Jan. 1997 of the Hanbo steel firm triggered a new round of corruption scandals. With currency and stock values plummeting, the nation averted default by agreeing, Dec. 4, on a $57 billion bailout from the IMF. Kim Dae Jung, a longtime dissident, won the presidential election Dec. 18. Chun and Roh were released and pardoned Dec. 22, 1997.

At an unprecedented summit meeting in Pyongyang, June 13-15, 2000, Pres. Kim Dae Jung and North Korean leader Kim Jong Il agreed to work for reconciliation and eventual reunification of their 2 countries. On Oct. 13, 2000, Kim Dae Jung was named the winner of the 2000 Nobel Peace Prize. Embarrassed by a naval clash with North Korea June 29, 2002, and by corruption probes targeting his family, he revamped his cabinet July 11. The legislature, controlled by opposition parties, rejected 2 of his nominees for prime min., July 31 and Aug. 28.

Kuwait

State of Kuwait

People: Population: 2,111,561. **Age distrib.** (%): <15: 28.8; 65+: 2.4. **Pop. density:** 306 per sq. mi. **Urban:** 98%. **Ethnic groups:** Kuwaiti 45%, other Arab 35%. **Principal languages:** Arabic (official), English. **Chief religion:** Muslim 85%.

Geography: Area: 6,900 sq. mi. **Location:** In Middle East, at N end of Persian Gulf. **Neighbors:** Iraq on N, Saudi Arabia on S. **Topography:** The country is flat, very dry, and extremely hot. **Capital:** Kuwait City: 888,000.

Government: Type: Constitutional monarchy. **Head of state:** Emir Sheikh Jabir al-Ahmad al-Jabir as-Sabah; b 1928; in office: Jan. 1, 1978. **Head of gov.:** Prime Min. Sheikh Saad Abdulla as-Salim as-Sabah; b 1930; in office: Feb. 8, 1978. **Local divisions:** 5 governorates. **Defense budget:** (2001) $2.6 bil. **Active troops:** 15,500.

Economy: Industries: Oil, petrochemicals. **Minerals:** Oil, gas. **Crude oil reserves** (2001): 98.8 bil bbls. **Livestock** (2001): cattle: 21,000; chickens: 32.46 mil.; goats: 130,000; sheep: 630,000. **Electricity prod.:** 31.20 bil. kWh. **Labor force:** 50% gov't. and social services; 40% services; 10% industry and agric.

Finance: Monetary unit: Dinar (Sept. 2002: 0.30 = $1 U.S.). **GDP** (2000 est.): $29.3 bil. **Per capita GDP:** $15,000. **Imports** (2000 est.): $7.6 bil.; partners (1999): U.S. 15%, Japan 10%. **Exports** (2000 est.): $23.2 bil.; partners (1999): Japan 23%, U.S. 12%. **Tourism** (1998): $207 mil. **Budget** (FY01/02): $17.2 bil. **Intl. reserves less gold** (end 2000): $5.44 bil. **Gold:** 2.54 mil oz t. **Consumer prices** (change in 2000): 1.8%.

Transport: Motor vehicles: 538,000 pass. cars, 155,000 comm. vehicles. **Civil aviation:** 3.7 bil pass.-mi.; 1 airport. **Chief port:** Mina al-Ahmadi.

Communications: TV sets: 505 per 1,000 pop. **Radios:** 678 per 1,000 pop. **Telephones:** 961,600. **Daily newspaper circ.:** 377 per 1,000 pop.

Health: Life expectancy: 75.6 male; 77.4 female. **Births** (per 1,000 pop.): 21.8. **Deaths** (per 1,000 pop.): 2.5. **Natural inc.:** 1.94%. **Infant mortality** (per 1,000 live births): 10.9.

Education: Free, compulsory: ages 6-14. **Literacy**: 79%.

Major Intl. Organizations: UN (FAO, IBRD, ILO, IMF, IMO, WHO, WTrO), AL, OPEC.

Embassy: 2940 Tilden St. NW 20008; 966-0702.

Website: www.moinfo.gov.kw

Kuwait is ruled by the Al-Sabah dynasty, founded 1759. Britain ran foreign relations and defense from 1899 until independence in 1961. The majority of the population is non-Kuwaiti, with many Palestinians, and cannot vote.

Oil is the fiscal mainstay, providing most of Kuwait's income. Oil pays for free medical care, education, and social security. There are no taxes, except customs duties.

Kuwaiti oil tankers came under frequent attack by Iran because of Kuwait's support of Iraq in the Iran-Iraq War. In July 1987, U.S. Navy warships began escorting Kuwaiti tankers in the Persian Gulf.

Kuwait was attacked and overrun by Iraqi forces Aug. 2, 1990. The emir and senior members of the ruling family fled to Saudi Arabia to establish a government in exile. On Aug. 28, Iraq announced that Kuwait was its 19th province. Following several weeks of aerial attacks on Iraq and Iraqi forces in Kuwait, a U.S.-led coalition began a ground attack Feb. 23, 1991. By Feb. 27, Iraqi forces were routed and Kuwait liberated. Following liberation, there were reports of abuse of Palestinians and others suspected of collaborating with Iraqi occupiers.

Former U.S. Pres. George Bush visited Kuwait, Apr. 14-16, 1993, and was honored as the leader of the Persian Gulf War alliance that expelled Iraqi troops. Kuwaiti authorities arrested 14 Iraqis and Kuwaitis for allegedly plotting to assassinate Bush during his visit; 13 were convicted and sentenced to prison or death, June 4, 1994. The UN Security Council ruled, Sept. 27, 2000, that Iraq had to pay the Kuwait Petroleum Corp. $15.9 billion for damage to Kuwaiti oil fields during the Persian Gulf War. Iraq recognized Kuwait's territorial integrity Mar. 28, 2002.

Kyrgyzstan

Kyrgyz Republic

People: Population: 4,822,166. **Age distrib. (%):** <15: 35.0; 65+: 6.1. **Pop density:** 63 per sq. mi. **Urban:** 33%. **Ethnic groups:** Kyrgyz 52%, Russian 18%, Uzbek 13%. **Principal languages:** Kyrgyz, Russian (both official). **Chief religions:** Muslim 75%, Russian Orthodox 20%.

Geography: Area: 76,600 sq. mi. **Location:** In Central Asia. **Neighbors:** Kazakhstan on N, China on E, Uzbekistan on W, Tajikistan on S. **Capital:** Bishkek: 736,000.

Government: Type: Republic. **Head of state:** Pres. Askar Akayev; b Nov. 10, 1944; in office: Oct. 28, 1990. **Head of gov.:** Prime Min. Nikolay Tanayev; b Nov. 5, 1945; in office: May 30, 2002. **Local divisions:** 6 oblasts, 1 city. **Defense budget (2001):** $40.8 mil. **Active troops:** 9,000.

Economy: Industries: Small machinery, textiles, food processing, cement. **Chief crops:** Tobacco, cotton, fruits. **Minerals:** Gold, coal, oil. **Crude oil reserves** (2000): 40 mil bbls. **Arable land:** 7%. **Livestock** (2001): cattle: 985,000; chickens: 3.12 mil.; goats: 236,000; pigs: 117,000; sheep: 4.16 mil. **Electricity prod.:** 14.68 bil. kWh. **Labor force:** agri. 55%, ind. 15%, services 30%.

Finance: Monetary unit: Som (Sept. 2002: 46.16 = $1 U.S.). **GDP** (2000 est.): $12.6 bil. **Per capita GDP:** $2,700. **Imports** (2000 est.): $579 mil.; partners (1999): Russia 18%, Kazakhstan 12%. **Exports** (2000 est.): $482 mil.; partners (1999): Germany 33%, Russia 16%. **Tourism** (1998): $7 mil. **Budget** (1999 est.): $238.7 mil. **Intl. reserves less gold** (end 2000): $183 mil. **Gold:** 83,100 oz t. **Consumer prices** (change in 2000): 18.7%.

Transport: Railroad: Length: 249 mi. **Motor vehicles:** 164,000 pass. cars. **Civil aviation:** 280.7 mil pass.-mi.; 2 airports. **Chief port:** Ysyk-Kol.

Communications: TV sets: 238 per 1,000 pop. **Telephones** (2000): 385,100. **Daily newspaper circ.:** 11 per 1,000 pop.

Health: Life expectancy: 59.4 male; 68 female. **Births** (per 1,000 pop.): 26.1. **Deaths** (per 1,000 pop.): 9.1. **Natural inc.:** 1.7%. **Infant mortality** (per 1,000 live births): 75.9.

Education: Compulsory: ages 6-15. **Literacy** (1993): 97%.

Major Intl. Organizations: UN (FAO, IBRD, ILO, IMF, WHO), CIS, OSCE.

Embassy: 1732 Wisconsin Ave. NW, 20007; 338-5141.

Website: www.kyrgyzstan.org

The region was inhabited around the 13th century by the Kyrgyz. It was annexed to Russia 1864. After 1917, it was nominally a Kara-Kyrgyz autonomous area, which was reorganized 1926, and made a constituent republic of the USSR in 1936. Kyrgyzstan declared independence Aug. 31, 1991. It became an independent state when the USSR disbanded Dec. 26, 1991. A constitution was adopted May 5, 1993.

Reelected Dec. 24, 1995, Pres. Askar Akayev gained approval by referendum of a constitutional amendment expanding his presidential powers, Feb. 10, 1996. Amendments restricting the powers of parliament and allowing private ownership of land were ratified by referendum Oct. 17, 1998. Akayev won a 3d 5-year term in the Oct. 29, 2000, election. The U.S. military presence in Kyrgyzstan has been expanding since Dec. 2001.

Laos

Lao People's Democratic Republic

People: Population: 5,777,180. **Age distrib.** (%): <15: 42.7; 65+: 3.3. **Pop. density:** 65 per sq. mi. **Urban:** 23%. **Ethnic groups:** Lao Loum 68%, Lao Theung 22%, Lao Soung (includes Hmong and Yao) 9%. **Principal languages:** Lao (official), French, English. **Chief religions:** Buddhism 60%, animist and other 40%.

Geography: Area: 89,100 sq. mi. **Location:** In Indochina Peninsula in SE Asia. **Neighbors:** Myanmar and China on N, Vietnam on E, Cambodia on S, Thailand on W. **Topography:** Landlocked, dominated by jungle. High mountains along eastern border are the source of the E-W rivers slicing across the country to the Mekong R., which defines most of the western border. **Capital:** Vientiane 663,000.

Government: Type: Communist. **Head of state:** Pres. Khamtai Siphandon; b Feb. 8, 1924; in office: Feb. 24, 1998. **Head of gov.:** Prime Min. Boungnang Vorachith; b Aug. 15, 1937; in office: Mar. 27, 2001. **Local divisions:** 16 provinces, 1 municipality, 1 special zone. **Defense budget (2001):** $15.8 mil. **Active troops:** 29,100.

Economy: Industries: Tin and gypsum mining, timber, electric power, agricultural processing. **Chief crops:** Sweet potatoes, corn, cotton, vegetables, coffee. **Minerals:** Gypsum, tin, gold. **Arable land:** 3%. **Livestock** (2001): cattle: 1.10 mil; chickens: 14.00 mil.; goats: 240,000; pigs: 1.50 mil. **Fish catch:** (1999): 40,000 metric tons. **Electricity prod.:** 1.02 bil. kWh. **Labor force:** agri. 80%.

Finance: Monetary unit: Kip (Sept. 2002: 7,600.00 = $1 U.S.). **GDP** (2000 est.): $9 bil. **Per capita GDP:** $1,700. **Imports** (2000 est.): $540 mil.; partners: Thailand, Japan, Vietnam, China, Singapore, Hong Kong. **Exports** (2000 est.): $323 mil.; partners: Vietnam, Thailand, Germany, France, Belgium. **Tourism:** $103 mil. **Budget** (FY98/99 est.): $462 mil. **Intl. reserves less gold** (end 2000): $107 mil. **Gold:** 17,100 oz t. **Consumer prices** (change in 2000): 25.1%.

Transport: Motor vehicles: 9,000 pass. cars, 9,000 comm. vehicles. **Civil aviation:** 29.9 mil pass.-mi.; 11 airports.

Communications: TV sets: 17 per 1,000 pop. **Radios:** 116 per 1,000 pop. **Telephones:** 82,200.

Health: Life expectancy: 52 male; 55.9 female. **Births** (per 1,000 pop.): 37.4. **Deaths** (per 1,000 pop.): 12.7. **Natural inc.:** 2.47%. **Infant mortality** (per 1,000 live births): 91.

Education: Compulsory for 5 years between ages 6-15. **Literacy:** 57%.

Major Intl. Organizations: UN (FAO, IBRD, ILO, IMF, WHO), ASEAN.

Embassy: 2222 S St. NW 20008; 332-6416.

Website: www.laoembassy.com/discover/index.htm

Laos became a French protectorate in 1893, but regained independence as a constitutional monarchy July 19, 1949.

Conflicts among neutralist, Communist, and conservative factions created a chaotic political situation. Armed conflict increased after 1960.

The 3 factions formed a coalition government in June 1962, with neutralist Prince Souvanna Phouma as premier. A 14-nation conference in Geneva signed agreements, 1962, guaranteeing neutrality and independence. By 1964 the Pathet Lao had withdrawn from the coalition, and, with aid from North Vietnamese troops, renewed sporadic attacks. U.S. planes bombed the Ho Chi Minh trail, supply line from North Vietnam to Communist forces in Laos and South Vietnam.

In 1970 the U.S. stepped up air support and military aid. After Pathet Lao military gains, Souvanna Phouma in May 1975 ordered government troops to cease fighting; the Pathet Lao took control. The Lao People's Democratic Republic was proclaimed Dec. 3, 1975.

From the mid-1970s through the 1980s, the Laotian government relied on Vietnam for military and financial aid. Since easing its foreign investment laws in 1988, Laos has attracted more than $5 billion from Thailand, the U.S., and other nations. Laos was admitted to ASEAN on July 23, 1997.

Latvia

Republic of Latvia

People: Population: 2,366,515. **Age distrib.** (%): <15: 16.6 65+: 15.3. **Pop density:** 95 per sq. mi. **Urban:** 69%. **Ethnic groups:** Latvian 57%, Russian 30%. **Principal languages:** Lettish (official), Lithuanian, Russian. **Chief religions:** Lutheran, Roman Catholic, Russian Orthodox.

Geography: Area: 24,900 sq. mi. **Location:** E Europe, on the Baltic Sea. **Neighbors:** Estonia on N, Lithuania and Belarus on S, Russia on E. **Capital:** Riga 756,000.

Government: Type: Republic. **Head of state:** Pres. Vaira Vike-Freiberga; b Dec. 1, 1937; in office: July 8, 1999. **Head of gov.:** Prime Min. Andris Berzins; b Aug. 4, 1951; in office; May 5, 2000. **Local divisions:** 26 counties, 7 municipalities. **Defense budget (2001):** $76 mil. **Active troops:** 6,500.

Economy: Industries: Vehicles, street and railroad cars, synthetic fibers. **Chief crops:** Grains, sugar beets, potatoes. **Minerals:** Amber, peat. **Arable land:** 27%. **Livestock** (2001): cattle: 366,700; chickens: 3.11 mil.; goats: 10,400; pigs: 393,500; sheep: 28,600. **Electricity prod.:** 3.30 bil. kWh. **Labor force:** agri. 10%, ind. 25%, services 65%.

Finance: Monetary unit: Lat (Sept. 2002: 0.61 = $1 U.S.). **GDP** (2000 est.): $17.3 bil. **Per capita GDP:** $7,200. **Imports** (2000): $3.2 bil.; partners (1999): Russia 15%, Germany 10%. **Exports** (2000): $2.1 bil.; partners (1999): Germany 16%, UK 11%. **Tourism:** $111 mil. **Budget** (1998 est.): $1.27 bil. **Intl. reserves less gold** (end 2000): $653 mil. **Gold:** 248,700 oz t. **Consumer prices** (change in 2000): 2.7%.

Transport: Railroad: Length: 1,499 mi. **Motor vehicles:** 252,000 pass. cars, 74,000 comm. vehicles. **Civil aviation:** 135.0 mil pass.-mi.; 1 airport. **Chief port:** Riga.

Communications: TV sets: 452 per 1,000 pop. **Radios:** 560 per 1,000 pop. **Telephones:** 1,381,600. **Daily newspaper circ.:** 235 per 1,000 pop.

Health: Life expectancy: 63.1 male; 75.2 female. **Births** (per 1,000 pop.): 8.3. **Deaths** (per 1,000 pop.): 14.7. **Natural inc.:** -0.65%. **Infant mortality** (per 1,000 live births): 15.

Education: Compulsory: ages 7-16. **Literacy** (1989): 100%.

Major Intl. Organizations: UN (FAO, IBRD, ILO, IMF, IMO, WHO), OSCE.

Embassy: 4325 17th St. NW 20011; 726-8213.

Websites: www.latvia-usa.org;
www.csb.lvavidus.cfm

Prior to 1918, Latvia was occupied by the Russians and Germans. It was an independent republic, 1918-39. The Aug. 1939 Soviet-German agreement assigned Latvia to the Soviet sphere of influence. It was officially accepted as part of the USSR on Aug. 5, 1940. It was overrun by the German army in 1941, but retaken in 1945.

During an abortive Soviet coup, Latvia declared independence, Aug. 21, 1991. The Soviet Union recognized Latvia's independence in Sept. 1991. The last Russian troops in Latvia withdrew by Aug. 31, 1994. Responding to international pressure, Latvian voters on Oct. 3, 1998, eased citizenship laws that had discriminated against some 500,000 ethnic Russians. On June 17, 1999, the legislature elected Vaira Vike-Freiberga as Latvia's 1st woman president.

Lebanon

Republic of Lebanon

People: Population: 3,667,780. **Age distrib.** (%): <15: 27.6; 65+: 6.7. **Pop. density:** 943 per sq. mi. **Urban:** 89%. **Ethnic groups:** Arab 95%, Armenian 4%. **Principal languages:** Arabic (official), French, English, Armenian. **Chief religions:** Islam 70%, Christian 30%.

Geography: Area: 3,900 sq. mi. **Location:** In Middle East, on E end of Mediterranean Sea. **Neighbors:** Syria on E, Israel on S. **Topography:** There is a narrow coastal strip, and 2 mountain ranges running N-S enclosing the fertile Beqaa Valley. The Litani R. runs S through the valley, turning W to empty into the Mediterranean. **Capital:** Beirut: 2,115,000.

Government: Type: Republic. **Head of state:** Pres. Emile Lahoud; b 1936; in office: Nov. 24, 1998. **Head of gov.:** Prime Min. Rafiq al-Hariri; b 1944; in office: Oct. 23, 2000. **Local divisions:** 5 governorates. **Defense budget (2001):** $594 mil (1999). **Active troops:** 71,380.

Economy: Industries: Banking, food processing, jewelry, cement, textiles. **Chief crops:** Citrus, olives, tobacco, potatoes, vegetables. **Minerals:** Limestone, iron. **Arable land:** 21%. **Livestock** (2001): cattle: 74,000; chickens: 32.00 mil.; goats: 445,000; pigs: 63,500; sheep: 380,000. **Electricity prod.:** 7.95 bil. kWh. **Labor force:** 62% services; 31% industry; 7% agric.

Finance: Monetary unit: Pound (Sept. 2002: 1,513.75 = $1 U.S.). **GDP** (2000 est.): $18.2 bil. **Per capita GDP:** $5,000. **Imports** (2000 est.): $6.2 bil.; partners (1999): Italy 13%, France 11%. **Exports** (2000 est.): $700 mil.; partners (1999): UAE 9%, Saudi Arabia 8%. **Tourism:** $807 mil. **Budget** (2000 est.): $5.55 bil. **Intl. reserves less gold** (end 2000): $4.56 bil. **Gold:** 9.22 mil oz t.

Transport: Railroad: Length: 138 mi. **Motor vehicles:** 1.1 mil pass. cars, 83,000 comm. vehicles. **Civil aviation:** 1.3 bil pass.-mi.; 1 airport. **Chief ports:** Beirut, Tripoli, Sidon.

Communications: TV sets: 291 per 1,000 pop. **Radios:** 608 per 1,000 pop. **Telephones** (2000): 1,424,500. **Newspaper circ.:** 172 per 1,000 pop.

Health: Life expectancy: 69.4 male; 74.3 female. **Births** (per 1,000 pop.): 20. **Deaths** (per 1,000 pop.): 6.3. **Natural inc.:** 1.36%. **Infant mortality** (per 1,000 live births): 27.4.

Education: Literacy: 92%.

Major Intl. Organizations: UN (FAO, IBRD, ILO, IMF, IMO, WHO), AL.

Embassy: 2560 28th St. NW 20008; 939-6300.

Formed from 5 former Turkish Empire districts, Lebanon became an independent state Sept. 1, 1920, administered under French mandate 1920-41. French troops withdrew in 1946.

Under the 1943 National Covenant, all public positions were divided among the various religious communities, with Christians in the majority. By the 1970s, Muslims became the majority and demanded a larger political and economic role.

U.S. Marines intervened, May-Oct. 1958, during a Syrian-aided revolt. Continued raids against Israeli civilians, 1970-75, brought Israeli attacks against guerrilla camps and villages. Israeli troops occupied S Lebanon, Mar. 1978, and again in Apr. 1980.

An estimated 60,000 were killed and billions of dollars in damage inflicted in a 1975-76 civil war. Palestinian units and leftist Muslims fought against the Maronite militia, the Phalange, and other Christians. Several Arab countries provided political and arms support to the various factions, while Israel aided Christian forces. Up to 15,000 Syrian troops intervened in 1976 to fight Palestinian groups. A cease-fire was mainly policed by Syria.

New clashes between Syrian troops and Christian forces erupted, Apr. 1, 1981. By Apr. 22, fighting had also broken out between two Muslim factions. In July, Israeli air raids on Beirut killed or wounded some 800 persons.

Israeli forces invaded Lebanon June 6, 1982, in a coordinated land, sea, and air attack aimed at crushing strongholds of the Palestine Liberation Organization (PLO). Israeli and Syrian forces engaged in the Bekaa Valley. By June 14, Israeli troops had encircled Beirut. On Aug. 21, the PLO evacuated west Beirut after massive Israeli bombings there. Israeli troops entered west Beirut following the Sept. 14 assassination of newly elected Lebanese Pres. Bashir Gemayel. On Sept. 16, Lebanese Christian troops entered 2 refugee camps and massacred hundreds of Palestinian refugees. An agreement May 17, 1983, between Lebanon, Israel, and the U.S. (but not Syria) provided for the withdrawal of Israeli troops; at least 30,000 Syrian troops remained in Lebanon, and Israeli forces continued to occupy a "security zone" in the south.

In 1983, terrorist bombings became a way of life in Beirut as some 50 people were killed in an explosion at the U.S. Embassy, Apr. 18; 241 U.S. servicemen and 58 French soldiers died in separate Muslim suicide attacks, Oct. 23.

Kidnapping of foreign nationals by Islamic militants became common in the 1980s. U.S., British, French, and Soviet citizens were victims. All were released by 1992.

A treaty signed May 22, 1991, between Lebanon and Syria recognized Lebanon as a separate state for the first time since the 2 countries gained independence in 1943.

Israeli forces conducted air raids and artillery strikes against guerrilla bases and villages in S Lebanon, causing over 200,000 to flee their homes July 25-29, 1993. Some 500,000 civilians fled their homes in Apr. 1996 when Israel again struck suspected guerrilla bases in the south. Pope John Paul II visited Lebanon May 10-11, 1997. During May-June 1998 the nation held its 1st municipal elections in 35 years. With Syria's approval, the legislature unanimously elected Lebanese armed forces chief Emile Lahoud as president Oct. 15.

Israel withdrew virtually all its troops from S Lebanon by May 24, 2000, leaving Hezbollah, an Iranian-backed guerrilla group, in control of much of the region.

Lesotho

Kingdom of Lesotho

People: Population: 2,207,954. **Age distrib.** (%): <15: 39.3; 65+: 4.7. **Pop. density:** 189 per sq. mi. **Urban:** 27%. **Ethnic groups:** Sotho 99.7%. **Principal languages:** English, Sesotho (both official). **Chief religions:** Christian 80%, indigenous beliefs 20%.

Geography: Area: 11,700 sq. mi. **Location:** In southern Africa. **Neighbors:** Completely surrounded by Republic of South Africa. **Topography:** Landlocked and mountainous, altitudes from 5,000 to 11,000 ft. **Capital:** Maseru: 271,000.

Government: Type: Modified constitutional monarchy. **Head of state:** King Letsie III; b July 17, 1963; in office: Feb. 7, 1996. **Head of gov.:** Pakalitha Mosisili; b Mar. 14, 1945; in office: May 29, 1998. **Local divisions:** 10 districts. **Defense budget (2001):** $21 mil. **Active troops:** 2,000.

Economy: Industries: Food, beverages, textiles, handicrafts, construction. **Chief crops:** Corn, grains, pulses, sorghum. **Other resources:** Diamonds. **Arable land:** 11%. **Livestock** (2001): cattle: 510,000; chickens: 1.70 mil.; goats: 570,000; pigs: 60,000; sheep: 730,000. **Labor force:** 86% subsistence agric.

Finance: Monetary unit: Maluti (Sept. 2002: 10.57 = $1 U.S.). **GDP** (2000 est.): $5.1 bil. **Per capita GDP:** $2,400. **Imports** (2000 est.): $700 mil.; partners (1998): South African Customs Union 90%, Asia 7%. **Exports** (2000 est.): $175 mil.; partners (1998): South African Customs Union 65%, North America 34%. **Tourism:** $19 mil. **Budget** (FY99/00 est.): $80 mil. **Intl. reserves less gold** (end 2000): $321 mil. **Consumer prices** (change in 2000): 6.1%.

Transport: Motor vehicles: 5,000 pass. cars, 18,000 comm. vehicles. **Civil aviation:** 5.7 mil pass.-mi.

Communications: TV sets: 7 per 1,000 pop. **Radios:** 558 per 1,000 pop. **Telephones** (2000): 43,800. **Daily newspaper circ.:** 7 per 1,000 pop.

Health: Life expectancy: 46.3 male; 47.8 female. **Births** (per 1,000 pop.): 30.7. **Deaths** (per 1,000 pop.): 16.8. **Natural inc.:** 1.39%. **Infant mortality** (per 1,000 live births): 82.6.

Education: Free, compulsory: ages 6-13. **Literacy**: 71%.

Major Intl. Organizations: UN (FOA, IBRD, ILO, IMF, WHO, WTrO), the Commonwealth, AU.

Embassy: 2511 Massachusetts Ave. NW 20008; 797-5533.

Website: www.lesotho.gov.ls

Lesotho (once called Basutoland) became a British protectorate in 1868 when Chief Moshesh sought protection against the Boers. Independence came Oct. 4, 1966. Elections were suspended in 1970. Most of Lesotho's GNP is provided by citizens working in South Africa. Livestock raising is the chief industry; diamonds are the chief export.

South Africa imposed a blockade, Jan. 1, 1986, because Lesotho had given sanctuary to anti-apartheid groups. The blockade sparked a Jan. 20 military coup, and was lifted, Jan. 25, when the new leaders agreed to expel the rebels.

In Mar. 1990, King Moshoeshoe was exiled by the military government. Letsie III became king Nov. 12. In Mar. 1993, Ntsu Mokhehle, a civilian, was elected prime minister, ending 23 years of military rule. After a series of violent disturbances, the king dismissed the Mokhele government Aug. 17, 1994; constitutional rule was restored Sept. 14. Letsie abdicated and Moshoeshoe was reinstated Jan. 25, 1995.

Moshoeshoe died in an automobile accident, Jan. 15, 1996. Letsie was reinstated Feb. 7; his formal coronation was Oct. 31, 1997. South Africa and Botswana sent troops Sept. 22, 1998, to help suppress violent antigovernment protests.

According to UN estimates, nearly one-fourth of the adult population has HIV/AIDS.

Liberia

Republic of Liberia

People: Population: 3,228,198. **Age distrib.** (%): <15: 43.2; 65+: 3.5. **Pop. density:** 88 per sq. mi. **Urban:** 44%. **Ethnic groups:** Indigenous tribes 95%, Americo-Liberians 2.5%. **Principal languages:** English (official), tribal languages. **Chief religions:** Traditional beliefs 70%, Muslim 20%, Christian 10%.

Geography: Area: 37,200 sq. mi. **Location:** On SW coast of W Africa. **Neighbors:** Sierra Leone on W, Guinea on N, Côte d'Ivoire on E. **Topography:** Marshy Atlantic coastline rises to low mountains and plateaus in the forested interior; 6 major rivers flow in parallel courses to the ocean. **Capital:** Monrovia 491,000.

Government: Type: Republic. **Head of state and gov.:** Pres. Charles Taylor; b Jan. 29, 1948; in office: Aug. 2, 1997. **Local divisions:** 13 counties. **Defense budget (2001):** $15 mil. **Active troops:** 11-15,000.

Economy: Industries: Rubber/palm oil processing, diamonds. **Chief crops:** Rice, cassava, coffee, cocoa, sugar. **Minerals:** Iron, diamonds, gold. **Other resources:** Rubber, timber. **Arable land:** 1%. **Livestock** (2001): cattle: 36,000; chickens: 4.00 mil.; goats: 220,000; pigs: 130,000; sheep: 210,000. **Electricity prod.:** 0.45 bil. kWh. **Labor force:** agri. 70%, ind. 8%, services 22%.

Finance: Monetary unit: Dollar (Sept. 2002: 1.00 = $1 U.S.). **GDP** (2000 est.): $3.35 bil. **Per capita GDP:** $1,100. **Imports** (2000 est.): $170 mil.; partners (1999): South Korea 30%, Italy 24%. **Exports** (2000 est.): $55 mil.; partners (1999): Belgium 53%, Switzerland 9%. **Budget:** NA.

Transport: Motor vehicles: 17,400 pass. cars, 10,700 comm. vehicles. **Civil aviation:** 4.3 mil pass.-mi; 1 airport. **Chief ports:** Monrovia, Buchanan, Greenville, Harper.

Communications: TV sets: 20 per 1,000 pop. **Radios:** 263 per 1,000 pop. **Telephones:** 6,700 main lines. **Daily newspaper circ.:** 15 per 1,000 pop.

Health: Life expectancy: 50.3 male; 53.3 female. **Births** (per 1,000 pop.): 46. **Deaths** (per 1,000 pop.): 16.1. **Natural inc.:** 2.99%. **Infant mortality** (per 1,000 live births): 130.2.

Education: Free, compulsory: ages 7-16. **Literacy:** 38%.

Major Intl. Organizations: UN and most of its specialized agencies, AU.

Embassy: 5201 16th St. NW 20011; 723-0437.

Website: www.liberiaemb.org

Liberia was founded in 1822 by U.S. black freedmen who settled at Monrovia with the aid of colonization societies. It became a republic July 26, 1847, with a constitution modeled on that of the U.S. Descendants of freedmen dominated politics.

Charging rampant corruption, an Army Redemption Council of enlisted men staged a bloody predawn coup, April 12, 1980, in which Pres. Tolbert was killed and replaced as head of state by Sgt. Samuel Doe. Doe was chosen president in a disputed election, and survived a subsequent coup, in 1985.

A civil war began Dec. 1989. Rebel forces seeking to depose Pres. Doe made major territorial gains and advanced on the capital, June 1990. In Sept., Doe was captured and put to death. Despite the introduction of peacekeeping forces from several countries, factional fighting intensified, and a series of cease-fires failed. A transitional Council of State was instituted Sept. 1, 1995. Factional fighting flared up again in Apr. 1996, devastating Monrovia.

On Sept. 3, 1996, Ruth Perry became modern Africa's first female head of state, leading another transitional government. By then, the civil war had claimed more than 150,000 lives and uprooted over half the population.

Former rebel leader Charles Taylor was elected president July 19, 1997, in Liberia's 1st national election in 12 years. The UN imposed sanctions May 4, 2001, to punish Liberia for aiding the Revolutionary United Front (RUF) insurgency in Sierra Leone. Taylor declared a state of emergency Feb. 8, 2002, after Liberian rebels launched raids near Monrovia.

Libya

Great Socialist People's Libyan Arab Jamahiriya

People: Population: 5,368,585. **Age distrib.** (%): <15: 35.4; 65+: 3.9. **Pop. density:** 8 per sq. mi. **Urban:** 87%. **Ethnic groups:** Arab-Berber 97%. **Principal language:** Arabic (official), Italian, English. **Chief religion:** Sunni Muslim 97%.

Geography: Area: 679,400 sq. mi. **Location:** On Mediterranean coast of N Africa. **Neighbors:** Tunisia, Algeria on W; Niger, Chad on S; Sudan, Egypt on E. **Topography:** Desert and semi-desert regions cover 92% of the land, with low mountains in N, higher mountains in S, and a narrow coastal zone. **Capital:** Tripoli. **Cities** (urban aggr.): Benghazi 829,000; Tripoli 1,776,000.

Government: Type: Islamic Arabic Socialist "Mass-State." **Head of state and gov.:** Col. Muammar al-Qaddafi; b Sept. 1942; in power: Sept. 1969. **Local divisions:** 25 municipalities. **Defense budget (2001):** $1.2 bil. **Active troops:** 76,000.

Economy: Industries: Oil, food processing, textiles, handicrafts, cement. **Chief crops:** Dates, olives, citrus, barley, wheat. **Minerals:** Gypsum, oil, gas. **Crude oil reserves** (2001): 30.0 bil bbls. **Arable land:** 1%. **Livestock** (2001): cattle: 220,000; chickens: 25.00 mil.; goats: 1.95 mil.; sheep: 5.10 mil. **Fish catch:** (1999): 32,849 metric tons. **Electricity prod.:** 19.40 bil. kWh. **Labor force:** services and government 54%, ind. 29%, agri. 17%.

Finance: Monetary unit: Dinar (Sept. 2002: 1.24 = $1 U.S.). **GDP** (2000 est.): $45.4 bil. **Per capita GDP:** $8,900. **Imports** (2000 est.): $7.6 bil.; partners (1999): Italy 24%, Germany 12%. **Exports** (2000 est.): $13.9 bil.; partners (1999): Italy 33%, Germany 24%. **Tourism:** $28 mil. **Budget** (2000 est.): $4.4 bil. **Intl. reserves less gold** (end 2000): $9.56 bil. Gold: 4.62 mil oz t.

Transport: Motor vehicles: 592,000 pass. cars, 312,000 comm. vehicles. **Civil aviation:** 234.1 mil pass.-mi. **Chief ports:** Tripoli, Banghazi.

Communications: TV sets: 105 per 1,000 pop. **Radios:** 191 per 1,000 pop. **Telephones:** 660,000. **Daily newspaper circ.:** 15 per 1,000 pop.

Health: Life expectancy: 73.7 male; 78.1 female. **Births** (per 1,000 pop.): 27.6. **Deaths** (per 1,000 pop.): 3.5. **Natural inc.:** 2.41%. **Infant mortality** (per 1,000 live births): 27.9.

Education: Compulsory: ages 6-15. **Literacy:** 76%.

Major Intl. Organizations: UN (FAO, IBRD, ILO, IMF, IMO, WHO), AL, AU, OPEC.

Website: www.libya–un.org

First settled by Berbers, Libya was ruled in succession by Carthage, Rome, the Vandals, and the Ottomans. Italy ruled from 1912, and Britain and France after WW II. Libya became an independent constitutional monarchy Jan. 2, 1952. In 1969 a junta led by Col. Muammar al-Qaddafi seized power.

Libya and Egypt fought several air and land battles along their border in July 1977. Chad charged Libya with military occupation of its uranium-rich northern region in 1977. Libyan troops were driven from their last major stronghold by Chad forces in 1987, leaving over $1 billion in military equipment behind.

Libya reportedly helped arm violent revolutionary groups in Egypt and Sudan and aided terrorists of various nationalities.

On Jan. 7, 1986, the U.S. imposed economic sanctions against Libya, ordered all Americans to leave that country, and froze all Libyan assets in the U.S. The U.S. commenced flight operations over the Gulf of Sidra, Jan. 27, and a U.S. Navy task force began conducting exercises in the Gulf, Mar. 23. When Libya fired antiaircraft missiles at American warplanes, the U.S. responded by sinking 2 Libyan ships and bombing a missile site in Libya. The U.S. withdrew from the Gulf, Mar. 27.

The U.S. accused Qaddafi of ordering the Apr. 5, 1986, bombing of a West Berlin discotheque, which killed 3, including a U.S. serviceman. In response, the U.S. sent warplanes to attack terrorist-related targets in Tripoli and Banghazi, Libya, Apr. 14.

The UN imposed limited sanctions, Apr. 15, 1992, for Libya's failure to extradite 2 agents linked to the 1988 bombing of Pan American World Airways Flight 103 over Lockerbie, Scotland, and 4 others linked to an airplane bombing over Niger. Sanctions were tightened Dec. 1, 1993. The international embargo ended, although U.S. sanctions remained, after Libya, Apr. 5, 1999, handed over two Lockerbie suspects for trial in the Netherlands under Scottish law. One of the two defendants, a Libyan intelligence official, Abdel Basset Ali al-Meghri, was convicted of murder Jan. 31, 2001.

Liechtenstein

Principality of Liechtenstein

People: Population: 32,842. **Age distrib.** (%): <15: 18.4; 65+: 11.0. **Pop. density:** 528 per sq. mi. **Urban:** 22%. **Ethnic groups:** Alemannic 88%. **Principal languages:** German (official), Alemannic dialect. **Chief religions:** Roman Catholic 80%, Protestant 7.4%.

Geography: Area: 62 sq. mi. **Location:** Central Europe, in the Alps. **Neighbors:** Switzerland on W, Austria on E. **Topography:** The Rhine Valley occupies one-third of the country, the Alps cover the rest. **Capital:** Vaduz: 5,000.

Government: Type: Hereditary constitutional monarchy. **Head of state:** Prince Hans-Adam II; b Feb. 14, 1945; in office: Nov. 13, 1989. **Head of gov.:** Otmar Hasler; b Sept. 28, 1953; in office: Apr. 5, 2001. **Local divisions:** 11 communes.

Economy: Industries: Electronics, metal manufacturing, textiles, ceramics, pharmaceuticals. **Chief crops:** Grain, corn, potatoes. **Arable land:** 24%. **Livestock: (2001): cattle: 6,000; goats: 280; pigs: 3,000; sheep: 2,900. Labor force:** ind., trade and building 45%, services 53%, agri., fishing, forestry, and horticulture 2%.

Finance: Monetary unit: Swiss Franc (Sept. 2002: 1.50= $1 U.S.). **GDP** (1998 est.): $730 mil. **Per capita GDP:** $23,000. **Imports** (1996): $917.3 mil.; partners (1996): EU countries, Switzerland. **Exports** (1996): $2.47 bil.; partners (1995): EU and EFTA countries 60.57%. **Budget** (1998 est.): $414.1 mil.

Transport: Railroad: Length: 12 mi.

Communications: TV sets: 371 per 1,000 pop. **Radios:** 384 per 1,000 pop. **Daily newspaper circ.:** 564 per 1,000 pop.

Health: Life expectancy: 75.5 male; 82.7 female. **Births** (per 1,000 pop.): 11.2. **Deaths** (per 1,000 pop.): 6.8. **Natural inc.:** 0.45%. **Infant mortality** (per 1,000 live births): 4.9.

Education: Compulsory: ages 7-16. **Literacy** (1997): 100%.

Major Intl. Organizations: UN (WTrO), EFTA, OSCE.

Website: www.news.li

Liechtenstein became sovereign in 1806. Austria administered Liechtenstein's ports up to 1920; Switzerland has administered its postal services since 1921. Liechtenstein is united with Switzerland by a customs and monetary union. Taxes are low; many international corporations have headquarters there. Foreign workers comprise 60% of the labor force.

Lithuania

Republic of Lithuania

People: Population: 3,601,138. **Age distrib.** (%): <15: 18.7; 65+: 13.6. **Pop. density:** 143 per sq. mi. **Urban:** 68%. **Ethnic groups:** Lithuanian 80.6%, Russian 8.7%, Polish 7%. **Principal languages:** Lithuanian (official), Polish, Russian. **Chief religions:** Primarily Roman Catholic.

Geography: Area: 25,200 sq. mi. **Location:** In E Europe, on SE coast of Baltic. **Neighbors:** Latvia on N, Belarus on E, S, Poland and Russia on W. **Capital:** Vilnius. **Cities** (urban aggr.): Vilnius 579,000; Kaunas 412,639.

Government: Type: Republic. **Head of state:** Pres. Valdas Adamkus; b Nov. 3, 1926; in office: Feb. 26, 1998. **Head of gov.:** Prime Min. Algirdas Brazauskas; b Sept. 22, 1932; in office: July 3, 2001. **Local divisions:** 10 provinces. **Defense budget** (2001): $184.3 mil. **Active troops:** 12,190.

Economy: Industries: Machine tools, electric motors, television sets. **Chief crops:** Sugar beets, grain, potatoes, vegetables. **Crude oil reserves** (2000): 12 mil bbls. **Arable land:** 35%. **Livestock** (2001): cattle: 748,300; chickens: 5.58 mil.; goats: 23,000; pigs: 855,600; sheep: 11,500. **Fish catch:** (1999): 19,837 metric tons. **Electricity prod.:** 10.97 bil. kWh. **Labor force:** ind. 30%, agri. 20%, services 50%.

Finance: Monetary unit: Litas (Sept. 2002: 3.54 = $1 U.S.). **GDP** (2000 est.): $26.4 bil. **Per capita GDP:** $7,300. **Imports** (2000): $4.9 bil.; partners (1999): Russia 20.4%, Germany 16.5%. **Exports** (2000): $3.7 bil.; partners (1999): Germany 15.8%, Latvia 12.6%. **Tourism:** $550 mil. **Budget** (1997 est.): $1.7 bil. **Intl. reserves less gold** (end 2000): $1.01 bil. **Gold:** 186,300 oz t. **Consumer prices** (change in 2000): 1.0%.

Transport: Railroad: Length: 1,802 mi. **Motor vehicles:** 653,000 pass. cars, 111,000 comm. vehicles. **Civil aviation:** 187.2 mil pass.-mi; 3 airports. **Chief port:** Klaipeda.

Communications: TV sets: 364 per 1,000 pop. **Radios:** 404 per 1,000 pop. **Telephones:** 2,083,700. **Daily newspaper circ.:** 136 per 1,000 pop.

Health: Life expectancy: 63.5 male; 75.6 female. **Births** (per 1,000 pop.): 10.2. **Deaths** (per 1,000 pop.): 12.9. **Natural inc.:** -0.27%. **Infant mortality** (per 1,000 live births): 14.3.

Education: Free, compulsory: ages 7-16. Literacy (1989): 98%.

Major Intl. Organizations: UN (FAO, IBRD, ILO, IMF, IMO, WHO), OSCE.

Embassy: 2622 16th St. NW 20009; 234-5860.

Websites: www.lruk.lt/anglu/home_anglo.htm
www.ltembassyus.org

Lithuania was occupied by the German army, 1914-18. It was annexed by the Soviet Russian army, but the Soviets were overthrown, 1919. Lithuania was a democratic republic until 1926, when the regime was ousted by a coup. In 1939 the Soviet-German treaty assigned most of Lithuania to the Soviet sphere of influence. Lithuania was annexed by the USSR Aug. 3, 1940.

Lithuania formally declared its independence from the Soviet Union Mar. 11, 1990. During an abortive Soviet coup in Aug., the Western nations recognized Lithuania's independence, which was ratified by the Soviet Union in Sept. 1991.

The last Russian troops withdrew on Aug. 31, 1993. Lithuania applied to join the European Union, Dec. 8, 1995. The conservative Homeland Union defeated the former Communists in parliamentary elections Oct. 20 and Nov. 10, 1996. A Lithuanian-American, Valdas Adamkus, won the presidency in a runoff election Jan. 4, 1998. Parliamentary elections Oct. 8, 2000, dealt conservatives a major setback.

Luxembourg

Grand Duchy of Luxembourg

People: Population: 448,569. **Age distrib.** (%): <15: 18.9; 65+: 14.1. **Pop. density:** 449 per sq. mi. **Urban:** 91%. **Ethnic groups:** Mixture of French and Germans predominates. **Principal languages:** French, German, Luxembourgian, English. **Chief religion:** Roman Catholic 97%.

Geography: Area: 998 sq. mi. **Location:** In W Europe. **Neighbors:** Belgium on W, France on S, Germany on E. **Topography:** Heavy forests (Ardennes) cover N, S is a low, open plateau. **Capital:** Luxembourg-Ville: 82,000.

Government: Type: Constitutional monarchy. **Head of state:** Grand Duke Henri; b Apr. 16, 1955; in office: Oct. 7, 2000. **Head of gov.:** Prime Min. Jean-Claude Juncker; b Dec. 9, 1954; in office: Jan. 19, 1995. **Local divisions:** 3 districts. **Defense budget (2001):** $93.5 mil. **Active troops:** 900.

Economy: Industries: Banking, iron and steel, food processing, chemicals, metal products, engineering. **Chief crops:** Grains, potatoes, wine grapes. **Arable land:** 24%. **Electricity prod.:** 0.47 bil. kWh. **Labor force:** services 83.2%, ind. 14.3%, agri. 2.5%.

Finance: Monetary unit: Euro (Sept. 2002: 1.03 = $1 U.S.). **GDP** (2000 est.): $15.9 bil. **Per capita GDP:** $36,400. **Imports** (2000): $10 bil.; partners (1999): EU 81%, U.S. 9%. **Exports** (2000): $7.6 bil.; partners (1999): EU 75%,U.S. 4%. **Budget** (2000 est.): $5.6 bil. **Intl. reserves less gold** (end 2000): $59 mil. **Gold:** 76,000 oz t. **Consumer prices** (change in 2000): 3.1%.

Transport: Railroad: Length: 170 mi. **Motor vehicles:** 231,666 pass. cars, 16,665 comm. vehicles. **Civil aviation:** 174.8 mil pass.-mi; 1 airport. **Chief port:** Mertert.

Communications: TV sets: 916 per 1,000 pop. **Radios:** 586 per 1,000 pop. **Telephones:** 782,400. **Daily newspaper circ.:** 381 per 1,000 pop.

Health: Life expectancy: 74.2 male; 81 female. **Births** (per 1,000 pop.): 12.1. **Deaths** (per 1,000 pop.): 8.8. **Natural inc.:** 0.32%. **Infant mortality** (per 1,000 live births): 4.7.

Education: Compulsory: ages 6-15. **Literacy**: 100%.

Major Intl. Organizations: UN (FAO, IBRD, ILO, IMF, IMO, WHO, WTrO), EU, NATO, OECD, OSCE.

Embassy: 2200 Massachusetts Ave. NW 20008; 265-4171.

Website: www.gouvernement.lu/

Luxembourg, founded about 963, was ruled by Burgundy, Spain, Austria, and France from 1448 to 1815. It left the Germanic Confederation in 1866. Overrun by Germany in 2 world wars, Luxembourg ended its neutrality in 1948, when a customs union with Belgium and Netherlands was adopted.

Macedonia

Former Yugoslav Republic of Macedonia

People: Population: 2,054,800. **Age distrib.** (%): <15: 22.9; 65+: 10.1. **Pop. density:** 208 per sq. mi. **Urban:** 62%. **Ethnic groups:** Macedonian 66%, Albanian 23%. **Principal languages:** Macedonian (official), Albanian, Serbo-Croatian. **Chief religions:** Eastern Orthodox 67%, Muslim 30%.

Geography: Area: 9,900 sq. mi. **Location:** In SE Europe. **Neighbors:** Bulgaria on E, Greece on S, Albania on W, Serbia on N. **Capital:** Skopje: 437,000.

Government: Type: Republic. **Head of state:** Pres. Boris Trajkovski; b June 25, 1956; in office: Dec. 15, 1999. **Head of gov.:** Prime Min. Ljupco Georgievski; b Jan. 17, 1966; in office: Nov. 30, 1998. **Local divisions:** 123 municipalities. **Defense budget (2001):** $71.6 mil. **Active troops:** 16,000.

Economy: Industries: Mining, textiles, wood products, tobacco. **Chief crops:** Wheat, rice, cotton, tobacco. **Minerals:** Chromium, lead, zinc. **Arable land:** 24%. **Livestock** (2001): cattle: 265,000; chickens: 3.35 mil.; goats: 204,000; sheep: 1.25 mil. **Electricity prod.:** 6.40 bil. kWh.

Finance: Monetary unit: Denar (Sept. 2002: 62.42 = $1 U.S.). **GDP** (2000 est.): $9 bil. **Per capita GDP:** $4,400. **Imports** (2000 est.): $2 bil.; partners (2000): Germany 13%, Ukraine 13%. **Exports** (2000 est.): $1.4 bil.; partners (2000): Germany 22%, Yugoslavia 22%. **Tourism** (1998): $15 mil. **Budget** (1996 est.): $1.0 bil. **Intl. reserves less gold** (end 2000): $330 mil. **Gold:** 108,000 oz t. **Consumer prices** (change in 1999): –1.3%.

Transport: Railroad: Length: 573 mi. **Motor vehicles:** 263,000 pass. cars, 23,000 comm. vehicles. **Civil aviation:** 161.1 mil pass.-mi; 2 airports.

Communications: TV sets: 179 per 1,000 pop. **Radios:** 179 per 1,000 pop. **Telephones:** 761,800. **Daily newspaper circ.:** 21 per 1,000 pop.

Health: Life expectancy: 72 male; 76.7 female. **Births** (per 1,000 pop.): 13.3. **Deaths** (per 1,000 pop.): 7.7. **Natural inc.:** 0.56%. **Infant mortality** (per 1,000 live births): 12.5.

Education: Free, compulsory: ages 7-15. **Literacy** (1996): 89%.

Major Intl. Organizations: UN (FAO, IBRD, ILO, IMF, IMO, WHO).

Embassy: 3050 K St. NW 20007; 337-3063.
Website: www.gov.mk

Macedonia, as part of a larger region also called Macedonia, was ruled by Muslim Turks from 1389 to 1912, when native Greeks, Bulgarians, and Slavs won independence. Serbia received the largest part of the territory, with the rest going to Greece and Bulgaria. In 1913, the area was incorporated into Serbia, which in 1918 became part of the Kingdom of Serbs, Croats, and Slovenes (later Yugoslavia). In 1946, Macedonia became a constituent republic of Yugoslavia.

Macedonia declared its independence Sept. 8, 1991, and was admitted to the UN under a provisional name in 1993. A UN force, which included several hundred U.S. troops, was deployed there to deter the warring factions in Bosnia from carrying their dispute into other areas of the Balkans.

In Feb. 1994 both Russia and the U.S. recognized Macedonia. Greece, which objected to Macedonia's use of what it considered a Hellenic name and symbols, imposed a trade blockade on the landlocked nation; the 2 countries agreed to normalize relations Sept. 13, 1995. A car bombing, Oct. 3, seriously injured Pres. Kiro Gligorov. Macedonia and Yugoslavia signed a treaty normalizing relations Apr. 8, 1996.

By the end of NATO's air war against Yugoslavia, Mar.-June 1999, Macedonia had a Kosovar refugee population of more than 250,000; over 90% had been repatriated by Sept. 1. Boris Trajkovski, candidate of the ruling center-right coalition, won a presidential runoff vote Nov. 14.

Ethnic Albanian guerrillas launched an offensive Mar. 2001 in NW Macedonia. An accord signed Aug. 13 paved the way for the introduction of a NATO peacekeeping force. A law broadening the rights of ethnic Albanians was enacted Jan. 24, 2002.

Madagascar

Republic of Madagascar

People: Population: 16,473,477. **Age distrib.** (%): <15: 45.0; 65+: 3.2. **Pop. density:** 73 per sq. mi. **Urban:** 29%. **Ethnic groups:** Malayo-Indonesian, Cotiers, French, Indian, Creole, Comoran. **Principal languages:** Malagasy, French (both official). **Chief religions:** Indigenous beliefs 52%, Christian 41%, Muslim 7%.

Geography: Area: 224,500 sq. mi. **Location:** In the Indian O., off the SE coast of Africa. **Neighbors:** Comoro Isls. to NW, Mozambique to W. **Topography:** Humid coastal strip in the E, fertile valleys in the mountainous center plateau region, and a wider coastal strip on the W. **Capital:** Antananarivo 1,689,000.

Government: Type: Republic. **Head of state:** Pres. Marc Ravalomanana; b Dec. 12, 1949; in office: Feb. 22, 2002 (de facto). **Head of gov.:** Prime Min. Jacques Sylla; b 1946; in office: Feb. 26, 2002 (de facto). **Local divisions:** 6 provinces. **Defense budget (2001):** $46 mil. **Active troops:** 13,500.

Economy: Industries: Meat processing, soap, breweries, tanneries, sugar, textiles. **Chief crops:** Coffee, cloves, vanilla beans, rice, sugar, cassava, peanuts. **Minerals:** Chromite, graphite, coal, bauxite. **Arable land:** 4%. **Livestock** (2001): cattle: 10.30 mil; chickens: 19.00 mil.; goats: 1.35 mil.; pigs: 850,000; sheep: 790,000. **Fish catch** (1999): 124,973 metric tons. **Electricity prod:** 0.82 bil. kWh.

Finance: Monetary unit: Malagasy franc (Sept. 2002: 6,480.00 = $1 U.S.). **GDP** (2000 est.): $12.3 bil. **Per capita GDP:** $800. **Imports** (1998): $693 mil.; partners (1999): France 34%, Hong Kong 6%, China 6%. **Exports** (1998): $538 mil.; partners (1999): France 41%, U.S. 19%. **Tourism:** $100 mil. **Budget** (1998 est.): $735 mil. **Intl. reserves less gold** (end 2000): $219 mil. **Consumer prices** (change in 2000): 12.0%.

Transport: Railroad: Length: 640 mi. **Motor vehicles:** 58,100 pass. cars, 15,860 comm. vehicles. **Civil aviation:** 471.0 mil pass.-mi; 44 airports. **Chief ports:** Toamasina, Antsiranana, Mahajanga, Toliara, Antsohimbondrona.

Communications: TV sets: 20 per 1,000 pop. **Radios:** 193 per 1,000 pop. **Telephones:** 205,900. **Daily newspaper circ.:** 4 per 1,000 pop.

Health: Life expectancy: 53.5 male; 58.1 female. **Births** (per 1,000 pop.): 42.4. **Deaths** (per 1,000 pop.): 12.2. **Natural inc.:** 3.03%. **Infant mortality** (per 1,000 live births): 81.9.

Education: Compulsory for 5 years between ages 6 and 13. **Literacy:** 46%.

Major Intl. Organizations: UN (FAO, IBRD, ILO, IMF, IMO, WHO, WTrO), AU.

Embassy: 2374 Massachusetts Ave. NW 20008; 265-5525.
Website: madagascar–gov.net

Madagascar was settled 2,000 years ago by Malayan-Indonesian people, whose descendants still predominate. A unified kingdom ruled the 18th and 19th centuries. The island became a French protectorate, 1885, and a colony 1896. Independence came June 26, 1960.

Discontent with inflation and French domination led to a coup in 1972. The new regime nationalized French-owned financial interests, closed French bases and a U.S. space-tracking station, and obtained Chinese aid. The government conducted a program of arrests, expulsion of foreigners, and repression of strikes, 1979.

In 1990, Madagascar ended a ban on multiparty politics that had been in place since 1975. Albert Zafy was elected president in 1993, ending the 17-year rule of Adm. Didier Ratsiraka. After Zafy was impeached by the legislature, Madagascar's constitutional court removed him from office, Sept. 5, 1996. Prime Min. Norbert Ratsirahonana then became interim president pending national elections, Nov. 3 and Dec. 29, in which Ratsiraka edged Zafy. A cholera epidemic, exacerbated by cyclones in Feb. and Apr. 2000, claimed at least 1,600 lives.

Marc Ravalomanana won a power struggle with Ratsiraka that followed a disputed presidential election Dec. 16, 2001.

Malawi

Republic of Malawi

People: Population: 10,701,824. **Age distrib.** (%): <15: 44.4; 65+: 2.8. **Pop. density:** 295 per sq. mi. **Urban:** 24%. **Ethnic groups:** Chewa, Nyanja, Lomwe, other Bantu tribes. **Principal languages:** English, Chichewa (both official). **Chief religions:** Protestant 55%, Muslim 20%, Roman Catholic 20%.

Geography: Area: 36,300 sq. mi. **Location:** In SE Africa. **Neighbors:** Zambia on W, Mozambique on S and E, Tanzania on N. **Topography:** Malawi stretches 560 mi. N-S along Lake Malawi (Lake Nyasa), most of which belongs to Malawi. High plateaus and mountains line the Rift Valley the length of the nation. **Capital:** Lilongwe. **Cities** (urban aggr., 1998 est.): : Blantyre 2,000,000; Lilongwe 523,000.

Government: Type: Multiparty democracy. **Head of state and gov.:** Pres. Bakili Muluzi; b Mar. 17, 1943; in office: May 21, 1994. **Local divisions:** 3 regions, 26 districts. **Defense budget (2001):** $19 mil. **Active troops:** 5,300.

Economy: Industries: Tobacco, tea, sugar, sawmill products, cement. **Chief crops:** Tea, tobacco, sugar, cotton, corn, potatoes. **Arable land:** 18%. **Livestock** (2001): cattle: 750,000; chickens: 15.20 mil.; goats: 1.45 mil.; pigs: 250,000; sheep: 110,000. **Fish catch** (1999): 56,564 metric tons. **Electricity prod.:** 0.83 bil. kWh. **Labor force:** agri. 86%.

Finance: Monetary unit: Kwacha (Sept. 2002: 79.85 = $1 U.S.). **GDP** (2000 est.): $9.4 bil. **Per capita GDP:** $900. **Imports** (2000): $435 mil.; partners (1999): South Africa 43%, Zimbabwe 14%. **Exports** (2000): $416 mil.; partners (1999): South Africa 16%, Germany 16%. . **Tourism:** $20 mil. **Budget** (FY99/00 est.): $523 mil. **Intl. reserves less gold** (end 2000): $190 mil. **Gold:** 10,000 oz t. **Consumer prices** (change in 2000): 29.5%.

Transport: Railroad: Length: 490 mi. **Motor vehicles:** 25,400 pass. cars, 28,900 comm. vehicles. **Civil aviation:** 208.6 mil pass.-mi; 5 airports.

Communications: Radios: 112 per 1,000 pop. **Telephones:** 109,800.

Health: Life expectancy: 36 male; 37.1 female. **Births** (per 1,000 pop.): 37.1. **Deaths** (per 1,000 pop.): 23.2. **Natural inc.:** 1.39%. **Infant mortality** (per 1,000 live births): 120.

Education: Compulsory: ages 6-14. **Literacy:** 56%.

Major Intl. Organizations: UN (FAO, IBRD, ILO, IMF, IMO, WHO, WTrO), the Commonwealth, AU.

Embassy: 2408 Massachusetts Ave. NW 20008; 797-1007.
Website: www.maform.malawi.net/MAIN.htm

Bantus came to the land in the 16th century, Arab slavers in the 19th. The area became the British protectorate Nyasaland in 1891. It became independent July 6, 1964, and a republic in 1966. After 3 decades as a one-party state under Pres. Hastings Kamuzu Banda, Malawi adopted a new constitution and, in multiparty elections held May 17, 1994, chose a new leader, Bakili Muluzi. Banda was acquitted, Dec. 23, 1995, of complicity in the deaths of 4 political opponents in 1983; he died Nov. 25, 1997.

According to UN estimates, more than 15% of the adult population has HIV/AIDS.

Malaysia

People: Population: 22,662,365. **Age distrib.** (%): <15: 34.5; 65+: 4.2. **Pop. density:** 179 per sq. mi. **Urban:** 57%. **Ethnic groups:** Malay and other indigenous 58%, Chinese 26%, Indian 7%. **Principal languages:** Malay (official), English, Chinese dialects. **Chief religions:** Muslim, Hindu, Buddhist, Christian.

Geography: Area: 126,900 sq. mi. **Location:** On the SE tip of Asia, plus the N coast of the island of Borneo. **Neighbors:** Thailand on N, Indonesia on S. **Topography:** Most of W Malaysia is covered by tropical jungle, including the central mountain range that runs N-S through the peninsula. The western coast is marshy, the eastern, sandy. E Malaysia has a wide, swampy coastal plain, with interior jungles and mountains. **Capital:** Kuala Lumpur 1,410,000.

Government: Type: Federal parliamentary democracy with a constitutional monarch. **Head of state:** Paramount Ruler Syed Sirajuddin Syed Putra Jamalullail; b May 16, 1943; in office: Dec. 13, 2001. **Head of gov.:** Prime Min. Datuk Seri Mahathir bin Mohamad; b Dec. 20, 1925; in office: July 16, 1981. **Local divisions:** 13 states, 2 federal territories. **Defense budget (2001):** $1.9 bil. **Active troops:** 100,500.

Economy: Industries: Rubber/oil palm goods, light manufacturing, electronics, logging **Chief crops:** Palm oil (world's leading producer), rice. **Minerals:** Tin (a leading producer), oil, gas, bauxite, copper, iron. **Crude oil reserves** (2001): 5.1 bil bbls. **Other resources:** Rubber, timber. **Arable land:** 3%. **Livestock** (2001): cattle: 723,346; chickens: 125.00 mil.; goats: 231,834; pigs: 1.83 mil; sheep: 174,661. **Fish catch** (1999): 1.28 mil metric tons. **Electricity prod.:** 63.07 bil. kWh. **Labor force:** local trade and tourism 28%, manufacturing 27%, agri. forestry and fisheries 16%, services 10%, government 10%, construction 9%.

Finance: Monetary unit: Ringgit (Sept. 2002: 3.80 = $1 U.S.). **GDP** (2000 est.): $223.7 bil. **Per capita GDP:** $10,300. **Imports** (2000 est.): $82.6 bil.; partners (2000 est.): Japan 21%, U.S. 17%. **Exports** (2000 est.): $97.9 bil.; partners (2000 est.): U.S. 21%, Singapore 18%. . **Tourism:** $2.82 bil. **Budget** (2000 est.): $17.8 bil **Intl. reserves less gold** (end 2000): $22.66 bil. **Gold:** 1.17 mil oz t. **Consumer prices** (change in 2000): 1.5%.

Transport: Railroad: Length: 1,113 mi. **Motor vehicles** (1997): 3.33 mil pass. cars, 618,066 comm. vehicles. **Civil aviation:** 17.8 bil pass.-mi; 39 airports. **Chief ports:** Kuantan, Kelang, Kota Kinabalu, Kuching.

Communications: TV sets: 424 per 1,000 pop. **Radios:** 442 per 1,000 pop. **Telephones:** 11,866,000. **Daily newspaper circ.:** 163 per 1,000 pop.

Health: Life expectancy: 68.8 male; 74.2 female. **Births** (per 1,000 pop.): 24.2. **Deaths** (per 1,000 pop.): 5.2. **Natural inc.:** 1.91%. **Infant mortality** (per 1,000 live births): 19.7.

Education: Free, compulsory: ages 6-16. **Literacy**: 83%.

Major Intl. Organizations: UN (FAO, IBRD, ILO, IMF, IMO, WHO, WTrO), APEC, ASEAN, the Commonwealth.

Embassy: 2401 Massachusetts Ave. NW 20008; 328-2700.

Websites: www.embassy.org/embassies/my.html
www.tour ism.gov.my/

European traders appeared in the 16th century; Britain established control in 1867. Malaysia was created Sept. 16, 1963. It included Malaya (which had become independent in 1957 after the suppression of Communist rebels), plus the formerly British Singapore, Sabah (N Borneo), and Sarawak (NW Borneo). Singapore was separated in 1965, in order to end tensions between Chinese, the majority in Singapore, and Malays in control of the Malaysian government.

A monarch is elected by a council of hereditary rulers of the Malayan states every 5 years.

Abundant natural resources have bolstered prosperity, and foreign investment has aided industrialization. Work on a new federal capital at Putrajaya, south of Kuala Lumpur, began in 1995. However, sagging stock and currency prices forced the postponement of major development projects in Sept. 1997.

As the recession deepened and political unrest grew, Prime Min. Mahathir bin Mohamad imposed new currency controls and fired his popular deputy prime minister, Anwar bin Ibrahim, Sept. 2, 1998. Anwar, who then called for Mahathir's resignation, was arrested Sept. 20; he was convicted of corruption, Apr. 14, 1999, and sentenced to 6 years in prison. Another conviction, Aug. 8, 2000, for sodomy, resulted in an additional 9-year sentence.

Maldives

Republic of Maldives

People: Population: 320,165. **Age distrib.** (%): <15: 45.6; 65+: 3.0. **Pop. density:** 2,764 per sq. mi. **Urban:** 26%. **Ethnic groups:** Sinhalese, Dravidian, Arab, African. **Principal languages:** Maldivian Divehi (Sinhalese dialect; official), English. **Chief religion:** Sunni Muslim.

Geography: Area: 116 sq. mi. **Location:** In the Indian O., SW of India. **Neighbors:** Nearest is India on N. **Topography:** 19 atolls with 1,190 islands, 198 inhabited. None of the islands are over 5 sq. mi. in area, and all are nearly flat. **Capital:** Male: 84,000.

Government: Type: Republic. **Head of state and gov.:** Pres. Maumoon Abdul Gayoom; b Dec. 29, 1937; in office: Nov. 11, 1978. **Local divisions:** 19 atolls and Male. **Defense budget:** NA. **Active troops:** NA.

Economy: Industries: Fish processing, tourism, shipping. **Chief crops:** Coconuts, corn, sweet potatoes. **Arable land:** 10%. **Fish catch** (1999): 107,676 metric tons. **Electricity prod.:** 0.11 bil. kWh. **Labor force:** agri. 22%, ind. 18%, services 60%.

Finance: Monetary unit: Rufiya (Sept. 2002: 11.77 = $1 U.S.). **GDP** (2000 est.): $594 mil. **Per capita GDP:** $2,000. **Imports** (2000 est.): $372 mil.; partners: Singapore, India, Sri Lanka, Japan, Canada. **Exports** (2000 est.): $88 mil.; partners: U.S., UK, Sri Lanka, Japan. **Tourism:** $334 mil. **Budget** (1999 est.): $192 mil. **Intl. reserves less gold** (end 2000): $94 mil. **Consumer prices** (change in 2000): –1.1%.

Transport: Civil aviation: 181.2 mil pass.-mi; 5 airports. **Chief ports:** Male, Gan.

Communications: TV sets: 19 per 1,000 pop. **Radios:** 96 per 1,000 pop. **Telephones:** 45,700. **Daily newspaper circ.:** 12 per 1,000 pop.

Health: Life expectancy: 61.7 male; 64.2 female. **Births** (per 1,000 pop.): 37.4. **Deaths** (per 1,000 pop.): 7.9. **Natural inc.:** 2.96%. **Infant mortality** (per 1,000 live births): 61.9.

Education: Literacy: 93%.

Major Intl. Organizations: UN (FAO, IBRD, IMF, IMO, WHO, WTrO), the Commonwealth.

Website: www.un.int/maldives

The islands had been a British protectorate since 1887. The country became independent July 26, 1965. Long a sultanate, the Maldives became a republic in 1968. Natural resources and tourism are being developed; however, the Maldives remains one of the world's poorest countries.

Mali

Republic of Mali

People: Population: 11,340,480. **Age distrib.** (%): <15: 47.2; 65+: 3.1. **Pop. density:** 24 per sq. mi. **Urban:** 29%. **Ethnic groups:** Mande (Bambara, Malinke, Sarakole) 50%, Peul 17%, Voltaic 12%, Tuareg and Moor 10%, Songhai 6%. **Principal languages:** French (official), Bambara, numerous African languages. **Chief religions:** Muslim 90%, indigenous beliefs 9%.

Geography: Area: 471,000 sq. mi. **Location:** In the interior of W Africa. **Neighbors:** Mauritania, Senegal on W; Guinea, Côte d'Ivoire, Burkina Faso on S; Niger on E; Algeria on N. **Topography:** A landlocked grassy plain in the upper basins of the Senegal and Niger rivers, extending N into the Sahara. **Capital:** Bamako: 1,161,000.

Government: Type: Republic. **Head of state:** Pres. Amadou Toumani Touré; b Nov. 4, 1948; in office: June 8, 2002. **Head of gov.:** Prime Min. Ahmed Mohamed Ag Hamani; in office: June 9, 2002. **Local divisions:** 8 regions, 1 capital district. **Defense budget (2001):** $28 mil. **Active troops:** 7,350.

Economy: Industries: Consumer goods and food processing, construction, mining. **Chief crops:** Millet, rice, peanuts, corn, vegetables, cotton. **Minerals:** Gold, phosphates, kaolin. **Arable land:** 2%. **Livestock** (2001): cattle: 6.82 mil; chickens: 25.00 mil.; goats: 9.90 mil.; pigs: 66,000; sheep: 6.40 mil. **Electricity prod.:** 0.46 bil. kWh. **Labor force**: agri. and fishing 80%.

Finance: Monetary unit: CFA Franc (Sept. 2002: 671.78 = $1 U.S.). **GDP** (2000 est.): $9.1 bil. **Per capita GDP:** $850. **Imports** (2000 est.): $575 mil.; partners (1999): Cote d'Ivoire 19%, France 19%. **Exports** (2000 est.): $480 mil.; partners (1999): Italy 18%, Thailand 15%. **Tourism** (1998): $50 mil. **Budget** (1997 est.): $770 mil. **Intl. reserves less gold** (end 2000): $293 mil. **Gold:** 19,000 oz t. **Consumer prices** (change in 2000): –0.7%.

Transport: Railroad: Length: 398 mi. **Motor vehicles:** 24,700 pass. cars, 17,100 comm. vehicles. **Civil aviation:** 150.5 mil pass.-mi; 9 airports. **Chief port:** Koulikoro.

Communications: TV sets: 12 per 1,000 pop. **Radios:** 168 per 1,000 pop. **Telephones:** 95,200.

Health: Life expectancy: 46.2 male; 48.6 female. **Births** (per 1,000 pop.): 48.4. **Deaths** (per 1,000 pop.): 18.3. **Natural inc.:** 3%. **Infant mortality** (per 1,000 live births): 119.6.

Education: Free, compulsory: ages 7-16. **Literacy**: 31%.

Major Intl. Organizations: UN and most of its specialized agencies, AU.

Embassy: 2130 R St. NW 20008; 332-2249.

Website: www.maliembassy–usa.org

Until the 15th century the area was part of the great Mali Empire. Timbuktu (Tombouctou) was a center of Islamic study. French rule was secured, 1898. The Sudanese Rep. and Senegal became independent as the Mali Federation June 20, 1960, but Senegal withdrew, and the Sudanese Rep. was renamed Mali.

Mali signed economic agreements with France and, in 1963, with Senegal. In 1968, a coup ended the socialist regime. Famine struck in 1973-74, killing as many as 100,000 people. Drought conditions returned in the 1980s.

The military, Mar. 26, 1991, overthrew the government of Pres. Moussa Traoré, who had been in power since 1968. Oumar Konare, a coup leader, was elected president, Apr. 26, 1992. A peace accord between the government and a Tuareg rebel group was signed in June 1994. Konare and his party won a series of flawed elections, Apr.-Aug. 1997. Twice condemned to death for crimes committed in office, Traoré had his sentences commuted to life imprisonment in Dec. 1997 and Sept. 1999.

Amadou Toumani Touré, who led the 1991 coup, won a presidential runoff election May 12, 2002.

AP/WIDE WORLD PHOTOS

AP/WIDE WORLD PHOTOS

MIDEAST VIOLENCE

From top: A bus destroyed by a car bomb in northern Israel, June 5 (the Palestinian bomber and 17 others were killed, 45 wounded); Palestinian women survey destruction at the Jenin refugee camp on the West Bank, after an Israeli incursion and occupation in early April in which at least 52 Palestinians died; photo of Wafa Idris, a Palestinian suicide bomber from a refugee camp who killed an Israeli man and wounded 100 in a Jan. 27 Jerusalem bombing; Pnina Eizenman, at funeral for her daughter, 5, at a West Bank settlement—Eizenman's mother and 5 others were also killed, in a suicide bombing in Jerusalem June 19.

AP/WIDE WORLD PHOTOS

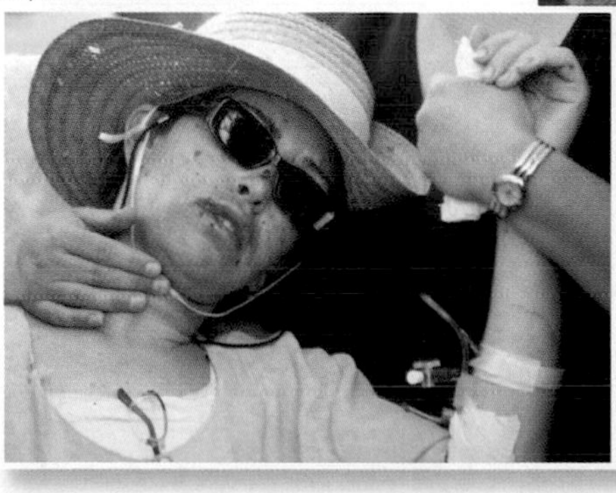

AP/WIDE WORLD PHOTOS

2003 WORLD SCENE

AP/WIDE WORLD PHOTOS

◄ BORDER TENSION
An Indian (left) and Pakistani border guard, June 1, during the daily closing ceremony at a border post near Lahore, Pakistan. Tensions between the 2 nuclear-armed nations ran high during exchanges of artillery fire in their escalating dispute over the status of Kashmir.

AP/WIDE WORLD PHOTOS

FRENCH ELECTIONS ►
A campaign flyer for controversial far-right National Party leader Jean-Marie Le Pen (top) portrays French Pres. Jacques Chirac as a jack of spades. Le Pen had earned the right to challenge Chirac by finishing a surprising 2nd in the 1st round of French elections, Apr. 21. Chirac was ultimately reelected, May 5, with 82% of the vote.

AP/WIDE WORLD PHOTOS

◄ A NEW NATION
East Timor's new president, Jose Alexandre (Xanana) Gusmao (right), embraces UN Sec. Gen. Kofi Annan at an independence celebration May 20 in the capital, Dili, after the UN officially ended its temporary sovereignty over the former Indonesian territory.

▼ REPORTER ABDUCTED AND SLAIN

Wall Street Journal reporter Daniel Pearl was abducted in Karachi by Pakistani militants on Jan. 23 and later murdered. Four defendants were convicted and sentenced (3 to life imprisonment, 1 to death) July 15 in an antiterrorism court in Pakistan.

AP/WIDE WORLD PHOTOS

AP/WIDE WORLD PHOTOS

HUSSEIN ON THE PODIUM ►

On the anniversary of the end of the bloody 1980-88 war with Iran, Aug. 8, Iraqi Pres. Saddam Hussein addresses the nation; he said he was not frightened by reports that the U.S. might seek to oust him from power through a military attack.

▼ HISTORIC FLOODS

Below Prague Castle, the swollen Vltava River surges through the Czech capital in mid-August. Flooding across central and eastern Europe during the summer led to more than 100 deaths and caused damages estimated at over $20 billion.

AP/WIDE WORLD PHOTOS

AP/WIDE WORLD PHOTOS

◄ A ROYAL WELCOME
Queen Elizabeth II (also shown below) and her husband, Prince Philip, ride in the Gold State Coach to St. Paul's Cathedral in London June 4, for a service celebrating her Golden Jubilee.

AP/WIDE WORLD PHOTOS

AP/WIDE WORLD PHOTOS

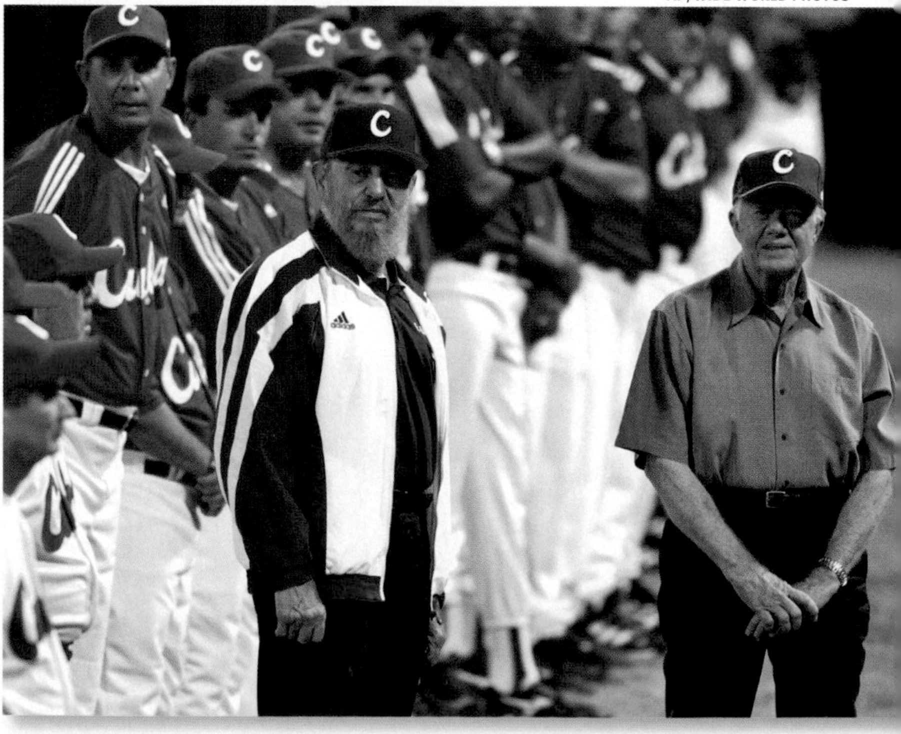

PLAY BALL! ►
Former Pres. Jimmy Carter (right) waits with Cuban Pres. Fidel Castro before throwing out the first pitch for an all-star baseball game in Havana May 14. Carter was the 1st U.S. president to visit Cuba since Calvin Coolidge in 1928.

AP/WIDE WORLD PHOTOS

◄ ODD COUPLE IN AFRICA
U.S. Treasury Sec. Paul O'Neill (right) and Irish rock star Bono wear garb given to them by villagers in Ghana May 22. Their 10-day fact-finding mission was aimed at improving the impact of Western aid in Africa.

IN HOT WATER ►
Martha Stewart (CEO of Martha Stewart Living Omnimedia) was among those investigated in connection with selling ImClone stock in December 2001, a day before the FDA declined to review ImClone's application for a new cancer drug.

AP/WIDE WORLD PHOTOS

AP/WIDE WORLD PHOTOS

◄ . . . WHEN I'M 64?
Former Beatle Sir Paul McCartney and new wife Heather Mills, seen in Liverpool, England, a few weeks after their June 11 wedding. McCartney turned 60 on June 18; Mills was 34.

AP/WIDE WORLD PHOTOS

AROUND THE WORLD ►
Millionaire adventurer Steve Fossett prepares to launch his balloon, *Spirit of Freedom*, in western Australia June 19. After 5 failed tries in 5 years, he became the 1st balloonist to circle the globe solo, landing July 4 in the Australian outback.

WORLD CUP WONDER ►
German Thomas Linke's hard tackle sends Brazil's Ronaldo (left) to the ground during the World Cup Final, June 30. But Ronaldo's 2 goals gave Brazil a 2-0 win and a record 5th World Cup title. He also won the Golden Shoe Award for most goals in the tournament (8, the most since 1970).

AP/WIDE WORLD PHOTOS

▼ EIGHT IS GREAT
Tiger Woods won his 8th major golf title on June 16, at the U.S. Open in Farmingdale, NY. He was the 1st player since Jack Nicklaus in 1972 to win the Masters and U.S. Open the same year.

AP/WIDE WORLD PHOTOS

▲ BASEBALL STRIKE
A father and daughter express their views at a game in Philadelphia, a day before the Aug. 30 deadline for a possible baseball strike. After all-night negotiations, players and owners reached agreement without a work stoppage—a first for major league baseball.

AP/WIDE WORLD PHOTOS

IT'S GOOD! ►

Kicker Adam Vinatieri leaps as his 48-yd field goal in the final seconds of Super Bowl XXXVI gives the underdog New England Patriots a 20-17 win over the St. Louis Rams, Feb. 3.

AP/WIDE WORLD PHOTOS

▼ LAKERS THREE-PEAT

L.A. Lakers teammates (left to right) Kobe Bryant, Rick Fox, Lindsey Hunter, and Shaquille O'Neal celebrate their 3rd NBA title in a row after sweeping the N.J. Nets with a 113-107 victory in Game 4 of the NBA Finals, June 12. O'Neal won his 3rd straight Finals MVP Award.

AP/WIDE WORLD PHOTOS

MAGNIFIQUE!! ►

On July 28, Lance Armstrong won the Tour de France for the 4th straight year. He finished the 3-week, 2,032-mi tour with a time of 82 hrs, 5 mins, 12 secs. Runner-up Joseba Beloki of Spain was 7:17 behind.

AP/WIDE WORLD PHOTOS

AP/WIDE WORLD PHOTOS

◄ SISTER SLAMS

Serena (left) and Venus Williams await serve in a 1st round match at Wimbledon, June 27, en route to their 2nd doubles title in 3 years. In the singles final, Serena defeated Venus, the 2-time defending champ (as she had in the French Open June 8), and replaced her as #1 in the world. Serena beat Venus again at the U.S. Open finals, Sept. 7.

2003 OLYMPIC HIGHLIGHTS

AP/WIDE WORLD PHOTOS

◄ SKATING SCANDAL

The pairs figure skating event at the 2002 Winter Olympics ended in an uproar, Feb. 11, when Russians Yelena Berezhnaya and Anton Sikharulidze (left), were named winners over flawless Canadians Jamie Salé and David Pelletier. It was later revealed that a French judge had been pressured to vote for the Russians. Duplicate gold medals were awarded to the Canadians.

► GOLDEN GIRL

In a stunning upset, American Sarah Hughes, 16, won the women's figure skating gold Feb. 21, after doing 2 triple-triple leaps. Favorite Michelle Kwan (U.S.) settled for the bronze after falling out of a triple jump.

AP/WIDE WORLD PHOTOS

AP/WIDE WORLD PHOTOS

◄ OLYMPIC HERITAGE

Celebrating his gold medal run in the skeleton, 3rd generation Olympian Jim Shea holds up a picture of his grandfather, Jack, a double gold-medalist in the 1932 Games. Jack Shea was killed in an auto accident just before the 2002 Games.

Malta

Republic of Malta

People: Population: 397,499. **Age distrib.** (%): <15: 20.0; 65+: 12.5. **Pop. density:** 3,207 per sq. mi. **Urban:** 90%. **Ethnic group:** Maltese. **Principal languages:** Maltese, English (both official). **Chief religion:** Roman Catholic 98%.

Geography: Area: 124 sq. mi. **Location:** In center of Mediterranean Sea. **Neighbors:** Nearest is Italy on N. **Topography:** Island of Malta is 95 sq. mi.; other islands in the group: Gozo, 26 sq. mi.; Comino, 1 sq. mi. The coastline is heavily indented. Low hills cover the interior. **Capital:** Valletta: 82,000.

Government: Type: Parliamentary democracy. **Head of state:** Pres. Guido de Marco; b July 22, 1931; in office: Apr. 4, 1999. **Head of gov.:** Prime Min. Edward Fenech-Adami; b Feb. 7, 1934; in office: Sept. 6, 1998. **Local divisions:** 3 regions comprising 67 local councils. **Defense budget (2001):** $25.6 mil. **Active troops:** 2,140.

Economy: Industries: Tourism, electronics, ship building/repair, construction, food and beverages. **Chief crops:** Potatoes, cauliflower, tomatoes. **Minerals:** Salt, limestone. **Arable land:** 38%. **Livestock** (2001): cattle: 19,200; chickens: 820,000; goats: 9,000; pigs: 80,074; sheep: 16,000. **Electricity prod.:** 1.75 bil. kWh. **Labor force:** ind. 24%, services 71%, agri. 5%.

Finance: Monetary unit: Maltese Lira (Sept. 2002: .42 = $1 U.S.). **GDP** (2000 est.): $5.6 bil. **Per capita GDP:** $14,300. **Imports** (1999): $2.6 bil.; partners (1999): France 19.1%, Italy 16.7%. **Exports** (1999): $2 bil.; partners (1999): U.S. 21.4%, France 15.2%. **Tourism:** $675 mil. **Budget** (1999): $1.73 bil. **Intl. reserves less gold** (end 2000): $1.13 bil. **Gold:** 6,000 oz t. **Consumer prices** (change in 2000): 2.4%.

Transport: Motor vehicles: 122,100 pass. cars, 19,100 comm. vehicles. **Civil aviation:** 1.0 bil pass.-mi; 1 airport. **Chief ports:** Valletta, Marsaxlokk.

Communications: TV sets: 739 per 1,000 pop. **Radios:** 525 per 1,000 pop. **Telephones:** 346,500. **Daily newspaper circ.:** 145 per 1,000 pop.

Health: Life expectancy: 75.8 male; 81 female. **Births** (per 1,000 pop.): 12.8. **Deaths** (per 1,000 pop.): 7.8. **Natural inc.:** 0.5%. **Infant mortality** (per 1,000 live births): 5.7.

Education: Free, compulsory: ages 5-16. **Literacy:** 91%.

Major Intl. Organizations: UN (FAO, IBRD, ILO, IMF, IMO, WHO, WTrO), the Commonwealth, OSCE.

Embassy: 2017 Connecticut Ave. NW 20008; 462-3611.

Website: www.gov.mt/index./asp?1-2

Malta was ruled by Phoenicians, Romans, Arabs, Normans, the Knights of Malta, France, and Britain (since 1814). It became independent Sept. 21, 1964. Malta became a republic in 1974. The withdrawal of the last British sailors, Apr. 1, 1979, ended 179 years of British military presence on the island. From 1971 to 1987 and again from 1996 to 1998, Malta was governed by the socialist Labour Party. The Nationalist Party, which held office 1987-96 and favors Malta's entry into the EU, returned to power after elections Sept. 5, 1998.

Marshall Islands

Republic of the Marshall Islands

People: Population: 73,630. **Age. distrib.** (%): <15: 49.3; 65+: 2.1. **Pop. density:** 1,054 per sq. mi. **Urban:** 70%. **Ethnic groups:** Micronesian. **Principal languages:** English (official), Marshallese, Japanese. **Chief religion:** Protestant 63%.

Geography: Area: 70 sq. mi. **Location:** In N Pacific Ocean; composed of two 800-mi-long parallel chains of coral atolls. **Neighbors:** Nearest are Micronesia to W, Nauru and Kiribati to S. **Capital:** Majuro: 25,000.

Government: Type: Republic. **Head of state and gov.:** Pres. Kessai Note; b 1950; in office: Jan. 10, 2000. **Local divisions:** 33 municipalities.

Economy: Industries: Copra, fish, tourism.

Finance: Monetary unit: U.S. Dollar. **GDP** (1998 est.): $105 mil. (supplemented by approximately $65 mil. annual U.S. aid) . **Per capita GDP:** $1,670. **Imports** (1997 est.): $58 mil.; partners: U.S., Japan, Australia, NZ, Guam, Singapore. **Exports** (1997 est.): $28 mil.; partners: U.S., Japan, Australia. **Tourism:** $4 mil. **Budget** (FY95/96 est.): $77.4 mil.

Transport: Civil aviation: 16.1 mil pass.-mi; 25 airports. **Chief port:** Majuro.

Communications: Telephones: 4,700.

Health: Life expectancy: 64.3 male; 68.1 female. **Births** (per 1,000 pop.): 45. **Deaths** (per 1,000 pop.): 6.1. **Natural inc.:** 3.89%. **Infant mortality** (per 1,000 live births): 38.7.

Education: Compulsory: ages 6-14. **Literacy** (1994): 93%.

Major Intl. Organizations: UN (IBRD, IMF, WHO).

Embassy: 2433 Massachusetts Ave. NW 20008; 234-5414.

Website: www.miembassyus.org/

The Marshall Islands were a German possession until World War I and were administered by Japan between the World Wars. After WW II, they were administered as part of the UN Trust Territory of the Pacific Islands by the U.S.

The Marshall Islands secured international recognition as an independent nation on Sept. 17, 1991. Amata Kabua, the islands' first and only president since 1979, died Dec. 19, 1996. His cousin Imata Kabua, elected president Jan. 13, 1997, was succeeded by Kessai Note on Jan. 10, 2000.

Mauritania

Islamic Republic of Mauritania

People: Population: 2,828,858. **Age distrib.** (%): <15: 46.1; 65+: 2.3. **Pop. density:** 7 per sq. mi. **Urban:** 56%. **Ethnic groups:** Mixed Maur/black 40%, Maur 30%, black 30%. **Principal languages:** Hasaniya Arabic, Wolof (both official), Pular, Soninke. **Chief religion:** Muslim 100%.

Geography: Area: 397,800 sq. mi. **Location:** In NW Africa. **Neighbors:** Morocco on N, Algeria and Mali on E, Senegal on S. **Topography:** The fertile Senegal R. valley in the S gives way to a wide central region of sandy plains and scrub trees. The N is arid and extends into the Sahara. **Capital:** Nouakchott: 626,000.

Government: Type: Islamic republic. **Head of state:** Pres. Maaouya Ould Sidi Ahmed Taya; b 1941; in office: Apr. 18, 1992. **Head of gov.:** Prime Min. Cheikh El Afia Ould Mohamed Khouna; b 1956; in office: Nov. 16, 1998. **Local divisions:** 12 regions, 1 capital district. **Defense budget (2001):** $25.6 mil. **Active troops:** 15,650.

Economy: Industries: Fish processing, iron and gypsum mining. **Chief crops:** Dates, millet. **Minerals:** Iron ore, gypsum. **Livestock** (2001): cattle: 1.50 mil; chickens: 4.10 mil.; goats: 5.10 mil.; sheep: 7.60 mil. **Fish catch** (1999): 82,000 metric tons. **Electricity prod.:** 0.15 bil. kWh. **Labor force:** agric. 47%, services 39%, ind. 14%.

Finance: Monetary unit: Ouguiya (Sept. 2002: 272.55 = $1 U.S.). **GDP** (2000 est.): $5.4 bil. **Per capita GDP:** $2,000. **Imports** (1999): $305 mil.; partners (1998): France 27%, Benelux 9%. **Exports** (1999): $333 mil.; partners (1998): Japan 18%, France 17%. **Tourism** (1998): $21 mil. **Budget** (1996 est.): $265 mil. **Intl. reserves less gold** (May 2000): $193.9 mil. **Gold:** 12,000 oz t. **Consumer prices** (change in 2000): 3.3%.

Transport: Railroad: Length: 437 mi. **Motor vehicles:** 17,300 pass. cars, 9,210 comm. vehicles. **Civil aviation:** 201.1 mil pass.-mi; 9 airports. **Chief ports:** Nouakchott, Nouadhibou.

Communications: Radios: 428 per 1,000 pop. **Telephones** (2000): 26,100.

Health: Life expectancy: 49.4 male; 53.7 female. **Births** (per 1,000 pop.): 42.5. **Deaths** (per 1,000 pop.): 13.3. **Natural inc.:** 2.92%. **Infant mortality** (per 1,000 live births): 75.2.

Education: Compulsory: ages 6-12. **Literacy:** 38%.

Major Intl. Organizations: UN (FAO, IBRD, ILO, IMF, IMO, WHO, WTrO), AL, AU.

Embassy: 2129 Leroy Pl. NW 20008; 232-5700.

Website: www.embassy.org/mauritania

Mauritania was a French protectorate from 1903. It became independent Nov. 28, 1960 and annexed the south of former Spanish Sahara (now Western Sahara) in 1976. Saharan guerrillas of the Polisario Front stepped up attacks in 1977; 8,000 Moroccan troops and French bomber raids aided the government. Mauritania signed a peace treaty with the Polisario Front, 1979, resumed diplomatic relations with Algeria while breaking a defense treaty with Morocco, and renounced sovereignty over its share of Western Sahara. Opposition parties were legalized and a new constitution approved in 1991.

Although slavery has been repeatedly abolished, most recently in 1980, thousands of Mauritanians continued to live under conditions of servitude.

Mauritius

Republic of Mauritius

People: Population: 1,200,206. **Age distrib.** (%): <15: 25.5; 65+: 6.2. **Pop. density:** 1,681 per sq. mi. **Urban:** 41%. **Ethnic groups:** Indo-Mauritian 68%, Creole 27%. **Principal languages:** English (official), French, Creole, Hindi, Bojpoori. **Chief religions:** Hindu 52%, Christian 28.3%, Muslim 16.6%.

Geography: Area: 714 sq. mi. **Location:** In the Indian O., 500 mi. E of Madagascar. **Neighbors:** Nearest is Madagascar to W. **Topography:** A volcanic island nearly surrounded by coral reefs. A central plateau is encircled by mountain peaks. **Capital:** Port Louis: 176,000.

Government: Type: Republic. **Head of state:** Pres. Karl Auguste Offmann; b Nov. 25, 1940; in office: Feb. 25, 2002. **Head of gov.:** Prime Min. Anerood Jugnauth; b Mar. 29, 1930; in office: Sept. 17, 2000. **Local divisions:** 9 districts, 3 dependencies. **Defense budget (2001):** $9 mil.

Economy: Industries: Food processing, textiles, clothing, chemicals. **Chief crops:** Sugarcane, corn, potatoes, tea. **Arable land:** 49%. **Livestock** (2001): cattle: 28,000; chickens: 4.50 mil.;

goats: 95,000; pigs: 21,000; sheep: 7,300. **Electricity prod.:** 1.29 bil. kWh. **Labor force:** construction and ind. 36%, services 24%, agri. and fishing 14%, trade restaurants hotels 16%, transportation and communication 7%, finance 3%.

Finance: Monetary unit: Rupee (Sept. 2002: 29.73 = $1 U.S.). **GDP** (2000 est.): $12.3 bil. **Per capita GDP:** $10,400. **Imports** (1999): $2.3 bil.; partners (1999 est.): France 14%, South Africa 11%. **Exports** (1999): $1.6 bil.; partners (1999 est.): UK 32%, France 19%. **Tourism:** $545 mil. **Budget** (1999 est.): $1.2 bil. **Intl. reserves less gold** (end 2000): $689 mil. **Gold:** 62,000 oz t. **Consumer prices** (change in 2000): 4.2%.

Transport: Motor vehicles: 69,945 pass. cars, 12,328 comm. vehicles. **Civil aviation:** 2.4 bil pass.-mi; 1 airport. **Chief port:** Port Louis.

Communications: TV sets: 150 per 1,000 pop. **Radios:** 353 per 1,000 pop. **Telephones:** 606,800. **Daily newspaper circ.:** 49 per 1,000 pop.

Health: Life expectancy: 67.5 male; 75.6 female. **Births** (per 1,000 pop.): 16.3. **Deaths** (per 1,000 pop.): 6.8. **Natural inc.:** 0.95%. **Infant mortality** (per 1,000 live births): 16.6.

Education: Compulsory: ages 5-12. **Literacy**: 83%.

Major Intl. Organizations: UN and all of its specialized agencies, the Commonwealth, AU.

Embassy: 4301 Connecticut Ave. NW, Suite 441, 20008; 244-1491.

Website: www.ncb.intnet.mu/govt/

Mauritius was uninhabited when settled in 1638 by the Dutch, who introduced sugarcane. France took over in 1721, bringing African slaves. Britain ruled from 1810 to Mar. 12, 1968, bringing Indian workers for the sugar plantations.

Mauritius formally severed its association with the British crown Mar. 12, 1992.

Mexico

United Mexican States

People: Population: 103,400,165. **Age distrib.** (%): <15: 33.3; 65+: 4.4. **Pop. density:** 139 per sq. mi. **Urban:** 74%. **Ethnic groups:** Mestizo 60%, Amerindian 30%, Caucasian 9%. **Principal languages:** Spanish (official), Mayan dialects. **Chief religions:** Roman Catholic 89%, Protestant 6%.

Geography: Area: 742,500 sq. mi. **Location:** In southern North America. **Neighbors:** U.S. on N, Guatemala and Belize on S. **Topography:** The Sierra Madre Occidental Mts. run NW-SE near the west coast; the Sierra Madre Oriental Mts. run near the Gulf of Mexico. They join S of Mexico City. Between the 2 ranges lies the dry central plateau, 5,000 to 8,000 ft. alt., rising toward the S, with temperate vegetation. Coastal lowlands are tropical. About 45% of land is arid. **Capital:** Mexico City. **Cities (urban aggr.):** Mexico City 18,268,000; Guadalajara 3,697,000; Monterrey 3,267,000; Puebla 1,888,000.

Government: Type: Federal republic. **Head of state and gov.:** Pres. Vicente Fox Quesada; b July 2, 1942; in office: Dec. 1, 2000. **Local divisions:** 31 states, 1 federal district. **Defense budget (2000):** $3 bil. **Active troops:**192,770.

Economy: Industries: Food and beverages, tobacco, chemicals, iron and steel, oil, mining. **Chief crops:** Cotton, coffee, wheat, rice, beans, soybeans, corn. **Minerals:** Silver, lead, zinc, gold, oil, gas, copper. **Crude oil reserves** (2001): 26.9 bil bbls. **Arable land:** 12%. **Livestock** (2001): cattle: 30.60 mil; chickens: 495.70 mil.; goats: 9.10 mil.; pigs: 17.75 mil; sheep: 6.15 mil. **Electricity prod.:** 194.37 bil. kWh. **Labor force**: agri. 20%, ind. 24%, services 56%.

Finance: Monetary unit: New Peso (Sept. 2001: 10.18 = $1 U.S.). **GDP** (2000 est.): $915 bil. **Per capita GDP:** $9,100. **Imports** (2000), includes in-bond industries $176 bil.; partners (2000 est.): U.S. 73.6%, Japan 3.7%, Germany 3.3%. **Exports** (2000): $168 bil.; partners (2000 est.): U.S. 88.6%, Canada 2%. **Tourism:** $7.59 bil. **Budget** (2000 est.): $130 bil. **Intl. reserves less gold** (end 2000): $27.25 bil. **Gold:** 250,000 oz t. **Consumer prices** (change in 2000): 9.5%.

Transport: Railroad: Length: 16,543 mi. **Motor vehicles:** 8.2 mil pass. cars, 4.03 mil comm. vehicles. **Civil aviation:** 14.7 bil pass.-mi; 83 airports. **Chief ports:** Coatzacoalcos, Mazatlan, Tampico, Veracruz.

Communications: TV sets: 257 per 1,000 pop. **Radios:** 329 per 1,000 pop. **Telephones:** 35,530,000. **Daily newspaper circ.:** 97 per 1,000 pop.

Health: Life expectancy: 69 male; 75.2 female. **Births** (per 1,000 pop.): 22.4. **Deaths** (per 1,000 pop.): 5. **Natural inc.:** 1.74%. **Infant mortality** (per 1,000 live births): 24.5.

Education: Free, compulsory: ages 6-12. **Literacy**: 90%.

Major Intl. Organizations: UN (FAO, IBRD, ILO, IMF, IMO, WHO, WTrO), APEC, OAS, OECD.

Embassy: 1911 Pennsylvania Ave. NW 20006; 728-1600.

Website: www.presidencia.gob.mx/?NLang=en

Mexico was the site of advanced Indian civilizations. The Mayas, an agricultural people, moved up from Yucatan, built immense stone pyramids, invented a calendar. The Toltecs were overcome by the Aztecs, who founded Tenochtitlan AD 1325, now Mexico City. Hernando Cortes, Spanish conquistador, destroyed the Aztec empire, 1519-21.

After 3 centuries of Spanish rule the people rose, under Fr. Miguel Hidalgo y Costilla, 1810, Fr. Morelos y Payon, 1812, and Gen. Agustin Iturbide, who made himself emperor as Agustin I, 1821. A republic was declared in 1823.

Mexican territory extended into the present American Southwest and California until Texas revolted and established a republic in 1836; the Mexican legislature refused recognition but was unable to enforce its authority there. After numerous clashes, the U.S.-Mexican War, 1846-48, resulted in the loss by Mexico of the lands north of the Rio Grande.

French arms supported an Austrian archduke on the throne of Mexico as Maximilian I, 1864-67, but pressure from the U.S. forced France to withdraw. Dictatorial rule by Porfirio Diaz, president 1877-80, 1884-1911, led to a period of rebellion and factional fighting. A new constitution, Feb. 5, 1917, brought social reform.

The Institutional Revolutionary Party (PRI) dominated politics from 1929 until the late 1990s. Radical opposition, including some guerrilla activity, was contained by strong measures. Some gains in agriculture, industry, and social services were achieved, but much of the work force remained jobless or underemployed. Although prospects brightened with the discovery of vast oil reserves, inflation and a drop in world oil prices aggravated Mexico's economic problems in the 1980s.

Mexico reached agreement with the U.S. and Canada on the North American Free Trade Agreement (NAFTA) Aug. 12, 1992; it took effect Jan. 1, 1994.

Guerrillas of the Zapatista National Liberation Army (EZLN) launched an uprising, Jan. 1, 1994, in southern Mexico. A tentative peace accord was reached Mar. 2. The presidential candidate of the governing PRI, Luis Donaldo Colosio Murrieta, was assassinated at a political rally in Tijuana, Mar. 23. The new PRI candidate, Ernesto Zedillo Ponce de León, won election Aug. 21 and was inaugurated Dec. 1, 1994.

An austerity plan and pledges of aid from the U.S. saved Mexico's currency from collapse in early 1995. Popular Revolutionary Army guerrillas launched coordinated attacks on government targets in Aug. 1996. In elections July 6, 1997, the PRI failed to win a congressional majority for the first time since 1929. An armed gang massacred 45 peasants in Chiapas on Dec. 22, 1997. In the presidential election of July 2, 2000, the PRI lost for the 1st time in over 7 decades; the winner, opposition candidate Vicente Fox Quesada, took office Dec. 1, 2000.

Micronesia

Federated States of Micronesia

People: Population: 135,869. **Pop. density:** 501 per sq. mi. **Urban:** 28%. **Ethnic groups:** 9 ethnic Micronesian and Polynesian groups. **Principal languages:** English (official), Trukese, Pohnpeian, Yapese. **Chief religions:** Roman Catholic 50%, Protestant 47%.

Geography: Area: 271 sq. mi. **Location:** Consists of 607 islands in the W Pacific Ocean. **Capital:** Palikir, on Pohnpei; (1994 island pop.) 33,372.

Government: Type: Republic. **Head of state and gov.:** Pres. Leo A. Falcam; b Nov. 20, 1935; in office: May 11, 1999. **Local divisions:** 4 states.

Economy: Industries: Tourism, construction, fish processing. **Chief crops:** Tropical fruits, vegetables, black pepper. **Livestock** (2001): cattle: 13,900; chickens: 185,000; goats: 4,000; pigs: 32,000. **Labor force:** 67% govt.

Finance: Monetary unit: U.S. Dollar. **GDP** (1999 est.): $263 mil. **Per capita GDP:** $2,000. **Imports** (1996 est.): $168 mil.; partners: U.S., Japan, Australia. **Exports** (1996 est.): $73 mil.; partners: Japan, U.S., Guam. **Budget** (1998 est.): $160 mil. **Intl. reserves less gold** (end 2000): $87 mil.

Transport: 4 airports. **Chief ports:** Colonia (Yap), Kolonia (Pohnpei), Lele, Moen.

Communications: TV sets: 19 per 1,000 pop. **Radios:** 664 per 1,000 pop. **Telephones:** 10,000.

Health: Life expectancy: NA. **Births** (per 1,000 pop.): NA. **Deaths** (per 1,000 pop.): NA. **Natural inc.:** NA. **Infant mortality** (per 1,000 live births): NA.

Education: Compulsory: ages 6-14. **Literacy** (1991): 90%.

Major Intl. Organizations: UN (IBRD, IMF, WHO).

Embassy: 1725 N St. NW 20036; 223-4383.

Website: www.fsmgov.org/

The Federated States of Micronesia, formerly known as the Caroline Islands, was ruled successively by Spain, Germany, Japan, and the U.S. It was internationally recognized as an independent nation Sept. 17, 1991. Tropical Storm Chata'an July 1-2, 2002, left 47 people dead and over 1,000 homeless in Chuuk.

Moldova

Republic of Moldova

People: Population: 4,434,547. **Age distrib.** (%): <15: 22.4; 65+: 9.9. **Pop. density:** 341 per sq. mi. **Urban:** 46%. **Ethnic groups:** Moldovan/Romanian 64.5%, Ukrainian 13.8%, Russian 13%. **Principal languages:** Moldovan (official), Russian. **Chief religion:** Eastern Orthodox 98.5%.

Geography: Area: 13,000 sq. mi. **Location:** In E Europe. **Neighbors:** Romania on W; Ukraine on N, E, and S. **Capital:** Kishinev 662,000.

Government: Type: Republic. **Head of state:** Pres. Vladimir Voronin; b May 25, 1941; in office: Apr. 7, 2001. **Head of gov.:** Prime Min. Vasile Tarlev; b Oct. 9, 1963; in office: Apr. 19, 2001. **Local divisions:** 21 cities and towns, 48 urban settlements, more than 1,600 villages. **Defense budget (2001):** $5.9 mil. **Active troops:** 8,220.

Economy: Industries: Food processing, agricultural machinery, foundry equipment. **Chief crops:** Grain, vegetables, fruits, wine. **Minerals:** Lignite, phosphorites, gypsum. **Arable land:** 53%. **Livestock** (2001): cattle: 402,000; chickens: 13.00 mil.; goats: 93,000; pigs: 543,000; sheep: 866,000. **Electricity prod.:** 3.32 bil. kWh. **Labor force:** agri. 40%, ind. 14%, other 46%.

Finance: Monetary unit: Leu (Sept. 2002: 13.58 = $1 U.S.). **GDP** (2000 est.): $11.3 bil. **Per capita GDP:** $2,500. **Imports** (2000): $761 mil.; partners (1999): Russia 21%, Romania 16%. **Exports** (2000): $500 mil.; partners (1999): Russia 41%, Romania 9%. **Tourism** (1998): $2 mil. **Budget** (1998 est.): $594 mil. **Intl. reserves less gold** (end 2000): $177 mil. **Consumer prices** (change in 2000): 31.3%.

Transport: Railroad: Length: 746 mi. **Motor vehicles:** 169,000 pass. cars, 71,000 comm. vehicles. **Civil aviation:** 37.8 mil pass.-mi; 1 airport.

Communications: TV sets: 30 per 1,000 pop. **Radios:** 209 per 1,000 pop. **Telephones:** 886,100. **Daily newspaper circ.:** 24 per 1,000 pop.

Health: Life expectancy: 60.4 male; 69.3 female. **Births** (per 1,000 pop.): 13.8. **Deaths** (per 1,000 pop.): 12.6. **Natural inc.:** 0.12%. **Infant mortality** (per 1,000 live births): 42.2.

Education: Compulsory: ages 7-16. **Literacy**: 96%.

Major Intl. Organizations: UN (FAO, IBRD, ILO, IMF, WHO, WTrO), CIS, OSCE.

Embassy: 2101 S St. NW 20008; 667 1130.

Website: www.moldova.md

In 1918, Romania annexed all of Bessarabia that Russia had acquired from Turkey in 1812 by the Treaty of Bucharest. In 1924, the Soviet Union established the Moldavian Autonomous Soviet Socialist Republic on the eastern bank of the Dniester. It was merged with the Romanian-speaking districts of Bessarabia in 1940 to form the Moldavian SSR.

During World War II, Romania, allied with Germany, occupied the area. It was recaptured by the USSR in 1944. Moldova declared independence Aug. 27, 1991. It became an independent state when the USSR disbanded Dec. 26, 1991.

Fighting erupted Mar. 1992 in the Dnestr (Dniester) region between Moldovan security forces and Slavic separatists—ethnic Russians and ethnic Ukrainians—who feared Moldova would merge with neighboring Romania. In a plebiscite on Mar. 6, 1994, voters in Moldova supported independence, without unification with Romania.

Defying the Moldovan government, voters in the breakaway Dnestr region held legislative elections and approved a separatist constitution Dec. 24, 1995. Petru Lucinschi, a former Communist, won a presidential runoff election Dec. 1, 1996. A peace accord with Dnestr separatists was signed in Moscow May 8, 1997. The Communists won the most seats in parliamentary elections Mar. 22, 1998, but a coalition of three center-right parties formed the government. New elections Feb. 25, 2001, brought a decisive Communist victory.

Monaco

Principality of Monaco

People: Population: 31,987. **Age distrib.** (%): <15: 15.3; 65+: 22.5. **Pop. density:** 41,423 per sq. mi. **Urban:** 100%. **Ethnic groups:** French 47%, Italian 16%, Monegasque 16%. **Principal languages:** French (official), English, Italian, Monegasque. **Chief religion:** Roman Catholic 95%.

Geography: Area: 1 sq. mi. **Location:** On the NW Mediterranean coast. **Neighbors:** France to W, N, E. **Topography:** Monaco-Ville sits atop a high promontory, the rest of the principality rises from the port up the hillside. **Capital:** Monaco-ville: 34,000.

Government: Type: Constitutional monarchy. **Head of state:** Prince Rainier III; b May 31, 1923; in office: May 9, 1949. **Head of gov.:** Min. of State Patrick Leclercq; b 1938; in office: Jan. 5, 2000. **Local divisions:** 4 quarters.

Economy: Industries: Tourism, gambling, construction.

Finance: Monetary unit: French Franc (Sept. 2002: 6.72 = $1 U.S.) or Monegasque Franc. **GDP** (1999 est.): $870 mil. **Per capita GDP:** $27,000. **Imports**: NA. **Exports** NA. **Budget** (1995): $531 mil.

Transport: Motor vehicles: 17,000 pass. cars, 4,000 comm. vehicles. **Civil aviation:** 820,000 pass.-mi; 1 airport. **Chief port:** Monaco.

Communications: TV sets: 690 per 1,000 pop. **Radios:** 941 per 1,000 pop.

Health: Life expectancy: 75.2 male; 83.2 female. **Births** (per 1,000 pop.): 9.6. **Deaths** (per 1,000 pop.): 12.9. **Natural inc.:** -0.33%. **Infant mortality** (per 1,000 live births): 5.7.

Education: Compulsory: ages 6-16.

Major Intl. Organizations: UN (IMO, WHO), OSCE.

Website: www.gouv.mc/PortGb

An independent principality for over 300 years, Monaco has belonged to the House of Grimaldi since 1297, except during the French Revolution. It was placed under the protectorate of Sardinia in 1815, and under France, 1861. The Prince of Monaco was an absolute ruler until the 1911 constitution. Monaco was admitted to the UN on May 28, 1993.

Monaco's fame as a tourist resort is widespread. It is noted for its mild climate, magnificent scenery, and elegant casinos.

Mongolia

People: Population: 2,694,432. **Age distrib.** (%): <15: 33.0; 65+: 3.9. **Pop. density:** 4 per sq. mi. **Urban:** 63%. **Ethnic groups:** Mongol 90%. **Principal language:** Khalkha Mongol (official). **Chief religion:** Mostly Tibetan Buddhist.

Geography: Area: 604,200 sq. mi. **Location:** In E Central Asia. **Neighbors:** Russia on N, China on E, W, and S. **Topography:** Mostly a high plateau with mountains, salt lakes, and vast grasslands. Arid lands in the S are part of the Gobi Desert. **Capital:** Ulan Bator: 781,000.

Government: Type: Republic. **Head of state:** Pres. Natsagiyn Bagabandi; b Apr. 22, 1950; in office: June 20, 1997. **Head of gov.:** Nambaryn Enkhbayar; b June 1, 1958; in office: July 26, 2000. **Local divisions:** 18 provinces, 3 municipalities. **Defense budget (2001):** $30.2 mil. **Active troops:** 9,100.

Economy: Industries: Construction materials, mining, food and beverages. **Chief crops:** Grain, potatoes. **Minerals:** Coal, oil, tungsten, copper, molybdenum, gold, phosphates, tin. **Arable land:** 1%. **Livestock** (2001): cattle: 2.48 mil; chickens: 90,000; goats: 11.80 mil.; pigs: 16,000; sheep: 15.67 mil. **Electricity prod.:** 2.77 bil. kWh. **Labor force:** primarily agricultural.

Finance: Monetary unit: Tugrik (Sept. 2002: 1,116.00 = $1 U.S.). **GDP** (2000 est.): $4.7 bil. **Per capita GDP:** $1,780. **Imports** (1999): $510.7 mil.; partners (1999): Russia 33%, China 21%. **Exports** (1999): $454.3 mil.; partners (2000 est.): China 60%, U.S. 20%. **Tourism:** $28 mil. **Budget** (2000 est.): $328 mil. **Intl. reserves less gold** (end 2000): $137 mil. **Gold:** 80,000 oz t. **Consumer prices** (change in 1999): 7.6%.

Transport: Railroad: Length: 1,294 mi. **Motor vehicles:** 21,000 pass. cars, 27,000 comm. vehicles. **Civil aviation:** 121.0 mil pass.-mi; 1 airport.

Communications: TV sets: 60.7 per 1,000 pop. **Radios:** 74 per 1,000 pop. **Telephones:** 318,000. **Daily newspaper circ.:** 92 per 1,000 pop.

Health: Life expectancy: 62.5 male; 66.9 female. **Births** (per 1,000 pop.): 21.8. **Deaths** (per 1,000 pop.): 7. **Natural inc.:** 1.48%. **Infant mortality** (per 1,000 live births): 52.

Education: Compulsory: ages 6-16. **Literacy** (1991): 83%.

Major Intl. Organizations: UN (FAO, IBRD, ILO, IMF, IMO, WHO, WTrO).

Embassy: 2833 M St. NW 20007; 333-7117.

Website: www.pmis.gov.mn/engmain.htm

One of the world's oldest countries, Mongolia reached the zenith of its power in the 13th century when Genghis Khan and his successors conquered all of China and extended their influence as far west as Hungary and Poland. In later centuries, the empire dissolved and Mongolia became a province of China.

With the advent of the 1911 Chinese revolution, Mongolia, with Russian backing, declared its independence. A Communist regime was established July 11, 1921.

In 1990, the Mongolian Communist Party yielded its monopoly on power but won election in July. A new constitution took effect Feb. 12, 1992. A democratic alliance won legislative elections, June 30, 1996. Natsagiyn Bagabandi, a former Communist, won the presidential election of May 18, 1997. A protracted political crisis took a violent turn Oct. 2, 1998, with the murder of Sanjaasuregiyn Zorig, a popular cabinet member seeking to become prime minister. The former Communists won 72 of 76 seats in parliamentary elections, July 2, 2000. Pres. Bagabandi was reelected May 20, 2001.

Morocco

Kingdom of Morocco

People: Population: 31,167,783. **Age distrib.** (%): <15: 34.4; 65+: 4.7. **Pop. density:** 181 per sq. mi. **Urban:** 55%. **Ethnic groups:** Arab-Berber 99%. **Principal languages:** Arabic (official), Berber dialects. **Chief religion:** Muslim 98.7%.

Geography: Area: 172,300 sq. mi. **Location:** On NW coast of Africa. **Neighbors:** Western Sahara on S, Algeria on E. **Topography:** Consists of 5 natural regions: mountain ranges (Riff in the N, Middle Atlas, Upper Atlas, and Anti-Atlas); rich plains in the W; alluvial plains in SW; well-cultivated plateaus in the center; a pre-Sahara arid zone extending from SE. **Capital:** Rabat. **Cities (urban aggr.):** Casablanca 3,357,000; Rabat 1,668,000; Fes 907,000.

Government: Type: Constitutional monarchy. **Head of state:** King Mohammed VI; b Aug. 21, 1963; in office: Jul 23, 1999. **Head of gov.:** Prime Min. Abderrahmane El Youssoufi; b Mar. 8, 1924; in office: Feb. 4, 1998. **Local divisions:** 16 regions. **Defense budget** (2000): $1.7 bil. **Active troops:** 198,500.

Economy: Industries: Mining, food processing, leather goods, textiles, construction, tourism. **Chief crops:** Grain, citrus, wine grapes, olives. **Minerals:** Phosphates, iron ore, manganese, lead, zinc. **Crude oil reserves** (2000): 1.9 mil bbls. **Arable land:** 21%. **Livestock** (2001): cattle: 2.66 mil; chickens: 137.00 mil.; goats: 5.20 mil.; pigs: 8,000; sheep: 17.30 mil. **Fish catch** (1999): 785,843 metric tons. **Electricity prod.:** 14.24 bil. kWh. **Labor force:** agri. 50%, services 35%, ind. 15%.

Finance: Monetary unit: Dirham (Sept. 2002: 10.73 = $1 U.S.). **GDP** (2000 est.): $105 bil. **Per capita GDP:** $3,500. **Imports** (1999 est.): $12.2 bil.; partners (1999): France 32%, Spain 12%. **Exports** (2000 est.): $7.6 bil.; partners (1999): France 35%, Spain 9%. **Tourism:** $1.96 bil. **Budget** (2001 est.): $8.6 bil. **Intl. reserves less gold** (end 2000): $3.70 bil. **Gold:** 710,000 oz t. **Consumer prices** (change in 2000): 1.9%.

Transport: Railroad: Length: 1,099 mi. **Motor vehicles** (1997): 1.10 mil pass. cars, 333,152 comm. vehicles. **Civil aviation:** 3.3 bil pass.-mi; 11 airports. **Chief ports:** Tangier, Casablanca, Kenitra.

Communications: TV sets: 92.7 per 1,000 pop. **Radios:** 222 per 1,000 pop. **Telephones:** 5,963,100. **Daily newspaper circ.:** 14.5 per 1,000 pop.

Health: Life expectancy: 67.5 male; 72.1 female. **Births** (per 1,000 pop.): 23.7. **Deaths** (per 1,000 pop.): 5.9. **Natural inc.:** 1.78%. **Infant mortality** (per 1,000 live births): 46.5.

Education: Compulsory: ages 7-13. **Literacy**: 44%.

Major Intl. Organizations: UN (FAO, IBRD, ILO, IMF, IMO, WHO, WTrO), AL.

Embassy: 1601 21st St. NW 20009; 462-7979.

Website: www.mincom.gov.ma/

Berbers were the original inhabitants, followed by Carthaginians and Romans. Arabs conquered in 683. In the 11th and 12th centuries, a Berber empire ruled all NW Africa and most of Spain from Morocco.

Part of Morocco came under Spanish rule in the 19th century; France controlled the rest in the early 20th. Tribal uprisings lasted from 1911 to 1933. The country became independent Mar. 2, 1956. Tangier, an internationalized seaport, was turned over to Morocco, 1956. Ifni, a Spanish enclave, was ceded in 1969. Morocco annexed the disputed territory of Western Sahara during the second half of the 1970s.

King Hassan II assumed the throne in 1961, reigning until his death on July 23, 1999; he was immediately succeeded by his eldest son. Political reforms in the 1990s included the establishment of a bicameral legislature in 1997.

Western Sahara

Western Sahara, formerly the protectorate of Spanish Sahara, is bounded the in N by Morocco, the NE by Algeria, the E and S by Mauritania, and on the W by the Atlantic Ocean. Phosphates are the major resource. Population (2002 est.): 256,177; capital: Laayoune (El Aaiun). Area: 102,600 sq mi.

Spain withdrew from its protectorate in Feb. 1976. On Apr. 14, 1976, Morocco annexed over 70,000 sq. mi, with the remainder annexed by Mauritania. A guerrilla movement, the Polisario Front, which had proclaimed the region independent Feb. 27, launched attacks with Algerian support. After Mauritania signed a treaty with Polisario on Aug. 5, 1979, Morocco occupied Mauritania's portion of Western Sahara.

After years of bitter fighting, Morocco controlled the main urban areas, but Polisario guerrillas moved freely in the vast, sparsely populated deserts. The 2 sides implemented a cease-fire in 1991, when a UN peacekeeping force was deployed. A UN-sponsored referendum on self-determination for Western Sahara has been repeatedly postponed.

Mozambique

Republic of Mozambique

People: Population: 19,607,519. **Age distrib.** (%): <15: 42.7; 65+: 2.8. **Pop. density:** 65 per sq. mi. **Urban:** 39%. **Ethnic groups:** Indigenous tribal groups. **Principal languages:** Portuguese (official), indigenous dialects. **Chief religions:** Indigenous beliefs 50%, Christian 30%, Muslim 20%.

Geography: Area: 302,700 sq. mi. **Location:** On SE coast of Africa. **Neighbors:** Tanzania on N; Malawi, Zambia, Zimbabwe on W; South Africa, Swaziland on S. **Topography:** Coastal lowlands comprise nearly half the country with plateaus rising in steps to the mountains along the western border. **Capital:** Maputo 1,134,000.

Government: Type: Republic. **Head of state:** Pres. Joaquim Chissano; b Oct. 22, 1939; in office: Oct. 19, 1986. **Head of gov.:** Prime Min. Pascoal Mocumbi; b Apr. 10, 1941; in office: Dec. 21, 1994. **Local divisions:** 10 provinces. **Defense budget (2001):** $82 mil **Active troops:** 10,600–11,600.

Economy: Industries: Food, beverages, chemicals, petroleum products, textiles. **Chief crops:** Cashews, cotton, sugar, corn, cassava, tea. **Minerals:** Coal, titanium. **Arable land:** 4%. **Livestock** (2001): cattle: 1.32 mil; chickens: 28.00 mil.; goats: 392,000; pigs: 180,000; sheep: 125,000. **Electricity prod.:** 7.02 bil. kWh. **Labor force:** agri. 81%, ind. 6%, services 13%

Finance: Monetary unit: Metical (Sept. 2002: 23,333 = $1 U.S.). **GDP** (2000 est.): $19.1 bil. **Per capita GDP:** $1,000. **Imports** (2000 est.): $1.4 bil.; partners (1999 est.): South Africa 44%, EU 16%. **Exports** (2000 est.): $390 mil.; partners (1999 est.): EU 27%, South Africa 26%. **Budget** (2000 est.): $1.004 bil. **Intl. reserves less gold** (end 2000): $557 mil. **Gold: 70,000 oz t. Consumer prices** (change in 1999): 2.0%.

Transport: Railroad: Length: 1,940 mi. **Motor vehicles:** 67,600 pass. cars, 21,200 comm. vehicles. **Civil aviation:** 180.6 mil pass.-mi; 7 airports. **Chief ports:** Maputo, Beira, Nacala, Inhambane.

Communications: TV sets: 3.5 per 1,000 pop. **Radios:** 38 per 1,000 pop. **Telephones:** 259,300. **Daily newspaper circ.:** 8 per 1,000 pop.

Health: Life expectancy: 36.2 male; 34.6 female. **Births** (per 1,000 pop.): 36.4. **Deaths** (per 1,000 pop.): 25.1. **Natural inc.:** 1.13%. **Infant mortality** (per 1,000 live births): 138.6.

Education: Compulsory: ages 7-14. **Literacy:** 40%.

Major Intl. Organizations: UN (FAO, IBRD, ILO, IMF, IMO, WHO, WTrO), the Commonwealth, AU.

Embassy: 1990 M St. NW, Suite 570, 20036; 293-7146.

Website: www.mozambique.mz/eindex.htm

The first Portuguese post on the Mozambique coast was established in 1505, on the trade route to the East. Mozambique became independent June 25, 1975, after a ten-year war against Portuguese colonial domination. The 1974 revolution in Portugal had paved the way for the orderly transfer of power to Frelimo (Front for the Liberation of Mozambique). Frelimo took over local administration Sept. 20, 1974, although opposed, in part violently, by some blacks and whites.

The new government, led by Maoist Pres. Samora Machel, provided for a gradual transition to a Communist system. Economic problems included the emigration of most of the country's whites, a politically untenable economic dependence on white-ruled South Africa, and a large external debt.

In the 1980s, severe drought and civil war caused famine and heavy loss of life. Pres. Machel was killed in a plane crash just inside the South African border, Oct. 19, 1986.

The ruling party formally abandoned Marxist-Leninism in 1989, and a new constitution, effective Nov. 30, 1990, provided for multiparty elections and a free-market economy.

On Oct. 4, 1992, a peace agreement was signed aimed at ending hostilities between the government and the rebel Mozambique National Resistance (MNR). Repatriation of 1.7 million Mozambican refugees officially ended June 1995. In Mar. 1999 the heaviest floods in 4 decades left nearly 200,000 people stranded. Even worse flooding in Feb.-Mar. 2000 claimed more than 600 lives, displaced over 1 million people, and devastated the economy. A train crash May 25, 2002, in S Mozambique killed 196 people.

Myanmar (*formerly* Burma)

Union of Myanmar

People: Population: 42,238,224. **Age distrib.** (%): <15: 29.8; 65+: 4.7. **Pop. density:** 166 per sq. mi. **Urban:** 27%. **Ethnic groups:** Burman 68%, Shan 9%, Karen 7%, Rakhine 4%. **Principal language:** Burmese (official). **Chief religions:** Buddhist 89%, Christian 4%, Muslim 4%.

Geography: Area: 254,000 sq. mi. **Location:** Between S and SE Asia, on Bay of Bengal. **Neighbors:** Bangladesh, India on W; China, Laos, Thailand on E. **Topography:** Mountains surround Myanmar on W, N, and E, and dense forests cover much of the nation. N-S rivers provide habitable valleys and communications, especially the Irrawaddy, navigable for 900 miles. The country has a tropical monsoon climate. **Capital:** Yangon (Rangoon). **Cities (urban aggr.):** Yangon 4,504,00; Mandalay 770,000.

Government: Type: Military. **Head of state and gov.:** Gen. Than Shwe; b Feb. 2, 1933; in office: Apr. 24, 1992. **Local divisions:** 7 states, 7 divisions. **Defense budget** (2000): $2.1 bil. **Active troops:** 444,000.

Economy: Industries: Agric. processing, textiles and footwear, wood and wood products, mining. **Chief crops:** Rice, sugarcane, corn, pulses. **Minerals:** Oil, lead, copper, tin, tungsten, precious stones. **Crude oil reserves** (2001): 0.2 bil bbls. **Arable land:** 15%. **Livestock** (2001): cattle: 11.22 mil; chickens: 48.27 mil.; goats: 1.44 mil.; pigs: 4.14 mil; sheep: 402,892. **Fish catch** (1999): 917,666 metric tons. **Electricity prod.:** 4.77 bil. kWh. **Labor force:** agri. 65%, ind. 10%, services 25%.

Finance: Monetary unit: Kyat (Sept. 2002: 6.45 = $1 U.S.). **GDP** (2000 est.): $63.7 bil. **Per capita GDP:** $1,500. **Imports** (1999): $2.5 bil.; partners (1999 est.): Singapore 28%, Thailand 12%. **Exports** (1999): $1.3 bil.; partners (1999 est.): India 13%, Singapore 11%, China 11%. **Tourism:** $35 mil. **Budget** (FY96/97): $12.2 bil. **Intl. reserves less gold** (end 2000): $171 mil. **Gold:** 231,000 oz t. **Consumer prices** (change in 2000): –0.1%.

Transport: Railroad: Length: 3,144 mi. **Motor vehicles:** 35,000 pass. cars, 34,000 comm. vehicles. **Civil aviation:** 91.5 mil pass.-mi; 19 airports. **Chief ports:** Bassein, Moulmein.

Communications: TV sets: 22 per 1,000 pop. **Radios:** 72 per 1,000 pop. **Telephones:** 295,000. **Daily newspaper circ.:** 23 per 1,000 pop.

Health: Life expectancy: 53.9 male; 57.1 female. **Births** (per 1,000 pop.): 19.6. **Deaths** (per 1,000 pop.): 12.2. **Natural inc.:** 0.74%. **Infant mortality** (per 1,000 live births): 72.1.

Education: Free, compulsory: ages 5-10. **Literacy:** 83%.

Major Intl. Organizations: UN (FAO, IBRD, ILO, IMF, IMO, WHO, WTrO), ASEAN.

Embassy: 2300 S St. NW 20008; 332-9044.

Website: www.myanmar.com/eng

The Burmese arrived from Tibet before the 9th century, displacing earlier cultures, and a Buddhist monarchy was established by the 11th. Burma was conquered by the Mongol dynasty of China in 1272, then ruled by Shans as a Chinese tributary, until the 16th century.

Britain subjugated Burma in 3 wars, 1824-84, and ruled the country as part of India until 1937, when it became self-governing. Independence outside the Commonwealth was achieved Jan. 4, 1948.

Gen. Ne Win dominated politics from 1962 to 1988, first as military ruler then as constitutional president. His regime drove Indians from the civil service and Chinese from commerce. Economic socialization was advanced, isolation from foreign countries enforced. In 1987 Burma, once the richest nation in SE Asia, was granted less-developed status by the UN.

Ne Win resigned July 1988, following waves of antigovernment riots. Rioting and street violence continued, and in Sept. the military seized power, under Gen. Saw Maung. In 1989 the country's name was changed to Myanmar.

The first free multiparty elections in 30 years took place May 27, 1990, with the main opposition party winning a decisive victory, but the military refused to hand over power. A key opposition leader, Aung San Suu Kyi, awarded the Nobel Peace Prize in 1991, was held under house arrest from July 20, 1989, to July 10, 1995; after her release, the military government continued to restrict her activities and to harass and imprison her supporters. New U.S. economic sanctions took effect on May 21, 1997. Myanmar was admitted to ASEAN July 23, 1997.

Confined again in Sept. 2000, Aung San Suu Kyi was freed May 6, 2002.

Namibia

Republic of Namibia

People: Population: 1,820,916. **Age distrib.** (%): <15: 42.7; 65+: 3.7. **Pop. density:** 6 per sq. mi. **Urban:** 30%. **Ethnic groups:** Ovambo 50%, Kavangos 9%, Herero 7%, Damara 7%. **Principal languages:** Afrikaans, English (official), German, indigenous languages. **Chief religions:** Lutheran 50%, other Christian 30%.

Geography: Area: 317,900 sq. mi. **Location:** In S Africa on the coast of the Atlantic Ocean. **Neighbors:** Angola on N, Botswana on E, South Africa on S. **Capital:** Windhoek: 216,000.

Government: Type: Republic. **Head of state:** Pres. Sam Nujoma; b May 12, 1929; in office: Mar. 21, 1990. **Head of gov.:** Prime Min. Theo-Ben Gurirab; b Jan. 23, 1939; in office: Aug. 28, 2002. **Local divisions:** 13 regions. **Defense budget (2001):** $87 mil. **Active troops:** 9,000.

Economy: Meatpacking, fish processing, dairy products, mining. **Minerals:** Diamonds, copper, gold, tin, lead, uranium. **Arable land:** 1%. **Livestock** (2001): cattle: 2.10 mil; chickens: 2.35 mil.; goats: 1.70 mil.; pigs: 18,000; sheep: 2.20 mil. Electricity prod.: **0.03 bil. kWh. Labor force:** agri. 47%, ind. 20%, services 33%.

Finance: Monetary unit: Dollar (Sept. 2002: 10.57 = $1 U.S.). **GDP** (2000 est.): $7.6 bil. **Per capita GDP:** $4,300. **Imports** (2000 est.): $1.6 bil.; partners (1997 est.): South Africa 81%, U.S. 4%. **Exports** (2000 est.): $1.4 bil.; partners (1998 est.): UK 43%, South Africa 26%. **Tourism** (1998): $288 mil. **Budget** (1998): $950 mil. **Intl. reserves less gold** (end 2000): $200 mil. **Consumer prices** (change in 1999): 8.6%.

Transport: Railroad: Length: 1,480 mi. **Motor vehicles:** 62,500 pass. cars, 66,500 comm. vehicles. **Civil aviation:** 563.0 mil pass.-mi; 11 airports. **Chief ports:** Luderitz, Walvis Bay.

Communications: TV sets: 27.6 per 1,000 pop. **Radios:** 152 per 1,000 pop. **Telephones:** 217,400. **Daily newspaper circ.:** 27.4 per 1,000 pop.

Health: Life expectancy: 40.8 male; 37.1 female. **Births** (per 1,000 pop.): 34.2. **Deaths** (per 1,000 pop.): 22.3. **Natural inc.:** 1.19%. **Infant mortality** (per 1,000 live births): 72.4.

Education: Compulsory: ages 6-16. **Literacy** (1993): 76%.

Major Intl. Organizations: UN (FAO, IBRD, ILO, IMF, IMO, WHO, WTrO), the Commonwealth, AU.

Embassy: 1605 New Hampshire Ave. NW 20009; 986-0540.

Namibia was declared a German protectorate in 1890 and officially called South-West Africa. South Africa seized the territory from Germany in 1915 during World War I; the League of Nations gave South Africa a mandate over the territory in 1920. In 1966, the Marxist South-West Africa People's Organization (SWAPO) launched a guerrilla war for independence. The UN General Assembly named the area Namibia in 1968.

Website: www.grnnet.gov.ng/intro.htm

After many years of guerrilla warfare and failed diplomatic efforts, South Africa, Angola, and Cuba signed a U.S.-mediated agreement Dec. 22, 1988, to end South African administration of Namibia and provide for a cease-fire and transition to independence, in accordance with a 1978 UN plan. A separate accord between Cuba and Angola provided for a phased withdrawal of Cuban troops from Namibia. A constitution providing for multiparty government was adopted Feb. 9, 1990, and Namibia gained independence Mar. 21.

Walvis Bay, the principal deepwater port, had been turned over to South African administration in 1922. It remained in South African hands after independence, but South Africa turned control of the port back to Namibia, as of Mar. 1, 1994. Separatist violence flared in the Caprivi Strip in the late 1990s.

According to UN estimates, about one-fifth of the adult population has HIV/AIDS.

Nauru

Republic of Nauru

People: Population: 12,329. **Age distrib. (%): <15: 40.3; 65+: 1.7. Pop. density:** 1,521 per sq. mi. **Urban:** 100%. **Ethnic groups:** Nauruan 58%, other Pacific Islander 26%, Chinese 8%, European 8%. **Principal languages:** Nauruan (official), English. **Chief religion:** Predominantly Christian.

Geography: Area: 8 sq. mi. **Location:** In W Pacific O. just S of the Equator. **Neighbors:** Nearest is Kiribati to E. **Topography:** Mostly a plateau bearing high-grade phosphate deposits, surrounded by a sandy shore and coral reef in concentric rings. **Capital:** Govt. offices in Yaren district.

Government: Type: Republic. **Head of state and gov.:** Pres. Rene Harris; b 1948; in office: Mar. 30, 2001. **Local divisions:** 14 districts.

Economy: Industries: Phosphate mining. **Minerals:** Phosphates. **Livestock:** (2001): chickens: 5,000; pigs: 2,800. **Electricity prod.:** 0.03 bil. kWh.

Finance: Monetary unit: Australian Dollar (Sept. 2002: 1.84 = $1 U.S.). **GDP** (2000 est.): $59 mil. **Per capita GDP:** $5,000. **Imports** (1991): $21.1 mil.; partners: Australia, UK, NZ, Japan. **Exports** (1991): $25.3 mil.; partners: Australia, NZ. **Budget** (FY95/96): $64.8 mil.

Transport: Civil aviation: 151.0 mil pass.-mi. **Chief port:** Nauru.

Communications: Radios: 385 per 1,000 pop.

Health: Life expectancy: 58 male; 65.3 female. **Births** (per 1,000 pop.): 26.6. **Deaths** (per 1,000 pop.): 7.1. **Natural inc.:** 1.95%. **Infant mortality** (per 1,000 live births): 10.5.

Education: Free, compulsory: ages 6-16. **Literacy:** 99%.

Major Intl. Organizations: UN (WHO), the Commonwealth.

The island was discovered in 1798 by the British but was formally annexed to the German Empire in 1886. After World War I, Nauru became a League of Nations mandate administered by Australia. During World War II the Japanese occupied the island and shipped 1,200 Nauruans to the fortress island of Truk as slave laborers.

In 1947 Nauru was made a UN trust territory, administered by Australia. It became an independent republic Jan. 31, 1968, and was admitted to the UN Sept. 14, 1999.

Phosphate exports have provided Nauru with per capita revenues that are among the highest in the Third World. Phosphate reserves, however, are nearly depleted, and environmental damage from strip-mining has been severe. Lax banking practices have made Nauru a haven for money laundering.

Nepal

Kingdom of Nepal

People: Population: 25,873,917. **Age distrib.** (%): <15: 40.3; 65+: 3.5. **Pop. density:** 490 per sq. mi. **Urban:** 12%. **Ethnic groups:** Newars, Indians, Tibetans, Gunings, Sherpas, others. **Principal languages:** Nepali (official), many dialects. **Chief religions:** Hindu (official) 90%, Buddhist 5%, Muslim 3%.

Geography: Area: 52,800 sq. mi. **Location:** Astride the Himalaya Mts. **Neighbors:** China on N, India on S. **Topography:** The Himalayas stretch across the N, the hill country with its fertile valleys extends across the center, while the S border region is part of the flat, subtropical Ganges Plain. **Capital:** Kathmandu. **Cities (urban aggr.):** Kathmandu 755,000; (1995 metro. est.) Lalitpur 190,000; Biratnagar 132,000.

Government: Type: Constitutional monarchy. **Head of state:** King Gyanendra Bir Bikram Shah Dev; b July 7, 1947; in office: June 4, 2001. **Head of gov.:** Prime Min. Sher Bahadur Deuba; b June 13, 1946; in office: July 22, 2001. **Local divisions:** 5 regions subdivided into 14 zones. **Defense budget (2000):** $50 mil. **Active troops:** 46,000.

Economy: Industries: Tourism, carpet, textile, rice, jute, sugar, and oilseed mills. **Chief crops:** Sugar, rice, grain. **Minerals:** Quartz. **Other resources:** Forests. **Arable land:** 17%. **Livestock** (2001): cattle: 6.98 mil; chickens: 19.79 mil.; goats: 6.48 mil.; pigs: 912,530; sheep: 850,172. **Fish catch:** (1999): 23,206 metric tons. **Electricity prod.:** 1.45 bil. kWh. **Labor force:** agric. 81%, services 16%, ind. 3%.

Finance: Monetary unit: Rupee (Sept. 2002: 76.84 = $1 U.S.). **GDP** (2000 est.): $33.7 bil. **Per capita GDP:** $1,360. **Imports** (1998): $1.2 bil.; partners: (FY97/98): India 31%, China/Hong Kong 16%. **Exports** (1998): $485 mil.; partners: India 33%, U.S. 26%, Germany 25% (FY97/98):. **Tourism:** $168 mil. **Budget** (FY96/97 est.): $818 mil. **Intl. reserves less gold** (end 2000): $727 mil. **Gold:** 153,000 oz t. **Consumer prices** (change in 2000): 1.5%.

Transport: Railroad: Length: 63 mi. **Civil aviation:** 564.3 mil pass.-mi; 24 airports.

Communications: TV sets: 12 per 1,000 pop. **Radios:** 30 per 1,000 pop. **Telephones:** 315,300. **Daily newspaper circ.:** 8 per 1,000 pop.

Health: Life expectancy: 59 male; 58.2 female. **Births** (per 1,000 pop.): 32.9. **Deaths** (per 1,000 pop.): 10. **Natural inc.:** 2.29%. **Infant mortality** (per 1,000 live births): 72.4.

Education: Free, compulsory: ages 6-11. **Literacy:** 27%.

Major Intl. Organizations: UN (FAO, IBRD, ILO, IMF, IMO, WHO).

Embassy: 2131 Leroy Pl. NW 20008; 667-4550.

Website: www.nepalembassy/usa.org

Nepal was originally a group of petty principalities, the inhabitants of one of which, the Gurkhas, became dominant about 1769. In 1951 King Tribhubana Bir Bikram, member of the Shah family, ended the system of rule by hereditary premiers of the Ranas family, who had kept the kings virtual prisoners, and established a cabinet system of government.

Virtually closed to the outside world for centuries, Nepal is now linked to India and Pakistan by roads and air service and to Tibet by road. Polygamy, child marriage, and the caste system were officially abolished in 1963.

The government announced the legalization of political parties in 1990. Elections on Nov. 15, 1994, led to the installation of Nepal's first Communist government, which held power until a no-confidence vote Sept. 10, 1995.

Nine members of Nepal's royal family, including King Birendra and Queen Aishwarya, died as the result of a massacre on the night of June 1, 2001. An official inquiry blamed the carnage on a 10th member of the family, Crown Prince Dipendra, who reportedly shot himself that night and died 3 days later, allowing Birendra's brother Gyanendra to assume the throne. Maoist rebels launched a wave of attacks Nov. 24 against Nepal's army and police; the insurgency has claimed more than 4,000 lives since 1996.

Netherlands

Kingdom of the Netherlands

People: Population: 16,067,754. **Age distrib.** (%): <15: 18.4; 65+: 13.7. **Pop. density:** 1,227 per sq. mi. **Urban:** 89%. **Ethnic groups:** Dutch 94%. **Principal language:** Dutch (official). **Chief religions:** Roman Catholic 34%, Protestant 25%.

Geography: Area: 13,100 sq. mi. **Location:** In NW Europe on North Sea. **Neighbors:** Germany on E, Belgium on S. **Topography:** The land is flat, an average alt. of 37 ft. above sea level, with much land below sea level reclaimed and protected by some 1,500 miles of dikes. Since 1920 the government has been draining the IJsselmeer, formerly the Zuider Zee. **Capital:** Amsterdam. **Cities (urban aggr.):** Amsterdam 1,105,151; Rotterdam 1,078,000; The Hague 442,799.

Government: Type: Parliamentary democracy under a constitutional monarch. **Head of state:** Queen Beatrix; b Jan. 31, 1938; in office: Apr. 30, 1980. **Head of gov.:** Prime Min. Jan Peter Balkenende; b May 7, 1956; in office: July 22, (designated): July 4, 2002. **Seat of govt.:** The Hague. **Local divisions:** 12 provinces. **Defense budget (2001):** $5.6 bil. **Active troops:** 50,430.

Economy: Industries: Agroindustry, metal and engineering products, electrical machinery and equip., chemicals. **Chief crops:** Grains, potatoes, sugar beets, vegetables, fruits. **Minerals:** Natural gas, oil. **Crude oil reserves** (2001): 0.1 bil bbls. **Arable land:** 25%. **Livestock** (2001): cattle: 4.05 mil; chickens: 107.00 mil.; goats: 180,000; pigs: 12.82 mil; sheep: 1.40 mil. **Electricity prod.:** 87.95 bil. kWh. **Labor force:** services 73%, ind. 23%, agri. 4%.

Finance: Monetary unit: Euro (Sept. 2002: 1.03 = $1 U.S.). **GDP** (2000 est.): $388.4 bil. **Per capita GDP:** $24,400. **Imports** (2000 est.): $201.2 bil.; partners (2000): EU 56%, U.S. 9%, Central and Eastern Europe. **Exports** (2000): $210.3 bil.; partners (2000): EU 78%,Central and Eastern Europe, U.S.. **Tourism:** $7.09 bil. **Budget** (2001 est.): $134 bil. **Intl. reserves less gold** (end 2000): $7.40 bil. **Gold:** 29.32 mil oz t. **Consumer prices** (change in 2000): 2.5%.

Transport: Railroad: Length: 1,702 mi. **Motor vehicles** (1997): 5.81 mil pass. cars, 715,000 comm. vehicles. **Civil aviation:** 41.4 bil pass.-mi; 6 airports. **Chief ports:** Rotterdam, Amsterdam, IJmuiden.

Communications: TV sets: 545 per 1,000 pop. **Radios:** 764 per 1,000 pop. **Telephones:** 21,900,000. **Daily newspaper circ.:** 306 per 1,000 pop.

Health: Life expectancy: 75.7 male; 81.6 female. **Births** (per 1,000 pop.): 11.6. **Deaths** (per 1,000 pop.): 8.7. **Natural inc.:** 0.29%. **Infant mortality** (per 1,000 live births): 4.3.

Education: Compulsory: ages 5-18. **Literacy:** 100%.

Major Intl. Organizations: UN and all of its specialized agencies, EU, NATO, OECD, OSCE.

Embassy: 4200 Linnean Ave. NW 20008; 244-5300.

Website: www.cbs.nl/enindex.htm

Julius Caesar conquered the region in 55 BC, when it was inhabited by Celtic and Germanic tribes.

After the empire of Charlemagne fell apart, the Netherlands (Holland, Belgium, Flanders) split among counts, dukes, and bishops, passed to Burgundy and thence to Charles V of Spain. His son, Philip II, tried to check the Dutch drive toward political freedom and Protestantism (1568-1573). William the Silent, prince of Orange, led a confederation of the northern provinces, called Estates, in the Union of Utrecht, 1579. The Estates retained individual sovereignty, but were represented jointly in the States-General, a body that had control of foreign affairs and defense. In 1581 they repudiated allegiance to Spain. The rise of the Dutch republic to naval, economic, and artistic eminence came in the 17th century.

The United Dutch Republic ended 1795 when the French formed the Batavian Republic. Napoleon made his brother Louis king of Holland, 1806; Louis abdicated 1810 when Napoleon annexed Holland. In 1813 the French were expelled. In 1815 the Congress of Vienna formed a kingdom of the Netherlands, including Belgium, under William I. In 1830, the Belgians seceded and formed a separate kingdom.

The constitution, promulgated 1814, and subsequently revised, provides for a hereditary constitutional monarchy.

The Netherlands maintained its neutrality in World War I, but was invaded and brutally occupied by Germany, 1940-45.

In 1949, after several years of fighting, the Netherlands granted independence to Indonesia. In 1963, West New Guinea (now Irian Jaya) was turned over to Indonesia. Immigration from former Dutch colonies has been substantial.

The murder May 6, 2002, of right-wing populist leader Pim Fortuyn, 9 days before legislative elections, marked the 1st political assassination in modern Dutch history.

Netherlands Dependencies

The **Netherlands Antilles,** constitutionally on a level of equality with the Netherlands homeland within the kingdom, consist of 2 groups of islands in the West Indies. **Curaçao** and **Bonaire** are near the coast of Venezuela; **St. Eustatius, Saba,** and the southern part of **St. Maarten** are SE of Puerto Rico. The northern two-thirds of St. Maarten belongs to French Guadeloupe; the French call the island St. Martin. Total area of the 2 groups is 309 sq. mi., including Bonaire (111), Curaçao (171), St. Eustatius (8), Saba (5), St. Maarten (Dutch part) (13). St. Maarten suffered extensive damage from Hurricane Luis, Sept. 1995. Total pop. of the Netherlands Antilles (2002 est.) was 214,258. Willemstad, on Curaçao, is the capital. The principal industry is the refining of crude oil from Venezuela. Tourism is also an important industry, as is shipbuilding.

Aruba, about 26 mi. W of Curaçao, was separated from the Netherlands Antilles on Jan. 1, 1986; it is an autonomous member of the Netherlands, the same status as the Netherland Antilles. Area 75 sq. mi.; pop. (2002 est.) 70,441; capital Oranjestad. Chief industries are oil refining and tourism.

New Zealand

People: Population: 3,908,037. **Age distrib.** (%): <15: 22.4; 65+: 11.5. **Pop. density:** 38 per sq. mi. **Urban:** 86%. **Ethnic groups:** New Zealand European 75%, Maori 10%. **Principal languages:** English (official), Maori. **Chief religions:** Anglican 24%, Presbyterian 18%, Roman Catholic 15%.

Geography: Area: 103,700 sq. mi. **Location:** In SW Pacific O. **Neighbors:** Nearest are Australia on W, Fiji and Tonga on N. **Topography:** Each of the 2 main islands (North and South Isls.) is mainly hilly and mountainous. The east coasts consist of fertile plains, especially the broad Canterbury Plains on South Isl. A volcanic plateau is in center of North Isl. South Isl. has glaciers and 15 peaks over 10,000 ft. **Capital:** Wellington. **Cities (urban aggr.):** Auckland 1,102,000; Wellington 345,000; Christchurch 331,443.

Government: Type: Parliamentary democracy. **Head of state:** Queen Elizabeth II, represented by Gov.-Gen. Dame Silvia Cartwright; b Nov. 7, 1943; in office: Apr. 4, 2001. **Head of gov.:** Prime Min. Helen Clark; b Feb. 26, 1950; in office: Dec. 10, 1999. **Local divisions:** 93 counties, 9 districts, 3 town districts. **Defense budget (2001):** $678 mil. **Active troops:** 9,230.

Economy: Industries: Food processing, wood and paper products, textiles, machinery. **Chief crops:** Grains, potatoes, fruits. **Minerals:** Gold, gas, iron, coal. **Crude oil reserves** (2001): 0.2 bil bbls. **Other resources:** Wool, timber. **Arable land:** 9%. **Livestock** (2001): cattle: 9.37 mil; chickens: 13.00 mil.; goats: 183,000; pigs: 354,489; sheep: 43.99 mil. **Electricity prod.:** 35.82 bil. kWh. **Labor force:** services 65%, ind. 25%, agri. 10%.

Finance: Monetary unit: N.Z. Dollar (Sept. 2002: 2.13 = $1 U.S.). **GDP** (2000 est.): $67.6 bil. **Per capita GDP:** $17,700. **Imports** (2000 est.): $14.3 bil.; partners (1999): Australia 24%, U.S. 17%. **Exports** (2000 est.): $14.6 bil.; partners (1999): Australia 22%, U.S. 14%. **Tourism** (1998): $1.73 bil. **Budget** (1999 est.): $19.2 bil. **Intl. reserves less gold** (end 2000): $2.56 bil. **Consumer prices** (change in 2000): 2.6%.

Transport: Railroad: Length: 2,433 mi. **Motor vehicles** (1997): 1.50 mil pass. cars, 322,809 comm. vehicles. **Civil aviation:** 13.0 bil pass.-mi; 36 airports. **Chief ports:** Auckland, Christchurch, Wellington, Dunedin, Tauranga.

Communications: TV sets: 496.5 per 1,000 pop. **Radios:** 1,027 per 1,000 pop. **Telephones:** 4,250,600. **Daily newspaper circ.:** 223 per 1,000 pop.

Health: Life expectancy: 75.2 male; 81.3 female. **Births** (per 1,000 pop.): 14.2. **Deaths** (per 1,000 pop.): 7.5. **Natural inc.:** 0.67%. **Infant mortality** (per 1,000 live births): 6.2.

Education: Free, compulsory: ages 6-16. **Literacy** (1997): 100%.

Major Intl. Organizations: UN (FAO, IBRD, ILO, IMF, IMO, WHO, WTrO), APEC, the Commonwealth, OECD.

Embassy: 37 Observatory Cir. NW 20008; 328-4800.

Websites: www.govt.nz; www.stats.govt.nz/statsweb.nsf

The Maoris, a Polynesian group from the eastern Pacific, reached New Zealand before and during the 14th century. The first European to sight New Zealand was Dutch navigator Abel Janszoon Tasman, but Maoris refused to allow him to land. British Capt. James Cook explored the coasts, 1769-1770.

British sovereignty was proclaimed in 1840, with organized settlement beginning in the same year. Representative institutions were granted in 1853. Maori Wars ended in 1870 with British victory. The colony became a dominion in 1907, and is an independent member of the Commonwealth.

A progressive tradition in politics dates back to the 19th century, when New Zealand was internationally known for social experimentation; much of the nation's economy has been deregulated in recent years. The National Party, led by Jim Bolger, won general elections in 1990 and 1993. After inconclusive elections, Oct. 12, 1996, Bolger remained as prime minister, heading a National/New Zealand First party coalition. When Bolger lost his party's support, Jenny Shipley became the nation's first female prime minister, Dec. 8, 1997. The Labour Party won the general elections of Nov. 27, 1999, and July 27, 2002.

The native Maoris number about 550,000. Six of 120 members of the House of Representatives are elected directly by the Maori people.

New Zealand comprises **North Island,** 44,702 sq. mi.; **South Island,** 58,384 sq. mi.; **Stewart Island,** 674 sq. mi.; **Chatham Islands,** 372 sq. mi.; and several groups of smaller islands.

In 1965, the **Cook Islands** (pop., 2002 est., 20,811; area 100 sq. mi.), located halfway between New Zealand and Hawaii, became self-governing although New Zealand retains responsibility for defense and foreign affairs. **Niue** attained the same status in 1974; it lies 400 mi. to W (pop., 1995 est., 1,800; area 100 sq. mi.). **Tokelau** (pop., 1995 est., 1,500; area 4 sq. mi.) comprises 3 atolls 300 mi. N of Samoa.

Ross Dependency, administered by New Zealand since 1923, comprises 160,000 sq. mi. of Antarctic territory.

Nicaragua

Republic of Nicaragua

People: Population: 5,023,818. **Age distrib.** (%): <15: 39.0; 65+: 2.9. **Pop. density:** 108 per sq. mi. **Urban:** 56%. **Ethnic groups:** Mestizo 69%, white 17%, black 9%, Amerindian 5%. **Principal languages:** Spanish (official). **Chief religion:** Roman Catholic 95%.

Geography: Area: 46,400 sq. mi. **Location:** In Central America. **Neighbors:** Honduras on N, Costa Rica on S. **Topography:** Both Caribbean and Pacific coasts are over 200 mi. long. The Cordillera Mts., with many volcanic peaks, run NW-SE through the middle of the country. Between this and a volcanic range to the E lie Lakes Managua and Nicaragua. **Capital:** Managua 1,039,000.

Government: Type: Republic. **Head of state and gov.:** Pres. Enrique Bolaños Geyer; b May 13, 1928; in office Jan. 10, 2002. **Local divisions:** 15 departments, 2 autonomous regions. **Defense budget (2001):** $27 mil. **Active troops:** 16,000.

Economy: Industries: Food processing, chemicals, machinery and metal products, textiles. **Chief crops:** Bananas, cotton, citrus, coffee, sugar, corn, rice. **Minerals:** Gold, silver, copper, tungsten. **Other resources:** Forests, seafood. **Arable land:** 9%. **Livestock** (2001): cattle: 2.28 mil; chickens: 17.00 mil.; goats: 6,600; pigs: 400,000; sheep: 4,250. **Fish catch:** (1999): 16,130 metric tons. **Electricity prod.:** 2.23 bil. kWh. **Labor force:** services 43%, agri. 42%, ind. 15%.

Finance: Monetary unit: Gold Cordoba (Sept. 2002: 14.47 = $1 U.S.). **GDP** (2000 est.): $13.1 bil. **Per capita GDP:** $2,700. **Imports** (2000 est.): $1.6 bil.; partners (1999): U.S. 34.5%, Costa Rica 11.4%. **Exports** (2000 est.): $631 mil.; partners (1999): U.S. 37.7%, El Salvador 12.5%. **Tourism:** $113 mil. **Budget** (1999 est.): $836 mil. **Intl. reserves less gold** (end 2000): $375 mil. **Gold: 20,000 oz t. Consumer prices** (change in 1999): 11.2%.

Transport: Motor vehicles: 72,413 pass. cars, 72,227 comm. vehicles. **Civil aviation:** 52.8 mil pass.-mi; 10 airports. **Chief ports:** Corinto, Puerto Sandino, San Juan del Sur

Communications: TV sets: 48 per 1,000 pop. **Radios:** 206 per 1,000 pop. **Telephones** (2000): 248,800. **Daily newspaper circ.:** 31 per 1,000 pop.

Health: Life expectancy: 67.4 male; 71.4 female. **Births** (per 1,000 pop.): 27. **Deaths** (per 1,000 pop.): 4.8. **Natural inc.:** 2.22%. **Infant mortality** (per 1,000 live births): 32.5.

Education: Free, compulsory: ages 7-13. **Literacy:** 66%.

Major Intl. Organizations: UN and most of its specialized agencies, OAS.

Embassy: 1627 New Hampshire Ave. NW 20009; 939-6570.

Nicaragua, inhabited by various Indian tribes, was conquered by Spain in 1552. After gaining independence from Spain, 1821, Nicaragua was united for a short period with Mexico, then with the United Provinces of Central America, finally becoming an independent republic, 1838.

Website: www.embassy.org/embassies/ni.html

U.S. Marines occupied the country at times in the early 20th century, the last time from 1926 to 1933.

Gen. Anastasio Somoza Debayle was elected president in 1967. He resigned in 1972, but was re-elected president in 1974. Martial law was imposed in Dec. 1974, after officials were kidnapped by the Marxist Sandinista guerrillas. Violent opposition spread to nearly all classes in 1978; nationwide strikes called against the government touched off a civil war, which ended when Somoza fled Nicaragua and the Sandinistas took control of Managua in July 1979. Somoza was assassinated in Paraguay, Sept. 17, 1980.

Relations with the U.S. were strained as a result of Nicaragua's aid to leftist guerrillas in El Salvador and U.S. backing of anti-Sandinista contra guerrilla groups. In 1983 the contras launched a major offensive; the Sandinistas imposed rule by decree. In 1985 the U.S. House rejected Pres. Reagan's request for military aid to the contras. The subsequent diversion of funds to the contras from the proceeds of a secret arms sale to Iran caused a major scandal in the U.S.

In a stunning upset, Violeta Barrios de Chamorro defeated Sandinista leader Daniel Ortega Saavedra in national elections, Feb. 25, 1990. Arnoldo Alemán Lacayo, a conservative former mayor of Managua, defeated Ortega in the presidential election of Oct. 20, 1996. Up to 2,000 people died in W Nicaragua Oct. 30, 1998, in a mudslide caused by rains from Hurricane Mitch. Drought and a drop in coffee prices plunged Nicaragua into an economic crisis in 2001. Enrique Bolaños Geyer, a conservative businessman, defeated Ortega in a presidential election Nov. 4. Bolaños Aug. 7, 2002, accused Alemán of having stolen nearly $95 million while he was president.

Niger

Republic of Niger

People: Population: 10,639,744. **Age distrib.** (%): <15: 48.0; 65+: 2.3. **Pop. density:** 22 per sq. mi. **Urban:** 20%. **Ethnic groups:** Hausa 56%, Djerma 22%, Fula 9%, Tuareg 8%. **Principal languages:** French (official), Hausa, Djerma. **Chief religion:** Muslim 80%.

Geography: Area: 489,100 sq. mi. **Location:** In the interior of N Africa. **Neighbors:** Libya, Algeria on N; Mali, Burkina Faso on W; Benin, Nigeria on S; Chad on E. **Topography:** Mostly arid desert and mountains. A narrow savanna in the S and the Niger R. basin in the SW contain most of the population. **Capital:** Niamey: 821,000.

Government: Type: Republic. **Head of state:** Pres. Tandja Mamadou; b 1938; in office: Dec. 22, 1999. **Head of gov.:** Prime Min. Hama Amadou; b 1950; in office: Jan. 3, 2000. **Local divisions:** 7 departments, 1 capital district. **Defense budget** (2001): $29 mil. **Active troops:** 5,300.

Economy: Industries: Uranium mining, cement, brick, textiles. Chief crops: Peanuts, cowpeas, cotton. **Minerals:** Uranium, coal, iron. **Arable land:** 3%. **Livestock** (2001): cattle: 2.26 mil; chickens: 24.00 mil.; goats: 6.90 mil.; pigs: 39,000; sheep: 4.50 mil. **Electricity prod.:** 0.22 bil. kWh. **Labor force:** agric. 90%, ind. and commerce 6%, government 4%.

Finance: Monetary unit: CFA Franc (Sept. 2002: 671.78 = $1 U.S.). **GDP** (2000 est.): $10 bil. **Per capita GDP:** $1,000. **Imports** (1999): $317 mil.; partners (1999): France 22%, Cote d'Ivoire 15%,. **Exports** (1999): $385 mil.; partners (1999): France 45%, Nigeria 27%. **Tourism:** $21 mil. **Budget** (1999 est.): $377 mil. **Intl. reserves less gold** (end 2000): $62 mil. **Gold:** 11,000 oz t. **Consumer prices** (change in 2000): 2.9%.

Transport: Motor vehicles: 37,500 pass. cars, 14,100 comm. vehicles. **Civil aviation:** 150.5 mil pass.-mi; 6 airports.

Communications: TV sets: 2.8 per 1,000 pop. **Radios:** 48 per 1,000 pop. **Telephones:** 23,500.

Health: Life expectancy: 42 male; 41.8 female. **Births** (per 1,000 pop.): 50. **Deaths** (per 1,000 pop.): 22.2. **Natural inc.:** 2.77%. **Infant mortality** (per 1,000 live births): 122.2.

Education: Free, compulsory: ages 7-15. **Literacy**: 14%.

Major Intl. Organizations: UN (FAO, IBRD, ILO, IMF, WHO, WTrO), AU.

Embassy: 2204 R St. NW 20008; 483-4224.

Website: www.nigerembassyusa.org

Niger was part of ancient and medieval African empires. European explorers reached the area in the late 18th century. The French colony of Niger was established 1900-22, after the defeat of Tuareg fighters, who had invaded the area from the N a century before. The country became independent Aug. 3, 1960. The next year it signed a bilateral agreement with France.

In 1993, Niger held its first free and open elections since independence; an opposition leader, Mahamane Ousmane, won the presidency. A peace accord Apr. 24, 1995, ended a Tuareg rebellion that began in 1990. A coup, Jan. 27, 1996, followed by a disputed presidential election in July, left the military in control of Niger. On Apr. 9, 1999, Gen. Ibrahim Bare Mainassara, Niger's president since 1996, was assassinated, apparently by members of his security team. Elections were held Oct. 17 and Nov. 24, 1999, under a new constitution, approved by referendum July 18, that provided for a return to civilian rule.

Nigeria

Federal Republic of Nigeria

People: Population: 129,934,911. **Age distrib.** (%): <15: 43.7; 65+: 2.8. **Pop. density:** 369 per sq. mi. **Urban:** 43%. **Ethnic groups:** Hausa, Yoruba, Ibo, Fulani, others. **Principal languages:** English (official), Hausa, Yoruba, Ibo. **Chief religions:** Muslim (in N) 50%, Christian (in S) 40%.

Geography: Area: 351,700 sq. mi. **Location:** On the S coast of W Africa. **Neighbors:** Benin on W, Niger on N, Chad and Cameroon on E. **Topography:** 4 E-W regions divide Nigeria: a coastal mangrove swamp 10-60 mi. wide, a tropical rain forest 50-100 mi. wide, a plateau of savanna and open woodland, and semidesert in the N. **Capital:** Abuja. **Cities (urban aggr.):** Lagos 8,665,000; Ibadan 1,549,000; Ogbomosho 809,000; Abuja 420,000.

Government: Type: Republic. **Head of state and gov.:** Pres. Olusegun Obasanjo; b Mar. 6, 1935; in office: May 29, 1999. **Local divisions:** 36 states, 1 capital territory. **Defense budget (2000):** $340 mil. **Active troops:** 78,500.

Economy: Industries: Crude oil, mining, palm oil, peanuts, cotton. **Chief crops:** Cocoa (main export crop), palm products, corn, rice, yams, cassava. **Minerals:** Oil, gas, lead, zinc, coal, iron, limestone, columbite, tin. **Crude oil reserves** (2001): 24.1 bil bbls. **Other resources:** Timber, rubber, hides. **Arable land:** 33%. **Livestock** (2001): cattle: 19.83 mil; chickens: 126.00 mil.; goats: 24.30 mil.; pigs: 4.86 mil; sheep: 20.50 mil. **Fish catch** (1999): 383,417 metric tons. **Electricity prod.:** 15.90 bil. kWh. **Labor force:** agri. 70%, ind. 10%, services 20%.

Finance: Monetary unit: Naira (Sept. 2002: 127.00 = $1 U.S.). **GDP** (2000 est.): $117 bil. **Per capita GDP:** $950. **Imports** (2000 est.): $10.7 bil.; partners (1999): UK 11%, Germany 10%. **Exports** (2000 est.): $22.2 bil.; partners (1999): U.S. 36%, India 9%. **Tourism** (1998): $142 mil. **Budget** (2000 est.): $3.6 bil. **Consumer prices** (change in 2000): 6.9%.

Transport: Railroad: Length: 2,178 mi. **Motor vehicles:** 589,600 pass. cars, 363,900 comm. vehicles. **Civil aviation:** 137.2 mil pass.-mi; 12 airports. **Chief ports:** Port Harcourt, Lagos, Warri, Calabar.

Communications: TV sets: 61 per 1,000 pop. **Radios:** 197 per 1,000 pop. **Telephones:** 830,000. **Daily newspaper circ.:** 24 per 1,000 pop.

Health: Life expectancy: 50.6 male; 50.6 female. **Births** (per 1,000 pop.): 39.2. **Deaths** (per 1,000 pop.): 14.1. **Natural inc.:** 2.51%. **Infant mortality** (per 1,000 live births): 72.5.

Education: Free, compulsory: ages 6-15. **Literacy**: 57%.

Major Intl. Organizations: UN (FAO, IBRD, ILO, IMF, IMO, WHO, WTrO), the Commonwealth, AU, OPEC.

Embassy: 1333 16th St. NW 20036; 986-8400.

Website: www.nigeriaembassyusa.org

Early cultures in Nigeria date back to at least 700 BC. From the 12th to the 14th centuries, more advanced cultures developed in the Yoruba area, at Ife, and in the north, where Muslim influence prevailed. Portuguese and British slavers appeared from the 15th-16th centuries. Britain seized Lagos, 1861, and gradually extended control inland until 1900. Nigeria became independent Oct. 1, 1960, and a republic Oct. 1, 1963.

On May 30, 1967, the Eastern Region seceded, proclaiming itself the Republic of Biafra, plunging the country into civil war. Casualties in the war were estimated at over 1 million, including many "Biafrans" (mostly Ibos) who died of starvation despite international efforts to provide relief. The secessionists, after steadily losing ground, capitulated Jan. 12, 1970.

Nigeria emerged as one of the world's leading oil exporters in the 1970s, but much of the revenue has been squandered through corruption and mismanagement.

After 13 years of military rule, the nation made a peaceful return to civilian government, Oct. 1979. Military rule resumed, Dec. 31, 1983; a second coup came in 1985.

Headed by Gen. Ibrahim Babangida, the military regime held elections June 12, 1993, but annulled the vote June 23 when it appeared that Moshood Abiola would win. Riots followed and many were killed. Babangida resigned and appointed a civilian to head an interim government, Aug. 26, but that government was ousted Nov. 17 in a coup led by Gen. Sani Abacha. On June 11, 1994, Abiola declared himself president; he was jailed June 23.

Abacha's brutal rule ended June 8, 1998, when he died of an apparent heart attack. Abiola died in prison July 7, as Abacha's successor, Gen. Abdulsalam Abubakar, was reportedly preparing to free him. Abiola's death sparked riots in Lagos and other cities; on July 20, Abubakar promised early elections and a return to civilian rule. Olusegun Obasanjo (a former military ruler) won the presidential vote Feb. 27, 1999, Nigeria's 1st civilian government in 15 years.

An oil fire that exploded from a ruptured pipeline in S. Nigeria, Oct. 17, 1998, killed at least 700 people who were scavenging for fuel. The imposition of strict Islamic law in northern states led to clashes, Jan.-Mar. 2000, in which at least 800 people died. U.S. Pres. Bill Clinton visited Nigeria Aug. 26-27, 2000, the 1st visit there by a U.S. head of state in 22 years. Clashes between Muslims and Christians Sept. 7-12 and Oct. 13-14 claimed an estimated 600 lives; another 200 people died when soldiers went on a rampage in SE Nigeria Oct. 22-24.

At least 1,000 people were killed Jan. 27, 2002, when an army weapons depot in Lagos exploded; many of the victims drowned in a drainage canal while fleeing the blasts.

By 2002, the strict Islamic legal code of sharia had been adopted by about one-third of Nigeria's 36 states.

Norway

Kingdom of Norway

People: Population: 4,525,116. **Age distrib.** (%): <15: 20.0; 65+: 15.1. **Pop. density:** 38 per sq. mi. **Urban:** 75%. **Ethnic groups:** Germanic (Nordic, Alpine, Baltic), Lapps. **Principal languages:** Norwegian (official). **Chief religion:** Evangelical Lutheran 87.8%.

Geography: Area: 118,900 sq. mi. **Location:** W part of Scandinavian peninsula in NW Europe (extends farther north than any European land). **Neighbors:** Sweden, Finland, Russia on E. **Topography:** A highly indented coast is lined with tens of thousands of islands. Mountains and plateaus cover most of the country, which is only 25% forested. **Capital:** Oslo. **Cities (urban aggr.):** Oslo 787,000 (city proper 2000 est., 507,467); Bergen (1996 est.) 223,773.

Government: Type: Hereditary constitutional monarchy. **Head of state:** King Harald V; b Feb. 21, 1937; in office: Jan. 17, 1991. **Head of gov.:** Prime Min. Kjell Magne Bondevik; b Sept. 3, 1947; in office: Oct. 19, 2001. **Local divisions:** 19 provinces. **Defense budget** (2001): $2.8 bil. **Active troops:** 26,700.

Economy: Industries: Oil & gas, food processing, shipbuilding, pulp and paper products. **Chief crops:** Grains, oats. **Minerals:** Oil, gas, copper, pyrites, nickel, iron, zinc, lead. **Crude oil reserves** (2001): 10.1 bil bbls. **Other resources:** Fish, livestock. **Arable land:** 3%. **Livestock** (2001): cattle: 979,800; chickens: 3.20 mil.; goats: 50,600; pigs: 391,100; sheep: 2.40 mil . **Fish catch** (1999): 3.22 mil metric tons. **Electricity prod.:** 141.16 bil. kWh. **Labor force:** services 74%, ind. 22%, agri., forestry, and fishing 4%.

Finance: Monetary unit: Krone (Sept. 2002: 7.49 = $1 U.S.). **GDP** (1999 est.): $124.1 bil. **Per capita GDP:** $27,700. **Imports** (2000 est.): $35.2 bil.; partners (1999): EU 66%, U.S. 10%, Japan. **Exports** (2000 est.): $59.2 bil.; partners (1999): EU 73%,U.S. 5%. **Budget** (2000 est.): $57.6 bil. **Tourism:** $2.23 bil. **Intl. reserves less gold** (end 2000): $15.48 bil. **Gold:** 1.18 mil oz t. **Consumer prices** (change in 2000): 3.1%.

Transport: Railroad: Length: 2,485 mi. **Motor vehicles** (1997): 1.76 mil pass. cars, 412,183 comm. vehicles. **Civil aviation:** 5.7 bil pass.-mi; 50 airports. **Chief ports:** Bergen, Stavanger, Oslo, Kristiansand.

Communications: TV sets: 579 per 1,000 pop. **Radios:** 913 per 1,000 pop. **Telephones:** 6,999,000. **Daily newspaper circ.:** 588 per 1,000 pop.

Health: Life expectancy: 76 male; 82.1 female. **Births** (per 1,000 pop.): 12.4. **Deaths** (per 1,000 pop.): 9.8. **Natural inc.:** 0.26%. **Infant mortality** (per 1,000 live births): 3.9.

Education: Compulsory: ages 6-16. **Literacy** (1994): 100%.

Major Intl. Organizations: UN and all of its specialized agencies, EFTA, NATO, OECD, OSCE.

Embassy: 2720 34th St. NW 20008; 333-6000.

Websites: www.norway.org; odin.dep.no/smk/engelsk

The first ruler of Norway was Harald the Fairhaired, who came to power in AD 872. Between 800 and 1000, Norway's Vikings raided and occupied widely dispersed parts of Europe.

The country was united with Denmark 1381-1814, and with Sweden, 1814-1905. In 1905, the country became independent with Prince Charles of Denmark as king.

Norway remained neutral during World War I. Germany attacked Norway Apr. 9, 1940, and held it until liberation May 8, 1945. The country abandoned its neutrality after the war, and joined NATO. In a referendum Nov. 28, 1994, Norwegian voters rejected European Union membership.

Abundant hydroelectric resources provided the base for industrialization, giving Norway one of the highest living standards in the world. The country is a leading producer and exporter of crude oil, with extensive reserves in the North Sea. Norway's merchant marine is one of the world's largest.

Svalbard is a group of mountainous islands in the Arctic O., area 23,957 sq. mi., pop. (1997 est.) 3,231. The largest, Spitsbergen (formerly called West Spitsbergen), 15,060 sq. mi., seat of the governor, is about 370 mi. N of Norway. By a treaty signed in Paris, 1920, major European powers recognized the sovereignty of Norway, which incorporated it in 1925.

Jan Mayen, area 144 sq. mi., is a volcanic island located about 565 mi. WNW of Norway; it was annexed in 1929.

Oman

Sultanate of Oman

People: Population: 2,713,462. **Age distrib.** (%): <15: 41.5; 65+: 2.4. **Pop. density:** 33 per sq. mi. **Urban:** 83%. **Ethnic groups:** Arab, Indian. **Principal languages:** Arabic (official). **Chief religion:** Ibadhi Muslim 75%.

Geography: Area: 82,000 sq. mi. **Location:** On SE coast of Arabian peninsula. **Neighbors:** United Arab Emirates, Saudi Arabia, Yemen on W. **Topography:** Oman has a narrow coastal plain up to 10 mi. wide, a range of barren mountains reaching 9,900 ft., and a wide, stony, mostly waterless plateau, avg. alt. 1,000 ft. Also, an exclave at the tip of the Musandam peninsula controls access to the Persian Gulf. **Capital:** Muscat: 540,000.

Government: Type: Absolute monarchy. **Head of state and gov.:** Sultan Qabus bin Said; b Nov. 18, 1940; in office: July 23, 1970 (also prime min. since Jan. 2, 1972). **Local divisions:** 6 regions and 2 governorates. **Defense budget (2001):** $2.4 bil. **Active troops:** 43,400.

Economy: Industries: Oil & gas, construction, cement, copper. **Chief crops:** Dates, limes, vegetables, alfalfa, bananas. **Minerals:** Oil (75% of exports). **Crude oil reserves** (2001): 5.8 bil bbls. **Livestock** (2001): cattle: 290,000; chickens: 3.40 mil.; goats: 980,000; sheep: 335,000. **Fish catch:** (1999): 117,049 metric tons. **Electricity prod.:** 8.10 bil. kWh.

Finance: Monetary unit: Rial Omani (Sept. 2002: 0.39 = $1 U.S.). **GDP** (2000 est.): $19.6 bil. **Per capita GDP:** $7,700. **Imports** (2000 est.): $4.5 bil.; partners (1999): UAE 26%, Japan 16%. **Exports** (2000 est.): $11.1 bil.; partners (1999): Japan 27%, China 12%, Thailand 18%, UAE 12%, South Korea 12%. **Tourism:** $104 mil. **Budget** (1999): $5.9 bil. **Intl. reserves less gold** (end 2000): $1.83 bil. **Gold:** 291,000 oz t. **Consumer prices** (change in 2000): –1.1%.

Transport: Motor vehicles (1997): 246,097 pass. cars, 101,223 comm. vehicles. **Civil aviation:** 2.0 bil pass.-mi; 6 airports. **Chief ports:** Matrah, Mina' al Fahl.

Communications: TV sets: 711 per 1,000 pop. **Radios:** 426 per 1,000 pop. **Telephones:** 559,800. **Daily newspaper circ.:** 31 per 1,000 pop.

Health: Life expectancy: 70.2 male; 74.6 female. **Births** (per 1,000 pop.): 37.8. **Deaths** (per 1,000 pop.): 4. **Natural inc.:** 3.37%. **Infant mortality** (per 1,000 live births): 21.8.

Education: Literacy (1993): 59%.

Major Intl. Organizations: UN (FAO, IBRD, ILO, IMF, IMO, WHO), AL.

Embassy: 2535 Belmont Rd. NW 20008; 387-1980.

Website: www.omanet.com

Oman was originally called Muscat and Oman. A long history of rule by other lands, including Portugal in the 16th century, ended with the ouster of the Persians in 1744. By the early 19th century, Muscat and Oman was one of the most important countries in the region, controlling much of the Persian and Pakistan coasts, and also ruling far-away Zanzibar, which was separated in 1861 under British mediation.

British influence was confirmed in a 1951 treaty, and Britain helped suppress an uprising by traditionally rebellious interior tribes against control by Muscat in the 1950s.

On July 23, 1970, Sultan Said bin Taimur was overthrown by his son, who changed the nation's name to Sultanate of Oman.

Oil is the major source of income.

Oman opened its air bases to Western forces following the Iraqi invasion of Kuwait on Aug. 2, 1990.

Pakistan

Islamic Republic of Pakistan

People: Population: 147,663,429. **Age distrib.** (%): <15: 40.5; 65+: 4.1. **Pop. density:** 491 per sq. mi. **Urban:** 37%. **Ethnic groups:** Punjabi, Sindhi, Pashtun (Pathan), Baloch. **Principal languages:** Urdu, English (both official), Punjabi, Sindhi, Pashtu. **Chief religions:** Sunni Muslim 77%, Shi'a Muslim 20%.

Geography: Area: 300,700 sq. mi. **Location:** In W part of South Asia. **Neighbors:** Iran on W, Afghanistan and China on N, India on E. **Topography:** The Indus R. rises in the Hindu Kush and Himalaya Mts. in the N (highest is K2, or Godwin Austen, 28,250 ft., 2d highest in world), then flows over 1,000 mi. through fertile valley and empties into Arabian Sea. Thar Desert, Eastern Plains flank Indus Valley. **Capital:** Islamabad. **Cities (urban aggr.):** Karachi 10,032,000; Lahore 5,452,000; Faisalabad 2,142,000; Islamabad 636,000.

Government: Type: In transition. **Head of state and gov:** Pres. Pervez Musharraf; b Aug. 11, 1943; in office: Oct. 15, 1999 (as pres. from June 20, 2001). **Local divisions:** 4 provinces and 1 capital territory, plus federally administered tribal areas. **Defense budget (2001):** $2.6 bil. **Active troops:** 620,000.

Economy: Industries: Textiles, food processing, beverages. **Chief crops:** Rice, wheat, cotton. **Minerals:** Natural gas. **Crude oil reserves** (2001): 0.3 bil bbls. **Arable land:** 27%. **Livestock** (2001): cattle: 22.40 mil; chickens: 155.00 mil.; goats: 49.10 mil.; sheep: 24.20 mil . **Fish catch** (1999): 597,201 metric tons. **Electricity prod.:** 62.69 bil. kWh. **Labor force:** agri. 44%, ind. 17%, services 39%.

Finance: Monetary unit: Rupee (Sept. 2002: 59.18 = $1 U.S.). **GDP** (2000 est.): $282 bil. **Per capita GDP:** $2,000. **Imports** (FY99/00): $9.6 bil.; partners: Saudi Arabia 8%, UAE 8%. **Exports** (FY99/00): $8.6 bil.; partners: (FY99/00): U.S. 24%, Hong Kong 7%. **Tourism** (1998): $98 mil. **Budget** (FY00/01 est.): $11.6 bil. **Intl. reserves less gold** (end 2000): $1.16 bil. **Gold:** 2.09 mil oz t. **Consumer prices** (change in 2000): 4.4%.

Transport: Railroad: Length: 5,453 mi. **Motor vehicles:** 800,000 pass. cars, 300,000 comm. vehicles. **Civil aviation:** 7.2 bil pass.-mi; 35 airports. **Chief port:** Karachi.

Communications: TV sets: 62 per 1,000 pop. **Radios:** 92 per 1,000 pop. **Telephones:** 4,200,000. **Daily newspaper circ.:** 21 per 1,000 pop.

Health: Life expectancy: 61 male; 62.7 female. **Births** (per 1,000 pop.): 30.4. **Deaths** (per 1,000 pop.): 9. **Natural inc.:** 2.14%. **Infant mortality** (per 1,000 live births): 78.5.

Education: Literacy: 38%.

Major Intl. Organizations: UN (FAO, IBRD, ILO, IMF, IMO, WHO, WTrO).

Embassy: 2315 Massachusetts Ave. NW 20008; 939-6200.

Website: www.pakistan-embassy.com/index.asp

Present-day Pakistan shares the 5,000-year history of the India-Pakistan subcontinent. At present-day Harappa and Mohenjo Daro, the Indus Valley Civilization, with large cities and elaborate irrigation systems, flourished c. 4,000-2,500 BC.

Aryan invaders from the NW conquered the region around 1,500 BC, forging a Hindu civilization that dominated Pakistan as well as India for 2,000 years.

Beginning with the Persians in the 6th century BC, and continuing with Alexander the Great and with the Sassanians, successive nations to the west ruled or influenced Pakistan. The first Arab invasion, AD 712, introduced Islam. Under the Mogul empire (1526-1857), Muslims ruled most of India, yielding to British encroachment and resurgent Hindus.

After World War I the Muslims of British India began agitation for minority rights in elections. Muhammad Ali Jinnah (1876-1948) was the principal architect of Pakistan. A leader of the Muslim League from 1916, he worked for dominion status for India; from 1940 he advocated a separate Muslim state.

When the British withdrew Aug. 14, 1947, the Islamic majority areas of India acquired self-government as Pakistan, with dominion status in the Commonwealth. Pakistan was divided into 2 sections, West Pakistan and East Pakistan. The 2 areas were nearly 1,000 mi. apart on opposite sides of India. Pakistan became a republic in 1956.

In Oct. 1958, Gen. Mohammad Ayub Khan took power in a coup. He was elected president in 1960, reelected in 1965. He resigned Mar. 25, 1969, after several months of violent rioting and unrest, most of it in East Pakistan, which demanded autonomy. The government was turned over to Gen. Agha Mohammad Yahya Khan and martial law was declared.

The Awami League, which sought regional autonomy for East Pakistan, won a majority in Dec. 1970 elections to a constituent assembly. In March 1971 Yahya postponed the assembly. Rioting and strikes broke out in the East.

On Mar. 25, 1971, government troops launched attacks in the East. The Easterners, aided by India, proclaimed the independent nation of Bangladesh. In months of widespread fighting, countless thousands were killed. Some 10 million Easterners fled into India. Full-scale war between India and Pakistan had spread to both the East and West fronts by Dec. 3. Pakistan troops in the East surrendered Dec. 16; Pakistan agreed to a cease-fire in the West Dec. 17. On July 3, 1972, Pakistan and India signed a pact agreeing to withdraw troops from their borders and seek peaceful solutions to all problems.

Zulfikar Ali Bhutto, leader of the Pakistan People's Party, which had won the most West Pakistan votes in Dec. 1970 elections, became president Dec. 20. Bhutto was overthrown in a military coup July 1977. Convicted of complicity in a 1974 political murder, he was executed Apr. 4, 1979. Over 3 million Afghan refugees flooded into Pakistan after the USSR invaded Afghanistan Dec. 1979; over 1.2 million remained in 1999.

Pres. Mohammad Zia ul-Haq was killed when his plane exploded in Aug. 1988. Following Nov. elections, Benazir Bhutto, daughter of Zulfikar Ali Bhutto, was named prime minister, becoming the first woman leader of a Muslim nation. She was accused of corruption and dismissed by the president, Aug. 1990; her party was soundly defeated in Oct. 1990 elections, and Nawaz Sharif became prime minister. She regained power after elections in Oct. 1993. Opposition to Bhutto centered around Karachi, which was crippled by violent strikes and ethnic clashes during 1995 and 1996. Accusing the Bhutto government of corruption and mismanagement, Pres. Farooq Leghari appointed a caretaker prime minister Nov. 5, 1996. Elections on Feb. 3, 1997, gave Sharif a parliamentary majority.

Responding to nuclear weapons tests by India, Pakistan conducted its own tests, May 28-30, 1998; the U.S. imposed economic sanctions on both countries. Tried in absentia, the exiled Bhutto was convicted Apr. 15, 1999, of receiving kickbacks; the conviction was overturned and a new trial ordered Apr. 6, 2001.

In mid-1999, Muslim infiltrators, apparently including Pakistani troops, seized Indian-held positions in the disputed territory of Kashmir, which witnessed its heaviest fighting in over 2 decades. After meeting with Pres. Bill Clinton on July 4, Sharif agreed to a Pakistani pullback. Growing conflict between Sharif and the military climaxed in his firing on Oct. 12 of army chief Gen. Pervez Musharraf, whose supporters staged a bloodless coup later that day. Martial law was imposed and the constitution suspended Oct. 15. Because of the military takeover, Pakistan was suspended, Oct. 18, from the Commonwealth. Sharif was sentenced to life imprisonment on Apr. 6, 2000; he was released and exiled to Saudi Arabia Dec. 10. Musharraf assumed the presidency June 20, 2001.

Following the Sept. 11, 2001, terrorist attack on the U.S., Pres. Musharraf, Sept. 19, pledged cooperation with the U.S. in actions against the Taliban and al-Qaeda in neighboring Afghanistan; in return, the U.S. offered Pakistan financial aid and debt relief. To defuse mounting tensions with India, Musharraf in late Dec. 2001 ordered the arrest of members of Islamic militant groups that India blamed for a Dec. 13 attack on the parliament in New Delhi. Guerrilla violence in Kashmir and Pakistani missile tests May 25-28, 2002, heightened fears of war with India, but the crisis was eased in June with U.S. mediation.

Militants kidnapped *Wall Street Journal* reporter Daniel Pearl Jan. 23, 2002, and eventually killed him. A Pakistani judge, July 15, convicted 4 militants in the crime.

A referendum Apr. 30, 2002, extended Musharraf's rule for another 5 years; many observers called the vote rigged. Musharraf amended the constitution Aug. 21 to increase the military's formal role in governing the country.

During 2002 there was evidence of growing al-Qaeda activity within Pakistan. Car bombings in Karachi attributed to al-Qaeda killed 11 French engineers in May and 12 Pakistanis at the U.S. Embassy in June. Several alleged al-Qaeda operatives, including Ramzi bin al-Shibh, believed to have been a close associate of 9-11 ringleader Mohamed Atta, were captured in a shootout in Karachi, Sept. 11, 2002.

Palau

Republic of Palau

People: Population: 19,409. **Age distrib.** (%): <15: 26.9; 65+: 4.7. **Pop. density:** 110 per sq. mi. **Urban:** 72%. **Ethnic groups:** Polynesian, Malayan, Melanesian. **Principal languages:** English (official), Palauan, Sonsorolese, Angaur, Japanese, Tobi (all official within certain states). **Chief religions:** Catholic, Modekngei.

Geography: Area: 177 sq. mi. **Location:** Archipelago (26 islands, more than 300 islets) in the W Pacific Ocean, about 530 mi SE of the Philippines. **Neighbors:** Micronesia to E, Indonesia to S. **Capital:** Koror: 14,000. (Note: a new capital is being built in Babelthuap.)

Government: Type: Republic. **Head of state and gov.:** Pres. Tommy Remengesau; b 1956; in office: Jan. 19, 2001. **Local divisions:** 18 states..

Economy: Industries: Tourism, crafts, construction. **Chief crops:** Coconuts, copra, cassava, sweet potatoes. **Minerals:** Gold.

Finance: Monetary unit: U.S. Dollar. **GDP** (1998 est.): $129 mil. **Per capita GDP:** $7,100. **Imports** (FY99/00): $126 mil.; partners: U.S.. **Exports** (1996): $14.3 mil.; partners: U.S., Japan. **Budget** (FY98/99 est.): $80.8 mil.

Transport: 1 airport.

Communications: TV sets: 98 per 1,000 pop. **Radios:** 550 per 1,000 pop.

Health: Life expectancy: 66.1 male; 72.5 female. **Births** (per 1,000 pop.): 19.3. **Deaths** (per 1,000 pop.): 7.1. **Natural inc.:** 1.22%. **Infant mortality** (per 1,000 live births): 16.2.

Education: Compulsory: ages 6-14. **Literacy** (1990): 98%.

Major Intl. Organizations: UN (WHO).

Embassy: 1150 18th Street NW, Suite 750, 20036; 452-6814.

Spain acquired the Palau Islands in 1886 and sold them to Germany in 1899. Japan seized them in 1914. American forces occupied the islands in 1944; in 1947, they became part of the U.S.-administered UN Trust Territory of the Pacific Islands. In 1981 Palau became an autonomous republic; in 1993 the republic ratified a compact of free association with the U.S., which provides financial aid in return for U.S. use of Palauan military facilities over 15 years. Palau became an independent nation on Oct. 1, 1994. Vice-Pres. Tommy Remengesau won the presidential election held Nov. 7, 2000.

Panama

Republic of Panama

People: Population: 2,882,329 **Age distrib.** (%): <15: 30.1; 65+: 6.0. **Pop. density:** 98 per sq. mi. **Urban:** 56%. **Ethnic groups:** Mestizo 70%, West Indian 14%, white 10%, Amerindian 6%. **Principal languages:** Spanish (official), English. **Chief religions:** Roman Catholic 85%, Protestant 15%.

Geography: Area: 29,300 sq. mi. **Location:** In Central America. **Neighbors:** Costa Rica on W, Colombia on E. **Topography:** 2 mountain ranges run the length of the isthmus. Tropical rain forests cover the Caribbean coast and eastern Panama. **Capital**: Panama City 1,202,000.

Government: Type: Constitutional republic. **Head of state and gov.:** Pres. Mireya Elisa Moscoso; b July 1, 1946; in office: Sept. 1, 1999. **Local divisions:** 9 provinces, 3 territories. **Defense budget:** Nil. **Active troops:** Nil. (11,800 paramilitary).

Economy: Industries: Construction, oil refining, brewing, cement. **Chief crops:** Bananas, rice, corn, coffee, sugar. **Minerals:** Copper. **Other resources:** Forests (mahogany), shrimp. **Arable land:** 7%. **Livestock** (2001): cattle: 1.34 mil; chickens: 14.45 mil.; goats: 5,200; pigs: 277,900. **Fish catch:** (1999): 169,718 metric tons. **Electricity prod.:** 4.89 bil. kWh. **Labor force:** agri. 20.8%, ind. 18%, services 61.2%.

Finance: Monetary unit: Balboa (Sept. 2002: 1.00 = $1 U.S.). **GDP** (2000 est.): $16.6 bil. **Per capita GDP:** $6,000. **Imports** (2000 est.): $6.9 bil.; partners (1999): U.S. 39%, Colon Free Zone 14%. **Exports** (2000 est.): $5.7 bil.; partners (1999): U.S. 42%, Germany 11%. **Tourism** (1998): $379 mil. **Budget** (2000 est.): $2.9 bil. **Intl. reserves less gold** (May 2000): $797.1 mil. **Consumer prices** (change in 2000): 1.4%.

Transport: Railroad: Length: 220 mi. **Motor vehicles:** 144,000 pass. cars, 82,800 comm. vehicles. **Civil aviation:** 679.9 mil pass.-mi; 10 airports. **Chief ports:** Balboa, Cristobal.

Communications: TV sets: 13 per 1,000 pop. **Radios:** 5.1 per 1,000 pop. **Telephones:** 1,030,000. **Daily newspaper circ.:** 62 per 1,000 pop.

Health: Life expectancy: 73.1 male; 78.7 female. **Births** (per 1,000 pop.): 18.6. **Deaths** (per 1,000 pop.): 5. **Natural inc.:** 1.36%. **Infant mortality** (per 1,000 live births): 19.6.

Education: Free, compulsory for 6 years between ages 6-15. **Literacy**: 91%.

Major Intl. Organizations: UN (FAO, IBRD, ILO, IMF, IMO, WHO), OAS.

Embassy: 2862 McGill Terrace NW 20008; 483-1407.

The coast of Panama was sighted by Rodrigo de Bastidas, sailing with Columbus for Spain in 1501, and was visited by Columbus in 1502. Vasco Nunez de Balboa crossed the isthmus and "discovered" the Pacific Ocean, Sept. 13, 1513. Spanish colonies were ravaged by Francis Drake, 1572-95, and Henry Morgan, 1668-71. Morgan destroyed the old city of Panama which had been founded in 1519. Freed from Spain, Panama joined Colombia in 1821.

Panama declared its independence from Colombia Nov. 3, 1903, with U.S. recognition. In support of Panama, U.S. naval forces deterred action by Colombia. Panama granted use, occupation, and control of the Canal Zone to the U.S. by treaty, ratified Feb. 26, 1904. In 1978, a new treaty provided for a gradual takeover by Panama of the canal, and withdrawal of U.S. troops, to be completed before the end of the century. U.S. payments were substantially increased in the interim.

President Delvalle was ousted by the National Assembly, Feb. 26, 1988, after he tried to fire the head of the Panama Defense Forces, Gen. Manuel Antonio Noriega, who was under U.S. federal indictment on drug charges. U.S. troops invaded Panama Dec. 20, 1989, and Noriega surrendered Jan. 3, 1990.

On Aug. 30, 1998, voters rejected a constitutional change that would have allowed Pres. Ernesto Pérez Balladares to run for reelection in 1999. Mireya Moscoso, widow of former Pres. Arnulfo Arias, was elected president May 2, 1999, becoming Panama's first female head of state. The U.S. handed over control of the Panama Canal to Panama Dec. 31, 1999.

Papua New Guinea

Independent State of Papua New Guinea

People: Population: 5,172,033. **Age distrib.** (%): <15: 38.7; 65+: 3.7. **Pop. density:** 30 per sq. mi. **Urban:** 17%. **Ethnic groups:** Papuan, Melanesian. **Principal languages:** English (official), Motu, 715 indigenous dialects. **Chief religions:** Indigenous beliefs 34%, Roman Catholic 22%, Lutheran 16%.

Geography: Area: 174,400 sq. mi. **Location:** SE Asia, occupying E half of island of New Guinea and about 600 nearby islands. **Neighbors:** Indonesia (West Irian) on W, Australia on S. **Topography:** Thickly forested mts. cover much of the center of the country, with lowlands along the coasts. Included are some islands of Bismarck and Solomon groups, such as the Admiralty Isls., New Ireland, New Britain, and Bougainville. **Capital:** Port Moresby: 259,000.

Government: Type: Parliamentary democracy. **Head of state:** Queen Elizabeth II, represented by Gov-Gen. Silas Atopare; in office: Nov. 1997. **Head of gov.:** Prime Min. Sir Michael Somare; b Apr. 9, 1936; in office: Aug. 5, 2002. **Local divisions:** 20 provinces. **Defense budget (2001):** $30 mil. **Active troops:** 4,400.

Economy: Industries: Copra and palm oil processing, wood products. **Chief crops:** Coffee, coconuts, cocoa. **Minerals:** Gold, copper, silver. **Crude oil reserves** (2001): 0.6 bil bbls. **Livestock** (2001): cattle: 88,000; chickens: 3.70 mil.; goats: 2,200; pigs: 1.60 mil; sheep: 6,200. **Fish catch:** (1999): 45,025 metric tons. **Electricity prod.:** 1.65 bil. kWh.

Finance: Monetary unit: Kina (Sept. 2002: 3.96 = $1 U.S.). **GDP** (2000 est.): $12.2 bil. **Per capita GDP:** $2,500. **Imports** (2000 est.): $1 bil.; partners (1999): Australia 53%, Singapore 13%. **Exports** (2000 est.): $2.1 bil.; partners (1999): Australia 30%, Japan 12%. **Tourism:** $104 mil. **Budget** (1998 est.): $1.9 bil. **Intl. reserves less gold** (end 2000): $237.0 mil. **Gold:** 63,000 oz t. **Consumer prices** (change in 1999): 15.6%.

Transport: Motor vehicles: 21,600 pass. cars, 77,700 comm. vehicles. **Civil aviation:** 456.5 mil pass.-mi; 129 airports. **Chief ports:** Port Moresby, Lae.

Communications: TV sets: 23 per 1,000 pop. **Radios:** 68 per 1,000 pop. **Telephones** (2000): 73,400. **Daily newspaper circ.:** 15 per 1,000 pop.

Health: Life expectancy: 61.7 male; 66 female. **Births** (per 1,000 pop.): 31.6. **Deaths** (per 1,000 pop.): 7.8. **Natural inc.:** 2.39%. **Infant mortality** (per 1,000 live births): 56.5.

Education: Literacy: 72%.

Major Intl. Organizations: UN (FAO, IBRD, ILO, IMF, IMO, WHO, WTrO), the Commonwealth, APEC.

Embassy: 1779 Massachusetts Ave NW, 20036; 745-3680.

Websites: www.pngonline.gov.pg; www.pngembassy.org

Human remains have been found in the interior of New Guinea dating back at least 10,000 years and possibly much earlier. Successive waves of peoples probably entered the country from Asia through Indonesia. The indigenous population consists of a huge number of tribes, many living in almost complete isolation with mutually unintelligible languages.

Europeans visited in the 15th century, but actual land claims did not begin until the 19th century, when the Dutch took control of the island's western half. The southern half of eastern New Guinea was first claimed by Britain in 1884, and transferred to Australia in 1905. The northern half was claimed by Germany in 1884, but captured in World War I by Australia, which was first granted a League of Nations mandate and then a UN trusteeship over the area. The 2 territories were administered jointly after 1949, given self-government Dec. 1, 1973, and became independent Sept. 16, 1975.

Secessionist rebels clashed with government forces on Bougainville beginning in 1988; a truce signed Oct. 10, 1997, brought a halt to the fighting, which had claimed an estimated 20,000 lives. The country suffered from a severe drought in 1997. A tsunami killed at least 3,000 people July 17, 1998. A Bougainville autonomy agreement was signed Aug. 30, 2001. Army mutinies were suppressed in Mar. 2001 and Mar. 2002.

Paraguay

Republic of Paraguay

People: Population: 5,884,491. **Age distrib.** (%): <15: 38.9; 65+: 4.7. **Pop. density:** 38 per sq. mi. **Urban:** 55%. **Ethnic groups:** Mestizo 95%, white & Amerindian 5%. **Principal languages:** Spanish (official), Guarani. **Chief religion:** Roman Catholic 90%.

Geography: Area: 153,400 sq. mi. **Location:** Landlocked country in central South America. **Neighbors:** Bolivia on N, Argentina on S, Brazil on E. **Topography:** Paraguay R. bisects the country. To E are fertile plains, wooded slopes, grasslands. To W is the Gran Chaco plain, with marshes and scrub trees. Extreme W is arid. **Capital**: Asunción 1,302,000.

Government: Type: Republic. **Head of state and gov.:** Pres. Luis Angel González Macchi; b Dec. 13, 1947; in office: Mar. 28, 1999. **Local divisions:** 18 departments and capital city. **Defense:** 1.4% of GDP. **Active troops:** 20,200.

Economy: Industries: Sugar, cement, textiles, beverages, wood products. **Chief crops:** Corn, cotton, soybeans, sugarcane. **Minerals:** Iron, manganese, limestone. **Other resources:** Forests. **Arable land:** 6%. **Livestock** (2001): cattle: 9.74 mil; chickens: 15.20 mil.; goats: 122,992; pigs: 2.70 mil; sheep: 402,092. **Fish catch:** (1999): 28,000 metric tons. **Electricity prod.:** 53.06 bil. kWh. **Labor force:** 45% agric.

Finance: Monetary unit: Guarani (Sept. 2002: 6,085.00 = $1 U.S.). **GDP** (2000 est.): $26.2 bil. **Per capita GDP:** $4,750. **Imports** (2000 est.): $3.3 bil.; partners: Brazil, U.S., Argentina, Uruguay, EU, Hong Kong. **Exports** (2000 est.): $3.5 bil.; partners: Brazil, Argentina, EU. **Tourism** (1998): $595 mil. **Budget** (1999 est.): $2 bil. **Intl. reserves less gold** (end 2000): $584 mil. **Gold:** 30,000 oz t. **Consumer prices** (change in 2000): 9.0%.

Transport: Railroad: Length: 274 mi. **Motor vehicles:** 71,000 pass. cars, 50,000 comm. vehicles. **Civil aviation:** 133.7 mil pass.-mi; 5 airports. **Chief port:** Asunción.

Communications: TV sets: 144 per 1,000 pop. **Radios:** 141 per 1,000 pop. **Telephones:** 1,438,800. **Daily newspaper circ.:** 40 per 1,000 pop.

Health: Life expectancy: 71.7 male; 76.8 female. **Births** (per 1,000 pop.): 30.5. **Deaths** (per 1,000 pop.): 4.7. **Natural inc.:** 2.58%. **Infant mortality** (per 1,000 live births): 28.8.

Education: Compulsory: ages 6-12. **Literacy**: 92%.

Major Intl. Organizations: UN (FAO, IBRD, ILO, IMF, IMO, WHO, WTrO), OAS.

Embassy: 2400 Massachusetts Ave. NW, 20008; 483-6960.

Website: www.embassy.org/embassies/py.html

The Guarani Indians were settled farmers speaking a common language before the arrival of Europeans.

Visited by Sebastian Cabot in 1527 and settled as a Spanish possession in 1535, Paraguay gained its independence from Spain in 1811. It lost much of its territory to Brazil, Uruguay, and Argentina in the War of the Triple Alliance, 1865-1870. Large areas were won from Bolivia in the Chaco War, 1932-35.

Gen. Alfredo Stroessner, who had ruled since 1954, was ousted in a military coup led by Gen. Andrés Rodríguez on Feb. 3, 1989. Rodríguez was elected president May 1. Juan Carlos Wasmosy was elected president May 9, 1993, becoming the nation's first civilian head of state in many years.

A prolonged power struggle involving a popular military leader, Gen. Lino César Oviedo, who was accused of insubordination, culminated in his surrender Dec. 12, 1997. He was freed Aug. 18, 1998, following the inauguration of Pres. Raúl Cubas Grau, Oviedo's successor as Colorado Party nominee. The assassination of Vice Pres. Luis María Argaña, Mar. 23, 1999, by an unidentified gunman, was widely attributed to Cubas and triggered protests and an impeachment vote; Cubas resigned Mar. 28 and was succeeded by Senate leader Luis Angel González Macchi. An attempted military coup was suppressed May 18, 2000. Mass protests over the weak economy led to the proclamation of a state of emergency July 15, 2002.

Peru

Republic of Peru

People: Population: 27,949,639. **Age distrib.** (%): <15: 34.4; 65+: 4.8. **Pop. density:** 57 per sq. mi. **Urban:** 72%. **Ethnic groups:** Amerindian 45%, mestizo 37%, white 15%. **Principal languages:** Spanish, Quechua (both official), Aymara. **Chief religion:** Roman Catholic.

Geography: Area: 494,200 sq. mi. **Location:** On the Pacific coast of South America. **Neighbors:** Ecuador, Colombia on N; Brazil, Bolivia on E; Chile on S. **Topography:** An arid coastal strip, 10 to 100 mi. wide, supports much of the population thanks to widespread irrigation. The Andes cover 27% of land area. The uplands are well-watered, as are the eastern slopes reaching the Amazon basin, which covers half the country with its forests and jungles. **Capital:** Lima. **Cities (urban aggr.):** Lima 7,594,000; Arequipa 710,103; Callao 424,294.

Government: Type: Republic. **Head of state:** Pres. Alejandro Toledo; b Mar. 28, 1946; in office: July 28, 2001. **Head of gov.:** Prime Min. Luis Solari; b 1948; in office: July 12, 2002. **Local divisions:** 12 regions, 24 departments, 1 constitutional province. **Defense budget (2001):** $827 mil. **Active troops:** 125,000.

Economy: Industries: Metal mining, oil, fishing, textiles, clothing. **Chief crops:** Cotton, sugar, coffee, rice. **Minerals:** Copper, silver, gold, iron, oil. **Crude oil reserves** (2001): 0.9 bil bbls. **Other resources:** Wool, fish. **Arable land:** 3%. **Livestock** (2001): cattle: 4.93 mil; chickens: 90.00 mil.; goats: 2.00 mil.; pigs: 2.80 mil; sheep: 14.50 mil. **Fish catch** (1999): 7.88 mil metric tons. **Electricity prod.:** 19.68 bil. kWh. Labor force: NA

Finance: Monetary unit: New Sol (Sept. 2002: 3.64 = $1 U.S.). **GDP** (2000 est.): $123 bil. **Per capita GDP:** $4,550. **Imports** (2000 est.): $7.4 bil.; partners (1999): U.S. 32%, EU 21%. **Exports** (2000 est.): $7 bil.; partners (1999): U.S. 29%, EU 25%, Andean Community 6%. **Tourism** (1998): $913 mil. **Budget** (1996 est.): $9.3 bil. **Intl. reserves less gold** (end 2000): $6.43 bil. **Gold:** 1.10 mil oz t. **Consumer prices** (change in 2000): 3.8%.

Transport: Railroad: Length: 1,318 mi. **Motor vehicles:** 500,000 pass. cars, 275,000 comm. vehicles. **Civil aviation:** 1.8 bil pass.-mi; 27 airports. **Chief ports:** Callao, Chimbote, Matarani, Salaverry.

Communications: TV sets: 85 per 1,000 pop. **Radios:** 221 per 1,000 pop. **Telephones:** 3,567,300. **Daily newspaper circ.:** 87 per 1,000 pop.

Health: Life expectancy: 68.2 male; 73.1 female. **Births** (per 1,000 pop.): 23.4. **Deaths** (per 1,000 pop.): 5.7. **Natural inc.:** 1.76%. **Infant mortality** (per 1,000 live births): 38.2.

Education: Free, compulsory: ages 6-11. **Literacy:** 89%.

Major Intl. Organizations: UN and all of its specialized agencies, APEC, OAS.

Embassy: 1700 Massachusetts Ave. NW 20036; 833-9860.

Website: www.peruemb.org

The powerful Inca empire had its seat at Cuzco in the Andes and covered most of Peru, Bolivia, and Ecuador, as well as parts of Colombia, Chile, and Argentina. Building on the achievements of 800 years of Andean civilization, the Incas had a high level of skill in architecture, engineering, textiles, and social organization.

A civil war had weakened the empire when Francisco Pizarro, Spanish conquistador, began raiding Peru for its wealth, 1532. In 1533 he seized the ruling Inca, Atahualpa, filled a room with gold as a ransom, then executed him and enslaved the natives.

Lima was the seat of Spanish viceroys until the Argentine liberator, José de San Martin, captured it in 1821; Spanish forces were ultimately routed by Simón Bolívar, 1824.

On Oct. 3, 1968, a military coup ousted Pres. Fernando Belaunde Terry. In 1968-74, the military government started socialist programs. Food shortages, escalating foreign debt, and strikes led to another coup, Aug. 29, 1976.

After 12 years of military rule, Peru returned to democratic leadership in 1980 but was plagued by economic problems and by leftist Shining Path (Sendero Luminoso) guerrillas.

Elected president in June 1990, Alberto Fujimori, the son of Japanese immigrants, dissolved the National Congress, suspended parts of the constitution, and initiated press censorship, Apr. 5, 1992. The leader of Shining Path was captured Sept. 12.

With the economy booming and signs of significant progress in curtailing guerrilla activity, Fujimori won reelection Apr. 9, 1995. Repressive antiterrorism tactics, however, drew international criticism. On Dec. 17, 1996, leftist Tupac Amaru guerrillas infiltrated a reception at the Japanese ambassador's residence in Lima and took hundreds of hostages, most of whom were later released. Peruvian soldiers stormed the embassy Apr. 22, 1997, rescuing 71 of the remaining hostages; 1 hostage, 2 soldiers, and all 14 guerrillas were killed.

Fujimori's path to a 3d term was cleared when his lone remaining challenger withdrew, charging electoral fraud, 6 days before a runoff vote on May 28, 2000. Scandals involving his top aide and intelligence chief, Vladimiro Montesinos, led Fujimori to resign his office Nov. 20, while on a visit to Japan; instead of accepting his resignation, Congress ousted him as "morally unfit."

Alejandro Toledo won a presidential runoff election June 3, 2001. Montesinos was captured in Venezuela June 23 and extradited to Peru and sentenced on abuse of power charges July 1, 2002. Charges were filed Sept. 5 against the exiled Fujimori, alleging his complicity in the killings by a paramilitary death squad of at least 25 people during 1991-92.

Fireworks explosions killed 291 people in a crowded Lima commercial district Dec. 29, 2001.

Philippines

Republic of the Philippines

People: Population: 84,525,639. **Age distrib.** (%): <15: 36.9; 65+: 3.7. **Pop. density:** 734 per sq. mi. **Urban:** 58%. **Ethnic groups:** Christian Malay 92%, Muslim Malay 4%. **Principal languages:** Pilipino, English (both official). **Chief religions:** Roman Catholic 83%, Protestant 9%, Muslim 5%.

Geography: Area: 115,100 sq. mi. **Location:** An archipelago off the SE coast of Asia. **Neighbors:** Nearest are Malaysia and Indonesia on S, Taiwan on N. **Topography:** The country consists of some 7,100 islands stretching 1,100 mi. N-S. About 95% of area and population are on 11 largest islands, which are mountainous, except for the heavily indented coastlines and for the central plain on Luzon. **Capital:** Manila. **Cities (urban aggr.):** Manila 10,069,000; Quezon City 2,160,000; Davao 1,146,000.

Government: Type: Republic. **Head of state and gov.:** Pres. Gloria Macapagal Arroyo; b Apr. 5, 1947; in office: Jan. 20, 2001. **Local divisions:** 72 provinces, 61 chartered cities. **Defense budget (2001):** $1.1 bil. **Active troops:** 107,000.

Economy: Industries: Textiles, pharmaceuticals, chemicals, wood products, food processing. **Chief crops:** Sugar, rice, pineapples, corn, coconuts. **Minerals:** Cobalt, copper, gold, nickel, silver, oil. **Other resources:** Forests (46% of area). **Crude oil reserves** (2001): 0.3 bil bbls. **Arable land:** 19%. **Livestock** (2001): cattle: 2.49 mil; chickens: 115.07 mil.; goats: 6.95 mil.; pigs: 11.06 mil; sheep: 30,000. **Fish catch** (1999): 2.14 mil metric tons. **Electricity prod.:** 40.67 bil. kWh. **Labor force:** agri. 39.8%, government and social services 19.4%, services 17.7%, manufacturing 9.8%, construction 5.8%, other 7.5%.

Finance: Monetary unit: Peso (Sept. 2002: 52.48 = $1 U.S.). **GDP** (2000 est.): $310 bil. **Per capita GDP:** $3,800. **Imports** (2000 est.): $35 bil.; partners (1998 est.): U.S. 22%, Japan 20%. **Exports** (2000 est.): $38 bil.; partners (1998): U.S. 34%, Japan 14%, Netherlands 8%. **Tourism:** $2.53 bil. **Budget** (1998 est.): $12.6 bil. **Intl. reserves less gold** (end 2000): $10.02 bil. **Gold:** 7.23 mil oz t. **Consumer prices** (change in 2000): 4.4%.

Transport: Railroad: Length: 557 mi. **Motor vehicles:** 702,578 pass. cars, 1.35 mil comm. vehicles. **Civil aviation:** 10.1 bil pass.-mi; 21 airports. **Chief ports:** Cebu, Manila, Iloilo, Davao.

Communications: TV sets: 109 per 1,000 pop. **Radios:** 113 per 1,000 pop. **Telephones:** 13,668,000. **Daily newspaper circ.:** 82 per 1,000 pop.

Health: Life expectancy: 65.3 male; 71.1 female. **Births** (per 1,000 pop.): 26.9. **Deaths** (per 1,000 pop.): 6. **Natural inc.:** 2.09%. **Infant mortality** (per 1,000 live births): 27.9.

Education: Free, compulsory: ages 7-12. **Literacy:** 95%.

Major Intl. Organizations: UN (FAO, IBRD, ILO, IMF, IMO, WHO, WTrO), ASEAN.

Embassy: 1600 Massachusetts Ave. NW 20036; 467-9300.

Websites: www.philippineembassy-usa.org; www.gov.ph

The Malay peoples of the Philippine Islands, whose ancestors probably migrated from Southeast Asia, were mostly hunters, fishers, and unsettled cultivators.

The archipelago was visited by Magellan, 1521. The Spanish founded Manila, 1571. The islands, named for King Philip II of Spain, were ceded by Spain to the U.S. for $20 million, 1898, following the Spanish-American War. U.S. troops suppressed a guerrilla uprising in a brutal 6-year war, 1899-1905.

Japan attacked the Philippines Dec. 8, 1941, and occupied the islands during WW II. On July 4, 1946, independence was proclaimed in accordance with an act passed by the U.S. Congress in 1934. A republic was established.

On Sept. 21, 1972, Pres. Ferdinand Marcos declared martial law. Marcos proclaimed a new constitution, Jan. 17, 1973, with himself as president. His wife, Imelda, received wide powers in 1978 to supervise planning and development. Political corruption was widespread. Martial law was lifted Jan. 17, 1981, but Marcos retained broad emergency powers. He was reelected in June to a new 6-year term as president.

The assassination of prominent opposition leader Benigno S. Aquino Jr., Aug. 21, 1983, sparked demonstrations calling for the resignation of Marcos. After a bitter presidential campaign, amid allegations of widespread election fraud, Marcos was declared the victor Feb. 16, 1986, over Corazon Aquino, widow of the slain opposition leader. With his support collapsing, Marcos fled the country Feb. 25.

Recognized as president by the U.S. and other nations, Aquino was plagued by a weak economy, widespread poverty, Communist and Muslim insurgencies, and lukewarm military support. Rebel troops seized military bases and TV stations and bombed the presidential palace, Dec. 1, 1989. Government forces defeated the attempted coup aided by air cover provided by U.S. F-4s. Aquino endorsed Fidel Ramos in the May 1992 presidential election, which he won.

The U.S. vacated the Subic Bay Naval Station at the end of 1992, ending its long military presence in the Philippines.

The government signed a cease-fire agreement, Jan. 30, 1994, with Muslim separatist guerrillas, but some rebels refused to abide by the accord. A new treaty providing for expansion and development of an autonomous Muslim region on Mindanao was signed Sept. 2, 1996, formally ending a rebellion that had claimed more than 120,000 lives since 1972.

Running as a populist, Joseph (Erap) Estrada, a former movie actor, won the presidential election of May 11, 1998. Charged with bribery and corruption, he was impeached Nov. 13, 2000. When the Supreme Court ruled the presidency vacant Jan. 20, 2001, Vice-Pres. Gloria Macapagal Arroyo became president.

As part of the war on terrorism, the U.S. assisted Filipino troops in combating Abu Sayyaf, an Islamic guerrilla group; the leader of the extremists, Abu Sabaya, was killed June 21, 2002.

Poland

Republic of Poland

People: Population: 38,625,478. **Age distrib.** (%): <15: 18.4, 65+: 12.4. **Pop. density:** 328 per sq. mi. **Urban:** 65%. **Ethnic groups:** Polish 98%. **Principal language:** Polish (official). **Chief religion:** Roman Catholic 95%.

Geography: Area: 117,600 sq. mi. **Location:** On the Baltic Sea in E central Europe. **Neighbors:** Germany on W; Czech Rep., Slovakia on S; Lithuania, Belarus, Ukraine on E; Russia on N. **Topography:** Mostly lowlands forming part of the Northern European Plain. The Carpathian Mts. along the S border rise to 8,200 ft. **Capital:** Warsaw. **Cities (urban aggr., 1997):** Katowice 3,494,000; Warsaw 2,282,000; Lodz 1,053,000; Krakow 859,000.

Government: Type: Republic. **Head of state:** Pres. Aleksander Kwasniewski; b Nov. 15, 1954; in office: Dec. 23, 1995. **Head of gov.:** Prime Min. Leszek Miller; b July 3, 1946; in office: Oct. 19, 2001. **Local divisions:** 16 provinces. **Defense budget (2001):** $3.7 bil. **Active troops:** 206,045.

Economy: Industries: Machinery, iron and steel, coal mining, chemicals, shipbuilding. **Chief crops:** Grains, potatoes, fruits, vegetables. **Minerals:** Coal, copper, silver, lead, sulfur, natural gas. **Crude oil reserves** (2001): 0.1 bil bbls. **Arable land:** 47%. **Livestock** (2001): cattle: 5.72 mil; chickens: 48.27 16.99 mil; sheep: 337,000. **Fish catch** (1999): 390,586 metric tons. **Electricity prod.:** 135.16 bil. kWh. **Labor force:** ind. 22.1%, agri. 27.5%, services 50.4%.

Finance: Monetary unit: Zloty (Sept. 2002: 4.16 = $1 U.S.). **GDP** (2000 est.): $327.5 bil. **Per capita GDP:** $8,500. **Imports** (2000): $42.7 bil.; partners (1999): Germany 25.2%, Italy 9.4%. **Exports** (2000): $28.4 bil.; partners (1999): Germany 36.1%, Italy 6.5%. **Tourism:** $6.10 bil. **Budget** (1999): $52.3 bil. **Intl. reserves less gold** (end 2000): $19.69 bil. **Gold:** 3.31 mil oz t. **Consumer prices** (change in 2000): 10.1%.

Transport: Railroad: Length: 14,904 mi. **Motor vehicles:** 7.52 mil pass. cars, 1.55 mil comm. vehicles. **Civil aviation:** 2.6 bil pass.-mi; 8 airports. **Chief ports:** Gdansk, Gdynia, Ustka, Szczecin.

Communications: TV sets: 414 per 1,000 pop. **Radios:** 522.6 per 1,000 pop. **Telephones:** 21,450,000. **Daily newspaper circ.:** 113 per 1,000 pop.

Health: Life expectancy: 69.5 male; 78 female. **Births** (per 1,000 pop.): 10.3. **Deaths** (per 1,000 pop.): 10. **Natural inc.:** 0.03%. **Infant mortality** (per 1,000 live births): 9.2.

Education: Free, compulsory: ages 7-14. **Literacy** (1994): 99%.

Major Intl. Organizations: UN (FAO, IBRD, ILO, IMF, IMO, WHO, WTrO), NATO, OECD, OSCE.

Embassy: 2640 16th St. NW 20009; 234-3800.

Websites: www.polandembassy.org; www.poland.pl

Slavic tribes in the area were converted to Latin Christianity in the 10th century. Poland was a great power from the 14th to the 17th centuries. In 3 partitions (1772, 1793, 1795) it was apportioned among Prussia, Russia, and Austria. Overrun by the Austro-German armies in World War I, it declared its independence on Nov. 11, 1918, and was recognized as independent by the Treaty of Versailles, June 28, 1919. Large territories to the east were taken in a war with Russia, 1921.

Germany and the USSR invaded Poland Sept. 1-27, 1939, and divided the country. During the war, some 6 million Polish citizens, half of them Jews, were killed by the Nazis. With Germany's defeat, a Polish government-in-exile in London was recognized by the U.S., but the USSR pressed the claims of a rival group. The election of 1947 was completely dominated by the Communists.

In compensation for 69,860 sq. mi. ceded to the USSR, in 1945 Poland received approx. 40,000 sq. mi. of German territory E of the Oder-Neisse line comprising Silesia, Pomerania, West Prussia, and part of East Prussia.

In 12 years of rule by Stalinists, large estates were abolished, industries nationalized, schools secularized, and Roman Catholic prelates jailed. Farm production fell off. Harsh working conditions caused a riot in Poznan, June 28-29, 1956. A new Politburo, committed to a more independent Polish Communism, was named Oct. 1956, with Wladyslaw Gomulka as first secretary of the party. Collectivization of farms was ended. Gomulka agreed to permit religious liberty and religious publications, provided the church kept out of politics.

In Dec. 1970 workers in port cities rioted because of price rises and new incentive wage rules. On Dec. 20 Gomulka resigned as party leader; he was succeeded by Edward Gierek. The rules were dropped and price rises revoked.

After 2 months of labor turmoil had crippled the country, the Polish government, Aug. 30, 1980, met the demands of striking workers at the Lenin Shipyard, Gdansk. Among the 21 concessions granted were the right to form independent trade unions and the right to strike. By 1981, 9.5 mil workers had joined the independent trade union (Solidarity). Solidarity leaders proposed, Dec. 12, a nationwide referendum on establishing a non-Communist government if the government failed to agree to a series of demands.

Spurred by fear of Soviet intervention, the government, Dec. 13, imposed martial law. Lech Walesa and other Solidarity leaders were arrested. The U.S. imposed sanctions, which were lifted when martial law was suspended Dec. 1982

On Apr. 5, 1989, an accord was reached between the government and opposition factions on political and economic reforms, including free elections. Candidates endorsed by Solidarity swept the parliamentary elections, June 4. Lech Walesa became president Dec. 22, 1990.

A radical economic program designed to transform the economy into a free-market system led to inflation and unemployment. In Sept. 1993, former Communists and other leftists won a majority in the lower house of Parliament. Walesa lost to a former Communist, Aleksander Kwasniewski, in a presidential runoff election, Nov. 19, 1995.

A new constitution was approved by referendum May 25, 1997. Flooding in July caused more than $1 billion in property damage. Solidarity won parliamentary elections held Sept. 21. Poland became a full member of NATO on Mar. 12, 1999. Pres. Kwasniewski was reelected Oct. 8, 2000. The former Communists won a plurality in parliamentary voting Sept. 23, 2001.

Portugal

Portuguese Republic

People: Population: 10,084,245. **Age distrib.** (%): <15: 17.0; 65+: 15.6. **Pop. density:** 285 per sq. mi. **Urban:** 63%. **Ethnic groups:** Homogeneous Mediterranean stock, small African minority. **Principal languages:** Portuguese (official). **Chief religion:** Roman Catholic 97%.

Geography: Area: 35,400 sq. mi., incl. the Azores and Madeira Islands. **Location:** At SW extreme of Europe. **Neighbors:** Spain on N, E. **Topography:** Portugal N of Tajus R., which bisects the country NE-SW, is mountainous, cool and rainy. To the S there are drier, rolling plains, and a warm climate. **Capital:** Lisbon. **Cities (urban agg.):** Lisbon 3,942,000; Porto 1,940,000.

Government: Type: Republic. **Head of state:** Pres. Jorge Sampaio; b Sept. 18, 1939; in office: Mar. 9, 1996. **Head of gov.:** Prime Min. José Manuel Durão Barroso; b 1956; in office: Apr. 6, 2002. **Local divisions:** 18 districts, 2 autonomous regions. **Defense budget (2001):** $1.3 bil. **Active troops:** 43,600.

Economy: Industries: Textiles and footwear, wood pulp, paper, cork, metalworking, oil refining. **Chief crops:** Grains, potatoes, grapes, olives. **Minerals:** Tungsten, uranium, iron. **Other resources:** Forests (world leader in cork production). **Arable land:** 26%. **Livestock** (2001): cattle: 1.25 mil; chickens: 35.00

mil.; goats: 760,000; pigs: 2.35 mil; sheep: 5.90 mil. **Fish catch** (1999): 229,108 metric tons. **Electricity prod.:** 43.24 bil. kWh. **Labor force:** services 60%, ind. 30%, agri. 10%.

Finance: Monetary unit: Euro (Sept. 2002: 1.03 = $1 U.S.). **GDP** (2000 est.): $159 bil. **Per capita GDP:** $15,800. **Imports** (2000 est.): $41 bil.; partners (1998): EU 78%, U.S. 3%, Japan 3%. **Exports** (2000 est.): $26.1 bil.; partners (1999): EU 83%,U.S. 5%. **Tourism:** $5.17 bil. **Budget** (2000 est.): $50.7 bil. **Intl. reserves less gold** (end 2000): $6.84 bil. **Gold:** 19.51 mil oz t. **Consumer prices** (change in 2000): 2.9%.

Transport: Railroad: Length: 1,909 mi. **Motor vehicles** (1997): 2.95 mil pass. cars, 960,300 comm. vehicles. **Civil aviation:** 5.23 bil pass.-mi; 16 airports. **Chief ports:** Lisbon, Setubal, Leixoes.

Communications: TV sets: 523 per 1,000 pop. **Radios:** 306 per 1,000 pop. **Telephones:** 12,374,900. **Daily newspaper circ.:** 75 per 1,000 pop.

Health: Life expectancy: 72.7 male; 79.9 female. **Births** (per 1,000 pop.): 11.5. **Deaths** (per 1,000 pop.): 10.2. **Natural inc.:** 0.13%. **Infant mortality** (per 1,000 live births): 5.8.

Education: Free, compulsory: ages 6-15. **Literacy:** 90%.

Major Intl. Organizations: UN (FAO, IBRD, ILO, IMF, IMO, WHO, WTrO), EU, NATO, OECD, OSCE.

Embassy: 2125 Kalorama Rd. NW 20008; 328-8610.

Website: www.presidenciarepublica.pt/en/main.html

Portugal, an independent state since the 12th century, was a kingdom until a revolution in 1910 drove out King Manoel II and a republic was proclaimed.

From 1932 a strong, repressive government was headed by Premier Antonio de Oliveira Salazar. Illness forced his retirement in Sept. 1968.

On Apr. 25, 1974, the government was seized by a military junta led by Gen. Antonio de Spinola, who became president. The new government reached agreements providing independence for Guinea-Bissau, Mozambique, Cape Verde Islands, Angola, and São Tomé and Príncipe. Banks, insurance companies, and other industries were nationalized.

Parliament approved, June 1, 1989, a package of reforms that did away with the socialist economy and created a "democratic" economy, denationalizing industries. Portugal returned Macao to China on Dec. 20, 1999.

Azores Islands, in the Atlantic, 740 mi. W of Portugal, have an area of 868 sq. mi. and a pop. (1993 est.) of 238,000. A 1951 agreement gave the U.S. rights to use defense facilities in the Azores. The **Madeira Islands,** 350 mi. off the NW coast of Africa, have an area of 306 sq. mi. and a pop. (1993 est.) of 437,312. Both groups were offered partial autonomy in 1976.

Qatar

State of Qatar

People: Population: 793,341. **Age distrib.** (%): <15: 25.8; 65+: 2.5. **Pop. density:** 189 per sq. mi. **Urban:** 92%. **Ethnic groups:** Arab 40%, Pakistani 18%, Indian 18%, Iranian 10%. **Principal languages:** Arabic (official), English. **Chief religion:** Muslim 95%.

Geography: Area: 4,200 sq. mi. **Location:** Middle East, occupying peninsula on W coast of Persian Gulf. **Neighbors:** Saudi Arabia on S. **Topography:** Mostly a flat desert, with some limestone ridges; vegetation of any kind is scarce. **Capital:** Doha: 285,000.

Government: Type: Traditional monarchy. **Head of state:** Emir Hamad bin Khalifa ath-Thani; b 1950; in office: June 27, 1995. **Head of gov.:** Prime Min. Abdullah bin Khalifa ath-Thani; in office: Oct. 29, 1996. **Local divisions:** 9 municipalities. **Defense budget (2001):** $1.5 bil. **Active troops:** 12,330.

Economy: Industries: Oil production and refining, fertilizers, petrochemicals. **Minerals:** Oil, gas. **Crude oil reserves** (2001): 5.6 bil bbls. **Livestock** (2001): cattle: 15,000; chickens: 4.00 mil.; goats: 179,000; sheep: 214,531. **Electricity prod.:** 9.20 bil. kWh. **Arable land:** 10%.

Finance: Monetary unit: Riyal (Sept. 2002: 3.64 = $1 U.S.). **GDP** (2000 est.): $15.1 bil. **Per capita GDP:** $20,300. **Imports** (2000 est.): $3.8 bil.; partners (1998): UK 10%, Japan 8%. **Exports** (2000 est.): $9.8 bil.; partners (1998): Japan 52%, Singapore 9%. **Tourism:** $5.17 bil. **Budget** (2000 est.): $4 bil. **Intl. reserves less gold** (end 2000): $889 mil. **Gold:** 150,000 oz t. **Consumer prices** (change in 2000): –1.0%

Transport: Motor vehicles: 96,800 pass. cars, 85,600 comm. vehicles. **Civil aviation:** 1.6 bil pass.-mi; 1 airport. **Chief ports:** Doha, Umm Sáid.

Communications: TV sets: 451 per 1,000 pop. **Radios:** 322 per 1,000 pop. **Telephones:** 346,200. **Daily newspaper circ.:** 143 per 1,000 pop.

Health: Life expectancy: 70.4 male; 75.5 female. **Births** (per 1,000 pop.): 15.8. **Deaths** (per 1,000 pop.): 4.3. **Natural inc.:** 1.14%. **Infant mortality** (per 1,000 live births): 20.7.

Education: Literacy: 79%.

Major Intl. Organizations: UN (FAO, IBRD, ILO, IMF, IMO, WHO, WTrO), AL, OPEC.

Embassy: 4200 Wisconsin Ave. NW 20016; 274-1600.

Website: www.english.mofa.gov.qa

Qatar was under Bahrain's control until the Ottoman Turks took power, 1872 to 1915. In a treaty signed 1916, Qatar gave Great Britain responsibility for its defense and foreign relations. After Britain announced it would remove its military forces from the Persian Gulf area by the end of 1971, Qatar sought a federation with other British-protected states in the area; this failed and Qatar declared itself independent, Sept. 1, 1971. Crown Prince Hamad bin Khalifa ath-Thani ousted his father, Emir Khalifa bin Hamad ath-Thani, June 27, 1995. In municipal elections held Mar. 8, 1999, women participated for the 1st time as candidates and voters.

Oil and natural gas revenues give Qatar a per capita income among the world's highest. Military ties with the U.S. have been expanding.

Romania

People: Population: 22,317,730. **Age distrib.** (%): <15: 17.9; 65+: 13.5. **Pop. density:** 251 per sq. mi. **Urban:** 56%. **Ethnic groups:** Romanian 89.1%, Hungarian 8.9%. **Principal languages:** Romanian (official), Hungarian, German. **Chief religions:** Romanian Orthodox 70%, Roman Catholic 6%, Protestant 6%.

Geography: Area: 88,900 sq. mi. **Location:** SE Europe, on the Black Sea. **Neighbors:** Moldova on E, Ukraine on N, Hungary and Serbia and Montenegro on W, Bulgaria on S. **Topography:** The Carpathian Mts. encase the north-central Transylvanian plateau. There are wide plains S and E of the mountains, through which flow the lower reaches of the rivers of the Danube system. **Capital:** Bucharest 1,998,000.

Government: Type: Republic. **Head of state:** Pres. Ion Iliescu; b Mar. 3, 1930; in office: Dec. 20, 2000. **Head of gov.:** Prime Min. Adrian Nastase; b June 22, 1950; in office: Dec. 28, 2000. **Local divisions:** 40 counties, 1 municipality. **Defense budget (2001):** $1 bil. **Active troops:** 103,000.

Economy: Industries: Textiles and footwear, light machinery and auto assembly, mining, timber. **Chief crops:** Grains, grapes, sunflower seeds, sugar beets, potatoes. **Minerals:** Oil, gas, coal, iron. **Crude oil reserves** (2001): 1.2 bil bbls. **Other resources:** Timber. **Arable land:** 41%. **Livestock** (2001): cattle: 2.97 mil; chickens: 73.50 mil.; goats: 573,900; pigs: 5.08 mil; sheep: 7.80 mil. **Fish catch** (1999): 19,322 metric tons. **Electricity prod.:** 49.79 bil. kWh. **Labor force:** agri. 40%, ind. 25%, services 35%.

Finance: Monetary unit: Leu (Sept. 2002: 33,065 = $1 U.S.). **GDP** (2000 est.): $132.5 bil. **Per capita GDP:** $5,900. **Imports** (2000 est.): $11.9 bil.; partners (1999): Italy 20%, Germany 19%. **Exports** (2000 est.): $11.2 bil.; partners (1999): Italy 23%, Germany 18%. **Tourism:** $254 mil. **Budget** (1999 est.): $12.4 bil. **Intl. reserves less gold** (end 2000): $3.01 bil. **Gold:** 3.37 mil oz t. **Consumer prices** (change in 2000): 45.7%.

Transport: Railroad: Length: 7,062 mi. **Motor vehicles:** 2.39 mil pass. cars; 513,312 comm. vehicles. **Civil aviation:** 1.1 bil pass.-mi; 8 airports. **Chief ports:** Constanta, Braila.

Communications: TV sets: 201 per 1,000 pop. **Radios:** 198 per 1,000 pop. **Telephones:** 7,954,000. **Daily newspaper circ.:** 297 per 1,000 pop.

Health: Life expectancy: 66.6 male; 74.4 female. **Births** (per 1,000 pop.): 10.8. **Deaths** (per 1,000 pop.): 12.3. **Natural inc.:** -0.15%. **Infant mortality** (per 1,000 live births): 18.9.

Education: Compulsory: ages 6-16. **Literacy** (1992): 97%.

Major Intl. Organizations: UN (FAO, IBRD, ILO, IMF, IMO, WHO, WTrO), OSCE.

Embassy: 1607 23d St. NW 20008; 332-4846.

Websites: www.roembus.org; www.gov.ro/engleza/index.html

Romania's earliest known people merged with invading Proto-Thracians, preceding by centuries the Dacians. The Dacian kingdom was occupied by Rome, AD 106-271; people and language were Romanized. The principalities of Wallachia and Moldavia, dominated by Turkey, were united in 1859, became Romania in 1861. In 1877 Romania proclaimed independence from Turkey, and became an independent state by the Treaty of Berlin, 1878; a kingdom under Carol I, 1881; and a constitutional monarchy with a bicameral legislature, 1886.

Romania helped Russia in its war with Turkey, 1877-78. After World War I it acquired Bessarabia, Bukovina, Transylvania, and Banat. In 1940 it ceded Bessarabia and Northern Bukovina to the USSR, part of southern Dobrudja to Bulgaria, and northern Transylvania to Hungary.

In 1941, Prem. Marshal Ion Antonescu led Romania in support of Germany against the USSR. In 1944 he was overthrown by King Michael and Romania joined the Allies.

After occupation by Soviet troops a People's Republic was proclaimed, Dec. 30, 1947; Michael was forced to abdicate.

On Aug. 22, 1965, a new constitution proclaimed Romania a Socialist Republic. Pres. Nicolae Ceausescu maintained an independent course in foreign affairs, but his domestic policies were repressive. All industry was state-owned, and state farms and cooperatives owned almost all arable land.

On Dec. 16, 1989, security forces opened fire on antigovernment demonstrators in Timisoara; hundreds were buried in mass graves. Ceausescu declared a state of emergency as protests spread to other cities. On Dec. 21, in Bucharest, security forces fired on protesters. Army units joined the rebellion, Dec. 22, and a group known as the Council of National Salvation announced that it had overthrown the government. Fierce fighting took place between the army, which backed the new government, and forces loyal to Ceausescu.

Ceausescu and his wife were captured and, following a trial in which they were found guilty of genocide, were executed Dec. 25, 1989. Former Communists dominated the government in succeeding years. A new constitution providing for a multiparty system took effect Dec. 8, 1991. Many of Romania's state-owned companies were privatized in 1996. The former Communists were swept from power in elections Nov. 3 and 17, 1996, but made a comeback in balloting Nov. 26 and Dec. 10, 2000.

Russia

Russian Federation

People: Population: 144,978,573. **Age distrib.** (%): <15: 17.4; 65+: 12.8 . **Pop. density:** 22 per sq. mi. **Urban:** 77%. **Ethnic groups:** Russian 81.5%, Tatar 3.8%. **Principal languages:** Russian (official), many others. **Chief religions:** Russian Orthodox, Muslim, others.

Geography: Area: 6,592,800 sq. mi., more than 76% of total area of the former USSR and the largest country in the world. **Location:** Stretches from E Europe across N Asia to the Pacific O. **Neighbors:** Finland, Norway, Estonia, Latvia, Belarus, Ukraine on W; Georgia, Azerbaijan, Kazakhstan, China, Mongolia, North Korea on S; Kaliningrad exclave bordered by Poland on the S, Lithuania on the N and E. **Topography:** Russia contains every type of climate except the distinctly tropical, and has a varied topography. The European portion is a low plain, grassy in S, wooded in N, with Ural Mts. on the E, and Caucasus Mts. on the S. Urals stretch N-S for 2,500 mi. The Asiatic portion is also a vast plain, with mountains on the S and in the E; tundra covers extreme N, with forest belt below; plains, marshes are in W, desert in SW. **Capital:** Moscow. **Cities (urban aggr.):** Moscow 8,316,000; St. Petersburg 4,635,000; Nizhniy Novgorod 1,332,000; Novosibirsk 1,321,000.

Government: Type: Federal republic. **Head of state:** Vladimir Putin; b Oct. 7, 1952; in office: May 7, 2000. **Head of gov.:** Prime Min. Mikhail Kasyanov; b Dec. 8, 1957; in office: May 17, 2000. **Local divisions:** 21 autonomous republics, 68 autonomous territories and regions. **Defense budget (2001):** $44 bil. **Active troops:** 977,100.

Economy: Industries: Coal, oil, gas, chemicals, metals; machinery, shipbuilding, vehicles, communications equipment, electric power, medical/scientific instruments. **Chief crops:** Grains, sugar beets, vegetables, sunflowers. **Minerals:** Manganese, mercury, potash, bauxite, cobalt, chromium, copper, coal, gold, lead, molybdenum, nickel, phosphates, silver, tin, tungsten, zinc, oil, gas, iron, potassium. **Crude oil reserves** (2001): 54.3 bil bbls. **Other resources:** Forests. **Arable land:** 8%. **Livestock** (2001): cattle: 27.30 mil; chickens: 325.00 mil.; goats: 1.70 mil.; pigs: 15.70 mil; sheep: 11.00 mil . **Fish catch** (2000). 4.72 mil metric tons. **Electricity prod.:** 835.57 bil. kWh. **Labor force:** agri. 15%, ind. 30%, services 55%.

Finance: Monetary unit: Ruble (Sept. 2002: 31.67 = $1 U.S. NOTE: On Jan 1, 1998, Russia eliminated 3 digits from the ruble.) **GDP** (2000 est.): $1.12 tril. **Per capita GDP:** $7,700. **Imports** (2000 est.): $44.2 bil.; partners (1999): Germany 13.8%, Belarus 10.7%. **Exports** (2000 est.): $105.1 bil.; partners (1999): U.S. 8.8%, Germany 8.5%. **Tourism:** $7.77 bil. **Budget** (2000 est.): $33.7 bil. **Intl. reserves less gold** (end 2000): $18.62 bil. **Gold:** 12.36 mil oz t. **Consumer prices** (change in 2000): 20.8%.

Transport: Railroad: Length: 94,400 mi. **Motor vehicles:** 13.71 mil pass. cars, 9.86 mil comm. vehicles. **Civil aviation:** 30.6 bil pass.-mi; 75 airports. **Chief ports:** St. Petersburg, Murmansk, Arkhangelsk.

Communications: TV sets: 389 per 1,000 pop. **Radios:** 417 per 1,000 pop. **Telephones:** 41,260,000. **Daily newspaper circ.:** 105 per 1,000 pop.

Health: Life expectancy: 62.3 male; 73 female. **Births** (per 1,000 pop.): 9.7. **Deaths** (per 1,000 pop.): 13.9. **Natural inc.:** -0.42%. **Infant mortality** (per 1,000 live births): 19.8.

Education: Free, compulsory: ages 7-17. **Literacy:** 99%.

Major Intl. Organizations: UN (IBRD, ILO, IMF, IMO, WHO), APEC, CIS, OSCE.

Embassy: 2650 Wisconsin Ave. NW 20007; 298-5700.

Website: www.un.int/russia

History. Slavic tribes began migrating into Russia from the W in the 5th century AD. The first Russian state, founded by Scandinavian chieftains, was established in the 9th century, centering in Novgorod and Kiev. In the 13th century the Mongols overran the country. It recovered under the grand dukes and princes of Muscovy, or Moscow, and by 1480 freed itself from the Mongols. Ivan the Terrible was the first to be formally proclaimed Tsar (1547). Peter the Great (1682-1725) extended the domain and, in 1721, founded the Russian Empire.

Western ideas and the beginnings of modernization spread through the huge Russian empire in the 19th and early 20th centuries. But political evolution failed to keep pace.

Military reverses in the 1905 war with Japan and in World War I led to the breakdown of the Tsarist regime. The 1917 Revolution began in March with a series of sporadic strikes for higher wages by factory workers. A provisional democratic government under Prince Georgi Lvov was established but was quickly followed in May by the second provisional government, led by Alexander Kerensky. The Kerensky government and the freely-elected Constituent Assembly were overthrown in a Communist coup led by Vladimir Ilyich Lenin Nov. 7.

Soviet Union

Lenin's death Jan. 21, 1924, resulted in an internal power struggle from which Joseph Stalin eventually emerged on top. Stalin secured his position at first by exiling opponents, but from the 1930s to 1953, he resorted to a series of "purge" trials, mass executions, and mass exiles to work camps. These measures resulted in millions of deaths, according to most estimates.

Germany and the Soviet Union signed a non-aggression pact Aug. 1939; Germany launched a massive invasion of the Soviet Union, June 1941. Notable heroic episode was the "900 days" siege of Leningrad (now St. Petersburg), lasting to Jan. 1944, and causing a million deaths; the city was never taken. Russian winter counterthrusts, 1941-42 and 1942-43, stopped the German advance. Turning point was the failure of German troops to take and hold Stalingrad (now Volgograd), Sept. 1942 to Feb. 1943. With British and U.S. Lend-Lease aid and sustaining great casualties, the Russians drove the German forces from eastern Europe and the Balkans in the next 2 years.

After Stalin died, Mar. 5, 1953, Nikita Khrushchev was elected first secretary of the Central Committee. In 1956 he condemned Stalin and "de-Stalinization" began.

Under Khrushchev the open antagonism of Poles and Hungarians toward domination by Moscow was brutally suppressed in 1956. He advocated peaceful co-existence with the capitalist countries, but continued arming the Soviet Union with nuclear weapons. He aided the Cuban revolution under Fidel Castro but withdrew Soviet missiles from Cuba during confrontation by U.S. Pres. Kennedy, Sept.-Oct. 1962. Khrushchev was suddenly deposed, Oct. 1964, and replaced by Leonid I. Brezhnev.

In Aug. 1968 Russian, Polish, East German, Hungarian, and Bulgarian military forces invaded Czechoslovakia to put a curb on liberalization policies of the Czech government.

Massive Soviet military aid to North Vietnam in the late 1960s and early 1970s helped assure Communist victories throughout Indo-China. Soviet arms aid and advisers were sent to several African countries in the 1970s.

In Dec. 1979, Soviet forces entered Afghanistan to support that government against rebels. In Apr. 1988, the Soviets agreed to withdraw their troops, ending a futile 8-year war.

Mikhail Gorbachev was chosen gen. secy. of the Communist Party, Mar. 1985. He held 4 summit meetings with U.S. Pres. Ronald Reagan. In 1987, in Washington, a treaty was signed eliminating intermediate-range nuclear missiles from Europe.

In 1987, Gorbachev initiated a program of reforms, including expanded freedoms and the democratization of the political process, through openness (*glasnost*) and restructuring (*perestroika*). The reforms were opposed by some Eastern bloc countries and many old-line Communists in the USSR. Gorbachev faced economic problems as well as ethnic and nationalist unrest in the republics.

When an apparent coup against Gorbachev became known on Aug. 19, 1991, the pres. of the Russian Republic, Boris Yeltsin, denounced it and called for a general strike. Some 50,000 demonstrated at the Russian Parliament in support of Yeltsin. By Aug. 21, the coup had failed and Gorbachev was restored as president. On Aug. 24, Gorbachev resigned as leader of the Communist Party. Several republics declared their independence, including Russia, Ukraine, and Kazakhstan. On Aug. 29, the Soviet Parliament voted to suspend all activities of the Communist Party.

The Soviet Union officially broke up Dec. 26, 1991, one day after Gorbachev resigned. The Soviet hammer and sickle flying over the Kremlin was lowered and replaced by the flag of Russia, ending the domination of the Communist Party over all areas of national life since 1917.

Russian Federation

In a first major step in radical economic reform, Russia eliminated state subsidies of most goods and services, Jan. 1992. The effect was to allow prices to soar far beyond the means of ordinary workers. In June, Pres. Yeltsin and U.S. Pres. George Bush agreed to massive arms reductions.

Russia launched a drive to privatize thousands of large and medium-sized state-owned enterprises in 1993. Yeltsin narrowly survived an impeachment vote by the Congress of People's Deputies, Mar. 28. He received strong support from voters in a referendum Apr. 25, but he continued to face a legislature dominated by conservatives and former Communists.

On Sept. 21, 1993, Yeltsin called for early elections and dissolved Parliament, which in turn declared him deposed. Anti-Yeltsin legislators then barricaded themselves in the Parliament building. On Oct. 3, anti-Yeltsin forces attacked some facilities in Moscow and broke into the Parliament building. Yeltsin ordered the army to attack and seize the building. About 140 people were killed in the fighting, according to medical authorities. More than 150 were arrested.

In elections Dec. 12, 1993, a Yeltsin-supported constitution was approved, but ultranationalists and Communist hard-liners made strong showings in legislative contests. In Dec. 1994 the Russian government sent troops into the breakaway republic of Chechnya. Grozny, the Chechen capital, fell in Feb. 1995 after heavy fighting, but Chechen rebels continued to resist.

Despite poor health, Yeltsin won a presidential runoff election over a Communist opponent, July 3, 1996. On Aug. 14, after rebels embarrassed the Russian military by retaking Grozny, Yeltsin gave his security chief, Alexander Lebed, broad powers to negotiate an end to the Chechnya war. Lebed and Chechen leaders signed a peace accord Aug. 31. On Oct. 17, Yeltsin dismissed Lebed for insubordination. Yeltsin survived quintuple-bypass heart surgery Nov. 5.

Russian troops remaining in Chechnya were pulled out Jan. 1997. A revitalized Yeltsin revamped his cabinet in Mar. to strengthen the hand of reformers. On May 27, he signed a "founding act" increasing cooperation with NATO and paving the way for NATO to admit Eastern European nations.

Russia's economic crisis deepened throughout 1998; in Aug. the ruble plummeted and the country defaulted on its debt. Yeltsin dismissed Prime Min. Viktor Chernomyrdin on Mar. 23 and Chernomyrdin's successor, Sergei Kiriyenko, on Aug. 23. Each move triggered a confrontation with parliament. Yevgeny Primakov became premier Sept. 11, 1998; in subsequent cabinet upheavals, Sergei Stepashin took over on May 19, 1999, followed by Vladimir Putin on Aug. 16. Disagreements over the war in Kosovo strained relations with the U.S. and NATO. Russia moved forcibly in Aug. 1999 to suppress Islamic rebels in Dagestan; the conflict soon spread to neighboring Chechnya, where Russia launched a full-scale assault. A series of 5 bombings in Moscow and Dagestan, which the Russian government attributed to Chechen rebels, killed over 300 people.

Yeltsin unexpectedly resigned Dec. 31, 1999, naming Putin as his interim successor. Russian troops took control of Grozny in early Feb. 2000. Putin defeated 10 opponents in a presidential election Mar. 26. The Russian parliament ratified 2 nuclear weapons treaties, the START II arms-reduction accord Apr. 14 and the Comprehensive Test Ban Treaty Apr. 21. A reorganization plan announced May 17 sought to reassert Moscow's control over Russia's regional governments. The Russian nuclear submarine *Kursk* sank in the Barents Sea Aug. 12, killing 118 sailors.

Russia and China signed a 20-year friendship and cooperation treaty July 16, 2001. With a deadline approaching for U.S. withdrawal from the 1972 Antiballistic Missile (ABM) Treaty, Putin and Bush signed May 24, 2002, an agreement calling for a 2/3 reduction in nuclear weapons stockpiles; the deal also replaced Start II, from which Russia pulled out June 14. Russia joined a new partnership agreement with NATO May 28, 2002.

Russian forces continued a campaign against Islamic separatists in Chechnya; meanwhile, in May 2002, a bomb blast in Dagestan killed 42 people.

Rwanda

Republic of Rwanda

People: Population: 7,398,074. **Age distrib.** (%): <15: 42.4; 65+: 2.9. **Pop. density:** 771 per sq. mi. **Urban:** 6%. **Ethnic groups:** Hutu 80%, Tutsi 19%, Twa (Pygmoid) 1%. **Principal languages:** French, Kinyarwanda, English (all official). **Chief religions:** Roman Catholic 65%, indigenous beliefs 25%.

Geography: Area: 9,600 sq. mi. **Location:** In E central Africa. **Neighbors:** Uganda on N, Congo (formerly Zaire) on W, Burundi on S, Tanzania on E. **Topography:** Grassy uplands and hills cover most of the country, with a chain of volcanoes in the NW. The source of the Nile R. has been located in the headwaters of the Kagera (Akagera) R., SW of Kigali. **Capital:** Kigali: 412,000.

Government: Type: Republic. **Head of state:** Pres. Paul Kagame; b Oct. 1957; in office: Apr. 22, 2000 (de facto from Mar. 24). **Head of gov.:** Prime Min. Bernard Makuza; b 1961; in office: Mar. 8, 2000. **Local divisions:** 12 prefectures subdivided into 155 communes. **Defense budget (2001):** $104 mil. **Active troops:** 56,000-71,000.

Economy: Industries: Cement, agricultural products. **Chief crops:** Coffee, tea, pyrethrum, bananas. **Minerals:** Tin, gold, wolframite. **Arable land:** 35%. **Livestock** (2001): cattle: 800,000; chickens: 1.20 mil.; goats: 700,000; pigs: 180,000; sheep: 260,000. **Electricity prod.:** 0.11 bil. kWh. **Labor force:** agric 90%.

Finance: Monetary unit: Franc (Sept. 2002: 475.35 = $1 U.S.). **GDP** (2000 est.): $6.4 bil. **Per capita GDP:** $900. **Imports** (2000 est.): $245.9 mil.; partners: Kenya, Tanzania, U.S., Benelux, France, India. **Exports** (2000 est.): $68.4 mil.; partners: Germany, Belgium, Pakistan, Italy, Kenya. **Tourism** (1998): $19 mil. **Budget** (2000 est.): $411 mil. **Intl. reserves less gold** (end 2000): $146.0 mil. **Consumer prices** (change in 2000): 4.3%.

Transport: Motor vehicles: 11,900 pass. cars, 15,900 comm. vehicles. **Civil aviation:** 1.2 mil pass.-mi; 2 airports. **Chief ports:** Gisenyi, Cyangugu. **Communications: Radios:** 78.4 per 1,000 pop. **Telephones:** 86,500.

Health: Life expectancy: 38.1 male; 39.2 female. **Births** (per 1,000 pop.): 33.3. **Deaths** (per 1,000 pop.): 21.4. **Natural inc.:** 1.19%. **Infant mortality** (per 1,000 live births): 117.8.

Education: Compulsory: ages 7-14. **Literacy**: 60%.

Major Intl. Organizations: UN (FAO, IBRD, ILO, IMF, WHO, WTrO), AU.

Embassy: 1714 New Hampshire Ave. NW 20009; 232-2882.

Website: www.rwanda1.com

For centuries, the Tutsi (an extremely tall people) dominated the Hutu (90% of the population). A civil war broke out in 1959 and Tutsi power was ended. Many Tutsi went into exile. A referendum in 1961 abolished the monarchic system. Rwanda, which had been part of the Belgian UN trusteeship of Rwanda-Urundi, became independent July 1, 1962.

In 1963 Tutsi exiles invaded in an unsuccessful coup; a large-scale massacre of Tutsi followed. Rivalries among Hutu led to a bloodless coup July 1973 in which Juvénal Habyarimana took power. After an invasion and coup attempt by Tutsi exiles in 1990, a multiparty democracy was established.

Renewed ethnic strife led to an Aug. 1993 peace accord between the government and rebels of the Tutsi-led Rwandan Patriotic Front (RPF). But after Habyarimana and the president of Burundi were killed Apr. 6, 1994, in a suspicious plane crash, massive violence broke out. More than 1 million may have died in massacres, mostly of Tutsi by Hutu militias, and in civil warfare as the RPF sought power. About 2 million Tutsi and Hutu fled to camps in Zaire (now Congo) and other countries, where many died of cholera and other natural causes. French troops under a UN mandate moved into SW Rwanda June 23 to establish a so-called safe zone. The RPF claimed victory, installing a government in July led by a moderate Hutu president. French troops pulled out Aug. 22. A UN peacekeeping mission ended Mar. 8, 1996, but the Rwandan government and a UN-sponsored tribunal in Tanzania continued to gather evidence against those responsible for genocide. More than 1 million refugees (mostly Hutu) flooded back to Rwanda from Tanzania and Zaire in Nov. and Dec. 1996.

Firing squads in Rwanda on Apr. 24, 1998, executed 22 people convicted of genocide. Former Prime Min. Jean Kambanda pleaded guilty May 1 before the UN tribunal and received a life sentence Sept. 4, 1998. Maj. Gen. Paul Kagame, leader of the RPF, was sworn in as Rwanda's 1st Tutsi president Apr. 22, 2000. A Belgian court June 8, 2001, convicted 2 Roman Catholic nuns and 2 other Rwandans for their role in the 1994 genocide.

Rwanda and the Congo signed an accord July 30, 2002, in which Rwanda agreed to withdraw troops from the Congo and the Congo agreed to stop harboring Hutu guerrilas.

Saint Kitts and Nevis

Federation of Saint Kitts and Nevis

People: Population: 38,736. **Age distrib.** (%):<15: 29.8; 65+: 8.8. **Pop. density:** 279 per sq. mi. **Urban:** 34%. **Ethnic group:** Black. **Principal language:** English (official). **Chief religion:** Protestant.

Geography: Area: 139 sq. mi. **Location:** In the N part of the Leeward group of the Lesser Antilles in the E Caribbean Sea. **Neighbors:** Antigua and Barbuda to E. **Capital:** Basseterre: 12,000.

Government: Constitutional monarchy. **Head of state:** Queen Elizabeth II, represented by Gov.-Gen. Frederick Ballantyne; in office: Sept. 2, 2002. **Head of gov.:** Prime Min. Ralph Gonsalves; b Aug. 8, 1946; in office: Mar. 29, 2001. **Local divisions:** 6 parishes.

Economy: Industries: Sugar, tourism, cotton. **Arable land:** 22%. **Livestock** (2001): cattle: 3,600; chickens: 60,000; goats: 14,500; pigs: 3,000; sheep: 7,400. **Electricity prod.:** 0.10 bil. kWh.

Finance: Monetary unit: East Caribbean Dollar (Sept. 2002: 2.70 = $1 U.S.). **GDP** (2000 est.): $274 mil. **Per capita GDP:** $7,000. **Imports** (2000 est.): $151.5 mil.; partners (1995 est.): U.S. 42.4%, Caricom countries 17.2%. **Exports** (2000 est.): $53.2 mil.; partners (1995 est.): U.S. 68.5%, UK 22.3%. **Tourism:** $66 mil. **Budget** (1997 est.) $73.3 mil. **Intl. reserves less gold** (end 2000): $35 mil. **Consumer prices** (change in 1999): 3.9%.

Transport: Civil aviation: 2 airports. **Chief ports:** Basseterre, Charlestown.

Communications: TV sets: 241 per 1,000 pop. **Radios:** 659 per 1,000 pop. **Telephones** (2000): 23,100.

Health: Life expectancy: 68.5 male; 74.3 female. **Births** (per 1,000 pop.): 18.6. **Deaths** (per 1,000 pop.): 9. **Natural inc.:** 0.96%. **Infant mortality** (per 1,000 live births): 15.8.

Education: Compulsory, ages 5-17. **Literacy** (1992): 90%.

Major Intl. Organizations: UN (FAO, IBRD, ILO, IMF, WHO, WTrO), Caricom, the Commonwealth, OAS, OECS.

Embassy: 3216 New Mexico Ave., NW 20016; 686-2636.

Website: www.stkittsnevis.net

St. Kitts (formerly St. Christopher; known by the natives as Liamuiga) and Nevis were reached (and named) by Columbus in 1493. They were settled by Britain in 1623, but ownership was disputed with France until 1713. They were part of the Leeward Islands Federation, 1871-1956, and the Federation of the West Indies, 1958-62. The colony achieved self-government as an Associated State of the UK in 1967, and became fully independent Sept. 19, 1983. A secession referendum on Nevis, Aug. 10, 1998, fell short of the two-thirds majority required.

Saint Lucia

People: Population: 160,145. **Age distrib.** (%): <15: 32.1; 65+: 5.3. **Urban:** 38%. **Pop. density:** 679 per sq. mi. **Ethnic groups:** Black 90%. **Principal languages:** English (official), French patois. **Chief religions:** Roman Catholic 90%, Protestant 7%.

Geography: Area: 236 sq. mi. **Location:** In E Caribbean, 2d largest of the Windward Isls. **Neighbors:** Martinique to N, St. Vincent to S. **Topography:** Mountainous, volcanic in origin; Soufriere, a volcanic crater, in the S. Wooded mountains run N-S to Mt. Gimie, 3,145 ft., with streams through fertile valleys. **Capital:** Castries: 57,000.

Government: Type: Parliamentary democracy. **Head of state:** Queen Elizabeth II, represented by Gov.-Gen. Calliopa Pearlette Louisy; b June 8, 1946; in office: Sept. 17, 1997. **Head of gov.:** Prime Min. Kenny Anthony; b Jan. 8, 1951; in office: May 24, 1997. **Local divisions:** 11 quarters.

Economy: Industries: Clothing, electronics assembly, beverages. **Chief crops:** Bananas, coconuts, vegetables, root crops, cocoa, citrus. **Other resources:** Forests. **Arable land:** 8%. **Livestock** (2001): cattle: 12,400; chickens: 210,000; goats: 9,800; pigs: 14,750; sheep: 12,500. **Electricity prod.:** 0.12 bil. kWh. **Labor force:** agri. 43.4%, services 38.9%, ind. and commerce 17.7%.

Finance: Monetary unit: East Caribbean Dollar (Sept. 2002: 2.70 = $1 U.S.). **GDP** (2000 est.): $700 mil. **Per capita GDP:** $4,500. **Imports** (2000 est.): $319.4 mil.; partners (1995): U.S. 36%, Caricom countries 22%. **Exports** (2000 est.): $68.3 mil.; partners (1995): UK 50%, U.S. 24%. **Tourism** (1998): $291 mil. **Budget** (FY97/98 est.): $146.7 mil. **Intl. reserves less gold** (end 2000): $61 mil. **Consumer prices** (change in 1999): 5.4%.

Transport: Motor vehicles: 10,000 pass. cars, 9,100 comm. vehicles. **Civil aviation:** 2 airports. **Chief ports:** Castries, Vieux Fort.

Communications: TV sets: 172 per 1,000 pop. **Radios:** 619 per 1,000 pop. **Telephones** (1999): 44,500 main lines.

Health: Life expectancy: 69.3 male; 76.6 female. **Births** (per 1,000 pop.): 21.4. **Deaths** (per 1,000 pop.): 5.3. **Natural inc.:** 1.61%. **Infant mortality** (per 1,000 live births): 14.8.

Education: Compulsory: ages 5-15. **Literacy** (1993): 80%.

Major Intl. Organizations: UN (FAO, IBRD, ILO, IMF, IMO, WHO, WTrO), Caricom, the Commonwealth, OAS, OECS.

Embassy: 3216 New Mexico Ave. NW 20016; 364-6792.

Website: www.stlucia.gov.lc

St. Lucia was ceded to Britain by France at the Treaty of Paris, 1814. Self-government was granted with the West Indies Act, 1967. Independence was attained Feb. 22, 1979.

Saint Vincent and the Grenadines

People: Population: 116,394. **Age distrib.** (%):<15: 29.6; 65+: 6.3. **Pop. density:** 889 per sq. mi. **Urban:** 54%. **Ethnic groups:** Black 82%, mixed 14%. **Principal languages:** English (official), French patois. **Chief religions:** Anglican, Methodist, Roman Catholic.

Geography: Area: 131 sq. mi. **Location:** In the E Caribbean, St. Vincent (133 sq. mi.) and the northern islets of the Grenadines form a part of the Windward chain. **Neighbors:** St. Lucia to N, Barbados to E, Grenada to S. **Topography:** St. Vincent is volcanic, with a ridge of thickly wooded mountains running its length. **Capital:** Kingstown: 28,000.

Government: Constitutional monarchy. **Head of State:** Queen Elizabeth II, represented by Gov.-Gen. Frederick Ballantyne; in office: Sept. 2, 2002. **Head of gov.:** Prime Min. Ralph Gonsalves; b Aug.. 8, 1946; in office: Mar. 29, 2001. **Local divisions:** 6 parishes.

Economy: Industries: Food processing, cement, furniture, clothing. **Chief crops:** Bananas, coconuts, sweet potatoes. **Arable land:** 10%. **Livestock** (2001): cattle: 6,200; chickens: 200,000; goats: 6,000; pigs: 9,500; sheep: 13,000. **Electricity prod.:** 0.09 bil. kWh. **Labor force**: agri. 26%, ind. 17%, services 57%.

Finance: Monetary unit: East Caribbean Dollar (Sept. 2002: 2.70 = $1 U.S.). **GDP** (2000 est.): $322 mil. **Per capita GDP:** $2,800. **Imports** (2000 est.): $185.6 mil.; partners (1995): U.S. 36%, Caricom countries 28%. **Exports** (2000 est.): $53.7 mil.; partners (1995): Caricom countries 49%, UK 16%. **Tourism:** $77 mil. **Budget** (1997 est.): $98.6 mil. **Intl. reserves less gold** (end 2000): $42 mil. **Consumer prices** (change in 2000): 0.2%.

Transport: Motor vehicles: 5,000 pass. cars, 3,200 comm. vehicles. **Civil aviation:** 5 airports. **Chief port:** Kingstown.

Communications: TV sets: 161 per 1,000 pop. **Radios:** 591 per 1,000 pop. **Telephones** (2000): 27,300.

Health: Life expectancy: 71.1 male; 74.6 female. **Births** (per 1,000 pop.): 17.5. **Deaths** (per 1,000 pop.): 6.1. **Natural inc.:** 1.14%. **Infant mortality** (per 1,000 live births): 16.1.

Education: Literacy (1994): 82%.

Major Intl. Organizations: UN (FAO, IBRD, ILO, IMF, IMO, WHO, WTrO), Caricom, the Commonwealth, OAS, OECS.

Embassy: 3216 New Mexico Ave. NW 20016; 364-6730.

Columbus landed on St. Vincent on Jan. 22, 1498 (St. Vincent's Day). Britain and France both laid claim to the island in the 17th and 18th centuries; the Treaty of Versailles, 1783, finally ceded it to Britain. Associated State status was granted 1969; independence was attained Oct. 27, 1979.

Samoa (*formerly* Western Samoa)

Independent State of Samoa

People: Population: 178,631. **Age distrib.** (%): <15: 31.9; 65+: 5.7. **Pop. density:** 162 per sq. mi. **Urban:** 21%. **Ethnic groups:** Samoan 92.6%, Euronesian (mixed) 7%. **Principal languages:** Samoan, English (both official). **Chief religion:** Christian 99.7%.

Geography: Area: 1,100 sq. mi. **Location:** In the S Pacific O. **Neighbors:** Nearest are Fiji to SW, Tonga to S. **Topography:** Main islands, Savaii (659 sq. mi.) and Upolu (432 sq. mi.), both ruggedly mountainous, and small islands Manono and Apolima. **Capital:** Apia: 35,000.

Government: Type: Constitutional monarchy. **Head of state:** Malietoa Tanumafili II; b Jan. 4, 1913; in office: Jan. 1, 1962. **Head of gov.:** Prime Min. Tuilaepa Sailele Malielegaoi; b Apr. 14, 1945; in office: Nov. 23, 1998. **Local divisions:** 11 districts.

Economy: Industries: Food processing, building materials, auto parts. **Chief crops:** Coconuts, taro, yams, bananas. **Other resources:** Hardwoods, fish. **Arable land:** 19%. **Livestock** (2001): cattle: 28,000; chickens: 450,000; pigs: 170,000. **Electricity prod.:** 0.10 bil. kWh. **Labor force:** agri. 65%, services 30%, ind. 5%.

Finance: Monetary unit: Tala (Sept. 2002: 3.31 = $1 U.S.). **GDP** (2000 est.): $571 mil. **Per capita GDP:** $3,200. **Imports** (2000): $90 mil.; partners (2000 est.): New Zealand 37%, Australia 24%. **Exports** (2000): $17 mil.; partners (2000 est.): American Samoa 59%, U.S. 18%. **Tourism:** $42 mil. **Budget** (1999 est.): $81.4 mil. **Intl. reserves less gold** (end 2000): $49 mil. **Consumer prices** (change in 2000): 1.0%.

Transport: Motor vehicles (1997): 1,200 pass. cars, 1,400 comm. vehicles. **Civil aviation:** 3 airports. **Chief ports:** Apia, Asau.

Communications: TV sets: 30 per 1,000 pop. **Radios:** 448 per 1,000 pop. **Telephones:** 13,000.

Health: Life expectancy: 67.1 male; 72.7 female. **Births** (per 1,000 pop.): 15.5. **Deaths** (per 1,000 pop.): 6.3. **Natural inc.:** 0.92%. **Infant mortality** (per 1,000 live births): 30.7.

Education: Free, compulsory: ages 6-16. **Literacy** (1989): 100%.

Major Intl. Organizations: UN (FAO, IBRD, IMF, IMO, WHO), the Commonwealth.

Embassy: 820 2nd Ave., Suite 800D, New York, NY 10017; (212) 599-6196.

Website: www.samoa.ws/govtsamoapress/

Samoa (formerly known as Western Samoa to distinguish it from American Samoa, a small U.S. territory) was a German colony, 1899 to 1914, when New Zealand landed troops and took over. It became a New Zealand mandate under the League of Nations and, in 1945, a New Zealand UN Trusteeship.

An elected local government took office in Oct. 1959, and the country became fully independent Jan. 1, 1962.

San Marino

Republic of San Marino

People: Population: 27,730. **Age distrib.** (%): <15: 15.9; 65+: 16.2. **Pop. density:** 1,197 per sq. mi. **Urban:** 89%. **Ethnic groups:** Sammarinese, Italian. **Principal language:** Italian. **Chief religion:** Roman Catholic.

Geography: Area: 23 sq. mi. **Location:** In N central Italy near Adriatic coast. **Neighbors:** Completely surrounded by Italy. **Topography:** The country lies on the slopes of Mt. Titano. **Capital:** San Marino: 5,000.

Government: Type: Republic. **Heads of state and gov.:** Two co-regents appt. every 6 months. **Local divisions:** 9 castelli.

Economy: Industries: Tourism, banking, textiles, electronics, ceramics, cement, wine. **Chief crops:** Wheat, grapes, maize. **Arable land:** 17%. **Labor force:** services 60%, ind. 38%, agri. 2%.

Finance: Monetary unit: Italian Lira (Sept. 2002: 1,982.97 = $1 U.S.). **GDP** (2000 est.): $860 mil. **Per capita GDP:** $32,000. **Imports**: trade data are included with the statistics for Italy . **Exports** . **Budget** (2000 est.): $400 mil.

Transport: Motor vehicles (1997): 24,825 pass. cars, 4,149 comm. vehicles.

Communications: Radios: 514 per 1,000 pop. **Daily newspaper circ.:** 82 per 1,000 pop.

Health: Life expectancy: 77.8 male; 85.2 female. **Births** (per 1,000 pop.): 10.6. **Deaths** (per 1,000 pop.): 7.8. **Natural inc.:** 0.28%. **Infant mortality** (per 1,000 live births): 6.1.

Education: Compulsory: ages 6-13. **Literacy** (1997): 99%.

Major Intl. Organizations: UN (ILO, IMF, WHO), OSCE.

San Marino claims to be the oldest state in Europe and to have been founded in the 4th century. A Communist-led coalition ruled 1947-57; a similar coalition ruled 1978-86. It has had a treaty of friendship with Italy since 1862.

São Tomé and Príncipe

Democratic Republic of São Tomé and Príncipe

People: Population: 170,372. **Age distrib.** (%): <15: 47.7; 65+: 4.0. **Pop. density:** 460 per sq. mi. **Urban:** 46%. **Ethnic groups:** Mestico (Portuguese-African), African minority (Angola, Mozambique immigrants). **Principal language:** Portuguese (official). **Chief religions:** Roman Catholic, Protestant.

Geography: Area: 371 sq. mi. **Location:** In the Gulf of Guinea about 125 miles off W central Africa. **Neighbors:** Gabon, Equatorial Guinea to E. **Topography:** São Tomé and Príncipe islands, part of an extinct volcano chain, are both covered by lush forests and croplands. **Capital:** São Tomé: 67,000.

Government: Type: Republic. **Head of state:** Pres. Fradique Melo de Menezes; b. Mar. 21, 1942; in office: Sept. 3, 2001. **Head of gov.:** Prime Min. Gabriel da Costa; b Dec. 11, 1954; in office: Apr. 8, 2002. **Local divisions:** 2 provinces.

Economy: Industries: Light construction, textiles, soap, beer. **Chief crops:** Cocoa, coconuts. **Arable land:** 2%. **Livestock** (2001): cattle: 4,100; chickens: 350,000; goats: 4,800; pigs: 2,200; sheep: 2,600. **Electricity prod.:** 0.02 bil. kWh.

Finance: Monetary unit: Dobra (Sept. 2002: 9,019.70 = $1 U.S.).

GDP (2000 est.): $178 mil. **Per capita GDP:** $1,100. **Imports** (2000 est.): $40 mil.; partners (1998): Portugal 42%, U.S. 20%. **Exports** (2000 est.): $3.2 mil.; partners (1998): Netherlands 18%, Germany 9%, Portugal 9%. **Tourism** (1998): $2 mil. **Budget (1993 est.): $114 mil. Intl. reserves less gold** (Dec. 1999): $8.0 mil.

Transport: Civil aviation: 5.8 mil pass.-mi; 2 airports. **Chief ports:** São Tomé, Santo Antonio.

Communications: TV sets: 154 per 1,000 pop. **Radios:** 232 per 1,000 pop. **Telephones:** 5,400.

Health: Life expectancy: 64.5 male; 67.5 female. **Births** (per 1,000 pop.): 42.3. **Deaths** (per 1,000 pop.): 7.3. **Natural inc.:** 3.5%. **Infant mortality** (per 1,000 live births): 47.5.

Education: Compulsory for 4 years between ages 7-14. **Literacy** (1991): 73%.

Major Intl. Organizations: UN (FAO, IBRD, ILO, IMF, IMO, WHO), AU.

The islands were discovered in 1471 by the Portuguese, who brought the first settlers—convicts and exiled Jews. Sugar planting was replaced by the slave trade as the chief economic activity until coffee and cocoa were introduced in the 19th century.

Portugal agreed, 1974, to turn the colony over to the Gabon-based Movement for the Liberation of São Tomé and Príncipe, which proclaimed as first president its East German-trained leader, Manuel Pinto da Costa. Independence came July 12, 1975. Democratic reforms were instituted in 1987. In 1991 Miguel Trovoada won the first free presidential election following da Costa's withdrawal. A military coup that ousted Trovoada Aug. 15, 1995, was reversed a week later after Angolan mediation. Trovoada defeated da Costa in a presidential runoff election, July 21, 1996. Fradique de Menezes, a wealthy cocoa exporter, easily beat da Costa in the presidential election of July 29, 2001.

Saudi Arabia

Kingdom of Saudi Arabia

People: Population: 23,513,330. **Age distrib.** (%): <15: 42.5; 65+: 2.7. **Pop. density:** 28 per sq. mi. **Urban:** 85%. **Ethnic groups:** Arab 90%, Afro-Asian 10%. **Principal language:** Arabic (official). **Chief religion:** Muslim 100%.

Geography: Area: 830,000 sq. mi. **Location:** Occupies most of Arabian Peninsula in Mid-East. **Neighbors:** Kuwait, Iraq, Jordan on N; Yemen, Oman on S; United Arab Emirates, Qatar on E. **Topography:** Bordered by Red Sea on the W. The highlands on W, up to 9,000 ft., slope as an arid, barren desert to the Persian Gulf on the E. **Capital:** Riyadh. **Cities (urban aggr.):** Riyadh 4,761,000; Jeddah 3,192,000; Mecca 1,335,000.

Government: Type: Monarchy with council of ministers. **Head of state and gov.:** King Fahd ibn Abdul Aziz; b 1923; in office: June 13, 1982 (prime min. since 1982). **Local divisions:** 13 provinces. **Defense budget (2001):** $27.2 bil. **Active troops:** 126,500.

Economy: Industries: Oil, oil products. **Chief crops:** Dates, wheat, barley, tomatoes, melon, citrus. **Minerals:** Oil, gas, gold, copper, iron. **Crude oil reserves** (2001): 265.3 bil bbls. **Arable land:** 2%. **Livestock** (2001): cattle: 297,000; chickens: 130.00 mil.; goats: 4.31 mil.; sheep: 7.58 mil. **Fish catch:** (1999): 54,085 metric tons. **Electricity prod.:** 123.50 bil. kWh. **Labor force:** agri. 12%, ind. 25%, services 63%.

Finance: Monetary unit: Riyal (Sept. 2002: 3.75 = $1 U.S.). **GDP** (2000 est.): $232 bil. **Per capita GDP:** $10,500. **Imports** (2000): $30.1 bil.; partners (1999): U.S. 25%, Japan 10%. **Exports** (2000): $81.2 bil.; partners (1999): Japan 18%, U.S. 18%. **Tourism** (1998): $1.46 bil. **Budget** (2000 est.): $66 bil. **Intl. reserves less gold** (end 2000): $15.39 bil. **Gold:** 4.60 mil oz t. **Consumer prices** (change in 2000): –0.8%.

Transport: Railroad: Length: 864 km. **Motor vehicles:** 1.71 mil pass. cars, 1.17 mil comm. vehicles. **Civil aviation:** 11.8 bil pass.-mi; 25 airports. **Chief ports:** Jiddah, Ad Dammam.

Communications: TV sets: 252 per 1,000 pop. **Radios:** 309 per 1,000 pop. **Telephones:** 5,761,600. **Daily newspaper circ.:** 59 per 1,000 pop.

Health: Life expectancy: 66.7 male; 70.2 female. **Births** (per 1,000 pop.): 37.2. **Deaths** (per 1,000 pop.): 5.9. **Natural inc.:** 3.14%. **Infant mortality** (per 1,000 live births): 49.6.

Education: Literacy: 63%.

Major Intl. Organizations: UN (FAO, IBRD, ILO, IMF, IMO, WHO), AL, OPEC.

Embassy: 601 New Hampshire Ave. NW 20037; 342-3800.

Website: www.saudiembassy.net

Before Muhammad, Arabia was divided among numerous warring tribes and small kingdoms and was at times dominated by larger Arabian and non-Arabian kingdoms. It was united for the first time by Muhammad, in the early 7th century AD. His successors conquered the entire Near East and North Africa, bringing Islam and the Arabic language. But Arabia itself soon returned to its former status.

Nejd, in central Arabia, long an independent state and center of the Wahhabi sect, fell under Turkish rule in the 18th century. In 1913 Ibn Saud, founder of the Saudi dynasty, overthrew the Turks and captured the Turkish province of Hasa in E Arabia; he took the Hejaz region in W Arabia in 1925 and most of Asir, in SW Arabia, by 1926. The discovery of oil in the 1930s transformed the new country.

Ibn Saud reigned until his death, Nov. 1953. Subsequent kings have been sons of Ibn Saud. The king exercises authority together with a Council of Ministers. The Islamic religious code is the law of the land. Alcohol and public entertainments are restricted, and women have an inferior legal status. There is no constitution and no parliament, although a Consultative Council was established by the king in 1993.

Saudi Arabia has often allied itself with the U.S. and other Western nations, and billions of dollars of advanced arms have been purchased from Britain, France, and the U.S.; however, Western support for Israel has often strained relations. Saudi units fought against Israel in the 1948 and 1973 Arab-Israeli wars. Beginning with the 1967 Arab-Israeli war, Saudi Arabia provided large annual financial gifts to Egypt; aid was later extended to Syria, Jordan, and Palestinian groups, as well as to other Islamic countries.

King Faisal played a leading role in the 1973-74 Arab oil embargo against the U.S. and other nations. Crown Prince Khalid was proclaimed king on Mar. 25, 1975, after the assassination of Faisal. Fahd became king on June 13, 1982, following Khalid's death.

The Hejaz contains the holy cities of Islam—Medina, where the Mosque of the Prophet enshrines the tomb of Muhammad, and Mecca, his birthplace. More than 2 million Muslims make pilgrimage to Mecca annually. In 1987, Iranians making a pilgrimage to Mecca clashed with anti-Iranian pilgrims and Saudi police; more than 400 were killed. Some 1,426 Muslim pilgrims died July 2, 1990, in a stampede in a pedestrian tunnel leading to Mecca. Nearly 300 pilgrims were killed in a stampede in Mecca, May 26, 1994. More than 340 pilgrims died in a tent fire near Mecca, Apr. 15, 1997.

Following Iraq's attack on Kuwait, Aug. 2, 1990, Saudi Arabia accepted the Kuwait royal family and more than 400,000 Kuwaiti refugees. King Fahd invited Western and Arab troops to deploy on its soil in support of Saudi defense forces. During the Persian Gulf War, 28 U.S. soldiers were killed when an Iraqi missile hit their barracks in Dhahran, Feb. 25, 1991. The nation's northern Gulf coastline suffered severe pollution as a result of Iraqi sabotage of Kuwaiti oil fields. Islamic extremists were blamed for truck bombs that killed 7 (5 from the U.S.) at a military training center in Riyadh, Nov. 13, 1995, and 19 Americans at a base in Dhahran, June 25, 1996. U.S. officials repeatedly chided the Saudi government for failing to cooperate fully in the investigation.

The presence of 15 Saudis among the 19 hijackers who took part in the Sept. 11, 2001, attacks on the U.S.raised new tensions between the U.S. and Saudi governments. Policy differences over Iraq and the Israeli-Palestinian dispute were further irritants. With King Fahd ailing, his half-brother, Crown Prince Abdullah, has taken a leading role in recent years.

Senegal

Republic of Senegal

People: Population: 10,589,571. **Age distrib.** (%): <15: 44.1; 65+: 3.1. **Pop. density:** 143 per sq. mi. **Urban:** 47%. **Ethnic groups:** Wolof 43.3%, Serer 14.7%, Diola 3.7%. **Principal languages:** French (official), Wolof, Pulaar, Diola, Mandingo. **Chief religions:** Muslim 92%, indigenous beliefs 6%, Christian 2%.

Geography: Area: 74,100 sq. mi. **Location:** At W extreme of Africa. **Neighbors:** Mauritania on N, Mali on E, Guinea and Guinea-Bissau on S; surrounds Gambia on three sides. **Topography:** Low rolling plains cover most of Senegal, rising somewhat in the SE. Swamp and jungles are in SW. **Capital:** Dakar 2,160,000.

Government: Type: Republic. **Head of state:** Pres. Abdoulaye Wade; b May 29, 1926; in office: Apr. 1, 2000. **Head of gov.:** Prime Min. Mame Madior Boye; b 1940; in office: Mar. 3, 2001. **Local divisions:** 10 regions. **Defense (2001):** $61 mil. **Active troops:** 9,400–10,000.

Economy: Industries: Agricultural and fish processing, phosphate mining. **Chief crops:** Peanuts, millet, corn, sorghum, rice. **Minerals:** Phosphates, iron. **Arable land:** 12%. **Livestock:** (2001): cattle: 3.23 mil; chickens: 45.00 mil.; goats: 4.00 mil.; pigs: 280,000; sheep: 4.82 mil . **Fish catch** (1999): 507,040 metric tons. **Electricity prod.:** 1.32 bil. kWh. **Labor force:** 60% agric.

Finance: Monetary unit: CFA Franc (Sept. 2002: 671.78 = $1 U.S.). **GDP** (2000 est.): $16 bil. **Per capita GDP:** $1,600. **Imports** (2000): $1.3 bil.; partners (1999): France 30%, Nigeria 7%. **Exports** (2000): $959 mil.; partners (1999): France 17%, India 17%. **Tourism:** $166 mil. **Budget** (1996 est.): $885 mil. **Intl. reserves less gold** (end 2000): 294 mil. **Gold:** 29,000 oz t. **Consumer prices** (change in 2000): 0.7%.

Transport: Railroad: Length: 562 mi. **Motor vehicles:** 110,000 pass. cars, 50,000 comm. vehicles. **Civil aviation:** 164.6 mil pass.-mi; 7 airports. **Chief ports:** Dakar, Saint-Louis.

Communications: TV sets: 6.9 per 1,000 pop. **Radios:** 93 per 1,000 pop. **Telephones:** 628,000.

Health: Life expectancy: 61.3 male; 64.6 female. **Births** (per 1,000 pop.): 37. **Deaths** (per 1,000 pop.): 8.1. **Natural inc.:** 2.88%. **Infant mortality** (per 1,000 live births): 55.4.

Education: Compulsory: ages 7-13. **Literacy**: 33%.

Major Intl. Organizations: UN and all of its specialized agencies, AU.

Embassy: 2112 Wyoming Ave. NW 20008; 234-0540.

Portuguese settlers arrived in the 15th century, but French control grew from the 17th century. The last independent Muslim state was subdued in 1893. Dakar became the capital of French West Africa.

Independence as part, along with the Sudanese Rep., of the Mali Federation, came June 20, 1960. Senegal withdrew Aug. 20. French political and economic influence remained strong.

Senegal, Dec. 17, 1981, signed an agreement with The Gambia for confederation of the 2 countries, without loss of individual sovereignty, under the name of Senegambia. The confederation collapsed in 1989, although in 1991 the 2 nations signed a friendship and cooperation treaty.

Separatists in Casamance Province of S Senegal have clashed with government forces since 1982. Senegal sent troops in June 1998 to help the Guinea-Bissau government suppress an army uprising. Forty years of Socialist Party rule ended when Abdoulaye Wade, leader of the Senegalese Democratic Party, won a presidential runoff election Mar. 19, 2000. A Senegalese ferry capsized off the coast of The Gambia Sept. 26, 2002, killing almost 1,000 people.

Serbia and Montenegro (*formerly* Yugoslavia)

People: Population: 9,979,752. **Age distrib.** (%): <15: 20.2; 65+: 13.1. **Pop. density:** 293 per sq. mi. **Urban:** 52%. **Ethnic groups:** Serbian 63%, Albanian 14%, Montenegrin 6%. **Principal languages:** Serbo-Croatian (official) 95%, Albanian 5%. **Chief religions:** Orthodox 65%, Muslim 19%, Roman Catholic 4%.

Geography: Area: 34,100 sq. mi. **Location:** On the Balkan Peninsula in SE Europe. **Neighbors:** Croatia, Bosnia and Herzegovina on W; Hungary on N; Romania, Bulgaria on E; Albania, Macedonia on S. **Capital:** Belgrade. **Cities (urban aggr.):** Belgrade 1,687,000.

Government: Type: Republic. **Head of state:** Pres. Vojislav Kostunica; b Mar. 24, 1944; in office: Oct. 7, 2000. **Head of gov.:** Prime Min. Dragisa Pesic; b 1954; in office: July 24, 2001. **Local divisions:** 2 republics, 2 autonomous provinces. **Defense budget:** $1.3 bil. **Active troops:** 97,700.

Economy: Industries: Machinery, metallurgy, mining, consumer goods, electronics. **Chief crops:** Cereals, fruits, vegetables. **Minerals:** Oil, gas, coal, antimony, lead, nickel, gold, zinc, pyrite, copper, chrome. **Crude oil reserves** (2000): 48.57 bil bbls. **Livestock** (2000): cattle: 1.45 mil; chickens: 21.12 mil; goats: 241,000; pigs: 4.09 mil; sheep: 1.92 mil. **Electricity prod.:** 32.98 bil kWh. **Labor force:** N/A

Finance: Monetary unit: New Dinar (Sept. 2002: 62.28 = $1 U.S.). **GDP** (2000 est.): $24.2 bil. **Per capita GDP:** $2,300. **Imports** (1999): $3.3 bil.; partners (1998): Germany, Italy, Russia, Macedonia. **Exports** (2000 est.): $4.2 bil.; partners (1998): Bosnia and Herzegovina, Italy, Macedonia, Germany. **Tourism:** $17 mil. **Budget** NA.

Transport: Railroad: Length: 2,505 mi. **Motor vehicles:** 1.00 mil pass. cars, 331,000 comm. vehicles. **Civil aviation:** 93 mil pass.-mi; 4 airports. **Chief ports:** Bar, Novi Sad.

Communications: TV sets: 27 per 1,000 pop. **Radios:** 118 per 1,000 pop. **Telephones:** 4,441,700. **Daily newspaper circ.:** 256 per 1,000 pop.

Health: (Serbia only) Life expectancy: 70.7 male; 76.7 female. **Births** (per 1,000 pop.): 12.7. **Deaths** (per 1,000 pop.): 10.8. **Natural inc.:** 0.19%. **Infant mortality** (per 1,000 live births): 17.9.

Education: Free, compulsory; ages 7-15. **Literacy:** 98%.

Major Intl. Organizations: Currently suspended from UN and its agencies.

Embassy: 2410 California St. NW 20008; 462-6566.

Website: www.gov.yu

Serbia, which had since 1389 been a vassal principality of Turkey, was established as an independent kingdom by the Treaty of Berlin, 1878. Montenegro, independent since 1389, also obtained international recognition in 1878. After the Balkan wars, Serbia's boundaries were enlarged by the annexation of Old Serbia and Macedonia, 1913.

When the Austro-Hungarian empire collapsed after World War I, the Kingdom of Serbs, Croats, and Slovenes was formed from the former provinces of Croatia, Dalmatia, Bosnia, Herzegovina, Slovenia, Vojvodina, and the independent state of Montenegro. The name became Yugoslavia in 1929.

Nazi Germany invaded in 1941. Many Yugoslav partisan troops continued to operate. Among these were the Chetniks led by Draja Mikhailovich, who fought other partisans led by Josip Broz, known as Marshal Tito. Tito, backed by the USSR and Britain from 1943, was in control by the time the Germans had been driven from Yugoslavia in 1945. Mikhailovich was executed July 17, 1946, by the Tito regime.

A constituent assembly proclaimed Yugoslavia a republic Nov. 29, 1945. It became a federal republic Jan. 31, 1946, with Tito, a Communist, heading the government. Tito rejected Stalin's policy of dictating to all Communist nations, and he accepted economic and military aid from the West.

Pres. Tito died May 4, 1980. After his death, Yugoslavia was governed by a collective presidency, with a rotating succession. On Jan. 22, 1990, the Communist Party renounced its leading role in society.

Croatia and Slovenia formally declared independence June 25, 1991. In Croatia, fighting began between Croats and ethnic Serbs. Serbia sent arms and medical supplies to the Serb rebels in Croatia. Croatian forces clashed with Yugoslav army units and their Serb supporters.

The republics of Serbia and Montenegro proclaimed a new "Federal Republic of Yugoslavia" Apr. 17, 1992. Serbia, under Pres. Slobodan Milosevic, was the main arms supplier to ethnic Serb fighters in Bosnia and Herzegovina. The UN imposed sanctions May 30 on the newly reconstituted Yugoslavia as a means of ending the bloodshed in Bosnia.

A peace agreement initialed in Dayton, Ohio, Nov. 21, 1995, was signed in Paris, Dec. 14, by Milosevic and leaders of Bosnia and Croatia. In May 1996, a UN tribunal in the Netherlands began trying suspected war criminals from the former Yugoslavia.

The UN lifted sanctions against Yugoslavia Oct. 1, 1996, after elections were held in Bosnia. Mass protests erupted when Milosevic refused to accept opposition victories in local elections Nov. 17; non-Communist governments took office in Belgrade and other cities in Feb. 1997. Barred from running for a 3d term as Serbian president, Milosevic had himself inaugurated as president of Yugoslavia on July 23, 1997.

Defeated in a presidential election Sept. 24, 2000, by opposition leader Vojislav Kostunica, Milosevic initially refused to accept the result. A rising tide of mass demonstrations forced him to resign Oct. 6, and Kostunica was sworn in the next day. Charged with corruption and abuse of power, Milosevic surrendered to Serbian authorities Apr. 1, 2001. He was extradited June 28, 2001, to The Hague, where a UN tribunal had indicted him for war crimes. A pact to reconstitute Yugoslavia as a new union of Serbia and Montenegro was signed Mar. 14, 2002.

Kosovo: A nominally autonomous province in southern Serbia (4,203 sq. mi.), with a population of about 2,000,000, mostly Albanians. The capital is Pristina. Revoking provincial autonomy, Serbia began ruling Kosovo by force in 1989. Albanian secessionists proclaimed an independent Republic of Kosovo in July 1990. Guerrilla attacks by the Kosovo Liberation Army in 1997 brought a ferocious counteroffensive by Serbian authorities.

Fearful that the Serbs were employing "ethnic cleansing" tactics, as they had in Bosnia, the U.S. and its NATO allies sought to pressure the Yugoslav government. When Milosevic refused to comply, NATO launched an air war against Yugoslavia, Mar.-June 1999; the Serbs retaliated by terrorizing the Kosovars and forcing hundreds of thousands to flee, mostly to Albania and Macedonia. A 50,000-member multinational force (KFOR) entered Kosovo in June, and most of the Kosovar refugees had returned by Sept. 1.

Vojvodina: A nominally autonomous province in northern Serbia (8,304 sq. mi.), with a population of about 2,000,000, mostly Serbian. The capital is Novi Sad.

Seychelles

Republic of Seychelles

People: Population: 80,098. **Age distrib.** (%): <15: 28.3; 65+: 6.3. **Pop. density:** 455 per sq. mi. **Urban:** 63%. **Ethnic groups:** Seychellois (mixture of Asians, Africans, Europeans). **Principal languages:** English, French (both official), Creole. **Chief religions:** Roman Catholic 90%, Anglican 8%.

Geography: Area: 176 sq. mi. **Location:** In the Indian O. 700 miles NE of Madagascar. **Neighbors:** Nearest are Madagascar on SW, Somalia on NW. **Topography:** A group of 86 islands, about half of them composed of coral, the other half granite, the latter predominantly mountainous. **Capital:** Victoria: 30,000.

Government: Type: Republic. **Head of state and gov.:** Pres. France-Albert René, b. Nov. 16, 1935; in office: June 5, 1977. **Local divisions:** 23 districts. **Defense budget (2001):** $11 mil. **Active troops:** 450.

Economy: Industries: Fishing, tourism, coconuts and vanilla processing. **Chief crops:** Coconuts, cinnamon, vanilla. **Arable land:** 2%. **Livestock** (2001): cattle: 1,500; chickens: 560,000; goats: 5,250; pigs: 18,400. **Electricity prod.:** 0.16 bil. kWh. **Labor force: ind. 19%, services 71%, agri. 10%..**

Finance: Monetary unit: Rupee (Sept. 2002: 5.62 = $1 U.S.). **GDP** (2000 est.): $610 mil. **Per capita GDP:** $7,700. **Imports** (1999): $440 mil.; partners: South Africa, UK, China, Singapore, France, Italy. **Exports** (1999): $111 mil.; partners: France, UK, Netherlands, Italy, China, Germany, Japan. **Budget** (1998 est.): $262 mil. **Tourism** (1998): $111 mil. **Intl. reserves less gold** (end 2000): $34 mil. **Consumer prices** (change in 2000): 6.3%.

Transport: Motor vehicles: 6,620 pass. cars, 1,880 comm. vehicles. **Civil aviation:** 526.5 mil pass.-mi; 2 airports. **Chief port:** Victoria.

Communications: TV sets: 173.4 per 1,000 pop. **Radios:** 667 per 1,000 pop. **Telephones:** 65,500. **Daily newspaper circ.:** 41 per 1,000 pop.

Health: Life expectancy: 65.5 male; 76.6 female. **Births** (per 1,000 pop.): 17.3. **Deaths** (per 1,000 pop.): 6.6. **Natural inc.:** 1.07%. **Infant mortality** (per 1,000 live births): 16.9.

Education: Free, compulsory: ages 6-15. **Literacy**: 84%.

Major Intl. Organizations: UN (FAO, IBRD, ILO, IMF, IMO, WHO), the Commonwealth, AU.

Embassy: 800 2d Ave., Suite 400C, New York, NY 10017; 212-972-1785.

Website: www.seychelles-online.com.sc/governement.htm

The islands were occupied by France in 1768, and seized by Britain in 1794. Ruled as part of Mauritius from 1814, the Seychelles became a separate colony in 1903. The ruling party had opposed independence as impractical, but pressure from the AU and the UN became irresistible, and independence was declared June 29, 1976. The first president was ousted in a coup a year later by a socialist leader. A new çonstitution, approved June 1993, provided for a multiparty state.

Sierra Leone

Republic of Sierra Leone

People: Population: 5,614,743. **Age distrib.** (%): <15: 44.7; 65+: 3.1. **Pop. density:** 203 per sq. mi. **Urban:** 36%. **Ethnic groups:** Temne 30%, Mende 30%, other tribes 30%. **Principal languages:** English (official), Mende, Temne, Krio. **Chief religions:** Muslim 60%, indigenous beliefs 30%, Christian 10%.

Geography: Area: 27,700 sq. mi. **Location:** On W coast of W Africa. **Neighbors:** Guinea on N and E, Liberia on S. **Topography:** The heavily-indented, 210-mi. coastline has mangrove swamps. Behind are wooded hills, rising to a plateau and mountains in the E. **Capital:** Freetown: 837,000.

Government: Type: Republic. **Head of state and gov.:** Ahmad Tejan Kabbah; b Feb. 16, 1932; in office: Mar. 10, 1998. **Local divisions:** 3 provinces, 1 area. **Defense budget (2001):** $10 mil. **Active troops:** 6,000+.

Economy: Industries: Mining, light manufacturing. **Chief crops:** Cocoa, coffee, palm kernels, rice. **Minerals:** Diamonds, titanium, bauxite. **Arable land:** 7%. **Livestock** (2001): cattle: 420,000; chickens: 6.00 mil.; goats: 200,000; pigs: 52,000; sheep: 365,000 . **Fish catch** (1999): 68,739 metric tons. **Electricity prod.:** 0.25 bil. kWh.

Finance: Monetary unit: Leone (Sept. 2002: 2,045.00 = $1 U.S.). **GDP** (2000 est.): $2.7 bil. **Per capita GDP:** $510. **Imports** (2000 est.): $145 mil.; partners (1999): UK 34%, U.S. 8%. **Exports** (2000 est.): $65 mil.; partners (1999): Belgium 38%, U.S. 6%. **Budget** (2000 est.): $351 mil. **Intl. reserves less gold** (end 2000): $39 mil. **Consumer prices** (change in 2000): –0.8%.

Transport: Railroad: Length: 52 mi. **Motor vehicles:** 20,860 pass. cars, 21,074 comm. vehicles. **Civil aviation:** 14.9 mil pass.-mi; 1 airport. **Chief ports:** Freetown, Bonthe.

Communications: Radios: 72 per 1,000 pop. **Telephones:** 49,600.

Health: Life expectancy: 43 male; 49 female. **Births** (per 1,000 pop.): 44.6. **Deaths** (per 1,000 pop.): 18.8. **Natural inc.:** 2.58%. **Infant mortality** (per 1,000 live births): 144.4.

Education: Literacy: 31%.

Major Intl. Organizations: UN (FAO, IBRD, ILO, IMF, IMO, WHO, WTrO), the Commonwealth, AU.

Embassy: 1701 19th St. NW 20009; 939-9261.

Website: www.Sierra-Leone.org

Freetown was founded in 1787 by the British government as a haven for freed slaves. Their descendants, known as Creoles, number more than 60,000.

Successive steps toward independence followed the 1951 constitution. Ten years later, full independence arrived Apr. 27, 1961. Sierra Leone declared itself a republic Apr. 19, 1971. A one-party state approved by referendum in 1978 brought political stability, but mismanagement and corruption plagued the economy.

Mutinous soldiers ousted Pres. Joseph Momoh Apr. 30, 1992. Another coup, Jan. 16, 1996, paved the way for multiparty elections and a return to civilian rule. A peace accord, signed Nov. 30 with the Revolutionary United Front (RUF), brought a temporary halt to a civil war that had claimed over 10,000 lives in 5 years.

A coup on May 25, 1997, was met with widespread international opposition. Armed intervention by Nigeria restored Pres. Ahmad Tejan Kabbah to power on Mar. 10, 1998, but RUF rebels mounted a guerrilla counteroffensive, reportedly killing thousands of civilians and mutilating thousands more. The Kabbah government signed a power-sharing agreement with the RUF on July 7, 1999. The accord collapsed in early May 2000, as RUF guerrillas took more than 500 UN peacekeepers hostage. Rebel leader Foday Sankoh was captured in Freetown May 17. The hostages were freed by the end of May, and 233 more UN personnel behind rebel lines were rescued July 15. A UN-sponsored disarmament program in 2001 reduced the level of violence. The UN authorized establishment of a war crimes tribunal Jan. 3, 2002. Government and rebel leaders declared an official end to the war Jan. 18. Kabbah won the May 14 presidential election.

Singapore

Republic of Singapore

People: Population: 4,452,732. **Age distrib.** (%): <15: 17.9; 65+: 7.0. **Pop. density:** 18,482 per sq. mi. **Urban:** 100%. **Ethnic groups:** Chinese 76.4%, Malay 14.9%, Indian 6.4%. **Principal languages:** Chinese, Malay, Tamil, English (all official). **Chief religions:** Buddhist, Taoist, Muslim, Christian, Hindu.

Geography: Area: 241 sq. mi. **Location:** Off tip of Malayan Peninsula in SE Asia. **Neighbors:** Nearest are Malaysia on N, Indonesia on S. **Topography:** Singapore is a flat, formerly swampy island. The nation includes 40 nearby islets. **Capital:** Singapore 4,108,000.

Government: Type: Republic. **Head of state:** Pres. S. R. Nathan; b July 3, 1924; in office: Sept. 1, 1999. **Head of gov.:**

Prime Min. Goh Chok Tong; b May 20, 1941; in office: Nov. 28, 1990. **Defense budget (2001):** $4.43 bil. **Active troops:** 60,500.

Economy: Industries: Electronics, chemicals, financial services, oil drilling equip., oil refining. **Chief crops:** Copra, rubber, fruit, vegetables. **Arable land:** 2%. **Livestock** (2001): cattle: 200; chickens: 2.00 mil.; goats: 300; pigs: 190,000. **Fish catch** (1999): 13,338 metric tons. **Electricity prod.:** 27.90 bil. kWh. **Labor force:** business, and other services 35%, manufacturing 21%, construction 13%, transportation and communication 9%.

Finance: Monetary unit: Dollar (Sept. 2002: 1.78 = $1 U.S.). **GDP** (2000 est.): $109.8 bil. **Per capita GDP:** $26,500. **Imports** (2000): $127 bil.; partners (1999): U.S. 17%, Japan 17%,. **Exports** (2000): $137 bil.; partners (1999): U.S. 19%, Malaysia 17%. **Tourism:** $5.79 bil. **Budget** (FY99/00 est.): $17.1 bil. **International reserves** (end 2000): $61.50 bil. **Consumer prices** (change in 2000): 1.4%.

Transport: Railroad: Length: 52 mi. **Motor vehicles** (1997): 379,497 pass. cars, 140,827 comm. vehicles. **Civil aviation:** 34.5 bil pass.-mi; 1 airport. **Chief port:** Singapore.

Communications: TV sets: 223 per 1,000 pop. **Radios:** 260 per 1,000 pop. **Telephones:** 4,939,100. **Daily newspaper circ.:** 360 per 1,000 pop.

Health: Life expectancy: 77.3 male; 83.5 female. **Births** (per 1,000 pop.): 12.8. **Deaths** (per 1,000 pop.): 4.3. **Natural inc.:** 0.85%. **Infant mortality** (per 1,000 live births): 3.6.

Education: Literacy: 91%.

Major Intl. Organizations: UN (IBRD, ILO, IMF, IMO, WHO, WTrO), the Commonwealth, APEC, ASEAN.

Embassy: 3501 International Pl. NW 20008; 537-3100.

Website: www.gov.sg

Founded in 1819 by Sir Thomas Stamford Raffles, Singapore was a British colony until 1959, when it became autonomous within the Commonwealth. On Sept. 16, 1963, it joined with Malaya, Sarawak, and Sabah to form the Federation of Malaysia. Tensions between Malayans, dominant in the federation, and ethnic Chinese, dominant in Singapore, led to an accord under which Singapore became a separate nation, Aug. 9, 1965.

Singapore is one of the world's largest ports. Standards in health, education, and housing are generally high. International banking has grown rapidly in recent years. The government, dominated by a single party, has taken strong actions to suppress dissent.

In Dec. 2001, the government thwarted an alleged plot to blow up the U.S. Embassy; in Sept. 2002, authorities reported arrests of 21 militants identified as members of Jemaah Islamiyah, a radical Muslim group active in Southeast Asia.

Slovakia

Slovak Republic

People: Population: 5,422,366. **Age distrib.** (%): <15: 18.9; 65+: 11.5. **Pop. density:** 288 per sq. mi. **Urban:** 57%. **Ethnic groups:** Slovak 85.7%, Hungarian 10.7%. **Principal languages:** Slovak (official), Hungarian. **Chief religions:** Roman Catholic 60%, Protestant 8%.

Geography: Area: 18,800 sq. mi. **Location:** In E central Europe. **Neighbors:** Poland on N, Hungary on S, Austria and Czech Rep. on W, Ukraine on E. **Topography:** Mountains (Carpathians) in N, fertile Danube plane in S. **Capital:** Bratislava. **Cities (urban aggr.):** Bratislava 464,000; (1997 est.): Kosice 242,000.

Government: Type: Republic. **Head of state:** Rudolf Schuster; b Jan. 4, 1934; in office: June 15, 1999. **Head of gov.:** Prime Min. Mikulás Dzurinda; b Feb. 4, 1955; in office: Oct. 30, 1998. **Local divisions:** 8 departments. **Defense budget (2001):** $369 mil. **Active troops:** 33,000.

Economy: Industries: Metal and metal products, food and beverages; electricity, gas. **Chief crops:** Grains, potatoes, sugar beets, hops, fruit. **Minerals:** Coal, lignite, iron, copper. **Crude oil reserves** (2000): 9.0 mil bbls. **Arable land:** 31%. **Livestock** (2001): cattle: 646,100; chickens: 13.58 mil.; goats: 51,419; pigs: 1.49 mil; sheep: 347,983. **Electricity prod.:** 27.53 bil. kWh. **Labor force:** ind. 29.3%, agri. 8.9%, construction 8%, transport and communication 8.2%, services 45.6%.

Finance: Monetary unit: Koruna (Sept. 2002: 43.00 = $1 U.S.). **GDP** (2000 est.): $55.3 bil. **Per capita GDP:** $10,200. **Imports** (2000 est.): $12.8 bil.; partners (1999): EU 51.4%, Czech Republic 16.6%,. **Exports** (2000 est.): $12 bil.; partners (1999): EU 59.7%,Czech Republic 18.1%. **Tourism:** $461 mil. **Budget** (1999): $5.6 bil. **Intl. reserves less gold** (end 2000): $3.09 bil. **Gold:** 1.29 mil oz t. **Consumer prices** (change in 2000): 12.0%.

Transport: Railroad: Length: 2,277 mi. **Motor vehicles:** 994,000 pass. cars, 94,000 comm. vehicles. **Civil aviation:** 63.8 mil pass.-mi; 2 airports. **Chief ports:** Bratislava, Komarno.

Communications: TV sets: 216 per 1,000 pop. **Telephones:** 3,703,600. **Daily newspaper circ.:** 256 per 1,000 pop.

Health: Life expectancy: 70.2 male; 78.4 female. **Births** (per 1,000 pop.): 10.1. **Deaths** (per 1,000 pop.): 9.2. **Natural inc.:** 0.09%. **Infant mortality** (per 1,000 live births): 8.8.

Education: Compulsory: ages 6-14. **Literacy** (1994): 100%.

Major Intl. Organizations: UN (FAO, IBRD, ILO, IMF, IMO, WHO, WTrO), OSCE.

Embassy: 2201 Wisconsin Ave. NW 20007; 965-5161.

Website: www.government.gov.sk/english/

Slovakia was originally settled by Illyrian, Celtic, and Germanic tribes and was incorporated into Great Moravia in the 9th century. It became part of Hungary in the 11th century. Overrun by Czech Hussites in the 15th century, it was restored to Hungarian rule in 1526. The Slovaks disassociated themselves from Hungary after World War I and joined the Czechs of Bohemia to form the Republic of Czechoslovakia, Oct. 28, 1918.

Germany invaded Czechoslovakia, 1939, and declared Slovakia independent. Slovakia rejoined Czechoslovakia in 1945.

Czechoslovakia split into 2 separate states—the Czech Republic and Slovakia—on Jan. 1, 1993. Slovakia, with its less developed economy, applied to join the European Union in 1995. A prolonged parliamentary standoff left the country without a president for much of 1998.

Prime Min. Vladimir Meciar, a nationalist, suffered a setback in legislative elections Sept. 25-26, 1998, and was defeated in a presidential runoff vote by Rudolf Schuster, May 29, 1999. A center-right coalition governed Slovakia after parliamentary elections Sept. 20-21, 2002.

Slovenia

Republic of Slovenia

People: Population: 1,932,917. **Age distrib.** (%): <15: 16.1; 65+: 14.3. **Pop. density:** 248 per sq. mi. **Urban:** 50%. **Ethnic groups:** Slovene 91%, Croat 3%. **Principal languages:** Slovenian (official), Serbo-Croatian. **Chief religion:** Roman Catholic 70.8%.

Geography: Area: 7,800 sq. mi. **Location:** In SE Europe. **Neighbors:** Italy on W, Austria on N, Hungary on NE, Croatia on SE, S. **Topography:** Mostly hilly; 42% of the land is forested. **Capital:** Ljubljana: 250,000.

Government: Type: Republic. **Head of state:** Pres. Milan Kucan; b Jan. 14, 1941; in office: Apr. 1990. **Head of gov.:** Prime Min. Janez Drnovsek; b May 17, 1950; in office: Nov. 17, 2000. **Local divisions:** 136 municipalities, 11 urban municipalities. **Defense budget** (2001): $269 mil. **Active troops:** 7,600.

Economy: Industries: Metallurgy and metal products, electronics, trucks. **Chief crops:** Potatoes, hops, wheat. **Arable land:** 12%. **Livestock** (2001): cattle: 493,670; chickens: 7.15 mil.; goats: 22,041; pigs: 603,594; sheep: 96,227. **Electricity prod.:** 12.82 bil. kWh.

Finance: Monetary unit: Tolar (Sept. 2002: 233.44 = $1 U.S.). **GDP** (2000 est.): $22.9 bil. **Per capita GDP:** $12,000. **Imports** (2000): $9.9 bil.; partners (1999): Germany 21%, Italy 17%. **Exports** (2000): $8.9 bil.; partners (1999): Germany 31%, Italy 14%. **Tourism:** $1.01 bil. **Budget** (1997 est.): $8.32 bil. **Intl. reserves less gold** (end 2000): $2.45 bil. **Gold:** 3,000 oz t. **Consumer prices** (change in 2000): 10.8%.

Transport: Railroad: Length: 746 mi. **Motor vehicles:** 657,000 pass. cars, 37,000 comm. vehicles. **Civil aviation:** 233.0 mil pass.-mi; 1 airport. **Chief ports:** Izola, Koper, Piran.

Communications: TV sets: 352 per 1,000 pop. **Radios:** 317 per 1,000 pop. **Telephones:** 2,315,400. **Daily newspaper circ.:** 199 per 1,000 pop.

Health: Life expectancy: 71.4 male; 79.4 female. **Births** (per 1,000 pop.): 9.3. **Deaths** (per 1,000 pop.): 10.1. **Natural inc.:** -0.08%. **Infant mortality** (per 1,000 live births): 4.5.

Education: Free, compulsory: ages 6-15. **Literacy** (1993): 99%.

Major Intl. Organizations: UN (FAO, IBRD, ILO, IMF, IMO, WHO, WTrO), OSCE.

Embassy: 1525 New Hampshire Ave. NW 20036; 667-5363.

Website: www.sigov.si

The Slovenes settled in their current territory during the period from the 6th to the 8th century. They fell under German domination as early as the 9th century. Modern Slovenian political history began after 1848 when the Slovenes, who were divided among several Austrian provinces, began their struggle for political and national unification. In 1918 a majority of Slovenes became part of the Kingdom of Serbs, Croats, and Slovenes, later renamed Yugoslavia.

Slovenia declared independence June 25, 1991, and joined the UN May 22, 1992. Linked by trade with the European Union, Slovenia applied for full membership June 10, 1996.

Solomon Islands

People: Population: 494,786. **Age distrib.** (%): <15: 43.8; 65+: 3.1. **Pop. density:** 47 per sq. mi. **Urban:** 19%. **Ethnic groups:** Melanesian 93%, Polynesian 4%. **Principal languages:** English (official); Melanesian, Polynesian languages. **Chief religions:** Anglican 34%, Roman Catholic 19%, Baptist 17%, other Christian 26%.

Geography: Area: 10,600 sq. mi. **Location:** Melanesian Archipelago in the W Pacific O. **Neighbors:** Nearest is Papua New Guinea to W. **Topography:** 10 large volcanic and rugged islands and 4 groups of smaller ones. **Capital:** Honiara: 78,000.

Government: Type: Parliamentary democracy within the Commonwealth of Nations. **Head of state:** Queen Elizabeth II, represented by Gov.-Gen. Sir John Lapli; b 1955; in office: July 7, 1999. **Head of gov.:** Prime Min. Sir Allan Kemakeza; b 1951; in office: Dec. 17, 2001. **Local divisions:** 9 provinces and Honiara.

Economy: Industries: Tuna, mining, timber. **Chief crops:** Coconuts, rice, cocoa, beans. **Minerals:** Gold, bauxite. **Other resources:** Forests. **Arable land:** 1%. **Livestock** (2001): cattle: 12,500; chickens: 200,000; pigs: 67,000. **Fish catch** (1999): 53,442 metric tons. **Electricity prod.:** 0.03 bil. kWh.

Finance: Monetary unit: Dollar (Sept. 2002: 7.25 = $1 U.S.). **GDP** (2000 est.): $900 mil. **Per capita GDP:** $2,000. **Imports** (1999 est.): $152 mil.; partners (1999): Australia 38.5%, Singapore 15%. **Exports** (1999 est.): $165 mil.; partners (1999): Japan 35.5%, other Asian countries 47.3%. **Tourism** (1998): $13 mil. **Budget** (1997 est.): $168 mil. **Intl. reserves less gold** (end 2000): $24 mil. **Consumer prices:** (change in 1999): 8.3%.

Transport: Civil aviation: 46.0 mil pass.-mi; 21 airports. **Chief port:** Honiara.

Communications: TV sets: 16 per 1,000 pop. **Radios:** 96 per 1,000 pop. **Telephones:** 8,400.

Health: Life expectancy: 69.4 male; 74.4 female. **Births** (per 1,000 pop.): 33.3. **Deaths** (per 1,000 pop.): 4.2. **Natural inc.:** 2.91%. **Infant mortality** (per 1,000 live births): 23.7.

Education: Literacy (1994): 54%.

Major Intl. Organizations: UN (FAO, IBRD, ILO, IMF, IMO, WHO, WTrO), the Commonwealth.

Embassy: 800 Second Ave., Suite 400L, New York, NY 10017; (212) 599-6193.

Website: www.commerce.gov.sb

The Solomon Islands were sighted in 1568 by an expedition from Peru. Britain established a protectorate in the 1890s over most of the group, inhabited by Melanesians.

The islands saw major World War II battles. Self-government came Jan. 2, 1976, and independence was formally attained July 7, 1978.

A coup attempt June 5, 2000, sparked factional fighting in Honiara.

Somalia

People: Population: 7,753,310. **Age distrib.** (%): <15: 44.5; 65+: 2.8. **Pop. density:** 32 per sq. mi. **Urban:** 27%. **Ethnic groups:** Somali 85%, Bantu, Arab. **Principal languages:** Somali (official), Arabic, Italian, English. **Chief religion:** Sunni Muslim.

Geography: Area: 242,200 sq. mi. **Location:** Occupies the eastern horn of Africa. **Neighbors:** Djibouti, Ethiopia, Kenya on W. **Topography:** The coastline extends for 1,700 mi. Hills cover the N; the center and S are flat. **Capital:** Mogadishu 1,212,000.

Government: Type: In transition. **Head of state:** Abdiqassim Salad Hassan; b 1942; in office: Aug. 27, 2000. **Head of gov.:** Prime Min. Hassan Abshir Farah; b June 20, 1945; in office: Nov. 12, 2001. Local divisions: 18 regions. **Defense budget (2001):** $15 mil. **Active troops:** Nil.

Economy: Chief crops: Sugar, textiles, wireless comm. **Minerals:** Uranium, iron, tin, gypsum, bauxite. **Arable land:** 2%. **Livestock** (2001): cattle: 5.20 mil; chickens: 3.30 mil.; goats: 12.50 mil.; pigs: 4,000; sheep: 13.20 mil. **Fish catch** (1999): 15,700 metric tons. **Electricity prod.:** 0.25 bil. kWh. **Labor force:** 71% nomadic agric.; 29% industry & services.

Finance: Monetary unit: Shilling (Sept. 2002: 2,620.00 = $1 U.S.).**GDP** (2000 est.): $4.3 bil. **Per capita GDP:** $600. **Imports** (1999 est.): $314 mil.; partners (1999): Djibouti 24%, Kenya 14%. **Exports** (1999 est.): $186 mil.; partners (1999): Saudi Arabia 53%, Yemen 19%. **Budget** NA.

Transport: Motor vehicles: 10,000 pass. cars, 10,000 comm. vehicles. **Civil aviation:** 86.9 mil pass.-mi; 1 airport. **Chief ports:** Mogadishu, Berbera.

Communications: TV sets: 18 per 1,000 pop. **Radios:** 45 per 1,000 pop. **Telephones:** 15,000 main lines.

Health: Life expectancy: 45.3 male; 48.6 female. **Births** (per 1,000 pop.): 46.8. **Deaths** (per 1,000 pop.): 18. **Natural inc.:** 2.88%. **Infant mortality** (per 1,000 live births): 122.2.

Education: Free, compulsory: ages 6-14. **Literacy** (1990): 24%.

Major Intl. Organizations: UN (FAO, IBRD, ILO, IMF, IMO, WHO), AL, AU.

British Somaliland (present-day N Somalia) was formed in the 19th century, as was Italian Somaliland (now central and S Somalia). Italy lost its African colonies in World War II. In 1949, the UN approved eventual independence for the former Italian colony (designated the UN Trust Territory of Somalia) after a 10-year period under Italian administration.

British Somaliland gained independence, June 26, 1960, and by prearrangement, merged July 1 with the trust territory of Somalia to create the independent Somali Republic (Somalia).

On Oct. 16, 1969, Pres. Abdi Rashid Ali Shirmarke was assassinated. On Oct. 21, a military group led by Maj. Gen. Muhammad Siad Barre seized power. In 1970, Barre declared the country a socialist state—the Somali Democratic Republic.

Somalia has laid claim to Ogaden, the huge eastern region of Ethiopia, peopled mostly by Somalis. Ethiopia battled Somali rebels in 1977. Some 11,000 Cuban troops with Soviet arms defeated Somali army troops and ethnic Somali rebels in Ethiopia, 1978. As many as 1.5 million refugees entered Somalia. Guerrilla fighting in Ogaden continued until 1988, when a peace agreement was reached with Ethiopia.

The civil war intensified again and Barre was forced to flee the capital, Jan. 1991. Fighting between rival factions caused 40,000 casualties in 1991 and 1992, and by mid-1992 the civil war, drought, and banditry combined to produce a famine that threatened some 1.5 million people with starvation.

In Dec. 1992 the UN accepted a U.S. offer of troops to safeguard food delivery to the starving. The UN took control of the multinational relief effort from the U.S. May 4, 1993. While the operation helped alleviate the famine, efforts to reestablish order foundered, and there were significant U.S. and other casualties; a failed mission Oct. 3-4 left 18 U.S. troops and more than 500 Somalis dead. The U.S. withdrew its peacekeeping forces Mar. 25, 1994.

When the last UN troops pulled out Mar. 3, 1995, Mogadishu had no functioning central government, and armed factions controlled different regions. By 1999 a joint police force was operating in the capital, but much of the country, especially in S Somalia, faced continued violence and food shortages. U.S. officials believe Somalia has been a base of operations for Al Qaeda terrorists.

South Africa

Republic of South Africa

People: Population: 43,647,658. **Age distrib.** (%): <15: 32.0; 65+: 4.9. **Pop. density:** 93 per sq. mi. **Urban:** 50%. **Ethnic groups:** Black 75.2%, white 13.6%, colored 8.6%. **Principal languages:** 11 official languages incl. Afrikaans, English, Ndebele, Pedi, Sotho. **Chief religions:** Christian 68%; traditional, animistic 28.5%.

Geography: Area: 471,400 sq. mi. **Location:** At the southern extreme of Africa. **Neighbors:** Namibia, Botswana, Zimbabwe on N; Mozambique, Swaziland on E; surrounds Lesotho. **Topography:** The large interior plateau reaches close to the country's 2,700-mi. coastline. There are few major rivers or lakes; rainfall is sparse in W, more plentiful in E. **Capitals:** Cape Town (legislative), Pretoria (administrative), and Bloemfontein (judicial). **Cities (urban aggr.):** Cape Town 2,993,000; Durban 2,391,000; Johannesburg 2,950,000; Pretoria 1,590,000; Bloemfontein 364,000.

Government: Type: Republic. **Head of state and gov.:** Pres. Thabo Mvuyelwa Mbeki; b: June 18, 1942; in office: June 16 1999. **Local divisions:** 9 provinces. **Defense budget (2001):** $2.0 bil. **Active troops:** 61,500.

Economy: Industries: Mining, auto assembly, metalworking, machinery, textile. **Chief crops:** Corn, wheat, vegetables, sugar, fruit. **Minerals:** Platinum, chromium, antimony, coal, iron, manganese, nickel, phosphates, tin, uranium, gem diamonds, copper, vanadium; world's largest producer of gold (approx. 30% of total world prod.) **Crude oil reserves** (2000): 29.36 mil bbls. **Other resources:** Wool, dairy products. **Arable land:** 10%. **Livestock** (2001): cattle: 13.74 mil; chickens: 119.00 mil.; goats: 6.55 mil.; pigs: 1.54 mil; sheep: 28.80 mil. **Fish catch** (1999): 513,586 metric tons. **Electricity prod.:** 194.38 bil. kWh. **Labor force:** agri. 30%, ind. 25%, services 45%.

Finance: Monetary unit: Rand (Sept. 2002: 10.57 = $1 U.S.). **GDP** (2000 est.): $369 bil. **Per capita GDP:** $8,500. **Imports** (2000 est.): $27.6 bil.; partners: Germany, U.S., UK, Japan. **Exports** (2000 est.): $30.8 bil.; partners: UK, Italy, Japan, U.S., Germany. **Tourism:** $2.74 bil. **Budget** (FY01/02): $34.4 bil. **Intl. reserves less gold** (end 2000): $4.67 bil. **Gold:** 5.91 mil oz t. **Consumer prices** (change in 2000): 5.3%.

Transport: Railroad: Length: 13,418 mi. **Motor vehicles** (1997): 4.35 mil pass. cars, 1.65 mil comm. vehicles. **Civil aviation:** 10.5 bil pass.-mi; 24 airports. **Chief ports:** Durban, Cape Town, East London, Port Elizabeth.

Communications: TV sets: 128 per 1,000 pop. **Radios:** 322 per 1,000 pop. **Telephones:** 14,166,000. **Daily newspaper circ.:** 31 per 1,000 pop.

Health: Life expectancy: 45.2 male; 45.7 female. **Births** (per 1,000 pop.): 20.6. **Deaths** (per 1,000 pop.): 18.9. **Natural inc.:** 0.18%. **Infant mortality** (per 1,000 live births): 61.8.

Education: Compulsory: ages 7-16. **Literacy:** 82%.

Major Intl. Organizations: UN (FAO, IBRD, ILO, IMF, IMO, WHO, WTrO), the Commonwealth, AU.

Embassy: 3051 Massachusetts Ave. NW 20008; 232-4400.

Website: www.gov.za

Bushmen and Hottentots were the original inhabitants. Bantus, including Zulu, Xhosa, Swazi, and Sotho, had occupied the area from NE to S South Africa before the 17th century.

The Cape of Good Hope area was settled by Dutch, beginning in the 17th century. Britain seized the Cape in 1806. Many Dutch trekked north and founded 2 republics, Transvaal and Orange Free State. Diamonds were discovered, 1867, and gold, 1886. The Dutch (Boers) resented encroachments by the British and others; the Anglo-Boer War followed, 1899-1902. Britain won and, effective May 31, 1910, created the Union of South Africa, incorporating 2 British colonies (Cape and Natal) with Transvaal and Orange Free State. After a referendum, the Union became the Republic of South Africa, May 31, 1961, and withdrew from the Commonwealth.

With the election victory of Daniel Malan's National Party in 1948, the policy of separate development of the races, or apartheid, already existing unofficially, became official. Under apartheid, blacks were severely restricted to certain occupations, and paid far lower wages than whites for similar work. Only whites could vote or run for public office. Persons of Asian Indian ancestry and those of mixed race (Coloureds) had limited political rights. In 1959 the government passed acts providing for the eventual creation of several Bantu nations, or Bantustans.

Protests against apartheid were brutally suppressed. At Sharpeville on Mar. 21, 1960, 69 black protesters were killed by government troops. At least 600 persons, mostly Bantus, were killed in 1976 riots protesting apartheid. In 1981, South Africa launched military operations in Angola and Mozambique to combat guerrilla groups.

A new constitution was approved by referendum, Nov. 1983, extending the parliamentary franchise to the Coloured and Asian minorities. Laws banning interracial sex and marriage were repealed in 1985.

In 1986, Nobel Peace Prize winner Bishop Desmond Tutu called for Western nations to apply sanctions against South Africa to force an end to apartheid. Pres. P. W. Botha announced in Apr. the end to the nation's system of racial pass laws and offered blacks an advisory role in government. On May 19, South Africa attacked 3 neighboring countries—Zimbabwe, Botswana, Zambia—to strike at guerrilla strongholds of the black nationalist African National Congress (ANC). A nationwide state of emergency was declared June 12, giving almost unlimited power to the security forces.

Some 2 million South African black workers staged a massive strike, June 6-8, 1988. Pres. Botha, head of the government since 1978, resigned Aug. 14, 1989, and was replaced by F. W. de Klerk. In 1990 the government lifted its ban on the ANC. Black nationalist leader Nelson Mandela was freed Feb. 11 after more than 27 years in prison. In Feb. 1991, Pres. de Klerk announced plans to end all apartheid laws.

In 1993 negotiators agreed on basic principles for a new democratic constitution. South Africa's partially self-governing black territories, or "homelands," were dissolved and incorporated into a national system of 9 provinces. In elections Apr. 26-29, 1994, the ANC won 62.7% of the vote, making Mandela president. The National Party won 20.4%. The Inkatha Freedom Party won 10.5% and control of the legislature in a mainly Zulu province. By then, fighting between the ANC and Inkatha (aided, during the apartheid era, by South African defense forces) had killed more than 14,000 people in the Zulu region since the mid-1980s.

In 1995, Mandela appointed a truth commission, led by Desmond Tutu, to document human rights abuses under apartheid. A post-apartheid constitution, modified to meet the objections of the Constitutional Court, became law Dec. 10, 1996, with provisions to take effect over a 3-year period.

The ANC won a landslide victory in elections held June 2, 1999. ANC leader Thabo Mbeki, Mandela's deputy president, thus became South Africa's 2d popularly elected president.

According to UN estimates, more than 4 million South Africans, including 20% of all adults, have HIV/AIDS. South Africa was the site, in July 2000, of an international AIDS conference. Pharmaceutical firms, Apr. 19, 2001, dropped their challenge to a 1997 law that allowed cheaper, generic versions of patented AIDS drugs to be imported. Johannesburg hosted the UN World Summit on Sustainable Development, Aug. 26-Sept. 4, 2002.

Spain

Kingdom of Spain

People: Population: 40,077,100. **Age distrib.** (%): <15: 14.6; 65+: 17.2. **Pop. density:** 208 per sq. mi. **Urban:** 77%. **Ethnic groups:** Mix of Mediterranean and Nordic types. **Principal languages:** Castilian Spanish (official), Catalan, Galician, Basque. **Chief religion:** Roman Catholic 99%.

Geography: Area: 192,800 sq. mi. **Location:** In SW Europe. **Neighbors:** Portugal on W, France on N. **Topography:** The interior is a high, arid plateau broken by mountain ranges and river valleys. The NW is heavily watered, the S has lowlands and a Mediterranean climate. **Capital:** Madrid. **Cities (urban agg.):** Madrid 3,969,000, (1998 city proper: 2,881,506); Barcelona 2,729,000; Valencia 754,000.

Government: Type: Constitutional monarchy. **Head of state:** King Juan Carlos I de Borbon y Borbon; b Jan. 5, 1938; in office: Nov. 22, 1975. **Head of gov.:** Prime Min. José María Aznar; b Feb. 25, 1953; in office: May 5, 1996. **Local divisions:** 17 automonous communities. **Defense budget (2001):** $6.9 bil. **Active troops:** 143,450.

Economy: Industries: Textiles and apparel, food and beverages, metals and metal products, chemicals, shipbuilding. **Chief crops:** Grains, olives, grapes, citrus, vegetables. **Minerals:** Lignite, uranium, iron, mercury, pyrites, fluorspar, gypsum, zinc, lead, coal. **Crude oil reserves** (2000): 14 mil bbls. **Other resources:** Forests. **Arable land:** 30%. **Livestock** (2001): cattle: 6.16 mil; chickens: 128.00 mil.; goats: 2.83 mil.; pigs: 23.35 mil; sheep: 24.40 mil. **Fish catch** (1999): 1.34 mil metric tons. **Electricity prod.:** 211.64 bil. kWh. **Labor force:** services 64%, manufacturing mining and construction 28%, agri. 8%.

Finance: Monetary unit: Euro (Sept. 2002: 1.03 = $1 U.S.) **GDP** (2000 est.): $720.8 bil. **Per capita GDP:** $18,000. **Imports** (2000 est.): $153.9 bil.; partners (1999): EU 68%, U.S. 8%,. **Exports** (2000 est.): $120.5 bil.; partners (2000): EU 71%,Latin America 6%, U.S. 5%. **Tourism:** $32.91 bil. **Budget** (2000 est.): $109 bil. **Intl. reserves less gold** (end 2000): $23.78 bil. **Gold:** 16.83 mil oz t. **Consumer prices** (change in 2000): 3.4%.

Transport: Railroad: Length: 8,252 mi. **Motor vehicles** (1997): 15.30 mil pass. cars, 3.36 mil comm. vehicles. **Civil aviation:** 23.1 bil pass.-mi; 25 airports. **Chief ports:** Barcelona, Bilbao, Valencia, Cartagena.

Communications: TV sets: 500 per 1,000 pop. **Radios:** 332 per 1,000 pop. **Telephones:** 43,921,200. **Daily newspaper circ.:** 99 per 1,000 pop.

Health: Life expectancy: 75.6 male; 82.8 female. **Births** (per 1,000 pop.): 9.3. **Deaths** (per 1,000 pop.): 9.2. **Natural inc.:** 0.01%. **Infant mortality** (per 1,000 live births): 4.8.

Education: Free, compulsory: ages 6-16. **Literacy:** 97%.

Major Intl. Organizations: UN and all of its specialized agencies, EU, NATO, OECD, OSCE.

Embassy: 2375 Pennsylvania Ave. NW 20037; 452-0100.

Website: www.spainemb.org/ingles/indexing.htm

Initially settled by Iberians, Basques, and Celts, Spain was successively ruled (wholly or in part) by Carthage, Rome, and the Visigoths. Muslims invaded Iberia from North Africa in 711. Reconquest of the peninsula by Christians from the N laid the foundations of modern Spain. In 1469 the kingdoms of Aragon and Castile were united by the marriage of Ferdinand II and Isabella I. Moorish rule ended with the fall of the kingdom of Granada, 1492. Spain's large Jewish community was expelled the same year.

Spain obtained a colonial empire with the "discovery" of America by Columbus, 1492, the conquest of Mexico by Cortes, and Peru by Pizarro. It also controlled the Netherlands and parts of Italy and Germany. Spain lost its American colonies in the early 19th century. It lost Cuba, the Philippines, and Puerto Rico during the Spanish-American War, 1898.

Primo de Rivera became dictator in 1923. King Alfonso XIII revoked the dictatorship, 1930, but was forced to leave the country in 1931. A republic was proclaimed, which disestablished the church, curtailed its privileges, and secularized education. During 1936-39 a Popular Front composed of socialists, Communists, republicans, and anarchists governed Spain.

Army officers under Francisco Franco revolted against the government, 1936. In a destructive 3-year war, in which some one million died, Franco received massive help and troops from Italy and Germany, while the USSR, France, and Mexico supported the republic. The war ended Mar. 28, 1939. Franco was named caudillo, leader of the nation. Spain was officially neutral in World War II, but its cordial relations with fascist countries caused its exclusion from the UN until 1955.

In July 1969, Franco and the Cortes (Parliament) designated Prince Juan Carlos as the future king and chief of state. After Franco's death, Nov. 20, 1975, Juan Carlos was sworn in as king. In free elections June 1977, moderates and democratic socialists emerged as the largest parties.

In 1981 a coup attempt by right-wing military officers was thwarted by the king. The Socialist Workers' Party, under Felipe

González Márquez, won 4 consecutive general elections, from 1982 to 1993, but lost to a coalition of conservative and regional parties in the election of Mar. 3, 1996.

Catalonia and the Basque country were granted autonomy, Jan. 1980, following overwhelming approval in home-rule referendums. Basque extremists, however, have pushed for independence. The militant Basque separatist group ETA proclaimed a cease-fire as of Sept. 18, 1998, but announced an end to the truce Nov. 28, 1999. The Popular Party of conservative Prime Min. José María Aznar won a majority in the parliamentary election of Mar. 12, 2000.

The **Balearic Islands** in the W Mediterranean, 1,927 sq. mi., are a province of Spain; they include **Majorca** (Mallorca; capital Palma de Mallorca), **Minorca, Cabrera, Ibiza,** and **Formentera.** The **Canary Islands,** 2,807 sq. mi., in the Atlantic W of Morocco, form 2 provinces, and include the islands of **Tenerife, Palma, Gomera, Hierro, Grand Canary, Fuerteventura,** and **Lanzarote;** Las Palmas and Santa Cruz are thriving ports. **Ceuta** and **Melilla,** small Spanish enclaves on Morocco's Mediterranean coast, gained limited autonomy in Sept. 1994.

Spain has sought the return of Gibraltar, in British hands since 1704.

Sri Lanka

Democratic Socialist Republic of Sri Lanka

People: Population: 19,576,783. **Age distrib.** (%): <15: 26.0; 65+: 6.6. **Pop. density:** 783 per sq. mi. **Urban:** 23%. **Ethnic groups:** Sinhalese 74%, Tamil 18%, Moor 7%. **Principal languages:** Sinhala (official), Tamil, English. **Chief religions:** Buddhist 69%, Hindu 15%, Christian 8%, Muslim 8%.

Geography: Area: 25,000 sq. mi. **Location:** In Indian O. off SE coast of India. **Neighbors:** India on NW. **Topography:** The coastal area and the northern half are flat; the S-central area is hilly and mountainous. **Capital:** Colombo: 681,000.

Government: Type: Republic. **Head of state:** Pres. Chandrika Bandaranaike Kumaratunga; b June 29, 1945; in office: Nov. 12, 1994. **Head of gov.:** Prime Min. Ranil Wickremesinghe; b Mar. 24, 1949; in office: Dec. 9, 2001. **Local divisions:** 8 provinces. **Defense budget (2000):** $700 mil. **Active troops:** 118,000–123,000.

Economy: Industries: Agric. processing, clothing, cement, oil refining. **Chief crops:** Tea, coconuts, rice, sugar. **Minerals:** Graphite, limestone, gems, phosphates. **Other resources:** Forests, rubber. **Arable land:** 14%. **Livestock** (2001): cattle: 1.56 mil; chickens: 11.00 mil.; goats: 500,000; pigs: 68,000; sheep: 11,000. **Fish catch** (1999): 247,000 metric tons. **Electricity prod.** 6.62 bil. kWh. **Labor force:** services 45%, agri. 38%, ind. 17%.

Finance: Monetary unit: Rupee (Sept. 2002: 96.27 = $1 U.S.). **GDP** (2000 est.): $62.7 bil. **Per capita GDP:** $3,250. **Imports** (2000): $6.1 bil.; partners (1999): Japan 10%, India 9%. **Exports** (2000): $5.2 bil.; partners (1999): U.S. 39%, UK 13%. **Tourism:** $275 mil. **Budget** (2000 est.): $3 bil. **Intl. reserves less gold** (end 2000): $797 mil. **Gold:** 630,000 oz t. **Consumer prices** (change in 2000): 6.2%.

Transport: Railroad: Length: 928 mi. **Motor vehicles:** 220,000 pass. cars, 248,900 comm. vehicles. **Civil aviation:** 2.6 bil pass.-mi; 1 airport. **Chief ports:** Colombo, Trincomalee, Galle.

Communications: TV sets: 91 per 1,000 pop. **Radios:** 210 per 1,000 pop. **Telephones:** 1,548,000. **Daily newspaper circ.:** 29 per 1,000 pop.

Health: Life expectancy: 69.8 male; 75 female. **Births** (per 1,000 pop.): 16.4. **Deaths** (per 1,000 pop.): 6.5. **Natural inc.:** 0.99%. **Infant mortality** (per 1,000 live births): 15.7.

Education: Free, compulsory: ages 5-12. **Literacy:** 88%.

Major Intl. Organizations: UN (FAO, IBRD, ILO, IMF, IMO, WHO, WTrO), the Commonwealth.

Embassy: 2148 Wyoming Ave. NW 20008; 483-4025.

Website: www.priv.gov.lk

The island was known to the ancient world as Taprobane (Greek for copper-colored) and later as Serendip (from Arabic). Colonists from N India subdued the indigenous Veddahs about 543 BC; their descendants, the Buddhist Sinhalese, still form most of the population. Hindu descendants of Tamil immigrants from S India account for about one-fifth of the population.

Parts were occupied by the Portuguese in 1505 and the Dutch in 1658. The British seized the island in 1796. As Ceylon it became an independent member of the Commonwealth in 1948, and the Republic of Sri Lanka May 22, 1972.

Prime Min. W. R. D. Bandaranaike was assassinated Sept. 25, 1959. In new elections, the Freedom Party was victorious under Mrs. Sirimavo Bandaranaike, widow of the former prime minister. After May 1970 elections, Mrs. Bandaranaike became prime minister again. In 1971 the nation suffered economic problems and terrorist activities by ultra-leftists, thousands of whom were executed. Massive land reform and nationalization of foreign-owned plantations were undertaken in the mid-1970s. Mrs. Bandaranaike was ousted in 1977 elections. Presidential powers were increased in 1978 in an effort to restore stability.

Tensions between Sinhalese and Tamil separatists erupted into violence in the early 1980s. More than 64,000 died in the civil war, which continued through the late 1990s; another 20,000, mostly young Tamils, "disappeared" after they were taken into custody by government security forces.

Pres. Ranasinghe Premadasa was assassinated May 1, 1993, by a Tamil rebel. Mrs. Bandaranaike's daughter, Chandrika Bandaranaike Kumaratunga, became prime minister after the Aug. 16, 1994, general elections. Elected president Nov. 9, Kumaratunga appointed her mother prime minister. Kumaratunga, who was injured in a suicide bomb attack at a campaign rally Dec. 18, 1999, won a 2nd 6-year term 3 days later. In failing health, Mrs. Bandaranaike resigned Aug. 10 and died Oct. 10, 2000. Facing a possible no-confidence motion, Pres. Kumaratunga suspended parliament July 10, 2001. Elections Dec. 5 resulted in a victory for the United National Party, headed by Ranil Wickremesinghe. A truce accord intended to bring an end to the 18-year-long civil war was signed Feb. 22, 2002.

Sudan

Republic of the Sudan

People: Population: 37,090,298. **Age distrib.** (%): <15: 44.6; 65+: 2.1. **Pop. density:** 40 per sq. mi. **Urban:** 35%. **Ethnic groups:** Black 52%, Arab 39%, Beja 6%. **Principal languages:** Arabic (official), Nubian, Ta Bedawie. **Chief religions:** Sunni Muslim 70%, indigenous beliefs 25%.

Geography: Area: 917,400 sq. mi., the largest country in Africa. **Location:** At the E end of Sahara desert zone. **Neighbors:** Egypt on N; Libya, Chad, Central African Republic on W; Congo (formerly Zaire), Uganda, Kenya on S; Ethiopia, Eritrea on E. **Topography:** The N consists of the Libyan Desert in the W, and the mountainous Nubia Desert in E, with narrow Nile valley between. The center contains large, fertile, rainy areas with fields, pasture, and forest. The S has rich soil, heavy rain. **Capital:** Khartoum. **Cities (urban aggr.):** Khartoum 2,853,000; Omdurman (1993) 1,271,403.

Government: Type: Republic with strong military influence. **Head of state and gov.:** Pres. Gen. Omar Hassan Ahmad Al-Bashir; b Jan. 1, 1944; in office: June 30, 1989. **Local divisions:** 26 states. **Defense budget (2001):** $581 mil. **Active troops:** 117,000.

Economy: Industries: Cotton ginning, textiles, cement. **Chief crops:** Gum arabic, sorghum, cotton (main export), wheat. **Minerals:** Petroleum, iron, chromium, copper. **Crude oil reserves** (2001): 0.6 bil bbls. **Arable land:** 5%. **Livestock** (2001): cattle: 38.33 mil; chickens: 37.50 mil.; goats: 39.00 mil.; sheep: 47.00 mil. **Electricity prod.:** 1.97 bil. kWh. **Labor force:** agri. 80%, ind. and commerce 10%, government 6%, unemployed 4%.

Finance: Monetary unit: Dinar (Sept. 2002: 258.70 = $1 U.S.), Dinar (Oct. 2000: 256.00 = $1 U.S.). **GDP** (2000 est.): $35.7 bil. **Per capita GDP:** $1,000. **Imports** (2000 est.): $1.2 bil.; partners (1999): China 14.7%, Libya 14.7%. **Exports** (2000 est.): $1.7 bil.; partners (1999): Saudi Arabia 16%, Italy 10%. **Tourism** (1998): $8 mil. **Budget** (2000 est.): $1.3 bil. **Intl. reserves less gold** (Apr. 2000): $238.4 mil. **Consumer prices** (change in 1999): 16.0%.

Transport: Railroad: Length: 2,960 mi. **Motor vehicles:** 35,000 pass. cars, 40,000 comm. vehicles. **Civil aviation:** 292.8 mil pass.-mi; 3 airports. **Chief port:** Port Sudan.

Communications: TV sets: 8.2 per 1,000 pop. **Radios:** 182 per 1,000 pop. **Telephones:** 558,000. **Daily newspaper circ.:** 21 per 1,000 pop.

Health: Life expectancy: 56.2 male; 58.5 female. **Births** (per 1,000 pop.): 37.2. **Deaths** (per 1,000 pop.): 9.8. **Natural inc.:** 2.74%. **Infant mortality** (per 1,000 live births): 67.1.

Education: Literacy: 46%.

Major Intl. Organizations: UN (FAO, IBRD, ILO, IMF, IMO, WHO), AL, AU.

Embassy: 2210 Massachusetts Ave. NW 20008; 338-8565.

Website: www.sudanembassy.org

Northern Sudan, ancient Nubia, was settled by Egyptians in antiquity. The population was converted to Coptic Christianity in the 6th century. Arab conquests brought Islam to the area in the 15th century.

In the 1820s Egypt took over Sudan, defeating the last of earlier empires, including the Fung. In the 1880s a revolution was led by Muhammad Ahmad, who called himself the Mahdi (leader of the faithful), and his followers, the dervishes.

In 1898 an Anglo-Egyptian force crushed the Mahdi's successors. In 1951 the Egyptian Parliament abrogated its 1899 and 1936 treaties with Great Britain and amended its constitution to provide for a separate Sudanese constitution. Sudan voted for complete independence as a parliamentary government effective Jan. 1, 1956.

In 1969, a Revolutionary Council took power, but a civilian premier and cabinet were appointed; the government announced it would create a socialist state.

Economic problems plagued the nation in the 1980s and 1990s, aggravated by civil war and influxes of refugees from neighboring countries. After 16 years in power, Pres. Jaafar al-Nimeiry was overthrown in a bloodless military coup, Apr. 6, 1985. Sudan held its first democratic parliamentary elections in 18 years in 1986, but the elected government was overthrown in a bloodless coup June 30, 1989.

In the mid-1980s, rebels in the south (populated largely by black Christians and followers of tribal religions) took up arms against government domination by northern Sudan, mostly Arab-Muslim. War and related famine cost an estimated 2 million lives and displaced millions of southerners. A preliminary peace pact was signed July 20, 2002, but talks broke off Sept. 2. In 1993, Amnesty International accused Sudan of "ethnic cleansing" against the Nuba people in the South.

Egypt publicly blamed Sudan for an attempted assassination of Egyptian Pres. Hosni Mubarak in Ethiopia, June 26, 1995.

A new constitution based on Islamic law took effect June 30, 1998. On Aug. 20, in retaliation for bombings in Kenya and Tanzania, U.S. missiles destroyed a Khartoum pharmaceutical plant the U.S. alleged was associated with terrorist activities; independent inquiries later cast some doubt on the U.S. claim. Embroiled in a power struggle, Pres. Omar Hassan Ahmad Al-Bashir dissolved parliament and declared a state of emergency Dec. 12, 1999. The main opposition parties boycotted presidential and legislative elections Dec. 13-22, 2000, won by Bashir.

Suriname

Republic of Suriname

People: Population: 436,494. **Age distrib.** (%): <15: 31.6; 65+: 5.7. **Pop. density:** 7 per sq. mi. **Urban:** 74%. **Ethnic groups:** Hindustani 37%, Creole 31%, Javanese 15%. **Principal languages:** Dutch (official), Sranang Tongo, English, Hindustani. **Chief religions:** Hindu 27%, Protestant 25%, Roman Catholic 23%, Muslim 20%.

Geography: Area: 62,300 sq. mi. **Location:** On N shore of South America. **Neighbors:** Guyana on W, Brazil on S, French Guiana on E. **Topography:** A flat Atlantic coast, where dikes permit agriculture. Inland is a forest belt; to the S, largely unexplored hills cover 75% of the country. **Capital:** Paramaribo: 240,000.

Government: Type: Republic. **Head of state and gov.:** Pres. Runaldo Ronald Venetiaan; b June 18, 1936; in office: Aug. 12, 2000. **Local divisions:** 10 districts. **Defense budget (2001):** (2001) $11 mil. **Active troops:** 2,040.

Economy: Industries: Mining, aluminum, lumbering. **Chief crops:** Rice, bananas, palm kernels. **Minerals:** Kaolin, bauxite, gold. **Crude oil reserves** (2000): 74 mil bbls. **Other resources:** Forests, fish, shrimp. **Livestock** (2001): cattle: 135,000; chickens: 2.90 mil.; goats: 7,400; pigs: 23,000; sheep: 7,500. **Fish catch:** (1999): 13,001 metr. t. **Electricity prod.:** 1.41 bil. kWh.

Finance: Monetary unit: Guilder (Sept. 2002: 2178.50 = $1 U.S.). **GDP** (1999 est.): $1.48 bil. **Per capita GDP:** $3,400. **Imports** (1999): $525 mil.; partners (1999): U.S. 35%, Netherlands 15%. **Exports** (1999): $443 mil.; partners (1999): U.S. 23%, Norway 19%. **Tourism** (1998): $44 mil. **Budget** (1997 est.): $403 mil. Intl. reserves less gold (1999): $28 mil. **Gold**: 250,000 oz t. **Consumer prices** (change in 2000): 64.3%.

Transport: Railroad: Length: 187 mi. **Motor vehicles:** 46,408 pass. cars, 19,255 comm. vehicles. **Civil aviation:** 663.5 mil pass.-mi; 3 airports. **Chief ports:** Paramaribo, New Nickerie, Albina.

Communications: TV sets: 146 per 1,000 pop. **Radios:** 719 per 1,000 pop. **Telephones:** 161,400. **Daily newspaper circ.:** 107 per 1,000 pop.

Health: Life expectancy: 69.2 male; 74.7 female. **Births** (per 1,000 pop.): 20. **Deaths** (per 1,000 pop.): 5.7. **Natural inc.:** 1.43%. **Infant mortality** (per 1,000 live births): 23.5.

Education: Free, compulsory: ages 6-16. **Literacy**: 93%.

Major Intl. Organizations: UN (FAO, IBRD, ILO, IMF, IMO, WHO, WTrO), Caricom, OAS.

Embassy: 4301 Connecticut Ave. NW 20008; 244-7488.

The Netherlands acquired Suriname in 1667 from Britain, in exchange for New Netherlands (New York). The 1954 Dutch constitution raised the colony to a level of equality with the Netherlands and the Netherlands Antilles. Independence was granted Nov. 25, 1975, despite objections from East Indians. Some 40% of the population (mostly East Indians) immigrated to the Netherlands in the months before independence.

The National Military Council took control of the government, Feb. 1982. Civilian rule was restored in 1987, but political turmoil continued until 1992, disrupting the nation's economy.

Swaziland

Kingdom of Swaziland

People: Population: 1,123,605. **Age distrib.** (%): <15: 45.5; 65+: 2.6. **Pop. density:** 170 per sq. mi. **Urban:** 26%. **Ethnic groups:** African 97%, European 3%. **Principal languages:** siSwati, English (both official). **Chief religions:** Christian 60%, indigenous beliefs 40%.

Geography: Area: 6,600 sq. mi. **Location:** In southern Africa, near Indian O. coast. **Neighbors:** South Africa on N, W, S; Mozambique on E. **Topography:** The country descends from W-E in broad belts, becoming more arid in the low veld region, then rising to a plateau in the E. **Capitals:** Mbabane (administrative), Lobamba (legislative). **Cities (urban aggr.):** Mbabane: 80,000.

Government: Type: Constitutional monarchy. **Head of state:** King Mswati III; b Apr. 19, 1968; in office: Apr. 25, 1986. **Head of gov.:** Prime Min. Barnabas Sibusiso Dlamini; b May 15, 1942; in office: July 26, 1996. **Local divisions:** 4 districts.

Economy: Industries: Mining, wood pulp, sugar. **Chief crops:** Sugar, corn, cotton, rice, pineapples, tobacco, citrus, peanuts. **Minerals:** Asbestos, clay, coal. **Other resources:** Forests. **Arable land:** 11%. **Livestock** (2001): cattle: 615,000; chickens: 3.20 mil.; goats: 445,000; pigs: 34,000; sheep: 32,000. **Electricity prod.:** 0.36 bil. kWh. **Labor force:** private sector: 70%, public sector: 30%.

Finance: Monetary unit: Lilangeni (Sept. 2002: 10.57 = $1 U.S.). **GDP** (2000 est.): $4.4 bil. **Per capita GDP:** $4,000. **Imports** (2000): $928 mil.; partners (1998): South Africa 84%, EU 5%. **Exports** (2000): $881 mil.; partners (1998): South Africa 65%, EU 12%. **Tourism** (1998): $37 mil. **Budget** (FY96/97): $450 mil. **Intl. reserves less gold** (end 2000): $270 mil. **Consumer prices** (change in 2000): 16.7%.

Transport: Railroad: Length: 187 mi. **Motor vehicles:** 28,523 pass. cars, 8,232 comm. vehicles. **Civil aviation:** 26.5 mil pass.-mi; 1 airport.

Communications: TV sets: 96 per 1,000 pop. **Radios:** 129 per 1,000 pop. **Telephones:** 98,000. **Daily newspaper circ.:** 40 per 1,000 pop.

Health: Life expectancy: 36.4 male; 37.7 female. **Births** (per 1,000 pop.): 39.6. **Deaths** (per 1,000 pop.): 23.3. **Natural inc.:** 1.63%. **Infant mortality** (per 1,000 live births): 109.4.

Education: Literacy: 77%.

Major Intl. Organizations: UN (FAO, IBRD, ILO, IMF, WHO, WTrO), the Commonwealth, AU.

Embassy: 3400 International Dr. NW 20008; 362-6683.

Website: www.swazi.com/government

The royal house of Swaziland traces back 400 years, and is one of Africa's last ruling dynasties. The Swazis, a Bantu people, were driven to Swaziland from lands to the N by the Zulus in 1820. Their autonomy was later guaranteed by Britain and Transvaal (later part of South Africa), with Britain assuming control after 1903. Independence came Sept. 6, 1968. In 1973 the king repealed the constitution and assumed full powers.

A new constitution banning political parties took effect Oct. 13, 1978. As Swaziland slowly moved toward political reform, student and labor unrest grew in the 1990s. The UN estimates that about one-fourth of the adult population has HIV/AIDS.

Sweden

Kingdom of Sweden

People: Population: 8,876,744. **Age distrib.** (%): <15: 18.2; 65+: 17.3. **Pop. density:** 56 per sq. mi. **Urban:** 83%. **Ethnic groups:** Swedish 89%, Finnish 2%. **Principal language:** Swedish. **Chief religion:** Evangelical Lutheran 94%.

Geography: Area: 158,900 sq. mi. **Location:** On Scandinavian Peninsula in N Europe. **Neighbors:** Norway on W, Denmark on S (across Kattegat), Finland on E. **Topography:** Mountains along NW border cover 25% of Sweden, flat or rolling terrain covers the central and southern areas, which include several large lakes. **Capital:** Stockholm. **Cities (urban aggr.):** Stockholm 1,626,000; Göteborg 778,000.

Government: Type: Constitutional monarchy. **Head of state:** King Carl XVI Gustaf; b Apr. 30, 1946; in office: Sept. 19, 1973. **Head of gov.:** Prime Min. Goran Persson; b June 20, 1949; in office: Mar. 21, 1996. **Local divisions:** 21 counties. **Defense budget** (2001): $4.2 bil. **Active troops:** 33,900.

Economy: Industries: Iron and steel, precision equipment, pulp and paper products, processed foods, vehicles. **Chief crops:** Grains, potatoes, sugar beets. **Minerals:** Zinc, iron, lead, copper, silver. **Other resources:** Forests (half the country); yield about 17% of exports. **Arable land:** 7%. **Livestock** (2001): cattle: 1.65 mil; chickens: 7.41 1.89 mil; sheep: 451,594. **Fish catch** (1999): 364,115 metric tons. **Electricity prod.:** 144.62 bil. kWh. **Labor force**: agri. 2%, ind. 24%, services 74%..

Finance: Monetary unit: Krona (Sept. 2002: 9.37 = $1 U.S.). **GDP** (2000 est.): $197 bil. **Per capita GDP:** $22,200. **Imports** (2000): $80 bil.; partners (1999): EU 67%, Norway 8%. **Exports** (2000): $95.5 bil.; partners (1999): EU 55%,U.S. 9%. **Tourism:**

$3.89 bil. **Budget** (2000 est.): $125.2 bil. **Intl. reserves less gold** (end 2000): $11.41 bil. **Gold:** 5.96 mil oz t. **Consumer prices** (change in 2000): 1.0%.

Transport: Railroad: Length: 6,756 mi. **Motor vehicles** (1997): 3.70 mil pass. cars, 336,593 comm. vehicles. **Civil aviation:** 5.54 bil pass.-mi; 48 airports. **Chief ports:** Göteborg, Stockholm, Malmö.

Communications: TV sets: 531 per 1,000 pop. **Radios:** 904 per 1,000 pop. **Telephones:** 13,627,000. **Daily newspaper circ.:** 484 per 1,000 pop.

Health: Life expectancy: 77.2 male; 82.6 female. **Births** (per 1,000 pop.): 9.8. **Deaths** (per 1,000 pop.): 10.6. **Natural inc.:** -0.08%. **Infant mortality** (per 1,000 live births): 3.4.

Education: Compulsory: ages 6-15. **Literacy:** 100%.

Major Intl. Organizations: UN and all of its specialized agencies, EU, OECD, OSCE.

Embassy: 1501 M St. NW 20005; 467-2600.

Website: www.swedish-embassy.org

The Swedes have lived in present-day Sweden for at least 5,000 years, longer than nearly any other European people. Gothic tribes from Sweden played a major role in the disintegration of the Roman Empire. Other Swedes helped create the first Russian state in the 9th century.

The Swedes were Christianized from the 11th century, and a strong centralized monarchy developed. A parliament, the Riksdag, was first called in 1435, the earliest parliament on the European continent, with all classes of society represented.

Swedish independence from rule by Danish kings (dating from 1397) was secured by Gustavus I in a revolt, 1521-23; he built up the government and military and established the Lutheran Church. In the 17th century Sweden was a major European power, gaining most of the Baltic seacoast, but its international position subsequently declined.

The Napoleonic wars, 1799-1815, in which Sweden acquired Norway (it became independent 1905), were the last in which Sweden participated. Armed neutrality was maintained in both world wars.

More than 4 decades of Social Democratic rule ended in the 1976 parliamentary elections; the party returned to power in the 1982 elections. After Prime Min. Olof Palme was shot to death in Stockholm, Feb. 28, 1986, Ingvar Carlsson took office. Carl Bildt, a non-Socialist, became prime minister Oct. 1991, with a mandate to restore Sweden's economic competitiveness. The Social Democrats returned to power following 1994 elections.

Swedish voters approved membership in the European Union Nov. 13, 1994, and Sweden entered the EU as of Jan. 1, 1995. Carlsson retired and was succeeded by Goran Persson in Mar. 1996. Persson and his Social Democrats led coalition governments after the elections of Sept. 20, 1998, and Sept. 15, 2002.

Switzerland

Swiss Confederation

People: Population: 7,301,994. **Age distrib.** (%): <15: 17.0; 65+: 15.3. **Pop. density:** 474 per sq. mi. **Urban:** 68%. **Ethnic groups:** German 65%, French 18%, Italian 10%, Romansch 1%. **Principal languages:** German, French, Italian, Romansch (all official). **Chief religions:** Roman Catholic 46.1%, Protestant 40%.

Geography: Area: 15,400 sq. mi. **Location:** In the Alps Mts. in central Europe. **Neighbors:** France on W, Italy on S, Austria on E, Germany on N. **Topography:** The Alps cover 60% of the land area; the Jura, near France, 10%. Running between, from NE to SW, are midlands, 30%. **Capitals:** Bern (administrative), Lausanne (judicial). **Cities (urban aggr.):** Zurich 939,000; Basel 166,700; Geneva 398,910; Bern 316,000.

Government: Type: Federal republic. **Head of state and gov.:** The president is elected by the Federal Assembly to a non-renewable 1-year term. **Local divisions:** 20 full cantons, 6 half cantons. **Defense budget** (2001): $2.7 bil. **Active troops:** 3,600.

Economy: Industries: Machinery, chemicals, watches, textiles, precision instruments. **Chief crops:** Grains, fruits, vegetables. **Minerals:** Salt. **Other resources:** Hydropower potential, timber. **Arable land:** 10%. **Livestock** (2001): cattle: 1.61 mil; chickens: 6.66 mil.; goats: 67,500; pigs: 1.56 mil; sheep: 460,000. **Electricity prod.:** 64.18 bil. kWh. **Labor force:** services 69.1%, ind. 26.3%, agri. 4.6%.

Finance: Monetary unit: Franc (Sept. 2002: 1.50 = $1 U.S.). **GDP** (2000 est.): $207 bil. **Per capita GDP:** $28,600. **Imports** (2000): $91.6 bil.; partners (1999): EU 77.7%, U.S. 7.1%, Japan 2.9%. **Exports** (2000): $91.3 bil.; partners (1999): EU 65.8%,U.S. 12.4%. **Tourism:** $7.36 bil. **Budget** (1998 est.): $34.89 bil. **Intl. reserves less gold** (end 2000): $24.77 bil. **Gold:** 77.79 mil oz t. **Consumer prices** (change in 2000): 1.6%.

Transport: Railroad: Length: 3,132 mi. **Motor vehicles (1997):** 3.32 mil pass. cars, 302,707 comm. vehicles. **Civil aviation:** 13.83 bil pass.-mi; 5 airports. **Chief port:** Basel.

Communications: TV sets: 536 per 1,000 pop. **Radios:** 990 per 1,000 pop. **Telephones:** 10,409,000. **Daily newspaper circ.:** 337 per 1,000 pop.

Health: Life expectancy: 77 male; 82.9 female. **Births** (per 1,000 pop.): 9.8. **Deaths** (per 1,000 pop.): 8.8. **Natural inc.:** 0.1%. **Infant mortality** (per 1,000 live births): 4.4.

Education: Compulsory: ages 7-16. **Literacy** (1994): 100%.

Major Intl. Organizations: UN and most of its specialized agencies, EFTA, OECD, OSCE.

Embassy: 2900 Cathedral Ave. NW 20008; 745-7900.

Website: www.admin.ch/index.en.html

Switzerland, the former Roman province of Helvetia, traces its modern history to 1291, when 3 cantons created a defensive league. Other cantons were subsequently admitted to the Swiss Confederation, which obtained its independence from the Holy Roman Empire through the Peace of Westphalia (1648). The cantons were joined under a federal constitution in 1848, with large powers of local control retained by each.

Switzerland has maintained an armed neutrality since 1815, and has not been involved in a foreign war since 1515. It is the seat of many UN and other international agencies but did not become a full member of the UN until Sept. 10, 2002.

Switzerland is a world banking center. In an effort to crack down on criminal transactions, the nation's strict bank-secrecy rules have been eased since 1990. Stung by charges that assets seized by the Nazis and deposited in Swiss banks in World War II had not been properly returned, the government announced, March 5, 1997, a $4.7 billion fund to compensate victims of the Holocaust and other catastrophies. Swiss banks agreed Aug. 12, 1998, to pay $1.25 billion in reparations. Abortion was decriminalized by a June 2, 2002 referendum.

Syria

Syrian Arab Republic

People: Population: 17,155,814. **Age distrib.** (%): <15: 39.9; 65+: 3.2. **Pop. density:** 241 per sq. mi. **Urban:** 54%. **Ethnic groups:** Arab 90%. **Principal languages:** Arabic (official), Kurdish, Armenian. **Chief religions:** Sunni Muslim 74%, other Muslims 16%, Christian 10%.

Geography: Area: 71,100 sq. mi. **Location:** Middle East, at E end of Mediterranean Sea. **Neighbors:** Lebanon and Israel on W, Jordan on S, Iraq on E, Turkey on N. **Topography:** Syria has a short Mediterranean coastline, then stretches E and S with fertile lowlands and plains, alternating with mountains and large desert areas. **Capital:** Damascus. **Cities (urban aggr.):** Damascus 2,195,000; Aleppo 2,229,000; Homs 811,000.

Government: Type: Republic (under military regime). **Head of state:** Pres. Bashar al-Assad; b Sept. 1965; in office: July 17, 2000. **Head of gov.:** Prime Min. Muhammad Mustafa Mero; b 1941; in office: Mar. 13, 2000. **Local divisions:** 14 provinces. **Defense budget (2001):** $838 mil. **Active troops:** 321,000.

Economy: Industries: Oil, textiles, food processing, beverages, tobacco, phosphate mining. **Chief crops:** Cotton, grains, lentils, chickpeas. **Minerals:** Oil, phosphates, chrome, manganese, asphalt, iron. **Crude oil reserves** (2001): 2.2 bil bbls. **Other resources:** Wool, dairy prods. **Arable land:** 28%. **Livestock** (2001): cattle: 836,868; chickens: 21.01 mil.; goats: 979,325; pigs: 770; sheep: 12.36 mil . **Electricity prod.:** 19.70 bil. kWh. **Labor force:** agri. 40%, ind. 20%, services 40%.

Finance: Monetary unit: Pound (Sept. 2002: 48.85 = $1 U.S.).**GDP** (2000 est.): $50.9 bil. **Per capita GDP:** $3,100. **Imports** (2000 est.): $3.5 bil.; partners (1999 est.): France 11%, Italy 8%. **Exports** (2000 est.): $4.8 bil.; partners (1999 est.): Germany 21%, Italy 12%. **Tourism:** $1.36 bil. **Budget** (2000 est.): $5.4 bil. **Gold:** 833,000 oz t. **Consumer prices** (change in 2000): –0.4%.

Transport: Railroad: Length: 1,097 mi. **Motor vehicles:** 134,000 pass. cars, 218,900 comm. vehicles. **Civil aviation:** 767.6 mil pass.-mi; 5 airports. **Chief ports:** Latakia, Tartus.

Communications: TV sets: 49 per 1,000 pop. **Radios:** 211 per 1,000 pop. **Telephones:** 2,007,600. **Daily newspaper circ.:** 19 per 1,000 pop.

Health: Life expectancy: 67.9 male; 70.3 female. **Births** (per 1,000 pop.): 30.1. **Deaths** (per 1,000 pop.): 5.1. **Natural inc.:** 2.5%. **Infant mortality** (per 1,000 live births): 32.7.

Education: Compulsory: ages 6-12. **Literacy:** 79%.

Major Intl. Organizations: UN (FAO, IBRD, ILO, IMF, IMO, WHO), AL.

Embassy: 2215 Wyoming Ave. NW 20008; 232-6313.

Syria contains some of the most ancient remains of civilization. It was the center of the Seleucid empire, but later became absorbed in the Roman and Arab empires. Ottoman rule prevailed for 4 centuries, until the end of World War I.

The state of Syria was formed from former Turkish districts, separated by the Treaty of Sevres, 1920, and divided into the states of Syria and Greater Lebanon. Both were administered under a French League of Nations mandate 1920-1941.

Syria was proclaimed a republic by the occupying French Sept. 16, 1941, and exercised full independence Apr. 17, 1946. Syria joined the Arab invasion of Israel in 1948.

Syria joined Egypt Feb. 1958 in the United Arab Republic but seceded Sept. 1961. The Socialist Baath party and military leaders seized power Mar. 1963. The Baath, a pan-Arab organization, became the only legal party. The government has been dominated by the Alawite minority.

In the Arab-Israeli war of June 1967, Israel seized and occupied the Golan Heights, from which Syria had shelled Israeli settlements. On Oct. 6, 1973, Syria joined Egypt in an attack on Israel. Arab oil states agreed in 1974 to give Syria $1 billion a year to aid anti-Israel moves. Some 30,000 Syrian troops entered Lebanon in 1976 to mediate in a civil war. They fought Palestinian guerrillas and, later, Christian militiamen. Syrian troops again battled Christian forces in Lebanon, Apr. 1981.

Following Israel's invasion of Lebanon, June 6, 1982, Israeli planes destroyed 17 Syrian antiaircraft missile batteries in the Bekaa Valley, June 9. Some 25 Syrian planes were downed during the engagement. Israel and Syria agreed to a cease-fire June 11. In 1983, Syria backed the PLO rebels who ousted Yasir Arafat's forces from Tripoli.

Syria's role in promoting international terrorism led to the breaking of diplomatic relations with Great Britain and to limited sanctions by the European Community in 1986.

Syria condemned the Aug. 1990 Iraqi invasion of Kuwait and sent troops to help Allied forces in the Gulf War. In 1991, Syria accepted U.S. proposals for the terms of an Arab-Israeli peace conference. Syria subsequently participated in negotiations with Israel, but progress toward peace was slow. Turkey has accused Syria of aiding Kurdish separatists.

Former Prime Min. Mahmoud Al-Zoubi killed himself May 21, 2000, after being charged with corruption. Hafez al-Assad, president of Syria since 1971, died June 10, 2000, and was succeeded by his son Bashar al-Assad.

Taiwan

Republic of China

People: Population: 22,548,009. **Age distrib.** (%): <15: 21.2; 65+: 8.8. **Pop. density:** 1,804 per sq. mi. **Urban:** 75%. **Ethnic groups:** Taiwanese 84%, mainland Chinese 14%. **Principal languages:** Mandarin Chinese (official), Taiwanese. **Chief religions:** Buddhist, Taoist, and Confucian 93%, Christian 5%.

Geography: Area: 12,500 sq. mi. **Location:** Off SE coast of China, between East and South China seas. **Neighbors:** Nearest is China. **Topography:** A mountain range forms the backbone of the island; the eastern half is very steep and craggy, the western slope is flat, fertile, and well cultivated. **Capital:** Taipei. **Cities (urban aggr., 1997 est.):** Taipei 2,595,699; Kaohsiung 1,434,907; Taichung 881,870.

Government: Type: Democracy. **Head of state:** Pres. Chen Shui-bian; b 1950; in office: May 20, 2000. **Head of gov.:** Prime Min. Yu Shyi-kun; b 1948; in office: Feb. 1, 2002. **Local divisions:** 16 counties, 5 municipalities, 2 special municipalities (Taipei, Kaohsiung). **Defense budget (2001):** $8.2 bil. **Active troops:** 370,000.

Economy: Industries: Electronics, oil refining, chemicals, textiles, iron and steel. **Chief crops:** Vegetables, rice, fruit, tea. **Minerals:** Coal, gas, limestone, marble. **Crude oil reserves** (2000): 4 mil bbls. **Arable land:** 24%. **Fish catch** (1997): 1.04 mil metric tons. **Electricity prod.:** 149.78 bil. kWh. **Labor force:** services 55%, ind. 37%, agri. 8%.

Finance: Monetary unit: New Taiwan Dollar (Sept. 2002: 34.98 = $1 U.S.). **GDP** (2000 est.): $386 bil. **Per capita GDP:** $17,400. **Imports** (2000): $140.01 bil.; partners (2000): Japan 27.5%, U.S. 17.9%. **Exports** (2000): $148.38 bil.; partners (2000): U.S. 23.5%, Hong Kong 21.1%. **Tourism:** $3.57 bil. **Budget** (2001 est.): $48.8 bil.

Transport: Railroad: Length: 2,410 mi. **Motor vehicles (1997):** 4.40 mil pass. cars, 833,545 comm. vehicles. **Civil aviation:** 22.8 bil pass.-mi; 13 airports. **Chief ports:** Kaohsiung, Chilung (Keelung), Hualien, Taichung.

Communications: TV sets: 327 per 1,000 pop. **Radios:** 402 per 1,000 pop. **Telephones:** 34,479,900. **Daily newspaper circ.:** 20.2 per 1,000 pop.

Health: Life expectancy: 74 male; 79.7 female. **Births** (per 1,000 pop.): 14.2. **Deaths** (per 1,000 pop.): 6.1. **Natural inc.:** 0.81%. **Infant mortality** (per 1,000 live births): 6.8.

Education: Free, compulsory: ages 6-15. **Literacy:** 94%.

Major Intl. Organizations: APEC.

Website: www.taiwan.gov.tw/ENGLISH/

Large-scale Chinese immigration began in the 17th century. The island came under mainland control after an interval of Dutch rule, 1620-62. Taiwan (also called Formosa) was ruled by Japan 1895-1945. Two million Kuomintang supporters fled to the island in 1949, establishing Taiwan as the seat of the Republic of China. The U.S., upon recognizing the People's Republic of China, Dec. 15, 1978, severed diplomatic ties with Taiwan. The U.S. and Taiwan maintain contact via quasi-official agencies.

Land reform, government planning, U.S. aid and investment, and free universal education brought huge advances in industry, agriculture, and living standards. In 1987 martial law was lifted after 38 years, and in 1991 the 43-year period of emergency rule ended. Taiwan held its first direct presidential election Mar. 23, 1996. An earthquake on Sept. 21, 1999, killed more than 2,300 people and injured thousands more. Five decades of Nationalist Party rule ended with the presidential election of Mar. 18, 2000, won by Chen Shui-bian, leader of the pro-independence Democratic Progressive Party.

Both the Taipei and Beijing governments long considered Taiwan an integral part of China, although Taiwanese officials appeared to signal a departure from that policy in July 1999. Taiwan has resisted Beijing's efforts at reunification, including military pressure, but economic ties with the mainland expanded in the 1990s. Taiwan has one of the world's strongest economies and is among the 10 leading capital exporters.

The **Penghu Isls.** (Pescadores), 49 sq. mi., pop. (1996 est.) 90,142, lie between Taiwan and the mainland. **Quemoy** and **Matsu,** pop. (1996 est.) 53,286, lie just off the mainland.

Tajikistan

Republic of Tajikistan

People: Population: 6,719,567. **Age distrib.** (%): <15: 41.2; 65+: 4.6. **Pop. density:** 122 per sq. mi. **Urban:** 32%. **Ethnic groups:** Tajik 65%, Uzbek 25%. **Principal languages:** Tajik (official), Russian. **Chief religion:** Sunni Muslim 80%.

Geography: Area: 55,300 sq. mi. **Location:** Central Asia. **Neighbors:** Uzbekistan on N and W, Kyrgyzstan on N, China on E, Afghanistan on S. **Topography:** Mountainous region that contains the Pamirs, Trans-Alai mountain system. **Capital:** Dushanbe: 522,000.

Government: Type: Republic. **Head of state:** Pres. Imomali Rakhmonov; b Oct. 5, 1952; in office: Nov. 19, 1994. **Head of gov.:** Akil Akilov; b 1944; in office: Dec. 20, 1999. **Local divisions:** 2 viloyats, 1 autonomous viloyat. **Defense budget** (2000): $19 mil. **Active troops:** 6,000.

Economy: Industries: Aluminum, zinc, lead, chemicals and fertilizers. **Chief crops:** Cotton, grains, fruits, vegetables. **Minerals:** Oil, uranium, mercury, coal, lead, zinc. **Crude oil reserves** (2000): 12 mil bbls. **Arable land:** 6%. **Livestock** (2001): cattle: 1.05 mil; chickens: 900,000; goats: 575,000; pigs: 900; sheep: 1.36 mil. **Electricity prod.:** 14.25 bil. kWh. **Labor force:** agri. 50%, ind. 20%, services 30%.

Finance: Monetary unit: Rouble (Sept. 2002: 31.67 = $1 U.S.). **GDP** (2000 est.): $7.3 bil. **Per capita GDP:** $1,140. **Imports** (2000 est.): $782 mil.; partners (1998): Europe 32.3%, Uzbekistan 29%,. **Exports** (2000 est.): $761 mil.; partners (1998): Liechtenstein 26%, Uzbekistan 20%. **Budget** (2000 est.): $196 mil.

Transport: Railroad: Length: 294.5 mi. **Motor vehicles:** 185,000 pass. cars, 3,600 comm. vehicles. **Civil aviation:** 1.1 bil pass.-mi; 1 airport.

Communications: TV sets: 259 per 1,000 pop. **Telephones:** 224,600. **Daily newspaper circ.:** 13.7 per 1,000 pop.

Health: Life expectancy: 61.2 male; 67.5 female. **Births** (per 1,000 pop.): 33. **Deaths** (per 1,000 pop.): 8.5. **Natural inc.:** 2.45%. **Infant mortality** (per 1,000 live births): 114.8.

Education: Compulsory for 9 years between ages 7-17. **Literacy:** 100%.

Major International Organizations: UN (FAO, IBRD, ILO, IMF, WHO), CIS, OSCE.

There were settled societies in the region from about 3000 BC. Throughout history, it has undergone invasions by Iranians (Arabs who converted the population to Islam), Mongols, Uzbeks, Afghans, and Russians. The USSR gained control of the region 1918-25. In 1924, the Tajik ASSR was created within the Uzbek SSR. The Tajik SSR was proclaimed in 1929.

Tajikistan declared independence Sept. 9, 1991. It became an independent state when the Soviet Union disbanded Dec. 26, 1991. Conservative Communist Pres. Rakhmon Nabiyev was forced to resign, Sept. 1992, by a coalition of Islamic, nationalist, and Western-oriented parties.

Factional fighting led to the installation of a pro-Communist regime, Jan. 1993. A new constitution establishing a presidential system was approved by referendum Nov. 6, 1994. Clashes between Muslim rebels, reportedly armed by Afghanistan, and troops loyal to the government and supported by Russia, claimed an estimated 55,000 lives by mid-1997, despite a series of peace accords. Constitutional changes including legalization of Islamic political parties were approved by referendum Sept. 26, 1999. Pres. Imomali Rakhmonov won a Nov. 6 election called "a farce" by human-rights observers.

Tanzania

United Republic of Tanzania

People: Population: 37,187,939. **Age distrib.** (%): <15: 44.8; 65+: 2.9. **Pop. density:** 109 per sq. mi. **Urban:** 32%. **Ethnic groups:** African 99%. **Principal languages:** Swahili, English (both official), many others. **Chief religions:** Christian 45%, Muslim 35%, indigenous beliefs 20%; Zanzibar is 99% Muslim.

Geography: Area: 342,100 sq. mi. **Location:** On coast of E Africa. **Neighbors:** Kenya, Uganda on N; Rwanda, Burundi, Congo (formerly Zaire) on W; Zambia, Malawi, Mozambique on S. **Topography:** Hot, arid central plateau, surrounded by the lake region in the W, temperate highlands in N and S, the coastal plains. Mt. Kilimanjaro, 19,340 ft., is highest in Africa. **Capital:** Dodoma. **Cities (urban aggr.):** Dar-es-Salaam 2,347,000; Dodoma 180,000.

Government: Type: Republic. **Head of state:** Pres. Benjamin William Mkapa; b Nov. 12, 1938; in office: Nov. 23, 1995. **Head of gov.:** Prime Min. Frederick Tluway Sumaye; b May 29, 1950; in office: Nov. 28, 1995. **Local divisions:** 25 regions. **Defense budget (2001):** $140 mil. **Active troops:** 27,000.

Economy: Industries: Agric. processing, mining, oil refining. **Chief crops:** Sisal, cotton, coffee, tea, tobacco, corn, cloves. **Minerals:** Tin, phosphates, iron, coal, gemstones, diamonds, gold. **Other resources:** Pyrethrum (insecticide made from chrysanthemums). **Arable land:** 3%. **Livestock** (2001): cattle: 14.40 mil; chickens: 30.00 mil.; goats: 10.00 mil.; pigs: 355,000; sheep: 4.25 mil **Fish catch** (1999): 357,210 metric tons. **Electricity prod.:** 2.77 bil. kWh. **Labor force:** agri. 80%, ind. and commerce 20%.

Finance: Monetary unit: Shilling (Sept. 2002: 972.00 = $1 U.S.). **GDP** (2000 est.): $25.1 bil. **Per capita GDP:** $710. **Imports** (2000 est.): $1.57 bil.; partners (1998): South Africa 8%, Japan 8%. **Exports** (2000 est.): $937 mil.; partners (1998): India 20%, UK 10%. **Tourism:** $733 mil. **Budget** (1999 est.): $1.36 bil. **Intl. reserves less gold** (end 2000): $748 mil. **Consumer prices** (change in 2000): 5.9%.

Transport: Railroad: Length: 2,218 mi. **Motor vehicles:** 55,000 pass. cars; 78,800 comm. vehicles. **Civil aviation:** 143.4 mil pass.-mi; 11 airports. **Chief ports:** Dar-es-Salaam, Mtwara, Tanga.

Communications: TV sets: 2.8 per 1,000 pop. **Radios:** 20 per 1,000 pop. **Telephones:** 575,400.

Health: Life expectancy: 50.8 male; 52.7 female. **Births** (per 1,000 pop.): 39.1. **Deaths** (per 1,000 pop.): 13. **Natural inc.:** 2.61%. **Infant mortality** (per 1,000 live births): 77.8.

Education: Free, compulsory: ages 7-14. **Literacy**: 68%.

Major Intl. Organizations: UN and all of its specialized agencies, the Commonwealth, AU.

Embassy: 2139 R St. NW 20008; 518-6647.

Website: www.tanzania.go.tz/index2E.html

The Republic of Tanganyika in E Africa and the island Republic of Zanzibar, off the coast of Tanganyika, both of which had recently gained independence, joined into a single nation, the United Republic of Tanzania, Apr. 26, 1964. Zanzibar retains internal self-government.

Until resigning as president in 1985, Julius K. Nyerere, a former Tanganyikan independence leader, dominated Tanzania's politics, which emphasized government planning and control of the economy, with single-party rule. In 1992 the constitution was amended to establish a multiparty system. Privatization of the economy was undertaken in the 1990s.

At least 500 people died when an overcrowded Tanzanian ferry sank in Lake Victoria, May 21, 1996. About 460,000 Rwandan refugees, mostly Hutu, returned from Tanzania to Rwanda in Dec. 1996. A bomb at the U.S. embassy in Dar-es-Salaam, Aug. 7, 1998, killed 11 people and injured at least 70 others. The U.S. blamed the attack and a near-simultaneous embassy bombing in Kenya on Islamic terrorists associated with Osama bin Laden. After a trial in New York City, 4 conspirators were convicted May 29, 2001.

Former Pres. Nyerere died in London Oct. 14, 1999. President since 1995, Benjamin Mkapa was reelected Oct. 29, 2000. Over 280 people died in a train wreck June 24, 2002, SE of Dodoma.

Tanganyika. Arab colonization and slaving began in the 8th century AD; Portuguese sailors explored the coast by about 1500. Other Europeans followed.

In 1885 Germany established German East Africa of which Tanganyika formed the bulk. It became a League of Nations mandate and, after 1946, a UN trust territory, both under Britain. It became independent Dec. 9, 1961, and a republic within the Commonwealth a year later.

Zanzibar, the Isle of Cloves, lies 23 mi. off mainland Tanzania; area 640 sq. mi. and pop. (1995 est.) 456,934. The island of **Pemba,** 25 mi. to the NE, area 380 sq. mi. and pop. (1995 est.) 322,466, is included in the administration.

Chief industry is cloves and clove oil production, of which Zanzibar and Pemba produce most of the world's supply.

Zanzibar was for centuries the center for Arab slave traders. Portugal ruled the region for 2 centuries until ousted by Arabs around 1700. Zanzibar became a British Protectorate in 1890; independence came Dec. 10, 1963. Revolutionary forces overthrew the Sultan Jan. 12, 1964. The new government ousted Western diplomats and newsmen, slaughtered thousands of Arabs, and nationalized farms. Union with Tanganyika followed.

Thailand

Kingdom of Thailand

People: Population: 62,354,402. **Age distrib.** (%): <15: 23.4; 65+: 6.6. **Pop. density:** 316 per sq. mi. **Urban:** 21%. **Ethnic groups:** Thai 75%, Chinese 14%. **Principal languages:** Thai (official), English. **Chief religions:** Buddhist 95%, Muslim 4%.

Geography: Area: 197,600 sq. mi. **Location:** On Indochinese and Malayan peninsulas in SE Asia. **Neighbors:** Myanmar on W and N, Laos on N, Cambodia on E, Malaysia on S. **Topography:** A plateau dominates the NE third of Thailand, dropping to the fertile alluvial valley of the Chao Phraya R. in the center. Forested mountains are in the N, with narrow fertile valleys. The S peninsula region is covered by rain forests. **Capital:** Bangkok 7,527,000.

Government: Type: Constitutional monarchy. **Head of state:** King Bhumibol Adulyadej; b Dec. 5, 1927; in office: June 9, 1946. **Head of gov.:** Prime Min. Thaksin Shinawatra; b July 26, 1949; in office: Feb. 18, 2001. **Local divisions:** 76 provinces. **Defense budget:** (2001) $1.7 bil. **Active troops:** 306,000.

Economy: Industries: Tourism, textiles and garments, agric. processing, beverages, tobacco. **Chief crops:** Rice (world's largest exporter), corn, cassava, sugarcane. **Minerals:** Tin, tungsten, gas. **Crude oil reserves** (2000): 296.25 mil bbls. **Other resources:** Forests, rubber, seafood (world's largest exporter of farmed shrimp). **Arable land:** 34%. **Livestock** (2001): cattle: 6.30 mil; chickens: 190.00 mil.; goats: 132,000; pigs: 8.30 mil; sheep: 43,000. **Fish catch** (1999): 3.49 mil metric tons. **Electricity prod.:** 94.31 bil. kWh. **Labor force:** agri. 54%, ind. 15%, services 31%.

Finance: Monetary unit: Baht (Sept. 2002: 43.52 = $1 U.S.). **GDP** (2000 est.): $413 bil. **Per capita GDP:** $6,700. **Imports** (2000 est.): $61.8 bil.; partners (1999): Japan 26%, U.S. 14%. **Exports** (2000 est.): $68.2 bil.; partners (1999): U.S. 22%, Japan 14%. **Tourism:** $7.00 bil. **Budget** (2000 est.): $21 bil. **Intl. reserves less gold** (end 2000): $24.57 bil. **Gold:** 2.37 mil oz t. **Consumer prices** (change in 2000): 1.5%.

Transport: Railroad: Length: 2,471 mi. **Motor vehicles:** 1.55 mil pass. cars, 4.15 mil comm. vehicles. **Civil aviation:** 19.2 bil pass.-mi; 25 airports. **Chief ports:** Bangkok, Sattahip.

Communication: TV sets: 54 per 1,000 pop. **Radios:** 163 per 1,000 pop. **Telephones:** 13,523,500. **Daily newspaper circ.:** 63 per 1,000 pop.

Health: Life expectancy: 66 male; 72.5 female. **Births** (per 1,000 pop.): 16.4. **Deaths** (per 1,000 pop.): 7.5. **Natural inc.:** 0.88%. **Infant mortality** (per 1,000 live births): 29.5.

Education: Compulsory: ages 6-15. **Literacy**: 94%.

Major Intl. Organizations: UN (FAO, IBRD, ILO, IMF, IMO, WHO, WTrO), ASEAN, APEC.

Embassy: 1024 Wisconsin Ave. NW 20007; 944-3600.

Website: www.thaigov.go.th/index-eng.htm

Thais began migrating from southern China during the 11th century. A unified Thai kingdom was established in 1350.

Thailand, known as Siam until 1939, is the only country in SE Asia never taken over by a European power, thanks to King Mongkut and his son King Chulalongkorn. Ruling successively from 1851 to 1910, they modernized the country and signed trade treaties with Britain and France. A bloodless revolution in 1932 limited the monarchy. Thailand was an ally of Japan during World War II and of the U.S. during the postwar period.

The military took over the government in a bloody 1976 coup. Kriangsak Chomanan, prime minister, resigned Feb. 1980 because of soaring inflation, oil price increases, labor unrest, and growing crime. Vietnamese troops crossed the border but were repulsed by Thai forces in the 1980s.

Chatichai Choonhavan was chosen prime minister in a democratic election, Aug. 1988. In Feb. 1991, the military ousted Choonhavan in a bloodless coup. A violent crackdown on street demonstrations in May 1992 led to more than 50 deaths. AIDS reached epidemic proportions in Thailand in the mid-1990s.

A steep downturn in the economy forced Thailand to seek more than $15 billion in emergency international loans in Aug. 1997. A new constitution won legislative approval Sept. 27. As the economic crisis deepened, Chuan Leekpai became prime minister Nov. 9, 1997, and implemented financial reforms.

Following elections in Jan. 2001, Thaksin Shinawatra, a wealthy former telecommunications executive, became prime minister. Thailand's Constitutional Court acquitted him Aug. 3 of corruption while he was deputy prime minister in 1997.

By the end of the 1990s, according to UN estimates, more than 750,000 people in Thailand had HIV/AIDS.

Togo

Togolese Republic

People: Population: 5,285,501. **Age distrib.** (%): <15: 45.6; 65+: 2.4. **Pop. density:** 252 per sq. mi. **Urban:** 33%. **Ethnic groups:** Ewe, Mina, Kabre, 37 other tribes. **Principal languages:** French (official), Ewe, Mina, Dagomba, Kabye. **Chief religions:** Indigenous beliefs 70%, Christian 20%, Muslim 10%.

Geography: Area: 21,000 sq. mi. **Location:** On S coast of W Africa. **Neighbors:** Ghana on W, Burkina Faso on N, Benin on E. **Topography:** A range of hills running SW-NE splits Togo into 2 savanna plains regions. **Capital:** Lomé: 732,000.

Government: Type: Republic. **Head of state:** Pres. Gnassingbé Eyadéma; b Dec. 26, 1937; in office: Apr. 14, 1967. **Head of gov.:** Prime Min. Koffi Sama; b 1944; in office: June 29, 2002. **Local divisions:** 5 regions. **Defense budget (2001):** $30 mil. **Active troops:** 9,450.

Economy: Industries: Phosphate mining, agric. processing, cement. handicrafts. **Chief crops:** Coffee, cocoa, yams, cotton, millet, rice. **Minerals:** Phosphates, limestone, marble. **Arable land:** 38%. **Livestock** (2001): cattle: 277,200; chickens: 8.50 mil.; goats: 1.42 mil.; pigs: 289,200; sheep: 1.00 mil. **Fish catch:** (1999): 14,310 metric tons. **Electricity prod.:** 0.10 bil. kWh. **Labor force:** agri. 65%, ind. 5%, services 30%.

Finance: Monetary unit: CFA Franc (Sept. 2002: 671.78 = $1 U.S.). **GDP** (2000 est.): $7.3 bil. **Per capita GDP:** $1,500. **Imports** (2000): $452 mil.; partners (1999): Ghana, China, France, Cote d'Ivoire. **Exports** (2000): $336 mil.; partners (1999): Nigeria, Brazil, Canada, Philippines. **Budget** (1997 est.): $252 mil. **Intl. reserves less gold** (end 2000): $117 mil. **Gold:** 13,000 oz t. **Consumer prices** (change in 2000): 1.9%.

Transport: Railroad: Length: 245 mi. **Motor vehicles:** 74,662 pass. cars, 34,605 comm. vehicles. **Civil aviation:** 150.5 mil pass.-mi; 2 airports. **Chief port:** Lomé.

Communications: TV sets: 36 per 1,000 pop. **Radios:** 212 per 1,000 pop. **Telephones:** 143,100.

Health: Life expectancy: 52 male; 56.1 female. **Births** (per 1,000 pop.): 36.1. **Deaths** (per 1,000 pop.): 11.3. **Natural inc.:** 2.48%. **Infant mortality** (per 1,000 live births): 69.3.

Education: Compulsory: ages 6-12. **Literacy:** 52%.

Major Intl. Organizations: UN (FAO, IBRD, ILO, IMF, IMO, WHO, WTrO), AU.

Embassy: 2208 Massachusetts Ave. NW 20008; 234-4212.

Website: www.republicoftogo.com/english/index.htm

The Ewe arrived in southern Togo several centuries ago. The country later became a major source of slaves. Germany took control in 1884. France and Britain administered Togoland as UN trusteeships. The French sector became the republic of Togo Apr. 27, 1960.

The population is divided between Bantus in the S and Hamitic tribes in the N. Togo has actively promoted regional integration, as a means of stimulating the economy.

In Jan. 1993 police fired on antigovernment demonstrators, killing at least 22. Some 25,000 people fled to Ghana and Benin as a result of civil unrest. In Jan. 1994 at least 40 people were killed when gunmen reportedly attacked an army base. Further violence marred Togo's 1st multiparty legislative elections, held Feb. 1994. In office since 1967, Pres. Gnassingbé Eyadéma was reelected June 21, 1998, in a vote that was disputed as in previous elections.

Tonga

Kingdom of Tonga

People: Population: 106,137. **Age distrib. (%): <15: 40.9; 65+: 4.1. Pop. density:** 383 per sq. mi. **Urban:** 37%. **Ethnic groups:** Polynesian. **Principal languages:** Tongan, English (both official). **Chief religions:** Free Wesleyan 41%, Roman Catholic 16%, Mormon 14%.

Geography: Area: 277 sq. mi. **Location:** In western South Pacific O. **Neighbors:** Nearest are Fiji to W, Samoa to NE. **Topography:** Tonga comprises 170 volcanic and coral islands, 36 inhabited. **Capital:** Nuku'alofa: 33,000.

Government: Type: Constitutional monarchy. **Head of state:** King Taufa'ahau Tupou IV; b July 4, 1918; in office: Dec. 16, 1965. **Head of gov.:** Prime Min. Prince Ulukalala Lavaka Ata; b July 12, 1959; in office: Jan. 3, 2000. **Local divisions:** 5 divisions, 23 districts.

Economy: Industries: Tourism, fishing. **Chief crops:** Coconuts, copra, bananas, vanilla beans. **Arable land:** 24%. **Livestock** (2001): cattle: 11,250; chickens: 300,000; goats: 12,500; pigs: 80,853. **Electricity prod.:** 0.03 bil. kWh. **Labor force:** agri. 65%.

Finance: Monetary unit: Pa'anga (Sept. 2002: 1.84 = $1 U.S.). **GDP** (2000 est.): $225 mil. **Per capita GDP:** $2,200. **Imports** (1998): $69 mil.; partners (1997 est.): NZ 30%, Australia 19%. **Exports** (1998): $8 mil.; partners (1997 est.): Japan 53%, U.S. 18%. **Tourism** (1998): $15 mil. **Budget** (FY96/97 est.): $120 mil. **Intl. reserves less gold** (end 2000): $21 mil. **Consumer prices** (change in 2000): 5.9%.

Transport: Motor vehicles: 3,400 pass. cars, 3,900 comm. vehicles. **Civil aviation:** 6.4 mil pass.-mi; 6 airports. **Chief port:** Nuku'alofa.

Communications: TV sets: 20 per 1,000 pop. **Radios:** 397 per 1,000 pop. **Telephones:** 9,200. **Daily newspaper circ.:** 70 per 1,000 pop.

Health: Life expectancy: 66.1 male; 71.1 female. **Births** (per 1,000 pop.): 24.1. **Deaths** (per 1,000 pop.): 5.6. **Natural inc.:** 1.84%. **Infant mortality** (per 1,000 live births): 13.7.

Education: Free, compulsory: ages 5-14. **Literacy** (1992): 93%.

Major Intl. Organizations: UN (FAO, IBRD, IMF, WHO), the Commonwealth.

Website: www.pmo.gov.to

The islands were first visited by the Dutch in the early 17th century. A series of civil wars ended in 1845 with establishment of the Tupou dynasty. In 1900 Tonga became a British protectorate. On June 4, 1970, Tonga became independent and a member of the Commonwealth. It joined the UN on Sept. 14, 1999.

Trinidad and Tobago

Republic of Trinidad and Tobago

People: Population: 1,163,724. **Age distrib.** (%): <15: 24.1; 65+: 6.7. **Pop. density:** 582 per sq. mi. **Urban:** 74%. **Ethnic groups:** Black 40%, East Indian 40%, mixed 14%. **Principal languages:** English (official), Hindi, French, Spanish. **Chief religions:** Roman Catholic 32%, Protestant 14%, Hindu 24%.

Geography: Area: 2,000 sq. mi. **Location:** In Caribbean, off E coast of Venezuela. **Neighbors:** Nearest is Venezuela to SW. **Topography:** Three low mountain ranges cross Trinidad E-W, with a well-watered plain between N and central ranges. Parts of E and W coasts are swamps. Tobago, 116 sq. mi., lies 20 mi. NE. **Capital:** Port-of-Spain: 54,000.

Government: Type: Parliamentary democracy. **Head of state:** Pres. Arthur N. R. Robinson; b Dec. 16, 1926; in office: Mar. 19, 1997. **Head of gov.:** Prime Min. Patrick Augustus Mervyn Manning; b Aug. 17, 1946; in office: Dec. 24, 2001. **Local divisions:** 8 counties, 3 municipalities, 1 ward. **Defense budget** (2001): $64 mil. **Active troops:** 2,700.

Economy: Industries: Oil products, chemicals, tourism. **Chief crops:** Sugar, cocoa, coffee, citrus, rice. **Minerals:** Asphalt, oil, gas. **Crude oil reserves** (2001): 0.7 bil bbls. **Arable land:** 15%. **Livestock** (2001): cattle: 35,000; chickens: 10.00 mil.; goats: 59,000; pigs: 41,000; sheep: 12,000. **Fish catch:** (1999): 15,012 metric tons. **Electricity prod.:** 5.15 bil. kWh. **Labor force:** construction and utilities 12.4%, manufacturing mining and quarrying 14%, agri. 9.5%, services 64.1%.

Finance: Monetary unit: Dollar (Sept. 2002: 6.09 = $1 U.S.). **GDP** (2000 est.): $11.2 bil. **Per capita GDP:** $9,500. **Imports** (2000 est.): $3 bil.; partners (1999): U.S. 39.8%, Venezuela 11.9%, EU 11%,. **Exports** (2000): $3.2 bil.; partners (1999): U.S. 39.3%, Caricom countries 26.1%. **Tourism** (1998): $201 mil. **Budget** (1998): $1.6 bil. **Intl. reserves less gold** (end 2000): $1.06 bil. **Gold:** 58,000 oz t. **Consumer prices** (change in 2000): 3.6%.

Transport: Motor vehicles: 128,000 pass. cars, 27,000 comm. vehicles. **Civil aviation:** 1.5 bil pass.-mi; 2 airports. **Chief ports:** Port-of-Spain, Scarborough.

Communications: TV sets: 198 per 1,000 pop. **Radios:** 433 per 1,000 pop. **Telephones:** 537,200. **Daily newspaper circ.:** 139 per 1,000 pop.

Health: Life expectancy: 66 male; 71.2 female. **Births** (per 1,000 pop.): 13.7. **Deaths** (per 1,000 pop.): 8.8. **Natural inc.:** 0.48%. **Infant mortality** (per 1,000 live births): 24.2.

Education: Free, compulsory: ages 5-12. **Literacy:** 98%.

Major Intl. Organizations: UN (FAO, IBRD, ILO, IMF, IMO, WHO, WTrO), Caricom, the Commonwealth, OAS.

Embassy: 1708 Massachusetts Ave. NW 20036; 467-6490.

Columbus sighted Trinidad in 1498. A British possession since 1802, Trinidad and Tobago won independence Aug. 31, 1962. It became a republic in 1976.

Website: www.gov.tt

The nation is one of the most prosperous in the Caribbean. Oil production has increased with offshore finds. Middle Eastern oil is refined and exported, mostly to the U.S.

In July 1990, some 120 Muslim extremists captured the Parliament building and TV station and took about 50 hostages, including Prime Min. Arthur N. R. Robinson, who was beaten, shot in the legs, and tied to explosives. After a 6-day siege, the rebels surrendered.

Basdeo Panday, the country's first prime minister of East Indian ancestry, took office Nov. 9, 1995. Robinson became president on Mar. 19, 1997. Patrick Manning of the People's National Movement became prime minister after elections Dec. 10, 2001.

Tunisia

Republic of Tunisia

People: Population: 9,815,644. **Age distrib.** (%) <15: 28.7; 65+: 6.1. **Pop. density:** 164 per sq. mi. **Urban:** 65%. **Ethnic groups:** Arab 98%. **Principal languages:** Arabic (official), French. **Chief religion:** Muslim 98%.

Geography: Area: 60,000 sq. mi. **Location:** On N coast of Africa. **Neighbors:** Algeria on W, Libya on E. **Topography:** The N is wooded and fertile. The central coastal plains are given to grazing and orchards. The S is arid, approaching Sahara Desert. **Capital:** Tunis 1,927,000.

Government: Type: Republic. **Head of state:** Pres. Gen. Zine al-Abidine Ben Ali; b Sept. 3, 1936; in office: Nov. 7, 1987. **Head of gov.:** Prime Min. Mohamed Ghannouchi; b Aug. 18, 1941; in office: Nov. 17, 1999. **Local divisions:** 23 governorates. **Defense budget:** (2000) $365 mil. **Active troops:** 35,000.

Economy: Industries: Oil, mining, tourism, textiles, footwear, food. **Chief crops:** Grains, dates, olives, sugar beets, grapes. **Minerals:** Phosphates, iron, oil, lead, zinc. **Crude oil reserves** (2001): 0.3 bil bbls. **Arable land:** 19%. **Livestock** (2001): cattle: 795,000; chickens: 43.00 mil.; goats: 1.45 mil.; pigs: 6,000; sheep: 6.60 mil. **Fish catch** (1999): 89,027 metric tons. **Electricity prod.:** 10.30 bil. kWh. **Labor force:** services 55%, ind. 23%, agri. 22%.

Finance: Monetary unit: Dinar (Sept. 2002: 1.40 = $1 U.S.). **GDP** (2000 est.): $62.8 bil. **Per capita GDP:** $6,500. **Imports** (2000 est.): $8.4 bil.; partners (1999): France 23%, Germany 23%,. **Exports** (2000 est.): $6.1 bil.; partners (1999): Germany 28%, France 22%. **Tourism:** $1.61 bil. **Budget** (2000 est.): $8.1 bil. **Intl. reserves less gold** (end 1999): $1.65 bil. **Gold:** 218,000 oz t. **Consumer prices** (change in 2000): 2.9%.

Transport: Railroad: Length: 1,337 mi. **Motor vehicles:** 248,000 pass. cars, 283,000 comm. vehicles. **Civil aviation:** 1.5 bil pass.-mi; 5 airports. **Chief ports:** Tunis, Sfax, Bizerte.

Communications: TV sets: 156 per 1,000 pop. **Radios:** 188 per 1,000 pop. **Telephones:** 1,445,400. **Daily newspaper circ.:** 45 per 1,000 pop.

Health: Life expectancy: 72.6 male; 75.9 female. **Births** (per 1,000 pop.): 16.8. **Deaths** (per 1,000 pop.): 5. **Natural inc.:** 1.18%. **Infant mortality** (per 1,000 live births): 28.

Education: Compulsory: ages 6-16. **Literacy**: 67%.

Major Intl. Organizations: UN (FAO, IBRD, ILO, IMF, IMO, WHO, WTrO), AL, AU.

Embassy: 1515 Massachusetts Ave. NW 20005; 862-1850.

Website: www.ministeres.tn/index.html

Site of ancient Carthage and a former Barbary state under the suzerainty of Turkey, Tunisia became a protectorate of France under a treaty signed May 12, 1881. The nation became independent Mar. 20, 1956, and ended the monarchy the following year. Habib Bourguiba, an independence leader, served as president until 1987, when he was deposed by his prime minister, Zine al-Abidine Ben Ali.

Tunisia has actively repressed Islamic fundamentalism. A synagogue blast on Djerba Is., Apr. 11, 2002, apparently set off by al-Qaeda, killed 17 people, including 12 German tourists.

Turkey

Republic of Turkey

People: Population: 67,308,928. **Age distrib.** (%): <15: 28.4; 65+: 6.1. **Pop. density:** 226 per sq. mi. **Urban:** 74%. **Ethnic groups:** Turk 80%, Kurd 20%. **Principal languages:** Turkish (official), Kurdish, Arabic. **Chief religion:** Muslim 99.8%.

Geography: Area: 297,600 sq. mi. **Location:** Occupies Asia Minor, stretches into continental Europe; borders on Mediterranean and Black seas. **Neighbors:** Bulgaria, Greece on W; Georgia, Armenia on N; Iran on E; Iraq, Syria on S. **Topography:** Central Turkey has wide plateaus, with hot, dry summers and cold winters. High mountains ring the interior on all but W, with more than 20 peaks over 10,000 ft. Rolling plains are in W; mild, fertile coastal plains are in S, W. **Capital:** Ankara. **Cities (urban aggr.):** Istanbul 8,953,000; Ankara 3,208,000; Izmir 2,214,000.

Government: Type: Republic. **Head of state:** Pres. Ahmet Necdet Sezer; b Sept. 13, 1941; in office: May 16, 2000. **Head of gov.:** Prime Min. Bülent Ecevit; b 1925; in office: Jan. 11, 1999. **Local divisions:** 80 provinces. **Defense budget (2001):** $5.1 bil. **Active troops:** 515,100.

Economy: Industries: Textiles, food processing, autos, mining , steel, oil. **Chief crops:** Tobacco, grains, cotton, pulses, citrus, olives, sugar beets. **Minerals:** Antimony, chromium, mercury, copper, coal. **Crude oil reserves** (2001): 0.3 bil bbls. **Arable land:** 32%. **Livestock** (2001): cattle: 10.80 mil; chickens: 220.00 mil.; goats: 8.06 mil.; pigs: 5,000; sheep: 29.44 mil. **Fish catch** (1999): 500,260 metric tons. **Electricity prod.:** 119.18 bil. kWh. **Labor force:** agri. 38%, services 38%, ind. 24%.

Finance: Monetary unit: Lira (Sept. 2002: 1,657,450.00 = $1 U.S.). **GDP** (2000 est.): $444 bil. **Per capita GDP:** $6,800. **Imports** (2000 est.): $55.7 bil.; partners (2000 est.): Germany 13.1%, Italy 7.9%, U.S. 7.2%, Russia 7.0%. **Exports** (2000 est.): $26.9 bil.; partners (2000 est.): Germany 18.7%, U.S. 11.4%. **Tourism:** $5.20 bil. **Budget** (2000): $75.2 bil. **Intl. reserves less gold** (end 2000): $17.26 bil. **Gold:** 3.74 mil oz t. **Consumer prices** (change in 2000): 54.9%.

Transport: Railroad: Length: 5,348 mi. **Motor vehicles:** 3.27 mil pass. cars, 1.05 mil comm. vehicles. **Civil aviation:** 7.7 bil pass.-mi; 26 airports. **Chief ports:** Istanbul, Izmir, Mersin.

Communications: TV sets: 288 per 1,000 pop. **Radios:** 181 per 1,000 pop. **Telephones:** 38,900,900. **Daily newspaper circ:** 111 per 1,000 pop.

Health: Life expectancy: 69.2 male; 74 female. **Births** (per 1,000 pop.): 17.9. **Deaths** (per 1,000 pop.): 6. **Natural inc.:** 1.2%. **Infant mortality** (per 1,000 live births): 45.8.

Education: Free, compulsory: ages 6-14. **Literacy**: 82%.

Major Intl. Organizations: UN (FAO, IBRD, ILO, IMF, IMO, WHO, WTrO), NATO, OECD, OSCE.

Embassy: 1714 Massachusetts Ave. NW 20036; 659-8200.

Website: www.turkey.org

Ancient inhabitants of Turkey were among the world's first agriculturalists. Such civilizations as the Hittite, Phrygian, and Lydian flourished in Asiatic Turkey (Asia Minor), as did much of Greek civilization. After the fall of Rome in the 5th century, Constantinople (now Istanbul) was the capital of the Byzantine Empire for 1,000 years. It fell in 1453 to Ottoman Turks, who ruled a vast empire for over 400 years.

Just before World War I, Turkey, or the Ottoman Empire, ruled what is now Syria, Lebanon, Iraq, Jordan, Israel, Saudi Arabia, Yemen, and islands in the Aegean Sea.

Turkey joined Germany and Austria in World War I, and its defeat resulted in the loss of much territory and the fall of the sultanate. A republic was declared Oct. 29, 1923, with Mustafa Kemal (later Kemal Ataturk) as its first president. Ataturk led Turkey until his death in 1938. The Caliphate (spiritual leadership of Islam) was renounced in 1924.

Long embroiled with Greece over Cyprus, off Turkey's south coast, Turkey invaded the island July 20, 1974, after Greek officers seized the Cypriot government as a step toward unification with Greece. Turkey sought a new government for Cyprus, with Greek Cypriot and Turkish Cypriot zones. In reaction to Turkey's moves, the U.S. cut off military aid in 1975. Turkey, in turn, suspended the use of most U.S. bases. Aid was restored in 1978. There was a military takeover, Sept. 12, 1980.

Religious and ethnic tensions and active left and right extremists have caused endemic violence. The military formally transferred power to an elected Parliament in 1983. Martial law, imposed in 1978, was lifted in 1984.

Turkey was a member of the Allied forces that ousted Iraq from Kuwait, 1991. In the aftermath of the war, millions of Kurdish refugees fled to Turkey's border to escape Iraqi forces. The Turkish government mounted sporadic offensives against separatist Kurds in this border area and in N Iraq, causing heavy casualties among guerrillas and civilians.

Kurdish militants, demanding an independent state for the Kurds, raided Turkish diplomatic missions in some 25 Western European cities June 24, 1993. Tansu Ciller officially became Turkey's first woman prime minister July 5, 1993. The Welfare Party, an Islamic group, gained strength in the 1990s but was unable to form a government until June 1996, when it came to power in coalition with Ciller's True Path Party.

The pro-Islamic government resigned June 18, 1997, under pressure from the military. The European Union rebuffed Turkey's membership bid Dec. 12, 1997. The military stepped up its campaign against Islamic fundamentalism in 1998.

Kurdish rebel leader Abdullah Öcalan was captured Feb. 15, 1999; convicted of terrorism June 29, he was sentenced to death by a Turkish security court. His organization, the Kurdistan Workers' Party, announced Aug. 5 that it would abandon its 14-year-old armed insurgency. A major earthquake Aug. 17 in NW Turkey killed over 17,000 people and injured thousands more. Another quake in the same region Nov. 12 claimed at least 675 lives.

The IMF announced $7.5 billion in emergency loans Dec. 6, 2000, to help Turkey cope with a severe financial crisis. The death penalty was abolished Aug. 3, 2002, and Öcalan's sentence was commuted to life in prison Oct. 3. With his coalition crumbling, the ailing Prime Min. Bülent Ecevit agreed to call elections for Nov. 3, 2002, 18 months ahead of schedule.

Turkmenistan

People: Population: 4,688,963. **Age distrib.** (%): <15: 37.9; 65+: 4.0. **Pop. density:** 25 per sq. mi. **Urban:** 45%. **Ethnic groups:** Turkmen 77%, Uzbek 9%, Russian 7%. **Principal languages:** Turkmen (official), Russian, Uzbek. **Chief religions:** Muslim 89%, Eastern Orthodox 9%.

Geography: Area: 188,500 sq. mi. **Neighbors:** Kazakhstan on N, Uzbekistan on N and E, Afghanistan and Iran on S. **Topography:** The Kara Kum Desert occupies 80% of the area. Bordered on W by Caspian Sea. **Capital:** Ashgabat: 558,000.

Government: Type: Republic. **Head of state and gov.:** Pres. Saparmurad Niyazov; b Feb. 18, 1940; in office: Oct. 27, 1990.

Local divisions: 5 regions. **Defense budget:** (2000) $157 mil. **Active troops:** 17,500.

Economy: Industries: Natural gas, oil and oil products, textiles, food processing. **Chief crops:** Grain, cotton. **Minerals:** Coal, sulfur, oils, gas, salt. **Crude oil reserves** (2000): 546 mil bbls. **Arable land:** 3%. **Livestock** (2001): cattle: 860,000; chickens: 4.80 mil.; goats: 375,000; pigs: 45,000; sheep: 6.00 mil. **Electricity prod.:** 9.26 bil. kWh. **Labor force:** agri. 44%, ind. 19%, services 37%.

Finance: Monetary unit: Manat (Sept. 2002: 5.25 = $1 U.S.). **GDP** (2000 est.): $19.6 bil. **Per capita GDP:** $4,300. **Imports** (2000 est.): $1.65 bil.; partners: Ukraine, Turkey, Russia, Germany, U.S., Kazakhstan, Uzbekistan. **Exports** (2000 est.): $2.4 bil.; partners: Ukraine, Iran, Turkey, Russia, Kazakhstan, Tajikistan, Azerbaijan. **Tourism** (1999 est.): $192 mil. **Budget** (1999 est.): $658.2 mil

Transport: Railroad: Length: 1,317 mi. **Civil aviation:** 679.2 mil pass.-mi; 1 airport. **Chief port:** Turkmenbashi.

Communications: TV sets: 189 per 1,000 pop. **Radios:** 189 per 1,000 pop. **Telephones** (2000): 373,900.

Health: Life expectancy: 57.6 male; 64.8 female. **Births** (per 1,000 pop.): 28.3. **Deaths** (per 1,000 pop.): 8.9. **Natural inc.:** 1.94%. **Infant mortality** (per 1,000 live births): 73.2.

Education: Literacy: 100%.

Major Intl. Organizations: UN (FAO, IBRD, ILO, IMF, IMO, WHO), CIS, OSCE.

Embassy: 2207 Massachusetts Ave., NW 20008; 588-1500.

Website: www.turkmenistanembassy.org

The region has been inhabited by Turkic tribes since the 10th century. It became part of Russian Turkestan in 1881, and a constituent republic of the USSR in 1925. Turkmenistan declared independence Oct. 27, 1991, and became an independent state when the USSR disbanded Dec. 26, 1991.

Extensive oil and gas reserves place Turkmenistan in a more favorable economic position than other former Soviet republics. A new rail line linking Iran and Turkmenistan was inaugurated May 13, 1996. Political power centered around the former Communist Party apparatus, and Pres. Saparmurad Niyazov became the object of a personality cult.

Tuvalu

People: Population: 11,146. **Age distrib.** (%): <15: 33.3; 65+: 5.1. **Pop. density:** 1,110 per sq. mi. **Urban:** 51%. **Ethnic group:** Polynesian 96%. **Principal languages:** Tuvaluan, English. **Chief religion:** Church of Tuvalu (Congregationalist) 97%.

Geography: Area: 10 sq. mi. **Location:** 9 islands forming a NW-SE chain 360 mi. long in the SW Pacific O. **Neighbors:** Nearest are Kiribati to N, Fiji to S. **Topography:** The islands are all low-lying atolls, nowhere rising more than 15 ft. above sea level, composed of coral reefs. **Capital:** Funafuti: 5,000.

Government: Head of state: Queen Elizabeth II, represented by Gov.-Gen. Tomasi Puapua; b 1938; in office: June 26, 1998. **Head of gov.:** Prime Min. Saufatu Sopoaga; in office: Aug. 2, 2002.

Economy: Industries: Fishing, tourism, copra. **Chief crops:** Coconuts. **Livestock:** (2001): chickens: 40,000; pigs: 13,200. Labor force: people make a living mainly through exploitation of the sea reefs and atolls and from wages sent home by those working abroad

Finance: Monetary unit: Australian Dollar (Sept. 2002: 1.84 = $1 U.S.). **GDP** (1999 est.): $11.6 mil. **Per capita GDP:** $1,100. **Imports** (1989): $4.4 mil.; partners: Fiji, Australia, NZ. **Exports** (1989): $165,000; partners: Fiji, Australia, NZ. **Budget** (1998 est.): $6.1 mil.

Transport: Civil aviation: 1 airport. **Chief port:** Funafuti.

Communications: Radios: 320 per 1,000 pop.

Health: Life expectancy: 64.8 male; 69.2 female. **Births** (per 1,000 pop.): 21.4. **Deaths** (per 1,000 pop.): 7.5. **Natural inc.:** 1.4%. **Infant mortality** (per 1,000 live births): 22.

Education: Compulsory: ages 7-15. **Literacy** (1990): 95%.

Major Intl. Organizations: UN, WHO, the Commonwealth.

The Ellice Islands separated from the British Gilbert and Ellice Islands Colony in 1975 and became Tuvalu; independence came Oct. 1, 1978. In 2000, Tuvalu joined the United Nations.

Uganda

Republic of Uganda

People: Population: 24,699,073. **Age distrib.** (%): <15: 51.1; 65+: 2.1. **Pop. density:** 320 per sq. mi. **Urban:** 14%. **Ethnic groups:** Baganda 17%, Karamojong 12%, many others. **Principal languages:** English (official), Luganda, Swahili. **Chief religions:** Protestant 33%, Roman Catholic 33%, indigenous beliefs 18%, Muslim 16%.

Geography: Area: 77,100 sq. mi. **Location:** In E Central Africa. **Neighbors:** Sudan on N, Congo (formerly Zaire) on W, Rwanda and Tanzania on S, Kenya on E. **Topography:** Most of Uganda is a high plateau 3,000-6,000 ft. high, with high Ruwenzori range in W (Mt. Margherita 16,750 ft.), volcanoes in SW; NE is arid, W and SW rainy. Lakes Victoria, Edward, Albert form much of borders. **Capital:** Kampala 1,274,000.

Government: Type: Republic. **Head of state:** Pres. Yoweri Kaguta Museveni; b Mar. 1944; in office: Jan. 29, 1986. **Head of gov.:** Prime Min. Apollo Nsibambi; b Nov. 27, 1938; in office: Apr. 5, 1999. **Local divisions:** 39 districts. **Defense budget (2001):** $115 mil. **Active troops:** 50,000–60,000.

Economy: Industries: Sugar, brewing, tobacco, cotton textiles. **Chief crops:** Coffee, cotton, tea, corn, tobacco. **Minerals:** Copper, cobalt. **Arable land:** 25%. **Livestock** (2001): cattle: 5.90 mil; chickens: 25.50 mil.; goats: 6.20 mil.; pigs: 1.55 mil; sheep: 1.10 mil. **Fish catch** (1999): 218,236 metric tons. **Electricity prod.:** 1.60 bil. kWh. **Labor force:** agri. 82%, ind. 5%, services 13%.

Finance: Monetary unit: Shilling (Sept. 2002: 1,818.85 = $1 U.S.). **GDP** (2000 est.): $26.2 bil. **Per capita GDP:** $1,100. **Imports** (1999): $1.1 bil.; partners (1999): Kenya 27.5%, U.S. 21.2%. **Exports** (1999): $500.1 mil.; partners (1999): Spain, Germany, Belgium, Netherlands, Hungary, Kenya. **Tourism:** $142 mil. **Budget** (FY98/99 est.): $1.04 bil. **Intl. reserves less gold** (end 2000): $620 mil. **Consumer prices** (change in 2000): 2.8%.

Transport: Railroad: Length: 771 mi. **Motor vehicles:** 24,400 pass. cars, 26,600 comm. vehicles. **Civil aviation:** 68.4 mil pass.-mi; 1 airport. **Chief ports:** Entebbe, Jinja.

Communications: TV sets: 27 per 1,000 pop. **Radios:** 485 per 1,000 pop. **Telephones:** 380,500.

Health: Life expectancy: 43 male; 44.7 female. **Births** (per 1,000 pop.): 47.1. **Deaths** (per 1,000 pop.): 17.5. **Natural inc.:** 2.96%. **Infant mortality** (per 1,000 live births): 89.3.

Education: Literacy: 62%.

Major Intl. Organizations: UN (FAO, IBRD, ILO, IMF, WHO, WTrO), the Commonwealth, AU.

Embassy: 5911 16th St. NW 20011; 726-7100.

Website: www.government.go.ug

Britain obtained a protectorate over Uganda in 1894. The country became independent Oct. 9, 1962, and a republic within the Commonwealth a year later. In 1967, the traditional kingdoms, including the powerful Buganda state, were abolished and the central government strengthened.

Gen. Idi Amin seized power from Prime Min. Milton Obote in 1971. During his eight years of dictatorial rule, he was responsible for the deaths of up to 300,000 of his opponents. In 1972 he expelled nearly all of Uganda's 45,000 Asians. Amin was named president for life in 1976. Tanzanian troops and Ugandan exiles and rebels ousted Amin, Apr. 11, 1979.

Obote held the presidency from Dec. 1980 until his ouster in a military coup July 27, 1985. Guerrilla war and rampant human rights abuses plagued Uganda under Obote's regime.

Conditions improved after Yoweri Museveni took power in Jan. 1986. In 1993 the government authorized restoration of the Buganda and other monarchies, but only for ceremonial purposes. Under a constitution ratified Oct. 1995, nonparty presidential and legislative elections were held in 1996. Uganda helped Laurent Kabila seize power in the Congo (formerly Zaire) in 1997 but sent troops in 1998 to aid insurgents seeking his ouster. A withdrawal agreement was made Sept. 6, 2002. Museveni faced several regional insurgencies in the late 1990s.

At least 330 members of the Movement for the Restoration of the Ten Commandments of God died in a church fire in Kanungu, Mar. 17, 2000; in all, over 900 deaths were associated with the cult. An ebola virus outbreak Oct.-Dec. 2000 killed more than 150 people. Pres. Museveni won reelection Mar. 12, 2001.

Ukraine

People: Population: 48,396,470. **Age distrib.** (%): <15: 17.3; 65+: 14.1. **Pop. density:** 208 per sq. mi. **Urban:** 68%. **Ethnic groups:** Ukrainian 73%, Russian 22%. **Principal languages:** Ukrainian, Russian. **Chief religions:** Ukrainian Orthodox, Ukrainian Catholic.

Geography: Area: 233,100 sq. mi. **Location:** In E Europe. **Neighbors:** Belarus on N; Russia on NE and E; Moldova and Romania on SW; Hungary, Slovakia, and Poland on W. **Topography:** Part of the E European plain. Mountainous areas include the Carpathians in the SW and Crimean chain in the S. Arable black soil constitutes a large part of the country. **Capital:** Kiev. **Cities (urban aggr.):** Kiev (Kyiv) 2,488,000; Kharkov 1,416,000; Dnepropetrovsk 1,069,000.

Government: Type: Constitutional republic. **Head of state:** Pres. Leonid Danylovich Kuchma; b Aug. 9, 1938; in office: July 19, 1994. **Head of gov.:** Prime Min. Anatoly Kinakh; b Aug. 4, 1954; in office: May 29, 2001. **Local divisions:** 24 oblasts, 2 municipalities, 1 autonomous republic. **Defense budget (2001):** $582 mil. **Active troops:** 303,800.

Economy: Industries: Coal, electric power, metals, machinery **Chief crops:** Grains, sugar beets, vegetables. **Minerals:** Iron, manganese, coal, gas, oil, sulfur, salt. **Other resources:**

Forests. **Crude oil reserves** (2000): 395 mil bbls. **Arable land:** 58%. **Livestock** (2001): cattle: 9.91 mil; chickens: 108.00 mil.; goats: 775,000; pigs: 9.08 mil; sheep: 995,000. **Fish catch** (1999): 403,005 metric tons. **Electricity prod.:** 163.57 bil. kWh. **Labor force:** ind. 32%, agri. 24%, services 44%.

Finance: Monetary unit: Hryvna (Sept. 2002: 5.33 = $1 U.S.). **GDP** (2000 est.): $189.4 bil. **Per capita GDP:** $3,850. **Imports** (2000 est.): $15 bil.; partners (2000 est.): Russia 42%, Europe 29%. **Exports** (2000 est.): $14.6 bil.; partners (2000 est.): Russia 24%, Europe 30%. **Tourism:** $541 mil. **Budget** (1999 est.): $8.8 bil. **Intl. reserves less gold** (end 2000): $1.04 bil. **Gold:** 437,800 oz t. **Consumer prices** (change in 1999): 22.7%.

Transport: Railroad: Length: 14,100 mi. **Motor vehicles:** 4.5 mil pass. cars. **Civil aviation:** 1.2 bil pass.-mi; 12 airports. **Chief ports:** Odesa, Kiev, Berdiansk.

Communications: TV sets: 233 per 1,000 pop. **Radios:** 346 per 1,000 pop. **Telephones:** 12,894,200. **Daily newspaper circ.:** 118 per 1,000 pop.

Health: Life expectancy: 60.9 male; 72.1 female. **Births** (per 1,000 pop.): 9.6. **Deaths** (per 1,000 pop.): 16.4. **Natural inc.:** -0.68%. **Infant mortality** (per 1,000 live births): 21.1.

Education: Compulsory: ages 7-15. **Literacy**: 99%.

Major Intl. Organizations: UN (IBRD, ILO, IMF, IMO, WHO), CIS, OSCE.

Embassy: 3350 M St. NW 20007; 333-0606.

Websites: www.ukremb.com; www.kmu.gov.ua

Trypilians flourished along the Dnieper River, Ukraine's main artery, from 6000-1000 BC. Ukrainians' Slavic ancestors inhabited modern Ukrainian territory well before the first century AD.

In the 9th century, the princes of Kiev established a strong state called Kievan Rus, which included much of present-day Ukraine. A strong dynasty was established, with ties to virtually all major European royal families. St. Vladimir the Great, ruler of Kievan Rus, accepted Christianity as the national faith in 988. At the crossroads of European trade routes, Kievan Rus reached its zenith under Yaroslav the Wise (1019-1054). Internal conflicts led to the disintegration of the Ukrainian state by the 13th century. Mongol rule was supplanted by Poland and Lithuania in the 14th and 15th centuries. The N Black Sea coast and Crimea came under the control of the Turks in 1478.

Ukrainian Cossacks, starting in the late 16th century, waged numerous wars of liberation against the occupiers of Ukraine: Russia, Poland, and Turkey. By the late 18th century, Ukrainian independence was lost. Ukraine's neighbors once again divided its territory. At the turn of the 19th century, Ukraine was occupied by Russia and Austria-Hungary.

An independent Ukrainian National Republic was proclaimed on January 22, 1918. In 1921, Ukraine's neighbors occupied and divided Ukrainian territory. In 1922, Ukraine became a constituent republic of the USSR as the Ukrainian SSR. In 1932-33, the Soviet government engineered a man-made famine in eastern Ukraine, resulting in the deaths of 7-10 million Ukrainians.

In March 1939, independent Carpatho-Ukraine was the first European state to wage war against Nazi-led aggression in the region. During World War II the Ukrainian nationalist underground fought both Nazi and Soviet forces. Restoration of Ukrainian independence was declared June 30, 1941. Over 5 million Ukrainians died in the war. With the reoccupation of Ukraine by Soviet troops in 1944 came a renewed wave of mass arrests, executions, and deportations.

The world's worst nuclear power plant disaster occurred in Chernobyl, Ukraine, in April 1986; many thousands were killed or disabled as a result of the radiation leak.The plant was finally shut down Dec. 15, 2000.

Ukrainian independence was restored in Dec. 1991 with the dissolution of the Soviet Union. In the post-Soviet period Ukraine was burdened with a deteriorating economy. Following a 1994 accord with Russia and the U.S., Ukraine's large nuclear arsenal was transferred to Russia for destruction. A new constitution legalizing private property and establishing Ukrainian as the sole official language was approved by parliament June 29, 1996. In May 1997, Russia and Ukraine resolved disputes over the Black Sea fleet and the future of Sevastopol and signed a long-delayed treaty of friendship. President since 1994, Leonid Kuchma won a 2nd 5-year term in a runoff vote Nov. 14, 1999; a referendum expanding his powers passed Apr. 16, 2000.

A blast from an errant Ukrainian missile caused a Russian jetliner to plunge into the Black Sea Oct. 4, 2001, killing all 78 people on board. A Russian Su-27 fighter plane crashed at a military airshow in W. Ukraine, July 27, 2002, killing 83.

United Arab Emirates

People: Population: 2,445,989. **Age distrib.** (%): <15: 28.9; 65+: 2.4. **Pop. density:** 76 per sq. mi. **Urban:** 86%. **Ethnic groups:** Arab, Iranian, Pakistani, Indian. **Principal languages:** Arabic (official), Persian, English, Hindi, Urdu. **Chief religions:** Muslim 96%, Christian, Hindu.

Geography: Area: 32,300 sq. mi. **Location:** Middle East, on the S shore of the Persian Gulf. **Neighbors:** Saudi Arabia on W and S, Oman on E. **Topography:** A barren, flat coastal plain gives way to uninhabited sand dunes on the S. Hajar Mts. are on E. **Capital:** Abu Dhabi 471,000.

Government: Type: Federation of emirates. **Head of state:** Pres. Zaid ibn Sultan an-Nahayan; b 1918; in office: Dec. 2, 1971. **Head of gov.:** Prime Min. Sheik Maktum ibn Rashid al-Maktum; b 1946; in office: Nov. 20, 1990. **Local divisions:** 7 autonomous emirates: Abu Dhabi, Ajman, Dubai, Fujaira, Ras al-Khaimah, Sharjah, Umm al-Qaiwain. **Defense budget (2000):** $3.9 bil. **Active troops:** 65,000.

Economy: Industries: Oil, fishing, petrochemicals. **Chief crops:** Vegetables, dates. **Minerals:** Oil, natural gas. **Crude oil reserves** (2001): 62.8 bil bbls. **Livestock** (2001): cattle: 110,000; chickens: 14.65 mil.; goats: 1.20 mil.; sheep: 467,281. **Fish catch:** (1999): 114,358 metric tons. **Electricity prod.:** 38.70 bil. kWh. **Labor force:** services 60%, ind. 32%, agri. 8%.

Finance: Monetary unit: Dirham (Sept. 2002: 3.67 = $1 U.S.). **GDP** (2000 est.): $54 bil. **Per capita GDP:** $22,800. **Imports** (2000 est.): $34 bil.; partners (1999): Japan 9%, U.S. 8%, UK 8%. **Exports** (2000 est.): $46 bil.; partners (1999): Japan 30%, India 7%. **Budget** (2000 est.): $7.3 bil. **Intl. reserves less gold** (end 2000): $10.38 bil. **Gold:** 397,000 oz t.

Transport: Motor vehicles: 320,000 pass. cars, 80,000 comm. vehicles. **Civil aviation:** 8.4 bil pass.-mi; 6 airports. **Chief ports:** Ajman, Das Island.

Communications: TV sets: 260 per 1,000 pop. **Radios:** 206 per 1,000 pop. **Telephones:** 2,962,200. **Daily newspaper circ.:** 170 per 1,000 pop.

Health: Life expectancy: 72.1 male; 77.1 female. **Births** (per 1,000 pop.): 18.3. **Deaths** (per 1,000 pop.): 3.9. **Natural inc.:** 1.44%. **Infant mortality** (per 1,000 live births): 16.1.

Education: Compulsory: ages 6-12. **Literacy**: 79%.

Major Intl. Organizations: UN (FAO, IBRD, ILO, IMF, IMO, WHO, WTrO), AL, OPEC.

Embassy: Suite 700, 1255 22nd Street NW, 20037, 955-7999.

Websites: www.uae.org.ae; www.emirates.org

The 7 "Trucial Sheikdoms" gave Britain control of defense and foreign relations in the 19th century. They merged to become an independent state Dec. 2, 1971.

The Abu Dhabi Petroleum Co. was fully nationalized in 1975. Oil revenues have given the UAE one of the highest per capita GDPs in the world. International banking has grown in recent years.

United Kingdom

United Kingdom of Great Britain and Northern Ireland

People: Population: 59,778,002. **Age distrib.** (%): <15: 18.9; 65+: 15.7. **Pop. density:** 641 per sq. mi. **Urban:** 89%. **Ethnic groups:** English 81.5%, Scottish 9.6%, Irish 2.4%, Welsh 1.9%, Ulster 1.8%; West Indian, Indian, Pakistani, others 2.8%. **Principal languages:** English, Welsh, Scottish, Gaelic. **Chief religions:** Anglican, Roman Catholic, other Christian, Muslim.

Geography: Area: 93,300 sq. mi. **Location:** Off the NW coast of Europe, across English Channel, Strait of Dover, and North Sea. **Neighbors:** Ireland to W, France to SE. **Topography:** England is mostly rolling land, rising to Uplands of southern Scotland; Lowlands are in center of Scotland, granite Highlands are in N. Coast is heavily indented, especially on W. British Isles have milder climate than N Europe due to the Gulf Stream and ample rainfall. Severn, 220 mi., and Thames, 215 mi., are longest rivers. **Capital:** London. **Cities (urban aggr.):** London 7,640,000; Birmingham 2,272,000; Manchester 2,252,000 Leeds 1,433,000; Liverpool 915,000.

Government: Type: Constitutional monarchy. **Head of state:** Queen Elizabeth II; b Apr. 21, 1926; in office: Feb. 6, 1952. **Head of gov.:** Prime Min. Tony Blair; b May 6, 1953; in office: May 2, 1997. **Local divisions:** 467 local authorities, including England: 387; Wales: 22; Scotland: 32; Northern Ireland: 26. **Defense budget** (2001): $34.0 bil. **Active troops:** 211,430.

Economy: Industries: Machine tools, electric power and automation equip., rail, shipbuilding, aircraft, vehicles, electronics and comm. equip. **Chief crops:** Cereals, oilseeds, potatoes, vegetables. **Minerals:** Coal, tin, oil, gas, limestone, iron, salt, clay. **Crude oil reserves** (2001): 4.7 bil bbls. **Arable land:** 25%. **Livestock** (2001): cattle: 10.60 mil; chickens: 167.55 mil.; goats: 5.85 mil; sheep: 36.70 mil. **Fish catch** (1999): 1.03 mil metric tons. **Electricity prod.:** 355.76 bil. kWh. **Labor force:** agri. 1%, ind. 19%, services 80%.

Finance: Monetary unit: Pound (Sept. 2002: .64 = $1 U.S.). **GDP** (2000 est.): $1.36 tril. **Per capita GDP:** $22,800. **Imports** (2000): $324 bil.; partners (1999): EU 53%, U.S. 13%, Japan 5%. **Exports** (2000): $282 bil.; partners (1999): EU 58%,U.S. 15%. **Tourism:** $20.97 bil. **Budget** (FY00): $510.8 bil. **Intl. reserves**

less gold (end 2000): $33.69 bil. **Gold:** 15.67 mil oz t. **Consumer prices** (change in 2000): 2.9%.

Transport: Railroad: Length: 23,518 mi. **Motor vehicles (1997):** 25.59 mil pass. cars, 3.22 mil comm. vehicles. **Civil aviation:** 98.1 bil pass.-mi; 57 airports. **Chief ports:** London, Liverpool, Cardiff, Belfast.

Communications: TV sets: 641 per 1,000 pop. **Radios:** 1,445 per 1,000 pop. **Telephones:** 82,352,000. **Daily newspaper circ.:** 332 per 1,000 pop.

Health: Life expectancy: 75.3 male; 80.8 female. **Births** (per 1,000 pop.): 11.3. **Deaths** (per 1,000 pop.): 10.3. **Natural inc.:** 0.1%. **Infant mortality** (per 1,000 live births): 5.5.

Education: Compulsory: ages 5-16. **Literacy** (1993): 100%.

Major Intl. Organizations: UN and all of its specialized agencies, the Commonwealth, EU, NATO, OECD, OSCE.

Embassy: 3100 Massachusetts Ave. NW 20008; 588-6500.

Website: www.britainusa.com

The United Kingdom of Great Britain and Northern Ireland comprises England, Wales, Scotland, and Northern Ireland.

Queen and Royal Family. The ruling sovereign is Elizabeth II of the House of Windsor, b Apr. 21, 1926, elder daughter of King George VI. She succeeded to the throne Feb. 6, 1952, and was crowned June 2, 1953. She was married Nov. 20, 1947, to Lt. Philip Mountbatten, b June 10, 1921, former Prince of Greece. He was created Duke of Edinburgh, and given the title H.R.H., Nov. 19, 1947; he was named Prince of the United Kingdom and Northern Ireland Feb. 22, 1957. Prince Charles Philip Arthur George, b Nov. 14, 1948, is the Prince of Wales and heir apparent. His 1st son, William Philip Arthur Louis, b June 21, 1982, is second in line to the throne.

Parliament is the legislative body for the UK, with certain powers over dependent units. It consists of 2 houses: The **House of Commons** has 659 members, elected by direct ballot and divided as follows: England 529; Wales 40; Scotland 72; Northern Ireland 18. Following a drastic reduction in the number of hereditary peerages, the **House of Lords** (Aug. 2002) comprised 91 hereditary peers, 584 life peers, and 2 archbishops and 24 bishops of the Church of England, for a total of 701.

Resources and Industries. Great Britain's major occupations are manufacturing and trade. Metals and metal-using industries contribute more than 50% of exports. Of about 60 million acres of land in England, Wales, and Scotland, 46 million are farmed, of which 17 million are arable, the rest pastures.

Large oil and gas fields have been found in the North Sea. Commercial oil production began in 1975. There are large deposits of coal.

Britain imports all of its cotton, rubber, sulphur, about 80% of its wool, half of its food and iron ore, also certain amounts of paper, tobacco, chemicals. Manufactured goods made from these basic materials have been exported since the industrial age began. Main exports are machinery, chemicals, textiles, clothing, autos and trucks, iron and steel, locomotives, ships, jet aircraft, farm machinery, drugs, radio, TV, radar and navigation equipment, scientific instruments, arms, whisky.

Religion and Education. The Church of England is Protestant Episcopal. The queen is its temporal head, with rights of appointments to archbishoprics, bishoprics, and other offices. There are 2 provinces, Canterbury and York, each headed by an archbishop. The most famous church is Westminster Abbey (1050-1760), site of coronations, tombs of Elizabeth I, Mary, Queen of Scots, kings, poets, and of the Unknown Warrior.

The most celebrated British universities are Oxford and Cambridge, each dating to the 13th century. There are about 70 other universities.

History. Britain was part of the continent of Europe until about 6,000 BC, but migration across the English Channel continued long afterward. Celts arrived 2,500 to 3,000 years ago. Their language survives in Welsh, and Gaelic enclaves.

England was added to the Roman Empire in AD 43. After the withdrawal of Roman legions in 410, waves of Jutes, Angles, and Saxons arrived from German lands. They contended with Danish raiders for control from the 8th through 11th centuries. The last successful invasion was by French speaking Normans in 1066, who united the country with their dominions in France.

Opposition by nobles to royal authority forced King John to sign the Magna Carta in 1215, a guarantee of rights and the rule of law. In the ensuing decades, the foundations of the parliamentary system were laid.

English dynastic claims to large parts of France led to the Hundred Years War, 1338-1453, and the defeat of England. A long civil war, the War of the Roses, lasted 1455-85, and ended with the establishment of the powerful Tudor monarchy. A distinct English civilization flourished. The economy prospered over long periods of domestic peace unmatched in continental Europe. Religious independence was secured when the Church of England was separated from the authority of the pope in 1534.

Under Queen Elizabeth I, England became a major naval power, leading to the founding of colonies in the new world and the expansion of trade with Europe and the Orient. Scotland was united with England when James VI of Scotland was crowned James I of England in 1603.

A struggle between Parliament and the Stuart kings led to a bloody civil war, 1642-49, and the establishment of a republic under the Puritan Oliver Cromwell. The monarchy was restored in 1660, but the "Glorious Revolution" of 1688 confirmed the sovereignty of Parliament: a Bill of Rights was granted 1689.

In the 18th century, parliamentary rule was strengthened. Technological and entrepreneurial innovations led to the Industrial Revolution. The 13 North American colonies were lost, but replaced by growing empires in Canada and India. Britain's role in the defeat of Napoleon, 1815, strengthened its position as the leading world power.

The extension of the franchise in 1832 and 1867, the formation of trade unions, and the development of universal public education were among the drastic social changes that accompanied the spread of industrialization and urbanization in the 19th century. Large parts of Africa and Asia were added to the empire during the reign of Queen Victoria, 1837-1901.

Though victorious in World War I, Britain suffered huge casualties and economic dislocation. Ireland became independent in 1921, and independence movements became active in India and other colonies. The country suffered major bombing damage in World War II, but held out against Germany singlehandedly for a year after France fell in 1940.

Industrial growth continued in the postwar period, but Britain lost its leadership position to other powers. Labor governments passed socialist programs nationalizing some basic industries and expanding social security. Prime Min. Margaret Thatcher's Conservative government, however, tried to increase the role of private enterprise. In 1987, Thatcher became the first British leader in 160 years to be elected to a 3d consecutive term as prime minister. Falling on unpopular times, she resigned as prime minister in Nov. 1990. Her successor, John Major, led Conservatives to an upset victory at the polls, Apr. 9, 1992.

The UK supported the UN resolutions against Iraq and sent military forces to the Persian Gulf War.

The Channel Tunnel linking Britain to the Continent was officially inaugurated May 6, 1994. Britain's relations with the European Union were frayed in 1996 when the EU banned British beef because of the threat of "mad cow" disease.

On May 1, 1997, the Labour Party swept into power in a landslide victory, the largest of any party since 1935. Labour Party leader Tony Blair, 43, became Britain's youngest prime minister since 1812. Diana, Princess of Wales, died in a car crash in Paris, Aug. 31. Britain played a leading role in the NATO air war against Yugoslavia, Mar.-June 1999, and contributed 12,000 troops to the multinational security force in Kosovo (KFOR).

Farming and tourism were hit hard in Mar.-Apr. 2001 by an epidemic of foot-and-mouth disease. Blair led Labour to another landslide election victory June 7, 2001. After the Sept. 11 attack on the U.S., Britain took an important role in the U.S.-led war against terrorism. The U.K. participated in the bombing of Afghanistan that began Oct. 7 and was the 1st to lead a multinational peacekeeping force, based in Kabul, authorized by the UN Dec. 20, 2001. Visiting the U.S. in Sept. 2002, Prime Min. Blair backed military action against Iraq to eliminate weapons of mass destruction.

Wales

The Principality of Wales in western Britain has an area of 8,019 sq. mi. and a population (1997 est.) of 2,927,000. Cardiff is the capital, pop. (1996 est.; city proper) 315,040.

Less than 20% of Wales residents speak English and Welsh; about 32,000 speak Welsh solely. A 1979 referendum rejected, 4-1, the creation of an elected Welsh assembly; a similar proposal passed by a thin margin on Sept. 18, 1997. Elections were held May 6, 1999.

Early Anglo-Saxon invaders drove Celtic peoples into the mountains of Wales, terming them Waelise (Welsh, or foreign). There they developed a distinct nationality. Members of the ruling house of Gwynedd in the 13th century fought England but were crushed, 1283. Edward of Caernarvon, son of Edward I of England, was created Prince of Wales, 1301.

Scotland

Scotland, a kingdom now united with England and Wales in Great Britain, occupies the northern 37% of the main British island, and the Hebrides, Orkney, Shetland, and smaller islands. Length 275 mi., breadth approx. 150 mi., area 30,418 sq. mi., population (1992 est.) 5,111,000.

The Lowlands, a belt of land approximately 60 mi. wide from the Firth of Clyde to the Firth of Forth, divide the farming region of the Southern Uplands from the granite Highlands of the North; they contain 75% of the population and most of the industry. The Highlands, famous for hunting and fishing, have been opened to industry by many hydroelectric power stations.

Edinburgh, pop. (1996 est., city proper) 448,850, is the capital. Glasgow, pop. (1996 est.; city proper) 616,430, is Britain's greatest industrial center. It is a shipbuilding complex on the Clyde and an ocean port. Aberdeen, pop. (1996 est.) 227,430, NE of Edinburgh, is a major port, center of granite industry, fish-processing, and North Sea oil exploration. Dundee, pop. (1996 est.) 150,250, NE of Edinburgh, is an industrial and fish-processing center. About 90,000 persons speak Gaelic as well as English.

History. Scotland was called Caledonia by the Romans who battled early Celtic tribes and occupied southern areas from the 1st to the 4th centuries. Missionaries from Britain introduced Christianity in the 4th century; St. Columba, an Irish monk, converted most of Scotland in the 6th century.

The Kingdom of Scotland was founded in 1018. William Wallace and Robert Bruce both defeated English armies 1297 and 1314, respectively.

In 1603 James VI of Scotland, son of Mary, Queen of Scots, succeeded to the throne of England as James I, and effected the Union of the Crowns. In 1707 Scotland received representation in the British Parliament, resulting from the union of former separate Parliaments. Its executive in the British cabinet is the Secretary of State for Scotland. The growing Scottish National Party urges independence. A 1979 referendum on the creation of an elected Scottish assembly was defeated, but a proposal to create a regional legislature with limited taxing authority passed by a landslide Sept. 11, 1997. Elections were held May 6, 1999.

Memorials of Robert Burns, Sir Walter Scott, John Knox, and Mary, Queen of Scots, draw many tourists, as do the beauties of the Trossachs, Loch Katrine, Loch Lomond, and abbey ruins.

Industries. Engineering products are the most important industry, with growing emphasis on office machinery, autos, electronics, and other consumer goods. Oil has been discovered offshore in the North Sea, stimulating on-shore support industries.

Scotland produces fine woolens, worsteds, tweeds, silks, fine linens, and jute. It is known for its special breeds of cattle and sheep. Fisheries have large hauls of herring, cod, whiting. Whisky is the biggest export.

The Hebrides are a group of c. 500 islands, 100 inhabited, off the W coast. The Inner Hebrides include **Skye, Mull,** and **Iona,** the last famous for the arrival of St. Columba, AD 563. The Outer Hebrides include **Lewis** and **Harris.** Industries include sheep raising and weaving. The **Orkney Islands,** c. 90, are to the NE. The capital is Kirkwall, on Pomona Isl. Fish curing, sheep raising, and weaving are occupations. NE of the Orkneys are the 200 **Shetland Islands,** 24 inhabited, home of Shetland pony. The Orkneys and Shetlands are centers for the North Sea oil industry.

Northern Ireland

Northern Ireland was constituted in 1920 from 6 of the 9 counties of Ulster, the NE corner of Ireland. Area 5,452 sq. mi., pop. (1996 est.) 1,663,300. Capital and chief industrial center, Belfast, pop. (1996 est.; city proper) 297,300.

Industries. Shipbuilding, including large tankers, has long been an important industry, centered in Belfast, the largest port. Linen manufacture is also important, along with apparel, rope, and twine. Growing diversification has added engineering products, synthetic fibers, and electronics. There are large numbers of cattle, hogs, and sheep. Potatoes, poultry, and dairy foods are also produced.

Government. An act of the British Parliament, 1920, divided Northern from Southern Ireland, each with a parliament and government. When Ireland became a dominion, 1921, and later a republic, Northern Ireland chose to remain a part of the United Kingdom. It elects 18 members to the British House of Commons.

During 1968-69, large demonstrations were conducted by Roman Catholics who charged they were discriminated against in voting rights, housing, and employment. The Catholics, a minority comprising about a third of the population, demanded abolition of property qualifications for voting in local elections. Violence and terrorism intensified, involving branches of the Irish Republican Army (outlawed in the Irish Republic), Protestant groups, police, and British troops.

A succession of Northern Ireland prime ministers pressed reform programs but failed to satisfy extremists on both sides. Between 1969 and 1994 more than 3,000 were killed in sectarian violence, many in England itself. Britain suspended the Northern Ireland parliament Mar. 30, 1972, and imposed direct British rule. A coalition government was formed in 1973 when moderates won election to a new one-house Assembly. But a Protestant general strike overthrew the government in 1974 and direct rule was resumed.

The agony of Northern Ireland was dramatized in 1981 by the deaths of 10 Irish nationalist hunger strikers in Maze Prison near Belfast. In 1985 the Hillsborough agreement gave the Rep. of Ireland a voice in the governing of Northern Ireland; the accord was strongly opposed by Ulster loyalists. On Dec. 12, 1993, Britain and Ireland announced a declaration of principles to resolve the Northern Ireland conflict.

On Aug. 31, 1994, the IRA announced a cease-fire, saying it would rely on political means to achieve its objectives; the IRA resumed its terrorist tactics on Feb. 9, 1996. Reinstatement of the IRA cease-fire as of July 20, 1997, led to the resumption of peace talks Sept. 15.

A settlement reached on Good Friday, April 10, 1998, provided for restoration of home rule and election of a 108-member assembly with safeguards for minority rights. Both Ireland and Great Britain agreed to give up their constitutional claims on Northern Ireland. The accord was approved May 22 by voters in Northern Ireland and the Irish Republic, and elections to the assembly were held June 25. IRA dissidents seeking to derail the agreement were responsible for a bomb at Omagh Aug. 15 that killed 29 people and injured over 330.

London transferred authority to a Northern Ireland power-sharing government Dec. 2, 1999. Self-rule was suspended several times because of IRA reluctance to disarm; the IRA finally began destroying its arsenal Oct. 23, 2001.

Education and Religion. Northern Ireland is about 58% Protestant, 42% Roman Catholic. Education is compulsory between the ages of 5 and 16 years.

Channel Islands

The Channel Islands, area 75 sq. mi., pop. (1997 est.) 152,241, off the NW coast of France, the only parts of the one-time Dukedom of Normandy belonging to England, are Jersey, Guernsey and the dependencies of Guernsey—Alderney, Brechou, Great Sark, Little Sark, Herm, Jethou and Lihou. Jersey and Guernsey have separate legal existences and lieutenant governors named by the Crown. The islands were the only British soil occupied by German troops in World War II.

Isle of Man

The Isle of Man, area 227 sq. mi., pop. (2001 est.) 73,489, is in the Irish Sea, 20 mi. from Scotland, 30 mi. from Cumberland. It is rich in lead and iron. The island has its own laws and a lieutenant governor appointed by the Crown. The Tynwald (legislature) consists of the Legislative Council, partly elected, and House of Keys, elected. Capital: Douglas. Farming, tourism, and fishing (kippers, scallops) are chief occupations. Man is famous for the Manx tailless cat.

Gibraltar

Gibraltar, a dependency on the southern coast of Spain, guards the entrance to the Mediterranean. The Rock of Gibraltar has been in British possession since 1704. The Rock is 2.75 mi. long, 3/4 of a mi. wide and 1,396 ft. in height; a narrow isthmus connects it with the mainland. Pop. (2002 est.) 27,714.

Gibraltar has historically been an object of contention between Britain and Spain. Residents voted with near unanimity to remain under British rule, in a 1967 referendum held in pursuance of a UN resolution on decolonization. A new constitution, May 30, 1969, increased Gibraltarian control of domestic affairs (the UK continues to handle defense and internal security matters). Following a 1984 agreement between Britain and Spain, the border, closed by Spain in 1969, was fully reopened in Feb. 1985. A UN General Assembly resolution requested Britain to end Gibraltar's colonial status by Oct. 1, 1996. No settlement has been reached.

British West Indies

Swinging in a vast arc from the coast of Venezuela NE, then N and NW toward Puerto Rico are the Leeward Islands, forming a coral and volcanic barrier sheltering the Caribbean from the open Atlantic. Many of the islands are self-governing British possessions. Universal suffrage was instituted 1951-54; ministerial systems were set up 1956-1960.

The **Leeward Islands** still associated with the UK are **Montserrat**, area 32 sq. mi., pop. (2002 est.) 8,437, capital Plymouth; the **British Virgin Islands,** 59 sq. mi., pop. (2002 est.) 21,272, capital Road Town; and **Anguilla**, the most northerly of the Leeward Islands, 60 sq. mi., pop. (2002 est.) 12,446, capital The Valley. Montserrat has been devastated by the Soufrière Hills volcano, which began erupting July 18, 1995.

The three **Cayman Islands,** a dependency, lie S of Cuba, NW of Jamaica. Pop. (2002 est.) 36,273, most of it on Grand Cayman. It is a free port; in the 1970s Grand Cayman became a tax-free refuge for foreign funds and branches of many Western banks were opened there. Total area 102 sq. mi., capital Georgetown.

The **Turks and Caicos Islands** are a dependency at the SE end of the Bahama Islands. Of about 30 islands, only 6 are inhabited; area 193 sq. mi., pop. (2002 est.) 18,378; capital Grand Turk. Salt, shellfish, and conch shells are the main exports.

Bermuda

Bermuda is a British dependency governed by a royal governor and an assembly, dating from 1620, the oldest legislative body among British dependencies. Capital is Hamilton.

It is a group of about 150 small islands of coral formation, 20 inhabited, comprising 20.0 sq. mi. in the western Atlantic, 580 mi. E of North Carolina. Pop. (2002 est.) 63,960 (about 61% of African descent). Pop. density is high.

The U.S. maintains a NASA tracking facility; a U.S. naval air base was closed in 1995.

Tourism is the major industry; Bermuda boasts many resort hotels. The government raises most revenue from import duties.

Exports: petroleum products, medicine. In a referendum Aug. 15, 1995, voters rejected independence by nearly a 3-to-1 majority.

South Atlantic

The **Falkland Islands,** a dependency, lie 300 mi. E of the Strait of Magellan at the southern end of South America.

The Falklands or Islas Malvinas include 2 large islands and about 200 smaller ones, area 4,700 sq. mi., pop. (1995 est.) 2,317, capital Stanley. The licensing of foreign fishing vessels has become the major source of revenue. Sheep grazing is a main industry; wool is the principal export. There are indications of large oil and gas deposits. The islands are also claimed by Argentina, though 97% of inhabitants are of British origin. Argentina invaded the islands Apr. 2, 1982. The British responded by sending a task force to the area, landing their main force on the Falklands, May 21, and forcing an Argentine surrender at Port Stanley, June 14. A pact resuming commercial air service with Argentina was signed July 14, 1999.

British Antarctic Territory, south of 60° S lat., formerly a dependency of the Falkland Isls., was made a separate colony in 1962 and includes the **South Shetland Islands,** the **South Orkneys**, and the Antarctic Peninsula. A chain of meteorological stations is maintained.

South Georgia and the South Sandwich Islands, formerly administered by the Falklands Isls., became a separate dependency in 1985. South Georgia, 1,450 sq. mi., with no permanent population, is about 800 mi. SE of the Falklands; the South Sandwich Isls., 130 sq. mi., are uninhabited, about 470 mi. SE of South Georgia.

St. Helena, an island 1,200 mi. off the W. coast of Africa and 1,800 mi. E of South America, 47 sq. mi. and pop. (2001 est.) 7,266. Flax, lace, and rope-making are the chief industries. After Napoleon Bonaparte was defeated at Waterloo the Allies exiled him to St. Helena, where he lived from Oct. 16, 1815, to his death, May 5, 1821. Capital is Jamestown.

Tristan da Cunha is the principal of a group of islands of volcanic origin, total area 40 sq. mi., halfway between the Cape of Good Hope and South America. A volcanic peak 6,760 ft. high erupted in 1961. The 262 inhabitants were removed to England, but most returned in 1963. The islands are dependencies of St. Helena. Pop. (1993) 300.

Ascension is an island of volcanic origin, 34 sq. mi. in area, 700 mi. NW of St. Helena, through which it is administered. It is a communications relay center for Britain, and has a U.S. satellite tracking center. Pop. (1993) was 1,117, half of them communications workers. The island is noted for sea turtles.

Hong Kong

(See **China/Hong Kong**)

British Indian Ocean Territory

Formed Nov. 1965, embracing islands formerly dependencies of Mauritius or Seychelles: the Chagos Archipelago (including Diego Garcia), Aldabra, Farquhar, and Des Roches. The latter 3 were transferred to Seychelles, which became independent in 1976. Area 23 sq. mi. No permanent civilian population remains; the U.K. and the U.S. maintain a military presence.

Pacific Ocean

Pitcairn Island is in the Pacific, halfway between South America and Australia. The island was discovered in 1767 by Philip Carteret but was not inhabited until 23 years later when the mutineers of the *Bounty* landed there. The area is 1.7 sq. mi. and 1995 pop. was 54. It is a British dependency and is administered by a British High Commissioner in New Zealand and a local Council. The uninhabited islands of **Henderson, Ducie,** and **Oeno** are in the Pitcairn group.

United States

United States of America

People: Population: 280,562,489 (incl. 50 states & Dist. of Columbia). (Note: U.S. pop. figures may differ elsewhere in *The World Almanac.*) **Age distrib.** (%): <15: 21.1; 65+: 12.6. **Pop. density:** 79 per sq. mi. **Urban:** 76%.

Geography: Area: 3,539,200 sq. mi. (incl. 50 states and DC). **Topography:** Vast central plain, mountains in west, hills and low mountains in east. **Capital:** Washington, D.C.: 3,997,000

Government: Federal republic, strong democratic tradition. **Head of state and gov.:** Pres. George W. Bush; b July 6, 1946; in office: Jan. 20, 2001. **Local divisions:** 50 states and Dist. of Columbia. **Defense budget (2002):** $343.3 bil. **Active troops:** 1,367,700.

Economy: Industries: Oil, steel, vehicles, aerospace, telecomm., chemicals, electronics, food processing, consumer goods, lumber, mining. **Minerals:** Coal, oil, gas, copper, lead, molybdenum, phosphates, uranium, bauxite, gold, iron, mercury, nickel, potash, silver, tungsten, zinc. **Crude oil reserves** (2001): 22.0 bil bbls. **Other resources:** forests. **Arable land:** 19%. **Livestock** (2001): cattle: 97.28 mil; chickens: 1.83 bil.; goats:. 1.35 mil.; pigs: 59.14 mil; sheep: 6.97 mil. **Fish catch** (1999): 5.45 mil metric tons. **Electricity prod.:** 3,799.94 bil. kWh. **Labor force:** managerial and professional 30.2%, technical sales and administrative support 29.2%, services 13.5%, manufacturing mining and crafts 24.6%, farming forestry and fishing 2.5%.

Finance: GDP (2000 est.): $9.963 tril. **Per capita GDP:** $36,200. **Imports** (2000 est.): $1.223 tril.; partners (2000): Canada 19%, Japan 11%. **Exports** (2000 est.): $776 bil.; partners (2000): Canada 23%, Mexico 14%. **Budget** (1999): $1.703 tril. **Tourism:** $74.49 bil. **Budget** (1998): $1.653 tril. **Intl. reserves less gold** (end 2000): $43.44 bil. **Gold:** 261.61 mil oz t. **Consumer prices** (change in 2000): 3.4%.

Transport: Railroad: Length: 137,900 mi. **Motor vehicles:** 129.73 mil pass. cars, 76.64 mil comm. vehicles. **Civil aviation:** 599.4 bil pass.-mi; 834 airports. **Communications: TV sets:** 847 per 1,000 pop. **Radios:** 2,115 per 1,000 pop. **Telephones:** 317,000,000. **Daily newspaper circ.:** 215 per 1,000 pop.

Health: Life expectancy: 74.5 male; 80.2 female. **Births** (per 1,000 pop.): 14.1. **Deaths** (per 1,000 pop.): 8.7. **Natural inc.:** 0.54%. **Infant mortality** (per 1,000 live births): 6.7.

Education: Free, compulsory: ages 7-16. **Literacy** (1994): 97%.

Major Intl. Organizations: UN (FAO, IBRD, ILO, IMF, IMO, WHO, WTrO), APEC, NATO, OAS, OECD, OSCE.

Websites: www.census.gov; www.whitehouse.gov
www.firstgov.gov

See also United States History chapter.

Uruguay

Oriental Republic of Uruguay

People: Population: 3,386,575. **Age distrib.** (%): <15: 24.4; 65+: 13.0. **Pop. density:** 51 per sq. mi. **Urban:** 91%. **Ethnic groups:** White 88%, mestizo 8%, black 4%. **Principal language:** Spanish. **Chief religion:** Roman Catholic 66%.

Geography: Area: 67,000 sq. mi. **Location:** In southern South America, on the Atlantic O. **Neighbors:** Argentina on W, Brazil on N. **Topography:** Uruguay is composed of rolling, grassy plains and hills, well watered by rivers flowing W to Uruguay R. **Capital:** Montevideo 1,329,000.

Government: Type: Republic. **Head of state and gov.:** Pres. Jorge Batlle Ibáñez; b Oct. 25, 1927; in office: Mar. 1, 2000. **Local divisions:** 19 departments. **Defense budget (2001):** $367 mil. **Active troops:** 23,900.

Economy: Industries: Food processing, electrical machinery, transp. equipment, petroleum products. **Chief crops:** Corn, wheat, sorghum, rice. **Arable land:** 7%. **Livestock** (2001): cattle: 10.80 mil; chickens: 13.00 mil.; goats: 14,800; pigs: 380,000; sheep: 13.03 mil. **Fish catch** (1999): 136,912 metric tons. **Electricity prod.:** 7.53 bil. kWh. **Labor force:** N/A

Finance: Monetary unit: Peso (Oct. 2001: 27.15 = $1 U.S.). **GDP** (2000 est.): $31 bil. **Per capita GDP:** $9,300. **Imports** (2000 est.): $3.4 bil.; partners (1999 est.): MERCOSUR; partners 43%, EU 20%. **Exports** (2000 est.): $2.6 bil.; partners (1999 est.): MERCOSUR; partners 45%, EU 20%, U.S. 7%. **Tourism:** $653 mil. **Budget** (2000 est.): $4.6 bil. **Intl. reserves less gold** (end 2000): $1.88 bil. **Gold:** 1.08 mil oz t. **Consumer prices** (change in 2000): 4.8%.

Transport: Railroad: Length: 1,288 mi. **Motor vehicles:** 475,000 pass. cars, 50,000 comm. vehicles. **Civil aviation:** 470.0 mil pass.-mi; 1 airport. **Chief port:** Montevideo.

Communications: TV sets: 191 per 1,000 pop. **Radios:** 586 per 1,000 pop. **Telephones:** 1,470,900. **Daily newspaper circ.:** 241 per 1,000 pop.

Health: Life expectancy: 72.3 male; 79.2 female. **Births** (per 1,000 pop.): 17.3. **Deaths** (per 1,000 pop.): 9. **Natural inc.:** 0.83%. **Infant mortality** (per 1,000 live births): 14.2.

Education: Free, compulsory for 6 years between ages 6-14. **Literacy**: 97%.

Major Intl. Organizations: UN (FAO, IBRD, ILO, IMF, IMO, WHO, WTrO), OAS.

Embassy: 2715 M St. NW 20007; 331-1313.

Website: www.embassy.org/uruguay

Spanish settlers began to supplant the indigenous Charrua Indians in 1624. Portuguese from Brazil arrived later, but Uruguay was attached to the Spanish Viceroyalty of Rio de la Plata in the 18th century. Rebels fought against Spain beginning in 1810. An independent republic was declared Aug. 25, 1825.

Terrorist activities led Pres. Juan María Bordaberry to agree to military control of his administration Feb. 1973. In June he abolished Congress and set up a Council of State in its place. Bordaberry was removed by the military in a 1976 coup. Civilian government was restored in 1985.

Socialist measures were adopted in the early 1900s. The state retains a dominant role in the power, telephone, railroad, cement, oil-refining, and other industries, although some privatization began in the early 2000s. Uruguay's standard of living remains one of the highest in South America, and political and labor conditions among the freest. The U.S. agreed Aug. 4, 2002, to provide a short-term loan of $1.5 billion to help Uruguay weather a financial crisis.

Uzbekistan

Republic of Uzbekistan

People: Population: 25,563,441. **Age distrib.** (%): <15: 36.3; 65+: 4.6. **Pop. density:** 148 per sq. mi. **Urban:** 37%. **Ethnic groups:** Uzbek 80%, Russian 6%, Tajik 5%. **Principal languages:** Uzbek, Russian. **Chief religions:** Muslim (mostly Sunni) 88%, Eastern Orthodox 9%.

Geography: Area: 172,700 sq. mi. **Location:** Central Asia. **Neighbors:** Kazakhstan on N and W, Kyrgyzstan and Tajikistan on E, Afghanistan and Turkmenistan on S. **Topography:** Mostly plains and desert. **Capital:** Tashkent 2,157,000.

Government: Type: Republic. **Head of state:** Pres. Islam A. Karimov; b Jan. 30, 1938; in office: Mar. 24, 1990. **Head of gov.:** Prime Min. Utkir Sultanov; b July 14, 1939; in office: Dec. 21, 1995. **Local divisions:** 12 regions, 1 autonomous republic, 1 city. **Defense budget** (2000): $300 mil. **Active troops:** 50,000–55,000.

Economy: Industries: Textiles, food processing, machine building, metallurgy **Chief crops:** Vegetables, cotton, fruits, grain. **Minerals:** Gas, oil, coal, gold, uranium, silver, copper. **Crude oil reserves** (2000): 594 mil bbls. **Arable land:** 9%. **Livestock (2001): cattle: 5.34 mil; chickens: 14.42 mil.; goats: 830,000; pigs: 89,000; sheep: 8.10 mil. Fish catch:** (1999): 10,565 metric tons. **Electricity prod.:** 44.08 bil. kWh. **Labor force:** agri. 44%, ind. 20%, services 36%.

Finance: Monetary unit: Som (Sept. 2001: 788.69 = $1 U.S.). **GDP** (2000 est.): $60 bil. **Per capita GDP:** $2,400. **Imports** (2000 est.): $2.6 bil.; partners (1999): Russia 14%, South Korea 14%. **Exports** (2000 est.): $2.9 bil.; partners (1999): Russia 13%, Switzerland 10%, UK 10%. **Tourism** (1998): $21 mil. **Budget** (1999 est.): $4.1 bil.

Transport: Railroad: Length: 2,100 mi. **Motor vehicles:** 865,000 pass. cars, 14,500 comm. vehicles. **Civil aviation:** 2.2 bil pass.-mi; 9 airports. **Chief port:** Termiz.

Communications: TV sets: 176 per 1,000 pop. **Telephones:** 1,725,700.

Health: Life expectancy: 60.4 male; 67.6 female. **Births** (per 1,000 pop.): 26.1. **Deaths** (per 1,000 pop.): 8. **Natural inc.:** 1.81%. **Infant mortality** (per 1,000 live births): 71.7.

Education: Compulsory: ages 6-14. **Literacy** (1993): 97%.

Major Intl. Organizations: UN (IBRD, ILO, IMF, WHO), CIS, OSCE.

Embassy: 1746 Massachusetts Ave. NW 20036; 887-5300.

The region was overrun by the Mongols under Genghis Khan in 1220. In the 14th century, Uzbekistan became the center of a native empire—that of the Timurids. In later centuries Muslim feudal states emerged. Russian military conquest began in the 19th century.

The Uzbek SSR became a Soviet Union republic in 1925. Uzbekistan declared independence Aug. 29, 1991. It became an independent republic when the Soviet Union disbanded Dec. 26, 1991. Subsequently, the government of Uzbekistan was led by former Communists. U.S. forces used bases in Uzbekistan during military action in Afghanistan in 2001. A pact tightening military and economic ties with the U.S. was signed Mar. 12, 2002.

Vanuatu

Republic of Vanuatu

People: Population: 196,178. **Age distrib.** (%): <15: 36.3; 65+: 3.2. **Pop. density:** 34 per sq. mi. **Urban:** 20%. **Ethnic groups:** Melanesian 94%, French 4%. **Principal languages:** French, English, Bislama (all official). **Chief religions:** Presbyterian 37%, Anglican 15%, Catholic 15%, other Christian 10%, indigenous beliefs 8%.

Geography: Area: 5,700 sq. mi. **Location:** SW Pacific, 1,200 mi. NE of Brisbane, Australia. **Neighbors:** Fiji to E, Solomon Isls. to NW. **Topography:** Dense forest with narrow coastal strips of cultivated land. **Capital:** Vila: 31,000.

Government: Type: Republic. **Head of state:** Pres. John Bani; b. July 1, 1941; in office: Mar. 24, 1999. **Head of gov.:** Prime Min. Edward Natapei; b 1955; in office: Apr. 13, 2001. **Local divisions:** 6 provinces

Economy: Industries: Food and fish freezing, wood processing, meat canning. **Chief crops:** Copra, coconuts, cocoa, coffee. **Minerals:** Manganese. **Arable land:** 2%. **Other resources:** Forests, cattle. **Fish catch** (1996): 2,729 metric tons. **Livestock** (2001): cattle: 151,000; chickens: 340,000; goats: 12,000; pigs: 62,000. **Electricity prod.:** 0.04 bil. kWh. **Labor force:** agri. 65%, services 32%, ind. 3%.

Finance: Monetary unit: Vatu (Sept. 2002: 137.75 = $1 U.S.). **GDP** (1999 est.): $245 mil. **Per capita GDP:** $1,300. **Imports** (1999): $77.2 mil.; partners (1997 est.): Japan 52%, Australia 20%. **Exports** (1999): $25.3 mil.; partners (1997 est.): Japan 32%, Germany 14%. **Tourism:** $56 mil. **Budget** (1996 est.): $99.8 mil. **Intl. reserves less gold** (end 2000): $30 mil. **Consumer prices** (change in 1999): 2.0%.

Transport: Motor vehicles: 4,000 pass. cars, 2,500 comm. vehicles. **Civil aviation:** 93.2 mil pass.-mi; 29 airports. **Chief ports:** Forai, Port-Vila.

Communications: Radios: 319 per 1,000 pop. **Telephones:** 7,100.

Health: Life expectancy: 59.9 male; 62.8 female. **Births** (per 1,000 pop.): 24.8. **Deaths** (per 1,000 pop.): 8.2. **Natural inc.:** 1.66%. **Infant mortality** (per 1,000 live births): 59.6.

Education: Literacy (1997): 36%.

Major Intl. Organizations: UN (FAO, IBRD, IMF, IMO, WHO), the Commonwealth.

Website: www.vanuatugovernment.gov.vu

The Anglo-French condominium of the New Hebrides, administered jointly by France and Great Britain since 1906, became the independent Republic of Vanuatu on July 30, 1980.

Vatican City (The Holy See)

People: Population: 880. **Urban:** 100%. **Ethnic groups:** Italian, Swiss. **Principal languages:** Italian, Latin. **Chief religion:** Roman Catholic.

Geography: Area: 108.7 acres. **Location:** In Rome, Italy. **Neighbors:** Completely surrounded by Italy.

Monetary unit: Vatican Lira, Italian Lira (equal value) (Sept. 2002: 1,982.97 = $1 U.S.).

Apostolic Nunciature in U.S.: 3339 Massachusetts Ave. NW 20008; 333-7121.

Website: www.vatican.va

The popes for many centuries, with brief interruptions, held temporal sovereignty over mid-Italy (the so-called Papal States), comprising an area of some 16,000 sq. mi., with a population in the 19th century of more than 3 million. This territory was incorporated in the new Kingdom of Italy (1861), the sovereignty of the pope being confined to the palaces of the Vatican and the Lateran in Rome and the villa of Castel Gandolfo, by an Italian law, May 13, 1871. This law also guaranteed to the pope and his successors a yearly indemnity of over $620,000. The allowance, however, remained unclaimed.

A Treaty of Conciliation, a concordat, and a financial convention were signed Feb. 11, 1929, by Cardinal Gasparri and Premier Mussolini. The documents established the independent state of Vatican City and gave the Roman Catholic church special status in Italy. The treaty (Lateran Agreement) was made part of the Constitution of Italy (Article 7) in 1947. Italy and the Vatican signed an agreement in 1984 on revisions of the concordat; the accord eliminated Roman Catholicism as the state religion and ended required religious education in Italian schools.

Vatican City includes the Basilica of Saint Peter, the Vatican Palace and Museum covering over 13 acres, the Vatican gardens, and neighboring buildings between Viale Vaticano and the church. Thirteen buildings in Rome, outside the boundaries, enjoy extraterritorial rights; these buildings house congregations or officers necessary for the administration of the Holy See.

The legal system is based on the code of canon law, the apostolic constitutions, and laws especially promulgated for the Vatican City by the pope. The Secretariat of State represents the Holy See in its diplomatic relations. By the Treaty of Conciliation the pope is pledged to a perpetual neutrality unless his mediation is specifically requested. This, however, does not prevent the defense of the Church whenever it is persecuted.

The present sovereign of the State of Vatican City is the Supreme Pontiff John Paul II, born Karol Wojtyla in Wadowice, Poland, May 18, 1920, elected Oct. 16, 1978 (the first non-Italian to be elected pope in 456 years).

The U.S. restored formal relations in 1984 after the U.S. Congress repealed an 1867 ban on diplomatic relations with the Vatican. The Vatican and Israel agreed to establish formal relations Dec. 30, 1993.

Venezuela

Bolivarian Republic of Venezuela

People: Population: 24,287,670. **Age distrib.** (%): <15: 32.1; 65+: 4.7. **Pop. density:** 71 per sq. mi. **Urban:** 87%. **Ethnic groups:** Spanish, Portuguese, Italian. **Principal language:** Spanish (official). **Chief religion:** Roman Catholic 96%.

Geography: Area: 340,600 sq. mi. **Location:** On Caribbean coast of South America. **Neighbors:** Colombia on W, Brazil on S, Guyana on E. **Topography:** Flat coastal plain and Orinoco Delta are bordered by Andes Mts. and hills. Plains, called llanos, extend between mountains and Orinoco. Guiana Highlands and plains are S of Orinoco, which stretches 1,600 mi. and drains 80% of Venezuela. **Capital:** Caracas. **Cities (urban aggr.):** Caracas 3,177,000; Maracaibo 1,901,000; Valencia 1,893,000.

Government: Type: Federal republic. **Head of state and gov.:** Pres. Hugo Rafael Chávez Frías; b July 28, 1954; in office: Feb. 2, 1999. **Local divisions:** 22 states, 1 federal district (Caracas), 1 federal dependency (72 islands). **Defense budget (2001):** $1.7 bil. **Active troops:** 82,300.

Economy: Industries: Oil, iron mining, construction materials, food processing. **Chief crops:** Rice, corn, sorghum, bananas, sugar. **Minerals:** Oil, gas, iron, gold. **Crude oil reserves** ((2001): 47.6 bil bbls. **Arable land:** 4%. **Livestock** (2001): cattle: 16.00 mil; chickens: 115.00 mil.; goats: 4.00 mil.; pigs: 5.40 mil; sheep: 820,000. **Fish catch** (1999): 502,728 metric tons. **Electricity prod.:** 80.75 bil. kWh. **Labor force:** services 64%, ind. 23%, agri. 13%.

Finance: Monetary unit: Bolivar (Sept. 2002: 1,476.76 = $1 U.S.). **GDP** (2000 est.): $146.2 bil. **Per capita GDP:** $6,200. **Imports** (2000): $14.7 bil.; partners (1999): U.S. 53%. **Exports** (2000): $32.8 bil.; partners (1999): U.S. and Puerto Rico 57%, Colombia, Brazil, Japan, Germany, Netherlands, Italy. **Tourism:** $656 mil. **Budget** (2000 est.): $27 bil. **Intl. reserves less gold** (end 2000): $10.05 bil. **Gold:** 10.24 mil oz t. **Consumer prices** (change in 2000): 16.2%.

Transport: Railroad: Length: 390 mi. **Motor vehicles:** 1.50 mil pass. cars, 525,000 comm. vehicles. **Civil aviation:** 2.8 bil pass.-mi; 20 airports. **Chief ports:** Maracaibo, La Guaira, Puerto Cabello.

Communications: TV sets: 183 per 1,000 pop. **Radios:** 372 per 1,000 pop. **Telephones:** 9,248,200. **Daily newspaper circ.:** 215 per 1,000 pop.

Health: Life expectancy: 70.5 male; 76.8 female. **Births** (per 1,000 pop.): 20.2. **Deaths** (per 1,000 pop.): 4.9. **Natural inc.:** 1.53%. **Infant mortality** (per 1,000 live births): 24.6.

Education: Free, compulsory: ages 5-15. **Literacy**: 91%.

Major Intl. Organizations: UN (FAO, IBRD, ILO, IMF, IMO, WHO, WTrO), OAS, OPEC.

Embassy: 1099 30th St. NW 20007; 342-2214.

Website: www.embavenez-us.org

Columbus first set foot on the South American continent on the peninsula of Paria, Aug. 1498. Alonso de Ojeda, 1499, was the first European to see Lake Maracaibo. He called the land Venezuela, or Little Venice, because the Indians had houses on stilts. Spain dominated Venezuela until Simón Bolívar's victory near Carabobo in June 1821. The republic was formed after secession from the Colombian Federation in 1830.

Military strongmen ruled Venezuela for most of the 20th century. They promoted the oil industry; some social reforms were implemented. Since 1959, the country has had democratically elected governments.

Venezuela helped found the Organization of Petroleum Exporting Countries (OPEC). The government, Jan. 1, 1976, nationalized the oil industry with compensation. Oil accounts for most of Venezuela's export earnings; the economy suffered a severe cash crisis in the 1980s and 1990s as a result of depressed oil revenues. Government attempts to reduce dependence on oil have met with limited success.

An attempted coup by midlevel military officers was thwarted by loyalist troops Feb. 4, 1992. A second coup attempt was thwarted in Nov. Pres. Carlos Andrés Pérez was removed from office on corruption charges, May 1993; he was convicted, May 1996, of mismanaging a $17 million secret government security fund. Citing an economic crisis, Pres. Rafael Caldera, a populist elected Dec. 5, 1993, suspended many civil liberties June 27, 1994; rights were restored in most regions July 6, 1995.

A 1992 coup leader, Hugo Chávez, who ran as a populist, was elected president Dec. 6, 1998. A constitutional assembly elected July 25, 1999, and controlled by Chávez supporters slashed the powers of Congress and moved to dismiss corrupt judges. Voters on Dec. 15 approved a new constitution greatly increasing the powers of the president. Floods and mudslides in Dec. 1999 killed, by official estimates, at least 30,000 people.

Popular among the poor, Chávez alienated some middle- and upper-class Venezuelans with his program of economic and political reform, and his foreign policy antagonized the U.S. After capital outflows led to a budget crisis, the currency was allowed to float Feb. 13, 2002. Mounting opposition to Chávez among the military, business leaders, and the media climaxed with a mass protest Apr. 11 in Caracas at which gunfire erupted, killing at least 17 people. Chávez was forced to relinquish power, but when an interim government issued decrees suspending the constitution and dissolving the legislature and supreme court, Chávez loyalists rebelled; the coup fell apart, and the president reclaimed his office Apr. 14.

Vietnam

Socialist Republic of Vietnam

People: Population: 81,098,416. **Age distrib.** (%): <15: 32.1; 65+: 5.4. **Pop. density:** 646 per sq. mi. **Urban:** 20%. **Ethnic groups:** Vietnamese 85-90%, Chinese 3%, Muong, Tai, Meo, Khmer, Man, Cham. **Principal languages:** Vietnamese (official), French, Chinese, English. **Chief religions:** Buddhist, Taoist, Roman Catholic, indigenous beliefs.

Geography: Area: 125,600 sq. mi. **Location:** SE Asia, on the E coast of the Indochinese Peninsula. **Neighbors:** China on N, Laos and Cambodia on W. **Topography:** Vietnam is long and narrow, with a 1,400-mi. coast. About 22% of country is readily arable, including the densely settled Red R. valley in the N, narrow coastal plains in center, and the wide, often marshy Mekong R. Delta in the S. The rest consists of semi-arid plateaus and barren mountains, with some stretches of tropical rain forest. **Capital:** Hanoi. **Cities (urban aggr.):** Ho Chi Minh City 4,619,000; Hanoi 3,822,000; Hai Phong 1,676,000.

Government: Type: Communist. **Head of state:** Pres. Tran Duc Luong; b May 1937; in office: Sept. 24, 1997. **Head of gov.:** Prime Min. Phan Van Khai; b Dec. 1933; in office: Sept. 25, 1997. **Local divisions:** 58 provinces, 3 cities, 1 capital region. **Defense budget (2001):** 1.8 bil. **Active troops:** 484,000.

Economy: Industries: Food processing, garments, shoes, machine building. **Chief crops:** Rice, potatoes, soybeans, coffee, tea, corn. **Minerals:** Phosphates, coal, gas, manganese, bauxite, chromate, oil. **Crude oil reserves** (2001): 1.8 bil bbls. **Other resources:** Forests. **Arable land:** 17%. **Livestock** (2001): cattle: 4.20 mil; chickens: 150.00 mil.; goats: 600,000; pigs: 20.20 mil. **Fish catch** (1999): 1.55 mil metric tons. **Electricity prod.:** 25.78 bil. kWh. **Labor force:** agri. 67%, ind. and services 33%.

Finance: Monetary unit: Dong (Sept. 2002: 15,341.50 = $1 U.S.). **GDP** (2000 est.): $154.4 bil. **Per capita GDP:** $1,950. **Imports** (2000 est.): $15.2 bil.; partners: Japan, Singapore, South Korea, Taiwan, China, Thailand, Hong Kong, Malaysia, Indonesia, France, U.S., Sweden. **Exports** (2000 est.): $14.3 bil.; partners: China, Japan, Germany, Australia, U.S., France, Singapore, UK, Taiwan. **Tourism** (1998): $86 mil. **Budget** (1999 est.): $5.6 bil. Intl. reserves less gold (end 2000): 2.62 bil.

Transport: Railroad: Length: 1,619 mi. **Motor vehicles:** 79,079 pass. cars, 97,104 comm. vehicles. **Civil aviation:** 2.4 bil pass.-mi; 12 airports. **Chief ports:** Ho Chi Minh City, Haiphong, Da Nang.

Communications: TV sets: 182 per 1,000 pop. **Radios:** 109 per 1,000 pop. **Telephones:** 4,301,100. **Daily newspaper circ.:** 4.1 per 1,000 pop.

Health: Life expectancy: 67.4 male; 72.5 female. **Births** (per 1,000 pop.): 20.9. **Deaths** (per 1,000 pop.): 6.1. **Natural inc.:** 1.48%. **Infant mortality** (per 1,000 live births): 29.3.

Education: Compulsory: ages 6-11. **Literacy**: 94%.

Major Intl. Organizations: UN (FAO, IBRD, ILO, IMF, IMO, WHO), APEC, ASEAN.

Embassy: Suite 400, 1233 20th St. NW 20036; 861-0737.

Website: www.vietnamembassy-usa.org

Vietnam's recorded history began in Tonkin before the Christian era. Settled by Viets from central China, Vietnam was held by China, 111 BC-AD 939, and was a vassal state during subsequent periods. Vietnam defeated the armies of Kublai Khan, 1288. Conquest by France began in 1858 and ended in 1884 with the protectorates of Tonkin and Annam in the N and the colony of Cochin-China in the S.

Japan occupied Vietnam in 1940; nationalist aims gathered force. A number of groups formed the Vietminh (Independence) League, headed by Ho Chi Minh, Communist guerrilla leader. In Aug. 1945 the Vietminh forced out Bao Dai, former emperor of Annam, head of a Japan-sponsored regime. France, seeking to reestablish colonial control, battled Communist and nationalist forces, 1946-1954, and was defeated at Dienbienphu, May 8, 1954. Meanwhile, on July 1, 1949, Bao Dai had formed a State of Vietnam, with himself as chief of state, with French approval. China backed Ho Chi Minh.

A cease-fire signed in Geneva July 21, 1954, provided for a buffer zone, withdrawal of French troops from the North, and elections to determine the country's future. Under the agreement the Communists gained control of territory north of the 17th parallel, with its capital at Hanoi and Ho Chi Minh as president. South Vietnam came to comprise the 39 southern provinces. Some 900,000 North Vietnamese fled to South Vietnam.

On Oct. 26, 1955, Ngo Dinh Diem, premier of the interim government of South Vietnam, proclaimed the Republic of Vietnam and became its first president.

The North adopted a constitution Dec. 31, 1959, based on Communist principles and calling for reunification of all Vietnam. North Vietnam sought to take over South Vietnam beginning in 1954. Fighting persisted from 1956, with the Communist Vietcong, aided by North Vietnam, pressing war in the South. Northern aid to Vietcong guerrillas was intensified in 1959, and large-scale troop infiltration began in 1964, with Soviet and Chinese arms assistance. Large Northern forces were stationed in border areas of Laos and Cambodia.

A serious political conflict arose in the South in 1963 when Buddhists denounced authoritarianism and brutality. This paved the way for a military coup Nov. 1-2, 1963, which overthrew Diem. Several other military coups followed.

In 1964, the U.S. began air strikes against North Vietnam. Beginning in 1965, the raids were stepped up and U.S. troops became combatants. U.S. troop strength in Vietnam, which reached a high of 543,400 in Apr. 1969, was ordered reduced by President Nixon in a series of withdrawals, beginning in June 1969. U.S. bombings were resumed in 1972-73.

A cease-fire agreement was signed in Paris Jan. 27, 1973 by the U.S., North and South Vietnam, and the Vietcong. It was never implemented.

North Vietnamese forces attacked remaining government outposts in the Central Highlands in the first months of 1975. Government retreats turned into a rout, and the Saigon regime surrendered April 30. North Vietnam assumed control, and began transforming society along Communist lines.

The war's toll included—Combat deaths: U.S. 47,369; South Vietnam more than 200,000; other allied forces 5,225. Total U.S. fatalities numbered more than 58,000. Vietnamese civilian casualties were more than a million. Displaced war refugees in South Vietnam totaled more than 6.5 million.

The country was officially reunited July 2, 1976. The Northern capital, flag, anthem, emblem, and currency were applied to the new state. Nearly all major government posts went to officials of the former Northern government.

Heavy fighting with Cambodia took place, 1977-80, amid mutual charges of aggression and atrocities against civilians. Increasing numbers of Vietnamese civilians, ethnic Chinese, escaped the country, via the sea or the overland route across Cambodia. Vietnam launched an offensive against Cambodian refugee strongholds along the Thai-Cambodian border in 1985; they also engaged Thai troops.

Relations with China soured as 140,000 ethnic Chinese left Vietnam charging discrimination; China cut off economic aid. Reacting to Vietnam's invasion of Cambodia, China attacked 4 Vietnamese border provinces, Feb. 1979.

Vietnam announced reforms aimed at reducing central control of the economy in 1987, as many of the old revolutionary followers of Ho Chi Minh were removed from office.

Citing Vietnamese cooperation in returning remains of U.S. soldiers killed in the Vietnam War, the U.S. announced an end, Feb. 3, 1994, to a 19-year-old U.S. embargo on trade with Vietnam. The U.S. extended full diplomatic recognition to Vietnam July 11, 1995. The Communist Party replaced the country's ill and aging leadership in Sept. 1997.

Floods in central Vietnam, Oct.-Nov. 1999, killed some 550 people and left over 600,000 families homeless. The U.S. and Vietnam signed a comprehensive trade deal July 13, 2000. U.S. Pres. Bill Clinton made a historic visit to Vietnam Nov. 17-19. Nong Duc Manh, a moderate, was named to head the Communist Party Apr. 22, 2001.

Western Samoa

See Samoa

Yemen

Republic of Yemen

People: Population: 18,701,257. **Age distrib.** (%): <15: 47.2; 65+: 3.0. **Pop. density:** 92 per sq. mi. **Urban:** 24%. **Ethnic groups:** Predominantly Arab, Afro-Arab, South Asian. **Principal language:** Arabic. **Chief religions:** Muslim (Sha'fi-Sunni, Zaydi-Shi'a).

Geography: Area: 203,800 sq. mi. **Location:** Middle East, on the S coast of the Arabian Peninsula. **Neighbors:** Saudi Arabia on N, Oman on the E. **Topography:** A sandy coastal strip leads to well-watered fertile mountains in interior. **Capital:** Sana'a. **Cities (urban aggr.):** Sana'a 1,410,000; Aden (1995 est.): 562,000.

Government: Type: Republic. **Head of state:** Pres. Ali Abdullah Saleh; b. 1942; in office: July 17, 1978. **Head of gov.:** Prime Min. Abd-al-Qadir Bajamal; b 1946; in office: Apr. 4, 2001. **Local divisions:** 17 governorates and capital region. **Defense budget** (2000): $435 mil. **Active troops:** 54,000

Economy: Industries: Oil, cotton textiles and leather goods. **Chief crops:** Grains, fruits, qat, coffee, cotton. **Minerals:** Oil, salt. **Crude oil reserves** (2001): 2.1 bil bbls. **Arable land:** 3%. **Livestock** (2001): cattle: 1.34 mil; chickens: 29.60 mil.; goats: 4.25 mil.; sheep: 4.80 mil. **Fish catch** (1999): 115,654 metric tons. **Electricity prod.:** 3.20 bil. kWh. Labor force: most are employed in agric. and herding; constr., ind. and commerce < 25%.

Finance: Monetary unit: Rial (Sept. 2002: 176.39 = $1 U.S.). **GDP** (2000 est.): $14.4 bil. **Per capita GDP:** $820. **Imports** (2000 est.): $2.7 bil.; partners (1999): Saudi Arabia 10%, UAE 8%, U.S. 7%, France 7%. **Exports** (2000 est.): $6 tril.; partners (1999): Thailand 34%, China 26%. **Tourism** (1998): $84 mil. **Budget** (2001 est.): $3.1 bil. **Intl. reserves less gold** (end 2000): $2.23 bil. **Gold:** 50,000 oz t. **Consumer prices** (change in 1998): 7.9%.

Transport: Motor vehicles: 229,084 pass. cars, 282,615 comm. vehicles. **Civil aviation:** 650.0 mil pass.-mi; 11 airports. **Chief ports:** Al Hudaydah, Al Mukalla, Aden.

Communications: TV sets: 6.5 per 1,000 pop. **Radios:** 43 per 1,000 pop. **Telephones:** 575,200.

Health: Life expectancy: 58.8 male; 62.5 female. **Births** (per 1,000 pop.): 43.3. **Deaths** (per 1,000 pop.): 9.3. **Natural inc.:** 3.4%. **Infant mortality** (per 1,000 live births): 66.8.

Education: Compulsory: ages 6-15. **Literacy** (1994): 43%.

Major Intl. Organizations: UN (FAO, IBRD, ILO, IMF, IMO, WHO), AL.

Embassy: Suite 705, 2600 Virginia Ave. NW 20037; 965-4760.

Website: www.yemenembassy.org

Yemen's territory once was part of the ancient Kingdom of Sheba, or Saba, a prosperous link in trade between Africa and India. The Bible speaks of its gold, spices, and precious stones as gifts borne by the Queen of Sheba to King Solomon.

Yemen became independent in 1918, after years of Ottoman Turkish rule, but remained politically and economically backward. Imam Ahmed ruled 1948-1962. Army officers headed by Brig. Gen. Abdullah al-Salal declared the country to be the Yemen Arab Republic.

The Imam Ahmed's heir, the Imam Mohamad al-Badr, fled to the mountains where tribesmen joined royalist forces; internal warfare between them and the republican forces continued. About 150,000 people died in the fighting.

There was a bloodless coup Nov. 5, 1967. In April 1970 hostilities ended with an agreement between Yemen and Saudi Arabia. On June 13, 1974, an army group, led by Col. Ibrahim al-Hamidi, seized the government. He was killed in 1977.

Meanwhile, South Yemen won independence from Britain in 1967, formed out of the British colony of Aden and the British protectorate of South Arabia. It became the Arab world's only Marxist state, taking the name People's Democratic Republic of Yemen in 1970 and signing a friendship treaty with the USSR in 1979 that allowed for the stationing of Soviet troops.

More than 300,000 Yemenis fled from the south to the north after independence, contributing to 2 decades of hostility between the 2 states that flared into warfare twice in the 1970s.

An Arab League-sponsored agreement between North and South Yemen on unification of the 2 countries was signed Mar. 29, 1979. An agreement providing for widespread political and economic cooperation was signed in 1988.

The 2 countries were formally united May 21, 1990, but regional clan-based rivalries led to full-scale civil war in 1994. Secessionists declared a breakaway state in S Yemen, May 21, 1994, but northern troops captured the former southern capital of Aden in July.

A new constitution was approved Sept. 28. Parliamentary elections were held Apr. 27, 1997.

A dispute between Yemen and Eritrea over the Hanish Isls. in the Red Sea, which led to armed clashes in 1995, was resolved by arbitration in 1998.

While on a refueling stop in Aden, Oct. 12, 2000, the destroyer U.S.S. *Cole* was bombed, leaving 17 Americans dead and more than 3 dozen injured; the U.S. government blamed the attack on terrorists associated with Osama bin Laden. The U.S. sent troops in 2002 to help track down members of al-Qaeda.

WORLD ALMANAC QUICK QUIZ

One of Tanzania's major products is an insecticide, Pyrethrum, made from what source?

(a) seaweed (b) cloves
(c) sisal (d) chrysanthemum

For the answer look in this chapter, or see page 1008.

Yugoslavia

See Serbia and Montenegro

Zaire

See Congo

Zambia

Republic of Zambia

People: Population: 9,959,037. **Age distrib.** (%): <15: 47.4; 65+: 2.5. **Pop. density:** 35 per sq. mi. **Urban:** 40%. **Ethnic groups:** African 98.7%, European 1.1%. **Principal languages:** English (official), indigenous. **Chief religions:** Christian 50-75%, Hindu and Muslim 24-49%.

Geography: Area: 286,000 sq. mi. **Location:** In S central Africa. **Neighbors:** Congo (formerly Zaire) on N; Tanzania, Malawi, Mozambique on E; Zimbabwe, Namibia on S; Angola on W. **Topography:** Zambia is mostly high plateau country covered with thick forests, and drained by several important rivers, including the Zambezi. **Capital:** Lusaka 1,718,000.

Government: Type: Republic. **Head of state and gov.:** Pres. Levy Patrick Mwanawasa; b Sept. 3, 1948; in office: Jan. 2, 2002. **Local divisions:** 9 provinces. **Defense budget (2001):** $64 mil. **Active troops:** 21,600.

Economy: Industries: Mining, construction, foodstuffs. **Chief crops:** Corn, cassava, sorghum, sugar. **Minerals:** Cobalt, copper, zinc, emeralds, gold, lead, silver, uranium, coal. **Arable land:** 7%. **Livestock** (2001): cattle: 2.40 mil; chickens: 30.00 mil.; goats: 1.27 mil.; pigs: 340,000; sheep: 150,000. **Fish catch** (1999): 70,702 metric tons. **Electricity prod.:** 7.82 bil. kWh. **Labor force:** agric. 85%, ind. 6%, services 9%.

Finance: Monetary unit: Kwacha (Sept. 2002: 4,500.00 = $1 U.S.). **GDP** (2000 est.): $8.5 bil. **Per capita GDP:** $880. **Imports** (2000 est.): $1.05 bil.; partners (1997): South Africa 48%, Saudi Arabia, UK, Zimbabwe. **Exports** (1999): $1.5 bil.; partners (1997): Japan, Saudi Arabia, India, Thailand, South Africa, U.S., Malaysia. **Tourism:** $85 mil. **Budget** (1999 est.): $1 bil. **Intl. reserves less gold** (end 2000): $188.0 mil. **Consumer prices** (change in 1997): 24.8%.

Transport: Railroad: Length: 791 mi. **Motor vehicles:** 142,000 pass. cars, 73,500 comm. vehicles. **Civil aviation:** 27.7 mil pass.-mi; 4 airports. **Chief port:** Mpulungu.

Communications: TV sets: 32 per 1,000 pop. **Radios:** 99 per 1,000 pop. **Telephones:** 183,700. **Daily newspaper circ.:** 13 per 1,000 pop.

Health: Life expectancy: 37 male; 37.7 female. **Births** (per 1,000 pop.): 41. **Deaths** (per 1,000 pop.): 21.9. **Natural inc.:** 1.91%. **Infant mortality** (per 1,000 live births): 89.4.

Education: Compulsory: ages 7-14. **Literacy**: 78%.

Major Intl. Organizations: UN (FAO, IBRD, ILO, IMF, WHO, WTrO), the Commonwealth, AU.

Embassy: 2419 Massachusetts Ave. NW 20008; 265-9717.

As Northern Rhodesia, the country was under the administration of the South Africa Company, 1889 until 1924, when the office of governor was established, and, subsequently, a legislature. The country became an independent republic within the Commonwealth Oct. 24, 1964.

After the white government of Rhodesia (now Zimbabwe) declared its independence from Britain Nov. 11, 1965, relations between Zambia and Rhodesia became strained.

As part of a program of government participation in major industries, a government corporation in 1970 took over 51% of the ownership of 2 foreign-owned copper-mining companies. Privately-held land and other enterprises were nationalized in 1975. In the 1980s and 1990s lowered copper prices hurt the economy and severe drought caused famine.

Food riots erupted in June 1990, as the nation suffered its worst violence since independence. Elections held Oct. 1991 brought an end to one-party rule. The new government sought to sell state enterprises, including the copper industry. Pres. Frederick Chiluba won reelection Nov. 18, 1996, but international observers cited harassment of opposition parties. A coup attempt was suppressed Oct. 28, 1997. Thwarted in his effort to change the constitution to allow himself to run for a 3d term, Chiluba endorsed Levy Patrick Mwanawasa, who won a disputed election Dec. 27, 2001.

According to UN estimates, the AIDS epidemic had orphaned some 650,000 children in Zambia by the end of the 1990s; at that time, about 20% of the adult population had HIV/AIDS. Food shortages threatened more than 2 million Zambians in 2002; the government refused to distribute shipments of U.S. food because the grain was genetically modified.

Zimbabwe

Republic of Zimbabwe

People: Population: 11,376,676. **Age distrib.** (%): <15: 38.7; 65+: 3.6. **Pop. density:** 76 per sq. mi. **Urban:** 35%. **Ethnic groups:** Shona 71%, Ndebele 16%. **Principal languages:** English (official), Shona, Sindebele. **Chief religions:** Syncretic (Christian-indigenous mix) 50%, Christian 25%, indigenous beliefs 24%.

Geography: Area: 149,300 sq. mi. **Location:** In southern Africa. **Neighbors:** Zambia on N, Botswana on W, South Africa on S, Mozambique on E. **Topography:** Zimbabwe is high plateau country, rising to mountains on eastern border, sloping down on the other borders. **Capital:** Harare. **Cities (urban aggr.):** Harare 1,868,000; Bulawayo 824,000.

Government: Type: Republic. **Head of state and gov.:** Pres. Robert Mugabe; b Feb. 21, 1924; in office: Dec. 31, 1987. **Local divisions:** 8 provinces, 2 cities. **Defense budget (2001):** $142 mil. **Active troops:** 39,000

Economy: Industries: Mining, steel, wood products, cement. **Chief crops:** Tobacco, sugar, cotton, wheat, corn. **Minerals:** Chromium, gold, nickel, asbestos, copper, iron, coal. **Arable land:** 7%. **Livestock** (2001): cattle: 5.55 mil; chickens: 16.50 mil.; goats: 2.80 mil.; pigs: 278,000; sheep: 535,000. **Fish catch** (1999): 18,241 metric tons. **Electricity prod.:** 6.43 bil. kWh. **Labor force:** agri. 66%, services 24%, ind. 10%.

Finance: Monetary unit: Dollar (Sept. 2002: 55.45 = $1 U.S.). **GDP** (2000 est.): $28.2 bil. **Per capita GDP:** $2,500. **Imports** (2000 est.): $1.3 bil.; partners (1999 est.): South Africa 46%, UK 6%, China 4%, Germany 4%. **Exports** (2000 est.): $928 mil.; partners (1999 est.): South Africa 10%, UK 9%. **Tourism:** $145 mil. **Budget** (FY96/97 est.): $2.9 bil. **Intl. reserves less gold** (end 2000): $148 mil. **Gold:** 470,000 oz t. **Consumer prices** (change in 1999): 58.5%.

Transport: Railroad: Length: 1,714 mi. **Motor vehicles:** 250,000 pass. cars, 108,000 comm. vehicles. **Civil aviation:** 582.7 mil pass.-mi; 7 airports. **Chief ports:** Binga, Kariba.

Communications: TV sets: 12 per 1,000 pop. **Radios:** 113 per 1,000 pop. **Telephones:** 582,400. **Daily newspaper circ.:** 17 per 1,000 pop.

Health: Life expectancy: 37.9 male; 35.1 female. **Births** (per 1,000 pop.): 24.6. **Deaths** (per 1,000 pop.): 24.1. **Natural inc.:** 0.05%. **Infant mortality** (per 1,000 live births): 63.

Education: Compulsory: ages 6-13. **Literacy**: 85%.

Major Intl. Organizations: UN (FAO, IBRD, ILO, IMF, WHO, WTrO), the Commonwealth, AU.

Embassy: 1608 New Hampshire Ave. NW 20009; 332-7100.

Website: www.gta.gov.zw

Britain took over the area as Southern Rhodesia in 1923 from the British South Africa Co. (which, under Cecil Rhodes, had conquered it by 1897) and granted internal self-government. Under a 1961 constitution, voting was restricted to keep whites in power. On Nov. 11, 1965, Prime Min. Ian D. Smith announced his country's unilateral declaration of independence.

Britain termed the act illegal and demanded that the country (known as Rhodesia until 1980) broaden voting rights to provide for eventual rule by the black African majority. The UN imposed sanctions and, in May 1968, a trade embargo.

Intermittent negotiations between the government and various black nationalist groups failed to prevent increasing guerrilla warfare. An "internal settlement" signed Mar. 1978 in which Smith and 3 popular black leaders would share control of the government until a transfer of power to the black majority was rejected by guerrilla leaders.

In the country's first universal-franchise election, Apr. 21, 1979, Bishop Abel Muzorewa's United African National Council gained a bare majority of the black-dominated Parliament. A cease-fire was accepted by all parties, Dec. 5. Independence as Zimbabwe was finally achieved Apr. 18, 1980.

On Mar. 6, 1992, Pres. Robert Mugabe declared a national disaster because of drought and appealed to foreign donors for food, money, and medicine. An economic adjustment program caused widespread hardship. Mugabe was reelected Mar. 1996 after opposition candidates withdrew. A land redistribution campaign launched by Mugabe triggered violent attacks in Apr. 2000 against some white farmers; whites make up less than 1% of the population but hold 70% of the land. Mugabe's opponents gained in legislative elections June 24-25, 2000. International observers criticized Mugabe for relying on fraud and intimidation to win the presidential election of Mar. 9-11, 2002. The government set a deadline of Aug. 8 for most white farmers to leave their farms.

According to UN estimates, about one-fourth of the adult population has HIV/AIDS.

National Rankings by Population, Area, Population Density, 2002

Source: Bureau of the Census, U.S. Dept. of Commerce

The world had an estimated population of 6,234,250,000 as of mid-2002. China was the largest country in population, with an estimated 1.3 billion inhabitants, 1/5 of the total. India, the 2nd-largest, passed the 1-billion mark in 1999. The U.S. ranked 3rd, with about 280 million in 2002. Russia is the largest country in land area, followed by China and Canada.

Largest Populations

Rank	Country	Population
1.	China[1]	1,284,303,705
2.	India	1,045,845,226
3.	United States	280,562,489
4.	Indonesia	232,073,071
5.	Brazil	176,029,560
6.	Pakistan	147,663,429
7.	Russia	144,978,573
8.	Bangladesh	133,376,684
9.	Nigeria	129,934,911
10.	Japan	126,974,628
11.	Mexico	103,400,165
12.	Philippines	84,525,639
13.	Germany	83,251,851
14.	Vietnam	81,098,416
15.	Egypt	70,712,345
16.	Ethiopia	67,673,031
16.	Turkey	67,308,928
17.	Iran	66,622,704
19.	Thailand	62,354,402
20.	United Kingdom	59,778,002

(1) Excluding Hong Kong, population 7,303,000.

Smallest Populations

Rank	Country	Population
1.	Vatican City	880
2.	Tuvalu	11,146
3.	Nauru	12,329
4.	Palau	19,409
5.	San Marino	27,730
6.	Monaco	31,987
7.	Liechtenstein	32,842
8.	Saint Kitts and Nevis	38,736
9.	Antigua and Barbuda	67,448
10.	Andorra	68,403

Largest Land Areas

Rank	Country	Area (sq km)
1.	Russia	17,075,400
2.	China	9,326,411
3.	Canada	9,220,970
4.	United States	9,166,601
5.	Brazil	8,456,511
6.	Australia	7,617,931
7.	India	2,973,190
8.	Argentina	2,736,690
9.	Kazakhstan	2,717,300
10.	Algeria	2,381,741

Smallest Land Areas

Rank	Country	Area (sq km)
1.	Vatican City	0.4
2.	Monaco	2
3.	Nauru	21
4.	Tuvalu	26
5.	San Marino	60
6.	Liechtenstein	161
7.	Marshall Islands	181
8.	Maldives	300
9.	Malta	321
10.	Grenada	339
	St. Vincent & the Grenadines	339

Most Densely Populated

Rank	Country	Persons per sq km
1.	Monaco	15,993.5
2.	Singapore	7,135.8
3.	Vatican City	2,200.0
4.	Malta	1,238.3
5.	Maldives	1,067.2
6.	Bahrain	1,060.4
7.	Bangladesh	996.0
8.	Taiwan	698.9
9.	Mauritius	649.1
10.	Barbados	643.3

Most Sparsely Populated

Rank	Country	Persons per sq km
1.	Mongolia	1.7
2.	Namibia	2.2
3.	Australia	2.6
4.	Suriname	2.7
5.	Botswana	2.7
6.	Mauritania	2.7
7.	Iceland	2.8
8.	Libya	3.1
9.	Guyana	3.5
10.	Canada	3.5

WORLD ALMANAC QUICK QUIZ

According to UN population projections, which metropolitan area will be the 2nd largest in the world, behind Tokyo, by 2015?

(a) New York, NY (b) Mexico City, Mexico (c) Dhaka, Bangladesh (d) Beijing, China

For the answer look in this chapter, or see page 1008.

Current Population and Projections for All Countries: 2002, 2025, and 2050

Source: Bureau of the Census, U.S. Dept. of Commerce

(midyear figures, in thousands)

COUNTRY	2002	2025	2050
Afghanistan	27,756	48,045	76,231
Albania	3,545	4,306	4,609
Algeria	32,278	47,676	58,880
Andorra	68	88	69
Angola	10,593	21,598	34,465
Antigua and Barbuda	67	65	51
Argentina	37,813	48,351	56,258
Armenia	3,330	3,434	3,428
Australia	19,547	22,191	22,846
Austria	8,170	7,822	6,136
Azerbaijan	7,798	9,429	10,585
Bahamas	301	369	404
Bahrain	656	923	1,098
Bangladesh	133,377	179,129	211,020
Barbados	277	279	266
Belarus	10,335	10,248	9,100
Belgium	10,275	9,533	7,609
Belize	263	383	489
Benin	6,788	13,541	22,171
Bhutan	2,094	3,341	4,935
Bolivia	8,445	12,007	15,240
Bosnia and Herzegovina	3,964	3,471	2,833
Botswana	1,591	1,634	2,146
Brazil	176,030	209,587	228,145
Brunei	351	530	704
Bulgaria	7,621	7,292	5,905
Burkina Faso	12,603	21,360	34,956
Burma (Myanmar)	42,238	68,107	87,778
Burundi	6,373	10,469	17,304
Cambodia	12,775	21,434	35,065
Cameroon	16,185	29,108	48,606
Canada	31,902	37,987	40,491
Cape Verde	409	532	545
Central African Republic	3,643	5,545	7,915
Chad	8,997	14,360	22,504
Chile	15,499	18,681	19,453
China (excl. Hong Kong)	1,284,304	1,407,739	1,322,435
Colombia	41,008	58,287	73,349
Comoros	614	1,160	1,953
Congo (Brazzaville)	2,958	4,246	6,081
Congo (Kinshasa)	55,225	105,737	184,456
Costa Rica	3,835	5,327	6,321
Côte d'Ivoire	16,805	27,840	44,509
Croatia	4,391	4,348	3,486
Cuba	11,224	11,722	10,594
Cyprus	767	870	878
Czech Republic	10,257	10,128	8,626
Denmark	5,369	5,334	4,476
Djibouti	473	841	1,329
Dominica	70	67	69
Dominican Republic	8,722	11,781	14,586
East Timor	825	NA	NA
Ecuador	13,447	17,800	21,059
Egypt	70,712	97,431	117,121
El Salvador	6,354	8,382	10,814
Equatorial Guinea	498	876	1,394
Eritrea	4,466	8,438	13,736
Estonia	1,416	1,237	1,047
Ethiopia	67,673	98,763	159,170
Fiji	856	1,085	1,285

IT'S A FACT: According to projections by the U.S. Census Bureau, India will surpass China as the world's biggest country in population, around 2025.

COUNTRY	2002	2025	2050
Finland	5,184	5,009	4,170
France	59,766	57,806	48,219
Gabon	1,233	1,800	2,518
Gambia, The	1,450	2,678	4,038
Georgia	4,961	4,718	4,365
Germany	83,252	75,372	57,429
Ghana	20,244	28,191	34,324
Greece	10,645	10,473	8,362
Grenada	89	154	210
Guatemala	13,314	22,344	32,185
Guinea	7,775	13,135	20,034
Guinea-Bissau	1,345	2,102	2,970
Guyana	698	710	726
Haiti	7,064	10,171	12,746
Honduras	6,561	8,612	11,001
Hong Kong S.A.R.	7,303	7,816	6,647
Hungary	10,075	9,374	7,684
Iceland	279	298	279
India	1,045,845	1,415,274	1,706,951
Indonesia	232,073	287,985	330,566
Iran	66,623	91,889	110,326
Iraq	24,002	44,146	65,529
Ireland	3,883	3,913	3,600
Israel	6,030	7,778	8,961
Italy	57,716	50,352	38,290
Jamaica	2,680	3,355	3,712
Japan	126,975	119,865	101,334
Jordan	5,307	8,223	11,303
Kazakhstan	16,742	18,565	20,426
Kenya	31,139	34,774	43,852
Kiribati	96	99	100
Kuwait	2,112	3,559	4,159
Kyrgyzstan	4,822	6,066	7,394
Laos	5,777	9,805	13,844
Latvia	2,367	1,965	1,659
Lebanon	3,678	4,001	5,508
Lesotho	2,208	2,724	3,533
Liberia	3,288	6,524	10,992
Libya	5,369	8,297	10,704
Liechtenstein	33	36	31
Lithuania	3,601	3,417	3,063
Luxembourg	449	447	360
Macao	462	644	762
Macedonia, The Former Yugo. Rep. of	2,055	2,171	1,977
Madagascar	16,473	29,306	48,327
Malawi	10,702	12,475	16,884
Malaysia	22,662	34,248	47,289
Maldives	320	623	949
Mali	11,340	22,647	40,433
Malta	397	391	325
Marshall Islands	74	171	348
Mauritania	2,829	5,446	9,329
Mauritius	1,200	1,488	1,614
Mexico	103,400	141,593	167,479
Micronesia, Federated States of	136	143	143
Moldova	4,435	4,830	4,811
Monaco	32	34	34
Mongolia	2,694	3,555	4,057
Morocco	31,168	43,228	52,069
Mozambique	19,608	33,308	47,805
Namibia	1,821	2,310	3,757
Nauru	12	12	12
Nepal	25,874	42,576	60,661
Netherlands	16,068	15,852	12,974
New Zealand	3,908	4,445	4,561
Nicaragua	5,024	8,112	10,817
Niger	10,640	20,424	33,896
Nigeria	129,935	203,423	337,591
North Korea	22,224	25,485	25,930
Norway	4,525	4,592	4,012
Oman	2,713	5,307	8,453
Pakistan	147,663	211,675	260,247
Palau	19	24	26
Panama	2,882	3,796	4,418
Papua New Guinea	5,172	7,597	10,049
Paraguay	5,884	9,929	15,001
Peru	27,950	39,170	47,899
Philippines	84,526	120,519	150,272
Poland	38,625	40,117	36,465
Portugal	10,084	9,012	7,256
Qatar	793	1,208	1,348
Romania	22,318	21,417	18,483
Russia	144,979	138,842	121,777
Rwanda	7,398	12,159	19,607
Saint Kitts and Nevis	39	60	69
Saint Lucia	160	203	224
Saint Vincent and the Grenadines	116	151	163
Samoa	179	367	471
San Marino	28	27	27
São Tomé and Príncipe	170	331	518
Saudi Arabia	23,513	50,374	97,120
Senegal	10,590	22,456	39,690
Serbia & Montenegro	9,980	10,552	9,105
Seychelles	80	91	95
Sierra Leone	5,615	11,010	18,369
Singapore	4,453	4,231	4,161
Slovakia	5,422	5,718	5,215
Slovenia	1,933	1,864	1,484
Solomon Islands	495	840	1,158
Somalia	7,753	15,192	26,243
South Africa	43,648	49,851	58,972
South Korea	48,324	54,256	52,625
Spain	40,077	36,841	29,405
Sri Lanka	19,577	24,088	26,146
Sudan	37,090	64,757	93,625
Suriname	436	460	380
Swaziland	1,124	1,589	3,059
Sweden	8,877	9,158	8,052
Switzerland	7,302	7,064	5,614
Syria	17,156	31,684	43,463
Taiwan	22,548	25,897	25,189
Tajikistan	6,720	9,634	13,261
Tanzania	37,188	50,661	76,500
Thailand	62,354	70,316	69,741
Togo	5,286	11,712	20,725
Tonga	106	133	156
Trinidad and Tobago	1,164	1,083	1,057
Tunisia	9,816	12,760	14,399
Turkey	67,309	89,736	103,656
Turkmenistan	4,689	6,514	8,422
Tuvalu	11	15	20
Uganda	24,699	49,181	91,398
Ukraine	48,396	45,096	39,096
United Arab Emirates	2,446	3,444	4,057
United Kingdom	59,778	59,985	54,116
United States	280,562	335,360	394,241
Uruguay	3,387	3,916	4,256
Uzbekistan	25,563	34,348	42,762
Vanuatu	196	282	347
Vatican City	(1)	NA	NA
Venezuela	24,288	32,474	37,773
Vietnam	81,098	103,909	119,464
Yemen	18,701	40,439	76,008
Zambia	9,959	16,156	26,967
Zimbabwe	11,377	12,366	16,064
REGIONS			
Asia	3,785,470	4,765,675	5,368,505
Africa	841,628	1,273,302	1,845,701
Europe	728,950	714,309	642,447
South America	355,068	435,601	480,270
North America	491,519	611,876	722,284
Oceania, incl. Australia	31,617	39,897	44,999
WORLD	**6,234,250**	**7,840,660**	**9,104,206**

NA = Not available. (1) Population in 2002 estimated at 880.

IT'S A FACT: According to an annual survey by Freedom House, a non-partisan organization that tracks freedoms and democratic reform globally, 121 of the world's 192 independent countries, or 63%, were democracies in 2002. In its 1987-1988 survey, it found just 66 democracies out of 164 independent countries, or 40%

Population of the World's Largest Cities

Source: United Nations, Dept. for Economic and Social Information and Policy Analysis

Population figures are revised UN estimates and projections for "urban agglomerations"—that is, contiguous densely populated urban areas, not demarcated by administrative boundaries. Data may differ from figures for cities elsewhere in *The World Almanac*.

Rank	City, Country	Pop. (thousands) 2000	Pop. (thousands, projected) 2015	Annual growth rate (percent) 1995-2000	Percentage increase for: 1975-2000	Percentage increase for: 2000-2015[1]	Pop. of city as percentage of nation's 2000 pop.
1.	Tokyo, Japan	26,444	27,190	0.51	34	3	21
2.	Mexico City, Mexico	18,066	20,434	1.52	69	13	18
3.	Sao Paulo, Brazil	17,962	21,229	1.81	74	18	10
4.	New York City, U.S.	16,732	17,944	0.48	5	7	6
5.	Mumbai (Bombay), India	16,086	22,577	2.80	119	40	2
6.	Los Angeles, U.S.	13,213	14,494	1.28	48	10	5
7.	Kolkata (Calcutta), India	13,058	16,747	1.90	66	28	1
8.	Shanghai, China	12,887	13,598	–0.34	13	6	1
9.	Dhaka, Bangladesh	12,519	22,766	6.62	476	82	10
10.	Delhi, India	12,441	20,884	4.65	181	68	1
11.	Buenos Aires, Argentina	12,024	13,185	0.70	31	10	33
12.	Jakarta, Indonesia	11,018	17,268	4.05	129	57	5
13.	Osaka, Japan	11,013	11,013	–0.05	12	0	9
14.	Beijing, China	10,839	11,671	0.02	27	8	1
15.	Karachi, Pakistan	10,032	16,197	3.69	151	61	7

(1) Projected.

The World's Refugees, 2001

Source: *World Refugee Survey 2002,* U.S. Committee for Refugees, a nonprofit corp.

These estimates are conservative. The refugees in this table include only those considered in need of protection and/or assistance and generally do not include those who have achieved permanent resettlement.

(as of Dec. 31, 2001; only countries estimated to host 50,000 or more refugees are listed)

Place of asylum	Origin of Most	Number
AFRICA		**3,002,000***
Algeria	Western Sahara, Palestinians	85,000
Democratic Republic of the Congo	Angola, Sudan, Burundi, Central African Republic, Uganda, Rep. of the Congo, Rwanda	305,000*
Republic of the Congo	Democratic Rep. of the Congo, Angola, Rwanda and Burundi, Central African Republic	102,000
Côte d'Ivoire	Liberia, Sierra Leone	103,000
Egypt	Palestinians, Sudan, Somalia	75,000*
Ethiopia	Sudan, Somalia, Eritrea	114,000*
Guinea	Sierra Leone , Liberia	190,000*
Kenya	Somalia, Sudan, Ethiopia, Uganda	243,000*
Liberia	Sierra Leone	60,000*
Sudan	Eritrea, Uganda, Ethiopia	307,000*
Tanzania	Burundi, Democratic Rep. of the Congo, Rwanda, Somalia	498,000*
Uganda	Sudan, Rwanda, Democratic Rep. of the Congo, Somalia	174,000
Zambia	Angola, Democratic Rep. of the Congo, Rwanda, Burundi	270,000*
EUROPE		**972,800**
Germany	Yugoslavia, Bosnia and Herzegovina	116,000
Switzerland	Yugoslavia, Turkey, Iraq	57,900
Yugoslavia	Croatia, Bosnia and Herzegovina, Macedonia (in Kosovo)	400,000
AMERICAS AND THE CARIBBEAN		**597,000**
Canada		70,000
United States	El Salvador, Guatemala, Haiti	492,500**
EAST ASIA AND THE PACIFIC		**815,700**
China	Vietnam, North Korea	345,000
Indonesia	East Timor	81,300
Malaysia	Philippines,	57,500
Thailand	Myanmar	277,000
MIDDLE EAST		**6,830,200**
Gaza Strip	Palestinians	852,600
Iran	Afghanistan, Iraq	2,558,000*
Iraq	Palestinians, Iran, Turkey	128,100
Jordan	Palestinians, Iraq, Sudan	1,643,900
Lebanon	Palestinians, Iraq, Sudan	389,500
Saudi Arabia	Palestinians, Iraq, Afghanistan	128,500
Syria	Palestinians	397,600
West Bank	Palestinians	607,800
Yemen	Somalia, Ethiopia, Iraq, Palestinians	69,500
SOUTH AND CENTRAL ASIA		**2,702,800**
Bangladesh	Myanmar	122,200*
India	Sri Lanka, China (Tibet), Burma, Bhutan, Bangladesh, Afghanistan	345,800*
Nepal	Bhutan, China (Tibet)	131,000
Pakistan	Afghanistan, India	2,018,000*
TOTAL		**14,921,000**

*Estimates vary widely in number reported. **Includes asylum seekers with cases pending in the United States.

Principal Sources of Refugees, 2001

Sources: *World Refugee Survey 2002,* U.S. Committee for Refugees (as of Dec. 31, 2001)

Afghanistan	4,500,000*
Palestinians	4,123,000*
Burma	450,000*
Angola	445,000
Sudan	440,000
Burundi	375,000
Dem. Rep. of the Congo	355,000
Eritrea	305,000*
Iraq	300,000*
Somalia	300,000*
Vietnam	295,000
Croatia	272,000*
El Salvador	217,000**
Liberia	215,000*
Bosnia and Herzegovina	210,000
Sierra Leone	185,000*
China (including Tibet)	151,000
Sri Lanka	144,000
Guatemala	129,000**
Bhutan	126,000
Western Sahara	110,000*
East Timor	80,000
Rwanda	60,000*
Yugoslavia	60,000*
Philippines	57,000
Tajikistan	55,000*
Mauritania	50,000
North Korea	50,000*
Turkey	43,000
Chad	35,000
Iran	34,000*
Rep. of the Congo	30,000
Haiti	25,000**
Colombia	23,000
Macedonia	23,000
Central African Republic	22,000
Georgia	21,000
Uganda	20,000
Russian Federation	18,000
India	17,000*
Cambodia	16,000
Ethiopia	13,000*
Algeria	10,000*
Ghana	10,000
Nigeria	10,000
Pakistan	10,000
Senegal	10,000
Ukraine	10,000
Armenia	9,000
Indonesia	5,000
Guinea	5,000

*Estimates vary widely in number reported. **Includes asylum seekers with cases pending in the United States.

Estimated HIV Infection and Reported AIDS Cases, Year-end 2001

Source: UNAIDS, Joint United Nations Program on HIV/AIDS

The spread of AIDS (acquired immune deficiency syndrome) has had a major impact on life expectancies in developing countries in Africa, and has begun to take a similar toll in other regions. In Botswana, for instance, life expectancy at birth has dropped to its pre-1950 level (about 35 years), due primarily to AIDS. In June 2001, the UN General Assembly held its 1st-ever special session devoted to a health issue, producing a Declaration of Commitment on HIV/AIDS. Among the stated goals was a 25% reduction in HIV (human immunodeficiency virus) among people 15 to 24 in the most affected countries by 2005, and globally by 2010.

The number of people living with HIV/AIDS worldwide as of Dec. 2001 was an estimated 40 million, with the largest number in sub-Saharan Africa. The total includes about 3 million children (under 15 years old); most children are believed to have acquired their HIV infection from their mother before or at birth, or through breastfeeding. UNAIDS estimates that nearly 5 million new HIV infections occurred in 2001 and that 3 million people died of AIDS that year, including roughly 580,000 children. Studies, primarily in industrialized nations, have indicated that approximately 60% of adults infected by HIV develop AIDS within 12-13 years of becoming infected; development of the disease may be more rapid in Third World countries.

Since the start of the global epidemic in the late 1970s, HIV has infected more than 60 million people; an estimated 24.8 million people have died of AIDS, including 4.9 million children.

Estimated Current HIV/AIDS Cases by Region, Year-end 2001

Region	Current cases[1]	Percent[2]	Region	Current cases[1]	Percent[2]
Sub-Saharan Africa	28,500,000	71.3	Western Europe	550,000	1.4
South/Southeast Asia	5,600,000	14.0	North Africa/Middle East	500,000	1.3
Latin America	1,500,000	3.8	Caribbean	420,000	1.1
East Asia/Pacific	1,000,000	2.5	Australasia	15,000	—
Eastern Europe/Central Asia	1,000,000	2.5			
North America	950,000	2.4	**WORLD[3]**	**40,000,000**	**100**

(1) Adults and children living with HIV/AIDS. (2) Percentage of total number of people worldwide living with HIV. (3) Details do not add to total because of rounding. (—) Dash means less than 1%.

Naturalization: How to Become an American Citizen

Source: Federal Statutes

A person who wishes to be naturalized as a citizen of the U.S. may obtain the necessary application form as well as detailed information from the nearest office of the Immigration and Naturalization Service. An applicant must be at least 18 years old and have been continuously resident in the U.S. for at least 5 years after admission for permanent residence. For husbands and wives of U.S. citizens the period is 3 years in most instances. Special provisions apply to certain veterans. An applicant must have been physically present in the country for at least half of the required 5 years before filing an application and must:

(1) have been of good moral character, attached to the principles of the Constitution, and well disposed to the good order and happiness of the U.S. for whatever period of residence is required;

(2) demonstrate an understanding of the English language, including an ability to read, write, and speak words in ordinary usage in English. Exceptions apply in case of handicaps or mental impairment. (Persons who, on the date of filing the application, are over 50 years of age and have been lawful permanent residents for at least 20 years, or who are over 55 and have been residents for at least 15 years, are also exempt);

(3) demonstrate a knowledge and understanding of the fundamentals of the history, and the principles and form of government, of the U.S. This must be done before an INS officer at the interview. Certain exemptions apply. The applicant may be represented by a lawyer or other representative. If action is favorable, there is a swearing in ceremony.

The following oath of allegiance is given:

I hereby declare, on oath, that I absolutely and entirely renounce and abjure all allegiance and fidelity to any foreign prince, potentate, state or sovereignty, to whom or which I have heretofore been a subject or citizen; that I will support and defend the Constitution and laws of the United States of America against all enemies, foreign and domestic; that I will bear true faith and allegiance to the same; that I will bear arms on behalf of the United States when required by the law; that I will perform noncombatant service in the armed forces of the United States when required by the law; that I will perform work of national importance under civilian direction when required by the law; and that I take this obligation freely without any mental reservation or purpose of evasion; so help me God.

Major International Organizations

African Union (AU), officially inaugurated July 9, 2002, in Durban, South Africa, following disbanding of the Organization of African Unity, and consisting of the same 35 members; i.e., all the countries of Africa, including the territory of Western Sahara. The new organization was intended to focus on fighting poverty and corruption in Africa. The founders endorsed an economic recovery plan, and provided for a peer review committee to oversee member states' adherence to standards of good government, respect for human rights, and financial transparency. The AU's founding document authorized the organization to intervene to stop genocide, war crimes, or human rights abuses within individual member nations. Headquarters: Ethiopia. Website: www.africa-union.org/home.asp

Asia-Pacific Economic Cooperation (APEC), founded Nov. 1989 as a forum to further cooperation on trade and investment between nations of the region and the rest of the world. Members of APEC in 2002 were Australia, Brunei, Canada, Chile, China, Hong Kong, Indonesia, Japan, Malaysia, Mexico, New Zealand, Papua New Guinea, Peru, Philippines, Russia, Singapore, South Korea, Taiwan, Thailand, the United States, and Vietnam. Headquarters: Singapore. Website: www.apecsec.org.sg

Association of Southeast Asian Nations (ASEAN), formed Aug. 8, 1967, to promote economic, social, and cultural cooperation and development among states of the Southeast Asian region. Members in 2002 were Brunei, Cambodia, Indonesia, Laos, Malaysia, Myanmar, Philippines, Singapore, Thailand, and Vietnam. Annual ministerial meetings set policy; the organization has a central Secretariat and specialized intergovernmental committees. Headquarters: Jakarta. Website: www.asean.or.id

Caribbean Community and Common Market (CARICOM), established July 4, 1973. Its aim is to further cooperation in economics, health, education, culture, science and technology, and tax administration, as well as the coordination of foreign policy. Members in 2002 were Antigua and Barbuda, Bahamas (Community only), Barbados, Belize, Dominica, Grenada, Guyana, Haiti (provisional), Jamaica, Montserrat, Saint Kitts and Nevis, Saint Lucia, Saint Vincent and the Grenadines, Suriname, and Trinidad and Tobago. Headquarters: Georgetown, Guyana. Website: www.caricom.org

The Commonwealth, originally called the British Commonwealth of Nations, then the Commonwealth of Nations; an association of nations and dependencies that were once parts of the former British Empire. The British monarch is the symbolic head of the Commonwealth.

There are 54 independent nations in the Commonwealth. As of 2002, regular members included the United Kingdom and 14 other nations recognizing the British monarch, represented by a governor-general, as their head of state: Antigua and Barbuda, Australia, Bahamas, Barbados, Belize, Canada, Grenada, Jamaica, New Zealand, Papua New Guinea, Saint Kitts and Nevis, Saint Lucia, Saint Vincent and the Grenadines, and the Solomon Islands. Also members in good standing were 37 countries with their own heads of state: Bangladesh, Botswana, Brunei, Cameroon, Cyprus, Dominica, Fiji, The Gambia, Ghana, Guyana, India, Kenya, Kiribati, Lesotho, Malawi, Malaysia, Maldives, Malta, Mauritius, Mozambique, Namibia, Nauru, Nigeria, Samoa, Seychelles, Sierra Leone, Singapore, South Africa, Sri Lanka, Swaziland, Tanzania, Tonga, Trinidad and Tobago, Tuvalu, Uganda, Vanuatu, and Zambia.

Following a military coup in Oct. 1999, Pakistan was suspended from the councils of the Commonwealth. In Mar. 2002, following election violence, Zimbabwe was suspended for a year. The Commonwealth facilitates consultation among members through meetings of ministers and through a permanent Secretariat. Headquarters: London. Website: www.thecommonwealth.org

Commonwealth of Independent States (CIS), created Dec. 1991 upon the disbanding of the Soviet Union. An alliance of independent states, it is made up of former Soviet constituent republics. Members in 2002 were 12 of the 15: Armenia, Azerbaijan, Belarus, Georgia, Kazakhstan, Kyrgyzstan, Moldova, Russia, Tajikistan, Turkmenistan, Ukraine, and Uzbekistan. Policy is set through coordinating bodies such as a Council of Heads of State and Council of Heads of Government. Capital of the commonwealth: Minsk, Belarus. Website: www.cis.minsk.by

European Free Trade Association (EFTA), created May 3, 1960, to promote expansion of free trade. By Dec. 31, 1966, tariffs and quotas between member nations had been eliminated. Members entered into free trade agreements with the EU in 1972 and 1973. In 1992, EFTA and EU agreed to create a single market—with free flow of goods, services, capital, and labor—among nations of the 2 organizations. Members in 2002 were Iceland, Liechtenstein, Norway, and Switzerland. Many former EFTA members are now EU members. Headquarters: Geneva. Website: www.efta.int/structure/main/index.html

European Union (EU)—known as the European Community (EC) until 1994—the collective designation of 3 organizations with common membership: the European Economic Community (Common Market), European Coal and Steel Community, and European Atomic Energy Community (Euratom). Austria, Finland, and Sweden entered the EU on Jan. 1, 1995. The 15 full members in 2002 were Austria, Belgium, Denmark, Finland, France, Germany, Greece, Ireland, Italy, Luxembourg, Netherlands, Portugal, Spain, Sweden, and UK. Some 70 nations in Africa, the Caribbean, and the Pacific are affiliated under the Lomé Convention. Website: europa.eu.int/index.htm

A merger of the 3 communities' executives went into effect July 1, 1967. The Council of the Union, European Commission, European Parliament, and European Courts of Justice and of Auditors comprise the permanent structure. The EU aims to integrate the economies, coordinate social developments, and bring about political union of the member states. Effective Dec. 31, 1992, there are no restrictions on the movement of goods, services, capital, workers, and tourists within the EU. There are also common agricultural, fisheries, and nuclear research policies.

Leaders of member nations (12 at the time) met Dec. 9-11, 1991, in Maastricht, the Netherlands. They committed the organization to launching a common currency (the euro) by 1999; sought to establish common foreign policies; laid the groundwork for a common defense policy; gave the organization a leading role in social policy (Britain was not included in this plan); pledged increased aid for poorer member nations; and slightly increased the powers of the 567-member European Parliament. The treaties went into effect Nov. 1, 1993, following ratification by all 12 members.

In June 1998 the European Central Bank was established. In Jan. 1999, 11 of the 15 EU countries began using the euro for some purposes: Austria, Belgium, Finland, France, Germany, Ireland, Italy, Luxembourg, Netherlands, Portugal, and Spain. On Jan. 1, 2002, a 6-week phasing out period began during which national currencies in these 11 countries and Greece were removed from circulation and replaced with the euro. At the end of the period, the euro became their only currency of legal tender.

Group of Eight (G-8), established Sept. 22, 1985; organization of 7 major industrial democracies (Canada, France, Germany, Italy, Japan, UK, and U.S.) and (later) Russia, meeting periodically to discuss economic and other issues. At its annual economic summit in May 1998, the name was changed to G-8 from G-7. The 7 were still free to meet without Russia on some issues, especially those relating to global finance. Website: www.g8online.org

International Criminal Police Organization (Interpol), created June 13, 1956, to promote mutual assistance among all police authorities within the limits of the law existing in the different countries. There were 179 members (independent nations), plus 14 subbureaus (dependencies) in 2002. Website: www.interpol.com

League of Arab States (Arab League), created Mar. 22, 1945. The League promotes economic, social, political, and military cooperation, mediates disputes, and represents Arab states in certain international negotiations. Members in 2002 were Algeria, Bahrain, Comoros, Djibouti, Egypt, Iraq, Jordan, Kuwait, Lebanon, Libya, Mauritania, Morocco, Oman, Palestine (considered an independent state by the League), Qatar, Saudi Arabia, Somalia, Sudan, Syria, Tunisia, United Arab Emirates, and Yemen. Headquarters: Cairo. Website: www.arabji.com/ArabGovt/ArabLeague.htm

North Atlantic Treaty Organization (NATO), created by treaty (signed Apr. 4, 1949; in effect Aug. 24, 1949). Members in 2002 were Belgium, Canada, Czech Republic, Denmark, France, Germany, Greece, Hungary, Iceland, Italy, Luxembourg, Netherlands, Norway, Poland, Portugal, Spain, Turkey, United Kingdom, and United States. Members agreed to settle disputes by peaceful means, develop their individual and collective capacity to resist armed attack, to regard an attack on one as an attack on all, and take necessary action to repel an attack under Article 51 of the UN Charter. Headquarters: Brussels. Website: www.nato.int

The NATO structure consists of a Council, the Defense Planning Committee, the Military Committee (consisting of 2 commands: Allied Command Europe, Allied Command Atlantic), Nuclear Planning Group, and Canada-U.S. Regional Planning Group. France detached itself from the military command structure in 1966.

With the dissolution of the Soviet Union and the end of the cold war in the early 1990s, members sought to modify the NATO mission, putting greater stress on political action and creating a rapid deployment force to react to local crises. By the mid-1990s, 27 nations, including Russia and other former Soviet republics, had joined with NATO in the so-called Partnership for Peace (PfP; drafted Dec. 1993), which provided for limited joint military exercises, peace-keeping missions, and information exchange. NATO has proceeded gradually toward extending full membership to former Eastern bloc nations. On Mar. 12, 1999, 3 former Warsaw Pact members, Hungary, Poland, and the Czech Republic, formally became members.

In Dec. 1995, a NATO-led multinational force was deployed to help keep the peace in Bosnia and Herzegovina. In response to the terrorist attack on the U.S., Sept. 11, 2001, the NATO Council agreed, Sept. 12, that each member state would take whatever actions it deemed necessary to restore and maintain the security of the North Atlantic area. This was the first instance of terrorism motivating NATO to invoke Article 5 of the 1949 treaty, which stipulates the conditions for collective defense.

Organization of African Unity (OAU), formed May 25, 1963, by 32 African countries to support the struggle for independence of all Africa from white colonial rule and promote "a better life for the people of Africa." In July 2002, the group, with 53 members, disbanded and re-formed as the African Union; see above.

Organization of American States (OAS), formed in Bogotá, Colombia, Apr. 30, 1948. It has a Permanent Council, Inter-American Council for Integral Development, Juridical Committee, and Commission on Human Rights. The Permanent Council can call meetings of foreign ministers to deal with urgent security matters. A General Assembly meets annually.

Members in 2002 were Antigua and Barbuda, Argentina, Bahamas, Barbados, Belize, Bolivia, Brazil, Canada, Chile, Colombia, Costa Rica, Cuba, Dominica, Dominican Republic, Ecuador, El Salvador, Grenada, Guatemala, Guyana, Haiti, Honduras, Jamaica, Mexico, Nicaragua, Panama, Paraguay, Peru, Saint Kitts and Nevis, Saint Lucia, Saint Vincent and the Grenadines, Suriname, Trinidad and Tobago, United States, Uruguay, and Venezuela. In 1962, the OAS suspended Cuba from participation in OAS activities but not from OAS membership. Headquarters: Washington, DC. Website: www.oas.org

Organization for Economic Cooperation and Development (OECD), established Sept. 30, 1961, to promote the economic and social welfare of all its member countries and to stimulate efforts on behalf of developing nations. The OECD also collects and disseminates economic and environmental information.

Members in 2002 were Australia, Austria, Belgium, Canada, Czech Republic, Denmark, Finland, France, Germany, Greece, Hungary, Iceland, Ireland, Italy, Japan, Luxembourg, Mexico, Netherlands, New Zealand, Norway, Poland, Portugal, Slovak Republic, South Korea, Spain, Sweden, Switzerland, Turkey, United Kingdom, and the United States. Headquarters: Paris. Website: www.oecd.org

Organization of Petroleum Exporting Countries (OPEC), created Sept. 14, 1960. The group attempts to set world oil prices by controlling oil production. It also pursues members' interests in trade and development dealings with industrialized oil-consuming nations. Members in 2002 were Algeria, Indonesia, Iran, Iraq, Kuwait, Libya, Nigeria, Qatar, Saudi Arabia, United Arab Emirates, and Venezuela. Headquarters: Vienna. Website: www.opec.org

Organization for Security and Cooperation in Europe (OSCE), established in 1972 as the Conference on Security and Cooperation in Europe; current name adopted Jan. 1, 1995. The group, formed by NATO and Warsaw Pact members, is interested in furthering East-West relations through a commitment to nonaggression and human rights as well as cooperation in economics, science and technology, cultural exchange, and environmental protection.

There were 54 member states in 2002. Headquarters: Vienna. Website: www.osce.org

United Nations

The 57th regular session of United Nations General Assembly opened Sept. 10, 2002, attended by world leaders and other delegates from 189 nations. On that day, Switzerland was admitted as the 190th member nation. On Sept. 27, the newly formed country of East Timor (Democratic Republic of Timor-Leste) joined as the 191st member.

UN headquarters is in New York, NY, between First Ave. and Roosevelt Drive and E. 42d St. and E. 48th St. The General Assembly Bldg., Secretariat, Conference and Library bldgs. are interconnected.

The 6 main organs of the UN are the: General Assembly, Security Council, Economic and Social Council, Trusteeship Council, International Court of Justice, and Secretariat. The UN family is much larger, encompassing 15 agencies and several programmes and bodies.

The UN has a post office originating its own stamps.

Proposals to establish an organization of nations for maintenance of world peace led to convening of the United Nations Conference on International Organization at San Francisco, Apr. 25-June 26, 1945, where the charter of the UN was drawn up. The charter was signed June 26 by 50 nations, and by Poland, one of the original 51 members, on Oct. 15, 1945. It came into effect Oct. 24, 1945, upon ratification by the permanent members of the Security Council and a majority of other signatories.

Purposes: To maintain international peace and security; to develop friendly relations among nations; to achieve international cooperation in solving economic, social, cultural, and humanitarian problems and in promoting respect for human rights and basic freedoms; to be a center for harmonizing the actions of nations in attaining these common ends.

Visitors to the UN: Headquarters is open to the public every day except Thanksgiving, Christmas, and New Year's Day. Guided tours are given approximately every half hour from 9:30 A.M. to 4:45 P.M. daily, except on weekends in January and February.

Groups of 12 or more should write to the Group Program Unit, Public Services Section, Room GA-63, United Nations, New York, NY 10017, or telephone (212) 963-4440. Children under 5 not permitted on tours.

Roster of the United Nations

The 191 members of the United Nations, with the years in which they became members; as of Oct. 2002.

Member	Year	Member	Year	Member	Year	Member	Year
Afghanistan	1946	Burundi	1962	El Salvador	1945	Ireland	1955
Albania	1955	Cambodia	1955	Equatorial Guinea	1968	Israel	1949
Algeria	1962	Cameroon	1960	Eritrea	1993	Italy	1955
Andorra	1993	Canada	1945	Estonia	1991	Jamaica	1962
Angola	1976	Cape Verde	1975	Ethiopia	1945	Japan	1956
Antigua and Barbuda	1981	Central African Rep.	1960	Fiji	1970	Jordan	1955
Argentina	1945	Chad	1960	Finland	1955	Kazakhstan	1992
Armenia	1992	Chile	1945	France	1945	Kenya	1963
Australia	1945	China[1]	1945	Gabon	1960	Kiribati	1999
Austria	1955	Colombia	1945	Gambia, The	1965	Korea, North	1991
Azerbaijan	1992	Comoros	1975	Georgia	1992	Korea, South	1991
Bahamas	1973	Congo, Democratic Rep. of the (Zaire)	1960	Germany	1973	Kuwait	1963
Bahrain	1971			Ghana	1957	Kyrgyzstan	1992
Bangladesh	1974	Congo, Republic of the	1960	Greece	1945	Laos	1955
Barbados	1966	Costa Rica	1945	Grenada	1974	Latvia	1991
Belarus	1945	Côte d'Ivoire	1960	Guatemala	1945	Lebanon	1945
Belgium	1945	Croatia	1992	Guinea	1958	Lesotho	1966
Belize	1981	Cuba	1945	Guinea-Bissau	1974	Liberia	1945
Benin	1960	Cyprus	1960	Guyana	1966	Libya	1955
Bhutan	1971	Czech Republic[2]	1993	Haiti	1945	Liechtenstein	1990
Bolivia	1945	Denmark	1945	Honduras	1945	Lithuania	1991
Bosnia & Herzegovina	1992	Djibouti	1977	Hungary	1955	Luxembourg	1945
Botswana	1966	Dominica	1978	Iceland	1946	Macedonia[5]	1993
Brazil	1945	Dominican Republic	1945	India	1945	Madagascar	1960
Brunei	1984	East Timor	2002	Indonesia[4]	1950	Malawi	1964
Bulgaria	1955	Ecuador	1945	Iran	1945	Malaysia[6]	1957
Burkina Faso	1960	Egypt[3]	1945	Iraq	1945	Maldives	1965

Member	Year	Member	Year	Member	Year	Member	Year
Mali	1960	Oman	1971	Saudi Arabia	1945	Togo	1960
Malta	1964	Pakistan	1947	Senegal	1960	Tonga	1999
Marshall Islands	1991	Palau	1994	Seychelles	1976	Trinidad and Tobago	1962
Mauritania	1961	Panama	1945	Sierra Leone	1961	Tunisia	1956
Mauritius	1968	Papua New Guinea	1975	Singapore[6]	1965	Turkey	1945
Mexico	1945	Paraguay	1945	Slovakia[2]	1993	Turkmenistan	1992
Micronesia	1991	Peru	1945	Slovenia	1992	Tuvalu	2000
Moldova	1992	Philippines	1945	Solomon Islands	1978	Uganda	1962
Monaco	1993	Poland	1945	Somalia	1960	Ukraine	1945
Mongolia	1961	Portugal	1955	South Africa[8]	1945	United Arab Emirates	1971
Morocco	1956	Qatar	1971	Spain	1955	United Kingdom	1945
Mozambique	1975	Romania	1955	Sri Lanka	1955	United States	1945
Myanmar (Burma)	1948	Russia[7]	1945	Sudan	1956	Uruguay	1945
Namibia	1990	Rwanda	1962	Suriname	1975	Uzbekistan	1992
Nauru	1999	Saint Kitts and Nevis	1983	Swaziland	1968	Vanuatu	1981
Nepal	1955	Saint Lucia	1979	Sweden	1946	Venezuela	1945
Netherlands	1945	Saint Vincent and the Grenadines	1980	Switzerland	2002	Vietnam	1977
New Zealand	1945	Samoa (formerly Western Samoa)	1976	Syria[3]	1945	Yemen[10]	1947
Nicaragua	1945	San Marino	1992	Tajikistan	1992	Yugoslavia[11]	1945
Niger	1960	São Tomé and Príncipe	1975	Tanzania[9]	1961	Zambia	1964
Nigeria	1960			Thailand	1946	Zimbabwe	1980
Norway	1945						

(1) The General Assembly voted in 1971 to expel the Chinese government on Taiwan and admit the Beijing government in its place. (2) Czechoslovakia, which split into the separate nations of the Czech Republic and Slovakia on Jan. 1, 1993, was a UN member from 1945 to 1992. (3) Egypt and Syria were original members of the UN. In 1958, the United Arab Republic was established by a union of Egypt and Syria and continued as a single member of the UN. In 1961, Syria resumed its separate membership. (4) Indonesia withdrew from the UN in 1965 and rejoined in 1966. (5) Admitted under the provisional name of The Former Yugoslav Republic of Macedonia. (6) Malaya joined the UN in 1957. In 1963, its name was changed to Malaysia following the accession of Singapore, Sabah, and Sarawak. Singapore became an independent UN member in 1965. (7) The Union of Soviet Socialist Republics was an original member of the UN from 1945. After the USSR's dissolution in 1991, Russia informed the UN it would be continuing the USSR's membership in the Security Council and all other UN organs with the support of the Commonwealth of Independent States (comprised of most of the former Soviet republics). (8) In 1994, the General Assembly accepted the credentials of the South African delegation, which had been rejected for 24 years because of the country's former apartheid policies. (9) Tanganyika was a member of the UN from 1961 and Zanzibar was a member from 1963. Following the ratification in 1964 of Articles of Union between Tanganyika and Zanzibar, the United Republic of Tanganyika and Zanzibar continued as a single member of the UN, later changing its name to United Republic of Tanzania. (10) The Yemen Arab Republic was admitted in 1947; the People's Republic of Yemen, in 1967. The 2 nations merged in 1990. (11) The Socialist Federal Republic of Yugoslavia became a member in 1945. After 4 of its 6 republics (Bosnia and Herzegovina, Croatia, Macedonia, and Slovenia) declared independence in 1991-92, the 2 remaining republics, Montenegro and Serbia, reconstituted themselves as the Federal Republic of Yugoslavia, which assumed Yugoslavia's UN seat Apr. 8, 1992. In Sept. 1992, the General Assembly decided the Federal Republic of Yugoslavia could not automatically take the seat of the former Yugoslavia. Membership was granted in Nov. 2000 by a vote of the General Assembly. **NOTE:** The following sovereign countries are not members of the UN: China (Taiwan), Vatican City (Holy See). Vatican City is a permanent observer.

United Nations Secretaries General

Took Office	Secretary, Nation	Took Office	Secretary, Nation	Took Office	Secretary, Nation
1946	Trygve Lie, Norway	1972	Kurt Waldheim, Austria	1992	Boutros Boutros-Ghali, Egypt
1953	Dag Hammarskjold, Sweden	1982	Javier Perez de Cuellar, Peru	1997	Kofi Annan, Ghana
1961	U Thant, Burma				

U.S. Representatives to the United Nations

The U.S. Representative to the United Nations is the Chief of the U.S. Mission to the United Nations in New York and holds the rank and status of Ambassador Extraordinary and Plenipotentiary (A.E.P.). Year given is the year each took office.

Year	Representative	Year	Representative	Year	Representative
1946	Edward R. Stettinius, Jr.	1968	James Russell Wiggins	1981	Jeane J. Kirkpatrick
1946	Herschel V. Johnson (act.)	1969	Charles W. Yost	1985	Vernon A. Walters
1947	Warren R. Austin	1971	George H. W. Bush	1989	Thomas R. Pickering
1953	Henry Cabot Lodge, Jr.	1973	John A. Scali	1992	Edward J. Perkins
1960	James J. Wadsworth	1975	Daniel P. Moynihan	1993	Madeleine K. Albright
1961	Adlai E. Stevenson	1976	William W. Scranton	1997	Bill Richardson
1965	Arthur J. Goldberg	1977	Andrew Young	1999	Richard C. Holbrooke
1968	George W. Ball	1979	Donald McHenry	2001	John D. Negroponte

Organization of the United Nations

The text of the UN Charter may be obtained from the Public Inquiries Unit, Department of Public Information, United Nations, New York, NY 10017. (212) 963-4475.

General Assembly. The General Assembly is composed of representatives of all the member nations. Each nation is entitled to one vote. The General Assembly meets in regular annual sessions and in special session when necessary. Special sessions are convoked by the secretary general at the request of the Security Council or of a majority of the members of the UN. On important questions a two-thirds majority of members present and voting is required; on other questions a simple majority is sufficient.

The General Assembly must approve the UN budget and apportion expenses among members. A member in arrears can lose its vote if the amount of arrears equals or exceeds the amount of the contributions due for the preceding 2 full years.

Security Council. The Security Council consists of 15 members, 5 with permanent seats. The remaining 10 are elected for 2-year terms by the General Assembly; they are not eligible for immediate reelection.

Permanent members of the Council are: China, France, Russia, United Kingdom, and the United States.

Nonpermanent members are: (with terms expiring Dec. 31, 2002) Colombia, Ireland, Mauritius, Norway, and Singapore; (with terms expiring Dec. 31, 2003) Bulgaria, Cameroon, Guinea, Mexico, and Syria.

The Security Council has the primary responsibility within the UN for maintaining international peace and security. The Council may investigate any dispute that threatens international peace and security.

Any member of the UN at UN headquarters may, if invited by the Council, participate in its discussions and a nation not a member of the UN may appear if it is a party to a dispute.

Decisions on procedural questions are made by an affirmative vote of 9 members. On all other matters the affirmative vote of 9 members must include the concurring votes of all permanent members; (giving them veto power). A party to a dispute must refrain from voting.

The Security Council directs the various peacekeeping forces deployed throughout the world.

Ongoing UN Peacekeeping Missions, 2002

Source: United Nations Cartographic Section, Map No. 4000(E) Rev. 19

(Year given is the year each mission began operation)

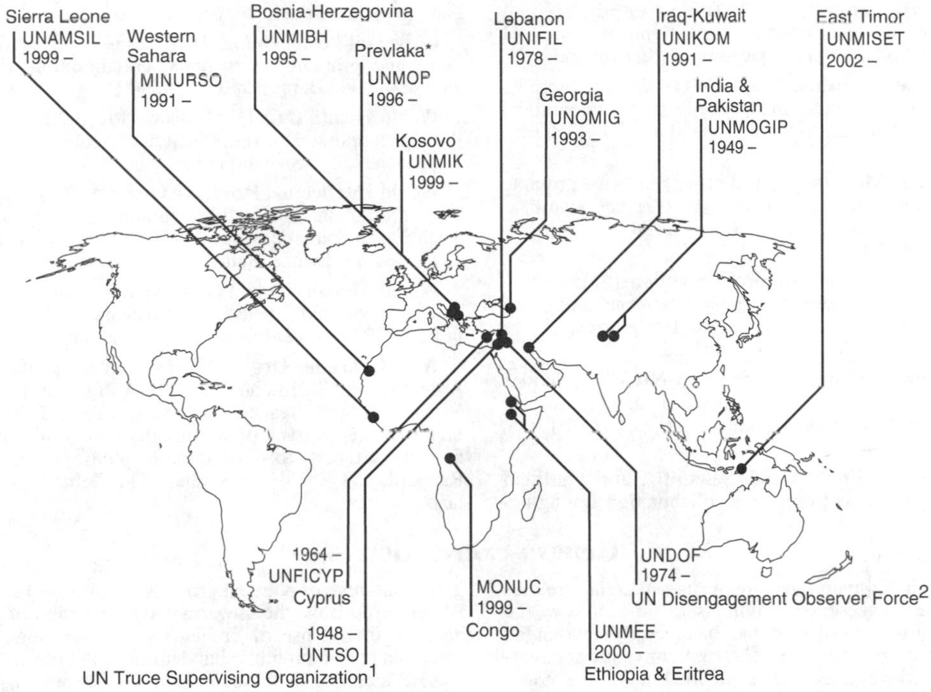

*Prevlaka is on border between Croatia and Montenegro. (1) Functions in 5 Mideast nations. (2) Golan Heights.

Economic and Social Council. The Economic and Social Council consists of 54 members elected by the General Assembly for 3-year terms.

The council is responsible for carrying out UN functions with regard to international economic, social, cultural, educational, health, and related matters. It meets once a year.

Trusteeship Council. The administration of trust territories was under UN supervision; however, all 11 Trust Territories have attained their right to self-determination. The work of the Council has, therefore, been suspended.

Secretariat. The Secretary General is the chief administrative officer of the UN. The Secretary General reports to the General Assembly and may bring to the attention of the Security Council any matter that threatens international peace.

Budget: The General Assembly approved a total budget for the biennium 2002–2003 of $2.6 billion.

International Court of Justice (World Court). The International Court of Justice is the principal judicial organ of the United Nations. All members are *ipso facto* parties to the statute of the Court. Other states may become parties to the Court's statute.

The Court has jurisdiction over cases which the parties submit to it and matters especially provided for in the charter or in treaties. The Court gives advisory opinions and renders judgments. Its decisions are binding only between parties concerned and in respect to a particular dispute. If any party to a case fails to heed a judgment, the other party may have recourse to the Security Council.

The 15 judges are elected for 9-year terms by the General Assembly and the Security Council. Retiring judges are eligible for reelection. The Court remains permanently in session, except during vacations. All questions are decided by majority. The International Court of Justice sits in The Hague, Netherlands.

Selected Specialized and Related Agencies

These specialized agencies are autonomous, with their own memberships and organs, and at the same time have a functional relationship or working agreement with the UN (headquarters), except for UNICEF and UNHCR, which report directly to the Economic and Social Council and to the General Assembly.

Food and Agriculture Organization (FAO) aims to increase production from farms, forests, and fisheries; improve food distribution and marketing, nutrition, and the living conditions of rural people. (Viale delle Terme di Caracalla, 100100 Rome, Italy.)

International Atomic Energy Agency (IAEA) aims to promote the safe, peaceful uses of atomic energy. (Vienna International Centre, PO Box 100, Wagramerstrasse 5, A-1400, Vienna, Austria.)

International Bank for Reconstruction and Development (IBRD) (World Bank) provides loans and technical assistance for projects in developing member countries; encourages cofinancing for projects from other public and private sources.

The IBRD has 4 affiliates: (1) The **International Development Association (IDA)** provides funds for development projects on concessionary terms to the poorer developing member countries. (2) The **International Finance Corporation (IFC)** promotes the growth of the private sector in developing member countries; encourages the development of local capital markets; stimulates the international flow of private capital. (3) The **Multilateral Investment Guarantee Agency (MIGA)** promotes private investment in developing countries; guarantees investments to protect investors from noncommercial risks, such as nationalization; advises governments on attracting private investment. (4) The **International Center for Settlement of Investment Disputes (ICSID)** provides conciliation and arbitration services for disputes between foreign investors and host governments which arise out of an investment. (1818 H St., NW, Washington, DC 20433.)

International Civil Aviation Org. (ICAO) promotes international civil aviation standards and regulations. (999 University St., Montreal, Quebec, Canada H3C 5H7.)

International Fund for Agricultural Development (IFAD) aims to mobilize funds for agricultural and rural projects in developing countries. (107 Via del Seratico, 00142 Rome, Italy.)

International Labor Org. (ILO) aims to promote employment; improve labor conditions and living standards. (4 route des Morillons, CH-1211 Geneva 22, Switzerland.)

International Maritime Org. (IMO) aims to promote cooperation on technical matters affecting international shipping. (4 Albert Embankment, London SE1 7SR, England.)

International Monetary Fund (IMF) aims to promote international monetary cooperation and currency stabilization and expansion of international trade. (700 19th St., NW, Washington, DC 20431.)

International Telecommunication Union (ITU) establishes regulations for radio, telegraph, telephone, and space radio-communications, allocates radio frequencies. (Place des Nations, 1211 Geneva 20, Switzerland.)

United Nations Children's Fund (UNICEF) provides financial aid and development assistance to programs for children and mothers in developing countries. (3 UN Plaza, New York, NY 10017.)

United Nations Educational, Scientific, and Cultural Org. (UNESCO) aims to promote collaboration among nations through education, science, and culture. (7 Place de Fontenoy, 75352 Paris 07SP, France.)

United Nations High Commissioner for Refugees (UNHCR) provides essential assistance for refugees. (Place des Nations, 1211 Geneva 10, Switzerland.)

Universal Postal Union (UPU) aims to perfect postal services and promote international collaboration. (Weltpoststrasse 4, 3000 Berne 15 Switzerland.)

World Health Org. (WHO) aims to aid the attainment of the highest possible level of health. (Avenue Appia 20, CH-1211 Geneva 27, Switzerland.)

World Intellectual Property Org. (WIPO) seeks to protect, through international cooperation, literary, industrial, scientific, and artistic works. (34, Chemin des Colom Bettes, 1211 Geneva, Switzerland.)

World Meteorological Org. (WMO) aims to coordinate and improve world meteorological work. (7 bis Avenue de la Paix, CP2300, 1211 Geneva 2, Switzerland.)

World Trade Org. (WTrO) replacing the General Agreement on Tariffs and Trade (GATT), administers trade agreements and treaties, examines the trade regimes of members, keeps track of various trade measures and statistics, and attempts to settle trade disputes. (Centre William Rappard, 154 Rue de Lausanne, 1211 Geneva 21, Switzerland.)

Geneva Conventions

The Geneva Conventions are 4 international treaties governing the protection of civilians in time of war, the treatment of prisoners of war, and the care of the wounded and sick in the armed forces. The first convention, covering the sick and wounded, was concluded in Geneva, Switzerland, in 1864; it was amended and expanded in 1906. A third convention, in 1929, covered prisoners of war. Outrage at the treatment of prisoners and civilians during World War II by some belligerents, notably Germany and Japan, prompted the conclusion, in Aug. 1949, of 4 new conventions. Three of these restated and strengthened the previous conventions, and the fourth codified general principles of international law governing the treatment of civilians in wartime.

The 1949 convention for civilians provided for special safeguards for the following categories of people: wounded persons, children under 15 years of age, pregnant women, and the elderly. Discrimination was forbidden on racial, religious, national, or political grounds. Torture, collective punishment, reprisals, the unwarranted destruction of property, and the forced use of civilians for an occupier's armed forces were also prohibited under the 1949 conventions.

Also included in the new 1949 treaties was a pledge to treat prisoners humanely, feed them adequately, and deliver relief supplies to them. They were not to be forced to disclose more than minimal information.

Most countries have formally accepted all or most of the humanitarian conventions as binding. A nation is not free to withdraw its ratification of the conventions during wartime. However, there is no permanent machinery in place to apprehend, try, or punish violators.

Officials in Switzerland scheduled a meeting on Jan. 27-29, 2003, with representatives from different nations to reach a possible consensus on how to apply the principles of the Geneva Conventions to the world of the early 21st century.

Major Foreign Develoment Aid Donors, 2000-2001

Source: Organization for Economic Cooperation and Development; ranked by percent of GNP in 2001.

In 2001, the U.S. gave the highest total amount of development aid but ranked 22nd by percent of GNP.

Country	ODA[1], as % of GNP 2000	ODA[1], as % of GNP 2001	ODA[1] in U.S. dollars (millions) 2000	ODA[1] in U.S. dollars (millions) 2001
1. Denmark	1.06	1.01	$1,664	$1,599
2. Norway	0.8	0.83	1,264	1,346
3. Netherlands	0.82	0.82	3,075	3,155
4. Luxembourg	0.7	0.8	116	142
5. Sweden	0.81	0.76	1,813	1,576
6. Belgium	0.36	0.37	812	866
7. France	0.33	0.34	4,221	4,293
Switzerland	0.34	0.34	888	908
9. Finland	0.31	0.33	371	389
Ireland	0.3	0.33	239	285
11. United Kingdom	0.31	0.32	4,458	4,659
12. Spain	0.24	0.3	$1,321	$1,748
13. Germany	0.27	0.27	5,034	4,879
14. Australia	0.27	0.25	995	852
Austria	0.25	0.25	461	457
Portugal	0.26	0.25	261	267
New Zealand	0.26	0.25	116	111
18. Canada	0.25	0.23	1,722	1,572
Japan	0.27	0.23	13,062	9,678
20. Greece	0.19	0.19	216	194
21. Italy	0.13	0.14	1,368	1,493
22. United States	0.1	0.11	9,581	10,884

(1) ODA = official development assistance.

Top 10 Recipients of U.S. Development Aid, 1999-2000

Source: Organization for Economic Cooperation and Development

Country	Millions of U.S. $ (avg. 1999-2000)
1. Russia	$1,154
2. Israel	967
3. Egypt	799
4. Ukraine	282
5. Indonesia	$194
6. Jordan	179
7. Colombia	169
8. Bosnia and Herzegovina	$152
9. India	148
10. Peru	136

SPORTS

SPORTS HIGHLIGHTS OF 2002

Brazil defeated Germany, 2-0, in the World Cup soccer final June 30 in Yokohama, Japan, to win a record 5th title. Turkey took 3rd with a 3-2 win over co-host South Korea. Last in 1998, the U.S. had its best World Cup showing since 1930, defeating Portugal 3-2 and tying co-host South Korea 1-1 in the 1st round, then upsetting Mexico 2-0 in the 2nd round, before losing to Germany, 1-0, in the quarterfinals.

The 2002 Winter Olympic Games, held in Salt Lake City, UT, Feb. 8-24, were the most successful ever for the U.S, which won 34 medals, 1 fewer than Germany; Norway was 3rd with 24. A judging controversy in pairs figure skating grew into an international scandal which led the Int'l Skating Union to award gold medals to both Russians and Canadians. In all, athletes from a record 18 nations earned gold medals. Among the winners were the Canadian men's and women's hockey teams, Croatian alpine skier Janica Kostelic (3 golds and a silver), and Americans Sarah Hughes (figure skating) and Jim Shea (skeleton). A 3rd generation Olympian, Shea dedicated his win to his grandfather, Jack, killed in an auto accident just before the Games.

The Los Angeles Lakers won their 3rd NBA championship in a row, sweeping the New Jersey Nets with a 113-107 victory in Game Four of the NBA Finals June 12, in East Rutherford, NJ. Center Shaquille O'Neal joined Michael Jordan as the only NBA players to win 3 straight Finals MVP Awards.

The New England Patriots upset the St. Louis Rams, 20-17, in Super Bowl XXXVI in New Orleans Feb. 3. St. Louis had trailed 17-3 with 10 mins. left to play, but scored 2 touchdowns, the 2nd with 1:37 remaining, to tie the score. Quarterback Tom Brady, the Super Bowl MVP, drove the Patriots from their own 17-yard line to the Rams' 30, where Adam Vinatieri kicked a 48-yard field goal as time ran out.

Major League Baseball owners and players agreed to a new contract, Aug. 30, averting what would have been the sport's 9th work stoppage since 1972. For the 1st time, they settled their differences without a strike or a lockout. The deal runs through the 2006 season and stipulates that no teams will be eliminated.

Serena Williams, 20, won the French Open, Wimbledon, and U.S. Open tennis championships, each time defeating her sister Venus, 22, in the finals. The sisters became the first siblings ever to hold the top 2 spots in the WTA tour rankings.

Lance Armstrong, leader of the U.S. Postal Service team, dominated the Tour de France, winning the world's premier cycling event for the 4th straight year. He finished the 3-week, 2,032-mile tour July 28, with an overall time of 82 hrs, 5 mins., 12 sec. Runner-up Joseba Beloki of Spain was 7:17 behind.

In the women's NCAA basketball championship game on Mar. 31, undefeated Connecticut topped Oklahoma, 82-70. Swin Cash, of Connecticut, was named Most Outstanding Player of the tournament. In the men's NCAA final, Maryland defeated Indiana, 64-52, for the national championship on Apr. 1. Maryland's Juan Dixon was named Most Outstanding Player.

On Apr. 14, golfer Tiger Woods won his 3rd Masters title at Augusta National. He went on to win the 2nd U.S. Open of his career on June 16, becoming the 1st player since Jack Nicklaus in 1972 to win both tournaments in the same year. That win gave Woods his 8th career major championship.

On Sept. 14, at the IAAF Grand Prix Final in Paris, American Tim Montgomery became the "World's Fastest Human," running the 100 meters in 9.78 secs., shaving one hundredth of a second off the previous world record set in 1999 by Maurice Greene. Britain's Dwain Chambers finished 2nd in a European record of 9.87.

Winter Olympic Games

Sites of Winter Olympic Games

1924 Chamonix, France
1928 St. Moritz, Switzerland
1932 Lake Placid, New York
1936 Garmisch-Partenkirchen, Germany
1948 St. Moritz, Switzerland
1952 Oslo, Norway
1956 Cortina d'Ampezzo, Italy
1960 Squaw Valley, California
1964 Innsbruck, Austria
1968 Grenoble, France
1972 Sapporo, Japan
1976 Innsbruck, Austria
1980 Lake Placid, New York
1984 Sarajevo, Yugoslavia
1988 Calgary, Alberta
1992 Albertville, France
1994 Lillehammer, Norway
1998 Nagano, Japan
2002 Salt Lake City, Utah
2006 Turin, Italy

Winter Olympic Games in 2002—Highlights

Salt Lake City, Utah, Feb. 8-24, 2002

The 2002 games opened with an honor guard of U.S. Olympians and New York City police officers and firefighters carrying a tattered U.S. flag, removed from the World Trade Center site, into Rice-Eccles Stadium. Mike Eruzione, captain of the gold-medal 1980 U.S. hockey team, lit the Olympic torch to begin the games. Over 16 days, 2,200 athletes from 77 nations competed. Some 2.1 billion viewers worldwide made these the most watched Winter Games ever.

Snowboarder Kelly Clark, 18, won the 1st gold medal for the U.S., in the halfpipe; in the men's event, Ross Powers led a U.S. sweep. Controversy hovered over the pairs figure skating competition when Canadians Jamie Sale and David Pelletier placed 2nd after a seemingly flawless long program. Russia's Yelena Berezhnaya and Anton Sikharulidze were awarded the gold, but an investigation concluded that a French judge had been pressured to vote for the Russians in exchange for a 1st-place vote for a French pair in ice dancing; the IOC awarded a 2nd gold medal to Sale and Pelletier. There was no controversy as 16-year-old Sarah Hughes upset fellow American Michelle Kwan and Russian Irina Slutskaya for the gold in women's figure skating. Croatia's Janica Kostelic became the 1st alpine skier to win 4 medals, 3 gold, in a single Olympics. Americans Jill Bakken and Vonetta Flowers won the 1st-ever women's bobsled event—Flowers was the 1st African-American to win a Winter Olympic medal. American Jim Shea Jr. won gold in the skeleton, an event not held in 44 years. In men's ice hockey, the U.S. team took the silver, losing to Canada, 5-2, in the final, the best U.S. finish since 1980. Canada also won gold in women's ice hockey, defeating the U.S., 3-2.

As in 1998, Germany led the medal count, edging the U.S. by 1. But U.S.'s 34 medals (10 gold) was its highest total in Winter Games history.

2002 Final Medal Standings

	Gold	Silver	Bronze	Total
Germany	12	16	7	35
United States	10	13	11	34
Norway	11	7	6	24
Canada	6	3	8	17
Austria	2	4	11	17
Russia	6	6	4	16
Italy	4	4	4	12
France	4	5	2	11
Switzerland	3	2	6	11
Netherlands	3	5	0	8
China	2	2	4	8
Finland	4	2	1	7
Sweden	0	2	4	6
Croatia	3	1	0	4
South Korea	2	2	0	4
Estonia	1	1	1	3
Bulgaria	0	1	2	3
Australia	2	0	0	2
Spain	2	0	0	2
Czech Republic	1	0	1	2
Great Britain	1	0	1	2
Japan	0	1	1	2
Poland	0	1	1	2
Belarus	0	0	1	1
Slovenia	0	0	1	1
TOTAL	**79**	**78**	**77**	**234**

WORLD ALMANAC QUICK QUIZ

Besides Carl Lewis, who is the only track and field athlete ever to win an event in 4 straight Olympics?

(a) Michael Johnson (b) Jackie Joyner-Kersee
(c) Al Oerter (d) Jan Zelezny

For the answer look in this chapter, or see page 1008.

2002 Winter Olympics Medal Winners

(G = Gold, S = Silver, B = Bronze)

ALPINE SKIING

Men

Downhill—G-Fritz Strobl, Austria, S-Lasse Kjus, Norway, B-Stephan Eberharter, Austria
Super Giant Slalom—G-Kjetil Andre Aamodt, Norway, S-Stephan Eberharter, Austria, B-Andreas Schifferer, Austria
Giant Slalom—G-Stephan Eberharter, Austria, S-Bode Miller, U.S., B-Lasse Kjus, Norway
Slalom—G-Jean-Pierre Vidal, France, S-Sebastien Amiez, France, B-Benjamin Raich, Austria*
Combined—G-Kjetil Andre Aamodt, Norway, S-Bode Miller, U.S., B-Benjamin Raich, Austria
*Raich was awarded bronze after the IOC disqualified Britain's Alain Baxter Mar. 21, 2002, for steriod use.

Women

Downhill—G-Carole Montillet, France, S-Isolde Kostner, Italy, B-Renate Goetschl, Austria
Super Giant Slalom—G-Daniela Ceccarelli, Italy, S-Janica Kostelic, Croatia, B-Karen Putzer, Italy
Giant Slalom—G-Janica Kostelic, Croatia, S-Anja Paerson, Sweden, B-Sonja Nef, Switzerland
Slalom—G-Janica Kostelic, Croatia, S-Laure Pequegnot, France, B-Anja Paerson, Sweden
Combined—G-Janica Kostelic, Croatia, S-Renate Goetschl, Austria, B-Martina Ertl, Germany

BIATHLON

Men

10KM—G-Ole Einar Bjoerndalen, Norway, S-Sven Fischer, Germany, B-Wolfgang Perner, Austria
12.5KM—G-Ole Einar Bjoerndalen, Norway, S-Raphael Poiree, France, B-Ricco Gross, Germany
20KM—G-Ole Einar Bjoerndalen, Norway, S-Frank Luck, Germany, B-Victor Maigourov, Russia
30KM Relay—G-Norway, S-Germany, B-France

Women

7.5KM—G-Kati Wilhelm, Germany, S-Uschi Disl, Germany, B-Magdalena Forsberg, Sweden
10KM—G-Olga Pyleva, Russia, S-Kati Wilhelm, Germany, B-Irina Nikoultchina, Bulgaria
15KM—G-Andrea Henkel, Germany, S-Liv Grete Poiree, Norway, B-Magdalena Forsberg, Sweden
30KM Relay—G-Germany, S-Norway, B-Russia

BOBSLEDDING

4-Man Bob—G-Germany II, S-U.S. I, B-U.S. II
2-Man Bob—G-Germany I, S-Switzerland I, B-Switzerland II
2-Woman Bob—G-U.S. II, S-Germany I, B-Germany II

CURLING

Men—G-Norway, S-Canada, B-Switzerland
Women—G-Great Britain, S-Switzerland, B-Canada

FIGURE SKATING

Men's Singles—G-Alexei Yagudin, Russia, S-Evgeni Plushenko, Russia, B-Timothy Goebel, U.S.
Women's Singles—G-Sarah Hughes, U.S., S-Irina Slutskaya, Russia, B-Michelle Kwan, U.S.
Pairs*—G-(tie) Elena Berezhnaya & Anton Sikharulidze, Russia, Jamie Sale & David Pelletier, Canada, B-Shen Xue & Zhao Hongbo, China
Ice Dancing—G-Marina Anissina & Gwendal Peizerat, France, S-Irina Lobacheva & Ilia Averbukh, Russia, B-Barbara Fusar Poli & Maurizio Margaglio, Italy
*On Feb. 15, 2002, the International Skating Union discarded one judge's scores and awarded a second pair of gold medals to Sale and Pelletier, who had initially been awarded the silver.

FREESTYLE SKIING

Men's Moguls—G-Janne Lahtela, Finland, S-Travis Mayer, U.S., B-Richard Gay, France
Men's Aerials—G-Ales Valenta, Czech Republic, S-Joe Pack, U.S., B-Alexei Grichin, Belarus
Women's Moguls—G-Kari Traa, Norway, S-Shannon Bahrke, U.S., B-Tae Satoya, Japan
Women's Aerials—G-Alisa Camplin, Australia, S-Veronica Brenner, Canada, B-Deidra Dionne, Canada

ICE HOCKEY

Men's—G-Canada, S-U.S., B-Russia
Women's—G-Canada, S-U.S., B-Sweden

LUGE

Men's Singles—G-Armin Zoeggeler, Italy, S-Georg Hackl, Germany, B-Markus Prock, Austria
Men's Doubles—G-Patric-Fritz Leitner & Alexander Resch, Germany, S-Brian Martin & Mark Grimmette, U.S., B-Chris Thorpe & Clay Ives, U.S.
Women's Singles—G-Sylke Otto, Germany, S-Barbara Niedernhuber, Germany, B-Silke Kraushaar, Germany

NORDIC SKIING

Cross-Country Events

Men

1.5KM—G-Tor Arne Hetland, Norway, S-Peter Schlickenrieder, Germany, B-Christian Zovzi, Italy
10KM—G-Johann Muehlegg, Spain, S-Thomas Alsgaard, Norway, B-Frode Estil, Norway
15KM—G-Andrus Veerpalu, Estonia, S-Frode Estil, Norway, B-Jaak Mae, Estonia
30KM—G-Johann Muehlegg, Spain, S-Christian Hoffmann, Austria, B-Mikhail Botvinov, Austria
50KM—G-Mikhail Ivanov, Russia, S-Andrus Veerpalu, Estonia, B-Odd-Bjoern Hjelmeset, Norway
40KM Relay—G-Norway, S-Italy, B-Germany

Women

1.5KM—G-Juliya Tchepalova, Russia, S-Evi Sachenbacher, Germany, B-Anita Moen, Norway
5KM—G-Olga Danilova, Russia, S-Larissa Lazutina, Russia, B-Beckie Scott, Canada
10KM—G-Bente Skari, Norway, S-Olga Danilova, Russia, B-Juliya Tchepalova, Russia
15KM—G-Stefania Belmondo, Italy, S-Larissa Lazutina, Russia, B-Katerina Neumannova, Czech Republic
30KM—G-Gabriella Paruzzi, Italy, S-Stefania Belmondo, Italy, B-Bente Skari, Norway
20KM Relay—G-Germany, S-Norway, B-Switzerland

Combined Cross-Country & Jumping Events (Men)

Nordic Combined 7.5—G-Samppa Lajunen, Finland, S-Ronny Ackermann, Germany, B-Felix Gottwald, Austria
Nordic Combined 15—G-Samppa Lajunen, Finland, S-Jaakko Tallus, Finland, B-Felix Gottwald, Austria
Team Nordic Combined—G-Finland, S-Germany, B-Austria

Ski Jumping (Men)

90M (Normal hill)—G-Simon Ammann, Switzerland, S-Sven Hannawald, Germany, B-Adam Malysz, Poland
120M (Large hill)—G-Simon Ammann, Switzerland, S-Adam Malysz, Poland, B-Matti Hautamaeki, Finland
Team 120M—G-Germany, S-Finland, B-Slovenia

SKELETON

Men—G-Jim Shea, U.S., S-Marin Rettl, Austria, B-Gregor Staehli, Switzerland
Women—G-Tristan Gale, U.S., S-Lea Ann Parsley, U.S., B-Alex Coomber, Britain

SNOWBOARDING

Men's Giant Slalom—G-Philipp Schoch, Switzerland , S-Richard Richardsson, Sweden, B-Chris Klug, U.S.
Men's Halfpipe—G-Ross Powers, U.S., S-Danny Kass, U.S., B-Jarret (J.J.) Thomas, U.S.
Women's Giant Slalom—G-Isabelle Blanc, France S-Karine Ruby, France, B-Lidia Trettel, Italy
Women's Halfpipe—G-Kelly Clark, U.S., S-Doriane Vidal, France, B-Fabienne Reuteler, Switzerland

SPEED SKATING

Men

500M—G-Casey FitzRandolph, U.S., S-Hiroyasu Shimizu, Japan, B-Kip Carpenter, U.S.
1,000M—G-Gerard van Velde, Netherlands, S-Jan Bos, Netherlands, B-Joey Cheek, U.S.
1,500M—G-Derek Parra, U.S., S-Jochem Uytdehaage, Netherlands, B-Adne Sondral, Norway
5,000M—G-Jochem Uytdehaage, Netherlands, S. Derek Parra, U.S., B-Jens Boden, Germany
10,000M—G-Jochem Uytdehaage, Netherlands, S-Gianni Romme, Netherlands, B-Lasse Saetre, Norway

Women

500M—G-Catriona LeMay Doan, Canada, S-Monique Garbrecht-Enfeldt, Germany, B-Sabine Voelker, Germany
1,000M—G-Chris Witty, U.S., S-Sabine Voelker, Germany, B-Jennifer Rodriguez, U.S.
1,500M—G-Anni Friesinger, Germany, B-Sabine Voelker, Germany, S-Jennifer Rodriguez, U.S.
3,000M—G-Claudia Pechstein, Germany, S-Renate Groenewold, Netherlands, B-Cindy Klassen, Canada
5,000M—G-Claudia Pechstein, Germany, S-Gretha Smit, Netherlands, B-Clara Hughes, Canada

SHORT-TRACK SPEED SKATING

Men's 500M—G-Marc Gagnon, Canada, S-Jonathan Guilmette, Canada, B-Rusty Smith, U.S.
Men's 1,000M—G-Steven Bradbury, Australia, S-Apolo Anton Ohno, U.S., B-Mathieu Turcotte, Canada
Men's 1,500M—G-Apolo Anton Ohno, U.S., S-Li Jiajun, China, B-Marc Gagnon, Canada
Men's 5,000M Relay—G-Canada, S-Italy, B-China
Women's 500M—G-Yang Yang (A), China, S-Evgenia Radanova, Bulgaria, B-Wang Chunlu, China
Women's 1,000M—G-Yang Yang (A), China, S-Ko Gi-Hyun, South Korea, B-Yang Yang (S), China
Women's 1,500M—G-Ko Gi-Hyun, South Korea, B-Choi Eun-Kyung, South Korea, S-Evgenia Radanova, Bulgaria
Women's 3,000M Relay—G-South Korea, S-China, B-Canada

Winter Olympic Games Champions, 1924-2002

In 1992, the Unified Team represented the former Soviet republics of Russia, Ukraine, Belarus, Kazakhstan, and Uzbekistan.

ALPINE SKIING

	Men's Downhill	Time
1948	Henri Oreiller, France	2:55.0
1952	Zeno Colo, Italy	2:30.8
1956	Toni Sailer, Austria	2:52.2
1960	Jean Vuarnet, France	2:06.0
1964	Egon Zimmermann, Austria	2:18.16
1968	Jean-Claude Killy, France	1:59.85
1972	Bernhard Russi, Switzerland	1:51.43
1976	Franz Klammer, Austria	1:45.73
1980	Leonhard Stock, Austria	1:45.50
1984	Bill Johnson, U.S.	1:45.49
1988	Pirmin Zurbriggen, Switzerland	1:59.63
1992	Patrick Ortlieb, Austria	1:50.37
1994	Tommy Moe, U.S.	1:45.75
1998	Jean-Luc Cretier, France	1:50.11
2002	Fritz Strobl, Austria	1:39.13

	Men's Super Giant Slalom	Time
1988	Franck Piccard, France	1:39.66
1992	Kjetil-Andre Aamodt, Norway	1:13.04
1994	Markus Wasmeier, Germany	1:32.53
1998	Hermann Maier, Austria	1:34.82
2002	Kjetil Andre Aamodt, Norway	1:21.58

	Men's Giant Slalom	Time
1952	Stein Eriksen, Norway	2:25.0
1956	Toni Sailer, Austria	3:00.1
1960	Roger Staub, Switzerland	1:48.3
1964	Francois Bonlieu, France	1:46.71
1968	Jean-Claude Killy, France	3:29.28
1972	Gustavo Thoeni, Italy	3:09.62
1976	Heini Hemmi, Switzerland	3:26.97
1980	Ingemar Stenmark, Sweden	2:40.74
1984	Max Julen, Switzerland	2:41.18
1988	Alberto Tomba, Italy	2:06.37
1992	Alberto Tomba, Italy	2:06.98
1994	Markus Wasmeier, Germany	2:52.46
1998	Hermann Maier, Austria	2:38.51
2002	Stephan Eberharter, Austria	2:23.28

	Men's Slalom	Time
1948	Edi Reinalter, Switzerland	2:10.3
1952	Othmar Schneider, Austria	2:00.0
1956	Toni Sailer, Austria	3:14.7
1960	Ernst Hinterseer, Austria	2:08.9
1964	Josef Stiegler, Austria	2:11.13
1968	Jean-Claude Killy, France	1:39.73
1972	Francisco Fernandez-Ochoa, Spain	1:49.27
1976	Piero Gros, Italy	2:03.29
1980	Ingemar Stenmark, Sweden	1:44.26
1984	Phil Mahre, U.S.	1:39.41
1988	Alberto Tomba, Italy	1:39.47
1992	Finn Christian Jagge, Norway	1:44.39
1994	Thomas Stangassinger, Austria	2:02.02
1998	Hans-Petter Buraas, Norway	1:49.31
2002	Jean-Pierre Vidal, France	1:41.06

	Men's Combined	Time
1936	Franz-Pfnuer, Germany	99.25 (pts.)
1948	Henri Oreiller, France	3.27 (pts.)
1988	Hubert Strolz, Austria	36.55 (pts.)
1992	Josef Polig, Italy	14.58 (pts.)
1994	Lasse Kjus, Norway	3:17.53
1998	Mario Reiter, Austria	3:08.06
2002	Kjetil Andre Aamodt, Norway	3:17.56

	Women's Downhill	Time
1948	Hedi Schlunegger, Switzerland	2:28.3
1952	Trude Jochum-Beiser, Austria	1:47.1
1956	Madeleine Berthod, Switzerland	1:40.7
1960	Heidi Biebl, Germany	1:37.6
1964	Christl Haas, Austria	1:55.39
1968	Olga Pall, Austria	1:40.87
1972	Marie-Theres Nadig, Switzerland	1:36.68
1976	Rosi Mittermaier, W. Germany	1:46.16
1980	Annemarie Moser-Proell , Austria	1:37.52
1984	Michela Figini, Switzerland	1:13.36
1988	Marina Kiehl, W. Germany	1:25.86
1992	Kerrin Lee-Gartner, Canada	1:52.55
1994	Katja Seizinger, Germany	1:35.93
1998	Katja Seizinger, Germany	1:28.89
2002	Carole Montillet, France	1:39.56

	Women's Super Giant Slalom	Time
1988	Sigrid Wolf, Austria	1:19.03
1992	Deborah Compagnoni, Italy	1:21.22
1994	Diann Roffe (Steinrotter), U.S.	1:22.15
1998	Picabo Street, U.S.	1:18.02
2002	Daniela Ceccarelli, Italy	1:13.59

	Women's Giant Slalom	Time
1952	Andrea Mead Lawrence, U.S.	2:06.8
1956	Ossi Reichert, Germany	1:56.5
1960	Yvonne Ruegg, Switzerland	1:39.9
1964	Marielle Goitschel, France	1:52.24
1968	Nancy Greene, Canada	1:51.97
1972	Marie-Theres Nadig, Switzerland	1:29.90
1976	Kathy Kreiner, Canada	1:29.13
1980	Hanni Wenzel, Liechtenstein (2 runs)	2:41.66
1984	Debbie Armstrong, U.S.	2:20.98
1988	Vreni Schneider, Switzerland	2:06.49
1992	Pernilla Wiberg, Sweden	2:12.74
1994	Deborah Compagnoni, Italy	2:30.97
1998	Deborah Compagnoni, Italy	2:50.59
2002	Janica Kostelic, Croatia	2:30.01

	Women's Slalom	Time
1948	Gretchen Fraser, U.S.	1:57.2
1952	Andrea Mead Lawrence, U.S.	2:10.6
1956	Renee Colliard, Switzerland	1:52.3
1960	Anne Heggtveit, Canada	1:49.6
1964	Christine Goitschel, France	1:29.86
1968	Marielle Goitschel, France	1:25.86
1972	Barbara Ann Cochran, U.S.	1:31.24
1976	Rosi Mittermaier, W. Germany	1:30.54
1980	Hanni Wenzel, Liechtenstein	1:25.09
1984	Paoletta Magoni, Italy	1:36.47
1988	Vreni Schneider, Switzerland	1:36.69
1992	Petra Kronberger, Austria	1:32.68
1994	Vreni Schneider, Switzerland	1:56.01
1998	Hilde Gerg, Germany	1:32.40
2002	Janica Kostelic, Croatia	1:46.10

	Women's Combined	Time
1936	Christl Cranz, Germany	97.06 (pts.)
1948	Trude Beiser-Jochum, Austria	6.58 (pts.)
1988	Anita Wachter, Austria	29.25 (pts.)
1992	Petra Kronberger, Austria	2.55 (pts.)
1994	Pernilla Wiberg, Sweden	3:05.16
1998	Katja Seizinger, Germany	2:40.74
2002	Janica Kostelic, Croatia	2:43.28

BIATHLON

	Men's 10 Kilometers	Time
1980	Frank Ullrich, E. Germany	32:10.69
1984	Eirik Kvalfoss, Norway	30:53.80
1988	Frank-Peter Roetsch, E. Germany	25:08.10
1992	Mark Kirchner, Germany	26:02.30
1994	Serguei Tchepikov, Russia	28:07.00
1998	Ole Einar Bjoerndalen, Norway	27:16.20
2002	Ole Einar Bjoerndalen, Norway	24:51.3

	Men's 12.5 Kilometers	Time
2002	Ole Einar Bjoerndalen, Norway	32:34.6

	Men's 20 Kilometers	Time
1960	Klas Lestander, Sweden	1:33:21.6
1964	Vladimir Melanin, USSR	1:20:26.8
1968	Magnar Solberg, Norway	1:13:45.9
1972	Magnar Solberg, Norway	1:15:55.50
1976	Nikolai Kruglov, USSR	1:14:12.26
1980	Anatoly Aljabiev, USSR	1:08:16.31
1984	Peter Angerer, W. Germany	1:11:52.7
1988	Frank-Peter Roetsch, E. Germany	0:56:33.33
1992	Yevgeny Redkine, Unified Team	0:57:34.4
1994	Serguei Tarasov, Russia	0:57:25.3
1998	Halvard Hanevold, Norway	0:56:16.4
2002	Ole Einar Bjoerndalen, Norway	0:51:03.3

Men's 30-Kilometer Relay		Time
1968	USSR, Norway, Sweden (40 km)	2:13:02.4
1972	USSR, Finland, E. Germany (40 km)	1:51:44.92
1976	USSR, Finland, E. Germany (40 km)	1:57:55.64
1980	USSR, E. Germany, W. Germany	1:34:03.27
1984	USSR, Norway, W. Germany	1:38:51.70
1988	USSR, W. Germany, Italy	1:22:30.00
1992	Germany, Unified Team, Sweden	1:24:43.50
1994	Germany, Russia, France	1:30:22.1
1998	Germany, Norway, Russia	1:19:43.3
2002	Norway, Germany, France	1:23:42.3

Women's 7.5 Kilometers		Time
1992	Anfissa Restsova, Unified Team	24:29.20
1994	Myriam Bedard, Canada	26:08.8
1998	Galina Koukleva, Russia	23:08.0
2002	Kati Wilhelm, Germany	20:41.4

Women's 10 Kilometers		Time
2002	Olga Pyleva, Russia	31:07.7

Women's 15 Kilometers		Time
1992	Antje Misersky, Germany	51:47.2
1994	Myriam Bedard, Canada	52:06.6
1998	Ekaterina Dafovska, Bulgaria	54:52.0
2002	Andrea Henkel, Germany	47:29.1

Women's 22.5-Kilometer Relay		Time
1992	France, Germany, Unified Team	1:15:55.6

Women's 30-Kilometer Relay		Time
1994	Russia, Germany, France	1:47:19.5
1998	Germany, Russia, Norway	1:40:13.6
2002	Germany, Norway, Russia	1:27:55.0

BOBSLEDDING

(Driver in parentheses)

4-Man Bob		Time
1924	Switzerland (Eduard Scherrer)	5:45.54
1928	United States (William Fiske) (5-man)	3:20.50
1932	United States (William Fiske)	7:53.68
1936	Switzerland (Pierre Musy)	5:19.85
1948	United States (Francis Tyler)	5:20.10
1952	Germany (Andreas Ostler)	5:07.84
1956	Switzerland (Franz Kapus)	5:10.44
1964	Canada (Victor Emery)	4:14.46
1968	Italy (Eugenio Monti) (2 races)	2:17.39
1972	Switzerland (Jean Wicki)	4:43.07
1976	E. Germany (Meinhard Nehmer)	3:40.43
1980	E. Germany (Meinhard Nehmer)	3:59.92
1984	E. Germany (Wolfgang Hoppe)	3:20.22
1988	Switzerland (Ekkehard Fasser)	3:47.51
1992	Austria (Ingo Appelt)	3:53.90
1994	Germany (Wolfgang Hoppe)	3:27.28
1998	Germany II (Christoph Langen)	2:39.41
2002	Germany II (Andre Lange)	3:07.51

2-Man Bob		Time
1932	United States (Hubert Stevens)	8:14.74
1936	United States (Ivan Brown)	5:29.29
1948	Switzerland (F. Endrich)	5:29.20
1952	Germany (Andreas Ostler)	5:24.54
1956	Italy (Dalla Costa)	5:30.14
1964	Great Britain (Anthony Nash)	4:21.90
1968	Italy (Eugenio Monti)	4:41.54
1972	W. Germany (Wolfgang Zimmerer)	4:57.07
1976	E. Germany (Meinhard Nehmer)	3:44.42
1980	Switzerland (Erich Schaerer)	4:09.36
1984	E. Germany (Wolfgang Hoppe)	3:25.56
1988	USSR (Janis Kipours)	3:54.19
1992	Switzerland (Gustav Weber)	4:03.26
1994	Switzerland (Gustav Weber)	3:30.81
1998	Canada (Pierre Lueders), Italy (Guenther Huber) (tie)	3:37.24
2002	Germany II (Christoph Langen)	3:10.11

2-Woman Bob		
2002	United States II (Jill Bakken)	1:37.76

CURLING

MEN

1998	Switzerland, Canada, Norway
2002	Norway, Canada, Switzerland

WOMEN

1998	Canada, Denmark, Sweden
2002	Britain, Switzerland, Canada

FIGURE SKATING

Men's Singles

1908#	Ulrich Salchow, Sweden
1920#	Gillis Grafstrom, Sweden
1924	Gillis Grafstrom, Sweden
1928	Gillis Grafstrom, Sweden
1932	Karl Schaefer, Austria
1936	Karl Schaefer, Austria
1948	Richard Button, U.S.
1952	Richard Button, U.S.
1956	Hayes Alan Jenkins, U.S.
1960	David W. Jenkins, U.S.
1964	Manfred Schnelldorfer, Germany
1968	Wolfgang Schwartz, Austria
1972	Ondrej Nepela, Czechoslovakia
1976	John Curry, Great Britain
1980	Robin Cousins, Great Britain
1984	Scott Hamilton, U.S.
1988	Brian Boitano, U.S.
1992	Viktor Petrenko, Unified Team
1994	Aleksei Urmanov, Russia
1998	Ilya Kulik, Russia
2002	Alexei Yagudin, Russia

(#) Event was held at Summer Olympics.

Women's Singles

1908#	Madge Syers, Great Britain
1920#	Magda Julin-Mauroy, Sweden
1924	Herma von Szabo-Planck, Austria
1928	Sonja Henie, Norway
1932	Sonja Henie, Norway
1936	Sonja Henie, Norway
1948	Barbara Ann Scott, Canada
1952	Jeanette Altwegg, Great Britan
1956	Tenley Albright, U.S.
1960	Carol Heiss, U.S.
1964	Sjoukje Dijkstra, Netherlands
1968	Peggy Fleming, U.S.
1972	Beatrix Schuba, Austria
1976	Dorothy Hamill, U.S.
1980	Anett Poetzsch, E. Germany
1984	Katarina Witt, E. Germany
1988	Katarina Witt, E. Germany
1992	Kristi Yamaguchi, U.S.
1994	Oksana Baiul, Ukraine
1998	Tara Lipinski, U.S.
2002	Sarah Hughes, U.S.

(#) Event was held at Summer Olympics.

Pairs

1908#	Anna Hubler & Heinrich Burger, Germany
1920#	Ludovika & Walter Jakobsson, Finland
1924	Helene Engelman & Alfred Berger, Austria
1928	Andree Joly & Pierre Brunet, France
1932	Andree Joly & Pierre Brunet, France
1936	Maxi Herber & Ernst Baier, Germany
1948	Micheline Lannoy & Pierre Baugniet, Belgium
1952	Ria and Paul Falk, Germany
1956	Elisabeth Schwartz & Kurt Oppelt, Austria
1960	Barbara Wagner & Robert Paul, Canada
1964	Ludmila Beloussova & Oleg Protopopov, USSR
1968	Ludmila Beloussova & Oleg Protopopov, USSR
1972	Irina Rodnina & Alexei Ulanov, USSR
1976	Irina Rodnina & Aleksandr Zaitzev, USSR
1980	Irina Rodnina & Aleksandr Zaitzev, USSR
1984	Elena Valova & Oleg Vassiliev, USSR
1988	Ekaterina Gordeeva & Sergei Grinkov, USSR
1992	Natalia Mishkutienok & Artur Dimitriev, Unified Team
1994	Ekaterina Gordeeva & Sergei Grinkov, Russia
1998	Oksana Kazakova & Artur Dmitriev, Russia
2002	Elena Berezhnaya & Anton Sikharulidze, Russia; Jamie Sale & David Pelletier, Canada (tie)

(#) Event was held at Summer Olympics.

Ice Dancing

1976	Ludmila Pakhomova & Aleksandr Gorschkov, USSR
1980	Natalya Linichuk & Gennadi Karponosov, USSR
1984	Jayne Torvill & Christopher Dean, Great Britain
1988	Natalia Bestemianova & Andrei Bukin, USSR
1992	Marina Klimova & Sergei Ponomarenko, Unified Team
1994	Pasha Grishuk & Evgeny Platov, Russia
1998	Pasha Grishuk & Evgeny Platov, Russia
2002	Marina Anissina & Gwendal Peizerat, France

FREESTYLE SKIING

Men's Moguls		Points
1992	Edgar Grospiron, France	25.81
1994	Jean-Luc Brassard, Canada	27.24
1998	Jonny Moseley, U.S.	26.93
2002	Janne Lahtela, Finland	27.97

Men's Aerials		Points
1994	Andreas Schoenbaechler, Switzerland	234.67
1998	Eric Bergoust, U.S.	255.64
2002	Ales Valenta, Czech Republic	257.02

Women's Moguls		Points
1992	Donna Weinbrecht, U.S.	23.69
1994	Stine Lise Hattestad, Norway	25.97
1998	Tae Satoya, Japan	25.06
2002	Kari Traa, Norway	25.94

	Women's Aerials	Points
1994	Lina Tcherjazova, Uzbekistan	166.84
1998	Nikki Stone, U.S.	193.00
2002	Alisa Camplin, Australia	193.47

ICE HOCKEY

MEN

1920#	Canada, U.S., Czechoslovakia
1924	Canada, U.S., Great Britain
1928	Canada, Sweden, Switzerland
1932	Canada, U.S., Germany
1936	Great Britain, Canada, U.S.
1948	Canada, Czechoslovakia, Switzerland
1952	Canada, U.S., Sweden
1956	USSR, U.S., Canada
1960	U.S., Canada, USSR
1964	USSR, Sweden, Czechoslovakia
1968	USSR, Czechoslovakia, Canada
1972	USSR, U.S., Czechoslovakia
1976	USSR, Czechoslovakia, W. Germany
1980	U.S., USSR, Sweden
1984	USSR, Czechoslovakia, Sweden
1988	USSR, Finland, Sweden
1992	Unified Team, Canada, Czechoslovakia
1994	Sweden, Canada, Finland
1998	Czech Republic, Russia, Finland
2002	Canada, U.S., Russia

(#) Event was held at Summer Olympics.

WOMEN

1998	U.S., Canada, Finland
2002	Canada, U.S., Sweden

LUGE

	Men's Singles	Time
1964	Thomas Keohler, E. Germany	3:26.77
1968	Manfred Schmid, Austria	2:52.48
1972	Wolfgang Scheidel, E. Germany	3:27.58
1976	Detlef Guenther, E. Germany	3:27.688
1980	Bernhard Glass, E. Germany	2:54.796
1984	Paul Hildgartner, Italy	3:04.258
1988	Jens Mueller, E. Germany	3:05.548
1992	Georg Hackl, Germany	3:02.363
1994	Georg Hackl, Germany	3:21.571
1998	Georg Hackl, Germany	3:18.436
2002	Armin Zoeggeler, Italy	2:57.941

	Women's Singles	Time
1964	Ortun Enderlein, Germany	3:24.67
1968	Erica Lechner, Italy	2:28.66
1972	Anna M. Muller, E. Germany	2:59.18
1976	Margit Schumann, E. Germany	2:50.621
1980	Vera Zozulya, USSR	2:36.537
1984	Steffi Martin, E. Germany	2:46.570
1988	Steffi Walter, E. Germany	3:03.973
1992	Doris Neuner, Austria	3:06.696
1994	Gerda Weissensteiner, Italy	3:15.517
1998	Silke Kraushaar, Germany	3:23.779
2002	Sylke Otto, Germany	2:52.464

	Men's Doubles	Time
1964	Austria	1:41.62
1968	E. Germany	1:35.85
1972	Italy, E. Germany (tie)	1:28.35
1976	E. Germany	1:25.604
1980	E. Germany	1:19.331
1984	W. Germany	1:23.620
1988	E. Germany	1:31.940
1992	Germany	1:32.053
1994	Italy	1:36.720
1998	Germany	1:41.105
2002	Germany	1:26.082

SKELETON

	Men	Time
1928	Jennison Heaton, U.S.	3:01.8
1948	Nino Bibbia, Italy	5:23.2
2002	Jim Shea, U.S.	1:41.96

	Women	Time
2002	Tristan Gale, U.S.	1:45.11

NORDIC SKIING

Cross-Country Events

	Men's 1.5 Kilometers (0.93 miles)	Time
2002	Tor Arne Hetland, Norway	2:56.9

	Men's 10 Kilometers (6.2 miles)	Time
1992	Vegard Ulvang, Norway	27:36.0
1994	Bjoern Daehlie, Norway	24:20.1
1998	Bjoern Daehlie, Norway	27:24.5
2002	Johann Muehlegg, Spain	49:20.4

	Men's 15 Kilometers (9.3 miles)	Time
1924	Thorleif Haug, Norway	1:14:31
1928	Johan Grottumsbraaten, Norway	1:37:01
1932	Sven Utterstrom, Sweden	1:23:07
1936	Erik-August Larsson, Sweden	1:14:38
1948	Martin Lundstrom, Sweden	1:13:50
1952	Hallgeir Brenden, Norway	1:01:34
1956	Hallgeir Brenden, Norway	0:49:39.0
1960	Haakon Brusveen, Norway	0:51:55.5
1964	Eero Maentyranta, Finland	0:50:54.1
1968	Harald Groenningen, Norway	0:47:54.2
1972	Sven-Ake Lundback, Sweden	0:45:28.24
1976	Nikolai Balukov, USSR	0:43:58.47
1980	Thomas Wassberg, Sweden	0:41:57.63
1984	Gunde Svan, Sweden	0:41:25.6
1988	Mikhail Deviatiarov, USSR	0:41:18.9
1992	Bjoern Daehlie, Norway	0:38:01.9
1994	Bjoern Daehlie, Norway	0:35:48.8
1998	Thomas Alsgaard, Norway	1:07:01.7
2002	Andrus Veerpalu, Estonia	0:37:07.4

(Note: approx. 18-km course 1924-1952)

	Men's 30 Kilometers (18.6 miles)	Time
1956	Veikko Hakulinen, Finland	1:44:06.0
1956	Veikko Hakulinen, Finland	1:44:06.0
1960	Sixten Jernberg, Sweden	1:51:03.9
1964	Eero Maentyranta, Finland	1:30:50.7
1968	Franco Nones, Italy	1:35:39.2
1972	Vyacheslav Vedenine, USSR	1:36:31.15
1976	Sergei Saveliev, USSR	1:30:29.38
1980	Nikolai Zimyatov, USSR	1:27:02.80
1984	Nikolai Zimyatov, USSR	1:28:56.3
1988	Aleksei Prokourorov, USSR	1:24:26.3
1992	Vegard Ulvang, Norway	1:22:27.8
1994	Thomas Alsgaard, Norway	1:12:26.4
1998	Mika Myllylae, Finland	1:33:55.8
2002	Johann Muehlegg, Spain	1:09:28.9

	Men's 50 Kilometers (31.2 miles)	Time
1924	Thorleif Haug, Norway	3:44:32.0
1928	Per Erik Hedlund, Sweden	4:52:03.0
1932	Veli Saarinen, Finland	4:28:00.0
1936	Elis Wiklund, Sweden	3:30:11.0
1948	Nils Karlsson, Sweden	3:47:48.0
1952	Veikko Hakulinen, Finland	3:33:33.0
1956	Sixten Jernberg, Sweden	2:50:27.0
1960	Kalevi Hamalainen, Finland	2:59:06.3
1964	Sixten Jernberg, Sweden	2:43:52.6
1968	Ole Ellefsaeter, Norway	2:28:45.8
1972	Paal Tyldum, Norway	2:43:14.75
1976	Ivar Formo, Norway	2:37:30.05
1980	Nikolai Zimyatov, USSR	2:27:24.60
1984	Thomas Wassberg, Sweden	2:15:55.8
1988	Gunde Svan, Sweden	2:04:30.9
1992	Bjoern Daehlie, Norway	2:03:41.5
1994	Vladimir Smirnov, Kazakhstan	2:07:20.3
1998	Bjoern Daehlie, Norway	2:05:08.2
2002	Mikhail Ivanov, Russia	2:06:20.8

	Men's 40-Kilometer Relay	Time
1936	Finland, Norway, Sweden	2:41:33.0
1948	Sweden, Finland, Norway	2:32:08.0
1952	Finland, Norway, Sweden	2:20:16.0
1956	USSR, Finland, Sweden	2:15:30.0
1960	Finland, Norway, USSR	2:18:45.6
1964	Sweden, Finland, USSR	2:18:34.6
1968	Norway, Sweden, Finland	2:08:33.5
1972	USSR, Norway, Switzerland	2:04:47.94
1976	Finland, Norway, USSR	2:07:59.72
1980	USSR, Norway, Finland	1:57:03.46
1984	Sweden, USSR, Finland	1:55:06.30
1988	Sweden, USSR, Czechoslovakia	1:43:58.60
1992	Norway, Italy, Finland	1:39:26.00
1994	Italy, Norway, Finland	1:41:15.00
1998	Norway, Italy, Finland	1:40:55.70
2002	Norway, Italy, Germany	1:32:45.5

	Women's 1.5 Kilometers (0.93 miles)	Time
2002	Julia Tchepalova, Russia	3:10.6

	Women's 5 Kilometers (3.1 miles)	Time
1964	Claudia Boyarskikh, USSR	17:50.5
1968	Toini Gustafsson, Sweden	16:45.2
1972	Galina Koulacova, USSR	17:00.50
1976	Helena Takalo, Finland	15:48.69
1980	Raisa Smetanina, USSR	15:06.92
1984	Marja-Liisa Haemaelainen, Finland	17:04.0
1988	Marjo Matikainen, Finland	15:04.0
1992	Marjut Lukkarinen, Finland	14:13.8
1994	Ljubov Egorova, Russia	14:08.8
1998	Larissa Lazutina, Russia	17:37.9
2002	Olga Danilova, Russia	24:52.1

	Women's 10 Kilometers (6.2 miles)	Time
1952	Lydia Wideman, Finland	41:40.0
1956	Lyubov Kosyreva, USSR	38:11.0
1960	Maria Gusakova, USSR	39:46.6
1964	Claudia Boyarskikh, USSR	40:24.3
1968	Toini Gustafsson, Sweden	36:46.5
1972	Galina Koulacova, USSR	34:17.82
1976	Raisa Smetanina, USSR	30:13.41
1980	Barbara Petzold, E. Germany	30:31.54
1984	Marja-Liisa Haemaelainen, Finland	31:44.2
1988	Vida Ventsene, USSR	30:08.3
1992	Lyubov Egorova, Unified Team	25:53.7
1994	Lyubov Egorova, Russia	27:30.1
1998	Larissa Lazutina, Russia	46.06.9
2002	Bente Skari, Norway	28:05.6

	Women's 15 Kilometers (9.3 miles)	Time
1992	Lyubov Egorova, Unified Team	42:20.8
1994	Manuela Di Centa, Italy	39:44.5
1998	Olga Danilova, Russia	46:55.4
2002	Stefania Belmondo, Italy	39:54.4

	Women's 30 Kilometers (18.6 miles)	Time
1992	Stefania Belmondo, Italy	1:22:30.1
1994	Manuela Di Centa, Italy	1:25:41.6
1998	Julija Tchepalova, Russia	1:22:01.5
2002	Gabriella Paruzzi, Italy	1:30:57.1

	Women's 20-Kilometer Relay	Time
1956	Finland, USSR, Sweden (15 km)	1:09:01.0
1960	Sweden, USSR, Finland (15 km)	1:04:21.4
1964	USSR, Sweden, Finland (15 km)	0:59:20.2
1968	Norway, Sweden, USSR (15 km)	0:57:30.0
1972	USSR, Finland, Norway (15 km)	0:48:46.15
1976	USSR, Finland, E. Germany	1:07:49.75
1980	E. Germany, USSR, Norway	1:02:11.1
1984	Norway, Czechoslovakia, Finland	1:06:49.7
1988	USSR, Norway, Finland	0:59:51.1
1992	United Team, Norway, Italy	0:59:34.8
1994	Russia, Norway, Italy	0:57:12.5
1998	Russia, Norway, Italy	0:55:13.5
2002	Germany, Norway, Switzerland	0:49:30.6

Combined Cross-Country & Jumping (Men)

	7.5 Kilometer Nordic Combined*
2002	Samppa Lajunen, FInland

	15 Kilometer Nordic Combined*
1924	Thorleif Haug, Norway
1928	Johan Grottumsbraaten, Norway
1932	Johan Grottumsbraaten, Norway
1936	Oddbjorn Hagen, Norway
1948	Heikki Hasu, Finland
1952	Simon Slattvik, Norway
1956	Sverre Stenersen, Norway
1960	Georg Thoma, W. Germany
1964	Tormod Knutsen, Norway
1968	Franz Keller, W. Germany
1972	Ulrich Wehling, E. Germany
1976	Ulrich Wehling, E. Germany
1980	Ulrich Wehling, E. Germany
1984	Tom Sandberg, Norway
1988	Hippolyt Kempf, Switzerland
1992	Fabrice Guy, France
1994	Fred Barre Lundberg, Norway
1998	Bjarte Engen Vik, Norway
2002	Samppa Lajunen, Finland

	Team Nordic Combined*
1988	W. Germany, Switzerland, Austria
1992	Japan, Norway, Austria
1994	Japan, Norway, Switzerland
1998	Norway, Finland, France
2002	Finland, Germany, Austria

*Medals based on combination of points for jumping events and time for cross-country events.

Ski Jumping (Men)

	Normal Hill	Points
1964	Veikko Kankkonen, Finland	229.9
1968	Jiri Raska, Czechoslovakia	216.5
1972	Yukio Kasaya, Japan	244.2
1976	Hans-Georg Aschenbach, E. Germany	252.0
1980	Toni Innauer, Austria	266.3
1984	Jens Weissflog, E. Germany	215.2
1988	Matti Nykaenen, Finland	230.5
1992	Ernst Vettori, Austria	222.8
1994	Espen Bredesen, Norway	282.0
1998	Jani Soininen, Finland	234.5
2002	Simon Ammann, Switzerland	269.0

	Large Hill	Points
1924	Jacob Tullin Thams, Norway	18.960
1928	Alfred Andersen, Norway	19.208
1932	Birger Ruud, Norway	228.1
1936	Birger Ruud, Norway	232.0
1948	Petter Hugsted, Norway	228.1
1952	Arnfinn Bergmann, Norway	226.0
1956	Antti Hyvarinen, Finland	227.0
1960	Helmut Recknagel, E. Germany	227.2
1964	Toralf Engan, Norway	230.7
1968	Vladimir Beloussov, USSR	231.3
1972	Wojciech Fortuna, Poland	219.9
1976	Karl Schnabl, Austria	234.8
1980	Jouko Tormanen, Finland	271.0
1984	Matti Nykaenen, Finland	231.2
1988	Matti Nykaenen, Finland	224.0
1992	Toni Nieminen, Finland	239.5
1994	Jens Weissflog, Germany	274.5
1998	Kazuyoshi Funaki, Japan	272.3
2002	Simon Ammann, Switzerland	281.4

	Team Large Hill	Points
1988	Finland, Yugoslavia, Norway	634.4
1992	Finland, Austria, Czechoslovakia	644.4
1994	Germany, Japan, Austria	970.1
1998	Japan, Germany, Austria	933.0
2002	Germany, FInland, Slovenia	974.1

SNOWBOARDING

	Men's Giant Slalom	Time
1998	Ross Rebagliati, Canada	2:03.96
2002	Philipp Schoch, Switzerland	

	Men's Halfpipe	Points
1998	Gian Simmen, Switzerland	85.2
2002	Ross Powers	46.1

	Women's Giant Slalom	Time
1998	Karine Ruby, France	2:17.34
2002	Isabelle Blanc, France	

	Women's Halfpipe	Points
1998	Nicola Thost, Germany	74.6
2002	Kelly Clark, U.S.	47.9

SPEED SKATING

*indicates Olympic record

	Men's 500 Meters	Time[1]
1924	Charles Jewtraw, U.S.	0:44.0
1928	Thunberg, Finland & Evensen, Norway (tie)	0:43.4
1932	John A. Shea, U.S.	0:43.4
1936	Ivar Ballangrud, Norway	0:43.4
1948	Finn Helgesen, Norway	0:43.1
1952	Kenneth Henry, U.S.	0:43.2
1956	Evgeniy Grishin, USSR	0:40.2
1960	Evgeniy Grishin, USSR	0:40.2
1964	Terry McDermott, U.S.	0:40.1
1968	Erhard Keller, W. Germany	0:40.3
1972	Erhard Keller, W. Germany	0:39.44
1976	Evgeny Kulikov, USSR	0:39.17
1980	Eric Heiden, U.S.	0:38.03
1984	Sergei Fokichev, USSR	0:38.19
1988	Uwe-Jens Mey, E. Germany	0:36.45
1992	Uwe-Jens Mey, Germany	0:37.14
1994	Aleksandr Golubev, Russia	0:36.33
1998	Hiroyasu Shimizu, Japan	0:35.59
2002	Casey FitzRandolph, U.S.	0:34.42*

(1) Better time of two runs. Medals based on combined times.

	Men's 1,000 Meters	Time
1976	Peter Mueller, U.S	1:19.32
1980	Eric Heiden, U.S.	1:15.18
1984	Gaetan Boucher, Canada	1:15.80
1988	Nikolai Guiliaev, USSR	1:13.03
1992	Olaf Zinke, Germany	1:14.85
1994	Dan Jansen, U.S.	1:12.43
1998	Ids Postma, Netherlands	1:10.64
2002	Gerard van Velde, Netherlands	1:07.18*

	Men's 1,500 Meters	Time
1924	Clas Thunberg, Finland	2:20.8
1928	Clas Thunberg, Finland	2:21.1
1932	John A. Shea, U.S.	2:57.5
1936	Charles Mathiesen, Norway	2:19.2
1948	Sverre Farstad, Norway	2:17.6
1952	Hjalmar Andersen, Norway	2:20.4
1956	Grishin, & Mikhailov, both USSR (tie)	2:08.6
1960	Aas, Norway & Grishin, USSR (tie)	2:10.4
1964	Ants Anston, USSR	2:10.3
1968	Cornetis Verkerk, Netherlands	2:03.4
1972	Ard Schenk, Netherlands	2:02.96
1976	Jan Egil Storholt, Norway	1:59.38
1980	Eric Heiden, U.S.	1:55.44
1984	Gaetan Boucher, Canada	1:58.36

	Men's 1,500 Meters	Time
1988	Andre Hoffmann, E. Germany	1:52.06
1992	Johann Koss, Norway	1:54.81
1994	Johann Koss, Norway	1:51.29
1998	Aadne Sondral, Norway	1:47.87
2002	Derek Parra, U.S.	1:43.95*

	Men's 5,000 Meters	Time
1924	Clas Thunberg, Finland	8:39.0
1928	Ivar Ballangrud, Norway	8:50.5
1932	Irving Jaffee, U.S.	9:40.8
1936	Ivar Ballangrud, Norway	8:19.6
1948	Reidar Liaklev, Norway	8:29.4
1952	Hjalmar Andersen, Norway	8:10.6
1956	Boris Shilkov, USSR	7:48.7
1960	Viktor Kosichkin, USSR	7:51.3
1964	Knut Johannesen, Norway	7:38.4
1968	F. Anton Maier, Norway	7:22.4
1972	Ard Schenk, Netherlands	7:23.61
1976	Sten Stensen, Norway	7:24.48
1980	Eric Heiden, U.S.	7:02.29
1984	Sven Tomas Gustafson, Sweden	7:12.28
1988	Tomas Gustafson, Sweden	6:44.63
1992	Geir Karlstad, Norway	6:59.97
1994	Johann Koss, Norway	6:34.96
1998	Gianni Romme, Netherlands	6:22.20
2002	Jochem Uytdehaage, Netherlands	6:14.66*

	Men's 10,000 Meters	Time
1924	Julius Skutnabb, Finland	18:04.8
1928	Event not held because of thawing of ice	
1932	Irving Jaffee, U.S.	19:13.6
1936	Ivar Ballangrud, Norway	17:24.3
1948	Ake Seyffarth, Sweden	17:26.3
1952	Hjalmar Andersen, Norway	16:45.8
1956	Sigvard Ericsson, Sweden	16:35.9
1960	Knut Johannesen, Norway	15:46.6
1964	Jonny Nilsson, Sweden	15:50.1
1968	Jonny Hoeglin, Sweden	15:23.6
1972	Ard Schenk, Netherlands	15:01.35
1976	Piet Kleine, Netherlands	14:50.59
1980	Eric Heiden, U.S.	14:28.13
1984	Igor Malkov, USSR	14:39.90
1988	Tomas Gustafson, Sweden	13:40.20
1992	Bart Veldkamp, Netherlands	14:12.12
1994	Johann Koss, Norway	13:30.55
1998	Gianni Romme, Netherlands	13:15.33
2002	Jochem Uytdehaage, Netherlands	12:58.92*

	Women's 500 Meters	Time[1]
1960	Helga Haase, Germany	0:45.9
1964	Lydia Skoblikova, USSR	0:45.0
1968	Ludmila Titova, USSR	0:46.1
1972	Anne Henning, U.S.	0:43.33
1976	Sheila Young, U.S.	0:42.76
1980	Karin Enke, E. Germany	0:41.78
1984	Christa Rothenburger, E. Germany	0:41.02
1988	Bonnie Blair, U.S.	0:39.10
1992	Bonnie Blair, U.S.	0:40.33
1994	Bonnie Blair, U.S.	0:39.25
1998	Catriona Le May-Doan, Canada	0:38.21
2002	Catriona Le May Doan, Canada	0:37.30

(1) Better time of two runs. Medals based on combined times.

	Women's 1,000 Meters	Time
1960	Klara Guseva, USSR	1:34.1
1964	Lydia Skoblikova, USSR	1:33.2
1968	Carolina Geijssen, Netherlands	1:32.6
1972	Monika Pflug, W. Germany	1:31.40
1976	Tatiana Averina, USSR	1:28.43
1980	Natalya Petruseva, USSR	1:24.10
1984	Karin Enke, E. Germany	1:21.61
1988	Christa Rothenburger, E. Germany	1:17.65
1992	Bonnie Blair, U.S.	1:21.90
1994	Bonnie Blair, U.S.	1:18.74
1998	Marianne Timmer, Netherlands	1:16.51
2002	Chris Witty, U.S.	1:13.83*

	Women's 1,500 Meters	Time
1960	Lydia Skoblikova, USSR	2:52.2
1964	Lydia Skoblikova, USSR	2:22.6
1968	Kaija Mustonen, Finland	2:22.4
1972	Dianne Holum, U.S.	2:20.85
1976	Galina Stepanskaya, USSR	2:16.58
1980	Anne Borckink, Netherlands	2:10.95
1984	Karin Enke, E. Germany	2:03.42
1988	Yvonne van Gennip, Netherlands	2:00.68
1992	Jacqueline Boerner, Germany	2:05.87
1994	Emese Hunyady, Austria	2:02.19
1998	Marianne Timmer, Netherlands	1:57.58
2002	Anni Friesinger, Germany,	1:54.02*

	Women's 3,000 Meters	Time
1960	Lydia Skoblikova, USSR	5:14.3
1964	Lydia Skoblikova, USSR	5:14.9
1968	Johanna Schut, Netherlands	4:56.2
1972	Christina Baas-Kaiser, Netherlands	4:52.14
1976	Tatiana Averina, USSR	4:45.19
1980	Bjoerg Eva Jensen, Norway	4:32.13
1984	Andrea Schoene, E. Germany	4:24.79
1988	Yvonne van Gennip, Netherlands	4:11.94
1992	Gunda Niemann, Germany	4:19.90
1994	Svetlana Bazhanova, Russia	4:17.43
1998	Gunda Niemann-Stirnemann, Germany	4:07.29
2002	Claudia Pechstein, Germany,	3:57.70*

	Women's 5,000 Meters	Time
1988	Yvonne van Gennip, Netherlands	7:14.13
1992	Gunda Niemann, Germany	7:31.57
1994	Claudia Pechstein, Germany	7:14.37
1998	Claudia Pechstein, Germany	6:59.61
2002	Claudia Pechstein, Germany	6:46.91*

SHORT-TRACK SPEED SKATING

*indicates Olympic record

	Men's 500 Meters	Time
1998	Takafumi Nishitani, Japan	42.862
2002	Marc Gagnon, Canada	41.802*

	Men's 1,000 Meters	Time
1992	Kim Ki-Hoon, S. Korea	1:30.76
1994	Kim Ki-Hoon, S. Korea	1:34.57
1998	Dong-Sung Kim, S. Korea	1:32.375
2002	Steven Bradbury, Australia	1:29.109

	Men's 1,500 Meters	Time
2002	Apolo Anton Ohno, U.S.	2:18.541

	Men's 5,000-Meter Relay	Time
1992	S. Korea, Canada, Japan	7:14.02
1994	Italy, U.S., Australia	7:11.74
1998	Canada, S. Korea, China	7:06.075
2002	Canada, Italy, China	6:51.579

	Women's 500 Meters	Time
1992	Cathy Turner, U.S.	47.04
1994	Cathy Turner, U.S.	45.98
1998	Annie Perreault, Canada	46.568
2002	Yang Yang (A)	44.187

	Women's 1,000 Meters	Time
1998	Chun Lee-Kyung, S. Korea	1:42.776
2002	Yang Yang (A), China	1:36.391

	Women's 1,500 Meters	Time
2002	Gi-Hyun Ko, S. Korea	2:31.581

	Women's 3,000 Meter Relay	Time
1992	Canada, U.S., Unified Team	4:36.62
1994	S. Korea, Canada, U.S.	4:26.64
1998	S. Korea, China, Canada	4:16.26
2002	S. Korea, China, Canada	4:12.793*

Summer Olympic Games

Summer Olympic Games in 2000

Sydney, Australia, Sept. 15-Oct. 1, 2000

About 11,000 athletes from 199 countries competed in 300 events in 28 sports at the 2000 Summer Games. New sports introduced in Sydney included synchronized diving, trampoline, taekwondo, and triathlon. For the 1st time, women also competed in water polo, weight lifting, the pole vault, the hammer throw, and the modern pentathlon.

Australia's Cathy Freeman won the women's 400m dash, becoming the 1st Aborigine to earn an individual gold medal. U.S. sprinter Marion Jones won 3 golds and 2 bronze medals, the most ever in track and field by a woman at a single Olympics. American wrestler Rulon Gardner provided the biggest upset of the Games when he defeated 3-time Olympic champion Aleksandr Karelin of Russia in the Greco-Roman super heavyweight final. The U.S. baseball team won its 1st-ever gold medal. In swimming, Sydney hometown favorite Ian Thorpe helped set 3 relay world records and improved his own record in the 400m freestyle.

Summer Olympic Games Champions, 1896-2000

(*indicates Olympic record; w indicates wind-aided)

The 1980 games were boycotted by 62 nations, including the U.S. The 1984 games were boycotted by the USSR and by most Eastern bloc nations. E and W Germany competed separately, 1968-88. The 1992 Unified Team consisted of 12 former Soviet republics. The 1992 Independent Olympic Participants (I.O.P.) were from Serbia, Montenegro, and Macedonia.

TRACK AND FIELD—Men

100-Meter Run

1896	Thomas Burke, United States	12.0s
1900	Francis W. Jarvis, United States	11.0s
1904	Archie Hahn, United States	11.0s
1908	Reginald Walker, South Africa	10.8s
1912	Ralph Craig, United States	10.8s
1920	Charles Paddock, United States	10.8s
1924	Harold Abrahams, Great Britain	10.6s
1928	Percy Williams, Canada	10.8s
1932	Eddie Tolan, United States	10.3s
1936	Jesse Owens, United States	10.3s
1948	Harrison Dillard, United States	10.3s
1952	Lindy Remigino, United States	10.4s
1956	Bobby Morrow, United States	10.5s
1960	Armin Hary, Germany	10.2s
1964	Bob Hayes, United States	10.0s
1968	Jim Hines, United States	9.95s
1972	Valery Borzov, USSR	10.14s
1976	Hasely Crawford, Trinidad	10.06s
1980	Allan Wells, Great Britain	10.25s
1984	Carl Lewis, United States	9.99s
1988	Carl Lewis, United States	9.92s
1992	Linford Christie, Great Britain	9.96s
1996	Donovan Bailey, Canada	9.84s*
2000	Maurice Greene, United States	9.87s

200-Meter Run

1900	Walter Tewksbury, United States	22.2s
1904	Archie Hahn, United States	21.6s
1908	Robert Kerr, Canada	22.6s
1912	Ralph Craig, United States	21.7s
1920	Allan Woodring, United States	22.0s
1924	Jackson Scholz, United States	21.6s
1928	Percy Williams, Canada	21.8s
1932	Eddie Tolan, United States	21.2s
1936	Jesse Owens, United States	20.7s
1948	Mel Patton, United States	21.1s
1952	Andrew Stanfield, United States	20.7s
1956	Bobby Morrow, United States	20.6s
1960	Livio Berruti, Italy	20.5s
1964	Henry Carr, United States	20.3s
1968	Tommie Smith, United States	19.83s
1972	Valeri Borzov, USSR	20.00s
1976	Donald Quarrie, Jamaica	20.23s
1980	Pietro Mennea, Italy	20.19s
1984	Carl Lewis, United States	19.80s
1988	Joe DeLoach, United States	19.75s
1992	Mike Marsh, United States	20.01s
1996	Michael Johnson, United States	19.32s*
2000	Konstantinos Kenteris, Greece	20.09s

400-Meter Run

1896	Thomas Burke, United States	54.2s
1900	Maxey Long, United States	49.4s
1904	Harry Hillman, United States	49.2s
1908	Wyndham Halswelle, Great Brit., walkover	50.0s
1912	Charles Reidpath, United States	48.2s
1920	Bevil Rudd, South Africa	49.6s
1924	Eric Liddell, Great Britain	47.6s
1928	Ray Barbuti, United States	47.8s
1932	William Carr, United States	46.2s
1936	Archie Williams, United States	46.5s
1948	Arthur Wint, Jamaica	46.2s
1952	George Rhoden, Jamaica	45.9s
1956	Charles Jenkins, United States	46.7s
1960	Otis Davis, United States	44.9s
1964	Michael Larrabee, United States	45.1s
1968	Lee Evans, United States	43.86s
1972	Vincent Matthews, United States	44.66s
1976	Alberto Juantorena, Cuba	44.26s
1980	Viktor Markin, USSR	44.60s
1984	Alonzo Babers, United States	44.27s
1988	Steven Lewis, United States	43.87s
1992	Quincy Watts, United States	43.50s
1996	Michael Johnson, United States	43.49s*
2000	Michael Johnson, United States	43.84s

800-Meter Run

1896	Edwin Flack, Australia	2m. 11s
1900	Alfred Tysoe, Great Britain	2m. 1.2s
1904	James Lightbody, United States	1m. 56s
1908	Mel Sheppard, United States	1m. 52.8s
1912	James Meredith, United States	1m. 51.9s
1920	Albert Hill, Great Britain	1m. 53.4s
1924	Douglas Lowe, Great Britain	1m. 52.4s
1928	Douglas Lowe, Great Britain	1m. 51.8s
1932	Thomas Hampson, Great Britain	1m. 49.8s
1936	John Woodruff, United States	1m. 52.9s
1948	Mal Whitfield, United States	1m. 49.2s
1952	Mal Whitfield, United States	1m. 49.2s
1956	Thomas Courtney, United States	1m. 47.7s
1960	Peter Snell, New Zealand	1m. 46.3s
1964	Peter Snell, New Zealand	1m. 45.1s
1968	Ralph Doubell, Australia	1m. 44.3s
1972	Dave Wottle, United States	1m. 45.9s
1976	Alberto Juantorena, Cuba	1m. 43.50s
1980	Steve Ovett, Great Britain	1m. 45.40s
1984	Joaquim Cruz, Brazil	1m. 43.00s
1988	Paul Ereng, Kenya	1m. 43.45s
1992	William Tanui, Kenya	1m. 43.66s
1996	Vebjoern Rodal, Norway	1m. 42.58s*
2000	Nils Schumann, Germany	1m. 45.08

1,500-Meter Run

1896	Edwin Flack, Australia	4m. 33.2s
1900	Charles Bennett, Great Britain	4m. 6.2s
1904	James Lightbody, United States	4m. 5.4s
1908	Mel Sheppard, United States	4m. 3.4s
1912	Arnold Jackson, Great Britain	3m. 56.8s
1920	Albert Hill, Great Britain	4m. 1.8s
1924	Paavo Nurmi, Finland	3m. 53.6s
1928	Harry Larva, Finland	3m. 53.2s
1932	Luigi Beccali, Italy	3m. 51.2s
1936	Jack Lovelock, New Zealand	3m. 47.8s
1948	Henri Eriksson, Sweden	3m. 49.8s
1952	Joseph Barthel, Luxembourg	3m. 45.2s
1956	Ron Delany, Ireland	3m. 41.2s
1960	Herb Elliott, Australia	3m. 35.6s
1964	Peter Snell, New Zealand	3m. 38.1s
1968	Kipchoge Keino, Kenya	3m. 34.9s
1972	Pekka Vasala, Finland	3m. 36.3s
1976	John Walker, New Zealand	3m. 39.17s
1980	Sebastian Coe, Great Britain	3m. 38.4s
1984	Sebastian Coe, Great Britain	3m. 32.53s
1988	Peter Rono, Kenya	3m. 35.96s
1992	Fermin Cacho Ruiz, Spain	3m. 40.12s
1996	Noureddine Morceli, Algeria	3m. 35.78s
2000	Noah Kiprono Ngenyi, Kenya	3m. 32.07s*

5,000-Meter Run

1912	Hannes Kolehmainen, Finland	14m. 36.6s
1920	Joseph Guillemot, France	14m. 55.6s
1924	Paavo Nurmi, Finlands	14m. 31.2
1928	Willie Ritola, Finland	14m. 38s
1932	Lauri Lehtinen, Finland	14m. 30s
1936	Gunnar Hockert, Finland	14m. 22.2s
1948	Gaston Reiff, Belgium	14m. 17.6s
1952	Emil Zatopek, Czechoslovakia	14m. 6.6s
1956	Vladimir Kuts, USSR	13m. 39.6s
1960	Murray Halberg, New Zealand	13m. 43.4s
1964	Bob Schul, United States	13m. 48.8s
1968	Mohamed Gammoudi, Tunisia	14m. 05.0s
1972	Lasse Viren, Finland	13m. 26.4s
1976	Lasse Viren, Finland	13m. 24.76s
1980	Miruts Yifter, Ethiopia	13m. 21.0s
1984	Said Aouita, Morocco	13m. 05.59s*
1988	John Ngugi, Kenya	13m. 11.70s
1992	Dieter Baumann, Germany	13m. 12.52s
1996	Venuste Niyongabo, Burundi	13m. 07.96s
2000	Millon Wolde, Ethiopia	13m. 35.49s

10,000-Meter Run

1912	Hannes Kolehmainen, Finland	31m. 20.8s
1920	Paavo Nurmi, Finland	31m. 45.8s
1924	Willie Ritola, Finland	30m. 23.2s
1928	Paavo Nurmi, Finland	30m. 18.8s
1932	Janusz Kusocinski, Poland	30m. 11.4s
1936	Ilmari Salminen, Finland	30m. 15.4s
1948	Emil Zatopek, Czechoslovakia	29m. 59.6s
1952	Emil Zatopek, Czechoslovakia	29m. 17.0s
1956	Vladimir Kuts, USSR	28m. 45.6s
1960	Pyotr Bolotnikov, USSR	28m. 32.2s
1964	Billy Mills, United States	28m. 24.4s
1968	Naftali Temu, Kenya	29m. 27.4s
1972	Lasse Viren, Finland	27m. 38.4s
1976	Lasse Viren, Finland	27m. 40.4s
1980	Miruts Yifter, Ethiopia	27m. 42.7s
1984	Alberto Cova, Italy	27m. 47.54s

10,000-Meter Run

1988	Brahim Boutaib, Morocco	27m. 21.46s
1992	Khalid Skah, Morocco	27m. 46.70s
1996	Haile Gebrselassie, Ethiopia	27m. 07.34s*
2000	Haile Gebrselassie, Ethiopia	27m. 18.20s

110-Meter Hurdles

1896	Thomas Curtis, United States	17.6s
1900	Alvin Kraenzlein, United States	15.4s
1904	Frederick Schule, United States	16.0s
1908	Forrest Smithson, United States	15.0s
1912	Frederick Kelly, United States	15.1s
1920	Earl Thomson, Canada	14.8s
1924	Daniel Kinsey, United States	15.0s
1928	Sydney Atkinson, South Africa	14.8s
1932	George Saling, United States	14.6s
1936	Forrest Towns, United States	14.2s
1948	William Porter, United States	13.9s
1952	Harrison Dillard, United States	13.7s
1956	Lee Calhoun, United States	13.5s
1960	Lee Calhoun, United States	13.8s
1964	Hayes Jones, United States	13.6s
1968	Willie Davenport, United States	13.3s
1972	Rod Milburn, United States	13.24s
1976	Guy Drut, France	13.30s
1980	Thomas Munkelt, E. Germany	13.39s
1984	Roger Kingdom, United States	13.20s
1988	Roger Kingdom, United States	12.98s
1992	Mark McCoy, Canada	13.12s
1996	Allen Johnson, United States	12.95s*
2000	Anier Garcia, Cuba	13.00s

400-Meter Hurdles

1900	J.W.B. Tewksbury, United States	57.6s
1904	Harry Hillman, United States	53.0s
1908	Charles Bacon, United States	55.0s
1920	Frank Loomis, United States	54.0s
1924	F. Morgan Taylor, United States	52.6s
1928	Lord Burghley, Great Britain	53.4s
1932	Robert Tisdall, Ireland	51.7s
1936	Glenn Hardin, United States	52.4s
1948	Roy Cochran, United States	51.1s
1952	Charles Moore, United States	50.8s
1956	Glenn Davis, United States	50.1s
1960	Glenn Davis, United States	49.3s
1964	Rex Cawley, United States	49.6s
1968	Dave Hemery, Great Britain	48.12s
1972	John Akii-Bua, Uganda	47.82s
1976	Edwin Moses, United States	47.64s
1980	Volker Beck, E. Germany	48.70s
1984	Edwin Moses, United States	47.75s
1988	Andre Phillips, United States	47.19s
1992	Kevin Young, United States	46.78s*
1996	Derrick Adkins, United States	47.54s
2000	Angelo Taylor, Atlanta	47.50s

400-Meter Relay

1912	Great Britain	42.4s
1920	United States	42.2s
1924	United States	41.0s
1928	United States	41.0s
1932	United States	40.0s
1936	United States	39.8s
1948	United States	40.6s
1952	United States	40.1s
1956	United States	39.5s
1960	Germany (U.S. disqualified)	39.5s
1964	United States	39.0s
1968	United States	38.2s
1972	United States	38.19s
1976	United States	38.33s
1980	USSR	38.26s
1984	United States	37.83s
1988	USSR (U.S. disqualified)	38.19s
1992	United States	37.40s*
1996	Canada	37.69s
2000	United States	37.61s

1,600-Meter Relay

1908	United States	3m. 29.4s
1912	United States	3m. 16.6s
1920	Great Britain	3m. 22.2s
1924	United States	3m. 16s
1928	United States	3m. 14.2s
1932	United States	3m. 8.2s
1936	Great Britain	3m. 9s
1948	United States	3m. 10.4s
1952	Jamaica	3m. 03.9s
1956	United States	3m. 04.8s
1960	United States	3m. 02.2s
1964	United States	3m. 00.7s
1968	United States	2m. 56.16s
1972	Kenya	2m. 59.8s
1976	United States	2m. 58.65s
1980	USSR	3m. 01.1s
1984	United States	2m. 57.91s
1988	United States	2m. 56.16s
1992	United States	2m. 55.74s*
1996	United States	2m. 55.99s
2000	United States	2m. 56.35s

3,000-Meter Steeplechase

1920	Percy Hodge, Great Britain	10m. 0.4s
1924	Willie Ritola, Finland	9m. 33.6s
1928	Toivo Loukola, Finland	9m. 21.8s
1932	Volmari Iso-Hollo, Finland (About 3,450 m; extra lap by error.)	10m. 33.4s
1936	Volmari Iso-Hollo, Finland	9m. 3.8s
1948	Thore Sjoestrand, Sweden	9m. 4.6s
1952	Horace Ashenfelter, United States	8m. 45.4s
1956	Chris Brasher, Great Britain	8m. 41.2s
1960	Zdzislaw Krzyszkowiak, Poland	8m. 34.2s
1964	Gaston Roelants, Belgium	8m. 30.8s
1968	Amos Biwott, Kenya	8m. 51s
1972	Kipchoge Keino, Kenya	8m. 23.6s
1976	Anders Garderud, Sweden	8m. 08.2s
1980	Bronislaw Malinowski, Poland	8m. 09.7s
1984	Julius Korir, Kenya	8m. 11.8s
1988	Julius Kariuki, Kenya	8m. 05.51s*
1992	Matthew Birir, Kenya	8m. 08.84s
1996	Joseph Keter, Kenya	8m. 07.12s
2000	Reuben Kosgei, Kenya	8m. 21.43s

20-Kilometer Walk

1956	Leonid Spirin, USSR	1h. 31m. 27.4s
1960	Vladimir Golubnichy, USSR	1h. 33m. 7.2s
1964	Kenneth Mathews, Great Britain	1h. 29m. 34.0s
1968	Vladimir Golubnichy, USSR	1h. 33m. 58.4s
1972	Peter Frenkel, E. Germany	1h. 26m. 42.4s
1976	Daniel Bautista, Mexico	1h. 24m. 40.6s
1980	Maurizio Damilano, Italy	1h. 23m. 35.5s
1984	Ernesto Canto, Mexico	1h. 23m. 13.0s
1988	Josef Pribilinec, Czechoslovakia	1h. 19m. 57.0s
1992	Daniel Plaza Montero, Spain	1h. 21m. 45.0s
1996	Jefferson Perez, Ecuador	1h. 20m.7s
2000	Robert Korzeniowski, Poland	1h. 18m. 59.0s*

50-Kilometer Walk

1932	Thomas W. Green, Great Britain	4h. 50m. 10s
1936	Harold Whitlock, Great Britain	4h. 30m. 41.4s
1948	John Ljunggren, Sweden	4h. 41m. 52s
1952	Giuseppe Dordoni, Italy	4h. 28m. 07.8s
1956	Norman Read, New Zealand	4h. 30m. 42.8s
1960	Donald Thompson, Great Britain	4h. 25m. 30s
1964	Abdon Pamich, Italy	4h. 11m. 12.4s
1968	Christoph Hohne, E. Germany	4h. 20m. 13.6s
1972	Bern Kannenberg, W. Germany	3h. 56m. 11.6s
1980	Hartwig Gauter, E. Germany	3h. 49m. 24.0s
1984	Raul Gonzalez, Mexico	3h. 47m. 26.0s
1988	Vayachselav Ivanenko, USSR	3h. 38m. 29.0s*
1992	Andrei Perlov, Unified Team	3h. 50m. 13.0s
1996	Robert Korzeniowski, Poland	3h. 43m. 30s
2000	Robert Korzeniowski, Poland	3h. 42m. 22s

Marathon

1896	Spiridon Loues, Greece	2h. 58m. 50s
1900	Michel Theato, France	2h. 59m. 45s
1904	Thomas Hicks, United States	3h. 28m. 63s
1908	John J. Hayes, United States	2h. 55m. 18.4s
1912	Kenneth McArthur, South Africa	2h. 36m. 54.8s
1920	Hannes Kolehmainen, Finland	2h. 32m. 35.8s
1924	Albin Stenroos, Finland	2h. 41m. 22.6s
1928	A.B. El Ouafi, France	2h. 32m. 57s
1932	Juan Zabala, Argentina	2h. 31m. 36s
1936	Kijung Son, Japan (Korean)	2h. 29m. 19.2s
1948	Delfo Cabrera, Argentina	2h. 34m. 51.6s
1952	Emil Zatopek, Czechoslovakia	2h. 23m. 03.2s
1956	Alain Mimoun, France	2h. 25m.
1960	Abebe Bikila, Ethiopia	2h. 15m. 16.2s
1964	Abebe Bikila, Ethiopia	2h. 12m. 11.2s
1968	Mamo Wolde, Ethiopia	2h. 20m. 26.4s
1972	Frank Shorter, United States	2h. 12m. 19.8s
1976	Waldemar Cierpinski, E. Germany	2h. 09m. 55s
1980	Waldemar Cierpinski, E. Germany	2h. 11m. 03s
1984	Carlos Lopes, Portugal	2h. 09m. 21s*
1988	Gelindo Bordin, Italy	2h. 10m. 32s
1992	Hwang Young-Cho, S. Korea	2h. 13m. 23s
1996	Josia Thugwane, South Africa	2h. 12m. 36s
2000	Gezahgne Abera, Ethiopia	2h. 10m. 11s

High Jump

1896	Ellery Clark, United States	1.81m. (5'11¼ ")
1900	Irving Baxter, United States	1.90m. (6' 2¾")
1904	Samuel Jones, United States	1.80m. (5' 11")

High Jump

1908	Harry Porter, United States	1.90m. (6' 2¾ ")
1912	Alma Richards, United States	1.93m. (6' 4")
1920	Richmond Landon, United States	1.93m. (6' 4")
1924	Harold Osborn, United States	1.98m. (6' 6")
1928	Robert W. King, United States	1.94m. (6' 4¼ ")
1932	Duncan McNaughton, Canada	1.97m. (6' 5½")
1936	Cornelius Johnson, United States	2.03m. (6' 8")
1948	John L. Winter, Australia	1.98m. (6' 6")
1952	Walter Davis, United States	2.04m. (6' 8¼")
1956	Charles Dumas, United States	2.12m. (6' 11½")
1960	Robert Shavlakadze, USSR	2.16m. (7' 1")
1964	Valery Brumel, USSR	2.18m. (7' 1¾)
1968	Dick Fosbury, United States	2.24m. (7' 4¼")
1972	Jüri Tarmak, USSR	2.23m. (7' 3¾")
1976	Jacek Wszola, Poland	2.25m. (7' 4½")
1980	Gerd Wessig, E. Germany	2.36m. (7' 8¾")
1984	Dietmar Mögenburg, W. Germany	2.35m. (7' 8½")
1988	Hennady Avdeyenko, USSR	2.38m. (7' 9¾")
1992	Javier Sotomayor Sanabria, Cuba	2.34m. (7' 8")
1996	Charles Austin, United States	2.39m. (7' 10")*
2000	Sergey Kliugin, Russia	2.35m. (7' 8½")

Long Jump

1896	Ellery Clark, United States	6.35m. (20' 10")
1900	Alvin Kraenzlein, United States	7.18m. (23' 6¾")
1904	Meyer Prinstein, United States	7.34m. (24' 1")
1908	Frank Irons, United States	7.48m. (24' 6½")
1912	Albert Gutterson, United States	7.60m. (24' 11¼")
1920	William Petterssen, Sweden	7.15m. (23' 5½")
1924	William DeHart Hubbard, U.S.	7.44m. (24' 5")
1928	Edward B. Hamm, United States	7.73m. (25' 4½")
1932	Edward Gordon, United States	7.64m. (25' ¾")
1936	Jesse Owens, United States	8.06m. (26' 5½")
1948	Willie Steele, United States	7.82m. (25' 8")
1952	Jerome Biffle, United States	7.57m. (24' 10")
1956	Gregory Bell, United States	7.83m. (25' 8¼")
1960	Ralph Boston, United States	8.12m. (26' 7¾")
1964	Lynn Davies, Great Britain	8.07m. (26' 5¾")
1968	Bob Beamon, United States	8.90m. (29' 2½")*
1972	Randy Williams, United States	8.24m. (27' ½")
1976	Arnie Robinson, United States	8.35m. (27' 4¾")
1980	Lutz Dombrowski, E. Germany	8.54m. (28' ¼")
1984	Carl Lewis, United States	8.54m. (28' ¼")
1988	Carl Lewis, United States	8.72m. (28' 7½")
1992	Carl Lewis, United States	8.67m. (28' 5½")
1996	Carl Lewis, United States	8.50m. (27' 10¾")
2000	Ivan Pedroso, Cuba	8.55m. (28' ¾")

Triple Jump

1896	James Connolly, United States	13.71m.(44' 11¾")
1900	Meyer Prinstein, United States	14.47m.(47' 5¾")
1904	Meyer Prinstein, United States	14.35m.(47' 1")
1908	Timothy Ahearne, G.B.-Ireland	14.92m.(48' 11½")
1912	Gustaf Lindblom, Sweden	14.76m.(48' 5")
1920	Vilho Tuulos, Finland	14.50m.(47' 7")
1924	Anthony Winter, Australia	15.52m.(50' 11")
1928	Mikio Oda, Japan	15.21m.(49' 11")
1932	Chuhei Nambu, Japan	15.72m.(51' 7")
1936	Naoto Tajima, Japan	16.00m.(52' 6")
1948	Arne Ahman, Sweden	15.40m.(50' 6¼")
1952	Adhemar Ferreira da Silva, Brazil	16.22m.(53' 2¾")
1956	Adhemar Ferreira da Silva, Brazil	16.35m.(53' 7¾")
1960	Jozef Schmidt, Poland	16.81m.(55' 1½")
1964	Jozef Schmidt, Poland	16.85m.(55' 3½")
1968	Viktor Saneyev, USSR	17.39m.(57' ¾")
1972	Viktor Saneyev, USSR	17.35m.(56' 11¼")
1976	Viktor Saneyev, USSR	17.29m.(56' 8¾")
1980	Jaak Uudmae, USSR	17.35m.(56' 11")
1984	Al Joyner, United States	17.26m.(56' 7½")
1988	Khristo Markov, Bulgaria	17.61m.(57' 9½")
1992	Mike Conley, United States	18.17m.(59' 7½")w
1996	Kenny Harrison, United States	18.09m.(59' 4¼")*
2000	Jonathan Edwards, Britain	17.71m.(58' 1¼")

Discus Throw

1896	Robert Garrett, United States	29.15m.(95' 7")
1900	Rudolf Bauer, Hungary	36.04m.(118' 3")
1904	Martin Sheridan, United States	39.28m.(128' 10")
1908	Martin Sheridan, United States	40.89m.(134' 1")
1912	Armas Taipale, Finland	45.21m.(148' 3")
1920	Elmer Niklander, Finland	44.68m.(146' 7")
1924	Clarence Houser, United States	46.15m.(151' 4")
1928	Clarence Houser, United States	47.32m.(155' 3")
1932	John Anderson, United States	49.49m.(162' 4")
1936	Ken Carpenter, United States	50.48m.(165' 7")
1948	Adolfo Consolini, Italy	52.78m.(173' 2")
1952	Sim Iness, United States	55.03m.(180' 6")
1956	Al Oerter, United States	56.36m.(184' 11")
1960	Al Oerter, United States	59.18m.(194' 2")
1964	Al Oerter, United States	61.00m.(200' 1")
1968	Al Oerter, United States	64.78m.(212' 6")

Discus Throw

1972	Ludvik Danek, Czechoslovakia	64.40m.(211' 3")
1976	Mac Wilkins, United States	67.50m.(221' 5")
1980	Viktor Rashchupkin, USSR	66.64m.(218' 8")
1984	Rolf Dannenberg, W. Germany	66.60m.(218' 6")
1988	Jurgen Schult, E. Germany	68.82m.(225' 9")
1992	Romas Ubartas, Lithuania	65.12m.(213' 8")
1996	Lars Riedel, Germany	69.40m.(227' 8")*
2000	Virgilijus Alekna, Lithuania	69.30m.(227' 4")

Hammer Throw

1900	John Flanagan, United States	49.73m.(163' 1")
1904	John Flanagan, United States	51.22m.(168' 0")
1908	John Flanagan, United States	51.92m.(170' 4")
1912	Matt McGrath, United States	54.74m.(179' 7")
1920	Pat Ryan, United States	52.86m.(173' 5")
1924	Fred Tootell, United States	53.28m.(174' 10")
1928	Patrick O'Callaghan, Ireland	51.38m.(168' 7")
1932	Patrick O'Callaghan, Ireland	53.92m.(176' 11")
1936	Karl Hein, Germany	56.48m.(185' 4")
1948	Imre Németh, Hungary	56.06m.(183' 11")
1952	József Csérmák, Hungary	60.34m.(197' 11")
1956	Harold Connolly, United States	63.18m.(207' 3")
1960	Vasily Rudenkov, USSR	67.10m.(202' 0")
1964	Romuald Klim, USSR	69.74m.(228' 10")
1968	Gyula Zsivótsky, Hungary	73.36m.(240' 8")
1972	Anatoly Bondarchuk, USSR	75.50m.(247' 8")
1976	Yuri Syedykh, USSR	77.52m.(254' 4")
1980	Yuri Syedykh, USSR	81.80m.(268' 4")
1984	Juha Tiainen, Finland	78.08m.(256' 2")
1988	Sergei Litvinov, USSR	84.80m.(278' 2")*
1992	Andrey Abduvaliyev, Unified Team	82.54m.(270' 9")
1996	Balázs Kiss, Hungary	81.24m.(266' 6")
2000	Szymon Ziolkowski, Poland	80.02m.(262' 6")

Javelin Throw

1908	Erik Lemming, Sweden	54.82m. (179' 10")
1912	Erik Lemming, Sweden	60.64m. (198' 11")
1920	Jonni Myyrä, Finland	64.78m. (215' 10")
1924	Jonni Myyrä, Finland	62.96m. (206' 7")
1928	Eric Lundkvist, Sweden	66.60m. (218' 6")
1932	Matti Järvinen, Finland	72.70m. (238' 6")
1936	Gerhard Stöck, Germany	71.84m. (235' 8")
1948	Kai Tapio Rautavaara, Finland	69.76m. (228' 11")
1952	Cy Young, United States	73.78m. (242' 1")
1956	Egil Danielsen, Norway	85.70m. (281' 2")
1960	Viktor Tsibulenko, USSR	84.64m. (277' 8")
1964	Pauli Nevala, Finland	82.66m. (271' 2")
1968	Janis Lusis, USSR	90.10m. (295' 7")
1972	Klaus Wolfermann, W. Germany	90.48m. (296' 10")
1976	Miklós Németh, Hungary	94.58m. (310' 4")
1980	Dainis Kula, USSR	91.20m. (299' 2")
1984	Arto Härkönen, Finland	86.76m. (284' 8")
1988	Tapio Korjus, Finland	84.28m. (276' 6")
1992	Jan Zelezny, Czechoslovakia (a)	89.66m. (294' 2")
1996	Jan Zelezny, Czech Republic	88.16m. (289' 3")
2000	Jan Zelezny, Czech Republic	90.17m. (295' 9½")*

(a) New records were kept after javelin was modified in 1986.

Pole Vault

1896	William Welles Hoyt, United States	3.30m.(10' 10")
1900	Irving Baxter, United States	3.30m.(10' 10")
1904	Charles Dvorak, United States	3.50m.(11' 6")
1908	A. C. Gilbert, United States Edward Cooke Jr., United States	3.71m (12' 2")
1912	Harry Babcock, United States	3.95m.(12' 11½")
1920	Frank Foss, United States	4.09m.(13' 5")
1924	Lee Barnes, United States	3.95m.(12' 11½")
1928	Sabin W. Carr, United States	4.20m.(13' 9¼")
1932	William Miller, United States	4.31m.(14' 1¾")
1936	Earle Meadows, United States	4.35m.(14' 3¼")
1948	Guinn Smith, United States	4.30m.(14' 1¼")
1952	Robert Richards, United States	4.55m.(14' 11¼")
1956	Robert Richards, United States	4.56m.(14' 11½")
1960	Don Bragg, United States	4.70m.(15' 5")
1964	Fred Hansen, United States	5.10m.(16' 8¾")
1968	Bob Seagren, United States	5.40m.(17' 8½")
1972	Wolfgang Nordwig, E. Germany	5.50m.(18' ½")
1976	Tadeusz Slusarski, Poland	5.50m.(18' ½")
1980	Wladyslaw Kozakiewicz, Poland	5.78m.(18' 11½")
1984	Pierre Quinon, France	5.75m.(18' 10¼")
1988	Sergei Bubka, USSR	5.90m.(19' 4¼")
1992	Maksim Tarassov, Unified Team	5.80m.(19' ¼")
1996	Jean Galfione, France	5.92m.(19' 5")*
2000	Nick Hysong, United States	5.90m.(19' 4¼")

16-lb. Shot Put

1896	Robert Garrett, United States	11.22m.(36' 9¾")
1900	Richard Sheldon, United States	14.10m.(46' 3¼")
1904	Ralph Rose, United States	14.81m.(48' 7")
1908	Ralph Rose, United States	14.21m.(46' 7½")
1912	Pat McDonald, United States	15.34m.(50' 4")

16-lb. Shot Put

1920	Ville Pörhölä, Finland	14.81m.(48' 7¼")
1924	L. Clarence Houser, United States	14.99m.(49' 2¼")
1928	John Kuck, United States	15.87m.(52' ¾")
1932	Leo Sexton, United States	16.00m.(52' 6")
1936	Hans Woellke, Germany	16.20m.(53' 1¾")
1948	Wilbur Thompson, United States	17.12m.(56' 2")
1952	W. Parry O'Brien, United States	17.41m.(57' 1½")
1956	W. Parry O'Brien, United States	18.57m.(60' 11¼")
1960	William Nieder, United States	19.68m.(64' 6¾")
1964	Dallas Long, United States	20.33m.(66' 8½")
1968	Randy Matson, United States	20.54m.(67' 4¾")
1972	Wladyslaw Komar, Poland	21.18m.(69' 6")
1976	Udo Beyer, E. Germany	21.05m.(69' ¾")
1980	Vladimir Kyselyov, USSR	21.35m.(70' ½")
1984	Alessandro Andrei, Italy	21.26m.(69' 9")
1988	Ulf Timmermann, E. Germany	22.47m.(73' 8¾")*
1992	Michael Stulce, United States	21.70m.(71' 2½")
1996	Randy Barnes, United States	21.62m.(70' 11¼")
2000	Arsi Harju, Finland	21.29m.(69' 10¼")

Decathlon (not held 1908)

1904	Thomas Kiely, Ireland	6,036 pts.
1912	Hugo Wieslander, Sweden (a)	7,724.49 pts.
1920	Helge Lovland, Norway	6,804.35 pts.
1924	Harold Osborn, United States	7,710.77 pts.
1928	Paavo Yrjola, Finland	8,053.29 pts.
1932	James Bausch, United States	8,462.23 pts.
1936	Glenn Morris, United States	7,900 pts.
1948	Robert Mathias, United States	7,139 pts.
1952	Robert Mathias, United States	7,887 pts.
1956	Milton Campbell, United States	7,937 pts.
1960	Rafer Johnson, United States	8,392 pts.
1964	Willi Holdorf, Germany (b)	7,887 pts.
1968	Bill Toomey, United States	8,193 pts.
1972	Nikolai Avilov, USSR	8,454 pts.
1976	Bruce Jenner, United States	8,617 pts.
1980	Daley Thompson, Great Britain	8,495 pts.
1984	Daley Thompson, Great Britain (c)	8,798 pts.*
1988	Christian Schenk, E. Germany	8,488 pts.
1992	Robert Zmelik, Czechoslovakia	8,611 pts.
1996	Dan O'Brien, United States	8,824 pts.
2000	Erki Nool, Estonia	8,641 pts.

(a) Jim Thorpe of the U.S. won the 1912 Decathlon with 8,413 pts. but was disqualified and had to return his medals because he had played pro baseball prior to the Olympics. The IOC in 1982 posthumously restored his decathlon and pentathlon golds. (b) Former point systems used prior to 1964. (c) Scoring change effective Apr. 1985; Thompson's readjusted score is 8,847 pts.

TRACK AND FIELD—Women

(*indicates Olympic record; w indicates wind-aided)

100-Meter Run

1928	Elizabeth Robinson, United States	12.2s
1932	Stella Walsh, Poland (a)	11.9s
1936	Helen Stephens, United States	11.5s
1948	Francina Blankers-Koen, Netherlands	11.9s
1952	Marjorie Jackson, Australia	11.5s
1956	Betty Cuthbert, Australia	11.5s
1960	Wilma Rudolph, United States	11.0s
1964	Wyomia Tyus, United States	11.4s
1968	Wyomia Tyus, United States	11.0s
1972	Renate Stecher, E. Germany	11.07s
1976	Annegret Richter, W. Germany	11.08s
1980	Lyudmila Kondratyeva, USSR	11.6s
1984	Evelyn Ashford, United States	10.97s
1988	Florence Griffith-Joyner, United States	10.54s*
1992	Gail Devers, United States	10.82s
1996	Gail Devers, United States	10.94s
2000	Marion Jones, United States	10.75s

(a) A 1980 autopsy determined that Walsh was a man.

200-Meter Run

1948	Francina Blankers-Koen, Netherlands	24.4s
1952	Marjorie Jackson, Australia	23.7s
1956	Betty Cuthbert, Australia	23.4s
1960	Wilma Rudolph, United States	24.0s
1964	Edith McGuire, United States	23.0s
1968	Irena Szewinska, Poland	22.5s
1972	Renate Stecher, E. Germany	22.40s
1976	Barbel Eckert, E. Germany	22.37s
1980	Barbel Wockel, E. Germany	22.03s
1984	Valerie Brisco-Hooks, United States	21.81s
1988	Florence Griffith-Joyner, United States	21.34s*
1992	Gwen Torrence, United States	21.81s
1996	Marie-Jose Perec, France	22.12s
2000	Marion Jones, United States	21.84s

400-Meter Run

1964	Betty Cuthbert, Australia	52.0s
1968	Colette Besson, France	52.0s
1972	Monika Zehrt, E. Germany	51.08s
1976	Irena Szewinska, Poland	49.29s
1980	Marita Koch, E. Germany	48.88s
1984	Valerie Brisco-Hooks, United States	48.83s
1988	Olga Bryzgina, USSR	48.65s
1992	Marie-Jose Perec, France	48.83s
1996	Marie-Jose Perec, France	48.25s*
2000	Cathy Freeman, Australia	49.11s

800-Meter Run

1928	Lina Radke, Germany	2m. 16.8s
1960	Ludmila Shevtsova, USSR	2m. 4.3s
1964	Ann Packer, Great Britain	2m. 1.1s
1968	Madeline Manning, United States	2m. 0.9s
1972	Hildegard Falck, W. Germany	1m. 58.6s
1976	Tatyana Kazankina, USSR	1m. 54.94s
1980	Nadezhda Olizayrenko, USSR	1m. 53.5s*
1984	Doina Melinte, Romania	1m. 57.6s
1988	Sigrun Wodars, E. Germany	1m. 56.10s
1992	Ellen Van Langen, Netherlands	1m. 55.54s
1996	Svetlana Masterkova, Russia	1m. 57.73s
2000	Maria Mutola, Mozambique	1m. 56.15s

1,500-Meter Run

1972	Lyudmila Bragina, USSR	4m. 01.4s
1976	Tatyana Kazankina, USSR	4m. 05.48s
1980	Tatyana Kazankina, USSR	3m. 56.6s
1984	Gabriella Dorio, Italy	4m. 03.25s
1988	Paula Ivan, Romania	3m. 53.96s*
1992	Hassiba Boulmerka, Algeria	3m. 55.30s
1996	Svetlana Masterkova, Russia	4m. 00.83s
2000	Nouria Benida Merah, Algeria	4m. 05.10s

3,000-Meter Run

1984	Maricica Puica, Romania	8m. 35.96s
1988	Tatyana Samolenko, USSR	8m. 26.53s*
1992	Elena Romanova, Unified Team	8m. 46.04s

5,000-Meter Run

1996	Wang Junxia, China	14m. 59.88s
2000	Gabriela Szabo, Romania	14m. 40.79s*

10,000-Meter Run

1988	Olga Boldarenko, USSR	31m. 44.69s
1992	Derartu Tulu, Ethiopia	31m. 06.02s
1996	Fernanda Ribeiro, Portugal	31m. 01.63s
2000	Derartu Tulu, Ethiopia	30m. 17.49s*

100-Meter Hurdles

1972	Annelie Ehrhardt, E. Germany	12.59s
1976	Johanna Schaller, E. Germany	12.77s
1980	Vera Komisova, USSR	12.56s
1984	Benita Brown-Fitzgerald, United States	12.84s
1988	Jordanka Donkova, Bulgaria	12.38s*
1992	Paraskevi Patoulidou, Greece	12.64s
1996	Ludmila Enquist, Sweden	12.58s
2000	Olga Shishigina, Kazakhstan	12.65s

400-Meter Hurdles

1984	Nawal el Moutawakii, Morocco	54.61s
1988	Debra Flintoff-King, Australia	53.17s
1992	Sally Gunnell, Great Britain	53.23s
1996	Deon Hemmings, Jamaica	52.82s*
2000	Irina Privalova, Russia	53.02s

1,600-Meter Relay

1972	East Germany	3m. 23s
1976	East Germany	3m. 19.23s
1980	USSR	3m. 20.02s
1984	United States	3m. 18.29s
1988	USSR	3m. 15.18s*
1992	Unified Team	3m. 20.20s
1996	United States	3m. 20.91s
2000	United States	3m. 22.62s

400-Meter Relay

1928	Canada	48.4s
1932	United States	46.9s
1936	United States	46.9s
1948	Netherlands	47.5s
1952	United States	45.9s
1956	Australia	44.5s
1960	United States	44.5s
1964	Poland	43.6s
1968	United States	42.8s
1972	West Germany	42.81s
1976	East Germany	42.55s
1980	East Germany	41.60s*
1984	United States	41.65s
1988	United States	41.98s
1992	United States	42.11s
1996	United States	41.95s
2000	Bahamas	41.95s

10 Kilometer Walk

1992	Chen Yueling, China	44m. 32s
1996	Elena Nikolayeva, Russia	41m. 49s*

20 Kilometer Walk

2000	Wang Liping, China	1m. 29.05s*

Marathon

1984	Joan Benoit, United States	2h. 24m. 52s
1988	Rosa Mota, Portugal	2h. 25m. 40s
1992	Valentina Yegorova, Unified Team	2h. 32m. 41s
1996	Fatuma Roba, Ethiopia	2h. 26m. 05s
2000	Naoko Takahashi, Japan	2h. 23m. 14s*

High Jump

1928	Ethel Catherwood, Canada	1.59m.	(5' 2½")
1932	Jean Shiley, United States	1.65m.	(5' 5")
1936	Ibolya Csák, Hungary	1.60m.	(5' 3")
1948	Alice Coachman, U. S.	1.68m.	(5' 6")
1952	Esther Brand, South Africa	1.67m.	(5' 5¾ ")
1956	Mildred L. McDaniel, U. S.	1.76m.	(5' 9¼")
1960	Iolanda Balas, Romania	1.85m.	(6' ¾ ")
1964	Iolanda Balas, Romania	1.90m.	(6' 2¾ ")
1968	Miloslava Resková, Czech.	1.82m.	(5' 11½")
1972	Ulrike Meyfarth, W. Germany	1.92m.	(6' 3½")
1976	Rosemarie Ackermann, E. Ger.	1.93m.	(6' 4")
1980	Sara Simeoni, Italy	1.97m.	(6' 5½")
1984	Ulrike Meyfarth, W. Germany	2.02m.	(6' 7½")
1988	Louise Ritter, United States	2.03m.	(6' 8")
1992	Heike Henkel, Germany	2.02m.	(6' 7½")
1996	Stefka Kostadinova, Bulgaria	2.05m.	(6' 8¾")*
2000	Yelena Yelesina, Russia	2.01m.	(6' 7")

Long Jump

1948	Olga Gyarmati, Hungary	5.69m.	(18' 8")
1952	Yvette Williams, New Zealand	6.24m.	(20' 5¼")
1956	Elzbieta Krzeskinska, Poland	6.35m.	(20' 10")
1960	Vira Krepkina, USSR	6.37m.	(20' 10¾)
1964	Mary Rand, Great Britain	6.76m.	(22' 2¼")
1968	Viorica Viscopoleanu, Romania	6.82m.	(22' 4½")
1972	Heidemarie Rosendahl, W. Ger.	6.78m.	(22' 3")
1976	Angela Voigt, E. Germany	6.72m.	(22' ¾")
1980	Tatyana Kolpakova, USSR	7.06m.	(23' 2")
1984	Anisoara Cusmir-Stanciu, Rom.	6.96m.	(22' 10")
1988	Jackie Joyner-Kersee, United States	7.40m.	(24' 3½")*
1992	Heike Drechsler, Germany	7.14m.	(23' 5¼")
1996	Chioma Ajunwa, Nigeria	7.12m.	(23' 4½"
2000	Heike Drechsler, Germany	6.99m.	(22' 11¼")

Triple Jump

1996	Inessa Kravets, Ukraine	15.33m	(50' 3½")*
2000	Tereza Marinova, Bulgaria	15.20m	(49' 10½")

Discus Throw

1928	Halina Konopacka, Poland	39.62m.	(130' 0")
1932	Lillian Copeland, United States	40.58m.	(133' 2")
1936	Gisela Mauermayer, Germany	47.62m.	(156' 3")
1948	Micheline Ostermeyer, France	41.92m.	(137' 6")
1952	Nina Ponomareva, USSR	51.42m.	(168' 8")
1956	Olga Fikotová, Czech.	53.68m.	(176' 1")
1960	Nina Ponomareva, USSR	55.10m.	(180' 9")
1964	Tamara Press, USSR	57.26m.	(187' 10")
1968	Lia Manoliu, Romania	58.28m.	(191' 2")
1972	Faina Melnik, USSR	66.62m.	(218' 7")
1976	Evelin Jahl, E. Germany	69.00m.	(226' 4")
1980	Evelin Jahl, E. Germany	69.96m.	(229' 6")
1984	Ria Stalman, Netherlands	65.36m.	(214' 5")
1988	Martina Hellmann, E. Germany	72.30m.	(237' 2")*
1992	Maritza Martén Garcia, Cuba	70.06m.	(229' 10")
1996	Ilke Wyludda, Germany	69.66m.	(228' 6")
2000	Ellina Zvereva, Belarus	68.40m.	(224' 5")

Hammer Throw

2000	Kamila Skolimowska, Poland	71.16m.	(233' 5¾")*

Pole Vault

2000	Stacy Dragila, United States	4.60m.	(15' 1")*

Shot Put (8 lb., 13 oz.)

1948	Micheline Ostermeyer, France	13.75m.	(45' 1½")
1952	Galina Zybina, USSR	15.28m.	(50' 1½")
1956	Tamara Tyshkyevich, USSR	16.59m.	(54' 5¼")
1960	Tamara Press, USSR	17.32m.	(56' 10")
1964	Tamara Press, USSR	18.14m.	(59' 6¼")
1968	Margitta Gummel, E. Germany	19.61m.	(64' 4")
1972	Nadezhda Chizova, USSR	21.03m.	(69' 0")
1976	Ivanka Khristova, Bulgaria	21.16m.	(69' 5¼")
1980	Ilona Slupianek, E. Germany	22.41m.	(73' 6¼")*
1984	Claudia Losch, W. Germany	20.49m.	(67' 2¼")
1988	Natalya Lisovskaya, USSR	22.24m.	(72' 11¾")
1992	Svetlana Krivelyova, Unified Team	21.06m.	(69' 1¼")
1996	Astrid Kumbernuss, Germany	20.56m.	(67' 5½")
2000	Yanina Karolchik, Belarus	20.56m.	(67' 5½")

Javelin Throw

1932	"Babe" Didrikson, United States	43.68m.	(143' 4")
1936	Tilly Fleischer, Germany	45.18m.	(148' 3")
1948	Herma Bauma, Austria	45.56m.	(149' 6")
1952	Dana Zátopková, Czech.	50.46m.	(165' 7")
1956	Inese Jaunzeme, USSR	53.86m.	(176' 8")
1960	Elvira Ozolina, USSR	55.98m.	(183' 8")
1964	Mihaela Penes, Romania	60.54m.	(198' 7")
1968	Angéla Németh, Hungary	60.36m.	(198' 0")
1972	Ruth Fuchs, E. Germany	63.88m.	(209' 7")
1976	Ruth Fuchs, E. Germany	65.94m.	(216' 4")
1980	Maria Colón Ruenes, Cuba	68.40m.	(224' 5")
1984	Tessa Sanderson, Great Britain	69.56m.	(228' 2")
1988	Petra Felke, E. Germany	74.68m.	(245' 0")
1992	Silke Renke, Germany	68.34m.	(224' 2")
1996	Heli Rantanen, Finland	67.94m.	(222' 11")
2000	Trine Hattestad, Norway	68.91m.	(226' 1")*

Heptathlon

1984	Glynis Nunn, Australia	6,390 pts.
1988	Jackie Joyner-Kersee, U.S.	7,215 pts.*
1992	Jackie Joyner-Kersee, U.S.	7,044 pts.
1996	Ghada Shouaa, Syria	6,780 pts.
2000	Denise Lewis, Britain	6,584 pts.

SWIMMING AND DIVING—Men

(*indicates Olympic record)

50-Meter Freestyle

1988	Matt Biondi, U.S.	22.14
1992	Aleksandr Popov, Unified Team	21.91*
1996	Aleksandr Popov, Russia	22.13
2000	Anthony Ervin, U.S.	21.98
2000	Gary Hall Jr., U.S.	21.98

100-Meter Freestyle

1896	Alfred Hajos, Hungary	1:22.2
1904	Zoltan de Halmay, Hungary (100 yards)	1:02.8
1908	Charles Daniels, U.S.	1:05.6
1912	Duke P. Kahanamoku, U.S.	1:03.4
1920	Duke P. Kahanamoku, U.S.	1:01.4
1924	John Weissmuller, U.S.	59.0
1928	John Weissmuller, U.S.	58.6
1932	Yasuji Miyazaki, Japan	58.2
1936	Ferenc Csik, Hungary	57.6
1948	Wally Ris, U.S.	57.3
1952	Clark Scholes, U.S.	57.4
1956	Jon Henricks, Australia	55.4
1960	John Devitt, Australia	55.2
1964	Don Schollander, U.S.	53.4
1968	Mike Wenden, Australia	52.2
1972	Mark Spitz, U.S.	51.22
1976	Jim Montgomery, U.S.	49.99
1980	Jorg Woithe, E. Germany	50.40
1984	Rowdy Gaines, U.S.	49.80
1988	Matt Biondi, U.S.	48.63
1992	Aleksandr Popov, Unified Team	49.02
1996	Aleksandr Popov, Russia	48.74
2000	Pieter van den Hoogenband, Netherlands	48.30

200-Meter Freestyle

1968	Mike Wenden, Australia	1:55.2
1972	Mark Spitz, U.S.	1:52.78
1976	Bruce Furniss, U.S.	1:50.29
1980	Sergei Kopliakov, USSR	1:49.81
1984	Michael Gross, W. Germany	1:47.44
1988	Duncan Armstrong, Australia	1:47.25
1992	Yevgeny Sadovyi, Unified Team	1:46.70
1996	Danyon Loader, New Zealand	1:47.63
2000	Pieter van den Hoogenband, Netherlands	1:45.35*

400-Meter Freestyle

1904	C. M. Daniels, U.S. (440 yards)	6:16.2
1908	Henry Taylor, Great Britain	5:36.8
1912	George Hodgson, Canada	5:24.4
1920	Norman Ross, U.S.	5:26.8
1924	John Weissmuller, U.S.	5:04.2
1928	Albert Zorilla, Argentina	5:01.6
1932	Clarence Crabbe, U.S.	4:48.4
1936	Jack Medica, U.S.	4:44.5
1948	William Smith, U.S.	4:41.0
1952	Jean Boiteux, France	4:30.7
1956	Murray Rose, Australia	4:27.3
1960	Murray Rose, Australia	4:18.3
1964	Don Schollander, U.S.	4:12.2
1968	Mike Burton, U.S.	4:09.0
1972	Brad Cooper, Australia	4:00.27
1976	Brian Goodell, U.S.	3:51.93
1980	Vladimir Salnikov, USSR	3:51.31
1984	George DiCarlo, U.S.	3:51.23
1988	Ewe Dassler, E. Germany	3:46.95
1992	Yevgeny Sadovyi, Unified Team	3:45.00
1996	Danyon Loader, New Zealand	3:47.97
2000	Ian Thorpe, Australia	3:40.59*

1,500-Meter Freestyle

1908	Henry Taylor, Great Britain	22:48.4
1912	George Hodgson, Canada	22:00.0
1920	Norman Ross, U.S.	22:23.2
1924	Andrew Charlton, Australia	20:06.6
1928	Arne Borg, Sweden	19:51.8
1932	Kusuo Kitamura, Japan	19:12.4
1936	Noboru Terada, Japan	19:13.7
1948	James McLane, U.S.	19:18.5
1952	Ford Konno, U.S.	18:30.3
1956	Murray Rose, Australia	17:58.9
1960	Jon Konrads, Australia	17:19.6
1964	Robert Windle, Australia	17:01.7
1968	Mike Burton, U.S.	16:38.9
1972	Mike Burton, U.S.	15:52.58
1976	Brian Goodell, U.S.	15:02.40
1980	Vladimir Salnikov, USSR	14:58.27
1984	Michael O'Brien, U.S.	15:05.20
1988	Vladimir Salnikov, USSR	15:00.40
1992	Kieren Perkins, Australia	14:43.48*
1996	Kieren Perkins, Australia	14:56.40
2000	Grant Hackett, Australia	14:48.33

100-Meter Backstroke

1904	Walter Brack, Germany (100 yds.)	1:16.8
1908	Arno Bieberstein, Germany	1:24.6
1912	Harry Hebner, U.S.	1:21.2
1920	Warren Kealoha, U.S.	1:15.2
1924	Warren Kealoha, U.S.	1:13.2
1928	George Kojac, U.S.	1:08.2
1932	Masaji Kiyokawa, Japan	1:08.6
1936	Adolph Kiefer, U.S.	1:05.9
1948	Allen Stack, U.S.	1:06.4
1952	Yoshi Oyakawa, U.S.	1:05.4
1956	David Thiele, Australia	1:02.2
1960	David Thiele, Australia	1:01.9
1968	Roland Matthes, E. Germany	58.7
1972	Roland Matthes, E. Germany	56.58
1976	John Naber, U.S.	55.49
1980	Bengt Baron, Sweden	56.33
1984	Rick Carey, U.S.	55.79
1988	Daichi Suzuki, Japan	55.05
1992	Mark Tewksbury, Canada	53.98
1996	Jeff Rouse, U.S.	54.10
2000	Lenny Krayzelburg, U.S.	53.72*

200-Meter Backstroke

1964	Jed Graef, U.S.	2:10.3
1968	Roland Matthes, E. Germany	2:09.6
1972	Roland Matthes, E. Germany	2:02.82
1976	John Naber, U.S.	1:59.19
1980	Sandor Wladar, Hungary	2:01.93
1984	Rick Carey, U.S.	2:00.23
1988	Igor Polianski, USSR	1:59.37
1992	Martin Lopez-Zubero, Spain	1:58.47
1996	Brad Bridgewater, U.S.	1:58.54
2000	Lenny Krayzelburg, U.S.	1:56.76*

100-Meter Breaststroke

1968	Don McKenzie, U.S.	1:07.7
1972	Nobutaka Taguchi, Japan	1:04.94
1976	John Hencken, U.S.	1:03.11
1980	Duncan Goodhew, Great Britain	1:03.44
1984	Steve Lundquist, U.S.	1:01.65
1988	Adrian Moorhouse, Great Britain	1:02.04
1992	Nelson Diebel, U.S.	1:01.50
1996	Fred Deburghgraeve, Belgium	1:00.60
2000	Domenico Fioravanti, Italy	1:00.46*

200-Meter Breaststroke

1908	Frederick Holman, Great Britain	3:09.2
1912	Walter Bathe, Germany	3:01.8
1920	Haken Malmroth, Sweden	3:04.4
1924	Robert Skelton, U.S.	2:56.6
1928	Yoshiyuki Tsuruta, Japan	2:48.8
1932	Yoshiyuki Tsuruta, Japan	2:45.4
1936	Tetsuo Hamuro, Japan	2:41.5
1948	Joseph Verdeur, U.S.	2:39.3
1952	John Davies, Australia	2:34.4
1956	Masura Furukawa, Japan	2:34.7
1960	William Mulliken, U.S.	2:37.4
1964	Ian O'Brien, Australia	2:27.8
1968	Felipe Munoz, Mexico	2:28.7
1972	John Hencken, U.S.	2:21.55
1976	David Wilkie, Great Britain	2:15.11
1980	Robertas Zhulpa, USSR	2:15.85
1984	Victor Davis, Canada	2:13.34
1988	Jozsef Szabo, Hungary	2:13.52
1992	Mike Barrowman, U.S.	2:10.16*
1996	Norbert Rozsa, Hungary	2:12.57
2000	Domenico Fioravanti, Italy	2:10.87

100-Meter Butterfly

1968	Doug Russell, U.S.	55.9
1972	Mark Spitz, U.S.	54.27
1976	Matt Vogel, U.S.	54.35
1980	Par Arvidsson, Sweden	54.92
1984	Michael Gross, W. Germany	53.08
1988	Anthony Nesty, Suriname	53.00
1992	Pablo Morales, U.S.	53.32
1996	Denis Pankratov, Russia	52.27
2000	Lars Froelander, Sweden	52.00

200-Meter Butterfly

1956	William Yorzyk, U.S.	2:19.3
1960	Michael Troy, U.S.	2:12.8
1964	Kevin J. Berry, Australia	2:06.6
1968	Carl Robie, U.S.	2:08.7
1972	Mark Spitz, U.S.	2:00.70
1976	Mike Bruner, U.S.	1:59.23
1980	Sergei Fesenko, USSR	1:59.76
1984	Jon Sieben, Australia	1:57.04
1988	Michael Gross, W. Germany	1:56.94
1992	Mel Stewart, U.S.	1:56.26
1996	Denis Pankratov, Russia	1:56.51
2000	Tom Malchow, U.S.	1:55.35*

200-Meter Individual Medley

1968	Charles Hickcox, U.S.	2:12.0
1972	Gunnar Larsson, Sweden	2:07.17
1984	Alex Baumann, Canada	2:01.42
1988	Tamas Darnyi, Hungary	2:00.17
1992	Tamas Darnyi, Hungary	2:00.76
1996	Attila Czene, Hungary	1:59.91
2000	Massimiliano Rosolino, Italy	1:58.98*

400-Meter Individual Medley

1964	Dick Roth, U.S.	4:45.4
1968	Charles Hickcox, U.S.	4:48.4
1972	Gunnar Larsson, Sweden	4:31.98
1976	Rod Strachan, U.S.	4:23.68
1980	Aleksandr Sidorenko, USSR	4:22.89
1984	Alex Baumann, Canada	4:17.41
1988	Tamas Darnyi, Hungary	4:14.75
1992	Tamas Darnyi, Hungary	4:14.23
1996	Tom Dolan, U.S.	4:14.90
2000	Tom Dolan, U.S.	4:11.76*

400-Meter Freestyle Relay

1964	United States	3:31.2
1968	United States	3:31.7
1972	United States	3:26.42
1984	United States	3:19.03
1988	United States	3:16.53
1992	United States	3:16.74
1996	United States	3:15.41
2000	Australia	3:13.67*

800-Meter Freestyle Relay

1908	Great Britain	10:55.6
1912	Australia	10:11.6
1920	United States	10:04.4
1924	United States	9:53.4
1928	United States	9:36.2
1932	Japan	8:58.4
1936	Japan	8:51.5
1948	United States	8:46.0
1952	United States	8:31.1
1956	Australia	8:23.6
1960	United States	8:10.2
1964	United States	7:52.1
1968	United States	7:52.33
1972	United States	7:35.78
1976	United States	7:23.22
1980	USSR	7:23.50
1984	United States	7:15.69
1988	United States	7:12.51
1992	Unified Team	7:11.95
1996	United States	7:14.84
2000	Australia	7:07.05*

400-Meter Medley Relay

1960	United States	4:05.4
1964	United States	3:58.4
1968	United States	3:54.9
1972	United States	3:48.16
1976	United States	3:42.22
1980	Australia	3:45.70
1984	United States	3:39.30
1988	United States	3:36.93
1992	United States	3:36.93
1996	United States	3:34.84
2000	United States	3:33.73*

Springboard Diving — Points

1908	Albert Zurner, Germany	85.5
1912	Paul Guenther, Germany	79.23
1920	Louis Kuehn, U.S	675.40
1924	Albert White, U.S.	97.46
1928	Pete Desjardins, U.S.	185.04
1932	Michael Galitzen, U.S.	161.38
1936	Richard Degener, U.S.	163.57
1948	Bruce Harlan, U.S.	163.64
1952	David Browning, U.S.	205.29
1956	Robert Clotworthy, U.S.	159.56
1960	Gary Tobian, U.S.	170.00
1964	Kenneth Sitzberger, U.S.	159.90
1968	Bernie Wrightson, U.S.	170.15
1972	Vladimir Vasin, USSR	594.09
1976	Phil Boggs, U.S.	619.52
1980	Aleksandr Portnov, USSR	905.02
1984	Greg Louganis, U.S.	754.41
1988	Greg Louganis, U.S.	730.80
1992	Mark Lenzi, U.S.	676.53
1996	Xiong Ni, China	701.46
2000	Xiong Ni, China	708.72

Platform Diving — Points

1904	Dr. G.E. Sheldon, U.S.	112.75
1908	Hjalmar Johansson, Sweden	183.75
1912	Erik Adlerz, Sweden	73.94
1920	Clarence Pinkston, U.S.	100.67
1924	Albert White, U.S.	97.46
1928	Pete Desjardins, U.S.	98.74
1932	Harold Smith, U.S.	124.80
1936	Marshall Wayne, U.S.	113.58
1948	Sammy Lee, U.S.	130.05
1952	Sammy Lee, U.S.	156.28
1956	Joaquin Capilla, Mexico	152.44
1960	Robert Webster, U.S.	165.56
1964	Robert Webster, U.S.	148.58
1968	Klaus Dibiasi, Italy	164.18
1972	Klaus Dibiasi, Italy	504.12
1976	Klaus Dibiasi, Italy	600.51
1980	Falk Hoffmann, E. Germany	835.65
1984	Greg Louganis, U.S.	710.91
1988	Greg Louganis, U.S.	638.61
1992	Sun Shuwei, China	677.31
1996	Dmitri Sautin, Russia	692.34
2000	Tian Liang, China	724.53

SWIMMING AND DIVING—Women

(*indicates Olympic record)

50-Meter Freestyle

1988	Kristin Otto, E. Germany	25.49
1992	Yang Wenyi, China	24.76*
1996	Amy Van Dyken, U.S.	24.87
2000	Inge de Bruijn, Netherlands	24.32

100-Meter Freestyle

1912	Fanny Durack, Australia	1:22.2
1920	Ethelda Bleibtrey, U.S.	1:13.6
1924	Ethel Lackie, U.S.	1:12.4
1928	Albina Osipowich, U.S.	1:11.0
1932	Helene Madison, U.S.	1:06.8
1936	Hendrika Mastenbroek, Holland	1:05.9
1948	Greta Andersen, Denmark	1:06.3
1952	Katalin Szoke, Hungary	1:06.8
1956	Dawn Fraser, Australia	1:02.0
1960	Dawn Fraser, Australia	1:01.2
1964	Dawn Fraser, Australia	59.5
1968	Jan Henne, U.S.	1:00.0
1972	Sandra Neilson, U.S.	58.59
1976	Kornelia Ender, E. Germany	55.65
1980	Barbara Krause, E. Germany	54.79
1984	(tie) Carrie Steinseifer, U.S.	55.92
	Nancy Hogshead, U.S.	55.92
1988	Kristin Otto, E. Germany	54.93
1992	Zhuang Yong, China	54.64
1996	Li Jingyi, China	54.50
2000	Inge de Bruijn, Netherlands	53.83

200-Meter Freestyle

1968	Debbie Meyer, U.S.	2:10.5
1972	Shane Gould, Australia	2:03.56
1976	Kornelia Ender, E. Germany	1:59.26
1980	Barbara Krause, E. Germany	1:58.33
1984	Mary Wayte, U.S.	1:59.23
1988	Heike Friedrich, E. Germany	1:57.65*
1992	Nicole Haislett, U.S.	1:57.90
1996	Claudia Poll, Costa Rica	1:58.16
2000	Susie O'Neill, Australia	1:58.24

400-Meter Freestyle

1924	Martha Norelius, U.S.	6:02.2
1928	Martha Norelius, U.S.	5:42.8
1932	Helene Madison, U.S.	5:28.5
1936	Hendrika Mastenbroek, Netherlands	5:26.4
1948	Ann Curtis, U.S.	5:17.8
1952	Valerie Gyenge, Hungary	5:12.1
1956	Lorraine Crapp, Australia	4:54.6
1960	Susan Chris von Saltza, U.S.	4:50.6
1964	Virginia Duenkel, U.S.	4:43.3
1968	Debbie Meyer, U.S.	4:31.8
1972	Shane Gould, Australia	4:19.44
1976	Petra Thuemer, E. Germany	4:09.89
1980	Ines Diers, E. Germany	4:08.76
1984	Tiffany Cohen, U.S.	4:07.10
1988	Janet Evans, U.S.	4:03.85*
1992	Dagmar Hase, Germany	4:07.18
1996	Michelle Smith, Ireland	4:07.25
2000	Brooke Bennett, U.S.	4:05.80

800-Meter Freestyle

1968	Debbie Meyer, U.S.	9:24.0
1972	Keena Rothhammer, U.S.	8:53.68
1976	Petra Thuemer, E. Germany	8:37.14
1980	Michelle Ford, Australia	8:28.90
1984	Tiffany Cohen, U.S.	8:24.95
1988	Janet Evans, U.S.	8:20.20
1992	Janet Evans, U.S.	8:25.52
1996	Brooke Bennett, U.S.	8:27.89
2000	Brooke Bennett, U.S.	8:19.67*

100-Meter Backstroke

1924	Sybil Bauer, U.S.	1:23.2
1928	Marie Braun, Netherlands	1:22.0
1932	Eleanor Holm, U.S.	1:19.4
1936	Dina Senff, Netherlands	1:18.9
1948	Karen Harup, Denmark	1:14.4
1952	Joan Harrison, South Africa	1:14.3
1956	Judy Grinham, Great Britain	1:12.9
1960	Lynn Burke, U.S.	1:09.3
1964	Cathy Ferguson, U.S.	1:07.7
1968	Kaye Hall, U.S.	1:06.2
1972	Melissa Belote, U.S.	1:05.78
1976	Ulrike Richter, E. Germany	1:01.83
1980	Rica Reinisch, E. Germany	1:00.86
1984	Theresa Andrews, U.S.	1:02.55
1988	Kristin Otto, E. Germany	1:00.89
1992	Krisztina Egerszegi, Hungary	1:00.68
1996	Beth Botsford, U.S.	1:01.19
2000	Diana Mocanu, Romania	1:00.21*

200-Meter Backstroke

1968	Pokey Watson, U.S.	2:24.8
1972	Melissa Belote, U.S.	2:19.19
1976	Ulrike Richter, E. Germany	2:13.43
1980	Rica Reinisch, E. Germany	2:11.77
1984	Jolanda De Rover, Netherlands	2:12.38
1988	Krisztina Egerszegi, Hungary	2:09.29
1992	Krisztina Egerszegi, Hungary	2:07.06*
1996	Krisztina Egerszegi, Hungary	2:07.83
2000	Diana Mocanu, Romania	2:08.16

100-Meter Breaststroke

1968	Djurdjica Bjedov, Yugoslavia	1:15.8
1972	Cathy Carr, U.S.	1:13.58
1976	Hannelore Anke, E. Germany	1:11.16
1980	Ute Geweniger, E. Germany	1:10.22
1984	Petra Van Staveren, Netherlands	1:09.88
1988	Tania Dangalakova, Bulgaria	1:07.95
1992	Elena Roudkovskaia, Unified Team	1:08.00
1996	Penny Heyns, South Africa	1:07.73
2000	Megan Quann, U.S.	1:07.05

200-Meter Breaststroke

1924	Lucy Morton, Great Britain	3:33.2
1928	Hilde Schrader, Germany	3:12.6
1932	Clare Dennis, Australia	3:06.3
1936	Hideko Maehata, Japan	3:03.6
1948	Nelly Van Vliet, Netherlands	2:57.2
1952	Eva Szekely, Hungary	2:51.7
1956	Ursula Happe, Germany	2:53.1
1960	Anita Lonsbrough, Great Britain	2:49.5
1964	Galina Prozumenschikova, USSR	2:46.4
1968	Sharon Wichman, U.S.	2:44.4
1972	Beverly Whitfield, Australia	2:41.71
1976	Marina Koshevaia, USSR	2:33.35
1980	Lina Kachushite, USSR	2:29.54
1984	Anne Ottenbrite, Canada	2:30.38
1988	Silke Hoerner, E. Germany	2:26.71
1992	Kyoko Iwasaki, Japan	2:26.65
1996	Penny Heyns, South Africa	2:25.41
2000	Agnes Kovacs, Hungary	2:24.35

100-Meter Butterfly

1956	Shelley Mann, U.S.	1:11.0
1960	Carolyn Schuler, U.S.	1:09.5
1964	Sharon Stouder, U.S.	1:04.7

100-Meter Butterfly

1968	Lynn McClements, Australia	1:05.5
1972	Mayumi Aoki, Japan	1:03.34
1976	Kornelia Ender, E. Germany	1:00.13
1980	Caren Metschuck, E. Germany	1:00.42
1984	Mary T. Meagher, U.S.	59.26
1988	Kristin Otto, E. Germany	59.00
1992	Qian Hong, China	58.62
1996	Amy Van Dyken, U.S.	59.13
2000	Inge de Bruijn, Netherlands	56:61*

200-Meter Butterfly

1968	Ada Kok, Netherlands	2:24.7
1972	Karen Moe, U.S.	2:15.57
1976	Andrea Pollack, E. Germany	2:11.41
1980	Ines Geissler, E. Germany	2:10.44
1984	Mary T. Meagher, U.S.	2:06.90
1988	Kathleen Nord, E. Germany	2:09.51
1992	Summer Sanders, U.S.	2:08.67
1996	Susan O'Neill, Australia	2:07.76
2000	Misty Hyman, U.S.	2:05.88*

200-Meter Individual Medley

1968	Claudia Kolb, U.S.	2:24.7
1972	Shane Gould, Australia	2:23.07
1984	Tracy Caulkins, U.S.	2:12.64
1988	Daniela Hunger, E. Germany	2:12.59
1992	Lin Li, China	2:11.65
1996	Michelle Smith, Ireland	2:13.93
2000	Yana Klochkova, Ukraine	2:10.68*

400-Meter Individual Medley

1964	Donna de Varona, U.S.	5:18.7
1968	Claudia Kolb, U.S.	5:08.5
1972	Gail Neall, Australia	5:02.97
1976	Ulrike Tauber, E. Germany	4:42.77
1980	Petra Schneider, E. Germany	4:36.29
1984	Tracy Caulkins, U.S.	4:39.24
1988	Janet Evans, U.S.	4:37.76
1992	Krisztina Egerszegi, Hungary	4:36.54
1996	Michelle Smith, Ireland	4:39.18
2000	Yana Klochkova, Ukraine	4:33.59*

400-Meter Freestyle Relay

1912	Great Britain	5:52.8
1920	United States	5:11.6
1924	United States	4:58.8
1928	United States	4:47.6
1932	United States	4:38.0
1936	Netherlands	4:36.0
1948	United States	4:29.2
1952	Hungary	4:24.4
1956	Australia	4:17.1
1960	United States	4:08.9
1964	United States	4:03.8
1968	United States	4:02.5
1972	United States	3:55.19
1976	United States	3:44.82
1980	East Germany	3:42.71
1984	United States	3:43.43
1988	East Germany	3:40.63
1992	United States	3:39.46
1996	United States	3:39.29
2000	United States	3:36.61*

800-Meter Freestyle Relay

1996	United States	7:59.87
2000	United States	7:57.80*

400-Meter Medley Relay

1960	United States	4:41.1
1964	United States	4:33.9
1968	United States	4:28.3
1972	United States	4:20.75
1976	East Germany	4:07.95
1980	East Germany	4:06.67
1984	United States	4:08.34
1988	East Germany	4:03.74
1992	United States	4:02.54
1996	United States	4:02.88
2000	United States	3:58.30*

Springboard Diving Points

1920	Aileen Riggin, U.S.	539.90
1924	Elizabeth Becker, U.S.	474.50
1928	Helen Meany, U.S.	78.62
1932	Georgia Coleman U.S.	87.52
1936	Marjorie Gestring, U.S.	89.27
1948	Victoria M. Draves, U.S.	108.74
1952	Patricia McCormick, U.S.	147.30
1956	Patricia McCormick, U.S.	142.36
1960	Ingrid Kramer, Germany	155.81
1964	Ingrid Engel-Kramer, Germany	145.00
1968	Sue Gossick, U.S.	150.77
1972	Micki King, U.S.	450.03
1976	Jenni Chandler, U.S.	506.19
1980	Irina Kalinina, USSR	725.91
1984	Sylvie Bernier, Canada	530.70
1988	Gao Min, China	580.23
1992	Gao Min, China	572.40
1996	Fu Mingxia, China	547.68
2000	Fu Mingxia, China	609.42

Platform Diving Points

1912	Greta Johansson, Sweden	39.90
1920	Stefani Fryland-Clausen, Denmark	34.60
1924	Caroline Smith, U.S.	33.20
1928	Elizabeth B. Pinkston, U.S.	31.60
1932	Dorothy Poynton, U.S.	40.26
1936	Dorothy Poynton Hill, U.S.	33.93
1948	Victoria M. Draves, U.S.	8.87
1952	Patricia McCormick, U.S.	79.37
1956	Patricia McCormick, U.S.	84.85
1960	Ingrid Kramer, Germany	91.28
1964	Lesley Bush, U.S.	99.80
1968	Milena Duchkova, Czech.	109.59
1972	Ulrika Knape, Sweden	390.00
1976	Elena Vaytsekhouskaya, USSR	406.59
1980	Martina Jaschke, E. Germany	596.25
1984	Zhou Jihong, China	435.51
1988	Xu Yanmei, China	445.20
1992	Fu Mingxia, China	461.43
1996	Fu Mingxia, China	521.58
2000	Laura Wilkinson, U.S.	543.75

BOXING

Lt. Flyweight (48 kg/106 lbs)

1968	Francisco Rodriguez, Venezuela
1972	Gyorgy Gedo, Hungary
1976	Jorge Hernandez, Cuba
1980	Shamil Sabyrov, USSR
1984	Paul Gonzalez, U.S.
1988	Ivailo Hristov, Bulgaria
1992	Rogelio Marcelo, Cuba
1996	Daniel Petrov, Bulgaria
2000	Brahim Asloum, France

Flyweight (51 kg/112 lbs)

1904	George Finnegan, U.S.
1920	William Di Gennara, U.S.
1924	Fidel LaBarba, U.S.
1928	Antal Kocsis, Hungary
1932	Istvan Enekes, Hungary
1936	Willi Kaiser, Germany
1948	Pascual Perez, Argentina
1952	Nathan Brooks, U.S.
1956	Terence Spinks, Great Britain
1960	GyulaTorok, Hungary
1964	Fernando Atzori, Italy
1968	Ricardo Delgado, Mexico
1972	Georgi Kostadinov, Bulgaria
1976	Leo Randolph, U.S.
1980	Peter Lessov, Bulgaria
1984	Steve McCrory, U.S.
1988	Kim Kwang Sun, S. Korea
1992	Su Choi Choi, N. Korea
1996	Maikro Romero, Cuba
2000	Wijan Ponlid, Thailand

Bantamweight (54 kg /119 lbs)

1904	Oliver Kirk, U.S.
1908	A. Henry Thomas, Great Britain
1920	Clarence Walker, South Africa
1924	William Smith, South Africa
1928	Vittorio Tamagnini, Italy
1932	Horace Gwynne, Canada
1936	Ulderico Sergo, Italy
1948	Tibor Csik, Hungary
1952	Pentti Hamalainen, Finland
1956	Wolfgang Behrendt, E. Germany
1960	Oleg Grigoryev, USSR
1964	Takao Sakurai, Japan
1968	Valery Sokolov, USSR
1972	Orlando Martinez, Cuba
1976	Yong-Jo Gu, N. Korea
1980	Juan Hernandez, Cuba
1984	Maurizio Stecca, Italy
1988	Kennedy McKinney, U.S.
1992	Joel Casamayor, Cuba
1996	Istvan Kovacs, Hungary
2000	Guillermo Rigondeaux, Cuba

Featherweight (57 kg/125 lbs)

1904	Oliver Kirk, U.S.
1908	Richard Gunn, Great Britain
1920	Paul Fritsch, France
1924	John Fields, U.S.
1928	Lambertus van Klaveren, Netherlands
1932	Carmelo Robledo, Argentina
1936	Oscar Casanovas, Argentina
1948	Ernesto Formenti, Italy
1952	Jan Zachara, Czechoslovakia
1956	Vladimir Safronov, USSR
1960	Francesco Musso, Italy
1964	Stanislav Stephashkin, USSR
1968	Antonin Roldan, Mexico
1972	Boris Kousnetsov, USSR
1976	Angel Herrera, Cuba
1980	Rudi Fink, E. Germany
1984	Meldrick Taylor, U.S.
1988	Giovanni Parisi, Italy
1992	Andreas Tews, Germany
1996	Somluck Kamsing, Thailand
2000	Bekzat Sattarkhanov, Kazakhstan

Lightweight (60 kg/132 lbs)

1904	Harry Spanger, U.S.
1908	Frederick Grace, Great Britain
1920	Samuel Mosberg, U.S.

1924 Hans Nielsen, Denmark
1928 Carlo Orlandi, Italy
1932 Lawrence Stevens, South Africa
1936 Imre Harangi, Hungary
1948 Gerald Dreyer, South Africa
1952 Aureliano Bolognesi, Italy
1956 Richard McTaggart, Great Britain
1960 Kazimierz Pazdzior, Poland
1964 Jozef Grudzien, Poland
1968 Ronald Harris, U.S.
1972 Jan Szczepanski, Poland
1976 Howard Davis, U.S.
1980 Angel Herrera, Cuba
1984 Pernell Whitaker, U.S.
1988 Andreas Zuelow, E. Germany
1992 Oscar De La Hoya, U.S.
1996 Hocine Soltani, Algeria
2000 Mario Kindelan, Cuba

Lt. Welterweight (63.5 kg/139 lbs)

1952 Charles Adkins, U.S.
1956 Vladimir Yengibaryan, USSR
1960 Bohumil Nemecek, Czechoslovakia
1964 Jerzy Kulej, Poland
1968 Jerzy Kulej, Poland
1972 Ray Seales, U.S.
1976 Ray Leonard, U.S.
1980 Patrizio Oliva, Italy
1984 Jerry Page, U.S.
1988 Viatcheslav Janovski, USSR
1992 Hector Vinent, Cuba
1996 Hector Vinent, Cuba
2000 Mahamadkadyz Abdullaev, Uzbekistan

Welterweight (67 kg/147 lbs)

1904 Albert Young, U.S.
1920 Albert Schneider, Canada
1924 Jean Delarge, Belgium
1928 Edward Morgan, New Zealand
1932 Edward Flynn, U.S.
1936 Sten Suvio, Finland
1948 Julius Torma, Czechoslovakia
1952 Zygmunt Chychia, Poland
1956 Nicolae Linca, Romania
1960 Giovanni Benvenuti, Italy
1964 Marian Kasprzyk, Poland
1968 Manfred Wolke, E. Germany
1972 Emilio Correa, Cuba
1976 Jochen Bachfeld, E. Germany
1980 Andres Aldama, Cuba
1984 Mark Breland, U.S.
1988 Robert Wangila, Kenya
1992 Michael Carruth, Ireland
1996 Oleg Saitov, Russia
2000 Oleg Saitov, Russia

Lt. Middleweight (71 kg/156 lbs)

1952 Laszlo Papp, Hungary
1956 Laszlo Papp, Hungary
1960 Wilbert McClure, U.S.
1964 Boris Lagutin, USSR
1968 Boris Lagutin, USSR
1972 Dieter Kottysch, W. Germany
1976 Jerzy Rybicki, Poland
1980 Armando Martinez, Cuba
1984 Frank Tate, U.S.
1988 Park Si Hun, S. Korea
1992 Juan Lemus, Cuba
1996 David Reid, U.S.
2000 Yermakhan Ibraimov, Kazakhstan

Middleweight (75 kg/165 lbs)

1904 Charles Mayer, U.S.
1908 John Douglas, Great Britain
1920 Harry Mallin, Great Britain
1924 Harry Mallin, Great Britain
1928 Piero Toscani, Italy
1932 Carmen Barth, U.S.
1936 Jean Despeaux, France
1948 Laszlo Papp, Hungary
1952 Floyd Patterson, U.S.
1956 Gennady Schatkov, USSR
1960 Edward Crook, U.S.
1964 Valery Popenchenko, USSR
1968 Christopher Finnegan, Great Britain
1972 Vyacheslav Lemechev, USSR
1976 Michael Spinks, U.S.
1980 Jose Gomez, Cuba
1984 Joon-Sup Shin, S. Korea
1988 Henry Maske, E. Germany
1992 Ariel Hernandez, Cuba
1996 Ariel Hernandez, Cuba
2000 Jorge Gutierrez, Cuba

Lt. Heavyweight (81 kg/178 lbs)

1920 Edward Eagan, U.S.
1924 Harry Mitchell, Great Britain
1928 Victor Avendano, Argentina
1932 David Carstens, South Africa
1936 Roger Michelot, France
1948 George Hunter, South Africa
1952 Norvel Lee, U.S.
1956 James Boyd, U.S.
1960 Cassius Clay, U.S.
1964 Cosimo Pinto, Italy
1968 Dan Poznyak, USSR
1972 Mate Parlov, Yugoslavia
1976 Leon Spinks, U.S.
1980 Slobodan Kacar, Yugoslavia
1984 Anton Josipovic, Yugoslavia
1988 Andrew Maynard, U.S.
1992 Torsten May, Germany
1996 Vassili Jirov, Kazakhstan
2000 Alexander Lebziak, Russia

Heavyweight (91 kg/201 lbs)

1984 Henry Tillman, U.S.
1988 Ray Mercer, U.S.
1992 Felix Savon, Cuba
1996 Felix Savon, Cuba
2000 Felix Savon, Cuba

Super Heavyweight (91+ kg/201+ lbs)

(known as heavyweight, 1904-80)

1904 Samuel Berger, U.S.
1908 Albert Oldham, Great Britain
1920 Ronald Rawson, Great Britain
1924 Otto von Porat, Norway
1928 Arturo Rodriguez Jurado, Argentina
1932 Santiago Lovell, Argentina
1936 Herbert Runge, Germany
1948 Rafael Iglesias, Argentina
1952 H. Edward Sanders, U.S.
1956 T. Peter Rademacher, U.S.
1960 Franco De Piccoli, Italy
1964 Joe Frazier, U.S.
1968 George Foreman, U.S.
1972 Teofilo Stevenson, Cuba
1976 Teofilo Stevenson, Cuba
1980 Teofilo Stevenson, Cuba
1984 Tyrell Biggs, U.S.
1988 Lennox Lewis, Canada
1992 Roberto Balado, Cuba
1996 Vladimir Klitchko, Ukraine
2000 Audley Harrison, Britain

Sites of Summer Olympic Games

1896	Athens, Greece	**1924**	Paris, France	**1956**	Melbourne, Australia	**1984**	Los Angeles, U.S.
1900	Paris, France	**1928**	Amsterdam, Netherlands	**1960**	Rome, Italy	**1988**	Seoul, South Korea
1904	St. Louis, U.S.			**1964**	Tokyo, Japan	**1992**	Barcelona, Spain
1906*	Athens, Greece	**1932**	Los Angeles, U.S.	**1968**	Mexico City, Mexico	**1996**	Atlanta, U.S.
1908	London, England	**1936**	Berlin, Germany	**1972**	Munich, W. Germany	**2000**	Sydney, Australia
1912	Stockholm, Sweden	**1948**	London, England	**1976**	Montreal, Canada	**2004**	Athens, Greece
1920	Antwerp, Belgium	**1952**	Helsinki, Finland	**1980**	Moscow, USSR	**2008**	Beijing, China

*Games not recognized by International Olympic Committee. Games 6 (1916), 12 (1940), and 13 (1944) were not celebrated.

Olympic Information

The modern Olympic Games, first held in Athens, Greece, in 1896, were the result of efforts by Baron Pierre de Coubertin, a French educator, to promote interest in education and culture and to foster better international understanding through love of athletics. His source of inspiration was the ancient Greek Olympic Games, most notable of the 4 Panhellenic celebrations. The games were combined patriotic, religious, and athletic festivals held every 4 years. The first such recorded festival was held in 776 BC, the date from which the Greeks began to keep their calendar by "Olympiads," or 4-year spans between the games.

Baron de Coubertin enlisted 13 nations to send athletes to the first modern Olympics in 1896; now athletes from nearly 200 nations and territories compete in the Summer Olympics. The Winter Olympic Games were started in 1924.

Symbol: Five rings or circles, linked together to represent the sporting friendship of all peoples. They also symbolize 5 geographic areas—Europe, Asia, Africa, Australia, and America. Each ring is a different color—blue, yellow, black, green, or red.

Flag: The symbol of the 5 rings on a plain white background.

Creed: "The most important thing in the Olympic Games is not to win but to take part, just as the most important thing in life is not the triumph but the struggle. The essential thing is not to have conquered but to have fought well."

Motto: "Citius, Altius, Fortius." Latin meaning "swifter, higher, stronger."

Oath: "In the name of all competitors I promise that we will take part in these Olympic Games, respecting and abiding by the rules which govern them, in the true spirit of sportsmanship for the glory of sport and the honor of our teams."

Flame: The modern version of the flame was adopted in 1936. The torch used to kindle it is first lit by the sun's rays at Olympia, Greece, then carried to the site of the Games by relays of runners. Ships and planes are used when necessary.

PARALYMPICS

The first Olympic games for the disabled were held in Rome after the 1960 Summer Olympics; use of the name "paralympic" began with the 1964 games in Tokyo. The Paralympics are held by the Olympic host country in the same year and usually same city or venue. A goal of the Paralympics is to provide elite competition to athletes with functional disabilities that prevent their involvement in the Olympics. In 1976 the first Winter Paralympic Games were held, in Ornskoldsvik, Sweden.

The VIII Paralympic Winter Games were held Mar. 7-16, 2002, in Salt Lake City, Utah. Some 417 athletes from 35 countries competed in Alpine and Nordic skiing and ice sledge hockey. The U.S. led the medal standings with 43 (10 gold), followed by Germany, 33 (17 gold), and Austria 29 (9 gold). U.S. highlights included a gold medal for the sledge hockey team after a 4-3 overtime shootout victory over Norway and 4 gold medals for Alpine skier Sarah Will.

The XII Paralympic Games were scheduled for Sept. 17-28, 2004, in Athens, Greece. The IX Paralympic Winter Games were to be held Mar. 10-19, 2006, in Torino, Italy, where wheelchair curling was to be contested for the first time.

SPECIAL OLYMPICS

Special Olympics is an international program of year-round sports training and athletic competition dedicated to "empowering individuals with mental retardation." All 50 U.S. states, Washington, DC, and Guam have chapter offices. In addition, there are accredited Special Olympics programs in nearly 150 countries. Persons wishing to volunteer or find out more about Special Olympics can contact Special Olympics International Headquarters, 1325 G St. NW, Suite 500, Washington, DC 20005, or access the Special Olympics website at www.specialolympics.org

Special Olympics: 2001 World Winter Games, 2003 World Summer Games

The 7th Special Olympics World Winter Games were held Mar. 4-11, 2001, in Anchorage, AK. About 2,400 athletes from 69 countries competed for the 1,894 medals that were awarded. Also participating were more than 3,000 coaches and family members as well as some 6,000 volunteers. The competition included Alpine Skiing, Cross-Country Skiing, Floor Hockey, Figure Skating, Speed Skating, and Snowshoeing; and for the first time, Snowboarding was held as a demonstration sport.

The 11th Special Olympics World Summer Games, the first to be held outside the U.S., were scheduled for June 20-29, 2003, in Dublin, Ireland. More than 7,000 athletes, 3,000 coaches and official delegates, and 28,000 friends and family members were expected to participate. Scheduled individual competition included Athletics, Aquatics, Badminton, Bocce, Bowling, Cycling, Equestrian Sports, Golf, Gymnastics (Artistic and Rhythmic), Power lifting, Rollerskating, Table Tennis, and Tennis. Scheduled team sports were Basketball, Handball, Sailing, Soccer, and Volleyball. Kayaking and Pitch-and-Putt (a form of golf) were to be included as demonstration sports.

TRACK AND FIELD

World Track and Field Outdoor Records

As of Oct. 2002

The International Amateur Athletic Federation, the world body of track and field, recognizes only records in metric distances, except for the mile. *Pending ratification.**World best; marathon records not officially recognized by IAAF.

Men's Records

Running

Event	Record	Holder	Country	Date	Where made
100 meters	**9.78* s.**	Tim Montgomery	U.S.	Sept. 14, 2002	Paris, France
200 meters	**19.32 s.**	Michael Johnson	U.S.	Aug. 1, 1996	Atlanta, GA
400 meters	**43.18 s.**	Michael Johnson	U.S.	Aug. 26, 1999	Seville, Spain
800 meters	**1 m., 41.11 s.**	Wilson Kipketer	Denmark	Aug. 24, 1997	Cologne, Germany
1,000 meters	**2 m., 11.96 s.**	Noah Ngeny	Kenya	Sept. 5, 1999	Rieti, Italy
1,500 meters	**3 m., 26.00 s.**	Hicham El Guerrouj	Morocco	July 14, 1998	Rome, Italy
1 mile	**3 m., 43.13 s.**	Hicham El Guerrouj	Morocco	July 7, 1999	Rome, Italy
2,000 meters	**4 m., 44.79 s.**	Hicham El Guerrouj	Morocco	Sept. 7, 1999	Berlin, Germany
3,000 meters	**7 m., 20.67 s.**	Daniel Komen	Kenya	Sept. 1, 1996	Rieti, Italy
5,000 meters	**12 m., 39.36 s.**	Haile Gebrselassie	Ethiopia	June 13, 1998	Helsinki, Finland
10,000 meters	**26 m., 22.75 s.**	Haile Gebrselassie	Ethiopia	June 1,1998	Hengelo, Netherlands
20,000 meters	**56 m., 55.6 s.**	Arturo Barrios	Mexico	Mar. 30, 1991	La Fléche, France
25,000 meters	**1 hr., 13 m., 55.8 s.**	Toshihiko Seko	Japan	Mar. 22, 1981	Christchurch, NZ
3,000 meter stpl.	**7 m., 55.28 s.**	Brahim Boulami	Morocco	Aug. 8, 2001	Brussels, Belgium
Marathon**	**2 hr., 5m., 38s.**	Khalid Khannouchi	U.S.	April 14, 2002	London, England

Hurdles

Event	Record	Holder	Country	Date	Where made
110 meters	**12.91 s.**	Colin Jackson	Gr. Britain	Aug. 20, 1993	Stuttgart, Germany
400 meters	**46.78 s.**	Kevin Young	U.S.	Aug. 6, 1992	Barcelona, Spain

Relay Races

Event	Record	Holder	Country	Date	Where made
400 mtrs. (4x100)	**37.40 s.**	(Marsh, Burrell, Mitchell, Lewis)	U.S.	Aug. 8, 1992	Barcelona, Spain
		(Drummond, Cason, Mitchell, Burrell)	U.S.	Aug. 21, 1993	Stuttgart, Germany
800 mtrs. (4×200)	**1 m., 18.68 s.**	(Marsh, Burrell, Heard, Lewis)	U.S.	Apr. 17, 1994	Walnut, CA
1,600 mtrs. (4×400)	**2 m., 54.20 s.**	(Young, Pettigrew, Washington, Johnson)	U.S.	July 22, 1998	Long Island, NY
3,200 mtrs. (4×800)	**7 m., 03.89 s.**	(Elliott, Cook, Cram, Coe)	Gr. Britain	Aug. 30, 1982	London, England

Field Events

Event	Record	Holder	Country	Date	Where made
High jump	**2.45m** (8' ½")	Javier Sotomayor	Cuba	July 27, 1993	Salamanca, Spain
Long jump	**8.95m** (29' 4½")	Mike Powell	U.S.	Aug. 30, 1991	Tokyo, Japan
Triple jump	**18.29m** (60' ¼")	Jonathan Edwards	Gr. Britain	Aug. 7, 1995	Göteborg, Sweden
Pole vault	**6.14m** (20' 1¾")	Sergei Bubka	Ukraine	July 31, 1994	Sestriere, Italy
16-lb. shot put	**23.12m** (75' 10¼")	Randy Barnes	U.S.	May 20, 1990	Los Angeles, CA
Discus	**74.08m** (243' 0")	Juergen Schult	E. Germany	June 6, 1986	Neubrandenburg, Germany
Javelin	**98.48m** (323' 1")*	Jan Zelezny	Czech Rep.	May 25, 1996	Jena, Germany
16-lb. hammer	**86.74m** (284' 7")	Yuri Sedykh	USSR	Aug. 30, 1986	Stuttgart, W. Germany
Decathlon	**9,026 pts.**	Roman Sebrle	Czech Rep.	May 27, 2001	Götzis, Austria

Women's Records

Running

Event	Record	Holder	Country	Date	Where made
100 meters	**10.49 s.**	Florence Griffith Joyner	U.S.	July 16, 1988	Indianapolis, IN
200 meters	**21.34 s.**	Florence Griffith Joyner	U.S.	Sept. 29, 1988	Seoul, S. Korea
400 meters	**47.60 s.**	Marita Koch	E. Germany	Oct. 6, 1985	Canberra, Australia

Event	Record	Holder	Country	Date	Where made
800 meters	**1 m., 53.28 s.**	Jarmila Kratochvilova	Czech Rep.	July 26, 1983	Munich, Germany
1,000 meters	**2 m., 28.98 s.**	Svetlana Masterkova	Russia	Aug. 23, 1996	Brussels, Belgium
1,500 meters	**3 m., 50.46 s.**	Qu Yunxia	China	Sept. 11, 1993	Beijing, China
1 mile	**4 m., 12.56 s.**	Svetlana Masterkova	Russia	Aug. 14, 1996	Zurich, Switzerland
2,000 meters	**5 m., 25.36 s.**	Sonia O'Sullivan	Ireland	July 8, 1994	Edinburgh, Scotland
3,000 meters	**8 m., 06.11 s.**	Junxia Wang	China	Sept. 13, 1993	Beijing, China
3,000 meter stpl.	**9 m., 16.51* s.**	Alesya Turova	Belarus	July 27, 2002	Gdansk, Poland
5,000 meters	**14 m., 28.09 s.**	Bo Jiang	China	Oct. 23, 1997	Shanghai, China
10,000 meters	**29 m., 31.78 s.**	Junxia Wang	China	Sept. 8, 1993	Beijing, China
Marathon**	**2 h., 18 m., 47 s.**	Catherine Ndereba	Kenya	Oct. 7, 2001	Chicago, IL

Hurdles

Event	Record	Holder	Country	Date	Where made
100 meters	**12.21 s.**	Yordanka Donkova	Bulgaria	Aug. 20, 1988	Stara Zagora, Bulgaria
400 meters	**52.61 s.**	Kim Batten	U.S.	Aug. 11, 1995	Göteborg, Sweden

Relay Races

Event	Record	Holder	Country	Date	Where made
400 mtrs. (4×100)	**41.37 s.**	(Gladisch, Rieger, Auerswald, Goehr)	E. Germany	Oct. 6, 1985	Canberra, Australia
800 mtrs. (4×200)	**1 m., 27.46 s.**	U.S. "Blue" (Jenkins, Clarke, Richardson, Jamieson)	U.S.	Sept. 28, 2000	Philadelphia, PA
1,600 mtrs. (4×400)	**3 m., 15.17 s.**	(Ledovskaya, Nazarova, Pinigina, Bryzgina)	USSR	Oct. 1, 1988	Seoul, S. Korea
3,200 mtrs. (4×800)	**7 m., 50.17 s.**	(Olizarenko, Gurina, Borisova, Podyalovskaya)	USSR	Aug. 5, 1984	Moscow

Field Events

Event	Record	Holder	Country	Date	Where made
High jump	**2.09m** (6' 10¼")	Stefka Kostadinova	Bulgaria	Aug. 30, 1987	Rome, Italy
Long jump	**7.52m** (24' 8¼")	Galina Chistyakova	USSR	June 11, 1988	Leningrad
Triple jump	**15.50m** (50' 10¼1")	Inessa Kravets	Ukraine	Aug. 10, 1995	Göteborg, Sweden
Pole vault	**4.81m** (15' 9¼")	Stacy Dragila	U.S.	June 9, 2001	Palo Alto, CA
Shot put	**22.63m** (74' 3")	Natalya Lisovskaya	USSR	June 7, 1987	Moscow, Russia
Discus	**76.80m** (252' 0")	Gabriele Reinsch	E. Germany	July 9, 1988	Neubrandenburg,Germany
Hammer	**76.07m** (249' 7")	Mihaela Melinte	Romania	Aug. 29, 1999	Rüdlingen, Switzerland
Javelin	**71.54m** (234' 8")*	Osleidys Menéndez	Cuba	July 1, 2001	Réthymno, Greece
Heptathlon	**7,291 pts.**	Jackie Joyner-Kersee	U.S.	Sept. 23-24, 1988	Seoul, S. Korea

World Track and Field Indoor Records

As of Oct. 2002

The International Amateur Athletic Federation first recognized world indoor track and field records on Jan. 1, 1987. World indoor bests set prior to Jan. 1, 1987, are subject to approval as world records providing they meet the IAAF world records criteria, including drug testing. Criteria for indoor and outdoor records are the same, except that a track performance cannot be set on an indoor track larger than 200 meters. (a)=altitude. * Pending ratification.

Men's Records

Event	Record	Holder	Country	Date	Where made
50 meters	**5.56** (a)	Donovan Bailey	Canada	Feb. 9, 1996	Reno, NV
	5.56	Maurice Greene	U.S.	Feb. 13, 1999	Los Angeles, CA
60 meters	**6.39**	Maurice Greene	U.S.	Mar. 3, 2001	Atlanta, GA
	6.39	Maurice Greene	U.S.	Feb. 3, 1998	Madrid, Spain
200 meters	**19.92**	Frankie Fredericks	Namibia	Feb. 18, 1996	Lievin, France
400 meters	**44.63**	Michael Johnson	U.S.	Mar. 4, 1995	Atlanta, GA
800 meters	**1:42.67**	Wilson Kipketer	Denmark	Mar. 9, 1997	Paris, France
1,000 meters	**2:14.96**	Wilson Kipketer	Denmark	Feb. 20, 2000	Birmingham, England
1,500 meters	**3:31.18**	Hicham El Guerrouj	Morocco	Feb. 2, 1997	Stuttgart, Germany
1 mile	**3:48.45**	Hicham El Guerrouj	Morocco	Feb. 12, 1997	Ghent, Belgium
3,000 meters	**7:24.90**	Daniel Komen	Kenya	Feb. 6, 1998	Budapest, Hungary
5,000 meters	**12:50.38**	Haile Gebrselassie	Ethiopia	Feb. 14, 1999	Birmingham, England
50-meter hurdles	**6.25**	Mark McKoy	Canada	Mar. 5, 1986	Kobe, Japan
60-meter hurdles	**7.30**	Colin Jackson	Gr. Britain	Mar. 6, 1994	Sindelfingen, Germany
High jump	**2.43m** (7' 11½")	Javier Sotomayor	Cuba	Mar. 4, 1989	Budapest, Hungary
Pole vault	**6.15m** (20' 2")	Sergei Bubka	Ukraine	Feb. 21, 1993	Donyetsk, Ukraine
Long jump	**8.79m** (28' 10¼")	Carl Lewis	U.S.	Jan. 27, 1984	New York, NY
Triple jump	**17.83** (58' 6")	Aliecer Urrutia	Cuba	Mar. 1, 1997	Sindelfingen, Germany
Shot put	**22.66m** (74' 4¼")	Randy Barnes	U.S.	Jan. 20, 1989	Los Angeles, CA

Women's Records

Event	Record	Holder	Country	Date	Where made
50 meters	**5.96**	Irina Privalova	Russia	Feb. 9, 1995	Madrid, Spain
60 meters	**6.92**	Irina Privalova	Russia	Feb. 9, 1995	Madrid, Spain
		Irina Privalova	Russia	Feb. 11, 1993	Madrid, Spain
200 meters	**21.87**	Merlene Ottey	Jamaica	Feb. 13, 1993	Lievin, France
400 meters	**49.59**	Jarmila Kratochvilova	Czechoslov.	Mar. 7, 1982	Milan, Italy
800 meters	**1:55.82***	Jolanda Ceplak	Slovenia	Mar. 3, 2002	Vienna, Austria
1,000 meters	**2:30.94**	Maria Mutola	Mozambique	Feb. 25, 1999	Stockholm, Sweden
1,500 meters	**4:00.27**	Doina Melinte	Romania	Feb. 9, 1990	E. Rutherford, NJ
1 mile	**4:17.14**	Doina Melinte	Romania	Feb. 9, 1990	E. Rutherford, NJ
3,000 meters	**8:29.15**	Berhane Adere	Ethiopia	Mar. 3, 2002	Stuttgart, Germany
5,000 meters	**14:47.35**	Gabriela Szabo	Romania	Feb. 13, 1999	Dortmund, Germany
50-meter hurdles	**6.58**	Cornelia Oschkenat	E. Germany	Feb. 20, 1988	Berlin, Germany
60-meter hurdles	**7.69**	Lyudmila Engquist	USSR	Feb. 4, 1990	Chelyabinsk, USSR
High jump	**2.07m** (6' 9½")	Heike Henkel	Germany	Feb. 8, 1992	Karlsruhe, Germany
Pole vault	**4.75*m** (15' 7")	Svetlana Feofanova	Russia	Mar. 3, 2002	Vienna, Austria
Long jump	**7.37m** (24' 2¼")	Heike Drechsler	E. Germany	Feb. 13, 1988	Vienna, Austria
Triple jump	**15.16m** (49' 9")	Ashia Hansen	Gr. Britain	Feb. 28, 1998	Valencia, Spain
Shot put	**22.50m** (73' 10")	Helena Fibingerova	Czechoslovakia	Feb. 19, 1977	Jablonec, Czechoslovakia

BASEBALL

No Strike!; All-Star Tie; Bonds Joins 600-Homer Club

With round-the-clock negotiations on the eve of the Aug. 30 deadline, Major League Baseball avoided its 9th work stoppage. Still feeling the effects of the season-ending strike of 1994, both sides feared the public relations fallout of another strike. The deal was announced minutes before the noon deadline. Players agreed to random drug testing for the 1st time, and accepted greater revenue sharing and higher "luxury taxes" on payrolls, designed in part to limit salary growth. The owners agreed to more revenue sharing and no contraction of teams for the duration of the deal, which runs through the 2006 season. Division winners in the regular season included Atlanta (who won a record 11th straight NL East title), Oakland (AL West champs who won an AL-record 20 straight games in Aug./Sept.), and Minnesota (who topped the AL Central after having been targeted by baseball owners for contraction in the off-season). Anaheim won the AL wildcard just 1 season after finishing 41 games out of 1st. For the 2nd time since 1961, the All-Star Game ended in a tie. Comm. Bud Selig was forced to call the 7-7 game at Milwaukee's Miller Park in the 11th inning, when both managers ran out of available pitchers. The newly named Ted Williams MVP Award was not given. San Francisco's Barry Bonds reached the World Series for the 1st time in his 17-year career. The 4-time MVP won the NL batting title (.370) and broke his own record for walks in a season (198). His .582 on-base percentage broke Ted Williams' 1941 mark of .553. On Aug. 9, Bonds hit his 600th home run, only the 4th player to do so. He finished the season with 613. John Smoltz of the Braves set an NL record with 55 saves.

Major League Pennant Winners, 1901–1968

National League						American League					
Year	Winner	Won	Lost	Pct	Manager	Year	Winner	Won	Lost	Pct	Manager
1901	Pittsburgh	90	49	.647	Clarke	1901	Chicago	83	53	.610	Griffith
1902	Pittsburgh	103	36	.741	Clarke	1902	Philadelphia	83	53	.610	Mack
1903	Pittsburgh	91	49	.650	Clarke	1903	Boston	91	47	.659	Collins
1904	New York	106	47	.693	McGraw	1904	Boston	95	59	.617	Collins
1905	New York	105	48	.686	McGraw	1905	Philadelphia	92	56	.622	Mack
1906	Chicago	116	36	.763	Chance	1906	Chicago	93	58	.616	Jones
1907	Chicago	107	45	.704	Chance	1907	Detroit	92	58	.613	Jennings
1908	Chicago	99	55	.643	Chance	1908	Detroit	90	63	.588	Jennings
1909	Pittsburgh	110	42	.724	Clarke	1909	Detroit	98	54	.645	Jennings
1910	Chicago	104	50	.675	Chance	1910	Philadelphia	102	48	.680	Mack
1911	New York	99	54	.647	McGraw	1911	Philadelphia	101	50	.669	Mack
1912	New York	103	48	.682	McGraw	1912	Boston	105	47	.691	Stahl
1913	New York	101	51	.664	McGraw	1913	Philadelphia	96	57	.627	Mack
1914	Boston	94	59	.614	Stallings	1914	Philadelphia	99	53	.651	Mack
1915	Philadelphia	90	62	.592	Moran	1915	Boston	101	50	.669	Carrigan
1916	Brooklyn	94	60	.610	Robinson	1916	Boston	91	63	.591	Carrigan
1917	New York	98	56	.636	McGraw	1917	Chicago	100	54	.649	Rowland
1918	Chicago	84	45	.651	Mitchell	1918	Boston	75	51	.595	Barrow
1919	Cincinnati	96	44	.686	Moran	1919	Chicago	88	52	.629	Gleason
1920	Brooklyn	93	60	.604	Robinson	1920	Cleveland	98	56	.636	Speaker
1921	New York	94	56	.614	McGraw	1921	New York	98	55	.641	Huggins
1922	New York	93	61	.604	McGraw	1922	New York	94	60	.610	Huggins
1923	New York	95	58	.621	McGraw	1923	New York	98	54	.645	Huggins
1924	New York	93	60	.608	McGraw	1924	Washington	92	62	.597	Harris
1925	Pittsburgh	95	58	.621	McKechnie	1925	Washington	96	55	.636	Harris
1926	St. Louis	89	65	.578	Hornsby	1926	New York	91	63	.591	Huggins
1927	Pittsburgh	94	60	.610	Bush	1927	New York	110	44	.714	Huggins
1928	St. Louis	95	59	.617	McKechnie	1928	New York	101	53	.656	Huggins
1929	Chicago	98	54	.645	McCarthy	1929	Philadelphia	104	46	.693	Mack
1930	St. Louis	92	62	.597	Street	1930	Philadelphia	102	52	.662	Mack
1931	St. Louis	101	53	.656	Street	1931	Philadelphia	107	45	.704	Mack
1932	Chicago	90	64	.584	Grimm	1932	New York	107	47	.695	McCarthy
1933	New York	91	61	.599	Terry	1933	Washington	99	53	.651	Cronin
1934	St. Louis	95	58	.621	Frisch	1934	Detroit	101	53	.656	Cochrane
1935	Chicago	100	54	.649	Grimm	1935	Detroit	93	58	.616	Cochrane
1936	New York	91	62	.597	Terry	1936	New York	102	51	.667	McCarthy
1937	New York	95	57	.625	Terry	1937	New York	102	52	.662	McCarthy
1938	Chicago	89	63	.586	Hartnett	1938	New York	99	53	.651	McCarthy
1939	Cincinnati	97	57	.630	McKechnie	1939	New York	106	45	.702	McCarthy
1940	Cincinnati	100	53	.654	McKechnie	1940	Detroit	90	64	.584	Baker
1941	Brooklyn	100	54	.649	Durocher	1941	New York	101	53	.656	McCarthy
1942	St. Louis	106	48	.688	Southworth	1942	New York	103	51	.669	McCarthy
1943	St. Louis	105	49	.682	Southworth	1943	New York	98	56	.636	McCarthy
1944	St. Louis	105	49	.682	Southworth	1944	St. Louis	89	65	.578	Sewell
1945	Chicago	98	56	.636	Grimm	1945	Detroit	88	65	.575	O'Neill
1946	St. Louis	98	58	.628	Dyer	1946	Boston	104	50	.675	Cronin
1947	Brooklyn	94	60	.610	Shotton	1947	New York	97	57	.630	Harris
1948	Boston	91	62	.595	Southworth	1948	Cleveland	97	58	.626	Boudreau
1949	Brooklyn	97	57	.630	Shotton	1949	New York	97	57	.630	Stengel
1950	Philadelphia	91	63	.591	Sawyer	1950	New York	98	56	.636	Stengel
1951	New York	98	59	.624	Durocher	1951	New York	98	56	.636	Stengel
1952	Brooklyn	96	57	.627	Dressen	1952	New York	95	59	.617	Stengel
1953	Brooklyn	105	49	.682	Dressen	1953	New York	99	52	.656	Stengel
1954	New York	97	57	.630	Durocher	1954	Cleveland	111	43	.721	Lopez
1955	Brooklyn	98	55	.641	Alston	1955	New York	96	58	.623	Stengel
1956	Brooklyn	93	61	.604	Alston	1956	New York	97	57	.630	Stengel
1957	Milwaukee	95	59	.617	Haney	1957	New York	98	56	.636	Stengel
1958	Milwaukee	92	62	.597	Haney	1958	New York	92	62	.597	Stengel
1959	Los Angeles	88	68	.564	Alston	1959	Chicago	94	60	.610	Lopez
1960	Pittsburgh	95	59	.617	Murtaugh	1960	New York	97	57	.630	Stengel
1961	Cincinnati	93	61	.604	Hutchinson	1961	New York	109	53	.673	Houk
1962	San Francisco	103	62	.624	Dark	1962	New York	96	66	.593	Houk
1963	Los Angeles	99	63	.611	Alston	1963	New York	104	57	.646	Houk

National League

Year	Winner	Won	Lost	Pct	Manager
1964	St. Louis	93	69	.574	Keane
1965	Los Angeles	97	65	.599	Alston
1966	Los Angeles	95	67	.586	Alston
1967	St. Louis	101	60	.627	Schoendienst
1968	St. Louis	97	65	.599	Schoendienst

American League

Year	Winner	Won	Lost	Pct	Manager
1964	New York	99	63	.611	Berra
1965	Minnesota	102	60	.630	Mele
1966	Baltimore	97	63	.606	Bauer
1967	Boston	92	70	.568	Williams
1968	Detroit	103	59	.636	Smith

Major League Pennant Winners, 1969-2002

National League

	East					West					Pennant
Year	Winner	W	L	Pct	Manager	Winner	W	L	Pct	Manager	Winner
1969	N.Y. Mets	100	62	.617	Hodges	Atlanta	93	69	.574	Harris	New York
1970	Pittsburgh	89	73	.549	Murtaugh	Cincinnati	102	60	.630	Anderson	Cincinnati
1971	Pittsburgh	97	65	.599	Murtaugh	San Francisco	90	72	.556	Fox	Pittsburgh
1972	Pittsburgh	96	59	.619	Virdon	Cincinnati	95	59	.617	Anderson	Cincinnati
1973	N.Y. Mets	82	79	.509	Berra	Cincinnati	99	63	.611	Anderson	New York
1974	Pittsburgh	88	74	.543	Murtaugh	Los Angeles	102	60	.630	Alston	Los Angeles
1975	Pittsburgh	92	69	.571	Murtaugh	Cincinnati	108	54	.667	Anderson	Cincinnati
1976	Philadelphia	101	61	.623	Ozark	Cincinnati	102	60	.630	Anderson	Cincinnati
1977	Philadelphia	101	61	.623	Ozark	Los Angeles	98	64	.605	Lasorda	Los Angeles
1978	Philadelphia	90	72	.556	Ozark	Los Angeles	95	67	.586	Lasorda	Los Angeles
1979	Pittsburgh	98	64	.605	Tanner	Cincinnati	90	71	.559	McNamara	Pittsburgh
1980	Philadelphia	91	71	.562	Green	Houston	93	70	.571	Virdon	Philadelphia
1981(a)	Philadelphia	34	21	.618	Green	Los Angeles	36	21	.632	Lasorda	(c)
1981(b)	Montreal	30	23	.566	Williams, Fanning	Houston	33	20	.623	Virdon	Los Angeles
1982	St. Louis	92	70	.568	Herzog	Atlanta	89	73	.549	Torre	St. Louis
1983	Philadelphia	90	72	.556	Corrales, Owens	Los Angeles	91	71	.562	Lasorda	Philadelphia
1984	Chicago	96	65	.596	Frey	San Diego	92	70	.568	Williams	San Diego
1985	St. Louis	101	61	.623	Herzog	Los Angeles	95	67	.586	Lasorda	St. Louis
1986	N.Y. Mets	108	54	.667	Johnson	Houston	96	66	.593	Lanier	New York
1987	St. Louis	95	67	.586	Herzog	San Francisco	90	72	.556	Craig	St. Louis
1988	N.Y. Mets	100	60	.625	Johnson	Los Angeles	94	67	.584	Lasorda	Los Angeles
1989	Chicago	93	69	.571	Zimmer	San Francisco	92	70	.568	Craig	San Francisco
1990	Pittsburgh	95	67	.586	Leyland	Cincinnati	91	71	.562	Piniella	Cincinnati
1991	Pittsburgh	98	64	.605	Leyland	Atlanta	94	68	.580	Cox	Atlanta
1992	Pittsburgh	96	66	.593	Leyland	Atlanta	98	64	.605	Cox	Atlanta
1993	Philadelphia	97	65	.599	Fregosi	Atlanta	104	58	.642	Cox	Philadelphia

Year	Division	Winner	W	L	Pct	Manager	Playoffs	Pennant Winner
1994(d)	East	Montreal	74	40	.649	Alou	—	—
	West	Cincinnati	66	48	.579	Johnson		
	Central	Los Angeles	58	56	.509	Lasorda		
1995	East	Atlanta	90	54	.625	Cox	Atlanta 3, Colorado* 1	Atlanta
	Central	Cincinnati	85	59	.590	Johnson	Cincinnati 3, Los Angeles 0	
	West	Los Angeles	78	66	.542	Lasorda	Atlanta 4, Cincinnati 0	
1996	East	Atlanta	96	66	.593	Cox	Atlanta 3, Los Angeles* 0	Atlanta
	Central	St. Louis	88	74	.543	La Russa	St. Louis 3, San Diego 0	
	West	San Diego	91	71	.562	Bochy	Atlanta 4, St. Louis 3	
1997	East	Atlanta	101	61	.623	Cox	Atlanta 3, Houston 0	Florida* (e)
	Central	Houston	84	78	.519	Dierker	Florida* 3, San Francisco 0	
	West	San Francisco	90	72	.556	Baker	Florida* 4, Atlanta 2	
1998	East	Atlanta	106	56	.654	Cox	Atlanta 3, Chicago* 0	San Diego
	Central	Houston	102	60	.630	Dierker	San Diego 3, Houston 1	
	West	San Diego	97	64	.602	Bochy	San Diego 4, Atlanta 2	
1999	East	Atlanta	103	59	.636	Cox	Atlanta 3, Houston 1	Atlanta
	Central	Houston	97	65	.599	Dierker	New York* 3, Arizona 1	
	West	Arizona	100	62	.617	Showalter	Atlanta 4, New York 2	
2000	East	Atlanta	95	67	.586	Cox	St. Louis 3, Atlanta 0	New York* (f)
	Central	St. Louis	95	67	.586	La Russa	New York* 3, San Francisco 1	
	West	San Francisco	97	65	.599	Baker	New York* 4, St. Louis 1	
2001	East	Atlanta	88	74	.543	Cox	Atlanta 3, Houston 0	Arizona
	Central	Houston	93	69	.574	Dierker	Arizona 3, St. Louis* 2	
	West	Arizona	92	70	.568	Brenly	Arizona 4, Atlanta 1	
2002	East	Atlanta	101	59	.631	Cox	St. Louis 3, Arizona 0	San Francisco* (g)
	Central	St. Louis	97	65	.599	La Russa	San Francisco* 3, Atlanta 2	
	West	Arizona	98	64	.605	Brenly	San Francisco 4, St. Louis 1	

American League

	East					West					Pennant
Year	Winner	W	L	Pct	Manager	Winner	W	L	Pct	Manager	Winner
1969	Baltimore	109	53	.673	Weaver	Minnesota	97	65	.599	Martin	Baltimore
1970	Baltimore	108	54	.667	Weaver	Minnesota	98	64	.605	Rigney	Baltimore
1971	Baltimore	101	57	.639	Weaver	Oakland	101	60	.627	Williams	Baltimore
1972	Detroit	86	70	.551	Martin	Oakland	93	62	.600	Williams	Oakland
1973	Baltimore	97	65	.599	Weaver	Oakland	94	68	.580	Williams	Oakland
1974	Baltimore	91	71	.562	Weaver	Oakland	90	72	.556	Dark	Oakland
1975	Boston	95	65	.594	Johnson	Oakland	98	64	.605	Dark	Boston
1976	New York	97	62	.610	Martin	Kansas City	90	72	.556	Herzog	New York
1977	New York	100	62	.617	Martin	Kansas City	102	60	.630	Herzog	New York
1978	New York	100	63	.613	Martin, Lemon	Kansas City	92	70	.568	Herzog	New York
1979	Baltimore	102	57	.642	Weaver	California	88	74	.543	Fregosi	Baltimore
1980	New York	103	59	.636	Howser	Kansas City	97	65	.599	Frey	Kansas City
1981(a)	New York	34	22	.607	Michael	Oakland	37	23	.617	Martin	(c)
1981(b)	Milwaukee	31	22	.585	Rodgers	Kansas City	30	23	.566	Frey, Howser	New York
1982	Milwaukee	95	67	.586	Rodgers, Kuenn	California	93	69	.574	Mauch	Milwaukee
1983	Baltimore	98	64	.605	Altobelli	Chicago	99	63	.611	La Russa	Baltimore

	East					West					Pennant
Year	Winner	W	L	Pct	Manager	Winner	W	L	Pct	Manager	Winner
1984	Detroit	104	58	.642	Anderson	Kansas City	84	78	.519	Howser	Detroit
1985	Toronto	99	62	.615	Cox	Kansas City	91	71	.562	Howser	Kansas City
1986	Boston	95	66	.590	McNamara	California	92	70	.568	Mauch	Boston
1987	Detroit	98	64	.605	Anderson	Minnesota	85	77	.525	Kelly	Minnesota
1988	Boston	89	73	.549	McNamara, Morgan	Oakland	104	58	.642	La Russa	Oakland
1989	Toronto	89	73	.549	Williams, Gaston	Oakland	99	63	.611	La Russa	Oakland
1990	Boston	88	74	.543	Morgan	Oakland	103	59	.636	La Russa	Oakland
1991	Toronto	91	71	.562	Gaston	Minnesota	95	67	.586	Kelly	Minnesota
1992	Toronto	96	66	.593	Gaston	Oakland	96	66	.593	La Russa	Toronto
1993	Toronto	95	67	.586	Gaston	Chicago	94	68	.580	Lamont	Toronto

Year	Division	Winner	W	L	Pct	Manager	Playoffs	Pennant Winner
1994(d)	East	New York	70	43	.619	Showalter	—	—
	Central	Chicago	67	46	.593	Lamont		
	West	Texas	52	62	.456	Kennedy		
1995	East	Boston	86	58	.597	Kennedy	Cleveland 3, Boston 0	Cleveland
	Central	Cleveland	100	44	.694	Hargrove	Seattle 3, New York* 2	
	West	Seattle	79	66	.545	Piniella	Cleveland 4, Seattle 2	
1996	East	New York	92	70	.568	Torre	Baltimore* 3, Cleveland 1	New York
	Central	Cleveland	99	62	.615	Hargrove	New York 3, Texas 1	
	West	Texas	90	72	.556	Oates	New York 4, Baltimore* 1	
1997	East	Baltimore	98	64	.605	Johnson	Baltimore 3, Seattle 1	Cleveland
	Central	Cleveland	86	75	.534	Hargrove	Cleveland 3, New York* 2	
	West	Seattle	90	72	.556	Piniella	Cleveland 4, Baltimore 2	
1998	East	New York	114	48	.704	Torre	New York 3, Texas 0	New York
	Central	Cleveland	89	73	.549	Hargrove	Cleveland 3, Boston* 1	
	West	Texas	88	74	.543	Oates	New York 4, Cleveland 2	
1999	East	New York	98	64	.605	Torre	New York 3, Texas 0	New York
	Central	Cleveland	97	65	.599	Hargrove	Boston* 3, Cleveland 2	
	West	Texas	95	67	.586	Oates	New York 4, Boston* 1	
2000	East	New York	87	74	.540	Torre	New York 3, Oakland 2	New York
	Central	Chicago	95	67	.586	Manuel	Seattle* 3, Chicago 0	
	West	Oakland	91	70	.565	Howe	New York 4, Seattle* 2	
2001	East	New York	95	65	.594	Torre	Seattle 3, Cleveland 2	New York
	Central	Cleveland	91	71	.562	Manuel	New York 3, Oakland 2	
	West	Seattle	116	46	.716	Piniella	New York 4, Seattle* 1	
2002	East	New York	103	58	.640	Torre	Anaheim* 3, New York 1	Anaheim* (h)
	Central	Minnesota	94	67	.584	Gardenhire	Minnesota 3, Oakland 2	
	West	Oakland	103	59	.636	Howe	Anaheim* 4, Minnesota 1	

*Wild card team. (a) First half. (b) Second half. (c) Montreal, L.A., N.Y. Yankees, and Oakland won the divisional playoffs. (d) In Aug. 1994, a players' strike began that caused the cancellation of the remainder of the season, the playoffs, and the World Series. Teams listed as division "winners" for 1994 were leading their divisions at the time of the strike. (e) Florida manager: Jim Leyland. (f) New York manager Bobby Valentine. (g) San Francisco manager: Dusty Baker. (h) Anaheim manager: Mike Scioscia.

Home Run Leaders

Note: Asterisk (*) indicates the all-time single-season record for each league.

National League

Year	Player, Team	HR
1901	Sam Crawford, Cincinnati	16
1902	Thomas Leach, Pittsburgh	6
1903	James Sheckard, Brooklyn	9
1904	Harry Lumley, Brooklyn	9
1905	Fred Odwell, Cincinnati	9
1906	Timothy Jordan, Brooklyn	12
1907	David Brain, Boston	10
1908	Timothy Jordan, Brooklyn	12
1909	Red Murray, New York	7
1910	Fred Beck, Boston; Frank Schulte, Chicago	10
1911	Frank Schulte, Chicago	21
1912	Henry Zimmerman, Chicago	14
1913	Gavvy Cravath, Philadelphia	19
1914	Gavvy Cravath, Philadelphia	19
1915	Gavvy Cravath, Philadelphia	24
1916	Dave Robertson, N.Y.; Fred (Cy) Williams, Chi.	12
1917	Dave Robertson, N.Y.; Gavvy Cravath, Phi.	12
1918	Gavvy Cravath, Philadelphia	8
1919	Gavvy Cravath, Philadelphia	12
1920	Cy Williams, Philadelphia	15
1921	George Kelly, New York	23
1922	Rogers Hornsby, St. Louis	42
1923	Cy Williams, Philadelphia	41
1924	Jacques Fournier, Brooklyn	27
1925	Rogers Hornsby, St. Louis	39
1926	Hack Wilson, Chicago	21
1927	Hack Wilson, Chicago; Cy Williams, Philadelphia	30
1928	Hack Wilson, Chicago; Jim Bottomley, St. Louis	31
1929	Chuck Klein, Philadelphia	43
1930	Hack Wilson, Chicago	56
1931	Chuck Klein, Philadelphia	31
1932	Chuck Klein, Philadelphia; Mel Ott, New York	38
1933	Chuck Klein, Philadelphia	28
1934	Rip Collins, St. Louis; Mel Ott, New York	35
1935	Walter Berger, Boston	34
1936	Mel Ott, New York	33

American League

Year	Player, Team	HR
1901	Napoleon Lajoie, Philadelphia	13
1902	Socks Seybold, Philadelphia	16
1903	Buck Freeman, Boston	13
1904	Harry Davis, Philadelphia	10
1905	Harry Davis, Philadelphia	8
1906	Harry Davis, Philadelphia	12
1907	Harry Davis, Philadelphia	8
1908	Sam Crawford, Detroit	7
1909	Ty Cobb, Detroit	9
1910	Jake Stahl, Boston	10
1911	J. Franklin Baker, Philadelphia	9
1912	J. Franklin Baker, Philadelphia; Tris Speaker, Boston	10
1913	J. Franklin Baker, Philadelphia	13
1914	J. Franklin Baker, Philadelphia	9
1915	Robert Roth, Chicago-Cleveland	7
1916	Wally Pipp, New York	12
1917	Wally Pipp, New York	9
1918	Babe Ruth, Boston; Tilly Walker, Philadelphia	11
1919	Babe Ruth, Boston	29
1920	Babe Ruth, New York	54
1921	Babe Ruth, New York	59
1922	Ken Williams, St. Louis	39
1923	Babe Ruth, New York	41
1924	Babe Ruth, New York	46
1925	Bob Meusel, New York	33
1926	Babe Ruth, New York	47
1927	Babe Ruth, New York	60
1928	Babe Ruth, New York	54
1929	Babe Ruth, New York	46
1930	Babe Ruth, New York	49
1931	Babe Ruth, Lou Gehrig, both New York	46
1932	Jimmie Foxx, Philadelphia	58
1933	Jimmie Foxx, Philadelphia	48
1934	Lou Gehrig, New York	49
1935	Jimmie Foxx, Philadelphia; Hank Greenberg, Detroit	36
1936	Lou Gehrig, New York	49

National League

Year	Player, Team	HR
1937	Mel Ott, New York; Joe Medwick, St. Louis	31
1938	Mel Ott, New York	36
1939	John Mize, St. Louis	28
1940	John Mize, St. Louis	43
1941	Dolph Camilli, Brooklyn	34
1942	Mel Ott, New York	30
1943	Bill Nicholson, Chicago	29
1944	Bill Nicholson, Chicago	33
1945	Tommy Holmes, Boston	28
1946	Ralph Kiner, Pittsburgh	23
1947	Ralph Kiner, Pittsburgh; John Mize, New York	51
1948	Ralph Kiner, Pittsburgh; John Mize, New York	40
1949	Ralph Kiner, Pittsburgh	54
1950	Ralph Kiner, Pittsburgh	47
1951	Ralph Kiner, Pittsburgh	42
1952	Ralph Kiner, Pittsburgh; Hank Sauer, Chicago	37
1953	Ed Mathews, Milwaukee	47
1954	Ted Kluszewski, Cincinnati	49
1955	Willie Mays, New York	51
1956	Duke Snider, Brooklyn	43
1957	Hank Aaron, Milwaukee	44
1958	Ernie Banks, Chicago	47
1959	Ed Mathews, Milwaukee	46
1960	Ernie Banks, Chicago	41
1961	Orlando Cepeda, San Francisco	46
1962	Willie Mays, San Francisco	49
1963	Hank Aaron, Milwaukee; Willie McCovey, S.F.	44
1964	Willie Mays, San Francisco	47
1965	Willie Mays, San Francisco	52
1966	Hank Aaron, Atlanta	44
1967	Hank Aaron, Atlanta	39
1968	Willie McCovey, San Francisco	36
1969	Willie McCovey, San Francisco	45
1970	Johnny Bench, Cincinnati	45
1971	Willie Stargell, Pittsburgh	48
1972	Johnny Bench, Cincinnati	40
1973	Willie Stargell, Pittsburgh	44
1974	Mike Schmidt, Philadelphia	36
1975	Mike Schmidt, Philadelphia	38
1976	Mike Schmidt, Philadelphia	38
1977	George Foster, Cincinnati	52
1978	George Foster, Cincinnati	40
1979	Dave Kingman, Chicago	48
1980	Mike Schmidt, Philadelphia	48
1981	Mike Schmidt, Philadelphia	31
1982	Dave Kingman, New York	37
1983	Mike Schmidt, Philadelphia	40
1984	Mike Schmidt, Phi.; Dale Murphy, Atlanta	36
1985	Dale Murphy, Atlanta	37
1986	Mike Schmidt, Philadelphia	37
1987	Andre Dawson, Chicago	49
1988	Darryl Strawberry, New York	39
1989	Kevin Mitchell, San Francisco	47
1990	Ryne Sandberg, Chicago	40
1991	Howard Johnson, New York	38
1992	Fred McGriff, San Diego	35
1993	Barry Bonds, San Francisco	46
1994	Matt Williams, San Francisco	43
1995	Dante Bichette, Colorado	40
1996	Andres Galarraga, Colorado	47
1997[1]	Larry Walker, Colorado	49
1998	Mark McGwire, St. Louis	70
1999	Mark McGwire, St. Louis	65
2000	Sammy Sosa, Chicago	50
2001	Barry Bonds, San Francisco	*73
2002	Sammy Sosa, Chicago	49

American League

Year	Player, Team	HR
1937	Joe DiMaggio, New York	46
1938	Hank Greenberg, Detroit	58
1939	Jimmie Foxx, Boston	35
1940	Hank Greenberg, Detroit	41
1941	Ted Williams, Boston	37
1942	Ted Williams, Boston	36
1943	Rudy York, Detroit	34
1944	Nick Etten, New York	22
1945	Vern Stephens, St. Louis	24
1946	Hank Greenberg, Detroit	44
1947	Ted Williams, Boston	32
1948	Joe DiMaggio, New York	39
1949	Ted Williams, Boston	43
1950	Al Rosen, Cleveland	37
1951	Gus Zernial, Chicago-Philadelphia	33
1952	Larry Doby, Cleveland	32
1953	Al Rosen, Cleveland	43
1954	Larry Doby, Cleveland	32
1955	Mickey Mantle, New York	37
1956	Mickey Mantle, New York	52
1957	Roy Sievers, Washington	42
1958	Mickey Mantle, New York	42
1959	Rocky Colavito, Cleve.; Harmon Killebrew, Wash.	42
1960	Mickey Mantle, New York	40
1961	Roger Maris, New York	*61
1962	Harmon Killebrew, Minnesota	48
1963	Harmon Killebrew, Minnesota	45
1964	Harmon Killebrew, Minnesota	49
1965	Tony Conigliaro, Boston	32
1966	Frank Robinson, Baltimore	49
1967	Carl Yastrzemski, Boston; Harmon Killebrew, Minn.	44
1968	Frank Howard, Washington	44
1969	Harmon Killebrew, Minnesota	49
1970	Frank Howard, Washington	44
1971	Bill Melton, Chicago	33
1972	Dick Allen, Chicago	37
1973	Reggie Jackson, Oakland	32
1974	Dick Allen, Chicago	32
1975	George Scott, Milwaukee; Reggie Jackson, Oakland	36
1976	Graig Nettles, New York	32
1977	Jim Rice, Boston	39
1978	Jim Rice, Boston	46
1979	Gorman Thomas, Milwaukee	45
1980	Reggie Jackson, New York; Ben Oglivie, Milwaukee	41
1981	Bobby Grich, California; Tony Armas, Oakland; Dwight Evans, Boston; Eddie Murray, Baltimore	22
1982	Gorman Thomas, Milwaukee; Reggie Jackson, Cal.	39
1983	Jim Rice, Boston	39
1984	Tony Armas, Boston	43
1985	Darrell Evans, Detroit	40
1986	Jesse Barfield, Toronto	40
1987	Mark McGwire, Oakland	49
1988	Jose Canseco, Oakland	42
1989	Fred McGriff, Toronto	36
1990	Cecil Fielder, Detroit	51
1991	Cecil Fielder, Detroit; Jose Canseco, Oakland	44
1992	Juan Gonzalez, Texas	43
1993	Juan Gonzalez, Texas	46
1994	Ken Griffey Jr., Seattle	40
1995	Albert Belle, Cleveland	50
1996	Mark McGwire, Oakland	52
1997[1]	Ken Griffey Jr., Seattle	56
1998	Ken Griffey Jr., Seattle	56
1999	Ken Griffey Jr., Seattle	48
2000	Troy Glaus, Anaheim	47
2001	Alex Rodriguez, Texas	52
2002	Alex Rodriguez, Texas	57

(1) In 1997, Mark McGwire hit 58 home runs; 34 with the Oakland Athletics (AL) and 24 with the St. Louis Cardinals (NL).

Runs Batted In Leaders

Note: Asterisk (*) indicates the all-time single-season record for each league since beginning of "modern" era in 1901.

National League

Year	Player, Team	RBI
1907	Sherwood Magee, Philadelphia	85
1908	Honus Wagner, Pittsburgh	109
1909	Honus Wagner, Pittsburgh	100
1910	Sherwood Magee, Philadelphia	123
1911	Frank Schulte, Chicago	121
1912	Henry Zimmerman, Chicago	103
1913	Gavvy Cravath, Philadelphia	128
1914	Sherwood Magee, Philadelphia	103
1915	Gavvy Cravath, Philadelphia	115
1916	Henry Zimmerman, Chicago-NewYork	83
1917	Henry Zimmerman, New York	102

American League

Year	Player, Team	RBI
1907	Ty Cobb, Detroit	116
1908	Ty Cobb, Detroit	108
1909	Ty Cobb, Detroit	107
1910	Sam Crawford, Detroit	120
1911	Ty Cobb, Detroit	144
1912	J. Franklin Baker, Philadelphia	133
1913	J. Franklin Baker, Philadelphia	126
1914	Sam Crawford, Detroit	104
1915	Sam Crawford, Detroit; Robert Veach, Detroit	112
1916	Del Pratt, St. Louis	103
1917	Robert Veach, Detroit	103

National League			American League		
Year	**Player, Team**	**RBI**	**Year**	**Player, Team**	**RBI**
1918	Sherwood Magee, Philadelphia	76	1918	Robert Veach, Detroit	78
1919	Hi Myers, Boston	73	1919	Babe Ruth, Boston	114
1920	George Kelly, N.Y.; Rogers Hornsby, St. Louis	94	1920	Babe Ruth, New York	137
1921	Rogers Hornsby, St. Louis	126	1921	Babe Ruth, New York	171
1922	Rogers Hornsby, St. Louis	152	1922	Ken Williams, St. Louis	155
1923	Emil Meusel, New York	125	1923	Babe Ruth, New York	131
1924	George Kelly, New York	136	1924	Goose Goslin, Washington	129
1925	Rogers Hornsby, St. Louis	143	1925	Bob Meusel, New York	138
1926	Jim Bottomley, St. Louis	120	1926	Babe Ruth, New York	145
1927	Paul Waner, Pittsburgh	131	1927	Lou Gehrig, New York	175
1928	Jim Bottomley, St. Louis	136	1928	Babe Ruth, New York; Lou Gehrig, New York	142
1929	Hack Wilson, Chicago	159	1929	Al Simmons, Philadelphia	157
1930	Hack Wilson, Chicago	*191	1930	Lou Gehrig, New York	174
1931	Chuck Klein, Philadelphia	121	1931	Lou Gehrig, New York	*184
1932	Don Hurst, Philadelphia	143	1932	Jimmie Foxx, Philadelphia	169
1933	Chuck Klein, Philadelphia	120	1933	Jimmie Foxx, Philadelphia	163
1934	Mel Ott, New York	135	1934	Lou Gehrig, New York	165
1935	Walter Berger, Boston	130	1935	Hank Greenberg, Detroit	170
1936	Joe Medwick, St. Louis	138	1936	Hal Trosky, Cleveland	162
1937	Joe Medwick, St. Louis	154	1937	Hank Greenberg, Detroit	183
1938	Joe Medwick, St. Louis	122	1938	Jimmie Foxx, Boston	175
1939	Frank McCormick, Cincinnati	128	1939	Ted Williams, Boston	145
1940	John Mize, St. Louis	137	1940	Hank Greenberg, Detroit	150
1941	Adolph Camilli, Brooklyn	120	1941	Joe DiMaggio, New York	125
1942	John Mize, New York	110	1942	Ted Williams, Boston	137
1943	Bill Nicholson, Chicago	128	1943	Rudy York, Detroit	118
1944	Bill Nicholson, Chicago	122	1944	Vern Stephens, St. Louis	109
1945	Dixie Walker, Brooklyn	124	1945	Nick Etten, New York	111
1946	Enos Slaughter, St. Louis	130	1946	Hank Greenberg, Detroit	127
1947	John Mize, New York	138	1947	Ted Williams, Boston	114
1948	Stan Musial, St. Louis	131	1948	Joe DiMaggio, New York	155
1949	Ralph Kiner, Pittsburgh	127	1949	Ted Williams, Bos.; Vern Stephens, Bos.	159
1950	Del Ennis, Philadelphia	126	1950	Walt Dropo, Bos.; Vern Stephens, Bos.	144
1951	Monte Irvin, New York	121	1951	Gus Zernial, Chicago-Philadelphia	129
1952	Hank Sauer, Chicago	121	1952	Al Rosen, Cleveland	105
1953	Roy Campanella, Brooklyn	142	1953	Al Rosen, Cleveland	145
1954	Ted Kluszewski, Cincinnati	141	1954	Larry Doby, Cleveland	126
1955	Duke Snider, Brooklyn	136	1955	Ray Boone, Detroit; Jackie Jensen, Boston	116
1956	Stan Musial, St. Louis	109	1956	Mickey Mantle, New York	130
1957	Hank Aaron, Milwaukee	132	1957	Roy Sievers, Washington	114
1958	Ernie Banks, Chicago	129	1958	Jackie Jensen, Boston	122
1959	Ernie Banks, Chicago	143	1959	Jackie Jensen, Boston	112
1960	Hank Aaron, Milwaukee	126	1960	Roger Maris, New York	112
1961	Orlando Cepeda, San Francisco	142	1961	Roger Maris, New York	142
1962	Tommy Davis, Los Angeles	153	1962	Harmon Killebrew, Minnesota	126
1963	Hank Aaron, Milwaukee	130	1963	Dick Stuart, Boston	118
1964	Ken Boyer, St. Louis	119	1964	Brooks Robinson, Baltimore	118
1965	Deron Johnson, Cincinnati	130	1965	Rocky Colavito, Cleveland	108
1966	Hank Aaron, Atlanta	127	1966	Frank Robinson, Baltimore	122
1967	Orlando Cepeda, St. Louis	111	1967	Carl Yastrzemski, Boston	121
1968	Willie McCovey, San Francisco	105	1968	Ken Harrelson, Boston	109
1969	Willie McCovey, San Francisco	126	1969	Harmon Killebrew, Minnesota	140
1970	Johnny Bench, Cincinnati	148	1970	Frank Howard, Washington	126
1971	Joe Torre, St. Louis	137	1971	Harmon Killebrew, Minnesota	119
1972	Johnny Bench, Cincinnati	125	1972	Dick Allen, Chicago	113
1973	Willie Stargell, Pittsburgh	119	1973	Reggie Jackson, Oakland	117
1974	Johnny Bench, Cincinnati	129	1974	Jeff Burroughs, Texas	118
1975	Greg Luzinski, Philadelphia	120	1975	George Scott, Milwaukee	109
1976	George Foster, Cincinnati	121	1976	Lee May, Baltimore	109
1977	George Foster, Cincinnati	149	1977	Larry Hisle, Minnesota	119
1978	George Foster, Cincinnati	120	1978	Jim Rice, Boston	139
1979	Dave Winfield, San Diego	118	1979	Don Baylor, California	139
1980	Mike Schmidt, Philadelphia	121	1980	Cecil Cooper, Milwaukee	122
1981	Mike Schmidt, Philadelphia	91	1981	Eddie Murray, Baltimore	78
1982	Dale Murphy, Atlanta; Al Oliver, Montreal	109	1982	Hal McRae, Kansas City	133
1983	Dale Murphy, Atlanta	121	1983	Cecil Cooper, Milwaukee; Jim Rice, Boston	126
1984	Gary Carter, Montreal; Mike Schmidt, Phi.	106	1984	Tony Armas, Boston	123
1985	Dave Parker, Cincinnati	125	1985	Don Mattingly, New York	145
1986	Mike Schmidt, Philadelphia	119	1986	Joe Carter, Cleveland	121
1987	Andre Dawson, Chicago	137	1987	George Bell, Toronto	134
1988	Will Clark, San Francisco	109	1988	Jose Canseco, Oakland	124
1989	Kevin Mitchell, San Francisco	125	1989	Ruben Sierra, Texas	119
1990	Matt Williams, San Francisco	122	1990	Cecil Fielder, Detroit	132
1991	Howard Johnson, New York	117	1991	Cecil Fielder, Detroit	133
1992	Darren Daulton, Philadelphia	109	1992	Cecil Fielder, Detroit	124
1993	Barry Bonds, San Francisco	123	1993	Albert Belle, Cleveland	129
1994	Jeff Bagwell, Houston	116	1994	Kirby Puckett, Minnesota	112
1995	Dante Bichette, Colorado	128	1995	Albert Belle, Cleveland; Mo Vaughn, Boston	126
1996	Andres Galarraga, Colorado	150	1996	Albert Belle, Cleveland	148
1997	Andres Galarraga, Colorado	140	1997	Ken Griffey Jr., Seattle	147
1998	Sammy Sosa, Chicago	158	1998	Juan Gonzalez, Texas	157
1999	Mark McGwire, St. Louis	147	1999	Manny Ramirez, Cleveland	165
2000	Todd Helton, Colorado	147	2000	Edgar Martinez, Seattle	145
2001	Sammy Sosa, Chicago	160	2001	Bret Boone, Seattle	141
2002	Lance Berkman, Houston	128	2002	Alex Rodriguez, Texas	142

Batting Champions

Note: Asterisk (*) indicates the all-time single-season record for each league since the beginning of the "modern" era in 1901.

National League

Year	Player	Team	Avg.
1901	Jesse C. Burkett	St. Louis	**.382**
1902	Clarence Beaumont	Pittsburgh	**.357**
1903	Honus Wagner	Pittsburgh	**.355**
1904	Honus Wagner	Pittsburgh	**.349**
1905	James Seymour	Cincinnati	**.377**
1906	Honus Wagner	Pittsburgh	**.339**
1907	Honus Wagner	Pittsburgh	**.350**
1908	Honus Wagner	Pittsburgh	**.354**
1909	Honus Wagner	Pittsburgh	**.339**
1910	Sherwood Magee	Philadelphia	**.331**
1911	Honus Wagner	Pittsburgh	**.334**
1912	Henry Zimmerman	Chicago	**.372**
1913	Jacob Daubert	Brooklyn	**.350**
1914	Jacob Daubert	Brooklyn	**.329**
1915	Larry Doyle	New York	**.320**
1916	Hal Chase	Cincinnati	**.339**
1917	Edd Roush	Cincinnati	**.341**
1918	Zach Wheat	Brooklyn	**.335**
1919	Edd Roush	Cincinnati	**.321**
1920	Rogers Hornsby	St. Louis	**.370**
1921	Rogers Hornsby	St. Louis	**.397**
1922	Rogers Hornsby	St. Louis	**.401**
1923	Rogers Hornsby	St. Louis	**.384**
1924	Rogers Hornsby	St. Louis	***.424**
1925	Rogers Hornsby	St. Louis	**.403**
1926	Eugene Hargrave	Cincinnati	**.353**
1927	Paul Waner	Pittsburgh	**.380**
1928	Rogers Hornsby	Boston	**.387**
1929	Lefty O'Doul	Philadelphia	**.398**
1930	Bill Terry	New York	**.401**
1931	Chick Hafey	St. Louis	**.349**
1932	Lefty O'Doul	Brooklyn	**.368**
1933	Chuck Klein	Philadelphia	**.368**
1934	Paul Waner	Pittsburgh	**.362**
1935	Arky Vaughan	Pittsburgh	**.385**
1936	Paul Waner	Pittsburgh	**.373**
1937	Joe Medwick	St. Louis	**.374**
1938	Ernie Lombardi	Cincinnati	**.342**
1939	John Mize	St. Louis	**.349**
1940	Debs Garms	Pittsburgh	**.355**
1941	Pete Reiser	Brooklyn	**.343**
1942	Ernie Lombardi	Boston	**.330**
1943	Stan Musial	St. Louis	**.357**
1944	Dixie Walker	Brooklyn	**.357**
1945	Phil Cavarretta	Chicago	**.355**
1946	Stan Musial	St. Louis	**.365**
1947	Harry Walker	St.L.-Phi.	**.363**
1948	Stan Musial	St. Louis	**.376**
1949	Jackie Robinson	Brooklyn	**.342**
1950	Stan Musial	St. Louis	**.346**
1951	Stan Musial	St. Louis	**.355**
1952	Stan Musial	St. Louis	**.336**
1953	Carl Furillo	Brooklyn	**.344**
1954	Willie Mays	New York	**.345**
1955	Richie Ashburn	Philadelphia	**.338**
1956	Hank Aaron	Milwaukee	**.328**
1957	Stan Musial	St. Louis	**.351**
1958	Richie Ashburn	Philadelphia	**.350**
1959	Hank Aaron	Milwaukee	**.355**
1960	Dick Groat	Pittsburgh	**.325**
1961	Roberto Clemente	Pittsburgh	**.351**
1962	Tommy Davis	Los Angeles	**.346**
1963	Tommy Davis	Los Angeles	**.326**
1964	Roberto Clemente	Pittsburgh	**.339**
1965	Roberto Clemente	Pittsburgh	**.329**
1966	Matty Alou	Pittsburgh	**.342**
1967	Roberto Clemente	Pittsburgh	**.357**
1968	Pete Rose	Cincinnati	**.335**
1969	Pete Rose	Cincinnati	**.348**
1970	Rico Carty	Atlanta	**.366**
1971	Joe Torre	St. Louis	**.363**
1972	Billy Williams	Chicago	**.333**
1973	Pete Rose	Cincinnati	**.338**
1974	Ralph Garr	Atlanta	**.353**
1975	Bill Madlock	Chicago	**.354**
1976	Bill Madlock	Chicago	**.339**
1977	Dave Parker	Pittsburgh	**.338**
1978	Dave Parker	Pittsburgh	**.334**
1979	Keith Hernandez	St. Louis	**.344**
1980	Bill Buckner	Chicago	**.324**
1981	Bill Madlock	Pittsburgh	**.341**

American League

Year	Player	Team	Avg.
1901	Napoleon Lajoie	Philadelphia	***.426**
1902	Ed Delahanty	Washington	**.376**
1903	Napoleon Lajoie	Cleveland	**.355**
1904	Napoleon Lajoie	Cleveland	**.381**
1905	Elmer Flick	Cleveland	**.306**
1906	George Stone	St. Louis	**.358**
1907	Ty Cobb	Detroit	**.350**
1908	Ty Cobb	Detroit	**.324**
1909	Ty Cobb	Detroit	**.377**
1910[1]	Ty Cobb	Detroit	**.385**
1911	Ty Cobb	Detroit	**.420**
1912	Ty Cobb	Detroit	**.410**
1913	Ty Cobb	Detroit	**.390**
1914	Ty Cobb	Detroit	**.368**
1915	Ty Cobb	Detroit	**.369**
1916	Tris Speaker	Cleveland	**.386**
1917	Ty Cobb	Detroit	**.383**
1918	Ty Cobb	Detroit	**.382**
1919	Ty Cobb	Detroit	**.384**
1920	George Sisler	St. Louis	**.407**
1921	Harry Heilmann	Detroit	**.394**
1922	George Sisler	St. Louis	**.420**
1923	Harry Heilmann	Detroit	**.403**
1924	Babe Ruth	New York	**.378**
1925	Harry Heilmann	Detroit	**.393**
1926	Henry Manush	Detroit	**.378**
1927	Harry Heilmann	Detroit	**.398**
1928	Goose Goslin	Washington	**.379**
1929	Lew Fonseca	Cleveland	**.369**
1930	Al Simmons	Philadelphia	**.381**
1931	Al Simmons	Philadelphia	**.390**
1932	Dale Alexander	Detroit-Boston	**.367**
1933	Jimmie Foxx	Philadelphia	**.356**
1934	Lou Gehrig	New York	**.363**
1935	Buddy Myer	Washington	**.349**
1936	Luke Appling	Chicago	**.388**
1937	Charlie Gehringer	Detroit	**.371**
1938	Jimmie Foxx	Boston	**.349**
1939	Joe DiMaggio	New York	**.381**
1940	Joe DiMaggio	New York	**.352**
1941	Ted Williams	Boston	**.406**
1942	Ted Williams	Boston	**.356**
1943	Luke Appling	Chicago	**.328**
1944	Lou Boudreau	Cleveland	**.327**
1945	George Stirnweiss	New York	**.309**
1946	Mickey Vernon	Washington	**.353**
1947	Ted Williams	Boston	**.343**
1948	Ted Williams	Boston	**.369**
1949	George Kell	Detroit	**.343**
1950	Billy Goodman	Boston	**.354**
1951	Ferris Fain	Philadelphia	**.344**
1952	Ferris Fain	Philadelphia	**.327**
1953	Mickey Vernon	Washington	**.337**
1954	Roberto Avila	Cleveland	**.341**
1955	Al Kaline	Detroit	**.340**
1956	Mickey Mantle	New York	**.353**
1957	Ted Williams	Boston	**.388**
1958	Ted Williams	Boston	**.328**
1959	Harvey Kuenn	Detroit	**.353**
1960	Pete Runnels	Boston	**.320**
1961	Norm Cash	Detroit	**.361**
1962	Pete Runnels	Boston	**.326**
1963	Carl Yastrzemski	Boston	**.321**
1964	Tony Oliva	Minnesota	**.323**
1965	Tony Oliva	Minnesota	**.321**
1966	Frank Robinson	Baltimore	**.316**
1967	Carl Yastrzemski	Boston	**.326**
1968	Carl Yastrzemski	Boston	**.301**
1969	Rod Carew	Minnesota	**.332**
1970	Alex Johnson	California	**.329**
1971	Tony Oliva	Minnesota	**.337**
1972	Rod Carew	Minnesota	**.318**
1973	Rod Carew	Minnesota	**.350**
1974	Rod Carew	Minnesota	**.364**
1975	Rod Carew	Minnesota	**.359**
1976	George Brett	Kansas City	**.333**
1977	Rod Carew	Minnesota	**.388**
1978	Rod Carew	Minnesota	**.333**
1979	Fred Lynn	Boston	**.333**
1980	George Brett	Kansas City	**.390**
1981	Carney Lansford	Boston	**.336**

National League				American League			
Year	**Player**	**Team**	**Avg.**	**Year**	**Player**	**Team**	**Avg.**
1982	Al Oliver	Montreal	**.331**	1982	Willie Wilson	Kansas City	**.332**
1983	Bill Madlock	Pittsburgh	**.323**	1983	Wade Boggs	Boston	**.361**
1984	Tony Gwynn	San Diego	**.351**	1984	Don Mattingly	New York	**.343**
1985	Willie McGee	St. Louis	**.353**	1985	Wade Boggs	Boston	**.368**
1986	Tim Raines	Montreal	**.334**	1986	Wade Boggs	Boston	**.357**
1987	Tony Gwynn	San Diego	**.370**	1987	Wade Boggs	Boston	**.363**
1988	Tony Gwynn	San Diego	**.313**	1988	Wade Boggs	Boston	**.366**
1989	Tony Gwynn	San Diego	**.336**	1989	Kirby Puckett	Minnesota	**.339**
1990	Willie McGee	St. Louis	**.335**	1990	George Brett	Kansas City	**.329**
1991	Terry Pendleton	Atlanta	**.319**	1991	Julio Franco	Texas	**.341**
1992	Gary Sheffield	San Diego	**.330**	1992	Edgar Martinez	Seattle	**.343**
1993	Andres Galarraga	Colorado	**.370**	1993	John Olerud	Toronto	**.363**
1994	Tony Gwynn	San Diego	**.394**	1994	Paul O'Neill	New York	**.359**
1995	Tony Gwynn	San Diego	**.368**	1995	Edgar Martinez	Seattle	**.356**
1996	Tony Gwynn	San Diego	**.353**	1996	Alex Rodriguez	Seattle	**.358**
1997	Tony Gwynn	San Diego	**.372**	1997	Frank Thomas	Chicago	**.347**
1998	Larry Walker	Colorado	**.363**	1998	Bernie Williams	New York	**.339**
1999	Larry Walker	Colorado	**.379**	1999	Nomar Garciaparra	Boston	**.357**
2000	Todd Helton	Colorado	**.372**	2000	Nomar Garciaparra	Boston	**.372**
2001	Larry Walker	Colorado	**.350**	2001	Ichiro Suzuki	Seattle	**.350**
2002	Barry Bonds	San Francisco	**.370**	2002	Manny Ramirez	Boston	**.349**

(1) Some baseball researchers have concluded that Ty Cobb actually hit .382 in 1910 while Napoleon Lajoie, Cleveland, hit .383.

Cy Young Award Winners

Year	Player, Team
1956	Don Newcombe, Dodgers
1957	Warren Spahn, Braves
1958	Bob Turley, Yankees
1959	Early Wynn, White Sox
1960	Vernon Law, Pirates
1961	Whitey Ford, Yankees
1962	Don Drysdale, Dodgers
1963	Sandy Koufax, Dodgers
1964	Dean Chance, Angels
1965	Sandy Koufax, Dodgers
1966	Sandy Koufax, Dodgers
1967	(NL) Mike McCormick, Giants
	(AL) Jim Lonborg, Red Sox
1968	(NL) Bob Gibson, Cardinals
	(AL) Dennis McLain, Tigers
1969	(NL) Tom Seaver, Mets
	(AL) (tie) Dennis McLain, Tigers
	Mike Cuellar, Orioles
1970	(NL) Bob Gibson, Cardinals
	(AL) Jim Perry, Twins
1971	(NL) Ferguson Jenkins, Cubs
	(AL) Vida Blue, A's
1972	(NL) Steve Carlton, Phillies
	(AL) Gaylord Perry, Indians
1973	(NL) Tom Seaver, Mets
	(AL) Jim Palmer, Orioles
1974	(NL) Mike Marshall, Dodgers
	(AL) Jim (Catfish) Hunter, A's
1975	(NL) Tom Seaver, Mets
	(AL) Jim Palmer, Orioles
1976	(NL) Randy Jones, Padres
	(AL) Jim Palmer, Orioles
1977	(NL) Steve Carlton, Phillies
	(AL) Sparky Lyle, Yankees
1978	(NL) Gaylord Perry, Padres
	(AL) Ron Guidry, Yankees
1979	(NL) Bruce Sutter, Cubs
	(AL) Mike Flanagan, Orioles
1980	(NL) Steve Carlton, Phillies
	(AL) Steve Stone, Orioles
1981	(NL) Fernando Valenzuela, Dodgers
	(AL) Rollie Fingers, Brewers
1982	(NL) Steve Carlton, Phillies
	(AL) Pete Vuckovich, Brewers
1983	(NL) John Denny, Phillies
	(AL) LaMarr Hoyt, White Sox
1984	(NL) Rick Sutcliffe, Cubs
	(AL) Willie Hernandez, Tigers
1985	(NL) Dwight Gooden, Mets
	(AL) Bret Saberhagen, Royals
1986	(NL) Mike Scott, Astros
	(AL) Roger Clemens, Red Sox
1987	(NL) Steve Bedrosian, Phillies
	(AL) Roger Clemens, Red Sox
1988	(NL) Orel Hershiser, Dodgers
	(AL) Frank Viola, Twins
1989	(NL) Mark Davis, Padres
	(AL) Bret Saberhagan, Royals
1990	(NL) Doug Drabek, Pirates
	(AL) Bob Welch, A's
1991	(NL) Tom Glavine, Braves
	(AL) Roger Clemens, Red Sox
1992	(NL) Greg Maddux, Cubs
	(AL) Dennis Eckersley, A's
1993	(NL) Greg Maddux, Braves
	(AL) Jack McDowell, White Sox
1994	(NL) Greg Maddux, Braves
	(AL) David Cone, Royals
1995	(NL) Greg Maddux, Braves
	(AL) Randy Johnson, Mariners
1996	(NL) John Smoltz, Braves
	(AL) Pat Hentgen, Blue Jays
1997	(NL) Pedro Martinez, Expos
	(AL) Roger Clemens, Blue Jays
1998	(NL) Tom Glavine, Braves
	(AL) Roger Clemens, Blue Jays
1999	(NL) Randy Johnson, Diamondbacks
	(AL) Pedro Martinez, Red Sox
2000	(NL) Randy Johnson, Diamondbacks
	(AL) Pedro Martinez, Red Sox
2001	(NL) Randy Johnson, Diamondbacks
	(AL) Roger Clemens, Yankees

Most Valuable Player

(As selected by the Baseball Writers' Assoc. of America. Prior to 1931, MVP honors were named by various sources.)

National League

Year	Player, team
1931	Frank Frisch, St. Louis
1932	Chuck Klein, Philadelphia
1933	Carl Hubbell, New York
1934	Dizzy Dean, St. Louis
1935	Gabby Hartnett, Chicago
1936	Carl Hubbell, N.Y.
1937	Joe Medwick, St. Louis
1938	Ernie Lombardi, Cincinnati
1939	Bucky Walters, Cincinnati
1940	Frank McCormick, Cincinnati
1941	Dolph Camilli, Brooklyn
1942	Mort Cooper, St. Louis
1943	Stan Musial, St. Louis
1944	Martin Marion, St. Louis
1945	Phil Cavarretta, Chicago
1946	Stan Musial, St. Louis
1947	Bob Elliott, Boston
1948	Stan Musial, St. Louis
1949	Jackie Robinson, Brooklyn
1950	Jim Konstanty, Philadelphia
1951	Roy Campanella, Brooklyn
1952	Hank Sauer, Chicago
1953	Roy Campanella, Brooklyn
1954	Willie Mays, N.Y.
1955	Roy Campanella, Brooklyn
1956	Don Newcombe, Brooklyn
1957	Hank Aaron, Milwaukee
1958	Ernie Banks, Chicago
1959	Ernie Banks, Chicago
1960	Dick Groat, Pittsburgh
1961	Frank Robinson, Cincinnati
1962	Maury Wills, L.A.
1963	Sandy Koufax, L.A.
1964	Ken Boyer, St. Louis
1965	Willie Mays, San Francisco
1966	Roberto Clemente, Pittsburgh
1967	Orlando Cepeda, St. Louis
1968	Bob Gibson, St. Louis
1969	Willie McCovey, San Francisco
1970	Johnny Bench, Cincinnati
1971	Joe Torre, St. Louis
1972	Johnny Bench, Cincinnati
1973	Pete Rose, Cincinnati
1974	Steve Garvey, L.A.
1975	Joe Morgan, Cincinnati
1976	Joe Morgan, Cincinnati
1977	George Foster, Cincinnati
1978	Dave Parker, Pittsburgh
1979	Willie Stargell, Pittsburgh
(tie)	Keith Hernandez, St. Louis
1980	Mike Schmidt, Philadelphia
1981	Mike Schmidt, Philadelphia
1982	Dale Murphy, Atlanta
1983	Dale Murphy, Atlanta
1984	Ryne Sandberg, Chicago
1985	Willie McGee, St. Louis
1986	Mike Schmidt, Philadelphia
1987	Andre Dawson, Chicago
1988	Kirk Gibson, L.A.
1989	Kevin Mitchell, San Francisco
1990	Barry Bonds, Pittsburgh
1991	Terry Pendleton, Atlanta
1992	Barry Bonds, Pittsburgh
1993	Barry Bonds, San Francisco
1994	Jeff Bagwell, Houston
1995	Barry Larkin, Cincinnati
1996	Ken Caminiti, San Diego
1997	Larry Walker, Colorado
1998	Sammy Sosa, Chicago
1999	Chipper Jones, Atlanta
2000	Jeff Kent, San Francisco
2001	Barry Bonds, San Francisco

American League

Year	Player, team
1931	Lefty Grove, Philadelphia
1932	Jimmie Foxx, Philadelphia
1933	Jimmie Foxx, Philadelphia
1934	Mickey Cochrane, Detroit
1935	Hank Greenberg, Detroit
1936	Lou Gehrig, N.Y.
1937	Charley Gehringer, Detroit
1938	Jimmie Foxx, Boston
1939	Joe DiMaggio, N.Y.
1940	Hank Greenberg, Detroit
1941	Joe DiMaggio, N.Y.
1942	Joe Gordon, N.Y.
1943	Spurgeon Chandler, N.Y.
1944	Hal Newhouser, Detroit
1945	Hal Newhouser, Detroit
1946	Ted Williams, Boston
1947	Joe DiMaggio, N.Y.
1948	Lou Boudreau, Cleveland
1949	Ted Williams, Boston
1950	Phil Rizzuto, N.Y.
1951	Yogi Berra, N.Y.
1952	Bobby Shantz, Philadelphia
1953	Al Rosen, Cleveland
1954	Yogi Berra, N.Y.
1955	Yogi Berra, N.Y.
1956	Mickey Mantle, N.Y.
1957	Mickey Mantle, N.Y.
1958	Jackie Jensen, Boston
1959	Nellie Fox, Chicago
1960	Roger Maris, N.Y.
1961	Roger Maris, N.Y.
1962	Mickey Mantle, N.Y.
1963	Elston Howard, N.Y.
1964	Brooks Robinson, Baltimore
1965	Zoilo Versalles, Minnesota
1966	Frank Robinson, Baltimore
1967	Carl Yastrzemski, Boston
1968	Denny McLain, Detroit
1969	Harmon Killebrew, Minnesota
1970	John (Boog) Powell, Baltimore
1971	Vida Blue, Oakland
1972	Dick Allen, Chicago
1973	Reggie Jackson, Oakland
1974	Jeff Burroughs, Texas
1975	Fred Lynn, Boston
1976	Thurman Munson, N.Y.
1977	Rod Carew, Minnesota
1978	Jim Rice, Boston
1979	Don Baylor, California
1980	George Brett, Kansas City
1981	Rollie Fingers, Milwaukee
1982	Robin Yount, Milwaukee
1983	Cal Ripken, Jr., Baltimore
1984	Willie Hernandez, Detroit
1985	Don Mattingly, N.Y.
1986	Roger Clemens, Boston
1987	George Bell, Toronto
1988	Jose Canseco, Oakland
1989	Robin Yount, Milwaukee
1990	Rickey Henderson, Oakland
1991	Cal Ripken, Jr., Baltimore
1992	Dennis Eckersley, Oakland
1993	Frank Thomas, Chicago
1994	Frank Thomas, Chicago
1995	Mo Vaughn, Boston
1996	Juan Gonzalez, Texas
1997	Ken Griffey Jr., Seattle
1998	Juan Gonzalez, Texas
1999	Ivan Rodriguez, Texas
2000	Jason Giambi, Oakland
2001	Ichiro Suzuki, Seattle

Rookie of the Year

(As selected by the Baseball Writers' Assoc. of America)

1947—Combined selection—Jackie Robinson, Brooklyn, 1b; 1948—Combined selection—Alvin Dark, Boston, N.L., ss

National League

Year	Player, team
1949	Don Newcombe, Brooklyn, p
1950	Sam Jethroe, Boston, of
1951	Willie Mays, N.Y., of
1952	Joe Black, Brooklyn, p
1953	Jim Gilliam, Brooklyn, 2b
1954	Wally Moon, St. Louis, of
1955	Bill Virdon, St. Louis, of
1956	Frank Robinson, Cincinnati, of
1957	Jack Sanford, Philadelphia, p
1958	Orlando Cepeda, S.F., 1b
1959	Willie McCovey, S.F., 1b
1960	Frank Howard, L.A., of
1961	Billy Williams, Chicago, of
1962	Ken Hubbs, Chicago, 2b
1963	Pete Rose, Cincinnati, 2b
1964	Richie Allen, Philadelphia, 3b
1965	Jim Lefebvre, L.A., 2b
1966	Tommy Helms, Cincinnati, 2b
1967	Tom Seaver, N.Y., p
1968	Johnny Bench, Cincinnati, c
1969	Ted Sizemore, L.A., 2b
1970	Carl Morton, Montreal, p
1971	Earl Williams, Atlanta, c
1972	Jon Matlack, N.Y., p
1973	Gary Matthews, S.F., of
1974	Bake McBride, St. Louis, of
1975	John Montefusco, S.F., p
1976	Butch Metzger, San Diego, p
(tie)	Pat Zachry, Cincinnati, p
1977	Andre Dawson, Montreal, of
1978	Bob Horner, Atlanta, 3b
1979	Rick Sutcliffe, L.A., p
1980	Steve Howe, L.A., p
1981	Fernando Valenzuela, L.A., p
1982	Steve Sax, L.A., 2b
1983	Darryl Strawberry, N.Y., of
1984	Dwight Gooden, N.Y., p
1985	Vince Coleman, St. Louis, of
1986	Todd Worrell, St. Louis, p
1987	Benito Santiago, San Diego, c
1988	Chris Sabo, Cincinnati, 3b
1989	Jerome Walton, Chicago, of
1990	Dave Justice, Atlanta, 1b
1991	Jeff Bagwell, Houston, 1b
1992	Eric Karros, L.A., 1b
1993	Mike Piazza, L.A., c
1994	Raul Mondesi, L.A., of
1995	Hideo Nomo, L.A., p
1996	Todd Hollandsworth, L.A., of
1997	Scott Rolen, Philadelphia, 3b
1998	Kerry Wood, Chicago, p
1999	Scott Williamson, Cincinnati, p
2000	Rafael Furcal, Atlanta, ss
2001	Albert Pujols, St. Louis, of

American League

Year	Player, team
1949	Roy Sievers, St. Louis, of
1950	Walt Dropo, Boston, 1b
1951	Gil McDougald, N.Y., 3b
1952	Harry Byrd, Philadelphia, p
1953	Harvey Kuenn, Detroit, ss
1954	Bob Grim, N.Y., p
1955	Herb Score, Cleveland, p
1956	Luis Aparicio, Chicago, ss
1957	Tony Kubek, N.Y., if-of
1958	Albie Pearson, Washington, of
1959	Bob Allison, Washington, of
1960	Ron Hansen, Baltimore, ss
1961	Don Schwall, Boston, p
1962	Tom Tresh, N.Y., if-of
1963	Gary Peters, Chicago, p
1964	Tony Oliva, Minnesota, of
1965	Curt Blefary, Baltimore, of
1966	Tommie Agee, Chicago, of
1967	Rod Carew, Minnesota, 2b
1968	Stan Bahnsen, N.Y., p
1969	Lou Piniella, Kansas City, of
1970	Thurman Munson, N.Y., c
1971	Chris Chambliss, Cleveland, 1b
1972	Carlton Fisk, Boston, c
1973	Al Bumbry, Baltimore, of
1974	Mike Hargrove, Texas, 1b
1975	Fred Lynn, Boston, of
1976	Mark Fidrych, Detroit, p
1977	Eddie Murray, Baltimore, dh
1978	Lou Whitaker, Detroit, 2b
1979	John Castino, Minnesota, 3b
(tie)	Alfredo Griffin, Toronto, ss
1980	Joe Charboneau, Cleveland, of
1981	Dave Righetti, N.Y., p
1982	Cal Ripken, Jr., Baltimore, ss
1983	Ron Kittle, Chicago, of
1984	Alvin Davis, Seattle, 1b
1985	Ozzie Guillen, Chicago, ss
1986	Jose Canseco, Oakland, of
1987	Mark McGwire, Oakland, 1b
1988	Walt Weiss, Oakland, ss
1989	Gregg Olson, Baltimore, p
1990	Sandy Alomar, Jr., Cleveland, c
1991	Chuck Knoblauch, Minnesota, 2b
1992	Pat Listach, Milwaukee, ss
1993	Tim Salmon, California, of
1994	Bob Hamelin, Kansas City, dh
1995	Marty Cordova, Minnesota, of
1996	Derek Jeter, N.Y., ss
1997	Nomar Garciaparra, Boston, ss
1998	Ben Grieve, Oakland, of
1999	Carlos Beltran, Kansas City, of
2000	Kazuhiro Sasaki, Seattle, p
2001	Ichiro Suzuki, Seattle, of

Manager of the Year

Year	Manager
1983	(NL) Tommy Lasorda, L.A.
	(AL) Tony La Russa, Chicago
1984	(NL) Jim Frey, Chicago
	(AL) Sparky Anderson, Detroit
1985	(NL) Whitey Herzog, St. Louis
	(AL) Bobby Cox, Toronto
1986	(NL) Hal Lanier, Houston
	(AL) John McNamara, Boston
1987	(NL) Buck Rodgers, Montreal
	(AL) Sparky Anderson, Detroit
1988	(NL) Tommy Lasorda, L.A.
	(AL) Tony La Russa, Oakland
1989	(NL) Don Zimmer, Chicago
	(AL) Frank Robinson, Blatimore
1990	(NL) Jim Leyland, Pittsburgh
	(AL) Jeff Torborg, Chicago
1991	(NL) Bobby Cox, Atlanta
	(AL) Tom Kelly, Minnesota
1992	(NL) Jim Leyland, Pittsburgh
	(AL) Tony La Russa, Oakland
1993	(NL) Dusty Baker, San Francisco
	(AL) Gene Lamont, Chicago
1994	(NL) Felipe Alou, Montreal
	(AL) Buck Showalter, N.Y.
1995	(NL) Don Baylor, Colorado
	(AL) Lou Piniella, Seattle
1996	(NL) Bruce Bochy, San Diego
	(AL) (tie) Joe Torre, N.Y. Johnny Oates, Texas
1997	(NL) Dusty Baker, San Francisco
	(AL) Davey Johnson, Baltimore
1998	(NL) Larry Dierker, Houston
	(AL) Joe Torre, N.Y.
1999	(NL) Jack McKeon, Cincinnati
	(AL) Jimy Williams, Boston
2000	(NL) Dusty Baker, San Francisco
	(AL) Jerry Manuel, Chicago
2001	(NL) Larry Bowa, Philadelphia
	(AL) Lou Piniella, Seattle

WORLD ALMANAC QUICK QUIZ

Who is the only player from a losing team to be named World Series Most Valuable Player?
(a) Bobby Richardson (b) Lenny Dykstra (c) Duke Snyder (d) Bob Gibson
For the answer look in this chapter, or see page 1008.

The Rawlings Gold Glove Awards: 2001 and All-Time Leaders

American League

Greg Maddux, Atlanta, p
Brad Ausmus, Houston, c
Todd Helton, Colorado, 1b
Fernando Vina, St. Louis, 2b
Scott Rolen, Philadelphia, 3b
Orlando Cabrera, Montr., ss
Jim Edmonds, St. Louis, of
Andruw Jones, Atlanta, of
Larry Walker, Colorado, of
Mike Mussina, N.Y., p

National League

Ivan Rodriguez, Texas, c
Doug Mientkiewicz, Minnesota, 1b
Roberto Alomar, Cleveland, 2b
Eric Chavez, Oakland, 3b
Omar Vizquel, Cleveland, ss
Mike Cameron, Seattle, of
Torii Hunter, Minnesota, of
Ichiro Suzuki, Seattle, of

The following are the players at each position who have won the most Gold Gloves since the award was instituted in 1957.

Position	Player	Gold Gloves
Pitcher:	Jim Kaat	16
	Greg Maddux	12
Catcher:	Johnny Bench	10
	Ivan Rodriguez	10
First base:	Keith Hernandez	11
	Don Mattingly	9
Second base:	Roberto Alomar	10
	Ryne Sandberg	9
	Bill Mazeroski	8
	Frank White	8
Third base:	Brooks Robinson	16
	Mike Schmidt	10
Shortstop:	Ozzie Smith	13
	Luis Aparicio	9
Outfield:	Roberto Clemente	12
	Willie Mays	12
	Al Kaline	10
	Ken Griffey Jr.	10

National League Final Standings, 2002

Eastern Division

	W	L	Pct.	GB	Home	vs. East	vs. Central	vs. West	vs. AL
Atlanta	101	59	.631	—	52-28	47-28	24-12	15-16	15-3
Montreal	83	79	.512	19	49-32	37-39	21-15	13-19	12-6
Philadelphia	80	81	.497	21½	40-40	34-41	22-14	14-18	10-8
Florida	79	83	.488	23	46-35	36-40	18-18	15-17	10-8
New York	75	86	.466	26½	38-43	35-41	20-15	10-22	10-8

Central Division

	W	L	Pct.	GB	Home	vs. East	vs. Central	vs. West	vs. AL
St. Louis	97	65	.599	—	52-29	11-19	57-33	21-09	8-4
Houston	84	78	.519	13	47-34	16-14	49-41	14-16	5-7
Cincinnati	78	84	.481	19	38-43	12-18	50-40	14-16	2-10
Pittsburgh	72	89	.447	24½	38-42	16-13	43-47	10-20	3-9
Chicago	67	95	.414	30	36-45	12-18	36-54	13-17	6-6
Milwaukee	56	106	.346	41	31-50	07-23	35-55	12-18	2-10

Western Division

	W	L	Pct.	GB	Home	vs. East	vs. Central	vs. West	vs. AL
Arizona	98	64	.605	—	55-26	21-11	23-13	43-33	11-7
San Francisco*	95	66	.590	2½	50-31	17-14	23-13	47-29	8-10
Los Angeles	92	70	.568	6	46-35	20-12	20-16	40-36	12-6
Colorado	73	89	.451	25	47-34	18-14	17-19	31-45	7-11
San Diego	66	96	.407	32	41-40	16-16	13-23	29-47	8-10

*Wild card team.

National League Statistics, 2002

(Individual Statistics: Batting—at least 150 at-bats; Pitching—at least 70 innings or 10 saves; *changed teams within NL during season; entry includes statistics for more than 1 team; # changed teams to or from AL during season; entry includes only NL stats)

Team Batting

Team	BAT	AB	R	H	HR	RBI
Colorado	.274	5,512	778	1,508	152	726
St. Louis	.268	5,505	787	1,475	175	758
Arizona	.267	5,508	819	1,471	165	783
San Francisco	.267	5,497	783	1,465	198	751
Los Angeles	.264	5,554	713	1,464	155	693
Houston	.262	5,503	749	1,441	167	719
Montreal	.261	5,479	735	1,432	162	695
Florida	.261	5,496	699	1,433	146	653
Atlanta	.260	5,495	708	1,428	164	669
Philadelphia	.259	5,523	710	1,428	165	676
New York	.256	5,496	690	1,409	160	650
Cincinnati	.253	5,470	709	1,386	169	678
Milwaukee	.253	5,415	627	1,369	139	597
San Diego	.253	5,515	662	1,393	136	627
Chicago	.246	5,496	706	1,351	200	676
Pittsburgh	.244	5,330	641	1,300	142	610

Team Pitching

Team	ERA	IP	H	SO	BB	SV
Atlanta	3.13	1,467.1	1,302	1,058	554	57
San Francisco	3.54	1,437.1	1,349	992	523	43
Los Angeles	3.69	1,457.2	1,311	1,132	555	56
St. Louis	3.70	1,446.1	1,355	1,009	547	42
New York	3.89	1,442.2	1,408	1,107	543	36
Arizona	3.92	1,446.2	1,361	1,303	421	40
Montreal	3.97	1,453.0	1,475	1,088	508	39
Houston	4.00	1,445.0	1,423	1,219	546	43
Philadelphia	4.17	1,449.2	1,381	1,075	570	47
Pittsburgh	4.23	1,412.2	1,447	920	572	47
Cincinnati	4.27	1,453.2	1,502	980	550	42
Chicago	4.29	1,441.1	1,373	1,333	606	23
Florida	4.36	1,456.1	1,449	1,104	631	36
San Diego	4.62	1,436.1	1,522	1,108	582	40
Milwaukee	4.73	1,432.1	1,468	1,026	666	32
Colorado	5.20	1426.2	1,554	920	582	43

Arizona Diamondbacks

BATTERS	BA	AB	R	H	HR	RBI	SO	SB
G. Colbrunn	.333	171	30	57	10	27	19	0
D. Bautista	.325	154	22	50	6	23	21	4
Q. McCracken	.309	349	60	108	3	40	68	5
J. Spivey	.301	538	103	162	16	78	100	11
L. Gonzalez	.288	524	90	151	28	103	76	9
S. Finley	.287	505	82	145	25	89	73	16
C. Counsell	.282	436	63	123	2	51	52	7
T. Womack	.271	590	90	160	5	57	80	29
E. Durazo	.261	222	46	58	16	48	60	0
M. Williams	.260	215	29	56	12	40	41	3
M. Grace	.252	298	43	75	7	48	30	2
D. Miller	.249	297	40	74	11	42	88	0
D. Dellucci	.245	229	34	56	7	29	55	2
R. Barajas	.234	154	12	36	3	23	25	1

PITCHERS	W-L	ERA	IP	H	BB	SO	SV
B. Kim	8-3	2.04	84.0	64	26	92	36
R. Johnson	24-5	2.32	260.0	197	71	334	0
C. Schilling	23-7	3.23	259.1	218	33	316	0
M. Batista	8-9	4.29	184.2	172	70	112	0
M. Myers	4-3	4.38	37.0	39	17	31	4
R. Helling	10-12	4.51	175.2	180	48	120	0
B. Anderson	6-11	4.79	156.0	174	32	81	0

Manager-Bob Brenly

Atlanta Braves

BATTERS	BA	AB	R	H	HR	RBI	SO	SB
C. Jones	.327	548	90	179	26	100	89	8
M. Franco	.317	205	25	65	6	30	31	1
G. Sheffield	.307	492	82	151	25	84	53	12
M. DeRosa	.297	212	24	63	5	23	24	2
J. Franco	.284	338	51	96	6	30	75	5
R. Furcal	.275	636	95	175	8	47	114	27
D. Bragg	.269	212	34	57	3	15	52	5
A. Jones	.264	560	91	148	35	94	135	8
W. Helms	.243	210	20	51	6	22	57	1
J. Lopez	.233	347	31	81	11	52	63	0
V. Castilla	.232	543	56	126	12	61	69	4
M. Giles	.230	213	27	49	8	23	41	1
K. Lockhart	.216	296	34	64	5	32	50	0
H. Blanco	.204	221	17	45	6	22	51	0

PITCHERS	W-L	ERA	IP	H	BB	SO	SV
C. Hammond	7-2	0.95	76.0	53	31	63	0
G. Maddux	16-6	2.62	199.1	194	45	118	0
T. Glavine	18-11	2.96	224.2	210	78	127	0
K. Millwood	18-8	3.24	217.0	186	65	178	0
J. Smoltz	3-2	3.25	80.1	59	24	85	55
D. Moss	12-6	3.42	179.0	140	89	111	0
J. Marquis	8-9	5.04	114.1	127	49	84	0

Manager-Bobby Cox

Chicago Cubs

BATTERS	BA	AB	R	H	HR	RBI	SO	SB
S. Sosa	.288	556	122	160	49	108	144	2
M. Alou	.275	484	50	133	15	61	61	8
F. McGriff	.273	523	67	143	30	103	99	1
M. Bellhorn	.258	445	86	115	27	56	144	7
C. Patterson	.253	592	71	150	14	54	142	18
B. Hill	.253	190	26	48	4	20	42	6
A. Gonzalez	.248	513	58	127	18	61	136	5
C. Stynes	.241	195	25	47	5	26	29	1
J. Girardi	.226	234	19	53	1	13	35	1
R. Brown	.211	204	14	43	3	23	50	2
T. Hundley	.211	266	32	56	16	35	80	0
C. Hermansen*	.207	237	25	49	8	18	82	7

PITCHERS	W-L	ERA	IP	H	BB	SO	SV
J. Borowski	4-4	2.73	95.2	84	29	97	2
M. Prior	6-6	3.32	116.2	98	38	147	0
M. Clement	12-11	3.60	205.0	162	85	215	0
C. Zambrano	4-8	3.66	108.1	94	63	93	0
K .Wood	12-11	3.66	213.2	169	97	217	0
J. Lieber	6-8	3.70	141.0	153	12	87	0
J. Cruz	3-11	3.98	97.1	84	59	81	1
A. Alfonseca	2-5	4.00	74.1	73	36	61	19
J. Bere	1-10	5.67	85.2	98	28	65	0

Managers-Don Baylor, Bruce Kimm

Cincinnati Reds

BATTERS	BA	AB	R	H	HR	RBI	SO	SB
A. Kearns	.315	372	66	117	13	56	81	6
T. Walker	.299	612	79	183	11	64	81	8
K. Griffey	.264	197	17	52	8	23	39	1
S. Casey	.261	425	56	111	6	42	47	2
R. Taylor	.254	287	41	73	9	38	79	11
J. LaRue	.249	353	42	88	12	52	117	1
A. Dunn	.249	535	84	133	26	71	170	19
B. Larkin	.245	507	72	124	7	47	57	13
R. Branyan#	.244	217	34	53	16	39	86	3
A. Boone	.241	606	83	146	26	87	111	32
J. Guillen	.238	240	25	57	8	31	43	4

PITCHERS	W-L	ERA	IP	H	BB	SO	SV
S. Williamson	3-4	2.92	74.0	46	36	84	8
E. Dessens	7-8	3.03	178.0	173	49	93	0
D. Graves	7-3	3.19	98.2	99	25	58	32
C. Reitsma	6-12	3.64	138.1	144	45	84	0
J. Haynes	15-10	4.12	196.2	210	81	126	0
S. Estes*	5-12	5.10	160.2	171	83	109	0
J. Rijo	5-4	5.14	77.0	89	20	38	0
J. Hamilton	4-10	5.27	124.2	136	50	85	1
R. Dempster*	10-13	5.38	209.0	228	93	153	0
B. Chen*	2-5	5.56	77.2	85	43	80	0
S. Sullivan	6-5	6.06	78.2	93	31	78	1

Manager-Bob Boone

Colorado Rockies

BATTERS	BA	AB	R	H	HR	RBI	SO	SB
L. Walker	.338	477	95	161	26	104	73	6
T. Helton	.329	553	107	182	30	109	91	5
J. Payton*	.303	445	69	135	16	59	54	7
T. Hollandsworth#	.295	298	39	88	11	48	71	7
J. Pierre	.287	592	90	170	1	35	52	47
T. Zeile	.273	506	61	138	18	87	92	1
G. Bennett	.265	291	26	77	4	26	45	1
B. Butler	.259	344	55	89	9	42	40	2
J. Ortiz	.250	192	22	48	1	12	30	2
J. Uribe	.240	566	69	136	6	49	120	9
T. Shumpert	.235	234	30	55	6	21	41	4
G. Norton	.220	168	19	37	7	37	52	2

PITCHERS	W-L	ERA	IP	H	BB	SO	SV
J. Jimenez	2-10	3.56	73.1	76	11	47	41
D. Stark	11-4	4.00	128.1	108	64	64	0
J. Jennings	16-8	4.52	185.1	201	70	127	0
T. Jones	1-4	4.70	82.1	84	28	73	1
D. Neagle	8-11	5.26	164.1	170	63	111	0
S. Chacon	5-11	5.73	119.1	122	60	67	0
S. Lowe	5-3	5.79	79.1	101	41	64	0
M. Hampton	7-15	6.15	178.2	228	91	74	0

Managers-Buddy Bell, Clint Hurdle

Florida Marlins

BATTERS	BA	AB	R	H	HR	RBI	SO	SB
K. Millar	.306	438	58	134	16	57	74	0
L. Castillo	.305	606	86	185	2	39	76	48
M. Redmond	.305	256	19	78	2	28	34	0
M. Lowell	.276	597	88	165	24	92	92	4
J. Encarnacion*	.271	584	77	158	24	85	113	21
D. Lee	.270	581	95	157	27	86	164	19
E. Owens	.270	385	44	104	4	37	33	26
A. Fox	.251	435	55	109	4	41	94	31
M. Mordecai	.243	151	19	37	0	11	27	2
P. Wilson	.243	510	80	124	23	65	140	20
A. Gonzalez	.225	151	15	34	2	18	32	3
C. Johnson	.217	244	18	53	6	36	61	0

PITCHERS	W-L	ERA	IP	H	BB	SO	SV
B. Looper	2-5	3.14	86.0	73	28	55	13
A. Burnett	12-9	3.30	204.1	153	90	203	0
V. Nunez	6-5	3.41	97.2	80	37	73	20
J. Beckett	6-7	4.10	107.2	93	44	113	0
M. Tejera	8-8	4.45	139.2	144	60	95	1
B. Penny	8-7	4.66	129.1	148	50	93	0
C. Pavano*	6-10	5.16	136.0	174	45	92	0
J. Tavarez	10-12	5.39	153.2	188	74	67	0

Manager-Jeff Torborg

Houston Astros

BATTERS	BA	AB	R	H	HR	RBI	SO	SB
M. Loretta*	.304	283	33	86	4	27	37	1
J. Vizcaino	.303	406	53	123	5	37	40	3
L. Berkman	.292	578	106	169	42	128	118	8
J. Bagwell	.291	571	94	166	31	98	130	7
O. Merced	.287	251	35	72	6	30	50	4
G. Blum	.283	368	45	104	10	52	70	2
D. Ward	.276	453	41	125	12	72	82	1
B. Hunter	.269	201	32	54	3	20	39	5
J. Lugo	.261	322	45	84	8	35	74	9
B. Ausmus	.257	447	57	115	6	50	71	2
C. Biggio	.253	577	96	146	15	58	111	16
R. Hidalgo	.235	388	54	91	15	48	85	6
G. Zaun	.222	185	18	41	3	24	36	1

PITCHERS	W-L	ERA	IP	H	BB	SO	SV
O. Dotel	6-4	1.85	97.1	58	27	118	6
B. Wagner	4-2	2.52	75.0	51	22	88	35
R. Oswalt	19-9	3.01	233.0	215	62	208	0
W. Miller	15-4	3.28	164.2	151	62	144	0
P. Munro	5-5	3.57	80.2	89	23	45	0
R. Stone	3-3	3.61	77.1	78	34	63	1
C. Hernandez	7-5	4.38	111.0	112	61	93	0
N. Cruz	2-6	4.48	78.1	90	29	61	0
S. Reynolds	3-6	4.86	74.0	80	26	47	0
D. Mlicki	4-10	5.34	86.0	101	34	57	0
T. Redding	3-6	5.40	73.1	78	35	63	0
K. Saarloos	6-7	6.01	85.1	100	27	54	0

Manager-Jimy Williams

Los Angeles Dodgers

BATTERS	BA	AB	R	H	HR	RBI	SO	SB
A. Cora	.291	258	37	75	5	28	38	7
S. Green	.285	582	110	166	42	114	112	8
B. Jordan	.285	471	65	134	18	80	86	2
T. Houston*	.281	320	34	90	7	40	62	1
P. Lo Duca	.281	580	74	163	10	64	31	3
D. Roberts	.277	422	63	117	3	34	51	45
M. Grissom	.277	343	57	95	17	60	68	5
E. Karros	.271	524	52	142	13	73	74	4
M. Grudzielanek	.271	536	56	145	9	50	89	4
A. Beltre	.257	587	70	151	21	75	96	7
C. Izturis	.232	439	43	102	1	31	39	7

PITCHERS	W-L	ERA	IP	H	BB	SO	SV
E. Gagne	4-1	1.97	82.1	55	16	114	52
P. Quantrill	5-4	2.70	76.2	80	25	53	1
O. Perez	15-10	3.00	222.1	182	38	155	0
G. Carrara	6-3	3.28	90.2	83	32	56	1
H. Nomo	16-6	3.39	220.1	189	101	193	0
O. Daal	11-9	3.90	161.1	142	54	105	0
A. Ashby	9-13	3.91	181.2	179	65	107	0
K. Ishii	14-10	4.27	154.0	137	106	143	0

Manager-Jim Tracy

Milwaukee Brewers

BATTERS	BA	AB	R	H	HR	RBI	SO	SB
L. Harris	.305	197	23	60	3	17	17	4
A. Sanchez	.289	394	55	114	1	33	62	37
J. Hernandez	.288	525	72	151	24	73	188	3
E. Young	.280	496	57	139	3	28	38	31
R. Sexson	.279	570	86	159	29	102	136	0
R. Machado*	.261	211	19	55	3	22	41	0
J. Hammonds	.257	448	47	115	9	41	86	4
A. Ochoa#	.256	215	32	55	6	21	30	8
R. Thompson	.248	137	16	34	8	24	38	1
M. Stairs	.244	270	41	66	16	41	50	2
G. Jenkins	.243	243	35	59	10	29	60	1
P. Bako	.235	234	24	55	4	20	46	0
R. Belliard	.211	289	30	61	3	26	46	2

PITCHERS	W-L	ERA	IP	H	BB	SO	SV
L. Vizcaino	5-3	2.99	81.1	55	30	79	5
M. DeJean	1-5	3.12	75.0	66	39	65	27
B. Sheets	11-16	4.15	216.2	237	70	170	0
G. Rusch	10-16	4.70	210.2	227	76	140	0
N. Figueroa	1-7	5.03	93.0	96	37	51	0
R. Quevedo	6-11	5.76	139.0	159	68	93	0
J. Cabrera	6-10	6.79	103.1	131	36	61	0

Managers-Davey Lopes, Jerry Royster

Montreal Expos

BATTERS	BA	AB	R	H	HR	RBI	SO	SB
V. Guerrero	.336	614	106	206	39	111	70	40
J. Vidro	.315	604	103	190	19	96	70	2
T. O'Leary	.286	273	27	78	3	37	47	1
C. Floyd#	.275	349	56	96	21	61	78	11
B. Schneider	.275	207	21	57	5	29	41	1
B. Wilkerson	.266	507	92	135	20	59	161	7
M. Barrett	.263	376	41	99	12	49	65	6
O. Cabrera	.263	563	64	148	7	56	53	25
A. Galarraga	.260	292	30	76	9	40	81	2
J. Macias	.255	231	33	59	7	33	44	5
F. Tatis	.228	381	43	87	15	55	90	2
L. Stevens#	.190	205	28	39	10	31	57	1

PITCHERS	W-L	ERA	IP	H	BB	SO	SV
S. Stewart	4-2	3.09	64.0	49	22	67	17
T. Ohka	13-8	3.18	192.2	194	45	118	0
B. Colon#	10-4	3.31	117.0	115	39	74	0
J. Vazquez	10-13	3.91	230.1	243	49	179	0
M. Yoshii	4-9	4.11	131.1	143	32	74	0
J. Brower	3-2	4.37	80.1	77	32	57	0
T. Armas, Jr.	12-12	4.44	164.1	149	78	131	0

Manager-Frank Robinson

New York Mets

BATTERS	BA	AB	R	H	HR	RBI	SO	SB
E. Alfonzo	.308	490	78	151	16	56	55	6
T. Perez	.295	444	52	131	8	47	36	10
M. Piazza	.280	478	69	134	33	98	82	0
R. Alomar	.266	590	73	157	11	53	83	16
R. Cedeno	.260	511	65	133	7	41	92	25
M. Vaughn	.259	487	67	126	26	72	145	0
R. Ordonez	.254	460	53	117	1	42	46	2
V. Wilson	.245	163	19	40	5	26	32	0
J. Valentin	.240	208	18	50	3	30	37	0
J. Burnitz	.215	479	65	103	19	54	135	10
J. McEwing	.199	196	22	39	3	26	50	4

PITCHERS	W-L	ERA	IP	H	BB	SO	SV
A. Benitez	1-0	2.27	67.1	46	25	79	33
D. Weathers	6-3	2.91	77.1	69	36	61	0
S. Trachsel	11-11	3.37	173.2	170	69	105	0
A. Leiter	13-13	3.48	204.1	194	69	172	0
J. Thomson*	9-14	4.71	181.2	201	44	107	0
P. Astacio	12-11	4.79	191.2	192	63	152	0
J. D'Amico	6-10	4.94	145.2	152	37	101	0

Manager-Bobby Valentine

Philadelphia Phillies

BATTERS	BA	AB	R	H	HR	RBI	SO	SB
B. Abreu	.308	572	102	176	20	85	117	31
P. Polanco*	.288	548	75	158	9	49	41	5
P. Burrell	.282	586	96	165	37	116	153	1
M. Lieberthal	.279	476	46	133	15	52	58	0
T. Lee	.265	536	55	142	13	70	104	5
M. Anderson	.258	539	64	139	8	48	71	5
T. Perez	.250	212	22	53	5	20	40	1
D. Glanville	.249	422	49	105	6	29	57	19
J. Rollins	.245	637	82	156	11	60	103	31
J. Giambi#	.244	156	32	38	12	28	54	0
R. Ledee	.227	203	33	46	8	23	50	1

PITCHERS	W-L	ERA	IP	H	BB	SO	SV
J. Mesa	4-6	2.97	75.2	65	39	64	45
M. Timlin*	4-6	2.98	96.2	75	14	50	0
R. Wolf	11-9	3.20	210.2	172	63	172	0
C. Silva	5-0	3.21	84.0	88	22	41	1
V. Padilla	14-11	3.28	206.0	198	53	128	0
J. Roa	4-4	4.04	71.1	78	13	35	0
B. Myers	4-5	4.25	72.0	73	29	34	0
T. Adams	7-9	4.35	136.2	132	58	96	0
D. Coggin	2-5	4.68	77.0	65	51	64	0
B. Duckworth	8-9	5.41	163.0	167	69	167	0
R. Person	4-5	5.44	87.2	79	51	61	0

Manager-Larry Bowa

Pittsburgh Pirates

BATTERS	BA	AB	R	H	HR	RBI	SO	SB
B. Giles	.297	497	95	148	38	103	74	15
J. Kendall	.283	545	59	154	3	44	29	15
A. Rios	.264	208	20	55	1	24	39	1
P. Reese	.264	421	46	111	4	50	81	12
C. Wilson	.264	368	48	97	16	57	116	2
J. Wilson	.252	527	77	133	4	47	74	5
K. Young	.246	468	60	115	16	51	101	4
R. Mackowiak	.244	385	57	94	16	48	120	9
A. Ramirez	.234	522	51	122	18	71	95	2
A. Nunez	.233	253	28	59	2	15	44	3
A. Hyzdu	.232	155	24	36	11	34	44	0
A. Brown	.216	208	20	45	1	21	34	10

PITCHERS	W-L	ERA	IP	H	BB	SO	SV
M. Williams	2-6	2.93	61.1	54	21	43	46
M. Lincoln	2-4	3.11	72.1	80	27	50	0
B. Boehringer	4-4	3.39	79.2	65	33	65	1
K. Wells	12-14	3.58	198.1	197	71	134	0
J. Fogg	12-12	4.35	194.1	199	69	113	0
J. Beimel	2-5	4.64	85.1	88	44	53	0
K. Benson	9-6	4.70	130.1	152	50	79	0
J. Anderson	8-13	5.44	140.2	167	63	47	0
R. Villone	4-6	5.81	93.0	95	34	55	0

Manager-Lloyd McClendon

St. Louis Cardinals

BATTERS	BA	AB	R	H	HR	RBI	SO	SB
A. Pujols	.314	590	118	185	34	127	69	2
J. Edmonds	.311	476	96	148	28	83	134	4
E. Renteria	.305	544	77	166	11	83	57	22
F. Vina	.270	622	75	168	1	54	36	17
S. Rolen*	.266	580	89	154	31	110	102	8
T. Martinez	.262	511	63	134	21	75	71	3
E. Marrero	.262	397	63	104	18	66	72	14
K. Robinson	.260	181	27	47	1	15	29	7
J. Drew	.252	424	61	107	18	56	104	8
M. Cairo	.250	184	28	46	2	23	36	1
M. Matheny	.244	315	31	77	3	35	49	1
M. DiFelice	.230	174	17	40	4	19	42	0
E. Perez	.201	154	22	31	10	26	36	0

PITCHERS	W-L	ERA	IP	H	BB	SO	SV
J. Isringhausen	3-2	2.48	65.1	46	18	68	32
W. Williams	9-4	2.53	103.1	84	25	76	0
A. Benes	5-4	2.78	97.0	80	51	64	0
M. Morris	17-9	3.42	210.1	210	64	171	0
D. Veres	5-8	3.48	82.2	67	39	68	4
D. Kile	5-4	3.72	84.2	82	28	50	0
C. Finley#	7-4	3.80	85.1	69	30	83	0
J. Simontacchi	11-5	4.02	143.1	134	54	72	0
L. Hackman	5-4	4.11	81.0	90	39	46	0
J. Wright*	7-13	5.29	129.1	130	75	77	0

Manager-Tony LaRussa

San Diego Padres

BATTERS	BA	AB	R	H	HR	RBI	SO	SB
R. Klesko	.300	540	90	162	29	95	86	6
M. Kotsay	.292	578	82	169	17	61	89	11
P. Nevin	.285	407	53	116	12	57	87	4
G. Kingsale#	.278	216	27	60	2	28	47	9
R. Vazquez	.274	423	50	116	2	32	79	7
S. Burroughs	.271	192	18	52	1	11	30	2
D. Cruz	.263	514	49	135	7	47	58	2
R. Gant	.262	309	58	81	18	59	59	4
B. Trammell	.243	403	54	98	17	56	71	1
D. Jimenez#	.240	321	39	77	3	33	63	4
J. Matos	.238	185	19	44	2	19	33	1
R. Lankford	.224	205	20	46	6	26	61	2
W. Gonzalez	.220	164	16	36	1	20	24	0
T. Lampkin	.217	281	32	61	10	37	59	4

PITCHERS	W-L	ERA	IP	H	BB	SO	SV
T. Hoffman	2-5	2.73	59.1	52	18	69	38
O. Perez	4-5	3.50	90.0	71	48	94	0
B. Lawrence	12-12	3.69	210.0	230	52	149	0
B. Tomko	10-10	4.49	204.1	212	60	126	0
J. Peavy	6-7	4.52	97.2	106	33	90	0
B. Jones	7-8	5.50	108.0	134	21	60	0

Manager-Bruce Bochy

San Francisco Giants

BATTERS	BA	AB	R	H	HR	RBI	SO	SB
B. Bonds	.370	403	117	149	46	110	47	9
J. Kent	.313	623	102	195	37	108	101	5
B. Santiago	.278	478	56	133	16	74	73	4
R. Martinez	.271	181	26	49	4	25	26	2
K. Lofton#	.267	180	30	48	3	9	22	7
B. Mueller*	.262	366	51	96	7	38	42	0
D. Bell	.261	552	82	144	20	73	80	1
T. Goodwin	.260	154	23	40	1	17	25	16
R. Aurilia	.257	538	76	138	15	61	90	1
R. Sanders	.250	505	75	126	23	85	121	18
J. T. Snow	.246	422	47	104	6	53	90	0
T. Shinjo	.238	362	42	86	9	37	46	5
D. Minor	.237	173	21	41	10	24	34	0

PITCHERS	W-L	ERA	IP	H	BB	SO	SV
R. Nen	6-2	2.20	73.2	64	20	81	43
T. Worrell	8-2	2.25	72.0	55	30	55	0
K. Rueter	14-8	3.23	203.2	204	54	76	0
J. Schmidt	13-8	3.45	185.1	148	73	196	0
R. Ortiz	14-10	3.61	214.2	191	94	137	0
L. Hernandez	12-16	4.38	216.0	233	71	134	0
R. Jensen	13-8	4.51	171.2	183	66	105	0

Manager-Dusty Baker

IT'S A FACT: For the 2nd year in a row, Texas Ranger Alex Rodriguez set the home run record for shortstops. He led the AL in 2002 (57) and 2001 (52). Ernie Banks of the Chicago Cubs had held the record of 47 since 1958.

American League Final Standings, 2002

Eastern Division

	W	L	Pct.	GB	Home	vs. East	vs. Central	vs. West	vs. NL
New York	103	58	.640	—	52-28	46-29	29-07	17-15	8-2
Boston	93	69	.574	10½	42-39	51-25	19-17	18-14	7-3
Toronto	78	84	.481	25½	42-39	41-35	16-16	12-24	8-2
Baltimore	67	95	.414	36½	34-47	26-50	18-14	14-22	0-10
Tampa Bay	55	106	.342	48	30-51	25-50	13-19	10-26	5-5

Central Division

	W	L	Pct.	GB	Home	vs. East	vs. Central	vs. West	vs. NL
Minnesota	94	67	.584	—	54-27	15-17	50-25	19-17	10-8
Chicago	81	81	.500	13½	47-34	18-14	40-36	15-21	8-10
Cleveland	74	88	.457	20½	39-42	19-17	37-39	12-20	6-12
Kansas City	62	100	.383	32½	37-44	10-22	33-43	14-22	5-13
Detroit	55	106	.342	39	33-47	11-25	29-46	09-23	6-12

Western Division

	W	L	Pct.	GB	Home	vs. East	vs. Central	vs. West	vs. NL
Oakland	103	59	.636	—	54-27	23-22	32-09	32-36	16-2
Anaheim*	99	63	.611	4	54-27	28-13	30-15	30-28	11-7
Seattle	93	69	.574	10	48-33	25-20	23-18	34-24	11-7
Texas	72	90	.444	31	42-39	25-16	18-27	20-38	9-9

*Wild card team.

American League Team Statistics, 2002

(Individual Statistics: Batting—at least 150 at-bats; Pitching—at least 70 innings or 10 saves; *changed teams within AL during season, entry includes statistics for more than one team; # changed teams to or from NL during season, entry includes only AL stats)

Team Batting

Team	BAT	AB	R	H	HR	RBI
Anaheim	.282	5678	851	1603	152	811
Boston	.277	5640	859	1560	177	810
New York	.275	5601	897	1540	223	857
Seattle	.275	5569	814	1531	152	771
Minnesota	.272	5582	768	1518	167	731
Texas	.269	5618	843	1510	230	806
Chicago	.268	5502	856	1475	217	819
Toronto	.261	5581	813	1457	187	771
Oakland	.261	5558	800	1450	205	772
Kansas City	.256	5535	737	1415	140	695
Tampa Bay	.253	5604	673	1418	133	640
Cleveland	.249	5423	739	1349	192	706
Detroit	.248	5406	575	1340	124	546
Baltimore	.246	5491	667	1353	165	636

Team Pitching

Team	ERA	IP	H	SO	BB	SV
Oakland	3.68	1452.0	1391	1021	474	48
Anaheim	3.69	1452.1	1345	999	509	54
Boston	3.75	1446.0	1339	1157	430	51
New York	3.87	1452.0	1441	1135	403	53
Seattle	4.07	1445.1	1422	1063	441	43
Minnesota	4.12	1444.2	1454	1026	439	47
Baltimore	4.46	1450.2	1491	967	549	31
Chicago	4.53	1423.0	1422	945	528	35
Toronto	4.80	1438.1	1504	991	590	41
Cleveland	4.91	1424.2	1508	1058	603	34
Detroit	4.93	1414.0	1593	794	463	33
Texas	5.15	1439.2	1528	1030	669	33
Kansas City	5.21	1441.0	1587	909	572	30
Tampa Bay	5.29	1440.1	1567	925	620	25

Anaheim Angels

BATTERS	BA	AB	R	H	HR	RBI	SO	SB
A. Kennedy	.312	474	65	148	7	52	80	17
G. Anderson	.306	638	93	195	29	123	80	6
O. Palmeiro	.300	263	35	79	0	31	22	7
D. Eckstein	.293	608	107	178	8	63	44	21
B. Fullmer	.289	429	75	124	19	59	44	10
T. Salmon	.286	483	84	138	22	88	102	6
S. Spiezio	.285	491	80	140	12	82	52	6
D. Erstad	.283	625	99	177	10	73	67	23
T. Glaus	.250	569	99	142	30	111	144	10
B. Molina	.245	428	34	105	5	47	34	0

PITCHERS	W-L	ERA	IP	H	BB	SO	SV
T. Percival	4-1	1.92	56.1	38	25	68	40
B. Weber	7-2	2.54	78.0	70	22	43	7
J. Washburn	18-6	3.15	206.0	183	59	139	0
J. Lackey	9-4	3.66	108.1	113	33	69	0
R. Ortiz	15-9	3.77	217.1	188	68	162	0
K. Appier	14-12	3.92	188.1	191	64	132	0
S. Schoeneweis	9-8	4.88	118.0	119	49	65	1
A. Sele	8-9	4.89	160.0	190	49	82	0

Manager-Mike Scioscia

Baltimore Orioles

BATTERS	BA	AB	R	H	HR	RBI	SO	SB
G. Matthews, Jr.#	.276	344	54	95	7	38	69	15
J. Conine	.273	451	44	123	15	63	66	8
J. Hairston	.268	426	55	114	5	32	55	21
C. Singleton	.262	466	67	122	9	50	83	20
M. Cordova	.253	458	55	116	18	64	111	1
J. Gibbons	.247	490	71	121	28	69	66	1
T. Batista	.244	615	90	150	31	87	107	5
M. Mora	.233	557	86	130	19	64	108	16
C. Richard	.232	155	15	36	4	21	30	0
G. Gil	.232	422	33	98	12	45	88	2
M. Bordick	.232	367	37	85	8	36	63	7

PITCHERS	W-L	ERA	IP	H	BB	SO	SV
J. Julio	5-6	1.99	68.0	55	27	55	25
W. Roberts	5-4	3.36	75.0	79	32	51	1
R. Lopez	15-9	3.57	196.2	172	62	136	0
R. Bauer	6-7	3.98	83.2	84	36	45	1
S. Ponson	7-9	4.09	176.0	172	63	120	0
J. Johnson	5-14	4.59	131.1	141	41	97	0
T. Driskill	8-8	4.95	132.2	150	48	78	0
S. Erickson	5-12	5.55	160.2	192	68	74	0

Manager-Mike Hargrove

Boston Red Sox

BATTERS	BA	AB	R	H	HR	RBI	SO	SB
M. Ramirez	.349	436	84	152	33	107	85	0
C. Floyd#	.316	171	30	54	7	18	28	4
N. Garciaparra	.310	635	101	197	24	120	63	5
S. Hillenbrand	.293	634	94	186	18	83	95	4
C. Baerga	.286	182	17	52	2	19	20	6
J. Damon	.286	623	118	178	14	63	70	31
R. Sanchez	.286	357	46	102	1	38	31	2
B. Daubach	.266	444	62	118	20	78	126	2
J. Varitek	.266	467	58	124	10	61	95	4
T. Nixon	.256	532	81	136	24	94	109	4
L. Merloni	.247	194	28	48	4	18	35	1
D. Mirabelli	.225	151	17	34	7	25	33	0
R. Henderson	.223	179	40	40	5	16	47	8
T. Clark	.207	275	25	57	3	29	57	0

PITCHERS	W-L	ERA	IP	H	BB	SO	SV
P. Martinez	20-4	2.26	199.1	144	40	239	0
D. Lowe	21-8	2.58	219.2	166	48	127	0
T. Wakefield	11-5	2.81	163.1	121	51	134	3
U. Urbina	1-6	3.00	60.0	44	20	71	40
C. Fossum	5-4	3.46	106.2	113	30	101	1

Manager–Grady Little

Chicago White Sox

BATTERS	BA	AB	R	H	HR	RBI	SO	SB
M. Ordonez	.320	590	116	189	38	135	77	7
P. Konerko	.304	570	81	173	27	104	72	0
S. Alomar Jr.#	.287	167	21	48	7	25	14	0
J. Crede	.285	200	28	57	12	35	40	0
C. Lee	.264	492	82	130	26	80	73	1
T. Graffanino	.262	229	35	60	6	31	38	2
K. Lofton#	.259	352	68	91	8	42	51	22
A. Rowand	.258	302	41	78	7	29	54	0
F. Thomas	.252	523	77	132	28	92	115	3
R. Clayton	.251	342	51	86	7	35	67	5
J. Valentin	.249	474	70	118	25	75	99	3
W. Harris	.233	163	14	38	2	12	21	8
J. Liefer	.230	204	28	47	7	26	60	0
M. Johnson	.209	263	31	55	4	18	52	0

PITCHERS	W-L	ERA	IP	H	BB	SO	SV
D. Marte	1-1	2.83	60.1	44	18	72	10
K. Foulke	2-4	2.90	77.2	65	13	58	11
M. Buehrle	19-12	3.58	239.0	236	61	134	0
A. Osuna	8-2	3.86	67.2	64	28	66	11
R. Biddle	3-4	4.06	77.2	72	39	64	1
J. Garland	12-12	4.58	192.2	188	83	112	0
M. Porzio	2-2	4.81	43.0	40	23	33	0
D. Wright	14-12	5.18	196.1	200	71	136	0
G. Glover	7-8	5.20	138.1	136	52	70	1
T. Ritchie	5-15	6.06	133.2	176	52	77	0

Manager-Jerry Manuel

Cleveland Indians

BATTERS	BA	AB	R	H	HR	RBI	SO	SB
J. Thome	.304	480	101	146	52	118	139	1
E. Burks	.301	518	92	156	32	91	108	2
K. Garcia	.297	202	30	60	16	52	41	0
O. Vizquel	.275	582	85	160	14	72	64	18
R. Gutierrez	.275	353	38	97	4	38	48	0
J. McDonald	.250	264	35	66	1	12	50	3
M. Bradley	.249	325	48	81	9	38	58	6
M. Lawton	.236	416	71	98	15	57	34	8
L. Stevens#	.222	153	22	34	5	26	32	0
C. Magruder*	.217	258	34	56	6	29	55	2
T. Fryman	.217	397	42	86	11	55	82	0
B. Selby	.214	159	15	34	6	21	27	0
E. Diaz	.206	320	34	66	2	16	27	0
R. Branyan#	.205	161	16	33	8	17	65	1

PITCHERS	W-L	ERA	IP	H	BB	SO	SV
B. Colon#	10-4	2.55	116.1	104	31	75	0
C. Sabathia	13-11	4.37	210.0	198	88	149	0
D. Baez	10-11	4.41	165.1	160	82	130	6
C. Finley#	4-11	4.44	105.1	114	48	91	0
B. Wickman	1-3	4.46	34.1	42	10	36	20
M. Wohlers	3-4	4.79	71.1	71	26	46	7
D. Burba	5-5	5.20	145.1	155	57	95	0
R. Drese	10-9	6.55	137.1	176	62	102	0

Managers-Charlie Manuel, Joel Skinner

Detroit Tigers

BATTERS	BA	AB	R	H	HR	RBI	SO	SB
R. Simon	.301	482	51	145	19	82	30	0
D. Young	.284	201	25	57	7	27	39	0
B. Higginson	.282	444	50	125	10	63	45	12
W. Magee,Jr.	.271	347	34	94	6	35	64	2
R. Fick	.270	556	66	150	17	63	90	0
D. Jackson	.257	245	31	63	1	25	36	12
R. Santiago	.243	222	33	54	4	20	48	8
C. Pena*	.242	397	43	96	19	52	111	2
G. Lombard	.241	241	34	58	5	13	78	13
S. Halter	.239	410	46	98	10	39	92	0
D. Easley	.224	304	29	68	8	30	43	1
B. Inge	.202	321	27	65	7	24	101	1
C. Truby#	.199	277	23	55	2	15	71	1
C. Paquette	.194	252	20	49	4	20	53	1

PITCHERS	W-L	ERA	IP	H	BB	SO	SV
J. Acevedo	1-5	2.65	74.2	68	23	43	28
M. Redman	8-15	4.21	203.0	211	51	109	0
M. Maroth	6-10	4.48	128.2	136	36	58	0
S. Sparks	8-16	5.52	189.0	238	67	98	0
J. Farnsworth	2-3	5.79	70.0	100	29	28	0
A. Bernero	4-7	6.20	101.2	128	31	69	0

Managers-Phil Garner, Luis Pujols

Kansas City Royals

BATTERS	BA	AB	R	H	HR	RBI	SO	SB
M. Sweeney	.340	471	81	160	24	86	46	9
R. Ibanez	.294	497	70	146	24	103	76	5
J. Randa	.282	549	63	155	11	80	69	2
C. Beltran	.273	637	114	174	29	105	135	35
A. Hinch	.249	197	25	49	7	27	35	3
M. Tucker	.248	475	65	118	12	56	105	23
C. Febles	.245	351	44	86	4	26	63	16
N. Perez	.236	554	65	131	3	37	53	8
B. Mayne	.236	326	35	77	4	30	54	4
A. Guiel	.233	240	30	56	4	38	61	1
L. Alicea	.228	237	28	54	1	23	34	2
C. Knoblauch	.210	300	41	63	6	22	32	19

PITCHERS	W-L	ERA	IP	H	BB	SO	SV
P. Byrd	17-11	3.90	228.1	224	38	129	0
J. Grimsley	4-7	3.91	71.1	64	37	59	1
R. Hernandez	1-3	4.33	52.0	62	12	39	26
R. Hernandez	4-4	4.36	74.1	79	22	45	0
J. Affeldt	3-4	4.64	77.2	85	37	67	0
M. Asencio	4-7	5.11	123.1	136	64	58	0
J. Suppan	9-16	5.32	208.0	229	68	109	0
D. May	4-10	5.35	131.1	144	50	95	0
R. Bukvich	1-0	6.12	25.0	26	19	20	0
S. Sedlacek	3-5	6.72	84.1	99	36	52	0
W. Obermueller	0-2	11.74	7.2	14	2	5	0

Managers-Tony Muser, John Mizerock, Tony Pena

Minnesota Twins

BATTERS	BA	AB	R	H	HR	RBI	SO	SB
A. Pierzynski	.300	440	54	132	6	49	61	1
J. Jones	.300	577	96	173	27	85	129	6
B. Kielty	.291	289	49	84	12	46	66	4
T. Hunter	.289	561	89	162	29	94	118	23
C. Guzman	.273	623	80	170	9	59	79	12
D. Ortiz	.272	412	52	112	20	75	87	1
D. Mohr	.269	383	55	103	12	45	86	6
C. Koskie	.267	490	71	131	15	69	127	10
D. Mientkiewicz	.261	467	60	122	10	64	69	1
M. LeCroy	.260	181	19	47	7	27	38	0
L. Rivas	.256	316	46	81	4	35	51	9
D. Hocking	.250	260	28	65	2	25	44	0

PITCHERS	W-L	ERA	IP	H	BB	SO	SV
J. Romero	9-2	1.89	81.0	62	36	76	1
L. Hawkins	6-0	2.13	80.1	63	15	63	0
E. Guardado	1-3	2.93	67.2	53	18	70	45
J. Santana	8-6	2.99	108.1	84	49	137	1
T. Fiore	10-3	3.16	91.0	74	43	55	0
R. Reed	15-7	3.78	188.0	192	26	121	0
K. Lohse	13-8	4.23	180.2	181	70	124	0
B. Radke	9-5	4.72	118.1	124	20	62	0
E. Milton	13-9	4.84	171.0	173	30	121	0
J. Mays	4-8	5.38	95.1	113	25	38	0

Manager-Ron Gardenhire

New York Yankees

BATTERS	BA	AB	R	H	HR	RBI	SO	SB
B. Williams	.333	612	102	204	19	102	97	8
J. Giambi	.314	560	120	176	41	122	112	2
A. Soriano	.300	696	128	209	39	102	157	41
D. Jeter	.297	644	124	191	18	75	114	32
J. Posada	.268	511	79	137	20	99	143	1
J. Vander Wal	.260	219	30	57	6	20	58	1
R. Ventura	.247	465	68	115	27	93	101	3
S. Spencer	.247	288	32	71	6	34	62	0
N. Johnson	.243	378	56	92	15	58	98	1
R. White	.240	455	59	109	14	62	86	1
R. Mondesi*	.232	569	90	132	26	88	103	15

PITCHERS	W-L	ERA	IP	H	BB	SO	SV
M. Rivera	1-4	2.74	46.0	35	11	41	28
M. Stanton	7-1	3.00	78.0	73	28	44	6
S. Karsay	6-4	3.26	88.1	87	30	65	12
A. Pettitte	13-5	3.27	134.2	144	32	97	0
R. Mendoza	8-4	3.44	91.2	102	16	61	4
J. Weaver*	11-11	3.52	199.2	193	48	132	2
O. Hernandez	8-5	3.64	146.0	131	36	113	1
D. Wells	19-7	3.75	206.1	210	45	137	0
M. Mussina	18-10	4.05	215.2	208	48	182	0
R. Clemens	13-6	4.35	180.0	172	63	192	0

Manager-Joe Torre

Oakland Athletics

BATTERS	BA	AB	R	H	HR	RBI	SO	SB
M. Tejada	.308	662	108	204	34	131	84	7
R. Durham*	.289	564	114	163	15	70	93	26
S. Hatteberg	.280	492	58	138	15	61	56	0
O. Saenz	.276	156	15	43	6	18	31	1
E. Chavez	.275	585	87	161	34	109	119	8
J. Mabry	.275	193	27	53	11	40	37	1
J. Giambi#	.274	157	26	43	8	17	40	0
M. Ellis	.272	345	58	94	6	35	54	4
D. Justice	.266	398	54	106	11	49	66	4
J. Dye	.252	488	74	123	24	86	108	2
T. Long	.240	587	71	141	16	67	96	3
R. Hernandez	.233	403	51	94	7	42	64	0

PITCHERS	W-L	ERA	IP	H	BB	SO	SV
B. Zito	23-5	2.75	229.1	182	78	182	0
T. Hudson	15-9	2.98	238.1	237	62	152	0
C. Bradford	4-2	3.11	75.1	73	14	56	2
B. Koch	11-4	3.27	93.2	73	46	93	44
M. Mulder	19-7	3.47	207.1	182	55	159	0
T. Lilly*	5-7	3.69	100.0	80	31	77	0
C. Lidle	8-10	3.89	192.0	191	39	111	0
A. Harang	5-4	4.83	78.1	78	45	64	0

Manager-Art Howe

Seattle Mariners

BATTERS	BA	AB	R	H	HR	RBI	SO	SB
I. Suzuki	.321	647	111	208	8	51	62	31
J. Olerud	.300	553	85	166	22	102	66	0
D. Wilson	.295	359	35	106	6	44	81	1
B. Boone	.278	608	88	169	24	107	102	12
E. Martinez	.277	328	42	91	15	59	69	1
M. McLemore	.270	337	54	91	7	41	63	18
R. Sierra	.270	419	47	113	13	60	66	4
D. Relaford	.267	329	55	88	6	43	51	10
C. Guillen	.261	475	73	124	9	56	91	4
B. Davis	.259	228	24	59	7	43	58	1
J. Cirillo	.249	485	51	121	6	54	67	8
M. Cameron	.239	545	84	130	25	80	176	31
J. Offerman*	.232	284	48	66	5	31	38	9

PITCHERS	W-L	ERA	IP	H	BB	SO	SV
K. Sasaki	4-5	2.52	60.2	44	20	73	37
S. Hasegawa	8-3	3.20	70.1	60	30	39	1
J. Pineiro	14-7	3.24	194.1	189	54	136	0
J. Moyer	13-8	3.32	230.2	198	50	147	0
J. Halama	6-5	3.56	101.0	112	33	70	0
R. Franklin	7-5	4.02	118.2	117	22	65	0
I. Valdes*	8-12	4.18	196.0	194	47	102	0
F. Garcia	16-10	4.39	223.2	227	63	181	0
J. Baldwin	7-10	5.28	150.0	179	49	88	0

Manager-Lou Piniella

Tampa Bay Devil Rays

BATTERS	BA	AB	R	H	HR	RBI	SO	SB
A. Huff	.313	454	67	142	23	59	55	4
R. Winn	.298	607	87	181	14	75	109	27
C. Gomez	.265	461	51	122	10	46	58	1
J. Flaherty	.260	281	27	73	4	33	50	2
C. Crawford	.259	259	23	67	2	30	41	9
T. Hall	.258	330	37	85	6	42	27	0
J. Conti	.257	222	26	57	3	21	55	4
S. Cox	.254	560	65	142	16	72	116	5
B. Grieve	.251	482	62	121	19	64	121	8
B. Abernathy	.242	463	46	112	2	40	46	10
J. Sandberg	.229	358	55	82	18	54	139	3
F. Escalona	.217	157	17	34	0	9	44	7
J. Tyner	.214	168	17	36	0	9	19	7
G. Vaughn	.163	251	28	41	8	29	82	3

PITCHERS	W-L	ERA	IP	H	BB	SO	SV
E. Yan	7-8	4.30	69.0	70	29	53	19
J. Kennedy	8-11	4.53	196.2	204	55	109	0
P. Wilson	6-12	4.83	193.2	219	67	111	0
T. Sturtze	4-18	5.18	224.0	271	89	137	0
W. Alvarez	2-3	5.28	75.0	80	36	56	1
T. Harper	5-9	5.46	85.2	101	27	60	1
V. Zambrano	8-8	5.53	114.0	120	68	73	1
J. Sosa	2-7	5.53	99.1	88	54	48	0
R. Rupe	5-10	5.60	90.0	83	25	67	0

Manager-Hal McRae

Texas Rangers

BATTERS	BA	AB	R	H	HR	RBI	SO	SB
I. Rodriguez	.314	408	67	128	19	60	71	5
A. Rodriguez	.300	624	125	187	57	142	122	9
R. Greer	.296	199	24	59	1	17	17	1
M. Lamb	.283	314	54	89	9	33	48	0
J. Gonzalez	.282	277	38	78	8	35	56	2
H. Perry	.276	450	64	124	22	77	66	4
R. Palmeiro	.273	546	99	149	43	105	94	2
F. Catalanotto	.269	212	42	57	3	23	27	9
C. Everett	.267	374	47	100	16	62	77	2
M. Young	.262	573	77	150	9	62	112	6
G. Kapler#	.260	196	25	51	0	17	30	5
K. Mench	.260	366	52	95	15	60	83	1
B. Haselman	.246	179	16	44	3	18	25	0
R. Rivera	.209	158	17	33	4	14	45	4

PITCHERS	W-L	ERA	IP	H	BB	SO	SV
F. Cordero	2-0	1.79	45.1	33	13	41	10
K. Rogers	13-8	3.84	210.2	212	70	107	0
J. Benoit	4-5	5.31	84.2	91	58	59	1
T. Van Poppel	3-2	5.45	72.2	80	29	85	1
H. Irabu	3-8	5.74	47.0	51	16	30	16
C. Park	9-8	5.75	145.2	154	78	121	0
R. Bell	4-3	6.22	94.0	113	35	70	0

Manager-Jerry Narron

Toronto Blue Jays

BATTERS	BA	AB	R	H	HR	RBI	SO	SB
J. Phelps	.309	265	41	82	15	58	82	0
S. Stewart	.303	577	103	175	10	45	60	14
E. Hinske	.279	566	99	158	24	84	138	13
C. Delgado	.277	505	103	140	33	108	126	1
O. Hudson	.276	192	20	53	4	23	27	0
C. Woodward	.276	312	48	86	13	45	72	3
V. Wells	.275	608	87	167	23	100	85	9
D. Berg	.270	374	42	101	4	39	57	0
T. Wilson	.257	265	33	68	8	37	79	0
K. Huckaby	.245	273	29	67	3	22	44	0
J. Cruz	.245	466	64	114	18	70	106	7
F. Lopez	.227	282	35	64	8	34	90	5
J. Lawrence	.180	150	16	27	2	15	38	2

PITCHERS	W-L	ERA	IP	H	BB	SO	SV
R. Halladay	19-7	2.93	239.1	223	62	168	0
K. Escobar	5-7	4.27	78.0	75	44	85	38
P. Walker#	10-5	4.33	139.1	143	51	80	1
C. Carpenter	4-5	5.28	73.1	89	27	45	0
J. Miller	9-5	5.54	102.1	103	66	68	0
E. Loaiza	9-10	5.71	151.1	192	38	87	0
S. Parris	5-5	5.97	75.1	96	35	48	0
L. Prokopec	2-9	6.78	71.2	90	25	41	0

Managers-Buck Martinez, Carlos Tosca

National Baseball Hall of Fame and Museum, Cooperstown, NY[1]

- #Aaron, Hank
- Alexander, Grover Cleveland
- Alston, Walt
- Anderson, Sparky
- Anson, Cap
- Aparicio, Luis
- Appling, Luke
- Ashburn, Richie
- Averill, Earl
- Baker, Home Run
- Bancroft, Dave
- #Banks, Ernie
- Barlick, Al
- Barrow, Edward G.
- Beckley, Jake
- Bell, Cool Papa
- #Bench, Johnny
- Bender, Chief
- Berra, Yogi
- Bottomley, Jim
- Boudreau, Lou
- Bresnahan, Roger
- #Brett, George
- #Brock, Lou
- Brouthers, Dan
- Brown, Mordecai (Three Finger)
- Bulkeley, Morgan C.
- Bunning, Jim
- Burkett, Jesse C.
- Campanella, Roy
- #Carew, Rod
- Carey, Max
- #Carlton, Steve
- Cartwright, Alexander
- Cepeda, Orlando
- Chadwick, Henry
- Chance, Frank
- Chandler, Happy
- Charleston, Oscar
- Chesbro, John
- Chylak, Nestor
- Clarke, Fred
- Clarkson, John
- Clemente, Roberto
- Cobb, Ty[2]
- Cochrane, Mickey
- Collins, Eddie
- Collins, James
- Combs, Earle
- Comiskey, Charles A.
- Conlan, Jocko
- Connolly, Thomas H.
- Connor, Roger
- Coveleski, Stan
- Crawford, Sam
- Cronin, Joe
- Cummings, Candy
- Cuyler, Kiki
- Dandridge, Ray
- Davis, George "Gorgeous"
- Day, Leon
- Dean, Dizzy
- Delahanty, Ed
- Dickey, Bill
- DiHigo, Martin
- DiMaggio, Joe
- Doby, Larry
- Doerr, Bobby
- Drysdale, Don
- Duffy, Hugh
- Durocher, Leo
- Evans, Billy
- Evers, John
- Ewing, Buck
- Faber, Urban
- #Feller, Bob
- Ferrell, Rick
- Fingers, Rollie
- Fisk, Carlton
- Flick, Elmer H.
- Ford, Whitey
- Foster, Andrew (Rube)
- Foster, Bill
- Fox, Nellie
- Foxx, Jimmie
- Frick, Ford
- Frisch, Frank
- Galvin, Pud
- Gehrig, Lou
- Gehringer, Charles
- #Gibson, Bob
- Gibson, Josh
- Giles, Warren
- Gomez, Lefty
- Goslin, Goose
- Greenberg, Hank
- Griffith, Clark
- Grimes, Burleigh
- Grove, Lefty
- Hafey, Chick
- Haines, Jesee
- Hamilton, Bill
- Hanlon, Ned
- Harridge, Will
- Harris, Bucky
- Hartnett, Gabby
- Heilmann, Harry
- Herman, Billy
- Hooper, Harry
- Hornsby, Rogers
- Hoyt, Waite
- Hubbard, Cal
- Hubbell, Carl
- Huggins, Miller
- Hulbert, William
- Hunter, Catfish
- Irvin, Monte
- #Jackson, Reggie
- Jackson, Travis
- Jenkins, Ferguson
- Jennings, Hugh
- Johnson, Byron
- Johnson, William (Judy)
- Johnson, Walter[2]
- Joss, Addie
- #Kaline, Al
- Keefe, Timothy
- Keeler, William
- Kell, George
- Kelley, Joe
- Kelly, George
- Kelly, King
- Killebrew, Harmon
- Kiner, Ralph
- Klein, Chuck
- Klem, Bill
- #Koufax, Sandy
- Lajoie, Napoleon
- Landis, Kenesaw M.
- Lasorda, Tom
- Lazzeri, Tony
- Lemon, Bob
- Leonard, Buck
- Lindstrom, Fred
- Lloyd, Pop
- Lombardi, Ernie
- Lopez, Al
- Lyons, Ted
- Mack, Connie
- MacPhail, Larry
- MacPhail, Lee
- #Mantle, Mickey
- Manush, Henry
- Maranville, Rabbit
- Marichal, Juan
- Marquard, Rube
- Mathews, Eddie
- Mathewson, Christy[2]
- #Mays, Willie
- Mazeroski, Bill
- McCarthy, Joe
- McCarthy, Thomas
- #McCovey, Willie
- McGinnity, Joe
- McGowan, Bill
- McGraw, John
- McKechnie, Bill
- McPhee, John "Bid"
- Medwick, Joe
- Mize, Johnny
- #Morgan, Joe
- #Musial, Stan
- Newhouser, Hal
- Nichols, Kid
- Niekro, Phil
- O'Rourke, James
- Ott, Mel
- Paige, Satchel
- #Palmer, Jim
- Pennock, Herb
- Perez, Tony
- Perry, Gaylord
- Plank, Ed
- #Puckett, Kirby
- Radbourn, Charlie
- Reese, Pee Wee
- Rice, Sam
- Rickey, Branch
- Rixey, Eppa
- Rizzuto, Phil (Scooter)
- Roberts, Robin
- #Robinson, Brooks
- #Robinson, Frank
- #Robinson, Jackie
- Robinson, Wilbert
- Rogan, Joe "Bullet"
- Roush, Edd
- Ruffing, Red
- Rusie, Amos
- Ruth, Babe[2]
- #Ryan, Nolan
- Schalk, Ray
- #Schmidt, Mike
- Schoendienst, Red
- #Seaver, Tom
- Selee, Frank
- Sewell, Joe
- Simmons, Al
- Sisler, George
- Slaughter, Enos
- Smith, Hilton
- *#Smith, Ozzie
- Snider, Duke
- #Spahn, Warren
- Spalding, Albert
- Speaker, Tris
- #Stargell, Willie
- Stearnes, Norman "Turkey"
- Stengel, Casey
- Sutton, Don
- Terry, Bill
- Thompson, Sam
- Tinker, Joe
- Traynor, Pie
- Vance, Dazzy
- Vaughan, Arky
- Veeck, Bill
- Waddell, Rube
- Wagner, Honus[2]
- Wallace, Roderick
- Walsh, Ed
- Waner, Lloyd
- Waner, Paul
- Ward, John
- Weaver, Earl
- Weiss, George
- Welch, Mickey
- Wells, Willie
- Wheat, Zach
- Wilhelm, Hoyt
- Williams, Billy
- Williams, Smokey Joe
- #Williams, Ted
- Williams, Vic
- Wilson, Hack
- #Winfield, Dave
- Wright, George
- Wright, Harry
- Wynn, Early
- #Yastrzemski, Carl
- Yawkey, Tom
- Young, Cy
- Youngs, Ross
- #Yount, Robin

(1) Player must generally be retired for five complete seasons before being eligible for induction. (2) Players inducted in 1936 (the year the Hall of Fame began). # Denotes players chosen in first year of Hall of Fame eligibility. *Denotes 2002 inductees. **NOTE:** Four players, Babe Ruth (1936), Lou Gehrig (1939), Joe DiMaggio (1955), and Roberto Clemente (1973), were inducted less than five years after retirement or, in Clemente's case, death.

Major League Leaders in 2002

American League

Batting: M. Ramirez, Boston, .349; M. Sweeney, Kansas City, .340; B. Williams, New York, .333; I. Suzuki, Seattle, .321; M. Ordonez, Chicago, .320

Runs: A. Soriano, New York, 128; A. Rodriguez, Texas, 125; D. Jeter, New York, 124; J. Giambi, New York, 120; J. Damon, Boston, 118.

Runs Batted In: A. Rodriguez, Texas, 142; M. Ordonez, Chicago, 135; M. Tejada, Oakland, 131; G. Anderson, Anaheim, 123; J. Giambi, New York, 122.

Hits: A. Soriano, New York, 209; I. Suzuki, Seattle, 208; B. Williams, New York, 204; M. Tejada, Oakland, 204; N. Garciaparra, Boston, 197; G. Anderson, Anaheim, 195.

Doubles: G. Anderson, Anaheim, 56; N. Garciaparra, Boston, 56; A. Soriano, New York, 51; M. Ordonez, Chicago, 47; C. Beltran, Kansas City, 44; S. Hillenbrand, Boston 43

Triples: J. Damon, Boston,11; R. Winn, Tampa Bay, 9; M. Young, Texas, 8; I. Suzuki, Seattle 8; C. Beltran, Kansas City, 7

Home Runs: A. Rodriguez, Texas, 57; J. Thome, Cleveland, 52; R. Palmeiro, Texas, 43; J. Giambi, New York, 41; A. Soriano, New York, 39.

Stolen Bases: A. Soriano, New York, 41; C. Beltran,: Kansas City, 35; D. Jeter, New York, 32; J. Damon, Seattle, 31; M. Cameron, Seattle, 31; I. Suzuki, Boston, 31.

Pitching (Most wins: W-L, Pct., ERA): B. Zito, Oakland, 23-5, .821, 2.75; D. Lowe, Boston, 21-8, .724, 2.58; P. Martinez, Boston, 20-4, .833, 2.26; R. Halladay, Toronto, 19-7, .731, 2.93, M. Mulder, Oakland, 19-7, .731, 3.47; D. Wells, New York, 19-7, .731, 3.75; M. Buehrle, Chicago, 19-12, .613, 3.58.

Strikeouts: P. Martinez, Boston, 239; R. Clemens, New York, 192; M. Mussina, New York, 182; B. Zito, Oakland, 182; F. Garcia, Seattle, 181; R. Halladay, Toronto, 168.

Saves: E. Guardado, Minnesota, 45; B. Koch, Oakland, 44; T. Percival, Anaheim, 40; U. Urbina, Boston, 40; K. Escobar, Toronto, 38; K. Sasaki, Seattle, 37.

National League

Batting: B. Bonds, San Francisco, .370; L. Walker, Colorado, .338; V. Guerrero, Montreal, .336, T. Helton, Colorado, .329; C. Jones, Atlanta, .327.

Runs: S. Sosa, Chicago, 122; A. Pujols, St. Louis, 118; B. Bonds, San Francisco, 117; S. Green, Los Angeles, 110; T. Helton, Colorado, 107.

Runs Batted In: L. Berkman, Houston, 128; A. Pujols, St. Louis, 127; P. Burrell, Philadelphia, 116; S. Green, Los Angeles, 114; V. Guerrero, Montreal, 111

Hits: V. Guerrero, Montreal, 206; J. Kent, San Francisco, 195; J. Vidro, Montreal, 190; L. Castillo, Florida, 185; A. Pujols, St. Louis, 185; T. Walker, Cincinnati, 183.

Doubles: B. Abreu, Philadelphia, 50; M. Lowell, Florida 44; J. Vidro, Montreal, 43; O. Cabera, Montreal, 43; T. Walker, Cincinnati, 43; J. Kent, San Francisco, 42; K. Millar, Florida, 41.

Triples: J. Rollins, Philadelphia, 10; Q. McCracken, Arizona, 8; S. Rolen, Philadelphia/St. Louis, 8; R. Furcal, Atlanta, 8; B. Wilkerson, Montreal, 8; J. Payton, New York/Colorado, 7; J. Uribe, Colorado, 7; M. Kostay, San Diego, 7; D. Lee, Florida, 7; D. Roberts, Los Angeles, 7; A. Sanchez, Milwaukee, 7.

Home Runs: S. Sosa, Chicago, 49; B. Bonds, San Francisco, 46; S. Green, Los Angeles, 42; L. Berkman, Houston, 42; V. Guerrero, Montral, 39.

Stolen Bases: L. Castillo, Florida, 48; J. Pierre, Colorado, 47; D. Roberts, Los Angeles, 45; V. Guerrero, Montreal, 40; A. Sanchez, Milwaukee, 37.

Pitching (Most wins: W-L, Pct., ERA): R. Johnson, Arizona, 24-5, .828, 2.32; C. Schilling, Arizona, 23-7, .767, 3.23; R. Oswalt, Houston, 19-9, .679, 3.01; K. Millwood, Atlanta, 18-8, .692, 3.24; T. Glavine, Atlanta, 18-11, .621, 2.96; M. Morris, St. Louis, 17-9, .654, 3.42.

Strikeouts: R. Johnson, Arizona, 334; C. Schilling, Arizona, 316; K. Wood, Chicago, 217; M. Clement, Chicago, 215; R. Oswalt, Houston, 208.

Saves: J. Smoltz, Atlanta, Atlanta, 55; E. Gagne, Los Angeles, 52; M. Williams, Pittsburgh, 46; J. Mesa, Philadelphia, 45; R. Nen, San Francisco, 43.

50 Home Run Club

Only Mark McGwire and Barry Bonds have ever hit 70 or more home runs in a season. Five players—including Babe Ruth and Roger Maris—have hit 60 or more, a feat Sammy Sosa accomplished for the 3d time in 2001. These 5 are at the pinnacle of a select group of players to have hit 50 or more homers in a season. The following list shows each time a player achieved this mark.

HR	Player, team	Year
73	Barry Bonds, San Francisco Giants	2001
70	Mark McGwire, St. Louis Cardinals	1998
66	Sammy Sosa, Chicago Cubs	1998
65	Mark McGwire, St. Louis Cardinals	1999
64	Sammy Sosa, Chicago Cubs	2001
63	Sammy Sosa, Chicago Cubs	1999
61	Roger Maris, N.Y. Yankees	1961
60	Babe Ruth, N.Y. Yankees	1927
59	Babe Ruth, N.Y. Yankees	1921
58	Jimmie Foxx, Philadelphia Athletics	1932
58	Hank Greenberg, Detroit Tigers	1938
58	Mark McGwire, Oakland A's/St. Louis Cardinals	1997
57	Luis Gonzalez, Arizona Diamondbacks	2001
57	Alex Rodriguez, Texas Rangers	2002
56	Hack Wilson, Chicago Cubs	1930
56	Ken Griffey Jr., Seattle Mariners	1997
56	Ken Griffey Jr., Seattle Mariners	1998
54	Babe Ruth, N.Y. Yankees	1920
54	Babe Ruth, N.Y. Yankees	1928
54	Ralph Kiner, Pittsburgh Pirates	1949
54	Mickey Mantle, N.Y. Yankees	1961
52	Mickey Mantle, N.Y. Yankees	1956
52	Willie Mays, San Francisco Giants	1965
52	George Foster, Cincinnati Reds	1977
52	Mark McGwire, Oakland A's	1996
52	Alex Rodriguez, Texas Rangers	2001
52	Jim Thome, Cleveland Indians	2002
51	Ralph Kiner, Pittsburgh Pirates	1947
51	Johnny Mize, N.Y. Giants	1947
51	Willie Mays, N.Y. Giants	1955
51	Cecil Fielder, Detroit Tigers	1990
50	Jimmie Foxx, Boston Red Sox	1938
50	Albert Belle, Cleveland Indians	1995
50	Brady Anderson, Baltimore Orioles	1996
50	Greg Vaughn, San Diego Padres	1998
50	Sammy Sosa, Chicago Cubs	2000

Earned Run Average Leaders

National League

Year	Player, team	G	IP	ERA
1977	John Candelaria, Pittsburgh	33	231	**2.34**
1978	Craig Swan, New York	29	207	**2.43**
1979	J. R. Richard, Houston	38	292	**2.71**
1980	Don Sutton, Los Angeles	32	212	**2.21**
1981	Nolan Ryan, Houston	21	149	**1.69**
1982	Steve Rogers, Montreal	35	277	**2.40**
1983	Atlee Hammaker, San Francisco	23	172	**2.25**
1984	Alejandro Pena, Los Angeles	28	199	**2.48**
1985	Dwight Gooden, New York	35	276	**1.53**
1986	Mike Scott, Houston	37	275	**2.22**
1987	Nolan Ryan, Houston	34	211	**2.76**
1988	Joe Magrane, St. Louis	24	165	**2.18**
1989	Scott Garrelts, San Francisco	30	193	**2.28**
1990	Danny Darwin, Houston	48	162	**2.21**
1991	Dennis Martinez, Montreal	31	222	**2.39**
1992	Bill Swift, San Francisco	30	164	**2.08**
1993	Greg Maddux, Atlanta	36	267	**2.36**
1994	Greg Maddux, Atlanta	25	202	**1.56**
1995	Greg Maddux, Atlanta	28	209	**1.63**
1996	Kevin Brown, Florida	32	233	**1.89**
1997	Pedro Martinez, Montrea	31	241	**1.90**
1998	Greg Maddux, Atlanta	34	251	**2.22**
1999	Randy Johnson, Arizona	35	271	**2.48**
2000	Kevin K. Brown, Los Angeles	33	230	**2.58**
2001	Randy Johnson, Arizona	35	249	**2.49**
2002	Randy Johnson, Arizona	35	260	**2.32**

American League

Year	Player, team	G	IP	ERA
1977	Frank Tanana, California	31	241	**2.54**
1978	Ron Guidry, New York	35	274	**1.74**
1979	Ron Guidry, New York	33	236	**2.78**
1980	Rudy May, New York	41	175	**2.47**
1981	Steve McCatty, Oakland	22	186	**2.32**
1982	Rick Sutcliffe, Cleveland	34	216	**2.96**
1983	Rick Honeycutt, Texas	25	174	**2.42**
1984	Mike Boddicker, Baltimore	34	261	**2.79**
1985	Dave Stieb, Toronto	36	265	**2.48**
1986	Roger Clemens, Boston	33	254	**2.48**
1987	Jimmy Key, Toronto	36	261	**2.76**
1988	Allan Anderson, Minnesota	30	202	**2.45**
1989	Bret Saberhagen, Kansas City	36	262	**2.16**
1990	Roger Clemens, Boston	31	228	**1.93**
1991	Roger Clemens, Boston	35	271	**2.62**
1992	Roger Clemens, Boston	32	246	**2.41**
1993	Kevin Appier, Kansas City	34	238	**2.56**
1994	Steve Ontiveros, Oakland	27	115	**2.65**
1995	Randy Johnson, Seattle	30	214	**2.48**
1996	Juan Guzman, Toronto	27	187	**2.93**
1997	Roger Clemens, Toronto	34	264	**2.05**
1998	Roger Clemens, Toronto	33	234	**2.65**
1999	Pedro Martinez, Boston	31	213	**2.07**
2000	Pedro Martinez, Boston	29	217	**1.74**
2001	Freddy Garcia, Seattle	34	238	**3.05**
2002	Pedro Martinez, Boston	30	199	**2.26**

ERA is computed by multiplying earned runs allowed by 9, then dividing by innings pitched.

Strikeout Leaders

Note: Asterisk (*) indicates the all-time single-season record for each league.

National League

Year	Pitcher, Team	SO
1901	Noodles Hahn, Cincinnati	239
1902	Vic Willis, Boston	225
1903	Christy Mathewson, New York	267
1904	Christy Mathewson, New York	212
1905	Christy Mathewson, New York	206
1906	Fred Beebe, Chicago-St. Louis	171
1907	Christy Mathewson, New York	178
1908	Christy Mathewson, New York	259
1909	Orval Overall, Chicago	205
1910	Earl Moore, Philadelphia	185
1911	Rube Marquard, New York	237
1912	Grover Alexander, Philadelphia	195
1913	Tom Seaton, Philadelphia	168
1914	Grover Alexander, Philadelphia	214
1915	Grover Alexander, Philadelphia	241
1916	Grover Alexander, Philadelphia	167
1917	Grover Alexander, Philadelphia	201
1918	Hippo Vaughn, Chicago	148
1919	Hippo Vaughn, Chicago	141
1920	Grover Alexander, Chicago	173
1921	Burleigh Grimes, Brooklyn	136
1922	Dazzy Vance, Brooklyn	134

American League

Year	Pitcher, Team	SO
1901	Cy Young, Boston	158
1902	Rube Waddell, Philadelphia	210
1903	Rube Waddell, Philadelphia	302
1904	Rube Waddell, Philadelphia	349
1905	Rube Waddell, Philadelphia	287
1906	Rube Waddell, Philadelphia	196
1907	Rube Waddell, Philadelphia	232
1908	Ed Walsh, Chicago	269
1909	Frank Smith, Chicago	177
1910	Walter Johnson, Washington	313
1911	Ed Walsh, Chicago	255
1912	Walter Johnson, Washington	303
1913	Walter Johnson, Washington	243
1914	Walter Johnson, Washington	225
1915	Walter Johnson, Washington	203
1916	Walter Johnson, Washington	228
1917	Walter Johnson, Washington	188
1918	Walter Johnson, Washington	162
1919	Walter Johnson, Washington	147
1920	Stan Coveleski, Cleveland	133
1921	Walter Johnson, Washington	143
1922	Urban Shocker, St. Louis	149

	National League			American League	
Year	Pitcher, Team	SO	Year	Pitcher, Team	SO
1923	Dazzy Vance, Brooklyn	197	1923	Walter Johnson, Washington	130
1924	Dazzy Vance, Brooklyn	262	1924	Walter Johnson, Washington	158
1925	Dazzy Vance, Brooklyn	221	1925	Lefty Grove, Philadelphia	116
1926	Dazzy Vance, Brooklyn	140	1926	Lefty Grove, Philadelphia	194
1927	Dazzy Vance, Brooklyn	184	1927	Lefty Grove, Philadelphia	174
1928	Dazzy Vance, Brooklyn	200	1928	Lefty Grove, Philadelphia	183
1929	Pat Malone, Chicago	166	1929	Lefty Grove, Philadelphia	170
1930	Bill Hallahan, St. Louis	177	1930	Lefty Grove, Philadelphia	209
1931	Bill Hallahan, St. Louis	159	1931	Lefty Grove, Philadelphia	175
1932	Dizzy Dean, St. Louis	191	1932	Red Ruffing, New York	190
1933	Dizzy Dean, St. Louis	199	1933	Lefty Gomez, New York	163
1934	Dizzy Dean, St. Louis	195	1934	Lefty Gomez, New York	158
1935	Dizzy Dean, St. Louis	190	1935	Tommy Bridges, Detroit	163
1936	Van Lingle Mungo, Brooklyn	238	1936	Tommy Bridges, Detroit	175
1937	Carl Hubbell, New York	159	1937	Lefty Gomez, New York	194
1938	Clay Bryant, Chicago	135	1938	Bob Feller, Cleveland	240
1939	Claude Passeau, Philadelphia-Chicago Bucky Walters, Cincinnati	137	1939	Bob Feller, Cleveland	246
1940	Kirby Higbe, Philadelphia	137	1940	Bob Feller, Cleveland	261
1941	John Vander Meer, Cincinnati	202	1941	Bob Feller, Cleveland	260
1942	John Vander Meer, Cincinnati	186	1942	Tex Hughson, Boston Bobo Newsom, Washington	113
1943	John Vander Meer, Cincinnati	174	1943	Allie Reynolds, Cleveland	151
1944	Bill Voiselle, New York	161	1944	Hal Newhouser, Detroit	187
1945	Preacher Roe, Pittsburgh	148	1945	Hal Newhouser, Detroit	212
1946	Johnny Schmitz, Cincinnati	135	1946	Bob Feller, Cleveland	348
1947	Ewell Blackwell, Cincinnati	193	1947	Bob Feller, Cleveland	196
1948	Harry Brecheen, St. Louis	149	1948	Bob Feller, Cleveland	164
1949	Warren Spahn, Boston	151	1949	Virgil Trucks, Detroit	153
1950	Warren Spahn, Boston	191	1950	Bob Lemon, Cleveland	170
1951	Warren Spahn, Boston Don Newcombe, Brooklyn	164	1951	Vic Raschi, New York	164
1952	Warren Spahn, Boston	183	1952	Allie Reynolds, New York	160
1953	Robin Roberts, Philadelphia	198	1953	Billy Pierce, Chicago	186
1954	Robin Roberts, Philadelphia	185	1954	Bob Turley, Baltimore	185
1955	Sam Jones, Chicago	198	1955	Herb Score, Cleveland	245
1956	Sam Jones, Chicago	176	1956	Herb Score, Cleveland	263
1957	Jack Sanford, Philadelphia	188	1957	Early Wynn, Cleveland	184
1958	Sam Jones, St. Louis	225	1958	Early Wynn, Chicago	179
1959	Don Drysdale, Los Angeles	242	1959	Jim Bunning, Detroit	201
1960	Don Drysdale, Los Angeles	246	1960	Jim Bunning, Detroit	201
1961	Sandy Koufax, Los Angeles	269	1961	Camilo Pacual, Minnesota	221
1962	Don Drysdale, Los Angeles	232	1962	Camilo Pacual, Minnesota	206
1963	Sandy Koufax, Los Angeles	306	1963	Camilo Pacual, Minnesota	202
1964	Bob Veale, Pittsburgh	250	1964	Al Downing, New York	217
1965	Sandy Koufax, Los Angeles	*382	1965	Sam McDowell, Cleveland	325
1966	Sandy Koufax, Los Angeles	317	1966	Sam McDowell, Cleveland	225
1967	Jim Bunning, Philadelphia	253	1967	Jim Lonborg, Boston	246
1968	Bob Gibson, St. Louis	268	1968	Sam McDowell, Cleveland	283
1969	Ferguson Jenkins, Chicago	273	1969	Sam McDowell, Cleveland	279
1970	Tom Seaver, New York	283	1970	Sam McDowell, Cleveland	304
1971	Tom Seaver, New York	289	1971	Mickey Lolich, Detroit	308
1972	Steve Carlton, Philadelphia	310	1972	Nolan Ryan, California	329
1973	Tom Seaver, New York	251	1973	Nolan Ryan, California	*383
1974	Steve Carlton, Philadelphia	240	1974	Nolan Ryan, California	367
1975	Tom Seaver, New York	243	1975	Frank Tanana, California	269
1976	Tom Seaver, New York	235	1976	Nolan Ryan, California	327
1977	Phil Niekro, Atlanta	262	1977	Nolan Ryan, California	341
1978	J.R. Richard, Houston	303	1978	Nolan Ryan, California	260
1979	J.R. Richard, Houston	313	1979	Nolan Ryan, California	223
1980	Steve Carlton, Philadelphia	286	1980	Len Barker, Cleveland	187
1981	Fernando Valenzuela, Los Angeles	180	1981	Len Barker, Cleveland	127
1982	Steve Carlton, Philadelphia	286	1982	Floyd Bannister, Seattle	209
1983	Steve Carlton, Philadelphia	275	1983	Jack Morris, Detroit	232
1984	Dwight Gooden, New York	276	1984	Mark Langston, Seattle	204
1985	Dwight Gooden, New York	268	1985	Bert Blyleven, Cleveland-Minnesota	206
1986	Mike Scott, Houston	306	1986	Mark Langston, Seattle	245
1987	Nolan Ryan, Houston	270	1987	Mark Langston, Seattle	262
1988	Nolan Ryan, Houston	228	1988	Roger Clemens, Boston	291
1989	Jose DeLeon, St. Louis	201	1989	Nolan Ryan, Texas	301
1990	David Cone, New York	233	1990	Nolan Ryan, Texas	232
1991	David Cone, New York	241	1991	Roger Clemens, Boston	241
1992	John Smotlz, Atlanta	215	1992	Randy Johnson, Seattle	241
1993	Jose Rijo, Cincinnati	227	1993	Randy Johnson, Seattle	308
1994	Andy Benes, San Diego	189	1994	Randy Johnson, Seattle	204
1995	Hideo Nomo, Los Angeles	236	1995	Randy Johnson, Seattle	294
1996	John Smotlz, Atlanta	276	1996	Roger Clemens, Boston	257
1997	Curt Schilling, Philadelphia	319	1997	Roger Clemens, Toronto	292
1998	Curt Schilling, Philadelphia	300	1998	Roger Clemens, Toronto	271
1999	Randy Johnson, Arizona	364	1999	Pedro Martinez, Boston	313
2000	Randy Johnson, Arizona	347	2000	Pedro Martinez, Boston	284
2001	Randy Johnson, Arizona	372	2001	Hideo Nomo, Boston	220
2002	Randy Johnson, Arizona	334	2002	Pedro Martinez, Boston	239

Victory Leaders

Note: Asterisk (*) indicates the all-time single-season record for each league in the "modern" era beginning in 1901.

National League			American League		
Year	Pitcher, Team	Wins	Year	Pitcher, Team	Wins
1901	Bill Donavan, Brooklyn	25	1901	Cy Young, Boston	33
1902	Jack Chesbro, Pittsburgh	28	1902	Cy Young, Boston	32
1903	Joe McGinnity, New York	31	1903	Cy Young, Boston	28
1904	Joe McGinnity, New York	35	1904	Jack Chesbro, New York	*41
1905	Christy Mathewson, New York	31	1905	Rube Waddell, Philadelphia	27
1906	Joe McGinnity, New York	27	1906	Al Orth, New York	27
1907	Christy Mathewson, New York	24	1907	Doc White, Chicago	27
1908	Christy Mathewson, New York	*37	1908	Ed Walsh, Chicago	40
1909	Mordecai Brown, Chicago	27	1909	George Mullin, Detroit	29
1910	Christy Mathewson, New York	27	1910	Jack Coombs, Philadelphia	31
1911	Grover Alexander, Chicago	28	1911	Jack Coombs, Philadelphia	28
1912	Rube Marquard, New York	26	1912	Joe Wood, Boston	34
1913	Tom Seaton, Philadelphia	27	1913	Walter Johnson, Washington	36
1914	Grover Alexander, Philadelphia	27	1914	Walter Johnson, Washington	28
1915	Grover Alexander, Philadelphia	31	1915	Walter Johnson, Washington	27
1916	Grover Alexander, Philadelphia	33	1916	Walter Johnson, Washington	25
1917	Grover Alexander, Philadelphia	30	1917	Eddie Cicotte, Chicago	28
1918	Hippo Vaughn, Chicago	22	1918	Walter Johnson, Washington	23
1919	Jesse Barnes, New York	25	1919	Eddie Cicotte, Chicago	29
1920	Grover Alexander, Philadelphia	27	1920	Jim Bagby, Cleveland	31
1921	Burleigh Grimes, Brooklyn	22	1921	Urban Shocker, St. Louis	27
1922	Eppa Rixey, Cincinnati	25	1922	Eddie Rommel, Philadelphia	27
1923	Dolf Luque, Cincinnati	27	1923	George Uhle, Cleveland	26
1924	Dazzy Vance, Brooklyn	28	1924	Walter Johnson, Washington	23
1925	Dazzy Vance, Brooklyn	22	1925	Eddie Rommel, Philadelphia	21
1926	Flint Rhem, St. Louis	20	1926	George Uhle, Cleveland	27
1927	Charlie Root, Chicago	26	1927	Ted Lyons, Chicago	22
1928	Burleigh Grimes, Pittsburgh	25	1928	George Pipgras, New York	24
1929	Pat Malone, Chicago	22	1929	George Earnshaw, Philadelphia	24
1930	Pat Malone, Chicago	20	1930	Lefty Grove, Philadelphia	28
1931	Heine Meine, Pittsburgh	19	1931	Lefty Grove, Philadelphia	31
1932	Lon Warneke, Chicago	22	1932	Alvin Crowder, Washington	26
1933	Carl Hubbell, New York	23	1933	Lefty Grove, Philadelphia	24
1934	Dizzy Dean, St. Louis	30	1934	Lefty Gomez, New York	26
1935	Dizzy Dean, St. Louis	28	1935	Wes Ferrell, Boston	25
1936	Carl Hubbell, New York	26	1936	Tommy Bridges, Detroit	23
1937	Carl Hubbell, New York	22	1937	Lefty Gomez, New York	21
1938	Bill Lee, Chicago	22	1938	Red Ruffing, New York	21
1939	Bucky Walters, Cincinnati	27	1939	Bob Feller, Cleveland	24
1940	Bucky Walters, Cincinnati	22	1940	Bob Feller, Cleveland	27
1941	Whit Wyatt, Brooklyn	22	1941	Bob Feller, Cleveland	25
1942	Mort Cooper, St. Louis	22	1942	Tex Hughson, Boston	22
1943	Rip Sewell, Pittsburgh	21	1943	Dizzy Trout, Detroit	20
1944	Bucky Walters, Cincinnati	23	1944	Hal Newhouser, Detroit	29
1945	Red Barrett, Boston-St. Louis	23	1945	Hal Newhouser, Detroit	25
1946	Howie Pollet, St. Louis	21	1946	Hal Newhouser, Detroit	26
1947	Ewell Blackwell, Cincinnati	22	1947	Bob Feller, Cleveland	20
1948	Johnny Sain, Boston	24	1948	Hal Newhouser, Detroit	21
1949	Warren Spahn, Boston	21	1949	Mel Parnell, Boston	25
1950	Warren Spahn, Boston	21	1950	Bob Lemon, Cleveland	23
1951	Sal Maglie, New York	23	1951	Bob Feller, Cleveland	22
1952	Robin Roberts, Philadelphia	28	1952	Bobby Shantz, Philadelphia	24
1953	Warren Spahn, Milwaukee	23	1953	Bob Porterfield, Washington	22
1954	Robin Roberts, Philadelphia	23	1954	Early Wynn, Cleveland	23
1955	Robin Roberts, Philadelphia	23	1955	Frank Sullivan, Boston	18
1956	Don Newcombe, Brooklyn	27	1956	Frank Lary, Detroit	21
1957	Warren Spahn, Milwaukee	21	1957	Billy Pierce, Chicago	20
1958	Warren Spahn, Milwaukee	22	1958	Bob Turley, New York	21
1959	Warren Spahn, Milwaukee	21	1959	Early Wynn, Chicago	22
1960	Warren Spahn, Milwaukee	21	1960	Jim Perry, Cleveland	18
1961	Warren Spahn, Milwaukee	21	1961	Whitey Ford, New York	25
1962	Don Drysdale, Los Angeles	25	1962	Ralph Terry, New York	23
1963	Juan Marichal, San Francisco	25	1963	Whitey Ford, New York	24
1964	Larry Jackson, Chicago	24	1964	Gary Peters, Chicago	20
1965	Sandy Koufax, Los Angeles	26	1965	Mudcat (Jim) Grant, Minnesota	21
1966	Sandy Koufax, Los Angeles	27	1966	Jim Kaat, Minnesota	25
1967	Mike McCormick, San Francisco	22	1967	Earl Wilson, Detroit	22
1968	Juan Marichal, San Francisco	26	1968	Denny McLain, Detroit	31
1969	Tom Seaver, New York	25	1969	Denny McLain, Detroit	24
1970	Gaylord Perry, San Francisco	23	1970	Jim Perry, Minnesota	24
1971	Fergie Jenkins, Chicago	24	1971	Mickey Lolich, Detroit	25
1972	Steve Carlton, Philadelphia	27	1972	Wilbur Wood, Chicago	24
1973	Ron Bryant, San Francisco	24	1973	Wilbur Wood, Chicago	24
1974	Phil Niekro, Atlanta	20	1974	Fergie Jenkins, Texas	25
1975	Tom Seaver, New York	22	1975	Jim Palmer, Baltimore	23
1976	Randy Jones, San Diego	22	1976	Jim Palmer, Baltimore	22
1977	Steve Carlton, Philadelphia	23	1977	Jim Palmer, Baltimore	20
1978	Gaylord Perry, San Diego	21	1978	Ron Guidry, New York	25
1979	Phil Niekro, Atlanta	21	1979	Mike Flanagan, Baltimore	23
1980	Steve Carlton, Philadelphia	24	1980	Steve Stone, Baltimore	25

National League			American League		
Year	**Pitcher, Team**	**Wins**	**Year**	**Pitcher, Team**	**Wins**
1981	Tom Seaver, Cincinnati	14	1981	Pete Vuckovich, Milwaukee	14
1982	Steve Carlton, Philadelphia	23	1982	La Marr Hoyt, Chicago	19
1983	John Denny, Philadelphia	19	1983	La Marr Hoyt, Chicago	24
1984	Joaquin Andujar, St. Louis	20	1984	Mike Boddicker, Baltimore	20
1985	Dwight Gooden, New York	24	1985	Ron Guidry, New York	22
1986	Fernando Valezuela, Los Angeles	21	1986	Roger Clemens, Boston	24
1987	Rick Sutcliffe, Chicago	18	1987	Dave Stewart, Oakland	20
1988	Danny Jackson, Cincinnati	23	1988	Frank Viola, Minnesota	24
1989	Mike Scott, Houston	20	1989	Bret Saberhagen, Kansas City	23
1990	Doug Drabek, Pittsburgh	22	1990	Bob Welch, Oakland	27
1991	John Smiley, Pittsburgh	20	1991	Bill Gullickson, Detroit	20
1992	Greg Maddux, Chicago	20	1992	Jack Morris, Toronto	21
1993	Tom Glavine, Atlanta	22	1993	Jack McDowell, Chicago	22
1994	Greg Maddux, Atlanta	16	1994	Jimmy Key, New York	17
1995	Greg Maddux, Atlanta	19	1995	Mike Mussina, Baltimore	19
1996	John Smotz, Atlanta	24	1996	Andy Pettitte, New York	21
1997	Denny Neagle, Atlanta	20	1997	Roger Clemens, Toronto	21
1998	Tom Glavine, Atlanta	20	1998	Rick Helling, Texas; Roger Clemens, Toronto	20
1999	Mike Hampton, Houston	22	1999	Pedro Martinez, Boston	23
2000	Tom Glavine, Atlanta	21	2000	David Wells, Toronto	20
2001	Matt Morris, St. Louis; Curt Schilling, Arizona	22	2001	Mark Mulder, Oakland	21
2002	Randy Johnson, Arizona	24	2002	Barry Zito, Oakland	23

World Series Results, 1903-2001

1903	Boston AL 5, Pittsburgh NL 3
1904	No series
1905	New York NL 4, Philadelphia AL 1
1906	Chicago AL 4, Chicago NL 2
1907	Chicago NL 4, Detroit AL 0, 1 tie
1908	Chicago NL 4, Detroit AL 1
1909	Pittsburgh NL 4, Detroit AL 3
1910	Philadelphia AL 4, Chicago NL 1
1911	Philadelphia AL 4, New York NL 2
1912	Boston AL 4, New York NL 3, 1 tie
1913	Philadelphia AL 4, New York NL 1
1914	Boston NL 4, Philadelphia AL 0
1915	Boston AL 4, Philadelphia NL 1
1916	Boston AL 4, Brooklyn NL 1
1917	Chicago AL 4, New York NL 2
1918	Boston AL 4, Chicago NL 2
1919	Cincinnati NL 5, Chicago AL 3
1920	Cleveland AL 5, Brooklyn NL 2
1921	New York NL 5, New York AL 3
1922	New York NL 4, New York AL 0, 1 tie
1923	New York AL 4, New York NL 2
1924	Washington AL 4, New York NL 3
1925	Pittsburgh NL 4, Washington AL 3
1926	St. Louis NL 4, New York AL 3
1927	New York AL 4, Pittsburgh NL 0
1928	New York AL 4, St. Louis NL 0
1929	Philadelphia AL 4, Chicago NL 1
1930	Philadelphia AL 4, St. Louis NL 2
1931	St. Louis NL 4, Philadelphia AL 3
1932	New York AL 4, Chicago NL 0
1933	New York NL 4, Washington AL 1
1934	St. Louis NL 4, Detroit AL 3
1935	Detroit AL 4, Chicago NL 2
1936	New York AL 4, New York NL 2
1937	New York AL 4, New York NL 1
1938	New York AL 4, Chicago NL 0
1939	New York AL 4, Cincinnati NL 0
1940	Cincinnati NL 4, Detroit AL 3
1941	New York AL 4, Brooklyn NL 1
1942	St. Louis NL 4, New York AL 1
1943	New York AL 4, St. Louis NL 1
1944	St. Louis NL 4, St. Louis AL 2
1945	Detroit AL 4, Chicago NL 3
1946	St. Louis NL 4, Boston AL 3
1947	New York AL 4, Brooklyn NL 3
1948	Cleveland AL 4, Boston NL 2
1949	New York AL 4, Brooklyn NL 1
1950	New York AL 4, Philadelphia NL 0
1951	New York AL 4, New York NL 2
1952	New York AL 4, Brooklyn NL 3
1953	New York AL 4, Brooklyn NL 2
1954	New York NL 4, Cleveland AL 0
1955	Brooklyn NL 4, New York AL 3
1956	New York AL 4, Brooklyn NL 3
1957	Milwaukee NL 4, New York AL 3
1958	New York AL 4, Milwaukee NL 3
1959	Los Angeles NL 4, Chicago AL 2
1960	Pittsburgh NL 4, New York AL 3
1961	New York AL 4, Cincinnati NL 1
1962	New York AL 4, San Francisco NL 3
1963	Los Angeles NL 4, New York AL 0
1964	St. Louis NL 4, New York AL 3
1965	Los Angeles NL 4, Minnesota AL 3
1966	Baltimore AL 4, Los Angeles NL 0
1967	St. Louis NL 4, Boston AL 3
1968	Detroit AL 4, St. Louis NL 3
1969	New York NL 4, Baltimore AL 1
1970	Baltimore AL 4, Cincinnati NL 1
1971	Pittsburgh NL 4, Baltimore AL 3
1972	Oakland AL 4, Cincinnati NL 3
1973	Oakland AL 4, New York NL 3
1974	Oakland AL 4, Los Angeles NL 1
1975	Cincinnati NL 4, Boston AL 3
1976	Cincinnati NL 4, New York AL 0
1977	New York AL 4, Los Angeles NL 2
1978	New York AL 4, Los Angeles NL 2
1979	Pittsburgh NL 4, Baltimore AL 3
1980	Philadelphia NL 4, Kansas City AL 2
1981	Los Angeles NL 4, New York AL 2
1982	St. Louis NL 4, Milwaukee AL 3
1983	Baltimore AL 4, Philadelphia NL 1
1984	Detroit AL 4, San Diego NL 1
1985	Kansas City AL 4, St. Louis NL 3
1986	New York NL 4, Boston AL 3
1987	Minnesota AL 4, St. Louis NL 3
1988	Los Angeles NL 4, Oakland AL 1
1989	Oakland AL 4, San Francisco NL 0
1990	Cincinnati NL 4, Oakland AL 0
1991	Minnesota AL 4, Atlanta NL 3
1992	Toronto AL 4, Atlanta NL 2
1993	Toronto AL 4, Philadelphia NL 2
1994	No series
1995	Atlanta NL 4, Cleveland AL 2
1996	New York AL 4, Atlanta NL 2
1997	Florida NL 4, Cleveland AL 3
1998	New York AL 4, San Diego NL 0
1999	New York AL 4, Atlanta NL 0
2000	New York AL 4, New York NL 1
2001	Arizona NL 4, New York AL 3

World Series MVP

Year	Player, Position, Team
1955	Johnny Podres, p, Brooklyn
1956	Don Larsen, p, New York, AL
1957	Lew Burdette, p, Milwaukee, NL
1958	Bob Turley, p, NY AL
1959	Larry Sherry, p, LA
1960[1]	Bobby Richardson, 2b, NY, AL
1961	Whitey Ford, p, NY, AL
1962	Ralph Terry, p, NY, AL
1963	Sandy Koufax, p, Los Angeles, NL
1964	Bob Gibson, p, St. Louis
1965	Sandy Koufax, p, Los Angeles, NL
1966	Frank Robinson, of, Baltimore
1967	Bob Gibson, p, St. Louis
1968	Mickey Lolich, p, Detroit
1969	Donn Clendenon, 1b, NY, NL
1970	Brooks Robinson, 3b, Baltimore
1971	Roberto Clemente, of, Pittsburgh
1972	Gene Tenace, c, Oakland
1973	Reggie Jackson, of, Oakland
1974	Rollie Fingers, p, Oakland
1975	Pete Rose, 3b, Cincinnati
1976	Johnny Bench, c, Cincinnati
1977	Reggie Jackson, of, NY, AL
1978	Bucky Dent, ss, NY, AL
1979	Willie Stargell, 1b, Pittsburgh
1980	Mike Schmidt, 3b, Philadelphia
1981	Ron Cey, 3b, LA
	Pedro Guerrero, of, LA
	Steve Yeager, c, LA
1982	Darrell Porter, c, St. Louis
1983	Rick Dempsey, c, Baltimore
1984	Alan Trammell, ss, Detroit
1985	Bret Saberhagen, p, Kansas City
1986	Ray Knight, 3b, NY, NL
1987	Frank Viola, p, Minnesota
1988	Orel Hershiser, p, LA
1989	Dave Stewart, p, Oakland
1990	Jose Rijo, p, Cincinnati
1991	Jack Morris, p, Minnesota
1992	Pat Borders, c, Toronto
1993	Paul Molitor, dh, Toronto
1994	no series
1995	Tom Glavine, p, Atlanta
1996	John Wetteland, p, NY, AL
1997	Livan Hernandez, p, Florida
1998	Scott Brosius, 3b, NY, AL
1999	Mariano Rivera, p, NY, AL
2000	Derek Jeter, ss, NY, AL
2001	Curt Schilling, p, Arizona
	Randy Johnson, p, Arizona

(1) Bobby Richardson won the MVP although Pittsburgh beat New York.

World Series Won-Lost Records, by Franchise[1]

Team	Wins	Losses
New York Yankees	26	12
Philadelphia/Kansas City/Oakland A's	9	5
St. Louis Cardinals	9	6
Brooklyn/Los Angeles Dodgers	6	12
Pittsburgh Pirates	5	2
Boston Red Sox	5	4
Cincinnati Reds	5	4
New York/San Francisco Giants	5	11
Detroit Tigers	4	5
Washington Senators/Minnesota Twins	3	3
St. Louis Browns/Baltimore Orioles	3	4
Boston/Milwaukee/Atlanta Braves	3	6
Toronto Blue Jays	2	0
New York Mets	2	2
Chicago White Sox	2	2
Cleveland Indians	2	3
Chicago Cubs	2	8
Arizona Diamondbacks	1	0
Florida Marlins	1	0
Kansas City Royals	1	1
Philadelphia Phillies	1	4
Seattle Pilots/Milwaukee Brewers	0	1
San Diego Padres	0	2

(1) Through 2001.

All-Time Major League Leaders

(*player in 2002 season)

Games	
Pete Rose	3,562
Carl Yastrzemski	3,308
Hank Aaron	3,298
Rickey Henderson*	3,051
Ty Cobb	3,035
Eddie Murray	3,026
Stan Musial	3,026
Cal Ripken Jr.	3,001
Willie Mays	2,992
Dave Winfield	2,973

At Bats	
Pete Rose	14,053
Hank Aaron	12,364
Carl Yastrzemski	11,988
Cal Ripken Jr.	11,551
Ty Cobb	11,434
Eddie Murray	11,336
Robin Yount	11,008
Dave Winfield	11,003
Stan Musial	10,972
Rickey Henderson*	10,889

Runs Batted In	
Hank Aaron	2,297
Babe Ruth	2,213
Lou Gehrig	1,995
Stan Musial	1,951
Ty Cobb	1,937
Jimmie Foxx	1,922
Eddie Murray	1,917
Willie Mays	1,903
Cap Anson	1,879
Mel Ott	1,860

Runs	
Rickey Henderson*	2,288
Ty Cobb	2,246
Hank Aaron	2,174
Babe Ruth	2,174
Pete Rose	2,165
Willie Mays	2,062
Stan Musial	1,949
Lou Gehrig	1,888
Tris Speaker	1,882
Mel Ott	1,859

Stolen Bases	
Rickey Henderson*	1,403
Lou Brock	938
Billy Hamilton	912
Ty Cobb	892
Tim Raines*	808
Vince Coleman	752
Eddie Collins	744
Arlie Latham	739
Max Carey	738
Honus Wagner	722

Triples	
Sam Crawford	309
Ty Cobb	295
Honus Wagner	252
Jake Beckley	243
Roger Connor	233
Tris Speaker	222
Fred Clarke	220
Dan Brouthers	205
Joe Kelley	194
Paul Waner	191

Doubles	
Tris Speaker	792
Pete Rose	746
Stan Musial	725
Ty Cobb	724
George Brett	665
Nap Lajoie	657
Carl Yastrzemski	646
Honus Wagner	640
Hank Aaron	624
Paul Moliter	605
Paul Waner	605

Walks	
Rickey Henderson*	2,179
Babe Ruth	2,062
Ted Williams	2,019
Barry Bonds*	1,724
Joe Morgan	1,865
Carl Yastrzemski	1,845
Mickey Mantle	1,733
Mel Ott	1,708
Eddie Yost	1,614
Darrell Evans	1,605

Strikeouts	
Nolan Ryan	5,714
Steve Carlton	4,136
Roger Clemens*	3,909
Randy Johnson*	3,746
Bert Blyleven	3,701
Tom Seaver	3,640
Don Sutton	3,574
Gaylord Perry	3,534
Walter Johnson	3,509
Phil Niekro	3,342

Saves	
Lee Smith	478
John Franco	422
Dennis Eckersley	390
Jeff Reardon	367
Trevor Hoffman	352
Randy Myers	347
Rollie Fingers	341
John Wetteland	330
Roberto Hernandez	320
Rick Aguilera	318

Shutouts	
Walter Johnson	110
Grover Alexander	90
Christy Mathewson	79
Cy Young	76
Eddie Plank	69
Warren Spahn	63
Nolan Ryan	61
Tom Seaver	61
Bert Blyleven	60
Don Sutton	58

Losses	
Cy Young	316
Jim Galvin	308
Nolan Ryan	292
Walter Johnson	279
Phil Niekro	274
Gaylord Perry	265
Don Sutton	256
Jack Powell	254
Eppa Rixey	251
Bert Blyleven	250

All-Time Home Run Leaders

Player	HR
Hank Aaron	755
Babe Ruth	714
Willie Mays	660
Barry Bonds*	613
Frank Robinson	586
Mark McGwire	583
Harmon Killebrew	573
Reggie Jackson	563
Mike Schmidt	548
Mickey Mantle	536
Jimmie Foxx	534
Willie McCovey	521
Ted Williams	521
Ernie Banks	512
Ed Mathews	512
Mel Ott	511
Eddie Murray	504
Sammy Sosa*	499
Lou Gehrig	493
Rafael Palmeiro*	490
Fred McGriff*	478
Stan Musial	475
Willie Stargell	475
Ken Griffey Jr.*	468
Dave Winfield	465
Jose Canseco	462
Carl Yastrzemski	452
Dave Kingman	442
Andre Dawson	438
Cal Ripken Jr.	431
Billy Williams	426
Darrell Evans	414
Duke Snider	407
Juan Gonzalez*	405
Al Kaline	399
Dale Murphy	398
Joe Carter	396
Andres Galarraga*	396
Graig Nettles	390
Johnny Bench	389
Dwight Evans	385
Harold Baines	384
Frank Howard	382
Jim Rice	382
Albert Belle	381
Orlando Cepeda	380
Jeff Bagwell*	379
Norm Cash	377
Tony Perez	379
Carlton Fisk	376
Frank Thomas*	376

Players With 3,000 Major League Hits

Player	Hits
Pete Rose	4,256
Ty Cobb	4,189
Hank Aaron	3,771
Stan Musial	3,630
Tris Speaker	3,514
Carl Yastrzemski	3,419
Honus Wagner	3,415
Paul Molitor	3,319
Eddie Collins	3,315
Willie Mays	3,283
Eddie Murray	3,255
Nap Lajoie	3,242
Cal Ripken Jr.	3,184
George Brett	3,154
Paul Waner	3,152
Robin Yount	3,142
Tony Gwynn	3,141
Dave Winfield	3,110
Rod Carew	3,053
Rickey Henderson*	3,040
Lou Brock	3,023
Wade Boggs	3,010
Al Kaline	3,007
Roberto Clemente	3,000

Pitchers With 300 Major League Wins

Cy Young	511
Walter Johnson	417
Grover Alexander	373
Christy Mathewson	373
Warren Spahn	363
Kid Nichols	361
Pud Galvin	360
Tim Keefe	342
Steve Carlton	329
John Clarkson	328
Eddie Plank	326
Nolan Ryan	324
Don Sutton	324
Phil Niekro	318
Gaylord Perry	314
Tom Seaver	311
Charley Radbourn	309
Mickey Welch	307
Lefty Grove	300
Early Wynn	300

All-Time Major League Single-Season Leaders

(*player active in 2002 season; records for "modern" era beginning 1901)

Home Runs

Barry Bonds* (2001)	73
Mark McGwire (1998)	70
Sammy Sosa* (1998)	66
Mark McGwire (1999)	65
Sammy Sosa* (2001)	64

Runs

Babe Ruth (1921)	177
Lou Gehrig (1936)	167
Lou Gehrig (1931)	163
Babe Ruth (1928)	163
Chuck Klein (1930)	158
Babe Ruth (1920, 1927)	158

Hits

George Sisler (1920)	257
Bill Terry (1930)	254
Lefty O'Doul (1929)	254
Al Simmons (1925)	253
Chuck Klein (1930)	250
Rogers Hornsby (1922)	250

Runs Batted In

Hack Wilson (1930)	191
Lou Gehrig (1931)	184
Hank Greenberg (1937)	183
Jimmie Foxx (1938)	175
Lou Gehrig (1927)	175

Batting Average

Nap Lajoie (1901)	.426
Rogers Hornsby (1924)	.424
George Sisler (1922)	.420
Ty Cobb (1911)	.420
Ty Cobb (1912)	.409

Stolen Bases

Rickey Henderson* (1982)	130
Lou Brock (1974)	118
Vince Coleman (1985)	110
Vince Coleman (1987)	109
Rickey Henderson* (1983)	108

Walks (Batter)

Barry Bonds* (2002)	198
Barry Bonds* (2001)	177
Babe Ruth (1923)	170
Mark McGwire* (1998)	162
Ted Williams (1949)	162
Ted Williams (1947)	162

Strikeouts (Batter)

Bobby Bonds (1970)	189
Jose Hernandez* (2002)	188
Preston Wilson* (2000)	187
Bobby Bonds (1969)	187
Rob Deer (1987)	186
Jim Thome* (2001)	185
Jose Hernandez* (2001)	185
Pete Incaviglia (1986)	185

Earned Run Average

Dutch Leonard (1914)	0.96
Mordecai Brown (1906)	1.04
Bob Gibson (1968)	1.12
Walter Johnson (1913)	1.14
Christy Mathewson (1909)	1.14

Wins

Jack Chesbro (1904)	41
Ed Walsh (1908)	40
Christy Mathewson (1908)	37
Walter Johnson (1913)	36
Joe McGinnity (1904)	35

Strikeouts

Nolan Ryan (1973)	383
Sandy Koufax (1965)	382
Randy Johnson* (2001)	372
Nolan Ryan (1974)	367
Randy Johnson* (1999)	364

Saves

Bobby Thigpen (1990)	57
John Smoltz* (2002)	55
Trevor Hoffman* (1998)	53
Randy Myers (1993)	53
Eric Gagne* (2002)	52
Rod Beck* (1998)	51

All-Star Baseball Games, 1933-2002

Year	Winner, Score	Host team
1933*	American, 4-2	Chicago (AL)
1934*	American, 9-7	New York (NL)
1935*	American, 4-1	Cleveland
1936*	National, 4-3	Boston (NL)
1937*	American, 8-3	Washington
1938*	National, 4-1	Cincinnati
1939*	American, 3-1	New York (AL)
1940*	National, 4-0	St. Louis (NL)
1941*	American, 7-5	Detroit
1942	American, 3-1	New York (NL)
1943	American, 5-3	Philadelphia (AL)
1944	National, 7-1	Pittsburgh
1945	(Not played)	
1946*	American, 12-0	Boston (AL)
1947*	American, 2-1	Chicago (NL)
1948*	American, 5-2	St. Louis (AL)
1949*	American, 11-7	Brooklyn
1950*	National, 4-3[1]	Chicago (AL)
1951*	National, 8-3	Detroit
1952*	National, 3-2	Philadelphia (NL)
1953*	National, 5-1	Cincinnati
1954*	American, 11-9	Cleveland
1955*	National, 6-5[2]	Milwaukee
1956*	National, 7-3	Washington
1957*	American, 6-5	St. Louis
1958*	American, 4-3	Baltimore
1959*	National, 5-4	Pittsburgh
1959*	American, 5-3	Los Angeles
1960*	National, 5-3	Kansas City
1960*	National, 6-0	New York (AL)
1961*	National, 5-4[3]	San Francisco
1961*	Called–rain, 1-1	Boston
1962*	National, 3-1[3]	Washington
1962*	American, 9-4	Chicago (NL)
1963*	National, 5-3	Cleveland
1964*	National, 7-4	New York (NL)
1965*	National, 6-5	Minnesota
1966*	National, 2-1[3]	St. Louis
1967*	National, 2-1[4]	California
1968	National, 1-0	Houston
1969*	National, 9-3	Washington
1970	National, 5-4[2]	Cincinnati
1971	American, 6-4	Detroit
1972	National, 4-3[3]	Atlanta
1973	National, 7-1	Kansas City
1974	National, 7-2	Pittsburgh
1975	National, 6-3	Milwaukee
1976	National, 7-1	Philadelphia
1977	National, 7-5	New York (AL)
1978	National, 7-3	San Diego
1979	National, 7-6	Seattle
1980	National, 4-2	Los Angeles
1981	National, 5-4	Cleveland
1982	National, 4-1	Montreal
1983	American, 13-3	Chicago (AL)
1984	National, 3-1	San Francisco
1985	National, 6-1	Minnesota
1986	American, 3-2	Houston
1987	National, 2-0[5]	Oakland
1988	American, 2-1	Cincinnati
1989	American, 5-3	California
1990	American, 2-0	Chicago (NL)
1991	American, 4-2	Toronto
1992	American, 13-6	San Diego
1993	American, 9-3	Baltimore
1994	National, 8-7[3]	Pittsburgh
1995	National, 3-2	Texas
1996	National, 6-0	Philadelphia
1997	American, 3-1	Cleveland
1998	American, 13-8	Colorado
1999	American, 4-1	Boston
2000	American, 6-3	Atlanta
2001	American, 4-1	Seattle
2002	Called–Comm. decision, 7-7[6]	

*Denotes day game. (1) 14 innings. (2) 12 innings. (3) 10 innings. (4) 15 innings. (5) 13 innings. (6) Game called in the 11th inning when both teams ran out of pitchers.

Major League Franchise Shifts and Additions

1953—Boston Braves (NL) became Milwaukee Braves.
1954—St. Louis Browns (AL) became Baltimore Orioles.
1955—Philadelphia Athletics (AL) became Kansas City Athletics.
1958—New York Giants (NL) became San Francisco Giants.
1958—Brooklyn Dodgers (NL) became L.A. Dodgers.
1961—Washington Senators (AL) became Minnesota Twins.
1961—L.A. Angels (renamed California Angels in 1965 and Anaheim Angels in 1997) enfranchised by the American League.
1961—Washington Senators enfranchised by the American League (a new team, replacing the former Washington club, whose franchise was moved to Minneapolis-St. Paul).
1962—Houston Colt .45's (renamed the Houston Astros in 1965) enfranchised by the National League.
1962—New York Mets enfranchised by the National League.
1966—Milwaukee Braves (NL) became Atlanta Braves.
1968—Kansas City Athletics (AL) became Oakland Athletics.
1969—Kansas City Royals and Seattle Pilots enfranchised by the American League; Montreal Expos and San Diego Padres enfranchised by the National League.
1970—Seattle Pilots became Milwaukee Brewers.
1971—Washington Senators became Texas Rangers (Dallas-Fort Worth area).
1977—Toronto Blue Jays and Seattle Mariners enfranchised by the American League.
1993—Colorado Rockies (Denver) and Florida Marlins (Miami) enfranchised by the National League.
1998—Tampa Bay Devil Rays began play in the American League; Arizona Diamondbacks (Phoenix) began play in the National League (both teams enfranchised in 1995). Milwaukee Brewers moved from the AL to the NL.

Baseball Stadiums[1]

National League

Team	Stadium (year opened)	Surface	Home run distances (ft.) LF	Center	RF	Seating capacity
Arizona Diamondbacks	Bank One Ballpark (1998)	Grass	330	407	334	49,033
Atlanta Braves	Turner Field (1997)	Grass	335	401	330	50,062
Chicago Cubs	Wrigley Field (1914)	Grass	355	400	353	38,902
Cincinnati Reds	Cinergy Field (1970)	Artificial	330	404	330	52,953
Colorado Rockies	Coors Field (1995)	Grass	347	415	350	50,381
Florida Marlins	Pro Player Stadium (1987)	Grass	325	410	345	42,531
Houston Astros	Minute Maid Park (2000)	Grass	315	435	326	42,000
Los Angeles Dodgers	Dodger Stadium (1962)	Grass	330	395	330	56,000
Milwaukee Brewers	Miller Park (2001)	Grass	342	400	356	43,000
Montreal Expos	Olympic Stadium (1976)	Artificial	325	404	325	46,500
New York Mets	Shea Stadium (1964)	Grass	338	410	338	55,775
Philadelphia Phillies	Veterans Stadium (1971)	Artificial	330	408	330	62,409
Pittsburgh Pirates	PNC Park (2001)	Grass	325	399	320	38,365
St. Louis Cardinals	Busch Stadium (1966)	Grass	330	402	330	49,625
San Diego Padres	Qualcomm Stadium (1967)	Grass	327	405	330	56.133
San Francisco Giants	Pacific Bell Park (2000)	Grass	335	404	307	41,059

American League

Team	Stadium (year opened)	Surface	LF	Center	RF	Seating capacity
Anaheim Angels	Edison Intl. Field of Anaheim (1966)	Grass	333	408	333	45,050
Baltimore Orioles	Oriole Park at Camden Yards (1992)	Grass	333	400	318	48,876
Boston Red Sox	Fenway Park (1912)	Grass	310	420	302	33,871
Chicago White Sox	Comiskey Park (1991)	Grass	347	400	347	45,936
Cleveland Indians	Jacobs Field (1994)	Grass	325	405	325	43,368
Detroit Tigers	Comerica Park (2000)	Grass	345	402	330	40,000
Kansas City Royals	Kauffman Stadium (1973)	Grass	330	400	330	40,625
Minnesota Twins	Hubert H. Humphrey Metrodome (1982)	Artificial	343	408	327	48,678
New York Yankees	Yankee Stadium (1923)	Grass	318	408	314	55,070
Oakland A's	Network Associates Coliseum (1968)	Grass	330	400	330	43,662
Seattle Mariners	Safeco Field (1999)	Grass	331	405	327	47,116
Tampa Bay Devil Rays	Tropicana Field (1990)	Artificial	315	407	322	45,200
Texas Rangers	The Ballpark in Arlington (1994)	Grass	332	400	325	49,166
Toronto Blue Jays	SkyDome (1989)	Artificial	328	400	328	50,516

(1) As of 2002 season.

Little League World Series

The Little League World Series is played annually in Williamsport, PA. Pitcher Aaron Alvey hit a home run and struck out 11 batters to lead Louisville (KY) to a 1-0 win over Sendai, Japan, in the 2002 LLWS final, Aug. 25. Alvey's 44 strikeouts and 21 scoreless innings in the tournament were LLWS records. He also tied the mark for consecutive no-hit innings, with 12.

Year	Winning / Losing Team	Score
1947	Williamsport, PA; Lock Haven, PA	16-7
1948	Lock Haven, PA; St. Petersburg, FL	6-5
1949	Hammonton, NJ; Pensacola, FL	5-0
1950	Houston, TX; Bridgeport, CT	2-1
1951	Stamford, CT; Austin, TX	3-0
1952	Norwalk, CT; Monongahela, PA	4-3
1953	Birmingham, AL; Schenectady, NY	1-0
1954	Schenectady, NY; Colton, CA	7-5
1955	Morrisville, PA; Merchantville, NJ	4-3
1956	Roswell, NM; Delaware, NJ	3-1
1957	Mexico; La Mesa, CA	4-0
1958	Mexico; Kankakee, IL	10-1
1959	Hamtramck, MI; Auburn, CA	12-0
1960	Levittown, PA; Ft. Worth, TX	5-0
1961	El Cajon, CA; El Campo, TX	4-2
1962	San Jose, CA; Kankakee, IL	3-0
1963	Granada Hills, CA; Stratford, CT	2-1
1964	Staten Island, NY; Mexico	4-0
1965	Windsor Locks, CT; Ontario, Canada	3-1
1966	Houston, TX; W. New York, NJ	8-2
1967	Tokyo, Japan; Chicago, IL	4-1
1968	Osaka, Japan; Richmond, VA	1-0
1969	Taiwan; Santa Clara, CA	5-0
1970	Wayne, NJ; Campbell, CA	2-0
1971	Taiwan; Gary, IN	12-3
1972	Taiwan; Hammond, IN	6-0
1973	Taiwan; Tucson, AZ	12-0
1974	Taiwan; Red Bluff, CA	12-1
1975	Lakewood, NJ; Tampa, FL	4-3
1976	Tokyo, Japan; Campbell, CA	10-3
1977	Taiwan; El Cajon, CA	7-2
1978	Taiwan; Danville, CA	11-1
1979	Taiwan; Campbell, CA	2-1
1980	Taiwan; Tampa, FL	4-3
1981	Taiwan; Tampa, FL	4-2
1982	Kirkland, WA; Taiwan	6-0
1983	Marietta, GA; Dominican Rep.	3-1
1984	South Korea; Altamonte Springs, FL	6-2
1985	South Korea; Mexico	7-1
1986	Taiwan; Tucson, AZ	12-0
1987	Chinese Taipei; Irvine, CA	21-1
1988	Chinese Taipei; Pearl City, HI	10-0
1989	Trumbull, CT; Chinese Taipei	5-2
1990	Chinese Taipei; Shippensburg, PA	9-0
1991	Chinese Taipei; Danville, CA	11-0
1992	Long Beach, CA; Philippines*	6-0
1993	Long Beach, CA; Panama	3-2
1994	Venezuela; Northridge, CA	4-3
1995	Taiwan; Spring, TX	17-3
1996	Taiwan; Cranston, RI	13-3
1997	Mexico; Mission Viejo, CA	5-4
1998	Toms River, NJ; Japan	12-9
1999	Japan; Phenix City, AL	5-0
2000	Venezuela; Bellaire, TX	3-2
2001	Japan; Apopka, FL	2-1
2002	Louisville, KY; Japan	1-0

*Philippines won 15-4, but was disqualified for using ineligible players. Long Beach was awarded title by forfeit 6-0 (1 run per inning).

NCAA Baseball Champions

1960	Minnesota
1961	USC
1962	Michigan
1963	USC
1964	Minnesota
1965	Arizona St.
1966	Ohio St.
1967	Arizona St.
1968	USC
1969	Arizona St.
1970	USC
1971	USC
1972	USC
1973	USC
1974	USC
1975	Texas
1976	Arizona
1977	Arizona St.
1978	USC
1979	Cal. St.-Fullerton
1980	Arizona
1981	Arizona St.
1982	Miami (FL)
1983	Texas
1984	Cal. St.-Fullerton
1985	Miami (FL)
1986	Arizona
1987	Stanford
1988	Stanford
1989	Wichita St.
1990	Georgia
1991	LSU
1992	Pepperdine
1993	LSU
1994	Oklahoma
1995	Cal. St.-Fullerton
1996	LSU
1997	LSU
1998	USC
1999	Miami (FL)
2000	LSU
2001	Miami (FL)
2002	Texas

NATIONAL BASKETBALL ASSOCIATION

2001-2002 Season: Lakers 3-peat, NBA Goes Global, Jordan Ails, Hornets Move

The L.A. Lakers claimed a 3rd straight NBA title and 14th in team history in 2002. After surviving an epic 7-game series with the Sacramento Kings in the Western Conference Finals, the Lakers swept the N.J. Nets in 4 games. The surprising Nets won 52 games, doubling their previous season's total en route to their 1st Atlantic Division title and 1st appearance in the NBA Finals.

The success of Dirk Nowitzki (Germany), Pau Gasol (Spain), and Predrag Stojakovic (former Yugoslavia) has led the NBA to broaden its search for talent. The Houston Rockets made headlines in June by making China's 7'5" Yao Ming (Shanghai Sharks), the 1st foreign-born top pick in the NBA draft. A record 17 international players—6 in the 1st round—were drafted in 2002.

In a much publicized move from the front office to the backcourt, superstar Michael Jordan helped the Washington Wizards win 37 games, up from 19 in 2000-2001. The Wizards were in playoff contention midway through the season before a knee injury benched Jordan for the final 2 months.

On May 10, the NBA board of governors approved relocation of the Hornets from Charlotte, NC, to New Orleans, starting in 2002-2003.

Final Standings, 2001-2002 Season

(playoff seedings in parentheses; in each conference the 2 division winners automatically get the number 1 and 2 seeds)

Eastern Conference

Atlantic Division

	W	L	Pct	GB
New Jersey(1)	52	30	.634	—
Boston(3)	49	33	.598	3
Orlando (5)	44	38	.537	8
Philadelphia (6)	43	39	.524	9
Washington	37	45	.451	15
Miami	36	46	.439	16
New York	30	52	.366	22

Central Division

	W	L	Pct	GB
Detroit (2)	50	32	.610	—
Charlotte (4)	44	38	.537	6
Toronto (5)	42	40	.512	8
Indiana (8)	42	40	.512	8
Milwaukee	41	41	.500	9
Atlanta	33	49	.402	17
Cleveland	29	53	.354	21
Chicago	21	61	.256	29

Western Conference

Midwest Division

	W	L	Pct	GB
San Antonio (2)	58	24	.707	—
Dallas (4)	57	25	.695	1
Minnesota (5)	50	32	.610	8
Utah (8)	44	38	.537	14
Houston	28	54	.341	30
Denver	27	55	.329	31
Memphis	23	59	.280	35

Pacific Division

	W	L	Pct	GB
Sacramento (1)	61	21	.744	—
L.A. Lakers (3)	58	24	.707	3
Portland(6)	49	33	.598	12
Seattle (7)	45	37	.549	16
L.A. Clippers	39	43	.476	22
Phoenix	36	46	.439	25
Golden State	21	61	.256	40

NBA Regular Season Individual Highs in 2001-2002

Minutes, game: 57, Michael Finley, Dal. at Ind., Feb. 5.
Points, game: 58, Allen Iverson, Phil. v. Houston, Jan. 15.
Field goals, game: 21, 4 players tied (Allen Iverson, Kobe Bryant, Michael Jordan, Shareef Abdur-Rahim).
FG attempts, game: 42, Allen Iverson, Phil. v. Houston, Jan. 15.
3-pointers, game: 10, Ray Allen, Mil. v. Char., Apr. 14.
3-pt. attempts, game: 17, Antoine Walker, Boston v. N.Y., Dec. 11.
Free throws, game: 18, Kobe Bryant, L.A. Lakers at Phoenix, Mar. 27; Steve Francis, Houston v. Utah, Feb. 4.
FT attempts, game: 28, Shaquille O'Neal, L.A. Lakers at Golden St., Mar. 14.
Rebounds, game: 28, Ben Wallace, Det. v. Boston, Mar. 24.
Assists, game: 23, Jamaal Tinsley, Ind. v. Wash., Nov. 22.
Steals, game: 9, Andre Miller, Clev. v. Phil., Dec. 15.
Blocks, game: 10, Ben Wallace, Det. at Mil., Feb. 24; Dikembe Mutombo, Phil. at Chicago, Dec. 1.
Minutes, season: 3,406: Antoine Walker, Boston.
Off. rebounds, season: 396, Elton Brand, L.A. Clippers.
Def. rebounds, season: 774, Tim Duncan, San Antonio.

2001 NBA Playoff Results

Eastern Conference

New Jersey defeated Indiana 3 games to 2
Detroit defeated Toronto 3 games to 2
Boston defeated Philadelphia 3 games to 2
Charlotte defeated Orlando 3 games to 1
New Jersey defeated Charlotte 4 games to 1
Boston defeated Detroit 4 games to 1
New Jersey defeated Boston 4 games to 2

Western Conference

Sacramento defeated Utah 3 games to 1
San Antonio defeated Seattle 3 games to 2
L.A. Lakers defeated Portland 3 games to 0
Dallas defeated Minnesota 3 games to 0
Sacramento defeated Dallas 4 games to 1
L.A. Lakers defeated San Antonio 4 games to 1
L.A. Lakers defeated Sacramento 4 games to 3

Championship

Los Angeles defeated New Jersey 4 games to 0 [99-94, 106-83, 106-103, 113-107].

Lakers Sweep in 2002

The L.A. Lakers swept the NBA Finals for the 1st time in franchise history, defeating the New Jersey Nets, 113-107, in Game 4 on June 12, at the Continental Airlines Arena in East Rutherford, NJ. The Lakers were the 3rd team in history to win at least 3 NBA titles in a row. L.A. center Shaquille O'Neal, who led all scorers in the series with 36.3 points per game, was also named MVP of the Finals a 3rd consecutive time. Teammate Kobe Bryant added 24.6 per game. Kenyon Martin led the Nets, averaging 22 points. L.A. coach Phil Jackson won his 9th NBA title in 12 years (he won 6 with Chicago), tying him with legendary Boston Celtic coach Red Auerbach for most career championships.

NBA Finals Composite Box Scores

L.A. Lakers	FG M-A	FT M-A	Reb O-T	Ast	Avg
Shaquille O'Neal	50-84	45-68	13-49	15	36.3
Kobe Bryant	36-70	29-36	3-23	21	26.8
Derek Fisher	17-33	9-14	2-14	15	12.0
Rick Fox	12-23	10-12	6-25	14	9.8
Robert Horry	11-24	5-6	6-29	17	8.0
Devean George	10-23	3-3	5-19	0	6.5
Brian Shaw	6-21	0-0	3-7	10	3.5
Mitch Richmond	1-1	0-0	0-0	0	2.0
S. Medvendenko	1-1	0-0	1-1	0	1.0
Samaki Walker	1-4	2-2	3-8	0	1.0
Lindsey Hunter	1-5	0-0	1-1	0	0.7
Mark Madsen	0-0	0-0	0-0	0	0.0

New Jersey Nets	FG M-A	FT M-A	Reb O-T	Ast	Avg
Kenyon Martin	35-75	17-26	8-26	10	22.0
Jason Kidd	35-80	7-11	12-29	39	20.8
Kerry Kittles	19-42	7-10	4-8	10	12.5
Keith Van Horn	17-44	3-4	7-23	9	10.5
Lucious Harris	11-32	8-10	5-11	8	7.8
Todd MacCulloch	14-28	2-4	12-20	2	7.5
Richard Jefferson	11-21	5-11	2-18	5	6.8
Jason Collins	5-10	7-8	5-10	1	4.3
Aaron Williams	6-16	2-2	4-9	1	3.5
Anthony Johnson	2-6	1-2	1-2	1	1.3
Donny Marshall	0-1	0-0	0-0	0	0.0
Brian Scalabrine	0-0	0-0	0-0	0	0.0

NBA Finals MVP

1969 Jerry West, Los Angeles
1970 Willis Reed, New York
1971 Lew Alcindor (Kareem Abdul-Jabbar), Milwaukee
1972 Wilt Chamberlain, Los Angeles
1973 Willis Reed, New York
1974 John Havlicek, Boston
1975 Rick Barry, Golden State
1976 Jo Jo White, Boston
1977 Bill Walton, Portland
1978 Wes Unseld, Washington
1979 Dennis Johnson, Seattle
1980 Magic Johnson, Los Angeles
1981 Cedric Maxwell, Boston
1982 Magic Johnson, Los Angeles
1983 Moses Malone, Philadelphia
1984 Larry Bird, Boston
1985 Kareem Abdul-Jabbar, L.A. Lakers
1986 Larry Bird, Boston
1987 Magic Johnson, L.A. Lakers
1988 James Worthy, L.A. Lakers
1989 Joe Dumars, Detroit
1990 Isiah Thomas, Detroit
1991 Michael Jordan, Chicago
1992 Michael Jordan, Chicago
1993 Michael Jordan, Chicago
1994 Hakeem Olajuwon, Houston
1995 Hakeem Olajuwon, Houston
1996 Michael Jordan, Chicago
1997 Michael Jordan, Chicago
1998 Michael Jordan, Chicago
1999 Tim Duncan, San Antonio
2000 Shaquille O'Neal, L.A. Lakers
2001 Shaquille O'Neal, L.A. Lakers
2002 Shaquille O'Neal, L.A. Lakers

NBA Finals All-Time Statistical Leaders

(at the end of the 2002 NBA season finals; *denotes active in 2001-2002)

Scoring Average (Minimum 10 games)

	G	FG	FT	Pts.	Avg
Rick Barry	10	138	87	363	36.3
*Shaquille O'Neal	19	253	144	650	34.2
*Michael Jordan	35	438	258	1,176	33.6
Jerry West	55	612	455	1,679	30.5
Bob Pettit	25	241	227	709	28.4
*Hakeem Olajuwon	17	187	91	467	27.5
Elgin Baylor	44	442	277	1,161	26.4
Julius Erving	22	216	128	561	25.5
Joe Fulks	11	84	104	272	24.7
Clyde Drexler	15	126	108	367	24.5

Games Played

Bill Russell	70
Sam Jones	64
Kareem Abdul-Jabbar	56
Jerry West	55
Tom Heinsohn	52

Rebounds

Bill Russell	1,718
Wilt Chamberlain	862
Elgin Baylor	593
Kareem Abdul-Jabbar	507
Tom Heinsohn	473

Assists

Magic Johnson	584
Bob Cousy	400
Bill Russell	315
Jerry West	306
Dennis Johnson	228

NBA Scoring Leaders

Year	Scoring champion	Pts	Avg
1947	Joe Fulks, Philadelphia	1,389	23.2
1948	Max Zaslofsky, Chicago	1,007	21.0
1949	George Mikan, Minneapolis	1,698	28.3
1950	George Mikan, Minneapolis	1,865	27.4
1951	George Mikan, Minneapolis	1,932	28.4
1952	Paul Arizin, Philadelphia	1,674	25.4
1953	Neil Johnston, Philadelphia	1,564	22.3
1954	Neil Johnston, Philadelphia	1,759	24.4
1955	Neil Johnston, Philadelphia	1,631	22.7
1956	Bob Pettit, St. Louis	1,849	25.7
1957	Paul Arizin, Philadelphia	1,817	25.6
1958	George Yardley, Detroit	2,001	27.8
1959	Bob Pettit, St. Louis	2,105	29.2
1960	Wilt Chamberlain, Philadelphia	2,707	37.9
1961	Wilt Chamberlain, Philadelphia	3,033	38.4
1962	Wilt Chamberlain, Philadelphia	4,029	50.4
1963	Wilt Chamberlain, San Francisco	3,586	44.8
1964	Wilt Chamberlain, San Francisco	2,948	36.5
1965	Wilt Chamberlain, San Francisco, Phil.	2,534	34.7
1966	Wilt Chamberlain, Philadelphia	2,649	33.5
1967	Rick Barry, San Francisco	2,775	35.6
1968	Dave Bing, Detroit	2,142	27.1
1969	Elvin Hayes, San Diego	2,327	28.4
1970	Jerry West, Los Angeles	2,309	31.2
1971	Lew Alcindor (Kareem Abdul-Jabbar), Milwaukee	2,596	31.7
1972	Kareem Abdul-Jabbar, Milwaukee	2,822	34.8
1973	Nate Archibald, Kans. City-Omaha	2,719	34.0
1974	Bob McAdoo, Buffalo	2,261	30.6
1975	Bob McAdoo, Buffalo	2,831	34.5
1976	Bob McAdoo, Buffalo	2,427	31.1
1977	Pete Maravich, New Orleans	2,273	31.1
1978	George Gervin, San Antonio	2,232	27.2
1979	George Gervin, San Antonio	2,365	29.6
1980	George Gervin, San Antonio	2,585	33.1
1981	Adrian Dantley, Utah	2,452	30.7
1982	George Gervin, San Antonio	2,551	32.3
1983	Alex English, Denver	2,326	28.4
1984	Adrian Dantley, Utah	2,418	30.6
1985	Bernard King, New York	1,809	32.9
1986	Dominique Wilkins, Atlanta	2,366	30.3
1987	Michael Jordan, Chicago	3,041	37.1
1988	Michael Jordan, Chicago	2,868	35.0
1989	Michael Jordan, Chicago	2,633	32.5
1990	Michael Jordan, Chicago	2,753	33.6
1991	Michael Jordan, Chicago	2,580	31.5
1992	Michael Jordan, Chicago	2,404	30.1
1993	Michael Jordan, Chicago	2,541	32.6
1994	David Robinson, San Antonio	2,383	29.8
1995	Shaquille O'Neal, Orlando	2,315	29.3
1996	Michael Jordan, Chicago	2,465	30.4
1997	Michael Jordan, Chicago	2,431	29.6
1998	Michael Jordan, Chicago	2,357	28.7
1999	Allen Iverson, Philadelphia	1,284	26.8
2000	Shaquille O'Neal, L.A. Lakers	2,344	29.7
2001	Allen Iverson, Philadelphia	2,207	31.1
2002	Allen Iverson, Philadelphia	1,883	31.4

NBA Most Valuable Player

1956 Bob Pettit, St. Louis
1957 Bob Cousy, Boston
1958 Bill Russell, Boston
1959 Bob Pettit, St. Louis
1960 Wilt Chamberlain, Philadelphia
1961 Bill Russell, Boston
1962 Bill Russell, Boston
1963 Bill Russell, Boston
1964 Oscar Robertson, Cincinnati
1965 Bill Russell, Boston
1966 Wilt Chamberlain, Philadelphia
1967 Wilt Chamberlain, Philadelphia
1968 Wilt Chamberlain, Philadelphia
1969 Wes Unseld, Baltimore
1970 Willis Reed, New York
1971 Lew Alcindor (Kareem Abdul-Jabbar), Milwaukee
1972 Kareem Abdul-Jabbar, Milwaukee
1973 Dave Cowens, Boston
1974 Kareem Abdul-Jabbar, Milwaukee
1975 Bob McAdoo, Buffalo
1976 Kareem Abdul-Jabbar, L.A. Lakers
1977 Kareem Abdul-Jabbar, L.A. Lakers
1978 Bill Walton, Portland
1979 Moses Malone, Houston
1980 Kareem Abdul-Jabbar, L.A. Lakers
1981 Julius Erving, Philadelphia
1982 Moses Malone, Houston
1983 Moses Malone, Philadelphia
1984 Larry Bird, Boston
1985 Larry Bird, Boston
1986 Larry Bird, Boston
1987 Magic Johnson, L.A. Lakers
1988 Michael Jordan, Chicago
1989 Magic Johnson, L.A. Lakers
1990 Magic Johnson, L.A. Lakers
1991 Michael Jordan, Chicago
1992 Michael Jordan, Chicago
1993 Charles Barkley, Phoenix
1994 Hakeem Olajuwon, Houston
1995 David Robinson, San Antonio
1996 Michael Jordan, Chicago
1997 Karl Malone, Utah
1998 Michael Jordan, Chicago
1999 Karl Malone, Utah
2000 Shaquille O'Neal, L.A. Lakers
2001 Allen Iverson, Philadelphia
2002 Tim Duncan, San Antonio

NBA Champions, 1947-2002

Year	Regular season Eastern Conference	Western Conference	Playoffs Champion	Coach	Runner-up
1947	Washington Capitols	Chicago Stags	Philadelphia	Ed Gottlieb	Chicago
1948	Philadelphia Warriors	St. Louis Bombers	Baltimore	Buddy Jeannette	Philadelphia
1949	Washington Capitols	Rochester	Minneapolis	John Kundla	Washington
1950	Syracuse	Minneapolis	Minneapolis	John Kundla	Syracuse
1951	Philadelphia Warriors	Minneapolis	Rochester	Lester Harrison	New York
1952	Syracuse	Rochester	Minneapolis	John Kundla	New York
1953	New York	Minneapolis	Minneapolis	John Kundla	New York
1954	New York	Minneapolis	Minneapolis	John Kundla	Syracuse
1955	Syracuse	Ft. Wayne	Syracuse	Al Cervi	Ft. Wayne
1956	Philadelphia Warriors	Ft. Wayne	Philadelphia	George Senesky	Ft. Wayne
1957	Boston	St. Louis	Boston	Red Auerbach	St. Louis
1958	Boston	St. Louis	St. Louis	Alex Hannum	Boston
1959	Boston	St. Louis	Boston	Red Auerbach	Minneapolis
1960	Boston	St. Louis	Boston	Red Auerbach	St. Louis
1961	Boston	St. Louis	Boston	Red Auerbach	St. Louis
1962	Boston	Los Angeles	Boston	Red Auerbach	Los Angeles
1963	Boston	Los Angeles	Boston	Red Auerbach	Los Angeles
1964	Boston	San Francisco	Boston	Red Auerbach	San Francisco
1965	Boston	Los Angeles	Boston	Red Auerbach	Los Angeles
1966	Philadelphia	Los Angeles	Boston	Red Auerbach	Los Angeles
1967	Philadelphia	San Francisco	Philadelphia	Alex Hannum	San Francisco
1968	Philadelphia	St. Louis	Boston	Bill Russell	Los Angeles
1969	Baltimore	Los Angeles	Boston	Bill Russell	Los Angeles
1970	New York	Atlanta	New York	Red Holzman	Los Angeles

Year	Atlantic	Central	Midwest	Pacific	Champion	Coach	Runner-up
1971	New York	Baltimore	Milwaukee	Los Angeles	Milwaukee	Larry Costello	Baltimore
1972	Boston	Baltimore	Milwaukee	Los Angeles	Los Angeles	Bill Sharman	New York
1973	Boston	Baltimore	Milwaukee	Los Angeles	New York	Red Holzman	Los Angeles
1974	Boston	Capital	Milwaukee	Los Angeles	Boston	Tom Heinsohn	Milwaukee
1975	Boston	Washington	Chicago	Golden State	Golden State	Al Attles	Washington
1976	Boston	Cleveland	Milwaukee	Golden State	Boston	Tom Heinsohn	Phoenix
1977	Philadelphia	Houston	Denver	Los Angeles	Portland	Jack Ramsay	Philadelphia
1978	Philadelphia	San Antonio	Denver	Portland	Washington	Dick Motta	Seattle
1979	Washington	San Antonio	Kansas City	Seattle	Seattle	Len Wilkens	Washington
1980	Boston	Atlanta	Milwaukee	Los Angeles	Los Angeles	Paul Westhead	Philadelphia
1981	Boston	Milwaukee	San Antonio	Phoenix	Boston	Bill Fitch	Houston
1982	Boston	Milwaukee	San Antonio	Los Angeles	Los Angeles	Pat Riley	Philadelphia
1983	Philadelphia	Milwaukee	San Antonio	Los Angeles	Philadelphia	Billy Cunningham	Los Angeles
1984	Boston	Milwaukee	Utah	Los Angeles	Boston	K.C. Jones	Los Angeles
1985	Boston	Milwaukee	Denver	L.A. Lakers	L.A. Lakers	Pat Riley	Boston
1986	Boston	Milwaukee	Houston	L.A. Lakers	Boston	K.C. Jones	Houston
1987	Boston	Atlanta	Dallas	L.A. Lakers	L.A. Lakers	Pat Riley	Boston
1988	Boston	Detroit	Denver	L.A. Lakers	L.A. Lakers	Pat Riley	Detroit
1989	New York	Detroit	Utah	L.A. Lakers	Detroit	Chuck Daly	L.A. Lakers
1990	Philadelphia	Detroit	San Antonio	L.A. Lakers	Detroit	Chuck Daly	Portland
1991	Boston	Chicago	San Antonio	Portland	Chicago	Phil Jackson	L.A. Lakers
1992	Boston	Chicago	Utah	Portland	Chicago	Phil Jackson	Portland
1993	New York	Chicago	Houston	Phoenix	Chicago	Phil Jackson	Phoenix
1994	New York	Atlanta	Houston	Seattle	Houston	Rudy Tomjanovich	New York
1995	Orlando	Indiana	San Antonio	Phoenix	Houston	Rudy Tomjanovich	Orlando
1996	Orlando	Chicago	San Antonio	Seattle	Chicago	Phil Jackson	Seattle
1997	Miami	Chicago	Utah	Seattle	Chicago	Phil Jackson	Utah
1998	Miami	Chicago	Utah	L.A. Lakers	Chicago	Phil Jackson	Utah
1999	Miami	Indiana	San Antonio	Portland	San Antonio	Gregg Popovich	New York
2000	Miami	Indiana	Utah	L.A. Lakers	L.A. Lakers	Phil Jackson	Indiana
2001	Philadelphia	Milwaukee	San Antonio	L.A. Lakers	L.A. Lakers	Phil Jackson	Philadelphia
2002	New Jersey	Detroit	San Antonio	Sacramento	L.A. Lakers	Phil Jackson	New Jersey

NBA Coach of the Year, 1963-2002

1963 Harry Gallatin, St. Louis Hawks
1964 Alex Hannum, San Francisco Warriors
1965 Red Auerbach, Boston Celtics
1966 Dolph Schayes, Philadelphia 76ers
1967 Johnny Kerr, Chicago Bulls
1968 Richie Guerin, St. Louis Hawks
1969 Gene Shue, Baltimore Bullets
1970 Red Holzman, New York Knicks
1971 Dick Motta, Chicago Bulls
1972 Bill Sharman, Los Angeles Lakers
1973 Tom Heinsohn, Boston Celtics
1974 Ray Scott, Detroit Pistons
1975 Phil Johnson, Kansas City-Omaha Kings
1976 Bill Fitch, Cleveland Cavaliers
1977 Tom Nissalke, Houston Rockets
1978 Hubie Brown, Atlanta Hawks
1979 Cotton Fitzsimmons, Kansas City Kings
1980 Bill Fitch, Boston Celtics
1981 Jack McKinney, Indiana Pacers
1982 Gene Shue, Washington Bullets
1983 Don Nelson, Milwaukee Bucks
1984 Frank Layden, Utah Jazz
1985 Don Nelson, Milwaukee Bucks
1986 Mike Fratello, Atlanta Hawks
1987 Mike Schuler, Portland Trail Blazers
1988 Doug Moe, Denver Nuggets
1989 Cotton Fitzsimmons, Phoenix Suns
1990 Pat Riley, Los Angeles Lakers
1991 Don Chaney, Houston Rockets
1992 Don Nelson, Golden State Warriors
1993 Pat Riley, New York Knicks
1994 Lenny Wilkens, Atlanta Hawks
1995 Del Harris, Los Angeles Lakers
1996 Phil Jackson, Chicago Bulls
1997 Pat Riley, Miami Heat
1998 Larry Bird, Indiana Pacers
1999 Mike Dunleavy, Portland Trail Blazers
2000 Glenn "Doc" Rivers, Orlando Magic
2001 Larry Brown, Philadelphia 76ers
2002 Rick Carlisle, Detroit Pistons

NBA All-League and All-Defensive Teams, 2001-2002

All-League Team First team	All-League Team Second team	Position	All-Defensive Team First team	All-Defensive Team Second team
Tim Duncan, San Antonio	Kevin Garnett, Minnesota	Forward	Tim Duncan, San Antonio	Bruce Bowen, Miami
Tracy McGrady, Orlando	Chris Webber, Sacramento	Forward	Kevin Garnett, Minnesota	Clifford Robinson, Detroit
Shaquille O'Neal, L.A. Lakers	Dirk Nowitzki, Dallas	Center	Ben Wallace, Detroit	Dikembe Mutombo, Philadelphia
Kobe Bryant, L.A. Lakers	Gary Payton, Seattle	Guard	Gary Payton, Seattle	Kobe Bryant, L.A. Lakers
Jason Kidd, New Jersey	Allen Iverson, Philadelphia	Guard	Jason Kidd, New Jersey	Doug Christie, Sacramento

NBA Statistical Leaders, 2001-2002

Scoring Average
(Minimum 70 games or 1,400 pts)

	G	FG	FT	Pts	Avg
Allen Iverson, Philadelphia	60	665	475	1,883	31.4
Shaquille O'Neal, L.A. Lakers	67	712	398	1,822	27.2
Paul Pierce, Boston	82	707	520	2,144	26.1
Tracy McGrady, Orlando	76	715	415	1,948	25.6
Tim Duncan, San Antonio	82	764	560	2,089	25.5
Kobe Bryant, L.A. Lakers	80	749	488	2,019	25.2
Dirk Nowitzki, Dallas	76	600	440	1,779	23.4
Karl Malone, Utah	80	635	509	1,788	22.4
Antoine Walker, Boston	81	666	240	1,794	22.1
Gary Payton, Seattle	82	737	267	1,815	22.1

3-Point Field Goal Percentage
(Minimum 55 3-point field goals made)

	FG	FGA	Pct
Steve Smith, San Antonio	116	246	.472
Jon Barry, DetroitStockton, Utah	121	258	.469
Eric Piatkowski, L.A. Clippers	111	238	.466
Wally Szczerbiak, Minnesota	87	191	.455
Steve Nash, Dallas	156	343	.455
Hubert Davis, Washington	57	126	.452
Tyronn Lue, Washington	63	141	.447
Michael Redd, Milwaukee	88	198	.444
Wesley Person, Cleveland	143	322	.444
Ray Allen, Milwaukee	229	528	.434

Rebounds per Game
(Minimum 70 games or 800 rebounds)

	G	Off	Def	Tot	Avg
Ben Wallace, Detroit	80	318	721	1,039	13.0
Tim Duncan, San Antonio	82	268	774	1,042	12.7
Kevin Garnett, Minnesota	81	243	738	981	12.1
Danny Fortson, Golden State	77	290	609	899	11.7
Elton Brand, L.A. Clippers	80	396	529	925	11.6
Dikembe Mutombo, Philadelphia	80	254	609	863	10.8
Jermaine O'Neal, Indiana	72	188	569	757	10.5
Dirk Nowitzki, Dallas	76	120	635	755	9.9
Shawn Marion, Phoenix	81	211	592	803	9.9
P.J. Brown, Charlotte	80	273	513	786	9.8

Assists per Game
(Minimum 70 games or 400 assists)

	G	No	Avg
Andre Miller, Cleveland	81	882	10.9
Jason Kidd, New Jersey	82	808	9.9
Gary Payton, Seattle	82	737	9.0
Baron Davis, Charlotte	82	698	8.5
John Stockton, Utah	82	674	8.2
Stephon Marbury, Phoenix	82	666	8.1
Jamall Tinsley, Indiana	80	647	8.1
Jason Williams, Memphis	65	519	8.0
Steve Nash, Dallas	82	634	7.7
Mark Jackson, New York	82	605	7.4

Field Goal Percentage
(Minimum 300 field goals made)

	FGM	FGA	Pct
Shaquille O'Neal, L.A. Lakers	712	1,229	.579
Elton Brand, L.A. Clippers	532	1,010	.527
Donyell Marshall, Utah	343	661	.519
Pau Gasol, Memphis	551	1,064	.518
John Stockton, Utah	401	775	.517
Alonzo Mourning, Miami	447	866	.516
Ruben Patterson, Portland	319	619	.515
Corliss Williamson, Detroit	411	806	.510
Tim Duncan, San Antonio	764	1,504	.508
Brent Barry, Seattle	401	790	.508
Wally Szczerbiak, Minnesota	609	1,200	.508

Steals per Game
(Minimum 70 games or 125 steals)

	G	No	Avg
Allen Iverson, Philadelphia	60	168	2.80
Ron Artest, Indiana	55	141	2.56
Jason Kidd, New Jersey	82	175	2.13
Baron Davis, Charlotteo	82	172	2.10
Doug Christie, Sacramento	81	160	1.98
Darrell Armstrong, Orlando	82	157	1.91
Karl Malon, Utah	80	152	1.90
Paul Pierce, Boston	82	154	1.88
Kenny Anderson, Boston	76	141	1.86
John Stockton, Utah	82	152	1.85
Jason Terry, Atlanta	78	144	1.85

Free Throw Percentage
(Minimum 125 free throws made)

	FTM	FTA	Pct
Reggie Miller, Indiana	296	325	.911
Richard Hamilton, Washington	300	337	.890
Darrell Armstrong, Orlando	182	205	.888
Damon Stoudamire, Portland	174	196	.888
Steve Nash, Dallas	260	293	.887
Chauncey Billups, Minnesota	207	234	.885
Chris Whitney, Washington	154	175	.880
Steve Smith, San Antonio	159	181	.878
Pedrag Stojakovic, Sacramento	283	323	.876
Troy Hudson, Orlando	176	201	.876
Jamal Mashburn, Charlotte	211	241	.876

Blocked Shots per Game
(Minimum 70 games or 100 blocked shots)

	G	Blk	Avg
Ben Wallace, Detroit	80	278	3.48
Raef LaFrentz, Dallas	78	213	2.73
Alonzo Movurning, Miami	75	186	2.48
Tim Duncan, San Antonio	82	203	2.48
Dikembe Mutombo, Philadelphia	80	190	2.38
Jermaine O'Neal, Indiana	72	166	2.31
Erick Dampier, Golden State	73	167	2.29
Adonal Foyle, Golden State	79	168	2.13
Pau Gasol, Memphis	82	169	2.06
Shaquille O'Neal, L.A. Lakers	67	137	2.04
Elton Brand, L.A. Clippers	80	163	2.04

NBA Rookie of the Year

Year	Player
1953	Don Meineke, Ft. Wayne
1954	Ray Felix, Baltimore
1955	Bob Pettit, Milwaukee
1956	Maurice Stokes, Rochester
1957	Tom Heinsohn, Boston
1958	Woody Sauldsberry, Philadelphia
1959	Elgin Baylor, Minneapolis
1960	Wilt Chamberlain, Philadelphia
1961	Oscar Robertson, Cincinnati
1962	Walt Bellamy, Chicago
1963	Terry Dischinger, Chicago
1964	Jerry Lucas, Cincinnati
1965	Willis Reed, New York
1966	Rick Barry, San Francisco
1967	Dave Bing, Detroit
1968	Earl Monroe, Baltimore
1969	Wes Unseld, Baltimore
1970	Lew Alcindor, Milwaukee
1971	Dave Cowens, Boston; Geoff Petrie, Portland (tie)
1972	Sidney Wicks, Portland
1973	Bob McAdoo, Buffalo
1974	Ernie DiGregorio, Buffalo
1975	Keith Wilkes, Golden State
1976	Alvan Adams, Phoenix
1977	Adrian Dantley, Buffalo
1978	Walter Davis, Phoenix
1979	Phil Ford, Kansas City
1980	Larry Bird, Boston
1981	Darrell Griffith, Utah
1982	Buck Williams, New Jersey
1983	Terry Cummings, San Diego
1984	Ralph Sampson, Houston
1985	Michael Jordan, Chicago
1986	Patrick Ewing, New York
1987	Chuck Person, Indiana
1988	Mark Jackson, New York
1989	Mitch Richmond, Golden State
1990	David Robinson, San Antonio
1991	Derrick Coleman, New Jersey
1992	Larry Johnson, Charlotte
1993	Shaquille O'Neal, Orlando
1994	Chris Webber, Golden State
1995	Grant Hill, Detroit; Jason Kidd, Dallas (tie)
1996	Damon Stoudamire, Toronto
1997	Allen Iverson, Philadelphia
1998	Tim Duncan, San Antonio
1999	Vince Carter, Toronto
2000	Elton Brand, Chicago; Steve Francis, Houston (tie)
2001	Mike Miller, Orlando
2002	Pau Gasol, Memphis

NBA Defensive Player of the Year

1983 Sidney Moncrief, Milwaukee
1984 Sidney Moncrief, Milwaukee
1985 Mark Eaton, Utah
1986 Alvin Robertson, San Antonio
1987 Michael Cooper, L.A. Lakers
1988 Michael Jordan, Chicago
1989 Mark Eaton, Utah
1990 Dennis Rodman, Detroit
1991 Dennis Rodman, Detroit
1992 David Robinson, San Antonio
1993 Hakeem Olajuwon, Houston
1994 Hakeem Olajuwon, Houston
1995 Dikembe Mutombo, Denver
1996 Gary Payton, Seattle
1997 Dikembe Mutombo, Atlanta
1998 Dikembe Mutombo, Atlanta
1999 Alonzo Mourning, Miami
2000 Alonzo Mourning, Miami
2001 Dikembe Mutombo, Philadelphia
2002 Ben Wallace, Detroit

NBA Sixth Man Award

1983 Bobby Jones, Philadelphia
1984 Kevin McHale, Boston
1985 Kevin McHale, Boston
1986 Bill Walton, Boston
1987 Ricky Pierce, Milwaukee
1988 Roy Tarpley, Dallas
1989 Eddie Johnson, Phoenix
1990 Ricky Pierce, Milwaukee
1991 Detlef Schrempf, Seattle
1992 Detlef Schrempf, Seattle
1993 Clifford Robinson, Portland
1994 Dell Curry, Charlotte
1995 Anthony Mason, New York
1996 Toni Kukoc, Chicago
1997 John Starks, New York
1998 Danny Manning, Phoenix
1999 Darrell Armstrong, Orlando
2000 Rodney Rogers, Phoenix
2001 Aaron McKie, Philadelphia
2002 Corliss Williamson, Detroit

2002 NBA Player Draft, First-Round Picks

(held June 26, 2002)

	Team	Player, College/Team
1.	Houston	Yao Ming, C, Shanghai Sharks (China)
2.	Chicago	Jay Williams, G, Duke
3.	Golden State	Mike Dunleavy, F, Duke
4.	Memphis	Drew Gooden, F, Kansas
5.	Denver	Nikoloz Tskitishvili, F/C, Italy
6.	Cleveland	Dajuan Wagner, G, Memphis
7.	New York	Maybyner "Nene" Hilario[1], F/G, Brazil
8.	L.A. Clippers[2]	Chris Wilcox, F, Maryland
9.	Phoenix	Amare Stoudemire, F, Cypress Creek HS (FL)
10.	Miami	Caron Butler, G/F, Connecticut
11.	Washington	Jared Jeffries, F, Indiana
12.	L.A. Clippers	Melvin Ely, F/C, Fresno State
13.	Milwaukee	Marcus Haislip, F, Tennessee
14.	Indiana	Fred Jones, G, Oregon
15.	Houston[3]	Bostjan Nachbar, F, Italy
16.	Philadelphia	Jiri Welsch[4], G, Slovenia
17.	Washington[5]	Juan Dixon, G, Maryland
18.	Orlando	Curtis Borchardt[6], C, Stanford
19.	Utah	Ryan Humphrey[7], F, Notre Dame
20.	Toronto[8]	Kareem Rush[9], G, Missouri
21.	Portland	Qyntel Woods, F, NE Mississippi CC
22.	Phoenix[10]	Casey Jacobsen, G/F, Stanford
23.	Detroit	Tayshaun Prince, F, Kentucky
24.	New Jersey	Nenad Krstic, F/C, Kentucky
25.	Denver[11]	Frank Williams[12], G, Illinois
26.	San Antonio	John Salmons[13], G, Miami
27.	L.A. Lakers	Chris Jeffries[14], F, Fresno State
28.	Sacramento	Dan Dickau[15], G, Gonzaga

(1) Rights traded to Denver. (2) From Atlanta. (3) From Toronto. (4) Rights traded to Golden St. (5) From New Orleans. (6) Rights traded to Utah. (7) Rights traded to Orlando. (8) From Seattle through New York. (9) Rights traded to L.A. Lakers. (10) From Boston. (11) From Dallas. (12) Rights traded to New York. (13) Rights traded to Philadelphia. (14) Rights traded to Toronto. (15) Rights traded to Atlanta.

Number-One First-Round NBA Draft Picks, 1966-2002

Year	Team	Player, college
1966	New York	Cazzie Russell, Michigan
1967	Detroit	Jimmy Walker, Providence
1968	Houston	Elvin Hayes, Houston
1969	Milwaukee	Lew Alcindor[1], UCLA
1970	Detroit	Bob Lanier, St. Bonaventure
1971	Cleveland	Austin Carr, Notre Dame
1972	Portland	LaRue Martin, Loyola-Chicago
1973	Philadelphia	Doug Collins, Illinois St.
1974	Portland	Bill Walton, UCLA
1975	Atlanta	David Thompson[2], N.C. State
1976	Houston	John Lucas, Maryland
1977	Milwaukee	Kent Benson, Indiana
1978	Portland	Mychal Thompson, Minnesota
1979	L.A. Lakers	Magic Johnson, Michigan St.
1980	Golden State	Joe Barry Carroll, Purdue
1981	Dallas	Mark Aguirre, DePaul
1982	L.A. Lakers	James Worthy, North Carolina
1983	Houston	Ralph Sampson, Virginia
1984	Houston	Akeem Olajuwon, Houston
1985	New York	Patrick Ewing, Georgetown
1986	Cleveland	Brad Daugherty, North Carolina
1987	San Antonio	David Robinson, Navy
1988	L.A. Clippers	Danny Manning, Kansas
1989	Sacramento	Pervis Ellison, Louisville
1990	New Jersey	Derrick Coleman, Syracuse
1991	Charlotte	Larry Johnson, UNLV
1992	Orlando	Shaquille O'Neal, LSU
1993	Orlando	Chris Webber[3], Michigan
1994	Milwaukee	Glenn Robinson, Purdue
1995	Golden State	Joe Smith, Maryland
1996	Philadelphia	Allen Iverson, Georgetown
1997	San Antonio	Tim Duncan, Wake Forest
1998	L.A. Clippers	Michael Olowokandi, Pacific
1999	Chicago Bulls	Elton Brand, Duke
2000	New Jersey	Kenyon Martin, Cincinnati
2001	Washington	Kwame Brown, Glynn Academy (HS)
2002	Houston	Yao Ming, Shanghai Sharks (China)

(1) Later Kareem Abdul-Jabbar. (2) Signed with Denver of the ABA. (3) Traded to Golden State.

All-Time NBA Statistical Leaders

(At the end of the 2001-2002 season. *Player active in 2001-2002 season.)

Scoring Average
(Minimum 400 goals or 10,000 points)

	G	Pts.	Avg
*Michael Jordan	990	30,652	31.0
Wilt Chamberlain	1,045	31,419	30.1
*Shaquille O'Neal	675	18,634	27.6
Elgin Baylor	846	23,149	27.4
Jerry West	932	25,192	27.0
*Allen Iverson	405	10,908	26.9
Bob Pettit	792	20,880	26.4
George Gervin	791	20,708	26.2
*Karl Malone	1,353	34,707	25.7
Oscar Robertson	1,040	26,710	25.7

Free Throw Percentage
(Minimum 1,200 free throws made)

	FTA	FTM	Pct.
Mark Price	2,362	2,135	.904
Rick Barry	4,243	3,818	.900
Calvin Murphy	3,864	3,445	.892
Scott Skiles	1,741	1,548	.889
Larry Bird	4,471	3,960	.886
*Reggie Miller	6,363	5,634	.885
Bill Sharman	3,559	3,143	.883
Jeff Hornacek	3,390	2,973	.877
*Ray Allen	1,870	1,638	.876
Ricky Pierce	3,871	3,389	.875

Field Goal Percentage
(Minimum 2,000 field goals made)

	FGA	FGM	Pct.
Artis Gilmore	9,570	5,732	.599
Mark West	4,356	2,528	.580
*Shaquille O'Neal	12,861	7,421	.577
Steve Johnson	4,965	2,841	.572
Darryl Dawkins	6,079	3,477	.572
James Donaldson	5,442	3,105	.571
Jeff Ruland	3,734	2,105	.564
Kareem Abdul-Jabbar	28,307	15,837	.559
Kevin McHale	12,334	6,830	.554
Bobby Jones	6,199	3,412	.550

3-Point Field Goal Percentage
(Minimum 250 3-point field goals made)

	3-FGA	3-FGM	Pct.
*Steve Kerr	1,475	677	.459
*Hubert Davis	1,614	716	.444
Drazen Petrovic	583	255	.437
Tim Legler	603	260	.431
B.J. Armstrong	1,026	436	.425
*Pat Garrity	835	352	.422
*Steve Nash	1,092	458	.419
*Wesley Person	2,296	954	.416
*Dana Barros	2,652	1,090	.411
Trent Tucker	1,410	575	.408
*Ray Allen	2,276	928	.408

Games Played

Robert Parish	1,611
Kareem Abdul-Jabbar	1,560
*John Stockton	1,422
*Karl Malone	1,353
Moses Malone	1,329
Buck Williams	1,307
Elvin Hayes	1,303
Sam Perkins	1,286
A.C. Green	1,278
*Terry Porter	1,274

Minutes Played

Kareem Abdul-Jabbar	57,446
*Karl Malone	50,543
Elvin Hayes	50,000
Wilt Chamberlain	47,859
John Havlicek	46,471
Robert Parish	45,704
*John Stockton	45,489
Moses Malone	45,071
*Hakeem Olajuwon	44,222
Oscar Robertson	43,886

Personal Fouls

Kareem Abdul-Jabbar	4,657
Robert Parish	4,443
*Hakeem Olajuwon	4,383
*Charles Oakley	4,323
Buck Williams	4,267
*Karl Malone	4,258
Elvin Hayes	4,193
Otis Thorpe	4,146
James Edwards	4,042
*Patrick Ewing	4,034

Blocked Shots

*Hakeem Olajuwon	3,830
Kareem Abdul-Jabbar	3,189
Mark Eaton	3,064
*Patrick Ewing	2,894
*David Robinson	2,843
*Dikembe Mutombo	2,836
Tree Rollins	2,542
Robert Parish	2,361
Manute Bol	2,086
George T. Johnson	2,082

Field Goals Attempted

Kareem Abdul-Jabbar	28,307
*Karl Malone	24,521
Elvin Hayes	24,272
John Havlicek	23,930
Wilt Chamberlain	23,497
*Michael Jordan	23,010
Dominique Wilkins	21,589
Alex English	21,036
*Hakeem Olajuwon	20,991
Elgin Baylor	20,171

Field Goals Made

Kareem Abdul-Jabbar	15,837
*Karl Malone	12,740
Wilt Chamberlain	12,681
*Michael Jordan	11,513
Elvin Hayes	10,976
*Hakeem Olajuwon	10,749
Alex English	10,659
John Havlicek	10,513
Dominique Wilkins	9,963
*Patrick Ewing	9,702

3- Point Field Goals Attempted

*Reggie Miller	5,536
*Tim Hardaway	4,314
Dale Ellis	4,266
Vernon Maxwell	3,931
*Mookie Blaylock	3,816
*Dan Majerle	3,798
*Glen Rice	3,614
*John Starks	3,591
*Mitch Richmond	3,417
*Nick Van Exel	3,405

3- Point Field Goals Made

*Reggie Miller	2,217
Dale Ellis	1,719
*Tim Hardaway	1,531
*Glen Rice	1,453
*Dan Majerle	1,360
*Mitch Richmond	1,326
*Terry Porter	1,297
*Mookie Blaylock	1,283
Vernon Maxwell	1,256
*Dell Curry	1,245

Points

Kareem Abdul-Jabbar	38,387
*Karl Malone	34,707
Wilt Chamberlain	31,419
*Michael Jordan	30,652
Moses Malone	27,409
Elvin Hayes	27,313
*Hakeem Olajuwon	26,946
Oscar Robertson	26,710
Dominique Wilkins	26,668
John Havlicek	26,395

Rebounds

Wilt Chamberlain	23,924
Bill Russell	21,620
Kareem Abdul-Jabbar	17,440
Elvin Hayes	16,279
Moses Malone	16,212
Robert Parish	14,715
Nate Thurmond	14,464
Walt Bellamy	14,241
*Karl Malone	13,973
Wes Unseld	13,769

Assists

*John Stockton	15,177
Magic Johnson	10,141
Oscar Robertson	9,887
*Mark Jackson	9,840
Isiah Thomas	9,061
*Rod Strickland	7,489
Maurice Cheeks	7,392
Lenny Wilkens	7,211
*Terry Porter	7,160
*Tim Hardaway	7,071

Steals

*John Stockton	3,128
*Michael Jordan	2,391
Maurice Cheeks	2,310
Clyde Drexler	2,207
*Scottie Pippen	2,181
*Hakeem Olajuwon	2,162
Alvin Robertson	2,112
*Mookie Blaylock	2,075
*Gary Payton	2,014
Derek Harper	1,957

WORLD ALMANAC QUICK QUIZ

Since the first NBA Finals MVP Award was given out in 1969, several players have won both the Finals MVP and the NBA MVP Awards in the same year. Who is the only player to win both awards in consecutive years?

(a) Larry Bird (b) Magic Johnson (c) Michael Jordan (d) Shaquille O'Neal

For the answer look in this chapter, or see page 1008.

All-Time NBA Coaching Victories

(At the end of the 2001-2002 season. *Active through 2001-2002 season.)

Coach	W-L	Pct.
Lenny Wilkens*	1,268-1,056	.546
Pat Riley*	1,085-512	.679
Don Nelson*	1,036-806	.562
Bill Fitch	944-1,106	.460
Red Auerbach	938-479	.662
Dick Motta	935-1,017	.479
Jack Ramsay	864-783	.525
Cotton Fitzsimmons	832-775	.518
Larry Brown*	831-651	.561
Jerry Sloan*	828-486	.630
Gene Shue	784-861	.477
Phil Jackson*	726-258	.738
John MacLeod	707-657	.518
Red Holzman	696-604	.535
George Karl*	666-459	.592
Chuck Daly	638-437	.593
Doug Moe	628-529	.543
Mike Fratello	572-465	.552
Alvin Attles	557-518	.518
Del Harris	556-457	.549

Basketball Hall of Fame, Springfield, MA

(2002 inductees have an asterisk*)

PLAYERS

Abdul-Jabbar, Kareem
Archibald, Nate
Arizin, Paul
Barlow, Thomas
Barry, Rick
Baylor, Elgin
Beckman, John
Bellamy, Walt
Belov, Sergei
Bing, Dave
Bird, Larry
Blazejowski, Carol
Borgmann, Bennie
Bradley, Bill
Brennan, Joseph
Cervi, Al
Chamberlain, Wilt
Cooper, Charles
Cosic, Kresimir
Cousy, Bob
Cowens, Dave
Crawford, Joan
Cunningham, Billy
Curry, Denise
Davies, Bob
DeBernardi, Forrest
DeBusschere, Dave
Denhart, Dutch
Donovan, Anne
Endacott, Paul
English, Alex
Erving, Julius (Dr. J)
Foster, Bud
Frazier, Walt
Friedman, Max
Fulks, Joe
Gale, Lauren
Gallatin, Harry
Gates, Pop
Gervin, George
Gola, Tom
Goodrich, Gail
Greer, Hal
Gruenig, Ace
Hagan, Cliff
Hanson, Victor
Harris-Stewart, Luisa
Havlicek, John
Hawkins, Connie
Hayes, Elvin
Haynes, Marques
Heinsohn, Tom
Holman, Nat
Houbregs, Bob
Howell, Bailey
Hyatt, Chuck
Issel, Dan
Jeannette, Buddy
*Johnson, Earvin "Magic"
Johnson, William
Johnston, Neil
Jones, K.C.
Jones, Sam
Krause, Moose
Kurland, Bob
Lanier, Bob
Lapchick, Joe
Lieberman-Cline, Nancy
Lovellette, Clyde
Lucas, Jerry
Luisetti, Hank
Macauley, Ed
Malone, Moses
Maravich, Pete
Martin, Slater
McAdoo, Bob
McCracken, Branch
McCracken, Jack
McDermott, Bobby
McGuire, Dick
McHale, Kevin
Meyers, Ann
Mikan, George
Mikkelsen, Vern
Miller, Cheryl
Monroe, Earl
Murphy, Calvin
Murphy, Stretch
Page, Pat
*Petrovic, Drazen
Pettit, Bob
Phillip, Andy
Pollard, Jim
Ramsey, Frank
Reed, Willis
Risen, Arnie
Robertson, Oscar
Roosma, John S.
Russell, Bill
Russell, Honey
Schayes, Adolph
Schmidt, Ernest
Schommer, John
Sedran, Barney
Semjonova, Uljana
Sharman, Bill
Steinmetz, Christian
Thomas, Isiah
Thompson, Cat
Thompson, David
Thurmond, Nate
Twyman, Jack
Unseld, Wes
Vandivier, Fuzzy
Wachter, Edward
Walton, Bill
Wanzer, Bobby
West, Jerry
White, Nera
Wilkens, Lenny
Wooden, John
Yardley, George

COACHES

Allen, Forrest (Phog)
Anderson, Harold
Auerbach, Red
Barry, Sam
Blood, Ernest
*Brown, Larry
Cann, Howard
Carlson, Dr. H. C.
Carnesecca, Lou
Carnevale, Ben
Carril, Pete
Case, Everett
Chaney, John
Conradt, Jody
Crum, Denny
Daly, Chuck
Dean, Everett
Diaz-Miguel, Antonio
Diddle, Edgar
Drake, Bruce
Gaines, Clarence
Gardner, Jack
Gill, Slats
Gomelsky, Aleksandr
Hannum, Alex
Harshman, Marv
Haskins, Don
Hickey, Edgar
Hobson, Howard
Holzman, Red
Iba, Hank
Julian, Alvin
Keaney, Frank
Keogan, George
Knight, Bob
Krzyzewski, Mike
Kundla, John
Lambert, Ward
Litwack, Harry
Loeffler, Kenneth
Lonborg, Dutch
McCutchan, Arad
McGuire, Al
McGuire, Frank
McLendon, John
Meanwell, Dr. W. E.
Meyer, Ray
Miller, Ralph
Moore, Billie
Newell, Pete
Nikolic, Aleksandar
*Olson, Lute
Ramsay, Jack
Rubini, Cesare
Rupp, Adolph
Sachs, Leonard
Shelton, Everett
Smith, Dean
Summitt, Pat
Taylor, Fred
Thompson, John
Wade, Margaret
Watts, Stan
Wilkens, Lenny
Wooden, John
Woolpert, Phil
Wootten, Morgan
*Yow, Kay

TEAMS

First Team
Original Celtics
Buffalo Germans
NY Renaissance
*Harlem Globetrotters

REFEREES

Enright, James
Hepbron, George
Hoyt, George
Kennedy, Matthew
Leith, Lloyd
Mihalik, Red
Nucatola, John
Quigley, Ernest
Shirley, J. Dallas
Strom, Earl
Tobey, David
Walsh, David

CONTRIBUTORS

Abbott, Senda B.
Bee, Clair
Biasone, Danny
Brown, Walter
Bunn, John
Douglas, Bob
Duer, Al O.
Embry, Wayne
Fagan, Cliff
Fisher, Harry
Fleisher, Larry
Gottlieb, Edward
Gulick, Dr. L. H.
Harrison, Lester
Hepp, Dr. Ferenc
Hickox, Edward
Hinkle, Tony
Irish, Ned
Jones, R. W.
Kennedy, Walter
Liston, Emil
Mokray, Bill
Morgan, Ralph
Morgenweck, Frank
Naismith, Dr. James
Newton, C. M.
O'Brien, John
O'Brien, Larry
Olsen, Harold
Podoloff, Maurice
Porter, H. V.
Reid, William
Ripley, Elmer
St. John, Lynn
Saperstein, Abe
Schabinger, Arthur
Stagg, Amos Alonzo
Stankovich, Boris
Steitz, Edward
Taylor, Chuck
Teague, Bertha
Tower, Oswald
Trester, Arthur
Wells, Clifford
Wilke, Lou
Zollner, Fred

NBA Home Courts[1]

Team	Name (built)	Capacity
Atlanta	Philips Arena (1999)	20,000
Boston	FleetCenter (1995)	18,624
Charlotte	Charlotte Coliseum[2] (1988)	23,799
Chicago	United Center (1994)	21,500
Cleveland	Gund Arena (1994)	20,562
Dallas	American Airlines Center (2001)	18,026
Denver	Pepsi Center (1999)	19,099
Detroit	The Palace of Auburn Hills (1988)	22,076
Golden State	Arena in Oakland[3] (1966)	19,596
Houston	Compaq Center[4] (1975)	16,285
Indiana	Conseco Fieldhouse (1999)	18,345
L.A. Clippers	Staples Center (1999)	19,060
L.A. Lakers	Staples Center (1999)	19,282
Memphis	The Pyramid (1991)	20,142
Miami	American Airlines Arena (1999)	19,600

Team	Name (built)	Capacity
Milwaukee	Bradley Center (1988)	18,600
Minnesota	Target Center (1990)	19,006
New Jersey	Continental Airlines Arena[5] (1981)	20,049
New York	Madison Square Garden (1968)	19,763
Orlando	TD Waterhouse Centre[6] (1989)	17,248
Philadelphia	First Union Center[7] (1996)	20,444
Phoenix	America West Arena (1992)	19,023
Portland	The Rose Garden (1995)	19,980
Sacramento	ARCO Arena (1988)	17,317
San Antonio	Alamodome[8] (1993)	20,557
Seattle	KeyArena at Seattle Center[9] (1962)	17,072
Toronto	Air Canada Centre (1999)	19,800
Utah	Delta Center (1991)	19,911
Washington	MCI Center (1997)	20,674

(1) At the end of the 2001-2002 season. (2) Prior to the 2002-2003 season, the Hornets moved to New Orleans and were to play in the 18,500-seat New Orleans Arena. (3) Oakland Coliseum Arena, 1966-96; renovated and renamed in 1997. (4) The Summit, 1975-97. (5) Brendan Byrne/Meadowlands Arena, 1981-96. (6) Orlando Arena, 1989-2000. (7) CoreStates Center, 1996-98. (8) The 18,500-seat SBC Center was scheduled to open for the 2002-2003 season. (9) Seattle Center Coliseum, 1962-94; renovated, expanded, and renamed in 1995.

WOMEN'S PROFESSIONAL BASKETBALL

WNBA 2002: L.A. Sparks Repeat, Sheryl Swoopes Makes MVP Comeback

A year after dethroning 4-time champion Houston, Lisa Leslie and the L.A. Sparks started their own dynasty, winning a 2nd WNBA title by defeating the New York Liberty, 69-66, in game 2 of the best-of-3 WNBA finals at the Staples Center in Los Angeles, Aug. 31. Rookie Nikki Teasley hit a 3-pointer with 2.4 seconds left in the game to give L.A. the win and only the 2nd undefeated run through the playoffs (Houston, 2000). For perennial runner-up New York, the loss marked the 4th time in the league's 6-year history that the team had made the finals and come away without the title. Lisa Leslie, who led L.A. with 17 points, was named MVP of the Finals for the 2nd straight year. Leslie also won her 3rd All-Star MVP Award in 2002.

Sheryl Swoopes, who missed the entire 2001 season with a knee injury, came back in 2002 to finish 3rd in scoring (18.5 points per game) and 2nd in steals (2.75 per game). Swoopes, who led Houston to the WNBA's 2nd best record (24-8), was named league MVP for the 2nd time in her career and was also named the 2002 Defensive Player of the Year.

WNBA Final Standings, 2002 Season

x-clinched playoff berth; y-clinched top seed

Eastern Conference

	W-L	Pct	GB
y-New York Liberty	18-14	0.563	—
x-Charlotte Sting	18-14	0.563	—
x-Washington Mystics	17-15	0.531	1
x-Indiana Fever	16-16	0.500	2
Orlando Miracle	16-16	0.500	2
Miami Sol	15-17	0.469	3
Cleveland Rockers	10-22	0.313	8
Detroit Shock	9-23	0.281	9

Western Conference

	W	Pct	GB
y-Los Angeles Sparks	25-7	0.781	—
x-Houston Comets	24-8	0.750	1
x-Utah Starzz	20-12	0.625	5
x-Seattle Storm	17-15	0.531	8
Portland Fire	16-16	0.500	9
Sacramento Monarchs	14-18	0.438	11
Phoenix Mercury	11-21	0.344	14
Minnesota Lynx	10-22	0.313	15

2002 WNBA Playoffs

(Playoff seeding in parentheses; Conference winner automatically gets top seed)

Eastern Conference

New York (1) defeated Indiana (4) 2 games to 1
Washington (3) defeated Charlotte (2) 3 games to 0
New York defeated Washington 2 games to 1

Western Conference

Los Angeles (1) defeated Seattle (4) 2 games to 0
Utah (3) defeated Houston (2) 2 games to 1
Los Angeles defeated Utah 2 games to 0

WNBA Championship (Best of 3)

Los Angeles defeated New York 2 games to 0 [71-63, 69-66].

2002 All-WNBA Teams

First Team	Position	Second Team
Sheryl Swoopes, Houston	Forward	Chamique Holdsclaw, Washington
Tamika Catchings, Indiana	Forward	Tina Thompson, Houston
Lisa Leslie, Los Angeles	Center	Tari Phillips, New York
Sue Bird, Seattle	Guard	Shannon Johnson, Orlando
Mwadi Mabika, Los Angeles	Guard	Katie Smith, Minnesota

WNBA Statistical Leaders and Awards in 2002

Minutes played — 1,167, Tamika Catchings, Indiana
Total points — 594, Tamika Catchings, Indiana
Points per game — 19.9, Chamique Holdsclaw, Washington
Highest field goal % — .629, Alisa Burras, Portland
Highest 3-pt. field goal % — .471, Kelly Miller, Charlotte
Highest free throw % — .911, Sue Bird, Seattle
Total rebounds — 322, Lisa Leslie, Los Angeles
Rebounds per game — 11.6, Chamique Holdsclaw, Washington
Total assists — 192, Ticha Penicheiro, Sacramento
Assists per game — 8.0, Ticha Penicheiro, Sacramento
Total steals — 94, Tamika Catchings, Indiana
Steals per game — 2.94, Tamika Catchings, Indiana
Total blocked shots — 107, Margo Dydek, Utah
Coach of the year — Marianne Stanley, Washington
Defensive player of year — Sheryl Swoopes, Houston
Most improved player of the year — Coco Miller, Washington

WNBA Champions

	Regular season		Playoffs		
Year	Eastern Conference	Western Conference	Champion	Coach	Runner-up
1997	Phoenix Mercury	Houston Comets	Houston	Van Chancellor	New York
1998	Cleveland Rockers	Houston Comets	Houston	Van Chancellor	Phoenix
1999	New York Liberty	Houston Comets	Houston	Van Chancellor	New York
2000	New York Liberty	Los Angeles Sparks	Houston	Van Chancellor	New York
2001	Cleveland Rockers	Los Angeles Sparks	Los Angeles	Michael Cooper	Charlotte
2002	New York Liberty	Los Angeles Sparks	Los Angeles	Michael Cooper	New York

WNBA Scoring Leaders

Year	Scoring champion	Pts	Avg
1997	Cynthia Cooper, Houston	621	22.2
1998	Cynthia Cooper, Houston	680	22.7
1999	Cynthia Cooper, Houston	686	22.1
2000	Sheryl Swoopes, Houston	643	20.7
2001	Katie Smith, Minnesota	739	23.1
2002	Chamique Holdsclaw, Washington	397	19.9

WNBA Finals MVP

1997	Cynthia Cooper, Houston
1998	Cynthia Cooper, Houston
1999	Cynthia Cooper, Houston
2000	Cynthia Cooper, Houston
2001	Lisa Leslie, Los Angeles
2002	Lisa Leslie, Los Angeles

WNBA Most Valuable Player

1997	Cynthia Cooper, Houston
1998	Cynthia Cooper, Houston
1999	Yolanda Griffith, Sacramento
2000	Sheryl Swoopes, Houston
2001	Lisa Leslie, Los Angeles
2002	Sheryl Swoopes, Houston

WNBA Rookie of the Year

1997	no award
1998	Tracy Reid, Charlotte
1999	Chamique Holdsclaw, Washington
2000	Betty Lennox, Minnesota
2001	Jackie Stiles, Portland
2002	Tamika Catchings, Indiana

COLLEGE BASKETBALL

Men's Final NCAA Division I Conference Standings, 2001-2002

(*conference tournament champion)

	Conf. W	Conf. L	All W	All L
America East				
Vermont	13	3	21	8
Boston U.*	13	3	22	9
Hartford	10	6	14	18
New Hampshire	8	8	11	17
Maine	7	9	12	18
Binghamton	6	10	9	19
Albany	5	11	8	20
Northeastern	5	11	7	21
Stony Brook	5	11	6	22
Atlantic Coast				
Maryland	15	1	26	4
Duke*	13	3	29	3
North Carolina St.	9	7	22	10
Wake Forest	9	7	20	12
Virginia	7	9	17	11
Georgia Tech	7	9	15	16
Clemson	4	12	13	17
Florida St.	4	12	12	17
North Carolina	4	12	8	20
Atlantic 10				
East Division				
St. Joseph's	12	4	18	11
Temple	12	4	15	14
St. Bonaventure	8	8	17	12
Massachusetts	6	10	13	16
Rhode Island	4	12	8	20
Fordham	4	12	8	20
West Division				
Xavier*	14	2	25	5
Richmond	11	5	19	13
Dayton	10	6	20	10
La Salle	6	10	15	17
George Washington	5	11	12	16
Duquesne	4	12	9	19
Big East				
East Division				
Connecticut*	13	3	24	6
Miami (FL)	10	6	24	7
St. John's	9	7	20	11
Boston College	8	8	20	11
Villanova	7	9	17	12
Providence	6	10	15	16
Virginia Tech	4	12	10	18
West Division				
Pittsburgh	13	3	27	5
Notre Dame	10	6	21	10
Syracuse	9	7	20	11
Georgetown	9	7	19	11
Rutgers	8	8	18	12
Seton Hall	5	11	12	18
West Virginia	1	15	8	20
Big Sky				
Montana St.	12	2	19	9
Eastern Wash.	10	4	17	13
Weber St.	8	6	18	11
Montana*	7	7	16	14
Northern Arizona	7	7	14	14
Portland St.	6	8	12	16
Idaho St.	3	11	10	17
Sacramento St.	3	11	9	19
Big South				
Winthrop*	10	4	19	11
UNC Asheville	10	4	13	15
Radford	9	5	15	16
Charleston Southern	8	6	12	17
Elon	7	7	13	16
High Point	5	9	11	19
Coastal Carolina	5	9	8	20
Liberty	2	12	5	25
Big Ten				
Ohio St.*	11	5	23	7
Illinois	11	5	24	8
Indiana	11	5	20	11
Wisconsin	11	5	18	12
Michigan St.	10	6	19	11
Minnesota	9	7	17	12
Northwestern	7	9	16	13
Iowa	5	11	19	15
Purdue	5	11	13	18
Michigan	5	11	11	18
Penn St.	3	13	7	21
Big 12				
Kansas	16	0	29	3
Oklahoma*	13	3	27	4
Oklahoma St.	10	6	23	8
Texas Tech	10	6	23	8
Texas	10	6	20	11
Missouri	9	7	21	11
Nebraska	6	10	13	15
Kansas St.	6	10	13	16
Colorado	5	11	15	14
Baylor	4	12	14	16
Iowa St.	4	12	12	19
Texas A&M	3	13	9	22
Big West				
Utah St.	13	5	23	7
UC Irvine	13	5	21	10
Pacific (CA)	11	7	20	10
UC Santa Barbara*	11	7	20	10
Cal St. Northridge	11	7	12	16
Cal. Poly	9	9	15	12
Long Beach St.	9	9	13	17
Idaho	6	12	9	19
UC Riverside	5	13	8	18
Cal. St. Fullerton	2	16	5	22
Colonial Athletic Association				
UNC Wilmington*	14	4	22	9
George Mason	13	5	19	9
Va. Commonwealth	11	7	21	11
Drexel	11	7	14	14
Delaware	9	9	14	16
Old Dominion	7	11	13	16
Towson	7	11	11	18
William & Mary	7	11	10	19
James Madison	6	12	14	15
Hofstra	5	13	12	20
Conference USA				
American Division				
Cincinnati*	14	2	30	3
Marquette	13	3	26	6
UNC Charlotte	11	5	18	11
St. Louis	9	7	15	16
Louisville	8	8	18	12
East Carolina	5	11	12	18
DePaul	2	14	9	19
National Division				
Memphis	12	4	22	9
Houston	9	7	18	14
South Florida	8	8	19	12
Texas Christian	6	10	16	15
Alabama-Birmingham	6	10	13	17
Tulane	5	11	14	15
So. Mississippi	4	12	10	17
Ivy Group[1]				
Pennsylvania	11	3	25	6
Yale	11	3	20	10
Princeton	11	3	16	11
Brown	8	6	17	10
Harvard	7	7	14	12
Columbia	4	10	11	17
Dartmouth	2	12	9	18
Cornell	2	12	5	22
Metro Atlantic Athletic				
Marist	13	5	19	9
Rider	13	5	17	11
Manhattan	12	6	20	8
Niagara	12	6	17	14
Iona	10	8	13	17
Siena*	9	9	16	18
Fairfield	9	9	12	17
Canisius	5	13	10	19
Loyola (MD)	4	14	5	23
St. Peter's	3	15	4	24
Mid-American				
East Division				
Kent St.*	17	1	27	5
Bowling Green	12	6	24	8
Ohio U.	11	7	17	11
Miami (OH)	9	9	13	18
Marshall	8	10	15	15
Buffalo	7	11	12	18
Akron	5	13	10	21
West Division				
Ball St.	12	6	20	11
Toledo	11	7	16	14
Western Michigan	10	8	17	13
Northern Illinois	8	10	12	16
Central Michigan	5	13	9	19
Eastern Michigan	2	16	6	24
Mid-Continent				
Valparaiso*	12	2	25	7
Oakland	10	4	17	13
Oral Roberts	10	4	16	14
Southern Utah	8	6	11	16
Missouri-K.C.	7	7	18	11
Indiana-Purdue	6	8	15	15
Western Illinois	3	11	12	15
Chicago St.	0	14	2	26
Mid-Eastern Athletic				
Hampton*	17	1	26	6
Delaware St.	12	6	16	13
South Carolina St.	12	7	16	16
Howard	11	7	18	13
North Carolina A&T	10	9	11	18
Norfolk St.	9	9	10	19
Florida A&M	9	9	9	19
Bethune-Cookman	8	10	12	17
MD-Eastern Shore	7	11	11	18
Coppin St.	3	15	6	25
Morgan St.	2	16	3	25
Horizon League				
Butler	12	4	25	5
Detroit	11	5	18	12
Wisconsin-Milwaukee	11	5	16	13
Wright St.	9	7	17	11
Loyola (IL)	9	7	17	13
Illinois-Chicago*	8	8	20	13
Cleveland St.	6	10	12	16
Wisconsin-Green Bay	4	12	9	21
Youngstown St.	2	14	5	23
Missouri Valley				
Southern Illinois	14	4	26	7
Creighton*	14	4	22	8
Illinois St.	12	6	17	14
SW Missouri St.	11	7	17	15
Wichita St.	9	9	15	15
Drake	9	9	14	15
Northern Iowa	8	10	14	15
Bradley	5	13	9	20
Evansville	4	14	7	21
Indiana St.	4	14	6	22
Mountain West				
Wyoming	11	3	21	8
Utah	10	4	21	8
UNLV	9	5	20	10
San Diego St.*	7	7	21	11
BYU	7	7	17	11
New Mexico	6	8	16	13
Colorado St.	3	11	12	18
Air Force	3	11	9	19
Northeast				
Cent. Connecticut St.*	19	1	27	4
MD-Baltimore County	15	5	20	9
Wagner	15	5	19	9
Monmouth (NJ)	14	6	18	12
St. Francis (NY)	13	7	18	11
Robert Morris	11	9	12	18
Quinnipiac	10	10	14	16
Sacred Heart	7	13	8	20
St. Francis (PA)	5	15	6	21
LIU-Brooklyn	5	15	5	22
Fairleigh Dickinson	4	16	4	25
Mt. St. Mary's (MD)	2	18	3	24

Team	Conf. W	Conf. L	All W	All L
Ohio Valley				
Tennessee Tech	15	1	24	6
Morehead St.	11	5	18	11
Murray St.*	10	6	19	12
Austin Peay	8	8	14	18
Tennessee-Martin	7	9	15	14
Eastern Illinois	7	9	15	16
Tennessee St.	7	9	11	17
SE Missouri St.	4	12	6	22
Eastern Kentucky	3	13	7	20
Pacific-10[1]				
Oregon	14	4	23	8
California	12	6	22	8
Arizona*	12	6	22	9
USC	12	6	22	9
Stanford	12	6	19	9
UCLA	11	7	19	11
Arizona St.	7	11	14	14
Washington	5	13	11	18
Oregon St.	4	14	12	17
Washington St.	1	17	6	21
Patriot League				
American	10	4	18	12
Holy Cross*	9	5	18	14
Colgate	8	6	17	11
Lafayette	8	6	15	14
Bucknell	8	6	13	16
Army	6	8	12	16
Navy	5	9	10	20
Lehigh	2	12	5	23
Southeastern				
Eastern Division				
Florida	10	6	22	8
Georgia	10	6	21	9
Kentucky	10	6	20	9
Tennessee	7	9	15	16
South Carolina	6	10	18	14
Vanderbilt	6	10	16	14
Western Division				
Alabama	12	4	26	7
Mississippi St.*	10	6	26	7
Mississippi	9	7	20	10
LSU	6	10	18	14
Arkansas	6	10	14	15
Auburn	4	12	12	16
Southern				
North Division				
Davidson*	11	5	21	9
UNC-Greensboro	11	5	20	10
East Tennessee St.	11	5	18	10
Western Carolina	6	10	12	16
Appalachian St.	5	11	10	18
VMI	5	11	10	18
South Division				
Col. Of Charleston	9	7	21	9
Georgia Southern	9	7	16	12
Tenn-Chattanooga	9	7	16	14
The Citadel	8	8	17	12
Furman	7	9	17	14
Wofford	5	11	11	18
Southland				
McNeese St.*	17	3	21	8
Louisiana-Monroe	15	5	20	12
Texas-San Antonio	13	7	19	10
Lamar	11	9	15	14
Stephen F. Austin	10	10	13	15
SW Texas St.	10	10	12	16
Texas-Arlington	9	10	12	14
Sam Houston St.	9	11	14	14
Northwestern St.	8	11	12	18
SE Louisiana	6	14	7	20
Nicholls St.	1	19	2	25
Southwestern Athletic				
Alcorn St.*	16	2	20	9
Alabama A&M	12	6	19	10
Alabama St.	12	6	19	13
Texas Southern	10	8	11	17
Mississippi Valley St.	9	9	12	17
Prairie View	8	10	10	20
Jackson St.	8	10	9	19
Grambling	7	11	9	19
Southern	6	12	7	20
Arkansas-Pine Bluff	2	16	2	26
Sun Belt				
East Division				
Western Kentucky*	13	1	28	3
Arkansas-Little Rock	8	6	18	11
Middle Tennessee St.	6	8	14	15
Arkansas St.	5	9	15	16
Florida International	4	10	10	20
West Division				
La. Lafayette	11	4	20	10
New Mexico St.	11	4	20	11
New Orleans	9	6	15	14
North Texas	8	7	15	14
Denver	3	12	8	20
South Alabama	2	13	7	21
Atlantic Sun[2]				
Georgia St.	14	6	20	10
Troy St.	14	6	17	10
Florida Atlantic*	13	7	19	11
Jacksonville	12	8	18	12
Central Florida	12	8	17	12
Samford	12	8	15	14
Jacksonville St.	8	12	13	16
Belmont	8	12	11	17
Stetson	7	13	10	16
Campbell	6	14	8	19
Mercer	4	16	6	23
West Coast				
Gonzaga*	13	1	29	3
Pepperdine	13	1	22	8
San Francisco	8	6	13	15
Santa Clara	8	6	13	15
San Diego	7	7	16	13
St. Mary's (CA)	3	11	9	20
Loyola Marymount	2	12	9	20
Portland	2	12	6	24
Western Athletic				
Hawaii*	15	3	27	5
Tulsa	15	3	26	6
Louisiana Tech	14	4	20	9
SMU	10	8	15	14
Fresno St.	9	9	19	14
Nevada	9	9	17	13
Boise St.	6	12	13	17
Rice	5	13	10	19
San Jose St.	4	14	10	22
Texas-El Paso	3	15	10	22

(1) Conference does not hold a tournament. (2) Trans America Athletic Conference, 1979-2001.

All-Time Winningest Division I College Teams by Percentage

(through 2001-2002 season)

TEAM	Yrs	Won	Lost	Pct.
Kentucky	99	1,815	567	.762
N. Carolina	92	1,789	650	.733
UNLV	44	906	351	.721
Kansas	104	1,767	743	.704
UCLA	83	1,508	653	.698
St. John's-NY	95	1,641	749	.687
Duke	97	1,678	767	.686
Syracuse	101	1,569	730	.682
Utah	94	1,467	716	.672
W. Kentucky	83	1,442	713	.669
Indiana	102	1,514	811	.651
Temple	106	1,586	857	.649
Louisville	88	1,405	770	.646
Notre Dame	97	1,504	827	.645
Illinois	97	1,431	790	.644
Weber State	40	730	407	.642
Arizona	97	1,408	784	.642
Purdue	104	1,457	815	.641
Arkansas	79	1,368	773	.639
DePaul	79	1,242	703	.639
Pennsylvania	102	1,533	869	.638
Villanova	82	1,344	771	.635

Major College Basketball Tournaments

The National Invitation Tournament (NIT), first played in 1938, is the nation's oldest basketball tournament. The first National Collegiate Athletic Association (NCAA) national championship tournament was played one year later. Selections for both tournaments are made in March, with the NCAA selecting first from among the top Division I teams.

National Invitation Tournament Champions

Year	Champion	Year	Champion	Year	Champion	Year	Champion	Year	Champion
1938	Temple	1951	Brigham Young	1964	Bradley	1977	St. Bonaventure	1990	Vanderbilt
1939	Long Island Univ.	1952	LaSalle	1965	St. John's	1978	Texas	1991	Stanford
1940	Colorado	1953	Seton Hall	1966	Brigham Young	1979	Indiana	1992	Virginia
1941	Long Island Univ.	1954	Holy Cross	1967	Southern Illinois	1980	Virginia	1993	Minnesota
1942	West Virginia	1955	Duquesne	1968	Dayton	1981	Tulsa	1994	Villanova
1943	St. John's	1956	Louisville	1969	Temple	1982	Bradley	1995	Virginia Tech
1944	St. John's	1957	Bradley	1970	Marquette	1983	Fresno State	1996	Nebraska
1945	De Paul	1958	Xavier (Ohio)	1971	North Carolina	1984	Michigan	1997	Michigan
1946	Kentucky	1959	St. John's	1972	Maryland	1985	UCLA	1998	Minnesota
1947	Utah	1960	Bradley	1973	Virginia Tech	1986	Ohio State	1999	California
1948	St. Louis	1961	Providence	1974	Purdue	1987	So. Mississippi	2000	Wake Forest
1949	San Francisco	1962	Dayton	1975	Princeton	1988	Connecticut	2001	Tulsa
1950	CCNY	1963	Providence	1976	Kentucky	1989	St. John's	2002	Memphis

2002 MEN'S NCAA BASKETBALL TOURNAMENT

EAST

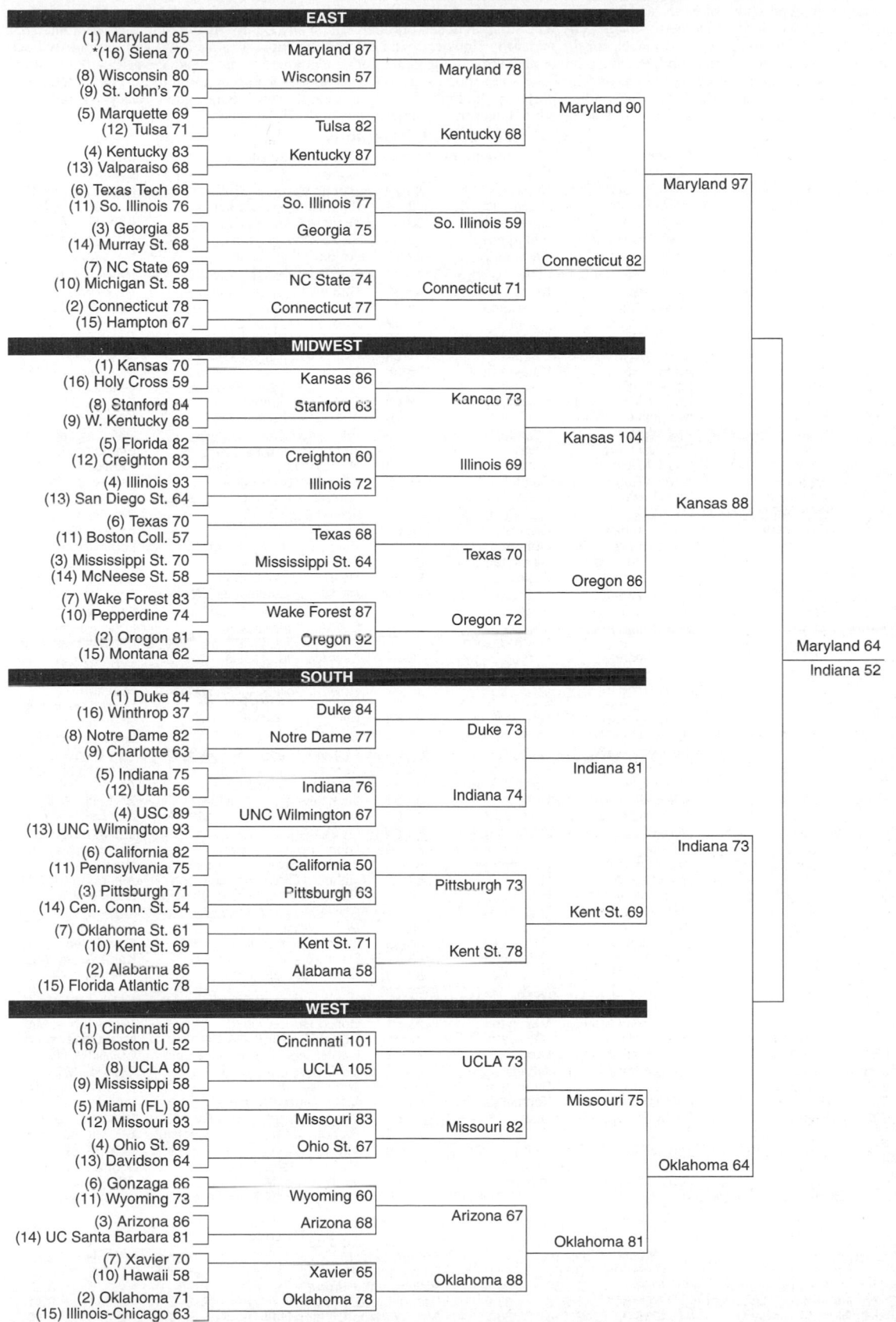

First round
- (1) Maryland 85, *(16) Siena 70
- (8) Wisconsin 80, (9) St. John's 70
- (5) Marquette 69, (12) Tulsa 71
- (4) Kentucky 83, (13) Valparaiso 68
- (6) Texas Tech 68, (11) So. Illinois 76
- (3) Georgia 85, (14) Murray St. 68
- (7) NC State 69, (10) Michigan St. 58
- (2) Connecticut 78, (15) Hampton 67

Second round
- Maryland 87, Wisconsin 57
- Tulsa 82, Kentucky 87
- So. Illinois 77, Georgia 75
- NC State 74, Connecticut 77

Regional semifinals
- Maryland 78, Kentucky 68
- So. Illinois 59, Connecticut 71

Regional final
- Maryland 90, Connecticut 82

MIDWEST

First round
- (1) Kansas 70, (16) Holy Cross 59
- (8) Stanford 84, (9) W. Kentucky 68
- (5) Florida 82, (12) Creighton 83
- (4) Illinois 93, (13) San Diego St. 64
- (6) Texas 70, (11) Boston Coll. 57
- (3) Mississippi St. 70, (14) McNeese St. 58
- (7) Wake Forest 83, (10) Pepperdine 74
- (2) Oregon 81, (15) Montana 62

Second round
- Kansas 86, Stanford 63
- Creighton 60, Illinois 72
- Texas 68, Mississippi St. 64
- Wake Forest 87, Oregon 92

Regional semifinals
- Kansas 73, Illinois 69
- Texas 70, Oregon 72

Regional final
- Kansas 104, Oregon 86

SOUTH

First round
- (1) Duke 84, (16) Winthrop 37
- (8) Notre Dame 82, (9) Charlotte 63
- (5) Indiana 75, (12) Utah 56
- (4) USC 89, (13) UNC Wilmington 93
- (6) California 82, (11) Pennsylvania 75
- (3) Pittsburgh 71, (14) Cen. Conn. St. 54
- (7) Oklahoma St. 61, (10) Kent St. 69
- (2) Alabama 86, (15) Florida Atlantic 78

Second round
- Duke 84, Notre Dame 77
- Indiana 76, UNC Wilmington 67
- California 50, Pittsburgh 63
- Kent St. 71, Alabama 58

Regional semifinals
- Duke 73, Indiana 74
- Pittsburgh 73, Kent St. 78

Regional final
- Indiana 81, Kent St. 69

WEST

First round
- (1) Cincinnati 90, (16) Boston U. 52
- (8) UCLA 80, (9) Mississippi 58
- (5) Miami (FL) 80, (12) Missouri 93
- (4) Ohio St. 69, (13) Davidson 64
- (6) Gonzaga 66, (11) Wyoming 73
- (3) Arizona 86, (14) UC Santa Barbara 81
- (7) Xavier 70, (10) Hawaii 58
- (2) Oklahoma 71, (15) Illinois-Chicago 63

Second round
- Cincinnati 101, UCLA 105
- Missouri 83, Ohio St. 67
- Wyoming 60, Arizona 68
- Xavier 65, Oklahoma 78

Regional semifinals
- UCLA 73, Missouri 82
- Arizona 67, Oklahoma 88

Regional final
- Missouri 75, Oklahoma 81

NATIONAL SEMIFINALS
- Maryland 97, Kansas 88
- Indiana 73, Oklahoma 64

CHAMPIONSHIP
- Maryland 64, Indiana 52

*Siena defeated Alcorn St., 81-77, in a special play-in game on Mar. 12 to earn the 16th seed in the East.

2002 Men's NCAA Tournament: Maryland Overpowers Indiana, Captures First Title

The top-seeded Univ. of Maryland Terrapins won their first NCAA men's title as they defeated the Indiana Hoosiers, 64-52, Apr. 1, at the Georgia Dome in Atlanta, GA. The strength of seniors Juan Dixon and Lonny Baxter, and their combined 33 points and 19 rebounds, were too much for the underdog Hoosiers, who entered the game as a 5th seed and previously beat top-ranked Duke in the 3rd round. Playing from behind most of the game, Indiana grabbed its first lead at 44-42 with less than 10 minutes left in regulation. However, on Maryland's next possession, Dixon nailed a 3-pointer and put Maryland on top for good. Dixon was named the Most Outstanding Player in the Final Four, averaging 25.8 points per game. Gary Williams became the 9th coach in NCAA history to lead his alma mater to a championship in the Final Four.

NCAA Division I Champions

Year	Champion	Coach	Final opponent	Score	Outstanding player	Site
1939	Oregon	Howard Hobson	Ohio St.	46-33	None	Evanston, IL
1940	Indiana	Branch McCracken	Kansas	60-42	Marvin Huffman, Indiana	Kansas City, MO
1941	Wisconsin	Harold Foster	Washington St.	39-34	John Kotz, Wisconsin	Kansas City, MO
1942	Stanford	Everett Dean	Dartmouth	53-38	Howard Dallmar, Stanford	Kansas City, MO
1943	Wyoming	Everett Shelton	Georgetown	46-34	Ken Sailors, Wyoming	New York, NY
1944	Utah	Vadal Peterson	Dartmouth	42-40[1]	Arnold Ferrin, Utah	New York, NY
1945	Oklahoma St.[2]	Henry Iba	NYU	49-45	Bob Kurland, Oklahoma St.	New York, NY
1946	Oklahoma St.[2]	Henry Iba	North Carolina	43-40	Bob Kurland, Oklahoma St.	New York, NY
1947	Holy Cross	Alvin Julian	Oklahoma	58-47	George Kaftan, Holy Cross	New York, NY
1948	Kentucky	Adolph Rupp	Baylor	58-42	Alex Groza, Kentucky	New York, NY
1949	Kentucky	Adolph Rupp	Oklahoma St.	46-36	Alex Groza, Kentucky	Seattle, WA
1950	CCNY	Nat Holman	Bradley	71-68	Irwin Dambrot, CCNY	New York, NY
1951	Kentucky	Adolph Rupp	Kansas St.	68-58	None	Minneapolis, MN
1952	Kansas	Forrest Allen	St. John's	80-63	Clyde Lovellette, Kansas	Seattle, WA
1953	Indiana	Branch McCracken	Kansas	69-68	B.H. Born, Kansas	Kansas City, MO
1954	La Salle	Kenneth Loeffler	Bradley	92-76	Tom Gola, La Salle	Kansas City, MO
1955	San Francisco	Phil Woolpert	LaSalle	77-63	Bill Russell, San Francisco	Kansas City, MO
1956	San Francisco	Phil Woolpert	Iowa	83-71	Hal Lear, Temple	Evanston, IL
1957	North Carolina	Frank McGuire	Kansas	54-53[1]	Wilt Chamberlain, Kansas	Kansas City, MO
1958	Kentucky	Adolph Rupp	Seattle	84-72	Elgin Baylor, Seattle	Louisville, KY
1959	California	Pete Newell	West Virginia	71-70	Jerry West, West Virginia	Louisville, KY
1960	Ohio St.	Fred Taylor	California	75-55	Jerry Lucas, Ohio St.	San Francisco, CA
1961	Cincinnati	Edwin Jucker	Ohio St.	70-65[1]	Jerry Lucas, Ohio St.	Kansas City, MO
1962	Cincinnati	Edwin Jucker	Ohio St.	71-59	Paul Hogue, Cincinnati	Louisville, KY
1963	Loyola (IL)	George Ireland	Cincinnati	60-58[1]	Art Heyman, Duke	Louisville, KY
1964	UCLA	John Wooden	Duke	98-83	Walt Hazzard, UCLA	Kansas City, MO
1965	UCLA	John Wooden	Michigan	91-80	Bill Bradley, Princeton	Portland, OR
1966	Texas-El Paso[3]	Don Haskins	Kentucky	72-65	Jerry Chambers, Utah	College Park, MD
1967	UCLA	John Wooden	Dayton	79-64	Lew Alcindor, UCLA	Louisville, KY
1968	UCLA	John Wooden	North Carolina	78-55	Lew Alcindor, UCLA	Los Angeles, CA
1969	UCLA	John Wooden	Purdue	92-72	Lew Alcindor, UCLA	Louisville, KY
1970	UCLA	John Wooden	Jacksonville	80-69	Sidney Wicks, UCLA	College Park, MD
1971	UCLA	John Wooden	Villanova*	68-62	Howard Porter, Villanova*	Houston, TX
1972	UCLA	John Wooden	Florida St.	81-76	Bill Walton, UCLA	Los Angeles, CA
1973	UCLA	John Wooden	Memphis St.	87-66	Bill Walton, UCLA	St. Louis, MO
1974	North Carolina St.	Norm Sloan	Marquette	76-64	David Thompson, N.C. St.	Greensboro, NC
1975	UCLA	John Wooden	Kentucky	92-85	Richard Washington, UCLA	San Diego, CA
1976	Indiana	Bob Knight	Michigan	86-68	Kent Benson, Indiana	Philadelphia, PA
1977	Marquette	Al McGuire	North Carolina	67-59	Butch Lee, Marquette	Atlanta, GA
1978	Kentucky	Joe Hall	Duke	94-88	Jack Givens, Kentucky	St. Louis, MO
1979	Michigan St.	Jud Heathcote	Indiana St.	75-64	Magic Johnson, Michigan St.	Salt Lake City, UT
1980	Louisville	Denny Crum	UCLA*	59-54	Darrell Griffith, Louisville	Indianapolis, IN
1981	Indiana	Bob Knight	North Carolina	63-50	Isiah Thomas, Indiana	Philadelphia, PA
1982	North Carolina	Dean Smith	Georgetown	63-62	James Worthy, N. Carolina	New Orleans, LA
1983	North Carolina St.	Jim Valvano	Houston	54-52	Hakeem Olajuwon, Houston	Albuquerque, NM
1984	Georgetown	John Thompson	Houston	84-75	Patrick Ewing, Georgetown	Seattle, WA
1985	Villanova	Rollie Massimino	Georgetown	66-64	Ed Pinckney, Villanova	Lexington, KY
1986	Louisville	Denny Crum	Duke	72-69	Pervis Ellison, Louisville	Dallas, TX
1987	Indiana	Bob Knight	Syracuse	74-73	Keith Smart, Indiana	New Orleans, LA
1988	Kansas	Larry Brown	Oklahoma	83-79	Danny Manning, Kansas	Kansas City, MO
1989	Michigan	Steve Fisher	Seton Hall	80-79[1]	Glen Rice, Michigan	Seattle, WA
1990	UNLV	Jerry Tarkanian	Duke	103-73	Anderson Hunt, UNLV	Denver, CO
1991	Duke	Mike Krzyzewski	Kansas	72-65	Christian Laettner, Duke	Indianapolis, IN
1992	Duke	Mike Krzyzewski	Michigan	71-51	Bobby Hurley, Duke	Minneapolis, MN
1993	North Carolina	Dean Smith	Michigan	77-71	Donald Williams, N. Carolina	New Orleans, LA
1994	Arkansas	Nolan Richardson	Duke	76-72	Corliss Williamson, Arkansas	Charlotte, NC
1995	UCLA	Jim Harrick	Arkansas	89-78	Ed O'Bannon, UCLA	Seattle, WA
1996	Kentucky	Rick Pitino	Syracuse	76-67	Tony Delk, Kentucky	E. Rutherford, NJ
1997	Arizona	Lute Olson	Kentucky	84-79[1]	Miles Simon, Arizona	Indianapolis, IN
1998	Kentucky	Tubby Smith	Utah	78-69	Jeff Sheppard, Kentucky	San Antonio, TX
1999	Connecticut	Jim Calhoun	Duke	77-74	Richard Hamilton, Connecticut	St. Petersburg, FL
2000	Michigan St.	Tom Izzo	Florida	89-76	Mateen Cleaves, Michigan St.	Indianapolis, IN
2001	Duke	Mike Krzyzewski	Arizona	82-72	Shane Battier, Duke	Minneapolis, MN
2002	Maryland	Gary Williams	Indiana	64-52	Juan Dixon, Maryland	Atlanta, GA

*Declared ineligible after the tournament. (1) Overtime. (2) Then known as Oklahoma A&M. (3) Then known as Texas Western.

Top Division I Career Scorers

(minimum 1,500 points; ranked by average)

Player, school	Years	Points	Avg.
Pete Maravich, LSU	1968-70	3,667	44.2
Austin Carr, Notre Dame	1969-71	2,560	34.6
Oscar Robertson, Cincinnati	1958-60	2,973	33.8
Calvin Murphy, Niagara	1968-70	2,548	33.1
Dwight Lamar, SW Louisiana	1972-73	1,862	32.7
Frank Selvy, Furman	1952-54	2,538	32.5
Rick Mount, Purdue	1968-70	2,323	32.3
Darrell Floyd, Furman	1954-56	2,281	32.1
Nick Werkman, Seton Hall	1962-64	2,273	32.0
Willie Humes, Idaho State	1970-71	1,510	31.5

John R. Wooden Award

Awarded to the nation's outstanding college basketball player by the Los Angeles Athletic Club.

1977	Marques Johnson, UCLA	1986	Walter Berry, St. John's	1995	Ed O'Bannon, UCLA
1978	Phil Ford, North Carolina	1987	David Robinson, Navy	1996	Marcus Camby, Massachusetts
1979	Larry Bird, Indiana State	1988	Danny Manning, Kansas	1997	Tim Duncan, Wake Forest
1980	Darrell Griffith, Louisville	1989	Sean Elliott, Arizona	1998	Antawn Jamison, North Carolina
1981	Danny Ainge, Brigham Young	1990	Lionel Simmons, La Salle	1999	Elton Brand, Duke
1982	Ralph Sampson, Virginia	1991	Larry Johnson, UNLV	2000	Kenyon Martin, Cincinnati
1983	Ralph Sampson, Virginia	1992	Christian Laettner, Duke	2001	Shane Battier, Duke
1984	Michael Jordan, North Carolina	1993	Calbert Cheaney, Indiana	2002	Jay Williams, Duke
1985	Chris Mullin, St. John's	1994	Glenn Robinson, Purdue		

Most Coaching Victories in the NCAA Tournament Through 2002

(Coaches active in 2001-2002 season in bold)

Coach, School(s), First/Last appearance	Wins	Tourns.
Dean Smith, North Carolina, 1967/1997	65	27
Mike Krzyzewski, Duke, 1984/2002	58	18
John Wooden, UCLA, 1950/1975	47	16
Denny Crum, Louisville, 1972/2000	42	23
Bob Knight, Indiana, Texas Tech, 1973/2002	42	25
Lute Olson, Iowa, Arizona, 1979/2002	39	23
John Thompson, Georgetown, 1975/1997	34	20
Jim Boeheim, Syracuse, 1977/2001	32	21
Eddie Sutton, Creighton, Arkansas, Kentucky, Oklahoma St., 1974/2002	32	23
Jerry Tarkanian, Long Beach St., UNLV, Fresno St.,1970/2001	32*	15

*Does not include 6 wins in the 1971-73 tournaments which were later vacated for NCAA rule violations.

Women's College Basketball

2002 Women's NCAA Tournament: UConn Finishes Undefeated, Beats Oklahoma for Title

The Univ. of Connecticut Huskies outgunned the Oklahoma Sooners, 82-70, March 31, at the Alamo Dome in San Antonio, TX, to complete their 2nd undefeated season and claim their 3rd NCAA women's title. Wade Trophy winner and AP Player of the Year Sue Bird contributed 14 points and 4 assists to the victory. However, Swin Cash led the Huskies with 20 points and 13 rebounds and was named the Most Outstanding Player of the Final Four. Considered one of the top women's teams ever, the 2001-2002 Huskies won their 39 games by an average margin of 35.4 points, an NCAA record.

NCAA Division I Women's Champions

Year	Champion	Coach	Final opponent	Score	Outstanding player	Site
1982	Louisiana Tech	Sonja Hogg	Cheyney	76-62	Janice Lawrence, La. Tech	Norfolk, VA
1983	USC	Linda Sharp	Louisiana Tech	69-67	Cheryl Miller, USC	Norfolk, VA
1984	USC	Linda Sharp	Tennessee	72-61	Cheryl Miller, USC	Los Angeles, CA
1985	Old Dominion	Marianne Stanley	Georgia	70-65	Tracy Claxton, Old Dominion	Austin, TX
1986	Texas	Jody Conradt	USC	97-81	Clarissa Davis, Texas	Lexington, KY
1987	Tennessee	Pat Summitt	Louisiana Tech	67-44	Tonya Edwards, Tennessee	Austin, TX
1988	Louisiana Tech	Leon Barmore	Auburn	56-54	Erica Westbrooks, La. Tech	Tacoma, WA
1989	Tennessee	Pat Summitt	Auburn	76-60	Bridgette Gordon, Tennessee	Tacoma, WA
1990	Stanford	Tara VanDerveer	Auburn	88-81	Jennifer Azzi, Stanford	Knoxville, TN
1991	Tennessee	Pat Summitt	Virginia	70-67*	Dawn Staley, Virginia	New Orleans, LA
1992	Stanford	Tara VanDerveer	W. Kentucky	78-62	Molly Goodenbour, Stanford	Los Angeles, CA
1993	Texas Tech	Marsha Sharp	Ohio St.	84-82	Sheryl Swoopes, Texas Tech	Atlanta, GA
1994	North Carolina	Sylvia Hatchell	Louisiana Tech	60-59	Charlotte Smith, North Carolina	Richmond, VA
1995	Connecticut	Geno Auriemma	Tennessee	70-64	Rebecca Lobo, Connecticut	Minneapolis, MN
1996	Tennessee	Pat Summitt	Georgia	83-65	Michelle Marciniak, Tennessee	Charlotte, NC
1997	Tennessee	Pat Summitt	Old Dominion	68-59	Chamique Holdsclaw, Tennessee	Cincinnati, OH
1998	Tennessee	Pat Summitt	Louisiana Tech	93-75	Chamique Holdsclaw, Tennessee	Kansas City, MO
1999	Purdue	Carolyn Peck	Duke	62-45	Ukari Figgs, Purdue	San Jose, CA
2000	Connecticut	Geno Auriemma	Tennessee	71-52	Shea Ralph, Connecticut	Philadelphia, PA
2001	Notre Dame	Muffet McGraw	Purdue	68-66	Ruth Riley, Notre Dame	St. Louis, MO
2002	Connecticut	Geno Auriemma	Oklahoma	82-70	Swin Cash, Connecticut	San Antonio, TX

* Overtime.

Wade Trophy

Awarded by National Assn. for Girls and Women in Sport for academics, community service, and player performance.

Year	Player, school
1978	Carol Blazejowski, Montclair St.
1979	Nancy Lieberman, Old Dominion
1980	Nancy Lieberman, Old Dominion
1981	Lynette Woodard, Kansas
1982	Pam Kelly, Louisiana Tech
1983	LaTaunya Pollard, Long Beach St.
1984	Janice Lawrence, Louisiana Tech
1985	Cheryl Miller, USC
1986	Kamie Ethridge, Texas
1987	Shelly Pennefeather, Villanova
1988	Teresa Weatherspoon, Louisiana Tech
1989	Clarissa Davis, Texas
1990	Jennifer Azzi, Stanford
1991	Daedra Charles, Tennessee
1992	Susan Robinson, Penn St.
1993	Karen Jennings, Nebraska
1994	Carol Ann Shudlick, Minnesota
1995	Rebecca Lobo, Connecticut
1996	Jennifer Rizzotti, Connecticut
1997	DeLisha Milton, Florida
1998	Chamique Holdsclaw, Tennessee
1999	Stephanie White-McCarty, Purdue
2000	Edwina Brown, Texas
2001	Jackie Stiles, SW Missouri St.
2002	Sue Bird, Connecticut

Top Division I Women's Career Scorers

(Minimum 1,500 points; ranked by average)

Player, school	Years	Points	Avg.
Patricia Hoskins, Miss. Valley St.	1985-89	3,122	28.4
Sandra Hodge, New Orleans	1981-84	2,860	26.7
Jackie Stiles, SW Missouri St.	1997-2001	3,393	26.3
Lorri Bauman, Drake	1981-84	3,115	26.0
Andrea Congreaves, Mercer	1989-93	2,796	25.9
Cindy Blodgett, Maine	1994-98	3,005	25.5
Valorie Whiteside, Appalachian St.	1984-88	2,944	25.4
Joyce Walker, LSU	1981-84	2,906	24.8
Tarcha Hollis, Grambling	1988-91	2,058	24.2
Korie Hlede, Duquesne	1994-98	2,631	24.1
Erma Jones, Bethune-Cookman	1982-84	2,095	24.1
Karen Pelphrey, Marshall	1983-86	2,746	24.1

2002 WOMEN'S NCAA BASKETBALL TOURNAMENT

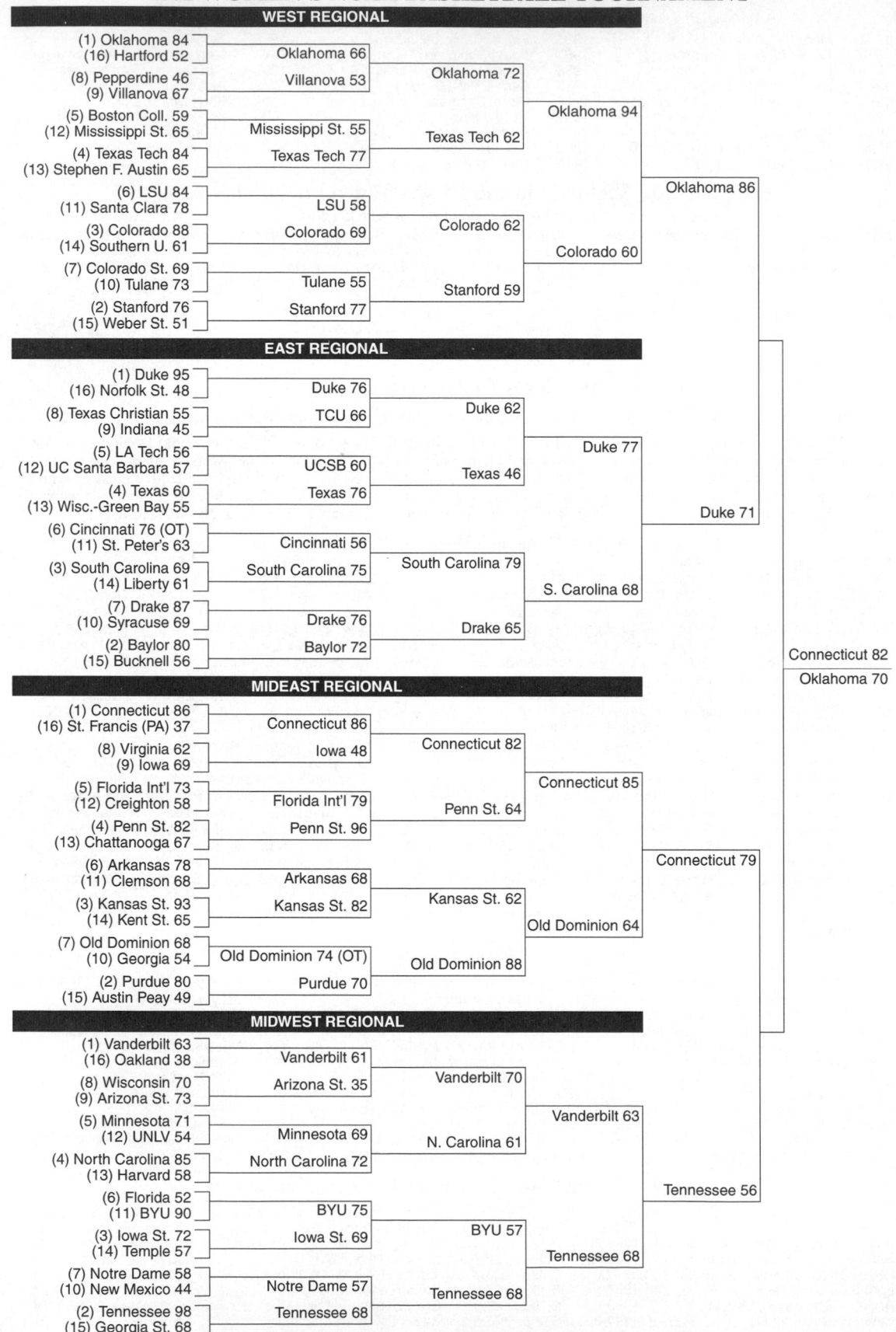

WEST REGIONAL

First round:
- (1) Oklahoma 84, (16) Hartford 52
- (8) Pepperdine 46, (9) Villanova 67
- (5) Boston Coll. 59, (12) Mississippi St. 65
- (4) Texas Tech 84, (13) Stephen F. Austin 65
- (6) LSU 84, (11) Santa Clara 78
- (3) Colorado 88, (14) Southern U. 61
- (7) Colorado St. 69, (10) Tulane 73
- (2) Stanford 76, (15) Weber St. 51

Second round:
- Oklahoma 66, Villanova 53
- Mississippi St. 55, Texas Tech 77
- LSU 58, Colorado 69
- Tulane 55, Stanford 77

Regional semifinals:
- Oklahoma 72, Texas Tech 62
- Colorado 62, Stanford 59

Regional final:
- Oklahoma 94, Colorado 60

EAST REGIONAL

First round:
- (1) Duke 95, (16) Norfolk St. 48
- (8) Texas Christian 55, (9) Indiana 45
- (5) LA Tech 56, (12) UC Santa Barbara 57
- (4) Texas 60, (13) Wisc.-Green Bay 55
- (6) Cincinnati 76 (OT), (11) St. Peter's 63
- (3) South Carolina 69, (14) Liberty 61
- (7) Drake 87, (10) Syracuse 69
- (2) Baylor 80, (15) Bucknell 56

Second round:
- Duke 76, TCU 66
- UCSB 60, Texas 76
- Cincinnati 56, South Carolina 75
- Drake 76, Baylor 72

Regional semifinals:
- Duke 62, Texas 46
- South Carolina 79, Drake 65

Regional final:
- Duke 77, S. Carolina 68

MIDEAST REGIONAL

First round:
- (1) Connecticut 86, (16) St. Francis (PA) 37
- (8) Virginia 62, (9) Iowa 69
- (5) Florida Int'l 73, (12) Creighton 58
- (4) Penn St. 82, (13) Chattanooga 67
- (6) Arkansas 78, (11) Clemson 68
- (3) Kansas St. 93, (14) Kent St. 65
- (7) Old Dominion 68, (10) Georgia 54
- (2) Purdue 80, (15) Austin Peay 49

Second round:
- Connecticut 86, Iowa 48
- Florida Int'l 79, Penn St. 96
- Arkansas 68, Kansas St. 82
- Old Dominion 74 (OT), Purdue 70

Regional semifinals:
- Connecticut 82, Penn St. 64
- Kansas St. 62, Old Dominion 88

Regional final:
- Connecticut 85, Old Dominion 64

MIDWEST REGIONAL

First round:
- (1) Vanderbilt 63, (16) Oakland 38
- (8) Wisconsin 70, (9) Arizona St. 73
- (5) Minnesota 71, (12) UNLV 54
- (4) North Carolina 85, (13) Harvard 58
- (6) Florida 52, (11) BYU 90
- (3) Iowa St. 72, (14) Temple 57
- (7) Notre Dame 58, (10) New Mexico 44
- (2) Tennessee 98, (15) Georgia St. 68

Second round:
- Vanderbilt 61, Arizona St. 35
- Minnesota 69, North Carolina 72
- BYU 75, Iowa St. 69
- Notre Dame 57, Tennessee 68

Regional semifinals:
- Vanderbilt 70, N. Carolina 61
- BYU 57, Tennessee 68

Regional final:
- Vanderbilt 63, Tennessee 68

FINAL FOUR

Semifinals:
- Oklahoma 86, Duke 71
- Connecticut 79, Tennessee 56

Championship:
- Connecticut 82, Oklahoma 70

NATIONAL FOOTBALL LEAGUE

NFL 2001-2002: Patriots Super, Strahan Sacks Record, Resurgent Bears

The New England Patriots, on a last-second field goal by Adam Vinatieri, upset the St. Louis Rams, 20-17, to win Super Bowl XXXVI, Feb. 3, 2002, in New Orleans. This was the first time the Super Bowl was held in February—a result of the season being delayed one week because of the Sept. 11 attacks. The victory gave the Patriots their first-ever world championship. For the 2nd time in 3 years, Rams quarterback Kurt Warner won the NFL's MVP award. He led the league in passing yds. (4,830), TD passes (36), and QB rating (101.4). NY Giants' DE Michael Strahan set an NFL record of 22.5 sacks for the season, eclipsing Mark Gastineau's (NY Jets) 22 in 1984. Last in the NFC Central division each year since 1997, the Chicago Bears—bolstered by a defense that allowed a league-low 12.7 points per game—finished with the NFL's 2nd-best record (13-3) and won their 1st division title since 1990. In 2002, the expansion Houston Texans began play on Sept. 8 at Reliant Stadium in Houston, with a 19-10 win over the Dallas Cowboys. Also in 2002, the NFL's 32nd team joined the newly created AFC South division. The Texans made Fresno State QB David Carr the top pick in the NFL Draft on April 20.

Final 2001 Standings

American Football Conference

Eastern Division	W	L	T	Pct.	Pts.	Opp.
New England	11	5	0	.688	371	272
Miami*	11	5	0	.688	344	290
NY Jets*	10	6	0	.625	308	295
Indianapolis	6	10	0	.375	413	486
Buffalo	3	13	0	.188	265	420
Central Division	**W**	**L**	**T**	**Pct.**	**Pts.**	**Opp.**
Pittsburgh	13	3	0	.812	352	212
Baltimore*	10	6	0	.625	303	265
Cleveland	7	9	0	.438	285	319
Tennessee	7	9	0	.438	336	388
Jacksonville	6	10	0	.375	294	286
Cincinnati	6	10	0	.375	226	309
Western Division	**W**	**L**	**T**	**Pct.**	**Pts.**	**Opp.**
Oakland	10	6	0	.625	399	327
Seattle	9	7	0	.562	301	324
Denver	8	8	0	.500	340	339
Kansas City	6	10	0	.375	320	344
San Diego	5	11	0	.312	332	321

National Football Conference

Eastern Division	W	L	T	Pct.	Pts.	Opp.
Philadelphia	11	5	0	.688	343	208
Washington	8	8	0	.500	256	303
NY Giants	7	9	0	.438	294	321
Arizona	7	9	0	.438	295	343
Dallas	5	11	0	.312	246	338
Central Division	**W**	**L**	**T**	**Pct.**	**Pts.**	**Opp.**
Chicago	13	3	0	.812	338	203
Green Bay*	12	4	0	.750	390	266
Tampa Bay*	9	7	0	.562	324	280
Minnesota	5	11	0	.312	290	390
Detroit	2	14	0	.125	270	424
Western Division	**W**	**L**	**T**	**Pct.**	**Pts.**	**Opp.**
St. Louis	14	2	0	.875	503	273
San Francisco*	12	4	0	.750	409	282
New Orleans	7	9	0	.438	333	409
Atlanta	7	9	0	.438	291	377
Carolina	1	15	0	.062	253	410

* Wild card team.

AFC Playoffs—Oakland 38, NY Jets 24; Baltimore 20, Miami 3; New England 16, Oakland 13; Pittsburgh 27, Baltimore 10; **Championship:** New England 24, Pittsburgh 17.

NFC Playoffs—Philadelphia 31, Tampa Bay 9; Green Bay 25, San Francisco 15; Philadelphia 33, Chicago 19; St. Louis 45, Green Bay 17; Championship: St. Louis 29, Philadelphia 24.

Super Bowl—New England 20, St. Louis 17.

National Football League Champions

Year	East Winner (W-L-T)	West Winner (W-L-T)	Playoff
1933	New York Giants (11-3-0)	Chicago Bears (10-2-1)	Chicago Bears 23, New York 21
1934	New York Giants (8-5-0)	Chicago Bears (13-0-0)	New York 30, Chicago Bears 13
1935	New York Giants (9-3-0)	Detroit Lions (7-3-2)	Detroit 26, New York 7
1936	Boston Redskins (7-5-0)	Green Bay Packers (10-1-1)	Green Bay 21, Boston 6
1937	Washington Redskins (8-3-0)	Chicago Bears (9-1-1)	Washington 28, Chicago Bears 21
1938	New York Giants (8-2-1)	Green Bay Packers (8-3-0)	New York 23, Green Bay 17
1939	New York Giants (9-1-1)	Green Bay Packers (9-2-0)	Green Bay 27, New York 0
1940	Washington Redskins (9-2-0)	Chicago Bears (8-3-0)	Chicago Bears 73, Washington 0
1941	New York Giants (8-3-0)	Chicago Bears (10-1-1)(a)	Chicago Bears 37, New York 9
1942	Washington Redskins (10-1-1)	Chicago Bears (11-0-0)	Washington 14, Chicago Bears 6
1943	Washington Redskins (6-3-1)	Chicago Bears (8-1-1)	Chicago Bears, 41, Washington 21
1944	New York Giants (8-1-1)	Green Bay Packers (8-2-0)	Green Bay 14, New York 7
1945	Washington Redskins (8-2-0)	Cleveland Rams (9-1-0)	Cleveland 15, Washington 14
1946	New York Giants (7-3-1)	Chicago Bears (8-2-1)	Chicago Bears 24, New York 14
1947	Philadelphia Eagles (8-4-0)(a)	Chicago Cardinals (9-3-0)	Chicago Cardinals 28, Philadelphia 21
1948	Philadelphia Eagles (9-2-1)	Chicago Cardinals (11-1-0)	Philadelphia 7, Chicago Cardinals 0
1949	Philadelphia Eagles (11-1-0)	Los Angeles Rams (8-2-2)	Philadelphia 14, Los Angeles 0
1950	Cleveland Browns (10-2-0)(a)	Los Angeles Rams (9-3-0)(a)	Cleveland 30, Los Angeles 28
1951	Cleveland Browns (11-1-0)	Los Angeles Rams (8-4-0)	Los Angeles 24, Cleveland 17
1952	Cleveland Browns (8-4-0)	Detroit Lions (9-3-0)(a)	Detroit 17, Cleveland 7
1953	Cleveland Browns (11-1-0)	Detroit Lions (10-2-0)	Detroit 17, Cleveland 16
1954	Cleveland Browns (9-3-0)	Detroit Lions (9-2-1)	Cleveland 56, Detroit 10
1955	Cleveland Browns (9-2-1)	Los Angeles Rams (8-3-1)	Cleveland 38, Los Angeles 14
1956	New York Giants (8-3-1)	Chicago Bears (9-2-1)	New York 47, Chicago Bears 7
1957	Cleveland Browns (9-2-1)	Detroit Lions (8-4-0)(a)	Detroit 59, Cleveland 14
1958	New York Giants (9-3-0)(a)	Baltimore Colts (9-3-0)	Baltimore 23, New York 17(b)
1959	New York Giants (10-2-0)	Baltimore Colts (9-3-0)	Baltimore 31, New York 16
1960	Philadelphia Eagles (10-2-0)	Green Bay Packers (8-4-0)	Philadelphia 17, Green Bay 13
1961	New York Giants (10-3-1)	Green Bay Packers (11-3-0)	Green Bay 37, New York 0
1962	New York Giants (12-2-0)	Green Bay Packers (13-1-0)	Green Bay 16, New York 7
1963	New York Giants (11-3-0)	Chicago Bears (11-1-2)	Chicago 14, New York 10
1964	Cleveland Browns (10-3-1)	Baltimore Colts (12-2-0)	Cleveland 27, Baltimore 0
1965	Cleveland Browns (11-3-0)	Green Bay Packers (10-3-1)(a)	Green Bay 23, Cleveland 12
1966	Dallas Cowboys (10-3-1)	Green Bay Packers (12-2-0)	Green Bay 34, Dallas 27

(a) Won divisional playoff. (b) Won at 8:15 of sudden death overtime period.

Year	Conference	Division	Winner (W-L-T)	Playoffs(c)	Year
1967	East	Century	Cleveland Browns (9-5-0)	Dallas 52, Cleveland 14	1967
		Capitol	Dallas Cowboys (9-5-0)		
	West	Central	Green Bay Packers (9-4-1)	Green Bay 28, Los Angeles 7	
		Coastal	Los Angeles Rams (11-1-2)(a)	Green Bay 21, Dallas 17	
1968	East	Century	Cleveland Browns (10-4-0)	Cleveland 31, Dallas 20	1968
		Capitol	Dallas Cowboys (12-2-0)		
	West	Central	Minnesota Vikings (8-6-0)	Baltimore 24, Minnesota 14	
		Coastal	Baltimore Colts (13-1-0)	Baltimore 34, Cleveland 0	
1969	East	Century	Cleveland Browns (10-3-1)	Cleveland 38, Dallas 14	1969
		Capitol	Dallas Cowboys (11-2-1)		
	West	Central	Minnesota Vikings (12-2-0)	Minnesota 23, Los Angeles 20	
		Coastal	Los Angeles Rams (11-3-0)	Minnesota 27, Cleveland 7	
1970	American	Eastern	Baltimore Colts (11-2-1)	Baltimore 17, Cincinnati 0	1970
		Central	Cincinnati Bengals (8-6-0)	Oakland 21, Miami* 14	
		Western	Oakland Raiders (8-4-2)	Baltimore 27, Oakland 17	
	National	Eastern	Dallas Cowboys (10-4-0)	Dallas 5, Detroit* 0	
		Central	Minnesota Vikings (12-2-0)	San Francisco 17, Minnesota 14	
		Western	San Francisco 49ers (10-3-1)	Dallas 17, San Francisco 10	
1971	American	Eastern	Miami Dolphins (10-3-1)	Miami 27, Kansas City* 24	1971
		Central	Cleveland Browns (9-5-0)	Baltimore 20, Cleveland 3	
		Western	Kansas City Chiefs(10-3-1)	Miami 21, Baltimore 0	
	National	Eastern	Dallas Cowboys (11-3-0)	Dallas 20, Minnesota 12	
		Central	Minnesota Vikings (11-3-0)	San Francisco 24, Washington* 20	
		Western	San Francisco 49ers (9-5-0)	Dallas 14, San Francisco 3	
1972	American	Eastern	Miami Dolphins (14-0-0)	Miami 20, Cleveland* 14	1972
		Central	Pittsburgh Steelers (11-3-0)	Pittsburgh 13, Oakland 7	
		Western	Oakland Raiders (10-3-1)	Miami 21, Pittsburgh 17	
	National	Eastern	Washington Redskins (11-3-0)	Washington 16, Green Bay 3	
		Central	Green Bay Packers (10-4-0)	Dallas* 30, San Francisco 28	
		Western	San Francisco 49ers (8-5-1)	Washington 26, Dallas* 3	
1973	American	Eastern	Miami Dolphins (12-2-0)	Miami 34, Cincinnati 16	1973
		Central	Cincinnati Bengals (10-4-0)	Oakland 33, Pittsburgh* 14	
		Western	Oakland Raiders (9-4-1)	Miami 27, Oakland 10	
	National	Eastern	Dallas Cowboys (10-4-0)	Dallas 27, Los Angeles 16	
		Central	Minnesota Vikings (12-2-0)	Minnesota 27, Washington* 20	
		Western	Los Angeles Rams (12-2-0)	Minnesota 27, Dallas 10	
1974	American	Eastern	Miami Dolphins (11-3-0)	Oakland 28, Miami 26	1974
		Central	Pittsburgh Steelers (10-3-1)	Pittsburgh 32, Buffalo* 14	
		Western	Oakland Raiders (12-2-0)	Pittsburgh 24, Oakland 13	
	National	Eastern	St. Louis Cardinals (10-4-0)	Minnesota 30, St. Louis 14	
		Central	Minnesota Vikings (10-4-0)	Los Angeles 19, Washington* 10	
		Western	Los Angeles Rams (10-4-0)	Minnesota 14, Los Angeles 10	
1975	American	Eastern	Baltimore Colts (10-4-0)	Pittsburgh 28, Baltimore 10	1975
		Central	Pittsburgh Steelers (12-2-0)	Oakland 31, Cincinnati* 28	
		Western	Oakland Raiders (11-3-0)	Pittsburgh 16, Oakland 10	
	National	Eastern	St. Louis Cardinals (11-3-0)	Dallas* 17, Minnesota 14	
		Central	Minnesota Vikings (12-2-0)	Los Angeles 35, St. Louis 23	
		Western	Los Angeles Rams (12-2-0)	Dallas* 37, Los Angeles 7	
1976	American	Eastern	Baltimore Colts (11-3-0)	Pittsburgh 40, Baltimore 14	1976
		Central	Pittsburgh Steelers (10-4-0)	Oakland 24, New England* 21	
		Western	Oakland Raiders (13-1-0)	Oakland 24, Pittsburgh 7	
	National	Eastern	Dallas Cowboys (11-3-0)	Minnesota 35, Washington* 20	
		Central	Minnesota Vikings (11-2-1)	Los Angeles 14, Dallas 12	
		Western	Los Angeles Rams (10-3-1)	Minnesota 24, Los Angeles 13	
1977	American	Eastern	Baltimore Colts (10-4-0)	Oakland* 37, Baltimore 31	1977
		Central	Pittsburgh Steelers (9-5-0)	Denver 34, Pittsburgh 21	
		Western	Denver Broncos (12-2-0)	Denver 20, Oakland* 17	
	National	Eastern	Dallas Cowboys (12-2-0)	Dallas 37, Chicago* 7	
		Central	Minnesota Vikings (9-5-0)	Minnesota 14, Los Angeles 7	
		Western	Los Angeles Rams (10-4-0)	Dallas 23, Minnesota 6	
1978	American	Eastern	New England Patriots (11-5-0)	Pittsburgh 33, Denver 10	1978
		Central	Pittsburgh Steelers (14-2-0)	Houston* 31, New England 14	
		Western	Denver Broncos (10-6-0)	Pittsburgh 34, Houston* 5	
	National	Eastern	Dallas Cowboys (12-4-0)	Dallas 27, Atlanta* 20	
		Central	Minnesota Vikings (8-7-1)	Los Angeles 34, Minnesota 10	
		Western	Los Angeles Rams (12-4-0)	Dallas 28, Los Angeles 0	
1979	American	Eastern	Miami Dolphins (10-6-0)	Houston* 17, San Diego 14	1979
		Central	Pittsburgh Steelers (12-4-0)	Pittsburgh 34, Miami 14	
		Western	San Diego Chargers (12-4-0)	Pittsburgh 27, Houston* 13	
	National	Eastern	Dallas Cowboys (11-5-0)	Tampa Bay 24, Philadelphia* 17	
		Central	Tampa Bay Buccaneers (10-6-0)	Los Angeles 21, Dallas 19	
		Western	Los Angeles Rams (9-7-0)	Los Angeles 9, Tampa Bay 0	
1980	American	Eastern	Buffalo Bills (11-5-0)	San Diego 20, Buffalo 14	1980
		Central	Cleveland Browns (11-5-0)	Oakland* 14, Cleveland 12	
		Western	San Diego Chargers (11-5-0)	Oakland* 34, San Diego 27	
	National	Eastern	Philadelphia Eagles (12-4-0)	Philadelphia 31, Minnesota 16	
		Central	Minnesota Vikings (9-7-0)	Dallas* 30, Atlanta 27	
		Western	Atlanta Falcons (12-4-0)	Philadelphia 20, Dallas* 7	
1981	American	Eastern	Miami Dolphins (11-4-1)	San Diego 41, Miami 38	1981
		Central	Cincinnati Bengals (12-4-0)	Cincinnati 28, Buffalo* 21	
		Western	San Diego Chargers (10-6-0)	Cincinnati 27, San Diego 7	
	National	Eastern	Dallas Cowboys (12-4-0)	Dallas 38, Tampa Bay 0	
		Central	Tampa Bay Buccaneers (9-7-0)	San Francisco 38, N.Y. Giants* 24	
		Western	San Francisco 49ers (13-3-0)	San Francisco 28, Dallas 27	
1982 (d)	American		Los Angeles Raiders (8-1-0)	Strike-shortened season (see playoff results after footnote)	1982 (d)
	National		Washington Redskins (8-1-0)		
1983	American	Eastern	Miami Dolphins (12-4-0)	Seattle* 27, Miami 20	1983
		Central	Pittsburgh Steelers (10-6-0)	L.A. Raiders 38, Pittsburgh 10	
		Western	Los Angeles Raiders (12-4-0)	L.A. Raiders 30, Seattle* 14	
	National	Eastern	Washington Redskins (14-2-0)	Washington 51, L.A. Rams* 7	
		Central	Detroit Lions (9-7-0)	San Francisco 24, Detroit 23	
		Western	San Francisico 49ers (10-6-0)	Washington 24, San Francisco 21	

Year	Conference	Division	Winner (W-L-T)	Playoffs(c)	Year
1984	American	Eastern	Miami Dolphins (14-2-0)	Miami 31, Seattle* 10	1984
		Central	Pittsburgh Steelers (9-7-0)	Pittsburgh 24, Denver 17	
		Western	Denver Broncos (13-3-0)	Miami 45, Pittsburgh 28	
	National	Eastern	Washington Redskins (11-5-0)	Chicago 23, Washington 19	
		Central	Chicago Bears (10-6-0)	San Francisco 21, N.Y. Giants* 10	
		Western	San Francisco 49ers (15-1-0)	San Francisco 23, Chicago 0	
1985	American	Eastern	Miami Dolphins (12-4-0)	New England* 27, L.A. Raiders 20	1985
		Central	Cleveland Browns (8-8-0)	Miami 24, Cleveland 21	
		Western	Los Angeles Raiders (12-4-0)	New England* 31, Miami 14	
	National	Eastern	Dallas Cowboys (10-6-0)	Chicago 21, N.Y. Giants* 0	
		Central	Chicago Bears (15-1-0)	L.A. Rams 20, Dallas 0	
		Western	Los Angeles Rams (11-5-0)	Chicago 24, L.A. Rams 0	
1986	American	Eastern	New England Patriots (11-5-0)	Denver 22, New England 17	1986
		Central	Cleveland Browns (12-4-0)	Cleveland 23, N.Y. Jets* 20	
		Western	Denver Broncos (11-5-0)	Denver 23, Cleveland 20	
	National	Eastern	New York Giants (14-2-0)	N.Y. Giants 49, San Francisco 3	
		Central	Chicago Bears (14-2-0)	Washington* 27, Chicago 13	
		Western	San Francisco 49ers (10-5-1)	N.Y. Giants 17, Washington* 0	
1987	American	Eastern	Indianapolis Colts (9-6-0)	Cleveland 38, Indianapolis 21	1987
		Central	Cleveland Browns (10-5-0)	Denver 34, Houston* 10	
		Western	Denver Broncos (10-4-1)	Denver 38, Cleveland 33	
	National	Eastern	Washington Redskins (11-4-0)	Washington 21, Chicago 17	
		Central	Chicago Bears (11-4-0)	Minnesota* 36, San Francisco 24	
		Western	San Francisco 49ers (13-2-0)	Washington 17, Minnesota* 10	
1988	American	Eastern	Buffalo Bills (12-4-0)	Buffalo 17, Houston* 10	1988
		Central	Cincinnati Bengals (12-4-0)	Cincinnati 21, Seattle 13	
		Western	Seattle Seahawks (9-7-0)	Cincinnati 21, Buffalo 10	
	National	Eastern	Philadelphia Eagles (10-6-0)	Chicago 20, Philadelphia 12	
		Central	Chicago Bears (12-4-0)	San Francisco 34, Minnesota* 9	
		Western	San Francisco 49ers (10-6-0)	San Francisco 28, Chicago 3	
1989	American	Eastern	Buffalo Bills (9-7-0)	Cleveland 34, Buffalo 30	1989
		Central	Cleveland Browns (9-6-1)	Denver 24, Pittsburgh* 23	
		Western	Denver Broncos (11-5-0)	Denver 37, Cleveland 21	
	National	Eastern	New York Giants (12-4-0)	San Francisco 41, Minnesota 13	
		Central	Minnesota Vikings (10-6-0)	L.A. Rams* 19, N.Y. Giants 13	
		Western	San Francisco 49ers (14-2-0)	San Francisco 30, L.A. Rams* 3	
1990	American	Eastern	Buffalo Bills (13-3-0)	L.A. Raiders 20, Cincinnati 10	1990
		Central	Cincinnati Bengals (9-7-0)	Buffalo 44, Miami* 34	
		Western	Los Angeles Raiders (12-4-0)	Buffalo 51, L.A. Raiders 3	
	National	Eastern	New York Giants (13-3-0)	San Francisco 28, Washington* 10	
		Central	Chicago Bears (11-5-0)	N.Y. Giants 31, Chicago 3	
		Western	San Francisco 49ers (14-2-0)	N.Y. Giants 15, San Francisco 13	
1991	American	Eastern	Buffalo Bills (13-3-0)	Denver 26, Houston 24	1991
		Central	Houston Oilers (11-5-0)	Buffalo 37, Kansas City* 14	
		Western	Denver Broncos (12-4-0)	Buffalo 10, Denver 7	
	National	Eastern	Washington Redskins (14-2-0)	Washington 24, Atlanta* 7	
		Central	Detroit Lions (12-4-0)	Detroit 38, Dallas* 6	
		Western	New Orleans Saints (11-5-0)	Washington 41, Detroit 10	
1992	American	Eastern	Miami Dolphins (11-5-0)	Miami 31, San Diego 0	1992
		Central	Pittsburgh Steelers (11-5-0)	Buffalo* 24, Pittsburgh 3	
		Western	San Diego Chargers (11-5-0)	Buffalo* 29, Miami 10	
	National	Eastern	Dallas Cowboys (13-3-0)	Dallas 34, Philadelphia* 10	
		Central	Minnesota Vikings (11-5-0)	San Francisco 20, Washington* 13	
		Western	San Francisco 49ers (14-2-0)	Dallas 30, San Francisco 20	
1993	American	Eastern	Buffalo Bills (12-4-0)	Buffalo 29, L.A. Raiders* 23	1993
		Central	Houston Oilers (12-4-0)	Kansas City 28, Houston 20	
		Western	Kansas City Chiefs (11-5-0)	Buffalo 30, Kansas City 13	
	National	Eastern	Dallas Cowboys (12-4-0)	Dallas 27, Green Bay* 17	
		Central	Detroit Lions (10-6-0)	San Francisco 44, N.Y. Giants* 3	
		Western	San Francisco 49ers (10-6-0)	Dallas 38, San Francisco 21	
1994	American	Eastern	Miami Dolphins (10-6-0)	Pittsburgh 29, Cleveland* 9	1994
		Central	Pittsburgh Steelers (12-4-0)	San Diego 22, Miami 21	
		Western	San Diego Chargers (11-5-0)	San Diego 17, Pittsburgh 13	
	National	Eastern	Dallas Cowboys (12-4-0)	San Francisco 44, Chicago* 15	
		Central	Minnesota Vikings (10-6-0)	Dallas 35, Green Bay* 9	
		Western	San Francisco 49ers (13-3-0)	San Francisco 38, Dallas 28	
1995	American	Eastern	Buffalo Bills (10 6 0)	Indianapolis* 10, Kansas City 7	1995
		Central	Pittsburgh Steelers (11-5-0)	Pittsburgh 40, Buffalo 21	
		Western	Kansas City Chiefs (13-3-0)	Pittsburgh 20, Indianapolis* 16	
	National	Eastern	Dallas Cowboys (12-4-0)	Dallas 30, Philadelphia* 11	
		Central	Green Bay Packers (11-5-0)	Green Bay 27, San Francisco 17	
		Western	San Francisco 49ers (11-5-0)	Dallas 38, Green Bay 27	
1996	American	Eastern	New England Patriots (11-5-0)	Jacksonville* 30, Denver 27	1996
		Central	Pittsburgh Steelers (10-6-0)	New England 28, Pittsburgh 3	
		Western	Denver Broncos (13-3-0)	New England 20, Jacksonville* 6	
	National	Eastern	Dallas Cowboys (10-6-0)	Green Bay 35, San Francisco* 14	
		Central	Green Bay Packers (13-3-0)	Carolina 26, Dallas 17	
		Western	Carolina Panthers (12-4-0)	Green Bay 30, Carolina 13	
1997	American	Eastern	New England Patriots (10-6-0)	Pittsburgh 7, New England 6	1997
		Central	Pittsburgh Steelers (11-5-0)	Denver* 14, Kansas City 10	
		Western	Kansas City Chiefs (13-3-0)	Denver* 24, Pittsburgh 21	
	National	Eastern	New York Giants (10-5-1)	San Francisco 38, Minnesota* 22	
		Central	Green Bay Packers (13-3-0)	Green Bay 21, Tampa Bay* 7	
		Western	San Francisco 49ers (13-3-0)	Green Bay 23, San Francisco 10	
1998	American	Eastern	N.Y. Jets (12-4-0)	Denver 38, Miami* 3	1998
		Central	Jacksonville Jaguars (11-5-0)	N.Y. Jets 34, Jacksonville 24	
		Western	Denver Broncos (14-2-0)	Denver 23, N.Y. Jets 10	
	National	Eastern	Dallas Cowboys (10-6-0)	Atlanta 20, San Francisco* 18	
		Central	Minnesota Vikings (15-1-0)	Minnesota 41, Arizona* 21	
		Western	Atlanta Falcons (14-2-0)	Atlanta 30, Minnesota 27 (OT)	

Year	Conference	Division	Winner (W-L-T)	Playoffs(c)	Year
1999	American	Eastern	Indianapolis Colts (13-3-0)	Jacksonville 62, Miami* 7	1999
		Central	Jacksonville Jaguars (14-2-0)	Tennessee* 19, Indianapolis 16	
		Western	Seattle Seahawks (9-7-0)	Tennessee* 33, Jacksonville 14	
	National	Eastern	Washington Redskins (10-6-0)	Tampa Bay 14, Washington 13	
		Central	Tampa Bay Buccaneers (11-5-0)	St. Louis 49, Minnesota* 37	
		Western	St. Louis Rams (13-3-0)	St. Louis 11, Tampa Bay 6	
2000	American	Eastern	Miami Dolphins (11-5-0)	Oakland 27, Miami 0	2000
		Central	Tennessee Titans (13-3-0)	Baltimore* 24, Tennessee 10	
		Western	Oakland (12-4-0)	Baltimore* 16, Oakland 3	
	National	Eastern	New York Giants (12-4-0)	Minnesota 34, New Orleans 16	
		Central	Minnesota Vikings (11-5-0)	N.Y. Giants 20, Philadelphia* 10	
		Western	New Orleans Saints (10-6-0)	N.Y. Giants 41, Minnesota 0	
2001	American	Eastern	New England(11-5-0)	New England 16, Oakland 13	2001
		Central	Pittsburgh(13-3-0)	Pittsburgh 27, Baltimore* 10	
		Western	Oakland (10-6-0)	New England 24, Pittsburgh 17	
	National	Eastern	Philadelphia(11-5-0)	Philadelphia 33, Chicago 19	
		Central	Chicago (13-3-0)	St. Louis 45, Green Bay* 17	
		Western	St. Louis (14-2-0)	St. Louis 29, Philadelphia 24	

*Wild card team. (c) From 1978 on, only the final 2 conference playoff rounds are shown. (d) A strike shortened the 1982 season from 16 to 9 games. The top 8 teams in each conference played in a tournament to determine the conference champion. See below. **AFC playoffs**—Miami 28, New England 13; L.A. Raiders 27, Cleveland 10; N.Y. Jets 44, Cincinnati 17; San Diego 31, Pittsburgh 28; N.Y. Jets 17, L.A. Raiders 14; Miami 34, San Diego 13; Miami 14, N.Y. Jets 0. **NFC playoffs**—Washington 31, Detroit 7; Green Bay 41, St. Louis 16; Dallas 30, Tampa Bay 17; Minnesota 30, Atlanta 24; Washington 21, Minnesota 7; Dallas 37, Green Bay 26; Washington 31, Dallas 17. **AFC Champion**—Miami Dolphins. **NFC Champion**—Washington Redskins.

New England Patriots Stun St. Louis Rams in Super Bowl XXXVI

The New England Patriots shocked the NFL and the St. Louis Rams en route to winning the Super Bowl, 20-17, Feb. 3, 2002, at the Super Dome in New Orleans. Adam Vinatieri's 48-yard field goal as time expired clinched the Patriots' first-ever NFL title. Second-year quarterback Tom Brady led the Patriots on a 53-yard, 9-play drive to set up Vinatieri's game-winning kick after the Rams battled back from a 17-3 deficit to tie the game with 90 seconds left. Brady, who completed 16 of 27 passes for 145 yards and no interceptions, was named the MVP. Despite Kurt Warner's 365 passing yards, turnovers doomed the Rams. Warner's 2 interceptions, and Ricky Proehl's fumble, led to 17 points for the Patriots, including Ty Law's 47-yard interception return in the 2nd quarter.

Score by Quarters

New England	0	14	3	3–20
St. Louis	3	0	0	14–17

Scoring

St. Louis—Wilkins 50 yd. field goal
New England—Law 47 yd. interception return (Vinatieri kick)
New England—Patten 8 yd. pass from Brady (Vinatieri kick)
New England—Vinatieri 37 yd. field goal
St. Louis—Warner 2 yd. run (Wilkins kick)
St. Louis—Proehl 26 yd. pass from Warner (Wilkins kick)
New England—Vinatieri 48 yd. field goal

Individual Statistics

Rushing–New England, An. Smith 18-92, Patten 1-22, K. Faulk 2-15, Marc Edwards 2-5, T. Brady 1-3, Redmond 1-(-4). St. Louis, M. Faulk 17-76, Warner 3-6, Hakim 1-5, Hodgins 1-3.

Passing–New England, T. Brady 16-27-0-145. St. Louis, Warner 28-44-2-365.

Receiving–New England, Troy Brown 6-89, Redmond 3-24, Wiggins 2-14, Patten 1-8, Marc Edwards 2-7, An. Smith 1-4, K. Faulk 1-(-1). St. Louis, Hakim 5-90, Proehl 3-71, Bruce 5-56, M. Faulk 4-54, Holt 5-49, Je. Robinson 2-18, Y. Murphy 1-11, Conwell 2-8, Hodgins 1-8.

Team Statistics	NE	STL
First downs	15	26
Total net yards	267	427
Rushes-yards	25-133	22-90
Passing yards, net	134	337
Punt returns-yards	1-4	3-6
Kickoff returns-yards	4-100	4-82
Interception returns-yards	2-77	0-0
Att.-comp.-int.	27-16-0	44-28-2
Field goals made-attempts	2-2	1-2
Sacked-yards lost	2-11	3-28
Punts-average	8-43	4-39
Fumbles-lost	0-0	2-1
Penalties-yards	5-31	6-39
Time of possession	26:30	33:30

Attendance—72,922. **Time**—3:24.

Super Bowl Single-Game Statistical Leaders

Passing Yards

	Year	Att/Comp	Yds	TDs
Kurt Warner, Rams	2000	45/24	414	2
Kurt Warner, Rams	2002	44/28	365	1
Joe Montana, 49ers	1989	36/23	357	2

Receiving Yards

	Year	Recept.	Yds	TDs
Jerry Rice, 49ers	1989	11	215	1
Ricky Sanders, Redskins	1988	9	193	2
Lynn Swann, Steelers	1976	4	161	1

Rushing Yards

	Year	Attempts	Yds	TDs
Timmy Smith, Redskins	1988	22	204	2
Marcus Allen, Raiders	1984	20	191	2
John Riggins, Redskins	1983	38	166	1

Passing Touchdowns

	Year	Att/Comp	Yds	TDs
Steve Young, 49ers	1995	36/24	325	6
Joe Montana, 49ers	1990	29/22	297	5
Troy Aikman, Cowboys	1993	30/22	273	4
Doug Williams, Redskins	1988	29/18	340	4
Terry Bradshaw, Steelers	1979	30/17	318	4

Scoring

	Year	Points	
Terrell Davis, Broncos	1998	18	3 TDs
Jerry Rice, 49ers	1995	18	3 TDs
Ricky Watters, 49ers	1995	18	3 TDs
Jerry Rice, 49ers	1990	18	3 TDs
Roger Craig, 49ers	1985	18	3 TDs
Don Chandler, Packers	1968	15	4 FG, 3PATs

Super Bowl Results

	Year	Winner	Loser	Winning coach	Site
I	1967	Green Bay Packers, 35	Kansas City Chiefs, 10	Vince Lombardi	Los Angeles Coliseum, CA
II	1968	Green Bay Packers, 33	Oakland Raiders, 14	Vince Lombardi	Orange Bowl, Miami, FL
III	1969	New York Jets, 16	Baltimore Colts, 7	Weeb Ewbank	Orange Bowl, Miami, FL
IV	1970	Kansas City Chiefs, 23	Minnesota Vikings, 7	Hank Stram	Tulane Stadium, New Orleans, LA
V	1971	Baltimore Colts, 16	Dallas Cowboys, 13	Don McCafferty	Orange Bowl, Miami, FL
VI	1972	Dallas Cowboys, 24	Miami Dolphins, 3	Tom Landry	Tulane Stadium, New Orleans, LA
VII	1973	Miami Dolphins, 14	Washington Redskins, 7	Don Shula	Los Angeles Coliseum, CA
VIII	1974	Miami Dolphins, 24	Minnesota Vikings, 7	Don Shula	Rice Stadium, Houston, TX
IX	1975	Pittsburgh Steelers, 16	Minnesota Vikings, 6	Chuck Noll	Tulane Stadium, New Orleans, LA
X	1976	Pittsburgh Steelers, 21	Dallas Cowboys, 17	Chuck Noll	Orange Bowl, Miami, FL
XI	1977	Oakland Raiders, 32	Minnesota Vikings, 14	John Madden	Rose Bowl, Pasadena, CA
XII	1978	Dallas Cowboys, 27	Denver Broncos, 10	Tom Landry	Superdome, New Orleans, LA
XIII	1979	Pittsburgh Steelers, 35	Dallas Cowboys, 31	Chuck Noll	Orange Bowl, Miami, FL

	Year	Winner	Loser	Winning coach	Site
XIV	1980	Pittsburgh Steelers, 31	Los Angeles Rams, 19	Chuck Noll	Rose Bowl, Pasadena, CA
XV	1981	Oakland Raiders, 27	Philadelphia Eagles, 10	Tom Flores	Superdome, New Orleans, LA
XVI	1982	San Francisco 49ers, 26	Cincinnati Bengals, 21	Bill Walsh	Silverdome, Pontiac, MI
XVII	1983	Washington Redskins, 27	Miami Dolphins, 17	Joe Gibbs	Rose Bowl, Pasadena, CA
XVIII	1984	Los Angeles Raiders, 38	Washington Redskins, 9	Tom Flores	Tampa Stadium, FL
XIX	1985	San Francisco 49ers, 38	Miami Dolphins, 16	Bill Walsh	Stanford Stadium, Palo Alto, CA
XX	1986	Chicago Bears, 46	New England Patriots, 10	Mike Ditka	Superdome, New Orleans, LA
XXI	1987	New York Giants, 39	Denver Broncos, 20	Bill Parcells	Rose Bowl, Pasadena, CA
XXII	1988	Washington Redskins, 42	Denver Broncos, 10	Joe Gibbs	San Diego Stadium, CA
XXIII	1989	San Francisco 49ers, 20	Cincinnati Bengals, 16	Bill Walsh	Joe Robbie Stadium, Miami, FL
XXIV	1990	San Francisco 49ers, 55	Denver Broncos, 10	George Seifert	Superdome, New Orleans, LA
XXV	1991	New York Giants, 20	Buffalo Bills, 19	Bill Parcells	Tampa Stadium, FL
XXVI	1992	Washington Redskins, 37	Buffalo Bills, 24	Joe Gibbs	Metrodome, Minneapolis, MN
XXVII	1993	Dallas Cowboys, 52	Buffalo Bills, 17	Jimmy Johnson	Rose Bowl, Pasadena, CA
XXVIII	1994	Dallas Cowboys, 30	Buffalo Bills, 13	Jimmy Johnson	Georgia Dome, Atlanta, GA
XXIX	1995	San Francisco 49ers, 49	San Diego Chargers, 26	George Seifert	Joe Robbie Stadium, Miami, FL
XXX	1996	Dallas Cowboys, 27	Pittsburgh Steelers, 17	Barry Switzer	Sun Devil Stadium, Tempe, AZ
XXXI	1997	Green Bay Packers, 35	New England Patriots, 21	Mike Holmgren	Superdome, New Orleans, LA
XXXII	1998	Denver Broncos, 31	Green Bay Packers, 24	Mike Shanahan	Qualcomm Stadium, San Diego, CA
XXXIII	1999	Denver Broncos, 34	Atlanta Falcons, 19	Mike Shanahan	Pro Player Stadium, Miami, FL
XXXIV	2000	St. Louis Rams, 23	Tennessee Titans, 16	Dick Vermeil	Georgia Dome, Atlanta, GA
XXXV	2001	Baltimore Ravens, 34	New York Giants, 7	Brian Billick	Raymond James Stad., Tampa, FL
XXXVI	2002	New England Patriots, 20	St. Louis Rams, 17	Bill Belichick	Superdome, New Orleans, LA

Super Bowl MVPs

1967	Bart Starr, Green Bay
1968	Bart Starr, Green Bay
1969	Joe Namath, N.Y. Jets
1970	Len Dawson, Kansas City
1971	Chuck Howley, Dallas
1972	Roger Staubach, Dallas
1973	Jake Scott, Miami
1974	Larry Csonka, Miami
1975	Franco Harris, Pittsburgh
1976	Lynn Swann, Pittsburgh
1977	Fred Biletnikoff, Oakland
1978	Randy White, Harvey Martin, Dallas
1979	Terry Bradshaw, Pittsburgh
1980	Terry Bradshaw, Pittsburgh
1981	Jim Plunkett, Oakland
1982	Joe Montana, San Francisco
1983	John Riggins, Washington
1984	Marcus Allen, L.A. Raiders
1985	Joe Montana, San Francisco
1986	Richard Dent, Chicago
1987	Phil Simms, N.Y. Giants
1988	Doug Williams, Washington
1989	Jerry Rice, San Francisco
1990	Joe Montana, San Francisco
1991	Ottis Anderson, N.Y. Giants
1992	Mark Rypien, Washington
1993	Troy Aikman, Dallas
1994	Emmitt Smith, Dallas
1995	Steve Young, San Francisco
1996	Larry Brown, Dallas
1997	Desmond Howard, Green Bay
1998	Terrell Davis, Denver
1999	John Elway, Denver
2000	Kurt Warner, St. Louis
2001	Ray Lewis, Baltimore
2002	Tom Brady, New England

American Football Conference Leaders

(American Football League, 1960 69)

Passing[1]						Receiving			
Player, team	Att	Com	YG	TD	Year	Player, team	Rec.	YG	TD
Jack Kemp, L.A. Chargers	406	211	3,018	20	**1960**	Lionel Taylor, Denver	92	1,235	12
George Blanda, Houston	362	187	3,330	36	**1961**	Lionel Taylor, Denver	100	1,176	4
Len Dawson, Dallas Texans	310	189	2,759	29	**1962**	Lionel Taylor, Denver	77	908	4
Tobin Rote, San Diego	286	170	2,510	20	**1963**	Lionel Taylor, Denver	78	1,101	10
Len Dawson, Kansas City	354	199	2,879	30	**1964**	Charley Hennigan, Houston	101	1,546	8
John Hadl, San Diego	348	174	2,798	20	**1965**	Lionel Taylor, Denver	85	1,131	6
Len Dawson, Kansas City	284	159	2,527	26	**1966**	Lance Alworth, San Diego	73	1,383	13
Daryle Lamonica, Oakland	425	220	3,228	30	**1967**	George Sauer, N.Y. Jets	75	1,189	6
Len Dawson, Kansas City	224	131	2,109	17	**1968**	Lance Alworth, San Diego	68	1,312	10
Greg Cook, Cincinnati	197	106	1,854	15	**1969**	Lance Alworth, San Diego	64	1,003	4
Daryle Lamonica, Oakland	356	179	2,516	22	**1970**	Marlin Briscoe, Buffalo	57	1,036	8
Bob Griese, Miami	263	145	2,089	19	**1971**	Fred Biletnikoff, Oakland	61	929	9
Earl Morrall, Miami	150	83	1,360	11	**1972**	Fred Biletnikoff, Oakland	58	802	7
Ken Stabler, Oakland	260	163	1,997	14	**1973**	Fred Willis, Houston	57	371	1
Ken Anderson, Cincinnati	328	213	2,667	18	**1974**	Lydell Mitchell, Baltimore Colts	72	544	2
Ken Anderson, Cincinnati	377	228	3,169	21	**1975**	Reggie Rucker, Cleveland	60	770	3
						Lydell Mitchell, Baltimore Colts	60	554	4
Ken Stabler, Oakland	291	194	2,737	27	**1976**	MacArthur Lane, Kansas City	66	686	1
Bob Griese, Miami	307	180	2,252	22	**1977**	Lydell Mitchell, Baltimore Colts	71	620	4
Terry Bradshaw, Pittsburgh	368	207	2,915	28	**1978**	Steve Largent, Seattle	71	1,168	8
Dan Fouts, San Diego	530	332	4,082	24	**1979**	Joe Washington, Baltimore Colts	82	750	3
Brian Sipe, Cleveland	554	337	4,132	30	**1980**	Kellen Winslow, San Diego	89	1,290	9
Ken Anderson, Cincinnati	479	300	3,754	29	**1981**	Kellen Winslow, San Diego	88	1,075	10
Ken Anderson, Cincinnati	309	218	2,495	12	**1982**	Kellen Winslow, San Diego	54	721	6
Dan Marino, Miami	296	173	2,210	20	**1983**	Todd Christensen, L.A. Raiders	92	1,247	12
Dan Marino, Miami	564	362	5,084	48	**1984**	Ozzie Newsome, Cleveland	89	1,001	5
Ken O'Brien, N.Y. Jets	488	297	3,888	25	**1985**	Lionel James, San Diego	86	1,027	6
Dan Marino, Miami	623	378	4,746	44	**1986**	Todd Christensen, L.A. Raiders	95	1,153	8
Bernie Kosar, Cleveland	389	241	3,033	22	**1987**	Al Toon, N.Y. Jets	68	976	5
Boomer Esiason, Cincinnati	388	223	3,572	28	**1988**	Al Toon, N.Y. Jets	93	1,067	5
Boomer Esiason, Cincinnati	455	258	3,525	28	**1989**	Andre Reed, Buffalo	88	1,312	9
Jim Kelly, Buffalo	346	219	2,829	24	**1990**	Haywood Jeffires, Houston	74	1,048	8
						Drew Hill, Houston	74	1,019	5
Jim Kelly, Buffalo	474	304	3,844	33	**1991**	Haywood Jeffires, Houston	100	1,181	7
Warren Moon, Houston	346	224	2,521	18	**1992**	Haywood Jeffires, Houston	90	913	9
John Elway, Denver	551	348	4,030	25	**1993**	Reggie Langhorne, Indianapolis	85	1,038	3
Dan Marino, Miami	615	385	4,453	30	**1994**	Ben Coates, New England	96	1,174	7
Jim Harbaugh, Indianapolis	314	200	2,575	17	**1995**	Carl Pickens, Cincinnati	99	1,234	17
John Elway, Denver	466	287	3,328	26	**1996**	Carl Pickens, Cincinnati	100	1,180	12
Mark Brunell, Jacksonville	435	264	3,281	18	**1997**	Tim Brown, Oakland	104	1,408	5
Vinny Testaverde, N.Y. Jets	421	259	3,256	29	**1998**	O.J. McDuffie, Miami	90	1,050	7
Peyton Manning, Indianapolis	533	331	4,135	26	**1999**	Jimmy Smith, Jacksonville	116	1,636	6
Brian Griese, Denver	336	216	2,688	19	**2000**	Marvin Harrison, Indianapolis	102	1,413	14
Rich Gannon, Oakland	549	361	3,828	27	**2001**	Marvin Harrison, Indianapolis	109	1,524	15

Scoring						Rushing			
Player, team	TD	PAT	FG	Pts	Year	Player, team	Yds	Att	TD
Gene Mingo, Denver	6	33	18	123	**1960**	Abner Haynes, Dallas Texans	875	156	9
Gino Cappelletti, Boston	8	48	17	147	**1961**	Billy Cannon, Houston	948	200	6
Gene Mingo, Denver	4	32	27	137	**1962**	Cookie Gilchrest, Buffalo	1,096	214	13
Gino Cappelletti, Boston	2	35	22	113	**1963**	Clem Daniels, Oakland	1,099	215	3
Gino Cappelletti, Boston	7	36	25	155	**1964**	Cookie Gilchrest, Buffalo	981	230	6
Gino Cappelletti, Boston	9	27	17	132	**1965**	Paul Lowe, San Diego	1,121	222	7
Gino Cappelletti, Boston	6	35	16	119	**1966**	Jim Nance, Boston	1,458	299	11
George Blanda, Oakland	0	56	20	116	**1967**	Jim Nance, Boston	1,216	269	7
Jim Turner, N.Y. Jets	0	43	34	145	**1968**	Paul Robinson, Cincinnati	1,023	238	8
Jim Turner, N.Y. Jets	0	33	32	129	**1969**	Dick Post, San Diego	873	182	6
Jan Stenerud, Kansas City	0	26	30	116	**1970**	Floyd Little, Denver	901	209	3
Garo Yepremian, Miami	0	33	28	117	**1971**	Floyd Little, Denver	1,133	284	6
Bobby Howfield, N.Y. Jets	0	40	27	121	**1972**	O.J. Simpson, Buffalo	1,251	292	6
Roy Gerela, Pittsburgh	0	36	29	123	**1973**	O.J. Simpson, Buffalo	2,003	332	12
Roy Gerela, Pittsburgh	0	33	20	93	**1974**	Otis Armstrong, Denver	1,407	263	9
O.J. Simpson, Buffalo	23	0	0	138	**1975**	O.J. Simpson, Buffalo	1,817	329	16
Toni Linhart, Baltimore Colts	0	49	20	109	**1976**	O.J. Simpson, Buffalo	1,503	290	8
Errol Mann, Oakland	0	39	20	99	**1977**	Mark van Eeghen, Oakland	1,273	324	7
Pat Leahy, N.Y. Jets	0	41	22	107	**1978**	Earl Campbell, Houston	1,450	302	13
John Smith, New England	0	46	23	115	**1979**	Earl Campbell, Houston	1,697	368	19
John Smith, New England	0	51	26	129	**1980**	Earl Campbell, Houston	1,934	373	13
Jim Breech, Cincinnati	0	49	22	115	**1981**	Earl Campbell, Houston	1,376	361	10
Nick Lowery, Kansas City	0	37	26	115					
Marcus Allen, L.A. Raiders	14	0	0	84	**1982**	Freeman McNeil, N.Y. Jets	786	151	6
Gary Anderson, Pittsburgh	0	38	27	119	**1983**	Curt Warner, Seattle	1,446	335	13
Gary Anderson, Pittsburgh	0	45	24	117	**1984**	Earnest Jackson, San Diego	1,179	296	8
Gary Anderson, Pittsburgh	0	40	33	139	**1985**	Marcus Allen, L.A. Raiders	1,759	380	11
Tony Franklin, New England	0	44	32	140	**1986**	Curt Warner, Seattle	1,481	319	13
Jim Breech, Cincinnati	0	25	24	97	**1987**	Eric Dickerson, L.A. Rams-Ind.	1,288*	283	6
Scott Norwood, Buffalo	0	33	32	129	**1988**	Eric Dickerson, Indianapolis	1,659	388	14
David Treadwell, Denver	0	39	27	120	**1989**	Christian Okoye, Kansas City	1,480	370	12
Nick Lowery, Kansas City	0	37	34	139	**1990**	Thurman Thomas, Buffalo	1,297	271	11
Pete Stoyanovich, Miami	0	28	31	121	**1991**	Thurman Thomas, Buffalo	1,407	288	7
Pete Stoyanovich, Miami	0	34	30	124	**1992**	Barry Foster, Pittsburgh	1,690	390	11
Jeff Jaeger, L.A. Raiders	0	27	35	132	**1993**	Thurman Thomas, Buffalo	1,315	355	6
John Carney, San Diego	0	33	34	135	**1994**	Chris Warren, Seattle	1,545	333	9
Norm Johnson, Pittsburgh	0	39	34	141	**1995**	Curtis Martin, New England	1,487	368	14
Cary Blanchard, Indianapolis	0	27	36	135	**1996**	Terrell Davis, Denver	1,538	345	13
Mike Hollis, Jacksonville	0	41	31	134	**1997**	Terrell Davis, Denver	1,750	369	15
Steve Christie, Buffalo	0	41	33	140	**1998**	Terrell Davis, Denver	2,008	392	21
Mike Vanderjagt, Indianapolis	0	43	34	145	**1999**	Edgerrin James, Indianapolis	1,553	369	13
Matt Stover, Baltimore	0	30	35	135	**2000**	Edgerrin James, Indianapolis	1,709	387	13
Mike Vanderjagt, Indianapolis	0	41	28	125	**2001**	Priest Holmes, Kansas City	1,555	325	8

*Includes 277 yards after being traded to NFC; 1,011 yards led AFC. (1) Based on quarterback ranking points.

National Football Conference Leaders

(National Football League, 1960-69)

Passing[1]						Receiving			
Player, team	Att	Com	YG	TD	Year	Player, team	Rec.	YG	TD
Milt Plum, Cleveland	250	151	2,297	21	**1960**	Raymond Berry, Baltimore Colts	74	1,298	10
Milt Plum, Cleveland	302	177	2,416	18	**1961**	Jim Phillips, L.A. Rams	78	1,092	5
Bart Starr, Green Bay	285	178	2,438	12	**1962**	Bobby Mitchell, Washington	72	1,384	11
Y.A. Tittle, N.Y. Giants	367	221	3,145	36	**1963**	Bobby Joe Conrad, St. Louis Cardinals	73	967	10
Bart Starr, Green Bay	272	163	2,144	15	**1964**	Johnny Morris, Chicago	93	1,200	10
Rudy Bukich, Chicago	312	176	2,641	20	**1965**	Dave Parks, San Francisco	80	1,344	12
Bart Starr, Green Bay	251	156	2,257	14	**1966**	Charley Taylor, Washington	72	1,119	12
Sonny Jurgensen, Washington	508	288	3,747	31	**1967**	Charley Taylor, Washington	70	990	9
Earl Morrall, Baltimore Colts	317	182	2,909	26	**1968**	Clifton McNeil, San Francisco	71	994	7
Sonny Jurgensen, Washington	442	274	3,102	22	**1969**	Dan Abramowicz, New Orleans	73	1,015	7
John Brodie, San Francisco	378	223	2,941	24	**1970**	Dick Gordon, Chicago	71	1,026	13
Roger Staubach, Dallas	211	126	1,882	15	**1971**	Bob Tucker, N.Y. Giants	59	791	4
Norm Snead, N.Y. Giants	325	196	2,307	17	**1972**	Harold Jackson, Philadelphia	62	1,048	4
Roger Staubach, Dallas	286	179	2,428	23	**1973**	Harold Carmichael, Philadelphia	67	1,116	9
Sonny Jurgensen, Washington	167	107	1,185	11	**1974**	Charles Young, Philadelphia	63	696	3
Fran Tarkenton, Minnesota	425	273	2,994	25	**1975**	Chuck Foreman, Minnesota	73	691	9
James Harris, L.A. Rams	158	91	1,460	8	**1976**	Drew Pearson, Dallas	58	806	6
Roger Staubach, Dallas	361	210	2,620	18	**1977**	Ahmad Rashad, Minnesota	51	681	2
Roger Staubach, Dallas	413	231	3,190	25	**1978**	Rickey Young, Minnesota	88	704	5
Roger Staubach, Dallas	461	267	3,586	27	**1979**	Ahmad Rashad, Minnesota	80	1,156	9
Ron Jaworski, Philadelphia	451	257	3,529	27	**1980**	Earl Cooper, San Francisco	83	567	4
Joe Montana, San Francisco	488	311	3,565	19	**1981**	Dwight Clark, San Francisco	85	1,105	4
Joe Thiesmann, Washington	252	161	2,033	13	**1982**	Dwight Clark, San Francisco	60	913	5
Steve Bartkowski, Atlanta	432	274	3,167	22	**1983**	Roy Green, St. Louis Cardinals	78	1,227	14
						Charlie Brown, Washington	78	1,225	8
						Earnest Gray, N.Y. Giants	78	1,139	5
Joe Montana, San Francisco	432	279	3,630	28	**1984**	Art Monk, Washington	106	1,372	7
Joe Montana, San Francisco	494	303	3,653	27	**1985**	Roger Craig, San Francisco	92	1,016	6
Tommy Kramer, Minnesota	372	208	3,000	24	**1986**	Jerry Rice, San Francisco	86	1,570	15
Joe Montana, San Francisco	398	266	3,054	31	**1987**	J.T. Smith, St. Louis Cardinals	91	1,117	8
Wade Wilson, Minnesota	332	204	2,746	15	**1988**	Henry Ellard, L.A. Rams	86	1,414	10
Joe Montana, San Francisco	386	271	3,521	26	**1989**	Sterling Sharpe, Green Bay	90	1,423	12
Phil Simms, N.Y. Giants	311	184	2,284	15	**1990**	Jerry Rice, San Francisco	100	1,502	13
Steve Young, San Francisco	279	180	2,517	17	**1991**	Michael Irvin, Dallas	93	1,523	8
Steve Young, San Francisco	402	268	3,465	25	**1992**	Sterling Sharpe, Green Bay	108	1,461	13
Steve Young, San Francisco	462	314	4,023	29	**1993**	Sterling Sharpe, Green Bay	112	1,274	11
Steve Young, San Francisco	461	324	3,969	35	**1994**	Cris Carter, Minnesota	122	1,256	7
Brett Favre, Green Bay	570	359	4,413	38	**1995**	Herman Moore, Detroit	123	1,686	14
Steve Young, San Francisco	316	214	2,410	14	**1996**	Jerry Rice, San Francisco	108	1,254	8
Steve Young, San Francisco	356	241	3,029	19	**1997**	Herman Moore, Detroit	104	1,293	8

Passing[1]						Receiving			
Player, team	Att	Com	YG	TD	Year	Player, team	Rec.	YG	TD
Randall Cunningham, Minnesota	425	259	3,704	34	**1998**	Frank Sanders, Arizona	89	1,145	3
Kurt Warner, St. Louis	499	325	4,353	41	**1999**	Muhsin Muhammad, Carolina	96	1,253	8
Trent Green, St. Louis	240	145	2,063	16	**2000**	Muhsin Muhammad, Carolina	102	1,183	6
Kurt Warner, St. Louis	546	375	4,830	36	**2001**	David Boston, Arizona	98	1,598	8

Scoring						Rushing			
Player, team	TD	PAT	FG	Pts	Year	Player, team	Yds	Att	TD
Paul Hornung, Green Bay	15	41	15	176	**1960**	Jim Brown, Cleveland	1,257	215	9
Paul Hornung, Green Bay	10	41	15	146	**1961**	Jim Brown, Cleveland	1,408	305	8
Jim Taylor, Green Bay	19	0	0	114	**1962**	Jim Taylor, Green Bay	1,474	272	19
Don Chandler, N.Y. Giants	0	52	18	106	**1963**	Jim Brown, Cleveland	1,863	291	12
Lenny Moore, Baltimore Colts	20	0	0	120	**1964**	Jim Brown, Cleveland	1,446	280	7
Gale Sayers, Chicago	22	0	0	132	**1965**	Jim Brown, Cleveland	1,544	289	17
Bruce Gossett, L.A. Rams	0	29	28	113	**1966**	Gale Sayers, Chicago	1,231	229	8
Jim Bakken, St. Louis Cardinals	0	36	27	117	**1967**	Leroy Kelly, Cleveland	1,205	235	11
Leroy Kelly, Cleveland	20	0	0	120	**1968**	Leroy Kelly, Cleveland	1,239	248	16
Fred Cox, Minnesota	0	43	26	121	**1969**	Gale Sayers, Chicago	1,032	236	8
Fred Cox, Minnesota	0	35	30	125	**1970**	Larry Brown, Washington	1,125	237	5
Curt Knight, Washington	0	27	29	114	**1971**	John Brockington, Green Bay	1,105	216	4
Chester Marcol, Green Bay	0	29	33	128	**1972**	Larry Brown, Washington	1,216	285	8
David Ray, L.A. Rams	0	40	30	130	**1973**	John Brockington, Green Bay	1,144	265	3
Chester Marcol, Green Bay	0	19	25	94	**1974**	Lawrence McCutcheon, L.A. Rams	1,109	236	3
Chuck Foreman, Minnesota	22	0	0	132	**1975**	Jim Otis, St. Louis Cardinals	1,076	269	5
Mark Moseley, Washington	0	31	22	97	**1976**	Walter Payton, Chicago	1,390	311	13
Walter Payton, Chicago	16	0	0	96	**1977**	Walter Payton, Chicago	1,852	339	14
Frank Corral, L.A. Rams	0	31	29	118	**1978**	Walter Payton, Chicago	1,395	333	11
Mark Moseley, Washington	0	39	25	114	**1979**	Walter Payton, Chicago	1,610	369	14
Ed Murray, Detroit	0	35	27	116	**1980**	Walter Payton, Chicago	1,460	317	6
Ed Murray, Detroit	0	46	25	121	**1981**	George Rogers, New Orleans	1,674	378	
Rafael Septien, Dallas	0	40	27	121					13
Wendell Tyler, L.A. Rams	13	0	0	78	**1982**	Tony Dorsett, Dallas	745	177	5
Mark Moseley, Washington	0	62	33	161	**1983**	Eric Dickerson, L.A. Rams	1,808	390	18
Ray Wersching, San Francisco	0	56	25	131	**1984**	Eric Dickerson, L.A. Rams	2,105	379	14
Kevin Butler, Chicago	0	51	31	144	**1985**	Gerald Riggs, Atlanta	1,719	397	10
Kevin Butler, Chicago	0	36	28	120	**1986**	Eric Dickerson, L.A. Rams	1,821	404	11
Jerry Rice, San Francisco	23	0	0	138	**1987**	Charles White, L.A. Rams	1,374	324	11
Mike Cofer, San Francisco	0	40	27	121	**1988**	Herschel Walker, Dallas	1,514	361	5
Mike Cofer, San Francisco	0	49	29	136	**1989**	Barry Sanders, Detroit	1,470	280	14
Chip Lohmiller, Washington	0	41	30	131	**1990**	Barry Sanders, Detroit	1,304	255	13
Chip Lohmiller, Washington	0	56	31	149	**1991**	Emmitt Smith, Dallas	1,563	365	12
Morten Andersen, New Orleans	0	33	29	120	**1992**	Emmitt Smith, Dallas	1,713	373	
Chip Lohmiller, Washington	0	30	30	120					18
Jason Hanson, Detroit	0	28	34	130	**1993**	Emmitt Smith, Dallas	1,486	283	9
Fuad Reveiz, Minnesota	0	30	34	132	**1994**	Barry Sanders, Detroit	1,883	331	
Emmitt Smith, Dallas	22	0	0	132					7
Emmitt Smith, Dallas	25	0	0	150	**1995**	Emmitt Smith, Dallas	1,773	377	25
John Kasay, Carolina	0	34	37	145	**1996**	Barry Sanders, Detroit	1,553	307	11
Richie Cunningham, Dallas	0	24	34	126	**1997**	Barry Sanders, Detroit	2,053	335	11
Gary Anderson, Minnesota	0	59	35	164	**1998**	Jamal Anderson, Atlanta	1,846	410	14
Jeff Wilkins, St. Louis	0	64	20	124	**1999**	Stephen Davis, Washington	1,405	290	17
Marshall Faulk, St. Louis	26	0	0	156	**2000**	Robert Smith, Minnesota	1,521	295	7
Marshall Faulk, St. Louis	21	0	0	128	**2001**	Stephen Davis, Washington	1,432	356	5

(1) Based on quarterback ranking points.

2001 NFL Individual Leaders

American Football Conference

PASSING	Att	Comp	Pct comp	Yds	Avg gain	Long	TD	Pct TD	Int	Rating points
Rich Gannon, Oakland	549	361	65.8	3,828	6.97	49	27	4.9	9	95.5
Steve McNair, Tennessee	431	264	61.3	3,350	7.77	71	21	4.9	12	90.2
Tom Brady, New England	413	264	63.9	2,843	6.88	91	18	4.4	12	86.5
Peyton Manning, Indianapolis	547	343	62.7	4,131	7.55	86	26	4.8	23	84.1
Mark Brunell, Jacksonville	473	289	61.1	3,309	7.00	44	19	4.0	13	84.1
Kordell Stewart, Pittsburgh	442	266	60.2	3,109	7.03	90	14	3.2	11	81.7
Jay Fiedler, Miami	450	273	60.7	3,290	7.31	74	20	4.4	19	80.3
Brian Griese, Denver	451	275	61.0	2,827	6.27	65	23	5.1	19	78.5
Alex Van Pelt, Buffalo	307	178	58.0	2,056	6.70	80	12	3.9	11	76.4
Vinny Testaverde, NY Jets	441	260	59.0	2,752	6.24	40	15	3.4	14	75.3

RUSHING	Att	Yds	Avg	Long	TD
Priest Holmes, Kansas City	327	1,555	4.8	41	8
Curtis Martin, NY Jets	333	1,513	4.5	47	10
Shaun Alexander, Seattle	309	1,318	4.3	88	14
Corey Dillon, Cincinnati	340	1,315	3.9	96	10
LaDainian Tomlinson, San Diego	339	1,236	3.6	54	10
Antowain Smith, New England	287	1,157	4.0	44	12
Dominic Rhodes, Indianapolis	233	1,104	4.7	77	9
Jerome Bettis, Pittsburgh	225	1,072	4.8	48	4
Lamar Smith, Miami	313	968	3.1	25	6
Eddie George, Tennessee	315	939	3.0	27	5

RECEIVING	Rec.	Yds	Avg	Long	TD
Marvin Harrison, Indianapolis	109	1,524	14.0	68	15
Jimmy Smith, Jacksonville	112	1,373	12.3	35	8
Rod Smith, Denver	113	1,343	11.9	65	11
Troy Brown, New England	101	1,199	11.9	60	5
Tim Brown, Oakland	91	1,165	12.8	46	9
Jerry Rice, Oakland	83	1,139	13.7	40	9
Derrick Mason, Tennessee	73	1,128	15.5	71	9
Curtis Conway, San Diego	71	1,125	15.8	72	6
Keenan McCardell,Jacksonville	93	1,110	11.9	45	6
Kevin Johnson, Cleveland	84	1,097	13.1	55	9

SCORING—KICKERS	PAT	FG	Long	Pts
Mike Vanderjagt, Indianapolis	41/42	28/34	52	125
Jason Elam, Denver	31/31	31/36	50	124
Kris Brown, Pittsburgh	34/37	30/44	55	124
Adam Vinatieri, New England	41/42	24/30	54	113
Sebastian Janikowski, Oakland	42/42	23/28	52	111

SCORING—NON-KICKERS	TD	Rush	Pass	2 Pt	Pts
Shaun Alexander, Seattle	16	14	2	0	96
Marvin Harrison, Indianapolis	15	0	15	0	90
Antowain Smith, New England	13	12	1	0	78
Corey Dillon, Cincinnati	13	10	3	0	78
Rod Smith, Denver	11	0	11	1	68
Derrick Mason, Tennessee	9	0	9	1	62

INTERCEPTIONS	No.	Yds	Avg	Long	TD
Anthony Henry, Cleveland	10	177	17.7	97	1
Deltha O'Neal, Denver	9	115	12.7	42	0
Ryan McNeil, San Diego	8	55	6.9	33	0
Chad Scott, Pittsburgh	5	204	40.8	62	2
Otis Smith, New England	5	181	36.2	78	2
Earl Little, Cleveland	5	33	6.6	78	2
Tory James, Oakland	5	72	14.4	33	0
Brock Marion, Miami	5	227	45.4	100	2

KICKOFF RETURNS	No.	Yds	Avg	Long	TD
Ronney Jenkins, San Diego	58	1,541	26.6	93	2
Jermaine Lewis, Baltimore	42	1,039	24.7	76	0
Chris Cole, Denver	48	1,127	23.5	52	0
Terry Kirby, Oakland	46	1,066	23.2	90	1
Troy Edwards, Pittsburgh	20	462	23.1	81	0

PUNT RETURNS	No.	Yds	Avg	Long	TD
Troy Brown, New England	29	413	14.2	85	2
Deltha O'Neal, Denver	31	405	13.1	86	1
Jermaine Lewis, Baltimore	42	519	12.4	62	0
Jeff Ogden, Miami	32	377	11.8	48	0
Tim Dwight, San Diego	24	271	11.3	84	1

PUNTING	No.	Yds	Long	Avg
Shane Lechler, Oakland	73	3,375	65	46.2
Tom Rouen, Denver	81	3,668	64	45.3
Hunter Smith, Indianapolis	68	3,023	65	44.5
Jeff Feagles, Seattle	85	3,730	68	43.9
Chris Hanson, Jacksonville	82	3,577	59	43.6

SACKS	No.
Peter Boulware, Baltimore	15
John Abraham, NY Jets	13
Marcellus Wiley, San Diego	13
Jamir Miller, Cleveland	13
Jason Gildon, Pittsburgh	12

National Football Conference

PASSING	Att	Comp	Pct comp	Yds	Avg gain	Long	TD	Pct TD	Int	Rating points
Kurt Warner, St. Louis	546	375	68.7	4830	8.85	65	36	6.6	22	101.4
Jeff Garcia, San Francisco	504	316	62.7	3538	7.02	61	32	6.3	12	94.8
Brett Favre, Green Bay	510	314	61.6	3921	7.69	67	32	6.3	15	94.1
Donovan McNabb, Philadelphia	493	285	57.8	3233	6.56	64	25	5.1	12	84.3
Chris Chandler, Atlanta	365	223	61.1	2847	7.80	94	16	4.4	14	84.1
Daunte Culpepper, Minnesota	366	235	64.2	2612	7.14	57	14	3.8	13	83.3
Jake Plummer, Arizona	525	304	57.9	3653	6.96	68	18	3.4	14	79.6
Brad Johnson, Tampa Bay	559	340	60.8	3406	6.09	47	13	2.3	11	77.7
Kerry Collins, NY Giants	568	327	57.6	3764	6.63	76	19	3.3	16	77.1
Charlie Batch, Detroit	341	198	58.1	2392	7.01	76	12	3.5	12	76.8

RUSHING	Att	Yds	Avg	Long	TD
Stephen Davis, Washington	356	1,432	4.0	32	5
Ahman Green, Green Bay	304	1,387	4.6	83	9
Marshall Faulk, St. Louis	260	1,382	5.3	71	12
Ricky Williams, New Orleans	313	1,245	4.0	46	6
Garrison Hearst, San Francisco	252	1,206	4.8	43	4
Anthony Thomas, Chicago	278	1,183	4.3	46	7
Emmitt Smith, Dallas	261	1,021	3.9	44	3
Tiki Barber, NY Giants	166	865	5.2	36	4
Michael Pittman, Arizona	241	846	3.5	42	5
Maurice Smith, Atlanta	237	760	3.2	58	5

RECEIVING	Rec.	Yds	Avg	Long	TD
David Boston, Arizona	98	1,598	16.3	61	8
Terrell Owens, San Francisco	93	1,412	15.2	60	16
Torry Holt, St. Louis	81	1,363	16.8	51	7
Keyshawn Johnson, Tampa Bay	106	1,266	11.9	47	1
Joe Horn, New Orleans	83	1,265	15.2	56	9
Randy Moss, Minnesota	82	1,233	15.0	73	10
Johnnie Morton, Detroit	77	1,154	15.0	76	4
Isaac Bruce, St. Louis	64	1,106	17.3	51	6
Marty Booker, Chicago	100	1,071	10.7	66	8
Amani Toomer, NY Giants	72	1,054	14.6	60	5

SCORING—KICKERS	PAT	FG	Long	Pts
Jeff Wilkins, St. Louis	58/58	23/29	54	127
David Akers, Philadelphia	37/38	26/31	50	115
Jay Feely, Atlanta	28/28	29/37	55	115
John Carney, New Orleans	32/32	27/31	50	113
Paul Edinger, Chicago	34/34	26/31	48	112

SCORING—NON-KICKERS	TD	Rush	Pass	2 Pt	Pts
Marshall Faulk, St. Louis	21	12	9	1	128
Terrell Owens, San Francisco	16	0	16	0	96
Mike Alstott, Tampa Bay	11	10	1	2	70
Ahman Green, Green Bay	11	9	2	0	66
Randy Moss, Minnesota	10	0	10	0	60
Bubba Franks, Green Bay	9	0	9	0	54

INTERCEPTIONS	No.	Yds	Avg	Long	TD
Ronde Barber, Tampa Bay	10	86	8.6	36	1
Kwamie Lassiter, Arizona	9	80	8.9	25	0
Doug Evans, Carolina	8	126	15.6	49	1
Ahmed Plummer, San Francisco	7	45	6.4	24	0
Zack Bronson, San Francisco	7	165	23.6	97	2
Dre' Bly, St. Louis	6	150	25.0	93	2
Sammy Knight, New Orleans	6	114	19.0	40	0
Darren Sharper, Green Bay	6	78	13.0	23	0

KICKOFF RETURNS	No.	Yds	Avg	Long	TD
Steve Smith, Carolina	56	1,431	25.6	99	2
Desmond Howard, Detroit	57	1,446	25.4	91	0
Brian Mitchell, Philadelphia	41	1,025	25.0	94	1
Darrick Vaughn, Atlanta	61	1,491	24.4	96	1
Deuce McAllister, New Orleans	45	1,091	24.2	63	0

PUNT RETURNS	No.	Yds	Avg	Long	TD
Darrien Gordon, Atlanta	31	437	14.1	74	0
Reggie Swinton, Dallas	31	414	13.4	65	1
Eric Metcalf, Washington	33	412	12.5	89	1
Brian Mitchell, Philadelphia	39	467	12.0	54	0
Arnold Jackson, Arizona	40	461	11.5	55	0

PUNTING	No.	Yds	Long	Avg
Todd Sauerbrun, Carolina	93	4,419	73	47.5
Mitch Berger, Minnesota	47	2,046	67	43.5
Sean Landeta, Philadelphia	97	4,221	64	43.5
John Jett, Detroit	58	2,512	62	43.3
Rodney Williams, NY Giants	91	3,905	90	42.9

SACKS	No.
Michael Strahan, NY Giants	22.5*
Leonard Little, St. Louis	14.5
Charlie Clemons, New Orleans	13.5
Kabeer Gbaja-Biamila, Green Bay	13.5
Patrick Kerney, Atlanta	12.0
Simeon Rice, Tampa Bay	11.0
Robert Porcher, Detroit	11.0

*NFL record.

First-Round Selections in the 2002 NFL Draft

Team	Player	Pos	College
1. Houston	David Carr	QB	Fresno St.
2. Carolina	Julius Peppers	DL	North Carolina
3. Detroit	Joey Harrington	QB	Oregon
4. Buffalo	Mike Williams	OL	Texas
5. San Diego	Quentin Jammer	DB	Texas
6. Kansas City[1]	Ryan Sims	DL	North Carolina
7. Minnesota	Bryant McKinnie	OL	Miami (FL)
8. Dallas[2]	Roy Williams	S	Oklahoma
9. Jacksonville	John Henderson	DL	Tennessee
10. Cincinnati	Levi Jones	OL	Arizona St.
11. Indianapolis	Dwight Freeney	DL	Syracuse
12. Arizona	Wendell Bryant	DL	Wisconsin
13. New Orleans	Donte' Stallworth	WR	Tennessee
14. N.Y. Giants[3]	Jeremy Shockey	TE	Miami (FL)
15. Tennessee[4]	Albert Haynesworth	DL	Tennessee
16. Cleveland	William Green	RB	Boston Coll.
17. Oakland[5]	Phillip Buchanon	DB	Miami (FL)
18. Atlanta[6]	T. J. Duckett	RB	Michigan St.
19. Denver	Ahsley Lelie	WR	Hawaii
20. Green Bay[7]	Javon Walker	WR	Florida St.
21. New England[8]	Daniel Graham	TE	Colorado
22. N.Y. Jets	Bryant Thomas	DL	Ala.-Birmingham
23. Oakland	Napoleon Harris	LB	Northwestern
24. Baltimore	Edward Reed	S	Miami (FL)
25. New Orleans[9]	Charles Grant	DL	Georgia
26. Philadelphia	Lito Sheppard	DB	Florida
27. San Francisco	Mike Rumph	DB	Miami (FL)
28. Seattle[10]	Jerramy Stevens	TE	Washington
29. Chicago	Marc Colombo	OL	Boston Coll.
30. Pittsburgh	Kendall Simmons	OL	Auburn
31. St. Louis	Robert Thomas	LB	UCLA
32. Washington[11]	Patrick Ramsey	QB	Tulane

(1) From Dallas. (2) From Kansas City. (3) From Tennessee. (4) From N.Y. Giants. (5) From Atlanta (6) From Washington through Oakland. (7) From Seattle. (8) From Tampa Bay through Oakland and Washington. (9) From Miami. (10) From Green Bay. (11) From New England.

Number One NFL Draft Choices, 1936-2002

Year	Team	Player, Pos., College	Year	Team	Player, Pos., College
1936	Philadelphia	Jay Berwanger, HB, Chicago	1970	Pittsburgh	Terry Bradshaw, QB, La.Tech
1937	Philadelphia	Sam Francis, FB, Nebraska	1971	New England	Jim Plunkett, QB, Stanford
1938	Cleveland Rams	Corbett Davis, FB, Indiana	1972	Buffalo	Walt Patulski, DE, Notre Dame
1939	Chicago Cards	Ki Aldrich, C, TCU	1973	Houston	John Matuszak, DE, Tampa
1940	Chicago Cards	George Cafego, HB, Tennessee	1974	Dallas	Ed "Too Tall" Jones, DE, Tenn. St.
1941	Chicago Bears	Tom Harmon, HB, Michigan	1975	Atlanta	Steve Bartkowski, QB, Cal.
1942	Pittsburgh	Bill Dudley, HB, Virginia	1976	Tampa Bay	Lee Roy Selmon, DE, Oklahoma
1943	Detroit	Frank Sinkwich, HB, Georgia	1977	Tampa Bay	Ricky Bell, RB, USC
1944	Boston Yanks	Angelo Bertelli, QB, Notre Dame	1978	Houston	Earl Campbell, RB, Texas
1945	Chicago Cards	Charley Trippi, HB, Georgia	1979	Buffalo	Tom Cousineau, LB, Ohio St.
1946	Boston Yanks	Frank Dancewicz, QB, Notre Dame	1980	Detroit	Billy Sims, RB, Oklahoma
1947	Chicago Bears	Bob Fenimore, HB, Okla. A&M	1981	New Orleans	George Rogers, RB, S.Carolina
1948	Washington	Harry Gilmer, QB, Alabama	1982	New England	Kenneth Sims, DT, Texas
1949	Philadelphia	Chuck Bednarik, C, Penn	1983	Baltimore Colts	John Elway, QB, Stanford
1950	Detroit	Leon Hart, E, Notre Dame	1984	New England	Irving Fryar, WR, Nebraska
1951	N.Y. Giants	Kyle Rote, HB, SMU	1985	Buffalo	Bruce Smith, DE, Va.Tech
1952	L.A. Rams	Bill Wade, QB, Vanderbilt	1986	Tampa Bay	Bo Jackson, RB, Auburn
1953	San Francisco	Harry Babcock, E, Georgia	1987	Tampa Bay	Vinny Testaverde, QB, Miami (FL)
1954	Cleveland	Bobby Garrett, QB, Stanford	1988	Atlanta	Aundray Bruce, LB, Auburn
1955	Baltimore Colts	George Shaw, QB, Oregon	1989	Dallas	Troy Aikman, QB, UCLA
1956	Pittsburgh	Gary Glick, DB, Col. A&M	1990	Indianapolis	Jeff George, QB, Illinois
1957	Green Bay	Paul Hornung, QB, Notre Dame	1991	Dallas	Russell Maryland, DL, Miami (FL)
1958	Chicago Cards	King Hill, QB, Rice	1992	Indianapolis	Steve Emtman, DL, Washington
1959	Green Bay	Randy Duncan, QB, Iowa	1993	New England	Drew Bledsoe, QB, Washington St.
1960	L.A. Rams	Billy Cannon, HB, LSU	1994	Cincinnati	Dan Wilkinson, DT, Ohio St.
1961	Minnesota	Tommy Mason, HB, Tulane	1995	Cincinnati	Ki-Jana Carter, RB, Penn State
1962	Washington	Ernie Davis, HB, Syracuse	1996	N.Y. Jets	Keyshawn Johnson, WR, USC
1963	L.A. Rams	Terry Baker, QB, Oregon St.	1997	St. Louis	Orlando Pace, T, Ohio St.
1964	San Francisco	Dave Parks, E, Texas Tech	1998	Indianapolis	Peyton Manning, QB, Tennessee
1965	N.Y. Giants	Tucker Frederickson, HB, Auburn	1999	Cleveland	Tim Couch, QB, Kentucky
1966	Atlanta	Tommy Nobis, LB, Texas	2000	Cleveland	Courtney Brown, DE, Penn State
1967	Baltimore Colts	Bubba Smith, DT, Michigan St.	2001	Atlanta	Michael Vick, QB, Virginia Tech
1968	Minnesota	Ron Yary, T, USC	2002	Houston	David Carr, QB, Fresno St.
1969	Buffalo	O.J. Simpson, RB, USC			

NFL MVP, Defensive Player of the Year, and Rookie of the Year

The Most Valuable Player and Defensive Player of the Year are two of many awards given out annually by the Associated Press. Rookie of the Year is one of many awards given out annually by *The Sporting News*. Many other organizations give out annual awards honoring the NFL's best players.

Most Valuable Player

1957	Jim Brown, Cleveland
1958	Gino Marchetti, Baltimore Colts
1959	Charley Conerly, N.Y. Giants
1960	Norm Van Brocklin, Philadelphia;
	Joe Schmidt, Detroit
1961	Paul Hornung, Green Bay
1962	Jim Taylor, Green Bay
1963	Y.A. Tittle, N.Y. Giants
1964	John Unitas, Baltimore Colts
1965	Jim Brown, Cleveland
1966	Bart Starr, Green Bay
1967	John Unitas, Baltimore Colts
1968	Earl Morrall, Baltimore Colts
1969	Roman Gabriel, L.A. Rams
1970	John Brodie, San Francisco
1971	Alan Page, Minnesota
1972	Larry Brown, Washington
1973	O.J. Simpson, Buffalo
1974	Ken Stabler, Oakland
1975	Fran Tarkenton, Minnesota
1976	Bert Jones, Baltimore
1977	Walter Payton, Chicago
1978	Terry Bradshaw, Pittsburgh
1979	Earl Campbell, Houston
1980	Brian Sipe, Cleveland
1981	Ken Anderson, Cincinnati
1982	Mark Moseley, Washington
1983	Joe Theismann, Washington
1984	Dan Marino, Miami
1985	Marcus Allen, L.A. Raiders
1986	Lawrence Taylor, N.Y. Giants
1987	John Elway, Denver
1988	Boomer Esiason, Cincinnati
1989	Joe Montana, San Francisco
1990	Joe Montana, San Francisco
1991	Thurman Thomas, Buffalo
1992	Steve Young, San Francisco
1993	Emmitt Smith, Dallas
1994	Steve Young, San Francisco
1995	Brett Favre, Green Bay
1996	Brett Favre, Green Bay
1997	(tie) Brett Favre, Green Bay
	Barry Sanders, Detroit
1998	Terrell Davis, Denver
1999	Kurt Warner, St. Louis
2000	Marshall Faulk, St. Louis
2001	Kurt Warner, St. Louis

Defensive Player of the Year

1966	Larry Wilson, St. Louis
1967	Deacon Jones, Los Angeles
1968	Deacon Jones, Los Angeles
1969	Dick Butkus, Chicago
1970	Dick Butkus, Chicago
1971	Carl Eller, Minnesota
1972	Joe Greene, Pittsburgh
1973	Alan Page, Minnesota
1974	Joe Greene, Pittsburgh
1975	Curley Culp, Houston
1976	Jerry Sherk, Cleveland
1977	Harvey Martin, Dallas
1978	Randy Gradishar, Denver
1979	Lee Roy Selmon, Tampa Bay
1980	Lester Hayes, Oakland
1981	Joe Klecko, N.Y. Jets
1982	Mark Gastineau, N.Y. Jets
1983	Jack Lambert, Pittsburgh
1984	Mike Haynes, L.A. Raiders
1985	Howie Long, L.A. Raiders
	Andre Tippett, New England
1986	Lawrence Taylor, N.Y. Giants
1987	Reggie White, Philadelphia
1988	Mike Singletary, Chicago
1989	Tim Harris, Green Bay
1990	Bruce Smith, Buffalo
1991	Pat Swilling, New Orleans
1992	Junior Seau, San Diego
1993	Bruce Smith, Buffalo
1994	Deion Sanders, San Francisco
1995	Bryce Paup, Buffalo
1996	Bruce Smith, Buffalo
1997	Dana Stubblefield, San Francisco
1998	Reggie White, Green Bay
1999	Warren Sapp, Tampa Bay
2000	Ray Lewis, Baltimore
2001	Michael Strahan, NY Giants

Rookie of the Year

1964	Charley Taylor, Washington
1965	Gale Sayers, Chicago
1966	Tommy Nobis, Atlanta
1967	Mel Farr, Detroit
1968	Earl McCullouch, Detroit
1969	Calvin Hill, Dallas
1970	NFC: Bruce Taylor, San Francisco
	AFC: Dennis Shaw, Buffalo
1971	NFC: John Brockington, Green Bay
	AFC: Jim Plunkett, New England
1972	NFC: Chester Marcol, Green Bay
	AFC: Franco Harris, Pittsburgh
1973	NFC: Chuck Foreman, Minnesota
	AFC: Boobie Clark, Cincinnati
1974	NFC: Wilbur Jackson, San Francisco
	AFC: Don Woods, San Diego
1975	NFC: Steve Bartkowski, Atlanta
	AFC: Robert Brazile, Houston
1976	NFC: Sammy White, Minnesota
	AFC: Mike Haynes, New England
1977	NFC: Tony Dorsett, Dallas
	AFC: A. J. Duhe, Miami
1978	NFC: Al Baker, Detroit
	AFC: Earl Campbell, Houston
1979	NFC: Ottis Anderson, St. Louis
	AFC: Jerry Butler, Buffalo
1980	Billy Sims, Detroit
1981	George Rogers, New Orleans
1982	Marcus Allen, L.A. Raiders
1983	Dan Marino, Miami
1984	Louis Lipps, Pittsburgh
1985	Eddie Brown, Cincinnati
1986	Rueben Mayes, New Orleans
1987	Robert Awalt, St. Louis
1988	Keith Jackson, Philadelphia
1989	Barry Sanders, Detroit
1990	Richmond Webb, Miami
1991	Mike Croel, Denver
1992	Santana Dotson, Tampa Bay
1993	Jerome Bettis, L.A. Rams
1994	Marshall Faulk, Indianapolis
1995	Curtis Martin, New England
1996	Eddie George, Houston
1997	Warrick Dunn, Tampa Bay
1998	Randy Moss, Minnesota
1999	Edgerrin James, Indianapolis
2000	Brian Urlacher, Chicago
2001	Kendrell Bell, Pittsburgh

The Sporting News 2001 NFL All-Pro Team

Offense—Quarterback: Kurt Warner, St. Louis. Running Backs: Marshall Faulk, St. Louis; Curtis Martin, NY Jets. Wide Receivers: David Boston, Arizona; Terrell Owens, San Francisco. Tight End: Tony Gonzalez, Kansas City. Tackles: Jonathan Ogden, Baltimore; Orlando Pace, St. Louis. Guards: Larry Allen, Dallas; Alan Faneca, Pittsburgh. Center: Kevin Mawae, NY Jets.

Defense—Linebackers: Ray Lewis, Baltimore; Jamir Miller, Cleveland; Brian Urlacher, Chicago. Defensive Ends: John Abraham, NY Jets; Michael Strahan, NY Giants. Defensive Tackles: Warren Sapp, Tampa Bay; Ted Washington, Chicago. Cornerbacks: Aeneas Williams, St. Louis; Charles Woodson, Oakland. Safeties: Brian Dawkins, Philadelphia; Rodney Harrison, San Diego.

Special Teams—Kicker: David Akers, Philadelphia. Punter: Todd Sauerbrun, Carolina. Punt Returner: Jermaine Lewis, Baltimore. Kick Returner: Steve Smith, Carolina.

All-Time NFL Coaching Victories

(at end of 2001 season; ranked by career wins; *active in 2001)

			Regular Season				Career			
Coach	Years	Teams	W	L	T	Pct	W	L	T	Pct
Don Shula	33	Colts, Dolphins	328	156	6	.676	347	173	6	.665
George Halas	40	Bears	318	148	31	.671	324	151	31	.671
Tom Landry	29	Cowboys	250	162	6	.605	270	178	6	.601
Curly Lambeau	33	Packers, Cardinals, Redskins	226	132	22	.624	229	134	22	.623
Chuck Noll	23	Steelers	193	148	1	.566	209	156	1	.572
Chuck Knox	22	Rams, Bills, Seahawks	186	147	1	.558	193	158	1	.550
Dan Reeves*	21	Broncos, Giants, Falcons	178	149	1	.544	188	157	1	.545
Paul Brown	21	Browns, Bengals	166	100	6	.621	170	109	6	.607
Bud Grant	18	Vikings	158	96	5	.620	168	108	5	.607
M. Schottenheimer*	16	Browns, Chiefs, Redskins	153	93	1	.621	158	104	1	.603
Steve Owen	23	Giants	153	100	17	.598	155	108	17	.584
Marv Levy	17	Chiefs, Bills	143	112	0	.561	154	120	0	.562
Bill Parcells	15	Giants, Patriots, Jets	138	100	1	.579	149	106	1	.584
Joe Gibbs	12	Redskins	124	60	0	.674	140	65	0	.683
Hank Stram	17	Chiefs, Saints	131	97	10	.571	136	100	10	.573
Weeb Ewbank	20	Colts, Jets	130	129	7	.502	134	130	7	.507
Mike Ditka	14	Bears, Saints	121	95	0	.560	127	101	0	.557
Jim Mora*	15	Saints, Colts	125	106	0	.541	125	112	0	.527
George Seifert*	11	49ers, Panthers	114	62	0	.648	124	67	0	.649
Sid Gillman	18	Rams, Chargers, Oilers	122	99	7	.550	123	104	7	.541

All-Time Professional (NFL and AFL) Football Records

(at end of 2001 season; *active in 2001; (a) includes AFL statistics)

Leading Lifetime Scorers

Player	Yrs	TD	PAT	FG	Total
Gary Anderson*	20	0	705	476	2,133
Morten Andersen*	20	0	644	464	2,036
George Blanda (a)	26	9	943	335	2,002
Norm Johnson	18	0	638	366	1,736
Nick Lowery	18	0	562	383	1,711
Jan Stenerud (a)	19	0	580	373	1,699
Eddie Murray	19	0	538	352	1,594
Al Del Greco	17	0	543	347	1,584
Pat Leahy	18	0	558	304	1,470
Jim Turner (a)	16	1	521	304	1,439
Matt Bahr	17	0	522	300	1,422
Mark Moseley	16	0	482	300	1,382
Jim Bakken	17	0	534	282	1,380
Fred Cox	15	0	519	282	1,365
Lou Groza	17	1	641	234	1,349
Jim Breech	14	0	517	243	1,246
Pete Stoyanovich	12	0	420	272	1,236
Chris Bahr	14	0	490	241	1,213
Kevin Butler	13	0	413	265	1,208
Steve Christie*	12	0	364	281	1,207

Leading Lifetime Touchdown Scorers

Player	Yrs	Rush	Rec	Ret	Total
Jerry Rice*	17	10	185	1	196
Emmit Smith*	12	148	11	0	159
Marcus Allen	16	123	21	1	145
Cris Carter*	15	0	129	1	130
Jim Brown	9	106	20	0	126
Walter Payton	13	110	15	0	125
John Riggins	14	104	12	0	116
Lenny Moore	12	63	48	2	113
Marshall Faulk*	8	79	31	0	110
Barry Sanders	10	99	10	0	109
Don Hutson	11	3	99	3	105
Steve Largent	14	1	100	0	101
Tim Brown*	14	1	95	4	100
Franco Harris	13	91	9	0	100
Eric Dickerson	11	90	6	0	96
Jim Taylor	10	83	10	0	93
Tony Dorsett	12	77	13	1	91
Bobby Mitchell	11	18	65	8	91
Ricky Watters*	10	78	13	0	91
Leroy Kelly	10	74	13	3	90
Charley Taylor	13	11	79	0	90

Most Points, Season — 176, Paul Hornung, Green Bay Packers, 1960 (15 TDs, 41 PATs, 15 FGs).
Most Points, Game — 40, Ernie Nevers, Chicago Cardinals vs. Chicago Bears, Nov. 28, 1929 (6 TDs, 4 PATs).
Most Touchdowns, Season — 26, Marshall Faulk, St. Louis Rams, 2000 (18 rushing, 8 receiving).
Most Touchdowns, Game — 6, Ernie Nevers, Chicago Cardinals vs. Chicago Bears, Nov. 28, 1929 (6 rushing); Dub Jones, Cleveland Browns vs. Chicago Bears, Nov. 25, 1951 (4 rushing, 2 pass receptions); Gale Sayers, Chicago Bears vs. San Francisco 49ers, Dec. 12, 1965 (4 rushing, 1 pass reception, 1 punt return).
Most Points After TD, Season — 66, Uwe von Schamann, Miami Dolphins, 1984.
Most Consecutive Points After TD — 344, Jason Elam, Denver Broncos, 1993-2001.
Most Field Goals, Season — 39, Olindo Mare, Miami Dolphins, 1999.
Most Field Goals, Game — 7, Jim Bakken, St. Louis Cardinals vs. Pittsburgh Steelers, Sept. 24, 1967; Rich Karlis, Minnesota vs. L.A. Rams, Nov. 5, 1989 (OT); Chris Boniol, Dallas vs. Green Bay, Nov. 18, 1996.
Most Field Goals Career — 476, Gary Anderson, Pitts. Steelers-Phil. Eagles-SF 49ers-Minn. Vikings, 1982-2001.
Longest Field Goal — 63 yds., Tom Dempsey, New Orleans Saints vs. Detroit Lions, Nov. 8, 1970; Jason Elam, Denver Broncos vs. Jacksonville Jaguars, Oct. 25, 1998.

Defensive Records

Most Interceptions, Career — 81, Paul Krause, Washington Redskins-Minnesota Vikings, 1964-79.
Most Interceptions, Season — 14, Dick "Night Train" Lane, L. A. Rams, 1952.
Most Touchdowns, Career — 10, Rod Woodson, Pittsburgh Steelers-San Francisco 49ers-Baltimore Ravens, 1987-2001.
Most Touchdowns, Season — 4, Ken Houston, Houston Oilers, 1971; Jim Kearney, Kansas City Chiefs, 1972; Eric Allen, Philadelphia Eagles, 1993.
Most Sacks, Career (Since 1982) — 198, Reggie White, Philadelphia Eagles-Green Bay Packers, 1985-2000.
Most Sacks, Season (Since 1982) — 22.5, Michael Strahan, N.Y. Giants, 2002.
Most Sacks, Game (Since 1982) — 7, Derrick Thomas, Kansas City Chiefs vs. Seattle Seahawks, Nov. 11, 1990.

Leading Lifetime Rushers

(ranked by rushing yards)

Player	Yrs	Att	Yards	Avg	Long	TD	Player	Yrs	Att	Yards	Avg	Long	TD
Walter Payton	13	3,838	16,726	4.4	76	110	O.J. Simpson (a)	11	2,404	11,236	4.7	94	61
Emmitt Smith*	12	3,798	16,187	4.3	75	148	Jerome Bettis*	9	2,686	10,876	4.0	71	53
Barry Sanders	10	3,062	15,269	5.0	85	99	Ricky Watters*	10	2,622	10,643	4.1	57	78
Eric Dickerson	11	2,996	13,259	4.4	85	90	Ottis Anderson	14	2,562	10,273	4.0	76	81
Tony Dorsett	12	2,936	12,739	4.3	99	77	Marshall Faulk*	8	2,155	9,442	4.4	71	79
Jim Brown	9	2,359	12,312	5.2	80	106	Earl Campbell	8	2,187	9,407	4.3	81	74
Marcus Allen	16	3,022	12,243	4.1	61	123	Curtis Martin*	7	2,343	9,267	4.0	70	64
Franco Harris	13	2,949	12,120	4.1	75	91	Terry Allen*	10	2,152	8,614	4.0	55	73
Thurman Thomas	13	2,877	12,074	4.2	80	65	Jim Taylor	10	1,941	8,597	4.4	84	83
John Riggins	14	2,916	11,352	3.9	66	104	Joe Perry	14	1,737	8,378	4.8	78	53

Most Yards Gained, Season — 2,105, Eric Dickerson, L.A. Rams, 1984.
Most Yards Gained, Game — 278, Corey Dillon, Cincinnati Bengals vs. Denver Broncos, Oct. 22, 2000.
Most Touchdowns Rushing, Career — 148, Emmitt Smith, Dallas Cowboys, 1990-2001.
Most Touchdowns Rushing, Season — 25, Emmitt Smith, Dallas Cowboys, 1995.
Most Touchdowns Rushing, Game — 6, Ernie Nevers, Chicago Cardinals vs. Chicago Bears, Nov. 28, 1929.
Most Rushing Attempts, Game — 45, Jamie Morris, Washington Redskins vs. Cincinnati Bengals, Dec. 17, 1988 (overtime).
Longest Run From Scrimmage — 99 yds., Tony Dorsett, Dallas Cowboys vs. Minnesota Vikings, Jan. 3, 1983 (touchdown).

Leading Lifetime Receivers

(ranked by number of receptions)

Player	Yrs	No.	Yards	Avg	Long	TD	Player	Yrs	No.	Yards	Avg	Long	TD
Jerry Rice*	17	1,364	20,386	14.9	96	185	Michael Irvin	12	750	11,904	15.9	87	65
Cris Carter*	15	1,093	13,833	12.7	80	129	Charlie Joiner (a)	18	750	12,146	16.2	87	65
Andre Reed	16	951	13,198	13.9	83	87	Andre Rison	12	743	10,205	13.7	80	84
Art Monk	16	940	12,721	13.5	79	68	Gary Clark	11	699	10,856	15.5	84	65
Tim Brown*	14	937	13,237	14.1	80	95	Shannon Sharpe*	12	692	8,604	12.4	68	51
Irving Fryar	17	851	12,785	15.0	80	84	Herman Moore*	11	670	9,174	13.7	93	62
Steve Largent	14	819	13,089	16.0	74	100	Terence Mathis*	12	666	8,591	12.9	81	61
Henry Ellard	16	814	13,777	16.9	81	65	Ozzie Newsome	13	662	7,980	12.1	74	47
Larry Centers*	11	765	6,303	8.2	54	27	Charley Taylor	13	649	9,110	14.0	88	79
James Lofton	16	764	14,004	18.3	80	75	Drew Hill	15	634	9,831	15.5	81	60

Most Yards Gained, Career — 20,386, Jerry Rice, San Francisco 49ers, Oakland Raiders, 1985-2001.
Most Yards Gained, Season — 1,848, Jerry Rice, San Francisco 49ers, 1995.
Most Yards Gained, Game — 336, Willie "Flipper" Anderson, L. A. Rams vs. New Orleans, Nov. 26, 1989 (overtime).
Most Pass Receptions, Season — 123, Herman Moore, Detroit Lions, 1995.
Most Pass Receptions, Game — 20, Terrell Owens, San Francisco 49ers vs. Chicago Bears, Dec. 17, 2000 (283 yards).
Most Touchdown Receptions, Career — 185, Jerry Rice, San Francisco 49ers, Oakland Raiders, 1985-2001.
Most Touchdown Receptions, Season — 22, Jerry Rice, San Francisco 49ers, 1987.
Most Touchdown Receptions, Game — 5, Bob Shaw, Chicago Cardinals vs. Baltimore Colts, Oct. 2, 1950; Kellen Winslow, San Diego Chargers vs. Oakland Raiders, Nov. 22, 1981; Jerry Rice, San Francisco 49ers vs. Atlanta Falcons, Oct. 14, 1990.

Leading Lifetime Passers

(minimum 1,500 attempts; ranked by quarterback rating points)

Player	Yrs	Att	Comp	Yds	TD	Int	Pts[1]	Player	Yrs	Att	Comp	Yds	TD	Int	Pts[1]
Steve Young	15	4,149	2,667	33,124	232	107	96.8	Neil Lomax	8	3,153	1,817	22,771	136	90	82.7
Joe Montana	15	5,391	3,409	40,551	273	139	92.3	S. Jurgensen	18	4,262	2,433	32,224	255	189	82.63
Brett Favre*	11	5,442	3,311	38,627	287	172	86.8	Len Dawson (a)	19	3,741	2,136	28,711	239	183	82.56
Dan Marino	17	8,358	4,967	61,361	420	252	86.4	Ken Anderson	16	4,475	2,654	32,838	197	160	81.85
Peyton Manning*	4	2,226	1,357	16,418	111	81	85.1	Bernie Kosar	12	3,365	1,994	23,301	124	87	81.82
Mark Brunell*	8	3,145	1,897	22,521	125	79	85.0	Danny White	13	2,950	1,761	21,959	155	132	81.71
Jim Kelly	11	4,779	2,874	35,467	237	175	84.4	Neil O'Donnell*	12	3,197	1,844	21,434	118	67	81.66
Roger Staubach	11	2,958	1,685	22,700	153	109	83.4	Troy Aikman	12	4,715	2,898	32,942	165	141	81.61
Brad Johnson*	8	2,380	1,466	16,379	92	68	83.07	Dave Krieg	19	5,311	3,105	38,147	261	199	81.49
Rich Gannon*	13	3,295	1,949	22,256	145	88	83.06	R. Cunningham*	16	4,289	2,429	29,979	207	134	81.47

(1) Rating points based on performances in the following categories: Percentage of completions, percentage of touchdown passes, percentage of interceptions, and average gain per pass attempt.

Most Yards Gained, Career — 61,361, Dan Marino, Miami Dolphins, 1983-99.
Most Yards Gained, Season — 5,084, Dan Marino, Miami Dolphins, 1984.
Most Yards Gained, Game — 554, Norm Van Brocklin, L. A. Rams vs. N.Y. Yanks, Sept. 18, 1951 (27 completions in 41 attempts).
Most Touchdowns Passing, Career — 420, Dan Marino, Miami Dolphins, 1983-99.
Most Touchdowns Passing, Season — 48, Dan Marino, Miami Dolphins, 1984.
Most Touchdowns Passing, Game — 7, Sid Luckman, Chicago Bears vs. N.Y. Giants, Nov. 14, 1943; Adrian Burk, Phil. Eagles vs. Washington Redskins, Oct. 17, 1954; George Blanda, Houston Oilers vs. N.Y. Titans, Nov. 19, 1961; Y.A. Tittle, N.Y. Giants vs. Washington Redskins, Oct. 28, 1962; Joe Kapp, Minnesota Vikings vs. Baltimore Colts, Sept. 28, 1969.
Most Passes Completed, Career — 4,967, Dan Marino, Miami Dolphins, 1983-99.
Most Passes Completed, Season — 404, Warren Moon, Houston Oilers, 1991.
Most Passes Completed, Game — 45, Drew Bledsoe, New England Patriots vs. Minnesota Vikings, Nov. 13, 1994 (overtime).

National Football League Franchise Origins

(founding year, league; home stadium location; subsequent history)

Arizona Cardinals—1920, American Professional Football Association (APFA)[1]. Chicago, 1920-59; St. Louis, 1960-87; Tempe, AZ, 1988-present.
Atlanta Falcons—1996, NFL. Atlanta, 1966-present.
Baltimore Ravens—1996, NFL. Baltimore, 1996-present.
Buffalo Bills—1969, American Football League (AFL)[2]. Buffalo, 1960-72; Orchard Park, NY, 1972-present.
Carolina Panthers—1995, NFL. Clemson, SC, 1995; Charlotte, NC, 1996-present.
Chicago Bears—1920 APFA. Decatur, IL, 1920; Chicago, 1921-present.
Cincinnati Bengals—1968, AFL. Cincinnati, 1968-present.
Cleveland Browns—1946, All-America Football Conference (AAFC)[3]. Cleveland, 1946-95; 1999-present.
Dallas Cowboys—1960, NFL. Dallas, 1960-70; Irving, TX, 1971-present.
Denver Broncos—1960, AFL. Denver, 1960-present.
Detroit Lions—1930, NFL. Portsmouth, OH, 1930-33; Detroit, 1934-74; Pontiac, MI, 1975-present.
Green Bay Packers—1921, APFA. Green Bay, WI, 1921-present.
Houston Texans—2002, NFL. Houston 2002-present.
Indianapolis Colts—1953, NFL. Baltimore, 1953-83; Indianapolis, 1984-present.
Jacksonville Jaguars—1995, NFL. Jacksonville, FL, 1995-present.
Kansas City Chiefs—1960, AFL. Dallas, 1960-62; Kansas City, 1963-present.
Miami Dolphins—1966, AFL. Miami, 1966-present.
Minnesota Vikings—1961, NFL. Bloomington, MN, 1961-81; Minneapolis, 1982-present.
New England Patriots—1960, AFL. Boston, 1960-70; Foxboro, MA, 1982-present.
New Orleans Saints—1967, NFL. New Orleans, 1967-present.
New York Giants—1925, NFL. New York, 1925-73, 1975; New Haven, CT, 1973-74; E. Rutherford, NJ, 1976-present.
New York Jets—1960, AFL. New York, 1960-83; E. Rutherford, NJ, 1984-present.
Oakland Raiders—1960, AFL. Oakland, CA, 1960-81, 1995-present; Los Angeles, 1982-94.
Philadelphia Eagles—1933, NFL. Piladelphia, 1933-present.
Pittsburgh Steelers—1933, NFL. Pittsburgh, 1933-present.
St. Louis Rams—1937, NFL. Cleveland, 1936-45; Los Angeles, 1946-79; Anaheim, 1980-94; St. Louis, 1995-present.
San Diego Chargers—1960, AFL. Los Angeles, 1960; San Diego, 1961-present.
Seattle Seahawks—1976, NFL. Seattle, 1976-present.
San Francisco 49ers—1946, AAFC. San Francisco, 1946-present.
Tampa Bay Buccaneers—1976, NFL. Tampa, 1976-present.
Tennessee Titans—1960, AFL. Houston, 1969-96; Memphis, 1997; Nashville, 1998-present.
Washington Redskins—1932, NFL. Boston, 1932-36, Washinton, DC, 1937-96; Landover, MD, 1997-present.

(1) The American Professional Football Association (APFA) was formed in 1920 to standardize the rules of professional football. In 1922, the name was changed to the National Football League. (2) The most successful of 4 separate leagues called the "American Football League" (1926; 1936-37; 1940-41, 1960-69). Congress approved an NFL/AFL merger in 1966. Baltimore, Cleveland, and Pittsburgh agreed to join the 10 incoming AFL teams to form the American Football Conference. The NFL began play in 1970 with 26 teams. (3) The All-America Football Conference, 1946-49. In 1950, 3 of its teams joined the NFL (Baltimore, Cleveland, and San Francisco). The Baltimore franchise failed, but the NFL awarded the city a 2nd one, also called the Colts, in 1953.

American Football League Champions

Year	Eastern Division	Western Division	Championship
1960	Houston Oilers (10-4-0)	Los Angeles Chargers (10-4-0)	Houston 24, Los Angeles 16
1961	Houston Oilers (10-3-1)	San Diego Chargers (12-2-0)	Houston 10, San Diego 3
1962	Houston Oilers (11-3-0)	Dallas Texans (11-3-0)	Dallas 20, Houston 17 (2 overtimes)
1963	Boston Patriots (7-6-1)(a)	San Diego Chargers (11-3-0)	San Diego 51, Boston 10
1964	Buffalo Bills (12-2-0)	San Diego Chargers (8-5-1)	Buffalo 20, San Diego 7
1965	Buffalo Bills (10-3-1)	San Diego Chargers (9-2-3)	Buffalo 23, San Diego 0
1966	Buffalo Bills (9-4-1)	Kansas City Chiefs (11-2-1)	Kansas City 31, Buffalo 7
1967	Houston Oilers (9-4-1)	Oakland Raiders (13-1-0)	Oakland 40, Houston 7
1968	New York Jets (11-3-0)	Oakland Raiders (12-2-0)(b)	New York 27, Oakland 23
1969	New York Jets (10-4-0)	Oakland Raiders (12-1-1)	Kansas City 17, Oakland 7 (c)

(a) Defeated Buffalo Bills in divisional playoff. (b) Defeated Kansas City Chiefs in divisional playoff. (c) Kansas City Chiefs defeated N.Y. Jets and Oakland Raiders defeated Houston Oilers in divisional playoffs.

Pro Football Hall of Fame, Canton, Ohio

(Asterisks indicate 2002 inductees.)

Herb Adderley
*George Allen
Lance Alworth
Doug Atkins
Morris "Red" Badgro
Lem Barney
Cliff Battles
Sammy Baugh
Chuck Bednarik
Bert Bell
Bobby Bell
Raymond Berry
Charles Bidwill
Fred Biletnikoff
George Blanda
Mel Blount
Terry Bradshaw
Jim Brown
Paul Brown
Roosevelt Brown
Willie Brown
Buck Buchanan
Nick Buoniconti
Dick Butkus
Earl Campbell
Tony Canadeo
Joe Carr
*Dave Casper
Guy Chamberlin
Jack Christiansen
Earl "Dutch" Clark
George Connor
Jim Conzelman
Lou Creekmur
Larry Csonka
Al Davis
Willie Davis
Len Dawson
Eric Dickerson
Dan Dierdorf
Mike Ditka
Art Donovan
Tony Dorsett
John "Paddy" Driscoll
Bill Dudley
Glen "Turk" Edwards
Weeb Ewbank
Tom Fears
Jim Finks
Ray Flaherty
Len Ford
Dr. Daniel Fortmann
Dan Fouts
Frank Gatski
Bill George
Joe Gibbs
Frank Gifford
Sid Gillman
Otto Graham
Red Grange
Bud Grant
Joe Greene
Forrest Gregg
Bob Griese
Lou Groza
Joe Guyon
George Halas
Jack Ham
*Dan Hampton
John Hannah
Franco Harris
Mike Haynes
Ed Healey
Mel Hein
Ted Hendricks
Wilbur "Pete" Henry
Arnold Herber
Bill Hewitt
Clarke Hinkle
Elroy "Crazylegs" Hirsch
Paul Hornung
Ken Houston
Cal Hubbard
Sam Huff
Lamar Hunt
Don Hutson
Jimmy Johnson
John Henry Johnson
Charlie Joiner
David "Deacon" Jones
Stan Jones
Henry Jordan
Sonny Jurgensen
*Jim Kelly
Leroy Kelly
Walt Kiesling
Frank "Bruiser" Kinard
Paul Krause
Earl "Curly" Lambeau
Jack Lambert
Tom Landry
Dick "Night Train" Lane
Jim Langer
Willie Lanier
Steve Largent
Yale Lary
Dante Lavelli
Bobby Layne
Alphonse "Tuffy" Leemans
Marv Levy
Bob Lilly
Larry Little
Vince Lombardi
Howie Long
Ronnie Lott
Sid Luckman
Roy "Link" Lyman
Tom Mack
John Mackey
Tim Mara
Wellington Mara
Gino Marchetti
George Preston Marshall
Ollie Matson
Don Maynard
George McAfee
Mike McCormack
Tommy McDonald
Hugh McElhenny
Johnny "Blood" McNally
Mike Michalske
Wayne Millner
Bobby Mitchell
Ron Mix
Joe Montana
Lenny Moore
Marion Motley
Mike Munchak

Anthony Munoz
George Musso
Bronko Nagurski
Joe Namath
Earle "Greasy" Neale
Ernie Nevers
Ozzie Newsome
Ray Nitschke
Chuck Noll
Leo Nomellini
Merlin Olsen
Jim Otto
Steve Owen
Alan Page
Clarence "Ace" Parker
Jim Parker
Walter Payton
Joe Perry
Pete Pihos
Hugh "Shorty" Ray
Dan Reeves
Mel Renfro
John Riggins
Jim Ringo
Andy Robustelli
Art Rooney
Dan Rooney
Pete Rozelle
Bob St. Clair
Gale Sayers
Joe Schmidt
Tex Schramm
Lee Roy Selmon
Billy Shaw
Art Shell
Don Shula
O.J. Simpson
Mike Singletary
Jackie Slater
Jackie Smith
*John Stallworth
Bart Starr
Roger Staubach
Ernie Stautner
Jan Stenerud
Dwight Stephenson
Ken Strong
Joe Stydahar
Lynn Swann
Fran Tarkenton
Charley Taylor
Jim Taylor
Lawrence "LT" Taylor
Jim Thorpe
Y.A. Tittle
George Trafton
Charley Trippi
Emlen Tunnell
Clyde "Bulldog" Turner
Johnny Unitas
Gene Upshaw
Norm Van Brocklin
Steve Van Buren
Doak Walker
Bill Walsh
Paul Warfield
Bob Waterfield
Mike Webster
Arnie Weinmeister
Randy White
Dave Wilcox
Bill Willis
Larry Wilson
Kellen Winslow
Alex Wojciechowicz
Willie Wood
Ron Yary
Jack Youngblood

NFL Stadiums[1]

Team—Stadium, Location, Turf (Year Built)	Capacity
Bears—Memorial Stad.[2], Champaign, IL, G (1924)	68,667
Bengals—Paul Brown Stad, Cincinnati, OH, G (2000)	65,600
Bills—Ralph Wilson Stad., Orchard Park, NY, A (1973)	73,967
Broncos—Invesco Field at Mile High, Denver, CO, G (2001)	76,125
Browns—Cleveland Browns Stad., Cleveland, OH, G (1999)	73,200
Buccaneers—Raymond James Stad., Tampa, FL, G (1998)	66,321
Cardinals—Sun Devil Stad., Tempe, AZ, G (1958)	73,273
Chargers—Qualcomm Stad.[3], San Diego, CA, G (1967)	71,500
Chiefs—Arrowhead Stad., Kansas City, MO, G (1972)	79,451
Colts—RCA Dome [4], Indianapolis, IN, A (1983)	56,127
Cowboys—Texas Stad., Irving, TX, A (1971)	65,675
Dolphins—Pro Player Stad.[5], Miami, FL, G (1987)	75,192
Eagles—Veterans Stad., Philadelphia, PA, A (1971)	65,352
Falcons—Georgia Dome, Atlanta, GA, A (1992)	71,149
49ers—3Com Park[6], San Francisco, CA, G (1960)	69,734
Giants—Giants Stad., E. Rutherford, NJ, G (1976)	79,466
Jaguars—ALLTEL Stad.[7], Jacksonville, FL, G (1946)	73,000
Jets—Giants Stad., E. Rutherford, NJ, G (1976)	79,466
Lions—Ford Field, Detroit, MI, A (2002)	65,000
Packers—Lambeau Field[8], Green Bay, WI, G (1957)	60,890
Panthers—Ericsson Stad., Charlotte, NC, G (1996)	73,367
Patriots—Gillette Stad., Foxboro, MA, G (2002)	68,000
Raiders—Network Associates Coliseum[9], Oakland, CA, G (1966)	63,132
Rams—Edward Jones Dome[10], St. Louis, MO, A (1995)	66,000
Ravens—Ravens Stad.[11], Baltimore, MD, SG (1998)	69,354
Redskins—FedEx Field[12], Landover, MD, G (1997)	80,116
Saints—Louisiana Superdome, New Orleans, A (1975)	70,200
Seahawks—Seahawks Stad., Seattle, WA, A (2002)	67,000
Steelers—Heinz Field, Pittsburgh, PA, A (2001)	65,000 est.
Texans—Reliant Stadium, Houston, TX, G (2002)	69,500
Titans—Adelphia Coliseum, Nashville, TN, G (1999)	67,000
Vikings—Hubert H. Humphrey Metrodome, Minn., MN, A (1982)	64,121

G=Grass. A=Artificial turf. SG=Sport Grass (hybrid of artificial and natural turf). (1) As of the start of the 2002 season. (2) Univ. of IL at Urbana-Champaign facility. Bears' new stad. was scheduled to open in 2003. (3) Formerly San Diego Stad. (1967-80), San Diego Jack Murphy Stad. (1981-97). (4) Formerly the Hoosier Dome (1983-94). (5) Formerly Joe Robbie Stad. (1987-96). (6) Formerly Candlestick Park; full name: 3Com Park at Candlestick Point. (7) Formerly Jacksonville Municipal Stad. (1946-97). (8) Formerly City Stadium (1957-65). (9) Formerly Oakland/Alameda County Coliseum. (10) Formerly Trans World Dome (1995-2001); full name: Edward Jones Dome at America's Center. (11) Formerly PSINet Stad. (1998-2002). (12) Formerly Jack Kent Cooke Stad. (1997-99).

Future Sites of the Super Bowl

(Information subject to change.)

No.	Site	Date
XXXVII	Qualcomm Stadium, San Diego, CA	Jan. 26, 2003
XXXVIII	Reliant Stadium, Houston, TX	Feb. 1, 2004
XXXIX	ALLTEL Stadium, Jacksonville, FL	Feb. 6, 2005
XL	Ford Field, Detroit, MI	Feb. 5, 2006

CANADIAN FOOTBALL LEAGUE

Grey Cup Championship Game, 1954-2001

1954 Edmonton Eskimos 26, Montreal Alouettes 25
1955 Edmonton Eskimos 34, Montreal Alouettes 19
1956 Edmonton Eskimos 50, Montreal Alouettes 27
1957 Hamilton Tiger-Cats 32, Winnipeg Blue Bombers 7
1958 Winnipeg Blue Bombers 35, Hamilton Tiger-Cats 28
1959 Winnipeg Blue Bombers 21, Hamilton Tiger-Cats 7
1960 Ottawa Rough Riders 16, Edmonton Eskimos 6
1961 Winnipeg Blue Bombers 21, Hamilton Tiger-Cats 14
1962 Winnipeg Blue Bombers 28, Hamilton Tiger-Cats 27
1963 Hamilton Tiger-Cats 21, British Columbia Lions 10
1964 British Columbia Lions 34, Hamilton Tiger-Cats 24
1965 Hamilton Tiger-Cats 22, Winnipeg Blue Bombers 16
1966 Saskatchewan Roughriders 29, Ottawa Rough Riders 14
1967 Hamilton Tiger-Cats 24, Saskatchewan Roughriders 1
1968 Ottawa Rough Riders 24, Calgary Stampeders 21
1969 Ottawa Rough Riders 29, Saskatchewan Roughriders 11
1970 Montreal Alouettes 23, Calgary Stampeders 10
1971 Calgary Stampeders 14, Toronto Argonauts 11
1972 Hamilton Tiger-Cats 13, Saskatchewan Roughriders 10
1973 Ottawa Rough Riders 22, Edmonton Eskimos 18
1974 Montreal Alouettes 20, Edmonton Eskimos 7
1975 Edmonton Eskimos 9, Montreal Alouettes 8
1976 Ottawa Rough Riders 23, Saskatchewan Roughriders 20
1977 Montreal Alouettes 41, Edmonton Eskimos 6
1978 Edmonton Eskimos 20, Montreal Alouettes 13
1979 Edmonton Eskimos 17, Montreal Alouettes 9
1980 Edmonton Eskimos 48, Hamilton Tiger-Cats 10
1981 Edmonton Eskimos 26, Ottawa Rough Riders 23
1982 Edmonton Eskimos 32, Toronto Argonauts 16
1983 Toronto Argonauts 18, British Columbia Lions 17
1984 Winnipeg Blue Bombers 47, Hamilton Tiger-Cats 17
1985 British Columbia Lions 37, Hamilton Tiger-Cats 24
1986 Hamilton Tiger-Cats 39, Edmonton Eskimos 15
1987 Edmonton Eskimos 38, Toronto Argonauts 36
1988 Winnipeg Blue Bombers 22, British Columbia Lions 21
1989 Saskatchewan Roughriders 43, Hamilton Tiger-Cats 40
1990 Winnipeg Blue Bombers 50, Edmonton Eskimos 11
1991 Toronto Argonauts 36, Calgary Stampeders 21
1992 Calgary Stampeders 24, Winnipeg Blue Bombers 10
1993 Edmonton Eskimos 33, Winnipeg Blue Bombers 23
1994 British Columbia Lions 26, Baltimore Football Club* 23
1995 Baltimore Stallions 37, Calgary Stampeders 20
1996 Toronto Argonauts 43, Edmonton Eskimos 37
1997 Toronto Argonauts 47, Saskatchewan Roughriders 23
1998 Calgary Stampeders 26, Hamilton Tiger-Cats 24
1999 Hamilton Tiger-Cats 32, Calgary Stampeders 21
2000 British Columbia Lions 28, Montreal Alouettes 26
2001 Calgary Stampeders 27, Winnipeg Blue Bombers 19

*Later Baltimore Stallions.

COLLEGE FOOTBALL

Miami Perfect With Rose Bowl Victory

The top-ranked and undefeated Miami (FL) Hurricanes overwhelmed the Nebraska Cornhuskers, 37-14, at the Rose Bowl in Pasadena, CA, Jan. 3, 2002, finishing 12-0 and winning their 5th national championship. The defeat eliminated Nebraska's hope of finishing with 1 loss and the possibility of a shared title with Oregon (11-1), who won the Fiesta Bowl Jan. 1. Miami quashed any doubt of their supremacy with a 34-0 halftime lead. Junior quarterback Ken Dorsey threw 3 TD passes, 2 to wide receiver Andre Johnson, as both players shared MVP honors. The Hurricane defense was equally dominant as they held Heisman winner Eric Crouch to 114 yds. rushing, 62 yds. passing, and 1 interception, which was returned 47 yards for a TD by Miami safety James Lewis.

National College Football Champions, 1936-2001

The unofficial champion as selected by the AP poll of writers and USA Today/ESPN (until 1991, UPI; 1991-1996 USA Today/CNN) poll of coaches. In years the polls disagreed, both teams are listed (AP winner first). The AP poll started in 1936; the UPI poll in 1950.

1936 Minnesota
1937 Pittsburgh
1938 Texas Christian
1939 Texas A&M
1940 Minnesota
1941 Minnesota
1942 Ohio St.
1943 Notre Dame
1944 Army
1945 Army
1946 Notre Dame
1947 Notre Dame
1948 Michigan
1949 Notre Dame
1950 Oklahoma
1951 Tennessee
1952 Michigan St.
1953 Maryland
1954 Ohio St., UCLA
1955 Oklahoma
1956 Oklahoma
1957 Auburn, Ohio St.
1958 Louisiana St.
1959 Syracuse
1960 Minnesota
1961 Alabama
1962 USC
1963 Texas
1964 Alabama
1965 Alabama, Mich. St.
1966 Notre Dame
1967 USC
1968 Ohio St.
1969 Texas
1970 Nebraska, Texas
1971 Nebraska
1972 USC
1973 Notre Dame, Alabama
1974 Oklahoma, USC
1975 Oklahoma
1976 Pittsburgh
1977 Notre Dame
1978 Alabama, USC
1979 Alabama
1980 Georgia
1981 Clemson
1982 Penn St.
1983 Miami (FL)
1984 Brigham Young
1985 Oklahoma
1986 Penn St.
1987 Miami (FL)
1988 Notre Dame
1989 Miami (FL)
1990 Colorado, Georgia Tech
1991 Miami (FL), Washington
1992 Alabama
1993 Florida St.
1994 Nebraska
1995 Nebraska
1996 Florida
1997 Michigan, Nebraska
1998 Tennessee
1999 Florida St.
2000 Oklahoma
2001 Miami (FL)

2001 Final Associated Press and USA Today/ESPN NCAA Football Polls

Associated Press Rankings

1. Miami (FL) (12-0)
2. Oregon (11-1)
3. Florida (10-2)
4. Tennessee (11-2)
5. Texas (11-2)
6. Oklahoma (11-2)
7. LSU (10-3)
8. Nebraska (11-2)
9. Colorado (10-3)
10. Washington St. (10-2)
11. Maryland (10-2)
12. Illinois (10-2)
13. S. Carolina (9-3)
14. Syracuse (10-3)
15. Florida St. (8-4)
16. Stanford (9-3)
17. Louisville (11-2)
18. Virginia Tech (8-4)
19. Washington (8-4)
20. Michigan (8-4)
21. Boston College (8-4)
22. Georgia (8-4)
23. Toledo (10-2)
24. Georgia Tech (8-5)
25. BYU (12-2)

USA Today/ESPN Rankings

1. Miami (FL)
2. Oregon
3. Florida
4. Tennessee
5. Texas
6. Oklahoma
7. Nebraska
8. LSU
9. Colorado
10. Maryland
11. Washington St.
12. Illinois
13. S. Carolina
14. Syracuse
15. Florida St.
16. Louisville
17. Stanford
18. Virginia Tech
19. Washington
20. Michigan
21. Marshall
22. Toledo
23. Boston College
24. BYU
25. Georgia

Note: Team records include bowl games. Won-loss records are listed in AP poll, except for Marshall (11-2).

Annual Results of Major Bowl Games

(Dates indicate year the game was played; bowl games are generally played in late December or early January.)

Rose Bowl, Pasadena, CA

1902	(Jan.) Michigan 49, Stanford 0
1916	Washington St. 14, Brown 0
1917	Oregon 14, Pennsylvania 0
1918-19	Service teams
1920	Harvard 7, Oregon 6
1921	California 28, Ohio St. 0
1922	Wash. & Jeff. 0, California 0
1923	USC 14, Penn St. 3
1924	Navy 14, Washington 14
1925	Notre Dame 27, Stanford 10
1926	Alabama 20, Washington 19
1927	Alabama 7, Stanford 7
1928	Stanford 7, Pittsburgh 6
1929	Georgia Tech 8, California 7
1930	USC 47, Pittsburgh 14
1931	Alabama 24, Wash. St. 0
1932	USC 21, Tulane 12
1933	USC 35, Pittsburgh 0
1934	Columbia 7, Stanford 0
1935	Alabama 29, Stanford 13
1936	Stanford 7, SMU 0
1937	Pittsburgh 21, Washington 0
1938	California 13, Alabama 0
1939	USC 7, Duke 3
1940	USC 14, Tennessee 0
1941	Stanford 21, Nebraska 13
1942*	Oregon St. 20, Duke 16
1943	Georgia 9, UCLA 0
1944	USC 29, Washington 0
1945	USC 25, Tennessee 0
1946	Alabama 34, USC 14
1947	Illinois 45, UCLA 14
1948	Michigan 49, USC 0
1949	Northwestern 20, California 14
1950	Ohio St. 17, California 14
1951	Michigan 14, California 6
1952	Illinois 40, Stanford 7
1953	USC 7, Wisconsin 0
1954	Mich. St. 28, UCLA 20
1955	Ohio St. 20, USC 7
1956	Mich. St. 17, UCLA 14
1957	Iowa 35, Oregon St. 19
1958	Ohio St. 10, Oregon 7
1959	Iowa 38, California 12
1960	Washington 44, Wisconsin 8
1961	Washington 17, Minnesota 7
1962	Minnesota 21, UCLA 3
1963	USC 42, Wisconsin 37
1964	Illinois 17, Washington 7
1965	Michigan 34, Oregon St. 7
1966	UCLA 14, Mich. St. 12
1967	Purdue 14, USC 13
1968	USC 14, Indiana 3
1969	Ohio St. 27, USC 16
1970	USC 10, Michigan 3
1971	Stanford 27, Ohio St. 17
1972	Stanford 13, Michigan 12
1973	USC 42, Ohio St. 17
1974	Ohio St. 42, USC 21
1975	USC 18, Ohio St. 17
1976	UCLA 23, Ohio St. 10
1977	USC 14, Michigan 6
1978	Washington 27, Michigan 20
1979	USC 17, Michigan 10
1980	USC 17, Ohio St. 16
1981	Michigan 23, Washington 6
1982	Washington 28, Iowa 0
1983	UCLA 24, Michigan 14
1984	UCLA 45, Illinois 9
1985	USC 20, Ohio St. 17
1986	UCLA 45, Iowa 28
1987	Arizona St. 22, Michigan 15
1988	Mich. St. 20, USC 17
1989	Michigan 22, USC 14
1990	USC 17, Michigan 10
1991	Washington 46, Iowa 34
1992	Washington 34, Michigan 14
1993	Michigan 38, Washington 31
1994	Wisconsin 21, UCLA 16
1995	Penn St. 38, Oregon 20
1996	USC 41, Northwestern 32
1997	Ohio St. 20, Arizona St. 17
1998	Michigan 21, Wash. St. 16
1999	Wisconsin 38, UCLA 31
2000	Wisconsin 17, Stanford 9
2001	Washington 34, Purdue 24
2002	Miami (FL) 37, Nebraska 14

*Played at Durham, NC.

Orange Bowl, Miami, FL

1935	(Jan.) Bucknell 26, Miami (FL) 0
1936	Catholic U. 20, Mississippi 19
1937	Duquesne 13, Mississippi St. 12
1938	Auburn 6, Michigan St. 0
1939	Tennessee 17, Oklahoma 0
1940	Georgia Tech 21, Missouri 7
1941	Mississippi St. 14, Georgetown 7
1942	Georgia 40, TCU 26
1943	Alabama 37, Boston Coll. 21
1944	LSU 19, Texas A&M 14
1945	Tulsa 26, Georgia Tech 12
1946	Miami (FL) 13, Holy Cross 6
1947	Rice 8, Tennessee 0
1948	Georgia Tech 20, Kansas 14
1949	Texas 41, Georgia 28
1950	Santa Clara 21, Kentucky 13
1951	Clemson 15, Miami (FL) 14
1952	Georgia Tech 17, Baylor 14

1953 Alabama 61, Syracuse 6
1954 Oklahoma 7, Maryland 0
1955 Duke 34, Nebraska 7
1956 Oklahoma 20, Maryland 6
1957 Colorado 27, Clemson 21
1958 Oklahoma 48, Duke 21
1959 Oklahoma 21, Syracuse 6
1960 Georgia 14, Missouri 0
1961 Missouri 21, Navy 14
1962 LSU 25, Colorado 7
1963 Alabama 17, Oklahoma 0
1964 Nebraska 13, Auburn 7
1965 Texas 21, Alabama 17
1966 Alabama 39, Nebraska 28
1967 Florida 27, Georgia Tech 12
1968 Oklahoma 26, Tennessee 24
1969 Penn St. 15, Kansas 14
1970 Penn St. 10, Missouri 3
1971 Nebraska 17, LSU 12
1972 Nebraska 38, Alabama 6
1973 Nebraska 40, Notre Dame 6
1974 Penn St. 16, LSU 9
1975 Notre Dame 13, Alabama 11
1976 Oklahoma 14, Michigan 6
1977 Ohio St. 27, Colorado 10
1978 Arkansas 31, Oklahoma 6
1979 Oklahoma 31, Nebraska 24
1980 Oklahoma 24, Florida St. 7
1981 Oklahoma 18, Florida St. 17
1982 Clemson 22, Nebraska 15
1983 Nebraska 21, LSU 20
1984 Miami (FL) 31, Nebraska 30
1985 Washington 28, Oklahoma 17
1986 Oklahoma 25, Penn St. 10
1987 Oklahoma 42, Arkansas 8
1988 Miami (FL) 20, Oklahoma 14
1989 Miami (FL) 23, Nebraska 3
1990 Notre Dame 21, Colorado 6
1991 Colorado 10, Notre Dame 9
1992 Miami (FL) 22, Nebraska 0
1993 Florida St. 27, Nebraska 14
1994 Florida St. 18, Nebraska 16
1995 Nebraska 24, Miami (FL) 17
1996 Florida St. 31, Notre Dame 26
1996 (Dec.) Nebraska 41, Virginia Tech 21
1998 (Jan.) Nebraska 42, Tennessee 17
1999 Florida 31, Syracuse 10
2000 Michigan 35, Alabama 34 (OT)
2001 Oklahoma 13, Florida St. 2
2002 Florida 56, Maryland 23

Sugar Bowl, New Orleans, LA

1935 (Jan.) Tulane 20, Temple 14
1936 TCU 3, LSU 2
1937 Santa Clara 21, LSU 14
1938 Santa Clara 6, LSU 0
1939 TCU 15, Carnegie Tech 7
1940 Texas A&M 14, Tulane 13
1941 Boston Col. 19, Tennessee 13
1942 Fordham 2, Missouri 0
1943 Tennessee 14, Tulsa 7
1944 Georgia Tech 20, Tulsa 18
1945 Duke 29, Alabama 26
1946 Oklahoma A&M 33, St. Mary's 13
1947 Georgia 20, N. Carolina 10
1948 Texas 27, Alabama 7
1949 Oklahoma 14, N. Carolina 6
1950 Oklahoma 35, LSU 0
1951 Kentucky 13, Oklahoma 7
1952 Maryland 28, Tennessee 13
1953 Georgia Tech 24, Mississippi 7
1954 Georgia Tech 42, West Virginia 19
1955 Navy 21, Mississippi 0
1956 Georgia Tech 7, Pittsburgh 0
1957 Baylor 13, Tennessee 7
1958 Mississippi 39, Texas 7
1959 LSU 7, Clemson 0
1960 Mississippi 21, LSU 0
1961 Mississippi 14, Rice 6
1962 Alabama 10, Arkansas 3
1963 Mississippi 17, Arkansas 13
1964 Alabama 12, Mississippi 7
1965 LSU 13, Syracuse 10
1966 Missouri 20, Florida 18
1967 Alabama 34, Nebraska 7
1968 LSU 20, Wyoming 13
1969 Arkansas 16, Georgia 2
1970 Mississippi 27, Arkansas 22
1971 Tennessee 34, Air Force 13
1972 Oklahoma 40, Auburn 22
1972 (Dec.) Oklahoma 14, Penn St. 0
1973 Notre Dame 24, Alabama 23
1974 Nebraska 13, Florida 10
1975 Alabama 13, Penn St. 6
1977 (Jan.) Pittsburgh 27, Georgia 3
1978 Alabama 35, Ohio St. 6
1979 Alabama 14, Penn St. 7
1980 Alabama 24, Arkansas 9
1981 Georgia 17, Notre Dame 10
1982 Pittsburgh 24, Georgia 20
1983 Penn St. 27, Georgia 23
1984 Auburn 9, Michigan 7
1985 Nebraska 28, LSU 10
1986 Tennessee 35, Miami (FL) 7
1987 Nebraska 30, LSU 15
1988 Syracuse 16, Auburn 16
1989 Florida St. 13, Auburn 7
1990 Miami (FL) 33, Alabama 25
1991 Tennessee 23, Virginia 22
1992 Notre Dame 39, Florida 28
1993 Alabama 34, Miami (FL) 13
1994 Florida 41, West Virginia 7
1995 Florida St. 23, Florida 17
1995 (Dec.) Virginia Tech 28, Texas 10
1997 (Jan.) Florida 52, Florida St. 20
1998 Florida St. 31, Ohio St. 14
1999 Ohio St. 24, Texas A&M 14
2000 Florida St. 46, Virginia Tech 29
2001 Miami (FL) 37, Florida 20
2002 LSU 47, Illinois 34

Cotton Bowl, Dallas, TX

1937 (Jan.) TCU 16, Marquette 6
1938 Rice 28, Colorado 14
1939 St. Mary's 20, Texas Tech 13
1940 Clemson 6, Boston Coll. 3
1941 Texas A&M 13, Fordham 12
1942 Alabama 29, Texas A&M 21
1943 Texas 14, Georgia Tech 7
1944 Randolph Field 7, Texas 7
1945 Oklahoma A&M 34, TCU 0
1946 Texas 40, Missouri 27
1947 Arkansas 0, LSU 0
1948 SMU 13, Penn St. 13
1949 SMU 21, Oregon 13
1950 Rice 27, North Carolina 13
1951 Tennessee 20, Texas 14
1952 Kentucky 20, TCU 7
1953 Texas 16, Tennessee 0
1954 Rice 28, Alabama 6
1955 Georgia Tech 14, Arkansas 6
1956 Mississippi 14, TCU 13
1957 TCU 28, Syracuse 27
1958 Navy 20, Rice 7
1959 TCU 0, Air Force 0
1960 Syracuse 23, Texas 14
1961 Duke 7, Arkansas 6
1962 Texas 12, Mississippi 7
1963 LSU 13, Texas 0
1964 Texas 28, Navy 6
1965 Arkansas 10, Nebraska 7
1966 LSU 14, Arkansas 7
1966 (Dec.) Georgia 24, SMU 9
1968 (Jan.) Texas A&M 20, Alabama 16
1969 Texas 36, Tennessee 13
1970 Texas 21, Notre Dame 17
1971 Notre Dame 24, Texas 11
1972 Penn St. 30, Texas 6
1973 Texas 17, Alabama 13
1974 Nebraska 19, Texas 3
1975 Penn St. 41, Baylor 20
1976 Arkansas 31, Georgia 10
1977 Houston 30, Maryland 21
1978 Notre Dame 38, Texas 10
1979 Notre Dame 35, Houston 34
1980 Houston 17, Nebraska 14
1981 Alabama 30, Baylor 2
1982 Texas 14, Alabama 12
1983 SMU 7, Pittsburgh 3
1984 Georgia 10, Texas 9
1985 Boston Coll. 45, Houston 28
1986 Texas A&M 36, Auburn 16
1987 Ohio St. 28, Texas A&M 12
1988 Texas A&M 35, Notre Dame 10
1989 UCLA 17, Arkansas 3
1990 Tennessee 31, Arkansas 27
1991 Miami (FL) 46, Texas 3
1992 Florida St. 10, Texas A&M 2
1993 Notre Dame 28, Texas A&M 3
1994 Notre Dame 24, Texas A&M 21
1995 USC. 55, Texas Tech 14
1996 Colorado 38, Oregon 6
1997 Brigham Young 19, Kansas St. 15
1998 UCLA 29, Texas A&M 23
1999 Texas 38, Mississippi St. 11
2000 Arkansas 27, Texas 6
2001 Kansas St. 35, Tennessee 21
2002 Oklahoma 10, Arkansas 3

Sun Bowl, El Paso, TX (John Hancock Bowl, 1989-93)

1936 (Jan.) Hardin-Simmons 14, New Mexico St. 14
1937 Hardin-Simmons 34, Texas Mines 6
1938 West Virginia 7, Texas Tech 6
1939 Utah 26, New Mexico 0
1940 Catholic U. 0, Arizona St. 0
1941 Western Reserve 26, Arizona St. 13
1942 Tulsa 6, Texas Tech 0
1943 2d Air Force 13, Hardin-Simmons 7
1944 Southwestern (TX) 7, New Mexico 0
1945 Southwestern (TX) 35, Univ. of Mexico 0
1946 New Mexico 34, Denver 24
1947 Cincinnati 18, Virginia Tech 6
1948 Miami (OH) 13, Texas Tech 12
1949 West Virginia 21, Texas Mines 12
1950 Texas Western 33, Georgetown 20
1951 West Texas St. 14, Cincinnati 13
1952 Texas Tech 25, Pacific (CA) 14
1953 Pacific (CA) 26, S. Mississippi 7
1954 Texas Western 37, S. Miss. 14
1955 Texas Western 47, Florida St. 20
1956 Wyoming 21, Texas Tech 14
1957 Geo. Washington 13, TX Western 0
1958 Louisville 34, Drake 20
1958 (Dec.) Wyoming 14, Hardin-Simmons 6
1959 New Mexico St. 28, N. Texas St. 8
1960 New Mexico St. 20, Utah St. 13
1961 Villanova 17, Wichita 9
1962 West Texas St. 15, Ohio U. 14
1963 Oregon 21, SMU 14
1964 Georgia 7, Texas Tech 0
1965 Texas Western 13, TCU 12
1966 Wyoming 28, Florida St. 20
1967 UTEP 14, Mississippi 7
1968 Auburn 34, Arizona 10
1969 Nebraska 45, Georgia 6
1970 Georgia Tech. 17, Texas Tech 9
1971 LSU 33, Iowa St. 15
1972 North Carolina 32, Texas Tech 28
1973 Missouri 34, Auburn 17
1974 Mississippi St. 26, North Carolina 24
1975 Pittsburgh 33, Kansas 19
1977 (Jan.) Texas A&M 37, Florida 14
1977 (Dec.) Stanford 24, LSU 14
1978 Texas 42, Maryland 0
1979 Washington 14, Texas 7
1980 Nebraska 31, Mississippi St. 17
1981 Oklahoma 40, Houston 14
1982 North Carolina 26, Texas 10
1983 Alabama 28, SMU 7
1984 Maryland 28, Tennessee 27
1985 Georgia 13, Arizona 13
1986 Alabama 28, Washington 6
1987 Oklahoma St. 35, West Virginia 33
1988 Alabama 29, Army 28
1989 Pittsburgh 31, Texas A&M 28
1990 Michigan St. 17, USC 16
1991 UCLA 6, Illinois 3
1992 Baylor 20, Arizona 15
1993 Oklahoma 41, Texas Tech 10
1994 Texas 35, North Carolina 31
1995 Iowa 38, Washington 18
1996 Stanford 38, Michigan St. 0
1997 Arizona St. 17, Iowa 7
1998 TCU 28, USC 19
1999 Oregon 24, Minnesota 20
2000 Wisconsin 21, UCLA 20
2001 Washington St. 33, Purdue 27

Fiesta Bowl, Tempe, AZ

1971 (Dec.) Arizona St. 45, Florida St. 38
1972 Arizona St. 49, Missouri 35
1973 Arizona St. 28, Pittsburgh 7
1974 Okla. St. 16, Brigham Young 6
1975 Arizona St. 17, Nebraska 14
1976 Oklahoma 41, Wyoming 7
1977 Penn St. 42, Arizona St. 30
1978 UCLA 10, Arkansas 10
1979 Pittsburgh 16, Arizona 10
1980 Penn St. 31, Ohio St. 19
1982 (Jan.) Penn St. 26, USC 10
1983 Arizona St. 32, Oklahoma 21
1984 Ohio St. 28, Pittsburgh 23
1985 UCLA 39, Miami (FL) 37
1986 Michigan 27, Nebraska 23
1987 Penn St. 14, Miami (FL) 10
1988 Florida St. 31, Nebraska 28
1989 Notre Dame 34, W. Virginia 21
1990 Florida St. 41, Nebraska 17
1991 Louisville 34, Alabama 7
1992 Penn St. 42, Tennessee 17
1993 Syracuse 26, Colorado 22
1994 Arizona 29, Miami (FL) 0
1995 Colorado 41, Notre Dame 24
1996 Nebraska 62, Florida 24
1997 Penn St. 38, Texas 15
1997 (Dec.) Kansas St. 35, Syracuse 18
1999 (Jan.) Tennessee 23, Florida St. 16
2000 Nebraska 31, Tennessee 21
2001 Oregon St. 41, Notre Dame 9
2002 Oregon 38, Colorado 16

Gator Bowl, Jacksonville, FL

1946 (Jan.) Wake Forest 26, S. Carolina 14
1947 Oklahoma 34, N. Carolina St. 13
1948 Maryland 20, Georgia 20
1949 Clemson 24, Missouri 23
1950 Maryland 20, Missouri 7
1951 Wyoming 20, Washington & Lee 7
1952 Miami (FL) 14, Clemson 0
1953 Florida 14, Tulsa 13
1954 Texas Tech 35, Auburn 13
1954 (Dec.) Auburn 33, Baylor 13
1955 Vanderbilt 25, Auburn 13
1956 Georgia Tech 21, Pittsburgh 14
1957 Tennessee 3, Texas A&M 0
1958 Mississippi 7, Florida 3
1960 (Jan.) Arkansas 14, Georgia Tech 7
1960 (Dec.) Florida 13, Baylor 12
1961 Penn St. 30, Georgia Tech 15
1962 Florida 17, Penn St. 7
1963 N. Carolina 35, Air Force 0
1965 (Jan.) Florida St. 36, Okla.19
1965 (Dec.) GA Tech 31, Texas Tech 21
1966 Tennessee 18, Syracuse 12
1967 Penn St. 17, Florida St. 17
1968 Missouri 35, Alabama 10
1969 Florida 14, Tennessee 13
1971 (Jan.) Auburn 35, Mississippi 28
1971 (Dec.) Georgia 7, N. Carolina 3
1972 Auburn 24, Colorado 3
1973 Texas Tech 28, Tennessee 19
1974 Auburn 27, Texas 3
1975 Maryland 13, Florida 0
1976 Notre Dame 20, Penn St. 9
1977 Pittsburgh 34, Clemson 3
1978 Clemson 17, Ohio St. 15
1979 N. Carolina 17, Michigan 15
1980 Pittsburgh 37, S. Carolina 9
1981 N. Carolina 31, Arkansas 27
1982 Florida St. 31, West Virginia 12
1983 Florida 14, Iowa 6
1984 Oklahoma St. 21, S. Carolina 14
1985 Florida St. 34, Oklahoma St. 23
1986 Clemson 27, Stanford 21
1987 LSU 30, S. Carolina 13
1989 (Jan.) Georgia 34, Michigan St. 27
1989 (Dec.) Clemson 27, W. Virginia 7
1991 (Jan.) Michigan 35, Mississippi 3
1991 (Dec.) Oklahoma 48, Virginia 14
1992 Florida 27, N. Carolina St. 10
1993 Alabama 24, N. Carolina 10
1994 Tennessee 45, Virginia Tech 23
1996 (Jan.) Syracuse 41, Clemson 0
1997 N. Carolina 20, W. Virginia 13
1998 N. Carolina 42, Virginia Tech 3
1999 Georgia Tech 35, Notre Dame 28
2000 Miami (FL) 28, Georgia Tech 13
2001 Virginia Tech 41, Clemson 20
2002 Florida St. 30, Virginia Tech 17

Liberty Bowl, Memphis, TN

1959 (Dec.) Penn St. 7, Alabama 0
1960 Penn St. 41, Oregon 12
1961 Syracuse 15, Miami (FL) 14
1962 Oregon St. 6, Villanova 0
1963 Mississippi St. 16, N. Carolina St. 12
1964 Utah 32, West Virginia 6
1965 Mississippi 13, Auburn 7
1966 Miami (FL) 14, Virginia Tech 7
1967 N. Carolina St. 14, Georgia 7
1968 Mississippi 34, Virginia Tech 17
1969 Colorado 47, Alabama 33
1970 Tulane 17, Colorado 3
1971 Tennessee 14, Arkansas 13
1972 Georgia Tech 31, Iowa St. 30
1973 N. Carolina St. 31, Kansas 18
1974 Tennessee 7, Maryland 3
1975 USC 20, Texas A&M 0
1976 Alabama 36, UCLA 6
1977 Nebraska 21, N. Carolina 17
1978 Missouri 20, LSU 15
1979 Penn St. 9, Tulane 6
1980 Purdue 28, Missouri 25
1981 Ohio St. 31, Navy 28
1982 Alabama 21, Illinois 15
1983 Notre Dame 19, Boston Coll. 18
1984 Auburn 21, Arkansas 15
1985 Baylor 21, LSU 7
1986 Tennessee 21, Minnesota 14
1987 Georgia 20, Arkansas 17
1988 Indiana 34, S. Carolina 10
1989 Mississippi 42, Air Force 29
1990 Air Force 23, Ohio St. 11
1991 Air Force 38, Mississippi St. 15
1992 Mississippi 13, Air Force 0
1993 Louisville 18, Michigan St. 7
1994 Illinois 30, East Carolina 0
1995 East Carolina 19, Stanford 13
1996 Syracuse 30, Houston 17
1997 So. Mississippi 41, Pittsburgh 7
1998 Tulane 41, Brigham Young 27
1999 So. Mississippi 23, Colorado St. 17
2000 Colorado St. 22, Louisville 17
2001 Louisville 28, BYU 10

Florida Citrus Bowl, Orlando, FL (Tangerine Bowl until 1983)

1947 (Jan.) Catawba 31, Maryville 6
1948 Catawba 7, Marshall 0
1949 Murray St. 21, Sul Ross St. 21
1950 St. Vincent 7, Emory & Henry 6
1951 Morris Harvey 35, Emory & Henry 14
1952 Stetson 35, Arkansas St. 20
1953 East Texas St. 33, Tenn. Tech 0
1954 East Texas St. 7, Arkansas St. 7
1955 Neb.-Omaha 7, E. Kentucky 6
1956 Juniata 6, Missouri Valley 6
1957 West Texas St. 20, So. Miss. 13
1958 East Texas St. 10, So. Miss. 9
1958 (Dec.) East Texas St. 26, Missouri Valley 7
1960 (Jan.) Middle Tennessee 21, Presbyterian 12
1960 (Dec.) Citadel 27, Tenn. Tech 0
1961 Lamar 21, Middle Tennessee 14
1962 Houston 49, Miami (OH) 21
1963 Western Ky. 27, Coast Guard 0
1964 E. Carolina 14, Massachusetts 13
1965 E. Carolina 31, Maine 0
1966 Morgan St. 14, West Chester 6
1967 Tenn.-Martin 25, West Chester 8
1968 Richmond 49, Ohio U. 42
1969 Toledo 56, Davidson 33
1970 Toledo 40, William & Mary 12
1971 Toledo 28, Richmond 3
1972 Tampa 21, Kent St. 18
1973 Miami (OH) 16, Florida 7
1974 Miami (OH) 21, Georgia 10
1975 Miami (OH) 20, S. Carolina 7
1976 Okla. St. 49, Brigham Young 21
1977 Florida St. 40, Texas Tech 17
1978 N. Carolina St. 30, Pittsburgh 17
1979 LSU 34, Wake Forest 10
1980 Florida 35, Maryland 20
1981 Missouri 19, So. Mississippi 17
1982 Auburn 33, Boston College 26
1983 Tennessee 30, Maryland 23
1984 Georgia 17, Florida St. 17
1985 Ohio St. 10, Brigham Young 7
1987 (Jan.) Auburn 16, USC 7
1988 Clemson 35, Penn St. 10
1989 Clemson 13, Oklahoma 6
1990 Illinois 31, Virginia 21
1991 Georgia Tech 45, Nebraska 21
1992 California 37, Clemson 13
1993 Georgia 21, Ohio St. 14
1994 Penn St. 31, Tennessee 13
1995 Alabama 24, Ohio St. 17
1996 Tennessee 20, Ohio St. 14
1997 Tennessee 48, Northwestern 28
1998 Florida 21, Penn St. 6
1999 Michigan 45, Arkansas 31
2000 Michigan St. 37, Florida 34
2001 Michigan 31, Auburn 28
2002 Tennessee 45, Michigan 17

Peach Bowl, Atlanta, GA

1968 (Dec.) LSU 31, Florida St. 27
1969 W. Virginia 14, S. Carolina 3
1970 Arizona St. 48, N. Carolina 26
1971 Mississippi 41, Georgia Tech 18
1972 N. Carolina St. 49, W. Virginia 13
1973 Georgia 17, Maryland 16
1974 Vanderbilt 6, Texas Tech 6
1975 W. Virginia 13, N. Carolina St. 10
1976 Kentucky 21, N. Carolina 0
1977 N. Carolina St. 24, Iowa St. 14
1978 Purdue 41, Georgia Tech. 21
1979 Baylor 24, Clemson 18
1981 (Jan.) Miami (FL) 20, Virginia Tech 10
1981 (Dec.) W. Virginia 26, Florida 6
1982 Iowa 28, Tennessee 22
1983 Florida St. 28, N. Carolina 3
1984 Virginia 27, Purdue 22
1985 Army 31, Illinois 29
1986 Va. Tech 25, N. Carolina St. 24
1988 (Jan.) Tennessee 28, Indiana 22
1988 (Dec.) N. Carolina St. 28, Iowa 23
1989 Syracuse 19, Georgia 18
1990 Auburn 27, Indiana 23
1992 (Jan.) E. Carolina 37, NC St. 34
1993 N. Carolina 21, Mississippi St. 17
1993 (Dec.) Clemson 14, Kentucky 13
1995 (Jan.) N. Carolina St. 28, Miss. St. 24
1995 (Dec.) Virginia 34, Georgia 27
1996 LSU 10, Clemson 7
1998 (Jan.) Auburn 21, Clemson 17
1998 (Dec.) Georgia 35, Virginia 33
1999 Mississippi St. 27, Clemson 7
2000 LSU 28, Georgia Tech 14
2001 North Carolina 16, Auburn 10

Other Bowl Results, Late 2001- Early 2002

Alamo Bowl, San Antonio, TX: Iowa 19, Texas Tech 16
Galleryfurniture.com Bowl, Houston, TX: Texas A&M 28, Texas Christian 9
GMAC Bowl, Mobile, AL: Marshall 64, East Carolina 61
Holiday Bowl, San Diego, CA: Texas 47, Washington 43
Humanitarian Bowl, Boise, ID: Clemson 49, La. Tech 24
Independence Bowl, Shreveport, LA: Alabama 14, Iowa St. 13
Insight.com Bowl, Phoenix, AZ: Syracuse 26, Kansas St. 3
Las Vegas Bowl, Las Vegas, NV: Utah 10, USC 6
Motor City Bowl, Pontiac, MI: Toledo 23, Cincinnati 16
Music City Bowl, Nashville, TN: Boston Col. 20, Georgia 16
New Orleans Bowl, New Orleans, LA: Colorado St. 45, North Texas 20
Outback Bowl, Tampa, FL: South Carolina 31, Ohio St. 28
Seattle Bowl, Seattle, WA: Georgia Tech 24, Stanford 14
Silicon Valley Bowl, San Jose, CA: Michigan St. 44, Fresno St. 35
Tangerine Bowl, Orlando, FL: Pittsburgh 34, NC St. 19

All-Time NCAA Division I-A Statistical Leaders

(at end of 2000 season)

Career Rushing Yards

Player, team	Yrs	Carries	Yds	Avg
Ron Dayne, Wisconsin	1996-99	1,115	6,397	5.74
Ricky Williams, Texas	1995-98	1,011	6,279	6.21
Tony Dorsett, Pittsburgh	1973-76	1,074	6,082	5.66
Charles White, USC	1976-79	1,023	5,598	5.47
Travis Prentice, Miami (OH)	1996-99	1,138	5,596	4.92

Career Rushing Yard/Game (min. 2,500 yds.)

Player, team	Yrs	Carries	Yds	Avg/ Game
Ed Marinaro, Cornell	1969-71	918	4,715	174.6
O.J. Simpson, USC	1967-68	621	3,124	164.4
Herschel Walker, Georgia	1980-82	994	5,259	159.4
LeShon Johnson, N. Illinois	1992-93	592	3,314	150.6
Ron Dayne, Wisconsin	1996-99	1,115	6,397	148.8

Career Passing Yards

Player, team	Yrs	Comp/Att	Yds
Ty Detmer, BYU	1988-91	958/1,530	15,031
Tim Rattay, Louisiana Tech	1997-99	1,015/1,552	12,746
Chris Redman, Louisville	1996-99	1,031/1,679	12,541
Todd Santos, San Diego St.	1984-87	910/1,484	11,425
Tim Lester, Western Mich.	1996-99	875/1,507	11,299

Career Receiving Yards

Player, team	Yrs	Rec	Yds	Avg
Trevor Insley, Nevada	1996-99	298	5,005	16.8
Marcus Harris, Wyoming	1993-96	259	4,518	17.4
Ryan Yarborough, Wyoming	1990-93	229	4,357	19.0
Troy Edwards, Louisiana Tech	1996-98	280	4,352	15.5
Aaron Turner, Pacific (CA)	1989-92	266	4,345	16.3

Selected College Division I Football Teams in 2001

(2001 record does not include bowl games or Division I-AA playoff games; coaches at the start of 2002 season)

Team	Nickname	Team colors	Conference	Coach	2001 record (W-L)
Air Force	Falcons	Blue & silver	Mountain West	Fisher DeBerry	6-6
Akron	Zips	Blue & gold	Mid-American	Lee Owens	4-7
Alabama	Crimson Tide	Crimson & white	Southeastern	Dennis Franchione	7-5
Arizona	Wildcats	Cardinal & navy	Pacific Ten	John Mackovic	5-6
Arizona State	Sun Devils	Maroon & gold	Pacific Ten	Dirk Koetter	4-7
Arkansas	Razorbacks	Cardinal & white	Southeastern	Houston Nutt	7-5
Arkansas State	Indians	Scarlet & black	Big West	Joe Hollis	2-9
Army	Cadets, Black Knights	Black, gold, gray	Conference USA	Todd Berry	3-8
Auburn	Tigers	Burnt orange & navy	Southeastern	Tommy Tuberville	7-5
Ball State	Cardinals	Cardinal & white	Mid-American	Bill Lynch	5-6
Baylor	Bears	Green & gold	Big Twelve	Kevin Steele	3-8
Boston College	Eagles	Maroon & gold	Big East	Tom O'Brien	8-4
Bowling Green	Falcons	Orange & brown	Mid-American	Urban Meyer	8-3
Brigham Young (BYU)	Cougars	Royal blue, white, tan	Mountain West	Gary Crowton	12-2
Brown	Bears	Brown, cardinal, white	Ivy League	Phil Estes	6-3
California	Golden Bears	Blue & gold	Pacific Ten	Jeff Tedford	1-10
Central Michigan	Chippewas	Maroon & gold	Mid-American	Mike DeBord	3-8
Cincinnati	Bearcats	Red & black	Conference USA	Rick Minter	7-5
Citadel	Bulldogs	Blue & white	Southern	Ellis Johnson	3-7
Clemson	Tigers	Purple & orange	Atlantic Coast	Tommy Bowden	6-5
Colgate	Red Raiders	Maroon, gray, & white	Patriot League	Dick Biddle	7-3
Colorado	Buffaloes	Silver, gold, & black	Big Twelve	Gary Barnett	10-3
Colorado State	Rams	Green & gold	Mountain West	Sonny Lubick	7-5
Columbia	Lions	Columbia blue & white	Ivy League	Ray Tellier	3-7
Connecticut	Huskies	Blue & white	Independent	Randy Edsall	2-9
Cornell	Big Red	Carnelian & white	Ivy League	Tim Pendergast	2-7
Dartmouth	Big Green	Dartmouth green & white	Ivy League	John Lyons	1-8
Delaware	Fightin' Blue Hens	Blue & gold	Atlantic Ten	Harold Raymond	4-6
Delaware State	Hornets	Red & blue	Mid-Eastern Athletic	Ben Blacknall	5-6
Duke	Blue Devils	Royal blue & white	Atlantic Coast	Carl Franks	0-11
East Carolina	Pirates	Purple & gold	Conference USA	Steve Logan	6-6
East Tennessee State	Buccaneers	Blue & gold	Southern	Paul Hamilton	6-5
Eastern Illinois	Panthers	Blue & gray	Ohio Valley	Bob Spoo	9-2
Eastern Kentucky	Colonels	Maroon & white	Ohio Valley	Roy Kidd	8-2
Eastern Michigan	Eagles	Dark green & white	Mid-American	Jeff Woodruff	2-9
Eastern Washington	Eagles	Red & white	Big Sky	Paul Wulff	7-4
Florida	Gators	Orange & blue	Southeastern	Ron Zook	10-2
Florida A&M	Rattlers	Orange & green	Mid-Eastern Athletic	Billy Joe	7-4
Florida State	Seminoles	Garnet & gold	Atlantic Coast	Bobby Bowden	8-4
Fresno State	Bulldogs	Cardinal & blue	Western Athletic	Pat Hill	12-2
Furman	Paladins	Purple & white	Southern	Bobby Johnson	12-3
Georgia	Bulldogs	Red & black	Southeastern	Mark Richt	8-4
Georgia Southern	Eagles	Blue & white	Southern	Paul Johnson	12-2
Georgia Tech	Yellow Jackets	Old gold & white	Atlantic Coast	Chan Gailey	8-5
Grambling State	Tigers	Black & gold	Southwestern	Doug Williams	10-1
Harvard	Crimson	Crimson, black, white	Ivy League	Tim Murphy	9-0
Holy Cross	Crusaders	Royal purple	Patriot League	Dan Allen	4-6
Houston	Cougars	Scarlet & white	Conference USA	Dana Dimel	0-11
Howard	Bison	Blue, white & red	Mid-Eastern Athletic	Steve Wilson	2-9
Idaho	Vandals	Silver & gold	Big West	Tom Cable	1-10
Idaho State	Bengals	Orange & black	Big Sky	Larry Lewis	4-7
Illinois	Fighting Illini	Orange & blue	Big Ten	Ron Turner	10-2
Illinois State	Redbirds	Red & white	Gateway	Denver Johnson	2-9

Team	Nickname	Team colors	Conference	Coach	2001 record (W-L)
Indiana	Hoosiers	Cream & crimson	Big Ten	Gerry DiNardo	5-6
Indiana State	Sycamores	Blue & white	Gateway	Tim McGuire	3-8
Iowa	Hawkeyes	Old gold & black	Big Ten	Kirk Ferentz	7-5
Iowa State	Cyclones	Cardinal & gold	Big Twelve	Dan McCarney	7-5
Jackson State	Tigers	Blue & white	Southwestern	Robert Hughes	7-4
James Madison	Dukes	Purple & gold	Atlantic Ten	Mickey Matthews	2-9
Kansas	Jayhawks	Crimson & blue	Big Twelve	Mark Mangino	3-8
Kansas State	Wildcats	Purple & white	Big Twelve	Bill Snyder	6-6
Kent State	Golden Flashes	Navy blue & gold	Mid-American	Dean Pees	6-5
Kentucky	Wildcats	Blue & white	Southeastern	Guy Morriss	2-9
Lafayette	Leopards	Maroon & white	Patriot League	Frank Tavani	2-8
Lehigh	Mountain Hawks	Brown & white	Patriot League	Pete Lembo	11-1
Liberty	Flames	Red, white, blue	Independent	Ken Karcher	3-8
Louisiana-Lafayette	Ragin' Cajuns	Vermilion & white	Independent	Rickey Bustle	3-8
Louisiana-Monroe	Indians	Maroon & gold	Independent	Bobby Keasler	2-9
Louisiana State (LSU)	Fighting Tigers	Purple & gold	Southeastern	Nick Saban	10-3
Louisiana Tech	Bulldogs	Red & blue	Independent	Jack Bicknell III	7-4
Louisville	Cardinals	Red, black, white	Conference USA	John L. Smith	11-2
Maine	Black Bears	Blue & white	Atlantic Ten	Jack Cosgrove	9-3
Marshall	Thundering Herd	Green & white	Mid-American	Bob Pruett	11-2
Maryland	Terrapins	Red, white, black, gold	Atlantic Coast	Ralph Friedgen	10-2
Massachusetts	Minutemen	Maroon & white	Atlantic Ten	Mark Whipple	3-8
McNeese State	Cowboys	Blue & gold	Southland	Tommy Tate	8-4
Memphis	Tigers	Blue & gray	Conference USA	Tommy West	5-6
Miami (Florida)	Hurricanes	Orange, green, white	Big East	Larry Coker	12-0
Miami (Ohio)	RedHawks	Red & white	Mid-American	Terry Hoeppner	7-5
Michigan	Wolverines	Maize & blue	Big Ten	Lloyd Carr	8-3
Michigan State	Spartans	Green & white	Big Ten	Bobby Williams	6-6
Middle Tennessee St.	Blue Raiders	Blue & white	Independent	Andy McCollum	8-3
Minnesota	Golden Gophers	Maroon & gold	Big Ten	Glen Mason	4-7
Mississippi	Rebels	Cardinal red & navy	Southeastern	David Cutcliffe	7-4
Mississippi State	Bulldogs	Maroon & white	Southeastern	Jackie Sherrill	3-8
Mississippi Valley	Delta Devils	Green & white	Southwestern	LaTraia Jones	0-11
Missouri	Tigers	Old gold & black	Big Twelve	Gary Pinkel	4-7
Montana	Grizzlies	Copper, silver, gold	Big Sky	Joe Glenn	14-1
Montana State	Bobcats	Blue & gold	Big Sky	Mike Kramer	5-6
Morehead State	Eagles	Blue & gold	Independent	Matt Ballard	6-5
Morgan State	Bears	Blue & orange	Mid-Eastern Athletic	Stanley Mitchell	2-9
Murray State	Racers	Blue & gold	Ohio Valley	Joe Pannunzio	4-6
Navy	Midshipmen	Navy blue & gold	Independent	Paul Johnson	0-10
Nebraska	Cornhuskers	Scarlet & cream	Big Twelve	Frank Solich	11-2
Nevada	Wolf Pack	Silver & blue	Western Athletic	Chris Tormey	3-8
Nev.-Las Vegas (UNLV)	Runnin' Rebels	Scarlet & gray	Mountain West	John Robinson	4-7
New Hampshire	Wildcats	Blue & white	Atlantic Ten	Sean McDonnell	4-7
New Mexico	Lobos	Cherry & silver	Mountain West	Rocky Long	6-5
New Mexico State	Aggies	Crimson & white	Big West	Tony Samuel	5-7
Nicholls St.	Colonels	Red & gray	Southland	Daryl Daye	3-8
North Carolina	Tar Heels	Carolina blue & white	Atlantic Coast	John Bunting	8-5
North Carolina A & T	Aggies	Blue & gold	Mid-Eastern Athletic	Bill Hayes	8-3
North Carolina State	Wolfpack	Red & white	Atlantic Coast	Chuck Amato	7-5
North Texas	Mean Green Eagles	Green & white	Big West	Darrell Dickey	5-7
Northeastern	Huskies	Red & black	Atlantic Ten	Don Brown	5-6
Northern Arizona	Lumberjacks	Blue & gold	Big Sky	Jerome Souers	8-4
Northern Illinois	Huskies	Cardinal & black	Mid-American	Joe Novak	6-5
Northern Iowa	Panthers	Purple & old gold	Gateway	Mark Farley	11-3
Northwestern	Wildcats	Purple & white	Big Ten	Randy Walker	4-7
Northwestern State	Demons	Purple, white, & burnt orange	Southland	Steve Roberts	8-4
Notre Dame	Fighting Irish	Gold & blue	Independent	Tyrone Willingham	5-6
Ohio	Bobcats	Hunter green & white	Mid-American	Brian Knorr	1-10
Ohio State	Buckeyes	Scarlet & gray	Big Ten	Jim Tressel	7-5
Oklahoma	Sooners	Crimson & cream	Big Twelve	Bob Stoops	11-2
Oklahoma State	Cowboys	Orange & black	Big Twelve	Les Miles	4-7
Oregon	Ducks	Green & yellow	Pacific Ten	Mike Bellotti	11-1
Oregon State	Beavers	Orange & black	Pacific Ten	Dennis Erickson	5-6
Penn State	Nittany Lions	Blue & white	Big Ten	Joe Paterno	5-6
Pennsylvania	Quakers	Red & blue	Ivy League	Al Bagnoli	8-1
Pittsburgh	Panthers	Blue & gold	Big East	Walt Harris	7-5
Princeton	Tigers	Orange & black	Ivy League	Roger Hughes	3-6
Purdue	Boilermakers	Old gold & black	Big Ten	Joe Tiller	6-6
Rhode Island	Rams	Light & dark blue, white	Atlantic Ten	Tim Stowers	8-3
Rice	Owls	Blue & gray	Western Athletic	Ken Hatfield	8-4
Richmond	Spiders	Red & white	Atlantic Ten	Jim Reid	3-8
Rutgers	Scarlet Knights	Scarlet	Big East	Greg Schiano	2-9
Sam Houston State	Bearkats	Orange & white	Southland	Ron Randleman	10-3
Samford	Bulldogs	Crimson & blue	Independent	Pete Hurt	5-5
San Diego State	Aztecs	Scarlet & black	Mountain West	Tom Craft	3-8
San Jose State	Spartans	Gold, white, blue	Western Athletic	Fitz Hill	3-9
South Carolina	Fighting Gamecocks	Garnet & black	Southeastern	Lou Holtz	9-3
South Carolina State	Bulldogs	Garnet & blue	Mid-Eastern Athletic	Willie E. Jeffries	6-5
SE Missouri State	Indians	Red & white	Ohio Valley	Tim Billings	4-7
Southern California (USC)	Trojans	Cardinal & gold	Pacific Ten	Pete Carroll	6-6
Southern Illinois	Salukis	Maroon & white	Gateway	Jerry Kill	1-11
Southern Methodist (SMU)	Mustangs	Red & blue	Western Athletic	Mike Cavan	4-7
Southern Mississippi	Golden Eagles	Black & gold	Conference USA	Jeff Bower	6-5
SW Missouri State	Bears	Maroon & white	Gateway	Randy Ball	6-5
SW Texas State	Bobcats	Maroon & gold	Southland	Bob DeBesse	4-7
Stanford	Cardinal	Cardinal & white	Pacific Ten	Buddy Teevens	9-3
Stephen F. Austin	Lumberjacks	Purple & white	Southland	Mike Santiago	6-5

Team	Nickname	Team colors	Conference	Coach	2001 record (W-L)
Syracuse	Orangemen	Orange	Big East	Paul Pasqualoni	10-3
Temple	Owls	Cherry & white	Big East	Bobby Wallace	4-7
Tennessee	Volunteers	Orange & white	Southeastern	Phillip Fulmer	10-2
Tennessee-Chattanooga	Mocs	Navy blue & gold	Southern	Donnie Kirkpatrick	3-8
Tennessee-Martin	Skyhawks	Orange, white, blue	Ohio Valley	Sam McCorkle	1-10
Tennessee State	Tigers	Royal blue & white	Ohio Valley	James Reese	8-3
Tennessee Tech	Golden Eagles	Purple & gold	Ohio Valley	Mike Hennigan	7-3
Texas	Longhorns	Burnt orange & white	Big Twelve	Mack Brown	11-2
Texas A & M	Aggies	Maroon & white	Big Twelve	R. C. Slocum	8-4
Texas Christian (TCU)	Horned Frogs	Purple & white	Western Athletic	Gary Patterson	6-6
Texas Southern	Tigers	Maroon & gray	Southwestern	Bill Thomas	3-7
Texas Tech	Red Raiders	Scarlet & black	Big Twelve	Mike Leach	7-5
Toledo	Rockets	Blue, gold, crimson	Mid-American	Tom Amstutz	9-2
Troy State	Trojans	Cardinal & black	Southland	Larry Blakeney	7-4
Tulane	Green Wave	Olive green & sky blue	Conference USA	Chris Scelfo	3-9
Tulsa	Golden Hurricane	Blue, gold, crimson	Western Athletic	Keith Burns	1-10
UCLA	Bruins	Blue & gold	Pacific Ten	Bob Toledo	7-4
Utah	Utes	Crimson & white	Mountain West	Ron McBride	8-4
Utah State	Aggies	Navy blue & white	Big West	Mick Dennehy	4-7
UTEP (Texas-El Paso)	Miners	Orange, blue, silver	Western Athletic	Gary Nord	2-9
Vanderbilt	Commodores	Black & gold	Southeastern	Bobby Johnson	2-9
Villanova	Wildcats	Blue & white	Atlantic Ten	Andy Talley	8-3
Virginia	Cavaliers	Orange & blue	Atlantic Coast	Al Groh	5-7
Virginia Military Inst. (VMI)	Keydets	Red, white, yellow	Southern	Cal McCombs	1-10
Virginia Tech	Gobblers, Hokies	Orange & maroon	Big East	Frank Beamer	8-4
Wake Forest	Demon Deacons	Old gold & black	Atlantic Coast	Jim Grobe	6-5
Washington	Huskies	Purple & gold	Pacific Ten	Rick Neuheisel	8-4
Washington State	Cougars	Crimson & gray	Pacific Ten	Mike Price	10-2
Weber State	Wildcats	Royal purple & white	Big Sky	Jerry Graybeal	3-8
West Virginia	Mountaineers	Old gold & blue	Big East	Rich Rodriquez	3-8
Western Carolina	Catamounts	Purple & gold	Southern	Bill Bleil	7-4
Western Illinois	Leathernecks	Purple & gold	Gateway	Don Patterson	5-5
Western Kentucky	Hilltoppers	Red & white	Ohio Valley	Jack Harbaugh	8-4
Western Michigan	Broncos	Brown & gold	Mid-American	Gary Darnell	5-6
William & Mary	Tribe	Green, gold, silver	Atlantic Ten	Jimmye Laycock	8-4
Wisconsin	Badgers	Cardinal & white	Big Ten	Barry Alvarez	5-7
Wyoming	Cowboys	Brown & gold	Mountain West	Vic Koenning	2-9
Yale	Bulldogs, Elis	Yale blue & white	Ivy League	Jack Siedlecki	3-6
Youngstown State	Penguins	Red & white	Gateway	Jon Heacock	8-3

Heisman Trophy Winners

Awarded annually to the nation's outstanding college football player by the Downtown Athletic Club.

1935 Jay Berwanger, Chicago, HB
1936 Larry Kelley, Yale, E
1937 Clinton Frank, Yale, HB
1938 David O'Brien, Texas Christian, QB
1939 Nile Kinnick, Iowa, HB
1940 Tom Harmon, Michigan, HB
1941 Bruce Smith, Minnesota, HB
1942 Frank Sinkwich, Georgia, HB
1943 Angelo Bertelli, Notre Dame, QB
1944 Leslie Horvath, Ohio St., QB
1945 Felix Blanchard, Army, FB
1946 Glenn Davis, Army, HB
1947 John Lujack, Notre Dame, QB
1948 Doak Walker, SMU, HB
1949 Leon Hart, Notre Dame, E
1950 Vic Janowicz, Ohio St., HB
1951 Richard Kazmaier, Princeton, HB
1952 Billy Vessels, Oklahoma, HB
1953 John Lattner, Notre Dame, HB
1954 Alan Ameche, Wisconsin, FB
1955 Howard Cassady, Ohio St., HB
1956 Paul Hornung, Notre Dame, QB
1957 John Crow, Texas A & M, HB
1958 Pete Dawkins, Army, HB
1959 Billy Cannon, LSU, HB
1960 Joe Bellino, Navy, HB
1961 Ernest Davis, Syracuse, HB
1962 Terry Baker, Oregon St., QB
1963 Roger Staubach, Navy, QB
1964 John Huarte, Notre Dame, QB
1965 Mike Garrett, USC, HB
1966 Steve Spurrier, Florida, QB
1967 Gary Beban, UCLA, QB
1968 O. J. Simpson, USC, RB
1969 Steve Owens, Oklahoma, RB
1970 Jim Plunkett, Stanford, QB
1971 Pat Sullivan, Auburn, QB
1972 Johnny Rodgers, Nebraska, RB-WR
1973 John Cappelletti, Penn St., RB
1974 Archie Griffin, Ohio St., RB
1975 Archie Griffin, Ohio St., RB
1976 Tony Dorsett, Pittsburgh, RB
1977 Earl Campbell, Texas, RB
1978 Billy Sims, Oklahoma, RB
1979 Charles White, USC, RB
1980 George Rogers, S. Carolina, RB
1981 Marcus Allen, USC, RB
1982 Herschel Walker, Georgia, RB
1983 Mike Rozier, Nebraska, RB
1984 Doug Flutie, Boston College, QB
1985 Bo Jackson, Auburn, RB
1986 Vinny Testaverde, Miami, QB
1987 Tim Brown, Notre Dame, WR
1988 Barry Sanders, Oklahoma St., RB
1989 Andre Ware, Houston, QB
1990 Ty Detmer, BYU, QB
1991 Desmond Howard, Michigan, WR
1992 Gino Torretta, Miami, QB
1993 Charlie Ward, Florida St., QB
1994 Rashaan Salaam, Colorado, RB
1995 Eddie George, Ohio St., RB
1996 Danny Wuerffel, Florida, QB
1997 Charles Woodson, Michigan, CB
1998 Ricky Williams, Texas, RB
1999 Ron Dayne, Wisconsin, RB
2000 Chris Weinke, Florida St., QB
2001 Eric Crouch, Nebraska, QB

Outland Award Winners

Honoring the outstanding interior lineman selected by the Football Writers Association of America.

1946 George Connor, Notre Dame, T
1947 Joe Steffy, Army, G
1948 Bill Fischer, Notre Dame, G
1949 Ed Bagdon, Michigan St., G
1950 Bob Gain, Kentucky, T
1951 Jim Weatherall, Oklahoma, T
1952 Dick Modzelewski, Maryland, T
1953 J. D. Roberts, Oklahoma, G
1954 Bill Brooks, Arkansas, G
1955 Calvin Jones, Iowa, G
1956 Jim Parker, Ohio St., G
1957 Alex Karras, Iowa, T
1958 Zeke Smith, Auburn, G
1959 Mike McGee, Duke, T
1960 Tom Brown, Minnesota, G
1961 Merlin Olsen, Utah St., T
1962 Bobby Bell, Minnesota, T
1963 Scott Appleton, Texas, T
1964 Steve Delong, Tennessee, T
1965 Tommy Nobis, Texas, G
1966 Loyd Phillips, Arkansas, T
1967 Ron Yary, Southern Cal, T
1968 Bill Stanfill, Georgia, T
1969 Mike Reid, Penn St., DT
1970 Jim Stillwagon, Ohio St., MG
1971 Larry Jacobson, Nebraska, DT
1972 Rich Glover, Nebraska, MG
1973 John Hicks, Ohio St., OT
1974 Randy White, Maryland, DE
1975 Lee Roy Selmon, Oklahoma, DT
1976 Ross Browner, Notre Dame, DE
1977 Brad Shearer, Texas, DT
1978 Greg Roberts, Oklahoma, G
1979 Jim Ritcher, North Carolina St., C
1980 Mark May, Pittsburgh, OT
1981 Dave Rimington, Nebraska, C
1982 Dave Rimington, Nebraska, C
1983 Dean Steinkuhler, Nebraska, G
1984 Bruce Smith, Virginia Tech, DT
1985 Mike Ruth, Boston College, NG
1986 Jason Buck, BYU, DT
1987 Chad Hennings, Air Force, DT
1988 Tracy Rocker, Auburn, DT
1989 Mohammed Elewonibi, BYU, G
1990 Russell Maryland, Miami (FL), DT
1991 Steve Emtman, Washington, DT
1992 Will Shields, Nebraska, G
1993 Rob Waldrop, Arizona, NG
1994 Zach Wiegert, Nebraska, OT
1995 Jonathan Ogden, UCLA, OT
1996 Orlando Pace, Ohio St., OT
1997 Aaron Taylor, Nebraska, OT
1998 Kris Farris, UCLA, OT
1999 Chris Samuels, Alabama, OT
2000 John Henderson, Tennessee, DT
2001 Bryant McKinnie, Miami (FL), OT

All-Time Division I-A Percentage Leaders

(Classified as Division I-A for the last 10 years; record includes bowl games; ties computed as half won and half lost)

	Years	Won	Lost	T	Pct.	Bowl Games** W	L	T
Notre Dame	113	781	247	42	.0.750	13	11	0
Michigan	122	813	266	36	.0.745	17	16	0
Alabama	107	744	281	43	.0.717	29	19	3
Nebraska	112	764	301	40	.0.710	20	20	0
Oklahoma	107	713	280	33	.0.707	22	12	1
Texas	109	754	304	53	.0.706	19	20	2
Ohio State	112	731	292	53	.0.704	14	19	0
Tennessee	105	718	294	41	.0.699	23	19	0
Penn St.	115	744	318	52	.0.693	23	11	2
USC	109	684	294	54	.0.689	25	15	0
Florida St.*	55	400	189	17	.0.674	18	9	2
Washington*	112	625	340	44	.0.640	14	13	1
Miami (OH)*	113	604	337	50	.0.636	5	2	0

	Years	Won	Lost	T	Pct.	Bowl Games** W	L	T
Georgia*	108	649	365	54	.0.633	19	15	3
Miami (FL)*	75	484	282	36	.0.629	15	11	1
LSU	108	628	363	36	.0.628	16	16	1
Arizona St.	89	494	297	24	.0.621	10	8	1
C. Michigan*	101	515	309	47	.0.620	0	2	0
Auburn*	109	617	370	47	.0.619	14	12	2
Florida	95	574	349	40	.0.617	14	15	0
Colorado	112	621	379	51	.0.617	11	13	0
Army	112	621	382	19	.0.613	2	2	0
Texas A&M	107	616	390	48	.0.607	13	14	0
Syracuse	112	648	414	49	.0.605	12	8	1
UCLA	83	491	318	37	.0.602	11	11	1

*Includes games that were forfeited or changed by action of NCAA Council and/or Committee on Infractions. **Includes major bowl games only; that is, those where team's opponent was classified as a major college team that season or at the time of the bowl game.

College Football Coach of the Year

The Division I-A Coach of the Year has been selected by the American Football Coaches Assn. since 1935 and selected by the Football Writers Assn. of America since 1957. When polls disagree, both winners are indicated.

1935 Lynn Waldorf, Northwestern
1936 Dick Harlow, Harvard
1937 Edward Mylin, Lafayette
1938 Bill Kern, Carnegie Tech
1939 Eddie Anderson, Iowa
1940 Clark Shaughnessy, Stanford
1941 Frank Leahy, Notre Dame
1942 Bill Alexander, Georgia Tech
1943 Amos Alonzo Stagg, Pacific
1944 Carroll Widdoes, Ohio St.
1945 Bo McMillin, Indiana
1946 Earl "Red" Blaik, Army
1947 Fritz Crisler, Michigan
1948 Bennie Oosterbaan, Michigan
1949 Bud Wilkinson, Oklahoma
1950 Charlie Caldwell, Princeton
1951 Chuck Taylor, Stanford
1952 Biggie Munn, Michigan St.
1953 Jim Tatum, Maryland
1954 Henry "Red" Sanders, UCLA
1955 Duffy Daugherty, Michigan St.
1956 Bowden Wyatt, Tennessee
1957 Woody Hayes, Ohio St.
1958 Paul Dietzel, LSU
1959 Ben Schwartzwalder, Syracuse
1960 Murray Warmath, Minnesota
1961 Paul "Bear" Bryant, Ala. (AFCA); Darrell Royal, Texas (FWAA)
1962 John McKay, USC
1963 Darrell Royal, Texas
1964 Ara Parseghian, Notre Dame, & Frank Broyles, Arkansas (AFCA); Ara Parseghian (FWAA)
1965 Tommy Prothro, UCLA (AFCA); Duffy Daugherty, Mich. St. (FWAA)
1966 Tom Cahill, Army
1967 John Pont, Indiana
1968 Joe Paterno, Penn St. (AFCA); Woody Hayes, Ohio St. (FWAA)
1969 Bo Schembechler, Michigan
1970 Charles McClendon, LSU, & Darrell Royal, Texas (AFCA); Alex Agase, Northwestern (FWAA)
1971 Paul "Bear" Bryant, Alabama (AFCA); Bob Devaney, Nebraska (FWAA)
1972 John McKay, USC
1973 Paul "Bear" Bryant, Alabama (AFCA); Johnny Majors, Pittsburgh (FWAA)
1974 Grant Teaff, Baylor
1975 Frank Kush, Arizona St. (AFCA); Woody Hayes, Ohio St. (FWAA)
1976 Johnny Majors, Pittsburgh
1977 Don James, Washington (AFCA); Lou Holtz, Arkansas (FWAA)
1978 Joe Paterno, Penn St.
1979 Earle Bruce, Ohio St.
1980 Vince Dooley, Georgia
1981 Danny Ford, Clemson
1982 Joe Paterno, Penn St.
1983 Ken Hatfield, Air Force (AFCA); Howard Schnellenberger, Miami (FL) (FWAA)
1984 LaVell Edwards, Brigham Young
1985 Fisher De Berry, Air Force
1986 Joe Paterno, Penn St.
1987 Dick MacPherson, Syracuse
1988 Don Nehlen, W. Virginia (AFCA); Lou Holtz, Notre Dame (FWAA)
1989 Bill McCartney, Colorado
1990 Bobby Ross, Georgia Tech
1991 Don James, Washington
1992 Gene Stallings, Alabama
1993 Barry Alvarez, Wisconsin (AFCA); Terry Bowden, Auburn (FWAA)
1994 Tom Osborne, Nebraska (AFCA) Rich Brooks, Oregon (FWAA)
1995 Gary Barnett, Northwestern
1996 Bruce Snyder, Arizona St.
1997 Mike Price, Washington St.
1998 Phillip Fulmer, Tennessee
1999 Frank Beamer, Virginia Tech
2000 Bob Stoops, Oklahoma
2001 Larry Coker, Miami (FL), Ralph Friedgen, Maryland (AFCA); Ralph Friedgen, Maryland (FWAA)

All-Time Division I-A Coaching Victories (Including Bowl Games)

*Joe Paterno 327
*Bobby Bowden 323
Paul "Bear" Bryant 323
Glenn "Pop" Warner 319
Amos Alonzo Stagg 314
*LaVell Edwards 257
Tom Osborne 255
Woody Hayes 238
Bo Schembechler 234
*Lou Holtz 233
Hayden Fry 232
Jess Neely 207
Warren Woodson 203
Don Nehlen 202
Eddie Anderson 201
Vince Dooley 201
Jim Sweeney 200
Dana X. Bible 198
Dan McGugin 197
Fielding Yost 196
Howard Jones 194
John Cooper 192
John Vaught 190
George Welsh 189
John Heisman 185
Johnny Majors 185
Darrell Royal 184
Gil Dobie 180
Carl Snavely 180
Jerry Claiborne 179
Ben Schwartzwalder 178
Frank Kush 176
Don James 176
Ralph Jordan 176

Coaches active in 2001 are denoted by an asterisk(*). Eddie Robinson of Grambling State Univ. (Div. I-AA) , who retired after the 1997 season, holds the record for most college football victories, with 408.

NCAA Div. I-A Football Conference Champions (1980-2001)

Atlantic Coast

1980 North Carolina
1981 Clemson
1982 Clemson
1983 Maryland
1984 Maryland
1985 Maryland
1986 Clemson
1987 Clemson
1988 Clemson
1989 Virginia, Duke
1990 Georgia Tech
1991 Clemson
1992 Florida St.
1993 Florida St.
1994 Florida St.
1995 Virginia, Florida St.
1996 Florida St.
1997 Florida St.
1998 Florida St., Georgia Tech
1999 Florida St.
2000 Florida St.
2001 Maryland

Big 12*

1996 Texas
1997 Nebraska
1998 Texas A&M
1999 Nebraska
2000 Oklahoma
2001 Colorado

Big East

1991 Miami (FL), Syracuse
1992 Miami (FL)
1993 West Virginia
1994 Miami (FL)
1995 Virginia Tech, Miami (FL)
1996 Virginia Tech, Miami (FL), Syracuse
1997 Syracuse
1998 Syracuse
1999 Virginia Tech
2000 Miami (FL)
2001 Miami (FL)

Big Ten

1980 Michigan
1981 Iowa, Ohio St.
1982 Michigan
1983 Illinois
1984 Ohio St.
1985 Iowa
1986 Michigan, Ohio St.
1987 Michigan St.
1988 Michigan
1989 Michigan
1990 Iowa, Ill., Mich., Mich. St.
1991 Michigan
1992 Michigan
1993 Ohio St., Wisconsin
1994 Penn St.
1995 Northwestern
1996 Ohio St., Northwestern
1997 Michigan
1998 Ohio St., Wisconsin, Michigan
1999 Wisconsin
2000 Michigan, Northwestern, Purdue
2001 Illinois

Big West**
1980 Long Beach St.
1981 San Jose St.
1982 Fresno St.
1983 Cal St.-Fullerton
1984 Cal St.-Fullerton
1985 Fresno St.
1986 San Jose St.
1987 San Jose St.
1988 Fresno St.
1989 Fresno St.
1990 San Jose St.
1991 San Jose St., Fresno St.
1992 Nevada
1993 SW Louisiana, Utah St.
1994 Nevada, SW Louisiana, UNLV
1995 Nevada
1996 Nevada, Utah St.
1997 Nevada, Utah St.
1998 Idaho
1999 Boise St.
2000 Boise St.

Conference USA
1996 So. Mississippi, Houston
1997 So. Mississippi
1998 Tulane
1999 So. Mississippi
2000 Louisville
2001 Louisville

Mid-American Athletic
1980 Central Michigan
1981 Toledo
1982 Bowling Green
1983 Northern Illinois
1984 Toledo
1985 Bowling Green
1986 Miami (OH)
1987 E. Michigan
1988 W. Michigan
1989 Ball St.
1990 Central Michigan
1991 Bowling Green
1992 Bowling Green
1993 Ball St.
1994 Central Michigan
1995 Toledo
1996 Ball St.
1997 Marshall
1998 Marshall
1999 Marshall
2000 Marshall
2001 Toledo

Mountain West***
1999 BYU, Colorado St., Utah
2000 Colorado St.
2001 BYU

Pacific Ten
1980 Washington
1981 Washington
1982 UCLA
1983 UCLA
1984 USC
1985 UCLA
1986 Arizona St.
1987 UCLA, USC
1988 USC
1989 USC
1990 Washington
1991 Washington
1992 Washington, Stanford
1993 UCLA, Arizona, USC
1994 Oregon
1995 USC, Washington
1996 Arizona St.
1997 Washington St., UCLA
1998 UCLA
1999 Stanford
2000 Washington, Oregon St., Oregon
2001 Oregon

Southeastern
1980 Georgia
1981 Georgia, Alabama
1982 Georgia
1983 Auburn
1984 Florida (title vacated)
1985 Tennessee
1986 LSU
1987 Auburn
1988 Auburn, LSU
1989 Ala., Tenn., Auburn
1990 Tennessee
1991 Florida
1992 Alabama
1993 Florida
1994 Florida
1995 Florida
1996 Florida
1997 Tennessee
1998 Tennessee
1999 Alabama
2000 Florida
2001 LSU

Sun Belt**
2001 LSU

Western Athletic
1980 Brigham Young (BYU)
1981 Brigham Young
1982 Brigham Young
1983 Brigham Young
1984 Brigham Young
1985 BYU, Air Force
1986 San Diego St.
1987 Wyoming
1988 Wyoming
1989 Brigham Young
1990 Brigham Young
1991 Brigham Young
1992 Hawaii, BYU, Fresno St.
1993 Wyoming, Fresno St., BYU
1994 Colorado St.
1995 Colorado St., Air Force, Utah, BYU
1996 Brigham Young
1997 Colorado St.
1998 Air Force
1999 Fresno St., Hawaii, TCU
2000 Texas Christian, UTEP
2001 Louisiana Tech

(*) In 1996 all former Big Eight teams joined with 4 of the 8 Southwest Conf. teams to form the Big 12. (**) In 2001, former Big West teams Ark. St., Idaho, New Mexico St., and N. Texas joined La.-Lafayette, La.-Monroe (Southland), and Middle Tenn. (Ohio Valley) to form the Sun Belt Conf. Boise St. moved to the WAC, and Utah St. became an independent. (***) In 1999, 8 Western Athletic teams formed the Mountain West Conf.

NCAA Div. I-AA Football Conference Champions (1990-2001)

Atlantic 10
1990 Massachusetts
1991 Delaware, Villanova
1992 Delaware
1993 Boston U.
1994 New Hampshire
1995 Delaware
1996 William & Mary
1997 Villanova
1998 Richmond
1999 J. Madison, Mass.
2000 Delaware, Richmond
2001 Hofstra, Maine, Villanova, Will. & Mary

Big Sky
1990 Nevada
1991 Nevada
1992 Idaho, Eastern Wash.
1993 Montana
1994 Boise St.
1995 Montana
1996 Montana
1997 Eastern Wash.
1998 Montana
1999 Montana
2000 Montana
2001 Montana

Gateway
1990 Northern Iowa
1991 Northern Iowa
1992 Northern Iowa
1993 Northern Iowa
1994 Northern Iowa
1995 N. Iowa, Eastern Ill.
1996 Northern Iowa
1997 Western Illinois
1998 Western Illinois
1999 Illinois St.
2000 Western Illinois
2001 Northern Iowa

Ivy Group
1990 Cornell, Dartmouth
1991 Dartmouth
1992 Dartmouth, Princeton
1993 Penn
1994 Penn
1995 Princeton
1996 Dartmouth
1997 Harvard
1998 Penn
1999 Brown, Yale
2000 Penn
2001 Harvard

Metro Atlantic
1993 Iona
1994 Marist, St. John's (NY)
1995 Duquesne
1996 Duquesne
1997 Georgetown
1998 Fairfield, Georgetown
1999 Duquesne
2000 Duquesne
2001 Duquesne

Mid-East Athletic
1990 Florida A&M
1991 North Carolina A&T
1992 North Carolina A&T
1993 Howard
1994 South Carolina St.
1995 Florida A&M
1996 Florida A&M
1997 Hampton
1998 Florida A&M, Hampton
1999 North Carolina A&T
2000 Florida A&M
2001 Florida A&M

Northeast
1996 R. Morris, Monmouth
1997 Robert Morris
1998 R.Morris, Monmouth
1999 Robert Morris
2000 Robert Morris
2001 Sacred Heart

Ohio Valley
1990 E. Ky., Middle Tenn.
1991 Eastern Kentucky
1992 Middle Tennessee
1993 Eastern Kentucky
1994 Eastern Kentucky
1995 Murray St.
1996 Murray St.
1997 Eastern Kentucky
1998 Tennessee St.
1999 Tennessee St.
2000 Western Kentucky
2001 Eastern Illinois

Patriot
1990 Holy Cross
1991 Holy Cross
1992 Lafayette
1993 Lehigh
1994 Lafayette
1995 Lehigh
1996 Bucknell
1997 Colgate
1998 Lehigh
1999 Colgate, Lehigh
2000 Lehigh
2001 Lehigh

Pioneer
1993 Dayton
1994 Dayton, Butler
1995 Drake
1996 Dayton
1997 Dayton
1998 TK
1999 Dayton
2000 Dayton, Drake, Valparaiso
2001 Dayton

Southern
1990 Furman
1991 Appalachian St.
1992 Citadel
1993 Georgia Southern
1994 Marshall
1995 Appalachian St.
1996 Marshall
1997 Georgia Southern
1998 Georgia Southern
1999 Appalachian St., GA Southern, Furman
2000 Georgia Southern
2001 Georgia Southern

Southland
1990 La.-Monroe
1991 McNeese St.
1992 La.-Monroe
1993 McNeese St.
1994 North Texas
1995 McNeese St.
1996 Troy St.
1997 McNeese St., Northwestern St.
1998 Northwestern St.
1999 Troy St., S. F. Austin
2000 Troy St.
2001 Sam Houston St., McNeese St.

Southwestern Athletic
1990 Jackson St.
1991 Alabama St.
1992 Alcorn St.
1993 Southern U.
1994 Grambling, Alcorn St.
1995 Jackson St.
1996 Jackson St.
1997 Southern U.
1998 Southern U.
1999 Southern U.
2000 Grambling
2001 Grambling

NATIONAL HOCKEY LEAGUE

2001-2002: Detroit Dominates; Bowman, Hasek Retire as Champions

The Detroit Red Wings defeated the Carolina Hurricanes in the Stanley Cup Finals, 4 games to 1, with a 3-1 victory in Game 5, at Joe Louis Arena in Detroit, June 13, 2002. It was Detroit's 10th overall title and 3rd cup in the last 5 years. The Red Wings' Nicklas Lidstrom won the Conn Smythe Trophy, becoming the 7th defenseman to earn playoff MVP honors. Superstar goaltender Dominik Hasek won his 1st Stanley Cup, allowing only 6 goals in the series and held the Hurricanes scoreless over 166 consecutive minutes between Games 3 and 5. Hasek announced his retirement 12 days later on June 25 and finished with a lifetime goals-against average of 2.23 and 61 shutouts. After winning his record 9th cup as a head coach, Scotty Bowman, the NHL's winningest coach, also ended his illustrious career, at age 68. Bowman left the game with 1,224 victories and a .654 winning percentage. The title capped a season of dominance for Detroit, with 9 potetntial Hall of Famers, who led the NHL with 116 points.

Final Standings 2001-2002

(playoff seeding in parentheses; division winners automatically seeded 1, 2, or 3; overtime losses [OTL] worth 1 point.)

Eastern Conference

Atlantic Division	W	L	T	OTL	GF	GA	Pts
Philadelphia (2)	42	27	10	3	234	192	97
N.Y. Islanders (5)	42	28	8	4	239	220	96
New Jersey (6)	41	28	9	4	205	187	95
N.Y. Rangers	36	38	4	4	227	258	80
Pittsburgh	28	41	8	5	198	249	69
Northeast Division	**W**	**L**	**T**	**OTL**	**GF**	**GA**	**Pts**
Boston (1)	43	24	6	9	236	201	101
Toronto (4)	43	25	10	4	249	207	100
Ottawa (7)	39	27	9	7	243	208	94
Montreal (8)	36	31	12	3	207	209	87
Buffalo	35	35	11	1	213	200	82
Southeast Division	**W**	**L**	**T**	**OTL**	**GF**	**GA**	**Pts**
Carolina (3)	35	26	16	5	217	217	91
Washington	36	33	11	2	228	240	85
Tampa Bay	27	40	11	4	178	219	69
Florida	22	44	10	6	180	250	60
Atlanta	19	47	11	5	187	288	54

Western Conference

Central Division	W	L	T	OTL	GF	GA	Pts
Detroit (1)	51	17	10	4	251	187	116
St. Louis (4)	43	27	8	4	227	188	98
Chicago (5)	41	7	13	1	216	207	96
Nashville	28	41	13	0	196	230	69
Columbus	22	47	8	5	194	255	57
Northwest Division	**W**	**L**	**T**	**OTL**	**GF**	**GA**	**Pts**
Colorado (2)	45	28	18	1	212	169	99
Vancouver (8)	42	30	7	3	254	211	94
Edmonton	38	28	12	4	205	182	92
Calgary	32	35	12	3	201	220	79
Minnesota	26	35	12	9	195	238	73
Pacific Division	**W**	**L**	**T**	**OTL**	**GF**	**GA**	**Pts**
San Jose (3)	44	27	8	3	248	199	99
Los Angeles (7)	40	27	11	4	214	190	95
Phoenix (6)	40	27	9	6	228	210	95
Dallas	36	28	13	5	215	213	90
Anaheim	29	42	8	3	175	198	69

2002 Stanley Cup Playoff Results

Eastern Conference

Ottawa defeated Philadelphia 4 games to 1
Carolina defeated New Jersey 4 games to 2
Montreal defeated Boston 4 games to 2
Toronto defeated N.Y. Islanders 4 games to 3
Carolina defeated Montreal 4 games to 2
Toronto defeated Ottawa 4 games to 3
Carolina defeated Toronto 4 games to 2

Western Conference

St. Louis defeated Chicago 4 games to 1
San Jose defeated Phoenix 4 games to 1
Detroit defeated Vancouver 4 games to 2
Colorado defeated Los Angeles 4 games to 3
Detroit defeated St. Louis 4 games to 1
Colorado defeated San Jose 4 games to 3
Detroit defeated Colorado 4 games to 3

Finals

Detroit defeated Carolina 4 games to 1 [2-3 (OT), 3-1, 3-2 (3 OT), 3-0, 3-1].

Stanley Cup Champions Since 1927

Year	Champion	Coach	Final opponent
1927	Ottawa	Dave Gill	Boston
1928	N.Y. Rangers	Lester Patrick	Montreal
1929	Boston	Cy Denneny	N.Y. Rangers
1930	Montreal	Cecil Hart	Boston
1931	Montreal	Cecil Hart	Chicago
1932	Toronto	Dick Irvin	N.Y. Rangers
1933	N.Y. Rangers	Lester Patrick	Toronto
1934	Chicago	Tommy Gorman	Detroit
1935	Montreal Maroons	Tommy Gorman	Toronto
1936	Detroit	Jack Adams	Toronto
1937	Detroit	Jack Adams	N.Y. Rangers
1938	Chicago	Bill Stewart	Toronto
1939	Boston	Art Ross	Toronto
1940	N.Y. Rangers	Frank Boucher	Toronto
1941	Boston	Cooney Weiland	Detroit
1942	Toronto	Hap Day	Detroit
1943	Detroit	Jack Adams	Boston
1944	Montreal	Dick Irvin	Chicago
1945	Toronto	Hap Day	Detroit
1946	Montreal	Dick Irvin	Boston
1947	Toronto	Hap Day	Montreal
1948	Toronto	Hap Day	Detroit
1949	Toronto	Hap Day	Detroit
1950	Detroit	Tommy Ivan	N.Y. Rangers
1951	Toronto	Joe Primeau	Montreal
1952	Detroit	Tommy Ivan	Montreal
1953	Montreal	Dick Irvin	Boston
1954	Detroit	Tommy Ivan	Montreal
1955	Detroit	Jimmy Skinner	Montreal
1956	Montreal	Toe Blake	Detroit
1957	Montreal	Toe Blake	Boston
1958	Montreal	Toe Blake	Boston
1959	Montreal	Toe Blake	Toronto
1960	Montreal	Toe Blake	Toronto
1961	Chicago	Rudy Pilous	Detroit
1962	Toronto	Punch Imlach	Chicago
1963	Toronto	Punch Imlach	Detroit
1964	Toronto	Punch Imlach	Detroit
1965	Montreal	Toe Blake	Chicago
1966	Montreal	Toe Blake	Detroit
1967	Toronto	Punch Imlach	Montreal
1968	Montreal	Toe Blake	St. Louis
1969	Montreal	Claude Ruel	St. Louis
1970	Boston	Harry Sinden	St. Louis
1971	Montreal	Al MacNeil	Chicago
1972	Boston	Tom Johnson	N.Y. Rangers
1973	Montreal	Scotty Bowman	Chicago
1974	Philadelphia	Fred Shero	Boston
1975	Philadelphia	Fred Shero	Buffalo
1976	Montreal	Scotty Bowman	Philadelphia
1977	Montreal	Scotty Bowman	Boston
1978	Montreal	Scotty Bowman	Boston
1979	Montreal	Scotty Bowman	N.Y. Rangers
1980	N.Y. Islanders	Al Arbour	Philadelphia
1981	N.Y. Islanders	Al Arbour	Minnesota
1982	N.Y. Islanders	Al Arbour	Vancouver
1983	N.Y. Islanders	Al Arbour	Edmonton
1984	Edmonton	Glen Sather	N.Y. Islanders
1985	Edmonton	Glen Sather	Philadelphia
1986	Montreal	Jean Perron	Calgary
1987	Edmonton	Glen Sather	Philadelphia
1988	Edmonton	Glen Sather	Boston
1989	Calgary	Terry Crisp	Montreal
1990	Edmonton	John Muckler	Boston
1991	Pittsburgh	Bob Johnson	Minnesota
1992	Pittsburgh	Scotty Bowman	Chicago
1993	Montreal	Jacques Demers	Los Angeles
1994	N.Y. Rangers	Mike Keenan	Vancouver
1995	New Jersey	Jacques Lemaire	Detroit
1996	Colorado	Marc Crawford	Florida
1997	Detroit	Scotty Bowman	Philadelphia
1998	Detroit	Scotty Bowman	Washington
1999	Dallas	Ken Hitchcock	Buffalo
2000	New Jersey	Larry Robinson	Dallas
2001	Colorado	Bob Hartley	New Jersey
2002	Detroit	Scotty Bowman	Carolina

IT'S A FACT: In the 2001-2002 season Jarome Iginla of the Calgary Flames became the 1st black player to lead the NHL in scoring—40 years after the NHL's 1st black player, fellow African-Canadian Willie O'Ree, scored his 1st goal on Jan. 1, 1961.

Individual Leaders, 2001-2002

Points

Jarome Iginla, Calgary, 96; Markus Naslund, Vancouver, 90; Todd Bertuzzi, Vancouver, 85; Mats Sundin, Toronto, 80; Jaromir Jagr, Washington, 79; Joe Sakic, Colorado, 79.

Goals

Jarome Iginla, Calgary, 52; Bill Guerin, Boston, 41; Glen Murray, Boston, 41; Mats Sundin, Toronto, 41, Markus Naslund, Vancouver, 40; Peter Bondra, Washington, 39.

Assists

Adam Oates, Wash.-Phil., 64; Jason Allison, Los Angeles, 54; Joe Sakic, Colorado, 53; Markus Naslund, Vancouver, 50; Ron Francis, Carolina, 50; Nicklas Lidstrom, Detroit, 50; Jozef Stumpel, Boston, 50.

Power-play goals

Peter Bondra, Washington, 17; Jarome Iginla, Calgary, 16; Miroslav Satan, Buffalo, 15; Alexei, Yashin, N.Y. Islanders, 15; Todd Bertuzzi, Vancouver, 14; Zigmund Palffy, Los Angeles, 14; Ron Francis, Carolina, 14.

Shorthanded goals

Brian Rolston, Boston, 9; Michael Peca, N.Y. Islanders, 6; Miroslav Satan, Buffalo, 5; Shawn Bates, N.Y. Islanders, 4; Stacy Roest, Minnesota, 4; 9 players tied with 3.

Shooting percentage

(minimum 82 shots)

Daniel Briere, Phoenix, 21.5; Jan Hrdina, Pittsburgh, 20.9; Adam Deadmarsh, Los Angeles, 20.9; Zigmund Palffy, Los Angeles, 19.9; Andrew Brunette, Minnesota, 19.8.

Plus/Minus

Chris Chelios, Detroit, 42; Jeremy Roenick, Philadelphia, 33; Glen Murray, Boston, 31; Simon Gagne, Philadelphia, 31; Zdeno Chara, Ottawa, 30.

Penalty minutes

Peter Worrell, Florida, 352; Brad Ference, Florida, 248; Chris Neil, Ottawa, 254; Kevin Sawyer, Anaheim, 216; Theo Fleury, N.Y. Rangers, 216; Andrei Nazarov, Phoenix, 215.

Goaltending Leaders

(minimum 25 games)

Goals against average

Patrick Roy, Colorado, 1.94; Roman Cechmanek, Philadelphia, 2.05; Marty Turco, Dallas, 2.11; Jose Theodore, Montreal, 2.11; Dominik Hasek, Detroit, 2.12; Jean-Sebastian Giguere, Anaheim, 2.15; Martin Brodeur, New Jersey, 2.15.

Wins

Dominik Hasek, Detroit, 41; Martin Brodeur, New Jersey, 38; Evgeni Nabokov, San Jose, 37; Byron Dafoe, Boston, 35; Brent Johnson, St. Louis, 34.

Save percentage

Jose Theodore, Montreal, .931; Patrick Roy, Colorado, .925; Roman Cechmanek, Philadelphia, .921; Sean Burke, Phoenix .920; Jean-Sebastian Giguere, Anaheim, .920; Nikolai Khabibulin, Tampa Bay, .920; Marty Turco, Dallas, .920.

Shutouts

Patrick Roy, Colorado, 9; Dan Cloutier, Vancouver, 7; Nikolai Khabibulin, Tampa Bay, 7; Patrick Lalime, Ottawa, 7; Evgeni Nabokov, San Jose, 7; Jose Theodore, Montreal, 7.

All-Time Leading Scorers

Player	Goals	Assists	Points	Player	Goals	Assists	Points	Player	Goals	Assists	Points
Wayne Gretzky	894	1,963	2,857	Phil Esposito	717	873	1,590	Doug Gilmour*	439	945	1,384
Gordie Howe	801	1,049	1,850	Ray Bourque	410	1,169	1,579	John Bucyk	556	813	1,369
Mark Messier*	658	1,146	1,804	Paul Coffey	396	1,135	1,531	Adam Oates*	330	1027	1,357
Marcel Dionne	731	1,040	1,771	Stan Mikita	541	926	1,467	Guy Lafleur	560	793	1,353
Ron Francis*	514	1,187	1,701	Bryan Trottier	524	901	1,425	Denis Savard	473	865	1,338
Steve Yzerman*	658	1,004	1,662	Dale Hawerchuk	518	891	1,409	Mike Gartner	708	627	1,335
Mario Lemieux*	654	947	1,601	Jari Kurri	601	797	1,398				

Note: Through end of 2001-2002 season. *Active in the 2001-2002 season.

Most NHL Goals in a Season

Player	Team	Season	Goals	Player	Team	Season	Goals
Wayne Gretzky	Edmonton	1981-82	92	Jari Kurri	Edmonton	1984-85	71
Wayne Gretzky	Edmonton	1983-84	87	Brett Hull	St. Louis	1991-92	70
Brett Hull	St. Louis	1990-91	86	Mario Lemieux	Pittsburgh	1987-88	70
Mario Lemieux	Pittsburgh	1988-89	85	Bernie Nicholls	Los Angeles	1988-89	70
Phil Esposito	Boston	1971-72	76	Mike Bossy	N.Y. Islanders	1978-79	69
Alexander Mogilny	Buffalo	1992-93	76	Mario Lemieux	Pittsburgh	1992-93	69
Teemu Selanne	Winnipeg	1992-93	76	Mario Lemieux	Pittsburgh	1995-96	69
Wayne Gretzky	Edmonton	1984-85	73	Mike Bossy	N.Y. Islanders	1980-81	68
Brett Hull	St. Louis	1989-90	72	Phil Esposito	Boston	1973-74	68
Wayne Gretzky	Edmonton	1982-83	71	Jari Kurri	Edmonton	1985-86	68

Art Ross Trophy (Leading Points Scorer)

1927 Bill Cook, N.Y. Rangers
1928 Howie Morenz, Montreal
1929 Ace Bailey, Toronto
1930 Cooney Weiland, Boston
1931 Howie Morenz, Montreal
1932 Harvey Jackson, Toronto
1933 Bill Cook, N.Y. Rangers
1934 Charlie Conacher, Toronto
1935 Charlie Conacher, Toronto
1936 Dave Schriner, N.Y. Americans
1937 Dave Schriner, N.Y. Americans
1938 Gordie Drillon, Toronto
1939 Toe Blake, Montreal
1940 Milt Schmidt, Boston
1941 Bill Cowley, Boston
1942 Bryan Hextall, N.Y. Rangers
1943 Doug Bentley, Chicago
1944 Herbie Cain, Boston
1945 Elmer Lach, Montreal
1946 Max Bentley, Chicago
1947 Max Bentley, Chicago
1948 Elmer Lach, Montreal
1949 Roy Conacher, Chicago
1950 Ted Lindsay, Detroit
1951 Gordie Howe, Detroit
1952 Gordie Howe, Detroit
1953 Gordie Howe, Detroit
1954 Gordie Howe, Detroit
1955 Bernie Geoffrion, Montreal
1956 Jean Beliveau, Montreal
1957 Gordie Howe, Detroit
1958 Dickie Moore, Montreal
1959 Dickie Moore, Montreal
1960 Bobby Hull, Chicago
1961 Bernie Geoffrion, Montreal
1962 Bobby Hull, Chicago
1963 Gordie Howe, Detroit
1964 Stan Mikita, Chicago
1965 Stan Mikita, Chicago
1966 Bobby Hull, Chicago
1967 Stan Mikita, Chicago
1968 Stan Mikita, Chicago
1969 Phil Esposito, Boston
1970 Bobby Orr, Boston
1971 Phil Esposito, Boston
1972 Phil Esposito, Boston
1973 Phil Esposito, Boston
1974 Phil Esposito, Boston
1975 Bobby Orr, Boston
1976 Guy Lafleur, Montreal
1977 Guy Lafleur, Montreal
1978 Guy Lafleur, Montreal
1979 Bryan Trottier, N.Y. Islanders
1980 Marcel Dionne, Los Angeles
1981 Wayne Gretzky, Edmonton
1982 Wayne Gretzky, Edmonton
1983 Wayne Gretzky, Edmonton
1984 Wayne Gretzky, Edmonton
1985 Wayne Gretzky, Edmonton
1986 Wayne Gretzky, Edmonton
1987 Wayne Gretzky, Edmonton
1988 Mario Lemieux, Pittsburgh
1989 Mario Lemieux, Pittsburgh
1990 Wayne Gretzky, Los Angeles
1991 Wayne Gretzky, Los Angeles
1992 Mario Lemieux, Pittsburgh
1993 Mario Lemieux, Pittsburgh
1994 Wayne Gretzky, Los Angeles
1995 Jaromir Jagr, Pittsburgh
1996 Mario Lemieux, Pittsburgh
1997 Mario Lemieux, Pittsburgh
1998 Jaromir Jagr, Pittsburgh
1999 Jaromir Jagr, Pittsburgh
2000 Jaromir Jagr, Pittsburgh
2001 Jaromir Jagr, Pittsburgh
2002 Jarome Iginla, Calgary

Maurice "Rocket" Richard Trophy (Most Goals)

1999 Teemu Selanne, Anaheim
2000 Pavel Bure, Florida
2001 Pavel Bure, Florida
2002 Jarome Iginla, Calgary

James Norris Memorial Trophy (Outstanding Defenseman)

1954 Red Kelly, Detroit
1955 Doug Harvey, Montreal
1956 Doug Harvey, Montreal
1957 Doug Harvey, Montreal
1958 Doug Harvey, Montreal
1959 Tom Johnson, Montreal
1960 Doug Harvey, Montreal
1961 Doug Harvey, Montreal
1962 Doug Harvey, N.Y. Rangers
1963 Pierre Pilote, Chicago
1964 Pierre Pilote, Chicago
1965 Pierre Pilote, Chicago
1966 Jacques Laperriere, Montreal
1967 Harry Howell, N.Y. Rangers
1968 Bobby Orr, Boston
1969 Bobby Orr, Boston
1970 Bobby Orr, Boston
1971 Bobby Orr, Boston
1972 Bobby Orr, Boston
1973 Bobby Orr, Boston
1974 Bobby Orr, Boston
1975 Bobby Orr, Boston
1976 Denis Potvin, N.Y. Islanders
1977 Larry Robinson, Montreal
1978 Denis Potvin, N.Y. Islanders
1979 Denis Potvin, N.Y. Islanders
1980 Larry Robinson, Montreal
1981 Randy Carlyle, Pittsburgh
1982 Doug Wilson, Chicago
1983 Rod Langway, Washington
1984 Rod Langway, Washington
1985 Paul Coffey, Edmonton
1986 Paul Coffey, Edmonton
1987 Ray Bourque, Boston
1988 Ray Bourque, Boston
1989 Chris Chelios, Montreal
1990 Ray Bourque, Boston
1991 Ray Bourque, Boston
1992 Brian Leetch, N.Y. Rangers
1993 Chris Chelios, Chicago
1994 Ray Bourque, Boston
1995 Paul Coffey, Detroit
1996 Chris Chelios, Chicago
1997 Brian Leetch, N.Y. Rangers
1998 Rob Blake, Los Angeles
1999 Al MacInnis, St. Louis
2000 Chris Pronger, St. Louis
2001 Nicklas Lidstrom, Detroit
2002 Nicklas Lidstrom, Detroit

Vezina Trophy (Outstanding Goalie)*

1927 George Hainsworth, Montreal
1928 George Hainsworth, Montreal
1929 George Hainsworth, Montreal
1930 Tiny Thompson, Boston
1931 Roy Worters, N.Y. Americans
1932 Charlie Gardiner, Chicago
1933 Tiny Thompson, Boston
1934 Charlie Gardiner, Chicago
1935 Lorne Chabot, Chicago
1936 Tiny Thompson, Boston
1937 Normie Smith, Detroit
1938 Tiny Thompson, Boston
1939 Frank Brimsek, Boston
1940 Dave Kerr, N.Y. Rangers
1941 Turk Broda, Toronto
1942 Frank Brimsek, Boston
1943 Johnny Mowers, Detroit
1944 Bill Durnan, Montreal
1945 Bill Durnan, Montreal
1946 Bill Durnan, Montreal
1947 Bill Durnan, Montreal
1948 Turk Broda, Toronto
1949 Bill Durnan, Montreal
1950 Bill Durnan, Montreal
1951 Al Rollins, Toronto
1952 Terry Sawchuk, Detroit
1953 Terry Sawchuk, Detroit
1954 Harry Lumley, Toronto
1955 Terry Sawchuk, Detroit
1956 Jacques Plante, Montreal
1957 Jacques Plante, Montreal
1958 Jacques Plante, Montreal
1959 Jacques Plante, Montreal
1960 Jacques Plante, Montreal
1961 John Bower, Toronto
1962 Jacques Plante, Montreal
1963 Glenn Hall, Chicago
1964 Charlie Hodge, Montreal
1965 Sawchuk, Bower, Toronto
1966 Worsley, Hodge, Montreal
1967 Hall, DeJordy, Chicago
1968 Worsley, Vachon, Montreal
1969 Hall, Plante, St. Louis
1970 Tony Esposito, Chicago
1971 Giacomin, Villemure, N.Y. Rangers
1972 Esposito, Smith, Chicago
1973 Ken Dryden, Montreal
1974 Bernie Parent, Philadelphia; Tony Esposito, Chicago
1975 Bernie Parent, Philadelphia
1976 Ken Dryden, Montreal
1977 Dryden, Larocque, Montreal
1978 Dryden, Larocque, Montreal
1979 Dryden, Larocque, Montreal
1980 Sauve, Edwards, Buffalo
1981 Sevigny, Larocque, Herron, Montreal
1982 Bill Smith, N.Y. Islanders
1983 Pete Peeters, Boston
1984 Tom Barrasso, Buffalo
1985 Pelle Lindbergh, Philadelphia
1986 John Vanbiesbrouck, N.Y. Rangers
1987 Ron Hextall, Philadelphia
1988 Grant Fuhr, Edmonton
1989 Patrick Roy, Montreal
1990 Patrick Roy, Montreal
1991 Ed Belfour, Chicago
1992 Patrick Roy, Montreal
1993 Ed Belfour, Chicago
1994 Dominik Hasek, Buffalo
1995 Dominik Hasek, Buffalo
1996 Jim Carey, Washington
1997 Dominik Hasek, Buffalo
1998 Dominik Hasek, Buffalo
1999 Dominik Hasek, Buffalo
2000 Olaf Kolzig, Washington
2001 Dominik Hasek, Buffalo
2002 Jose Theodore, Montreal

*Before 1982, awarded to the goalie or goalies who played a minimum of 25 games for the team that allowed the fewest goals; since 1982, awarded to the outstanding goalie, as determined by a vote of NHL general managers.

Frank J. Selke Trophy (Best Defensive Forward)

1978 Bob Gainey, Montreal
1979 Bob Gainey, Montreal
1980 Bob Gainey, Montreal
1981 Bob Gainey, Montreal
1982 Steve Kasper, Boston
1983 Bobby Clarke, Philadelphia
1984 Doug Jarvis, Washington
1985 Craig Ramsay, Buffalo
1986 Troy Murray, Chicago
1987 Dave Poulin, Philadelphia
1988 Guy Carbonneau, Montreal
1989 Guy Carbonneau, Montreal
1990 Rick Meagher, St. Louis
1991 Dirk Graham, Chicago
1992 Guy Carbonneau, Montreal
1993 Doug Gilmour, Toronto
1994 Sergei Fedorov, Detroit
1995 Ron Francis, Pittsburgh
1996 Sergei Federov, Detroit
1997 Michael Peca, Buffalo
1998 Jere Lehtinen, Dallas
1999 Jere Lehtinen, Dallas
2000 Steve Yzerman, Detroit
2001 John Madden, New Jersey
2002 Michael Peca, N.Y. Islanders

Calder Memorial Trophy (Rookie of the Year)

1933 Carl Voss, Detroit
1934 Russ Blinco, Montreal Maroons
1935 Dave Schriner, N.Y. Americans
1936 Mike Karakas, Chicago
1937 Syl Apps, Toronto
1938 Cully Dahlstrom, Chicago
1939 Frank Brimsek, Boston
1940 Kilby Macdonald, N.Y. Rangers
1941 John Quilty, Montreal
1942 Grant Warwick, N.Y. Rangers
1943 Gaye Stewart, Toronto
1944 Gus Bodnar, Toronto
1945 Frank McCool, Toronto
1946 Edgar Laprade, N.Y. Rangers
1947 Howie Meeker, Toronto
1948 Jim McFadden, Detroit
1949 Pentti Lund, N.Y. Rangers
1950 Jack Gelineau, Boston
1951 Terry Sawchuk, Detroit
1952 Bernie Geoffrion, Montreal
1953 Gump Worsley, N.Y. Rangers
1954 Camille Henry, N.Y. Rangers
1955 Ed Litzenberger, Chicago
1956 Glenn Hall, Detroit
1957 Larry Regan, Boston
1958 Frank Mahovlich, Toronto
1959 Ralph Backstrom, Montreal
1960 Bill Hay, Chicago
1961 Dave Keon, Toronto
1962 Bobby Rousseau, Montreal
1963 Kent Douglas, Toronto
1964 Jacques Laperriere, Montreal
1965 Roger Crozier, Detroit
1966 Brit Selby, Toronto
1967 Bobby Orr, Boston
1968 Derek Sanderson, Boston
1969 Danny Grant, Minnesota
1970 Tony Esposito, Chicago
1971 Gilbert Perreault, Buffalo
1972 Ken Dryden, Montreal
1973 Steve Vickers, N.Y. Rangers
1974 Denis Potvin, N.Y. Islanders
1975 Eric Vail, Atlanta
1976 Bryan Trottier, N.Y. Islanders
1977 Willi Plett, Atlanta
1978 Mike Bossy, N.Y. Islanders
1979 Bobby Smith, Minnesota
1980 Ray Bourque, Boston
1981 Peter Stastny, Quebec
1982 Dale Hawerchuk, Winnipeg
1983 Steve Larmer, Chicago
1984 Tom Barrasso, Buffalo
1985 Mario Lemieux, Pittsburgh
1986 Gary Suter, Calgary
1987 Luc Robitaille, Los Angeles
1988 Joe Nieuwendyk, Calgary
1989 Brian Leetch, N.Y. Rangers
1990 Sergei Makarov, Calgary
1991 Ed Belfour, Chicago
1992 Pavel Bure, Vancouver
1993 Teemu Selanne, Winnipeg
1994 Martin Brodeur, New Jersey
1995 Peter Forsberg, Quebec
1996 Daniel Alfredsson, Ottawa
1997 Bryan Berard, N.Y. Islanders
1998 Sergei Samsonov, Boston
1999 Chris Drury, Colorado
2000 Scott Gomez, New Jersey
2001 Evgeni Nabokov, San Jose
2002 Dany Heatley, Atlanta

Lady Byng Memorial Trophy (Most Gentlemanly Player)

1925 Frank Nighbor, Ottawa
1926 Frank Nighbor, Ottawa
1927 Billy Burch, N.Y. Americans
1928 Frank Boucher, N.Y. Rangers
1929 Frank Boucher, N.Y. Rangers
1930 Frank Boucher, N.Y. Rangers
1931 Frank Boucher, N.Y. Rangers
1932 Joe Primeau, Toronto
1933 Frank Boucher, N.Y. Rangers
1934 Frank Boucher, N.Y. Rangers
1935 Frank Boucher, N.Y. Rangers
1936 Doc Romnes, Chicago
1937 Marty Barry, Detroit
1938 Gordie Drillon, Toronto
1939 Clint Smith, N.Y. Rangers
1940 Bobby Bauer, Boston
1941 Bobby Bauer, Boston
1942 Syl Apps, Toronto
1943 Max Bentley, Chicago
1944 Clint Smith, Chicago
1945 Bill Mosienko, Chicago
1946 Toe Blake, Montreal
1947 Bobby Bauer, Boston
1948 Buddy O'Connor, N.Y. Rangers
1949 Bill Quackenbush, Detroit
1950 Edgar Laprade, N.Y. Rangers
1951 Red Kelly, Detroit
1952 Sid Smith, Toronto
1953 Red Kelly, Detroit
1954 Red Kelly, Detroit
1955 Sid Smith, Toronto
1956 Earl Reibel, Detroit
1957 Andy Hebenton, N.Y. Rangers
1958 Camille Henry, N.Y. Rangers
1959 Alex Delvecchio, Detroit
1960 Don McKenney, Boston
1961 Red Kelly, Toronto
1962 Dave Keon, Toronto
1963 Dave Keon, Toronto
1964 Ken Wharram, Chicago
1965 Bobby Hull, Chicago
1966 Alex Delvecchio, Detroit
1967 Stan Mikita, Chicago
1968 Stan Mikita, Chicago
1969 Alex Delvecchio, Detroit
1970 Phil Goyette, St. Louis
1971 John Bucyk, Boston
1972 Jean Ratelle, N.Y. Rangers
1973 Gil Perreault, Buffalo
1974 John Bucyk, Boston
1975 Marcel Dionne, Detroit
1976 Jean Ratelle, N.Y.R.-Boston
1977 Marcel Dionne, Los Angeles
1978 Butch Goring, Los Angeles
1979 Bob MacMillan, Atlanta
1980 Wayne Gretzky, Edmonton
1981 Rick Kehoe, Pittsburgh
1982 Rick Middleton, Boston
1983 Mike Bossy, N.Y. Islanders
1984 Mike Bossy, N.Y. Islanders
1985 Jari Kurri, Edmonton
1986 Mike Bossy, N.Y. Islanders
1987 Joe Mullen, Calgary
1988 Mats Naslund, Montreal
1989 Joe Mullen, Calgary
1990 Brett Hull, St. Louis
1991 Wayne Gretzky, Los Angeles
1992 Wayne Gretzky, Los Angeles
1993 Pierre Turgeon, N.Y. Islanders
1994 Wayne Gretzky, Los Angeles
1995 Ron Francis, Pittsburgh
1996 Paul Kariya, Anaheim
1997 Paul Kariya, Anaheim
1998 Ron Francis, Pittsburgh
1999 Wayne Gretzky, N.Y. Rangers
2000 Pavol Demitra, St. Louis
2001 Joe Sakic, Colorado
2002 Ron Francis, Carolina

Hart Memorial Trophy (MVP)

1927 Herb Gardiner, Montreal
1928 Howie Morenz, Montreal
1929 Roy Worters, N.Y. Americans
1930 Nels Stewart, Montreal Maroons
1931 Howie Morenz, Montreal
1932 Howie Morenz, Montreal
1933 Eddie Shore, Boston
1934 Aurel Joliat, Montreal
1935 Eddie Shore, Boston
1936 Eddie Shore, Boston
1937 Babe Siebert, Montreal
1938 Eddie Shore, Boston
1939 Toe Blake, Montreal
1940 Ebbie Goodfellow, Detroit
1941 Bill Cowley, Boston
1942 Tom Anderson, N.Y. Americans
1943 Bill Cowley, Boston
1944 Babe Pratt, Toronto
1945 Elmer Lach, Montreal
1946 Max Bentley, Chicago
1947 Maurice Richard, Montreal
1948 Buddy O'Connor, N.Y. Rangers
1949 Sid Abel, Detroit
1950 Chuck Rayner, N.Y. Rangers
1951 Milt Schmidt, Boston
1952 Gordie Howe, Detroit
1953 Gordie Howe, Detroit
1954 Al Rollins, Chicago
1955 Ted Kennedy, Toronto
1956 Jean Beliveau, Montreal
1957 Gordie Howe, Detroit
1958 Gordie Howe, Detroit
1959 Andy Bathgate, N.Y. Rangers
1960 Gordie Howe, Detroit
1961 Bernie Geoffrion, Montreal
1962 Jacques Plante, Montreal
1963 Gordie Howe, Detroit
1964 Jean Beliveau, Montreal
1965 Bobby Hull, Chicago
1966 Bobby Hull, Chicago
1967 Stan Mikita, Chicago
1968 Stan Mikita, Chicago
1969 Phil Esposito, Boston
1970 Bobby Orr, Boston
1971 Bobby Orr, Boston
1972 Bobby Orr, Boston
1973 Bobby Clarke, Philadelphia
1974 Phil Esposito, Boston
1975 Bobby Clarke, Philadelphia
1976 Bobby Clarke, Philadelphia
1977 Guy Lafleur, Montreal
1978 Guy Lafleur, Montreal
1979 Bryan Trottier, N.Y. Islanders
1980 Wayne Gretzky, Edmonton
1981 Wayne Gretzky, Edmonton
1982 Wayne Gretzky, Edmonton
1983 Wayne Gretzky, Edmonton
1984 Wayne Gretzky, Edmonton
1985 Wayne Gretzky, Edmonton
1986 Wayne Gretzky, Edmonton
1987 Wayne Gretzky, Edmonton
1988 Mario Lemieux, Pittsburgh
1989 Wayne Gretzky, Los Angeles
1990 Mark Messier, Edmonton
1991 Brett Hull, St. Louis
1992 Mark Messier, N.Y. Rangers
1993 Mario Lemieux, Pittsburgh
1994 Sergei Fedorov, Detroit
1995 Eric Lindros, Philadelphia
1996 Mario Lemieux, Pittsburgh
1997 Dominik Hasek, Buffalo
1998 Dominik Hasek, Buffalo
1999 Jaromir Jagr, Pittsburgh
2000 Chris Pronger, St. Louis
2001 Joe Sakic, Colorado
2002 Jose Theodore, Montreal

Conn Smythe Trophy (MVP in Playoffs)

1965 Jean Beliveau, Montreal
1966 Roger Crozier, Detroit
1967 Dave Keon, Toronto
1968 Glenn Hall, St. Louis
1969 Serge Savard, Montreal
1970 Bobby Orr, Boston
1971 Ken Dryden, Montreal
1972 Bobby Orr, Boston
1973 Yvan Cournoyer, Montreal
1974 Bernie Parent, Philadelphia
1975 Bernie Parent, Philadelphia
1976 Reg Leach, Philadelphia
1977 Guy Lafleur, Montreal
1978 Larry Robinson, Montreal
1979 Bob Gainey, Montreal
1980 Bryan Trottier, N.Y. Islanders
1981 Butch Goring, N.Y. Islanders
1982 Mike Bossy, N.Y. Islanders
1983 Billy Smith, N.Y. Islanders
1984 Mark Messier, Edmonton
1985 Wayne Gretzky, Edmonton
1986 Patrick Roy, Montreal
1987 Ron Hextall, Philadelphia
1988 Wayne Gretzky, Edmonton
1989 Al MacInnis, Calgary
1990 Bill Ranford, Edmonton
1991 Mario Lemieux, Pittsburgh
1992 Mario Lemieux, Pittsburgh
1993 Patrick Roy, Montreal
1994 Brian Leetch, N.Y. Rangers
1995 Claude Lemieux, New Jersey
1996 Joe Sakic, Colorado
1997 Mike Vernon, Detroit
1998 Steve Yzerman, Detroit
1999 Joe Nieuwendyk, Dallas
2000 Scott Stevens, New Jersey
2001 Patrick Roy, Colorado
2002 Nicklas Lidstrom, Detroit

National Hockey Hall of Fame, Toronto, Ontario

(2002 inductees have an asterisk*)

PLAYERS
Abel, Sid
Adams, Jack
Apps, Syl
Armstrong, George
Bailey, Ace
Bain, Dan
Baker, Hobey
Barber, Bill
Barry, Marty
Bathgate, Andy
Bauer, Bobby
Beliveau, Jean
Benedict, Clint
Bentley, Doug
Bentley, Max
Blake, Toe
Boivin, Leo
Boon, Dickie
Bossy, Mike
Bouchard, Butch
Boucher, Frank
Boucher, George
Bower, Johnny
Bowie, Dubbie
Brimsek, Frank
Broadbent, Punch
Broda, Turk
Bucyk, John
Burch, Billy
Cameron, Harry
Cheevers, Gerry
Clancy, King
Clapper, Dit
Clarke, Bobby
Cleghorn, Sprague
Colville, Neil
Conacher, Charlie
Conacher, Lionel
Conacher, Roy
Connell, Alex
Cook, Bill
Cook, Bun
Coulter, Art
Cournoyer, Yvan
Cowley, Bill
Crawford, Rusty
Darragh, Jack
Davidson, Scotty
Day, Hap
Delvecchio, Alex
Denneny, Cy
Dionne, Marcel
Drillon, Gordie
Drinkwater, Graham
Dryden, Ken
Dumart, Woody
Dunderdale, Tommy
Durnan, Bill
Dutton, Red
Dye, Babe
Esposito, Phil
Esposito, Tony
Farrel, Arthur
*Federko, Bernie
Fetisov, Vlacheslav
Flaman, Fernie
Foyston, Frank
Fredrickson, Frank
Gadsby, Bill
Gainey, Bob
Gardiner, Chuck
Gardiner, Herb
Gardiner, Jimmy
Gartner, Mike

Geoffrion, Bernie
Gerard, Eddie
Giacomin, Eddie
Gilbert, Rod
*Gillies, Clark
Gilmour, Billy
Goheen, Moose
Goodfellow, Ebbie
Goulet, Michel
Grant, Mike
Green, Shorty
Gretzky, Wayne
Griffis, Si
Hainsworth, George
Hall, Glenn
Hall, Joe
Harvey, Doug
Hawerchuk, Dale
Hay, George
Hern, Riley
Hextall, Bryan
Holmes, Hap
Hooper, Tom
Horner, Red
Horton, Tim
Howe, Gordie
Howe, Syd
Howell, Harry
Hull, Bobby
Hutton, Bouse
Hyland, Harry
Irvin, Dick
Jackson, Busher
Johnson, Ching
Johnson, Ernie
Johnson, Tom
Joliat, Aurel
Keats, Duke
Kelly, Red
Kennedy, Ted
Keon, Dave
Kurri, Jari
Lach, Elmer
Lafleur, Guy
Lalonde, Newsy
*Langway, Rod
Laperriere, Jacques
Lapointe, Guy
Laprade, Edgar
Laviolette, Jack
LeSueur, Percy
Lehman, Hughie
Lemaire, Jacques
Lemieux, Mario
Lewis, Herbie
Lindsay, Ted
Lumley, Harry
MacKay, Mickey
Mahovlich, Frank
Malone, Joe
Mantha, Sylvio
Marshall, Jack
Maxwell, Fred
McDonald, Lanny
McGee, Frank
McGimsie, Billy
McNamara, George
Mikita, Stan
Moore, Dickie
Moran, Paddy
Morenz, Howie
Mosienko, Bill
Mullen, Joe
Nighbor, Frank
Noble, Reg
O'Connor, Buddy
Oliver, Harry
Olmstead, Bert
Orr, Bobby
Parent, Bernie
Park, Brad
Patrick, Lester
Patrick, Lynn
Perreault, Gilbert
Phillips, Tom
Pilote, Pierre
Pitre, Didier
Plante, Jacques
Potvin, Denis
Pratt, Babe
Primeau, Joe
Pronovost, Marcel
Pulford, Bob
Pulford, Harvey
Quackenbush, Bill
Rankin, Frank
Ratelle, Jean
Rayner, Chuck
Reardon, Kenny
Richard, Henri
Richard, Maurice
Richardson, George
Roberts, Gordie
Robinson, Larry
Ross, Art
Russel, Blair
Russell, Ernie
Ruttan, Jack
Salming, Borje
Savard, Denis
Savard, Serge
Sawchuk, Terry
Scanlan, Fred
Schmidt, Milt
Schriner, Sweeney
Seibert, Earl
Seibert, Oliver
Shore, Eddie
Shutt, Steve
Siebert, Babe
Simpson, Joe
Sittler, Darryl
Smith, Alf
Smith, Billy
Smith, Clint
Smith, Hooley
Smith, Tommy
Stanley, Allan
Stanley, Barney
Stastny, Peter
Stewart, Jack
Stewart, Nels
Stuart, Bruce
Stuart, Hod
Taylor, Cyclone
Thompson, Tiny
Tretiak, Vladislav
Trihey, Harry
Trottier, Bryan
Ullman, Norm
Vezina, Georges
Walker, Jack
Walsh, Marty
Watson, Harry (Moose)
Watson, Harry Percival
Weiland, Cooney
Westwick, Harry
Whitcroft, Fred
Wilson, Phat
Worsley, Gump
Worters, Roy

BUILDERS

Adams, Charles
Adams, Weston
Ahearn, Bunny
Ahearn, Frank
Allan, Sir Montagu
Allen, Keith
Arbour, Al
Ballard, Harold
Bauer, Father David
Bickell, J.P.
Bowman, Scotty
Brown, George
Brown, Walter
Buckland, Frank
Bush, Walter, Jr.
Butterfield, Jack
Calder, Frank
Campbell, Angus
Campbell, Clarence
Cattarinich, Joseph
Dandurand, Leo
Dilio, Frank
Dudley, George
Dunn, James
Francis, Emile
Gibson, Jack
Gorman, Tommy
Griffiths, Frank
Hanley, Bill
Hay, Charles
Hendy, Jim
Hewitt, Foster
Hewitt, William
Hume, Fred
Imlach, Punch
Ivan, Tommy
Jennings, William
Johnson, Bob
Juckes, Gordon
Kilpatrick, John
Knox, Seymour
LeBel, Robert
Leader, Al
Lockhart, Thomas
Loicq, Paul
Mariucci, John
Mathers, Frank
McLaughlin, Frederic
Milford, Jake
Molson, Sen. Hartland
Morrison, Ian "Scotty"
Murray, Pere Athol
*Neilson, Roger
Nelson, Francis
Norris, Bruce
Norris, James
Norris, James Sr.
Northey, William
O'Brien, J. Ambrose
O'Neill, Brian Francis
Page, Frederick
Patrick, Craig
Patrick, Frank
Pickard, Allan
Pilous, Rudy
Poile, Bud
Pollock, Sam
Raymond, Sen. Donat
Robertson, John Ross
Robinson, Claude
Ross, Phillip
Sabetzki, Gunther
Sather, Glen
Selke, Frank
Sinden, Harry
Smith, Frank
Smythe, Conn
Snider, Ed
Stanley, Lord (of Preston)
Sutherland, Capt. James T.
Tarasov, Anatoli
Torrey, Bill
Turner, Lloyd
Tutt, William
Voss, Carl
Waghorne, Fred
Wirtz, Arthur
Wirtz, Bill
Ziegler, John A., Jr.

REFEREES AND LINESMEN

Armstrong, Neil
Ashley, John
Chadwick, Bill
D'Amico, John
Elliott, Chaucer
Hayes, George
Hewiston, Bobby
Ion, Mickey
Pavelich, Matt
Rodden, Mike
Smeaton, Cooper
Storey, Red
Udvari, Frank
Van Hellemond, Andy

NHL Home Ice

Team	Name (built)	Capacity
Anaheim	The Arrowhead Pond of Anaheim (1993)	17,174
Atlanta	Philips Arena (1999)	18,750
Boston	FleetCenter (1995)	17,565
Buffalo	HSBC Arena[1] (1996)	18,690
Calgary	Pengrowth Saddledome (1983)	17,139
Carolina	Entertainment & Sports Arena (1999)	18,730
Chicago	United Center (1994)	20,500
Colorado	Pepsi Center (1999)	22,076
Columbus	Nationwide Arena (2000)	18,500
Dallas	American Airlines Center (1980)	18,000
Detroit	Joe Louis Arena (1979)	19,983
Edmonton	Skyreach Centre[2] (1974)	17,100
Florida	National Car Rental Center (1998)	19,250
Los Angeles	Staples Center (1999)	18,118
Minnesota	Xcel Energy Arena (2000)	18,600
Montreal	Le Centre Molson (1996)	21,273
Nashville	Gaylord Entertainment Center[3] (1996)	17,500
New Jersey	Continental Airlines Arena[4] (1981)	19,040
N.Y. Islanders	Nassau Veterans Memorial Col. (1972)	16,297
N.Y. Rangers	Madison Square Garden (1968)	18,200
Ottawa	Corel Centre (1996)	18,500
Philadelphia	First Union Center (1996)	19,519
Phoenix	America West Arena (1992)	16,210
Pittsburgh	Mellon Arena[5] (1961)	16,958
St. Louis	Savvis Center[6] (1994)	21,000
San Jose	HP Pavilion[7] (1993)	17,513
Tampa Bay	Ice Palace (1996)	19,758
Toronto	Air Canada Centre (1999)	18,800
Vancouver	GM Place (1995)	18,422
Washington	MCI Center (1997)	18,672

(1) Marine Midland Arena, 1996-2000. (2) Northlands Col., 1974-79; Edmonton Col., 1979-98. (3) Nashville Arena, 1997-1999. (4) Brendan Byrne/Meadowlands Arena, 1981-96. (5) Civic Arena, 1961-99. (6) Kiel Center, 1994-2000. (7) San Jose Arena, 1993-2000; Compaq Center, 2001.

NCAA HOCKEY CHAMPIONS

1948 Michigan
1949 Boston College
1950 Colorado College
1951 Michigan
1952 Michigan
1953 Michigan
1954 RPI
1955 Michigan
1956 Michigan
1957 Colorado College
1958 Denver
1959 North Dakota
1960 Denver
1961 Denver
1962 Michigan Tech
1963 North Dakota
1964 Michigan
1965 Michigan Tech
1966 Michigan State
1967 Cornell
1968 Denver
1969 Denver
1970 Cornell
1971 Boston Univ.
1972 Boston Univ.
1973 Wisconsin
1974 Minnesota
1975 Michigan Tech
1976 Minnesota
1977 Wisconsin
1978 Boston Univ.
1979 Minnesota
1980 North Dakota
1981 Wisconsin
1982 North Dakota
1983 Wisconsin
1984 Bowling Green
1985 RPI
1986 Michigan State
1987 North Dakota
1988 Lake Superior St.
1989 Harvard
1990 Wisconsin
1991 N. Michigan
1992 Lake Superior St.
1993 Maine
1994 Lake Superior St.
1995 Boston Univ.
1996 Michigan
1997 North Dakota
1998 Michigan
1999 Maine
2000 North Dakota
2001 Boston College
2002 Minnesota

SOCCER

World Cup

2002 Men's World Cup

Soccer superpower Brazil won 7 straight matches, including a 2-0 win over Germany on June 30, to claim a record 5th World Cup. Favorites France, Argentina, and Portugal failed to advance to the 2nd round, while the U.S. had an unexpectedly strong showing, defeating Mexico, 2-0, before losing 1-0 to Germany in the quarterfinals. Co-host S. Korea also played well, finishing 4th overall. A total of 198 teams vied for the 29 of 32 spots in the competition. (Co-hosts Japan and S. Korea, and 1998 winner France had automatic bids.) Brazilian forward Ronaldo won the Golden Shoe for most goals, 8, including 2 in the final. Germany's Oliver Kahn became the 1st goalkeeper to win the Golden Ball as the tournament's best player.

First Round Results

Group A

COUNTRY	W	L	T	GF	GA	Pts
Denmark	2	0	1	5	2	7
Senegal	1	0	2	5	4	5
Uruguay	0	1	2	4	5	2
France	0	2	1	0	3	1

Group B

COUNTRY	W	L	T	GF	GA	Pts
Spain	3	0	0	9	4	9
Paraguay	1	1	1	6	6	4
S. Africa	1	1	1	5	5	4
Slovenia	0	3	0	2	7	0

Group C

COUNTRY	W	L	T	GF	GA	Pts
Brazil	3	0	0	11	3	9
Turkey	1	1	1	5	3	4
Costa Rica	1	1	1	5	6	4
China	0	3	0	0	9	0

Group D

COUNTRY	W	L	T	GF	GA	Pts
S. Korea	2	0	1	4	1	7
U.S.	1	1	1	5	6	4
Portugal	1	2	0	6	4	3
Poland	1	2	0	3	7	3

Group E

COUNTRY	W	L	T	GF	GA	Pts
Germany	2	0	1	11	1	7
Ireland	1	0	2	5	2	5
Cameroon	1	1	1	2	3	4
Saudi Arabia	0	3	0	0	12	0

Group F

COUNTRY	W	L	T	GF	GA	Pts
Sweden	1	0	2	4	3	5
England	1	0	2	2	1	5
Argentina	1	1	1	2	2	4
Nigeria	0	2	1	1	3	1

Group G

COUNTRY	W	L	T	GF	GA	Pts
Mexico	2	0	1	4	2	7
Italy	1	1	1	4	3	4
Croatia	1	2	0	2	3	3
Ecuador	1	2	0	2	4	3

Group H

COUNTRY	W	L	T	GF	GA	Pts
Japan	2	0	1	5	2	7
Belgium	1	0	2	6	5	5
Russia	1	2	0	4	4	3
Tunisia	0	0	1	1	5	1

Final Round Results

June 15: Seogwipo (S. Korea)
Germany 1, Paraguay 0

June 16: Suwon (S. Korea)
Spain 1, Ireland 1
(Spain won 3-2, penalty kicks)

June 17: Jeonju (S. Korea)
U.S. 2, Mexico 0

June 18: Daejeon (S. Korea)
S. Korea 2, Italy 1 (OT)

June 15: Niigata (Japan)
England 3, Denmark 0

June 16: Oita (Japan)
Senegal 2, Sweden 1 (OT)

June 17: Kobe (Japan)
Brazil 2, Belgium 0

June 18: Miyagi (Japan)
Turkey 1, Japan 0

June 21: Ulsan (S. Korea)
Germany 1, U.S. 0

June 22: Gwangju (S. Korea)
S. Korea 0, Spain 0
(S. Korea won 5-3, penalty kicks)

June 21: Shizuoka (Japan)
Brazil 2, England 1

June 22: Osaka (Japan)
Turkey 1, Senegal 0

June 25: Seoul (S. Korea)
Germany 1, S. Korea 0

June 26: Saitama (Japan)
Brazil 1, Turkey 0

June 30: Yokohama (Japan)
Brazil 2, Germany 0

Third Place Final
June 29: Daegu (S. Korea)
Turkey 3, S. Korea 2

Men's World Cup, 1930-2002

Year	Winner	Final opponent	Site
1930	Uruguay	Argentina	Uruguay
1934	Italy	Czechoslovakia	Italy
1938	Italy	Hungary	France
1950	Uruguay	Brazil	Brazil
1954	W. Germany	Hungary	Switzerland
1958	Brazil	Sweden	Sweden
1962	Brazil	Czechoslovakia	Chile
1966	England	W. Germany	England
1970	Brazil	Italy	Mexico
1974	W. Germany	Netherlands	W. Germany
1978	Argentina	Netherlands	Argentina
1982	Italy	W. Germany	Spain
1986	Argentina	W. Germany	Mexico
1990	W. Germany	Argentina	Italy
1994	Brazil	Italy	U.S.
1998	France	Brazil	France
2002	Brazil	Germany	Japan/S. Korea

1999 Women's World Cup

The U.S. defeated China, 5-4, on penalty kicks, July 10, 1999, in the Rose Bowl in Pasadena, CA, in front of 90,185 fans, the largest crowd ever at a U.S. women's sporting event. The 2003 Women's World Cup was scheduled to be held in China.

Women's World Cup, 1991-99

Year	Winner	Final Opponent	Score	Site	Third Place
1991	U.S.	Norway	2-1	China	Germany
1995	Norway	Germany	2-0	Sweden	U.S.
1999	U.S.	China	0-0*	U.S.	Brazil

* U.S. 5-4, penalty kicks

Major League Soccer

2002 Final Standings

Eastern Division

	W	L	T	GF	GA	Pts
New England Revolution*	12	14	2	49	49	38
Columbus Crew*	11	12	5	44	43	38
Chicago Fire*	11	13	4	43	38	37
NY/NJ MetroStars	11	15	2	41	47	35
Washington, DC United	9	14	5	31	40	32

Western Division

	W	L	T	GF	GA	Pts
Los Angeles Galaxy*	16	9	3	44	33	51
San Jose Earthquakes*	14	11	3	45	35	45
Colorado Rapids*	13	11	4	43	48	43
Dallas Burn*	12	9	7	44	43	43
Kansas City Wizards*	9	10	9	37	45	36

*Clinched playoff berth. **Note:** 3 points for a win, 1 point for a tie.

2002 MLS Scoring Leaders

(2 pts for a goal, 1 pt for an assist)

	Name	Team	GP	G	A	Pts
1.	Taylor Twellman	N. England	28	23	6	52
2.	Carlos Ruiz	Los Angeles	26	24	1	49
3.	Jeff Cunningham	Columbus	27	16	5	37
4.	Ante Razov	Chicago	25	14	8	36
5.	Ariel Graziani	San Jose	28	14	5	33
6.	Mark Chung	Colorado	27	11	10	32
7.	Jason Kreis	Dallas	27	13	4	30
8.	Mamadou Diallo	MetroStars*	24	12	5	29
	Rodrigo Faria	MetroStars	28	12	5	29
	Chris Henderson	Colorado	28	11	7	29
	Steve Ralston	N. England	27	5	19	29

* Played for more than 1 team, most recent shown.

2002 Goalkeeping Leaders

(minimum 1,000 minutes played)

	Name	Team	Games	Minutes	Shots[1]	Saves	GA	GAA	W	L	T
1.	Kevin Hartman	Los Angeles	18	1,648	108	83	20	1.09	11	6	1
	Jon Busch	Columbus	14	1,236	80	63	15	1.09	8	3	2
3.	Joe Cannon	San Jose	26	2,375	136	100	29	1.10	13	10	3
4.	Zach Thornton	Chicago	27	2,483	164	124	34	1.23	10	13	4
5.	Adin Brown	N. England	16	1,460	102	72	20	1.23	9	6	1

Note: GA = goals against; GAA = goals against average. (1) Not shots on goal; includes shots over the goal or just past the post.

MLS Cup Champions, 1996-2001

Year	Winner	Final opponent	Score	Site	MVP
1996	Washington, DC	Los Angeles	3–2 (OT)	Foxboro, MA	Marco Etcheverry
1997	Washington, DC	Colorado	2–1	Washington, DC	Jaime Moreno
1998	Chicago	Washington, DC	2–0	Pasadena, CA	Peter Nowak
1999	Washington, DC	Los Angeles	2–0	Foxboro, MA	Ben Olsen
2000	Kansas City	Chicago	1-0	Washington, DC	Tony Meola
2001	San Jose	Los Angeles	2-1 (OT)	Columbus, OH	Dwayne DeRosario

2002 Women's United Soccer Association

The Carolina Courage defeated the Washington Freedom, 3-2, in the WUSA Founders Cup II at Atlanta's Herndon Stadium on Aug. 24. The game's MVP was Carolina forward Birgit Prinz, who scored 1 goal and set up another. Philadelphia's Marinette Pichon was the 2002 WUSA MVP and Offensive Player of the Year. For champion Carolina, Danielle Slaton was named Defensive Player of the Year, and Kristin Luckenbill took home Goalkeeper of the Year honors. Rookie of the Year was Washington's Abby Wambach, and Mark Krikorian was named Coach of the Year for Philadelphia.

NCAA Soccer Champions, 1982-2001

Year[1]	Men	Women
1982	Indiana	North Carolina
1983	Indiana	North Carolina
1984	Clemson	North Carolina
1985	UCLA	George Mason
1986	Duke	North Carolina
1987	Clemson	North Carolina
1988	Indiana	North Carolina
1989	Santa Clara (tie, 2 ot) Virginia	North Carolina
1990	UCLA	North Carolina
1991	Virginia	North Carolina
1992	Virginia	North Carolina
1993	Virginia	North Carolina
1994	Virginia	North Carolina
1995	Wisconsin	Notre Dame
1996	St. John's (NY)	North Carolina
1997	UCLA	North Carolina
1998	Indiana	Florida
1999	Indiana	North Carolina
2000	Connecticut	North Carolina
2001	North Carolina	Santa Clara

(1) NCAA Championships began in 1959 for men, in 1982 for women.

GOLF

Men's All-Time Major Professional Championship Leaders

(Through the 2002 season; *active PGA player; (a)=amateur.)

Player	Masters	U.S. Open	British Open	PGA	Total
Jack Nicklaus*	1963, '65-66, '72, '75, '86	1962, '67, '72, '80	1966, '70, '78	1963, '71, '73, '75, '80	18
Walter Hagen	—	1914, '19	1922, '24, '28-29	1921, '24-27	11
Ben Hogan	1951, '53	1948, '50-51, '53	1953	1946, '48	9
Gary Player	1961, '74, '78	1965	1959, '68, '74	1962, '72	9
Tom Watson*	1977, '81	1982	1975, '77, '80, '82-83	—	8
Tiger Woods*	1997, 2001, 2002	2000, 2002	2000	1999, 2000	8
Bobby Jones(a)	—	1923, '26, '29-30	1926-27, '30	—	7
Arnold Palmer	1958, '60, '62, '64	1960	1961-62	—	7
Gene Sarazen	1935	1922, '32	1932	1922-23, '33	7
Sam Snead	1949, '52, '54	—	1946	1942, '49, '51	7
Harry Vardon	—	1900	1896, '98-99, 1903, '11, '14	—	7
Nick Faldo*	1989-90, '96	—	1987, '90, '92	—	6
Lee Trevino	—	1968, '71	1971-72	1974, '84	6

Professional Golfers' Association Leading Money Winners, by Year

Year	Player	Earnings	Year	Player	Earnings	Year	Player	Earnings
1946	Ben Hogan	$42,556	1965	Jack Nicklaus	$140,752	1984	Tom Watson	$476,260
1947	Jimmy Demaret	27,936	1966	Billy Casper	121,944	1985	Curtis Strange	542,321
1948	Ben Hogan	36,812	1967	Jack Nicklaus	188,988	1986	Greg Norman	653,296
1949	Sam Snead	31,593	1968	Billy Casper	205,168	1987	Curtis Strange	925,941
1950	Sam Snead	35,758	1969	Frank Beard	175,223	1988	Curtis Strange	1,147,644
1951	Lloyd Mangrum	26,088	1970	Lee Trevino	157,037	1989	Tom Kite	1,395,278
1952	Julius Boros	37,032	1971	Jack Nicklaus	244,490	1990	Greg Norman	1,165,477
1953	Lew Worsham	34,002	1972	Jack Nicklaus	320,542	1991	Corey Pavin	979,430
1954	Bob Toski	65,819	1973	Jack Nicklaus	308,362	1992	Fred Couples	1,344,188
1955	Julius Boros	65,121	1974	Johnny Miller	353,201	1993	Nick Price	1,478,557
1956	Ted Kroll	72,835	1975	Jack Nicklaus	323,149	1994	Nick Price	1,499,927
1957	Dick Mayer	65,835	1976	Jack Nicklaus	266,438	1995	Greg Norman	1,654,959
1958	Arnold Palmer	42,407	1977	Tom Watson	310,653	1996	Tom Lehman	1,780,159
1959	Art Wall, Jr.	53,167	1978	Tom Watson	362,429	1997	Tiger Woods	2,066,833
1960	Arnold Palmer	75,262	1979	Tom Watson	462,636	1998	David Duval	2,591,031
1961	Gary Player	64,540	1980	Tom Watson	530,808	1999	Tiger Woods	6,616,585
1962	Arnold Palmer	81,448	1981	Tom Kite	375,699	2000	Tiger Woods	9,188,321
1963	Arnold Palmer	128,230	1982	Craig Stadler	446,462	2001	Tiger Woods	5,687,777
1964	Jack Nicklaus	113,284	1983	Hal Sutton	426,668			

IT'S A FACT: Prize money has increased so much over the years that the PGA's all-time leaders in career wins, Sam Snead (82) and Jack Nicklaus (70), are not even in the top 75 on the career money list. Snead won $620,126 and Nicklaus, as of Oct. 2002, had won $5,772,901. The top all-time money winner is Tiger Woods, who by Oct. 2002 had taken in $32,687,252 for 34 wins.

Masters Golf Tournament Winners

Year	Winner	Year	Winner	Year	Winner	Year	Winner
1934	Horton Smith	1953	Ben Hogan	1970	Billy Casper	1987	Larry Mize
1935	Gene Sarazen	1954	Sam Snead	1971	Charles Coody	1988	Sandy Lyle
1936	Horton Smith	1955	Cary Middlecoff	1972	Jack Nicklaus	1989	Nick Faldo
1937	Byron Nelson	1956	Jack Burke	1973	Tommy Aaron	1990	Nick Faldo
1938	Henry Picard	1957	Doug Ford	1974	Gary Player	1991	Ian Woosnam
1939	Ralph Guldahl	1958	Arnold Palmer	1975	Jack Nicklaus	1992	Fred Couples
1940	Jimmy Demaret	1959	Art Wall Jr.	1976	Ray Floyd	1993	Bernhard Langer
1941	Craig Wood	1960	Arnold Palmer	1977	Tom Watson	1994	Jose Maria Olazabal
1942	Byron Nelson	1961	Gary Player	1978	Gary Player	1995	Ben Crenshaw
1943-45	not played	1962	Arnold Palmer	1979	Fuzzy Zoeller	1996	Nick Faldo
1946	Herman Keiser	1963	Jack Nicklaus	1980	Seve Ballesteros	1997	Tiger Woods
1947	Jimmy Demaret	1964	Arnold Palmer	1981	Tom Watson	1998	Mark O'Meara
1948	Claude Harmon	1965	Jack Nicklaus	1982	Craig Stadler	1999	Jose Maria Olazabal
1949	Sam Snead	1966	Jack Nicklaus	1983	Seve Ballesteros	2000	Vijay Singh
1950	Jimmy Demaret	1967	Gay Brewer, Jr.	1984	Ben Crenshaw	2001	Tiger Woods
1951	Ben Hogan	1968	Bob Goalby	1985	Bernhard Langer	2002	Tiger Woods
1952	Sam Snead	1969	George Archer	1986	Jack Nicklaus		

United States Open Winners

(First contested in 1895)

Year	Winner	Year	Winner	Year	Winner	Year	Winner
1934	Olin Dutra	1954	Ed Furgol	1971	Lee Trevino	1987	Scott Simpson
1935	Sam Parks, Jr.	1955	Jack Fleck	1972	Jack Nicklaus	1988	Curtis Strange
1936	Tony Manero	1956	Cary Middlecoff	1973	Johnny Miller	1989	Curtis Strange
1937	Ralph Guldahl	1957	Dick Mayer	1974	Hale Irwin	1990	Hale Irwin
1938	Ralph Guldahl	1958	Tommy Bolt	1975	Lou Graham	1991	Payne Stewart
1939	Byron Nelson	1959	Billy Casper	1976	Jerry Pate	1992	Tom Kite
1940	Lawson Little	1960	Arnold Palmer	1977	Hubert Green	1993	Lee Janzen
1941	Craig Wood	1961	Gene Littler	1978	Andy North	1994	Ernie Els
1942-45	Not Played	1962	Jack Nicklaus	1979	Hale Irwin	1995	Corey Pavin
1946	Lloyd Mangrum	1963	Julius Boros	1980	Jack Nicklaus	1996	Steve Jones
1947	L. Worsham	1964	Ken Venturi	1981	David Graham	1997	Ernie Els
1948	Ben Hogan	1965	Gary Player	1982	Tom Watson	1998	Lee Janzen
1949	Cary Middlecoff	1966	Billy Casper	1983	Larry Nelson	1999	Payne Stewart
1950	Ben Hogan	1967	Jack Nicklaus	1984	Fuzzy Zoeller	2000	Tiger Woods
1951	Ben Hogan	1968	Lee Trevino	1985	Andy North	2001	Retief Goosen
1952	Julius Boros	1969	Orville Moody	1986	Ray Floyd	2002	Tiger Woods
1953	Ben Hogan	1970	Tony Jacklin				

WORLD ALMANAC QUICK QUIZ

In 2001, the British Open replaced the du Maurier Classic as the LPGA's 4th major. Which golfer has won all 4 current LPGA majors as well as the du Maurier?

(a) Karrie Webb (b) Juli Inskter (c) Pat Bradley (d) Annika Sorenstam

For the answer look in this chapter, or see page 1008.

British Open Winners

(First contested in 1860)

Year	Winner	Year	Winner	Year	Winner	Year	Winner
1934	Henry Cotton	1955	Peter Thomson	1971	Lee Trevino	1987	Nick Faldo
1935	Alf Perry	1956	Peter Thomson	1972	Lee Trevino	1988	Seve Ballesteros
1936	Alf Padgham	1957	Bobby Locke	1973	Tom Weiskopf	1989	Mark Calcavecchia
1937	T.H. Cotton	1958	Peter Thomson	1974	Gary Player	1990	Nick Faldo
1938	R.A. Whitcombe	1959	Gary Player	1975	Tom Watson	1991	Ian Baker-Finch
1939	Richard Burton	1960	Kel Nagle	1976	Johnny Miller	1992	Nick Faldo
1940-45	not played	1961	Arnold Palmer	1977	Tom Watson	1993	Greg Norman
1946	Sam Snead	1962	Arnold Palmer	1978	Jack Nicklaus	1994	Nick Price
1947	Fred Daly	1963	Bob Charles	1979	Seve Ballesteros	1995	John Daly
1948	Henry Cotton	1964	Tony Lema	1980	Tom Watson	1996	Tom Lehman
1949	Bobby Locke	1965	Peter Thomson	1981	Bill Rogers	1997	Justin Leonard
1950	Bobby Locke	1966	Jack Nicklaus	1982	Tom Watson	1998	Mark O'Meara
1951	Max Faulkner	1967	Roberto de Vicenzo	1983	Tom Watson	1999	Paul Lawrie
1952	Bobby Locke	1968	Gary Player	1984	Seve Ballesteros	2000	Tiger Woods
1953	Ben Hogan	1969	Tony Jacklin	1985	Sandy Lyle	2001	David Duval
1954	Peter Thomson	1970	Jack Nicklaus	1986	Greg Norman	2002	Ernie Els

PGA Championship Winners

(First contested in 1916)

Year	Winner	Year	Winner	Year	Winner	Year	Winner
1934	Paul Runyan	1952	James Turnesa	1969	Ray Floyd	1986	Bob Tway
1935	Johnny Revolta	1953	Walter Burkemo	1970	Dave Stockton	1987	Larry Nelson
1936	Denny Shute	1954	Melvin Harbert	1971	Jack Nicklaus	1988	Jeff Sluman
1937	Denny Shute	1955	Doug Ford	1972	Gary Player	1989	Payne Stewart
1938	Paul Runyan	1956	Jack Burke	1973	Jack Nicklaus	1990	Wayne Grady
1939	Henry Picard	1957	Lionel Hebert	1974	Lee Trevino	1991	John Daly
1940	Byron Nelson	1958	Dow Finsterwald	1975	Jack Nicklaus	1992	Nick Price
1941	Victor Ghezzi	1959	Bob Rosburg	1976	Dave Stockton	1993	Paul Azinger
1942	Sam Snead	1960	Jay Hebert	1977	Lanny Wadkins	1994	Nick Price
1943	not played	1961	Jerry Barber	1978	John Mahaffey	1995	Steve Elkington
1944	Bob Hamilton	1962	Gary Player	1979	David Graham	1996	Mark Brooks
1945	Byron Nelson	1963	Jack Nicklaus	1980	Jack Nicklaus	1997	Davis Love III
1946	Ben Hogan	1964	Bob Nichols	1981	Larry Nelson	1998	Vijay Singh
1947	Jim Ferrier	1965	Dave Marr	1982	Ray Floyd	1999	Tiger Woods
1948	Ben Hogan	1966	Al Geiberger	1983	Hal Sutton	2000	Tiger Woods
1949	Sam Snead	1967	Don January	1984	Lee Trevino	2001	David Toms
1950	Chandler Harper	1968	Julius Boros	1985	Hubert Green	2002	Rich Beem
1951	Sam Snead						

Women's All-Time Major Professional Championship Leaders

(Through the 2002 season; *active LPGA player.)

Player	Nabisco[1]	LPGA	U.S. Open[2]	du Maurier[3]	Titleholders[4]	Western Open[5]	Total
Patty Berg	—	—	1946	—	1937-39, '48, '53, '55, '57	1941, '43, '48, '51, '55, '57-58	15
Mickey Wright	—	1958, '60-61, '63	1958-59, '61, '64	—	1961-62	1962-63, '66	13
Louise Suggs	—	1957	1949, '52	—	1946, '54, '56, '59	1946-47, '49, '53	11
Babe Zaharias	—	—	1948, '50, '54	—	1947, '50, '52	1940, '44-45, '50	10
Betsy Rawls	—	1959, '69	1951, '53, '57, '60	—	—	1952, '59	8
Juli Inkster*	1984, '89	1999, 2000	1999, 2002	1984	—	—	7
Pat Bradley*	1986	1986	1981	1980, '85-86	—	—	6
Betsy King*	1987, '90, '97	1992	1989-90	—	—	—	6
Patty Sheehan*	1996	1983-84, '93	1992, '94	—	—	—	6
Kathy Whitworth	—	1967, '71, '75	—	—	1965-66	1967	6
Karrie Webb*[3]	2000	2001	2000-2001	1999[3]	—	—	6

Tournaments: (1) Nabisco Championship, formerly Nabisco Dinah Shore (1982-1999), designated major in 1983. (2) U.S. Women's Open (3) In 2001, the British Open replaced the du Maurier Classic as the LPGA's 4th major. Karrie Webb won the 2002 Brit. Open. (4) Titleholders Championship; major from 1930 to 1972. (5) Western Open; major from 1937 to 1967.

Ladies Professional Golf Association Leading Money Winners

Year	Player	Earnings	Year	Player	Earnings	Year	Player	Earnings
1954	Patty Berg	$16,011	1970	Kathy Whitworth	$30,235	1986	Pat Bradley	$492,021
1955	Patty Berg	16,492	1971	Kathy Whitworth	41,181	1987	Ayako Okamoto	466,034
1956	Marlene Hagge	20,235	1972	Kathy Whitworth	65,063	1988	Sherri Turner	347,255
1957	Patty Berg	16,272	1973	Kathy Whitworth	82,854	1989	Betsy King	654,132
1958	Beverly Hanson	12,629	1974	JoAnne Carner	87,094	1990	Beth Daniel	863,578
1959	Betsy Rawls	26,774	1975	Sandra Palmer	94,805	1991	Pat Bradley	763,118
1960	Louise Suggs	16,892	1976	Judy Rankin	150,734	1992	Dottie Mochrie	693,335
1961	Mickey Wright	22,236	1977	Judy Rankin	122,890	1993	Betsy King	595,992
1962	Mickey Wright	21,641	1978	Nancy Lopez	189,813	1994	Laura Davies	687,201
1963	Mickey Wright	31,269	1979	Nancy Lopez	215,987	1995	Annika Sorenstam	666,533
1964	Mickey Wright	29,800	1980	Beth Daniel	231,000	1996	Karrie Webb	1,002,000
1965	Kathy Whitworth	28,658	1981	Beth Daniel	206,977	1997	Annika Sorenstam	1,236,789
1966	Kathy Whitworth	33,517	1982	JoAnne Carner	310,399	1998	Annika Sorenstam	1,092,748
1967	Kathy Whitworth	32,937	1983	JoAnne Carner	291,404	1999	Karrie Webb	1,591,959
1968	Kathy Whitworth	48,379	1984	Betsy King	266,771	2000	Karrie Webb	1,876,853
1969	Carol Mann	49,152	1985	Nancy Lopez	416,472	2001	Annika Sorenstam	2,105,868

Nabisco Championship Winners[1]

Year	Winner	Year	Winner	Year	Winner	Year	Winner
1983	Amy Alcott	1988	Amy Alcott	1993	Helen Alfredsson	1998	Pat Hurst
1984	Juli Inkster	1989	Juli Inkster	1994	Donna Andrews	1999	Dottie Pepper
1985	Alice Miller	1990	Betsy King	1995	Nanci Bowen	2000	Karrie Webb
1986	Pat Bradley	1991	Amy Alcott	1996	Patty Sheehan	2001	Annika Sorenstam
1987	Betsy King	1992	Dottie Pepper	1997	Betsy King	2002	Annika Sorenstam

(1) Formerly the Colgate Dinah Shore (1972-81), the Nabisco Dinah Shore (1982-99). Designated as a major championship in 1983.

LPGA Championship Winners

Year	Winner	Year	Winner	Year	Winner	Year	Winner
1955	Beverly Hanson	1967	Kathy Whitworth	1979	Donna Caponi	1991	Meg Mallon
1956	Marlene Hagge	1968	Sandra Post	1980	Sally Little	1992	Betsy King
1957	Louise Suggs	1969	Betsy Rawls	1981	Donna Caponi	1993	Patty Sheehan
1958	Mickey Wright	1970	Shirley Englehorn	1982	Jan Stephenson	1994	Laura Davies
1959	Betsy Rawls	1971	Kathy Whitworth	1983	Patty Sheehan	1995	Kelly Robbins
1960	Mickey Wright	1972	Kathy Ahern	1984	Patty Sheehan	1996	Laura Davies
1961	Mickey Wright	1973	Mary Mills	1985	Nancy Lopez	1997	Chris Johnson
1962	Judy Kimball	1974	Sandra Haynie	1986	Pat Bradley	1998	Se Ri Pak
1963	Mickey Wright	1975	Kathy Whitworth	1987	Jane Geddes	1999	Juli Inkster
1964	Mary Mills	1976	Betty Burfeindt	1988	Sherri Turner	2000	Juli Inkster
1965	Sandra Haynie	1977	Chako Higuchi	1989	Nancy Lopez	2001	Karrie Webb
1966	Gloria Ehret	1978	Nancy Lopez	1990	Beth Daniel	2002	Se Ri Pak

U.S. Women's Open Winners

Year	Winner	Year	Winner	Year	Winner	Year	Winner
1946	Patty Berg	1961	Mickey Wright	1975	Sandra Palmer	1989	Betsy King
1947	Betty Jameson	1962	Murle Lindstrom	1976	JoAnne Carner	1990	Betsy King
1948	"Babe" Zaharias	1963	Mary Mills	1977	Hollis Stacy	1991	Meg Mallon
1949	Louise Suggs	1964	Mickey Wright	1978	Hollis Stacy	1992	Patty Sheehan
1950	"Babe" Zaharias	1965	Carol Mann	1979	Jerilyn Britz	1993	Lauri Merten
1951	Betsy Rawls	1966	Sandra Spuzich	1980	Amy Alcott	1994	Patty Sheehan
1952	Louise Suggs	1967	Catherine Lacoste (amateur)	1981	Pat Bradley	1995	Annika Sorenstam
1953	Betsy Rawls			1982	Janet Alex	1996	Annika Sorenstam
1954	"Babe" Zaharias	1968	Susie Maxwell Berning	1983	Jan Stephenson	1997	Alison Nicholas
1955	Fay Crocker	1969	Donna Caponi	1984	Hollis Stacy	1998	Se Ri Pak
1956	Mrs. K. Cornelius	1970	Donna Caponi	1985	Kathy Baker	1999	Juli Inkster
1957	Betsy Rawls	1971	JoAnne Carner	1986	Jane Geddes	2000	Karrie Webb
1958	Mickey Wright	1972	Susie Maxwell Berning	1987	Laura Davies	2001	Karrie Webb
1959	Mickey Wright	1973	Susie Maxwell Berning	1988	Liselotte Neumann	2002	Juli Inkster
1960	Betsy Rawls	1974	Sandra Haynie				

du Maurier Classic Winners[1]

Year	Winner	Year	Winner	Year	Winner	Year	Winner
1979	Amy Alcott	1985	Pat Bradley	1991	Nancy Scranton	1996	Laura Davies
1980	Pat Bradley	1986	Pat Bradley	1992	Sherri Steinhauer	1997	Colleen Walker
1981	Jan Stephenson	1987	Jody Rosenthal	1993	Brandie Burton	1998	Brandie Burton
1982	Sandra Haynie	1988	Sally Little	1994	Martha Nause	1999	Karrie Webb
1983	Hollis Stacy	1989	Tammie Green	1995	Jenny Lidback	2000	Meg Mallon
1984	Juli Inkster	1990	Cathy Johnston				

(1) Formerly the Peter Jackson Classic (1974-82). Designated a major championship from 1979-2000. In 2001, the Women's British Open became the LPGA's 4th major and was won by South Korea's Se Ri Pak. Karrie Webb, of Australia, was the 2002 winner.

International Golf

Ryder Cup

Began as a biennial team competition between pro golfers from the U.S. and Great Britain. The British team was expanded in 1973 to include players from Ireland and in 1979 to include players from the rest of Europe. In 2002, the score was tied at 8 going into the singles competition on the final day at The Belfry in Sutton Coldfield, Eng., Sept. 29. Europe opened with 3 straight wins and went on to outscore the U.S. 7½ to 4½ in singles play. The 2004 Cup was scheduled for Sept. 14-19, at Oakland Hills CC, Bloomfield Hills, MI.

Year	Winner	Year	Winner	Year	Winner	Year	Winner
1927	U.S., 9½-2½	1951	U.S., 9½-2½	1967	U.S., 23½-8½	1985	Europe, 16½-11½
1929	Britain-Ireland, 7-5	1953	U.S., 6½-5½	1969	Draw, 16-16	1987	Europe, 15-13
1931	U.S., 9-3	1955	U.S., 8-4	1971	U.S., 18½-13½	1989	Draw, 14-14
1933	Britain, 6½-5½	1957	Britain-Ireland, 7½-4½	1973	U.S., 19-13	1991	U.S., 14½-13½
1935	U.S., 9-3			1975	U.S., 21-11	1993	U.S., 15-13
1937	U.S., 8-4	1959	U.S., 8½-3½	1977	U.S., 12½-7½	1995	Europe, 14½-13½
1939-45	Not played	1961	U.S., 14½-9½	1979	U.S., 17-11	1997	Europe, 14½-13½
1947	U.S., 11-1	1963	U.S., 23-9	1981	U.S., 18½-9½	1999	U.S., 14½-13½
1949	U.S., 7-5	1965	U.S., 19½-12½	1983	U.S., 14½-13½	2002	Europe, 15½, 12½

Solheim Cup

The Solheim Cup began in 1990 as a biennial team competition between women professional golfers from Europe and the U.S. In 2002, the U.S. trailed 9-7 going into the final round on Sept. 22, in Edina, MN, but won 7 matches and tied 3 to surpass the 14½ points needed to win. Competition was scheduled to move to odd years in 2003 to alternate with the Ryder Cup, which was postponed and moved permanently to even years after the 2001 terrorist attacks. The 2003 Cup was scheduled to be held Sept. 12-14, at Barsebäck Golf and Country Club in Sweden.

Year	Winner	Year	Winner	Year	Winner	Year	Winner
1990	U.S., 11½-4½	1994	U.S., 13-7	1998	U.S., 16-12	2002	U.S., 15½-12½
1992	Europe, 11½-6½	1996	U.S., 17-11	2000	Europe, 14½-11½		

TENNIS

All-Time Grand Slam Singles Titles Leaders

Men	Australian Open	French Open[1]	Wimbledon	U.S. Open	Total
Pete Sampras*	1994, '97	—	1993-95, '97-2000	1990, '93, '95-96, 2002	14
Roy Emerson	1961, '63-67	1963, '67	1964-65	1961, '64	12
Bjorn Borg	—	1974-75, 1978-81	1976-80	—	11
Rod Laver	1960, '62, '69	1962, '69	1961-62, '68-69	1962, '69	11
Bill Tilden	—	—	1920-21, '30	1920-25, '29	10
Jimmy Connors	1974	—	1974, '82	1974, '76, '78, '82-83	8
Ivan Lendl	1989-90	1984, '86-87	—	1985-87	8
Fred Perry	1934	1935	1934-36	1933-34, '36	8
Ken Rosewall	1953, '55, '71-72	1953, '68	—	1956, '70	8
Women					
Margaret Smith Court	1960-66, '69-71, '73	1962, '64, '69-70, '73	1963, '65, '70	1962, '65, '69-70, '73	24
Steffi Graf	1988-90, '94	1987-88, '93, '95-96, '99	1988-89, '91-93, '95-96	1988-89, '93, '95-96	22
Helen Wills Moody	—	1928-30, '32	1927-30, '32-33, '35, '38	1923-25, '27-29, '31	19
Chris Evert Lloyd	1982, '84	1974-75, '79-80, '83, '85-86	1974, '76, '81	1975-78, '80, '82	18
Martina Navratilova	1981, '83, '85	1982, '84	1978-79, '82-87, '90	1983-84, '86-87	18
Billie Jean King	1968	1972	1966-68, '72-73, '75	1967, '71-72, '74	12
Suzanne Lenglen	—	1920-23, '25-26	1919-23, '25	—	12
Maureen Connolly	1953	1953-54	1952-54	1951-53	9
Monica Seles*	1991-93, '96	1990-92	—	1991-92	9

*active player (1) Prior to 1925, French Open entry was limited to members of French clubs.

Australian Open Singles Champions, 1969-2002

(First contested 1905 for men, 1922 for women)

*2 tournaments held in 1977 (Jan. & Dec.). **In 1986 tournament moved to Jan. 1987; no championship in 1986.

Men's Singles

Year	Champion	Final Opponent	Year	Champion	Final Opponent
1969	Rod Laver	Andres Gimeno	1985**	Stefan Edberg	Mats Wilander
1970	Arthur Ashe	Dick Crealy	1987	Stefan Edberg	Pat Cash
1971	Ken Rosewall	Arthur Ashe	1988	Mats Wilander	Pat Cash
1972	Ken Rosewall	Mal Anderson	1989	Ivan Lendl	Miloslav Mecir
1973	John Newcombe	Onny Parun	1990	Ivan Lendl	Stefan Edberg
1974	Jimmy Connors	Phil Dent	1991	Boris Becker	Ivan Lendl
1975	John Newcombe	Jimmy Connors	1992	Jim Courier	Stefan Edberg
1976	Mark Edmondson	John Newcombe	1993	Jim Courier	Stefan Edberg
1977*	Roscoe Tanner	Guillermo Vilas	1994	Pete Sampras	Todd Martin
	Vitas Gerulaitis	John Lloyd	1995	Andre Agassi	Pete Sampras
1978	Guillermo Vilas	John Marks	1996	Boris Becker	Michael Chang
1979	Guillermo Vilas	John Sadri	1997	Pete Sampras	Carlos Moya
1980	Brian Teacher	Kim Warwick	1998	Petr Korda	Marcelo Rios
1981	Johan Kriek	Steve Denton	1999	Yevgeny Kafelnikov	Thomas Enqvist
1982	Johan Kriek	Steve Denton	2000	Andre Agassi	Yevgeny Kafelnikov
1983	Mats Wilander	Ivan Lendl	2001	Andre Agassi	Arnaud Clement
1984	Mats Wilander	Kevin Curren	2002	Thomas Johansson	Marat Safin

Women's Singles

Year	Champion	Final Opponent	Year	Champion	Final Opponent
1969	Margaret Smith Court	Billie Jean King	1985**	Martina Navratilova	Chris Evert Lloyd
1970	Margaret Smith Court	Kerry Melville Reid	1987	Hana Mandlikova	Martina Navratilova
1971	Margaret Smith Court	Evonne Goolagong	1988	Steffi Graf	Chris Evert
1972	Virginia Wade	Evonne Goolagong	1989	Steffi Graf	Helena Sukova
1973	Margaret Smith Court	Evonne Goolagong	1990	Steffi Graf	Mary Joe Fernandez
1974	Evonne Goolagong	Chris Evert	1991	Monica Seles	Jana Novotna
1975	Evonne Goolagong	Martina Navratilova	1992	Monica Seles	Mary Joe Fernandez
1976	Evonne Goolagong	Renata Tomanova	1993	Monica Seles	Steffi Graf
1977*	Kerry Reid	Dianne Balestrat	1994	Steffi Graf	Arantxa Sánchez Vicario
	Evonne Goolagong	Helen Gourlay	1995	Mary Pierce	Arantxa Sánchez Vicario
1978	Chris O'Neill	Betsy Nagelsen	1996	Monica Seles	Anke Huber
1979	Barbara Jordan	Sharon Walsh	1997	Martina Hingis	Mary Pierce
1980	Hana Mandlikova	Wendy Turnbull	1998	Martina Hingis	Conchita Martínez
1981	Martina Navratilova	Chris Evert Lloyd	1999	Martina Hingis	Amelie Mauresmo
1982	Chris Evert Lloyd	Martina Navratilova	2000	Lindsay Davenport	Martina Hingis
1983	Martina Navratilova	Kathy Jordan	2001	Jennifer Capriati	Martina Hingis
1984	Chris Evert Lloyd	Helena Sukova	2002	Jennifer Capriati	Martina Hingis

French Open Singles Champions, 1968-2002

(First contested 1925)

Men's Singles

Year	Champion	Final Opponent	Year	Champion	Final Opponent
1968	Ken Rosewall	Rod Laver	1986	Ivan Lendl	Mikael Pernfors
1969	Rod Laver	Ken Rosewall	1987	Ivan Lendl	Mats Wilander
1970	Jan Kodes	Zeljko Franulovic	1988	Mats Wilander	Henri Leconte
1971	Jan Kodes	Ilie Nastase	1989	Michael Chang	Stefan Edberg
1972	Andres Gimeno	Patrick Proisy	1990	Andres Gomez	Andre Agassi
1973	Ilie Nastase	Nikki Pilic	1991	Jim Courier	Andre Agassi
1974	Bjorn Borg	Manuel Orantes	1992	Jim Courier	Petr Korda
1975	Bjorn Borg	Guillermo Vilas	1993	Sergi Bruguera	Jim Courier
1976	Adriano Panatta	Harold Solomon	1994	Sergi Bruguera	Alberto Berasategui
1977	Guillermo Vilas	Brian Gottfried	1995	Thomas Muster	Michael Chang
1978	Bjorn Borg	Guillermo Vilas	1996	Yevgeny Kafelnikov	Michael Stich
1979	Bjorn Borg	Victor Pecci	1997	Gustavo Kuerten	Sergei Bruguera
1980	Bjorn Borg	Vitas Gerulaitis	1998	Carlos Moya	Alex Corretja
1981	Bjorn Borg	Ivan Lendl	1999	Andre Agassi	Andrei Medvedev
1982	Mats Wilander	Guillermo Vilas	2000	Gustavo Kuerten	Magnus Norman
1983	Yannick Noah	Mats Wilander	2001	Gustavo Kuerten	Alex Corretja
1984	Ivan Lendl	John McEnroe	2002	Albert Costa	Juan Carlos Ferrero
1985	Mats Wilander	Ivan Lendl			

Women's Singles

Year	Champion	Final Opponent
1968	Nancy Richey	Ann Jones
1969	Margaret Smith Court	Ann Jones
1970	Margaret Smith Court	Helga Niessen
1971	Evonne Goolagong	Helen Gourlay
1972	Billie Jean King	Evonne Goolagong
1973	Margaret Smith Court	Chris Evert
1974	Chris Evert	Olga Morozova
1975	Chris Evert	Martina Navratilova
1976	Sue Barker	Renata Tomanova
1977	Mima Jausovec	Florenza Mihai
1978	Virginia Ruzici	Mima Jausovec
1979	Chris Evert Lloyd	Wendy Turnbull
1980	Chris Evert Lloyd	Virginia Ruzici
1981	Hana Mandlikova	Sylvia Hanika
1982	Martina Navratilova	Andrea Jaeger
1983	Chris Evert Lloyd	Mima Jausovec
1984	Martina Navratilova	Chris Evert Lloyd
1985	Chris Evert Lloyd	Martina Navratilova
1986	Chris Evert Lloyd	Martina Navratilova
1987	Steffi Graf	Martina Navratilova
1988	Steffi Graf	Natalia Zvereva
1989	Arantxa Sánchez Vicario	Steffi Graf
1990	Monica Seles	Steffi Graf
1991	Monica Seles	Arantxa Sánchez Vicario
1992	Monica Seles	Steffi Graf
1993	Steffi Graf	Mary Joe Fernandez
1994	Arantxa Sánchez Vicario	Mary Pierce
1995	Steffi Graf	Arantxa Sánchez Vicario
1996	Steffi Graf	Arantxa Sánchez Vicario
1997	Iva Majoli	Martina Hingis
1998	Arantxa Sánchez Vicario	Monica Seles
1999	Steffi Graf	Martina Hingis
2000	Mary Pierce	Conchita Martinez
2001	Jennifer Capriati	Kim Clijsters
2002	Serena Williams	Venus Williams

All-England Champions, Wimbledon, 1925-2002

Men's Singles

(First contested 1877)

Year	Champion	Final Opponent
1925	Rene Lacoste	Jean Borotra
1926	Jean Borotra	Howard Kinsey
1927	Henri Cochet	Jean Borotra
1928	Rene Lacoste	Henri Cochet
1929	Henri Cochet	Jean Borotra
1930	Bill Tilden	Wilmer Allison
1931	Sidney B. Wood	Francis X. Shields
1932	Ellsworth Vines	Henry Austin
1933	Jack Crawford	Ellsworth Vines
1934	Fred Perry	Jack Crawford
1935	Fred Perry	Gottfried von Cramm
1936	Fred Perry	Gottfried von Cramm
1937	Donald Budge	Gottfried von Cramm
1938	Donald Budge	Henry Austin
1939	Bobby Riggs	Elwood Cooke
1940-45	Not held	Not held
1946	Yvon Petra	Geoff E. Brown
1947	Jack Kramer	Tom P. Brown
1948	Bob Falkenburg	John Bromwich
1949	Ted Schroeder	Jaroslav Drobny
1950	Budge Patty	Frank Sedgman
1951	Dick Savitt	Ken McGregor
1952	Frank Sedgman	Jaroslav Drobny
1953	Vic Seixas	Kurt Nielsen
1954	Jaroslav Drobny	Ken Rosewall
1955	Tony Trabert	Kurt Nielsen
1956	Lew Hoad	Ken Rosewall
1957	Lew Hoad	Ashley Cooper
1958	Ashley Cooper	Neale Fraser
1959	Alex Olmedo	Rod Laver
1960	Neale Fraser	Rod Laver
1961	Rod Laver	Chuck McKinley
1962	Rod Laver	Martin Mulligan
1963	Chuck McKinley	Fred Stolle
1964	Roy Emerson	Fred Stolle
1965	Roy Emerson	Fred Stolle
1966	Manuel Santana	Dennis Ralston
1967	John Newcombe	Wilhelm Bungert
1968	Rod Laver	Tony Roche
1969	Rod Laver	John Newcombe
1970	John Newcombe	Ken Rosewall
1971	John Newcombe	Stan Smith
1972	Stan Smith	Ilie Nastase
1973	Jan Kodes	Alex Metreveli
1974	Jimmy Connors	Ken Rosewall
1975	Arthur Ashe	Jimmy Connors
1976	Bjorn Borg	Ilie Nastase
1977	Bjorn Borg	Jimmy Connors
1978	Bjorn Borg	Jimmy Connors
1979	Bjorn Borg	Roscoe Tanner
1980	Bjorn Borg	John McEnroe
1981	John McEnroe	Bjorn Borg
1982	Jimmy Connors	John McEnroe
1983	John McEnroe	Chris Lewis
1984	John McEnroe	Jimmy Connors
1985	Boris Becker	Kevin Curren
1986	Boris Becker	Ivan Lendl
1987	Pat Cash	Ivan Lendl
1988	Stefan Edberg	Boris Becker
1989	Boris Becker	Stefan Edberg
1990	Stefan Edberg	Boris Becker
1991	Michael Stich	Boris Becker
1992	Andre Agassi	Goran Ivanisevic
1993	Pete Sampras	Jim Courier
1994	Pete Sampras	Goran Ivanisevic
1995	Pete Sampras	Boris Becker
1996	Richard Krajicek	MaliVai Washington
1997	Pete Sampras	Cedric Pioline
1998	Pete Sampras	Goran Ivanisevic
1999	Pete Sampras	Andre Agassi
2000	Pete Sampras	Patrick Rafter
2001	Goran Ivanisevic	Patrick Rafter
2002	Lleyton Hewitt	David Nalbandian

Women's Singles

(First contested 1884)

Year	Champion	Final Opponent
1925	Suzanne Lenglen	Joan Fry
1926	Kathleen McKane Godfree	Lili de Alvarez
1927	Helen Wills	Lili de Alvarez
1928	Helen Wills	Lili de Alvarez
1929	Helen Wills	Helen Jacobs
1930	Helen Wills Moody	Elizabeth Ryan
1931	Cilly Aussem	Hilde Kranwinkel
1932	Helen Wills Moody	Helen Jacobs
1933	Helen Wills Moody	Dorothy Round
1934	Dorothy Round	Helen Jacobs
1935	Helen Wills Moody	Helen Jacobs
1936	Helen Jacobs	Hilde Kranwinkel Sperling
1937	Dorothy Round	Jadwiga Jedrzejowska
1938	Helen Wills Moody	Helen Jacobs
1939	Alice Marble	Kay Stammers
1940-45	Not held	Not held
1946	Pauline Betz	Louise Brough
1947	Margaret Osborne	Doris Hart
1948	Louise Brough	Doris Hart
1949	Louise Brough	Margaret Osborne duPont
1950	Louise Brough	Margaret Osborne duPont
1951	Doris Hart	Shirley Fry
1952	Maureen Connolly	Louise Brough
1953	Maureen Connolly	Doris Hart
1954	Maureen Connolly	Louise Brough
1955	Louise Brough	Beverly Fleitz
1956	Shirley Fry	Angela Buxton
1957	Althea Gibson	Darlene Hard
1958	Althea Gibson	Angela Mortimer
1959	Maria Bueno	Darlene Hard
1960	Maria Bueno	Sandra Reynolds
1961	Angela Mortimer	Christine Truman
1962	Karen Hantze-Susman	Vera Sukova
1963	Margaret Smith	Billie Jean Moffitt
1964	Maria Bueno	Margaret Smith
1965	Margaret Smith	Maria Bueno
1966	Billie Jean King	Maria Bueno
1967	Billie Jean King	Ann Haydon Jones
1968	Billie Jean King	Judy Tegart
1969	Ann Haydon-Jones	Billie Jean King
1970	Margaret Smith Court	Billie Jean King
1971	Evonne Goolagong	Margaret Smith Court
1972	Billie Jean King	Evonne Goolagong
1973	Billie Jean King	Chris Evert
1974	Chris Evert	Olga Morozova
1975	Billie Jean King	Evonne Goolagong Cawley

Year	Champion	Final Opponent
1976	Chris Evert	Evonne Goolagong Cawley
1977	Virginia Wade	Betty Stove
1978	Martina Navratilova	Chris Evert
1979	Martina Navratilova	Chris Evert Lloyd
1980	Evonne Goolagong	Chris Evert Lloyd
1981	Chris Evert Lloyd	Hana Mandlikova
1982	Martina Navratilova	Chris Evert Lloyd
1983	Martina Navratilova	Andrea Jaeger
1984	Martina Navratilova	Chris Evert Lloyd
1985	Martina Navratilova	Chris Evert Lloyd
1986	Martina Navratilova	Hana Mandlikova
1987	Martina Navratilova	Steffi Graf
1988	Steffi Graf	Martina Navratilova
1989	Steffi Graf	Martina Navratilova
1990	Martina Navratilova	Zina Garrison
1991	Steffi Graf	Gabriela Sabatini
1992	Steffi Graf	Monica Seles
1993	Steffi Graf	Jana Novotna
1994	Conchita Martinez	Martina Navratilova
1995	Steffi Graf	Arantxa Sánchez Vicario
1996	Steffi Graf	Arantxa Sánchez Vicario
1997	Martina Hingis	Jana Novotna
1998	Jana Novotna	Nathalie Tauziat
1999	Lindsay Davenport	Steffi Graf
2000	Venus Williams	Lindsay Davenport
2001	Venus Williams	Justine Henin
2002	Serena Williams	Venus Williams

U.S. Open Champions, 1925-2002

Men's Singles

(First contested 1881)

Year	Champion	Final Opponent
1925	Bill Tilden	William Johnston
1926	Rene Lacoste	Jean Borotra
1927	Rene Lacoste	Bill Tilden
1928	Henri Cochet	Francis Hunter
1929	Bill Tilden	Francis Hunter
1930	John Doeg	Francis Shields
1931	H. Ellsworth Vines	George Lott
1932	H. Ellsworth Vines	Henri Cochet
1933	Fred Perry	John Crawford
1934	Fred Perry	Wilmer Allison
1935	Wilmer Allison	Sidney Wood
1936	Fred Perry	Don Budge
1937	Don Budge	Baron G. von Cramm
1938	Don Budge	C. Gene Mako
1939	Robert Riggs	S. Welby Van Horn
1940	Don McNeill	Robert Riggs
1941	Robert Riggs	F. L. Kovacs
1942	F. R. Schroeder Jr.	Frank Parker
1943	Joseph Hunt	Jack Kramer
1944	Frank Parker	William Talbert
1945	Frank Parker	William Talbert
1946	Jack Kramer	Thomas Brown Jr.
1947	Jack Kramer	Frank Parker
1948	Pancho Gonzales	Eric Sturgess
1949	Pancho Gonzales	F. R. Schroeder Jr.
1950	Arthur Larsen	Herbert Flam
1951	Frank Sedgman	E. Victor Seixas Jr.
1952	Frank Sedgman	Gardnar Mulloy
1953	Tony Trabert	E. Victor Seixas Jr.
1954	E. Victor Seixas Jr.	Rex Hartwig
1955	Tony Trabert	Ken Rosewall
1956	Ken Rosewall	Lewis Hoad
1957	Malcolm Anderson	Ashley Cooper
1958	Ashley Cooper	Malcolm Anderson
1959	Neale A. Fraser	Alejandro Olmedo
1960	Neale A. Fraser	Rod Laver
1961	Roy Emerson	Rod Laver
1962	Rod Laver	Roy Emerson
1963	Rafael Osuna	F. A. Froehling 3d
1964	Roy Emerson	Fred Stolle
1965	Manuel Santana	Cliff Drysdale
1966	Fred Stolle	John Newcombe
1967	John Newcombe	Clark Graebner
1968	Arthur Ashe	Tom Okker
1969	Rod Laver	Tony Roche
1970	Ken Rosewall	Tony Roche
1971	Stan Smith	Jan Kodes
1972	Ilie Nastase	Arthur Ashe
1973	John Newcombe	Jan Kodes
1974	Jimmy Connors	Ken Rosewall
1975	Manuel Orantes	Jimmy Connors
1976	Jimmy Connors	Bjorn Borg
1977	Guillermo Vilas	Jimmy Connors
1978	Jimmy Connors	Bjorn Borg
1979	John McEnroe	Vitas Gerulaitis
1980	John McEnroe	Bjorn Borg
1981	John McEnroe	Bjorn Borg
1982	Jimmy Connors	Ivan Lendl
1983	Jimmy Connors	Ivan Lendl
1984	John McEnroe	Ivan Lendl
1985	Ivan Lendl	John McEnroe
1986	Ivan Lendl	Miloslav Mecir
1987	Ivan Lendl	Mats Wilander
1988	Mats Wilander	Ivan Lendl
1989	Boris Becker	Ivan Lendl
1990	Pete Sampras	Andre Agassi
1991	Stefan Edberg	Jim Courier
1992	Stefan Edberg	Pete Sampras
1993	Pete Sampras	Cedric Pioline
1994	Andre Agassi	Michael Stich
1995	Pete Sampras	Andre Agassi
1996	Pete Sampras	Michael Chang
1997	Patrick Rafter	Greg Rusedski
1998	Patrick Rafter	Mark Philippoussis
1999	Andre Agassi	Todd Martin
2000	Marat Safin	Pete Sampras
2001	Lleyton Hewitt	Pete Sampras
2002	Pete Sampras	Andre Agassi

Women's Singles

(First contested 1887)

Year	Champion	Final Opponent
1925	Helen Willis	Kathleen McKane
1926	Molla B. Mallory	Elizabeth Ryan
1927	Helen Wills	Betty Nuthall
1928	Helen Wills	Helen Jacobs
1929	Helen Wills	M. Watson
1930	Betty Nuthall	L. A. Harper
1931	Helen Wills Moody	E. B. Whittingstall
1932	Helen Jacobs	Carolin A. Babcock
1933	Helen Jacobs	Helen Wills Moody
1934	Helen Jacobs	Sarah H. Palfrey
1935	Helen Jacobs	Sarah Palfrey Fabyan
1936	Alice Marble	Helen Jacobs
1937	Anita Lizana	Jadwiga Jedrzejowska
1938	Alice Marble	Nancye Wynne
1939	Alice Marble	Helen Jacobs
1940	Alice Marble	Helen Jacobs
1941	Sarah Palfrey Cooke	Pauline Betz
1942	Pauline Betz	Louise Brough
1943	Pauline Betz	Louise Brough
1944	Pauline Betz	Margaret Osborne
1945	Sarah Palfrey Cooke	Pauline Betz
1946	Pauline Betz	Doris Hart
1947	Louise Brough	Margaret Osborne
1948	Margaret Osborne duPont	Louise Brough
1949	Margaret Osborne duPont	Doris Hart
1950	Margaret Osborne duPont	Doris Hart
1951	Maureen Connolly	Shirley Fry
1952	Maureen Connolly	Doris Hart
1953	Maureen Connolly	Doris Hart
1954	Doris Hart	Louise Brough
1955	Doris Hart	Patricia Ward
1956	Shirley Fry	Althea Gibson
1957	Althea Gibson	Louise Brough
1958	Althea Gibson	Darlene Hard
1959	Maria Bueno	Christine Truman
1960	Darlene Hard	Maria Bueno
1961	Darlene Hard	Ann Haydon
1962	Margaret Smith	Darlene Hard
1963	Maria Bueno	Margaret Smith
1964	Maria Bueno	Carole Graebner
1965	Margaret Smith	Billie Jean Moffitt
1966	Maria Bueno	Nancy Richey
1967	Billie Jean King	Ann Haydon Jones
1968	Virginia Wade	Billie Jean King
1969	Margaret Smith Court	Nancy Richey
1970	Margaret Smith Court	Rosemary Casals
1971	Billie Jean King	Rosemary Casals
1972	Billie Jean King	Kerry Melville
1973	Margaret Smith Court	Evonne Goolagong
1974	Billie Jean King	Evonne Goolagong

Year	Champion	Final Opponent
1975	Chris Evert	Evonne Goolagong
1976	Chris Evert	Evonne Goolagong
1977	Chris Evert	Wendy Turnbull
1978	Chris Evert	Pam Shriver
1979	Tracy Austin	Chris Evert Lloyd
1980	Chris Evert Lloyd	Hana Mandlikova
1981	Tracy Austin	Martina Navratilova
1982	Chris Evert Lloyd	Hana Mandlikova
1983	Martina Navratilova	Chris Evert Lloyd
1984	Martina Navratilova	Chris Evert Lloyd
1985	Hana Mandlikova	Martina Navratilova
1986	Martina Navratilova	Helena Sukova
1987	Martina Navratilova	Steffi Graf
1988	Steffi Graf	Gabriela Sabatini
1989	Steffi Graf	Martina Navratilova
1990	Gabriela Sabatini	Steffi Graf
1991	Monica Seles	Martina Navratilova
1992	Monica Seles	Arantxa Sanchez Vicario
1993	Steffi Graf	Helena Sukova
1994	Arantxa Sanchez Vicario	Steffi Graf
1995	Steffi Graf	Monica Seles
1996	Steffi Graf	Monica Seles
1997	Martina Hingis	Venus Williams
1998	Lindsay Davenport	Martina Hingis
1999	Serena Williams	Martina Hingis
2000	Venus Williams	Lindsay Davenport
2001	Venus Williams	Serena Williams
2002	Serena Williams	Venus Williams

Davis Cup Challenge Round, 1900-2001

Year	Result
1900	United States 3, British Isles 0
1901	Not held
1902	United States 3, British Isles 2
1903	British Isles 4, United States 1
1904	British Isles 5, Belgium 0
1905	British Isles 5, United States 0
1906	British Isles 5, United States 0
1907	Australia 3, British Isles 2
1908	Australasia 3, United States 2
1909	Australasia 5, United States 0
1910	Not held
1911	Australasia 5, United States 0
1912	British Isles 3, Australasia 2
1913	United States 3, British Isles 2
1914	Australasia 3, United States 2
1915-18	Not held
1919	Australasia 4, British Isles 1
1920	United States 5, Australasia 0
1921	United States 5, Japan 0
1922	United States 4, Australasia 1
1923	United States 4, Australasia 1
1924	United States 5, Australasia 0
1925	United States 5, France 0
1926	United States 4, France 1
1927	France 3, United States 2
1928	France 4, United States 1
1929	France 3, United States 2
1930	France 4, United States 1
1931	France 3, Great Britain 2
1932	France 3, United States 2
1933	Great Britain 3, France 2
1934	Great Britain 4, United States 1
1935	Great Britain 5, United States 0
1936	Great Britain 3, Australia 2
1937	United States 4, Great Britain 1
1938	United States 3, Australia 2
1939	Australia 3, United States 2
1940-45	Not held
1946	United States 5, Australia 0
1947	United States 4, Australia 1
1948	United States 5, Australia 0
1949	United States 4, Australia 1
1950	Australia 4, United States 1
1951	Australia 3, United States 2
1952	Australia 4, United States 1
1953	Australia 3, United States 2
1954	United States 3, Australia 2
1955	Australia 5, United States 0
1956	Australia 5, United States 0
1957	Australia 3, United States 2
1958	United States 3, Australia 2
1959	Australia 3, United States 2
1960	Australia 4, Italy 1
1961	Australia 5, Italy 0
1962	Australia 5, Mexico 0
1963	United States 3, Australia 2
1964	Australia 3, United States 2
1965	Australia 4, Spain 1
1966	Australia 4, India 1
1967	Australia 4, Spain 1
1968	United States 4, Australia
1969	United States 5, Romania 0
1970	United States 5, W. Germany 0
1971	United States 3, Romania 2
1972	United States 3, Romania 2
1973	Australia 5, United States 0
1974	South Africa (default by India)
1975	Sweden 3, Czechoslovakia 2
1976	Italy 4, Chile 1
1977	Australia 3, Italy 1
1978	United States 4, Great Britain 1
1979	United States 5, Italy 0
1980	Czechoslovakia 4, Italy 1
1981	United States 3, Argentina 1
1982	United States 4, France, 1
1983	Australia 3, Sweden 2
1984	Sweden 4, United States 1
1985	Sweden 3, W. Germany 2
1986	Australia 3, Sweden 2
1987	Sweden 5, India 0
1988	W. Germany 4, Sweden 1
1989	W. Germany 3, Sweden 2
1990	United States 3, Australia 2
1991	France 3, United States 1
1992	United States 3, Switzerland 1
1993	Germany 4, Australia 1
1994	Sweden 4, Russia 1
1995	United States 3, Russia 2
1996	France 3, Sweden 2
1997	Sweden 5, United States 0
1998	Sweden 4, Italy 1
1999	Australia 3, France 2
2000	Spain 3, Australia 1
2001	France 3, Australia 2

RIFLE AND PISTOL INDIVIDUAL CHAMPIONSHIPS

Source: National Rifle Association

National Outdoor Rifle and Pistol Championships in 2002

Pistol—GYSG Brian Zins, USMC, Quantico, VA, 2611-110x
Civilian Pistol—Lawrence B. Carter, Portland, ME, 2611-101x
Woman Pistol—Kimberly Hobart, New Philadelphia, OH, 2528-67x
Smallbore Rifle Prone—Lawrence Wigger, Colorado Springs, CO, 6377-468x
Civilian Smallbore Rifle Prone—Lawrence Wigger, Colorado Springs, CO, 6377-468x
Woman Smallbore Rifle Prone—Carolyn D. Sparks, Dunwoody, GA, 6370-127x
Smallbore Rifle NRA 3-Position—SPC Shane M. Barnhart, USA, Phenix City, AL, 2290-83x
Civilian Smallbore Rifle NRA 3-Position—Jeffrey Doerschler, Wetherfield, CT, 2285-95x
Woman Smallbore Rifle NRA 3-Position—Jamie L. Beyerle, Lebanon, PA, 2279-76x
High Power Rifle—G. David Tubb, Canadian, TX, 2365-121x
Civilian High Power Rifle—G. David Tubb, Canadian, TX, 2365-121x
Woman High Power Rifle—Robin Maly, Lodi, WI, 2315-72x
High Power Rifle Long Range—Joshua K. Harless, Fountain, CO, 1438-79x
Civilian High Power Rifle Long Range—Joshua K. Harless, Fountain, CO, 1438-79x
Woman High Power Rifle Long Range—Sherri J. Gallagher, Prescott, AZ, 1438-63x

National Indoor Rifle and Pistol Championships in 2002

Smallbore Rifle 4-Position—Jason Parker, Cusseta, GA, 800-68x
Woman Smallbore Rifle 4-Position—Karyn Manges, Waverly Hall, GA, 797-67x
Smallbore Rifle NRA 3-Position—Michael Anti, Ft. Benning, GA, 1189-76x
Woman Smallbore Rifle NRA 3-Position—Jamie Beyerle, Lebanon, PA, 1176-77x
International Smallbore Rifle—Michael Anti, Ft. Benning, GA, 1190-89x
Woman International Smallbore Rifle—Amber Darland, Fairbanks, AK, 1178-75x
Air Rifle—Matthew Emmons, Browns Mill, NJ, 598
Woman Air Rifle—Gerda Szakonyi, Denver, CO, 585
Conventional Pistol—Gary Spear, Harpursville, NY, 884-34x
Woman Conventional Pistol—Kathy Chatterton, Glen Rock, NJ, 866-31x
International Free Pistol—Tony Silva, Merced, CA, 537
Woman International Free Pistol—Kathy Chatterton, Glen Rock, NJ, 501
International Standard Pistol—Eric Weeldreyer, Kalamazoo, MI, 569
Woman International Standard Pistol—Kathy Chatterton, Glen Rock, NJ, 544
Air Pistol—Chris Alto, Portland, OR, 576
Woman Air Pistol—Laura Tyler, Craig, CO, 540

NRA Bianchi Cup National Action Pistol Championships in 2002

Action Pistol—Doug Koenig, Albertus, PA, 1920.184
Woman Action Pistol—Vera Koo, Menlo Park, CA, 1905.151
Junior Action Pistol—Mitch Conrad, Tulsa, OK, 1903.166

AUTO RACING

Indianapolis 500 Winners

Year	Winner, Car (Chassis-Engine)	MPH[1]
1911	Ray Harroun, Marmon	74.602
1912	Joe Dawson, National	78.719
1913	Jules Goux, Peugeot	75.933
1914	Rene Thomas, Delage	82.474
1915	Ralph DePalma, Mercedes	89.840
1916	Dario Resta, Peugeot	84.001
1917-18	—Not held	
1919	Howdy Wilcox, Peugeot	88.050
1920	Gaston Chevrolet, Frontenac	88.618
1921	Tommy Milton, Frontenac	89.621
1922	Jimmy Murphy, Duesenberg-Miller	94.484
1923	Tommy Milton, Miller	90.954
1924	L.L. Corum-Joe Boyer, Duesenberg	98.234
1925	Peter DePaolo, Duesenberg	101.127
1926	Frank Lockhart, Miller	95.904
1927	George Souders, Duesenberg	97.545
1928	Louie Meyer, Miller	99.482
1929	Ray Keech, Miller	97.585
1930	Billy Arnold, Summers-Miller	100.448
1931	Louis Schneider, Stevens-Miller	96.629
1932	Fred Frame, Wetteroth-Miller	104.144
1933	Louie Meyer, Miller	104.162
1934	Bill Cummings, Miller	104.863
1935	Kelly Petillo, Wetteroth-Offy	106.240
1936	Louie Meyer, Stevens-Miller	109.069
1937	Wilbur Shaw, Shaw-Offy	113.580
1938	Floyd Roberts, Wetteroth-Miller	117.200
1939	Wilbur Shaw, Maserati	115.035
1940	Wilbur Shaw, Maserati	114.277
1941	Floyd Davis-Mauri Rose, Wetteroth-Offy	115.117
1942-45	—Not held	
1946	George Robson, Adams-Sparks	114.820
1947	Mauri Rose, Deidt-Offy	116.338
1948	Mauri Rose, Deidt-Offy	119.814
1949	Bill Holland, Deidt-Offy	121.327
1950	Johnnie Parsons, Kurtis-Offy	124.002
1951	Lee Wallard, Kurtis-Offy	126.244
1952	Troy Ruttman, Kuzma-Offy	128.922
1953	Bill Vukovich, KK500A-Offy	128.740
1954	Bill Vukovich, KK500A-Offy	130.840
1955	Bob Sweikert, KK500C-Offy	128.213
1956	Pat Flaherty, Watson-Offy	128.490
1957	Sam Hanks, Salih-Offy	135.601
1958	Jimmy Bryan, Salih-Offy	133.791
1959	Rodger Ward, Watson-Offy	135.857
1960	Jim Rathmann, Watson-Offy	138.767
1961	A.J. Foyt Jr., Trevis-Offy	139.130
1962	Rodger Ward, Watson-Offy	140.293
1963	Parnelli Jones, Watson-Offy	143.137
1964	A.J. Foyt Jr., Watson-Offy	147.350
1965	Jim Clark, Lotus-Ford	150.686
1966	Graham Hill, Lola-Ford	144.317
1967	A.J. Foyt Jr., Coyote-Ford	151.207
1968	Bobby Unser, Eagle-Offy	152.882
1969	Mario Andretti, Hawk-Ford	156.867
1970	Al Unser, P.J. Colt-Ford	155.749
1971	Al Unser, P.J. Colt-Ford	157.735
1972	Mark Donohue, McLaren-Offy	162.962
1973	Gordon Johncock, Eagle-Offy	159.036
1974	Johnny Rutherford, McLaren-Offy	158.589
1975	Bobby Unser, Eagle-Offy	149.213
1976	Johnny Rutherford, McLaren-Offy	148.725
1977	A.J. Foyt Jr., Coyote-Foyt	161.331
1978	Al Unser, Lola-Cosworth	161.363
1979	Rick Mears, Penske-Cosworth	158.899
1980	Johnny Rutherford, Chaparral-Cosworth	142.862
1981	Bobby Unser, Penske-Cosworth	139.084
1982	Gordon Johncock, Wildcat-Cosworth	162.029
1983	Tom Sneva, March-Cosworth	162.117
1984	Rick Mears, March-Cosworth	163.612
1985	Danny Sullivan, March-Cosworth	152.982
1986	Bobby Rahal, March-Cosworth	170.722
1987	Al Unser, March-Cosworth	162.175
1988	Rick Mears, Penske-Chevy Indy V8	144.809
1989	Emerson Fittipaldi, Penske-Chevy Indy V8	167.581
1990	Arie Luyendyk, Lola-Chevy Indy V8	185.981*
1991	Rick Mears, Penske-Chevy Indy V8	176.457
1992	Al Unser Jr., Galmer-Chevy Indy V8A	134.477
1993	Emerson Fittipaldi, Penske-Chevy Indy V8C	157.207
1994	Al Unser Jr., Penske-Mercedes Benz	160.872
1995	Jacques Villeneuve, Reynard-Ford Cosworth XB	153.616
1996	Buddy Lazier, Reynard-Ford Cosworth	147.956
1997	Arie Luyendyk, G Force-Aurora	145.827
1998	Eddie Cheever, Dallara-Aurora	145.155
1999	Kenny Brack, Dallara-Aurora	153.176
2000	Juan Montoya, G Force-Aurora	167.607
2001	Helio Castroneves, Reynard-Honda	131.294
2002	Helio Castroneves, Reynard-Honda	166.499

*Race record. **Note:** The race was less than 500 mi in the following years: 1916 (300 mi), 1926 (400 mi), 1950 (345 mi), 1973 (332.5 mi), 1975 (435 mi), 1976 (255 mi). (1) Average speed.

FedEx Championship Series PPG Cup Winners

(U.S. Auto Club Champions prior to 1979; Championship Auto Racing Teams [CART] Champions, 1979-2001)

Year	Driver
1959	Roger Ward
1960	A. J. Foyt
1961	A. J. Foyt
1962	Rodger Ward
1963	A. J. Foyt
1964	A. J. Foyt
1965	Mario Andretti
1966	Mario Andretti
1967	A. J. Foyt
1968	Bobby Unser
1969	Mario Andretti
1970	Al Unser
1971	Joe Leonard
1972	Joe Leonard
1973	Roger McCluskey
1974	Bobby Unser
1975	A. J. Foyt
1976	Gordon Johncock
1977	Tom Sneva
1978	Tom Sneva
1979	Rick Mears
1980	Johnny Rutherford
1981	Rick Mears
1982	Rick Mears
1983	Al Unser
1984	Mario Andretti
1985	Al Unser
1986	Bobby Rahal
1987	Bobby Rahal
1988	Danny Sullivan
1989	Emerson Fittipaldi
1990	Al Unser Jr.
1991	Michael Andretti
1992	Bobby Rahal
1993	Nigel Mansell
1994	Al Unser Jr.
1995	Jacques Villeneuve
1996	Jimmy Vasser
1997	Alex Zanardi
1998	Alex Zanardi
1999	Juan Montoya
2000	Gil de Ferran
2001	Gil de Ferran

Notable One-Mile Land Speed Records

Andy Green, a Royal Air Force pilot, broke the sound barrier and set the first supersonic world speed record on land, Oct. 15, 1997, in Black Rock Desert, NV. Green, driving a car built by Richard Noble, had 2 runs at an average speed of 763.035 mph, as calculated according to the rules of the Federation Internationale Automobiliste (FIA). This record and speed exceeded the speed of sound, calculated at 751.251 mph for that place and time. On Sept. 25, 1997, Green had set a new world mark at 714.144 mph, which eclipsed the old record of 633.468 mph. Both records were recorded by the U.S. Auto Club and recognized by the FIA.

Date	Driver	Car	MPH
1/26/06	Marriott	Stanley (Steam)	127.659
3/16/10	Oldfield	Benz	131.724
4/23/11	Burman	Benz	141.732
2/12/19	DePalma	Packard	149.875
4/27/20	Milton	Dusenberg	155.046
4/28/26	Parry-Thomas	Thomas Spl.	170.624
3/29/27	Seagrave	Sunbeam	203.790
4/22/28	Keech	White Triplex	207.552
3/11/29	Seagrave	Irving-Napier	231.446
2/05/31	Campbell	Napier-Campbell	246.086
2/24/32	Campbell	Napier-Campbell	253.96
2/22/33	Campbell	Napier-Campbell	272.109
9/03/35	Campbell	Bluebird Special	301.13
11/19/37	Eyston	Thunderbolt 1	311.42
9/16/38	Eyston	Thunderbolt 1	357.5
8/23/39	Cobb	Railton	368.9
9/16/47	Cobb	Railton-Mobil	394.2
8/05/63	Breedlove	Spirit of America	407.45
10/27/64	Arfons	Green Monster	536.71
11/15/65	Breedlove	Spirit of America	600.601
10/23/70	Gabelich	Blue Flame	622.407
10/09/79	Barrett	Budweiser Rocket	638.637*
10/04/83	Noble	Thrust 2	633.468
9/25/97	Green	Thrust SSC	714.144
10/15/97	Green	Thrust SSC	763.035

*Not recognized as official by sanctioning bodies.

2002 Le Mans 24 Hours Race

Frank Biela (Germany), Tom Kristensen (Denmark), and Emanuele Pirro (Italy) drove their Audi R8 to a 3rd-consecutive victory in the "24 Hours of Le Mans" race held June 15, 2002, completing a record 375 laps around the 8.48-mile (13.65-km) track, eclipsing their mark of 368 set in 2000. The winning car averaged 132 mph (213 km/hour) for the 3,180 miles (5,118 km). Audi cars also finished 2nd (374 laps) and 3rd (372 laps). Bentley was 4th, with 362 laps. Biela, Kristensen, and Pirro were the 1st driving team to win Le Mans 3 times in a row.

World Formula One Grand Prix Champions, 1950-2002

Year	Driver	Year	Driver	Year	Driver
1950	Nino Farini, Italy	1968	Graham Hill, England	1985	Alain Prost, France
1951	Juan Fangio, Argentina	1969	Jackie Stewart, Scotland	1986	Alain Prost, France
1952	Alberto Ascari, Italy	1970	Jochen Rindt, Austria	1987	Nelson Piquet, Brazil
1953	Alberto Ascari, Italy	1971	Jackie Stewart, Scotland	1988	Ayrton Senna, Brazil
1954	Juan Fangio, Argentina	1972	Emerson Fittipaldi, Brazil	1989	Alain Prost, France
1955	Juan Fangio, Argentina	1973	Jackie Stewart, Scotland	1990	Ayrton Senna, Brazil
1956	Juan Fangio, Argentina	1974	Emerson Fittipaldi, Brazil	1991	Ayrton Senna, Brazil
1957	Juan Fangio, Argentina	1975	Niki Lauda, Austria	1992	Nigel Mansell, Britain
1958	Mike Hawthorne, England	1976	James Hunt, England	1993	Alain Prost, France
1959	Jack Brabham, Australia	1977	Niki Lauda, Austria	1994	Michael Schumacher, Germany
1960	Jack Brabham, Australia	1978	Mario Andretti, United States	1995	Michael Schumacher, Germany
1961	Phil Hill, United States	1979	Jody Scheckter, South Africa	1996	Damon Hill, England
1962	Graham Hill, England	1980	Alan Jones, Australia	1997	Jacques Villeneuve, Canada
1963	Jim Clark, Scotland	1981	Nelson Piquet, Brazil	1998	Mika Hakkinen, Finland
1964	John Surtees, England	1982	Keke Rosberg, Finland	1999	Mika Hakkinen, Finland
1965	Jim Clark, Scotland	1983	Nelson Piquet, Brazil	2000	Michael Schumacher, Germany
1966	Jack Brabham, Australia	1984	Niki Lauda, Austria	2001	Michael Schumacher, Germany
1967	Denis Hulme, New Zealand			2002	Michael Schumacher, Germany

NASCAR Racing

Winston Cup Champions, 1949-2001

Year	Driver	Year	Driver	Year	Driver	Year	Driver
1949	Red Byron	1963	Joe Weatherly	1976	Cale Yarborough	1989	Rusty Wallace
1950	Bill Rexford	1964	Richard Petty	1977	Cale Yarborough	1990	Dale Earnhardt
1951	Herb Thomas	1965	Ned Jarrett	1978	Cale Yarborough	1991	Dale Earnhardt
1952	Tim Flock	1966	David Pearson	1979	Richard Petty	1992	Alan Kulwicki
1953	Herb Thomas	1967	Richard Petty	1980	Dale Earnhardt	1993	Dale Earnhardt
1954	Lee Petty	1968	David Pearson	1981	Darrell Waltrip	1994	Dale Earnhardt
1955	Tim Flock	1969	David Pearson	1982	Darrell Waltrip	1995	Jeff Gordon
1956	Buck Baker	1970	Bobby Isaac	1983	Bobby Allison	1996	Terry Labonte
1957	Buck Baker	1971	Richard Petty	1984	Terry Labonte	1997	Jeff Gordon
1958	Lee Petty	1972	Richard Petty	1985	Darrell Waltrip	1998	Jeff Gordon
1959	Lee Petty	1973	Benny Parsons	1986	Dale Earnhardt	1999	Dale Jarrett
1960	Rex White	1974	Richard Petty	1987	Dale Earnhardt	2000	Bobby Labonte
1961	Ned Jarrett	1975	Richard Petty	1988	Bill Elliott	2001	Jeff Gordon
1962	Joe Weatherly						

NASCAR Rookie of the Year, 1958-2001

Year	Driver	Year	Driver	Year	Driver	Year	Driver
1958	Shorty Rollins	1969	Dick Brooks	1980	Jody Riley	1991	Bobby Hamilton
1959	Richard Petty	1970	Bill Dennis	1981	Ron Bouchard	1992	Jimmy Hensley
1960	David Pearson	1971	Walter Ballard	1982	Geoff Bodine	1993	Jeff Gordon
1961	Woodie Wilson	1972	Larry Smith	1983	Sterling Martin	1994	Jeff Burton
1962	Tom Cox	1973	Lennie Pond	1984	Rusty Wallace	1995	Ricky Craven
1963	Billy Wade	1974	Earl Ross	1985	Ken Schrader	1996	Johnny Benson
1964	Doug Cooper	1975	Bruce Hill	1986	Alan Kulwicki	1997	Mike Skinner
1965	Sam McQuagg	1976	Skip Manning	1987	Davey Allison	1998	Kenny Irwin
1966	James Hylton	1977	Ricky Rudd	1988	Ken Bouchard	1999	Tony Stewart
1967	Donnie Allison	1978	Ronnie Thomas	1989	Dick Trickle	2000	Matt Kenseth
1968	Pete Hamilton	1979	Dale Earnhardt	1990	Rob Moroso	2001	Kevin Harvick

IT'S A FACT: With 6 races left in the 2002 season, Germany's Michael Schumacher won the French Grand Prix July 21 to clinch the Formula One world driving championship earlier than any driver in history. Schumacher's 3rd consecutive world title, and 5th overall, tied him with Argentina's legendary Juan Fangio, who won his 5th in 1957.

Daytona 500 Winners, 1959-2002

Year	Driver, car	Avg. MPH	Year	Driver, car	Avg. MPH
1959	Lee Petty, Oldsmobile	135.521	1981	Richard Petty, Buick	169.651
1960	Junior Johnson, Chevrolet	124.740	1982	Bobby Allison, Buick	153.991
1961	Marvin Panch, Pontiac	149.601	1983	Cale Yarborough, Pontiac	155.979
1962	Fireball Roberts, Pontiac	152.529	1984	Cale Yarborough, Chevrolet	150.994
1963	Tiny Lund, Ford	151.566	1985	Bill Elliott, Ford	172.265
1964	Richard Petty, Plymouth	154.334	1986	Geoff Bodine, Chevrolet	148.124
1965	Fred Lorenzen, Ford (a)	141.539	1987	Bill Elliott, Ford	176.263
1966	Richard Petty, Plymouth (b)	160.627	1988	Bobby Allison, Buick	137.531
1967	Mario Andretti, Ford	146.926	1989	Darrell Waltrip, Chevrolet	148.466
1968	Cale Yarborough, Mercury	143.251	1990	Derrike Cope, Chevrolet	165.761
1969	Lee Roy Yarborough, Ford	160.875	1991	Ernie Irvan, Chevrolet	148.148
1970	Pete Hamilton, Plymouth	149.601	1992	Davey Allison, Ford	160.256
1971	Richard Petty, Plymouth	144.456	1993	Dale Jarrett, Chevrolet	154.972
1972	A. J. Foyt, Mercury	161.550	1994	Sterling Marlin, Chevrolet	156.931
1973	Richard Petty, Dodge	157.205	1995	Sterling Marlin, Chevrolet	141.710
1974	Richard Petty, Dodge (c)	140.894	1996	Dale Jarrett, Ford	154.308
1975	Benny Parsons, Chevrolet	153.649	1997	Jeff Gordon, Chevrolet	148.295
1976	David Pearson, Mercury	152.181	1998	Dale Earnhardt, Chevrolet	172.712
1977	Cale Yarborough, Chevrolet	153.218	1999	Jeff Gordon, Chevrolet	161.551
1978	Bobby Allison, Ford	159.730	2000	Dale Jarrett, Ford	155.669
1979	Richard Petty, Oldsmobile	143.977	2001	Michael Waltrip, Chevrolet	161.794
1980	Buddy Baker, Oldsmobile	177.602	2002	Ward Burton, Dodge	142.971

(a) 322.5 mi. (b) 495 mi. (c) 450 mi.

BOXING

Champions by Classes

There are many governing bodies in boxing, including the World Boxing Council, World Boxing Assn., International Boxing Federation, World Boxing Org., U.S. Boxing Assn., North American Boxing Federation, and European Boxing Union. Others are recognized by TV networks and the print media. All the governing bodies have their own champions and assorted boxing divisions.

The following are the recognized champions—as of Oct. 10, 2002—in the principal divisions of the WBA, WBC, and IBF.

Class, Weight limit	WBA	WBC	IBF
Heavyweight	John Ruiz, U.S.	Lennox Lewis, U.K.	Vacant
Cruiserweight (190 lb)	Jean-Marc Mormeck, France	Juan Carlos Gomez, Cuba/Germany	Vassiliy Jirov, U.S./Kazakhstan
Light Heavyweight (175 lb)	Roy Jones, U.S.[1]	Roy Jones Jr., U.S.	Roy Jones Jr., U.S.
Super Middleweight (168 lb)	Byron Mitchell, U.S	Eric Lucas, Canada	Sven Ottke, Germany
Middleweight (160 lb)	Bernard Hopkins, U.S.[2]	Bernard Hopkins, U.S.	Bernard Hopkins, U.S.
Jr. Middleweight (154 lb)	Oscar de la Hoya, U.S.[3]	Oscar de la Hoya, U.S.	Ronald Wright, U.S.
Welterweight (147 lb)	Ricardo Mayorga, Nicaragua	Vernon Forrest, U.S.	Vernon Forrest, U.S.
Jr. Welterweight (140 lb)	Kostya Tszyu, Australia[4]	Kostya Tszyu, Australia	Zab Judah, U.S.
Lightweight (135 lb)	Leonard Dorin, Canada	Floyd Mayweather, U.S.	Paul Spadafora, U.S.
Jr. Lightweight (130 lb)	Acelino Freitas, Brazil[5]	S. Singmanassak, Thailand	Vacant
Featherweight (126 lb)	Derrick Gainer, U.S.	Erik Morales, Mexico	Johnny Tapia, U.S.
Jr. Featherweight (122 lb)	Salim Medjkoune, France	Willie Jorrin, U.S.	Manny Pacquiao, Philippines
Bantamweight (118 lb)	Johnny Bredahl, Denmark	Veeraphol Sahaprom, Thailand	Tim Austin, U.S.
Jr. Bantamweight (115 lb)	Alexander Munoz, Venezuela	Masanori Tokuyama, Japan	Felix Machado, Venezuela
Flyweight (112 lb)	Eric Morel, U.S./P.R.	P.S. Wonjongkam, Thailand	Irene Pacheco, Colombia
Jr. Flyweight (108 lb)	Rosendo Alvarez, Nicaragua	Jorge Arce, Mexico	Ricardo Lopez, Mexico
Strawweight (105 lb)	Noel Arambulent, Venezuela	Jose Antonio Aguirre, Mexico	Miguel Barrera, Mexico

Note: The WBA designates multiple title holders as "Super World Champs" and permits a concurrent "World" champ: (1) Bruno Girard, France (2) William Joppy, U.S. (3) Santiago Samaniego, Panama. (4) Diobelys Hurtado, Cuba. (5) Yodsanan Nanthachai, Thailand.

Ring Champions by Years

(*abandoned the title or was stripped of it; IBF champions listed only for heavyweight division)

Heavyweights

1882-1892	John L. Sullivan (a)
1892-1897	James J. Corbett (b)
1897-1899	Robert Fitzsimmons
1899-1905	James J. Jeffries* (c)
1905-1906	Marvin Hart
1906-1908	Tommy Burns
1908-1915	Jack Johnson
1915-1919	Jess Willard
1919-1926	Jack Dempsey
1926-1928	Gene Tunney*
1928-1930	Vacant
1930-1932	Max Schmeling
1932-1933	Jack Sharkey
1933-1934	Primo Carnera
1934-1935	Max Baer
1935-1937	James J. Braddock
1937-1949	Joe Louis*
1949-1951	Ezzard Charles
1951-1952	Joe Walcott
1952-1956	Rocky Marciano*
1956-1959	Floyd Patterson
1959-1960	Ingemar Johansson
1960-1962	Floyd Patterson
1962-1964	Sonny Liston
1964-1967	Cassius Clay* (Muhammad Ali) (d)
1970-1973	Joe Frazier
1973-1974	George Foreman
1974-1978	Muhammad Ali
1978-1979	Muhammad Ali* (WBA)
1978	Leon Spinks (WBC*, WBA) (e); Ken Norton (WBC)
1978-1983	Larry Holmes* (WBC) (f)
1979-1980	John Tate (WBA)
1980-1982	Mike Weaver (WBA)
1982-1983	Michael Dokes (WBA)
1983-1984	Gerrie Coetzee (WBA)
1983-1985	Larry Holmes (IBF) (f)
1984	Tim Witherspoon (WBC)
1984-1985	Greg Page (WBA)
1984-1986	Pinklon Thomas (WBC)
1985-1986	Tony Tubbs (WBA)
1985-1987	Michael Spinks* (IBF)
1986	Tim Witherspoon (WBA) Trevor Berbick (WBC)
1986-1987	Mike Tyson (WBC); James "Bonecrusher" Smith (WBA)
1987	Tony Tucker (IBF)
1987-1990	Mike Tyson (WBC, WBA, IBF)
1990	"Buster" Douglas (WBA, WBC, IBF)
1990-1992	Evander Holyfield (WBA, WBC, IBF)
1992-1993	Riddick Bowe (WBA, IBF, WBC*)
1992-1994	Lennox Lewis (WBC)
1993-1994	Evander Holyfield (WBA, IBF)
1994	Michael Moorer (WBA, IBF)
1994-1995	Oliver McCall (WBC); George Foreman (WBA*, IBF*)
1995	Frans Botha* (IBF)
1995-1996	Bruce Seldon (WBA); Frank Bruno (WBC)
1996	Mike Tyson (WBC*, WBA)
1996-1997	Michael Moorer (IBF)
1996-1999	Evander Holyfield (WBA, IBF)
1997-2001	Lennox Lewis (WBC)
1999-2001	Lennox Lewis (WBA*, WBC, IBF)
2000-2001	Evander Holyfield (WBA)
2001	John Ruiz (WBA); Hasim Rahman (WBC, IBF); Lennox Lewis (WBC, IBF*)

(a) London Prize Ring (bare knuckle champion). (b) First Marquis of Queensberry champion. (c) Jeffries vacated title (1905), designated Marvin Hart and Jack Root as logical contenders. Hart def. Root in 12 rounds (1905), in turn was def. by Tommy Burns (1906), who claimed the title. Jack Johnson def. Burns (1908) and was recognized as champ. Johnson won the title by defeating Jeffries in the latter's attempted comeback (1910). (d) Title declared vacant by the WBA and others in 1967 after Ali refused military induction. Joe Frazier recognized as champ by 6 states, Mexico, and South America. Jimmy Ellis declared champ by the WBA. Frazier KOd Ellis, Feb. 16, 1970. (e) After Spinks defeated Ali, the WBC recognized Ken Norton as champ. Ali def. Spinks in 1978 rematch for WBA title, retired in 1979. (f) Holmes relinquished WBC title in Dec. 1983, to fight as champ of the new IBF.

Light Heavyweights

1903	Jack Root, George Gardner
1903-1905	Bob Fitzsimmons
1905-1912	Philadelphia Jack O'Brien*
1912-1916	Jack Dillon
1916-1920	Battling Levinsky
1920-1922	George Carpentier
1922-1923	Battling Siki
1923-1925	Mike McTigue
1925-1926	Paul Berlenbach
1926-1927	Jack Delaney*
1927-1929	Tommy Loughran*
1930-1934	Maxey Rosenbloom
1934-1935	Bob Olin
1935-1939	John Henry Lewis*
1939	Melio Bettina
1939-1941	Billy Conn*
1941	Anton Christoforidis (won NBA title)
1941-1948	Gus Lesnevich, Freddie Mills
1948-1950	Freddie Mills
1950-1952	Joey Maxim
1952-1962	Archie Moore
1962-1963	Harold Johnson
1963-1965	Willie Pastrano
1965-1966	Jose Torres
1966-1968	Dick Tiger
1968-1974	Bob Foster*
1974-1977	John Conteh (WBC)
1974-1978	Victor Galindez (WBA)
1977-1978	Miguel Cuello (WBC)
1978	Mate Parlov (WBC)
1978-1979	Mike Rossman (WBA); Marvin Johnson (WBC)
1979-1981	Matthew Saad Muhammad (WBC)
1979-1980	Marvin Johnson (WBA)
1980-1981	Eddie Mustafa Muhammad (WBA)
1981-1983	Michael Spinks (WBA); Dwight Braxton (WBC)
1983-1985	Michael Spinks*
1985-1986	J. B. Williamson (WBC)
1986-1987	Marvin Johnson (WBA); Dennis Andries (WBC)
1987	Leslie Stewart (WBA)
1987-1991	Virgil Hill (WBA)
1987	Thomas Hearns* (WBC)
1987-1988	Don Lalonde (WBC)
1988	Sugar Ray Leonard* (WBC)
1989	Dennis Andries (WBC)
1989-1990	Jeff Harding (WBC)
1990-1991	Dennis Andries (WBC)
1991-1994	Jeff Harding (WBC)
1991-1992	Thomas Hearns (WBA)
1992	Iran Barkley* (WBA)
1992-1997	Virgil Hill (WBA)
1994-1995	Mike McCallum (WBC)
1995-1996	Fabrice Tiozzo* (WBC)
1996-1997	Roy Jones Jr. (WBC)
1997	Montell Griffin (WBC); Roy Jones Jr. (WBC); Darius Michalczewski*(WBA)
1997-1998	Lou Del Valle (WBA)
1998	Roy Jones Jr. (WBA,WBC)
2001	Bruno Girard (WBA) (a)

(a) Jones is the WBA "super world champion." Girard TKO'd Robert Koon for vacant WBA title in Dec. 2001.

Middleweights

1884-1891	Jack "Nonpareil" Dempsey
1891-1897	Bob Fitzsimmons*
1897-1907	Tommy Ryan*
1907-1908	Stanley Ketchel; Billy Papke
1908-1910	Stanley Ketchel
1911-1913	vacant
1913	Frank Klaus; George Chip
1914-1917	Al McCoy
1917-1920	Mike O'Dowd
1920-1923	Johnny Wilson
1923-1926	Harry Greb
1926-1931	Tiger Flowers; Mickey Walker
1931-1932	Gorilla Jones (NBA)
1932-1937	Marcel Thil
1938	Al Hostak (NBA); Solly Krieger (NBA)
1939-1940	Al Hostak (NBA)
1941-1947	Tony Zale
1947-1948	Rocky Graziano
1948	Tony Zale; Marcel Cerdan
1949-1951	Jake LaMotta
1951	Ray Robinson; Randy Turpin; Ray Robinson*
1953-1955	Carl (Bobo) Olson
1955-1957	Ray Robinson
1957	Gene Fullmer; Ray Robinson
1957-1958	Carmen Basilio
1958	Ray Robinson
1959	Gene Fullmer (NBA); Ray Robinson (NY)
1960	Gene Fullmer (NBA); Paul Pender (NY and MA)
1961	Gene Fullmer (NBA); Terry Downes (NY, MA, Europe)
1962	Gene Fullmer; Dick Tiger (NBA); Paul Pender (NY and MA)*
1963	Dick Tiger (universal)
1963-1965	Joey Giardello
1965-1966	Dick Tiger
1966-1967	Emile Griffith
1967	Nino Benvenuti
1967-1968	Emile Griffith
1968-1970	Nino Benvenuti
1970-1977	Carlos Monzon*
1977-1978	Rodrigo Valdez
1978-1979	Hugo Corro
1979-1980	Vito Antuofermo
1980	Alan Minter
1980-1987	Marvin Hagler
1987	Sugar Ray Leonard* (WBC)
1987-1989	Sumbu Kalambay (WBA)
1987-1988	Thomas Hearns (WBC)
1988-1989	Iran Barkley (WBC)
1989-1990	Roberto Duran* (WBC)
1989-1991	Mike McCallum (WBA)
1990-1993	Julian Jackson (WBC)
1992-1993	Reggie Johnson (WBA)
1993-1995	Gerald McClellan* (WBC)
1993-1994	John David Jackson (WBA)
1994-1997	Jorge Castro (WBA)
1995	Julian Jackson (WBC)
1995-1996	Quincy Taylor (WBC); Shinji Takehara (WBA)
1996-1998	Keith Holmes (WBC)
1996-1997	William Joppy (WBA)
1997	Julio Cesar Green (WBA)
1998-2001	William Joppy (WBA)
1998-1999	Hassine Cherifi (WBC)
1999-2001	Keith Holmes (WBC)
2001	Felix Trinidad (WBA); Bernard Hopkins (WBC, WBA); William Joppy (WBA) (a)

(a) Hopkins is the WBA "super world champion." Joppy def. Howard Eastman for vacant WBA title in Nov. 2001.

Welterweights

1892-1894	Mysterious Billy Smith
1894-1896	Tommy Ryan
1896	Kid McCoy*
1900	Rube Ferns; Matty Matthews
1901	Rube Ferns
1901-1904	Joe Walcott
1904-1906	Dixie Kid; Joe Walcott; Honey Mellody
1907-1911	Mike Sullivan
1911-1915	Vacant
1915-1919	Ted Lewis
1919-1922	Jack Britton
1922-1926	Mickey Walker
1926	Pete Latzo
1927-1929	Joe Dundee
1929	Jackie Fields
1930	Jack Thompson; Tommy Freeman
1931	Tommy Freeman; Jack Thompson; Lou Brouillard
1932	Jackie Fields
1933	Young Corbett; Jimmy McLarnin
1934	Barney Ross; Jimmy McLarnin
1935-1938	Barney Ross
1938-1940	Henry Armstrong
1940-1941	Fritzie Zivic
1941-1946	Fred Cochrane
1946	Marty Servo*
1946-1951	Ray Robinson* (a)
1951	Johnny Bratton (NBA)
1951-1954	Kid Gavilan
1954-1955	Johnny Saxton
1955	Tony De Marco
1955-1956	Carmen Basilio
1956	Johnny Saxton
1956-1957	Carmen Basilio*
1958	Virgil Akins
1958-1960	Don Jordan
1960-1961	Benny Paret
1961	Emile Griffith
1961-1962	Benny Paret
1962-1963	Emile Griffith
1963	Luis Rodriguez
1963-1966	Emile Griffith*
1966-1969	Curtis Cokes
1969-1970	Jose Napoles
1970-1971	Billy Backus
1971-1975	Jose Napoles
1975-1976	John Stracey (WBC); Angel Espada (WBA)
1976-1979	Carlos Palomino (WBC)
1976-1980	Jose Cuevas (WBA)
1979	Wilfredo Benitez (WBC)
1979-1980	Sugar Ray Leonard (WBC)
1980	Roberto Duran (WBC)
1980-1981	Thomas Hearns (WBA)
1980-1982	Sugar Ray Leonard*
1983-1985	Donald Curry (WBA); Milton McCrory (WBC)
1985-1986	Donald Curry
1986-1987	Lloyd Honeyghan (WBC)
1987	Mark Breland (WBA)
1987-1988	Marlon Starling (WBA); Jorge Vaca (WBC)
1988-1989	Tomas Molinares (WBA); Lloyd Honeyghan (WBC)
1989-1990	Marlon Starling (WBC); Mark Breland (WBA)
1990-1991	Maurice Blocker (WBC); Aaron Davis (WBA)
1991	Simon Brown (WBC)
1991-1992	Meldrick Taylor (WBA)
1991-1993	Buddy McGirt (WBC)
1992-1994	Crisanto Espana (WBA)
1993-1997	Pernell Whitaker (WBC)
1994-1998	Ike Quartey* (WBA)
1997-1999	Oscar De La Hoya* (WBC)
1998	James Page (WBA*)
1999-2000	Felix Trinidad* (WBC)
2000	Oscar De La Hoya (WBC) (b)
2000-2002	Shane Mosley (WBC)
2001-2002	Andrew Lewis (WBA)
2002	Vernon Forrest (WBC); Ricardo Mayorga (WBA)

(a) Robinson gained the title by defeating Tommy Bell in an elimination agreed to by the New York Commission and the National Boxing Association. Both claimed Robinson waived his title when he won the middleweight crown from LaMotta in 1951. (b) Trinidad was stripped of the WBC title when he moved up to super welterweight; De La Hoya def. Derrell Coley for the title in Feb. 2000.

Lightweights

1896-1899	Kid Lavigne
1899-1902	Frank Erne
1902-1908	Joe Gans
1908-1910	Battling Nelson
1910-1912	Ad Wolgast
1912-1914	Willie Ritchie
1914-1917	Freddie Welsh
1917-1925	Benny Leonard*
1925	Jimmy Goodrich; Rocky Kansas
1926-1930	Sammy Mandell
1930	Al Singer; Tony Canzoneri
1930-1933	Tony Canzoneri
1933-1935	Barney Ross*
1935-1936	Tony Canzoneri
1936-1938	Lou Ambers
1938	Henry Armstrong
1939	Lou Ambers
1940	Lew Jenkins
1941-1943	Sammy Angott
1944	S. Angott (NBA); J. Zurita (NBA)
1945-1951	Ike Williams (NBA: later universal)
1951-1952	James Carter
1952	Lauro Salas; James Carter
1953-1954	James Carter
1954	Paddy De Marco; James Carter
1955	James Carter; Bud Smith
1956	Bud Smith; Joe Brown
1956-1962	Joe Brown
1962-1965	Carlos Ortiz
1965	Ismael Laguna
1965-1968	Carlos Ortiz
1968-1969	Teo Cruz
1969-1970	Mando Ramos
1970	Ismael Laguna
1970-1972	Ken Buchanan (WBA)
1971-1972	Pedro Carrasco (WBC)
1972-1979	Roberto Duran* (WBA)
1972	Mando Ramos (WBC); Chango Carmona (WBC)
1972-1974	Rodolfo Gonzalez (WBC)
1974-1976	Ishimatsu Suzuki (WBC)
1976-1978	Esteban De Jesus (WBC)
1979-1981	Jim Watt (WBC)
1979-1980	Ernesto Espana (WBA)
1980-1981	Hilmer Kenty (WBA)
1981	Sean O'Grady (WBA); Claude Noel (WBA)
1981-1983	Alexis Arguello* (WBC)
1981-1982	Arturo Frias (WBA)
1982-1984	Ray Mancini (WBA)
1983-1984	Edwin Rosario (WBC)
1984-1986	Livingstone Bramble (WBA)
1984-1985	Jose Luis Ramirez (WBC)
1985-1986	Hector (Macho) Camacho (WBC)
1986-1987	Edwin Rosario (WBA)
1987-1988	Julio Cesar Chavez (WBA); Jose Luis Ramirez (WBC)
1988-1989	Julio Cesar Chavez (WBA, WBC)
1989-1990	Edwin Rosario (WBA); Pernell Whitaker (WBC)
1990	Juan Nazario (WBA)
1990-1992	Pernell Whitaker*
1992	Joey Gamache (WBA)
1992-1996	Miguel Angel Gonzalez* (WBC)
1992-1993	Tony Lopez (WBA)
1993	Dingaan Thobela (WBA)
1993-1998	Orzubek Nazarov (WBA)
1996-1997	Jean-Baptiste Mendy (WBC)
1997-1998	Steve Johnston (WBC)
1998-1999	Jean-Baptiste Mendy (WBA); Cesar Bazan (WBC)
1999	Julian Lorcy (WBA); Stefano Zoff (WBA)
1999-2000	Gilberto Serrano (WBA); Steve Johnston (WBC)
2000-2001	Takanori Hatakeyama (WBA);
2000-2002	Jose Luis Castillo (WBC)
2001	Julien Lorcy (WBA)
2001-2002	Raul Balbi (WBA)
2002	Leonard Dorin (WBA); Floyd Mayweather (WBC)

Featherweights

1892-1900	George Dixon (disputed)	1963-1964	Sugar Ramos	1984	Wilfredo Gomez (WBC)
1900-1901	Terry McGovern; Young Corbett*	1964-1967	Vicente Saldivar*	1984-1988	Azumah Nelson (WBC)
1901-1912	Abe Attell	1968	Paul Rojas (WBA)	1985-1986	Barry McGuigan (WBA)
1912-1923	Johnny Kilbane	1968-1969	Jose Legra (WBC)	1986-1987	Steve Cruz (WBA)
1923	Eugene Criqui; Johnny Dundee	1968-1971	Shozo Saijyo (WBA)	1987-1991	Antonio Esparragoza (WBA)
1923-1925	Johnny Dundee*	1969-1970	Johnny Famechon (WBC)	1988-1990	Jeff Fenech* (WBC)
1925-1927	Kid Kaplan*	1970	Vicente Salvidar (WBC)	1990-1991	Marcos Villasana (WBC)
1927-1928	Benny Bass; Tony Canzoneri	1970-1972	Kuniaki Shibata (WBC)	1991-1993	Park Yung Kyun (WBA); Paul Hodkinson (WBC)
1928-1929	Andre Routis	1971-1972	Antonio Gomez (WBA)	1993	Goyo Vargas (WBC)
1929-1932	Battling Battalino*	1972	Clemente Sanchez* (WBC)	1993-1995	Kevin Kelley (WBC)
1932-1934	Tommy Paul (NBA)	1972-1974	Ernesto Marcel* (WBA)	1993-1996	Eloy Rojas (WBA)
1933-1936	Freddie Miller	1972-1973	Jose Legra (WBC)	1995	Alejandro Gonzalez (WBC)
1936-1937	Petey Sarron	1973-1974	Eder Jofre* (WBC)	1995-1996	Manuel Medina (WBC)
1937-1938	Henry Armstrong*	1974	Ruben Olivares (WBA)	1995-1999	Luisito Espinosa (WBC)
1938-1940	Joey Archibald (a)	1974-1975	Bobby Chacon (WBC)	1996-1997	Wilfredo Vasquez* (WBA)
1940-1941	Harry Jeffra	1974-1976	Alexis Arguello* (WBA)	1998	Freddie Norwood (WBA)
1942-1948	Willie Pep	1975	Ruben Olivares (WBC)	1998-1999	Antonio Ceremeno (WBA)
1948-1949	Sandy Saddler	1975-1976	David Kotey (WBC)	1999	Cesar Soto (WBC); Naseem Hamed* (WBC); Freddie Norwood (WBA)
1949-1950	Willie Pep	1976-1980	Danny Lopez (WBC)	2000-2001	Guty Espadas (WBC); Derrick Gaines (WBA)
1950-1957	Sandy Saddler*	1977	Rafael Ortega (WBA)	2001-2002	Erik Morales (WBC)(b)
1957-1959	Hogan (Kid) Bassey	1977-1978	Cecilio Lastra (WBA)		
1959-1963	Davey Moore	1978-1985	Eusebio Pedrosa (WBA)		
		1980-1982	Salvador Sanchez (WBC)		
		1982-1984	Juan LaPorte (WBC)		

(a) After Petey Scalzo knocked out Archibald in an overweight match and was refused a title bout, the NBA named Scalzo champion. NBA title succession: Scalzo, 1938-1941; Richard Lemos, 1941; Jackie Wilson, 1941-1943; Jackie Callura, 1943; Phil Terranova, 1943-1944; Sal Bartolo, 1944-1946. (b) Marco Antonio Barrera won a unanimous dec. over Morales on June 22, 2002, but refused the WBC title.

History of Heavyweight Championship Bouts

(bouts in which title changed hands)

1889—July 8—John L. Sullivan def. Jake Kilrain, 75, Richburg, MS. (Last championship bare knuckles bout.)

1892—Sept. 7—James J. Corbett def. John L. Sullivan, 21, New Orleans. (Big gloves used for first time.)

1897—Bob Fitzsimmons def. James J. Corbett, 14, Carson City, NV.

1899—June 9, James J. Jeffries def. Bob Fitzsimmons, 11, Coney Island, NY. (Jeffries retired as champion in 1905.)

1905—July 3, Marvin Hart KOd Jack Root, 12, Reno, NV. (Jeffries refereed and gave the title to Hart. Jack O'Brien also claimed the title.)

1906—Feb. 23, Tommy Burns def. Marvin Hart, 20, Los Angeles.

1908—Dec. 26, Jack Johnson KOd Tommy Burns, 14, Sydney, Australia. (Police halted contest.)

1915—April 5, Jess Willard KOd Jack Johnson, 26, Havana, Cuba.

1919—July 4, Jack Dempsey KOd Jess Willard, Toledo, OH. (Willard failed to answer bell for 4th round.)

1926—Sept. 23, Gene Tunney def. Jack Dempsey, 10, Philadelphia. (Tunney retired as champion in 1928.)

1930—June 12, Max Schmeling def. Jack Sharkey, 4, NY. (Sharkey fouled Schmeling in a bout generally considered to have resulted in the election of a successor to Tunney.)

1932—June 21, Jack Sharkey def. Max Schmeling, 15, NY.

1933—June 29, Primo Carnera KOd Jack Sharkey, 6, NY.

1934—June 14, Max Baer KOd Primo Carnera, 11, NY.

1935—June 13, James J. Braddock def. Max Baer, 15, NY.

1937—June 22, Joe Louis KOd James J. Braddock, 8, Chicago. (Louis retired as champion in 1949.)

1949—June 22, Ezzard Charles def. Joe Walcott, 15, Chicago; NBA recognition only.

1951—July 18, Joe Walcott KOd Ezzard Charles, 7, Pittsburgh.

1952—Sept. 23, Rocky Marciano KOd Joe Walcott, 13, Philadelphia. (Marciano retired as champion in 1956.)

1956—Nov. 30, Floyd Patterson KOd Archie Moore, 5, Chicago.

1959—June 26, Ingemar Johansson KOd Floyd Patterson, 3, NY.

1960—June 20, Floyd Patterson KOd Ingemar Johansson, 5, NY. (Patterson was 1st heavyweight to regain title.)

1962—Sept. 25, Sonny Liston KOd Floyd Patterson, 1, Chicago.

1964—Feb. 25, Cassius Clay (Muhammad Ali) KOd Sonny Liston, 7, Miami Beach, FL. (In 1967, Ali was stripped of his title by the WBA and others for refusing military service.)

1970—Feb. 16, Joe Frazier KOd Jimmy Ellis, 5, NY. (Frazier def. Ali in 15 rounds, Mar. 8, 1971, in NY.)

1973—Jan. 22, George Foreman KOd Joe Frazier, 2, Kingston, Jamaica

1974—Oct. 30, Muhammad Ali KOd George Foreman, 8, Kinshasa, Zaire.

1978—Feb. 15, Leon Spinks def. Muhammad Ali, 15, Las Vegas. (WBC recognized Ken Norton as champion after Spinks refused to fight him before his rematch with Ali.)

1978—June 9, (WBC) Larry Holmes def. Ken Norton, 15, Las Vegas. (Holmes gave up title in Dec. 1983.)

1978—Sept. 15, (WBA) Muhammad Ali def. Leon Spinks, 15, New Orleans. (Ali retired as champion in 1979.)

1979—Oct. 20, (WBA) John Tate def. Gerrie Coetzee, 15, Pretoria, South Africa.

1980—Mar. 31, (WBA) Mike Weaver KOd John Tate, 15, Knoxville.

1982—Dec. 10, (WBA) Michael Dokes KOd Mike Weaver, 1, Las Vegas.

1983—Sept. 23, (WBA) Gerrie Coetzee KOd Michael Dokes, 10, Richfield, OH.

1983—In Dec., Larry Holmes relinquished the WBC title and was named champion of the newly formed IBF.

1984—Mar. 9, (WBC) Tim Witherspoon def. Greg Page, 12, Las Vegas.

1984—Aug. 31, (WBC) Pinklon Thomas def. Tim Witherspoon, 12, Las Vegas.

1984—Dec. 2, WBA) Greg Page KOd Gerrie Coetzee, 8, Sun City, Bophuthatswana.

1985—Apr. 29, (WBA) Tony Tubbs def. Greg Page, 15, Buffalo, NY.

1985—Sept. 21, (IBF) Michael Spinks def. Larry Holmes, 15, Las Vegas. (Spinks relinquished title in Feb. 1987.)

1986—Jan. 17, (WBA) Tim Witherspoon def. Tony Tubbs, 15, Atlanta, GA.

1986—Mar. 23, (WBC) Trevor Berbick def. Pinklon Thomas, 12, Miami.

1986—Nov. 22, (WBC) Mike Tyson KOd Trevor Berbick, 2, Las Vegas.

1986—Dec. 12, (WBA) James "Bonecrusher" Smith KOd Tim Witherspoon, 1, NY.

1987—Mar. 7, (WBA, WBC) Mike Tyson def. James "Bonecrusher" Smith, 12, Las Vegas.

1987—May 30, (IBF) Tony Tucker KO'd James "Buster" Douglas, 10, Las Vegas.

1987—Aug. 1, (WBA, WBC, IBF) Mike Tyson def. Tony Tucker, 12, Las Vegas. (Tyson became undisputed champion.)

1990—Feb. 11, (WBA, WBC, IBF) James "Buster" Douglas KOd Mike Tyson, 10, Tokyo.

1990—Oct. 25, (WBA, WBC, IBF) Evander Holyfield KOd James "Buster" Douglas, 3, Las Vegas.

1992—Nov. 13, (WBA, WBC, IBF) Riddick Bowe def. Evander Holyfield, 12, Las Vegas. (Lennox Lewis was later named WBC champion when Bowe refused to fight him.)

1993—Nov. 6, (WBA, IBF) Evander Holyfield def. Riddick Bowe, 12, Las Vegas.

1994—Apr. 22, (WBA, IBF) Michael Moorer def. Evander Holyfield, 12, Las Vegas.

1994—Sept. 24, (WBC) Oliver McCall KOd Lennox Lewis, 2, London.

1994—Nov. 5, (WBA, IBF) George Foreman KOd Michael Moorer, 10, Las Vegas. (In Mar. 1995, Foreman was stripped of the WBA title. In June, Foreman relinquished the IBF title.)

1995—Sept. 2, (WBC) Frank Bruno def. Oliver McCall, 12, London.

1995—Dec. 9, (IBF) Frans Botha def. Axel Schulz, 12, Las Vegas. (Botha was subsequently stripped of title.)

1996—Mar. 16, (WBC) Mike Tyson KOd Frank Bruno, 3, Las Vegas.

1996—June 22, (IBF) Michael Moorer def. Axel Schulz, 12, Dortmund, Germany.

1996—Sept. 7, (WBA, WBC) Mike Tyson KOd Bruce Seldon, 1, Las Vegas. (Tyson was subsequently stripped of WBC title.)

1996—Nov. 9, (WBA) Evander Holyfield KOd Mike Tyson, 11, Las Vegas.

1997—Feb. 7, (WBC) Lennox Lewis KOd Oliver McCall, 5, Las Vegas.

1997—Nov. 8, (IBF) Evander Holyfield def. Michael Moorer, 8, Las Vegas.

1999—Nov. 13, (WBA, WBC, IBF) Lennox Lewis def. Evander Holyfield, 12, Las Vegas. (Lewis became undisputed champion. In April 2000, Lewis was stripped of his WBA title.)

2000—Aug. 12, (WBA) Evander Holyfield def. John Ruiz, 12, Las Vegas.

2001—Mar. 3, (WBA) John Ruiz def. Evander Holyfield, 12, Las Vegas.

2001—Apr. 21, (WBC, IBF) Hasim Rahman KOd Lennox Lewis, 5, Brakpan, South Africa.

2001—Nov. 17, (WBC, IBF) Lennox Lewis KOd Hasim Rahman, 4, Las Vegas.

THOROUGHBRED RACING

Triple Crown Winners

Since 1920, colts have carried 126 lb. in triple crown events; fillies, 121 lb.
(Kentucky Derby, Preakness, and Belmont Stakes)

Year	Horse	Jockey	Trainer
1919	Sir Barton	J. Loftus	H. G. Bedwell
1930	Gallant Fox	E. Sande	J. Fitzsimmons
1935	Omaha	W. Sanders	J. Fitzsimmons
1937	War Admiral	C. Kurtsinger	G. Conway
1941	Whirlaway	E. Arcaro	B. A. Jones
1943	Count Fleet	J. Longden	G. D. Cameron
1946	Assault	W. Mehrtens	M. Hirsch
1948	Citation	E. Arcaro	H. A. Jones
1973	Secretariat	R. Turcotte	L. Laurin
1977	Seattle Slew	J. Cruguet	W. H. Turner Jr.
1978	Affirmed	S. Cauthen	L. S. Barrera

Kentucky Derby

Churchill Downs, Louisville, KY; inaug. 1875; distance 1-1/4 mi; 1-1/2 mi until 1896. 3-year-olds.
Best time: 1:59 2/5, by Secretariat, 1973; 2002 time: 2:01.13.

Year	Winner	Jockey
1875	Aristides	O. Lewis
1876	Vagrant	R. Swim
1877	Baden Baden	W. Walker
1878	Day Star	Carter
1879	Lord Murphy	C. Schauer
1880	Fonso	G. Lewis
1881	Hindoo	J. McLaughlin
1882	Apollo	B. Hurd
1883	Leonatus	W. Donohue
1884	Buchanan	I. Murphy
1885	Joe Cotton	E. Henderson
1886	Ben Ali	P. Duffy
1887	Montrose	I. Lewis
1888	Macbeth II.	G. Covington
1889	Spokane	T. Kiley
1890	Riley	I. Murphy
1891	Kingman	I. Murphy
1892	Azra	A. Clayton
1893	Lookout	E. Kunze
1894	Chant	F. Goodale
1895	Halma	J. Perkins
1896	Ben Brush	W. Simms
1897	Typhoon II.	F. Garner
1898	Plaudit	W. Simms
1899	Manuel	F. Taral
1900	Lieut. Gibson	J. Boland
1901	His Eminence	J. Winkfield
1902	Alan-a-Dale	J. Winkfield
1903	Judge Himes	H. Booker
1904	Elwood	F. Prior
1905	Agile	J. Martin
1906	Sir Huon	R. Troxler
1907	Pink Star	A. Minder
1908	Stone Street	A. Pickens
1909	Wintergreen	V. Powers
1910	Donau	F. Herbert
1911	Meridian	G. Archibald
1912	Worth	C.H. Shilling
1913	Donerail	R. Goose
1914	Old Rosebud	J. McCabe
1915	Regret*	J. Notter
1916	George Smith	J. Loftus
1917	Omar Khayyam	C. Borel
1918	Exterminator	W. Knapp
1919	Sir Barton	J. Loftus
1920	Paul Jones	T. Rice
1921	Behave Yourself	C. Thompson
1922	Morvich	A. Johnson
1923	Zev	E. Sande
1924	Black Gold	J. D. Mooney
1925	Flying Ebony	E. Sande
1926	Bubbling Over	A. Johnson
1927	Whiskery	L. McAtee
1928	Reigh Count	C. Lang
1929	Clyde Van Dusen	L. McAtee
1930	Gallant Fox	E. Sande
1931	Twenty Grand	C. Kurtsinger
1932	Burgoo King	E. James
1933	Brokers Tip	D. Meade
1934	Cavalcade	M. Garner
1935	Omaha	W. Saunders
1936	Bold Venture	I. Hanford
1937	War Admiral	C. Kurtsinger
1938	Lawrin	E. Arcaro
1939	Johnstown	J. Stout
1940	Gallahadion	C. Bierman
1941	Whirlaway	E. Arcaro
1942	Shut Out	W. D. Wright
1943	Count Fleet	J. Longden
1944	Pensive	C. McCreary
1945	Hoop, Jr.	E. Arcaro
1946	Assault	W. Mehrtens
1947	Jet Pilot	E. Guerin
1948	Citation	E. Arcaro
1949	Ponder	S. Brooks
1950	Middleground	W. Boland
1951	Count Turf	C. McCreary
1952	Hill Gail	E. Arcaro
1953	Dark Star	H. Moreno
1954	Determine	R. York
1955	Swaps	W. Shoemaker
1956	Needles	D. Erb
1957	Iron Liege	W. Hartack
1958	Tim Tam	I. Valenzuela
1959	Tomy Lee	W. Shoemaker
1960	Venetian Way	W. Hartack
1961	Carry Back	J. Sellers
1962	Decidedly	W. Hartack
1963	Chateaugay	B. Baeza
1964	Northern Dancer	W. Hartack
1965	Lucky Debonair	W. Shoemaker
1966	Kauai King	D. Brumfield
1967	Proud Clarion	R. Ussery
1968	Dancer's Image#	R. Ussery
1969	Majestic Prince	W. Hartack
1970	Dust Commander	M. Manganello
1971	Canonero II	G. Avila
1972	Riva Ridge	R. Turcotte
1973	Secretariat	R. Turcotte
1974	Cannonade	A. Cordero
1975	Foolish Pleasure	J. Vasquez
1976	Bold Forbes	A. Cordero
1977	Seattle Slew	J. Cruguet
1978	Affirmed	S. Cauthen
1979	Spectacular Bid	R. Franklin
1980	Genuine Risk*	J. Vasquez
1981	Pleasant Colony	J. Velasquez
1982	Gato del Sol	E. Delahoussaye
1983	Sunny's Halo	E. Delahoussaye
1984	Swale	L. Pincay
1985	Spend a Buck	A. Cordero
1986	Ferdinand	W. Shoemaker
1987	Alysheba	C. McCarron
1988	Winning Colors*	G. Stevens
1989	Sunday Silence	P. Valenzuela
1990	Unbridled	C. Perret
1991	Strike the Gold	C. Antley
1992	Lil E. Tee	P. Day
1993	Sea Hero	J. Bailey
1994	Go for Gin	C. McCarron
1995	Thunder Gulch	G. Stevens
1996	Grindstone	J. Bailey
1997	Silver Charm	G. Stevens
1998	Real Quiet	K. Desormeaux
1999	Charismatic	C. Antley
2000	Fusaichi Pegasus	K. Desormeaux
2001	Monarchos	J. Chavez
2002	War Emblem	V. Espinoza

*Regret, Genuine Risk, and Winning Colors are the only fillies to have won the Derby. # Dancer's Image was disqualified from purse money after tests disclosed that he had run with a pain-killing drug, phenylbutazone, in his system. All wagers were paid on Dancer's Image. Forward Pass was awarded first place money. The Kentucky Derby has been won 5 times by 2 jockeys: Eddie Arcaro, 1938, 1941, 1945, 1948, and 1952; and Bill Hartack, 1957, 1960, 1962, 1964, and 1969. It was won 4 times by Willie Shoemaker, 1955, 1959, 1965, and 1986; and 3 times by each of 4 jockeys: Isaac Murphy, 1884, 1890, and 1891; Earle Sande, 1923, 1925, and 1930; Angel Cordero, 1974, 1976, and 1985; and Gary Stevens, 1988, 1995, and 1997.

Top 10 Fastest Winning Times for the Kentucky Derby

(Official Kentucky Derby times measured in fifths of a second.)

Time	Horse	Jockey	Year
1m. 59 2/5 s.	Secretariat	Ron Turcotte	1973
1m. 59 4/5 s.	Monarchos	Jorge Chavez	2001
2m.	Northern Dancer	Bill Hartack	1964
2m. 1/5 s.	Spend a Buck	Angel Cordero Jr.	1985
2m. 2/5 s.	Decidedly	Bill Hartack	1962
2m. 3/5 s.	Proud Clarion	Bill Shoemaker	1967
2m. 1 s.	War Emblem	Victor Espinoza	2002
	Fusaichi Pegasus	Kent Desormeaux	2000
	Grindstone	Jerry Bailey	1996
2m. 1 1/5 s.	Thunder Gulch	Gary Stevens	1995
	Affirmed	Steve Cauthen	1978
	Lucky Debonair	Bill Shoemaker	1965
2m. 1 2/5 s.	Whirlaway	Eddie Arcaro	1941
2m. 1 3/5 s.	Bold Forbes	Angel Cordero Jr.	1976
	Hill Gail	Eddie Arcaro	1952
	Middleground	William Boland	1950

Preakness Stakes

Pimlico Race Course, Baltimore, MD; inaug. 1873; distance 1-3/16 mi. 3-year-olds.
Best time: 1:53 2/5, by Tank's Prospect (1985) and Louis Quatorze (1996); 2002 time: 1:56.36.

Year	Winner	Jockey
1873	Survivor	G. Barbee
1874	Culpepper	M. Donohue
1875	Tom Ochiltree	L. Hughes
1876	Shirley	G. Barbee
1877	Cloverbrook	C. Holloway
1878	Duke of Magenta	C. Holloway
1879	Harold	L. Hughes
1880	Grenada	L. Hughes
1881	Saunterer	W. Costello
1882	Vanguard	W. Costello
1883	Jacobus	G. Barbee
1884	Knight of Ellerslie	S. H. Fisher
1885	Tecumseh	J. McLaughlin
1886	The Bard	S. H. Fisher
1887	Dunboyne	W. Donohue
1888	Refund	F. Littlefield
1889	Buddhist	G. Anderson
1890	Montague	W. Martin
1894	Assignee	F. Taral
1895	Belmar	F. Taral
1896	Margrave	H. Griffin
1897	Paul Kauvar	C. Thorpe
1898	Sly Fox	W. Simms
1899	Half Time	R. Clawson
1900	Hindus	H. Spencer
1901	The Parader	F. Landry
1902	Old England	L. Jackson
1903	Flocarline	W. Gannon
1904	Bryn Mawr	E. Hildebrand
1905	Cairngorm	W. Davis
1906	Whimsical	W. Miller
1907	Don Enrique	G. Mountain
1908	Royal Tourist	E. Dugan
1909	Effendi	W. Doyle
1910	Layminster	R. Estep
1911	Watervale	E. Dugan
1912	Colonel Holloway	C. Turner
1913	Buskin	J. Butwell
1914	Holiday	A. Schuttinger
1915	Rhine Maiden	D. Hoffman
1916	Damrosch	L. McAtee
1917	Kalitan	E. Haynes
1918	War Cloud	J. Loftus
	Jack Hare	Jr. C. Peak
1919	Sir Barton	J. Loftus
1920	Man o' War	C. Kummer
1921	Broomspun	F. Coltiletti
1922	Pillory	L. Morris
1923	Vigil	B. Marinelli
1924	Nellie Morse	J. Merimee
1925	Coventry	C. Kummer
1926	Display	J. Malben
1927	Bostonian	A. Abel
1928	Victorian	R. Workman
1929	Dr. Freeland	L. Schaefer
1930	Gallant Fox	E. Sande
1931	Mate	G. Ellis
1932	Burgoo King	E. James
1933	Head Play	C. Kurtsinger
1934	High Quest	R. Jones
1935	Omaha	W. Saunders
1936	Bold Venture	G. Woolf
1937	War Admiral	C. Kurtsinger
1938	Dauber	M. Peters
1939	Challedon	G. Seabo
1940	Bimelech	F.A. Smith
1941	Whirlaway	E. Arcaro
1942	Alsab	B. James
1943	Count Fleet	J. Longden
1944	Pensive	C. McCreary
1945	Polynesian	W.D. Wright
1946	Assault	W. Mehrtens
1947	Faultless	D. Dodson
1948	Citation	E. Arcaro
1949	Capot	T. Atkinson
1950	Hill Prince	E. Arcaro
1951	Bold	E. Arcaro
1952	Blue Man	C. McCreary
1953	Native Dancer	E. Guerin
1954	Hasty Road	J. Adams
1955	Nashua	E. Arcaro
1956	Fabius	W. Hartack
1957	Bold Ruler	E. Arcaro
1958	Tim Tam	I. Valenzuela
1959	Royal Orbit	W. Harmatz
1960	Bally Ache	R. Ussery
1961	Carry Back	J. Sellers
1962	Greek Money	J.L. Rotz
1963	Candy Spots	W. Shoemaker
1964	Northern Dancer	W. Hartack
1965	Tom Rolfe	R. Turcotte
1966	Kauai King	D. Brumfield
1967	Damascus	W. Shoemaker
1968	Forward Pass	I. Valenzuela
1969	Majestic Prince	W. Hartack
1970	Personality	E. Belmonte
1971	Canonero II	G. Avila
1972	Bee Bee Bee	E. Nelson
1973	Secretariat	R. Turcotte
1974	Little Current	M. Rivera
1975	Master Derby	D. McHargue
1976	Elocutionist	J. Lively
1977	Seattle Slew	J. Cruguet
1978	Affirmed	S. Cauthen
1979	Spectacular Bid	R. Franklin
1980	Codex	A. Cordero
1981	Pleasant Colony	J. Velasquez
1982	Aloma's Ruler	J. Kaenel
1983	Deputed Testamony	D. Miller
1984	Gate Dancer	A. Cordero
1985	Tank's Prospect	P. Day
1986	Snow Chief	A. Solis
1987	Alysheba	C. McCarron
1988	Risen Star	E. Delahoussaye
1989	Sunday Silence	P. Valenzuela
1990	Summer Squall	P. Day
1991	Hansel	J. Bailey
1992	Pine Bluff	C. McCarron
1993	Prairie Bayou	M. Smith
1994	Tabasco Cat	P. Day
1995	Timber Country	P. Day
1996	Louis Quatorze	P. Day
1997	Silver Charm	G. Stevens
1998	Real Quiet	K. Desormeaux
1999	Charismatic	C. Antley
2000	Red Bullet	J. Bailey
2001	Point Given	G. Stevens
2002	War Emblem	V. Espinoza

Belmont Stakes

Belmont Park, Elmont, NY; inaug. 1867; distance 1-1/2 mi. 3-year-olds. Best time: 2:24, Secretariat, 1973; 2002 time: 2:29.71.

Year	Winner	Jockey
1867	Ruthless	J. Gilpatrick
1868	General Duke	R. Swim
1869	Fenian	C. Miller
1870	Kingfisher	W. Dick
1871	Harry Bassett	W. Miller
1872	Joe Daniels	J. Rowe
1873	Springbok	J. Rowe
1874	Saxon	G. Barbee
1875	Calvin	R. Swim
1876	Algerine	W. Donohue
1877	Cloverbrook	C. Holloway
1878	Duke of Magenta	L. Hughes
1879	Spendthrift	S. Evans
1880	Grenada	L. Hughes
1881	Saunterer	T. Costello
1882	Forester	J. McLaughlin
1883	George Kinney	J. McLaughlin
1884	Panique	J. McLaughlin
1885	Tyrant	P. Duffy
1886	Inspector	B.J. McLaughlin
1887	Hanover	J. McLaughlin
1888	Sir Dixon	J. McLaughlin
1889	Eric	W. Hayward
1890	Burlington	S. Barnes
1891	Foxford	E. Garrison
1892	Patron	W. Hayward
1893	Comanche	W. Simms
1894	Henry of Navarre	W. Simms
1895	Belmar	F. Taral
1896	Hastings	H. Griffin
1897	Scottish Chieftain	J. Scherrer
1898	Bowling Brook	F. Littlefield
1899	Jean Bereaud	R. R. Clawson
1900	Ildrim	N. Turner
1901	Commando	H. Spencer
1902	Masterman	J. Bullman
1903	Africander	J. Bullman
1904	Delhi	G. Odom
1905	Tanya	E. Hildebrand
1906	Burgomaster	L. Lyne
1907	Peter Pan	G. Mountain
1908	Colin	J. Notter
1909	Joe Madden	E. Dugan
1910	Sweep	J. Butwell
1913	Prince Eugene	R. Troxler
1914	Luke McLuke	M. Buxton
1915	The Finn	G. Byrne
1916	Friar Rock	E. Haynes
1917	Hourless	J. Butwell
1918	Johren	F. Robinson
1919	Sir Barton	J. Loftus
1920	Man o' War	C. Kummer
1921	Grey Lag	E. Sande
1922	Pillory	C. H. Miller
1923	Zev	E. Sande
1924	Mad Play	E. Sande
1925	American Flag	A. Johnson
1926	Crusader	A. Johnson
1927	Chance Shot	E. Sande
1928	Vito	C. Kummer
1929	Blue Larkspur	M. Garner
1930	Gallant Fox	E. Sande
1931	Twenty Grand	C. Kurtsinger
1932	Faireno	T. Malley
1933	Hurryoff	M. Garner
1934	Peace Chance	W. D. Wright
1935	Omaha	W. Saunders
1936	Granville	J. Stout
1937	War Admiral	C. Kurtsinger
1938	Pasteurized	J. Stout
1939	Johnstown	J. Stout
1940	Bimelech	F. A. Smith
1941	Whirlaway	E. Arcaro
1942	Shut Out	E. Arcaro
1943	Count Fleet	J. Longden
1944	Bounding Home	G. L. Smith
1945	Pavot	E. Arcaro
1946	Assault	W. Mehrtens
1947	Phalanx	R. Donoso
1948	Citation	E. Arcaro
1949	Capot	T. Atkinson
1950	Middleground	W. Boland
1951	Counterpoint	D. Gorman
1952	One Count	E. Arcaro
1953	Native Dancer	E. Guerin
1954	High Gun	E. Guerin
1955	Nashua	E. Arcaro
1956	Needles	D. Erb
1957	Gallant Man	W. Shoemake
1958	Cavan	P. Anderson
1959	Sword Dancer	W. Shoemaker
1960	Celtic Ash	W. Hartack
1961	Sherluck	B. Baeza
1962	Jaipur	W. Shoemaker
1963	Chateaugay	B. Baeza
1964	Quadrangle	M. Ycaza
1965	Hail to All	J. Sellers
1966	Amberoid	W. Boland
1967	Damascus	W. Shoemaker
1968	Stage Door Johnny	H. Gustines
1969	Arts and Letters	B. Baeza
1970	High Echelon	J. L. Rotz
1971	Pass Catcher	W. Blum
1972	Riva Ridge	R. Turcotte
1973	Secretariat	R. Turcotte

Year	Winner	Jockey	Year	Winner	Jockey	Year	Winner	Jockey
1974	Little Current	M. Rivera	1984	Swale	L. Pincay	1994	Tabasco Cat	P. Day
1975	Avatar	W. Shoemaker	1985	Creme Fraiche	E. Maple	1995	Thunder Gulch	G. Stevens
1976	Bold Forbes	A. Cordero	1986	Danzig Connection	C. McCarron	1996	Editor's Note	R. Douglas
1977	Seattle Slew	J. Cruguet	1987	Bet Twice	C. Perret	1997	Touch Gold	C. McCarron
1978	Affirmed	S. Cauthen	1988	Risen Star	E. Delahoussaye	1998	Victory Gallop	G. Stevens
1979	Coastal	R. Hernandez	1989	Easy Goer	P. Day	1999	Lemon Drop Kid	J. Santos
1980	Temperence Hill	E. Maple	1990	Go and Go	M. Kinane	2000	Commendable	P. Day
1981	Summing	G. Martens	1991	Hansel	J. Bailey	2001	Point Given	G. Stevens
1982	Conquistador Cielo	L. Pincay	1992	A.P. Indy	E. Delahoussaye	2002	Sarava	E. Prado
1983	Caveat	L. Pincay	1993	Colonial Affair	J. Krone			

Annual Leading Jockey — Money Won[1]

Year	Jockey	Earnings	Year	Jockey	Earnings	Year	Jockey	Earnings
1957	Bill Hartack	$3,060,501	1972	Laffit Pincay, Jr.	$3,225,827	1987	Jose Santos	$12,375,433
1958	Willie Shoemaker	2,961,693	1973	Laffit Pincay, Jr.	4,093,492	1988	Jose Santos	14,877,298
1959	Willie Shoemaker	2,843,133	1974	Laffit Pincay, Jr.	4,251,060	1989	Jose Santos	13,838,389
1960	Willie Shoemaker	2,123,961	1975	Braulio Baeza	3,695,198	1990	Gary Stevens	13,881,198
1961	Willie Shoemaker	2,690,819	1976	Angel Cordero, Jr.	4,709,500	1991	Chris McCarron	14,441,083
1962	Willie Shoemaker	2,916,844	1977	Steve Cauthen	6,151,750	1992	Kent Desormeaux	14,193,006
1963	Willie Shoemaker	2,526,925	1978	Darrel McHargue	6,029,885	1993	Mike Smith	14,024,815
1964	Willie Shoemaker	2,649,553	1979	Laffit Pincay, Jr.	8,193,535	1994	Mike Smith	15,979,820
1965	Braulio Baeza	2,582,702	1980	Chris McCarron	7,663,300	1995	Jerry Bailey	16,311,876
1966	Braulio Baeza	2,951,022	1981	Chris McCarron	8,397,604	1996	Jerry Bailey	19,465,376
1967	Braulio Baeza	3,088,888	1982	Angel Cordero, Jr.	9,483,590	1997	Jerry Bailey	18,320,743
1968	Braulio Baeza	2,835,108	1983	Angel Cordero, Jr.	10,116,697	1998	Gary Stevens	19,622,855
1969	Jorge Velasquez	2,542,315	1984	Chris McCarron	12,045,813	1999	Pat Day	18,092,845
1970	Laffit Pincay, Jr.	2,626,526	1985	Laffit Pincay, Jr.	13,353,299	2000	Pat Day	17,479,838
1971	Laffit Pincay, Jr.	3,784,377	1986	Jose Santos	11,329,297	2001	Jerry Bailey	22,597,720

(1) Total earnings for all horses that jockey raced in year listed; does not reflect jockey's earnings.

Breeders' Cup

The Breeders' Cup was inaugurated in 1984 and consists of 7 races at one track on one day late in the year to determine Thoroughbred racing's champion contenders. It has been held at the following locations:

1984	Hollywood Park, CA	1990	Belmont Park, NY	1996	Woodbine Racetrack, Ontario
1985	Aqueduct Racetrack, NY	1991	Churchill Downs, KY	1997	Hollywood Park, CA
1986	Santa Anita Park, CA	1992	Gulfstream Park, FL	1998	Churchill Downs, KY
1987	Hollywood Park, CA	1993	Santa Anita Park, CA	1999	Gulfstream Park, FL
1988	Churchill Downs, KY	1994	Churchill Downs, KY	2000	Churchill Downs, KY
1989	Gulfstream Park, FL	1995	Belmont Park, NY	2001	Belmont Park, NY

Juvenile

Distances: 1 mi 1984-85, 1987; 1-1/16 mi 1986 and since 1988

Year		Jockey	Year		Jockey	Year		Jockey
1984	Chief's Crown	D. MacBeth	1990	Fly So Free	J. Santos	1996	Boston Harbor	J. Bailey
1985	Tasso	L. Pincay, Jr.	1991	Arazi	P. Valenzuela	1997	Favorite Trick	P. Day
1986	Capote	L. Pincay, Jr.	1992	Gilded Time	C. McCarron	1998	Answer Lively	J. Bailey
1987	Success Express	J. Santos	1993	Brocco	G. Stevens	1999	Anees	G. Stevens
1988	Is It True	L. Pincay, Jr.	1994	Timber Country	P. Day	2000	Macho Uno	J. Bailey
1989	Rhythm	C. Perret	1995	Unbridled's Song	M. Smith	2001	Johannesburg	M. Kinane

Juvenile Fillies

Distances: 1 mi 1984-85, 1987; 1-1/16 mi 1986 and since 1988

Year		Jockey	Year		Jockey	Year		Jockey
1984	*Outstandingly	W. Guerra	1990	Meadow Star	J. Santos	1996	Storm Song	C. Perret
1985	Twilight Ridge	J. Velasquez	1991	Pleasant Stage	E. Delahoussaye	1997	Countess Diana	S. Sellers
1986	Brave Raj	P. Valenzuela	1992	Eliza	P. Valenzuela	1998	Silverbulletday	G. Stevens
1987	Epitome	P. Day	1993	Phone Chatter	L. Pincay, Jr.	1999	Cash Run	J. Bailey
1988	Open Mind	A. Cordero, Jr.	1994	Flanders	P. Day	2000	Caressing	J. Velazquez
1989	Go for Wand	R. Romero	1995	My Flag	J. Bailey	2001	Tempera	D. Flores

*By disqualification.

Filly & Mare Turf

Distance: 1-3/8 mi 1999-2000, 1-1/4 mi 2002

Year		Jockey	Year		Jockey	Year		Jockey
1999	Soaring Softly	J. Bailey	2000	Perfect Sting	J. Bailey	2001	Banks Hill	O. Peslier

Sprint

Distance: 6 furlongs

Year		Jockey	Year		Jockey	Year		Jockey
1984	Eillo	C. Perret	1990	Safely Kept	C. Perret	1996	Lit De Justice	C. Nakatani
1985	Precisionist	C. McCarron	1991	Sheikh Albadou	P. Eddery	1997	Elmhurst	C. Nakatani
1986	Smile	J. Vasquez	1992	Thirty Slews	E. Delahoussaye	1998	Reraise	C. Nakatani
1987	Very Subtle	P. Valenzuela	1993	Cardmania	E. Delahoussaye	1999	Artax	J. Chaves
1988	Gulch	A. Cordero, Jr.	1994	Cherokee Run	M. Smith	2000	Kona Gold	A. Solis
1989	Dancing Spree	A. Cordero, Jr.	1995	Desert Stormer	K. Desormeaux	2001	Squirtle Squirt	J. Bailey

Mile

Year		Jockey	Year		Jockey	Year		Jockey
1984	Royal Heroine	F. Toro	1990	Royal Academy	L. Piggott	1996	Da Hoss	G. Stevens
1985	Cozzene	W. Guerra	1991	Opening Verse	P. Valenzuela	1997	Spinning World	C. Asmussan
1986	Last Tycoon	Y. St.-Martin	1992	Lure	M. Smith	1998	Da Hoss	J. Velazquez
1987	Miesque	F. Head	1993	Lure	M. Smith	1999	Silic	C. Nakatani
1988	Miesque	F. Head	1994	Barathea	L. Dettori	2000	War Chant	G. Stevens
1989	Steinlen	J. Santos	1995	Ridgewood Pearl	J. Murtagh	2001	Val Royal	J. Valdivia Jr.

Distaff

Distances: 1-1/4 mi 1984-87; 1-1/8 mi since 1988

Year	Winner	Jockey
1984	Princess Rooney	E. Delahoussaye
1985	Life's Magic	A. Cordero, Jr.
1986	Lady's Secret	P. Day
1987	Sacahuista	R. Romero
1988	Personal Ensign	R. Romero
1989	Bayakoa	L. Pincay, Jr.
1990	Bayakoa	L. Pincay, Jr.
1991	Dance Smartly	P. Day
1992	Paseana	C. McCarron
1993	Hollywood Wildcat	E. Delahoussaye
1994	One Dreamer	G. Stevens
1995	Inside Information	M. Smith
1996	Jewel Princess	C. Nakatani
1997	Ajina	M. Smith
1998	Escena	G. Stevens
1999	Beautiful Pleasure	J. Chaves
2000	Spain	V. Espinoza
2001	Unbridled Elaine	P. Day

Turf

Distance: 1-1/2 mi

Year	Winner	Jockey
1984	Lashkari	Y. St.-Martin
1985	Pebbles	P. Eddery
1986	Manila	J. Santos
1987	Theatrical	P. Day
1988	Great Communicator	R. Sibille
1989	Prized	E. Delahoussaye
1990	In The Wings	G. Stevens
1991	Miss Alleged	E. Legrix
1992	Fraise	P. Valenzuela
1993	Kotashaan	K. Desormeaux
1994	Tikkanen	M. Smith
1995	Northern Spur	C. McCarron
1996	Pilsudski	W. Swinburn
1997	Chief Bearhart	J. Santos
1998	Buck's Boy	S. Sellers
1999	Daylami	L. Dettori
2000	Kalanisi	J. Murtagh
2001	Fantastic Light	L. Dettori

Classic

Distance: 1-1/4 mi

Year	Winner	Jockey
1984	Wild Again	P. Day
1985	Proud Truth	J. Velasquez
1986	Skywalker	L. Pincay, Jr.
1987	Ferdinand	W. Shoemaker
1988	Alysheba	C. McCarron
1989	Sunday Silence	C. McCarron
1990	Unbridled	P. Day
1991	Black Tie Affair	J. Bailey
1992	A.P. Indy	E. Delahoussaye
1993	Arcangues	J. Bailey
1994	Concern	J. Bailey
1995	Cigar	J. Bailey
1996	Alphabet Soup	C. McCarron
1997	Skip Away	M. Smith
1998	Awesome Again	P. Day
1999	Cat Thief	P. Day
2000	Tiznow	C. McCarron
2001	Tiznow	C. McCarron

Eclipse Awards

The Eclipse Awards, honoring the Horse of the Year and other champions of the sport, began in 1971 and are sponsored by the *Daily Racing Form,* the Thoroughbred Racing Associations, and the National Turf Writers Assn. Prior to 1971, the *DRF* (1936-70) and the TRA (1950-70) issued separate selections for Horse of the Year.

Eclipse Awards for 2001

Horse of the Year—Point Given
2-year-old colt or gelding—Johannesburg
2-year-old filly—Tempera
3-year-old colt or gelding—Point Given
3-year-old filly—Xtra Heat
Older male (4-year-olds & up)—Tiznow
Older female (4-year-olds & up)—Gourmet Girl
Male turf horse—Fantastic Light
Turf filly or mare—Banks Hill
Sprinter—Squirtle Squirt
Steeplechase horse—Pompeyo
Trainer—Bobby Frankel
Jockey—Jerry Bailey
Apprentice jockey—Jeremy Rose
Breeder—Juddmonte Farms
Owner—Richard Englander

Horse of the Year

1936	Granville
1937	War Admiral
1938	Seabiscuit
1939	Challedon
1940	Challedon
1941	Whirlaway
1942	Whirlaway
1943	Count Fleet
1944	Twilight Tear
1945	Busher
1946	Assault
1947	Armed
1948	Citation
1949	Capot
1950	Hill Prince
1951	Counterpoint
1952	One Count (DRF)
	Native Dancer (TRA)
1953	Tom Fool
1954	Native Dancer
1955	Nashua
1956	Swaps
1957	Bold Ruler (DRF)
	Dedicate (TRA)
1958	Round Table
1959	Sword Dancer
1960	Kelso
1961	Kelso
1962	Kelso
1963	Kelso
1964	Kelso
1965	Roman Brother (DRF)
	Moccasin (TRA)
1966	Buckpasser
1967	Damascus
1968	Dr. Fager
1969	Arts and Letters
1970	Fort Marcy (DRF)
	Personality (TRA)
1971	Ack Ack
1972	Secretariat
1973	Secretariat
1974	Forego
1975	Forego
1976	Forego
1977	Seattle Slew
1978	Affirmed
1979	Affirmed
1980	Spectacular Bid
1981	John Henry
1982	Conquistador Cielo
1983	All Along
1984	John Henry
1985	Spend A Buck
1986	Lady's Secret
1987	Ferdinand
1988	Alysheba
1989	Sunday Silence
1990	Criminal Type
1991	Black Tie Affair
1992	A.P. Indy
1993	Kotashaan
1994	Holy Bull
1995	Cigar
1996	Cigar
1997	Favorite Trick
1998	Skip Away
1999	Charismatic
2000	Tiznow
2001	Point Given

HARNESS RACING

Harness Horse of the Year

(Chosen by the U.S. Trotting Assn. and the U.S. Harness Writers Assn.)

1947	Victory Song
1948	Rodney
1949	Good Time
1950	Proximity
1951	Pronto Don
1952	Good Time
1953	Hi Lo's Forbes
1954	Stenographer
1955	Scott Frost
1956	Scott Frost
1957	Torpid
1958	Emily's Pride
1959	Bye Bye Byrd
1960	Adios Butler
1961	Adios Butler
1962	Su Mac Lad
1963	Speedy Scot
1964	Bret Hanover
1965	Bret Hanover
1966	Bret Hanover
1967	Nevele Pride
1968	Nevele Pride
1969	Nevele Pride
1970	Fresh Yankee
1971	Albatross
1972	Albatross
1973	Sir Dalrae
1974	Delmonica Hanover
1975	Savoir
1976	Keystone Ore
1977	Green Speed
1978	Abercrombie
1979	Niatross
1980	Niatross
1981	Fan Hanover
1982	Cam Fella
1983	Cam Fella
1984	Fancy Crown
1985	Nihilator
1986	Forrest Skipper
1987	Mack Lobell
1988	Mack Lobell
1989	Matt's Scooter
1990	Beach Towel
1991	Precious Bunny
1992	Artsplace
1993	Staying Together
1994	Cam's Card Shark
1995	CR Kay Suzie
1996	Continentalvictory
1997	Malabar Man
1998	Moni Maker
1999	Moni Maker
2000	Gallo Blue Chip
2001	Bunny Lake

NCAA WRESTLING CHAMPIONS

Year	Champion	Year	Champion	Year	Champion	Year	Champion
1964	Oklahoma State	1974	Oklahoma	1984	Iowa	1994	Oklahoma State
1965	Iowa State	1975	Iowa	1985	Iowa	1995	Iowa
1966	Oklahoma State	1976	Iowa	1986	Iowa	1996	Iowa
1967	Michigan State	1977	Iowa State	1987	Iowa State	1997	Iowa
1968	Oklahoma State	1978	Iowa	1988	Arizona State	1998	Iowa
1969	Iowa State	1979	Iowa	1989	Oklahoma State	1999	Iowa
1970	Iowa State	1980	Iowa	1990	Oklahoma State	2000	Iowa
1971	Oklahoma State	1981	Iowa	1991	Iowa	2001	Minnesota
1972	Iowa State	1982	Iowa	1992	Iowa	2002	Minnesota
1973	Iowa State	1983	Iowa	1993	Iowa		

CHESS

World Chess Champions

Source: U.S. Chess Federation

Official world champions since the title was first used are as follows:

1866-1894	Wilhelm Steinitz, Austria
1894-1921	Emanuel Lasker, Germany
1921-1927	Jose R. Capablanca, Cuba
1927-1935	Alexander A. Alekhine, France
1935-1937	Max Euwe, Netherlands
1937-1946	Alexander A. Alekhine, France (a)
1948-1957	Mikhail Botvinnik, USSR
1957-1958	Vassily Smyslov, USSR
1958-1959	Mikhail Botvinnik, USSR
1960-1961	Mikhail Tal, USSR
1961-1963	Mikhail Botvinnik, USSR
1963-1969	Tigran Petrosian, USSR
1969-1972	Boris Spassky, USSR
1972-1975	Bobby Fischer, U.S. (b)
1975-1985	Anatoly Karpov, USSR
1985-1993	Garry Kasparov, USSR/Russia (c)
1993-1995	Garry Kasparov, Russia (PCA) (d)
1993-1999	Anatoly Karpov, Russia (FIDE)
1999	Aleksandr Khalifman, Russia (FIDE)
2000	Viswanathan Anand, India (FIDE)
2001	Ruslan Ponomariov, Ukraine (FIDE)

(a) After Alekhine died in 1946, the title was vacant until 1948, when Botvinnik won the 1st championship match sanctioned by the International Chess Federation (FIDE). (b) Defaulted championship after refusal to accept FIDE rules for a championship match, Apr. 1975. (c) Kasparov broke with FIDE, Feb. 26, 1993. FIDE stripped Kasparov of his title Mar. 23. Kasparov defeated Nigel Short of Great Britain in a world championship match played Sept.-Oct. 1993 under the auspices of a new organization the two had founded, the Professional Chess Association (PCA). FIDE held a championship match between Anatoly Karpov (Russia) and Jan Timman (the Netherlands), which Karpov won in Nov. 1993. (d) The PCA folded in 1995.

Recent matches: In Feb. 1996, Kasparov defeated Deep Blue (3 wins, 1 loss, 2 draws), a computer designed by IBM, in the 1st multigame regulation match between a world chess champion and a computer. In a May 1997 rematch, however, Kasparov was defeated by the computer; he scored 1 win, 2 losses, 3 draws. Karpov successfully defended the FIDE title in June-July 1996 against 1991 U.S. chess champion Gata Kamsky of New York City, 10 to 7. In Aug. 1999, after Karpov had refused to play under the controversial format, Aleksandr Khalifman (Russia) earned the FIDE title by defeating Vladmir Akopian (Armenia), 3 to 2, in Las Vegas. In Nov. 2000, Vladimir Kramnik (Russia) defeated Garry Kasparov (Russia), widely recognized as the unofficial world champion, 8½-6½, at the Braingames World Chess Championships in London. In Dec. 2000, Viswanathan Anand (India) def. Alexi Shirov (Spain), 3½-½, in Tehran, Iran, for the FIDE title. In Jan. 2002, 18-year-old Ruslan Ponomariov (Ukraine) def. Vassily Ivanchuk (Ukraine), 4½-2½, in Moscow, Russia, to become the youngest world chess champion. (Anand had lost to Ivanchuk in the semifinals.) The next FIDE World Chess Championship was scheduled for Nov.-Dec. 2003, in London.

Further information: More information on chess and chess champions may be accessed on the U.S. Chess Federation's Internet site: www.uschess.org

BOWLING

Professional Bowlers Association

Hall of Fame

PERFORMANCE

Bill Allen
Glenn Allison
Earl Anthony
Barry Asher
Mike Aulby
Tom Baker
Parker Bohn III
Roy Buckley
Nelson Burton, Jr.
Don Carter
Pat Colwell
Steve Cook
Dave Davis
Gary Dickinson
Mike Durbin
Buzz Fazio
Dave Ferraro
Skee Foremsky
Jim Godman
Johnny Guenther
Billy Hardwick
Tommy Hudson
Dave Husted
Don Johnson
Joe Joseph
Larry Laub
Mike Limongello
Don McCune
Mike McGrath
Amleto Monacelli
David Ozio
George Pappas
Johnny Petraglia
Dick Ritger
Mark Roth
Jim St. John
Carmen Salvino
Ernie Schlegel
Teata Semiz
Bob Strampe
Harry Smith
Dave Soutar
Jim Stefanich
Brian Voss
Wayne Webb
Dick Weber
Pete Weber
Billy Welu
Walter Ray Williams, Jr.
Wayne Zahn

MERITORIOUS SERVICE

Joe Antenora
John Archibald
Chuck Clemens
Eddie Elias
Frank Esposito
Dick Evans
Raymond Firestone
E. A. "Bud" Fisher
Jim Fitzgerald
Lou Frantz
Harry Golden
Ted Hoffman, Jr.
John Jowdy
Joe Kelley
Larry Lichstein
Steve Nagy
Keijiro Nakano
Chuck Pezzano
Jack Reichert
Joe Richards
Chris Schenkel
Lorraine Stilzlein
Al Thompson
Roger Zeller
Chuck Pezzano

Tournament of Champions

Year	Winner	Year	Winner	Year	Winner	Year	Winner
1965	Billy Hardwick	1974	Earl Anthony	1983	Joe Berardi	1992	Marc McDowell
1966	Wayne Zahn	1975	Dave Davis	1984	Mike Durbin	1993	George Branham, 3rd
1967	Jim Stefanich	1976	Marshall Holman	1985	Mark Williams	1994	Norm Duke
1968	Dave Davis	1977	Mike Berlin	1986	Marshall Holman	1996	Dave D'Entremont
1969	Jim Godman	1978	Earl Anthony	1987	Pete Weber	1997	John Gant
1970	Don Johnson	1979	George Pappas	1988	Mark Williams	1998	Bryan Goebel
1971	Johnny Petraglia	1980	Wayne Webb	1989	Del Ballard, Jr.	1999	Jason Couch
1972	Mike Durbin	1981	Steve Cook	1990	Dave Ferraro	2000	Jason Couch
1973	Jim Godman	1982	Mike Durbin	1991	David Ozio	2001	Walter Ray Williams Jr.

PBA Leading Money Winners

Total winnings are from PBA, ABC Masters, and BPAA All-Star tournaments only and do not include numerous other tournaments or earnings from special television shows and matches. In 2001, the PBA began an Oct.-Mar. season schedule. After 2000, year shown is year the season ended.

Year	Bowler	Amount	Year	Bowler	Amount	Year	Bowler	Amount
1962	Don Carter	$49,972	1976	Earl Anthony	$110,833	1989	Mike Aulby	$298,237
1963	Dick Weber	46,333	1977	Mark Roth	105,583	1990	Amleto Monacelli	204,775
1964	Bob Strampe	33,592	1978	Mark Roth	134,500	1991	David Ozio	225,585
1965	Dick Weber	47,674	1979	Mark Roth	124,517	1992	Marc McDowell	174,215
1966	Wayne Zahn	54,720	1980	Wayne Webb	116,700	1993	Walter Ray Williams, Jr.	296,370
1967	Dave Davis	54,165	1981	Earl Anthony	164,735	1994	Norm Duke	273,753
1968	Jim Stefanich	67,377	1982	Earl Anthony	134,760	1995	Mike Aulby	219,792
1969	Billy Hardwick	64,160	1983	Earl Anthony	135,605	1996	Walter Ray Williams, Jr.	241,330
1970	Mike McGrath	52,049	1984	Mark Roth	158,712	1997	Walter Ray Williams, Jr.	240,544
1971	Johnny Petraglia	85,065	1985	Mike Aulby	201,200	1998	Walter Ray Williams, Jr.	238,225
1972	Don Johnson	56,648	1986	Walter Ray Williams, Jr.	145,550	1999	Parker Bohn III	240,912
1973	Don McCune	69,000	1987	Pete Weber	175,491	2000	Norm Duke	143,325
1974	Earl Anthony	99,585	1988	Brian Voss	225,485	2002	Parker Bohn III	245,200
1975	Earl Anthony	107,585						

Leading PBA Averages by Year

Year	Bowler	Average	Year	Bowler	Average	Year	Bowler	Average
1962	Don Carter	212.844	1976	Mark Roth	215.970	1989	Pete Weber	215.432
1963	Billy Hardwick	210.346	1977	Mark Roth	218.174	1990	Amleto Monacelli	218.158
1964	Ray Bluth	210.512	1978	Mark Roth	219.834	1991	Norm Duke	218.208
1965	Dick Weber	211.895	1979	Mark Roth	221.662	1992	Dave Ferraro	219.702
1966	Wayne Zahn	208.663	1980	Earl Anthony	218.535	1993	Walter Ray Williams, Jr.	222.980
1967	Wayne Zahn	212.342	1981	Mark Roth	216.699	1994	Norm Duke	222.830
1968	Jim Stefanich	211.895	1982	Marshall Holman	212.844	1995	Mike Aulby	225.490
1969	Bill Hardwick	212.957	1983	Earl Anthony	216.645	1996	Walter Ray Williams, Jr.	225.370
1970	Nelson Burton, Jr.	214.908	1984	Marshall Holman	213.911	1997	Walter Ray Williams, Jr.	222.008
1971	Don Johnson	213.977	1985	Mark Baker	213.718	1998	Walter Ray Williams, Jr.	226.130
1972	Don Johnson	215.290	1986	John Gant	214.378	1999	Parker Bohn III	228.040
1973	Earl Anthony	215.799	1987	Marshall Holman	216.801	2000	Chris Barnes	220.930
1974	Earl Anthony	219.394	1988	Mark Roth	218.036	2002	Parker Bohn III	221.546
1975	Earl Anthony	219.060						

American Bowling Congress

ABC Masters Tournament Champions

Year	Winner	Year	Winner	Year	Winner
1980	Neil Burton, St. Louis, MO	1988	Del Ballard, Jr., Richardson, TX	1996	Ernie Schlegel, Vancouver, WA
1981	Randy Lightfoot, St. Charles, MO	1989	Mike Aulby, Indianapolis, IN	1997	Jason Queen, Decatur, IL
1982	Joe Berardi, Brooklyn, NY	1990	Chris Warren, Dallas, TX	1998	Mike Aulby, Indianapolis, IN
1983	Mike Lastowski, Havre de Grace, MD	1991	Doug Kent, Canandaigua, NY	1999	Brian Boghosian, Middletown, CT
1984	Earl Anthony, Dublin, CA	1992	Ken Johnson, N. Richmond Hills, TX	2000	MIka Koivuniemi, Finland
1985	Steve Wunderlich, St. Louis, MO	1993	Norm Duke, Oklahoma City, OK	2001	Parker Bohn III, Jackson, NJ
1986	Mark Fahy, Chicago, IL	1994	Steve Fehr, Cincinnati, OH	2002	Brett Wolfe, Reno, NV
1987	Rick Steelsmith, Wichita, KS	1995	Mike Aulby, Indianapolis, IN		

Champions in 2002

Regular Singles . . . . .Mark Millsap, Portage, IN
Regular Doubles. . . . .Fred Mattson, Tacoma, WA & Chris Warren, Puyallup, WA
Regular All Events . . .Stephen A. Hardy, Manchester, NH
Regular Team . . . . . . .Bruno's Pizza #1, Lafayette, IN

Classified Singles . . . Bob Winston, Lexington, NC
Classified Doubles . . Ralph Spencer, Des Plaines, IL & Tom Mangan, Schaumburg, IL
Classified All Events. Joe Lemmon, Milaca, MN
Classified Team . . . . . Magic, Sallisaw, OK

Most Sanctioned 300 Games

Jeff Carter, Springfield, IL 70
Joe Jimenez, Saginaw, MI 62
Robert Faragon, Albany, NY 59
Bob Learn Jr., Erie PA 57
Jeff Jensen, Wichita, KS 55
Jim Johnson Jr., Tampa, FL. 54
Dean Wolf, Reading, PA. 54
Mike Whalin, Cincinnati, OH 53
Randy Choat, Granite City, IL 53
Bob Buckery, McAdoo, PA 52
Jerry Kessler, Dayton, OH 50
Ralph Burley Jr., Dayton, OH. 49
Ken Hall, Schenectady, NY 47
John Wilcox Jr., Lewisburg, PA 46
Ron Krippelcz, St. Louis, MO 46
Jason Hurd, Tulare, CA. 44
Dave Frascatore Jr., Amsterdam, NY . 44
John Delp III, West Lawn, PA 43
John Chacko Jr., Larksville, PA. 43
Bob J. Johnson, Dayton, OH. 42
Randy Lightfoot, St. Charles, MO 42
Steve Gehringer, Reading, PA. 42

Women's International Bowling Congress

Champions in 2002

Queens Tournament: Kim Terrell, Daly City, CA
Classic Singles: Theresa Smith, Indianapolis, IN
Classic Doubles: Jody Ellis, Pembroke Pines, FL & Kathy Tribbey, Newberg, OR
Classic All Events: Cara Honeychurch, Australia
Classic Team: High Rollers, Henderson, NV

Div. I Singles: Kathy Pausch, Moorhead, MN
Div. I Doubles: Tosca Cobbien, Euclid, OH & Zelma Barnes, S. Euclid, OH
Div. I All Events: Karleen Reynolds, Carrollton, TX
Div. I Team: Fargo Sports, E. Moline, IL

Most Sanctioned 300 Games

Tish Johnson, Panorama City, CA 28
Aleta Sill, Dearborn, MI 25
Jodi Musto, Schenectady, NY. 24
Jeanne Naccarato, Tacoma, WA 23
Leanne Barrette, Yukon, OK. 23
Dede Davidson, Woodland Hills, CA . . 23
Vicki Fischel, Wheat Ridge, CO 21
Debbie McMullen, Denver, CO. 21
Anne-Marie Duggan, Edmond, OK . . . 20
Jodi Hughes, Greenville, SC 19
Cheryl Daniels, Detroit, MI. 18
Shannon Duplantis, New Orleans, LA . 18
Carolyn Dorin-Ballard, N. Richland Hills, TX 18
Mandy Wilson, Dayton, OH 17
Kim Terrell, San Francisco, CA 17
Marianne DiRupo, Succasunna, NJ . . 15
Cindy Coburn-Carroll, Tonawanda, NY 14
Donna Adamek, Apple Valley, CA. . . . 12
Jackie Mitskavich, DuBois, PA 12
Stacy Rider, LaHabra, CA. 12
Charita Williams, Indianapolis, IN 12

FIGURE SKATING

U.S. and World Individual Champions, 1952-2002

U.S. Champions MEN	U.S. Champions WOMEN	YEAR	World Champions MEN	World Champions WOMEN
Dick Button	Tenley Albright	1952	Dick Button, U.S.	Jacqueline du Bief, France
Hayes Jenkins	Tenley Albright	1953	Hayes Jenkins, U.S.	Tenley Albright, U.S.
Hayes Jenkins	Tenley Albright	1954	Hayes Jenkins, U.S.	Gundi Busch, W. Germany
Hayes Jenkins	Tenley Albright	1955	Hayes Jenkins, U.S.	Tenley Albright, U.S.
Hayes Jenkins	Tenley Albright	1956	Hayes Jenkins, U.S.	Carol Heiss, U.S.
Dave Jenkins	Carol Heiss	1957	Dave Jenkins, U.S.	Carol Heiss, U.S.
Dave Jenkins	Carol Heiss	1958	Dave Jenkins, U.S.	Carol Heiss, U.S.
Dave Jenkins	Carol Heiss	1959	Dave Jenkins, U.S.	Carol Heiss, U.S.
Dave Jenkins	Carol Heiss	1960	Alain Giletti, France	Carol Heiss, U.S.
Bradley Lord	Laurence Owen	1961	none	none
Monty Hoyt	Barbara Roles Pursley	1962	Don Jackson, Canada	Sjoukje Dijkstra, Netherlands
Tommy Litz	Lorraine Hanlon	1963	Don McPherson, Canada	Sjoukje Dijkstra, Netherlands
Scott Allen	Peggy Fleming	1964	Manfred Schnelldorfer, W. Germany	Sjoukje Dijkstra, Netherlands
Gary Visconti	Peggy Fleming	1965	Alain Calmat, France	Petra Burka, Canada
Scott Allen	Peggy Fleming	1966	Emmerich Danzer, Austria	Peggy Fleming, U.S.
Gary Visconti	Peggy Fleming	1967	Emmerich Danzer, Austria	Peggy Fleming, U.S.
Tim Wood	Peggy Fleming	1968	Emmerich Danzer, Austria	Peggy Fleming, U.S.
Tim Wood	Janet Lynn	1969	Tim Wood, U.S.	Gabriele Seyfert, E. Germany
Tim Wood	Janet Lynn	1970	Tim Wood, U.S.	Gabriele Seyfert, E. Germany
John Misha Petkevich	Janet Lynn	1971	Ondrej Nepela, Czechoslovakia	Beatrix Schuba, Austria
Ken Shelley	Janet Lynn	1972	Ondrej Nepela, Czechoslovakia	Beatrix Schuba, Austria
Gordon McKellen, Jr.	Janet Lynn	1973	Ondrej Nepela, Czechoslovakia	Karen Magnussen, Canada
Gordon McKellen, Jr.	Dorothy Hamill	1974	Jan Hoffmann, E. Germany	Christine Errath, E. Germany
Gordon McKellen, Jr.	Dorothy Hamill	1975	Sergei Volkov, USSR	Dianne de Leeuw, Neth.-U.S.
Terry Kubicka	Dorothy Hamill	1976	John Curry, Gr. Britain	Dorothy Hamill, U.S.
Charles Tickner	Linda Fratianne	1977	Vladimir Kovalev, USSR	Linda Fratianne, U.S.
Charles Tickner	Linda Fratianne	1978	Charles Tickner, U.S.	Anett Poetzsch, E. Germany
Charles Tickner	Linda Fratianne	1979	Vladimir Kovalev, USSR	Linda Fratianne, U.S.
Charles Tickner	Linda Fratianne	1980	Jan Hoffmann, E. Germany	Anett Poetzsch, E. Germany
Scott Hamilton	Elaine Zayak	1981	Scott Hamilton, U.S.	Denise Biellmann, Switzerland
Scott Hamilton	Rosalynn Sumners	1982	Scott Hamilton, U.S.	Elaine Zayak, U.S.
Scott Hamilton	Rosalynn Sumners	1983	Scott Hamilton, U.S.	Rosalynn Sumners, U.S.
Scott Hamilton	Rosalynn Sumners	1984	Scott Hamilton, U.S.	Katarina Witt, E. Germany
Brian Boitano	Tiffany Chin	1985	Aleksandr Fadeev, USSR	Katarina Witt, E. Germany
Brian Boitano	Debi Thomas	1986	Brian Boitano, U.S.	Debi Thomas, U.S.
Brian Boitano	Jill Trenary	1987	Brian Orser, Canada	Katarina Witt, E. Germany
Brian Boitano	Debi Thomas	1988	Brian Boitano, U.S.	Katarina Witt, E. Germany
Christopher Bowman	Jill Trenary	1989	Kurt Browning, Canada	Midori Ito, Japan
Todd Eldredge	Jill Trenary	1990	Kurt Browning, Canada	Jill Trenary, U.S.
Todd Eldredge	Tonya Harding	1991	Kurt Browning, Canada	Kristi Yamaguchi, U.S.
Christopher Bowman	Kristi Yamaguchi	1992	Viktor Petrenko, Ukraine	Kristi Yamaguchi, U.S.
Scott Davis	Nancy Kerrigan	1993	Kurt Browning, Canada	Oksana Baiul, Ukraine
Scott Davis	vacant(1)	1994	Elvis Stojko, Canada	Yuka Sato, Japan
Todd Eldredge	Nicole Bobek	1995	Elvis Stojko, Canada	Chen Lu, China
Rudy Galindo	Michelle Kwan	1996	Todd Eldredge, U.S.	Michelle Kwan, U.S.
Todd Eldredge	Tara Lipinski	1997	Elvis Stojko, Canada	Tara Lipinski, U.S.
Todd Eldredge	Michelle Kwan	1998	Alexei Yagudin, Russia	Michelle Kwan, U.S.
Michael Weiss	Michelle Kwan	1999	Alexei Yagudin, Russia	Maria Butyrskaya, Russia
Michael Weiss	Michelle Kwan	2000	Alexei Yagudin, Russia	Michelle Kwan, U.S.
Timothy Goebel	Michelle Kwan	2001	Yevgeny Plushchenko, Russia	Michelle Kwan, U.S.
Todd Eldredge	Michelle Kwan	2002	Alexei Yagudin, Russia	Irina Slutskaya, Russia

(1) Tonya Harding was stripped of title.

SKIING

World Cup Alpine Champions, 1967-2002

Men

1967 Jean Claude Killy, France
1968 Jean Claude Killy, France
1969 Karl Schranz, Austria
1970 Karl Schranz, Austria
1971 Gustavo Thoeni, Italy
1972 Gustavo Thoeni, Italy
1973 Gustavo Thoeni, Italy
1974 Piero Gros, Italy
1975 Gustavo Thoeni, Italy
1976 Ingemar Stenmark, Sweden
1977 Ingemar Stenmark, Sweden
1978 Ingemar Stenmark, Sweden
1979 Peter Luescher, Switzerland
1980 Andreas Wenzel, Liechtenstein
1981 Phil Mahre, U.S.
1982 Phil Mahre, U.S.
1983 Phil Mahre, U.S.
1984 Pirmin Zurbriggen, Switzerland
1985 Marc Girardelli, Luxembourg
1986 Marc Girardelli, Luxembourg
1987 Pirmin Zurbriggen, Switzerland
1988 Pirmin Zurbriggen, Switzerland
1989 Marc Girardelli, Luxembourg
1990 Pirmin Zurbriggen, Switzerland
1991 Marc Girardelli, Luxembourg
1992 Paul Accola, Switzerland
1993 Marc Girardelli, Luxembourg
1994 Kjetil Andre Aamodt, Norway
1995 Alberto Tomba, Italy
1996 Lasse Kjus, Norway
1997 Luc Alphand, France
1998 Hermann Maier, Austria
1999 Lasse Kjus, Norway
2000 Hermann Maier, Austria
2001 Hermann Maier, Austria
2002 Stephan Eberharter, Austria

Women

1967	Nancy Greene, Canada	1979	Annemarie Proell Moser, Austria	1991	Petra Kronberger, Austria
1968	Nancy Greene, Canada	1980	Hanni Wenzel, Liechtenstein	1992	Petra Kronberger, Austria
1969	Gertrud Gabl, Austria	1981	Marie-Theres Nadig, Switzerland	1993	Anita Wachter, Austria
1970	Michele Jacot, France	1982	Erika Hess, Switzerland	1994	Vreni Schneider, Switzerland
1971	Annemarie Proell, Austria	1983	Tamara McKinney, U.S.	1995	Vreni Schneider, Switzerland
1972	Annemarie Proell, Austria	1984	Erika Hess, Switzerland	1996	Katja Seizinger, Germany
1973	Annemarie Proell, Austria	1985	Michela Figini, Switzerland	1997	Pernilla Wiberg, Sweden
1974	Annemarie Proell, Austria	1986	Maria Walliser, Switzerland	1998	Katja Seizinger, Germany
1975	Annemarie Proell, Austria	1987	Maria Walliser, Switzerland	1999	Alexandra Meissnitzer, Austria
1976	Rose Mittermaier, W. Germany	1988	Michela Figini, Switzerland	2000	Renate Goetschl, Austria
1977	Lise-Marie Morerod, Switzerland	1989	Vreni Schneider, Switzerland	2001	Janica Kostelic, Croatia
1978	Hanni Wenzel, Liechtenstein	1990	Petra Kronberger, Austria	2002	Michaela Dorfmeister, Austria

LACROSSE

Lacrosse Champions in 2002

World Lacrosse Championship—Perth, Australia, July 14: U.S. def. Canada 18-15.

U.S. Club Lacrosse Association Championship—New Hyde Park, NY, June 16: Single Source Solutions def. M.A.B. Philadelphia 15-6.

National Lacrosse League Championship—Albany, NY, Apr. 13: Toronto def. Albany 13-12.

NCAA Men's Division I Championship—Piscataway, NJ, May 27: Syracuse 13, Princeton 12.

NCAA Women's Division I Championship—Baltimore, MD, May 19: Princeton 12, Georgetown 7.

2002 Men's NCAA Division I All-America Team

Attack: Mike Powell, Syracuse; Steve Dusseau, Georgetown; Josh Coffman, Syracuse.

Midfield: Kevin Cassese, Duke; Kyle Sweeney, Georgetown; Adam Donegar, Johns Hopkins; Chris Rotelli, Virginia.

Defense: John Glatzel, Syracuse; Nick Polanco, Hofstra; Ryan McClay, Cornell.

Goal: Nick Murtha, Johns Hopkins.

Coach of the Year: Dave Pietramala, Johns Hopkins.

2002 Women's NCAA Division I All-America Team

Attack: Erin Elbe, Georgetown; Jessie Groszkowski, UNH; Courtney Hobbs, Maryland; Megan Mirick, Ohio State; Stacey Morlang, Loyola; Lauren Simone, Princeton.

Midfield: Lauren Aumiller, Virginia; Jen Newitt, Dartmouth; Christine McPike, North Carolina; Jaimee Reynolds, Cornell; Theresa Sherry, Princeton.

Defense: Rachael Becker, Princeton; Melissa Biles, Georgetown; Tiffany Schummer, Virginia; Porter Wilkinson, North Carolina.

Goal: Tricia Dabrowski, Loyola.

Coach of the Year: Jenny Graap, Cornell.

NCAA Division I Lacrosse Champions 1982-2002

Year[1]	Men	Women	Year[1]	Men	Women	Year[1]	Men	Women
1982	North Carolina	Massachusetts	1989	Syracuse	Penn St.	1996	Princeton	Maryland
1983	Syracuse	Delaware	1990	vacated	Harvard	1997	Princeton	Maryland
1984	Johns Hopkins	Temple	1991	North Carolina	Virginia	1998	Princeton	Maryland
1985	Johns Hopkins	New Hampshire	1992	Princeton	Maryland	1999	Virginia	Maryland
1986	North Carolina	Maryland	1993	Syracuse	Virginia	2000	Syracuse	Maryland
1987	Johns Hopkins	Penn St.	1994	Princeton	Princeton	2001	Princeton	Maryland
1988	Syracuse	Temple	1995	Syracuse	Maryland	2002	Syracuse	Princeton

(1) NCAA Championships began in 1971 for men, in 1982 for women.

SWIMMING

World Swimming Records

(Long course, as of Oct. 2, 2002, * pending FINA ratification)

Men's Records

Distance	Time	Holder	Country	Where made	Date
Freestyle					
50 meters	**0:21.64**	Alexander Popov	Russia	Moscow, Russia	June 16, 2000
100 meters	**0:47.84**	Pieter van den Hoogenband	Netherlands	Sydney, Australia	Sept. 19, 2000
200 meters	**1:44.06**	Ian Thorpe	Australia	Fukuoka, Japan	July 25, 2001
400 meters	**3:40.08***	Ian Thorpe	Australia	Manchester, England	July 30, 2002
800 meters	**7:39.16**	Ian Thorpe	Australia	Fukuoka, Japan	July 24, 2001
1,500 meters	**14:34:56**	Grant Hackett	Australia	Fukuoka, Japan	July 29, 2001
Breaststroke					
50 meters	**0:27.18**	Oleg Lisogor	Ukraine	Berlin, Germany	Aug. 2, 2002
100 meters	**0:59.94**	Roman Sloudnov	Russia	Fukuoka, Japan	July 23, 2001
200 meters	**2:09.97***	Kosuke Kitajima	Japan	Busan, S. Korea	Oct. 2, 2002
Butterfly					
50 meters	**0:23.44**	Geoffrey Huegill	Australia	Fukuoka, Japan	July 27, 2001
100 meters	**0:51.81**	Michael Klim	Australia	Canberra, Australia	Dec. 12, 1999
200 meters	**1:54.58**	Michael Phelps	U.S.	Fukuoka, Japan	July 24, 2001
Backstroke					
50 meters	**0:24.99**	Lenny Krayzelburg	U.S.	Sydney, Australia	Aug. 28, 1999
100 meters	**0:53.60**	Lenny Krayzelburg	U.S.	Sydney, Australia	Aug. 24, 1999
200 meters	**1:55.15**	Aaron Peirsol	U.S.	Minneapolis, MN	Mar. 20, 2002
Individual Medley					
200 meters	**1:58.16**	Jani Sievinen	Finland	Rome, Italy	Sept. 11, 1994
400 meters	**4:11.09**	Michael Phelps	U.S.	Ft. Lauderdale, FL	Aug. 15, 2002
Medley Relay					
400 m. (4×100)	**3:33.48**	(Peirsol, Hansen, Phelps, Lezak)	U.S.	Yokohama, Japan	Aug. 29, 2002
Freestyle Relays					
400 m. (4×100)	**3:13.67**	(Klim, Fydler, Callus, Thorpe)	Australia	Sydney, Australia	Sept. 16, 2000
800 m. (4×200)	**7:04.66**	(Hackett, Klim, Kirby, Thorpe)	Australia	Fukuoka, Japan	July 27, 2001

Women's Records

Freestyle

Distance	Time	Holder	Country	Where made	Date
50 meters	**0:24.13**	Inge de Bruijn	Netherlands	Sydney, Australia	Sept. 22, 2000
100 meters	**0:53.77**	Inge de Bruijn	Netherlands	Sydney, Australia	Sept. 20, 2000
200 meters	**1:56.64**	Franziska Van Almsick	Germany	Berlin, Germany	Aug. 3, 2002
400 meters	**4:03.85**	Janet Evans	U.S.	Seoul, South Korea	Sept. 22, 1988
800 meters	**8:16.22**	Janet Evans	U.S.	Tokyo, Japan	Aug. 20, 1989
1,500 meters	**15:52.10**	Janet Evans	U.S.	Orlando, FL	Mar. 26, 1988
Breaststroke					
50 meters	**0:30.57***	Zoe Baker	U.K.	Manchester, England	July 30, 2002
100 meters	**1:06.52**	Penny Heyns	South Africa	Canberra, Australia	Aug. 23, 1999
200 meters	**2:22.79**	Hui Ql	China	Hangzhou, China	Apr. 13, 2001
Butterfly					
50 meters	**0:25.57**	Anna-Karin Kammerling	Sweden	Berlin, Germany	July 30, 2000
100 meters	**0:56.61**	Inge de Bruijn	Netherlands	Sydney, Australia	Sept. 17, 2000
200 meters	**2:05.78**	Otylia Jedrzejczak	Poland	Berlin, Germany	Aug. 4, 2002
Backstroke					
50 meters	**0:28.25**	Sandra Voelker	Germany	Berlin, Germany	June 17, 2000
100 meters	**0:59.58**	Natalie Coughlin	U.S.	Ft. Lauderdale, FL	Aug. 13, 2002
200 meters	**2:06.62**	Krisztina Egerszegi	Hungary	Athens, Greece	Aug. 25, 1991
Individual Medley					
200 meters	**2:09.72**	Yanyan Wu	China	Shanghai, China	Oct. 17, 1997
400 meters	**4:33.59**	Yana Klochkova	Ukraine	Sydney, Australia	Sept. 16, 2000
Freestyle Relays					
400 m. (4×100)	**3:36.00**	(Meissner, Dallman, Volker, van Almsick)	Germany	Berlin, Germany	July 29, 2002
800 m. (4×200)	**7:55.47**	(Stellmach, Strauss, Mohring, Friedrich)	E. Germany.	Strasbourg, France	Aug. 18, 1987
Medley Relay					
400 m. (4×100)	**3:58.30**	(Bedford, Quann, Thompson, Torres)	U.S.	Sydney, Australia	Sept. 23, 2000

YACHTING

The America's Cup in 2000

In the 30th America's Cup, held in the Hauraki Gulf off the coast of Auckland, New Zealand, Team New Zealand defeated Italy's Prada Challenge to become the first non-American syndicate to successfully defend the oldest trophy in sports. On Mar. 2, 2000, the Kiwis' *New Zealand* sailed to a 48-sec. victory over Luna Rossa, to complete a 5-0 sweep in the best-of-nine series. Team New Zealand, which also swept the U.S. yacht Young America in 1995, set a record of 10 straight wins in Cup finals. In an surprising move, veteran skipper Russell Coutts stepped aside after his record-tying 9th consecutive Cup race victory to allow 26-year-old Dean Barker to take the helm in the final race. The 31st America's Cup was scheduled to be held in New Zealand in 2003.

Competition for the America's Cup grew out of the first contest to establish a world yachting championship, one of the carnival features of the London Exposition of 1851. The race covered a 60-mile course around the Isle of Wight; the prize was a cup worth about $500, donated by the Royal Yacht Squadron of England, known as the "America's Cup" because it was first won by the U.S. yacht *America*.

Winners of the America's Cup

1851 America
1870 Magic defeated Cambria, England, (1-0)
1871 Columbia (first three races) and Sappho (last two races) defeated Livonia, England, (4-1)
1876 Madeline defeated Countess of Dufferin, Canada, (2-0)
1881 Mischief defeated Atalanta, Canada, (2-0)
1885 Puritan defeated Genesta, England, (2-0)
1886 Mayflower defeated Galatea, England, (2-0)
1887 Volunteer defeated Thistle, Scotland, (2-0)
1893 Vigilant defeated Valkyrie II, England, (3-0)
1895 Defender defeated Valkyrie III, England, (3-0)
1899 Columbia defeated Shamrock, England, (3-0)
1901 Columbia defeated Shamrock II, England, (3-0)
1903 Reliance defeated Shamrock III, England, (3-0)
1920 Resolute defeated Shamrock IV, England, (3-2)
1930 Enterprise defeated Shamrock V, England, (4-0)
1934 Rainbow defeated Endeavour, England, (4-2)
1937 Ranger defeated Endeavour II, England, (4-0)
1958 Columbia defeated Sceptre, England, (4-0)
1962 Weatherly defeated Gretel, Australia, (4-1)
1964 Constellation defeated Sovereign, England, (4-0)
1967 Intrepid defeated Dame Pattie, Australia, (4-0)
1970 Intrepid defeated Gretel II, Australia, (4-1)
1974 Courageous defeated Southern Cross, Australia, (4-0)
1977 Courageous defeated Australia, Australia, (4-0)
1980 Freedom defeated Australia, Australia, (4-1)
1983 Australia II, Australia, defeated Liberty, (4-3)
1987 Stars & Stripes defeated Kookaburra III, Australia, (4-0)
1988 Stars & Stripes defeated New Zealand, New Zealand, (2-0)
1992 America^3 defeated Il Moro di Venezia, Italy, (4-1)
1995 Black Magic 1, New Zealand, defeated Young America, (5-0)
2000 New Zealand, NZ, defeated Luna Rossa, Italy, (5-0)

POWER BOATING

American Power Boat Assn. Gold Cup Champions, 1978-2002

Year	Boat	Driver
1978	Atlas Van Lines	Bill Muncey
1979	Atlas Van Lines	Bill Muncey
1980	Miss Budweiser	Dean Chenoweth
1981	Miss Budweiser	Dean Chenoweth
1982	Atlas Van Lines	Chip Hanauer
1983	Atlas Van Lines	Chip Hanauer
1984	Atlas Van Lines	Chip Hanauer
1985	Miller American	Chip Hanauer
1986	Miller American	Chip Hanauer
1987	Miller American	Chip Hanauer
1988	Circus Circus	Chip Hanauer
1989	Miss Budweiser	Tom D'Eath
1990	Miss Budweiser	Tom D'Eath
1991	Winston Eagle	Mark Tate
1992	Miss Budweiser	Chip Hanauer
1993	Miss Budweiser	Chip Hanauer
1994	Smokin' Joe's	Mark Tate
1995	Miss Budweiser	Chip Hanauer
1996	Pico American Dream	Dave Villwock
1997	Miss Budweiser	Dave Villwock
1998	Miss Budweiser	Dave Villwock
1999	Miss PICO	Chip Hanauer
2000	Miss Budweiser	Dave Villwock
2001	Miss Tubby's Subs	Mike Hanson
2002	Miss Budweiser	Dave Villwock

RODEO

Pro Rodeo Cowboy All-Around Champions, 1977-2001

Year	Winner	Money won	Year	Winner	Money won
1977	Tom Ferguson, Miami, OK	$76,730	1990	Ty Murray, Stephenville, TX	$213,772
1978	Tom Ferguson, Miami, OK	103,734	1991	Ty Murray, Stephenville, TX	244,230
1979	Tom Ferguson, Miami, OK	96,272	1992	Ty Murray, Stephenville, TX	225,992
1980	Paul Tierney, Rapid City, SD	105,568	1993	Ty Murray, Stephenville, TX	297,896
1981	Jimmie Cooper, Monument, NM	105,862	1994	Ty Murray, Stephenville, TX	246,170
1982	Chris Lybbert, Coyote, CA.	123,709	1995	Joe Beaver, Huntsville, TX	141,753
1983	Roy Cooper, Durant, OK	153,391	1996	Joe Beaver, Huntsville, TX	166,103
1984	Dee Pickett, Caldwell, ID.	122,618	1997	Dan Mortensen, Manhattan, MT	184,559
1985	Lewis Feild, Elk Ridge, UT	130,347	1998	Ty Murray, Stephenville, TX	264,673
1986	Lewis Feild, Elk Ridge, UT	166,042	1999	Fred Whitfield, Hockley, TX	217,819
1987	Lewis Feild, Elk Ridge, UT	144,335	2000	Joe Beaver, Huntsville, TX	225,396
1988	Dave Appleton, Arlington, TX	121,546	2001	Cody Ohl, Stephensville, TX	296,419
1989	Ty Murray, Odessa, TX	134,806			

DOGS

Westminster Kennel Club, 1989-2002

Year	Best-in-show	Breed	Owner(s)
1989	Ch. Royal Tudor's Wild As The Wind	Doberman	Sue & Art Kemp, Richard & Carolyn Vida, Beth Wilhite
1990	Ch. Wendessa Crown Prince	Pekingese	Ed Jenner
1991	Ch. Whisperwind on a Carousel	Poodle	Joan & Frederick Hartsock
1992	Ch. Registry's Lonesome Dove	Fox Terrier	Marion & Sam Lawrence
1993	Ch. Salilyn's Condor	English Springer Spaniel	Donna & Roger Herzig
1994	Ch. Chidley Willum	Norwich Terrier	Ruth Cooper & Patricia Lussier
1995	Ch. Gaelforce Post Script	Scottish Terrier	Dr. Vandra Huber & Dr. Joe Kinnarney
1996	Ch. Clussexx Country Sunrise	Clumber Spaniel	Judith & Richard Zaleski
1997	Ch. Parsifal Di Casa Netzer	Standard Schnauzer	Rita Holloway & Gabrio Del Torre
1998	Ch. Fairewood Frolic	Norwich Terrier	Sandina Kennels
1999	Ch. Loteki Supernatural Being	Papillon	John Oulton
2000	Ch. Salilyn 'N Erin's Shameless	English Springer Spaniel	Carl Blain, Fran Sunseri, & Julia Gasow
2001	Ch. Special Times Just Right	Bichons Frises	Cecilia Ruggles, E. McDonald, & F. Werneck
2002	Ch. Surrey Spice Girl	Poodle (Miniature)	Ron L. & Barbara Scott

2002 Iditarod Trail Sled Dog Race

Martin Buser of Big Lake, AK, won his 4th Iditarod Trail Sled Dog Race, Mar. 12, 2002, completing the 1,100-mile course from Anchorage to Nome, AK, in a record 8 days, 22 hours, 46 minutes, 2 seconds, becoming the first musher to break the hallowed 9-day barrier. The victory tied Buser with Doug Swingley (1995, 1999-2001) and Susan Butcher (1986-88, 1990) on the all-time list, behind 5-time winner Rick Swenson (1977, 1979, 1981-82, 1991). Ramy Brooks finished 2nd (9 d, 49 m) and also eclipsed the previous record (9 d, 58 m, 6s) set in 2000 by Swingley.

MARATHONS

Boston Marathon, 2002, and 1972-2002

In the 106th Boston Marathon, Apr. 15, 2002, Rodgers Rop of Kenya won in 2:09:02. Kenyans took the top 4 places and 6 out of the top 10. The 2001 winner, Lee Bong-Ju of South Korea, finished 5th in 2:10:30. The 1st U.S. finisher in 2002 was Keith Dowling (VA) who ranked in 15th place, with a time of 2:13:28. In the women's race, Kenya's Margaret Okayo was the winner, setting a course record of 2:20:43. Kenyan Catherine Ndereba, the 2000-2001 Boston winner and former course record holder (2:23:53), finished 29 seconds back. The top American woman was Jill Gaitenby (MA), who finished 13th in 2:38:55. All times in hour:minute:second format. *Course records.

Men's Winner	Time	Year	Women's Winner	Time
Olavi Suomalainen, Finland	2:15:39	**1972**	Nina Kuscsik, U.S.	3:10:26
Jon Anderson, U.S.	2:16:03	**1973**	Jacqueline Hansen, U.S.	3:05:59
Neil Cusack, Ir.	2:13:39	**1974**	Michiko Gorman, U.S.	2:47:11
Bill Rodgers, U.S.	2:09:55	**1975**	Liane Winter, West Ger.	2:42:24
Jack Fultz, U.S.	2:20:19	**1976**	Kim Merritt, U.S.	2:47:10
Jerome Drayton, Can.	2:14:46	**1977**	Michiko Gorman, U.S.	2:48:33
Bill Rodgers, U.S.	2:10:13	**1978**	Gayle S. Barron, U.S.	2:44:52
Bill Rodgers, U.S.	2:09:27	**1979**	Joan Benoit, U.S.	2:35:15
Bill Rodgers, U.S.	2:12:11	**1980**	Jacqueline Gareau, Can.	2:34:28
Toshihiko Seko, Japan	2:09:26	**1981**	Allison Roe, N. Zealand	2:26:46
Alaberto Salazar, U.S.	2:08:52	**1982**	Charlotte Teske, West Ger.	2:29:33
Greg Myer, U.S.	2:09:00	**1983**	Joan Benoit, U.S.	2:22:43
Geoff Smith, G.B.	2:10:34	**1984**	Lorraine Moller, N. Zealand	2:29:28
Geoff Smith, G.B.	2:14:05	**1985**	Lisa Larsen Weidenbach, U.S.	2:34:06
Robert de Castella, Australia	2:07:51	**1986**	Ingrid Kristiansen, Nor.	2:24:55
Toshihiko Seko, Japan	2:11:50	**1987**	Rosa Mota, Portugal	2:25:21
Ibrahim Hussein, Ken.	2:08:43	**1988**	Rosa Mota, Portugal	2:24:30
Abebe Mekonnen, Eth.	2:09:06	**1989**	Ingrid Kristiansen, Nor.	2:24:33
Gelindo Bordin, Italy	2:08:19	**1990**	Rosa Mota, Portugal	2:25:24
Ibrahim Hussein, Kenya	2:11:06	**1991**	Wanda Panfil, Poland	2:24:18
Ibrahim Hussein, Kenya	2:08:14	**1992**	Olga Markova, CIS	2:23:43
Cosmas Ndeti, Kenya	2:09:33	**1993**	Olga Markova, CIS	2:25:27
Cosmas Ndeti, Kenya	2:07:15*	**1994**	Uta Pippig, Germany	2:21:45*
Cosmas Ndeti, Kenya	2:09:22	**1995**	Uta Pippig, Germany	2:25:11
Moses Tanui, Kenya	2:09:15	**1996**	Uta Pippig, Germany	2:27:12
Lameck Aguta, Kenya	2:10:34	**1997**	Fatuma Roba, Ethiopia	2:26:23
Moses Tanui, Kenya	2:07:34	**1998**	Fatuma Roba, Ethiopia	2:23:21
Joseh Chebet, Kenya	2:09:52	**1999**	Fatuma Roba, Ethiopia	2:23:25
Elijah Lagat, Kenya	2:09:47	**2000**	Catherine Ndereba, Kenya	2:26:11
Lee Bong-ju, S. Korea	2:09:43	**2001**	Catherine Ndereba, Kenya	2:23:53
Rodgers Rop, Kenya	2:09:02	**2002**	Margaret Okayo, Kenya	2:20:43

Boston Marathon Winners, 1897-1971

The first Boston Marathon was held in 1897. Women were officially accepted into the race in 1972.

Year	Winner	Time	Year	Winner	Time
1897	John J. McDermott, New York	2:55:10	1935	John A. Kelley, Massachusetts	2:32:07
1898	Ronald J. MacDonald, Canada	2:42:00	1936	Ellison M. Brown, Rhode Island	2:33:40
1899	Lawrence Brignolia, Massachusetts	2:54:38	1937	Walter Young, Canada	2:33:20
1900	John Caffery, Canada	2:39:44	1938	Leslie S. Pawson, Rhode Island	2:35:34
1901	John Caffery, Canada	2:29:23	1939	Ellison M. Brown, Rhode Island	2:28:51
1902	Sammy Mellor, New York	2:43:12	1940	Gerard Cote, Canada	2:28:28
1903	John Lorden , Massachusetts	2:41:29	1941	Leslie S. Pawson, Rhode Island	2:30:38
1904	Michael Spring, New York	2:38:04	1942	Joe Smith, Massachusetts	2:26:51
1905	Frederick Lorz, New York	2:38:25	1943	Gerard Cote, Canada	2:28:25
1906	Tim Ford, Massachusetts	2:45:45	1944	Gerard Cote, Canada	2:31:50
1907	Thomas Longboat, Canada	2:24:24	1945	John A. Kelley, Massachusetts	2:30:40
1908	Thomas Morrissey, New York	2:25:43	1946	Stylianos Kyriakides, Greece	2:29:27
1909	Henri Renaud, New Hampshire	2:53:36	1947	Yun Bok Suh, Korea	2:25:39
1910	Fred Cameron, Canada	2:28:52	1948	Gerard Cote, Canada	2:31:02
1911	Clarence DeMar, Massachusetts	2:21:39	1949	Karl Leandersson, Sweden	2:31:50
1912	Michael Ryan, New York	2:21:18	1950	Kee Yong Ham, Korea	2:32:39
1913	Fritz Carlson, Minnesota	2:25:14	1951	Shigeki Tanaka, Japan	2:27:45
1914	James Duffy, Canada	2:25:14	1952	Doroteo Flores, Guatamela	2:31:53
1915	Edouard Fabre, Canada	2:31:41	1953	Keizo Yamada, Japan	2:18:51
1916	Arthur Roth, Massachusetts	2:27:16	1954	Veikko Karvonen, Finland	2:20:39
1917	Bill Kennedy, New York	2:28:37	1955	Hideo Hamamura, Japan	2:18:22
1918	Military Relay, Camp Devens	2:29:53	1956	Antti Viskari, Finland	2:14:14
1919	Carl Linder, Massachusetts	2:29:13	1957	John J. Kelley, Connecticut	2:20:05
1920	Peter Trivoulides, New York	2:29:31	1958	Franjo Mihalic, Yugoslavia	2:25:54
1921	Frank Zuna, New York	2:18:57	1959	Eino Oksanen, Finland	2:22:42
1922	Clarence DeMar, Massachusetts	2:18:10	1960	Paavo Kotila, Finland	2:20:54
1923	Clarence DeMar, Massachusetts	2:23:47	1961	Eino Oksanen, Finland	2:23:39
1924	Clarence DeMar, Massachusetts	2:29:40	1962	Eino Oksanen, Finland	2:23:48
1925	Charles Mellor, Illinois	2:33:00	1963	Aurele Vandendriessche, Belgium	2:18:58
1926	John C. Miles, Canada	2:25:40	1964	Aurele Vandendriessche, Belgium	2:19:59
1927	Clarence DeMar, Massachusetts	2:40:22	1965	Morio Shigematsu, Japan	2:16:33
1928	Clarence DeMar, Massachusetts	2:37:07	1966	Kenji Kemihara, Japan	2:17:11
1929	John C. Miles, Canada	2:33:08	1967	David McKenzie, New Zealand	2:15:45
1930	Clarence DeMar, Massachusetts	2:34:48	1968	Amby Burfoot, Connecticut	2:22:17
1931	James P. Henigan, Massachusetts	2:46:45	1969	Yoshiaki Unetani, Japan	2:13:49
1932	Paul DeBruyn, Germany	2:33:36	1970	Ron Hill, Great Britain	2:10:30
1933	Leslie S. Pawson, Rhode Island	2:31:01	1971	Alvaro Mejia, Colombia	2:18:45
1934	Dave Komonen, Canada	2:32:53			

New York City Marathon

All time in hour:minute:second format; *Course record.

Men's Winner	Time	Year	Women's Winner	Time
Gary Muhrcke, U.S.	2:31:38	**1970**	no finisher	—
Norman Higgins, U.S.	2:22:54	**1971**	Beth Bonner, U.S.	2:55:22
Sheldon Karlin, U.S.	2:27:52	**1972**	Nina Kuscsik, U.S.	3:08:41
Tom Fleming, U.S.	2:19:25	**1973**	Nina Kuscsik, U.S.	2:57:07
Norbert Sander, U.S.	2:26:30	**1974**	Katherine Switzer, U.S.	3:07:29
Tom Fleming, U.S.	2:19:27	**1975**	Kim Merritt, U.S.	2:46:14
Bill Rodgers, U.S.	2:10:10	**1976**	Miki Gorman, U.S.	2:39:11
Bill Rodgers, U.S.	2:11:28	**1977**	Miki Gorman, U.S.	2:43:10
Bill Rodgers, U.S.	2:12:12	**1978**	Grete Waitz, Norway	2:32:30
Bill Rodgers, U.S.	2:11:42	**1979**	Grete Waitz, Norway	2:27:33
Alberto Salazar, U.S.	2:09:41	**1980**	Grete Waitz, Norway	2:25:42
Alberto Salazar, U.S.	2:08:13	**1981**	Allison Roe, N. Zealand	2:25:29
Alberto Salazar, U.S.	2:09:29	**1982**	Grete Waitz, Norway	2:27:14
Rod Dixon, N.Z.	2:08:59	**1983**	Grete Waitz, Norway	2:27:00
Orlando Pizzolato, Italy	2:14:53	**1984**	Grete Waitz, Norway	2:29:30
Orlando Pizzolato, Italy	2:11:34	**1985**	Grete Waitz, Norway	2:28:34
Gianni Poli, Italy	2:11:06	**1986**	Grete Waitz, Norway	2:28:06
Ibrahim Hussein, Kenya	2:11:01	**1987**	Priscilla Welch, G.B.	2:30:17
Steve Jones, G.B.	2:08:20	**1988**	Grete Waitz, Norway	2:28:07
Juma Ikangaa, Tanz.	2:08:01	**1989**	Ingrid Kristiansen, Norway	2:25:30
Douglas Wakiihuri, Ken.	2:12:39	**1990**	Wanda Panfil, Poland	2:30:45
Salvador Garcia, Mexico	2:09:28	**1991**	Liz McColgan, G.B.	2:27:32
Willie Mtolo, S. Afr.	2:09:29	**1992**	Lisa Ondieki, Australia	2:24:40*
Andres Espinosa, Mex.	2:10:04	**1993**	Uta Pippig, Germany	2:26:24
German Silva, Mexico	2:11:21	**1994**	Tegla Loroupe, Kenya	2:27:37
German Silva, Mexico	2:11:00	**1995**	Tegla Loroupe, Kenya	2:28:06
Giacomo Leone, Italy	2:09:54	**1996**	Anuta Catuna, Romania	2:28:43
John Kagwe, Kenya	2:08:12	**1997**	F. Rochat-Moser, Switzerland	2:28:43
John Kagwe, Kenya	2:08:45	**1998**	Franca Fiacconi, Italy	2:25:17
Joseph Chebet, Kenya	2:09:14	**1999**	Adriana Fernandez, Mex.	2:25:06
Abdelkhader El Mouaziz, Morocco	2:10:09	**2000**	Ludmila Petrova, Russia	2:25:45
Tesfaye Jifar, Ethiopia	2:07:43*	**2001**	Margaret Okayo, Kenya	2:24:21*

Other Marathon Results in 2002

Los Angeles Marathon—Mar. 3. Men: Stephen Ndungu, Kenya, 2:10:27. Women: Lyubov Denisova, Russia, 2:28:49

Paris Marathon—Apr. 7. Men: Benoit Zwierchiewski, France, 2:08:18. Women: Marleen Renders, Belgium, 2:23:05

Fortis Rotterdam Marathon—Apr. 21. Men: Simon Biwott, Kenya, 2:08:39. Women: Takemi Ominami, Japan, 2:23:42

London Marathon—Apr. 14. Men: Khalid Khannouchi, U.S., 2:05:38 (world best). Women: Paula Radcliffe, U.K., 2:18:56

Berlin Marathon—Sept. 29. Men: Raymond Kipkoech, Kenya, 2:06:47. Women: Naoko Takahashi, Japan, 2:21:49

LaSalle Bank Chicago Marathon—Oct. 13. Men: Khalid Khannouchi, U.S., 2:05:55. Women: Paula Radcliffe, U.K., 2:17:18 (world best)

Ironman Triathlon World Championships

The Ironman Triathlon World Championships—a 2.4-mile ocean swim, 112-mile bike ride and 26.2-mile run—are held annually at Kailua-Kona, Hawaii. On Oct. 6, 2001, the men's race was won by American Tim DeBoom in 8:31:17. New Zealand's Cameron Brown won the women's race in 8:47:40. All times in hour:minute:second format. *Course records.

Men's Winner	Time	Year	Women's Winner	Time
Gordon Haller, U.S.	11:46:58	1978	no finisher	—
Tom Warren, U.S.	11:15:56	1979	Lyn Lemaire, U.S.	12:55:00
Dave Scott, U.S.	9:24:33	1980	Robin Beck, U.S.	11:21:24
John Howard, U.S.	9:38:29	1981	Linda Sweeney, U.S.	12:00:32
Dave Scott, U.S.	9:08:23	1982	Julie Leach, U.S.	10:54:08
Dave Scott, U.S.	9:05:57	1983	Sylviane Puntous, Canada	10:43:36
Dave Scott, U.S	8:54:20	1984	Sylvanie Puntous, Canada	10:25:13
ScottTinley, U.S.	8:50:54	1985	Joanne Ernst, U.S.	10:25:22
Dave Scott, U.S.	8:28:37	1986	Paula Newby-Fraser, Zimbabwe	9:49:14
Dave Scott, U.S.	8:34:13	1987	Erin Baker, New Zealand	9:35:25
Scott Molina, U.S.	8:31:00	1988	Paula Newby-Fraser, Zimbabwe	9:01:01
Mark Allen, U.S.	8:09:15	1989	Paula Newby-Fraser, Zimbabwe	9:00:56
Mark Allen, U.S.	8:28:17	1990	Erin Baker, New Zealand	9:13:42
Mark Allen, U.S.	8:18:32	1991	Paula Newby-Fraser, Zimbabwe	9:07:52
Mark Allen, U.S.	8:09:08	1992	Paula Newby-Fraser, Zimbabwe	8:55:28*
Mark Allen, U.S.	8:07:45	1993	Paula Newby-Fraser, Zimbabwe	8:58:23
Greg Welch, Australia	8:20:27	1994	Paula Newby-Fraser, Zimbabwe	9:20:14
Mark Allen, U.S.	8:20:34	1995	Karen Smyers, U.S.	9:16:46
Luc Van Lierde, Belgium	8:04:08*	1996	Paula Newby-Fraser, Zimbabwe	9:06:49
Thomas Hellriegel, Germany	8:33:01	1997	Heather Fuhr, Canada	9:31:43
Peter Reid, Canada	8:24:20	1998	Natascha Badmann, Switz.	9:24:16
Luc Van Lierde, Belgium	8:17:17	1999	Lori Bowden, U.S.	9:13:02
Peter Reid, Canada	8:21:01	2000	Natascha Badmann, Switz.	9:26:16
Timothy Deboom, U.S.	8:31:18	2001	Natascha Badmann, Switz.	9:28:37

CYCLING

2001 Tour de France

On July 28, 2002, Lance Armstrong became the 4th cyclist in history, and the 1st American, to win the Tour de France 4 straight years. He finished the 3-week, 2,032-mile tour with an overall time of 82 hrs, 5 mins, 12 secs, 7:17 ahead of Spain's Joseba Beloki (3rd in 2000 and 2001). Lithuanian Raimondas Rumsas was 8:17 back, in 3rd. The remaining riders trailed by over 13 mins. It was the 2nd-largest margin of victory for Armstrong, who beat Alex Zuelle by 7:37 in 1999. The 30-year-old Texan, who battled back from a near-fatal bout with cancer in 1996 before beginning his record run in 1999, announced plans to return in 2003 and 2004 to try to break Miguel Indurain's record of 5 straight wins (1991-95). In the team competition, Armstrong and the U.S. Postal Service finished 2nd behind the Spanish team, ONCE-Eroski.

Tour de France Winners, 1980-2002

Year	Winner
1980	Zoop Zoetemelk, The Netherlands
1981	Bernard Hinault, France
1982	Bernard Hinault, France
1983	Laurent Fignon, France
1984	Laurent Fignon, France
1985	Bernard Hinault, France
1986	Greg LeMond, U.S.
1987	Stephen Roche, Ireland
1988	Pedro Delgado, Spain
1989	Greg LeMond, U.S.
1990	Greg LeMond, U.S.
1991	Miguel Indurain, Spain
1992	Miguel Indurain, Spain
1993	Miguel Indurain, Spain
1994	Miguel Indurain, Spain
1995	Miguel Indurain, Spain
1996	Bjarne Riis, Denmark
1997	Jan Ullrich, Germany
1998	Marco Pantani, Italy
1999	Lance Armstrong, U.S.
2000	Lance Armstrong, U.S.
2001	Lance Armstrong, U.S.
2002	Lance Armstrong, U.S.

SULLIVAN AWARD

James E. Sullivan Memorial Trophy Winners

The James E. Sullivan Memorial Trophy, named after the former president of the Amateur Athletic Union (AAU) and inaugurated in 1930, is awarded annually by the AAU to the athlete who "by his or her performance, example and influence as an amateur, has done the most during the year to advance the cause of sportsmanship."

Year	Winner	Sport
1930	Bobby Jones	Golf
1931	Barney Berlinger	Track
1932	Jim Bausch	Track
1933	Glenn Cunningham	Track
1934	Bill Bonthron	Track
1935	Lawson Little	Golf
1936	Glenn Morris	Track
1937	Don Budge	Tennis
1938	Don Lash	Track
1939	Joe Burk	Rowing
1940	Greg Rice	Track
1941	Leslie MacMitchell	Track
1942	Cornelius Warmerdam	Track
1943	Gilbert Dodds	Track
1944	Ann Curtis	Swimming
1945	Doc Blanchard	Football
1946	Arnold Tucker	Football
1947	John Kelly, Jr.	Rowing
1948	Robert Mathias	Track
1949	Dick Button	Skating
1950	Fred Wilt	Track
1951	Rev. Robert Richards	Track
1952	Horace Ashenfelter	Track
1953	Dr. Sammy Lee	Diving
1954	Mal Whitfield	Track
1955	Harrison Dillard	Track
1956	Patricia McCormick	Diving
1957	Bobby Joe Morrow	Track
1958	Glenn Davis	Track
1959	Parry O'Brien	Track
1960	Rafer Johnson	Track
1961	Wilma Rudolph Ward	Track
1962	James Beatty	Track
1963	John Pennel	Track
1964	Don Schollander	Swimming
1965	Bill Bradley	Basketball
1966	Jim Ryun	Track
1967	Randy Matson	Track
1968	Debbie Meyer	Swimming
1969	Bill Toomey	Track
1970	John Kinsella	Swimming
1971	Mark Spitz	Swimming
1972	Frank Shorter	Track
1973	Bill Walton	Basketball
1974	Rick Wohlhutter	Track
1975	Tim Shaw	Swimming
1976	Bruce Jenner	Track
1977	John Naber	Swimming
1978	Tracy Caulkins	Swimming
1979	Kurt Thomas	Gymnastics
1980	Eric Heiden	Speed Skating
1981	Carl Lewis	Track
1982	Mary Decker	Track
1983	Edwin Moses	Track
1984	Greg Louganis	Diving
1985	Joan Benoit Samuelson	Marathon
1986	Jackie Joyner-Kersee	Track
1987	Jim Abbott	Baseball
1988	Florence Griffith Joyner	Track
1989	Janet Evans	Swimming
1990	John Smith	Wrestling
1991	Mike Powell	Track
1992	Bonnie Blair	Speed Skating
1993	Charlie Ward	Football, Basketball
1994	Dan Jansen	Speed Skating
1995	Bruce Baumgartner	Wrestling
1996	Michael Johnson	Track
1997	Peyton Manning	Football
1998	Chamique Holdsclaw	Basketball
1999	Kelly Miller and Coco Miller	Basketball
2000	Rulon Gardner	Wrestling
2001	Michelle Kwan	Figure Skating

FISHING

Selected IGFA Saltwater & Freshwater All-Tackle World Records

Source: International Game Fish Association; records confirmed to Oct. 1, 2002

Saltwater Fish Records

Species	Weight	Where caught	Date	Angler
Albacore	88 lbs. 2 oz.	Canary Islands, Spain	Nov. 19, 1977	Siegfried Dickemann
Amberjack, greater	155 lbs. 12 oz.	Bermuda	Aug. 16, 1992	Larry Trott
Barracuda, great	85 lbs.	Christmas Island, Kiribati	Apr. 11, 1992	John W. Helfrich
Barracuda, Mexican	21 lbs.	Phantom Isle, Costa Rica	Mar. 27, 1987	E. Greg Kent
Barracuda, Pacific	26 lbs. 8 oz.	Playa Matapalo, Costa Rica	Jan. 3, 1999	Doug Hettinger
Bass, barred sand	13 lbs. 3 oz.	Huntington Beach, CA	Aug. 29, 1988	Robert Halal
Bass, black sea	10 lbs. 4 oz.	Virginia Beach, VA	Jan. 1, 2000	Allan P. Paschall
Bass, giant sea	563 lbs. 8 oz.	Anacapa Island, CA	Aug. 20, 1968	James D. McAdam Jr.
Bass, striped	78 lbs. 8 oz.	Atlantic City, NJ	Sept. 21, 1982	Albert R. McReynolds
Bluefish	31 lbs. 12 oz.	Hatteras Inlet, NC	Jan. 30, 1972	James M. Hussey
Bonefish	19 lbs.	Zululand, South Africa	May 26, 1962	Brian W. Batchelor
Bonito, Atlantic	18 lbs. 4 oz.	Faial Island, Azores	July 8, 1953	D. Gama Higgs
Bonito, Pacific	21 lbs. 3 oz.	Malibu, CA	July 30, 1978	Gino M. Picciolo
Cabezon	23 lbs.	Juan De Fuca Strait, WA	Aug. 4, 1990	Wesley S. Hunter
Cobia	135 lbs. 9 oz.	Shark Bay, Australia	July 9, 1985	Peter W. Goulding
Cod, Atlantic	98 lbs. 12 oz.	Isle of Shoals, NH	June 8, 1969	Alphonse J. Bielevich
Cod, Pacific	35 lbs.	Unalaska Bay, AK	June 16, 1999	Jim Johnson
Conger	133 lbs. 4 oz.	Berry Head, S. Devon, England	June 5, 1995	Vic Evans
Dolphin	88 lbs.	Exuma, Bahamas	May 5, 1998	Richard D. Evans
Drum, black	113 lbs. 1 oz.	Lewes, DE	Sept. 15, 1975	Gerald M. Townsend
Drum, red	94 lbs. 2 oz.	Avon, NC	Nov. 7, 1984	David G. Deuel
Eel, American	9 lbs. 4 oz.	Cape May, NJ	Nov. 9, 1995	Jeff Pennick
Eel, marbled	36 lbs. 1 oz.	Hazelmere Dam, South Africa	June 10, 1984	Ferdie Van Nooten
Flounder, southern	20 lbs. 9 oz.	Nassau Sound, FL	Dec. 23, 1983	Larenza W. Mungin
Flounder, summer	22 lbs. 7 oz.	Montauk, NY	Sept. 15, 1975	Charles Nappi
Grouper, Goliath	680 lbs.	Fernandina Beach, FL	May 20, 1961	Lynn Joyner
Grouper, Warsaw	436 lbs. 12 oz.	Gulf of Mexico, Destin, FL	Dec. 22, 1985	Steve Haeusler
Halibut, Atlantic	355 lbs. 6 oz.	Valevag, Norway	Oct. 20, 1997	Odd Arve Gunderstad
Halibut, California	58 lbs. 9 oz.	Santa Rosa Island, CA	June 26, 1999	Roger W. Borrell
Halibut, Pacific	459 lbs.	Dutch Harbor, AK	June 11, 1996	Jack Tragis
Jack, crevalle	58 lbs. 6 oz.	Barra do Kwanza, Angola	Dec. 10, 2000	Nuno Abohbot Po da Silva
Jack, horse-eye	29 lbs. 8 oz.	Ascencion Island, South Atlantic	May 28, 1993	Mike Hanson
Jack, Pacific crevalle	39 lbs.	Playa Zancudo, Costa Rica	Mar. 3, 1997	Ingrid Callaghan
Kawakawa	29 lbs.	Clarion Island, Mexico	Dec. 17, 1986	Ronald Nakamura
Lingcod	76 lbs. 9 oz.	Gulf of Alaska, AK	Aug. 11, 2001	Antwan D. Tinsley
Mackerel, cero	17 lbs. 2 oz.	Islamorada, FL	Apr. 5, 1986	G. Michael Mills
Mackerel, king	93 lbs.	San Juan, PR	Apr. 18, 1999	Steve Perez Graulau
Mackerel, Spanish	13 lbs.	Ocracoke Inlet, NC	Nov. 4, 1987	Robert Cranton
Marlin, Atlantic blue	1,402 lbs. 2 oz.	Vitoria, Brazil	Feb. 29, 1992	Paulo Roberto A. Amorim
Marlin, black	1,560 lbs.	Cabo Blanco, Peru	Aug. 4, 1953	Alfred C. Glassell Jr.
Marlin, Pacific blue	1,376 lbs.	Kaaiwi Pt., Kona, HI	May 31, 1982	Jay W. deBeaubien
Marlin, striped	494 lbs.	Tutukaka, New Zealand	Jan. 16, 1986	Bill Boniface
Marlin, white	181 lbs. 14 oz.	Vitoria, Brazil	Dec. 8, 1979	Evandro Luiz Coser
Permit	56 lbs. 2 oz.	Ft. Lauderdale, FL	June 30, 1997	Thomas Sebestyen
Pollack, European	27 lbs. 6 oz.	Salcombe, Devon, England	Jan. 16, 1986	Robert Samuel Milkins
Pollock	50 lbs.	Salstraumen, Norway	Nov. 30, 1995	Thor-Magnus Lekang
Pompano, African	50 lbs. 8 oz.	Daytona Beach, FL	Apr. 21, 1990	Tom Sargent
Roosterfish	114 lbs.	La Paz, Baja Cal., Mexico	June 1, 1960	Abe Sackheim
Runner, blue	11 lbs. 2 oz.	Dauphin Isl., AL	June 28, 1997	Stacey Michelle Moiren
Runner, rainbow	37 lbs. 9 oz.	Clarion Island, Mexico	Nov. 21, 1991	Tom Pfleger
Sailfish, Atlantic	141 lbs. 1 oz.	Luanda, Angola	Feb. 19, 1994	Alfredo de Sousa Neves
Sailfish, Pacific	221 lbs.	Santa Cruz Island, Ecuador	Feb. 12, 1947	C. W. Stewart
Seabass, white	83 lbs. 12 oz.	San Felipe, Mexico	Mar. 31, 1953	L. C. Baumgardner
Seatrout, spotted	17 lbs. 7 oz.	Ft. Pierce, FL	May 11, 1995	Craig F. Carson
Shark, bigeye thresher	802 lbs.	Tutukaka, New Zealand	Feb. 8, 1981	Dianne North
Shark, bignose	369 lbs. 14 oz.	Markham R., Papua New Guinea	Oct. 23, 1993	Lester J. Rohrlach
Shark, blue	528 lbs.	Montauk Point, NY	Aug. 9, 2001	Joe Seidel
Shark, great hammerhead	991 lbs.	Sarasota, FL	May 30, 1982	Allen Ogle
Shark, Greenland	1,708 lbs. 9 oz.	Trondheimsfjord, Norway	Oct. 18, 1987	Terje Nordtvedt
Shark, porbeagle	507 lbs.	Caithness, Scotland	Mar. 9, 1993	Christopher Bennett
Shark, shortfin mako	1,221 lbs.	Chatham, MA	July 21, 2001	Luke Sweeney
Shark, tiger	1,780 lbs.	Cherry Grove, SC	June 14, 1964	Walter Maxwell
Shark, white	2,664 lbs.	Ceduna, S.A., Australia	Apr. 21, 1959	Alfred Dean
Sheepshead	21 lbs. 4 oz.	New Orleans, LA	Apr. 16, 1982	Wayne Desselle
Skipjack, black	26 lbs.	Thetis Bank, Baja Cal., Mexico	Oct. 23, 1991	Clifford Hamaishi
Snapper, cubera	121 lbs. 8 oz.	Cameron, LA	July 5, 1982	Mike Hebert
Snapper, red	50 lbs. 4 oz.	Gulf of Mexico, LA	June 23, 1996	Capt. Doc Kennedy
Snook, common	53 lbs. 10 oz.	Parismina Ranch, Costa Rica	Oct. 18, 1978	Gilbert Ponzi
Spearfish, Mediterranean	90 lbs. 13 oz.	Madeira Island, Portugal	June 2, 1980	Joseph Larkin
Swordfish	1,182 lbs.	Iquique, Chile	May 7, 1953	L. B. Marron
Tarpon	283 lbs. 4 oz.	Sherbro Island, Sierra Leone	Apr. 16, 1991	Yvon Sebag
Tautog	25 lbs.	Ocean City, NJ	Jan. 20, 1998	Anthony R. Monica
Trevally, bigeye	31 lbs. 8 oz.	Poivre Isl., Seychelles	Apr. 23, 1997	Les Sampson
Trevally, giant	145 lbs. 8 oz.	Makena, Maui, HI	Mar. 28, 1991	Russell Mori
Tuna, Atlantic bigeye	392 lbs. 6 oz.	Canary Islands, Spain	July 15, 1996	Dieter Vogel
Tuna, blackfin	45 lbs. 8 oz.	Key West, FL	May 4, 1996	Sam J. Burnett
Tuna, bluefin	1,496 lbs.	Aulds Cove, Nova Scotia	Oct. 26, 1979	Ken Fraser
Tuna, longtail	79 lbs. 2 oz.	Montague Isl., N.S.W., Australia	Apr. 12, 1982	Tim Simpson
Tuna, Pacific bigeye	435 lbs.	Cabo Blanco, Peru	Apr. 17, 1957	Dr. Russel V. A. Lee
Tuna, skipjack	45 lbs. 4 oz.	Flathead Bank, Baja Cal., Mexico	Nov. 16, 1996	Brian Evans

Species	Weight	Where caught	Date	Angler
Tuna, southern bluefin	348 lbs. 5 oz.	Whakatane, New Zealand	Jan. 16, 1981	Rex Wood
Tuna, yellowfin	388 lbs. 12 oz.	San Benedicto Island, Mexico	Apr. 1, 1977	Curt Wiesenhutter
Tunny, little	35 lbs. 2 oz.	Cap de Garde, Algeria	Dec. 14, 1988	Jean Yves Chatard
Wahoo	158 lbs. 8 oz.	Loreto, Baja Cal., Mexico	June 10, 1996	Keith Winter
Weakfish	19 lbs. 2 oz.	Jones Beach Inlet, NY	Oct. 11, 1984	Dennis Roger Rooney
		Delaware Bay, DE	May 20, 1989	William E. Thomas
Yellowtail, California	88 lbs. 3 oz.	Alijos Rocks, Baja Cal., Mexico	June 21, 2000	Ronald Tadashi Fujii
Yellowtail, southern	114 lbs. 10 oz.	Tauranga, New Zealand	Feb. 5, 1984	Mike Godfrey
		White Island, New Zealand	Jan. 9, 1987	David Lugton

Freshwater Fish Records

Species	Weight	Where caught	Date	Angler
Barramundi	83 lbs. 7 oz.	Lake Tinaroo, N. Queensland, Australia	Sept. 23, 1999	David Powell
Bass, largemouth	22 lbs. 4 oz.	Montgomery Lake, GA	June 2, 1932	George W. Perry
Bass, rock	3 lbs.	York River, Ontario	Aug. 1, 1974	Peter Gulgin
	3 lbs.	Lake Erie, PA	June 18, 1998	Herbert G. Ratner, Jr.
Bass, shoal	8 lbs. 12 oz.	Apalachicola River, FL	Jan. 28, 1995	Carl W. Davis
Bass, smallmouth	10 lbs. 14 oz.	Dale Hollow Lake, TN	Apr. 24, 1969	John T. Gorman
Bass, white	6 lbs. 13 oz.	Lake Orange, VA	July 31, 1989	Ronald L. Sprouse
Bass, whiterock	27 lbs. 5 oz.	Greers Ferry Lake, AR	April 24, 1997	Jerald C. Shaum
Bass, yellow	2 lbs. 9 oz.	Waverly, TN	Feb. 27, 1998	John T. Chappell
Bluegill	4 lbs. 12 oz.	Ketona Lake, AL	Apr. 9, 1950	T. S. Hudson
Bowfin	21 lbs. 8 oz.	Florence, SC	Jan. 29, 1980	Robert L. Harmon
Buffalo, bigmouth	70 lbs. 5 oz.	Bastrop, LA	Apr. 21, 1980	Delbert Sisk
Buffalo, black	63 lbs. 6 oz.	Mississippi River, IA	Aug. 14, 1999	Jim Winters
Buffalo, smallmouth	82 lbs. 3 oz.	Athens Lake, AR	June 6, 1993	Randy Collins
Bullhead, brown	6 lbs. 1 oz.	Waterford, NY	Apr. 26, 1998	Bobby Triplett
Bullhead, yellow	4 lbs. 4 oz.	Mormon Lake, AZ	May 11, 1984	Emily Williams
Burbot	18 lbs. 11 oz.	Angenmanalren, Sweden	Oct. 22, 1996	Margit Agren
Carp, common	75 lbs. 11 oz.	Lac de St. Cassien, France	May 21, 1987	Leo van der Gugten
Catfish, blue	116 lbs. 12 oz.	Mississippi R., AR	Aug 3, 2001	Charles Ashley Jr.
Catfish, channel	58 lbs.	Santee-Cooper Res., SC	July 7, 1964	W. B. Whaley
Catfish, flathead	123 lbs. 9 oz.	Independence, KS	May 14, 1998	Ken Paulie
Catfish, white	21 lbs. 8 oz.	Gorton Pond, CT	Apr. 22, 2001	Thomas Urguhart
Char, Arctic	32 lbs. 9 oz.	Tree River, Canada	July 30, 1981	Jeffrey L. Ward
Crappie, white	5 lbs. 3 oz.	Enid Dam, MS	July 31, 1957	Fred L. Bright
Dolly Varden	20 lbs. 11oz.	Wulik R., AK	July 7, 2001	Raz Reid
Dorado	51 lbs. 5 oz.	Toledo (Corrientes), Argentina	Sept. 27, 1984	Armando Giudice
Drum, freshwater	54 lbs. 8 oz.	Nickajack Lake, TN	Apr. 20, 1972	Benny E. Hull
Gar, alligator	279 lbs.	Rio Grande, TX	Dec. 2, 1951	Bill Valverde
Gar, Florida	10 lbs.	Everglades, FL	Jan. 28, 2002	Herbert G. Ratner Jr.
Gar, longnose	50 lbs. 5 oz.	Trinity River, TX	July 30, 1954	Townsend Miller
Gar, shortnose	5 lbs. 12 oz.	Ren Lake, IL	July 16, 1995	Donna K. Willmert
Gar, spotted	9 lbs. 12 oz.	Lake Mexia, TX	Apr. 7, 1994	Rick Rivard
Grayling, Arctic	5 lbs. 15 oz.	Katseyedie River, N.W.T.	Aug. 16, 1967	Jeanne P. Branson
Inconnu	53 lbs.	Pah River, AK	Aug. 20, 1985	Lawrence E. Hudnall
Kokanee	9 lbs. 6 oz.	Okanagan Lake, Vernon, B.C.	June 18, 1988	Norm Kuhn
Muskellunge	67 lbs. 8 oz.	Lake Court Oreilles, WI	July 24, 1949	Cal Johnson
Muskellunge, tiger	51 lbs. 3 oz.	Lac Vieux-Desert, MI	July 16, 1919	John Knobla
Perch, Nile	230 lbs.	Lake Nasser, Egypt	Dec. 20, 2000	William Toth
Perch, white	3 lbs. 1 oz.	Forest Hill Park, NJ	May 6, 1989	Edward Tango
Perch, yellow	4 lbs. 3 oz.	Bordentown, NJ	May, 1865	Dr. C. C. Abbot
Pickerel, chain	9 lbs. 6 oz.	Homerville, GA	Feb. 17, 1961	Baxley McQuaig Jr.
Pike, northern	55 lbs. 1 oz.	Lake of Grefeern, W. Germany	Oct. 16, 1986	Lothar Louis
Redhorse, greater	9 lbs. 3 oz.	Salmon River, Pulaski, NY	May 11, 1985	Jason Wilson
Redhorse, silver	11 lbs. 7 oz.	Plum Creek, WI	May 29, 1985	Neal Long
Salmon, Atlantic	79 lbs. 2 oz.	Tana River, Norway	1928	Henrik Henriksen
Salmon, chinook	97 lbs. 4 oz.	Kenai River, AK	May 17, 1985	Les Anderson
Salmon, chum	35 lbs.	Edye Pass, BC	July 11, 1995	Todd A. Johansson
Salmon, coho	33 lbs. 4 oz.	Salmon River, Pulaski, NY	Sept. 27, 1989	Jerry Lifton
Salmon, pink	14 lbs. 13 oz.	Monroe, WA	Sept. 30, 2001	Alexander Minerich
Salmon, sockeye	15 lbs. 3 oz.	Kenai River, AK	Aug. 9, 1987	Stan Roach
Sauger	8 lbs. 12 oz.	Lake Sakakawea, ND	Oct. 6, 1971	Mike Fischer
Shad, American	11 lbs. 4 oz.	Connecticut River, MA	May 19, 1986	Bob Thibodo
Sturgeon, beluga	224 lbs. 13 oz.	Guryev, Kazakhstan	May 3, 1993	Merete Lehne
Sturgeon, white	468 lbs.	Benicia, CA	July 9, 1983	Joey Pallotta 3d
Sunfish, green	2 lbs. 2 oz.	Stockton Lake, MO	June 18, 1971	Paul M. Dilley
Sunfish, redbreast	1 lb. 12 oz.	Suwannee River, FL	May 29, 1984	Alvin Buchanan
Sunfish, redear	5 lbs. 7oz.	Diverson Canal, GA	Nov. 6, 1998	Amos M. Gay
Tigerfish, giant	97 lbs.	Zaire River, Kinshasa, Zaire	July 9, 1988	Raymond Houtmans
Tilapia, Nile	13 lbs. 3 oz.	Antelope Isl., Karibe, Zimbabwe	July 5, 2002	Sorel van Rooyen
Trout, Apache	5 lb. 3 oz.	Apache Res., AZ	May 29, 1991	John Baldwin
Trout, brook	14 lbs. 8 oz.	Nipigon River, Ontario	July, 1916	Dr. W. J. Cook
Trout, bull	32 lbs.	Lake Pend Oreille, ID	Oct. 27, 1949	N. L. Higgins
Trout, cutthroat	41 lbs.	Pyramid Lake, NV	Dec., 1925	John Skimmerhorn
Trout, golden	11 lbs.	Cooks Lake, WY	Aug. 5, 1948	Charles S. Reed
Trout, lake	72 lbs.	Great Bear Lake, N.W.T.	Aug. 9, 1995	Lloyd E. Bull
Trout, rainbow	42 lbs. 2 oz.	Bell Island, AK	June 22, 1970	David Robert White
Trout, tiger	20 lbs. 13 oz.	Lake Michigan, WI	Aug. 12, 1978	Pete M. Friedland
Walleye	25 lbs.	Old Hickory Lake, TN	Aug. 2, 1960	Mabry Harper
Warmouth	2 lbs. 7 oz.	Yellow River, Holt, FL	Oct. 19, 1985	Tony D. Dempsey
Whitefish, lake	14 lbs. 6 oz.	Meaford, Ontario	May 21, 1984	Dennis M. Laycock
Whitefish, mountain	5 lbs. 8 oz.	Elbow River, Calgary, AB	Aug. 1, 1995	Randy G. Woo
Whitefish, round	6 lbs.	Putahow R., Manitoba, Can.	June 14, 1984	Allan J. Ristori
Zander	25 lbs. 2 oz.	Trosa, Sweden	June 12, 1986	Harry Lee Tennison

DIRECTORY OF SPORTS ORGANIZATIONS

Major League Baseball

Commissioner's Office 245 Park Ave., 31st Fl., New York, NY 10167
Website: www.mlb.com

American League

Anaheim Angels
2000 Gene Autry Way
Anaheim, CA 92806

Baltimore Orioles
333 W. Camden St.
Baltimore, MD 21201

Boston Red Sox
4 Yawkey Way
Boston, MA 02215

Chicago White Sox
333 W. 35th St.
Chicago, IL 60616

Cleveland Indians
2401 Ontario St.
Cleveland, OH 44115

Detroit Tigers
2100 Woodward Ave.
Detroit, MI 48201

Kansas City Royals
1 Royal Way
Kansas City, MO 64141

Minnesota Twins
34 Kirby Puckett Place
Minneapolis, MN 55415

New York Yankees
161st St. and River Ave.
Bronx, NY 10451

Oakland Athletics
7000 Coliseum Way
Oakland, CA 94621

Seattle Mariners
PO Box 4100
Seattle, WA 98104

Tampa Bay Devil Rays
One Tropicana Dr.
St. Petersburg, FL 33705

Texas Rangers
1000 Ballpark Way
Arlington, TX 76011

Toronto Blue Jays
1 Blue Jays Way, Suite 3200
Toronto, ON M5V 1J1

National League

Arizona Diamondbacks
401 E. Jefferson St.
Phoenix, AZ 85004

Atlanta Braves
755 Hank Aaron Drive
Atlanta, GA 30315

Chicago Cubs
1060 W. Addison
Chicago, IL 60613

Cincinnati Reds
100 Cinergy Field
Cincinnati, OH 45202

Colorado Rockies
2001 Blake St.
Denver, CO 80205

Florida Marlins
2269 Dan Marino Blvd.
Miami, FL 33056

Houston Astros
501 Crawford St.
Houston, TX 77002

Los Angeles Dodgers
1000 Elysian Park Ave.
Los Angeles, CA 90012

Milwaukee Brewers
One Brewers Way
Milwaukee, WI 53214

Montreal Expos
4549 Ave. Pierre de Coubertin
Montreal, QC H1V 3N7

New York Mets
123-01 Roosevelt Ave.
Flushing, NY 11368

Philadelphia Phillies
3501 S. Broad St.
Philadelphia, PA 19148

Pittsburgh Pirates
115 Federal St.
Pittsburgh, PA 15212

St. Louis Cardinals
250 Stadium Plaza
St. Louis, MO 63102

San Diego Padres
8880 Rio San Diego Dr., Ste. 400
San Diego, CA 92112

San Francisco Giants
24 Willie Mays Plaza
San Francisco, CA 94107

National Basketball Association

League Office, Olympic Tower, 645 5th Ave., New York, NY 10022
Website: www.nba.com

Atlanta Hawks
One CNN Center, Ste. 405, South Tower
Atlanta, GA 30303

Boston Celtics
151 Merrimac St.
Boston, MA 02114

Chicago Bulls
1901 W. Madison St.
Chicago, IL 60612

Cleveland Cavaliers
1 Center Court
Cleveland, OH 44115

Dallas Mavericks
2909 Taylor St.
Dallas, TX 75226

Denver Nuggets
1000 Chopper Pl.
Denver, CO 80204

Detroit Pistons
Two Championship Dr.
Auburn Hills, MI 48326

Golden State Warriors
1011 Broadway
Oakland, CA 94607

Houston Rockets
Two Greenway Plaza, Ste. 400
Houston, TX 77046

Indiana Pacers
125 S. Pennsylvania St.
Indianapolis, IN 46204

Los Angeles Clippers
1111 S. Figueroa St., Ste. 1100
Los Angeles, CA 90015

Los Angeles Lakers
555 Nash St.
El Segundo, CA 90245

Memphis Grizzlies
P.O. Box 3463
Memphis, TN 38173

Miami Heat
601 Biscayne Blvd.
Miami, FL 33132

Milwaukee Bucks
1001 N. 4th St.
Milwaukee, WI 53203

Minnesota Timberwolves
600 1st Ave. North
Minneapolis, MN 55403

New Jersey Nets
390 Murray Hill Parkway
E. Rutherford, NJ 07073

New Orleans Hornets
1501 Girod St.
New Orleans, LA 70113

New York Knickerbockers
Two Pennsylvania Plaza
New York, NY 10121

Orlando Magic
Two Magic Place
8701 Maitland Summit Blvd.
Orlando, FL 32810

Philadelphia 76ers
3601 S. Broad St.
Philadelphia, PA 19148

Phoenix Suns
201 E. Jefferson
Phoenix, AZ 85004

Portland Trail Blazers
7325 SW Childs Rd.
Portland, OR 97224

Sacramento Kings
One Sports Parkway
Sacramento, CA 95834

San Antonio Spurs
100 Montana St.
San Antonio, TX 78203

Seattle SuperSonics
351 Elliott Ave., West
Suite 500
Seattle, WA 98119

Toronto Raptors
40 Bay St., Ste. 400
Toronto, ON M5J 2X2

Utah Jazz
301 W. South Temple
Salt Lake City, UT 84101

Washington Wizards
601 F St., NW
Washington, DC 20004

National Hockey League

League Headquarters, 1251 Ave. of the Americas, 47th Fl., New York, NY 10020
Website: www.nhl.com

Mighty Ducks of Anaheim
2695 E. Katella Ave.
Anaheim, CA 92803

Atlanta Thrashers
1 CNN Ctr., 12th Fl., S. Tower
Atlanta, GA 30348

Boston Bruins
One FleetCenter, Ste. 250
Boston, MA 02114

Buffalo Sabres
HSBC Arena
One Seymour H. Knox III Plaza
Buffalo, NY 14203

Calgary Flames
PO Box 1540, Station M
Calgary, AB T2P 3B9

Carolina Hurricanes
1400 Edwards Mill Rd.
Raleigh, NC 27607

Chicago Blackhawks
1901 W. Madison St.
Chicago, IL 60612

Colorado Avalanche
1000 Chopper Cr.
Denver, CO 80204

Columbus Blue Jackets
200 W. Nationwide Blvd.
Columbus, OH 43215

Dallas Stars
211 Cowboys Parkway
Irving, TX 75063

Detroit Red Wings
600 Civic Center Dr.
Detroit, MI 48226

Edmonton Oilers
11230 110 St.
Edmonton, AB T5G 3H7

Florida Panthers
One Panther Parkway
Sunrise, FL 33323

Los Angeles Kings
1111 S. Figueroa St.
Los Angeles, CA 90015

Minnesota Wild
444 Cedar St.
St. Paul, MN 55101

Montreal Canadiens
1260 rue de La Gauchetière St. W
Montreal, QC H3B 5E8

Nashville Predators
501 Broadway
Nashville, TN 37203

New Jersey Devils
50 Rte. 120 N. PO Box 504
E. Rutherford, NJ 07073

New York Islanders
Nassau Veterans Memorial Coliseum
Uniondale, NY 11553

New York Rangers
Two Pennsylvania Plaza
New York, NY 10121

Ottawa Senators
1000 Prom. Palladium Dr.
Kanata, ON K2V 1A4

Philadelphia Flyers
First Union Center
3601 South Broad St.
Philadelphia, PA 19148

Phoenix Coyotes
9375 E. Bell Rd.
Scottsdale, AZ 85257

Pittsburgh Penguins
66 Mario Lemieux Place
Pittsburgh, PA 15219

St. Louis Blues
1401 Clark Ave.
St. Louis, MO 63103

San Jose Sharks
525 W. Santa Clara St.
San Jose, CA 95113

Tampa Bay Lightning
401 Channelside Dr.
Tampa, FL 33602

Toronto Maple Leafs
40 Bay St., Ste. 300
Toronto, ON M5J 2X2

Vancouver Canucks
800 Griffiths Way
Vancouver, BC V6B 6G1

Washington Capitals
601 F St. NW
Washington, DC 20004

National Football League

League Office, 280 Park Ave., New York, NY 10017
Website: www.nfl.com

Arizona Cardinals
PO Box 888
Phoenix, AZ 85001

Atlanta Falcons
4400 Falcon Parkway
Flowery Branch, GA 30542

Baltimore Ravens
11001 Owings Mills Blvd.
Owings Mills, MD 2117

Buffalo Bills
One Bills Drive
Orchard Park, NY 14127

Carolina Panthers
800 S. Mint St.
Charlotte, NC 28202

Chicago Bears
1000 Football Dr.
Lake Forest, IL 60045

Cincinnati Bengals
One Paul Brown Stadium
Cincinnati, OH 45202

Cleveland Browns
76 Lou Groza Blvd.
Berea, OH 44017

Dallas Cowboys
One Cowboys Parkway
Irving, TX 75063

Denver Broncos
13655 Broncos Parkway
Englewood, CO 80112

Detroit Lions
1200 Featherstone Rd.
Pontiac, MI 48342

Green Bay Packers
1265 Lombardi Dr.
Green Bay, WI 54304

Houston Texans
One Reliant Park
Houston, TX 77054

Indianapolis Colts
PO Box 535000
Indianapolis, IN 46253

Jacksonville Jaguars
One ALLTELL Stadium Place
Jacksonville, FL 32202

Kansas City Chiefs
One Arrowhead Drive
Kansas City, MO 64129

Miami Dolphins
7500 SW 30th St.
Davie, FL 33314

Minnesota Vikings
9520 Viking Dr.
Eden Prairie, MN 55344

New England Patriots
60 Washington St.
Foxboro, MA 02035

New Orleans Saints
5800 Airline Hwy.
Metairie, LA 70003

New York Giants
Giants Stadium
E. Rutherford, NJ 07073

New York Jets
1000 Fulton Ave.
Hempstead, NY 11550

Oakland Raiders
1220 Harbor Bay Parkway
Alameda, CA 94502

Philadelphia Eagles
One Novacare Way
Philadelphia, PA 19145

Pittsburgh Steelers
3400 S. Water St.
Pittsburgh, PA 15203

St. Louis Rams
One Rams Way
St. Louis, MO 63045

San Diego Chargers
PO Box 609609
San Diego, CA 92160

San Francisco 49ers
4949 Centennial Blvd.
Santa Clara, CA 95054

Seattle Seahawks
11220 NE 53d St.
Kirkland, WA 98033

Tampa Bay Buccaneers
One Buccaneer Place
Tampa, FL 33607

Tennessee Titans
460 Great Circle Rd.
Nashville, TN 37228

Washington Redskins
21300 Redskin Park Dr.
Ashburn, VA 20147

Other Sports Organizations

Amateur Athletic Union
PO Box 22409
Lake Buena Vista, FL 32830
www.aausports.org

Amateur Softball Assn.
2801 NE 50th St.
Oklahoma City, OK 73111
www.softball.org

American Kennel Club
260 Madison Ave., 4th Fl.
New York, NY 10016
www.akc.org

Canadian Football League
110 Eglinton Ave. W, 5th Fl.
Toronto, Ont. M4R 1A3
www.cfl.ca

CART (Championship Auto Racing Teams)
5350 Lakeview Pkwy.
South Dr.
Indianapolis, IN 46268
www.cart.com

Intl. Game Fish Assn.
300 Gulf Stream Way
Dania Beach, FL 33004
www.igfa.org

LPGA
100 International Golf Dr.
Daytona Beach, FL 32124
www.lpga.com

Little League Baseball
PO Box 3485
Williamsport, PA 17701
www.littleleague.org

Major League Soccer
110 E. 42d St., 10th Fl.
New York, NY 10017
www.mlsnet.com

NASCAR
P.O. Box 2875
Daytona Beach, FL 32120
www.nascar.com

NCAA (National Collegiate Athletic Association)
700 W. Washington St.
PO Box 6222
Indianapolis, IN 46206
www.ncaa.org

National Rifle Assn.
11250 Waples Mill Rd.
Fairfax, VA 22030
www.nra.org

Pro Bowlers Assn.
719 Second Ave., Ste. 701
Seattle, WA 98104
www.pbatour.com

PGA
100 Ave. of the Champions
Box 109601
Palm Beach Gardens, FL 33410
www.pga.com

Pro Rodeo Cowboys Assn.
101 Pro Rodeo Dr.
Colorado Springs, CO 80919
www.prorodeo.com

Special Olympics
1325 G St., NW, Ste. 500
Washington, DC 20005
www.specialolympics.org

Thoroughbred Racing Assn.
420 Fair Hill Dr.
Elkton, MD 21921
www.tra-online.com

USA Equestrian
4047 Iron Works Pkwy.
Lexington, KY 40511
www.equestrian.org

USA Swimming
One Olympic Plaza
Colorado Springs, CO 80909
www.usa-swimming.org

USA Track & Field
1 RCA Dome, Ste. 140
Indianapolis, IN 46225
www.usatf.org

U.S. Auto Club
4910 W. 16th St.
Speedway, IN 46227

U.S. Figure Skating Assn.
20 First St.
Colorado Springs, CO 80906
www.usfsa.org

U.S. Olympic Committee
One Olympic Plaza
Colorado Springs, CO 80909
www.usoc.org

U.S. Skiing Assn.
1500 Kearns Blvd.
PO Box 100
Park City, UT 84060
www.usskiteam.com

U.S. Soccer Federation
1801-1811 S. Prairie Ave.
Chicago, IL 60616
www.ussoccer.com

U.S. Tennis Assn.
70 W. Red Oak Lane
White Plains, NY 10604
www.usta.com

U.S. Trotting Assn.
750 Michigan Ave.
Columbus, OH 43215
www.ustrotting.com

WNBA
645 5th Ave., 10th Fl.
New York, NY 10022
www.wnba.com

NOTABLE SPORTS PERSONALITIES

Henry (Hank) Aaron, b. 1934: Milwaukee-Atlanta outfielder; hit record 755 home runs, led NL 4 times; record 2,297 RBIs.

Kareem Abdul-Jabbar, b. 1947: Milwaukee, L.A. Lakers center; MVP 6 times; all-time leading NBA scorer, 38,387 points.

Andre Agassi, b. 1970: won: Wimbledon, '92; U.S. Open, '94; Austral. Open, '95, 2000-01; French Open, '99.

Troy Aikman, b. 1966: quarterback, led Dallas Cowboys to Super Bowl wins in 1993-94, 1996; Super Bowl MVP, 1993.

Amy Alcott, b. 1956: golfer, 29 career wins (5 majors), inducted into World Golf Hall of Fame in 1999.

Grover Cleveland "Pete" Alexander (1887-1950): pitcher; won 373 NL games; pitched 16 shutouts, 1916.

Muhammad Ali, b. 1942: 3-time heavyweight champion.

Gary Anderson, b. 1959: kicker, NFL's career points leader, with 2,133 through the end of the 2001 seaon.

Sparky Anderson, b. 1934: only manager to win World Series in the NL (Cincinnati, 1975-76) and the AL (Detroit, 1984).

Mario Andretti, b. 1940: won Daytona 500 (1967), Indy 500 (1969); Formula 1 world title (1978).

Earl Anthony (1938-2001): bowler, won record 6 PBA Championships (1973-75, 1981-83), 41 career PBA tournaments.

Eddie Arcaro, (1916-97): only jockey to win racing's Triple Crown twice, 1941,1948; rode 4,779 winners in his career.

Henry Armstrong (1912-88): boxer, held feather-, welter-, lightweight titles simultaneously, 1937-38.

Lance Armstrong, b. 1971: cyclist, 4-time winner of the Tour de France (1999-2002).

Arthur Ashe (1943-93): tennis, won U.S. Open (1968); Wimbledon (1975); died of AIDS.

Evelyn Ashford, b.1957: sprinter, won 100m gold (1984) and silver (1988); member of 5 U.S. Olympic teams (1976-1992).

Red Auerbach, b. 1917: coached Boston to 9 NBA titles.

Tracy Austin, b. 1962: youngest player to win U.S. Open tennis title (age 16 in 1979), 2-time AP Female Athlete of the Year.

Ernie Banks, b. 1931: Chicago Cubs slugger; hit 512 NL homers; twice MVP; never played in World Series.

Roger Bannister, b. 1929: British physician, ran first sub 4-minute mile, May 6, 1954 (3 min. 59.4 sec.).

Charles Barkely, b. 1963: NBA MVP, 1993; 4th player ever to surpass 20,000 pts, 10,000 rebounds, and 4,000 assists.

Rick Barry, b. 1944: NBA scoring leader, 1967; ABA, 1969.

Sammy Baugh, b. 1914: Washington Redskins quarterback; held numerous records upon retirement after 16 pro seasons.

Elgin Baylor, b. 1934: L.A. Lakers forward; 10-time all-star.

Bob Beamon, b. 1946: Olympic long jump gold medalist in 1968; world record jump of 29' 2½" stood until 1991.

Boris Becker, b. 1967: German tennis star; won U.S. Open 1989; Wimbledon champ 3 times.

Jean Beliveau, b. 1931: Montreal Canadiens center; scored 507 goals; twice MVP.

Johnny Bench, b. 1947: Cincinnati Reds catcher; MVP twice; led league in home runs twice, RBIs 3 times.

Patty Berg, b. 1918: won more than 80 golf tournaments; AP Woman Athlete-of-the-Year 3 times.

Yogi Berra, b. 1925: Yankee catcher (1946-63); 3-time MVP.

Abebe Bikila (1932-73): Ethiopian runner, won consecutive Olympic marathon gold medals in 1960 (barefoot), 1964.

Matt Biondi, b. 1965: swimmer, won 5 golds, 1988 Olympics.

Larry Bird, b. 1956: Boston Celtics forward; chosen MVP 1984-86; 1998 coach of the year with Indiana Pacers.

Bonnie Blair, b. 1964: speed skater won 5 individual gold medals in 3 Olympics (1988, '92, '94).

George Blanda, b. 1927: quarterback, kicker; 26 years as active player, scored 2,002 career points.

Fanny Blankers-Koen, b. 1918: track, won 4 golds in 1948.

Wade Boggs, b. 1958: AL batting champ, 1983, 1985-88; reached 3,000 career hits, 1999 (3,010).

Barry Bonds, b. 1964: outfielder, set records for walks (198), on-base pct. (.582) in 2002; hit record 73 homers in 2001; NL MVP 1990, 1992-93, 2001; 4th all-time in home runs (613).

Bjorn Borg, b. 1956: led Sweden to first Davis Cup, 1975; Wimbledon champion 5 times.

Mike Bossy, b. 1957: N.Y. Islanders right wing scored more than 50 goals 8 times.

Ray Bourque, b. 1960: Boston defenseman,1979-2000, 5-time Norris Trophy winner; won Stanley Cup with Colorado, 2001.

Bill Bradley, b. 1943: basketball All-America at Princeton, 1965 Player of the Year; led NY Knicks to 2 NBA titles (1970, '73); U.S. senator, 1979-97.

Terry Bradshaw, b. 1948: quarterback, led Pittsburgh to 4 Super Bowl wins (1975-76, 1979-80); NFL MVP, 1978.

George Brett, b. 1953: Kansas City Royals infielder, led AL in batting, 1976, 1980, 1990; MVP, 1980.

Lou Brock, b. 1939: St. Louis Cardinals outfielder, stole NL record 118 bases, 1974; led NL 8 times.

Jim Brown, b. 1936: Clev. fullback, 12,312 yds.; 3-time MVP.

Paul Brown (1908-91): football owner, coach; led eponymous Cleveland Browns to 3 NFL championships.

Paul "Bear" Bryant (1913-83): college football coach with 323 wins; led Alabama to 5 national titles (1961, '64, '65, '78, '79).

Sergei Bubka, b. 1963: Ukrainian pole vaulter; first to clear 20 feet; gold medal, 1988 Olympics.

Don Budge, (1915-2000): won numerous amateur and pro tennis titles; "grand slam," 1938.

Maria Bueno, b. 1939: tennis, 4 U.S. titles, 3 Wimbledon.

Dick Butkus, b. 1942: Chicago Bears linebacker, twice chosen best NFL defensive player.

Dick Button, b. 1929: figure skater; won 1948, 1952 Olympic gold medals; world titlist, 1948-52.

Walter Camp, (1859-1925): Yale football player, coach, athletic director; established many rules.

Roy Campanella (1921-93): Hall of Fame catcher for the Brooklyn Dodgers (1948-57); 3-time NL MVP.

Earl Campbell, b. 1955: NFL running back; MVP 1978-79.

Jennifer Capriati, b. 1976: won Australian (2001-02) and French Opens (2001), Olympic gold (1992); in 1990, at age 14, became youngest top-10 player.

Rod Carew, b. 1945: AL infielder; 7 batting titles, 1977 MVP.

Steve Carlton, b. 1944: NL pitcher; won 20 games 5 times, Cy Young award 4 times.

Billy Casper, b. 1931: PGA Player-of-the-Year 3 times; U.S. Open champ twice.

Tracy Caulkins, b. 1963: swimmer, won 3 Olympic golds, 1984; set 63 U.S. and 5 world records; won 48 individual U.S. titles.

Wilt Chamberlain (1936-99): center; was NBA leading scorer 7 times, MVP 4 times; scored 100 pts. in a game, 1962.

Bobby Clarke, b. 1949: Philadelphia Flyers center; led team to 2 Stanley Cup championships; MVP 3 times.

Roger Clemens, b. 1962: pitcher, 1986 AL MVP; only 6-time Cy Young winner (1986-87, '91, '97-98; 2001); twice struck out record 20 batters in a game; all-time AL strikeout leader (3,909).

Roberto Clemente (1934-72): Pittsburgh Pirates outfielder; won 4 batting titles; MVP, 1966; killed in plane crash.

Ty Cobb (1886-1961): Detroit Tigers outfielder; had record .367 lifetime batting average, 12 batting titles.

Sebastian Coe, b. 1956: British runner, won Olympic 1,500m gold medal and 800m silver medal in 1980 and 1984.

Nadia Comaneci, b. 1961: Romanian gymnast, won 3 gold medals, achieved 7 perfect scores, 1976 Olympics.

Maureen Connolly (1934-69): won tennis "grand slam," 1953; AP Woman-Athlete-of-the-Year 3 times.

Jimmy Connors, b. 1952: tennis, 5 U.S. titles, 2 Wimbledon.

Cynthia Cooper, b. 1963: basketball, 4-time MVP of the WNBA finals and 2-time league MVP for the Houston Comets.

James J. Corbett (1866-1933): heavyweight champion, 1892-97; credited with being the first "scientific" boxer.

Angel Cordero, b. 1942: leading money winner, 1976, 1982-83; rode 3 Kentucky Derby winners.

Howard Cosell (1920-95): commentator for ABC's *Monday Night Football* and *Wide World of Sports.*

Margaret Smith Court, b. 1942: Australian tennis great, won 24 grand slam events.

Bob Cousy, b. 1928: Boston guard; 6 NBA titles; 1957 MVP.

Bjoern Daehlie, b. 1967: Norwegian cross-country skier; won record 8 Winter Olympic gold medals.

Lindsay Davenport, b. 1976: tennis, won Olympic gold (1996), U.S. Open (1998), Wimbledon (1999), Austral. Open (2000).

Dizzy Dean (1911-74): colorful pitcher for St. Louis Cardinals "Gashouse Gang" in the 30s; MVP, 1934.

Mary Decker Slaney, b. 1958: runner, has held 7 separate American records from the 800m to 10,000m.

Oscar De La Hoya, b. 1972: won IBF lightweight title, 1995; WBC super lightweight title, 1996; WBC welterweight title, 1997, 2000.

Donna de Varona, b. 1947: 2 Olympic swimming golds,1964; 1st female sportscaster at a major network (ABC), 1965.

Jack Dempsey (1895-1983): heavyweight champ, 1919-26.

Gail Devers, b. 1966: Olympic 100m gold medalist, 1992, '96.

Eric Dickerson, b. 1960: NFL record 2,105 rushing yds.,1984.

Joe DiMaggio (1914-99): N.Y. Yankees outfielder; hit safely in record 56 consecutive games, 1941; AL MVP 3 times.

Tony Dorsett, b. 1954: Heisman winner who led the Dallas Cowboys to an NFL title in his rookie year (1977); 5th all-time in career rushing yards (12,739).

Roberto Duran, b. 1951: Panamanian boxer, held titles at 3 weights; lost 1980 "no mas" fight to Sugar Ray Leonard.

Leo Durocher (1906-91): manager, won 3 NL pennants (Brooklyn-1941, NY Giants-1951, '54) and 1954 World Series.

Dale Earnhardt (1951-2001): 7-time NASCAR Winston Cup champ; died in a last-lap crash at 2001 Daytona 500.

Stefan Edberg, b. 1966: U.S. singles champ, 1991, 1992; Wimbledon champ, 1988, 1990.

Gertrude Ederle, b. 1906: first woman to swim English Channel, broke existing men's record, 1926.

Teresa Edwards, b. 1964: basketball, 5-time Olympian; gold medalist in 1984, '88, '96, 2000 and bronze medal in 1992.
Hicham El Guerrouj, b. 1974: Moroccan runner, holds world records in mile (3:43.13) and 1500m (3:26.0), as well as 7 of the top 10 times in the history of each event.
John Elway, b. 1960: quarterback; led Denver Broncos to 2 Super Bowl wins, 1998, 1999; regular-season MVP, 1987.
Julius Erving, b. 1950: 3-time ABA MVP, 1981 NBA MVP.
Phil Esposito, b. 1942: NHL scoring leader 5 times.
Janet Evans, b. 1971: 4 Olympic swimming golds, 1988-92.
Lee Evans, b. 1947: Olympic 400m gold medalist in 1968 with a 43.86 sec. world record not broken until 1988.
Chris Evert, b. 1954: U.S. Open tennis champ 6 times, Wimbledon champ 3 times.
Ray Ewry (1873-1937): track-and-field star, won 8 gold medals, 1900, 1904, and 1908 Olympics.
Nick Faldo, b. 1957: won Masters, British Open 3 times each.
Juan Fangio (1911-95): Argentinian, 5-time World Grand Prix driving champ (1951, 1954-57).
Marshall Faulk, b. 1973: 2000 NFL MVP, record 26 TDs in 2001; 2-time Off. Player of the Year (2000-01).
Brett Favre, b. 1969: led Green Bay to Super Bowl win, 1997; NFL regular-season MVP, 1995, 1996; co-MVP, 1997.
Bob Feller, b. 1918: Cleveland Indians pitcher; won 266 games; pitched 3 no-hitters, 12 one-hitters.
Rollie Fingers, b. 1946: pitcher, 341 career saves; AL MVP, Cy Young Award, 1982; World Series MVP, 1974.
Peggy Fleming, b. 1948: world figure skating champion, 1966-68; gold medalist, 1968 Olympics.
Whitey Ford, b. 1928: N.Y. Yankees pitcher, won record 10 World Series games.
George Foreman, b. 1949: heavyweight champion, 1973-74, 1994-95; at 45, the oldest to win a heavyweight title.
Dick Fosbury, b. 1947: high jumper; won 1968 Olympic gold medal; developed the "Fosbury Flop."
Dan Fouts, b. 1951: quarterback (San Diego), 5th in career passing yards (43,040); TV analyst on *Monday Night Football.*
Jimmie Foxx (1907-67): Red Sox, Athletics slugger; MVP 3 times; triple crown, 1933.
A. J. Foyt, b. 1935: won Indy 500 4 times; U.S. Auto Club champ 7 times.
Joe Frazier, b. 1944: heavyweight champion, 1970-73.
Walt Frazier, b. 1945: Hall of Fame guard for N.Y. Knicks NBA championship teams (1970, '73); NBA radio-TV commentator.
Haile Gebrselassie, b. 1973: Ethiopian, world record holder in 5,000m and 10,000m; 10,000m gold medalist in 1996, 2000.
Lou Gehrig (1903-41): N.Y. Yankees 1st baseman; MVP, 1927, 1936; triple crown, 1934; AL record 184 RBIs, 1931.
George Gervin, b. 1952: top NBA scorer, 1978-80, 1982.
Althea Gibson, b. 1927: 2-time U.S. and Wimbledon champ.
Bob Gibson, b. 1935: St. Louis Cardinals pitcher; won Cy Young award twice; struck out 3,117 batters.
Josh Gibson (1911-47): Hall of Fame catcher, known as "Babe Ruth of the Negro Leagues"; credited with as many as 84 homers in 1 season and about 800 in his career.
Marc Girardelli, b. 1963: skier (Lux.), won 5 World Cup titles.
Jeff Gordon, b. 1971: race car driver, youngest to win NASCAR Winston Cup 3 times (1995, 1997-98).
Steffi Graf, b. 1969: German; won tennis "grand slam," 1988; U.S. champ 5 times; Wimbledon champ 7 times.
Otto Graham, b. 1921: Cleveland quarterback, 4-time all-pro.
Red Grange (1903-91): All-America at Univ. of Illinois, 1923-25; played for Chicago Bears, 1925-35.
Joe Greene, b. 1946: Pittsburgh Steelers lineman; twice NFL outstanding defensive player.
Wayne Gretzky, b. 1961: top scorer in NHL history with record 894 goals, 1,963 assists, 2,857 points; MVP, 1980-87, 1989.
Bob Griese, b. 1945: All-Pro quarterback led Miami Dolphins to 17-0 season (1972) and 2 Super Bowl titles (1973-74).
Ken Griffey Jr., b. 1969: outfielder, led AL in homers 1994, 1997-1999; 1997 AL MVP; 10 gold gloves.
Archie Griffin, b. 1954: Ohio State running back is the only 2-time winner of the Heisman Trophy (1974-75).
Florence Griffith Joyner, (1959-98): sprinter; won 3 gold medals at 1988 Olympics; Olympic record for 100m.
Lefty Grove (1900-75): pitcher; won 300 AL games.
Janet Guthrie, b. 1938: 1st woman driver in Indy 500 (1977).
Tony Gwynn, b. 1960: 8-time NL batting champ, 1984, 1987-89, 1994-97; 3,141 career hits.
Walter Hagen (1892-1969): golf; 5 PGA, 4 British Open titles.
George Halas (1895-1983): founder-coach of Chicago Bears; won 5 NFL championships.
Dorothy Hamill, b. 1956: figure skater, gold medalist at the Olympics and World championships in 1976.
Scott Hamilton, b. 1958: U.S. and world figure skating champion, 1981-84; Olympic gold medalist, 1984.
Mia Hamm, b. 1972: led U.S. to World Cup (1991, '99) and Olympic ('96) titles; most career goals in women's soccer.
Franco Harris, b. 1950: running back, led Steelers to 4 Super Bowls (1975-76, 1979-80); 1,000+ yds. in a season 8 times.
Bill Hartack, b. 1932: jockey, rode 5 Kentucky Derby winners.
Dominik Hasek, b. 1965: Buffalo Sabres goalie; won Vezina Trophy, 1994-95, 1997-99, 2001; NHL MVP, 1997-98.
John Havlicek, b. 1940: Boston Celtics forward scored more than 26,000 NBA points.
Eric Heiden, b. 1958: speed skater, won 5 Olympic golds, 1980.
Rickey Henderson, b. 1958; outfielder, 1990 AL MVP; record 130 stolen bases, 1982; all-time leader in steals (1,403), runs (2,288), and walks (2,179); 4th all-time in games played (3,051).
Sonja Henie (1912-69): world champion figure skater, 1927-36; Olympic gold medalist, 1928, 1932, 1936.
Martina Hingis, b. 1980: won Australian Open, Wimbledon, and U.S. Open; youngest No. 1 player (16 yrs., 6 m.) in 1997.
Ben Hogan (1912-97): golfer, won 4 U.S. Open championships, 2 PGA, 2 Masters.
Chamique Holdsclaw, b. 1977: basketball, 2-time national player of the year, led Tennessee to 3 NCAA titles (1996-98).
Evander Holyfield, b. 1962: 4-time heavyweight champion.
Rogers Hornsby (1896-1963): NL 2nd baseman; batted record .424 in 1924; twice won triple crown; batting leader, 1920-25.
Paul Hornung, b. 1935: Green Bay Packers runner-placekicker, scored record 176 points, 1960.
Gordie Howe, b. 1928: hockey forward; NHL MVP 6 times; scored 801 goals in 26 NHL seasons.
Carl Hubbell (1903-88): N.Y. Giants pitcher; 20-game winner 5 consecutive years, 1933-37.
Sarah Hughes, b. 1985: figure skater, won Olympic gold, 2002; silver at U.S. and bronze at World Championships, 2001.
Bobby Hull, b. 1939: NHL all-star 10 times; MVP, 1965-66.
Brett Hull, b. 1964: St. Louis Blues forward; led NHL in goals, 1990-92; MVP, 1991.
Catfish Hunter (1946-99); pitched perfect game, 1968; 20-game winner 5 times.
Don Hutson (1913-97): Packers receiver, caught 99 TD passes; 2-time NFL MVP.
Julie Inkster, b. 1960: Hall of Fame golfer, 2nd to win all 4 of LPGA's modern majors; won 7 career major titles.
Phil Jackson, b. 1945: won 9 NBA titles as coach with Bulls (1991-93, 1996-98) and Lakers (2000-2002); NBA championship with Knicks as a player, 1973.
Reggie Jackson, b. 1946: slugger; led AL in home runs 4 times; MVP, 1973; hit 5 World Series home runs, 1977.
"Shoeless" Joe Jackson (1889-1951): outfielder, 3rd highest career batting average (.356); one of the "Black Sox" banned for allegedly throwing 1919 World Series.
Jaromir Jagr, b. 1972: Czech hockey player, NHL MVP in 1999; Art Ross Trophy (leading scorer) 1995, 1998-2001.
Bruce Jenner, b. 1949: Olympic decathlon gold medalist, 1976.
Lynn Jennings, b. 1960: runner, 3-time World and 9-time U.S. cross country champ; bronze at 1992 Olympics (10,000m).
Earvin (Magic) Johnson, b. 1959: NBA MVP, 1987, 1989, 1990; Playoff MVP, 1980, 1982, 1987; 2nd in career assists.
Jack Johnson (1878-1946): heavyweight champion, 1908-15.
Michael Johnson, b. 1967: 5-time Olympic gold medalist (1996, 2000); world and Olympic record holder, 200m and 400m.
Randy Johnson, b. 1963: 4-time Cy Young winner; strikeout leader: 1993-94, 1998-2002; 3,746 career strikeouts (4th).
Walter Johnson (1887-1946): Washington Senators pitcher; won 416 games; record 110 shutouts.
Bobby Jones (1902-71): won "grand slam of golf" 1930; U.S. Amateur champ 5 times, U.S. Open champ 4 times.
David "Deacon" Jones, b.1938: Hall of Fame defensive end; 5-time All-Pro with LA Rams (1965-69); quarterback "sack" specialist credited with inventing the term.
Marion Jones, b. 1975: 2000 Olympic 100m, 200m, 1,600m relay gold medalist, bronze in long jump and 400m relay; Most track and field medals won by a woman at 1 Olympics.
Roy Jones Jr., b. 1969: undisputed Light heavyweight champ.
Michael Jordan, b. 1963: leading NBA scorer, 1987-93, 1996-98; MVP, 1988, 1991-92, '96, '98; Playoff MVP, 1991-93, 1996-98; ESPN Athlete of the Century.
Dorothy Kamenshek, b. 1925: led Rockford (IL) Peaches to 4 All-American Girls Baseball League titles in the 1940s.
Jackie Joyner-Kersee, b. 1962: Olympic gold medalist in heptathlon (1988 ,'92) and long jump (1988).
Harmon Killebrew, b. 1936: Minnesota Twins slugger; led AL in home runs 6 times; 573 lifetime.
Jean Claude Killy, b. 1943: French skier; 3 1968 Olympic golds.
Ralph Kiner, b. 1922: Pittsburgh Pirates slugger, led NL in home runs 7 consecutive years, 1946-52.
Billie Jean King, b. 1943: U.S. singles champ 4 times; Wimbledon champ 6 times; beat Bobby Riggs, 1973.
Bob Knight, b. 1940: basketball coach, led Indiana U. to NCAA title in 1976, '81, '87.
Olga Korbut, b. 1955: Soviet gymnast; 3 1972 Olympic golds.
Sandy Koufax, b. 1935: 3-time Cy Young winner; lowest ERA in NL, 1962-66; pitched 4 no-hitters, one a perfect game.

Ingrid Kristiansen, b. 1956: Norwegian, only runner ever to hold world records in 5,000m, 10,000m, and marathon.
Julie Krone, b. 1963: winningest female jockey, only woman to ride a winner in a Triple Crown race (Belmont, 1993).
Michelle Kwan, b.1980: figure skater, U.S. Champion (1996, 1998-2002) and World Champion (1996, '98, 2000, 2001); silver medalist at 1998 Olympics, bronze in 2002.
Guy Lafleur, b. 1951: 3-time NHL scoring leader; 1977-78 MVP.
Kennesaw Mountain Landis (1866-1944): 1st commissioner of baseball (1920-44); banned the 8 "Black Sox" involved in the fixing of the 1919 World Series.
Tom Landry (1924-2000): Dallas Cowboys head coach, 1960-88; won 2 Super Bowls (1972, '78); 3rd in career wins (270).
Dick "Night train" Lane (1928-2002): Hall of Fame defensive back, intercepted an NFL single-season record 14 passes (1952).
Don Larsen, b. 1929: As NY Yankee, pitched only World Series perfect game, Oct. 8, 1956—a 2-0 win over Brooklyn.
Rod Laver, b. 1938: Australian; won tennis "grand slam" twice, 1962, 1969; Wimbledon champ 4 times.
Mario Lemieux, b. 1965: 6-time NHL leading scorer; MVP, 1988, 1993, 1996; Playoff MVP, 1991-92.
Greg Lemond, b. 1961: 3-time Tour de France winner (1986, '89-90); first American to win the event.
Ivan Lendl, b. 1960: U.S. Open tennis champ, 1985-87.
Sugar Ray Leonard, b. 1956: boxer, held titles in 5 different weight classes.
Carl Lewis, b. 1961: track-and-field star, won 9 Olympic gold medals in sprinting and the long jump.
Lennox Lewis, b. 1965: Brit. boxer, heavyweight champion, 1997-2002.
Tara Lipinski, b. 1982: youngest figure skater to win U.S. and world championships, 1997, and Winter Olympic gold, 1998.
Vince Lombardi (1913-70): Green Bay Packers coach, led team to 5 NFL championships and 2 Super Bowl victories.
Nancy Lopez, b. 1957: Hall of Fame golfer, 4-time LPGA Player of the Year, 3-time winner of the LPGA Championship.
Greg Louganis, b. 1960: won Olympic gold medals in both springboard and platform diving, 1984, 1988.
Joe Louis (1914-81): heavyweight champion, 1937-49.
Sid Luckman (1916-98): Chicago Bears quarterback; led team to 4 NFL championships; MVP, 1943.
Connie Mack (1862-1956): Philadelphia Athletics manager, 1901-50; won 9 pennants, 5 championships.
John Madden, b. 1936: won Super Bowl as coach of the Oakland Raiders (1977); NFL TV analyst since 1982.
Greg Maddux, b. 1966: NL pitcher, won 4 consecutive Cy Young awards, 1992-95.
Karl Malone, b. 1963: Utah Jazz forward; was MVP, 1997, 1999; 13-time All-Star; 34,707 career points (2nd all-time).
Moses Malone, b. 1955: NBA center, MVP, 1979, 1982-83.
Mickey Mantle (1931-95): N.Y. Yankees outfielder; triple crown, 1956; 18 World Series home runs; MVP 3 times.
Pete Maravich (1948-88): guard, scored NCAA record 44.2 ppg during collegiate career; led NBA in scoring, 1977.
Rocky Marciano (1923-69): heavyweight champion, 1952-56; retired undefeated.
Dan Marino, b. 1961: Miami Dolphins quarterback; passed for NFL record 5,084 yds and 48 touchdowns, 1984; career records for touchdowns, yds passing, completions.
Roger Maris (1934-85): N.Y. Yankees outfielder; hit AL record 61 home runs, 1961; MVP, 1960 and 1961.
Eddie Mathews (1931-2001): Milwaukee-Atlanta 3rd baseman, hit 512 career home runs.
Christy Mathewson (1880-1925): N.Y. Giants pitcher, 373 wins.
Bob Mathias, b. 1930: decathlon gold medalist, 1948, 1952.
Willie Mays, b. 1931: N.Y.-S.F. Giants center fielder; hit 660 home runs, led NL 4 times; had 3,283 hits; twice MVP.
Willie McCovey, b. 1938: S.F. Giants slugger; hit 521 home runs; led NL 3 times; MVP, 1969.
John McEnroe, b. 1959: U.S. Open tennis champ, 1979-81, 1984; Wimbledon champ, 1981, 1983-84.
John McGraw (1873-1934): N.Y. Giants manager, led team to 10 pennants, 3 championships.
Mark McGwire, b. 1963: hit then-record 70 home runs in 1998; 583 career home runs (5th).
Tamara McKinney, b. 1962: 1st U.S. skier to win overall Alpine World Cup championship (1983).
Mary T. Meagher, b. 1964: swimmer, "Madame Butterfly" won 3 Olympic gold medals in 1984.
Mark Messier, b. 1961: center, chosen NHL MVP, 1990, 1992; Conn Smythe Trophy, 1984.
Debbie Meyer, b. 1952: 1st swimmer to win 3 individual Olympic golds (1968).
George Mikan, b. 1924: Minn. Lakers center, considered the best basketball player of the first half of the 20th century.
Stan Mikita, b. 1940: Chicago Black Hawks center, led NHL in scoring 4 times; MVP twice.
Billy Mills, b. 1938: runner, upset winner of the 1964 Olympic 10,000m; only American man ever to win the event.
Joe Montana, b. 1956: S.F. 49ers quarterback; Super Bowl MVP, 1982, 1985, 1990.
Archie Moore (1913-98): light-heavyweight champ, 1952-62.
Howie Morenz (1902-37): Montreal Canadiens forward, considered best hockey player of first half of the 20th century.
Edwin Moses, b. 1955: undefeated in 122 consecutive 400m hurdles races, 1977-87; Olympic gold medalist, 1976, '84.
Shirley Muldowney, b. 1940: 1st woman to race National Hot Rod Assoc. Top Fuel dragsters; 3-time NHRA points champ.
Eddie Murray, b. 1956: durable slugger; 3rd player to combine 3,000+ hits with 500+ home runs.
Stan Musial, b. 1920: St. Louis Cardinals star; won 7 NL batting titles; MVP 3 times.
Bronko Nagurski (1908-90): Chicago Bears fullback and tackle; gained more than 4,000 yds. rushing.
Joe Namath, b. 1943: Jets quarterback, 1969 Super Bowl MVP.
Martina Navratilova, b. 1956: Wimbledon champ 9 times, U.S. Open champ 1983-84, 1986-87.
Byron Nelson, b. 1912: won 11 consecutive golf tournaments in 1945; twice Masters and PGA titlist.
Ernie Nevers (1903-76): Stanford star, selected as best college fullback to play between 1919-69.
Paula Newby-Fraser, b. 1972: 8-time winner of the Ironman Triathlon World Championships in Hawaii; holds course record.
John Newcombe, b. 1943: Australian; twice U.S. Open tennis champ; Wimbledon titlist 3 times.
Jack Nicklaus, b. 1940: PGA Player-of-the-Year, 1967, 1972; leading money winner 8 times; won 18 majors (6 Masters).
Chuck Noll, b. 1931: Pittsburgh coach; won 4 Super Bowls.
Paavo Nurmi (1897-1973): Finnish distance runner, won 6 Olympic gold medals, 1920, 1924, 1928.
Al Oerter, b. 1936: discus thrower, won gold medal at 4 consecutive Olympics, 1956-68.
Hakeem Olajuwon, b. 1963: Houston center; NBA MVP, 1994, Playoffs MVP, 1994-95; career leader in blocked shots (3,830).
Barney Oldfield, (1878-1946): pioneer auto racer was first to drive a car 60 mph (1903).
Shaquille O'Neal, b. 1972: center, led L.A. Lakers to NBA titles, 2000-2002; 2000, 2002 Finals MVP; 2000 NBA MVP.
Bobby Orr, b. 1948: Boston Bruins defenseman; Norris Trophy 8 times; led NHL in scoring twice, assists 5 times.
Mel Ott (1909-1958): N.Y. Giants outfielder hit 511 home runs; led NL 6 times.
Jesse Owens (1913-80): track and field star, won 4 1936 Olympic gold medals.
Satchel Paige (1906-82): pitcher, starred in Negro leagues, 1924-48; entered major leagues at age 42.
Arnold Palmer, b. 1929: golf's first $1 million winner; won 4 Masters, 2 British Opens.
Jim Palmer, b. 1945: Baltimore Orioles pitcher; Cy Young award 3 times; 20-game winner 8 times.
Joe Paterno, b. 1926: winningest NCAA Div. I football coach, 327 wins through 2001; led Penn St. to natl. titles, 1982, 1986.
Floyd Patterson, b. 1935: 2-time heavyweight champion.
Walter Payton (1954-1999): Chicago Bears running back; most rushing yards in NFL history; top NFC rusher, 1976-80.
Pelé, b. 1940: soccer star, led Brazil to 3 World Cup titles (1958, '62, '70); scored 1,281 goals in 22-year career.
Bob Pettit, b. 1932: first NBA player to score 20,000 points; twice NBA scoring leader.
Richard Petty, b. 1937: NASCAR national champ 7 times; 7-time Daytona 500 winner.
Laffit Pincay Jr., b. 1946: jockey, leading money-winner, 1970-74, 1979, 1985.
Jacques Plante (1929-86): goalie; 7 Vezina trophies; first goalie to wear a mask in a game.
Gary Player, b. 1936: South African golfer, won 3 Masters, 3 British Opens, 2 PGA Championships, and the U.S. Open.
Steve Prefontaine, (1951-75): runner, 1st to win 4 NCAA titles in same event (5,000m, 1970-73); died in auto accident.
Kirby Puckett, b. 1961: Minnesota Twins outfielder; won AL batting title, 1989; led AL in hits, 1987-89, 1992; RBIs, 1994.
Willis Reed, b. 1942: N.Y. Knicks center; MVP, 1970; Playoff MVP, 1970, 1973.
Mary Lou Retton, b. 1968: 1st American woman to win a gold medal in gymnastics (1984).
Jerry Rice, b. 1962: receiver, 1989 Super Bowl MVP; NFL record for career touchdowns (196), receptions (1,364).
Maurice Richard, (1921-2000): Montreal Canadiens forward scored 544 regular season goals, 82 playoff goals.
Branch Rickey (1881-1965): executive; helped break baseball's color barrier, 1947; initiated farm system, 1919.
Cal Ripken Jr., b. 1960: Baltimore shortstop; AL MVP 1983, 1991; most consecutive games played (2,632).
Oscar Robertson, b. 1938: guard; averaged career 25.7 points per game; 3rd most career assists; MVP, 1964.
Brooks Robinson, b. 1937: Baltimore Orioles 3rd baseman; played in 4 World Series; MVP, 1964; 16 gold gloves.
Frank Robinson, b. 1935: MVP in both NL and AL; triple crown, 1966; 586 career home runs; first black manager in majors.

Jackie Robinson (1919-72): broke baseball's color barrier with Brooklyn Dodgers, 1947; MVP, 1949.
Sugar Ray Robinson (1920-89): middleweight champion 5 times, welterweight champion.
Knute Rockne (1888-1931): Notre Dame football coach, 1918-31; revolutionized game by stressing forward pass.
Bill Rodgers, b. 1947: runner, won Boston and New York City marathons 4 time each, 1975-80.
Dennis Rodman, b. 1961: led NBA in rebounding 1991-98.
Pete Rose, b. 1941: won 3 NL batting titles; hit safely in 44 consecutive games, 1978; has most career hits, 4,256; banned from baseball for alleged gambling, 1989.
Ken Rosewall, b. 1934: Australian; 2-time U.S. Open champ, 8 grand slam singles titles.
Patrick Roy, b. 1965: Montreal-Colorado goalie; only 3-time NHL Playoffs MVP (Conn Smythe Trophy), 1986, '93, 2001.
Wilma Rudolph (1940-94): sprinter, won 3 1960 Olympic golds.
Adolph Rupp (1901-77): NCAA basketball coach; led Kentucky to 4 national titles, 1948-49, 1951, 1958.
Bill Russell, b. 1934: Boston Celtics center, led team to 11 NBA titles; MVP 5 times; first black coach of major pro sports team.
Babe Ruth (1895-1948): N.Y. Yankees outfielder; hit 60 home runs, 1927; 714 lifetime; led AL 12 times.
Johnny Rutherford, b. 1938: auto racer, won 3 Indy 500s.
Nolan Ryan, b. 1947: pitcher; holds season (383), career (5,714) strikeout records; won 324 games (7 no-hitters).
Pete Sampras, b. 1971: tennis star; 1st man in Open era to win 7 Wimbledons; most career Grand Slam wins (14).
Joan Benoit Samuelson, b. 1968: won 1st Olympic women's marathon (1984), Boston Marathon (1979, '83).
Barry Sanders, b. 1968: rushed for 2,053 yards in 1997; led NFL in rushing, 1990, 1994, 1996, 1997.
Gene Sarazen, (1902-99): won PGA championship 3 times, U.S. Open twice; developed the sand wedge.
Gale Sayers, b. 1943: Chicago back, twice led NFL in rushing.
Mike Schmidt, b. 1949: Phillies 3rd baseman; led NL in home runs 8 times; 548 lifetime; NL MVP, 1980, 1981, 1986.
Michael Schumacher, b. 1969: German driver, 5-time Formula 1 world champ (1994-95, 2000-2002).
Tom Seaver, b. 1944: pitcher; won NL Cy Young award 3 times; won 311 major league games.
Monica Seles, b. 1973: won U.S. ('91-92), Australian ('91-93, '96), French ('90-92) Opens; stabbed on court by fan, 1993.
Patty Sheehan, b. 1956: Hall of Fame golfer, 3 LPGA Championships (1983-84, '93).
Willie Shoemaker, b. 1931: jockey; rode 4 Kentucky Derby and 5 Belmont Stakes winners; leading career money winner.
Eddie Shore (1902-85): Boston Bruins defenseman; MVP 4 times, first-team all-star 7 times.
Frank Shorter, b. 1947: runner, only American to win men's Olympic marathon (1972) since 1908; silver medalist in 1976.
Don Shula, b. 1930: all-time winningest NFL coach (347 games).
Al Simmons (1902-56): AL outfielder batted .334 lifetime.
O. J. Simpson, b. 1947: running back; rushed for 2,003 yds., 1973; AFC leading rusher 4 times; acquitted of murder, 1995.
George Sisler (1893-1973): St. Louis Browns 1st baseman; had record 257 hits, 1920; batted .340 lifetime.
Dean Smith, b. 1931: basketball coach, most career Division I wins (879); led North Carolina to 2 NCAA titles (1982, '93).
Emmitt Smith, b. 1969: Dallas running back; NFL and Super Bowl MVP, 1993; record 25 rushing touchdowns, 1995.
Lee Smith, b. 1957: relief pitcher, all-time saves leader, 478.
Conn Smythe (1895-1980): won 7 Stanley Cups as Toronto GM (1929-1961); playoff MVP award named in his honor.
Sam Snead (1912-2002): PGA and Masters champ 3 times each, record 82 PGA tournament victories.
Annika Sorenstam, b. 1970: golfer, set LPGA 18-hole record of 59 (–13), and 72-hole record of 27-under-par in Mar. 2001.
Sammy Sosa, b. 1968: Cubs outfielder; 66 homers, NL MVP, 1998; 1st to hit 60+ homers 3 times (63 in 1999, 64 in 2001).
Warren Spahn, b. 1921: pitcher; won 363 NL games; 20-game winner 13 times; Cy Young award, 1957.
Tris Speaker (1885-1958): AL outfielder; batted .345 over 22 seasons; hit record 792 career doubles.
Mark Spitz, b. 1950: swimmer, won 7 golds at 1972 Olympics.
Amos Alonzo Stagg (1862-1965): football innovator; Univ. of Chicago football coach for 41 years, 5 undefeated seasons.
Bart Starr, b. 1934: Green Bay Packers quarterback, led team to 5 NFL titles and 2 Super Bowl victories.
Roger Staubach, b. 1942: Dallas Cowboys quarterback; leading NFC passer 5 times.
Casey Stengel (1890-1975): managed Yankees to 10 pennants, 7 championships, 1949-60.
Jackie Stewart, b. 1939: Scot auto racer, 27 Grand Prix wins.
John Stockton b. 1962: Utah Jazz guard; NBA career leader in assists, steals; NBA assists leader, 1988-96.
Picabo Street, b. 1971: skier, 2-time World Cup downhill champion (1995-96); Olympic super G gold medalist in 1998.
Louise Suggs, b. 1923: U.S. Women's Open champ., 1949, '52; 11 major victories, ranks 3rd all-time.
John L. Sullivan (1858-1918): last bareknuckle heavyweight champion, 1882-1892.
Pat Summit, b. 1952: basketball coach, led Tennessee Lady Vols to 6 NCAA titles (1987, '89, '91, '96-98).
Fran Tarkenton, b. 1940: quarterback, Minnesota, N.Y. Giants, 2nd in career touchdown passes; 1975 Player of the Year.
Lawrence Taylor, b. 1959; linebacker; led N.Y. Giants to 2 Super Bowl titles; played in 10 Pro Bowls.
Frank Thomas, b. 1968: Chicago White Sox 1st baseman; was AL MVP, 1993-94; won AL batting title, 1997.
Jenny Thompson, b. 1973: swimmer, most decorated U.S. woman with 10 Olympic medals (8 gold) in 1992, 1996, 2000.
Daley Thompson, b. 1958: British decathlete, Olympic gold medalist in 1980, '84.
Jim Thorpe (1888-1953): football All-America, 1911, 1912; won pentathlon and decathlon, 1912 Olympics.
Bill Tilden (1893-1953): won 7 U.S. tennis titles, 3 Wimbledon.
Y. A. Tittle, b. 1926: N.Y. Giants quarterback; MVP, 1961, 1963.
Alberto Tomba, b. 1966: Italian skier, all-time Olympic alpine medalist (3 golds, 2 silver).
Lee Trevino, b. 1939: golfer, won U.S., British Open twice.
Bryan Trottier, b. 1956: center for 6 Stanley Cup champs.
Gene Tunney, (1897-1978): heavyweight champion, 1926-28.
Mike Tyson, b. 1966: Undisputed heavyweight champ, 1987-1990; at 19, youngest to win a heavyweight title (WBC, 1986).
Wyomia Tyus, b. 1945: Olympic 100m gold medalist, 1964, '68.
Johnny Unitas, (1933-2002): Baltimore Colts quarterback; passed for more than 40,000 yds; MVP, 1957, 1967.
Al Unser, b. 1939: Indy 500 winner 4 times.
Bobby Unser, b. 1934: Indy 500 winner 3 times.
Norm Van Brocklin (1926-83): quarterback; passed for game record 554 yds., 1951; MVP, 1960.
Amy Van Dyken, b. 1973: swimmer, first American woman to win 4 gold medals in one Olympics (1996).
Lasse Viren, b. 1949: Finnish runner; Olympic 5,000m and 10,000m gold medalist in 1972 and 1976.
Honus Wagner (1874-1955): Pittsburgh Pirates shortstop, won 8 NL batting titles.
Grete Waitz, b. 1953: Norwegian, 9-time winner of the New York City Marathon (1978-80, 1982-86, '88).
"Jersey" Joe Walcott, (1914-94): boxer, became heavyweight champion at age 37, 1951-52.
Bill Walton, b. 1952: center led Portland Trail Blazers to 1977 NBA title; MVP, 1978; NBA TV commentator.
Kurt Warner, b. 1971: St. Louis Rams quarterback, NFL MVP 1999, 2001; Super Bowl MVP, 2000.
Tom Watson, b. 1949: 6-time PGA Player of the Year, won 5 British Opens, 2 Masters, U.S. Open.
Karrie Webb, b. 1974: Australian golfer; youngest (26 yrs. 6 mos.) to win career Grand Slam, 1999-2001.
Johnny Weissmuller (1903-84): swimmer; won 52 national championships, 5 Olympic gold medals; set 67 world records.
Jerry West, b. 1938: L.A. Lakers guard; had career average 27 points per game; first team all-star 10 times.
Byron "Whizzer" White (1917-2002): running back, led NCAA in scoring and rushing at Colorado (1937), led NFL in rushing twice (1938, '40); Supreme Court justice, 1962-93.
Reggie White, b. 1961: defensive end, all-time NFL sack leader.
Kathy Whitworth, b. 1939: 7-time LPGA Player of the Year (1966-69, 1971-73); 88 tour wins most on LPGA or PGA tour.
Lenny Wilkens, b. 1937: winningest coach in NBA history; in Hall of Fame as player and coach.
Serena Williams, b. 1981: won singles titles at French Open, Wimbledon, and U.S. Open over her sister, Venus, in 2002; won 1999 U.S. Open.
Ted Williams (1918-2002): Boston Red Sox outfielder; won 6 batting titles, two triple crowns; hit .406 in 1941.
Venus Williams, b. 1980: Wimbledon, U.S. Open, Olympic champ (2000); Wimbledon, U.S. Open champ (2001).
Helen Willis Moody (1905-98): tennis star; won U.S. Open 7 times, Wimbledon 8 times.
Katarina Witt, b. 1965: German figure skater; won Olympic gold medal, 1984, 1988; world champ, 1984-84, 1987-88.
John Wooden, b. 1910: UCLA basketball coach; 10 NCAA titles.
Tiger Woods, b. 1975: golfer, youngest ever to win the sport's career Grand Slam (all 4 majors), at age 24, when he won the British Open, 2000; 8 major titles.
Mickey Wright, b. 1935: won LPGA and U.S. Open championship 4 times; 82 career wins including 13 majors.
Kristi Yamaguchi, b. 1971: figure skater, won national, world, and Olympic titles in 1992.
Carl Yastrzemski, b. 1939: Boston Red Sox slugger; won 3 batting titles; triple crown, 1967.
Cy Young (1867-1955): pitcher, won record 511 games.
Steve Young, b. 1961: 49ers quarterback; led NFL in passing, 1991-94, 1996, 1997; Super Bowl MVP, 1995.
Babe Didrikson Zaharias (1914-56): track star; won 2 1932 Olympic gold medals; won numerous golf tournaments.
Emil Zátopek (1922-2000): Czech runner won 3 gold medals at 1952 Olympics (5,000m, 10,000m, and marathon).

GENERAL INDEX

Note: Page numbers in **boldface** indicate key reference. Page numbers in *italics* indicate photos.

–X–

–Y–

–Z–

SPORTS QUICK REFERENCE INDEX

FOR COMPLETE INDEX, SEE PAGES 979-1007.

WORLD ALMANAC QUICK QUIZ—ANSWERS

16–c; **40**–d; **61**–c; **80**–b; **96**–d; **149**–a; **164**–d; **217**–d; **219**–c; **236**–c; **281**–b; **305**–d; **307**–c, a, b, d; **335**–a; **358**–a; **366**–c; **380**–c; **396**–c; **444**–a; **469**–a, c, d, b; **489**–a; **523**–c; **528**–b; **569**–b; **607**–d; **615**–b; **617**–b; **629**–a; **636**–b; **652**–b; **655**–d; **693**–b; **699**–d, a, c, b; **706**–b; **716**–b; **751**–d; **757**–c; **854**–d; **856**–c; **865**–c; **891**–a; **910**–c; **948**–a.